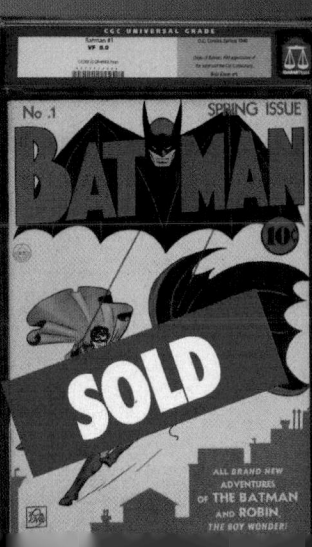

THE OVERSTREET® COMIC BOOK PRICE GUIDE

42nd Edition

COMICS FROM THE 1500s–PRESENT INCLUDED
FULLY ILLUSTRATED CATALOGUE
& EVALUATION GUIDE

by ROBERT M. OVERSTREET

GEMSTONE PUBLISHING

J.C. Vaughn, Associate Publisher & Executive Editor
Mark Huesman, Creative Director & Production Coordinator
Heather Winter, Office Manager

SPECIAL CONTRIBUTORS TO THIS EDITION

Robert Beerbohm • Dr. Arnold T. Blumberg • Melissa Bowersox • Scott Braden • Pat Calhoun
Michael Eury • Gene Gonzales • Rob Hughes • Richard D. Olson, Ph.D. • J.C. Vaughn

SPECIAL ADVISORS TO THIS EDITION

Grant Adey • Bill Alexander • David Alexander • Tyler Alexander • Lon Allen • Dave Anderson
David J. Anderson, DDS • Matt Ballesteros • Stephen Barrington • L.E. Becker • Robert L. Beerbohm
Jim Berry • Jon Bevans • Steve Borock • Kevin Boyd • Michael Browning • Shawn Caffrey
John Chruscinski • Gary Colabuono • Bill Cole • Frank Cwiklik • Brock Dickinson • Peter Dixon
Gary Dolgoff • Walter Durajlija • Ken Dyber • Bruce Ellsworth • Richard Evans • D'Arcy Farrell
Stephen Fishler • Dan Fogel • Steven Gentner • Steve Geppi • Douglas Gillock • Tom Gordon III
Andy Greenham • John Haines • Mark Haspel • Greg Holland, Ph.D. • Dennis Keum • Phil Levine
Ben Lichtenstein • Paul Litch • Jon McClure • Todd McDevitt • Mike McKenzie • John Jackson Miller
Steve Mortensen • Tom Nelson • Jamie Newbold • Terry O'Neill • Michael Pavlic • Jim Pitts • Bill Ponseti
Mick Rabin • Jeff Rader • Yolanda Ramirez • Greg Reece • Rob Reynolds • Barry Sandoval
Brian Schutzer • Alika Seki • Doug Simpson • Ben Smith • Mark Squirek • Tony Starks
West Stephan • Al Stoltz • Doug Sulipa • Chris Swartz • Michael Tierney • Ted VanLiew
Frank Verzyl • John Verzyl • Rose Verzyl • Mike Wilbur • Vincent Zurzolo, Jr.

See a full list of Overstreet Advisors on pages 1120-1123

NOTICE: Values for items pictured in this book are based on author's experience, consultations with a network of advisors including collectors specializing in various categories, and actual prices realized for specific items sold through private sales and auctions. The values offered in this book are approximations influences by many factors including condition, rarity and demand, and they should serve as only guidelines, presenting an average range of what one might expect to pay for the items. In the marketplace, knowledge and opinions held by both sellers and buyers determine prices asked and prices paid. This is not a price list of items for sale or items wanted by the author or publisher. The author and the publisher shall not be held responsible for losses that may occur in the purchase, sale or other transaction of property because of information contained herein. Efforts have been made to present accurate information, but the possibility of error exists. Readers who believe that have discovered an error are invited to mail corrective information to the author, Robert M. Overstreet at Gemstone Publishing, 1966 Greenspring Drive, Timonium, MD 21093. Verified corrections will be incorporated into future editions of this book.

Avengers Hardcover Edition ISBN: 978-1-60360-136-8
Avengers Soft Cover Edition ISBN: 978-1-60360-137-5

Catwoman Hardcover Edition ISBN: 978-1-60360-138-2
Catwoman Soft Cover Edition ISBN: 978-1-60360-139-9

Batman/Grendel Hardcover Edition ISBN: 978-1-60360-140-5

Printed in Canada

10 9 8 7 6 5 4 3 2 1

Forty-Second Edition: July 2012

TABLE OF CONTENTS

ACKNOWLEDGEMENTS

We've been fortunate in the last few years to feature some of the best covers we've ever had on *The Overstreet Comic Book Price Guide*. That tradition obviously continues with the forty-second edition.

Joe Jusko, an awesome cover artist in his own rite, brings all of his power into the spotlight with his simultaneously faithful and inventive recreation of John Buscema's cover for *The Avengers* #58 for our cover. He's well matched with the amazing Adam Hughes, who not only shows why he's a fan favorite, but also that he has great subtlety with his Catwoman cover (did you catch the shadow or what's in her bag?). Matt Wagner and colorist Ryan Brown also knocked their cover - the limited edition hardcover featuring Batman and Grendel created exclusively for The Hero Initiative - out of the park.

This year's edition includes new articles by Pat Calhoun and Rob Hughes, an interview with our old friend and founding *Comic Book Marketplace* editor Gary M. Carter, and the usual spectacular efforts by our Mark Huesman and J.C. Vaughn.

Special Thanks to the Overstreet Advisors who contributed to this edition, including Grant Adey, Bill Alexander, David Alexander, Tyler Alexander, Lon Allen, Dave Anderson, David J. Anderson, DDS, Matt Ballesteros, Stephen Barrington, L.E. Becker, Robert L. Beerbohm, Jim Berry, Jon Bevans, Dr. Arnold T. Blumberg, Steve Borock, Kevin Boyd, Michael Browning, Shawn Caffrey, Mike Carbonaro, John Chruscinski, Gary Colabuono, Bill Cole, Frank Cwiklik, Brock Dickinson, Peter Dixon, Gary Dolgoff, Walter Durajlija, Ken Dyber, Bruce Ellsworth, Richard Evans, D'Arcy Farrell, Stephen Fishler, Dan Fogel, Steven Gentner, Steve Geppi, Douglas Gillock, Tom Gordon III, Andy Greenham, John Haines, Jim Halperin, Mark Haspel, Ronnie Hayes, Greg Holland, Ph.D., Cat Jones, Dennis Keum, Phil Levine, Ben Lichtenstein, Paul Litch, Jon McClure, Todd McDevitt, Mike McKenzie, John Jackson Miller, Steve Mortensen, Tom Nelson, Jamie Newbold, Terry O'Neill, Michael Pavlic, Jim Pitts, Bill Ponseti, Mick Rabin, Jeff Rader, Yolanda Ramirez, Greg Reece, Rob Reynolds, Barry Sandoval, Brian Schutzer, Alika Seki, Doug Simpson, Marc Sims, Ben Smith, Mark Squirek, Tony Starks, West Stephan, Al Stoltz, Doug Sulipa, Chris Swartz, Michael Tierney, Ted VanLiew, Frank Verzyl, John Verzyl, Rose Verzyl, Eddie Wendt, Mike Wilbur, Vincent Zurzolo, Jr., as well as to our additional contributors, including Stephen Baer, Ron Ballard, Ivan Briggs, Mike Bromberg, Jonathan Calure, Bruce Darling, Peter Gaskin, Paul Howley, John Korfel, Ben Labonog, Jason Lohr, Rod Matlack, Bill Parker, Dan Paulun, James Pender, Dennis Petilli, Michael Proteau, David Singleton, Ron Stewart, Mel Taylor, and Tom Trombley. Without their active participation, this project would not have been possible.

Additionally, I would like to personally extend my thanks to all of those who encouraged and supported first the creation of and then subsequently the expansion of the *Guide* over the past four decades. While it's impossible in this brief space to individually acknowledge every individual, mention is certainly due to Lon Allen (Golden Age data); Mark Arnold (Harvey data); Larry Bigman (Frazetta-Williamson data); Bill Blackbeard (Platinum Age cover photos); Steve Borock and Mark Haspel (Grading); Glenn Bray (Kurtzman data); Gary Carter (DC data); J. B. Clifford Jr. (EC data); Gary Coddington (Superman data); Gary Colabuono (Golden Age ashcan data); Wilt Conine (Fawcett data); Chris Cormier (Miracleman data); Dr. S. M. Davidson (Cupples & Leon data); Al Dellinges (Kubert data); Stephen Fishler (10-Point Grading system); Chris Friesen (Glossary additions); David Gerstein (Walt Disney Comics data); Gene Gonzales (introduction illustrations); Kevin Hancer (Tarzan data); Charles Heffelfinger and Jim Ivey (March of Comics listing); R. C. Holland and Ron Pussell (Seduction and Parade of Pleasure data); Grant Irwin (Quality data); Richard Kravitz (Kelly data); Phil Levine (giveaway data); Paul Litch (Copper & Modern Age data); Dan Malan & Charles Heffelfinger (Classic Comics data); Jon McClure (Whitman data); Fred Nardelli (Frazetta data); Michelle Nolan (Love comics); Mike Nolan (MLJ, Timely, Nedor data); George Olshevsky (Timely data); Dr. Richard Olson (Grading and Yellow Kid info); Chris Pedrin (DC War data); Scott Pell ('50s data); Greg Robertson (National data); Don Rosa (Late 1940s to 1950s data); Matt Schiffman (Bronze Age data); Frank Scigliano (Little Lulu data); Gene Seger (Buck Rogers data); Rick Sloane (Archie data); David R. Smith, Archivist, Walt Disney Productions (Disney data); Bill Spicer and Zetta DeVoe (Western Publishing Co. data); Tony Starks (Silver and Bronze Age data); Al Stoltz (Golden Age & Promo data); Doug Sulipa (Bronze Age data); Don and Maggie Thompson (Four Color listing); Mike Tiefenbacher & Jerry Sinkovec (Atlas and National data); Raymond True & Philip J. Gaudino (Classic Comics data); Jim Vadeboncoeur Jr. (Williamson and Atlas data); Richard Samuel West (Victorian Age and Platinum Age data); Kim Weston (Disney and Barks data); Cat Yronwode (Spirit data); Andrew Zerbe and Gary Behymer (M. E. data).

Finally, thanks, as always, to our advertisers, whose support makes this project possible, and to all of you who have purchased this edition.

Comic link
AUCTIONS AND EXCHANGE

LOOKING FOR A
COMIC SHOP NEAR YOU?
COMIC SHOP LOCATOR SERVICE
COMICS
comicshoplocator.com
888-COMIC-BOOK

CREATING CLASSICS IN THE MODERN AGE

ASK YOUR LOCAL RETAILER ABOUT THE CGC VARIANT PROGRAM

ONLY FROM BOOM! STUDIOS

WWW.BOOM-STUDIOS.COM

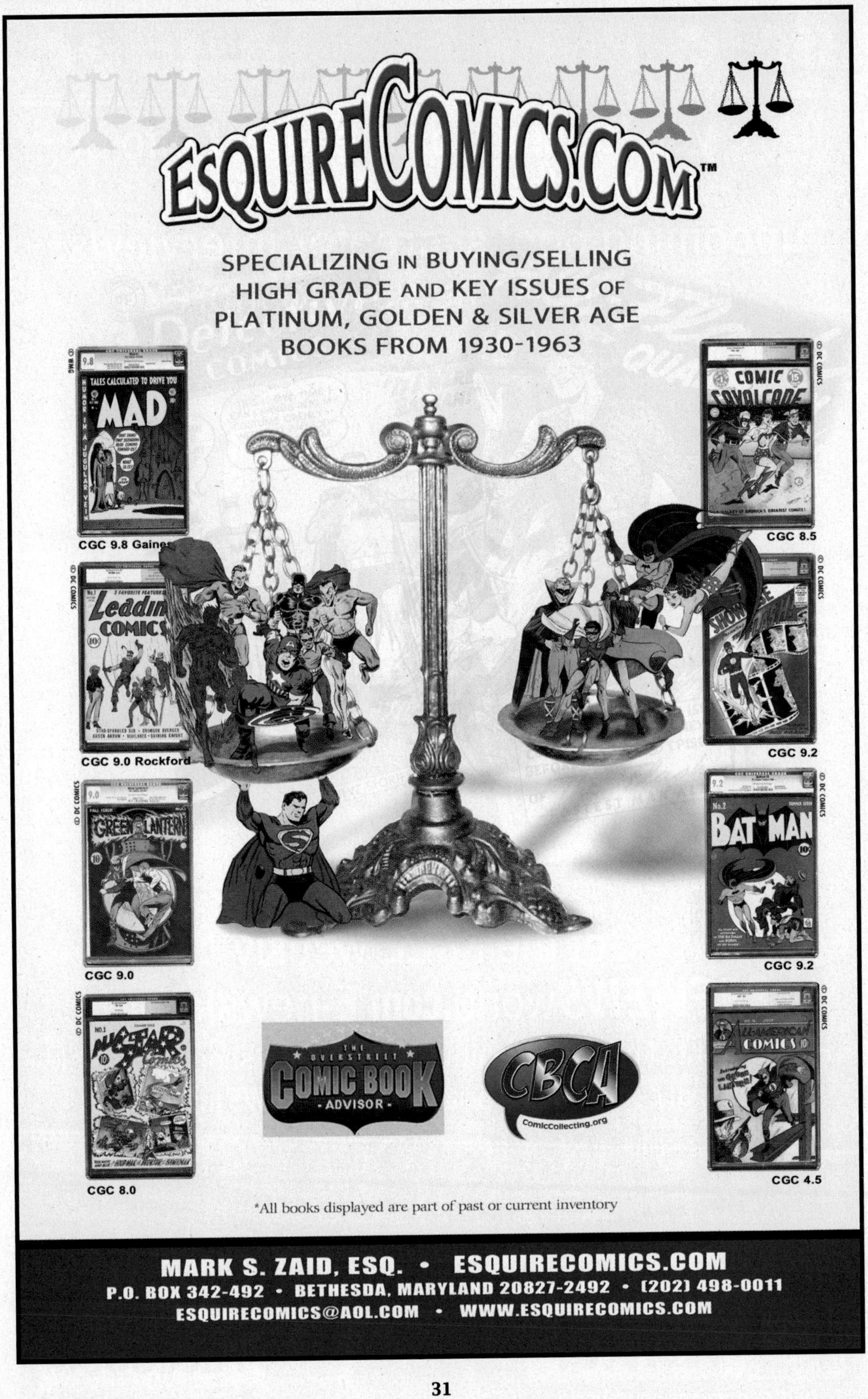

neatstuff

COLLECTIBLES LLC

BUYING ENTIRE COLLECTIONS!

What I buy...

- G.I. JOE/ BARBIES
- BIG LITTLE BOOKS
- MOVIE POSTERS
- PULPS
- ORIGINAL ART
- MARX PLAYSETS
- MARVEL MANIA
- DISNEY
- NON SPORTS CARDS
- STATUES
- BISQUE FIGURES
- TOY ROBOTS
- BOARD GAMES
- MOVIE MEMORABILIA
- BASEBALL & SPORTS
- ALL PAPER COLLECTIBLES
- STAR WARS
- MARILYN MONROE
- FLASH GORDON
- SPIDER-MAN
- KING KONG
- PETER MAX, BEATLES
- '60s ROCK & ROLL
- ROY ROGERS
- JAMES BOND
- JAMES DEAN
- BUCK ROGERS
- MARVEL SUPER HEROES
- TARZAN
- ELVIS PRESLEY
- KISS TOYS & COMICS
- LITTLE NEMO

Golden Age Comics › Silver Age Comics › Original Comic Art › Toys

Why do ALL the other dealers in this book sell to me?

Because over the past ten years or so I have been buying comics from dealers throughout the country. In fact, over the years I have bought comics from just about every dealer who advertises in this book. I spend millions of dollars a year buying. If professional dealers sell me comics, why can't you? A dealer is extremely knowledgeable, has shown his comics to all kinds of buyers from retail customers to every other dealer in the country at shows. They choose to sell to me because of honesty, financial reliability, and of course the prices I pay.

I travel to YOU!
Unlimited funds available!
Payment in full on the spot!

We buy it all in one FREE call

1 (800) 224.9588

buyingeverything@yahoo.com

sellmyneatstuff.com

visit us: www.geppismuseum.com!

SPORTS LEGENDS OPEN

Attend OUR
SUPER
HERO
CONVENTION EVERY DAY!
Visit us at www.comicsamerica.com
A BOUNTY OF:
Graphic Novels! Action Figures! Magazines! New Comics!
Books! Back Issue Comics! Collectibles!
Pop Culture! Posters & Prints and much more!

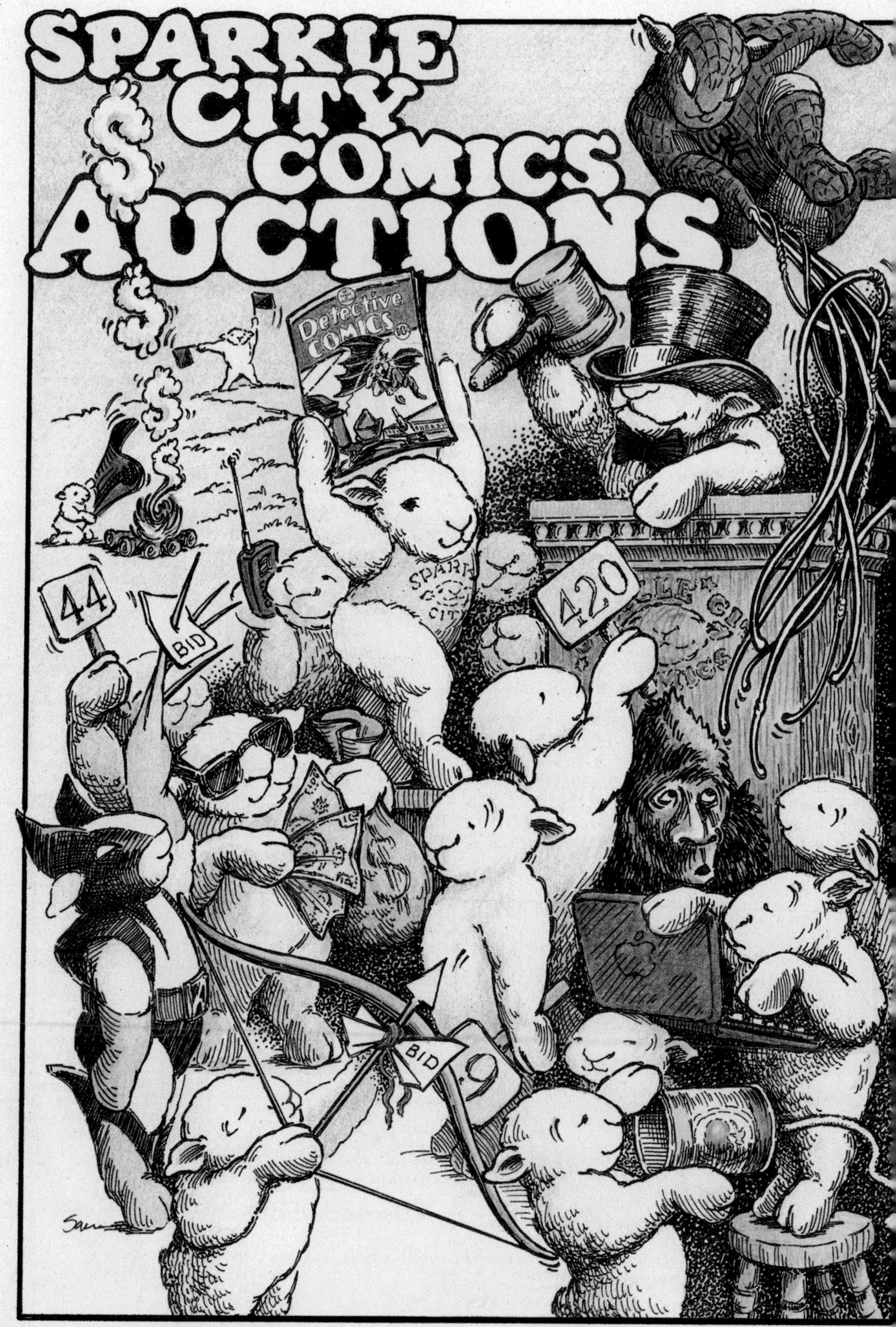

SPARKLE CITY COMICS AUCTIONS
Detective COMICS
44
BID
420
BID
9

HERITAGE

MORE EXPOSURE FOR SELLERS AT HERITAGE!

Beautiful printed catalogs entice bidders to bid higher.

Our **heavily advertised** Signature® auctions are among the biggest events in the comic book hobby. The live sessions have bidders participating by phone, in person, and over the Internet.

Auction archive of Comics and Original Art — every item we've ever auctioned with full descriptions, images and actual prices realized. We don't hide our past results (and we don't intermix retail sales with our auction records)!

EXCLUSIVE AUCTIONEER OF THESE OUTSTANDING PERSONAL COLLECTIONS:

The Kerby Confer Collection
$3.9 million **sold**

The Billy Wright Collection
$3.6 million **sold**

The Gary Dahlberg Collection
$2.4 million **sold** to date

Heritage's experts will guide you through the consignment process and help you get the most money for your treasured items. Call or email us today!

3500 Maple Avenue | Dallas, Texas 75219 | 800-872-6467 | Bid@HA.com

HERITAGE AUCTIONS 

Annual Sales Exceed $800 Million | 700,000+ Online Bidder-Members

DALLAS | NEW YORK | BEVERLY HILLS | SAN FRANCISCO | PARIS | GENEVA

Free catalog and *The Collector's Handbook* ($65 value) for new clients. Please submit auction invoices of $1000+ in this category, from any source. Include your contact information and mail to Heritage, fax 214-409-1425, email catalogorders@ha.com, or call 866-835-3243. For more details, go to HA.com/FCO.

TX Auctioneer licenses: Samuel Foose 11727; Robert Korver 13754; Andrea Voss 16406. • All comic auctions are subject to a 19.5% Buyer's Premium.

LAST YEAR PEOPLE WHO FANCY THEMSELVES IN THE "IN CROWD" IN HOLLYWOOD STARTED TALKING ABOUT HOW SUPERHERO FILMS WERE "OVER."

THEN *THE AVENGERS* HIT AND SO MANY RECORDS FELL... AND THE SUPERHERO MOVIE SUMMER BRINGS WITH IT A FAIR AMOUNT OF MEDIA ATTENTION.

AND ARCHIE GOT MARRIED. AGAIN.

SO WITH ALL OF THESE EVENTS IN AND AROUND COMICS, THERE WERE A WHOLE LOT OF EYES ON OUR INDUSTRY.

PICKING UP FROM 2011, WE'VE SEEN MORE RECORD PRICES FOR COMIC BOOKS AND ORIGINAL COMIC ART...
WE'VE SEEN THE FIRST GOLDEN AGE COMIC BOOK BREAK THE $2 MILLION MARK...

AND THERE'S POTENTIAL FOR A LOT MORE TO COME!

THE OVERSTREET
COMIC BOOK
PRICE GUIDE
42ND EDITION
2012 - 2013
ROBERT M. OVERSTREET
IT MIGHT BE HARD TO BELIEVE, BUT THIS IS THE 42ND EDITION OF *THE OVERSTREET COMIC BOOK PRICE GUIDE!*
ABOUT THIS BOOK
BY J.C. VAUGHN
ILLUSTRATED BY GENE GONZALES

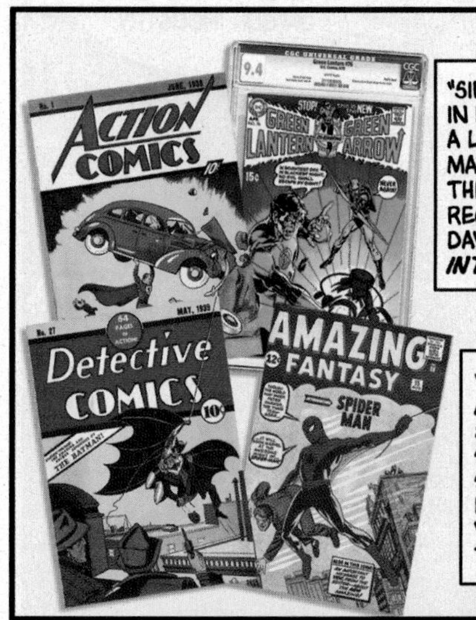
ACTION COMICS
GREEN LANTERN GREEN ARROW
Detective COMICS
AMAZING FANTASY
SPIDER MAN

"SINCE THE *GUIDE*'S DEBUT IN 1970, THERE HAVE BEEN A LOT OF CHANGES IN THE MARKETPLACE. FOR INSTANCE, THERE HAVE ALWAYS BEEN RECORD PRICES, BUT THESE DAYS THEY CAN MAKE ***INTERNATIONAL NEWS...***"

"WHEN YOU KEEP UP WITH ***RECORD PRICES***, WHAT'S ***SELLING***, WHAT'S ***NOT*** SELLING, AND WHAT'S SUDDENLY ***IN DEMAND***, IT HELPS YOU KNOW WHAT YOU SHOULD BE WILLING TO PAY OR WHEN TO SELL."

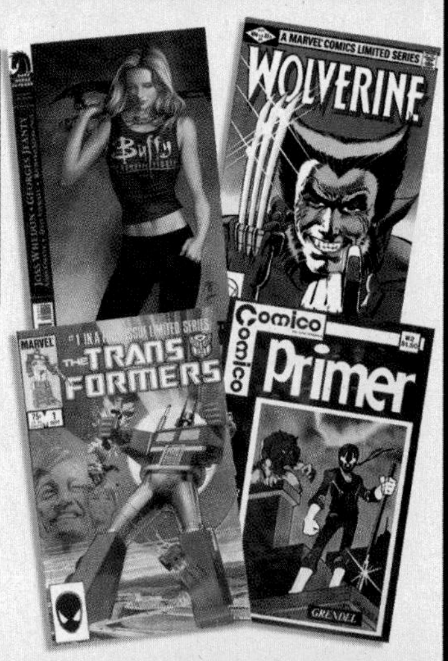
A MARVEL COMICS LIMITED SERIES
WOLVERINE
Buffy
THE TRANSFORMERS
Comico
Primer
GRENDEL

AND THERE HAVE BEEN LOTS OF OTHER CHANGES, TOO. WE'VE BEEN STUDYING THIS FOR *FOUR DECADES* NOW AND ONE THING IS REALLY CLEAR...

THE MORE YOU *KNOW* ABOUT COMICS, THE MORE YOU *WANT* TO KNOW. AND WE'VE BEEN HAPPY TO HELP PEOPLE LEARN FOR *42 YEARS.*

ONE OF THE COOL THINGS ABOUT COMIC BOOKS IS THAT THERE ARE LOTS OF NEW ONES TO DISCOVER...

AND THERE ARE LITERALLY HUNDREDS OF THOUSANDS OF DIFFERENT BACK ISSUES, TOO!

BACK ISSUE COMICS RANGE FROM LESS THAN COVER PRICE TO **$2,100,000.**
A COMIC BOOK FOR ***$2.1 MILLION?*** HARD TO BELIEVE, HUH?

THE FIRST COMIC TO HIT $1 MILLION WAS ***ACTION COMICS*** #1, THE FIRST APPEARANCE OF ***SUPERMAN***.
THE SECOND, JUST A FEW DAYS LATER, WAS ***DETECTIVE COMICS*** #27, THE FIRST APPEARANCE OF ***BATMAN***.
ANOTHER ACTION #1 SOLD FOR ***$1.5 MILLION*** JUST A SHORT WHILE AFTER THAT.

MANY OTHERS HAVE SOLD FOR RECORD PRICES IN THE LAST YEAR OR SO, EVEN WITH THE TOUGH ECONOMY NATIONALLY.

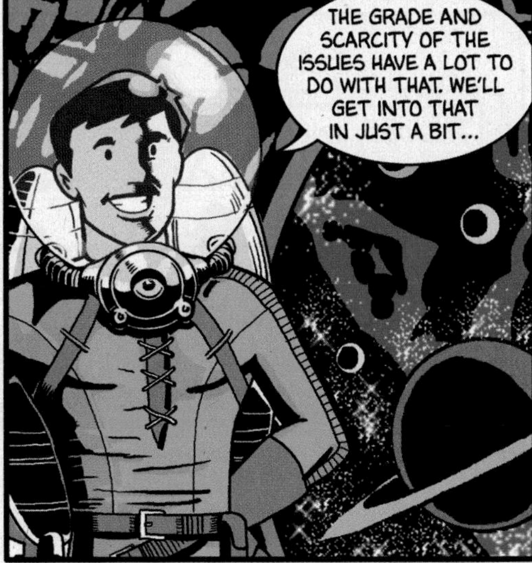
THE GRADE AND SCARCITY OF THE ISSUES HAVE A LOT TO DO WITH THAT. WE'LL GET INTO THAT IN JUST A BIT...

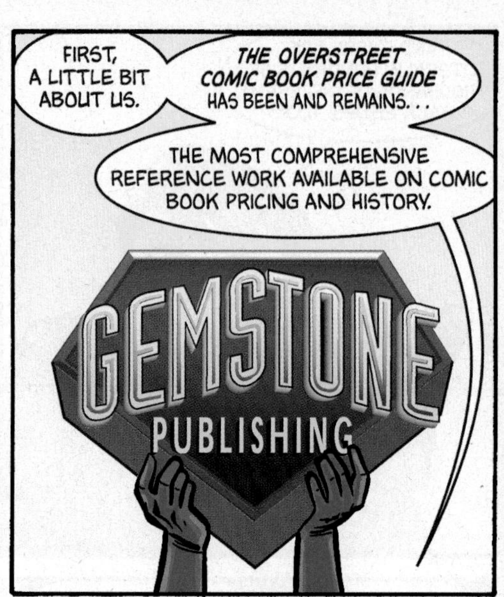

FIRST, A LITTLE BIT ABOUT US.
THE OVERSTREET COMIC BOOK PRICE GUIDE HAS BEEN AND REMAINS. . .
THE MOST COMPREHENSIVE REFERENCE WORK AVAILABLE ON COMIC BOOK PRICING AND HISTORY.
GEMSTONE PUBLISHING

IT'S RESPECTED AND USED BY DEALERS AND COLLECTORS EVERYWHERE.
OVERSTREET PRICING AND GRADING STANDARDS ARE THE ACCEPTED FOUNDATIONS OF THE COMIC BOOK MARKETPLACE AROUND THE WORLD.
THROUGH HARD WORK, DILIGENCE AND CONSTANT CONTACT WITH THE MARKET FOR DECADES, OVERSTREET HAS BECOME THE MOST TRUSTED NAME IN COMICS.

OUR BOOK IS A DETAILED ALPHABETICAL LIST OF COMIC BOOKS AND THEIR MARKET VALUES.

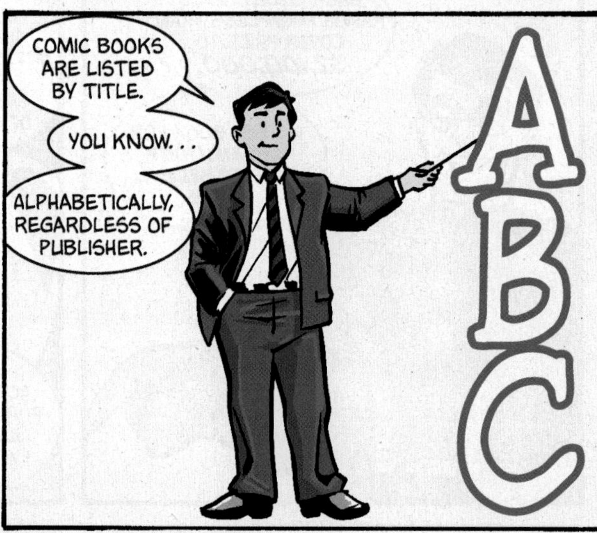

COMIC BOOKS ARE LISTED BY TITLE.
YOU KNOW. . .
ALPHABETICALLY, REGARDLESS OF PUBLISHER.
A
B
C

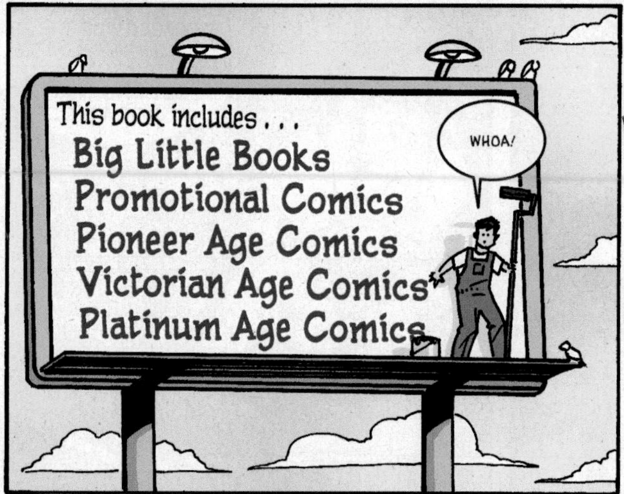

This book includes . . .
Big Little Books
Promotional Comics
Pioneer Age Comics
Victorian Age Comics
Platinum Age Comics
WHOA!

THE MAIN PRICING SECTION FEATURES COMICS FROM 1938 THROUGH THE PRESENT!

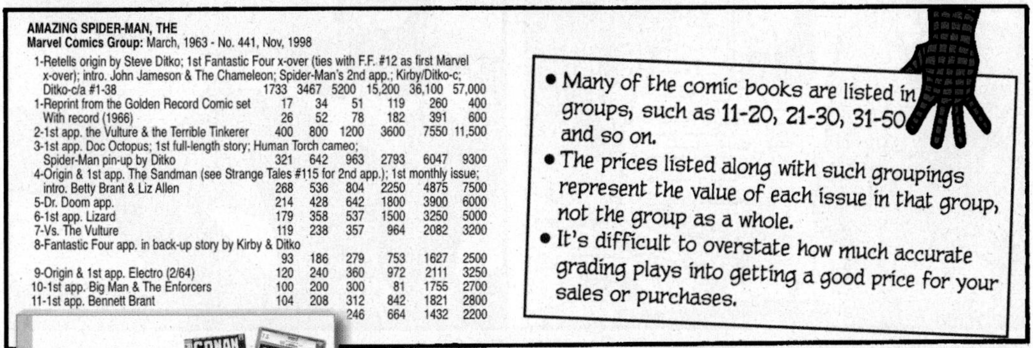

9.2
9.0
8.5
8.0
7.5
7.0
6.5
6.0
5.5
5.0
4.5
4.0
3.5
3.0
2.5
2.0

PRICES ARE LISTED IN SIX GRADES, RANGING FROM 2.0 TO 9.2 ON A 10.0 SCALE.

THERE ARE MORE GRADES THAN THE SIX WE HAVE LISTED, BUT THESE WILL GIVE YOU THE KEYS TO UNDERSTANDING THE MARKET.

WHILE PRICES BELOW 9.2 ARE FAIRLY STEADY, IT'S IMPORTANT TO NOTE THAT PRICES ABOVE 9.2 ARE FREQUENTLY CONSIDERED EXTREMELY VOLATILE.

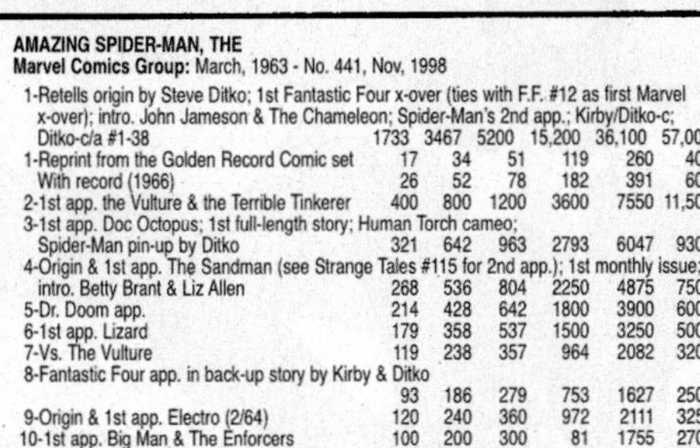

AMAZING SPIDER-MAN, THE
Marvel Comics Group: March, 1963 - No. 441, Nov, 1998

1-Retells origin by Steve Ditko; 1st Fantastic Four x-over (ties with F.F. #12 as first Marvel x-over); intro. John Jameson & The Chameleon; Spider-Man's 2nd app.; Kirby/Ditko-c; Ditko-c/a #1-38	1733	3467	5200	15,200	36,100	57,000
1-Reprint from the Golden Record Comic set	17	34	51	119	260	400
With record (1966)	26	52	78	182	391	600
2-1st app. the Vulture & the Terrible Tinkerer	400	800	1200	3600	7550	11,500
3-1st app. Doc Octopus; 1st full-length story; Human Torch cameo; Spider-Man pin-up by Ditko	321	642	963	2793	6047	9300
4-Origin & 1st app. The Sandman (see Strange Tales #115 for 2nd app.); 1st monthly issue; intro. Betty Brant & Liz Allen	268	536	804	2250	4875	7500
5-Dr. Doom app.	214	428	642	1800	3900	6000
6-1st app. Lizard	179	358	537	1500	3250	5000
7-Vs. The Vulture	119	238	357	964	2082	3200
8-Fantastic Four app. in back-up story by Kirby & Ditko	93	186	279	753	1627	2500
9-Origin & 1st app. Electro (2/64)	120	240	360	972	2111	3250
10-1st app. Big Man & The Enforcers	100	200	300	81	1755	2700
11-1st app. Bennett Brant	104	208	312	842	1821	2800
			246	664	1432	2200

- Many of the comic books are listed in groups, such as 11-20, 21-30, 31-50 and so on.
- The prices listed along with such groupings represent the value of each issue in that group, not the group as a whole.
- It's difficult to overstate how much accurate grading plays into getting a good price for your sales or purchases.

THE DEFINITIVE GUIDE TO GRADING COMIC BOOKS!
OFFICIAL
OVERSTREET® COMIC BOOK GRADING GUIDE
THIRD EDITION
FEATURING THE 10 POINT GRADING SYSTEM!
ROBERT M. OVERSTREET AND DR. ARNOLD T. BLUMBERG
HOUSE OF COLLECTIBLES
It's a good practice to develop relationships with dealers and other collectors who prove themselves trustworthy.
MANY PEOPLE HAVE STARTED USING INDEPENDENT, THIRD-PARTY GRADING SERVICES, SUCH AS CGC.
HEY, SOMEONE TOOK A BITE OUT OF THIS COMIC!

THE BEST PART IS THERE ARE MANY DIFFERENT WAYS TO COLLECT.

YOU CAN CHOOSE TO FOLLOW INDIVIDUAL PUBLISHERS, WRITERS, ARTISTS, CHARACTERS...

YOU CAN COLLECT SUPERHEROES, WAR COMICS, WESTERNS, ROMANCE OR WHATEVER YOU LIKE...

YOU CAN CHOOSE #1 ISSUES, FIRST APPEARANCES, CROSSOVERS, OR MANY OTHER VARIATIONS.

THE BEST THING TO COLLECT IS WHAT YOU LIKE, NOT WHAT SOMEONE ELSE LIKES.

WHETHER IT'S SPIDER-MAN OR EVERY COMIC THAT CAME OUT THE MONTH YOU WERE BORN, IT'S BEST TO DO IT WITH A PLAN.

THE BEST WAY TO HAVE A GOOD PLAN IS TO FIRST GET INFORMED.

THE BEST WAY TO GET INFORMED IS TO GO TO THE EXPERTS!
CAN'T I SAY "OR ELSE!" AFTER THAT?

LEARN THE INS AND OUTS OF COLLECTING, INCLUDING HOW TO TAKE CARE OF YOUR COLLECTION!

Learn how to grade your comics and why the grades make a difference!

LEARN WHAT TO EXPECT AT CONVENTIONS OR WHEN BUYING AND SELLING COMICS.
AND MAYBE HOW TO FIGHT ZOMBIES...

IT'S ALSO IMPORTANT TO REMEMBER THAT THIS BOOK IS A GUIDE, NOT A DEALER'S PRICE LIST. THE MARKET SETS THE PRICES.

WITH INPUT FROM A NETWORK OF EXPERIENCED ADVISORS INCLUDING WELL ESTABLISHED COLLECTORS, DEALERS AND HISTORIANS OF POPULAR CULTURE, WE HAVE UNDERTAKEN SIGNIFICANT EFFORT TO ASSEMBLE THIS PRICING INFORMATION.

THE RESULTING LISTINGS COME THROUGH THE OBSERVATION AND DOCUMENTATION OF PRICES REALIZED THROUGH HOBBY AND TRADE SHOWS, CATALOG SALES, RETAIL SALES, AND INTERNET, LIVE AND MAIL-IN AUCTIONS. DOCUMENTED PERSONAL SALES MAY ALSO BE INCLUDED.

WE HAVE EARNED OUR REPUTATION FOR OUR CAUTIOUS, CONSERVATIVE APPROACH TO PRICING.

WE ACTIVELY ENCOURAGE READERS WHO BELIEVE THEY HAVE DISCOVERED AN ERROR TO MAIL RELATED INFORMATION TO THE AUTHOR.
WRITE TO: ROBERT M. OVERSTREET GEMSTONE PUBLISHING, INC. 1966 GREENSPRING DRIVE TIMONIUM, MD 21093
OR EMAIL FEEDBACK@GEMSTONEPUB.COM
VERIFIED CORRECTIONS WILL BE INCORPORATED INTO FUTURE EDITIONS OF THIS BOOK.
Editor's note: For more updates, visit *Scoop* at http://scoop.diamondgalleries.com.

A YEAR OF RECORD-BREAKING SALES
IN A PERIOD OF ENTHUSIASM AND CAUTION
by Robert M. Overstreet

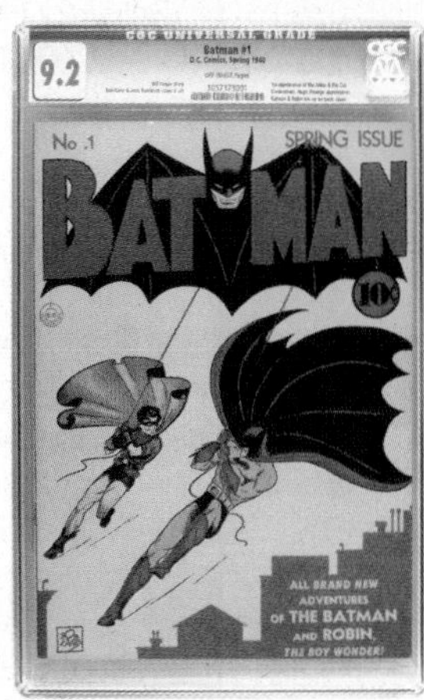

A record-setting price of $2,161,000 was paid for this CGC-certified 9.0 copy of ***Action Comics*** *#1, formerly belonging to Nicolas Cage. Also impressive were sales of a CGC-certified 9.2 copy of* ***Batman*** *#1 for a record $850,000 and this CGC-certified 9.4 copy of* ***Daredevil Battles Hitler*** *#1 which brought $38,837.*

Although most auction results in 2011 were mixed, the comics market again scored many record sales in both Golden Age and Silver Age comics. The news of the year (at least to date) was the $2,161,000 sale of a CGC-certified 9.0 copy of *Action Comics* #1 in November by ComicConnect. This turned out to be the copy stolen from Nicolas Cage's home over a decade ago which had resurfaced. As Rob Reynolds of ComicConnect remembered, "Eleven years ago, the comic was stolen out of a display vault at his house after a party. ComicConnect was contacted by a California entrepreneur hoping to make a few bucks buying the contents of auctioned-off storage units." Surprisingly, the *Action* #1 was found in one of these units and ended up in their November 2011 auction.

We continue to observe successes among rare, vintage, high grade comics, particularly those featuring characters that have broken through into other media, whether those of long standing such as Superman or more recent ones like Green Lantern (even though the movie didn't perform to the standards its enormous budget might have suggested). It's very important to note, however, that performance in other media – or lack thereof – is no guaranty of reciprocal performance for the comic book source material. In fact, this is clearly evident in the Golden Age marketplace.

In addition to the record-setting first $2 million comic, some key Golden Age sales of 2011-2012 included *Action Comics* #1 CGC 1.8 ($110,000), #1 CGC 3.0 ($298,750), #1 CGC 4.5 ($345,000), #10 CGC 9.0 ($258,000), #13 CGC 9.2 ($185,000), CGC 5.0 ($35,850), and #19 CGC 9.4 ($79,000), as well as *Adventure Comics* #40 (CGC 8.0 $59,750), *All American Comics* #16 CGC 8.0 ($203,150), #17 CGC 9.0 ($19,120), *All Star Comics* #3 CGC 8.5 ($49,294), *All Winners* #1 CGC 9.6 ($49,294), CGC 9.2 ($35,850), and *Archie Comics* #1 CGC 3.5 ($20,315).

The noteworthy Golden Age sales included *Batman* #1 CGC 9.2 ($850,000), CGC 8.5 ($274,850), *Captain America Comics* #1 CGC 6.0 ($65,725), CGC 7.0 ($90,000), CGC 9.2 ($343,057), #2 CGC 9.4 ($113,525), #3 CGC 9.2 ($50,787), *Daredevil Battles Hitler* #1 CGC 9.4 ($38,837), and *Detective Comics* #27 CGC 6.5 ($522,812), #28, CGC 7.5 ($32,265), #29 CGC 7.0 ($83,650), #33 CGC 8.0 ($92,612), and CGC 9.2 ($194,000).

Top highlights also included *Eerie* #1 CGC 9.2 ($13,145 and $9,560), *Fantastic Comics* #3 CGC 5.5 ($19,120), *Flash Comics* #2, CGC 9.0 ($168,000), *Marvel Comics* #1 CGC 7.5 ($113,525), *Marvel Mystery Comics* #4 CGC 9.2 ($50,787), #5 CGC 8.5 ($33,460), #9 CGC 4.0 ($10,157) and CGC 7.5 ($35,850), #40, CGC 9.0 ($21,510), *Red*

Raven #1 CGC 9.0 ($41,825), CGC 4.5 ($8,365), *Richie Rich* #1 CGC 9.6 ($23,900) #2, CGC 9.6 ($8,962), *Sub-Mariner* #1 CGC 8.5 ($44,812), *Superman* #1 CGC 2.5 ($36,500), #1 CGC 5.5 ($214,000), *Walt Disney Comics & Stories* #1 CGC 8.5 ($25,500), *Whiz Comics* #2(#1) CGC 6.0 ($176,007), and *Young Lovers* #18 CGC 7.5 ($1,314). Even with all the media hoopla, driving forces in the marketplace appear to be what they've been in previous years, particularly for Golden Age titles.

"Classic covers of the Golden Age sell in every grade and generally at above *Guide* prices. Hitler cover appearances are at an all time high and WWII covers are especially hot and show no signs of slowing down," West Stephan wrote. "Nice iconic covers, coveted titles, and important appearances fare better than the ordinary material around them, as it has always been," Stephen Gentner added.

Likewise, there have been plenty of notable sales of Silver Age comics as well. The Silver Age market tends to be somewhat more reflective of the characters' success in other media, but again this notion only serves as an indication, not a hard and fast rule. Among the more significant ones were *Action Comics* #242 CGC 7.5 ($3,734), #252 CGC 9.2 ($25,500) and CGC 9.0 ($13,145), *Amazing Fantasy* #15 CGC 7.0 ($33,460), CGC 8.5 ($107,300), and CGC 9.4 ($325,000), *Amazing Spider-Man* #1 CGC 9.0 ($38,837) and CGC 9.2 ($59,750), #129 CGC 9.0 ($539) and CGC 9.6 ($1,900 and $1,750), *Avengers* #1 CGC 9.2 ($60,000), CGC 9.4 ($100,000), CGC 9.6 ($250,000), and #4 CGC 9.6 ($80,000).

The Silver Age highlights also include *Brave & the Bold* #28 CGC 8.0 ($11,054) and CGC 8.5 ($20,000), *Daredevil* #1 CGC 9.6 ($37,344), *Fantastic Four* #1 CGC 5.5 ($19,120) and CGC 9.4 ($300,000), #4 CGC 9.6 ($44,812), #5 CGC 9.4 ($65,725), #12 CGC 9.4 ($48,201) and CGC 9.6 ($65,725), *Flash* #105 CGC 8.0 ($8,664), CGC 9.2 ($26,290) and CGC 9.4 ($38,837), *House of Secrets* #92 CGC 9.4 ($1,673), *Incredible Hulk* #1 CGC 8.0 ($34,500), *Iron Man* #1 CGC 9.6 ($2,749), *Journey Into Mystery* #83 CGC 8.5 ($26,500) and CGC 9.4 ($222,200), *Justice League* #1 (CGC 9.0) $18,000, and *Superman's Girlfriend Lois Lane* #1 CGC 8.0 ($8,963 and $16,730).

Also definitely worth a mention were such Silver Age sales as *Our Army At War* #81 CGC 8.5 ($6,573), #83 CGC 7.5 ($9,600) and CGC 8.0 ($16,783), #112 CGC 8.5 ($3,107), #128 CGC 9.4 ($2,629), *Sgt. Fury and His Howling Commandos* #1 CGC 8.0 ($2,629) and CGC 9.4 ($28,680), *Showcase* #4, CGC 8.0 ($23,900), CGC 9.0 ($38,837) and CGC 9.2 ($100,000), #22 CGC 8.0 ($23,900), *Tales of Suspense* #39 CGC 9.6 ($375,000), CGC 9.4 ($130,000) and CGC 9.2 ($72,100), and *X-Men* #1 CGC CGC 8.0 ($13,145) and 9.6 ($200,000), and #2 CGC 96 ($23,500).

You can find our top sales lists beginning on page 157 in this edition.

The tone and vigor of the market reports submitted by the Overstreet Advisors was varied, presenting a diverse and inconsistent view of the marketplace this year. As you read them for yourself, you will see there are many positive indications, but it is definitely not an across-the-board feeling of robustness. Given the state of the national and international economies, this should not be too surprising.

Bill Ponseti wrote, "Although there were a fair amount of big sales in 2011, the market clearly had cooled off some from the prior year's frenzied pace." He continued, "Even in a year of market correction downward, plenty of comics and cash changed hands in all segments that I track… Three million dollars for a comic book seems more and more likely as higher and higher graded copies of *Action Comics* #1 are released into the market."

Some notable Silver Age sales included this CGC-certified 9.6 copy of ***Tales of Suspense #39*** *selling for $375,000, a CGC-certified 9.2 copy of* ***Amazing Spider-Man #1*** *selling for $59,750, and this CGC-certified 9.2 copy of* ***Showcase #4*** *selling for $100,000.*

Terry O'Neill of Terry's Comics wrote, "Golden Age sales have been mixed. At some shows, high grade will sell well, at other shows lower grade will sell well." He continued, "Timely, DC, MLJ, and Quality are selling at or above *Guide*. Early Disney comics are selling well at *Guide*."

For every cautionary voice, though, there are also enthusiastic entries. As Frank Cwiklik of Metropolis Comics said in his market report, "Everyone wants in. The runaway success of high-profile books sold by us has attracted buyers who are looking for tangible investments that are not prey to the volatility of the stock market or real estate." He continues "The new buyers coming in are impressed by the stability and simplicity of the comics market, and like having an asset that they not only understand, but that brings them great pleasure."

Many times over the years, we've heard dealers and seasoned collectors speculate that all the great collections have already been found. As we've also seen over the span of the *Guide*'s history, we keep finding out that this isn't actually true. Major collections still turn up. As Jamie Newbold of Southern California Comics wrote, "We purchased several unique collections.... One collection consisted of 375 Golden Age comics from the mid-1930s to the early 1940s. The DCs and Centaurs went quickly." His company was hardly alone.

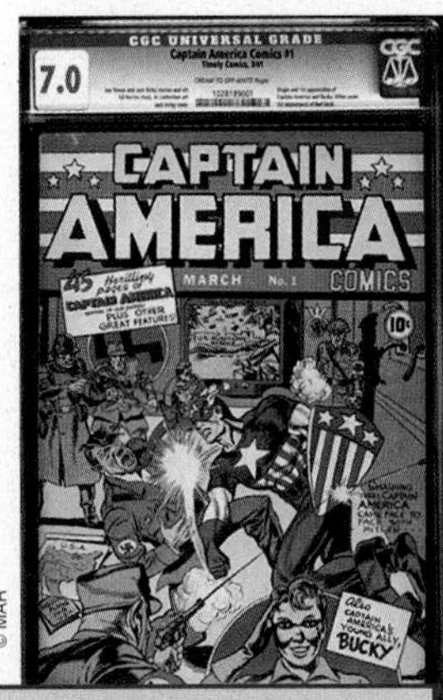

The emergence of the new Super Soldier and Billy Wright collections proved that all the great collections had not yet been found.

The Super Soldier collection of 250 Golden Age comics including many Timelys was sold by Metropolis and released simultaneously at Comic-Con International: San Diego and on the company's website. As Frank Cwiklik pointed out. "...nearly half the collection was sold within the first week."

Heritage Auctions offered the Billy Wright pedigree collection in February 2012, consisting of Golden Age comics including many #1 issues and high grade runs of top titles covering the period of 1936 through 1941. This collection of slightly over 340 issues sold for a record $3.9 million. And we're continuing to see the impact of Twin Cities pedigree collection, too. It's not only pedidgrees that are performing, though.

Brian Schutzer of Neat Stuff Collectibles and Sparkle City reported, "Golden Age was very strong in 2011. The Golden Age market appears to be poised for a big jump in interest and prices over the next few years."

Providing a grounding perspective, Dave Anderson pointed out that "the huge sales that get all the attention are very unique, exceptional books and those that have bought them paid those prices because they felt they may not soon get the opportunity to buy them again. The majority of the books sold throughout the year are not of that caliber and sell for much closer to *Guide* prices."

It has been reported to us that many of the Bronze Age key issues in 9.2 to 9.6 grade are being pressed to increase the grade to a higher level. This process is adding more 9.8 books to the census population. Consequently, because 9.8 copies have become more common, we have seen prices for many of them level off and even decrease.

"The Bronze Age has been affected in an adverse manner by the increase in the number of high-grade copies joining the census. I have found that the prices have plateaued to a certain extent," said Vincent Zurzolo of Metropolis Comics.

Brian Schutzer of Neat Stuff concurs. "2011 continued the downward trend of prices attained for high grade Bronze books. It now appears that a correction has taken place in the Bronze market and price stabilization seems to be taking place," he said.

However, Tom Nelson of Top Notch Comics writes "*Incredible Hulk* #181, first Wolverine, observed online sales of double *Guide* in the good to fine conditions."

A note on digital comic books from Stephen Gentner: "It's hard to read how the digital comic market will help or hurt our hobby. The newer and younger readers whose first blush with comics is in digital form, will remember looking at a computer screen to fondly remember their youth and favorite characters. To older collectors, the idea of reading a comic book is exactly that...a [periodical]. The tactile sensation of turning pages and smelling newsprint (or ink), is a big part of the experience. Yet, if the newer reader never knew what that was, they have no frame of reference to "miss it." Instead of taking a stack of books over to a buddies house and share and read, today's comicphile will meet their buddies either on-line, or go to Starbucks with their laptops to share."

© MAR

A price stabilization seems to be taking place for high grade Bronze Age books like this *Incredible Hulk* #181.

We know a number of our readers in both the consumer and dealer ranks are concerned about this topic. For our part, while we are following it closely, the wider dissemination offered by the internet should mean that more potential collectors than ever will be exposed to what our hobby offers. After all, if even a small percentage of the group not presently reading comics starts discovering what we have to offer, we could be in for the biggest growth we've ever seen. That's not to say it will happen, just that we should be skeptical of those who tell us they're certain of what will happen.

As has been recent history, 2011 was a volatile year for investments in the age-old, tried and true stock market. The stock market had many days last year on which it would jump up 200 points, but to go down 200 points the very next day. We were hit with continuous bad news coming out of Europe and the U.S. had its credit rating downgraded by S&P. In all, 2011 was a difficult year to navigate where investments were concerned. Could the alternative be comic books?

In recent years comic conventions across the country have grown in number of attendees. There are three giant shows – Comic-Con International: San Diego, the New York Comic Con, and Chicago's C2E2. There are also a number of thriving mid-level shows and a surprising number of small ones, and many of these latter two groups are comic-centric where the largest ones tend to have a more multi-media approach (there's even a new comic-centric one in San Diego starting this fall).

With San Diego presently around 130,000 attendees and NYCC at about 100,000, comic books are now firmly rooted in the consciousness of the general population. The old media and new media coverage of these events is growing (San Diego was even shown on Bloomburg TV). As the idea of collecting comic books reaches more and more people through all of these outlets, our hobby continues to grow and is today accepted as one of the top collectibles.

Will we as a hobby or industry capitalize on this time in the sun? That remains to be seen. In the meantime, while we're thinking about the market as it may be in the future, let's concentrate on the market as it is right now.

2011 showed thousands of price changes reflected in this edition. The following market reports were submitted from some of our many advisors and are published here for your information. While the opinions in these reports belong to each contributor and do not necessarily reflect the views of the publisher or the staff of *The Overstreet Comic Book Price Guide* or Gemstone Publishing, they will provide important insights into the thinking of many key players in the marketplace.

See you next year!

Bob

Robert M. Overstreet
Publisher

Artist's Editions

One of the interesting additions to the comic book market this past year also has some potentially strong implications for the already vibrant original comic art market. IDW Publishing's *Artist's Edition* books feature the complete black and white line art for stories which are scanned in full color so that blue pencil marks, paste-up components, editorial components in the margins, other corrections, and aging are all evident. The pages are reproduced at their original size, making for some big books (and very big in the case of the Wally Wood editions). They're hardcovers with relatively small print runs.

As we're working on this edition of the *Guide*, IDW has thus far released *Dave Stevens' The Rocketeer: Artist's Edition* (one version), *Walter Simonson's The Mighty Thor: Artist's Edition* (three versions – the standard featuring the cover art from *Thor* #337, a San Diego con variant featuring the cover art from *Thor* #338, and a blank cover edition featuring hand drawn Thor or Beta Ray Bill sketches by Simonson, which came in its own slipcase), *John Romita's Amazing Spider-Man* (two versions – a standard one and variant version with self-portrait cover of Romita and many of his characters. The limited version has signatures by both Romita and Stan Lee, and original drawings by Romita), and *Wally Wood's EC Stories: Artist's Edition* (three versions – a standard one, a variant cover edition of 100 copies featuring a self-portrait by Wood, and a second printing edition with a new cover, which we have not seen yet as I write this).

These are scheduled to be followed by *Will Eisner's The Spirit: Artist's Edition* and *David Mazzucchelli's Daredevil: Born Again – Artist's Edition* (which will have regular and signed, limited versions). As one would expect with success, at least one other publisher has announced a similar project.

We'll see if the strong prices (up to 3x cover, with cover $100 or higher) paid for some of these volumes stand up over time, particularly in the face of the second printing on the *Wally Wood* book. They are uniformly selling above their offering prices. Given what's been happening with select original art, perhaps these products we timed perfectly.

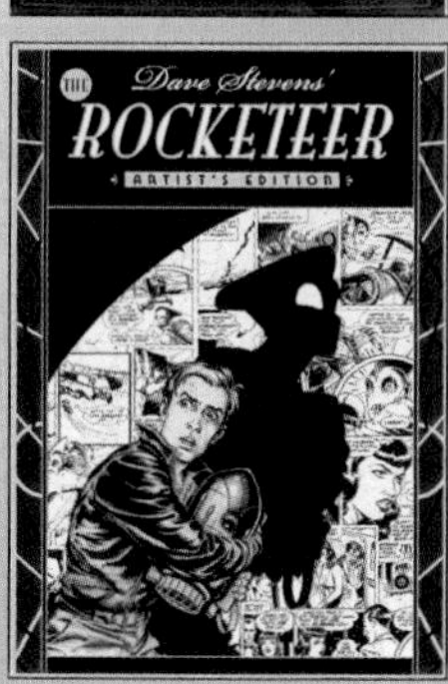

Regardless, we'll keep an eye on them..

OVERSTREET COVER SUBJECTS
FIRST APPEARANCES

CATWOMAN
BATMAN #1 SPRING 1940
2012 NM- PRICE: $350,000

OVERSTREET COMIC BOOK PRICE GUIDE
1ST EDITION - 1970
2012 NM- PRICE: $1825

THOR
JOURNEY INTO MYSTERY #83
AUGUST 1962
2012 NM- PRICE: $40,000

THE VISION
THE AVENGERS #57
OCTOBER 1968
2012 NM- PRICE: $425

IRON MAN
TALES OF SUSPENSE #39
MARCH 1963
2012 NM- PRICE: $32,000

CAPTAIN AMERICA
CAPTAIN AMERICA COMICS #1
MARCH 1941
2012 NM- PRICE: $275,000

GOLIATH
THE AVENGERS #28
MAY 1966
2012 NM- PRICE: $160

BLACK PANTHER
FANTASTIC FOUR #52
JULY 1966
2012 NM- PRICE: $700

HAWKEYE
TALES OF SUSPENSE #57
SEPTEMBER 1964
2012 NM- PRICE: $1400

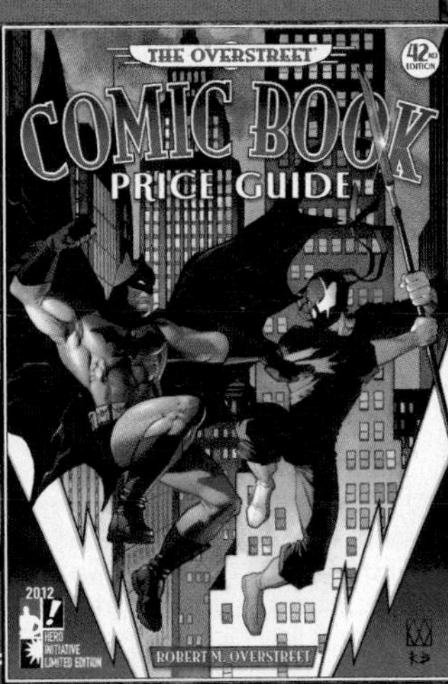

BATMAN
DETECTIVE COMICS #27
MAY 1939
2012 NM- PRICE: $1,350,000

GRENDEL
PRIMER #2
1982
2012 NM- PRICE: $160

PRICES: 1970 vs. TODAY

Action Comics #1
First appearance of Superman
1970 Mint Price: $300
2012 NM– Price: $1,750,000

All-American Comics #16
First appearance of Green Lantern
1970 Mint Price: $50
2012 NM– Price: $480,000

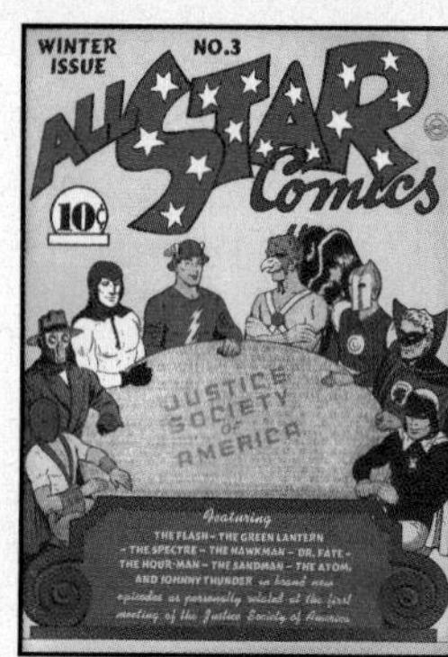

All Star Comics #3
First Justice Society of America
1970 Mint Price: $135
2012 NM– Price: $95,000

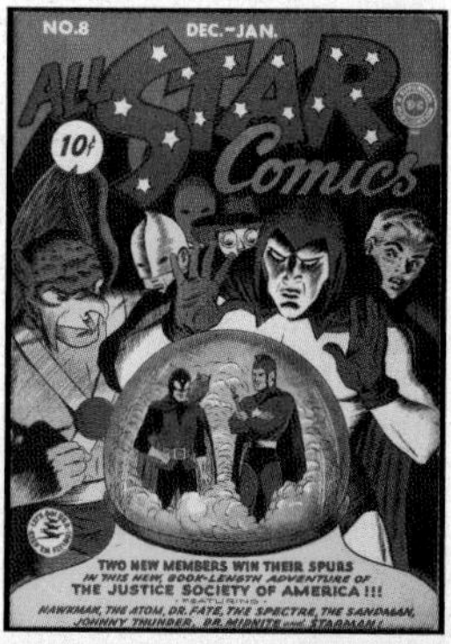

All Star Comics #8
First appearance of Womder Woman
1970 Mint Price: $45
2012 NM– Price: $80,000

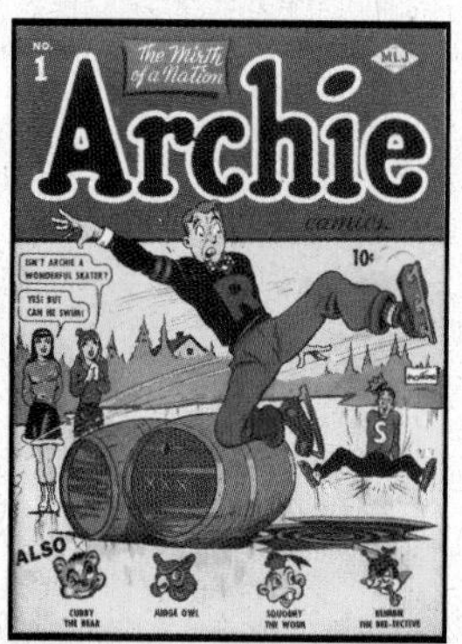

Archie Comics #1
First Teen-Age comic
1970 Mint Price: $10
2012 NM– Price: $90,000

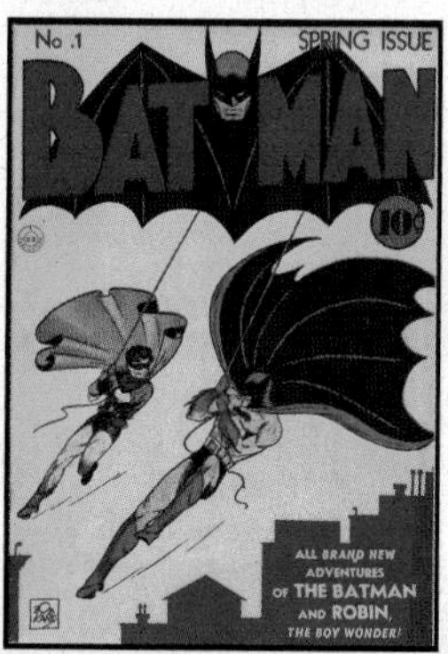

Batman #1
Debut of the Joker and Catwoman
1970 Mint Price: $175
2012 NM– Price: $350,000

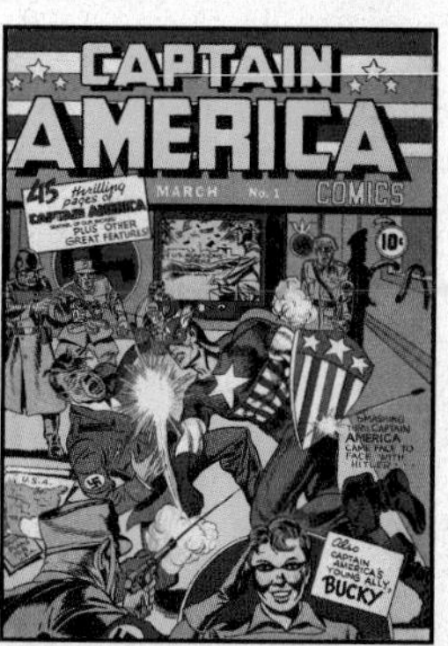

Captain America Comics #1
First appearance of Captain America
1970 Mint Price: $150
2012 NM– Price: $275,000

Crypt of Terror #17
First of the EC New Trend issues
1970 Mint Price: $30
2012 NM– Price: $5,200

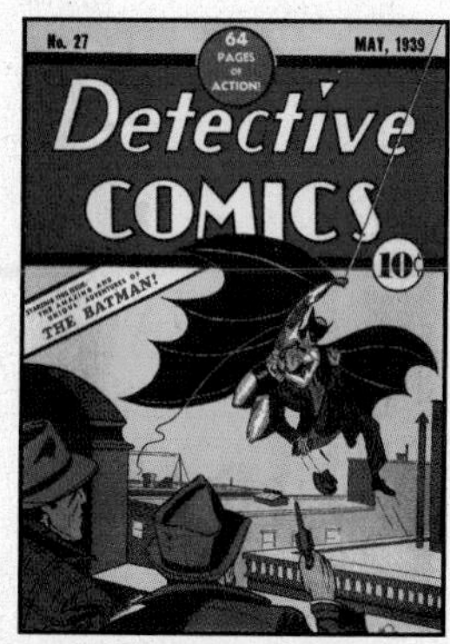

Detective Comics #27
First appearance of Batman
1970 Mint Price: $275
2012 NM– Price: $1,350,000

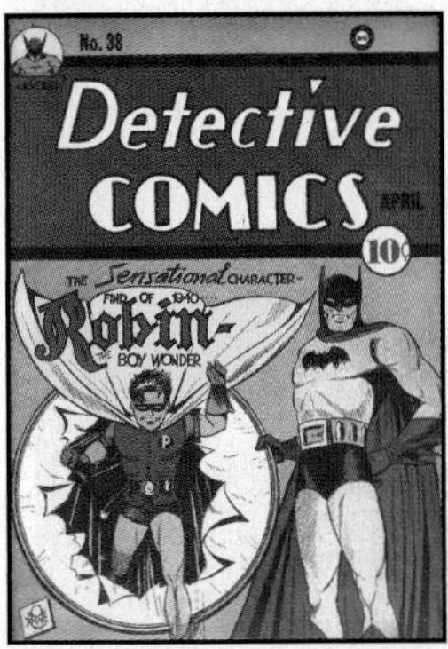

Detective Comics #38

First appearance of Robin
1970 Mint Price: $60
2012 NM– Price: $90,000

Flash Comics #1

Debut of the Flash and Hawkman
1970 Mint Price: $125
2012 NM– Price: $165,000

Marvel Comics #1

First Sub-Mariner and Human Torch
1970 Mint Price: $250
2012 NM– Price: $475,000

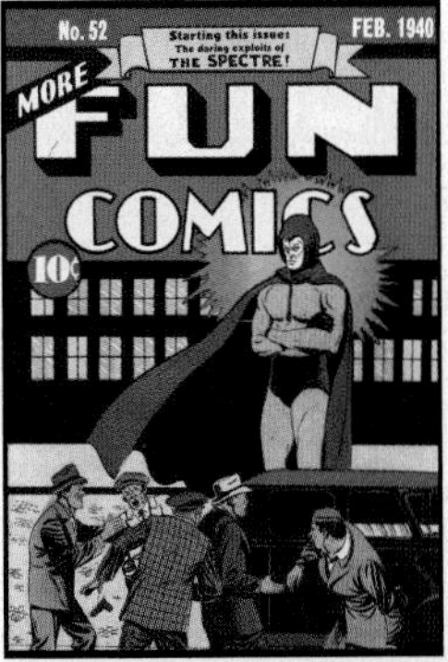

More Fun Comics #52

First appearance of The Spectre
1970 Mint Price: $100
2012 NM– Price: $150,000

More Fun Comics #56

First cover appearance of Dr. Fate
1970 Mint Price: $40
2012 NM– Price: $16,000

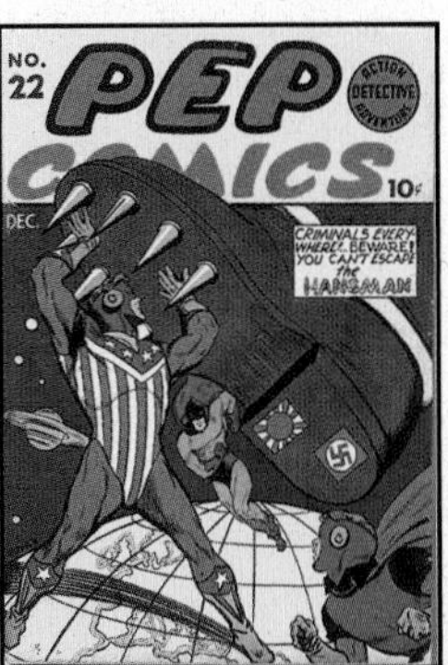

Pep Comics #22

First appearance of Archie
1970 Mint Price: $10
2012 NM– Price: $110,000

Superman #1

Superman's origin
1970 Mint Price: $250
2012 NM– Price: $650,000

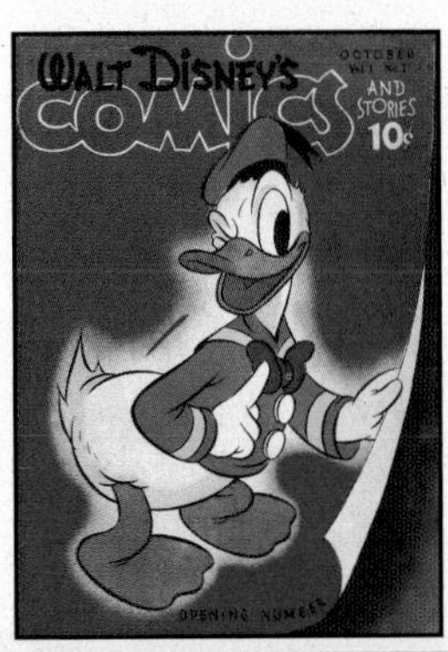

Walt Disney's Comics & Stories #1

Donald Duck, Mickey Mouse reprints
1970 Mint Price: $115
2012 NM– Price: $44,000

Whiz Comics #2 (#1)

First appearance of Captain Marvel
1970 Mint Price: $235
2012 NM– Price: $110,000

PRICES: 1970 vs. TODAY

Amazing Fantasy #15
First appearance of Spider-Man
1970 Mint Price: $16
2012 NM– Price: $150,000

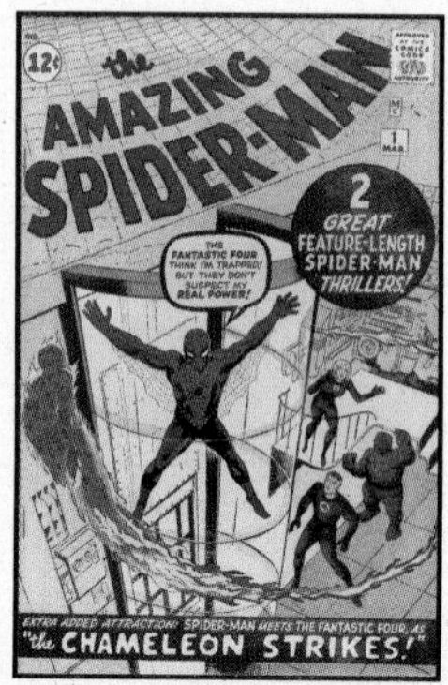

Amazing Spider-Man #1
Spider-Man's 2nd appearance
1970 Mint Price: $16
2012 NM– Price: $57,000

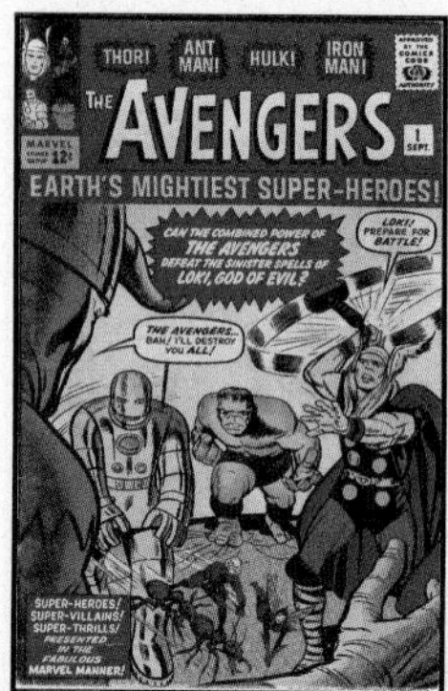

The Avengers #1
First appearance of the Avengers
1970 Mint Price: $6
2012 NM– Price: $25,000

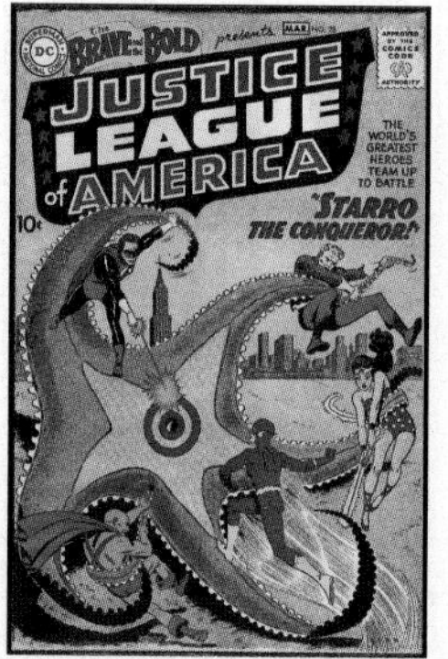

Brave and the Bold #28
First Justice League of America
1970 Mint Price: $5
2012 NM– Price: $23,000

Captain America #100
1st Silver Age Cap in his own title
1970 Mint Price: $1
2012 NM– Price: $675

Conan the Barbarian #1
Comic book debut of Conan
1970 Mint Price: 15¢
2012 NM– Price: $485

Fantastic Four #1
First appearance of the Fantastic Four
1970 Mint Price: $12
2012 NM– Price: $90,000

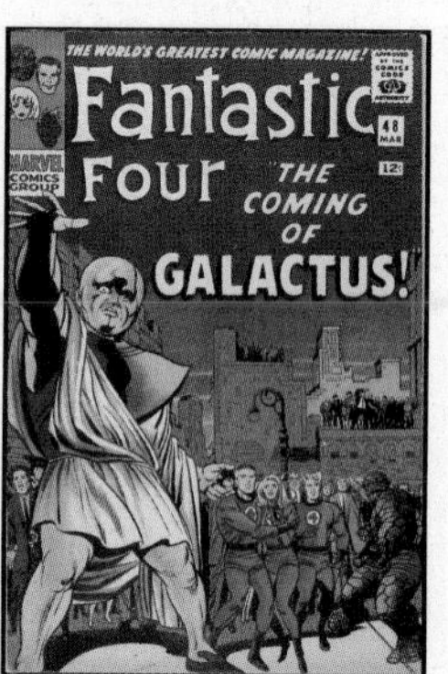

Fantastic Four #48
Debuts of Silver Surfer & Galactus
1970 Mint Price: $1
2012 NM– Price: $1,500

Green Lantern #76
O'Neil/Adams issues begin
1970 Mint Price: 65¢
2012 NM– Price: $2,600

Incredible Hulk #1

First appearance of the Hulk
1970 Mint Price: $14
2012 NM– Price: $90,000

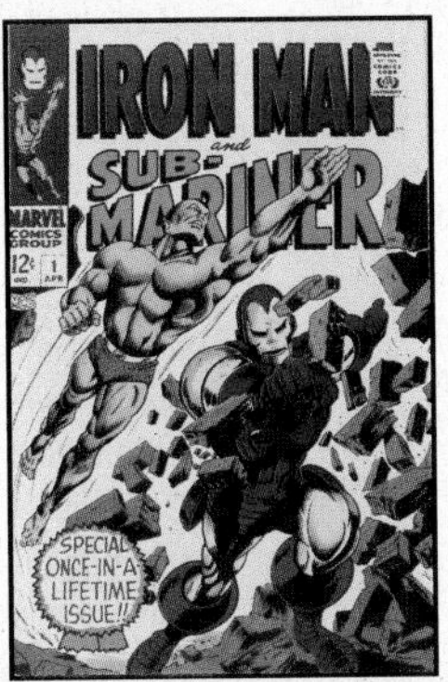

Iron Man & Sub-Mariner #1

Prelude to new #1 issues
1970 Mint Price: $1.15
2012 NM– Price: $325

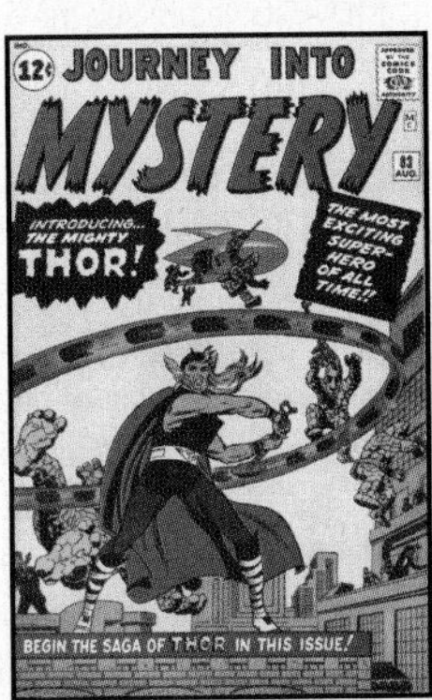

Journey Into Mystery #83

First appearance of Thor
1970 Mint Price: $10
2012 NM– Price: $40,000

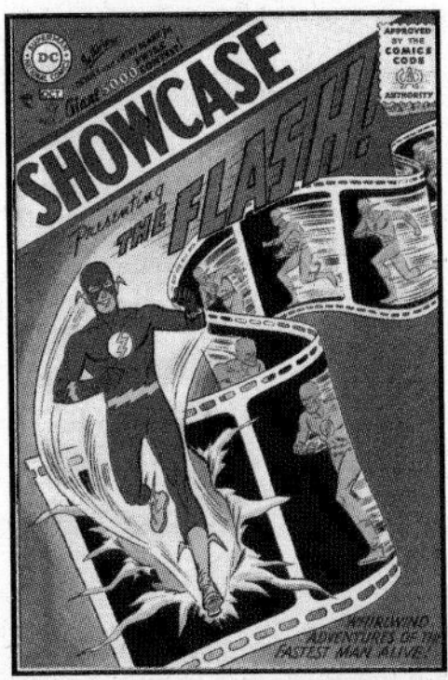

Showcase #4

First appearance of Silver Age Flash
1970 Mint Price: $12
2012 NM– Price: $60,000

Showcase #22

First Silver Age Green Lantern
1970 Mint Price: $6
2012 NM– Price: $24,000

Strange Tales #110

First appearance of Dr. Strange
1970 Mint Price: $3
2012 NM– Price: $4,800

Tales of Suspense #39

First appearance of Iron Man
1970 Mint Price: $6
2012 NM– Price: $32,000

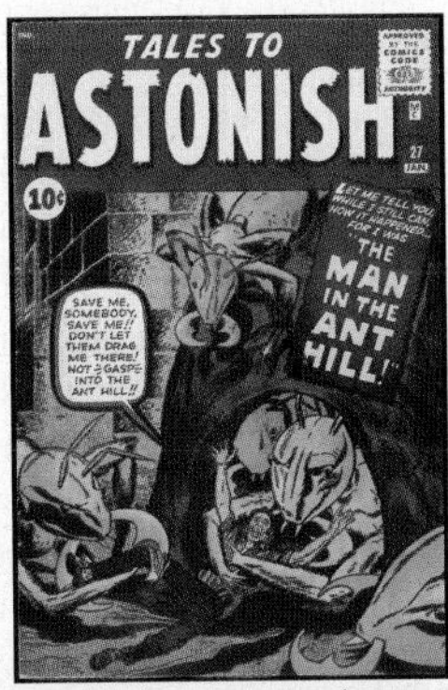

Tales to Astonish #27

First appearance of Ant-Man
1970 Mint Price: $12
2012 NM– Price: $20,000

X-Men #1

First appearance of the X-Men
1970 Mint Price: $6
2012 NM– Price: $35,000

Grant Adey
Fats Comics Australia

Some very exciting news for buying comics in Australia, 2011. I have started to see the first of eBay-bought collections arriving on the floor of my shop, high grade keys, CGCs, mid-grade Golden Age, pedigrees. What I have seen so far is very impressive. Most Australian comic book Internet collectors took to eBay in 2001 like ducks to water, and for the first time high grade U.S. comic books were being auctioned off by the droves. With plenty of talk rooms/forums to inform collectors on what to buy, the Internet buyer was well informed. It was an emerging market in the U.S. where anybody who had a computer could sell comics. The results here are nothing short of amazing.

For one reason or another, comic collections don't always remain in the hands of the collector. Also for one reason or another, the owner decides for a quick tasty sale on the lot here and now. More boxes of comics end up on my shop floor rather than eBayed. The other shops on the East Coast of Australia dumped vintage comics for the assurance of guaranteed sales of new issues rather than the unknown monthly figures of back issues. The last couple of months have been a bonanza for the Silver Age collectors who shop in my store. All of those U.S. "chuck 'em out" auctions from 2001 - 2008 have been a blessing. For the first time in 10 years, I have been able to compete with U.S. stores on price, and quality, sometimes better.

Here are some sale prices: *Action Comics* #1 Poor book-wormed $7000 (the *Action* #1 was a deal I brokered from one collector to another, neither asked for my advice, nor was it given), *Detective* #27 coverless $2500, *Amazing Fantasy* #15 (3 copies) all GD+ $2500 ea, *Amazing Spider-Man* #1 (3 copies) GD/VG $1500, *Mickey Mouse Magazine* #1 Good $800, *Avengers* #1 CGC 6.5 $1600, *Avengers* #1 CGC 1.5 $500, *Avengers* #2 FN $650, *Fantastic Four* #12 CGC 5.0 $300, *ASM* #4 VG $400, *Incredible Hulk* #2 to #6 GD+/VG $1200, *Incredible Hulk* #181 CGC 9.2 $1500 & 181 Fine $250, *Conan* #1 to 10 VF $300, *Strange Tales* #101 VG/FN $150, *Green Lantern* #1 VG $200, *Giant-Size X-Men* #1 FN/VF $350, *X-Men* #94 FN/VF $180, *Sub-Mariner* #1 FN/VF $200.

The tyranny of distance also played a role in what Australian collectors bought, and importation freight charges have always dictated that it's better to buy small and good rather than a big pile of ordinary stuff, locally called tipsy run. Along with every comic collection comes the associated trinkets, also bought along with comics are: Vintage Cereal rings, Syroco figures, toys and original art. I bought Bernie Wrightson's 4 water color covers for the cult with receipt from Bernie, a Dick Ayres *Strange Tales* page, a Jerry Robinson Joker sketch signed, a Kirby Captain America splash page, I'm handling things here that were never seen outside the USA.

Selling Comics: Australia is a very unique market, some books get way over the odds while other gems flounder. For example *Amazing Spider-Man* #300 I get $300 lucky if it lasts a week on the shelf, *Batman The Killing Joke* 1st print $100, *Transformers* '88 #1-4 set VF $85, *Predator* anything #1-4 $35, *Aliens* #1-4 set $35, Gold Keys double *Guide*, TV comics e.g., *Buffy* photo covers $20, *Angel* $15, *Battlestar Galactica* $15, *Wolverine* #1 '88 $100. I don't sell new issues so "new" meaning last 10 years or so. New comic sales are a value for money thing, I build sets from the collections I buy. If #9 is that month's hot book I don't care, there it is #1 to 10 $15 take em all. I have ended $1 comics. Shop rent, insurance and administration has put floor space at a premium and dollar boxes don't cut the mustard anymore. My used trade paperbacks at $15 to $20 fly out the door, priced same as a set of #1-4.

Selling, I tried some new approaches this year taking a trade booth at the Gold Coast Hot Rod Show, a 3-day indoor event at the Gold Coast Convention Centre. Booth cost was a reasonable $300, I must admit it did look a little odd with pop culture in a sea of chrome parts, but one thing hot rod owners have is wives and children with time and money. Sell out items were Charlton Hot Rod comics, Ed Roth books, how to draw books, Australian reprints of Matt Baker Romance comics, Movie comics, swinging '60/'70s comics with psychedelic covers, sold all Aragonés/Wolverton *Plop* comics, Horror, all these comics sold at $6 to $8 ea. Plus there was the associated toys, bobble heads, magazines etc.

It was a very successful weekend and it resulted in expanding shop customers. My shop has been in the one location since 1974, although I am the 4th owner, still I have reached local people who never gave comics a second thought. The marriage of convention to shop with website or eBay works well. I don't believe convention to Internet works, follow up sales for purely Internet sellers just doesn't happen, something gets lost. I think it's commitment to a product, let's face it, most websites that are selling comics today could change to ladies handbags and Tiffany lamps tomorrow and know one would really be surprised. The newspaper auction pages here are filled with "failed Internet business" ads. The bricks and mortar shop still holds lots of advantages over online businesses, in-house buying stock, in-house appraisals, insurance valuations, consignment with 1st owner insurance, warranty, money back or exchange, payment plan, trade up or down.

More on Selling Comics: This past year has seen some great things in comics, Marvel movies, TV's *Big Bang Theory* gaining more popularity, and closer to roots, record if not "science fiction" numbers being paid for comics at the big 2 auction houses. Vincent Zurzolo and the ComicConnect team has had many record sales of *Action* #1, chalked up 2 more pedigrees that is an enormous amount of work, plus a selling buying trip to Europe. I have sold comics at conventions on 3 continents, San Diego, London and home in Australia, and its tough traveling internationaly dealing with manifests forwarding freight C.O.s and customs specially in these uncertain times. Rick Milne from radio 4BC in Brisbane has invited me in for his talk back collectors show and I'm sure one of the topics will be *Action* #1.

I have invited Al Stoltz from Basement Comics to visit Australia next year, a simple 10 day meet and greet at all the major comic shops on the East Coast of Australia. Well known Phantom collector Pete Klaus from Baltimore visited us this August. It was great to see "Pistol Pete" talking comics and collecting, he is so passionate. The international network of comic retailers and collectors brings flavor and excitement to the industry. I would like to see a tightening up of comic retailers shops coming under certain big 2 brand names with a corporate uniform look and code of conduct. This is the next step for the industry.

A Little Bit of History: I spoke with Tony Albanese in Brisbane recently. Tony is one of the founding fathers of Australian comic book retailers. My question to him was why I couldn't find any early U.S. comics locally. His answer: During World War 2, all periodicals were no longer sold outside America. The stories were sold to Australia/England and reprinted in black & white. In Australia no imports were looked at until 1959, the first few available were Harveys like Casper, Wendy etc., Atlas TTA #24, *Strange Tales* #88 and some Westerns, Dell Four Colour series, Charlton Super Suspense and some assorted issues. DC stories sold well in reprints and only new titles were to be imported: *Justice League*, *Green Lantern*, and some issues of their war titles. In 1963 Dell split the licensed properties like Tarzan and the Disneys to a new imprint called Gold Key and concentrated Dell to promote company owned new titles. For the next few years Australian publications still sold well but once Stan and Jack filled the racks with all Marvel comics in colour no more new Australian comics were produced. The first US editions in Australia, I found, were *Amazing Spider-Man* #2 and *Fantastic Four* #4 in 1962.

So with no imports of U.S comics from 1939 (Australia joined the war in Europe in 1939) to 1959, this explains the huge amount of American reprints and lack of finding U.S editions.

Australian Phantom/Disney/Crime Reprints: Australian Frew Phantom comics consist of U.S newspaper strips reprinted in B&W, starting in 1948. Golden Age Phantoms continue to rise in value, high grade gaining about 10-15% a year. Very stable gains. On the other hand, Disneys seem to be falling slowly, losing 15-20%. Best buys are the U.S Crime and Romance reprints. Pre-code Crime reprint comics can be bought at a fraction of the U.S. print cost, no censorship here. Most are identical copies with the exception of b&w interiors, colour covers all printed on newsprint paper. I have sold a *Venus* #1 reprint, brutal covers, marijuana stories, Matt Baker romance covers/stories, Mary Worth love stories, torture covers, gangsters in drag, etc., etc. And there are some shocking advertisements that take the back covers. Most Australian comic collectors just don't see what's wrong on these covers, or don't care, I dunno. But a 50 year old man leering behind a young dancer back stage is a little different in my opinion.

Some of the Australian '50s comics I was able to buy are stamped "foreign file copy". The collection was the finest array of Australian comics ever brought to auction, 1930s *Buck Rogers*, *Kit Carson Indian Fighter*, *Prince Valiant*, *Jungle Jim*, *Popeye*, *Crime and Punishment*, *Police File*, *Brenda Starr*, *Felix the Cat*, *Ripley's*, *Teenage Love*, *Taxi O'Hara*, *Mandrake*, *Ben Bolt*, *Don Winslow*, *Secret Agent X-9* to name a few of these incredibly rare gems. Australian print runs are microscopic, so a lot of the '30s and '40s comics are very likely to be the only ones known.

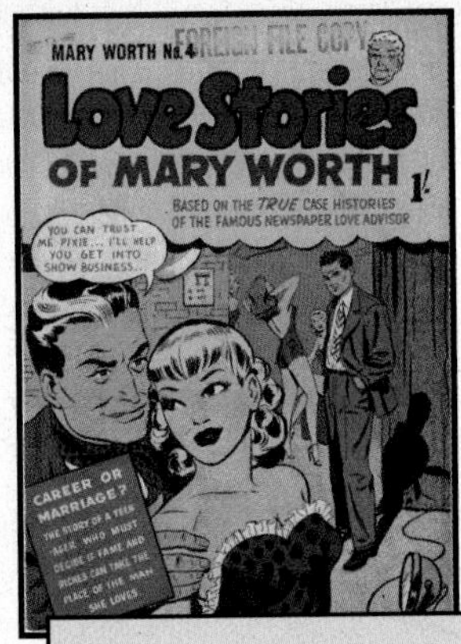

Foreign File Copies from the 1950s are incredibly rare reprint gems.

Comics printed in Australia during 1939 to 1945, the WWII years, are of the poorest quality paper and the b&w interiors change from black ink to blue to red (clearly a case of whatever a printer could lay his hands on at the time), none were stapled, just a glued spine and quite frequently the guillotine failed to cut leaving a folded comic uncut. I have found U.S. comics which have been bound into a 100 page giants by publishers, e.g. American Disneys with the covers torn off then 4 comics bound with a new wrapper saying *Donald Duck* bumper issue 1 shilling (10c). Same went for Westerns and Romance comics. Australian comics went to dollars and cents pricing in 1966.

Many thanks to Mike Clarke and Bruce (Rooster) Ellsworth for their help and support again this year, from the furthermost outpost this is Slim signing off till 2013.

Bill Alexander
Collector

Greetings from Central California. Well some good news for price variant collectors. It appears another 15¢ test market price variant has been discovered in the hobby. Dell's regular size comics that were published cover month dated 2/57-7/58 can be found with both 10¢ and 15¢ cover prices on them with the 15¢ editions being test market price variants that were test marketed regionally in the USA . Almost immediately after the 15c price variant test market period ended, Dell released another variant, a "10¢ Now" cover variant. The "10¢ Now" cover variant editions are found on Dell regular size comics cover month dated 9/58, 9-10/58 and 9-11/58. For example Dell's *Uncle Scrooge* #23 9-11/58, *Comic Album* #3 9-11/58 and *Walt Disney's Comics and Stories* #216 9/58 all exist as "10¢ Now" cover variants that I have seen.

I purchased in 2011 a *Pep Comics* #156 15¢ price variant (unslabbed) in VG+ for $95.00 about 7x *Guide*. Archie 15¢ price variants, still new to the hobby, are quite difficult to find, especially in mid to high grade and are mainly found in low grade VG or less when found as far as I can tell. One might note *Pep Comics* #153-159 15¢ price variants have all surfaced in the hobby and I believe all the Archie 15¢ price variants will in due time. I compiled a list of Dell 15¢ price variants seen below and hope it helps collectors out as to where to look for them. I hope everyone fills the holes in their collections.

Dell Comics 15¢ price variants 4/56, 2/57-9/58:
Andy Panda #37 through #42
Angel #9 through #14
Annie Oakley #11 through #16
Bambi #3 4/56 (Movie Classics)
Beetle Bailey #9 through #15
Ben Bowie and His Mountain Men #10 through #15
Bugs Bunny #53 through #61
Buffalo Bill Jr. #7 through #8
Cisco Kid #34 through #40
Cheyenne #4 through #7
Chip N Dale #9 through #14
Comic Album #1 through #2
Daffy #9 through #14
Dell Junior Treasury #8 though #9
Donald Duck #52 through #60
Flying A's Range Rider #17 through #22
Four Color #765 through #922
Fritz Ritz #56 through #58
Gene Autry and Champion #114 through #119
Gunsmoke #6 through #9
Henry #50 through #55
I Love Lucy #15 through #20
Indian Chief #26 through #31
Jace Pearson's Tales of the Texas Rangers #15 through #20
Jungle Jim #12 through #17
King of the Royal Mounted #24 through #28
Little Iodine #36 through #41
Lone Ranger #104 through #121
Lone Ranger's Companion Tonto #26 through #31
Lone Ranger's Horse Hi Yo Silver #22 through #27
Looney Tunes #184 through #201
M-G-M's Lassie #33 through #41
M-G-M's The Mouse Musketeers #8 through #13
M-G-M's Spike and Tyke #8 through #14
Marge's Little Lulu #104 through #121
Marge's Tubby #21 through #29
Mickey Mouse #52 through #60
Nancy #141 through #156
Popeye #40 through #45
Porky Pig #51 through #59
Queen of the West Dale Evans #15 through #20
Red Ryder Comics #150 through #151
Rex Allen #24 through #29
Rin Tin Tin and Rusty #18 through #25
Roy Rogers and Trigger #110 through #126
Scamp #5 through #6
Sergeant Preston of Yukon #22 through #27
Spin and Marty #5 through #6
Tarzan #89 through #106
Tip Top Comics #211 through #213
Tom and Jerry #151 through #168
Turok, Son of Stone #7 through #12
Tweety and Sylvester #16 through #21
Uncle Scrooge #17 through #22
Walt Disney's Comics and Stories #197 through #214
Walter Lantz New Funnies #240 through #257
Walter Lantz Woody Woodpecker #41 through #49
Zane Grey's Stories of the West #33 through #38

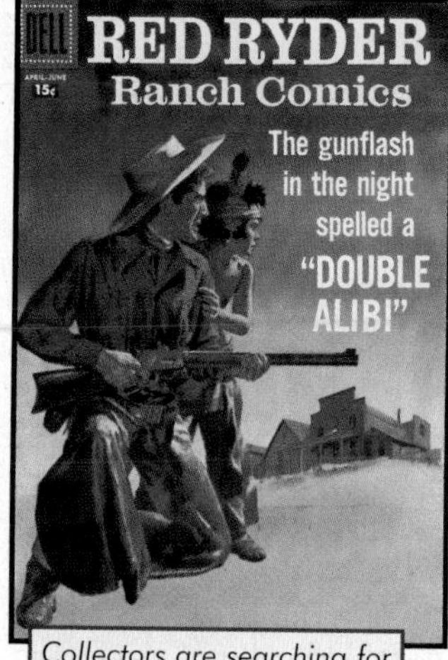

Collectors are searching for Dell 15¢ price variants like Red Ryder (Ranch Comics) #151.

David T. Alexander, Tyler Alexander and Eddie Wendt
DTACollectibles.com

While doing some research for one of our clients I had an occasion the reference past editions of *The Overstreet Comic Book Price Guide*. During an exhaustive study of the first 41 editions of the *Guide* one of our researchers pointed out the fact that among all the dealers that have placed ads in the *Guide* over the past 4 decades, no one has had ads in more editions than I have. I have had full page ads in every edition beginning with the second one that appeared in 1971. I would have placed an ad in the first edition but it seems that there was no solicitation of advertising for that issue. My earliest ads were directed towards mail order buyers and sellers and were generated from my office in Hollywood, CA. In 1973 I opened the American Comic Book Company, a retail store and mail order chain in Southern California, and ran ads under that name until my move back to Florida in 1989. We have always had one or two staff members as *Price Guide* advisors since the beginning.

I can fondly remember those early days of collecting and dealing with comic books before there was any reference material or historical documentation available to comic book fans. You had to physically get the material in your hands to track down origins, artist and character appearances, etc. To be able to dig out information from the long lost pages of the four color treasures that we still seek today just added to the thrill of the hunt. Early fanzines began to pick up speed in the early 1970s and were an important source of information and documentation for early comic book historians. Now there is a ton of information available about the history of comic books and collecting. Reprints of older comics give us all an opportunity to see the material first hand but there is still a lot of work to be done and ground to cover in documenting the phenomenon of collection.

In the past, collecting was looked down upon and considered to be "Americas Secret Hobby". With the advent of the internet and the proliferation of the comic book inspired movies, the hobby has become an acceptable part of mainstream America. With several comic books selling for million dollar prices, collectors now have to compete with investors.

The State Of The Market

We can sum this up by saying that 2011 had our biggest volume of sales, ever. Original owner collections popped up like never before. A few years ago we thought that virtually all the original owner collections had been unearthed. Fortunately our assumption was in error as we have had monsterous collections come in during the last 14 months. Two of the owners had just recently become aware that a collector's market existed. In both of these cases the original owners had amassed their collections during the 1940s and had gone on to other pursuits during the 1950s and beyond. Both lived in the North Eastern US and had large family homes where the collections stayed unmolested for decades. One of these fellows had moved back into the family home a couple decades earlier and had actually become a hoarder. His children had become concerned that he was headed for the TV program *Hoarders* and took on the task of cleaning the place up and in the process unearthed a shockingly valuable collection of comic books.

Considering these recent acquisitions I have come to realize that there are many more original owner collections that will come to the market in the next few years. As the population ages the folks who bought material as kids in the 1940s begin to expire and their heirs will be disposing of lots of valuable collector's items. Maybe those of us in Florida will finally have a geographic advantage as lots of old timers choose to spend their last days in the hospitable climate that our state offers. Actually one day after we submit this report we are headed to look at an original owner collection, the old timer has passed away and the heirs finally cleaned out the house and sold it. They were astute enough to gather all the collectibles and put them into a storage unit. They were visiting Florida and brought us several boxes of material, which proved to be excellent. Now that the weather has improved we will travel to their site and liberate the remainder of the collection.

Clearly the ongoing economic problems are a concern to all of us. When your house is worth only one half of what you owe on it you have a problem. When a lot of people are in this situation we all have a problem. The drag on real estate values has also put a strain on the values of some collectibles. This creates a unique economic triangle. Economic strain forces prices downward. As prices drop bargain hunters and bottom feeders thrive and compete for the available material. The increased competition drives prices upwards.

Even economic disasters cannot diminish the passion of the collector. The pride of ownership and the thrill of the hunt are not quenched by financial crisis. The intensity of the collector is a stronger force than an economic depression. Could it be that in hard times each acquisition is more precious? We have seen many record prices in the last year and this trend is not likely to stop and and will certainly improve with the economy. Expect price increases.

Golden Age And Other Comics Related Items

Timely: Pre-1955 comic books are still the backbone of the hobby. Relative to the number of books available the demand for vintage Timely comic books is without equal. Captain America is still the most popular Timely hero. Next in popularity come *Marvel Mystery*, *Human Torch* and *Sub-Mariner*. The multi-character titles are equally popular. Titles like *Daring Mystery*, *All-Winners*, *All Select*, *USA* and *Mystic* had short runs and seem that they could be collected as complete sets. This has not been the case as several of these issues are quite scarce and those collectors who have completed sets of any of these titles are to be congratulated. The fact that these multi-hero titles had many origins, first and single character appearances is only eclipsed by the fact that some of the top Golden Age artists worked on these books. Several have stories and covers by Joe Simon, Jack Kirby and Alex Schomburg in addition to editorial guidance from Stan Lee.

These books are regularly selling for 1-1/2 times listed *Guide* values and 2 or more times *Guide* value in higher grades. Certainly this is not breaking news to anyone, the important fact here is to recognize the consistent rate of appreciation that the Timely super-hero issues have had over the last four decades.

As the earlier issues get harder to find, the Timely collectors have taken a more serious approach to locating the Western, War, Romance and Funny Animal issues. Forty years ago very few people would have projected that *Super Rabbit* and *Annie Oakley* would be titles that are highly sought after in 2012. Ask yourself "how many copies of these titles have you seen at comic cons this year"?

DC Comics: Where would comic book collecting be today without DC Comics. They have had a major influence on the hobby, our culture and the world. Even terrorists in the remote areas of Afghanistan know who Batman, Superman and Wonder Woman are. Without a doubt DC Comics are the most collected of the Golden Age. The main titles are always in demand to the point that we often sell out of *Action*, *Detective*, *Batman* and *Superman* issues. We have recently seen increased want lists for *Flash*, *All-American*, *Sensation*, *Star-Spangled* and believe it or not, *Boy Commandos*.

The 1950s era DC issues with the best sell thru rate were the 5 major War titles. *Our Army At War* is the key series and seems rather low in *Guide* values resulting in many of the issues being snapped up at double *Guide* prices. The other War titles sold between full *Guide* and 1-1/2 x *Guide*. Key issues were the exception and many went for double *Guide*. In most cases prices drop for the 1966 and later issues. This time period drop does not apply to the DC Romance titles. Later issues have brought 3-5 x *Guide* values on a very consistent basis. One sleeper from DC is *Blackhawk*. This series began at the start of the Golden Age and was published originally by Quality Pubs. Although it started as a War title it morphed into a Sci-fi Super-hero series at about the time that most publishers were dropping the costumed characters. *Blackhawk* was continuously published when *Flash*, Hawkman, *Human Torch* and *Sub-Mariner* were being dropped in the late 1940s. As a War and Sci-fi title it fit in perfectly with the trends of the 1950s. The series enjoyed almost constant publication through 1984 and has had some mini-series and special issues hit the stands into the 1990s. This seems like the type of book that will always be available, but don't count on it. We have noticed a few investors quietly hoarding copies of this series.

The Silver Age DC keys are not cheap, but think what their values could be in 5 years. Investors are buying these now. They are also buying high grade DC digest titles.

Other Publishers: Among the fastest sellers are Fawcett and Fiction House. *Marvel Family* has been our best Fawcett title, we attribute this to multiple super-heroes appearing in a fairly low priced series. All the Fawcett Super-heroes are bargains when compared to DC and Timely. They are an acquired taste but we have seen a couple of convention investment buyers snapping up higher grade copies in the last 6 months of 2011.

Fiction House is still the top of the Good Girl Art publishers. Don't expect this to change and don't expect your local dealer to have copies in his inventory forever. The only *Planet Comics* we located all year long were ones that we took in trade from other dealers. They used to be easy to find. *Sheena* remains an American icon and everyone seems to love the issues that have girls stepping out of panels. We are not sure who started that concept, possibly it was Matt Baker.

Fox Comics: They are now the targets of many Good Girl Art collectors and still sell faster than they can be found. At some point every existing copy will be in the hands of collectors. How far are we away from that time? The early super-hero issues from Fox are fun to own and read. This inconsistent but entertaining publisher featured the Blue Beetle as their headline character. In the first issue of his title he had a different but similar costume in each of the 4 stories. The 1950s saw Fox trying to gain readers by producing comics with more adult themes such as *Phantom Lady*, *Rulah* and *All-Top*. Several Fox issues were cited in *Seduction Of The Innocent*, a book that attempted to show the deviant nature of comic books and their detrimental influence on children. Fox romance and crime titles were loaded with good artists and wild stories. All the Fox titles have had brisk sales and have brought at least full *Guide* values and in many cases they have sold for as high as double *Guide* for key issues.

Quality Comics: Strong sellers were the Blackhawk titles and early *Hit* and *National* issues. *Plastic Man*, *Spirit*, *Doll*man and *Kid Eternity* issues were consistent movers. Romance issues with Bill Ward art brought 1-1/2 x *Guide* with the other issues selling with little resistance at full *Guide*.

Archie Comics: These have been popular from the Golden Age to now. We see the $2.99 Archie Digests in the check out lines of the grocery store every week. Archies are the only comics that we ever see at the grocery store. What does that tell you?

We sell some of the Golden Age issues almost every week at full to 1-1/2 x *Guide*. Almost every time we offer them for sale we get several low-ball offers at 1/4 to 1/2 of the *Guide* prices. This must mean something.

St. John and Avon: These publishers produced lots of key issues. They are often overlooked because they did not have long runs of any of their series. The Matt Baker issues of the St. John Romance titles have been bringing 4,5 & 6 times *Guide*. Do you ever see them for sale at any conventions? Popular Avon issues have art by Wally Wood and Everett Raymond Kinstler. There were lots of Sci-fi, Romance and Crime issues that today are bargains at double *Guide* prices.

Pre-Code Horror Comics: These have made a comeback after a couple years of low demand activity. The more bizarre and lurid the issue, the more people want it. Prices are creeping up on these. I remember as a child seeing some of these issues on the newsstands and I was terrified. I never read one until I found a few EC comics around 1956. I have been collecting them ever since and it seems that a lot of collectors are in competition with me for the few issues that become available.

EC Comics: Although there are a multitude of reprint editions, the original comic books still have a loyal following of serious collectors. As one of them told me, "there is nothing like holding the original book and feeling the coarse newsprint paper with the slightly musty old book store odor". Reading the original satisfies the senses like no reprint ever can. We had several hundred original EC comics in stock in the past, now we have several hands full. Yes, we need more of them.

Silver Age Comics: Marvel titles are in heavy demand. The great thing is that all conditions sell well. *Amazing Spider-Man* is by far the most popular title of all time and is like money in the bank. *Fantastic Four*, *X-Men*, *Iron Man* and *Avengers* are extremely popular.

Batman far outpaces the other DC characters and Superman and Wonder Woman are also in high demand. Remember, these characters enjoyed continuous publication throughout the 1950s when all the other super-heroes had ceased to exist.

Warren Publications and Other Magazine Format Comics: *Vampirella* and *Mad* had both been in a slump in 2010 but had terrific rebounds in 2011. I'm not sure why they had a down year in 2010, maybe we did not do enough to promote them. *Creepy* and *Eerie* were again popular with back issue collectors. *Famous Monsters of Filmland*, which is not actually a comic book, is still the flagship Warren title and should be listed in the *Guide* since so many comic book collectors also cherish this title.

Eerie Publications remaned strong sellers. Their violent covers and stories appeal to collectors of the unusual and bizarre. Their key titles were *Witches Tales*, *Terror Tales*, *Weird* and *Horror Tales*. It is interesting to note that their titles were almost all swipes of previously used titles and their earliest issues reprinted Ajax/Farrell pre-code horror comics. These titles were created in 1966 as a reaction to the repressive Comics Code and there a lot of collectors for them. Many issues sell in the double *Guide* range and are hard to locate in higher grades.

Pulp Magazines: The super-hero pulps had a deep decline in popularity during 2011. We cut prices on many issues and still had trouble moving them. The Detective and Crime pulps were on fire and Science Fiction pulps could be considered hot items. As write this our shipping department is packing several thousand dollars in pulp orders. They are all sci-fi and Detective issues. As of early 2012 we had had a few orders for *Shadow*, *Doc Savage*, *The Spider* and *Operator* #5 pulps. We anticipate that the turn around for the super-hero pulps is underway.

Acquisitions: One year ago we did a market report stating that we would wholesale product rather than taking on additional storage space. We have received so many collections during the year that we have been forced to reverse our strategy and we are now receiving contractor proposals for enlargement of our current structures. We have several collections to pick up in early 2012 and need space for processing. Accordingly we have had to increase our staff and expand our management team. We did get a huge influx of inventory from a long time dealer who finally retired and placed his entire inventory and collection for sale with us. We will probably be offering this material over the next several years as we have only been able to move a small part of the comics to our location. As in the past we did a large volume of our business off of want lists, however internet sales still top all other areas.

Conventions: After several years of not setting up at any conventions our management team adopted an intensive convention schedule beginning in late 2011. If you see us at any of the future conventions please stop by our booth and introduce yourself, we are always interested in meeting other collectors. One hidden gem for convention attendees is the Tampa Bay Comic Con. I have nothing to do with this except as an exhibitor but I want to spread the word to collectors that this is one of the best local type cons for older comics in the U.S. It has recently had a new management team step in and expand it to a multi-day show. Many dealers from as far away as Canada have been setting up at this show and the variety of older books for sale is shocking compared to many similar size shows. If you have a chance to attend the Tampa Con you will not be disappointed.

In Appreciation: We want to take this opportunity to give a word of thanks to the Edgar Rice Burroughs and Frank Frazetta families. We have been through some tragedies and triumphs together and we just want to say "keep up the good work".

Dave Anderson, DDS
Collector

2011 was a very exciting year in the comic collecting world. Several new collections surfaced and nearly anything in high grade sold for well above *Guide* prices, and in many cases, for record prices. Despite the bad economy, there is no reason why this trend cannot continue. It is important to recognize however, that the huge sales that get all of the attention are very unique, exceptional books and those that have bought them paid those prices because they felt they may not soon get the opportunity to buy them again. The majority of the books sold throughout the year are not of that caliber and sell for much closer to *Guide* prices.

Mainline titles of recognizable characters sell for *Guide* or slightly above, second tier titles sell for 20-30% below *Guide* due to less demand, and very common low interest titles sell for 50% or less of *Guide* values especially if in lower grades.

Bob Overstreet has done a nice job over the years in making the *Guide* prices reflect the majority of the market and then reporting the record sales in his market report rather than have *Guide* values reflect the record sales.

Stephen Barrington
with Ronnie Hayes
Flea Market Comics

In 2011 the biggest news was DC's "New 52". And big it was with all of the #1 issues going into second or more printings. We underestimated the impact of this radical idea but DC kept us well supplied with additional copies. The entire concept was unprecedented.

Even after the first few issues of each title, sales have been very good for DC comics. Whole new groups of readers and collectors have been coming into our shop; including younger ones. The new interest in the Justice League, Batman titles and Superman titles have been tremendous. The $2.99 issues (plus a few $3.99 ones) have been very popular with the readers.

Marvel, however, has not been able to match the success of DC. For the most part, Marvel sales have been flat and even declining with too many X-titles glutting the market. Marvel needs a new and imaginative approach, like DC, to put

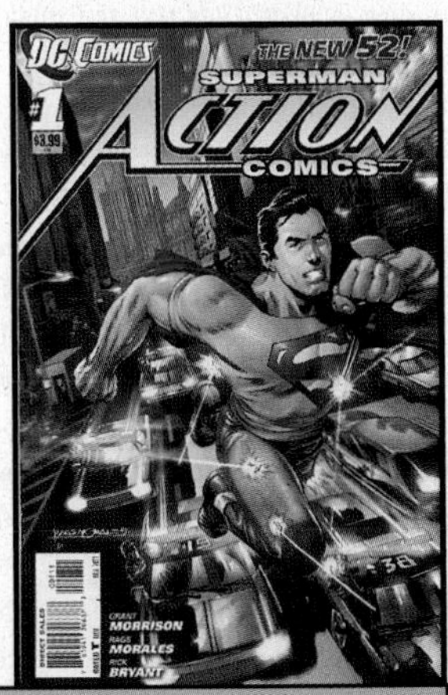

DC's "New 52" was a big hit with **Action Comics #1** and other issues going into multiple printings.

some life into its line of comics. Marvel's *Amazing Spider-Man*, Avengers line and main two X-Men comics are selling well but it seems future growth in these titles will be limited.

With the exception of *The Walking Dead*, we order very few Image comics. There is no demand for them, including *Spawn*. The Zenescope Entertainment Grimm Fairy Tales titles sell well especially with the variant covers that are offered. On a more adult theme, Broadsword's *Tarot, Witch of the Black Rose* is an incredible back issue seller. They are impossible to keep in stock.

Dark Horse doesn't do well but the quality of its comics is good. The lone exception is *Buffy, The Vampire Slayer*. This has a strong cult following. Our best sellers for IDW are the Godzilla titles. We were caught off guard when sales jumped quite a bit after their introduction.

Trade paperbacks and hardcover comics are difficult to sell. We only take special orders on these. Most comics published over the past 30 years are hard to sell with most winding up in the 25-cent or dollar boxes. The 25-cent section is red hot and sometimes hard to keep filled.

Silver Age Marvel keys do well when priced right. Issues such as *Tales of Suspense* #39, #52 (1st Black Widow) and #57 (1st Hawkeye) don't last long in the shop. Sales of early *Fantastic Four* are nearly comatose. The exceptions are the first appearance of Black Panther (#52) and issues 48-49-50 (Galactus-Silver Surfer). Miscellaneous *Tales To Astonish* and *Tales Of Suspense* just languish in the shop. *The Incredible Hulk* isn't much better with most collectors only looking for #181 (1st Wolverine).

X-Men from the 1960s are very hard to move; even in nice shape. The exception to this is #1. With *Avengers*, the most sought after are #1 and #4 (Captain America). *Amazing Spider-Man* key issues have slowed down quite a bit with most being out of our customers' price range.

Even 1960's *Batman* and *Detective* comics have experienced a slow-down. Issues from the 1970s do well, however. *Superman*, *World's Finest* and related titles (*Lois Lane*, *Jimmy Olsen* and *Superboy*) do OK marginally.

The high unemployment rate in our area has forced many collectors to sell their collections to us. Unfortunately, almost all the comics brought in are from the '80s on up and these we sell very cheaply. We did get an exceptional Silver Age collection (mostly Marvels) and the key issues sold very quickly. The collection totaled over 10,000 issues.

Sales of Golden Age and CGC comics are for the most part dead or on life support. Everyone wants a bargain on these titles but that's not going to happen on key issues. Sales of humor comics (Disney, Warner Bros., numerous other companies) from the 1940s and 1950s, are practically nonexistent. We had a large group of Carl Barks *Donald Duck* Four Colors from these eras but managed only to get 20 to 25 percent of *Guide* for them (we were glad to get it too!).

Ebay is a vast wasteland with most sellers not knowing what they are doing or expecting premium prices for their items. In some cases, though, eBay can be a buyers' paradise with established sellers. Heritage Auctions offers good deals from time to time with My Comic Shop.com and Metropolis Comics being in the exceptional range.

Wizard World Chicago (2011) saw a sharp drop in the number of comic book dealers from 2010. There were few bargains to be found. Metropolis, Graham Crackers and Harley Yee were the mainstays. Also, there were many copies of *Amazing Fantasy* #15, *Tales Of Suspense* #39 and *Tales To Astonish* #27 glutting the dealer room. Overall the convention was very well attended.

Sales of the 2011 *Overstreet Price Guide* were very strong and probably the best ever for us. We expect the 2012 edition sales to be even stronger.

Prices That Should Go Up: *Detective Comics* #359 (1st Barbara Gordon Batgirl, 1/67) has been a very hot item. Early *Lois Lane* issues and *Superboy* in top condition.

Prices That Should Go Down: All Dell titles, humor and otherwise, are vastly bloated and very hard to sell. Marvel's *Conan* (early issues) DON'T SELL! Anything past #24 goes in the 25-cent box. *X-Men* #5-115. The reprint issues (67-93) especially. 1960s *Adventure* and *World's Finest* comics. *Fantastic Four* #8-47, 51-on up; *Captain America* #101-up. *Journey Into Mystery/Thor* #101-on up. *Tales of Suspense* #40-49, 59-99; *Tales To Astonish* #35-on up. *Incredible Hulk* #103-179, 183-on up. All *Showcase* and *Green Lantern* #8-75; *The Atom* (All), and all Adam Strange *Mystery In Space*.

Sales: *Journey Into Mystery* #83 (Good-) $700. *Amazing Spider-Man* #3 (fair) $150; #4 (GD/VG) $300. *Tales of Suspense* #39 (VG-) $1100.

L. E. Becker
WARP 9 Comics

2012 already? The year has flown by quickly with record sales of Silver Age comics (*Amazing Fantasy* #15...$1.1 Million!!), publishers scrambling to raise their print runs, Big box stores starting to carry direct market product, and the ever "dangling threat" of digital comics. Hmmm...you know, looking at these three topics, I just realized...they were ALL items of interest that I had talked about for the last THREE years within Overstreet's market report. So what's next?

DC Comics: The New 52 Relaunch...Things must have been REALLY desperate at the WB office for them to even OK this. A desperate gamble that paid off...kinda. The first issues of almost all of the new DCs sold out for us. I say "almost" as a few of the titles were heavily ordered for the variants, or as we knew that a few would be great back issue sellers. Some no-brainers such as *Justice League* #1 sold out at our competitors instantly. We were getting phone calls from shops in OTHER STATES to supply them. A book by Geoff Johns AND Jim Lee, and many of the retailers I talked to didn't even bump their normal orders by at least 25%? After market prices have stabilized since #3 was released, but it still commands a $10.00 price The bigger *Justice League* #1 surprise was the 2nd printing fiasco. Everyone's orders were cut by 68%! So a smaller shop who ordered say 10 copies, only received a maximum of 3! Slap on a variant cover, and it's the second coming of *Batman* #608 second print! Right now we get an easy $20.00 for this one, but I can see this printing shoot as high as $50.00 in the next year or so when supply dries up more.

Other DC 52 titles that are selling well are *Batman* (due to Scott Snyder & Greg Capullo), *Action Comics*, *Detective Comics*, *Batgirl*, *Justice League Dark*, and *Aquaman*. The 2 surprise hits, however, are *Animal Man* and *Swamp Thing*! Written by Jeff Lemire and Scott Snyder, respectively, both of these titles have been exceptionally strong sellers, even outselling certain key Marvel titles. Of course, with the good comes the bad, as *Blue Beetle*, *Men of War*, *Static Shock*, and *Green Lantern Corps* are way under performing.

Talking to a few retailers, I was told by a few that many did not order crazy numbers (even though many of the 52 titles had future returnability, which we took full advantage of), because of the new digital release program. Many of my peers felt that there would be no need to order multiple copies due to same-day digital release. I am going to say the same thing as I said before about digital format vs. print format: as long as comics are perceived as a collectible, the print format is NEVER going to die. The digital target audience is for the casual or lapsed reader. The collector will ALWAYS buy the print format. Will that change years from now when the cost of print becomes so high that every publisher will begin producing on a digital format? Perhaps. But as of now, the print format (according to Dan Didio, EIC of DC Comics) outsells digital at 64,000,000 copies to 1,000,000 (or 64:1). Digital is a great format, true, but it still has a long way to go to catch up, or even surpass the print format. In my opinion, I don't think I will see it in MY lifetime (my grandkids might).

Marvel death issues like **Ultimate Spider-Man** *#160 were a great seller.*

Besides the new 52, DC has a minor hit on their hands with the various computer/gaming comics. Online sales of such titles as *God of War*, *Assassins Creed*, and *Batman Arkham City* are well beyond cover price for complete sets. For example, a full set of *Assassins Creed: The Fall* went for $40.00 and *Arkham City* has closed for about the same. I should reiterate however, that these sales are through the internet (ie: eBay). In the store, sales are non-existent.

Vertigo needs a shot in the arm. There are not many new projects coming out that are getting people excited. *Spaceman* did well, however the new main stays such as *Unwritten*, *Sweet Tooth*, and *I Zombie*, have fallen off, selling at the single digits. The one trend I am seeing with Vertigo titles (I have said before), is that the TPBs sell better than the normal issues. *Scalped* sells 10 copies within the store, however, we sell almost double that in the trades.

Marvel Comics: *Fear Itself*, although a very good story, fell kinda flat in its sales. The constant crossovers did NOTHING to help sales, and perhaps, arguably, hurt sales of the regular titles, as the trade dress for the series crossover, made each title look like it was a mini-series and NOT an issue of the regular on-going. For example, *Avengers* normally sells for us an average of 75 copies. Once the Fear Itself trade dress was placed though, sales dropped by 8-15%. Many regular customers missed an issue of the normal book because it looked like part of a mini-series.

Marvel had a few re-launches this year also, like DC. *Captain America*, *Daredevil*, *Uncanny X-Men*, *Wolverine and the X-Men*, and *Incredible Hulk*. All sold very well (of course the accompanied variant cover didn't hurt either). The biggest surprise however, was *Ultimate Comics Ultimate Spider-Man*! We heard MANY grumblings from our customers. "A ethnically different Spider-Man? How absurd/stupid/racist (that one I didn't understand)". "This title will be cancelled within 6 months!" Does NO ONE remember *Spider-Man 2099*? Long story short...a HUGE shot in the arm for the Ultimate series! Sales have almost doubled. #1s are all over the place, however, #2 commands $10.00, and #3 about $8.00.

Ultimate Spider-Man #160 and *Fantastic Four* #587, both death issues of Spider-Man and the Human Torch respectively, were also great sellers, although many fans did not/do not believe those characters will stay dead (SPOILER! *Fantastic Four* #600 came out...with a newly resurrected Human Torch...go figure).

Independents: Image leads the way again with such titles as *Severed*, and *The Vault*. Dark Horse's *Mass Effect* comics are still doing well (see the previous remarks about DC's video game lines), but the relaunch of Buffy and friends... well...they just ran out of steam. IDW actually had some great books that have sold well such as *Godzilla: King of Monsters* (which had a retailer variant that we participated in), *Next Men*, *True Blood*, and the biggest surprise of all, *TEENAGE MUTANT NINJA TURTLES*! Nice to see that the classics (and YES, I do believe that 1984 WAS a classic time for certain comics) are still sought after.

Jim Berry
Collector

Thank you to Mr. Overstreet and the staff at Gemstone for giving me the opportunity to share my observations and for continuing to publish the bible of comic collecting. One of the joys of spring is knowing that a new *Guide* is just around the corner.

I'm a collector and dealer in the Northwest, Seattle and Portland mainly, with about 25 years experience. I sell comics on eBay (As jb233 – always buying!) and, generally speaking, I have few gripes. I find it to be a fair marketplace and one that has allowed me to grow my personal collection and shift my inventory in a way I couldn't have imagined 15 years ago. Certainly, it would be great if the fees were less (we are the 99% after all) but, given the service, I can't really find the voice to object.

This year, I sold over 10,000 comics, working for one special client in my region who owns a massive collection. Our top books included summer sales on an *Action Comics* #24 in CGC 8.5 that sold for $4400, an *X-Men* #1 in CGC 4.0 for $1690, *Journey Into Mystery* #83 in CGC 3.5 for $1725, *Incredible Hulk* #181 in CGC 9.0 for $1325 and many nice CGC comics including 5 copies of *Marvel Premiere* #1, all in CGC 9.2 that went for between $66 - $116.

As I write this, Nic Cage's *Action Comics* #1 in CGC 9.0 has just become the champion money comic of all time. Can you believe it? Someone paid over two million dollars for a comic book. We've come very far, very fast and there is no end in sight for high-grade keys. It seems like all we hear about are records being broken by this or that auction house - and this highlights the most definitive trend in collecting old comics, the bifurcation of the hobby/business where slabbed, pedigreed "museum pieces" are bought and sold as serious investments versus . . . everything else.

While this observation is nothing new, I can confirm that while the big keys break records, the polar opposite end of the spectrum – the low-end books – continue a slight downward trend. Much of what I've sold this year consisted of 30-50 book lots, typically Bronze and Silver Age low-mid grade runs of titles from all publishers and genres but focusing mainly on your typical DC and Marvel super-heroes. Without exception, I saw a 10-20% price dip in mid-summer for these lots. Furthermore, the market for these books has not recovered despite an ever growing customer base, and a (knock-on-wood) perfect customer record with over 1800 feedbacks.

Last year I reported that Craigslist was a great avenue for collectors to pursue the hobby . . . Man, how quickly things change these days! Unfortunately, at least in my region, Craigslist is overrun with collectors and resellers who use apps and programs to alert them with instant messages whenever a comic listing is posted. This means that an iPhone message or email is instantly relayed when someone posts anything with 'comics' in the title. I've tried to keep up with this set of aggressive Craigslisters with little success. Where a few years ago, I routinely pulled great collections off of Craigslist, I now find that I am never (NEVER) the first to reply and typically the books are gone or going out the door. I've also noted that the quantity and quality of comics listed on Craigslist has dipped this year. Oh, well. It was fun while it lasted.

The highlight of the year for me was a private sale at a local comic shop, Excalibur Comics of Portland, owned and operated by Peter and Debbie Fagnant. Peter opened Excalibur in Portland in 1974 and he's kept his doors open for 37 consecutive years, focusing, primarily, on comic books.

In October, Peter invited me to a special sale on the very next evening after the shop was closed. I showed up to find twelve other collectors and dealers waiting as Peter carefully laid out around 700 comics in small stacks corresponding with titles. Then, when everything was set, he turned us loose. This collection of mostly high-grade comics, focusing on Good Girl Art from the 1942-48, with nearly all Fiction House and Quality titles represented, probably should have been submitted to CGC as a pedigree collection. In my 25 years of comic hunting, I've never seen a collection quite like it. Runs of *Phantom Lady*, *Blue Beetle*, *Planet*, *Hit*, *National* as well as complete runs of *Torchy*, *Seven Seas*, and all of the Fox jungle books – many in devastatingly high grade. I'm certain the only place I'll ever see more Matt Baker and Lou Fine covers in one place is my *Gerber* guides . . . It was quite a night! And made even more amazing because these books were nearly thrown away by the original owner's elderly wife but saved from the trash heap by a neighbor that suggested they call the local comic store. Thanks again Peter and Debbie.

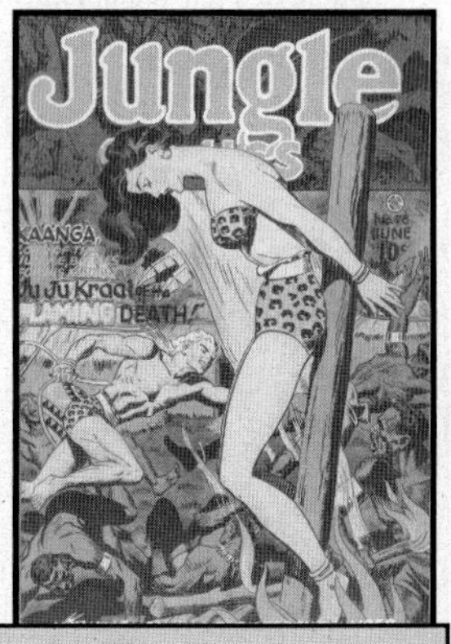

*Collectors still savor the Good Girl Art from Fiction House and Quality. (**Jungle Tales** #78 shown)*

Speaking of old collections, if you have an interest in the history of the pedigree collections, you owe it to yourself to click on over to Steven Ritter and Matt Nelson's site, (www.comicpedigrees.com.) There, they've painstakingly detailed the top comic collections ever found. Literally hours of great reading on this site and highly enjoyable. Thanks guys.

To further investigate the frequent fluctuations of recently sold books, check out the Stock Exchange column at the *Bleeding Cool* website (www.bleedingcool.com). This column – and the site in general – are highly recommended for news on comics and they frequently track the sales of old books in up-to-the minute articles.

Good hunting to all in 2012.

Steve Borock
Heritage Auctions

Before I talk about the market, I would like to thank Bob Overstreet for 42 years of greatness! Without Bob, the market would not be where it is today, happy and healthy. I would also like to give a shout out to J.C Vaughn and Mark Huesman for their hard work on the *Guide*. These fine folk never get the credit they deserve.

This year's market report can be summed up in just a few words: THE MARKET IS ON FIRE FOR THE RIGHT COMIC BOOKS AND COMIC ART! As I write this, we have just finished the current Heritage Signature Auction and it brought in almost nine million dollars! That blows away any auction in the history of our hobby and blows away the record that Heritage previously held before by about three million dollars, a new world record!!!

It has been three years since I left my position as President and Primary Grader at CGC and joined Heritage Auctions and I am still having a blast! The main reason is that I am able to go around the country helping collectors and many dealers of comics bring their collections to market and getting them the highest prices. In the last year, Heritage has brought most of the best material in our hobby to market, such as the Savannah Collection, the final pieces from the Edgar Church/Mile High collection, the Billy Wright collection, and many, many more, all realizing record prices.

Just a few Heritage world record prices from the most recent auction:
Action Comics #6 CGC 8.5 $34,655
Adventure Comics #320 CGC 9.8 $2,031
All-American Comics #16 CGC 8.0 $203,150
Batman #1 CGC 8.5 $274,850
Captain America Comics #3 CGC 9.2 $50,787
Daredevil Comics (Battles Hitler) #1 CGC 9.4 $38,837
Detective Comics #29 CGC 7.0 $83,650
Detective Comics #33 CGC 8.0 $92,612
Fantastic Four #4 CGC 9.6 $44,812
Fantastic Four #5 CGC 9.4 $65,725
Fantastic Four # 12 CGC 9.6 $65,725
Incredible Hulk #1 CGC 6.5 $11,950
Marvel Mystery Comics #40 CGC 9.0 $21,510
Star Trek (Gold Key) #1 CGC 9.6 $22,705
Tales of Suspense #69 CGC 9.6 $2,629
Tales to Astonish #50 CGC 9.8 $2,390
Wonder Woman #6 CGC 7.5 $5,975

Let's not forget the original art! Heritage has brought more amazing vintage original art to public auction in the last year than all the other auction houses combined. The prices realized have been through the roof! Three covers alone from the late, great Jerry Robinson's collection totaled almost half a million dollars!

As I mentioned before, the market is on fire for the right pieces. By "right pieces" I mean rare comics and high grade vintage comics (pre-1968), as well as classic original art. Will this trend last? I don't know, but I have been in our hobby since I was a kid and I have never seen more enthusiasm from collectors than I do at this point in time.

Much of what I will be writing next is some of the same things I have written in the past, but I think it is very important that I reiterate some of these points.

Modern comic books: I love them! I read at least one new comic a day and up to as many as ten. There is such great stuff being published, but like movies, TV shows, novels, and other entertainment, you still need to weed through the bad and mediocre to get to the good and the great. Now, about investing in Modern comics, I have to say: BE CAREFUL! If a comic book comes and you can't find it that week or that month, have some patience. If you are looking for a reading copy, most will be available as a collected trade within six months to a year. If you are looking to put a high grade copy in your collection, most of the time, when the "hype dies down, you will find it at a much lower price as well. I personally believe that most Modern comics will not be a good place to put your hard earned money as an investment. With a few exceptions, you are better off putting money into pre-1968 comic books.

Speaking of places to put your money....please check out The Hero Initiative (www.Heroinitiative.org). This is the one place where we can really help the people who bring and have brought us the many, many hours we have enjoyed with these wonderful comics. To quotes the website:
"The Hero Initiative is the first-ever federally chartered not-for-profit corporation dedicated strictly to helping comic book creators in need. Hero creates a financial safety net for yesterdays' creators who may need emergency medical aid, financial support for essentials of life, and an avenue back into paying work. Since its inception, The Hero Initiative (Formerly known as A.C.T.O.R., A Commitment To Our Roots) has had the good fortune to grant over $500,000 to over 50 comic book veterans who have paved the way for those in the industry today." This is fueled only by your contibutions. Remember: If you would accept help, you should give it as well, fair is fair. Let's hope most of us never need any financial help, but let's help those that do.

I will end my report they way I have for the last couple of years: Even though I believe in this market, there is no "free lunch". If you are going to invest in comics, you had better love what you buy. If the economy ever gets really bad, just like if you own stocks or precious metals, you will not be able to sell them for a really high price very quickly and you can certainly not use them to house or feed yourself or your family. The best advice I can give, and have been doing so for as long as I remember, is: "Buy what you love and can afford." It's really that simple. Enjoy collecting and reading comic books, enjoy the friendships we make in this wonderful hobby, look at and enjoy all the cool stuff around us, from original comic art to movies based on our favorite comics to comic book memorabilia, and it will all seem worthwhile in the end.

Thank you for taking the time to read this and
HAPPY COLLECTING! - Steve

Kevin Boyd
Director, Joe Shuster Awards

One highlight of the year for comics in general was DC's New 52 relaunch/reboot. First announced in the Spring and a reality in September, it seemed to both infuriate long-time readers but also caught the interest of lapsed readers - everyone wanted to know just what was happening to the DC Universe in general - causing a huge upswing of interest in DC Comics publications in September and October, and a lot of interest in the product at retail outlets and on the secondary market. As I write this, the books are cooling off, but there is no doubt that this attention-getting move improved the sales of many flagging titles such as *Justice League*, *Action Comics*, *Superman*, *Wonder Woman* and *The Flash*. Some number one issues were selling as high as $20. Demand definitely outstripped supply for a short time, but the heavy reprinting of the books will likely compromise any long-term collectability.

2011 was the year that most comics publishers embraced digital formats seriously. Unfortunately it was done without any visible strategy, but it is literally changing the business of comics, whether we like it or not. No publisher seems to quite know yet how to integrate the existing (yet declining) print markets with a complimentary digital strategy that doesn't throw out the direct market. My hope is that the highlight of 2012 is that someone comes up with a formula that integrates a proper multi-media roll-out strategy that wasn't ad hoc. Between digital publishing and intensive reprinting of back issues in various print formats such as hardcovers and trade paperbacks, we are in the midst of a period of immediate availability of almost all types of comics and comic strips. Basically if you are interested in reading it, it's probably available to you in some format.

Original Art collecting is still a fun and thriving aspect of our community. At events across the world every weekend it seems, fans are obtaining sketches, commissions and/or original published artwork from creators and a new breed of convention sketch artists has emerged.

I used to be the Director of CGC's Signature Series program, but work and changes to the program led to my stepping back and congratulations should go to the fine work of CGC's Signature Series Director Joe Pierson, who tirelessly works for fans and collectors at events big and small alike. The last couple of years we've seen tremendous growth and interest in sketch covers – comics printed with blank covers so that fans can get their favorite creators to draw on the cover for them, and there's been huge interest in getting these unique pieces of original art CGC graded. One quick visit to CGC's message boards will establish the preponderance and variety of sketch opportunities from artists of all kinds, professional and amateur alike.

What I see and hear from my friends and associates in the field is that there is still steady demand for quality Golden, Silver and Bronze Age comics. Record sales continue to be seen for key books in high grade, such as ComicConnect's recent sale of a CGC 9.0 *Action Comics* #1 for $2.16 million. Personally I seen a slight decline in the use of eBay for private sales, and a growing shift towards using alternate methods such as the CGC forums and the ComicArtFans website to sell original art and back issues, particularly CGC graded back issues, online. On a more prestigious level, auction houses such as Heritage, ComicConnect, and ComicLink continue to get record sale prices for key books and original comic art pieces.

As for comics in other media, the success of superhero movies does not seem to have that great of an effect on sales of new comics and back issues, however the massive success of the *Walking Dead* television show has created a lot of interest in the *Walking Dead* back issues.

I'm also here to wave the Canadian flag a little bit and promote the Canadian comics scene. Canadian creators were at the forefront of comics publishing on all fronts – webcomics, self-publishing, mainstream comics, comics for kids and alternative/artistic comics making this another banner year for Canadian creators. Some of the Canadian publishing highlights were: Chester Brown's *Paying for It*, Darwyn Cooke's *Parker: The Martini Edition*, Francis Manapul's *The Flash*, John-Paul Eid's *Le Fond de Trou*, Jeff Lemire's *Animal Man*, *Frankenstein* and *Sweet Tooth*, Stuart Immonen on Marvel's *Fear Itself*, Kate Beaton's *Hark! A Vagrant*, Michel Rabagliati's *Paul au Parc*, the amazing webcomics of people like Emily Carroll and Connor Willumsen, Jon Klassen's hilarious children's book *I Want My Hat Back*, Ramon Perez's adaptation of Jim Henson's *A Tale of Sand*, and the astounding collections of Hal Foster's *Prince Valiant* from Fantagraphics.

Canada has two official languages, and I'm happy to report a thriving French language comics scene based out of Quebec. There were dozens of high quality graphic albums published featuring the work of Quebecois creators like Michel Rabagliati, Jean-Paul Eid, Maryse Debuc and Marc Delafontaine, Guy Deslisle, François Miville-Deschênes, among others.

Certainly there is no better example of the diversification of the field than in the 2011 Joe Shuster Award winners, announced at the Calgary Comic & Entertainment Expo in June. Highlights include Francis Manapul (Outstanding Artist for *The Flash*), Fiona Staples (Outstanding Cover Artist for IDW's *Mystery Society* and others), Émilie Villeneuve (Outstanding Writer for the French language graphic novel *La Fille Invisible*), Tin Can Forest (Outstanding Cartoonist for graphic novel *Baba Yaga and the Wolf*), Koyama Press (Outstanding Publisher), Scott Chantler (Comics for Kids for his graphic novel *Three Thieves: Tower of Treasure*), Emily Carroll (Outstanding Webcomics Creator for *His Face All Red* and other stories), Montreal's Planète BD (Harry Kremer Retailer Award) and our Hall of Fame Inductees Todd McFarlane and Chester Brown.

We were saddened by the recent loss of two Golden Age creators and the Awards Association would like to thank Alvin Schwartz and particularly the ambassador of comics - Jerry Robinson for their contributions to comics and comics creators. Jerry was of great help to the organization when we launched the Joe Shuster Awards in 2004. Our condolences to their families and friends and to the generations of comics fans who mourn the loss of these great men.

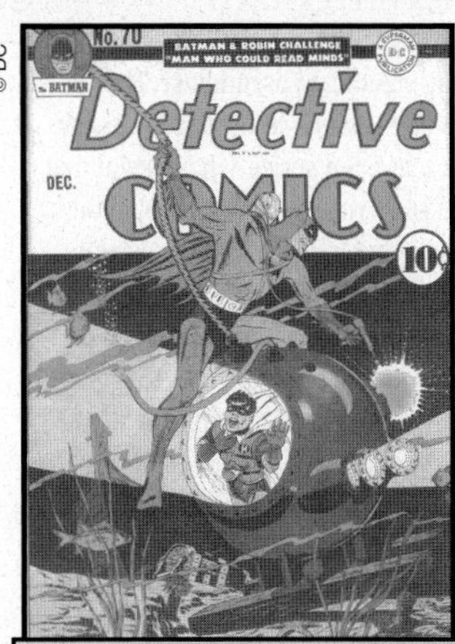

The comics world was saddened by the passing of Jerry Robinson. (His classic cover to **Detective Comics #70**)

Canadian comic events grew tremendously this year. The largest --- FanExpo Canada, continues as North America's third largest event (after San Diego and New York) with attendance above 80,000. Shows like the Calgary Comic & Entertainment Expo, The Montreal Comic-Con and the Central Canada Comic-Con (in Winnipeg) all saw major spikes in attendance and interest, and retailers at these events were fairly positive in their outlook on convention sales in general. Special mention should be made of the Toronto Comic Arts Festival and the Festival de la bande dessinée francophone de Québec (FBDFQ), two unique events which display the strengths of Canada's indie/artistic comics community and French language comics scene respectively. Finally, special mention should be made to the growing zine community that gathers regularly for events such as Canzine in Toronto and Vancouver, and Expozine in Montreal. The next generations of comics creators are cutting their teeth on zines and webcomics, and there are a lot of great comics being published.

I get the sense that we are on the verge of some major changes to the comics industry, so it will be interesting to see what will happen in 2012.

John Chruscinski
TropicComics.com

It's been another impressive year for comics and collectibles. We have all seen constant record prices for rare keys like *Action Comics* #1 and *Detective Comics* #27 in all grades. The news media has continued to follow these mega-sales and these have and will create new interest in the hobby. If it's rare and quality it continues to sell well and typically for strong prices. Lesser grade books with weaker demand continue to sell when priced fairly and discounted.

While Tropic Comics primarily deals in comics and related comic and entertainment collectibles we also deal in many historical items and collectibles in other fields including general Americana. It's been a solid year overall, even though the economy is not where it was a few years ago... The recovery continues and so does the passion for collecting and investing in comics and collectibles.

We can't say enough good things about CGC certified comics and the continued positive sales that third party independent grading has brought to the comic hobby. We are still in the early years in regards to certification when compared to coins or baseball cards. We are seeing a lot of success in Bronze Age and later certified comics. Collectors are buying these books to complete their runs or add to their registry collections. While some comics and titles in these eras have seen corrections when compared to prices several years ago there are numerous hidden gems that sell for real money compared to their non-certified counterparts.

This year will no doubt be a banner year for comic book movies with *The Avengers* and *The Dark Knight Rises* hitting theaters. We've seen solid interest in related titles and issues of these comics. Collectors are longing to finally see the Avengers assemble in May. It is a great time to be a comic fan!

Brock Dickinson
Collector

In last year's *Overstreet Comic Book Price Guide,* Ken Dyber of Cloud Nine Comics suggested that "I hope *Overstreet* will consider expanding the number of new advisors that have a good amount of knowledge of Copper – Present books, as these are the largest percentage of books bought/sold in the marketplace, yet, least represented by advisor reports in the *Guide*." Hopefully, this is an area where I'll be able to contribute some useful content.

Speculating on Modern comics has had a bad rap since the crash of the 1990s. And in some sense that's justified – if we all collect only those things that we personally love to read, rather than things we hope might become valuable, our hobby will likely be better off in the long run. However, that doesn't mean that the laws of supply and demand, the vagaries of the distribution system and the rising popularity of individual characters or creators won't still drive price increases, even in Modern comics!

I'll be focusing this report on the period from the late Bronze Age (say, about 1977 or 1978) through to the Modern period. There's actually been quite a bit of action in this area over the past year, and signs of more to come. Perhaps the key trend is a search for scarcity – anything that collectors believe to be rare or scarce (both relative terms in this context, of course) seems to be attracting significant interest. Here's a few ways this trend is playing itself out:

Small Press Successes: Over the past few years, we've seen a number of small or independent titles reach huge audiences. *Teenage Mutant Ninja Turtles* (with their multimedia presence) or *Bone* (with more than 7 million books in print) are classic examples. Often these titles have small initial print runs, and once they become hits, there's no way that supply can keep up with demand. The past year has continued to see strong growth on the original *Teenage Mutant Ninja Turtles*, with prices on #1 reaching the stratosphere, and #2-6 rising rapidly. *Bone* #1 also commands significant prices – but there are other titles also fitting this pattern:

Acme Novelty Library #1 ($50), #2-4 ($30 each)
Albedo #2 ($800 for the first Usagi Yojimbo appearance)
Caliber Presents #1 ($40 for the first Crow appearance)
Comic Primer #2 ($80 for the first Grendel), #5 ($40 for the first Maxx)
Creatures of the Id #1 ($30 for the first Madman)
Cursed Pirate Girl #1 ($80), #2 ($120), #3 ($30)
Dime Press #4 ($100 for the first Hellboy appearance)
Grendel 1983 series #1 ($100)
John's Byrne's Next Men #21 ($40 for early Hellboy)
Love and Rockets original black and white cover #1 ($250)
San Diego Comic-Con Comics #2 ($100 for early Hellboy)
30 Days of Night #1 ($80)

Last Issues: Perceptions of scarcity also drive this trend in the market, with many collectors believing these issues to be scarcer than other issues in a run. While this may or may not be true, it has caused demand for many issues to soar. Copper Age final issues of many War and Horror titles (like *Sgt. Rock* #422, *Weird War Tales* #124 and *House of Mystery* #321) are difficult books to find in strict high grade, while some titles (such as *Silver Surfer* #146) do seem to be scarcer. However, many final issues of popular 1990s titles (like *Captain America* #454, *Incredible Hulk* #474 and *Thor* #502) still had significant print runs, and supply is such that they command only a small premium. Some final issues of Marvel's Star imprint are seeing price increases, with *Masters of the Universe* #13 ($30) leading the way. The key issues in this area are probably *Conan* #275 ($40), Creepy #146 ($60), *G.I. Joe* #155 ($80), *Promethea* #32 ($15), *Savage Sword of Conan* #235 ($15), *Star Wars* #107 ($50), *Transformers* #80 ($80) and Vampirella #113 ($300).

Reprints: While most reprints tend not to be particularly collectable, the increasing interest in "scarcity" is driving some reprints to higher prices. The 2nd printings for *Batman* #608 and #612 often reach $40, and the 2nd printing of *Superman/Batman* #8 goes for $12; these prices are all much higher than for 1st printings. More pronounced examples of this activity are seen in issues like *Silver Surfer* #50 (3rd printing) which can reach $10 as its 1st printing counterpart collects dust in the dollar bin. *Incredible Hulk #377* (3rd printing) appears to be quite scarce, with copies often surpassing $50. Later printings of *Batman Adventures: Mad Love* will often fetch $30 or more, meaning they are priced roughly the same as copies of the 1st printing. *Wolverine* (3rd series) #66 2nd printings can reach $20.

"Scarce" Issues – Some issues are seen by collectors as scarce due to distribution issues, which can drive prices up. Examples currently heating up the market include recalled issues like the *Elektra* #3 nude variant ($30) and *All-Star Batman and Robin* #10 ($15), as well as the pulped *Elseworlds 80-Page Giant* #1 ($200). Of greater interest, though, are widely collected titles where past print runs are not sufficient to meet collector demand. This is most evident on *The Walking Dead* from Image Comics, where #1 is now a $600 book, followed closely by #2 at $350, with later printings also commanding significant premiums. The growing popularity of this title – and a boost this past year from its development as a television series – has meant that supply is inadequate to meet increasing demand. Numbers 3 through 10 are also skyrocketing in price, but this year's breakout book has been #19, the first appearance of the tough-as-nails character Michonne; this now routinely reaches $100. Walking Dead #63 (featuring the first appearance of *Chew* as a flipbook) also commands about $20. Other long-running books that have gone through "dry spells" are seeing similar (though certainly less pronounced) price hikes. *Amazing Spider-Man* remains one of Marvel's top sellers, but only a decade or so ago, this was not the case, and the relatively lower print runs of some issues are driving prices up; numbers 403, 410, 416, 430-432, 434, 435 and 437-439 and numbers 19 and 21-29 from its renumbered period are all commanding premiums. *Uncle Scrooge* comics continue to attract attention, especially the scarce Gladstone run from 1996; number 310 is a $120 book, while 309 and 311-318 all command significant premiums.

Variants: Variants are a source of constant debate among collectors of Modern comics. While they are less common than "regular" issues, there is a growing sense that this manufactured scarcity is somehow counterproductive to the hobby, or even destructive. To be fair, most variants have limited collectability. They may see an initial price spike before settling down to normal prices. Every now and then, though, something captures the imagination and takes off. The *Maxx* #3 black variant, of which less than 15 copies are thought to exist, is said to be worth $1,000 or more, though sales to back this claim up are lacking. The legendary *Miracleman* 2-D #1 (with some 100 copies released by Eclipse comics to readers with vision problems preventing them from seeing 3-D images) is the basis of many Holy Grail-style searches throughout fandom. With only a handful of known copies still in existence, this book in strict high grade could also break the $1,000 mark quite easily. But most variants – even those produced as 1 in 200 editions – are much more common, with more reasonable prices. Among those that seem to be developing some staying power in the market are the DC Whitman variants (especially tougher issues like *Sgt. Rock* and *Warlord*), *Amazing Spider-Man* #400 with a white cover ($75), #408 ($100) and #678 ($140), IDW's *Teenage Mutant Ninja Turtles* #1 variants (of which there are many!) and the *Adventures of Superman* #500 platinum edition ($50).

Image #1s: Following on the huge price increases in *Walking Dead* #1, Image Comics found a way to make the lightning strike again with *Chew* #1 ($200) and *Morning Glories* #1 ($40). This – and the generally high quality of story in many of its new launches – has prompted a speculator run on many first issues of new Image series. This has spurred repeated sell-outs of Image titles, and although prices are not stable, it is likely that some of these titles will see higher prices in the future as demand outstrips supply. Among the titles falling into this category are *Skull Kickers*, *27*, *Nonplayer*, *Prophet*, *Fatale*, and *Thief of Thieves*.

There were some other big stories in the past year in this Cooper to Modern segment of the market, though perhaps not so directly linked to perceptions of scarcity. These include:

Heroines: The 1950s gave us Good Girl Art, and the 1990s brought us Bad Girls – but comics featuring female leads were increasingly hot this year. Aspen's *Lady Mechanika* led the way, with price increases on #0 ($60), #1 ($40) and #2 ($8), while Zenescope's *Grimm Fairy Tales* continued to rise – issue #1 now commands $60 or more. Basement Comics *Cavewoman* is also in demand. Over at DC, *The Brave and the Bold* #33 (starring Wonder Woman, Zatanna and Batgirl) sells for $25 or more (as a prelude of sorts to *Batman: The Killing Joke*), as do *Batman: Harley Quinn* and *Batman Adventures #12* (with an early Harley Quinn appearance). The Brian Bolland covers on *Wonder Woman* #s 63 to 100 are heating up, with the iconic cover on #72 commanding $20. For Marvel, the first appearance of the Black Cat in *Amazing Spider-Man* #194 ($60)continues to be strong, while her more recent appearances in *Amazing Spider-Man* #606 and #607 are bot fetching $8-$10. Cover art by J. Scott Campbell is helping drive those latter two issues, and is also pushing up the variant cover of *Amazing Spider-Man Presents: Black Cat* #1 (prices vary widely, but average about $50). Variants are often key in this sector, where current interest levels are even heating up older variants on previously cold 1990s titles, including *Danger Girl* variants. And over at Archie, the early Cheryl Blossom appearances are through the roof – *Archie's Girls Betty and Veronica* #320 goes for $150 or more, while *Jughead* #325 (Cheryl's 2nd appearance) is almost as strong.

Television Tie-Ins – Fans of cult television have descended upon the back issue market, looking for fixes of their favourite television series. Hot comics in this area include *Futurama* #1 at $20 (with other issues heating up as well), *Simpsons/Futurama Crossover Crisis* #1 and #2 at $10 each, and *Jericho* (both the IDW and Devil's Due series) at about $10 each. Boom's *Adventure Time* #1 looks to be poised for similar success, with early sell-outs.

© Spencer & Eisma

Like *The Walking Dead*, Image Comics made lightning strike again with *Morning Glories*. (#1 shown)

Finally, here's a quick rundown of a few other Late Bronze and Copper to Modern issues that seem to be generating some activity in the current market: *Amazing Spider-Man* #252, 298, 300, 361; *Animal Man* (New 52) #1; *Batman* #357 & 497; *Batman: Vengeance of Bane* #1; *Birds of Prey* #8; *DC Comics Presents* #26, 27 & Annual 3; *DC Special* #29; *DC Special Series* – all issues except the Swamp Thing reprints; *Dead @ 17* #1; *Deadpool* #54, 55, 69; *Fables* #1; *Hack Slash* #1; *Harbinger* #1; *House of Mystery* #290; *Iron Man* #282; *New Mutants* #98; *New Teen Titans* #s 2, 10; *NYX* #3; *Powers* (first series) #1; *Spectacular Spider-Man* #64; *Uncanny X-Force* #4; *X-Men* #266 and *Y: The Last Man* #1.

Sales in this end of the market may not generate the excitement of a $2 million *Action Comics* #1, but the vast majority of collectors are active in the Modern market. While we all look to avoid the kind of speculator-driven bubbles of the past, its arguable that more quality material is being produced by more publishers in more genres than at any other time in the history of our hobby. With the relatively low print runs of Modern comics, the search for great reading and great art will continue to create situations in which demand outstrips supply – and in which the Modern market produces its own key books, hot titles and record-setting sales.

Gary Dolgoff
Gary Dolgoff Comics

2011 - The Year of the "Outbidding-Purchases":
I am pleased to say, that despite being known worldwide as a "strict grader" of comics, I was able to come out on top bidding on and winning a major collection, plus getting another major "score" because of other relevant buying factors. Details to follow...

2011 Buying Experience (From Winter to Winter):
In January of 2011, a fellow from a "small and friendly" town in Colorado called me with quite a nice offering: over 5 pallets (around 150 boxes) of older comics featuring a near-complete Marvel run (*Amazing Spider-Man*, *Avengers*, *Fantastic Four*, *Journey into Mystery* #83-up, *X-Men* #1-up, etc.) plus DCs from the 1960s and up and "nice-shaped multiples" of mid-'70s to late 1980s comics.

He didn't want the "hassle" of tons of folks pouring through his beloved treasures; instead, he wanted one "right guy" for his collection. I replied, enthusiastically, "Well, I could be that person." A couple weeks later, I was bound for Montrose, Colorado. The seller mentioned that one buying outfit was too pushy and he didn't want to feel like he was being force-fed into a deal he may not have been comfortable with. An auction house that brags of "big, aggressive buying" wanted him to sell them only the early keys (*Fantastic Four* #1, *Amazing Spider-Man* #1, etc.).

This is known in the industry as "cherry-picking". I prefer to buy the entire collection myself. They told the seller, "Simply ship us the whole collection, then we'll make an offer." Being a smart seller, he preferred not to be "cherry-picked," so I come along and I spend many hours looking over his collection. What really helped was that he took several digital pictures of some of the more prominent comics, as well as some of his multiple Bronze and Copper comics. That, and my conversations with the seller, convinced me that he was serious to sell and realistic: he wasn't about to give away the collection, but he understood that (a) the value of his treasured comics depended on the conditions (grades) of the books, and (b) that I must make a profit in order to justify the purchase.

The seller and his wife were very nice folks, and their books were "nice" too. The Silver Age comics were in Good to Fine shape, and many of his "later books" (1975-1990) were in awesome (9.4-9.8) shape. His 1960s DCs varied from "so-so, to nice." Since I truly enjoy buying comics in all conditions, low-to-high, I could maximize what I could offer him for the collection, which was close to $100,000. We made the deal – I had a shipper pick-up the 5 pallets, and then I found that due to extreme Winter conditions, I'd be stranded for a couple of days.

Although I missed my wife, I took advantage of these couple of days off and visited (along with my assistant on this trip who had never been to the U.S.A. "Mountain West" states before) nearby points of interest, including the Black Canyon of the Gunnison (a true scenic wonder, to be sure), and a "jewel of a town", Ouray, Colorado, as well as frequenting daily the local coffee house in Montrose.

When the comics came in, I worked with my small but capable staff, to lay out and totally organize the collection. I have eight aisles of 8-foot high steel-shelves in my 4,800 sq. ft warehouse, wherein reside over 4,000 boxes of comic books, magazines, and some original art and pulps. But, I always enjoy buying more, so I make sure to have space for incoming goodies! (We also have a nice view of Mount Tom, a local mountain, from our windows.)

So, we sold the major Marvel titles as "runs of an issue" over the months… and then, the "real work" of the collection began. I've been going through boxes, looking for comics that are potentially "CGC-worthy" (in some cases – such as *Amazing Spider-Man*s in the #201-251 range, they must be a potential 9.8 to qualify. *Amazing Spider-Man* issues in that number range in 9.6 or less just don't sell for enough to make it worthwhile to CGC 'em (and I must admit I've gotten pretty good at determining which of them would most likely be graded 9.8, or only a "mere 9.6" or less.)

As of this writing, I still have about 60 boxes from the collection to look through, and hopefully, will get through them by the time you read this.

Another collection I bought, later in the year, had runs of many titles from the late '40s to the present (one of my favorites being a run of *Superman* #45-423). For this collection, I was willing to pay 50% more than another prominent dealer, who charges twice as much as me. How can this be? It's because I have a "Ready Clientele" of customers who know they can depend on grading and purchasing satisfaction from me, and I can work on a much smaller profit margin than do many other comic dealers. Plus, I enjoy having a "multi-decade supply" of comics for my customers' continuing satisfaction!

eBay: It has become a larger part of my selling than I care to admit to myself (though my regular "year-after-year" buyers, and the "newer-recruits" to making GDC purchases are still the mainstay of my business.) eBay, in many ways, is a hassle: and very time-consuming. With over 4,000 boxes in my warehouse, I so far have less than 5,000 comics on eBay! Those are "Worthy oldies" being offered, for sure, but still... We have a "boss" staff, that is overall quite computer and eBay-literate and works well with eBay customers. Still, the eBay overhead can be a bit much, but on the other hand, it does bring in additional satisfied buyers (we presently have a 100% eBay-satisfaction rating.) I'm hoping to finally have our newly-revised website (www.gdcomics.com) ready by the time you read this.

I'm proud to say that my warehouse is more organized than ever, thanks largely to my "crack crew." Most of my 50,000+ Silver Age and back, as well as many of my 200,000 (or-so) Bronze Age comics, are now in order, as are over a thousand boxes of mid-'80s through 2000s. I love to buy collections, dealers' stock, and other "Warehouses" of comics, "lock, stock, and barrel", resulting in the "sick" amount of comics that I own. I am proud to say as well that when I am offered an Inheritance collection. I truly do give them, and the collection (or dealers' stock) the respect that it, and they, deserve. I realize that many of these sellers are putting their financial fate in the buyers' hands, so I pride myself in doing the right thing for them. In addition to making things a bit better at this difficult time for them, it adds to the credibility and respect for our treasured hobby.

Golden Age: I still do great with these, on comics like Timelys (especially *Captain America Comics*!). I find myself comfortable paying close to *Guide*. I can often sell them, somewhat over *Guide,* and I do well with Poor to Good condition Timely comics, as well as higher grade ones.

DC Comics: Ahhh... early *Action* and *Detective* comics, I can get over *Guide* for, so of course I pay for 'em accordingly. Mid to late '40s Super-hero DCs, I get *Guide* for, and non-Superhero DCs (*Boy Commandos* to *Gangbusters*) have, in my experience, suffered in sales over the last couple of years, so I often discount these. I'll still buy them, but I must take the above into account when I do so.

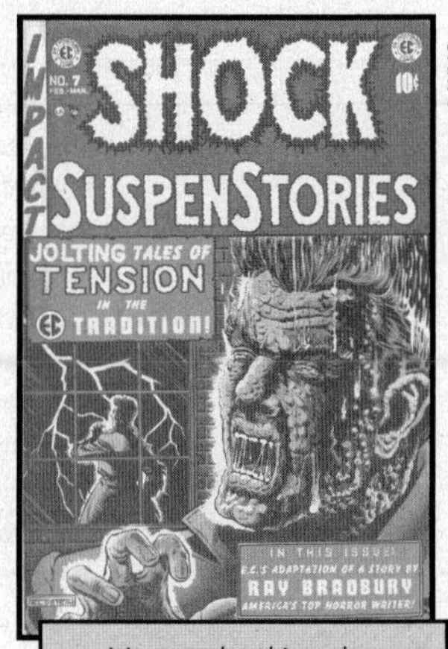

It's not shocking that Pre-code Horror is selling well. (*Shock SuspenStories* #7 shown)

Other Golden Age: Super-hero oldies sell, as do Pre-code Horror. I especially like buying EC collections (I scored many of them last year) and Super-hero Golden Age collections that include runs of 1930s and early '40s stuff.)

Silver Age Marvel: I do great with 1960s comics, especially Marvels. I've scored many runs of these this year, in all grades. The main problem for me is that, as I grade them, I can't help but re-read, or at least re-look through them. These great "1960s babies"… I never tire of them.

I find myself continually running low (and then replenishing) 1960s-1975 *Amazing Spider-Man*, *Captain America*, *Iron Man*, *X-Men*, etc. Those early Marvels I consider to be the true "brick and mortar" of today's comic market, in almost all grades.

DC Super-Hero Titles: *Green Lantern* issues are solid sellers (especially #1-20), as are Batman comics. Most other Super-hero 1960s DCs sell kinda slow, but I like "stockin' 'em" anyway!

DC War Titles: *Our Army at War* issues sell solidly enough.

DC Mystery and Horror Titles: They sell pretty steadily. In "sharp" shape, most Silver Age DCs do quite well as they are kinda tough to get in that condition.

Other Silver Age Genres: Well known TV Comics sell pretty well (Gold Key *Star Trek* and *I Love Lucy*, just to name a couple) and *Herbie Comics* (The Fat Fury!) move well enough.

Bronze Age: They've been, in general, slowly but steadily increasing in value. One can still, however, get many of them, for a dollar a piece, or less. Quite a bargain, I'd say, for comics over 30 years of age! I like being well-stocked in Bronze and early Copper comics, as for the generation immediately following the Baby Boomer generation, these are the books with which they grew up.

The best Bronze sellers are 1970-1975 *Amazing Spider-Man*, *Batman*, *Captain America*, *Detective*, *Fantastic Four*, *Hulk*, *Iron Man*, and *X-Men*, plus DC 1970s Horror comics.

Modern Age (1980s – 2000s): Folks, there are a lot of these out there, so, to really move them pretty well, the best way is in sets. I sell many of them on eBay, at around 60¢-$1.00 a book, and for that reason, I enjoy buying runs of comics from that era.

Original Art: These are the great "Wild West" of comic-related collectibles. Many 1960s "better artist" pages (such as Kirby, Ditko, etc.) that were worth $200 a piece or less in the 1980s, are now worth thousands of dollars per page. Of course, I love getting in these "unique-wonders."

Hey, have a grr-reat Comic book enjoying year! *G.D.*

Walter Durajlija and Marc Sims Big B Comics

Big B Comics had a great 2011! We had strong showings at the Toronto area conventions we attended, including our best Canadian Fan Expo ever in August 2011. The Montreal Comic-Con was also a huge surprise with the building over capacity both days! Back issue sales for us are always led by Spider-Man. I honestly don't know what we'd do without the guy. We bought and sold 2 copies of *Amazing Fantasy* #15, one was a CGC 3.5 and the other an un-graded 1.8, both went for about 15% above *Guide* and both to very happy local buyers. As always, if we had more of them we could have been selling them every month. Every issue of *Amazing Spider-Man* sells for us and sells quickly. We truly believe that there is no title that is more collected than *Amazing Spider-Man*.

We saw a pickup in Golden Age comic sales by the end of 2011. We sold about a half dozen mid-grade issues of *All-American* and *Green Lantern* that had been sitting for a while at our shop. Maybe it was a fluke but it does seem that there was a bit more interest locally for DC Golden Age than in years past. Golden Age Batman and Timelys sold well for us as well, which is never a surprise. The supply of original owner Golden Age in our region is relatively scarce so we don't see much coming into the shops anymore. As a result, any thing new and cool that we do get doesn't tend to last long.

Bronze Age keys did OK this year. We were able to get full *Guide* for nice copies of *Green Lantern* #76, *Amazing Spider-Man* #129 and *Incredible Hulk* #181 though we did see a softening in price on some of the lesser Bronze Age books in high grade. I think many investors are seeing that it's wiser to buy 5 copies of *Amazing Spider-Man* #129 than one each of 5 different lesser or equal Bronze keys. *X-Men* #94 and *Giant-Size X-Men* #1 especially couldn't sell for *Guide* unless in ultra high grade. They both appear frequently in collections that we have been buying for the last 5 years.

Our website comicbookdaily.com enjoyed strong growth in readership in 2011. The comic book collecting component of the site, which includes my weekly Undervalued Spotlights and my Auction Highlights columns, saw a twofold increase in regular readers. My Auction Highlights did reveal a negative trend in realized prices for a large part of the back issue market.

The price correction is still happening in the graded back issue comic market, especially for the Bronze Age to Modern Age. International press coverage of high profile sales like the $2.16 Million received for the CGC 9.0 copy of *Action Comics* #1 presented a rosy picture to those outside the collecting community. In reality there was, and still is, quite the drastic correction occurring just below the headlines. Seasoned collectors agree this correction is needed and it's my view that corrections like this weed out the sunny day speculators, ultimately leaving behind a more stable market.

Unfortunately there are still investors and collectors out there that overreact to a newly graded "highest grade" copy. Thankfully more and more collectors and investors are realizing (some the hard way) that CGC Census scarcity is not the same as actual scarcity. We need years and years of adding to the CGC Census before we can get even a remotely accurate handle on the general scarcity of a comic. We at Big B Comics advise all our customers investing in the graded back issue comic market to steer clear of the best graded or even second best graded copies. One need look no further than the $1.1 Million paid for a 9.6 *Amazing Fantasy* #15 in March 2011. At the time it was the only 9.6. Now at the time of this writing there are 3 (2 universal, one restored). Maybe there will be a 4th by the time you are reading this. What we can guarantee is that whoever shelled out over a million bucks for that 9.6 because it was the "only one" is going to be displeased with the result if that second one comes to market.

Another interesting trend that accelerated in 2011 was the market's refusal to blindly agree with the CGC grade. While I agree that CGC holds a critically important position in our market, many are now openly questioning some of the actual grades assigned. It's to the point where large fluctuations in realized prices can be seen for books with identical CGC grades. People plopping down large sums of money now more than ever want to agree with the grade before buying the book. Often advice is sought from industry experts (some of these 'experts' buy exclusively for high end buyers).

In a nutshell, issues like centering, which CGC for some reason tends to ignore, gloss and the overall feel are all aesthetic markers that help determine a person's willingness to pay. These markers are now actively being measured against the grade assigned by CGC. Books can have 8.0 looks with 7.0 grades while others can have 7.0 looks with 8.0 grades. More and more I'm seeing collectors grade with their wallets on the big monthly comic book auctions.

I expect the downward correction of prices to continue through 2012, especially for books that are known to be common. Here's where I give another compliment to the *Overstreet Comic Book Price Guide* (no, I don't get free ads though I do believe it is indispensible as a tool). *The Overstreet Guide* has been acting as a sort of safety net for many a comic book in freefall. Basically if the graded 9.8 and 9.6 prices start collapsing on any comic book published say, post 1970, the NM- or 9.2 *Overstreet Guide* price acts as the minimum point to where the value will tend to fall. This is a generalization and I'm sure you can find individual examples to refute this but collectors and investors are subconsciously exercising their faith in the goodwill the *Overstreet Guide* has built up through 40 plus years of doing a great job monitoring and reporting values for comic books. Let's face it, most of the comics from 1975 and up are in high grade. Just because there were only 5 graded at 9.8 by CGC in 2009 does not mean there are not 5000 more out there just as nice and ungraded. For comic books like this a 9.8 or a 9.6 is really a 9.2 price guide wise. These high grades are the expected standard for someone searching for a nice copy of any book from this era.

The trend to question the CGC grading could lead to a problematic near future for the collecting community. The back issue market needs total (and deserved) faith in the CGC grading process if there is to be renewed and sustained growth. It would be unrealistic to assume that CGC got all their grades right over the last 10+ years but we are entering a phase in the market where buyers will scrutinize the grades more thoroughly than ever and we can only hope CGC's consistency can carry the day.

Markets in correction can offer opportunities though. As a generalization I'd make these recommendations going forward. Chose key comics, chose high grades but not necessarily the highest, chose aesthetically pleasing books that are well centered and have strong page quality. and use the *Overstreet Price Guide* as a reference point.

Some great comic books will get overlooked at auctions because they may be trending downward on price tracking sites. Opportunities to buy wisely are all over the place. Happy hunting!

2011 was a pretty solid year for the back issue portion of our business, but it really shined for us on the retail side. In 2011 we operated two storefronts in Hamilton & Barrie Ontario. In 2012 we will add our third store in the heart of beautiful Niagara Falls, Ontario. Both our stores saw massive gains in 2011. Sales and people through the door both enjoyed record double digit gains. So much for the global recession!

The DC New 52 relaunch in September certainly helped the cause, allowing us to sell new, accessible comics to a whole new readership. We saw a big gain in both lapsed readers and brand new readers as a result. Now 6 months in, not everyone of course has stuck around but we continue to get new people coming in and trying books from the relaunch. I have to thank our partners at DC Comics, especially fellow advisor Bob Wayne, for a fantastically executed launch. DC made it easy for retailers to stock these products with numerous ordering incentives, limited returnability, and very quick reprints on all the sellouts. And most importantly, they got people excited about it and into our stores looking for the products! Retailers that failed to capitalize, and there were far too many of them, should think long and hard about who is really to blame.

We want to take this time to thank all of our wonderful customers and of course all of our hard-working staff. You're all awesome. In 2011 we celebrated our 15th anniversary of selling comics out of our retail stores, and over 25 years of buying and selling comics in total. The comic collecting community is a great place to call home and one that we feel forever fortunate to be a part of.

Ken Dyber
Cloud 9 Comics

Greetings. I've been buying and selling comics for 25 years now, starting on the East Coast in Connecticut, and now on the West Coast in Oregon. Feel free to visit Cloud 9 online at www.cloudninecomics.com or you can email me at ken@cloudninecomics.com. Contact me as well for a private showing if you're coming to the Portland area. The website continues to evolve and improve with more 1 to 1 ratio cover scans, better design, and now direct links from

GPAnalysis to our CGC slabbed books, as well as the acceptance of all major credit cards. Cloud 9 is also a CGC Authorized Dealer, so feel free to contact me if you have questions about CGC or would like to receive a discount on submitting your books to CGC.

This year I was able to travel to the East Coast and Midwest to shop, hitting about half a dozen stores in New England, and ones in Madison, Chicago, and Iowa City, which helped give me a sense of what was available across the country, and what things were selling at (or not selling).

The Year Overall: This year I believe I've found a new price variant for *Daredevil* #190. I've had this book in stock before, and always seen a cover price of $1.00, but this year I purchased a collection with a huge run of this title, with multiple copies of most issues, and there were 3 copies of this issue, 2 with $1 covers, and 1 with a $1.25 cover price. There was no listing inside the book of a "second printing" or "reprint" information. All text/artwork was the same. If anyone else has found other variants from the $1 cover time period, please email me, as I was not familiar with any from this period, as most identified in the *Guide* are from the Bronze Age.

eBay: Most non-keys are selling well below *Guide* of common books from Silver Age to present in lower & mid grade. This has been consistent for a while. So… good deals can be had if you're happy with buying a FN+ from the Silver Age or VF from the Bronze or a VF/NM from the Copper Age. Unless you buy regularly on eBay, there is quite a bit of risk on raw books here. Buy from people who are nationally known dealers with return policies, 1 to 1 ratio cover scans or high quality photos. Be wary of sellers offering raw high grade Silver and Bronze keys month after month, as there just are not that many of those books available. Some sellers on eBay will buy restored CGC books, crack them out of the case and sell them as unrestored. Check the CGC forums before dropping big bucks!

Below are some thoughts about specific time periods, some books I've purchased, some books I've sold, and some basic thoughts on pricing in our beloved price guide.

Golden Age: I continue finding myself buying more and more Archies. Great artwork and stories, and boy are these tough to find in Fine or better! I picked up a nice copy of issue #47 which I kept for myself which has a full page Veronica pin up, with a full page Betty pin up on the other side. Highest graded copy of this issue is only a 7.5, with only 3 graded copies! War comic sales are picking up for me as I continue to tell my regular customers about how scarce these are in Fine or higher - forget VF copies for many issues. In July, an *Our Army At War* #83 CGC 7.5 sold for $9,600, which isn't even the highest graded (a lone 9.0). Is this a steal or ridiculous amount to pay for a 7.5 of this book, who knows, only time will tell. Either way, this book seems quite scarce, and needs to move upward in *Guide* in all grades by a good percentage.

© AP

Golden Age Archies are tough to find in Fine or better (**Archie Comics** #50 shown).

Crime books have been slow for a while, but so was precode Horror for a while. Keep your eye on these, as many are quite scarce, and often contain quite violent covers and stories. *Fight Against Crime* #20 is a classic decapitation cover that hardly ever comes up for sale. This one needs a major upward price adjustment in *Guide* in all grades. *Thrilling Crime Cases* #49 (Classic L.B. Cole cover) also is selling well above *Guide* in all grades with a raw GD+/VG- selling on eBay for $128 (*Guide* is $72.50) and a CGC 8.0 selling for $1315 (*Guide* is $284, that's 5x *Guide* for upper mid grade!). Issue #41 (first issue) has only one graded copy, a 9.2, issues #45 and #47 have no graded copies and issue #44's highest graded copy is a 4.0 (the only graded copy). This entire series seems quite scarce & very undervalued in *Guide*.

Early Four Colors continue to be hard to track down as are early Dick Tracy issues, both of which sell quite fast at or slightly above *Guide* when I can find them.

Good Girl books have regained quite a bit of interest here in the Pacific Northwest with what I have called the "Hollywood Smokeshop Collection" being discovered by Peter Fagnant the owner of Excalibur Comics, Portland's oldest comic book shop. This collection contained around 600 higher grade Fox, Fiction House, Harvey, Timely, Avon and Quality books from such titles as *Phantom Lady* (entire series except for issue #23), *Jo-Jo Comics*, *Rulah*, *Zoot*, *Torchy*, *Jungle*, *Jumbo*, *Fight*, *Modern*, *Doll Man*, *Planet*, *Black Cat*, *Blond Phantom*, and *Blue Beetle*, to name only a handful. Almost the entire collection graded above Fine, with Very Fine- probably being the average grade. Cover gloss and page quality was excellent with many books having White or Off White to White pages.

I already knew many of these titles were less common, but after some research, it seems many of these books are quite scarce in any grade, let alone in high grade. CGC census for some of the *Modern Comics* I picked up had zero graded copies or only 1 graded usually around the 7.0 range (Often the "D" Crippen copy). For many of these books, the highest graded copy is between a 7.5 & 9.0. The savvy investor should keep their eye on this genre, as there could be a big upward swing in pricing in the near future on many of these.

Although not in this collection, I then researched *My Love Secret*, the title *Phantom Lady* switched to after issue #23. *My Love Secret* #24 (1st issue) has zero graded copies and even has Kamen and Feldstein artwork. The series only went seven issues to #30 before once again changing its name. At the time of this report, the CGC census had 1 graded copy of issue #25 (9.0) and 1 graded copy of issue #26

(4.5). That's it, no other graded copies of the entire series. I then checked eBay, 2 auction sites, and 2 other major retailers' sites (that's 5 of the largest comic retailers sites) and there were NO copies of this title for sale. So, not only are many of these Good Girl titles containing great stories and artwork, many of them are scarcer then I think people believe. The *Blue Beetle* Kamen/Baker run seems quite affordable compared with their horror counterparts from the early '50s. Issues #52 and #54 have been noted due to their bondage and headlight covers respectively, however issue #53 should also receive its own line listing with a strangulation cover.

Silver Age: So many great titles and investment opportunities here, where to begin.... How about with *Archie's Girls Betty & Veronica* #75 where they sell their souls to the devil? This is one to keep your eye out for. From what I've been told, right after this issue came out, a certain religious group nationally asked everyone in its faith to purchase this book and destroy it so no one else could buy it due to the storyline. To date only 1 copy has been graded by CGC, a 5.0/FN-. This book seems undervalued to me, and is probably much more scarce then people realize.

A few big ticket sales to note: A *Tales of Suspense* #39 CGC 9.2 sold for $72,100 in Sept. 2011 and the following month a *Journey Into Mystery* #83 CGC 9.2 sold for $100,000. *Detective Comics* #359 the intro. to Batgirl Barbara Gordon has become a super hot book selling well above *Guide* in all grades and needs a major upward swing in *Guide* to reflect its true value. *Iron Man* #1 continues to be one of the most liquid books from any time period for me. This book needs to go up in all grades in *Guide*, as does *Captain America* #100. I think both of these are still affordable keys compared with many other earlier Silver Age keys, as people can still buy these for $50-$200, unlike a *Journey Into Mystery* #83 or *Tales of Suspense* #39, which now seem to start at $1000.

The next Marvel key to keep your eye on for an explosion I think is *Sgt. Fury* #1, which seems fairly common in GD- to VG-, but finding it above VG or better seems quite difficult. As for DCs, *Showcase* #4 has been flat for several years now, so keep your eye on this one and *Flash* #105. *Adventure Comics* #210 (1st Krypto) and #247 (1st Legion) are both tough to track down, as is *Action* #252 (1st Supergirl), and all are quite liquid. Same goes for *Brave and the Bold* #28 (1st Justice League). Will one of these be the *Showcase* #22 for this next year? That book skyrocketed, then crashed!

Bronze Age: This period seems to be quite tricky from an investment standpoint, as books soar in price, then dip dramatically the following year. *Incredible Hulk* #181s in CGC 9.8 sell anywhere from $12,000 to $30,000! That's a huge range, and quite a gamble from an investment standpoint. Yes, it's a blue chip key, but that doesn't seem like a sure thing to me. *Hero For Hire* #1 needs to go up in *Guide* significantly in all grades. This is one of my more liquid keys, which sells above *Guide* in all grades. *Amazing Spider-Man* #123 seems undervalued as it ties for Luke Cage's 3rd appearance with *Hero For Hire* #3, and is his first crossover. *Amazing Spider-Man* #204, 205, 226 and 227 also seem undervalued as they are early appearances of the Black Cat (3rd, 4th, 5th & 6th appearances). *Detective Comics* 15¢ covers, especially Neal Adams ones, as well as 20¢ and 25¢ large logo covers seem quite cheap to me, and are pretty hard to find about VF in grade. Batman 15¢ and 20¢ covers also seem quite affordable. *Detective Comics* #425 is a cool Wrightson cover which should be highlighted in the *Guide*, and possibly a bit higher in Guide then other issues around it, although issue #426 with Batman holding a gun to his head is another desirable cover.

Independent titles from smaller publishers continue to be scarce and interesting. By now most people hopefully know about *Cerebus* and *Zap Comics*, but there are quite a few other titles, writers and artists to keep your eyes on that I feel are quite undervalued. The religious series titled *The Crusaders* by Jack T. Chick which on the cover says "Recommended reading for adults and teens" is spot on. This is some disturbing stuff regardless of what your religious beliefs may be from kidnapping, to sacrifices and maiming. I hardly ever see this series, let alone in grade. *The Big Betrayal* by Jack T. Chick (1981 Chick Publications, no cover price – possibly a promo?) currently isn't in the *Guide*. I'm guessing a $2-$25 spread would put it in line with his *Crusaders* series pricing, but with books like this and their limited sales history, who knows. Also, the Spire Christian books are also pretty interesting, and some command top dollar like *Hansi, The Girl Who Loved the Swastika* (I sold a raw mid grade copy for $40 at the first show I brought it to which is over double *Guide*).

House of Secrets #92 (1st Swamp Thing) is one to keep your eye on as sales have been flat for several years now, yet this iconic cover always draws people in at shows.

Copper/Modern Age: Teenage Mutant Ninja Turtles are hot again. In May 2011, a CGC 9.8 *TMNT* #1 sold for $22,752, with several CGC 9.6s going for $5600-$7000. The latest CGC 9.2 sales are $3107 and $2900. Prices do NOT vary wildly on this book anymore. The book sells consistently at strong prices in all grades and needs a line listing in the *Guide* at NM- of around $2600. This has been long overdue, and it should also be listed in the Top 10 Copper Age Books at #2 behind *Gobbledygook* #1. I also think more, if not a majority of the series deserves line listings, as many of the issues have lower print runs then their Marvel/DC counterparts, and come on, how many movies have there been, as well as the TV show, action figures, etc...? They even got referenced in the new Muppet Movie!

Amazing Spider-Man #294, the Death of Kraven the Hunter at $14 in NM- seems like an absurd bargain to me, as historically, he was one of Spidey's most difficult villains, and always an interesting character. *Amazing Spider-Man* issues at the end of volume 1 can be fairly scarce due to the lower print runs. Issue #430 with a Carnage & Silver Surfer cover and #431 a Carnage cover on the Surfer's board seem to be the least common and selling for the most, regularly going for $15-$25. I suggest line listings for these two at $12 & $15 at the NM- range respectively. Issues 432, 434, 440 & 441 all regularly sell for $5-$10 each, and warrant line listings with $7 - $10 at the NM- line. A mini-series I feel is undervalued is the 4-part *Vision and The Scarlet Witch* series from '82-'83, where in the last issue, Wanda and Pietro find out that their father is Magneto, some pretty important information in the Marvel Universe without even a line listing at present.

Other keys to keep your eye on are *The Crow* #1 (1st print, Caliber Press 1989), with a current NM- listing of $80 seems quite low for a book that doesn't appear at cons or on eBay very often, which is not the case for most Silver Age keys that are twice as old. *Cry For Dawn* #1 at $120 in NM- also seems like a steal, also from 1989. *Primer* #2 (1st Grendel) has been soft for too long, and interest should return back to it soon. Pick up one or two of these if you can find them in grade now.

For the third year in a row I must continue to, at the minimum, mention *The Walking Dead*. I feel after two years of pushing for a line listing for the early issues of this series, now it's time to give those listings upward movement. CGC 9.8's seem to be going consistently around $600, with CGC 9.2's around $300 to $350. Guide needs to come up for the entire series, with NM- listings around: #1 $300, #2 $100, #3 & #4 $50, #5 & #6 $30, #7-#10 $15, and #11-#20 $10, with #61 around $12. *Chew* #1 in NM- should be listed around $150 (very conservative starting line listing), as this book seem much less common for the 1st printing, and seems non-existent at cons. *Morning Glories* seemed quite hot, with NM- copies selling around $50 raw, but many readers (including myself) found the story amazing to begin with, then just seemed to go nowhere, and readership/interest started to fall off. How this series could go nowhere is really beyond me, as possibilities seemed limitless. Another key that needs a line listing is *Fables* #1 at $35. This book has sold at this price or higher consistently now for several years, and doesn't appear much at cons or in local shops. Another indie title to keep your eye on is *Fish Police* from 1985 on Fishwrap Productions. I bought a collection that had the first 8 issues in it all in NM which I sold for a lot on eBay in less than 24 hours as a Buy-It-Now.

Thanks to everyone that's read my market report, visited the website, and said hello at one of the cons. I look forward to meeting more of you, and another year in the hobby!

Bruce Ellsworth & Alika P. Seki
Bruce's Comics and Collectibles

Welcome to Bruce's Comics in Hawaii! Lots of things have changed since I left Australia. I found 5,000 Silver and Golden Age comics before I left the continent and they were all bagged and boarded so I threw them under my shipping container before I left. I attended San Diego this year and noticed that the comic book dealers were spread out all over the place and that mostly other items than comics were being sold. What started out as a comic book show has now become a major media event, an elaborate TV production. I noticed a lot of slabbed comic books going unsold while the "used" comics are being bought up steadily at a great pace. I found some great deals on slabbed merchandise which was in Very Fine (8.0) or worse condition way below *Guide*. Most dealers didn't seem to care that they sold for below *Guide*, even though they had gone through the trouble of getting it slabbed. They considered their merchandise worthless because it wasn't in Very Fine/NM (9.0) or better.

Onto the big trouble with San Diego: they don't have any aisles for handicapped people. People in wheelchairs had a difficult time finding access at the event, more so than any previous years. Really, really enjoyed running into all my friends in the comic industry. I hadn't seen many of them for over 6 years since I had gone to Australia. They made me feel very welcome.

Now onto new things I've been noticing on the internet with graded Modern comics. There is a variant that is becoming more prevalent in sales lately. The variant I speak of is the UPC variant. Many good examples can be found in the '80s and '90s, say *Incredible Hulk* #340. I saw two identically graded copies in Near Mint (9.6) condition, one with the bar code UPC and the other with the Spider-Man head. The one with the Spider-Man head in the place of the UPC was selling for 20% more than the bar code version. Also, *Amazing Spider-Man* #300 with this variant consistently sells for 20-30% higher than its bar code counterparts. In fact most comics with this variant have been going for over 20% more than their bar code counterparts. Perhaps it is the visual presentation of a comic that is unsoiled by that symbol of commercialism, the bar code. Or maybe it is a much rarer variant that we are aware of just yet. What do you think? Feel free to shoot me an email with your opinion.

Golden Age Sales: For this year in Hawaii, sales include *Batman* #2, 3 & 4 in Good condition for $3,500 together, *Batman* #92 in CGC 7.0 for $450, and *Superman* #14 in CGC 5.0 for $1,100.

Atomic Age: *Archie Annual* #2 & #3 in Fine condition for $600 together, and *Atomic Boy* #1 in Very Good condition for $400. Most Pre-code horror is selling for *Guide* price, where some of the nastier covers are going for double to triple the *Guide* price. ECs sell at a very steady pace. I can't keep 'em in stock!

Silver Age: *Amazing Spider-Man* #14 & #17 in Fine condition for $600 together (in Australia), *Amazing Spider-Man* #96-98 (non-code issues) in CGC 9.2 for $200 each, and *Amazing Spider-Man* #121 & #122 in CGC 9.4 condition for $2,000 together. Sales of *Daredevil* are slow, but *Avengers* is going through the roof along with *Captain America* and *Thor*.

Bronze Age: Sales are soaring, mostly in high grades, especially last appearances like *Star Wars*, *Tales of the Unexpected*, any major DC War/combat title, any Marvel title, along with many other long series that ended in the decade. DC War comics in general from the '50s, '60s and '70s are much sought after and sell briskly at *Guide* price, with *G.I. Combat* grey-tone covers leading the pack in requests. Most comics listed in the guides are put in groupings, and some fantastic covers just get lumped in with them, when they really stand out in terms of sales and popularity. They really should be separated out by cover appeal.

On the rise is Australian horror magazines (which are reprints of pre-code DC, ACG, Star, Standard, Atlas, etc.) sell like hotcakes. Also on the rise is *Heavy Metal*, published again after so many years. I was astounded by the caliber of the artists' work displayed in the magazines. Sci-Fi and Fantasy readers give it a shot, you'll love it.

Finally, a previously unknown comic has come to serendipitous fruition (with a certain dastardly dictator being deposed of!)...*Daffy Qaddafi*, *Malice in Wonderland* will surely see a spike in sales in the coming years.

Good news is that comic prices are still on the rise. Happy hunting to all you collectors out there; maybe you could be the next one to find the lost *Superman* #1 in CGC 9.2(or better!) condition. And if you're in Maui, be sure to come see us.

Aloha!

D'Arcy Farrell
Pendragon Comics

Overall review of the NEW comic releases market 2011:

What a year for DC! In a nutshell, everything DC increased in sales and demand. What DC did reminds me of what Marvel and Bendis did with the Ultimate stories 10+ years back. Marvel ushered in Ultimate Spider-Man to introduce a new alternate universe. A re-hash of original story lines of the 1960s to present. When many retailers saw the initial order forms for *Ultimate Spider-Man*, many were unsure of what to think. Is this sort of a reprint? Will it last as long as the Marvel 2099 line(a big bomb)? Needless to say, many retailers kept orders low. But, as we can see now, it took off quite well. It branched into new tiles and is still a force today.

How does DC compare to this? Well, it is a rehash. True. BUT one big difference. It is not meant to be an alternative universe! It is the real deal. Overall this big new 52 DC thing was huge! It created new fans, brought back some older fans, revitalized DC, and no one left! A huge hit!

As per Marvel, the Death of Spider-Man story with a new hero sold modestly well. But when new customers came in asking for the Death of Spider-Man storyline in 2011, I quipped, "do you mean the fake Spider-Man"? Then I'd have to explain it was a Spider-Man in the Ultimate universe. I know it was an opportunity to sell items and get people hooked, but those new to the comic fandom do not need to be deceived.

I do have some negative for DC this year though. Firstly, I disliked the way the variants were managed. Specifically the variant of the week. It forced retailers to bump up orders for regular titles that really didn't even belong in this universe. *Static Shock* was a big waste for me. Anything from the Milestone Universe was pointless. I can see bringing in *Grifter* or *Stormwatch* as decent sellers, but why not use this beginning for some of the under used characters from the '70s and '80s like Black Lightning or Red Tornado?

My other big negative this year for all companies is the digital format. Wow! What a store killer this is. Maybe it is inevitable, but do we really need to do this when many stores, especially in the US, are hurting from economic hardships? We are fine at least until my loyal customers start dying off in 10-30 years. Eventually, just like in the movie *WALL-E* , everything will be owned by one big corporation.

Now on to specifics.

DC in 2011: The new DC 52 is amazing! The "Bat" books are leading the way in popularity with almost everyone. *Detective* being the best and the regular *Batman* a close second. The storyline in *Batman* with the Court of Owls is fantastic. The reboot of Nightwing is a great book too. Dick is such an under-appreciated character in the DC universe considering he's almost as old as Batman and Superman. Great to see Babs as Batgirl again. The original is back better than ever. All the Batman titles, as well as the Lantern Titles, *Flash*, *Animal Man*, *Swamp Thing* and *Men of War* are big hits in our store. *Voodoo* and *I, Vampire* have been sleeper hits.

Having said all that, not all of the new DC 52 titles are good. *Static Shock*, *JLA International*, *Stormwatch*, *Hawk and Dove*, *Mr. Terrific*, *Superboy* and even *Teen Titans* have been sluggish in our store.

©DC

I, Vampire #1, one of the sleeper hits of DC's New 52.

There has also been some confusion about continuity in the DC Universe after the whole relaunch. Why is it that no one in the Justice League knows each other? Yet Batman is still basically running "Batman Inc." with his son Damian as his sidekick? Why does Hal Jordan remember being a Green Lantern before, and that Sinestro was the evil leader of the Yellow Lanterns, but doesn't know Superman? The idea was to relaunch all the titles without worrying about the 50+ years of back story for characters, yet they seem to have selectively removed some back stories (Superman apparently never met Doomsday and never died), while leaving other back stories mostly intact (Dick Grayson is still Nightwing, Jason Todd still lives, Tim Drake is Red Robin and Damian is still Robin).

Flashpoint was definitely an interesting prelude to the New 52 line. It sold well, despite the slight confusion as to what exactly was happening. DC did a decent job of tying up most plot lines in all their titles and dove-tailing them into the new launch, although there were some mini-series that were released late in the schedule and finished a bit out of continuity.

The *Mystery Men*, *American Vampire*, *Penguin Pain and Prejudice* and The Huntress mini-series were all good. The 5 issues of *Batman: The Dark Knight* before the relaunch are great books with the hardcover collection out now. Vertigo's resurrected *Sgt. Rock Between Hell and a Hard Place* was nice to see, with the trade of that being impossible to find. Highly recommended.

Marvel in 2011: *Captain America* was relaunched successfully, as well as *The Punisher*. Alpha Flight made a big splash with another new mini-series. Too bad they can't manage an ongoing series! *Daredevil* has seen mixed reviews (many online like the relaunch, but not so many of our customers). *Fear Itself* was another mega crossover event that saw mixed results. Red Hulk seems to have been rescued from Jeph Loeb and has become a decent title. We saw the end of Greg Pak's run on *The Incredible Hulk*, with the title relaunched late in the year. *Amazing Spider-Man* even appears to have brought back some readers who were put off by the whole "Brand New Day" debacle.

The X-Titles are still going strong. With yet another "regenesis" happening, it remains to be seen if they can continue. Wolverine continues to appear in every other title every other month (or so it seems). *Uncanny X-Force* really seems to have won over readers.

Surprising sleeper hits have been *Venom*, *Secret Avengers*, *FF/Fantastic Four*, *Vengeance* mini-series and even the new *Ultimate Spider-Man*. Other than *Moon Knight*, it doesn't seem that Bendis can write a bad comic. With the amount of titles he works on in any given month, we'll let him slide on that one.

Fear Itself was well received as a mini-series. The various tie-ins did not do so well and really just seemed to be tacked on to try and get more sales.

Marvel also has had some series missteps. *Moon Knight*, *Ghost Rider* and the new *Defenders* are forefront. Many fans are also not happy with the $3.99 price point on the majority of the titles, especially with DC mostly holding the line at $2.99.

Dark Horse in 2011: *Dark Horse Presents* - Welcome back. Anthologies are an unappreciated part of Comicdom. *DHP* has offered some interesting stories over the last year. Whenever customers ask for something new, other than the super-hero genre, I steer them towards books like this. Not every issue is great but there is enough variety to make it worthwhile.

Hellboy, *The Fury*, *B.P.R.D.*, *Witchfinder* et al - Continues the creepiness of the Hellboy universe. I like the stories and art and most customers have given positive feedback. "It is nice to have something other than zombies". Nice to have some Corben art too.

The Strange Case of Mister Hyde - A nice take on the classic. Good art and story which ties into the Jack the Ripper mythos It helps to know that Jekyll/Hyde is more than a man turning into a monster and the author works that angle which reminds me: see the BBC series *Jekyll*(I know this has nothing to do with comics but still, a good story)

Solomon Kane (Red Shadows) - I don't know why but every time I see this art I think of the movie *Hellsinger*. The style is much the same so I think the set designer must have read this series. It is very much evocative of the Robert E. Howard stories. Liked the art and story but look at the source material so it was hard to go wrong.

The Strain - Great story. A vampire/detective story which starts off with a a plane of dead passengers and crew. So this time it is a plane that shows up on the tarmac instead of a ship on the coast. It still works. Waiting to see how it turns out.

Creepy - Did I mention that I still like anthologies? Especially horror?

Criminal Macabre/The Goon - Only a one shot but worth the read especially if you like Cal and The Goon humour.

Avatar in 2011: Avatar has established itself as the studio for horror with titles like *Crossed*, *Caligula* and *Night of the Living Dead*. *Caligula* pushing the envelope is an understatement. Great interpretation of the Caligula story plus a talking horse and no it's not Mister Ed. This is one that is definitely for adults and not for the squeamish. *Crossed: Psychopath* has a great story and art but this one is not for the squeamish. It touches on very sensitive subjects: rape torture etc. Admittance for over 18 only.

BOOM! Studios: They continue to be solid, despite the Stan Lee titles. *Irredeemable* and *Incorruptible* lead the way. *Malignant Man* initially it seems to be about a terminally ill patient then spins off in to superhero sci-fi. I liked the beginning but it seemed to derail near the end. Worth a quick look. *Hellraiser* was a so/so story like but I do like the variant covers. *The Rinse* is definitely one to add to your list of must reads. Good story and art.

Dynamite Entertainment: They continue to grow. *Jennifer Blood* was huge and *The Boys* remains strong. Many of their other licensed titles are doing well.

IDW Publishing: *Crawl to Me* is as good as *Hangers*. If you like horror get this.

Locke & Key Clockworks - There are really no comments for this except that if you haven't read the series, get the back issues/trades and do so. Well crafted story and art that complements it. As the ad said, "Only a few issues left".

Doctor Who: A Fairy Tale Life - Most customers are not really impressed by this series. The art, to quote a customer, seemed rather sketchy and over simplified as if the title was all that was required to sell the book.

Suicide Girls - Once again secret organization and tough minded girls eager to battle them. Most interested customers asked about the variant cover NOT the series. Go to the web site and you'll know what they were looking for.

The Rocketeer - Most customers who saw this take on the Rocketeer liked it. It provided simple stories with good art and dialogue.

The Cape - Get it. It is one of the best stories in the "What would you really do if you got super powers?" genre.

Wormwood: Bingo Night in Valhalla - It is always difficult to describe the Wormwood stories. Suffice to say more of the same BUT in this this case, it's all good.

That Hellbound Train - For those who are familiar/like Robert Bloch's stories, this doesn't disappoint. Nice art and it is true to the original.

Image Comics: *The Big Lie* - If you really want to feed your paranoia, read this.

Blue Estate - Good crime story which pulls several disparate type into a the Big Job. This time to steal from a Hollywood action star. Customers who like the crime stories definitely liked this story line and the art.

Breed III Book of Revelations - A fitting continuance of the Breed story line. Very good art and story.

Green Wake - A story of people in transition from this life to ??. Reminiscent of *Fallen Angel* and *Bete Noir* which is not a bad thing. The art is not to all tastes but definitely suits the material. It is worth the time investment to read at least the opening story line

Last Mortal - An unusual story of attempted murder and suicide. Well worth the effort to track down and read.

Moriarty - Enjoyable addition to the Moriarty storyline.

Near Death - Killer seeks redemption after nearly dying. So far so good. I'll give it another couple of issues before making up my mind or recommending it.

Pigs - A definite yes. Nicely done story about what happens to the sleeper agents and what happens when they awake.

Undying Love - Hey this beats Twilight but again anything could. Once again a story of how the path of love can be rough. He's mortal; she's a vampire. Great art and story. It washes the bad taste of those shiny vampires away. Get it.

The Vault - Nicely done story with the moral that things that are buried should stay buried. Good read,

Severed - The BEST horror story of the last few years. Great story, great art. Everyone who picked this up was sorry that it wasn't weekly. If any customer likes horror, recommend this.

68 - A very interesting take on the zombie story. Art is very good. One of the few times I looked for the variant covers because I remembered what they were based on. Unfortunately, none of this generation got the references: " What Vietnam War? "

Memoir - Black and white art only add to thie story. Totally enjoyable but I'm not certain exactly where it was going but it gradually clicked.

Screamland - Loved it and customers who are familiar with the Hammer Horror series felt the same. Mixture of humour and pathos with the has been's of the horror movie world. And an interesting commentary on how the classic horror can't compete against the modern.

The Mission - Man comes up and commands you to kill someone or there will be disastrous consequences. Ok , that had me from the start. I'm just waiting to see where it goes. Again good story and art.

The Red Wing - Really liked the art and the story. Worth taking a look at

Who is Jake Ellis - At first it appears to be a guy talking to another agent then it gradually the truth emerges. Good story, good art. Feedback was positive.

Witch Doctor - Not overly impressed. Seemed to be trying too hard. The humour seemed to be laboured but maybe that is just how it struck me. No feedback from customers on this one.

Radical: Radical remained dedicated to quality over quantity, releasing few titles but doing well with each.

Abattoir - Great, great story and art; very well done. I recommend this to any customer that is interested in horror but not necessarily in buckets of blood.

Damaged - Brutal story of crossing the line and the men on either side of it. Well done and good value.

Top Cow: *Echoes* - A terrifying story of a man on the edge of a complete breakdown but also more than that. I recommend this to anyone who likes well written psychological pieces.

Zenescope Entertainment: The Dream Eater Saga - Great story which pulls in most of the Grimm Fairy Tale characters. Worth the read.

VALIANT Returns!!!: Watch out! Original company of the early 1990s, headed by the creative genius of comic prodigy Jim Shooter and BW Smith. This fantastic collaboration issued in one of the few shining points of the 1990s (the biggest would be Death of Sup and Bane vs Bat)! It lasted quite the while bringing fresh stories and some innovation. It did crash and burn after a few years with BW Smith and Shooter parting ways. It resurfaced somewhat under Acclaim, then died again. Now it has a new fresh start albeit without the superb creative forces that spawned it. So, 20 years later, *X-O Manowar* is about to debut. How well will it do? Most diehard fans most likely will buy the #1. Writing is very key as these fans expect it. This is not a company like Image of the 1990s where fancy variants and redundant #1s were typical and had mostly a teen demographic. These Valiant fans are mature Vertigo-*esque* readers, and expect great stories. Try #1 and see for yourself!

2011 Movies: It was another summer filled with superhero movies. We saw *Green Lantern*, *Captain America*, *Thor* and the First Class of *X-Men*. All the movies were good if you're a comic book fan but were not appreciated by movie critics. *Thor* and *Captain America: The First Avenger* were probably the best. Marvel has been fairly consistent with solid stories and decent acting for the majority of their films. I think that the *Thor* movie was the most well done as far as storyline and CGI are concerned.

Green Lantern was not a bad movie, despite what the critics thought. It relied a little too heavily on CGI effects, but it is difficult to create such a movie without them. The breadth of the alien Corps is staggering. What was really disappointing was the decision to cut the early back story of Hal Jordan as a child from the Theatrical release. Watching it on the extended Blu-ray really added to the story and for the extra 10 minutes, it should have been included in the theatrical release.

Conan was another movie trashed by the critics, but was an alright movie. Better than expected. Let's face it, trying to follow up Arnold in the Dino De Laurentis original is damned difficult to do.

Comic book movies don't seem to be slowing down any time soon. In 2012 we have *Dark Knight Rising*, the reboot of Spider-Man, *Ghost Rider: Spirit of Vengeance*, *The Avengers*, *G.I. Joe: Retaliation* and a re-make of *Judge Dredd* starring Karl Urban.

Trades for 2011/2012: Trade Paperbacks by all companies remain strong sellers for us. Many customers just want to read a story and don't want to spend time waiting for individual issues to ship. Some miss the initial issues and simply catch up on the story with the TPB. In today's society of Instant Gratification, these are a great way to satisfy that requirement.

Walking Dead TV/Trades: *The Walking Dead* trades sell like crazy and the show has only added interest in the comics for people. People who watch the show are coming to buy the books and trades now, which is awesome. We are continually sold out of Volume One of the trade. I've seen people come in and buy two trades, take them home and read them and then come back 3 hours later and buy the next two trades! *TWD* has always sold well enough. With success of the show new interest in the comics and trades is happening. It will only become more and more popular. Some fans have complained about the disconnect in the story line of the TV show and that of the comics, but what works in a comic does not necessarily translate well to the screen.

The success of the TV show has **The Walking Dead** trades flying off the shelves. (Volume#1 shown)

Expect *Batman: Knightfall* trades to start selling once fans of the movie get wind of Bane's existence from 20 years ago. Don't expect the same lame character from that 1997 movie disaster *Batman and Robin*. This promises to be great.

Batman: Earth One is coming out. *Superman: Earth One* was a great success, selling out in our store.

DMZ has ended its successful run and the trades will likely continue to be strong sellers for the foreseeable future. We're hoping to see more collections of the old EC titles as well, as they do very well for us.

Marvel's various Omnibus collections do well as do DC's Absolute titles. They are affordable collections that allow readers to catch up on character histories without having to track down high priced individual issues.

Overall review of the Vintage comic market for 2011:

We have had fantastic sales overall. Marvel (almost anything) moves and for DC mostly Batman and Green Lantern! I have sold about four runs of *The Avengers* in the past 3 months alone! As usual, Timely and Golden Age DCs and Atomic Age Horrors all fly. The only genre that sold little in 2011 was War books, except for DC (which ROCKS!).

Normally I spend nearly a page of this report on sales, but to be honest, it really is about the same as 2010 sales. Timely, DC, Marvel will always sell. Sometimes things change, such as the hotness of the AVENGERS. But that is a moment in time and has been mentioned. I wish to talk about future thoughts in the marketplace this time. To help vintage investors to look ahead instead of telling them what they missed. Far more productive. Firstly, as mentioned earlier, the AVENGERS are hot. As is anything related like Captain America, Iron Man, Thor and so on.

Early issues have been going over *Guide* since the beginning of 2010 till when you read this in summer 2012. *Avengers* #4 (first Silver Age Captain America), *Tales of Suspense* #39 (first Iron Man), *Journey Into Mystery* #83 (first Thor), and *Avengers* #1 (first Avengers) are probably the hottest keys out there right now!!! They will cost premiums for high grades, and little deals will be found. Now is that good investing? Well yes, in the long long run. But if I could suggest something to all you investors, why not look to the JLA? *Brave and the Bold* #28 (first JLA) is not only 3 years older (1960), but more valuable, important and the scarcer key issue. It is also a few years away from a movie. Now a good movie, and the hype that goes with it, will skyrocket this issue. And not just the first appearance , but *Brave and the Bold* #29+30, *JLA* #1 and the whole run. Compare, using your trusty *Overstreet Guide*, *The Avengers* to the *JLA*. Look not just at the huge issues, look at the typical minor keys that are very affordable. When I look, I see a TON of minor keys in *JLA* I'd prefer way over *The Avengers*. Examples you ask? *JLA* #s 5,9,12,21!!,22!!,34,37,38,46,47,55!!!,56!!,64,73!!, and so much more all the way to final issue of #261! So many Crisis issues too! Now *The Avengers* has some nice keys, but nothing in quantity or importance compared to *JLA*! Avenger #s 6-11,16,19!!,48,57,58,71,83, and maybe some others. Overall the cost of a *JLA* run is more, and harder to come by, but the sheer quantity of keys, major and minor not to mention a potential big movie in the making, make *JLA* worthy of any investor.

Concluson: Sales in the vintage market are amazing. What other marketplace has such a great way to invest and reap rewards? It does not take decades like stocks, bonds, funds, stamps, coins, and other collectibles. The only risk really is how you store your investments. Personally, I like using the following: BCE copper pages (these go on your inner covers front and back!), then using a mylite or arklite 1mil (mylar D acid free bag), use a real acid-free backboard (we use

BCE version 24mil only), then I like to use an Ultra-Pro comic Top Loader. This combination will run around $3-$4 a comic. It protects within and structurally as well. Far superior to CGC slabs (great for resale and restoration checks but hardly good for long term, hence make sure you resubmit ALL your CGC slabs on a regular basis, like every 3-5 years?). You can get by without the top loader, but make sure you keep your comics in a box upright and take care.

But really, for a big book, even a $100 book, what's $3 or $4? Protect your investment! Do it RIGHT! BTW, BCE is Bill Cole Enterprises, and they specialize in archival protective products. There are others, but we prefer them. Overall we saw new fans in the marketplace, and there is room to grow. Digital comics are good for the big companies, but not much for anyone else.

Sales in new DC are fabulous! Marvel still sells quite well. Dynamite keeps putting out nice new Americana related items like *Lone Ranger*. Image is excellent for the true Indies like *Walking Dead*, as is Avatar, BOOM!, and IDW. Dark Horse and Zenescope are slipping huge. And Radical, great a couple years back, have disappeared, and that's a shame. You can never go wrong buying anything that is DC/Vertigo. And for long run great collections of DC or Marvel, buy the Absolute or Omnibus editions. They usually cost $99, but you are getting 40+ issues in each volume, and that's about 3 times a Marvel Masterworks or DC Archives which costs around $50 each. Also, we need a Quarterly price guide from someone that also deals with issues hot on the marketplace. Restoration, CGC to do or not, spotlights on artists or companies, list of back issues like Neal Adams everything and so on. *Comic Book Marketplace*, defunct now, but redone would be great if kept topical to the NOW! Restoration must be addressed sometime soon by the big players like Overstreet, CGC, Heritage, ComicLink. A guide or rating system should be put in place. There is such a huge difference in so many things/factors, it cannot just use the simple tags CGC uses. Major or Minor? Professional or Amateur? Not enough. If grading can go decimal 0.5-10.0, why not restoration?

Happy reading, because that is what comics are all about!

Dan Fogel
Hippy Comix, Inc.

Writing my Annual Market Report this year on my birthday leads me to wax nostalgic, although current events in the Comics Biz are exciting enough to feel these could be someone's "Good Old Days"! The $2,000,000 barrier was broken last week (as of this writing) for actor Nic Cage's slabbed 9.0 *Action Comics* #1, and many other records (which I'll leave Unca Bob to cover as always) have fallen since three books cleared a million bucks in 2010! Perhaps ironically, my theme this year is intrinsic, not financial, riches, "Recovering the Love" of comic books that originally Seduced us Innocents into this colorful art form, marketplace, and community. "Psst! Wanna buy a funnybook, keed?"

This past journey around the sun has not only seen my retail volume pick up at conventions and my wholesaling to other dealers increase, but I've officially begun my second comic book collection! I'm now once more on both sides of the vending trenches, providing me an increased (one can hope!) perspective on the marketplace. Collection #1 spanned my first newsstand titles (cover dates November-December 1968) through decades of weekly title addiction and multiple distributor accounts, culminating in 2005. Since then, I've peeked into the new book market occasionally, but jumping off the current continuity merry-go-round has freed me to revisit my personal "Golden Age", the 1970s!

What's the main difference collecting back issues today? Now, as never before: High Grade Rules! For the truly pristine books -say the top 1% ;) - it's a Seller's Market. The vast majority, say 99%, of mostly mid to low grade books, are ruled by a growing Buyer's Market. Steep discounts off *Guide* are required and expected to move most titles. There are many, many more Silver & Bronze Age books out there than previously available or thought to exist. The exception to the rule is that True Keys in any shape sell quickly when priced reasonably, and sometimes for amounts formerly thought "unreasonable". The upshot is that the past 40-45 years of mainstream back issues are available for the same cover prices of ever-more expensive new titles! I don't begrudge modern fans their New 52s and other reboots, but this time I'm sticking to what I love: Pre-Crisis DC, Marvel through the Shooterverse, and a smattering of Dennis the Menace, Richie Rich, Ducks, and Charltons!

The end of 2012 will also see the new, expanded edition of *Fogel's Underground Price Guide*! As a true Overstreet fanboy, I consider my humble efforts a corollary to the "bible" you hold in your hands, and am honored to follow in the footsteps of Bob Overstreet, Steve Geppi, J.C. Vaughn, and Mark Huesman, bringing knowledge, enthusiasm, and, yes, LOVE of our shared four-color (and black and white) universes! Thanks Again to those worthy gentlemen and to all you all reading this!

Stephen Gentner
Collector

The tumult of the U.S. and world economies has not destroyed our hobby. Collectible automobiles (the right ones), and many other collectible fields have attracted substantial sums of money. The volatility and uncertainty of the U.S. Stock Market, and the collapse of the housing market, have driven money into our hobby as a safer place to park it. Money market and interest rates generally are so low, the savvy investor can garner greater returns buying and holding high grade, desirable comics. In the hobby for the mid-grade or lower run-of-the-mill books, the market has softened somewhat. High grade, desirable Gold, Silver, and Bronze keys still attract buyers, not only in the hobby, but in the greater market as a whole.

Last year's stunning million dollar books, *Detective*

Comics #27 and *Action Comics* #1, illustrate the level to which value has risen in the hobby. Nice icon covers, coveted titles, and important appearances fare better than the ordinary material around them, as it has always been. As the hobby recognizes how difficult some books are to find in grade, the money will pursue them. It's hard to read how the "digital" comic market will help or hurt our hobby. The newer and younger readers whose first brush with comics is in digital form will remember looking at a computer screen to fondly remember their youth and favorite characters. To collectors in my generation, the idea of reading a comic book is exactly that... a book. The tactile sensation of turning pages and smelling newsprint (or ink) is a big part of the experience. Yet, if the newer readers never knew what that was, they have no frame of reference to "miss" it. Instead of taking a stack of books over to a buddy's house to share and read, today's comic-phile will meet their buddies either online, or go to Starbucks with their laptops to share. I think this is sad. It's just not the same. I know... I'm a dinosaur.

My targets of opportunity collecting-wise this year were pretty good! My colleagues will ask what I'm after... and I have reached the point now that I truthfully say, "I'll know it when I see it!" I picked up a *House of Mystery* #143 in 8.0+ for $110, and a *Tales of the Unexpected* #66, 8.5+ for $155 in one buy. I never really pursued *Tales of the Unexpected* before, preferring Adam Strange to Space Ranger. But that cover to #66 was advertised a lot "in house" at DC at the time, and what a cool cover it was (maybe the best for him!).

A collection of Golden Age books presented themselves, with lots of "good-girl" material. I snapped up *Wings* #90 in VF+ for $144, *Wings* #91 in VF for $144, both Bob Lubbers covers. *Jo-Jo* #8 in 8.0 for $275 (the "Mountain of Skulls" cover), *Jo-Jo* #11 in 8.0 for $385 and *Zoot* #11 in VF- for $300 (the breaking branch bondage cover in the cobra pit by "bone-in-the-nose" natives!) Really nice stuff!

Best of luck this coming year finding great books.

Douglas Gillock
ComicLink

ComicLink marked its 15th year online in 2011 and it was another year of record results and expansion in the hobby. Despite the general economic uncertainty in the larger financial markets in the U.S. and abroad, the vintage comic book market continues to shock and surprise with its vigor and vitality. Long time collectors continue to take great pleasure and pride in acquiring new additions to their collections, and new buyers are constantly entering the hobby looking for an investment that brings a satisfaction of ownership despite the specifics of the return. At the same time, several high profile sales have resulted in more collections coming to light, and the release of several long-held hordes has meant that a tremendous amount of high quality material was made available in a relatively short amount of time.

With 4 Featured Auctions, 7 Focused Auctions, and ComicLink's Comic Book Exchange running 24/7, there were far too many impressive and record sales in 2011 to list any more than just a small fraction. There were some notable standouts, however, that are worth pointing out as evidence of certain market trends. Superman is truly the greatest of all superheroes and the market has clearly decided that his earliest appearances are among the most coveted collectibles in the world. A CGC 6.5 example of *Action Comics #1*, one of only 2 at this grade level, traded hands for $625,000 and a solid CGC 4.5 example of the premiere issue of his own run, *Superman* #1 found a new home at $126,111 – both are record prices in the conditions sold. Other early *Action Comics* sales included a #5 CGC 8.5 for $52,500, #10 CGC 3.0 for $20,351, and #54 CGC 8.5 for $4459. Sales on Golden Age Batman appearances were not far behind with strong interest in examples across all grade ranges for early and important appearances in *Batman* and *Detective Comics*. *Detective Comics* #31 CGC 3.0 sold for $20,250, while a stunning CGC 9.4 example of issue #142 (second Riddler appearance) traded hands for $21,250. Meanwhile a very sharp example of *Batman* #47 featuring Batman's origin story graded at 8.0 and brought a record $10,099.

Interest also rose sharply on Golden Age appearances of Captain America with the build up to and release of the feature film. A *Captain America Comics* #32 in CGC 9.4 went for $11,750 while a 7.0 example of issue #46 which features a distinctive WWII-themed Concentration Camp cover sold for $8101. This interest carried over to other Golden Age Timelys with sales like *Marvel Mystery Comics* #9 CGC 5.5 for $19,801 and *All Winners #7 CGC 6.5 for $3,736* also setting records.

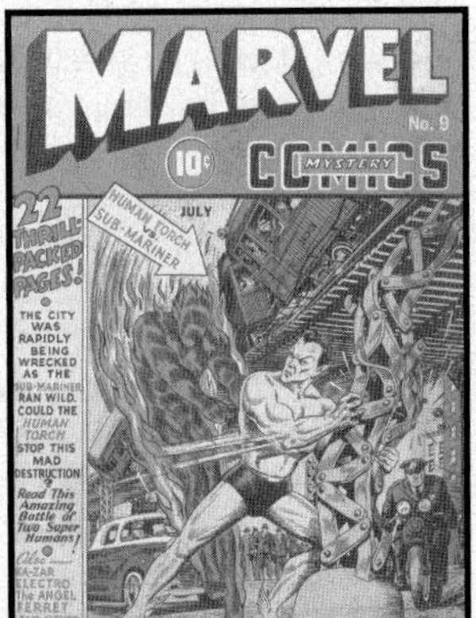

Sales of Golden Age Timelys like **Marvel Mystery Comics #9** are setting records.

Scarcity, either in grade or in general also drove the Golden Age market in 2011, along with the appeal of classic cover art. Just a few examples included *Weird Science Fantasy* #29 CGC 9.4 for $8315 (classic Frank Frazetta cover), *Archie Comics* #50 CGC 6.5 at $1100 (classic Betty cover), *Terrific Comics* #5 CGC 1.8 for $5033 (scarce with a classic Schomburg bondage cover), *Blue Beetle* #54 CGC 6.0 at $2700 (lingerie "Good Girl Art" cover), and *New Adventure Comics* #26 CGC 1.0 for $7956 (considered one of the toughest issues in any condition from this run).

Key Silver Age issues featuring the first appearances of major heroes and villains make up what is perhaps the most dynamic end of the vintage comic book market. Just as in the Golden Age, interest in Captain America issues from the

1960s rose sharply this year. Leading the way was a record-setting $91,501 sale of a CGC 9.6 example of *Avengers* #4, the hero's first appearance in the Silver Age. With an Avengers movie on the way, there was also interest in early issues from the "World's Greatest Heroes" run. A CGC 9.4 example of *Avengers* #1 found a new home for $100,000, a substantial record in grade while a CGC 8.5 went for $15,259. Other heroes that benefited from movie releases in 2011 were Thor, with *Journey Into Mystery* #83 (his first appearance) in CGC 9.0 selling for $52,102, and Green Lantern, with a CGC 8.0 *Green Lantern* #1 trading hands for $5799. Additionally, with a reboot of the Amazing Spider-Man film franchise right around the corner, the Web-Slinger seems poised for yet another upswing in the market. Examples of notable Spider-Man sales in 2011 included, but of course were not nearly limited to, *Amazing Spider-Man* #7 CGC 9.4 for $7757, #13 CGC 9.6 at $45,000, and #25 CGC 9.8 for $26,500. These Hollywood films are here to stay and the characters featured in them are getting nearly unprecedented "mainstream" exposure. This will likely continue to drive the market for years to come. A few other examples of notable record-busting Silver Age sales included *Flash* #105 CGC 9.2 for $36,888, and *Fantastic Four* #1 CGC 8.5 for $83,022. Iron Man comic books also continued to blast through the roof with his first appearance in *Tales of Suspense* #39 selling for $150,000 in CGC 9.4 and the debut of the title bearing his name, *Iron Man* #1, selling for $69,600 in CGC 9.9.

Availability has affected much of the Bronze Age market, with large increases in the number certified in the highest grades for many issues adjusting market expectations. That said, key issues and books from significant runs that have proven to be very tough to find in the highest grades remain extremely desirable. A great example of this is the $150,000 sale of the single highest certified CGC 9.9 MINT of the first full appearance of Wolverine in *Incredible Hulk* #181. This was the very first comic from the 1970s to ever sell for six-figures and an impressive demonstration of just how important this comic is to collectors of that era. Examples of other Bronze Age record breakers included *X-Men* #81 CGC 9.8 Double Cover for $3333, *Giant-Size Daredevil* #1 CGC 9.8 for $1459, and *House of Secrets* #92 CGC 9.8 (first Swamp Thing) for $16,350.

If I had to place a distinct moniker on 2011 for the vintage comic book market as a whole it would be "The Year of the Educated Buyer". The Web, and specifically ComicLink, has served as a virtual marketplace for comics books practically since its very inception and in the years since, the amount of accumulated information seems to have increased annually at an exponential rate. At this point, it would seem that most established collectors are deeply immersed in the flow of data permeating the hobby and are keeping up with what is happening on the ComicLink Exchange and within ComicLink auction venues on a weekly and at times even a *daily* basis. It is becoming increasingly important to anyone deciding to make an investment in vintage comics or beginning the process of selling their treasured collection, to have accurate information. I advise those that cannot keep up with it all, and are ready to sell, or make a significant investment decision, to be in touch with me, or other contacts at ComicLink, for information and guidance.

The sea of information, data, and opinion can be very difficult to navigate at times even for the most savvy buyer or seller, however, and it can be especially so for collectors new to the market and those just starting to actively sell. Understanding why certain titles, issue numbers, eras, and genres sell for more than others can be difficult enough to understand for the uninitiated. For decades, great resources like the *Overstreet Comic Book Price Guide* have gone a long way in levelling the playing field, but in the current market, buyers and sellers often need to make sense of questions like why one example of a comic book in a certified grade, might sell for 20% more or less than another one in the same grade. Some of this might have to do with the "upside" or "downside" potential of a particular selling environment. Other cases might be the results of "mainstream" influences from outside the core of the hobby, such as the bump many runs and specific issues have seen over the past few years from major movie releases such as *Iron Man*, *Captain America*, *Green Lantern*, and the upcoming *Avengers* film. It can even be as simple as realizing that even with certification, comic book grading retains an element of subjectivity, and that not every book in a given CGC grade is considered equal by every buyer.

Whatever the reasons, this variability underscores the importance of being well-informed and the quickest route to this is finding advocacy. The online and print resources are great, but gathering and making sense of the information can not only be time-consuming, but it can also require expert analysis based on years of experience in the hobby. I can't count the number of times where a seller has come to us looking to list a book on ComicLink for substantially less money than I knew I could get for it in short order; or where even the most aggressive market estimate on a comic was greatly exceeded at auction. Under different circumstances, such as going it alone online without ComicLink's reach, reputation, and guidance, the seller's net return might have been much less. As the comic book hobby continues to mature, the market becomes more established, and the record results escalate year after year, the benefit of expert council for buyers and sellers will grow right along with them.

Tom Gordon III
Collector

The comic book market continues to be a robust market across the board with sales in the back issue marketplace. Record sales are continuing for truly rare and key items. We are very fortunate to see this as some other fields in collecting are continuing to see "graying" with age and are not seeing the infusion of new collectors/investors. Some areas once strong with collectors are seeing less interest than previously. Unless there are dramatic changes in these collecting fields, they will continue to stagnate without new blood.

For years we have categorized key comics by era including Golden Age, Silver, and Bronze. With the past few years of record sales in six-figure and seven-figure territory. I think it's easy to see that there is a list of these books which cross the boundaries of comic eras. The list includes in order *Action Comics* #1, *Detective Comics* #27, *Superman* #1, *Batman* #1, *Action Comics* #7, *Amazing Fantasy* #15, *Fantastic Four* #1, *Amazing Spider-Man* #1, *Showcase* #4, *X-Men* #1, *Avengers* #1, and several others. I think now would be the ideal time to create a new Top Comic list for these books.

The words "Avengers Assemble" are without a doubt on the forefront of comic fans minds as May 4, 2012 and the *Avengers* movie is released. This movie will definitely take its place as one of the all-time greatest films in the comic book genre. *The Dark Knight Rises* is also probably a close second or tied evenly on fans' minds depending on the day and which film has released the latest trailer or movie poster. Both films will no doubt break box office records, but Marvel may honestly edge out DC a bit as they have truly set up the *Avengers* as the ultimate superhero team movie. Marvel carefully and strategically built the film from the individual superhero films. Regardless, it will be another banner year for comic book movies and we can only appreciate that the general public will take interest in comics.

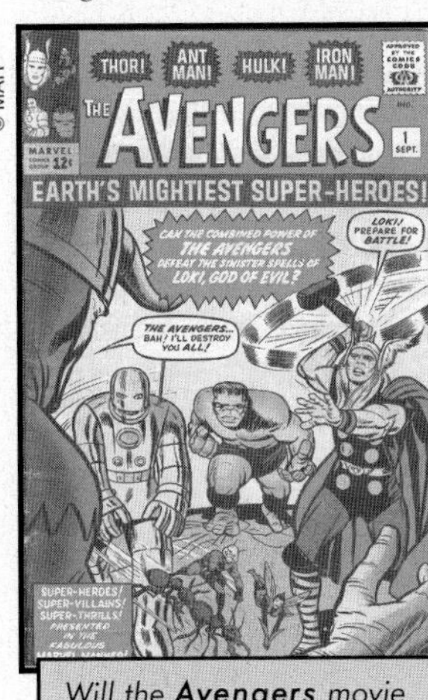

Will the **Avengers** movie be one of the all-time greatest films in the comic book genre? (#1 shown)

CGC continues to be a major force in the marketplace whether it's a 9.6 Mile High pedigree comic or a record price for a 9.9 Modern Age book. The certified market has truly changed the way comics are bought and sold and also assisted in bringing in buyers at levels that seemed impossible not too many years ago. Comic books are getting to be on par with certified coins, currency, and sports cards.

When it comes to comics, rarity is continuing to be key. In the 1990s the idea of breaking a million dollar auction total was something of a dream and today it's a reality on a consistent basis. There are numerous auctions which are easily exceeding these amounts. Also, as we all know comic books in the past few years have broken the ceiling of million dollar sales and appear to have no slowdown in sight! We should continue to see a banner year in 2012.

John Haines
John Haines Rare Comics

Any discussion of the 2011 comic book marketplace has to begin with the event of the year: The DC New 52. Our brick and mortar store, Comics and Friends, experienced explosive growth in both subscribers and the raw number of comics sold from the start of the *Flashpoint* limited series right through the second issues of the New 52 titles with things stabilizing somewhat by the third issues. The excitement and energy that this retooling of the DCU has brought to the hobby cannot be understated. We ordered multiple times the normal copies we would get for DC titles and have nearly sold through by the third month – in many cases we only have second or third printings of the 1st issues, and in fact, just sold our last first print *Action* #1 the week after Thanksgiving.

Many of our new subscribers are readers who had left comics in the '90s but were attracted back by media reports of the event. Others are simply long-time readers who were tired of not being able to get copies of comics they wanted at their regular store and have decided to give us a try. When we heard the responses from our customers to the new books, we ordered even more of the second issues and were not disappointed. For the main Batman, Superman, and Flash titles, we sold even more #2s than we did #1s – and continued to add more subscribers.

What else has the New 52 done? Well, it generated a lot of interest in the last year's worth of issues of the titles that they were replacing. We had to reorder runs of *Batman and Robin*, *Flash*, *Superman*, etc. due to new readers asking to see what happened prior to the New titles. It has also sparked an interest in vintage DC comics as well. We now have collectors who check in weekly to see what new "old" DC comics we've gotten in since their last visit. And, we should also note that demand for first printings of the New 52 titles have pushed prices on the regular issues up to the $10 range and fans do not seem to be complaining at all. Not all of the titles have been successful of course, but the excitement it has generated is very welcome. Thanks DC!

New Comics and Products: After the DC New 52, the most consistent seller for the year has to be *The Walking Dead*. New subscribers add this title every month, and the trade paperbacks just keep on selling. We try to keep at least three copies of every *Walking Dead* softcover trade on the shelf at all times and have trouble doing it. Once someone starts with Volume 1, we see them again and again until they have read them all. Back issues are gone as soon as we put them on the shelf. The exception to this is the *Walking Dead Weekly* which is not a good seller at all for us. No other Image title comes close to this one but *Spawn*, *Hack/Slash*, and *Haunt* do sell as well as most Marvel and DC Titles. A pleasant surprise this summer was the *Carbon Grey* miniseries. We had a good feeling about this one, and ordered plenty of the first issue. It sold out so quickly that we had to get copies from dealers at shows in order to have some for the shelves. At this time the *Carbon Grey Origins* two issue run is beginning and we are hearing the same raves from the fans that we heard about the first one.

Another pleasant trend for us is the reader/fan response to the Dynamite titles. *Jennifer Blood* sells at around the level that *Deadpool* sells for us – amazing! I guess there has been untapped demand for a soccer-mom contract assassin that we weren't aware of. Of course the Garth Ennis scripts and those sexy covers don't hurt either. Ninjettes! Other solid Dynamite titles are: *Warlord of Mars, Deja Thoris*, *Red Sonja*, *The Boys*, and *Stargate*. Kirby Genesis has tailed off for us, likewise *Vampirella* and *Green Hornet*.

Some things never change and Good-Girl art has always been a fan favorite. The Golden Age had Matt Baker and Bill Ward. Current readers have the Zenescope *Grimm Fairy Tales* titles and *Tarot Witch of the Black Rose*. Both are solid sellers with loyal readers – and the first issue of the new Big Dog title *Oz The Wicked West* has outsold both of those. Likewise, there has always been demand for Teenage Mutant Ninja Turtles and the new IDW version with Eastman on board has been a hit. These Turtles are not for kids and that's what people like about them. Most of the other IDW movie/TV tie-ins are modest sellers with *Godzilla* doing slightly better.

Marvel's perennial top dogs continue to be Deadpool and Wolverine. The Astonishing titles are doing well and the new Ultimates line with the new Spider-Man are also doing very well. The Ultimate Spidey is growing on readers who seemed at first hesitant to check him out and fans seem impressed with Ultimate Hawkeye as well. Mark Waid was a welcome addition to *Daredevil* which had dwindling sales for a while but is now regaining readers who are enjoying the current storyline. *Fear Itself* was fun, readers liked it for the most part, but they are beginning to feel that Marvel is taking the bucket to the well once too often. There are **alot** of titles/crossovers/ one shots for *Fear Itself* and many customers are finding it hard to justify the expense of purchasing them all. Conversely, the Spider-Island titles seemed just about right. A good storyline to draw readers in and then a few crossovers and specials to round things out.

Kids comics are on the move. The last *Sonic the Hedgehog* story arc was a monster with issues selling out in the first week. The new *Mega Man* series is also a huge hit – they sell so fast it's hard to determine how many to order! Archie titles continue to sell decently with the *Life With Archie Magazine* and the *Double Digest* series leading the way. Archies have generally slowed since the Archie Gets Married issues a few years back so we hope big things are in store for the new Archie/Kiss crossover.

Scooby-Doo has solid readership along with the DC Cartoon Network related comics. Sales on the current Disney books have slowed somewhat. *Richie Rich* has done well – especially since there hadn't been a new title for so long. Bongo is going great guns – all of the *Simpsons* related titles fly off the shelves. And back issues for all of these are quick to go – we have three spin racks set up in the store all filled with back-issue kids books. We hear that tell-tale squeak and we know someone is looking for an elusive back issue! The biggest seller, bar none, in the kids' genre this year has been *Mad Magazine*. The new TV cartoon show has breathed new life into the venerable institution. It's not the Mad that those over 40 remember, but the new readers adore it just as much as the old readers did theirs.

Bronze/Copper Age: Bronze Age remains the biggest seller of all the time periods by volume. We sell more comics from 1969 to 1984 than we do from any other category. This is surely due to the fact that there are a lot of these available, the prices are relatively low (and have been pretty stable in common grade), and there are just tons and tons of great stories with great art from this period. Most asked for are Neal Adams issues – collectors all want his *Green Lantern* and *X-Men* issues, while Deadman and the DC cover issues are a bit slower, they still sell steadily. Adams' short run on *The Avengers* during the Kree-Skrull war continues to be in demand, ditto those great Ra's Al Ghul and Joker Batmans! After that it's anybody's game. In this arena it all sells: Movie/TV, Western, War, Cartoon Characters, Horror, and Super-Hero – they all have fans looking to fill holes. Mid-grade issues actually sell the quickest, with real low-grade issues only moving at bargain prices. True high-grade issues from this period are in demand but to a smaller segment of collectors. These individuals are dogged in their pursuit of high-grade gems and will spend money commensurate with condition and scarcity.

We are asking, and getting, up to 20 times top *Guide* for raw (unslabbed) copies of mainstay titles like *Flash*, *Amazing Spider-Man*, and *Scooby-Doo*. Also of note is the increased demand, and decreased supply, of square bound giant-size issues from the Bronze Age. Collectors are looking for solid copies of DC 100 page giants along with the Marvel *Giant-Size* series and are frustrated to find them not available. Surprisingly, Treasury Editions have taken off again. The *Superman Vs. Muhammad Ali* reprint from last year has seemingly ignited a dormant demand for these over-sized oddities. Because these are so large and do not fit into normal comic boxes, high grade copies of these are very hard to find – and that's what collectors want! We sell these steadily at all the conventions we bring them to. Marvel black and white magazines are on the move again along with Atlas/Seaboard titles – we are always asked for them and we buy them whenever they are offered to us.

The big ticket sellers everyone knows: *Teenage Mutant Ninja Turtles* #1, *Hulk* #181, *Tomb of Dracula* #10, *Marvel Spotlight* #5, *Amazing Spider-Man* #121, #122, and #129, *Marvel Preview* #2, *X-Men* #94, *Giant-Size X-Men* #1, *Batman* #232, *Green Lantern* #76, *Star Wars* #1 variant, *House of Secrets* #92, and *Cerebus* #1 (anyone seen one? We counted ourselves lucky to get a collection in recently that started with #4! Forget about that #1.)

Silver Age: Everyone loves Spider-Man! The Silver Age really is a Spider-Man centered universe. We just cannot keep issues in stock. All grades, all issues – there is demand across the board. The really low-grade issues have actually started to sell the quickest which was a bit of a change from previous years. But really, all *ASM* issues are in demand. Next up is *The Avengers* – with the impending movie, folks are filling holes quickly anticipating price increases – followed closely by Batman. Superman issues are going strong but *Adventure* has slowed to a crawl. *Flash*, *Green Lantern*, *Justice League*, *Tales of Suspense*, and *Thor* are going strong. In general it's the same every year – superhero titles from the Silver Age always have a solid following.

Anyone have a decent copy of Gold Key's *Scarecrow of Romney Marsh*? We are constantly asked for it, and when we do get one, it sells right away. The first issue seems to be the easiest to find with the second and third issues rarely showing up. This is possibly the most in demand non-superhero comic of the Silver Age. Another oddball comic that always commands an audience is *Mad Monster Party* from Dell. This is a relatively scarce item that is based on a Harvey Kurtzman premise. See how many you can spot during convention season.

Charlton comics are on the upswing. The late 1950s issues have solid demand - mostly the oddball titles but also the Western and War. Watch for Matt Baker reprints in the Charlton War comics. ACG titles are all very slow – we have long runs of *Forbidden Worlds* and *Adventures into the Unknown* with relatively few takers. The exception being issues containing Herbie which have modest demand. Tower comics are steady – we get groups of *Thunder Agents* in every spring and by year's end most are gone – this year was no exception.

Gold Key movie/TV comics had a strong showing for the year but their superhero issues like *Magnus* and *Solar* were just so-so. *Classics Illustrated* are red hot – we sell these as fast as we can get them – almost all in mid- to low-grade – high grade *Classics* do not seem to have a following at this time. Warren magazines have shown increased demand – we have sold multiple runs of *Creepy*, *Eerie*, and *Vampirella* and are always looking to get more.

Golden Age: We have seen an uptick in demand for the later Fiction House issues of *Jungle*, *Jumbo*, and *Planet* with those great good-girl covers. In fact, most good girl issues from this period are solid sellers. Archie comics are highly sought and we receive want lists for them constantly. Dell movie comics with photo covers are very solid – the grade is not terribly important – collectors just want solid copies with decent looking covers. Westerns had been slow for a while but have picked up over the summer – low-grade reading copies go first and high-grade copies are just sitting. Non-EC Horror and Sci-Fi comics have slowed greatly for us but thankfully that has been offset by interest in the Atlas War titles like *Combat Casey* and *Battlefront*. These are great reads and are still fairly inexpensive compared with their super hero counterparts.

EC comics have always been in demand and will continue to always be in demand because they are just so darn good! We used to get them in frequently but have not really been able to restock for a few years now –still those that we do get in sell right away. DC comics from this period are just plain hard to find – we were lucky to get a batch in and most are already gone – again! Timely – forget about it. We sell them right around guide and cannot keep them – we just picked up a few *Miss America* and *Daring Mystery* issues and expect them to be gone by the time this sees print.

Early issues of Gleason titles sell well but the later 1950's issues do not – they just gather dust – eventually someone will trip over these and realize how ridiculously cheap they are. Fox issues are slow. Dells are selling very well with a focus on Disney titles right now.

Classics Illustrated are solid with demand for first prints the strongest although later printings do sell based on price. Fawcett issues have slowed from previous years and there seem to be enough Captain Marvel comics to go around right now. Quality comics are actually hot – *Feature*, *Police*, *Smash*, *Hit*, and *Crack* are all selling very well in all grades.

Spirit sections are hot – with price increases due in the not too distant future. Has anyone seen any of the early Harvey super-hero issues? We have been looking for *Green Hornet*, *Prize*, *Speed*, and *Champ* with no luck.

We actually see more Centaur issues than we do these Harveys. Speaking of Centaur - they are maybe the hottest section of the market. *Guide* prices seem very low on these, and we sell them right away at well over *Guide*. We also watch them sell for crazy prices at auction. If you have Centaurs out there, this may be the time to bring them to market.

Greg Holland, Ph.D.
Collector

Valiant Comics: The market for Valiant comics has been fairly stable for a few years, with a few books consistently selling for prices that might shock those who view all comics from the 1990s as bargain bin material. For example, *Harbinger* #1 consistently sells for $40+ online 'unslabbed', and $500+ in CGC 9.8. That's right, $500+. Those prices are down from the $1,000+ prices seen in a dozen sales in 2008 and 2009. The majority of books printed by Valiant in 1993-94 are bargain bin material, but earlier and later Valiant comics are still quite collectible for first appearances and lower print runs relative to other 1990s comics. ValiantFans.com continues to be a busy site and message-board for collectors. By the time this report is printed, Valiant will have returned to publication, starting with Free Comic Book Day 2012. It will be interesting to see what impact Valiant's return has on the back issue market. Twenty years ago, collectors were kicking themselves for missing out on *Harbinger* #1. Will something similar occur with the new Valiant comics?

CGC Census: Since 2003, I have been compiling the population data from the CGC census website. A variety of search options are available on my website - CGCdata.com - allowing visitors to see how many copies of comics have received what grades over the past decade. A few numbers that may be of interest are (as of December 2010): 1,686,347 CGC-graded comics with an average grade of 8.84. Universal grades make up 90.3%, Signature Series are 7%, Restored are 1.6%, Qualified are 1.1%. 2,039 books have received the CGC 10 grade, or about 1-in-827 slabs. The average Universal grades by decade are: 9.7 for the 2000s, 9.6 for the 1990s, 9.4 for the 1980s, 8.9 for the 1970s, 7.7 for the 1960s, 7.2 for the 1950s, 6.8 for the 1940s, and 5.5 for the 1930s. The most often submitted books are *Wolverine Limited Series* #1 (1982) and *Amazing Spider-Man* #300 (1988). Marvel leads all publishers submitted with 61%, and DC is next with 19%. Comics from 2006 (led by *Civil War* #1 and *Amazing Spider-Man* #529) were submitted more than any other year, but the second most popular comic year for submissions is 1968, the year that gave us *Iron Man* #1, *Silver Surfer* #1, *Captain America* #100 and *Incredible Hulk* #102.

Comic Ages: Though it is a controversial topic, I feel compelled to offer a suggestion to the comic collecting community regarding comic ages. Traditional names like Golden Age and Silver Age serve their purpose well, but we're quickly approaching an end to the usefulness of such labels. Debating the beginning and end of more recent ages such as Copper seems like a waste of time. If we're talking about comic books from the 1980s, why don't we simply call them "1980s comics"? There's no confusion about what comics are being discussed, and there's no debate about which dates are included. While major content, style, or culture shifts are often cited as the beginning and ending events for comic ages, I'm sure we all agree that those shifts never happened on the same date for all publishers. We can either continue to debate whether the Bronze Age started with a book from early 1970, or late 1970, or sometime in 1971, and debate whether the Bronze Age ended before 1980 or as late as the mid-1980s, and ultimately never reach a unanimous decision, or we could just call them "1970s comics". If you mean to focus on comics from 1970-1984, just say so. Modern Age is a moving target that doesn't work either. 1980s, 1990s, 2000s, 2010s. So simple. I'm sure I'm not the only collector who thinks years make more sense than naming decreasingly-valued metals and arguing about start and end points. The confusion is really unnecessary.

Dennis Keum
Fantasy-Comics

Our sales continue to grow in both volume and higher dollar totals with steady demand throughout the year. Big premiums are being paid for certain high demand books while more common material continues to have a high degree of buyer price sensitivity. Demand is out there but for low to mid-grade Silver and Bronze along with Moderns, discounts and free shipping were key components to drive strong sales. The fact is with stagnant or dropping incomes, the vast majority are being squeezed by rising costs. While certain prices have decreased such as everyday electronics like TVs and smart phones, others more important to long term health of society, such as quality healthcare and education, are seemingly becoming more out of reach for more people everyday. It is no wonder in a difficult economy, collectors are looking for deals and taking respite reading and collecting comics.

© MAR

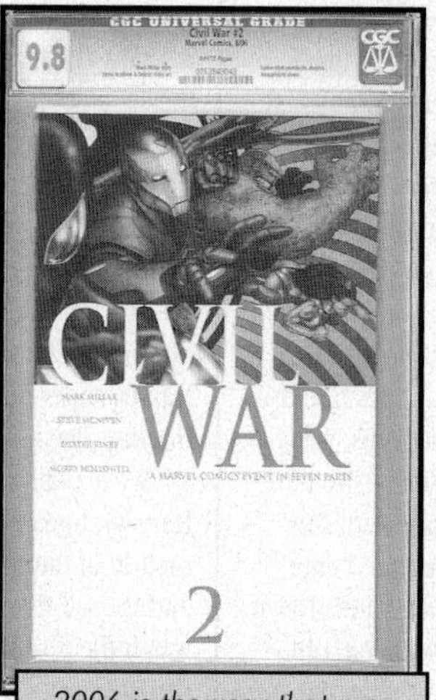

2006 is the year that produced the most comics submitted to CGC for grading. (Civil War #2 shown)

eBay vs. Individual Websites: Successful sales on individual company websites were varied through the year. With an individual website, keeping things fresh with new inventory, newsletters, discounts and other promotions are a must. Comparatively, with eBay one thing is certain in that you really don't have to worry about attracting buyers. As a marketplace, eBay is tough to match with its vast number of global buyers and sellers in one place as compared to any other single website. A particular challenge for sellers is in complying with their constant company policy updates. While these changes have been ongoing, that is generally true with any business and with the world in general. It is amazing to see certain businesses becoming overnight successes. Did anyone hear of Google 10 years ago? Or Facebook 5 years ago? Yet both have become huge business successes and have brought about important social change throughout the world. It is sad to see other businesses that have been around for generations suddenly cease to exist. Where did Borders go? In today's environment, businesses can come and go faster than ever. Seemingly the world keeps changing at a faster pace and you have to adapt quickly to survive.

CGC Books: For the certified market, as comic dealers and collectors we can all say that CGC helps make this a very exciting hobby. Not only does the company help safely buy and sell a book that has gone through a restoration check but also be assured of a comic that is generally accurately graded and presented in a safe, professional looking holder. This trust is why collectors are willing to pay huge premiums for the certification. For the year we sent in more books to CGC for certification than in any previous year. When sending books in for certification, being the owner, there are always many books that come back with grades less than expected, there may be a few better, with the vast majority around what you would expect. It is interesting that there is a huge dichotomy in perception of value once a comic book is in a holder. Collectors are still excited about 9.9s and 10s and are willing to pay staggering premiums over their raw counterparts. On the other hand, most Modern books graded less than a 9.8 are generally viewed as having no value, despite there being an actual comic in the holder. At certain lesser grades many Silver and Bronze books have no premium value over *Guide* and often sell at a discount which is especially true when sold in an auction format. There is also a huge segment out there that will not purchase a book because it is CGC graded. It is difficult to convince these collectors that there is an actual comic in a holder that can be taken out.

Collections and Pricing: With regards to new material entering the market, it was amazing to see the number of original owner Golden Age material that was offered. While this material caused a lot of excitement, it also shows if these early books are still being found, it must be asked, how many more high grade original owner collections and other just plain nice books are out there. While certification is a must when buying and selling high grade books, in terms of relative value of certain high grade CGC books there are variables of supply and demand that should play an important role in the coming years. On the supply side there are yet to be found original owner collections and additional high grade population growth coming from pressing and attaining certification upgrades. On the demand side there may be a general declining collector base for collecting full high grade certified runs. This trend has been seen in softening or declining prices in certified non-key Silver Age, most Bronze and Modern Age books and we should expect this trend to continue.

With huge premiums paid and decreases in value in other certified books, this leads to a more general question of what is the accurate price for any comic book graded vs. raw, and how do you assess value at any given time. The difficulty in fully understanding an accurate valuation can sometimes be better understood looking back at historical price movements of many assets. With housing over the past 10 years, we saw unprecedented price appreciation and at a certain point most thought there was a new era of no risk where prices would only go up. Then there was a major crash which most people and even market experts did not see coming. During the price run-up years, it was easier to understand market value but more difficult to understand or believe in inherent value.

Certainly in the uncertified comic market the *Guide* currently reflects a good general benchmark of what most comics are bought and sold for. In the certified market, we can see market value quickly with tools such as GPA and though the *Guide* only lists prices up to 9.2 in most cases, it may be observed that prices tend to be undervalued in the *Guide*. The flip side is there are many collectors out there that say the *Guide* value is inaccurate because too many books are overpriced and can be found for a discount at shows. Here though the transaction may not necessarily represent accurate value just because there was a wholesale transaction between two parties in one part of the country. The book usually has a completely different and usually higher value in another part of the country or in the international market. The conclusion is there's no doubt that the *Guide* has taken a more conservative approach towards reflecting price increases. However with premiums and spreads paid for non-key and high grade common certified books generally coming down, a longer term trend may show the conservative valuation and spreads shown in the *Guide* may have been more accurate than certain market prices after all.

Conventions: Shows can be a lot of work but also a place to find some quality material at great prices. Whether you buy and sell high grade or are looking for low grade reader copies, artwork, or looking to meet your favorite celebrity or get your books signed, it really is an exciting place to spend money and have a good time. While the buying and selling makes this business seem like work it can be easily forgotten that this is supposed to be a fun hobby. At the end of the day though it's all the people involved in comics that make this an exciting hobby. Many I've met through this business are some of the most wonderful people out there and whom today I can call friends. It's the people and of course the hunt for the next collection. In every new collection there's always something you haven't seen before and the excitement of finding a book that looks extraordinarily nice that you want to send in for certification.

Ben Lichtenstein
Zapp Comics

Greetings from New Jersey. As this is my first report, some background information. We are a brick and mortar operation with 2 shops, open since 1993. We devote a lot of effort and space to back issues and other secondary market lines, like toys and cards. In addition, we set up at most of the major East Coast conventions, as well as Chicago. eBay sales also play a part in our business, albeit a smaller one.

Trade Paperbacks/Hardcovers: We're experiencing much price resistance on collected editions. It is hard to justify a $19.99 cover price for a mediocre 5-issue mini-series. Our customers are willing to buy TPBs at cover price, but only for the very best material by the best creators. We have also seen a surge in interest in out of print TPBs, with many fetching double to triple cover when they fall out of print, however temporary. Everything else has been a struggle to sell unless placed on extreme sale.

New Releases: DC scored a huge hit with the New 52. Of the 52 new titles, at least half have shown consistent sales, with about 10 of them in our topsellers consistently.

In our neck of the woods, the new #1s were severely under-ordered by other shops and first prints were scarce across the state. We are encouraging the readers by stocking every issue of every title at cover price, while also providing first prints for the collectors, making everyone happy.

It felt like 1993 all over again for a few weeks, as tons of new faces came in to purchase them. Also, many dealers/shop owners came snooping around to buy them from us at cover. Interesting times indeed.

While we happily kept all on the shelves at cover price, once new printings arrived, we sold 1st prints at generally $4, with *Batgirl*, *Detective*, *Justice League*, *Nightwing* and *Animal Man* commanding $8 to $10 each. *Justice League* #1 2nd prints sold out at $20 each, due to a low print run and a gorgeous cover.

Similarly at the New York Comic Con, our racks of DC 52 #1 1st prints sold extremely well at $4 to $10 each. Even more positive, the new 52 series are showing legs, with continued interest through #5 on and many new readers coming in and purchasing all available issues on specific titles. An interesting trend is that we're seeing many confirmed Marvel readers make the switch to DC because of this relaunch. This made for a tremendous September for us, with sales about 25% higher than September 2010.

On the Marvel side, *Kick Ass* has been a big hit, selling in bigger numbers than most of their superhero fare. Marvel has relaunched *Uncanny X-Men*, with little interest from readers. Reader feedback is an overwhelming one of confusion/boredom with the Marvel Universe at this time. *Fear Itself* startedoff well and sold respectable numbers, but those were way down from the days of *Civil War*. *Incredible Hulk* #1 with Silvestri art did well and continues to have legs. *Wolverine* has sold better due to the writing of Jason Aaron, of *Scalped* fame.

Image had many sleeper hits, with strong interest in many oftheir new #1s. Titles such as *Blue Estate*, *Carbon Grey*, and *Fatale* have drawn good interest, though they're not huge sellers. We've seen a trend of high interest in almost all Image #1s, with some titles continuing and others not quite hooking their readers.

Chew and *Morning Glories* still selling consistently as new and back issues, while *Invincible* has cooled somewhat. We sold many *Invincible* #1 1st prints this year for $25 to $50 each, but most of the other back issues have cooled greatly. *The Walking Dead*, thanks to the excellent TV series, showed a big spike in new comics sales, and back issues sell as fast as we can get them.

Anything Bane-related is hot right now, as he is the main villain in the next Dark Knight movie. We broke out those Knightfall issues from 1993 and sell loads of them at over cover price. *Batman* #497(Bane breaks Batman's back) sells well at $4.00 to $5.00. I'm serious. Similarly, the *Vengeance of Bane* one-shot sells easily at $20 to $25 and Vengeance of Bane II, $12.

Bronze Age: We've experienced very strong sales in almost all Bronze Age Marvels and DCs. We sell tons of below 9.0 copies to readers/completists. Generally, we're selling them for 25 to 50% of *Guide*, depending on title. On the flipside, anytime we get clean, high grade Bronze Marvels, they are gobbled up at *Guide* and over by buyers who will press and slab them. I definitely have more buyers than supply for high-grade Bronze. Pricing on Keys is always 1.2 to 1.6 *Guide* in various lower grades, with no price resistance.

While Marvel is king, DC Bronze does very well for us as well, with highest demand for anl Neal Adams work, any Batmans, *Green Lantern* and *Wonder Woman* to name a few.

We do a brisk business in Charltons/Gold Keys and Archies, priced about 20% to 30% of *Guide* on average. Overall, we can sell any and all Bronze Age when priced appropriately.

Silver Age: We've been very lucky to pick up some nice Silver Age inventory, with very good turnover. We've moved several copies of *Amazing Fantasy* #15, *Amazing Spider-Man* #1, *X-Men* #1, *Avengers* #1, etc. In general, they have moved well in line. I won't bore you with lots of statistics on our Silver Age sales, as the more focused dealers in this book will do it far better than I can.

Golden Age: It always sells well for us, and we can never get enough.

When we set up at conventions, we bring a wide mixture of categories. Our $1 stock turns over very well, and boxes of $2 and $3 low-grade oldies doing very, very well. We find there's plenty of demand out there for almost anything before 1980, as long as it's priced right.

2011 was an excellent year for us, with sales on new issues and back issues markedly up over 2010. With the full advent of digital comics here to stay, we've seen only increases in our overall print new comic sales. It remains to be seen how and when the migration to digital will begin.

Overall, it's been a hectic, exciting year. If you're in the New Jersey area or attending one of the East Coast conventions, please look us up.

Jon McClure
Collector

For the record, I generally sell low end keys and pre-1980 comics of all types, in all grades Fair and up, under $1000, and virtually all of those for under $500. Despite the ongoing recession, comics have set amazing records with Golden Age keys like *Action* #1 and *Detective* #27. Paradoxically, more modern high-grade keys like *Green Lantern* #76 have plummeted from previously achieved stellar heights. The rarest of Bronze Age books (such as 1977 35 cent variant Marvel Westerns) would bring more than common keys like *Incredible Hulk* #181, even in mid-grade, if a single copy were to surface for sale, but some books in runs such as *Kid Colt Outlaw* #218-220 have only one known copy in existence, which makes this highly improbable, and it serves as a perfect example of why the first appearance of Superman and Batman, although rarely exchanging hands in high grade, were discussed in the million-dollar plus range for many years before any actual sales occurred. It is difficult to nail down reasonable market value on truly rare and desirable items, regardless of the virtual certainty of such, without such gems actually changing hands.

Dell "Now 10c" Variants turn out to be all books with

cover dates of 9/58,9-10/58 and 9-11/58, which are the latest uncommon test market variants to hit the radar, but these pale in comparison to the rarity of Archie 15 cent test market variants (of which 112 are currently known to exist, with cover dates ranging from 2/62 to 4/63), especially keys such as *Madhouse* #22, another example of a killer gem with only one variant copy currently confirmed to exist. The *Madhouse* #22 15 cent test market variant has yet to change hands, and such ultra-rare items, with standard 12 cent copies of the same issue already vastly undervalued in the *Guide* could, and likely would, bring at least 5-10K in a major comic book auction, at least on any day without a nuclear war announced in the news. One must read between the lines when it comes to such super-collectibles, and people with financial motives often work to keep such matters under wraps until it profits them to do otherwise, which is only one reason for my ceaseless efforts to disseminate information to collectors worldwide on the broad and complex subject of Variant comics.

So-called "foreign editions," being U.S. copies printed simultaneously for foreign distribution are actually cover variants, with UK priced copies being only one example, will continue to remain lost in the self-serving mists and midst of obfuscation at the hands of big money and influence, despite the inarguable truth of the matter, and overall scarcity of same. My lengthy article in the *Overstreet Guide* #40, pages #1010-1038, was an attempt to jump start understanding across the board, and it is working. A number of new variant types have surfaced in the last two years, and I will revisit the subject in detail once again in the not-too-distant future, when further stones have been overturned by collectors, at least enough to justify such efforts.

As is almost always the case with such rarities, dealers have no financial interest to pursue "new" collectibles until they stumble upon them or possess knowledge of them, and even then, they must literally pursue and bring such items to market with full disclosure, which is difficult at best to prompt; the search for truth is too impractical for most dealers to take the time to expand their understanding without customer requests, and such efforts may in fact work against investments they and others have already made. Belief systems already solidly in place are difficult to change both within and outside of collectibles markets, so for now, my factual observations have been oft received much as Copernicus' works were when argued by Galileo, but unlike yesteryear's starstruck pioneers, you'll hear no apologies nor recantments from me, for the truth has a way of winning out over time. That's right, I'm once again arguing against the status quo: The most common copies of key comic book issues may one day not be the most valuable examples, based on the laws of scarcity and demand. Hey, someone has to rock the boat!

Notable sales this year include *Conan* #1 VG+ $95, *Iron Man* #55 GD+ $27, *Madhouse* #22 GD/VG $95, *Tomb of Dracula* #10 GD/VG $19, *Weird War Tales* #1 GD/VG $90 and *Iron Fist* #14 (35¢-c variant) VG/FN $2075.79.

Todd McDevitt
New Dimension Comics

Since I think it's valuable to know where the insight in these market reports is coming from, here is a little history on me. I just celebrated my 25th anniversary in the comic book business! New Dimension Comics has grown to 5 stores surrounding the Pittsburgh, PA area. When I started, I thought I thought it would be just me in 1 store having fun selling comics. I never expected to grow to 5 stores and 40-some employees. All this time dedicating my life to comics seems to have earned me the chance to rant here once a year. The good folks at Overstreet keep askin' me to come back! This is my 5th market report!

Buying Overview: One of my rules has always been to buy everything I can. I think keeping a fresh and relentless flow of new material through my stores has been a huge component to my success. With the purchase of a giant warehouse, nothing holds me back from taking on loads of comics, sometimes hundreds of thousands at a time. And with 5 store locations, attending conventions, wholesale activity, and other venues, they go out the door quickly as well. My job most days is just to keep the NDC machine fed with cool comics!

Selling Overview: While in past years people with comics for sale have turned to eBay or some internet outlet, more and more come to me with the realization that selling comics is a lot of work. I know better than most! So recently, the tide has turned. People value their time and leave the comic selling to the experts. You don't cut your own hair, do you? Collections flow in literally faster than I can get through them. My new trick is to burn through collections, pull the high profile stuff that is needed, and toss the rest out for $1.00 each in my Ellwood City location where I have a giant store that doubles as a warehouse. Then, if I get time, I go through them again later, but that never happens. They sit for $1.00 each until somebody takes time to comb through them and find the treasures. In addition, I have a sorted inventory of about 400,000 comics that I open to the public twice a year for $1.00 each. Folks come from all over (even Canada!) to shop these. For high-end vintage material, the same is true. Most folks realize that trying to squeeze out that extra money themselves isn't worth the risk or effort. I can pay premiums for good books like *Hulk* #181 or other keys because I have a list of clients waiting for them. And they want to buy them from a reputable source such as I have established with a long history in my region. If I know I have a book sold for $500 tomorrow, I can certainly pay $400 for it today.

Golden Age: Let's start old and work our way forward. As always, the Marvels/Timelys rule here. The small handful that I have seen in the past year sell easily within a week. In my 25 years of aggressively buying in the Western PA region, I bet I have only seen a couple dozen of these gems surface. It seems that collectors know how scarce they are and save up to buy one book when they finally do see it to make it a highlight of their collection. If you are Captain America fan and have most of the Silver Age and up, you have to have just one Golden Age issue just to show off. In my years buying, I have seen more sizable collections of DC Comics, but even those have been slow this past year. I like to think this is the calm before the storm, and that big find is just a phone call away!

As for more obscure publishers from the Golden Age, I had some great luck selling scarce L.B. Cole covers, but most others have such a limited market that the only real way to get them moving is at lower prices. In fact, I think a general statement can be made that popular books from this era can sell for over *Guide* price, while slow movers need price breaks to attract buyers. For example, *Classics Illustrated* and Westerns. It seems these buyers all know that these are slow sellers for all dealers and expect a discount. I have had 2 copies of *Roy Rogers* #1 for years that I can't sell for $95.

Silver Age: My main outlet for these is my $3 inventory. I have been doing this for several years now and I'm starting to earn the nickname "that $3 guy" at some shows. It's my favorite to bring with me to conventions with about 12,000 comics. Many are low grade, but many are just my overstock, so into the cheapies they go! Since they do so well, and I buy so much stuff, I keep it very full. Why should I fight to get $8-12 for a book that I can get $3 for quickly? This keeps both my $3 stock looking good and my "real" inventory too since I'm more selective about what I will take time bag, tag, price, and sort.

For good stuff, no surprise, high grade still rules. I don't do much with CGC, so I end up having guys who do hit my high grade stuff pretty hard. But low grades still sell well on popular key issues. There are all types of buyers when it comes to wanting a key book. Some collectors want nice copies for high dollars, others are just happy to have one in their collection even if it's banged up.

Modern Age: Wow. What a crazy year for new comics. DC rocked the industry with 52 new #1 issues. While there were lots of gripes leading up to this September 2011 event, when it finally hit, it was gobbled up! The trick is that we are seeing mixed reactions as the #2s & #3s are arriving. Will the boost of the relaunches keep these titles riding at higher circulation? Or will the typical curse of later issues dipping off still apply? As I write this, we are just seeing the #3s come in, so the real answer will be evident once the new *Overstreet* is released!

Digital Threat (?): A lot of brick-n-mortar comic shop retailers are feeling the creep of the digital comics. Many worry they will be the end of comic shops. Publishers make more and more efforts to woo readers in that direction as well. Everyone is positioning themselves for the future. I believe the advent of digital comics should be compared to the newsstand of 30 years ago or more. When I was a kid, comics were everywhere. That mass exposure kept some readers interested enough to keep up with the hobby into their adult life, creating many of the collectors I enjoy as customers today. Now, you practically have to fight to find a place that sells comic books. But the internet is easy. I think that of the masses that get hooked on comics online, some percentage of them will become diehard fans. And diehard fans shop at comic book shops. Digital comics may be the marketing stroke that keeps comic shops thriving for the next several decades.

John Jackson Miller
Curator, The Comic Chronicles

While I covered comics pricing for many years for various publications, my main area of expertise — and ongoing research — is on the supply side. How many copies of comics existed originally? This is an important question, and my Comics Chronicles website (http://www.comichron.com) has for several years provided a public stream of data not just for people interested in the health of the business over time, but also for collectors interested in the number of copies that originally existed. We can see the role of original supply in the prices of many titles over the years; the dynamics that boosted *Giant-Size X-Men* #1 and *Teenage Mutant Ninja Turtles* #1 have been more recently on very visible display in the prices paid for *Walking Dead*. It's worth knowing about.

Back at the beginning of the 2000s, Mile High Comics owner Chuck Rozanski noted that the sales of many new comics had reached levels where they would be immediately scarcer, on publication, than issues of the same title from earlier periods. This continued to be the trend for many ongoing series in 2011. While the new comics market in aggregate sold slightly more copies in 2011 as in 2010 — a little more than 70 million copies in Direct Market comics shops in North America — circulations on many marquee titles continued to decline.

But while the initial supplies of many top-selling comics have declined against previous years, the aggregate number of comics sold in the Direct Market has stayed the same or increased slightly. How is that possible? The bench is deeper. The largest publishers are producing more titles between themselves than they did a decade ago, and with the addition of strong middle-tier publishers including IDW, Boom, and Dynamite, titles past 200th place on the charts each month are regularly selling three to four times what similarly ranked titles sold ten years earlier. It's not that specific lower-tier titles have grown in sales — rather, a title in that lower grouping is much more likely now to be from a major or mid-sized publisher. There's simply more out there, and, as with the proliferation of television channels, we have seen a fragmentation of audience.

Again, for the collector or dealer, this means that many marquee titles exist in very small quantities, relative to the past. Marvel's *Amazing Spider-Man* had an average monthly circulation of 79,844 copies across all channels, as compared with 113,557 ten years earlier during a similar slowdown — when the now three-issue-a-month title was only shipping once a month. Several times in 2011, the top-selling title in the industry had sales that didn't reach six digits. If we assume that "mortality" rates on comics began to collapse in the 1980s with the proliferation of comics shops and the easy availability of storage media, we might well conclude that there are more Near Mint copies of, say, *Amazing Spider-Man* #375 (when sales were over half a million copies) than there are of *Amazing Spider-Man* #675!

The major deviation from that in 2011, of course, can be found in the DC "New 52" reboot. DC sold more than 4 million copies of the first issues of its rebooted titles in September and October, the first two months of the program. Ten "New 52" first issues had domestic Direct Market sales in their first two months exceeding 100,000 copies — *Justice League*, *Batman*, *Action*, *Green Lantern*, *Flash*, *Superman*, *Detective*, *Batman: The Dark Knight*, *Batman and Robin*, and *Aquaman* — with *Justice League*, *Batman*, and *Action* exceeding 200,000 copies. The scarcest New 52 #1s are *Static Shock*, *Omac*, and *Men of War*, all with fewer than 40,000 copies sold into the Direct Market in their first two months on the racks.

That's the #1s — but what about the #2s? Interestingly, while the second issues of series have, historically, been much scarcer than the first given how retailers order comics — *G.I. Joe: A Real American Hero* #2 in the 1980s famously becoming more valuable than its first issue — the DC effort is bucking that trend. The falloff in first-month orders from the average DC "new 52" #1 to #2 was only 6%, and some titles actually went up in sales. Once all reorders are tabulated, there will probably still be more #1 first printings than #2s on most titles, but the gap will be small. A lot has to do with retailer confidence in the effort prompting higher orders, but the logistical advances in comics ordering have also greatly shortened the time it takes for series demand to be reflected in print runs.

The highest-circulation comic book of 2011 is the one that started it all, *Justice League* #1. First-day domestic orders for the first printing were 171,000 copies, with a Combo Pack variant adding 15,000 copies; overseas sales add about 10% to the known supply. Retailers went on to order another 70,000 copies in the succeeding two months, although it is expected that most of those were of later printings. Topping a quarter-million copies in combined printings puts the issue in the dozen best-selling issues of the 21st Century; most *Civil War* issues and the Barack Obama *Amazing Spider-Man* had higher initial first printing sales, but *Justice League* #1 should still be one of the more plentiful big-event titles out there.

Where retailers might see opportunity, as has happened with many relaunched series, is on the final issues of the series that were replaced. *Batman* #713 had first-month orders of 51,760, less than a quarter of the eventual sales of the *Batman* #1 that followed it; *Action Comics* #904 went from around 40,000 copies up to more than five times that. *Supergirl* went from less than 20,000 copies to more than three times as many. So there's both a significant bump — and an opportunity, should those last issues be seen as attractively scarce.

While the renumberings of DC series were traumatic for some collectors, recent history has shown that such changes are, regardless of what publishers may say at any one time, only as permanent as the publishers' desire to keep them going. We've seen various Marvel renumberings undone — and then redone — and yet collectors do find a way to keep things straight, just as they imposed their own sequential numbering on *Walt Disney's Comics & Stories* years ago when the title did not have it. It seems hard to believe that #96 of the new *Action Comics* won't have a #1000 on it somewhere; it would be a missed bet if it didn't.

© DC

DC's New 52 **Justice League #1** was *the highest-circulation comic book of 2011.*

Perhaps most interestingly, from a historical perspective — the 200,000-copy sales of the new *Action Comics* #1 are very close to what the sales of the original *Action Comics* #1 were, in the 1930s, judging from Audit Bureau of Circulation reports!

And on that topic of returning to the past: increasingly, more and more information is becoming available about how many copies were originally sold on many titles. In addition to the data that I've continued to post on www.comichron.com (where I have nearly 3,000 Statements of Ownership since 1960 which I expect to post in the near future), a number of new resources are becoming available. Recently, former Marvel editor-in-chief Jim Shooter began posting on his blog (www.jimshooter.com) archival internal documents from that publisher, including not just tracking of Marvel's own sales, but inside information about what other publishers were doing. How many comics initially existed is a major factor in how many exist now — and a little at a time, those blanks are filling in.

Steve Mortensen
Miracle Comics

2011 was another banner year for comics, especially in the CGC market. Prices seem to be stabilizing, but as more supply enters the market, prices have been affected on key books. *Wolverine* Limited Series #1 is an example of a book that is highly submitted and frequently sold. As of December 2011, the median price for a CGC 9.8 for this book was around $150. There are more than 6,000 graded copies but demand continues to keep the price afloat. In 2002, the book in CGC 9.8 reached a high of $215; in 2006, the book in CGC 9.8 reached an all-time high of $410. 2011 brought its greatest volatility with a high of $263 and a low of $61. Of course these numbers don't consider the page quality or the centering of the book, which also has a great deal of influence on the price. CGC 9.8s can still be miscut and have page quality below White, which can lower the value.

The Year in Review (based on observations first made in my monthly columns for *Comics Buyer's Guide*):

In December 2010, I noted how more and more books are being re-certified. Pressing has become more prevalent and many collectors are re-submitting books for higher grades. Some collectors will try to determine if the book is a "9.5" or a "9.7" and take their chances resubmitting the book for a possible higher grade. There has been lots of controversy about this in the comic market among collectors and dealers and some feel that this technique is considered restoration and should be given a purple label by CGC.

From my experience, it's very difficult to determine if a book has been professionally pressed or if the book has been stored tightly in a box. I have bought collections that have been stored for 30+ years and each books looks as if it has been professionally pressed. That said, the prices have already fallen on CGC 9.8s of key books such as *Incredible Hulk* #181 (a popular pressing candidate). Once it was a $25,000 book, but the last recorded sale in December 2011 was for $13,500. Collectors savvy in pressing are finding nice 9.4/9.6 candidates, pressing them, and then re-submitting them for higher grades. This has created a greater supply in the 9.8 markets and has lowered prices.

In January 2011, I noticed that Deadpool back issues from the late 1990s are gaining ground, but as of this writing prices have dropped. *Deadpool* #1 in CGC 9.8 sold in January for $129 but in December 2011 the last few sales have been in the $40-80 range. Issue #54, a Punisher appearance, has gained ground in CGC 9.8. The last sale in December 2011 was for $146. Prices for common issues have dropped to $25-35 in CGC 9.8.

In February 2011, I noted that Image Comics had become a great pipeline for investment grade moderns. *Walking Dead* #1 in CGC 9.8 sold for $525 in February 2011 and last sold in December 2011 for $850. I think the popularity of the new TV show has sparked new interest in the back issue market for the book. *Chew* #1 in CGC 9.8 sold in February for $220 and in December 2011 the last sale was for $450. *Morning Glories* #1 in CGC 9.8 sold in February for $83 and in December the last sale was for $100.

In March, I noticed that many of my customers were favoring Auctions over Buy-It-Nows. As of my March writing, there were 85,617 auctions and 1,689,582 Buy-It-Nows for a total of 1,775,199 comics for sale on eBay. In December the totals were 75,918 auctions and 1,473,842 Buy-It-Nows for a total of 1,534,224 comics for sale on eBay. About a year ago eBay decided to make Buy-It-Nows searchable on the same level as auctions.

In April 2011, I talked about how local flea markets have become a great place to pick up old comics. One of my prizes was an *Uncle Scrooge* #1 for two dollars. The copy was in Fair/Good condition, but complete. From the same seller I found *Uncle Scrooge* #17-19 and 21-22, the 15-cent variant editions released in the San Francisco Bay Area during 1957. I sent those in to CGC and they came back with an average grade of CGC 7.0, eventually selling on ComicLink for about $100 each.

In May 2011, I noted that Witchblade and Darkness comics were good sellers for me in CGC 9.8. In May, I sold a *Darkness Special Preview Edition* in CGC 9.8 for $269 and a *Darkness* #3 in CGC 9.8 for $50. Many of these issues can still be picked up for cover price at comic stores. In December I sold a *Darkness* #3 in CGC 9.8 for $42.

In June 2011, I discussed the Teenage Mutant Ninja Turtles' return to comics. I have strong ties to the characters – remembering when I bought #3 of the original series off the shelf. In November a copy of #3 in CGC 9.8 sold for $200. Issue #1 of the original series in first print is extremely hard to find in any grade since very few were printed. In February a CGC 9.6 sold for $7,000 and in December a CGC 9.8 copy sold for $22,752.

In July 2011, I predicted that the new *Justice League* was going to be in high demand. In December the regular cover last sold for $61 in CGC 9.8 and the retail incentive cover sold for $500 in CGC 9.8. The Justice League of America first appeared in *Brave and the Bold* #28 in 1960. A CGC 9.0 sold in February for $21,510. A CGC 9.4 copy sold for $60,375 back in 2004. According to the CGC census the CGC 9.4 is the highest graded copy

In August 2011, *Futurama* back issues caught my eye. *Futurama* has been a great cult favorite both on and off TV. It has been a great year for *Futurama* back issues. Issue #1 in CGC 9.8 last sold for $110; #3 last sold in CGC 9.8 for $70; #8 last sold in CGC 9.8 for $80; #10 last sold in CGC 9.8 for $70; #11 last sold in CGC 9.8 for $70. As of December, issue #1 last sold for $100 in CGC 9.8.

In September 2011, I reflected on the death of a friend in the comic community and thought about how we can best prepare our comic collections for our loved ones. Along with being a lot of fun, comics are a financial asset that can be a great resource to our families if something happens to us. But without friends to guide our families in the selling process it can end up more of a burden than an asset. I think it's a good idea for us collectors to have a few experts in the community that our families can go to in case something happens to us.

In October 2011, I noted how DC's new 52 titles have been doing really well. The variant covers in particular have held strong; issues have been popping up in CGC 9.8 less than a month after they came out. *Action Comics* #1 sketch cover in CGC 9.8 sold in October for $600. *Batman* #1 sketch cover in CGC 9.8 sold in October for $510. In December 2011, *Action Comics* #1 sketch cover sold for $405 in CGC 9.8 and *Batman* #1 sketch cover sold for $521.

In November 2010, I saw a pickup of popularity of *Ultimate Spider-Man* #1 from 2000. Prices for *Ultimate Spider-Man* #1 appear to be on the rise after about a four year slump. The 90-day average for the regular red cover in CGC 9.8 is about $350 however it has dropped to $300 in December. Prices for a CGC 9.8 copy of the white cover are about $700.

In conclusion, collecting and selling comic books is a great hobby. I have personally been enriched this year by my monthly sales on eBay and my purchases for my personal collection. While *X-Men* and *Iron Man* were my staples when I was a kid, I've found a new favorite in Conan over the past several years. I enjoy CGC graded comics and ungraded reader copies. Collectors can enjoy both! Although CGC has changed the hobby from the investment market, it's hard to beat picking up and reading a nice Bronze Age Barry Smith Conan where you can smell the pages and enjoy the story and art.

Tom Nelson
Top Notch Comics

We are an online back issue comic book dealer who has been selling on eBay since 1999 (our ID is topnotchcomics). We primarily sell comics from the Silver Age through around 2005, and we occasionally get Golden Age and current Moderns. We run weekly eBay auctions with high value CGC certified books. We also stock around 2000 books in our fixed price eBay store that are lower value in low to high grade. Sales have been strong for us in 2011, up over 2010. We constantly see new collectors on eBay with new accounts entering the online collecting hobby.

My market report will be skewed towards the non-typical high profile auction house sales, eBay sales, plus our actual sales. I will also cover high volume popular comics from the Bronze to Modern Ages. I believe the largest number of collectors are buying popular Bronze and Modern keys for their collections.

In 2011, I attended 12 of the larger comic book conventions as a buyer. Four on the West Coast, six in the Midwest, and four on the East Coast. Going to this many conventions has given me knowledge on how dealers price there books with regional selling market conditions. Attendance was strong at the long running established conventions I attended. Dealers who brought fresh new collections were well received with strong sales. Some dealers who literally haul around the same picked over books did not have as much success. For those who set up at shows, those old foggy plastic bags and old labels just gives the impression of picked over stale inventory. It would be a wise idea to invest in some new bags to freshen things up a bit, also its nice to leave enough room in the boxes for customers to actually look through the comics. Since my outlet for books is entirely online I constantly do extensive research of completed eBay auction sales. I also follow the high end CGC market of Heritage weekly and Signature auctions, and ComicLink's monthly auctions. This keeps me familiar with liquid value of books from the Silver Age through hot Modern books.

Golden Age: We do not specialize in this era, but when we do run across them in low grade they make great stock for our eBay store fixed price listings. They eventually move at *Guide*, but if they start to hang around, a 30% discount moves them quicker.

Silver Age: Early Silver Age DC 1955-1961 which are the 10 centers, I have seen strong demand in 8.0 or better condition in virtually every title regardless of how common. This includes War titles, Sci-Fi, Superheroes and even Humor. The paper quality was poor in this era and buyers will pay a premium for off white and white pages.

For the later Silver Age DC (the 12 centers 1962-1969), there is strong demand in the NM 9.4 and higher range as they are still very scarce compared to their Marvel counterparts from the same era. We have seen a strong demand for the *Strange Adventures* Deadman run starting at #205 (with Infantino art) which is scarce in 8.0 or better, through the Neal Adams issues.

DC 10-centers in Fair to Fine, sell OK in our eBay store. Some need 20-30% discount to move, but still sell able books. DC 12 centers need a little more discounting to move for the common runs, 25-50% off for the low to mid grades. Low and mid grade keys and first appearances sell closer to *Guide*.

© DC

*There's a strong demand for the Deadman run that started in **Strange Adventures** #205.*

For Marvel and Atlas Silver, there's no need for me to rehash the same reports you can see elsewhere. Late Marvel Silver, which is almost Bronze books. *Iron Man* #1, *Silver Surfer* #1, *Captain America* #100, *Sub-Mariner* #1, all have been hot sellers in our eBay listings. They sell at *Guide* as quick as I post them in low grade and high CGC grades.

Silver Age Dell and Gold key, we sold a number of books. Some of our better sellers in our eBay store were *Magnus Robot Fighter*, *Doctor Solar*, *Turok*, *Munsters*, *Uncle Scrooge*, *Star Trek*, and *Peanuts*.

Bronze Marvels from the 1970s: This made up the bulk of our volume this year. One of the hottest books for us was *Amazing Spider-Man* #129. We sold copies from Good 2.0 all the way up to CGC 9.6. I can monitor the number of hits and bookmarks in our eBay listings. The surprising thing I noticed was the volume of interest in the lowest grades of Good to Very Good. They had more interest than the high CGC grade of 9.0 and 9.6. This is a great example of the sheer depth and volume of interest in the Bronze keys. Sales of this book; two copies in Good 2.0 $80.00 each, VG 4.0 $125.00, CGC 5.0 $180.00, CGC 7.0 $270.00, CGC 9.0 $539.00, CGC 9.6 $1750.00. Other Spider-Man books that were hot are #121, #194, #122 and #135, in that order. Some of our eBay sales: #121 CGC 8.0 $180.00, #121 CGC 9.4 $535.00, #194 GD/VG 3.0 $10.00, #194 VG 4.0 $10.00, #194 VF+ 8.5 $50.00, #194 CGC 9.6 $200.00, #194 CGC 9.8 $400.00, #194 CGC 9.8 SS by Stan Lee $650.00, #135 VG 4.0 $12.00, #135 CGC 9.6 $430.00.

Incredible Hulk #181 with the first Wolverine is another mega key. I observed online sales of double Guide prices in the Good to Fine conditions, while VF to NM were at around *Guide*. Getting the book CGC graded helped it sell even faster. This book provides another example of collectors who just want an affordable copy in low to mid grade.

Werewolf By Night #32, the first Moon Knight, is a hot book with tremendous demand in all grades, especially mid grades of VG to VF. Some sales we had of this comic, GD/VG 3.0 $35.00, VG $50.00, VG+ 4.5 $70.00, CGC 7.0 $150.00, CGC 8.5 $200.00.

Marvel and DC Horror non keys were a little softer than a couple years ago.

Batman #200-#300 were our best sellers from the Bronze Age in mid grade Fine to Very Fine, selling at *Guide* value in our eBay store. The Adams covers lead the way in value and demand with many (#227, #234, #232, #222, and #251) selling over *Guide*. Joker covers were highly sought after. *Detective* Adams and Joker covers were sought after also, although the common non-Adams issues were slower to move.

Neal Adams' *Green Lantern* issues (#76-#89) have leveled off in sales after the film was released. It's still a collectable run but not quite as Hot.

X-Men always sell, although some discounting gets them to move quicker this year.

Some of the more popular Gold Key comics from our eBay fixed price store were *Scooby Doo*, *Pink Panther*, *Star Trek*, *Uncle Scrooge*, and *Turok*.

The scarce Marvel Price variants continued to be hot in CGC grades. The most elusive issues are *Star Wars* #1 and *Iron Fist* #14. Some notable sales from auction sites were: *Iron Fist* #14 CGC 8.5 $2,850.00, CGC 6.5 $900.00, *Star Wars* #1 CGC 9.0 $3,850.00, CGC 4.0 $332.00.

1980s comics: I have seen strong demand for mini or limited series which are instant collections. *Batman Dark Knight* #1-4, *Wolverine* Limited #1-4, *Punisher* Limited #1-5. Collectors buy them in CGC 9.8 or clean raw copies to read. The *Amazing Spider-Man* keys of #300 and #238 are both hot in grades of Fine to CGC 9.8. #300 VF 8.0 $70.00, #300 CGC 9.6 $200.00, #300 CGC 9.8 $550.00, #238 CGC 9.8 $450.00, #238 CGC 9.6 $170.00. Another collectable run is the *Daredevil* Miller run #158-191. The keys of #158 and #168 sell well in all grades. Daredevil #168 VG 4.0 $25.00, CGC 9.6 $250.00, CGC 9.8 $700.00.

The McFarlane *Amazing Spider-Man* run is also a popular run to collect. *Miracleman* #1-24 is in demand with the #15 leading with way with sales in CGC 9.6 $180.0, CGC 9.8 $450.00. The entire *Miracleman* run is collectable with the #14, #15, #16, #23 and #24 being the toughest to find. *The Crow* #1-4 are rare in high grade. The *Uncanny X-Men* run is relatively cool in price and needs to be discounted. Except for the #266 which continues to sell in all grades, VG/FN 5.5 $10.00 FN/VF 7.0 $25.00, CGC 9.8 $150.00.

Transformers #1 and *G.I. Joe* #1 both sell for around $25.00 in NM. *G.I. Joe* #21 goes for around $35.00 in NM. *Batman* #357 (1st Jason Todd) is a hot book selling for $35.00 in VF 8.0 $100.00 in CGC 9.6 $200.00 in CGC 9.8. *Batman* #426-428 is a collectable run in collector grade and CGC 9.8 grade.

There are many hidden treasures mixed through Independents in the 1980s with the Dave Stevens covers. These have become very popular in CGC 9.8 as they display well and are some of my favorite cover art. Try finding *3-D Zone* #16 Space Vixens, an amazing cover. Online sales have been around $35.00 for VF copies.

1990s Comics: An era with high print runs and the collapse of Marvel along with thousands of comic book stores. Will there ever be any long term hot in demand books from the 1990s. The sifting has been going on for 12-20 years already, so what nuggets will get sifted out of all the clutter of overprinted hoarded books. Start looking at the lower print runs of the late 1990s and limited variants and Platinum editions. We have seen strong demand for *Superman* #75 Platinum sealed $100.00, CGC 9.6 $150.00, CGC 9.8 $450.00, *Spider-Man* #1 Platinum NM $100.00, CGC 9.6 $180.00, CGC 9.8 $500.00.

There should be some line corrections to the *Amazing Spider-Man* run in Near Mint- condition: #400 White $35.00, #406 Variant $100.00, #430 $10.00 #431 $25.00 #432 Variant $25.00. *Uncanny X-Men* #297 Gold Pressman variant is very scarce, sales realized of CGC 9.6 $650.00, CGC 9.4 $315.00. *Batman: Vengeance of Bane* turned into an overnight hot book when they announced Bane was in the upcoming Batman film. Near Mint copies go for around $35.00, with CGC 9.6 going for $80.00 and CGC 9.8 around $200.00. *Batman Adventures* #12 is the first comic appearance of Harley Quinn and this should have a line item as it sells for around $25.00 in Near Mint, and $125.00 in CGC 9.8.

New Mutants #98, first Deadpool, is still a mega key of the decade, with raw NM copies selling for $60.00 to $80.00, CGC 9.6 $100.00-$120.00, CGC 9.8 $200.00. *New Mutants* #87 has taken second fiddle to the #98 as it sells $25.00-$35.00 raw and $125.00 in CGC 9.8. A rare variant is the *Wolverine* #145 Nabisco variant, there are over 250 copies graded by CGC. NM copies sell in the $200.00-$300.00 range, CGC 9.8 $700.00, CGC 9.6 $300.00, CGC 9.4 $250.00. Some other hot books are the final run of *G.I. Joe* #150-155, and *Transformers* #70-80, CGC 9.8 copies sell for a premium. The *Deadpool* run from 1997 has cooled from a year ago, the *Punisher* issues #54 and #55 sell in the $20.00 per book range in NM, the other common issues are in the $3.00-$5.00 NM range.

Oh those pesky *Super Mario Brothers* by Valiant, cool nostalgia comic books, they move well for us at $10.00-$20.00 each. *The Legend of Zelda* issues are also popular in the $10.00-$20.00 range for NM copies.

2000-2005 Comics: An era where print runs are lower as stores try to sell through all copies while back issue space is eliminated from many stores. The mega key is *Walking Dead* #1, with raw copies in NM selling for $300.00-$400.00, CGC 9.2 $300.00, CGC 9.4 $350.00, CGC 9.6 $450.00, CGC 9.8 $600.00; #2 NM selling for $150.00, CGC 9.6 $150.00, CGC 9.8 $300.00; #3 NM $80.00, CGC 9.8 $200.00; #4 NM $70.00 CGC 9.8 $150.00; #5 NM $50.00 CGC 9.8 $100.00; #19 NM $50.00 CGC 9.8 $150.00.

Another mega key is *Batman* #608 retailer incentive, very scarce and is a hot book on eBay. Some sales observed this year: CGC 9.8 $2,000-2500.00, 9.6 $800-1000.00, 9.4 $500.00, 9.2 $500.00, 9.0 $500.00, 8.5 $350.00. This book is 10 years old and estimated print run is higher than 200.

Spawn is one of the most collected runs in the past 20 years. I have yet to go to a comic book store or a booth at a show where they had the entire run for sale individually. Issues #1-99 are for the most part common and can be found for $1.00-$3.00 each without too much effort, and #18 and #21 are not low distribution. Dealers typically have huge gaps when you get from issue #100-199. There are some scarce issues in that era as print runs were a fraction of the high print runs of the first 50 copies. Common issues are going for $5.00-$10.00 per book. The #150 has 5 variant covers and they sell in the $35.00-$50.00 range each in NM on eBay. *Spawn* #185 had McFarlane returning to the run, there are two variants, a headless McFarlane variant which goes for $80.00-$100.00 in NM, and the extremely rare Sketch Variant by Portacio has recorded sales this year of CGC 9.2 $390.00, and a CGC 9.4 signed by McFarlane $725.00 and a NM raw copy signed by McFarlane sold on eBay for $495.00. *Spawn* #1 Black and White Edition from 1997 had a limited print run with NM copies selling for $100.00 CGC 9.6 $250.00, CGC 9.8 $600.00.

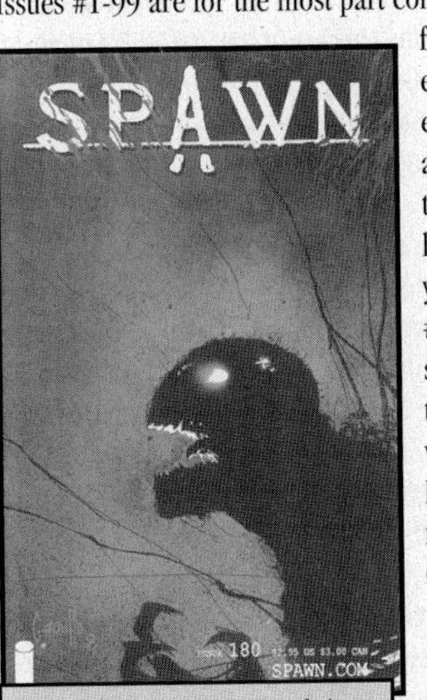

Spawn is still one of the most collected runs in the past 20 years. (Spawn #180 shown)

In closing I would like to motivate everyone to support your local comic book store. Try to find a cousin, nephew, or neighbor friend and invite them to tag along to the comic store. It's also a trend to pay with credit or debit, but make an effort to pay for your purchase with cash as margins can be tight on new release material.

Jamie Newbold
Southern California Comics

Greetings! I begin this market report with a general overview of our comic book business as of November 2011. The end of 2010 brought a slight boost in business at the store. Following Christmas, our store saw a larger increase in walk-in traffic that lasted right up through the summer. Business dampened a bit after the start of the fall school semester and remained relatively flat up to the date of this article. The DC New 52 made quite a sales impact with the number one issues. The financial pump in the arm off-set waning recent back issue sales (I'm sure just a momentary stall in sales).

The transitory nature of the population of San Diego is always suspect as reason for declining sales. That state of being may be thankfully changing. I watched a news source on television say that fewer Americans are relocating throughout the country this year. Customers exiting San Diego may not be as common through 2012 and we may be able to hold onto them longer.

Our local popularity is supported by the quantity and frequency of traditional back-issue sales. Our competition to acquire and sell Gold/Silver/Bronze comics has expanded our reach into the US market and kept us active over the years. Our proof is the increased frequency of sales outside of San Diego. As for the market- nothing major has changed in overall back issue sales. The usual stuff is selling for the usual prices. Pressed books are more accepted in the market and studies have shown no ill effects to pressed comics. We've dabbled in pressed books and seen quality improvements in their suppleness and appearance. Those changes have translated into better books with higher sticker prices. Still, haggling and discounting have not gone out of fashion. *Overstreet* prices are starting points but often fail to accommodate for discounted sales. Some constants still remain in place:

CGC books sell better for us on eBay than raw books. Raw books sell better for us at the store than CGC books. Raw books sell better for us at Comic Con. CGC books sell for closer to the mark than raw books(less demand for discounting with CGC books). Our web site sees more hits for raw books than CGC books.

EBay has become a little less friendly to sellers and with the newly applied rules. Also, common back issues that used to sell cheap on eBay are barely selling at all now. Our raw Marvel back issues commonly sell for about one-third of *Overstreet*. DCs sell at about one-quarter of *Overstreet*, if they sell at all. That outlet may finally have peaked for us. CGC material sells well but the flood of CGC material in high-grade (pressed, minty fresh copies that did not exist two years ago) has dramatically reduced the prices we would have seen in the past.

New comic sales rise and fall with the same inconsistency as previous years. The revamped DC line caused quite a stir with our customers. The numbers initially sold were outstanding. Then, issue 2 happened. Some titles remained popular and sold in numbers vastly larger than previous counterparts. Others dropped off slightly when the buyers did not return. The "issue number one" speculators made DC and our store a lot of money. Then, they did what they do best: they left. The quality of the titles, stories, and art were wonderful. Top-notch stuff! Usually Marvel is the annual go-to comic company; the leader of the pack. Marvel still has dominance in the face of DC's recent successes. Marvel sold in equal or slightly less proportions to DC these past two months. Not because Marvel slipped or did anything wrong, It's because DC did something more dynamic. My customers have overwhelmingly given DC a thumbs-up for their new direction. Here's hoping the quality does not sink with exiting first string writers and artists.

2011 dropped three cool Marvel movies into the theaters and one DC movie. Our expectations were that the Marvel movies would be quality and well attended. The Green Lantern movie had some plotting disappointments and was received as average movie fare, more or less. Our business is strictly print-driven: new and old comics, trade books and the like. Our selection does not necessarily lead to movie tie-in sales. The occasional key book related to a specific movie still drives buyers to find us. The upcoming Avengers movie will most certainly generate buyers for our Avengers number ones. New reader interest following the recent movie releases was minimal.

Conversely, *Walking Dead* trades and comics flew out the store with the broadcasted television series. Sales on trades were constant for months. Other comic book-to-trade favorites like *Y, The Last Man*, *Chew* and *Fables* are ripe for this kind of exploitation. I see rip-off/adaptations of *Fables* are on television now.

Important Sales/Purchases: We purchased several unique collections since the summer of 2010. One collection consisted of about 375 Golden Age comics from the mid-1930s to the early 1940s we acquired from the deceased owner's middle aged son. The DCs and Centaurs went quickly. Large runs of *Famous Funnies*, *Ace Comics*, *King Comics* and the like will hang around for awhile and slowly sell at comic conventions. Many of the books did not place high enough to send off to CGC. Those that did were sold quickly, mostly to other dealers. There are still a number of 1930s books that just don't show up often. Fun stuff.

Near the end of 2010, I sealed the deal with a local collector looking to get out. He sold us hundreds of comics but he led with the best. Sixty-Five Timelys! An improbable dream of mine to acquire such a collection finally came true. We've since sold more than half. Once again, many went to other dealers. *Marvel Mystery* and *Human Torch* made up a majority of the titles.

Finally, we picked up an original owner collection of about 2,000 1950s to early 1960s comics: Dell, Disney, and DC. A few key books like *Mystery in Space* #53 and *Flash* #105. The cheap Disneys turned out to be the most popular when I brought them to a show in Denmark! It was fun seeing hundreds of covers I don't normally see. Most of the books were VG-ish in grade. Many were better from Fine to VFs. Lots of stuff destined to reach more receptive audiences at shows.

© DIS

Cheap copies of old Disney comics are also quite popular in Denmark. (*Donald Duck* #60 shown)

Throughout the year, we have purchased small and large collections of Silver Age…mostly Marvel. Consistent buying opportunities abound. Bronze/Silver and Gold walk into the store every week, in all manner of varieties and conditions. The totality of these collections was important to the success of the 2011 SD Comic Con; important to purchasers at our store who're always looking for the next, new thing to buy.

Speaking of shows…

Comic Cons: We rarely do shows. We did four shows between last summer and now. Terry O'Neill's Orange County show was entertaining and profitable. More customers show up with each show and our increased sales reflect that. Guests were there doing signings and sketches. Terry's raffles were popular and back issues were everywhere. Too bad he's maxed out on exhibitor space. All comic dealers should take advantage of this all back-issue venue.

Oceanside, which is just north of San Diego, held its second annual one-day comic con. We retained a booth from last year and did surprisingly well for such a small, localized show. Rey and Doug (the founders) would like to expand the venue in another location. I hope their growing pains are met with increased dealer/attendee attention. I like their show.

Terry O'Neill also put on a comic con in Copenhagen, Denmark. Four American exhibitors travelled to set up at his show. Terry, Vinnie Zurzulo, Harley Yee, and me (with my loving and sales-savvy wife). The show was small but well attended. Don Rosa, Mike Ploog and Barry Kitson wowed attendees with signatures and sketches. We dealers tested the back-issue market to see what would sell. I got caught up in helping Terry with the multiple tasks he needed to perform. My wife learned her English to Danish cash and coin conversion tables as she sold inexpensive 1950s and 60s low-grade Disneys and funny animal comics to the locals. I wasn't sure if there would be any market for old US comics. I know of the western European fascination with Disney stuff so I loaded for bear with those comics. It turned out to be the right call...I only wish I'd brought more of it.

San Diego International Comic Con: Enormous, packed, overwhelming. And that's just the lobby! We had our best show ever. In terms of sales and little stress, this show was a winner. We sold a little bit of everything and a whole lot of specific things. Our commitment to the back issue market was reaffirmed at this show. Our sales to other dealers were large because of the significant collections we picked up beforehand. I spoke to some of my peers who confirmed they also did well.

Strangely, when I audited our inventory after the show, I was surprised at what didn't sell. Mid-60's Marvels are always some of our strongest inventory. *Amazing Spider-Man* is the most beefed up inventory we had going into the show. Yet *Amazing Spider-Man* from the mid-60s was one of our weakest selling titles at Comic Con. Over-saturated or over-priced? They barely sold at a show we were set up to operate for six days. I think I sold more funny animal comics than Spideys this year. Silver Age DCs were a hit for us. They sold well at Terry's Orange County show and they sold well here in San Diego. Raw comics are handled by everyone trying to corner a potential CGC-worthy book. The "Your Book Is Not Mint Enough" crowd was busy looking for their golden opportunities. Don't they think we've already tried our own stock?

One problem that was dealt with this year at San Diego was the theft factor. Several dealers pooled their money and hired a retired police officer to work undercover in the Gold/Silver Age Pavilion. His job was to do what all the security in the building could not - protect the dealers from theft. The job included an exhausting 5 days, at ten hours each - but we believe it paid off. I heard of maybe one booth that got hit. Our security watched a couple of known thieves but could not catch them in the act. The dealers were hyper-sensitive this year and made things tougher on potential thieves. We did watch several attempts by people that were identified in the past. Our undercover guy watched crooks make attempts and taught us how to better protect ourselves. A major aid to theft at the Con is the large tote bags handed out upon entry. We learned that the thieves use them to catch objects on display by holding the bag at hip height and just scooping items right in! It makes them very swift and hard to catch. I wish the Con would stop distributing those "Grand Theft Bags"!

Many of us can't complain about it in person, though. The Con still schedules the in-person feedback opportunity at the most inopportune period of the show. One hour on Sunday afternoon when we are either (a) in line to pay for next year's show, (b) busy protecting our booth from the most intense period of theft, or (c) packing out our inventory to beat the mass exodus that begins less than one hour later. Very frustrating!

Some Comic Sales of Note:

All-Winners Squad #17 GD $210
Batman #22 CGC 6.0 $348
Captain America #43 VG/F $720
Captain America #48 VG+ $450
Funny Pages #10 CGC 5.0 $350
Funny Picture Stories V2/#10 CGC 6.5 $300
Mad #1 CGC 6.5 $1,200
Star Comics #14 CGC 5.5 $300
USA Comics #15 FN $509
Amazing Spider-Man #1 GD $1,700
Amazing Spider-Man #38 CGC 9.0 $350
Fantastic Four #5 CGC 3.5 $674
Fantastic Four #60 CGC 9.6 $467
Strange Tales #140 CGC 9.6 $317
X-Men #7 CGC 6.0 $145
X-Men #24 CGC 9.6 $587
X-Men #25 CGC 9.6 $723
X-Men #26 CGC 9.6 $623
Amazing Spider-Man #129 CGC 9.2 $800
Giant-Size X-Men #1 CGC 8.5 $507

Terry O'Neill
Terry's Comics/Nationwide Comics
CalComicCon

Sales from 2010 to 2011 have been mostly strong, although sales in certain geographic regions reflect particularly weak economies. Our convention attendance has continued to be high. It seems all comic book conventions have experienced high attendance, although this did not always translate into strong sales. Collectors had enough cash to go through the door but used credit cards for early and low dollar purchases. Shows that were particularly strong this year: Wizard World in Chicago, Wondercon in San Francisco, and Midwest Comicbook Association's SpringCon in St. Paul Minnesota. Catalog orders have been slightly down, but we have made up for this with an increase in our eBay store sales, (we only list CGC graded comics and offer free shipping on all U.S. orders).

Golden Age: Sales have been mixed. At some shows high grade will sell well, at other shows lower grade will sell well. I am befuddled by collectors who, assuming that Golden Age comics are too expensive, will then buy a copy of *Amazing Spider-Man* #300 or *Wolverine* V1#1 for hundreds of dollars. We have been selling less Golden Age through our mail order business; this is a new trend. Lower grade comics are still selling at around 85% of *Guide*. Unfortunately, more collectors want higher grade comics at greater discounts. This trend may cause us to adjust how much we pay for acquiring this material. Mid-to-higher grade Timely, DC, MLJ, and Quality are selling at or above *Guide*. Short-run titles and lesser known characters like "Green Lama" and "Steel Sterling" are not in demand and, unless very rare, unlikely to end up in collections. *Classics*, even first prints, are not moving for us at all, although they contain great stories and art. Early Disney comics are selling well at *Guide*. Some sales of note: *Jackpot Comics* #1 CGC 7.5@$1,600, *Captain America Comics* #75 3.5@$585, *Hyper Mystery Comics* #1

VG+ @$285, *Leading Comics* #2 VG-@$261, *Speed Comics* #20 GD-@$255, *Sub-Mariner Comics* #4 VG@$765, *Witness* #1 GD+@$405, *Green Lantern* #17 VG/FN@$350, *Phantom Lady* #19 VG-@$450.

Atom Age: Many comics from this era are still on collectors' want lists. We try to stock as much as possible, but the supply is limited because print runs were lower, or more likely, many issues were just thrown out. Humor titles with offbeat titles like *Crazy*, *Nuts* and *Get Lost* are selling. Many comics from this era are great reads and have wonderful artwork, and compared to Silver Age Super-hero titles, they are real bargains. Mid-grade Westerns still sell well from the catalog, so if you are having a hard time selling your Westerns, call us.

Teen/Romance comics sell well at less than $30 unless they have Baker art; then the price can be quite high. War comics, mostly Atlas and DC titles, are selling well at *Guide* prices. Some sales of note: *Joker* #18 FN+@$150, *Joker* #22 FN/VF@$185, *Dennis the Menace* #1 VG+@$145, *Cow Puncher* #3 VG/FN@$108, *Journey into Mystery* #1 VG-@$550, *Strange Tales* #9 FN@$200, *Young Men* #27 VG-@$319, *Phantom Stranger* V1#1 GD/VG@$300, *Moon Girl* #4 GD/VG@$250, *Tarzan* #1 FN-@$240, *Two Gun Kid* #3 CGC 9.4@$1200.

Silver Age: Super-hero Marvels are still our best sellers. That being said, we are starting to heavily discount many common issues in VF- or lower grade. Low grade Marvel comics are not selling well unless priced at $5 or less, even if they *Guide* up to $20. DC comics in lower grade sell a little closer to *Guide*. We did get a couple of original-owner collections and did well selling higher grade *Batman* and *Detectives*. We have not purchased many DC keys in the past year, but the few we got sold fast at near *Guide*.

Marvel keys are still offered on a regular basis, and they usually sell well at around *Guide*. *Amazing Fantasy* #15 is a comic that we have had bad luck with lately. We were paying up to 85% of *Guide* (in lower grades) but found price resistance while trying to get above *Guide*. This may be because the *Guide* price increased so quickly. TV/Movie comics from the Silver Age are selling well at near *Guide* and Archie comics are selling well if priced right. Some sales of note: *Journey into Mystery* #83 PGX 4.0@$2500, *Tales of Suspense* #39 FR/GD@$500, *Fantastic Four* #5 VG/FN@$900, *Avengers* #4 FN@$500, *Incredible Hulk* #1 GVG@$2000, *Daredevil* #1 FN/VF@$2200, *Tales of Suspense* #39 VG-@$1400, *Avengers* #1 GD/VG@$850, *Tales to Astonish* #43 VF/NM $900, *Batman* #222 CGC 9.4@$1200, #227 CGC 9.4@$1100, *Green Lantern* #86 CGC 9.6@$800.

Bronze Age: Most of these comics are very common in all but the highest grades. The exceptions are off-beat titles such as Charlton humor and the few remaining TV comics from that era. However a few odd Marvel and DC titles may be the next big surprise as far as prices go. As always, *Hulk* #181 is the most requested comic at shows. Interest has increased in *Iron Man* #55 and *Amazing Spider-Man* #121,#122 and #129. Some sales of note: *Amazing Spider-Man* #129 CGC 9.6@ $1900, *Giant-Size X-Men* #1 CGC 9.2@$1000, *X-Men* #94 FN/VF@$400, *Tomb of Dracula* #10 CGC 9.0@$195, *Werewolf by Night* #32 CGC 9.2@$475, *Conan the Barbarian* #1 VF-@$186, *Iron Fist* #14 CGC 9.6@$500.

Magazines: We finally got a collection of Warren magazines in higher-grade. Most early and scarce issues sold fast at slightly above *Guide*. *Savage Sword of Conan* in high grade sell at or above *Guide*. Titles like *Rampaging Hulk* and *Planet of the Apes* are beginning to sell again. Horror and Monster titles are still on a lot of want lists, and are steady sellers, especially magazines by Eerie Pubs. Some sales of note: *Vampirella* #100 NM-@$170, #101 NM@$170, *Vampire Tales* V1#2 NM+@$110, *Dracula Lives!* #12@$60, *Tales of Voodoo* V7#1 FN@$48, *Savage Sword of Conan* #7 CGC 9.8@$425, #11 CGC 9.6@$100.

Horror and Monster Magazines are on a lot of want lists. (**Dracula Lives! #12 shown**)

Modern Age & Independents: We only sell very high grade comics from this era; anything less gets wholesaled or put in bargain boxes. Marvel titles like *Wolverine*, *Daredevil*, *Spider-Man* and *X-Men* are still selling at or above *Guide*. DC titles like *Batman* and *Detective* sell well near *Guide*. *The Crow* and *Miracleman* are also good Indy sellers. Some sales of note: *Amazing Spider-Man* #198 CGC 9.8@$550, #300 NM+@$170, *New Teen Titans* #2 CGC 9.8@$200, *Daredevil* #168 CGC 9.6 @$275, #169 CGC 9.8@$250, *New Mutants* #98 CGC 9.8@$190, *Ms. Marvel* #1 CGC 9.6@$135, *Spectacular Spider-Man* #2 CGC 9.6@$275, #27 CGC 9.8@$225, *Miracleman* #15 CGC 9.8@$306.

Graded books: The best way to sell pre-1975 comics is in very high grade, and it's the only way to get good money out of super high grade Modern comics. It is also the best way to keep really nice comics from getting damaged and to determine if any repairs or restoration was done. If you are looking for a solid investment with a great track record of appreciation, I recommend you consider third party graded comics. Some sales of note: *Captain America Comics* #46 CGC 5.0 @$4,000, #18 CGC 5.0@$2800, *DC 100 Page Super Spectacular* #4 CGC 9.6@$5250, *Sgt. Fury* #3 CGC 9.6@ $5975, #4 CGC 9.6@ $3734, *Amazing Spider-Man* #28 CGC 4.5@ $6800.

Internet Sales: Most of our Internet sales have been through our eBay store, although we have two websites with over 45,000 items listed. We have had steady sales of our graded comics through this venue. We usually sell only CGC graded books on eBay; we have our entire inventory at www.Terryscomics.com and www.NationwideKomics.com.

In summary, despite the continuing recession of the past three years, our sales remain strong. I want to thank the *Overstreet Price Guide* staff, our customers, show promoters, and comic sellers that have helped to make the past year a success. I also want to thank all the investors that included comics as tangible assets in their portfolios. If you are collecting for fun, profit, or nostalgia you are participating in a truly great American hobby.

Michael Pavlic
Purple Gorilla Comics

Purple Gorilla Comics is for people who love comics! People who love to read, collect and talk about them. I've made it my mission to create new readers, to bring back the lapsed ones and to accomodate the current ones. Since my store is located in a weekend only flea market and all I sell are back issues, I've had to work hard over the last three years to establish a good reputation and to stand out from the other comic stores in town.

I look at and count every page of every comic I sell. It wouldn't matter if it's an *Amazing Spider-Man* #1 or a *Dazzler* #23, I would treat and grade them the same way. So far, I've gone through more than 35 000 comics, with more being counted every week! I've been called crazy for doing so, but I've yet to have a single comic returned due to condition. It's what I'd expect when I buy comics for me, why would I give my customers any less?

I try to have a diverse selection of comics, from the most popular to the most obscure. Newer or older, high grade or low, Archie or Underground, all are welcomed to Purple Gorilla Comics with a new bag and board. If I can find it, I will carry it, no matter the publisher, genre or age.

Being in a flea market has shown me that the proper display of comics will not only attract comic collectors, but people who have never read a comic in their life. Sometimes, you can even turn non-readers into collectors! I believe there is a comic for every person, many of them just don't know it yet!

Purple Gorilla Comics is a celebration of a unique North American art form: comic books. I enjoy talking to people about comics, answering any question, if I can, suggesting comics they might like or listening to their stories of comics long since thrown out by their Mom. These connections are important to me and because of this, I've chosen to never buy or sell on-line. Never will. Maybe I've missed out on some great comics or sales, but, somehow, I've managed to amass 100,000 comics and sales have doubled every year. So, I think I'm doing all right!

Many comic stores have abandoned the back issues, unless it's a key book or it's expensive. The average $2-$20 comic, which comic stores were drowning in, were shoved aside for trade paperbacks and toys (which comic stores seem to be drowning in now, but that's another topic!). Many comics were dumped into $1 (or less) bins, usually unsorted and unloved by the owners. I always thought this was a mistake. Done right, back issues can be more profitable than trades ever could!

While Purple Gorilla Comics does have older comics, the majority of my stock is from 1982-1996. These are, for the most part, the easiest comics to find. Fortunately for me, my best selling titles, either as single issues or as sets, read like a top twenty list from *Wizard Magazine* circa 1994!

I'm finding a noticeable difference between the buying habits of comic collectors and casual readers: collectors generally buy superhero comics while readers are more interested in comics with pop culture tie-ins (movies, TV, music, video games). Collectors mostly buy single issues, readers prefer sets.

Bronze/Copper/Modern Age: In terms of single issue sales, Marvel greatly outsells every other publisher. As you would expect, any key issue like *Secret Wars* #8, *Incredible Hulk* #340, *Wolverine* #1 (1988) sell easily for *Guide* as do the *Amazing Spider-Man* and *Uncanny X-Men* titles. Other good selling Marvels include: *Hulk*, *Silver Surfer*, *Wolverine*, *Spider-Man* (1990), *Iron Man*, *Thor*, *Ghost Rider* (1990), *G.I. Joe* and *Transformers*. Any non-key issue of these titles can sell in the $3-$5 range. Surprisingly popular are: *Cloak and Dagger*, *Rom*, *Alpha Flight*, *Micronauts*, *Dreadstar*, *Warlock* and *What If?* (1st and 2nd series.).

DC's strong sellers include: *Batman*, *Swamp Thing*, *Hellblazer*, *Sandman*, *Green Lantern*, *Flash* and anything by Alan Moore and Neil Gaiman. I sell far more DCs as sets than I do as single issues. As for the other Modern publishers, *Buffy*, *Hellboy*, *Spawn*, *Evil Ernie*, *Lady Death* and anything by Alan Moore and Frank Miller all move briskly.

Silver Age: Like everywhere else in the world, high grade anything sells well. So does *Amazing Spidey* and *X-Men*. For the most part, my experiences mirror the market's as a whole. I will mention that I do sell a fair amount of lower grade Silver Age to people who want an original comic but are unwilling to spend huge money on a high grade copy. These people want to read, to enjoy their comic! In the case of Dell westerns, I've had beautiful copies of *Lone Ranger* comics gather dust at the $70-$100 range while "well-loved" copies in the $15-$40 range fly out the door! In fact, most non-super hero comics in this era are an easier sell in lower grades.

That covers what the "hard core" collectors are buying. Since I'm located in a flea market, I have hundreds of people walking by my store every weekend, representing every socio-economic demographic you can imagine. For these folks, nostalgia is the driving force behind their comic purchases. From the 70 year old man who loved Tarzan comics as a kid to the 25 year old woman who loves Ren and Stimpy and had no idea there was a comic, these are the kinds of people who buy from me. In every case, they did not come to the flea market to buy comics, it was the furthest thing from their minds, yet they leave with a comic or two or a set. *Classics Illustrated*, any Dell/Gold Key movie or TV tie-in,

Little Lulu, Flintstones, Jetsons, Sabrina, Josie and the Pussycats, Scooby-Doo, Sgt. Rock, Sgt. Fury, Rawhide Kid (and other Marvel westerns) are popular with the over-50 crowd. High grade is not a concern to these folks, indeed, more often it would scare them off due to the high price. The younger buyers like *TMNT, Sonic the Hedgehog*, anything to do with the WWF/WWE, *Buffy, Archie, Sailor Moon, Pokemon* and *Freak Bros.*

Sets: In one short year, sets of comics have become an integral part of my business. Sets are either a complete story (eg. Frank Miller's "Born Again" story in *Daredevil*), a mini-series or five sequential issues of a title. Sales of sets really took off once I had amassed about 200 of them (I have more than 350 now, more being created every week!). The selection became diverse enough to offer something to almost everyone. Sets are an easy entry point for casual readers and new collectors. Sets account for anywhere between 20%-40% of total sales, depending on the week. Prices for sets range between $10-$50.

Again, comics from the 1980s-1990s dominate sales. *Venom, Spawn, Spider-Man* (1990), *X-Men, Wolverine, Lobo, Batman, Infinity Gauntlet/War/Crusade, Secret Wars 2, Star Wars* (Dark Horse), *Silver Surfer, Buffy, Hellboy, Ren n Stimpy, Beavis & Butt-Head, Sandman, Superman, Lady Death, Dawn* and *Deadpool* all consistently sell at $15-25 per set. Many titles sell only as sets: *Aliens, Predator, Terminator, Hellraiser* and *Lone Wolf and Cub* are examples. I also find that five packs of titles like *Marvel Tales, Marvel's Greatest Comics* and other reprint titles sell quickly to parents of 8-12 year olds who want kid-friendly comics. The same holds true for the various Batman titles spun-off from the cartoons.

More than three years ago Purple Gorilla Comics began with eight long boxes. Today there are 35 000 comics for sale, with more coming all the time! A lot of hard work went into making the store what it is today, and I've loved every minute of it!

Jim Pitts
Avalon Collectibles

A tough, and wacky, year in the world of paper that saw me having to be more resourceful in finding shows to do that money can be made at. While the big companies seem to rake in all the biz these days, there is still stuff to find, and a few bucks to be made along the way. With signs of economic improvement, hopefully people start shopping for more collectibles in the coming year. Here's a quick overview of my last year.

Golden Age: A year where I scored more than usual, though mostly Humor and Funny Animal. I also got a wooden trunk full of low to mid grade Archie titles from around the end of WWII to the early '50s. Sales in this area included: *Adventure Comics* #62 GD $250, *Adventures of Bob Hope* #1 FR/GD $200, *Adventures of Bob Hope* #3 GD $60, *Airboy Comics* V3#9 VG $75, *Air Fighters Comics* #7 FR/GD $150, *Air Fighters Comics* #9 GD $80, about 25 issues of *Archie* between #18 and #60 with an average grade of VG on 'em going for between $60 and $100 each on eBay, *Archie's Pal Jughead* just over 20 issues in GD/VG between #3 and #35 that went for an average of $60 each, some first edition *Classics* (many with clipped order forms) #24 VG (clipped) $40, *Classic Comics* #26 VG (pencil) $200, *Classic Comics* #27 VG (clipped) $35, *Classic Comics* #33 GD/VG (pencil) $150, a small batch of *Four Colors* that were highlighted by a VG #108 (brown pages) $280, and 29 issues of *Walt Disney's Comics and Stories* between issues #37 and #100 with an average grade of GD on those. A small amount of Horror comics, Movie titles, and Atlas war also crossed my path over the year!

Silver Age: An area where competition for key books has hit an all time high! I had a couple of key Marvels this year that were on consignment. They included: *Avengers* #4 VG $400, #5 VG $80, *Incredible Hulk* #6 VG $200, *Journey Into Mystery* #83 FR/GD $1000. The key DCs I had included *Adventure* #247 GD/VG (Rest.) $500, *Brave and the Bold* #34 VG (Am. Rest.) $250, *The Flash* #110 VG- $300, *Justice League of America* #2 GD $110, several other early issues of *Superboy*, and *World's Finest* Silver Age issues. Low grade issues of *Fantastic Four* below #100, *X-Men* below #50, *Captain America* below #150 and *Avengers* below #50 didn't stay long in my boxes. Low grade DC War titles seemed to be in constant demand from people with big want lists! There were also some early Silver Age Archie titles left over from the collection I picked up with those issues selling decently in the $15 to $20 range.

Bronze Age: No massive sales for me in this area, but titles keep on moving! Both DC and Marvel Horror and War books seem to be the anchor of sales for me in this area. Conan titles do well, and when I can find them High Grade Harvey comics from the late '60s through the mid '70s have lots of people looking to fill their want lists. The Atlas/Seaboard titles have a lot of interest as well in FN or better. *Swamp Thing, Conan, Batman, Incredible Hulk, X-Men*, War, and Horror were what I was asked for all year long.

Modern Age: Not an area I make a lot of money off of, but these were the things I was asked for a LOT during the year: Alan Moore titles, War titles, Zombie books, Iron Man, and Thor were books people couldn't get enough of.

Big Little Books: I only had a few to sell this year, all in great shape though! They included: *Andy Panda's Vacation* FN/VF $60, *Blondie and Dagwood Some Fun* FN/VF $40, *Bugs Bunny the Masked Marvel* VF $75, and several of the early '70s ones in VF/NM for $15 to $25 each.

Undergrounds: My best seller year round as I have people looking for something at every show! While I didn't have any record setting sales I sold several copies of early (tabloid) issues of *Yellow Dog* at $50 to $75 each. *Cherry Poptart* has slowed, but demand for early first printings still outstrips supply. I sold most of the issues from a run I purchased where every issue was signed, first prints up through the 3D issue. Issue #1 VF (signed) $185, #2 (signed) $50, #11 3D issue (signed) $40. Several copies of *Spains Trashman Tabloid* went through my hands this year in the $30 to $60 range. Crumb titles remain the "King of the Jungle" with the cheaper priced first printings of his books moving quickly in the $15 to $100 range!

See ya at the shows everybody!

Bill Ponseti
Collector

2011 was, in many ways, very dissimilar to 2010. 2010 was the year of record sale after record sale. Although, there were a fair amount of big sales in 2011 the market clearly had cooled off some from the prior year's frenzied pace. Throughout the year, I often heard negative sentiment about the overall sales health of the hobby, but some incredible individual sales of high grade Golden Age key comics provided a distraction from some of the nay saying. However, even in a year of market correction downward, plenty of comics and cash changed hands in all segments that I track. My one question for the year is when will the flood of big collections and super high grade big key issues slow down? Based on what has surfaced in the final quarter of the year, my guess is not for a while.

Golden Age: As alluded to above, record prices are still being realized for the truly important comics form this period. Pop culture will always have a place for Superman, Batman and Captain America, and comic collectors with big wallets are finding more incredible copies featuring these characters to spend record sums of money on. Three million dollars for a comic book seems more and more likely as higher and higher graded copies of *Action Comics* #1 are released into the market. One very pleasant observation from 2011 in this segment was the migration into Golden Age collecting by Silver Age collectors continuing to happen month after month. Folks are finding the challenge of collecting Golden Age, and the wide variety of genres and titles out there, an appealing change from the silver age. The upward spiral of the aforementioned iconic heroes has not brought their lesser regarded brethren along with them. In fact, I can't remember a year when some of the titles and issues that were once so hot and sought after could be had for a better bargain than in 2011. I don't think this is a one year syndrome either. These books have been trending downwards for a while now. As much as I love them, *All-American* #16, *Adventure Comics* #40, #48, #61, and especially #73 are due for considerable downward correction in the *Guide*. The same is true for *Flash Comics* #1, *All Star Comics* #3 and #8, *Sensation Comics* #1, *Wonder Woman* #1, *Whiz Comics* #2(#1), and yes even the once much coveted and highly regarded *Marvel Comics* #1. All of these books are more affordable now than they have been in many years. For collectors this is a nice change, for dealers, not so much.

Silver Age: One thing that has always been true about Silver Age key comics, especially Marvels, is that they are basically currency in the hobby. No other sub-segment of the hobby has been as liquid as these books have been over the years. While this is still very true, some of them have been a bit less liquid than in years past. High grade examples still continue to sell for nosebleed and record prices. Mid-grade issues for some titles have trended up as well. However lower grade copies of *X-Men* #1, *Fantastic Four* #1, *Amazing Spider-Man* #1, *Brave and the Bold* #28, *Justice League* #1, *Showcase* #8, #22 and *Adventure Comics* #247 all are selling at much lower prices than recent years. *Journey into Mystery* #83 has gotten pretty expensive in mid to high grades, and I don't think it was due to the movie hype. As with any year, mid-run Silver Age comics in mid to low grades simply don't sell anywhere near *Guide* levels and all need to be priced 30-50% lower than they are listed.

Original Comic Art: The bargain train here left a long time ago. Unlike comics, large caches of original comic art aren't sprouting from trees and entering the market. We did see some fantastic Golden Age covers come to market thanks to Jerry Robinson, but for the most part much of what can be found has been found. When a previously complete book of art is broken up and offered for sale, I advise you take advantage of that opportunity and buy a nice page when it does happen. The few times I've tracked this in the past, these pages seem to disappear for a while after such an event and when they do resurface, the prices are much higher. You can't go wrong collecting the great artists as they never seem to go out of style.

Outlook: 2012 is looking to be similar to 2010 as far as record sales for big books. From what I've seen this last quarter of 2011 and what has been previewed for the first quarter of 2012, stand by for action! If you have been on the fence about going after a key Silver Age or Golden Age book due to price, 2012 should be a good year for you to get off that fence and scoop it up. I don't see the downward trend in the areas that went down in 2011 being reversed next year. Yet, I am very optimistic about the overall health of the hobby and still find it to be a ton of fun to collect comics. Life offers enough stress, so comics should not be part of that stress. Not worrying about the value of my collection has taken the stress out of the hobby altogether. So buy what you love and you can afford and you'll always smile when you look at your comic collection.

Jeff Rader and Cat Jones
Offbeat-Archives Auctions and Consignments

My last report was met with wonderful feedback, so thanks so much to all that wrote or called. Hopefully we can keep the momentum going this year, and many years following.

Not to disparage popular High Grade stuff, but it just is not our area of expertise. We won't be reporting any earth-shaking prices (not yet at least) – there are others far more suited for that. Our thrill is reporting on the neglected areas in which a collector on a budget can find truly enjoyable books without taking out a second mortgage. There are still bargains out there to be had. I have always specialized in the esoteric, arcane, rare, unlisted, unknown, etc. There's nothing like opening a book and finding something that has gone overlooked for decades of fandom.

On top of our own stock of crazy stuff we have started taking consignments this year, with sellers happy to have their books listed in the "Offbeat" fashion, and realizing "Offbeat" prices, many times ending at multiples of *Guide*.

Our report is not primarily set out to show what prices can/should be, but how much more enjoyable our hobby can be for those collectorss that love to read through their accumulations and see how much fun has been overlooked over the ages, along with how such gems can be had for a pittance This is what keeps collecting comics the thrilling hobby that it is to me. Following is only a handful of observances, including some un-noted appearances, artwork, drugs, atomic bombs, from the past year but check in next year as I will be passing on a lot of info to the *Guide*'s editors.

If you do enjoy reading, and digging through, your books there's always that chance that you can make a discovery first-hand instead of letting the market dictate your purchases. Our aim is to let you know what lies inside those books, to seek out info, and spread the word.

Different niche collectors make darn near everything collectible (*Dazzler* #1 excluded!) Foreign comics have a following that rivals nearly anything going on in mainstream comicdom. Just try to land early copies of Australia's *The Phantom*. Australian DCs have been causing a bit of a stir lately themselves, though information is lacking, and there are not enough left to meet demand. Canadian Whites are rare, and highly coveted, while their versions of U.S. titles had print runs that were dwarfed by their U.S. counterparts, and the variations in covers, stories, and ads, make for interesting comparisons. British comics have finally started getting some recognition with titles that never made it to the States, or variations that fit perfectly with their Stateside titles.

Non-comic collectors don't care what the "*Guide* value" is on something that had cross-over interest to them. Golf covers bring out the duffers like it's the PGA tour. Barbers will bid far fiercer for a Barber Pole cover than most comic collectors, and they do not care what the grade is. Other niches that sell well are those with covers featuring playing cards, Universal monsters (Archie Comics had some great ones in the late '50s and early '60s), gorillas, hot rods, chess, Indians (and please, no PC comments – I *am* Native, and the covers and stories do not offend me in the slightest), and too many more to list. Holiday covers have come into their own and there is a complete different group of collectors that battle it out for covers with Christmas, Halloween, Thanksgiving, Easter, etc. themes. This is another type of collector that often cares less about condition and current value than run collectors. Genre collectors often overlook Platinum, also. I could go on listing un-heralded gems for pages but in deference to my fave marketplace reporter, Doug Sulipa, I'm gonna keep it to a low uproar, but there will be countless more next year.

While there will be some input into prices we have sold books for, and a few purchases, much will be primarily for those looking for those fun bits that are primary unknown and/or overlooked, and are a load of fun to seek out and read. We hope to add to your want lists with the info below, and go out of our way to fill those same lists.

Platinum tidbits: *Buster Brown His Dog Tige & Their Jolly Times*, from 1906, has yet another version to go along with the two already listed. The version we sold, a Good+ for $153.00, is the larger size of the earlier version but had 58 pages (we thoroughly checked this book and there were no pages missing). The later version had 46 pages so maybe this was a transitional issue between the two. A *Buster Brown On His Travels*, from 1910, in stunning, bright shape went for $249.50. *Buster Brown's Happy Days*, 1911, has a very early aviation cover, with Buster, Tige, and Buster's uncle (looking a lot like Thomas Edison), in flight on an early Wright Brothers glider. *Hawkshaw the Detective*, was popular enough at the time to run thorugh 3 printings and our Very Good- 1st print sold for $43.00

You think Good Girl artwork started in the Golden Age? Nope! Grab a *Bringing Up Father*. Many have flappers galore and they were just as Good Girl, for being a century old, as much that qualified later.

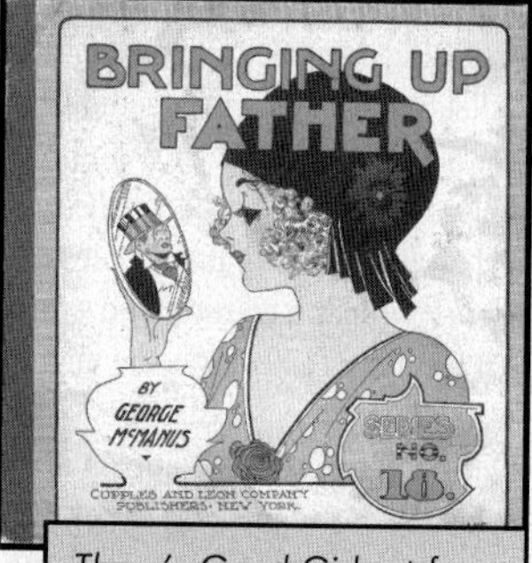

© C&L

There's Good Girl art from nearly a century ago to be found in **Bringing Up Father**. (#18 shown)

Your collection of Commie-themes comics will never be complete without a copy of *Mutt and Jeff* #7, from 1920, in which Jeff violently pounds a guy for being a Red Bolshevik.

For those avid Archie collectors out there, give *Harold Teen* a shot. The first issue, from 1929, has all the makings that made Archie and the Gang what they became. It also has a great early avaiation theme with a couple mentions of Charles Lindbergh, and Harold trying to emulate his hero, not very long after Man took to winged flight.

There are also volumes of great stuff to be found in the Golden Age. While much has been researched, there is just as much, if not more, that is still to be noted. We went through an huge collection of ACG and Charlton titles and there were cameos, appearances, artwork, etc. that deserves acclaim but has been overlooked until now. We also sold countless Romance comics, Humor, Funny Animal, and even Superhero, and there are items of note in just about everything...but they do not get noticed until the comic gets read. That's where our propensity for reading everything (GEN-

TLY) that comes through our hands comes in handy to us, and our consignors.

Adventures Into the Unknown #15 has a tale in which the Goths come to get vengeance on Hitler in an unlisted, post-war appearance. #38 has an atomic bomb panel, #80 has a Hydrogen bomb/mushroom cloud panel.

Cookie is another title for those that love vintage Archies but can get loads of the same hilarity, and GGA galore – much by Al Hartley, for a fraction of the price. This title is also full of great celebrity cameos and appearances that have gone under the radar. #2 features the unlisted 1st appearance of Tee-Pee Tim, who later took over *Ha Ha Comics*, and converted it into his own title. Bing Crosby makes a guest appearance in #8, while #12 has a sexy Hawaiian cannibal gal, Cookie in blackface drag, and a Hedy Lamarr mention all in the same story! #13 has what is probably the 1st comic book mention of "Jackie Robinson of the Dodgers" as he had just crossed the baseball color line. Gregory Peck makes an appearance on the cover of #15, and in #16 a photography studio lists "U.B. Iwerks", the true creator of Mickey Mouse, as the photographer. #18 has a Jane Russell-type, Jane Bustle, by Al Hartley, and he sure got her anatomically correct, while Cookie takes a dog to see a Lassie movie in #19. #26 has an unlisted story by Milt Gross, along with an unlisted Starlet O'Hara tale. Starlet also has unlisted appearances in #28, and #30. This title is ripe for the picking for the curious.

ACG's horror entry, *Forbidden Worlds* has some gems. Issue #3 is stated as having artwork by Al Williamson, and Joe Orlando, but after checking with a few experts it has been determined that Williamson's work was definitely inked by Wallace Wood. The artistic mastery of this story, with a panel by Frazetta even, rivals that of any of the other work these gents did over at EC Comics. A Fair copy sold for $33.00. #5 has all that makes for a must-have book with a Sub-Mariner-looking "monster" that seeks revenge on Red Communists that decimated his people with an atomic bomb. The kicker is that to help revive him, after killing the Russians, an American sub commander shoots him up with speed to revive him. ?!?! A Good- went for $16.88. ACG's editor, Richard Hughes, supposedly wrote the vast majority of ACG stories, and in this one there's a story of a writer that sells his soul for Satan's typewriter and the last couple pages take place in Hughes' office at ACG. A Good- sold for $25.76.

For the Western collector, Gene Autry makes a 4-panel appearance in *Funny Films* #4, and there are mentions of Jack Dempsey, Hedy Lamarr, Milton Berle, Gorgeous George, and Joseph Stalin.

Operation Peril was to ACG what *Venus* was to Atlas, in that they just couldn't figure out what they wanted to do with the title. Their indecisiveness worked out to our benefit because this title hit quite a few great genres and makes for one of the coolest short-run (meaning: attainable) titles around. In a short pre-Code 16-issue run they worked in adventure, crime, mystery, war, science fiction, and horror, so in this one you get everything from gun-toting adventurers, time-travelers, dead commies, bug-eyed monsters, dinosaurs, aliens, cave men, undersea adventure, some Good Girl Art thrown in for good measure, and a heck of a lot more. The Time Travelers feature, in #1-12, beat out Rip Hunter by a decade. Harry S. Truman makes a cameo and talks about atomic war in #2, and #3 has a horror tales about Jivaros and shrunken heads. #6 should be of interest the DC Big Five war collectors as it has a tank vs. a T-Rex cover a whole 9 years before *Star Spangled War Stories* combined war and dinosaurs in #90.

Out of the Night #1 has a story in which a werewolf dies of...a drug overdose! How can you beat that? It also features ACG's 1st editor's page, with Richard Hughes soliciting feedback from the readers. #2 is a doozie in that, after consulting a few experts, we have come to the conclusion that the 5-page story by Al Williamson had some inking assistance from his pal, Frank Frazetta, just as he did in *Forbidden Worlds* #3 but with quite a bit more. For the gore-hounds, #12 has an Arabian slave trader that pays a hell of a price for cutting the tongues out of a caravan of nomads.

Lev Gleason's *Boy Loves Girl* #28 (#4) has a great heroin story, and a bright pink cover that is notoriously difficult to find unfaded.

We have no problem selling copies of the EC/Charlton 1st variant of *Impact* #1. The relatively unknown story behind this one makes it a must-have curiosity. Grant Geissman, EC expert-extraordinaire told me that there was mention of it in *Overstreet* by Bob and Russ Cochran "opening the Gaines File Copy packages for sale, around 1990 or so. This report has it a bit wrong, because it concluded that the one copy of the Charlton printing found in Gaines's files was the only copy extant, which of course is not correct. Jerry Weist and Roger Hill were the first people to discover the *Impact* #1 first printing, which they brought in and showed to Gaines some time in the late 1960s. Gaines then related to them the story that you see in *Collectibly Mad*." That story is that Gaines, looking to save money, originally farmed the printing job out to Charlton. The quality was so atrocious that Gaines ordered the entire run destroyed. Obviously a few escaped mass extinction because there are still some out there to be found. The logo is white instead of yellow, the quality is far inferior, and they have that "Charlton feel" to them.

Charlton's *Danger and Adventure* #22 (#1) happens to feature the last Golden Age appearnce of Ibis, who went into hibernation until he was revived by DC years later.

For the lover of pre-code horror and crime, *Fight Against Crime* #12 has a story of a doctor that gets his patient addicted to morphine on purpose, along with a violent tale of some thugs that work over a fortune teller and light his turban on fire. What the...???

Even incomplete comics have seekers nowadays as we sold a *Wings* #1 with a partial cover, no staples, and last 6 pages missing for over $50.00.

Giggle Comics is another wonderland for unknown oddities and awesomeness. They are also full of covers and artwork by the extremely under-rated Ken Hultgren, who has a quiet fan base that do just about anything for his work. Along with the 1st appearance of the long-running Superkatt, #9 also features the 1st appearance of many of his racist depiction of an big-lipped African-American maid. *Giggle* #10 had Superkatt shooting Japanese planes, and in #10 he goes up against a Nazi robot. *Giggle* #14 has Superkatt on the splash page getting ready to put a medal on a Nazi kommandant's chest...with a huge nail and hammer right over his heart. Superkatt takes on a Nazi U-boat and a bunch of Nazis. Spencer Spook, who eventually took over this title, makes his 2nd appearance in #22. Bob Hope and Bing Crosby make an appearance at the 1947 Academy Awards on the splash page of Superkatt in #46. *Giggle* #44 features "Mussel-Man", a Superman parody, and Witch Hazel makes her 1st appearance in #45. Want to see how an evil Santa Claus with an atomic bomb would look? Try issue #49, which has a great Christmas cover as well. *Giggle* #61 has some unlisted artwork by Milt Gross, along with a nice Christmas cover, and both Bob Hope, and Frank Buck appear in the Superkatt story. Another great Christmas cover, #69, sold for $26.55 in VG. In #70 Superkatt's island pals get relocated to the States so that they can use their island for atomic bomb tests.

Ha Ha was the companion title to *Giggle*, and just as fun. *Ha Ha* #44 has a racist Little Black Sambo appearance, with a huge bone in his hair, and big lips, and also has what I think is the 1st Tee-Pee Tim appearance. *Ha Ha* #95 is an oddball book with its 3-D effect cover and the fact that, as is the same in #96, the borders on all the interior pages are all colored either red, green, or blue. It looks pretty cool but must not have gone over too well because it didn't last long.

For the connoisseur of hillbilly love, *Romantic Adventures* #7 is the one for you. This one has a great story about a city slicker who takes on a bet that he can't take a hillbilly gal from her shotgun-toting Pa and civilize her. Her Pa smacks her until she agrees so she leaves with the rich guy to get scrubbed in a tub, taught to speak properly, festooned with jewelry, and taught to be a lady. After her conversion, and she becomes a TV star, they end up back in the swamp fighting a gator and finding love.

While it has been surmised that the first issue of *Li'l Genius* has been #5, we have corresponded with a couple of the leading Charlton collectors and have come to the conclusion that #5 does not exist, and that #6 is actually (#1). #11 has an appearance by Li'l Tomboy, that is tied with her 1st appearance in her own title in 10/56. You collectors of atomic bombs, and Communist spies will find a must-have in this title too, as #34 has Li'l Genius up against Commie terrorists trying to blow up a dam, and has an atomic bomb/mushroom cloud...??? Yep, it's gotta be a Charlton.

Along with #1 and #2, *My Little Margie* #3, #4 and #14 have photo front and back covers as well. Issue #44 includes everything that made Charlton so crazily unique. It has a great UFO cover and story, but that was not enough. There is an ad for "Wate-On" featuring a scantily-clad June "The Bosom" Wilkinson, better known for her *Playboy* appearances. Issue #52 has a strip, "The American Way", with a panel of Nikita Khrushchev ranting like he had just been denied entry to Disneyland.

If you are a Turok fan then you must give the scarce *Space Western* #45 a gander. It has a story, The Valley That Time Forgot, that was a pre-Turok story about a valley that has escaped the ravages of time and is occupied by battling dinosaurs, and a bow-toting Indian. Sound familiar? It sure looks familiar. I really would not doubt if someone over at Dell got a gander at this story a year before Turok made his debut in *Four Color* #596, in 12/54. This one is easily more of a prototype issue than many of the pre-hero Marvel prototypes can claim to be. Our glossy, Off-White Fine+/Very Fine-copy sold for $132.45.

Some other sales we made were *Planet Comics* #47 in GD/VG- for $44.33, #57 in Fine- $103.51, #58 in VG-$56.00, #62 in GD+ $38.95, and #63, with a wild phallic cover, in VG $73.55. *Blue Bolt* v9 #5, with a Fish-In-Face cover by L.B. Cole in VG+ $36.01. *Baffling Mysteries* #14, glossy Fine $56.55. *Battle Stories* #8, with a Commie Colonel murdering U.S. POWs – Fine $26.30. A nice, complete *Donald Duck Fun Book* #1 in VG+ $57.89. *United States Marines* #2, with a racist bloddy Tojo cover in VG+ $57. *Black Knight* #1 in VG $96.00. *Marvel Mystery Comics* #88, with the second appearance of Sun Girl in VG-$165.72. *Strange Adventures* #1 in VG+ $379.01. *Superman* #32 in VG+ $173.51. *Green Mask* v2 #5 in Fine+ 41.00. *Racket Squad* #12, with a classic Ditko bomb cover, Fine+ $79.00. We also sold two rare format books that are always in high demand. Our Good copy of *It Rhymes With Lust* went for $206.00 with some fervent bidding, and a VG+ copy of the Dell *Told in Pictures – Four Frightened Women* went $54.11.

Silver and Bronze Age did well for us also, and there are still countless discoveries to be made there as well. In last year's report we listed what we had done with the first half of a near-complete run of Charltons. For the collector that finds their kicks in comics with pin-ups and posters Charlton wins hands-down. This year we wrapped them up and what we found is listed below, along with other finds and sales.

Attack #6 a great commie Russian nuclear (that's "nucular" for all you news commentators and politicians) submarine story and #8 has an unlisted Richard Nixon make a brief appearance as his General fills him in on the situation.

While the previous two issues of *Atomic Mouse* featured Hoppy the Marvel Bunny, something must have gone awry with the rights to Hoppy because in #16 the red-suited Hoppy is gone and "Happy the Magic Bunny" appeared. It must be a heck of a coincidence because when Happy yells, "Alizam!" a marvelous bunny in a blue super-suit shows up. Yep, coincidence. *Blondie* #212 has a GREAT Super-Dagwood cover & story. The best thing about *Bo* #1 and #3, other than the fact that they are definitely NOT common, are the unlisted Noodnik the Eskimo stories that Charlton must have picked up the rights to after Noodnik's own title was canceled the year before.

Fightin' Air Force #22 has a President Dwight D. Eisenhower cameo, and #27 has a great "Area 51"-type USAF vs "UFO" story, until the pilot is shown "the best kept secret in the world today!" *Fightin' Army* #48 has a Cuban "Power-Mad Dictator" trying to kidnap the current anti-Communist leader to kill him. The lunatic even looks *exactly* like a ranting Fidel Castro, while #51 has an Adolf Hitler cover and appearances in "Hitler's Private Paradise". *Fightin' Army* #75 is not the 1st appearance of "The Lonely War of Captain Willy Shultz!". #76 contains the 1st cover, and 1st appearance of the awesome series, "The Lonely War of Capt. Willy Schultz", along with Willy's origin. Willy was falsely framed for a traitorous murder by crooked Captain Wilkes, and spends the series playing the part of a Nazi to avoid execution, and the part of a G.I. when he can to help.

In *The Flintstones* #38 Pebbles finds a genie and flies to 20th century New York, they see a war at some point in time where an atomic bomb is dropped and they get a gander at a mushroom cloud, and land on the moon. You can't get too much more sci-fi than that!

You a KISS fan? You need to look a bit earlier than *Howard the Duck* to nab a swipe/1st comic book appearance. *Ghostly Haunts* #46 has a make-up laden heavy metal band story singing, "Kiss me..Kiss me". In '75 this could not be a take on any other band than KISS.

Go-Go was definitely aimed at the hippie teen set, and is fun from beginning to end, but a few cool things worthy of note are that in #2 Blooperman appears along with a parody of Batman, and a cigar-chomping Robin, and Alfred, along with "The Bestest League of America" with parodies of Green Lantern, Flash, Wonder Woman, the Atom, and Aquaman. *Go-Go* #6 has a Marvel vs. DC parody "The BLA vs The Marvelous Super-Heroes with swipes at the Human Torch, Captain America, the Wasp, Giant-Man Iron Man, The Hulk, Mr. Fantastic, Thor, Spider-Man, and The Thing vs. twisted versions of the Flash, Hawkman, Wonder Woman, Green Arrow, Green Lantern, Aquaman. Plastic Man, Blackhawk, and more.

Get your hippie teen fun with a splash of super-hero parody in **Go-Go** #6 from Charlton.

Haunted #5 has a Ditko story with characters that look exactly like Peter Parker and Norman Osborn...was Ditko thumbing his nose at Marvel yet again?? (for more examples, a couple blatant, check out my report in last year's *Guide*). In #26 there is a story with some crazy wife-beating going on - how that got past the Comics Code Authority is anybody's guess. *Haunted* #39 has a shotgun blast point-blank in the face panel, a Sutton story with over-the-top SEXY Good Girl Art throughout and a topless panel. *Haunted Love* #4 has got what must be the weirdest dead headlight cover ever.

Jetsons #9 is a must for any Good Girl Art fancier. Judy Jetson drawn in a way we *never* got to see her on TV...skimpy bikini, and quite a bit bustier than I remember...wooooooo hooooo! *Jetsons* #9 has a great Flintstones crossover story, "A Visit to Bedrock".

Just Married #72 has a wild cover and story about swingers and the one newlywed bride that didn't really want to play along. Only in Charlton... #102 has a crazy story about a guy that ODs on uppers and downers and later knocks his wife's tooth out with a right hook before his final overdose...?! *Love Diary* #89 has a text story "Is Your Boyfriend Getting Hooked?" with all the signs to tell if someone is loaded, while #92 has a psychedelic story with a heroin overdose.

Marines Attack #8 is not noted in the Guide but this is probably the 1st Vietnam War cover on a comic, and one of the very first stories. *Marine War Heroes* #11 has "First Contact", one of the earliest Vietnam stories - features VC tunnels and moles, and #17 has a story of Tojo's war plans prior to Pearl Harbor, the bombing of Pearl Harbor while Japanese were in Washington discussing "peace", and the bombing of Hiroshima and Nagasaki - with an atomic bomb/mushroom cloud panel.

Midnight Tales #5 has a SEXY centerfold pin-up of cover-girl Arachne, by Howard. I have never heard of a horror comic having a hot centerfold but WOW!!!

The last issue of *My Secret Life*, #47, has the unheralded 1st appearance of Sue and Sally Smith, Flying Nurses, who took over the title after this issue.

You like "interactive" stories? *Mysteries of Unexplored Worlds* #16 has an alien that interacts with the powers-that-were at Derby, Conn. by selling his story to Charlton Comics. Issue #28 has a Communist A-Bomb story in which Khrushchev does his usual tantrum throwing and dies just as he is reaching to push "The Button". If only... #43 also has an atomic bomb panel.

Want an inexpensive alternative to *Showcase* #4 for the dawn of the Silver Age? *Nature Boy* #3 (#1) was Charlton's shot at an original superhero from 03/56. When the Golden Age of comics came to a halt, publishers were scrambling to come up with new titles, ideas, and characters to get sales going again. DC's revamping of the Flash, in *Showcase* #4, from 09-10/56, is usually looked at as kicking off the Silver Age but this new character, by John Buscema, beat the Flash's re-intro by a half a year. This book features Nature Boy's 1st appearance, origin, and even a Nature Man story depicting him after he had matured a bit. This also features the last "Golden Age" appearance of the Blue Beetle and he disappeared for 10 years until his 2nd incarnation in '65.

While the *Guide* states that *Outer Space* #17 (#1) contains "Williamson/Wood style art; not by them" the concensus of those in the know is that this story truly was done by Al Williamson and Wallace Wood. I concur, and the artwork is AMAZING! While Sid Check could do some pretty accurate impressions of some of the comic masters, the artwork in this story is unmistakable. A Good copy sold for $19.02. Are you absolutely positive that your Matt Baker collection is complete? If you do not have *Out of This World* #14 then you're missing one. It has a signed, 7-page unlisted story by the legendary Baker that was one of the last done in his lifetime since his untimely passing was probably very soon after he drew this story. If you are the Baker completionist odds are this book has eluded you, so nab it now. A GD+/VG- copy sold for #13.50

Pebbles and Bamm Bamm #26 has unlisted EARLY pro Mike Zeck artwork in text illos. His only prior fan "pro" non-fanzine work were also unlisted illos. in one issue each of *Savage Sword of Conan*, and *Savage Tales* magazines for Marvel.

Charlton's run of *The Phantom* is one of the most amazing overlooked titles around. The painted covers, artwork by Newton, and storylines are unbeatable. *The Phantom* #51 has a grey-tone bondage/sacrifice cover, and a 3-page grey-tone story. #52-54 also have grey-tone covers. #67 has a 5-star painted cover, by Newton that is worthy of framing, and Humphrey Bogart, Lauren Bacall, and Peter Lorre are drawn (and drawn very well) into the whole book-length story that has a *Maltese Falcon/Casablanca* noir-feel to it. The painted flag cover on #74 is second in all of comicdom only to *Superman* #14. This artwork is absolutely breathtaking! If this were a DC or a Marvel book the price would be through the stratosphere. I can't keep this one in stock.

I have no idea how *Popeye* #108 has eluded mention before but it has the greatest "Story of..." origin of any character imaginable. It kicks off with Elzie Segar's conception of Popeye in 1929, his transformation over the years, and goes up to the point where George Wildman (wearing a Charlton shirt) draws himself on a full-page panel along with Popeye and many of his cohorts. In #123 Wimpy beats Neil Armstrong to the moon and interrupts his, "One small step for man..." with, "Greetings! You didn't happen to bring a hamburger with you, did you?" #130 has the 1st appearance (and hopefully only) of SuperStuff - A Gorgeous George-looking superhero that Sea Hag conjures up to kick Popeye's tail. #137 is the closest you are going to get to a GGA cover and story with Popeye as Sea Hag turns herself, then all other women, into curvy beauties.

For a wild dino-love tale grab *Reptisaurus* #5 where he takes a hit from an atomic bomb, pounds the hell out of Beijing, and falls in love with a paper parade dragon from the People's Republic of China.

Romantic Story #26 has a story just as risque as any Fox jungle girl story and the lead gal looks like – and is dressed like – Sheena. The crazy part is that in one panel the artist drew her with half of her leopard bikini off, exposing her, but the colorist did not dare color her correctly. In #105 there is a crazy woman-beater cover and story in which a doctor smacks a gal for calling him a draft dodger...then she marries him. Go figure...

For the collector of the U.S. Space program *Space Adventures* #43 is a must. It has an awesome cover featuring Alan Shephard (name misspelled on cover but corrected on splash page) Freedom 7 - cover and story about the second man in space, and 1st American astronaut. This 13-page story, about Shephard – his training – the mission and everything else in detail.

You up for yet another Matt Baker previously unlisted discovery? Who wouldn't be?! *Strange Suspense Stories* #47 has an 8-page story by Baker. This story was one of the last done by Baker due to his untimely death in '59.

Submarine Attack #16 and #47 have atomic bomb/mushroom cloud panels while #43 has a Cuban Missile Crisis story.

Charlton must have had some brutal writers and artists as the cover of *Summer Love* #48 says it all...the story title is "The Swingers" and some "groovy" dude is man-handling some gal into submission by her ponytail...what the...??? The story is just as off-the-wall. *Sweethearts* #44 has a Pat Boone photo cover that has escaped notice until now.

Trying to complete your Judomaster collection? Well things just got switched up a bit for you. *Thunderbolt* #52 has an unlisted Judomaster story, his 4th appearance that was on the stands the same time as *Judomaster* #89 (#1). *Thunderbolt* #53 has an unlisted 2-page Captain Atom story telling the history of atomic power with a panel of the atomic bomb dropped on Hiroshima. Lastly, #60 has the 1st appearance, and last, of The Prankster which was Dennis O'Neil's 1st story and drawn by Jim Aparo. The story is pretty funny and, despite the announcement of Prankster's return in the next issue, he disappeared into comic oblivion. Even DC didn't bring him back to life like they did with most other Charlton superheroes.

Just when you think you've seen it all...Charlton pulls another wild stunt. *Tiger* #3 has an ad for a life-size inflatable doll, with optional bikini, pajamas and wig(?!?!?!) but I really think they missed their target audience by a million miles with this one! Only Charlton!!!

The LAST place you would expect to find a Nazi story is in *Timmy the Timid Ghost* but #27 has a Nazi story with the ghost of a U-Boat captain – swastika and all...yikes!

Self-potrait comics? Try *Unusual Tales* #13 has great cover of a comic book artist by Dick Giordano (self-portrait?).

War at Sea #26 features "Pearl Harbor...The Day of Infamy" story with an unlisted Franklin Roosevelt appearance while #42 has a story of U.S. occupation in Cuba with countless appearances of a loud-mouth Fidel Castro, and some of his obnoxious "Yanqui"-hating commie cohorts. *War Heroes* #22 has the true story about the plot to kill Hitler.

Other books that we have sold over this past year include *Journey Into Mystery* #76, the non-blacked out price version in GD/VG $21.01. *Hansi the Girl Who Loved the Swastika* in VG 1st printing $16.56. *Captain America* #100 VF/VF+ $177.50. *Daredevil* #1 - Beautiful Bright VF-

$769.00. A near-perfect *Iron Man* #55 - SHARP Glossy Off-White NM+ $270.56. *Silver Surfer* #1 in Fine+ $160.00. *Silver Surfer* #4 in VF $157.50. The crazy giveaway *Sardineland*, 1967 version – indisputable Mint (and in nearly 4 decades I have very rarely ever used that term) $21.06.

Other offbeat comic-related goodies we sold include a rare 1949 copy of *Love & Death*, by Gershon Legman. While *Seduction of the Innocent* seems to have brought on the Comics Code Authority, five years before that comics were already under scrutiny and Gershon Legman (nope, I didn't make that up) self-published this tome, *Love & Death - A Study in Censorship*, making the argument that in America the "Glorification of crime" led to the repression of sexuality. The dialogue in this book is far beyond anything Wertham did and Legman did not pull a single punch. Our copy sold for $78.00. A VG copy of the scarce CCA censorship booklet *Facts About Code Approved Comics Magazines* sold for $67.00.

Our VG+ copy of *Americana in Four Colors* '72 (copyright states 1964, but this is the '72 version) sold for $151.38. There was one from '74 as well. It was written by John L. Goldwater, one of the founders of MLJ/Archie Comics, and President of the CCA for 25 years. It is a narrative about the comic book industry, its history, how the Code operates, the "Educational Values in Code-Approved Comics Magazines, self-regulation, and the code of the CCA. There is a 2-page comic, "The Comics Technique" that details the A-Z steps of producing a comic, with a couple panels by Archie good girl artist, Dan DeCarlo.

A killer Near Mint+ copy of the 1st print of the truly offbeat *DC Super Heroes Super Healthy Cookbook* from 1981, went to a very pleased buyer for $36.99.

A VG+/FN- 1st print of the hotter-than-hell *Super Dictionary* from 1978 went for $68.77. This popular book contains the vast majority of the DC line-up, along with obscure characters like Conjura - an African-American lass that speaks backward to cast spells and travel through time, Jonna Crisp - a spaceship pilot, El Dragón - a Mexican hero that has power over electricity, Wilson Forbes - an African-American reporter, Jody - Tomahawk's African-American scout pal, SR-12 - a small purple-haired gal from another planet, and Ted & Teri Trapper - an African-American husband and wife detective team. Joe Kubert, Neal Adams, Kurt Schaffenberger, Murphy Anderson, Ross Andru & Mike Esposito, Jim Aparo, Carmine Infantino, Wayne Boring, Curt Swan, Al Plastino, and H.G. Peter, all have artwork represented in this one.

We also did quite a bit of buying this year including a coveted copy of the VERY RARE (I looked for years before finding, and buying, my copy from a gent that looked just as long as I did) *Super Duper Comics* #3, from 1947, featuring the first appearance of Mr. Monster. I also finally landed a copy of the also VERY RARE *Kid Colt Album*. One thing that is noted in the *Guide* that needs an update is that this book is NOT rebound books, so the contents will not vary. There is actually a table of contents that lists all of the stories included. Another fun score was a beautiful copy of *World's Finest Comics* #44. Now why would I be so happy about that? This issue is a newly-discovered *Seduction of the Innocent* comic that Wertham referred to as Batman and Robin being gay, along with his mention of a cop getting shot in the face...by Batman!

We are just now starting to sell an amazing run of one of the lesser-known areas of comic books, Chick tracts. These little tracts, from Jack T. Chick, have been around for decades and have more variants than *Classics Illustrated*. Next year we will have a full report on those, but just to give you an idea of how much interest there is in them, our GD/VG copy of 1962's *A Demon's Nightmare* just sold for $89.21, with some serious competition butting heads.

We truly want to thank everybody that has made this our best, and funnest, year by far. As always, if anybody has any questions, or just want to chat about comics, please do write, or give us a call!

Greg Reece
Greg Reece's Rare Comics

By the time you read this report our redesigned website (www.gregreececomics.com) will have launched. This area of our business has seen the largest growth in the last year and it stands to reason that trend will continue so we really wanted to upgrade the shopping experience. Every book listed has a scan that can be enlarged along with a zoom feature that allows you to magnify any part of the book you wish. Other new features include an automated want list feature that will notify you of any book that meets your preset criteria and a new consignment option where you can upload your books directly to the site for sale.

I feel like a broken record but last year was like all of the years prior in that we cannot keep keys in stock in any grade. *Amazing Fantasy* #15, in particular, just defies gravity. I remember thinking 2 years ago, the book had nowhere to go. That was 30% ago across all grades. It is a must have and collectors are scrambling to get a copy before even the lower grades move totally out of sight. A book that had slowed in the last half of 2010 but really picked up as we closed out 2011 was *Avengers* #1, particularly in 6.0+. It is one of the few keys that is relatively affordable even in grade. I think the *Avengers* movie will fuel interest in this book, along with *Avengers* #4 (1st Silver Age appearance of Captain America) and *Strange Tales* #135 (1st appearance Nick Fury).

Journey Into Mystery #83 was another book we got lots of interest in and we sold them as fast as we got them. The *Thor* movie was a hit and that didn't hurt interest at all. *Flash* #105 is an undervalued key in better grades along with *Showcase* #4. The Bronze Age book to have is *Incredible Hulk* #181. While we handle multiple copies of *Giant-Size X-Men* #1 and *X-Men* #94, we rarely get *Incredible Hulk* #181 and when we do, it flies out. *Incredible Hulk* #1 looks ready to breakout. Next time you're at a major convention, count the number (in any grade) of *Incredible Hulk* #1s in the room vs. other Marvel keys.

Books that really slowed for us this year included *Showcase* #22 and *Green Lantern* #1. I suspect that was because the movie was not well received (although I must confess, I enjoyed it. Metropolis shattered all sales records with their incredible *Action Comics* #1 CGC 9.0 selling for just shy of $2.2 million. This can only translate into good things for the hobby and its acceptance as a legitimate investment alternative.

Notable Sales:
Amazing Fantasy #15 CGC 7.0 $39,500
Batman #1 CGC 3.0 $32,500
Atom #1 CGC 9.4 (Twin Cities Pedigree) $10,800
Brave And The Bold #28 CGC 7.5 $10,000
Journey Into Mystery #106 CGC 9.6 $6,000
Avengers #1 CGC 7.0 $5500
Amazing Spider-Man #1 CGC 5.0 $6000
Avengers #18 CGC 9.8 $4800
Amazing Spider-Man #50 CGC 9.4 $4200
Avengers #1 CGC 6.0 $3300
Avengers #4 CGC 8.5 $3200
Avengers #1 CGC 6.0 $3000

Notable Purchases: We were able to buy an incredible original owner collection out of Philadelphia, PA. We got a call the day before Hurricane Irene ripped up the Atlantic Seaboard but there was just enough time to drive up and see the books. A man brought books in plastic grocery bags, unbagged and unboarded for all of these years. They were uniformly spectacular and we were thrilled to make the purchase. Of the books sent off to CGC, these were some of the highlights: *Fantastic Four* #72 CGC 9.6, *Green Lantern #32* and #33 both CGC 9.6, *Green Lantern* #40 CGC 9.4, *Journey Into Mystery* #106 CGC 9.6, *Journey Into Mystery* #118 CGC 9.4, *Amazing Spider-Man Annual* #1 CGC 9.0 and many, many more.

At the close of 2011, we purchased a beautiful run of books out of Chicago. Many of these are off to be certified including a *Tales Of Suspense* #40 that will be in the 9.0 range and many other very high grade books. Other highlights from the collection include high grade examples of DC's from the tough 1950-1956 era.

Chicago, IL - C2E2: The 2011 show season started for us in March in Chicago and we were lucky to catch good weather. We met many customers for the first time and let me tell you, Midwest charm is alive and well. Some of the nicest guys you could ever want to meet stopped by the booth. We went out to Spiaggia's (an Italian restaurant) and it was an awesome experience. If you are looking to splurge on something other than or in addition to comic books in Chicago, this might be the place for you. We bought the nicest group of Bronze we'd ever laid eyes on and many of those books ended up in CGC 9.8 holders with several as the stand alone highest graded examples.

Pittsburgh, PA: This show continues its struggles but is very close to home and we have just enough customers to justify coming back. Thankfully, Stan Lee is scheduled for 2012 so hopefully that moves the needle for Pittsburgh. We are also able to buy here so all in all, worth the effort.

New York, NY - Wizard World: This was a solid 2 day show that Wizard just took over from legendary promoter, Michael Carbonaro. The AC didn't work Saturday and that was also the day the world was supposed to end. Someone was playing "It's the end of the world as we know it", "1999", and many other apocalyptic songs. We even had a countdown. Very solid show as we sold numerous Jerry Robinson signature series/archive edition books, a gorgeous *Daredevil* #2 CGC 9.4 and many other high grade books. There truly is no place like NY.

Philadelphia, PA - Wizard World: Another great Philly show and it was nice to see so many of our Philadelphia area customers again. Sales were brisk. We sold a very bright *Amazing Spider-Man* #1 CGC 5.0. Went out to Pat's Steak n Cheese (was ok but will try Gino's next year). One of our favorite shows on the circuit. Center City Philadelphia is just a fun place to hang out.

Chicago, IL - Wizard World: Another one of the more enjoyable shows on the tour. Hotels are located conveniently to the convention center and there are lots of great spots to eat close by. We sold it all in Chicago, high grade CGCs, fillers for runs and quite a bit of Golden Age. We chose venerable Gibson's one night and if you are a steak lover, it doesn't get any better than that.

Baltimore, MD: Can this show get any better? I don't know how but each year somehow tops the year before and 2011 was no exception. Sunday was busier for us than Saturday for the 2nd year in a row. The only negative was we were too busy to get out and walk the floor and bought very little as a result. Just flat out too busy selling. There was tons of great material in the room so we would've loved to look. Is it time for Baltimore to go to a 3 day venue?

New York, NY- C2E2: Wow! We broke all sales records at this one-of-a-kind event. For those of us that don't set up at San Diego, there simply is no other venue like C2E2 New York. We debuted The Philadelphia Story collection (more on this in our buy report) at NY so it was a perfect storm scenario. The promoters did a nice job of spacing out the aisles in the comic book section. Even though there were tons of people there, it wasn't the cramped madhouse it was in 2010.

Columbus, OH - Wizard World: Solid, middle of the road show. We were able to reload some stock after the blitzkrieg of NY, buying a nice DC collection and some stellar Marvel Bronze. Sold quite a bit of raw, but CGC sales were practically non-existent. Columbus has a fun downtown area with every kind of cuisine you can think of.

We will set up at all of the shows listed above in 2012 and are also adding Megacon in Orlando, FL and Heroes in Charlotte, NC

In closing, I wish everyone a safe, happy year of collecting and I hope to see you on the road in 2012.

Barry Sandoval
Heritage Auctions

"Finds": One of the most interesting things about vintage comic collecting is that you never know what undiscovered collections might still be out there.

As we write this, we're about to introduce an original-owner Golden Age collection to the market that features almost all of the major keys: *Action* #1, *Detective* #27, *All-American Comics* #16, *All Star* #3, etc. CGC has designated it a pedigree collection, named after the collector, Billy Wright. Is this the last such collection that will ever surface, or are there several more, or many more?

When it comes to Silver Age books, on the other hand, it's a certainty that outstanding original-owner collections exist that haven't yet come to market. Collectors of the early 1960s are still relatively young for the most part. However, Heritage did introduce one such excellent collection to the market in the past year, the Gary Dahlberg Collection (aka the Twin Cities pedigree). It went to auction because Mr. Dahlberg died tragically while only in his early sixties, but his meticulous collecting was validated by the total sales of $2 million and counting.

Mile High copies: The Edgar Church/Mile High collection remains unsurpassed as the greatest of the pedigree collections, and we got a special treat last August as Chuck Rozanski of Mile High Comics consigned the last 150 or so comics which he had held onto for personal reasons. We were certainly honored that Chuck, himself a comic seller of great renown, entrusted the collection to Heritage. While the Mile High *Red Raven* #1 was the traditionally "big" book of the group, it was particularly interesting to see the results of the *Spirit* run. Issue #22 of *The Spirit* fetched $25,095 – a strong number for a book perhaps not thought of as a major key. But maybe this book with its femme fatale cover deserves to rank with *Brenda Starr* #14, *Blue Beetle* #54, *Phantom Lady* #17, etc. Incidentally, the covers for *Spirit* #20 and #21 are also by Eisner and have a similar feel.

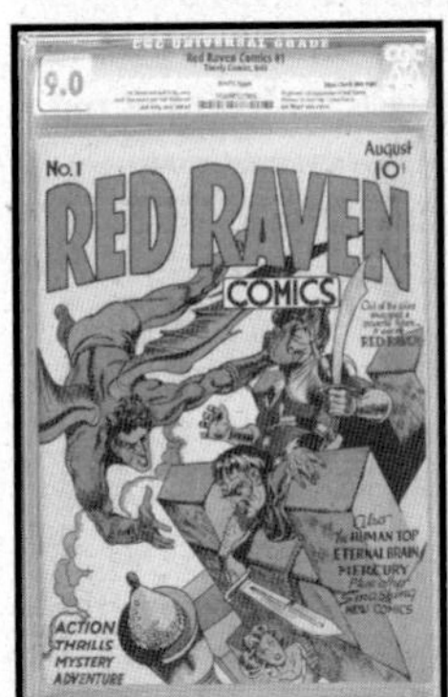

Red Raven Comics #1 was the "big book" of Chuck Rozanski's consignment of the last of his Mile High copies.

***Archie Comics* #1:** Every *Archie Comics* #1 that we have offered to date has sold for over *Guide*, and last August a VG- 3.5 copy followed suit by selling for $20,315. The question is, what is the current market value of issues #2-9? We have not seen one single copy of these issues since the last market report we wrote, but we would be interested in letting our bidders fight over some.

Sgt. Rock: Since the *Guide* has an extensive annual "War Report" these days we needn't go into much detail here, but the sale of a VF 8.0 copy of *Our Army at War* #83 for $16,730 (an unheard-of price for a DC War comic) deserves mention – there are several books that lay claim to being the first appearance of Sgt. Rock, but the bidding public seems to have settled on #83 as the key book to have. And while the hardcore guts-and-glory war collector might not think of Marvel's *Sgt. Fury* as a true war book, a NM copy of #1 sold for $28,680 this year, partly because this book is much tougher to find in the highest grade than other Marvel keys of the same era like *X-Men* #1 .

Keys break away from the pack: We wish we had a dollar for everyone we talk to who says he's looking for a *Detective* #27... heck, we wish we had a *Detective* #27 for each of those worthies! The top key books have distanced themselves from the rest of the comic world. In particular, restored copies of these big books, which were not hot items even two years ago, have really come on. The first time we sold a restored comic for over $100,000 it made news, but in the meantime we have sold several.

Original comic art: How much more expensive can original art get? We are looking forward to finding out. Here are a few of the most notable recent results:

Carl Barks The Sport of Tycoons $262,900
Jerry Robinson *Detective Comics* #67 cover art $239,000
John Romita Sr. *Amazing Spider-Man* #49 original cover art $167,300
Joe Simon and Jack Kirby *Adventure Comics* #73 cover art $119,500
John Byrne and Terry Austin *X-Men* #137 page 44 panel page $65,725
Alex Ross Superman: 20th Century painting $52,281

A trend worth noting here is that the most frenzied bidding tends to be for pieces that have been in collector's hands over the years and haven't been shopped around at the San Diego and Chicago shows, posted on the web, etc. Some collectors who picked up pieces in the 1970s or 1980s and kept them ever since have done very well in our auctions. Here too, the uncertainty as to whether a given piece of art still exists and where it might be keeps the hobby interesting.

My colleagues and I look forward to helping more collectors maximize the value of their four-color treasures in the coming year.

Brian Schutzer
Sparkle City Comics
Neat Stuff Collectibles

Given the past few years and how tough they have been for people across the world, I can't help but feel thankful for being in the position of doing what I love and succeeding at it. If it were not for all of the friends, collectors and colleagues I've met through this great hobby none of it would be possible. Thank you everyone.

2011 was a very strong year across the board for comics

and comic book artwork. For me, this year was a key transitional point in this hobby and business. Having fine tuned Neat Stuff Collectibles, I spent the past few years focusing on building my Original Comic Art collection and inventory. The Comic Art hobby remains to be strong and 2011 proved to be a great year to acquire quality pieces. In 2011, I again shifted my focus back to comic books, this time on the high grade CGC niche. I revived and launched Sparkle City Comics, and the success and impact has exceeded even my optimistic expectations. My goal was simply to offer real auctions on eBay in honest no-reserve format as well as an alternative for consignors. My 10% flat rate commission, 10 days to sell, 10 days to get paid model really resonated with collectors. However, the real fun in launching Sparkle City Comics came from the non-stop spree of sourcing and buying impressive collections. It seemed like this year was the year when collectors finally starting letting go of things that were holding onto, and there seemed to be no shortage of buyers waiting to gobble it all up. In times of such economic uncertainty it's always interesting to see where people are investing.

Whereas in the past couple of years I witnessed a drop in wholesale sales of large collections/lots, 2011 really picked up steam. Neat Stuff Collectibles could barely amass enough inventory to satisfy our buyers and they seemed to keep coming back so that would indicate success on their part in breaking up and re-selling these collections. The only exception appeared to be in bulk Modern stuff, which got much tougher to deal in. Neat Stuff Collectibles handles all types of collectibles from cards to toys and everywhere in between, all of which were plentiful and selling well.

Sparkle City Comics has a long history in the comic book hobby and holds a special place for me in that it was the first business I ever bought a vintage comic book from. When I set forth to launch a new entity that would focus solely on honest auctions of high grade CGC books I couldn't think of anything but re-establishing Sparkle City at the pinnacle of the hobby. So far, I think I'm doing the name and the collectors who remember it fondly well. Sparkle City Comics came onto the scene this year with a bang. We premiered an Original Owner collection purchased in Saginaw Michigan. The Saginaw Collection, as it became known, featured ultra high grade examples of early issues from the most sought after Marvel runs such as *Amazing Spider-Man*, *Fantastic Four*, *X-Men*, *Tales to Astonish*, *Tales of Suspense*, and *Daredevil*. As I write this I'm looking around at the stacks of amazing Golden Age and Silver Age books from recent purchases and can't help but feel that 2012 is going to be even more fun.

Golden Age: Golden Age was very strong in 2011. With the preponderance of High Dollar Silver Age books in the market, more collectors seemed to be flocking towards quality Golden Age books. The Golden Age market appears to be poised for a big jump in interest and prices over the next few years. As new original owner collections hit the marketplace and long time collectors start to let go, the prospects for Golden Age seem bright. Particularly hot were the first 20 issues of *Action Comics* and pre-Robin *Detectives*. World War II covers continued to be in high demand, with *Action Comics* World War II covers gaining some ground on their Timely counterparts.

Sparkle City Comics held our first Golden Age auction in October of 2011. By all accounts the auction was a great success with several record prices achieved and very strong interest across the board. Sparkle City also unearthed 3 Original Owner Golden Age collections in the last months of 2011, which are in the process of being brought to the market as I write this. Some ultra-rare books were acquired in these collections, including but not limited to: *New Adventure* #26, *Wonder Comics* #2 and the *Marvel Mystery* 128 page Annual; ALL were the highest graded copies. I am very excited about the amount of rare and high quality fresh to market Golden Age stuff in 2011 and I expect this to continue into 2012.

Silver Age: The past year has been a very exciting time for Silver Age comics. In 2011 we witnessed both the Savannah and Twin Cities Pedigree collections brought to the marketplace. Sparkle City Comics unearthed the Saginaw Collection, which featured many highest graded early Marvel issues and resulted in MANY record sales. A few of the many notable Saginaw sales were: *Amazing Fantasy* #15 CGC 8.5 - $107,300, *Tales of Suspense* #39 CGC 9.2 - $72,100, *Fantastic Four* #12 CGC 9.4 - $48,201, *Tales To Astonish* #44 CGC 9.6 - $10,900 and *Avengers* #16 CGC 9.6 - $11,100. Silver Age key issues continue to sell quickly and at increasing values across all grade levels. Early Marvels continue to command premium prices, however due to increased availability of books at the highest grades we are starting to see some price erosion. The drop in prices of High Grade Bronze CGC books experienced in 2010 seems to have spread into the late Silver Age period (1966-1969), resulting in slightly decreased prices in 2011. I view these minor examples of price erosion as a necessary correction in the market and I don't believe it will be as significant or lengthy as what happened with Bronze Age books. Overall, the Silver Age market is booming and was the most exciting and significant niche for me in 2011.

Silver Age DC sales have in general been flat to slightly lower in 2011, with the exception of key issues and highest graded copies. Collectors are willing to pay big money for High Grade DC key issues and Highest Graded copies, which are much scarcer than their Marvel counterparts. This is supported by Sparkle City Comics sales of Saginaw copies of *Flash* #118 and *Flash* #128 (single highest graded copies) which sold for over $6,000 each. In my opinion, the trend of new Silver Age collections coming to market will continue in 2012 and will present many opportunities for collectors to acquire fresh high quality books.

Bronze Age: Despite the fact that High Grade Bronze continues to be a popular area of the hobby, 2011 continued the downward trend of prices attained for High Grade Bronze books. It now appears that a correction has taken place in the Bronze market and price stabilization seems to be taking place, especially at the 9.2-9.4 levels. We are still seeing some price erosion on highest graded copies, probably due to the fact that speculators and investors are not as heavily involved in the Bronze market. Bronze Age key issues have not escaped the slide with *Green Lantern* #76 and *Giant-Size X-Men* #1 among issues that have dropped substantially in 2011, at the highest grades.

One of the key driving forces in the drop in prices is the constant fresh supply of high-grade issues arriving at CGC. It doesn't seem like there is much scarcity of Bronze Age books, even at the highest grades. High Grade DC Bronze is scarcer than their Marvel counterparts, however demand is generally lower. Bronze Age Neal Adams covers have appeared to calm a bit in 2011, but still remain relatively strong. Despite some price pressure, Bronze Age CGC books sell fast and are eagerly snagged by collectors every time they are offered. I believe that the Bronze Age market is healthier today than it was a couple of years ago and after the necessary corrections, there are good times ahead in 2012 and beyond.

Overall, the comic book hobby and market was undeniably strong in 2011. With the ever-increasing mainstream interest in comics, from movies to video games, it seems that the stories and characters that we all love will continue to captivate people worldwide, with no end in sight. Walking around comic conventions I can already see the next generation of collectors sharpening their teeth. With the amount of new collections being brought to market and the abundance of buyers waiting for stuff, I expect 2012 to be even better than 2011 on all fronts.

Doug Simpson
Paradise Comics

Without any doubt, 2011 was a transition year for our business and the hobby in Canada. We saw the smallest growth in over a decade, our total sales increased by only 3% with graphic novels making the largest contribution at 8% growth.

Not surprisingly Hollywood has helped our sales with the increasing visibility of its mainstream comic movies including (*Thor*, *Captain America*, *Green Lantern*, and *X-Men: First Class* that were all released in 2011). Let's hope the Avengers and Batman releases in 2012 continue the trend by bringing more buyers into the market.

In general Golden Age sales were very sluggish this year and, with so many collectors pursuing high-grade Silver Age, sales have been exceptionally slow. There is always a market for Timelys in any grade, but most Golden Age Hero comics are selling well below *Guide* with the exception of *Batman* and *Detective Comics*.

Silver Age sales continue to dominate our market, with most high-grade copies selling within hours of arriving in the shop.

DC Silver Age shows the greatest demand in the usual suspects Batman, Green Lantern and Superman, but Wonder Woman is showing some signs of life as well. War Comics continue to be slow sellers and demand for Horror and Romance comics has slowed right down. Unfortunately DC bin stock sells way less in volume than its Marvel counterpart.

X-Men *issues #108-142 help Marvel lead the way in Bronze Age sales.* *(***X-Men** *#125 shown)*

Marvel Silver Age is selling very well, with *Amazing Spider-Man* and *X-Men* leading the way, and demand for *Avengers* and *Captain America* steadily growing. The Marvel Silver Age market is always strong and doesn't look to be slowing down anytime soon.

Bronze Age comic sales continue to be through the roof in high grade, and demand for mid-grade copies have increased as well. Marvel leads the way in this category primarily because of *X-Men* issues #108-#142 with all *Amazing Spider-Man* issues between #100 and #150 following closely behind. We are starting to see more demand for *Avengers* and *Daredevil* issues as well.

Generally with the exception of the "New 52" launch by DC Comics in September, our new issue sales are on the decline. The impact of digital comics is starting to be felt by many retailers for the first time, and it looks like they will be a major part of the hobby in the years to come.

Our website sales have been very strong in 2011 and we hope that this continues throughout 2012 and beyond.

Some recent CGC sales include:

Amazing Spider-Man #1 CGC 3.0 $2600.00
Amazing Spider-Man #2 CGC 4.5 $750.00
Amazing Spider-Man #3 CGC 6.0 $1,000.00
Amazing Spider-Man #129 CGC 9.0 $900.00
Daredevil #1 CGC 7.0 $1,600.00
Batman #49 CGC 6.0 $1000.00
Silver Surfer #1 CGC 9.0 $900.00
Planet Comics #68 CGC 9.0 $750.00
X-Men #1 CGC 7.0 $5500.00
X-Men #28 CGC 9.4 $1000.00
X-Men #94 CGC 9.2 $1050.00
CGC Signature Series *Amazing Fantasy* #15 CGC 2.5 $5500.00

The Convention season never seems to end and as a result Paradise has a very busy convention schedule planned for 2012 with the first show being Wizard World Toronto 2012 on April 14-15, 2012. We also plan on doing at least three U.S. shows this summer along with the usual Canadian conventions. Let's hope 2012 turns out to be an amazing year for everyone in the industry.

Tony Starks Comics Ina Flash!

Well, there is both good and bad in my 2011 Market Report. The market remains very mixed. The best of the best – the high grade key issues – continue to sell at ever-increasing record prices. If one has for sale (or in their collection) a lot of high grade key issues, or books like *Action Comics* #1, *Amazing Fantasy* #15, *Detective Comics* #27, or *Captain America Comics* #1 in any grade, then it's been another banner year. Reach for the champagne. If you are trying to sell "run" issues of Gold/Silver or Bronze – in just about any condition besides near perfect - you are left wondering where the floor is at on pricing and reaching for the aspirin instead.

I mentioned it last year and I will repeat it this year. *The Overstreet Price Guide* needs to list real market values for the run books I speak of. I would guess that the editorial staff at the *OPG* face tremendous push back from dealers and collectors alike at the thought of devaluing by 50-65% huge swaths of their inventory or collection. But the *OPG* does not create the value of comic books, it reports the value. The deflation in value has already taken place and pretending it has not both compromises the *Price Guide* and further damages the marketplace.

Here are a handful of representative sales from the past year: *Action Comics* #220 VG- @ $30 (*Guide* $100), *Amazing Spider-Man* #119 FN+ @ $26 (*Guide* $37), *Archie Comics* #167 VG, #193 VG (swim suit covers) @ $3 each (*Guide* $6), *Avengers* #102 VF/NM @ $11.00 (*Guide* $34) *Batman* #251 FN/VF @ $39 (*Guide* $50 – Adams Joker issue), *Black Lightning* #1 FN @ $3.25 (*Guide* $6.00), *Bonanza* #24 VF+ @ $16.75 (*Guide* $37), *Brave & Bold* #79 VG @ $9.75 (*Guide* $18), *DC Comics Presents* #3 NM @ $6.50 (*Guide* $12), *Detective Comics* #425-430 @ $4 each (*Guide* $15 each), *Doctor Strange* (1974) #2 NM @ $16 (*Guide* $65), *Hero for Hire* #1 VG+ @ $18 (*Guide* $26), *Howard the Duck* #12 FN @ $2.75 (*Guide* $12) ...Tired yet? I'll keep going... *Justice League* #5 GD+ @ $26 (*Guide* $65), *Logan's Run* #2-4 NM @ $3.25 each (*Guide* $8), *Marvel Two In One* #1 VG @ $8 (*Guide* $14), *Psychoanalysis* #2 VG @ $13 (*Guide* $28), *Special Marvel Edition* #15 FN/VF @ $11.50 (*Guide* $66), *Swamp Thing* #1 VG/FN @ $21 (*Guide* $40), *Tales of Suspense* #65 FN+ @ 24.50 (*Guide* $84), *Thor* #225 FN+ @ $8 (*Guide* $11 – a bright spot – 1st Firelord), *Walt Disney's Comics & Stories* #100 VG/FN @ $25 (*Guide* $55), *Where Monsters Dwell* #1 FN @ $7.50 (*Guide* $12.00), and *X-Men* #133 VG/FN @ $5 (*Guide* $12.50).

I have tried to list a wide range of examples. I sold thousands of comics last year and the vast majority were at similar prices. High grade, low grade, mainstream superhero, Archie or Western. Published 1950s, '60s, '70s or later. Doesn't seem to matter. If it is not a key issue in nice shape 50% off *OPG* is pretty much a given and 65% off is not uncommon

Yet all of the examples I've listed above sold for well above their original cover price. I'm still selling collectibles, not used books. I can sell VG Silver and VF Bronze comics - just not at *OPG* prices. The real problem becomes buying collections for resale. *OPG* in hand, individuals selling comics they found in the attic view offers based on the real market value as thievery. Because "The Guide" says it they are worth a lot more.

Perhaps you ask what is driving the prices down on run type books: First, eBay has made it apparent that run type books are common. Then add professional grading where buyers can count on the grade they purchase at being the grade they later sell at. Whereas eBay has made run books look common, CGC has proven that high grade keys and super high grade most anythings are scarce. So the prices of those books have risen dramatically as the moneyed class now views them as good investments.

Collectors – rightly concerned that they will never own high grade copies of the big books if they do not move fast - continue to sell their run type books to raise the money to buy the keys. So the common issues have yet more downward pricing pressure as still more copies enter the market

Speaking of books that are selling well – I should mention a few of those sales. It's not all bottom feeding here at Comics Ina Flash! Before doing so I should note the impact professional grading has had here as well. Some really hot books (like *Amazing Fantasy* #15) - in lower grades especially - sell for about as much raw as they do professionally graded. Routinely though if you want to obtain market value on key, not so key and/or high grade books, they need to be professionally graded. The problem here is obvious - grading and slabbing costs money and takes time. I find myself routinely doing the math on this: How much might it sell for raw? How much slabbed? What will it to cost to get it professionally graded and how long before I have it back to sell?

While doing this mental math I often think of the Gold rushes of the 19th and early 20th centuries. The smart money was made by those selling picks and shovels, not those digging for gold. But I digress.

Anyway, some recent sales that reflect the healthy side of the market: *G.I. Combat* #168 CGC 9.8 @ $400 (great Adams cover), *Giant-Size Kid Colt* #1 CGC 9.4 @ $140, *Amazing Adventures* #1 PGX 9.4 @ $125, *Flash* #225 PGX 9.4 @ $45, *Amazing Spider-Man* #40 CGC 7.5 @ $172, *Captain*

The healthy side of the market is reflected in hearty sale prices for issues like **G.I. Combat #168**

America #113 CGC 9.4 @ $281, #117 CGC 9.2 @ $312, *Machine Man* #19 CGC 9.8 @ $150, *Special Marvel Edition* #15 CGC 9.4 @ $160, *Superman* #273 CGC 9.8 @ $138, *Justice League of America* #1 PGX 8.5 @ $4550, #138 CGC 9.6 @ $71, *Sgt. Fury* #1 PGX 3.0 @ $350, *Champions* #1 CGC 9.6 @ $104, *Strange Adventures* #208 PGX 9.0 $80, *Phantom* #1 CGC 8.0 (GK) @ $245, *Tales From the Crypt* #35 CGC 8.5 $788, *Batman* #244 CGC 9.2 $215, *Adventure Comics* #300 CGC 9.0 $1166, *Brave & Bold* #54 CGC 9.4 @ $2300, CGC 9.0 $665, *Tales of Suspense* #39 CGC 6.5 $3320, #59 CGC 7.0 @ $173, #63 CGC 8.5 @ $231, *Tales to Astonish* #35 PGX 5.0 $327, *Demon* #1 CGC 9.4 @ $111, *Strange Tales* #110 CGC 4.0 @ $325, *Green Lantern* #87 CGC 9.0 $169, and *Conan the Barbarian* #3 CGC 9.2 @ $189.

Some of these sales are over *Guide* or market highs (*Brave and the Bold* #54, *G.I. Combat* #168, *Tales From the Crypt* #35), a few were a bit low, but most sold for around *Guide*. But the trend here is that books are selling well when professionally graded and slabbed. High grade keys selling exceedingly well. Technically, the *OPG* doesn't list prices for professionally graded books nor does it list prices for books in grades of 9.4 and higher. Which is another challenge the *OPG* needs to address if they wish to be remain the industry standard.

So what to take away from the roller coaster ride that is the market today? Well in Adversity, Opportunity always exists.

If you like collecting long runs of your favorite characters, if you enjoy reading your books so don't want them in perfect shape locked up in an impenetrable holder, now is a fantastic time to buy. It's like having a time machine and purchasing comics at 1990s prices.

If you have money, it certainly appears that high grade key issues are solid investments. *Avengers* #1 CGC 9.4 has gone from 17K to 100K in ten years. We don't know if it will increase in value another six-fold in the next 10 years. But with only seven 9.4s and three 9.6s in the CGC census, we do know that the demand will continue to greatly exceed the supply.

If you want to cast your eyes about for other books with potential to appreciate nicely in value, a number come to mind. The key DC issues are still overlooked – though the Green Lantern movie has brought some attention to *Showcase* #22. Historically the key DCs have constantly trailed, then played catch up with the key Marvels. The early Marvels have a larger fan base for sure – but Stan and company only started doing superhero books in the early '60s because DC was making money with costumed heroes for years before that. Plus the DCs are substantially scarcer in high grade. Also tempting are the better Gold Key first issues. *Magnus*, *Lost in Space*, *Doctor Solar*, *Phantom*, *Star Trek*, and *Turok* (OK –*Turok* #1 is a Dell). These books are CHEAP, they have solid fan bases (TV shows/Movies/Video Game franchise) and are often even scarcer in high grade than comparable DCs.

West Stephan
Collector

Mainline publishers such as Timely and DC are still the blue chips of the Golden Age. After that, classic covers sell in every grade and generally at above *Guide* prices. Hitler cover appearances are at an all-time high. World War II covers are especially hot and show no signs of slowing down. 1930s DC Super-hero books are alway a quick sale. Centaur titles are getting a boost in popularity as collectors are realizing how truly scarce most of them are. Fiction House is red hot, especially titles where the *Guide* is far too low, such as *Fight Comics* #25-28 and the Good Girl covers of *Wings Comics* #82-89. The hottest Golden Age book on the planet has to be *Marvel Mystery Comics* #46 with the classic Hitler cover. A CGC-graded 2.0 copy sold for $2868 (almost 10 times *Guide*) at auction, and a restored 7.0 copy sold on eBay for $1500 as a "Buy it now".

Sci-fi titles of the '50s are also doing well, but mostly with the covers that really stand out. More and more collectors are "cover collecting", meaning they are more interested in what is depicted on the cover than the interior story. For instance, *Action Comics* #43-46 are all valued the same in the *Guide*, but reality is that *Action Comics* #43 and #44 with their classic War covers will always outsell *Action* #45 and #46.

Al Stoltz
Basement Comics

Yes, here we are again, another year of buying and selling under our belts and many great books were found and sold to happy collectors and investors. Yes, it was a good year for us and far better than the dark days of 2008, changes can be seen taking place online and at shows if you just take a look. I am pretty sure that 2011 was the real year of re-alignment of prices for the other 80-90% of the comic back issues out there. Seems like every show that I attended this year was full of dealers flying signs signaling sales of 30-80% off boxed stock that was sitting on the tables at their booths. I see it as real life catching up with "whatever we feel like pricing" of the '80s and early '90s finally reflecting the fact that customers will buy lower grade items...BUT...at a greatly reduced price.

Books listed under *Overstreet* value on our eBay store sell, but really sell with a 20% discount offered during sale periods. So the price point is there and if a value is there for lower grade items, then the happy buyer spends away. I also always like to point out that most of my buyers at conventions are of the late Baby Boomer age and very few are under the age of twenty five. As an industry we need to keep finding ways to pull in new buyers of back issues and keep the interest in building collections so this art form can be appreciated for many more decades to come. Hopefully the plethora of movies related to DC and Marvel characters will keep the wheel of comic collecting moving forward.

Shows: I was happy to set up at just five major shows this year but did attend a few others including San Diego Comic Con for my 11th time! As a comic buyer and seller at San Diego I now trim my time there down to Tuesday to Friday and get out of town..literally..as the monster crowds grow and the act of just walking the show floor becomes more of an impossibility. I was actually stunned by the amount of Marvel keys that were for sale at SDCC this year and by my ability to spend lots of money for online inventory at this year's show. I normally do not get a chance to buy lots of comics at SDCC but dealers both large and small were in the mood to make as many dollars as they could before the weekend came to a close. Wizard Chicago and Baltimore Comic-Con rounded out my top three shows to buy both High Grade and wacky stuff that I have interest in by the box full. MegaCon in Florida was super good as usual and Beth and her group do a fantastic job. Wizard Philly was as crowded as I ever saw and was a great show and is only an hour from my house. NYCC by Reed is fast becoming the SDCC of the East and could potentially pull even more attendees when they take over the whole building and we all get more elbow room after the 2012 show. This is also the "Official " 20th year of Basement Comics, but I traded and sold far before that and cannot believe that 20 years has now flown by working for the meanest Boss I have ever had...myself !

eBay Sales: While a great amount of my income does come from online selling both to customers on eBay and those clients I have built up over the many years, it is eBay that constantly confounds me as a business. Constant changes and new rules makes selling on eBay a gigantic chore and it seems that the new CEO is pushing to sweep all the "junk" sellers from their universe. So far we keep up with the new nutty rule changes and try to stay ahead by offering 30 day returns and we pay the shipping for that return. So far not one item has been returned and it seems our grading and service are still dead on for the buying public. Our sales were on path to well exceed 2010 sales and our constant injection of minor keys and odd ball items kept the machine humming along. One of our best buys was a load of high grade Spanish Harvey Horror books from the 1950s that are selling very well to many Spanish speaking countries around the world. The South American market has exploded for us with these items and much more and I can see this as a very expanding base in the future. We have also starting shipping boxes of Bronze Age comics to accounts in China. Hey, if they have to enjoy the culture of America then why not do it reading a copy of *Howard the Duck* #1 with a Coke!

eBay sales are always a blend of all items selling at different times of the year, but overall it always seems to be oddball weird items we are known for listing selling the best and Dell Comics other than Westerns bringing up the rear in sales. Auctions aren't really a risk anymore unless you want to just get the opening price on some books. We just hope to get our listings well above 10,000 and keep a pulse on what is selling in the online world and stay competitive in 2012.

What is selling?: As much as it makes me crazy to have to work hard to find flawless books, they do sell and they do not sit around long enough to gather dust. But a recent amount paid for a *Fantastic Four* #12 in CGC 9.6 of $75,000...really? Come on guys....let's get our feet back on Earth. We slabbed no books for resell this year and have adopted the business model to base price on GPA or other sources and have sold every nice key book we have purchased raw and let the speculator have their own fun. I always wish them the very best and hope they hit their perceived grades...a future customer in the making if they get their surprise grade numbers.

Another surprise was the ease at selling high grade Treasury Editions this year at the shows we did set up at. We bagged and tagged a large box full of them and I am guessing a weird sense of nostalgia gripped the buyers and they smiled and bought up just about all of the original load we brought out to sell. Legion issues and the Ali-Superman issue lead the way for the DC Treasury issues and Hulk and Thor seemed to be always looked for as far as Marvel Treasury issues go. We were glad to see an interest in items that for many years just languished back at the warehouse.

Big Little Books and older material seem to have died yet again! We bought lots of BLBs this year and never paid more than five bucks for any title even in higher grade. We will begin listing the hundreds of BLBs on our eBay store in 2012 and will price them to go away quickly. Same goes for Platinum and Victorian books...is anyone actually looking for all the different titles that are listed? I have zero customers asking me to find any of these.

The most asked question I fielded this year was when is the *Overstreet Guide* going to be available as a searchable data base on smart phones and computers? Have no idea and it seems like a natural way to go in the 21st century and the info contained in this collectors tool could really be enjoyed and used more easily. I would download a version to my iPhone in 2 seconds if it finally becomes available!

I guess in conclusion I feel happy that I saw lots of energy and activity at the major shows this year and personally moved loads of material both at shows and online in 2011. My concern of the slashing of prices may actually be a good thing in the end since the dumping of product may just in the end create new collectors that need to fill in those gaps in the new collection...I can only hope so. Perhaps the new wave of comic related movies and convention coverage on shows like G4 will push the interest along on comics and related material for the next generation.

Douglas W. Sulipa
Doug Sulipa's Comic World

We sold a lot of comics this year, but still below our pre-Recession (pre-Summer 2008) levels. The main trend I have seen changed is below-average demand for items priced at over $50.00, especially in High Grade. In many genres, I have noticed sales on Low Grade and affordable copies have actually increased. The biggest area of increased demand was for affordable copies of KEY issues (First, Last, Origin, Giants, Anniversary, better Artists, Low Print etc.) with current Good thru Fine *Guide* prices in the $5 to $50 price range. Price spreads between GD-FN vs. VF-NM- are now so wide, many of these are now very undervalued in GD-FN in the *Overstreet Guide* and often bring premiums of +25% to +100% over *Guide*, with many eager buyers.

Many DC and especially Marvel KEY issue comics in GD-FN are near impossible to keep in stock and the current *Guide* prices are now wholesale prices. (Other sellers and I now more regularly buy KEY issues at 70-125% *Guide* in GD-FN to mark-up by 50% or more over cost for immediate re-sale to want list buyers.) Similarly, affordable copies of hard-to-find issues from uncommon to scarcer popular titles (especially 1950-1980 era) are sold out in most major dealer inventories and often bring premiums of +25% to +100% over *Guide*. Just a few examples: *Amazing Fantasy* #15, *Amazing Spider-Man* (most Key issues from #1-300), *Archie* #1-100, *Archie's Girls Betty & Veronica* #1-100, Batmans by Neal Adams, *Conan the Barbarian* #1, *Creepy* #31-80, 121-146 in GD-FN, *Dizzy Dames* #1-6, *Dracula Lives* in GD-FN, *Eerie* #17-80, 121-139 in GD-FN, Hanna-Barbera #1s, *Iron Man* (1968) #1, *Laugh* #20-150, *Little Lulu* #1-30, *Magnus* (GK) #1, *Marvel Spotlight* #5 (1st Ghost Rider), *Millie the Model* #18-93 with DeCarlo-a, *Our Army at War* #83-130 (Sgt. Rock), *Pep* #22-161, *Scooby Doo* (1970s to 1990s), *Tarzan* (Dell) #1-20, *Turok* (Dell) #1-5, *Vampire Tales* in GD-FN, *Vampirella* #1-33, 91-113 in GD-FN, *Werewolf by Night* #32 and many More.

Non-KEY issues of common 1965-1980 Marvel & DC Super-Hero comics in VG to FN/VF are still quite plentiful and many were slower sellers. We have started selling large quantities in discounted bargain sets to force sales on many of these, as our warehouse is bursting at the seams with overstock on many of these. Since I have specialized in and gone out of my way to re-stock affordable comics that are hard to find in ANY grade for over 30 years, I have always done quite well with these. I actually search out to re-stock sold out issues of comics other dealers on carry only if they walk in the door. I try to keep near complete inventories of (1960 and newer, with good selection of older issues): ACG, Archie, Charlton, Classics, Comic Digests, *Cracked*, Dell, Dennis the Menace, Gold Key, Harvey, IW/Super, King, *Mad*, *National Lampoon*, Religious, Treasury, Walt Disney, Whitman, etc.

The shortage of copies in dealer inventories for these uncommon to scarce Oddball comics is usually not reported by most *Overstreet* advisors (high priced and Superhero comics are "sexier" in market reports) thus prices tend to remain unrealistically low, and the "higher demand than supply" shortage continues on year after year. I have a loyal following of regular repeat customers who love my giganic selection (world's biggest in many catagories). This once again was the area that brought in the most sales this year.

High Grade investment copies were still good sellers, but mostly items in the $5 to $50 price ranges, thus a lot of Bronze Age (1970-1984) comics, with increased interest in Copper Age (1985-1992) comics. Many many buyers have finally caught on to the fact that 1980s comics in strict VF/NM or better are getting harder and harder to find, as they are already 23-32 years old. Decades of dumping these comics in Bargain Bins and constant handling have lowered the grade of copies of 1980s comics in most dealer inventories to around a FN/VF average. In addition, many major dealers grade averything in VF or better as NM, while the actual grades (if submitted to CGC) would be a strict 7.0 to 9.0, with only a handful in actual 9.4. Since most of the 1980s comics *Guide* at between $2 to $10, this has become a widespread practice, considered acceptable by the majority of buyers. It has in fact persuaded many uninformed collectors that VF copies are in fact NM copies. For the advanced and informed collector, it can be a frustrating market to buy in if you collect only strict High Grade in 9.2 or better. Because I have over 20,000 strictly graded (with CGC in mind) affordable High Grade comics in stock, especially those from the Manitoba Pedigree quality collection, I sell many hundreds of these at premium prices. My average asking price, as a percentage of *Overstreet Guide* 9.2 price, for comics that *Guide* at $50 or less is: 9.8=400%, 9.6=300%, 9.4=200%, 9.2=150% and with VF/NM copies bringing 9.2 *Guide* prices.

Our 8000 square foot warehouse is still bursting at the seams with 1,300,000 comics, magazines, digests, paperbacks, records, movies, posters and other related items. Since I hope to retire in 10-15 years, I have continued to list more items on our overstock clearance sales, so far mostly overstock comics sets in 10-25 item groups at 25-75% off *Guide* range. By far the most popular set of the year was *Captain Canuck* (1975-81) #1-4 and Special #1 VF for $39 (almost 50 sets sold), surpassing the previous best seller *ROM Spaceknight* #1-75 and Annual #1-4. *Booster Gold* (1986-88) #1-25 became a surprise bestseller and I am currently sold out. (He appeared in the final season of TV's *Smallville* and rumor has it that the character may be getting his own SyFy channel TV pilot and potential series.) Other unexpected good sellers included: *Amethyst* (1983) #1-12, *Captain Britain* (1976 UK) #1-11, *Capt. Planet* #1-12, *Further Adv. of Indiana Jones* #1-34, *Groo* #61-120, *John Carter* #1-28 and Annual 1-3, *Savage She-Hulk* #1-25, *2001: A Space Odyssey* #1-10, etc.

Many collectors view the prices in *Overstreet* as set in

© MAR

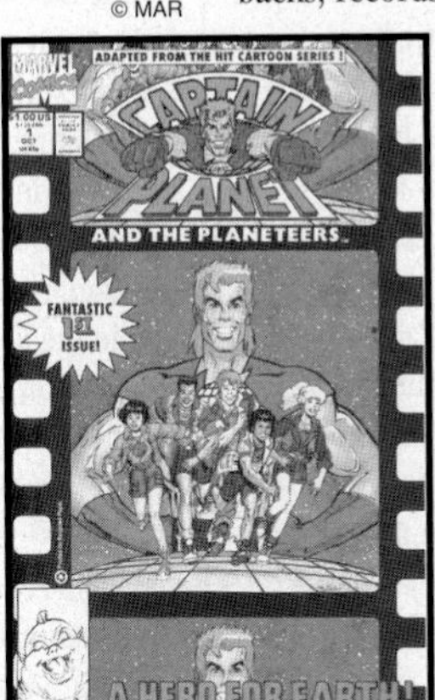

Titles like **Captain Planet**, when sold in groups, were unexpected good sellers. (#1 shown)

stone, so they will not pay more, but are still happy when they get items for less. They miss out on buying High Demand items that might have potential for future price escalations and so they often end up buying slower selling items. Many do not fully understand that it is a price GUIDE, and is more an average of the approximate retail price you should expect to have to pay to a professional dealer. Pro dealers are willing to pay more for High Demand items and then need to charge more, often well over *Guide*. There are many discount places where you can readily buy common items at 25-75% off *Guide* (eBay, conventions, small dealers, fellow collectors, flea markets, garage sales, auctions, etc.), but these (often transient) sellers usually have: low overhead, smaller selections, off-condition items, questionable condition/grading, etc. Thus, this leaves discounting and/or selling to captive buyers (local only, eBay only, flea market only, non-internet etc.) as their main selling tool. There is nothing wrong with buying discounted comics (as long as you are careful), but these type of sales should NOT be used to judge current values of collectible comics.

On the flip side, many collectors blindly buy comics (especially new comics) for years and decades, without thought about how much they will be able to sell them for, when that time inevitably arrives (often old age) to sell. Many are shocked to hear offers like 25, 10 or even 5 cents each for their common newer comics. For example, I get many emails from sellers wanting to liquidate collections of 1986-1994 era comics that are "Bagged & Boarded" (implying that they are "MINT" because they bought them new). One collector spent presumably 100+ Hours methodically cataloging over 10,000 post-1980 comics by exact condition and price in *Guide* and came up with a value of over $35,000. He was asking only $20,000 and sent the list to dozens of dealers, but could not understand why he was getting no replies. So I finally emailed him and explained that 95% of his collection consisted of items that all major dealers were already overstocked on and they were already a hard sell. After several email exchanges, he began to understand that he would be lucky to get an offer of 10% *Guide* on his common slow selling comics and if he wanted more, he would need to become a dealer himself. Getting good money was extremely labour intensive and would take him hundreds of hours of work. Unfortunately a collector cannot just take his $12 *Spawn* #1 to the grocery store and get a meal for it. He would instead have a hard time getting $4 on eBay for it and even less from a dealer who already has 10 copies in stock. He thanked me for explaining, but soon after, there were still more similar sellers.

Archie Comics: Our Archie inventory is the world's biggest selection (35,000+ Archie comics and 10,000+ Digests in stock). About 85% of what we sell falls into the $2 to $20 each FR/GD to FN condition range items. About 15% sells in the FN/VF to VF/NM condition. We would sell more pre-1988 in High Grade if we had more, but most are scarce in strict VF or better. Everything Betty & Veronica were easily our #1 bestsellers. Golden Age 1941-1950 Archie titles are in high demand (at 120%-150% *Guide* in any grade. Archies with Dan DeCarlo art issues are always top sellers. 1951-1964 Archie titles are steady sellers. Most GD-FN copies sell at 120-140% *Guide*. The circa-1960 Horror and Sci-Fi cover issues have 2-3 times the demand as compared to other issues of the period (at 120-135% *Guide*).

All the other girls of Archie titles still have strong demand (Cheryl Blossom, Ginger, Josie & the Pussycats, Katy Keene, Sabrina, Suzie, etc.) Cheryl Blossom 1982-1993 (pre-1994 and Love Showdown) appearances are in demand when identified and sell for 125-150% *Guide*. The 1970s Red Circle Horror, 1980s Red Circle/Archie Adventure titles were the most requested in VF or better, and they are in steady demand. All the LAST Issues are still in high demand and even lower supply as minor-Key issues: *Archie and Me* #161 (2/87), *Archie at Riverdale High* #113(2/87), *Archie Giant Series* #632 (7/92), *Archie's Girls B&V* #347 (4/1987), *Archie's Pals N Gals* #224 (9/1991), *Archie's TV Laughout* #105 (2/86), *Betty & Me* #200 (8/92), *Everything's Archie* #157 (9/91), *Jughead* #352 (6/87), *Laugh* #400 (4/87), *Life with Archie* #286 (9/91), *Pep* #411 (3/87), all bringing 150-200% *Guide*.

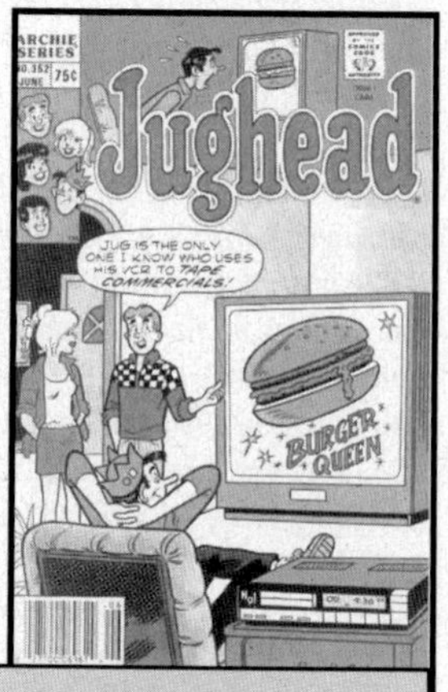

Last issues on Archie titles are in high demand. (*Jughead #352* shown)

© AP

All the Archie brand Teenage Mutant Ninja Turtles Adventures titles are in high demand (while the original Mirage titles are slow sellers) with all the high number and later issues having LOW print runs and being scarcer. The 1990s Hanna-Barbera titles are already hard to find, are in high demand, sold out with almost all dealers, and very undervalued in the *Guide*, with #1-5 issues being uncommon (selling at 150% *Guide*) with most #6-up issues being scarce (selling at 200-400% *Guide*).

The Archie 15¢-c test market variants (2/1962-4/1963) are 50-100 scarcer than regular editions and still bring a very conservative 150-200% *Guide* (*Archie's Madhouse* #22 is the major Key issue); Canadian Newsstand Cover Price Variants (10-20 scarcer than USA editions) include: Archie Comics and Digests (35 cent Giants from late 1950s through the mid '60s.) All comics and Digests from 9/1982-4/1997 with Digests up to 12/1997 have a modest demand at about 120% *Guide*.

This year's bestsellers include: *Archie Comics* #1-120 (120-150%), *Archie All-Star Special - Series*; (Winter/1975; 164 Pages, 4 different = 200%), *Archie as Pureheart* (120%), *Archie at Riverdale High* (#1-20 = 120% *Guide*; early appearances of Cheryl Blossom in

#89,90,92,96,99,103 = 150%), #113(200%), *Archie Giant* #26, 32(150%), *Archie Giant* series (#1-32, 136-200; GD-FN= 125-150%; VF-NM- = 110-125%); *Archie Giant* series (all issues with B&V, Josie & Sabrina issues = 125-150%), *Archie's Girls Betty & Veronica* #1-30(125-150%), 31-200, 329-346(120-135%), (#320-322,327,328 Cheryl Blossom & 347 Last issue = 200%), *Archie & Big Ethyl*(150%), *Archie & Mr Weatherbee*(150%), *Archie's Circus*(200%), *Archie's Date Book* (150%), *Archie's Festival* (150%), *Archie's Roller Coaster* (200%), *Archie's Roller Sports Scene* (200%), *Christmas with Archie* (Giant; Spire Edition 250%), *Archie's Jokebook* (#1-43 = 110-120%; #44-48 Neal Adams = 125-135%), 288(200%), *Archie's Madhouse* [#1-21 = 110-120%; #22(150%), Sabrina issues(125-135%)], *Archie's Mechanics*(135%), *Archie's Pal Jughead* (#1-20 = 120-130%; #21-76 = 110-120%; #79 Creature-c 150%; #77,78,80-82,85,86, 88 = 125-135%), *Archie's Pals N Gals* [#1-20 = 115-130%; #23(1st Josie = 200%), #29(Beatles 150%), #161(1st Cheryl Blossom Solo 200%], *Archie's Ten Issue Collectors Set* #1-10(Giveaway 125-150%), *Archie's TV Laughout* #1-23(120-130%), 91(200%), 92-106(120-150%), *Betty & Me* #1-15(120-130%), 16(300%), 23(150%), 40(125%), 79-86(125%), 200(150%), *Black Hood* (1983 = 150%), *Cartoon Network Presents Space Ghost* #1(200%), *Cheryl Blossom* Mini-Series (13 issues total from 1995-1996 = 150-200%), *Chilling Advs. in Sorcery* (130-150%), *Christmas with Archie Treasury* (200%), *Cosmo the Merry Martian* (125%), *Flintstones* #1-10(150%), 11-22(200%), *The Fly* (1983-84 = 150%), Horror/Science Fiction cover issues (circa 1962 = 125-135%), *Ginger* (120-135%), *Hanna-Barbera All Stars*(200%), *Hanna-Barbera Presents*(200%), *Jetsons* (200%), *Josie* #1(150%), 2-20(125%), 45(150%), 46-74(125-150%), 100-106 (Low Print = 150%), *JCP Presents Thunder Agents* (200%), *Jughead* #325(Cheryl Blossom = 300%), 352(200%), *Jughead as Capt. Hero*(125%), *Jughead's Folly* #1(1st Elvis in comics 125%), *Jughead Soul Food*(150%), *Katy Keene* (1950's/1950's; GD-FN = #110-120%; VF-NM- = 90-110%); *Katy Keene*(1983-1990 = 150%), *Laugh Comics* #20-168(120-150%), *Life with Archie* #1-66(120-130%), *Little Archie* #1-66(120-130%), *Madhouse* #95-97(Horror 150%), *Mighty Crusaders*(1983-85 = 150%), *Pep Comics* #22-180(120-135%), *Red Circle Sorcery* (150%), *Sabrina* (#1-17, 71-77 = 135-150%; #18-70 = 110-120%), *Scooby Doo*(200%), *The Shield* (1983-84 = 150%); *Sonic the Hedgehog* #1-50(120-150%), *Suzie* (120-135%), *Tales Calculated to Drive you Bats*(120%), *TMNT Advs.* #19,50-72, Special #6-10, Sourcebook 1-2, Digests, & *Mighty Mutant Animals* #5-9 which are low Print items (sell at 200-400% Guide), *That Wilkin Boy* (all are undervalued = 150%), *Thunder Agents* (Archie; 150%), *Whiz Kids* (Archie & Radio Shack $5-10 ea), *Wilbur* (Katy Keene #5-56,58-69 & DeCarlo art in later issues = 110-125%).

Charlton Comics: With over 25,000 in stock, we have the world's biggest selection of Charlton comics (95% of 1960-1986 issues and about 50% of the 1940's-1959 issues). Our selection makes our site the first destination for many Charlton fans, from readers to advanced collectors. The TV, Horror and Sci-Fi titles are the bestsellers in both Lower & High Grades, with all issues from 1966-1986 in High Demand. Second most requested are the better artist issues, including; Aparo, Boyette, Buscema, John Byrne, Ditko, Glanzman, Himes, Wayne Howard, Severin, Sanho Kim, Larson, Morisi, Don Newton, Staton, Tom Sutton, Wood, Williamson and Mike Zeck. Hanna Barbera comics are always consistent good sellers. The moderate sellers included: Superhero, War, Western titles, mostly sold to fans and readers that enjoy those genres in multiple publishers. We always do well with Charlton, but most other comic dealers do not bother with them. Everything sells eventually, with no really dead titles. Completonists and collectors who like hard-to-find and unusual items are often fascinated with the Charlton magazines, including: Adult Cartoon titles (*Cartoon Carnival*, *Comedy Capers*, *Good Humor*, *150 Cartoons*), *Charlton Bullseye*, CPL (Fanzine), *Horror Monsters*, *Mad Monsters*, *Monsters Attack*, *Sick* mag, and other non-Comic mags by Charlton (*True Western*, Romance, Movie/TV, Puzzle, etc). The 17 different known Charlton / Xerox Comic Digests (*Barney & Betty*, *Bugs Bunny*, *Dino*, *Dr. Graves*, *Flintstones*, *Jetsons*, *Pebbles & Bamm-Bamm*, *Road Runner*, *Scooby Doo*, *Space 1999*, *Tweety and Sylvester*, *Woody Woodpecker*, *Yogi Bear*, etc.) are still very scarce, rarely found in better than FN and sell for 200-300% *Guide*.

Bestsellers this year included (at 115-135% *Guide*): *Abbott & Costello*, *Barney & Betty*, *Beetle Bailey*, *Beyond the Grave*, *Bionic Woman*, *Blondie*, *Blue Beetle*, *Bobby Sherman*, *Bugaloos*, *Bullwinkle*, *Capt. Atom*, *Charlton Bullseye* (comic and magazine), *Charlton Premiere*, *Cheyenne Kid*, *Cowboy Western*, *David Cassidy*, *Dino*, *Doomsday + 1* (John Byrne), *Dudley Do-Right*, *EH!*, *E-Man*, *Emergency* (comic and magazine), *Flash Gordon*, *Flintstones*, *Ghostly Haunts*, *Ghostly Tales*, *Ghost Manor*, *Go-Go*, *Gorgo*, *Great Gazoo*, *Gunfighters*, *Hanna-Barbera Parade*, *Haunted*, *Haunted Love*, *Hercules*, *Hong Kong Phooey*, *Huckleberry Hound*, *Jetsons*, *Judo Master*, *Jungle Jim*, *Jungle Tales of Tarzan*, *Kid Montana*, *Konga*, *Korg*, *Magilla Gorilla*, *Many Ghosts of Dr. Graves*, *Masked Raider*, *Midnight Tales*, *Monster Hunters*, *Mysterious Suspense*, *Outer Space*, *Outlaws of the West*, *Partridge Family*, *Pebbles*, *Phantom*, *Ponytail*, *Popeye*, *Primus*, *Ronald McDonald*, *Quick Draw McGraw*, *Reptisaurus*, *Ronald McDonald*, *Sarge Steel*, *Scary Tales*, *Scooby Doo*, *Six Million Dollar Man* (comic and magazine), *Son of Vulcan*, *Space Adventures*, *Space 1999* (comic and magazine), *Space War*, *Speed Buggy*, *Static*, *Strange Suspense*, *Thane*, *Thunderbolt*, *Top Cat*, *Underdog*, *Unusual Tales*, *Valley of Dinosaurs*, *Vengeance Squad*, *War*, War comics (most 1950-1970), Western comics (most 1950-1970), *Wheelie & Chopper Bunch*, *Wyatt Earp*, *Yang*, & *Yogi Bear*.

DC Comics: DC Comics back issue sales are dominated by their long-standing classic characters and teams, especially

Batman, Flash, Green Lantern, JLA, JSA, Legion, Superman and Wonder Woman, so it might shock readers to realize all their titles were poor sellers with low print runs in the early 1980s. Circulation statements reveal these Low Print Runs; *Batman* #357-402 (75,303 to 97,741/month), *Detective* #482-569 (64,635 to 89,635/month), *Flash* (1959) #317-350 (72,771 to 69,881/month), *Green Lantern* (1960) #150-195 (89,657 to 80,765/month), *Justice League* (1960) #234-257 (96,281 to 82,406/month), *Superman* (1939-1986) #403-423 (98,767/month) and *Wonder Woman* (1942) #299-329 (73,256 to 52,145/month). Frank Miller revived Batman, John Byrne revived Superman and *Crisis* revived the others, with sales of these backbone characters never again low since the mid-1980s. Batman is by far the most collected DC character, as Spider-Man is to Marvel, yet 1960s Batman prices are far more affordable. Justice League is easily the mostly collected DC Team series, yet prices remain more affordable when compared to Marvel's Fantastic Four of the same time period. Since *Crisis* and George Pérez resurrected Wonder Woman in 1987, she has become arguably the most important female character in comics history. *Wonder Woman* (1942) #51-130 are in very low supply on the marketplace, a very tough run to complete, with GD-FN condition copies often bringing 125-200% *Guide*. *Wonder Woman* (1942) #177-220 are in steady demand. *Wonder Woman* (1987) #50-100, 121-226 are hard to keep in stock and usually sell at 25-100% over *Guide*.

DC War comics have never been more collected, with most 1950s issues in very low supply in any grade. *Our Army at War* #83(1st true Sgt. Rock) and *G.I. Combat* #68 are extremely undervalued and on many want lists (expect to pay 150-200% *Guide*). *OAAW* #81-82 (Sgt. Rock prototypes) are now slower sellers. *OAAW* #84-120 are tough to keep in stock in any grade and most major dealers are usually sold out. All Sgt. Rock comics are in demand, with #401-422 having Low Print Runs and being scarcer. *All American Men of War*, *G.I. Combat*, *Our Fighting Forces* and *Star Spangled War* are all in demand, with 1950s and 1970s issues being most requested. Bronze Age DC War in VF/NM or better are among the fastest selling investment grade copies of the period.

DC Horror and Sci-Fi comics are also in constantly good demand, with low grade reading copies being the bestsellers. Better artist issues of the 1968-1975 era are the most requested. Many investors are having a tough time completing runs of 1970-1985 era Horror titles in VF/NM or better. They are much more uncommon to scarce than many would think. All the Oddball titles (Cartoon, Digests, Humor, Love, Teen, Treasuries, Western etc.) still have a good following and always do well with these, as many dealers do not bother to carry them.

Bestselling DC comics this year included: (GD-FN = 120-140% *Guide*; FN/VF-VF+ = 100-135% *Guide*; VF/NM, 9.0 to NM-, 9.2 = 120-150% *Guide*); *Action* #377-450, 583, *Adventure* #381-440, 491-503, *All American Men of War* #38-117, *All New Collectors' Edition* C-53 to C-60; *All Star Comics* #58-74, *All-Star Western* #1-11, *Angel & the Ape* #1-7, *Aquaman* #48-63, *Amazing World of DC* #1-4, 9,14-17, *Bat Lash* 1-7, *Batman* #103-429, *Batman Family* #1-20, *Best of DC Digest* #1-10, 41-71, *Beware the Creeper* #1-6, *Blitzkrieg* #1-5, *Brave & the Bold* #50-120, 181-197, *Challengers of the Unknown* #74, 81-87, *Dark Mansion* #1-4, *DC Comics Presents* #1,2,26,47,85- 97, *DC 100 Page Super Spectacular* #4-14, *DC Special* #2-4,6,11,28,29, *DC Special Series* #1-27, *DC Special Blue Ribbon Digest* #1-24, *DC Superstars* #17, *Detective* #298-600, *Doorway to Nightmare* #1-5, *1st Issue Special* #1-13, *Flash* #105-130, 201-232,289-350, *Flex Mentallo* #1-4, *Freedom Fighters* #1-15, *Ghosts* #1-40, 97-99, *G.I. Combat* #55-210, *Green Lantern* (1960-1986) #76-123, 181-205, *GL Corps Annual* #2,3(Alan Moore), *Hawk & Dove* #1-6, *Hot Wheels* #1-6, *House of Mystery* #174-256, *House of Secrets* #61-154, *Joker* #1-9, *Jonah Hex* #1-20, 81-92 & Digest #1-3, *Justice League of America* #94-261 (especially JSA issues), *Legion* (1980) #290-300, *Limited Collectors' Edition* C#21 thru C-59, *Men of War* #1-26, *New Teen Titans* #1-10, *New Titans* #101-130, *Our Army at War* #51-301, *Our Fighting Forces* #41-100, 123-150, *Phantom Stranger* #1-14,31-41, *Rima* #1-7, *Sandman* (1989) #1-27, *Secret Society of Super-Villains* #1-15, *Secrets of Haunted House* #1-10, *Sgt. Rock* #302-350,400-422; *Shazam!* #1,8,12-17, 25-35, *Sinister House* #1-4, *Star Spangled War Stories* #45-183, *Strange Adventures* #205-217, *Superboy* #197-245, *Super DC Giant* #S-13 thru S-26, *Super Friends* #1-10, *Supergirl* (1972) #1-10, *Superman* #233-300, 400-423, *Superman Family* #164, *Superman's Pal Jimmy Olsen* #133-150, *Swamp Thing* (1982) #20-64 (Alan Moore), *Tales of New Teen Titans* #42-44 & Annual #3, *Tomahawk* #116-119, 121,123-130 (Adams covers), *Unexpected* #105-162, *Unknown Soldier* #205- 220, 265-268, *V for Vendetta* #1-10, *Watchmen* #1-12, *Weird Mystery* #1-24, *Weird War* #1-124, *Weird Western* #12-20,39-50, Whitman Variants of DC Comics (150-200% *Guide*), *Witching Hour* #1-20, *Wonder Woman* (1942-86) #51-130, 177-220, 281-329 and *Wonder Woman* (1987) #50-100.

Dell Comics: This year I went through my entire Dell inventory and identifed hundreds of Variants that are NOT yet listed in the *Guide* and sold over 60% of what I found at premium prices. These include Dell Variants: (2/1957-7/1958 = 15 Cent variants and September 1958 "10¢ Now" Cover Date Variants = These sell for a 50% premium over *Guide*); (1956-1962 Back Cover Variants with Strips in place of ads and Dell Giants with 30-35¢ Variant cover prices = These sell for a 10-30% Premium over *Guide*). Those back cover Variants with illustrations instead of ads are especially popular, as many have bonus features on the title character. Identified Variants are 2-10 times more saleable as compared to a standard issue (and at a premium too). In addition, I also sold most of my Canadian Editions of Dell comics. These are 10-20 times scarcer than the U.S. editions, but in the past these sold at discounts below *Guide*. With Variant collectors interest, I sold most of my remaining copies at U.S. *Guide* prices with no premiums.

VF or better and High Grade CGC copies of Dell comics (with the exception of high demand Key issues and titles) were once again slow sellers. Many sold at heavy discounts off *Guide* prices at eBay auctions. Meanwhile about 95% of our Dell sales were in the FR/GD (Reading Copies) thru FN (presentable, but still affordable) condition ranges. FN/VF and better copies were slower moving than usual this year. Most Dell comics in GD-FN are still undervalued in the *Guide*, while many VF-NM Dells are still overvalued in the *Guide.* This problem occurs because the "Price to Condition" spreads are far too wide. Wide price spreads for Marvel comics make sense, but do not apply well to Cartoon, Western and TV comics.

The bestselling titles (GD-FN = 120-140% *Guide*; FN/VF-VF/NM= 90-110% *Guide*) included: *Adventures of Mighty Mouse*, *Air War*, *Annie Oakley*, *Bat Masterson*, *Beetle Bailey*, *Ben Bowie*, *Beverly Hillbillies*, *Bewitched*, *Big Valley*, *Bullwinkle*, *Cheyenne*, *Chilly Willy*, *Cisco Kid*, *Colt 45*, *Combat*, Dell Giants, Dell Variants, *Dunc & Loo*, *Flintstones*, *Flying Nun*, *Flying Saucers*, *Fritzi Ritz* (with *Peanuts*), *F-Troop*, *Gene Autry* #101-121, *Get Smart*, *Ghost Stories*, *Gidget*, *Have Gun Will Travel*, *Hogan's Heroes*, *Huckleberry Hound*, *I Dream of Jeannie*, *I Love Lucy*, *Indian Chief*, *Jetsons*, *John Carter of Mars*, John Wayne titles, *King of Royal Mounted*, *Kona*, *Laramie*, *Lawman*, *Leave It to Beaver*, *Little Lulu*, *Lone Ranger* #112-145 & *Tonto*, *March of Comics*, *Maverick*, *McHale's Navy*, *Melvin Monster*, *Monkees*, *Movie Classics* (Western, SF & Horror), *Nancy* (*Peanuts*, Oona, and Stanley issues), *Outer Limits*, *Peanuts*, *Pogo*, *Ponytail*, *Popeye*, *Quick Draw McGraw*, *Rawhide*, *Real McCoys*, *Red Ryder* #1-118, *Ricky Nelson*, *Rifleman*, *Rin Tin Tin* #18-38(TV's Rusty), *Rocky & Friends*, *Roy Rogers* #121-145, *Sgt. Preston*, *Smokey Stover*, *Tarzan* #1-30, 80-131, *Thirteen*, *Tip Top* #211-225, *Top Cat*, *Turok*, *Twilight Zone*, *Voyage to the Bottom of the Sea*, *Wyatt Earp*, *Yogi Bear* and *Zorro*.

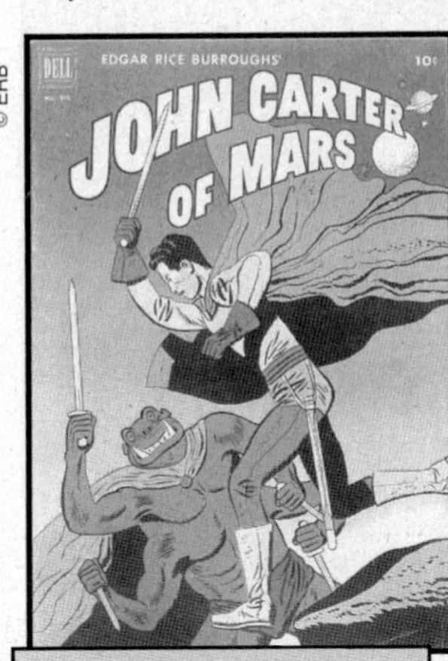

John Carter of Mars is a popular Dell title. (Four Color #375 shown)

Gold Key Comics (see also Walt Disney Comics)**:** We have over 35,000 in stock (world's biggest selection) thus these are always consistantly good solid sellers. 90% of our inventory is GD-FN range grades, but we have a decent selection of FN/VF to VF/NM copies. Luckily, the GD-FN copies are the most popular and bestsellers for us. Titles most requested in VF or better include: *Boris Karloff*, *Dr. Solar*, Hanna-Barbera titles, *Magnus*, *Tarzan*, *Turok*, *Twilight Zone*, plus Key issues, Horror/SF, TV, #1s and one-shots.

Gold Key Variants are still popular sellers. Whitman Variants of the Gold Key comics (11/1971 thru 4/1980 = 125-200% of GK issue values)(Canadian Newsstand Variant cover price issues (4-8/1968 with 15¢-c prices, 3/1972-4/1973 with 20¢-c prices; 12/1977-3/1978 with reverse 30¢-c prices) bring 125-150% *Guide*). (Whitman Variant 75¢-c price issues of 1984 Comics that are 60¢-c in USA bring 200-300% *Guide*).

The bestsellers this year included: (at VF-NM= 110-130% *Guide*; GD-FN=120-140% *Guide*) *Addams Family*, *Amazing Chan*, *Atom Ant*, *Astro Boy*, *Auggie Doggie*, *Avengers* (TV) #1(photo back-c), *Bamm Bamm*, *Banana Splits*, *Battle of the Planets*, *Beatles Yellow Submarine*, *Beneath Planet of Apes*, *Beetle Bailey*, *Boris Karloff*, *Bullwinkle*, *Cave Kids*, *Close Shaves of Pauline Peril*, *Daffy Duck* #31-50, *Dagar*, Dan Curtis (Giveaways) #1-9, *Daniel Boone*, *Dark Shadows*, *Doc Savage*, *Dr. Solar*, *Family Affair*, *Flash Gordon*, *Flintstones*, *Frankenstein Jr.*, *Fun-In*, *Funky Phantom*, *George of the Jungle*, *Gold Key Spotlight*, *Gomer Pyle*, *Grimm's Ghost*, *Hair Bear Bunch*, *Hanna-Barbera Bandwagon*, *Hanna Barbera Super TV Heroes*, *Happy Days*, *Honey West*, *H.R. Pufnstuf*, *Huckleberry Hound*, *Inspector*, *Jetsons*, *John Carter*, *Jonny Quest*, *Korak*, *Kroft Supershow*, *Lancelot Link*, *Land of Giants*, *Laredo*, *Lidsville*, *Little Lulu* #207 up, *Little Monsters*, *Lone Ranger*, *Lucy Show*, *Magilla Gorilla*, *Magnus Robot Fighter*, *Marge's Little Lulu* #165-206, *Mars Patrol*, *Mighty Hercules*, *Mighty Mouse*, *Mighty Samson*, *Milton Monster*, *Mr. Ed*, *Mr. & Mrs. J Evil Scientist*, *Munsters*, *My Favorite Martian*, *Nancy & Sluggo*, *Occult Files of Dr. Spector*, *Peanuts*, *Peter Potomus*, *Phantom*, *Pink Panther*, Popeye, *Quick Draw McGraw*, *Rifleman*, *Ripley's Believe it or Not*, *Rocky & Fiendish Friends*, *Scooby Doo*, *Secret Squirrel*, *Snagglepuss*, *Snooper & Blabber*, *Space Family Robinson*, *Space Ghost*, *Space Mouse*, *Spine Tingling Tales*, *Star Stream*, *Star Trek* #1-9, *Supercar*, *Tarzan*, *Tasmanian Devil* #1, *Three Stooges*, *Time Tunnel*, *Top Cat*, *Turok*, *Twilight Zone*, *UFO Flying Saucers*, *Underdog*, *Wacky Races*, *Wacky Witch* and *Wagon Train*.

Harvey Comics: All 1975 and older Cartoon titles were in good steady demand, in FR/GD through FN grades. Most 1976-1990 titles were in moderate demand (mostly in VG to VF grades). 1991-1994 titles all had low print runs (except for issue #1s) and are scarcer, with most issues always sold out with most major dealers. My minimum price for any of these is: VF/NM=$6; VF=$5; FN=$4; VG=$3; G=$2.

Bestselling titles (9.2=150% *Guide*; VF-VF/NM=115-130% *Guide*; GD-FN=120-150% *Guide*) include: all square-bound Giants, *Alarming Tales*, *Alarming Adventures*, *Alvin*, *Astro Comics*, *Baby Huey*, *Black Cat*, *Blast-Off*, *Blondie* (undervalued), *Bunny*, *Casper the Friendy Ghost* #1-20, Casper (assorted titles, 1961-1974), *Casper's Ghostland*, *Casper & Nightmare*, *Chamber of Chills*, *Dagwood*, *Devil Kids*, *Dotty Dribble*, *Family Funnies*, *Felix the Cat*, *First*

Love, First Romance, Flintstones, Friendy Ghost Casper, Fruitman, Hanna-Barbera Giant Size, Harvey Collectors Comics, Harvey Hits, Harvey Pop, Hot Stuff the Little Devil, Jetsons, Joe Palooka, Little Audrey, Little Dot, Little Dot's Uncles & Aunts, Little Lotta, Little Max, Man in Black, Mazie, Mutt & Jeff, Playful Little Audrey, Pebbles & Bamm-Bamm, Richie Rich (all 1960-1974), *Sad Sack* (all pre-1975), *Scooby Doo, Spooky, Stumbo Tinytown, Tastee-Freez, Thrill-O-Rama, Tomb of Terror, Tuff Ghosts, TV Casper & Co., Underdog, Unearthly Spectacular, Warfront, Wendy, Witches Tales* and *Yogi Bear*.

Marvel Comics: To many collectors and dealers alike, back issue Marvels are the only comics really worth having. This narrow view is actually quite widespread, and Marvel comics are so much hoarded, that they have inevitably become the most common comics on the marketplace for the given time period. There are almost 5000 CGC graded copies of *Incredible Hulk* #181 and presumably 2-4 times as many still ungraded copies, yet it *Guide*s at $1700 in 9.2. There are hundreds of other 1974 comics that are scarcer, yet they *Guide* at under 1% of that price. Although Marvel has published less than 5% of all extant comics, more dealer inventories have over 50% Marvel than otherwise. Incredibly, supply and demand is so high that prices continue to climb. For about 35 years now Marvel has been viewed by many as the safest publisher to collect and deal in.

How do you make a popular but common or uncommon comic into a Scarce to Rare Comic?? Not with magic, but by seeking only the highest graded copies! When everyone wants high grade, prices keep increasing like a Juggernaut, thus the current state of the Market. High Grade Silver Age Marvel have priced many collectors out of that maket toward Bronze Age, and now High Grade Bronze prices are driving many to Copper Age comics. In stamps, coins, sports cards and other hobbies, most of the money in the market is focused only on high grade slabbed copies. But in comics, this has not happened, because it is also a media artform, with probably still over 75% of the buyers still want them for story and art, not just for investment. Thus the comic collecting hobby is here to stay for the long haul. Quantity wise, over 90% of my Marvel comic sales are Good through VF condition copies, while only about 10% of my sale quantities are VF/NM or better "investment grade" copies.

Bestselling Marvels this year (GD-FN = 120-140% *Guide*; FN/VF-VF+ = 100-135% *Guide*; VF/NM, 9.0 to NM-, 9.2 = 120-150% *Guide*) included: *Amazing Adventures* #1,5-8, 11,18, *Amazing Spider-Man* #50, 96-150,194,300 and Annual #1,2, *Astonishing Tales* #1,12,25, *Avengers* #57-200 and Annual #1-10, *Captain America* #100,109-113,117,140-255 and Annual #1-4, *Captain Britain* (1976 UK) #1,8(1st Psylocke), *Cat* #1-4, *Chamber of Chills* #1-25, *Champions* #11-17, *Conan* #1, 3, 271-275, *Creatures on the Loose* #10-16, 30-37, *Daredevil* #50-158, 168 and Annual #1-4, *Dead of Night* #1-11, *Deadly Hands of Kung Fu* #1,14,17,28, *Defenders* #1-11, *Dr. Strange*(1974) #1,14,58-62, *Dracula Lives* #1-13, *Fear* #1-31, *Fantastic Four* #110-167, *Foom* #1-15, 22, *Frankenstein* #1,8,9,18, *Ghost Rider* (1973) #1-20, 81, *Ghost Rider* (1990) #81-93, *Giant-Size...* (1974-1975 most titles), *G.I. Joe* #1-21, 93, 139-155, *Haunt of Horror* (Mag) #1-5, *Hero For Hire* #1, *Incredible Hulk* #102, 121-250 and Annual #1-10, *Invaders* #1-10, 31-33, *Iron Fist* #1-15, *Iron Man* #1-10, 31-150 and Annual #1-5, *Journey into Mystery* #83-112 and Annual #1, *Jungle Action* #5-10, *Kull the Conqueror* (1971) #1-15, *Man-Thing* (1974) #1-10, *Marvel Chillers* #3-7, *Marvel Feature*(1971) #1-12, *Marvel Feature* (1975) #1-7, *Marvel Premiere* #1-28, *Marvel Preview* #1-8, *Marvel Spotlight* (1971) #1-33, *Marvel Super-Heroes* #1,12-50, *Marvel Tales* #1,31-50 *Marvel Team-Up* #1-20, 53, John Byrne issues, 141, and Annual #1, *Marvel Treasury* #1-20, *Marvel Two-in-One* #1-20,46 and all Byrne, Perez, Miller art issues, *Master of Kung Fu* #15-30, *Masters of the Universe* #1-13, *Monsters of the Prowl* #9-30, *Monsters Unleashed* #1-11, *My Love* #1-39, *Nick Fury* (1968) #1-5, *Our Love Story* #1-38, *Planet of the Apes* mag #21-29, *Power Man* #17-20,48-50, Price Variants (1970s 30¢-c Variants; 150-200% *Guide*); (1970s 35¢-c Variants; 200-400% *Guide*); *Rampaging Hulk* #1-9, *Red Sonja* (1977) #1-15, *Savage Sword* #181-235, *Savage Tales* #1, *Shanna* #1-5, *Silver Surfer*(1968) #1-7,14,15,18, *Spidey Super Stories* #1-20, *Spider-Man Digest* #1-13, *Strange Tales* #101-115, 169-181, *Superman vs. Spider-Man* #1, *Supernatural Thrillers* #1-15, *Super Villain Team-Up* #1-17, *Tales of the Zombie* #1-10, *Tales of Suspense* #39-66, *Tales to Astonish* #27,35-60, *Thor* #180-250, 332,333,337, *Tomb of Darkness* #9-23, *Tomb of Dracula* #1-13, *Transformers* #71-80, *Vampire Tales* #1-11, *War is Hell* #1-15, *Warlock* #1,9-15, *Werewolf by Night* #1-10, 32,33, *What If* (1977) #1-10, *X-Men* #50-66, 94-111, 120,121.

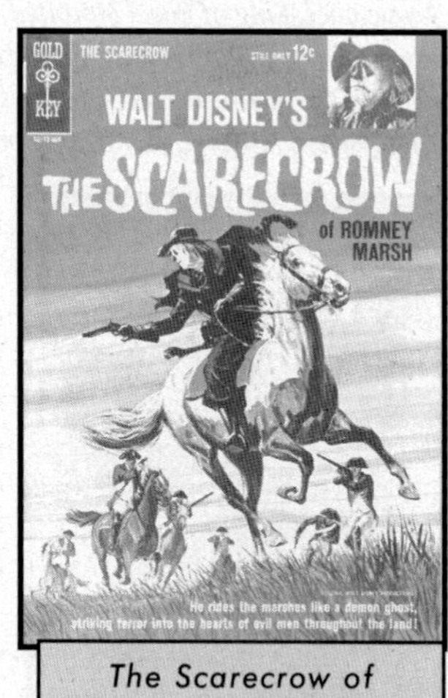

The Scarecrow of Romney Marsh (#1 shown) is still one of the most requested of all Disney comics.

Walt Disney Comics: We have a large selection of about 20,000 Walt Disney comics in stock from all their publishers (Dell, Disney, Gemstone, Gladstone, Gold Key, March of Comics, Marvel, Whitman, etc.). Especially popular are all the Live Action TV Series and Movie Classic (both Cartoon and Live Action) comics. *Scarecrow of Romney Marsh* #1-3 are by far the most requested and impossible to keep in stock even at 200% *Guide*. The *WD Showcase* #53 reprint is also in high demand at 200% *Guide*. Pre-1950 Golden Age Disney titles were in steady demand and hard to re-stock.

Dell titles, the Four Color one-shot titles, Live Action comics (TV and Movie) were above-average sellers (except for the nature and science titles).

Bestselling pre-1985 comics this year (GD-FN = 120-140% *Guide*; FN/VF-VF+ = 100-135% *Guide*; VF/NM, 9.0 to NM-, 9.2 = 120-135% *Guide*) included: *Annette* (Funicello - all titles), *Beagle Boys*, *Black Hole*, *Chip N' Dale*, *Condorman*, *Darby O'Gill*, *Davy Crockett* (Fess Parker), many Dell Giants, *Donald Duck*, *Dynabrite*, *Goofy* FC, *Greyfriars Bobby*, Hayley Mills (all titles), *Hardy Boys*, *Huey Dewie & Louie*, *Ludwig Von Drake*, *Mickey Mouse*, *Moby Duck*, *Movie Classics* (most Live Action), *Phantom Blot*, *Scamp*, *Scarecrow of Romney Marsh*, *Spin & Marty*, *Super Goof*, *Tinker Bell*, *Uncensored Mouse*, *Uncle Scrooge* #1-60, 174-197, 285-320, *Walt Disney Presents* (hot title), *Walt Disney Showcase*, *Winnie the Pooh*, *World of Adventure* and *Zorro* (Guy Williams).

Warren, Skywald & Misc. Horror Comic Magazines - Warren: It seems strange now, but only about a decade ago Warren magazines were on the "Slow Selling List", and the market still had a lot of leftover Warren warehouse copies. As demand picked up, they all got absorbed into the marketplace and they have been in high demand ever since. Due to handling wear, the average Warren warehouse copy was in the FN through VF condition range, with only a small percentage in strict VF/NM range. The Warehouse copies have made them uncommon and still affordable (*Creepy* #1 with Frazetta art lists at only $230 in 9.2, but might currently be worth 10 times that, if it were not for the Warehouse copies). The issues that sold out earlier in the 1970s and 1980s warehouse, are still the scarcest issues today and many are consistently sold out and in short supply with most dealers.

Creepy, *Eerie*, *Famous Monsters* and *Vampirella* usually make up 90% of Warren sales, yet are less than 50% of the magazines they printed. There are more and more Warren completionists each year, thus the Scarce issues are very difficult to keep in stock. Low Grade Reading copies are amazingly fast sellers and actually bring good premiums. Middle Grade copies are the slower sellers. *Creepy* and *Eerie* #41-80 were the most requested issues in High Grades. Investors still want VF/NM or better copies and they get harder to restock each year.

The Highest Demand Warren magazines and scarcer issues include: *Blazing Combat* #1 & Anthology (GD-FN=300% *Guide*; VF-NM- = 200%), *Comix International* #1(200%), *Creepy* #32(200%), #9, 11, 19, 29, 76, 79, 146(150%), *Creepy* #10,14,17,18,34,39,46,47,50,53,63, 70,71,78,85, 91,113,132-145 (125% *Guide*); *Best of Creepy* paperback (VF $30), *Dracula* TPB (Maroto-a; 150%), *Dracula* (UK New English Library mag. editions #1-12; VF = $14; FN=$10; VG=$7 ea); *Edgar Allan Poe's Fall of the House of Usher* (Hardcover or Softcover 150%); *Eerie* #17(GD-FN=300%; VF-NM- = 200%); #1, 23(200%); #8, 25, 48, 135(150%); *Eerie* #18, 24, 28, 38-41,45, 60, 81,125,128, 130-134,136-139 (125% *Guide*); *Famous Monsters* #1(VF=$1800; FN=$900; VG=$600), 2-10(VF = $300-$900 ea), 11-30(VF = $150-$300 ea), (scarcer numbers = #32,38,114 (VF+ = $100-$200 ea); (uncommon numbers = #31,33,37,48,51, 56,82,92,93,100,108; VF = $40-$60); 1962 Yearbook #1(VF $250), *Famous Monsters* Convention Books (1974, 1975; VF = $75+ ea), *Famous Monsters* Paperbacks (VF = $100; FN=$60; G=$25), *Flintstones at New York World's Fair 1964* (150%), *Help* magazine (Kurtzman) (Note: spines split easily, thus tough in VF or better) #1(VF $80); #2-5, 9, 13,15, 16,21-26(VF=$35-$50; others= $25-35); *Help* paperbacks #1,2(VF $35); *Heidi Saha* (500 printed?, very rare; FN = $500+); *Monsters & Heroes* (Warren related; publ. by Larry Ivie; 1967-1969; VF = $30-$50); *Monsterland / Forrest J. Ackerman's Monsterland* (1984-1987) #1-17(VF= $12-24); *Monster World* (replaces *Famous Monsters* #70-79) #3(VF $60+); #4(VF $35+); *Odd World of Richard Corben* TPB (200%), *On the Scene / Freakout* nn (#1; Fall 1967 = 125%); *Screen Thrills* (1962-1965) #1,10(VF $75+); 2-4 (VF $50); *Spacemen* (Note: spines split easily, thus tough in VF or better) #1,3(VF=$200+); #2,4-8 and Yearbook (VF=$50-$75); *Spirit Special* (mail only, approx. 1500 printed = 150%), *Outer Space Spirit* (TPB; VF $35); *Teen Love Stories* #1-3 (115-125%), *Tiny Tim*(125%); *Vampirella* #1,3,112,113 (GD-FN=125-150% *Guide*; VF-NM- = 110-125%), #2,4-8,11,12,16,19,32-34,36,41, 45,46,48,49, 51,52,61,63,64,77,78,89,90, 100-111 (GD-FN=125-150% *Guide*; VF-NM- = 110-125%); #32-34 (spines split easily); Annual #1(125%), Special #1(Softcover=125%; rare Hardcover=200%), *Vampirella* paperbacks #1-3(VF=$30; FN=$20; GD=$10), 4-6(VF=$50; FN=$30; GD=$15); *Vampirella* UK mags #1-4(VF $50 ea); *Warren Presents* #13, 14(150%); *Wildest Westerns/Favorite Westerns of Filmland* (Note: spines split easily, thus tough in VF or better) #1 (VF=$200; GD=$50); #2(VF=$100; GD=$35); #3-6 (VF=$60; GD=$20).

Skywald: The Skywald magazines (*Crime-Machine*, *Hell-Rider*, *Nightmare*, *Psycho* and *Scream*) are in constant demand, are 3-6 times harder to find than Warren magazines and are very hard to keep in stock. These are great horror comics and a "must try" for fans of the Genre. Fans especially like the issues with: Al Hewetson stories, Dracula, Edgar Allan Poe, Frankenstein, Heap, "Horror-Mood", H.P. Lovecraft, Human Gargoyles, Lady Satan, Nosferatu, Werewolfs, etc. Especially in demand are issues with art by: John Byrne, Everett, Jeff Jones, Bruce Jones, Kaluta, Marcos, Segrelles, Boris Vallejo, Wrightson, etc. The Horror-Mood issues are said to have inspired Stephen King. VF or better copies are especially difficult to find and are in very high demand. Reading copies sell as fast as we get them. *King* mags (3-7/1971; Boris-a) are rare (#1 VF =$75; #2 VF=$50); *Crime-Machine* and *Hell-Rider* are also decent sellers (#1s = 150%; #2s = 120%). *Nightmare*, *Psycho* and *Scream* (GD-FN= 140-165%; VF-NM- = 120-140%).

Miscellaneous Horror Magazines: Those by Eerie Pub, Globe, Hamilton, Major, Modern Day, Stanley, Tempest Pub and World Famous are in steady demand. Affordable Reading copies are in very high demand and sell as fast as we find them. VF/NM or better copies are getting scarcer and are usually good sellers, but a bit slower this year due to the economy. The Eerie Pub and Stanley magazines feature "Wild Shocking Gruesome" colorful covers that are the biggest appeal in these. The interiors also include: Blood & Gore, Bloody Stake Through the Heart, Bondage, Decapitations, Severed Heads & Limbs, Skeletons, Torture, Vampires, Werewolves and more. Stanley Pub magazines have a lot of pre-Code horror reprints, with less copies on the marketplace, making them faster sellers. The 1966-1970 issues and the Low Print 1980-1983 issues are the Scarcest and the toughest issues for completionists.

Bestsellers this year (VF-VF/NM=110-125% *Guide*; GD-FN=130-160% *Guide*) included: *Castle of Frankenstein* #1-25, *Chilling Tales of Horror*, *Dread of Night*, *Ghoul Tales*, *Grace Tales*, Hammer magazines (UK), *Horror Tales*, *Maggots*, *Monsters Attack*, *Murder Tales*, *Shock*, *Stark Terror*, *Tales From The Crypt*, *Tales of the Killers*, *Tales From the Tomb* (1969-70 issues), *Tales of Voodoo*(1968-70 issues), *Terrors of Dracula* (all), *Terror Tales* (1969-70 issues), *Web of Horror*, *Weird* (1966-1970, 1979-1981), *Weird Vampire Tales* (all) and *Witches Tales*(1969-70).

Christopher Swartz
Collector

This past year has been a turbulent time for the back issue comic book market, for all issues, from all ages, with the exception of key Golden Age and key mid to high grade Silver Age issues. All other issues need to decrease or stay at their current *Guide* value. Even some keys from these eras have been affected by slow sales and troubling economic times. There were three major comic book based movies that came out in 2011 (*Thor*, *Green Lantern*, *Captain America*) which increased demand in key books from these characters, even if the movies didn't live up to fan based expectations.

This being my third year as an Overstreet Advisor, an alarming trend that I have noticed is many advisors, although not all, tend to report overinflated prices for comics and state that year every is a tremendous year for comic sales. This troubling trend can hurt the integrity of the *Overstreet Price Guide* for the simple fact, that anyone can log on to Heritage, ComicLink, GPA, and even eBay to see the actual fair market value for certain comic books. No one is going to pay $6,000 for an CGC 4.0 *Fantastic Four* #1 when you can see from any of the above mentioned sites, that copies of that book have been selling for well below that price. I know from experience that the majority of advisors are dealers, and selling comic books is their livelihood, but trying to increase values on certain books to make a profit without actual market facts to support these claims is going to turn people away from utilizing the *Overstreet Guide* as a resource. Let's dive into the comic book market for 2011.

Golden Age – DC: No big changes here with what issues have been in demand: *Action Comics* #1-23, *Detective Comics* #27-40, *Batman* #1-5, *All-American* #16, *More Fun Comics* #52,73, and *Wonder Woman* #1-6. *Action Comics* Superman covers (#7,10,13,15) have been selling well above *Guide* value, with an *Action* #10 CGC 3.0 selling for $20,000. Same trend with *Detective Comics* Batman covers (#29,31,33,35,36,37) all selling for a premium. The most popular Golden Age issues this past year have been pre-Robin *Detective* #27-37, which have been selling for around three times current *Guide* value.

There have been many keys that have been on a downward spiral, except in high grade, such as *All Star Comics* #3, *Adventure Comics* #40, *Flash Comics* #1, and even *Superman* #1 selling for below *Guide* value. *Superman* #1 is and always will be a desirable book, but I think collectors are not as willing to spend outlandish prices, as in the past, on a book that just reprints the first four issues of *Action Comics*.

Golden Age – Timely/Marvel: *Captain America Comics* #1-10 (Kirby issues) have had an increase in demand this past year, most likely because of the feature film of the Captain. The only other Timely that has been consistently selling at or above *Guide* value, has been *Marvel Mystery Comics* #9, but even this has seen a decrease in sales price in the later part of 2011. Recently in November, a CGC 2.5 copy of *Marvel Mystery* #9 sold for $5,300, a far cry from what earlier prices of this book have fetched. All other Timely issues have been in demand but selling for under *Guide* value, with *Marvel Comics* #1 still being a "for sure" sell if it is priced right. I anticipate *All-American Comics* #16 or *Batman* #1 taking over the 4th most valuable comic book spot from *Marvel Comics* #1 within the next few years.

All other Golden Age: *Pep Comics* #22 and *Archie Comics* #1 have sold very well whenever copies arise. Other books such as *Whiz Comics* #1 have been easy to sell, but only at below *Guide* value. EC Horror comics always sell really well, along with Good Girl issues of *Phantom Lady* #17 and *Blue Beetle* #54 being in high demand.

Silver Age - DC: The main DC key books during this timeframe that had the most interest this past year are: *Showcase* #4, 22, *Brave & the Bold* #28 (1st JLA), *Adventure Comics* #247 (1st Legion), and *Flash* #105. All of these books have sold quite well during 2011 and can be had for a fraction of their Marvel counterparts. Finding a mid to high grade copy of any of these issues is far more difficult then finding a *X-Men* #1 or *Tales of Suspense* #39 in the same grade. War issues such as *Our Army at War* #81-83 (1st Sgt. Rock) have shown an increase in interest, with prices reflecting the demand.

Silver Age – Marvel: *Amazing Fantasy* #15 has continued to be the top book from this era, with prices in all grades, especially 5.0 VG/FN and above, consistently selling for many times above *Guide*. A CGC 6.0 Twin Cities pedigree copy sold for $20,000 this past November. *Journey Into Mystery* #83 has been a strong seller this past year as well as *Avengers* #1, *Incredible Hulk* #1, *Fantastic Four* #5, and *Tales to Astonish* #27. However, *Fantastic Four* #1 and *Amazing*

Spider-Man #1 have been selling under *Guide* value in mid-to-low grades and the *Guide* needs to reflect this. *Sgt. Fury and His Howling Commandos* #1 is still the most undervalued Silver Age Marvel. If you are able to obtain a VF or better copy for a fair price, jump on it!

Sgt. Fury #1 is possibly the most undervalued Silver Age Marvel.

Bronze Age - Marvel: Within recent years there has been an increase in supply of high grade books from the Bronze Age. This is because many key books from the Bronze Age are being pressed. Eight years ago there were maybe 20 copies of *Incredible Hulk* #181 in CGC 9.6, now there are hundreds of copies in 9.6 or higher, with many being pressed. While it may seem like a good idea right now to press a key book to obtain a higher grade, what affect will this have on the comic market when it becomes saturated with pressed books? *Incredible Hulk* #181, *Amazing Spider-Man* #129, *Ghost Rider* #1, and *Marvel Spotlight* #5 in high grade have been selling well, but for all other issues the *Guide* needs to lower their values, such as *Giant-Size X-Men* #1 and *X-Men* #94. Both of these books supply has exceeded demand.

Bronze Age - DC: The only books during this time that deserve a price increase are high grade copies of *Green Lantern* #76, *Batman* #227-251, *Detective Comics* #400, and *All-Star Western* #10.

San Diego Comic-Con: The best way I can describe this year's past Con is, way too many people that aren't comic book fans. There are less and less comic book dealers and collectors that show up to Con because it has lost touch with its roots, which is a love of comic books. Con has become too Hollywood for its own good, while starting to alienate true comic book fans. I don't feel the need to fight my way through thousands of Twilight tweens in order to get an autograph from my favorite comic book artist. I would like to see the Con administrators plan more comic book related events and panels, as opposed to the current regimen of everything but comics. As for obtaining any significant comics during Con this year, I did not make any purchases. I did obtain a Jim Aparo *Brave & the Bold* #174 original cover art, but there were no deals on any key books at the show. As a side note, if you are looking to attend a comic show that has a good amount of dealers and a comic fan friendly atmosphere, contact Terry O'Neill of Terry's Comics. For the past few years now Terry O'Neill has been conducting a show in Yorba Linda, CA, which has been a great venue to purchase back-issues, while not having to deal with non-comic fans.

Important Sales or Purchases:
Action Comics #40 CGC 2.5 $325
Adventure Comics #247 CGC 5.0 $1,200
Batman #59 CGC 5.0 $280
Brave and the Bold #28 CGC 3.5 $950
Captain America Comics #7 CGC 5.0 (Joe Simon Signature Series) $2,300
Fantastic Four #1 CGC 4.5 $4,300
Incredible Hulk #1 CGC 1.5 $1,300
Amazing Spider-Man #2 CGC 2.5 $375
Detective Comics #36 CGC 4.0 (restored) $3,050
Detective Comics #140 CGC 4.0 $1,250
More Fun Comics #55 CGC 1.0 (restored) $900
More Fun Comics #60 CGC 2.0 $500
More Fun Comics #62 CGC 3.0 $500
More Fun Comics #73 CGC 7.5 (restored) $3,100
Showcase #22 CGC 3.0 $1,100
Superman #3 CGC 3.5 $1,500
Tales of Suspense #39 CGC 4.5 $1,750
X-Men #1 CGC 4.0 $1,350

On an end note, collectors need to realize that the *Overstreet Price Guide* is exactly that, a guide. The prices contained in this book are not the end all or be all of comic book prices, but should be used as a reference to the current comic book market place. The *Overstreet Price Guide* has been the one true comic book price guide since 1970 and hopefully for the foreseeable future, but if the *Guide* does not reflect the actual market activity, then I can see some collectors opting to stop using the *Guide* as a resource. Until next year, stay fan-boys my friends.

Michael Tierney Collector's Edition & The Comic Book Store

The traditional selling seasons for new comics were flip-flopped in 2011 when the mainstream DC universe ended with little pomp or fanfare, and was replaced by the alternate reality universe of Flashpoint for what turned out to be a summer of filler when DC announced that once Flashpoint concluded there would be a complete reboot. DC then confused the message when they added that it was really more of a relaunch of titles like *Batman* and *Green Lantern*, which would retain some of their history, but not all. Many long-term fans were angered, especially with the abandonment of *Action Comics*' numbering that was nearing #1000, and ended their collections immediately. The normally strongest new comic sales months of the Summer were a disappointment.

But when the actual launch hit in September, it was well supported by a media campaign that reached new and lapsed readers alike. Having started making my own TV commercials, I had fortuitous timing when my commercial plugging the event, and the 29th anniversary of my first store, Collector's Edition, ran on the same programming.

For the first time ever, September was the best month of

the year. But, to put it in proper perspective, it was only my 6th best September out of 30, showing how far new comic sales had fallen.

Marvel's plan for the year was much the same as it has been for years. The longer running series got relaunched with #1 issues, and a Super-Hero died every few months. The first to die, while achieving decent sales numbers, was the Human Torch, who'd soon return in a special that reverted to the original numbering of #600. I figured wrong when I thought that the death of the Ultimate Spider-Man would have even greater demand. It didn't. There was no interest from non-regulars, as the general public apparently knew the difference between the Amazing and Ultimate Spider-Men.

But Marvel's relaunches, including the introduction of Peter Parker's replacement of half-black/half-hispanic Miles Morales as the Ultimate Spider-Man, only achieved temporary boosts, and subsequently fell to numbers less than the original series they had replaced.

Marvel's big summer crossover event of Fear Itself sold well with the core titles, but poorly with the spin-off mini-series. It's clear that fans are no longer enamored with either big Event series or the now common #1 issues, and many would actually prefer the continuity of high numbers. DC's success in spite of this trend was largely due to their mass media ad campaign, shown by the way those characters featured in their commercials are the ones who did well, while the rest of the New 52 quickly slipped back to pre-Flashpoint numbers and lower. This fact is illustrated by how all of the #1 issues were reprinted, sometimes multiple times, but for the #2 issues there were only a handful.

New readers are what pushed sales up on *Justice League*, *Superman*, *Batman*, *Aquaman*, and *Wonder Woman*. But creating new readers remains the area where publishers still need more improvement.

When DC made their switch to digital, they finally adopted a grading system. The only problem with this was that every single title of DC's new 52 was rated Teen Plus. The all-important new customer market of the Tweeners was completely ignored, with everything aimed either at older readers or the Kiddie books of Johnny DC, with nothing for ages 9 through early Teens. Marvel did only a smattering of books, as true All-Ages material was as scarce as ever, despite the enthusiasm of youth for comics being as great as ever. This year's crowds for our annual "Halloween On the Hill" at Collector's Edition numbered in the thousands. One young girl was so excited about her Strawberry Shortcake comic that she threw down her candy pail and walked off, so engrossed in reading that she fell twice within a few steps, but kept popping back up with unbroken attention.

Tiny Titans was a bright spot in a market that offers few new books for young readers.

As much as digital is now being touted, holding an actual comic in your hands is something that will provide a unique experience long after the current digital platforms have become obsolete, like 8-track or VHS tapes. It is clear that text conversion to digital is impacting the chain booksellers, who had previously wiped out all the independent bookstores, so much so that the local Yellow Pages informed me that next year they were dropping the "Book Dealers -- Retail" listing. But, just as the piano survived technological evolutions in music, the combination of graphics and words in comic books makes this a format best presented in print. Then there's the whole collectability aspect that digital can never compete with.

So, given how obvious it is that back issue sales in 2011 were not driven by new comics sales, and how last year I didn't see a single back issue sale for over $300.00, you might think that this year would be a repeat. But the exact opposite happened as back issues were hot in 2011, with extra sizzle being provided by this year's batch of Super-Hero movies.

Thor hammered the registers twice, first with the theatrical release and again with Blu-Ray and DVD, selling many dozens of Jack Kirby issues in *Journey Into Mystery* and *Thor* in the $15 to $45 range. Captain America might have done the same but, outside of his first appearance in *Avengers* #4, there really aren't a lot of high-dollar Captain America comics from the Silver Age, and much less Kirby.

Green Lantern back issue sales were also way up thanks to a movie adaptation. Key sales include a Fair copy of #1 for $60.00, and Hector Hammond's first appearance in *Green Lantern* #5 in GD+ for $60.00

But it wasn't just movie related back issues that were selling. It seemed that the more customers were disappointed with the summer's slate of new comics, the more they delved into the past.

The *Amazing Spider-Man* was hopping, selling the 1st appearance of the Lizard in a Poor copy of #3 for $45.00, #13 in VG- for $67.50, and the three controversial drug issues of #96 in FN for $27.00, #97 in VF for $28.00, and #98 in VF+ for $37.50. Sold two copies of Morbius' 1st appearance in #101, one in GD+ for $15.00 and another in VG+ for $38.00. The Death of Gwen Stacy in #121 in FN+ went for $70.00, the 1st appearance of the Punisher in #129 in VG sold lightning fast for $60.00, and the 1st Tarantula in #134 in VF went for $26.25.

First appearances were a key as ever. The 1st appearances of the Silver Surfer and Galactus in *Fantastic Four* #48 sold in FN for $116.25, their 2nd appearance in #49 went in VF for $120.00, and their 3rd in #50 in FN went for $97.50.

I sold a number of key appearances in the *Brave and the*

Bold, including #12 with the 4th Challengers of the Unknown in GD for $86.00, and #31 with Aquaman in VF- for $157.50. Sold two copies of #54 featuring the 1st appearance and origin of the Teen Titans, one in VG for $55.00 and a FN+ for $60.00. In *Showcase*, I sold the 2nd appearance of the Sea Devils in #28 in VF for $125.00, and the 1st Silver Age Spectre in #60 in VG for $36.00. Another key 1st appearance was that of Darkseid in *Superman's Pal Jimmy Olsen* #134 in FN+ for $17.25.

The 1st Appearance of Iron Fist in *Marvel Premiere* #15 sold in VF+ for $55.00, and the origin of the Venom Costume in *Marvel Super-Heroes Secret Wars* #8 sold in NM for $25.00. The origin of the Watcher told in *Tales of Suspense* #53 went in GD for $24.75. Sold an entire run of the reprint issues of *X-Men* in issues #67 through #93. X-Men as a whole sold very well this year.

My best sales were from the Golden Age, starting with Lex Luthor's second appearance in *Superman* #4, with a Good copy selling for $650.00. I also sold two copies of *Superman* #18, one in Good for $275.00 and another in GD- $200.00. Other notable Superman sales were issue #69 in Good for $52.50, and *Superman's Pal Jimmy Olsen* #7 in FN- for $71.25.

Batman also had some good Golden Age activity with #24 in GD $90.00, #35 in GD for $80.00, #41 in VG for $155.00, and #98 in FN- for $175.00. Batman in *Detective Comics* #95 sold in VG+ for $150.00, and #136 in VG+ for $100.00.

Just about everything was moving. Simon & Kirby's *Adventures of the Fly* #1 sold in VG+ for $67.75. And the Western comics even saw some action with *Gunsmoke* #1 selling in FN+ for $62.50, the *Real Life Story of Fess Parker* #1 in VG for $18.00, and *Roy Rogers* #10 in VF for $77.75.

Funny Animals were not to be ignored, as *Fox & Crow* #1 sold in VG+ for $62.50 and Quick Draw McGraw (*Four Color*) #1040 in VG- for $21.00. Even the TV puppet *Howdy Doody* #6 sold in FN+ for $78.00.

Those were the bigger books. Eighties comics also moved very well, and I literally sold a ton of 'reading material' out of my 50 cent boxes. Here the Comics Code Approval was heavily sought out by parents, making even the cheapest Nineties and early New Millennium comics difficult to move without any kind of ratings guidelines.

One Nineties comic that did move was *New Mutants* #98, featuring the 1st appearance of Deadpool. Sold a copy in NM for $40.00 and a MT copy for $50.00.

All in all, it was a banner year for old comic sales!

Ted VanLiew
Superworld Comics

Overall, people are being more cautious. High grade and really significant pieces are very strong, but regular stuff is hit or miss. For example, *Fantastic Four* #5 in VF condition is going to sell quickly at a healthy price, but *Fantastic Four* #42 in Fine will have to be discounted for it to move in a reasonable amount of time.

I believe the internet, as time goes by, shows what's truly scarce and special and what isn't. Certain Golden Age books and titles, such as *Speed* and *Prize Comics*, are genuinely tough to find in any grade, while nearly all Silver and Bronze Age books are available plentifully. Of course demand is a huge driver. *Incredible Hulk* #181 and *Amazing Spider-Man* #129 are common, but there's endless demand for them!

The market's strong at the core, with an ever larger amount of material needing to be discounted, some to get it sold. Certified books remain very strong, although the standard multiples of *Guide* prices no longer apply. It's become more complex, as certain issues are preceived as harder to locate than others, driving the price on those upward. So, an *Amazing Spider-Man* #10 in CGC 9.2 will go for above *Guide* price, but not much, while *Amazing Spider-Man* #9 in CGC 9.2 will go for much more. Just doesn't turn up as often. Also page quality has become more important. We had an *Incredible Hulk* #181 CGC 9.8 with off-white pages. A copy in 9.8 with white pages had sold for $24,000, and a copy with off-white to white pages sold for $20,000. Our copy sold for $17,000. That's quite a difference for the same grade!

The Original Art market has been steadily growing. It's a bit of a star system. Regular decent pages will sell for very reasonable prices, while outstanding or historic pages sell for big $$. Covers and splash pages which are most "poster-like" sell for by far the most, and pages with good characters and action do very well. Artists such as Kirby, Ditko, Steranko, Smith, Wrightson, Wood lead the way.

Vincent Zurzolo, Frank Cwiklik & Rob Reynolds
Metropolis/ComicConnect.com

Vincent Zurzolo - ComicConnect.com / Metropolis Collectibles, Inc.

When I came into this business, I didn't know where it would take me or how things would work out. I was and continue to be a very competitive person. Every day I feel like I am climbing a mountain. Every day I am almost at the top, yet the next day the mountain is taller. My companies have accomplished some amazing things over the last few years. After selling the first $1,000,000.00 comic book in 2010 (*Action Comics* #1 CGC 8.0) and the most expensive comic ever sold for $1,500,000.00 (*Action Comics* #1 CGC 8.5), I challenged my partner, my employees and myself with the task of topping 2010. It was no easy task, but we did it! In 2011, we sold the first Silver Age comic book to break the million mark with the sale of *Amazing Fantasy* #15 CGC 9.6 for $1,100,000.00 and broke our own record with the sale of the 9.0 *Action Comics* #1 CGC 9.0 at $2,161,000.00. 2012 is coming and it will receive the same challenge. I am hopeful that by the time you read this market report, we will have changed the collecting world once more.

2011 will be remembered for the debut of the Atlantic

City Collection. It was one of the most exciting auctions of the year. The sales of the *Captain America Comics* #1 CGC 9.2 for $343,057.00 and the *Action Comics* #10 CGC 9.2 for $258,000.00 were astounding highlights. This original owner collection proved that there were still fresh, high-grade Golden Age collections out there that could change the comic collecting landscape.

The Silver Age market has dominated the headlines for a number of years. This is due to the popularity of the characters, the movies, the abundance of high-grade material, and of course, the record prices realized. This year we made news with the aforementioned *Amazing Fantasy* #15 9.6 sale, the *Amazing Fantasy* #15 CGC 9.4 at $325,000.00, the *Avengers* #1 CGC 9.6 for $250,000.00, the *X-Men* #1 CGC 9.6 for $200,000.00 and *Showcase* #4 CGC 9.2 for $100,000.00.

The Golden Age market continues to percolate and grow in its importance. Aside from the major six and seven figure priced sales mentioned in the preceding paragraphs, we have also noticed an increasing demand for low- and mid-priced Golden Age titles. We are seeing sales increases across many publishers and titles, not just Timely and DC. A growing number of astute collectors are buying these truly rare comic books. This is a trend I confidently expect to see more of in 2012.

© MAR

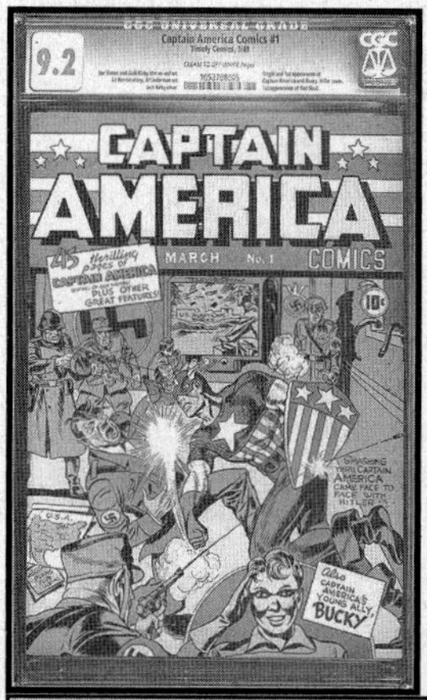

One of the highlights of the new Atlantic City Collection was this CGC-certified 9.4 copy of **Captain America Comics #1.**

One last incredibly important auction result to take note of is that of the first appearance of the original Captain Marvel in *Whiz* #1 CGC 6.0 for $176,007.000. Many have often said this book, whose character outsold Superman for years, was under-valued and under-appreciated. With this price realized, this is no longer the case. This is another indicator that the Golden Age of Comics has returned.

The Bronze Age has been affected in an adverse manner by the increase in the number of high-grade copies joining the census. I have found that the prices have plateaued to a certain extent, and stability and slight growth has been restored. I grew up during the Bronze Age of comics and never get tired of seeing super high grade copies of 1970s *Avengers* and *Green Lantern*. I know there are many people out there who feel the same way and continue to put Bronze Age runs together. Don't be afraid to do this. Enjoy, have fun, you will get some great deals and better yet, it will put a big smile on your face.

I sincerely want to thank every one of you who has made a purchase from us in the recent or distant past. You have given me a profession about which I am very passionate and something I am proud to do. In return, I will continue to do my very best to promote our hobby, and to expound upon its virtues as a true American art form, a dynamic form of entertainment and a valuable method of growing one's wealth. From the bottom of my heart, thank you all.

In closing, I'd like to share a little bit about my background. My parents came to the United States from Italy in the 1960s. They spoke very little English, had next to no money and were basically living in a cousin's basement sleeping on lawn furniture. My father worked three jobs washing dishes in restaurants and pizzerias all over New York City trying to build a future for his family. He learned how to make pizza and the very next day, got a job as a pizzaiolo. From there he learned how to butcher and cook classic southern Italian dishes. He saved and saved and eventually opened his own pizzeria in Brooklyn. From there he would open a number of well-received restaurants with names like Napoli, In Roma Di Notte, Il Pescatore and Villa Venezia. My mother, an amazing woman, great cook, seamstress and super home-maker, raised me and my two older brothers in Rockaway Beach, Queens. I share this story to give you an insight into who I am and where I come from. From a very early age, my parents instilled in me the idea that if you studied and worked hard, you could become anything you wanted in this great country of ours. I believe these are the key ingredients that have led to my success. Thanks mom and dad. And again, I thank all of you for your support and patronage.

Frank Cwiklik - Metropolis Collectibles, Inc.

I spend most of my days sitting in a wheely chair surrounded by boxes of old comics answering hundreds of emails and occasionally getting up to grab lunch or another stack of Golden Age bags. I do far less phone work now than I did when I first started, and the majority of my client contact comes via email or the website. Because of this, I have become very attuned to crowds and clientele at conventions, as these have become the few times I can really interact one-on-one in person with our busy customer base, and to make new contacts. It also means I notice big changes in interest and interaction with comics customers on the whole, as I only see them a few times a year and the little changes that other folks might miss become more pronounced to me. Here's what I've noticed, all of which are very positive for the vintage comics market.

First, the age and gender of vintage comics buyers is changing. In a market predominantly made up of males in their 30s through 50s, it really stands out when you have a number of women, both old and young, stopping by and buying books with knowledge and a clear sense of what they like and what comics will suit them, not to mention the influx of relatively younger buyers who are flush with their first real money and are looking to start collecting long-term. I made several new client contacts at Chicago and San

Diego this year, all women, who collect everything from Black Canary to St. John's titles, to Baker and Heath art, and who are all knowledgeable and ready to buy. The stereotype of the Golden and Silver Age comics collector (see: *The Simpsons*), never really accurate to begin with, is finally starting to crumble as these new buyers enter the market with confidence and enthusiasm. Much of this can be attributed to the second observation I've made this year...

The vintage comics market has penetrated the mainstream consciousness in a big way. Unlike the speculator boom of the '90s, when the cheap faddishness of modern collecting tarnished the perceptions and appearance of comic book collecting, the price tags of high-profile books and the professional appearance put forth through internet, TV and convention appearances, have made an indelible impact on the average person's perceptions of our business. Our COO, Vincent Zurzolo, has diligently made the rounds of major media outlets, giving a public face to the overall comics market that wipes out the misperceptions that have previously made it hard to attract collectors from other fields such as fine art or rare books. When I first started doing conventions some years ago (you kids get off my lawn), I would spend half my day at the booth fielding questions from people who had no idea of the value of the books, or waving away lookie-loos who would paw at the booth not knowing that they were touching thousands of dollars worth of material. What I saw this past year in San Diego, especially, but also in Chicago and New York, were hundreds of people stopping before our booth and quietly explaining to each other, as though they were in a library or museum, that these were the books they saw on CNN, or that they read about on *Scoop*, etc. The average person is now more likely to understand the value and significance of what we do and what we sell than at any time in our business' history. This is instrumental to the third point I've discovered this past year...

Everyone wants in. I have no less than a dozen new clients in our database who explicitly and specifically sought us out this past year to move their money into vintage comics, either for long-term investment or for pleasure, but usually both. The runaway success of high-profile books sold by us has attracted buyers who are looking for tangible investments that are not prey to the volatility of the stock market or real estate, and not choked by the erratic regulatory environment that is unnerving so many other markets and spooking investors. The new buyers coming in are impressed by the stability and simplicity of the comics market, and like having an asset that they not only understand, but that brings them great pleasure. Again, the newfound and hard-earned respect given to our field is the reason this is possible, and it hasn't happened overnight. One new client told me he loves the idea of simply having a book he really likes, keeping it tucked away, pulling it out to enjoy it, and knowing that when he's ready to sell, all he has to do is come to us, name a price, and we'll get it sold for him. (Yes, I know, there are a few extra steps in there, but you must admit it's easier than selling real estate. And more fun.)

Speaking of fun, this brings me to the last observation, which seems counterintuitive, but not really...

The pop culture monster that swallowed San Diego may not be such a monster after all. Every year, I hear a few older buyers or more determined comic nerds bemoan the size of San Diego or Chicago's pop culture areas, complaining that the comics have been forgotten. And yet, the number of calls I've gotten this year from clients, or emails, or messages over the site, mentioning that they saw us on their local news promoting one of the big cons, or that they got our card from our booth at Wizard or C2E2, or just new customers finding us through one of these big popular culture cons, tells me that the old-school comics booths are finding their way into their consciousness just as much as the enormous movie and TV booths are spreading across the sales floor. I'd always hoped that the increased attention from mainstream culture to the world of comics would translate into sales for our end of the business, and slowly but surely, it seems to be happening. I have a small group of new solid buyers who we only met because they were intrigued by the size and scale of the Chicago or San Diego or New York shows, and who came to check them out. Would I have met those buyers without their showing up to see an *Avengers* movie display or to see the Batmobile? Maybe, maybe not. What I can tell you is that without the media saturation that Reed, San Diego, and Wizard all attract for their shows, our business may not have been able to get the leg up on other collectibles that it has.

Speaking of conventions, an experiment Metropolis conducted in San Diego was one of the most enjoyable sales events we've organized yet, and one of the most successful. A longtime friend and client of Metropolis amassed an impressive mid- and high-grade Timely collection, including a full *Captain America* run and extensive runs of most other Timely titles like *All Winners*, *All Select*, *Human Torch*, *Marvel Mystery* and *USA Comics*. It was an awesome run of books, and knowing that we needed to give it the exposure it deserved, we brainstormed on how to make the biggest impact. Vincent knew that San Diego would be the ideal show at which to sell the books, but we took it much further, making it a full event, waiting until Preview Night of San Diego Con to reveal the books at both the show and on the website. It took some coordination and luck, as there was the risk that the books would fire too early on the site, or that technical glitches would make them available too late and books would be sold at the show before online buyers had a chance to grab them. Thankfully, I was able to stay on the phone with our Vice President Ben Smith at the office while our team pulled down the curtains on the display booth, and the sale went live simultaneously at San Diego and on MetropolisComics.com. The night went off without a hitch, as I pulled books from the wall as they sold on site, and removed books from site inventory as we sold them at the booth. There was a buzz at the con and a major frenzy ensured. I discovered later that some extremely eager Timely collectors were buying on their smart phones while standing by the booth in case one or the other method failed them!

The promotion, coordination and excitement that was generated led us to the best single-day con sales in our history, and nearly half the collection was sold within the first week. This made our client, who was in San Diego to watch the fun from a front row seat, very pleased indeed. It was one of the most rewarding evenings I've had in this business, and I'm now trying to come up with an even better opening-night event for next year!

Sales from the Super-Soldier collection generated enough heat to make the Wizard World Chicago show the strongest yet. In fact, many of the sales at Wizard Chicago this year were Timely sales, though there were some old standbys making strong showings, as Fiction House, EC, and even Prize titles sold very well, in both high grades and reader grades, showing that this con has become the go-to place for specialized and scholarly collectors looking for merchandise that might seem lost in the shuffle of key issues and high-grade auctions. I'd also note that our sales in general, both at shows and on our site, have reflected a return to more rare titles and publishers, and obscure Golden Age inventory that sat unjustly neglected for some years is now once again generating interest. Most of the books I brought to conventions per request this year tended to be "caviar" books, which are the kind I really enjoy seeing and selling, so it made me a very happy camper indeed.

As for the other two monster shows of the year, Big Apple, as always, is a hometown favorite that hearkens back to the glory days of Seuling shows and church-basement swap meets. Not that the sale of a 7.5 *Amazing Fantasy* #15 for $48,000 is anything to sniff at, so it's not like the Penn Plaza shows don't attract their fair share of killer sales. Again, strong sales of titles like *Hit Comics*, *Smash Comics*, and a *Silver Streak* #1 goes to prove that the classic Golden Age scarcities are coming back into play in an increasingly specialized and educated market.

New York Comic Con was, as always, an impressive and audience-gobbling show. We scored some impressive sales, including the Super Soldier copy of the ultra-scarce *All-American Comics* #61, *Plastic Man* #1 VF/NM and a solid 9.4 PGX *Incredible Hulk* #181. Again, at this show, we met serious buyers from all over the U.S. and overseas who came specifically because of the hype over record-breaking comics and the size of the convention, and who had not been buyers to that point. Something is working!

Finally, Reed's feisty and colorful upstart, C2E2, once again proved that Chicago can support a San Diego-sized con, and again, unexpected and unusual titles anchored our sales, with solid books from ACG, Quality, Better, and others. Of course, there was no shortage of terrific key sales, such as the ubiquitous *Amazing Fantasy* #15, this time selling in 5.5 CGC, plus the 9.8 Boston copy of *Captain America* #109, a really handsome *Journey Into Mystery* #83 in 8.5 CGC, and a nice *Fantastic Four* #20 in 9.4 CGC. We made many new contacts at this show thanks to strong prices and a general public awareness of the seriousness of the comics investing market.

I'd said last year that there was no one magic bullet for our business. The popularity and success of our web site, the changing nature of conventions, and the new customers resulting from both require us to think smart and adapt to a changing landscape. The excitement seen in our new clients, the media and "civilian" attention paid to our business, and the long-term goodwill and business created, make everything worthwhile. It's my hope that some of the folks reading this now are the new collectors who've been enticed into the market by these changes and successes. If so, welcome. The best is yet to come! For those of you who've been collecting for years through thick and thin, congratulations. I think we've all finally hit the big time. As always, feel free to drop me a line at orders@metropoliscomics.com or call 1-800-229-METRO extension 10.

Robert Reynolds - ComicConnect.com

When ComicConnect.com launched in the summer of 2007, we had no idea that the business would one day hold the records for the three most expensive comic book sales in history. On November 30, 2011, we set the world record for a comic book sale with *Action Comics* #1 CGC 9.0 at $2,161,000, beating out our previous world record of a CGC 8.5 copy for $1,500,000, and making it the first and only comic book to ever break the $2 million dollar mark. This was not ComicConnect.com's only 7-figure sale for the record books in 2011. Earlier in March, we set the record for the most expensive Silver Age comic book ever sold with the highest graded copy of *Amazing Fantasy* #15 CGC 9.6 for $1,100,000.00. Our quarterly Event Auctions, our Monthly Auctions, and our fixed price marketplace have become a destination for smart collectors and dealers alike.

In April of this year, there was much excitement and the industry was abuzz when we helped recover the stolen copy of *Action Comics* #1 that belonged to our client, actor Nicolas Cage. Eleven years ago, the comic was stolen out of a display vault at his house after a party. ComicConnect.com was contacted by a California entrepreneur hoping to make a few bucks buying the contents of auctioned-off storage units. He had stumbled across a once-in-a-lifetime find: a high-grade copy of *Action Comics* #1. Unfortunately for the California man, it was THE Action Comics #1—the same one that was stolen in 2000. Stephen Fishler, our CEO, flew to California and recovered the comic with the help of the LAPD.

2011 also saw ComicConnect.com's addition of four-color print catalogs to promote our online Event Auctions. The positive feedback we received from both buyers and sellers was overwhelming. Collectors loved having something tangible in their hands to help them pinpoint the comics and original art lots they wanted to bid upon. Consignors were overjoyed to have the benefit of a print catalog, but still only pay a 10% seller's commission with no buyer's premiums. The debut of our auction catalogs has truly created a "cake and eat it too" phenomenon helping to make ComicConnect.com a very viable selling option for collectors everywhere.

This year ComicConnect.com debuted the Atlantic City Collection as well as the Oregon Collection in our August and November Event Auctions. The Atlantic City Collection was comprised of some of the highest graded Golden Age Comics such as *Action Comics* #10 CGC 9.0, *Action Comics* #13 CGC 9.2, *Action Comics* #19 CGC 9.4 and *Detective Comics* #25 CGC 9.0. I was blown away when I saw the comics in person. It's almost easier to believe the owner had a time machine. For a collector to have kept these amazing comics in such pristine shape and off the market for 70 years is simply incredible.

High grade Silver Age DC collectors were also happy to see ComicConnect.com's introduction of The Oregon Collection: a 1950's Superman-centric collection kept in perfect climate conditions. Collectors know that it is nearly impossible to find this material in high grade with superior page quality. The collection contained both the highest graded first appearance of Supergirl in *Action Comics* #252 CGC 9.2 as well as the highest graded *Superman's Girlfriend Lois Lane* #1 CGC 8.0. Professional graders who had a chance to view the collection in person described the comics as "stunning" and "freakishly well-preserved."

For the happy surprise of the year, on December 3rd, *Whiz Comics* #2 (#1) CGC 6.0 hammered at an astounding $176,007. The comic features the first appearance and origin of Captain Marvel. SHAZAM!

©FAW

No matter the economy, blue chip keys like **Whiz Comics #2 (#1)** are always in demand.

ComicConnect.com sold fifteen comics each for over $100,000 in 2011 including five copies of *Action Comics* #1, four copies of *Amazing Fantasy* #15 and two *Superman* #1's.

Noteworthy Golden Age comic sales:
Action Comics #1 CGC 9.0 $2,161,000
Action Comics #1 CGC 4.5 $345,000
Action Comics #1 CGC 1.8 $110,000
Action Comics #1 CGC 1.8 $110,000
Action Comics #1 CGC 1.5 R $63,000
Action Comics #10 CGC 9.0 $258,000 Atlantic City Copy
Action Comics #13 CGC 9.2 $185,000 Atlantic City Copy
Action Comics #13 CGC 8.0 $67,435 Larson Copy
Action Comics #19 CGC 9.4 $79,000 Atlantic City Copy
Action Comics #20 CGC 9.0 $60,000
Action Comics #252 CGC 9.2 $25,500 Oregon Copy
Batman #1 CGC 9.2 R $37,000
Batman #5 CGC 9.4 $30,000
Captain America Comics #1 CGC 9.2 $343,057 Atlantic City Copy
Captain America Comics #1 CGC 7.0 $90,000 Super Soldier Collection
Detective Comics #27 CGC 8.5 R $105,000
Detective Comics #33 CGC 9.2 $194,000 Atlantic City Copy
Flash Comics #1 CGC 9.0 $168,000 Atlantic City Copy
Master Comics #21 CGC 9.6 $35,000 Church Copy
Special Edition Comics #1 CGC 9.8 $30,003 Allentown Copy
Superman #1 CGC 5.5 $214,000 Jerry Siegel's Personal Copy
Superman #1 CGC 5.0 $148,000
Superman #3 CGC 9.0 $33,500 Atlantic City Copy
Superman #14 CGC 9.0 $26,600 Rockford Copy
Walt Disney Comics & Stories #1 CGC 8.5 $25,500

ComicConnect.com had a run of success with keys and first appearances, as sales records were smashed each month. March brought the sale of the *Amazing Fantasy* #15 CGC 9.6 at $1.1 Million. In May, we sold Flash's first appearance, *Showcase* #4 CGC 9.2 for $100,000. Coming off the *Amazing Fantasy* #15 world record sale, a CGC-certified 9.4 copy of *Amazing Fantasy* #15 sold at $325,000 in August of this year. No matter the economy, blue chip keys are always in demand.

Noteworthy Silver, Bronze, and Modern comic sales:
Amazing Fantasy #15 CGC 9.4 $345,000
Amazing Fantasy #15 CGC 9.0 $151,555
Amazing Fantasy #15 CGC 8.5 $110,000
Amazing Fantasy #15 CGC 8.0 $70,000
Amazing Fantasy #15 CGC 6.5 $29,600 Stan Lee Sig.
Avengers #1 CGC 9.2 $60,000
Avengers #4 CGC 9.4 $28,500
Fantastic Four #1 CGC 9.4 $300,000
Journey into Mystery #83 CGC 8.5 $26,500
Showcase #4 CGC 9.2 $100,000
Tales of Suspense #39 CGC 9.4 $130,000
X-Men #1 CGC 9.6 $200,000
X-Men #1 CGC 9.0 $28,000
X-Men #2 CGC 9.6 $23,500

We enjoyed several high quality consignments in the original art section of our auctions with original *Peanuts* strips, Golden Age art, and original Will Eisner pieces.

Noteworthy Original Art sales include:
Bob Kane Original Batman Art $8,600
Flash Comics #72 Page $5,050
Ghost Rider #8 Cover $5,500
Peanuts Sunday Page $29,500
Peanuts Daily Strip $15,200
Spirit Magazine #28 Cover $7,755
Superman's Girlfriend Lois Lane #95 Cover $7,300

With each Event Auction consisting of roughly 1,500 lots spread over five nights, space is extremely limited to just the best material and consignments. It's been an incredible few years for this company and it feels like it has only begun.

Again, my thanks go out to all of our customers and consignors. I can't do this without you and I am forever grateful for your participation. To sell through ComicConnect.com, e-mail me at support@comicconnect.com or call me at 212.895.3999. I am ready for more amazing consignments.

THE WAR REPORT

by Matt Ballesteros & the War Correspondents

Richard Evans, Andy Greenham, and Mick Rabin

Welcome to the fourth edition of the War Report! A comprehensive chronicle specifically focused on the War comic genre; composed by devoted collectors, enthusiasts, and subject matter experts who have toiled to provide you with an annual account of the activities within the War comic book marketplace. The report includes ruminations on the creative forces behind the War comic classification, speculations on the medium's collectability, and opinions on the War comic field as a whole.

I want to thank returning War Correspondents Richard Evans, Andy Greenham, and Mick Rabin. Three renowned and knowledgeable veterans of the genre, whose overall eruditions and contributions give this report substance, and more importantly aid in qualifying it as a bona fide resource for the collecting industry. Should you ever want direct input from any of these authoritative experts (among other War connoisseurs); I encourage you to visit the "War Thread" on the CGC Forum.

As we do each year, this report typically covers topics such as market highlights and books on the move, discussions about characters or the artists that created them, deliberations on the actual stories and the art that drives them, War comic rankings in the marketplace, and other related subjects. This year, we also endeavor to test out a new feature – a short segment that will dabble in investment opportunities from our point of view. We hope you enjoy all our submissions and welcome your feedback on any part of our report.

© DC

Definition of a "War Book" Very, Very Briefly Revisited

We characterized War comics as "Stories centered on the military, which is involved in major armed conflicts" (*i.e., no Cold War, police actions, spy stories, etc.*)

We eliminated war stories with super-heroes *(by employing the notion that "a war story with a super-hero is by definition a 'fantasy' story")*

We defined classifications for specific war themes. We selected "War Battle Tales" (*i.e., stories that were predominantly centered on characters engulfed in battle).* Therefore, for now, we purged classifications such as War Adventure, War Propaganda, and Tragedy in Wartime, etc.

We categorized two main comic book ages:

- The Golden Age
- The Atom/Silver Age/Bronze Age

If you would like an in-depth look at our comprehensive classification process, I encourage you to pick up a copy of the *Overstreet Comic Book Price Guide* #39, #40 or simply visit *www.warcomicreport.com* for more details.

News from the Front - A Market Report

We have beguiling intel from the market. If you had the opportunity to read our report from last year you may recall that we talked about a softening in the market. A drop in middle and low grade books that we attributed not to economic reasons, or lack of interest in the genre, but to the fact that the market was suddenly flooded with a greater supply of low to mid grade War books (an opinion that we still steadfastly hold). What we were interested in understanding however, was how the market would behave through the ensuing year. In short, the fledgling collecting year began much like the previous year ended: low to mid grade War books had reached a plateau in supply and demand and high grade keys were still fetching moderately high prices. Overall, there is, was, and still is one constant—buyers are gunning after books in all war titles across the board: DC, Marvel, EC, Atlas, Charlton, Fiction House, St. John… you name it.

The War niche, however, was temporarily affected by yet another pivotal event. For a second time in five years, Keith Marlow decided to unload his extensive high grade War collection. Surprisingly, Keith had managed to amass a heady collection of high grade key books (we wonder when the man sleeps). However, this time his collection, primarily made up of DC War, was larger and the key books (which were great in number) were all, for the most part, highest census across the board. How he accomplished the feat of acquiring these pedigree books in half a decade is still a wonder to us hardcore War books collectors.

Nevertheless, and back to the point, right in the middle of a year that had seemed to level off, this pedigree collection gets dropped on the market's proverbial lap courtesy of Heritage Auctions. As aforementioned, this stockpile dwarfed his previous collection not only in size but in overall grade. OK, in most cases we were only talking about a half grade or full grade differential, but in our niche, where a 9.0 is highest census, a full grade tick is a tremendous upgrade. What I'm getting at is that this auction was a market first for our genre. Interestingly, this auction coincided with contemporaneous sales of additional key books through ComicLink, eBay, and other well known sales channels. It was a gold rush. Consequently, what transpired was quite fascinating....

Although, Keith recouped a moderate gross return on his books overall, individual sales were wildly divergent. There were some amazing prices actualized and there were some downright and surprising disasters. From our point of view only the prime key books and the high-grade/low-census books garnered exceptionally formidable prices, the rest took a sizeable hit. Now, for the books that experienced losses, they were still commanding four figures on average (so, these aren't inexpensive books), but compared to where they stood in the market the previous year, they were underperforming as a whole. Obviously, the War Correspondents were watching closely as this event unfolded. More importantly, we were able to circle back and study the phenomenon, reviewing the events of this and other near simultaneous auctions, evaluating prices, comparing results against census reports and discussing amongst ourselves. After the usual deliberation on our part, we came to this inevitable conclusion: **the existing market could not bear the weight of multiple auctions and the sale of such a large collection all at one time.**

After all, only so many hardcore DC War enthusiasts exist that can play at the dollar level that these types of books command. It's not that there wasn't wide general interest. The interest was there, and every book sold for higher prices than anyone would have believed several years ago. But too many high-end DC War books were released at once for each to extract its full maturated potential. This is very useful tactical information for us long term collectors, and certainly if you understand its impact, valuable intel for those of you toying with the idea of getting into the War comic market.

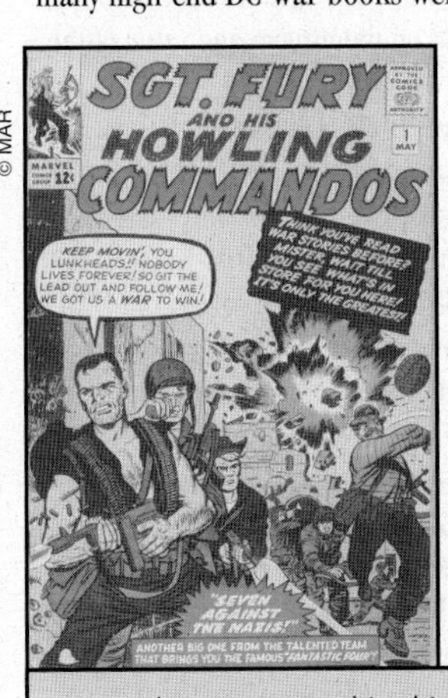

Interest has not waned in this key Marvel War book, *Sgt. Fury and His Howling Commandos #1*.

Let's not forget, a good number of individual sales still broke every record of our genre and transcended the values and prices comparable to key superhero books (more on that later in this report). Nevertheless, we witnessed a veritable brouhaha of auctions unfold, showering books down onto our genre. And when it was done, we were left wondering how the War category was affected overall.

Consequently, after watching the market attentively for the ensuing six months after the auctions, we noticed something that we have not seen or experienced since before 2007. We had our answer... **There seems to be little to nothing left**. I repeat—a complete dearth of high grade War books remain in the market (particularly high grade DC War). Is there anything left? Ironically, after such an onslaught of books hit the market a mere nine months ago, we feel that there really isn't. Certainly a new outcrop could emerge at some point, but for now the market has in essence gobbled everything up. The fact is, these auctions did such a good job of gaining a vast purchasing audience, we feel that the War books in those auctions and sales have been spread out among a greater number of collectors, not lumped in concentrated pockets. Our conclusion: the likelihood of a large mass of high grade War books hitting the market again in the next few years and in the same manner is highly unlikely—possible, but unlikely. You can't discount a new major find or other anomalous factors of course; but, this past year was a doozy.

So, after all that transpired, we sat gazing out into the market, and what did we see as the net result of this depleted market? This is where we got our final elucidation: With a market now barren of high grade War, **when anything of notable caliber does appear—it goes for big, big, big dollars**. That makes sense of course with more buyers and fewer high grade books to go around. Trolling our typical War book sources and channels, it is evident that only a few gems remain available—and when they do go on the block, we witness fireworks! This has been the case for weeks now. Whether it continues or not will certainly be dependent on many factors. But at least you have our opinion as to why.

Our recommendation: shop carefully, try to find unslabbed copies of key books, and hang on to them. If you are in the market to sell ... well, this is a very opportune moment to do so. Our recommendation, however, is to sell in small controlled bursts. In that manner, you will maximize your return. Good luck out there.

Other Battlefield Ops

Sgt. Marvel: Last year we pointed out that *Sgt. Fury* #1 was doing extremely well, with sales for CGC 8.5s and 9.0s commanding $6k to $10k per book. Well, we are pleased to report that interest in this key Marvel war hero has not waned. Since our last report, there have been numerous sales that ran the spectrum of prices, solidifying its importance to the niche and the overall comic hobby. Although there were some outright steals (like an 8.0 finding a new home for less than $3K), there were also monumental prices achieved for the book. A notable sale to mention was the auction of one of the top census 9.4s which hammered in at nearly $30K! Wow! A pretty explosive price considering that there are four more 9.4 copies of the book on census! Nevertheless, Sgt. Fury aficionados have spoken—the book is hot. The War Correspondents still feel that *Sgt. Fury* #1 has not found its true value rhythm however, and we may see some varying sales recorded over the next year or so. It will be interesting to witness if it maintains its intensity, or even better, surpasses current expectations. We'll see and compare notes next year.

With all the interest in #1, a couple other *Sgt. Fury* issues have inevitably gained some momentum, particularly issue

#2 and, of course, the infamous #13 Captain America crossover. We anticipate that these books will continue to perform well overall, so we will also be keeping an eye on them.

It must be mentioned however that mid-grade copies of the entire *Sgt. Fury* run are available by the veritable truckload. There seems to be an endless supply available everywhere. We of course feel that this may potentially produce an adverse halo effect on the overall value of the title, but perhaps the singular gems of the run can still hold their own. Nevertheless, if you are interested in the title for investment sake, we recommend sticking with the three aforementioned issues or only ultra high grade copies of the remaining title. Otherwise, benefit from the cornucopia of low grade *Fury* books out there and get yourself an entire run to read and enjoy.

Lifting the Fog of War

A benefit of writing the War Report is our opportunity to correspond with Bob Overstreet directly about our avocation. In one such communication the topic arose regarding the descriptions related to Sgt Rock's first appearance. There has been heavily conflicting conjecture on this subject in the past and we jointly felt it would be good to get to the bottom of the matter. Bob had his suspicions about the precision of the existing information, and welcomed our ideas on the subject. Consequently, Bob invited us to help redefine and illuminate details on Sgt Rock's first appearance in the succession of books credited with the character's origination. I am of course referring to the shroud of mystery surrounding the first "true" appearance of Rock in *G.I. Combat* #68, *Our Army at War* #81, #82 and #83—the issues recognized with the distinction of directly accounting for his origin.

It has been our pleasure and honor to write the War Report these last few years (and we are equally thrilled to contribute to the advancement of the comic hobby in whatever capacity). Thus, when tasked with such a commission, we proceed cautiously with the suggestion of any wide sweeping modifications. The fact remains, however, that some confusion persists in the industry regarding this matter, and we feel honored (and duty-bound) to bring much needed clarity to the subject. When discussing the matter with Bob, we proposed presenting him with evidence that would support our findings in the actualization of the story arc and on how those story arcs may impact values on the books. He was graciously amenable to our thoughts and charged us to move forward.

I understand that Sgt. Rock as a character receives a tremendous amount of attention from this report and from other war collectors in general. It's not that there aren't other memorable and key figures that grace the pages of alternative and exceptional war tiles (e.g., Sgt. Fury, Don Winslow, Enemy Ace, Iron Corporal, Jeb Stuart, The Unknown Soldier and many more). It's just that compared to Rock, no other character in the War comic genre is so equally indelibly imprinted within the psyche of War comic fans and in pop culture as whole. That said, Sgt. Fury is certainly giving Rock a run for his money lately, but it will take years of exposure before Fury could garner anywhere near the same recognition and status. At present, Sgt. Rock is unequivocally the most important character in the entirety of the War comic genre (Golden, Silver or Bronze Age). Ergo, among other factors, Sgt. Rock's prominence largely influences the growing popularity of the War genre within the overall comic industry. It is for this reason that Bob and the War Correspondents feel it essential to share what we have definitively identified as Rock's true originations, and in which comic book issues they manifested.

In short, the team went to work. We researched and itemized any book credited with a Sgt. Rock prototype or early appearance (including minor prototypes such as *All-American Men of War* #28 or *G.I. Combat* #56). After compiling a complete list we pulled out and reread each of the books carefully, making notes on key details panel by panel. We contemporaneously dug into any historical data that we could get our hands on to ensure we were considering any anomalous factors (including articles, interviews with the creators, and published subject matter expert opinions).

Our threshold inquiry in this process was to satisfy ourselves that the books most significantly tied to Sgt. Rock's first appearance— *i.e.*, *G.I. Combat* #68, *Our Army at War* #81, #82 and #83—were indeed the best, most appropriate and undeniable sources of Rock's origins. That we concluded they were should be of no surprise to anyone, but it did bear scrutiny as we wanted to be thorough in our research. What is far more interesting is the data we compiled regarding these four key books. Here again, while ardent War book collectors will not likely be shocked to read what emerged from our efforts, one or two important factors have come to light that may have an impact on the esteem and value of the books overall. Here is what we found:

• ***G.I. Combat* #68 – "The Rock"** (Jan 1959). A character named Jimmy referred to as "The Rock" appears as a sergeant on the cover, but as a private in the story. And although DC later reprints the story in early 1972 (see *OAAW* #242), editors have to modify the reprinted issue to fit DC's needs by editing Jimmy's name out. In brief, *G.I. Combat* #68 is definitely a key Sgt. Rock prototype, but undeniably not his first true appearance.

• ***Our Army at War* #81 – "The Rock of Easy"** (April 1959). Three months after *G.I. Combat* #68, OAAW #81 features a story with a character named "Sgt. Rocky", who is referred to as "The Rock of Easy". However, Sgt Rocky is a "4th grade rate" sergeant (only has three chevrons / stripes) and not the Master Sergeant we all know the true Sgt. Rock to be. Nevertheless, with the editor's promise of more stories of a "...Rock-like Sergeant", it is clear that the creative team has something in mind, making *OAAW* #81 a significant prototype issue.

• ***Our Army at War* #82 – "Hold up Easy"** (May 1959). Appearance of a character named Sgt. Rock ...Wait! Appearance of "a" Sgt. Rock?! What does that mean? And why isn't this issue credited with his "first" appearance? Well, in this final Kanigher and Drucker prototype amalgam, we get a character that is still short of the Kanigher and Kubert creation, and who appears in a supporting "motivator" role to the main characters of the story. Moreover, and of particular significance, he appears again only as the prototyped 4th grade rate sergeant (three stripes/chevrons). Nonetheless, it is important to state that the character does actually physically "appear" in the issue, and is not merely appearing "in name only" as widely believed in the industry. With this clarification, his key prototype appearance in six panels in the six-page story "Hold up Easy" should have a considerable impact on the importance of this book from this point forward.

• ***Our Army at War* #83 – "The Rock and Wall"** (June 1959). As a demonstratively key determinant, Sgt. Rock is finally introduced as the main character of the title story, and more importantly, as a "Master Sergeant" (six stripes—three chevrons and three rockers) by what is the 1st actual collaboration on Rock between creators Kanigher and Kubert (who are credited as the true progenitors of the defined character). Further, readers are finally given the 1st definitive narration, as compared to all the other previous issues, that unequivocally defines the "Rock of Easy" as Sgt. Rock in the actual storyline. All these key elements combined make *OAAW* #83 the indisputable issue to furnish the 1st "true appearance" of Sgt. Rock.

• ***Our Army at War* #84 – "Laughter on Snakehead Hill"** (July 1959). Story advances true Sgt. Rock continuity in the 13-page title story featuring Sgt. Rock and Easy Co. And with this being his 2nd true appearance, it is a significant issue.

Not that we didn't already know of the existence of this key data, but now we had these facts distinctly memorialized. The task then was to put those details in a format that Bob could use for the *OCBPG*. One matter that was important to address as we conveyed this information was how we saw the chronicling of the prototype books *GIC* #68, *OAAW* #81 and *OAAW* #82. The fact is, that while each of the power trio have fluctuated in prominence over the years (with *G.I. Combat* #68 originally being credited with Rock's first appearance, a credit that was then later bestowed on *Our Army at War* #81, and now *OAAW* #82's significant relevance has come more into light), the trait that they all share is that each leads up to the true first appearance in *OAAW* #83. Stated differently, while on their own, each is fairly important for various reasons;—they are ALL key **prototype** issues that lead up to the 1st definitive Rock in *OAAW* #83. Once we reached that conclusion, we compiled the remaining key descriptors for Bob to utilize as he saw fit for the price guide. Below is what we produced in list form:

***G.I. Combat* #68 – "The Rock"**
- Sgt. Rock Prototype (Jan 1959)
- Part of lead-up trio to 1st definitive Sgt. Rock
- A character named Jimmy is referred to as "The Rock" (nickname)
- Jimmy is portrayed as a sergeant on the cover and a private in the story
- Mythos includes Jimmy as a pre-war boxer (similar to Frank Rock's past)
- DC later edits Jimmy's name out and reprints story in *OAAW* #242
- Art by Kubert and story by Kanigher
- Editor – Kanigher

***Our Army at War* #81 – "The Rock of Easy"**
- Sgt. Rock Prototype (April 1959)
- Part of lead-up trio to 1st definitive Sgt. Rock
- Main character is referred to as "The Rock of Easy"
- Story features main character named "Sgt. Rocky"
- Sgt. Rocky is a "4th grade rate" sergeant (three stripes/chevrons)
- Editor's closing notes promises more stories of "...Rock-like Sergeant"
- Art by Andru & Esposito and story by Haney
- Editor – Kanigher

***Our Army at War* #82 – "Hold up Easy"**
- 1st Appearance of a Sgt. Rock (May 1959)
- Part of lead-up trio to 1st definitive Sgt. Rock
- Sgt. Rock character appears as a "4th grade rate" sergeant (three stripes/chevrons)
- Sgt. Rock character appears in a supporting role throughout the storyline
- In a supporting role, Sgt. Rock character plays as a motivator to main characters
- Sgt. Rock character appears in six panels throughout six page story
- Art by Drucker and story by Haney
- Editor – Kanigher

***Our Army at War* #83 – "The Rock and the Wall"**
- 1st true appearance of Sgt. Rock (June 1959)
- Sgt. Rock is finally introduced as a Master Sergeant (three chevrons and three rockers)
- Sgt. Rock is the main character and focus of storyline
- 1st actual Sgt. Rock collaboration between creators Kanigher and Kubert
- 1st demonstrative narration "Hear...about the Rock of Easy Co?" "You Mean Sgt. Rock?"
- Narration sustains "The man in Easy who was... it's Rock... Sgt. Rock"
- Art by Kubert and story by Kanigher
- Editor – Kanigher

***Our Army at War* #84 – "Laughter on Snakehead Hill"**
- 2nd appearance of Sgt. Rock (July 1959)
- 13 page title story features Sgt. Rock and Easy Co.
- Story advances true Sgt. Rock continuity
- Sgt Rock is referred to as "Sgt. Rock" and "The Rock of Easy"
- Art by Novick and story by Kanigher
- Editor – Kanigher

We hope you found this segment intriguing and we look forward to seeing how our data is not only utilized by

Overstreet, but how the market reacts over time to our assertions and our suppositions.

Taking Cover

We are very fortunate to have Andy Greenham in our ranks. He is a specialist who truly fights to keep the genre thriving and you can witness his efforts directly on the CGC Forums. Thanks to him the boards have been treated to several War comic "best cover polls" over the years that have aided in putting crosshairs on the most coveted War comic covers in the genre. This year was no exception. Utilizing willing and contributing members of the forum, Andy organized and moderated the polling of an entire new 2012 poll. This year however there was a twist. Because every poll thus far had washtone covers dominating the field, he disallowed them in this latest poll. His request was simple. Using the guidelines of what we deem a "War book"—no superheroes, etc.— he asked voters to nominate the top 100+ War comic covers and then pare them down to the best. What you see below are the top 10 issues from the poll, and it's great to see so many Atlas books make the list and an EC war book topping it out! Better yet, you can now use this as a great cheat sheet for chasing down what will most likely be highly sought after cool War cover books. Happy recon missions!

2012 COOL WAR COVER POLL RESULTS

1st - *Two-Fisted Tales* #30 (EC)
2nd - *G. I. Combat* #46 (DC)
3rd - *Star Spangled War Stories* #81 (DC)
4th - *Star Spangled War Stories* #138 (DC)
5th - *War Comics* #11 (Atlas)
6th - *Battlefront* #15 (Atlas)
7th - *War Comics* #23 (Atlas)
8th (tied) - *Navy Action* #2 (Atlas)
8th (tied) - *Our Army at War* #70 (DC)
8th (tied) - *Star Spangled War Stories* #67 (DC)

A Medal of Honor for *Our Army at War* #83

Yes, we are spotlighting this book again. My apologies to non-DC War collectors, but the impact this book has had on the entire genre is too important not to spotlight. It is a comic that, whether you are a fan of DC War or not, continues to do its part in bringing deserved attention to our niche of the hobby. It is clear that the market agrees. *OAAW* #83 is the reigning King of the War comic genre. This is supported by the fact that in the last 12 months we witnessed incredible leaps in prices actualized for the key book—regardless of its grade!

The most significant sale being that of Keith's CGC 8.0 copy sold via Heritage in November 2011. There was great speculation as to what price it would grab, as mid-grade issues were performing incredibly well prior to the year-end auction. I don't believe, however, that anyone could have predicted the book would bring in nearly $17,000! This even had us hardcore War collectors shell-shocked, especially since it is still 2nd to the CGC 9.0 copy on the census! Furthermore, ensuing sales on ANY grade of the book have continued to go for way over *Guide*. Nonetheless, we are incredibly pleased that this very important book is receiving highly warranted action and interest.

Recent confirmed sales figures since our last report:
Our Army At War #83 CGC 8.0 $17,000
Our Army At War #83 CGC 7.5 $9,600
Our Army At War #83 CGC 7.0 Qualified $967
Our Army At War #83 CGC 6.0 $1,600
Our Army At War #83 CGC 5.5 $1,100
Our Army At War #83 CGC 4.5 $2,350
Our Army At War #83 CGC 4.0 $1,135
Our Army At War #83 CGC 4.0 $900
Our Army At War #83 CGC 3.0 $710
Our Army At War #83 CGC 2.5 $480
Our Army At War #83 CGC 1.8 $500

All these, along with a few equally commanding sales that we did not list, truly support the notion that *Our Army at War* #83 and the 1st true appearance of Sgt. Rock is a key book in the annals of the overall comic book market. More importantly, these sales show that the book is consistently getting prices that make it a long term winner and that the recent larger-scale sales are no anomaly.

© WMG

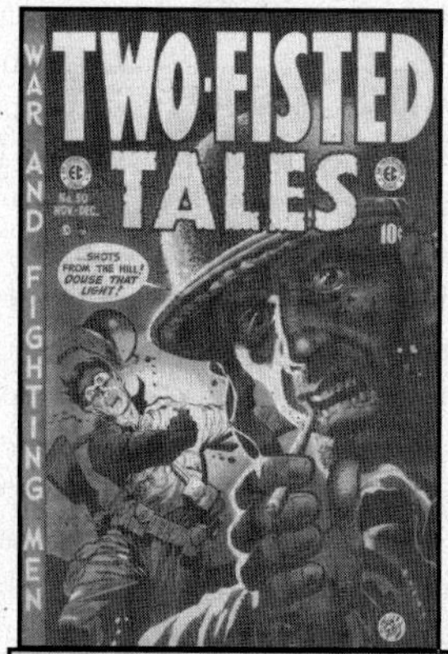

Two-Fisted Tales #30, the well-deserved winner of the 2012 Cool War Cover Poll. Art by Jack Davis.

And although #83 is making big noise in the market, relatively few #83s are for sale (as it is a fairly difficult book to find in general). A good example of its rarity is the fact that since the high profile sale of the CGC 8.0 copy in Nov 2011, only a handful of books have been slabbed and added to the CGC census—This is the opposite phenomenon of what one normally sees, as when a book becomes an obvious overnight powerhouse in the market, typically the census numbers soar in the subsequent months. In this case, other than two books, there have been maybe less than 10 low grade copies added to the census ranks. In sum, as far as we can tell, other than a single CGC 7.5 and a lone 6.0, nothing else submitted has received a higher grade than a CGC 3.5. A tough book indeed!

When considering all I just mentioned, you may now want to contemplate this: When put side by side to comparable super-hero books, *OAAW* #83 not only holds its own, but quite frankly outpaces a good number of the top 20 Silver Age books listed by the *Guide*. When you look at what the market is garnering for super-hero books of equal grade and then measure that against the current *OCBPG* Top 20 list, you will see that the book is at least in contention with *Showcase* #22 (ranked 12th in 2011) and, dare we say, is quite possibly approaching the performance of *Brave and the Bold* #28 (ranked 9th in 2011). OK, we know that this is not going to happen overnight, that the comic will need continued performance over the next few years, and that Bob Overstreet will need to carefully scrutinize its market growth and significance… But, we strongly feel that this book is merely a few years away from making the top 20 list in some manner. Watch out super-hero books - a War comic is invading!

The Spoils of War

As War comic enthusiasts we are asked some fairly similar questions every year: "What is your favorite title or series?" "What do you feel are the top 3 War books?" "Which War book do you think has the best cover?" And of course, there is the often repeated "Is this a good investment?"

Well, with this being our fourth year producing the War Report, we felt we may dare broach the subject of potential investment strategies. It's not that the "News from the Front" segment isn't filled with our opinions on how the genre is fairing overall in the comic book market. But here, we are specifically spotlighting a book or two that we feel are very good buys for the enthusiast who may be dabbling with the idea of a potential return on their purchase.

Colossal Disclaimer: THE INFORMATION PROVIDED IN THIS SEGMENT MAY BE WHOLLY INACCURATE. NONE OF THE WRITERS, CONTRIBUTORS, OR PUBLISHERS OF THIS REPORT CAN BE RESPONSIBLE FOR THE ACCURACY OF THIS INFORMATION OR FOR HOW YOU USE THIS INFORMATION, NONE ARE FINANCIAL OR INVESTMENT ADVISORS AND NONE CAN PREDICT HOW THE MARKETPLACE WILL ULTIMATELY VALUE THESE BOOKS. USE AT YOUR OWN RISK.

These are merely the opinions of seasoned War comic collectors. We are not financial analysts, we are not soothsayers, and we are obviously biased to our genre. We urge you to use caution when taking heed to any of our investment opinions.

OK, on to our prognostication…

This first statement is going to seem rather obvious. Although there may be a hidden exception, most superior investment books will likely be a known key book of some nature. So, I don't think we are going to surprise anyone here with a filler issue from a title. Rather, we will spotlight a gem that we feel has the potential to move positively.

Long Term Return

• ***Don Winslow* #1 (Four Color Comics - Series 1 nn (#2) (Dell, 1939)** – a Golden Age character and series that has not yet had a chance to blossom to its full potential. Although not heavily sought after, we feel that the character and series helped pave the way to war and war adventure lines in the ensuing years. It's not an easy book to find, but if you do and if you have patience, this issue should bring you back a small return in 5+ years.

Don Winslow #1 has plenty of long term investment potential.

• ***Our Army At War* #100** – Also a tough book to get, so that will be your first problem, but we believe the market does not yet reflect nor understand the substance and rich potential of this book. Even low grade copies would be a good investment here. Obviously your return will be commensurate with the grade level of the book. But, we see this book steadily gaining momentum over the next 4 to 5 years.

• ***Our Army At War* #83** – obvious pick. Yet, with the dollar values this book is bringing in, it is still a costly investment. We feel strongly about the inherent and enduring growth of this book, but you may have to sit on it for 2-3+ years before you can get a solid return. Unless of course you find a low to moderate deal on a raw copy… then your return will be immediately worth bragging about.

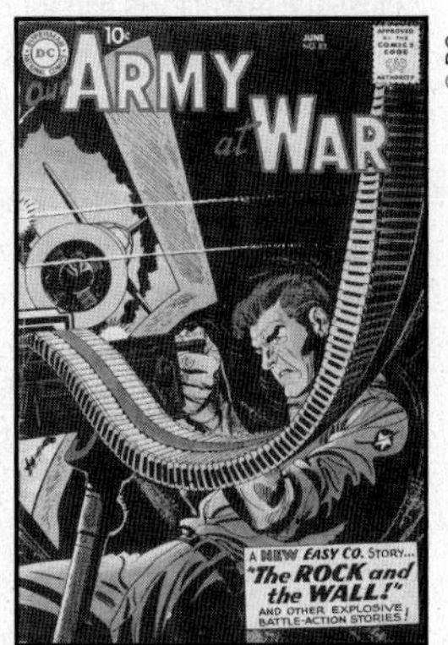

Short Term Return

• ***Our Army At War* #82** – This is the spotlight pick of this report. If you have not read our segment in this report on the classification of Sgt. Rock's first appearance, take a moment and read above. It in essence lays down the foundation as to why we think this book is such an incredible buy. Part of the benefit of this report is that we are cleaning the rafters of misnomers, and because this is still early in our crusade we could be bringing to center stage a book that has been woefully misunderstood, giving it the most potential to climb aggressively. Bottom-line, for such an important and pivotal book, in our opinion, it is simply greatly undervalued.

First of all, it is the opinion of the War Correspondents that *OAAW* #82 holds as much weight, value and importance in the incubation of the Sgt. Rock character as *G.I. Combat* #68 and *OAAW* #81, one could even argue that it may even be a bit stronger if you consider that it **IS** the **first** appearance of a character named *Sgt Rock*, as opposed to #81's "prototyped" *Sgt. Rocky*.

As you may have known, or now know, there has been a misconception in the market for many years about *OAAW* #82, that in our eyes has reduced this book's true potential. I'm of course referring to the accepted concept that the issue was the - *1st Sgt. Rock appearance, **in name only**..."* Where in actuality, Sgt Rock physically appears six different times in the six-page story *"Hold up Easy"*. This is a fairly fundamental difference. And this key differentiator should have a strong impact on its value.

By the way, if you compare this unique circumstance to say, Wolverine's appearance in *Incredible Hulk* #180, the distinction here is that in *Incredible Hulk* #180, Wolverine appears briefly on the last page, however, in *OAAW* #82, Sgt Rock, albeit still in prototype form, appears several times throughout the six page story. Except now imagine that it was not even widely known that Wolverine even appeared in *Incredible Hulk* #180... and we just pointed it out. Food for thought!

Buy this book, and buy it now – at the current and generally agreed upon low values presently bestowed on it—before the market has had an opportunity to correct itself. Of course, this article is not making it easier for you, but you have two things to your advantage: 1) How many people have actually read this far into this report, and 2) This *Guide* and potentially other market reports will be careful not to make a sudden change in their valuing of #82, as they will typically need to adjust pricing in a controlled and governed manner.
We envision good returns on this book in as soon as 12 months. Happy chasing!

Losing Ground

There are a few books that we see fluctuating in performance. Just as we identify movers, it is only fair that we mention books that have shown some slowing. We would like to point out two keys that have slipped a little in the last year.

The first is *OAAW* #81. We have witnessed some backsliding in value on the book. Not because of what we disclosed above about *OAAW* #82, but mainly because the market has recently realigned its core focus onto *OAAW* #83, undermining the value of #81 in the short term. The book is still very important and has some great long term potential and, when compared to super-hero books, is still a tough one to get, so don't be frustrated if you own a copy. But, it is going to take a few years for the market to correct itself in light of the market share the other Sgt. Rock books are commanding. If you are thinking about buying a copy, this would actually be a good time to do some picky shopping. The book is garnering a bit lower sales figure as of late and it may be a good time to snap one up. However, do not expect any return in the short term. This is a book you will need to be happy to own just because it's a damn good comic and hard to get in anything above CGC 6.5. Let's see where it stands in 5 years.

The other book is *G.I. Combat* #91. There was a recent rush on this book as there were few copies in market circulation, and with its classic 1st Haunted Tank cover, it gained momentum because of cool cover speculators. However, its recent attention has brought a good number of copies out. It's not an inordinate amount of copies, but again, the market is correcting itself as the once obscure book now seems more readily available in mid-grades. Good luck finding an 8.5 or higher though....

Gaining Rank

Since our first report in *Overstreet* #39, we have been watchful of the market and its fluctuations and movements, providing a ranking of the top books in the War category. After developing the initial rank listing in 2008 we've been careful not to make any abrupt changes to the position of the books. However, we are continuously making small tweaks as we either gather new intel on the books or see activity or changes in the market. We are delighted to report that we have been able to expand our rankings this year to include some more issues (and their corresponding ranks). After careful deliberation we present the following War books rankings:

GAINING RANK

TOP 50 ATOM / SILVER / BRONZE AGE WAR COMICS

ISSUE	2012 RANK	2011 RANK
Our Army at War #83	**1**	1
G.I. Combat #87	**2**	2
Sgt. Fury #1	**3**	6
Our Army at War #81	**4**	3
G.I. Combat #68	**5 (Tied)**	4
Our Army at War #82	**5 (Tied)**	5
Two-Fisted Tales #18	**7**	7
Our Army at War #1	**8**	9
Frontline Combat #1	**9**	8
Our Army at War #90	**10**	10
Our Fighting Forces #1	**11**	12
G.I. Combat #44	**12**	11
Star Spangled War Stories #131	**13**	14
Our Army at War #88	**14**	13
All American Men of War #127	**15**	15
Our Fighting Forces #45	**16**	16
Our Army at War #91	**17**	17
Star Spangled War Stories #84	**18**	20
Our Army at War #151	**19**	18
Our Army at War #85	**20**	19

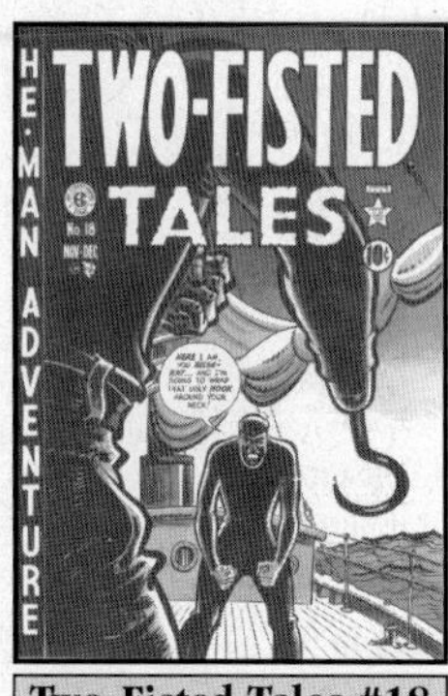

© WMG

Two-Fisted Tales #18

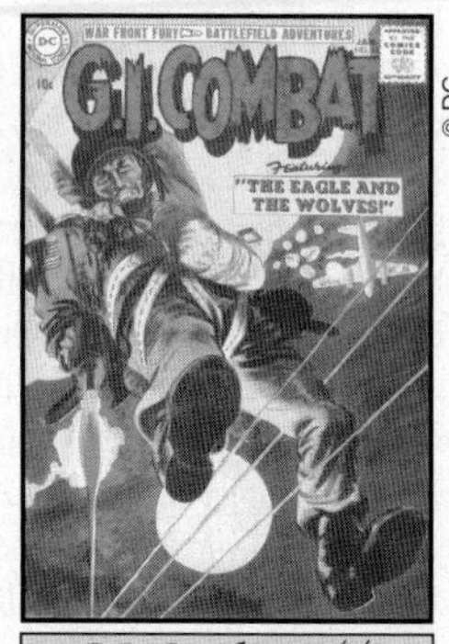

© DC

G.I. Combat #44

Our Army at War #84	21	20
Our Army at War #112	22	24
G.I. Combat #1	23	23
All American Men of War #28	24	20
Star Spangled War Stories #90	25	27
Two-Fisted Tales Annual #1	26	25
Our Army at War #86	27	26
Fightin' Marines #15 (#1)	28	29
All American Men of War #67	29	27
G.I. Combat #91	30	32

© DC

Our Army at War #84

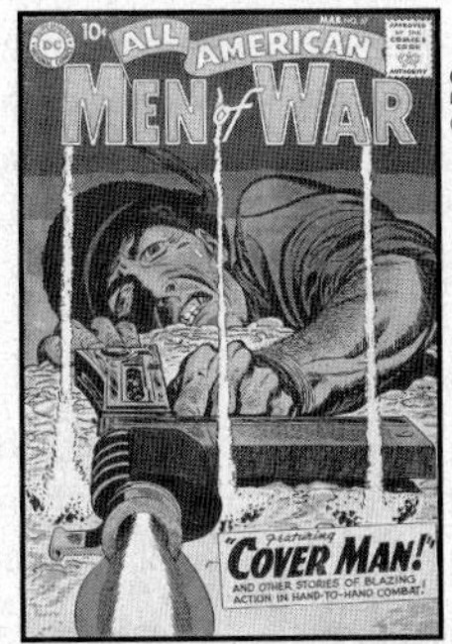

© DC

All American Men of War #67

Blazing Combat #1	31	30
Star Spangled War Stories #151	32	33
G.I. Combat #75	33 (Tied)	34
Our Army at War #100	33 (Tied)	34
All American Men of War #82	35	31
G.I. Combat #69	36	35
Battle #1	37	35
Weird War Tales #1	38	na
Our Fighting Forces #49	39 (Tied)	na
Combat #1	39 (Tied)	na
Foxhole #1	41 (Tied)	na
Our Army at War #95	41 (Tied)	na
Our Army at War #128	43	na
G.I. Combat #83	44	na
Fightin' Marines #2	45	na
G.I. Combat #80	46 (Tied)	na
All American Men of War #18	46 (Tied)	na
Combat Kelly #1	48 (Tied)	na
Our Army at War #168	48 (Tied)	na
Sgt Rock's Prize Battle Tales #1	48 (Tied)	na

© DC

Weird War Tales #1

© MAR

Foxhole #1

© DC

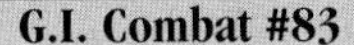
G.I. Combat #83

© MAR

Combat Kelly #1

GAINING RANK

TOP 14 GOLDEN AGE WAR COMICS

The titles and corresponding ranking for Golden Age War comics had very little movement since last year and nearly hold steadfast in their original positions. We are also introducing two new issues and expanding our list to 14. The Top Golden Age War books for 2012 are as follows:

ISSUE	2012 RANK	2011 RANK
Wings Comics #1	1	1
War Comics #1	2	2
Real Life #3	3	3
Contact Comics #1	4	4
Real Life Comics #1	5	5
Rangers Comics #8	6	7
Bill Barnes Comics #1	7	6
Wings Comics #2	8	8
Remember Pearl Harbor (nn)	9	9
US Marines #2	10	10
Don Winslow #1 (1937)	11	11
American Library nn (#1)	12 (Tied)	12
Don Winslow #1 (1939)	12 (Tied)	na
American Library nn (#2)	14	na

© FH

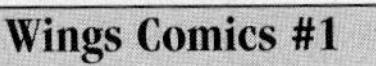
Wings Comics #1

© Nedor

Real Life Comics #43

TOP 5 ATLAS AND CHARLTON WAR COMICS

There was no movement on the Charlton ranks, they remain unvarying. But Atlas was another story. The Correspondents had previously not included the illustrious Atlas/Marvel title "*Battle*" on earlier Atlas listings because we considered it primarily a Marvel production. After some serious deliberation, we determined it was too prominent of an Atlas publication to overlook, so we decided to include it, and to rank it appropriately. Below is the result:

TOP 5 ATLAS WAR BOOKS OF 2011

ISSUE	2012 RANK	2011 RANK
Battle #1	1	na
Combat #1	2	1
War Comics #1	3	2
War Action #1	4	3
Battleground #1	5	4

TOP 5 CHARLTON WAR BOOKS OF 2011

ISSUE	2012 RANK	2011 RANK
Fightin' Marines #15 (#1)	1	1
Soldier & Marine #1	2	2
Attack #54	3	3
US Air Force #1	4	4
Fightin' Air Force #3	5	5

Intel from the War Correspondents

In this section of our report we typically supply whatever useful and helpful musings and advice that we can muster in hopes that it aids collectors through their pursuit of the War comic book collecting hobby. We consider key questions that we typically discuss amongst ourselves or with fans of the genre and then summarize our deliberations to share with you. Some of the information offered might even shed light on how certain titles or issues work their way up on to our top war lists. Due to space limitations, this year's Intel segment will be brief, but there are still a couple of topics worth mentioning....

War Books that Are Underrated

• ***Our Fighting Forces* #49** – The first Pooch book has not gained the market value that we believe it deserves (and we stated this last year). Andy even mentioned that if you were to compare it to the 1st Krypto, our war dog is not getting a fair shake. We believe that this book has got as much bite as bark.

• ***Star Spangled War Stories* #84** – Mlle. Marie's first appearance is selling cheap for what it is. Even though her run in *Star Spangled* only lasted six issues, the impact she made on the genre is undeniable. Plus, this is a very tough book to find in grade. If you can get this book in any condition snap it up, we believe it will only have to gain stature in the long run.

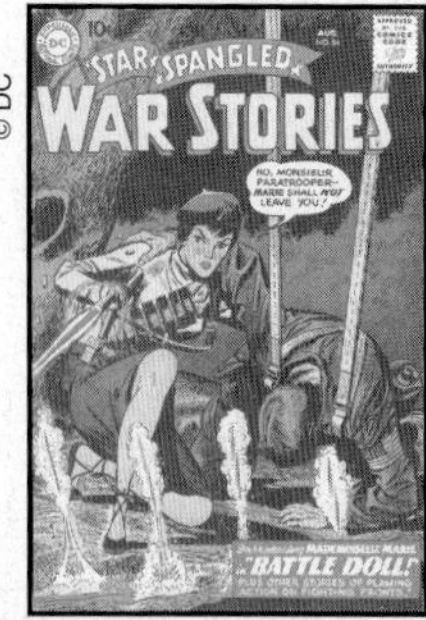

War Books that Are Tough to Find

• ***Wings* #2 through #20** are incredibly tough to find. In a recent auction some of these books in high grade finally did make their way into the market; however, they went for some fairly sizeable prices. Richard pointed out that the hammer prices of those books were influenced by the fact that they were being fought over by not just War comic fans, but by Fiction House enthusiasts as well. Interestingly, although *Wings* #1 still commands some high prices itself, it is a much more common book and easier to locate. Make note.

There are truly not that many **Gunner and Sarge** collectors, but good luck finding these books in grade. Whether these books gain financial momentum making them larger investment contenders is still to be determined, but... you just have to find them first.

War Stories with Impact

• ***Our Fighting Forces* #40 –** "The Silent Ones" is a stand out tale that is worthy of you searching it out. Mick summed up his feelings about it in two words: "It's killer!"

• ***Unknown Soldier* #21** (2010) – A tale worthy of reading by anyone regardless of your penchant of a particular genre. It's a wonderfully crafted story about the life of an AK47, starting with creator Avtomat Kalashnikov's concept for the weapon in 1941, and the production of it in 1947. The story then follows the same weapon from conflict to conflict, changing from owner to owner as war rages and people die. The weapon lives on, enduring by design. The tale, told from the gun's point-of-view is a stark and profound contrast from what we usually ingest. It is a modern book that is already a classic. Find it, read it.

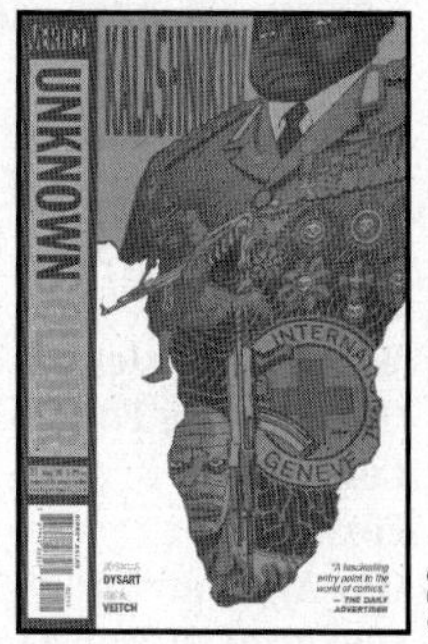

Over and Out

Thanks again for perusing the War Report. We hope that you found the information useful and entertaining. I would like to thank everyone who contacted us throughout the year with their thoughts and comments. Although we are not always able to work everyone's opinions into the report, your input is still appreciated and quite frankly, makes an impact on the whole of what we address. As always, if you would like to support or challenge any of our deliberations, or would just like to share your own musings; please do not hesitate to contact the War Correspondents at *hq@warcomicreport.com* .

As always, we want to extend our thanks to the staff and crew at Overstreet, Bob Overstreet, JC Vaughn and Mark Huesman, and for not busting us down to buck privates.

A special salute to the War Correspondents themselves, Richard Evans, Andy Greenham and Mick Rabin for sharing rations and ammunition freely and making this dispatch possible!

KEY SALES FROM 2011-2012

The following lists of sales were reported to Gemstone during the year and represent only a small portion of the total amount of important books that have sold.

PLATINUM AGE SALES

All the Funny Folks nn GD/VG $74
Barney Google and Spark Plug #4 VG $95.60
Buster Brown #1908 Amusing Capers VG $125.48
Buster Brown And His Resolutions GD/VG $507.88
Buster Brown Muslin Series - Plays Cowboy VG $84
Buster Brown My Resolutions VG+ $107.55
Charlie Chaplin #318 GD $79
Clancy the Cop #1 GD/VG $50
F. Fox's Funny Folk nn GD+ $69
Gumps, The #5 VG/FN $59
Hans und Fritz #193 VG $95.60
Happy Hooligan #1906 GD $191.20
Keeping Up With The Jones #2 VG $107.55
Little Orphan Annie #1 VG $30
Mickey Mouse #948 VF $418.25
Mickey Mouse, Adventures of Book 1 SC FN $215.10
Mickey Mouse Book (not 1st printing) VG- $717
Moon Mullins Big Book 1 VG+ $191.20
Mutt and Jeff Book 1 GD/VG $36
Pore Li'l Mose nn PR $310.70

GOLDEN AGE - ATOM AGE SALES

Action Comics #27 VF/NM $1,200 (restored)
Action Funnies Ashcan VF+ $10,157.50
Adventures of Detective Ace King VG $750
All Star Comics #13 GD/VG $375
Animal Antics Ashcan Cover NM $1,000
Batman #24 GD $90
Batman #35 GD $80
Batman #41 VG $155
Batman #98 FN- $175
Blackhawk #52 VG+ $11.25
Dell Giant Lone Ranger Golden West FN $55
Detective Comics #95 VG+ $150
Detective Comics #136 VG+ $100
Detective Comics #140 VG $1,434
Fox & Crow #1 VG+ $62.50
Howdy Doody #6 FN+ $78
Looney Tunes & M.M. #84 VG+ $18.75
Mighty Mouse #41 VG+ $11.25
Mister Mystery #17 GD $21
New Fun Comics #6 GD $2,629
Porky Pig (Four Color) #420 VG+ $11.25
Roy Rogers Comics #10 VF $77.75
Roy Rogers Comics #73 VG $8.25
Screen Gems Ashcan Cover # VF $775
Superman #4 GD $650
Superman #18 GD $275
Superman #18 GD- $200
Superman #69 GD $52.50
Vic Torry and His Flying Saucer #1 GD+ $85.75
Whiz Comics #124 VG- $30

SILVER AGE SALES

Action Comics #346 VF- $32.99
Adventures of the Fly #1 VG+ $67.75
Amazing Spider-Man #3 PR $45
Amazing Spider-Man #13 VG- $67.50
Amazing Spider-Man #20 VF $495
Amazing Spider-Man #29 VG+ $36
Amazing Spider-Man #30 VG $21
Amazing Spider-Man #52 FN $37
Amazing Spider-Man #63 VG+ $24
Amazing Spider-Man #70 VG- $12.75
Amazing Spider-Man #84 VG- $12.50
Amazing Spider-Man #86 VG- $11.25
Aquaman #3 VG+ $16
Aquaman #43 VG+ $10.50
Atom #2 FR/GD- $18.75
Atom #7 VG/FN $23
Avengers #1 FN/VF $4,500
Batman #136 GD+ $41.25
Batman #137 FR $10.50
Batman #141 FR $10.50
Brave and the Bold #10 FN/VF $270
Brave and the Bold #12 GD $86
Brave and the Bold #22 VF- $280
Brave and the Bold #23 VF- $340

Brave and the Bold #31 VF- $157.50
Brave and the Bold #31 GD/VG $56.99
Brave and the Bold #32 VG+ $49.99
Brave and the Bold #35 GD/VG $64.99
Brave and the Bold #42 GD+ $33.75
Brave and the Bold #54 FN+ $60
Brave and the Bold #54 VG $55
Brave and the Bold #55 VG+ $16.50
Brave and the Bold #79 FN/VF $44.99
Captain Venture #1 VF- $12.75
Creepy #1 VG $27
Creepy #1 VG+ $21.75
Daredevil #14 VG- $42
Detective Comics #283 VG+ $15.75
Detective Comics #295 VG+ $45
Detective Comics #298 VG/FN $62.99
Doctor Strange #182 VF $16.50
Fantastic Four #1 FN/VF $16,000
Fantastic Four #2 VF+ $7,500
Fantastic Four #3 VF+ $6,500
Fantastic Four #6 VF/NM $4,200
Fantastic Four #7 NM $4,800
Fantastic Four #8 NM- $4,000
Fantastic Four #14 NM- $1,600
Fantastic Four #48 FN $116.25
Fantastic Four #49 VF $120
Fantastic Four #50 FN $97.50
Fantastic Four #55 VG $35
Fantastic Four #73 FN- $25
Flash #137 FN $63.75
Flash #137 VG+ $55
Flash #137 VG $41.25
Flash #176 FN $19.50
Green Lantern #1 FR $60
Green Lantern #5 GD+ $60
Green Lantern #14 GD- $12
Green Lantern #20 VG+ $29
Green Lantern #68 VG+ $14.25
Gunsmoke #1 FN+ $62.50
Hawkman #17 VF- $35
Hawkman #25 FN $15
Incredible Hulk #1 FN/VF $12,000
Iron Man #5 FN/VF $40.99
Iron Man #7 VG- $12
Iron Man #8 VG $12
Journey Into Mystery #93 GD- $16.25
Journey Into Mystery #99 GD $34.50
Journey Into Mystery #100 GD- $9
Journey Into Mystery #108 VG+ $27.50
Journey Into Mystery #109 GD $17
Journey Into Mystery #110 VG- $24
Journey Into Mystery #111 FN- $33.75
Journey Into Mystery #111 GD $17.25
Journey Into Mystery #114 GD+ $32.50
Journey Into Mystery #118 GD+ $26.25
Journey Into Mystery #119 FN- $45
Journey Into Mystery #120 VG+ $32.50
Journey Into Mystery #121 VG- $28.75
Journey Into Mystery #122 VG+ $34.50
Journey Into Mystery #123 GD+ $21
Journey Into Mystery #124 VG+ $18.50
Journey Into Mystery #124 VG $18
Justice League of America #1 VF+ $10,000
Justice League of America #24 GD+ $16
Justice League of America #65 VF- $16
Magnus, Robot Fighter #7 VF- $49.99
Millie The Model #147 VG $12
My Greatest Adventure #82 VG/FN $42.99
My Greatest Adventure #83 VG $34.99
Mystery In Space #85 VG $19.50
New Funnies #203 VG $11.50
Quick Draw McGraw (Four Color) #1040 VG- $21
Sgt. Fury and His H.C. #1 GD $150
Sgt. Fury Annual #1 F/VF $70.99
Showcase #28 VF $125
Showcase #36 GD 2.0 $43.99
Showcase #60 VG $36
Strange Adventures #145 VG+ $19
Superboy #53 VG- $13.25
Superman's Girlfriend Lois Lane #70 VG/FN $62.99
Superman's Girlfriend Lois Lane #70 VG $47.99
Superman's Girlfriend Lois Lane #86 VF- $31.99
Superman's Pal Jimmy Olsen #7 FN- $71.25
Superman's Pal Jimmy Olsen #8 FN $78.75
Tales of Suspense #14 VG $16
Tales of Suspense #19 GD- $16.50
Tales of Suspense #39 FR $700
Tales of Suspense #53 GD $24.75
Tales of the Unexpected #50 GD+ $14
Tales to Astonish #27 VF $7,000
Tales to Astonish #100 VG- $13.75
Thor #126 VG- $38.50
Thor #128 FN+ $38.50
Thor #128 VG+ $21.75
Thor #130 FN+ $30
Thor #132 VG+ $22.50
Thor #144 FN+ $26.25
Uncle Scrooge #8 VG $37.99
Unknown Worlds #1 GD $12.75
X-Men #14 FN- $74.50
X-Men #17 VG $40
X-Men #47 VG+ $20
X-Men #48 FN- $22
X-Men #53 FN- $27
X-Men #90 VG- $16
X-Men #93 VG+ $19.50

BRONZE AGE TO MODERN AGE SALES

Bronze Age Sales:

Amazing Spider-Man #96 FN $27
Amazing Spider-Man #97 VF $28
Amazing Spider-Man #98 VF+ $37.50
Amazing Spider-Man #101 VG+ $38
Amazing Spider-Man #101 GD+ $15
Amazing Spider-Man #108 VG- $13
Amazing Spider-Man #112 VG- $12.50
Amazing Spider-Man #115 FN- $17
Amazing Spider-Man #121 FN+ $70
Amazing Spider-Man #129 VG $60
Amazing Spider-Man #134 VF $26.25
Amazing Spider-Man #201 FN+ $10.50
Avengers #100 VG+ $18
Detective Comics #458 FN+ $11.25
G.I. Joe (Marvel) #26 VF+ $20
G.I. Joe (Marvel) #26 VF+ $16
Giant-Size Spider-Man #6 VF/NM $33.99
Giant-Size Thor #1 FN+ $14.50
Green Lantern #76 FN- $300
House of Secrets #92 FN/VF $260
Incredible Hulk #180 GD- $14.25
Incredible Hulk #181 FR- $20
Iron Fist #14 VF+ $150
Jonah Hex #15 NM+ $49.99
Jonah Hex #20 NM- $30.99
Marvel Feature #11 VG+ $19.50
Marvel Premiere #15 VF+ $55
Marvel Spotlight #5 VG/FN $47
Our Army At War #275 VG+ $13
Shadow #1 VG- $16
Spectacular Spider-Man #1 NM- $76.99
Speed Buggy #1 FN+ $10
Spider-Woman #1 VF/NM $16
Strange Adventures #209 VF- $57.99
Strange Adventures #210 FN/VF $53.99
Superman's Pal Jimmy Olsen #134 FN+ $17.25
Thor #200 VF $10
Tomb of Dracula #1 VG $26.50
Vampirella #31 VF- $31.99
Witching Hour #38 VF/NM $51.99
Wolverine (v1) #3 VF+ $34
Wolverine (v1) #4 FN+ $18
X-Men #100 FN- $22.50
X-Men #122 FN+ $22
X-Men #123 NM $12
X-Men #129 FN+ $22

Copper Age Sales:

Amazing Spider-Man #310 VF/NM $11
Batman #404 NM $13
Crisis on Infinite Earths #8 NM $14.25
Gobbledygook #1 VF $1,912
Marvel Super-Heroes Secret Wars #8 NM $25
New Mutants #87 VF+ $16
New Mutants #98 MT $50
New Mutants #98 NM $40
Transformers #8 VF+ $10
Vampirella #80 VF/NM $36.99
Vampirella #82 VF/NM $36.99
Wolverine (1988) #1 NM- $34.99
Wolverine (1988) #1 VF/NM $34.99
Wolverine (1988) #10 NM $34.99
X-Men (Uncanny) #248 NM $14.25
X-Men (Uncanny) #244 VF+ $25
X-Men (Uncanny) #268 NM $12

Modern Age Sales:

Batman Adventures #12 NM- $79.99
Brave and the Bold #33 NM $36
Chew #1 NM $520
Miracleman TPB #4 NM $124.99

GOLDEN AGE - SALES OF CGC-CERTIFIED COMICS

Action Comics #1 VF/NM (9.0) $2,161,000
Action Comics #1 FN/VF (7.0) $120,100 (restored)
Action Comics #1 FN+ (6.5) $625,000
Action Comics #1 GD/VG (3.0) $298,750 Billy Wright
Action Comics #1 GD- (1.8) $110,000
Action Comics #5 VF+ (8.5) $52,500
Action Comics #6 VF+ (8.5) $34,655
Action Comics #10 VF/NM (9.0) $258,000
Action Comics #10 GD/VG (3.0) $20,351
Action Comics #13 NM- (9.2) $185,000
Action Comics #19 VG+ (4.5) $2,785
Action Comics #24 VF+ (8.5) $4,400
Action Comics #50 VG- (3.5) $310
Action Comics #54 VF+ (8.5) $4,459
All-American Comics #16 VF (8.0) $203,150 Billy Wright
All Star Comics #8 FN/VF (7.0) $3,750 (restored)
All Winners Comics #1 NM+ (9.6) $49,293 Chicago
All Winners Comics #7 FN+ (6.5) $3,736
All Winners Comics #8 FN (6.0) $2,100
All Winners Comics #12 NM (9.4) $11,500 San Fran.
America's Best Comics #7 FN/VF (7.0) $2,250

Archie Comics #1 VG- (3.5) $20,315
Archie Comics #50 FN+ (6.5) $1,100
Batman #1 NM- (9.2) $850,000
Batman #1 VF+ (8.5) $274,850 Billy Wright
Batman #1 GD/VG (3.0) $32,500
Batman #9 FN/VF (7.0) $2,151
Batman #37 FN (6.0) $295 (restored)
Batman #47 VF (8.0) $10,099
Batman #49 FN (6.0) $1,000
Blue Beetle #54 FN (6.0) $2,700
Bulletman #2 NM (9.4) $4,481.25 Mile High
Captain America Comics #1 NM- (9.2) $343,057
Captain America Comics #1 FN/VF (7.0) $90,000 Super Soldier
Captain America Comics #1 FN (6.0) $65,725
Captain America Comics #2 NM (9.4) $113,525 Billy Wright
Captain America Comics #2 VF+ (8.5) $22,705
Captain America Comics #3 NM- (9.2) $508,787
Captain America Comics #32 NM (9.4) $11,750
Captain America Comics #46 FN/VF (7.0) $8,101
Captain America Comics #46 VG (4.0) $4,000
Cisco Kid Comics #1 NM+ (9.6) $2,031.50 Carson
Comic Cavalcade #2 VF (8.0) $1,314 Pennsylvania
Crime Does Not Pay #23 FN+ (6.5) $805
Crime Does Not Pay #24 VG/FN (5.0) $2,200
Crime Does Not Pay #25 VG/FN (5.0) $235
Crypt of Terror #17 NM (9.4) $5,825.63 Gaines File
Daredevil #1 NM (9.4) $38,837
Detective Comics #24 VF (8.0) $1,450 (restored)
Detective Comics #27 VF+ (8.5) $130,000 (restored)
Detective Comics #27 VF- (7.5) $101,575 (restored)
Detective Comics #27 FN+ (6.5) $522,812.50 Billy Wright
Detective Comics #27 GD (2.0) $116,512.50
Detective Comics #29 FN/VF (7.0) $83,650
Detective Comics #31 VG (4.0) $26,100
Detective Comics #31 GD/VG (3.0) $20,250
Detective Comics #33 NM- (9.2) $194,000
Detective Comics #33 VF (8.0) $92,612
Detective Comics #33 VG/FN (5.0) $16,250
Detective Comics #41 FN/VF (7.0) $680
Detective Comics #142 NM (9.4) $21,250
Detective Comics #168 VF- (7.5) $5,078.75
Fairy Tale Parade #2 NM+ (9.6) $1,553.50
Famous Funnies #2 VG (4.0) $1,374.25
Feature Comics #69 NM (9.4) $445
Flash Comics #1 VF/NM (9.0) $168,000
Flash Comics #5 NM (9.4) $15,535
Four Color #16 Mickey Mouse FN/VF (7.0) $5,377.50
Four Most Vol. 2 #5 VG/FN (5.0) $119
Frontline Combat #1 NM+ (9.6) $2,629 Gaines File
Ghost #1 NM- (9.2) $3,107 Mile High
Green Lantern #9 NM- (9.2) $5,078.75 Mile High
Guns Against Gangsters #4 NM (9.4) $650
Haunt of Fear #7 NM+ (9.6) $1,434 Gaines File
Hit Comics #3 VG/FN (5.0) $750
Kewpies #1 FN- (5.5) $334.60 Mile High
Mad #1 VF (8.0) $2,031.50 (restored)
Marvel Comics #1 VF- (7.5) $113,525
Marvel Mystery Comics #9 FN- (5.5) $19,801
Marvel Mystery Comics #15 VF (8.0) $4,100
Marvel Mystery Comics #17 VF (8.0) $4,000 Penn
Marvel Mystery Comics #20 VF (8.0) $3,600
Marvel Mystery Comics #40 VF/NM (9.0) $21,510
Marvel Mystery Comics #45 VF (8.0) $3,000
More Fun Comics #101 FN/VF (7.0) $2,330.25
Mystery Men Comics #3 VF- (7.5) $4,630.63
Mystic Comics #8 NM+ (9.6) $12,500
Mystic Comics Vol. 2 #2 NM (9.4) $6,400 "D" copy, double-c
New Adventure Comics #26 FR (1.0) $7,956
New York World's Fair Comics 1939 VG- (3.5) $1,434
Our Army at War #2 VF- (7.5) $836.50 Carson City
Phantom Lady #23 VG+ (4.5) $625
Planet Comics #68 VF/NM (9.0) $750
Popular Comics #1 GD- (1.8) $376
Red Raven Comics #1 VF/NM (9.0) $74,687.50 Mile High
Sensation Comics #1 GD/VG (3.0) $4,361.75
Shock SuspenStories #6 NM+ (9.6) $5,526.88 Gaines
Spirit nn (#1) NM+ (9.6) $5,377.50 Mile High
Startling Comics #49 FN/VF (7.0) $3,107
Strange Adventures #17 VF- (7.5) $225
Sub-Mariner Comics #1 VG (4.0) $4,182.50
Sunny #11 VF+ (8.5) $1,750
Superman #1 VG+ (4.5) $126,111
Superman #14 VF- (7.5) $6,572.50
Superman #14 VG+ (4.5) $1,600
Superman #28 VF+ (8.5) $1,000
Superman #34 VF/NM (9.0) $1,150
Superman #46 VF+ (8.5) $1,125
Tales From the Crypt #21 NM (9.4) $2,270.50 Gaines
Terrific Comics #5 GD- (1.8) $5,033
Terry-Toons Comics #54 VF/NM (9.0) $189
USA Comics #1 VF (8.0) $5,078.75
USA Comics #4 VF/NM (9.0) $3,500
USA Comics #13 VG (4.0) $1,350
Walt Disney's Comics & Stories #1 VG/FN (5.0) $4,780
Weird Fantasy #10 NM/MT (9.8) $2,868 Gaines File
Weird Science-Fantasy #29 NM (9.4) $8,315
Whiz Comics #2 (#1) FN (6.0) $176,007
Wonder Comics #1 GD+ (2.5) $3,883.75
Wonder Woman #6 VF- (7.5) $5,975
World's Best Comics #1 VG (4.0) $1,673
Young Allies Comics #1 FN- (5.5) $2,987.50

Action Comics #242 VF- (7.5) $3,734
Action Comics #252 FN+ (6.5) $1,912
Adventure Comics #247 VG/FN (5.0) $1,314.50
Adventure Comics #320 NM/MT (9.8) $2,031 Twin Cities
Adventure Comics #366 NM/MT (9.8) $2,031 Twin Cities
Amazing Fantasy #15 NM (9.4) $325,000
Amazing Fantasy #15 VF+ (8.5) $110,000
Amazing Fantasy #15 VF+ (8.5) $107,300
Amazing Fantasy #15 VF (8.0) $70,000
Amazing Fantasy #15 VF- (7.5) $48,000
Amazing Fantasy #15 VG/FN (5.0) $9,000
Amazing Fantasy #15 GD+ (2.5) $5,500 Sig Series
Amazing Spider-Man #1 NM- (9.2) $90,000 Massachusetts
Amazing Spider-Man #1 GD/VG (3.0) $2,600
Amazing Spider-Man #2 VF (8.0) $3,400
Amazing Spider-Man #2 VG+ (4.5) $750
Amazing Spider-Man #3 NM- (9.2) $8,601
Amazing Spider-Man #3 FN (6.0) $1,000
Amazing Spider-Man #7 NM (9.4) $7,757
Amazing Spider-Man #11 NM (9.4) $12,700
Amazing Spider-Man #13 NM+ (9.6) $45,000
Amazing Spider-Man #13 NM+ (9.6) $33,500
Amazing Spider-Man #13 NM+ (9.6) $16,878
Amazing Spider-Man #13 NM (9.4) $7,300
Amazing Spider-Man #14 NM+ (9.6) $36,000
Amazing Spider-Man #14 NM (9.4) $5,325
Amazing Spider-Man #18 NM+ (9.6) $8,200
Amazing Spider-Man #20 NM (9.4) $3,150
Amazing Spider-Man #22 NM+ (9.6) $5,100
Amazing Spider-Man #25 NM/MT (9.8) $26,500
Amazing Spider-Man #28 NM (9.4) $6,800
Amazing Spider-Man #45 NM/MT (9.8) $4,100
Amazing Spider-Man #68 NM (9.4) $285
Aquaman #1 NM- (9.2) $2,390
Avengers #1 NM+ (9.6) $250,000
Avengers #1 NM (9.4) $100,000
Avengers #1 NM- (9.2) $60,000
Avengers #1 NM- (9.2) $57,000 Northland
Avengers #1 VF+ (8.5) $15,259
Avengers #2 NM+ (9.6) $10,600
Avengers #3 NM (9.4) $6,001
Avengers #4 NM+ (9.6) $91,501
Avengers #4 NM+ (9.6) $80,000
Avengers #4 NM+ (9.6) $69,500
Avengers #5 NM (9.4) $2,501
Avengers #6 NM+ (9.6) $5,755
Avengers #12 NM (9.4) $1,275
Avengers #16 NM+ (9.6) $11,000
Avengers #16 NM+ (9.6) $9,100
Avengers #28 NM+ (9.6) $3,294
Avengers #29 NM+ (9.6) $924 Pacific Coast
Avengers #53 NM (9.4) $300
Avengers #84 NM (9.4) $225
Batman #145 NM (9.4) $1,135.25
Batman #211 NM/MT (9.8) $1,553.50 Twin Cities
Brave and the Bold #28 VF (8.0) $11,054
Brave and the Bold #28 FN (6.0) $2,031.50
Brave and the Bold #28 VG/FN (5.0) $1,792.50
Brave and the Bold #61 NM+ (9.6) $776.75
Captain America #104 NM/MT (9.8) $929.71
Captain America #115 NM (9.4) $135
Chalengers of the Unknown #1 FN/VF (7.0) $956
Daredevil #1 NM+ (9.6) $37,384
Daredevil #1 NM (9.4) $15,050
Daredevil #1 NM- (9.2) $8,801
Daredevil #1 FN/VF (7.0) $1,600
Daredevil #2 NM+ (9.6) $4,060
Detective Comics #255 VF (8.0) $3,049
Detective Comics #267 VF+ (8.5) $3,466
Detective Comics #359 NM- (9.2) $1,613.25
Devil Kids Starring Hot Stuff #1 NM+ (9.6) $1,912 Harvey File Copy
Double Life of Private Strong #2 NM (9.4) $478 Bethlehem
Fantastic Four #1 VF+ (8.5) $83,022
Fantastic Four #1 VF- (7.5) $30,000 CGC Sig Series Stan Lee
Fantastic Four #2 NM+ (9.6) $87,000 White Mountain
Fantastic Four #2 NM+ (9.6) $82,500
Fantastic Four #3 NM (9.4) $38,000
Fantastic Four #3 NM- (9.2) $13,500
Fantastic Four #4 NM+ (9.6) $44,812
Fantastic Four #5 NM (9.4) $65,725
Fantastic Four #5 NM- (9.2) $22,020
Fantastic Four #12 NM+ (9.6) $65,725
Fantastic Four #12 NM (9.4) $48,300
Fantastic Four #13 NM- (9.2) $5,900
Fantastic Four #26 NM (9.4) $3,140
Fantastic Four #28 NM+ (9.6) $6,450
Fantastic Four #32 NM+ (9.6) $2,800
Fantastic Four #48 NM/MT (9.8) $9,200
Fantastic Four #59 NM/MT (9.8) $975
Fantastic Four #98 NM+ (9.6) $240
Flash #105 NM- (9.2) $36,888
Flash #105 NM- (9.2) $26,290
Flash #105 VF (8.0) $8,664
Flintstones on the Rocks nn NM (9.4) $507.88
G.I. Combat #68 VF (8.0) $3,107
G.I. Combat #87 VF+ (8.5) $3,883.75

Green Hornet #3 NM/MT (9.8) $1,075.50 Boston
Green Lantern #1 VF (8.0) $5,799
Green Lantern #1 FN+ (6.5) $1,254.75
Green Lantern #40 NM- (9.2) $1,375
Green Lantern #40 VF/NM (9.0) $507.88
Green Lantern #43 NM/MT (9.8) $2,987.50 Twin Cities
Hawkman #1 NM+ (9.6) $4,182.50 Twin Cities
House of Mystery #143 NM+ (9.6) $657.25
I Love Lucy #20 NM/MT (9.8) $717
Incredible Hulk #1 FN+ (6.5) $11,950
Incredible Hulk #6 NM+ (9.6) $17,251
Incredible Hulk #103 NM (9.4) $295
Invaders #6 NM+ (9.6) $125
Iron Man #1 MT (9.9) $69,600
Iron Man #1 NM+ (9.6) $3,250 Pacific Coast
Journey Into Mystery #83 NM (9.4) $222,200
Journey Into Mystery #83 NM- (9.2) $100,000
Journey Into Mystery #83 VF/NM (9.0) $52,102
Journey Into Mystery #83 VF/NM (9.0) $46,501 Twin Cities
Journey Into Mystery #83 VG- (3.5) $1,725
Journey into Mystery #87 NM (9.4) $4,301
Journey into Mystery #89 NM (9.4) $11,433
Journey into Mystery #95 NM (9.4) $5,989
Journey into Mystery #96 NM+ (9.6) $3,050
Justice League of America #5 NM- (9.2) $2,270.50
Metal Men #1 NM+ (9.6) $1,792.50
Millie the Model #148 NM/MT (9.8) $131.45
Mystery in Space #53 VF+ (8.5) $3,107
Our Army at War #81 VF+ (8.5) $6,500
Our Army at War #81 VF+ (8.5) $4,481.25
Our Army at War #83 VF (8.0) $16,730
Our Army At War #83 VF- (7.5) $9,600
Our Army at War #112 VF+ (8.5) $3,107
Our Army at War #113 VF+ (8.5) $1,613.25
Our Fighting Forces #72 NM (9.4) $380
Phantom #1 NM+ (9.6) $1,912 Boston
Secret Agent #1 NM+ (9.6) $657.25 Boston
Sgt. Fury and His H.C. #1 NM (9.4) $28,680
Sgt. Fury and His H.C. #3 NM+ (9.6) $5,975
Sgt. Fury and His H.C. #4 NM+ (9.6) $3,734
Sgt. Fury and His H.C. #5 NM (9.4) $1,553
Sgt. Fury and His H.C. #6 NM+ (9.6) $3,107
Sgt. Fury and His H.C. #13 NM (9.4) $3,301
Shadow #1 (1964) NM+ (9.6) $448.13 Pac. Coast
Showcase #4 NM- (9.2) $100,000
Showcase #4 VF/NM (9.0) $38,837.50 Bethlehem
Showcase #4 VF (8.0) $23,900
Showcase #4 VF- (7.5) $1,800 (restored)
Showcase #8 GD/VG (3.0) $717
Showcase #22 VF (8.0) $23,900
Showcase #27 VF/NM (9.0) $1,434
Showcase #36 NM+ (9.6) $4,780
Showcase #45 NM+ (9.6) $2,629
Silver Surfer #1 VF/NM (9.0) $900
Star Trek #1 NM+ (9.6) $22,705
Star Trek #4 NM/MT (9.8) $3,107 Twin Cities
Strange Adventures #190 NM+ (9.6) $956 Pac. Coast
Strange Tales #103 NM (9.4) $4,551
Strange Tales #104 NM (9.4) $5,037
Strange Tales #109 NM+ (9.6) $3,151
Strange Tales #110 VF+ (8.5) $3,200
Strange Tales #119 NM (9.4) $2,901
Strange Tales Annual #2 NM (9.4) $5,322
Sub-Mariner #1 NM/MT (9.8) $2,450
Superman #181 NM+ (9.6) $657.25 Boston
Superman #184 NM (9.4) $239
Superman #209 NM/MT (9.8) $1,015 Pacific Coast
Superman's GF Lois Lane #1 VF (8.0) $8,963
Tales of Suspense #39 NM+ (9.6) $375,000
Tales of Suspense #39 NM (9.4) $150,000
Tales of Suspense #39 NM (9.4) $145,000
Tales of Suspense #39 NM (9.4) $130,000
Tales of Suspense #39 NM (9.4) $102,500
Tales of Suspense #44 NM- (9.2) $2,449
Tales of Suspense #59 NM+ (9.6) $5,107
Tales of Suspense #69 NM+ (9.6) $2,629
Tales to Astonish #35 NM- (9.2) $30,000
Tales to Astonish #37 NM (9.4) $3,500
Tales to Astonish #38 NM (9.4) $2,551
Tales to Astonish #44 NM+ (9.6) $10,900
Tales to Astonish #44 NM+ (9.6) $7,888
Tales to Astonish #50 NM/MT (9.8) $2,390
Tales to Astonish #60 NM+ (9.6) $5,900
Thor #171 NM (9.4) $162 Pacific Coast
Three Stooges FC #1170 NM/MT (9.8) $896.25 Dell File Copy
Wonder Woman #147 NM/MT (9.8) $1,374.25 Savannah
World's Finest Comics #141 NM+ (9.6) $507.88
X-Men #1 NM+ (9.6) $200,000
X-Men #1 NM (9.4) $137,500
X-Men #1 NM (9.4) $90,000
X-Men #1 NM (9.4) $90,000
X-Men #1 NM (9.4) $124,000
X-Men #1 FN/VF (7.0) $5,500
X-Men #1 VG (4.0) $1,690
X-Men #3 NM- (9.2) $2,150
X-Men #4 NM (9.4) $9,201
X-Men #8 NM (9.4) $2,007
X-Men #13 NM (9.4) $2,432
X-Men #16 NM+ (9.6) $2,550 Pacific Coast
X-Men #28 NM (9.4) $1,000
X-Men #38 NM- (9.2) $195
X-Men #81 NM/MT (9.8) $3,333 Double-c

BRONZE AGE - SALES OF CGC-CERTIFIED COMICS

All-Star Squadron #1 NM/MT (9.8) $54.99
Amazing Spider-Man #100 NM- (9.2) $295
Amazing Spider-Man #106 NM- (9.2) $175
Amazing Spider-Man #117 NM (9.4) $225
Amazing Spider-Man #129 VF/NM (9.0) $900
Amazing Spider-Man #133 NM+ (9.6) $200
Amazing Spider-Man #134 NM (9.4) $135
Avengers #93 NM+ (9.6) $2,031.50 Twin Cities
Avengers #100 NM/MT (9.8) $717
Batman #227 NM/MT (9.8) $6,273.75 Twin Cities
Batman #232 NM/MT (9.8) $2,031.50 Twin Cities
Cerebus the Aardvark #1 VF/NM (9.0) $1,434
Conan the Barbarian #1 NM/MT (9.8) $4,780
DC 100 Page Super Spect. #4 NM+ (9.6) $5,250
Fantastic Four #119 NM- (9.2) $77
Giant-Size X-Men #1 NM/MT (9.8) $5,377.50
G.I. Joe, A Real American Hero #21 NM/MT (9.8) $310.55
G.I. Joe, A Real American Hero #21 NM+ (9.6) $85.55
Giant-Size Daredevil #1 NM/MT (9.8) $1,459
Giant-Size X-Men #1 NM/MT (9.8) $4,611
Giant-Size X-Men #1 NM+ (9.6) $2,650
Green Lantern #76 NM+ (9.6) $9,560 Twin Cities
House of Secrets #92 NM/MT (9.8) $16,350
Incredible Hulk #180 NM/MT (9.8) $1,912
Incredible Hulk #181 MT (9.9) $150,000
Incredible Hulk #181 NM/MT (9.8) $12,750
Incredible Hulk #181 VF/NM (9.0) $1,325
Iron Fist #14 NM+ (9.6) $500
Power Man and Iron Fist #57 NM (9.4) $39.99
Silver Surfer #14 NM+ (9.6) $1,792.50 Twin Cities
Tomb of Dracula #1 NM/MT (9.8) $1,553.50
Uncanny X-Men #173 NM/MT (9.8) $32.50
X-Men #94 NM (9.4) $2,750
X-Men #94 NM- (9.2) $1,050

COPPER AGE - SALES OF CGC-CERTIFIED COMICS

Crisis on Infinite Earths #7 NM/MT (9.8) $54.99
Detective Comics #556 NM/MT (9.8) $34.99
Detective Comics #566 NM/MT (9.8) $49.99
Detective Comics #572 NM/MT (9.8) $49.99
G.I. Joe, A Real American Hero #98 NM/MT (9.8) $45.55
Miracleman #15 NM/MT (9.8) $306
Punisher #50 NM/MT (9.8) $39.99
Tales of the Teen Titans #44 NM/MT (9.8) $119.99
Tales of the Teen Titans #44 NM/MT (9.8) $95
Tales of the Teen Titans #44 NM/MT (9.8) $75
Tales of the Teen Titans #44 NM/MT (9.8) $52
Uncanny X-Men #207 NM/MT (9.8) $36.87
Uncanny X-Men #212 NM/MT (9.8) $105
Uncanny X-Men #266 NM+ (9.6) $61.50
Uncanny X-Men #268 NM/MT (9.8) $39
Uncanny X-Men #268 NM/MT (9.8) $31.66
Uncanny X-Men #269 NM/MT (9.8) $39.99

MODERN AGE - SALES OF CGC-CERTIFIED COMICS

Batman #609 NM/MT (9.8) $39.99
Batman #610 NM/MT (9.8) $39.99
Batman #611 NM/MT (9.8) $39.99
Batman Adventures #12 NM/MT (9.8) $249.99
Batman: Vengeance of Bane #1 NM/MT (9.8) $335
Brave and the Bold #33 NM/MT (9.8) $30
Chew #1 NM/MT (9.8) $799.99 Sig. Series
Encyclopaedia Deadpoolica #1 NM/MT (9.8) $74.99
Ghost Rider V2 #19 NM/MT (9.8) $34.99
Green Lantern V3 #48 NM/MT (9.8) $44.99
Green Lantern V3 #51 NM/MT (9.8) $34.99
Invincible #16 NM/MT (9.8) $39.99
Invincible #19 MT (9.9) $33.22
John Byrne's Next Men #21 NM+ (9.6) $74.99
John Byrne's Next Men #21 NM+ (9.6) $39
New Mutants #98 NM/MT (9.8) $241.34
NYX #3 NM/MT (9.8) $172.50
Preacher #1 NM/MT (9.8) $105.50
Sonic the Hedgehog #18 NM/MT (9.8) $59.99
Spawn #1 NM/MT (9.8) $49.99
Superman #79 NM/MT (9.8) $39.99
Superman: The Man of Steel #30 MT (9.9) $34 Collector's Ed
Uncanny X-Men #377 NM/MT (9.8) $39.99
Venom: Lethal Protector #1 NM/MT (9.8) $690 Black Cover Variant
Walking Dead #1 MT (9.9) $7,750
Walking Dead #1 NM/MT (9.8) $2,275 Sig. Series
Walking Dead #19 NM/MT (9.8) $1,299 Sig. Series
Wolverine (1988) #156 NM/MT (9.8) $44.99
X-Men #1C NM/MT (9.8) $39.99
X-Men #1D NM/MT (9.8) $39.99

TOP BOOKS

The following tables denote the rate of appreciation of the top Golden Age, Platinum Age, Silver Age and Bronze Age books, as well as selected genres over the past year. The retail value for a Near Mint- copy of each book (or VF where a Near Mint- copy is not known to exist) in 2012 is compared to its Near Mint- value in 2011. The rate of return for 2012 over 2011 is given. The place in rank is given for each comic by year, with its corresponding value in highest known grade. These tables can be very useful in forecasting trends in the market place. For instance, the investor might want to know which book is yielding the best dividend from one year to the next, or one might just be interested in seeing how the popularity of books changes from year to year. For instance, *Pep Comics* #22 was in 23rd place in 2011 and has increased to 14th place in 2012. Premium books are also included in these tables and are denoted with an asterisk(*).

The following tables are meant as a guide to the investor. However, it should be pointed out that trends may change at anytime and that some books can meet market resistance with a slowdown in price increases, while others can develop into real comers from a presently dormant state. In the long run, if the investor sticks to the books that are appreciating steadily each year, he shouldn't go very far wrong.

TOP 100 GOLDEN AGE BOOKS

TITLE/ISSUE#	2012 RANK	2012 NM- PRICE	2011 RANK	2011 NM- PRICE	$ INCR.	% INCR.
Action Comics #1	1	$1,750,000	1	$1,400,000	$350,000	25%
Detective Comics #27	2	$1,350,000	2	$1,200,000	$150,000	13%
Superman #1	3	$650,000	3	$560,000	$90,000	16%
All-American Comics #16	4	$480,000	5	$400,000	$80,000	20%
Marvel Comics #1	5	$475,000	4	$460,000	$15,000	3%
Batman #1	6	$350,000	6	$285,000	$65,000	23%
Captain America Comics #1	7	$275,000	7	$240,000	$35,000	15%
Action Comics #7	8	$165,000	10	$125,000	$40,000	32%
Flash Comics #1	8	$165,000	8	$155,000	$10,000	6%
More Fun Comics #52	10	$150,000	9	$145,000	$5,000	3%
Adventure Comics #40	11	$125,000	11	$120,000	$5,000	4%
Detective Comics #31	11	$125,000	12	$100,000	$25,000	25%
Detective Comics #33	13	$115,000	12	$100,000	$15,000	15%
Action Comics #2	14	$110,000	15	$95,000	$15,000	16%
Detective Comics #29	14	$110,000	17	$88,000	$22,000	25%
Pep Comics #22	14	$110,000	23	$70,000	$40,000	57%
Whiz Comics #2 (#1)	14	$110,000	12	$100,000	$10,000	10%
Action Comics #10	18	$95,000	26	$66,000	$29,000	44%
All Star Comics #3	18	$95,000	16	$90,000	$5,000	6%
Archie Comics #1	20	$90,000	23	$70,000	$20,000	29%
Detective Comics #38	20	$90,000	17	$88,000	$2,000	2%
Detective Comics #1	22	VF $88,000	19	VF $84,000	$4,000	5%
Marvel Mystery Comics #9	23	$85,000	20	$80,000	$5,000	6%
All Star Comics #8	24	$80,000	21	$75,000	$5,000	7%
More Fun Comics #53	25	$77,000	21	$75,000	$2,000	3%
Action Comics #3	26	$70,000	31	$60,000	$10,000	17%
Marvel Mystery Comics #2	26	$70,000	25	$68,000	$2,000	3%
Sub-Mariner Comics #1	28	$68,000	27	$65,000	$3,000	5%
Human Torch #2 (#1)	29	$66,000	27	$65,000	$1,000	2%
Detective Comics #28	30	$65,000	34	$56,000	$9,000	16%
Green Lantern #1	31	$64,000	29	$64,000	$0	0%
Sensation Comics #1	32	$62,000	30	$62,000	$0	0%
Captain Marvel Adventures #1	33	$60,000	32	$57,000	$3,000	5%
Detective Comics #35	33	$60,000	39	$46,000	$14,000	30%
Marvel Mystery Comics #5	33	$60,000	32	$57,000	$3,000	5%
Wonder Woman #1	36	$58,000	35	$55,000	$3,000	5%
Adventure Comics #48	37	$55,000	36	$54,000	$1,000	2%
Suspense Comics #3	37	$55,000	38	$50,000	$5,000	10%
New Fun Comics #1	39	VF $53,000	37	VF $52,000	$1,000	2%
Action Comics #13	40	$45,000	59	$30,000	$15,000	50%
Superman #2	40	$45,000	42	$38,000	$7,000	18%

TITLE/ISSUE#	2012 RANK	2012 NM- PRICE	2011 RANK	2011 NM- PRICE	$ INCR.	% INCR.
Walt Disney's Comics & Stories #1	42	$44,000	40	$42,000	$2,000	5%
Captain America Comics #2	43	$42,000	42	$38,000	$4,000	11%
*Marvel Mystery Comics 132 pg. #	43	VF $42,000	42	VF $38,000	$4,000	11%
Action Comics #4	45	$40,000	50	$34,000	$6,000	18%
Action Comics #5	45	$40,000	50	$34,000	$6,000	18%
Action Comics #6	45	$40,000	50	$34,000	$6,000	18%
All-American Comics #19	45	$40,000	41	$39,000	$1,000	3%
Marvel Mystery Comics #3	45	$40,000	42	$38,000	$2,000	5%
Batman #2	50	$38,000	47	$35,000	$3,000	9%
Daring Mystery Comics #1	50	$38,000	42	$38,000	$0	0%
Marvel Mystery Comics #4	50	$38,000	54	$33,000	$5,000	15%
Captain America Comics 132 pg.	53	VF $36,000	47	VF $35,000	$1,000	3%
More Fun Comics #54	53	$36,000	50	$34,000	$2,000	6%
All Winners Comics #1	55	$35,000	47	$35,000	$0	0%
More Fun Comics #55	56	$34,000	54	$33,000	$1,000	3%
Captain America Comics #3	57	$33,000	59	$30,000	$3,000	10%
Motion Picture Funn. Wkly #1	57	$33,000	54	$33,000	$0	0%
Amazing Man Comics #5	59	$32,000	59	$30,000	$2,000	7%
Famous Funnies-Series 1	59	VF $32,000	57	VF $31,000	$1,000	3%
All-Select Comics #1	61	$31,000	59	$30,000	$1,000	3%
More Fun Comics #73	61	$31,000	57	$31,000	$0	0%
New Book of Comics #1	63	VF $30,000	59	VF $30,000	$0	0%
Wonder Comics #1	63	$30,000	65	$28,000	$2,000	7%
Mystic Comics #1	65	$29,000	65	$28,000	$1,000	4%
New York World's Fair 1939	65	VF/NM $29,000	64	VF/NM $29,000	$0	0%
Detective Comics #2	67	VF $28,000	78	VF $24,000	$4,000	17%
Four Color Ser. 1 (Donald Duck) #4	67	$28,000	72	$25,000	$3,000	12%
Marvel Mystery Comics #8	67	$28,000	67	$27,000	$1,000	4%
Red Raven Comics #1	67	$28,000	78	$24,000	$4,000	17%
Silver Streak Comics #6	67	$28,000	69	$26,500	$1,500	6%
Action Comics #8	72	$27,000	88	$22,000	$5,000	23%
Action Comics #9	72	$27,000	88	$22,000	$5,000	23%
Wow Comics (FAW) #1	72	$27,000	67	$27,000	$0	0%
All-Flash #1	75	$26,000	70	$26,000	$0	0%
Marvel Mystery Comics #10	75	$26,000	72	$25,000	$1,000	4%
Young Allies Comics #1	75	$26,000	70	$26,000	$0	0%
Adventure Comics #73	78	$25,000	72	$25,000	$0	0%
All-American Comics #17	78	$25,000	88	$22,000	$3,000	14%
New Fun Comics #6	78	VF $25,000	76	VF $24,500	$500	2%
Planet Comics #1	78	$25,000	76	$24,500	$500	2%
Superman #3	78	$25,000	88	$22,000	$3,000	14%
World's Best Comics #1	78	$25,000	72	$25,000	$0	0%
Adventure Comics #61	84	$24,000	78	$24,000	$0	0%
All Star Comics #1	84	$24,000	81	$23,500	$500	2%
All-American Comics #18	84	$24,000	83	$23,000	$1,000	4%
Famous Funnies #1	84	VF $24,000	83	VF $23,000	$1,000	4%
Green Giant Comics #1	84	$24,000	83	$23,000	$1,000	4%
Daredevil #1	89	$23,500	81	$23,500	$0	0%
All-American Comics #25	90	$23,000	88	$22,000	$1,000	5%
Looney Tunes and Merrie Melodies #1	90	$23,000	86	$22,500	$500	2%
New Fun Comics #2	90	VF $23,000	86	VF $22,500	$500	2%
Daring Mystery Comics #2	93	$22,000	94	$21,000	$1,000	5%
Dick Tracy-Feature Book nn (#1)	93	$22,000	94	$21,000	$1,000	5%
Jumbo Comics #1	93	VF $22,000	93	VF $21,500	$500	2%
Batman #3	96	$21,000	97	$20,000	$1,000	5%
Comics Magazine #1	96	VF $21,000	97	VF $20,000	$1,000	5%
Detective Comics #3	96	VF $21,000	107	VF $18,000	$3,000	17%
Double Action Comics #2	96	$21,000	96	$20,500	$500	2%
Exciting Comics #9	96	$21,000	97	$20,000	$1,000	5%

TOP 20 SILVER AGE BOOKS

TITLE/ISSUE#	2012 RANK	2012 NM- PRICE	2011 RANK	2011 NM- PRICE	$ INCR.	% INCR.
Amazing Fantasy #15	1	$150,000	1	$125,000	$25,000	20%
Fantastic Four #1	2	$90,000	2	$80,000	$10,000	13%
Incredible Hulk #1	2	$90,000	3	$75,000	$15,000	20%
Showcase #4 (The Flash)	4	$60,000	4	$56,000	$4,000	7%
Amazing Spider-Man #1	5	$57,000	5	$54,000	$3,000	6%
Journey Into Mystery #83 (Thor)	6	$40,000	6	$30,000	$10,000	33%
X-Men #1	7	$35,000	6	$30,000	$5,000	17%
Tales of Suspense #39 (Iron Man)	8	$32,000	8	$25,000	$7,000	28%
Avengers #1	9	$25,000	13	$15,000	$10,000	67%
Showcase #22 (Green Lantern)	10	$24,000	12	$16,000	$8,000	50%
Brave and the Bold #28	11	$23,000	9	$20,000	$3,000	15%
Tales To Astonish #27 (Ant-Man)	12	$20,000	13	$15,000	$5,000	33%
The Flash #105	13	$19,000	11	$18,000	$1,000	6%
Showcase #8 (The Flash)	14	$18,500	10	$18,500	$0	0%
Fantastic Four #5	15	$16,500	17	$14,000	$2,500	18%
Adventure Comics #247 (Legion)	16	$16,000	13	$15,000	$1,000	7%
Justice League of America #1	16	$16,000	13	$15,000	$1,000	7%
Green Lantern #1	18	$14,000	19	$12,500	$1,500	12%
Showcase #9 (Lois Lane)	18	$14,000	17	$14,000	$0	0%
Fantastic Four #2	20	$12,000	20	$11,000	$1,000	9%

TOP 10 BRONZE AGE BOOKS

TITLE/ISSUE#	2012 RANK	2012 NM- PRICE	2011 RANK	2011 NM- PRICE	$ INCR.	% INCR.
Star Wars #1 (35¢ price variant)	1	$3,500	1	$3,000	$500	17%
Green Lantern #76	2	$2,600	2	$2,500	$100	4%
Incredible Hulk #181	3	$1,725	3	$1,700	$25	1%
Iron Fist #14 (35¢ price variant)	4	$1,700	4	$1,650	$50	3%
Cerebus #1	5	$1,500	7	$1,200	$300	25%
Giant-Size X-Men #1	6	$1,300	5	$1,300	$0	0%
X-Men #94	7	$1,275	6	$1,250	$25	2%
House of Secrets #92	8	$1,175	8	$1,150	$25	2%
DC 100 Page Super Spectacular #5	9	$1,150	8	$1,150	$0	0%
Amazing Spider-Man #129	10	$950	10	$925	$25	3%

TOP 10 COPPER AGE BOOKS

TITLE/ISSUE#	2012 RANK	2012 NM- PRICE	2011 RANK	2011 NM- PRICE	$ INCR.	% INCR.
Gobbledygook #1	1	$5,500	1	$5,000	$500	10%
Gobbledygook #2	2	$2,100	2	$2000	$100	5%
Miracleman #1 Gold Edition	3	$1,500	3	$1,500	$0	0%
Miracleman #1 Blue Edition	4	$800	4	$800	$0	0%
Albedo #2	4	$800	5	$750	$50	7%
Vampirella #113	6	$550	6	$550	$0	0%
Grendel #1	7	$190	7	$190	$0	0%
Primer #2	8	$160	8	$160	$0	0%
Spider-Man #1 (Platinum)	9	$130	9	$130	$0	0%
Spider-Man #1 (2nd pr. w/Gold UPC)	10	$120	10	$120	$0	0%

*Teenage Mutant Ninja Turtles #1 - Recent sales of this book include a CGC 9.6 for $5,975 and a CGC 9.4 for $3,585

TOP 20 BIG LITTLE BOOKS

BOOK #	TITLE	2012 RANK	2012 VF/NM PRICE	2011 RANK	2011 VF/NM PRICE	$ INCR.	% INCR.
731	Mickey Mouse the Mail Pilot (variant version of Mickey Mouse #717)	(Fine copy sold at auction for $5,090)					
nn	Mickey Mouse and Minnie Mouse at Macy's	2	$3,600	2	$3,500	$100	3%
717	Mickey Mouse (skinny Mickey on-c)	3	$3,135	3	$3,135	$0	0%
nn	Mickey Mouse and Minnie March to Macy's	4	$2,400	5	$2,400	$0	0%
725	Big Little Mother Goose HC	4	$2,400	5	$2,400	$0	0%
W-707	Dick Tracy The Detective	6	$2,200	4	$2,500	-$300	-12%
717	Mickey Mouse (reg. Mickey on-c)	7	$1,750	7	$1,750	$0	0%
4063	Popeye Thimble Theater Starring... (2nd printing)	8	$1,620	8	$1,620	$0	0%
721	Big Little Paint Book (336 pg.)	9	$1,500	9	$1,500	$0	0%
725	Big Little Mother Goose SC	9	$1,500	9	$1,500	$0	0%
nn	Mickey Mouse the Mail Pilot (Great Big Midget Book)	9	$1,500	9	$1,500	$0	0%
nn	Mickey Mouse (Great Big Midget Book)	12	$1,485	12	$1,485	$0	0%
4062	Mickey Mouse and the Smugglers	13	$1,430	13	$1,430	$0	0%
4063	Popeye Thimble Theater Starring...(1st pr.)	14	$1,385	14	$1,385	$0	0%
nn	Mickey Mouse Silly Symphonies	15	$1,320	15	$1,320	$0	0%
nn	Buck Rogers	16	$1,250	15	$1,320	-$70	-5%
4062	Mickey Mouse, The Story of...	17	$1,210	17	$1,210	$0	0%
721	Big Little Paint Book (330 pg.)	18	$1,200	18	$1,200	$0	0%
nn	Mickey Mouse Sails For Treasure Island (Great Big Midget Book)	18	$1,200	18	$1,200	$0	0%
nn	Mickey Mouse and the Magic Carpet	20	$1,050	20	$1,050	$0	0%

TOP 10 PLATINUM AGE BOOKS

TITLE/ISSUE#	2012 RANK	2012 PRICE	2011 RANK	2011 PRICE	$ INCR.	% INCR.
Yellow Kid in McFadden Flats	1	FN $14,000	1	FN $14,000	$0	0%
Mickey Mouse Book (2nd printing)-variant	2	FN $8,000	2	FN $12,000	-$4,000	-33%
Little Sammy Sneeze	3	FN $6,000	5	FN $6,000	$0	0%
Mickey Mouse Book (1st printing)	3	VF $6,000	2	VF $12,000	-$6,000	-50%
Little Nemo 1906	5	FN $5,000	8	FN $5,000	$0	0%
Buster Brown and His Resolutions 1903	6	FN $4,500	7	FN $5,500	-$1,000	-18%
Pore Li'l Mose	6	FN $4,500	6	FN $5,775	-$1,275	-22%
Little Nemo 1909	8	FN $4,000	9	FN $4,000	$0	0%
Mickey Mouse Book (2nd printing)	9	VF $3,500	4	VF $10,000	-$6,500	-65%
Yellow Kid #1	9	FN $3,500	10	FN $3,500	$0	0%

TOP 10 CRIME BOOKS

TITLE/ISSUE#	2012 RANK	2012 NM- PRICE	2011 RANK	2011 NM- PRICE	$ INCR.	% INCR.
Crime Does Not Pay #22	1	$9,000	1	$8,200	$800	10%
Crime Does Not Pay #24	2	$7,000	2	$5,200	$1,800	35%
Crime Does Not Pay #23	3	$4,000	3	$3,600	$400	11%
True Crime Comics #2	4	$2,900	4	$2,800	$100	4%
The Killers #1	5	$2,100	5	$2,000	$100	5%
Crimes By Women #1	6	$2,000	6	$1,950	$50	3%
True Crime Comics #3	7	$1,950	7	$1,900	$50	3%
The Killers #2	8	$1,700	8	$1,600	$100	6%
True Crime Comics #4	9	$1,575	9	$1,550	$25	2%
Crime Does Not Pay, Best of ('44)	10	$1,500	10	$1,400	$100	7%

TOP 10 HORROR BOOKS

TITLE/ISSUE#	2012 RANK	2012 NM- PRICE	2011 RANK	2011 NM- PRICE	$ INCR.	% INCR.
Eerie #1	1	$9,000	2	$8,500	$500	6%
Vault of Horror #12	2	$8,700	1	$8,700	$0	0%
Tales of Terror Annual #1	3	VF $7,200	3	VF $6,600	$600	9%
Journey into Mystery #1	4	$6,200	4	$5,800	$400	7%
Strange Tales #1	5	$5,700	5	$5,500	$200	4%
Crypt of Terror #17	6	$5,200	6	$5,200	$0	0%
Haunt of Fear #15	7	$5,100	7	$5,100	$0	0%
Crime Patrol #15	8	$4,700	8	$4,700	$0	0%
Tales to Astonish #1	9	$4,600	9	$4,200	$400	10%
House of Mystery #1	10	$3,900	10	$3,900	$0	0%

TOP 10 ROMANCE BOOKS

TITLE/ISSUE#	2012 RANK	2012 NM- PRICE	2011 RANK	2011 NM- PRICE	$ INCR.	% INCR.
Giant Comics Edition #12	1	$5,500	1	$4,800	$700	15%
Negro Romance #1	2	$2,500	2	$2,200	$300	14%
Negro Romance #2	3	$2,000	3	$1,700	$300	18%
Negro Romance #3	3	$2,000	3	$1,700	$300	18%
Intimate Confessions #1	5	$1,800	5	$1,600	$200	13%
Giant Comics Edition #9	6	$1,500	6	$1,400	$100	7%
Giant Comics Edition #15	7	$1,400	10	$1,250	$150	12%
Modern Love #1	8	$1,350	7	$1,300	$50	4%
A Moon, A Girl...Romance #9	9	$1,285	8	$1,275	$10	1%
A Moon, A Girl...Romance #12	9	$1,285	8	$1,275	$10	1%

TOP 10 SCI-FI BOOKS

TITLE/ISSUE#	2012 RANK	2012 NM- PRICE	2011 RANK	2011 NM- PRICE	$ INCR.	% INCR.
Mystery In Space #1	1	$6,500	1	$6,400	$100	2%
Showcase #17 (Adam Strange)	2	$5,700	3	$5,200	$500	10%
Strange Adventures #1	3	$4,500	2	$5,900	-$1,400	-24%
Showcase #15 (Space Ranger)	4	$4,300	5	$4,200	$100	2%
Weird Science-Fantasy Annual 1952	4	$4,300	4	$4,300	$0	0%
Journey Into Unknown Worlds #36	6	$4,200	6	$4,100	$100	2%
Fawcett Movie #15 (Man From Planet X)	7	$3,800	7	$3,800	$0	0%
Weird Fantasy #13 (#1)	8	$3,500	9	$3,500	$0	0%
Weird Science #12 (#1)	8	$3,500	9	$3,500	$0	0%
Strange Adventures #9	10	$2,800	8	$3,550	-$750	-21%

TOP 10 WESTERN BOOKS

TITLE/ISSUE#	2012 RANK	2012 NM- PRICE	2011 RANK	2011 NM- PRICE	$ INCR.	% INCR.
Gene Autry Comics #1	1	$7,500	1	$10,000	-$2,500	-25%
Hopalong Cassidy #1	2	$6,000	2	$6,000	$0	0%
*Lone Ranger Ice Cream 1939 2nd	2	VF $6,000	2	VF $6,000	$0	0%
*Lone Ranger Ice Cream 1939	4	VF $4,200	4	VF $4,200	$0	0%
Roy Rogers Four Color #38	5	$4,100	5	$4,000	$100	3%
Red Ryder Comics #1	6	$3,800	6	$3,800	$0	0%
*Tom Mix Ralston #1	7	$3,600	7	$3,600	$0	0%
Western Picture Stories #1	8	$3,200	9	$3,100	$100	3%
John Wayne Adventure Comics #1	9	$2,500	12	$2,500	$0	0%
*Red Ryder Victory Patrol '42	9	$2,500	8	$3,500	-$1,000	-29%

GRADING DEFINITIONS

When grading a comic book, common sense must be employed. The overall eye appeal and beauty of the comic book must be taken into account along with its technical flaws to arrive at the appropriate grade.

10.0 GEM MINT (GM): This is an exceptional example of a given book - the best ever seen. The slightest bindery defects and/or printing flaws may be seen only upon very close inspection. The overall look is "as if it has never been handled or released for purchase." Only the slightest bindery or printing defects are allowed, and these would be imperceptible on first viewing. No bindery tears. Cover is flat with no surface wear. Inks are bright with high reflectivity. Well centered and firmly secured to interior pages. Corners are cut square and sharp. No creases. No dates or stamped markings allowed. No soiling, staining or other discoloration. Spine is tight and flat. No spine roll or split allowed. Staples must be original, centered and clean with no rust. No staple tears or stress lines. Paper is white, supple and fresh. No hint of acidity in the odor of the newsprint. No interior autographs or owner signatures. Centerfold is firmly secure. No interior tears.

9.9 MINT (MT): Near perfect in every way. Only subtle bindery or printing defects are allowed. No bindery tears. Cover is flat with no surface wear. Inks are bright with high reflectivity. Generally well centered and firmly secured to interior pages. Corners are cut square and sharp. No creases. Small, inconspicuous, lightly penciled, stamped or inked arrival dates are acceptable as long as they are in an unobtrusive location. No soiling, staining or other discoloration. Spine is tight and flat. No spine roll or split allowed. Staples must be original, generally centered and clean with no rust. No staple tears or stress lines. Paper is white, supple and fresh. No hint of acidity in the odor of the newsprint. Centerfold is firmly secure. No interior tears.

9.8 NEAR MINT/MINT (NM/MT): Nearly perfect in every way with only minor imperfections that keep it from the next higher grade. Only subtle bindery or printing defects are allowed. No bindery tears. Cover is flat with no surface wear. Inks are bright with high reflectivity. Generally well centered and firmly secured to interior pages. Corners are cut square and sharp. No creases. Small, inconspicuous, lightly penciled, stamped or inked arrival dates are acceptable as long as they are in an unobtrusive location. No soiling, staining or other discoloration. Spine is tight and flat. No spine roll or split allowed. Staples must be original, generally centered and clean with no rust. No staple tears or stress lines. Paper is off-white to white, supple and fresh. No hint of acidity in the odor of the newsprint. Centerfold is firmly secure. Only the slightest interior tears are allowed.

9.6 NEAR MINT+ (NM+): Nearly perfect with a minor additional virtue or virtues that raise it from Near Mint. The overall look is "as if it was just purchased and read once or twice." Only subtle bindery or printing defects are allowed. No bindery tears are allowed, although on Golden Age books bindery tears of up to 1/8" have been noted. Cover is flat with no surface wear. Inks are bright with high reflectivity. Well centered and firmly secured to interior pages. One corner may be almost imperceptibly blunted, but still almost sharp and cut square. Almost imperceptible indentations are permissible, but no creases, bends, or color break. Small, inconspicuous, lightly penciled, stamped or inked arrival dates are acceptable as long as they are in an unobtrusive location. No soiling, staining or other discoloration. Spine is tight and flat. No spine roll or split allowed. Staples must be original, generally centered, with only the slightest discoloration. No staple tears, stress lines, or rust migration. Paper is off-white, supple and fresh. No hint of acidity in the odor of the newsprint. Centerfold is firmly secure. Only the slightest interior tears are allowed.

9.4 NEAR MINT (NM): Nearly perfect with only minor imperfections that keep it from the next higher grade. Minor feathering that does not distract from the overall beauty of an otherwise higher grade copy is acceptable for this grade. The overall look is "as if it was just purchased and read once or twice." Subtle bindery defects are allowed. Bindery tears must be less than 1/16" on Silver Age and later books, although on Golden Age books bindery tears of up to 1/4" have been noted. Cover is flat with no surface wear. Inks are bright with high reflectivity. Generally well centered and secured to interior pages. Corners are cut square and sharp with ever-so-slight blunting permitted. A 1/16" bend is permitted with no color break. No creases. Small, inconspicuous, lightly penciled, stamped or inked arrival dates are acceptable as long as they are in an unobtrusive location. No soiling, staining or other discoloration apart from slight foxing. Spine is tight and flat. No spine roll or split allowed. Staples are generally centered; may have slight discoloration. No staple tears are allowed; almost no stress lines. No rust migration. In rare cases, a comic was not stapled at the bindery and therefore has a missing staple; this is not considered a defect. Any staple can be replaced on books up to Fine, but only vintage staples can be used on books from Very Fine to Near Mint. Mint books must have original staples. Paper is cream to off-white, supple and fresh. No hint of acidity in the odor of the newsprint. Centerfold is secure. Slight interior tears are allowed.

9.2 NEAR MINT– (NM–): Nearly perfect with only a minor additional defect or defects that keep it from Near Mint. A limited number of minor bindery defects are allowed. A light, barely noticeable water stain or minor foxing that does not distract from the beauty of the book is acceptable for this grade. Cover is flat with no surface wear. Inks are bright with only the slightest dimming of reflectivity. Generally well centered and secured to interior pages. Corners are cut square and sharp with ever-so-slight blunting permitted. A 1/16"-1/8" bend is permitted with no color break. No creases. Small, inconspicuous, lightly penciled, stamped or inked arrival dates are acceptable as long as they are in an unobtrusive location. No soiling, staining or other discoloration apart from slight foxing. Spine is tight and flat. No spine roll or split allowed. Staples may show some discoloration. No staple tears are allowed; almost no stress lines. No rust migration. In rare cases, a comic was not stapled at the bindery and therefore has a missing staple; this is not considered a defect. Any staple can be replaced on books up to Fine, but only vintage staples can be used on books from Very Fine to Near Mint. Mint books must have original staples. Paper is cream to off-white, supple and fresh. No hint of acidity in the odor of the newsprint. Centerfold is secure. Slight interior tears are allowed.

9.0 VERY FINE/NEAR MINT (VF/NM): Nearly perfect with outstanding eye appeal. A limited number of bindery defects are allowed. Almost flat cover with almost imperceptible wear. Inks are bright with slightly diminished reflectivity. An 1/8" bend is allowed if color is not broken. Corners are cut square and sharp with ever-so-slight blunting permitted but no creases. Several lightly penciled, stamped or inked arrival dates are acceptable. No obvious soiling, staining or other discoloration, except for very minor foxing. Spine is tight and flat. No spine roll or split allowed. Staples may show some discoloration. Only the slightest staple tears are allowed. A very minor accumulation of stress lines may be present if they are nearly imperceptible. No rust migration. In rare cases, a comic was not stapled at the bindery and therefore has a missing staple; this is not considered a defect. Any staple can be replaced on books up to Fine, but only vintage staples can be used on books from Very Fine to Near Mint. Mint books must have original staples. Paper is cream to off-white and supple. No hint of acidity in the odor of the newsprint. Centerfold is secure. Very minor interior tears may be present.

8.5 VERY FINE+ (VF+): Fits the criteria for Very Fine but with an additional virtue or small accumulation of virtues that improves the book's appearance by a perceptible amount.

8.0 VERY FINE (VF): An excellent copy with outstanding eye appeal. Sharp, bright and clean with supple pages. A comic book in this grade has the appearance of having been carefully handled. A limited accumulation of minor bindery defects is allowed. Cover is relatively flat with minimal surface wear beginning to show, possibly including some minute wear at corners. Inks are generally bright with moderate to high reflectivity. A 1/4" crease is acceptable if color is not broken. Stamped or inked arrival dates may be present. No obvious soiling, staining or other discoloration, except for minor foxing. Spine is almost flat with no roll. Possible minor color break allowed. Staples may show some discoloration. Very slight staple tears and a few almost very minor to minor stress lines may be present. No rust migration. In rare cases, a comic was not stapled at the bindery and therefore has a missing staple; this is not considered a defect. Any staple can be replaced on books up to Fine, but only vintage staples can be used on books from Very Fine to Near Mint. Mint books must have original staples. Paper is tan to cream and supple. No hint of acidity in the odor of the newsprint. Centerfold is mostly secure. Minor interior tears at the margin may be present.

7.5 VERY FINE– (VF–): Fits the criteria for Very Fine but with an additional defect or small accumulation of defects that detracts from the book's appearance by a perceptible amount.

7.0 FINE/VERY FINE (FN/VF): An above-average copy that shows minor wear but is still relatively flat and clean with outstanding eye appeal. A small accumulation of minor bindery defects is allowed. Minor cover wear beginning to show with interior yellowing or tanning allowed, possibly including minor creases. Corners may be blunted or abraded. Inks are generally bright with a moderate reduction in reflectivity. Stamped or inked arrival dates may be present. No obvious soiling, staining or other discoloration, except for minor foxing. The slightest spine roll may be present, as well as a possible moderate color break. Staples may show some discoloration. Slight staple tears and a slight accumulation of light stress lines may be present. Slight rust migration. In rare cases, a comic was not stapled at the bindery and therefore has a missing staple; this is not considered a defect. Any staple can be replaced on books up to Fine, but only vintage staples can be used on books from Very Fine to Near Mint. Mint books must have original staples. Paper is tan to cream, but not brown. No hint of acidity in the odor of the newsprint. Centerfold is mostly secure. Minor interior tears at the margin may be present.

6.5 FINE+ (FN+): Fits the criteria for Fine but with an additional virtue or small accumulation of virtues that improves the book's appearance by a perceptible amount.

6.0 FINE (FN): An above-average copy that shows minor wear but is still relatively flat and clean with no significant creasing or other serious defects. Eye appeal is somewhat reduced because of slight surface wear and the accumulation of small defects, especially on the spine and edges. A FINE condition comic book appears to have been read a few times and has been handled with moderate care. Some accumulation of minor bindery defects is allowed. Minor cover wear apparent, with minor to moderate creases. Inks show a major reduction in reflectivity. Blunted or abraded corners are more common, as is minor staining, soiling, discoloration, and/or foxing. Stamped or inked arrival dates may be present. A minor spine roll is allowed. There can also be a 1/4" spine split or severe color break. Staples show minor discoloration. Minor staple tears and an accumulation of stress lines may be present, as well as minor rust migration. In rare cases, a comic was not stapled at the bindery and therefore has a missing staple; this is not considered a defect. Any staple can be replaced on books up to Fine, but only vintage staples can be used on books from Very Fine to Near Mint. Mint books must have original staples. Paper is brown to tan and fairly supple with no signs of brittleness. No hint of acidity in the odor of the newsprint. Minor interior tears at the margin may be present. Centerfold may be loose but not detached.

5.5 FINE– (FN–): Fits the criteria for Fine but with an additional defect or small accumulation of defects that detracts from the book's appearance by a perceptible amount.

5.0 VERY GOOD/FINE (VG/FN): An above-average but well-used comic book. A comic in this grade shows some moderate wear; eye appeal is somewhat reduced because of the accumulation of defects. Still a desirable copy that has been handled with some care. An accumulation of bindery defects is allowed. Minor to moderate cover wear apparent, with minor to moderate creases and/or dimples. Inks have major to extreme reduction in reflectivity. Blunted or abraded corners are increasingly common, as is minor to moderate staining, discoloration, and/or foxing. Stamped or inked arrival dates may be present. A minor to moderate spine roll is allowed. A spine split of up to 1/2" may be present. Staples show minor discoloration. A slight accumulation of minor staple tears and an accumulation of minor stress lines may also be present, as well as minor rust migration. In rare cases, a comic was not stapled at the bindery and therefore has a missing staple; this is not considered a defect. Any staple can be replaced on books up to Fine, but only vintage staples can be used on books from Very Fine to Near Mint. Mint books must have original staples. Paper is brown to tan with no signs of brittleness. May have the faintest trace of an acidic odor. Centerfold may be loose but not detached. Minor tears may also be present.

4.5 VERY GOOD+ (VG+): Fits the criteria for Very Good but with an additional virtue or small accumulation of virtues that improves the book's appearance by a perceptible amount.

4.0 VERY GOOD (VG): The average used comic book. A comic in this grade shows some significant moderate wear, but still has not accumulated enough total defects to reduce eye appeal to the point that it is not a desirable copy. Cover shows moderate to significant wear, and may be loose but not completely detached. Moderate to extreme reduction in reflectivity. Can have an accumulation of creases or dimples. Corners may be blunted or abraded. Store stamps, name stamps, arrival dates, initials, etc. have no effect on this grade. Some discoloration, fading, foxing, and even minor soiling is allowed. As much as a 1/4" triangle can be missing out of the corner or edge; a missing 1/8" square is also acceptable. Only minor unobtrusive tape and other amateur repair allowed on otherwise high grade copies. Moderate spine roll may be present and/or a 1" spine split. Staples discolored. Minor to moderate staple tears and stress lines may be present, as well as some rust migration. Paper is brown but not brittle. A minor acidic odor can be detectable. Minor to moderate tears may be present. Centerfold may be loose or detached at one staple.

3.5 VERY GOOD– (VG–): Fits the criteria for Very Good but with an additional defect or small accumulation of defects that detracts from the book's appearance by a perceptible amount.

3.0 GOOD/VERY GOOD (GD/VG): A used comic book showing some substantial wear. Cover shows significant wear, and may be loose or even detached at one staple. Cover reflectivity is very low. Can have a book-length crease and/or dimples. Corners may be blunted or even rounded. Discoloration, fading, foxing, and even minor to moderate soiling is allowed. A triangle from 1/4" to 1/2" can be missing out of the corner or edge; a missing 1/8" to 1/4" square is also acceptable. Tape and other amateur repair may be present. Moderate spine roll likely. May have a spine split of anywhere from 1" to 1-1/2". Staples may be rusted or replaced. Minor to moderate staple tears and moderate stress lines may be present, as well as some rust migration. Paper is brown but not brittle. Centerfold may be loose or detached at one staple. Minor to moderate interior tears may be present.

2.5 GOOD+ (GD+): Fits the criteria for Good but with an additional virtue or small accumulation of virtues that improves the book's appearance by a perceptible amount.

2.0 GOOD (GD): Shows substantial wear; often considered a "reading copy." Cover shows significant wear and may even be detached. Cover reflectivity is low and in some cases completely absent. Book-length creases and dimples may be present. Rounded corners are more common. Moderate soiling, staining, discoloration and foxing may be present. The largest piece allowed missing from the front or back cover is usually a 1/2" triangle or a 1/4" square, although some Silver Age books such as 1960s Marvels have had the price corner box clipped from the top left front cover and may be considered Good if they would otherwise have graded higher. Tape and other forms of amateur repair are common in Silver Age and older books. Spine roll is likely. May have up to a 2" spine split. Staples may be degraded, replaced or missing. Moderate staple tears and stress lines may be present, as well as rust migration. Paper is brown but not brittle. Centerfold may be loose or detached. Moderate interior tears may be present.

1.8 GOOD– (GD–): Fits the criteria for Good but with an additional defect or small accumulation of defects that detracts from the book's appearance by a perceptible amount.

1.5 FAIR/GOOD (FR/GD): A comic showing substantial to heavy wear. A copy in this grade still has all pages and covers, although there may be pieces missing. Books in this grade are commonly creased, scuffed, abraded, soiled, and possibly unattractive, but still generally readable. Cover shows considerable wear and may be detached. Nearly no reflectivity to no reflectivity remaining. Store stamp, name stamp, arrival date and initials are permitted. Book-length creases, tears and folds may be present. Rounded corners are increasingly common. Soiling, staining, discoloration and foxing is generally present. Up to 1/10 of the back cover may be missing. Tape and other forms of amateur repair are increasingly common in Silver Age and older books. Spine roll is common. May have a spine split between 2" and 2/3 the length of the book. Staples may be degraded, replaced or missing. Staple tears and stress lines are common, as well as rust migration. Paper is brown and may show brittleness around the edges. Acidic odor may be present. Centerfold may be loose or detached. Interior tears are common.

1.0 FAIR (FR): A copy in this grade shows heavy wear. Some collectors consider this the lowest collectible grade because comic books in lesser condition are usually incomplete and/or brittle. Comics in this grade are usually soiled, faded, ragged and possibly unattractive. This is the last grade in which a comic remains generally readable. Cover may be detached, and inks have lost all reflectivity. Creases, tears and/or folds are prevalent. Corners are commonly rounded or absent. Soiling and staining is present. Books in this condition generally have all pages and most of the covers, although there may be up to 1/4 of the front cover missing or no back cover, but not both. Tape and other forms of amateur repair are more common. Spine roll is more common; spine split can extend up to 2/3 the length of the book. Staples may be missing or show rust and discoloration. An accumulation of staple tears and stress lines may be present, as well as rust migration. Paper is brown and may show brittleness around the edges but not in the central portion of the pages. Acidic odor may be present. Accumulation of interior tears. Chunks may be missing. The centerfold may be missing if readability is generally preserved (although there may be difficulty). Coupons may be cut.

0.5 POOR (PR): Most comic books in this grade have been sufficiently degraded to the point where there is little or no collector value; they are easily identified by a complete absence of eye appeal. Comics in this grade are brittle almost to the point of turning to dust with a touch, and are usually incomplete. Extreme cover fading may render the cover almost indiscernible. May have extremely severe stains, mildew or heavy cover abrasion to the point that some cover inks are indistinct/absent. Covers may be detached with large chunks missing. Can have extremely ragged edges and extensive creasing. Corners are rounded or virtually absent. Covers may have been defaced with paints, varnishes, glues, oil, indelible markers or dyes, and may have suffered heavy water damage. Can also have extensive amateur repairs such as laminated covers. Extreme spine roll present; can have extremely ragged spines or a complete, book-length split. Staples can be missing or show extreme rust and discoloration. Extensive staple tears and stress lines may be present, as well as extreme rust migration. Paper exhibits moderate to severe brittleness (where the comic book literally falls apart when examined). Extreme acidic odor may be present. Extensive interior tears. Multiple pages, including the centerfold, may be missing that affect readability. Coupons may be cut.

PUBLISHERS' CODES

The following abbreviations are used with cover reproductions throughout the book for copyright purposes:

ABC-America's Best Comics
AC-AC Comics
ACE-Ace Periodicals
ACG-American Comics Group
AJAX-Ajax-Farrell
AP-Archie Publications
BP-Better Publications
C & L-Cupples & Leon
CC-Charlton Comics
CEN-Centaur Publications
CCG-Columbia Comics Group
CG-Catechetical Guild
CHES-Harry 'A' Chesler
CLDS-Classic Det. Stories
CM-Comics Magazine
CN-Cartoon Network
CPI-Conan Properties Inc.
DC-DC Comics, Inc.
DELL-Dell Publishing Co.
DH-Dark Horse
DIS-Disney Enterprises, Inc.
DMP-David McKay Publishing
DS-D. S. Publishing Co.
EAS-Eastern Color Printing Co.
EC-E. C. Comics
ECL-Eclipse Comics
ENWIL-Enwil Associates
EP-Elliott Publications
ERB-Edgar Rice Burroughs
FAW-Fawcett Publications
FC-First Comics
FF-Famous Funnies
FH-Fiction House Magazines
FOX-Fox Features Syndicate
GIL-Gilberton
GK-Gold Key
GP-Great Publications
HARV-Harvey Publications
H-B-Hanna-Barbera
HILL-Hillman Periodicals
HOKE-Holyoke Publishing Co.
IM-Image Comics
KING-King Features Syndicate
LEV-Lev Gleason Publications
MAL-Malibu Comics
MAR-Marvel Characters, Inc.
ME-Magazine Enterprises
MLJ-MLJ Magazines
MS-Mirage Studios
NOVP-Novelty Press
NYNS-New York News Syndicate
PG-Premier Group
PINE-Pines
PMI-Parents' Magazine Institute
PRIZE-Prize Publications
QUA-Quality Comics Group
REAL-Realistic Comics
RH-Rural Home
S & S-Street and Smith Publishers
SKY-Skywald Publications
STAR-Star Publications
STD-Standard Comics
STJ-St. John Publishing Co.
SUPR-Superior Comics
TC-Tower Comics
TM-Trojan Magazines
TMP-Todd McFarlane Prods.
TOBY-Toby Press
TOPS-Tops Comics
UFS-United Features Syndicate
VAL-Valiant
VITL-Vital Publications
WB-Warner Brothers.
WEST-Western Publishing Co.
WHIT-Whitman Publishing Co.
WHW-William H. Wise
WMG-William M. Gaines (E. C.)
WP-Warren Publishing Co.
YM-Youthful Magazines
Z-D-Ziff-Davis Publishing Co.

OVERSTREET ADVISORS

Even before the first edition of *The Overstreet Comic Book Price Guide* was printed, author Robert M. Overstreet solicited pricing data, historical notations, and general information from a variety of sources. What was initially an informal group offering input quickly became an organized field of comic book collectors, dealers and historians whose opinions are actively solicited in advance of each edition of this book. Some of these Overstreet Advisors are specialists who deal in particular niches within the comic book world, while others are generalists who are interested in commenting on the broader marketplace. Each advisor provides information from their respective areas of interest and expertise, spanning the history of American comics.

While some choose to offer pricing and historical information in the form of annotated sales catalogs, auction catalogs, or documented private sales, assistance from others comes in the form of the market reports such as those beginning on page 74 in this book. In addition to those who have served as Overstreet Advisors almost since *The Guide*'s inception, each year new contributors are sought.

With that in mind, we are pleased to present our newest Overstreet Advisors:

THE CLASS OF 2012

SHAWN CAFFREY
Finalizer/Modern Age Specialist
Certified Guaranty Co., LLC

JESSE JAMES CRISCIONE
Jesse James Comics
Glendale, AZ

BROCK DICKINSON
Collector
St. Catharines, ONT
Canada

JOSEPH FIORE
ComicWiz.com
Toronto, ONT Canada

DOUGLAS GILLOCK
ComicLink
Portland, ME

BEN LICHTENSTEIN
Zapp Comics
Wayne, NJ

TOM NELSON
Top Notch Comics
Yankton, SD

MICHAEL PAVLIC
Purple Gorilla Comics
Calgary, AB Canada

BRIAN SCHUTZER
Sparkle City Comics
Neat Stuff Collectibles
North Bergen, NJ

ALIKA SEKI
Bruce's Comics and Collectibles
Waihee, HI

A complete listing of our Overstreet Advisors can be found on our title page and beginning on page 1120.

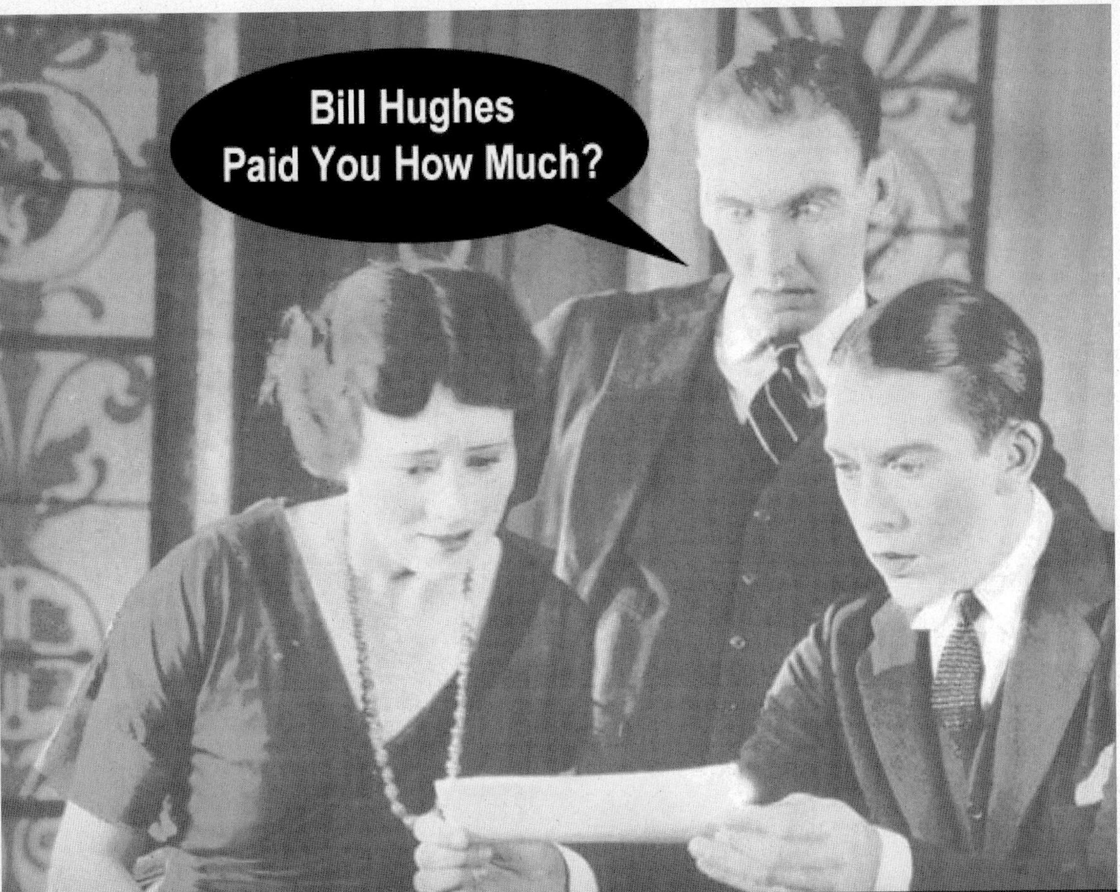

THE AMAZON.COM
OF COMIC BOOKS
THE NATION'S LARGEST COMIC DEALER
METROPOLIS
METROPOLIS COLLECTIBLES
DISCOUNT SECTION!
DAREDEVIL, THE MAN WITHOUT FEAR!
©DC
HOME OF
COMIC ZONE RADIO
TUNE IN TO FREE INTERNET INVERVIEW ARCHIVES FEATURING LEGENDS SUCH AS STAN LEE, WILL EISNER, JIM STERANKO, CARMINE INFANTINO, TODD MCFARLANE, JOE KUBERT, GENE COLAN, JOHN ROMITA NEAL ADAMS, MARV WOLFMAN & MORE!

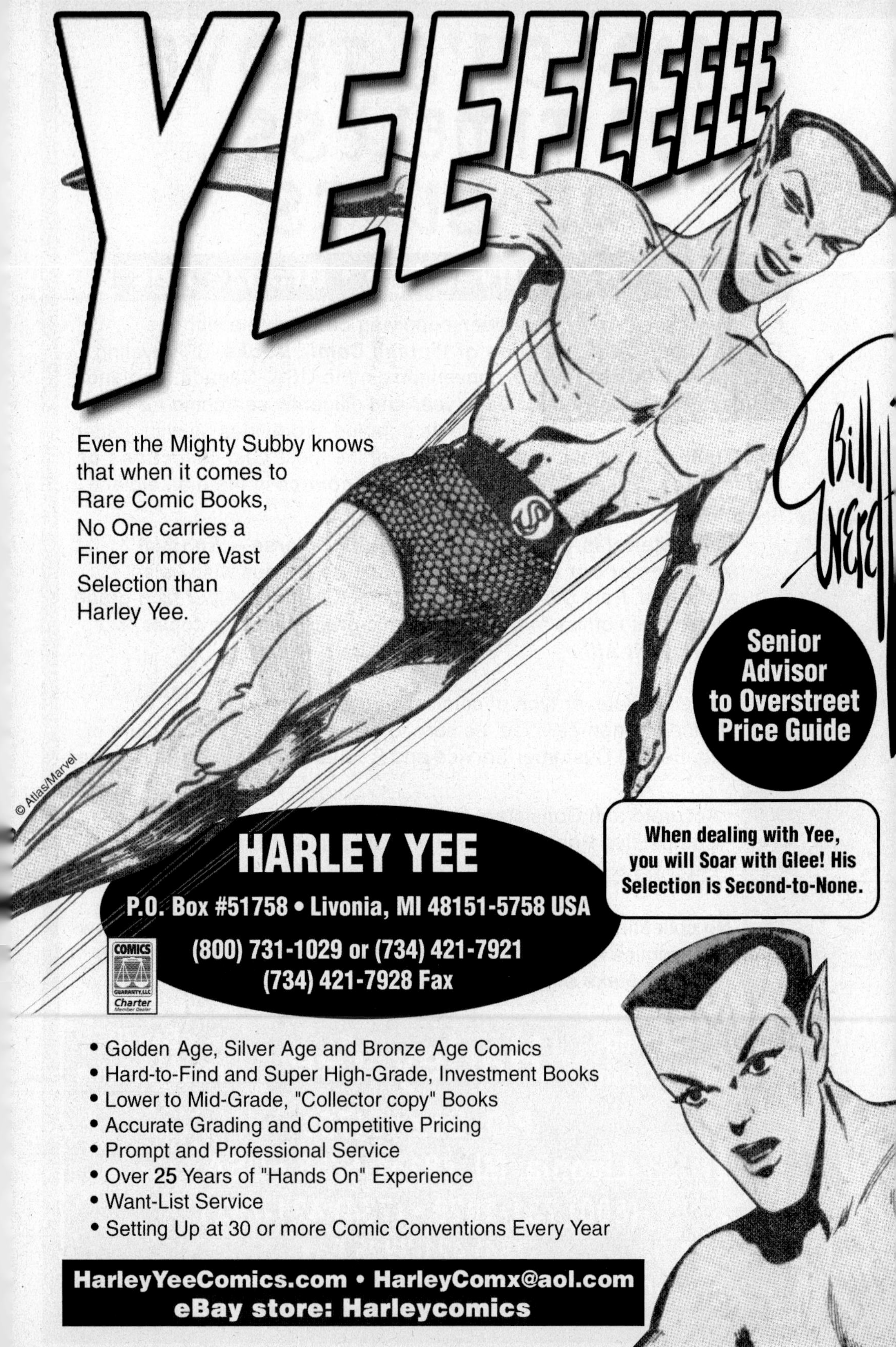
YEEEEEEEE
Even the Mighty Subby knows that when it comes to Rare Comic Books, No One carries a Finer or more Vast Selection than Harley Yee.
Bill Everett
Senior Advisor to Overstreet Price Guide
© Atlas/Marvel
HARLEY YEE
P.O. Box #51758 • Livonia, MI 48151-5758 USA
(800) 731-1029 or (734) 421-7921
(734) 421-7928 Fax
COMICS GUARANTY, LLC Charter Member Dealer
When dealing with Yee, you will Soar with Glee! His Selection is Second-to-None.
• Golden Age, Silver Age and Bronze Age Comics
• Hard-to-Find and Super High-Grade, Investment Books
• Lower to Mid-Grade, "Collector copy" Books
• Accurate Grading and Competitive Pricing
• Prompt and Professional Service
• Over 25 Years of "Hands On" Experience
• Want-List Service
• Setting Up at 30 or more Comic Conventions Every Year
HarleyYeeComics.com • HarleyComx@aol.com
eBay store: Harleycomics

COMIC COLLECTOR/DEALER

Paying up to **100% or more** of guide for many comics of interest

▼ POINTS TO CONSIDER ▼

TO SELL ON EBAY OR NOT TO SELL ON EBAY—THAT IS YOUR QUESTION?

- Consigning your comics to an eBay seller or an auction may not let you realize your collection's potential. EBay sellers and auctions charge 15% to 35% on every transaction regardless if they sell for less than guide. Many items sell for way below guide and you still pay all related charges. Many dealers buy these items well below market value. After you consider all charges and the final selling price you will generally net much less then we would pay. Selling to us there will be no charges, no waiting for payment. It's easy, and you will be treated with honesty and fairness.
- We have over 25 years experience in comic fandom. We have purchased many well-known collections while competing against other interested parties. Give us the chance to show you your top price.
- Being a collector/dealer gives us the ability to buy your entire collection and pay you the most for it. You will maximize your collection's value.

You have everything to gain by contacting us. WHY miss out on your BEST OFFER? Call 603-869-2097 today!

JAMES PAYETTE
Rare Books & Comics
P.O. Box 750 • Bethlehem, NH 03574
Tel (603) 869-2097 • Fax (603) 869-3475
www.jamespayettecomics.com
jimpayette@msn.com

CREDENTIALS

Special Advisor to Overstreet Guide	1985–present
Member AACBC	1990–present
Sotheby's Authenticating, Certification, and Grading committee	1991–2002
Experience as a Dealer/Collector	since 1975
CBG Customer Service Award Winner for many years	

PLEASE SEE OUR OTHER ADS FOR FURTHER REFERENCE

THE SELLER'S GUIDE

Yes, here are the pages you're looking for. These percentages will help you determine the sale value of your collection. If you do not find your title, call with any questions. We have purchased many of the major well-known collections. We are serious about buying your comics and paying you the most for them.

If you have comics or related items for sale call or send your list for a quote. No collection is too large or small. Immediate funds available of 500K and beyond.

These are some of the high prices we will pay. Percentages stated will be paid for any grade unless otherwise noted. All percentages based on this Overstreet Guide.

—JAMES PAYETTE

We are paying 100% of Guide for the following:

Title	Issues
All Select	1-up
All Winners	6-up
America's Best	1-up
Black Terror	1-25
Captain Aero	3-25
Captain America	11-up
Catman	1-up
Dynamic	2-15
Exciting	3-50
Human Torch	6-35
Marvel Mystery	11-up
Pep	22-45
Prize	2-50
Reform School Girl	1
Speed	10-30
Startling	2-up
Sub-Mariner	3-32
Thrilling	2-52
U.S.A.	6-up
Wonder (Nedor)	1-up

We are paying 75% of Guide for the following:

Action 1-15
Adventure 247
All New 2-13
All Winners 1-5
Amazing Man all
Amazing Mystery Funnies all
Andy Devine
Arrow all
Captain America 1-10
Daredevil (2nd) 1
Detective 2-26
Detective Eye all
Detective Picture Stories all
Fantastic Four 1-2
Four Favorites 3-27
Funny Pages all
Funny Picture Stories all
Hangman all
Jumbo 1-10
Journey into Mystery 83
Keen Detective Funnies all
Marvel Mystery 1-10
Mystery Men all
Showcase 4
Spiderman 1-2
Superman 1
Superman's Pal 1
Tim McCoy all
Wonder (Fox)
Young Allies all

BUYING & SELLING GOLDEN & SILVER AGE COMICS SINCE 1975

AMAZING FANTASY
SPIDER MAN
© MARVEL COMICS

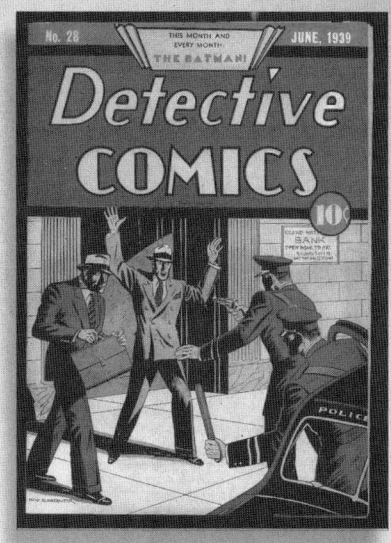

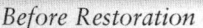

STOP!

If you have a comic collection to sell
BIG or SMALL, Please Read:

I am a comic collector with deep pockets and I love buying new collections and meeting new people every day.

Contact me FIRST before you contact anyone else in this book. I WILL pay more!

I will NOT be reselling your comics like 99% of the people in this book.

I will NOT tell you lies and undergrade your comics like some dealers.

I WILL give you the price that you deserve for your comics. You put so much effort into collecting over the years. Don't get ripped off in the end!

CONTACT JIM at (914) 523-7491
or JamesVarco@yahoo.com

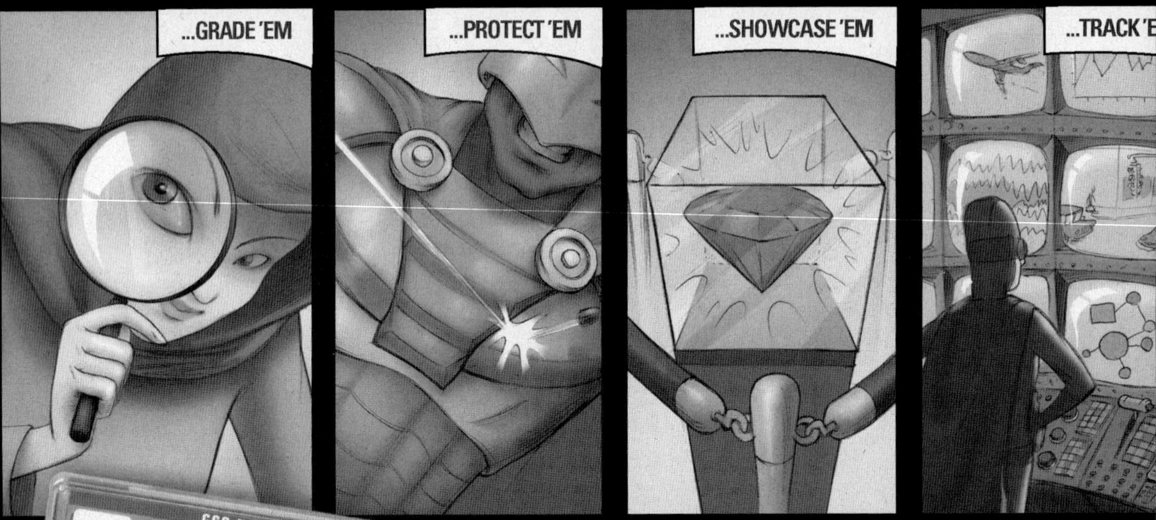

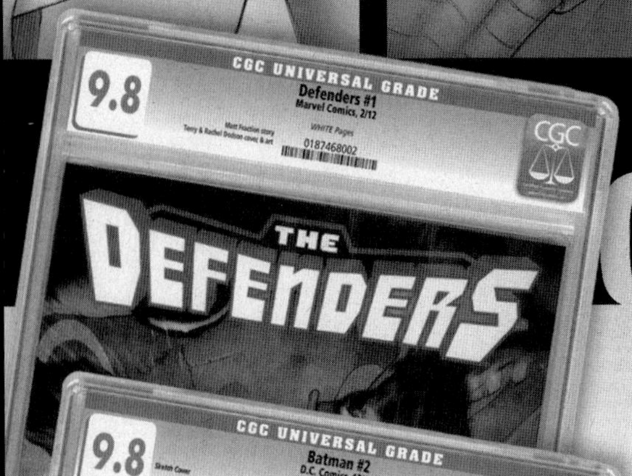

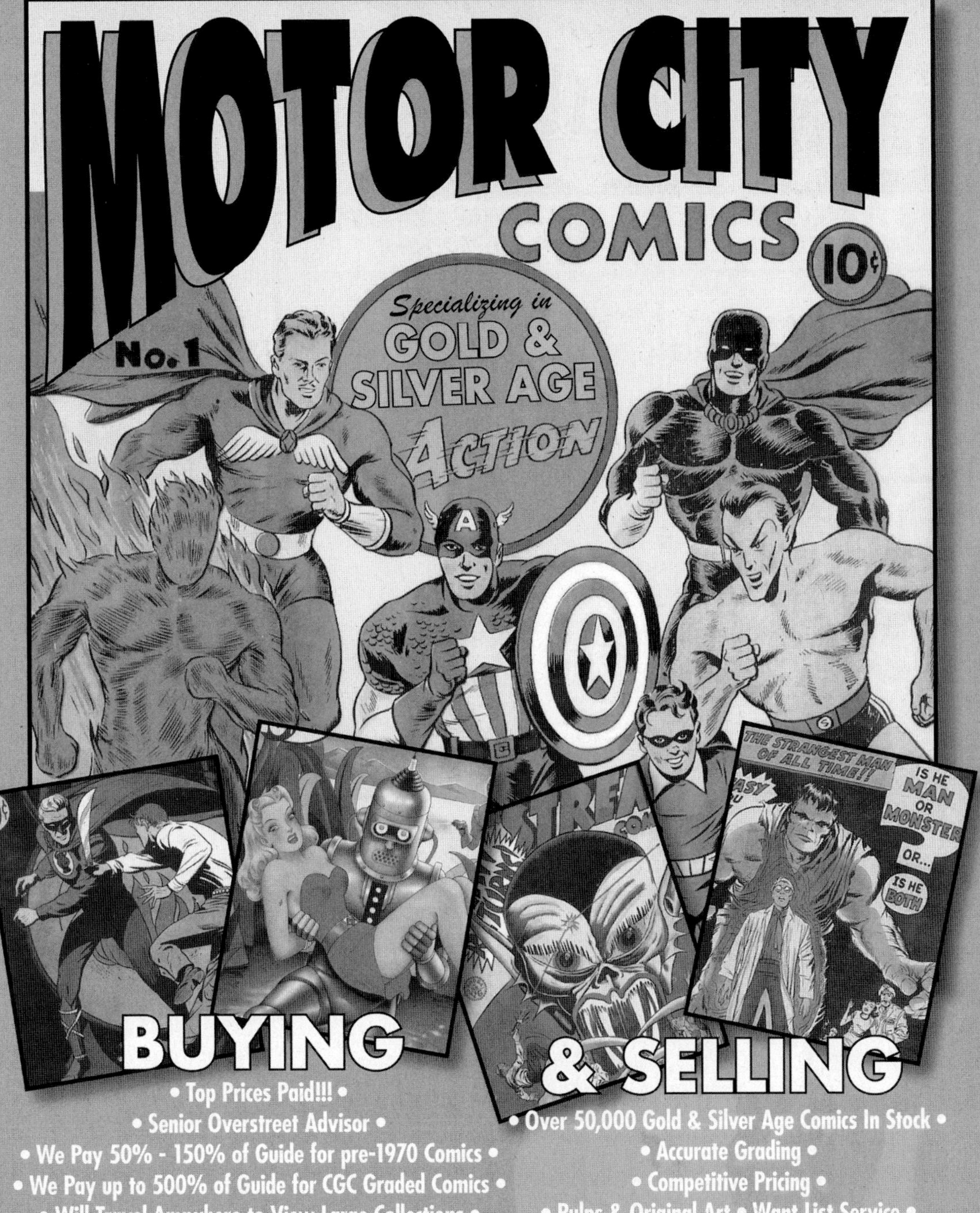
MOTOR CITY
COMICS
10¢
No. 1
Specializing in
GOLD &
SILVER AGE
ACTION
THE STRANGEST MAN OF ALL TIME!!
IS HE MAN OR MONSTER
OR...
IS HE BOTH
BUYING
& SELLING
• Top Prices Paid!!! •
• Senior Overstreet Advisor •
• We Pay 50% - 150% of Guide for pre-1970 Comics •
• We Pay up to 500% of Guide for CGC Graded Comics •
• Will Travel Anywhere to View Large Collections •
• Consignment Sales •
• Over 50,000 Gold & Silver Age Comics In Stock •
• Accurate Grading •
• Competitive Pricing •
• Pulps & Original Art • Want List Service •
• Free Catalogs: call or write for your copy •

. . . A CAR WITHOUT A
PROFESSIONAL'S OPINIO

So, why buy comics without CGC's certification?

When you purchase a comic certified by CGC, you know that it has been graded by the hobby's most experienced and trusted team, according to an established grading standard. Furthermore, every book graded by CGC undergoes a thorough restoration check by leading professionals. When restoration is detected, it's clearly noted on the certification label.

Once certified by CGC, every comic is encapsulated in a state-of-the-art, tamper-evident holder, providing superior protection and stability for long-term enjoyment. **For your comic books, you deserve certification from CGC, the only impartial, third-party grading service.**

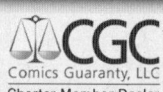

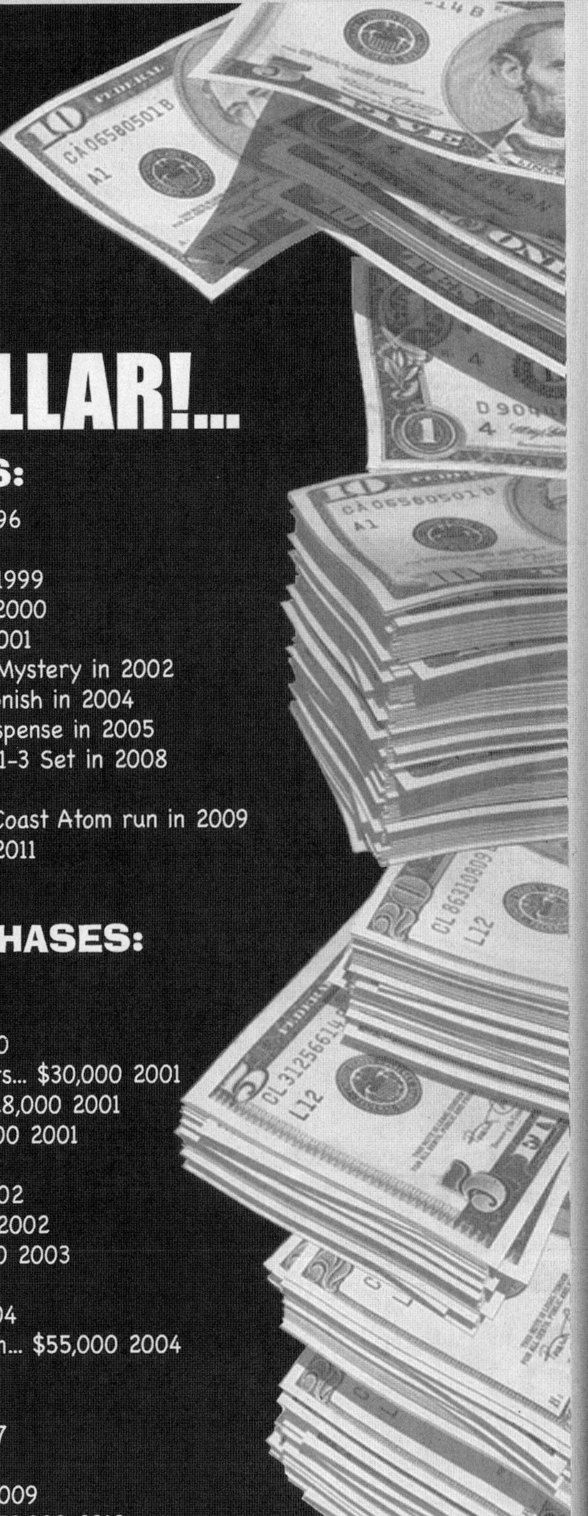

COMICS TO ASTONISH
WE SELL!
-COMICS OLD AND NEW!
-MAGIC THE GATHERING!
-WIZKIDS!
-NON SPORT CARDS!
-GRADED COMICS!
-STATUES!
-ACTION FIGURES!
-TPB'S!
-MANGA AND ANIME!
-DC DIRECT!
-COMIC SUPPLIES!
9400 SNOWDEN RIVER PKWY
COLUMBIA, MD 21045
MONDAY-SATURDAY 12-8PM
SUNDAY 12-6 PM
410-381-2732
VBBB
Check out our new website w/h tons of CGC books
CONTACT:
KEEGAN F. CONRAD
410-381-2732
COMICS2U@AOL.COM
WE BUY!
-ALL COMICS 30'S TO 80'S!
-ENTIRE COLLECTIONS!
-BRONZE TO GOLDEN AGE!
-GRADED BOOKS!
WE HAVE OVER 80,000 BACK ISSUES!
WWW.COMICSTOASTONISH.COM

BACK ISSUE GUIDES

Since 1970, *The Overstreet Comic Book Price Guide* has been the Bible of serious comic book collectors. Over the four decades since, the *Guide* itself has become collectible. Gemstone Publishing has a limited supply of some editions of the *Guide* available for sale on our website. Maybe we have the one you're looking for!

www.gemstonepub.com

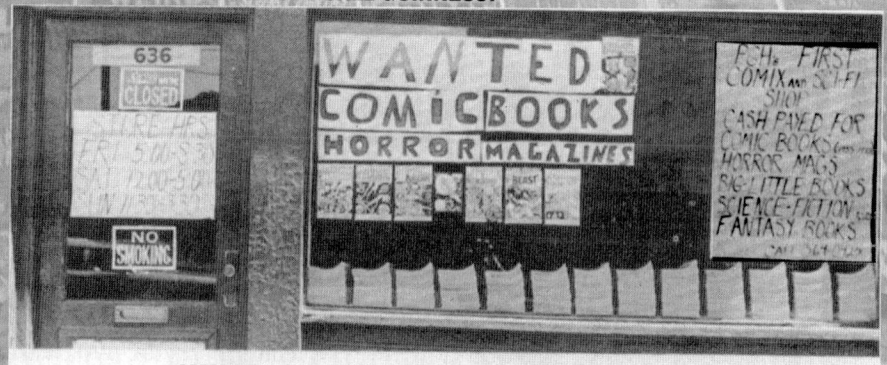

4. BUYING - THERE ARE PLENTY OF DEALERS WHO WILL ALWAYS CLAIM TO PAY THE "HIGHEST PRICES". WHEN PURCHASING A COLLECTION THEY TAKE A QUANTITY COUNT & THEN ASSIGN A PRICE PER BOOK MULTIPLIER. AT EIDE'S, WE SEPARATE YOUR BETTER ITEMS FROM YOUR COMMON PIECES, INDIVIDUALLY GRADE & PRICE EACH ITEM OF VALUE, AND ASSIGN A PERCENTAGE OF VALUE BASED ON QUALITY, QUANTITY AND DEMAND. ALL PAPERWORK IS SHOWN AND FULLY EXPLAINED TO THE SELLER. WHICH METHOD WOULD YOU PREFER TO USE WHEN SELLING YOUR VALUABLES? ALSO, WITH EIDE'S YOU WILL ALSO GET CASH ON HAND AND NO BOUNCED CHECKS.

3. LEGENDARY ANNIVERSARY SALE - 40% OFF ALL BACK ISSUES, 30% OFF ALL NEW PRODUCT. A TRUE SALE ON CORRECTLY GRADED AND PRICED ITEMS NOT THE USUAL CONVENTION SCAM OF 50% OFF ITEMS ALREADY PRICED AT OVER DOUBLE GUIDE VALUE.

2. STAFF - MOST COMIC SHOPS ARE 1-3 MAN OPERATIONS: EIDE'S EMPLOYS 7 FULL TIME AND 3 PART TIME EMPLOYEES IN ITS COMIC DEPT. EACH HAS A LONG HISTORY OF COLLECTING (COMBINED 390+ YEARS) AND PARTICULAR AREAS OF EXPERTISE. AS FOR YEARS IN THE ACTUAL BUSINESS OF BUYING AND SELLING COMICS, THE COMBINED TOTAL EXCEEDS 230 YEARS. ONE PRE-EMINENT DEALERSHIP ADVERTISES THAT IT HAS A COMBINED BUSINESS EXPERIENCE OF A PALTRY 50 YEARS. REALLY! WE HAVE 5 EMPLOYEES ALONE THAT HAVE OVER 30 YEARS EACH IN THE BUSINESS. DO THE MATH.

1. BECAUSE IT SAYS SO ON THE WALL - WE CLAIMED THE TITLE 20 YEARS AGO AND NO ONE HAS EVER DISPUTED IT. IN FACT, OUR CUSTOMERS, AND ANYONE WHO HAS EVER BEEN TO EIDE'S ENTERTAINMENT, CONCUR. NUFF SAID!

FULL TIME PROFESSIONALS HONESTY INTEGRITY DISCLOSURE

OVER 230 COMBINED YEARS SELLING COMICS

EIDE'S ENTERTAINMENT, LLC
1121 PENN AVE
PITTSBURGH PA 15222
PHONE: (412) 261-0900

WEBSITE www.eides.com
EBAY STORE eides_entertainment
E-MAIL eides@eides.com
FAX: (412) 261-3102

JOHN VERZYL AND DAUGHTER ROSE, "HARD AT WORK."

John Verzyl started collecting comic books in 1965, and within ten years he had amassed thousands of Golden and Silver Age comic books. In 1979, with his wife Nanette, he opened "COMIC HEAVEN," a retail store devoted entirely to the buying and selling of comic books.

Over the years, John Verzyl has come to be recognized as an authority in the field of comic books. He has served as a special advisor to the "Overstreet Comic Book Price Guide" for the last 25 years. Thousands of his "mint" comics were photographed for Ernst Gerber's "Photo-Journal Guide to Comic Books." His tables and displays at the annual San Diego Comic Convention and the Chicago Comic Convention draw customers from all over the country.

The first COMIC HEAVEN AUCTION was held in 1987, and today his Auction Catalogs are mailed out to more than ten thousand interested collectors and dealers.

Comic Heaven
John and Nanette Verzyl
P.O. Box 900
Big Sandy, TX 75755
www.comicheaven.net
1-903-636-5555

THESE DIDN'T HAPPEN WITHOUT YOUR HELP.

The Overstreet Comic Book Price Guide doesn't happen by magic. A network of advisors – made up of experienced dealers, collectors and comics historians – gives us input for every edition we publish. If you spot an error or omission in this edition or any of our publications, let us know!

Write to us at Gemstone Publishing Inc., 1966 Greenspring Dr., Timonium, MD 21093. Or e-mail **feedback@gemstonepub.com**.

We want your help!

BIG LITTLE BOOKS

INTRODUCTION

In 1932, at the depths of the Great Depression, comic books were not selling despite their successes in the previous two decades. Desperate publishers had already reduced prices to 25¢, but this was still too much for many people to spend on entertainment.

Comic books quickly evolved into two newer formats, the comics magazine and the Big Little Book. Both types retailed for 10¢.

Big Little Books began by reprinting the art (and adapting the stories) from newspaper comics. As their success grew and publishers began commissioning original material, movie adaptations and other entertainment-derived stories became commonplace.

GRADING

Before a Big Little Book's value can be assessed, its condition or state of preservation must be determined. A book in **Near Mint** condition will bring many times the price of the same book in **Poor** condition. Many variables influence the grading of a Big Little Book and all must be considered in the final evaluation. Due to the way they are constructed, damage occurs with very little use - usually to the spine, book edges and binding. More important defects that affect grading are: Split spines, pages missing, page browning or brittleness, writing, crayoning, loose pages, color fading, chunks missing, and rolling or out of square. The following grading guide is given to aid the novice:

9.4 Near Mint: The overall look is as if it was just purchased and maybe opened once; only subtle defects are allowed; paper is cream to off-white, supple and fresh; cover is flat with no surface wear or creases; inks and colors are bright; small penciled or inked arrival dates are acceptable; very slight blunting of corners at top and bottom of spine are common; outside corners are cut square and sharp. Books in this grade could bring prices of guide and a half or more.

9.0 Very Fine/Near Mint: Limited number of defects; full cover gloss with only very slight wear on book corners and edges; very minor foxing; very minor tears allowed, binding still square and tight with no pages missing; paper quality still fresh from cream to off-white. Dates, stamps or initials allowed on cover or inside.

8.0 Very Fine: Most of the cover gloss retained with minor wear appearing at corners and around edges; spine tight with no pages missing; cream/tan paper allowed if still supple; up to 1/4" bend allowed on covers with no color break; cover relatively flat; minor tears allowed.

6.0 Fine: Slight wear beginning to show; cover gloss reduced but still clean, pages tan/brown but still supple (not brittle); up to 1/4" split or color break allowed; minor discoloration and/or foxing allowed.

4.0 Very Good: Obviously a read copy with original printing luster almost gone; some fading and discoloration, but not soiled; some signs of wear such as corner splits and spine rolling; paper can be brown but not brittle; a few pages can be loose but not missing; no chunks missing; blunted corners acceptable.

2.0 Good: An average used copy complete with only minor pieces missing from the spine, which may be partially split; slightly soiled or marked with spine rolling; color flaking and wear around edges, but perfectly sound and legible; could have minor tape repairs but otherwise complete.

1.0 Fair: Very heavily read and soiled with small chunks missing from cover; most or all of spine could be missing; multiple splits in spine and loose pages, but still sound and legible, bringing 50 to 70 percent of good price.

0.5 Poor: Damaged, heavily weathered, soiled or otherwise unsuited for collecting purposes.

IMPORTANT

Most BLBs on the market today will fall in the **Good** to **Fine** grade category. When **Very Fine** to **Near Mint** BLBs are offered for sale, they usually bring premium prices.

A WORD ON PRICING

The prices are given for **Good**, **Fine** and **Very Fine/ Near Mint** condition. A book in **Fair** would be 50-70% of the **Good** price. **Very Good** would be halfway between the **Good** and **Fine** price, and **Very Fine** would be halfway between the **Fine** and **Very Fine/**

Near Mint price. The prices listed were averaged from convention sales, dealers' lists, adzines, auctions, and by special contact with dealers and collectors from coast to coast. The prices and the spreads were determined from sales of copies in available condition or the highest grade known. Since most available copies are in the **Good** to **Fine** range, neither dealers nor collectors should let the **Very Fine/Near Mint** column influence the prices they are willing to charge or pay for books in less than near perfect condition.

The prices listed reflect a six times spread from **Good** to **Very Fine/ Near Mint** (1 - 3 - 6). We feel this spread accurately reflects the current market, especially when you consider the scarcity of books in **Very Fine/Near Mint** condition. When one or both end sheets are missing, the book's value would drop about a half grade.

Books with movie scenes are of double importance due to the high crossover demand by movie collectors.

Abbreviations: a-art; c-cover; nn-no number; p-pages; r-reprint.

Publisher Codes: BRP-Blue Ribbon Press; **ERB**-Edgar Rice Burroughs; **EVW**-Engel van Wiseman; **FAW**-Fawcett Publishing Co.; **Gold**-Goldsmith Publishing Co.; **Lynn**-Lynn Publishing Co.; **McKay**-David McKay Co.; **Whit**-Whitman Publishing Co.; **World**-World Syndicate Publishing Co.

Terminology: *All Pictures Comics*-no text, all drawings; *Fast-Action*-A special series of Dell books highly collected; *Flip Pictures*-upper right corner of interior pages contain drawings that are put into motion when rifled; *Movie Scenes*-book illustrated with scenes from the movie. *Soft Cover*-A thin single sheet of cardboard used in binding most of the giveaway versions.

"Big Little Book" and "Better Little Book" are registered trademarks of Whitman Publishing Co. "Little Big Book" is a registered trademark of the Saalfield Publishing Co.

"Pop-Up" is a registered trademark of Blue Ribbon Press. "Little Big Book" is a registered trademark of the Saalfield Co.

Top 20 Big Little Books and related size books*

Issue#	Rank	Title	Price
731	1	Mickey Mouse the Mail Pilot (variant version of Mickey Mouse #717) (Fine copy sold at auction for $5,090)	
nn	2	Mickey Mouse and Minnie Mouse at Macy's	$3,600
717	3	Mickey Mouse (skinny Mickey on-c)	$3,135
nn	4	Mickey Mouse and Minnie March to Macy's	$2,400
725	4	Big Little Mother Goose HC	$2,400
W-707	6	Dick Tracy The Detective	$2,200
717	7	Mickey Mouse (reg. Mickey on-c)	$1,750
4063	8	Popeye Thimble Theater Starring... (2nd printing)	$1,620
721	9	Big Little Paint Book (336 pg.)	$1,500
725	9	Big Little Mother Goose SC	$1,500
nn	9	Mickey Mouse Mail Pilot (Great Big Midget Book)	$1,500
nn	12	Mickey Mouse (Great Big Midget Book)	$1,485
4062	13	Mickey Mouse and the Smugglers	$1,430
4063	14	Popeye Thimble Theater Starring... (1st printing)	$1,385
nn	15	Mickey Mouse Silly Symphonies	$1,320
nn	16	Buck Rogers	$1,250
4062	17	Mickey Mouse, The Story of...	$1,210
721	18	Big Little Paint Book (320 pg.)	$1,200
nn	18	Mickey Mouse Sails For Treasure Island (Great Big Midget Book)	$1,200
nn	20	Mickey Mouse and the Magic Carpet	$1,050

*Includes only the various sized BLBs; no premiums, giveaways or other divergent forms are included.

1182 - Abbie an' Slats-and Becky © Saalfield

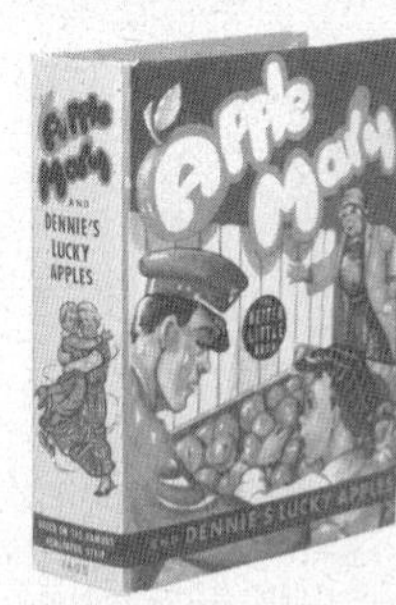

1403 - Apple Mary and Dennie's Lucky Apples © WHIT

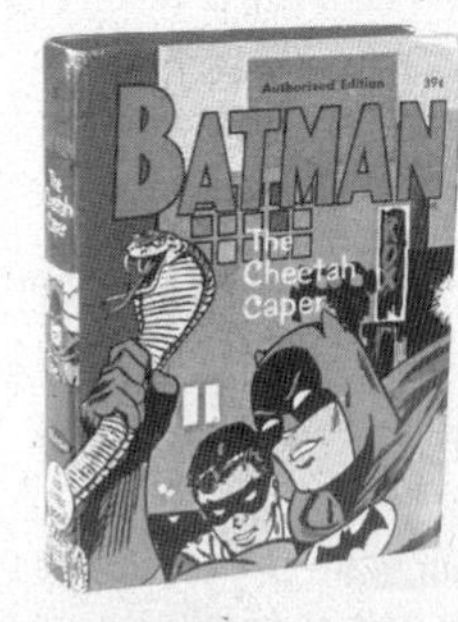

2031 - Batman and Robin in the Cheetah Caper © DC

	GD	FN	VF/NM
1175-0- **Abbie an' Slats**, 1940, Saalfield, 400 pgs.	12.00	30.00	80.00
1182- **Abbie an' Slats-and Becky**, 1940, Saalfield, 400 pgs.	12.00	30.00	80.00
1177- **Ace Drummond**, 1935, Whitman, 432 pgs.	12.00	30.00	85.00
Admiral Byrd (See Paramount Newsreel ...)			
nn- **Adventures of Charlie McCarthy and Edgar Bergen, The**, 1938, Dell, 194 pgs., Fast-Action Story, soft-c	26.00	65.00	185.00
1422- **Adventures of Huckleberry Finn, The**, 1939, Whitman, 432 pgs., Henry E. Vallely-a	12.00	30.00	75.00
1648- **Adventures of Jim Bowie** (TV Series), 1958, Whitman, 280 pgs.	5.00	12.50	33.00
1056- **Adventures of Krazy Kat and Ignatz Mouse in Koko Land**, 1934, Saalfield, 160 pgs., oblong size, hard-c, Herriman-c/a	72.00	180.00	505.00
1306- **Adventures of Krazy Kat and Ignatz Mouse in Koko Land**, 1934, Saalfield, 164 pgs., oblong size, soft-c, Herriman-c/a	79.00	197.00	550.00
1082- **Adventures of Pete the Tramp, The**, 1935, Saalfield, hard-c, by C. D. Russell	12.00	30.00	75.00
1312- **Adventures of Pete the Tramp, The**, 1935, Saalfield, soft-c, by C. D. Russell	12.00	30.00	75.00
1053- **Adventures of Tim Tyler**, 1934, Saalfield, hard-c, oblong size, by Lyman Young	26.00	65.00	180.00
1303- **Adventures of Tim Tyler**, 1934, Saalfield, soft-c, oblong size, by Lyman Young	26.00	65.00	180.00
1058- **Adventures of Tom Sawyer, The**, 1934, Saalfield, 160 pgs., hard-c, Park Sumner-a	12.00	30.00	75.00
1308- **Adventures of Tom Sawyer, The**, 1934, Saalfield, 160 pgs., soft-c, Park Sumner-a	12.00	30.00	75.00
1448- **Air Fighters of America**, 1941, Whitman, 432 pgs., flip picture	12.00	30.00	85.00
Alexander Smart, ESQ. (See Top Line Comics)			
759- **Alice in Wonderland**, 1933, Whitman, 160 pgs., hard-c, photo-c, movie scenes	46.00	115.00	325.00
1481- **Allen Pike of the Parachute Squad U.S.A.**, 1941, Whitman, 432 pgs.	12.00	30.00	85.00
763- **Alley Oop and Dinny**, 1935, Whitman, 384 pgs., V. T. Hamlin-a	21.00	52.50	145.00
1473- **Alley Oop and Dinny in the Jungles of Moo**, 1938, Whitman, 432 pgs., V. T. Hamlin-a	21.00	52.50	145.00
nn- **Alley Oop and the Missing King of Moo**, 1938, Whitman, 36 pgs., 2 1/2" x 3 1/2", Penny Book	12.00	30.00	85.00
nn- **Alley Oop in the Kingdom of Foo**, 1938, Whitman, 68 pgs., 3 1/4" x 3 1/2", Pan-Am premium	29.00	73.00	200.00
nn- **"Alley Oop the Invasion of Moo,"** 1935, Whitman, 260 pgs., Cocomalt premium, soft-c; V. T. Hamlin-a	22.00	52.50	155.00
Andy Burnette (See Walt Disney's...)			
Andy Panda (Also see Walter Lantz ...)			
531- **Andy Panda**, 1943, Whitman, 3 3/4x8 3/4", Tall Comic Book, All Pictures Comics	26.00	65.00	180.00
1425- **Andy Panda and Tiny Tom**, 1944, Whitman, All Pictures Comics	12.00	30.00	85.00
1431- **Andy Panda and the Mad Dog Mystery**, 1947, Whitman, 288 pgs., by Walter Lantz	12.00	30.00	80.00
1441- **Andy Panda in the City of Ice**, 1948, Whitman, All Picture Comics, by Walter Lantz	12.00	30.00	85.00
1459- **Andy Panda and the Pirate Ghosts**, 1949, Whitman, 88 pgs., by Walter Lantz	12.00	30.00	80.00
1485- **Andy Panda's Vacation**, 1946, Whitman, All Pictures Comics, by Walter Lantz	12.00	30.00	85.00
15- **Andy Panda (The Adventures of)**, 1942, Dell, Fast-Action Story	26.00	65.00	180.00
707-10 - **Andy Panda and Presto the Pup**, 1949, Whitman	12.00	30.00	80.00
1130- **Apple Mary and Dennie Foil the Swindlers**, 1936, Whitman, 432 pgs. (Forerunner to Mary Worth)	12.00	30.00	80.00
1403- **Apple Mary and Dennie's Lucky Apples**, 1939, Whitman, 432 pgs.	12.00	30.00	80.00
2017- **(#17)-Aquaman-Scourge of the Sea**, 1968, Whitman, 260 pgs., 39 cents, hard-c, color illos	4.00	10.00	27.00

	GD	FN	VF/NM
1192- **Arizona Kid on the Bandit Trail, The**, 1936, Whitman, 432 pgs.	11.00	27.50	70.00
1469- **Bambi** (Walt Disney's), 1942, Whitman, 432 pgs.	26.00	65.00	180.00
1497- **Bambi's Children** (Disney), 1943, Whitman, 432 pgs., Disney Studios-a	26.00	65.00	180.00
1138- **Bandits at Bay**, 1938, Saalfield, 400 pgs.	10.00	25.00	65.00
1459- **Barney Baxter in the Air with the Eagle Squadron**, 1938, Whitman, 432 pgs.	12.00	30.00	80.00
1083- **Barney Google**, 1935, Saalfield, hard-c	21.00	52.50	145.00
1313- **Barney Google**, 1935, Saalfield, soft-c	21.00	52.50	145.00
2031-(#31)- **Batman and Robin in the Cheetah Caper**, 1969, Whitman, 258 pgs.	4.00	10.00	27.00
5771- **Batman and Robin in the Cheetah Caper**, 1974, Whitman, 258 pgs., 49 cents	2.00	5.00	12.00
5771-1- **Batman and Robin in the Cheetah Caper**, 1974, Whitman, 258 pgs., 69 cents	2.00	5.00	12.00
5771-2- **Batman and Robin in the Cheetah Caper**, 1975?, Whitman, 258 pgs.	2.00	5.00	12.00
nn- **Beauty and the Beast**, nd (1930s), np (Whitman), 36 pgs., 3" x 3 1/2" Penny Book	4.00	10.00	27.00
Beep Beep The Road Runner (See Road Runner)			
760- **Believe It or Not!**, 1933, Whitman, 160 pgs., by Ripley (c. 1931)	12.00	30.00	80.00
Betty Bear's Lesson (See Wee Little Books)			
1119- **Betty Boop in Snow White**, 1934, Whitman, 240 pgs., hard-c; adapted from Max Fleischer Paramount Talkartoon	86.00	215.00	600.00
1119- **Betty Boop in Snow White**, 1934, Whitman, 240 pgs., soft-c; same contents as hard-c (Rare)	128.00	320.00	900.00
1158- **Betty Boop in "Miss Gullivers Travels,"** 1935, Whitman, 288 pgs., hard-c (Scarce)	100.00	250.00	700.00
2070- **Big Big Paint Book**, 1936, Whitman, 432 pgs., 8 1/2" x 11 3/8", B&W pages to color	25.00	62.00	175.00
1432- **Big Chief Wahoo and the Lost Pioneers**, 1942, Whitman, 432 pgs., Elmer Woggon-a	12.00	30.00	80.00
1443- **Big Chief Wahoo and the Great Gusto**, 1938, Whitman, 432 pgs., Elmer Woggon-a	12.00	30.00	80.00
1483- **Big Chief Wahoo and the Magic Lamp**, 1940, Whitman, 432 pgs., flip pictures, Woggon-c/a	12.00	30.00	80.00
725- **Big Little Mother Goose, The**, 1934, Whitman, 580 pgs. (Rare) Hardcover	300.00	750.00	2400.00
725- **Big Little Mother Goose, The**, 1934, Whitman, 580 pgs. (Rare) Softcover	188.00	470.00	1500.00
1005- **Big Little Nickel Book**, 1935, Whitman, 144 pgs., Blackie Bear stories and Donna the Donkey	11.00	27.50	70.00
1006- **Big Little Nickel Book**, 1935, Whitman, 144 pgs., Blackie Bear stories, folk tales in primer style	11.00	27.50	70.00
1007- **Big Little Nickel Book**, 1935, Whitman, 144 pgs., Peter Rabbit, etc.	11.00	27.50	70.00
1008- **Big Little Nickel Book**, 1935, Whitman, 144 pgs., Wee Wee Woman, etc.	11.00	27.50	70.00
721- **Big Little Paint Book**, The, 1933, Whitman, 320 pgs., 3 3/4" x 8 1/2", for crayoning; first printing has green page ends; second printing has purple page ends (both are rare)	150.00	375.00	1200.00
721- **Big Little Paint Book**, The, 1933, Whitman, 336 pgs., 3 3/4" x 8 1/2", for crayoning; first printing has green page ends; second printing has purple page ends (both are rare)	188.00	470.00	1500.00
1178- **Billy of Bar-Zero**, 1940, Saalfield, 400 pgs.	11.00	27.50	70.00
773- **Billy the Kid**, 1935, Whitman, 432 pgs., Hal Arbo-a	12.00	30.00	80.00
1159- **Billy the Kid on Tall Butte**, 1939, Saalfield, 400 pgs.	11.00	27.50	70.00
1174- **Billy the Kid's Pledge**, 1940, Saalfield, 400 pgs.	11.00	27.50	70.00
nn- **Billy the Kid, Western Outlaw**, 1935, Whitman, 260 pgs., Cocomalt premium, Hal Arbo-a, soft-c	12.00	30.00	85.00
1057- **Black Beauty**, 1934, Saalfield, hard-c	10.00	25.00	65.00
1307- **Black Beauty**, 1934, Saalfield, soft-c	10.00	25.00	65.00
1414- **Black Silver and His Pirate Crew**, 1937, Whitman, 300 pgs.	12.00	30.00	75.00

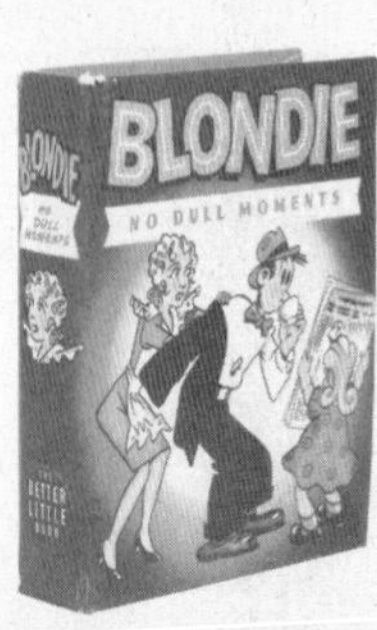

1450 - Blondie No Dull Moments © WHIT

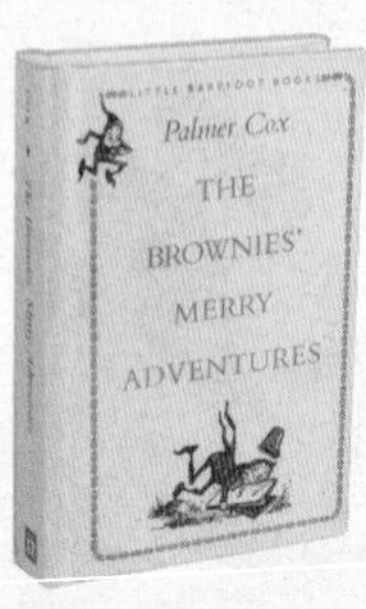

The Brownies' Merry Adventures © Barefoot Books

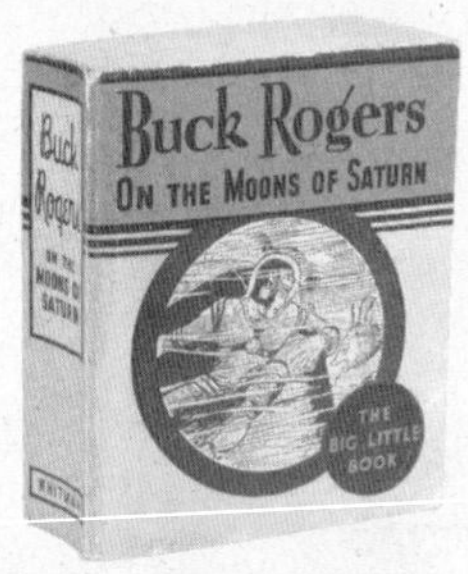

Buck Rogers on the Moons of Saturn (3-color premium) © KING

GD FN VF/NM

1447- **Blaze Brandon with the Foreign Legion**, 1938, Whitman, 432 pgs. 12.00 30.00 75.00
1410- **Blondie and Dagwood in Hot Water**, 1946, Whitman, 352 pgs., by Chic Young 12.00 30.00 80.00
1415- **Blondie and Baby Dumpling**, 1937, Whitman, 432 pgs., by Chic Young 12.00 30.00 85.00
1419- **Oh, Blondie the Bumsteads Carry On**, 1941, Whitman, 432 pgs., flip pictures, by Chic Young 12.00 30.00 85.00
1423- **Blondie Who's Boss?**, 1942, Whitman, 432 pgs., flip pictures, by Chic Young 12.00 30.00 85.00
1429- **Blondie with Baby Dumpling and Daisy**, 1939, Whitman, 432 pgs., by Chic Young 12.00 30.00 85.00
1430- **Blondie Count Cookie in Too!**, 1947, Whitman, 288 pgs., by Chic Young 12.00 30.00 80.00
1438- **Blondie and Dagwood Everybody's Happy**, 1948, Whitman, 288 pgs., by Chic Young 12.00 30.00 80.00
1450- **Blondie No Dull Moments**, 1948, Whitman, 288 pgs., by Chic Young 12.00 30.00 80.00
1463- **Blondie Fun For All**, 1949, Whitman, 288 pgs., by Chic Young 12.00 30.00 80.00
1466- **Blondie or Life Among the Bumsteads**, 1944, Whitman, 352 pgs., by Chic Young 12.00 30.00 85.00
1476- **Blondie and Bouncing Baby Dumpling**, 1940, Whitman, 432 pgs., by Chic Young 12.00 30.00 85.00
1487- **Blondie Baby Dumpling and All!**, 1941, Whitman, 432 pgs. flip pictures, by Chic Young 12.00 30.00 85.00
1490- **Blondie Papa Knows Best**, 1945, Whitman, 352 pgs., by Chic Young 12.00 30.00 80.00
1491- **Blondie-Cookie and Daisy's Pups**, 1943, Whitman, 1st printing, 432 pgs. 12.00 30.00 85.00
1491- **Blondie-Cookie and Daisy's Pups**, 1943, Whitman,. 2nd printing with different back-c & 352 pgs. 12.00 30.00 75.00
703-10- **Blondie and Dagwood Some Fun!**, 1949, Whitman, by Chic Young 10.00 25.00 65.00
21- **Blondie and Dagwood**, 1936, Lynn, by Chic Young 21.00 52.50 145.00
1108- **Bobby Benson on the H-Bar-O Ranch**, 1934, Whitman, 300 pgs., based on radio serial 13.00 32.50 90.00
Bobby Thatcher and the Samarang Emerald (See Top-Line Comics)
1432- **Bob Stone the Young Detective**, 1937, Whitman, 240 pgs., movie scenes 12.00 30.00 85.00
2002- **(#2)-Bonanza-The Bubble Gum Kid**, 1967, Whitman, 260 pgs., 39 cents, hard-c, color illos 4.00 10.00 27.00
1139- **Border Eagle, The**, 1938, Saalfield, 400 pgs. 10.00 25.00 65.00
1153- **Boss of the Chisholm Trail**, 1939, Saalfield, 400 pgs. 10.00 25.00 65.00
1425- **Brad Turner in Transatlantic Flight**, 1939, Whitman, 432 pgs. 11.00 27.50 70.00
1058- **Brave Little Tailor, The** (Disney), 1939, Whitman, 5" x 5 1/2", 68 pgs., hard-c (Mickey Mouse) 16.00 40.00 115.00
1427- **Brenda Starr and the Masked Impostor**, 1943, Whitman, 352 pgs., Dale Messick-a 15.00 37.50 105.00
1426- **Brer Rabbit** (Walt Disney's ...), 1947, Whitman, All Picture Comics, from "Song Of The South" movie 22.00 52.50 155.00
704-10- **Brer Rabbit**, 1949, Whitman 19.00 47.50 135.00
1059- **Brick Bradford in the City Beneath the Sea**, 1934, Saalfield, hard-c, by William Ritt & Clarence Gray 18.00 45.00 125.00
1309- **Brick Bradford in the City Beneath the Sea**, 1934, Saalfield, soft-c, by Ritt & Gray 18.00 45.00 125.00
1468- **Brick Bradford with Brocco the Modern Buccaneer**, 1938, Whitman, 432 pgs., by Wm. Ritt & Clarence Gray 12.00 30.00 80.00
1133- **Bringing Up Father**, 1936, Whitman, 432 pgs., by George McManus 16.00 40.00 115.00
1100- **Broadway Bill**, 1935, Saalfield, photo-c, 4 1/2" x 5 1/4", movie scenes (Columbia Pictures, horse racing) 12.00 30.00 85.00
1580- **Broadway Bill**, 1935, Saalfield, soft-c, photo-c, movie scenes 12.00 30.00 85.00
1181- **Broncho Bill**, 1940, Saalfield, 400 pgs. 11.00 27.50 70.00
nn- **Broncho Bill**, 1935, Whitman, 148 pgs., 3 1/2" x 4", Tarzan Ice Cream cup lid premium 36.00 90.00 255.00
nn- **Broncho Bill in Suicide Canyon** (See Top-Line Comics)
1417- **Bronc Peeler the Lone Cowboy**, 1937, Whitman, 432 pgs., by Fred Harman, forerunner of Red Ryder (also see Red Death on the Range) 12.00 30.00 80.00
nn- **Brownies' Merry Adventures, The**, 1993, Barefoot Books, 202 pgs., reprints from Palmer Cox's late 1800s books 3.00 7.50 18.00
1470- **Buccaneer, The**, 1938, Whitman, 240 pgs., photo-c, movie scenes 13.00 32.50 90.00
1646- **Buccaneers, The** (TV Series), 1958, Whitman, 4 1/2" x 5 1/4", 280 pgs., Russ Manning-a 5.00 12.50 33.00
1104- **Buck Jones in the Fighting Code**, 1934, Whitman, 160 pgs., hard-c, movie scenes 19.00 47.50 135.00
1116- **Buck Jones in Ride 'Em Cowboy** (Universal Presents), 1935, Whitman, 240 pgs., photo-c, movie scenes 19.00 47.50 135.00
1174- **Buck Jones in the Roaring West** (Universal Presents), 1935, Whitman, 240 pgs., movie scenes 19.00 47.50 135.00
1188- **Buck Jones in the Fighting Rangers** (Universal Presents), 1936, Whitman, 240 pgs., photo-c, movie scenes 19.00 47.50 135.00
1404- **Buck Jones and the Two-Gun Kid**, 1937, Whitman, 432 pgs. 13.00 32.50 90.00
1451- **Buck Jones and the Killers of Crooked Butte**, 1940, Whitman, 432 pgs. 13.00 32.50 90.00
1461- **Buck Jones and the Rock Creek Cattle War**, 1938, Whitman, 432 pgs. 13.00 32.50 90.00
1486- **Buck Jones and the Rough Riders in Forbidden Trails**, 1943, Whitman, flip pictures, based on movie; Tim McCoy app. 18.00 45.00 125.00
3- **Buck Jones in the Red Rider**, 1934, EVW, 160 pgs., movie scenes 39.00 98.00 275.00
8- **Buck Jones Cowboy Masquerade**, 1938, Whitman, 132 pgs., soft-c, 3 3/4" x 3 1/2", Buddy Book premium 43.00 108.00 300.00
15- **Buck Jones in Rocky Rhodes**, 1935, EVW, 160 pgs., photo-c, movie scenes 57.00 142.00 400.00
4069- **Buck Jones and the Night Riders**, 1937, Whitman, 7" x 9", 320 pgs., Big Big Book 79.00 198.00 550.00
nn- **Buck Jones on the Six-Gun Trail**, 1939, Whitman, 36 pgs., 2 1/2" x 3 1/2", Penny Book 12.00 30.00 80.00
nn- **Buck Jones Big Thrill Chewing Gum**, 1934, Whitman, 8 pgs., 2 1/2" x 3 1/2" (6 diff.) each... 20.00 50.00 140.00
742- **Buck Rogers in the 25th Century A.D.**, 1933, Whitman, 320 pgs., Dick Calkins-a 47.00 118.00 330.00
nn- **Buck Rogers in the 25th Century A.D.**, 1933, Whitman, 204 pgs.,Cocomalt premium, Calkins-a 30.00 75.00 210.00
765- **Buck Rogers in the City Below the Sea**, 1934, Whitman, 320 pgs., Dick Calkins-a 36.00 90.00 255.00
765- **Buck Rogers in the City Below the Sea**, 1934, Whitman, 324 pgs., soft-c, Dick Calkins-c/a (Rare) 82.00 205.00 575.00
1143- **Buck Rogers on the Moons of Saturn**, 1934, Whitman, 320 pgs., Dick Calkins-a 38.00 95.00 255.00
nn- **Buck Rogers on the Moons of Saturn**, 1934, Whitman, 324 pgs., premium w/no ads, soft 3-color-c, Dick Calkins-a 64.00 160.00 450.00
1169- **Buck Rogers and the Depth Men of Jupiter**, 1935, Whitman, 432 pgs., Calkins-a 36.00 90.00 255.00
1178- **Buck Rogers and the Doom Comet**, 1935, Whitman, 432 pgs., Calkins-a 34.00 85.00 240.00
1197- **Buck Rogers and the Planetoid Plot**, 1936, Whitman, 432 pgs., Calkins-a 34.00 85.00 240.00
1409- **Buck Rogers Vs. the Fiend of Space**, 1940, Whitman, 432 pgs., Calkins-a 45.00 113.00 315.00
1437- **Buck Rogers in the War with the Planet Venus**, 1938, Whitman, 432 pgs., Calkins-a 34.00 85.00 240.00
1474- **Buck Rogers and the Overturned World**, 1941, Whitman, 432 pgs., flip pictures, Calkins-a 36.00 90.00 250.00
1490- **Buck Rogers and the Super-Dwarf of Space**, 1943, Whitman, 11 Pictures Comics, Calkins-a 34.00 85.00 240.00
4057- **Buck Rogers, The Adventures of**, 1934, Whitman, 7" x 9 1/2", 320 pgs., Big Big Book, "The Story of Buck Rogers on the Planet Eros," Calkins-c/a 125.00 313.00 1000.00

2007 - Bugs Bunny-Double Trouble on Diamond Island © WB

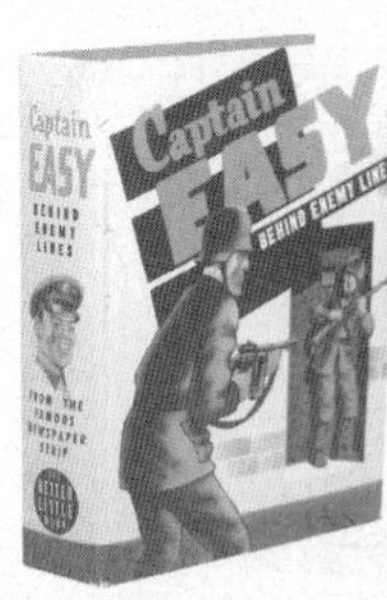

1474 - Captain Easy Behind Enemy Lines © WHIT

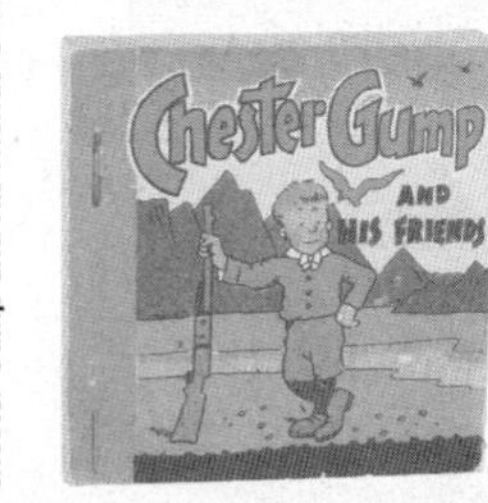

5 - Chester Gump and His Friends © WHIT

GD FN VF/NM

nn- Buck Rogers, 1935, Whitman, 4" x 3 1/2", Tarzan Ice Cream cup premium (Rare) 156.00 390.00 1250.00
nn- Buck Rogers in the City of Floating Globes, 1935, Whitman, 258 pgs., Cocomalt premium, soft-c, Dick Calkins-a 115.00 287.00 810.00
nn- Buck Rogers Big Thrill Chewing Gum, 1934, Whitman, 8 pgs., 2 1/2" x 3 " (6 diff.) each... 29.00 73.00 200.00
1135- Buckskin and Bullets, 1938, Saalfield, 400 pgs. 11.00 27.50 70.00
Buffalo Bill (See Wild West Adventures of ...)
nn- Buffalo Bill, 1934, World Syndicate, All pictures, by J. Carroll Mansfield 11.00 27.50 70.00
713- Buffalo Bill and the Pony Express, 1934, Whitman, hard-c, 384 pgs., Hal Arbo-a 12.00 30.00 80.00
nn- Buffalo Bill and the Pony Express, 1934, Whitman, soft-c, 384 pgs., Hal Arbo-a; three-color premium (Rare) 71.00 178.00 500.00
1194- Buffalo Bill Plays a Lone Hand, 1936, Whitman, 432 pgs., Hal Arbo-a 11.00 27.50 70.00
530- Bugs Bunny, 1943, Whitman, All Pictures Comics, Tall Comic Book, 3 1/4" x 8 1/4", reprints/Looney Tunes 1 & 5 31.00 78.00 215.00
1403- Bugs Bunny and the Pirate Loot, 1947, Whitman, All Pictures Comics 12.00 30.00 80.00
1435- Bugs Bunny, 1944, Whitman, All Pictures Comics 12.00 30.00 85.00
1440- Bugs Bunny in Risky Business, 1948, Whitman, All Pictures & Comics 12.00 30.00 80.00
1455- Bugs Bunny and Klondike Gold, 1948, Whitman, 288 pgs. 12.00 30.00 80.00
1465- Bugs Bunny The Masked Marvel, 1949, Whitman, 288 pgs. 12.00 30.00 80.00
1496- Bugs Bunny and His Pals, 1945, Whitman, All Pictures Comics; r/Four Color Comics #33 12.00 30.00 80.00
13- Bugs Bunny and the Secret of Storm Island, 1942, Dell,194 pgs., Fast-Action Story 36.00 90.00 255.00
706-10- Bugs Bunny and the Giant Brothers, 1949, Whitman 11.00 27.50 70.00
2007- (#7)-Bugs Bunny-Double Trouble on Diamond Island, 1967, Whitman, 260 pgs., 39 cents, hard-c, color illos 5.00 12.50 33.00
2029-(#29)- Bugs Bunny, Accidental Adventure, 1969, Whitman, 256 pgs., hard-c, color illos. 4.00 10.00 22.00
2952- Bugs Bunny's Mistake, 1949, Whitman, 3 1/4" x 4", 24 pgs., Tiny Tales, full color (5 cents) (1030-5 on back-c) 11.00 27.50 70.00
5757-2- Bugs Bunny in Double Trouble on Diamond Island,1967, (1980-reprints #2007), Whitman, 260 pgs., soft-c, 79 cents, B&W 2.00 5.00 14.00
5758- Bugs Bunny, Accidental Adventure, 1973, Whitman, 256 pgs., soft-c, B&W illos. 2.00 5.00 14.00
5758-1- Bugs Bunny, Accidental Adventure, 1973, Whitman, 256 pgs., soft-c, B&W illos. 2.00 5.00 14.00
5772- Bugs Bunny the Last Crusader, 1975, Whitman, 49 cents, flip-it book 2.00 5.00 14.00
5772-2- Bugs Bunny the Last Crusader, 1975, Whitman, $1.50, flip-it book 1.00 2.50 6.00
1169- Bullet Benton, 1939, Saalfield, 400 pgs. 11.00 27.50 70.00
nn- Bulletman and the Return of Mr. Murder, 1941, Fawcett, 196 pgs., Dime Action Book 54.00 135.00 375.00
1142- Bullets Across the Border (A Billy The Kid story), 1938, Saalfield, 400 pgs. 11.00 27.50 70.00
Bunky (See Top-Line Comics)
837- Bunty (Punch and Judy), 1935, Whitman, 28 pgs., Magic-Action with 3 pop-ups 16.00 40.00 115.00
1091- Burn 'Em Up Barnes, 1935, Saalfield, hard-c, movie scenes 15.00 37.50 105.00
1321- Burn 'Em Up Barnes, 1935, Saalfield, soft-c, movie scenes 15.00 37.50 105.00
1415- Buz Sawyer and Bomber 13,1946, Whitman, 352 pgs., Roy Crane-a 15.00 37.50 105.00
1412- Calling W-1-X-Y-Z, Jimmy Kean and the Radio Spies, 1939, Whitman, 300 pgs. 12.00 30.00 80.00

GD FN VF/NM

Call of the Wild (See Jack London's...)
1107- Camels are Coming, 1935, Saalfield, movie scenes 12.00 30.00 75.00
1587- Camels are Coming, 1935, Saalfield, movie scenes 12.00 30.00 75.00
nn- Captain and the Kids, Boys Vill Be Boys, The, 1938, 68 pgs., Pan-Am Oil premium, soft-c 15.00 37.50 105.00
1128- Captain Easy Soldier of Fortune, 1934, Whitman, 432 pgs., Roy Crane-a 15.00 37.50 105.00
nn- Captain Easy Soldier of Fortune, 1934, Whitman, 436 pgs., Premium, no ads, soft 3-color-c, Roy Crane-a 26.00 65.00 180.00
1474- Captain Easy Behind Enemy Lines, 1943, Whitman, 352 pgs., Roy Crane-a 13.00 32.50 90.00
nn- Captain Easy and Wash Tubbs, 1935, 260 pgs., Cocomalt premium, Roy Crane-a 13.00 32.50 90.00
1444- Captain Frank Hawks Air Ace and the League of Twelve, 1938, Whitman, 432 pgs. 12.00 30.00 80.00
nn- Captain Marvel, 1941, Fawcett, 196 pgs., Dime Action Book 65.00 163.00 460.00
1402- Captain Midnight and Sheik Jomak Khan, 1946, Whitman, 352 pgs. 26.00 65.00 180.00
1452- Captain Midnight and the Moon Woman, 1943, Whitman, 352 pgs. 28.00 70.00 195.00
1458- Captain Midnight Vs. The Terror of the Orient, 1942, Whitman, 432 pgs., flip pictures, Hess-a 28.00 70.00 195.00
1488- Captain Midnight and the Secret Squadron, 1941, Whitman, 432 pgs. 28.00 70.00 195.00
Captain Robb of.. (See Dirigible ZR90 ...)
nn- Cauliflower Catnip Pearls of Peril, 1981, Teacup Tales, 290 pgs., Joe Wehrle Jr.-s/a; deliberately printed on aged-looking paper to look like an old BLB 4.00 10.00 27.00
20- Ceiling Zero, 1936, Lynn, 128 pgs., 7 1/2" x 5", hard-c, James Cagney, Pat O'Brien photos on-c, movie scenes, Warner Bros. Pictures 12.00 30.00 80.00
1093- Chandu the Magician, 1935, Saalfield, 5" x 5 1/4", 160 pgs., hard-c, Bela Lugosi photo-c, movie scenes 16.00 40.00 115.00
1323- Chandu the Magician, 1935, Saalfield, 5" x 5 1/4", 160 pgs., soft-c, Bela Lugosi photo-c 18.00 45.00 125.00
Charlie Chan (See Inspector ...)
1459- Charlie Chan Solves a New Mystery (See Inspector..), 1940, Whitman, 432 pgs., Alfred Andriola-a 16.00 40.00 110.00
1478- Charlie Chan of the Honolulu Police, Inspector, 1939, Whitman, 432 pgs., Andriola-a 16.00 40.00 110.00
Charlie McCarthy (See Story Of ...)
734- Chester Gump at Silver Creek Ranch, 1933, Whitman, 320 pgs., Sidney Smith-a 15.00 37.50 105.00
nn- Chester Gump at Silver Creek Ranch, 1933, Whitman, 204 pgs., Cocomalt premium, soft-c, Sidney Smith-a 18.00 45.00 125.00
nn- Chester Gump at Silver Creek Ranch, 1933, Whitman, 52 pgs., 4" x 5 1/2", premium-no ads, soft-c, Sidney Smith-a 26.00 65.00 180.00
766- Chester Gump Finds the Hidden Treasure, 1934, Whitman, 320 pgs., Sidney Smith-a 15.00 37.50 105.00
nn- Chester Gump Finds the Hidden Treasure, 1934, Whitman, 52 pgs., 3 1/2" x 5 3/4", premium-no ads, soft-c, Sidney Smith-a 26.00 65.00 180.00
nn- Chester Gump Finds the Hidden Treasure, 1934, Whitman, 52 pgs., 4" x 5 1/2", premium-no ads, Sidney Smith-a 26.00 65.00 180.00
1146- Chester Gump in the City Of Gold, 1935, Whitman, 432 pgs., Sidney Smith-a 15.00 37.50 105.00
nn- Chester Gump in the City Of Gold, 1935, Whitman, 436 pgs., premium-no ads, 3-color, soft-c, Sidney Smith-a 30.00 75.00 210.00
1402- Chester Gump in the Pole to Pole Flight, 1937, Whitman, 432 pgs. 13.00 32.50 90.00
5- Chester Gump and His Friends, 1934, Whitman, 132 pgs., 3 1/2" x 3 1/2", soft-c, Tarzan Ice Cream cup lid premium 29.00 73.00 200.00
nn- Chester Gump at the North Pole, 1938, Whitman, 68 pgs.

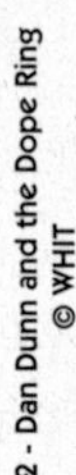
1446 - Convoy Patrol © WHIT

1492 - Dan Dunn and the Dope Ring © WHIT

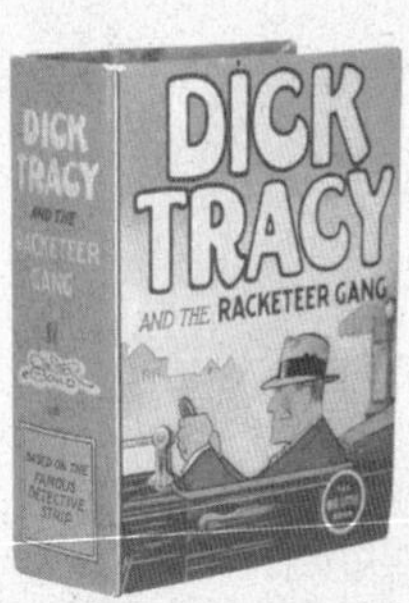

1112 - Dick Tracy and the Racketeer Gang © UFS

	GD	FN	VF/NM
soft-c, 3 3/4" x 3 1/2", Pan-Am giveaway	29.00	73.00	200.00
nn- **Chicken Greedy**, nd(1930s), np (Whitman), 36 pgs., 3" x 2 1/2", Penny Book	4.00	10.00	22.00
nn- **Chicken Licken**, nd (1930s), np (Whitman), 36 pgs., 3" x 2 1/2", Penny Book	4.00	10.00	22.00
1101- **Chief of the Rangers**, 1935, Saalfield, hard-c, Tom Mix photo-c, movie scenes from "The Miracle Rider"	21.00	52.50	145.00
1581- **Chief of the Rangers**, 1935, Saalfield, soft-c, Tom Mix photo-c, movie scenes	21.00	52.50	145.00
Child's Garden of Verses (See Wee Little Books)			
L14- **Chip Collins' Adventures on Bat Island**, 1935, Lynn, 192 pgs.	12.00	30.00	85.00
2025- **Chitty Chitty Bang Bang**, 1968, Whitman, movie photos	4.00	10.00	27.00
Chubby Little Books, 1935, Whitman, 3" x 2 1/2", 200 pgs.			
W803- **Golden Hours Story Book, The**	7.00	17.50	40.00
W803- **Story Hours Story Book, The**	7.00	17.50	40.00
W804- **Gay Book of Little Stories, The**	7.00	17.50	40.00
W804- **Glad Book of Little Stories, The**	7.00	17.50	40.00
W804- **Joy Book of Little Stories, The**	7.00	17.50	40.00
W804- **Sunny Book of Little Stories, The**	7.00	17.50	40.00
1453- **Chuck Malloy Railroad Detective on the Streamliner**, 1938, Whitman, 300 pgs.	12.00	30.00	75.00
Cinderella (See Walt Disney's...)			
Clyde Beatty (See The Steel Arena)			
1410- **Clyde Beatty Daredevil Lion and Tiger Tamer**, 1939, Whitman, 300 pgs.	14.00	35.00	95.00
1480- **Coach Bernie Bierman's Brick Barton and the Winning Eleven**, 1938, 300 pgs.	11.00	27.50	70.00
1446- **Convoy Patrol** (A Thrilling U.S. Navy Story), 1942, Whitman, 432 pgs., flip pictures	11.00	27.50	70.00
1127- **Corley of the Wilderness Trail**, 1937, Saalfield, hard-c	11.00	27.50	70.00
1607- **Corley of the Wilderness Trail**, 1937, Saalfield, soft-c	11.00	27.50	70.00
1- **Count of Monte Cristo**, 1934, EVW, 160 pgs., (Five Star Library), movie scenes, hard-c (Rare)	43.00	108.00	300.00
1457- **Cowboy Lingo Boys' Book of Western Facts**, 1938, Whitman, 300 pgs., Fred Harman-a	12.00	30.00	75.00
1171- **Cowboy Malloy**, 1940, Saalfield, 400 pgs.	10.00	25.00	65.00
1106- **Cowboy Millionaire**, 1935, Saalfield, movie scenes with George O'Brien, photo-c, hard-c	15.00	37.50	105.00
1586- **Cowboy Millionaire**, 1935, Saalfield, movie scenes with George O'Brien, photo-c, soft-c	15.00	37.50	105.00
724- **Cowboy Stories**, 1933, Whitman, 300 pgs., Hal Arbo-a	12.00	30.00	85.00
nn- **Cowboy Stories**, 1933, Whitman, 52 pgs., soft-c, premium-no ads, 4" x 5 1/2" Hal Arbo-a	15.00	37.50	105.00
1161- **Crimson Cloak, The**, 1939, Saalfield, 400 pgs.	11.00	27.50	70.00
L19- **Curley Harper at Lakespur**, 1935, Lynn, 192 pgs.	11.00	27.50	70.00
5785-2- **Daffy Duck in Twice the Trouble**, 1980, Whitman, 260 pgs., 79 cents soft-c	1.00	2.50	6.00
2018-(#18)-**Daktari-Night of Terror**, 1968, Whitman, 260 pgs., 39 cents, hard-c, color illos	4.00	10.00	27.00
1010- **Dan Dunn And The Gangsters' Frame-Up**, 1937, Whitman, 7 1/4" x 5 1/2", 64 pgs., Nickel Book	45.00	114.00	320.00
1116- **Dan Dunn "Crime Never Pays,"** 1934, Whitman, 320 pgs., by Norman Marsh	14.00	35.00	95.00
1125- **Dan Dunn on the Trail of the Counterfeiters**, 1936, Whitman, 432 pgs., by Norman Marsh	14.00	35.00	95.00
1171- **Dan Dunn and the Crime Master**, 1937, Whitman, 432 pgs., by Norman Marsh	14.00	35.00	95.00
1417- **Dan Dunn and the Underworld Gorillas**, 1941, Whitman, All Pictures Comics, flip pictures, by Norman Marsh	14.00	35.00	95.00
1454- **Dan Dunn on the Trail of Wu Fang**, 1938, Whitman, 432 pgs., by Norman Marsh	16.00	40.00	115.00
1481- **Dan Dunn and the Border Smugglers**, 1938, Whitman, 432 pgs., by Norman Marsh	13.00	32.50	90.00
1492- **Dan Dunn and the Dope Ring**, 1940, Whitman, 432 pgs., by Norman Marsh	12.00	30.00	85.00
nn- **Dan Dunn and the Bank Hold-Up**, 1938, Whitman, 36 pgs., 2 1/2" x 3 1/2", Penny Book	11.00	27.50	70.00
nn- **Dan Dunn and the Zeppelin Of Doom**, 1938, Dell, 196 pgs., Fast-Action Story, soft-c	33.00	83.00	230.00
nn- **Dan Dunn Meets Chang Loo**, 1938, Whitman, 66 pgs., Pan-Am premium, by Norman Marsh	29.00	73.00	200.00
nn- **Dan Dunn Plays a Lone Hand**, 1938, Whitman, 36 pgs., 2 1/2" x 3 1/2", Penny Book	11.00	27.50	70.00
3 3/4" x 3 1/2", Buddy book	39.00	98.00	275.00
6- **Dan Dunn Secret Operative 48 and the Counterfeiter Ring**, 1938, Whitman, 132 pgs., soft-c, 3 3/4" x 3 1/2", Buddy Book premium	39.00	98.00	275.00
9- **Dan Dunn's Mysterious Ruse**, 1936, Whitman, 132 pgs., soft-c, 3 1/2" x 3 1/2", Tarzan Ice Cream cup lid premium	39.00	98.00	275.00
1177- **Danger Trail North**, 1940, Saalfield, 400 pgs.	11.00	27.50	70.00
1151- **Danger Trails in Africa**, 1935, Whitman, 432 pgs.	18.00	45.00	125.00
nn- **Daniel Boone**, 1934, World Syndicate, High Lights of History Series, hard-c, All in Pictures	11.00	27.50	70.00
1160- **Dan of the Lazy L**, 1939, Saalfield, 400 pgs.	11.00	27.50	70.00
1148- **David Copperfield**, 1934, Whitman, hard-c, 160 pgs., photo-c, movie scenes (W. C. Fields)	19.00	47.50	130.00
nn- **David Copperfield**, 1934, Whitman, soft-c, 164 pgs., movie scenes	19.00	47.50	130.00
1151- **Death by Short Wave**, 1938, Saalfield	12.00	30.00	75.00
1156- **Denny the Ace Detective**, 1938, Saalfield, 400 pgs.	10.00	25.00	65.00
1431- **Desert Eagle and the Hidden Fortress, The**, 1941, Whitman, 432 pgs., flip pictures	12.00	30.00	75.00
1458- **Desert Eagle Rides Again, The**, 1939, Whitman, 300 pgs.	12.00	30.00	75.00
1136- **Desert Justice**, 1938, Saalfield, 400 pgs.	10.00	25.00	65.00
1484- **Detective Higgins of the Racket Squad**, 1938, Whitman, 432 pgs.	12.00	30.00	75.00
1124- **Dickie Moore in the Little Red School House**, 1936, Whitman, 240 pgs., photo-c, movie scenes (Chesterfield Motion Picts. Corp)	13.00	32.50	90.00
W-707- **Dick Tracy the Detective, The Adventures of**, 1933, Whitman, 320 pgs. (The 1st Big Little Book), by Chester Gould (Scarce)	259.00	648.00	2200.00
nn- **Dick Tracy Detective, The Adventures of**, 1933, Whitman, 52 pgs., 4" x 5 1/2", premium-no ads, soft-c, by Chester Gould	93.00	233.00	650.00
nn- **Dick Tracy Detective, The Adventures of**, 1933, Whitman, 52 pgs., 4" x 5 1/2", inside back-c & back-c ads for Sundial Shoes, soft-c, by Chester Gould	100.00	250.00	700.00
710- **Dick Tracy and Dick Tracy, Jr.** (The Advs. of ...), 1933, Whitman, 320 pgs., by Chester Gould	71.00	178.00	500.00
nn- **Dick Tracy and Dick Tracy, Jr.** (The Advs. of ...), 1933, Whitman, 52 pgs., premium-no ads, soft-c, 4" x 5 1/2", by Chester Gould	71.00	178.00	500.00
nn- **Dick Tracy the Detective and Dick Tracy, Jr.**, 1933, Whitman, 52 pgs., premium-no ads, 3 1/2"x 5 1/4", soft-c, by Chester Gould	71.00	178.00	500.00
723- **Dick Tracy Out West**, 1933, Whitman, 300 pgs., by Chester Gould	46.00	115.00	325.00
749- **Dick Tracy from Colorado to Nova Scotia**, 1933, Whitman, 320 pgs., by Chester Gould	43.00	108.00	300.00
nn- **Dick Tracy from Colorado to Nova Scotia**, 1933, Whitman, 204 pgs., premium-no ads, soft-c, by Chester Gould	46.00	115.00	325.00
1105- **Dick Tracy and the Stolen Bonds**, 1934, Whitman, 320 pgs., by Chester Gould	26.00	65.00	185.00
1112- **Dick Tracy and the Racketeer Gang**, 1936, Whitman, 432 pgs., by Chester Gould	21.00	52.50	145.00
1137- **Dick Tracy Solves the Penfield Mystery**, 1934, Whitman, 320 pgs., by Chester Gould	26.00	65.00	185.00

1445 - Dick Tracy and the Bicycle Gang © UFS

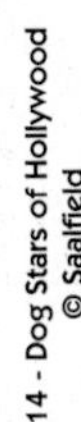

1114 - Dog Stars of Hollywood © Saalfield

1432 - Donald Duck and the Green Serpent © WDC

GD FN VF/NM

nn- Dick Tracy Solves the Penfield Mystery, 1934, Whitman, 324 pgs., premium-no ads, 3-color, soft-c, by Chester Gould 61.00 153.00 425.00

1163- Dick Tracy and the Boris Arson Gang, 1935, Whitman, 432 pgs., by Chester Gould 24.00 60.00 165.00

1170- Dick Tracy on the Trail of Larceny Lu, 1935, Whitman, 432 pgs., by Chester Gould 21.00 52.50 145.00

1185- Dick Tracy in Chains of Crime, 1936, Whitman, 432 pgs., by Chester Gould 24.00 60.00 165.00

1412- Dick Tracy and Yogee Yamma, 1946, Whitman, 352 pgs., by Chester Gould 21.00 52.50 145.00

1420- Dick Tracy and the Hotel Murders, 1937, Whitman, 432 pgs., by Chester Gould 24.00 60.00 165.00

1434- Dick Tracy and the Phantom Ship, 1940, Whitman, 432 pgs., by Chester Gould 24.00 60.00 165.00

1436- Dick Tracy and the Mad Killer, 1947, Whitman, 288 pgs., by Chester Gould 18.00 45.00 125.00

1439- Dick Tracy and His G-Men, 1941, Whitman, 432 pgs., flip pictures, by Chester Gould 24.00 60.00 165.00

1445- Dick Tracy and the Bicycle Gang, 1948, Whitman, 288 pgs., by Chester Gould 18.00 45.00 125.00

1446- Detective Dick Tracy and the Spider Gang, 1937, Whitman, 240 pgs., movie scenes from "Adventures of Dick Tracy" (Republic serial) 29.00 73.00 200.00

1449- Dick Tracy Special F.B.I. Operative, 1943, Whitman, 432 pgs. by Chester Gould 24.00 60.00 165.00

1454- Dick Tracy on the High Seas, 1939, Whitman, 432 pgs., by Chester Gould 24.00 60.00 165.00

1460- Dick Tracy and the Tiger Lilly Gang, 1949, Whitman, 288 pgs., by Chester Gould 18.00 45.00 125.00

1478- Dick Tracy on Voodoo Island, 1944, Whitman, 352 pgs., by Chester Gould 18.00 45.00 125.00

1479- Detective Dick Tracy Vs. Crooks in Disguise, 1939, Whitman, 432 pgs., flip pictures, by Chester Gould 24.00 60.00 165.00

1482- Dick Tracy and the Wreath Kidnapping Case, 1945, Whitman, 352 pgs. 20.00 50.00 140.00

1488- Dick Tracy the Super-Detective, 1939, Whitman, 432 pgs., by Chester Gould 24.00 60.00 165.00

1491- Dick Tracy the Man with No Face, 1938, Whitman, 432 pgs. 24.00 60.00 165.00

1495- Dick Tracy Returns, 1939, Whitman, 432 pgs., based on Republic Motion Picture serial, Chester Gould-a 24.00 60.00 165.00

2001- (#1)-Dick Tracy-Encounters Facey, 1967, Whitman, 260 pgs., 39 cents, hard-c, color illos 4.00 10.00 27.00

4055- Dick Tracy, The Adventures of, 1934, Whitman, 7" x 9 1/2", 320 pgs., Big Big Book, by Chester Gould 107.00 268.00 750.00

4071- Dick Tracy and the Mystery of the Purple Cross, 1938, 7" x 9 1/2", 320 pgs., Big Big Book, by Chester Gould (Scarce) 100.00 250.00 700.00

nn- Dick Tracy and the Invisible Man, 1939, Whitman, 3 1/4" x 3 3/4", 132 pgs., stapled, soft-c, Quaker Oats premium; NBC radio play script, Chester Gould-a 41.00 103.00 285.00

Vol. 2- Dick Tracy's Ghost Ship, 1939, Whitman, 3 1/2" x 3 1/2", 132 pgs., soft-c, stapled, Quaker Oats premium; NBC radio play script episode from actual radio show; Gould-a 41.00 103.00 285.00

3- Dick Tracy Meets a New Gang, 1934, Whitman, 3" x 3 1/2", 132 pgs., soft-c, Tarzan Ice Cream cup lid premium 70.00 175.00 490.00

11- Dick Tracy in Smashing the Famon Racket, 1938, Whitman, 3 3/4" x 3 1/2", Buddy Book-ice cream premium, by Chester Gould 70.00 175.00 490.00

nn- Dick Tracy Gets His Man, 1938, Whitman, 36 pgs., 2 1/2" x 3 1/2", Penny Book 12.00 30.00 75.00

nn- Dick Tracy the Detective, 1938, Whitman, 36 pgs., 2 1/2" x 3 1/2", Penny Book 12.00 30.00 75.00

9- Dick Tracy and the Frozen Bullet Murders, 1941, Dell, 196 pgs., Fast-Action Story, soft-c, by Gould 41.00 103.00 285.00

6833- Dick Tracy Detective and Federal Agent, 1936, Dell, 244 pgs., Cartoon Story Books, hard-c, by Gould 49.00 122.00 345.00

nn- Dick Tracy Detective and Federal Agent, 1936, Dell, 244 pgs., Fast-Action Story, soft-c, by Gould 46.00 115.00 320.00

GD FN VF/NM

nn- Dick Tracy and the Blackmailers, 1939, Dell, 196 pgs., Fast-Action Story, soft-c, by Gould 46.00 115.00 320.00

nn- Dick Tracy and the Chain of Evidence, Detective, 1938, Dell, 196 pgs., Fast-Action Story, soft-c, by Chester Gould 46.00 115.00 320.00

nn- Dick Tracy and the Crook Without a Face, 1938, Whitman, 68 pgs., 3 1/4" x 3 1/2", Pan-Am giveaway, Gould-c/a 49.00 122.00 345.00

nn- Dick Tracy and the Maroon Mask Gang, 1938, Dell, 196 pgs., Fast-Action Story, soft-c, by Gould 46.00 115.00 320.00

nn- Dick Tracy Cross-Country Race, 1934, Whitman, 8 pgs., 2 1/2" x 3", Big Thrill chewing gum premium (6 diff.) 18.00 45.00 125.00

nn- Dick Whittington and his Cat, nd(1930s), np(Whitman), 36 pgs., Penny Book 5.00 12.50 33.00

Dinglehoofer und His Dog Adolph (See Top-Line Comics)

Dinky (See Jackie Cooper in ...)

1464- Dirigible ZR90 and the Disappearing Zeppelin (Captain Robb of ...), 1941, Whitman, 300 pgs., Al Lewin-a 20.00 50.00 140.00

1167- Dixie Dugan Among the Cowboys, 1939, Saalfield, 400 pgs. 12.00 30.00 85.00

1188- Dixie Dugan and Cuddles, 1940, Saalfield, 400 pgs., by Striebel & McEvoy 12.00 30.00 85.00

Doctor Doom (See Foreign Spies... & International Spy...)

Dog of Flanders, A (See Frankie Thomas in ...)

1114- Dog Stars of Hollywood, 1936, Saalfield, photo-c, photo-illos 16.00 40.00 115.00

1594- Dog Stars of Hollywood, 1936, Saalfield, photo-c, soft-c, photo-illos 16.00 40.00 115.00

Donald Duck (See Silly Symphony... & Walt Disney's ...)

800- Donald Duck in Bringing Up the Boys, 1948, Whitman, hard-c, Story Hour series 12.00 30.00 85.00

1404- Donald Duck (Says Such a Life) (Disney), 1939, Whitman, 432 pgs., Taliaferro-a 31.00 78.00 220.00

1411- Donald Duck and Ghost Morgan's Treasure (Disney), 1946, Whitman, All Pictures Comics, Barks-a; reprints Four Color #9 38.00 95.00 255.00

1422- Donald Duck Sees Stars (Disney), 1941, Whitman, 432 pgs., flip pictures, Taliaferro-a 31.00 78.00 215.00

1424- Donald Duck Says Such Luck (Disney), 1941, Whitman, 432 pgs., flip pictures, Taliaferro-a 31.00 78.00 215.00

1430- Donald Duck Headed For Trouble (Disney), 1942, Whitman, 432 pgs., flip pictures, Taliaferro-a 31.00 78.00 215.00

1432- Donald Duck and the Green Serpent (Disney), 1947, Whitman, All Pictures Comics, Barks-a; reprints Four Color #108 34.00 85.00 240.00

1434- Donald Duck Forgets To Duck (Disney), 1939, Whitman, 432 pgs., Taliaferro-a 31.00 78.00 215.00

1438- Donald Duck Off the Beam (Disney), 1943, Whitman, 352 pgs., flip pictures, Taliaferro-a 31.00 78.00 215.00

1438- Donald Duck Off the Beam (Disney), 1943, Whitman, 432 pgs., flip pictures, Taliaferro-a 31.00 78.00 215.00

1449- Donald Duck Lays Down the Law, 1948, Whitman, 288 pgs., Barks-a 31.00 78.00 215.00

1457- Donald Duck in Volcano Valley (Disney), 1949, Whitman, 288 pgs., Barks-a 31.00 78.00 215.00

1462- Donald Duck Gets Fed Up (Disney), 1940, Whitman, 432 pgs.,Taliaferro-a 31.00 78.00 215.00

1478- Donald Duck-Hunting For Trouble (Disney), 1938, Whitman, 432 pgs., Taliaferro-a 31.00 78.00 215.00

1484- Donald Duck is Here Again!, 1944, Whitman, All Pictures Comics, Taliaferro-a 31.00 78.00 215.00

1486- Donald Duck Up in the Air (Disney), 1945, Whitman, 352 pgs., Barks-a 34.00 85.00 240.00

705-10- Donald Duck and the Mystery of the Double X, (Disney), 1949, Whitman, Barks-a 16.00 40.00 115.00

2033-(#33)- Donald Duck, Luck of the Ducks, 1969, Whitman, 256 pgs., hard-c, 39 cents, color illos. 4.00 10.00 22.00

2009-(#9)-Donald Duck-The Fabulous Diamond Fountain, (Walt Disney), 1967, Whitman, 260 pgs., 39 cents, hard-c, color illos 4.00 10.00 27.00

5756- Donald Duck-The Fabulous Diamond Fountain,

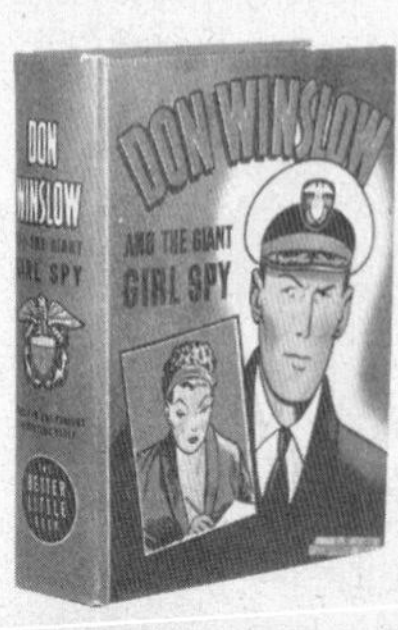

1408 - Don Winslow and the Giant Girl Spy © WHIT

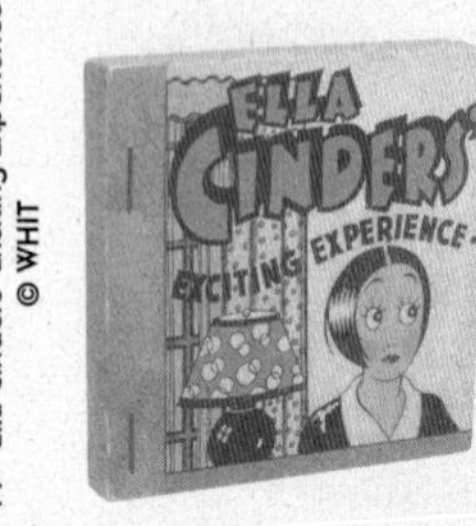

11 - Ella Cinders' Exciting Experience © WHIT

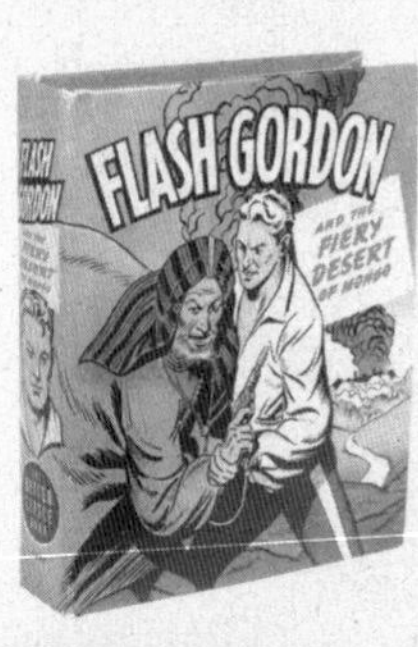

1447 - Flash Gordon and the Fiery Desert of Mongo © KING

	GD	FN	VF/NM
(Walt Disney), 1973, Whitman, 260 pgs., 79 cents, soft-c, color illos	3.00	7.50	20.00
5756-1- Donald Duck-The Fabulous Diamond Fountain, (Walt Disney), 1973, Whitman, 260 pgs., 79 cents, soft-c, color illos	3.00	7.50	20.00
5756-2- Donald Duck-The Fabulous Diamond Fountain, (Walt Disney), 1973, Whitman, 260 pgs., 79 cents, soft-c, color illos	3.00	7.50	20.00
5760- Donald Duck in Volcano Valley (Disney), 1973, Whitman, 39 cents, flip-it book	3.00	7.50	20.00
5760-2- Donald Duck in Volcano Valley (Disney), 1973, Whitman, 79 cents, flip-it book	2.00	5.00	14.00
5764- Donald Duck, Luck of the Ducks, 1969, Whitman, 256 pgs., soft-c, 49 cents, color illos.	3.00	7.50	20.00
5773- Donald Duck - The Lost Jungle City, 1975, Whitman, 49 cents, flip-it book; 6 printings through 1980	2.00	5.00	14.00
nn- Donald Duck and the Ducklings, 1938, Dell, 194 pgs., Fast-Action Story, soft-c, Taliaferro-a	58.00	146.00	410.00
nn- Donald Duck Out of Luck (Disney), 1940, Dell, 196 pgs., Fast-Action Story, has Four Color #4 on back-c, Taliaferro-a	58.00	146.00	410.00
8- Donald Duck Takes It on the Chin (Disney), 1941, Dell, 196 pgs., Fast-Action Story, soft-c, Taliaferro-a	58.00	146.00	410.00
L13- Donnie and the Pirates, 1935, Lynn, 192 pgs.	12.00	30.00	85.00
1438- Don O'Dare Finds War, 1940, Whitman, 432 pgs.	11.00	27.50	70.00
1107- Don Winslow, U.S.N., 1935, Whitman, 432 pgs.	20.00	50.00	140.00
nn- Don Winslow, U.S.N., 1935, Whitman, 436 pgs., premium-no ads, 3-color, soft-c	31.00	78.00	220.00
1408- Don Winslow and the Giant Girl Spy, 1946, Whitman, 352 pgs.	13.00	32.50	90.00
1418- Don Winslow Navy Intelligence Ace, 1942, Whitman, 432 pgs., flip pictures	18.00	45.00	125.00
1419- Don Winslow of the Navy Vs. the Scorpion Gang, 1938, Whitman, 432 pgs.	18.00	45.00	125.00
1453- Don Winslow of the Navy and the Secret Enemy Base, 1943, Whitman, 352 pgs.	18.00	45.00	125.00
1489- Don Winslow of the Navy and the Great War Plot, 1940, Whitman, 432 pgs.	18.00	45.00	125.00
nn- Don Winslow U.S. Navy and the Missing Admiral, 1938, Whitman, 36 pgs., 2 1/2" x 3 1/2", Penny Book	11.00	27.50	70.00
1137- Doomed To Die, 1938, Saalfield, 400 pgs.	11.00	27.50	70.00
1140- Down Cartridge Creek, 1938, Saalfield, 400 pgs.	11.00	27.50	70.00
1416- Draftie of the U.S. Army, 1943, Whitman, All Pictures Comics	12.00	30.00	75.00
1100B- Dreams (Your dreams & what they mean), 1938, Whitman, 36 pgs., 2 1/2" x 3 1/2", Penny Book	4.00	10.00	27.00
24- Dumb Dora and Bing Brown, 1936, Lynn	14.00	35.00	95.00
1400- Dumbo, of the Circus - Only His Ears Grew! (Disney), 1941, Whitman, 432 pgs., based on Disney movie	28.00	70.00	195.00
10- Dumbo the Flying Elephant (Disney), 1944, Dell, 194 pgs., Fast-Action Story, soft-c	46.00	115.00	320.00
nn- East O' the Sun and West O' the Moon, nd (1930s), np (Whitman), 36 pgs., 3" x 2 1/2", Penny Book	4.00	10.00	27.00
774- Eddie Cantor in An Hour with You, 1934, Whitman, 154 pgs., 4 1/4" x 5 1/4", photo-c, movie scenes	16.00	40.00	115.00
nn- Eddie Cantor in Laughland, 1934, Goldsmith, 132 pgs., soft-c, photo-c, Vallely-a	16.00	40.00	115.00
1106- Ella Cinders and the Mysterious House, 1934, Whitman, 432 pgs.	15.00	37.50	105.00
nn- Ella Cinders and the Mysterious House, 1934, Whitman, 52 pgs., premium-no ads, soft-c, 3 1/2" x 5 3/4"	22.00	52.50	155.00
nn- Ella Cinders, 1935, Whitman, 148 pgs., 3 1/4" x 4", Tarzan Ice Cream cup lid premium	36.00	90.00	255.00
nn- Ella Cinders Plays Duchess, 1938, Whitman, 68 pgs., 3 3/4" x 3 1/2", Pan-Am Oil premium	16.00	40.00	115.00
nn- Ella Cinders Solves a Mystery, 1938, Whitman, 68 pgs., Pan-Am Oil premium, soft-c	16.00	40.00	115.00

	GD	FN	VF/NM
11- Ella Cinders' Exciting Experience, 1934, Whitman, 3 1/2" x 3 1/2", 132 pgs., Tarzan Ice Cream cup lid giveaway	36.00	90.00	255.00
1406- Ellery Queen the Adventure of the Last Man Club, 1940, Whitman, 432 pgs.	15.00	37.50	105.00
1472- Ellery Queen the Master Detective, 1942, Whitman, 432 pgs., flip pictures	15.00	37.50	105.00
1081- Elmer and his Dog Spot, 1935, Saalfield, hard-c	11.00	27.50	70.00
1311- Elmer and his Dog Spot, 1935, Saalfield, soft-c	11.00	27.50	70.00
722- Erik Noble and the Forty-Niners, 1934, Whitman, 384 pgs.	11.00	27.50	70.00
nn- Erik Noble and the Forty-Niners, 1934, Whitman, 386 pgs., 3-color, soft-c (Rare)	64.00	160.00	450.00
2019-(#19)- Fantastic Four in the House of Horrors, 1968, Whitman, 256 pgs., hard-c, color illos.	4.00	10.00	27.00
5775 - Fantastic Four in the House of Horrors, 1976, Whitman, 256 pgs., soft-c, color illos.	3.00	7.50	20.00
5775-1 - Fantastic Four in the House of Horrors, 1976, Whitman, 256 pgs., soft-c, color illos.	3.00	7.50	20.00
1058- Farmyard Symphony, The (Disney), 1939, 5" X 5 1/2", 68 pgs., hard-c	15.00	37.50	105.00
1129- Felix the Cat, 1936, Whitman, 432 pgs., Messmer-a	33.00	83.00	230.00
1439- Felix the Cat, 1943, Whitman, All Pictures Comics, Messmer-a	28.00	70.00	195.00
1465- Felix the Cat, 1945, Whitman, All Pictures Comics, Messmer-a	24.00	60.00	165.00
nn- Felix (Flip book), 1967, World Retrospective of Animation Cinema, 188 pgs., 2 1/2" x 4" by Otto Messmer	4.00	10.00	27.00
nn- Fighting Cowboy of Nugget Gulch, The, 1939, Whitman, 2 1/2" x 3 1/2", Penny Book	7.00	17.50	45.00
1401- Fighting Heroes Battle for Freedom, 1943, Whitman, All Pictures Comics, from "Heroes of Democracy" strip, by Stookie Allen	11.00	27.50	70.00
6- Fighting President, The, 1934, EVW (Five Star Library), 160 pgs., photo-c, photo ill., F. D. Roosevelt	12.00	30.00	85.00
nn- Fire Chief Ed Wynn and "His Old Fire Horse," 1934, Goldsmith, 132 pgs., H. Vallely-a, photo, soft-c	12.00	30.00	85.00
1464- Flame Boy and the Indians' Secret, 1938, Whitman, 300 pgs., Sekakuku-a (Hopi Indian)	11.00	27.50	70.00
22- Flaming Guns, 1935, EVW, with Tom Mix, movie scenes — Hardcover	78.00	195.00	550.00
(Scarce) — Softcover	85.00	212.00	600.00
1110- Flash Gordon on the Planet Mongo, 1934, Whitman, 320 pgs., by Alex Raymond	49.00	122.00	345.00
1166- Flash Gordon and the Monsters of Mongo, 1935, Whitman, 432 pgs., by Alex Raymond	41.00	103.00	290.00
nn- Flash Gordon and the Monsters of Mongo, 1935, Whitman, 436 pgs., premium-no ads, 3-color, soft-c, by Raymond	61.00	153.00	430.00
1171- Flash Gordon and the Tournaments of Mongo, 1935, Whitman, 432 pgs., by Alex Raymond	43.00	108.00	300.00
1190- Flash Gordon and the Witch Queen of Mongo, 1936, Whitman, 432 pgs., by Alex Raymond	43.00	108.00	300.00
1407- Flash Gordon in the Water World of Mongo, 1937, Whitman, 432 pgs., by Alex Raymond	38.00	95.00	255.00
1423- Flash Gordon and the Perils of Mongo, 1940, Whitman, 432 pgs., by Alex Raymond	33.00	83.00	230.00
1424- Flash Gordon in the Jungles of Mongo, 1947, Whitman, 352 pgs., by Alex Raymond	24.00	60.00	170.00
1443- Flash Gordon in the Ice World of Mongo, 1942, Whitman, 432 pgs., flip pictures, by Alex Raymond	36.00	90.00	250.00
1447- Flash Gordon and the Fiery Desert of Mongo, 1948, Whitman, 288 pgs., Raymond-a	24.00	60.00	170.00
1469- Flash Gordon and the Power Men of Mongo, 1943, Whitman, 352 pgs., by Alex Raymond	36.00	90.00	250.00
1479- Flash Gordon and the Red Sword Invaders, 1945, Whitman, 352 pgs., by Alex Raymond	34.00	85.00	240.00

Flintstones: The Great Balloon Race
© H-B

1434 - Gene Autry and the Gun-Smoke Reckoning © WHIT

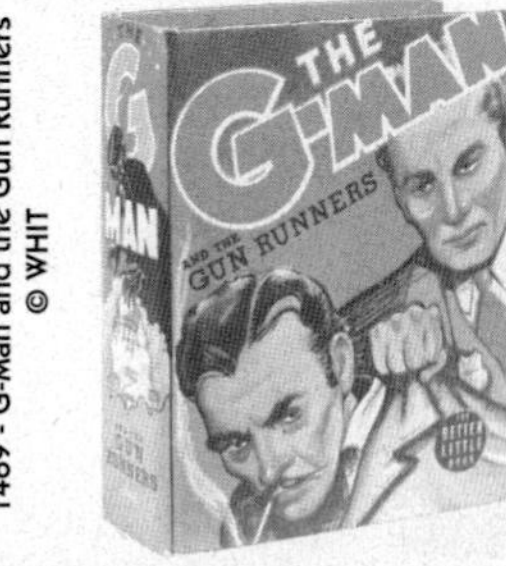

1469 - G-Man and the Gun Runners © WHIT

GD FN VF/NM

1484- Flash Gordon and the Tyrant of Mongo, 1941, Whitman, 432 pgs., flip pictures, by Alex Raymond 36.00 90.00 250.00
1492- Flash Gordon in the Forest Kingdom of Mongo, 1938, Whitman, 432 pgs., by Alex Raymond 46.00 115.00 320.00
12- Flash Gordon and the Ape Men of Mor, 1942, Dell, 196 pgs., Fast-Action Story, by Alex Raymond 64.00 160.00 450.00
6833- Flash Gordon Vs. the Emperor of Mongo, 1936, Dell, 244 pgs., Cartoon Story Books, hard-c, Alex Raymond-c/a 79.00 198.00 550.00
nn- Flash Gordon Vs. the Emperor of Mongo, 1936, Dell, 244 pgs., Fast-Action Story, soft-c, Alex Raymond-c/a 62.00 155.00 440.00
1467- Flint Roper and the Six-Gun Showdown, 1941, Whitman, 300 pgs. 11.00 27.50 70.00
2014-(#14)- Flintstones-The Case of the Many Missing Things, 1968, Whitman, 260 pgs., 39 cents, hard-c, color illos 4.00 10.00 27.00
nn- Flintstones: A Friend From the Past, 1977, Modern Promotions, 244 pgs., 49 cents, soft-c, flip pictures 2.00 5.00 11.00
nn- Flintstones: It's About Time, 1977, Modern Promotions, 244 pgs., 49 cents, soft-c, flip pictures 2.00 5.00 11.00
nn- Flintstones: Pebbles & Bamm-Bamm Meet Santa Claus, 1977, Modern Promotions, 244 pgs., 49 cents, soft-c, flip pictures 2.00 5.00 11.00
nn- Flintstones: The Great Balloon Race, 1977, Modern Promotions, 244 pgs., 49 cents, soft-c, flip pictures 2.00 5.00 11.00
nn- Flintstones: The Mystery of the Many Missing Things, 1977, Modern Promotions, 244 pgs., 49 cents, soft-c, flip pictures 2.00 5.00 11.00
2003-(#3)- Flipper-Killer Whale Trouble, 1967, Whitman, 260 pgs., hard-c, 39 cents, color illos 3.00 7.50 20.00
2032-(#32)- Flipper, Deep-Sea Photographer, 1969, Whitman, 256 pgs., hard-c, color illos. 3.00 7.50 20.00
1108- Flying the Sky Clipper with Winsie Atkins, 1936, Whitman, 432 pgs. 11.00 27.50 70.00
1460- Foreign Spies Doctor Doom and the Ghost Submarine, 1939, Whitman, 432 pgs., Al McWilliams-a 13.00 32.50 90.00
1100B- Fortune Teller, 1938, Whitman, 36 pgs., 2 1/2" x 3 1/2", Penny Book 5.00 12.50 33.00
1175- Frank Buck Presents Ted Towers Animal Master, 1935, Whitman, 432 pgs. 12.00 30.00 80.00
2015-(#15)-Frankenstein, Jr. - The Menace of the Heartless Monster, 1968, Whitman, 260 pgs., 39 cents, hard-c, color illos. 4.00 10.00 27.00
16- Frankie Thomas in A Dog of Flanders, 1935, EVW, movie scenes 15.00 37.50 105.00
1121- Frank Merriwell at Yale, 1935, 432 pgs. 11.00 27.50 70.00
Freckles and His Friends in the North Woods (See Top-Line Comics)
nn- Freckles and His Friends Stage a Play, 1938, Whitman, 36 pgs., 2 1/2" x 3 1/2", Penny Book 11.00 27.50 70.00
1164- Freckles and the Lost Diamond Mine, 1937, Whitman, 432 pgs., Merrill Blosser-a 12.00 30.00 85.00
nn- Freckles and the Mystery Ship, 1935, Whitman, 66 pgs., Pan-Am premium 16.00 40.00 115.00
1100B- Fun, Puzzles, Riddles, 1938, Whitman, 36 pgs., 2 1/2" x 3 1/2", Penny Book 4.00 10.00 27.00
1433- Gang Busters Step In, 1939, Whitman, 432 pgs., Henry E. Vallely-a 13.00 32.50 90.00
1437- Gang Busters Smash Through, 1942, Whitman, 432 pgs. 13.00 32.50 90.00
1451- Gang Busters in Action!, 1938, Whitman, 432 pgs. 13.00 32.50 90.00
nn- Gang Busters and Guns of the Law, 1940, Dell, 4" x 5", 194 pgs., Fast-Action Story, soft-c 41.00 103.00 285.00
nn- Gang Busters and the Radio Clues, 1938, Whitman, 36 pgs., 2 1/2" x 3 1/2", Penny Book 11.00 27.50 70.00
1409- Gene Autry and Raiders of the Range, 1946, Whitman, 352 pgs. 15.00 37.50 105.00
1425- Gene Autry and the Mystery of Paint Rock Canyon, 1947, Whitman, 288 pgs. 15.00 37.50 105.00
1428- Gene Autry Special Ranger, 1941, Whitman, 432 pgs., Erwin Hess-a 20.00 50.00 140.00

GD FN VF/NM

1433- Gene Autry in Public Cowboy No. 1, 1938, Whitman, 240 pgs., photo-c, movie scenes (1st Autry BLB) 38.00 95.00 255.00
1434- Gene Autry and the Gun-Smoke Reckoning, 1943, Whitman, 352 pgs. 19.00 47.50 135.00
1439- Gene Autry and the Land Grab Mystery, 1948, Whitman, 290 pgs. 14.00 35.00 95.00
1456- Gene Autry in Special Ranger Rule, 1945, Whitman, 352 pgs., Henry E. Vallely-a 19.00 47.50 135.00
1461- Gene Autry and the Red Bandit's Ghost, 1949, Whitman, 288 pgs. 13.00 32.50 90.00
1483- Gene Autry in Law of the Range, 1939, Whitman, 432 pgs. 19.00 47.50 135.00
1493- Gene Autry and the Hawk of the Hills, 1942, Whitman, 428 pgs., flip pictures, Vallely-a 19.00 47.50 135.00
1494- Gene Autry Cowboy Detective, 1940, Whitman, 432 pgs., Erwin Hess-a 19.00 47.50 135.00
700-10- Gene Autry and the Bandits of Silver Tip, 1949, Whitman 12.00 30.00 80.00
714-10- Gene Autry and the Range War, 1950, Whitman 12.00 30.00 80.00
nn- Gene Autry in Gun-Smoke, 1938, Dell, 196 pgs., Fast-Action story, soft-c 46.00 115.00 320.00
2035-(#35)- Gentle Ben, Mystery of the Everglades, 1969, Whitman, 256 pgs., hard-c, color illos. 3.00 7.50 20.00
1176- Gentleman Joe Palooka, 1940, Saalfield, 400 pgs. 16.00 40.00 115.00
George O'Brien (See The Cowboy Millionaire)
1101- George O'Brien and the Arizona Badman, 1936?, Whitman 15.00 37.50 105.00
1418- George O'Brien in Gun Law, 1938, Whitman, 240 pgs., photo-c, movie scenes, RKO Radio Pictures 15.00 37.50 105.00
1457- George O'Brien and the Hooded Riders, 1940, Whitman, 432 pgs., Erwin Hess-a 11.00 27.50 70.00
nn- George O'Brien and the Arizona Bad Man, 1939, Whitman, 36 pgs., 2 1/2" x 3 1/2", Penny Book 11.00 27.50 70.00
1462- Ghost Avenger, 1943, Whitman, 432 pgs., flip pictures, Henry Vallely-a 11.00 27.50 70.00
nn- Ghost Gun Gang Meet Their Match, The, 1939. Whitman, 2 1/2" x 3 1/2", Penny Book 10.00 25.00 65.00
nn- Gingerbread Boy, The, nd(1930s), np(Whitman), 36 pgs., Penny Book 4.00 10.00 22.00
1118- G-Man on the Crime Trail, 1936, Whitman, 432 pgs. 12.00 30.00 80.00
1147- G-Man Vs. the Red X, 1936, Whitman, 432 pgs. 14.00 35.00 95.00
1162- G-Man Allen, 1939, Saalfield, 400 pgs. 11.00 27.50 70.00
1173- G-Man in Action, A, 1940, Saalfield, 400 pgs., J.R. White-a 11.00 27.50 70.00
1434- G-Man and the Radio Bank Robberies, 1937, Whitman, 432 pgs. 13.00 32.50 90.00
1469- G-Man and the Gun Runners, The, 1940, Whitman, 432 pgs. 13.00 32.50 90.00
1470- G-Man vs. the Fifth Column, 1941, Whitman, 432 pgs., flip pictures 13.00 32.50 90.00
1493- G-Man Breaking the Gambling Ring, 1938, Whitman, 432 pgs., James Gary-a 13.00 32.50 90.00
nn- G-Man on Lightning Island, 1936, Dell, 244 pgs., Fast-Action Story, soft-c, Henry E. Vallely-a 33.00 83.00 230.00
nn- G-Man, Underworld Chief, 1938, Whitman, Buddy Book premium, 50.00 125.00 350.00
6833- G-Man on Lightning Island, 1936, Dell, 244 pgs., Cartoon Story Book, hard-c, Henry E. Vallely-a 29.00 73.00 200.00
4- G-Men Foil the Kidnappers, 1936, Whitman, 132 pgs., 3 1/2" x 3 1/2", soft-c, Tarzan Ice Cream cup lid premium 36.00 90.00 255.00
1157- G-Men on the Trail, 1938, Saalfield, 400 pgs. 11.00 27.50 70.00
1168- G Men on the Job, 1935, Whitman, 432 pgs. 12.00 30.00 85.00
nn- G-Men on the Job Again, 1938, Whitman, 36 pgs., 2 1/2" x 3 1/2", Penny Book 11.00 27.50 70.00
nn- G-Men and Kidnap Justice, 1938, Whitman, 68 pgs., Pan-Am premium, soft-c 12.00 30.00 85.00

5778 - Grimm's Ghost Stories © WHIT

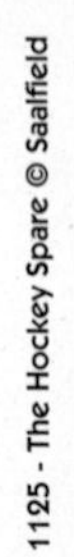

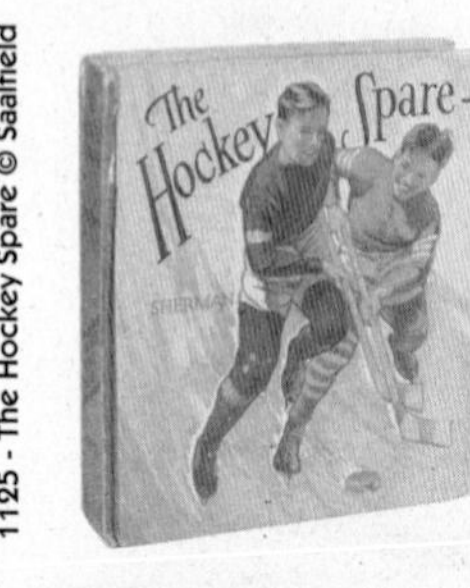

1125 - The Hockey Spare © Saalfield

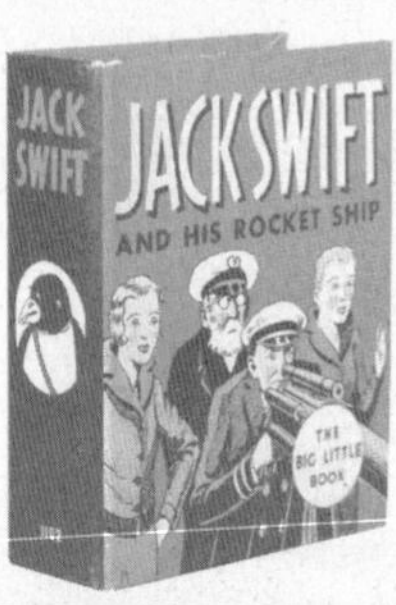

1102 - Jack Swift and His Rocket Ship © WHIT

No.	Title	GD	FN	VF/NM
nn-	**G-Men and the Missing Clues**, 1938, Whitman, 36 pgs., 2 1/2"x 3 1/2", Penny Book	11.00	27.50	70.00
1097-	**Go Into Your Dance**, 1935, Saalfield, 160 pgs.. photo-c, movie scenes with Al Jolson & Ruby Keeler	15.00	37.50	105.00
1577-	**Go Into Your Dance**, 1935, Saalfield, 160 pgs., photo-c, movie scenes, soft-c	15.00	37.50	105.00
2021-	**Goofy in Giant Trouble** (Walt Disney's ...), 1968, Whitman, hard-c, 260 pgs., 39 cents, color illos.	3.00	7.50	20.00
5751-	**Goofy in Giant Trouble** (Walt Disney's ...), 1968, Whitman, soft-c, 260 pgs., 39 cents, color illos.	3.00	7.50	20.00
5751-2-	**Goofy in Giant Trouble**, 1968 (1980-reprint of '67 version), Whitman, soft-c, 260 pgs., 79 cents, B&W	1.00	2.50	8.00
8-	**Great Expectations**, 1934, EVW, (Five Star Library), 160 pgs., photo-c, movie scenes	20.00	50.00	140.00
1453-	**Green Hornet Strikes!, The**, 1940, Whitman, 432 pgs., Robert Weisman-a	49.00	122.00	345.00
1480-	**Green Hornet Cracks Down, The**, 1942, Whitman, 432 pgs., flip pictures, Henry Vallely-a	46.00	115.00	320.00
1496-	**Green Hornet Returns, The**, 1941, Whitman, 432 pgs., flip pictures	49.00	122.00	345.00
5778-	**Grimm's Ghost Stories**, 1976, Whitman, 256 pgs., Laura French-s adapted from fairy tales; blue spine & back-c	2.00	5.00	13.00
5778-1-	**Grimm's Ghost Stories**, 1976, Whitman, 256 pgs., reprint of #5778; yellow spine & back-c	2.00	5.00	13.00
1172-	**Gullivers' Travels**, 1939, Saalfield, 320 pgs., adapted from Paramount Pict. Cartoons (Rare) Hardcover	50.00	125.00	350.00
	(Scarce) Softcover	57.00	142.00	400.00
nn-	**Gumps In Radio Land, The** (Andy Gump and the Chest of Gold), 1937, Lehn & Fink Prod. Corp., 100 pgs., 3 1/4" x 5 1/2", Pebeco Tooth Paste giveaway, by Gus Edson	24.00	60.00	165.00
nn-	**Gunmen of Rustlers' Gulch, The**, 1939, Whitman, 36 pgs., 2 1/2" x 3 1/2", Penny Book	11.00	27.50	70.00
1426-	**Guns in the Roaring West**, 1937, Whitman, 300 pgs.	11.00	27.50	70.00
1647-	**Gunsmoke** (TV Series), 1958, Whitman, 280 pgs., 4 1/2" x 5 3/4"	7.00	17.50	44.00
1101-	**Hairbreath Harry in Department QT**, 1935, Whitman, 384 pgs., by J. M. Alexander	12.00	30.00	85.00
1413-	**Hal Hardy in the Lost Land of Giants**, 1938, Whitman, 300 pgs., "The World 1,000,000 Years Ago"	12.00	30.00	85.00
1159-	**Hall of Fame of the Air**, 1936, Whitman, 432 pgs., by Capt. Eddie Rickenbacker	11.00	27.50	70.00
nn-	**Hansel and Grethel, The Story of**, nd (1930s), no publ., 36 pgs., Penny Book	4.00	10.00	22.00
1145-	**Hap Lee's Selection of Movie Gags**, 1935, Whitman, 160 pgs., photos of stars	15.00	37.50	105.00
	Happy Prince, The (See Wee Little Books)			
1111-	**Hard Rock Harrigan-A Story of Boulder Dam**, 1935, Saalfield, hard-c, photo-c, photo illos.	11.00	27.50	70.00
1591-	**Hard Rock Harrigan-A Story of Boulder Dam**, 1935, Saalfield, soft-c, photo-c, photo illos.	11.00	27.50	70.00
1418-	**Harold Teen Swinging at the Sugar Bowl**, 1939, Whitman, 432 pgs., by Carl Ed	12.00	30.00	80.00
nn-	**Hercules - The Legendary Journeys**, 1998, Chronicle Books, 310 pgs., based on TV series, 1-color (brown) illos	1.00	2.50	9.00
1100B-	**Hobbies**, 1938, Whitman, 36 pgs., 2 1/2" x 3 1/2", Penny Book	4.00	10.00	22.00
1125-	**Hockey Spare, The**, 1937, Saalfield, sports book	8.00	20.00	50.00
1605-	**Hockey Spare, The**, 1937, Saalfield, soft-c	8.00	20.00	50.00
728-	**Homeless Homer**, 1934, Whitman, by Dee Dobbin, for young kids	5.00	12.50	33.00
17-	**Hoosier Schoolmaster, The**, 1935, EVW, movie scenes	15.00	37.50	105.00
715-	**Houdini's Big Little Book of Magic**, 1927 (1933), 300 pgs.	16.00	40.00	115.00
nn-	**Houdini's Big Little Book of Magic**, 1927 (1933), 196 pgs., American Oil Co. premium, soft-c	16.00	40.00	115.00
nn-	**Houdini's Big Little Book of Magic**, 1927 (1933), 204 pgs., Cocomalt premium, soft-c	16.00	40.00	115.00
	Huckleberry Finn (See The Adventures of...)			
nn-	**Huckleberry Hound Newspaper Reporter**, 1977, Modern Promotions, 244 pgs., 49 cents, soft-c, flip pictures	2.00	5.00	13.00
1644-	**Hugh O'Brian TV's Wyatt Earp** (TV Series), 1958, Whitman, 280 pgs.	7.00	17.50	44.00
5782-2-	**Incredible Hulk Lost in Time**, 1980, 260 pgs., 79¢-c, soft-c, B&W	2.00	5.00	10.00
1424-	**Inspector Charlie Chan Villainy on the High Seas**, 1942, Whitman, 432 pgs., flip pictures	16.00	40.00	115.00
1186-	**Inspector Wade of Scotland Yard**, 1940, Saalfield, 400 pgs.	11.00	27.50	70.00
1194-	**Inspector Wade and The Feathered Serpent**, 1939, Saalfield, 400 pgs.	11.00	27.50	70.00
1448-	**Inspector Wade Solves the Mystery of the Red Aces**, 1937, Whitman, 432 pgs.	11.00	27.50	70.00
1148-	**International Spy Doctor Doom Faces Death at Dawn**, 1937, Whitman, 432 pgs., Arbo-a	12.00	30.00	85.00
1155-	**In the Name of the Law**, 1937, Whitman, 432 pgs., Henry E. Vallely-a	11.00	27.50	70.00
2012-(#12)-	**Invaders, The-Alien Missile Threat** (TV Series), 1967, Whitman, 260 pgs., hard-c, 39 cents, color illos.	4.00	10.00	27.00
1403-	**Invisible Scarlet O'Neil**, 1942, Whitman, All Pictures Comics, flip pictures	12.00	30.00	85.00
1406-	**Invisible Scarlet O'Neil Versus the King of the Slums**, 1946, Whitman, 352 pgs.	11.00	27.50	70.00
1098-	**It Happened One Night**, 1935, Saalfield, 160 pgs., Little Big Book, Clark Gable, Claudette Colbert photo-c, movie scenes from Academy Award winner	21.00	52.50	145.00
1578-	**It Happened One Night**, 1935, Saalfield, 160 pgs., soft-c	21.00	52.50	145.00
	Jack and Jill (See Wee Little Books)			
1432-	**Jack Armstrong and the Mystery of the Iron Key**, 1939, Whitman, 432 pgs., Henry E. Vallely-a	12.00	30.00	85.00
1435-	**Jack Armstrong and the Ivory Treasure**, 1937, Whitman, 432 pgs., Henry Vallely-a	12.00	30.00	85.00
	Jackie Cooper (See Story Of..)			
1084-	**Jackie Cooper in Peck's Bad Boy**, 1934, Saalfield, 160 pgs., hard, photo-c, movie scenes	15.00	37.50	105.00
1314-	**Jackie Cooper in Peck's Bad Boy**, 1934, Saalfield, 160 pgs., soft, photo-c, movie scenes	15.00	37.50	105.00
1402-	**Jackie Cooper in "Gangster's Boy,"** 1939, Whitman, 240 pgs., photo-c, movie scenes	15.00	37.50	105.00
13-	**Jackie Cooper in Dinky**, 1935, EVW, 160 pgs., movie scenes	15.00	37.50	105.00
nn-	**Jack King of the Secret Service and the Counterfeiters**, 1939, Whitman, 36 pgs., 2 1/2" x 3 1/2", Penny Book, by John G. Gray	11.00	27.50	70.00
L11-	**Jack London's Call of the Wild**, 1935, Lynn, 20th Cent. Pic., movie scenes with Clark Gable	15.00	37.50	105.00
nn-	**Jack Pearl as Detective Baron Munchausen**, 1934, Goldsmith, 132 pgs., soft-c	12.00	30.00	85.00
1102-	**Jack Swift and His Rocket Ship**, 1934, Whitman, 320 pgs.	24.00	60.00	165.00
1498-	**Jane Arden the Vanished Princess**, Whitman, 300 pgs.	11.00	27.50	70.00
1179-	**Jane Withers in This is the Life** (20th Century-Fox Presents...), 1935, Whitman, 240 pgs., photo-c, movie scenes	15.00	37.50	105.00
1463-	**Jane Withers in Keep Smiling**, 1938, Whitman, 240 pgs., photo-c, movie scenes	15.00	37.50	105.00
	Jaragu of the Jungle (See Rex Beach's ...)			
1447-	**Jerry Parker Police Reporter and the Candid Camera Clue**, 1941, Whitman, 300 pgs.	11.00	27.50	70.00
	Jim Bowie (See Adventures of ...)			
nn-	**Jim Brant of the Highway Patrol and the Mysterious Accident**, 1939, Whitman, 36 pgs., 2 1/2" x 3 1/2", Penny Book	10.00	25.00	65.00
1466-	**Jim Craig State Trooper and the Kidnapped Governor**, 1938, Whitman, 432 pgs.	11.00	27.50	70.00
nn-	**Jim Doyle Private Detective and the Train Hold-Up**, 1939, Whitman, 36 pgs., 2 1/2" x 3 1/2", Penny Book	12.00	30.00	75.00

1100B - Jokes © WHIT

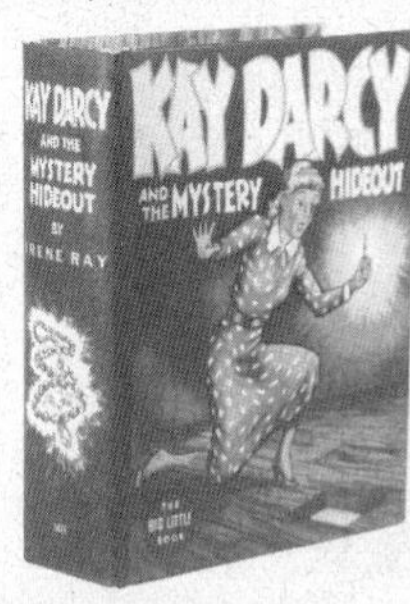

1411 - Kay Darcy and the Mystery Hideout © WHIT

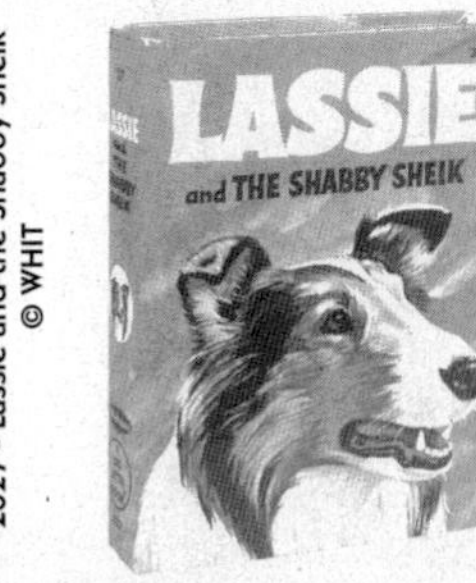

2027 - Lassie and the Shabby Sheik © WHIT

GD FN VF/NM

1180- Jim Hardy Ace Reporter, 1940, Saalfield, 400 pgs., Dick Moores-a 12.00 30.00 75.00

1143- Jimmy Allen in the Air Mail Robbery, 1936, Whitman, 432 pgs. 12.00 30.00 75.00

27- Jimmy Allen in The Sky Parade, 1936, Lynn, 130 pgs., 5 x 7 1/2", Paramount Pictures, movie scenes 13.00 32.50 90.00

L15- Jimmy and the Tiger, 1935, Lynn, 192 pgs. 12.00 30.00 75.00

1428- Jim Starr of the Border Patrol, 1937, Whitman, 432 pgs. 12.00 30.00 75.00

Joan of Arc (See Wee Little Books)

1105- Joe Louis the Brown Bomber, 1936, Whitman, 240 pgs., photo-c, photo-illos. 24.00 60.00 170.00

Joe Palooka (See Gentleman ...)

1123- Joe Palooka the Heavyweight Boxing Champ, 1934, Whitman, 320 pgs., Ham Fisher-a 22.00 52.50 155.00

1168- Joe Palooka's Great Adventure, 1939, Saalfield 18.00 45.00 125.00

nn- Joe Penner's Duck Farm, 1935, Goldsmith, Henry Vallely-a 12.00 30.00 85.00

1402- John Carter of Mars, 1940, Whitman, 432 pgs., John Coleman Burroughs-a 71.00 178.00 500.00

nn- John Carter of Mars, 1940, Dell, 194 pgs., Fast-Action Story, soft-c 93.00 233.00 650.00

1164- Johnny Forty Five, 1938, Saalfield, 400 pgs. 11.00 27.50 70.00

John Wayne (See Westward Ho!)

1100B- Jokes (A book of laughs galore), 1938, Whitman, 36 pgs., 2 1/2" x 3 1/2", Penny Book, laughing guy-c 4.00 10.00 22.00

1100B- Jokes (A book of side-splitting funny stories), 1938, Whitman, 36 pgs., 2 1/2" x 3 1/2", Penny Book, clowns on-c 4.00 10.00 22.00

2026-(#26)- Journey to the Center of the Earth, The Fiery Foe, 1968, Whitman 4.00 10.00 27.00

Jungle Jim (See Top-Line Comics)

1138- Jungle Jim, 1936, Whitman, 432 pgs., Alex Raymond-a 22.00 52.50 155.00

1139- Jungle Jim and the Vampire Woman, 1937, Whitman, 432 pgs., Alex Raymond-a 22.00 52.50 155.00

1442- Junior G-Men, 1937, Whitman, 432 pgs., Henry E. Vallely-a 12.00 30.00 80.00

nn- Junior G-Men Solve a Crime, 1939, Whitman, 36 pgs., 2 1/2" x 3 1/2", Penny Book 12.00 30.00 80.00

1422- Junior Nebb on the Diamond Bar Ranch, 1938, Whitman, 300 pgs., by Sol Hess 12.00 30.00 80.00

1470- Junior Nebb Joins the Circus, 1939, Whitman, 300 pgs. by Sol Hess 12.00 30.00 80.00

nn- Junior Nebb Elephant Trainer, 1939, Whitman, 68 pgs., Pan-Am Oil premium, soft-c 15.00 37.50 105.00

1052- "Just Kids" (Adventures of ...), 1934, Saalfield, oblong size, by Ad Carter 22.00 52.50 155.00

1094- Just Kids and the Mysterious Stranger, 1935, Saalfield, 160 pgs., by Ad Carter 15.00 37.50 105.00

1184- Just Kids and Deep-Sea Dan, 1940, Saalfield, 400 pgs., by Ad Carter 12.00 30.00 85.00

1302- Just Kids, The Adventures of, 1934, Saalfield, oblong size, soft-c, by Ad Carter 22.00 52.50 155.00

1324- Just Kids and the Mysterious Stranger, 1935, Saalfield, 160 pgs., soft-c, by Ad Carter , 15.00 37.50 105.00

1401- Just Kids, 1937, Whitman, 432 pgs., by Ad Carter 15.00 37.50 105.00

1055- Katzenjammer Kids in the Mountains, 1934, Saalfield, hard-c, oblong, H. H. Knerr-a 21.00 52.50 145.00

1305- Katzenjammer Kids in the Mountains, 1934, Saalfield, soft-c, oblong, H. H. Knerr-a 21.00 52.50 145.00

14- Katzenjammer Kids, The, 1942, Dell, 194 pgs., Fast-Action Story, H. H. Knerr-a 24.00 60.00 165.00

1411- Kay Darcy and the Mystery Hideout, 1937, Whitman, 300 pgs., Charles Mueller-a 13.00 32.50 90.00

1180- Kayo in the Land of Sunshine (With Moon Mullins), 1937, Whitman, 432 pgs., by Willard 15.00 37.50 105.00

1415- Kayo and Moon Mullins and the One Man Gang, 1939, Whitman, 432 pgs., by Frank Willard 12.00 30.00 85.00

7- Kayo and Moon Mullins 'Way Down South, 1938, Whitman, 132 pgs., 3 1/2" x 3 1/2", Buddy Book 31.00 78.00 220.00

1105- Kazan in Revenge of the North (James Oliver Curwood's...), 1937, Whitman, 432 pgs., Henry E. Vallely-a 11.00 27.50 70.00

1471- Kazan, King of the Pack (James Oliver Curwood's...), 1940, Whitman, 432 pgs. 10.00 25.00 65.00

1420- Keep 'Em Flying! U.S.A. for America's Defense, 1943, Whitman, 432 pgs., Henry E. Vallely-a, flip pictures 11.00 27.50 70.00

1133- Kelly King at Yale Hall, 1937, Saalfield 10.00 25.00 65.00

Ken Maynard (See Strawberry Roan & Western Frontier)

5- Ken Maynard in "Wheels of Destiny," 1934, EVW, 160 pgs., movie scenes (scarce) 57.00 142.00 400.00

776- Ken Maynard in "Gun Justice," 1934, Whitman, 160 pgs., hard-c, movie scenes (Universal Pic.) 21.00 52.50 145.00

776- Ken Maynard in "Gun Justice," 1934, Whitman, 160 pgs., soft-c, movie scenes (Universal Pic.) 21.00 52.50 145.00

1430- Ken Maynard in Western Justice, 1938, Whitman, 432 pgs., Irwin Myers-a 12.00 30.00 85.00

1442- Ken Maynard and the Gun Wolves of the Gila, 1939, Whitman, 432 pgs. 12.00 30.00 85.00

nn- Ken Maynard in Six-Gun Law, 1938, Whitman, 36 pgs., 2 1/2" x 3 1/2", Penny Book 10.00 25.00 65.00

1134- King of Crime, 1938, Saalfield, 400 pgs. 11.00 27.50 70.00

King of the Royal Mounted (See Zane Grey)

nn- Kit Carson, 1933, World Syndicate, by J. Carroll Mansfield, High Lights Of History Series, hard-c 11.00 27.50 70.00

nn- Kit Carson, 1933, World Syndicate, same as hard-c above but with a black cloth-c 11.00 27.50 70.00

1105- Kit Carson and the Mystery Riders, 1935, Saalfield, hard-c, Johnny Mack Brown photo-c, movie scenes 18.00 45.00 125.00

1585- Kit Carson and the Mystery Riders, 1935, Saalfield, soft-c, Johnny Mack Brown photo-c, movie scenes 18.00 45.00 125.00

Krazy Kat (See Adventures of...)

2004- (#4)-Lassie-Adventure in Alaska (TV Series), 1967, Whitman, hard-c, 260 pgs., 39 cents, color illos 4.00 10.00 27.00

5754- Lassie-Adventure in Alaska (TV Series), 1973, Whitman, soft-c, 260 pgs., 49 cents, color illos 2.00 5.00 15.00

2027- Lassie and the Shabby Sheik (TV Series), 1968, Whitman, hard-c, 260 pgs., 39 cents 4.00 10.00 25.00

5762- Lassie and the Shabby Sheik (TV Series), 1972, Whitman, soft-c, 260 pgs., 39 cents 2.00 5.00 15.00

5769- Lassie, Old One-Eye (TV Series), 1975, Whitman, soft-c, 260 pgs., 49 cents, three printings 2.00 5.00 15.00

1132- Last Days of Pompeii, The, 1935, Whitman, 5 1/4" x 6 1/4", 260 pgs., photo-c, movie scenes 15.00 37.50 105.00

1128- Last Man Out (Baseball), 1937, Saalfield, hard-c 11.00 27.50 70.00

L30- Last of the Mohicans, The, 1936, Lynn, 192 pgs., movie scenes with Randolph Scott, United Artists Pictures 16.00 40.00 115.00

1126- Laughing Dragon of Oz, The, 1934, Whitman 432 pgs., by Frank Baum (scarce) 118.00 295.00 825.00

1086- Laurel and Hardy, 1934, Saalfield, 160 pgs., hard-c, photo-c, movie scenes 21.00 52.50 145.00

1316- Laurel and Hardy, 1934, Saalfield, 160 pgs. soft-c, photo-c, movie scenes 21.00 52.50 145.00

1092- Law of the Wild, The, 1935, Saalfield, 160 pgs., photo-c, movie scenes of Rex, The Wild Horse & Rin-Tin-Tin Jr. 12.00 30.00 85.00

1322- Law of the Wild, The, 1935, Saalfield, 160 pgs., photo-c, movie scenes, soft-c 12.00 30.00 85.00

1100B- Learn to be a Ventriloquist, 1938, Whitman, 36 pgs. 2 1/2" x 3 1/2", Penny Book 4.00 10.00 22.00

1149- Lee Brady Range Detective, 1938, Saalfield, 400 pgs. 10.00 25.00 65.00

L10- Les Miserables (Victor Hugo's ...), 1935, Lynn, 192 pgs., movie scenes 15.00 37.50 105.00

1441- Lightning Jim U.S. Marshal Brings Law to the West, 1940, Whitman, 432 pgs., based on radio program 12.00 30.00 85.00

nn- Lightning Jim Whipple U.S. Marshal in Indian Territory, 1939, Whitman, 36 pgs., 2 1/2" x 3 1/2", Penny Book 11.00 27.50 70.00

653- Lions and Tigers (With Clyde Beatty), 1934, Whitman, 160 pgs.,

1149 - Little Big Shot © WHIT

1461 - Little Orphan Annie and the Underground Hide-Out © WHIT

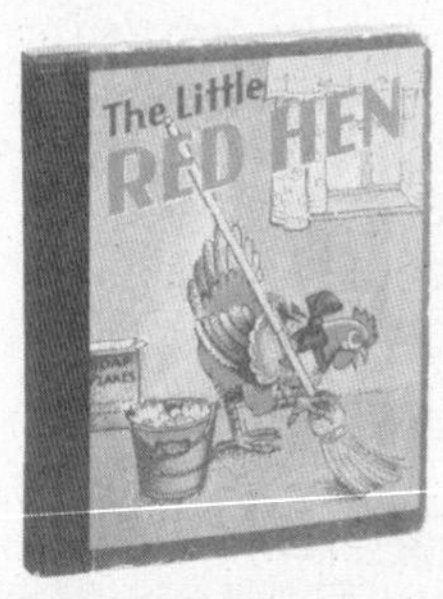

The Little Red Hen © WHIT

	GD	FN	VF/NM
photo-c movie scenes	15.00	37.50	105.00
1187- **Li'l Abner and the Ratfields**, 1940, Saalfield, 400 pgs., by Al Capp	19.00	47.50	135.00
1193- **Li'l Abner and Sadie Hawkins Day**, 1940, Saalfield, 400 pgs., by Al Capp	19.00	47.50	135.00
1198- **Li'l Abner in New York**, 1936, Whitman, 432 pgs., by Al Capp	21.00	52.50	145.00
1401- **Li'l Abner Among the Millionaires**, 1939, Whitman, 432 pgs., by Al Capp	21.00	52.50	145.00
1054- **Little Annie Rooney**, 1934, Saalfield, oblong - 4" x 8", All Pictures Comics, hard-c	20.00	50.00	140.00
1304- **Little Annie Rooney**, 1934, Saalfield, oblong - 4" x 8", All Pictures, soft-c	20.00	50.00	140.00
1117- **Little Annie Rooney and the Orphan House**, 1936, Whitman, 432 pgs.	12.00	30.00	80.00
1406- **Little Annie Rooney on the Highway to Adventure**, 1938, Whitman, 432 pgs.	12.00	30.00	80.00
1149- **Little Big Shot** (With Sybil Jason), 1935, Whitman, 240 pgs., photo-c, movie scenes	15.00	37.50	105.00
nn- **Little Black Sambo**, nd (1930s), np (Whitman), 36 pgs., 3" x 2 1/2", Penny Book	12.00	30.00	85.00
Little Bo-Peep (See Wee Little Books)			
Little Colonel, The (See Shirley Temple)			
1148- **Little Green Door, The**, 1938, Saalfield, 400 pgs.	11.00	27.50	70.00
1112- **Little Hollywood Stars**, 1935, Saalfield, movie scenes (Little Rascals, etc.), hard-c	15.00	37.50	105.00
1592- **Little Hollywood Stars**, 1935, Saalfield, movie scenes, soft-c	15.00	37.50	105.00
1087- **Little Jimmy's Gold Hunt**, 1935, Saalfield, 160 pgs., hard-c, Little Big Book, by Swinnerton	20.00	50.00	140.00
1317- **Little Jimmy's Gold Hunt**, 1935, Saalfield, 160 pgs., 4 1/4" x 5 3/4", soft-c, by Swinnerton	20.00	50.00	140.00
Little Joe and the City Gangsters (See Top-Line Comics)			
Little Joe Otter's Slide (See Wee Little Books)			
1118- **Little Lord Fauntleroy**, 1936, Saalfield, movie scenes, photo-c, 4 1/2" x 5 1/4", starring Mickey Rooney & Freddie Bartholomew, hard-c	12.00	30.00	85.00
1598- **Little Lord Fauntleroy**, 1936, Saalfield, photo-c, movie scenes, soft-c	12.00	30.00	85.00
1192- **Little Mary Mixup and the Grocery Robberies**, 1940, Saalfield	11.00	27.50	70.00
8- **Little Mary Mixup Wins A Prize**, 1936, Whitman, 132 pgs., 3 1/2" x 3 1/2", soft-c, Tarzan Ice Cream cup lid premium	36.00	90.00	255.00
1150- **Little Men**, 1934, Whitman, 4 3/4" x 5 1/4", movie scenes (Mascot Prod.), photo-c, hard-c	12.00	30.00	80.00
9- **Little Minister, The**,-Katharine Hepburn, 1935, 160 pgs., 4 1/4" x 5 1/2", EVW (Five Star Library), movie scenes (RKO)	16.00	40.00	115.00
1120- **Little Miss Muffet**, 1936, Whitman, 432 pgs., by Fanny Y. Cory	12.00	30.00	80.00
708- **Little Orphan Annie**, 1933, Whitman, 320 pgs., by Harold Gray, the 2nd Big Little Book	70.00	175.00	495.00
nn- **Little Orphan Annie**, 1928('33), Whitman, 52 pgs., 4" x 5 1/2", premium-no ads, soft-c, by Harold Gray	39.00	98.00	275.00
716- **Little Orphan Annie and Sandy**, 1933, Whitman, 320 pgs., by Harold Gray	33.00	83.00	230.00
716- **Little Orphan Annie and Sandy**, 1933, Whitman, 300 pgs., by Harold Gray	33.00	83.00	230.00
nn- **Little Orphan Annie and Sandy**, 1933, Whitman, 52 pgs., premium-no ads, 4" x 5 1/2", soft-c by Harold Gray	39.00	98.00	275.00
748- **Little Orphan Annie and Chizzler**, 1933, Whitman, 320 pgs., by Harold Gray	26.00	65.00	185.00
1010- **Little Orphan Annie and the Big Town Gunmen**, 1937, 7 1/4" x 5 1/2", 64 pgs., Nickel Book	15.00	37.50	105.00
nn- **Little Orphan Annie with the Circus**, 1934, Whitman, 320 pgs., same cover as L.O.A. 708 but with blue background, Ovaltine giveaway stamp inside front-c, by Harold Gray	58.00	146.00	410.00
1140- **Little Orphan Annie and the Big Train Robbery**, 1934, Whitman, 300 pgs., by Gray	20.00	50.00	140.00
1140- **Little Orphan Annie and the Big Train Robbery**, 1934, Whitman, 300 pgs., premium-no ads, soft-c, by Harold Gray	36.00	90.00	255.00
1154- **Little Orphan Annie and the Ghost Gang**, 1935, Whitman, 432 pgs. by Harold Gray	20.00	50.00	140.00
nn- **Little Orphan Annie and the Ghost Gang**, 1935, Whitman, 436 pgs., premium-no ads, 3-color, soft-c, by Harold Gray	36.00	90.00	255.00
1162- **Little Orphan Annie and Punjab the Wizard**, 1935, Whitman, 432 pgs., by Harold Gray	20.00	50.00	140.00
1186- **Little Orphan Annie and the $1,000,000 Formula**, 1936, Whitman, 432 pgs., by Gray	18.00	45.00	125.00
1414- **Little Orphan Annie and the Ancient Treasure of Am**, 1939, Whitman, 432 pgs., by Gray	16.00	40.00	115.00
1416- **Little Orphan Annie in the Movies**, 1937, Whitman, 432 pgs., by Harold Gray	16.00	40.00	115.00
1417- **Little Orphan Annie and the Secret of the Well**, 1947, Whitman, 352 pgs., by Gray	12.00	30.00	85.00
1435- **Little Orphan Annie and the Gooneyville Mystery**, 1947, Whitman, 288 pgs., by Gray	13.00	32.50	90.00
1446- **Little Orphan Annie in the Thieves' Den**, 1949, Whitman, 288 pgs., by Harold Gray	13.00	32.50	90.00
1449- **Little Orphan Annie and the Mysterious Shoemaker**, 1938, Whitman, 432 pgs., by Harold Gray	15.00	37.50	105.00
1457- **Little Orphan Annie and Her Junior Commandos**, 1943, Whitman, 352 pgs., by H. Gray	12.00	30.00	85.00
1461- **Little Orphan Annie and the Underground Hide-Out**, 1945, Whitman, 352 pgs., by Gray	12.00	30.00	85.00
1468- **Little Orphan Annie and the Ancient Treasure of Am**, 1949 (Misdated 1939), 288 pgs., by Gray	12.00	30.00	85.00
1482- **Little Orphan Annie and the Haunted Mansion**, 1941, Whitman, 432 pgs., flip pictures, by Harold Gray	16.00	40.00	115.00
3048- **Little Orphan Annie and Her Big Little Kit**, 1937, Whitman, 384 pgs., 4 1/2" x 6 1/2" box, includes miniature box of 4 crayons-red, yellow, blue and green	94.00	235.00	660.00
4054- **Little Orphan Annie, The Story of**, 1934, Whitman, 7" x 9 1/2", 320 pgs., Big Big Book, Harold Gray-c/a	102.00	255.00	715.00
nn- **Little Orphan Annie Gets into Trouble**, 1938, Whitman, 36 pgs., 2 1/2" x 3 1/2", Penny Book	11.00	27.50	70.00
nn- **Little Orphan Annie in Hollywood**, 1937, Whitman, 3 1/2" x 3 1/4", Pan-Am premium, soft-c	29.00	73.00	200.00
nn- **Little Orphan Annie in Rags to Riches**, 1939, Dell, 194 pgs., Fast-Action Story, soft-c	39.00	98.00	275.00
nn- **Little Orphan Annie Saves Sandy**, 1938, Whitman, 36 pgs., 2 1/2" x 3 1/2", Penny Book	11.00	27.50	70.00
nn- **Little Orphan Annie Under the Big Top**, 1938, Dell, 194 pgs., Fast-Action Story, soft-c	39.00	98.00	270.00
nn- **Little Orphan Annie Wee Little Books** (In open box) nn, 1934, Whitman, 44 pgs., by H. Gray			
L.O.A. And Daddy Warbucks	9.00	22.50	55.00
L.O.A. And Her Dog Sandy	9.00	22.50	55.00
L.O.A. And The Lucky Knife	9.00	22.50	55.00
L.O.A. And The Pinch-Pennys	9.00	22.50	55.00
L.O.A. At Happy Home	9.00	22.50	55.00
L.O.A. Finds Mickey	9.00	22.50	55.00
Complete set with box	57.00	143.00	400.00
nn- **Little Polly Flinders, The Story of**, nd (1930s), no publ., 36 pgs., 2 1/2" x 3", Penny Book	4.00	10.00	22.00
nn- **Little Red Hen, The**, nd(1930s), np(Whitman), 36 pgs., Penny Book	4.00	10.00	22.00
nn- **Little Red Riding Hood**, nd(1930s), np(Whitman), 36 pgs., 3" x 2 1/2", Penny Book	4.00	10.00	22.00
nn- **Little Red Riding Hood and the Big Bad Wolf** (Disney), 1934, McKay, 36 pgs., stiff-c, Disney Studio-a	33.00	83.00	230.00
757- **Little Women**, 1934, Whitman, 4 3/4" x 5 1/4", 160 pgs., photo-c, movie scenes, starring Katharine Hepburn	21.00	52.50	145.00

1407 - Lone Ranger and Dead Men's Mine
© Lone Ranger Inc.

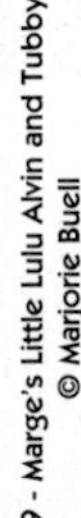

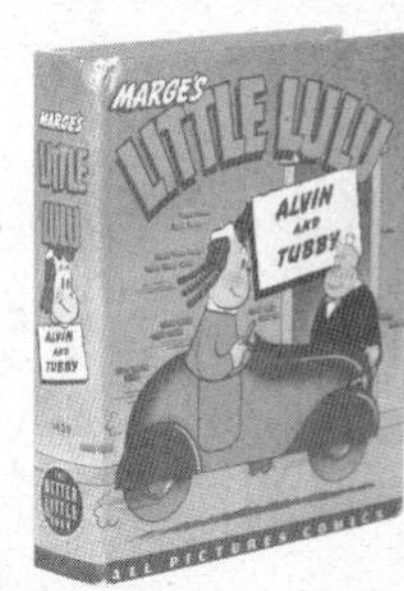

1429 - Marge's Little Lulu Alvin and Tubby
© Marjorie Buell

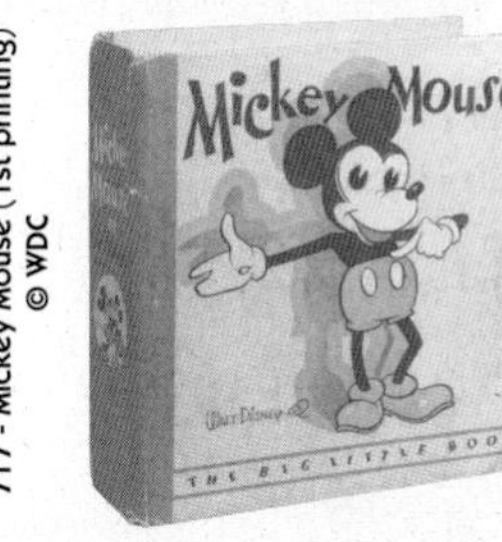

717 - Mickey Mouse (1st printing)
© WDC

	GD	FN	VF/NM
Littlest Rebel, The (See Shirley Temple)			
1181- **Lone Ranger and his Horse Silver**, 1935, Whitman, 432 pgs., Hal Arbo-a	29.00	73.00	200.00
1196- **Lone Ranger and the Vanishing Herd**, 1936, Whitman, 432 pgs.	24.00	60.00	165.00
1407- **Lone Ranger and Dead Men's Mine, The**, 1939, Whitman, 432 pgs.	22.00	52.50	155.00
1421- **Lone Ranger on the Barbary Coast, The**, 1944, Whitman, 352 pgs., Henry Vallely-a	19.00	47.50	135.00
1428- **Lone Ranger and the Secret Weapon, The**, 1943, Whitman,	19.00	47.50	135.00
1431- **Lone Ranger and the Secret Killer, The**, 1937, Whitman 432 pgs., H. Anderson-a	24.00	60.00	165.00
1450- **Lone Ranger and the Black Shirt Highwayman, The**, 1939, Whitman, 432 pgs.	22.00	52.50	155.00
1465- **Lone Ranger and the Menace of Murder Valley, The**, 1938, Whitman, 432 pgs., Robert Wiseman-a	21.00	52.50	145.00
1468- **Lone Ranger Follows Through, The**, 1941, Whitman, 432 pgs., H.E. Vallely-a	21.00	52.50	145.00
1477- **Lone Ranger and the Great Western Span, The**, 1942, Whitman, 424 pgs., H. E. Vallely-a	19.00	47.50	135.00
1489- **Lone Ranger and the Red Renegades, The**, 1939, Whitman, 432 pgs.	24.00	60.00	165.00
1498- **Lone Ranger and the Silver Bullets**, 1946, Whitman, 352 pgs., Henry E. Vallely-a	19.00	47.50	135.00
712-10- **Lone Ranger and the Secret of Somber Cavern, The**, 1950, Whitman	12.00	30.00	80.00
2013- (#13)-**Lone Ranger Outwits Crazy Cougar, The**, 1968, Whitman, 260 pgs., 39 cents, hard-c, color illos	4.00	10.00	27.00
5774- **Lone Ranger Outwits Crazy Cougar, The**, 1976, Whitman, 260 pgs., 49 cents, soft-c, color illos	4.00	10.00	22.00
5774-1- **Lone Ranger Outwits Crazy Cougar, The**, 1979, Whitman, 260 pgs., 69 cents, soft-c, color illos	4.00	10.00	22.00
nn- **Lone Ranger and the Lost Valley, The**, 1938, Dell, 196 pgs., Fast-Action Story, soft-c	43.00	108.00	300.00
1405- **Lone Star Martin of the Texas Rangers**, 1939, Whitman, 432 pgs.	18.00	45.00	125.00
19- **Lost City, The**, 1935, EVW, movie scenes	16.00	40.00	115.00
1103- **Lost Jungle, The** (With Clyde Beatty), 1936, Saalfield, movie scenes, hard-c	16.00	40.00	115.00
1583- **Lost Jungle, The** (With Clyde Beatty), 1936, Saalfield, movie scenes, soft -c	13.00	32.50	90.00
753- **Lost Patrol, The**, 1934, Whitman, 160 pgs., photo-c, movie scenes with Boris Karloff	15.00	37.50	105.00
nn- **Lost World, The - Jurassic Park 2**, 1997, Chronicle Books, 312 pgs., adapts movie, 1-color (green) illos	3.00	7.50	20.00
1189- **Mac of the Marines in Africa**, 1936, Whitman, 432 pgs.	12.00	30.00	80.00
1400- **Mac of the Marines in China**, 1938, Whitman, 432 pgs.	12.00	30.00	80.00
1100B- **Magic Tricks** (With explanations), 1938, Whitman, 36 pgs., 2 1/2" x 3 1/2", Penny Book, rabbit in hat-c	4.00	10.00	22.00
1100B- **Magic Tricks** (How to do them), 1938, Whitman, 36 pgs., 2 1/2" x 3 1/2", Penny Book, genie-c	4.00	10.00	22.00
Major Hoople (See Our Boarding House)			
2022-(#22)- **Major Matt Mason, Moon Mission**, 1968, Whitman, 256 pgs., hard-c, color illos.	4.00	10.00	27.00
1167- **Mandrake the Magician**, 1935, Whitman, 432 pgs., by Lee Falk & Phil Davis	24.00	60.00	170.00
1418- **Mandrake the Magician and the Flame Pearls**, 1946, Whitman, 352 pgs., by Lee Falk & Phil Davis	15.00	37.50	105.00
1431- **Mandrake the Magician and the Midnight Monster**, 1939, Whitman, 432 pgs., by Lee Falk & Phil Davis	16.00	40.00	115.00
1454- **Mandrake the Magician Mighty Solver of Mysteries**, 1941, Whitman, 432 pgs., by Lee Falk & Phil Davis, flip pictures	16.00	40.00	115.00
2011-(#11)-**Man From U.N.C.L.E., The**-The Calcutta Affair (TV Series), 1967, Whitman, 260 pgs., 39 cents, hard-c, color illos	4.00	10.00	27.00
1429- **Marge's Little Lulu Alvin and Tubby**, 1947, Whitman, All Pictures Comics, Stanley-a	31.00	78.00	215.00
1438- **Mary Lee and the Mystery of the Indian Beads**, 1937, Whitman, 300 pgs.	11.00	27.50	70.00
1165- **Masked Man of the Mesa, The**, 1939, Saalfield, 400 pgs.	10.00	25.00	65.00
nn- **Mask of Zorro, The**, 1998, Chronicle Books, 312 pgs., adapts movie, 1-color (yellow-green) illos	1.00	2.50	9.00
1436- **Maximo the Amazing Superman**, 1940, Whitman, 432 pgs., Henry E. Vallely-a	15.00	37.50	105.00
1444- **Maximo the Amazing Superman and the Crystals of Doom**, 1941, Whitman,432 pgs., Henry E. Vallely-a	15.00	37.50	105.00
1445- **Maximo the Amazing Superman and the Supermachine**, 1941, Whitman, 432 pgs.	15.00	37.50	105.00
755- **Men of the Mounted**, 1934, Whitman, 320 pgs.	15.00	37.50	105.00
nn- **Men of the Mounted**, 1933, Whitman, 52 pgs., 3 1/2" x 5 3/4", premium-no ads; other versions with Poll Parrot & Perkins ad; soft-c	21.00	52.50	145.00
nn- **Men of the Mounted**, 1934, Whitman, Cocomalt premium, soft-c, by Ted McCall	12.00	30.00	85.00
1475- **Men With Wings**, 1938, Whitman, 240 pgs., photo-c, movie scenes (Paramount Pics.)	12.00	30.00	85.00
1170- **Mickey Finn**, 1940, Saalfield, 400 pgs., by Frank Leonard	12.00	30.00	85.00
717- **Mickey Mouse** (Disney), (1st printing) 1933, Whitman, 320 pgs., Gottfredson-a, skinny Mickey on cover	392.00	980.00	3135.00
717- **Mickey Mouse** (Disney), (2nd printing)1933, Whitman, 320 pgs., Gottfredson-a, regular Mickey on cover	219.00	547.00	1750.00
nn- **Mickey Mouse** (Disney), 1933, Dean & Son, Great Big Midget Book, 320 pgs.	186.00	464.00	1485.00
731- **Mickey Mouse the Mail Pilot** (Disney), 1933, Whitman, (This is the same book as the 1st Mickey Mouse BLB #717(2nd printing) but with "The Mail Pilot" printed on the front. Lower left of back cover has a small box printed over the existing "No. 717." "No. 731" is printed next to it.) (sold at auction in 2001 in Fine condition for $5,090)			
726- **Mickey Mouse in Blaggard Castle** (Disney), 1934, Whitman, 320 pgs., Gottfredson-a	47.00	118.00	330.00
731- **Mickey Mouse the Mail Pilot** (Disney), 1933, Whitman, 300 pgs., Gottfredson-a	47.00	118.00	330.00
731- **Mickey Mouse the Mail Pilot** (Disney), 1933, Whitman, 300 pgs., soft cover; Gottfredson-a (Rare)	85.00	212.00	600.00
nn- **Mickey Mouse the Mail Pilot** (Disney), 1933, Whitman, 292 pgs., American Oil Co. premium, soft-c, Gottfredson-a; another version 3 1/2" x 4 3/4"	47.00	118.00	330.00
nn- **Mickey Mouse the Mail Pilot** (Disney), 1933, Dean & Son, Great Big Midget Book (Rare)	187.00	467.00	1500.00
750- **Mickey Mouse Sails for Treasure Island** (Disney), 1933, Whitman, 320 pgs., Gottfredson-a	47.00	118.00	330.00
nn- **Mickey Mouse Sails for Treasure Island** (Disney), 1935, Whitman, 196 pgs., premium-no ads, soft-c, Gottfredson-a (Scarce)	56.00	140.00	395.00
nn- **Mickey Mouse Sails for Treasure Island** (Disney), 1935, Whitman, 196 pgs., Kolynos Dental Cream premium (Scarce)	56.00	140.00	395.00
nn- **Mickey Mouse Sails for Treasure Island** (Disney), 1933, Dean & Son, Great Big Midget Book, 320 pgs.	150.00	375.00	1200.00
756- **Mickey Mouse Presents a Walt Disney Silly Symphony** (Disney), 1934, Whitman, 240 pgs., Bucky Bug app.	43.00	108.00	300.00
801- **Mickey Mouse's Summer Vacation**, 1948, Whitman, hard-c, Story Hour series	12.00	30.00	85.00
1111- **Mickey Mouse Presents Walt Disney's Silly Symphonies Stories**, 1936, Whitman, 432 pgs., Donald Duck app.	43.00	108.00	300.00
1128- **Mickey Mouse and Pluto the Racer** (Disney), 1936, Whitman, 432 pgs., Gottfredson-a	38.00	95.00	255.00
1139- **Mickey Mouse the Detective** (Disney), 1934, Whitman, 300 pgs., Gottfredson-a	43.00	108.00	300.00
1139- **Mickey Mouse the Detective** (Disney), 1934, Whitman, 304 pgs., premium-no ads, soft-c, Gottfredson-a (Scarce)	64.00	160.00	450.00
1153- **Mickey Mouse and the Bat Bandit** (Disney), 1935,			

1451 - Mickey Mouse and the Desert Palace © WDC

Mickey Mouse and Minnie March to Macy's © WDC

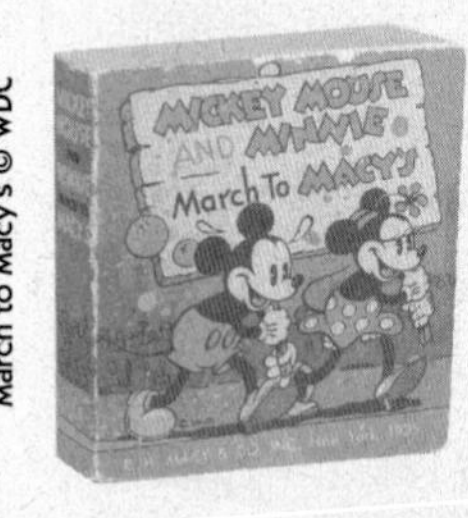

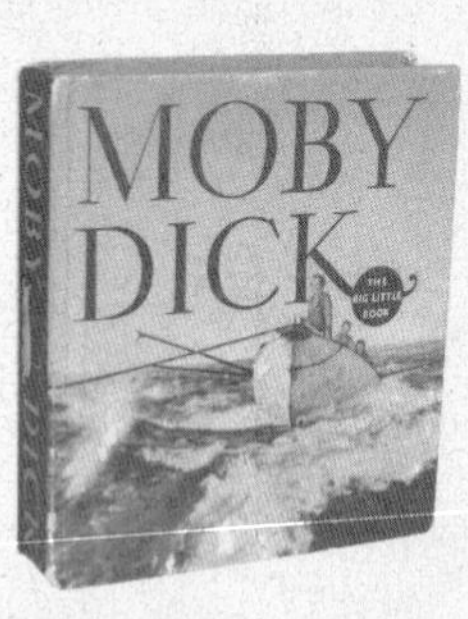

710 - Moby Dick the Great White Whale © WHIT

GD FN VF/NM

Whitman, 432 pgs., Gottfredson-a 39.00 98.00 275.00

nn- **Mickey Mouse and the Bat Bandit** (Disney), 1935, Whitman, 436 pgs., premium-no ads, 3-color, soft-c, Gottfredson-a (Scarce) 64.00 160.00 450.00

1160- **Mickey Mouse and Bobo the Elephant** (Disney), 1935, Whitman, 432 pgs., Gottfredson-a 39.00 98.00 275.00

1187- **Mickey Mouse and the Sacred Jewel** (Disney), 1936, Whitman, 432 pgs., Gottfredson-a 36.00 90.00 255.00

1401- **Mickey Mouse in the Treasure Hunt** (Disney), 1941, Whitman, 430 pgs., flip pictures of Pluto, Gottfredson-a 34.00 85.00 240.00

1409- **Mickey Mouse Runs His Own Newspaper** (Disney), 1937, Whitman, 432 pgs., Gottfredson-a 34.00 85.00 240.00

1413- **Mickey Mouse and the 'Lectro Box** (Disney), 1946, Whitman, 352 pgs., Gottfredson-a 24.00 60.00 165.00

1417- **Mickey Mouse on Sky Island** (Disney), 1941, Whitman, 432 pgs., flip pictures, Gottfredson-a; considered by Gottfredson to be his best Mickey story 34.00 85.00 240.00

1428- **Mickey Mouse in the Foreign Legion** (Disney), 1940, Whitman, 432 pgs., Gottfredson-a 34.00 85.00 240.00

1429- **Mickey Mouse and the Magic Lamp** (Disney), 1942, Whitman, 432 pgs., flip pictures 34.00 85.00 240.00

1433- **Mickey Mouse and the Lazy Daisy Mystery** (Disney), 1947, Whitman, 288 pgs. 24.00 60.00 165.00

1444- **Mickey Mouse in the World of Tomorrow** (Disney), 1948, Whitman, 288 pgs., Gottfredson-a 36.00 90.00 255.00

1451- **Mickey Mouse and the Desert Palace** (Disney), 1948, Whitman, 288 pgs. 24.00 60.00 165.00

1463- **Mickey Mouse and the Pirate Submarine** (Disney), 1939, Whitman, 432 pgs., Gottfredson-a 34.00 85.00 240.00

1464- **Mickey Mouse and the Stolen Jewels** (Disney), 1949, Whitman, 288 pgs. 33.00 83.00 230.00

1471- **Mickey Mouse and the Dude Ranch Bandit** (Disney), 1943, Whitman, 432 pgs., flip pictures 34.00 85.00 240.00

1475- **Mickey Mouse and the 7 Ghosts** (Disney), 1940, Whitman, 432 pgs., Gottfredson-a 34.00 85.00 240.00

1476- **Mickey Mouse in the Race for Riches** (Disney), 1938, Whitman, 432 pgs., Gottfredson-a 34.00 85.00 240.00

1483- **Mickey Mouse Bell Boy Detective** (Disney), 1945, Whitman, 352 pgs. 33.00 83.00 230.00

1499- **Mickey Mouse on the Cave-Man Island** (Disney), 1944, Whitman, 352 pgs. 33.00 83.00 230.00

2004- **Mickey Mouse, Here Comes** (Disney), 1936, Whitman, (Very Rare), 224 pgs., 12" x 8 1/4" box, with red, yellow and blue crayons, contains 224 loose pages to color, reprinted from early Mickey Mouse related movie and strip reprints 475.00 1187.00 3800.00

2020-(#20)- **Mickey Mouse, Adventure in Outer Space,** 1968, Whitman, 256 pgs.,hard-c, color illos. 4.00 10.00 27.00

5750- **Mickey Mouse, Adventure in Outer Space,** 1973, Whitman, 256 pgs.,soft-c, 39 cents, color illos. 2.00 5.00 15.00

3049- **Mickey Mouse and His Big Little Kit** (Disney), 1937, Whitman, 384 pgs., 4 1/2" x 6 1/2" box, includes miniature box of 4 crayons-red, yellow, blue and green 150.00 375.00 1210.00

3061- **Mickey Mouse to Draw and Color** (The Big Little Set), nd (early 1930s), Whitman, with crayons; box contains 320 loose pages to color, reprinted from early Mickey Mouse BLBs 123.00 308.00 880.00

4062- **Mickey Mouse, The Story Of**, 1935, Whitman, 7" x 9 1/2", 320 pgs., Big Big Book, Gottfredson-a 150.00 375.00 1210.00

4062- **Mickey Mouse and the Smugglers, The Story Of,** 1935, Whitman, (Scarce), 7" x 9 1/2", 320 pgs., Big Big Book, same contents as above version; Gottfredson-a 179.00 447.00 1430.00

708-10- **Mickey Mouse on the Haunted Island** (Disney), 1950, Whitman, Gottfredson-a 15.00 37.50 105.00

nn- **Mickey Mouse and Minnie at Macy's,** 1934 Whitman, 148 pgs., 3 1/4" x 3 1/2", soft-c, R. H. Macy & Co. Christmas giveaway (Rare, less than 20 known copies) 450.00 1125.00 3600.00

nn- **Mickey Mouse and Minnie March to Macy's,** 1935, Whitman, 148 pgs., 3 1/2" x 3 1/2", soft-c, R. H. Macy & Co. Christmas giveaway (scarce) 300.00 750.00 2400.00

GD FN VF/NM

nn- **Mickey Mouse and the Magic Carpet**, 1935, Whitman, 148 pgs., 3 1/2"x 4", soft-c, giveaway, Gottfredson-a, Donald Duck app. 131.00 328.00 1050.00

nn- **Mickey Mouse Silly Symphonies**, 1934, Dean & Son, Ltd (England), 48 pgs., with 4 pop-ups, Babes In The Woods, King Neptune
With dust jacket 165.00 412.00 1320.00
Without dust jacket 119.00 298.00 835.00

nn- **Mickey Mouse the Sheriff of Nugget Gulch** (Disney) 1938, Dell, 196 pgs., Fast-Action Story, soft-c, Gottfredson-a 56.00 140.00 395.00

nn- **Mickey Mouse Waddle Book**, 1934, BRP, 20 pgs., 7 1/2" x 10", forerunner of the Blue Ribbon Pop-Up books; with 4 removable articulated cardboard characters Book Only 100.00 200.00 500.00
(A complete copy in VG/FN w/VF dustjacket sold for $5676 in 2010)

nn- **Mickey Mouse with Goofy and Mickey's Nephews**, 1938, Dell, Fast-Action Story, Gottfredson-a 56.00 140.00 395.00

16- **Mickey Mouse and Pluto** (Disney), 1942, Dell, 196 pgs., Fast-Action story 56.00 140.00 395.00

512- **Mickey Mouse Wee Little Books** (In open box), nn, 1934, Whitman, 44 pgs., small size, soft-c
Mickey Mouse and Tanglefoot 13.00 32.50 90.00
Mickey Mouse at the Carnival 13.00 32.50 90.00
Mickey Mouse Will Not Quit! 13.00 32.50 90.00
Mickey Mouse Wins the Race! 13.00 32.50 90.00
Mickey Mouse's Misfortune 13.00 32.50 90.00
Mickey Mouse's Uphill Fight 13.00 32.50 90.00
Complete set with box 96.00 240.00 675.00

1493- **Mickey Rooney and Judy Garland and How They Got into the Movies**, 1941, Whitman, 432 pgs., photo-c 15.00 37.50 105.00

1427- **Mickey Rooney Himself**, 1939, Whitman, 240 pgs., photo-c, movie scenes, life story 15.00 37.50 105.00

532- **Mickey's Dog Pluto** (Disney), 1943, Whitman, All Picture Comics, A Tall Comic Book , 3 3/4" x 8 3/4" 41.00 103.00 285.00

284- **Midget Jumbo Coloring Book**, 1935, Saalfield 71.00 178.00 500.00

2113- **Midget Jumbo Coloring Book**, 1935, Saalfield, 240 pgs. 71.00 178.00 500.00

21- **Midsummer Night's Dream**, 1935, EVW, movie scenes 15.00 37.50 105.00

nn- **Minute-Man** (Mystery of the Spy Ring), 1941, Fawcett, Dime Action Book 57.00 143.00 400.00

710- **Moby Dick the Great White Whale, The Story of**, 1934, Whitman, 160 pgs., photo-c, movie scenes from "The Sea Beast" 15.00 37.50 105.00

746- **Moon Mullins and Kayo** (Kayo and Moon Mullins-inside), 1933, Whitman, 320 pgs., Frank Willard-c/a 16.00 40.00 115.00

nn- **Moon Mullins and Kayo**, 1933, Whitman, Cocomalt premium, soft-c, by Willard 16.00 40.00 115.00

1134- **Moon Mullins and the Plushbottom Twins**, 1935, Whitman, 432 pgs., Willard-c/a 16.00 40.00 115.00

nn- **Moon Mullins and the Plushbottom Twins**, 1935, Whitman, 436 pgs., premium-no ads, 3-color, soft-c, by Willard 29.00 73.00 200.00

1058- **Mother Pluto** (Disney), 1939, Whitman, 68 pgs., hard-c 13.00 32.50 90.00

1100B- **Movie Jokes** (From the talkies), 1938, Whitman, 36 pgs., 2 1/2" x 3 1/2", Penny Book 4.00 10.00 22.00

1408- **Mr. District Attorney on the Job**, 1941, Whitman, 432 pgs., flip pictures 12.00 30.00 75.00

nn- **Musicians of Bremen, The**, nd (1930s), np (Whitman), 36 pgs., 3" x 2 1/2", Penny Book 4.00 10.00 22.00

1113- **Mutt and Jeff**, 1936, Whitman, 300 pgs., by Bud Fisher 26.00 65.00 180.00

1116- **My Life and Times** (By Shirley Temple), 1936, Saalfield, Little Big Book, hard-c, photo-c/illos 16.00 40.00 115.00

1596- **My Life and Times** (By Shirley Temple), 1936, Saalfield, Little Big Book, soft-c, photo-c/illos 16.00 40.00 115.00

1497- **Myra North Special Nurse and Foreign Spies**, 1938, Whitman, 432 pgs. 12.00 30.00 85.00

1400- **Nancy and Sluggo**, 1946, Whitman, All Pictures Comics, Ernie Bushmiller-a 13.00 32.50 90.00

1487- **Nancy Has Fun**, 1946, Whitman, All Pictures Comics

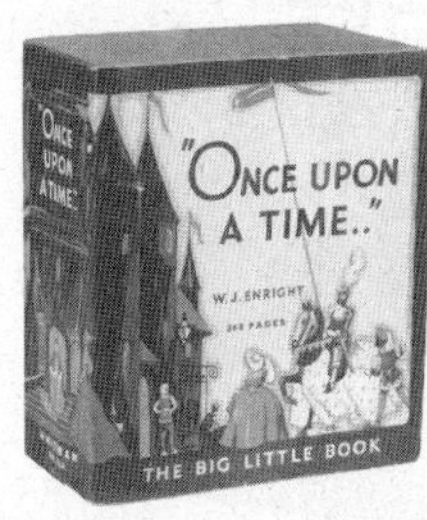

718 - Once Upon a Time © WHIT

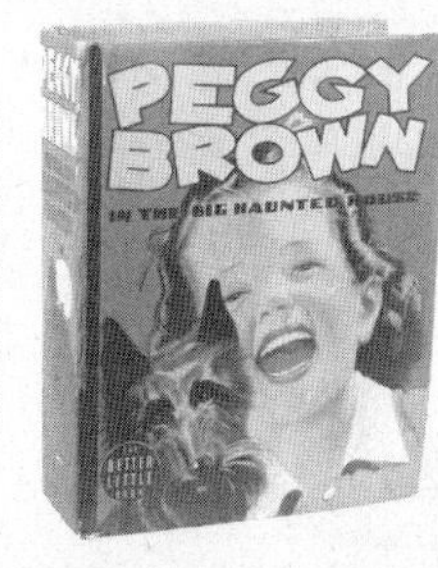

1491 - Peggy Brown in the Big Haunted House © WHIT

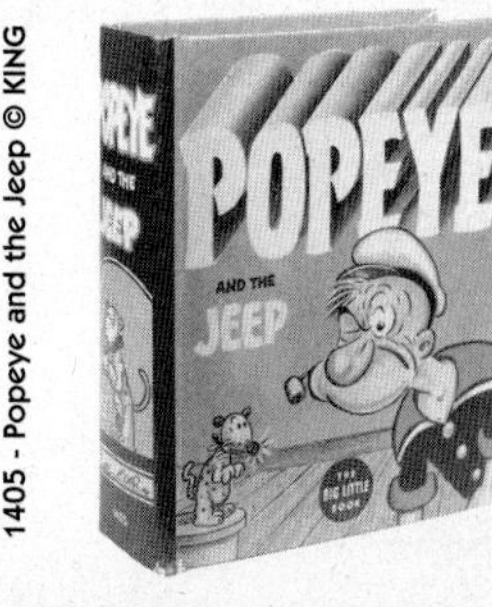

1405 - Popeye and the Jeep © KING

	GD	FN	VF/NM
	13.00	32.50	90.00
1150- **Napoleon and Uncle Elby**, 1938, Saalfield, 400 pgs., by Clifford McBride	12.00	30.00	85.00
1166- **Napoleon Uncle Elby And Little Mary**, 1939, Saalfield, 400 pgs., by Clifford McBride	12.00	30.00	85.00
1179- **Ned Brant Adventure Bound**, 1940, Saalfield, 400 pgs.	11.00	27.50	70.00
1146- **Nevada Rides The Danger Trail**, 1938, Saalfield, 400 pgs., J.R. White-a	11.00	27.50	70.00
1147- **Nevada Whalen, Avenger**, 1938, Saalfield, 400 pgs.	11.00	27.50	70.00
Nicodemus O'Malley (See Top-Line Comics)			
1115- **Og Son of Fire**, 1936, Whitman, 432 pgs.	16.00	40.00	115.00
1419- **Oh, Blondie the Bumsteads** (See Blondie)			
11- **Oliver Twist**, 1935, EVW (Five Star Library), movie scenes, starring Dickie Moore (Monogram Pictures)	15.00	37.50	105.00
718- **Once Upon a Time**, 1933, Whitman, 364 pgs., soft-c	15.00	37.50	105.00
712- **100 Fairy Tales for Children, The**, 1933, Whitman, 288 pgs., Circle Library	11.00	27.50	70.00
1099- **One Night of Love**, 1935, Saalfield, 160 pgs., hard-c, photo-c, movie scenes, Columbia Pictures, starring Grace Moore	15.00	37.50	105.00
1579- **One Night of Love**, 1935, Sat, 160 pgs., soft-c, photo-c, movie scenes, Columbia Pictures, starring Grace Moore	15.00	37.50	105.00
1155- **$1000 Reward**, 1938, Saalfield, 400 pgs.	11.00	27.50	70.00
Orphan Annie (See Little Orphan ...)			
L17- **O'Shaughnessy's Boy**, 1935, Lynn, 192 pgs., movie scenes, w/Wallace Beery & Jackie Cooper (Metro-Goldwyn-Mayer)	12.00	30.00	85.00
1109- **Oswald the Lucky Rabbit**, 1934, Whitman, 288 pgs.	21.00	52.50	145.00
1403- **Oswald Rabbit Plays G-Man**, 1937, Whitman, 240 pgs., movie scenes by Walter Lantz	22.00	52.50	155.00
1190- **Our Boarding House, Major Hoople and his Horse**, 1940, Saalfield, 400 pgs.	12.00	30.00	85.00
1085- **Our Gang**, 1934, Saalfield, 160 pgs., photo-c, movie scenes, hard-c	15.00	37.50	105.00
1315- **Our Gang**, 1934, Saalfield, 160 pgs., photo-c, movie scenes, soft-c	15.00	37.50	105.00
1451- **"Our Gang" on the March**, 1942, Whitman, 432 pgs., flip pictures, Vallely-a	15.00	37.50	105.00
1456- **Our Gang Adventures**, 1948, Whitman, 288 pgs.	12.00	30.00	85.00
nn- **Paramount Newsreel Men with Admiral Byrd in Little America**, 1934, Whitman, 96 pgs., 6 1/4" x 6 1/4", photo-c, photo ill.	16.00	40.00	115.00
nn- **Patch**, nd (1930s), np (Whitman), 36 pgs., 3" x 2 1/2", Penny Book	4.00	10.00	22.00
1445- **Pat Nelson Ace of Test Pilots**, 1937, Whitman, 432 pgs.	11.00	27.50	70.00
1411- **Peggy Brown and the Mystery Basket**, 1941, Whitman, 432 pgs., flip pictures, Henry E. Vallely-a	12.00	30.00	75.00
1423- **Peggy Brown and the Secret Treasure**, 1947, Whitman, 288 pgs., Henry E. Vallely-a	12.00	30.00	75.00
1427- **Peggy Brown and the Runaway Auto Trailer**, 1937, Whitman, 300 pgs., Henry E. Vallely-a	12.00	30.00	75.00
1463- **Peggy Brown and the Jewel of Fire**, 1943, Whitman, 352 pgs., Henry E. Vallely-a	12.00	30.00	75.00
1491- **Peggy Brown in the Big Haunted House**, 1940, Whitman, 432 pgs., Vallely-a	12.00	30.00	75.00
1143- **Peril Afloat**, 1938, Saalfield, 400 pgs.	11.00	27.50	70.00
1199- **Perry Winkle and the Rinkeydinks**, 1937, Whitman, 432 pgs., by Martin Branner	15.00	37.50	105.00
1487- **Perry Winkle and the Rinkeydinks get a Horse**, 1938, Whitman, 432 pgs., by Martin Branner	15.00	37.50	105.00
Peter Pan (See Wee Little Books)			
nn- **Peter Rabbit**, nd(1930s), np(Whitman), 36 pgs., Penny Book, 3" x 2 1/2"	5.00	12.50	33.00
Peter Rabbit's Carrots (See Wee Little Books)			
1100- **Phantom, The**, 1936, Whitman, 432 pgs., by Lee Falk & Ray Moore	47.00	118.00	330.00
1416- **Phantom and the Girl of Mystery, The**, 1947, Whitman, 352 pgs. by Falk & Moore	21.00	52.50	145.00
1421- **Phantom and Desert Justice, The**, 1941, Whitman, 432 pgs., flip pictures, by Falk & Moore	28.00	70.00	195.00
1468- **Phantom and the Sky Pirates, The**, 1945, Whitman, 352 pgs., by Falk & Moore	24.00	60.00	170.00
1474- **Phantom and the Sign of the Skull, The**, 1939, Whitman, 432 pgs., by Falk & Moore	29.00	73.00	205.00
1489- **Phantom, Return of the...**, 1942, Whitman, 432 pgs., flip pictures, by Falk & Moore	28.00	70.00	195.00
1130- **Phil Burton, Sleuth** (Scout Book), 1937, Saalfield, hard-c	9.00	22.50	55.00
Pied Piper of Hamlin (See Wee Little Books)			
1466- **Pilot Pete Dive Bomber**, 1941, Whitman, 432 pgs., flip pictures	11.00	27.50	70.00
5776- **Pink Panther Adventures in Z-Land, The**, 1976, Whitman, 260 pgs., soft-c, 49 cents, B&W	1.00	2.50	8.00
5776-2- **Pink Panther Adventures in Z-Land, The**, 1980, Whitman, 260 pgs., soft-c, 79 cents, B&W	1.00	2.50	8.00
5783-2- **Pink Panther at Castle Kreep, The**, 1980, Whitman, 260 pgs., soft-c, 79 cents, B&W	1.00	2.50	8.00
Pinocchio and Jiminy Cricket (See Walt Disney's ...)			
nn- **Pioneers of the Wild West** (Blue-c), 1933, World Syndicate, High Lights of History Series	10.00	25.00	65.00
With dustjacket	57.00	142.00	400.00
nn- **Pioneers of the Wild West** (Red-c), 1933, World Syndicate, High Lights of History Series	10.00	25.00	65.00
1123- **Plainsman, The**, 1936, Whitman, 240 pgs., photo-c, movie scenes with Gary Cooper (Paramount Pics.)	26.00	65.00	180.00
Pluto (See Mickey's Dog ... & Walt Disney's ...)			
2114- **Pocket Coloring Book**, 1935, Saalfield	39.00	98.00	270.00
1060- **Polly and Her Pals on the Farm**, 1934, Saalfield, 164 pgs., hard-c, by Cliff Sterrett	15.00	37.50	105.00
1310- **Polly and Her Pals on the Farm**, 1934, Saalfield, soft-c	15.00	37.50	105.00
1051- **Popeye, Adventures of...**, 1934, Saalfield, oblong-size, E.C. Segar-a, hard-c	58.00	146.00	410.00
1088- **Popeye in Puddleburg**, 1934, Saalfield, 160 pgs., hard-c, E. C. Segar-a	22.00	52.50	155.00
1113- **Popeye Starring in Choose Your Weppins**, 1936, Saalfield, 160 pgs., hard-c, Segar-a	46.00	115.00	320.00
1117- **Popeye's Ark**, 1936, Saalfield, 4 1/2" x 5 1/2", hard-c, Segar-a	24.00	60.00	165.00
1163- **Popeye Sees the Sea**, 1936, Whitman, 432 pgs., Segar-a	24.00	60.00	170.00
1301- **Popeye, Adventures of...**, 1934, Saalfield, oblong-size, Segar-a	58.00	146.00	410.00
1318- **Popeye in Puddleburg**, 1934, Saalfield, 160 pgs., soft-c, Segar-a	24.00	60.00	165.00
1405- **Popeye and the Jeep**, 1937, Whitman, 432 pgs., Segar-a	24.00	60.00	170.00
1406- **Popeye the Super-Fighter**, 1939, Whitman, All Pictures Comics, flip pictures, Segar-a	24.00	60.00	165.00
1422- **Popeye the Sailor Man**, 1947, Whitman, All Pictures Comics	16.00	40.00	115.00
1450- **Popeye in Quest of His Poopdeck Pappy**, 1937, Whitman, 432 pgs., Segar-c/a	24.00	60.00	170.00
1458- **Popeye and Queen Olive Oyl**, 1949, Whitman, 288 pgs., Sagendorf-a	16.00	40.00	115.00
1459- **Popeye and the Quest for the Rainbird**, 1943, Whitman, Winner & Zaboly-a	18.00	45.00	125.00
1480- **Popeye the Spinach Eater**, 1945, Whitman, All Pictures Comics	16.00	40.00	115.00
1485- **Popeye in a Sock for Susan's Sake**, 1940, Whitman, 432 pgs., flip pictures	18.00	45.00	125.00
1497- **Popeye and Caster Oyl the Detective**, 1941, Whitman, 432 pgs. flip pictures, Segar-a	21.00	52.50	145.00
1499- **Popeye and the Deep Sea Mystery**, 1939, Whitman, 432 pgs.,			

103 - "Pop-Up" Buck Rogers in the Dangerous Mission © KING

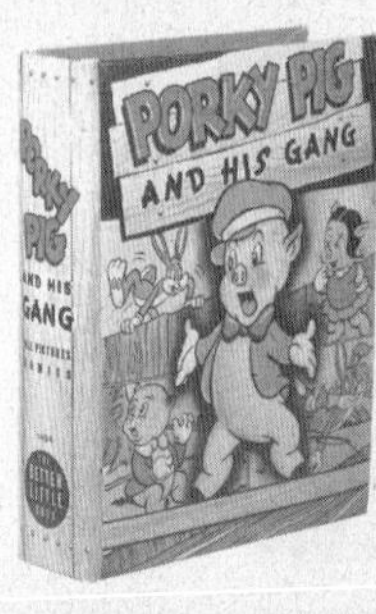

1404 - Porky Pig and His Gang © WB

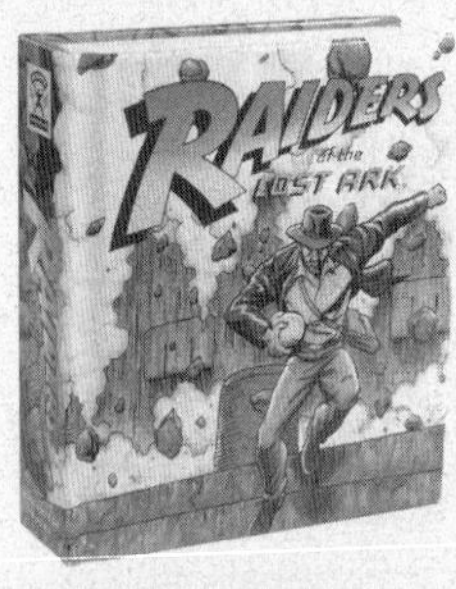

Raiders of the Lost Ark © 20th Century Fox

	GD	FN	VF/NM
Segar-c/a	21.00	52.50	145.00
1593- Popeye Starring in Choose Your Weppins, 1936, Saalfield, 160 pgs., soft-c, Segar-a	21.00	52.50	145.00
1597- Popeye's Ark, 1936, Saalfield, 4 1/2" x 5 1/2", soft-c, Segar-a	21.00	52.50	145.00
2008-(#8)- Popeye-Ghost Ship to Treasure Island, 1967, Whitman, 260 pgs., 39 cents, hard-c, color illos	4.00	10.00	27.00
5755- Popeye-Ghost Ship to Treasure Island, 1973, Whitman, 260 pgs., soft-c, color illos	2.00	5.00	15.00
2034-(#34)- Popeye, Danger Ahoy!, 1969, Whitman, 256 pgs., hard-c, color illos.	4.00	10.00	25.00
5768- Popeye, Danger Ahoy!, 1975, Whitman, 256 pgs., soft-c, color illos.	2.00	5.00	15.00
4063- Popeye, Thimble Theatre Starring, 1935, Whitman, 7" x 9 1/2", 320 pgs., Big Big Book, Segar-c/a; (Cactus cover w/yellow logo)	173.00	433.00	1385.00
4063- Popeye, Thimble Theatre Starring, 1935, Whitman, 7" x 9 1/2", 320 pgs., Big Big Book, Segar-c/a; (Big Balloon-c with red logo), (2nd printing w/same contents as above)	202.00	506.00	1620.00
5761- Popeye and Queen Olive Oyl, 1973, 260 pgs., B&W, soft-c	4.00	10.00	27.00
5761-2- Popeye and Queen Olive Oyl, 1973 (1980-reprint of 1973 version), 260 pgs., 79 cents, B&W, soft-c	2.00	5.00	15.00
103- "Pop-Up" Buck Rogers in the Dangerous Mission (with Pop-Up picture), 1934, BRP, 62 pgs., The Midget Pop-Up Book w/Pop-Up in center of book, Calkins-a	173.00	433.00	1385.00
206- "Pop-Up" Buck Rogers - Strange Adventures in the Spider Ship, The, 1935, BRP, 24 pgs., 8" x 9", 3 Pop-Ups, hard-c, by Dick Calkins	173.00	433.00	1385.00
nn- "Pop-Up" Cinderella, 1933, BRP, 7 1/2" x 9 3/4", 4 Pop-Ups, hard-c			
With dustjacket ($2.00)	100.00	250.00	700.00
Without dustjacket	79.00	198.00	550.00
207- "Pop-Up" Dick Tracy-Capture of Boris Arson, 1935, BRP, 24 pgs., 8" x 9", 3 Pop-Ups, hard-c, by Gould	100.00	250.00	700.00
210- "Pop-Up" Flash Gordon Tournament of Death, The, 1935, BRP, 24 pgs., 8" x 9", 3 Pop-Ups, hard-c, by Alex Raymond	156.00	390.00	1250.00
202- "Pop-Up" Goldilocks and the Three Bears, The, 1934, BRP, 24 pgs., 8" x 9", 3 Pop-Ups, hard-c	45.00	113.00	315.00
nn- "Pop-Up" Jack and the Beanstalk, 1933, BRP, hard-c (50 cents), 1 Pop-Up	45.00	113.00	315.00
nn- "Pop-Up" Jack the Giant Killer, 1933, BRP, hard-c (50 cents), 1 Pop-Up	45.00	113.00	315.00
nn- "Pop-Up" Jack the Giant Killer, 1933, BRP, 4 Pop-Ups, hard-c			
With dustjacket ($2.00)	100.00	250.00	700.00
Without dust jacket	79.00	198.00	550.00
nn- "Pop-Up" Little Black Sambo, (with Pop-Up picture), 1934, BRP, 62 pgs., The Midget Pop-Up Book, one Pop-Up in center of book	64.00	160.00	450.00
208- "Pop-Up" Little Orphan Annie and Jumbo the Circus Elephant, 1935, BRP, 24 pgs., 8" x 9 1/2", 3 Pop-Ups, hard-c, by H. Gray	100.00	250.00	700.00
nn- "Pop-Up" Little Red Ridinghood, 1933, BRP, hard-c (50 cents), 1 Pop-Up	57.00	143.00	400.00
nn- "Pop-Up" Mickey Mouse, The, 1933, BRP, 34 pgs., 6 1/2" x 9", 3 Pop-Ups, hard-c, Gottfredson-a (75 cents)	86.00	215.00	600.00
nn- "Pop-Up" Mickey Mouse in King Arthur's Court, The, 1933, BRP, 56 pgs., 7 1/2" x 9 1/4", 4 Pop-Ups, hard-c, Gottfredson-a			
With dust jacket ($2.00)	188.00	470.00	1500.00
Without dustjacket	150.00	375.00	1200.00
101- "Pop-Up" Mickey Mouse in "Ye Olden Days" (with Pop-Up picture), 1934, 62 pgs., BRP, The Midget Pop-Up Book, one Pop-Up in center of book, Gottfredson-a	121.00	303.00	850.00
nn- "Pop-Up" Minnie Mouse, The, 1933, BRP, 36 pgs., 6 1/2" x 9", 3 Pop-Ups, hard-c (75 cents), Gottfredson-a	86.00	215.00	600.00
203- "Pop-Up" Mother Goose, The, 1934, BRP, 24 pgs., 8" x 9 1/4", 3 Pop-Ups, hard-c	71.00	178.00	500.00
nn- "Pop-Up" Mother Goose Rhymes, The, 1933, BRP, 96 pgs., 7 1/2" x 9 1/4", 4 Pop-Ups, hard-c			
With dustjacket ($2.00)	82.00	205.00	575.00
Without dustjacket	71.00	178.00	500.00
209- "Pop-Up" New Adventures of Tarzan, 1935, BRP, 24 pgs., 8" x 9", 3 Pop-Ups, hard-c	121.00	303.00	850.00
104- "Pop-Up" Peter Rabbit, The (with Pop-Up picture), 1934, BRP, 62 pgs., The Midget Pop-Up Book, one Pop-Up in center of book	64.00	160.00	450.00
nn- "Pop-Up" Pinocchio, 1933, BRP, 7 1/2" x 9 3/4", 4 Pop-Ups, hard-c			
With dustjacket ($2.00)	96.00	240.00	675.00
Without dust jacket	75.00	188.00	525.00
102- "Pop-Up" Popeye among the White Savages (with Pop-Up picture), 1934, BRP, 62 pgs., The Midget Pop-Up Book, one Pop-Up in center of book, E. C. Segar-a	89.00	223.00	625.00
205- "Pop-Up" Popeye with the Hag of the Seven Seas, The, 1935, BRP, 24 pgs., 8" x 9", 3 Pop-Ups, hard-c, Segar-a	100.00	250.00	700.00
201- "Pop-Up" Puss In Boots, The, 1934, BRP, 24 pgs., 3 Pop-Ups, hard-c	46.00	115.00	320.00
nn- "Pop-Up" Silly Symphonies, The (Mickey Mouse Presents His ...), 1933, BRP, 56 pgs., 9 3/4" x 7 1/2", 4 Pop-Ups, hard-c			
With dust jacket ($2.00)	150.00	375.00	1200.00
Without dust jacket	93.00	233.00	650.00
nn- "Pop-Up" Sleeping Beauty, 1933, BRP, hard-c, (50 cents), 1 Pop-up	53.00	132.00	370.00
212- "Pop-Up" Terry and the Pirates in Shipwrecked, The, 1935, BRP, 24 pgs., 8" x 9", 3 Pop-Ups, hard-c	86.00	215.00	600.00
211- "Pop-Up" Tim Tyler in the Jungle, The, 1935, BRP, 24 pgs., 8" x 9", 3 Pop-Ups, hard-c	75.00	188.00	525.00
1404- Porky Pig and His Gang, 1946, Whitman, All Pictures Comics, Barks-a, reprints Four Color #48	24.00	60.00	165.00
1408- Porky Pig and Petunia, 1942, Whitman, All Pictures Comics, flip pictures, reprints Four Color #16 & Famous Gang Book of Comics	16.00	40.00	115.00
1176- Powder Smoke Range, 1935, Whitman, 240 pgs., photo-c, movie scenes, Hoot Gibson, Harey Carey app. (RKO Radio Pict.)	14.00	35.00	95.00
1058- Practical Pig!, The (Disney), 1939, Whitman, 68 pgs., 5" x 5 1/2", hard-c	12.00	30.00	85.00
758- Prairie Bill and the Covered Wagon, 1934, Whitman, 384 pgs., Hal Arbo-a	12.00	30.00	85.00
nn- Prairie Bill and the Covered Wagon, 1934, Whitman, 390 pgs., premium-no ads, 3-color, soft-c, Hal Arbo-a	18.00	45.00	125.00
1440- Punch Davis of the U.S. Aircraft Carrier, 1945, Whitman, 352 pgs.	10.00	25.00	65.00
nn- Puss in Boots, nd(1930s), np(Whitman), 36 pgs., Penny Book	4.00	10.00	22.00
1100B- Puzzle Book, 1938, Whitman, 36 pgs., 2 1/2" x 3 1/2", Penny Book	4.00	10.00	27.00
1100B- Puzzles, 1938, Whitman, 36 pgs., 2 1/2" x 3 1/2", Penny Book	4.00	10.00	27.00
1100B- Quiz Book, The, 1938, Whitman, 36 pgs., 2 1/2" x 3 1/2", Penny Book	4.00	10.00	27.00
1142- Radio Patrol, 1935, Whitman, 432 pgs., by Eddie Sullivan & Charlie Schmidt (#1)	12.00	30.00	85.00
1173- Radio Patrol Trailing the Safeblowers, 1937, Whitman, 432 pgs.	11.00	27.50	70.00
1496- Radio Patrol Outwitting the Gang Chief, 1939, Whitman, 432 pgs.	11.00	27.50	70.00
1498- Radio Patrol and Big Dan's Mobsters, 1937, Whitman, 432 pgs.	11.00	27.50	70.00
nn- Raiders of the Lost Ark, 1998, Chronicle Books, 304 pgs., adapts movie, 1-color (green) illos	4.00	10.00	22.00
1441- Range Busters, The, 1942, Whitman, 432 pgs., Henry E. Vallely-a	11.00	27.50	70.00
1163- Ranger and the Cowboy, The, 1939, Saalfield, 400 pgs.	11.00	27.50	70.00
1154- Rangers on the Rio Grande, 1938, Saalfield, 400 pgs.	11.00	27.50	70.00
1447- Ray Land of the Tank Corps, U.S.A., 1942, Whitman, 432 pgs., flip pictures, Hess-a	11.00	27.50	70.00
1157- Red Barry Ace-Detective, 1935, Whitman, 432 pgs., by Will Gould	15.00	37.50	105.00

1466 - Red Ryder and Circus Luck © WHIT

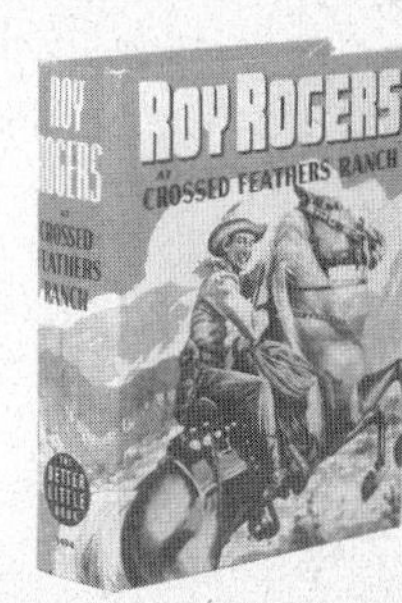

1494- Roy Rogers at Crossed Feathers Ranch © WHIT

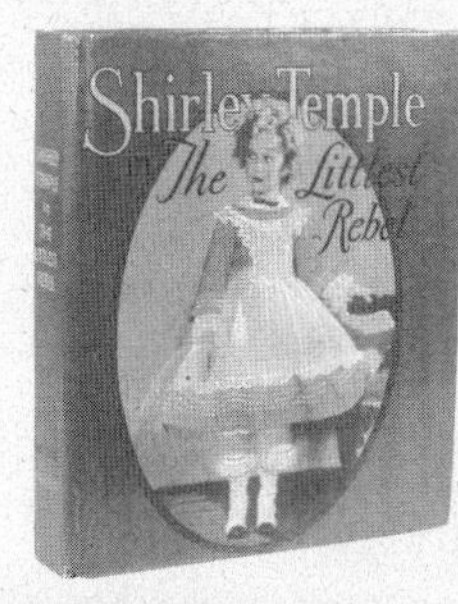

1115 - Shirley Temple in The Littlest Rebel © Saalfield

GD FN VF/NM

1426- Red Barry Undercover Man, 1939, Whitman, 432 pgs., by Will Gould 13.00 32.50 90.00
20- Red Davis, 1935, EVW, 160 pgs. 12.00 30.00 85.00
1449- Red Death on the Range, The, 1940, Whitman, 432 pgs., Fred Harman-a (Bronc Peeler) 12.00 30.00 85.00
nn- Red Falcon Adventures, The, 1937, Seal Right Ice Cream, 8 pgs., set of 50 books, circular in shape
Issue #1 87.00 218.00 605.00
Issue #2-5 60.00 150.00 420.00
Issue #6-10 49.00 122.00 345.00
Issue #11-50 31.00 78.00 220.00
nn- Red Hen and the Fox, The, nd(1930s), np(Whitman), 36 pgs., 3" x 2 1/2", Penny Book 4.00 10.00 22.00
1145- Red-Hot Holsters, 1938, Saalfield, 400 pgs. 11.00 27.50 70.00
1400- Red Ryder and Little Beaver on Hoofs of Thunder, 1939, Whitman, 432 pgs., Harman-c/a 20.00 50.00 140.00
1414- Red Ryder and the Squaw-Tooth Rustlers, 1946, Whitman, 352 pgs., Fred Harman-a 15.00 37.50 105.00
1427- Red Ryder and the Code of the West, 1941, Whitman, 432 pgs., flip pictures, by Harman 19.00 47.50 135.00
1440- Red Ryder the Fighting Westerner, 1940, Whitman, Harman-a 19.00 47.50 135.00
1443- Red Ryder and the Rimrock Killer, 1948, Whitman, 288 pgs., Harman-a 14.00 35.00 95.00
1450- Red Ryder and Western Border Guns, 1942, Whitman, 432 pgs., flip pictures, by Harman 19.00 47.50 135.00
1454- Red Ryder and the Secret Canyon, 1948, Whitman, 288 pgs., Harman-a 14.00 35.00 95.00
1466- Red Ryder and Circus Luck, 1947, Whitman, 288 pgs., by Fred Harman 14.00 35.00 95.00
1473- Red Ryder in War on the Range, 1945, Whitman, 352 pgs., by Fred Harman 15.00 37.50 105.00
1475- Red Ryder and the Outlaw of Painted Valley, 1943, Whitman, 352 pgs., by Harman 14.00 35.00 95.00
702-10- Red Ryder Acting Sheriff, 1949, Whitman, by Fred Hannan 12.00 30.00 85.00
nn- Red Ryder Brings Law to Devil's Hole, 1939, Dell, 196 pgs., Fast-Action Story, Harman-c/a 44.00 110.00 310.00
nn- Red Ryder and the Highway Robbers, 1938, Whitman, 36 pgs., 2 1/2" x 3 1/2", Penny Book 12.00 30.00 85.00
754- Reg'lar Fellers, 1933, Whitman, 320 pgs., by Gene Byrnes 13.00 32.50 90.00
nn- Reg'lar Fellers, 1933, Whitman, 202 pgs., Cocomalt premium, by Gene Byrnes 13.00 32.50 90.00
1424- Rex Beach's Jaragu of the Jungle, 1937, Whitman, 432 pgs. 11.00 27.50 70.00
12- Rex, King of Wild Horses in "Stampede," 1935, EVW, 160 pgs., movie scenes, Columbia Pictures 12.00 30.00 75.00
1100B- Riddles for Fun, 1938, Whitman, 36 pgs., 2 1/2" x 3 1/2", Penny Book 4.00 10.00 27.00
1100B- Riddles to Guess, 1938, Whitman, 36 pgs., 2 1/2" x 3 1/2", Penny Book 4.00 10.00 27.00
1425- Riders of Lone Trails, 1937, Whitman, 300 pgs. 12.00 30.00 75.00
1141- Rio Raiders (A Billy The Kid Story), 1938, Saalfield, 400 pgs. 12.00 30.00 75.00
2023-(#23)- The Road Runner, The Super Beep Catcher, 1968, Whitman, 256 pgs., hard-c, color illos. 1.00 2.50 9.00
5759- The Road Runner, The Super Beep Catcher, 1973, Whitman, 256 pgs., soft-c, 39 cents, B&W illos., and flip pictures 2.00 5.00 12.00
5767-2- Road Runner, The Lost Road Runner Mine, The, 1974 (1980), 260 pgs., 79 cents, B&W, soft-c 2.00 5.00 12.00
5784- The Road Runner and the Unidentified Coyote, 1974, Whitman, 260 pgs., soft-c, flip pictures 2.00 5.00 12.00
5784-2- The Road Runner and the Unidentified Coyote, 1980, Whitman, 260 pgs., soft-c, flip pictures 2.00 5.00 12.00
nn- Road To Perdition, 2002, Dreamworks, screenplay from movie, hard-c (Dreamworks and 20th Century Fox) 1.00 2.50 9.00
Robin Hood (See Wee Little Books)
10- Robin Hood, 1935, EVW, 160 pgs., movie scenes w/Douglas Fairbanks (United Artists), hard-c 18.00 45.00 125.00

GD FN VF/NM

719- Robinson Crusoe (The Story of...), nd (1933), Whitman, 364 pgs., soft-c 13.00 32.50 90.00
1421- Roy Rogers and the Dwarf-Cattle Ranch, 1947, Whitman, 352 pgs., Henry E. Vallely-a 18.00 45.00 125.00
1437- Roy Rogers and the Deadly Treasure, 1947, Whitman, 288 pgs. 18.00 45.00 125.00
1448- Roy Rogers and the Mystery of the Howling Mesa, 1948, Whitman, 288 pgs. 18.00 45.00 125.00
1452- Roy Rogers in Robbers' Roost, 1948, Whitman, 288 pgs. 18.00 45.00 125.00
1460- Roy Rogers Robinhood of the Range, 1942, Whitman, 432 pgs., Hess-a (1st) 21.00 52.50 145.00
1462- Roy Rogers and the Mystery of the Lazy M, 1949, Whitman 15.00 37.50 105.00
1476- Roy Rogers King of the Cowboys, 1943, Whitman, 352 pgs., Irwin Myers-a, based on movie 22.00 52.50 155.00
1494- Roy Rogers at Crossed Feathers Ranch, 1945, Whitman, 320 pgs., Erwin Hess-a , 3 1/4" x 5 1/2" 18.00 45.00 125.00
701-10- Roy Rogers and the Snowbound Outlaws, 1949, 3 1/4" x 5 1/2" 12.00 30.00 85.00
715-10- Roy Rogers Range Detective, 1950, Whitman, 2 1/2" x 5" 12.00 30.00 85.00
nn- Sandy Gregg Federal Agent on Special Assignment, 1939, Whitman, 36 pgs., 2 1/2" x 3 1/2", Penny Book 11.00 27.50 70.00
Sappo (See Top-Line Comics)
1122- Scrappy, 1934, Whitman, 288 pgs. 20.00 50.00 140.00
L12- Scrappy (The Adventures of...), 1935, Lynn, 192 pgs., movie scenes 20.00 50.00 140.00
1191- Secret Agent K-7,1940, Saalfield, 400 pgs., based on radio show 11.00 27.50 70.00
1144- Secret Agent X-9, 1936, Whitman, 432 pgs., Charles Flanders-a 15.00 37.50 105.00
1472- Secret Agent X-9 and the Mad Assassin, 1938, Whitman, 432 pgs., Charles Flanders-a 15.00 37.50 105.00
1161- Sequoia, 1935, Whitman, 160 pgs., photo-c, movie scenes 12.00 30.00 85.00
1430- Shadow and the Living Death, The, 1940, Whitman, 432 pgs., Erwin Hess-a 65.00 163.00 460.00
1443- Shadow and the Master of Evil, The, 1941, Whitman, 432 pgs., flip pictures, Hess-a 65.00 163.00 460.00
1495- Shadow and the Ghost Makers, The, 1942, Whitman, 432 pgs., John Coleman Burroughs-c 65.00 163.00 460.00
2024- Shazzan, The Glass Princess, 1968, Whitman, Hanna-Barbera 4.00 10.00 27.00
Shirley Temple (See My Life and Times & Story of..)
1095- Shirley Temple and Lionel Barrymore Starring In "The Little Colonel," 1935, Saalfield, photo hard-c, movie scenes 20.00 50.00 140.00
1115- Shirley Temple in "The Littlest Rebel," 1935, Saalfield, photo-c, movie scenes, hard-c 20.00 50.00 140.00
1575- Shirley Temple and Lionel Barrymore Starring In "The Little Colonel," 1935, Saalfield, photo soft-c, movie scenes 20.00 50.00 140.00
1595- Shirley Temple in "The Littlest Rebel," 1935, Saalfield, photo-c, movie scenes, soft-c 20.00 50.00 140.00
1195- Shooting Sheriffs of the Wild West, 1936, Whitman, 432 pgs. 11.00 27.50 70.00
1169- Silly Symphony Featuring Donald Duck (Disney), 1937, Whitman, 432 pgs., Taliaferro-a 38.00 95.00 255.00
1441- Silly Symphony Featuring Donald Duck and His (MIS) Adventures (Disney), 1937, Whitman, 432 pgs., Taliaferro-a 38.00 95.00 255.00
1155- Silver Streak, The, 1935, Whitman, 160 pgs., photo-c, movie scenes (RKO Radio Pict.) 12.00 30.00 75.00
Simple Simon (See Wee Little Books)
1649- Sir Lancelot (TV Series), 1958, Whitman, 280 pgs. 7.00 17.50 44.00
1112- Skeezix in Africa, 1934, Whitman, 300 pgs., Frank King-a 14.00 35.00 95.00
1408- Skeezix at the Military Academy, 1938, Whitman, 432 pgs., Frank King-a 14.00 35.00 95.00

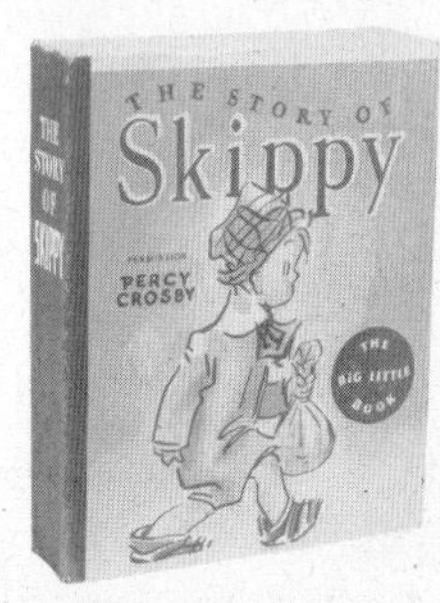
Skippy, The Story of © WHIT

2016 - Space Ghost-The Sorceress of Cyba-3 © H-B

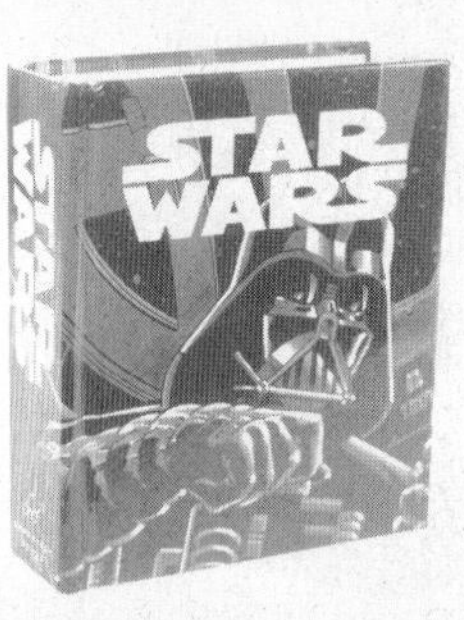
Star Wars - A New Hope © LucasFilm Ltd.

GD FN VF/NM

1414- Skeezix Goes to War, 1944, Whitman, 352 pgs., Frank King-a 14.00 35.00 95.00
1419- Skeezix on His Own in the Big City, 1941, Whitman, All Pictures Comics, flip pictures, Frank King-a 14.00 35.00 95.00
761- Skippy, 1934, Whitman, 320 pgs., by Percy Crosby 14.00 35.00 95.00
4056- Skippy, The Story of, 1934, Whitman, 320 pgs., 7" x 9 1/2", Big Big Book, Percy Crosby-a 70.00 175.00 490.00
nn- Skippy, The Story of, 1934, Whitman, Phillips Dental Magnesia premium, soft-c, by Percy Crosby 14.00 35.00 95.00
1439- Skyroads with Clipper Williams of the Flying Legion, 1938, Whitman, 432 pgs., by Lt. Dick Calkins, Russell Keaton-a 12.00 30.00 85.00
1127- Skyroads with Hurricane Hawk, 1936, Whitman, 432 pgs., by Lt. Dick Calkins, Russell Keaton-a 12.00 30.00 80.00
Smilin' Jack and his Flivver Plane (See Top-Line Comics)
1152- Smilin' Jack and the Stratosphere Ascent, 1937, Whitman, 432 pgs., Zack Mosley-a 16.00 40.00 115.00
1412- Smilin' Jack Flying High with "Downwind," 1942, Whitman, 432 pgs., Zack Mosley-a 15.00 37.50 105.00
1416- Smilin' Jack in Wings over the Pacific, 1939, Whitman, 432 pgs., Zack Mosley-a 15.00 37.50 105.00
1419- Smilin' Jack and the Jungle Pipe Line, 1947, Whitman, 352 pgs., Zack Mosley-a 12.00 30.00 85.00
1445- Smilin' Jack and the Escape from Death Rock, 1943, Whitman, 352 pgs., Mosley-a 12.00 30.00 85.00
1464- Smilin' Jack and the Coral Princess, 1945, Whitman, 352 pgs., Zack Mosley-a 12.00 30.00 85.00
1473- Smilin' Jack Speed Pilot, 1941, Whitman, 432 pgs., Zack Mosley-a 16.00 40.00 115.00
2- Smilin' Jack and his Stratosphere Plane, 1938, Whitman, 132 pgs., Buddy Book, soft-c, Zack Mosley-a 39.00 98.00 275.00
nn- Smilin' Jack Grounded on a Tropical Shore, 1938, Whitman, 36 pgs., 2 1/2" x 3 1/2", Penny Book 11.00 27.50 70.00
11- Smilin' Jack and the Border Bandits, 1941, Dell, 196 pgs., Fast-Action Story, soft-c, Zack Mosley-a 36.00 90.00 255.00
745- Smitty Golden Gloves Tournament, 1934, Whitman, 320 pgs., Walter Berndt-a 15.00 37.50 105.00
nn- Smitty Golden Gloves Tournament, 1934, Whitman, 204 pgs., Cocomalt premium, soft-c, Walter Berndt-a 16.00 40.00 115.00
1404- Smitty and Herby Lost Among the Indians, 1941, Whitman, All Pictures Comics 11.00 27.50 70.00
1477- Smitty in Going Native, 1938, Whitman, 300 pgs., Walter Berndt-a 11.00 27.50 70.00
2- Smitty and Herby, 1936, Whitman, 132 pgs., 3 1/2" x 3 1/2", soft-c, Tarzan Ice Cream cup lid premium 36.00 90.00 255.00
9- Smitty's Brother Herby and the Police Horse, 1938, Whitman, 132 pgs., 3 1/4" x 3 1/2", Buddy Book-ice cream premium, by Walter Berndt 36.00 90.00 255.00
1010- Smokey Stover Firefighter of Foo, 1937, Whitman, 7 1/4" x 5 1/2", 64 pgs., Nickel Book, Bill Holman-a 16.00 40.00 115.00
1413- Smokey Stover, 1942, Whitman, All Pictures Comics, flip pictures, Bill Holman-a 14.00 35.00 95.00
1421- Smokey Stover the Foo Fighter, 1938, Whitman, 432 pgs., Bill Holman-a 14.00 35.00 95.00
1481- Smokey Stover the Foolish Foo Fighter, 1942, Whitman, All Pictures Comics 14.00 35.00 95.00
1- Smokey Stover the Fireman of Foo, 1938, Whitman, 3 3/4" x 3 1/2", 132 pgs., Buddy Book-ice cream premium, by Bill Holman 41.00 103.00 285.00
1100A- Smokey Stover, 1938, Whitman, 36 pgs., 2 1/2" x 3 1/2", Penny Book 12.00 30.00 80.00
nn- Smokey Stover and the Fire Chief of Foo, 1938, Whitman, 36 pgs., 2 1/2" x 3 1/2", Penny Book, yellow shirt on-c 12.00 30.00 80.00
nn- Smokey Stover and the Fire Chief of Foo, 1938, Whitman, 36 pgs., Penny Book, green shirt on-c 12.00 30.00 80.00
1460- Snow White and the Seven Dwarfs (The Story of Walt Disney's ...), 1938, Whitman, 288 pgs. 29.00 73.00 200.00
1136- Sombrero Pete, 1936, Whitman, 432 pgs. 11.00 27.50 70.00
1152- Son of Mystery, 1939, Saalfield, 400 pgs. 11.00 27.50 70.00

GD FN VF/NM

1191- SOS Coast Guard, 1936, Whitman, 432 pgs., Henry E. Vallely-a 12.00 30.00 75.00
2016-(#16)-Space Ghost-The Sorceress of Cyba-3 (TV Cartoon), 1968, Whitman, 260 pgs., 39¢-c, hard-c, color illos 10.00 25.00 60.00
1455- Speed Douglas and the Mole Gang-The Great Sabotage Plot, 1941, Whitman, 432 pgs., flip pictures 11.00 27.50 70.00
5779- Spider-Man Zaps Mr. Zodiac, 1976, 260 pgs., soft-c, B&W 1.00 2.50 9.00
5779-2- Spider-Man Zaps Mr. Zodiac, 1980, 260 pgs., 79¢-c, soft-c, B&W 1.00 2.50 6.00
1467- Spike Kelly of the Commandos, 1943, Whitman, 352 pgs. 11.00 27.50 70.00
1144- Spook Riders on the Overland, 1938, Saalfield, 400 pgs. 11.00 27.50 70.00
768- Spy, The, 1936, Whitman, 300 pgs. 13.00 32.50 90.00
nn- Spy Smasher and the Red Death, 1941, Fawcett, 4" x 5 1/2", Dime Action Book 58.00 146.00 410.00
1120- Stan Kent Freshman Fullback, 1936, Saalfield, 148 pgs., hard-c 9.00 22.50 55.00
1132- Stan Kent, Captain, 1937, Saalfield 9.00 22.50 55.00
1600- Stan Kent Freshman Fullback, 1936, Saalfield, 148 pgs., soft-c 9.00 22.50 55.00
1123- Stan Kent Varsity Man, 1936, Saalfield, 160 pgs., hard-c 9.00 22.50 55.00
1603- Stan Kent Varsity Man, 1936, Saalfield, 160 pgs., soft-c 9.00 22.50 55.00
nn- Star Wars - A New Hope, 1997, Chronicle Books, 320 pgs., adapts movie, 1-color (blue) illos 3.00 7.50 20.00
nn- Star Wars - Empire Strikes Back, The, 1997, Chronicle Books, 296 pgs., adapts movie, 1-color (blue) illos 3.00 7.50 20.00
nn- Star Wars - Episode 1 - The Phantom Menace, 1999, Chronicle Books, 344 pgs., adapts movie, 1-color (blue) illos 1.00 2.50 9.00
nn- Star Wars - Episode 2 - Attack of the Clones, 2002, Chronicle Books, 340 pgs., adapts movie, 1-color (blue) illos 1.00 2.50 9.00
nn- Star Wars - Return of the Jedi, 1997, Chronicle Books, 312 pgs., adapts movie, 1-color (blue) illos 3.00 7.50 20.00
1104- Steel Arena, The (With Clyde Beatty), 1936, Saalfield, hard-c, movie scenes adapted from "The Lost Jungle" 12.00 30.00 85.00
1584- Steel Arena, The (With Clyde Beatty), 1936, Saalfield, soft-c, movie scenes 12.00 30.00 85.00
1426- Steve Hunter of the U.S. Coast Guard Under Secret Orders, 1942, Whitman, 432 pgs. 11.00 27.50 70.00
1456- Story of Charlie McCarthy and Edgar Bergen, The, 1938, Whitman, 288 pgs. 15.00 37.50 105.00
Story of Daniel, The (See Wee Little Books)
Story of David, The (See Wee Little Books)
1110- Story of Freddie Bartholomew, The, 1935, Saalfield, 4 1/2" x 5 1/4", hard-c, movie scenes (MGM) 12.00 30.00 75.00
1590- Story of Freddie Bartholomew, The, 1935, Saalfield, 4 1/2" x 5 1/4", soft-c, movie scenes (MGM) 12.00 30.00 75.00
Story of Gideon, The (See Wee Little Books)
W714- Story of Jackie Cooper, The, 1933, Whitman, 240 pgs., photo-c, movie scenes, "Skippy" & "Sooky" movie 15.00 37.50 105.00
Story of Joseph, The (See Wee Little Books)
Story of Moses, The (See Wee Little Books)
Story of Ruth and Naomi (See Wee Little Books)
1089- Story of Shirley Temple, The, 1934, Saalfield, 160 pgs., hard-c, photo-c, movie scenes 13.00 32.50 90.00
1319- Story of Shirley Temple, The, 1934, Saalfield, 160 pgs., soft-c, photo-c, movie scenes 13.00 32.50 90.00
1090- Strawberry-Roan, 1934, Saalfield, 160 pgs., hard-c, Ken Maynard photo-c, movie scenes 13.00 32.50 90.00
1320- Strawberry-Roan, 1934, Saalfield, 160 pgs., soft-c, Ken Maynard photo-c, movie scenes 13.00 32.50 90.00
Streaky and the Football Signals (See Top-Line Comics)
5780-2- Superman in the Phantom Zone Connection, 1980, 260 pgs., 79¢-c, soft-c, B&W 1.00 2.50 9.00
582- "Swap It" Book, The, 1949, Samuel Lowe Co., 260 pgs., 3 1/2" x 4 1/2"
1. Little Tex in the Midst of Trouble 7.00 17.50 44.00
2. Little Tex's Escape 7.00 17.50 44.00

Tailspin Tommy the Dirigible Flight to the North Pole (3-color premium) © WHIT

Tarzan and a Daring Rescue © ERB

1100B - Tell Your Fortune © WHIT

	GD	FN	VF/NM
3. Little Tex Comes to the XY Ranch	7.00	17.50	44.00
4. Get Them Cowboy	7.00	17.50	44.00
5. The Mail Must Go Through! A Story of the Pony Express	7.00	17.50	44.00
6. Nevada Jones, Trouble Shooter	7.00	17.50	44.00
7. Danny Meets the Cowboys	7.00	17.50	44.00
8. Flint Adams and the Stage Coach	7.00	17.50	44.00
9. Bud Shinners and the Oregon Trail	7.00	17.50	44.00
10. The Outlaws' Last Ride	7.00	17.50	44.00
Sybil Jason (See Little Big Shot)			
747- **Tailspin Tommy in the Famous Pay-Roll Mystery**, 1933, Whitman, hard-c, 320 pgs., Hal Forrest-a (# 1)	15.00	37.50	105.00
747- **Tailspin Tommy in the Famous Pay-Roll Mystery**, 1933, Whitman, soft-c, 320 pgs., Hal Forrest-a (# 1)	15.00	37.50	105.00
nn- **Tailspin Tommy the Pay-Roll Mystery**, 1934, Whitman, 52 pgs., 3 1/2" x 5 1/4", premium-no ads, soft-c; another version with Perkins ad, Hal Forrest-a	26.00	65.00	185.00
1110- **Tailspin Tommy and the Island in the Sky,** 1936, Whitman, 432 pgs., Hal Forrest-a	13.00	32.50	90.00
1124- **Tailspin Tommy the Dirigible Flight to the North Pole,** 1934, Whitman, 432 pgs., H. Forrest-a	15.00	37.50	105.00
nn- **Tailspin Tommy the Dirigible Flight to the North Pole,** 1934, Whitman, 436 pgs., 3-color, soft-c, premium-no ads, Hal Forrest-a	36.00	90.00	255.00
1172- **Tailspin Tommy Hunting for Pirate Gold**, 1935, Whitman, 432 pgs., Hal Forrest-a	13.00	32.50	90.00
1183- **Tailspin Tommy Air Racer**, 1940, Saalfield, 400 pgs., hard-c	13.00	32.50	90.00
1184- **Tailspin Tommy in the Great Air Mystery**, 1936, Whitman, 240 pgs., photo-c, movie scenes	15.00	37.50	105.00
1410- **Tailspin Tommy the Weasel and His "Skywaymen,"** 1941, Whitman, All Pictures Comics, flip pictures	12.00	30.00	80.00
1413- **Tailspin Tommy and the Lost Transport**, 1940, Whitman, 432 pgs., Hal Forrest-a	12.00	30.00	80.00
1423- **Tailspin Tommy and the Hooded Flyer**, 1937, Whitman, 432 pgs., Hal Forrest-a	13.00	32.50	90.00
1494- **Tailspin Tommy and the Sky Bandits**, 1938, Whitman 432 pgs., Hal Forrest-a	13.00	32.50	90.00
nn- **Tailspin Tommy and the Airliner Mystery**, 1938, Dell, 196 pgs., Fast-Action Story, soft-c, Hal Forrest-a	47.00	118.00	330.00
nn- **Tailspin Tommy in Flying Aces**, 1938, Dell, 196 pgs., Fast-Action Story, soft-c, Hal Forrest-a	47.00	118.00	330.00
nn- **Tailspin Tommy in Wings Over the Arctic**, 1934, Whitman, Cocomalt premium, Forrest-a	20.00	50.00	140.00
nn- **Tailspin Tommy Big Thrill Chewing Gum**, 1934, Whitman, 8 pgs., 2 1/2" x 3 " (6 diff.) each..	13.00	32.50	90.00
3- **Tailspin Tommy on the Mountain of Human Sacrifice**, 1938, Whitman, soft-c, Buddy Book	43.00	108.00	300.00
7- **Tailspin Tommy's Perilous Adventure**, 1934, Whitman, 132 pgs., 3 1/2" x 3 1/2" soft-c, Tarzan Ice Cream cup premium	43.00	108.00	300.00
nn- **Tailspin Tommy**, 1935, Whitman, 148 pgs., 3 1/2" x 4", Tarzan Ice Cream cup premium	54.00	135.00	385.00
L16- **Tale of Two Cities, A**, 1935, Lynn, movie scenes	15.00	37.50	105.00
744- **Tarzan of the Apes**, 1933, Whitman, 320 pgs., by Edgar Rice Burroughs (1st)	46.00	115.00	325.00
nn- **Tarzan of the Apes**, 1935, Whitman, 52 pgs., 3 1/2" x 5 1/4", soft-c, stapled, premium, no ad; another version with a Perkins ad	58.00	146.00	410.00
769- **Tarzan the Fearless**, 1934, Whitman, 240 pgs., Buster Crabbe photo-c, movie scenes, ERB	33.00	83.00	230.00
770- **Tarzan Twins, The**, 1934, Whitman, 432 pgs., ERB	118.00	295.00	825.00
770- **Tarzan Twins, The**, 1935, Whitman, 432 pgs., ERB	58.00	146.00	410.00
nn- **Tarzan Twins, The**, 1935, Whitman, 52 pgs., 3 1/2" x 5 3/4", premium-no ads, soft-c, ERB	79.00	198.00	550.00
nn- **Tarzan Twins, The**, 1935, Whitman, 436 pgs., 3-color, soft-c, premium-no ads, ERB	84.00	210.00	580.00
778- **Tarzan of the Screen** (The Story of Johnny Weissmuller), 1934, Whitman, 240 pgs., photo-c, movie scenes, ERB	34.00	85.00	240.00
1102- **Tarzan, The Return of**, 1936, Whitman, 432 pgs., Edgar Rice Burroughs	24.00	60.00	170.00
1180- **Tarzan, The New Adventures of**, 1935, Whitman, 160 pgs., Herman Brix photo-c, movie scenes, ERB	28.00	70.00	195.00
1182- **Tarzan Escapes**, 1936, Whitman, 240 pgs., Johnny Weissmuller photo-c, movie scenes, ERB	34.00	85.00	240.00
1407- **Tarzan Lord of the Jungle**, 1946, Whitman, 352 pgs., ERB	18.00	45.00	125.00
1410- **Tarzan, The Beasts of**, 1937, Whitman, 432 pgs., Edgar Rice Burroughs	21.00	52.50	145.00
1442- **Tarzan and the Lost Empire**, 1948, Whitman, 288 pgs., ERB	18.00	45.00	125.00
1444- **Tarzan and the Ant Men**, 1945, Whitman, 352 pgs., ERB	18.00	45.00	125.00
1448- **Tarzan and the Golden Lion**, 1943, Whitman, 432 pgs., ERB	22.00	52.50	155.00
1452- **Tarzan the Untamed**, 1941, Whitman, 432 pgs., flip pictures, ERB	22.00	52.50	155.00
1453- **Tarzan the Terrible**, 1942, Whitman, 432 pgs., flip pictures, ERB	22.00	52.50	155.00
1467- **Tarzan in the Land of the Giant Apes**, 1949, Whitman, ERB	18.00	45.00	125.00
1477- **Tarzan, The Son of**, 1939, Whitman, 432 pgs., ERB	22.00	52.50	155.00
1488- **Tarzan's Revenge**, 1938, Whitman, 432 pgs., ERB	22.00	52.50	155.00
1495- **Tarzan and the Jewels of Opar**, 1940, Whitman, 432 pgs.	22.00	52.50	155.00
4056- **Tarzan and the Tarzan Twins with Jad-Bal-Ja the Golden Lion**, 1936, Whitman, 7" x 9 1/2", 320 pgs., Big Big Book	115.00	288.00	810.00
709-10- **Tarzan and the Journey of Terror**, 1950, Whitman, 2 1/2" x 5", ERB, Marsh-a	12.00	30.00	75.00
2005- **(#5)-Tarzan: The Mark of the Red Hyena**, 1967, Whitman, 260 pgs., 39 cents, hard-c, color illos	4.00	10.00	27.00
nn- **Tarzan**, 1935, Whitman, 148 pgs., soft-c, 3 1/2" x 4", Tarzan Ice Cream cup premium, ERB (scarce)	130.00	327.00	1045.00
nn- **Tarzan and a Daring Rescue**, 1938, Whitman, 68 pgs., Pan-Am premium, soft-c, ERB (blank back-c version also exists)	71.00	178.00	500.00
nn- **Tarzan and his Jungle Friends**, 1936, Whitman, 132 pgs., soft-c, 3 1/2" x 3 1/2", Tarzan Ice Cream cup premium, ERB (scarce)	114.00	285.00	800.00
nn- **Tarzan in the Golden City**, 1938, Whitman, 68 pgs., Pan-Am premium, soft-c, ERB	71.00	178.00	500.00
nn- **Tarzan The Avenger**, 1939, Dell, 194 pgs., Fast-Action Story, ERB, soft-c	47.00	118.00	330.00
nn- **Tarzan with the Tarzan Twins in the Jungle**, 1938, Dell, 194 pgs., Fast-Action Story, ERB	47.00	118.00	330.00
1100B- **Tell Your Fortune**, 1938, Whitman, 36 pgs., 2 1/2" x 3 1/2", Penny Book	5.00	12.50	33.00
nn- **Terminator 2: Judgment Day**, 1998, Chronicle Books, 310 pgs., adapts movie, 1-color (blue-gray) illos	1.00	2.50	9.00
1156- **Terry and the Pirates**, 1935, Whitman, 432 pgs., Milton Caniff-a (#1)	18.00	45.00	125.00
nn- **Terry and the Pirates**, 1935, Whitman, 52 pgs., 3 1/2" x 5 1/4", soft-c, premium, Milton Caniff-a; 3 versions: No ad, Sears ad & Perkins ad	31.00	78.00	220.00
1412- **Terry and the Pirates Shipwrecked on a Desert Island**, 1938, Whitman, 432 pgs., Milton Caniff-a	15.00	37.50	105.00
1420- **Terry and War in the Jungle**, 1946, Whitman, 352 pgs., Milton Caniff-a	13.00	32.50	90.00
1436- **Terry and the Pirates The Plantation Mystery**, 1942, Whitman, 432 pgs., flip pictures, Milton Caniff-a	15.00	37.50	105.00
1446- **Terry and the Pirates and the Giant's Vengeance**, 1939, Whitman, 432 pgs., Caniff-a	15.00	37.50	105.00
1499- **Terry and the Pirates in the Mountain Stronghold**,			

7 - Texas Bad Man © EVW

1490 - Tim McCoy and the Sandy Gulch Stampede © WHIT

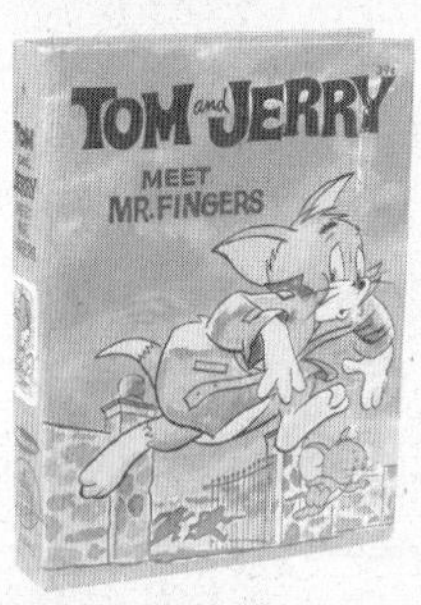

2006 - Tom and Jerry Meet Mr. Fingers © H-B

GD FN VF/NM

1941, Whitman, 432 pgs., Caniff-a 15.00 37.50 105.00

4073- Terry and the Pirates, The Adventures of, 1938, Whitman, 7" x 9 1/2", 320 pgs., Big Big Book, Milton Caniff-a 87.00 218.00 605.00

4- Terry and the Pirates Ashore in Singapore, 1938, Whitman, 132 pgs., 3 1/2" x 3 3/4", soft-c, Buddy Book premium 38.00 95.00 255.00

10- Terry and the Pirates Meet Again, 1936, Whitman, 132 pgs., 3 1/2" x 3 1/2", soft-c, Tarzan Ice Cream cup lid premium 58.00 146.00 410.00

nn- Terry and the Pirates, Adventures of, 1938, 36 pgs., 2 1/2" x 3 1/2", Penny Book, Caniff-a 11.00 27.50 70.00

nn- Terry and the Pirates and the Island Rescue, 1938, Whitman, 68 pgs., 3 1/4" x 3 1/2", Pan-Am premium 29.00 73.00 200.00

nn- Terry and the Pirates on Their Travels, 1938, 36 pgs., 2 1/2" x 3 1/2", Penny Book, Caniff-a 11.00 27.50 70.00

nn- Terry and the Pirates and the Mystery Ship, 1938, Dell, 194 pgs., Fast-Action Story, soft-c 39.00 98.00 275.00

1492- Terry Lee Flight Officer U.S.A., 1944, Whitman, 352 pgs., Milton Caniff-a 12.00 30.00 85.00

7- Texas Bad Man, The (Tom Mix), 1934, EVW, 160 pgs., (Five Star Library), movie scenes 24.00 60.00 165.00

1429- Texas Kid, The, 1937, Whitman, 432 pgs. 11.00 27.50 70.00

1135- Texas Ranger, The, 1936, Whitman, 432 pgs., Hal Arbo-a 11.00 27.50 70.00

nn- Texas Ranger, The, 1935, Whitman, 260 pgs., Cocomalt premium, soft-c, Hal Arbo-a 12.00 30.00 85.00

nn- Texas Ranger and the Rustler Gang, The, 1936, Whitman, Pan-Am giveaway 29.00 73.00 200.00

nn- Texas Ranger in the West, The, 1938, Whitman, 36 pgs., 2 1/2" x 3 1/2", Penny Book 10.00 25.00 65.00

nn- Texas Ranger to the Rescue, The, 1938, Whitman, 36 pgs., 2 1/2" x 3 1/2", Penny Book 10.00 25.00 65.00

12- Texas Ranger in Rustler Strategy, The, 1936, Whitman, 132 pgs., 3 1/2" x 3 1/2", soft-c, Tarzan Ice Cream cup lid premium 36.00 90.00 255.00

Tex Thorne (See Zane Grey)

Thimble Theatre (See Popeye)

26- 13 Hours By Air, 1936, Lynn, 128 pgs., 5" x 7 1/2", photo-c, movie scenes (Paramount Pictures) 14.00 35.00 95.00

nn- Three Bears, The, nd (1930s), np (Whitman), 36 pgs., 3" x 2 1/2", Penny Book 4.00 10.00 22.00

1129- Three Finger Joe (Baseball), 1937, Saalfield, Robert A. Graef-a 10.00 25.00 65.00

nn- Three Little Pigs, The, nd (1930s), np (Whitman), 36 pgs., 3" x 2 1/2", Penny Book 4.00 10.00 22.00

1131- Three Musketeers, 1935, Whitman, 182 pgs., 5 1/4" x 6 1/4", photo-c, movie scenes 18.00 45.00 125.00

1409- Thumper and the Seven Dwarfs (Disney), 1944, Whitman, All Pictures Comics 24.00 60.00 165.00

1108- Tiger Lady, The (The life of Mabel Stark, animal trainer), 1935, Saalfield, photo-c, movie scenes, hard-c 11.00 27.50 70.00

1588- Tiger Lady, The, 1935, Saalfield, photo-c, movie scenes, soft-c 11.00 27.50 70.00

1442- Tillie the Toiler and the Wild Man of Desert Island, 1941, Whitman, 432 pgs., Russ Westover-a 12.00 30.00 85.00

1058- "Timid Elmer" (Disney), 1939, Whitman, 5" x 5 1/2", 68 pgs., hard-c 12.00 30.00 85.00

1152- Tim McCoy in the Prescott Kid, 1935, Whitman, 160 pgs., hard-c, photo-c, movie scenes 20.00 50.00 140.00

1193- Tim McCoy in the Westerner, 1936, Whitman, 240 pgs., photo-c, movie scenes 18.00 45.00 125.00

1436- Tim McCoy on the Tomahawk Trail, 1937, Whitman, 432 pgs., Robert Weisman-a 12.00 30.00 85.00

1490- Tim McCoy and the Sandy Gulch Stampede, 1939, Whitman, 424 pgs. 12.00 30.00 75.00

2- Tim McCoy in Beyond the Law, 1934, EVW, Five Star Library, photo-c, movie scenes (Columbia Pict.) Hardcover 21.00 52.00 145.00
(Rare) Softcover 54.00 135.00 375.00

10- Tim McCoy in Fighting the Redskins, 1938, Whitman, 130 pgs., Buddy Book, soft-c 34.00 85.00 240.00

14- Tim McCoy in Speedwings, 1935, EVW, Five Star Library, 160 pgs., photo-c, movie scenes (Columbia Pictures) 24.00 60.00 165.00

nn- Tim the Builder, nd (1930s), np (Whitman), 36 pgs., 3" x 2 1/2", Penny Book 4.00 10.00 22.00

Tim Tyler (Also see Adventures of ...)

1140- Tim Tyler's Luck Adventures in the Ivory Patrol, 1937, Whitman, 432 pgs., by Lyman Young 13.00 32.50 90.00

1479- Tim Tyler's Luck and the Plot of the Exiled King, 1939, Whitman, 432 pgs., by Lyman Young 12.00 30.00 80.00

767- Tiny Tim, The Adventures of, 1935, Whitman, 384 pgs., by Stanley Link 15.00 37.50 105.00

1172- Tiny Tim and the Mechanical Men, 1937, Whitman, 432 pgs., by Stanley Link 13.00 32.50 90.00

1472- Tiny Tim in the Big, Big World, 1945, Whitman, 352 pgs., by Stanley Link 13.00 32.50 90.00

2006- (#6)-Tom and Jerry Meet Mr. Fingers, 1967, Whitman, 39¢-c 260 pgs., hard-c, color illos. 4.00 10.00 27.00

5752- Tom and Jerry Meet Mr. Fingers, 1973, Whitman, 39¢-c 260 pgs., soft-c, color illos., 5 printings 2.00 5.00 15.00

2030-(#30)- Tom and Jerry, The Astro-Nots, 1969, Whitman, 256 pgs., hard-c, color illos. 3.00 7.50 20.00

5765- Tom and Jerry, The Astro-Nots, 1974, Whitman, 256 pgs., soft-c, color illos. 2.00 5.00 15.00

5787-2- Tom and Jerry Under the Big Top, 1980, Whitman, 79¢-c, 260 pgs., soft-c, B&W 2.00 5.00 15.00

723- Tom Beatty Ace of the Service, 1934, Whitman, 256 pgs., George Taylor-a 13.00 32.50 90.00

nn- Tom Beatty Ace of the Service, 1934, Whitman, 260 pgs., soft-c 13.00 32.50 90.00

1165- Tom Beatty Ace of the Service Scores Again, 1937, Whitman, 432 pgs., Weisman-a 12.00 30.00 80.00

1420- Tom Beatty Ace of the Service and the Big Brain Gang, 1939, Whitman, 432 pgs. 12.00 30.00 80.00

nn- Tom Beatty Ace Detective and the Gorgon Gang, 1938?, Whitman, 36 pgs., 2 1/2" x 3 1/2", Penny Book 11.00 27.50 70.00

nn- Tom Beatty Ace of the Service and the Kidnapers, 1938?, Whitman, 36 pgs., 2 1/2" x 3 1/2", Penny Book 11.00 27.50 70.00

1102- Tom Mason on Top, 1935, Saalfield, 160 pgs., Tom Mix photo-c, from Mascot serial "The Miracle Rider," movie scenes, hard-c 20.00 50.00 140.00

1582- Tom Mason on Top, 1935, Saalfield, 160 pgs., Tom Mix photo-c, movie scenes, soft-c 20.00 50.00 140.00

Tom Mix (See Chief of the Rangers, Flaming Guns & Texas Bad Man)

762- Tom Mix and Tony Jr. in "Terror Trail," 1934, Whitman, 160 pgs., movie scenes 20.00 50.00 140.00

1144- Tom Mix in the Fighting Cowboy, 1935, Whitman, 432 pgs., Hal Arbo-a 15.00 37.50 105.00

nn- Tom Mix in the Fighting Cowboy, 1935, Whitman, 436 pgs., premium-no ads, 3 color, soft-c, Hal Arbo-a 29.00 73.00 200.00

1166- Tom Mix in the Range War, 1937, Whitman, 432 pgs., Hal Arbo-a 12.00 30.00 85.00

1173- Tom Mix Plays a Lone Hand, 1935, Whitman, 288 pgs., hard-c, Hal Arbo-a 12.00 30.00 85.00

1183- Tom Mix and the Stranger from the South, 1936, Whitman, 432 pgs. 12.00 30.00 85.00

1462- Tom Mix and the Hoard of Montezuma, 1937, Whitman, H. E. Vallely-a 12.00 30.00 85.00

1482- Tom Mix and His Circus on the Barbary Coast, 1940, Whitman, 432 pgs., James Gary-a 12.00 30.00 85.00

3047- Tom Mix and His Big Little Kit, 1937, Whitman, 384 pgs., 4 1/2" x 6 1/2" box, includes miniature box of 4 crayons-red, yellow, blue and green 100.00 250.00 700.00

4068- Tom Mix and the Scourge of Paradise Valley, 1937, Whitman, 7" x 9 1/2", 320 pgs., Big Big Book, Vallely-a 70.00 175.00 490.00

6833- Tom Mix in the Riding Avenger, 1936, Dell, 244 pgs., Cartoon Story Book, hard-c 31.00 78.00 220.00

nn- Tom Mix Rides to the Rescue, 1939, 36 pgs., 2 1/2" x 3", Penny Book 11.00 27.50 70.00

nn- Tom Mix Avenges the Dry Gulched Range King, 1939, Dell, 196 pgs., Fast-Action Story, soft-c 33.00 83.00 230.00

nn- Tom Mix in the Riding Avenger, 1936, Dell, 244 pgs.,

1126 - Tommy of Troop Six © Saalfield

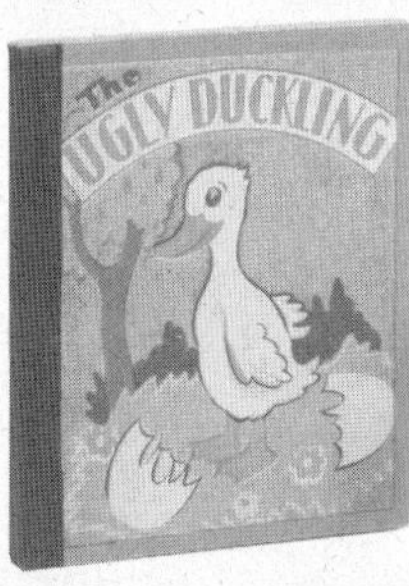

The Ugly Duckling © WHIT

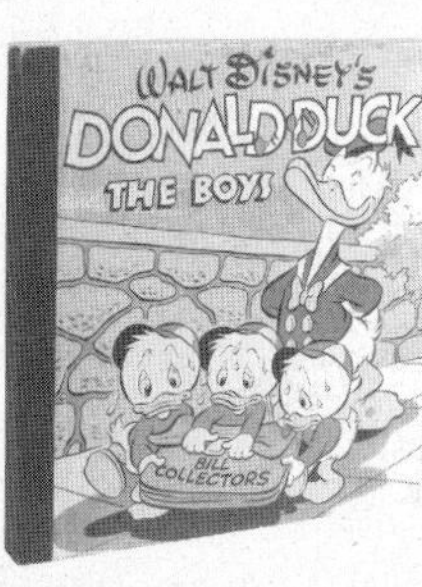

845 - Walt Disney's Donald Duck and the Boys © WDC

	GD	FN	VF/NM
Fast-Action Story	33.00	83.00	230.00
nn- **Tom Mix the Trail of the Terrible 6**, 1935, Ralston Purina Co., 84 pgs., 3" x 3 1/2", premium	24.00	60.00	170.00
4- **Tom Mix and Tony in the Rider of Death Valley**, 1934, EVW, Five Star Library, 160 pgs., movie scenes (Universal Pictures), hard-c	24.00	60.00	165.00
4- **Tom Mix and Tony in the Rider of Death Valley**, 1934, EVW, Five Star Library, 160 pgs., movie scenes (Universal Pictures), soft-c (Rare)	57.00	142.00	400.00
7- **Tom Mix in the Texas Bad Man**, 1934, EVW, Five Star Library, 160 pgs., movie scenes, hard-c	24.00	60.00	165.00
7- **Tom Mix in the Texas Bad Man**, 1934, EVW, Five Star Library, 160 pgs., movie scenes; soft-c (Rare)	50.00	142.00	400.00
10- **Tom Mix in the Tepee Ranch Mystery**, 1938, Whitman, 132 pgs., Buddy Book, soft-c	34.00	85.00	240.00
1126- **Tommy of Troop Six** (Scout Book), 1937, Saalfield, hard-c	10.00	25.00	65.00
1606- **Tommy of Troop Six** (Scout Book), 1937, Saalfield, soft-c	10.00	25.00	65.00
Tom Sawyer (See Adventures of ...)			
1437- **Tom Swift and His Magnetic Silencer**, 1941, Whitman, 432 pgs., flip pictures	50.00	125.00	350.00
1485- **Tom Swift and His Giant Telescope**, 1939, Whitman, 432 pgs., James Gary-a	36.00	90.00	250.00
540- **Top-Line Comics** (In Open Box), 1935, Whitman, 164 pgs., 3 1/2" x 3 1/2", 3 books in set, all soft-c:			
Bobby Thatcher and the Samarang Emerald	18.00	45.00	125.00
Broncho Bill in Suicide Canyon	18.00	45.00	125.00
Freckles and His Friends in the North Woods	18.00	45.00	125.00
Complete set with box	62.00	155.00	440.00
541- **Top-Line Comics** (In Open Box), 1935, Whitman, 164 pgs., 3 1/2" x 3 1/2", 3 books in set; all soft-c:			
Little Joe and the City Gangsters	18.00	45.00	125.00
Smilin' Jack and His Flivver Plane	18.00	45.00	125.00
Streaky and the Football Signals	18.00	45.00	125.00
Complete set with box	62.00	155.00	440.00
542- **Top-Line Comics** (In Open Box), 1935, Whitman, 164 pgs., 3 1/2" x 3 1/2", 3 books in set; all soft-c:			
Dinglehoofer Und His Dog Adolph by Knerr	18.00	45.00	125.00
Jungle Jim by Alex Raymond	22.00	52.50	155.00
Sappo by Segar	22.00	52.50	155.00
Complete set with box	79.00	198.00	550.00
543- **Top-Line Comics** (In Open Box), 1935, Whitman, 164 pgs., 3 1/2" x 3 1/2", 3 books in set; all soft-c:			
Alexander Smart, ESQ by Winner	18.00	45.00	125.00
Bunky by Billy de Beck	18.00	45.00	125.00
Nicodemus O'Malley by Carter	18.00	45.00	125.00
Complete set with box	62.00	155.00	440.00
1158- **Tracked by a G-Man**, 1939, Saalfield, 400 pgs.	10.00	25.00	65.00
25- **Trail of the Lonesome Pine, The**, 1936, Lynn, movie scenes	16.00	40.00	115.00
nn- **Trail of the Terrible 6** (See Tom Mix ...)			
1185- **Trail to Squaw Gulch, The**, 1940, Saalfield, 400 pgs.	11.00	27.50	70.00
720- **Treasure Island**, 1933, Whitman, 362 pgs.	21.00	52.50	145.00
1141- **Treasure Island**, 1934, Whitman, 164 pgs., hard-c, 4 1/4" x 5 1/4", Jackie Cooper photo-c, movie scenes	16.00	40.00	115.00
1141- **Treasure Island**, 1934, Whitman, 164 pgs., soft-c, 4 1/4" x 5 1/4", Jackie Cooper photo-c, movie scenes	16.00	40.00	115.00
1018- **Trick and Puzzle Book**, 1939, Whitman, 100 pgs., soft-c	4.00	10.00	22.00
1100B- **Tricks Easy to Do** (Slight of hand & magic), 1938, Whitman, 36 pgs., 2 1/2" x 3 1/2", Penny Book	4.00	10.00	22.00
1100B- **Tricks You Can Do**, 1938, Whitman, 36 pgs., 2 1/2" x 3 1/2", Penny Book	4.00	10.00	22.00
5777- **Tweety and Sylvester, The Magic Voice**, 1976, Whitman, 260 pgs., soft-c, flip-it feature; 5 printings	2.00	5.00	11.00
1104- **Two-Gun Montana**, 1936, Whitman, 432 pgs., Henry E. Vallely-a	11.00	27.50	70.00
nn- **Two-Gun Montana Shoots it Out**, 1939, Whitman, 36 pgs., 2 1/2" x 3 1/2", Penny Book	11.00	27.50	70.00
1058- **Ugly Duckling, The** (Disney), 1939, Whitman, 68 pgs., 5" x 5 1/2", hard-c	14.00	35.00	95.00
nn- **Ugly Duckling, The**, nd (1930s), np (Whitman), 36 pgs., 3" x 2 1/2", Penny Book	4.00	10.00	22.00
Unc' Billy Gets Even (See Wee Little Books)			
1114- **Uncle Don's Strange Adventures**, 1935, Whitman, 300 pgs., radio star-Uncle Don Carney	12.00	30.00	75.00
722- **Uncle Ray's Story of the United States**, 1934, Whitman, 300 pgs.	12.00	30.00	75.00
1461- **Uncle Sam's Sky Defenders**, 1941, Whitman, 432 pgs., flip pictures	11.00	27.50	70.00
1405- **Uncle Wiggily's Adventures**, 1946, Whitman, All Pictures Comics	16.00	40.00	115.00
1411- **Union Pacific**, 1939, Whitman, 240 pgs., photo-c, movie scenes	12.00	30.00	85.00
With Union Pacific letter	57.00	142.00	400.00
1189- **Up Dead Horse Canyon**, 1940, Saalfield, 400 pgs.	10.00	25.00	65.00
1455- **Vic Sands of the U.S. Flying Fortress Bomber Squadron**, 1944, Whitman, 352 pgs.	12.00	30.00	85.00
1645- **Walt Disney's Andy Burnett on the Trail** (TV Series), 1958, Whitman, 280 pgs.	4.00	10.00	27.00
803- **Walt Disney's Bongo**, 1948, Whitman, hard-c, Story Hour Series	12.00	30.00	85.00
711-10-**Walt Disney's Cinderella and the Magic Wand**, 1950, Whitman, 2 1/2" x 5", based on Disney movie	12.00	30.00	75.00
845- **Walt Disney's Donald Duck and his Cat Troubles** (Disney), 1948, Whitman, 100 pgs., 5" x 5 1/2", hard-c	12.00	30.00	85.00
845- **Walt Disney's Donald Duck and the Boys**, 1948, Whitman, 100 pgs., 5" x 5 1/2", hard-c, Barks-a	28.00	70.00	195.00
2952- **Walt Disney's Donald Duck in the Great Kite Maker**, 1949, Whitman, 24 pgs., 3 1/4" x 4", Tiny Tales, full color (5 cents)	11.00	27.50	70.00
804- **Walt Disney's Mickey and the Beanstalk**, 1948, Whitman, hard-c, Story Hour Series	12.00	30.00	85.00
845- **Walt Disney's Mickey Mouse and the Boy Thursday**, 194 pgs., Whitman, 5" x 5 1/2", 100 pgs.	12.00	30.00	85.00
845- **Walt Disney's Mickey Mouse the Miracle Maker**, 1948, Whitman, 5" x 5 1/2", 100 pgs.	12.00	30.00	85.00
2952- **Walt Disney's Mickey Mouse and the Night Prowlers**, Whitman, 1949, 24 pgs., 3 1/4" x 4", Tiny Tales, full color (5 ¢)	11.00	27.50	70.00
5770- **Walt Disney's Mickey Mouse - Mystery at Disneyland**, Whitman, 1975, 260 pgs., four printings	2.00	5.00	13.00
5781-2- **Walt Disney's Mickey Mouse - Mystery at Dead Man's Cove**, Whitman, 1980, 260 pgs., two printings	2.00	5.00	11.00
845- **Walt Disney's Minnie Mouse and the Antique Chair**, 1948, Whitman, 5" x 5 1/2", 100 pgs.	12.00	30.00	85.00
1435- **Walt Disney's Pinocchio and Jiminy Cricket**, 1940, Whitman, 432 pgs.	21.00	52.50	145.00
845- **Walt Disney's Poor Pluto**, 1948, Whitman, 5" x 5 1/2", 100 pgs., hard-c	12.00	30.00	85.00
1467- **Walt Disney's Pluto the Pup** (Disney), 1938, Whitman, 432 pgs., Gottfredson-a	18.00	45.00	125.00
1066- **Walt Disney's Story of Clarabelle Cow** (Disney), 1938, Whitman, 100 pgs.	12.00	30.00	85.00
66- **Walt Disney's Story of Dippy the Goof** (Disney), 1938, Whitman, 100 pgs.	12.00	30.00	85.00
1066- **Walt Disney's Story of Donald Duck** (Disney), 1938, Whitman, 100 pgs., hard-c, Taliaferro-a	12.00	30.00	85.00
1066- **Walt Disney's Story of Mickey Mouse** (Disney), 1938, Whitman, 100 pgs., hard-c, Gottfredson-a, Donald Duck app.	12.00	30.00	85.00
1066- **Walt Disney's Story of Minnie Mouse** (Disney), 1938, Whitman, 100 pgs., hard-c	12.00	30.00	85.00
1066- **Walt Disney's Story of Pluto the Pup**, (Disney), 1938, Whitman, 100 pgs., hard-c	12.00	30.00	85.00
2952- **Walter Lantz Presents Andy Panda's Rescue**, 1949, Whitman, Tiny Tales, full color (5 cents) (1030-5 on back-c)	11.00	27.50	70.00
751- **Wash Tubbs in Pandemonia**, 1934, Whitman, 320 pgs., Roy Crane-a			

1124 - The West Point Five © Saalfield

Xena - Warrior Princess © Universal Studios

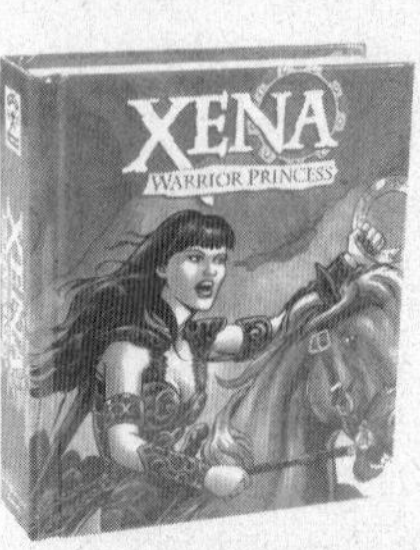

1486 - Zane Grey's King of the Royal Mounted and the Great Jewel Mystery © WHIT

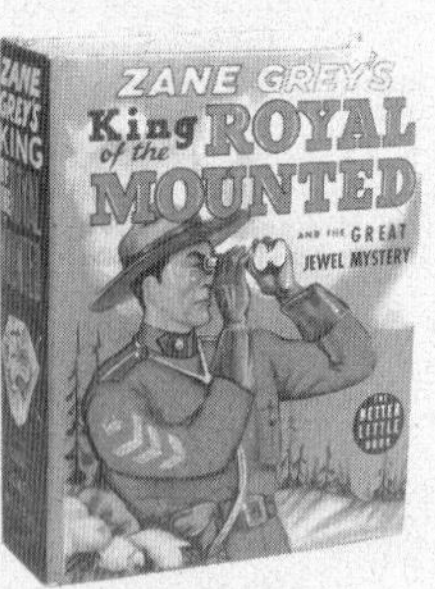

GD FN VF/NM

12.00 30.00 85.00
nn- Wash Tubbs in Pandemonia, 1934, Whitman, 52 pgs., 4" x 5 1/2", premium-no ads, soft-c, Roy Crane-a 20.00 50.00 140.00
1455- Wash Tubbs and Captain Easy Hunting For Whales, 1938, Whitman, 432 pgs., Roy Crane-a 12.00 30.00 85.00
6- Wash Tubbs in Foreign Travel, 1934, Whitman, soft-c, 3 1/2" x 3 1/2", Tarzan Ice Cream cup premium 34.00 85.00 240.00
513- Wee Little Books (In Open Box), 1934, Whitman, 44 pgs., small size, 6 books in set
Child's Garden of Verses 5.00 12.50 30.00
The Happy Prince (The Story of) 5.00 12.50 30.00
Joan of Arc (The Story of) 5.00 12.50 30.00
Peter Pan (The Story of) 5.00 12.50 30.00
Pied Piper Of Hamlin 5.00 12.50 30.00
Robin Hood (A Story of...) 5.00 12.50 30.00
Complete set with box 31.00 78.00 220.00
514- Wee Little Books (In Open Box), 1934, Whitman, 44 pgs., small size, 6 books in set
Jack And Jill 5.00 12.50 30.00
Little Bo-Peep 5.00 12.50 30.00
Little Tommy Tucker 5.00 12.50 30.00
Mother Goose 5.00 12.50 30.00
Old King Cole 5.00 12.50 30.00
Simple Simon 5.00 12.50 30.00
Complete set with box 33.00 83.00 230.00
518- Wee Little Books (In Open Box), 1933, Whitman, 44 pgs., small size, 6 books in set, written by Thornton Burgess
Betty Bear's Lesson-1930 5.00 12.50 30.00
Jimmy Skunk's Justice-1933 5.00 12.50 30.00
Little Joe Otter's Slide-1929 5.00 12.50 30.00
Peter Rabbit's Carrots-1933 5.00 12.50 30.00
Unc' Billy Gets Even-1930 5.00 12.50 30.00
Whitefoot's Secret-1933 5.00 12.50 30.00
Complete set with box 33.00 83.00 230.00
519- Wee Little Books (In Open Box) (Bible Stories), 1934, Whitman, 44 pgs., small size, 6 books in set, Helen Janes-a
The Story of David 5.00 12.50 30.00
The Story of Gideon 5.00 12.50 30.00
The Story of Daniel 5.00 12.50 30.00
The Story of Joseph 5.00 12.50 30.00
The Story of Ruth and Naomi 5.00 12.50 30.00
The Story of Moses 5.00 12.50 30.00
Complete set with box 33.00 83.00 230.00
1471- Wells Fargo, 1938, Whitman, 240 pgs., photo-c, movie scenes 14.00 35.00 95.00
L18- Western Frontier, 1935, Lynn, 192 pgs., starring Ken Maynard, movie scenes 21.00 52.50 145.00
1121- West Pointers on the Gridiron, 1936, Saalfield, 148 pgs., hard-c, sports book 10.00 25.00 65.00
1601- West Pointers on the Gridiron, 1936, Saalfield, 148 pgs., soft-c, sports book 10.00 25.00 65.00
1124- West Point Five, The, 1937, Saalfield, 4 3/4" x 5 1/4", sports book, hard-c 10.00 25.00 65.00
1604- West Point Five, The, 1937, Saalfield, 4 1/4" x 5 1/4", sports book, soft-c 10.00 25.00 65.00
1164- West Point of the Air, 1935, Whitman, 160 pgs., photo-c, movie scenes 12.00 30.00 85.00
18- Westward Ho!, 1935, EVW, 160 pgs., movie scenes, starring John Wayne (Scarce) 71.00 178.00 500.00
1109- We Three, 1935, Saalfield, 160 pgs., photo-c, movie scenes, by John Barrymore, hard-c 11.00 27.50 70.00
1589- We Three, 1935, Saalfield, 160 pgs., photo-c, movie scenes, by John Barrymore, soft-c 11.00 27.50 70.00
Whitefoot's Secret (See Wee Little Books)
nn- Who's Afraid of the Big Bad Wolf, "Three Little Pigs" (Disney), 1933, McKay, 36 pgs., 6" x 8 1/2", stiff-c, Disney studio-a 39.00 98.00 275.00
nn- Wild West Adventures of Buffalo Bill, 1935, Whitman, 260 pgs., Cocomalt premium, soft-c, Hal Arbo-a 15.00 37.50 105.00
1096- Will Rogers, The Story of, 1935, Saalfield, photo-hard-c 12.00 30.00 75.00

GD FN VF/NM

1576- Will Rogers, The Story of, 1935, Saalfield, photo-soft-c 12.00 30.00 75.00
1458- Wimpy the Hamburger Eater, 1938, Whitman, 432 pgs., E.C. Segar-a 24.00 60.00 165.00
1433- Windy Wayne and His Flying Wing, 1942, Whitman, 432 pgs., flip pictures 11.00 27.50 70.00
1131- Winged Four, The, 1937, Saalfield, sports book, hard-c 11.00 27.50 70.00
1407- Wings of the U.S.A., 1940, Whitman, 432 pgs., Thomas Hickey-a 11.00 27.50 70.00
nn- Winning of the Old Northwest, The, 1934, World Syndicate, High Lights of History Series, full color-c 11.00 27.50 70.00
nn- Winning of the Old Northwest, The, 1934, World Syndicate, High Lights of History Series; red & silver-c 11.00 27.50 70.00
1122- Winning Point, The, 1936, Saalfield, (Football), hard-c 9.00 22.50 58.00
1602- Winning Point, The, 1936, Saalfield, soft-c 9.00 22.50 58.00
nn- Wizard of Oz Waddle Book, 1934, BRP, 20 pgs., 7 1/2" x 10", forerunner of the Blue Ribbon Pop-Up books; with 6 removable articulated cardboard characters. Book only 54.00 135.00 375.00
Dust jacket only 61.00 153.00 490.00
Near Mint Complete - $12,500
710-10-Woody Woodpecker Big Game Hunter, 1950, Whitman, by Walter Lantz 10.00 25.00 65.00
2010-(#10)-Woody Woodpecker-The Meteor Menace, 1967, Whitman, 260 pgs., 39¢-c, hard-c, color illos. 4.00 10.00 27.00
5753- Woody Woodpecker-The Meteor Menace, 1973, Whitman, 260 pgs., no price, soft-c, color illos. 1.00 2.50 6.00
2028- Woody Woodpecker-The Sinister Signal, 1969, Whitman 4.00 10.00 22.00
5763- Woody Woodpecker-The Sinister Signal, 1974, Whitman, 1st printing-no price; 2nd printing-39¢-c 1.00 2.50 6.00
23- World of Monsters, The, 1935, EVW, Five Star Library, movie scenes 16.00 40.00 115.00
779- World War in Photographs, The, 1934, Whitman, photo-c, photo illus. 11.00 27.50 70.00
Wyatt Earp (See Hugh O'Brian ...)
nn- Xena - Warrior Princess, 1998, Chronicle Books, 310 pgs., based on TV series, 1-color (purple) illos 1.00 2.50 9.00
nn- Yogi Bear Goes Country & Western, 1977, Modern Promotions, 244 pgs., 49 cents, soft-c, flip pictures 2.00 5.00 13.00
nn- Yogi Bear Saves Jellystone Park, 1977, Modern Promotions, 244 pgs., 49 cents, soft-c, flip pictures 2.00 5.00 13.00
nn- Zane Grey's Cowboys of the West, 1935, Whitman, 148 pgs., 3 3/4" x 4", Tarzan Ice Cream Cup premium, soft-c, Arbo-a 39.00 98.00 275.00
Zane Grey's King of the Royal Mounted (See Men of the Mounted)
1010- Zane Grey's King of the Royal Mounted in Arctic Law, 1937, Whitman, 7 1/4" x 5 1/2", 64 pgs., Nickel Book 15.00 37.50 105.00
1103- Zane Grey's King of the Royal Mounted, 1936, Whitman, 432 pgs. 14.00 35.00 95.00
nn- Zane Grey's King of the Royal Mounted, 1935, Whitman, 260 pgs., Cocomalt premium, soft-c 18.00 45.00 125.00
1179- Zane Grey's King of the Royal Mounted and the Northern Treasure, 1937, Whitman, 432 pgs. 14.00 35.00 95.00
1405- Zane Grey's King of the Royal Mounted the Long Arm of the Law, 1942, Whitman, All Pictures Comics 14.00 35.00 95.00
1452- Zane Grey's King of the Royal Mounted Gets His Man, 1938, Whitman, 432 pgs. 14.00 35.00 95.00
1486- Zane Grey's King of the Royal Mounted and the Great Jewel Mystery, 1939, Whitman, 432 pgs. 14.00 35.00 95.00
5- Zane Grey's King of the Royal Mounted in the Far North, 1938, Whitman, 132 pgs., Buddy Book, soft-c (Rare) 50.00 125.00 350.00
nn- Zane Grey's King of the Royal Mounted in Law of the North, 1939, Whitman, 36 pgs., 2 1/2" x 3 1/2", Penny Book 9.00 22.50 58.00
nn- Zane Grey's King of the Royal Mounted Policing the Frozen North, 1938, Dell, 196 pgs., Fast-Action Story, soft-c 26.00 65.00 180.00
1440- Zane Grey's Tex Thorne Comes Out of the West, 1937, Whitman, 432 pgs. 11.00 27.50 70.00
1465- Zip Saunders King of the Speedway, 1939, 432 pgs., Weisman-a 11.00 27.50 70.00

PROMOTIONAL COMICS

THE MARKETING OF A MEDIUM

by Dr. Arnold T. Blumberg, DCD

with new material and additional research by Sol M. Davidson, PhD, and Robert L. Beerbohm

Everyone wants something for free. It's in our nature to look for the quick fix, the good deal, the complimentary gift. We long to hit the lottery and quit our job, to win the trip around the world, or find that pot of gold at the end of the proverbial rainbow. Collectors in particular are certainly built to appreciate the notion of the "free gift," since it not only means a new item to collect and enjoy, but no risk or obligation in order to acquire it.

Ah, but there's the rub. Because things are not always what they seem, and "free gifts" usually come with a price. As the saying goes, "there's no such thing as a free lunch," so if it seems too good to be true, it probably is. This is the case even in the world of comics, where premiums and giveaways have a familiar agenda hidden behind the bright colors and fanciful stories. But where did it all begin?

Some of the earliest characters that were used as successful tools in promotional comics were Palmer Cox's creation "The Brownies." The illustration shown here showcases them drinking and endorsing Seal Brand Coffee.

EXTRA EXTRA

As we learn more about the early history of the comic book industry through continual investigation and the publishing of articles like those regularly featured in this book, we gain a much greater understanding of the financial and creative forces at work in shaping the medium, but perhaps one of the most intriguing and least recognized factors that influenced the dawn of comics is the concept of the premium or giveaway. (Note: Some of the historical information referenced in this article is derived from material also presented in Robert L. Beerbohm's introductory articles to the Platinum Age and Modern Age sections.)

The birth of the comic book as we know it today is intimately connected with the development of the comic strip in American newspapers and their use as an advertising and marketing tool for staple products such as bread, milk, and cereal. From the very beginning, comic characters have played several roles in pop culture, entertaining the youth of the country while also (sometimes none too subtly) acting as hucksters for whatever corporation foots the bill. From important staples to frivolous material produced simply to make a buck, these products have utilized the comics medium to sell, sell, sell. And what better way to hook a prospective customer than to give them "something for nothing?"

Starting in the 1850s, comics were being used in free almanacs such as **Elton's**, **Hostetter's** and **Wright's** to lure readers for the little booklets to sell patent medicine, farm products, tobacco, shoe polish, etc. Most of these are exceedingly rare today, hence it is difficult to compile an accurate history. More mention of these early precursors can be found in the Victorian Comics Era essay following this one. But although comic characters themselves were already being aggressively merchandised all around the world by the mid-1890s--as with, for example, Palmer Cox's **The Brownies**--the real starting point for the success of comics as a giveaway marketing mechanism can be traced to the introduction of **The Yellow Kid**, Richard Outcault's now legendary newspaper strip.

Newspaper publishers had already recognized that comic strips could boost circulation as well as please sponsors and advertisers by drawing more eyes to the page, so Sunday "supplements" were introduced to entice fans. Outcault's creation cemented the theory with proof of comic characters' marketing and merchandising power.

This unused cover was designed as the second cover for "Motion Picture Funnies Weekly." While the concept for this promotional comic title never caught on, the inaugural issue did feature the origin and first printed appearance of the Sub-Mariner.

Soon after, Outcault (who had most likely been inspired by Cox's merchandising success with **The Brownies** in the first place) caught lightning in a bottle once more with **Buster Brown**, who has the distinction of being America's first nationally licensed comic strip character. Soon, comic strips proliferated throughout the nation's newspapers as tycoons like Hearst and Pulitzer recognized the drawing power of the new medium and fought circulation wars to capture the pennies of the nouveau readership. They paid exorbitant salaries to comic strip artists such as Rudolph Dirks (**Katzenjammer Kids**), and used the funnies as newspaper supplements and as premiums to attract readers. Corporations soon had the chance to license recognizable personas as their own personal pitchmen (or women or animals...). Comic character merchandise wasn't far behind, resulting in a boom of future collectibles now catalogued in volumes like **Hake's Price Guide to Character Toys**.

TWO BIRTHS FOR THE PRICE OF ONE

Comic books themselves were at the heart of this movement, and giveaway and premium collections of comic strips not only appealed to children and adults alike, but provided the impetus for the birth of the modern comic book format itself. It could be said that without the concept of the giveaway comic or the marketing push behind it, there would be no comic book industry as we have it today. Well-known now is the story of how in spring 1933 Harry Wildenberg of Eastern Color Printing Company convinced Proctor & Gamble to sponsor the first modern comic book, **Funnies on Parade**, as a premium. Its success led to the first continuing comic book, **Famous Funnies**, and the rest, as they say, is history.

In 1935, while working on the printing presses of Eastern Color developing how modern comic books get printed, Juliun J. Proskauer came up with an idea for printing "Comic-Books-For-Industry." In July 1936 he made his first sale through his newly formed William C. Popper & Co. to David M. Davies, then advertising manager for Seagram's Distillers Corp. for three million copies of **Seagram's Merrymakers** in time for the 1936-37 Christmas season. "Thus was a new industry born," wrote **Printing News** in August 1945.

Even a casual perusal of the listings in this section of the Guide will dazzle the reader with the endless variety of purposes that this medium has served. Yes, promos have been used to hawk products from athletic equipment to zithers and zip codes, but comics are too versatile an art form to be confined to a few uses. They've swayed elections in cities (**The O'Dwyer Story**, 1949), in states (**Giant for a Day**: Jacob Javits, 1946) and nationwide (**The Story of Harry Truman**, 1948); solicited for charities (**Donald Duck and the Red Feather**, 1948); addressed health issues (**Blondie**, 1949, mental hygiene); discouraged kids from smoking (**Captain America Meets the Asthma Monster**, 1987); coached youngsters in sports skills (**Circling the Bases**, 1947, A.G. Spaulding); explained scientific complexities (**Adventures in Science**, 1946-61, GE); pleaded for social justice (**Consumer Comics**, 1975); espoused religious causes (**Oral Roberts' True Stories**, 1950s); protected the environment (**Our Spaceship Earth**, 1947); encouraged tourism (**Wyoming, The Cowboy State**, 1954); conveyed a sense of history (**Louisiana Purchase**, 1953); taught about computers (**Superman Radio Shack Giveaway**, 1980); trained employees (**Dial Finance Dialogues**, 1961-70) and executives (**Beneficial Finance System, Managing New Employees**, 1950s); cautioned safety (**Willy Wing Flap**, 1944(?)); announced corporate annual results (**Motorola Annual Report**, 1952); defended free enterprise (**Steve Merritt**, 1949); hammered communism (**How Stalin Hopes to Destroy America**, 1951); fought discrimination (**Mammy Yokum & the Great Dogpatch Mystery**, 1956, B'nai Brith); aided young workers in job-hunting (**The Job Scene**, 1969); battled the scourge of sickle cell anemia (**Where's Herbie**, 1972, U.S. H.E.W.); inspired the overcoming of adversity (**Al Capp by Li'l Abner**, 1946); fostered reading (**Linus Gets a Library Card**, 1960); recruited for the armed forces (**Li'l Abner Joins the Navy**, 1950); beguiled readers into

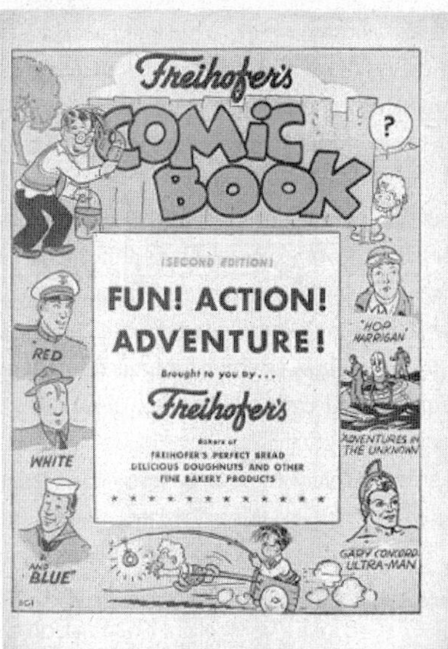

Every market and product has been on the promotional comic book bandwagon. Freihofer's Baking Company distributed a comic in the 1940s that featured reprinted pages from "All-American Comics."

learning languages (**Blondie**, 1949, Philadelphia public schools); and even instructed in such delicate matters as birth control (**Escape from Fear**, 1950 (revised 1959, etc.), for Planned Parenthood).

READ ALL ABOUT IT

The impact of this new approach to advertising was not lost on the business world. Contrary to modern belief, comic books were hardly discounted by the adults of the time...at least not those who had the marketing savvy to recognize an opportunity - or a threat - when they saw one. In the April 1933 issue of **Fortune** magazine, an article titled "The Funny Papers" trumpeted the arrival of comics as a force to be reckoned with in the world of advertising and business, and what's more, a force to fear as well. At first providing a brief survey of the newspaper comic strip business (which for many of the magazine's readers must have seemed a foreign topic for serious discussion), the article goes on to examine the incredible financial draw of comics and their characters:

"Between 70 and 75 per cent {sic} of the readers of any newspaper follow its comic sections regularly...Even the advertiser has succumbed to the comic, and in 1932 spent well over $1,000,000 for comic-paper space."

"**Comic Weekly** is the comic section of seventeen Hearst Sunday papers...Advertisers who market their wares through balloon-speaking manikins {sic} may enjoy the proximity of Jiggs, Maggie, Barney Google, and other funny Hearst headliners."

Although the article continues to cast the notion of relying on comic strip material to sell product in a negative light, actually suggesting that advertisers who utilize comics are violating unspoken rules of "advertising decorum" and bringing themselves "down to the level" of comics (and since when have advertisers been stalwart preservers of good taste and high moral standards), there is no doubt that they are viewing comics in a new light. The comic characters have arrived by 1933...and they're ready to help sell your merchandise too.

Fortune wasn't the only one to take notice as World War II came and went. In 1948, Louis P. Birk, the head of Brevity, Inc., an important promotional comics publisher said, "Comics are serious business." In an article in **Printers' Ink** magazine, he estimated that more than 80 different "comic booklets" had been produced and more than 45,000,000 million copies distributed in the five years before 1948. But of course, comics were serious business long before businessman/historian Birk noted the fact for posterity.

THE MARCH OF WAR AND BEYOND

Through the relentless currents of time, comic strips, books, and the characters that starred in them became more and more an intrinsic part of American culture. During the turmoil of the Great Depression and World War II, comic characters in print and celluloid form entertained while informing and selling at the same time, and premium and giveaway comics came well and truly into their own, pushing everything from loaves of bread to war bonds.

In the 1950s and '60s, there was a shift in focus as the power of giveaway and premium comics was applied to more altruistic endeavors than simply selling something. Comic book format pamphlets, fully illustrated and often inventively written, taught children about banking, money, the dangers of poison and other household products, and even chronicled moments in

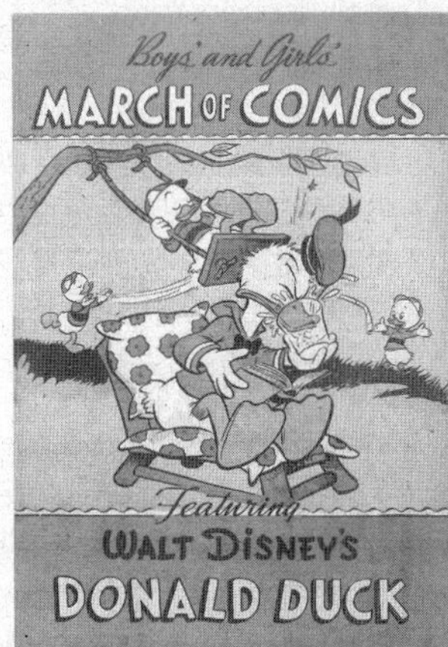

The promotional title "March of Comics" was a prolific comic that ran for 36 years and 488 issues featuring a variety of subjects and characters. (#20 shown)

American history. The comic book as giveaway was now not only a marketing gimmick--it was a tool for educating as well.

The 1970s and '80s saw another boom in premium and giveaway comics. Every product imaginable seemed to have a licensing deal with a comic book character, usually one of the prominent flag bearers of the Big Two, Marvel or DC. Spider-Man fought bravely against the Beetle for the benefit of All Detergent; Captain America allied himself with the Campbell Kids; and Superman helped a class of computer students beat a disaster-conjuring foe at his own game with the help of Radio Shack Tandy computers.

Newspapers rediscovered the power of comics, not just with enlarged strip supplements but with actual comic books. Spider-Man, the Hulk, and others turned up as giveaway comic extras in various American newspapers (including Chicago and Dallas publications), while a whole series of public information comics like those produced decades earlier used superheroes to caution children about the dangers of smoking, drugs, and child abuse.

Comics also turned up in a plethora of other toy products as the 1980s introduced kids to the joy of electronic games and action figures. Supplementary comics provided "free" with action figure and video game packages told the backstory about the product, adding depth to the play experience while providing an extra incentive to buy. Comics became an intrinsic part of the Atari line of video cartridges, for example, eventually spawning its own full-blown newsstand series as well.

As the twentieth century gave way to the twenty-first, giveaway comics were still being produced for inclusion in action figure and video game packages, as well as in conjunction with countless consumer items and corporations. It seems that the medium still has a lot to offer for all those companies desperate to make the most of their market share.

Today, promotional comics continue to be used as a marketing tool to reach both children and adults alike. This 2005 comic was produced by Marvel Comics as a salute to the men and women of the armed forces.

A COMIC BY ANY OTHER NAME

One of the earliest names for promotional comics was "special purpose comics." In their pursuit of superheroes, collectors have allowed promotional comics to lie fallow - underappreciated and uncollected. Without a legitimate name, these products were given sundry other appellations - industrial comics, promos, giveaways, premiums, promics - each accurate but only for a small segment of the unorganized but lusty and lively medium. Perhaps no one name can cover all the variations and purposes of this branch of comic art, but for practical reasons if we accept the general premise that these comics were created to promote an idea, a product or a person, then "Promotional Comics" is probably as convenient a catch-all title as we can come up with.

We used the phrase "for practical reasons" because the word "practical" goes to the heart of promotional comics more than it does for any other comics product. What greater testimony is there to the medium's impact on American culture than to note their use by hard-headed, profit-minded business people and corporations? They invest their money and they expect results.

Today, premium comics continue to thrive and are still utilized as a valuable marketing and promotional tool. "Free" comics are still packaged with action figures and video games, and offered as mail-away premiums from a variety of product manufacturers. The comic industry itself has expanded its use of giveaway comics to self-promote as well, with "ashcan" and other giveaway editions turning up at conventions and comic shops to advertise upcoming series and special events. Many of these function as old-fashioned premiums, with a coupon or other response required from the reader to receive the comic.

As for the supplements and giveaways printed all those years ago, they have spawned a collectible fervor all their own, thanks to their atypical distribution and frequent rarity. For that and the desire to delve deeper into comics history, we hope that by focusing more directly on this genre, we can enhance our understanding of this vital component in the development and history of the modern comic book.

Whether you're a collector or not, we're all motivated by that desire to get something for nothing. For as long as consumers are enticed by the notion of the "free gift," promotional comics will remain a vital marketing component in many business models, but they will also continue to fight the stigma that has long been associated with the industry as a whole. "Respectable" sources like **Fortune** may have taken notice of the power of comic-related advertising 71 years ago, but after all this time comics still fight an uphill battle to establish some measure of dignity for the medium. Perhaps the higher visibility of promotional comics will eventually prove to be a deciding factor in that intellectual war.

See ya in the funny papers.

Action Zone #1 © CBS

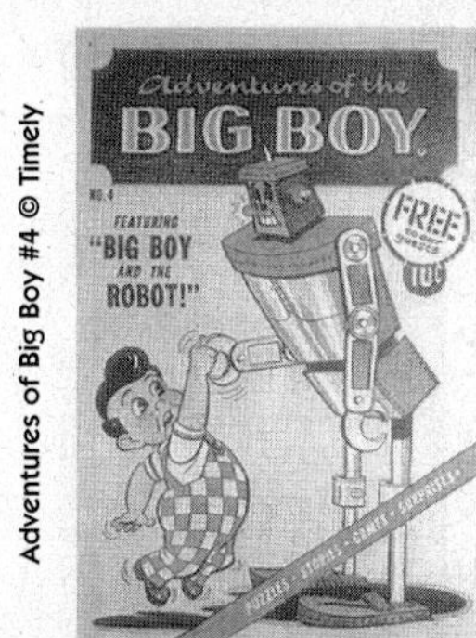

Adventures of Big Boy #4 © Timely

Amazing Spider-Man (Sony Pictures Edition) #50 © MAR

GD 2.0 VG 4.0 FN 6.0 VF 8.0 VF/NM 9.0 NM- 9.2

GD 2.0 VG 4.0 FN 6.0 VF 8.0 VF/NM 9.0 NM- 9.2

ACTION COMICS
DC Comics: 1947 - 1998 (Giveaway)

1 (1976) paper cover w/10¢ price, 16 pgs. in color; reprints complete Superman story from #1 ('38) 3 6 9 21 32 42
1 (1976) Safeguard Giveaway; paper cover w/"free", 16 pgs. in color; reprints complete Superman story from #1 ('38) 3 6 9 21 32 42
1 (1983) paper cover w/10¢ price, 16 pgs. in color; reprints complete Superman story from #1 ('38) 3 6 9 14 20 25
1 (1987 Nestle Quik; 1988, 50¢) 1 2 3 5 7 9
1 (1993)-Came w/Reign of Superman packs 4.00
1 (1998 U.S. Postal Service, $7.95) Reprints entire issue; extra outer half-cover contains First Day Issuance of 32¢ Superman stamp with Sept. 10, 1998 Cleveland, OH postmark 1 2 3 5 6 8
Theater (1947, 32 pgs., 5" x 7", nn)-Vigilante story based on Columbia Vigilante serial; no Superman-c or story 63 126 189 400 688 975

ACTION ZONE
CBS Television: 1994 (Promotes CBS Saturday morning cartoons)

1-WildC.A.T.s, T.M.N.Turtles, Skeleton Warriors stories; Jim Lee-c 4.00

ADVENTURE COMICS
IGA: No date (early 1940s) (Paper-c, 32 pgs.)

Two diff. issues; Super-Mystery-r from 1941 21 42 63 123 204 285

ADVENTURE IN DISNEYLAND
Walt Disney Productions (Dist. by Richfield Oil): May, 1955 (Giveaway, soft-c., 16 pgs)

nn 10 20 30 58 79 100

ADVENTURES @ EBAY
eBay: 2000 (6 3/4" x 4 1/2", 16 pgs.)

1-Judd Winick-a/Rucka & Van Meter-s; intro to eBay comic buying 2.50

ADVENTURES OF BIG BOY (Also titled Adventures of the Big Boy)
Timely Comics/Webs Adv. Corp./Illus. Features: 1956 - Present (Giveaway) (East & West editions of early issues)

1-Everett-c/a 108 216 324 686 1181 1675
2-Everett-c/a 37 74 111 222 361 500
3-5: 4-Robot-c 19 38 57 110 175 240
6-10: 6-Sci/fic issue 10 20 30 68 127 185
11-20: 11,13-DeCarlo-a 7 14 21 44 72 100
21-30 4 8 12 26 41 55
31-50 3 6 9 17 25 32
51-100 2 4 6 9 13 16
101-150 2 4 6 8 10 12
151-240 1 2 3 5 7 9
241-265,267-269,271-300: 6.00
266-Superman x-over 3 6 9 18 27 35
270-TV's Buck Rogers-c/s 3 6 9 14 20 25
301-400 4.00
401-500 3.00
1-(2nd series - '76-'84,Paragon Prod.) (...Shoney's Big Boy) 1 3 4 6 8 10
2-20 5.00
21-50 3.00
Summer, 1959 issue, large size 7 14 21 50 83 115

ADVENTURES OF G. I. JOE
1969 (3-1/4x7") (20 & 16 pgs.)

First Series: 1-Danger of the Depths. 2-Perilous Rescue. 3-Secret Mission to Spy Island. 4-Mysterious Explosion. 5-Fantastic Free Fall. 6-Eight Ropes of Danger. 7-Mouth of Doom. 8-Hidden Missile Discovery. 9-Space Walk Mystery. 10-Fight for Survival. 11-The Shark's Surprise.
Second Series: 2-Flying Space Adventure. 4-White Tiger Hunt. 7-Capture of the Pygmy Gorilla. 12-Secret of the Mummy's Tomb.
Third Series: Reprinted surviving titles of First Series. Fourth Series: 13-Adventure Team Headquarters. 14-Search For the Stolen Idol.
each.... 3 6 9 18 27 35

ADVENTURES OF JELL-O MAN AND WOBBLY, THE
Welsh Publishing Group: 1991 ($1.25)

1 4.00

ADVENTURES OF KOOL-AID MAN
Marvel Comics: 1983 - No. 3, 1985 (Mail order giveaway)
Archie Comics: No. 4, 1987 - No. 8, 1989

1-8: 4-8-Dan DeCarlo-a/c 1 2 3 5 7 9

ADVENTURES OF MARGARET O'BRIEN, THE
Bambury Fashions (Clothes): 1947 (20 pgs. in color, slick-c, regular size) (Premium)

In "The Big City" movie adaptation (scarce) 20 40 60 120 195 270

ADVENTURES OF QUIK BUNNY
Nestle's Quik: 1984 (Giveaway, 32 pgs.)

nn-Spider-Man app. 2 4 6 9 13 16

ADVENTURES OF STUBBY, SANTA'S SMALLEST REINDEER, THE
W. T. Grant Co.: nd (early 1940s) (Giveaway, 12 pgs.)

nn 7 14 21 37 46 55

ADVENTURES OF VOTEMAN, THE
Foundation For Citizen Education Inc.: 1968

nn 4 8 12 28 44 60

ADVENTURES WITH SANTA CLAUS
Promotional Publ. Co. (Murphy's Store): No date (early 50's) (9-3/4x 6-3/4", 24 pgs., giveaway, paper-c)

nn-Contains 8 pgs. ads 6 12 18 29 36 42
16 pg. version 6 12 18 33 41 48

AIR POWER (CBS TV & the U.S. Air Force Presents)
Prudential Insurance Co.: 1956 (5-1/4x7-1/4", 32 pgs., giveaway, soft-c)

nn-Toth-a? Based on 'You Are There' TV program by Walter Cronkite 10 20 30 56 76 95

ALASKA BUSH PILOT
Jan Enterprises: 1959 (Paper cover)

1-Promotes Bush Pilot Club (Value will be based on sale)
NOTE: *A CGC certified 9.9 Mint sold for $632.50 in 2005.*

ALICE IN BLUNDERLAND
Industrial Services: 1952 (Paper cover, 16 pgs. in color)

nn-Facts about government waste and inefficiency 14 28 42 80 115 150

ALICE IN WONDERLAND
Western Printing Company/Whitman Publ. Co.: 1965; 1969; 1982

Meets Santa Claus(1950s), nd, 16 pgs. 6 12 18 28 34 40
Rexall Giveaway(1965, 16 pgs., 5x7-1/4) Western Printing (TV, Hanna-Barbera) 3 6 9 16 23 30
Wonder Bakery Giveaway(1969, 16 pgs, color, nn, nd) (Continental Baking Company) 3 6 9 16 22 28

ALICE IN WONDERLAND MEETS SANTA
No publisher: nd (6-5/8x9-11/16", 16 pgs., giveaway, paper-c)

nn 9 18 27 50 65 80

ALL ABOARD, MR. LINCOLN
Assoc. of American Railroads: Jan, 1959 (16 pgs.)

nn-Abraham Lincoln and the Railroads 6 12 18 28 34 40

ALL NEW COMICS
Harvey Comics: Oct, 1993 (Giveaway, no cover price, 16 pgs.)(Hanna-Barbera)

1-Flintstones, Scooby Doo, Jetsons, Yogi Bear & Wacky Races previews for upcoming Harvey's new Hanna-Barbera line-up 1 2 3 4 5 7
NOTE: *Material previewed in Harvey giveaway was eventually published by Archie.*

AMAZING SPIDER-MAN, THE
Marvel Comics Group

Acme & Dingo Children's Boots (1980)-Spider-Woman app. 2 4 6 11 16 20
Adventures in Reading Starring... (1990,1991) Bogdanove & Romita-c/a 5.00
Aim Toothpaste Giveaway (36 pgs., reg. size)-1 pg. origin recap; Green Goblin-c/story 2 4 6 9 13 16
Aim Toothpaste Giveaway (16 pgs., reg. size)-Dr. Octopus app. 2 4 6 9 13 16
All Detergent Giveaway (1979, 36 pgs.), nn-Origin-r 2 4 6 9 13 16
Amazing Fantasy #15 (8/02) reprint included in Spider-Man DVD Collector's Gift Set 5.00
Amazing Fantasy #15 (2006) News America Marketing newspaper giveaway 4.00
Amazing Spider-Man nn (1990, 6-1/8x9", 28 pgs.)-Shan-Lon giveaway; retells origin of Spider-Man; Bagley-a/Saviuk-c 2 4 6 8 10 12
Amazing Spider-Man nn (1990, 6-1/8x9", 28 pgs.)-Shan-Lon giveaway; reprints Amazing Spider-Man #303 w/McFarlane-c/a 2 4 6 8 10 12
Amazing Spider-Man #1 Reprint (1990, 4-1/4x6-1/4", 28 pgs.)-Packaged with the book "Start Collecting Comic Books" from Running Press 4.00
Amazing Spider-Man #3 Reprint (2004)-Best Buy/Sony giveaway 2.50
Amazing Spider-Man #50 (Sony Pictures Edition) (8/04)-mini-comic included in Spider-Man 2

Amazing Spider-Man & the Incredible Hulk © MAR

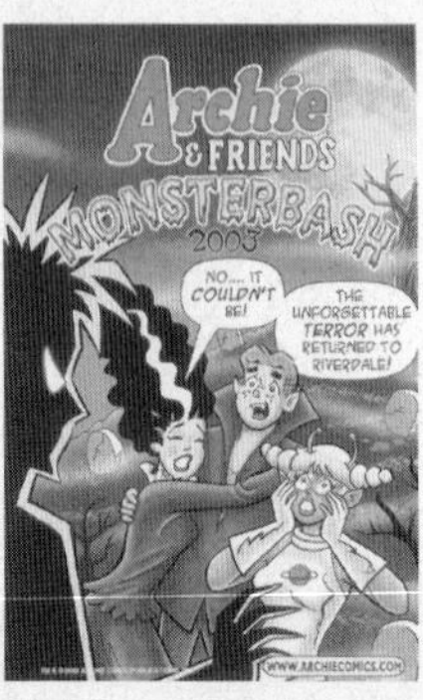

Archie and Friends Monster Bash 2003 © AP

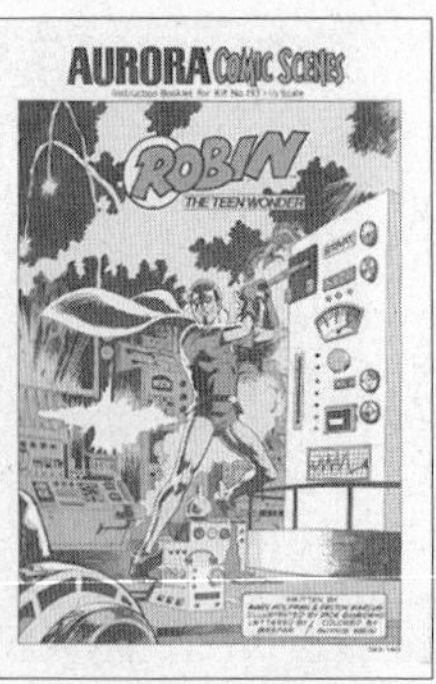

Aurora Comic Scenes Instruction Booklet - Robin © DC

GD 2.0 | VG 4.0 | FN 6.0 | VF 8.0 | VF/NM 9.0 | NM- 9.2

movie DVD Collector's Gift Set; r/#50 & various ASM covers with Dr. Octopus 2.50
Amazing Spider-Man #129 (Lion Gate Films) (6/04)-promotional comic given away at movie theaters on opening night for The Punisher 2.50
...& Power Pack (1984, nn)(Nat'l Committee for Prevention of Child Abuse) (two versions, mail offer & store giveaway)-Mooney-a; Byrne-c
Mail offer 2 4 6 9 11 14
Store giveaway 5.00
...& The Hulk (Special Edition)(6/8/80; 20 pgs.)-Supplement to Chicago Tribune 2 4 6 9 13 16
...& The Incredible Hulk (1981, 1982; 36 pgs.)-Sanger Harris or May D&F supplement to Dallas Times, Dallas Herald, Denver Post, Kansas City Star, Tulsa World; Foley's supplement to Houston Chronicle (1982, 16 pgs.)- "Great Rodeo Robbery"; The Jones Store-giveaway (1983, 16 pgs.) 2 4 6 13 18 22
...and the New Mutants Featuring Skids nn (National Committee for Prevention of Child Abuse/K-Mart giveaway)-Williams-c(i) 5.00
... Battles Ignorance (1992)(Sylvan Learning Systems) giveaway; Mad Thinker app. Kupperberg-a 1 2 3 5 7 9
...Captain America, The Incredible Hulk, & Spider-Woman (1981) (7-11 Stores giveaway; 36 pgs.) 2 4 6 10 14 18
...: Christmas in Dallas (1983) (Supplement to Dallas Times Herald) giveaway 2 4 6 10 14 18
...: Danger in Dallas (1983) (Supplement to Dallas Times Herald) giveaway 2 4 6 10 14 18
...: Danger in Denver (1983) (Supplement to Denver Post) giveaway for May D&F stores 2 4 6 10 14 18
..., Fire-Star, And Ice-Man at the Dallas Ballet Nutcracker (1983; supplement to Dallas Times Herald)-Mooney-p 2 4 6 10 14 18
Giveaway-Esquire Magazine (2/69)-Miniature-Still attached (scarce) 12 24 36 83 172 260
Giveaway-Eye Magazine (2/69)-Miniature-Still attached 10 20 30 65 118 170
...: Riot at Robotworld (1991; 16 pgs.)(National Action Council for Minorities in Engineering, Inc.) giveaway; Saviuk-c 1 2 3 5 6 8
..., Storm & Powerman (1982; 20 pgs.)(American Cancer Society) giveaway; also a 1991 2nd printing and a 1994 printing 1 2 3 5 6 8
...Vs. The Hulk (Special Edition; 1979, 20 pgs.)(Supplement to Columbus Dispatch) 2 4 6 13 18 22
...Vs. The Prodigy (Giveaway, 16 pgs. in color (1976, 5x6-1/2")-Sex education; (1 million printed; 35-50¢) 2 4 6 10 14 18
Spidey & The Mini-Marvels Halloween 2003 Ashcan (12/03, 8 1/2"x 5 1/2") Giarusso-s/a; Venom and Green Goblin app. 2.00

AMERICA MENACED!
Vital Publications: 1950 (Paper-c)
nn-Anti-communism 36 72 108 211 343 475

AMERICAN COMICS
Theatre Giveaways (Liberty Theatre, Grand Rapids, Mich. known): 1940's
Many possible combinations. "Golden Age" superhero comics with new cover added and given away at theaters. Following known: Superman #59, Capt. Marvel #20, 21, Capt. Marvel Jr. #5, Action #33, Classics Comics #8, Whiz #39. Value would vary with book and should be 70-80 percent of the original.

ANDY HARDY COMICS
Western Printing Co.:
...& the New Automatic Gas Clothes Dryer (1952, 5x7-1/4", 16 pgs.) Bendix Giveaway (soft-c) 6 12 18 31 38 45

ANIMANIACS EMERGENCY WORLD
DC Comics: 1995
nn-American Red Cross 4.00

APACHE HUNTER
Creative Pictorials: 1954 (18 pgs. in color) (promo copy) (saddle stitched)
nn-Severin, Heath stories 15 30 45 85 130 175

AQUATEERS MEET THE SUPER FRIENDS
DC Comics: 1979
nn 2 4 6 10 14 18

ARCHIE AND HIS GANG (Zeta Beta Tau Presents...)
Archie Publications: Dec. 1950 (St. Louis National Convention giveaway)
nn-Contains new cover stapled over Archie Comics #47 (11-12/50) on inside; produced for Zeta Beta Tau 20 40 60 114 182 250

ARCHIE COMICS (Also see Sabrina)
Archie Publications
... And Friends and the Shield (10/02, 8 1/2"x 5 1/2") Diamond Comic Dist. 4.00
... And Friends - A Halloween Tale (10/98, 8 1/2"x 5 1/2") Diamond Comic Dist.; Sabrina and Sonic app.; Dan DeCarlo-a 4.00
... And Friends - A Timely Tale (10/01, 8 1/2"x 5 1/2") Diamond Comic Dist. 4.00
... And Friends Monster Bash 2003 (8 1/2"x 5 1/2") Diamond Comic Dist. Halloween 4.00
...And His Friends Help Raise Literacy Awareness In Mississippi nn (3/94) 1 2 3 5 6 8
...And His Friends Vs. The Household Toxic Wastes nn (1993, 16 pgs.) produced for the San Diego Regional Household Hazardous Materials Program 1 2 3 5 6 8
...And His Pals in the Peer Helping Program nn (2/91, 7"x4 1/2") produced by the FBI 1 2 3 5 6 8
...And the History of Electronics nn (5/90, 36 pgs.)-Radio Shack giveaway; Bender-c/a 1 2 3 5 6 8
Fairmont Potato Chips Giveaway-Mini comics 1970 (6 issues-nn's.,6 7/8" x 2 1/4", 8 pgs. each) 3 6 9 19 29 38
Fairmont Potato Chips Giveaway-Mini comics 1971 (4 issues-nn's.,6 7/8" x 5", 8 pgs. each) 3 6 9 19 29 38
Little Archie, The House That Wouldn't Move ('07, 8-1/2" x 5-3/8" Halloween mini-comic) 2.00
Official Boy Scout Outfitter (1946, 9-1/2x6-1/2, 16 pgs.)-B. R. Baker Co. (Scarce) 48 96 144 302 514 725
...'s Ham Radio Adventure (1997) Morse code instruction; Goldberg-a 6.00
...'s Weird Mysteries (9/99, 8 1/2"x 5 1/2") Diamond Comic Dist. Halloween giveaway 3.00
Tales From Riverdale (2006, 8 1/2"x 5 1/2") Diamond Comic Dist. Halloween giveaway 3.00
...: The Dawn of Time ('10, 8-1/2" x 5-3/8" Halloween mini-comic) 3.00
...: The Mystery of the Museum Sleep-In ('08, 8-1/2" x 5-3/8" Halloween mini-comic) 3.00

ARCHIE SHOE-STORE GIVEAWAY
Archie Publications: 1944-50 (12-15 pgs. of games, puzzles, stories like Superman-Tim books, No nos. - came out monthly)

	GD	VG	FN	VF	VF/NM	NM-
(1944-47)-issues	19	38	57	111	176	240
2/48-Peggy Lee photo-c	19	38	57	111	176	240
3/48-Marylee Robb photo-c	16	32	48	94	147	200
4/48-Gloria De Haven photo-c	19	38	57	111	176	240
5/48,6/48,7/48	16	38	48	94	147	200
8/48-Story on Shirley Temple	20	40	60	114	182	250
10/48-Archie as Wolf on cover	17	34	51	100	158	215
5/49-Kathleen Hughes photo-c	15	30	45	86	133	180
7/49	15	30	45	84	127	170
8/49-Archie photo-c from radio show	22	44	66	132	216	300
10/49-Gloria Mann photo-c from radio show	17	34	51	100	158	215
11/49,12/49, 2/50, 3/50	15	30	45	85	130	175

ARCHIE'S JOKE BOOK MAGAZINE (See Joke Book ...)
Archie Publications
Drug Store Giveaway (No. 39 w/new-c) 7 14 21 35 43 50

ARCHIE'S TEN ISSUE COLLECTOR'S SET (Title inside of cover only)
Archie Publications: June, 1997 - No. 10, June, 1997 ($1.50, 20 pgs.)
1-10: 1,7-Archie. 2,8-Betty & Veronica. 3,9-Veronica. 4-Betty. 5-World of Archie. 6-Jughead. 10-Archie and Friends each... 5.00

ASTRO COMICS
American Airlines (Harvey): 1968 - 1979 (Giveaway)(Reprints of Harvey comics)
1968-Richie Rich, Hot Stuff, Casper, Wendy on-c only; Spooky and Nightmare app. inside 4 8 12 24 37 50
1970-Casper, Spooky, Hot Stuff, Stumbo the Giant, Little Audrey, Little Lotta, & Richie Rich reprints. Five different versions 3 6 9 20 30 40
1973,1975,1976: 1973-Three different versions 3 6 9 17 25 32
1977-r/Richie Rich & Casper #20. 1978-r/Richie Rich & Casper #25. 1979-r/Richie Rich & Casper #30 (scarce) 3 6 9 16 23 30

ATARI FORCE
DC Comics: 1982 - No. 5, 1983
1-3 (1982, 5X7", 52 pgs.)-Given away with Atari games 1 2 3 5 6 8
4,5 (1982-1983, 52 pgs.)-Given away with Atari games (scarcer) 2 4 6 9 12 15

AURORA COMIC SCENES INSTRUCTION BOOKLET (Included with superhero model kits)
Aurora Plastics Co.: 1974 (6-1/4x9-3/4," 8 pgs., slick paper)
181-140-Tarzan; Neal Adams-a 3 6 9 18 27 36
182-140-Spider-Man. 4 8 12 24 37 50
183-140-Tonto(Gil Kane art). 184-140-Hulk. 185-140-Superman. 186-140-Superboy. 187-140-Batman. 188-140-The Lone Ranger(1974-by Gil Kane). 192-140-Captain America(1975). 193-140-Robin 3 6 9 16 23 30

BACK TO THE FUTURE

Bionicle #9 © LEGO

Blind Justice © DC

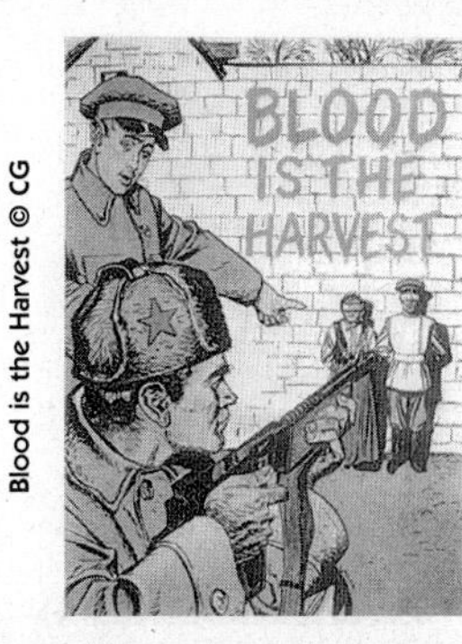

Blood is the Harvest © CG

GD VG FN VF VF/NM NM-
2.0 4.0 6.0 8.0 9.0 9.2

Harvey Comics
Special nn (1991, 20 pgs.)-Brunner-c; given away at Universal Studios in Florida 6.00

BALTIMORE COLTS
American Visuals Corp.: 1950 (Giveaway)
nn-Eisner-c 43 86 129 271 461 650

BAMBI (Disney)
K. K. Publications (Giveaways): 1941, 1942
1941-Horlick's Malted Milk & various toy stores; text & pictures; most copies mailed out with store stickers on-c 43 86 129 271 461 650
1942-Same as 4-Color #12, but no price (Same as '41 issue?) (Scarce) 90 180 270 576 988 1400

BATMAN
DC Comics: 1966 - Present
Act II Popcorn mini-comic(1998) 4.00
Batman #121 Toys R Us edition (1997) r/1st Mr. Freeze 4.00
Batman #279 Mini-comic with Monogram Model kit (1995) 4.00
Batman #362 Mervyn's edition (1989) 5.00
Batman #608 New York Post edition (2002) 4.00
Batman Adventures #25 Best Western edition (1997) 4.00
Batman and Other DC Classics 1 (1989, giveaway)-DC Comics/Diamond Comic Distributors; Batman origin-r/Batman #47, Camelot 3000-r, Justice League-r('87), New Teen Titans-r 5.00
Batman and Robin movie preview (1997, 8 pgs.) Kellogg's Cereal promo 3.00
Batman Beyond Six Flags edition 1 2 3 5 6 8
Batman: Canadian Multiculturalism Custom (1992) 5.00
Batman Claritan edition (1999) 3.00
Kellogg's Poptarts comics (1966, Set of 6, 16 pgs.); All were folded and placed in Poptarts boxes. Infantino art on Catwoman and Joker issues.
"The Man in the Iron Mask", "The Penguin's Fowl Play", "The Joker's Happy Victims", "The Catwoman's Catnapping Caper", "The Mad Hatter's Hat Crimes", "The Case of the Batman II"
each.... 5 10 15 30 48 65
Mask of the Phantasm (1993) Mini-comic released w/video 1 2 3 5 7 9
Onstar - Auto Show Special Edition (OnStar Corp., 2001, 8 pgs.) Riddler app. 3.00
Pizza Hut giveaway (12/77)-exact-r of #122,123; Joker-c/story 2 4 6 9 12 15
Prell Shampoo giveaway (1966, 16 pgs.)- "The Joker's Practical Jokes" (6-7/8x3-3/8") 8 16 24 51 86 120
Revell in pack (1995) 4.00
...: The 10-Cent Adventure (3/02, 10¢) intro. to the "Bruce Wayne: Murderer" x-over; Rucka-s/ Burchett & Janson-a/Dave Johnson-c; these are alternate copies with special outer half-covers (at least 10 different) promoting comics, toys and games shops 3.00

BATMAN RECORD COMIC
National Periodical Publications: 1966 (one-shot)
1-With record (still sealed) 12 24 36 83 172 260
Comic only 8 16 24 58 97 135

BEETLE BAILEY
Charlton Comics: 1969-1970 (Giveaways)
Armed Forces ('69)-same as regular issue (#68) 2 4 6 10 14 18
Armed Forces ('70) 2 4 6 10 14 18
Bold Detergent ('69)-same as regular issue (#67) 2 4 6 10 14 18
Cerebral Palsy Assn. V2#71('69) - V2#73(#1,1/70) 4.00
Red Cross (1969, 5x7", 16 pgs., paper-c) 2 4 6 10 14 18

BELLAIRE BICYCLE CO.
Bellaire Bicycle Co.: 1940 (promotional comic)
nn-Contains Wonderworld #12 w/new-c. Contents can vary w/diff. 1940's books 26 52 78 154 252 350

BEST WESTERN GIVEAWAY
DC Comics: 1999
nn-Best Western hotels 2.50

BETTER LIFE FOR YOU, A
Harvey Publications Inc.: (16 pgs., paper cover)
nn-Better living through higher productivity 3 6 9 16 22 28

BEWARE THE BOOBY TRAP
Malcolm Alter: 1970 (5" x 7")
nn-Deals with drug abuse 4 8 12 24 37 50

B-FORCE (Milwaukee Brewers and Wisconsin Dental Asso.)
Dark Horse Comics: 2001 (School and stadium giveaway)
nn-Brewers players combat the evils of smokeless tobacco 3.00

BIG BOY (see Adventures of...)

BIG JIM'S P.A.C.K.
Mattel, Inc. (Marvel Comics): No date (1975) (16 pgs.)
nn-Giveaway with Big Jim doll; Buscema/Sinnott-c/a 4 8 12 24 37 50

"BILL AND TED'S EXCELLENT ADVENTURE" MOVIE ADAPTATION
DC Comics: 1989 (No cover price)
nn-Torres-a 4.00

BIONICLE (LEGO robot toys)
DC Comics: Jun, 2001 - No. 27, Nov, 2005 ($2.25/$3.25, 16 pages, available to LEGO club members)
1 1 2 3 5 6 8
2-5 6.00
6-13 4.00
14-27 3.00
The Legend of Bionicle (McDonald's Mini-comic, 4-1/4 x 7") 4.00
Special Edition #0 (Six Heroes...One Destiny) '03 San Diego Comic Con; Ashley Wood-c 6.00

BLACK GOLD
Esso Service Station (Giveaway): 1945? (8 pgs. in color)
nn-Reprints from True Comics 6 12 18 27 33 38

BLADE SINS OF THE FATHER
Marvel Comics: Aug, 1996 (24 pgs. with paper cover)
1-Theatrical preview; possibly limited to 2000 copies (Value will be based on sale)

BLAZING FOREST, THE (See Forest Fire and Smokey Bear)
Western Printing: 1962 (20 pgs., 5x7", slick-c)
nn-Smokey The Bear fire prevention 3 6 9 14 20 26

BLESSED PIUS X
Catechetical Guild (Giveaway): No date (Text/comics, 32 pgs., paper-c)
nn 6 12 18 33 41 48

BLIND JUSTICE (Also see Batman: Blind Justice)
DC Comics/Diamond Comic Distributors: 1989 (Giveaway, squarebound)
nn-Contains Detective #598-600 by Batman movie writer Sam Hamm, w/covers; published same time as originals? 6.00

BLONDIE COMICS
Harvey Publications: 1950-1964
1950 Giveaway 8 16 24 40 50 60
1962,1964 Giveaway 3 6 9 16 23 30
N. Y. State Dept. of Mental Hygiene Giveaway-(1950) Regular size; 16 pgs.; no # 4 8 12 24 37 50
N. Y. State Dept. of Mental Hygiene Giveaway-(1956) Regular size; 16 pgs.; no # 3 6 9 17 25 32
N. Y. State Dept. of Mental Hygiene Giveaway-(1961) Regular size; 16 pgs.; no # 3 6 9 16 22 28

BLOOD IS THE HARVEST
Catechetical Guild: 1950 (32 pgs., paper-c)
(Scarce)-Anti-communism (21 known copies) 194 388 582 1242 2121 3000
Black & white version (5 known copies), saddle stitched 94 188 282 597 1024 1450
Untrimmed version (only one known copy); estimated value - $1000
NOTE: *In 1979 nine copies of the color version surfaced from the old Guild's files plus the five black & white copies.*

BLUE BIRD CHILDREN'S MAGAZINE, THE
Graphic Information Service: V1#2, 1957 - No. 10 1958 (16 pgs., soft-c, regular size)
V1#2-10: Pat, Pete & Blue Bird app. 2 4 6 8 11 14

BLUE BIRD COMICS
Various Shoe Stores: 1947 - 1950 (Giveaway, 36 pgs.)
Charlton Comics: 1959 - 1964 (Giveaway)
nn-(1947-50, not Charlton)(36 pgs.)-Several issues; Human Torch, Sub-Mariner app. in some 18 36 54 103 162 220
1959-(Charlton) Lil Genius, Wild Bill Hickok, Black Fury, Masked Raider, Timmy The Timid Ghost, Freddy (All #1) 3 6 9 15 21 26
1959-(Charlton, same 6 titles; all #2-5) except (#5) Masked Raider #21 3 6 9 14 20 25
1959-(#5) Masked Raider #21 3 6 9 16 22 28
1960-(6 titles, all #6-9) Black Fury, Masked Raider, Freddy, Timmy the Timid Ghost, Li'l Genius, Six Gun Heroes 3 6 9 14 19 24

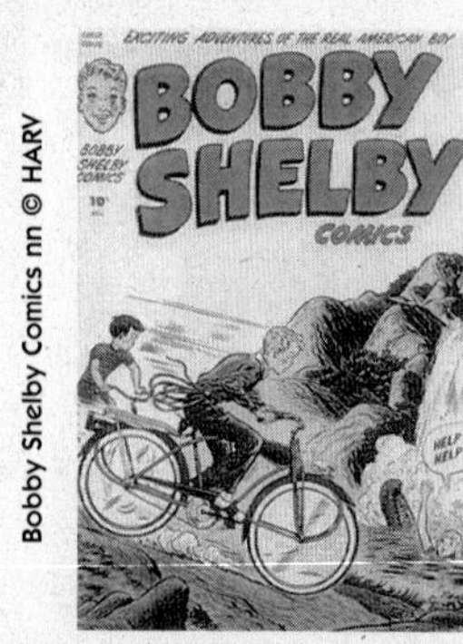

Bobby Shelby Comics nn © HARV

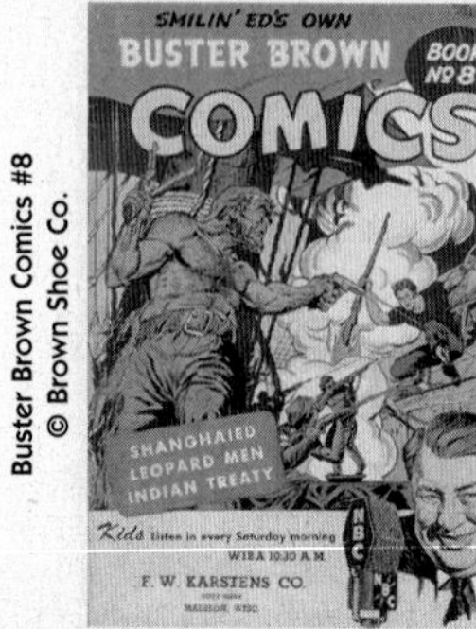

Buster Brown Comics #8 © Brown Shoe Co.

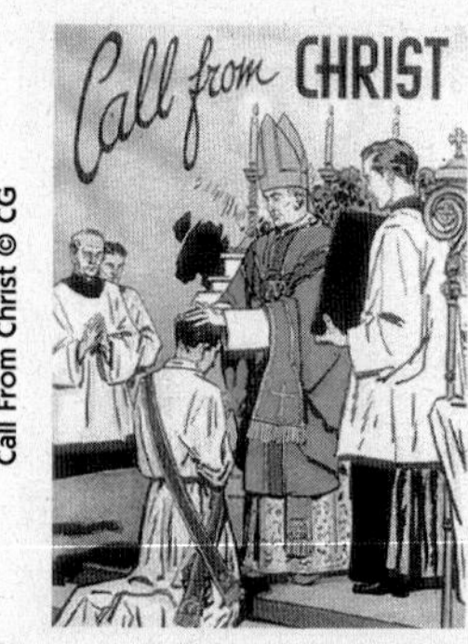

Call From Christ © CG

	GD 2.0	VG 4.0	FN 6.0	VF 8.0	VF/NM 9.0	NM- 9.2
1961-(All #10's) Black Fury, Masked Raider, Freddy, Timmy the Timid Ghost, Li'l Genius, Six Gun Heroes (Charlton)	2	4	6	13	18	22
1961-(All #11-13) Lil Genius, Wyatt Earp, Black Fury, Timmy the Timid Ghost, Atomic Mouse, Freddy	2	4	6	13	18	22
1962-(All #14) Lil Genius, Wyatt Earp, Black Fury, Timmy the Timid Ghost, Atomic Mouse, Freddy	2	4	6	13	18	22
1962-(6 titles, all #15) Lil Genius, Six Gun Heroes, Black Fury, Timmy the Timid Ghost, Texas Rangers, Freddy	2	4	6	13	18	22
1962-(7 titles, all #16) Lil Genius, Six Gun Heroes, Black Fury, Timmy the Timid Ghost, Texas Rangers, Wyatt Earp, Atomic Mouse	2	4	6	13	18	22
1963-(All #17) My Little Margie, Lil Genius, Timmy the Timid Ghost, Texas Rangers (Charlton)	2	4	6	9	13	16
1964-(All #18) Mysteries of Unexplored Worlds, Teenage Hotrodders, War Heroes, Wyatt Earp (Charlton)	2	4	6	9	13	16

NOTE: *Reprints comics of regular issue, with Blue Bird shoe promo on back cover, with upper front cover imprint of various shoe retailers. Printed from 1959 to 1962, with issues 1 thru 16. The 8 different front cover imprints for issues 1 thru 16 are, 1) Blue Bird Shoes, 2) Schiff's Shoes, 3) Big Shoe Store, 4) E.D. Edwards Shoe Store, 5) R & S Shoe store, 6) Federal Shoe Store, 7) Kirby's Shoes, 8) Gallenkamps.*

BOB & BETTY & SANTA'S WISHING WHISTLE
Sears Roebuck & Co.: 1941 (Christmas giveaway, 12 pgs.)

	GD	VG	FN	VF	VF/NM	NM-
nn	15	30	45	85	130	175

BOBBY BENSON'S B-BAR-B RIDERS (Radio)
Magazine Enterprises/AC Comics

	GD	VG	FN	VF	VF/NM	NM-
...in the Tunnel of Gold-(1936, 5-1/4x8"; 100 pgs.) Radio giveaway by Hecker-H.O. Company (H.O. Oats); contains 22 color pgs. of comics, rest in novel form	11	22	33	64	90	115
...And The Lost Herd-same as above	11	22	33	64	90	115

BOBBY SHELBY COMICS
Shelby Cycle Co./Harvey Publications: 1949

	GD	VG	FN	VF	VF/NM	NM-
nn	5	10	14	20	24	28

BONE
Cartoon Books: Halloween, 2008 (8-1/2" x 5-3/8" mini-comic giveaway)

nn-Jeff Smith-s/a 2.00

BOY SCOUT ADVENTURE
Boy Scouts of America: 1954 (16 pgs., paper cover)

	GD	VG	FN	VF	VF/NM	NM-
nn	5	10	14	20	24	28

BOYS' RANCH
Harvey Publications: 1951

	GD	VG	FN	VF	VF/NM	NM-
Shoe Store Giveaway #5,6 (Identical to regular issues except Simon & Kirby centerfold replaced with ad)	14	28	42	76	108	140

BOZO THE CLOWN (TV)
Dell Publishing Co.: 1961

	GD	VG	FN	VF	VF/NM	NM-
Giveaway-1961, 16 pgs., 3-1/2x7-1/4", Apsco Products	5	10	15	32	51	70

BRER RABBIT IN "ICE CREAM FOR THE PARTY"
American Dairy Association: 1955 (5x7-1/4", 16 pgs., soft-c) (Walt Disney) (Premium)

	GD	VG	FN	VF	VF/NM	NM-
nn-(Scarce)	37	74	111	222	361	500

BUCK ROGERS (In the 25th Century)
Kelloggs Corn Flakes Giveaway: 1933 (6x8", 36 pgs)

	GD	VG	FN	VF	VF/NM	NM-
370A-By Phil Nowlan & Dick Calkins; 1st Buck Rogers radio premium & 1st app. in comics (tells origin) (Reissued in 1995)	75	150	225	550	-	-
with envelope	95	190	285	700	-	-

BUGS BUNNY (Puffed Rice Giveaway)
Quaker Cereals: 1949 (32 pgs. each, 3-1/8x6-7/8")

A1-Traps the Counterfeiters, A2-Aboard Mystery Submarine, A3- Rocket to the Moon, A4-Lion Tamer, A5-Rescues the Beautiful Princess, B1-Buried Treasure, B2-Outwits the Smugglers, B3-Joins the Marines, B4-Meets the Dwarf Ghost, B5-Finds Aladdin's Lamp, C1-Lost in the Frozen North, C2-Secret Agent, C3-Captured by Cannibals, C4-Fights the Man from Mars, C5-And the Haunted Cave

	GD	VG	FN	VF	VF/NM	NM-
each....	9	18	27	52	69	85
Mailing Envelope (has illo of Bugs on front)(Each envelope designates what set it contains, A,B or C on front)	9	18	27	52	69	85

BUGS BUNNY (3-D)
Cheerios Giveaway: 1953 (Pocket size) (15 titles)

	GD	VG	FN	VF	VF/NM	NM-
each....	11	22	33	62	86	110
Mailing Envelope (has Bugs drawn on front)	11	22	33	62	86	110

BUGS BUNNY
DC Comics: May, 1997 ($4.95, 24 pgs., comic-sized)

1-Numbered ed. of 100,000; "1st Day of Issue" stamp cancellation on-c 6.00

BUGS BUNNY POSTAL COMIC
DC Comics: 1997 (64 pgs., 7.5" x 5")

nn -Mail Fan; Daffy Duck app. 4.50

BULLETMAN
Fawcett Publications

	GD	VG	FN	VF	VF/NM	NM-
Well Known Comics (1942)-Paper-c, glued binding; printed in red (Bestmaid/Samuel Lowe giveaway)	15	30	45	85	130	175

BULLS-EYE (Cody of The Pony Express No. 8 on)
Charlton: 1955

	GD	VG	FN	VF	VF/NM	NM-
Great Scott Shoe Store giveaway-Reprints #2 with new cover	18	36	54	103	162	220

BUSTER BROWN COMICS (Radio)(Also see My Dog Tige in Promotional sec.)
Brown Shoe Co.: 1945 - No. 43, 1959 (No. 5: paper-c)

	GD	VG	FN	VF	VF/NM	NM-
nn, nd (#1,scarce)-Featuring Smilin' Ed McConnell & the Buster Brown gang "Midnight" the cat, "Squeaky" the mouse & "Froggy" the Gremlin; covers mention diff. shoe stores. Contains adventure stories	60	120	180	381	653	925
2	19	38	57	111	178	245
3,5-10	13	26	39	74	105	135
4 (Rare)-Low print run due to paper shortage	17	34	51	98	154	210
11-20	9	18	27	47	61	75
21-24,26-28	6	12	18	31	38	45
25,33-37,40,41-Crandall-a in all	10	20	30	56	76	95
29-32-"Interplanetary Police Vs. the Space Siren" by Crandall (pencils only #29)	10	20	30	58	79	100
38,39,42,43	6	12	18	31	38	45

BUSTER BROWN COMICS (Radio)
Brown Shoe Co: 1950s

	GD	VG	FN	VF	VF/NM	NM-
...Goes to Mars (2/58-Western Printing), slick-c, 20 pgs., reg. size	13	26	39	74	105	135
...In "Buster Makes the Team!" (1959-Custom Comics)	8	16	24	44	57	70
...In The Jet Age ('50s), slick-c, 20 pgs., 5x7-1/4"	10	20	30	58	79	100
...Of the Safety Patrol ('60-Custom Comics)	3	6	9	18	27	35
...Out of This World ('59-Custom Comics)	7	14	21	35	43	50
...Safety Coloring Book ('58, 16 pgs.)-Slick paper	7	14	21	35	43	50

CALL FROM CHRIST
Catechetical Educational Society: 1952 (Giveaway, 36 pgs.)

	GD	VG	FN	VF	VF/NM	NM-
nn	6	12	18	33	41	48

CANCELLED COMIC CAVALCADE
DC Comics, Inc.: Summer, 1978 - No. 2, Fall, 1978 (8-1/2x11", B&W)
(Xeroxed pgs. on one side only w/blue cover and taped spine)(Only 35 sets produced)

1-(412 pgs.) Contains xeroxed copies of art for: Black Lightning #12, cover to #13; Claw #13,14; The Deserter #1; Doorway to Nightmare #6; Firestorm #6; The Green Team #2,3.

2-(532 pgs.) Contains xeroxed copies of art for: Kamandi #60 (including Omac), #61; Prez #5; Shade #9 (including The Odd Man); Showcase #105 (Deadman), 106 (The Creeper); Secret Society of Super Villains #16 & 17; The Vixen #1; and covers to Army at War #2, Battle Classics #3, Demand Classics #1 & 2, Dynamic Classics #3, Mr. Miracle #26, Ragman #6, Weird Mystery #25 & 26, & Western Classics #1 & 2.

(A FN set of Number 1 & 2 was sold in 2005 for $3680; a VG set sold in 2007 for $2629)

NOTE: *In June, 1978, DC cancelled several of their titles. For copyright purposes, the unpublished original art for these titles was xeroxed, bound in the above books, published and distributed. Only 35 copies were made. Beware of bootleg copies.*

CAP'N CRUNCH COMICS (See Quaker Oats)
Quaker Oats Co.: 1963; 1965 (16 pgs.; miniature giveaways; 2-1/2x6-1/2")

	GD	VG	FN	VF	VF/NM	NM-
(1963 titles)- "The Picture Pirates", "The Fountain of Youth", "I'm Dreaming of a Wide Isthmus". (1965 titles)- "Bewitched, Betwitched, & Betweaked", "Seadog Meets the Witch Doctor", "A Witch in Time"	5	10	15	35	55	75

CAPTAIN ACTION (Toy)
National Periodical Publications

	GD	VG	FN	VF	VF/NM	NM-
...& Action Boy('67)-Ideal Toy Co. giveaway (1st app. Captain Action)	11	22	33	74	145	215

CAPTAIN AMERICA
Marvel Comics Group

	GD	VG	FN	VF	VF/NM	NM-
...& The Campbell Kids (1980, 36pg. giveaway, Campbell's Soup/U.S. Dept. of Energy)	2	4	6	9	13	16
...Goes To War Against Drugs(1990, no #, giveaway)-Distributed to direct sales shops; 2nd printing exists	1	2	3	5	6	8

Captain Marvel and the Lieutenants of Safety #1 © FAW

Cardinal Mindszenty © CG

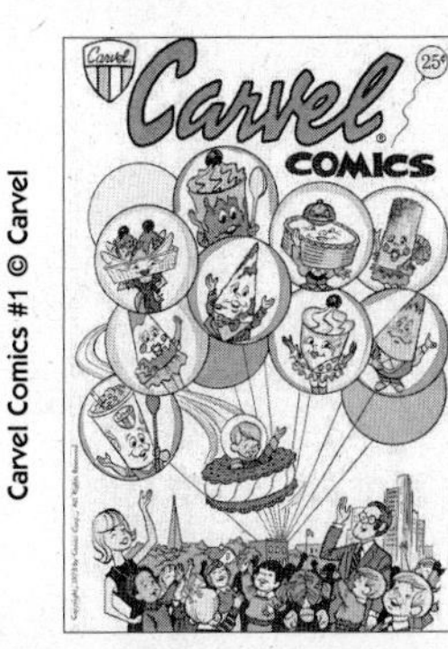

Carvel Comics #1 © Carvel

GD VG FN VF VF/NM NM-
2.0 4.0 6.0 8.0 9.0 9.2

...Meets The Asthma Monster (1987, no #, giveaway, Your Physician and Glaxo, Inc.) 1 2 3 5 6 8
Return of The Asthma Monster Vol. 1 #2 (1992, giveaway, Your Physician & Allen & Hanbury's) 1 2 3 5 6 8
...Vs. Asthma Monster (1990, no #, giveaway, Your Physician & Allen & Hanbury's) 1 2 3 5 6 8

CAPTAIN AMERICA COMICS
Timely/Marvel Comics: 1954
Shoestore Giveaway #77 87 174 261 553 952 1350

CAPTAIN ATOM
Nationwide Publishers
...- Secret of the Columbian Jungle (16 pgs. in color, paper-c, 3-3/4x5-1/8")-
Fireside Marshmallow giveaway 6 12 18 28 34 40

CAPTAIN BEN DIX
Bendix Aviation Corporation: 1943 (Small size)
nn 8 16 24 42 54 65

CAPTAIN BEN DIX IN ACTION WITH THE INVISIBLE CREW
Bendix Aviation Corp.: 1940s (nd), (20 pgs, 8-1/4"x11", heavy paper)
nn-WWII bomber-c; Japanese app. 7 14 21 35 43 50

CAPTAIN BEN DIX IN SECRETS OF THE INVISIBLE CREW
Bendix Aviation Corp.: 1940s (nd), (32 pgs, soft-c)
nn 6 12 18 31 38 45

CAPTAIN FORTUNE PRESENTS
Vital Publications: 1955 - 1959 (Giveaway, 3-1/4x6-7/8", 16 pgs.)
"Davy Crockett in Episodes of the Creek War", "Davy Crockett at the Alamo", "In Sherwood Forest Tells Strange Tales of Robin Hood" ('57), "Meets Bolivar the Liberator" ('59), "Tells How Buffalo Bill Fights the Dog Soldiers" ('57), "Young Davy Crockett" 4 7 9 14 17 20

CAPTAIN GALLANT (...of the Foreign Legion) (TV)
Charlton Comics
Heinz Foods Premium (#1?)(1955; regular size)-U.S. Pictorial; contains Buster Crabbe photos; Don Heck-a 1 3 4 6 8 10
Mailing Envelope 20.00

CAPTAIN JOLLY ADVENTURES
Johnston and Cushing: 1950's, nd (Post Corn Fetti cereal giveaway) (5-1/4" x 4-1/2")
1-3: 1-Captain Jolly Advs. 2-Captain Jolly and His Pirate Crew in Off To Treasure Island. 3-C.J. & His Pirate Crew in The Terror Of The Deep 2 4 5 7 8 10

CAPTAIN MARVEL ADVENTURES
Fawcett Publications
Bond Bread Giveaways-(24 pgs.; pocket size-7-1/4x3-1/2"; paper cover): "...& the Stolen City" ('48), "The Boy Who Never Heard of Capt. Marvel", "Meets the Weatherman" (1950) (reprint) each.... 21 42 63 126 208 290
...Well Known Comics (1944; 12 pgs.; 8-1/2x10-1/2")-printed in red & in blue; soft-c; glued binding - (Bestmaid/Samuel Lowe Co. giveaway) 15 30 45 94 147 200

CAPTAIN MARVEL ADVENTURES (Also see Flash and Funny Stuff)
Fawcett Publications (Wheaties Giveaway): 1945 (6x8", full color, paper-c)
nn- "Captain Marvel & the Threads of Life" plus 2 other stories (32 pgs.) 93 186 372 700 - -
NOTE: *All copies were taped at each corner to a box of Wheaties and are never found in Fine or Mint condition. Prices listed for each grade include tape.*

CAPTAIN MARVEL AND THE LTS. OF SAFETY
Ebasco Services/Fawcett Publications: 1950 - 1951 (3 issues - no No.'s)
nn (#1) "Danger Flies a Kite" ('50, scarce), 58 116 174 371 636 900
nn (#2)"Danger Takes to Climbing" ('50), 47 94 141 296 498 700
nn (#3)"Danger Smashes Street Lights" ('51) 47 94 141 296 498 700

CAPTAIN MARVEL, JR.
Fawcett Publications: (1944; 12 pgs.; 8-1/2x10-1/2")
...Well Known Comics (Printed in blue; paper-c, glued binding)-Bestmaid/Samuel Lowe Co. giveaway 14 28 42 76 108 140

CARDINAL MINDSZENTY (The Truth Behind the Trial of...)
Catechetical Guild Education Society: 1949 (24 pgs., paper cover)
nn-Anti-communism 11 22 33 62 86 110
Press Proof-(Very Rare)-(Full color, 7-1/2x11-3/4", untrimmed)
Only two known copies 300.00
Preview Copy (B&W, stapled), 18 pgs.; contains first 13 pgs. of Cardinal Mindszenty and was sent out as an advance promotion. Only one known copy 300.00 - 400.00
NOTE: *Regular edition also printed in French. There was also a movie released in 1949 called "Guilty of Treason" which is a fact-based account of the trial and imprisonment of Cardinal Mindszenty by the Communist regime in Hungary.*

CARNIVAL OF COMICS
Fleet-Air Shoes: 1954 (Giveaway)
nn-Contains a comic bound with new cover; several combinations possible; Charlton's Eh! known 5 10 15 24 30 35

CARTOON NETWORK
DC Comics: 1997 (Giveaway)
nn-reprints Cow and Chicken, Scooby-Doo, & Flintstones stories 4.00

CARVEL COMICS (Amazing Advs. of Capt. Carvel)
Carvel Corp. (Ice Cream): 1975 - No. 5, 1976 (25¢; #3-5: 35¢) (#4,5: 3-1/4x5")
1-3 1 2 3 5 6 8
4,5(1976)-Baseball theme 2 4 6 8 10 12

CASE OF THE WASTED WATER, THE
Rheem Water Heating: 1972? (Giveaway)
nn-Neal Adams-a 4 8 12 28 44 60

CASPER SPECIAL
Target Stores (Harvey): nd (Dec, 1990) (Giveaway with $1.00 cover)
Three issues-Given away with Casper video 6.00

CASPER, THE FRIENDLY GHOST (Paramount Picture Star...)(2nd Series)
Harvey Publications
American Dental Association (Giveaways):
...'s Dental Health Activity Book-1977 2 4 6 8 11 14
...Presents Space Age Dentistry-1972 2 4 6 9 13 16
..., His Den, & Their Dentist Fight the Tooth Demons-1974 2 4 6 9 13 16
Casper Rides the School Bus (1960, 7x3.5", 16 pgs.) 2 4 6 9 13 16

CELEBRATE THE CENTURY SUPERHEROES STAMP ALBUM
DC Comics: 1998 - No. 5, 2000 (32 pgs.)
1-5: Historical stories hosted by DC heroes 4.00

CENTIPEDE
DC Comics: 1983
1-Based on Atari video game 2 4 6 8 11 14

CENTURY OF COMICS
Eastern Color Printing Co.: 1933 (100 pgs.)
Bought by Wheatena, Malt-O-Milk, John Wanamaker, Kinney Shoe Stores, & others to be used as premiums and radio giveaways. No publisher listed.
nn-Mutt & Jeff, Joe Palooka, etc. reprints 2350 4700 7050 18,000 - -

CHEERIOS PREMIUMS (Disney)
Walt Disney Productions: 1947 (16 titles, pocket size, 32 pgs.)
Mailing Envelope for each set "W,X,Y & Z" (has Mickey illo on front)(each envelope designates the set it contains on the front) 11 22 33 60 83 105
Set "W"
W1-Donald Duck & the Pirates 11 22 33 60 83 105
W2-Bucky Bug & the Cannibal King 7 14 21 37 46 55
W3-Pluto Joins the F.B.I. 7 14 21 37 46 55
W4-Mickey Mouse & the Haunted House 8 16 24 42 54 65
Set "X"
X1-Donald Duck, Counter Spy 11 22 33 60 83 105
X2-Goofy Lost in the Desert 7 14 21 37 46 55
X3-Br'er Rabbit Outwits Br'er Fox 7 14 21 37 46 55
X4-Mickey Mouse at the Rodeo 8 16 24 42 54 65
Set "Y"
Y1-Donald Duck's Atom Bomb by Carl Barks. Disney has banned reprinting this book 76 152 228 483 829 1175
Y2-Br'er Rabbit's Secret 7 14 21 37 46 55
Y3-Dumbo & the Circus Mystery 7 14 21 37 46 55
Y4-Mickey Mouse Meets the Wizard 8 16 24 42 54 65
Set "Z"
Z1-Donald Duck Pilots a Jet Plane (not by Barks) 11 22 33 60 83 105
Z2-Pluto Turns Sleuth Hound 7 14 21 37 46 55
Z3-The Seven Dwarfs & the Enchanted Mtn. 8 16 24 42 54 65
Z4-Mickey Mouse's Secret Room 8 16 24 42 54 65

CHEERIOS 3-D GIVEAWAYS (Disney)
Walt Disney Productions: 1954 (24 titles, pocket size) (Glasses came in envelopes)

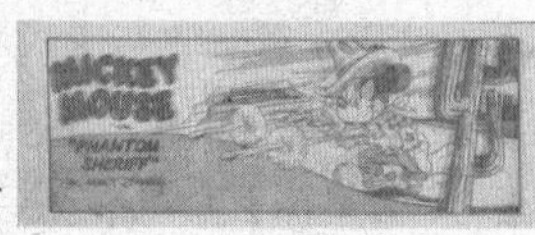

Cheerios 3-D Giveaways - Mickey Mouse, Phantom Sheriff © DIS

Christmas is Coming

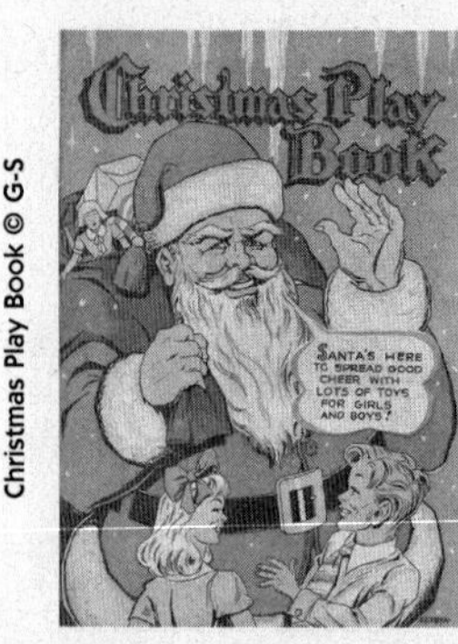

Christmas Play Book © G-S

	GD 2.0	VG 4.0	FN 6.0	VF 8.0	VF/NM 9.0	NM- 9.2
Glasses only...	8	16	24	40	50	60
Mailing Envelope (no art on front)	9	18	27	47	61	75
(Set 1)						
1-Donald Duck & Uncle Scrooge, the Firefighters	9	18	27	52	69	85
2-Mickey Mouse & Goofy, Pirate Plunder	9	18	27	47	61	75
3-Donald Duck's Nephews, the Fabulous Inventors	9	18	27	52	69	85
4-Mickey Mouse, Secret of the Ming Vase	9	18	27	47	61	75
5-Donald Duck with Huey, Dewey, & Louie; ...the Seafarers (title on 2nd page)	9	18	27	52	69	85
6-Mickey Mouse, Moaning Mountain	9	18	27	47	61	75
7-Donald Duck, Apache Gold	9	18	27	52	69	85
8-Mickey Mouse, Flight to Nowhere	9	18	27	47	61	75
(Set 2)						
1-Donald Duck, Treasure of Timbuktu	9	18	27	52	69	85
2-Mickey Mouse & Pluto, Operation China	9	18	27	47	61	75
3-Donald Duck and the Magic Cows	9	18	27	52	69	85
4-Mickey Mouse & Goofy, Kid Kokonut	9	18	27	47	61	75
5-Donald Duck, Mystery Ship	9	18	27	52	69	85
6-Mickey Mouse, Phantom Sheriff	9	18	27	47	61	75
7-Donald Duck, Circus Adventures	9	18	27	52	69	85
8-Mickey Mouse, Arctic Explorers	9	18	27	47	61	75
(Set 3)						
1-Donald Duck & Witch Hazel	9	18	27	52	69	85
2-Mickey Mouse in Darkest Africa	9	18	27	47	61	75
3-Donald Duck & Uncle Scrooge, Timber Trouble	9	18	27	52	69	85
4-Mickey Mouse, Rajah's Rescue	9	18	27	47	61	75
5-Donald Duck in Robot Reporter	9	18	27	52	69	85
6-Mickey Mouse, Slumbering Sleuth	9	18	27	47	61	75
7-Donald Duck in the Foreign Legion	9	18	27	52	69	85
8-Mickey Mouse, Airwalking Wonder	9	18	27	47	61	75
CHESTY AND COPTIE (Disney)						
Los Angeles Community Chest: 1946 (Giveaway, 4pgs.)						
nn-(One known copy) by Floyd Gottfredson	77	154	231	489	845	1200
CHESTY AND HIS HELPERS (Disney)						
Los Angeles War Chest: 1943 (Giveaway, 12 pgs., 5-1/2x7-1/4")						
nn-Chesty & Coptie	50	100	150	315	533	750
CHOCOLATE THE FLAVOR OF FRIENDSHIP AROUND THE WORLD						
The Nestle Company: 1955						
nn	6	12	18	28	34	40
CHRISTMAS ADVENTURE, THE						
S. Rose (H. L. Green Giveaway): 1963 (16 pgs.)						
nn	2	4	6	9	13	16
CHRISTMAS ADVENTURES WITH ELMER THE ELF						
1949 (paper-c)						
nn	4	7	10	14	17	20
CHRISTMAS AT THE ROTUNDA (Titled Ford Rotunda Christmas Book 1957 on) (Regular size)						
Ford Motor Co. (Western Printing): 1954 - 1961 (Given away every Christmas at one location)						
1954-56 issues (nn's)	8	16	24	40	50	60
1957-61 issues (nn's)	7	14	21	35	43	50
CHRISTMAS CAROL, A						
Sears Roebuck & Co.: No date (1942-43) (Giveaway, 32 pgs., 8-1/4x10-3/4", paper cover)						
nn-Comics & coloring book	19	38	57	111	176	240
CHRISTMAS CAROL, A						
Sears Roebuck & Co.: 1940s ? (Christmas giveaway, 20 pgs.)						
nn-Comic book & animated coloring book	18	36	54	105	165	225
CHRISTMAS CAROLS						
Hot Shoppes Giveaway: 1959? (16 pgs.)						
nn	4	8	11	16	19	22
CHRISTMAS COLORING FUN						
H. Burnside: 1964 (20 pgs., slick-c, B&W)						
nn	2	4	6	11	16	20
CHRISTMAS DREAM, A						
Promotional Publishing Co.: 1950 (Kinney Shoe Store Giveaway, 16 pgs.)						
nn	5	10	15	23	28	32
CHRISTMAS DREAM, A						
J. J. Newberry Co.: 1952? (Giveaway, paper cover, 16 pgs.)						
nn	4	8	12	18	22	25
CHRISTMAS DREAM, A						
Promotional Publ. Co.: 1952 (Giveaway, 16 pgs., paper cover)						
nn	4	8	12	18	22	25
CHRISTMAS FUN AROUND THE WORLD						
No publisher: No date (early 50's) (16 pgs., paper cover)						
nn	5	10	15	22	26	30
CHRISTMAS FUN BOOK						
G. C. Murphy Co.: 1950 (Giveaway, paper cover)						
nn-Contains paper dolls	6	12	18	28	34	40
CHRISTMAS IS COMING!						
No publisher: No date (early 50's?) (Store giveaway, 16 pgs.)						
nn	4	8	12	18	22	25
CHRISTMAS JOURNEY THROUGH SPACE						
Promotional Publishing Co.: 1960						
nn-Reprints 1954 issue Jolly Christmas Book with new slick cover	3	6	9	16	23	30
CHRISTMAS ON THE MOON						
W. T. Grant Co.: 1958 (Giveaway, 20 pgs., slick cover)						
nn	8	16	24	44	57	70
CHRISTMAS PLAY BOOK						
Gould-Stoner Co.: 1946 (Giveaway, 16 pgs., paper cover)						
nn	8	16	24	44	57	70
CHRISTMAS ROUNDUP						
Promotional Publishing Co.: 1960						
nn-Marv Levy-c/a	2	4	6	9	13	16
CHRISTMAS STORY CUT-OUT BOOK, THE						
Catechetical Guild: No. 393, 1951 (15¢, 36 pgs.)						
393-Half text & half comics	8	16	24	42	54	65
CHRISTMAS USA (Through 300 Years) (Also see Uncle Sam's...)						
Promotional Publ. Co.: 1956 (Giveaway)						
nn-Marv Levy-c/a	4	7	9	14	16	18
CHRISTMAS WITH SNOW WHITE AND THE SEVEN DWARFS						
Kobackers Giftstore of Buffalo, N.Y.: 1953 (16 pgs., paper-c)						
nn	8	16	24	42	54	65
CHRISTOPHERS, THE						
Catechetical Guild: 1951 (Giveaway, 36 pgs.) (Some copies have 15¢ sticker)						
nn-Stalin as Satan in Hell	22	44	66	128	209	290
CHUCKY JACK'S A-COMIN'						
Great Smoky Mountains Historical Assn., Gatlinburg, TN: 1956 (Reg. size)						
nn-Life of John Sevier, founder of Tennessee	8	16	24	40	50	60
CINDERELLA IN "FAIREST OF THE FAIR" (Walt Disney)						
American Dairy Association (Premium): 1955 (5x7-1/4", 16 pgs., soft-c)						
nn	10	20	30	56	76	95
CINEMA COMICS HERALD						
Paramount Pictures/Universal/RKO/20th Century Fox/Republic:						
1941 - 1943 (4-pg. movie "trailers", paper-c, 7-1/2x10-1/2")(Giveaway)						
"Mr. Bug Goes to Town" (1941)	15	30	45	90	140	190
"Bedtime Story"	11	22	33	64	90	115
"Lady For A Night", John Wayne, Joan Blondell ('42)	18	36	54	107	169	230
"Reap The Wild Wind" (1942)	12	24	36	69	97	125
"Thunder Birds" (1942)	11	22	33	64	90	115
"They All Kissed the Bride"	11	22	33	64	90	115
"Arabian Nights" (nd)	12	24	36	69	97	125
"Bombardie" (1943)	11	22	33	64	90	115
"Crash Dive" (1943)-Tyrone Power	12	24	36	69	97	125
NOTE: *The 1941-42 issues contain line art with color photos. 1943 issues are line art.*						
CLASSICS GIVEAWAYS (Classic Comics reprints)						
12/41–Walter Theatre Enterprises (Huntington, WV) giveaway containing #2 (orig.) w/new generic-c (only 1 known copy)	84	168	252	533	917	1300
1942–Double Comics containing CC#1 (orig.) (diff. cover) (not actually a giveaway) (very rare) (also see Double Comics) (only one known copy)	148	296	444	940	1620	2300

Comic Book Confidential #1 © Sphinx

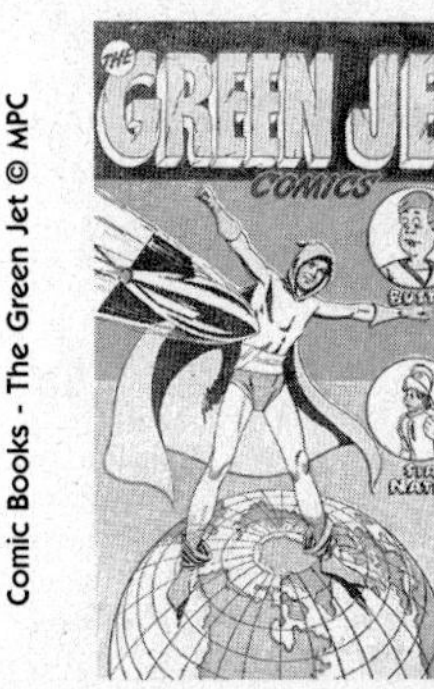

Comic Books - The Green Jet © MPC

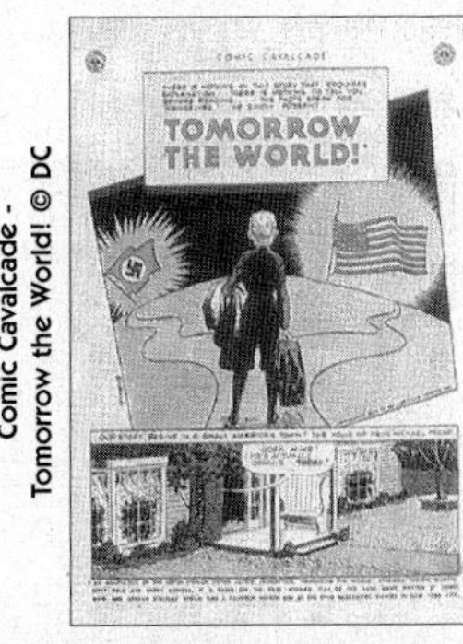

Comic Cavalcade - Tomorrow the World! © DC

	GD 2.0	VG 4.0	FN 6.0	VF 8.0	VF/NM 9.0	NM- 9.2

12/42–Saks 34th St. Giveaway containing CC#7 (orig.) (diff. cover)
(very rare; only 6 known copies) 300 600 900 2011 3506 5000
2/43–American Comics containing CC#8 (orig.) (Liberty Theatre giveaway) (different cover)
(only one known copy) (see American Comics) 97 194 291 616 1058 1500
12/44–Robin Hood Flour Co. Giveaway - #7-CC(R) (diff. cover) (rare)
(edition probably 5 [22]) 155 310 465 984 1692 2400
NOTE: How are above editions determined without CC covers? 1942 is dated 1942, and CC#1-first reprint did not come out until 5/43. 12/42 and 2/43 are determined by blue note at bottom of first text page only in original edition. 12/44 is estimated from page width each reprint edition had progressively slightly smaller page width.

1951–Shelter Thru the Ages (C.I. Educational Series) (actually Giveaway by the Ruberoid Co.) (16 pgs.) (contains original artwork by H. C. Kiefer) (there are 5 diff. back cover ad variations: "Ranch" house ad, "Igloo" ad, "Doll House" ad, "Tree House" ad & blank)
(scarce) 52 104 156 330 565 800
1952–George Daynor Biography Giveaway (CC logo) (partly comic book/pictures/newspaper articles) (story of man who built Palace Depression out of junkyard swamp in NJ) (64 pgs.) (very rare; only 3 known copies, one missing back-c)
360 720 1080 2556 4428 6300
1953–Westinghouse/Dreams of a Man (C.I. Educational Series) (Westinghousebio./ Westinghouse Co. giveaway) (contains original artwork by H. C. Kiefer) (16 pgs.)
(also French/Spanish/Italian versions) (scarce) 47 94 141 296 498 700
NOTE: Reproductions of 1951, 1952, and 1953 exist with color photocopy covers and black & white photocopy interior ("W.C.N. Reprint") 2 4 5 7 8 10

1951-53–Coward Shoe Giveaways (all editions very rare); 2 variations of back-c ad exist:
With back-c photo ad: 5 (87), 12 (89), 22 (85), 32 (85), 49 (85), 69 (87), 72 (no HRN), 80 (0), 91 (0), 92 (0), 96 (0), 98 (0), 100 (0), 101 (0), 103-105 (all Os)
29 58 87 170 278 385
With back-c cartoon ad: 106-109 (all 0s), 110 (111), 112 (0)
31 62 93 184 302 420
1956–Ben Franklin 5-10 Store Giveaway (#65-PC with back cover ad)
(scarce) 24 48 72 142 234 325
1956–Ben Franklin Insurance Co. Giveaway (#65-PC with diff. back cover ad)
(very rare) 47 94 141 296 498 700
11/56–Sealtest Co. Edition - #4 (135) (identical to regular edition except for Sealtest logo printed, not stamped, on front cover) (only two copies known to exist)
28 56 84 165 270 375
1958–Get-Well Giveaway containing #15-CI (new cartoon-type cover) (Pressman Pharmacy)
(only one copy known to exist) 27 54 81 162 266 370
1967-68–Twin Circle Giveaway Editions - all HRN 166, with back cover ad for National Catholic Press.

	GD	VG	FN	VF	VF/NM	NM-
2(R68), 4(R67), 10(R68), 13(R68)	3	6	9	21	32	42
48(R67), 128(R68), 535(576-R68)	4	8	12	22	34	45
16(R68), 68(R67)	5	10	15	30	48	65

12/69–Christmas Giveaway ("A Christmas Adventure") (reprints Picture Parade #4-1953, new cover) (4 ad variations)

	GD	VG	FN	VF	VF/NM	NM-
Stacey's Dept. Store	3	6	9	21	32	42
Anne & Hope Store	5	10	15	32	51	70
Gibson's Dept. Store (rare)	5	10	15	32	51	70
"Merry Christmas" & blank ad space	3	6	9	21	32	42

CLEAR THE TRACK!
Association of American Railroads: 1954 (paper-c, 16 pgs.)

	GD	VG	FN	VF	VF/NM	NM-
nn	5	10	15	22	26	30

CLIFF MERRITT SETS THE RECORD STRAIGHT
Brotherhood of Railroad Trainsmen: Giveaway (2 different issues)

	GD	VG	FN	VF	VF/NM	NM-
...and the Very Candid Candidate by Al Williamson	1	3	4	6	8	10
...Sets the Record Straight by Al Williamson (2 different-c: one by Williamson, the other by McWilliams)	1	3	4	6	8	10

CLYDE BEATTY COMICS (Also see Crackajack Funnies)
Commodore Productions & Artists, Inc.

...African Jungle Book('56)-Richfield Oil Co. 16 pg. giveaway, soft-c
10 20 30 56 76 95

C-M-O COMICS
Chicago Mail Order Co.(Centaur): 1942 - No. 2, 1942 (68 pgs., full color)

1-Invisible Terror, Super Ann, & Plymo the Rubber Man app. (all Centaur costume heroes)
90 180 270 576 988 1400
2-Invisible Terror, Super Ann app. 54 108 162 343 574 825

COCOMALT BIG BOOK OF COMICS
Harry 'A' Chesler (Cocomalt Premium): 1938 (Reg. size, full color, 52 pgs.)

1-(Scarce)-Biro-c/a; Little Nemo by Winsor McCay Jr., Dan Hastings; Jack Cole, Guardineer, Gustavson, Bob Wood-a 226 452 678 1446 2473 3500

COMIC BOOK (Also see Comics From Weatherbird)
American Juniors Shoe: 1954 (Giveaway)

Contains a comic rebound with new cover. Several combinations possible. Contents determine price.

COMIC BOOK CONFIDENTIAL
Sphinx Productions: 1988 (Givewaway, 16 pgs.)

1-Tie-in to a documentary about comic creators; creator biographies; Chester Brown-c 5.00

COMIC BOOK MAGAZINE
Chicago Tribune & other newspapers: 1940 - 1943 (Similar to Spirit sections) (7-3/4x10-3/4"; full color; 16-24 pgs. ea.)

	GD	VG	FN	VF	VF/NM	NM-
1940 issues	7	14	21	37	46	55
1941, 1942 issues	6	12	18	28	34	40
1943 issues	5	10	15	24	30	35

NOTE: *Published weekly. Texas Slim, Kit Carson, Spooky, Josie, Nuts & Jolts, Lew Loyal, Brenda Starr, Daniel Boone, Captain Storm, Rocky, Smokey Stover, Tiny Tim, Little Joe, Fu Manchu appear among others. Early issues had photo stories with pictures from the movies; later issues had comic art.*

COMIC BOOKS (Series 1)
Metropolitan Printing Co. (Giveaway): 1950 (16 pgs.; 5-1/4x8-1/2"; full color; bound at top; paper cover)

	GD	VG	FN	VF	VF/NM	NM-
1-Boots and Saddles; intro The Masked Marshal	6	12	18	28	34	40
1-The Green Jet; Green Lama by Raboy	19	38	57	112	181	250
1-My Pal Dizzy (Teen-age)	4	8	12	18	22	25
1-New World; origin Atomaster (costumed hero)	9	18	27	52	69	85
1-Talullah (Teen-age)	4	8	12	18	22	25

COMIC CAVALCADE
All-American/National Periodical Publications

Giveaway (1944, 8 pgs., paper-c, in color)-One Hundred Years of Co-operation-
r/Comic Cavalcade #9 47 94 141 296 498 700
Giveaway (1945, 16 pgs., paper-c, in color)-Movie "Tomorrow The World" (Nazi theme);
r/Comic Cavalcade #10 61 122 183 390 670 950
Giveaway (c. 1944-45; 8 pgs, paper-c, in color)-The Twain Shall Meet-r/Comic Cavalcade #8
47 94 141 296 498 700

COMIC SELECTIONS (Shoe store giveaway)
Parents' Magazine Press: 1944-46 (Reprints from Calling All Girls, True Comics, True Aviation, & Real Heroes)

	GD	VG	FN	VF	VF/NM	NM-
1	5	10	15	22	26	30
2-6	4	8	11	16	19	22

COMICS FROM WEATHER BIRD (Also see Comic Book, Edward's Shoes, Free Comics to You & Weather Bird)
Weather Bird Shoes: 1954 - 1957 (Giveaway)
Contains a comic bound with new cover. Many combinations possible. Contents would determine price. Some issues do not contain complete comics, but only parts of comics. Value equals 40 to 60 percent of contents.

COMICS READING LIBRARIES (Educational Series)
King Features (Charlton Publ.): 1973, 1977, 1979 (36 pgs. in color) (Giveaways)

	GD	VG	FN	VF	VF/NM	NM-
R-01-Tiger, Quincy	2	4	6	8	11	14
R-02-Beetle Bailey, Blondie & Popeye	2	4	6	10	14	18
R-03-Blondie, Beetle Bailey	2	4	6	8	11	14
R-04-Tim Tyler's Luck, Felix the Cat	3	6	9	16	23	30
R-05-Quincy, Henry	2	4	6	8	11	14
R-06-The Phantom, Mandrake	3	6	9	16	23	30
1977 reprint(R-04)	2	4	6	9	13	16
R-07-Popeye, Little King	2	4	6	13	18	22
R-08-Prince Valiant (Foster), Flash Gordon	3	6	9	18	27	36
1977 reprint	2	4	6	11	16	20
R-09-Hagar the Horrible, Boner's Ark	2	4	6	10	14	18
R-10-Redeye, Tiger	2	4	6	8	11	14
R-11-Blondie, Hi & Lois	2	4	6	8	11	14
R-12-Popeye-Swee'pea, Brutus	2	4	6	13	18	22
R-13-Beetle Bailey, Little King	2	4	6	8	11	14
R-14-Quincy-Hamlet	2	4	6	8	11	14
R-15-The Phantom, The Genius	2	4	6	13	18	22
R-16-Flash Gordon, Mandrake	3	6	9	18	27	36
1977 reprint	2	4	6	10	14	18
Other 1977 editions....	2	4	6	8	10	12
1979 editions (68 pgs.)	2	4	6	8	10	12

NOTE: *Above giveaways available with purchase of $45.00 in merchandise. Used as a reading skills aid for small children.*

COMMANDMENTS OF GOD
Catechetical Guild: 1954, 1958

	GD	VG	FN	VF	VF/NM	NM-
300-Same contents in both editions; diff-c	5	10	15	24	29	34

COMPLIMENTARY COMICS
Sales Promotion Publ.: No date (1950's) (Giveaway)

	GD	VG	FN	VF	VF/NM	NM-
1-Strongman by Powell, 3 stories	8	16	24	40	50	60

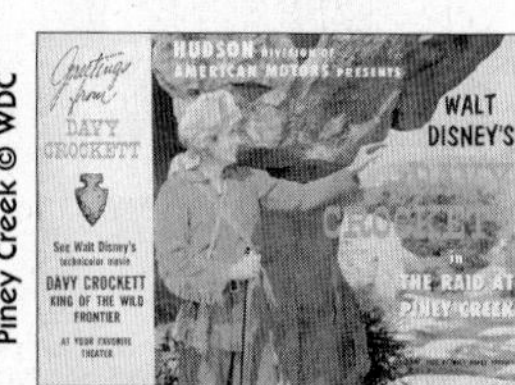

Davy Crockett In the Raid at Piney Creek © WDC

DC Spotlight #1 © DC

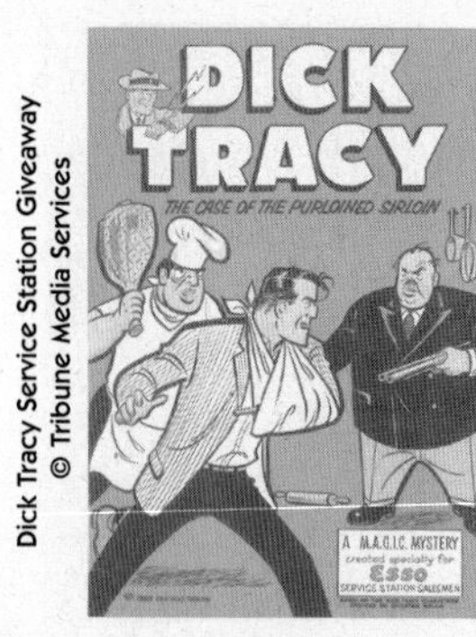

Dick Tracy Service Station Giveaway © Tribune Media Services

	GD 2.0	VG 4.0	FN 6.0	VF 8.0	VF/NM 9.0	NM- 9.2

COPPER - THE OLDEST AND NEWEST METAL
Commercial Comics: 1959
nn 2 4 6 9 12 15

CRACKAJACK FUNNIES (Giveaway)
Malto-Meal: 1937 (Full size, soft-c, full color, 32 pgs.)(Before No. 1?)
nn-Features Dan Dunn, G-Man, Speed Bolton, Buck Jones, The Nebbs, Clyde Beatty, Freckles, Major Hoople, Wash Tubbs 71 142 213 454 777 1100

CRISIS AT THE CARSONS
Pictorial Media: 1958 (Reg. size)
nn 5 10 15 23 28 32

CROSLEY'S HOUSE OF FUN (Also see Tee and Vee Crosley...)
Crosley Div. AVCO Mfg. Corp.: 1950 (Giveaway, paper cover, 32 pgs.)
nn-Strips revolve around Crosley appliances 5 10 15 22 26 30

DAGWOOD SPLITS THE ATOM (Also see Topix V8#4)
King Features Syndicate: 1949 (Science comic with King Features characters) (Giveaway)
nn-Half comic, half text; Popeye, Olive Oyl, Henry, Mandrake, Little King, Katzenjammer Kids app. 9 18 27 52 69 85

DAISY COMICS (Daisy Air Rifles)
Eastern Color Printing Co.: Dec, 1936 (5-1/4x7-1/2")
nn-Joe Palooka, Buck Rogers (2 pgs. from Famous Funnies No. 18, 1st full cover app.), Napoleon Flying to Fame, Butty & Fally 31 62 93 186 301 425

DAISY LOW OF THE GIRL SCOUTS
Girl Scouts of America: 1954, 1965 (16 pgs., paper-c)
1954-Story of Juliette Gordon Low 5 10 15 22 26 30
1965 2 4 6 9 12 15

DAN CURTIS GIVEAWAYS
Western Publishing Co.:1974 (3x6", 24 pgs., reprints)
1-Dark Shadows 3 6 9 16 23 30
2,6-Star Trek 3 6 9 16 23 30
3,4,7-9: 3-The Twilight Zone. 4-Ripley's Believe It or Not! 7-The Occult Files of Dr. Spektor. 8-Dagar the Invincible. 9-Grimm's Ghost Stories 2 4 6 11 16 20
5-Turok, Son of Stone (partial-r/Turok #78) 3 6 9 16 23 30

DANNY AND THE DEMOXICYCLE
Virginia Highway Safety Division: 1970s (Reg. size, slick-c)
nn 3 6 9 20 30 40

DANNY KAYE'S BAND FUN BOOK
H & A Selmer: 1959 (Giveaway)
nn 7 14 21 35 43 50

DAREDEVIL
Marvel Comics Group: 1993
...Vs. Vapora 1 (Engineering Show Giveaway, 16 pg.) - Intro Vapora 6.00

DAVY CROCKETT (TV)
Dell Publishing Co.
...Christmas Book (no date, 16 pgs., paper-c)-Sears giveaway 6 12 18 31 38 45
...Safety Trails (1955, 16pgs, 3-1/4x7")-Cities Service giveaway 8 16 24 40 50 60

DAVY CROCKETT
Charlton Comics
Hunting With... nn ('55, 16 pgs.)-Ben Franklin Store giveaway (Publ.-S. Rose) 5 10 15 24 30 35

DAVY CROCKETT
Walt Disney Prod.: (1955, 16 pgs., 5x7-1/4", slick, photo-c)
...In the Raid at Piney Creek-American Motors giveaway 8 16 24 40 50 60

DC SAMPLER
DC Comics: nn (#1) 1983 - No. 3, 1984 (36 pgs.; 6 1/2" x 10", giveaway)
nn(#1) -3: nn-Wraparound-c, previews upcoming issues. 3-Kirby-a 1 2 3 4 5 7

DC SPOTLIGHT
DC Comics: 1985 (50th anniversary special) (giveaway)
1-Includes profiles on Batman:The Dark Knight & Watchmen 6.00

DEATH JR. HALLOWEEN SPECIAL
Image Comics: Oct, 2006 (8-1/2"x 5-1/2", Halloween giveaway)
nn-Guy Davis-a/Joe Morrisey-s; wraparound-c 2.50

DENNIS THE MENACE
Hallden (Fawcett)
...& Dirt ('59)-Soil Conservation giveaway; r-# 36; Wiseman-c/a 3 6 9 14 20 26
...& Dirt ('68)-reprints '59 edition 2 4 6 8 11 14
...Away We Go('70)-Caladryl giveaway 2 4 6 8 10 12
...Coping with Family Stress-giveaway 2 4 6 8 10 12
...Takes a Poke at Poison('61)-Food & Drug Admin. giveaway; Wiseman-c/a 2 4 6 8 10 12
...Takes a Poke at Poison-Revised 1/66, 11/70 1 2 3 5 6 8
...Takes a Poke at Poison-Revised 1972, 1974, 1977, 1981 1 2 3 4 5 7

DESERT DAWN
E.C./American Museum of Natural History: 1935 (paper-c)
nn-Johnny Jackrabbit stars. Three known copies: A Fair copy (brittle) sold for $657 in 2007. A GD+ copy (brittle) sold for $2300 in 2005. Another Fair copy (brittle) sold for $690 in 2004

DETECTIVE COMICS (Also see other Batman titles)
National Periodical Publications/DC Comics
27 (1984)-Oreo Cookies giveaway (32 pgs., paper-c) r-/Det. #27,#38 & Batman #1 (1st Joker) 5 10 15 35 55 75
38 (1995) Blockbuster Video edition; reprints 1st Robin app. 3.00
38 (1997) Toys R Us edition 3.00
359 (1997) Toys R Us edition; reprints 1st Batgirl app. 3.00
373 (1997, 6 1/4" x 4") Warner Brothers Home Video 3.00

DICK TRACY GIVEAWAYS
1939 - 1958; 1990
Buster Brown Shoes Giveaway (1940s?, 36 pgs. in color); 1938-39-r by Gould 29 58 87 170 278 385
Gillmore Giveaway (See Superbook)
...Hatful of Fun (No date, 1950-52, 32pgs.; 8-1/2x10")-Dick Tracy hat promotion; Dick Tracy games, magic tricks. Miller Bros. premium 15 30 45 90 140 190
Motorola Giveaway (1953)-Reprints Harvey Comics Library #2; "The Case of the Sparkle Plenty TV Mystery" 7 14 21 37 46 55
Original Dick Tracy by Chester Gould, The (Aug, 1990, 16 pgs., 5-1/2x8-1/2")-Gladstone Publ.; Bread Giveaway 1 3 4 6 8 10
Popped Wheat Giveaway (1947, 16 pgs. in color)-1940-r; Sig Feuchtwanger Publ.; Gould-a 4 8 12 18 22 25
...Presents the Family Fun Book; Tip Top Bread Giveaway, no date or number (1940, Fawcett Publ., 16 pgs. in color)-Spy Smasher, Ibis, Lance O'Casey app. 43 86 129 271 461 650
Same as above but without app. of heroes & Dick Tracy on cover only 14 28 42 82 121 160
Service Station Giveaway (1958, 16 pgs. in color)(regular size, slick cover)-Harvey Info. Press 5 10 14 20 24 28
Shoe Store Giveaway (Weatherbird and Triangle Stores)(1939, 16 pgs.)-Gould-a 14 28 42 80 115 150

DICK TRACY SHEDS LIGHT ON THE MOLE
Western Printing Co.: 1949 (16 pgs.) (Ray-O-Vac Flashlights giveaway)
nn-Not by Gould 8 16 24 42 54 65

DICK WINGATE OF THE U.S. NAVY
Superior Publ./Toby Press: 1951; 1953 (no month)
nn-U.S. Navy giveaway 5 10 15 24 30 35
1(1953, Toby)-Reprints nn issue? (same-c) 5 10 14 20 24 28

DIG 'EM
Kellogg's Sugar Smacks Giveaway: 1973 (2-3/8x6", 16 pgs.)
nn-4 different issues 1 3 4 6 8 10

DOC CARTER VD COMICS
Health Publications Institute, Raleigh, N. C. (Giveaway): 1949 (16 pgs. in color) (Paper-c)
nn 19 38 57 110 175 250

DONALD AND MICKEY MERRY CHRISTMAS (Formerly Famous Gang Book Of Comics)
K. K. Publ./Firestone Tire & Rubber Co.: 1943 - 1949 (Giveaway, 20 pgs.)
Put out each Christmas; 1943 issue titled "Firestone Presents Comics" (Disney)
1943-Donald Duck-r/WDC&S #32 by Carl Barks 77 154 231 493 847 1200
1944-Donald Duck-r/WDC&S #35 by Barks 74 148 222 470 810 1150
1945- "Donald Duck's Best Christmas", 8 pgs. Carl Barks; intro. & 1st app. Grandma Duck in comic books 107 214 321 680 1165 1650
1946-Donald Duck in "Santa's Stormy Visit", 8 pgs. Carl Barks

Donald Duck in "The Litterbug" © WDC

Famous Comics nn © UFS

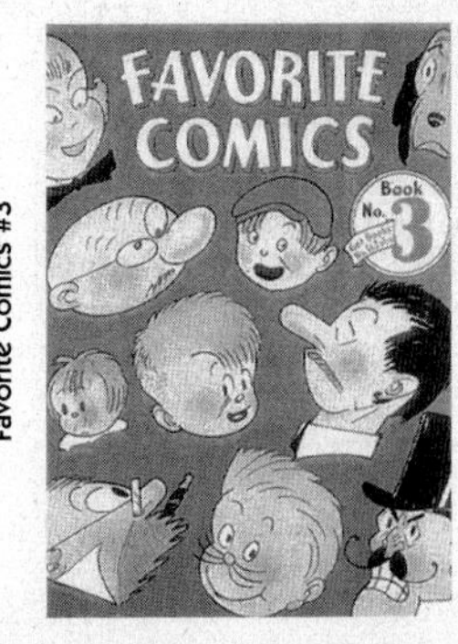

Favorite Comics #3

	GD 2.0	VG 4.0	FN 6.0	VF 8.0	VF/NM 9.0	NM- 9.2
	71	142	213	454	777	1100
1947-Donald Duck in "Three Good Little Ducks", 8 pgs. Carl Barks	71	142	213	454	777	1100
1948-Donald Duck in "Toyland", 8 pgs. Carl Barks	71	142	213	454	777	1100
1949-Donald Duck in "New Toys", 8 pgs. Barks	68	136	204	435	743	1050

DONALD DUCK
K. K. Publications: 1944 (Christmas giveaway, paper-c, 16 pgs.)(2 versions)
nn-Kelly cover reprint 103 206 309 659 1130 1600

DONALD DUCK AND THE RED FEATHER
Red Feather Giveaway: 1948 (8-1/2x11", 4 pgs., B&W)
nn 19 38 57 112 181 250

DONALD DUCK IN "THE LITTERBUG"
Keep America Beautiful: 1963 (5x7-1/4", 16 pgs., soft-c) (Disney giveaway)
nn 5 10 15 34 55 75

DONALD DUCK "PLOTTING PICNICKERS" (See Frito-Lay Giveaway)

DONALD DUCK'S SURPRISE PARTY
Walt Disney Productions: 1948 (16 pgs.) (Giveaway for Icy Frost Twins Ice Cream Bars)
nn-(Rare)-Kelly-c/a 219 438 657 1402 2401 3400

DOT AND DASH AND THE LUCKY JINGLE PIGGIE
Sears Roebuck Co.: 1942 (Christmas giveaway, 12 pgs.)
nn-Contains a war stamp album and a punch out Jingle Piggie bank
12 24 36 67 94 120

DOUBLE TALK (Also see Two-Faces)
Feature Publications: No date (1962?) (32 pgs., full color, slick-c)
Christian Anti-Communism Crusade (Giveaway)
nn-Sickle with blood-c 16 32 48 94 147 200

DRUMMER BOY AT GETTYSBURG
Eastern National Park & Monument Association: 1976
nn-Fred Ray-a 3 6 9 14 20 25

DUMBO (Walt Disney's..., The Flying Elephant)
Weatherbird Shoes/Ernest Kern Co.(Detroit)/ Wieboldt's (Chicago): 1941
(K.K. Publ. Giveaway)
nn-16 pgs., 9x10" (Rare) 42 84 126 265 445 625
nn-52 pgs., 5-1/2x8-1/2", slick cover in color; B&W interior; half text, half reprints 4-Color No. 17 (Dept. store) 22 44 66 131 216 300

DUMBO WEEKLY
Walt Disney Prod.: 1942 (Premium supplied by Diamond D-X Gas Stations)
1 41 82 123 256 428 600
2-16 14 28 42 82 121 160
Binder only 225
NOTE: *A cover and binder came separate at gas stations. Came with membership card.*

EAT RIGHT TO WORK AND WIN
Swift & Company: 1942 (16 pgs.) (Giveaway)
Blondie, Henry, Flash Gordon by Alex Raymond, Toots & Casper, Thimble Theatre(Popeye), Tillie the Toiler, The Phantom, The Little King, & Bringing up Father - original strips just for this book -(in daily strip form which shows what foods we should eat and why)
30 60 90 177 289 400

EDWARD'S SHOES GIVEAWAY
Edward's Shoe Store: 1954 (Has clown on cover)
Contains comic with new cover. Many combinations possible. Contents determines price, 50-60 percent of original. (Similar to Comics From Weatherbird & Free Comics to You)

ELSIE THE COW
D. S. Publishing Co.
Borden's cheese comic picture bk ('40, giveaway) 19 38 57 112 181 250
Borden Milk Giveaway-(16 pgs., nn) (3 ishs, 1957) 14 28 42 81 118 155
Elsie's Fun Book(1950; Borden Milk) 14 28 42 81 118 155
Everyday Birthday Fun With... (1957; 20 pgs.)(100th Anniversary); Kubert-a
14 28 42 81 118 155

ESCAPE FROM FEAR
Planned Parenthood of America: 1956, 1962, 1969 (Giveaway, 8 pgs., color) (On birth control)
1956 edition 11 22 33 60 83 105
1962 edition 4 8 12 24 37 50
1969 edition 3 6 9 14 20 25

EVEL KNIEVEL
Marvel Comics Group (Ideal Toy Corp.): 1974 (Giveaway, 20 pgs.)
nn-Contains photo on inside back-c 4 8 12 28 44 60

GD VG FN VF VF/NM NM-
2.0 4.0 6.0 8.0 9.0 9.2

FAMOUS COMICS (Also see Favorite Comics)
Zain-Eppy/United Features Syndicate: No date; Mid 1930's (24 pgs., paper-c)
nn-Reprinted from 1933 & 1934 newspaper strips in color; Joe Palooka, Hairbreadth Harry, Napoleon, The Nebbs, etc. (Many different versions known)
61 122 183 387 669 950

FAMOUS FAIRY TALES
K. K. Publ. Co.: 1942; 1943 (32 pgs.); 1944 (16 pgs.) (Giveaway, soft-c)
1942-Kelly-a 39 78 117 236 388 540
1943-r-/Fairy Tale Parade No. 2,3; Kelly-a 25 50 75 150 245 340
1944-Kelly-a 22 44 66 131 216 300

FAMOUS FUNNIES - A CARNIVAL OF COMICS
Eastern Color: 1933
36 pgs., no date given, no publisher, no number; contains strip reprints of The Bungle Family, Dixie Dugan, Hairbreadth Harry, Joe Palooka, Keeping Up With the Jones, Mutt & Jeff, Reg'lar Fellers, S'Matter Pop, Strange As It Seems, and others. This book was sold by M. C. Gaines to Wheatena, Malt-O-Milk, John Wanamaker, Kinney Shoe Stores, & others to be given away as premiums and radio giveaways (1933). Originally came with a mailing envelope.
486 972 1458 3550 6275 9000

FAMOUS GANG BOOK OF COMICS (Becomes Donald & Mickey Merry Christmas 1943 on)
Firestone Tire & Rubber Co.: Dec, 1942 (Christmas giveaway, 32 pgs., paper-c)
nn-(Rare)-Porky Pig, Bugs Bunny, Mary Jane & Sniffles, Elmer Fudd; r/Looney Tunes
68 136 204 432 741 1050

FANTASTIC FOUR
Marvel Comics
nn (1981, 32 pgs.) Young Model Builders Club 2 4 6 9 12 15
Vol. 3 #60 Baltimore Comic Book Show (10/02, newspaper supplement) 200,000 copies were distributed to Baltimore Sun home subscribers to promote Baltimore Comic Con 4.00

FATHER OF CHARITY
Catechetical Guild Giveaway: No date (32 pgs.; paper cover)
nn 5 10 15 24 29 34

FAVORITE COMICS (Also see Famous Comics)
Grocery Store Giveaway (Diff. Corp.) (detergent): 1934 (36 pgs.)
Book 1-The Nebbs, Strange As It Seems, Napoleon, Joe Palooka, Dixie Dugan, S'Matter Pop, Hairbreadth Harry, etc. reprints 100 200 300 635 1093 1550
Book 2,3 61 122 183 387 664 940

FAWCETT MINIATURES (See Mighty Midget)
Fawcett Publications: 1946 (3-3/4x5", 12-24 pgs.) (Wheaties giveaways)
Captain Marvel "And the Horn of Plenty"; Bulletman story
16 32 48 94 147 200
Captain Marvel "& the Raiders From Space"; Golden Arrow story
16 32 48 94 147 200
Captain Marvel Jr. "The Case of the Poison Press!" Bulletman story
16 32 48 94 147 200
Delecta of the Planets; C. C. Beck art; B&W inside; 12 pgs.; 3 printing variations (coloring) exist 20 40 60 120 198 275

FEARLESS FOSDICK
Capp Enterprises Inc.: 1951
...& The Case of The Red Feather 6 12 18 27 33 38

FIFTY WHO MADE DC GREAT
DC Comics: 1985 (Reg. size, slick-c)
nn 1 3 4 6 8 10

FIGHT FOR FREEDOM
National Assoc. of Mfgrs./General Comics: 1949, 1951 (Giveaway, 16 pgs.)
nn-Dan Barry-c/a; used in **POP**, pg. 102 6 12 18 31 38 45

FIRE AND BLAST
National Fire Protection Assoc.: 1952 (Giveaway, 16 pgs., paper-c)
nn-Mart Baily A-Bomb-c; about fire prevention 15 30 45 85 130 175

FIRE CHIEF AND THE SAFE OL' FIREFLY, THE
National Board of Fire Underwriters: 1952 (16 pgs.) (Safety brochure given away at schools) (produced by American Visuals Corp.)(Eisner)
nn-(Rare) Eisner-c/a 40 80 120 252 426 600

FLASH, THE
DC Comics
nn-(1990) Brochure for CBS TV series 4.00
The Flash Comes to a Standstill (1981, General Foods giveaway, 8 pages, 3-1/2 x 6-3/4", oblong) 2 4 6 10 14 18

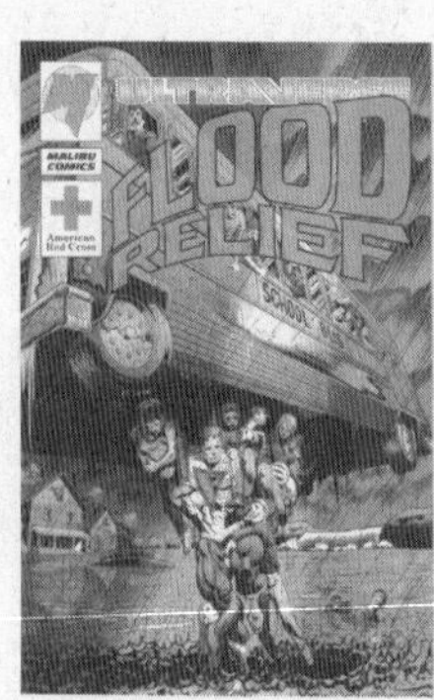

Flood Relief #1 © MAL

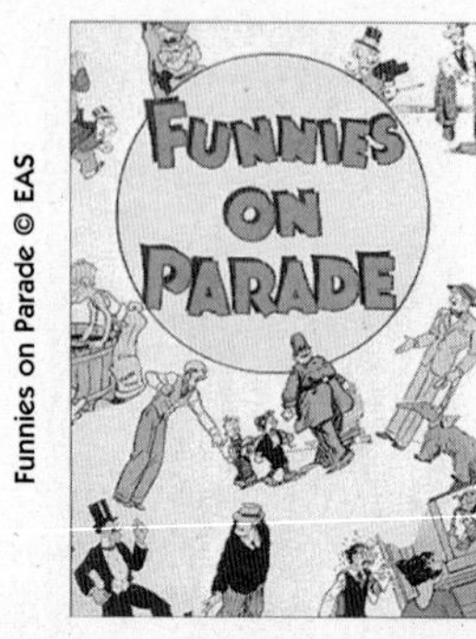

Funnies on Parade © EAS

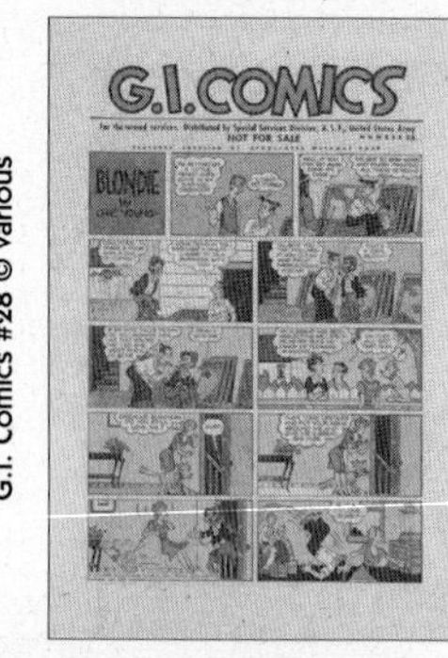

G.I. Comics #28 © various

	GD 2.0	VG 4.0	FN 6.0	VF 8.0	VF/NM 9.0	NM- 9.2
FLASH COMICS (Also see Captain Marvel and Funny Stuff)						
National Periodical Publications: 1946 (6-1/2x8-1/4", 32 pgs.)(Wheaties Giveaway)						
nn-Johnny Thunder, Ghost Patrol, The Flash & Kubert Hawkman app.; Irwin Hasen-c/a	190	380	900	-	-	-
NOTE: *All known copies were taped to Wheaties boxes and are never found in mint condition. Copies with light tape residue bring the listed prices in all grades*						
FLASH FORCE 2000						
DC Comics: 1984						
1-5						6.00
FLASH GORDON						
Dell Publishing Co.: 1943 (20 pgs.)						
Macy's Giveaway-(Rare); not by Raymond	58	116	174	368	634	900
FLASH GORDON						
Harvey Comics: 1951 (16 pgs. in color, regular size, paper-c) (Gordon Bread giveaway)						
1,2: 1-r/strips 10/24/37 - 2/6/38. 2-r/strips 7/14/40 - 10/6/40; Reprints by Raymond each....	2	4	6	10	14	18
NOTE: *Most copies have brittle edges.*						
FLINTSTONES FUN BOOK, THE						
Denny's giveaway: 1990						
1-20	1	2	3	5	6	8
FLOOD RELIEF						
Malibu Comics (Ultraverse): Jan, 1994 (36 pgs.)(Ordered thru mail w/$5.00 to Red Cross)						
1-Hardcase, Prime & Prototype app.						6.00
FOREST FIRE (Also see The Blazing Forest and Smokey Bear)						
American Forestry Assn.(Commerical Comics): 1949 (dated-1950) (16 pgs., paper-c)						
nn-Intro/1st app. Smokey The Forest Fire Preventing Bear; created by Rudy Wendelein; Wendelein/Sparling-a; 'Carter Oil Co.' on back-c of original	18	36	54	103	162	220
FOREST RANGER HANDBOOK						
Wrather Corp.: 1967 (5x7", 20 pgs., slick-c)						
nn-WIth Corey Stuart & Lassie photo-c	2	4	6	13	18	22
FORGOTTEN STORY BEHIND NORTH BEACH, THE						
Catechetical Guild: No date (8 pgs., paper-c)						
nn	5	10	15	23	28	32
FORK IN THE ROAD						
U.S. Army Recruiting Service: 1961 (16 pgs., paper-c)						
nn	2	4	6	11	16	20
48 FAMOUS AMERICANS						
J. C. Penney Co. (Cpr. Edwin H. Stroh): 1947 (Giveaway) (Half-size in color)						
nn - Simon & Kirby-a	10	20	30	58	79	100
FOXHOLE ON YOUR LAWN						
No Publisher: No date						
nn-Charles Biro art	4	7	10	14	17	20
FRANKIE LUER'S SPACE ADVENTURES						
Luer Packing Co.: 1955 (5x7", 36 pgs., slick-c)						
nn - With Davey Rocket	4	8	12	17	21	24
FREDDY						
Charlton Comics						
Schiff's Shoes Presents... #1 (1959)-Giveaway	4	8	11	16	19	22
FREE COMIC BOOK DAY EDITIONS (Now listed in the regular section)						
FREE COMICS TO YOU FROM... (name of shoe store) (Has clown on cover & another with a rabbit) (Like comics from Weather Bird & Edward's Shoes)						
Shoe Store Giveaway: Circa 1956, 1960-61						
Contains a comic bound with new cover - several combinations possible; some Harvey titles known. Contents determine price.						
FREEDOM TRAIN						
Street & Smith Publications: 1948 (Giveaway)						
nn-Powell-c w/mailer	18	36	54	103	162	220
FREIHOFER'S COMIC BOOK						
All-American Comics: 1940s (7 1/2 x 10 1/4")						
2nd edition-(Scarce) Cover features All-American Comics characters Ultra-Man, Hop Harrigan, Red, White and Blue and others	57	114	171	362	619	875
FRIENDLY GHOST, CASPER, THE						
Harvey Publications: 1967 (16 pgs.)						
American Dental Assoc. giveaway-Small size	3	6	9	17	25	32
FRITO-LAY GIVEAWAY						
Frito-Lay: 1962 (3-1/4x7", soft-c, 16 pgs.) (Disney)						
nn-Donald Duck "Plotting Picnickers"	5	10	15	32	51	70
nn-Ludwig Von Drake "Fish Stampede"	3	6	9	20	30	40
nn- Mickey Mouse & Goofy "Bicep Bungle"	4	8	12	22	34	45
FRONTIER DAYS						
Robin Hood Shoe Store (Brown Shoe): 1956 (Giveaway)						
1	4	7	10	14	17	20
FRONTIERS OF FREEDOM						
Institute of Life Insurance: 1950 (Giveaway, paper cover)						
nn-Dan Barry-a	8	16	24	44	57	70
FUNNIES ON PARADE (Premium)(See Toy World Funnies)						
Eastern Color Printing Co.: 1933 (36 pgs., slick cover)						
No date or publisher listed						
nn-Contains Sunday page reprints of Mutt & Jeff, Joe Palooka, Hairbreadth Harry, Reg'lar Fellers, Skippy, & others (10,000 print run). This book was printed for Proctor & Gamble to be given away & came out before Famous Funnies or Century of Comics.	1000	2000	3000	6000	10,500	15,000
FUNNY PICTURE STORIES						
Comics Magazine Co./Centaur Publications: 1930s (Giveaway, 16-20 pgs., slick-c)						
Promotes diff. laundries; has box on cover where "your Laundry Name" is printed	34	68	102	199	325	450
FUNNY STUFF (Also see Captain Marvel & Flash Comics)						
National Periodical Publications (Wheaties Giveaway): 1946 (6-1/2x8-1/4")						
nn-(Scarce)-Dodo & the Frog, Three Mouseketeers, etc.; came taped to Wheaties box; never found in better than fine	135	270	400	–	–	–
FUTURE COP: L.A.P.D. (Electronic Arts video game)						
DC Comics (WildStorm): 1998						
nn-Ron Lim-a/Dave Johnson-c						2.50
GABBY HAYES WESTERN (Movie star)						
Fawcett Publications						
Quaker Oats Giveaway nn's(#1-5, 1951, 2-1/2x7") (Kagran Corp.)-...In Tracks of Guilt, ...In the Fence Post Mystery, ...In the Accidental Sherlock, ...In the Frame-Up, ...In the Double Cross Brand known	10	20	30	54	72	90
Mailing Envelope (has illo of Gabby on front)	10	20	30	54	72	90
GARY GIBSON COMICS (Donut club membership)						
National Dunking Association: 1950 (Included in donut box with pin and card)						
1-Western soft-c, 16 pgs.; folded into the box	5	10	14	20	24	28
GENE AUTRY COMICS						
Dell Publishing Co.						
...Adventure Comics And Play-Fun Book ('47)-32 pgs., 8x6-1/2"; games, comics, magic (Pillsbury premium)	22	44	66	132	216	300
Quaker Oats Giveaway(1950)-2-1/2x6-3/4"; 5 different versions; "Death Card Gang", "Phantoms of the Cave", "Riddle of Laughing Mtn.", "Secret of Lost Valley", "Bond of the Broken Arrow" (came in wrapper) each...	10	20	30	58	79	100
Mailing Envelope (has illo. of Gene on front)	10	20	30	58	79	100
3-D Giveaway(1953)-Pocket-size; 5 different	10	20	30	58	79	100
Mailing Envelope (no art on front)	8	16	24	44	57	70
GENE AUTRY TIM (Formerly Tim) (Becomes Tim in Space)						
Tim Stores: 1950 (Half-size) (B&W Giveaway)						
nn-Several issues (All Scarce)	19	38	57	109	172	235
GENERAL FOODS SUPER-HEROES						
DC Comics: 1979, 1980						
1-4 (1979), 1-4 (1980) each...						12.00
G. I. COMICS (Also see Jeep & Overseas Comics)						
Giveaways: 1945 - No. 73?, 1946 (Distributed to U. S. Armed Forces)						
1-73-Contains Prince Valiant by Foster, Blondie, Smilin' Jack, Mickey Finn, Terry & the Pirates, Donald Duck, Alley Oop, Moon Mullins & Capt. Easy strip reprints (at least 73 issues known to exist)	8	16	24	42	54	65
GOLDEN ARROW						
Fawcett Publications						
...Well Known Comics (1944; 12 pgs.; 8-1/2x10-1/2"; paper-c; glued binding)- Bestmaid/Samuel Lowe giveaway; printed in green	10	20	30	54	72	90

Gulf Funny Weekly #375 © Gulf

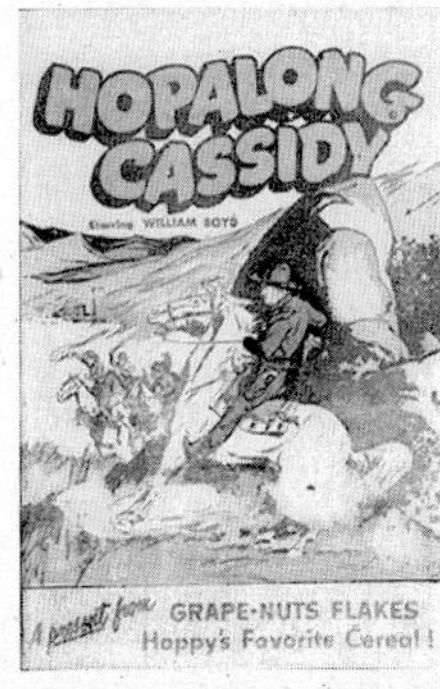

Hopalong Cassidy Grape Nuts Flakes © FAW

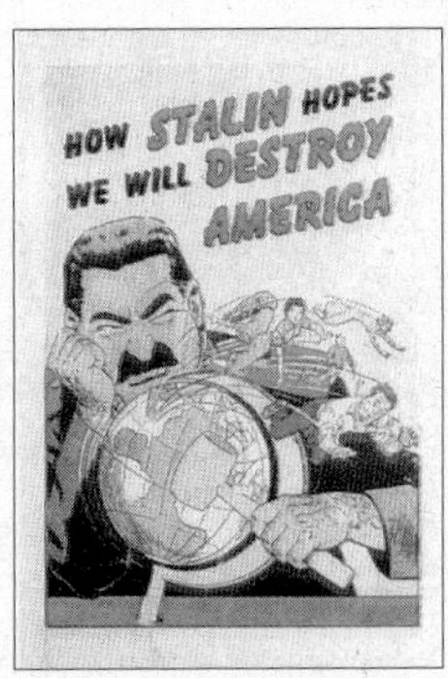

How Stalin Hopes We Will Destroy America © PM

	GD 2.0	VG 4.0	FN 6.0	VF 8.0	VF/NM 9.0	NM- 9.2

GOLDILOCKS & THE THREE BEARS
K. K. Publications: 1943 (Giveaway)
nn 13 26 39 74 105 135

GREAT PEOPLE OF GENESIS, THE
David C. Cook Publ. Co.: No date (Religious giveaway, 64 pgs.)
nn-Reprint/Sunday Pix Weekly 5 10 15 23 28 32

GREAT SACRAMENT, THE
Catechetical Guild: 1953 (Giveaway, 36 pgs.)
nn 5 10 15 22 26 30

GREEN JET COMICS, THE (See Comic Books, Series 1)

GRENADA
Commercial Comics Co.: 1983 (Giveaway produced by the CIA)
1-Air dropped over Grenada during the 1983 invasion 30.00

GRIT (YOU'VE GOT TO HAVE...)
GRIT Publishing Co.: 1959
nn-GRIT newspaper sales recruitment comic; Schaffenberger-a. Later version has altered artwork 5 10 15 22 26 30

GROWING UP WITH JUDY
1952
nn-General Electric giveaway 4 8 12 18 22 25

GULF FUNNY WEEKLY (Gulf Comic Weekly No. 1-4)(See Standard Oil Comics)
Gulf Oil Company (Giveaway): 1933 - No. 422, 5/23/41 (in full color; 4 pgs.; tabloid size to 2/3/39; 2/10/39 on, regular comic book size)(early issues undated)
1 65 130 195 416 708 1000
2-5 30 60 90 177 289 400
6-30 20 40 60 114 182 250
31-100 14 28 42 82 121 160
101-196 10 20 30 58 79 100
197-Wings Winfair begins(1/29/37); by Fred Meagher beginning in 1938 23 46 69 136 223 310
198-300 (Last tabloid size) 14 28 42 82 121 160
301-350 (Regular size) 9 18 27 52 69 85
351-422 8 16 24 42 54 65

GULLIVER'S TRAVELS
Macy's Department Store: 1939, small size
nn-Christmas giveaway 14 28 42 76 108 140

GUN THAT WON THE WEST, THE
Winchester-Western Division & Olin Mathieson Chemical Corp.: 1956 (Giveaway, 24 pgs.)
nn-Painted-c 5 10 15 24 30 35

HAPPINESS AND HEALING FOR YOU (Also see Oral Roberts'...)
Commercial Comics: 1955 (36 pgs., slick cover) (Oral Roberts Giveaway)
nn 9 18 27 52 69 85
NOTE: *The success of this book prompted Oral Roberts to go into the publishing business himself to produce his own material.*

HAPPY TOOTH
DC Comics: 1996
1 3.00

HARLEM YOUTH REPORT (Also see All-Negro Comics and Negro Romances)
Custom Comics, Inc.: 1964 (Giveaway)(No #1-4)
5-"Youth in the Ghetto" and "The Blueprint For Change"; distr. in Harlem only; has map of central Harlem on back-c (scarce) 59 118 177 478 1039 1600

HAWKMAN - THE SKY'S THE LIMIT
DC Comics: 1981 (General Foods giveaway, 8 pages, 3-1/2 x 6-3/4", oblong)
nn 2 4 6 10 14 18

HAWTHORN-MELODY FARMS DAIRY COMICS
Everybody's Publishing Co.: No date (1950's) (Giveaway)
nn-Cheerie Chick, Tuffy Turtle, Robin Koo Koo, Donald & Longhorn Legends 2 4 6 8 11 14

HENRY ALDRICH COMICS (TV)
Dell Publishing Co.
Giveaway (16 pgs., soft-c, 1951)-Capehart radio 3 6 9 17 25 35

HERE IS SANTA CLAUS
Goldsmith Publishing Co. (Kann's in Washington, D.C.): 1930s (16 pgs., 8 in color) (stiff paper covers)
nn 13 26 39 74 105 135

HERE'S HOW AMERICA'S CARTOONISTS HELP TO SELL U.S. SAVINGS BONDS
Harvey Comics: 1950? (16 pgs., giveaway, paper cover)
Contains: Joe Palooka, Donald Duck, Archie, Kerry Drake, Red Ryder, Blondie & Steve Canyon 19 38 57 112 181 250

HISTORY OF GAS
American Gas Assoc.: Mar, 1947 (Giveaway, 16 pgs.)
nn-Miss Flame narrates 7 14 21 35 43 50

HOME DEPOT, SAFETY HEROES
Marvel Comics.: Oct, 2005 (Giveaway)
nn-Spider-Man and the Fantastic Four on the cover; Olliffe-a/c; Roseman-s 2.50

HONEYBEE BIRDWHISTLE AND HER PET PEPI (Introducing...)
Newspaper Enterprise Assoc.: 1969 (Giveaway, 24 pgs., B&W, slick cover)
nn-Contains Freckles newspaper strips with a short biography of Henry Fornhals (artist) & Fred Fox (writer) of the strip 4 8 12 28 44 60

HOODS UP
Fram Corp.: 1953 (15¢, distributed to service station owners, 16 pgs.)
1-(Very Rare; only 2 known); Eisner-c/a in all (a CGC 9.0 copy sold for $1840 in 2006)
2-6-(Very Rare; only 1 known of #3, 2 known of #2,4) 48 96 144 302 514 725
NOTE: *Convertible Connie gives tips for service stations, selling Fram oil filters.*

HOOKED (Anti-drug comic distributed at NYC methadone clinics)
U.S. Dept. of Health: 1966 (giveaway, oblong)
nn-Distributed between May and July, 1966 3 6 9 20 30 40

HOPALONG CASSIDY
Fawcett Publications
Grape Nuts Flakes giveaway (1950,9x6") 14 28 42 78 112 145
...& the Mad Barber (1951 Bond Bread giveaway)-7x5"; used in **SOTI**, pgs. 308,309 18 36 54 103 162 220
...Meets the Brend Brothers Bandits (1951 Bond Bread giveaway, color, paper-c, 16 pgs., 3-1/2x7")- Fawcett Publ. 9 18 27 47 61 75
...Strange Legacy (1951 Bond Bread giveaway) 9 18 27 47 61 75
White Tower Giveaway (1946, 16pgs., paper-c) 9 18 27 52 69 85

HOPPY THE MARVEL BUNNY (WELL KNOWN COMICS)
Fawcett Publications: 1944 (8-1/2x10-1/2", paper-c)
Bestmaid/Samuel Lowe (printed in red or blue) 10 20 30 56 76 95

HOT STUFF, THE LITTLE DEVIL
Harvey Publications (Illustrated Humor):1963
Shoestore Giveaway 4 8 12 22 34 45

HOW KIDS ENJOY NEW YORK
American Airlines: 1966 (Giveaway, 40 pgs., 4x9")
nn-Includes 8 color pages by Bob Kane featuring a tour of New York and his studio (a VG copy sold for $180 and a FN+ sold for $250 in 2004)

HOW STALIN HOPES WE WILL DESTROY AMERICA
Joe Lowe Co. (Pictorial Media): 1951 (Giveaway, 16 pgs.)
nn 41 82 123 256 428 600

HURRICANE KIDS, THE (Also See Magic Morro, The Owl, Popular Comics #45)
R.S. Callender: 1941 (Giveaway, 7-1/2x5-1/4", soft-c)
nn-Will Ely-a. 8 16 24 44 57 70

IF THE DEVIL WOULD TALK
Roman Catholic Catechetical Guild/Impact Publ.: 1950; 1958 (32 pgs.; paper cover; in full color)
nn-(Scarce)-About secularism (20-30 copies known to exist); very low distribution 82 164 246 521 898 1275
1958 Edition-(Impact Publ.); art & script changed to meet church criticism of earlier edition; 80 plus copies known to exist 30 60 90 177 289 400
Black & White version of nn edition; small size; only 4 known copies exist 34 68 102 199 325 450
NOTE: *The original edition of this book was printed and killed by the Guild's board of directors. It is believed that a very limited number of copies were distributed. The 1958 version was a complete bomb with very limited, if any, circulation. In 1979, 11 original, 4 1958 reprints, and 4 B&W's surfaced from the Guild's old files in St. Paul, Minnesota.*

IN LOVE WITH JESUS
Catechetical Educational Society: 1952 (Giveaway, 36 pgs.)
nn 7 14 21 37 46 55

Is This Tomorrow? © CG

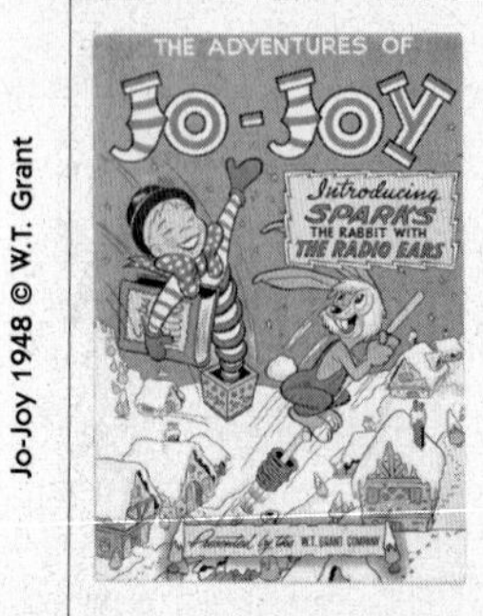

Jo-Joy 1948 © W.T. Grant

Kasco Komics #2 © Kasko

	GD	VG	FN	VF	VF/NM	NM-
	2.0	4.0	6.0	8.0	9.0	9.2

INTERSTATE THEATRES' FUN CLUB COMICS
Interstate Theatres: Mid 1940's (10¢ on cover) (B&W cover) (Premium)
Cover features MLJ characters looking at a copy of Top-Notch Comics, but contains an early Detective Comic on inside; many combinations possible 11 22 33 60 83 105

IN THE GOOD HANDS OF THE ROCKEFELLER TEAM
Country Art Studios: No date (paper cover, 8 pgs.)
nn-Joe Simon-a 8 16 24 42 54 65

IRON GIANT
DC Comics: 1999 (4 pages, theater giveaway)
1-Previews movie 3.00

IRON HORSE GOES TO WAR, THE
Association of American Railroads: 1960 (Giveaway, 16 pgs.)
nn-Civil War & railroads 3 6 9 14 20 25

IRON MAN
Marvel Comics
Marvel Halloween Ashcan 2007 (8-1/2" x 5-3/8") updated origin; Michael Golden-c 2.00

IS THIS TOMORROW?
Catechetical Guild: 1947 (One Shot) (3 editions) (52 pgs.)
1-Theme of communists taking over the USA; (no price on cover) Used in **POP**, pg. 102 26 52 78 154 252 350
1-(10¢ on cover) 28 56 84 165 270 375
1-Has blank circle with no price on cover 30 60 90 177 289 400
Black & White advance copy titled "Confidential" (52 pgs.)-Contains script and art edited out of the color edition, including one page of extreme violence showing mob nailing a Cardinal to a door; (only two known copies). A VF+ sold in 2/08 for $3346. A NM 9.6 sold in 1/07 for $5975
NOTE: *The original color version first sold for 10 cents. Since sales were good, it was later printed as a giveaway. Approximately four million in total were printed. The two black and white copies listed plus two other versions as well as a full color untrimmed version surfaced in 1979 from the Guild's old files in St. Paul, Minnesota.*

IT'S FUN TO STAY ALIVE
National Automobile Dealers Association: 1948 (Giveaway, 16 pgs., heavy stock paper)
Featuring: Bugs Bunny, The Berrys, Dixie Dugan, Elmer, Henry, Tim Tyler, Bruce Gentry, Abbie & Slats, Joe Jinks, The Toodles, & Cokey; all art copyright 1946-48 drawn especially for this book 15 30 45 86 133 180

IT'S TIME FOR REASON - NOT TREASON
Liberty Lobby: 1967 (Reg. size, soft-c) (Anti-communist)
nn 7 14 21 44 72 100

JACK AND CHUCK LEARN THE HARD WAY
Commercia Comics/Wagner Electric Co.: 1950s (Reg. size, soft-c)
nn-Automotive giveaway 9 18 27 47 61 75

JACK & JILL VISIT TOYTOWN WITH ELMER THE ELF
Butler Brothers (Toytown Stores): 1949 (Giveaway, 16 pgs., paper cover)
nn 5 10 15 22 26 30

JACK ARMSTRONG (Radio)(See True Comics)
Parents' Institute: 1949
12-Premium version (distr. in Chicago only); Free printed on upper right-c; no price (Rare) 18 36 54 107 169 230

JACKIE JOYNER KERSEE IN HIGH HURDLES (Kellogg's Tony's Sports Comics)
DC Comics: 1992 (Sports Illustrated)
nn 5.00

JACKPOT OF FUN COMIC BOOK
DCA Food Ind.: 1957, giveaway
nn-Features Howdy Doody 11 22 33 64 90 115

JEDLICKA SHOES
DC Comics: 1961 (Funny animal-c)
nn-Contains Superman #14 9 18 27 60 100 150

JEEP COMICS
R. B. Leffingwell & Co.: 1945 - 1946
1-46 (Giveaways)-Strip reprints in all; Tarzan, Flash Gordon, Blondie, The Nebbs, Little Iodine, Red Ryder, Don Winslow, The Phantom, Johnny Hazard, Katzenjammer Kids; distr. to U.S. Armed Forces from 1945-1946 6 12 18 31 38 45

JINGLE BELLS CHRISTMAS BOOK
Montgomery Ward (Giveaway): 1971 (20 pgs., B&W inside, slick-c)
nn 6.00

	GD	VG	FN	VF	VF/NM	NM-
	2.0	4.0	6.0	8.0	9.0	9.2

JOAN OF ARC
Catechetical Guild (Topix) (Giveaway): No date (28 pgs., blank back-c)
nn-Ingrid Bergman photo-c; Addison Burbank-a 12 24 36 69 97 125
NOTE: *Unpublished version exists which came from the Guild's files.*

JOE PALOOKA (2nd Series)
Harvey Publications
...Body Building Instruction Book (1958 B&M Sports Toy giveaway, 16 pgs., 5-1/4x7")-Origin 9 18 27 47 61 75
...Fights His Way Back (1945 Giveaway, 24 pgs.) Family Comics 15 30 45 85 130 175
...in Hi There! (1949 Red Cross giveaway, 12 pgs., 4-3/4x6") 9 18 27 50 65 80
...in It's All in the Family (1945 Red Cross giveaway, 16 pgs., regular size) 11 22 33 60 83 105

JOE THE GENIE OF STEEL (Also see "Return of...")
U.S. Steel Corp., Pittsburgh, PA: 1950 (16 pgs, reg size)
nn-Joe Magarac, the Paul Bunyan of steel 9 18 27 50 65 80

JOHNNY JINGLE'S LUCKY DAY
American Dairy Assoc.: 1956 (16 pgs.; 7-1/4x5-1/8") (Giveaway) (Disney)
nn 5 10 15 24 30 35

JOHNSON MAKES THE TEAM
B.F. Goodrich: 1950 (Reg. size) (Football giveaway)
nn 6 12 18 31 36 45

JO-JOY (The Adventures of...)
W. T. Grant Dept. Stores: 1945 - 1953 (Christmas gift comic, 16 pgs., 7-1/16x10-1/4")
1945-53 issues 7 14 21 37 46 55

JOLLY CHRISTMAS BOOK (See Christmas Journey Through Space)
Promotional Publ. Co.: 1951; 1954; 1955 (36 pgs.; 24 pgs.)
1951-(Woolworth giveaway)-slightly oversized; no slick cover; Marv Levy-c/a 7 14 21 37 46 55
1954-(Hot Shoppes giveaway)-regular size-reprints 1951 issue; slick cover added; 24 pgs.; no ads 6 12 18 31 38 45
1955-(J. M. McDonald Co. giveaway)-reg. size 6 12 18 28 34 40

JOURNEY OF DISCOVERY WITH MARK STEEL (See Mark Steel)

JUMPING JACKS PRESENTS THE WHIZ KIDS
Jumping Jacks Stores giveaway: 1978 (In 3-D) with glasses (4 pgs.)
nn 6.00

JUNGLE BOOK FUN BOOK, THE (Disney)
Baskin Robbins: 1978
nn-Ice Cream giveaway 2 4 6 9 12 15

JUSTICE LEAGUE OF AMERICA
DC Comics: 1999 (included in Justice League of America Monopoly game)
nn - Reprints 1st app. in Brave and the Bold #28 2.50

KASCO KOMICS
Kasko Grainfeed (Giveaway): 1945; No. 2, 1949 (Regular size, paper-c)
1(1945)-Similar to Katy Keene; Bill Woggon-a; 28 pgs.; 6-7/8x9-7/8" 17 34 51 100 158 215
2(1949)-Woggon-c/a 13 26 39 74 105 135

KATY AND KEN VISIT SANTA WITH MISTER WISH
S. S. Kresge Co. : 1948 (Giveaway, 16 pgs., paper-c)
nn 6 12 18 29 36 42

KELLOGG'S CINNAMON MINI-BUNS SUPER-HEROES
DC Comics: 1993 (4 1/4" x 2 3/4")
4 editions: Flash, Justice League America, Superman, Wonder Woman and the Star Riders each..... 4.00

KERRY DRAKE DETECTIVE CASES
Publisher's Syndicate
...in the Case of the Sleeping City-(1951)-16 pg. giveaway for armed forces; paper cover 6 12 18 29 36 42

KEY COMICS
Key Clothing Co./Peterson Clothing: 1951 - 1956 (32 pgs.) (Giveaway)
Contains a comic from different publishers bound with new cover. Cover changed each year. Many combinations possible. Distributed in Nebraska, Iowa, & Kansas. Contents would determine price, 40-60 percent of original.

KING JAMES "THE KING OF BASKETBALL"

King James © DC

Porky Pig's
Kite Fun Book
PORKY PIG'S KITE FUN BOOK

Kite Fun Book 1960 - Porky Pig © WB

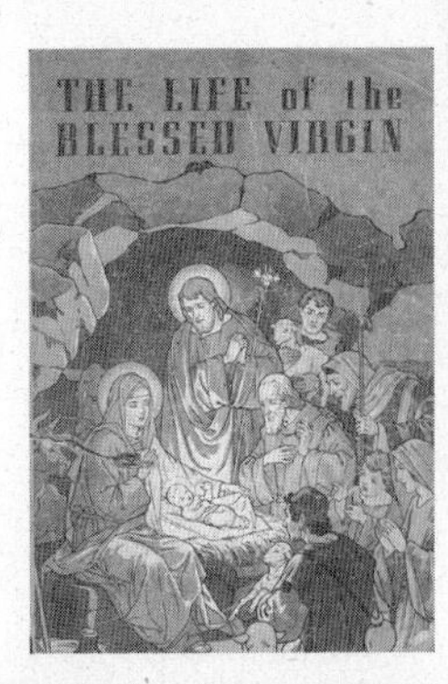

The Life of the Blessed Virgin © CG

	GD 2.0	VG 4.0	FN 6.0	VF 8.0	VF/NM 9.0	NM- 9.2

DC Comics: 2004 (Promo comic for LeBron James and Powerade Flava23 sports drink)

nn - Ten different covers by various artists; 4 covers for retail, 4 for mail-in, 1 for military commissaries, and 1 general market; Damion Scott-a/Gary Phillips-s						2.50

KIRBY'S SHOES COMICS
Kirby's Shoes: 1959 - 1961 (8 pgs., soft-c)

nn-Features Kirby the Golden Bear	3	5	7	10	12	14

KITE FUN BOOK
Pacific, Gas & Electric/Sou. California Edison/Florida Power & Light/ Missouri Public Service Co.: 1952 - 1998 (16 pgs, 5x7-1/4", soft-c)

1952-Having Fun With Kites (P.G.&E.)	12	24	36	69	97	125
1953-Pinocchio Learns About Kites (Disney)	41	82	123	256	428	600
1954-Donald Duck Tells About Kites-Fla. Power, S.C.E. & version with label issues -Barks pencils-8 pgs.; inks-7 pgs. (Rare)	258	516	774	1651	2826	4000
1954-Donald Duck Tells About Kites-P.G.&E. issue -7th page redrawn changing middle 3 panels to show P.G.&E. in story line; (All Barks-a) Scarce	206	412	618	1318	2259	3200
1955-Brer Rabbit in "A Kite Tail" (Disney)	27	54	81	158	259	360
1956-Woody Woodpecker (Lantz)	14	28	42	76	108	140
1957-Ruff and Reddy (exist?)						
1958-Tom And Jerry (M.G.M.)	9	18	27	52	69	85
1959-Bugs Bunny (Warner Bros.)	4	8	12	28	44	60
1960-Porky Pig (Warner Bros.)	5	10	15	30	48	65
1960-Bugs Bunny (Warner Bros.)	5	10	15	30	48	65
1961-Huckleberry Hound (Hanna-Barbera)	5	10	15	35	55	75
1962-Yogi Bear (Hanna-Barbera)	4	8	12	26	41	55
1963-Rocky and Bullwinkle (TV)(Jay Ward)	6	12	18	41	66	90
1963-Top Cat (TV)(Hanna-Barbera)	3	6	9	20	30	40
1964-Magilla Gorilla (TV)(Hanna-Barbera)	3	6	9	18	27	35
1965-Jinks, Pixie and Dixie (TV)(Hanna-Barbera)	3	6	9	16	22	28
1965-Tweety and Sylvester (Warner); S.C.E. version with Reddy Kilowatt app.	2	4	6	9	13	16
1966-Secret Squirrel (Hanna-Barbera); S.C.E. version with Reddy Kilowatt app.	5	10	15	32	51	70
1967-Beep! Beep! The Road Runner (TV)(Warner)	2	4	6	11	16	20
1968-Bugs Bunny (Warner Bros.)	2	4	6	13	18	22
1969-Dastardly and Muttley (TV)(Hanna-Barbera)	3	6	9	20	30	40
1970-Rocky and Bullwinkle (TV)(Jay Ward)	4	8	12	28	44	60
1971-Beep! Beep! The Road Runner (TV)(Warner)	2	4	6	11	16	20
1972-The Pink Panther (TV)	2	4	6	10	14	18
1973-Lassie (TV)	3	6	9	16	22	28
1974-Underdog (TV)	2	4	6	11	16	20
1975-Ben Franklin	2	4	6	8	10	12
1976-The Brady Bunch (TV)	3	6	9	16	23	30
1977-Ben Franklin (exist?)	2	4	6	8	10	12
1977-Popeye	2	4	6	9	13	16
1978-Happy Days (TV)	2	4	6	11	16	20
1979-Eight is Enough (TV)	2	4	6	9	13	16
1980-The Waltons (TV, released in 1981)	2	4	6	9	13	16
1982-Tweety and Sylvester	2	4	6	8	11	14
1984-Smokey Bear	1	3	4	6	8	10
1986-Road Runner	1	2	3	5	6	8
1997-Thomas Edison						4.00
1998-Edison Field (Anaheim Stadium)						3.00

KNOWING IS NOT ENOUGH
Commercial Comics: 1956 (Reg. size, paper-c) (Safety giveaway)

nn	7	14	21	35	43	50

KNOW YOUR MASS
Catechetical Guild: No. 303, 1958 (35¢, 100 Pg. Giant) (Square binding)

303-In color	7	14	21	35	43	50

KOLYNOS PRESENTS THE WHITE GUARD
Whitehall Pharmacal Co.: 1949 (paper cover, 8 pgs.)

nn	6	12	18	27	33	38

K. O. PUNCH, THE (Also see Lucky Fights It Through & Sidewalk Romance)
E. C. Comics: 1948 (VD Educational giveaway)

nn-Feldstein-splash; Kamen-a	84	168	252	538	919	1300

KOREA MY HOME (Also see Yalta to Korea)
Johnstone and Cushing: nd (1950s)

nn-Anti-communist; Korean War	20	40	60	116	191	265

KRIM-KO KOMICS
Krim-ko Chocolate Drink: 5/18/35 - No. 6, 6/22/35; 1936 - 1939 (weekly)

1-(16 pgs., soft-c, Dairy giveaways)-Tom, Mary & Sparky Advs. by Russell Keaton, Jim Hawkins by Dick Moores, Mystery Island! by Rick Yager begin	14	28	42	76	108	140
2-6 (6/22/35)	10	20	30	56	76	95
Lola, Secret Agent; 184 issues, 4 pg. giveaways - all original stories each....	7	14	21	37	46	55

LABOR IS A PARTNER
Catechetical Guild Educational Society: 1949 (32 pgs., paper-c)

nn-Anti-communism	20	40	60	116	191	265
Confidential Preview-(8-1/2x11", B&W, saddle stitched)-only one known copy; text varies from color version, advertises next book on secularism (If the Devil Would Talk)	24	48	72	142	234	325

LADIES - WOULDN'T IT BE BETTER TO KNOW
American Cancer Society: 1969 (Reg. size)

nn	4	8	12	22	34	45

LADY AND THE TRAMP IN "BUTTER LATE THAN NEVER"
American Dairy Assoc. (Premium): 1955 (16 pgs., 5x7-1/4", soft-c) (Disney)

nn	8	16	24	44	57	70

LASSIE (TV)
Dell Publ. Co

The Adventures of... nn-(Red Heart Dog Food giveaway, 1949)-16 pgs, soft-c; 1st app. Lassie in comics	31	62	93	184	302	420

LIFE OF THE BLESSED VIRGIN
Catechetical Guild (Giveaway): 1950 (68pgs.) (square binding)

nn-Contains "The Woman of the Promise" & "Mother of Us All" rebound	7	14	21	35	43	50

LIGHTNING RACERS
DC Comics: 1989

1						4.50

LI'L ABNER (Al Capp's) (Also see Natural Disasters!)
Harvey Publ./Toby Press

...& the Creatures from Drop-Outer Space-nn (Job Corps giveaway; 36 pgs., in color) (entire book by Frank Frazetta)	21	42	63	121	201	280
...Joins the Navy (1950) (Toby Press Premium)	11	22	33	62	86	110
Al Capp by Li'l Abner (Circa 1946, nd, giveaway) Al Capp bio and his life as an amputee	11	22	33	62	86	110

LITTLE ALONZO
Macy's Dept. Store: 1938 (B&W, 5-1/2x8-1/2")(Christmas giveaway)

nn-By Ferdinand the Bull's Munro Leaf	9	18	27	50	65	80

LITTLE ARCHIE (See Archie Comics)

LITTLE DOT
Harvey Publications

Shoe store giveaway 2	4	8	12	28	44	60

LITTLE FIR TREE, THE
W. T. Grant Co. : nd (1942) (8-1/2x11") (12 pgs. with cover, color & B&W, heavy paper) (Christmas giveaway)

nn-Story by Hans Christian Anderson; 8 pg. Kelly-r/Santa Claus Funnies (not signed); X-Mas-c	90	180	270	576	988	1400

LITTLE KLINKER
Little Klinker Ventures: Nov, 1960 (20 pgs.) (slick cover) (Montgomery Ward Giveaway)

nn - Christmas; Santa-c	2	4	6	11	16	20

LITTLE MISS SUNBEAM COMICS
Magazine Enterprises/Quality Bakers of America

Bread Giveaway 1-4(Quality Bakers, 1949-50)-14 pgs. each	6	12	18	31	38	45
Bread Giveaway (1957,61; 16pgs, reg. size)	5	10	15	24	30	35

LITTLE ORPHAN ANNIE
David McKay Publ./Dell Publishing Co.

Junior Commandos Giveaway (same-c as 4-Color #18, K.K. Publ.)(Big Shoe Store); same back cover as '47 Popped Wheat giveaway; 16 pgs; flag-c; r/strips 9/7/42-10/10/42	26	52	78	154	252	350
Popped Wheat Giveaway ('47)-16 pgs. full color; reprints strips from 5/3/40 to 6/20/40	4	8	12	18	22	25
Quaker Sparkies Giveaway (1940)	18	36	54	103	162	220

How the Lone Ranger Captured Silver © Lone Ranger Inc.

The Man Who Wouldn't Quit © HARV

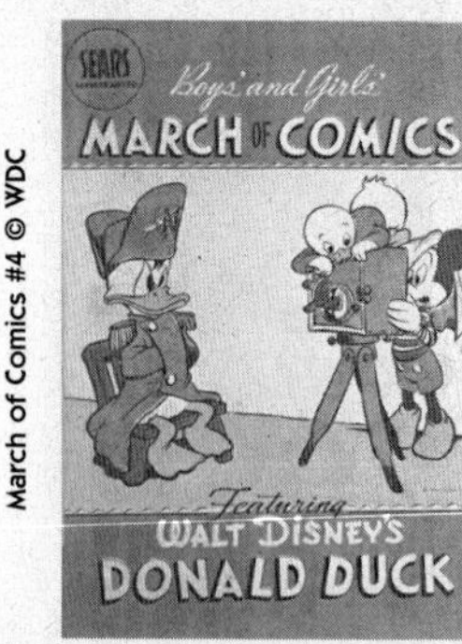

March of Comics #4 © WDC

GD 2.0 VG 4.0 FN 6.0 VF 8.0 VF/NM 9.0 NM- 9.2

Quaker Sparkies Giveaway (1941, full color, 20 pgs.); "LOA and the Rescue"; r/strips 4/13/39-6/21/39 & 7/6/39-7/17/39. "LOA and the Kidnappers"; r/strips 11/28/38-1/28/39 15 30 45 94 147 200
Quaker Sparkies Giveaway (1942, full color, 20 pgs.); "LOA and Mr. Gudge"; r/strips 2/13/38-3/21/38 & 4/18/37-5/30/37. "LOA and the Great Am" 15 30 45 88 137 185

LITTLE TREE THAT WASN'T WANTED, THE
W. T. Grant Co. (Giveaway): 1960, (Color, 28 pgs.)
nn-Christmas story, puzzles and games 4 8 12 22 34 45

LOADED (Also see Re-Loaded)
DC Comics: 1995 (Interplay Productions)
1-Garth Ennis-s; promotes video game 4.00

LONE RANGER, THE
Dell Publishing Co.
Cheerios Giveaways (1954, 16 pgs., 2-1/2x7", soft-c) #1- "The Lone Ranger, His Mask & How He Met Tonto". #2- "The Lone Ranger & the Story of Silver" each.... 15 30 45 85 130 175
Doll Giveaways (Gabriel Ind.)(1973, 3-1/4x5")- "The Story of The Lone Ranger," "The Carson City Bank Robbery" & "The Apache Buffalo Hunt" 2 4 6 12 16 20
How the Lone Ranger Captured Silver Book(1936)-Silvercup Bread giveaway 55 110 165 349 600 850
...In Milk for Big Mike (1955, Dairy Association giveaway), soft-c; 5x7-1/4", 16 pgs. 14 28 42 76 108 140
Legend of The Lone Ranger (1969, 16 pgs., giveaway)-Origin The Lone Ranger 4 8 12 22 34 45
Merita Bread giveaway (1954, 16 pgs., 5x7-1/4")- "How to Be a Lone Ranger Health & Safety Scout" 18 36 54 103 162 220

LONE RANGER COMICS, THE
Lone Ranger, Inc. : Book 1, 1939(inside) (shows 1938 on-c) (52 pgs. in color; regular size) (Ice cream mail order)
Book 1-(Scarce)-The first western comic devoted to a single character; not by Vallely 600 1200 1800 4200 - -
2nd version w/large full color promo poster pasted over centerfold & a smaller poster pasted over back cover; includes new additional premiums not originally offered (Rare) 857 1714 2571 6000 - -

LOONEY TUNES
DC Comics: 1991, 1998
Claritin promotional issue (1998) 3.00
Colgate mini-comic (1998) 3.00
Tyson's 1-10 (1991) 4.00

LUCKY FIGHTS IT THROUGH (Also see The K. O. Punch & Sidewalk Romance)
Educational Comics: 1949 (Giveaway, 16 pgs. in color, paper-c)
nn-(Very Rare)-1st Kurtzman work for E. C.; V.D. prevention 129 258 387 826 1413 2000
nn-Reprint in color (1977) 7.00
NOTE: *Subtitled "The Story of That Ignorant, Ignorant Cowboy". Prepared for Communications Materials Center, Columbia University.*

LUDWIG VON DRAKE (See Frito-Lay Giveaway)

MACO TOYS COMIC
Maco Toys/Charlton Comics: 1959 (Giveaway, 36 pgs.)
1-All military stories featuring Maco Toys 3 6 9 14 19 24

MAD MAGAZINE
DC Comics: 1997, 1999, 2008
Special Edition (1997, Tang giveaway) 3.00
Stocking Stuffer (1999) 3.00
San Diego Comic-Con Edition (2008) Watchmen parody with Fabry-a; Aragonés cartoons 3.00

MAGAZINELAND
DC Comics: 1977
nn-Kubert-c/a 3 6 9 16 22 28

MAGIC MORRO (Also see Super Comics #21, The Owl, & The Hurricane Kids)
K. K. Publications: 1941 (7-1/2 x 5-1/4", giveaway, soft-c)
nn-Ken Ernst-a. 10 20 30 54 72 90

MAGIC OF CHRISTMAS AT NEWBERRYS, THE
E. S. London: 1967 (Giveaway) (B&W, slick-c, 20 pgs.)
nn 1 3 4 6 8 10

GD 2.0 VG 4.0 FN 6.0 VF 8.0 VF/NM 9.0 NM- 9.2

MAGIC SHOE ADVENTURE BOOK
Western Publications: 1962 - No. 3, 1963 (Shoe store giveaway, Reg. size)
nn-(1962) 5 10 15 35 55 75
1 (1963)-And the Flaming Threat 4 8 12 28 44 60
2 (1963)-And the Winning Run 4 8 12 28 44 60
3 (1963)-And the Missing Masterpiece Mystery 4 8 12 28 44 60

MAJOR INAPAK THE SPACE ACE
Magazine Enterprises (Inapac Foods): 1951 (20 pgs.) (Giveaway)
1-Bob Powell-c/a 6.00
NOTE: *Many warehouse copies surfaced in 1973.*

MAMMY YOKUM & THE GREAT DOGPATCH MYSTERY
Toby Press: 1951 (Giveaway)
nn-Li'l Abner 15 30 45 88 137 185
nn-Reprint (1956) 5 10 15 22 26 30

MAN NAMED STEVENSON, A
Democratic National Committee: 1952 (20 pgs., 5 1/4 x 7")
nn 9 18 27 47 61 75

MAN OF PEACE, POPE PIUS XII
Catechetical Guild: 1950 (See Pope Pius XII... & To V2#8)
nn-All Powell-a 7 14 21 35 43 50

MAN OF STEEL BEST WESTERN
DC Comics: 1997 (Best Western hotels promo)
3-Reprints Superman's first post-Crisis meeting with Batman 4.00

MAN WHO RUNS INTERFERENCE
General Comics, Inc./Institute of Life Insurance: 1946 (Paper-c)
nn-Football premium 5 10 15 22 26 30

MAN WHO WOULDN'T QUIT, THE
Harvey Publications Inc.: 1952 (16 pgs., paper cover)
nn-The value of voting 4 8 12 18 22 25

MARCH OF COMICS (Boys' and Girls'...#3-353)
K. K. Publications/Western Publishing Co.: 1946 - No. 488, April, 1982 (#1-4 are not numbered) (K.K. Giveaway) (Founded by Sig Feuchtwanger)
Early issues were full size, 32 pages, and were printed with and without an extra cover of slick stock, just for the advertiser. The binding was stapled if the slick cover was added; otherwise, the pages were glued together at the spine. Most 1948 - 1951 issues were full size,24 pages, pulp covers. Starting in 1952 they were half-size (with a few exceptions) and 32 pages with slick covers.1959 and later issues had only 16 pages plus covers. 1952 -1959 issues read oblong; 1960 and later issues read upright. All have new stories except where noted.
nn (#1, 1946)-Goldilocks; Kelly back-c (16 pgs., stapled) 53 106 159 334 567 800
nn (#2, 1946)-How Santa Got His Red Suit; Kelly-a (11 pgs., r/4-Color #61 from 1944) (16pgs., stapled) 34 68 102 199 325 450
nn (#3, 1947)-Our Gang (Walt Kelly) 40 80 120 246 411 575
nn (#4)-Donald Duck by Carl Barks, "Maharajah Donald", 28 pgs.; Kelly-c? (Disney) 757 1514 2271 5602 9801 14,000
5-Andy Panda (Walter Lantz) 21 42 63 122 199 275
6-Popular Fairy Tales; Kelly-c; Noonan-a(2) 23 46 69 136 223 310
7-Oswald the Rabbit 21 42 63 126 206 285
8-Mickey Mouse, 32 pgs. (Disney) 50 100 150 315 533 750
9(nn)-The Story of the Gloomy Bunny 14 28 42 81 118 155
10-Out of Santa's Bag 14 28 42 78 112 145
11-Fun With Santa Claus 12 24 36 69 97 125
12-Santa's Toys 12 24 36 69 97 125
13-Santa's Surprise 12 24 36 69 97 125
14-Santa's Candy Kitchen 12 24 36 69 97 125
15-Hip-It-Ty Hop & the Big Bass Viol 11 22 33 64 90 115
16-Woody Woodpecker (1947)(Walter Lantz) 15 30 45 85 130 175
17-Roy Rogers (1948) 23 46 69 138 227 315
18-Popular Fairy Tales 14 28 42 80 115 150
19-Uncle Wiggily 13 26 39 72 101 130
20-Donald Duck by Carl Barks, "Darkest Africa", 22 pgs.; Kelly-c (Disney) 300 600 900 2010 3505 5000
21-Tom and Jerry 14 28 42 76 108 140
22-Andy Panda (Lantz) 12 24 36 67 94 120
23-Raggedy Ann & Andy; Kerr-a 14 28 42 82 121 160
24-Felix the Cat, 1932 daily strip reprints by Otto Messmer 20 40 60 117 189 260
25-Gene Autry 20 40 60 115 185 255
26-Our Gang; Walt Kelly 19 38 57 109 172 235
27-Mickey Mouse; r/in M. M. #240 (Disney) 34 68 102 199 325 450

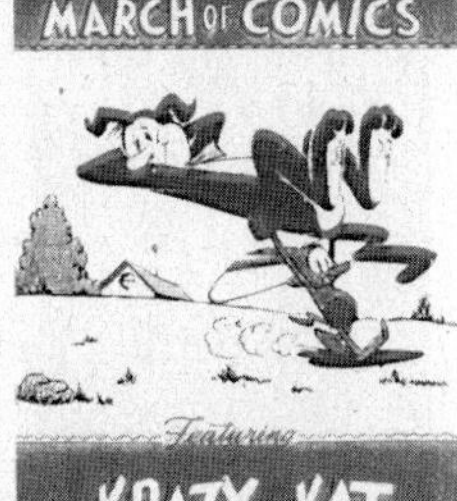

March of Comics #72 © KING

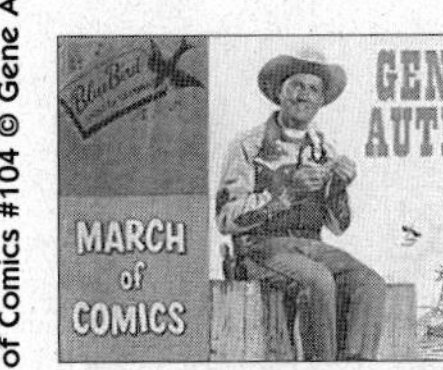

March of Comics #104 © Gene Autry

March of Comics #125 © ERB

	GD 2.0	VG 4.0	FN 6.0	VF 8.0	VF/NM 9.0	NM- 9.2
28-Gene Autry	20	40	60	114	182	250
29-Easter Bonnet Shop	9	18	27	47	61	75
30-Here Comes Santa	8	16	24	44	57	70
31-Santa's Busy Corner	8	16	24	44	57	70
32-No book produced						
33-A Christmas Carol (12/48)	9	18	27	47	61	75
34-Woody Woodpecker	13	26	39	74	105	135
35-Roy Rogers (1948)	21	42	63	122	199	275
36-Felix the Cat(1949); by Messmer; '34 strip-r	17	34	51	100	158	215
37-Popeye	15	30	45	85	130	175
38-Oswald the Rabbit	10	20	30	58	79	100
39-Gene Autry	19	38	57	111	176	240
40-Andy and Woody	10	20	30	58	79	100
41-Donald Duck by Carl Barks, "Race to the South Seas", 22 pgs.; Kelly-c	300	600	900	1950	3375	4800
42-Porky Pig	11	22	33	60	83	105
43-Henry	10	20	30	56	76	95
44-Bugs Bunny	11	22	33	64	90	115
45-Mickey Mouse (Disney)	24	48	72	140	230	320
46-Tom and Jerry	11	22	33	64	90	115
47-Roy Rogers	18	36	54	107	169	230
48-Greetings from Santa	6	12	18	31	38	45
49-Santa Is Here	6	12	18	31	38	45
50-Santa Claus' Workshop (1949)	6	12	18	31	38	45
51-Felix the Cat (1950) by Messmer	15	30	45	94	147	200
52-Popeye	14	28	42	76	108	140
53-Oswald the Rabbit	10	20	30	54	72	90
54-Gene Autry	16	32	48	94	147	200
55-Andy and Woody	9	18	27	52	69	85
56-Donald Duck; not by Barks; Barks art on back-c (Disney)	27	54	81	158	259	360
57-Porky Pig	10	20	30	54	72	90
58-Henry	8	16	24	44	57	70
59-Bugs Bunny	10	20	30	58	79	100
60-Mickey Mouse (Disney)	24	48	72	140	230	320
61-Tom and Jerry	10	20	30	54	72	90
62-Roy Rogers	18	36	54	105	165	225
63-Welcome Santa (1/2-size, oblong)	6	12	18	31	38	45
64(nn)-Santa's Helpers (1/2-size, oblong)	6	12	18	31	38	45
65(nn)-Jingle Bells (1950) (1/2-size, oblong)	6	12	18	31	38	45
66-Popeye (1951)	12	24	36	69	97	125
67-Oswald the Rabbit	9	18	27	52	69	85
68-Roy Rogers	17	34	51	100	158	215
69-Donald Duck; Barks-a on back-c (Disney)	22	44	66	132	216	300
70-Tom and Jerry	9	18	27	50	65	80
71-Porky Pig	9	18	27	52	69	85
72-Krazy Kat	10	20	30	58	79	100
73-Roy Rogers	15	30	45	90	140	190
74-Mickey Mouse (1951)(Disney)	20	40	60	114	182	250
75-Bugs Bunny	9	18	27	52	69	85
76-Andy and Woody	9	18	27	50	65	80
77-Roy Rogers	15	30	45	90	140	190
78-Gene Autry (1951); last regular size issue	15	30	45	86	133	180

Note: All pre #79 issues came with or without a slick protective wrap-around cover over the regular cover which advertised Poll Parrot Shoes, Sears, etc. This outer cover protects the inside pages making them in nicer condition.
Issues with the outer cover are worth 15-25% more

	GD 2.0	VG 4.0	FN 6.0	VF 8.0	VF/NM 9.0	NM- 9.2
79-Andy Panda (1952, 5x7" size)	7	14	21	35	43	50
80-Popeye	10	20	30	58	79	100
81-Oswald the Rabbit	6	12	18	29	36	42
82-Tarzan; Lex Barker photo-c	15	30	45	90	140	190
83-Bugs Bunny	7	14	21	37	46	55
84-Henry	6	12	18	29	36	42
85-Woody Woodpecker	6	12	18	29	36	42
86-Roy Rogers	14	28	42	76	108	140
87-Krazy Kat	8	16	24	44	57	70
88-Tom and Jerry	6	12	18	31	38	45
89-Porky Pig	6	12	18	29	36	42
90-Gene Autry	12	24	36	69	97	125
91-Roy Rogers & Santa	13	26	39	74	105	135
92-Christmas with Santa	5	10	15	24	30	35
93-Woody Woodpecker (1953)	5	10	15	23	28	32
94-Indian Chief	10	20	30	54	72	90
95-Oswald the Rabbit	5	10	15	23	28	32

	GD 2.0	VG 4.0	FN 6.0	VF 8.0	VF/NM 9.0	NM- 9.2
96-Popeye	10	20	30	54	72	90
97-Bugs Bunny	7	14	21	35	43	50
98-Tarzan; Lex Barker photo-c	15	30	45	86	133	180
99-Porky Pig	5	10	15	23	28	32
100-Roy Rogers	11	22	33	62	86	110
101-Henry	5	10	15	22	26	30
102-Tom Corbett (TV)('53, early app).; painted-c	14	28	42	76	108	140
103-Tom and Jerry	5	10	15	23	28	32
104-Gene Autry	11	22	33	60	83	105
105-Roy Rogers	11	22	33	60	83	105
106-Santa's Helpers	5	10	15	24	30	35
107-Santa's Christmas Book - not published						
108-Fun with Santa (1953)	5	10	15	24	30	35
109-Woody Woodpecker (1954)	5	10	15	24	30	35
110-Indian Chief	6	12	18	31	38	45
111-Oswald the Rabbit	5	10	15	22	26	30
112-Henry	4	9	13	18	22	26
113-Porky Pig	5	10	15	22	26	30
114-Tarzan; Russ Manning-a	15	30	45	86	133	180
115-Bugs Bunny	6	12	18	27	33	38
116-Roy Rogers	11	22	33	60	83	105
117-Popeye	10	20	30	54	72	90
118-Flash Gordon; painted-c	12	24	36	67	94	120
119-Tom and Jerry	5	10	15	22	26	30
120-Gene Autry	11	22	33	60	83	105
121-Roy Rogers	11	22	33	60	83	105
122-Santa's Surprise (1954)	5	10	15	22	26	30
123-Santa's Christmas Book	5	10	15	22	26	30
124-Woody Woodpecker (1955)	4	9	13	18	22	26
125-Tarzan; Lex Barker photo-c	15	30	45	83	124	165
126-Oswald the Rabbit	4	9	13	18	22	26
127-Indian Chief	7	14	21	35	43	50
128-Tom and Jerry	4	9	13	18	22	26
129-Henry	4	8	12	17	21	24
130-Porky Pig	4	9	13	18	22	26
131-Roy Rogers	11	22	33	60	83	105
132-Bugs Bunny	5	10	15	23	28	32
133-Flash Gordon; painted-c	11	22	33	60	83	105
134-Popeye	8	16	24	42	54	65
135-Gene Autry	10	20	30	56	76	95
136-Roy Rogers	10	20	30	56	76	95
137-Gifts from Santa	4	7	10	14	17	20
138-Fun at Christmas (1955)	4	7	10	14	17	20
139-Woody Woodpecker (1956)	4	9	13	18	22	26
140-Indian Chief	7	14	21	35	43	50
141-Oswald the Rabbit	4	9	13	18	22	26
142-Flash Gordon	11	22	33	60	83	105
143-Porky Pig	4	9	13	18	22	26
144-Tarzan; Russ Manning-a; painted-c	14	28	42	80	115	150
145-Tom and Jerry	4	9	13	18	22	26
146-Roy Rogers; photo-c	10	20	30	56	76	95
147-Henry	4	8	11	16	19	22
148-Popeye	8	16	24	42	54	65
149-Bugs Bunny	5	10	15	22	26	30
150-Gene Autry	10	20	30	56	76	95
151-Roy Rogers	10	20	30	56	76	95
152-The Night Before Christmas	4	8	11	16	19	22
153-Merry Christmas (1956)	4	9	13	18	22	26
154-Tom and Jerry (1957)	4	9	13	18	22	26
155-Tarzan; photo-c	14	28	42	78	112	145
156-Oswald the Rabbit	4	9	13	18	22	26
157-Popeye	7	14	21	35	43	50
158-Woody Woodpecker	4	9	13	18	22	26
159-Indian Chief	7	14	21	35	43	50
160-Bugs Bunny	5	10	15	22	26	30
161-Roy Rogers	9	18	27	52	69	85
162-Henry	4	8	11	16	19	22
163-Rin Tin Tin (TV)	8	16	24	42	54	65
164-Porky Pig	4	9	13	18	22	26
165-The Lone Ranger	10	20	30	54	72	90
166-Santa and His Reindeer	4	7	10	14	17	20
167-Roy Rogers and Santa	9	18	27	52	69	85
168-Santa Claus' Workshop (1957, full size)	4	8	11	16	19	22
169-Popeye (1958)	7	14	21	35	43	50

March of Comics #208 © Lone Ranger Inc.

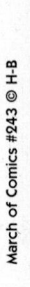

March of Comics #243 © H-B

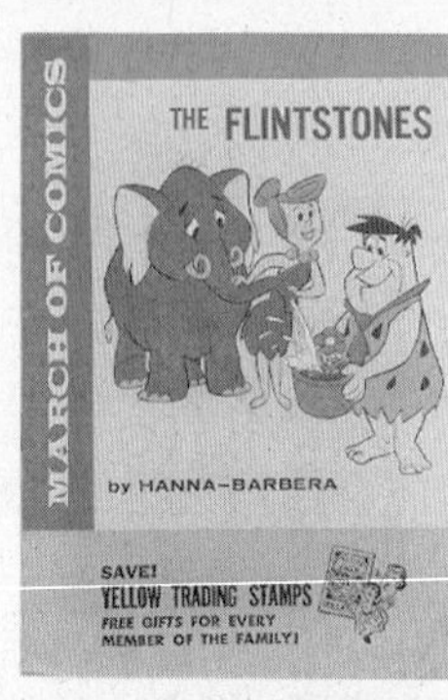

March of Comics #290 © WEST

	GD 2.0	VG 4.0	FN 6.0	VF 8.0	VF/NM 9.0	NM- 9.2
170-Indian Chief	7	14	21	35	43	50
171-Oswald the Rabbit	4	8	12	17	21	24
172-Tarzan	11	22	33	64	90	115
173-Tom and Jerry	4	8	12	17	21	24
174-The Lone Ranger	10	20	30	54	72	90
175-Porky Pig	4	8	12	17	21	24
176-Roy Rogers	9	18	27	47	61	75
177-Woody Woodpecker	4	8	12	17	21	24
178-Henry	4	8	11	16	19	22
179-Bugs Bunny	4	8	12	17	21	24
180-Rin Tin Tin (TV)	7	14	21	37	46	55
181-Happy Holiday	4	7	9	14	16	18
182-Happi Tim	4	8	11	16	19	22
183-Welcome Santa (1958, full size)	4	7	9	14	16	18
184-Woody Woodpecker (1959)	4	8	11	16	19	22
185-Tarzan; photo-c	11	22	33	60	83	110
186-Oswald the Rabbit	4	8	11	16	19	22
187-Indian Chief	6	12	18	28	34	40
188-Bugs Bunny	4	8	11	16	19	22
189-Henry	4	7	10	14	17	20
190-Tom and Jerry	4	8	11	16	19	22
191-Roy Rogers	8	16	24	44	57	70
192-Porky Pig	4	8	11	16	19	22
193-The Lone Ranger	9	18	27	52	69	85
194-Popeye	6	12	18	31	38	45
195-Rin Tin Tin (TV)	7	14	21	35	43	50
196-Sears Special - not published						
197-Santa Is Coming	4	7	10	14	17	20
198-Santa's Helpers (1959)	4	7	10	14	17	20
199-Huckleberry Hound (TV)(1960, early app.)	8	16	24	42	54	65
200-Fury (TV)	6	12	18	28	34	40
201-Bugs Bunny	4	8	11	16	19	22
202-Space Explorer	8	16	24	42	54	65
203-Woody Woodpecker	4	7	10	14	17	20
204-Tarzan	9	18	27	52	69	85
205-Mighty Mouse	6	12	18	33	41	48
206-Roy Rogers; photo-c	8	16	24	42	54	65
207-Tom and Jerry	4	7	10	14	17	20
208-The Lone Ranger; Clayton Moore photo-c	11	22	33	62	86	110
209-Porky Pig	4	7	10	14	17	20
210-Lassie (TV)	6	12	18	33	41	48
211-Sears Special - not published						
212-Christmas Eve	4	7	10	14	17	20
213-Here Comes Santa (1960)	4	7	10	14	17	20
214-Huckleberry Hound (TV)(1961)	7	14	21	35	43	50
215-Hi Yo Silver	8	16	24	40	50	60
216-Rocky & His Friends (TV)(1961); predates Rocky and His Fiendish Friends #1 (see Four Color #1128)	10	20	30	58	79	100
217-Lassie (TV)	6	12	18	31	38	45
218-Porky Pig	4	7	10	14	17	20
219-Journey to the Sun	5	10	15	24	30	35
220-Bugs Bunny	4	8	11	16	19	22
221-Roy and Dale; photo-c	8	16	24	42	54	65
222-Woody Woodpecker	4	7	10	14	17	20
223-Tarzan	9	18	27	52	69	85
224-Tom and Jerry	4	7	10	14	17	20
225-The Lone Ranger	8	16	24	40	50	60
226-Christmas Treasury (1961)	4	7	10	14	17	20
227-Letters to Santa (1961)	4	7	10	14	17	20
228-Sears Special - not published?						
229-The Flintstones (TV)(1962); early app.; predates 1st Flintstones Gold Key issue (#7)	11	22	33	60	83	105
230-Lassie (TV)	6	12	18	27	33	38
231-Bugs Bunny	4	8	11	16	19	22
232-The Three Stooges	10	20	30	54	72	90
233-Bullwinkle (TV) (1962, very early app.)	10	20	30	58	79	100
234-Smokey the Bear	5	10	15	23	28	32
235-Huckleberry Hound (TV)	7	14	21	35	43	50
236-Roy and Dale	7	14	21	35	43	50
237-Mighty Mouse	6	12	18	27	33	38
238-The Lone Ranger	8	16	24	40	50	60
239-Woody Woodpecker	4	7	10	14	17	20
240-Tarzan	8	16	24	44	57	70
241-Santa Claus Around the World	4	7	9	14	16	18
242-Santa's Toyland (1962)	4	7	9	14	16	18
243-The Flintstones (TV)(1963)	8	16	24	44	57	70
244-Mister Ed (TV); early app.; photo-c	7	14	21	35	43	50
245-Bugs Bunny	4	8	11	16	19	22
246-Popeye	6	12	18	27	33	38
247-Mighty Mouse	6	12	18	27	33	38
248-The Three Stooges	10	20	30	54	72	90
249-Woody Woodpecker	4	7	10	14	17	20
250-Roy and Dale	7	14	21	35	43	50
251-Little Lulu & Witch Hazel	12	24	36	67	94	120
252-Tarzan; painted-c	8	16	24	42	54	65
253-Yogi Bear (TV)	8	16	24	40	50	60
254-Lassie (TV)	6	12	18	27	33	38
255-Santa's Christmas List	4	7	10	14	17	20
256-Christmas Party (1963)	4	7	10	14	17	20
257-Mighty Mouse	6	12	18	27	33	38
258-The Sword in the Stone (Disney)	8	16	24	42	54	65
259-Bugs Bunny	4	8	11	16	19	22
260-Mister Ed (TV)	6	12	18	31	38	45
261-Woody Woodpecker	4	7	10	14	17	20
262-Tarzan	8	16	24	40	50	60
263-Donald Duck; not by Barks (Disney)	9	18	27	52	69	85
264-Popeye	6	12	18	27	33	38
265-Yogi Bear (TV)	6	12	18	31	38	45
266-Lassie (TV)	5	10	15	23	28	32
267-Little Lulu; Irving Tripp-a	10	20	30	56	76	95
268-The Three Stooges	9	18	27	47	61	75
269-A Jolly Christmas	3	6	8	12	14	16
270-Santa's Little Helpers	3	6	8	12	14	16
271-The Flintstones (TV)(1965)	8	16	24	44	57	70
272-Tarzan	8	16	24	40	50	60
273-Bugs Bunny	4	8	11	16	19	22
274-Popeye	6	12	18	27	33	38
275-Little Lulu; Irving Tripp-a	9	18	27	50	65	80
276-The Jetsons (TV)	14	28	42	76	108	140
277-Daffy Duck	4	8	11	16	19	22
278-Lassie (TV)	5	10	15	23	28	32
279-Yogi Bear (TV)	6	12	18	31	38	45
280-The Three Stooges; photo-c	9	18	27	47	61	75
281-Tom and Jerry	4	7	9	14	16	18
282-Mister Ed (TV)	6	12	18	31	38	45
283-Santa's Visit	4	7	9	14	16	18
284-Christmas Parade (1965)	4	7	9	14	16	18
285-Astro Boy (TV); 2nd app. Astro Boy	28	56	84	165	270	375
286-Tarzan	7	14	21	37	46	55
287-Bugs Bunny	4	8	11	16	19	22
288-Daffy Duck	4	7	10	14	17	20
289-The Flintstones (TV)	8	16	24	44	57	70
290-Mister Ed (TV); photo-c	5	10	15	24	30	35
291-Yogi Bear (TV)	6	12	18	27	33	38
292-The Three Stooges; photo-c	9	18	27	47	61	75
293-Little Lulu; Irving Tripp-a	8	16	24	42	54	65
294-Popeye	5	10	15	24	30	35
295-Tom and Jerry	4	7	9	14	16	18
296-Lassie (TV); photo-c	5	10	15	22	26	30
297-Christmas Bells	3	6	8	12	14	16
298-Santa's Sleigh (1966)	3	6	8	12	14	16
299-The Flintstones (TV)(1967)	8	16	24	44	57	70
300-Tarzan	7	14	21	37	46	55
301-Bugs Bunny	4	7	10	14	17	20
302-Laurel and Hardy (TV); photo-c	6	12	18	28	34	40
303-Daffy Duck	3	6	8	12	14	16
304-The Three Stooges; photo-c	8	16	24	44	57	70
305-Tom and Jerry	3	6	8	12	14	16
306-Daniel Boone (TV); Fess Parker photo-c	7	14	21	35	43	50
307-Little Lulu; Irving Tripp-a	7	14	21	37	46	55
308-Lassie (TV); photo-c	5	10	15	22	26	30
309-Yogi Bear (TV)	5	10	15	24	30	35
310-The Lone Ranger; Clayton Moore photo-c	11	22	33	62	86	110
311-Santa's Show	4	7	9	14	16	18
312-Christmas Album (1967)	4	7	9	14	16	18
313-Daffy Duck (1968)	3	6	8	12	14	16
314-Laurel and Hardy (TV)	6	12	18	27	33	38
315-Bugs Bunny	4	7	10	14	17	20

March of Comics #362 © Smokey Bear

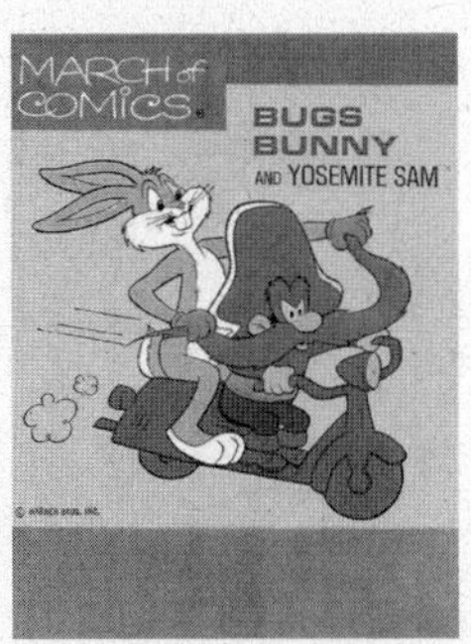

March of Comics #392 © WB

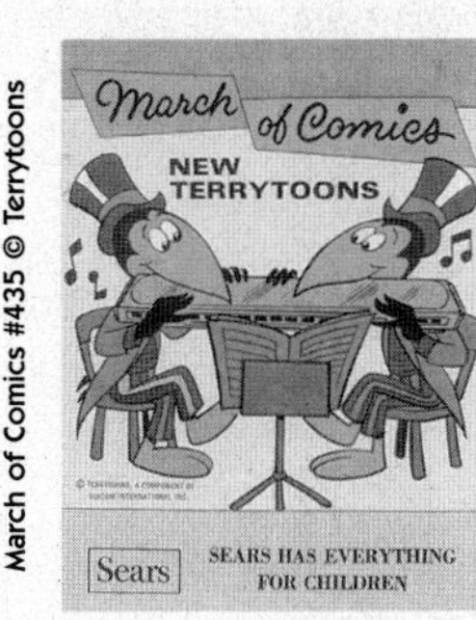

March of Comics #435 © Terrytoons

	GD 2.0	VG 4.0	FN 6.0	VF 8.0	VF/NM 9.0	NM- 9.2
316-The Three Stooges	8	16	24	40	50	60
317-The Flintstones (TV)	8	16	24	42	54	65
318-Tarzan	7	14	21	35	43	50
319-Yogi Bear (TV)	5	10	15	24	30	35
320-Space Family Robinson (TV); Spiegle-a	12	24	36	69	97	125
321-Tom and Jerry	3	6	8	12	14	16
322-The Lone Ranger	7	14	21	37	46	55
323-Little Lulu; not by Stanley	5	10	15	24	30	35
324-Lassie (TV); photo-c	5	10	15	22	26	30
325-Fun with Santa	4	7	9	14	16	18
326-Christmas Story (1968)	4	7	9	14	16	18
327-The Flintstones (TV)(1969)	8	16	24	42	54	65
328-Space Family Robinson (TV); Spiegle-a	12	24	36	69	97	125
329-Bugs Bunny	4	7	10	14	17	20
330-The Jetsons (TV)	10	20	30	56	76	95
331-Daffy Duck	3	6	8	12	14	16
332-Tarzan	6	12	18	28	34	40
333-Tom and Jerry	3	6	8	12	14	16
334-Lassie (TV)	4	9	13	18	22	26
335-Little Lulu	5	10	15	24	30	35
336-The Three Stooges	8	16	24	40	50	60
337-Yogi Bear (TV)	5	10	15	24	30	35
338-The Lone Ranger	7	14	21	37	46	55
339-(Was not published)						
340-Here Comes Santa (1969)	3	6	8	12	14	16
341-The Flintstones (TV)	8	16	24	42	54	65
342-Tarzan	3	6	9	20	30	40
343-Bugs Bunny	2	4	6	10	14	18
344-Yogi Bear (TV)	3	6	9	16	23	30
345-Tom and Jerry	2	4	6	9	13	16
346-Lassie (TV)	3	6	9	15	21	26
347-Daffy Duck	2	4	6	9	13	16
348-The Jetsons (TV)	6	12	18	39	62	85
349-Little Lulu; not by Stanley	3	6	9	16	23	30
350-The Lone Ranger	3	6	9	18	27	35
351-Beep-Beep, the Road Runner (TV)	2	4	6	11	16	20
352-Space Family Robinson (TV); Spiegle-a	8	16	24	53	89	125
353-Beep-Beep, the Road Runner (1971) (TV)	2	4	6	11	16	20
354-Tarzan (1971)	3	6	9	18	27	35
355-Little Lulu; not by Stanley	3	6	9	16	23	30
356-Scooby Doo, Where Are You? (TV)	6	12	18	42	69	95
357-Daffy Duck & Porky Pig	2	4	6	8	11	14
358-Lassie (TV)	3	6	9	14	19	24
359-Baby Snoots	2	4	6	10	14	18
360-H. R. Pufnstuf (TV); photo-c	6	12	18	42	69	95
361-Tom and Jerry	2	4	6	8	11	14
362-Smokey Bear (TV)	2	4	6	8	11	14
363-Bugs Bunny & Yosemite Sam	2	4	6	9	13	16
364-The Banana Splits (TV); photo-c	6	12	18	37	59	80
365-Tom and Jerry (1972)	2	4	6	8	11	14
366-Tarzan	3	6	9	18	27	35
367-Bugs Bunny & Porky Pig	2	4	6	9	13	16
368-Scooby Doo (TV)(4/72)	6	12	18	37	59	80
369-Little Lulu; not by Stanley	3	6	9	14	19	24
370-Lassie (TV); photo-c	3	6	9	14	19	24
371-Baby Snoots	2	4	6	9	13	16
372-Smokey the Bear (TV)	2	4	6	8	11	14
373-The Three Stooges	4	8	12	24	37	50
374-Wacky Witch	2	4	6	8	11	14
375-Beep-Beep & Daffy Duck (TV)	2	4	6	8	11	14
376-The Pink Panther (1972) (TV)	2	4	6	10	14	18
377-Baby Snoots (1973)	2	4	6	9	13	16
378-Turok, Son of Stone; new-a	8	16	24	56	93	130
379-Heckle & Jeckle New Terrytoons (TV)	2	4	6	8	11	14
380-Bugs Bunny & Yosemite Sam	2	4	6	8	11	14
381-Lassie (TV)	2	4	6	11	16	20
382-Scooby Doo, Where Are You? (TV)	5	10	15	32	51	70
383-Smokey the Bear (TV)	2	4	6	8	11	14
384-Pink Panther (TV)	2	4	6	8	11	14
385-Little Lulu	2	4	6	13	18	22
386-Wacky Witch	2	4	6	8	11	14
387-Beep-Beep & Daffy Duck (TV)	2	4	6	8	11	14
388-Tom and Jerry (1973)	2	4	6	8	11	14
389-Little Lulu; not by Stanley	2	4	6	13	18	22
390-Pink Panther (TV)	2	4	6	8	11	14
391-Scooby Doo (TV)	4	8	12	26	41	55
392-Bugs Bunny & Yosemite Sam	2	4	6	8	10	12
393-New Terrytoons (Heckle & Jeckle) (TV)	2	4	6	8	10	12
394-Lassie (TV)	2	4	6	9	13	16
395-Woodsy Owl	2	4	6	8	10	12
396-Baby Snoots	2	4	6	8	11	14
397-Beep-Beep & Daffy Duck (TV)	2	4	6	8	10	12
398-Wacky Witch	2	4	6	8	10	12
399-Turok, Son of Stone; new-a	7	14	21	49	82	115
400-Tom and Jerry	2	4	6	8	10	12
401-Baby Snoots (1975) (r/#371)	2	4	6	8	11	14
402-Daffy Duck (r/#313)	1	3	4	6	8	10
403-Bugs Bunny (r/#343)	2	4	6	8	10	12
404-Space Family Robinson (TV)(r/#328)	6	12	18	41	66	90
405-Cracky	1	3	4	6	8	10
406-Little Lulu (r/#355)	2	4	6	10	14	18
407-Smokey the Bear (TV)(r/#362)	2	4	6	8	10	12
408-Turok, Son of Stone; c-r/Turok #20 w/changes; new-a	6	12	18	39	62	85
409-Pink Panther (TV)	1	3	4	6	8	10
410-Wacky Witch	1	2	3	5	6	8
411-Lassie (TV)(r/#324)	2	4	6	9	13	16
412-New Terrytoons (1975) (TV)	1	2	3	5	6	8
413-Daffy Duck (1976)(r/#331)	1	2	3	5	6	8
414-Space Family Robinson (r/#328)	6	12	18	39	62	85
415-Bugs Bunny (r/#329)	1	2	3	5	6	8
416-Beep-Beep, the Road Runner (r/#353)(TV)	1	2	3	5	6	8
417-Little Lulu (r/#323)	2	4	6	10	14	18
418-Pink Panther (r/#384) (TV)	1	2	3	5	6	8
419-Baby Snoots (r/#377)	1	3	4	6	8	10
420-Woody Woodpecker	1	2	3	5	6	8
421-Tweety & Sylvester	1	2	3	5	6	8
422-Wacky Witch (r/#386)	1	2	3	5	6	8
423-Little Monsters	1	3	4	6	8	10
424-Cracky (12/76)	1	2	3	5	6	8
425-Daffy Duck	1	2	3	5	6	8
426-Underdog (TV)	4	8	12	22	34	45
427-Little Lulu (r/#335)	2	4	6	8	11	14
428-Bugs Bunny	1	2	3	4	5	7
429-The Pink Panther (TV)	1	2	3	4	5	7
430-Beep-Beep, the Road Runner (TV)	1	2	3	4	5	7
431-Baby Snoots	1	2	3	5	6	8
432-Lassie (TV)	2	4	6	8	10	12
433-437: 433-Tweety & Sylvester. 434-Wacky Witch. 435-New Terrytoons (TV). 436-Wacky Advs. of Cracky. 437-Daffy Duck	1	2	3	4	5	7
438-Underdog (TV)	3	6	9	20	30	40
439-Little Lulu (r/#349)	2	4	6	8	11	14
440-442,444-446: 440-Bugs Bunny. 441-The Pink Panther (TV). 442-Beep-Beep, the Road Runner (TV). 444-Tom and Jerry. 445-Tweety and Sylvester. 446-Wacky Witch	1	2	3	5	6	8
443-Baby Snoots	1	2	3	5	6	8
447-Mighty Mouse	2	4	6	8	10	12
448-455,457,458: 448-Cracky. 449-Pink Panther (TV). 450-Baby Snoots. 451-Tom and Jerry. 452-Bugs Bunny. 453-Popeye. 454-Woody Woodpecker. 455-Beep-Beep, the Road Runner (TV). 457-Tweety & Sylvester. 458-Wacky Witch	1	2	3	5	6	8
456-Little Lulu (r/#369)	2	4	6	8	10	12
459-Mighty Mouse	2	4	6	8	10	12
460-466: 460-Daffy Duck. 461-The Pink Panther (TV). 462-Baby Snoots. 463-Tom and Jerry. 464-Bugs Bunny. 465-Popeye. 466-Woody Woodpecker	1	2	3	5	6	8
467-Underdog (TV)	3	6	9	18	27	35
468-Little Lulu (r/#385)	1	2	3	5	6	8
469-Tweety & Sylvester	1	2	3	5	6	8
470-Wacky Witch	1	2	3	5	6	8
471-Mighty Mouse	1	3	4	6	8	10
472-474,476-478: 472-Heckle & Jeckle(12/80). 473-Pink Panther(1/81)(TV). 474-Baby Snoots. 476-Bugs Bunny. 477-Popeye. 478-Woody Woodpecker	1	2	3	5	6	8
475-Little Lulu (r/#323)	1	3	4	6	8	10
479-Underdog (TV)	3	6	9	16	23	30
480-482: 480-Tom and Jerry. 481-Tweety and Sylvester. 482-Wacky Witch	1	2	3	4	5	8
483-Mighty Mouse	1	3	4	6	8	10

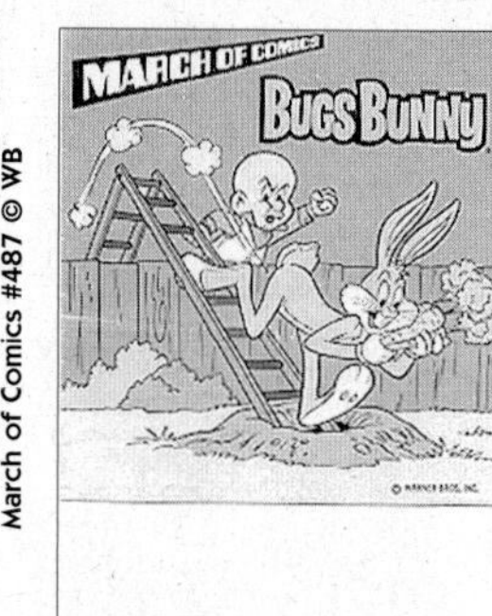

March of Comics #487 © WB

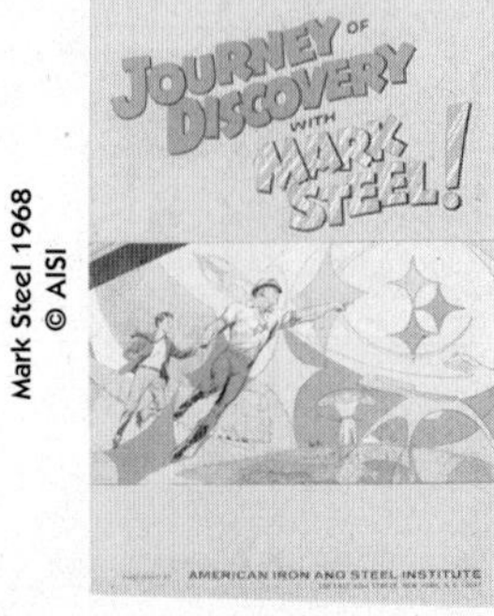

Mark Steel 1968 © AISI

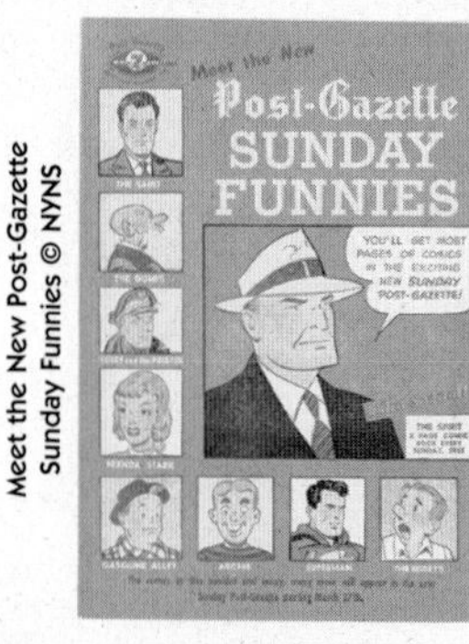

Meet the New Post-Gazette Sunday Funnies © NYNS

	GD 2.0	VG 4.0	FN 6.0	VF 8.0	VF/NM 9.0	NM- 9.2
484-487: 484-Heckle & Jeckle. 485-Baby Snoots. 486-The Pink Panther (TV).						
487-Bugs Bunny	1	2	3	4	5	8
488-Little Lulu (4/82) (r/#335) (Last issue)	2	4	6	10	14	18

MARCH TO MARKET, THE
Swift & Co.: 1950 (Giveaway)

	GD	VG	FN	VF	VF/NM	NM-
nn-The story of meat	3	6	8	11	13	15

MARGARET O'BRIEN (See The Adventures of...)

MARK STEEL
American Iron & Steel Institute: 1967, 1968, 1972 (Giveaway) (24 pgs.)

	GD	VG	FN	VF	VF/NM	NM-
1967,1968- "Journey of Discovery with..."; Neal Adams art	4	8	12	28	44	60
1972- "...Fights Pollution"; N. Adams-a	2	4	6	11	16	20

MARTIN LUTHER KING AND THE MONTGOMERY STORY
Fellowship Reconciliation: 1956 (Giveaway, 16 pgs.) (A Spanish edition also exists)
nn-In color with paper-c (a CGC 9.2 copy sold for $350 and a FN+ sold for $200 in 2004)

MARVEL COLLECTOR'S EDITION: X-MEN
Marvel Comics: 1993 (3-3/4x6-1/2")

	GD	VG	FN	VF	VF/NM	NM-
1-4-Pizza Hut giveaways						5.00

MARVEL COMICS PRESENTS
Marvel Comics: 1987, 1988 (4 1/4 x 6 1/4, 20 pgs.)
...Mini Comic Giveaway

	GD	VG	FN	VF	VF/NM	NM-
nn-(1988) Alf	1	2	3	5	6	8
nn-(1987) Captain America r/ #250	1	2	3	4	5	7
nn-(1987) Care Bears (Star Comics...)	1	2	3	4	5	7
nn-(1988) Flintstone Kids	1	2	3	5	6	8
nn-(1987) Heathcliffe (Star Comics...)	1	2	3	4	5	7
nn-(1987) Spider-Man-r/Spect. Spider-Man #21	1	2	3	4	5	7
nn-(1988) Spider-Man-r/Amazing Spider-Man #1	1	2	3	4	5	7
nn-(1988) X-Men-reprints X-Men #53; B. Smith-a	1	2	3	4	5	7

MARVEL GUIDE TO COLLECTING COMICS, THE
Marvel Comics: 1982 (16 pgs., newsprint pages and cover)

	GD	VG	FN	VF	VF/NM	NM-
1-Simonson-c	1	2	3	4	5	7

MARVEL HALLOWEEN ASHCAN 2006
Marvel Comics: 2006 (8-1/2"x 5-1/2", Halloween giveaway)

	GD	VG	FN	VF	VF/NM	NM-
nn-r/Marvel Adventures The Avengers #1						2.00

MARVEL MINI-BOOKS
Marvel Comics Group: 1966 (50 pgs., B&W; 5/8x7/8") (6 different issues)
(Smallest comics ever published) (Marvel Mania Giveaways)

	GD	VG	FN	VF	VF/NM	NM-
Captain America, Millie the Model, Sgt. Fury, Hulk, Thor each...	2	4	6	11	16	20
Spider-Man	3	6	9	14	20	25

NOTE: *Each came from gum machines in six different color covers, usually one color: Pink, yellow, green, etc.*

MARVEL SUPER-HERO ISLAND ADVENTURES
Marvel Comics: 1999 (Sold at the park polybagged with Captain America V3 #19, one other comic, 5 trading cards and a cloisonn'e pin)

	GD	VG	FN	VF	VF/NM	NM-
1-Promotes Universal Studios Islands of Adventures theme park						4.00

MARY'S GREATEST APOSTLE (St. Louis Grignion de Montfort)
Catechetical Guild (Topix) (Giveaway): No date (16 pgs.; paper cover)

	GD	VG	FN	VF	VF/NM	NM-
nn	5	10	15	23	28	32

MASK
DC Comics: 1985

	GD	VG	FN	VF	VF/NM	NM-
1-3						6.00

MASKED PILOT, THE (See Popular Comics #43)
R.S. Callender: 1939 (7-1/2x5-1/4", 16 pgs., premium, non-slick-c)

	GD	VG	FN	VF	VF/NM	NM-
nn-Bob Jenney-a	8	16	24	44	57	70

MASTERS OF THE UNIVERSE (He-Man)
DC Comics: 1982 (giveaways with action figures, at least 35 different issues, unnumbered)

	GD	VG	FN	VF	VF/NM	NM-
nn	2	4	6	8	10	12

MATRIX, THE (1999 movie)
Warner Brothers: 1999 (Recalled by Warner Bros. over questionable content)

	GD	VG	FN	VF	VF/NM	NM-
nn-Paul Chadwick-s/a (16 pgs.); Geof Darrow-c	1	2	3	5	6	8

McCRORY'S CHRISTMAS BOOK
Western Printing Co: 1955 (36 pgs., slick-c) (McCrory Stores Corp. giveaway)

	GD	VG	FN	VF	VF/NM	NM-
nn-Painted-c	5	10	15	22	26	30

McCRORY'S TOYLAND BRINGS YOU SANTA'S PRIVATE EYES
Promotional Publ. Co.: 1956 (16 pgs.) (Giveaway)

	GD	VG	FN	VF	VF/NM	NM-
nn-Has 9 pg. story plus 7 pgs. toy ads	4	8	11	16	19	22

McCRORY'S WONDERFUL CHRISTMAS
Promotional Publ. Co.: 1954 (20 pgs., slick-c) (Giveaway)

	GD	VG	FN	VF	VF/NM	NM-
nn	4	8	12	18	22	25

McDONALDS COMMANDRONS
DC Comics: 1985

	GD	VG	FN	VF	VF/NM	NM-
nn-Four editions						5.00

MEDAL FOR BOWZER, A (Giveaway)
American Visuals Corp.: 1966 (8 pgs.)

	GD	VG	FN	VF	VF/NM	NM-
nn-Eisner-c/script; Bowzer (a dog) survives untried pneumonia cure and earns his medal; (medical experimentation on animals)	15	30	45	104	227	350

MEET HIYA A FRIEND OF SANTA CLAUS
Julian J. Proskauer/Sundial Shoe Stores, etc.: 1949 (18 pgs.?, paper-c)(Giveaway)

	GD	VG	FN	VF	VF/NM	NM-
nn	6	12	18	31	38	45

MEET THE NEW POST-GAZETTE SUNDAY FUNNIES
Pittsburgh Post Gazette: 3/12/49 (7-1/4x10-1/4", 16 pgs., paper-c)
Commercial Comics (insert in newspaper) (Rare)
Dick Tracy by Gould, Gasoline Alley, Terry & the Pirates, Brenda Starr, Buck Rogers by Yager, The Gumps, Peter Rabbit by Fago, Superman, Funnyman by Siegel & Shuster, The Saint, Archie, & others done especially for this book. A fine copy sold at auction in 1985 for $276.00.

	GD	VG	FN	VF	VF/NM	NM-
	260	520	780	1700	-	-

MEN OF COURAGE
Catechetical Guild: 1949

	GD	VG	FN	VF	VF/NM	NM-
Bound Topix comics-V7#2,4,6,8,10,16,18,20	6	12	18	31	38	45

MEN WHO MOVE THE NATION
Publisher unknown: (Giveaway) (B&W)

	GD	VG	FN	VF	VF/NM	NM-
nn-Neal Adams-a	6	12	18	31	38	45

MERRY CHRISTMAS, A
K. K. Publications (Child Life Shoes): 1948 (Giveaway)

	GD	VG	FN	VF	VF/NM	NM-
nn	8	16	24	40	50	60

MERRY CHRISTMAS
K. K. Publications (Blue Bird Shoes Giveaway): 1956 (7-1/4x5-1/4")

	GD	VG	FN	VF	VF/NM	NM-
nn	4	8	12	18	22	25

MERRY CHRISTMAS FROM MICKEY MOUSE
K. K. Publications: 1939 (16 pgs.) (Color & B&W) (Shoe store giveaway)

	GD	VG	FN	VF	VF/NM	NM-
nn-Donald Duck & Pluto app.; text with art (Rare); c-reprint/Mickey Mouse Mag. V3#3 (12/37)(Rare)	245	490	735	1556	2678	3800

MERRY CHRISTMAS FROM SEARS TOYLAND (See Santa's Christmas Comic)
Sears Roebuck Giveaway: 1939 (16 pgs.) (Color)

	GD	VG	FN	VF	VF/NM	NM-
nn-Dick Tracy, Little Orphan Annie, The Gumps, Terry & the Pirates	103	206	309	654	1127	1600

MICKEY MOUSE (Also see Frito-Lay Giveaway)
Dell Publ. Co

	GD	VG	FN	VF	VF/NM	NM-
...& Goofy Explore Business(1978)	2	4	6	8	10	12
...& Goofy Explore Energy(1976-1978, 36 pgs.); Exxon giveaway in color; regular size	2	4	6	8	10	12
...& Goofy Explore Energy Conservation(1976-1978)-Exxon	2	4	6	8	10	12
...& Goofy Explore The Universe of Energy(1985, 20 pgs.); Exxon giveaway in color; regular size	1	2	3	5	7	9
The Perils of Mickey nn (1993, 5-1/4x7-1/4", 16 pgs.)-Nabisco giveaway w/ games, Nabisco coupons & 6 pgs. of stories; Phantom Blot app.						6.00

MICKEY MOUSE MAGAZINE
Walt Disney Productions: V1#1, Jan, 1933 - V1#9, Sept, 1933 (5-1/4x7-1/4")
No. 1-3 published by Kamen-Blair (Kay Kamen, Inc.)
(Scarce)-Distributed by dairies and leading stores through their local theatres.
First few issues had 5¢ listed on cover, later ones had no price.

	GD	VG	FN	VF	VF/NM	NM-
V1#1	460	920	1840	5500	-	-
2-4	220	440	880	1500	-	-
5-9	125	250	500	1000	-	-

MICKEY MOUSE MAGAZINE
Walt Disney Productions: V1#1, 11/33 - V2#12, 10/35 (Mills giveaways issued by different dairies)

Mr. Peanut (The Personal Story Of...) © Planters

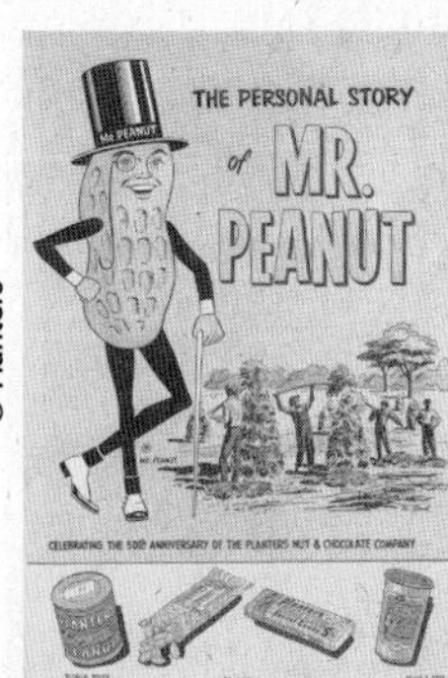

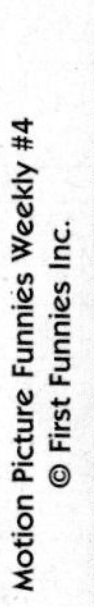
Motion Picture Funnies Weekly #4 © First Funnies Inc.

On the Air nn © NBC

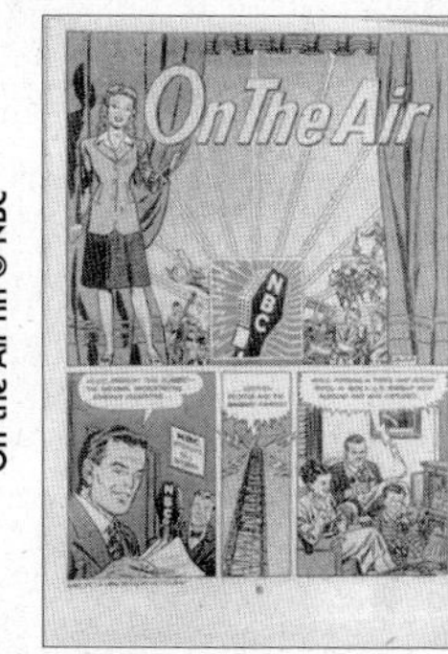

	GD 2.0	VG 4.0	FN 6.0	VF 8.0	VF/NM 9.0	NM- 9.2
V1#1	129	258	387	826	1413	2000
2-12: 2-X-Mas issue	43	86	129	271	461	650
V2#1-4,6-12: 2-X-Mas issue. 4-St. Valentine-c	34	68	102	199	325	450
V2#5 (3/35) 1st app. Donald Duck in sailor outfit on-c	90	180	270	576	988	1400

MICKEY MOUSE MAGAZINE
K.K. Publications: V4#1, Oct, 1938 (Giveaway)

	GD	VG	FN	VF	VF/NM	NM-
V4#1	40	80	120	252	426	600

MIGHTY ATOM, THE
Whitman

	GD	VG	FN	VF	VF/NM	NM-
Giveaway (1959, '63, Whitman)-Evans-a	3	6	9	16	23	30
Giveaway ('64r, '65r, '66r, '67r, '68r)-Evans-r?	2	4	6	10	14	18
Giveaway ('73r, '76r)	2	4	6	8	11	14

MILES THE MONSTER (Initially sold only at the Dover Speedway track)
Dover International Speedway, Inc.: 2006 ($3.00)

	GD	VG	FN	VF	VF/NM	NM-
1,2-Allan Gross & Mark Wheatley-s/Wheatley-a						3.00

MILITARY COURTESY
Harvey Publications: (16 pgs.)

	GD	VG	FN	VF	VF/NM	NM-
nn-Regulations and saluting instructions	5	10	14	20	24	28

MINUTE MAN
Sovereign Service Station giveaway: No date (16 pgs., B&W, paper-c blue & red)

	GD	VG	FN	VF	VF/NM	NM-
nn-American history	3	6	8	12	14	16

MINUTE MAN ANSWERS THE CALL, THE
By M. C. Gaines: 1942,1943,1944,1945 (4 pgs.) (Giveaway inserted in Jr. JSA Membership Kit)

	GD	VG	FN	VF	VF/NM	NM-
nn-Sheldon Moldoff-a	21	42	63	121	201	280

MIRACLE ON BROADWAY
Broadway Comics: Dec, 1995 (Giveaway)

	GD	VG	FN	VF	VF/NM	NM-
1-Ernie Colon-c/a; Jim Shooter & Co. story; 1st known digitally printed comic book; 1st app. Spire & Knights on Broadway (1150 print run)						20.00

NOTE: *Miracle on Broadway was a limited edition comic given to 1100 VIPs in the entertainment industry for the 1995 Holiday Season.*

MISS SUNBEAM (See Little Miss Sunbeam Comics)

MR. BUG GOES TO TOWN (See Cinema Comics Herald)
K.K. Publications: 1941 (Giveaway, 52 pgs.)

	GD	VG	FN	VF	VF/NM	NM-
nn-Cartoon movie (scarce)	68	136	204	432	741	1050

MR. PEANUT, THE PERSONAL STORY OF
Planters Nut & Chocolate Co.: 1956

	GD	VG	FN	VF	VF/NM	NM-
nn	4	8	12	22	34	45

MOTHER OF US ALL
Catechetical Guild Giveaway: 1950? (32 pgs.)

	GD	VG	FN	VF	VF/NM	NM-
nn	5	10	15	23	28	32

MOTION PICTURE FUNNIES WEEKLY (Amazing Man #5 on?)
First Funnies, Inc.: 1939 (Giveaway)(B&W, 36 pgs.) No month given; last panel in Sub-Mariner story dated 4/39 (Also see Colossus, Green Giant & Invaders No. 20)

	GD	VG	FN	VF	VF/NM	NM-
1-Origin & 1st printed app. Sub-Mariner by Bill Everett (8 pgs.); Fred Schwab-c; reprinted in Marvel Mystery #1 with color added over the craft tint which was used to shade the black & white version; Spy Ring, American Ace (reprinted in Marvel Mystery #3) app. (Rare)-only eight known copies, one near mint with white pages, the rest with brown pages.	4600	9200	13,800	18,860	33,000	-
Covers only to #2-4 (set)						700

NOTE: Eight copies (plus one coverless) were discovered in 1974 in the estate of the deceased publisher. Covers only to issues No. 2-4 were also found which evidently were printed in advance along with #1. #1 was to be distributed only through motion picture movie houses. However, it is believed that only advanced copies were sent out and the motion picture houses not going for the idea. Possible distribution at local theaters in Boston suspected. The "pay" copy (graded at 9.0) was discovered after 1974, bringing the total known to nine. The last panel of Sub-Mariner contains a rectangular box with "Continued Next Week" printed in it. When reprinted in Marvel Mystery, the box was left in with lettering omitted.

MY DOG TIGE (Buster Brown's Dog)
Buster Brown Shoes: 1957 (Giveaway)

	GD	VG	FN	VF	VF/NM	NM-
nn	5	10	15	24	30	35

MY GREATEST THRILLS IN BASEBALL
Mission of California: Date? (16 pg. Giveaway)

	GD	VG	FN	VF	VF/NM	NM-
nn-By Mickey Mantle	53	106	159	337	581	825

MYSTERIOUS ADVENTURES WITH SANTA CLAUS
Lansburgh's: 1948 (paper cover)

	GD	VG	FN	VF	VF/NM	NM-
nn	13	26	39	72	101	130

NAKED FORCE!

Commercial Comics: 1958 (Small size)

	GD 2.0	VG 4.0	FN 6.0	VF 8.0	VF/NM 9.0	NM- 9.2
nn	3	6	8	11	13	15

NATURAL DISASTERS!
Graphic Information Service/ Civil Defense: 1956 (16 pgs., soft-c)

	GD	VG	FN	VF	VF/NM	NM-
nn-Al Capp Li'l Abner-c; Li'l Abner cameo (1 panel); narrated by Mr. Civil Defense	10	20	30	54	72	90

NAVY: HISTORY & TRADITION
Stokes Walesby Co./Dept. of Navy: 1958 - 1961 (nn) (Giveaway)

	GD	VG	FN	VF	VF/NM	NM-
1772-1778, 1778-1782, 1782-1817, 1817-1865, 1865-1936, 1940-1945: 1772-1778-16 pg. in color	5	10	15	22	26	30
1861: Naval Actions of the Civil War: 1865-36 pg. in color; flag-c	5	10	15	22	26	30

NEW ADVENTURE OF WALT DISNEY'S SNOW WHITE AND THE SEVEN DWARFS, A
(See Snow White Bendix Giveaway)

NEW ADVENTURES OF PETER PAN (Disney)
Western Publishing Co.: 1953 (5x7-1/4", 36 pgs.) (Admiral giveaway)

	GD	VG	FN	VF	VF/NM	NM-
nn	14	28	42	76	108	140

NEW AVENGERS... (Giveaway for U.S Military personnel)
Marvel Comics: 2005 - Present (Distributed by Army & Air Force Exchange Service)

	GD	VG	FN	VF	VF/NM	NM-
... Guest Starring the Fantastic Four (4/05) Bendis-s/Jurgens-a/c						4.00
...: Pot of Gold (AAFES 110th Anniversary Issue) (10/05) Jenkins-s/Nolan-a/c						4.00
(#3) ...: Avengers & X-Men Time Trouble (4/06) Kirkman-s						4.00
(#4) ...: Letters Home (12/06) Capt. America, Punisher, Silver Surfer, Ghost Rider on-c						4.00
5-The Spirit of America (10/05) Captain America app.						4.00
6-Fireline (8/08) Spider-Man, Iron Man & Hulk app. Richards-a/Dave Ross-c						4.00
7-An Army of One (2009) Frank Cho pin-up on back-c						4.00
8-The Promise (12/09) Captain America (Bucky) app.						4.00

NEW FRONTIERS
Harvey Information Press (United States Steel Corp.) : 1958 (16 pgs., paper-c)

	GD	VG	FN	VF	VF/NM	NM-
nn-History of barbed wire	3	6	9	14	19	24

NEW TEEN TITANS, THE
DC Comics: Nov. 1983

	GD	VG	FN	VF	VF/NM	NM-
nn(11/83-Keebler Co. Giveaway)-In cooperation with "The President's Drug Awareness Campaign"; came in Presidential envelope w/letter from White House (Nancy Reagan)	1	2	3	4	5	7
nn-(re-issue of above on Mando paper for direct sales market); American Soft Drink Industry version; I.B.M. Corp. version						5.00

NEW USES FOR GOOD EARTH
Mined Land Conservation: 1960

	GD	VG	FN	VF	VF/NM	NM-
nn	3	6	9	20	30	40

NOLAN RYAN IN THE WINNING PITCH (Kellogg's Tony's Sports Comics)
DC Comics: 1992 (Sports Illustrated)

	GD	VG	FN	VF	VF/NM	NM-
nn						5.00

OLD GLORY COMICS
Chesapeake & Ohio Railway: 1944 (Giveaway)

	GD	VG	FN	VF	VF/NM	NM-
nn-Capt. Fearless reprint	8	16	24	40	50	60

ON THE AIR
NBC Network Comic: 1947 (Giveaway, paper-c)

	GD	VG	FN	VF	VF/NM	NM-
nn-(Rare)	18	36	54	105	165	225

OUT OF THE PAST A CLUE TO THE FUTURE
E. C. Comics (Public Affairs Comm.): 1946? (16 pgs.) (paper cover)

	GD	VG	FN	VF	VF/NM	NM-
nn-Based on public affairs pamphlet "What Foreign Trade Means to You"	20	40	60	116	191	265

OUTSTANDING AMERICAN WAR HEROES
The Parents' Institute: 1944 (16 pgs., paper-c)

	GD	VG	FN	VF	VF/NM	NM-
nn-Reprints from True Comics	5	10	15	22	26	30

OVERSEAS COMICS (Also see G.I. Comics & Jeep Comics)
Giveaway (Distributed to U.S. Armed Forces): 1944 - No. 105?, 1946 (7-1/4x10-1/4"; 16 pgs. in color)

	GD	VG	FN	VF	VF/NM	NM-
23-105-Bringing Up Father (by McManus), Popeye, Joe Palooka, Dick Tracy, Superman, Gasoline Alley, Buz Sawyer, Li'l Abner, Blondie, Terry & the Pirates, Out Our Way	7	14	21	35	43	50

OWL, THE (See Crackajack Funnies #25 & Popular Comics #72)(Also see The Hurricane Kids & Magic Morro)

Oxydol-Dreft #2 © TOBY

Poll Parrot #1 © K.K. Pub

Punisher: Countdown © MAR

	GD 2.0	VG 4.0	FN 6.0	VF 8.0	VF/NM 9.0	NM- 9.2
Western Pub. Co./R.S. Callender: 1940 (Giveaway)(7-1/2x5-1/4")(Soft-c, color)						
nn-Frank Thomas-a	15	30	45	86	133	180
OXYDOL-DREFT						
Toby Press:1950 (Set of 6 pocket-size giveaways; distributed through the mail as a set) (Scarce)						
1-3: 1-Li'l Abner. 2-Daisy Mae. 3-Shmoo	9	18	27	52	69	85
4-John Wayne; Williamson/Frazetta-c from John Wayne #3	13	26	39	72	101	130
5-Archie	12	24	36	67	94	120
6-Terrytoons Mighty Mouse	9	18	27	50	65	80
Mailing Envelope (has All Capp's Shmoo on front)	10	20	30	54	72	90
OZZIE SMITH IN THE KID WHO COULD (Kellogg's Tony's Sports Comics)						
DC Comics: 1992 (Sports Illustrated)						
nn-Ozzie Smith app.						5.00
PADRE OF THE POOR						
Catechetical Guild: nd (Giveaway) (16 pgs., paper-c)						
nn	5	10	15	24	30	35
PAUL TERRY'S HOW TO DRAW FUNNY CARTOONS						
Terrytoons, Inc. (Giveaway): 1940's (14 pgs.) (Black & White)						
nn-Heckle & Jeckle, Mighty Mouse, etc.	13	26	39	72	101	130
PEANUTS HALLOWEEN						
Fantagraphics Books: Sept, 2008 (8-1/2" x 5-3/8" ashcan giveaway)						
nn-Halloween themed reprints in color and B&W						2.00
PETER PAN (See New Adventures of Peter Pan)						
PETER PENNY AND HIS MAGIC DOLLAR						
American Bankers Association, N. Y. (Giveaway): 1947 (16 pgs.; paper-c; regular size)						
nn-(Scarce)-Used in **SOTI**, pg. 310, 311	15	30	45	88	137	185
Diff. version (7-1/4x11")-redrawn, 16 pgs., paper-c	10	20	30	56	76	95
PETER WHEAT (The Adventures of...)						
Bakers Associates Giveaway: 1948 - 1957? (16 pgs. in color) (paper covers)						
nn(No.1)-States on last page, end of 1st Adventure of...; Kelly-a	26	52	78	154	252	350
nn(4 issues)-Kelly-a	14	28	42	82	121	160
6-10-All Kelly-a	10	20	30	54	72	90
11-20-All Kelly-a	9	18	27	50	65	80
21-35-All Kelly-a	8	16	24	40	50	60
36-66	6	12	18	28	34	40
...Artist's Workbook ('54, digest size)	6	12	18	28	34	40
...Four-In-One Fun Pack (Vol. 2, '54), oblong, comics w/puzzles	7	14	21	35	43	50
...Fun Book ('52, 32 pgs., paper-c, B&W & color, 8-1/2x10-3/4")-Contains cut-outs, puzzles, games, magic & pages to color	8	16	24	44	57	70
NOTE: ***Al Hubbard** art #36 on; written by Del Connell.*						
PETER WHEAT NEWS						
Bakers Associates: 1948 - No. 30, 1950 (4 pgs. in color)						
Vol. 1-All have 2 pgs. Peter Wheat by Kelly	21	42	63	123	204	285
2-10	13	26	39	72	101	130
11-20	8	16	24	40	50	60
21-30	6	12	18	28	34	40
NOTE: *Early issues have no date & **Kelly** art.*						
PINOCCHIO						
Cocomalt/Montgomery Ward Co.: 1940 (10 pgs.; giveaway, linen-like paper)						
nn-Cocomalt edition	43	86	129	271	456	640
nn-store edition	36	72	108	215	350	485
PIUS XII MAN OF PEACE						
Catechetical Guild: No date (12 pgs.; 5-1/2x8-1/2") (B&W)						
nn-Catechetical Guild Giveaway	6	12	18	31	38	45
PLOT TO STEAL THE WORLD, THE						
Work & Unity Group: 1948, 16pgs., paper-c						
nn-Anti commumism	18	36	54	103	162	220
POCAHONTAS						
Pocahontas Fuel Company (Coal): 1941 - No. 2, 1942						
nn(#1), 2-Feat. life story of Indian princess Pocahontas & facts about Pocahontas coal, Pocahontas, VA.	15	30	45	85	130	175
POLL PARROT						

	GD 2.0	VG 4.0	FN 6.0	VF 8.0	VF/NM 9.0	NM- 9.2
Poll Parrot Shoe Store/International Shoe						
K. K. Publications (Giveaway): 1950 - No. 4, 1951; No. 2, 1959 - No. 16, 1962						
1 ('50)-Howdy Doody; small size	18	36	54	107	169	230
2-4('51)-Howdy Doody	15	30	45	88	137	185
2('59)-16('62): 2-The Secret of Crumbley Castle. 5-Bandit Busters. 7-The Make-Believe Mummy. 8-Mixed Up Mission('60). 10-The Frightful Flight. 11-Showdown at Sunup. 12-Maniac at Mubu Island. 13-...and the Runaway Genie. 14-Bully for You. 15-Trapped In Tall Timber. 16-...& the Rajah's Ruby('62)	3	6	9	16	23	30
POPEYE						
Whitman						
Bold Detergent giveaway (Same as regular issue #94)	2	4	6	9	13	16
Quaker Cereal premium (1989, 16pp, small size,4 diff.)(Popeye & the Time Machine, --On Safari, --& Big Foot, --vs. Bluto)	2	4	6	8	10	12
POPEYE						
Charlton (King Features) (Giveaway): 1972 - 1974 (36 pgs. in color)						
E-1 to E-15 (Educational comics)	2	4	6	9	13	16
nn-Popeye Gettin' Better Grades-4 pgs. used as intro. to above giveaways (in color)	2	4	6	9	13	16
POPSICLE PETE FUN BOOK (See All-American Comics #6)						
Joe Lowe Corp.: 1947, 1948						
nn-36 pgs. in color; Sammy 'n' Claras, The King Who Couldn't Sleep & Popsicle Pete stories, games, cut-outs	11	22	33	64	90	115
Adventure Book ('48)-Has Classics ad with checklist to HRN #343 (Great Expectations #43)	10	20	30	56	76	95
PORKY'S BOOK OF TRICKS						
K. K. Publications (Giveaway): 1942 (8-1/2x5-1/2", 48 pgs.)						
nn-7 pg. comic story, text stories, plus games & puzzles	53	106	159	334	567	800
POST GAZETTE (See Meet the New...)						
PUNISHER: COUNTDOWN (Movie)						
Marvel Comics: 2004 (7 1/4" X 4 3/4" mini-comic packaged with Punisher DVD)						
nn-Prequel to 2004 movie; Ennis-s/Dillon-a/Bradstreet-c						2.50
PURE OIL COMICS (Also see Salerno Carnival of Comics, 24 Pages of Comics, & Vicks Comics)						
Pure Oil Giveaway: Late 1930's (24 pgs., regular size, paper-c)						
nn-Contains 1-2 pg. strips; i.e., Hairbreadth Harry, Skyroads, Buck Rogers by Calkins & Yager, Olly of the Movies, Napoleon, S'Matter Pop, etc. Also a 16 pg. 1938 giveaway with Buck Rogers	34	68	102	204	332	460
QUAKER OATS (Also see Cap'n Crunch)						
Quaker Oats Co.: 1965 (Giveaway) (2-1/2x5-1/2") (16 pgs.)						
"Plenty of Glutton", starring Quake & Quisp;	3	6	9	14	19	24
"Lava Come-Back", "Kite Tale"	1	3	4	6	8	10
RAILROADS DELIVER THE GOODS!						
Assoc. of American Railroads: Dec, 1954; Sept, 1957 (16 pgs., paper-c)						
nn-The story of railway freight	6	12	18	28	34	40
RAILS ACROSS AMERICA!						
Assoc. of American Railroads: nd (16 pgs.)						
nn	6	12	18	28	34	40
READY THEN, READY NOW						
Western Publications: 1966 (National Guard military giveaway, regular size)						
nn	6	12	18	37	59	80
REAL FUN OF DRIVING!!, THE						
Chrysler Corp.: 1965, 1966, 1967 (Regular size, 16 pgs.)						
nn-Schaffenberger-a (12 pgs.)	1	2	3	5	6	8
REAL HIT						
Fox Features Publications: 1944 (Savings Bond premium)						
1-Blue Beetle-r; Blue Beetle on-c	15	30	45	90	140	190
NOTE: *Two versions exist, with and without covers. The coverless version has the title, No. 1 and price printed at top of splash page.*						
RED BALL COMIC BOOK						
Parents' Magazine Institute: 1947 (Red Ball Shoes giveaway)						
nn-Reprints from True Comics	4	8	11	16	19	22
REDDY GOOSE						
International Shoe Co. (Western Printing): No number, 1958?; No. 2, Jan, 1959 - No. 16, July, 1962 (Giveaway)						

Reddy Kilowatt nn © EC

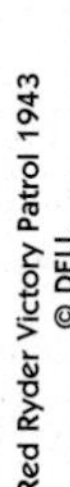
Red Ryder Victory Patrol 1943 © DELL

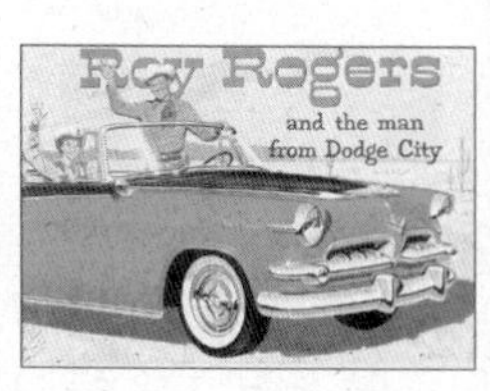

Roy Rogers and the Man From Dodge City © DELL

	GD 2.0	VG 4.0	FN 6.0	VF 8.0	VF/NM 9.0	NM- 9.2
nn (#1)	5	10	15	30	48	65
2-16	3	6	9	18	27	35

REDDY KILOWATT (5¢) (Also see Story of Edison)
Educational Comics (E. C.): 1946 - No. 2, 1947; 1956 - 1965 (no month) (16 pgs., paper-c)

	GD 2.0	VG 4.0	FN 6.0	VF 8.0	VF/NM 9.0	NM- 9.2
nn-A Visit With Reddy (1948-1954?)	9	18	27	50	65	80
nn-Reddy Made Magic (1946, 5¢)	13	26	39	72	101	130
nn-Reddy Made Magic (1958)	9	18	27	50	65	80
2-Edison, the Man Who Changed the World (3/4" smaller than #1) (1947, 5¢)	13	26	39	72	101	130
...Comic Book 2 (1954)- "Light's Diamond Jubilee"	9	18	27	54	72	90
...Comic Book 2 (1956, 16 pgs.)- "Wizard of Light"	9	18	27	52	69	85
...Comic Book 2 (1958, 16 pgs.)- "Wizard of Light"	9	18	27	50	65	78
...Comic Book 2 (1965, 16 pgs.)- "Wizard of Light"	4	8	12	28	44	60
...Comic Book 3 (1956, 8 pgs.)- "The Space Kite"; Orlando story; regular size	9	18	27	47	61	75
...Comic Book 3 (1960, 8 pgs.)- "The Space Kite"; Orlando story; regular size	4	8	12	28	44	60

NOTE: *Several copies surfaced in 1979.*

REDDY MADE MAGIC
Educational Comics (E. C.): 1956, 1958 (16 pgs., paper-c)

	GD 2.0	VG 4.0	FN 6.0	VF 8.0	VF/NM 9.0	NM- 9.2
1-Reddy Kilowatt-r (splash panel changed)	11	22	33	60	83	105
1 (1958 edition)	6	12	18	31	38	45

RED ICEBERG, THE
Impact Publ. (Catechetical Guild): 1960 (10¢, 16 pgs., Communist propaganda)

	GD 2.0	VG 4.0	FN 6.0	VF 8.0	VF/NM 9.0	NM- 9.2
nn-(Rare)- "We The People" back-c	27	54	81	196	423	650
2nd version- "Impact Press" back-c	23	46	69	161	343	525
3rd version- "Explains comic" back-c	23	46	69	161	343	525
4th version- "Impact Press w/World Wide Secret Heart Program ad"	23	46	69	161	343	525
5th version- "Chicago Inter-Student Catholic Action" back-c	23	46	69	161	343	525

NOTE: *This book was the Guild's last anti-communist propaganda book and had very limited circulation. 3 - 4 copies surfaced in 1979 from the defunct publisher's files. Other copies do turn up.*

RED RYDER COMICS
Dell Publ. Co.

	GD 2.0	VG 4.0	FN 6.0	VF 8.0	VF/NM 9.0	NM- 9.2
Buster Brown Shoes Giveaway (1941, color, soft-c, 32 pgs.)	18	36	54	105	165	225
Red Ryder Super Book of Comics (1944, paper-c, 32 pgs.; blank back-c) Magic Morro app.	20	40	60	114	182	250
Red Ryder Victory Patrol-nn(1942, 32 pgs.)(Langendorf bread; includes cut-out membership card and certificate, order blank and "Slide-Up" decoder, and a Super Book of Comics in color (same content as Super Book #4 w/diff. cover (Pan-Am)) (Rare)	161	322	483	1030	1765	2500
Red Ryder Victory Patrol-nn(1943, 32 pgs.)(Langendorf bread; includes cut-out "Rodeomatic" radio decoder, order coupon for "Magic V-Badge", cut-out membership card and certificate and a full color Super Book of comics comic book) (Rare)	129	258	387	826	1413	2000
Red Ryder Victory Patrol-nn(1944, 32 pgs.)-r-/#43,44; comic has a paper-c & is stapled inside a triple cardboard fold-out-c; contains membership card, decoder, map of R.R. home range, etc. Herky app. (Langendorf Bread giveaway; sub-titled 'Super Book of Comics') (Rare)	129	258	387	826	1413	2000
Wells Lamont Corp. giveaway (1950)-16 pgs. in color; regular size; paper-c; 1941-r	15	30	45	86	133	180

RETURN OF JOE THE GENIE OF STEEL (Also see Joe The Genie of Steel)
U. S. Steel Corp., Pittsburgh, PA/Commercial Comics: 1951 (U. S. Steel Corp. giveaway)

	GD 2.0	VG 4.0	FN 6.0	VF 8.0	VF/NM 9.0	NM- 9.2
nn-Joe Magarac, the Paul Bunyan of steel	5	10	15	30	48	65

REX MORGAN M.D. TALKS ABOUT YOUR UNBORN CHILD
(No publisher) Fetal Alcohol, Tobacco & Firearms giveaway, 1980 (Reg. size, paper-c)

	GD 2.0	VG 4.0	FN 6.0	VF 8.0	VF/NM 9.0	NM- 9.2
nn	6	12	18	28	34	40

RICHIE RICH, CASPER & WENDY NATIONAL LEAGUE
Harvey Publications: June, 1976 (52 pgs.) (newsstand edition also exists)

	GD 2.0	VG 4.0	FN 6.0	VF 8.0	VF/NM 9.0	NM- 9.2
1 (Released-3/76 with 6/76 date)	3	6	9	16	22	28
1 (6/76)-2nd version w/San Francisco Giants & KTVU 2 logos; has "Compliments of Giants and Straw Hat Pizza" on-c	3	6	9	16	22	28
1-Variants for other 11 NL teams, similar to Giants version but with different ad on inside front-c	3	6	9	16	22	28

RIDE THE HIGH IRON!
Assoc. of American Railroads: Jan, 1957 (16 pgs.)

	GD 2.0	VG 4.0	FN 6.0	VF 8.0	VF/NM 9.0	NM- 9.2
nn-The Story of modern passenger trains	5	10	15	24	30	35

RIPLEY'S BELIEVE IT OR NOT!
Harvey Publications

	GD 2.0	VG 4.0	FN 6.0	VF 8.0	VF/NM 9.0	NM- 9.2
J. C. Penney giveaway (1948)	9	18	27	50	65	80

ROBIN HOOD (New Adventures of...)
Walt Disney Productions: 1952 (Flour giveaways, 5x7-1/4", 36 pgs.)

	GD 2.0	VG 4.0	FN 6.0	VF 8.0	VF/NM 9.0	NM- 9.2
"New Adventures of Robin Hood", "Ghosts of Waylea Castle", & "The Miller's Ransom" each....	5	10	15	22	26	30

ROBIN HOOD'S FRONTIER DAYS (...Western Tales, Adventures of... #1)
Shoe Store Giveaway (Robin Hood Stores): 1956 (20 pgs., slick-c)(7 issues?)

	GD 2.0	VG 4.0	FN 6.0	VF 8.0	VF/NM 9.0	NM- 9.2
nn	6	12	18	28	34	40
nn-Issues with Crandall-a	8	16	24	40	50	60

ROCKETS AND RANGE RIDERS
Richfield Oil Corp.: May, 1957 (Giveaway, 16 pgs., soft-c)

	GD 2.0	VG 4.0	FN 6.0	VF 8.0	VF/NM 9.0	NM- 9.2
nn-Toth-a	15	30	45	84	127	170

ROUND THE WORLD GIFT
National War Fund (Giveaway): No date (mid 1940's) (4 pgs.)

	GD 2.0	VG 4.0	FN 6.0	VF 8.0	VF/NM 9.0	NM- 9.2
nn	11	22	33	64	90	115

ROY ROGERS COMICS
Dell Publishing Co.

	GD 2.0	VG 4.0	FN 6.0	VF 8.0	VF/NM 9.0	NM- 9.2
...& the Man From Dodge City (Dodge giveaway, 16 pgs., 1954)-Frontier, Inc. (5x7-1/4")	12	24	36	69	97	125
Official Roy Rogers Riders Club Comics (1952; 16 pgs., reg. size, paper-c)	21	42	63	122	199	275

RUDOLPH, THE RED-NOSED REINDEER
Montgomery Ward: 1939 (2,400,000 copies printed); Dec, 1951 (Giveaway)

	GD 2.0	VG 4.0	FN 6.0	VF 8.0	VF/NM 9.0	NM- 9.2
Paper cover-1st app. in print; written by Robert May; ill. by Denver Gillen	15	30	45	83	124	165
Hardcover version	19	38	57	109	172	235
1951 Edition (Has 1939 date)-36 pgs., slick-c printed in red & brown; pulp interior printed in four mixed-ink colors: red, green, blue & brown	11	22	33	62	86	110
1951 Edition with red-spiral promotional booklet printed on high quality stock, 8-1/2"x11", in red & brown, 25 pages composed of 4 fold outs, single sheets and the Rudolph comic book inserted (rare)	47	94	141	296	498	700

SABRINA THE TEENAGE WITCH
Archie Comic Publications: (8 1/2"x 5 1/2", Diamond Comic Dist. Halloween giveaway)

	GD 2.0	VG 4.0	FN 6.0	VF 8.0	VF/NM 9.0	NM- 9.2
... And The Archies (2004)-Tania Del Rio-s/a; manga-style; Josie and the Pussycats app.						2.50

SAD CASE OF WAITING ROOM WILLIE, THE
American Visuals Corp. (For Baltimore Medical Society): (nd, 1950?)
(14 pgs. in color; paper covers; regular size)

	GD 2.0	VG 4.0	FN 6.0	VF 8.0	VF/NM 9.0	NM- 9.2
nn-By Will Eisner (Rare)	44	88	132	277	469	660

SAD SACK COMICS
Harvey Publications: 1957-1962

	GD 2.0	VG 4.0	FN 6.0	VF 8.0	VF/NM 9.0	NM- 9.2
Armed Forces Complimentary copies, HD #1-40 (1957-1962)	3	6	9	16	22	28

SALERNO CARNIVAL OF COMICS (Also see Pure Oil Comics, 24 Pages of Comics, & Vicks Comics)
Salerno Cookie Co.: Late 1930s (Giveaway, 16 pgs, paper-c)

	GD 2.0	VG 4.0	FN 6.0	VF 8.0	VF/NM 9.0	NM- 9.2
nn-Color reprints of Calkins' Buck Rogers & Skyroads, plus other strips from Famous Funnies	42	84	126	265	445	625

SALUTE TO THE BOY SCOUTS
Association of American Railroads: 1960 (16 pgs., paper-c, regular size)

	GD 2.0	VG 4.0	FN 6.0	VF 8.0	VF/NM 9.0	NM- 9.2
nn-History of scouting and the railroad	3	6	9	16	22	28

SANTA AND POLLYANNA PLAY THE GLAD GAME
Western Publ.: Aug, 1960 (16 pgs.) (Disney giveaway)

	GD 2.0	VG 4.0	FN 6.0	VF 8.0	VF/NM 9.0	NM- 9.2
nn	2	4	6	13	18	22

SANTA & THE BUCCANEERS
Promotional Publ. Co.: 1959 (Giveaway, paper-c)

	GD 2.0	VG 4.0	FN 6.0	VF 8.0	VF/NM 9.0	NM- 9.2
nn-Reprints 1952 Santa & the Pirates	2	4	6	11	16	20

SANTA & THE CHRISTMAS CHICKADEE
Murphy's: 1974 (Giveaway, 20 pgs.)

	GD 2.0	VG 4.0	FN 6.0	VF 8.0	VF/NM 9.0	NM- 9.2
nn	2	4	6	8	10	12

SANTA & THE PIRATES
Promotional Publ. Co.: 1952 (Giveaway)

	GD 2.0	VG 4.0	FN 6.0	VF 8.0	VF/NM 9.0	NM- 9.2
nn-Marv Levy-c/a	4	8	12	17	21	24

Santa's Christmas Comic Variety Show © Sears

Santa's Toytown Fun Book © KK

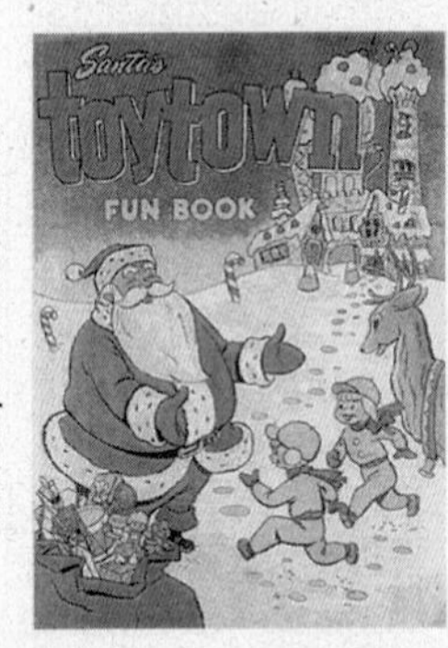

Sergeant Preston of the Yukon © DELL

	GD 2.0	VG 4.0	FN 6.0	VF 8.0	VF/NM 9.0	NM- 9.2
SANTA CLAUS FUNNIES (Also see The Little Fir Tree) **W. T. Grant Co./Whitman Publishing:** nd; 1940 (Giveaway, 8x10"; 12 pgs., color & B&W, heavy paper)						
nn-(2 versions- no date and 1940)	14	28	42	78	112	145
SANTA IS HERE! **Western Publ. (Giveaway):** 1949 (oblong, slick-c)						
nn	6	12	18	31	58	45
SANTA ON THE JOLLY ROGER **Promotional Publ. Co. (Giveaway):** 1965						
nn-Marv Levy-c/a	2	4	6	8	10	12
SANTA! SANTA! **R. Jackson:** 1974 (20 pgs.) (Montgomery Ward giveaway)						
nn	1	3	4	6	8	10
SANTA'S BUNDLE OF FUN **Gimbels:** 1969 (Giveaway, B&W, 20 pgs.)						
nn-Coloring book & games	2	4	6	8	10	12
SANTA'S CHRISTMAS COMIC VARIETY SHOW (See Merry Christmas From Sears Toyland) **Sears Roebuck & Co.:** 1943 (24 pgs.)						
Contains puzzles & new comics of Dick Tracy, Little Orphan Annie, Moon Mullins, Terry & the Pirates, etc.	52	104	156	325	555	785
SANTA'S CHRISTMAS TIME STORIES **Premium Sales, Inc.:** nd (Late 1940s) (16 pgs., paper-c) (Giveaway)						
nn	6	12	18	31	38	45
SANTA'S CIRCUS **Promotional Publ. Co.:** 1964 (Giveaway, half-size)						
nn-Marv Levy-c/a	2	4	6	8	11	14
SANTA'S FUN BOOK **Promotional Publ. Co.:** 1951, 1952 (Regular size, 16 pgs., paper-c) (Murphy's giveaway)						
nn	5	10	15	24	30	35
SANTA'S GIFT BOOK **No Publisher:** No date (16 pgs.)						
nn-Puzzles, games only	4	8	11	16	19	22
SANTA'S NEW STORY BOOK **Wallace Hamilton Campbell:** 1949 (16 pgs., paper-c) (Giveaway)						
nn	6	12	18	31	38	45
SANTA'S REAL STORY BOOK **Wallace Hamilton Campbell/W. W. Orris:** 1948, 1952 (Giveaway, 16 pgs.)						
nn	6	12	18	31	38	45
SANTA'S RIDE **W. T. Grant Co.:** 1959 (Giveaway)						
nn	3	6	9	14	19	24
SANTA'S RODEO **Promotional Publ. Co.:** 1964 (Giveaway, half-size)						
nn-Marv Levy-a	2	4	6	8	11	14
SANTA'S SECRET CAVE **W.T. Grant Co.:** 1960 (Giveaway, half-size)						
nn	2	4	6	11	16	20
SANTA'S SECRETS **Sam B. Anson Christmas giveaway:** 1951, 1952? (16 pgs., paper-c)						
nn-Has games, stories & pictures to color	4	8	12	17	21	24
SANTA'S STORIES **K. K. Publications (Klines Dept. Store):** 1953 (Regular size, paper-c)						
nn-Kelly-a	15	30	45	88	137	185
nn-Another version (1953, glossy-c, half-size, 7-1/4x5-1/4")-Kelly-a	11	22	33	62	86	110
SANTA'S SURPRISE **K. K. Publications:** 1947 (Giveaway, 36 pgs., slick-c)						
nn	8	16	24	40	50	60
SANTA'S TOYTOWN FUN BOOK **Promotional Publ. Co.:** 1953 (Giveaway)						
nn-Marv Levy-c	4	8	11	16	19	22
SANTA TAKES A TRIP TO MARS **Bradshaw-Diehl Co., Huntington, W.VA.:** 1950s (nd) (Giveaway, 16 pgs.)						
nn	4	8	11	16	19	22
SCHWINN BIKE THRILLS **Schwinn Bicycle Co.:** 1959 (Reg. size)						
nn	8	16	24	40	50	60
SCIENCE FAIR STORY OF ELECTRONICS **Radio Shack/Tandy Corp.:** 1975 - 1987 (Giveaway)						
11 different issues (approx. 1 per year) each....						3.00
SCOOBY-DOO! **DC Comics.:** 2002 (Burger King/Cartoon Network giveaway)						
1						2.50
SEEING WASHINGTON **Commercial Comics:** 1957 (also sold at 25¢)(Slick-c, reg. size)						
nn	6	12	18	28	34	40
SERGEANT PRESTON OF THE YUKON **Quaker Cereals:** 1956 (4 comic booklets) (Soft-c, 16 pgs., 7x2-1/2" & 5x2-1/2") Giveaways						
"How He Found Yukon King", "The Case That Made Him A Sergeant", "How Yukon King Saved Him From The Wolves", "How He Became A Mountie" each...	9	18	27	47	61	75
SHAZAM! (Visits Portland Oregon in 1943) **DC Comics:** 1989 (69¢ cover)						
nn-Promotes Super-Heroes exhibit at Oregon Museum of Science and Industry; reprints Golden Age Captain Marvel story	2	4	6	8	11	14
SHERIFF OF COCHISE, THE (TV) **Mobil:** 1957 (16 pgs.) Giveaway						
nn-Schaffenberger-a	4	9	13	18	22	26
SIDEWALK ROMANCE (Also see The K. O. Punch & Lucky Fights It Through) **Health Publications:** 1950						
nn-VD educational giveaway	34	68	102	199	325	450
SILLY PUTTY MAN **DC Comics:** 1978						
1	2	4	6	10	14	18
SKATING SKILLS **Custom Comics, Inc./Chicago Roller Skates:** 1957 (36 & 12 pgs.; 5x7", two versions) (10¢)						
nn-Resembles old ACG cover plus interior art	4	7	10	14	17	20
SKIPPY'S OWN BOOK OF COMICS (See Popular Comics) **No publisher listed:** 1934 (Giveaway, 52 pgs., strip reprints)						
nn-(Scarce)-By Percy Crosby	377	754	1131	2639	4620	6600
Published by Max C. Gaines for Phillip's Dental Magnesia to be advertised on the Skippy Radio Show and given away with the purchase of a tube of Phillip's Tooth Paste. This is the first four-color comic book of reprints about one character.						
SKY KING "RUNAWAY TRAIN" (TV) **National Biscuit Co.:** 1964 (Regular size, 16 pgs.)						
nn	6	12	18	41	66	90
SLAM BANG COMICS **Post Cereal Giveaway:** No. 9, No date						
9-Dynamic Man, Echo, Mr. E, Yankee Boy app.	9	18	27	50	65	80
SMILIN' JACK **Dell Publishing Co.**						
Popped Wheat Giveaway (1947)-1938 strip reprints; 16 pgs. in full color	2	4	6	8	11	14
Shoe Store Giveaway-1938 strip reprints; 16 pgs.	5	10	15	24	30	35
Sparked Wheat Giveaway (1942)-16 pgs. in full color	5	10	15	24	30	35
SMOKEY BEAR (See Forest Fire for 1st app.) **Dell Publ. Co.:** 1959,1960						
True Story of..., The -U.S. Forest Service giveaway-Publ. by Western Printing Co.; reprints 1st 16 pgs. of Four Color #932. Inside front-c differs slightly in 1959 & 1960 editions	6	12	18	28	34	40
1964,1969 reprints	3	6	9	14	19	24
SMOKEY STOVER **Dell Publishing Co.**						
General Motors giveaway (1953)	8	16	24	42	54	65
National Fire Protection giveaway(1953 & 1954)-16 pgs., paper-c						

Snow White and the Seven Dwarfs © WDC

Space Ghost Coast to Coast © Cartoon Network

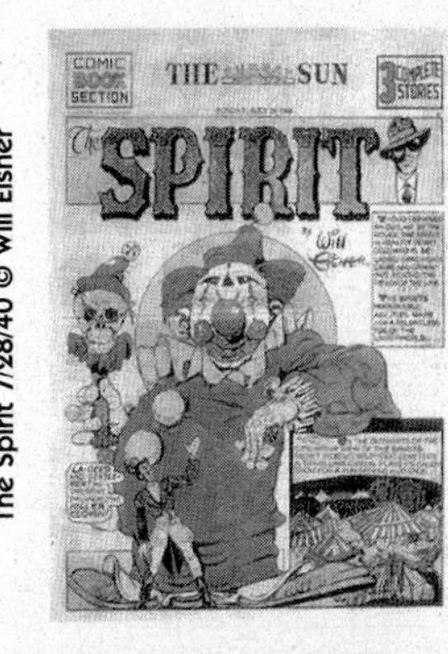

The Spirit 7/28/40 © Will Eisner

	GD 2.0	VG 4.0	FN 6.0	VF 8.0	VF/NM 9.0	NM- 9.2
	8	16	24	42	54	65

SNOW FOR CHRISTMAS
W. T. Grant Co.: 1957 (16 pgs.) (Giveaway)
nn 4 8 12 18 22 25

SNOW WHITE AND THE SEVEN DWARFS
Bendix Washing Machines: 1952 (32 pgs., 5x7-1/4", soft-c) (Disney)
nn 11 22 33 62 86 110

SNOW WHITE AND THE SEVEN DWARFS
Promotional Publ. Co.: 1957 (Small size)
nn 6 12 18 28 34 40

SNOW WHITE AND THE SEVEN DWARFS
Western Printing Co.: 1958 (16 pgs, 5x7-1/4", soft-c) (Disney premium)
nn- "Mystery of the Missing Magic" 6 12 18 31 38 45

SNOW WHITE AND THE 7 DWARFS IN "MILKY WAY"
American Dairy Assoc.: 1955 (16 pgs., soft-c, 5x7-1/4") (Disney premium)
nn 7 14 21 35 43 50

SOLDIER OF GOD
Conventual Franciscans of Marytown: 1982 ($1.00)
nn-Story of Father Maximilian Kobe, priest in WWII Poland; Ray Chatton-a 5.00

SPACE GHOST COAST TO COAST
Cartoon Network: Apr, 1994 (giveaway to Turner Broadcasting employees)
1-(8 pgs.); origin of Space Ghost 6.00

SPACE PATROL (TV)
Ziff-Davis Publishing Co. (Approved Comics)
...'s Special Mission (8 pgs., B&W, Giveaway) 45 90 135 284 480 675

SPARKY
Fire Protection Association: 1961 (Reg. size, paper-c)
nn 5 10 15 23 28 32

SPECIAL AGENT
Assoc. of American Railroads: Oct, 1959 (16 pgs.)
nn-The Story of the railroad police 6 12 18 28 34 40

SPECIAL DELIVERY
Post Hall Synd.: 1951 (32 pgs.; B&W) (Giveaway)
nn-Origin of Pogo, Swamp, etc.; 2 pg. biog. on Walt Kelly
(One copy sold in 1980 for $150.00)

SPECIAL EDITION (U. S. Navy Giveaways)
National Periodical Publications: 1944 - 1945 (Regular comic format with wording simplified, 52 pgs.)
1-Action (1944)-Reprints Action #80 55 110 165 352 601 850
2-Action (1944)-Reprints Action #81 55 110 165 352 601 850
3-Superman (1944)-Reprints Superman #33 55 110 165 352 601 850
4-Detective (1944)-Reprints Detective #97 55 110 165 352 601 850
5-Superman (1945)-Reprints Superman #34 55 110 165 352 601 850
6-Action (1945)-Reprints Action #84 55 110 165 352 601 850
NOTE: ***Wayne Boring** c-1, 2, 6. **Dick Sprang** c-4.*

SPIDER-MAN (See Amazing Spider-Man, The)

SPIRIT, THE (Weekly Comic Book)
Will Eisner: 6/2/40 - 10/5/52 (16 pgs.; 8 pgs.) (no cover) (in color)
(Distributed through various newspapers and other sources)
NOTE: **Eisner** script, pencils/inks for the most part from 6/2/40-4/26/42; a few stories assisted by Jack Cole, Fine, Powell and Kotsky.
6/2/40(#1)-Origin/1st app. The Spirit; reprinted in Police #11; Lady Luck (Brenda Banks) (1st app.) by Chuck Mazoujian & Mr. Mystic (1st. app.) by S. R. (Bob) Powell begin (rare) 213 426 639 1363 2332 3300
6/9/40(#2) 43 86 129 271 461 650
6/16/40(#3)-Black Queen app. in Spirit 32 64 96 188 307 425
6/23/40(#4)-Mr. Mystic receives magical necklace 24 48 72 142 234 325
6/30/40(#5) 24 48 72 142 234 325
7/7/40(#6)-1st app. Spirit carplane; Black Queen app. in Spirit 26 52 78 154 252 350
7/14/40(#7)-8/4/40(#10): 7/21/40-Spirit becomes fugitive wanted for murder 22 44 66 132 216 300
8/11/40-9/22/40: 9/15/40-Racist-c 21 42 63 122 199 275
9/29/40-Ellen drops engagement with Homer Creep 20 40 60 114 182 250
10/6/40-11/3/40 20 40 60 114 182 250
11/10/40-The Black Queen app. 20 40 60 114 182 250
11/17/40, 11/24/40 20 40 60 114 182 250
12/1/40-Ellen spanking by Spirit on cover & inside; Eisner-1st 3 pgs., J. Cole rest 24 48 72 142 234 325
12/8/40-3/9/41 16 32 48 94 147 200
3/16/41-Intro. & 1st app. Silk Satin 20 40 60 118 192 265
3/23/41-6/1/41: 5/11/41-Last Lady Luck by Mazoujian. 5/18/41-Lady Luck by Nick Viscardi begins, ends 2/22/42 15 30 45 90 140 190
6/8/41-2nd app. Satin; Spirit learns Satin is also a British agent 18 36 54 103 162 220
6/15/41-1st app. Twilight 17 34 51 98 154 210
6/22/41-Hitler app. in Spirit 16 32 48 94 147 200
6/29/41-1/25/42,2/8/42 14 28 42 81 118 155
2/1/42-1st app. Duchess 16 32 48 94 147 200
2/15/42-4/26/42-Lady Luck by Klaus Nordling begins 3/1/42 15 30 45 84 127 170
5/3/42-8/16/42-Eisner/Fine/Quality staff assists on Spirit 12 24 36 69 97 125
8/23/42-Satin cover splash; Spirit by Eisner/Fine although signed by Fine 17 34 51 98 154 210
8/30/42,9/27/42-10/11/42,10/25/42-11/8/42-Eisner/Fine/Quality staff assists on Spirit 12 24 36 67 94 120
9/6/42-9/20/42,10/18/42-Fine/Belfi art on Spirit; scripts by Manly Wade Wellman 9 18 27 50 65 80
11/15/42-12/6/42,12/20/42,12/27/42,1/17/43-4/18/43,5/9/43-8/8/43-Wellman/ Woolfolk scripts, Fine pencils, Quality staff inks 9 18 27 50 65 80
12/13/42,1/3/43,1/10/43,4/25/43,5/2/43-Eisner scripts/layouts; Fine pencils, Quality staff inks 10 20 30 54 72 90
8/15/43-Eisner script/layout; pencils/inks by Quality staff; Jack Cole-a 8 16 24 44 57 70
8/22/43-12/12/43-Wellman/Woolfolk scripts, Fine pencils, Quality staff inks; Mr. Mystic by Guardineer-10/10/43-10/24/43 8 16 24 44 57 70
12/19/43-8/13/44-Wellman/Woolfolk/Jack Cole scripts; Cole, Fine & Robin King-a; Last Mr. Mystic-5/14/44 8 16 24 42 54 65
8/20/44-12/16/45-Wellman/Woolfolk scripts; Fine art with unknown staff assists 8 16 24 42 54 65
NOTE: *Scripts/layouts by Eisner, or Eisner/Nordling, Eisner/Mercer or Spranger/Eisner; inks by Eisner or Eisner/Spranger in issues 12/23/45-2/2/47.*
12/23/45-1/6/46: 12/23/45-Christmas-c 9 18 27 52 69 85
1/13/46-Origin Spirit retold 13 26 39 72 101 130
1/20/46-1st postwar Satin app. 11 22 33 64 90 115
1/27/46-3/10/46: 3/3/46-Last Lady Luck by Nordling 9 18 27 52 69 85
3/17/46-Intro. & 1st app. Nylon 11 22 33 64 90 115
3/24/46,3/31/46,4/14/46 9 18 27 52 69 85
4/7/46-2nd app. Nylon 10 20 30 56 76 95
4/21/46-Intro. & 1st app. Mr. Carrion & His Pet Buzzard Julia 13 26 39 72 101 130
4/28/46-5/12/46,5/26/46-6/30/46: Lady Luck by Fred Schwab in issues 5/5/46-11/3/46 9 18 27 52 69 85
5/19/46-2nd app. Mr. Carrion 10 20 30 56 76 95
7/7/46-Intro. & 1st app. Dulcet Tone & Skinny 11 22 33 64 90 115
7/14/46-9/29/46 9 18 27 52 69 85
10/6/46-Intro. & 1st app. P'Gell 13 26 39 74 105 135
10/13/46-11/3/46,11/16/46-11/24/46 9 18 27 52 69 85
11/10/46-2nd app. P'Gell 11 22 33 62 86 110
12/1/46-3rd app. P'Gell 10 20 30 54 72 90
12/8/46-2/2/47 9 18 27 50 65 80
NOTE: *Scripts, pencils/inks by Eisner except where noted in issues 2/9/47-12/19/48.*
2/9/47-7/6/47: 6/8/47-Eisner self satire 9 18 27 50 65 80
7/13/47- "Hansel & Gretel" fairy tales 11 22 33 64 90 115
7/20/47-Li'L Abner, Daddy Warbucks, Dick Tracy, Fearless Fosdick parody; A-Bomb blast-c 13 26 39 72 101 130
7/27/47-9/14/47 9 18 27 50 65 80
9/21/47-Pearl Harbor flashback 10 20 30 56 76 95
9/28/47-1st mention of Flying Saucers in comics-3 months after 1st sighting in Idaho on 6/25/47 17 34 51 98 154 210
10/5/47- "Cinderella" fairy tales 11 22 33 64 90 115
10/12/47-11/30/47 9 18 27 50 65 80
12/7/47-Intro. & 1st app. Powder Pouf 13 26 39 72 101 130
12/14/47-12/28/47 9 18 27 50 65 80
1/4/48-2nd app. Powder Pouf 10 20 30 54 72 90
1/11/48-1st app. Sparrow Fallon; Powder Pouf app. 10 20 30 54 72 90
1/18/48-He-Man ad cover; satire issue 10 20 30 54 72 90
1/25/48-Intro. & 1st app. Castanet 13 26 39 72 101 130
2/1/48-2nd app. Castanet 9 18 27 52 69 85

The Spirit 1/09/49 © Will Eisner

The Spirit 3/12/50 © Will Eisner

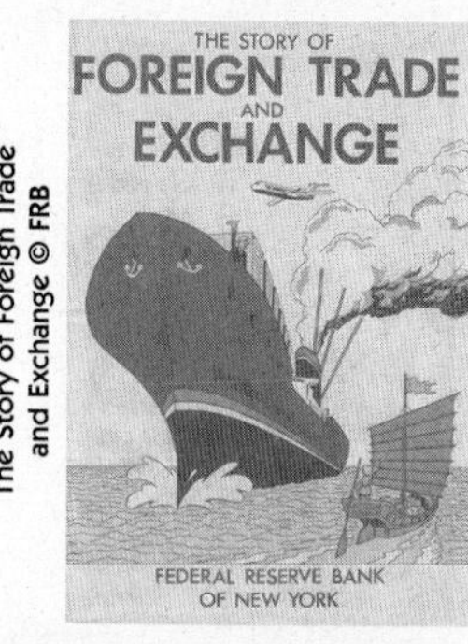

The Story of Foreign Trade and Exchange © FRB

	GD 2.0	VG 4.0	FN 6.0	VF 8.0	VF/NM 9.0	NM- 9.2
2/8/48-3/7/48	9	18	27	50	65	80
3/14/48-Only app. Kretchma	9	18	27	52	69	85
3/21/48,3/28/48,4/11/48-4/25/48	9	18	27	50	65	80
4/4/48-Only app. Wild Rice	9	18	27	52	69	85
5/2/48-2nd app. Sparrow	9	18	27	50	65	80
5/9/48-6/27/48,7/11/48,7/18/48: 6/13/48-TV issue	9	18	27	50	65	80
7/4/48-Spirit by Andre Le Blanc	8	16	24	42	54	65
7/25/48-Ambrose Bierce's "The Thing" adaptation classic by Eisner/Grandenetti	15	30	45	90	140	190
8/1/48-8/15/48,8/29/48-9/12/48	9	18	27	50	65	80
8/22/48-Poe's "Fall of the House of Usher" classic by Eisner/Grandenetti	15	30	45	90	140	190
9/19/48-Only app. Lorelei	10	20	30	54	72	90
9/26/48-10/31/48	9	18	27	50	65	80
11/7/48-Only app. Plaster of Paris	11	22	33	64	90	115
11/14/48-12/19/48	9	18	27	50	65	80

NOTE: *Scripts by Eisner or Feiffer or Eisner/Feiffer or Nordling. Art by Eisner with backgrounds by Eisner, Grandenetti, Le Blanc, Stallman, Nordling, Dixon and/or others in issues 12/26/48-4/1/51 except where noted.*

	GD 2.0	VG 4.0	FN 6.0	VF 8.0	VF/NM 9.0	NM- 9.2
12/26/48-Reprints some covers of 1948 with flashbacks	9	18	27	50	65	80
1/2/49-1/16/49	9	18	27	50	65	80
1/23/49,1/30/49-1st & 2nd app. Thorne	10	20	30	54	72	90
2/6/49-8/14/49	9	18	27	50	65	80
8/21/49,8/28/49-1st & 2nd app. Monica Veto	10	20	30	54	72	90
9/4/49,9/11/49	9	18	27	50	65	80
9/18/49-Love comic cover; has gag love comic ads on inside	10	20	30	54	72	90
9/25/49-Only app. Ice	9	18	27	52	69	85
10/2/49,10/9/49-Autumn News appears & dies in 10/9 issue	9	18	27	52	69	85
10/16/49-11/27/49,12/18/49,12/25/49	9	18	27	50	65	80
12/4/49,12/11/49-1st & 2nd app. Flaxen	9	18	27	52	69	85
1/1/50-Flashbacks to all of the Spirit girls-Thorne, Ellen, Satin, & Monica	4	28	42	76	108	140
1/8/50-Intro. & 1st app. Sand Saref	15	30	45	86	133	180
1/15/50-2nd app. Saref	13	26	39	72	101	130
1/22/50-2/5/50	9	18	27	50	65	80
2/12/50-Roller Derby issue	10	20	30	54	72	90
2/19/50-Half Dead Mr. Lox - Classic horror	11	22	33	64	90	115
2/26/50-4/23/50,5/14/50,5/28/50,7/23/50-9/3/50	9	18	27	50	65	80
4/30/50-Script/art by Le Blanc with Eisner framing	8	16	24	40	50	60
5/7/50,6/4/50-7/16/50-Abe Kanegson-a	8	16	24	40	50	60
5/21/50-Script by Feiffer/Eisner, art by Blaisdell, Eisner framing	8	16	24	40	50	60
9/10/50-P'Gell returns	10	20	30	54	72	90
9/17/50-1/7/51	9	18	27	50	65	80
1/14/51-Life Magazine cover; brief biography of Comm. Dolan, Sand Saref, Silk Satin, P'Gell, Sammy & Willum, Darling O'Shea, & Mr. Carrion & His Pet Buzzard Julia, with pin-ups by Eisner	11	22	33	64	90	115
1/21/51,2/4/51-4/1/51	9	18	27	50	65	80
1/28/51- "The Meanest Man in the World" by Eisner	11	22	33	64	90	115
4/8/51-7/29/51,8/12/51-Last Eisner issue	9	18	27	50	65	80
8/5/51,8/19/51-7/20/52-Not Eisner	8	16	24	40	50	60
7/27/52-(Rare)-Denny Colt in Outer Space by Wally Wood; 7 pg. S/F story of E.C. vintage	40	80	120	246	411	575
8/3/52-(Rare)- "Mission...The Moon" by Wood	40	80	120	246	411	575
8/10/52-(Rare)- "A DP On The Moon" by Wood	40	80	120	246	411	575
8/17/52-(Rare)- "Heart" by Wood/Eisner	37	74	111	222	361	500
8/24/52-(Rare)- "Rescue" by Wood	40	80	120	246	411	575
8/31/52-(Rare)- "The Last Man" by Wood	40	80	120	246	411	575
9/7/52-(Rare)- "The Man in The Moon" by Wood	40	80	120	246	411	575
9/14/52-(Rare)-Eisner/Wenzel-a	21	42	63	122	199	275
9/21/52-(Rare)- "Denny Colt, Alias The Spirit/Space Report" by Eisner/Wenzel	22	44	66	132	216	300
9/28/52-(Rare)- "Return From The Moon" by Wood	39	78	117	240	395	550
10/5/52-(Rare)- "The Last Story" by Eisner	20	40	60	114	182	250

Large Tabloid pages from 1946 on (Eisner) - Price 200 percent over listed prices.

NOTE: *Spirit sections came out in both large and small format. Some newspapers went to the 8-pg. format months before others. Some printed the pages so they cannot be folded into a small comic book section; these are worth less. (Also see Three Comics & Spiritman).*

SPY SMASHER
Fawcett Publications

	GD 2.0	VG 4.0	FN 6.0	VF 8.0	VF/NM 9.0	NM- 9.2
Well Known Comics (1944, 12 pgs., 8-1/2x10-1/2"), paper-c, glued binding, printed in green; Bestmaid/Samuel Lowe giveaway	15	30	45	83	124	165

STANDARD OIL COMICS (Also see Gulf Funny Weekly)
Standard Oil Co.: 1932-1934 (Giveaway, tabloid size, 4 pgs. in color)

	GD 2.0	VG 4.0	FN 6.0	VF 8.0	VF/NM 9.0	NM- 9.2
nn (Dec. 1932)	52	104	156	330	565	800
1-Series has original art	45	90	135	284	480	675
2-5	20	40	60	116	191	265
6-14: 14-Fred Opper strip, 1 pg.	14	28	42	76	108	140
1A (Jan 1933)	47	94	141	296	498	700
2A-14A (1933)	30	60	90	176	288	400
1B (1934)	37	74	111	222	361	500
2B-?B (1934)	30	60	90	176	288	400

NOTE: *Series A contains Frederick Opper's Si & Mirandi; Series B contains Goofus: He's From The Big City; McVittle by Walter O'Ehrle; interior strips include Pesty And His Pop & Smiling Slim by Sid Hicks.*

STAR TEAM
Marvel Comics Group: 1977 (6-1/2x5", 20 pgs.) (Ideal Toy Giveaway)

	GD 2.0	VG 4.0	FN 6.0	VF 8.0	VF/NM 9.0	NM- 9.2
nn	3	6	9	14	19	24

STEVE CANYON COMICS
Harvey Publications

	GD 2.0	VG 4.0	FN 6.0	VF 8.0	VF/NM 9.0	NM- 9.2
Dept. Store giveaway #3(6/48, 36pp)	10	20	30	54	72	90
...'s Secret Mission (1951, 16 pgs., Armed Forces giveaway); Caniff-a	9	18	27	47	61	75
Strictly for the Smart Birds (1951, 16 pgs.)-Information Comics Div. (Harvey) Premium	8	16	24	40	50	60

STORIES OF CHRISTMAS
K. K. Publications: 1942 (Giveaway, 32 pgs., paper cover)

	GD 2.0	VG 4.0	FN 6.0	VF 8.0	VF/NM 9.0	NM- 9.2
nn-Adaptation of "A Christmas Carol"; Kelly story "The Fir Tree"; Infinity-c	29	58	87	172	281	390

STORY HOUR SERIES (Disney)
Whitman Publ. Co.: 1948, 1949; 1951-1953 (36 pgs., paper-c) (4-3/4x6-1/2")
Given away with subscription to Walt Disney's Comics & Stories

	GD 2.0	VG 4.0	FN 6.0	VF 8.0	VF/NM 9.0	NM- 9.2
nn(1948)-Mickey Mouse and the Boy Thursday	12	24	36	67	94	120
nn(1948)-Mickey Mouse the Miracle Master	12	24	36	67	94	120
nn(1948)-Minnie Mouse and Antique Chair	12	24	36	67	94	120
nn(1949)-The Three Orphan Kittens(B&W & color)	9	18	27	47	61	75
nn(1949)-Danny-The Little Black Lamb	9	18	27	47	61	75
800(1948)-Donald Duck in "Bringing Up the Boys"	15	30	45	88	137	185
1953 edition	11	22	33	64	90	115
801(1948)-Mickey Mouse's Summer Vacation	10	20	30	56	76	95
1951, 1952 editions	7	14	21	35	43	50
802(1948)-Bugs Bunny's Adventures	9	18	27	50	65	80
803(1948)-Bongo	8	16	24	40	50	60
804(1948)-Mickey and the Beanstalk	9	18	27	47	61	75
805-15(1949)-Andy Panda and His Friends	8	16	24	40	50	60
806-15(1949)-Tom and Jerry	8	16	24	44	57	70
808-15(1949)-Johnny Appleseed	8	16	24	40	50	60

1948, 1949 Hard Cover Edition of each....30% - 40% more.

STOP AND GO, THE SAFETY TWINS
J.C. Penney: no date (giveaway)

	GD 2.0	VG 4.0	FN 6.0	VF 8.0	VF/NM 9.0	NM- 9.2
nn	5	10	15	24	30	35

STORY OF CHECKS THE
Federal Reserve Bank: 1979 (Reg. size)

	GD 2.0	VG 4.0	FN 6.0	VF 8.0	VF/NM 9.0	NM- 9.2
nn	1	3	4	6	8	10

STORY OF CHECKS AND ELECTRONIC PAYMENTS
Federal Reserve Bank: 1983 (Reg size)

	GD 2.0	VG 4.0	FN 6.0	VF 8.0	VF/NM 9.0	NM- 9.2
nn	1	2	3	5	6	8

STORY OF CONSUMER CREDIT
Federal Reserve Bank: 1980 (Reg. size)

	GD 2.0	VG 4.0	FN 6.0	VF 8.0	VF/NM 9.0	NM- 9.2
nn	1	2	3	5	6	8

STORY OF EDISON, THE
Educational Comics: 1956 (16 pgs.) (Reddy Killowatt)

	GD 2.0	VG 4.0	FN 6.0	VF 8.0	VF/NM 9.0	NM- 9.2
nn-Reprint of Reddy Kilowatt #2(1947)	7	14	21	35	43	50

STORY OF FOREIGN TRADE AND EXCHANGE
Federal Reserve Bank: 1985 (Reg. size)

	GD 2.0	VG 4.0	FN 6.0	VF 8.0	VF/NM 9.0	NM- 9.2
nn	1	2	3	5	6	8

STORY OF HARRY S. TRUMAN, THE
Democratic National Committee: 1948 (Giveaway, regular size, soft-c, 16 pg.)

	GD 2.0	VG 4.0	FN 6.0	VF 8.0	VF/NM 9.0	NM- 9.2
nn-Gives biography on career of Truman; used in **SOTI**, pg. 311	14	28	42	76	108	140

Super Book of Comics #4 © WEST

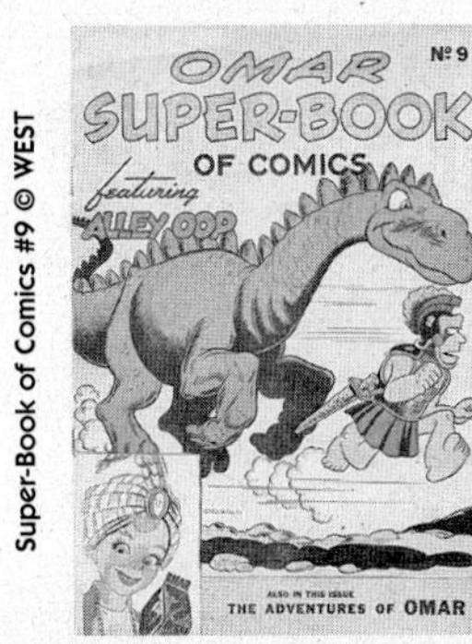

Super-Book of Comics #9 © WEST

Super Friends Special #1 © DC

	GD 2.0	VG 4.0	FN 6.0	VF 8.0	VF/NM 9.0	NM- 9.2

STORY OF INFLATION, THE
Federal Reserve Bank: 1980s (Reg size)

	GD	VG	FN	VF	VF/NM	NM-
nn	1	3	4	6	8	10

STORY OF MONEY
Federal Reserve Bank: 1984 (Reg. size)

	GD	VG	FN	VF	VF/NM	NM-
nn	1	3	4	6	8	10

STORY OF THE BALLET, THE
Selva and Sons, Inc.: 1954 (16 pgs., paper cover)

	GD	VG	FN	VF	VF/NM	NM-
nn	4	8	11	16	19	22

STRANGE AS IT SEEMS
McNaught Syndicate: 1936 (B&W, 5" x 7", 24 pgs.)

	GD	VG	FN	VF	VF/NM	NM-
nn-Ex-Lax giveaway	8	16	24	44	57	70

STRAY
Dark Horse Comics: 2004 (8 1/2"x 5 1/2", Diamond Comic Dist. Halloween giveaway)

	GD	VG	FN	VF	VF/NM	NM-
nn-Reprint from The Dark Horse Book of Hauntings; Evan Dorkin-s/Jill Thompson-a						2.50

SUGAR BEAR
Post Cereal Giveaway: No date, circa 1975? (2 1/2" x 4 1/2", 16 pgs.)

	GD	VG	FN	VF	VF/NM	NM-
"The Almost Take Over of the Post Office", "The Race Across the Atlantic", "The Zoo Goes Wild" each...	1	2	3	5	6	8

SUNDAY WORLD'S EASTER EGG FULL OF EASTER MEAT FOR LITTLE PEOPLE
Supplement to the New York World: 3/27/1898 (soft-c, 16pg, 4"x8" approx., opens at top, color & B&W)(Giveaway)(shaped like an Easter egg)

	GD	VG	FN	VF	VF/NM	NM-
nn-By R.F. Outcault	18	36	54	103	162	220

SUPER BOOK OF COMICS
Western Publishing Co.: nd (1942-1943?) (Soft-c, 32 pgs.) (Pan-Am/Gilmore Oil/Kelloggs premiums)

	GD	VG	FN	VF	VF/NM	NM-
nn-Dick Tracy (Gilmore)-Magic Morro app. (2 versions: Dick Tracy Jr. on cover and a filing cabinet cover)	32	64	96	190	310	430
1-Dick Tracy & The Smuggling Ring; Stratosphere Jim app. (Rare) (Pan-Am)	32	64	96	190	310	430
1-Smilin' Jack, Magic Morro (Pan-Am)	14	28	42	76	108	140
2-Smilin' Jack, Stratosphere Jim (Pan-Am)	14	28	42	76	108	140
2-Smitty, Magic Morro (Pan-Am)	14	28	42	76	108	140
3-Captain Midnight, Magic Morro (Pan-Am)	22	44	66	131	216	300
3-Moon Mullins?	13	26	39	74	105	135
4-Red Ryder, Magic Morro (Pan-Am). Same content as Red Ryder Victory Patrol comic w/diff. cover	15	30	45	85	130	175
4-Smitty, Stratosphere Jim (Pan-Am)	13	26	39	74	105	135
5-Don Winslow, Magic Morro (Gilmore)	15	30	45	85	130	175
5-Don Winslow, Stratosphere Jim (Pan-Am)	15	30	45	85	130	175
5-Terry & the Pirates	17	34	51	98	154	210
6-Don Winslow, Stratosphere Jim (Pan-Am)-McWilliams-a	15	30	45	85	130	175
6-King of the Royal Mounted, Magic Morro (Pan-Am)	15	30	45	85	130	175
7-Dick Tracy, Magic Morro (Pan-Am)	19	38	57	111	178	245
7-Little Orphan Annie	11	22	33	64	90	115
8-Dick Tracy, Stratosphere Jim (Pan-Am)	17	34	51	98	154	210
8-Dan Dunn, Magic Morro (Pan-Am)	11	22	33	64	90	115
9-Terry & the Pirates, Magic Morro (Pan-Am)	17	34	51	98	154	210
10-Red Ryder, Magic Morro (Pan-Am)	15	30	45	85	130	175

SUPER-BOOK OF COMICS
Western Publishing Co.: (Omar Bread & Hancock Oil Co. giveaways) 1944 - No. 30, 1947 (Omar); 1947 - 1948 (Hancock) (16 pgs.)

NOTE: The Hancock issues are all exact reprints of the earlier Omar issues. The issue numbers were removed in some of the reprints.

	GD	VG	FN	VF	VF/NM	NM-
1-Dick Tracy (Omar, 1944)	15	30	45	94	147	200
1-Dick Tracy (Hancock, 1947)	14	28	42	78	112	145
2-Bugs Bunny (Omar, 1944)	8	16	24	40	50	60
2-Bugs Bunny (Hancock, 1947)	6	12	18	32	39	46
3-Terry & the Pirates (Omar, 1944)	11	22	33	60	83	105
3-Terry & the Pirates (Hancock, 1947)	10	20	30	54	72	90
4-Andy Panda (Omar, 1944)	8	16	24	40	50	60
4-Andy Panda (Hancock, 1947)	6	12	18	32	39	46
5-Smokey Stover (Omar, 1945)	6	12	18	32	39	46
5-Smokey Stover (Hancock, 1947)	5	10	15	24	30	35
6-Porky Pig (Omar, 1945)	8	16	24	40	50	60
6-Porky Pig (Hancock, 1947)	6	12	18	32	39	46
7-Smilin' Jack (Omar, 1945)	8	16	24	40	50	60
7-Smilin' Jack (Hancock, 1947)	6	12	18	32	39	46
8-Oswald the Rabbit (Omar, 1945)	6	12	18	32	39	46
8-Oswald the Rabbit (Hancock, 1947)	5	10	15	24	30	35
9-Alley Oop (Omar, 1945)	11	22	33	64	90	115
9-Alley Oop (Hancock, 1947)	11	22	33	60	83	105
10-Elmer Fudd (Omar, 1945)	6	12	18	32	39	46
10-Elmer Fudd (Hancock, 1947)	5	10	15	24	30	35
11-Little Orphan Annie (Omar, 1945)	8	16	24	42	53	64
11-Little Orphan Annie (Hancock, 1947)	7	14	21	36	45	54
12-Woody Woodpecker (Omar, 1945)	6	12	18	32	39	46
12-Woody Woodpecker (Hancock, 1947)	5	10	15	24	30	35
13-Dick Tracy (Omar, 1945)	11	22	33	64	90	115
13-Dick Tracy (Hancock, 1947)	11	22	33	60	83	105
14-Bugs Bunny (Omar, 1945)	6	12	18	32	39	46
14-Bugs Bunny (Hancock, 1947)	5	10	15	24	30	35
15-Andy Panda (Omar, 1945)	6	12	18	28	34	40
15-Andy Panda (Hancock, 1947)	5	10	15	24	30	35
16-Terry & the Pirates (Omar, 1945)	11	22	33	60	83	105
16-Terry & the Pirates (Hancock, 1947)	9	18	27	47	61	75
17-Smokey Stover (Omar, 1946)	6	12	18	32	39	46
17-Smokey Stover (Hancock, 1948?)	5	10	15	24	30	35
18-Porky Pig (Omar, 1946)	6	12	18	28	34	40
18-Porky Pig (Hancock, 1948?)	5	10	15	24	30	35
19-Smilin' Jack (Omar, 1946)	6	12	18	32	39	46
nn-Smilin' Jack (Hancock, 1948)	5	10	15	24	30	35
20-Oswald the Rabbit (Omar, 1946)	6	12	18	28	34	40
nn-Oswald the Rabbit (Hancock, 1948)	5	10	15	24	30	35
21-Gasoline Alley (Omar, 1946)	8	16	24	42	53	64
nn-Gasoline Alley (Hancock, 1948)	7	14	21	36	45	54
22-Elmer Fudd (Omar, 1946)	6	12	18	28	34	40
nn-Elmer Fudd (Hancock, 1948)	5	10	15	24	30	35
23-Little Orphan Annie (Omar, 1946)	8	16	24	40	50	60
nn-Little Orphan Annie (Hancock, 1948)	6	12	18	32	39	46
24-Woody Woodpecker (Omar, 1946)	6	12	18	28	34	40
nn-Woody Woodpecker (Hancock, 1948)	5	10	15	24	30	35
25-Dick Tracy (Omar, 1946)	11	22	33	60	83	105
nn-Dick Tracy (Hancock, 1948)	9	18	27	50	65	80
26-Bugs Bunny (Omar, 1946))	6	12	18	28	34	40
nn-Bugs Bunny (Hancock, 1948)	5	10	15	24	30	35
27-Andy Panda (Omar, 1946)	6	12	18	28	34	40
27-Andy Panda (Hancock, 1948)	5	10	15	24	30	35
28-Terry & the Pirates (Omar, 1946)	11	22	33	60	83	105
28-Terry & the Pirates (Hancock, 1948)	9	18	27	47	61	75
29-Smokey Stover (Omar, 1947)	6	12	18	28	34	40
29-Smokey Stover (Hancock, 1948)	5	10	15	24	30	35
30-Porky Pig (Omar, 1947)	6	12	18	28	34	40
30-Porky Pig (Hancock, 1948)	5	10	15	24	30	35
nn-Bugs Bunny (Hancock, 1948)-Does not match any Omar book	6	12	18	28	34	40

SUPER CIRCUS (TV)
Cross Publishing Co.

	GD	VG	FN	VF	VF/NM	NM-
1-(1951, Weather Bird Shoes giveaway)	8	16	24	40	50	60

SUPER FRIENDS
DC Comics: 1981 (Giveaway, no ads, no code or price)

	GD	VG	FN	VF	VF/NM	NM-
...Special 1 -r/Super Friends #19 & 36	2	4	6	9	12	15

SUPERGEAR COMICS
Jacobs Corp.: 1976 (Giveaway, 4 pgs. in color, slick paper)

	GD	VG	FN	VF	VF/NM	NM-
nn-(Rare)-Superman, Lois Lane; Steve Lombard app. (500 copies printed, over half destroyed?)	19	38	57	128	277	425

SUPERGIRL
DC Comics: 1984, 1986 (Giveaway, Baxter paper)

	GD	VG	FN	VF	VF/NM	NM-
nn-(American Honda/U.S. Dept. Transportation) Torres-c/a	2	4	6	8	11	14

SUPER HEROES PUZZLES AND GAMES
General Mills Giveaway (Marvel Comics Group): 1979 (32 pgs., regular size)

	GD	VG	FN	VF	VF/NM	NM-
nn-Four 2-pg. origin stories of Spider-Man, Captain America, The Hulk, & Spider-Woman	3	6	9	14	20	26

SUPERMAN
National Periodical Publ./DC Comics

Superman - Radio Shack (7/80) © DC

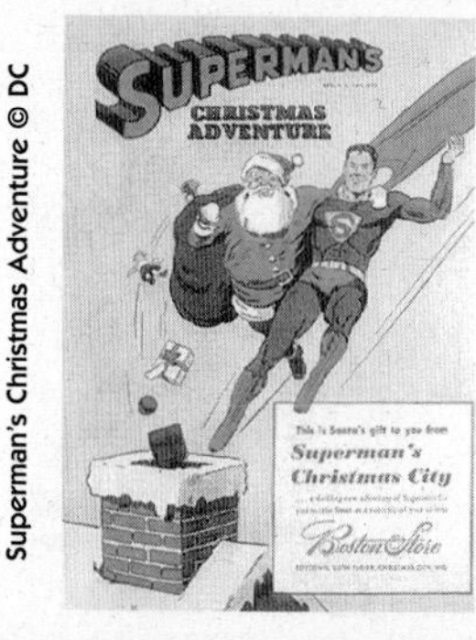

Superman's Christmas Adventure © DC

Swamp Fox © DIS

	GD	VG	FN	VF	VF/NM	NM-
	2.0	4.0	6.0	8.0	9.0	9.2

72-Giveaway(9-10/51)-(Rare)-Price blackened out; came with banner wrapped around book; without banner 73 146 219 467 796 1125
72-Giveaway with banner 116 232 348 742 1271 1800
Bradman birthday custom (1988)(extremely limited distribution) - a CGC 9.6 copy sold for $2600, a NM copy sold for $1125, and a FN/VF copy sold for $800 in 2011-2012
... For the Animals (2000, Doris Day Animal Foundation, 30 pgs.) polybagged with Gotham Adventures #22, Hourman #12, Impulse #58, Looney Tunes #62, Stars and S.T.R.I.P.E. #8 and Superman Adventures #41 2.50
Kelloggs Giveaway-(2/3 normal size, 1954)-r-two stories/Superman #55 28 56 84 165 270 375
Kenner: Man of Steel (Doomsday is Coming) (1995, 16 pgs.) packaged with set of Superman and Doomsday action figures 4.00
...Meets the Quik Bunny (1987, Nestles Quik premium, 36 pgs.) 1 2 3 5 6 8
Pizza Hut Premiums (12/77)-Exact reprints of 1950s comics except for paid ads (set of 6 exist?); Vol. 1-r#97 (#113-r also known) 1 3 4 6 8 10
Radio Shack Giveaway-36 pgs. (7/80) "The Computers That Saved Metropolis", Starlin/Giordano-a; advertising insert in Action #509, New Advs. of Superboy #7, Legion of Super-Heroes #265, & House of Mystery #282. (All comics were 68 pgs.) Cover of inserts printed on newsprint. Giveaway contains 4 extra pgs. of Radio Shack advertising that inserts do not have 1 2 3 5 6 8
Radio Shack Giveaway-(7/81) "Victory by Computer" 1 2 3 5 6 8
Radio Shack Giveaway-(7/82) "Computer Masters of Metropolis" 1 2 3 5 6 8

SUPERMAN ADVENTURES, THE (TV)
DC Comics: 1996 (Based on animated series)
1-(1996) Preview issue distributed at Warner Bros. stores 4.00
Titus Game Edition (1998) 2.50

SUPERMAN AND THE GREAT CLEVELAND FIRE
National Periodical Publ.: 1948 (Giveaway, 4 pgs., no cover) (Hospital Fund)
nn-In full color 65 130 195 416 708 1000

SUPERMAN AT THE GILBERT HALL OF SCIENCE
National Periodical Publ.: 1948 (Giveaway) (Gilbert Chemistry Sets / A.C. Gilbert Co.)
nn 37 74 111 222 361 500

SUPERMAN (Miniature)
National Periodical Publ.: 1942; 1955 - 1956 (3 issues, no #'s, 32 pgs.)
The pages are numbered in the 1st issue: 1-32; 2nd: 1A-32A, and 3rd: 1B-32B
No date-Py-Co-Pay Tooth Powder giveaway (8 pgs.; circa 1942) 45 90 135 284 480 675
1-The Superman Time Capsule (Kellogg's Sugar Smacks)(1955) 24 48 72 142 234 325
1A-Duel in Space (1955) 22 44 66 131 216 300
1B-The Super Show of Metropolis (also #1-32, no B)(1955) 22 44 66 131 216 300
NOTE: *Numbering variations exist. Each title could have any combination-#1, 1A, or 1B.*

SUPERMAN RECORD COMIC
National Periodical Publications: 1966 (Golden Records)
(With record)-Record reads origin of Superman from comic; came with iron-on patch, decoder, membership card & button; comic-r/Superman #125,146 12 24 36 81 166 250
Comic only 7 14 21 44 72 100

SUPERMAN'S BUDDY (Costume Comic)
National Periodical Publications: 1954 (4 pgs., slick paper-c; one-shot) (Came in box w/costume)
1-With box & costume 123 246 369 781 1341 1900
Comic only 55 110 165 349 600 850
1-(1958 edition)-Printed in 2 colors 17 34 51 98 154 210

SUPERMAN'S CHRISTMAS ADVENTURE
National Periodical Publications: 1940, 1944 (Giveaway, 16 pgs.)
Distributed by Nehi drinks, Bailey Store, Ivey-Keith Co., Kennedy's Boys Shop, Macy's Store, Boston Store
1(1940)-Burnley-a; F. Ray-c/r from Superman #6 (Scarce)-Superman saves Santa Claus. Santa makes real Superman Toys offered in 1940. 1st merchandising story; versions with Royal Crown Cola ad on front-c & Boston Store ad on front-c; cover art on each has the same layout but different art 360 720 1080 2520 4410 6300
nn(1944) w/Santa Claus & X-mas tree-c 97 194 291 616 1058 1500
nn(1944) w/Candy cane & Superman-c 90 180 270 572 986 1400

SUPERMAN-TIM (Becomes Tim)
Superman-Tim Stores/National Periodical Publ.: Aug, 1942 - May, 1950 (Half size) (B&W Giveaway w/2 color covers) (Publ. monthly 2/43 on)

	GD	VG	FN	VF	VF/NM	NM-
	2.0	4.0	6.0	8.0	9.0	9.2

8/42 (#1)-All have Superman illos. 113 226 339 718 1234 1750
1/43 (#2) 39 78 117 234 380 525
2/43 (#3) 37 74 111 222 361 500
3/43 (#4) 37 74 111 222 361 500
4/43, 5/43, 6/43, 7/43, 8/43 33 66 99 198 324 450
9/43, 10/43, 11/43, 12/43 28 56 84 165 270 375
1/44-12/44 24 48 72 140 230 320
1/45-5/45, 10-12/45, 1/46-8/46 21 42 63 126 208 290
6/45-Classic Superman-c 23 46 69 138 227 315
7/45-Classic Superman flag-c 23 46 69 138 227 315
9/45-1st stamp album issue 48 96 114 302 509 715
9/46-2nd stamp album issue 40 80 120 252 426 600
10/46-1st Superman story 29 58 87 170 278 385
11/46, 12/46, 1/47-8/47 issues-Superman story in each; 2/47-Infinity-c. All 36 pgs. 29 58 87 170 278 385
9/47-Stamp album issue & Superman story 40 80 120 245 410 575
10/47, 11/47, 12/47-Superman stories (24 pgs.) 29 58 87 170 278 385
1/48-7/48,10/48, 11/48, 2/49, 4/49-11/49 23 46 69 138 227 315
8/48-Contains full page ad for Superman-Tim watch giveaway 23 46 69 138 227 315
9/48-Stamp album issue 31 62 93 186 301 425
1/49-Full page Superman bank cut-out 23 46 69 138 227 315
3/49-Full page Superman boxing game cut-out 23 46 69 138 227 315
12/49-3/50, 5/50-Superman stories 25 50 75 150 245 340
4/50-Superman story, baseball stories; photo-c without Superman 29 58 87 170 278 385
NOTE: *All issues have Superman illustrations throughout. The page count varies depending on whether a Superman-Tim comic story is inserted. If it is, the page count is either 36 or 24 pages. Otherwise all issues are 16 pages. Each issue has a special place for inserting a full color Superman stamp. The stamp album issues had spaces for the stamps given away the past year. The books were mailed as a subscription premium. The stamps were given away free (or when you made a purchase) only when you physically came into the store.*

SUPER SEAMAN SLOPPY
Allied Pristine Union Council, Buffalo, NY: 1940s, 8pg., reg. size (Soft-c)
nn 4 8 12 17 21 24

SWAMP FOX, THE
Walt Disney Productions: 1960 (14 pgs, small size) (Canada Dry Premiums)
Titles: (A)-Tory Masquerade, (B)-Turnabout Tactics, (C)-Rindau Rampage; each came in paper sleeve, books 1,2 & 3;
Set with sleeves 5 10 15 34 55 75
Comic only 2 4 6 13 18 22

SWORDQUEST
DC Comics/Atari Pub.: 1982, 52pg., 5"x7" (Giveaway with video games)
1,2-Roy Thomas & Gerry Conway-s; George Pérez & Dick Giordano-c/a in all 2 4 6 10 14 18
3-Low print 3 6 9 16 22 28

SYNDICATE FEATURES (Sci/fi)
Harry A. Chesler Syndicate: V1#3, 11/15/37 (Tabloid size, 3 colors, 4 pgs.) (Editors premium) (Came folded)
V1#3-Dan Hastings daily strips-Guardineer-a 155 310 465 984 1692 2400

TAKING A CHANCE
American Cancer Society: no date (giveaway)
nn-Anti-smoking 2 4 6 11 16 20

TASTEE-FREEZ COMICS (Also see Harvey Hits and Richie Rich)
Harvey Comics: 1957 (10¢, 36 pgs.)(6 different issues given away)
1-Little Dot on cover; Richie Rich "Ride 'Em Cowboy" story published one year prior to being printed in Harvey Hits #9. 18 36 54 129 252 375
2,4,5: 2-Rags Rabbit. 4-Sad Sack. 5-Mazie 4 8 12 26 41 55
3-Casper 5 10 15 34 55 75
6-Dick Tracy 5 10 15 34 55 75

TAYLOR'S CHRISTMAS TABLOID
Dept. Store Giveaway: Mid 1930s, Cleveland, Ohio (Tabloid size; in color)
nn-(Very Rare)-Among the earliest pro work of Siegel & Shuster; one full color page called "The Battle in the Stratosphere", with a pre-Superman look; Shuster art thoughout. (Only 1 known copy) Estimated value... 4000.00

TAZ'S 40TH BIRTHDAY BLOWOUT
DC Comics: 1994 (K-Mart giveaway, 16 pgs.)
nn-Six pg. story, games and puzzles 4.00

TEE AND VEE CROSLEY IN TELEVISION LAND COMICS (Also see Crosley's House of Fun)
Crosley Division, Avco Mfg. Corp. : 1951 (52 pgs.; 8x11"; paper cover; in color) (Giveaway)

Titans Beat #1 © DC

Tom Mix Commandos Comics #11 © FAW

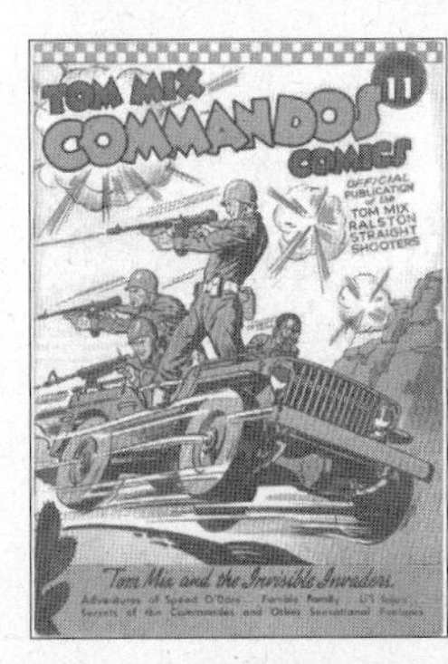

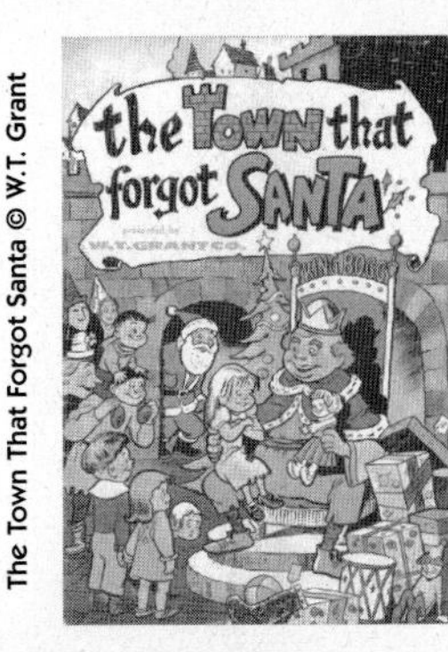

The Town That Forgot Santa © W.T. Grant

	GD 2.0	VG 4.0	FN 6.0	VF 8.0	VF/NM 9.0	NM- 9.2

Many stories, puzzles, cut-outs, games, etc. 7 14 21 35 43 50

TEEN-AGE BOOBY TRAP
Commercial Comics: 1970 (Small size)
nn 4 7 10 14 17 20

TENNESSEE JED (Radio)
Fox Syndicate? (Wm. C. Popper & Co.): nd (1945) (16 pgs.; paper-c; reg. size; giveaway)
nn 19 38 57 111 178 245

TENNIS (...For Speed, Stamina, Strength, Skill)
Tennis Educational Foundation: 1956 (16 pgs.; soft cover; 10¢)
Book 1-Endorsed by Gene Tunney, Ralph Kiner, etc. showing how tennis has helped them 6 12 18 28 34 40

TERRY AND THE PIRATES
Dell Publishing Co.: 1939 - 1953 (By Milton Caniff)
Buster Brown Shoes giveaway(1938)-32 pgs.; in color 19 38 57 112 181 250
Canada Dry Premiums-Books #1-3(1953, 36 pgs.; 2x5")-Harvey; #1-Hot Shot Charlie Flies Again; 2-In Forced Landing; 3-Dragon Lady in Distress) 14 28 42 78 112 145
Gambles Giveaway (1938, 16 pgs.) 9 18 27 50 65 80
Gillmore Giveaway (1938, 24 pgs.) 9 18 27 52 69 85
Popped Wheat Giveaway(1938)-Strip reprints in full color; Caniff-a 2 4 6 8 10 12
Shoe Store giveaway (Weatherbird & Poll-Parrot)(1938, 16 pgs., soft-c)(2-diff.) 9 18 27 52 69 85
Sparked Wheat Giveaway(1942, 16 pgs.)-In color 9 18 27 52 69 85

TERRY AND THE PIRATES
Libby's Radio Premium: 1941 (16 pgs.; reg. size)(shipped folded in the mail)
"Adventure of the Ruby of Genghis Khan" - Each pg. is a puzzle that must be completed to read the story 400 800 1200 2600 - -

THAT THE WORLD MAY BELIEVE
Catechetical Guild Giveaway: No date (16 pgs.) (Graymoor Friars distr.)
nn 4 8 12 18 22 25

3-D COLOR CLASSICS (Wendy's Kid's Club)
Wendy's Int'l Inc.: 1995 (5 1/2" x 8", comes with 3-D glasses)
The Elephant's Child, Gulliver's Travels, Peter Pan, The Time Machine, 20,000 Leagues Under the Sea: Neal Adams-a in all each.... 3.50

350 YEARS OF AMERICAN DAIRY FOODS
American Dairy Assoc.: 1957 (5x7", 16 pgs.)
nn-History of milk 3 6 8 12 14 16

THUMPER (Disney)
Grosset & Dunlap: 1942 (50¢, 32pgs., hardcover book, 7"x8-1/2" w/dust jacket)
nn-Given away (along with a copy of Bambi) for a $2.00, 2-year subscription to WDC&S in 1942. (Xmas offer). Book only 15 30 45 90 140 190
Dust jacket only 10 20 30 56 76 95

TILLY AND TED-TINKERTOTLAND
W. T. Grant Co.: 1945 (Giveaway, 20 pgs.)
nn-Christmas comic 7 14 21 37 46 55

TIM (Formerly Superman-Tim; becomes Gene Autry-Tim)
Tim Stores: June, 1950 - Oct, 1950 (B&W, half-size)
4 issues; 6/50, 9/50, 10/50 known 17 34 51 98 154 210

TIM AND SALLY'S ADVENTURES AT MARINELAND
Marineland Restaurant & Bar, Marineland, CA: 1957 (5x7", 16 pgs., soft-c)
nn-copyright Oceanarium, Inc. 2 4 6 8 11 14

TIME MACHINE, THE
DC Comics: 2002 (10 pgs.)
nn-Promotes the 2002 DreamWorks movie 6.00

TIME OF DECISION
Harvey Publications Inc.: (16 pgs., paper cover)
nn-ROTC recruitment 4 7 10 14 17 20

TIM IN SPACE (Formerly Gene Autry Tim; becomes Tim Tomorrow)
Tim Stores: 1950 (1/2 size giveaway) (B&W)
nn 14 28 42 78 112 145

TIM TOMORROW (Formerly Tim In Space)
Tim Stores: 8/51, 9/51, 10/51, Christmas, 1951 (5x7-3/4")
nn-Prof. Fumble & Captain Kit Comet in all 14 28 42 78 112 145

TIM TYLER'S LUCK
Standard Comics (King Feat. Syndicate): 1950s (Reg. size, slick-c)
nn-Felix the at app. 4 7 10 14 17 20

TITANS BEAT (Teen Titans)
DC Comics: Aug, 1996 (16 pgs., paper-c)
1-Intro./preview new Teen Titans members; Pérez-a 4.00

TOM MIX (...Commandos Comics #10-12)
Ralston-Purina Co.: Sept, 1940 - No. 12, Nov, 1942 (36 pgs.); 1983 (one-shot)
Given away for two Ralston box-tops; 1983 came in cereal box
1-Origin (life) Tom Mix; Fred Meagher-a 232 464 696 1473 2537 3600
2 52 104 156 330 565 800
3-9 40 80 120 252 426 600
10-12: 10-Origin Tom Mix Commando Unit; Speed O'Dare begins; Japanese sub-c. 12-Sci/fi-c 37 74 111 222 361 500
1983- "Taking of Grizzly Grebb", Toth-a; 16 pg. miniature 2 4 6 9 12 15

TOM SAWYER COMICS
Giveaway: 1951? (Paper cover)
nn-Contains a coverless Hopalong Cassidy from 1951; other combinations known 3 6 9 14 20 25

TOO MUCH, TOO LITTLE
Federal Reserve Bank: 1989 (Reg. size)
9-13 1 3 4 6 8 10

TOP-NOTCH COMICS
MLJ Magazines/Rex Theater: 1940s (theater giveaway, sepia-c)
1-Black Hood-c; content & covers can vary 42 84 126 265 445 625

TOPPS COMICS PRESENTS
Topps Comics: No. 0, 1993 (Giveaway, B&W, 36 pgs.)
0-Dracula vs. Zorro, Teenagents, Silver Star, & Bill the Galactic Hero 2.50

TOWN THAT FORGOT SANTA, THE
W. T. Grant Co.: 1961 (Giveaway, 24 pgs.)
nn 3 6 9 16 23 30

TOY LAND FUNNIES (See Funnies On Parade)
Eastern Color Printing Co.: 1934 (32 pgs., Hecht Co. store giveaway)
nn-Reprints Buck Rogers Sunday pages #199-201 from Famous Funnies #5. A rare variation of Funnies On Parade; same format, similar contents, same cover except for large Santa placed in center (value will be based on sale)

TOY WORLD FUNNIES (See Funnies On Parade)
Eastern Color Printing Co.: 1933 (36 pgs., slick cover, Golden Eagle and Wanamaker giveaway)
nn-Contains contents from Funnies On Parade/Century Of Comics. A rare variation of Funnies On Parade; same format, similar contents, same cover except for large Santa placed in center (value will be based on sale)

TRAPPED
Harvey Publications (Columbia Univ. Press): 1951 (Giveaway, soft-c, 16 pgs)
nn-Drug education comic (30,000 printed?) distributed to schools.; mentioned in SOTI, pgs. 256,350 2 4 6 8 10 12
NOTE: *Many copies surfaced in 1979 causing a setback in price; beware of trimmed edges, because many copies have a brittle edge.*

TRIPLE-A BASEBALL HEROES
Marvel Comics: 2007 (Minor league baseball stadium giveaway)
1-Special John Watson painted-c for Memphis, Durham and Buffalo; generic cover with team logos for each of the other 27 teams; Spider-Man, Iron Man, FF app. 3.00

TRIP TO OUTER SPACE WITH SANTA
Sales Promotions, Inc/Peoria Dry Goods: 1950s (paper-c)
nn-Comics, games & puzzles 5 10 15 22 26 30

TRIP WITH SANTA ON CHRISTMAS EVE, A
Rockford Dry Goods Co.: No date (Early 1950s) (Giveaway, 16 pgs., paper-c)
nn 5 10 15 22 26 30

TRUTH BEHIND THE TRIAL OF CARDINAL MINDSZENTY, THE (See Cardinal Mindszenty)

24 PAGES OF COMICS (No title) (Also see Pure Oil Comics, Salerno Carnival of Comics, & Vicks Comics)
Giveaway by various outlets including Sears: Late 1930s
nn-Contains strip reprints-Buck Rogers, Napoleon, Sky Roads, War on Crime

Two Faces of Communism © CACC

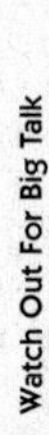
Watch Out For Big Talk

Wheaties B-1 © DIS

	GD 2.0	VG 4.0	FN 6.0	VF 8.0	VF/NM 9.0	NM- 9.2

31 62 93 184 302 420

TWO FACES OF COMMUNISM (Also see Double Talk)
Christian Anti-Communism Crusade, Houston, Texas: 1961 (Giveaway, paper-c, 36 pgs.)

nn 16 32 48 94 147 200

2001, A SPACE ODYSSEY (Movie)
Marvel Comics Group

Howard Johnson giveaway (1968, 8pp); 6 pg. movie adaptation, 2 pg. games, puzzles; McWilliams-a 2 4 6 9 12 15

UNCLE SAM'S CHRISTMAS STORY
Promotional Publ. Co.: 1958 (Giveaway)

nn-Reprints 1956 Christmas USA 2 4 6 10 13 16

UNCLE WIGGILY COMICS
Herberger's Clothing Store: 1942 (32 pgs., paper cover)

nn-Comic panels with 6 pages of puzzles 12 24 36 69 97 125

UNKEPT PROMISE
Legion of Truth: 1949 (Giveaway, 24 pgs.)

nn-Anti-alcohol 10 20 30 58 79 100

UNTOLD LEGEND OF THE BATMAN, THE
DC Comics: 1989 (28 pgs., 6X9", limited series of cereal premiums)

1-1st & 2nd printings known; Byrne-a 2 3 4 6 8 10
2,3: 1st & 2nd printings known 1 2 3 5 6 8

UNTOUCHABLES, THE (TV)
Leaf Brands, Inc.

Topps Bubblegum premiums produced by Leaf Brands, Inc.-2-1/2x4-1/2", 8 pgs. (3 diff. issues) "The Organization, Jamaica Ginger, The Otto Frick Story (drug), 3000 Suspects, The Antidote, Mexican Stakeout, Little Egypt, Purple Gang, Bugs Moran Story, & Lily Dallas Story" 3 6 9 16 23 30

VICKS COMICS (See Pure Oil Comics, Salerno Carnival of Comics & 24 Pages of Comics)
Eastern Color Printing Co. (Vicks Chemical Co.): nd (circa 1938) (Giveaway, 68 pgs. in color)

nn-Famous Funnies-r (before #40); contains 5 pgs. Buck Rogers (4 pgs. from F.F. #15, & 1 pg. from #16) Joe Palooka, Napoleon, etc. app. 54 108 162 343 592 840
nn-16 loose, untrimmed page giveaway; paper-c; r/Famous Funnies #14; Buck Rogers, Joe Palooka app. Has either "Vicks Comics" printed on cover or only a local store name as the logo. 22 44 66 131 216 300

WALT DISNEY'S COMICS & STORIES
K.K. Publications: 1942-1963 known (7-1/3"x10-1/4", 4 pgs. in color, slick paper) (folded horizontally once or twice as mailers) (Xmas subscription offer)

1942 mailer-r/Kelly cover to WDC&S 25; 2-year subscription + two Grosset & Dunlap hardcover books (32-pages each), of Bambi and of Thumper, offered for $2.00; came in an illustrated C&S envelope with an enclosed postage paid envelope
(Rare) Mailer only 21 42 63 123 204 285
with envelopes 27 54 81 158 259 360
1947,1948 mailer 17 34 51 98 154 210
1949 mailer-A rare Barks item: Same WDC&S cover as 1942 mailer, but with art changed so that nephew is handing teacher Donald a comic book rather than an apple, as originally drawn by Kelly. The tiny, 7/8"x1-1/4" cover shown was a rejected cover by Barks that was intended for C&S 110, but was redrawn by Kelly for C&S 111. The original art has been lost and this is its only app. (Rare) 39 78 117 233 377 520
1950 mailer-P.1 r/Kelly cover to Dell Xmas Parade 1 (without title); p.2 r/Kelly cover to C&S 101 (w/o title), but with the art altered to show Donald reading C&S 122 (by Kelly); hardcover book, "Donald Duck in Bringing Up the Boys" given with a $1.00 one-year subscription; P.4 r/full Kelly Xmas cover to C&S 99 (Rare) 17 34 51 98 154 210
1952 mailer-P1 r/cover WDC&S #88 14 28 42 80 115 150
1953 mailer-P.1 r/cover Dell Xmas Parade 4 (w/o title); insides offer "Donald Duck Full Speed Ahead," a 28-page, color, 5-5/8"x6-5/8" book, not of the Story Hour series; P.4 r/full Barks C&S 148 cover (Rare) 14 28 42 80 115 150
1963 mailer-Pgs. 1,2 & 4 r/GK Xmas art; P.3 r/a 1963 C&S cover (Scarce) 7 14 21 46 76 105

NOTE: *It is assumed a different mailer was printed each Xmas for at least twenty years.*

WALT DISNEY'S COMICS & STORIES
Walt Disney Productions: 1943 (36 pgs.) (Dept. store Xmas giveaway)

nn-X-Mas-c with Donald & the Boys; Donald Duck by Jack Hannah; Thumper by Ken Hultgren 43 86 129 271 461 650

WALT DISNEY'S DONALD DUCK
Gemstone Publishing: 2006

nn-(8-1/2"x 5-1/2", Halloween giveaway) r/"A Prank Above" -Barks-s/a; Rosa-s/a 2.50
nn-(2008, 8-1/2"x 5-1/2", Halloween giveaway) "The Halloween Huckster"; Rota-s/a 2.50

WALT DISNEY'S UNCLE SCROOGE
Gemstone Publishing

nn-(2007, 8-1/2"x 5-1/2", Halloween giveaway) Hound of the Whiskevilles; Barks-s/a 2.50

WARLORD
DC Comics: (Remco Toy giveaway, 2-3/4x4")

nn 5.00

WATCH OUT FOR BIG TALK
Giveaway: 1950

nn-Dan Barry-a; about crooked politicians 7 14 21 37 46 55

WEATHER-BIRD (See Comics From..., Dick Tracy, Free Comics to You..., Super Circus & Terry and the Pirates)
International Shoe Co./Western Printing Co.: 1958 - No. 16, July, 1962 (Shoe store giveaway)

1 4 8 12 25 39 52
2-16 3 6 9 14 19 24

NOTE: *The numbers are located in the lower bottom panel, pg. 1. All feature a character called Weather-Bird.*

WEATHER BIRD COMICS (See Comics From Weather Bird)
Weather Bird Shoes: 1957 (Giveaway)

nn-Contains a comic bound with new cover. Several combinations possible; contents determine price (40 - 60 percent of contents).

WEEKLY COMIC MAGAZINE
Fox Publications: May 12, 1940 (16 pgs.) (Others exist w/o super-heroes)

(1st Version)-8 pg. Blue Beetle story, 7 pg. Patty O'Day story; two copies known to exist. (a VF copy sold in 5/07 for $1553)
(2nd Version)-7 two-pg. adventures of Blue Beetle, Patty O'Day, Yarko, Dr. Fung, Green Mask, Spark Stevens, & Rex Dexter (two known copies, a FN sold in 2007 for $1912, other is GD)
(3rd version)-Captain Valor (only one known copy, in VG+; it sold in 2005 for $480) -

Discovered with business papers, letters and exploitation material promoting **Weekly Comic Magazine** for use by newspapers in the same manner of **The Spirit** weeklies. Interesting note: these are dated three weeks before the first Spirit comic. Letters indicate that samples may have been sent to a few newspapers. These sections were actually 15-1/2x22" pages which will fold down to an approximate 8x10" comic booklet. Other various comic sections were found with the above, but were more like the Sunday comic sections in format.

WE HIT THE JACKPOT
General Comics, Inc./American Affairs: 1947 (Promotional comic)

nn 6 12 18 31 38 45

WHAT DO YOU KNOW ABOUT THIS COMICS SEAL OF APPROVAL?
No publisher listed (DC Comics Giveaway): nd (1955) (4 pgs., slick paper-c)

nn-(Rare) 77 154 231 489 845 1200

WHAT'S BEHIND THESE HEADLINES
William C. Popper Co.: 1948 (16 pgs.)

nn-Comic insert "The Plot to Steal the World" 6 12 18 31 38 45

WHAT'S IN IT FOR YOU?
Harvey Publications Inc.: (16 pgs., paper cover)

nn-National Guard recruitment 4 7 10 14 17 20

WHEATIES (Premiums)
Walt Disney Productions: 1950 & 1951 (32 titles, pocket-size, 32 pgs.)

Mailing Envelope (no art on front)(Designates sets A,B,C or D on front) 7 14 21 37 46 55

(Set A-1 to A-8, 1950)

A-1-Mickey Mouse & the Disappearing Island, A-5-Mickey Mouse, Roving Reporter each... 6 12 18 28 34 40
A-2-Grandma Duck, Homespun Detective, A-6-Li'l Bad Wolf, Forest Ranger, A-7-Goofy, Tightrope Acrobat, A-8-Pluto & the Bogus Money each... 5 10 15 24 30 35
A-3-Donald Duck & the Haunted Jewels, A-4-Donald Duck & the Giant Ape each... 8 16 24 42 54 65

(Set B-1 to B-8, 1950)

B-1-Mickey Mouse & the Pharoah's Curse, B-4-Mickey Mouse & the Mystery Sea Monster each... 6 12 18 31 38 45
B-2-Pluto, Canine Cowpoke, B-5-Li'l Bad Wolf in the Hollow Tree Hideout, B-7-Goofy & the Gangsters each... 5 10 15 24 30 35
B-3-Donald Duck & the Buccaneers, B-6-Donald Duck,Trail Blazer, B-8 Donald Duck, Klondike Kid each... 8 16 24 42 54 65

(Set C-1 to C-8, 1951)

C-1-Donald Duck & the Inca Idol, C-5-Donald Duck in the Lost Lakes, C-8-Donald Duck Deep-Sea Diver each... 8 16 24 42 54 65
C-2-Mickey Mouse & the Magic Mountain, C-6-Mickey Mouse & the Stagecoach Bandits each... 6 12 18 31 38 45
C-3-Li'l Bad Wolf, Fire Fighter, C-4-Gus & Jaq Save the Ship, C-7-Goofy, Big Game Hunter

Wild Kingdom nn © WEST

Woody Woodpecker in Chevrolet Wonderland © Walter Lantz

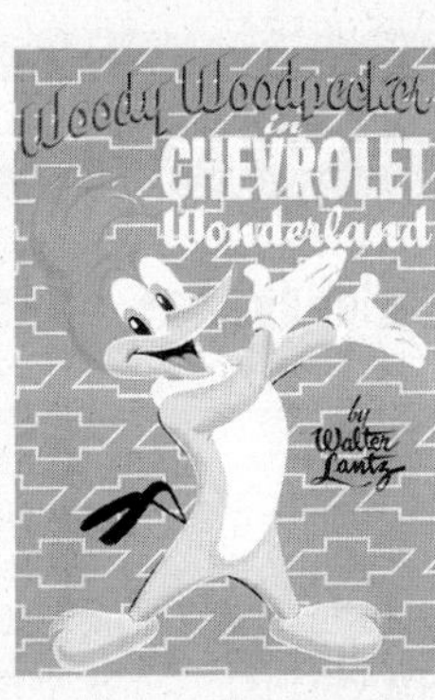

X2 Presents The Ultimate X-Men #2 © MAR

	GD 2.0	VG 4.0	FN 6.0	VF 8.0	VF/NM 9.0	NM- 9.2
each...	5	10	15	24	30	35

(Set D-1 to D-8, 1951)

D-1-Donald Duck in Indian Country, D-5-Donald Duck, Mighty Mystic each...	8	16	24	42	54	65
D-2-Mickey Mouse and the Abandoned Mine, D-6-Mickey Mouse & the Medicine Man each...	6	12	18	31	38	45
D-3-Pluto & the Mysterious Package, D-4-Bre'r Rabbit's Sunken Treasure, D-7-Li'l Bad Wolf and the Secret of the Woods, D-8-Minnie Mouse, Girl Explorer each...	5	10	15	24	30	35

NOTE: *Some copies lack the Wheaties ad.*

WHEEL OF PROGRESS, THE
Assoc. of American Railroads: Oct, 1957 (16 pgs.)

nn-Bill Bunce	6	12	18	28	34	40

WHIZ COMICS (Formerly Flash Comics & Thrill Comics #1)
Fawcett Publications

Wheaties Giveaway(1946, Miniature, 6-1/2x8-1/4", 32 pgs.); all copies were taped at each corner to a box of Wheaties and are never found in very fine or mint condition; "Capt. Marvel & the Water Thieves", plus Golden Arrow, Ibis, Crime Smasher stories	90	180	405	–	–	–

WILD KINGDOM (TV) (Mutual of Omaha's...)
Western Printing Co.: 1965, 1966 (Giveaway, regular size, slick-c, 16 pgs.)

nn-Front & back-c are different on 1966 edition	2	4	6	9	12	15

WISCO/KLARER COMIC BOOK (Miniature)
Marvel Comics/Vital Publ./Fawcett Publ.: 1948 - 1964 (3-1/2x6-3/4", 24 pgs.)
Given away by Wisco "99" Service Stations, Carnation Malted Milk, Klarer Health Wieners, Fleers Dubble Bubble Gum, Rodeo All-Meat Wieners, Perfect Potato Chips, & others; see ad in Tom Mix #21

Blackstone & the Gold Medal Mystery (1948)	8	16	24	42	54	65
Blackstone "Solves the Sealed Vault Mystery" (1950)	8	16	24	42	54	65
Blaze Carson in "The Sheriff Shoots It Out" (1950)	8	16	24	42	54	65
Captain Marvel & Billy's Big Game (r/Capt. Marvel Adv. #76)	24	48	72	145	238	330
(Prices vary widely on this book)						
China Boy in "A Trip to the Zoo" #10 (1948)	5	10	15	24	30	35
Indoors-Outdoors Game Book	4	7	10	14	17	20
Jim Solar Space Sheriff in "Battle for Mars", "Between Two Worlds", "Conquers Outer Space", "The Creatures on the Comet", "Defeats the Moon Missile Men", "Encounter Creatures on Comet", "Meet the Jupiter Jumpers", "Meets the Man From Mars", "On Traffic Duty", "Outlaws of the Spaceways", "Pirates of the Planet X", "Protects Space Lanes", "Raiders From the Sun", "Ring Around Saturn", "Robots of Rhea", "The Sky Ruby", "Spacetts of the Sky", "Spidermen of Venus", "Trouble on Mercury"	7	14	21	35	43	50
Johnny Starboard & the Underseas Pirates (1948)	5	10	15	22	26	30
Kid Colt in "He Lived by His Guns" (1950)	8	16	24	44	57	70
Little Aspirin as the "Crook Catcher" #2 (1950)	4	7	10	14	17	20
Little Aspirin in "Naughty But Nice" #6 (1950)	4	7	10	14	17	20
Return of the Black Phantom (not M.E. character)(Roy Dare)(1948)	6	12	18	28	34	40
Secrets of Magic	4	8	11	16	19	22
Slim Morgan "Brings Justice to Mesa City" #3	4	8	11	16	19	22
Super Rabbit(1950)-Cuts Red Tape, Stops Crime Wave!	9	18	27	50	65	80
Tex Farnum, Frontiersman (1948)	5	10	15	22	26	30
Tex Taylor in "Draw or Die, Cowpoke!" (1950)	7	14	21	35	43	50
Tex Taylor in "An Exciting Adventure at the Gold Mine" (1950)	6	12	18	31	38	45
Wacky Quacky in "All-Aboard"	3	6	8	12	14	16
When School Is Out	3	6	8	12	14	16
Willie in a "Comic-Comic Book Fall" #1	4	8	11	16	19	22
Wonder Duck "An Adventure at the Rodeo of the Fearless Quacker!" (1950)	9	18	27	47	61	75

Rare uncut version of three; includes Capt. Marvel, Tex Farnum, Black Phantom
Estimated value... 700.00
Rare uncut version of three; includes China Boy, Blackstone, Johnny Starboard & the Underseas Pirates Estimated value... 250.00
Rare uncut version of three; includes Willie in a "Comic-Comic Book Fall", Little Aspirin #2, Slim Morgan Brings Justice to Mesa City (a VF/FN copy sold for $54 in Nov. 2007)

WOLVERINE
Marvel Comics

145-(1999 Nabisco mail-in offer) Sienkiewicz-c	8	16	24	53	84	125
...Son of Canada (4/01, ed. of 65,000) Spider-Man & The Hulk app.; Lim-a						3.00

WOMAN OF THE PROMISE, THE
Catechetical Guild: 1950 (General Distr.) (Paper cover, 32 pgs.)

nn	6	12	18	28	34	40

WONDERFUL WORLD OF DUCKS (See Golden Picture Story Book)
Colgate Palmolive Co.: 1975

1-Mostly-r	1	3	4	6	8	10

WONDER WOMAN
DC Comics: 1977

Pizza Hut Giveaways (12/77)-Reprints #60,62	2	4	6	9	13	16
... - The Minotaur (1981, General Foods giveaway, 8 pages, 3-1/2 x 6-3/4", oblong)	2	4	6	13	18	22

WONDER WORKER OF PERU
Catechetical Guild: No date (5x7", 16 pgs., B&W, giveaway)

nn	5	10	15	27	33	38

WOODY WOODPECKER
Dell Publishing Co.

Clover Stamp-Newspaper Boy Contest('56)-9 pg. story-(Giveaway)	7	14	21	37	46	55
In Chevrolet Wonderland(1954-Giveaway)(Western Publ.)-20 pgs., full story line; Chilly Willy app.	18	36	54	103	162	220
...Meets Scotty MacTape(1953-Scotch Tape giveaway)-16 pgs., full size	18	36	54	103	162	220

WOOLWORTH'S CHRISTMAS STORY BOOK
Promotional Publ. Co.(Western Printing Co.): 1952 - 1954 (16 pgs., paper-c) (See Jolly Christmas Book)

nn: 1952 issue-Marv Levy c/a	6	12	18	33	41	48

WOOLWORTH'S HAPPY TIME CHRISTMAS BOOK
F. W. Woolworth Co. (Western Printing Co.): 1952 (Christmas giveaway)

nn-36 pgs.	6	12	18	31	38	45

WORLD'S FINEST COMICS
National Periodical Publ./DC Comics

Giveaway (c. 1944-45, 8 pgs., in color, paper-c)-Johnny Everyman-r/World's Finest	20	40	60	118	194	270
Giveaway (c. 1949, 8 pgs., in color, paper-c)- "Make Way For Youth" r/World's Finest; based on film of same name	18	36	54	107	169	230
#176, #179- Best Western reprint edition (1997)						3.00

WORLD'S GREATEST SUPER HEROES
DC Comics (Nutra Comics) (Child Vitamins, Inc.): 1977 (Giveaway, 3-3/4x3-3/4", 24 pgs.)

nn-Batman & Robin app.; health tips	2	4	6	9	13	16

WYOMING THE COWBOY STATE
1954 (Giveaway, slick-c)

nn	5	10	15	22	26	30

XMAS FUNNIES
Kinney Shoes: No date (Giveaway, paper cover, 36 pgs.?)

Contains 1933 color strip-r; Mutt & Jeff, etc.	29	58	87	172	281	390

X-MEN THE MOVIE
Marvel Comics/Toys R' Us: 2000

Special Movie Prequel Edition						5.00

X2 PRESENTS THE ULTIMATE X-MEN #2
Marvel Comics/New York Post: July, 2003

Reprint distributed inside issue of the New York Post						2.50

YALTA TO KOREA (Also see Korea My Home)
M. Phillip Corp. (Republican National Committee): 1952 (Giveaway, paper-c)

nn-(8 pgs.)-Anti-communist propaganda book	18	36	54	103	162	220

YOGI BEAR (TV)
Dell Publishing Co.

Giveaway ('84, '86)-City of Los Angeles, "Creative First Aid" & "Earthquake Preparedness for Children"	1	2	3	4	5	7

YOUR TRIP TO NEWSPAPERLAND
Philadelphia Evening Bulletin (Printed by Harvey Press): June, 1955 (14x11-1/2", 12 pgs.)

nn-Joe Palooka takes kids on newspaper tour	5	10	15	24	30	35

YOUR VOTE IS VITAL!
Harvey Publications Inc.: 1952 (5" x 7", 16 pgs., paper cover)

nn-The importance of voting	4	8	12	18	22	25

THE PIONEER AGE

The American Comic Book: 1500s-1828

For the last few years, we have featured a tremendous article by noted historian and collector Eric C. Caren on the foundations of what we now call "The Pioneer Age" of comics. We look forward to a new article on this significant topic in a future edition of *The Overstreet Comic Book Price Guide*. In the meantime, should you need it, Caren's article may be found in the 35th through 39th editions.

That said, even with the space constraints in this edition of the *Guide*, we could not possibly exclude reference to these incredible, formative works.

Why are these illustrations and sequences of illustrations important to the comic books of today?

German broadsheet, dated 1569.

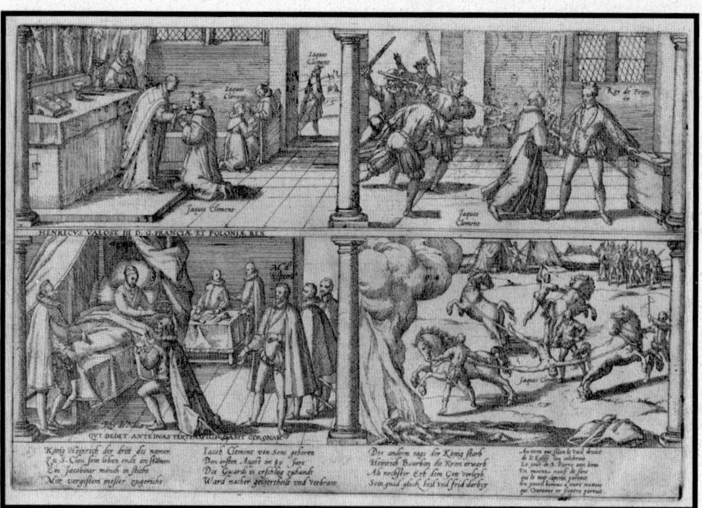

Quite frankly, because we can see in them the very building blocks of the comic art form.

The Murder of King Henry III (1589).

The shooting of the Italian Concini (1617).

Over the course of just a few hundred years, we the evolution of narration, word balloons, panel-to-panel progression of story, and so much more. If these stories aren't developed first, how would be every have reached the point that that *The Adventures of Mr. Obadiah Oldbuck* could have come along in 1842?

As the investigation of comic book history has blown away the notion that comic books were a 20 century invention, it hasn't been easy to convince some, even with the clear, linear progression of the artful melding of illustration and words.

"Want to avoid an argument in social discourse? Steer clear of politics and religion. In the latter category, the most controversial subject is human evolution. Collectors can become just as squeamish when you start messing with the evolution of a particular collectible," Eric Caren wrote in his article. "In most cases, the origin of a particular comic character will be universally agreed upon, but try tackling the origin of printed comics and you are asking for trouble."

"The Bubblers Medley" (1720).

"Join, or Die" from the Pennsylvania Gazette, May 9, 1754.

"Amusement for John Bull..." from The European Magazine (1783).

But the evidence is there for any who choose to look. Before the original comics of the Golden Age, there were comic strip reprints collected in comic book form. The practice dated back decades earlier, of course, but coalesced into the current form when the realities of the Great Depression spawned the modern incarnation of the comic book and its immediate cousin, the Big Little Book.

Everything that came later, though, did so because the acceptance of the visual language had already been worked out. Before Spider-Man and the Hulk, before Superman and Batman, before the Yellow Kid, Little Nemo, and the Brownies, cartoonists and editorial illustrators were working out how to tell a story or simply convey their ideas in this new artform.

Without this sort of work, without these pioneers, we simply wouldn't be where we are today.

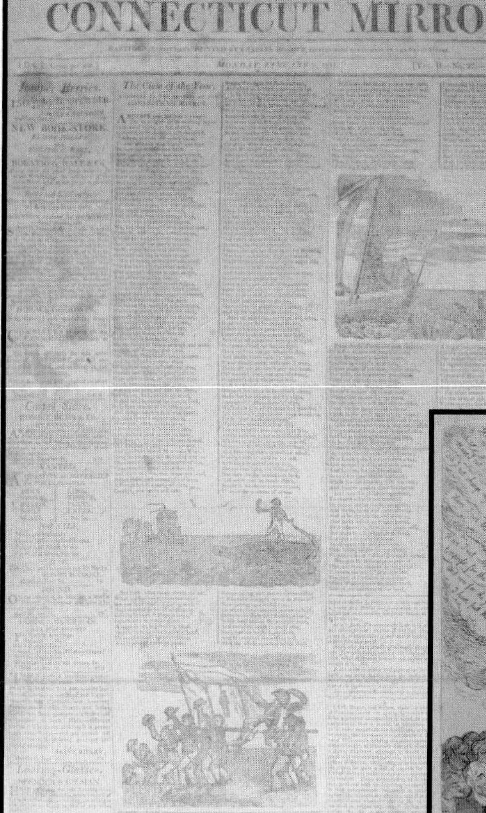
CONNECTICUT MIRROR.

Cartoons satirizing Napoleon on the front page of the Connecticut Mirror, dated January 7, 1811.

Another Napoleon cartoon, this time dubbing him "The Corsican Munchausen," from the London Strand, December 4, 1813.

"A Consultation at the Medical Board" from The Pasquin or General Satirist *(1821).*

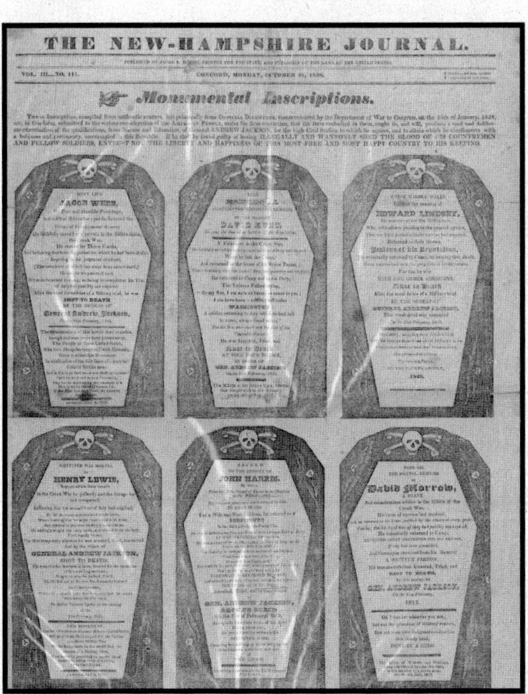

THE NEW-HAMPSHIRE JOURNAL.

CONCORD, MONDAY, OCTOBER 20, 1828.

Monumental Inscriptions.

ILLEGALLY AND WANTONLY SHED THE BLOOD OF HIS COUNTRYMEN AND FELLOW SOLDIERS, ENTRUST NOT THE LIBERTY AND HAPPINESS OF THIS MOST FREE AND MOST HAPPY COUNTRY TO HIS KEEPING.

JACOB WEBB,

EDWARD LINDSEY,

HENRY LEWIS,

JOHN HARRIS.

David Morrow,

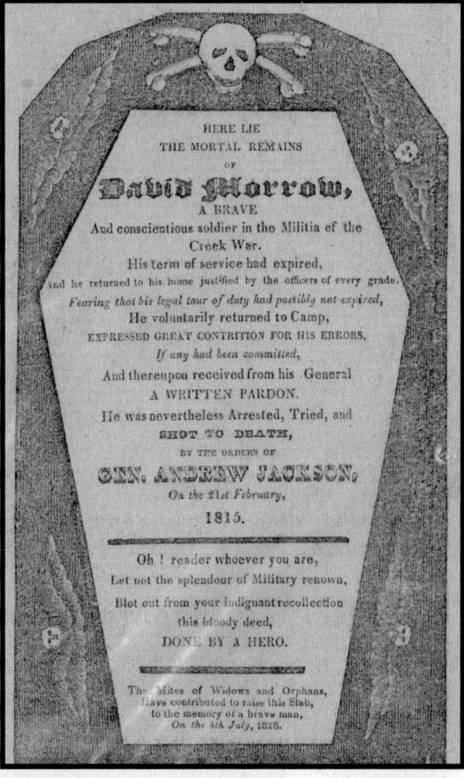

HERE LIE
THE MORTAL REMAINS
OF
David Morrow,
A BRAVE
And conscientious soldier in the Militia of the
Creek War.
His term of service had expired,
And he returned to his home justified by the officers of every grade.
Fearing that his legal tour of duty had possibly not expired,
He voluntarily returned to Camp,
EXPRESSED GREAT CONTRITION FOR HIS ERRORS,
If any had been committed,
And thereupon received from his General
A WRITTEN PARDON.
He was nevertheless Arrested, Tried, and
SHOT TO DEATH,
BY THE ORDERS OF
GEN. ANDREW JACKSON,
On the 21st February,
1815.

Oh! reader whoever you are,
Let not the splendour of Military renown,
Blot out from your indignant recollection
this bloody deed,
DONE BY A HERO.

The Mites of Widows and Orphans,
Have contributed to raise this Slab,
to the memory of a brave man,
On the 4th July, 1828.

Above left, the front page of The New Hampshire Journal, *dated October 20, 1828, with multiple tombstone "panels." To the right is a detail of the bottom right tombstone.*

THE VICTORIAN AGE

Comic Strips and Books: 1646-1900

A Concise History & Price Index Of The Field As Of 2012

ORIGINS OF EARLY AMERICAN COMIC STRIPS BEFORE THE YELLOW KID

by Robert Lee Beerbohm, Richard Samuel West & Richard D. Olson, PhD ©2012

(This article was originally created by Doug Wheeler, Robert Beerbohm and Richard D. Olson, PhD for CBPG #32 and continues to be revised annually by the current authors.) We welcome any and all corrections and additions. Special Thanks This Installment To Leonardo De Sa, Terrence Keegen, Gabriel Laderman and Joe Rainone.

Left: "The Burning of Mr. John Rogers," 1646 is the earliest-known North American cartoon printed on paper printed in the earliest children's primer in America.

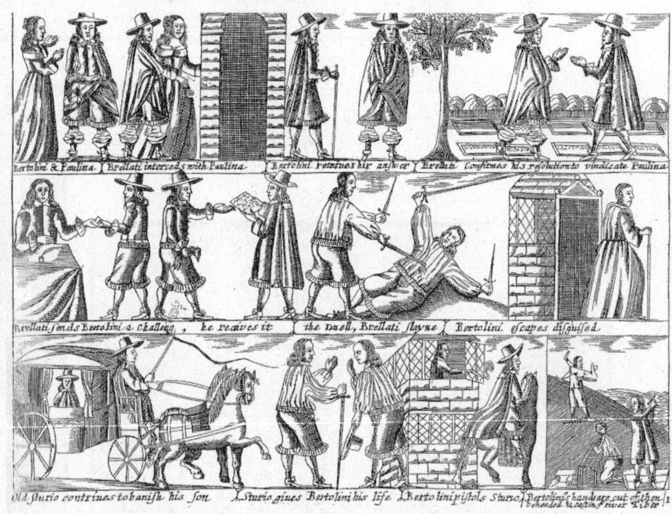

"God's Revenge For Murder" By John Reynolds, unknown artist, 1656. Earliest-known sequential comic "panel" strip created in the English language.

Left: From his pamphlet Plain Truth 1747 containing Ben Franklin's earliest-known cartoon titled "Heaven Helps Only Those Who Help Themselves" depicting ancient "super hero" Hercules in the upper right corner. Middle: "A Warm Place - Hell", one of two images definitely known to be drawn and engraved by Paul Revere, 1768. Word balloons had wide-spread usage in many cartoons in the 1700s. Right: The Tables Turned by James Gillray, 1797 com-menting on an "invasion" of England by 1400 French convicts. The use of word balloons was wide spread in many parts of the world long before the Yellow Kid's parrot uttered a few words in 1896.

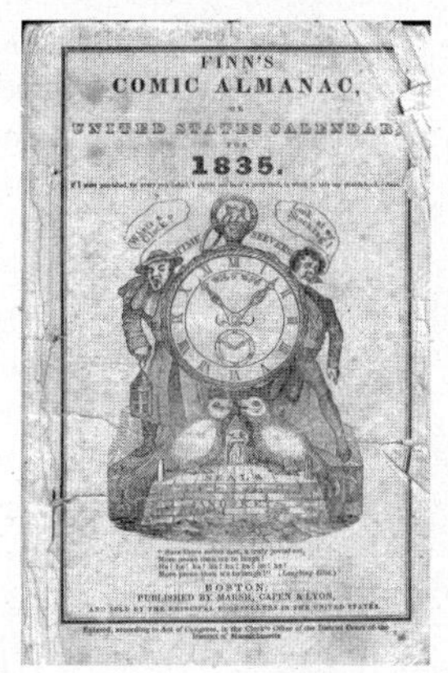

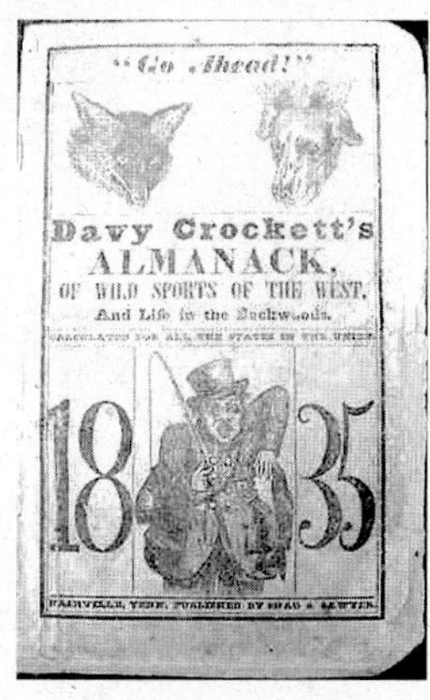

The Comic Almanac(k) debuted in America in 1831 with the earliest-known titles starting heavy with humor and sporting crude woodcut single panel cartoons. Ellm's American Comic Almanac was one of the first. By 1835 Davy Crockett, one of the nation's earliest national folk heroes, began issuing his own version. In the late 1840s the Comic Almanac(k)s began to offer tall-tale sequential comic strips which became somewhat commonplace in the 1850s, fueled by the advent of the California Gold Rush. They were instrumental in the development of the American comic strip and we will be reporting more new finds after further research into American folklore.

We have a lot of new discoveries to share with you again this year as amply evident in the price index which follows this year's history lesson. A quantum leap has finally been achieved in the area of introducing the comic book collecting world to *American Comic Almanac(k)s* as well as a huge multitude of American humor periodicals, many of which contained sequential comic strips.

This Victorian Era section is devoted to comic strips and books published during the years the United States expanded across the North American continent, fought a Civil War, shifted from an agrarian to an industrial society, "welcomed" waves of immigrants, and struggled over race, class, religion, temperance, and suffrage - and all of it depicted and satirized by generations of mostly now long-forgotten cartoonists. The social attitudes, beliefs, and conventions of 19th century America, the good as well as the bad, are to be found in abundance. Perhaps the first question to pop into most readers' minds will be, "What, beyond the happenstance of publication date, are Victorian Era comics?"

There has been a long slow-motion evolution of the comic strip which was not invented in America, contrary to many previous history books on the subject. One must examine many aspects of concurrent popular culture. The main aspect that we believe most distinguishes Victorian Era comic strips from those of later eras was the extremely rare use of word balloons within sequential (multi-picture) comic stories. When word balloons were used, it was nearly always within single-panel cartoons. On the occasions when they appeared inside a strip, with very few exceptions, the ballooned dialogue was inconsequential. Nineteenth-century comics tended to place both narration and dialogue beneath comic panels rather than within the panel's borders as they were thought by many to interfere with the art. Many of these comics are to the word balloon-strewn post-Yellow Kid comics of the 20th Century as silent movies are to the later "talkies." Just as sound changed how stories were structured on film, so too did comic strips change when the words were moved from beneath panels to inside them, and dialogue rather than narration drove the story in conjunction with the pictures.

The Victorian Era of actual comic strip books began on different dates in different nations, depending on when the first publication of a sequential comic book on their soil is known to have occurred. For the U.S. this happened when the American literary periodical *Brother Jonathan* printed the 40-page, 195-panel graphic novel *The Adventures of Mr. Obadiah Oldbuck* as a special extra dated September 14, 1842. Almost six decades later, America's Victorian comics came to their end, replaced by the onslaught of Platinum Age books reprinting newspaper strips from Bennett, Hearst, and Pulitzer Sunday comic sections, among many others.

There is considerable overlap between Victorian Era and Platinum Age comic books and strips. Those publications that continued from one century into the next, such as *Puck*, *Judge*, and *Life*, have their pre-1900 issues listed within the Victorian Age section, while their post-1899 issues can be found inside the Platinum Age. Some non-sequential (i.e., single-panel) American comic items existing prior to 1842 are also listed herein, going back to 1795. These belong to what could tentatively be called the Age of Caricature (1770s through 1830s). This was a fertile period for the art in England, when Gillray and Rowlandson, and, later, Cruikshank, Heath, and Seymour were that nation's top cartoonists. During the same period in the U.S., there were no artists who made their living as caricaturists, though William Charles, printer and engraver, did produce about two dozen spirited cartoon broadsides from 1805 to 1820, the most important ones concerning events of the War of 1812.

In addition, one can trace origins of American comic books to the humorous Comic Almanacs which began in earnest in the early 1830s.

The earliest known cartoon-like woodcut printed on paper in North America was in a Puritan children's book first published in 1646. Titled simply *The Burning of Mr. John*

The Comus Offering, 1830 sample page of single panel cartoons using word balloons in every panel. Very Rare.

Rogers, it showed in flaming graphic detail what happens to those who stray from the flock and have to be burned at the stake. Dr. Wertham would have had a field day with that one!

Cartoon broadsides and other single panel images, often using word balloons, appeared from pre-Revolution days through the end of the 19th Century. The earliest known attributed cartoon, designed by the ubiquitous Benjamin Franklin, was "Heaven Helps Only Those Who Help Themselves," which first appeared in his pamphlet *Plain Truth* in 1747.

The most popularly remembered 18th-Century American cartoons are likely Franklin's *"Join or Die"* in 1754, representing the American Colonies as severed snake parts, and *"The Bloody Massacre Perpetrated in King Street"* -- Paul Revere's 1770 depiction of the Boston Massacre, which he pirated from the earlier Henry Pelham broadsheet cartoon *"The Fruits of Arbitrary Power."*

In September 1826, John Warner Barber, New Haven, Ct. (1798-1885) designed and self-published the broadside *The Drunkard's Progress, Or The Direct Road to Poverty, Wretchedness and Ruin* showing in four stages sequentially "The Morning Dram" which is "The Beginning of Sorrow, " "The Grog Shop" with its "Bad Company," "The Confirmed Drunkard" in a state of "Beastly Intoxication," and the "Concluding Scene" with the family being driven off to the alms house. It is an interesting set of cuts, faintly reminiscent of Hogarth. Barber began his career in 1819, age 21, engraving on wood. He devoted most of his career to the multitude of art chores associated with book production. As late as 1870 he was issuing *Barber's Temperance Tracts,* which built upon his 1826 original plus four panels showing the positive effects of living without alcohol.

The first American whose fame was based primarily on his cartoons appears to be David Claypoole Johnston (1798-1865). Johnston provided illustrations for various almanacs, books, and periodicals, including the masthead for *Brother Jonathans*. Most notable of Johnston's comics work was his nine-issue series *Scraps*, which he self-published from 1828 to 1849. This series was highly influenced by George Cruikshank's series *Scraps and Sketches*, which first appeared in 1827. Because of the resemblance, Johnston became known in his day as "the American Cruikshank." Each issue of Johnston's *Scraps* consists of four large folio-sized pages, printed on one side, with nine to twelve single-panel cartoons per page, and each page often organized around a theme. Also popular was his comic album Outlines Illustrative of the Journal of F****** A*** K***** (1835), which parodied passages from the journal of recently published observations on America by British actress Fanny Kemble.

Johnston, himself a failed actor, had an interest in the theater his entire career. In addition to producing a number of prints depicting American actors in famous roles, he collaborated with actor Henry J. Finn to produce the 1831 *(American) Comic Annual*, with Finn as Editor and Johnston as artist, published by Richardson, Lord and Holbrook, Boston. It featured almost 30 full-page Johnston-designed copper engravings and woodcuts. Also that year, Finn solo produced *Finn's Comic Sketch Book*, a twelve-page album similar to Johnston's *Scraps* with upwards of half a dozen single-panel cartoons per page. It was published by Peabody and Co, of New York in business from 1831-1843. (Finn died tragically in a steamboat accident Jan. 13, 1840.)

Perhaps Johnston's most interesting contribution to the history of the comic strip in American came in 1837, when he produced the sequential comic broadside, *Illustrations of the Adventures & Achievements of the Renowned Don Quixote & his Doughty Squire Sancho Panza* (27.4 x 30.4 cm). This blank-reverse engraved print was an elaborate twelve-panel satire of the Andrew Jackson-Van Buren administration. It likely sold for 25 cents, seeing distribution in Boston, New York and Philadelphia. Much later, in 1863, Johnston drew another sequential comic broadside, *The House the Jeff Built* (27.5 x 36.7 cm), a bitter indictment of Jefferson Davis and the Southern slavocracy.

In July 1839, Wilson and Company, a newly formed New York printing firm, began publishing a mammoth newspaper by the name of *Brother Jonathan*. The publisher, J. Gregg Wilson had employed the newspaper format for *Brother Jonathan* to circumvent the higher postage rates imposed on magazines, but *Brother Jonathan* was a newspaper in format only -- it contained not a shred of news, instead specializing in serialized fiction, some of it written by Americans but most of it pirated from foreign sources. Despite the cost savings, the mammoth format had its limitations; when opened it measured a whopping three feet by four feet. So, once *Brother Jonathan* was an established success, Wilson and Day began in January 1841 the simultaneous publication of a magazine-sized quarto edition of *Brother Jonathan* that reprinted the contents of the mammoth edition.

Later that same year, to capitalize on the name recognition

of their successful twin publications, Wilson and Company started issuing book-length *Brother Jonathan Extras* in the same format as the quarto magazine. These reprints are counted among the earliest paperback books in America. Most of the *Extra* numbers were pirated European novels. For example their eighth extra was the first American printing of a Charles Dickens novel. But for their ninth *Extra*, they did something no American publisher had ever done before -- they pirated a graphic novel, Rodolphe Töpffer's *The Adventures of Mr. Obadiah Oldbuck*. By reformatting *Oldbuck* from its original small oblong strip design to fit *Brother Jonathan's* standard quarto format Wilson and Company inadvertently made this edition (alone) of *Obadiah Oldbuck* resemble a modern comic book. *Oldbuck's* arrival on the shores of the New World would directly inspire a wave of American imitators. [*This first Wilson printing of Oldbuck from 1842 was reprinted in same-size limited edition facsimile by the Naples Comicon in 2003. An English translation by Leonardo De Sá of Töpffer's original draft is at leonardo desa.interdinamica. net/comics/lds/*]

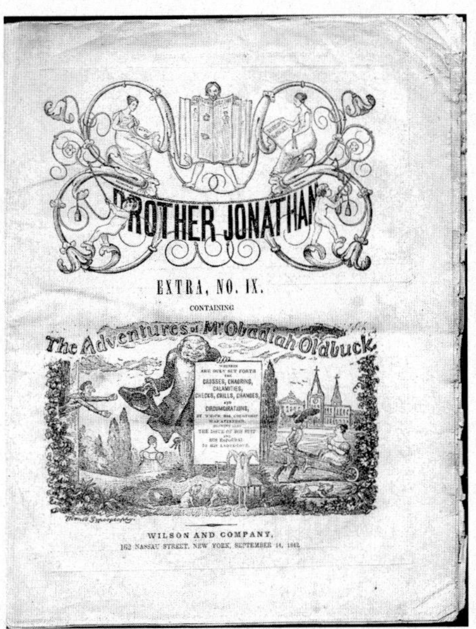

Cover to the subscriber version of the earliest-known sequential comic book published in America, The Adventures of Mr. Obadiah Oldbuck, Sept. 1842, Wilson & Co. New York, originally conceived in 1828 in Geneva Switzerland by creator Rodolphe Töpffer.

Even though in 1904 (in its September 3 edition), *The New York Times* accurately identified the *Brother Jonathan Extra* as the first American comic book as well as Wilson & Co. utilizing Tilt & Bougue's original printing plates as well as still being in print for sale in New York at such a late date, Töpffer has already been largely forgotten in the New World. It is high time Töpffer received credit long overdue as the inventor of the modern comic strip, laying previously long-held myths to rest.

Töpffer (1799-1846) was a playwright, novelist, artist, and teacher from Geneva, Switzerland, who in 1827 had begun producing what he called "picture novels," sharing them with his friends and students. His earliest editions were self-published via lithography on transfer paper as they use the word "autographie" in their imprints. The earliest printers were J. Freydig, Frutiger (1830s) and Schmidt (1840s). These first sequential comic books, scripted in Töpffer's native French language, found their way to Paris and became an instant hit. According to Gombrich in *Art and Illusion* (1960), "Töpffer recognized that he could rely on the reader to supplement from their own lives what was omitted between the panels. This is crucial in the development of the sequential comic strip."

The demand for his comic books soon outstripped the supply, and pirated editions, redrawn by others, were created by Parisian publisher Aubert to capitalize on this. In a world where international copyright conventions did not exist, this was perfectly legal, if morally questionable. Thus, in 1841, London publisher Tilt and Bogue commissioned George Cruikshank to create an English version of Töpffer's *Les Amours de M. Vieux Bois* by pirating Aubert's pirated edition of the Geneva original.

This English translation, co-financed by George Cruikshank himself, sported a new cover page by George's brother Robert, based on a montage of Töpffer's scenes. Confirmation of this fact came when George Cruikshank's personal copy surfaced in auction recently with the inscription "Copied from a French book by my Brother Robert" above the title page with the same scene. This is the translation that was reprinted by America's Wilson and Company as *The Adventures of Mr. Obadiah Oldbuck* utilizing the original Tilt and Bogue printing plates.

Tilt and Bogue followed up their success by translating into English two additional stories of Töpffer's seven published graphic novels: *Beau Ogleby*, circa 1843 (originally Histoire de M. Jabot), and *Bachelor Butterfly* two years later (from *Histoire de M. Cryptogame)*. David Bogue also published picture-story strip books by John Leighton using the pseudonym Luke Limner. He wrote and drew beautiful comic books titled *London Out of Town or The Adventures of the Browns At The Seaside; Comic Art-Manufactures; and The Ancient Story of the Old Dame and Her Pig* starting in 1847, but none of these seem to have ever been republished in America. They follow a definite Töpffer influence. This growing body of comic book production was made easier by the spreading understanding of transfer paper lithography, otherwise the panels would have had to have been drawn and lettered mirror reverse. Gombrich referred to Töpffer's comic books as "the innocent ancestors of today's manufactured dreams... everywhere in these countless episodes of almost surrealist inconsequence we find a mastery of physiognomic characterization which sets the standard for such influential humorous draftsmen in the 19th century as Wilhelm Busch in Germany."

A Register of The New York City Book Trades 1821-1842 by Sidney F. & Elizabeth Stege12, Huttner (The Bibliographical Society of America, NYC, 1993) mentions Benjamin H. Day bought into *Brother Jonathan*'s publisher,

Wilson and Company, in this year, becoming at some point an equal partner with owner J. Gregg Wilson. The Register lists them both as publishers of *Brother Jonathan* at the same address of 162 Nassau Street. Other historical artifacts state Day eventually became sole-owner and publisher. Exactly when has not yet been determined, though we have figured out with certainly before 1850.

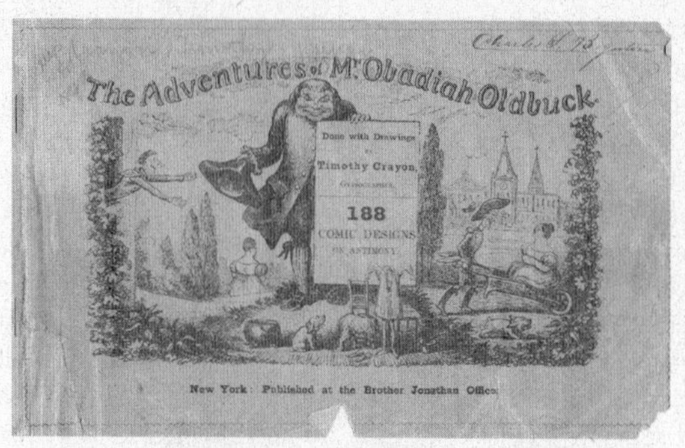

The Adventures of Obadiah Oldbuck, rare newly discovered 4th edition from mid 1850s. Says now "Published at Brother Jonathan Offices." Art & Story now accredited to the pseudonym "Timothy Crayon" - see Peter Piper ad previous page.

The Strange and Wonderful Adventures of Bachelor Butterfly by Rodolphe Töpffer (New York, 1846) was America's 3rd comic book; Wilson & Company's second comic book, this time out staying with the original European format.

This is the same Benjamin H. Day who started the first successful penny newspaper in 1833, *The (New York) Sun*, transforming it in four short years into the largest circulation daily in the world at that time. He sold out his ownership of the Sun to his brother-in-law during the financial "panic" of 1837, a mistake he regretted the rest of his life. He re-emerged heavily involved in *Brother Jonathan* definitely by 1840 and as a partner by 1841. *Brother Jonathan's* offices were right next door to Tamany Hall. (See the first 20 minutes of the 2002 movie *Gangs of New York* to visualize the period atmosphere and their customer base.) According to *The Brothers Harper* by Eugene Exmen (Harper & Row, 1965), on page 125, "*Brother Jonathan*... offered in its weekly edition and also in special supplements very cheap reprints of English novels. In effect, it began a price-cutting war against the older established 'pirates' among the book publishers..." Day, it appears, had found the perfect project on which to build a new empire.

Desirous of repeating the success they had with *Obadiah Oldbuck*, Wilson and Company published the first American edition of *Bachelor Butterfly* in 1846. Three years later, they reformatted *Obadiah Oldbuck* back into its original British shape using lithography, dropping a handful of comic panels and altering the text to hide these deletions. Soon thereafter, they published other comic books for a steadily growing market that they had helped to stimulate. In recognition of their significant role in the dissemination of sequential comics, Wilson and Company deserve to be remembered as the first comic book publisher in America.

Back in Europe, perhaps inspired by his involvement with Töpffer's *Obadiah Oldbuck*, George Cruikshank soon created several sequential comic books of his own. These too found their way to America. *The Bachelor's Own Book*, published first in Britain in 1844, became the second known U.S. published sequential comic book when it was reprinted by Burgess, Stringer and Company the following year. Next was Cruikshank's masterpiece *The Bottle*, the Hogarthian-style tale of a man whose addiction to alcohol brings himself and his family to ruin. After debuting in London in 1847, it was reprinted the same year in a British-American co-publication between David Bogue and Americans Wiley and Putnam. Both printings were in huge folio form, available in either black and white or professionally hand-tinted versions. In 1848, the story saw American print again, this time in smaller form, placed at the front of the otherwise prose volume *Temperance Tales; Or, Six Nights with the Washing-tonians*. It continued to be reprinted by a variety of publishers into the early 20th Century. *The Bottle* was even reproduced onto painted glass slides and then projected by magic lantern onto a screen for the moral edification of temperance audiences. *The Drunkard's Children, Cruikshank's sequel to The Bottle*, was issued July 1, 1848 as a British-American-Australian co-publishing venture, but was less successful, and had not nearly as many reprints.

The most clearly sequential, as well as fun, of George Cruikshank's comic books was *The Tooth-Ache*, first issued in London in 1849. It was reprinted in America later that same year by Philadelphia map maker J.L. Smith. An additional concurrent version was also issued from Boston.

When closed, this booklet appears an unassuming 5-1/4 inches tall by 3-1/4 inches wide. Its striking feature is that the book folds open accordion style, stretching the entire 43-panel story along one single strip of paper, which when fully extended is seven feet, three inches long! *The Tooth-Ache* was issued in both black and white and professionally hand-colored editions. Abridged editions of the story, printed in black and white and with a "normal" page-turning rather than foldout presentation, appeared inside promotional give-away comics issued by American companies in the 1880s.

Thanks to Töpffer, Cruikshank, and a handful of enterprising American publishers, the 1840s should be remembered as the decade when America first fell in love with the comics.

The Tooth-Ache by George Cruickshank 1849
© J. L. Smith, Philadelphia, PA. First American edition opens up accordian-like into a single continuous paper strip 7 feet, 3 inches long!

It had seen the U.S. publication of six sequential comic books, as well as the importation of other comics with foreign imprints. America's growing interest in graphic humor was further stimulated by the growth of two other fields: the cartoon broadside and the humor magazine.

As mentioned before, the cartoon broadside had been a part of the American scene since pre-Revolution days, but it did not flourish until stone lithography (introduced in 1818 and in wide use by the 1830s) made the reproduction of images relatively fast and cheap. From the early 1830s into the mid 1840s, the leading producer of cartoon broadsides in America was New York printer H. R. Robinson, who either drew his own cartoons or employed others, especially E. W. Clay, to do it. Clay is notable for having produced the first sequential comic broadside in America. Published in 1834 and entitled, "This Is the House that Jack Built" (50 x 32 cm), the nine-panel parody of the classic nursery rhyme was an attack on the Jackson Administration. The dominant theme of American cartoon broadsides was political, as befitted a nation where politics was the leading spectator sport. As the American electorate grew increasingly educated and prosperous, the demand for cartoon broadside also increased. During the 1840s, lithographers in New York, Boston, and Philadelphia, entered the field to satisfy that demand. The best known of these, Nathaniel Currier, later Currier and Ives, joined the fray in 1848. The firm employed many artists, but its chief political cartoonist was Louis Maurer and its chief comic artist was Thomas Worth.

Except for the three previously cited sequential cartoon broadsides, nearly all of the cartoon broadsides published in America from 1832 to 1876, its dominant era, were single panels. From the 1860s onward, broadside series on a single comic theme became common, the most famous being Thomas Worth's *Darktown* series. These can be loosely categorized as sequential comics since they employed the same characters and formed a story of sorts when hung together on a wall, as was the publisher's expectation. Sequential art or not, the cartoon broadsides nearly always employed the speech balloons that later became one of the defining characteristic of the American comic strip.

During the same decade that sequential comics and cartoon broadsides were growing in popularity, the illustrated American humor magazine made its debut. The British comic weekly *Punch*, founded in 1841, was an immediate success, both in England and the United States. It was a handsomely printed quarto, initially twelve pages and later sixteen, with a repeating cover design, backed by a page of small advertisements, humorous text interspersed with comic spot art, and a single panel full-page cartoon. A significant subset of *Punch*'s subscriber base was located in the U.S., to which thousands of copies were exported on an ongoing trans-Atlantic basis. Inevitably, enterprising American publishers attempted to repulse this invader with a home-grown comic weekly. The first, *Yankee Doodle*, came to town (New York, that is) on October 10, 1846, for one year. *Judy* (November 28, 1846 to February 20, 1847), *The John-Donkey* (January 1 to October 21, 1848), and *The Elephant* (January 22 to February 19, 1848) soon followed. None of them was successful, but all of them continued to feed the growing American interest in comic art.

By the late 1840s, comic art was flourishing in America. The conditions were right for the production of the earliest known American-created sequential comic book. Brothers James and Donald Read, who had worked for a time as cartoonists on *Yankee Doodle*, were the creators of *Journey to the Gold Diggins by Jeremiah Saddlebags*. This spirited send-up of the California gold rush craze was published in June 1849 by Stringer and Townsend, the late publishers of *Judy*, and, soon after, by U. P. James of Cincinnati. This Töpffer-influenced comic book chronicles the adventures of its hero *Jeremiah Saddlebags* in his get-rich-quick quest for gold in California. It is highly sought by collectors of Western Americana. Interestingly, the back cover of the Stringer and Townsend edition carries an advertisement for *Rose and Gertrude* - a Genevese Story, one of Rodolphe Töpffer's non-comics prose novels.

Stringer and Townsend was making something of a name for itself as a publisher of comic art. It will be remembered that it was one of the 1845 participants in the American publication of *The Bachelor's Own Book*. And, then, in 1846-47, it published *Judy*. Its decision to issue *Jeremiah Saddlebags* was all in due course.

The Gold Rush proved to be a gold mine for American comic artists. Aside from being a featured topic in the 1849 edition of David Claypool Johnston's *Scraps*, in comic almanacs, and in Currier cartoon prints, it was the subject of several other significant sequential series. The first, *The Adventures of Mr. Tom Plump* (a fat man who nearly starves to death in his failed attempt at California Gold riches), saw print in 1850. The second, *The Adventures of Jeremiah Old-Pot* (a twelve-part burlesque narrative of a New York businessman who attempts to get rich selling tin in price-inflated California), ran throughout 1852 in *Yankee Notions*. Though the narrative was distinctly American in its humor, the artwork was probably German in origin. *Yankee Notions*' Publisher, T. W. Strong, built his business on recycling old woodcuts with new captions attached. It should be noted that the *Old-Pot* series, borrowed or otherwise, was the first sequential art to appear in an American humor magazine. *Yankee Notions*, published from 1852 to 1875, also has the distinction of being the first comic monthly published in America.

"Moses Keyser the Bowery Bully's Trip to the California Gold Mines," was a 13-page comic story that appeared in *Elton's Californian Comic All-My-Nack* for 1850. It was reprinted at least twice in the circa 1850-51 booklet *The Clown, Or The Banquet of Wit* and later again in *Sam Slick's Comic Almanac* in 1857. *The Clown* is also notable as the earliest known anthology of sequential comics, with the bonus that each multi-panel story is by a different artist. Many of the artists are as yet unidentified, and how much of it is original American material versus that reprinted from Europe is presently unknown. But verified are cartoons by George Cruikshank, Elton (American), the Read brothers, Grandville (French), and Richard Doyle (British). The Doyle contribution reprints the comics story "Brown, Jones and Robinson and How They Went to a Ball," which originally saw print in the August 24, 1850 issue of *Punch*. This is the first known American appearance of these Doyle characters, and was almost certainly pirated.

Richard Doyle's *The Foreign Tour of Messrs. Brown, Jones, and Robinson* is basically a travelogue in illustrated form, told via humorous episodes, part sequential cartoon sequences, and part snapshots of moments jumping forward in time. This halfway sequential format was ideal for most 19th Century cartoonists, who, with rare exception, had not quite grasped how to maintain a single sequential story for much longer than two dozen successive panels. Doyle had simplified Töpffer's formula in a manner most artists could attempt to emulate. Episodes of "*Brown, Jones, and Robinson*" originally appeared in *Punch* in 1850, until a dispute between the Roman Catholic Doyle and Punch's editors over an anti-Papal joke ended with Doyle's resignation. Doyle redrew and expanded the story into a single album, first seeing print in 1854 from British publisher Bradbury and Evans.

New York Publisher D. Appleton brought the album to America, reprinting it in 1860, 1871, and 1877. Next, Dick and Fitzgerald of New York pirated Doyle's story sometime in the early 1870s. Doyle's format from *Foreign Tour* was emulated again and again. Examples include: the 1857 *Mr. Hardy Lee, His Yacht*, by Charles Stedman; the 1860s- 1870s G. W. Carleton-published *Our Artist In...* series, set in various Latin American countries; the Augustus Hoppin 1870s sketch novels *On the Nile, Crossing the Atlantic*, and *Ups and Downs on Land and Water*; and *Life* founder John Ames Mitchell's 1881 (pre-Life) *The Summer School of Philosophy at Mt. Desert*. D. Appleton, the official, authorized American publisher of *Foreign Tour*, even commissioned an American artist - Toby - to create a sequel comic album involving Doyle's characters visiting the U.S. and Canada, published in 1872 as *The American Tour of Messrs Brown, Jones and Robinson*. In terms of influencing the development of mid-19th Century American comics, Doyle's *Foreign Tour* ranks with the works of Töpffer, Cruikshank, and Busch.

Doyle was also the author of an equally popular earlier cartoon series for Punch, titled, *In Manners and Customs of Ye Englyshe, Mr. Pips Hys Diary*, which was reprinted in 1849. In this work, Doyle told his story using a deliberately primitive almost stick-figure art style, combined with the Hogarthian structure of large single panel cartoons leaping forward in time with each picture.

Manners and Customs of Ye Harvard Studente, which ran in the first year of the *Harvard Lampoon* (1876-current), shows the clearest influence. The series by then stu-

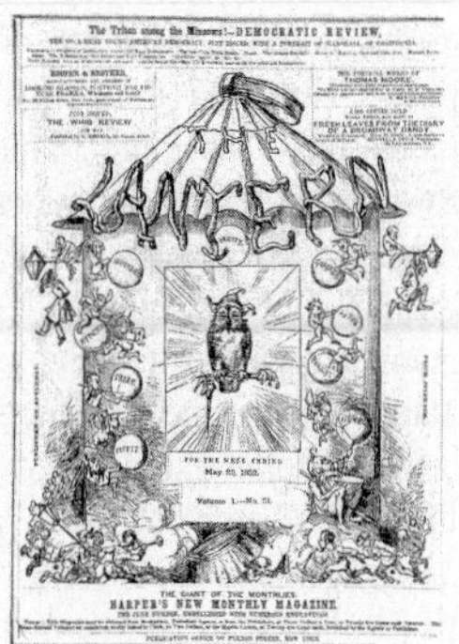

A few samples of the many humor magazines of the mid-1800s which ran cartoons. Wide-spread acceptance of the comic strip slowly evolved over the decades. Right: ***Yankee Doodle*** *#30, this title was the first American comic weekly which ran Oct 1846-Oct 1847; Second: Judy #1 ran Nov 28-Feb 20, 1847; Third:* ***The John-Donkey*** *#4 ran January-October 1848. Fourth:* ***The Lantern*** *#21, May 29, 1851 title ran Jan. 10, 1852-July 1853.*

dent Francis Gilbert Attwood was collected in 1877 by Houghton Mifflin. Attwood followed it up with *Manners and Customs of Ye Bostonians*, again in the pages of the *Harvard Lampoon*, but it is unknown whether that series was ever reprinted in book form. Attwood later became one of the regular artists in *Life*.

The Extraordinary and Mirth-provoking Adventures by Sea and Land of Oscar Shanghai, inspired by Bachelor Butterfly, was issued May 1855 by Garrett and Company, Publishers, No. 18 Ann Street, New York. Oscar Shanghai has many misadventures including being swallowed by a whale, making a trip in a flying machine to Africa, where he is shot out of a huge bow by a "Black Prince" for refusing to marry a local princess of color. After more adventures, he makes it back home.

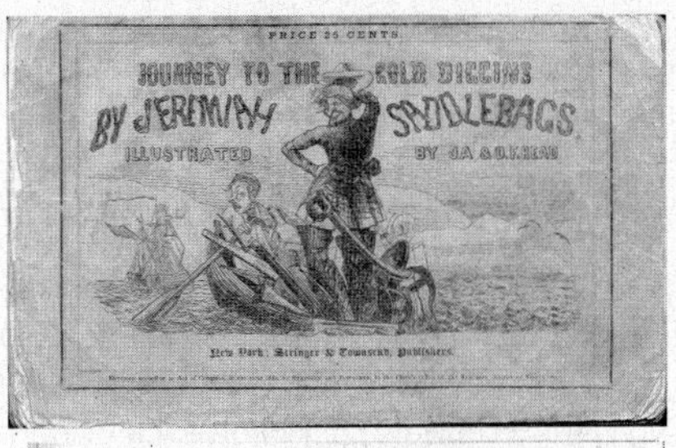

Journey to the Gold Diggins By Jeremiah Saddlebags, June 1849, so far the earliest known sequential comic book by American creators, J.A. and D.F. Read. Above: a couple sample pages. Note similarity to Töpffer's comics especially **Bachelor Butterfly**

Oscar Shanghai's first publisher was confirmed in 2002 with the discovery of a very rare 36-page catalog from 1856 of books, pamphlets and prints handled by B.H. Day (successor to Wilson and Company) who was by this time publishing *Brother Jonathan* as a twice-a-year holiday pictorial only. The catalog has a few crossover advertisement pages from an associate publisher, Garrett and Company. This rediscovered treasure, which sold for $750 in 2002, contains within a sequential strip of one panel per page over 32 of those pages titled "*Peter Piper in Bengal,*" by John Tenniel, reprinted from four 1853 issues of *Punch*. In the narrative, Peter Piper tries his hand hunting all different kinds of wild game with many misadventures.

Amongst the many varied types of "Cheap Books" for sale in this rare catalog are the comic books *The Adventures of Obadiah Oldbuck, Bachelor Butterfly's Queer Love Adventures and Misfortunes*, and *The Fortunes of Ferdinand Flipper*, plus the aforementioned *Oscar Shanghai*. All were priced at "25¢ per copy, postage free, refunds paid out in stamps." There is also an advertisement for a comic book entitled *A Day's Sport - Or, Hunting Adventures of S. Winks Wattles, a Shopkeeper, Thomas Titt, a "legal gent," and Major Nicholas Noggin, a Jolly Good Fellow Generally* by Henry L. Stephens (1824-1882) of Philadelphia.

Stephens, later the political cartoonist for *Vanity Fair* (New York, 1859-1863) and a leading children's book illustrator, produced his first work, *Illustrations of the Poets: From Passages in the Life of Little Billy Vidkins*, a small wrappered album of 32 comic woodcuts, in 1849. It was first published by S. Robinson, of Philadelphia, and reprinted with variant titles several times in the 1850s including *Yankee Notions*. It is likely that Little *Billy Vidkins* was printed before *Jeremiah Saddlebags*, though more research is needed before making this claim.

Garrett and Company was also responsible for the 1856 publication of *The Sad Tale of the Courtship of Chevalier Slyfox-Wikof, Showing His Heart-Rending Astounding and Most Wonderful Love Adventures with Fanny Elssler and Miss Gambol.* This book parodied the very public relationship between the then-famous wealthy American aristocrat Henry Wikoff, and the even more famous European actress/ dancer Fanny Elssler. It is dated thusly because Wikoff's memoir is pictured in the comic book.

Apparently in late 1854 Garrett and Company formed a brief two-year partnership with Dick and Fitzgerald, officially becoming Garrett, Dick and Fitzgerald in November 1856, while continuing to operate out of the same 18 Ann Street address in New York. One month later they issued Richard Doyle's British published graphic novel *The Foreign Tour of Messrs. Brown, Jones, and Robinson,* reformatting it into the same oblong shape as Garrett's two prior comic books (which in turn were formatted in imitation of Töpffer's albums). This information came to light just this year. The interested scholar is encouraged to check out the new listings for Garrett's The Home Circle in the index.

In 1858, Garrett appears to have dropped out, leaving Dick and Fitzgerald alone with the former's book stock, his place of business, and most importantly, the printing plates for his comic books. For reasons unknown, Dick and Fitzgerald steered away from reprinting Garrett's comic books for more than a decade. But in the 1870s they resumed publication - not only of the three albums published by Garrett, but also of *Obadiah Oldbuck and Bachelor Butterfly* from Wilson and Company, and *Ferdinand Flipper* from *Brother Jonathan* - all of them also making use of the original printing plates. The inclusion of books from *Brother Jonathan*, Wilson and Company, and Garrett and Company all within the same promotional Peter Piper catalog from B.H. Day suggests that these early publishers of comic books had many over-lapping fields of interest,, and that Dick and Fitzgerald became the inheritor/acquirer of all of it. Dick and Fitzgerald also reprinted in the 1870s the earlier William T. Peter published *Ichabod Academicus* (how that title might have connected, if at all, with B.H. Day's business remains unclear). We can now say, though, that an evolving group of a handful of publishers was responsible, over a span of 46 years, beginning with the very first graphic novel published in America in 1842, for keeping in print in America a cluster of slightly over half a dozen graphic novels.

Yankee Notions #1, January, 1852. This title began the first sequential comic strips in an American humor magazine, The Adventures of Jerimiah Old-Pot.

Tebbel's *History of Book Publishing* in the US (vol. 1, pages 351-2) states that Burgess and Stringer was dissolved in late 1840s and became two firms, Stringer and Townsend, and Burgess and Garrett. Burgess retired in 1850 and his nephew William Brisbane Dick stepped into the partnership, whereupon the new company was renamed Garrett, Dick and Fitzgerald. Garrett retired in 1851 and the firm became Dick and Fitzgerald. The firm persisted under that name until 1917.

Collections reprinting cartoons from Punch saw print in the U.S., such as *Merry Pictures by the Comic Hands*, imported for the 1859 Christmas Season, plus various John Leech, George Du Maurier, and Phil May books which appeared from the 1850s through 1910s. Finally, many American weekly newspapers and weekly and monthly magazines, humorous and non-humorous, reprinted cartoons from Punch. Such inclusions often became a prelude to switching to original material by American artists, if that publication find's cartoon section find American cartoonists of sufficient talent.

Harper's Monthly, the leading American monthly, was a prime example. Soon after it commenced publication in November 1850, it began to carry a few pages of single panel cartoons reprinted from *Punch* at the rear of each issue. This evolved into reprinting sequential comic pages from the British periodical *Town Talk*, and then, starting December 1853, original sequential comics by the great Frank Bellew.

Bellew (1828-1888) should be regarded as the "Father of American Sequential Comics." Born in India, educated in France and England, he emigrated to America in 1850. His earliest work shows an influence from Doyle, but he rapidly developed his own unique art style. Bellew's comics, both sequential and single panel, graced nearly every American comic periodical published from the 1850s into the 1870s.

A month after the publication of the anonymous first installment of *Jeremiah Old-Pot* in *Yankee Notions*, Bellew began contributing his six-part, 18-panel comic series, *"Mr. Blobb in Search of a Physician"* to *The Lantern*, a New York comic weekly published from January 10, 1852 to July 2, 1853. The series ran in six of the nine issues published from January 31 through March 27, 1852. This was followed in April and May by the 16-panel, three-issue comic sequence "*Mr. Bulbear's Dream*", which concluded with the main character awakened from his dream by falling out of bed, exactly like *Little Nemo* would do five decades later.

These two series were just the beginning for Bellew, who contributed a voluminous amount of work to the *New York Picayune* (1850-1860) (which he also edited for a time in 1857-58), *The Comic Monthly* (1859-1881), *Momus*, an 1860 comic daily, *The Phunniest of Awl* (1864-1867) (which he also edited), *Punchinello* (1870), and *Wild Oats* (1870-1881), to name the most prominent.

The Comic Monthly deserves special mention. Started in March 1859 and published by J. C. Haney and Company, of 119 Nassau Street, New York, *The Comic Monthly* was a profusely illustrated 16-page folio, the same size as *Harper's Weekly*. It focused its graphic satire on politics, the theater, and the comedy of everyday life. A preponderance of the purely comic satire took the form of sequential art. Here are random samplings of highlights from issues from 1860:

- February: "A Day of Humiliation, Fasting, Supplication, and Prayer (four panels, unsigned), "New Year Calls under the Influence of Hard Times" (twelve panels, unsigned), "Young Trouble-some; or, Master Jacky's Holidays" (nineteen panels covering three and half pages, unsigned);
- April: "Four Years After Marriage" (sixteen panels, unsigned), "Our Masked Ball" (twelve panel centerspread, Bellew), "Trials of a Witness" (eight panels, Bellew);
- May: "Precocities of Young Springles" (seven panels, unsigned), "The Fight for the Championship" (twenty-four panel centerspread, Bellew), "Steam Applied to Music" (three panels, unsigned), "The Course of True Love" (four panels, Bellew);
- June: "Further Particulars of the Fight" (nine panel cover, Bellew), "The Man Who Went to See the Fight" (twelve panels, unsigned);
- July: "Explaining American Politics to an Intelligent Foreigner" (twelve panels, unsigned), "The Meerschaum Mania" (two panels, Bellew), "The Art of Stump Speaking" (ten panels, unsigned), "Our Little Friend, Tom Noddy" (three panels, unsigned); "The Japanese in New York" (twelve panel centerspread, Bellew), "The Observant Child" (three panels, unsigned), "Mr. Dibbs Goes to Pike's Peak and Comes Back Again" (fourteen panel back cover, unsigned);
- September: "The Zouave Fever" (four panel cover, unsigned), "Mr. Lupell" (two panels, Bellew), "The Prince of Wales in America" (twenty-four panel centerspread, J. H. Howard), "D'ye Think It's True?" (three panels, Bellew);
- October: "The Duties of the Wide Awake" (four panels, Bellew), "Our Charley (two panels, unsigned), "The Three Young Friends" (eighteen panel back cover, unsigned);
- November: "The Hanlon's (sic) At Home" (nine panel

back cover, unsigned);

• December: "The Target Excursion" (seventeen panel centerspread, signed with an unidentifiable monogram); "The Sporting Critic" two panels, Bellew).

The Comic Monthly also published many multi-panel cartoons grouped under a single heading, which were not strictly sequential in nature. Bellew was the monthly's chief artist, assisted by Thomas Nast, A. R Waud, and others. Some of the unsigned art was certainly by Bellew, some by journeymen artists, and some of it pirated from European journals.

The Comic Monthly was not the first folio-sized humor magazine. Those laurels go to *The New York Picayune,* which began as a newspaper, switched to a folio in 1856, adopted *Punch's* format for thirty-five issues in 1857-58, and returned to a folio for the remainder of its run.

Frank Leslie's *Budget of Fun*, the greatest of the folio monthlies, began in January 1859 and was published until June 1878. Its star cartoonist during the sixties was William Newman (c. 1817-1870), one of the founding artists of Punch. As we have noted, *The Comic Monthly* began two months later.

Frank Leslie was born Henry Cart in Ipswich, England in 1821. He became a very skilled engraver before coming over to America in 1948. He first worked as manager for P.T. Barnum's *New York Illustrated News* for several years. in 1850 he legally had his name changed to Frank Leslie. He died in 1880 and his wife continued the numerous publications he was publishing. Many of Frank Leslie's periodicals had a lot of sequental comic art.

Quarto-sized monthlies to compete with the successful *Yankee Notions* were also proliferating. *Nick-Nax* was the first (May 1856 to December 1875), followed by *Phunny Phellow* (October 1859- 1876) and *Merryman's Comic Monthly* (January 1863 to December 1875), to name the most prominent.

Frank Leslie's Budget of Fun#19 June 1860 sports a comic strip on its front cover.

Enterprising publishers continued to attempt an American comic weekly in the style of *Punch*. The most notable efforts, *Vanity Fair* (1859-1863), *Mrs. Grundy* (1865), and *Punchinello* (1870), were distinguished but unsuccessful.

Nearly all of them, weeklies and monthlies, to varying degrees, featured sequential comic art. By the time of the American Civil War, sequential comic art was a part of the American graphic landscape.

While Bellew stood out for his sequential comics, Thomas Nast (1840-1902) brought a new style to American political cartoons, of which he is regarded the father. Even though he created several sequential strips early in his career (especially for Nick-Nax in 1859), Nast made his name in the pages of the national news periodical, *Harper's Weekly*, for which he worked from 1862 until 1886. Nast was influenced more by the dark wood engravings of Franco-German illustrator Gustave Dore than by the cartoonists of *Punch*. His somber cartoons were a novelty in American cartooning. Nast in the pages of *Harper's Weekly* (and Newman in the pages of the *Budget of Fun*) popularized the extravagant double-page folio-sized cartoon, which had no precedent in European or American cartooning, save for the separately published cartoon broadsides. This format would come to full maturity after 1876 in the pages of *Puck* (1876-1918) and then *Judge* (1881-1947).

As Nast grew in prominence and success, American cartoonists increasingly emulated him. U.S. humor publications evolved towards an amalgamation of Nast and Punch, rather than sheer imitation of the latter. After the War, with Nast's style of cartoons more entrenched in American readers' minds, efforts to launch *Punch*-like American periodicals floundered quickly. *Mrs. Grundy*, ironically most famous for its cover design by Nast, died after a mere twelve issues (running July 8 to September 23, 1865). *Punchinello* (April 2 to December 24, 1870) struggled nine months before its backers gave up. *Punchinello* had been financed by Tammany Hall politicians Tweed and Sweeney, as counter-propaganda against Nast's ongoing assault upon their corruption. They attempted to buy and threaten Nast into silence, to no avail.

American comics continued their pull away from Anglo-Franco imitation with the infusion of a third major European influence – the German humor magazine. The German-American community swelled significantly after the failed revolution of 1848. These émigrés brought with them a culture of humor, expressed most flamboyantly in their native humor magazines, the most famous being *Kladderadatsch, Fliegende Blätter*, and *Münchener Bilderbogen*. As high in quality, as were the graphic artists who contributed to them, one German comic artist in particular excelled beyond the rest, his stories breaking out and crossing over into English language translations, the demand for which resulted in numerous printings. This artist, of course, was Heinrich Christian Wilhelm Busch (1832-1908).

Busch's work appeared in English in the 1860s in both British and American periodicals, often uncredited. For example, four of Busch's strips appeared in English in the pages of *Merryman's Monthly* in 1864, while in 1879 his graphic story "Fipps der Affe" was serialized across a 10-issue run of Puck as "Troddledums the Simian." The earliest known English language appearance of Busch in book form was *The Flying Dutchman, or The Wrath of Herr von Stoppelnoze*, in 1862, from New York publisher G. W. Carleton. Carleton not only pirated Busch's strip, but went so far as to credit the entire story to American poet John G. Saxe, with Busch's cartoons mere illustrations accompanying Saxe's prose!

The next known English language Busch book was A *Bushel of Merry Thoughts*, an 1868 London-published anthology collecting various Busch strips. Some of these same stories later appeared in the U.S.-published *The Mischief Book* (1880), newly translated and with a few more Busch tales added. One of these additions was "Hans Huckebein," a tale of a mischievous pet raven who in the end gets drunk and accidentally hangs himself. It became, at least in the States, Busch's second most popular sequential comic story. The unrepentant bird was promoted to title character in two later collections: the rare *Hookeybeak the Raven and Other Tales* in 1878 and *Jack Huckaback, the Scapegrace Raven*, circa 1888. There were also at least three trade card series in the 1870s and 1880s that reprinted the ending sequence, as *Fritz Spindle-Shanks, The Raven Black.*

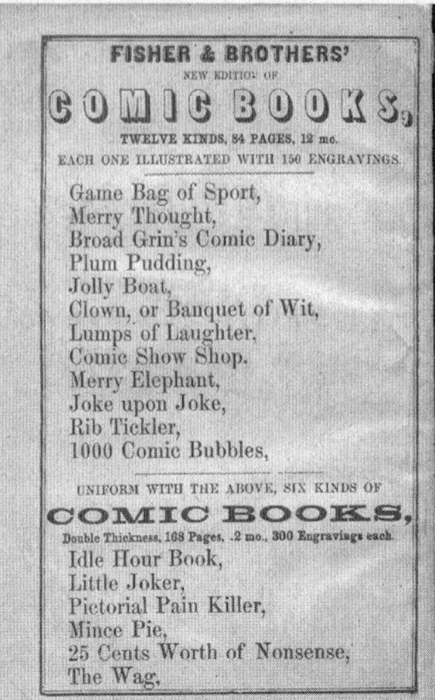
FISHER & BROTHERS'
NEW EDITION OF
COMIC BOOKS,
TWELVE KINDS, 84 PAGES, 12 mo.
EACH ONE ILLUSTRATED WITH 150 ENGRAVINGS.

Game Bag of Sport,
Merry Thought,
Broad Grin's Comic Diary,
Plum Pudding,
Jolly Boat,
Clown, or Banquet of Wit,
Lumps of Laughter,
Comic Show Shop.
Merry Elephant,
Joke upon Joke,
Rib Tickler,
1000 Comic Bubbles,

UNIFORM WITH THE ABOVE, SIX KINDS OF
COMIC BOOKS,
Double Thickness, 168 Pages, .2 mo., 300 Engravings each.
Idle Hour Book,
Little Joker,
Pictorial Pain Killer,
Mince Pie,
25 Cents Worth of Nonsense,
The Wag.

Earliest-known use of the description COMIC BOOKS dates from the early 1850s.

The most popular Busch tale, though, was easily Max und Moritz, which in the U.S. saw print as *Max and Maurice - A Juvenile History in Seven Tricks*. Published in Boston in 1871, this English language version saw at minimum of 60 reprintings by the century's end, plus countless more printings thereafter. A separate British translation debuted in 1874, under the title *Max and Moritz*. It is well known that the later Rudolph Dirks comic strip series, Katzenjammer Kids, beginning in late 1897, was based on *Max und Moritz*.

According to documents found by comics historian Alfredo Castelli, *Katzenjammer Kids* may not have been pirated as has been assumed but was licensed by William Randolph Hearst instead. Hearst's *New York Journal* was published in different language editions for New York City's immigrant communities. In the German edition, the strip was published under its original name, *Max und Moritz*. Numerous other translations of Busch were published in America - too many to name in this article. Several can be found in the Victorian Age Price Index.

The most significant humor magazine of the 1870s, prior to the founding of the German-language *Puck* in 1876, was *Wild Oats* (1870-1881), which for part of its run also published a German-language edition, *Schnedereddeng*. In terms of the quality of its cartoons and comics, this New York City publication was in 1872 at an artistic level *Puck* would not achieve until 1880. Published by Winchell and Small (later Collin and Small) and distributed through the New York News Company, *Wild Oats* carried a cross-section of old and new generation comic artists, from the more established W. M. Avery, Frank Beard, Frank Bellew, E.S. Bisbee, Michael Angelo Woolf, and Thomas Worth, to up-and-comers such as Livingston Hopkins, Frederick Burr Opper, Palmer Cox, and James A. Wales.

Wild Oats began carrying sequential comic strips as early as #26, dated March 14, 1872, with the Livingston Hopkins strip pictured on the next page (we do not know anything yet about the first 25 issues). The very next issue has a Worth double-page spread titled "The Political Humpty Dumpty... Horace Greeley" told in eleven panels plus the sequential fictional "Graphic Account of the Assassination of Queen Victoria" and "Love As the Angels Love." "The Doings of the Japanese Embassy At Washington" related in twelve panels by W. M. Avery follows up in #28 April 11, 1872. An unknown hand drew "The Physiology of Moving" in six panels in #30. Hopkins returns with a beautiful intense 28-panel double-page spread in #31 May 23. Hopkins and Worth alternated for many issues with sequential comic strips on baseball, horse racing and other pertinent subjects of the day. In #45 December 5, 1872, E.S. Bisbee contributed his first sequential in seventeen panels and Worth showed up in "Humor and Pathos of a New England Thanksgiving" in eleven panels. Issue 47 expands the concept with a twelve-panel job by Bisbee, twenty-panel effort on one page by Hopkins and a three-panel effort by Worth. And on it goes through 1873 as well - comic strip after comic strip. Issue 58 June 5, 1873, includes a particularly humorous nineteen-panel double-pager drawn by someone still unknown titled "The Terrible Adventures of Messrs. Buster and Stumps, with the Indians" which begins with two white men heading out west in an effort to exterminate Indians - and their misadventures of not quite getting the job done. It reads across both pages in a unique evolution similar to Popeye #2052 (found in the Platinum listings). Issue 65 contains two nine-panel Thomas Worth strips "Only a Mad Dog Scare - Another Lesson For Nervous People" and "Only a Cholera Scare - Something For Nervous People to Read and Ponder Over." Issue 66 Sept 18, 1873, has the very funny Hopkins twelve-panel strip as well as two more ten-panel Worth strips on the delights of Hunting and Fishing plus one by Hopkins titled "The Adventures of Mr Old Party with Jersey Mosquitoes" in twelve-panels. All told, four comic strips in this issue. They obviously liked what they were doing, judging from the exuberance of the work.

The next issue has Worth's nine-panel report on "The Adventures of Young Muttonhead among the Free Lovers" which was all about the "free sex" convention recently held in Chicago. Issue 68 has a nine-panel "An Adventure with a New Jersey Mosquito" which smacks of Winsor McCay in subject and even art style. Maybe McCay was inspired by this for his later animated cartoon as well as earlier Rarebit Fiend. We'll never know for sure. On through 1875, *Wild Oats* presented sequential comic strips issue after issue. With #148, October 27, 1875, Frederick Opper contributes his very first Wild Oats cover, a political cartoon on inflation then rampant in the US. He does covers through at least #161 before a short break and then comes back with many more. In #158, January 5, 1876, Palmer Cox - some five years before inventing The Brownies - begins a wonderful series of 24-panel double page spread comic strips, with a couple sample titles being "The Adventures of Mr. and Mrs. Sprowl And Their Christmas Turkey-A Crashing Chasing Tearful Tragedy But Happily Ending Well" and "Bachelor Broke and Widow Snuggi: A Pictorial Account of Their Sleigh Ride and What Became of It."

Even though he had been contributing many covers and interior single panel jobs to *Wild Oats* for years, Frank Bellew does not show up with his first comic strip until #190, August 16, 1876, with a nine-panel effort he titled, "Rodger's Patent Mosquito Armour." By this time America's "Father of the sequential comic strip" had inspired many other cartoonists to try their hand telling stories with words and pictures.

Another highly desirable American graphic novel, sought especially by collectors of Western lore, is *Quiddities of an Alaskan Trip* by William H. Bell which debuted in 1873. Bell was Timothy O'Sullivan's assistant photographer on the 1871-74 expeditions of Lt. George Wheeler, surveying and mapping the western territories for the U.S. government. The story panels are laid out within ornate frames like those of stereograph cards, such as Bell was involved in creating on the expedition. It involves a parody of a trip from Washington, D.C., to survey the newly purchased territory of Alaska, which at the time was derisively referred to as "Seward's Folly." Bell published *Quiddities* in Portland, Oregon, in 1873, meaning that he drew it while he was on just such an expedition.

The seemingly disparate influences of Thomas Nast and German comics came together in the work of Austrian immigrant Joseph Keppler (1838-1894). Like many cartoonists in America, Keppler desired to rival Nast. Unlike most, he possessed the talent and drive to accomplish it. Keppler, trained as an artist but working as an actor, began contributing comic art to *Kikeriki* (1861-1923) in his native Vienna. He emigrated to St. Louis in 1868, where he took his first stab at starting a comic weekly, the German language *Die Vehme* (Aug 28, 1869 - Aug. 20, 1870). Seven months later, still in St. Louis, he tried again, launching another German language humor periodical, titled *Puck*. This German *Puck* began on March 18, 1871, joined by an English language version one year later, but both ended on Aug. 24, 1872.

(1.) THE ALARM

"On Thursday night Mr. Lincoln was aroused, and informed that a stranger desired to see him on a matter of life and death. * * * A conversation elicited the fact that an organized body of men had determined that Mr. Lincoln should never leave Baltimore alive. * * * Statesmen laid the plan and bankers indorsed it."

(2.) THE COUNCIL

"Mr. Lincoln did not want to yield, and his friends cried with indignation. But they insisted, and he left."

(3.) THE SPECIAL TRAIN

"He wore a Scotch plaid cap and a very long military cloak, so that he was entirely unrecognizable."

(4.) THE OLD COMPLAINT

"Mr. Lincoln, accompanied by Mr. Seward, paid his respects to President Buchanan."

THE FLIGHT OF ABRAHAM

"The Flight of Abraham Lincoln," first appeared in ***Harper's Weekly**, March 9, 1861.*

Keppler moved to New York City and began working for Frank Leslie. His cartoons appeared in *Frank Leslie's Illustrated Newspaper*, Frank Leslie's *Budget of Fun*, and the Leslie-owned *Jolly Joker* and *Day's Doings*. (To capitalize on the 1876 Centennial Exposition in Philadelphia, Leslie published in that year a paperback collection of Centennial-related humor, *Centennial Fun*, most of which was Keppler's work.) Four years after the first *Puck* died, Keppler was ready to try again. He re-launched the German language edition of *Puck* in New York City on September 27, 1876.

This *Puck* was both familiar and exotic. Its format of an extravagant centerspread cartoon sandwiched between front and back cover cartoons had by this time become something of a comic periodical standard, certainly for the monthlies. But *Puck* was different from what had come before. The cartoons were lithographed, not engraved, which lent to them a softer, more pleasing quality, and they were in color, something virtually without precedent in American comic periodical literature.

Initially, the magazine's cartoons were tinted in just one color, but *Puck* appeared, ambitiously, every week, and the coloring set it apart from anything else on American stands. The parallel English language edition of *Puck* was launched six months after the German version, on March 14, 1877. This English edition of *Puck* was a money-loser for several years, kept afloat by the German edition's profits and the determination of the English edition's literary editor, H.C. Bunner, not to give up. By 1880, *Puck* was a huge success. It became the new model for American humor publications. In time, Keppler hired other artists, most notably Frederick Burr Opper, Eugene Zimmerman ("Zim") and F. M. Howarth, and added black and white sequential comics to the magazine's interior and then, with increasing frequency in the early 1890s to the magazine's back cover. *Funny Folks* by F. M. Howarth, 1899, collected many early sequential comics from *Puck;* one of the titles many consider bridges the Victorian and Platinum Ages of comics. *Puck* was the model that inspired William Randolph Hearst to add a color comics section to his Sunday Journal in 1895.

With the first issue dated October 29, 1881, *Puck's* chief rival, *Judge*, was born. Founded by *Puck* artist James A. Wales, it also featured the work of Thomas Worth and Livingston Hopkins. *Judge* made several forays into *Puck*'s talent pool over the years. Its best capture was Eugene Zimmerman ("Zim"), who became for Judge the star artist that Frederick Burr Opper was for Puck.

Judge struggled financially for

several years, and likely would have ceased publication had it not been for Puck's powerful performance during the 1884 election. *Puck*'s success galvanized Republican powerbrokers into recognizing the importance of the political cartoon weekly. They financed newspaperman W. J. Arkell's purchase of *Judge* in 1886 to turn it into a reliable Republican house organ.

Numerous other Puck imitators emerged in the 1880s but quickly died. Note should be made of two that did not: the *Puck*-like *San Francisco Wasp*, which debuted August 5, 1876 (too early for it to be considered a *Puck* knockoff), and the black and white *Texas Siftings*, which debuted on May 9, 1881. Though neither was as successful as *Puck* or *Judge*, both cut their own paths, managing to survive as cartoon humor magazines into the 1890s.

Also worthy of mention is the New York City newspaper *The Daily Graphic* (March 4, 1873 to Sept 23, 1889), which claims the distinction of being the first regularly illustrated daily newspaper in the world, published every day except Sundays and holidays. The majority of its illustrations were portraits or depictions of news events, but nearly every issue contained some comic drawing, many of them gracing the front cover.

With so many pages to fill on a daily basis, *The Daily Graphic* became a rotating door for many young American cartoonists in the early stages of their careers (making one suspect that it was not the best paying gig in town). Within its pages, like needles to be found in the haystack of its more than 4800 issues, is early work by Livingston Hopkins (who mysteriously appears, vanishes, reappears, etc., for months to whole years at a time, right up to his 1884 departure to Australia), pre-*Life* work by Kemble, pre-*Harper*'s appearances by A.B. Frost and W.A. Rogers, pre-Puck and Judge Opper, C.J. Taylor, Hamilton, and Gillam. Old hats, too, appear at times, such as Michael Woolf and Frank Bellew, Sr.

Further, *The Daily Graphic* regularly plundered British periodicals for its back and sometimes center pages, not only perpetrating the usual swipes of single-panel *Punch* cartoons, but also stealing sequential strips from Punch's two main rival publications, *Judy* and *Fun*. This included occasionally reprinting (albeit at random) episodes of continuing British strips "The British Workman" by James Sullivan, and "McNab of that Ilk" by James Brown, though, strangely enough, not Marie Duval's *Ally Sloper*, despite the fact that *The Daily Graphic* did reprint some of Duval's non-"Sloper" strips. ("Ally Sloper" was a continuing sequential strip character who debuted in 1867, lasting into the 1920s, and had very successful solo British book collections of his strip appearances published as early as 1873, more than two decades prior to *Yellow Kid in McFadden*'s Flats).

Livingston Hopkins, whose art style changed like a chameleon from one year to the next, exhibited a definite Duval influence in his work within a year following the publication of the first *Ally Sloper* collection. Given that Hopkins worked for *The Daily Graphic* during the same period in which this newspaper was stealing cartoons from *Sloper*'s home publication, *Judy*, this can hardly be considered coincidental. Hopkins contributed a daily comic strip to *The Daily Graphic* in 1874-75, complete with word balloons. By the time Hopkins was preparing to emigrate to Australia to become lead cartoonist for the Sydney Bulletin, his art style was an imitation of Kemble's, who was also working at *The Daily Graphic*.

Life debuted on January 4, 1883, founded by J.A. Mitchell, and modeled after the Harvard Lampoon. It quickly rose to become the third main pillar of late 1800s American humor periodicals. Smaller in size, black and white, and priced the same as *Puck* and *Judge*, it nevertheless succeeded by appealing to a more genteel audience. Its earliest artists included Kemble and Palmer Cox, but its foremost artist was Charles Dana Gibson, becoming world renowned as the hand behind the graceful, aristocratic "Gibson Girls."

Unlike *Judge*, which had to become a low-brow imitation of *Life* to survive in the next century, and *Puck*, which attempted but failed to become an American version of the highbrow European humor magazines, Life transitioned into the 20th century virtually unaltered, and thrived. By the mid-1880s, with *Puck, Judge*, and *Life* all solidly in place, American comics and cartoon humor had come very much into their own, no longer looking first at Europe to take their cues.

Almanacs began to appear in America starting in 1639. Humor was introduced as early as 1647 by Samuel Danforth. A very important one was *Leed Almanac* beginning in 1687. John Tulley produced the first humorous almanac in 1688. James Franklin, brother of Ben, began the *Rhode Island Almanac* in 1728 using the name "Poor Robin" and his younger brother began *Poor Richard's Almanac* in 1732. Farmer's Almanac began in 1792 and used some humor.

The first comic almanac totally devoted to humor was published by Charles Ellm in Boston in 1831 and featured the artwork of D.C. Johnston. Perhaps the most famous comic almanacs (certainly the most valuable) are the *Davy Crockett* series (1835-1856) which began in Nashville, Tennessee. The comic periodicals all ended up issuing comic almanacs beginning with *Yankee Notions* in 1856 and continuing into the 1890s with a one-shot comic almanac published by *Judge* for the year 1894.

Beginning in the 1850s, a new breed of almanacs appeared. Usually created by medicine and farm product companies, they were distributed for free to promote the company's product. Competition amongst companies, whose goal was to get customers to read the almanacs and the advertisements contained therein again and again, meant that attention-getting humorous cartoons soon found their way back into these giveaway pamphlets. Initially their cartoons were done cheap, either poorly drawn or pirated from elsewhere, such as those found in the Hostetter's and Wright's almanac series. More elaborate promotional almanacs eventually did evolve, though, and amongst the best of these was *Barker's Illustrated Almanac*, first produced for the year 1878, and annually into the 1930s. Each *Barker's Almanac* contained ten to twelve full page cartoons, wonderful and bizarre in design, frequently racist, but also comically manic and crammed with details in a manner similar to Outcault's much later *Yellow Kid* pages. The cartoons in *Barker's Almanac* were so popular that in 1892, The Barker, Moore, and Mein Medicine Company published their first edition of *Barker's Komic Picture Souvenir*, reprinting nearly 150 pages of cartoons from their almanacs.

Flag of Our Union, July 23, 1870, sample panels from Pt 1 of a 3 part comic strip depicting early baseball game.

This first *Barker's Souvenir* features a wraparound color cover depicting people headed towards the Columbian World's Fair Exposition, which was to be held in Chicago the next year. It is the earliest confirmed "premium" comic book, sent to customers who mailed in a box label and outside wrapper from two different Barker's products. The *Souvenir* album was *Barker's* most in-demand premium. It was reprinted as a thick unnumbered booklet three more times in the 1890s, with the contents reorganized each time. Later, between 1901 and 1903, *Barker's* broke the album into three separate "Parts," each of which required still more box labels and wrappers to obtain. The 3-part series of reprint albums expanded to four parts circa 1906 or 1907. Both the 3 and 4-part album series had multiple printings.

Also very American in character were the country's promotional comics, which flourished throughout the latter half of the 19th century. They trace their beginnings to Comic Almanacs, which flourished in England and the United States since they first appeared in the 1830s. The first promotional comics which did not double as almanacs began to appear in the 1870s. They included the aforementioned reprints of Cruikshank and Busch strips, reprints of strips lifted from American sources (A.B. Frost's strip "The Bull Calf" was a particular favorite), and original material placing the product being promoted as the focus of the story. These original short cartoon dramas were in many ways similar in storyline to those found in modern television advertisements, except that the clothing is Victorian, and the claims, pre-F.D.A. and F.C.C., were unabashedly wild, over-the-top, and blunt. Chewing tobacco and snuff saved romances, calmed crying babies, and made the sick well. Stove polish that propelled you to wealth and power. Corsets that brought you a husband. The objective, of course, in an era before TV or radio, was to make each comic handout so entertaining that customers would want to keep and read the advertisement again and again.

The more wonderful graphics and outrageous claims tended to come from tobacco companies, who were using comic books and strips to sell their products more than a century before cries against "Joe Camel." The most elaborate of these were printed full color, and unfolded into a single long strip, just like Cruikshank's *The Tooth-Ache* from the 1840s, though usually limited to just the cover plus seven panels.

Examples are the Jackson Chewing Tobacco comics *How Adolphus Slim-Jim Used Jackson's Best and Ye Veracious Chronicle of Gruff and Pompey, and Durham Smoking Tobacco's Home Made Happy - A Romance for Married Men*. The artists of these comics are mostly unidentified, but their level of skill was equal to anything in *Puck* and *Judge*. *The Home Made Happy Comic*, in fact, was produced for Durham by The Graphic Company -- the publisher of *The Daily Graphic*, the aforementioned 1870s illustrated newspaper which included cartoons.

The earliest known anthology devoted to collecting the comic strips of a single American artist was A.B. Frost's *Stuff and Nonsense* in 1884. The next known American collection came in 1888, the very rare Frederick Burr Opper anthology, *Puck's Opper Book*. Both proved popular, so more Frost and Opper collections followed, to be joined within a few years by reprints collecting the cartoons and strips of Keppler, Kemble, Zim, Gibson, Mayer, Taylor, Frank Bellew's son "Chip," Howarth, Woolf, etc.

Puck, Judge, and *Texas Siftings* all began monthly Library series - 8-1/2" x 11" magazines, mostly black and white, which organized previously published material around one theme or one artist. For example, the first *Puck's Library* (July 1887) was titled "The National Game," and gathered beneath one cover *Puck* material poking fun at the game of baseball. The third (March 1888) and ninth (November 1889) issues of *Judge's Serial (later named Judge's Library)* were devoted entirely to the work of Zim.

Life tended more towards hardcover collections, such as its annual ten-issue series *The Good Things of Life* (1884-1893), which included cartoons and strips by Palmer Cox, T.S. Sullivant, Hy Mayer, and others. *The Good Things of Life* was published initially by the firm of White, Stokes, and Allen, but which by the fourth book, had become simply Frederick A. Stokes. Stokes published a number of other cartoon books in the 1880s and 1890s, the majority of them reprint collections. The experience he gained at this time with these reprint albums placed Stokes in the perfect position to pick up the wealth of material about to be created for the comics supplements of William R. Hearst's newspapers, making Stokes the first major publisher of the coming Platinum Age.

In 1892, Charles Scribner's Sons published A. B. Frost's *Bull Calf and Other Tales*. It contains sequential comic strip art on quite a few pages as well as single panel cartoons. By 1898, Charles Scribner's Sons also issued Kemble's *The Billy Goat and Other Comicalities* as a 112-page hardcover, which also has sequential comic strips.

In the early 1890s, the slum children cartoons of artist Michael Woolf (many of which were reprinted in the 1896 collection *99 Woolfs from Truth* and in the posthumous 1899 collection *Sketches of Lowly Life in a Great City*) were popular. *Truth* magazine, which followed Puck's format of color front cover, back cover and centerspread cartoons, but in style was more akin to the aristocratic Life, was initially unable to secure Woolf's services, creating an opportunity for the young cartoonist Richard F. Outcault, who desired to break into one of the weekly comic periodicals.

It was in his Woolf-inspired slum children cartoons for *Truth* that Outcault's prototype of the *Yellow Kid* first emerged. The bald, sack-clothed youngster made four appearances in *Truth*, starting with #372 on June 2, 1894, prior to his newspaper debut.

During the rise of Yellow Kid's popularity, he appeared in American comic magazines in parodies drawn by others, with politicians, even Hearst and Pulitzer, dressed up as the *Yellow Kid*. Such cartoons are known to have appeared in *Judge, Life, The Bee*, and *Vim* plus various newspapers across the country. More about the *Yellow Kid's* importance can be found in the Platinum Age section of this book.

While comics definitely have their roots in Europe, and the earliest American comic books either reprinted or emulated those of Europe, the direction of influence was by no means one way. By at least the 1870s, American cartoons were being published and seen in the Old World, as evidenced by the arrest in Spain of the on-the-lamb corrupt Tammany Hall politician Boss Tweed by Spanish police who recognized Tweed from a Nast cartoon.

European piracy of American cartoons was just as lucrative as the American piracy of Europeans. In the 1880s and '90s, the comics of Zim, Chip Bellew, and Charles Dana Gibson all saw reprint in Europe. In April 1899, *Pictorial Comedy*, a monthly magazine destined for a ten-year run, commenced publication in London. It was made up entirely of cartoons reprinted with permission from *Puck* and *Life*. F.M. Howarth's domestic comedies from *Puck* were favorites in France. American Hy Mayer was commissioned to create original comics work for *Black and White* (Britain), *Le Rire* (France), and *Fliegende Blätter*. Michael Woolf's slum children cartoons saw print in the British periodical *Pick-Me-Up*, during the same years that top British artist Phil May's first published work debuted in that publication. May later became famous for his Woolf-inspired street children cartoons as well as his influence on the development of comics in Australia.

As the 19th Century ended, American comics were coming to the fore worldwide, soon to explode into a position of dominance with the Platinum Age revolution brought about by the emergence of the color comic supplement in America's newspapers and the arrival of Richard F. Outcault's *Yellow Kid*.

Judge #791, Dec 12, 1896, depicting Tammany Hall politicians as RFO's Yellow Kid & Cox's Brownies. Art by Hamilton.

END NOTE: Victorian Era comics were issued in many relatively obscure formats compared to what most of us are used to today. The Victorian Era section can only grow as there are many more heretofore undiscovered comics from the 1800s which have fallen off the radar of history. Some may wonder why some of the earlier items listed contain as of yet no prices. The reason is simple. These books are part of a relatively "new" market which is still establishing itself.

High-grade copies are almost unheard of in almost all instances. Some books may truly have only a handful left in existence. We are sure there are some known to have been published which no (as of yet) known copies have survived the ravages of time and neglect.

Each year expect another quantum leap in our ever-expanding knowledge of the fascinating earliest origins of the comic strip as it relates to North America. Your input in helping this section of the Guide grow and mature is most welcome!

Robert Lee Beerbohm first sold comics through the legendary RBCC beginning in 1966, set up at his first comicon in 1967, helped found the northern California Comics & Comix chain of stores in August 1972, co-hosted Berkeleycon 1973, the first UG creator-owned comix con and operated comic book stores from 1972-1994. He now owns Robert Beerbohm Comic Art that specializes in buying and selling scarce comics and related material from the 1840s-1980s. He has been compiling a detailed history book of the business of the American comic book for some time now and hopes to complete it soon.

Contact Robert directly at www.BLBComics.com

Richard Olson is an Research Professor Emeritus at the University of New Orleans. He published the Richard Outcault Collector for years. Reach Richard directly at: rolsonredoak@bellsouth.net

Richard Samuel West is the author of Satire on Stone: The Political Cartoons of Joseph Keppler (University of Illinois, 1988) and The San Francisco Wasp: An Illustrate History (Periodyssey Press, 2004) and editor of several cartoon collections. He is the owner of Periodyssey, a business that specializes in buying and selling significant and unusual American magazines. Richard can be reached at: www.oldmagazines.com

All three are life-long collectors and students of all forms of the comics who welcome corrections and additions to this concise compilation of our earliest American comics heritage dating back almost two centuries. Happy Hunting!

The American Comic Almanac #5
1835 © Charles Ellms, NYC

The Strange and Wonderful Adventures
of Bachelor Butterfly by Rodolphe Töpffer
1870s © Dick & Fitzgerald, NYC

Barker's "Komic" Picture Souvenir, 3rd Edition
1894 © Barker, Moore & Klein Medicine Co.

FR1.0 GD2.0 FN6.0

COLLECTOR'S NOTE: Most of the books listed in this section were published well over a century before organized comics fandom began archiving and helping to preserve these fragile popular culture artifacts. With some of these comics now over 160 years old, they almost never surface in Fine+ or better shape. Be happy when you simply find a copy.

This year has seen price growth in quite a few comic books in this era. Since this section began growing almost a decade now, comic books from Wilson, Brother Jonathan, Huestis & Cozans, Garrett, Dick & Fitzgerald, Frank Leslie, Street & Smith and others continue to be recognized by the more savvy in this fine hobby as legitimate comic book collectors' items. We had been more concerned with simply establishing what is known to exist. For the most part, that work is now a *fait accompli* in this section compiled, revised, and expanded by Robert Beerbohm with special thanks this year to Terrance Keegan plus acknowledgment to Bill Blackbeard, Chris Brown, Alfredo Castelli, Darrell Coons, Leonardo De Sá, Scott Deschaine, Joe Evans, Ron Friggle, Tom Gordon III, Michel Kempeneers, Andy Konkykru, Don Kurtz, Richard Olson, Robert Quesinberry, Joseph Rainone, Steve Rowe, Randy Scott, John Snyder, Art Spiegelman, Steve Thompson, Richard Samuel West, Doug Wheeler and Richard Wright. Special kudos to long-time collector and scholar Gabriel Laderman.

The prices given for Fair, Good and Fine categories are for strictly graded editions. If you need help grading your item, we refer you to the grading section in this book or contact the authors of this essay. Items marked Scarce, Rare or Very Rare we are still trying to figure out how many copies might still be in existence. We welcome additions and corrections from any interested collectors and scholars at robert@BLBcomics.com

For ease ascertaining the contents of each item of this listing and the Platinum index list, we offer the following list of categories found immediately following most of the titles:

E - EUROPEAN ORIGINAL COMICS MATERIAL; Printed in Europe or reprinted in USA
G - GRAPHIC NOVEL (LONGER FORMAT COMIC TELLING A SINGLE STORY)
H - "HOW TO DRAW CARTOONS" BOOKS
I - ILLUSTRATED BOOKS NOTABLE FOR THE ARTIST, BUT NOT A COMIC.
M - MAGAZINE / PERIODICAL COMICS MATERIAL REPRINTS
N - NEWSPAPER COMICS MATERIAL REPRINTS
O - ORIGINAL COMIC MATERIAL NOT REPRINTED FROM ANOTHER SOURCE
P - PROMOTIONAL COMIC, EITHER GIVEN AWAY FOR FREE, OR A PREMIUM GIVEN IN CONJUNCTION WITH THE PURCHASE OF A PRODUCT.
S - SINGLE PANEL / NON-SEQUENTIAL CARTOONS

Measurements are in inches. The first dimension given is Height and the second is Width. Some original British editions are included in the section, so as to better explain and differentiate their American counterparts.

ACROBATIC ANIMALS
R.H. Russell: 1899 (9x11-7/8", 72 pgs, B&W, hard-c)

nn (Scarce) 150.00 300.00 600.00
NOTE: *Animal strips by Gustave Verbeck, presented 1 panel per page.*

ALMY'S SANTA CLAUS (P,E)
Edward C. Almy & Co., Providence, R.I.: nd (1880's) (5-3/4x4-5/8", 20 pgs, B&W, paper-c

nn - (Rare) 12.50 40.00 80.00
NOTE: *Department store Christmas giveaway containing an abbreviated 28-panel reprinting of George Cruikshank's **The Tooth-ache**. Santa Claus cover.*

AMERICAN COMIC ALMANAC, THE (OLD AMERICAN COMIC ALMANAC 1839-1846)
Charles Ellms: 1831-1846 (5x8, 52 pgs, B&W)

1 first American comic almanac ever prrinted 600.00 1200.00 2200.00
2-16 100.00 200.00 400.00
NOTE:#1 from 1831 is the First American Comic Almanac

AMERICAN PUNCH
American Punch Publishing Co: Jan 1879-March 1881, J.A. Cummings Engraving Co (last 3 ussues) (Quarto Monthly)

Most issues 25.00 50.00 150.00

THE AMERICAN WIT
Richardson & Collins, NY: 1867-68 (18-1/2x13. 8 pgs, B&W)
2/3 Frank Bellew single panels 50.00 100.00 200.00

AMERICAN WIT AND HUMOR
Harper & Bros, NY: 1859 (

nn - numerous McLenan sequential comic strips 100.00 200.00 450.00

ATTWOOD'S PICTURES - AN ARTIST'S HISTORY OF THE LAST TEN YEARS OF THE NINETEENTH CENTURY (M,S)
Life Publishing Company, New York: 1900 (11-1/4x9-1/8", 156 pgs, B&W, gilted blue hard-c)

nn - By Attwood 40.00 80.00 160.00
NOTE: *Reprints monthly calendar cartoons which appeared in **LIFE**, for 1887 through 1899.*

BACHELOR BUTTERFLY, THE VERITABLE HISTORY OF MR. (E,G)
D. Bogue, London: 1845 (5-1/2x10-1/4", 74 pgs, B&W, gilted hardcover)

nn - By Rodolphe Töpffer (Scarce) 500.00 1250.00 2800.00
nn - Hand colored edition (Very Rare) (no known sales)
NOTE: *This is the British Edition, translated from the re-engraved by Cham serialization found in **L'Illustration** - a periodical from Paris publisher Dubochet. Predates the first French collected edition. Third Töpffer comic book published in English. The first story page is numbered Page 3. Page 17 shows Bachelor Butterfly being swallowed by a whale.*

BACHELOR BUTTERFLY, THE STRANGE ADVENTURES OF (E,G)
Wilson & Co., New York: 1846 (5-3/8x10-1/8", 68 pgs, B&W, soft-c)

FR1.0 GD2.0 FN6.0

nn - By Rodolphe Töpffer (Very Rare) 600.00 1500.00 3200.00
nn - At least one hand colored copy exists (Very Rare) (no known sales)
NOTE: *2nd Töpffer comic book printed in the U.S., 3rd earliest known sequential comic book in the USA. Reprinted from the British D. Bogue 1845 edition, itself from the earlier French language **Histoire de Mr. Cryptogame**. Released the same year as the French Dubochet edition. Two variations known, the earlier printing with Page number 17 placed on the inside (left) bottom corner in error, with slightly later printings corrected to place page number 17 on the outside (right) bottom corner of that page. Another first printing indicator is pages 17 and 20 are printed on the wrong side of the page. For both printings: the first story page is numbered 2. Page 17 shows Bachelor Butterfly already in the whale. In most panels with 3 lines of text, the third line is indented further than the second, which is in turn indented further than the first.*

BACHELOR BUTTERFLY, THE STRANGE ADVENTURES
Brother Jonathan Press, NY: 1854 (5-1/2x10-5/8", 68 pgs, paper-c, B&W) (Very Rare)

nn - By Rodolphe Töpffer 250.00 500.00 1100.00

BACHELOR BUTTERFLY,THE STRANGE & WONDERFUL ADVENTURES OF
Dick & Fitzgerald, New York: 1870s-1888 (various printings 30 Cent cover price, 68 pgs, B&W, paper cover) (all versions Rare) (E,G)

nn - Black print on blue cover (5-1/2x10-1/2"); string bound 112.00 225.00 450.00
nn - Black print on green cover (5-1/2x10-1/2"); string bound 100.00 200.00 400.00
NOTE: *Reprints the earlier Wilson & Co. edition. Page 2 is the first story page. Page 17 shows Bachelor Butterfly already in the whale. In most panels with 3 lines of text, the second and third lines are equally indented in from the first. Unknown which cover (blue or green) is earlier.*

BACHELOR'S OWN BOOK. BEING THE PROGRESS OF MR. LAMBKIN, (GENT.) IN THE PURSUIT OF PLEASURE AND AMUSEMENT (E,O,G)
(See also PROGRESS OF MR. LAMBKIN)
D. Bogue, London: August 1, 1844 (5x8-1/4", 28 pgs printed one side only, cardboard cover & interior) (all versions Rare)

nn - First printing hand colored 200.00 400.00 800.00
nn - First printing black & white 200.00 400.00 800.00
NOTE: *First printing has misspellings in the title. "PURSUIT" is spelled "PERSUIT", and "AMUSEMENT" is spelled "AMUSEMEMT".*
nn - Second printing hand colored 200.00 400.00 800.00
nn - Second printing black & white 200.00 400.00 800.00
NOTE: Second printing. The misspelling of "PURSUIT" has been corrected, but "AMUSEMEMT" error is still present.
nn - Third printing hand colored No misspellings 200.00 400.00 800.00
nn - Third printing black & white 200.00 400.00 800.00
NOTE: *By George Cruikshank. This is the British Edition. Issued both in black & white, and professionally hand-colored editions. Hand-colored editions have survived in higher quantities than uncolored. Originally made with thin paper sheets covering the plates.*

BACHELOR'S OWN BOOK; OR, THE PROGRESS OF MR. LAMBKIN, (GENT.), IN THE PURSUIT OF PLEASURE AND AMUSEMENT, AND ALSO IN SEARCH OF HEALTH AND HAPPINESS, THE (E,O,G)
David Bryce & Son: Glasgow: 1884 (one shilling; 7-5/8 x5-7/8", 62 pgs printed one side only, illustrated hardcover, page edges guilt

nn - Reprints the 1844 edition with altered title 17.50 35.00 70.00
nn - soft cover edition exists 15.00 30.00 60.00

BACHELOR'S OWN BOOK. BEIN-G TWENTY-FOUR PASSAGES IN THE LIFE OF MR. LAMBKIN, GENT. (E,G)
Burgess, Stringer & Co., New York on cover; Carey & Hart, Philadelphia on title page: 1845 (31-1/4 cents, 7-1/2x4-5/8", 52 pgs, B&W, paper cover)

nn - By George Cruikshank (Very Rare) (no known sales)
NOTE: *This is the second known sequential comic book story published in America. Reprints the earlier British edition. Pages printed on one side only. New cover art by an unknown artist.*

BAD BOY'S FIRST READER (O,S)
G.W. Carleton & Co.: 1881 (5-3/4 x 4-1/8", 44 pgs, B&W, paper cover)

nn - By Frank Bellew (Senior) 50.00 100.00 200.00
NOTE: *Parody of a children's ABC primer, one cartoon illustration plus text per page. Includes one panel of Boss Tweed. Frank Bellew is considered the "Father of the American Sequential Comics."*

BALL OF YARN OR, QUEER, QUIANT & QUIZZICAL STORIES, UNRAVELED WITH NEARLY 200 COMIC ENGRAVINGS OF FREAKS, FOLLIES & FOIBLES OF QUEER FOLKS BY THAT PRINCE OF COMICS, ELTON, THE (M)
Philip. J. Cozans, 116 Nassau St, NY: early 1850s (7-1/4x3-1/2", 76 pgs, yellow-wraps)

nn - sequential comic strips plus singles (no known sales)
NOTE: Mose Keyser-r, Jones, Smith & Robinson Goes To A Ball-r; The Adventures of Mr Goliah Starvemouse-r are all sequential comic strips printed in a number of sources

BARKER'S ILLUSTRATED ALMANAC (O,P,S)
Barker, Moore & Mein Medicine Co: 1878-1932+ (36 pgs, B&W, color paper-cr)

1878-1879 (Rare) 50.00 100.00 180.00
NOTE: *Not known yet what the cover art is.*
1880 Farmer Plowing Field-c 40.00 80.00 140.00
1881-1883 (Scarce,7-3/4x6-1/8") *4-mast ships & lighthouse-c* 40.00 80.00 140.00
1884-1889 (8x6-1/4") *Horse & Rider jumping picket fence-c* 30.00 50.00 100.00
1890-1897 (8-1/8x6-1/4") 30.00 50.00 100.00
1898-1899 (7-3/8x5-7/8") 30.00 50.00 100.00
1900+: see the Platinum Age Comics section (7x5-7/8")
NOTE: *Barker's Almanacs were actually issued in November of the year preceding the year which appears on the almanac. For example, the 1878 dated almanac was issued November 1877. They were given away to retailers of Barker's farm animal medicinal products, to in turn be given away to customers. Each Barker's Almanac contains 10 full page cartoons. These frequently included racist stereotypes of blacks. Each cartoon*

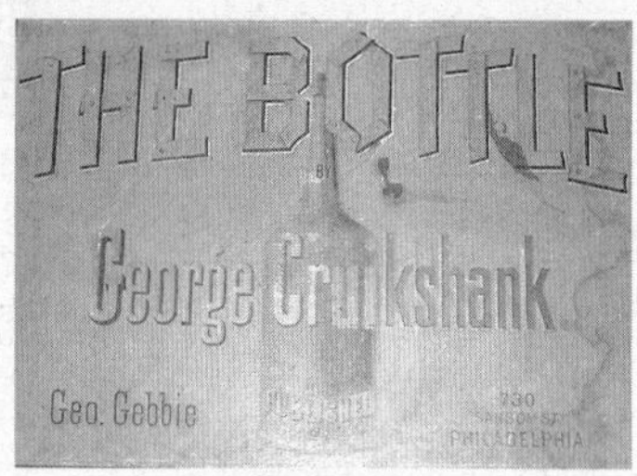

The Bottle by George Cruickshank
1871 © Geo. Gebbie, Philadelphia

The Story of The Man of Humanity
and The Bull Calf by A. B. Frost
1890 © C.H. Fargo & Co.

Buzz A Buzz Or The Bees By Wilhelm Busch
1873 © Henry Holt And Company, New York

contained advertisements for Barker's products. It is unknown whether the cartoons appeared only in the almanacs, or if they also ran as newspaper ads or flyers. Originally issued with a metal hook attached in the upper left hand corner, which could be used to hang the almanac.

BARKER'S "KOMIC" PICTURE SOUVENIR (P,S)
Barker, Moore & Mein Medicine Co: nd (1892-94) (color cardboard cover, B&W interior) (all unnumbered editions Very Rare)

nn - (1892) (1st edition, 6-7/8x10-1/2, 150 pgs) wraparound cover showing people headed towards Chicago for the 1893 World's Fair 150.00 300.00 700.00
nn - (1893) (2nd edition, ??? pgs) same cover as 1st edition 150.00 300.00 700.00
nn - (1894) (3rd edition, 180 pgs, 6-3/4x10-3/8") 150.00 300.00 700.00
NOTE: *New cover art showing crowd of people laughing with a copy of Barker's Almanac.The crowd picture is flanked on both sides by picture of a tall thin person.*
nn - (1894) (4th edition, 124 pgs, 6-3/8x9-3/8") same-c as 3rd edition 150.00 300.00 700.00
NOTE: *Essentially same-c as 3rd edition, except flanking picture on left edge is now gone. The 2nd through 4th editions state their printing on the first interior page, in the paragraph beneath the picture of the Barker's Building. These have been confirmed as premium comic books, predating the Buster Brown premiums. They reprint advertising cartoons from Barker's Illustrated Almanac. For the 50 page booklets by this same name, numbered as "Part"s, see the PLATINUM AGE SECTION. All "Editions in Parts", without exception, were published after 1900.*

BEAU OGLEBY, THE COMICAL ADVENTURES OF (E,G)
Tilt & Bogue: nd (c1843) (5-7/8x9-1/8", 72 pgs, printed one side only, green gilted hard-c, B&W)

nn - By Rodolphe Töpffer (Rare) 400.00 800.00 1800.00
nn - Hand coloured edition (Very Rare) (no known sales)
NOTE: *British Edition; no known American Edition. 2nd Töpffer comic book published in English. Translated from Paris publisher Aubert's unauthorized redrawn 1839 bootleg edition of Töpffer's* ***Histoire de Mr. Jabot****. The back most interior page is an advertisement for* ***Obadiah Oldbuck****, showing its comic book cover*

BEE, THE
Bee Publishing Co: May 16 1898-Aug 2 1898 (Chromolithographic Weekly)

most issues 50.00 100.00 200.00
8 June Yellow Kid Hearst cover issue 150.00 300.00 650.00

BEFORE AND AFTER. A LOCOFOCO CHRISTMAS PRESENT. (O, C)
D.C. Johnston, Boston: 1837 (4-3/4x3", 1 page, hand colored cardboard)

nn - (Very Rare) by David Claypoole Johnston (sold at auction for $400 in GD)
NOTE: *Pull-tab cartoon envelope, parodying the 1836 New York City mayoral election, picturing the candidate of the Locofoco Party smiling "Before the N.York election", then, when the tab is pulled, picturing him with an angry sneer "After the N.York election".*

BILLY GOAT AND OTHER COMICALITIES, THE (M)
Charles Scribner's Sons: 1898 (6-3/4x8-1/2", 116 pgs., B&W, Hardcover)

nn - By E. W. Kemble 125.00 250.00 600.00

BLACKBERRIES, THE (N,S) (see Coontown's 400)
R. H. Russell: 1897 (9"x12", 76 pgs, hard-c, every other page in color, every other page in one color sepia tone)

nn - By E. W. Kemble 162.00 325.00 1500.00
NOTE: *Tastefully done comics about Black Americana during the USA's Jim Crow days.*

BOOK OF BUBBLES, YE (S)
Endicott & Co., New York: March 1864 (6-1/4 x 9-7/8",160 pgs, guilt-illus. hard-c, B&W

nn - By unknown 150.00 300.00 600.00
NOTE: *Subtitle: A contribution to the New York Fair in aid of the Sanitary Commission; 68 single-sided pages of B&W cartoons, each with an accompanying limerick. A few are sequential.*

BOOK OF DRAWINGS BY FRED RICHARDSON (N,S)
Lakeside Press, Chicago: 1899 (13-5/8x10-1/2", 116 pgs, B&W, hard-c)

nn - 80.00 160.00 320.00
NOTE: *Reprinted from the* ***Chicago Daily News****. Mostly single panel. Includes one* ***Yellow Kid*** *parody, some Spanish-American War cartoons.*

BOTTLE, THE (E,O) (see also THE DRUNKARD'S CHILDREN, and TEA GARDEN TO TEA POT, and TEMPERANCE TALES; OR, SIX NIGHTS WITH THE WASHINGTONIANS)
D. Bogue, London, with others in later editions: nd (1846) (16-1/2x11-1/2", 16 pgs, printed one side only, paper cover)

D. Bogue, London (nd; 1846): first edition:
nn - Black & white (Scarce) 200.00 400.00 1000.00
nn - Hand colored (Rare) (no known sales)
D. Bogue, London, and Wiley and Putnam, New York (nd; 1847) : second edition, misspells American publisher "Putnam" as "Putman":
nn - Black & white (Scarce) 150.00 300.00 600.00
nn - Hand colored (Rare) (no known sales)
D. Bogue, London, and Wiley and Putnam, New York (nd; 1847) : third edition has "Putnam" spelled correctly.
nn - Black & white (Scarce) 150.00 300.00 600.00
nn - Hand colored (Rare) (no known sales)
D. Bogue, London, Wiley and Putnam, New York, and J. Sands, Sydney, New South Wales: (nd; 1847) : fourth edition with no misspellings
nn - Black & white (Scarce) 150.00 300.00 600.00
nn - Hand colored (Rare) (no known sales)
NOTE: *By George Cruikshank. Temperance/anti-alcohol story. All editions are in precisely identical format. The only difference is to be found on the cover, where it lists who published it. Cover is text only - no cover art.*

BOTTLE, THE HISTORY OF THE
J.C. Becket, 22 Grea St James St, Montreal, Canada: 1851 (9-1/8x6", B&W)

nn - From Engravings by Cruikshank 150.00 300.00 650.00
NOTE: *As published in The Canada Temperance Advocate.*

BOTTLE, THE (E)
W. Tweedie, London: nd (1862) (11-1/2x17-1/3", 16 pgs, printed one side only, paper cover)

nn - Black & white; By George Cruikshank (Scarce) 100.00 200.00 400.00
nn - Hand colored (Scarce) (no known sales)

BOTTLE, THE (E)
Geo. Gebbie, Philadelphia: nd (c.1871) (11-3/8x17-1/8", 42 pgs, tinted interior, hard-c)

nn - By George Cruikshank 100.00 200.00 400.00
NOTE: *New cover art (cover not by Cruikshank).*

BOTTLE, THE (E)
National Temperance, London: nd (1881) (11-1/2x16-1/2", 16 pgs, printed one side only, paper-c, color)

nn - By George Cruikshank 100.00 200.00 400.00
NOTE: *See Platinum Age section for 1900s printings.*

BOTTLE, THE (E)
Marques, Pittsburgh, PA: 1884/85 (6x8", 8 plates, full color, illustrated envelope)
nn - art not by Cruickshank; New Art 50.00 100.00 200.00
NOTE: Says Presented by J.M. Gusky, Dealer in Boots and Shoes

BROAD GRINS OF THE LAUGHING PHILOSOPHER
Dick & Fitzgerald,NY: 1870s
nn - (4) panel sequential strip 25.00 50.00 150.00

BROTHER JONATHAN
Wilson & Co/Benj H Day, 48 Beekman, NYC: 1839-???

July 4 1846 - ads for Obadiah & Butterfly 50.00 100.00 200.00
July 4 1856 catalog list - front cover comic strip 100.00 200.00 400.00
Xmas/New Years 1856 75.00 150.00 300.00
average large size issues 25.00 50.00 100.00
NOTE: *has full page advert for Fredinand Flipper comic book*116

BULL CALF, THE (P,M)
Various: nd (c1890's) (3-7/8x4-1/8", 16 pgs, B&W, paper-c)

nn - By A.B. Frost Creme Oatmeal Toilet Soap 25.00 50.00 150.00
nn - By A.B. Frost Thompson & Taylor Spice Co, Chicago 25.00 50.00 150.00
NOTE: *Reprints the popular strip story by Frost. with the art modified to place a sign for Creme Oatmeal Soap within each panel. The back cover advertises the specific merchant who gave this booklet away - multiple variations exist.*

BULL CALF AND OTHER TALES, THE (M)
Charles Scribner's Sons: 1892 (120 pgs., 6-3/4x8-7/8", B&W, illus. hard cover)

nn - By Arthur Burdett Frost 50.00 150.00 500.00
NOTE: *Blue, grey, tan hard covers known to exist.*

BULL CALF, THE STORY OF THE MAN OF HUMANITY AND THE (P,M)
C.H. Fargo & Co.: 1890 (5-1/4x6-1/4", 24 pgs, B&W, color paper-c)

nn - By A.B. Frost 50.00 100.00 200.00
NOTE: *Fargo shoe company giveaway; pages alternate between shoe advertisements and the strip story.*

BUSHEL OF MERRY THOUGHTS, A (see Mischief Book, The) (E)
Sampson Low Son & Marsten: 1868 (68 pgs, handcolored hardcover, B&W)

nn - (6-1/4 x 9-7/8", 138 pgs) red binding, publisher's name on title page only 200.00 400.00 800.00
nn - (6-1/2 x 10", 134 pgs) green binding, publisher's name on cover & title page 200.00 400.00 800.00
NOTE: *Cover plus story title pages designed by Leighton Brothers, based on Busch art. Translated by Harry Rogers (who is credited instead of Busch). This is a British publication, notable as the earliest known English language anthology collection of Wilhelm Busch comic strips. Page 13 of second story missing from all editions (panel dropped). Unknown which of the two editions was published first. A modern reprint, by Dover in 1971.*

BUTTON BURSTER, THE (M) (says on cover "ten cents hard cash")
M.J. Ivers & Co., 86 Nassau St., New York: 1873 (11x8-1/8", soft paper, B&W)

By various cartoonists (Very Rare) 125.00 250.00 500.00
NOTE: *Reprints from various 1873 issues of Wild Oats; has (5) different sequential comic strips: (3) by Livingston Hopkins, (1) by Thomas Worth, other one creator presently unknown; Bellew, Sr. single panel cartoons.*

BUZZ A BUZZ OR THE BEES (E)
Griffith & Farran, London: September 1872 (8-1/2x5-1/2", 168 pgs, printed one side only, orange, black & white hardcover, B&W interior)

nn - By Wilhelm Busch (Scarce) 112.00 225.00 450.00
NOTE: *Reprint published by Phillipson & Golder, Chester; text written by English to accompany Busch art.*

BUZZ A BUZZ OR THE BEES (E)
Henry Holt & Company, New York: 1873 (9x6", 96 pgs, gilted hardcover, hand colored)

nn - By Wilhelm Busch (Scarce) 100.00 200.00 450.00
NOTE: *Completely different translation than the Griffith & Farran version. Also, contains 28 additional illustrations by Park Benjamin. The lower page count is because the Henry Holt edition prints on both sides of each page, and the Griffith & Farran edition is printed one side only.*

CALENDAR FOR THE MONTH; YE PICTORIAL LYSTE OF YE MATTERS OF

The Carpet Bag #14
1851 © Snow & Wilder

The Clown, or The Banquet of Wit
1851 © Fisher & Brother

Comic Monthly v6 #8
March 1865 © J.C.Haney, NY

FR1.0 GD2.0 FN6.0

INTEREST FOR SUMMER READING (P,M)
S.E. Bridgman & Company, Northampton, Mass: nd (c. late 1880's-1890's) (5-5/8x7-1/4", 64 pgs, paper-c, B&W)

nn - (Very Rare) T.S. Sullivant-c/a 100.00 200.00 400.00
NOTE: Book seller's catalog, with every other page reprinting cartoons and strips (from Life??). Art by: Chips Bellew, Gibson, Howarth, Kemble, Sullivant, Townsend, Woolf.

CARICATURE AND OTHER COMIC ART
Harper & Brothers, NY: 1877 (9-5/16x7-1/8", 360 pgs, B&W, green hard-c)

nn - By James Parton (over 200 illustrations) 30.00 60.00 200.00
*NOTE: This is the earliest known serious history of comics & related genre from around the world produced by an American. Parton was a cousin of Thomas Nast's wife Sarah. A large portion of this book was first serialized in **Harper's Monthly** in 1875.*

CARPET BAG, THE
Snow & Wilder, later Wilder & Pickard, Boston: March 21 1851-March 26 1853

Each average issue 25.00 50.00 100.00
Samuel "Mark Twain" Clemmons issues (first app in print) 600.00 1200.00 2500.00
NOTE: Many issues contain cartoons by DC Johnston, Frank Bellew, others; literature includes Artemus Ward's Miss Partington who had a mischevious little Katzenjammer Kids-like brat. Carpet Bag was not considered derogatory pre-Civil War.

CARROT-POMADE (O.G)
James G. Gregory, Publisher, New York: 1864 (9x6-7/8", 36 pgs, B&W)

nn - By Augustus Hoppin 70.00 140.00 280.00
NOTE: The story of a quack remedy for baldness, sequentially told in the format parodying ABC primers. Has protective tissue pages (not part of page count).

CARTOONS BY HOMER C. DAVENPORT (M,N,S)
De Witt Publishing House: 1898 (16-1/8x12", 102 pgs, hard-c, B&W)

nn 100.00 200.00 400.00
NOTE: Reprinted from Harper's Weekly and the New York Journal. Includes cartoons about the Spanish-American War. Title page reads "Davenport's Cartoons".

CARTOONS BY WILL E. CHAPIN (P,N,S)
The Times-Mirror Printing and Binding House, Los Angeles: 1899 (15-1/4x12", 98 pgs, hard-c, B&W)

nn - scarce 100.00 200.00 400.00
NOTE: Premium item for subscribing to the Los-Angeles Times-Mirror newspaper, from which these cartoons were reprinted. Includes cartoons about the Spanish-American War.

CARTOONS OF OUR WAR WITH SPAIN (N,S)
Frederick A. Stokes Company: 1898 (11-1/2x10", 72 pgs, hardcover, B&W)

nn - By Charles Nelan (r-New York Herald) 40.00 100.00 200.00
nn - 2nd printing noted on copy right page 30.00 60.00 120.00

CARTOONS OF THE WAR OF 1898 (E,M,N,S)
Belford, Middlebrook & Co., Chicago: 1898 (7x10-3/8",190 pgs, B&W, hard-c)

nn 50.00 100.00 200.00
NOTE: Reprints single panel editorial cartoons on the Spanish-American War, from American, Spanish, Latino, and European newspapers and magazines, at rate of 2 to 6 cartoons per page. Art by Bart, Berryman, Bowman, Bradley, Chapin, Gillam, Nelan, Tenniel, others.

CENTENNIAL FUN (O,S) (Rare)
Frank Leslie, Philadelphia: (July) 1876 (25¢, 11x8", 32 pgs, paper cover, B&W)

nn - By Joseph Keppler-c/a;Thomas Worth-a 150.00 300.00 600.00
NOTE: Issued for the 1876 Centennial Exposition in Philadelphia. Exists with both black & white, and orange, black & white covers. One copy of the latter had an embossed newstand label from Partland, Maine, implying that the orange cover version, at least, was distributed and sold outside of Philadelphia.

CHAMPAIGNE
Frank Leslie: June-Dec 1871

1-7 scarce 150.00 225.00 350.00

CHIC
Chic Publishing Co: 1880-81 (Chromolithographic Weekly)

1-38 Livingston Hopkins, Charles Kendrick, CW Weldon 75.00 150.00 300.00

CHILDREN'S CHRISTMAS BOOK, THE
The New York Sunday World: 1897 (10-1/4x8-3/4", 16 pgs, full color)

Dec 12, 1897 - By George Luks, G.H. Grant, Will Crawford, others) (Rare)
50.00 100.00 280.00

CHIP'S DOGS (M)
R.H. Russell and Son Publishers: 1895 hardcover, B&W)

nn - By Frank P. W. "Chip" Bellew 25.00 50.00 100.00
Early printing 80 pgs, 8-7/8x11-7/8"; dark green border of hardcover surrounds all four sides of pasted on cover image; pages arranged in error -- see NOTE below. (more scarce)
nn - By Frank P. W. "Chip" Bellew 12.50 25.00 50.00
Later printing 72 pgs, 8-7/8x11-3/4";green border only on the binding side (one side) of the cover image.
*NOTE: Both are strip reprints from **LIFE**. The difference in page count is due to more blank pages in the first printing -- all printings have the same comics contents, but with the pages in the first printing arranged differently. This is noticeable particularly in the 2-page strip "Getting a Pointer", which appears on the 2nd & 3rd to last pages of the later printings, but in the early printing the first half of this strip is near the middle of the book, while the last half appears on the 2nd to last story page.*

CHIP'S OLD WOOD CUTS (M,S)
R.H. Russell & Son: 1895 (8-7/8x11-3/4", 72 pgs, hardcover, B&W)

nn - By Frank P. W. ("Chip") Bellew 25.00 50.00 100.00

FR1.0 GD2.0 FN6.0

nn - 1897 reprint 15.00 30.00 60.00

CHIP'S UN-NATURAL HISTORY (O,S)
Frederick A. Stokes & Brother: 1888 (7x5-1/4", 64 pgs, hardcover, B&W)

nn - By Frank P. W. ("Chip") Bellew 12.50 25.00 50.00
NOTE: Title page lists publisher as "Successors to White, Stokes & Allen."

CLOWN, OR THE BANQUET OF WIT, THE (E,M,O)
Fisher & Brother, Philadelphia, Baltimore, New York, Boston: nd (c.1851) (7-3/8x4-1/2", 88 pgs, paper cover, B&W)

nn - (Very Rare; 3 known copies) 500.00 1000.00 2000.00
NOTE: Earliest known multi-artist anthology of sequential comics; contains multiple sequential comics, plus numerous single panel cartoons. A mixture of reprinted and original material, involving both European and American artists. "Jones, Smith, and Robinson Goes to a Ball" by Richard Doyle (1st app. of Doyle's "Foreign Tour" in America, reprinted from PUNCH, August 24, 1850); "Moses Keyser The Bowery Bully's Trip to the Californian Gold Mines", by John H. Manning; "The Adventures of Mr. Gulp" (by the Read brothers?); more comics by artists unknown; cartoons by George Cruikshank, Grandville, Elton.

COLD CUTS AND PICKLED EELS' FEET; DONE BROWN BY JOHN BROWN
P.J. Cozans, New York: nd (c1855-60) (B&W)

nn (Very Rare) 100.00 200.00 300.00
NOTE: Mostly a children's book. But, pages 87 to 110, and 111 to 122, contain narrative sequential stories.

COLLEGE SCENES (O,G)
N. Hayward, Boston: 1850 (5x6-3/4", 72 pgs, printed one side only, B&W lithography)

nn - (Rare) by Nathan Hayward 200.00 400.00 600.00
NOTE: This is the 2nd such production for an American University; the first issued at Yale circa 1845, decent funny art of story about life of a Harvard student from his entrance thru graduation entirely in caricature. Has art on back cover as well.

COLLEGE CUTS Chosen From The Columbia Spectator 1880-81-82 (S)
White & Stokes, NY: 1882 (8x9-5/8", 92 pgs, B&W)

By F. Benedict Herzog, H. McVickar, W. Bard McVickar, others 20.00 40.00 100.00
nn - 2nd edition reprint (1888) (8-1/4x10-3/8) 10.00 20.00 50.00

COMICAL COONS (M)
R.H. Russell: 1898 (8-7/8 x 11-7/8", 68 pgs, hardcover, B&W)

nn - By E. W. Kemble 300.00 600.00 1300.00
NOTE: Black Americana collection of 2-panel stories.

COMICAL ALMANAC
Anton Bicker, Cinncinati, OH: 1885 (9x6, 260 pgs, B&W, illustrated-c)

nn - two (12) page sequential Busch comic strips 50.00 100.00 200.00

COMIC ALMANAC, THE
John Berger. Baltimore: 1854-? (7-1/2x6-1/4, 36 pgs, B&W)

nn - 60.00 120.00 240.00

COMIC ANNUAL, AMERICAN (O,I)
Richardson, Lord, & Holbrook, Boston: 1831 (6-7/8x4-3/8", 268 pgs, B&W, hard-c)

nn - (Scarce) 150.00 300.00 600.00
NOTE: Mostly text; front & back cover illustrations, 13 full page, and scattered smaller illustrations by David Claypoole Johnston; edited by Henry J. Finn.

COMIC HISTORY OF THE UNITED STATES, (I)
Carleton & Co., NY: 1876 (6-7/8x5-1/8", 336 pgs, hardcover, B&W)

nn - By Livingston Hopkins. 12.50 25.00 50.00
2nd printing: Cassell, Petter, Galpin & Co.: 1880 (6-7/8x5-1/8", 336 pgs, hardcover, B&W)
nn - By Livingston Hopkins. 12.50 25.00 50.00
*NOTE: Text with many B&W illustrations; some are multi-panel comics. Not to beconfused with **Bill Nye's Comic History Of The U.S.** which contains Frederick Opper illustrations.*

COMIC MONTHLY, THE
J.C. Haney, N.Y.: March 1859-1880 (16 x 11-1/2", 30 pgs average, B&W)

Certain average issues with sequential comics 50.00 100.00 200.00

11 (Jan 1860) Bellew-c 25.00 50.00 100.00
v2#2 (Apr 1860) Bellew-c 25.00 50.00 100.00
v2#3 (May 1860) Bellew-c 25.00 50.00 100.00
v2#4 (June 1860) Comic Strip Cover 50.00 100.00 200.00
v2#5 (July 1860) Bellew-c; (12) panel Explaining American Politics To An Intelligent Foreigner; (10) panel The Art of Stump Speaking; (15) panel Mr. Dibbs Goes to Pike's Peak and Comes Back Again 100.00 200.00 400.00
v2#7 (Sept 1860) Comic Strip Cover; (24) panel double page spread The Prince of Wales In America 50.00 100.00 200.00
v2#8 (18) panel The Three Young Friends Sillouette Strip 25.00 50.00 100.00
v2#9 (Nov 1860) (9) panel sequential 25.00 50.00 100.00
v2#10 11 not indexed 25.00 50.00 100.00
v2#12 (Jan 1861) (12) panel double page spread 25.00 50.00 100.00

COMIC TOKEN FOR 1836, A COMPANION TO THE COMIC ALMANAC, THE
Charles Ellms, Boston: 1836 (8x5', 48 pgs, B&W)
nn - 50.00 100.00 200.00

COMIC WEEKLY, THE
???, NYC: 1881-???

issues with comic strips (Chips, etc) 60.00 125.00 250.00

Comics From Scribner's Magazine
1891 © Scribner's

The Comus Offering
1830-31 © B. Franklin Edmands

Elton's Californian Comic All-My-Nack #17
1850 © Elton's, NY

FR1.0 GD2.0 FN6.0

COMIC WORLD
???: 1876-1879 (Quarto Monthly)
issues with comic strips 37.50 75.00 150.00

COMICS FROM SCRIBNER'S MAGAZINE (M)
Scribner's: nd (1891) (10 cents, 9-1/2x6-5/8", 24 pgs, paper cover, side stapled, B&W)
nn - (Rare) F.M.Howarth C&A 125.00 250.00 500.00
NOTE: *Advertised in SCRIBNER'S MAGAZINE in the June 1891 issue, page 793, as available by mail order for 10 cents. Collects together comics material which ran in the back pages of Scribner's Magazine. Art by Attwood, "Chip" Bellew, Dŏes, Frost, Gibson, Zim.*

COMUS OFFERING CONTAINING HUMOROUS SCRAPS OF DIVERTING COMICALITIES, THE (O, S)
B. Franklin Edmands, 25 Court St, Boston: c1830-31 (8-7/8x10-3/4", 16 pgs, thin brown paper-c, blank on backs,
nn - (William F Straton, Engraver, 15 Water St, Boston) (no known sales)
NOTE: All hand-colored single panel cartoons format definitely inspired by D.C. Johnston's Scraps with every panel character using well-defined word balloons. Might become a seminal step in the evolution of the American comic book. More research is needed.

CONTRASTS AND CONCEITS FOR CONTEMPLATION BY LUKE LIMNER (O)
Ackerman & Co, 96 Strand, London: c1848 (9-3/4x6-1/4, 48 pgs, B&W)
nn - By John Leighton 50.00 100.00 200.00

COONTOWN'S 400 (M) (see **Blackberries**) (M)
The Life (Magazine) Co.: 1899 (10-15/16x8-7/8, 68 pgs, cloth light-brown hard-c, B&W
nn - By E.W. Kemble (scarce) 250.00 500.00 1500.00
NOTE: *Tastefully drawn depictions of Black Americana over one hundred years ago during Jim Crow days.*

CROSSING THE ATLANTIC (O,G)
James R. Osgood & Co., Boston: 1872 (10-7/8x16", 68 pgs, hardcover, B&W);
Houghton, Osgood & Co., Boston: 1880
1st printing - by Augustus Hoppin 50.00 100.00 200.00
2nd printing (1880; 66 pgs; 8-1/8x11-1/8") 32.50 65.00 150.00

C.R. PITT'S COMIC ALMANAC
C.R. Pitt: 1880 (7-1/2x4-5/8", 28 pgs)
nn - contains (8) panel sequential 50.00 100.00 200.00

CRUIKSHANK'S OMNIBUS: A VEHICLE FOR FUN AND FROLIC (E,S)
E. Ferrett & Co., Philadelphia: 1845 (25 cents, 7-1/2" x 4-5/8", 96 pgs, B&W, paper-c)
nn - By George Cruikshank c/a (Very Rare) 150.00 300.00 650.00
NOTE: *Mostly prose, with 10 plates of cartoons printed on one-side (about half the plates with multiple cartoons), plus illustrated cover, all by George Cruikshank. First (perhaps only) American printing of Cruikshank's Omnibus, which was published first in Britain. It is only a partial reprinting.*

CYCLISTS' DICTIONARY (S)
Morgan & Wright, Chicago: 1894 (5 x3-3/4, 80 pgs, soft-c, B&W
nn - By Unknown 37.50 75.00 150.00

THE DAILY GRAPHIC
The Graphic Company, 39 Park Place, NY: 1873-Sept 23, 1889 (14x20-1/2, 8 pgs, B&W)
Average issues with comic strips 15.00 20.00 40.00
Average issues without comic strips 10.00 15.00 30.00
NOTE:

DAVY CROCKETT'S COMIC ALMANACK
???, Nashville, TN, then elsewhere: 1835-end (32 pages plus wraps)
1 500.00 1000.00 2000.00
2-13 15 end 250.00 500.00 1000.00
14 contains (17) panel Crocket comic strip bio 1848 1000.00 1500.00 3000.00

DAY'S DOINGS (was The Last Sensation) (Becomes New York Illustrated Times)
James Watts, NYC: #1 June 6 1868-early 1876 (11x16, 16 pgs, B&W)
average issue with comic strips 10.00 15.00 25.00
Paul Pry & Alley Sloper character issues 25.00 50.00 100.00
Aug 19 1871 - First Alley Sloper in America?? 50.00 100.00 200.00
NOTE: *James Watts was a shadow company for Frank Leslie; outright sold to Frank Leslie in 1873. There are a lot of issues with comic strips from 1868 up.*

DAY'S SPORT - OR, HUNTING ADVENTURES OF S. WINKS WATTLES, A SHOPKEEPER, THOMAS TITT, A "LEGAL GENT," AND MAJOR NICHOLAS NOGGIN, A JOLLY GOOD FELLOW GENERALLY, A (O)
Brother Jonathan, NY: c1850s (5-7/8x8-1/4, 44 pgs)
nn - By Henry L. Stephens, Philadelphia (Very Rare) (no known sales)

DEVIL'S COMICAL OLDMANICK WITH COMIC ENGRAVINGS OF THE PRINCIPAL EVENTS OF TEXAS, THE
Turner & Fisher, NY & Philadelphia: 1837 (7-7/8x5", 24 pgs)
nn - many single panel cartoons 100.00 200.00 400.00

DIE VEHME, ILLUSTRIRTES WOCHENBLATT FUR SCHERZ UND ERNEST (M,O)
Heinrich Binder, St. Louis: No.1 Aug 28, 1869 - No.?? Aug 20, 1870 (10 cents, 8 pgs, B&W, paper-c) (see also PUCK)
1-?? (Very Rare) by Joseph Keppler 100.00 200.00 400.00
NOTE: *Joseph Keppler's first attempt at a weekly American humor periodical. Entirely in German. The title translates into:* ***"The Star Chamber: An Illustrated Weekly Paper in Fun and Ernest"****.*

FR1.0 GD2.0 FN6.0

DOMESTIC MANNERS OF THE AMERICANS
The Imprint Society, Barre, Mass: 1969 (9-3/4 x 7-1/4", 390 pgs, hard-c in slipcase, B&W)
nn - 10.00 20.00 50.00
NOTE: *Reprints the 1832 edition of this book by Mrs. Trollope with an added insert. The 28-page insert is what is of primary interest to us -- it reproduces SCRAPS No. 4 (1833) by D.C. Johnston.*

DRUNKARD'S CHILDREN, THE (see also THE BOTTLE) (E,O)
David Bogue, London; John Wiley and G.P. Putnam, New York; J. Sands, Sydney, New South Wales: July 1, 1848 (16x11", 16 pgs, printed on one side only, paper-c)
nn - Black & white edition (Scarce) 300.00 600.00 950.00
nn - Hand colored edition (Rare) (no known sales)
NOTE: *Sequel story to THE BOTTLE, by George Cruikshank. Temperance/anti-alcohol story. British-American-Australian co-publication. Cover is text only - no cover art.*

DRUNKARD'S PROGRESS, OR THE DIRECT ROAD TO POVERTY, WRETCHEDNESS & RUIN, THE
J. W. Barber, New Haven, Conn.: Sept 1826 (single sheet)
nn - By John Warner Barber (Very Rare) (no known sales)
NOTE: *Broadside designed and printed by barber contains four large wood engravings showing "The Morning Dram" which is "The Beginning of Sorrow"; "The Grog Shop" with its "Bad Company"; "The Confirmed Drunkard" in a state of "Beastly Intoxication"; and the "Concluding Scene" with the family being drive off to the alms house. It is an interesting set of cuts, faintly reminiscent of Hogarth. Many modern reprints exist.*

DUEL FOR LOVE, A (O,P)
E.C. DeWitt & Co., Chicago: nd (c1880's) (3-3/8" x 2-5/8", 12 pgs, B&W, paper-c)
nn - Art by F.M. Howarth (Rare) 25.00 50.00 100.00
NOTE: *Advertising giveaway for DeWitt's Little Early Risers, featuring an 8-panel strip story, spread out 1 panel per page.*

DURHAM WHIFFS (O, P)
Blackwells Durham Tobacco Co: Jan 8 1878 (9x6.5", 8 pgs, color-c, B&W)
v1 #1 w/Trade Card Insert 37.50 75.00 150.00
NOTE: Sold in 2008 CGC 9.4 $1250

DYNALENE LAFLETS (P)
The Dynalene Company: nd (3 x 3-1/2", 16 pgs, B&W, paper cover)
nn - Dynalene Dyes promo (9) panel comic strip 25.00 50.00 75.00

ELEPHANT, THE
William H Graham, Tribune Building, NYC: Jan 22 1848-Feb 19 1848 (11x8.5", B&W)
1-5 Rare - single panel cartoons 150.00 300.00 600.00

ELTON'S COMIC ALL-MY-NACK (E,O.S)
Elton, Publisher, 18 Division & 98 Nassau St, NY: 1833-1852 (7-1/2x4-1/2", 36pgs, B&W
1-5 99% single panel cartoons 100.00 200.00 400.00
6 (1839) 100.00 200.00 400.00
NOTE: Two different covers & different interiors exist for this title and number
7-15 - 99% single panel cartoons 100.00 200.00 400.00
16 - contains 6 panel "A Tales of A Tayl-or" 1848-49 200.00 400.00 600.00
17 - contains "Moses Keyser, The Bowery Bully's Trip To the California Gold Mines" 1850 By John H. Manning, early comics creator, told in 15 panels 200.00 400.00 600.00
18-19 presently unknown contents 100.00 200.00 400.00
NOTE: *Contains both original American, and pirated European, cartoons. All single panel material, except where noted. Almanacs are published near the end of the year prior to that for which they are printed -- like calendars today. Thus, the 1833 No. 1 issue was really published in the last months of 1832. #17 has Elton's Californian Comic-All-My-Nack on the cover.*

ELTON'S COMIC ALMANAC (Publsiher change)
GW Cottrell & Co, Publishers & C Cornhill, Boston, Mass: 1853 (7-7/8x4-5/8,36pgs,B&W
20 - (2) sequential comic strips (9) panel "Jones, Smith and Robinson Goes To A Ball; (21) panel "The Adventures of Mr. Gulp" Rare 300.00 600.00 1200.00
NOTE: *Both strips appear in* The Clown, Or The Banquet of Wit

ELTON'S FUNNY ALMANACK (title change to Almanac)
Elton Publisher and Engraver, New York: 1846 (8x6-1/2", 36 pgs)
1 1846 50.00 100.00 200.00

ELTON'S FUNNY ALMANAC (#1 titled Almanack)
Elton & Co, New York: 1847-1853 (8x6-1/4, 36 pgs, B&W)
2 (1847) #3 (1848) 50.00 100.00 200.00
nn 1853 (8-1/8x4-7/8"; (5) panel comic strip "The Adventures of Mr. Goliah Starvemouse"

ELTON'S RIPSNORTER COMIC ALMANAC
Elton, 90 Nassau St, NY: 1850 (8x5, 24 pgs, B&W, paper-c)
nn - scarce 50.00 100.00 200.00

ENGLISH SOCIETY (S)
Harper & Brothers, Publishers, New York: 1897 (9-5/8x12-1/4", 206 pgs, B&W)
nn - by George Du Maurier 50.00 75.00 100.00

ENGLISH SOCIETY AT HOME (S)
James R. Osgood and Company: 1881 (10-7/8x8-5/8, 182 pgss, protective sheets on some pages - not included in pages count, hard-c, B&W 50.00 75.00 100.00
nn - by George Du Maurier

ENTER: THE COMICS (E,G)
University of Nebraska Press: 1965 (6-7/8x9-1/4", 120 pgs, hard-c)

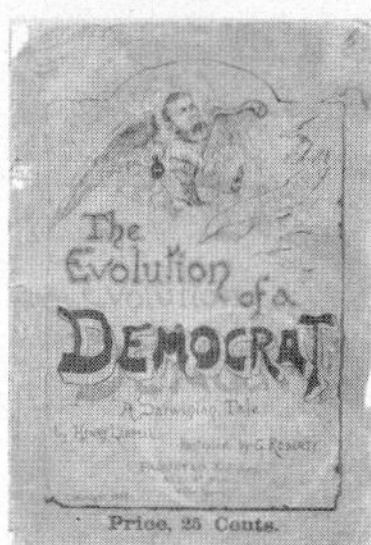
The Evolution Of A Democrat
1888 © Paquet & Co, NY

Flying Leaves
1880s © E.R. Herrick & Company, New York

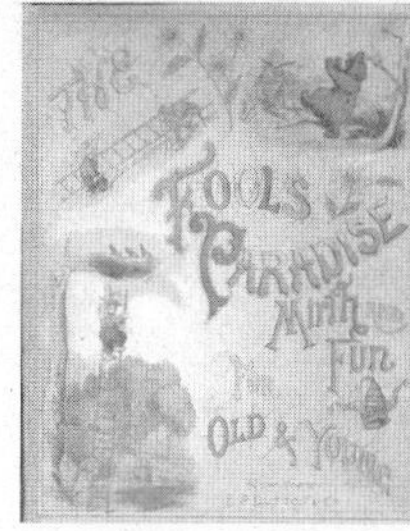
The Fools Paradise Mirth and Fun
For Old and Young
1883 © E.P. Dutton & Co, NYC

FR1.0 GD2.0 FN6.0

nn - By Ellen Weisse 25.00 50.00 100.00
NOTE: *Contains overview of Töpffer's life and career plus only published English translation of Töpffer's Monsieur Crepin (1837); appears to have been re-drawn by Weisse in the days before xerox machines.*

ESQUIRE BROWN AND HIS MULE, STORY OF
A.C. Meyer, Baltimore, Maryland: 1880s (5x3/7/8", 28 pgs, B&W)
Booklet (9 panel story plus cough remedies catalog) 25.00 50.00 100.00
Fold-Out of Booklet (9 panel version) 25.00 50.00 100.00

"EVENTS OF THE WEEK" REPRINTED FROM THE CHICAGO TRIBUNE
Henry O. Shepard Co, Chicago: 1894 (5-3/8x15-7/8", 110 pg, B&W, hard-c)
First Series, Second Series - By HR Heaton 37.50 75.00 150.00

EVERYBODY'S COMICK ALMANACK
Turner & Fisher, NY & Philadelphia: 1837 (7-7/8x5", 36 pgs, B&W)
nn 50.00 100.00 200.00

EVOLUTION OF A DEMOCRAT - A DARWINIAN TALE, THE (O,G)
Paquet & Co., New York: 1888 (25 cents, 7-7/8x5-1/2", 100 pgs, printed one side only, orange paper cover, B&W) (Very Rare)
nn - Written by Henry Liddell, art by G. Roberty 300.00 600.00 1200.00
NOTE: *Political parody about the rise of an Irishman through Tammany Hall. Grover Cleveland appears as linked with Tammany. Ireland becomes the next state in the USA.*

FABLES FOR THE TIMES (S, I)
R.H. Russell & Son, New York: 1896 (9-1/8x12-1/8", 52 pgs, yellow hard-c)
nn - By H.W. Phillips and T.S. Sullivant Scarce 75.00 150.00 300.00

FERDINAND FLIPPER, ESQ., THE FORTUNES OF (O,G)
Brother Jonathan, Publisher, NY: nd (1851) (5-3/4 x 9-3/8", 84 pgs, B&W, printed both sides)
nn - By Various (Very Rare) 700.00 1200.00 2800.00
NOTE: *Extended title: "...Commencing With A Period of Four Months And Anterior To His Birth Going Thru The Various Stages of His Infancy, Childhood, Verdant Years, Manhood, Middle Life, and Green and Ripe Old Age, And Ending A Short Time Subsequent to His Sudden Decease With His Final Exit, Funeral And Burial." Extremely unique comic book, put together by gathering 145 independent single illustrations and cartoons, by various artists, and stringing them together into a sequential story. The majority of panels are by Grandville. Also included are at least 19 signed Charles Martin, reprinted from 1847 issues of Yankee Doodle, 5 panels from D.C. Johnston, plus other panels by F.O.C. Darley, T.H. Matheson, and others. The story also contains several panels of Gold Rush content . Printed by E.A. Alverds. The 1851 date is derived from an advertisement found in the Oct-Dec 1851 issue of the Brother Jonathan newspaper. It ispossible, however, that it actually came out even earlier.*

FERDINAND FLIPPER, ESQ., THE FORTUNES OF (G)
Dick & Fitzgerald, New York: nd (1870's to 1888) (30 Cents, 84 pgs, B&W, paper cover)
nn - (Very Rare reprint - several editions possible) 375.00 750.00 1500.00

FINN'S COMIC ALMANAC
Marsh, Capen, & Lyon; Boston: 1835-??? (4.5x7.5, 36 pgs, B&W)
nn 100.00 200.00 400.00

FINN'S COMIC SKETCHBOOK (S)
Peabody & Co., 223 Broadway, NY: 1831 (10-1/2x16", 12 pgs, B&W)
nn - By Henry J. Finn (Very Rare) (no known sales)
NOTE: *Designs on copper plates; etched by J. Harris, NY; should have tissue paper in front of each plate.*

50 GREAT CARTOONS (M,P,S)
Ram's Horn Press: 1899 (14x10-3/4, 112 pgs, hard-c)
nn - By Frank Beard 30.00 60.00 120.00
NOTE: *Premium in return for a subscription to **The Ram's Horn** magazine.*

FISHER'S COMIC ALMANAC
Ames Fisher and Brother, No 12 North Sixth St, Philadelphia , Charles Small in NYC, Also in Boston: 1841-1868 (4-1/2 x 7-1/4, 36 pgs, B&W)
1-7 (1841-1847) 100.00 200.00 400.00
12 reprints mermaid-c with word balloon (1868) 100.00 200.00 400.00

F**** A*** K*****, OUTLINES ILLUSTRATIVE OF THE JOURNAL OF** (O,S)
D.C. Johnston, Boston: 1835 (9-5/16 x 6", 12 pgs, printed one side only, blue paper cover, B&W interior) (see also **SCRAPS**)
nn - by David Claypoole Johnston (Scarce) 600.00 1000.00 1600.00
NOTE: *This is a series of 8 plates parodying passages from the Journal of Fanny (Frances) A. Kemble, a British woman who wrote a highly negative book about American Culture after returning from the U.S. Though remembered now for her campaign against slavery, she was prejudiced against most everything American culture, thus inspiring Johnston's satire. Contains 4 protective sheets (not part of page count.)*

FLYING DUTCHMAN; OR, THE WRATH OF HERR VONSTOPPELNOZE, THE (E)
Carleton Publishing, New York: 1862 (7-5/8x5-1/4", 84 pgs, printed on one side only, gilted hardcover, B&W)
nn - By Wilhelm Busch (Scarce) 35.00 70.00 160.00
nn - 1975 Scarce 100 copy-r 74 pgs Visual Studies Workshop 5.00 10.00 20.00
NOTE: *This is the earliest known English language book publication of a Wilhelm Busch work. The story is plagiarized by American poet John G. Saxe, who is credited with the text, while the uncredited Busch cartoons are described merely as accompanying illustrations.*

FLYING LEAVES (E)
E.R. Herrick & Company, New York: nd (c1889/1890's) (8-1/4" x 11-1/2", 76 pgs, B&W interior, orange, b&w hard-c)
nn- (Scarce) 85.00 175.00 260.00

FR1.0 GD2.0 FN6.0

NOTE: *Reprints strips and single panel cartoons from 1888 Fliegende Blatter issues, translated into English. Various artists, including Bechstein, Adolf Hengeler, Lothar Meggendorfer, Emil Reinicke.*

FOOLS PARADISE WITH THE MANY ADVENTURES THERE AS SEEN IN THE STRANGE SURPRISING PEEP SHOW OF PROFESSOR WOLLEY COBBLE, THE (E)
(see also THE COMICAL PEEP SHOW)
John Camden Hotten, London: Nov 1871 (1 crown, 9-7/8x7-3/8", 172 pgs, printed one side only, gilted green hardcover, hand colored interior)
nn - By Wilhelm Busch (Rare) 400.00 800.00 1750.00
NOTE: *Title on cover is: **WALK IN! WALK IN!! JUST ABOUT TO BEGIN!!! the FOOLS PARADISE**; below the above title page. Anthology of Wilhelm Busch comics, translated into English.*

FOOLS PARADISE WITH THE MANY WONDERFUL SIGHTS AS SEEN IN THE STRANGE SURPRISING PEEP SHOW OF PROFESSOR WOLLEY COBBLE, FURTHER ADVENTURES IN (E)
Chatto & Windus, London: 1873 (10x7-3/8", 128 pgs, printed one side only, brown hardcover, hand colored interior)
nn - By Wilhelm Busch (Rare) 300.00 600.00 1320.00
NOTE: *Sequel to the 1871 **FOOLS PARADISE**, containing a completely different set of Busch stories, translated into English.*

FOOLS PARADISE MIRTH AND FUN FOR THE OLD & YOUNG (E)
Griffith & Farran, London: May 1883 (9-3/4x7-5/8", 78 pgs, color cover, color interior)
nn - By Wilhelm Busch (Rare) 100.00 200.00 420.00
NOTE: *Collection of selected stories reprinted from both the 1871 & 1873 **FOOLS PARADISE**.*

FOOLS PARADISE - MIRTH AND FUN FOR THE OLD & YOUNG (E)
E.P. Dutton and Co., NY: May 1883 (9-3/4x7-5/8", 78 pgs, color cover, color interior)
nn - By Wilhelm Busch (Rare) 100.00 200.00 420.00
NOTE: *Collection of selected stories reprinted from both the 1871 & 1873 **FOOLS PARADISE.***

FOREIGN TOUR OFMESSRS. BROWN, JONES, AND ROBINSON, THE (see Messrs...,)

FRANK LESLIE'S BOYS AND GIRLS
Frank Leslie, NYC: Oct 13 1866-#905 Feb 9 1884
average issue with comic strip 20.00 30.00 50.00

FRANK LESLIE'S BUDGET OF FUN
Frank Leslie, Ross & Tousey, 121 Nassau St, NYC: Jan 1859-1878 (newspaper size)
1-5 no comic strips 50.00 100.00 200.00
6 June 1859 (9) panel "The Wonderful Hunting Tour of Mr Borridge After the Deer" 75.00 150.00 300.00
7-9 no comic strips 25.00 50.00 100.00
10 Sept 1859 sequential comic strip 50.00 100.00 200.00
11 (8) panel sequential "Apropos of the Great Eastern" 50.00 100.00 200.00
12-14 25.00 50.00 100.00
15 Feb 1860 (12) panel "The Ballet Girl" strip 50.00 100.00 200.00
16-18 25.00 50.00 100.00
19 June 1860 comic strip front cover 100.00 200.00 300.00
NOTE: Cover is (11) panel "The Very Latest Fashionable Amusement..."; Back cover comic strip "Mr Jogg's Reasons For Preferring to Board to Keeping House" (7) panels using word balloons. Plus centerfold double page (18) panel spread "The New York May, Moving in General, and Mrs. Grundy's In Particular."
20 24 25 no comic strips 25.00 50.00 100.00
21 (7/15/60) (8) panel Mr Septimus Verdilater Visits the Baltimore Convention" 50.00 100.00 200.00
22 (8/1/60) (3) panel 25.00 50.00 100.00
23 (8/15/60) (12) panel "Superb Scheme For Perfecting of Dramatic Entertainment" 50.00 100.00 200.00
25 (9/15/60 (9) panel sequential 25.00 50,00 100.00
27 AbrahamLincoln Word Balloon cover 50.00 100.00 200.00
28 Wilhelm Busch sequential strip-r begin 50.00 100.00 200.00
29, 31-51 to be indexed next year 25.00 50.00 100.00
30 (12/15/60) (3) panel sequential strip 25.00 50.00 100.00
31 (Jan 1861) (12) panel The Boarding School Miss 25.00 50.00 100.00
32 (Feb 1861) (10) panel Telegraphic Horrors; Or, Mr Buchanan Undergoing A Series of Electric Shocks 50.00 100.00 200.00
35 (4/1/61) Abraham Lincoln Word Balloon cover 50.00 100.00 200.00
43 44 no sequential comic strips 25.00 50.00 100.00
45 (Nov 1861) (6) panel sequential; (11) panel The Budget Army and Infantry Tactics; First Bellew here? - Many Bellew full pagers begin 50.00 100.00 200.00
48 (Feb 1862) Bellew-c; (2) panel Bellew strip plus singles 50.00 100.00 200.00
49 (Mar 1862) Bellew-c; (16) panel Wilhelm Busch "The Fly Or The Disturbed Ducthman A Story without Words" 50.00 100.00 200.00
50 (April 1862) Bellew-c "Succession Bath" plus singles 25.00 50.00 100.00
51 (May 1862) Bellew-c; (25) panel Busch The Toothache (6) panel Definitions of the Day 50.00 100.00 200.00
52 (June 1862) Bellew-c; (9) panel A Cock & A Bull Expedition; (6) panel Bellew The First Campaign of the Home Guard 50.00 100.00 200.00
NOTE: Johnny Bull & Louis Napolean with Brother Jonathan
53-67 To Be Indexed in the Future 25.00 50.00 100.00
68 (11/18//63) (6) panel Bellew strip "Cuts On Cowards" 25.00 50.00 100.00
NOTE: contains (1) panel William Newman 1817-1870, mentor to Thomas Nast
71 (Feb 1864) Wiord Balloon Jefferson Davis-c 25.00 50.00 100.00
72 (Mar 1864) Word Balloon-c 25.00 50.00 100.00

Frank Tousey's Illustrated New York Monthly #9
June 1882 © Frank Tousey

Funny Fellow's Own Book
1852 © Philip Cozans

Funny Folk by F.M. Howarth
1899© E.P. Dutton

	FR1.0	GD2.0	FN6.0
73 (April 1864) Word Balloon-c in (6) panels	25.00	50.00	100.00
74 (May 1864) Newman Word Balloon-c	25.00	50.00	100.00
75 77 78 no sequentials	25.00	50.00	100.00
76 (July 1864) Newman Word Balloon-c	25.00	50.00	100.00
79 (Oct 1864) Word Balloon-c	25.00	50.00	100.00
80 (Nov 1864) Robt E Lee & JeffDavis-c; no sequentials	25.00	50.00	100.00
81 (Dec 1864) Word Balloon "Abyss of War"-c	25.00	50.00	100.00
83 (2/18/65) Back-c (6) panel "Petroleum"	25.00	50.00	100.00
84 (Mar 1865) (6) panel sequential	25.00	50.00	100.00
85 (Apr 1865) Word Balloon-c	25.00	50.00	100.00
86 89 90 92 no sequentials	25.00	50.00	100.00
88 (7/6/65) (6) panel "Marriage"	25.00	50.00	100.00
91 (Oct 1865) (6) panel "Brief Confab At The Corner	25.00	50.00	100.00
93-98 yet to be indexed	25.00	50.00	100.00
99 (June 1866) (18) panel Mr Paul Peters Adventures While Trout-Fishing In The Adirondacks	50.00	100.00	200.00
100 (July 1866) (4) panel sequential comic strip	25.00	50.00	100.00
102 (Sept 1866) (6) panel sequential comic strip	25.00	50.00	100.00
103 (Oct 1866) (9) panel strip; (12) pane;l back cover Adventures of McTiffin At Long Branch	50.00	100.00	200.00
104 (Nov 1866) (4) panel; (23) panel "The Budget Rebuses; (2) panel Glut On Treason Market;back-c; (6) sequential strip	25.00	50.00	100.00
105 (12/18/66) Word Balloon-c; (20) panel sequential back-c	37.50	65.00	130.00

NOTE: Artists include William Newman (1863-1868), William Henry Shelton, Joseph Keppler (1873-1876), James A. Wales (1876-1878), Frederick Burr Opper (1878)

FRANK LESLIE'S LADY'S MAGAZINE
Frank Leslie, NYC: Feb 1863-Dec 1882 (8.5x12", typically 152 pgs)

issues with comic strips	20.00	40.00	50.00

FRANK LESLIE'S PICTORIAL WEEKLY
Frank Leslie, Ross & Tousey, 121 Nassau St, NYC:

average issue (Very Rare)	50.00	100.00	200.00

FRANK TOUSEY'S NEW YORK COMIC MONTHLY
Frank Tousey, NYC: (no known sales)

FREAKS
???, Philadelphia: Jan 8, 1881-April? 1881 (Chromolithographic Weekly)

(Very Rare)	50.00	100.00	300.00

FREELANCE, THE
A.M. Soteldo Jr, Edito, 292 Broadway, NYC: 1874-75 (Folio Weekly)

(Rare)	25.00	50.00	100.00

FREE MASONRY EXPOSED
Winchell & Small, 113 Fulton, NY: 1871 (7-5/8x10-1/2", 36pgs, blue paper-c, B&W)

nn- Thomas Worth Scarce	100.00	200.00	400.00

NOTE: Scathing satircal look at Free Masons thru many cartoons, their power waning by the 1870s

FREETHINKERS' PICTORIAL TEXT-BOOK, THE (S,O)
The Truth Seeker Company, New York: 1890, 1896, 1898 (9x12, hard-c, B&W)

1 (1890 edition) - Scarce 382 pgs By Watson Heston	200.00	400.00	800.00
1 (1896 edition) - Scarce 378 pgs By Watson Heston (1890-r)	100.00	200.00	450.00
2 (1898 edition) - Scarce 408 pgs By Watson Heston	125.00	250.00	450.00

NOTE: *Sought after by collectors of Freethought/Atheism material. There is also 200 copy Modern Reprint.*

FRITZ SPINDLE-SHANKS, THE RAVEN BLACK
Cosack & C o, Buffalo, NY: 1870/80s (4-3/8x2-3/4", color)

(10) card comic strip set by Wilhelm Busch	25.00	50.00	100.00

FUN BY RALL
Unknown: circa 1865 (11x7-7/8", 68 pgs, soft-c, B&W)

nn - By presently unknown (Very Rare)	100.00	200.00	350.00

NOTE: *Wraparound soft cover like modern comic book; yellow paper cover with red & black ink.*

FUN FOR THE FAMILY IN PICTURES
D. Lothrop and Company: 1886 (4 x 7", 48 pgs, Silver & Red stiff-c; interior pages have various single color inks)

nn - By unknown hand	50.00	100.00	200.00

NOTE: *Single panel cartoons and sequential stories.*

FUN FROM LIFE
Frederick A Stokes & Brother, New York: 1889 (9 1/8 by 7 1/8, 72 pages, hard-c)

nn - Mostly by Frank "Chips" Bellew Jr	62.50	125.00	250.00

NOTE: *Contains both single panel and many sequential comics reprints from Life.*

FUNNYEST OF AWL AND THE FUNNIEST SORT OF PHUN, THE
AT Bellew Or W. Jennings Demorest, 121 Nassau St, NY : 1865-67 (30 issues, 16x11 tabloid 16 pgs B&W Monthly, 1-8 © American News; 9-on © A.T. Bellews)

1 (April 1864) Bellew-c	50.00	100.00	200.00
4 (1865) Bellew-c	50.00	100.00	200.00
5 (1865) Busch (20) panel comic srtip The Toothache	75.00	150.00	300.00
7 (1865) Bellew-c	50.00	100.00	200.00
8 (1865) Special Petroleum oil issue - much cartoon art	100.00	200.00	400.00
9 (July 1865) Bellew Bullfrog-c; centerfold double page spread hanging many Confederates; (6) panel strip hanging Jeff Davis	100.00	200.00	400.00
10 (Aug 1865) Bellew-c (13) panel Busch strip with two ducks, a frog and a butcher who gets the ducks in the end	100.00	200.00	400.00
11 (Sept 1865) Bellew Bull Frog Anti-French-c	50.00	100.00	200.00
13 14 15 (12/65-1/66) Bellew-c no sequential comic strips	50.00	100.00	200.00
16 (March 1866) address change to 39 Park Ave	50.00	100.00	200.00
22 (Sept 1866) 133 Nassau St	50.00	100.00	200.00
34 (Oct 1867) 133 Nassau St (7) panel Baseball comic strip; Last Known Issue - were there more?	100.00	200.00	400.00

NOTE: *Radical Republican politics distributed by Great American News Company; owned by Frank Bellew's wife as a front for her husband. When the Civil War ended, the brutal anti-Confederate comic strips and jokes switched to frogs and began attacking France. Funny thing, history says without France's help in the 1700s, there just might not have been a United States.*

FUNNY ALMANAC
Elton & Co., NY: 1853 (8-1/8x4-7/8, 36 pgs)

nn - sequential comic strip	50.00	100.00	200.00

NOTE: (5) panel strip "The Adventures of Mr. Goliah Starvemouse"

FUNNY FELLOWS OWN BOOK, A COMPANION FOR THE LOVERS OF FROLIC AND GLEE, THE (M,N)
Philip. J. Cozans, 116 Nassau ST, NY: 1852 (4-1/2x7-1/2", 196 pgs, burnt orange paper-c)

nn - contains many sequential comic strips (Very Rare) (no known sales)

NOTE: Collected from many different Comic Alamac(k)s including Mose Keyser (Calif Gold Rush); Jones, Smith and Robinson Goes To A Ball; Adventures of Mr. Gulp, Or the Effects of A Dinner Party; The Bowery Bully's Trip To The California Gold Mines plus lots more. This one is a sleeper so far.

FUNNY FOLK (M)
E. P. Dutton: 1899 (12x16-1/2", 90 pgs,14 strips in color-rest in b&w, hard-c)

nn - By Franklin Morris Howarth	162.50	325.00	1500.00
nn - London: J.M. Dent, 1899 embossed-c; same interior	200.00	450.00	900.00

NOTE: *Reprints many sequential strips & single panel cartoons from **Puck.** This is considered by many to be yet another "missing link" between Victorian & Platinum Age comic books. Most comic books 1900-1917 re-printing Sunday newspaper comic strips follow this size format, except using cardboard-c rather than hard-c.*

FUNNY SKETCHES...Also Embracing Comic Illustrations
Frank Harrison, New York: 1881 (6-5/8x5", 68 pgs, B&W, Color-c)

nn - contains (3) sequential comic strips; one strip is (6) pages long; plus one (3) pages; one more (2) pager	75.00	150.00	300.00

GIBSON BOOK, THE (M,S)
Charles Scribner's Sons & R.H. Russell, New York: 1906 (11-3/8x17-5/8", gilted red hard-c, B&W)

Book I	50.00	100.00	200.00

NOTE: *Reprints in whole the books: Drawings, Pictures of People, London,Sketches and Cartoons, Education of Mr. Pipp, Americans. 414 pgs. 1907 2nd editions exist same value.*

Book II	50.00	100.00	200.00

NOTE: *Reprints in whole the books: A Widow and Her Friends, The Weaker Sex, Everyday People, Our Neighbors. 314 pgs 1907 second edition for both also exists. Same value.*

GIBSON'S PUBLISHED DRAWINGS, MR. (M,S) (see Plat index for later issues post 1900)
R.H. Russell, New York: No.1 1894 - No. 9 1904 (11x17-3/4", hard-c, B&W)

nn (No.1; 1894) Drawings 96 pgs	30.00	60.00	120.00
nn (No.2; 1896) Pictures of People 92 pgs	30.00	60.00	120.00
nn (No.3; 1898) Sketches and Cartoons 94 pgs	30.00	60.00	120.00
nn (No.4; 1899) The Education of Mr. Pipp 88 pgs	30.00	60.00	120.00
nn (No.5; 1900) Americans	30.00	60.00	120.00

NOTE: *By Charles Dana Gibson cartoons, reprinted from magazines, primarily **LIFE**. The Education of Mr. Pipp tells a story. Series continues how long after 1904? Each of these books originally came in a boxx and are worth more with the box.*

GIRL WHO WOULDN'T MIND GETTING MARRIED, THE (O)
Frederick Warne & Co., London & New York: nd (c1870's) (9-1/2x11-1/2", 28 pgs, printed 1 side, paper-c, B&W)

nn - By Harry Parkes	62.50	125.00	250.00

NOTE: *Published simultaneously with its companion volume, **The Man Who Would Like to Marry**.*

GOBLIN SNOB, THE (O)
DeWitt & Davenport, New York: nd (c1853-56) (24 x 17 cm, 96 pgs, B&W, color hard-c)

nn - (Rare) by H.L. Stephens	250.00	500.00	1000.00

GOLDEN ARGOSY
Frank A. Munsey, 81 Warren St, NYC: 1880s (10-1/2x12, 16 pgs, B&W)

issues with full page comic strips by Chips and Bisbee	20.00	40.00	60.00

GOLDEN DAYS, THE
James Elverson, Publisher, NYC: March 6 1880-May 11 1907 weekly, 16 pgs

issues with comic strips	4.00	7.50	15.00
Horatio Alger issues	10.00	20.00	40.00
v10 #49-v11#1 1889 first Stratemeyer story	25.00	50.00	100.00

GOLDEN WEEKLY, THE
Frank Tousey, NYC: #1 Sept 25 1889-#145 Aug 18 1892 (10-3/4x14-1/2, 16 pgs, B&W)

average issue with comic striips	15.00	25.00	50.00

GREAT LOCOFOCO JUGGERNAUT, THE (S)
publisher unknown: Fall/Winter 1837 (7-5/8x3-1/4, handbill single page)

The Story of Han's The Swapper Cover & First Two Panels
1865 © L. Pranc & Co, Boston

Humpty Dumpty, The Adventures of...
© Gantz, Jones and Co.

Imagerie d'Epinal
1888 © Mumoristic Publishing Co.

FR1.0 GD2.0 FN6.0

nn - By David Claypoole Johnston (a VG copy sold for $2000 in 2005)
nn - **Imprint Society:** 1971 (reprint) 6.00 12.00 25.00

HALF A CENTURY OF ENGLISH HISTORY (S. M)
G.P. Putnam's Sons - The Knickerbocker Press, New York and London: 1884 (7-3/4 x 5-3/4", 316 pgs., illustrated hard-c)
nn - By Various 25.00 50.00 175.00
NOTE: *Subtitle: Pictorially Presented in a Series of Cartoons from the Collection of Mr. Punch. Comprising 150 plates by Doyle, Leech, Tenniel, and others, in which are portrayed the political careers of Peel, Palmerston, Russell, Cobden, Bright, Beaconsfield, Derby, Salisbury, Gladstone and other English statesmen.*

HAIL COLUMBIA! HISTORICAL, COMICAL, AND CENTENNIAL (O,S)
The Graphic Co., New York & Walter F. Brown, Providence, RI: 1876 (10x11-3/8", 60 pgs, red gilted hard-c, B&W)
nn - by Walter F. Brown (Scarce) 100.00 200.00 450.00

HANS HUCKEBEIN'S BATCH OF ODD STORIES ODDLY ILLUSTRATEDED
McLoughlin Bros., New York: 1880s (9-3/4x7-3/8, 36?? pg?
nn - By Wilhelm Busch (Rare) 75.00 150.00 300.00

HANS THE SWAPPER, THE STORY OF (O)
L. Pranc & Co., 159 Washington St, Boston: 1865 (33 inch long fold out in colors)
nn - unique fold out comic book on one long piece of paper 75.00 150.00 300.00

HARPER'S NEW MONTHLY MAGAZINE
Harper & Brothers, Franklin Square, NY: 1850-1870s (6-3/4x10, 140 pgs, paper-c, B&W)
1850s issues with comic strips in back advert section 20.00 30.00 50.00

HEALTH GUYED (I)
Frederick A. Stokes Company: 1890 (5-3/8 x 8-3/8, 56 pgs, hardcover, B&W)
nn - By Frank P.W. ("Chip") Bellew (Junior) 25.00 50.00 175.00
NOTE: *Text & cartoon illustration parody of a health guide.*

HEATHEN CHINEE, THE (O)
Western News Co.: 1870 (5-1/32x7-1/4, B&W, paper)
nn - 10 sheets printed on one side came in envelope 75.00 150.00 300.00

HITS AT POLITICS (M,S)
R.H. Russell, New York: 1899 (15" x 12", 156 pgs, B&W, hard-c)
nn - W.A. Rogers c/a 100.00 200.00 300.00
NOTE: *Collection of W.A. Rogers cartoons, all reprinted from Harper's Weekly. Includes Spanish-American War cartoons.*

THE HOME CIRCLE
Garrett & Co, NY: 1854-56 (26x19", 4 pgs, B&W)

	FR	GD	FN
1 (1/54) beautiful ad of Garrett Building	100.00	200.00	400.00
2/4 (4/66) Cover ad for Yale College Scraps	100.00	200.00	400.00
2/5 (5/55) First ad for Oscas Shanghai	75.00	150.00	300.00
2/6 (6/55) another ad forOscas Snanghai	75.00	150.00	300.00
2/8 (#20) (8/55) Oscar Shanghai comic book cover repro	200.00	400.00	800.00
3/1 (#25) (1/56)	200.00	400.00	800.00

NOTE: Garrett's 2nd comic book Courtship of Chavalier Slyfox-Wikoff

	FR	GD	FN
3/8 (#32) (8/56)	50.00	100.00	200.00

NOTE: First print ad for Foreign Tour of Messrs. Brown, Jones, and Robinson

	FR	GD	FN
35 (11/56) first official Garrett, Dick & Fitzgerald issue	50.00	100.00	200.00
37 (1/57)	100.00	200.00	400.00

NOTE: Front page comic strip repro ad for Messrs. Brown, Jones, and Robinson's Foreign Tour; Back cover full of short sequentials, singles panel

HOME MADE HAPPY. A ROMANCE FOR MARRIED MEN IN SEVEN CHAPTERS (O,P)
Genuine Durham Smoking Tobacco & The Graphic Co.: nd (c1870's) (5-1/4 tall x 3-3/8" wide folded, 27" wide unfolded, color cardboard)
nn - With all 8 panels attached (Scarce) 30.00 60.00 200.00
nn - Individual panels/cards 5.00 10.00 25.00
NOTE: *Consists of 8 attached cards, printed on one side, which unfold into a strip story of title card & 7 panels. Scrapbook hobbyists in the 19th Century tended to pull the panels apart to paste into their scrapbooks, making copies with all panels still attached scarce.*

HOME PICTURE BOOK FOR LITTLE CHILDREN (E,P)
Home Insurance Company, New York: July 1887 (8 x 6-1/8", 36 pgs, b&w, color paper-c)
nn (Scarce) 40.00 80.00 160.00
NOTE: *Contains an abbreviated 32-panel reprinting of "The Toothache" by George Cruikshank. Remainder of booklet does not contain comics. Some copies known to exist do not contain The Toothache - buyer beware!*

HOOD'S COMICALITIES. COMICAL PICTURES FROM HIS WORKS (E,S)
Porter & Coates: 1880 (8-1/2x10-3/8", 104 pgs, printed one side, hard-c, B&W)
nn 30.00 50.00 100.00
NOTE: *Reprints 4 cartoon illustrations per page from the British Hood's Comic Annuals, which were poetry books by Thomas Hood.*

HOOKEYBEAK THE RAVEN, AND OTHER TALES (see also JACK HUCKABACK, THE SCAPEGRACE RAVEN) (E)
George Routledge and Sons, London & New York: nd (1878) (7-1/4x5-5/8", 104 pgs, hardcover, B&W)
nn - By Wilhelm Busch (Rare) 100.00 200.00 400.00

HOW ADOLPHUS SLIM-JIM USED JACKSON'S BEST, AND WAS HAPPY. A LENGTHY TALE IN 7 ACTS. (O,P)
Jackson's Best Chewing Tobacco & Donaldson Brothers: nd(c1870's) (5-1/8 tall x 3-3/8" wide folded, 27" wide unfolded, color cardboard)
nn - With all 8 panels attached (Scarce) 30.00 60.00 200.00
nn - Individual panels/cards 5.00 10.00 25.00
NOTE: *Consists of 8 attached cards, printed on one side, which unfold into a strip story of title card & 7 panels. Scrapbook hobbyists in the 19th Century tended to pull the panels apart topaste into their scrapbooks, making copies with all panels still attached scarce.*

HOW DAYS' DURHAM STANDARD OF THE WORLD SMOKING TOBACCO MADE TWO PAIRS OF TWINS HAPPY (O,P)
J.R. Day & Bro. Standard Durham Smoking Tobacco, Durham, NC: nd (c late 1870's/early 1880's) (3-5/8" x 5-1/2", folded, 21-3/4" tall unfolded, color cardboard)
nn- With all 6 panels attached (Scarce) 120.00 240.00 480.00
nn- Individual panels/cards 20.00 40.00 60.00
NOTE: *Highly sought by both Black Americana and Tobacciana collectors. Recurring mid-19th Century story about two African-American twin brothers who romance and marry a pair of African-American twin sisters. Although the text is racist at points, the art is not. Consists of 6 attached cards, printed on one side, which unfold downwards into a strip story of title card & 5 panels. Scrapbook hobbyists in the 19th Century tended to pull the panels apart and paste into their scrapbooks, making copies with all panels attached scarce. Note, there are numerous cartoon tellings of this same story, including several card series versions (with different art, and story variations, each time). But, the above is the only version which unfolds as a strip of attached cards. The cards from all the unattached versions are smaller sized, and thus distinguishable.*

HUGGINIANA; OR, HUGGINS' FANTASY, BEING A COLLECTION OF THE MOST ESTEEMED MODERN LITERARY PRODUCTIONS (I,S,P)
H.C. Southwick, New York: 1808 (296 pgs, printed one side, B&W, hard-c)
nn - (Very Rare)) (no known sales)
NOTE: *The earliest known surviving collected promotional cartoons in America. This is a booklet collecting 7 folded plus 1 full page flyer advertisements for barber John Richard Desborus Huggins, who hired American artists Elkanah Tisdale and William S. Leney to modify previously published illustrations into cartoons referring to his barber shop.*

HUMOROUS MASTERPIECES - PICTURES BY JOHN LEECH (E,M)
Frederick A. Stokes: nd (late 1900's - early 1910's) No.1-2 (5-5/8x3-7/8", 68 pgs, cardboard covers, B&W)
1- John Leech (single panel cartoon-r from **Punch**) 20.00 40.00 80.00
2- John Leech (single panel cartoon-r from **Punch**) 20.00 40.00 80.00

HUMOURIST, THE (E,I,S)
C.V. Nickerson and Lucas and Deaver, Baltimore: No.1 Jan 1829 - No.12 Dec 1829 (5-3/4x3-1/2", B&W text w/hand colored cartoon pg.)
Bound volume No.1-12 (Very Rare; copies in libraries 270 pgs) (no known sales)
NOTE: *Earliest known American published periodical to contain a cartoon every issue. Surviving individual issues currently unknown -- all information comes from 1 surviving bound volume. Each issue is mostly text, with one full page hand-colored cartoon. Bound volume contains an additional hand-colored cartoons at front of each six month set (total of 14 cartoons in volume). Cartoons appear to be of British origin, possibly by George Cruikshank.*

HUMPTY DUMPTY, ADVENTURES OF...(I,P)
1877 (Promotional 4x3-1/2", 12 page chapbook from Gantz, Jones & Co, 10¢-c.)
nn-Promotes Gantz Sea Foam Baking Powder; early app. of a costumed character, dressed as Humpty Dumpty 50.00 100.00 400.00

HUSBAND AND WIFE, OR THE STORY OF A HAIR. (O,P)
Garland Stoves and Ranges, Michigan Stove Co.: 1883 (4-3/16 tall x 2-11/16" wide folded, 16" wide unfolded, color cardboard)
nn - With all 6 panels attached (Scarce) 25.00 50.00 125.00
nn - Individual panels/cards 5.00 10.00 25.00
NOTE: *Consists of 6 attached cards, printed on one side, which unfold into a strip story of title card & 5 panels. Scrapbook hobbyists in the 19th Century tended to pull the panels apart topaste into their scrapbooks, making copies with all panels still attached scarce.*

ICHABOD ACADEMICUS, THE COLLEGE EXPERIENCES OF (O,G)
William T. Peters, New Haven, CT: 1850 (5-1/2x9-3/4",108 pgs, B&W)
nn - By William T. Peters (Rare) 1000.00 2000.00 4000.00
NOTE: *Pages are not uniform in size. Also, a copy showed up on eBay with misspelled Academicus. Has "n" instead of "m" - not known yet which printing is earliest version.*

ICHABOD ACADEMICUS, THE COLLEGE EXPERIENCES OF (O,G)
Dick & Fitzgerald, New York: nd (1870s-1888) (paper-c, B&W)
nn - By William T. Peters (Very Rare) 250.00 500.00 1000.00
NOTE: *Pages are uniform in size.*

ILLUSTRATED SCRAP-BOOK OF HUMOR AND INTELLIGENCE (M)
John J. Dyer & Co.: nd (c1859-1860)
nn - Very Rare 200.00 400.00 800.00
NOTE: *A "printed scrapbook" of images culled from some unidentified periodical. About half of it is illustrations that would have accompanied prose pieces. There are pages of single panel cartoons (multiple per page). And there are roughly 8 to 12 pages of sequential comics (all different stories, but appears to all be by the same presently unidentified artist).*

THE ILLUSTRATED WEEKLY
Chars C Lucas & Co, 11 Dey St, NY: 1876 (15x18", 8pgs, 8¢ per issue)

	FR	GD	FN
2/8 (2/19/76) back-c all sequential comic strips	100.00	200.00	400.00
2/12 (3/18/76) full page of British-r sequentials	100.00	200.00	400.00
2/14 (4/1/76) April Fool Issue - (6) panel center; plus more	100.00	200.00	400.00
2/15 (4/8/76) (6) panel sequential	100.00	200.00	400.00
issues without comic strips	12.50	25.00	50.00

Jingo No. 3, Sept 24
1884 © Art Newspaper Co, Boston & NYC

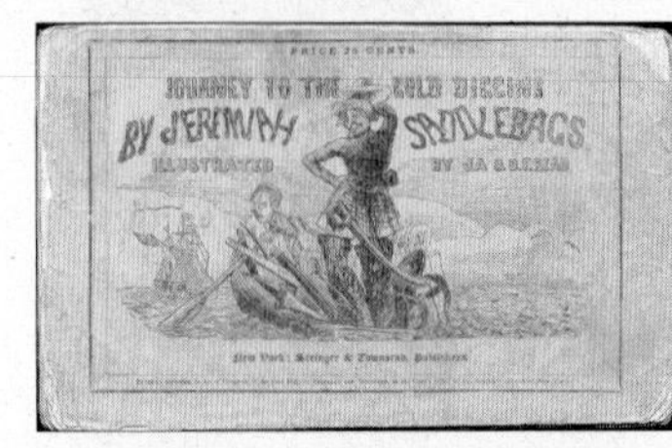

Journey To The Gold Diggings By Jeremiah Saddlebags
1849 © Various - First Original USA Comic Book

Judge, No. 1, October 29, 1881
1881 © Judge Publishing, NYC

ILLUSTRATIONS OF THE POETS: FROM PASSAGES IN THE LIFE OF LITTLE BILLY VIDKINS (See A Day's Sport...)
S. Robinson, Philadelphia: May 1849 (14.7 cm x 11.3 cm, 32 pgs, B&W)

nn - by Henry Stephens (very rare) (no known sales)
NOTE: *Predates Journey to the Gold Diggins By Jeremiah Saddlebags by a few months and is an original American proto-comic strip book. More research needs to be done. A later edition brought $800 in G/VG 2007*

IMAGERIE d'EPINAL (untrimmed individual sheets) (E)
Pellerin for Humoristic Publishing Co, Kansas City, Mo.: nd (1888) No.1-60 (15-7/8x11-3/4",single sheets, hand colored) (All are Rare)

1-14, 21, 22, 25-46, 49-60 - in the Album d'Images 17.50 35.00 70.00
15-20, 23,24, 47, 48 - not in the Album d'Images 30.00 60.00 120.00
NOTE: *Printed and hand colored in France expressly for the Humoristic Publishing Company . Printed on one side only. These are single sheets, sold separately. Reprints and translates the sheets from their original French.*

IMAGERIE d'EPINAL ALBUM d'IMAGES (E)
Pellerin for Humoristic Publishing Co., Kansas City. Mo: nd (1888) (15-1/2x11-1/2",108 pgs plus full color hard-c, hand colored interior)

nn - Various French artists (Rare) 400.00 800.00 2000.00
NOTE: *Printed and hand colored in France expressly for the Humoristic Publishing Company . Printed on one side only. This is supposedly a collection of sixty broadsheets, originally sold separately. All copies known only have fifty of the sixty known of these broadsheets (slightly bigger, before binding, trimming the margins in the process, down to 15-1/4x11-3/8".). Three slightly different covers known to exist, with or without the indication in French "Textes en Anglais" ("Texts in Englishi), with or without the general title "Contes de FEes" ("Fairy Tales"). All known copies were collected with sheets 15-20, 23,24, 47, and 48 missing.*

IN LAUGHLAND (M)
R.H. Russell, New York: 1899 (14-9/16x12", 72 pgs, hard-c)

nn - By Henry "Hy" Mayer (scarce) 150.00 300.00 600.00
NOTE: *Mostly strips plus single panel cartoon-r from various magazines. The majority are reprinted from Life, with the rest from: Truth, Dramatic Mirror, Black and White, Figaro Illustre, Le Rire, and Fliegende Blatter.*

IN THE "400" AND OUT (M,S) (see also **THE TAILOR-MADE GIRL**)
Keppler & Schwarzmann, New York: 1888 (8-1/4x12", 64 pgs, hardc, B&W)

nn - By C.J. Taylor 42.50 85.00 170.00
NOTE: *Cartoons reprinted from **Puck**. The "400" is a reference to New York City's aristocratic elite.*

IN VANITY FAIR (M,S)
R.H.Russell & Son, New York: 1896 (11-7/8x17-7/8", 80 pgs, hard-c, B&W)

nn - By A.B.Wenzell, r-LIFE and HARPER'S 45.00 90.00 180.00

JACK HUCKABACK, THE SCAPEGRACE RAVEN (see also HOOKEYBEAK THE RAVEN) (E)
Stroefer & Kirchner, New York: nd (c1877) (9-3/8x6-3/8", 56 pgs, printed one side only, hand colored hardcover, B&W interior)

nn - By Wilhelm Busch (Rare) 75.00 150.00 350.00
NOTE: *The 1877 date is derived from a gift signature on one known copy. The publication date might in truth be earlier.* There are also professionally hand colored copies known to exist which would be worth more.

JEFF PETTICOATS
American News Company, NY: July 1865 (23 inches folded out; 6-1/4x8 folded,, B&W)
nn - Very Rare Frank Bellew (6) panel sequential foldout (10¢) (no known sales)
NOTE: printed also in **FUNNYEST OF AWL AND THE FUNNIEST SORT OF PHUN** #9 (July 1865) (6) panel strip hanging Jeff Davis; This sold hundreds of thousand of copies in its day

JINGO (M,O)
Art Newspaper Co., Boston & New York: No.1 Sept 10, 1884 - No.11 Nov 19, 1884 (10 cents, 13-7/8" x 10-1/4",16 pgs, color front/back-c and center, remainder B&W, paper-c)

1-11(Rare) 50.00 100.00 200.00
NOTE: *Satirical Republican propaganda magazine, modeled after **Puck** and **Judge**, which was published during the last couple months of the 1884 Presidential Election campaign. The Republicans lost, **Jingo** ceased publication, and Republican backers soon after purchased **Judge** magazine.*

JOHN-DONKEY, THE (O, S)
George Dexter, Burgess, Stringer & Co., NYC: 1848 (10x7.5",16 pgs,B&W, 6¢

1 Jan 1 1848 75.00 150.00 300.00
2-end (last issue Aug 12 1848) 50.00 100.00 200.00

JOLLY JOKER
Frank Leslie, NY: 1862-1878 (B&W, 10¢)

20/6 (July 1877) (Bellew Opper cover & single panels 150.00 300.00 600.00

JOLLY JOKER, OR LAUGH ALL-ROUND
Dick & Fitzgerald, NY: 1870s? (8-1/4x4-7/8", 148, B&W, illustrated green cover)

nn - cartoons on every page 100.00 200.00 400.00

JONATHAN'S WHITTLINGS OF THE WAR (O, S)
T.W. Strong, 98 Nassau St, NYC: April 1854-July 8 1854 (11.5x8.5", 16 pgs, B&W)

1 April 1854 100.00 200.00 400.00
NOTE: *Begins Frank Bellew's sequential comic strip* "Mr. Hookemcumsnivey, A Russian Gentleman, Hears That His Country Is In A State of War"
2-12 (July 8 1854) Many Bellew & Hopkins 100.00 200.00 400.00

JOURNAL CARRIER'S GREETING
???, Minn, Minn: 1897-98? (giveaway promo, 10-1/8x8-1/4, 36, B&W, paper-c)
nn - rare 50.00 100.00 200.00

JOURNEY TO THE GOLD DIGGINS BY JEREMIAH SADDLEBAGS (O,G)
Various publishers: 1849 (25 cents, 5-5/8 x 8-3/4", 68 pgs, green & black paper cover, B&W interior)

nn -- New York edition, Stringer & Townsend, Publishers (Very Rare) By J.A. and D.F. Read. 5000.00 8000.00 13000.00
nn -- Cincinnati, Ohio edition, published by U.P. James (Very Rare) By J.A. and D.F. Read. 5000.00 8000.00 13000.00
nn -- 1950 reprint, with introduction, published by William P. Wreden, Burlingame, California: 1950 (5-7/8 x 9", 92 pgs, hardcover, color interior) (390 copies printed) By J.A. and D.F. Read. 67.50 125.00 250.00
NOTE: *Earliest known original sequential comic book by an American creator; directly inspired by Töpffer's **Obadiah Oldbuck** and **Bachelor Butterfly** The New York and Cincinnati editions were both published in 1849, one soon after the other. Antiquarian Book sources have traditionally cited that the Cincinnati edition preceded the New York, but without referencing their evidence. Conflicting with this, the Cincinnati edition lists the New York publishers' 1849 copyright, while the New York edition makes no reference to the Cincinnati publishers. Such would indicate that the New York edition was first. Both are very rare, and until resolved both will be regarded as published simultaneously. A New York copy with missing back cover, detached front cover, and G/VG interior sold for $2000 in 2000. Two copies sold at auction in 2006 for $11,500 and 12,000. (Prices vary widely.)*

JUDGE (M,O)
Judge Publishing, New York: No.1 Oct 29, 1881 - No. 950, Dec ??, 1899 (10 cents, color front/back c and centerspread, remainder B&W, paper-c)

1 (Scarce) (no known sales)
2-26 (Volume 1; Scarce) 30.00 50.00 100.00
27-790,792-950 12.50 25.00 50.00
791 (12/12/1896; Vol.31) - classic satirical-c depicting Tammany Hall politicians as the Yellow Kid & Cox's Brownies 75.00 200.00 400.00
Bound Volumes (six month, 26 issue run each):
Vol. 1 (Scarce) (no known sales)
Vol. 2-30,32-37 140.00 280.00 600.00
Vol. 31 - includes issue 791 **YK/Brownies** parody 200.00 250.00 750.00
NOTE: *Rival publication to Puck. Purchased by Republican Party backers, following their loss in the 1884 Presidential Election, to become a Republican propaganda satire magazine.*

JUDGE, GOOD THINGS FROM
Judge Publishing Co., NY: 1887 (13-3/4x10.5", 68 pgs, color paper-c)

1 first printing 50.00 100.00 200.00
NOTE: Zimmerman, Hamilton, Victor, Woolf, Beard, Ehrhart, De Meza, Howarth, Smith, Alfred Mitchell

JUDGE'S LIBRARY (M)
Judge Publishing, New York: No.1, April 1890 - No. 141, Dec 1899 (10 cents, 11x8-1/8", 36 pgs, color paper-c, B&W)

1 10.00 20.00 40.00
2-141 10.00 20.00 40.00
151-??? (post-1900 issues; see Platinum Age section)
NOTE: ***Judge's Library** was a monthly magazine reprinting cartoons & prose from **Judge**, with each issue's material organized around the same subject. The cover art was often original. All issues were kept in print for the duration of the series, so later issues are more scarce than earlier ones.*

JUDGE'S QUARTERLY (M)
Judge Publishing Company/Arkell Publishing Company, New York: No.1 April 1892 - 31 Oct 1899 (25¢, 13-3/4x10-1/4", 64 pgs, color paper-c, B&W)

1-11 13-31 contents presently unknown to us 15.00 30.00 60.00
12 ZIM Sketches From Judge Jan 1895 100.00 200.00 400.00
NOTE: *Similar to **Judge's Library**, except larger in size, and issued quarterly. All reprint material, except for the cover art.*

JUDGE'S SERIALS (M,S)
Judge Publishing, New York: March 1888 (10x7.5", 36 pgs)

#3 - Eugene Zimmerman 100.00 200.00 400.00
NOTE: *A bit of sequential comic strips; mostly single panel cartoons. This series runs to at least #8.*

JUDY
Burgess, Stringer & Co., 17 Ann St, NYC: Nov 28 1846-Feb 20 47 (11x8.5",12 pgs,B&W)

1 Nov 28 1846 67.50 125.00 250.00
2-13 50.00 100.00 200.00

JUVENILE GEM, THE (see also THE ADVENTURES OF MR. TOM PLUMP, and OLD MOTHER MITTEN) (O,I)
Huestis & Cozans: nd (1850-1852) (6x3-7/8", 64 pgs, hand colored paper-c, B&W) (all versions Very Rare)

nn - First printing(s) publisher's address is 104 Nassau Street (1850-1851) (1 copy sold for $800.00 in Fair)
nn - 2nd printing(s) publisher's address is 116 Nassau Street (1851-1852) (no known sales)
nn - 3rd printing(s) publisher's address is 107 Nassau Street (1852+) (no known sales)
NOTE: *The JUVENILE GEM is a gathering of multiple booklets under a single, hand colored cover (none of the interior booklets have the covers which they were given when sold separately). The publisher appears to have gathered whichever printings of each booklet were available when copies of THE JUVENILE GEM was assembled, so that the booklets within, and the corresponding cover, may be from a mixture of printings. Contains two sequential comic booklets: THE ADVENTURES OF MR. TOM PLUMP, and OLD MOTHER MITTEN AND HER FUNNY KITTEN, plus five heavily illustrated children's booklets - **The Pretty Primer**, **The Funny Book**, **The Picture Book**, **The Two Sisters**, and **Story Of The Little Drummer**. Six of these -- including the two comic books -- were reprinted in the 1960's by Americana Review as a set of individual booklets, and included in a folder collectively titled "Six Children's Books of the 1850's".*

LANTERN, THE
Stringer & Townsend:1852-1853 (11x8-3/8", 12 pgs, soft paper, 6 ¢)

Leslie's Young America #1
1881 © Leslie & Company, NYC

Life's Book of Animals
1888 © Doubleday & McClure Co.

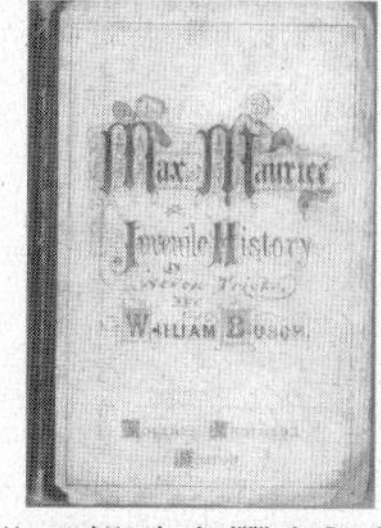

Max and Maurice by Wilhelm Busch
1871 © Roberts Bros, Boston

FR1.0 GD2.0 FN6.0

1 Jan 10, 1852 37.50 75.00 150.00
2 25.00 50.00 100.00
3 First Frank Bellew cartoons onwards each issue 37.50 75.00 150.00
4 Bellew 's Mr Blobb begins 1/31/52 50.00 100.00 200.00
NOTE: *Bellew serial sequential comic strip "Mr Blobb In Search Of A Physician" becomes 2nd earliest known recurring character in American comic strips plus full page single panel Bellew cartoon "The Modern Frankenstein" take-off on Shelly's story.*
5 Hunsdale 2-panel "The Horrors of Slavery"; Mr Blobb 50.00 100.00 200.00
6 DF Read 15 panel "A Volley of Valentines"; Mr Blobb 50.00 100.00 200.00
7-8 10 Bellew's Mr Blobb continues 25.00 50.00 100.00
9 (4) panel "The Perils of Leap Year" MrBlobb 50.00 100.00 200.00
11 no Mr Blobb 20.00 40.00 80.00
12 Bellew's Mr Blobb continues 3/27/52 50.00 100.00 200.00
13 Bellew (10) panel sequential "Stump Speaking Studied" 50.00 100.00 200.00
14 no comic strips 20.00 40.00 80.00
15 Bellew's Mr Blobb ends (5) panel 4/17/52 50.00 100.00 200.00
16 Bellew begins new comic strip serial, "Mr. Bulbear, A Stockbroker, After having Supped at Delmonicos, Has A Dream", Part One, (6) panels 50.00 100.00 200.00
17 Bellew's Mr Bulbear continues 25.00 50.00 100.00
18 Bellew (8) panel "Trials of a Witness" 50.00 100.00 200.00
19 Bellew's Mr Bulbear's Dream continues 25.00 50.00 100.00
20-23 no comic strips 20.00 40.00 80.00
24 Bellew "Trials of a Publisher" (6) panel 50.00 100.00 200.00
25 comic strip "Travels of Jonathan Verdant"recurring character 25.00 50.00 100.00
26-49 contents to be indexed soon
50 (12/18/52) (2) panel Impertinent Smile 25.00 50.00 100.00
58 (2/12/53) (6) panel Trip to California 25.00 50.00 100.00
66 (4/9/53) (3) panel sequential strip 25.00 50.00 100.00

LAST SENSATION, THE (Becomes Day's Doings)
James Watts, NYC: Dec 27 1867-May 30 1868 (11x16 folio-size, 16 pgs, B&W)
issues with comic strips 50.00 100.00 200.00

LAUGH AND GROW FAT COMIC ALMANAC
Fisher & Brother, Philadelphia, New York & Boston: 1860-? (36 pgs)
nn 60.00 120.00 240.00

LEGEND OF SAM'L OF POSEN (O)
M.B. Curtis Company: 1884-85 (8x3-3/8", 44 pgs, Color-c, B&W interior)
nn - By M.B. Curtis 50.00 100.00 200.00
NOTE: Cover blurb says: From Early Days in Fatherland to affluence And Success in the Land of His Adoption, America

LESLIE'S YOUNG AMERICA (O. S)
Leslie & Co, 98 Chamber St, NY: 1881-82 (11-1/2x8", 5¢, B&W)
1 (7/9/81) back cover (6) panel strip 125.00 250.00 500.00
2 (7/16/81) back cover (9) panel strip 50.00 100.00 200.00
3 (7/23/81) back cover (16) panel Busch strip 67.50 125.00 250.00
9 (9/3/81) sequentials; Hopkins singles 50.00 100.00 200.00
15 (10/15/81) Zim or Frost? (6) panel strip 50.00 100.00 200.00
19 (11/12/81) (9) panel back-c strip 50.00 100.00 200.00
24 (4) panel strip 25 (2) panel back-c strip 50.00 100.00 200.00
26 27 (6) panel back-c strip 50.00 100.00 200.00
29 31 (12) panel strip 50.00 100.00 200.00
32 (2/11/82) (8) panel strip 50.00 100.00 200.00
issues without comic strips or Jules Verne 25.00 50.00 100.00
NOTE: Jules Verne stories begin with #1 and run thru at least #42

LIFE (M,O) (continues with Vol.35 No. 894+ in the Platinum Age section)
J.A.Mitchell: Vol.1 No.1 Jan. 4, 1883 - Vol.1 No.26 June 29, 1883 (10-1/4x8", 16 pgs, B&W, paper cover); J.A. Mitchell: Vol. 2 No. 27, July 5, 1883 - Vol. 6 No.148, Oct 29, 1885 (10-1/4x8-1/4", 16 pgs., B&W, paper cover); Mitchell & Miller: Vol.6 No.149, Nov. 5, 1885 - Vol. 31, No. 796, March 17, 1898 (10-3/8x8-3/8", 16 pgs., B&W, paper cover); Life Publishing Company: Vol. 31 No. 797, March 24, 1898 - Vol. 34 No. 893, Dec 28, 1899 (10-3/8 x 8-1/2", 20 pgs., B&W, paper cover)
1-26 (Scarce) (no known sales)
27-799 5.00 10.00 20.00
800 (4/7/1898) parody Yellow Kid / Spanish-American War cover (not by Outcault) 67.50 125.00 250.00
801-893 5.00 10.00 20.00
NOTE: *All covers for issues 1 - 26 are identical, apart from issue number & date.*
Hard bound collected volumes:
V. 1 (No.1-26) (Scarce) 67.50 125.00 250.00
V. 2-34 45.00 90.00 180.00
V. 31 YK #800 parody-c not by RFO 70.00 140.00 280.00
NOTE: *Because the covers of all issues in Volume 1 are identical, it was common practice to remove the covers before binding the issues together. This is not true of later volumes, though, in all volumes it was common to drop the advertising pages which appeared at the rear of each issue. Information on many more individual issues will expand next Guide.*

LIFE AND ADVENTURES OF JEFF DAVIS (I)
J.C. Haney & Co., NY: 1865 (10 cents, 7-1/2" x 4", 36 pgs, B&W, paper-c)
nn - By McArone (Scarce) 150.00 300.00 650.00
nn - 1974 Reprint (350) copies 6-3/4x4-3/8 50.00 10.00 20.00
nn - 1997 Reprint (7th Fla. Sutler, Clearwater, 6-3/4x4-1/4") - - 2.00
NOTE: *Humorous telling of the capture of Confederate President Jeff Davis in women's clothing, from the publisher of Merryman's Monthly. It contains an ad page for that publication; the material is perhaps reprinted from it. J.C. Haney licensed it to local printers, and so various publishers are found -- all printings currently regarded as simultaneous. (The Geo. H. Hees printing, Oswego, NY, contains an ad for the upcoming October 1865 issue of Merryman's Monthly, thus placing that printing in September 1865). Modern facsimile editions have been produced.*

LIFE IN PHILADELPHIA
W. Simpson, 66 Chestnut, Philadelphia; Siltart, No. 65 South Third St, Philadelphia: 1830 (7-3/4x6-7/8", 15 loose plates, hand colored copies exist, maybe B&W also)
nn - By Edward Williams Clay (1799-1857) (Very Rare) (no known sales)
NOTE: *First 13 plates etched, with many word balloons; scenes of exaggerated Black Americana in Philadelphia viewed one by one as broadsides. Had several publishers over the years. Was also eventually collected into a book of same name but only with the first 13 plates used; the last two not used in book. Collected book not yet viewed to share info.*

LIFE'S BOOK OF ANIMALS (M.S)
Doubleday & McClure Co.: 1898 (7-1/4x10-1/8", 88 pgs, color hardcover, B&W)
nn 25.00 50.00 100.00
NOTE: *Reprints funny animal single panel and strip cartoons reprinted from LIFE. Art by Blaisdell, Chip Bellew, Kemble, Hy Mayer, Sullivant, Woolf.*

LIFE'S COMEDY (M,S)
Charles Scribner's Sons: Series 1 1897 - Series 3 1898 (12x9-3/8", hardcover, B&W)
1 (142 pgs). 2, 3 (138 pgs) 60.00 120.00 240.00
NOTE: *Gibson a-1-3; c-3. Hy Mayer a-1-3. Rose O'Neill a-2-3. Stanlaws a-2-3. Sullivant a-1-2. Verbeek a-2. Wenzell a-1-3; c(painted)-2.*

LIFE, THE GOOD THINGS OF (M,S)
White, Stokes, & Allen, NY: 1884 - No.3 1886 ; Frederick A. Stokes, NY: No.4 1887; Frederick Stokes & Brother, NY: No.5 1888 - No.6 1889; Frederick A. Stokes Company, NY: No. 7 1890 - No.10 1893 (8-3/8x10-1/2", 74 pgs, gilted hardcover, B&W)
nn - 1884 (most common issue) 32.50 65.00 130.00
2 - 1885 32.50 65.00 130.00
3 - 1886 (76 pgs) 32.50 65.00 130.00
4 - 1887 (76 pgs) 32.50 65.00 130.00
5 - 1888 32.50 65.00 130.00
6 - 1889 32.50 65.00 130.00
7 - 1890 32.50 65.00 130.00
8 - 1891 (scarce) 50.00 100.00 200.00
9 - 1892 32.50 65.00 130.00
10 - 1893 32.50 65.00 130.00
NOTE: *Contains mostly single panel, and some sequential, comics reprinted from LIFE. Attwood a-1-4,10. Roswell Bacon a-5. Chip Bellew a-4-6. Frank Bellew a-4,6. Palmer Cox a-1. H. E. Dey a-5. C. D. Gibson a-4-10. F.M. Howarth a-5-6. Kemble a-1-3. Klapp a-5. Walt McDougall a-1-2. H. McVickar a-5; J. A. Mitchell a-5. Peter Newell a-2-3. Gray Parker a-4-5,7. J. Smith a-5. Albert E. Steiner a-5; T. S. Sullivant a-7-9. Wenzell a-8-10. Wilder a-3. Woolf a-3-6.)*

LIFE, THE SPICE OF (E,M,)
White and Allen: NY & London: 1888 (8-3/8x10-1/2",76 pgs, hard-c, B&W)
nn 50.00 100.00 200.00
NOTE: *Resembles **THE GOOD THINGS OF LIFE** in layout and format, and appears to be an attempt to compete with their former partner Frederick A. Stokes. However, the material is not from **LIFE**, but rather is reprinted and translated German sequential and single panel comics.*

LIFE'S PICTURE GALLERY (becomes LIFE'S PRINTS) (M,S,P)
Life Publishing Company, New York: nd (1898-1899) (paper cover, B&W) (all are scarce)
nn - (nd; 1898, 100 pgs, 5-1/4x8-1/2") Gibson-c of a woman with closed umbrella; 1st interior page announcing that after January 1, 1899 Gibson will draw exclusively for LIFE; the word "SPECIMEN" is printed in red, diagonally, across every print; a-Gibson, Rose O'Neill, Sullivant 37.50 75.00 150.00
nn - (nd; 1899, 128 pgs, 4-7/8x7-3/8") Gibson-c of a woman golfer; 1st interior page announcing that Gibson & Hanna, Jr. draw exclusively for LIFE; the word "SPECIMEN" is printed in red, horizontally, across every print. Includes prints from Gibson's **THE EDUCATION OF MR. PIPP**; a-Gibson, Sullivant 37.50 75.00 150.00
NOTE: *Catalog of prints reprinted from **LIFE** covers & centerspreads. The first catalog was given away free to anyone requesting it, but after many people got the catalog without ordering anything, subsequent catalogs were sold at 10 cents.*

LITTLE SICK BEAR, THE
Edwin W. Joy Co, San Francisco, CA: 1897 (6-1/4x5", 20 pgs, B&W, Scarce)
nn - By James Swinnerton one long sequential comic strip 200.00 400.00 800.00

LIGHT AND SHADE
William Drey Doppel Soap: 1892 (3-3/4x5-3/8", 20 pgs, B&W, color cover)
nn - By J.C. 50.00 100.00 200.00
NOTE: Contains (8) panel comic strip of black boy whose skin turns white using this soap.

LONDON OUT OF TOWN, OR THE ADVENTURES OF THE BROWNS AT THE SEA SIDE BY LUKE LIMNER, ESQ. (O)
David Bogue, 86 Fleet St, London: c1847 (5-1/2x4-1/4, 32 pgs, yellow paper hard-c, B&W
nn - By John Leighton 150.00 300.00 600.00
NOTE: one long sequential comic strip multiple-panel per page story; each page crammed with panels inspired by the Töpffer comic books Bogue began several years earlier.

LORGNETTE, THE (S)

Merryman's Monthly v3#5 with Bellew strip
May 1865 © J. C. Haney & Co., New York

Minneapolis Journal Cartoons Second Series
1895 © Minneapolis Journal

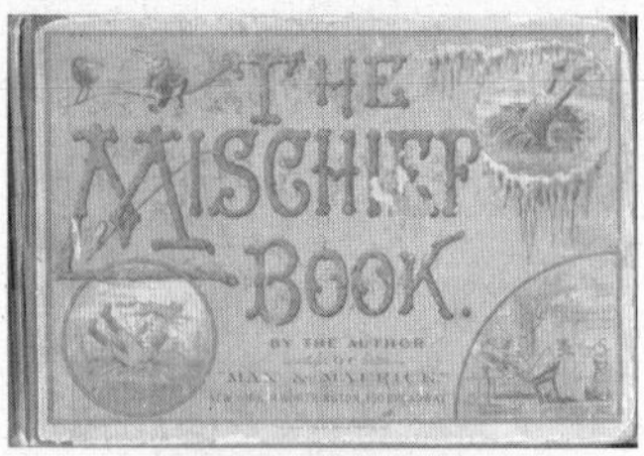

The Mischief Book by Wilhelm Busch
color cover art variation
1880 © R. Worthington, New York

George J Coombes, New York: 1886 (6-1/2x8-3/4, 38 pgs, hard-c, B&W)
nn - By J.K. Bangs 50.00 100.00 200.00

LOVING BALLAD OF LORD BATEMAN, THE (E,I)
G.W. Carleton & Co., Publishers, Madison Square, NY: 1871 (9x5-7/8",16 pgs, soft-c, 6¢)
nn - By George Cruikshank 50.00 100.00 200.00

MADISON'S EXPOSITION OF THE AWFUL & TERRIFYING CEREMONIES OF THE ODD FELLOWS
T.E. Peterson & Brothers, 306 Chestnut St, Phila: 1870s? (5-3/4x9-1/4, 68 pgs, B&W)
nn - single panel cartoons 50.00 100.00 200.00

MANNERS AND CUSTOMS OF YE HARVARD STUDENTE (M,S)
Houghton Mifflin & Co., Boston & Moses King, Cambridge: 1877 (7-7/8x11", 72 pgs, printed one side, hardc, B&W)
nn - by F.G. Attwood 75.00 150.00 300.00
NOTE: *Collection of cartoons originally serialized in the* ***Harvard Lampoon****. Attwood later became a major cartoonist for* ***Life****.*

MAN WHO WOULD LIKE TO MARRY, THE (O)
Frederick Warne & Co., London & New York: nd (c 1880's) (9-1/2x11-1/2", 28 pgs, printed 1 side, paper-c, B&W)
nn - By Harry Parkes 62.50 125.00 250.00
NOTE: *Published simultaneously with its companion volume,* ***The Girl Who Wouldn't Mind Getting Married****.*

MAX AND MAURICE: A JUVENILE HISTORY IN SEVEN TRICKS (E)
(see also Teasing Tom and Naughty Ned)
Roberts Brothers, Boston: 1871 first edition (8-1/8 x 5-1/2", 76 pgs, hard & soft-c B&W)
nn - By Wilhelm Busch (green or brown cloth hardbound) 275.00 550.00 1000.00
nn - exactly the same, but soft paper cover 162.00 325.00 650.00
NOTE: *Page count includes 56 pgs of art, two blank endpapers at the front (one colored), 8 pgs of ads at the back, two blank endpapers at the end (one colored), and the covers. Green or brown illustrated hardcover. The name of the author is given on the title page as "William Busch." We assume this to be the 1st edition. Back side of title page states: Entered according to Act of Congress, in the year 1870, by Roberts Brothers, In the office of the Librarian of Congress at Washington.*
nn - By Wilhelm Busch (1872 edition) 225.00 470.00 900.00
nn - 1875 reprint 100.00 200.00 450.00
nn - 1882 reprint (76 pgs, hand colored- c/a, 75¢) 100.00 200.00 400.00
nn- 1889 reprint with new art on cover printed in full color 100.00 200.00 400.00
NOTE: *Each of the above contains 56 pages of art and text in a transitional format between a regular children's book and a comic book (the page count difference is ad pages in back). Seminal inspiration for William Randolph Hearst to acquire as a "new comic" (following the wild success of Outcault's Yellow Kid) to license M&M from Busch and hire Rudolph Dirks in late 1897 to create a New York American newspaper incarnation. In Hearst's English language newspapers it was called The Katzenjammer Kids and in his German language NYC newspaper it was titled Max & Moritz, Busch's original title. At least 50 other reprints versions are reputed to exist printed thru 1900. Translated from the 1865 German original. We are still sorting out the edition confusion.*

MAX AND MAURICE: A JUVENILE HISTORY IN SEVEN TRICKS (E)
(see also Teasing Tom and Naughty Ned)
Little, Brown, and Company, Boston: 1898-1902 (8-1/8 x 5-3/4", 72 pgs, hardcover, black ink on orange paper) (various early reprints)
nn - 1898 , 1899 By Wilhelm Busch 50.00 100.00 200.00
nn - 1902 (64 pages, B&W) 10.00 30.00 90.00

MERRY MAPLE LEAVES Or A Summer In The Country (S)
E.P. Dutton And Company, New York: 1872 (9-3/8x7-3/8", 90 and 86 pgs pgs, hard-c)
nn - By Abner Perk 25.00 50.00 150.00
NOTE: *Each drawing contained in a maple leaf motif by Livingston Hopkins and others.*

MERRYMAN'S MONTHLY A COMIC MAGAZINE FOR THE FAMILY (M,O,E)
J.C. Haney & Co, NY: 1863-1875 (10-7/8x7-13/16", 30 pgs average, B&W)
Certain issues with sequential comics 100.00 200.00 400.00
NOTE: *Sequential strips by Frank Bellew Sr, Wilhelm Busch found so far; others?*

MERRYTHOUGHT, OR LAUGHTER FROM YEAR TO YEAR, THE
Fisher & Brother, Phila, Baltimore: early 1850s (4-1/2x7", B&W)
nn - many singles, some sequential (Very Rare) (no known sales)
NOTE: See Vict article for back cover pic which is earliest known use of the term Comic Book

MESSRS. BROWN, JONES, AND ROBINSON, THE FOREIGN TOUR OF
(see also **THE CLOWN, OR THE BANQUET OF WIT**) (E,M,O,G)
Bradbury & Evans, London: 1854 (11-5/8x9-1/2", 196 pgs, gilted hard-c, B&W)
nn - By Richard Doyle 35.00 70.00 200.00
nn - Bradbury & Evans 1900 reprint 20.00 40.00 80.00
NOTE: *Protective sheets between each page (not part of page count). Expanded and redrawn sequential comics story from the serialized episodes originally published in PUNCH. Also comes in a 174 pg 8-3/4x11" version.*

MESSRS. BROWN, JONES, AND ROBINSON, THE LAUGHABLE ADVENTURES OF (E,M,G)
Garrett, Dick & Fitzgerald, NY: nd (1856 or 1857) (5-3/4x9-1/4", 100 pgs, printed one side only, paper-c, B&W)
nn - (Very Rare) by Richard Doyle c/a 300.00 500.00 1100.00
NOTE: *1st American reprinting of the "Foreign Tour"; reformatted into a small oblong format. Links the earlier Garrett & Co. to the later Dick & Fitzgerald. Back cover reprints full size the Garrett & Co. version cover for Oscar Shanghai. Interior front cover reprints full size the Garrett & Co. version cover for Slyfox-Wikof. Issued without a title page.*

MESSRS. BROWN, JONES, AND ROBINSON, THE FOREIGN TOUR OF (E,M,G)
D. Appleton & Co., New York: 1860 & 1877 (11-5/8x9-1/2", 196 pgs, gilted hard-c, B&W)
nn - (1860 printing) by Richard Doyle 30.00 60.00 200.00
nn - (1871 printing) by Richard Doyle 30.00 60.00 150.00
nn - (1877 printing) by Richard Doyle 30.00 60.00 150.00
NOTE: *Protective sheets between each page (not part of page count). Reprints the Bradbury & Evans edition.*

MESSRS BROWN JONES AND ROBINSON, THE AMERICAN TOUR OF (O,G)
D. Appleton & Co., New York: 1872 (11-5/8x9-1/2", 158 pgs, printed one side only, B&W, green gilted hard-c)
nn - By Toby 70.00 140.00 400.00
NOTE: *Original American graphic novel sequel to Richard Doyle's Foreign Tour of Brown, Jones, and Robinson, with the same characters visiting New York, Canada, and Cuba. Protective sheets between each page (not part of page count).*

MESSRS. BROWN, JONES, AND ROBINSON, THE LAUGHABLE ADVEN. OF (E,M,G)
Dick & Fitzgerald, NY: nd (late 1870's - 1888) (5-3/4x9-1/4", 100 pgs, printed one side only, green paper-c, B&W)
nn - (Scarce) by Richard Doyle 100.00 200.00 450.00
NOTE: *Reprints the Garrett, Dick & Fitzgerald printing, with the following changes: Takes what had been page 12 in the Garrett, D&F printing (art by M.H. Henry), and makes it a title page, which is numbered page 1. The first story page, "Go to the Races", is numbered 2 (whereas it is numbered 1 in the Garrett, Dick & Fitzgerald version). Numbering stays ahead of the G,D&F edition by 1 page up through page 12, after which the page numbering becomes identical.*

MINNEAPOLIS JOURNAL CARTOONS (N,S)
Minneapolis Journal: nn 1894 - No.2 1895 (7-3/4" x 10-7/8", 76 pgs, B&W, paper-c)
nn (1894) (Rare) 50.00 100.00 200.00
Second Series (1895) (Rare) 50.00 100.00 200.00
nn- "War Cartoons" Jan 1899 (9x8", 160 pgs, paperback, punched & string bound) (Scarce) 24.00 96.00 170.00
NOTE: *Reprints single panel cartoons from the prior year, by Charles "Bart" L. Bartholomew.*

MISCHIEF BOOK, THE (E)
R. Worthington, New York: 1880 (7-1/8 x 10-3/4", 176 pgs, hard-c, B&W)
nn - Green cloth binding; green on brown cover; cover art by R. Lewis based on Busch art by Wilhelm Busch 175.00 350.00 735.00
nn - Blue cloth binding; hand colored cover; completely different cover art based on Busch by Wilhelm Busch 175.00 350.00 735.00
NOTE: *Translated by Abby Langdon Alger. American published anthology collection of Wilhelm Busch comic strips. Includes two of the strips found in the British "Bushel of Merry-Thoughts" collection, translated better, and with the dropped panel restored. Unknown which cover version was first.*

MISSES BROWN, JONES AND ROBINSON, THE FOREIGN TOUR OF THE (E,O,G)
Bickers & Sons, London: nd (c1850's) (12-1/4" x 9-7/8", 108 pgs, printed on one side, B&W, hard-c)
nn- "by Miss Brown" (Rare) 100.00 200.00 400.00
NOTE: *A female take on Doyle's Foreign Tour, by an unknown woman artist, using the pseudonym "Miss Brown."*

MISS MILLY MILLEFLEUR'S CAREER (S)
Sheldon & Co., NY: 1869 (10-3/4x9-7/8", 74 pgs, purple hard-c)
nn - Artist unknown (Rare) 75.00 150.00 300.00

MR PODGER AT COUP'S GREATEST SHOW ON EARTH HIS HAPS AND MISHAPS, THE ADVENTURES OF (O,S)
W.C. Coup, New York: 1884 (5-5/8x4-1/4", 20 pgs, color-c, B&W)
nn - Circus Themes; Similar to Barker's Comic Almanacs 25.00 50.00 100.00

MR. TOODLES' GREAT ELEPHANT HUNT (See Peter Piper in Bengal)
Brother Jonathan, NYC: 1850s (4-1/4x7-7/8", page count presently unknown)
nn - catalog contains comic strip (Very Rare) (no known sales)

MR. TOODLES' TERRIFIC ELEPHANT HUNT
Dick & Fitzgerald, NYC: 1860s (5-3/4x9-1/4", 32 pgs, paper-c, B&W) (Very Rare)
nn - catalog reprint contains 28 panel comic strip 150.00 300.00 600.00

MRS GRUNDY
Mrs Grundy Publishing Co, NYC: July 8 1865-Sept 30 1865 (weekly)
1-13 Thomas Nast, Hoppin, Stephens, 50.00 100.00 200.00

MUSEUM OF WONDERS, A (O,I)
Routledge & Sons: 1894 (13x10", 64 pgs, color-c, color thru out)
nn - By Frederick Opper 100.00 200.00 500.00

MY FRIEND WRIGGLES, A (Laughter) Moving Panorama, of His Fortunes And Misfortunes, Illustrated With Over 200 Engravings, of Most Comic Catastrophes And Side-Splitting Merriment) (O,G)
Stearn & Co, 202 Williams St, NY: 1850s (5-7/8x9-3/4", 100 pgs, B&W)
nn - By S. P. Avery (also the engraver) (Very Rare) 200.00 400.00 800.00

MY SKETCHBOOK (E,S)
Dana Estes & Charles E. Lauriat, Boston; J. Sabins & Sons, New York: circa 1880s (9-3/8x12", brown hard-c)
nn - By George Cruikshank 25.00 50.00 150.00
NOTE: *Reprints British editions 1834-36; extensive usage of word balloons.*

Nasby's Life Of Andy Jonson
1866 © Jesse Haney Company

99 "Woolf's" from Truth
1896 © Truth Company

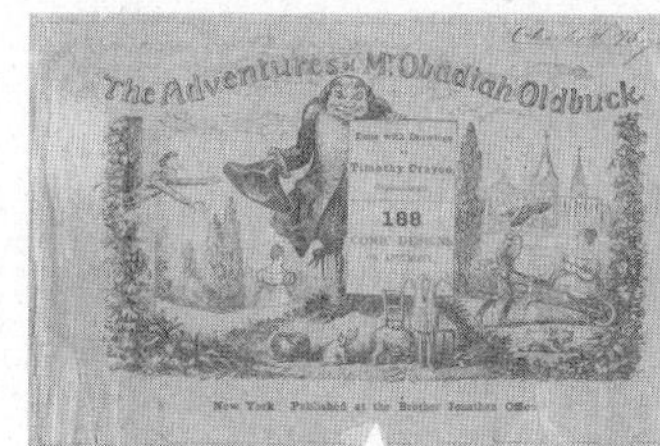

The Adventures of Obadiah Oldbuck 4th printing
mid-1850s © Brother Jonathan Offices, NY

NASBY'S LIFE OF ANDY JONSON (O, M)
Jesse Haney Co., Publishers No. 119 Nassau St, NY: 1866 (4-1/2x7-1/2, 48 pgs, B&W)
nn - President Andrew Johnson satire 100.00 200.00 450.00
NOTE: Blurb further reads: With a True Pictorial History of His STumping Tour Out West By Petroleum V. Nasby, A Dimmicrat of Thirty Years Standing, And Who Allus Tuk His Licker Straight. Front of book has long sequential comic strip satire on President Andrew Johnson, misspelling his name on the cover on purpose.

NAST'S ILLUSTRATED ALMANAC
Harper & Brothers, Franklin Square, NYC: 1872-1874 (8x5.5", 80 pgs, B&W, 35¢)
nn 60.00 120.00 240.00

NAST'S WEEKLY (O,S)
???: 1892-93 (Quarto Weekly)
all issues scarce 50.00 100.00 200.00

NATIONAL COMIC ALMANAC
An Association of Gentlemen, Boston: 1838-?? (8.25x4.75", 34 pgs, B&W)
nn 60.00 120.00 240.00

NEW AMERICAN COMIC ALL-IMAKE (ELTON'S BASKET OF COMICAL SCRAPS), THE
Elton, Publisher, New York: 1839 (7-1/2x4-5/8, 24 pgs)
1 100.00 200.00 400.00

NEW BOOK OF NONSENSE, THE: A Contribution To The Great Central Fair In Aid of the Sanitary Commission (O,S)
Ashmead & Evans, No. 724 Chestnut St, Philadelphia: June 1864 (red hard-c)
nn - Artists unknown (Scarce) 50.00 150.00 300.00

NEW YORK ILLUSTRATED NEWS
Frank Leslie, NYC: 10/14/76-June 1884
average issues with comic strips 20.00 40.00 80.00

NEW YORK PICAYUNE (see PHUN FOTOCRAFT)
Woodward & Hutchings: 1850-1855 newspaper-size weekly; 1856-1857 Folio Monthly 16x10.5; 1857-1858 Quarto Weekly; 1858-1860 Quarto Weekly
Average Issue With Comic Strips 50.00 100.00 200.00
Issues with Full Front Page Comic Strip 100.00 200.00 400.00
NOTE: *Many issues contain Frank Bellew sequential comic strips & single panel cartoons. Later issues published by Woodward, Levison & Robert Gun (1853-1857) ; Levison & Thompson (1857-1860)*

NICK-NAX
Levison & Haney, NY: 1857-1858? (11x7-3/4", 32 pgs, B&W, paper-c)
v2 #10 Feb 1858 has many single panel cartoons 50.00 100.00 200.00

99 "WOOLFS" FROM TRUTH (see Sketches of Lowly Life in a Great City, Truth)
Truth Company, NY: 1896 (9x5-1/2", 72 pgs, varnished paper-like cloth hard-c, 25 cents)
nn - By Michael Angelo Woolf (Rare) 150.00 300.00 600.00
NOTE: *Woolf's cartoons are regarded as a primary influence on R.F. Outcault in the later development of The Yellow Kid newspaper strip. Copy sold in 2002 on eBay for $800.00.*

NONSENSE OR, THE TREASURE BOX OF UNCONSIDERED TRIFLES
Fisher & Brother, 12 North Sixth St, Phila, PA, 64 Baltimore St, Baltimore, MD: early 1850s (4-1/2x7", 128 pgs, B&W)
nn - much Davy Crocket sequential story-telling comic strips 250.00 500.00 1000.00

OBADIAH OLDBUCK, THE ADVENTURES OF MR. (E,G)
Tilt & Bogue, London: nd (1840-41) (5-15/16x9-3/16", 176 pgs,B&W, gilted hard-c)
nn - By Rodolphe Töpffer 800.00 1300.00 2900.00
nn - Hand coloured edition (Very Rare) (no known sales)
NOTE: *This is the British edition, translating the unauthorized redrawn 1839 edition from Parisian publisher Aubert, adapted from Töpffer's "Les Amours de Mr. Vieux Bois" (aka "Histoire de Mr. Vieux Bois"), originally published in French in Switzerland, in 1837 (2nd ed. 1839). Early 19th century books are often found rebound, with original cover and/or title page gone. To distinguish editions having no cover or title page: the British oblong editions (published by Tilt & Bogue) use Roman Numerals to number pages. American oblong shaped editions use Arabic Numerals. British are printed on one side only. This is the earliest known English language sequential comic book. Has a new title page with art by Robert Cruikshank.*

OBADIAH OLDBUCK, THE ADVENTURES OF MR. (E,G)
Wilson and Company, New York: September 14, 1842 (11-3/4x9", 44 pgs, B&W, yellow paper-c on bookstand editions, hemp paper interior)
Brother Jonathan Extra No. IX - Rare bookstand edition 2600.00 5500.00 11000.00
Brother Jonathan Extra No. IX Very Rare subscriber/mailorder 2600.00 5500.00 11000.00
NOTE: *By Rodolphe Töpffer. Earliest known sequential American comic book, reprinting the 1841 British edition. Pages are numbered via Roman numerals. States "BROTHER JONATHAN EXTRA - ADVENTURES OF MR. OBADIAH OLDBUCK." at the top of each page. Prints 2 to 3 tiers of panels on both sides of each page. Copies could be had for ten cents according to adverts in* ***Brother Jonathan****. By Rodolphe Töpffer with cover masthead design by David Claypool Johnston, and cover art beneath the masthead reprinting Robert Cruikshank's title page art from the Tilt & Bogue edition. A special, additional cover was added for copies sold on stands (it was not issued with mail order or subscriber copies). Only 1 known copy possesses (partially) this very thin outer yellow cover. A decent (subscriber) copy sold on eBay in later October 2002 for over $3500.00. In 2005, a G/VG for $20,000; and a VG for $20,000. An apparent GD copy sold in auction in 2007 for $9560. A FA/GD copy sold in 2008 for $4182.50. A bound edition sold in 2010 for $2270.50. (Prices vary widely.)*

OBADIAH OLDBUCK, THE ADVENTURES OF MR. (E,G)
Wilson & Co, New York: nd (1849) (5-11/16x8-3/8", 84 pgs, B&W,paper-c)
nn - by Rodolphe Töpffer; title page by Robert Cruikshank (Very Rare)
500.00 1200.00 4200.00
NOTE: *2nd Wilson & Co printing, reformatted into a small oblong format, with nine panels edited out, and text modified to smooth out this removal. Results in four less printed tiers/strips. Pages are numbered via Arabic numerals. Every panel on Pages 11, 14, 19, 21, 24, 34, 35 has one line of text. Reformatted to conform with British first edition.*

OBADIAH OLDBUCK, THE ADVENTURES OF MR. (E,G)
Wilson & Co, 162 Nassau, NY: nd (early-1850s) (5-11/16x8-3/8", 84 pgs, B&W, yellow-c
nn - 3rd USA Printing by Rodolphe Töpffer; title page by Robert Cruikshank (Very Rare) Says By Timothy Crayon, an obvious pseudonym 800.00 1600.00 4200.00
NOTE: Front cover banner the giant is holding says "Done With Drawings By Timothy Crayon, Gypsographer, 188 Comic Etchings On Antimony" Title page changes address to No. 15 Spruce-Street. (Late 162 Nassau Street.)

OBADIAH OLDBUCK, THE ADVENTURES OF MR..
Brother Jonathan Offices: ND (mid-1850s) (5-11/16x8-3/8", 84 pages, B&W, oblong)
nn - 4th printing; Originally by Rodolphe Töpffer (Very Rare) 500.00 1200.00 4200.00
NOTE: *Cover States: "New York: Published at the Brother Jonathan Office". Front cover banner the giant is holding says "Done With Drawings By Timothy Crayon, Gypsographer, 188 Comic Designs On Antimony."*

OBADIAH OLDBUCK, THE ADVENTURES OF MR. (E,G)
Dick & Fitzgerald, New York: nd (various printings; est. 1870s to 1888) (Thirty Cents, 84 pgs, B&W, paper-c) (all versions scarce)
nn - Black print on green cover(5-11/16x8-15/16"); string bound 200.00 400.00 900.00
nn - Black print on blue cover; same format as green-c 200.00 400.00 900.00
nn - Black print on white cover(5-13/16x9-3/16"); staple bound beneath cover); this is a later printing than the blue or green-c 200.00 400.00 900.00
NOTE: *Reprints the abbreviated 1849 Wilson & Co. 2nd printing. Pages are numbered via Arabic numerals. Many of the panels on Pages 11, 14, 19, 21, 24, 34, 35 take two lines to print the same words found in the Wilson & Co version, which used only one text line for the same panels. Unknown whether the blue or green cover is earlier. White cover version has "thirty cents" line blackened out on the two copies known to exist. Robert Cruikshank's title page has been made the cover in the D&F editions.*

OLD FOGY'S COMIC ALMANAC
Philip J. Cozans, NY: 1858 (4-7/8x7-1/4, 48 pgs)
nn - sequential comic strip told one panel per page 50.00 100.00 200.00
NOTE: Contains (12) panel "Fourth of July in New York" sequential

OLD MOTHER MITTEN AND HER FUNNY KITTEN (see also **The Juvenile Gem**) (O)
Huestis & Cozans: nd(1850-1852) (6x3-7/8"12pgs, hand colored paper-c, B&W)
nn - first printing(s) publisher's address is 104 Nassau Street (1850-1851) (Very Rare) (no known sales)
NOTE: *A hand colored outer cover is highly rare, with only 1 recorded copy possessing it. Front cover image and text is repeated precisely on page 3 (albeit b&w), and only interior pages are numbered, together leading owners of coverless copies to believe they have the cover. The true back cover has ads for the publisher. Cover was issued only with copies which were sold separately - books which were bound together as part of THE JUVENILE GEM never had such covers.*

OLD MOTHER MITTEN AND HER FUNNY KITTEN (see JUVENILE GEM) (O)
Philip J. Cozans: nd (1850-1852) (6x3-7/8",12 pgs, hand colored paper-c, B&W)
nn - Second printing(s) publisher's address is 116 Nassau Street (1851-1852) (Very Rare) (no known sales)
nn - Third printing(s) publisher's address is 107 Nassau Street (1852+) (Very Rare) (no known sales)

OLD MOTHER MITTEN AND HER FUNNY KITTEN
Americana Review, Scotia, NY: nd (1960's) (6-1/4x4-1/8", 8 pgs, side-stapled, cardboard, B&W)
nn - Modern reprint 2.50 5.00 10.00
NOTE: *Issued within a folder titled SIX CHILDREN'S BOOKS OF THE 1850'S. States "Reprinted by American Review" at bottom of front cover. Reprints the 104 Nassau Street address.*

ON THE NILE (O,G)
James R. Osgood & Co., Boston: 1874 ; **Houghton, Osgood & Co., Boston:** 1880 (112 pgs, gilted green hardcover, B&W)
1st printing (1874; 10-3/4x16") - by Augustus Hoppin 45.00 90.00 180.00
2nd printing (1880; smaller sized) 32.50 65.00 130.00

OSCAR SHANGHAI, THE EXTRAORDINARY AND MIRTH-PROVKING ADVENTURES BY SEA & LAND OF (O, G)
Garrett & Co., Publishers, No. 18 Ann Street, New York: May 1855 (5-3/4x9-1/4", 100 pgs, printed one side only, paper-c, 25¢, B&W)
nn - Samuel Avery-c; interior by ALC Very Rare) 1000.00 2000.00 4000.00
NOTE: *Not much is known of this first edition as the data comes from a recently rediscovered* ***Brother Jonathan*** *catalog issued circa 1853-55. No original known yet to exist.*

OSCAR SHANGHAI, THE WONDERFUL AND AMUSING DOINGS BY SEA AND LAND OF (G)
Dick & Fitzgerald, 10 Ann St, NY: nd (1870s-1888) (25 ¢, 5-3/4x9-1/4", 100 pgs, printed one side only, green paper c, B&W)
nn - Cover by Samuel Avery; interior by ALC (Rare) 300.00 500.00 1000.00
NOTE: *Exact reprint of Garrett & Co original.*

OUR ARTIST IN CUBA (O)
Carleton, New York: 1865 (6-5/8x4-3/8", 120 pgs, printed one side only, gilted hard-c, B&W)
nn - By Geo. W. Carleton 37.50 75.00 150.00

OUR ARTIST IN CUBA, PERU, SPAIN, AND ALGIERS (O)
Carleton: 1877 (6-1/2x5-1/8", 156 pgs, hard-c, B&W)
nn - By Geo. W. Carleton 50.00 100.00 200.00
nn - By Geo. W. Carleton (wraps paper cover) (Rare) 45.00 90.00 180.00

The Wonderful and Amusing Doings by Sea & Land of Oscar Shanghai
1870s © Dick & Fitzgerald, New York

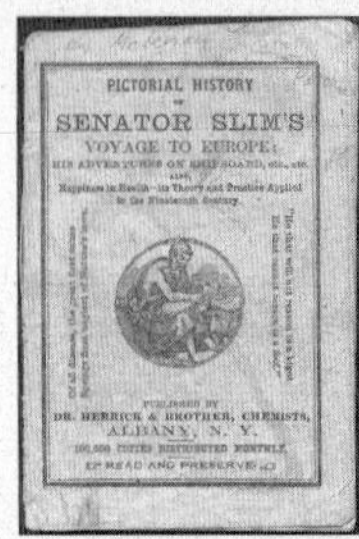

Pictorial History of Senator Slim's Voyage To Europe
1860 © Dr. Herrick & Brother, Albany, NY

PUCK
© Keppler & Schwarzman, NY

FR1.0 GD2.0 FN6.0

NOTE: *Reprints OUR ARTIST IN CUBA and OUR ARTIST IN PERU, then adds new section on Spain and Algiers.*

OUR ARTIST IN PERU (O)
Carleton, New York: 1866 (7-3/4x5-7/8", 68 pgs, gilted hardcover, B&W)
nn- By Geo. W. Carleton 37.50 75.00 150.00
NOTE: *Contains advertisement for the upcoming books* ***OUR ARTIST IN ITALY*** *and* ***OUR ARTIST IN FRANCE***, *but no such publications have been found to date.*

PARSON SOURBALL'S EUROPEAN TOUR (O)
Duff and Ashmead: 1867 (6x7-1/2", 76 pgs, blue embossed title hard-c)
nn - By Horace Cope 100.00 200.00 400.00
NOTE: see **REV. MR. SOURBALL'S EUROPEAN TOUR, THE** for the soft paper cover version

PEN AND INK SKETCHES OF YALE NOTABLES (O,S)
Soule, Thomas and Winsor, St. Louis: 1872 (12-1/4x9-3/4", B&W)
By Squills 25.00 50.00 100.00
NOTE: *Printed by Steamlith Press, The R.P. Studley Company, St Louis.*

PETER PIPER IN BENGAL
Bengamin H Day.Publisher, Brother Jonathan Cheap Book Establishment, 48 Beekman, NY: 1953-55 (6-5/8x4-1/4, 36 pgs, yellow paper-c, B&W, 3 cents - two dollars per hundred) (Very Rare)
nn - By John Tenniel - 32 panel comic strip Punch-r 500.00 1000.00 2000.00
NOTE: *Actually also a catalog of inexpensive books, prints, maps and half a dozen comic books for sale on separate pages from publishers Day and Garrett - see full story of this brand new find in the Victorian Era essay. A complete copy with split spine sold in November 2002 for $750.00. Published date most likely 1855.*

THE PHILADELPHIA COMIC ALMANAC (S)
G. Strong, 44 Strawberry St, NYC: 1835 (8-1/2x5", 36 pgs)
nn - 100.00 200.00 600.00
NOTE: 77 engravings full of recurring cartoon characters but not sequential; early use of recurring characters.

PHIL MAY'S SKETCH BOOK (E,S,M)
R.H. Russell, New York: 1899 (14-5/8x10", 64 pgs, brown hard-c, B&W)
nn - By Phil May 32.50 65.00 130.00
NOTE: *American reprint of the British edition.*

PHUNNY PHELLOW, THE
Oakie, Dayton & Jones: Oct 1859-1876; **Street & Smith** 1876: (Folio Monthly)
average issue with Thomas Nast 50.00 100.00 200.00

PHUN FOTOCRAFT, KEWREUS KONSEETS KOMICALLY ILLUSTRATED BY A KWEER FELLER (N) (see **NEW YORK PICAYUNE**)
The New York Picayune, NY: 1850s (104 pgs)
nn - Mostly Frank Bellew, some John Leach 250.00 500.00 1000.00
NOTE: Many sequential comic strips as well as single cartoons all collected from The New York Picayune. Ross & Tousey, Agents, 121 Nassau St, NY. The Picayune ran many sequential comic strips in its decade.

PICTORIAL HISTORY OF SENATOR SLIM'S VOYAGE TO EUROPE
Dr. Herrick & Brother, Chemists, Albany, NY: 1860 (3-1/4x4-3/4", 32 pgs, B&W)
nn - By John McLenan Very Rare 150.00 300.00 600.00

PICTURES OF ENGLISH SOCIETY (Parchment-Paper Series, No.4) (M,S,E)
D. Appleton & Co., New York: 1884 (5-5/8x4-3/8", 108 pgs, paper-c, B&W)
4 - By George du Maurier; Punch-r 30.00 60.00 120.00
NOTE: *Every other page is a full page cartoon, with the opposite page containing the cartoon's caption.*

PICTURES OF LIFE AND CHARACTER (M,S,E)
Bradbury and Evans, London: No.1 1855 - No.5 c1864 (12-1/2x18", 100 pgs, illustrated hard-c, B&W)
nn (No.1) (1855) 32.50 65.00 130.00
2 (1858), 3 (1860) 32.50 65.00 130.00
4 (nd; c1862) 5 (nd; c1864) 32.50 65.00 130.00
nn (nd (late 1860's) 32.50 65.00 130.00
NOTE: 2-1/2x18-1/4", 494 pgs, green gilted-c) reprints 1-5 in one book
1-3 John Leech's... (nd; 12-3/8x10", ? pgs, red gilted-c). 25.00 50.00 100.00
NOTE: *Reprints John Leech cartoons from* ***Punch***. *note that the Volume Number is mentioned only on the last page of these versions.*

PICTURES OF LIFE AND CHARACTER (E,M,S)
G.P. Putnam's Sons: 1880's (8-5/8x6-1/4", 218 pgs, hardcover, color-cr, B&W)
nn - John Leech (single panel **Punch** cartoon-r) 20.00 40.00 160.00
NOTE: *Leech reprints which extend back to the 1850s.*

PICTURES OF LIFE AND CHARACTER (Parchment-Paper Series) (E,M,S)
(see also Humerous Masterpieces)
D. Appleton & Co., NY: 1884 (30¢, 5-3/4 x 4-1/2", 104 pgs, paper-c, B&W)
nn - John Leech (single panel **Punch** cartoon-r) 20.00 40.00 160.00
NOTE: *An advertisment in the back refers to a cloth-bound edition for 50 cents.*

PIPPIN AMONG THE WIDE-AWAKES (O,S)
Werill & Chapin, 113 Nassau St, NYC, NY): 1860 (6x4-1/2", 36 pgs, 6 cents)
nn - Artist unknown (Very Rare) 100.00 200.00 400.00

PLISH AND PLUM (E.G)
Roberts Brothers, Boston: 1883 (8-1/8x5-3/4", 80 pgs, hardcover, B&W)
nn - By Wilhelm Busch 40.00 80.00 200.00
nn - Reprint (Roberts Brothers, 1895) 40.00 80.00 200.00
nn - Reprint (Little, Brown & Co., 1899) 40.00 80.00 200.00
NOTE: *The adventures of two dogs.*

POUNDS OF FUN
Frank Tousey, 34 North Moore St, NY: 1881 (6-1/2x9-1/2", 68pgs, B&W)
nn - Bellew, Worth, Woolf, Chips 40.00 80.00 200.00

PRESIDENTS MESSAGE, THE
G.P. Putnam's Sons, NY: 1887 (5-3/4x7-5/8, 44 pgs)
nn - (19) Thomas Nast single panel full page cartoons 40.00 80.00 200.00

PROTECT THE U.S. FROM JOHN BULL - PROTECTION PICTURES FROM JUDGE
Judge Publishing, New York: 1888 ((10 cents, 6-7/8x10-3/8", 36 pgs, paper-c, B&W)
nn - (Scarce) 25.00 50.00 100.00
NOTE: *Reprints both cartoons and commentary from* ***Puck***, *concerning the issue of tariffs which were then being debated in Congress. Art by Gillam, Hamilton, Victor.*

PUCK (German language edition, St. Louis) (M,O) (see also Die Vehme)
Publisher unknown, St. Louis: No.1, March 18, 1871 - No. ??, Aug. 24, 1872 (B&W, paper-c)
1-?? (Very Rare) by Joseph Keppler (no known sales)
NOTE: *Joseph Keppler's second attempt at a weekly humor periodical, following* ***Die Vehme*** *one year earlier. This was his first attempt to launch using the title* ***Puck***. *This German language version ran for a full year before being joined by an English language version.*

PUCK (English language edition, St. Louis) (M,O)
Publisher unknown, St. Louis: No.1, March ?? 1872 - No. ??, Aug. 24, 1872 (B&W, paper c)
1-?? (Very Rare) by Joseph Keppler (no known sales)
NOTE: *Same material as in the German language edition, but in English.*

PUCK, ILLUSTRIRTES HUMORISTISCHES WOCHENBLATT (German language edition, NYC) (M,O)
Keppler & Schwarzmann, New York: No.1 Sept (27) 1876 - 1164 Dec ?? 1899 (10 cents, color front/back-c and centerspread, remainder B&W, paper-c)
1-26 (Volume 1; Rare) by Joseph Keppler - these issues precede the English language version, and contain cartoons not found in them. Includes cartoons on the controversial Tilden-Hayes 1876 Presidential Election debacle. (no known sales)
27-52 (Volume 2; Rare) by Joseph Keppler - contains some cartoon material not found in the English language editions. Particularly in the earlier issues. (no known sales)
53-1164 10.00 20.00 50.00
Bound Volumes (six month, 26 issue run each):
Vol. 1 (Rare) (no known sales)
Vol. 2-4 (Rare) (no known sales)
Vol. 5-47 62.50 125.00 250.00
NOTE: *Joseph Keppler's second, and successful, attempt to launch* ***Puck***. *In German. The first six months precede the launch of the English language edition. Soon after (but not immediately after) the launch of the English edition, both editions began sharing the same cartoons, but, their prose material always remained different. The German language edition ceased publication at the end of 1899, while the English language edition continued into the early 20th Century. First American periodical to feature printed color every issue.*

PUCK (English language edition, NYC) (M,O)
Keppler & Schwarzmann, New York: No.1 March (14) 1877 - 1190 Dec ?? 1899 (10 cents, color front/back-c and centerspread, remainder B&W, paper-c)
1 (Rare) by Joseph Keppler (no known sales)
2-26 (Rare) by Joseph Keppler (no known sales)
27-1190 12.50 25.00 50.00
(see Platinum Age section for year 1900+ issues)
Bound volumes (six month, 26 issue run each):
Vol. 1 (Rare) (one set sold on eBay for $2300.00)
Vol. 2 (Scarce) (one set sold on eBay for $1500.00)
Vol. 3-6 (pre-1880 issues) 175.00 375.00 750.00
Vol. 7-46 140.00 300.00 600.00
NOTE: *The English language editions began six months after the German editions, and so the English edition numbering is always one volume number, and 26 issue numbers, behind its parallel German language edition. Pre-1880 & post-1900 issues are more scarce than 1880's & 1890's.*

PUCK (miniature) (M,P,I)
Keppler & Schwarzmann, New York: nd (c1895) (7x5-1/8", 12 pgs, color front & back paper-c, B&W interior)
nn - Scarce 25.00 50.00 110.00
NOTE: *C.J.Taylor-c; F.M.Howarth-a; F.Opper-a; giveaway item promoting* ***Puck's*** *various publications. Mostly text, with art reprinted from* ***Puck***.

PUCK, CARTOONS FROM (M,S)
Keppler & Schwarzmann, New York: 1893 (14-1/4x11-1/2", 244 pgs, hard-c, mostly B&W)
nn - by Joseph Keppler (Signed and Numbered) 100.00 200.00 400.00
NOTE: *Reprints Keppler cartoons from 1877 to 1893, mostly in B&W, though a few in color, with a text opposite each cartoon explaining the situation then being satirized. Issued only in an edition of 300 numbered issues, signed by Keppler. Only 1/4 of the pages are cartoons.*

PUCK'S LIBRARY (M)
Keppler & Schwarzmann, New York: No.1, July, 1887 - No. 174, Dec, 1899 (10 cents, 11-1/2x8-1/4", 36 pgs, color paper-c, B&W)
1- "The National Game" (Baseball) 50.00 100.00 200.00
2-149 10.00 20.00 40.00
NOTE: ***Puck's Library*** *was a monthly magazine reprinting cartoons & prose from* ***Puck***, *with each issue's*

Rays of Light
1886 © Morse Bros., Canton, Mass.

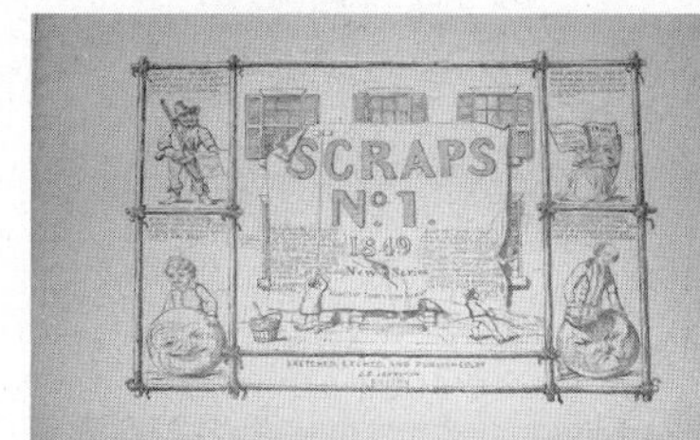

Scraps, New Series #1 by D.C. Johnston
1849 © D.C. Johnston, Boston

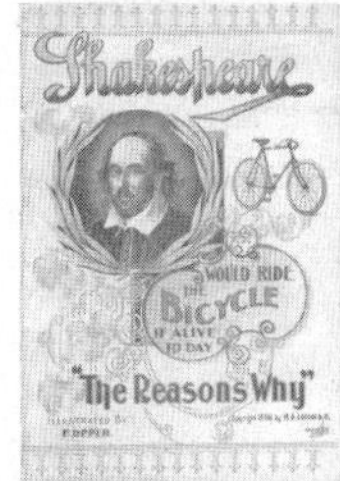

Shakespeare Would Ride The Bicycle If Alive Today
1896 © Cleveland Bicycles, Toledo, OH.

material organized around the same subject. The cover art was often original. All issues were kept in print for the duration of the series, so later issues are more scarce than earlier ones.

PUCK, PICKINGS FROM (M)
Keppler & Schwarzmann, New York: No.1, Sept, 1891 - No. 34, Dec, 1899 (25 cents, 13-1/4x10-1/4", 68 pgs, color paper-c, B&W)

1-34 Scarce 20.00 40.00 80.00
NOTE: *Similar to* **Puck's Library**, *except larger in size, and issued quarterly. All reprint material, except for the cover art. There also exist variations with "RAILROAD EDITION 30 CENTS" printed on the cover in place of the standard 25 cent price.*

PUCK'S OPPER BOOK (M)
Keppler & Schwarzmann, New York: 1888 (11-3/4x13-7/8", color paper-c, 68 pgs,interior B&W, 30¢)

nn - (Very Rare) by F. Opper 225.00 450.00 750.00
NOTE: *Puck's first book collecting work by a single artist.; mostly sequential comic strips.*

PUCK'S PRINTING BOOK FOR CHILDREN (S,O.I)
Keppler & Schwarzman, Pubs, NY: 1891 (10-3/8x7-7/8", 52 pgs, color-c, B&W and color)

nn - Frederick B Opper (Very Rare) (no known sales)

NOTE: *Left side printed in color; Right side B&W to be colored in.*

PUCK PROOFS (M,P,S)
Keppler & Schwarzmann, New York: nd (1906-1909) (74 pgs, paper cover; B&W) (all are Scarce)

nn - (c.1906, no price, 4-1/8x5-1/4") B&W painted -c of couple kissing over a chess board; 1905 & 1906-r 25.00 50.00 100.00
nn- (c.1909, 10 cents, 4-3/8x5-3/8") plain green paper-c; 76 pgs 1905-1909-r 25.00 50.00 100.00
NOTE: *Catalog of prints available from* **Puck**, *reprinting mostly cover & centerspread art from* **Puck**. *There likely exist more as yet unreported* **Puck Proofs** *catalogs. Art by Rose O'Neill.*

PUCK, THE TARIFF ?, CARTOONS AND COMMENTS FROM (M,S)
Keppler & Schwarzmann, New York: 1888 (10 cents, 6-7/8x10-3/8", 36 pgs, paper-c, B&W)

nn - (Scarce) 37.50 75.00 200.00
NOTE: *Reprints both cartoons and commentary from* **Puck**, *concerning the issue of tariffs which were then being debated in Congress. Art by Gillam, Keppler, Opper, Taylor.*

PUCK, WORLD'S FAIR
Keppler & Schwarzmann, PUCK BUILDING, World's Fair Grounds, Chicago: No.1 May 1, 1893 - No.26 Oct 30, 1893 (10 cents, 11-1/4x8-3/4, 14 pgs, paper-c, color front/back/center pages, rest B&W)(All issues Scarce to Rare)

1-26 30.00 60.00 130.00
1-26 bound volume: 500.00 1100.00 2200.00
NOTE: *Art by Joseph Keppler, F. Opper, F.M. Howarth, C.J. Taylor, W.A. Rogers. This was a separate, parallel run of* **Puck**, *published during the 1893 Chicago World's Fair from within the fairgrounds, and containing all new and different material than the regular weekly* **Puck**. *Smaller sized and priced the same, this originally sold poorly, and had not as wide distribution as* **Puck**, *and so consequently issues are much more rare than regular* **Puck** *issues from the same period. Not to be confused with the larger sized regular* **Puck** *issues from 1893 which sometimes also contained World's Fair related material, and sometimes had the words "World's Fair" appear on the cover. Can also be distinguished by the fact that* **Puck's** *issue numbering was in the 800's in 1893, while these issue number 1 through 26.*

PUNCHINELLO
Punchinello Publishing Co, NYC: April 2-Dec 24 1870 (weekly)

1-39 Henry L. Stephens, Frank Bellew, Bowlend 20.00 30.00 75.00
NOTE: *Funded by the Tweed Ring, mild politics attacking Grant Admin & other NYC newspapers. Bound copies exist.*

QUIDDITIES OF AN ALASKAN TRIP (O,G)
G.A. Steel & Co., Portland, OR: 1873 (6-3/4x10-1/2", 80 pgs, gilted hard-c, Red-c and Blue-c exist, B&W)

nn - By William H. Bell (Scarce) 350.00 750.00 1500.00
NOTE: *Highly sought Western Americana collectors. Parody of a trip from Washington DC to Alaska, by a member of the team which went to survey Alaska, purchase commonly known then as "Seward's Folly".*

"RAG TAGS" AND THEIR ADVENTURES, THE (N,S)
A. M. Robertson, San Francisco: 1899 (10-1/4x13-7/8, 84 pgs, color hard-c, B&W inside)

nn - By Arthur M. Lewis (SF Chronicle newspaper-r) (Scarce) 60.00 120.00 240.00

RAYS OF LIGHT (O,P)
Morse Bros., Canton, Mass.: No.1 1886 (7-1/8x5-1/8", 8 pgs, color paper-c, B&W)

1- (Rare) 50.00 100.00 200.00
NOTE: *Giveaway pamphlet in guise of an educational publication, consisting entirely of a sequential story in which a teacher instructs her classroom of young girls in the use of Rising Sun Stove Polish. Color front & back covers.*

RELIC OF THE ITALIAN REVOLUTION OF 1849, A
Gabici's Music Stores, New Orleans: 1849 (10-1/8x12-3/4", 144 pgs, hardcover)

nn - By G. Daelli (Scarce) 100.00 200.00 400.00
NOTE: *From the title page: "Album of fifty line engravings, executed on copper, by the most eminent artists at Rome in 1849; secreted from the papal police after the 'Restoration of Order,' And just imported into America."*

REMARKS ON THE JACOBINIAD (I,S)
E.W. Weld & W. Greenough, Boston: 1795-98 (8-1/4x5-1/8", 72 pgs, a number of B&W plates with text)

nn - Written by Rev. James Sylvester Gardner,artist unknown (Rare) (no known sales)
NOTE: *Early comics-type characters. Not sequential comics, but uses word balloons. Satire directed against "The Jacobin Club," supporters of the French Revolution and Radical Republicans. Gardner came to America from England in 1783, was minister of Trinity Church, Boston. There appears to be some reprints of this done as late as 1798.*

REV. MR. SOURBALL'S EUROPEAN TOUR, THE RECREATION OF A CITY, THE
Duffield Ashmead, Philadelphia: 1867 (7-5/8x6-1/4", 72 pgs, turquoise blue soft wrappers)

By Horace Cope (Rare) 50.00 100.00 200.00
NOTE: *see* **PARSON SOURBALL'S EUROPEAN TOUR** *for the hard cover version.*

RHYMES OF NONSENSE TRUTH & FICTION (S)
G.W. Carleton & Co, Publishers, NY: 1874 (10x7-3/4", 44 pgs, hard-c, B&W) (Very Rare)

nn - By Chaucer Jones and Michael Angelo Raphael Smith 100.00 200.00 400.00
NOTE: *Creator names obviously pseudonyms; looks like weak A.B. Frost.*

ROMANCE OF A HAMMOCK, THE - AS RECITED BY MR. GUS WILLIAMS IN "ONE OF THE FINEST" (O,P)
Unknown: 1880s (5-1/2x3-5/8" folded, 7 attached cardboard cards which fold out into a strip, color)

nn - By presently unknown Scarce 75.00 150.00 300.00
NOTE: *12-panel story, which one begins reading on one side of the folded-out strip, then flip to the other side to continue -- unlike the vast majority of folded strips, which are printed on only one side. This was a promotional handout, for a play titled "One of the Finest". The story pictured comes from a poem read in the play by then famous New York stage actor Gus Williams, who is pictured on the "cover"/title card."*

SAD TALE OF THE COURTSHIP OF CHEVALIER SLYFOX-WIKOF, SHOWING HIS HEART-RENDING ASTOUNDING & MOST WONDERFUL LOVE ADVENTURES WITH FANNY ELSSLER AND MISS GAMBOL, THE (O,G)
Garrett & Co., NY: Jan 1856 (25 ¢, 5-3/4x9-1/4", 100 pages, paper-c, B&W)

nn - By T.C. Bond ?? (Very Rare) 500.00 1000.00 2000.00
NOTE: *No surviving copies yet reported -- known via ads in Home Circle published by Garrett. Cover art by John McLenan and Samuel Avery. Graphic novel parodying the real-life romance between European actress/dancer Fanny Elssler and American aristocrat Henry Wikoff. The entire graphic novel is reprinted in the 1976 book "Fanny Elssler in America."*

SAD TALE OF THE COURTSHIP OF CHEVALIER SLYFOX-WIKOF, SHOWING HIS HEART-RENDING ASTOUNDING & MOST WONDERFUL LOVE ADVENTURES WITH FANNY ELSSLER AND MISS GUMBEL, THE (G) (25 cents printed on cover)
Dick And Fitzgerald, NY: 1870s-1888 (5-3/4x9-1/4", ??? pages, soft paper-c, B&W)

nn - By T.C. Bond ?? (Very Rare) 250.00 500.00 1000.00
NOTE: *Reprint of Garrett original printing before G,D&F partnership begins.*

SALT RIVER GUIDE FOR DISAPPOINTED POLITICIANS
Winchell, Small & Co., 113 Fulton St, NY: 1870s (16 pgs, 10¢)

nn - single panel cartoons from Wlld Oats (Rare) 75.00 150.00 300.00

SAM SLICK'S COMIC ALMANAC
Philip J. Cozans, NYC: 1857 (7.5x4.5, 48 pgs, B&W) 100.00 200.00 400.00
NOTE: *Contains reprint of* "Moses Keyser the Bowery Bully's Trip to the California Gold Mines" *from* Elton's Comic Almanac *#17 1850.*

SCRAPS (O,S) (see also **F****** A*** K*****)
D.C. Johnston, Boston: 1828 - No.8 1840; New Series No.1 1849 (12 pgs, printed one side only, paper-c, B&W)

1 - 1828 (9-1/4 x 11-3/4") (Very Rare) (no known sales)
2 - 1830 (9-3/4 x 12-3/4") (Very Rare) (no known sales)
3 - 1832 (10-7/8 x 13-1/8") (Very Rare) (no known sales)
4 - 1833 (11 x 13-5/8") (Very Rare) (no known sales)
5- 1834 (10-3/8 x 13-3/8") (Very Rare) (no known sales)
6 - 1835 (10-3/8 x 13-1/4") red lettering in title SCRAPS (Very Rare) 250.00 500.00 1000.00
6 - 1835 (10-3/8 x 13-1/4") no red lettering in title (Rare) 200.00 400.00 880.00
7 - 1837 (10-3/4 x 13-7/8") 1st Edition (Very Rare) 200.00 400.00 880.00
7 - 1837 (10-3/4 x 13-3/4") 2nd Edition (so stated) 100.00 175.00 375.00
NOTE: 20 pgs. of text (double-sided), 4 pgs. of art (single-sided), plus the covers. There are no protective sheets between the art pages.
8 - 1840 (10-1/2 x 13-7/8") (Rare) 200.00 400.00 880.00
New Series 1- 1849 (10-7/8 x 13-3/4") 125.00 250.00 475.00
NOTE: *By David Claypoole Johnston. All issues consist of four one-sided sheets with 9 to 12 single panel cartoons per sheet. The other pages are blank or text. With #1-5 the size of the pages can vary up to an inch. Contains 4 protective sheets (not part of page count) Only 1 3 4 and the 1849 New Series Number 1 has cover art along with 4 art pgs. (single sided) with 4 protective sheets and no text pages.New Series Number 1, as well as #6 with bo red lettering and the second printing of issue 7, have survived in higher numbers due to a 1940s warehouse discovery.*

THE SETTLEMENT OF RHODE ISLAND (O)
The Graphic Co. Photo-Lith 39 & 41, Park Place, New York: 1874 (11-3/8x10, 40 pgs, gilted blue hard-c

nn - Charles T. Miller & Walter F. Brown 50.00 100.00 250.00
NOTE: *This is also the Same Walter F. Brown that did "Hail Columbia".*

SHAKESPEARE WOULD RIDE THE BICYCLE IF ALIVE TODAY. "THE REASON WHY" (O,P,S)
Cleveland Bicycles H.A. Lozier & Co., Toledo, OH: 1896 (5-1/2x4",16 pgs, paper-c, color)

nn - By F. Opper (Rare) 70.00 140 .00 300.00
NOTE: *Original cartoons of Shakespearian characters riding bicycles; also popular amongst collectors of bicycle ephemera.*

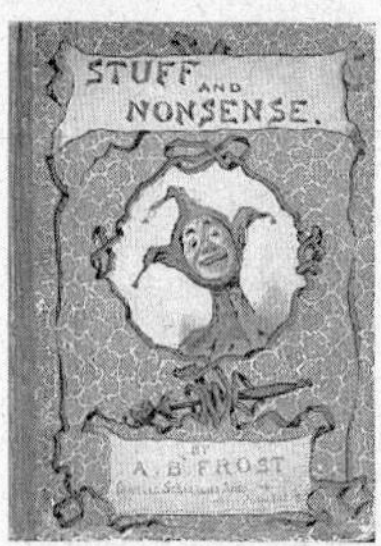

Stuff and Nonsense by A.B. Frost
1884 © Charles Scribner's Sons

Texas Siftings v6 #2 May 15
1886 ©Texas Siftings Publishing Co.

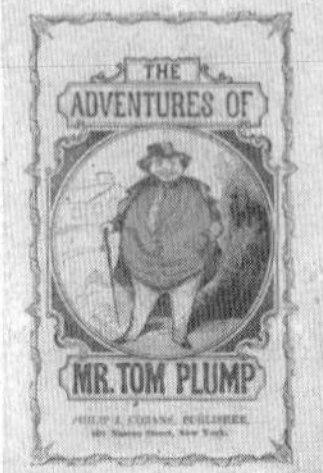

The Adventures Of Mr. Tom Plump
1851 © Huestis & Cozans, NY

SHAKINGS - ETCHINGS FROM THE NAVAL ACADEMY BY A MEMBER OF THE CLASS OF '67 (O,S)
Lee & Shepard, Boston: 1867 (7-7/8x10", 132 pages, blue hard-c)

By: Park Benjamin 38.00 75.00 150.00
NOTE: *Park Benjamin later became editor of Harper's Bazaar magazine.*

SHOO FLY PICTORIAL (S)
John Stetson, Chestnut sT Theatre, Phila, PA: June 1870 (15-1/2x11-1/2", 8 pgs, B&W)
1 67.50 125.00 250.00

SHYS AT SHAKSPEARE
J.P. and T.C.P., Philadelphia: 1869 (9-1/4x6", 52 pgs)

nn - Artist unknown 75.00 150.00 300.00

SKETCHES OF LOWLY LIFE IN A GREAT CITY (M,S) (See 99 "Woolfs" From Truth)
G. P. Puntam's Sons: 1899 (8-5/8x11-1/4", 200 pgs, hard-c, B&W)
(reprints from Life and Judge of Woolf's cartoons of NYC slum children)

nn - By Michael Angelo Woolf 75.00 150.00 350.00
NOTE: *Woolf's cartoons are regarded as a primary influence on R.F. Outcault in the later development of The Yellow Kid newspaper strip.*

SNAP (O,S)
Valentine & Townsend, Tribune Bldg, NYC: March 13,1885 (17x11, 8 pgs, B&W)

1-Contains a sequential comic strip 50.00 100.00 150.00

SOCIETY PICTURES (M,S,E)
Charles H. Sergel Company, Chicago: 1895 (5-1/4x7-3/4", 168 pgs, printed 1 side, paper-c, B&W)

nn - By George du Maurier; reprints from **Punch**. 25.00 50.00 100.00

SOLDIERS AND SAILORS HALF DIME TALES OF THE LATE REBELLION
Soldiers & Sailors Publishing Co: 1868 (5-1/4x7-7/8", 32 pgs)

v1#1-#16 v2#1-#10 15.00 30.00 60.00
v2 #11 contains (5) page comic strip 25.00 50.00 100.00
NOTE: *Changes to Soldiers & Sailors Half Dime Magazine with v2 #1.*

SOUVENIR CONTAINING CARTOONS ISSUED BY THE PRESS BUREAU OF THE OHIO STATE REPUBLICAN EXECUTIVE COMMITTEE, A (S)
Ohio State Republican Executive Committee, Columbus, OH: 1899 (10-3/8x13-1/2, 248 pgs, Hard-c, B&W

nn - By William L. Bloomer (Scarce) 100.00 200.00 400.00

SOUVENIR OF SOHMER CARTOONS FROM PUCK, JUDGE, AND FRANK LESLIE'S (M,S,P)
Sohmer Piano Co.: nd(c.1893) (6x4-3/4", 16 pgs, paper-c, B&W)

nn 25.00 50.00 100.00
NOTE: *Reprints painted "cartoon" Sohmer Piano advertisements which appeared in the above publications. Artists include Keppler, Gillam, others.*

SPORTING NEW YORKER, THE
Ornum & Co, Beekman ST, NYC: 1870s

issues with sequential comic strips (Rare) 50.00 100.00 200.00

STORY OF THE MAN OF HUMANITY AND THE BULL CALF, THE
(see Bull Calf, The Story of The Man Of Humanity And The)
NOTE: *Reprints of two of A. B. Frost's mostfamous sequential comic strips.*

STREET & SMITH'S LITERARY ALBUM
Street & Smith, NY: #1 Dec 23 1865-#225 Apr 9 1870 (11-3/4x16-3/4", 16 pgs, B&W)

1 (23 Dec 1865) 10.00 30.00 50.00
2-129 131-225 (issues with short sequential strips) 7.50 15.00 30.00
130 (Steam Man satire parody) 100.00 200.00 300.00

STUFF AND NONSENSE (Harper's Monthly strip-r) (M)
Charles Scribner's Sons: 1884 (10-1/4x7-3/4", 100 pgs, hardcover, B&W)

nn - By Arthur Burdett Frost 100.00 185.00 375.00
nn - By A.B. Frost (1888 reprint, 104 pgs) 40.00 80.00 180.00
NOTE: *Earliest known anthology devoted to collecting the comic strips of a single American artist. 1888 2nd printing has a different cover and is layed out somewhat differently inside with a new title page, 3 added pages of cartoons, and a couple more illustrations. For more Frost, the 2nd is worth checki ng out also.*

STUMPING IT (LAUGHING SERIES BRICKTOP STORIES #8) (O,S)
Collin & Small, NY: 1876 (6-5/8x9-1/4, 68 pgs, perfect bound, B&W)

nn - Thomas Worth art abounds (some sequentials) 75.00 150.00 300.00
NOTE: Mainly single panel cartoons w/text; however, some sequential comic strips inside worth picking up

SUMMER SCHOOL OF PHILOSOPHY AT MT. DESERT, THE
Henry Holt & Co.: 1881 (10-3/8x8-5/8", 60 pgs, illus. gilt hard-c, B&W)

nn - By J. A. Mitchell 60.00 120.00 240.00
NOTE: *J.A.Mitchell went on to found **LIFE** two years later in 1883. Also, the long-running mascot for **LIFE** was Cupid - which you see multitudes of Cupids flying around in this story.*

SURE WATER CURE, THE
Carey Grey & Hart, Phila, PA: c1841-43 (8-/2x5, 32 pgs, B&W

nn - proto-comic-strip Very Rare 150.00 300.00 600.00

TAILOR-MADE GIRL, HER FRIENDS, HER FASHIONS, AND HER FOLLIES, THE
(see also IN THE "400" AND OUT) (M)
Charles Scribner's Sons, New York: 1888 (8-3/8x10-1/2", 68 pgs, hard-c, B&W)

nn - Art by C.J. Taylor 20.00 40.00 80.00
NOTE: *Format is a full page cartoon on every other page, with a script style vignette, written by Philip H. Welch, on every page opposite the art.*

TALL STUDENT, THE
Roberts Brothers, Boston: 1873 (7x5", 48 pgs, printed one side only, gilted hard-c, B&W)

nn - By Wilhelm Busch (Scarce) 37.50 75.00 150.00

TARIFF ?, CARTOONS AND COMMENTS FROM PUCK, THE (see Puck, The Tariff...)

TEASING TOM AND NAUGHTY NED WITH A SPOOL OF CLARK'S COTTON, THE ADVENTURES OF (O,P)
Clark's O.N.T. Spool Cotton: 1879 (4-1/4x3", 12 pgs, B&W, paper-c)

nn 17.50 35.00 70.00
NOTE: *Knock-off of the "First Trick" in Wilhelm Busch's **Max and Maurice**, modified to involve Clark's Spool Cotton in the story, with similar but new art by an artist identified as "HB". The back cover advertises the specific merchant who gave this booklet away -- multiple variations of back cover suspected.*

TEMPERANCE TALES; OR, SIX NIGHTS WITH THE WASHINGTONIANS, VOL I & II
W.A. Leary & Co., Philadelphia: 1848 (50¢, 6-1/8x4", 328 pgs, B&W, hard-c)

nn 100.00 200.00 400.00
NOTE: *Mostly text. This edition gathers Volume I & II together. The first 8 pages reprints George Cruikshank's **THE BOTTLE**, re-drawn & re-engraved by Phil A. Pilliner. Later editions of this book do not include **THE BOTTLE** reprint and are therefore of little interest to comics collectors.*

TEXAS SIFTINGS
Texas Siftings Publishing Co, Austin, Texas (1881-1887), **NYC** (1887-1897): 1881-1885 newspaper-size weekly; 1886-1897 folio weekly (15x10-3/4", 16 pgs, B&W 10¢

1881-1885 issues 25.00 50.00 100.00
v6#1 (5/8/86) (8) panel strip Afterwhich He Emigrated;
(16) panel The Tenor's Triumph Veni Vidi Vici 12.50 25.00 50.00
v6#2 (5/16/86 (5) panel sewuential 12.50 25.00 50.00
v6#3 no sequentials 12.50 25.00 50.00
v6#4 (5/29/86) Worth-c (4) panel Worth strip; (2) panel 12.50 25.00 50.00
v6#5 no sequentials 12.50 25.00 50.00
v6#6 (6/12/86) Comic Strip Cover (11) panels The Rise of a Great Artist
(5) panel sequential 50.00 100.00 200.00
v6#7 (6/19/86) Worth-c (2) panel Wiorth;
(10) panel Ha! Ha! The Honest Youth & the Lordly Villain 25.00 50.00 100.00
v6#8 (6/26/86) Worth-c; (15) panel The Kangaroo Hunter 25.00 50.00 100.00
v6#9 (7/3/86) Worth-c; Bellew (2) panel How Wives Get What They Want
12.50 25.00 50.00
v6#10 ((7/10/86) Baseball-c; (3) panel;
(5) panel A Story Without Words from Fliegende Blätter 12.50 25.00 50.00
v6 #11 12 13 Worth-c no sequentials 12.50 25.00 50.00
v6#14 (8/7/86) Wiorth-c; (7) panel Mrs Cleveland Presents
The President With A New Rocking Chair 12.50 25.00 50.00
v6#15 (8/14/86) Worth-c; (6) panel Worth strip 12.50 25.00 50.00
v6#16 (8/21/86) Worth-c Asleep At Post USA/Mexico Border
(6) panel sequential 12.50 25.00 50.00
v6#17 no sequrntials 12.50 25.00 50.00
v6#18 (9/4/86) Worth-c; (3) panel from Fliegende 12.50 25.00 50.00
v6#19 (9/11/86) Worth Anarchist & Uncle Sam-c;
(5) panel Duel of the Dudes 12.50 25.00 50.00
v6#20 (9/18/86) Worth-c (6) panel sequential 12.50 25.00 50.00
v6#21 (9/25/86) Worth-c; Verbeck single panel; (9) panel 12.50 25.00 50.00
v6#22 (10/2/86) Verbeck-c plus interiors 12.50 25.00 50.00
v6#23 (10/9/86) Worth-c Geronimo & Devil cover;
Verbeck and Chips singles 25.00 50.00 100.00
v6#24 (10/16/86) Worth-c Verbeck strip "Evolution" 12.50 25.00 50.00
v6#25 no sequential strips 12.50 25.00 50.00
v6#26 (10/30/86) Worth-c; (6) panel Verbeck "A Warning To Smokers"
12.50 25.00 50.00
NOTE: *Many Thomas Worth sequential comic strips. Frank Bellew and Dan McCarthy appear. Wilhelm Busch-r from German Fligende Blaetter. Later issues in 1890s comics become sporadic*

THAT COMIC PRIMER (S)
G.W. Carleton & Co., Publishers: 1877 (6-5/8x5", 52 pgs, paper soft-c, B&W)

nn - By Frank Bellew 75.00 150.00 300.00
NOTE: *Premium for the United States Life Insurance Company, New York.*

TIGER, THE LEFTENANT AND THE BOSUN, THE
Prudential Insurance Home Office, 878 & 880 Broad St, Newark, NJ: 1889 (4.5x3.25", 12 pgs) (Scarce)

nn - 8 panel sequential story in color 50.00 100.00 200.00

TOM PLUMP, THE ADVENTURES OF MR. (see also The Juvenile Gem) (O)
Huestis & Cozans, New York: nd (c1850-1851) (6x3-7/8", 12 pgs, hand colored paper-c, B&W)

nn- First printing(s) publisher's address is 104 Nassau Street (1850-1851)
(Very Rare) 750.00 1500.00 2800.00
NOTE: *California Gold Rush story. The hand colored outer cover is highly rare, with only 1 recorded copy possessing it. The front cover image and text is repeated precisely on page 3 (albeit b&w), and only interior pages are numbered, together leading owners of coverless copies to believe they have the cover. The true back*

Truth #372 (first app. The Yellow Kid)
June 2 1894 © Truth Company, NY

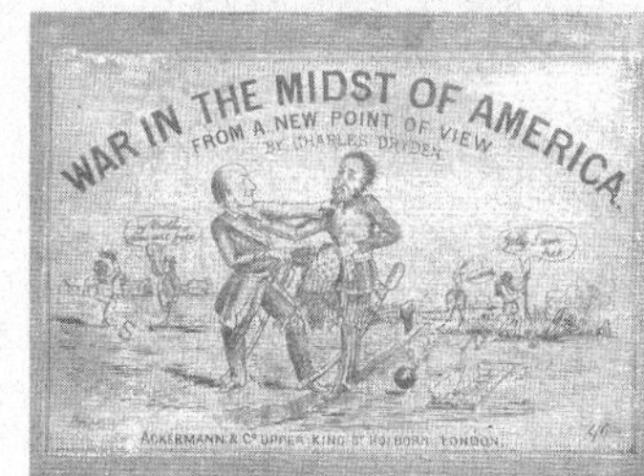

War in the Midst of America

Wild Oats #115 March 10
1875 © Winchell & Small, NYC

cover contains ads for the publisher. The cover was issued only with copies which were sold separately - booklets which were bound together as part of ***THE JUVENILE GEM*** *never had such covers.*

TOM PLUMP, THE ADVENTURES OF MR. (see also The Juvenile Gem) (O)
Philip J. Cozans: nd (1851-1852) (6x3-7/8", 12 pgs,hand colored paper-c, B&W)

nn- Second printing(s) publisher's address is 116 Nassau Street (1851-1852)
(Very Rare) 400.00 800.00 1600.00
nn- Third printing(s) publisher's address is 107 Nassau Street (1852+)
(Very Rare) 400.00 800.00 1600.00

TOM PLUMP, THE ADVENTURES OF MR.
Americana Review, Scotia, NY: nd(1960's) (6-1/4x4-1/8", 8 pgs, side-stapled, cardboard-c, B&W)

nn - Modern reprint - 12.00 24.00
NOTE: *Issued within a folder titled SIX CHILDREN'S BOOKS OF THE 1850'S. States "Reprinted by American Review" at bottom of front cover. Reprints the 104 Nassau Street address.*)
nn - Modern reprint (Scarce 1980s) (5-1/2x4-1/4", 8 pgs,side-stapled) - 5.00 10.00
NOTE: *Photocopy reprint by a comix zine publisher, from an Americana Review cop; vailable by mail order*

TOOTH-ACHE, THE (E,O)
D. Bogue, London: 1849 (5-1/4x3-3/4)

nn - By Cruikshank, B&W (Very Rare) 250.00 500.00 1100.00
nn - By Cruikshank, hand colored (Rare) (no known sales)
NOTE: *Scripted by Horace Mayhew, art by George Cruikshank. This is the British edition. Price 1/6 b&w, 3 hand colored. In British editions, the panels are not numbered. Publisher's name appears on cover. Booklet's "pages" unfold into a single, long, strip.*

J.L. Smith, Philadelphia, PA: nd (1849) (5-1/8"x 3-3/4" folded, 86-7/8" wide unfolded, 26 pgs, cardboard-c, color, 15¢)

nn - By Cruikshank, hand colored (Very Rare) 400.00 800.00 1600.00
NOTE: *Reprints the D. Bogue edition. In American editions, the panels are numbered (43 panels, not counting front & back cover). Publisher's name stamped on inside front cover, plus printed along left-hand side of first interior page. Page 1 is pasted to inside back cover, and unfolds from there. Front cover not attached to back cover by design. Booklet's "pages" unfold into a single, long, strip (made from four individual strips pasted together on the blank back side). There is a fairly common1974 British Arts Council reprint.*

TRAMP, THE: His Tricks, Tallies, and Tell-Tales, with His Signs, Countersigns, Grips, Passwords and Villainies Exposed (0,S)
Dick & Fitzgerald, New York: 1878 (11-3/8x8, 36 pgs, paper-c, B&W, 25¢) (Rare)

1 Frank Bellew 150.00 300.00 650.00
NOTE: *Edited by Frank Bellew, A Bee And A Chip (Bellew's daughter and son Frank).*

TRUTH (See Platinum Age section for 1900-1906 issues)
Truth Company, NY: 1886-1906? (13-11/16x10-5/16", 16 pgs, process color-c & centerfolds, rest B&W)

1886-1887 issues 20.00 40.00 100.00
1888-1895 issues non Outcault issues 15.00 30.00 80.00
Mar 10 1894 - precursor Yellow Kid RFO 60.00 180.00 400.00
#372 June 2 1894 - first app Yellow Kid RFO 215.00 650.00 1300.00
June 23 1894 - precursor Yellow Kid R. F. Outcault 60.00 180.00 400.00
July 14 1894 -2nd app Yellow Kid RFO 110.00 330.00 700.00
Sept 15 1894 - (2) 3rd app YK RFO plus YK precursor 110.00 330.00 700.00
Feb 9 1895 - 4th app Yellow Kid RFO 110.00 330.00 700.00
1896-1899 issues 10.00 20.00 55.00
NOTE: *This magazine contains the earliest known appearances of* ***The Yellow Kid*** *by Richard Felton Outcault. Feb 9 1895 issue's YK cartoon was reprinted one week later in the* ***New York World*** *Feb 17 1895 edition. We are still sorting out further Outcault appearances. Truth also contained full color sequential strips by Hy Mayer on the back plus Woolf, Verbeek, etc.*

TRUTH, SELECTIONS FROM
Truth Company, NY: 1894-Spr 1897 (13-11/16x10-1/4, color-c, quarterly)

1-4 25.00 50.00 100.00
5-Outcault's early Yellow Kid 100.00 200.00 400.00
6-13 20.00 40.00 80.00
NOTE: *#5 reprints all early Outcault Yellow Kid appearances*

TURNER'S COMIC ALMANAC
Charles Strong, 298 Pearl St, NYC: ???-1843 (7.25x4.5", 36 pgs, B&W)

nn 60.00 120.00 240.00

TURNER'S COMICK ALMA-NACK
Turner & Fisher, NYC: 1844-?? (7.25x4.5", 36 pgs, B&W)

nn 60.00 120.00 240.00

TWO HUNDRED SKETCHES, HUMOROUS AND GROTESQUE, BY GUSTAVE DORE (E)
Frederick Warne & Co, London: 1867 (13-3/4x11-3/8, 94 pgs, hard-c, B&W)

nn - (1867) by Gustave Dore 100.00 200.00 500.00
nn - (Second Edition; 1871)- by Gustave Dore 50.00 100.00 240.00
nn - (Third Edition; 1870's)- by Gustave Dore 50.00 100.00 240.00
nn - (Fourth Edition; 1870's- by Gustave Dore 50.00 100.00 240.00
NOTE: *Contains sequential comics stories, single panel cartoons, and sketches. Reprints and translates material which originally appeared in the French publications "Le Journal pour Rire", circa 1848-49. Although dated 1867, it was likely published & available for the 1866 Christmas Season, as has been confirmed for the American edition. Printed by Dalziel. The American & first British editions were printed simultaneously, the American edition is not a reprint of the British.*

TWO HUNDRED SKETCHES, HUMOROUS AND GROTESQUE, BY GUSTAVE DORE (E)
Roberts Brothers, Boston: 1867 (13-3/4x11-3/8", 96 pgs, hard-c, B&W)

nn - By Gustave Dore 100.00 200.00 500.00
NOTE: *Although dated 1867, it was published & available for the 1866 Christmas Season. Printed by Dalziel, in England, and imported to the USA expressly for a USA publisher.*

UNCLE JOSH'S TRUNK-FUL OF FUN
Dick & Fitzgerald, 18 Ann St, NY: 1870s (5-3/4x9", 68 pgs, B&W & Red-c, B&W inside)

nn - Rare 75.00 125.00 200.00
NOTE: *Many single panel cartoons; (2) pages of early boxing sequential strip*

UNCLE SAM'S COMIC ALMANAC
M.J. Meyers, NY: 1879 (11x8", 32 pgs)

nn - 50.00 100.00200.00

UNDER THE GASLIGHT
Gaslight Publishing Co (Frank Tousey): Oct 13 1878-Apr 12 1879 (Folio, 16pgs)

1-27 75.00 125.00 200.00

UNITED STATES COMIC ALMANAC
King & Baird, Philadelphia: 1851-?? (7.5x4.5", 36 pgs, B&W)

nn 60.00 120.00 240.00

UPS AND DOWNS ON LAND AND WATER (O.G)
James R. Osgood & Co., Boston: 1871 ; **Houghton, Osgood & Co., Boston:** 1880 (108 pgs, gilted hard-c, B&W)

1st printing (1871; 10-3/4x16") - By Augustus Hoppin 45.00 90.00 180.00
2nd printing (1880; smaller sized) 32.50 65.00 130.00
NOTE: *Exists as blue or orange hard covers.*

VANITY FAIR
William A. Stephens (for Thompson & Camac): Dec 29 1859-July 4 1863 Quarto Weekly

average issues with comic strips 20.00 30.00 75.00

VERDICT, THE
Verdict Publishing Co: Dec 19 1898-Nov 12 1900 (Chromolithographic Weekly)

Average Issues 50.00 100.00 200.00
NOTE: Artists included George B. Luks, Horace Taylor, MIRS. Striking anti-Republican weekly full o fsome of the most savage political cartoons of the era. The last brilliant burst of energy for the political cartoon weekly

VERY VERY FUNNY (M,S)
Dick & Fitzgerald, New York: nd(c1880's) (10¢, 7-1/2x5", 68 pgs, paper-c, B&W)

nn - (Rare) 75.00 150.00 300.00
NOTE: *Unauthorized reprints of prose and cartoons extracted from Puck, Texas Siftings, and other publications. Includes art by Chips Bellew, Bisbee, Graetz, Opper, Wales, Zim.*

VIM
H. Wimmel, NYC: June 22-Aug 24 1898 (Chromolithographic Weekly)

average issue 50.00 100.00 200.00
Yellow Kid by Leon Barritt issues 75.00 150.00 300.00

WAR IN THE MIDST OF AMERICA. FROM A NEW POINT OF VIEW. (E,O,G)
Ackermann & Co., London: 1864 (4-3/8" x 5-7/8", folded, 36 feet wide unfolded, 80 pgs, hard-c, B&W)

nn- by Charles Dryden (rare) 400.00 800.00 1600.00
NOTE: *British graphic novel about the American Civil War, with a pro-Confederate bent. Adventures of a British artist who decides to visually summarize the American Civil War for his countrymen, from newspaper accounts. Reaching current events, he finds he can not finish the story until the War ends, and so he travels to America, to end it. Book unfolds into a single long strip (binding was issued split, to enable the unfolding).*

WASP, THE ILLUSTRATED SAN FRANCISCO
F. Korbel & Bros and Numerous Others: August 5 1876-April 25 1941 (Chromolithographic Weekly)

average 1800s issues with comic strips 50.00 100.00 200.00

WHAT I KNOW OF FARMING: Founded On The Experience of Horace Greeley (S)
The American News Company, New York: 1871 (7-1/4x4-1/2", paper-c, B&W)

nn - By Joseph Hull (Scarce) 35.00 70.00 140.00
NOTE: *Pay & Cox, Printers & Engravers, NY; political tract regarding Presidential elections.*

WILD FIRE
Wild Fire Co, NYC: Nov 30 1877-at least#16 Mar 1878 (Folio, 16 pgs)

1-16 25.00 50.00 100.00

WILD OATS, An Illustrated Weekly Journal of Fun, Satire, Burlesque, and Nits at Persons and Events of the Day (O)
Winchell & Small, 113 Fulton St /48 Ann St, NYC: Feb 1870-1881 (16-1/4x11", generally 16 pages, B&W, began as monthly, then bi-weekly, then weekly) All loose issues Very Rare (See *The Overstreet Price Guide* #35 2005 for a detailed index of single issue contents)

1-25 Very Rare - contents to be indexed next year 50.00 100.00 200.00
26-28 30 32 35 36 39 40 41 43-46 1872 (sequential strips) 50.00 100.00 200.00
29 33 37 42 no sequential strips 40.00 80.00 160.00
31 34 38 47 Hopkins sequential comic strips 50.00 100.00 200.00
48 (1/16/73) Worth 13 panel sequential; first Woolf-c 50.00 100.00 200.00
49 51 53 54 60 62 61 64 65 66 67 69 1873 sequential strips 50.00 100.00 200.00
50 52 56 59 63 71 no sequential strips 40.00 80.00 160.00
51 (Worth 18 panel double page spread, Woolf 9 panel 50.00 100.00 200.00
55 Hopkins 22 panel double page spread; Bellew-c 50.00 150.00 300.00
57 intense unknown 6 panel "Two Relics of Barbarism, or A Few Contrasted Pictures,

Wild Oats #139 August 25 1875 © Winchell & Small, NY

Wild Oats Vol. XIV #181346 June 14, 1876 © Winchell & Small

Yankee Notions #7 (v2#1) July 1852 © T.W. Strong, NY

FR1.0 GD2.0 FN6.0

Showing the origin of the North American Indian 50.00 100.00 200.00
58 (6/5/73) unknown 19 panel double pager "The Terrible Adventures of Messrs Buster & Stumps, About Exterminating the Indians" reads across both pages like Popeye #2095 (1933); Woolf-c 100.00 200.00 400.00
68 (10/16/73) unknown 9 panel "Adv of New jersey Mosquito" looks like Winsor McCay type style: early inspiration for McCay's animated cartoon? 50.00 100.00 200.00
70 unknown 6 panel; Hopkins 6 panel "Hopkins novel: A Tale of True Love, with all the variations"; Bellew-c 50.00 100.00 200.00
72 (12/11/73) Worth 11 panel; Wales President Grant war-c 50.00 100.00 200.00
73 74 75 Hopkins sequential comic strip 75.00 150.00 300.00
76 77 sequential strips 50.00 100.00 200.00
78 Bellew 5 panel double pager 50.00 100.00 200.00
79-105 (March 1874-Dec 1874) contents presently unknown 50.00 100.00 200.00
106 107 111 no sequentials;Bellew-c #106 110;Wales-c #107 50.00 100.00 200.00
108 (1/20/75) Wales 12 panel double pg spread; Bellew-c 50.00 100.00 200.00
109 (1/27/75) unknown 6 panel; Wales-c 50.00 100.00 200.00
111 Busch 13 panel "The Conundrum of the Day - Is Lager Beer Intoxicating?"; Bellew-c 50.00 100.00 200.00
112 116 sequential comic strips 50.00 100.00 200.00
113 114 115 no sequentials Worth-c #114 40.00 80.00 160.00
117 intense Wales 6 panel "One of the Oppresions of the Civil Rights Laws"' Bellew-c 75.00 150.00 300.00
118-137 (3/31/75-8/4/75) no sequential comic strips 40.00 80.00 160.00
138 (8/18/75) Bellew Sr & Bellew "Chips" Jr singles appear 50.00 100.00 200.00
139-143 145-147 154-157 159 no sequentials 40.00 80.00 160.00
144 (9/29/75) Hopkins 8 panel sequential; Wales-c 50.00 100.00 200.00
148 (10/27/75) Opper's first cover; many Opper singles 75.00 150.00 300.00
149 150 151 152 153 all Opper-c and much interior work 50.00 100.00 200.00
158 (1/5/76) Palmer Cox 1rst comic strip 24 panel double page spread "The Adv of Mr & Mrs Sprowl And Their Christmas Turkey - A Crashing Chasing Tearful Tragedy But Happily Ending Well"; Opper-c 100.00 200.00 400.00
159 160 162 165 167 169-173 no sequentials 40.00 80.00 160.00
161 163 164 166 168 179 182 Palmer Cox sequential strips 100.00 200.00 400.00
174 (4/26/76) Cox 24 panel double pager "The Tramp's Progress; A Story of the West And the Union Pacific Railroad" 100.00 200.00 400.00
175-178 183-189 no sequentials 40.00 80.00 160.00
180 (6/7/76) Beard & Opper jam; Woolf, Bellew singles 50.00 100.00 200.00
181 more Mann two panel jobs; Opper-c 50.00 100.00 200.00
190 Bellew 9 panel "Rodger's Patent Mosquito Armour" 75.00 150.00 300.00
191-end contents to be indexed in the near future 40.00 80.00 160.00

NOTE: *There are very few lknown oose issues. All loose issues are Very Rare. Prices vary widely on this magazine. Issues with sequential comic strips would be in higher demand than issues with no comic strips. We present this index from the Library of Congress and New York Historical Society bound sets. We would love to hear from any one who turns up loose copies. This scarce humor bi-weekly contains easily a couple hundred original first-time published sequential comic strips found in most issues plus innumerable single panel cartoons in every issue*

WYMAN'S COMIC ALMANAC FOR THE TIMES
T.W.Strong, NY: 1854 (8x5", 24 pgs)
nn - 50.00 100.00 200.00

WOMAN IN SEARCH OF HER RIGHTS, THE ADVENTURES OF (G)
Lee & Shepard, Boston And New York: early 1870s (8-3/8x13", 40 pgs, hard-c)
By Florence Claxton (Very Rare) 450.00 900.00 1800.00
NOTE: *Earliest known original comic book sequential story by a woman; contains "nearly 100 original drawings by the author, which have been reproduced in fac-simile by the graphotype process of engraving." Tinted two color lithography; orange tint printed first, then printed 2nd time with black ink; early women's sufferage.*

WORLD OVER, THE (I)
G. W. Dillingham Company, New York: 1897 (192 pgs, hard-c)
nn - By Joe Kerr; 80 illustrations by R.F. Outcault (Rare) 300.00 600.00 1200.00
NOTE: soft cover editions also exist

WRECK-ELECTIONS OF BUSY LIFE (S)
Kellogg & Bulkeley: 1867 (9-1/4x11-3/4", ??? pages, soft-c)
nn - By J. Bowker (Rare) 100.00 200.00 400.00
NOTE: *Says "Sold by American News Company, New York" on cover.*

YANKEE DOODLE
W.H. Graham, Tribune Building, NYC: Oct 10 1846-Oct 2 1847 (Quarto weekly)
average issue 50.00 100.00 200.00

YANKEE NOTIONS, OR WHITTLINGS OF JONATHAN'S JACK-KNIFE
T.W. Strong, 98 Nassau St, NYC: Jan. 1852-1875 (11x8, 32 pgs, paper-c, 12.5¢, monthly)
1 Brother Jonathan character single panel cartoons 50.00 100.00 200.00
NOTE: *Begins continuing character sequential comic strip, "The Adventures of Jeremiah Oldpot" in "A Bird in the Hand Is Worth Two in The Bush"*
2-4 25.00 50.00 100.00
5 British X-Over 25.00 50.00 100.00
NOTE: *Single panel of John Bull & Brother Jonathan exchanging civilities (issues of Punch & Yankee Notions)*
6 end of Jeremiah Oldpot continued strip 25.00 50.00 100.00
v2#1 begin "Hoosier Bragg" sequential strip - six issue serial 25.00 50.00 100.00
v2#2 Feb 1853 two pg 12 panel sequential "Mr Vanity's Exploits, Arising Out Of A Valentine" 37.50 75.00 150.00
v2#3-v2#5 continues Hoosier Bragg 25.00 50.00 100.00
v2#6 Juen 1853 Lion Eats Hoosier Bragg, end of story 25.00 50.00 100.00
v3#1 begins referring to its cartoons as "Comic Art" 37.50 75.00 150.00

FR1.0 GD2.0 FN6.0

v4#1-V4#6 v5#1-v5#2 no sequential comic strips 20.00 40.00 80.00
v5#3 two sequential comic strips 37.50 75.00 150.00
NOTE: *Mr Take-A-Drop And The Maine Law (5) panels and The First Segar (7) panels (about smoking tobacco)*
v5#4 April 1856 begin Billy Vidkins 37.50 75.00 150.00
NOTE: *Begins reprinting "From Passages in the Life of Little Billy Vidkins, first issued as a stand alone proto-comic book in 1849 Illustrations of the Poets*
v5#5 The McBargem Guards (9) panel sequential; Vidkins 25.00 50.00 100.00
v5#6 v5 #9 no comics 20.00 40.00 80.00
v5#7 Billy Vidkins continues 25.00 50.00 100.00
v5#8 end of Vidkins By HL Stephens, Esq. 25.00 50.00 100.00
v5#10 (6) panel "How We Learn To Ride"; Timber is hero 25.00 50.00 100.00
v5#11 (7) panel "How Mr. Green Sparrowgrass Voted-A Warning For the Benefit of Quiet Citizens About To Excercize the Elective Franchise" plus Pt Two "How We Learn to Ride" 37.50 75.00 150.00
v5#12 (6) panel "How Mr Pipp Got Struck"; "The Eclipse" featuring Mr Phips; Pt 3 "How We Learn to Ride" 25.00 50.00 100.00
v6#1 (Jan 1857) (12) panel "A Tale of An Umbrella; (4) panel begins a serial "The Man Who Bought The Elephant; (8) panel How Our Young New Yorkers Celebrate New Years Day 25.00 50.00 100.00
v6#2 (Feb 1857) Pt 2 (4) panels The Man Who Bought the Elephant; (7) panel A Game of All Fours 25.00 50.00 100.00
v6#3 (Mar 1857) Pt 3 (4) panels The Man Who Bought the Elephant ending; (4) panel Ye Great Crinoline Monopoly 25.00 50.00 100.00
v6#4 no comic strips 25.00 50.00 100.00
v6#5 (May 1850) (3) panel A Short Trip to Mr Bumps, And How It Ended; (2) panel How mr Trembles Was Garrotted 25.00 50.00 100.00
v6#6 no comic strips 25.00 50.00 100.00
v6#7 (July 1857) (5) panel Alma Mater; (3) panel Three Tableaux In the Life of A Broadway Swell 25.00 50.00 100.00
v6 #8 9 no comic strips 25.00 50.00 100.00
v6#10 (Oct 1857) (3) panel Adv of Mr Near-Sight 25.00 50.00 100.00
v6#11 (Nov 1857) (11) panel Mrs Champignon's Dinner Party And the Way She Arranged Her Guests; (4) panel A Stroll in August 25.00 50.00 100.00
v6#12 (Dec 1857) (8) panel strip; (12) panel Young Fitz At A Blow Out in the Fifth Ave 25.00 50.00 100.00
v10#1 (Jan 1860) comic strip Bibbs at Central Park Skating Pond using word balloons 25.00 50.00 100.00

YE TRUE ACCOUNTE OF YE VISIT TO SPRINGFIELDE BY YE CONSTABEL HIS SPECIAL REPORTER
Frank Leslie: 1861 (5-1/8 x 5-1/4 or 93 inches when folded out, paper-c, B&W)
nn - Very Rare fold-out of 18 comic strip panels plus covers - - -
NOTE: *8 panels contain word balloons (Very Rare - only one copy known to exist.) First printed in Frank Leslie's Budget of Fun Jan 1 1861 issue. Abraham Lincoln Biography.*

YE VERACIOUS CHRONICLE OF GRUFF & POMPEY IN 7 TABLEAUX. (O,P)
Jackson's Best Chewing Tobacco & Donaldson Brothers: nd (c1870's) (5-1/8 tall x 3-3/8" wide folded, 27" wide unfolded, color cardboard)
nn - With all 8 panels attached (Scarce) 40.00 80.00 160.00
nn - Individual panels/cards 6.00 12.00 24.00
NOTE: *Black Americana interest. Consists of 8 attached cards, printed on one side, which unfold into a strip story of title card & 7 panels. Scrapbook hobbyists in the 19th Century tended to pull the panels apart and paste into their scrapbooks, making copies with all panels attached scarce.*

YOUNG AMERICA (continues as Yankee Doodle)
T.W. Strong, NYC: 1856
1-30 John McLennon 50.00 100.00 200.00

YOUNG AMERICA'S COMIC ALMANAC
T.W. Strong, NY: 1857 (7-1/2x5", 24 pgs)
nn 50.00 100.00 200.00

THE YOUNG MEN OF AMERICA (becomes Golden Weekly) (S)
Frank Tousey, NYC: 1887-88 (14x10-1/4", 16 pgs, B&W)
527 (10/13/87) Bellew strip "Story of A Black Eye" 25.00 50.00 100.00
530 (11/3/87) Thomas Worth (6) panel strip 125
531 (11/10/87) Thomas Worth(3) panel strip
537 (12/22/87) H.E. Patterson (3) panel strip
544 (2/9/88) Caran s'Ache (6) panel strip-r 37.50 75.00 100.00
555 (4/26/88) Thomas Worth (3) panel strip
556 (5/3/88) Thomas Worth (6) panel strip; Kit Carson-c 75.00 150.00 300.00
569 (8/21/88) Frank Bellew (2) panel strip
570 (8/9/88) Kemble (2) panel strip
571 (8/16/88) Kemble (2) panel strip; first Davy Crockett 75.00 150.00 300.00
Issues with just single panel cartoons 10.00 20.00 40.00

ZIM'S QUARTERLY (M)
(13-13/16x10-1/4", 60 pgs, color-c; most;y B&W, some interior color)
1 - Eugene Zimmerman 112.50 225.00 450.00
NOTE: *Approx. half sequential comic strips, other half single panel cartoons.*

Any addititions or corrections to this section are always welcome, very much encouraged and can be sent to **feedback@gemstonepub.com** to be processed for next year's Guide.

The American Comic Book: 1883-1938

Further Concise History & Price Index Of The Field As Of 2012

NEWSPAPERS HARNESS COMICS POWER MYRIAD FORMATS COMPETE

by Robert Lee Beerbohm and Richard D. Olson, PhD ©2012

(This article was originally created by Robert L. Beerbohm and Richard D. Olson beginning in CBPG #27 1997 and is revised annually as new information comes to light.)

The story of the success of the modern comic strip as we know it today is tied closely to the companies who sponsored and bought licenses from the copyright holder for the purpose of advertising products. Platinum Age comic books have come back into their own after languishing mostly forgotten for a few decades. With this series of comics history research updates now marking its first decade, these historically important books are seem by many now as very collectible. Online sources such as eBay and bookfinder.com have demonstrate that many of these Platinum books are actually not scarce at all as previously thought, though they are in any type of higher-grade condition. Even so, most Platinum Age books are much rarer than so-called Golden Age comic books, yet despite this scarcity, *Mutt & Jeff, Bringing Up Father, The Katzenjammer Kids*, and many more were more popular than say Superman and Batman when they were introduced. Recent research has come up with some more amazing rediscoveries. There is much that can be learned and applied to today's comics market by a simple historical examination of the medium's evolution over more than 160 years.

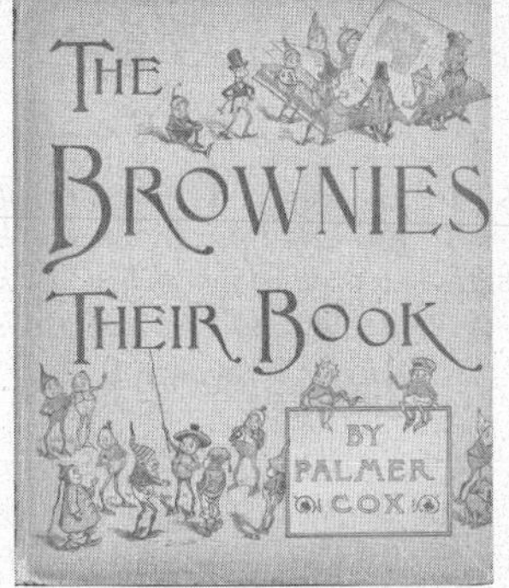

The Brownies' first book, 1887 by Palmer Cox, set a precedent for the Platinum Age, collecting and reprinting previously published material.

It should be noted that "ages" are applied to historical periods in the history of comics for convenience. In fact, ages typically overlap and there is no discrete beginning or ending for any given "age." This is the case with the Platinum Age, which clearly began with Palmer Cox's creation of *The Brownies* in 1883 even though it overlaps with the Victorian Age which ran through the end of the 19th Century. Cox introduced a qualitative change to the field, not an incremental quantitative change. Specifically, he produced art and verse for children in children's magazines and then merchandised those characters. He published work for children not only in books but in magazines and newspapers, and he merchandised his creations to an extent that had never been done previously.

Palmer Cox was born in 1840 near Granby, Quebec. He journeyed to Oakland, California in 1863, and began publishing cartoon, prose and poems in the local press and media outlets such as *The San Francisco Examiner* wherein by 1867 it has been reported he also began creating sequential comic strips, though none have yet surfaced.

His first book, *Squibs of California*, was published in 1874. He subsequently moved to New York in 1875 and almost immediately began working for the magazine *Wild Oats*, of which more is written about in the preceding Victorian Age history introduction as well as a sample of his sequential work. He drew dozens of sequential comic strips for *Wild Oats*, a humor magazine so scarce only one issue has been offered on eBay in the past six years.

Soon thereafter he became a major contributor to the Scribner publications, including *The St. Nicholas*, an illustrated magazine for young folk. His first cartoon for them was "The Wasp And The Bee," published in the March 1879 cover-date issue. While it is now clear that Cox used elves and brownie-like characters in his art for several different magazines as early as 1877 in *Harper's Young People* magazine as well as using Brownies-type characters beginning in the Feb

The Brownies in the Philippines by Palmer Cox, Oct 1904 - scarce original art from the book. President Roosevelt is pictured within these multitudes of Brownie madness, a Cox "signature trademark." Cox's stories are comic strip-oriented in nature of time sequence as he boldly took his Brownies around the world.

1881 issue of *Wide Awake*, the first true appearance of the Brownies in their own story using that title, a combination of art and verse was February, 1883, in *St. Nicholas*. Palmer Cox's *The Brownies* were the first North American comics-type characters to be internationally merchandised. Even though Cox was continuously doing sequential comic strips in magazines like *Wild Oats*, he left the popular medium of comics when he hit paydirt with *The Brownies*. For over a quarter of a century, Cox deftly combined the popular advertising motifs of animals and fairies into a wonderful, whimsical world of society at its best and worst.

The Brownies' first book was issued in 1887, titled *The Brownies: Their Book*; many more followed. Cox also added a run of his hugely popular characters in *Ladies Home Journal* from October 1891 through February 1895, as well as a special for December 1910. With the 1892-93 World's Fair, the merchandising exploded with a host of products, including pianos, paper dolls and other figurines, chairs, stoves, puzzles, cough drops, coffee, soap, boots, candy, and many more. *Brownies* material was being produced in Europe as well as the United States of America.

Chicago Inter Ocean Jr., May 27, 1894 Cover of The Ting-Lings by Charles W. Saalburg, was inspired by Palmer Cox's The Brownies and later provided inspiration for Outcault's Yellow Kid.

Cox tried out *The Brownies* as a newspaper strip in the *San Francisco Examiner* during 1898, where he had begun his newspaper career over 30 years before, and then in the *New York World* in 1900. It was then syndicated from 1903 through 1907. He seems to have retired from regularly drawing *The Brownies* with the January 1914 issue of *St. Nicholas* when he was 74. A wealthy man, he lived to the ripe old age of 84, spending his last decade in his home he affectionately called Brownie Castle, back in Granby, Quebec.

By the mid-1890s, while keeping careful track of steadily rising circulations of magazines with graphic humor such as *Harper's, Puck, St. Nicholas, Judge, Life* and *Truth*, New York based newspaper publishers began to recognize that illustrated humor would sell extra papers. This is what *The Yellow Kid* taught these publishers. Thus was born the Sunday "comic supplement." Most of the super star favorites were under contract with these magazines. However, there was an artist working for *Truth* who wasn't. Roy L McCardell, then a staffer at *Puck*, informed Morrill Goddard, Sunday Editor of *The New York World*, that he knew someone who could fit what was needed at the then-largest newspaper in America.

Richard F. Outcault (1863-1928) first introduced his street children strip in *Truth* #372, June 2, 1894, somewhat inspired by Michael Angelo Woolf's slum kids single panel cartoons in **Life** which had begun in the mid 1880s. The interested collector should seek out a copy of Woolf's *Sketches of Lowly Life In A Great City* (1899) listed in the *Guide* for comparison study. Edward Harrigan's play "O'Reilly and the Four Hundred," which had a song beginning with the words "Down in Hogan's Alley..." also likely provided direct inspiration.

It's also probable that Outcault's *Hogan's Alley* cast, including the *Yellow Kid*, was inspired by Charles W. Saalburg's *The Ting Lings*, which began in the *Chicago Inter Ocean Jr* supplement post-dated May 1, 1894 in the April 29, 1894 edition of Chicago Inter Ocean. That first episode is titled: "The Brownies Welcome The Ting-Lings."

There is also a definite similarity in Mickey Dugan's appearance and clothing style to Saalburg's creation which we will now examine in more detail thanks to welcome, on-going research by long time comics historian Allan Holtz supplemented by living comics history legend Bill Blackbeard .

Charles Saalzburg was an artist who was also the genius behind color printing in newspapers. He seems to have pioneered the concept from whom all others learned their craft.

On June 23, 1892 the *Chicago Inter Ocean* introduced a section with mostly editorial cartoons titled the *Illustrated Supplement*, commemorating the Democratic National Convention held in that city. Early regulars included Thomas Nast and Art Young. Starting June 26, the *Inter Ocean* began steadily issuing this weekly four page supplement, typically featuring full page editorial cartoons on its front and back covers. In May 1893 the supplement began coming out twice a week, and even greater frequency to daily during the *World Columbian Exposition* held in Chicago later that same year as it was used as a wrapper to attract sales from fair goers. Art Young did some of the color cover art and comic strips for the early Fair supplements, printing them right at the Fair to goggle-eyed fair tourists. Thomas Nast did some art as well during a visit he made to the Fair.

By September 10, 1893 the *Inter Ocean* introduced color, a multi-panel editorial comic strip by Charles Saalburg. The supplement used yellow ink, a further nail in the coffin of various Yellow Kid myths which had clouded serious comics scholarship in earlier decades before being proven wrong.

On October 1, Tom E. Powers introduced their first sequential non-political comic strip in color, a humorous pantomime.

As the Exposition ended in November, the contents were soon aimed more at children, enhanced with color added to the center as well by December 24, 1893, then changing its title to *Inter Ocean Jr* in January 1894. This was accomplished easily by folding the single four page sheet into eight pages.

In the January 1894 Saalburg began using Brownies-inspired characters in his color comic strips. The present theory is the *Ting-Ling* characters took over solo five months later in response to a presumed cease and desist letter which inevitably must have been issued from Palmer Cox to the *Inter Ocean.*

However, on July 8 1894, the *Inter Ocean Jr* stopped color and full page comics-type work in this supplement, devolving back to simple small spot art works. By mid-1894, color comics printing genius Saalburg had been lured to Pulitzer's New York World, becoming Art Director in charge of coloring for the new color printing press at the *New York World.* The color supplement was soon to be unleashed in the largest city in America.

By the November 18, 1894 issue of the *World*, Outcault was working for Goddard and Saalburg. Outcault produced a successful Sunday newspaper sequential comic strip in color with "The Origin of a New Species" on the back page in the World's first colored Sunday supplement. Long time pro Walt McDougall, a famous cartoonist reputed to have turned the 1884 Presidential race with a single cartoon that ran in the *World*, handled the cartoon art on the front page. Earlier, *The World* began running full page color single panels on May 21, 1893. McDougall did various other page panels during 1893, but it was Jan. 28, 1894 when the first sequence of comic pictures in a New York World newspaper appeared in panels in the same format as our comic strips today. It was a full page cut up into nine panels. This historic sequence was drawn entirely in pantomime, with no words, by Mark Fenderson.

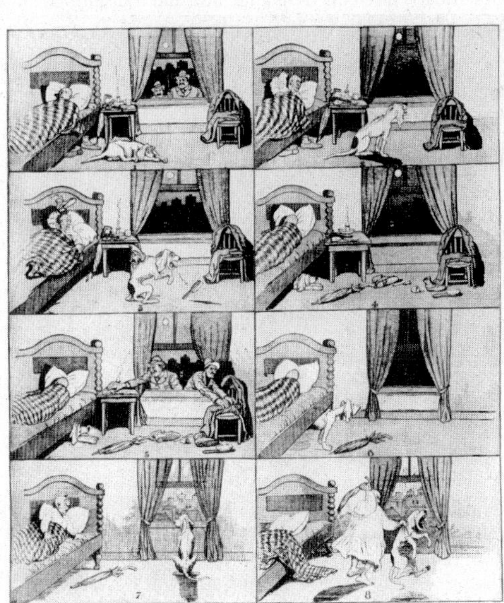

Walt McDougall & Mark Fenderson, the 2nd sequential comic strip in New York World, February 4, 1894, predates Yellow Kid in The World by over a year. Mark Fenderson drew the first NY World newspaper comic strip.

The second page to appear in panels was an eight panel strip from February 4, 1894, also lacking words except for the title. This page was a collaboration between Walt McDougall and Mark Fenderson titled "The Unfortunate Fate of a Well-Intentioned Dog." From then on, many full page color strips by McDougall and Fenderson appeared; they were the first cartoonists to draw for the Sunday newspaper comic section. It was Outcault, however, who soon became the most famous cartoonist featured. After first appearing in black and white in Pulitzer's *The New York World* on February 17, 1895 and again on March 10, 1895, *The Yellow Kid* was introduced to the public in color on May 5, 1895.

Some have erroneously reported in scholarly journals that perhaps it was Frank Ladendorf's "Uncle Reuben," first introduced May 26, 1895, which became the first regularly recurring comics character in newspapers. This is wrong, as even Outcault's "Yellow Kid" began in Pulitzer's paper a good three months before *Uncle Reuben*. Until firm evidence to the contrary comes to light, that honor will forever be enshrined with Jimmy Swinnerton's *Little Bears* cartoon characters, found all over inside Hearst's *San Francisco Examiner* beginning October 14, 1893 with the first one called "Baby Monarch. Though never actually a comic strip, they nonetheless were the earliest presently-known recurring comics-type characters in American newspapers. In June 1895, a semi-regular "Little Bears" feature began. On January 26, 1896, children were introduced, the title eventually changed to "Little Bears and Tykes," forever confusing some scholars decades later. There never was a strip titled *Little Bears and Tigers,* as the *Tigers* were strictly for New York consumption when Hearst ordered Swinnerton to move to the Big Apple to compete better in the brewing comic strip wars.

The Yellow Kid's importance is widely recognized today as the first newspaper comic strip to demonstrate without a doubt that the general public was ready for full color comics. *The Yellow Kid* was the first in the USA to show that comics could increase newspaper sales, and that comic characters could be merchandised. *The Yellow Kid* was the headlining spark of what was soon dubbed by Hearst as "eight pages of polychromatic effulgence that makes the rainbow look like a lead pipe."

Ongoing research suggests that Palmer Cox's fabulous success with *The Brownies* was a direct inspiration for Richard Outcault's future merchandising work. The ultimate proof lies in the fourth Yellow Kid cartoon, which appeared in the February 9, 1895 issue of *Truth*. It was reprinted in the *New York World* eight days later on February 17, 1895, becoming the first Yellow Kid cartoon in the newspapers. The caption read "FOURTH WARD BROWNIES. MICKEY, THE ARTIST (adding a finishing touch) Dere, Chimmy! If Palmer Cox wuz t' see yer, he'd git yer copyrighted in a minute." The Yellow Kid was widely licensed in the greater New York area for all kinds of products, including gum and cigarette cards, toys, pinbacks, cookies, postcards, tobacco products, and appliances. There was also a short-lived humor magazine from Street & Smith named *The Yellow Kid*, featuring exquisite Outcault covers, plus a 196-page comic book from Dillingham & Co. known as *The Yellow Kid in McFadden's Flats,* dated to early 1897. Check out the covers in "The Platinum Age" three-page comic strip elsewhere in this Guide. In addition, there were several Yellow Kid plays produced, spawning other collectibles like show posters, programs and illustrated sheet music. (For those interested in more information regarding the Yellow Kid, it is available on the Internet at www.neponset.com/yellowkid.)

Mickey Dugan burned brightly for a few years as Outcault secured a copyright on the character with the United States Government by September 1896. By the time he completed the necessary paperwork, however, hundreds of business people nationwide had pirated the image of The Yellow Kid and plastered it all over every product imaginable; mothers were even dressing their newborns to look like Dugan. Outcault, however, kept regularly utilizing images of *The Yellow Kid* in his comics style advertising work confirmed as late as 1915. Outcault soon found himself in a maelstrom not of his choosing, which probably pushed him to eventually drop the character. Outcault's creation went back and forth between newspaper giants Pulitzer and Hearst until Bennett's New York Herald mercifully snatched the cartoonist away in 1900 to do what amounted to a few relatively short-run strips. Later, he did one particular strip for a year–a satire of rural Black America titled *Pore Li'l Mose His Letters to his Mammy*, and then his newer creation, *Buster Brown*, debuted May 4, 1902. *Mose* had a very rare comic book collection published in 1902 by Cupples & Leon, now highly sought after by today's savvy collectors. Outcault continued drawing him in the background of occasional *Buster Brown* strips for many years to come.

William Randolph Hearst loved the comic strip medium ever since he was a little boy growing up on *Max & Moritz* by Wilhelm Busch in American collected book editions translated from the original German (these collections were first published in book form in 1871, serving as the influence for *The Katzenjammer Kids*). One of the ways Hearst responded to losing Outcault in 1900 was by purchasing the

"Fourth Ward Brownies," artwork by Richard F. Outcault, Feb. 17, 1895, the 4th Yellow Kid app. and 1st in Pulitzer's New York World. Note the Kid, second from left. This panel first saw print in Truth, Feb 9, 1895.

highly successful 23-year-old humor magazine *Puck* from the heirs of founder Joseph Keppler. With *Puck* and its exclusive cartoonist contracts, he commanded, among others, the very popular F. M. Howarth and Frederick Burr Opper's undivided attention. Opper first burst upon the comics scene in America back in 1880. Within a year Hearst had expanded this *National Lampoon* of its day into the colored Sunday comics section, *Puck-The Comic Weekly*. At first featuring Rudolph Dirk's *The Katzenjammer Kids* (1897), *Happy Hooligan* and other fine strips by the wildly popular Opper and a few others including Rudolph's brother Gus Dirks, the Hearst comic section steadily added more strips. For decades to come, there wasn't anything else that could compete with *Puck*. Hearst hired the best of the best and transformed *Puck* into the most popular comics section anywhere.

Left: The Yellow Kid #1, March 20, 1897, Street & Smith as Howard Ainslee, NY. Right: A rare full color "The Yellow Kid in McFadden's Flats" advertising sign promoting the first comic book featuring the Yellow Kid. The sign is from 1896 and measures 12x18".

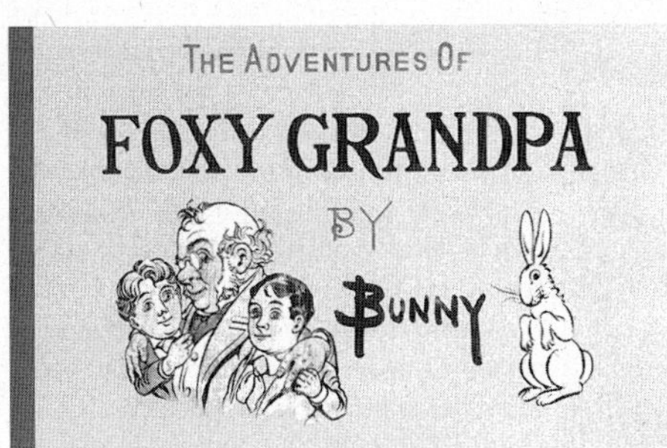

The Adventures of Foxy Grandpa, late 1900, cover for the rare earliest known first edition of Carl "Bunny" Schultze's famous creation. He was one of the newspaper comics' first superstars.

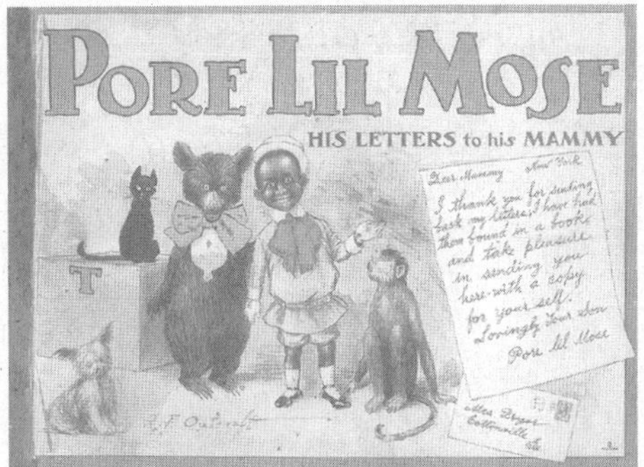

Pore Li'l Mose by Richard Outcault, 1901. Bridges in between Yellow Kid and Buster Brown. Becoming scarce because many copies have been cut up.

Outcault, meanwhile, followed in Palmer Cox's footprints a decade later by using the nexus of a World's Fair as a jumping off venue. *Buster Brown* was an instant sensation when he debuted as the new merchandising mascot of the Brown Shoe Company at the 1904 St. Louis World's Fair in a special Buster Brown Shoes pavilion. The character has the honor of being the first nationally licensed comic strip character in America with this time Outcault in almost full control. Many hundreds of different *Buster Brown* premiums have been issued. Comic books by Frederick A. Stokes Company featuring *Buster Brown & His Dog Tige* began as early as 1903 with *Buster Brown and His Resolutions*, simultaneously published in several different languages throughout the world.

After a few years, Buster and Outcault returned to Hearst in late 1905, joining what soon became the flagship of the comics world. Buster's popularity quickly spread all over the United States and then the world as he single-handedly spawned the first great comic strip licensing dynasty. For years, there were little people traveling from town to town performing as *Buster Brown* and selling shoes while accompanied by small dogs named Tige. Many other highly competitive licensed strips would soon follow. We suggest getting *Hake's Price Guide to Character Toys* for info on several hundred *Buster Brown* competitors, as well as several pages of the more fascinating *Buster Brown* material.

Soon there were many comic strip syndicates not only offering hundreds of various comic strips but also offering to license the characters for any company interested in paying the fee. The history of the comic strip with wide popularity since *The Yellow Kid* has been intertwined with giveaway premiums and character-based, store-bought merchandise of all kinds. Since its infancy as a profitable art form unto itself with *The Yellow Kid*, the comic strip world has profited from selling all sorts of "stuff" to the public featuring their favorite character or strip as its motif. American business gladly responded to the desire for comic character memorabilia with thousands of fun items to enjoy and collect. Most of the early comics were not aimed specifically at kids, though children understandably enjoyed them as well.

Comic books have generally been associated with almost all of the licensed merchandise in this century. In the Platinum Age section beginning right after this essay, you will find a great many comic books in varied formats and sizes published before the advent of the first successful monthly newsstand comic magazine, *Famous Funnies*. What drove each of these evolutionary format changes was the need by their producers to make money so more books could be issued.

A very significant format was F. M. Howarth's *Funny Folks*, published in 1899 by E. P. Dutton and drawn from color as well as black and white pages of *Puck*. This rather large hardcover volume measured 16 1/2" wide by 12" tall. It contains numerous sequential comic strip pages as well as single gag illustrations. Howarth's art was a joy to behold and deserves wider recognition.

By Oct. 1900, Hearst had already caused Opper's *Folks In Funnyville* to be collected by publisher R. H. Russell, NY in a 12x9 hard cover format from his *New York Journal American Humorist* section. At the end of 1900, Carl Shultze had a first edition of *Vaudevilles and Other Things* published by Isaac H. Blanchard Co., NY. It measures 10 1/2" wide by 13" tall with 22 pages including covers. Each interior page is a 2 to 7 panel comic strip with lots of color.

There were also recently unearthed format variation second and third printings of *Vaudevilles* with the inscription "From the Originator of the 'Foxy Grandpa' Series" at the bottom of its front cover of the third printing. This note is lacking on the earlier first two editions, and it also switches format size to 11" tall by 13" wide. Discovered last year was a heretofore undocumented *The Adventures of Foxy Grandpa* - also issued in 1900 - new to the Platinum listings. The second number dated 1901 drops the words "The Adventures of..." from the title.

E. W. Kemble's *The Blackberries* had a color collection by 1901, also published by R. H. Russell, NY, as well as a few other comic-related volumes by Kemble still to be unearthed and properly identified. An earlier one was titled *Coontown's 400* (1899) newly listed this year. While the title is definitely not "PC" by today's standards, Kemble's drawings are excellent slices of African-American life in the USA with some humor

HUGO HERCULES MISSES THE FOOTBALL, BUT—

The Chicago Tribune introduced a straight super hero with obvious super strength called "Hugo Hercules" by the unknown artist J. Koerner. This Sunday strip ran September 7, 1902 through January 11, 1903 and ran only in this one paper. It is entirely possible a very young Chicago-resident named Philip Wylie read "Hugo" since that was the same name he gave his super-heroic main character in his much-later book The Gladiator (1930). Other appearances have Hugo running with almost super speed.

injected. Kemble did a good job documenting aspects of life.

Confirmed is the exact format of Hearst's 1902 *The Katzenjammer Kids and Happy Hooligan And His Brother Gloomy Gus*. They both measure 15 5/16" wide by 10" tall and contain 88 pages including covers. Confirmed also is the fact that there are two separate editions with different covers for the pictured 1902 first edition and a 1903 Frederick Stokes edition of *Katzenjammer Kids* and *Happy Hooligan* with differing contents. They both are two different books entirely, and what confuses many collectors is that they have identical indicia title pages, but so does an entirely different *KK* from 1905.

Settling on a popular size of 17" wide by 11" tall, comic books were soon available that featured Charles "Bunny" Schultze's *Foxy Grandpa*, Rudolph Dirk's *The Katzenjammer Kids*, Winsor McCay's *Little Sammy Sneeze, Rarebit Fiend* and *Little Nemo*, and Fred Opper's *Happy Hooligan* and *Maud*, in addition to dozens of *Buster Brown* comic books. For well over a decade, these large-size, full-color volumes were the norm, retailing for 60¢. These collections offered full-size Sunday comics with the back side blank per page.

Though not the first daily newspaper strip, the very rare *Brainy Bowers and Drowsy Dugan* by R. W. Taylor is now crowned the first collection of strip reprints from a daily newspaper published in America. There are now four different collections of Brainy Bower known to exist.

The Outbursts of Everett True by A. D. Condo and J. W. Raper was first published by Saalfield in 1907 in an 88-page hardcover collection. It qualifies as the second daily comic strip collection as it predates the first *Mutt & Jeff* collection from Ball by three years. Condo & Raper's creation began its regular run several times a week in 1905 daily newspapers and lasted until 1927, when Condo became too sick to continue. This same *Everett True* collection was later truncated a bit by Saalfield in 1921 to 56 strips in just 32 pages measuring the standard 10"x10" Cupples & Leon size.

By 1908 Stokes had a large backlist of full color comic books for sale at 60¢ each. Some of these titles date back to 1903 and were reprinted over and over as demand warranted. Note the number of titles in the advertisement pulled from the back of *The Three Fun Makers* shown below.

With the ever-increasing popularity of Bud Fisher's new daily strip sensation, *Mutt & Jeff*, a new format was created for reprinting daily strips in black and white, a hardcover book about 15" wide by 5" tall, published by Ball starting in 1910 for five volumes. In 1912, Ball also branched out with at least the

Left, The Outbursts of Everett True. 2nd daily strip collection, published 1907 Right: The earliest known comic book display ad, from in the back of1908 Stokes comic books, 27 titles then in print. Cover prices are 60¢.

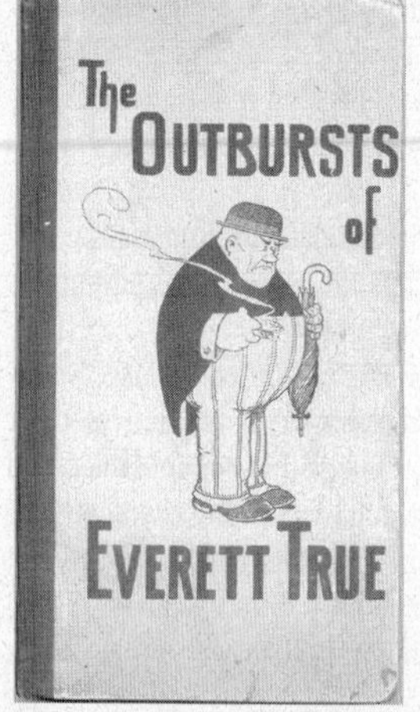

now-obscure *Doings of the Van Loons* by Fred I. Leipziger, a rare comic book in the same format as the *Mutt & Jeffs*.

Cartoons Magazine also began in 1912 and ran through 1921 before undergoing a radical format change. It is notable as a wonderful source for information on early comics and their creators. See also the Platinum index.

The next significant evolutionary change occurred in 1919, when Cupples & Leon began issuing their black and white daily strip reprint books in a new aforementioned format, about 10" wide by 10" tall, with four panels reprinted per page in a two by two matrix. These books were 52 pages for 25¢. The first ones featured *Bringing Up Father* and *Mutt & Jeff;* there were about 100 others.

By 1921, the last of the oblong (11"x15") color comic books were issued, with Cupples & Leon's *Jimmie Dugan* and *The Reg'lar Fellers* by Gene Byrne, and EmBee's *The Trouble Of Bringing Up Father* by self publisher George McManus. Of special historical interest, Embee issued the first 10¢ monthly comic book, *Comic Monthly*, with the first issue dated January 1922. A dozen 8-1/2"x9" issues were published, each featuring solo adventures of popular King Features strips. The monthly 10¢ comic book concept had finally arrived, though it would be more than a decade before it became truly successful.

Skippy by Percy Crosby debuted in the long-running humor magazine *Life* in the March 22, 1923 issue. By 1924 the first hard cover collection, *Life Presents Skippy*, was published. The newspaper comic strip debuted June 23, 1925 with the McClure syndicate. Hearst soon picked up a Sunday page a year later in mid-1926, then added a daily strip in 1929. By the 1930s it was red hot - think *Calvin & Hobbes or Peanuts* in popularity. In its day, it was one of the most popular comic strips ever created. Read the Modern era essay for more on *Skippy's* immense popularity.

In 1926, Cupples & Leon added a new 7" wide by 9" tall format with *Little Orphan Annie, Smitty,* and others. These were issued in both softcover and hardcover editions with dust jackets, and became extremely popular at 60¢ per copy.

Dell began publishing all original material in *The Funnies* in late 1929 in a larger tabloid format. At least three dozen issues were published before Delacorte threw in the towel. Even the extremely popular *Big Little Book*, introduced in 1932, can be viewed as a smaller version of the existing formats. The competition amongst publishers now included Dell, McKay, Sonnet, Saalfield and Whitman. The 1930s saw a definite shift in merchandising comic strip material from adults to children. This was the decade when Kellogg's placed *Buck Rogers* on the map, when Ovaltine issued tons of *Little Orphan Annie* material. Merchandising from such pioneers as Sam Gold and Kay Kamen spearheaded this next transformation of the comics biz beginning in the early 1930s.

Upwards of a thousand of these *Funnies On Parade* precursors, in all formats, were published through 1935 and were very popular. Towards the end of this era of once-popular comic book formats, beautiful collections of *Popeye, Mickey Mouse, Dick Tracy*, and many others were published which today command ever higher prices on the open market as they are rediscovered by the advanced collector who appreciates and enjoys truly great classic comics.

END NOTE: Each year we strive to add to the many 1930s variant formats. This Platinum Age section has grown as a result of advanced collectors who continue to report in with new finds. We encourage interested collectors and scholars to help with this section of the book, as each new data entry is very important for recovering our history. For corrections and additions to next year's next edition of *The Overstreet Guide* of some treasures you may have uncovered, please feel free to contact Gemstone Publishing at feedback@gemstonepub.com.

For further information on this era of American comic books, check out the previous evolving comics history essays in Guides #27,29-#40. Happy Hunting!

Comic Monthly #11 1922 (top), the first 10¢ monthly newsstand comic book title.

Banana Oil, a 1924 example of Cupples & Leon's then-revolutionary format from M.S. Publishers

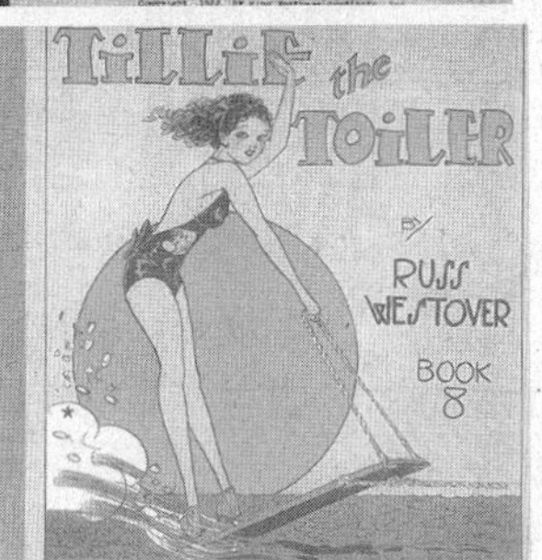

Tillie the Toiler #8 1933 from Cupples & Leon, another scarce number at the end of this once popular format.

David McKay published the last of the 10x10 comic books in 1935 as Famous Funnies grew in popularity.

The Platinum Age 1883–1938

by J.C. Vaughn & Gene Gonzales

OKAY, I'VE GOT A QUESTION FOR YOU.
WHY WOULD ANYONE IGNORE FACTS IN FAVOR OF OPINION?

WHY IN THE FACE OF OVERWHELMING EMPIRICAL EVIDENCE WOULD SOMEONE SAY THAT THE COMIC BOOKS OF *THE VICTORIAN AGE* AND *THE PLATINUM AGE* AREN'T COMIC BOOKS?
GOSH, I FEEL LIKE THE RIDDLER.

THE FIRST COLLECTION OF PREVIOUSLY PUBLISHED STRIPS FEATURING *THE BROWNIES* WAS PRINTED IN 1887.

THE BROWNIES BECAME THE ROAD MAP FOR SUCCESSFUL LICENSED CHARACTERS . . .

THE PATH THAT WAS LATER FOLLOWED BY THE *YELLOW KID*, *MICKEY MOUSE*, AND *SUPERMAN*.

THE YELLOW KID IN MCFADDEN'S FLATS WAS COLLECTED R.F. OUTCAULT'S SUCCESSFUL CHARACTER IN BOOK FORM.
LIKE MANY OTHERS IN THAT TIME, IT WAS A HUGE SUCCESS.
BUT NO ONE WOULD CALL THIS COLLECTION A COMIC BOOK, WOULD THEY?
50 Cents
THE YELLOW KID IN McFADDEN'S FLATS
BY E.W. TOWNSEND AUTHOR OF CHIMMIE FADDEN
AND R.F. OUTCAULT CREATOR OF THE YELLOW KID
DIS BOOK IS DE STORY OF ME SWEET YOUNG LIFE
G.W. DILLINGHAM Co. PUBLISHERS NEW YORK
THIRTIETH THOUSAND.

THE MOST *POPULAR COMIC BOOKS* EVER PUBLISHED.
ARTEMUS WARD. HIS COMPLETE COMIC WRITINGS, WITH BIOGRAPHY AND ONE HUNDRED ILLUSTRATIONS. THE BIOGRAPHICAL SKETCH BY "ELI PERKINS." CLOTH BOUND, PRICE $1.50.
JOSH BILLINGS. HIS WORKS COMPLETE (FOUR VOLUMES IN ONE), WITH ONE HUNDRED ILLUSTRATIONS, BY THOMAS NAST, AND OTHERS. CLOTH BOUND, PRICE $2.00.
VERDANT GREEN. A RACY ENGLISH COLLEGE STORY, BY CUTHBERT BEDE. PROFUSELY ILLUSTRATED, AND CLOTH BOUND. PRICE $1.50.
SOLD EVERYWHERE, AND SENT BY MAIL, POSTAGE FREE, ON RECEIPT OF PRICE, BY G.W. DILLINGHAM CO., PUBLISHERS, 33 WEST 23D STREET, NEW YORK.
THE MOST POPULAR COMIC BOOKS EVER PUBLISHED.
ARTEMUS WARD.
His complete comic writings, with biography and one hundred illustrations. The biographical sketch by "Eli Perkins." Cloth bound, price $1.50.
JOSH BILLINGS.
His works complete (four volumes in one), with one hundred illustrations, by Thomas Nast, and others. Cloth bound, price $2.00.
VERDANT GREEN.
A racy English college story, by Cuthbert Bede. Profusely illustrated, and cloth bound. Price $1.50.
Sold everywhere, and sent by mail, postage free, on receipt of price, by
G. W. Dillingham Co., Publishers, 33 West 23d Street, New York.

SO, LET'S GET THIS STRAIGHT . . .
IN 1897 THESE GUYS KNEW IT WAS A COMIC BOOK, BUT THERE ARE STILL PEOPLE OUT THERE IN 2012 WHO DON'T?

WHO ELSE MIGHT HAVE BEEN DOING COMIC BOOKS?
I CREATED LITTLE NEMO IN 1905 AND SOON IT WAS BEING COLLECTED INTO COMIC BOOK REPRINTS.
LADIES AND GENTLEMEN, WINSOR McCAY.
LATER, COMIC MONTHLY, WHICH DEBUTED IN 1922, WAS THE FIRST MONTHLY NEWSSTAND COMIC BOOK.
DREAM OF THE RAREBIT FIEND
BANG!
Comic Monthly
10¢
POLLY & HER PALS
BY CLIFF STERRETT.
BY GEORGE, THE REPRINTS OF MY STRIP, BRINGING UP FATHER, SOLD MORE THAN 4 MILLION COPIES EACH . . .
. . . IN A NATION OF ONLY 100 MILLION PEOPLE!
BRINGING UP FATHER
by GEO McMANUS
FUNNIES ON PARADE, WHICH IS LITTLE MORE THAN AN INTERESTING FOOTNOTE IN COMICS HISTORY, WAS PUBLISHED IN 1933 . . .
IT WAS, OF COURSE, A COLLECTION OF REPRINTS . . .
. . . AND THE ONLY DIFFERENCE, OF COURSE, THE FORMAT AND TYPE OF BINDING USED.
SO WHY IS ONE A COMIC BOOK AND THE OTHER IS NOT?
THE BROWNIES THEIR BOOK
BY PALMER COX
FUNNIES ON PARADE
IF YOU CAN FIGURE IT OUT, LET US KNOW.
IN THE MEANTIME, WE HOPE YOU ENJOY THIS YEAR'S LISTING OF PLATINUM AGE COMIC BOOKS.

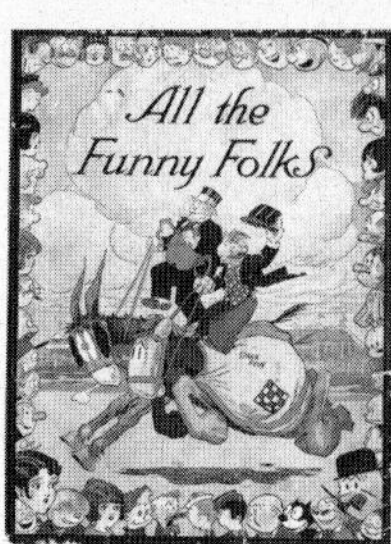

All the Funny Folks
© WPT

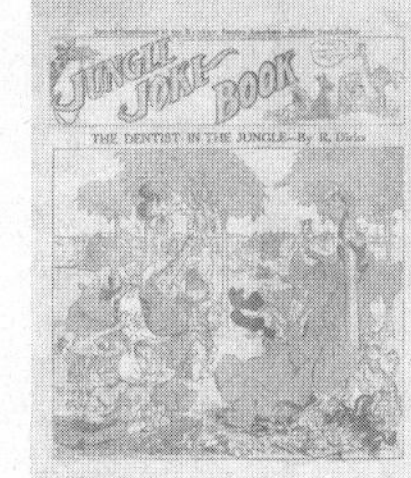

American-Journal-Examiner Joke Book
Special Supplement #12
1912 © New York American-Examiner

Banana Oil by Milt Gross
1924 © M.S. Publishing Company

GD2.0 FN6.0 VF8.0

COLLECTOR'S NOTE: The books listed in this section were published many decades before organized comics fandom began archiving and helping to preserve these fragile popular culture artifacts. Consequently, copies of most all of these comics do not often surface in Fine+ or better shape. eBay has proven after more than a decade that many items once considered rare actually are not, though they almost always are in higher grades. For items marked scarce, we are trying to ascertain how many copies might still be in existence. Your input is always welcome.

Most Platinum Age comic books are in the Fair to VG range. If you want to collect these only in high grade, your collection will be extremely small. The prices given for Good, Fine and Very Fine categories are for strictly graded editions. If you need help grading your item, we refer you to the grading section in the front of this price guide or contact the authors of the Platinum essay. Most measurements are in inches. A few measurements are in centimeters. The first dimension given is Height and the second is Width.

For ease of ascertaining the contents of each item of this listing, there is a code letter or two following most titles we have been adding in over the years to aid you. A helpful list of categories pertaining to these codes can be found at the beginning of the Victorian Age pricing sections.This section created, revised, and expanded by Robert Beerbohm and Richard Olson with able assistance from Ray Agricola, Jon Berk, Bill Blackbeard, Roy Bonario, Ray Bottorff Jr., Chris Brown, Alfredo Castelli, Darrell Coons, Sol Davidson, Leonardo De Sá, Scott Deschaine, Mitchell Duval, Joe Evans, Tom Gordon III, Bruce Hamilton, Andy Konkykru, Don Kurtz, Gabriel Laderman, Bruce Mason, Donald Puff, Robert Quesinberry, Steve Rowe, Randy Scott, John Snyder, Art Spiegelman, Steve Thompson, Joan Crosby Tibbets, Richard Samuel West, Doug Wheeler, Richard Wright and Craig Yoe.

ADVENTURES OF EVA, PORA AND TED (M)
Evaporated Milk Association: 1932 (5x15", 16 pgs, B&W)

nn - By Steve 20.00 40.00 80.00
NOTE: *Appears to have had green, blue or white paper cover versions.*

ADVENTURES OF HAWKSHAW (N) (See Hawkshaw The Detective)
The Saalfield Publishing Co.: 1917 (9-3/4x13-1/2", 48 pgs., color & two-tone)

nn - By Gus Mager (only 24 pgs. of strips, reverse of each pg. is blank) 50.00 175.00 300.00
nn - 1927 Reprints 1917 issue 30.00 150.00 260.00
NOTE: *Started Feb 23, 1913-Sept 4, 1922, then begins again Dec 13, 1931-Feb 11, 1952.*

ADVENTURES OF SLIM AND SPUD, THE (M)
Prairie Farmer Publ. Co.: 1924 (3-3/4x 9-3/4", 104 pgs., B&W strip reprints)

nn 21.00 84.00 150.00
NOTE: *Illustrated mailing envelope exists postmarked out of Chicago, add 50%.*

ADVENTURES OF WILLIE WINTERS, THE (O,P)
Kelloggs Toasted Corn Flake Co.: 1912 (6-7/8x9-1/2", 20 pgs, full color)

nn - By Byron Williams & Dearborn Melvill 54.00 189.00 350.00

ADVENTURES OF WILLIE GREEN, THE (N) (see The Willie Green Comics)
Frank M. Acton Co.: 1915 (50¢, 52 pgs, 8-1/2X16", B&W, soft-c)

Book 1 - By Harris Brown; strip-r 54.00 189.00 350.00

A. E. F. IN CARTOONS BY WALLY, THE (N)
Don Sowers & Co.: 1933 (12x10-1/8", 88 pgs, hardcover B&W)

nn - By Wally Wallgren (WW One Stars & Stripes-r) 25.00 90.00 150.00

AFTER THE TOWN GOES DRY (I)
The Howell Publishing Co, Chicago: 1919 (48 pgs, 6-1/2x4", hardbound two color-c)

nn - By Henry C. Taylor; illus by Frank King 25.00 75.00 150.00

AIN'T IT A GRAND & GLORIOUS FEELING? (N) (Also see Mr. & Mrs.)
Whitman Publishing Co.: 1922 (9x9-3/4", 52 pgs., stiff cardboard-c)

nn - 1921 daily strip-r; B&W, color-c; Briggs-a 36.00 143.00 250.00
nn -(9x9-1/2", 28pgs., stiff cardboard-c)-Sunday strip-r in color (inside front-c says "More of the Married Life of Mr. & Mrs".) 36.00 143.00 250.00
NOTE: *Strip started in 1917; This is the 2nd Whitman comic book, after Brigg's MR. & MRS.*

ALL THE FUNNY FOLKS (I)
World Press Today, Inc.: 1926 (11-1/2x8-1/2", 112 pgs., color, hard-c)

nn-Barney Google, Spark Plug, Jiggs & Maggie, Tillie The Toiler, Happy Hooligan, Hans & Fritz, Toots & Casper, etc. 100.00 400.00 650.00
With Dust Jacket By Louis Biedermann 200.00 800.00 1600.00
NOTE: *Booklength race horse story masterfully enveloping all major King Features characters.*

ALPHONSE AND GASTON AND THEIR FRIEND LEON (N)
Hearst's New York American & Journal: 1902,1903 (10x15-1/4", Sunday strip reprints in color)

nn - (1902) - By Frederick Opper (scarce) 500.00 1800.00 –
nn - (1903) - By Frederick Opper (scarce) (72 pages) 500.00 1800.00 –
NOTE: *Strip ran Sept 22, 1901to at least July 17, 1904.*

ALWAYS BELITTLIN' (see Skippy; That Rookie From the 13th Squad; Between Shots)
Henry Holt & Co.: 1927 (6x8", hard-c with DJ,

nn -By Percy Crosby (text with cartoons) 43.00 172.00 300.00

ALWAYS BELITTLIN' (I) (see Skippy; That Rookie From the 13th Squad, Between Shots)
Percy Crosby, Publisher: 1933 (14 1/4 x 11", 72 pgs, hard-c, B&W)

GD2.0 FN6.0 VF8.0

nn - By Percy Crosby 43.00 172.00 300.00
NOTE: *Self-published; primarily political cartoons with text pages denouncing prohibition's gang warfare effects and cuts in the national defense budget as Crosby saw war looming in Europe and with Japan.*

AMERICAN-JOURNAL-EXAMINER JOKE BOOK SPECIAL SUPPLEMENT (O)
New York American: 1911-12 (12 x 9 3/4", 16 pgs) (known issues) (Very Rare)

1 Tom Powers Joke Book(12/10/11) 80.00 280.00 –
2 Mutt & Jeff Joke Book (Bud Fisher 12/17/11) 100.00 350.00 –
3 TAD's Joke Book (Thomas Dorgan 12/24/11) 80.00 300.00 –
4 F. Opper's Joke Book (Frederick Burr Opper 12/31/11) (contains Happy Hooligan) 100.00 350.00 –
5 not known to exist
6 Swinnerton's Joke Book (Jimmy Swinnerton 01/14/12) (contains Mr. Jack) 100.00 350.00 –
7 The Monkey's Joke Book (Gus Mager 01/21/12) (contains Sherlocko the Monk) 100.00 350.00 –
8 Joys And Glooms Joke Book (T. E. Powers 01/28/12) 80.00 280.00 –
9 The Dingbat Family's Joke Book (George Herriman 02/04/12) (contains early Krazy Kat & Ignatz) 200.00 700.00 –
10 Valentine Joke Book, A (Opper, Howarth, Mager, T. E. Powers 02/11/12) 80.00 280.00 –
11 Little Hatchet Joke Book (T. E. Powers 02/18/12) 80.00 280.00 –
12 Jungle Joke Book (Dirks, McCay 02/25/12) 100.00 400.00 –
13 The Hayseeds Joke Book (03/03/12) 80.00 280.00 –
14 Married Life Joke Book (T.E. Powers 03/10/12) 80.00 280.00 –
NOTE: *These were insert newspaper supplements similar to Eisner's later Spirit sections. A Valentine Joke Book recently surfaced from Hearst's Boston Sunday American proving that other cities besides New York City had these special supplements. Each issue also contains work by other cartoonists besides the cover featured creator and those already listed above such as Sidney Smith, Winsor McCay, Hy Mayer, Grace Weiderseim (later Drayton), others.*

AMERICA'S BLACK & WHITE BOOK 100 Pictured Reasons Why We Are At War (N,S)
Cupples & Leon: 1917 (10 3/4 x 8", 216 pgs)

nn - W. A. Rogers (New York Herald-r) 32.00 114.00 195.00

AMONG THE FOLKS IN HISTORY
Rand McNally Print Guild: 1935 (192 pgs, 8-1/2x9-1/2", hard-c, B&W)

nn - By Gaar Williams 21.00 84.00 150.00

AMONG THE FOLKS IN HISTORY
The Book and Print Guild: 1935 (200 pgs, 8-1/2x9-1/2:,

nn - By Gaar Williams 21.00 84.00 150.00
NOTE: *Both the above are evidently different editions and contain largely full-page, single panel cartoons similar to Briggs' work of that sort. 8 or 10 pages are broken into panels, usually with a this is how it was in the old days, this is how it is today theme.*

ANGELIC ANGELINA (N)
Cupples & Leon Company: 1909 (11-1/2x17", 56 pgs., 2 colors)

nn - By Munson Paddock 67.00 233.00 400.00
NOTE: *Strip ran March 22, 1908-Feb 7, 1909.*

ANDY GUMP, HIS LIFE STORY (I)
The Reilly & Lee Co, Chicago: 1924 (192 pgs, hardbound)

nn - By Sidney Smith (over 100 illustrations) 20.00 80.00 150.00

ANIMAL CIRCUS, THE (from Puggery Wee)
Rand McNally + Company: 1908 (48 pgs, 11x8-1/2", color-c, 3-color insides)

nn - By unknown 20.00 80.00 150.00
NOTE: *Illustrated verse, many pages with multiple illustrations.*

ANIMAL SERIALS
T. Y. Crowell: 1906 (9x6-7/8", 214 pgs, hard-c, B&W)

nn - By E Warde Blaisdell 20.00 80.00 150.00
NOTE: *Multi-page comic strip stories. Reprints of Sunday strip "Bunny Bright He's All-Right".*

A NOBODY'S SCRAP BOOK
Frederik A. Stokes Co., New York: 1900 (11" x 8-5/8", hard-c, color)

nn- (Scarce) 67.00 233.00 400.00
NOTE: *Designed in England, printed in Holland, on English paper -- which likely explains the mispelling of Frederick Stokes' name. Highly fragile paper. Strips and cartoons, all by the same unidentified artist, "A Nobody", almost certainly reprinted from somewhere, as they are very professional.*

AT THE BOTTOM OF THE LADDER (M)
J.P. Lippincott Company: 1926 (11x8-1/4", 296 pgs, hardcover, B&W)

nn - By Camillus Kessler 45.00 157.50 300.00
NOTE: *Hilarious single panel cartoons showing first jobs of then important "captains of industry."*

AUTO FUN, PICTURES AND COMMENTS FROM "LIFE"
Thomas Y. Crowell & Co.: 1905 (152 pgs, 9x7", hard-c, B&W)

nn -By various 45.00 157.00 300.00
NOTE: *The cover just has "Auto Fun" but the title page also has the subheading listed here. This is similar to other reprint books of Life cartoons printed in the guide. Largely single panel cartoons but also several sequential. One or more cartoons by Kemble, Levering, Dirks, Flagg, Sullivant. Sequential cartoons by Kemble, Levering, Sullivant, and the highpoint, a 2 pg 6 panel piece by Winsor McCay.*

BANANA OIL (N) (see also HE DONE HER WRONG)

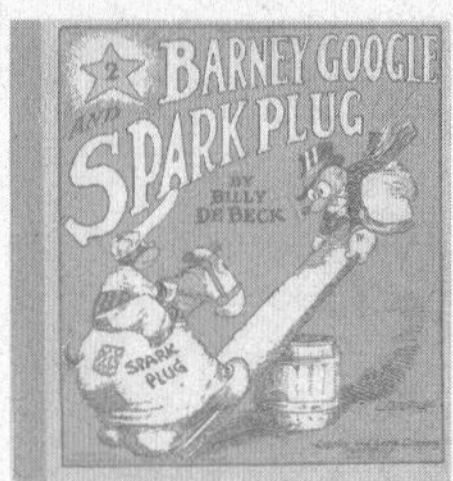

Barney Google and Spark Plug #2
© C&L

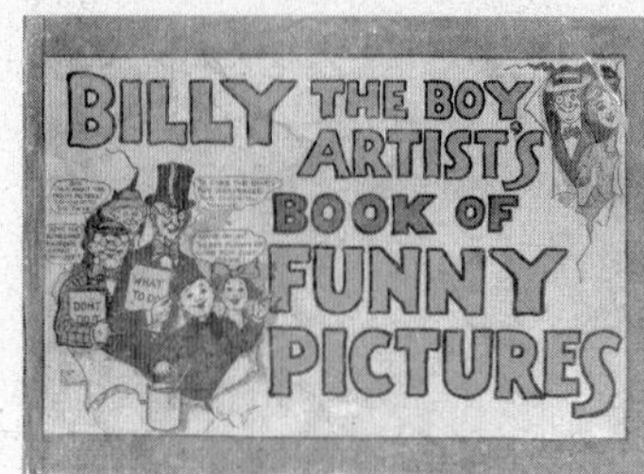

Bill the Boy Artist's Book by Ed Payne
1910 © C.M. Clark Publishing Co

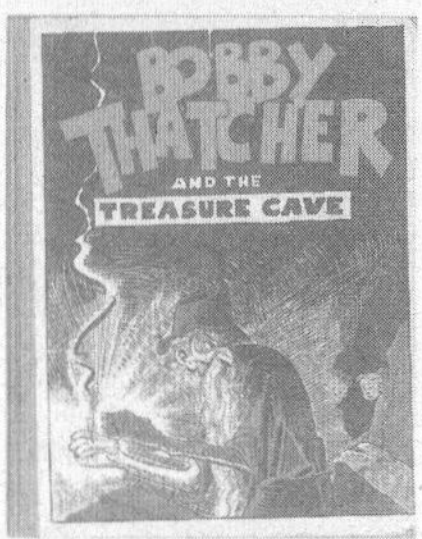

Bobby Thatcher and the Treasure Cave
1932 © Altemus Co.

MS Publ. Co.: 1924 (9-7/8x10", 52 pgs., B&W)
nn - Milt Gross comic strips; not reprints 150.00 450.00 750.00

BARKER'S ILLUSTRATED ALMANAC (O,P,S) (See Barkers in Victorian Era section)
Barker, Moore & Mein Medicine Co: 1900-1932+ (36 pgs, B&W, color paper-c)
1900-1932+ (7x5-7/8") 20.00 70.00 150.00

BARKER'S "KOMIC" PICTURE SOUVENIR (P,S) (see Barker's in Victorian)
Barker, Moore & Mein Medicine Co: nd (Parts 1-3, 1901-1903; Parts 1-4, 1906+) (color cardboard-c, B&W interior, 50 pages)
Parts 1-3 (Rare, earliest printing, nd (1901)) 60.00 300.00 600.00
NOTE: *Same cover as 4th edition in Victorian Age Section, except has "Part 1", "Part 2", or "Part 3" printed in the blank space beneath the crate on which central figure is sitting. States "Edition in 3 Parts" on the first interior page, beneath the picture of the Barker's Building.*
Parts 1-3 (nd, c1901-1903) 50.00 200.00 400.00
NOTE: *New cover art on all Parts. States "Edition in 3 Parts" on the first interior page.*
Parts 1-4 (nd, c1906+) 50.00 100.00 300.00
NOTE: *States "Edition in 4 Parts" on the first interior page. Various printings known.These have been confirmed as premium comic books, predating the Buster Brown premiums. They reprint advertising cartoons from Barker's Illustrated Almanac. For the 50 page booklets by this same name, numbered as "Part"s, without exception, were published after 1900. Some editions are found to have 54 pages.*

BARNEY GOOGLE AND SPARK PLUG (N) (See **Comic Monthly**)
Cupples & Leon Co.: 1923 - No.6, 1928 (9-7/8x9-3/4"; 52 pgs., B&W, daily-r)
1 (nn)-By Billy DeBeck 60.00 240.00 450.00
2-4 (#5 & #6 do not exist) 46.00 186.00 350.00
NOTE: *Started June 17, 1919 as newspaper strip; Spark Plug introduced July 17, 1922; strip still running making it one of the oldest still in existence.*

BART'S CARTOONS FOR 1902 FROM THE MINNEAPOLIS JOURNAL (N,S)
Minneapolis Journal: 1903 (11x9", 102 pgs, paperback, B&W)
nn - By Charles L. Bartholomew 28.00 99.00 170.00

BELIEVE IT OR NOT! by Ripley (N,S)
Simon & Schuster: 1929 (8x 5-1/4", 68 pgs, red, B&W cover, B&W interior)
nn - By Robert Ripley (strip-r text & art) 40.00 120.00 240.00
NOTE: *1929 was the first printing of many reprintings . Strip began Dec 19, 1918 and is still running.*

BEN WEBSTER (N)
Standard Printing Company: 1928-1931 (13-3/4x4-7/16", 768 pgs, soft-c)
1 - "Bound to Win" 40.00 120.00 280.00
2 - "...in old Mexico 40.00 120.00 280.00
3 - "...At Wilderness Lake 40.00 120.00 280.00
4 - "...in the Oil Fields 40.00 120.00 280.00
NOTE: *Self Published by Edwin Alger, also contains fan's letter pages.*

BIG SMOKER
W.T. Blackwell & Co.: 1908 (16 pgs, 5-1/2x3-1/2", color-c & interior)
nn - By unknown 12.00 48.00 80.00
NOTE: *Stated reprint of 1878 version. no known copies yet of original printing.*

BILLY BOUNCE (I)
Donohue & Co.: 1906 (288 pgs, hardbound)
nn - By W.W. Denslow & Dudley Bragdon 150.00 525.00 900.00
NOTE: *Billy Bounce was created in 1901 as a comic strip by W. W. Denslow (strip ran from 1901 NOV 11 to 1905 DEC 3), but the series is best remembered in the C. W. Kahles version (from 1902 SEP 28). Denslow resumed his character in the above illustrated book.*

BILLY HON'S FAMOUS CARTOON BOOK (H)
Wasley Publishing Co.: 1927 (7-1/2x10", 68 pgs, softbound wraparound)
nn - By Billy Hon 12.00 48.00 80.00

BILLY THE BOY ARTIST'S BOOK OF FUNNY PICTURES (N)
C.M.Clark Publishing Co.: 1910 (9x12", hardcover-c, Boston Globe strip-r)
nn - By Ed Payne 125.00 400.00 750.00
NOTE: *This long lived strip ran in **The Boston Globe** from Nov 5 1899-Jan 7 1955; one of the longer run strips.*

BILLY THE BOY ARTIST'S PAINTING BOOK OF FUNNY PICTURES
(known to exist; more data required) – – –

BIRD CENTER CARTOONS: A Chronicle of Social Happenings (N,S)
A. C. McClurg & Co.: 1904 (12-3/8x9-1/2", 216 pgs, hardcover, B&W, single panels)
nn - By John McCutcheon 40.00 140.00 260.00
NOTE: *Strip began in **The Chicago Tribune** in 1903. Satirical cartoons and text concerning a mythical town.*

BLASTS FROM THE RAM'S HORN
The Rams Horn Company: 1902 (330 pgs, 7x9", B&W)
nn - By various 20.00 70.00 120.00
NOTE: *Cartoons reprinted from what was, apparently, a religious newspaper. Many cartoons by Frank Beard. Mostly single panel but occasionally sequential. Allegorical cartoons similar to the Christian Cartoons book. This book mixes cartoons and text sort of like the Caricature books. One or more cartoons on every page.*

BOBBY THATCHER & TREASURE CAVE (N)
Altemus Co.: 1932 (9x7", 86 pgs., B&W, hard-c)
nn - Reprints; Storm-a 54.00 189.00 400.00

BOBBY THATCHER'S ROMANCE (N)
The Bell Syndicate/Henry Altemus Co.: 1931 (8-3/4x7", color cover, B&W)
nn - By Storm 54.00 189.00 400.00

BOOK OF CARTOONS, A (M,S)
Edward T. Miller: 1903 (12-1/4x9-1/4", 120 pgs, hardcover, B&W)
nn - By Harry J. Westerman (Ohio State Journal-r) 20.00 70.00 120.00

BOOK OF DRAWINGS BY A.B. FROST, A (M,S)
P.F. Collier & Son: 1904 (15-3/8 x 11", 96 pgs, B&W)
nn - A.B. Frost 50.00 100.00 300.00
NOTE: *Pages alternate verses by Wallace Irwin and full-page plated by A.B.Frost. 39 plates.*

BOTTLE, THE (E) (see Victorian Age section for earlier printings)
Gowans & Gray, London & Glasgow: June 1905 (3-3/4x6", 72 pgs, printed one side only, paper cover, B&W)
nn - 1st printing (June 1905) 20.00 40.00 80.00
nn - 2nd printing (March 1906) 20.00 40.00 80.00
nn - 3rd printing (January 1911) 20.00 40.00 80.00
NOTE: *By George Cruikshank. Reprints both THE BOTTLE and THE DRUNKARD'S CHILDREN. Cover is text only - no cover art.*

BOTTLE, THE (E)
Frederick A. Stokes: nd (c1906) (3-3/4x6", 72 pgs, printed one side only, paper-c, B&W)
nn- by George Cruikshank 17.50 35.00 70.00
NOTE: *Reprint of the Gowans & Gray edition. Reprints both THE BOTTLE and THE DRUNKARD'S CHILDREN. Cover is text only - no cover art.*

BOYS AND FOLKS (N).
George H. Dornan Company: 1917 (10-1/4 x 8-1/4", 232 pgs. (single-sided), B&W strip-r.
nn - By Webster 21.00 64.00 150.00
NOTE: *Four sections: Life's Darkest Moments, Mostly About Folks, The Thrill That Comes Once in a Lifetime, and Our Boyhood Ambitions. Most are single-panel cartoons, but there are some sequential comic strips.*

BOY'S & GIRLS' BIG PAINTING BOOK OF INTERESTING COMIC PICTURES (N)
M. A. Donohue & Co.: 1914-16 (9x15, 70 pgs)
nn - By Carl "Bunny" Schultze (Foxy Grandpa-r) 81.00 284.00 –
#2 (1914) 81.00 284.00 –
#337 (1914) (sez "Big Painting & Drawing Book") 81.00 284.00 –
nn - (1916) (sez "Big Painting Book")(9-1/4x15") 81.00 284.00 –
NOTE: *These are all **Foxy Grandpa** items.*

BRAIN LEAKS: Dialogues of Mutt & Flea (N)
O. K. Printing Co. (Rochester Evening Times): 1911 (76 pgs, 6-5/8x4-5/8, hard-c, B&W)
nn - By Leo Edward O'Melia; newspaper strip-r 29.00 100.00 171.00

BRAINY BOWERS AND DROWSY DUGGAN (N)
Star Publishing: 1905 (7-1/4 x 4-9/16", 98 pgs., blue, brown & white color cover, B&W interior, 25¢) (daily strip-r 1902-04 Chicago Daily News)
#74 - By R. W. Taylor (Scarce) 500.00 1700.00 –
NOTE: *Part of a series of Atlantic Library Heart Series. Strip begins in 1901 and runs thru 1915. Taylor also created Yen the Janitor for the **New York World.***

BRAIN BOWERS AND DROWSY DUGAN (N)
Max Stein Pub. House, Chicago: 1905 (6-3/16x4-3/8", 64 pgs, B&W)
nn - By R.W. Taylor (Scarce) 500.00 1700.00 –
NOTE: *A coverless copy of this surfaced on eBay in 2002 selling for $700.00.;*

BRAINY BOWERS AND DROWSY DUGGAN GETTING ON IN THE WORLD WITH NO VISIBLE MEANS OF SUPPORT (STORIES TOLD IN PICTURES TO MAKE THEIR TELLING SHORT) (N)
Max Stein/Star Publishing: 1905 (7-3/8x5 1/8", 164 pgs, slick black, red & tan color cover, interior newsprint) (daily strip-r 1902-04 Chicago Daily News)
nn - By R. W. Taylor (Scarce) 500.00 1700.00 –
nn - Possible hard cover edition also? – – –
NOTE: *These Brainy Bowers editions are the earliest known daily newspaper strip reprint books.*

BRINGING UP FATHER (N)
Star Co. (King Features): 1917 (5-1/2x16-1/2", 100 pgs., B&W, cardboard-c)
nn - (Scarcer)-Daily strip- by George McManus 158.00 553.00 950.00

BRINGING UP FATHER (N)
Cupples & Leon Co.: 1919 - No. 26, 1934 (10x10", 52 pgs., B&W, stiff cardboard-c) (No. 22 is 9-1/4x9-1/2")
1-Daily strip-r by George McManus in all 25.00 100.00 260.00
2-10 25.00 100.00 250.00
11-20 40.00 200.00 375.00
21-26 (Scarcer) 60.00 300.00 550.00
The Big Book 1 (1926)-Thick book (hardcover, 142 pgs.) 127.00 508.00 1000.00
w/dust jacket (rare) 183.00 732.00 1325.00
The Big Book 2 (1929) 96.00 384.00 700.00
w/dust jacket (rare) 183.00 732.00 1325.00
NOTE: *The Big Books contain 3 regular issues rebound. Strip began Jan 2 1913-May 28 2000.*

BRINGING UP FATHER, THE TROUBLE OF (N)
Embee Publ. Co.: 1921 (9-3/4x15-3/4", 46 pgs, Sunday-r in color)
nn - (Rare) 100.00 350.00 600.00
NOTE: *Ties with Mutt & Jeff (EmBee) and Jimmie Dugan And The Reg'lar Fellers (C&L) as the last of the*

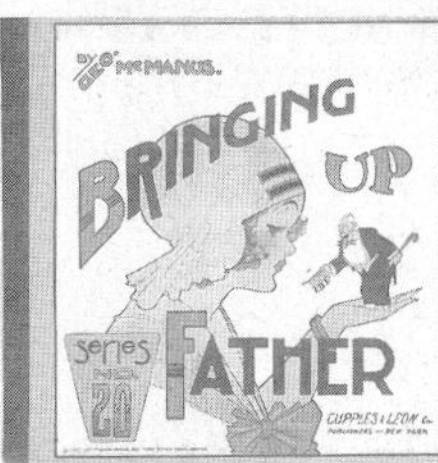

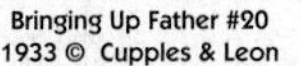
Bringing Up Father #20
1933 © Cupples & Leon

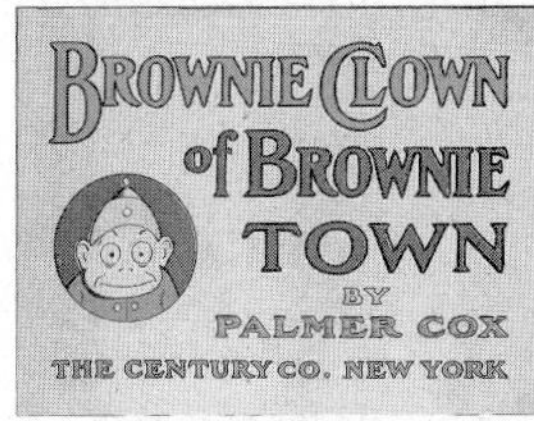

Brownie Clown of Brownie Town
© The Century Co.

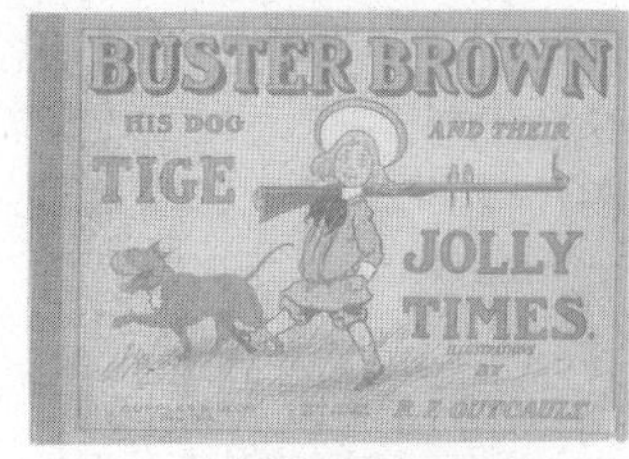

Buster Brown His Dog Tige And Their Jolly Times
1906 © Cupples & Leon

GD2.0 FN6.0 VF8.0

oblong size era. This was self published by George McManus.

BRINGING UP FATHER (N) (see SAGARA'S ENGLISH CARTOONS
Publisher unknown (actually, unreadable), Tokyo: October 1924 (9-7/8" x 7-1/2", 90 pgs, color hard-c, B&W)

nn- (Scarce) by George McManus C&A (no known sales)

NOTE: *Published in Tokyo, Japan, with all strips in both English and Japanese, to facilitate learning English. Introduction by George McManus. Scarce in USA.*

BRONX BALLADS (I)
Simon & Schuster, NY: 1927 (9-1/2x7-1/4", hard-c, B&W)

nn - By Robert Simon and Harry Hershfield 36.00 143.00 250.00

BROWNIES, THE (not sequential comic strips)
The Century Co.: 1887 - 1914 (all came with dust jackets; add $100-150 to value if original dust jacket is included and intact)

Book 1 - The Brownies: Their Book (1887) 200.00 850.00 1320.00
Book 2 - Another Brownies Book (1890) 150.00 635.00 1000.00
Book 3 - The Brownies at Home (1893) 125.00 530.00 825.00
Book 4 - The Brownies Around the World (1894) 100.00 425.00 660.00
Book 5 - The Brownies Through the Union (1895) 100.00 425.00 660.00
Book 6 - The Brownies Abroad (1899) 100.00 425.00 660.00
Book 7 - The Brownies in the Philippines (1904) 100.00 425.00 660.00
Book 8 - The Brownies' Latest Adventures (1910) 100.00 425.00 660.00
Book 9 - The Brownies Many More Nights (1914) 100.00 425.00 660.00
...Raid on Kleinmaier Bros. (c. 1910, 16 pages) Kleinmaier Bros. Clothing, Marion, Ohio (no known sales)

BROWNIE CLOWN OF BROWNIE TOWN (N)
The Century Co.: 1908 (6-7/8 x 9-3/8", 112 pgs, color hardcover & interior)

nn - By Palmer Cox (rare; 1907 newspaper comic strip-r) 250.00 800.00 1200.00

NOTE: *The Brownies created 1883 in* ***St Nicholas Magazine.***

BUDDY TUCKER & HIS FRIENDS (N) (Also see **Buster Brown Nuggets**)
Cupples & Leon Co.: 1906 (11-5/8 x17", 58 pgs, color) (Scarce)

nn - 1905 Sunday strip-r by R. F. Outcault 500.00 1500.00 2500.00

NOTE: *Strip began Apr 30, 1905 thru at least Oct 1905.*

BUFFALO BILL'S PICTURE STORIES
Street & Smith Publications: 1909 (Soft cardboard cover)

nn - Very rare 67.00 233.00 400.00

BUGHOUSE FABLES (N) (see also **Comic Monthly**)
Embee Distributing Co. (King Features): 1921 (10¢, 4x4-1/2", 48 pgs.)

1-By Barney Google (Billy DeBeck) 46.00 186.00 350.00

BUG MOVIES (O) (Also see Clancy The Cop & Deadwood Gulch)
Dell Publishing Co.: 1931 (9-13/16x9-7/8", 52 pgs., B&W)

nn - Original material; Stookie Allen-a 150.00 300.00 500.00

BULL
Bull Publishing Company, New York: No.1, March, 1916 - No.12, Feb, 1917 (10 cents, 10-3/4x8-3/4", 24 pgs, color paper-c, B&W)

1-12 (Very Rare) – – –

NOTE: *Pro-German, Anti-British cartoon/humor monthly, whose goal was to keep the U.S. neutral and out of World War I. We know of no copies which have sold in the past few years.*

BUNNY'S BLUE BOOK (see also Foxy Grandpa) (N)
Frederick A. Stokes Co.: 1911 (10x15, 60¢)

nn - By Carl "Bunny" Schultze strip-r 100.00 350.00 –

BUNNY'S RED BOOK (see also Foxy Grandpa) (N)
Frederick A. Stokes Co.: 1912 (10-1/4x15-3/4", 64 pgs.)

nn - By Carl "Bunny" Schultze strip-r 100.00 350.00 –

BUNNY'S GREEN BOOK (see also Foxy Grandpa) (N)
Frederick A. Stokes Co.: 1913 (10x15")

nn - By Carl "Bunny" Schultze 100.00 350.00 –

BUSTER BROWN (C) (Also see Brown's Blue Ribbon Book of Jokes and Jingles & Buddy Tucker & His Friends)
Frederick A. Stokes Co.: 1903 - 1916 (Daily strip-r in color)

1903...& His Resolutions (11-1/4x16", 66 pgs.) by R. F. Outcault (Rare)-1st nationally distributed comic. Distr. through Sears & Roebuck 1600.00 4500.00 –
1904...His Dog Tige & Their Troubles (11-1/4x16-1/4", 66 pgs.)(Rare) 600.00 1875.00 –
1905...Pranks (11-1/4x16-3/8", 66 pgs.) 400.00 1450.00 –
1906...Antics (11x16-3/8", 66 pgs.) 400.00 1450.00 –
1906...And Company (11x16-1/2", 66 pgs.) 300.00 1050.00 –
1906...Mary Jane & Tige (11-1/4x16, 66 pgs.) 300.00 1050.00 –

NOTE: ***Yellow Kid*** *pictured on two pages.*

1908 Collection of Buster Brown Comics 250.00 835.00 –
1909 Outcault's Real Buster and The Only Mary Jane (11x16, 66 pgs, Stokes) 250.00 835.00 –
1910...Up to Date (10-1/8x15-3/4", 66 pgs.) 208.00 729.00 1315.00
1911...Fun And Nonsense (10-1/8x15-3/4", 66 pgs.) 183.00 642.00 1150.00
1912...The Fun Maker (10-1/8x15-3/4", 66 pgs.) -Yellow Kid (4 pgs.) 183.00 642.00 1150.00
1913...At Home (10-1/8x15-3/4", 56 pgs.) 167.00 583.00 1050.00
1914...And Tige Here Again (10x16, 62 pgs, Stokes) 153.00 535.00 1000.00
1915...And His Chum Tige (10x16, Stokes) 153.00 535.00 1000.00
1916...The Little Rogue (10-1/8x15-3/4", 62 pgs.) 162.00 567.00 1025.00
1917...And the Cat (5-1/2x 6-1/2, 26 pgs, Stokes) 115.00 402.00 750.00
1917...Disturbs the Family (5-1/2x 6 1/2, 26 pgs, Stokes

NOTE: *Story featuring statue of "the Chinese Yellow Kid"* 115.00 402.00 750.00

1917...The Real Buster Brown (5-1/2x 6 -/2, 26 pgs, Stokes 115.00 402.00 750.00

Frederick A. Stokes Co. Hard Cover Series (I)

...Abroad (1904, 10-1/4x8", 86 pgs., B&W, hard-c)-R. F. Outcault-a (Rare) 200.00 700.00 1260.00
...Abroad (1904, B&W, 67 pgs.)-R. F. Outcault-a 200.00 700.00 1260.00

NOTE: *Buster Brown Abroad is not an actual comic book, but prose with illustrations.*

..."Tige" His Story 1905 (10x8", 63 pgs., B&W) (63 illos.)
nn-By RF Outcault 143.00 500.00 –
...My Resolutions 1906 (10x8", B&W, 68 pgs.)-R.F. Outcault-a (Rare) 233.00 817.00 1475.00
...Autobiography 1907 (10x8", B&W, 71 pgs.) (16 color plates & 36 B&W illos) 67.00 233.00 440.00
...And Mary Jane's Painting Book 1907 (10x13-1/4", 60 pgs, both card & hardcover versions exist
nn-RFO (first printing blank on top of cover) 67.00 233.00 440.00
First Series- this is a reprint if it says First Series 67.00 233.00 440.00
Volume Two - By RFO 67.00 233.00 440.00
... My Resolutions by Buster Brown (1907, 68 pgs, small size, cardboard covers) scarce 43.00 150.00 285.00

NOTE: *Not actual comic book per se, but a compilation of the Resolutions panels found at the end of Outcault's Buster Brown newspaper strips.*

BUSTER BROWN (N)
Cupples & Leon Co./N. Y. Herald Co.: 1906 - 1917 (11x17", color, strip-r)

NOTE: *Early issues by R. F. Outcault; most C&L editions are not by Outcault.*

1906...His Dog Tige And Their Jolly Times (11-3/8x16-5/8", 68 pgs.) 300.00 1100.00 1900.00
1906...His Dog Tige & Their Jolly Times (11x16, 46 pgs.) 163.00 600.00 1025.00
1907...Latest Frolics (11-3/8x16-5/8", 66 pgs., r/'05-06 strips) 163.00 600.00 1025.00
1908...Amusing Capers (58 pgs.) 129.00 475.00 815.00
1909...The Busy Body (11-3/8x16-5/8", 62 pgs.) 129.00 475.00 815.00
1910...On His Travels (11x16", 58 pgs.) 115.00 402.00 750.00
1911...Happy Days (11-3/8x16-5/8", 58 pgs.) 115.00 402.00 750.00
1912...In Foreign Lands (10x16", 58 pgs) 115.00 402.00 750.00
1913...And His Pets (11x16", 58 pgs.) STOKES???? 115.00 402.00 750.00
1913...And His Pets (26 pg partial reprint) – – –
1914...Funny Tricks (11-3/8x16-5/8", 58 pgs.) 115.00 402.00 750.00
1916...At Play (10x16, 58 pgs) 115.00 402.00 750.00

BUSTER BROWN NUGGETS (N)
Cupples & Leon Co./N.Y.Herald Co.: 1907 (1905, 7-1/2x6-1/2", 36 pgs., color, strip-r, hard-c)(By R. F. Outcault) (NOTE: books are all unnumbered)

Buster Brown Goes Fishing, Goes Swimming, Plays Indian, Goes Shooting, Plays Cowboy, On Uncle Jack's Farm, Tige And the Bull, And Uncle Buster 40.00 150.00 300.00
Buddy Tucker Meets Alice in Wonderland 56.00 200.00 400.00
Buddy Tucker Visits The House That Jack Built 40.00 150.00 300.00

BUSTER BROWN MUSLIN SERIES (N)
Saalfield: 1907 (also contain copyright Cupples & Leon)

...Goes Fishing, Plays Indian, And the Donkey (1907, 6-7/8x6-1/8", 24 pgs., color)-r/1905 Sunday comics page by Outcault (Rare) 50.00 175.00 315.00
...Plays Cowboy (1907, 6-3/4x6", 10 pgs., color)-r/1905 Sunday comics page by Outcault (Rare) 50.00 175.00 315.00

NOTE: *These are muslin versions of the C&L BB Nugget series. Muslin books are all cloth books, made to be washable so as not easily stained/destroyed by very young children. The Muslin books contain one strip each (the title strip), to the more common NUGGET's three strips.*

BUSTER BROWN PREMIUMS (Advertising premium booklets)
Various Publishers: 1904 - 1912 (3x5" to 5x7"; sizes vary)

American Fruit Product Company, Rochester, NY

Buster Brown Duffy's 1842 Cider (1904, 7x5". 12 pgs, C.E. Sherin Co, NYC)
nn - By R. F. Outcault (scarce) 100.00 350.00 600.00

The Brown Shoe Company, St. Louis, USA
Set of five books (5x7", 16 pgs., color)

Brown's Blue Ribbon Book of Jokes and Jingles Book 1 (nn, 1904)-By R. F. Outcault; Buster Brown & Tige, Little Tommy Tucker, Jack & Jill, Little Boy Blue, Dainty Jane; The Yellow Kid app. on back-c (1st BB comic book premium) 300.00 1050.00 1900.00

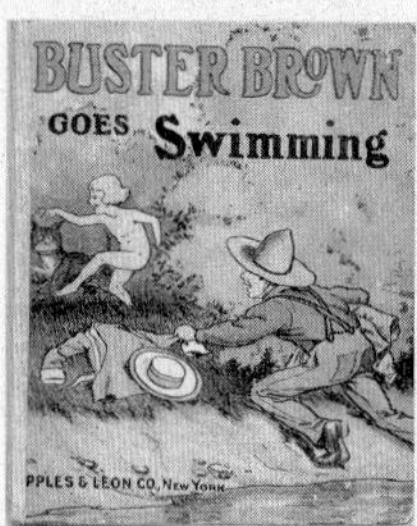

Buster Brown Goes Swimming Nuggets
1907 © Cupples & Leon

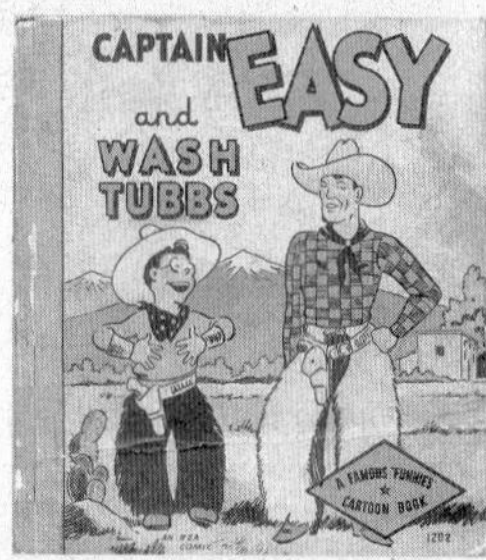

Captain Easy and Wash Tubbs by Roy Crane
1934 © Whitman Famous Comics Cartoon Book

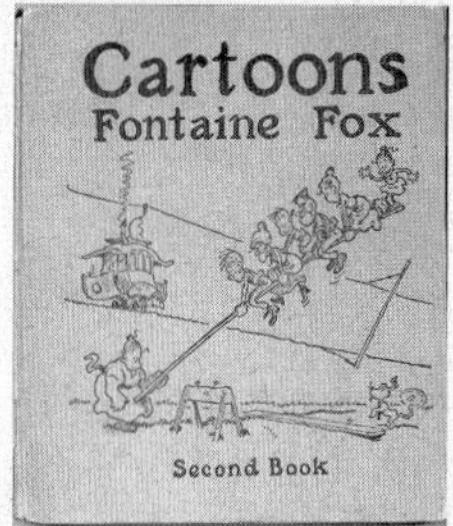

Cartoons Fontaine Fox Second Book
early 1920s © Harper & Bros, NY

	GD2.0	FN6.0	VF8.0
Buster Brown's Blue Ribbon Book of Jokes and Jingles Book 2 (1905)- Original color art by Outcault	200.00	600.00	1260.00
Buster's Book of Jokes & Jingles Book 3 (1909) not by R.F. Outcault	150.00	400.00	840.00

NOTE: *Reprinted from the Blue Ribbon post cards with advert jingles added.*

Buster's Book of Instructive Jokes and Jingles Book 4 (1910)-Original color art not by R.F. Outcault	150.00	585.00	1050.00
...Book of Travels nn (1912, 3x5")-Original color art not signed by Outcault	117.00	408.00	735.00

NOTE: *Estimated 5 or 6 known copies exist of books #1-4.*

The Buster Brown Bread Company

"Buster Brown" Bread Book of Rhymes, The (1904, 4x6", 12 pgs., half color, half B&W)- Original color art not signed by RFO — 158.00 553.00 1000.00

Buster Brown's Hosiery Mills

"How Buster Brown Got The Pie" nn (nd, 7x5-1/4". 16 pgs, color paper cover and color interior By R.F. Outcault — 83.00 292.00 525.00

"The Autobiography of Buster Brown" nn (nd,9x6-1/8", 36 pgs, text story & art by R.F. Outcault — 83.00 292.00 525.00

NOTE: *Similar to, but a distinctly different item than "Buster Brown's Autobiography."*

The Buster Brown Stocking Company

Buster Brown Drawing Book, The nn (nd, 5x6", 20 pgs.)-B&W reproductions of 1903 R.F. Outcault art to trace — 50.00 150.00 315.00

NOTE: *Reprints a comic strip from Burr McIntosh Magazine, which includes Buster, Yellow Kid, and Pore Li'l Mose (only known story involving all three.)*

Buster Brown Stocking Magazine nn (Jan. 1906, 7-3/4x5-3/8", 36 pgs.) R.F. Outcault — 50.00 100.00 200.00

NOTE: *This was actually a store bought item selling for 5 cents per copy.*

Collins Baking Company

Buster Brown Drawing Book nn (1904, 5x3", 12 pgs.)-Original B&W art to trace, not signed by R.F. Outcault — 50.00 150.00 315.00

C. H. Morton, St. Albans, VT

Merry Antics of Buster Brown, Buddy Tucker & Tige nn (nd, 3-1/2x5-1/2", 16 pgs.) -Original B&W art by R.F. Outcault — 83.00 292.00 525.00

Ivan Frank & Company

Buster Brown nn (1904, 3x5", 12 pgs.)-B&W repros of R. F. Outcault Sunday pages (First premium to actually reproduce Sunday comic pages – may be first premium comic strip-r book?) — 125.00 438.00 785.00

Buster Brown's Pranks (1904, 3-1/2x5-1/8", 12 pgs.)-reprints intro of Buddy Tucker into the BB newspaper strip before he was spun off into his own short lived newspaper strip — 125.00 438.00 785.00

Kaufmann & Strauss

Buster Brown Drawing Book (1906, 28 pages, 5x3-1/2") Color Cover, B+W original story signed by Outcault, tracing paper inserted as alternate pages. Back cover imprinted for Nox' Em All Shoes — 50.00 150.00 315.00

Pond's Extract

Buster Brown's Experiences With Pond's Extract nn (1904, 6-3/4x4-1/2", 28 pgs.) Original color art by R.F. Outcault (may be the first BB premium comic book with original art) — 100.00 250.00 525.00

C. A. Cross & Co.

Red Cross Drawing Book nn (1906, 4-7/8x3-1/2", color paper -c, B&W interior, 12 pgs.) — 50.00 150.00 315.00

NOTE: *This is for Red Cross coffee; not the health organization.*

Ringen Stove Company

Quick Meal Steel Ranges nn (nd, 5x3", 16 pgs.)-Original B&W art not signed by R.F. Outcault — 50.00 150.00 315.00

Steinwender Stoffregen Coffee Co.

"Buster Brown Coffee" (1905, 4-7/8x3", color paper cover, B&W interior, 12 printed pages, plus 1 tracing paper page above each interior image (total of 8 sheets) (Very Rare) — 83.00 292.00 525.00

NOTE: *Part of a BB drawing contest. If instructions had been followed, most copies would have ended up destroyed.*

U. S. Playing Card Company

Buster Brown - My Own Playing Cards (1906, 2-1/2x1-3/4", full color)
nn - By R. F. Outcault — 42.00 147.00 250.00

NOTE: *Series of full color panels tell stories, average about 5 cards per story.*

Publisher Unknown

The Drawing Book nn (1906, 3-9/16x5", 8 pgs.)-Original B&W art to trace not by R.F. Outcault — 50.00 150.00 300.00

BUTLER BOOK A Series of Clever Cartoons of Yale Undergraduate Life
Yale Record: June 16, 1913 (10-3/4 x 17", 34 pgs, paper cover B&W)

nn - By Alban Bernard Butler — 21.00 73.00 130.00

NOTE: *Cartoons and strips reprinted from The Yale Record student newspaper.*

BUTTONS & FATTY IN THE FUNNIES
Whitman Publishing Co.: nd 1927 (10-1/4x15-1/2", 28pg., color)

W936 - Signed "M.E.B.", probably M.E. Brady; strips in color copyright The Brooklyn Daily Eagle; (very rare) — 61.00 244.00 425.00

BY BRIGGS (M,N,P) (see also OLD GOLD THE SMOOTHER AND BETTER CIGARETTE)
Old Gold Cigarettes: nd (c1920's) (11" x 9-11/16", 44 pgs, cardboard-c, B&W)

nn- (Scarce) — 20.00 70.00 130.00

NOTE: *Collection reprinting strip cartoons by Clare Briggs, advertising Old Gold Cigarettes. These strips originally appeared in various magazines, play program booklets, newspapers, etc. Some of the strips involve regular Briggs strip series. Contains all of the strips in the smaller, color "OLD GOLD" giveaways, plus more.*

CAMION CARTOONS
Marshall Jones Company: 1919 (7-1/2x5", 136 pgs, B&W)

nn - By Kirkland H. Day (W.W.One occupation) — 20.00 70.00 120.00

CANYON COUNTRY KIDDIES (M)
Doubleday, Page & Co: 1923 (8x10-1/4", 88 pgs, hard-c, B&W)

nn - By James Swinnerton — 39.00 137.00 260.00

CARLO (H)
Doubleday, Page & Co.: 1913 (8 x 9-5/8, 120 pgs, hardcover, B&W)

nn - By A.B. Frost — 40.00 140.00 300.00

NOTE: *Original sequential strips about a dog. Became short lived newspaper comic strip in 1914. Originally published with a dust jacket which increases value 50%.*

CARTOON BOOK, THE
Bureau of Publicity, War Loan Organization, Treasury Department, Washington, D.C.: 1918 (6-1/2x4-7/8", 48 pgs, paper cover, B&W)

nn - By various artists — 31.00 108.00 185.00

NOTE: *U.S. government issued booklet of WW I propaganda cartoons by 46 artists promoting the third sale of Liberty Loan bonds. The artists include: Berryman, Clare Briggs, Cesare, J. N. "Ding" Darling, Rube Goldberg, Kemble, McCutcheon, George McManus, F. Opper, T. E. Powers, Ripley, Satterfield, H. T. Webster, Gaar Williams.*

CARTOON CATALOGUE (S)
The Lockwood Art School, Kalamazoo, Mich.: 1919 (11-5/8x9, 52 pgs, B&W)

nn - Edited by Mr. Lockwood — 20.00 60.00 140.00

NOTE: *Jammed with 100s of single panel cartoons and some sequential comics; Mr Lockwood began the very first cartoonist school back in 1892. Clare Briggs was one of his students.*

CARTOON COMICS
Lasco Publications, Detroit, Mich: #1, April 1930 - #2, May 1930 (8-3/6x5-1/5")

1, 2 - By Lu Harris — 20.00 60.00 100.00

NOTE: *Contains recurring characters Hollywood Horace, Campus Charlie, Pair-A-Dice Alley and Jocko Monkey. Not much is presently known about the creator(s) or publisher.*

CARTOON HISTORY OF ROOSEVELT'S CAREER, A
The Review of Reviews Company: 1910 (276 pgs, 8-1/4x11",

nn - By various — 43.00 129.00 325.00

NOTE: *Reprints editorial cartoons about Teddy Roosevelt from U.S. and international newspapers and cartoons from the humor magaines (Puck, Judge, etc.). A few cartoonists whose work is included are Dalrymple, Opper, McDougall, McCutcheon, Remington, Rogers, Kemble. Mostly single panel but 10 or so are sequential strips.*

CARTOON HUMOR
Collegian Press: 1938 (102 pgs, squarebound, B&W)

nn — 20.00 70.00 120.00

NOTE: *Contains cartoons & strips by Otto Soglow, Syd Hoff, Peter Arno, Abner Dean, others.*

CARTOONIST'S PHILOSOPHY, A
Percy Crosby: 1931, HC, 252 pgs, 5-1/2x7-1/2", hard-c, celluloid dust wrapper

nn - By Percy Crosby (10 plates, 6 are of Skippy) — 20.00 60.00 130.00

NOTE: *Crosby's partial autobiography regarding his return to France in 1929, and portrayals of Normandy, the "cliff dwellers" on Normandy cliffs (destroyed in WWII), his visit to London, comments on art, philosophy, several poems, and political dialogue. His description of his Cockney driver, " Harold" is amusing. Also describes his experience visiting Chicago to speak out against Capone, his concerns over the evils of Prohibition, and the economy prior to the 1929 crash. This book reveals he was aware of the dangers of his outspoken views, and is prophetic, re: his later years as political prisoner. Also reveals his religious beliefs.*

CARTOONS BY BRADLEY: CARTOONIST OF THE CHICAGO DAILY NEWS
Rand McNally & Company: 1917 (11-1/4x8-3/4", 112 pgs, hardcover, B&W)

nn - By Luther D. Bradley (editorial) — 20.00 70.00 120.00

CARTOONS BY FONTAINE FOX (Toonerville Trolley) (S)
Harper & Brothers Publishers: nd early '20s (9x7-7/8",102 pgs., hard-c, B&W)

Second Book- By Fontaine Fox (Toonerville-r) — 150.00 300.00 500.00

CARTOONS BY HALLADAY (N,S)
Providence Journal Co., Rhode Island: Dec 1914 (116 pgs, 10-1/2x 7-3/4", hard-c, B&W)

nn- (Scarce) — 50.00 125.00 250.00

NOTE: *Cartoons on Rhode Island politics, plus some Teddy Roosevelt & WW I cartoons.*

CARTOONS BY McCUTCHEON (S)
A. C. McClurg & Co.: 1903 (12-3/8x9-3/4", 212 pgs., hardcover, B&W)

nn - By John McCutcheon — 20.00 70.00 120.00

CARTOONS BY W. A. IRELAND (S)
The Columbus-Evening Dispatch: 1907 (13-3/4 x 10-1/2", 66 pgs, hardcover)

nn - By W. A. Ireland (strip-r) — 20.00 70.00 120.00

CARTOONS MAGAZINE (I,N,S)
H. H. Windsor, Publisher: Jan 1912-June 1921; July 1921-1923; 1923-1924; 1924-1927 (1912-July 1913 issues 12x9-1/4", 68-76 pgs; 1913-1921 issues 10x7", average 112 to 188 pgs, color covers)

1912-Jan-Dec — 30.00 75.00 125.00

Cartoons Magazine v9 #5 by various creators
May 1916 © H. H. Windsor, Chicago

Charlie Chaplin in the Movies by Segar
1917 © Essaney

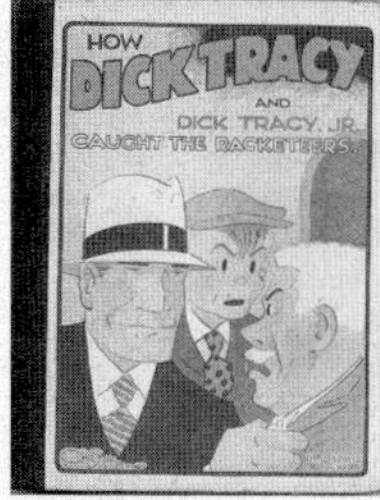

How Dick Tracy and Dick Tracy, Jr.
Caught the Racketeers by Chester Gould
1933 © Cupples & Leon

	GD2.0	FN6.0	VF8.0
1913-1917	30.00	75.00	125.00
1917-(Apr) "How Comickers Regard Their Characters"	30.00	105.00	150.00
1917-(June) "A Genius of the Comic Page" - long article on George Herriman, Krazy Kat, etc with lots of Herriman art; "Cartoonists and Their Cars"	125.00	250.00	500.00
1918-1919	30.00	75.00	125.00
1920-June 1921	30.00	75.00	125.00
July 1921-1923 titled Wayside Tales & Cartoons Magazine	30.00	75.00	125.00
1923-1924 becomes Cartoons Magazine again	30.00	75.00	125.00
1924-1927 becomes Cartoons & Movie Magazine	30.00	75.00	125.00

NOTE: *Many issues contain a wealth of historical background on then current cartoonists of the day with an international slant; each issue profusely illustrated with many cartoons. We are unsure if this magazine continued after 1927.*

CARTOONS BY J. N. DARLING (S,N - some sequential strips)
The Register & Tribune Co., Des Moines, Iowa: 1909?-1920 (12x8-7/8",B&W)

	GD2.0	FN6.0	VF8.0
Book 1	15.00	51.00	90.00
Book 2 Education of Alonzo Applegate (1910)	15.00	51.00	90.00
2nd printing	10.00	30.00	90.00
Book 3 Cartoons From The Files (1911)	15.00	51.00	90.00
Book 4	15.00	51.00	90.00
Book 5 In Peace And War (1916)	15.00	51.00	90.00
Book 6 Aces & Kings War Cartoons (Dec 1, 1918)	15.00	51.00	90.00
Book 7 The Jazz Era (Dec 1920)	15.00	51.00	90.00
Book 8 Our Own Outlines of History (1922)	15.00	51.00	90.00

NOTE: *Some of the most inspired hard hitting cartoons ever printed. Are there more?*

CARTOONS THAT MADE PRINCE HENRY FAMOUS, THE (N,S)
The Chicago Record-Herald: Feb/March 1902 (12-1/8" x 9", 32 pgs, paper-c, B&W)

	GD2.0	FN6.0	VF8.0
nn- (Scarce) by McCutcheon	15.00	51.00	90.00

NOTE: *Cartoons about the visit of the British Prince Henry to the U.S.*

CAVALRY CARTOONS (O)
R. Montalboddi: nd (c1918) (14-1/4" x 11", 30 pgs, printed on one side, olive & black construction paper-c, B&W interior)

	GD2.0	FN6.0	VF8.0
nn - By R.Montalboddi	20.00	55.00	100.00

NOTE: *Comics about life in the U.S.Cavalry during World War I, by a soldier who was in the 1st Cavalry.*

CHARLIE CHAPLIN (N)
Essanay/M. A. Donohue & Co.: 1917 (9x16", B&W, large size soft-c)

	GD2.0	FN6.0	VF8.0
Series 1, #315-Comic Capers (9-3/4x15-3/4")-20 pgs. by Segar; Series 1, #316-In the Movies	165.00	525.00	1200.00
#317-Up in the Air (20 pgs), #318-In the Army	165.00	525.00	1400.00
Funny Stunts-(12-1/2x16-3/8",16 color pgs)	165.00	525.00	1400.00

NOTE: *All contain pre-Thimble Theatre Segar art. The thin paper used makes high grade copies very scarce.*

CHASING THE BLUES
Doubleday Page: 1912 (7-1/2x10", 108 pgs., B&W, hard-c)

	GD2.0	FN6.0	VF8.0
nn - By Rube Goldberg	150.00	525.00	900.00

NOTE: *Contains a dozen Foolish Questions, baseball, a few Goldberg poems and lots of sequential strips.*

CHRISTIAN CARTOONS (N,S)
The Sunday School Times Company: 1922 (7-1/4 x 6-1/8,104 pgs, brown hard-c, B&W)

	GD2.0	FN6.0	VF8.0
nn - E.J. Pace	15.00	51.00	90.00

NOTE: *Religious cartoons reprinted from The Sunday School Times.*

CLANCY THE COP (O))
Dell Publishing Co.: 1930 - No. 2, 1931 (10x10", 52 pgs., B&W, cardboard-c)
(Also see Bug Movies & Deadwood Gulch)

	GD2.0	FN6.0	VF8.0
1, 2-By VEP Victor Pazimino (original material; not reprints)	10000	250.00	500.00

CLIFFORD MCBRIDE'S IMMORTAL NAPOLEON & UNCLE ELBY (N)
The Castle Press: 1932 (12x17"; soft-c cartoon book)

	GD2.0	FN6.0	VF8.0
nn - Intro. by Don Herod	36.00	144.00	250.00

COLLECTED DRAWINGS OF BRUCE BAIRNSFATHER, THE
W. Colston Leigh: 1931 (11-1/4x8-1/4 ", 168 pages, hardcover, B&W)

	GD2.0	FN6.0	VF8.0
nn - By Bruce Bairnsfather	24.00	96.00	165.00

COMICAL PEEP SHOW
McLoughlin Bros: 1902 (36 pgs, B&W)

	GD2.0	FN6.0	VF8.0
nn	24.00	96.00	165.00

NOTE: *Comic stories of Wilhelm Busch redrawn; two versions with green or gold front cover logos; back covers different.*

COMIC ANIMALS (I)
Charles E. Graham & Co.: 1903 (9-3/4x7-1/4", 90 pgs, color cover)

	GD2.0	FN6.0	VF8.0
nn - By Walt McDougall (not comic strips)	43.00	150.00	260.00

COMIC CUTS (O)
H. L. Baker Co., Inc.: 5/19/34-7/28/34 (Tabloid size 10-1/2x15-1/2", 24 pgs., 5¢)
(full color, not reprints; published weekly; created for news stand sales)

	GD2.0	FN6.0	VF8.0
V1#1 - V1#7(6/30/34), V1#8(7/14/34), V1#9(7/28/34)-Idle Jack strips	200.00	400.00	800.00

NOTE: *According to a 1958 Lloyd Jacquet interview, this short-lived comics mag was the direct inspiration for Major Malcolm Wheeler-Nicholson's **New Fun Comics**, not **Famous Funnies**.*

COMIC MONTHLY (N)
Embee Dist. Co.: Jan, 1922 - No. 12, Dec, 1922 (10¢, 8-1/2"x9", 28 pgs., 2-color covers)
(1st monthly newsstand comic publication) (Reprints 1921 B&W dailies)

	GD2.0	FN6.0	VF8.0
1-Polly & Her Pals by Cliff Sterrett	375.00	1125.00	2225.00
2-Mike & Ike by Rube Goldberg	140.00	490.00	1000.00
3-S'Matter, Pop?	140.00	490.00	1000.00
4-Barney Google by Billy DeBeck	140.00	490.00	1000.00
5-Tillie the Toiler by Russ Westover	140.00	490.00	1000.00
6-Indoor Sports by Tad Dorgan	140.00	490.00	1000.00

NOTE: *#6 contains more Judge Rummy than Indoor Sports.*

	GD2.0	FN6.0	VF8.0
7-Little Jimmy by James Swinnerton	140.00	490.00	1000.00
8-Toots and Casper b y Jimmy Murphy	140.00	490.00	1000.00
9-New Bughouse Fables by Barney Google	140.00	490.00	1000.00
10-Foolish Questions by Rube Goldberg	140.00	490.00	1000.00
11-Barney Google & Spark Plug by Billy DeBeck	140.00	490.00	1000.00
12-Polly & Her Pals by Cliff Sterrett	214.00	752.00	1500.00

NOTE: *This series was published by George McManus (Bringing Up Father) as Em & Rudolph Block, Jr., son of Hearst's cartoon editor for many years, as "Bee." One would have thought this series would have done very well considering the tremendous amount of talent assembled. All issues are extremely hard to find these days and rarely show up in any type of higher grade.*

COMIC PAINTING AND CRAYONING BOOK (H)
Saalfield Publ. Co.: 1917 (13-1/2x10", 32 pgs.) (No price on-c)

	GD2.0	FN6.0	VF8.0
nn - Tidy Teddy by F. M. Follett, Clarence the Cop, Mr. & Mrs. Butt-In; regular comic stories to read or color	50.00	175.00	300.00

COMPLETE TRIBUNE PRIMER, THE (I)
Mutual Book Company: 1901 (7 1/4 x 5", 152 pgs, red hard-c)

	GD2.0	FN6.0	VF8.0
nn - By Frederick Opper; has 75 Opper cartoons	25.00	88.00	150.00

COURTSHIP OF TAGS, THE (N)
McCormick Press: pre-1910 (9x4", 88 pgs, red & B&W-c, B&W interior)

	GD2.0	FN6.0	VF8.0
nn - By O. E. Wertz (strip-r Wichita Daily Beacon)	25.00	88.00	150.00

DAFFYDILS (N)
Cupples & Leon Co.: 1911 (5-3/4x7-7/8", 52 pgs., B&W, hard-c)

	GD2.0	FN6.0	VF8.0
nn - By "Tad" Dorgan	58.00	204.00	350.00

NOTE: *Also exists in self-published TAD edition: The T.A. Dorgan Company; unknown which is first printing.*

DAN DUNN SECRET OPERATIVE 48 (Also See Detective Dan) (N)
Whitman Publishing: 1937 ((5 1/2 x 7 1/4", 68pgs., color cardboard-c, B&W)

	GD2.0	FN6.0	VF8.0
1010 And The Gangsters' Frame-Up	50.00	150.00	300.00

NOTE: *There are two versions of the book the later printing has a 5 cent cover price. Dick Tracy look-alike character by Norman Marsh.*

DANGERS OF DOLLY DIMPLE, THE (N)
Penn Tobacco Co.: nd (1930's) (9-3/8x7-7/8", 28 pgs, red cardboard-c, B&W)

	GD2.0	FN6.0	VF8.0
nn - (Rare) by Walter Enright	25.00	88.00	150.00

NOTE: *Reprints newspaper comic strip advertisements, in which in every episode, Dolly Dimple's life is saved by Penn's Smoking Tobacco. - how very un-P.C. by today's standards.*

DEADWOOD GULCH (O) (See The Funnies 1929)(also see Bug Movies & Clancy The Cop)
Dell Publishing Co.: 1931 (10x10", 52 pgs., B&W, color covers, B&W interior)

	GD2.0	FN6.0	VF8.0
nn - By Charles "Boody" Rogers (original material)	150.00	300.00	600.00

DESTINY A Novel In Pictures (O)
Farrar & Rinehart: 1930 (8x7", 424 pgs, B&W, hard-c, dust jacket?)

	GD2.0	FN6.0	VF8.0
nn - By Otto Nuckel (original graphic novel)	25.00	100.00	175.00

DICK TRACY & DICK TRACY JR. CAUGHT THE RACKETEERS, HOW
Cupples & Leon Co.: 1933 (8-1/2x7", 88 pgs., hard-c) (See Treasure Box of Famous Comics) (N)

	GD2.0	FN6.0	VF8.0
2-(Numbered on pg. 84)-Continuation of Stooge Viller book (daily strip reprints from 8/3/33 thru 11/8/33)(Rarer than #1)	94.00	376.00	750.00
With dust jacket...	175.00	500.00	1000.00

DICK TRACY & DICK TRACY JR. AND HOW THEY CAPTURED "STOOGE" VILLER (N)
Cupples & Leon Co.: 1933 (8-1/2x7", 100 pgs., hard-c, one-shot)
Reprints 1932 & 1933 Dick Tracy daily strips

	GD2.0	FN6.0	VF8.0
nn(No.1)-1st app. of "Stooge" Viller	94.00	376.00	700.00
With dust jacket...	175.00	500.00	900.00

DIMPLES By Grace Drayton (N) (See Dolly Dimples)
Hearst's International Library Co.: 1915 (6 1/4 x 5 1/4, 12 pgs) (5 known)

	GD2.0	FN6.0	VF8.0
nn-Puppy and Pussy; nn-She Goes For a Walk; nn-She Had A Sneeze; nn-She Has a Naughty Play Husband; nn-Wait Till Fido Comes Home	21.00	74.00	150.00

DOINGS OF THE DOO DADS, THE (N)
Detroit News (Universal Feat. & Specialty Co.): 1922 (50¢, 7-3/4x7-3/4", 34 pgs, B&W, red & white-c, square binding)

	GD2.0	FN6.0	VF8.0
nn-Reprints 1921 newspaper strip "Text & Pictures" given away as prize in the Detroit News Doo Dads contest; by Arch Dale	43.00	173.00	360.00

DOING THE GRAND CANYON
Fred Harvey: 1922 (7 x 4-3/4", 24 pgs, B&W, paper cover)

'Erbie And 'Is Playmates By F. Opper
1932 © Democratic National Committee

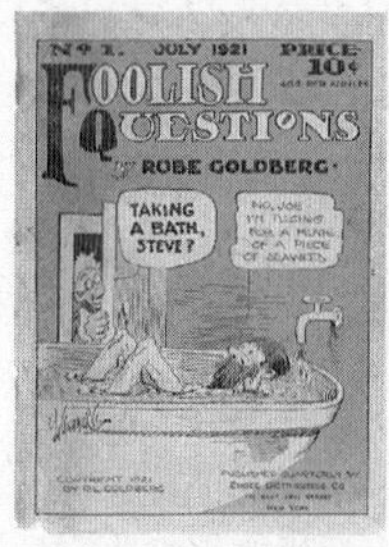

Foolish Questions by Rube Goldberg
1921 © EmBee Distributing Co., NY.

The Latest Adventures of Foxy Grandpa 1905
© Bunny Publ.

GD2.0 FN6.0 VF8.0

nn - John McCutcheon 20.00 40.00 100.00
NOTE: *Text & 8 cartoons about visiting the Grand Canyon.*

DOINGS OF THE VAN-LOONS (N) (from same company as Mutt & Jeff #1-#5)
Ball Publications: 1912 (5-3/4X15-1/2", 68pg., B&W, hard-c)
nn - By Fred I. Leipziger (scarce) 72.00 252.00 600.00

DOLLY DIMPLES & BOBBY BOUNCE (See Dimples)
Cupples & Leon Co.: 1933 (8-3/4x7", color hardcover, B&W)
nn - Grace Drayton-a 24.00 96.00 165.00

DOO DADS, THE (Sleepy Sam and Tiny the Elephant)
Universal Feature * Specialty Co: 1922 (5-1/4x14", 36 pgs.,B&W, R&W-c,square binding)
nn - By Arch Dale 35.00 125.00 250.00

DRAWINGS BY HOWARD CHANDLER CHRISTIE (S, M)
Moffat, Yard & Company, NY: 1905 (11-7/8x16-1/2", 68 pgs, hard-c, B&W)
nn - Howard C. Christie 30.00 60.00 120.00
NOTE: *Reprints1898-1905 from Haprer & Bros, Ch. Scribners Sons, Leslie's, MacMillians, McLurg, Russell.*

DREAMS OF THE RAREBIT FIEND (N)
Frederick A. Stokes Co.:1905 (10-1/4x7-1/2", 68 pgs, thin paper cover all B&W) newspaper reprints from the New York Evening Telegram printed on yellow paper
nn-By Winsor "Silas" McCay (Very Rare) (Five copies known to exist)
Estimated value.... 900.00 2600.00 –
NOTE: *A G/VG copy sold for $2,045 in May 2004. This item usually turns up with fragile paper.*

DRISCOLL'S BOOK OF PIRATES (O)
David McKay Publ.: 1934 (9x7", 124 pgs, B&W, hardcover)
nn - By Montford Amory ("Pieces of Eight strip-r) 21.00 64.00 150.00

DUCKY DADDLES
Frederick A. Stokes Co: July 1911 (15x10")
nn - By Grace Weiderseim (later Drayton) strip-r 50.00 175.00 300.00

DUMBUNNIES AND THEIR FRIENDS IN RABBITBORO, THE (O)
Albertine Randall Wheelan: 1931 (8-3/4x7-1/8", 82 pgs, color hardcover, B&W)
nn - By Albertine Randall Wheelan (self-pub) 34.00 103.00 240.00

EDISON - INSPIRATION TO YOUTH (N)(Also see Life of Thomas---)
Thomas A. Edison, Incorporated: 1939 (9-1/2 x 6-1/2, paper cover, B&W)
nn - Photo-c 50.00 150.00 200.00
NOTE: *Reprints strip material found in the 1928 Life of Thomas A. Edison in Word and Picture.*

'ERBIE AND 'IS PLAYMATES
Democratic National Committee: 1932 (8x9-1/2, 16 pgs, B&W)
nn - By Frederick Opper (Rare) 100.00 200.00 400.00
NOTE: *Anti-Hoover/Pro-Roosevelt political comics.*

EXPANSION BEING BART'S BEST CARTOONS FOR 1899
Minneapolis Journal: 1900 (10-1/4x8-1/4", 124 pgs, paperback, B&W)
v2#1 - By Charles L. Bartholomew 24.00 84.00 145.00

FAMOUS COMICS (N)
King Features Synd. (Whitman Pub. Co.): 1934 (100 pgs., daily newspaper-r) (3-1/2x8-1/2"; paper cover)(came in an illustrated box)
684 (#1) - Little Jimmy, Katz Kids & Barney Google 40.00 103.00 240.00
684 (#2) - Polly, Little Jimmy, Katzenjammer Kids 40.00 103.00 240.00
684 (#3) - Little Annie Rooney, Polly and Her Pals, Katzenjammer Kids
40.00 103.00 240.00
Box price... 75.00 150.00 375.00

FAMOUS COMICS CARTOON BOOKS (N)
Whitman Publishing Co.: 1934 (8x7-1/4", 72 pgs, B&W hard-c, daily strip-r)
1200-The Captain & the Kids; Dirks reprints credited to Bernard Dibble 29.00 86.00 200.00
1202-Captain Easy & Wash Tubbs by Roy Crane; 2 slightly different versions of cover exist 34.00 103.00 240.00
1203-Ella Cinders By Conselman & Plumb 28.00 84.00 195.00
1204-Freckles & His Friends 25.00 75.00 175.00
NOTE: *Called Famous Funnies Cartoon Books inside back area sales advertisement.*

FANTASIES IN HA-HA (M)
Meyer Bros & Co.: 1900 (14 x 11-7/8", 64 pgs, color cover hardcover, B&W)
nn - By Hy Mayer 50.00 150.00 300.00

FELIX (N)
Henry Altemus Company: 1931 (6-1/2"x8-1/4", 52 pgs., color, hard-c w/dust jacket)
1-3-Sunday strip reprints of Felix the Cat by Otto Messmer. Book No. 2 r/1931 Sunday panels mostly two to a page in a continuity format oddly arranged so each tier of panels reads across two pages, then drops to the next tier. (Books 1 & 3 have not been documented.)(Rare)
Each 250.00 500.00 1000.00
With dust jacket 250.00 750.00 1200.00

FELIX THE CAT BOOK (N)
McLoughlin Bros.: 1927 (8"x15-3/4", 52 pgs, half in color-half in B&W)
nn - Reprints 23 Sunday strips by Otto Messmer from 1926 & 1927, every other one in color, two pages per strip. (Rare) 200.00 800.00 1550.00
260-Reissued (1931), reformatted to 9-1/2"x10-1/4" (same color plates, but one strip per every three pages), retitled ("Book" dropped from title) and abridged (only eight strips repeated from first issue, 28 pgs.).(Rare) 79.00 316.00 600.00

F. FOX'S FUNNY FOLK (see Toonerville Trolley; Cartoons by Fontaine Fox) (C)
George H. Doran Company: 1917 (10-1/4x8-1/4", 228 pgs, red, B&W cover, B&W interior, hardcover; dust jacket?)
nn - By Fontaine Fox (Toonerville Trolley strip-r) 150.00 450.00 750.00

52 CAREY CARTOONS (O,S)
Carey Cartoon Service, NY: 1915 (25 cents, 6-3/4" x 10-1/2", 118 pgs, printed on one side, color cardboard-c, B&W)
nn - (1915) War – – –
NOTE: *The Carey Cartoon Service supplied a weekly, hand-colored single panel cartoon broadsheet, on current news events, starting in 1906 or 1907, for window display in Carey Fountain Pen chain stores. These broadsheets were 22-1/2" x 33" in size. Starting circa 1915, Carey Fountain Pens began offering subscriptions for the broadsheets to other merchants, for window display in their stores as well. This collects, in B&W, the cartoons for 1915. An "Edition Deluxe" was also advertised, with all cartoons hand colored. It is currently unknown whether a reprint collection was only issued in 1915, or if other editions exist.*

52 LETTERS TO SALESMEN
Steven-Davis Company: 1927 (???)
nn - (Rare) 25.00 100.00 150.00
NOTE: *52 motivational letters to salesmen, with page of comics for each week, bound into embossed leather binder.*

FOLKS IN FUNNYVILLE (S)
R.H. Russell: 1900 (12"x9-1/4", 48 pgs.)(cardboard-c)
nn - By Frederick Opper 271.00 950.00 –
NOTE: *Reprinted from Hearst's NY Journal American Humorist supplements.*

FOOLISH QUESTIONS (S)
Small, Maynard & Co.: 1909 (6-7/8 x 5-1/2", 174 pgs, hardcover, B&W)
nn - By Rube Goldberg (first Goldberg item) 100.00 300.00 500.00
NOTE: *Comic strip began Oct 23, 1908 running thru 1941. Also drawn by George Frink in 1909.*

FOOLISH QUESTIONS THAT ARE ASKED BY ALL
Levi Strauss & Co./Small, Maynard & Co.: 1909 (5-1/2x5-3/4", 24 pgs, paper-c, B&W)
nn- (Rare) by Rube Goldberg 65.00 175.00 350.00

FOOLISH QUESTIONS (Boxed card set) (S)
Wallie Dorr Co., N.Y.: 1919 (5-1/4x3-3/4")(box & card backs are red)
nn - Boxed set w/52 B&W comics on cards; each a single panel gag complete set w/box
75.00 263.00 450.00
NOTE: *There are two diff sets put out simultaneously with the first set, by the same company. One set continues/picks up the numbering of the cards from the other set.*

FOOLISH QUESTIONS (S)
EmBee Distributing Co.: 1921 (10¢, 4x5 1/2; 52 pgs, 3 color covers; B&W)
1-By Rube Goldberg 46.00 160.00 300.00

FOXY GRANDPA
Foxy Grandpa Company, 33 Wall St, NY : 1900 (9x15", 84 pgs, full color, cardboard-c)
nn - By Carl Schultze (By Permission of New York Herald) 271.00 1200.00 –
NOTE: *This seminal comic strip began Jan 7, 1900 and was collected later that same year.*

FOXY GRANDPA (Also see The Funnies, 1st series) (N)
N. Y. Herald/Frederick A. Stokes Co./M. A. Donahue & Co./Bunny Publ. (L. R. Hammersly Co.): 1901 - 1916 (Strip-r in color, hard-c)
1901- 9x15" in color-N. Y. Herald 313.00 1100.00 –
1902- "Latest Larks of...", 32 pgs., 9-1/2x15-1/2" 164.00 575.00 –
1902- "The Many Advs. of...", 9x12", 148 pgs., Hammersly Co.
179.00 625.00 –
1903- "Latest Advs.", 9x15", 24 pgs., Hammersly Co. 164.00 575.00 –
1903- "...'s New Advs.", 11x15", 66 pgs., Stokes 164.00 575.00 –
1904- "Up to Date", 10x15", 66 pgs., Stokes 146.00 510.00 900.00
1904- "The Many Adventures of...", 9x15, 144pgs, Donohue 146.00 510.00 900.00
1905- "& Flip-Flaps", 9-1/2x15-1/2", 52 pgs. 146.00 510.00 900.00
1905- "The Latest Advs. of...", 9x15", 28, 52, & 68 pgs, M.A. Donohue Co.; re-issue of 1902 issue 104.00 365.00 700.00
1905- "Latest Larks of...", 9-1/2x15-1/2", 52 pgs., Donahue; re-issue of 1902 issue with more pages added 104.00 365.00 700.00
1905- "Latest Larks of...", 9-1/2x15-1/2", 24 pgs. edition, Donahue; re-issue of 1902 issue 104.00 365.00 700.00
1905- "Merry Pranks of...", 9-1/2x15-1/2", 28, 52 & 62 pgs., Donahue
104.00 365.00 700.00
1905-"...Surprises",10x15", color, 64 pg,Stokes, 60¢ 104.00 365.00 700.00
1906- "Frolics", 10x15", 30 pgs., Stokes 104.00 365.00 700.00
1907?-"...& His Boys",10x15", 64 color pgs, Stokes 104.00 365.00 700.00
1907- "Triumphs", 10x15", 62 pgs, Stokes 104.00 365.00 700.00
1908-"...Mother Goose", Stokes 104.00 365.00 700.00

Gasoline Alley
1929 © Reilly & Lee

The Gumps #1 by Sidney Smith
1924 © Cupples & Leon

Hans and Fritz, Funny Larks of
1917 © Saalfield Publishing Co.

GD2.0 FN6.0 VF8.0

1909- "...& Little Brother", 10x15, 58 pgs, Stokes 104.00 365.00 700.00
1911- "Latest Tricks", r-1910,1911 Sundays-Stokes Co. 104.00 365.00 700.00
1914-(9-1/2x15-1/2", 24 pgs.)-6 color cartoons/page, Bunny Publ. Co. 88.00 306.00 575.00
1915 - ...Always Jolly (10x16, Stokes) 88.00 306.00 575.00
1916- "Merry Book", (10x15", 64 pgs, Stokes) 88.00 306.00 575.00
1917-"...Adventures (5 1/2 x 6 1/2, 26 pgs, Stokes) 57.00 200.00 400.00
1917-"...Frolics (5 1/2 x 6 1/2, 26 pgs, Stokes) 57.00 200.00 400.00
1917-"...Triumphs (5 1/2 x 6 1/2, 26 pgs, Stokes) 57.00 200.00 400.00

FOXY GRANDPA, FUNNY TRICKS OF (The Stump Books)
M.A. Donahue Co, Chicago: approx 1903 (1-7/8x6-3/8", 44 pgs, blue hardcover)
nn - By Carl Schultze 54.00 189.00 325.00
NOTE: *One of a series of ten "stump" books; the only comics one.*

FOXY GRANDPA'S MOTHER GOOSE (I)
Stokes: October 1903 (10-11/16x8-1/2", 86 pgs, hard-c)
nn - By Carl Schultze (not comics - illustrated book) 54.00 189.00 325.00

FOXY GRANDPA SPARKLETS SERIES (N)
M. A. Donahue & Co.: 1908 (7-3/4x6-1/2"; 24 pgs., color)
"... Rides the Goat", "...& His Boys", "...Playing Ball", "...Fun on the Farm", "...Fancy Shooting", "...Show His Boys Up-To-Date Sports", "...Plays Santa Claus" each.... 88.00 306.00 525.00
900- "Playing Ball"; Bunny illos; 8 pgs., linen like pgs., no date 73.00 254.00 435.00

FOXY GRANDPA VISITS RICHMOND (O,P)
Dietz Printing Co., Richmond, VA / Hotel Rueger: nd (c1920's) (5-7/8" x 4-1/2", 16 pgs, paper-c, B&W)
nn - (Scarce) By Bunny 25.00 88.00 175.00
NOTE: *Promotional comic given away to its guests by the Hotel Rueger, about Foxy Grandpa visiting and enjoying the Hotel. Originally came in an envelope, with the words "Foxy Grandpa Visits Richmond -- and Rueger's" printed on it.*

FOXY GRANDPA VISITS WASHINGTON, D.C. (P)
Dietz Printing Co., Richmond, VA / Hamilton Hotel: nd (c1920's) (5-7/8" x 4-1/2", 16 pgs, paper-c, B&W)
nn - (Scarce) By Bunny 25.00 88.00 150.00
NOTE: *Mostly reprints "... Visits Richmond", changing all references to Hotel Rueger, to Hamilton Hotel instead. Also, changes depictions of a waiter and a cook from black to white, plus incompletely erases the cover art on a book Foxy Grandpa falls asleep with (the latter is how we know that the Richmond version was first).*

FRAGMENTS FROM FRANCE (S)
G. P. Putnam & Sons: 1917 (9x6-1/4", 168 pgs, hardcover, $1.75)
nn - By Bruce Bairnsfather 25.00 88.00 150.00
NOTE: *WW1 trench warfare cartoons; color dust jacket.*

FUNNIES, THE (H) (See Clancy the Cop, Deadwood Gulch, Bug Movies)
Dell Publishing Co.: 1929 - No. 36, 10/18/30 (10¢; 5¢ No. 22 on) (16 pgs.)
Full tabloid size in color; not reprints; published every Saturday
1-My Big Brudder, Jonathan, Jazzbo & Jim, Foxy Grandpa, Sniffy, Jimmy Jams & other strips begin; first four-color comic newsstand publication; also contains magic, puzzles & stories 200.00 700.00 1500.00
2-21 (1930, 10¢) 150.00 300.00 600.00
22(nn-7/12/30-5¢) 150.00 300.00 600.00
23(nn-7/19/30-5¢), 24(nn-7/26/30-5¢), 25(nn-8/2/30), 26(nn-8/9/30), 27(nn-8/16/30), 28(nn-8/23/30), 29(nn-8/30/30), 30(nn-9/6/30), 31(nn-9/13/30), 32(nn-9/20/30), 33(nn-9/27/30), 34(nn-10/4/30), 35(nn-10/11/30), 36(nn, no date-10/18/30) each.... 150.00 300.00 600.00

GASOLINE ALLEY (Also see Popular Comics & Super Comics) (N)
Reilly & Lee Publishers: 1929 (8-3/4x7", B&W daily strip-r, hard-c)
nn - By King (96 pgs.) 125.00 300.00 600.00
with scarce Dust Wrapper 250.00 500.00 1000.00
NOTE: *Of all the Frank King reprint books, this is the only one to reprint actual complete newspaper strips - all others are illustrated prose text stories.*

GIBSON'S PUBLISHED DRAWINGS, MR. (M,S) (see Victorian index for earlier issues)
R.H. Russell, New York: No.1 1894 - No. 9 1904 (11x17-3/4", hard-c, B&W)
nn (No.6; 1901) A Widow and her Friends (90 pgs.) 30.00 60.00 120.00
nn (No.7; 1902) The Social Ladder (88 pgs.) 30.00 60.00 120.00
8 - 1903 The Weaker Sex (88 pgs.) 30.00 60.00 120.00
9 - 1904 Everyday People (88 pgs.) 30.00 60.00 120.00
NOTE: *By Charles Dana Gibson cartoons, reprinted from magazines, primarily LIFE. The Education of Mr. Pipp tells a story. Series continues how long after 1904?*

GIGGLES
Pratt Food Co., Philadelphia, PA: 1908-09? (12x9", 8 pgs, color, 5 cents-c)
1-8: By Walt McDougall (#8 dated March 1909) 40.00 175.00 -
NOTE: *Appears to be monthly; almost tabloid size; yearly subscriptions was 25 cents.*

GOD'S MAN (H)
Jonathan Cape and Harrison Smith Inc.: 1929 (8-1/4x6", 298 pgs, B&W hardcover w/dust jacket) (original graphic novel in wood cuts)
nn - By Lynd Ward 43.00 171.00 300.00

GOLD DUST TWINS
N. K. Fairbank Co.: 1904 (4-5/8x6-3/4", 18 pgs, color and B&W)
nn - By E. W. Kemble (Rare) 30.00 60.00 130.00
NOTE: *Promo comic for Gold DustWashing Powder; includes page of watercolor paints.*

GOLF
Volland Co.: 1916 (9x12-3/4", 132 pgs, hard-c, B&W)
nn - By Clair Briggs 100.00 200.00 400.00

GUMPS, THE (N)
Landfield-Kupfer: No. 1, 1918 - No. 6, 1921; (B&W Daily strip-r)
Book No. 1(1918)(scarce)-cardboard-c, 5-1/4x13-1/3", 64 pgs., daily strip-r by Sidney Smith 75.00 250.00 500.00
Book No.2(1918)-(scarce); 5-1/4x13-1/3"; paper cover; 36 pgs. daily strip reprints by Sidney Smith 75.00 250.00 500.00
Book No. 3 100.00 350.00 700.00
Book No. 4 (1918) 5-3/8x13-7/8", 20 pgs. Color card-c 100.00 350.00 700.00
Book No. 5 10-1/4x13-1/2", 20 pgs. Color paper-c 100.00 350.00 700.00
Book No. 6 (Rare, 20 pgs, 8x13-3/8, strip-r 1920-21) 121.00 423.00 725.00

GUMPS, ANDY AND MIN, THE (N)
Landfield-Kupfer Printing Co., Chicago/Morrison Hotel: nd (1920s) (Giveaway, 5-1/2"x14", 20 pgs., B&W, soft-c)
nn - Strip-r by Sidney Smith; art & logo embossed on cover w/hotel restaurant menu on back-c or a hotel promo ad; 4 different contents of issues known 50.00 175.00 300.00

GUMPS, THE (N)
Cupples & Leon: 1924-1930 (10x10, 52 pgs, B&W)
1 - By Sidney Smith 61.00 244.00 450.00
2-7 39.00 154.00 300.00

THE GUMPS (P)
Cupples & Leon Company: 1924 (9 x 7-1/2", 28 pgs, paper cover)
nn (1924) 50.00 175.00 300.00
NOTE: *Promotional comic for Sunshine Andy Gump Biscuits. Daily strip-r from 1922-24.*

GUMP'S CARTOON BOOK, THE (N)
The National Arts Company: 1931 (13-7/8x10", 36 pgs, color covers, B&W)
nn - By Sidney Smith 57.00 228.00 450.00

GUMPS PAINTING BOOK, THE (N)
The National Arts Company: 1931 (11 x 15 1/4", 20 pgs, half in full color)
nn - By Sidney Smith 57.00 228.00 450.00

HALT FRIENDS! (see also **HELLO BUDDY**)
???: 1918? (4-3/8x5-3/4", 36 pgs, color-c, B&W, no cover price listed)
nn - Unknown 20.00 40.00 80.00
NOTE: *Says on front cover: "Comics of War Facts of Service Sold on its merits by Unemployed or Disabled Ex-Service Men. Credentials Shown On Request. Price - Pay What You Please." These are very common; contents vary widely.*

HAMBONE'S MEDITATIONS
Jahl & Co.: no date 1920 (6-1/8 x 7-1/2, 108 pgs, paper cover, B&W)
nn - By J. P. Alley 33.00 132.00 250.00
NOTE: *Reprint of racist single panel newspaper series, 2 cartoons per page.*

HAN OLA OG PER (N)
Anundsen Publishing Co, Decorah, Iowa: 1927 (10-3/8 x 15-3/4", 54 pgs, paper-c, B&W)
nn - American origin Norwegian language strips-r 33.00 131.00 230.00
NOTE: *1940s and modern reprints exist.*

HANS UND FRITZ (N)
The Saalfield Publishing Co.: 1917, 1927-29 (10x13-1/2", 28 pgs., B&W)
nn - By R. Dirks (1917, r-1916 strips) 96.00 335.00 600.00
nn - By R. Dirks (1923 edition- reprint of 1917 edition) 58.00 204.00 350.00
nn - By R. Dirks (1926 edition- reprint of 1917 edition) 58.00 204.00 350.00
The Funny Larks Of... By R. Dirks (©1917 outside cover; ©1916 inside indicia) 96.00 335.00 600.00
The Funny Larks Of... (1927) reprints 1917 edition of 1916 strips Halloween-c 58.00 204.00 350.00
The Funny Larks Of... 2 (1929) 58.00 204.00 350.00
193 - By R. Dirks; contains 1916 Sunday strip reprints of Katzenjammer Kids & Hawkshaw the Detective - reprint of 1917 nn edition (1929) this edition is not rare 58.00 204.00 350.00

HAPPY DAYS (S)
Coward-McCann Inc.: 1929 (12-1/2x9-5/8", 110 pgs, hardcover B&W)
nn - By Alban Butler (WW 1 cartoons) 20.00 60.00 120.00

HAPPY HOOLIGAN (See Alphonse...) (N)
Hearst's New York American & Journal: 1902,1903
Book 1-(1902)-"And His Brother Gloomy Gus", By Fred Opper; has 1901-02-r;

Harold Teen #1 by Carl Ed
1929 © Cupples & Leon

Jimmy By Jimmy Swinnerton
1905 © Frederick A. Stokes

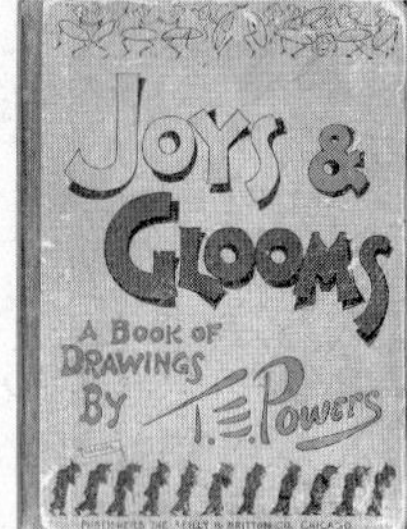

Joys & Glooms By T.E. Powers
1912 © Reilly & Britton Co.

GD2.0 FN6.0 VF8.0

(yellow & black)(86 pgs.)(10x15-1/4") 600.00 1800.00 3000.00
New Edition, 1903 -10x15" 82 pgs. in color 350.00 1400.00 –
NOTE: *Strip ran March 26, 1900-Aug 14, 1932 and is widely recognized as setting the format standard for all newspaper comic strips which came after it. Opper (1857-1937) was going blind towards the end.*

HAPPY HOOLIGAN (N) (By Fredrick Opper)
Frederick A. Stokes Co.: 1906-08 (10-1/4x15-3/4", cardboard color-c)
1906 - :Travels of...), 68 pgs,10-1/4x15-3/4", 1905-r 450.00 1000.00 –
1907 - "--Home Again", 68 pgs., 10x15-3/4", 60¢; full color-c 450.00 1000.00 –
1908 - "Handy--", 68 pgs, color 450.00 1000.00 –

HAPPY HOOLIGAN, THE STORY OF (G)
McLoughlin Bros.: No. 281, 1932 (12x9-1/2", 20 pgs., soft-c)
281-Three-color text, pictures on heavy paper 57.00 228.00 400.00
NOTE: *An homage to Opper's creation on its 30th Anniversary in 1932.*

HAROLD HARDHIKE'S REJUVENATION
O'Sullivan Rubber: 1917 (6-1/4x3-1/2, 16 pgs, B&W)
nn 25.00 100.00 175.00
NOTE: *Comic book to promote rubber shoe heels.*

HAROLD TEEN (N)
Cupples & Leon Co.: 1929 (9-7/8x9-7/8", 52 pgs, cardboard covers)
1 - By Carl Ed 50.00 200.00 500.00
nn - (1931, 8-11/16x6-7/8", 96 pgs, hardcover w/dj) 41.00 164.00 290.00
NOTE: *Title 2nd book:* ***HAROLD TEEN AND HIS OLD SIDE-KICK– POP JENKINS,*** *(Adv. of...). Precursor for Archie Andrews & crew; strip began May 4, 1919 running into 1959.*

HAROLD TEEN PAINT AND COLOR BOOK (N)
McLoughlin Bros Inc.: 1932 (13x9-3/4, 28 pgs, B&W and color)
#2054 25.00 100.00 175.00

HAWKSHAW THE DETECTIVE (See Advs. of..., Hans Und Fritz & Okay) (N)
The Saalfield Publishing Co.: 1917 (10-1/2x13-1/2", 24 pgs., B&W)
nn - By Gus Mager (Sunday strip-r) 54.00 190.00 350.00
nn - By Gus Mayer (1923 reprint of 1917 edition) 25.00 100.00 175.00
nn - By Gus Mager (1926 reprint of 1917 edition) 25.00 100.00 175.00
NOTE: *Runs Feb 23, 1913-Sept 4, 1922, starts again from Dec 13, 1931-Feb 11, 1952; Sherlock Holmes spoof.*

HEALTH IN PICTURES
American Public Health Association, NYC: 1930 (6-1/2" x 5-3/16", 76 pgs, green & black paper-c, B&W interior)
nn - By various 15.00 51.00 90.00
NOTE: *Collection of strips and cartoons put out by the Public Health Association, on topics ranging from boating and food safety, to small pox and typhoid prevention.*

HE DONE HER WRONG (O) (see also BANANA OIL)
Doubleday, Doran & Company: 1930 (8-1/4x 7-1/4", 276pgs, hard-c with dust jacket, B&W interiors)
nn - By Milt Gross 75.00 225.00 400.00
NOTE: *A seminal original-material wordless graphic novel, not reprints. Several modern reprints.*

HELLO BUDDY (see also **HALT FRIENDS**)
???: 1919? (4-3/8x5-3/4", 36 pgs, color-c, B&W, 15¢)
nn - Unknown 10.00 30.00 70.00
NOTE: *Says on front cover: "Comics of War Facts of Service Sold on its merits by Unemployed or Disabled Ex-Service Men." These are very common; contents vary widely.*

HENRY (N)
David McKay Co.: 1935 (25¢, soft-c)
Book 1 - By Carl Anderson 57.00 200.00 400.00
NOTE: *Strip began March 19 1932; this book ties with Popeye (David McKay) and Little Annie Rooney (David McKay) as the last of the 10x10" Platinum Age comic books.*

HENRY (M)
Greenberg Publishers Inc.: 1935 (11-1/4x 8-5/8", 72 pgs, red & blue color hard-c, dust jacket, B&W interiors) (strip-r from Saturday Evening Post)
nn - By Carl Anderson 57.00 200.00 400.00

HIGH KICKING KELLYS, THE (M)
Vaudeville News Corporation, NY: 1926 (5x11", B&W, two color soft-c)
nn - By Jack A. Ward (scarce) 40.00 160.00 280.00

HIGHLIGHTS OF HISTORY (N)
World Syndicate Publishing Co.: 1933-34 (4-1/2x4", 288 pgs)
nn - 5 different unnumbered issues; daily strip-r 10.00 40.00 70.00
NOTE: *Titles include Buffalo Bill, Daniel Boone, Kit Carson, Pioneers of the Old West, Winning of the Old Northwest. There are line drawing color covers and embossed hardcover versions. It is unknown which came out first.*

HOMER HOLCOMB AND MAY (N)
no publisher listed: 1920s (4 x 9-1/2", 40 pgs, paper cover, B&W)
nn - By Doc Bird Finch (strip-r) 10.00 40.00 70.00

HOME, SWEET HOME (N)
M.S. Publishing Co.: 1925 (10-1/4x10")

GD2.0 FN6.0 VF8.0

nn - By Tuthill 33.00 134.00 235.00

HOW THEY DRAW PROHIBITION (S)
Association Against Prohibition: 1930 (10x9", 100 pgs.)
nn - Single panel and multi-panel comics (rare) 71.00 285.00 500.00
NOTE: *Contains art by J.N. "Ding" Darling, James Flagg, Rollin Kirby, Winsor McCay, T.E. Powers, H.T. Webster, others. Also comes with a loose sheet listing all the newspapers where the cartoons originally appeared.*

HOW TO BE A CARTOONIST (H)
Saalfield Pub. Co: 1936 (10-3/8x12-1/2", 16 pgs, color-c, B&W)
nn - By Chas. H. Kuhn 10.00 40.00 70.00

HOW TO DRAW: A PRACTICAL BOOK OF INSTRUCTION (H)
Harper & Brothers: 1904 (9-1/4x12-3/8", 128 pgs, hardcover, B&W)
nn - Edited By Leon Barritt 57.00 228.00 400.00
NOTE: *Strips reprinted include: "Buster Brown" by Outcault, "Foxy Grandpa" by Bunny, "Happy Hooligan" by Opper, "Katzenjammer Kids" by Dirks, "Lady Bountiful" by Gene Carr, "Mr. Jack" by Swinnerton, "Panhandle Pete" by George McManus, "Mr E.Z. Mark" by F.M. Howarth others; non-character strips by Hy Mayer, Winsor McCay, T.E. Powers, others; single panel cartoons by Davenport, Frost, McDougall, Nast, W.A. Rogers, Sullivant, others.*

HOW TO DRAW CARTOONS (H)
Garden City Publishing Co.: 1926, 1937 (10 1/4 x 7 1/2, 150 pgs)
1926 first edition By Clare Briggs 25.00 75.00 150.00
1937 2nd edition By Clare Briggs 20.00 60.00 120.00
NOTE: *Seminal "how to" break into the comics syndicates with art by Briggs, Fisher, Goldberg, King, Webster, Opper, Tad, Hershfield, McCay, Ding, others. Came with Dust Jacket -add 50%.*

HOW TO DRAW FUNNY PICTURES: A Complete Course in Cartooning (H)
Frederick J. Drake & Co., Chicago: 1936 (10-3/8x6-7/8", 168 pgs, hardcover, B&W)
nn - By E.C. Matthews (200 illus by Eugene Zimmerman) 20.00 60.00 120.00

HY MAYER (M)
Puck Publishing: 1915 (13-1/2 x 20-3/4", 52 pgs, hardcover cover, color & B&W interiors)
nn - By Hy Mayer(strip reprints from Puck) 40.00 140.00 300.00

HYSTERICAL HISTORY OF THE CIVILIAN CONSERVATION CORPS
Peerless Engraving: 1934 (10-3/4x7-1/2", 104 pgs, soft-c, B&W)
nn - By various 20.00 60.00 120.00
NOTE: *Comics about CCC life, includes two color insert postcards in back.*

INDOOR SPORTS (N,S)
National Specials Co., New York: nd circa 1912 (25 cents, 6 x 9", 68 pgs, B&W)
nn - Tad 35.00 125.00 225.00
NOTE: *Cartoons reprinted from Hearst papers.*

IT HAPPENS IN THE BEST FAMILIES (N)
Powers Photo Engraving Co.: 1920 (52 pgs.)(9-1/2x10-3/4")
nn - By Briggs; B&W Sunday strips-r 29.00 114.00 200.00
Special Railroad Edition (30¢)-r/strips from 1914-1920 26.00 103.00 180.00

JIMMIE DUGAN AND THE REG'LAR FELLERS (N)
Cupples & Leon: 1921, 46 pgs. (11"x16")
nn - By Gene Byrne 71.00 284.00 500.00
NOTE: *Ties with EmBee's Mutt & Jeff and Trouble of Bringing Up Father as the last of this size.*

JIMMY (N) (see Little Jimmy Picture & Story Book)
N. Y. American & Journal: 1905 (10x15", 84 pgs., color)
nn - By Jimmy Swinnerton (scarce) 300.00 800.00 1500.00
NOTE: *James Swinnerton was one of the original first pioneers of the American newspaper comic strip.*

JIMMY AND HIS SCRAPES (N)
Frederick A. Stokes: 1906, (10-1/4x15-1/4", 66 pgs, cardboard-c, color)
nn - By Jimmy Swinnerton (scarce) 300.00 800.00 1500.00

JOE PALOOKA (N)
Cupples & Leon Co.: 1933 (9-13/16x10", 52 pgs., B&W daily strip-r)
nn - By Ham Fisher (scarce) 150.00 500.00 850.00

JOHN, JONATHAN AND MR. OPPER BY F. OPPER (S,I,N)
Grant, Richards, 48 Leicester Square, W.C.: 1903 (9-5/8x8-3/8", 108 pgs, hard-c B&W)
nn - Opper (Scarce) 50.00 200.00 380.00
NOTE: *British precursor-type companion to* WIllie And His Poppa *reprints from Hearst's* NY American & Journal *Opper cartoons interfacing* Uncle Sam *precursor* Brother Jonathan, John Bull. *Uses name* Happy Hooligan *in one cartoon, has* John Bull *smoking opium in another.*

JOLLY POLLY'S BOOK OF ENGLISH AND ETIQUETTE (S)
Jos. J. Frisch: 1931 (60 cents, 8 x 5-1/8, 88 pgs, paper-c, B&W)
nn - By Jos. J. Frisch 20.00 60.00 120.00
NOTE: *Reprint of single panel newspaper series, 4 per page, of English and etiquette lessons taught by a flapper.*

JOYS AND GLOOMS (N)
Reilly & Britton Co.: 1912 (11x8", 72 pgs, hard-c, B&W interior)
nn - By T. E. Powers (newspaper strip-r) 39.00 156.00 325.00

JUDGE - yet to be indexed

The Katzenjammer Kids
1921 © EmBee Publishing Co.

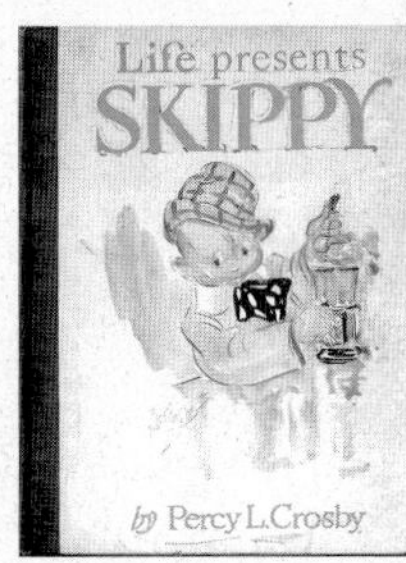

Life Presents Skippy by Percy L. Crosby
1924 © Life Publishing Company

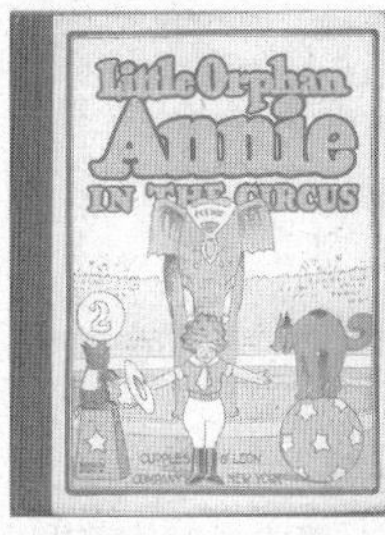

Little Orphan Annie by Harold Gray #2
1927© Cupples & Leon

GD2.0 FN6.0 VF8.0

JUDGE'S LIBRARY - yet to be indexed

JUST KIDS COMICS FOR CRAYON COLORING
King Features. NYC: 1928 (11x8-1/2, 16 pgs, soft-c)

nn - By Ad Carter 33.00 100.00 200.00
NOTE: *Porous better grade paper; top pics printed in color; lower in b&w to color.*

JUST KIDS, THE STORY OF (I)
McLoughlin Bros.: 1932 (12x9-1/2", 20 pgs., paper-c)

283-Three-color text, pictures on heavy paper 39.00 156.00 275.00

KAPTIN KIDDO AND PUPPO (N)
Frederick A. Stokes Co.: 1910-1913 (11x16-1/2", 62 pgs)

1910-By Grace Wiederseim (later Drayton) 40.00 140.00 240.00
1910-Turr-ble Tales of... By Grace Wiederseim (Edward Stern & Co., 11x16-1/2", 64 pgs.) 40.00 140.00 240.00
1913- ...'Speriences By Grace Drayton 40.00 140.00 240.00
NOTE: *Strip ran approx. 1909-1912.*

KATZENJAMMER KIDS, THE (Also see Hans Und Fritz) (N)
New York American & Journal: 1902,1903 (10x15-1/4", 86 pgs., color)
(By Rudolph Dirks; strip first appeared in 1897) © W.R. Hearst
NOTE: *All KK books 1902-1905 all have the same exact title page with a 1902 copyright by W.R. Hearst; almost always look instead on the front cover.*

1902 (Rare) (red & black); has 1901-02 strips 1000.00 2400.00 –
1903- **A New Edition** (Rare), 86 pgs 800.00 2100.00 –
1904- 10x15", 84 pgs 250.00 900.00 –
1905?-The Cruise of the, 10x15", 60¢, in color 250.00 900.00 –
1905-A Series of Comic Pictures, 10x15", 84 pgs. in color, possible reprint of 1904 edition 250.00 800.00 –
1905-Tricks of... (10x15", 66 pgs, Stokes) 250.00 800.00 –
1906-Stokes (10x16", 32 pgs. in color) 186.00 800.00 –
1907- The Cruise of the, 10x15", 62 pgs 1905-r? 186.00 800.00 –
1910-The Komical...(10x15) 150.00 450.00 800.00
1921-Embee Dist. Co., 10x16", 20 pgs. in color 150.00 450.00 800.00

KATZENJAMMER KIDS MAGIC DRAWING AND COLORING BOOK (N)
Sam L Gabriel Sons And Company: 1931 (8 1/2 x 12", 36 pages, stiff-c

838-By Knerr 50.00 200.00 350.00

KEEPING UP WITH THE JONESES (N)
Cupples & Leon Co.: 1920 - No. 2, 1921 (9-1/4x9-1/4",52 pgs.,B&W daily strip-r)

1,2-By Pop Momand 39.00 154.00 270.00

KID KARTOONS (N,S)
The Century Co.: 1922 (232 pgs, printed 1 side, 9-3/4 x 7-3/4", hard-c, B&W)

nn - By Gene Carr (Metropolitan Movies strip-r) 60.00 240.00 –

KING OF THE ROYAL MOUNTED (Also See Dan Dunn) (N)
Whitman Publishing: 1937 (5 1/2 x 7 1/4", 68 pgs., color cardboard-c, B&W)

1010 36.00 144.00 250.00

LADY BOUNTIFUL (N)
Saalfield Publ. Co./Press Publ. Co.: 1917 (13-3/8x10", 36 pgs, color cardboard-c, B&W interiors)

nn - By Gene Carr; 2 panels per page 50.00 175.00 300.00
193S - 2nd printing (13-1/8x10",28 pgs color-c, B&W) 33.00 117.00 200.00

LAUGHS YOU MIGHT HAVE HAD From The Comic Pages of Six Week Day Issues of the Post-Dispatch (N)
St. Louis Post-Dispatch: 1921 (9 x 10 1/2", 28 pgs, B&W, red ink cover)

nn - Various comic strips 39.00 154.00 270.00

LIFE, DOGS FROM (M)
Doubleday, Page & Company: nn 1920 - No.2 1926 (130 pgs, 11-1/4 x 9", color painted-c, hard-c, B&W)

nn (No.1) 120.00 360.00 –
Second Litter 80.00 320.00 –
NOTE: *Reprints strips & cartoons featuring dogs, from Life Magazine. Editted by Thomas L. Masson. Highly sought by collectors of dog ephemera. Art in both books is mostly by Robert L. Dickey. Other art: Carl Anderson-1,2; Barbes-1; Chip Bellew-1; Lang Campbell-1,2; Percy Crosby-1,2; Edwina-2; Frueh-2; R.B. Fuller-1; Gibson-1,2; Don Herold-2; Gus Mager-2; Orr-1; J.R. Shaver-1,2; T.S. Sullivant-2; Russ Westover-1,2; Crawford Young-1.*

LIFE OF DAVY CROCKETT IN PICTURE AND STORY, THE
Cupples & Leon: 1935 (8-3/4x7", 64 pgs, B&W hard-c, dust jacket)

nn - By C. Richard Schaare 29.00 116.00 200.00

LIFE OF THOMAS A. EDISON IN WORD AND PICTURE, THE (N)(Also see Edison...)
Thomas A. Edison Industries: 1928 (10x8", 56 pgs, paper cover, B&W)

nn - Photo-c 100.00 250.00 400.00
NOTE: *Reprints newspaper strip which ran August to November 1927.*

LIFE'S LITTLE JOKES (S)
M.S. Publ. Co.: No date (1924)(10-1/16x10", 52 pgs., B&W)

GD2.0 FN6.0 VF8.0

nn - By Rube Goldberg 64.00 257.00 525.00

LIFE, MINIATURE (see also LIFE (miniature reprint of of issue No. 1)) (M,P,S)
Life Publishing Co.: No. 1 - No. 4 1913, 1916, 1919 (5-3/4x4-5/8", 20 pgs, color paper-c

1- 3 (1913) 4 (1916) 5 (1919) (no known sales)
NOTE: *Giveaway item from Life, to promote subscriptions. All reprint material. No.2: James Montgomery Flagg-c; a-Chip Bellew, Gus Dirks, Gibson, F.M.Howarth, Art Young.*

LIFE'S PRINTS (was **LIFE'S PICTURE GALLERY -** See Victorian Age section) (M,S,P)
Life Publishing Company, New York: nd (c1907) (7x4-1/2", 132 pgs, paper cover, B&W)

nn - (nd; c1907) unillustrated black construction paper cover; reprints art from 1895-1907; art by J.M.Flagg, A.B.Frost, Gibson (Scarce) – – –
nn - (nd; c1908) b&w cardboard painted cover by Gibson, showing angel raising a champagne glass; reprints art from 1901-1908; art by J.M.Flagg, A.B.Frost, Gibson, Walt Kuhn, Art Young (Scarce) – – –
NOTE: *Catalog of prints reprinted from LIFE covers & centerspreads. There are likely more as yet unreported catalogs.*

LIFE, THE COMEDY OF LIFE
Life Publishing Company: 1907 (130 pgs, 11-3/4x9-1/4",embossed printed cloth covered board-c, B+W

nn - By various 20.00 80.00 120.00
NOTE: *Single cartoons and some sequential cartoons). Artists include Charles Dana Gibson, Harrison Cady, E.W. Kemble, James Montgomery Flagg.*

LILY OF THE ALLEY IN THE FUNNIES
Whitman Publishing Co.: No date (1927) (10-1/4x15-1/2"; 28 pgs., color)

W936 - By T. Burke (Rare) 57.00 228.00 400.00

LITTLE ANNIE ROONEY (N)
David McKay Co.: 1935 (25¢, soft-c)

Book 1 43.00 172.00 340.00
NOTE: *Ties with Henry & Popeye (David McKay) as the last of the 10x10" size Plat comic books.*

LITTLE ANNIE ROONEY WISHING BOOK (G) (See Happy Hooligan, Story of #281)
McLoughlin Bros.: 1932 (12x9-1/2", 16 pgs., soft-c, 3-color text, heavier paper)

282 - By Darrell McClure 41.00 144.00 250.00

LITTLE BIRD TOLD ME, A (E)
Life Publishing Co.: 1905? (96 pgs, hardbound)

nn - By Walt Kuhn (Life-r) 41.00 144.00 250.00

LITTLE FOLKS PAINTING BOOK (N)
The National Arts Company: 1931 (10-7/8 x 15-1/4", 20 pgs, half in full color)

nn - By "Tack" Knight (strip-r) 41.00 144.00 250.00

LITTLE JIMMY PICTURE AND STORY BOOK (I) (see Jimmy)
McLaughlin Bros., Inc.: 1932 (13-1/4 x 9-3/4", 20 pgs, cardstock color cover)

284 Text by Marion Kincaird; illus by Swinnerton 57.00 228.00 400.00

LITTLE JOHNNY & THE TEDDY BEARS (Judge-r) (M) (see Teddy Bear Books)
Reilly & Britton Co.: 1907 (10x14".; 68 pgs, green, red, black interior color)

nn - By J. R. Bray-a/Robert D. Towne-s 67.00 233.00 400.00

LITTLE JOURNEY TO THE HOME OF BRIGGS THE SKY-ROCKET, THE
Lockhart Art School: 1917 (10-3/4x7-7/8", 20 pgs, B&W) (I)

nn - About Clare Briggs (bio & lots of early art) 41.00 144.00 250.00

LITTLE KING, THE (see New Yorker Cartoon Albums for 1st appearance) (M)
Farrar & Reinhart, Inc: 1933 (10-1/4 x 8-3/4, 80 pgs, hardcover w/dust jacket

nn - By Otto Soglow (strip-r The New Yorker) 125.00 250.00 450.00
NOTE: *Copies with dust jacket are worth 50% more. Also exists in a 12x8-3/4 edition.*

LITTLE LULU BY MARGE (M)
Rand McNally & Company, Chicago: 1936 (6-9/16x6", 68 pgs, yellow hard-c, B&W)

nn - By Marjorie Henderson Buell 25.00 100.00 250.00
NOTE: *Begins reprinting single panel Little Lulu cartoons which began with Saturday Evening Post Feb. 23, 1935. This book was reprinted several times as late as 1940.*

LITTLE NAPOLEON
No publisher listed: 1924 , 50 pages, 10" by 10"; Color cardstock-c, B&W

nn - By Bud Counihan (Cupples &Leon format) 25.00 100.00 240.00

LITTLE NEMO (...in Slumberland) (N) (see also Little Sammy Sneeze, Dreams...Rarebit F)
Doffield & Co.(1906)/Cupples & Leon Co.(1909): 1906, 1909 (Sunday strip-r in color, cardboard covers)

1906-11x16-1/2" by Winsor McCay; 30 pgs. (scarce) 1500.00 5000.00 –
1909-10x14" by Winsor McCay (scarce) 1300.00 4000.00 –

LITTLE ORPHAN ANNIE (See Treasure Box of Famous Comics) (N)
Cupples & Leon Co.: 1926 - 1934 (8-3/4x7", 100 pgs., B&W daily strip-r, hard-c)

1 (1926)-Little Orphan Annie (softback see Treasure Box) 50.00 200.00 375.00
2 (1927)-In the Circus (softback see Wonder Box...) 36.00 144.00 275.00
3 (1928)-The Haunted House (softback see Wonder Box...) 36.00 144.00 275.00
4 (1929)-Bucking the World 36.00 144.00 275.00

The Trials of Lulu and Leander by Howarth
1906 © NY American & Journal

Maud by Frederick Opper
1906 © Frederick A. Stokes

Mickey Mouse Book
1930 © Bibo & Lang

5 (1930)-Never Say Die 30.00 120.00 225.00
6 (1931)-Shipwrecked 30.00 120.00 225.00
7 (1932)-A Willing Helper 25.00 100.00 200.00
8 (1933)-In Cosmic City 25.00 100.00 200.00
9 (1934)-Uncle Dan (not rare) 25.00 100.00 200.00
NOTE: *Each book reprints dailies from the previous year. Each hardcover came with a dust jacket. Books without dust jackets are worth 50% less. Many of copies of #9 Uncle Dan have been turning up on eBay recently.*

LITTLE ORPHAN ANNIE RUMMY CARDS (N)
Whitman Publishing Co., Racine: 1935 (box: 5 x 6 1/2" Cards: 3 1/2 x 2 1/4")
nn-Harold Gray 20.00 60.00 120.00
NOTE: *36 cards, including 1 instruction card, 5 character cards and 30 cards forming 5 sequential stories (6 cards each).*

LITTLE SAMMY SNEEZE (N) (see also Little Nemo, Dreams of A Rarebit Fiend)
New York Herald Co.: Dec 1905 (11x16-1/2", 72 pgs., color)
nn - By Winsor McCay (Very Rare) 3000.00 6000.00 –
NOTE: *Rarely found in fine to mint condition.*

LIVE AND LET LIVE
Travelers Insurance Co.: 1936 (5-3/4x7/3/4", 16 pgs. color and B&W)
nn - Bill Holman, Carl Anderson, etc 20.00 60.00 120.00

LULU AND LEANDER (N) (see also Funny Folk, 1899, in Victorian section)
New York American & Journal: 1904 (76 pgs); **William A Stokes & Co:** 1906
nn - By F.M. Howarth 300.00 750.00 1500.00
nn - The Trials of...(1906, 10x16", 68 pgs. in color) 300.00 750.00 1500.00
NOTE: *F. M. Howarth helped pioneer the American comic strip in the pages of PUCK magazine in the early 1890s before the Yellow Kid.*

MADMAN'S DRUM (O)
Jonathan Cape and Harrison Smith Inc.: 1930 (8-1/4x6", 274 pgs, B&W hardcover w/dust jacket) (original graphic novel in wood cuts)
nn - By Lynd Ward 50.00 175.00 300.00

MAMA'S ANGEL CHILD IN TOYLAND (I)
Rand McNally, Chicago: 1915 (128 pgs, hardbound)
nn - By M.T. "Penny" Ross & Marie C, Sadler 40.00 140.00 240.00
NOTE: *Mamma's Angel Child published as a comic strip by the "Chicago Tribune" 1908 Mar 1 to 1920 Oct 17.This novel dedicated to Esther Starring Richartz, "the original Mamma's Angel Kid."*

MAUD (N) (see also **Happy Hooligan**)
Frederick A. Stokes Co.: 1906 - 1908? (10x15-1/2", cardboard-c)
1906-By Fred Opper (Scarce), 66 pgs. color 400.00 1200.00 –
1907-The Matchless, 10x15" 70 pgs in color 300.00 900.00 –
1908-The Mirthful Mule, 10x15", 64 pgs in color 300.00 900.00 –
NOTE: *First run of strip began July 24, 1904 to at least Oct 6, 1907, spun out of* ***Happy Hooligan.***

MEMORIAL EDITION The Drawings of Clare Briggs (S)
Wm H. Wise & Company: 1930 (7-1/2x8-3/4", 284 pgs, pebbled false black leather, B&W) (posthumous boxed set of 7 books by Clare Briggs)
nn - The Days of Real Sport; nn-Golf; nn-Real Folks at Home; nn-Ain't it a Grand and Glorious Feeling?; nn-That Guiltiest Feeling; nn-Somebody's Always Taking the Joy Out of Life; nn-When a Feller Needs a Friend
Each book... 30.00 120.00 175.00
NOTE: *Also exists in a whitish cream colored paper back edition; first edition unknown presently.*

MENACE CARTOONS (M, S)
Menace Publishing Company, Aurora, Missouri: 1914 (10-3/8x8", 80 pgs, cardboard-c, B&W)
nn - (Rare) 50.00 150.00 450.00
NOTE: *Reprints anti-Catholic cartoons from K.K.K. related publication* ***The Menace.***

MEN OF DARING (N)
Cupples & Leon Co.: 1933 (8-3/4x7", 100 pgs)
nn - By Stookie Allen, intro by Lowell Thomas 30.00 90.00 200.00

MICKEY MOUSE BOOK
Bibo & Lang: 1930-1931 (12x9", stapled-c, 20 pgs., 4 printings)
nn - First Disney licensed publication (a magazine, not a book–see first book, Adventures of Mickey Mouse). Contains story of how Mickey met Walt and got his name; games, cartoons & song "Mickey Mouse (You Cute Little Feller)," written by Irving Bibo; Minnie, Clarabelle Cow, Horace Horsecollar & caricature of Walt shaking hands with Mickey. The changes made with the 2nd printing have been verified by billing affidavits in the Walt Disney Archives and include:Two Win Smith Mickey strips from 4/15/30 and 4/17/30 added to page 8 & back-c; "Printed in U.S.A." added to front cover; Bobette Bibo's age of 11 years added to title page; faulty type on the word "tail" corrected top of page 3; the word "start" added to bottom of page 7, removing the words "start 1 2 3 4" from the top of page 7; music and lyrics were rewritten on pages 12-14. A green ink border was added beginning with 2nd printing and some covers have inking variations. Art by Albert Barbelle, drawn in an Ub Iwerks style. Total circulation : 97,938 copies varying from 21,000 to 26,000 per printing.
1st printing. Contains the song lyrics **censored** in later printings, "When little Minnie's pursued by a big bad villain we feel so bad then we're glad when you up and kill him." Attached to the Nov. 15, 1930 issue of the Official Bulletin of the Mickey Mouse Club notes: "Attached to this Bulletin is a new Mickey Mouse Book that has just been published." This is thought to be the reason why a slightly disproportionate larger number of copies of the first printing still exist 800.00 1600.00 6000.00
2nd printing with a theater/advertising. Christmas greeting added to inside front cover (1 copy known with Dec. 27, 1930 date) – 8000.00 –
2nd-4th printings 600.00 1200.00 3500.00
NOTE: *Theater/advertising copies do not qualify as separate printings. Most copies are missing pages 9 & 10 which had a puzzle to be cut out. Puzzle (pages 9 and 10) cut out or missing, subtract 60% to 75%.*

MICKEY MOUSE COLORING BOOK (S)
Saalfield Publishing Company:1931 (15-1/4x10-3/4", 32 pgs, color soft cover, half printed in full color interior, rest B&W
871 - By Ub Iwerks & Floyd Gottfredson (rare) 400.00 1200.00 2520.00
NOTE: *Contains reprints of first MM daily strip ever, including the "missing" speck the chicken is after found only on the original daily strip art by Iwerks plus other very early MM art. There were several other Saalfield Mickey Mouse coloring books manufactured around the same time.*

MICKEY MOUSE, THE ADVENTURES OF (I)
David McKay Co., Inc.: Book I, 1931 - Book II, 1932 (5-1/2"x8-1/2", 32 pgs.)
Book I-First Disney book, by strict definition (1st printing-50,000 copies)(see Mickey Mouse Book by Bibo & Lang). Illustrated text refers to Clarabelle Cow as "Carolyn" and Horace Horsecollar as "Henry". The name "Donald Duck" appears with a non-costumed generic duck on back cover & inside, not in the context of the character that later debuted in the Wise Little Hen.
Hardback w/characters on back-c 75.00 300.00 650.00
Softcover w/characters on back-c 38.00 151.00 350.00
Version without characters on back-c 45.00 180.00 400.00
Book II-Less common than Book I. Character development brought into conformity with the Mickey Mouse cartoon shorts and syndicated strips. Captain Church Mouse, Tanglefoot, Peg-Leg Pete and Pluto appear with Mickey & Minnie 46.00 186.00 400.00

MICKEY MOUSE COMIC (N)
David McKay Co.: 1931 - No. 4, 1934 (10"x9-3/4", 52 pgs., card board-c)
(Later reprints exist)
1 (1931)-Reprints Floyd Gottfredson daily strips in black & white from 1930 & 1931, including the famous two week sequence in which Mickey tries to commit suicide 229.00 914.00 1680.00
2 (1932)-1st app. of Pluto reprinted from 7/8/31 daily. All pgs. from 1931 164.00 656.00 1200.00
3 (1933)-Reprints 1932 & 1933 Sunday pages in color, one strip per page, including the "Lair of Wolf Barker" continuity pencilled by Gottfredson and inked by Al Taliaferro & Ted Thwaites. First app. Mickey's nephews, Morty & Ferdie, one identified by name of Mortimer Fieldmouse, not to be confused with Uncle Mortimer Mouse who is introduced in the Wolf Barker story 214.00 856.00 1600.00
4 (1934)-1931 dailies, include the only known reprint of the infamous strip of 2/4/31 where the villainous Kat Nipp snips off the end of Mickey's tail with a pair of scissors 140.00 560.00 1050.00

MICKEY MOUSE (N)
Whitman Publishing Co.: 1933-34 (10x8-3/4", 34 pgs, cardboard-c)
948-1932 & 1933 Sunday strips in color, printed from the same plates as Mickey Mouse Book #3 by David McKay, but only pages 5-17 & 32-48 (including all of the "Wolf Barker" continuity) 157.00 629.00 1100.00
NOTE: *Some copies bound with back cover upside down. Variance doesn't affect value. Same art appears on front and back covers of all copies. Height of Whitman reissue trimmed 1/2 inch.*

MILITARY WILLIE
J. I. Austen Co.: 1907 (7x9-1/2", 12 pgs., every other page in color, stapled)
nn - By F. R. Morgan 70.00 245.00 400.00

MINNEAPOLIS TRIBUNE CARTOON BOOK (S)
Minneapolis Tribune: 1899-1903 (11-3/8x9-3/8", B&W, paper cover)
nn (#1) (1899) 28.00 99.00 170.00
nn (#2) (1900) 28.00 99.00 170.00
nn (#3) (1901) (published Jan 01, 1901) 28.00 99.00 170.00
nn (#4) (1902) (114 pgs) 28.00 99.00 170.00
nn (#5) (1903) (9x10-3/4",110 pgs, B&W; color-c) 28.00 99.00 170.00
NOTE: *All by Roland C. Bowman (editorial-r).*

MINUTE BIOGRAPHIES: INTIMATE GLIMPSES INTO THE LIVES OF 150 FAMOUS MEN AND WOMEN
Grossett & Dunlap: 1931, 1933 (10-1/4x7-3/4", 168 pgs, hardcover, B&W)
nn - By Nisenson (art) & Parker(text) 21.00 63.00 125.00
More.... (1933) 21.00 63.00 125.00

MISCHIEVOUS MONKS OF CROCODILE ISLE, THE (N)
J. I. Austen Co., Chicago: 1908 (8-1/2x11-1/2", 12 pgs., 4 pgs. in color)
nn - By F. R. Morgan; reads longwise 125.00 375.00 600.00

MR. & MRS. (Also see Ain't It A Grand and Glorious Feeling?) (N)
Whitman Publishing Co.: 1922 (9x9-1/2", 52 & 28 pgs., cardboard-c)
nn - By Briggs (B&W, 52 pgs.) 37.00 149.00 260.00
nn - 28 pgs.-(9x9-1/2")-Sunday strips-r in color 41.00 163.00 285.00

Moon Mullins #2 by Frank Willard
1928 @ Cupples & Leon

Mutt and Jeff #15 by Bud Fisher
1930 © Cupples & Leon

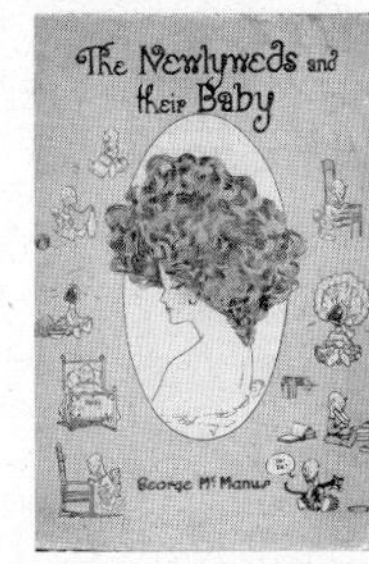

The Newlyweds by George McManus
1907 © Saalfield Publishing Co.

GD2.0 FN6.0 VF8.0

NOTE: *The earliest presently-known Whitman comic books*

MR. BLOCK (N)
Industrial Workers of the World (IWW): 1913, 1919

nn - By Ernest Riebe (C) 50.00 150.00 -
...And The Profiteers (original material) (H) 50.00 150.00 -
NOTE: *Mr Block was a daily strip published from 1912 NOV 7 to 1913 SEP ? by the socialist newspaper "Industrial Worker"; Mr Block was a "square" guy (his head was in fact a block) who enthusiastically supported the same system that exploited him. The noted Joe Hill wrote a song about him (Mr Block,1913, on the air of "It loooks me like a big time tonight") for the "Industrial Worker Songbook".*

MR. TWEE-DEEDLE (N)
Cupples & Leon: 1913, 1917 (11-3/8 x 16-3/4" color strips-r from NY Herald)

nn - By John B. Gruelle (later of Raggedy Ann fame) 350.00 900.00 1800.00
nn - "Further Adventures of..." By Gruelle 350.00 900.00 1800.00
NOTE: *Strip ran Feb 5, 1911-March 10, 1918.*

MONKEY SHINES OF MARSELEEN AND SOME OF HIS ADVENTURES (C)
McLaughlin Bros. New York: 1906 (10 x 12-3/8", 36 pgs, full color hardcover)

nn - By Norman E. Jennett strip-r NY Evening Telegram 100.00 250.00 450.00
NOTE: *Strip began in 1906 until at least March 13, 1910.*

MONKEY SHINES OF MARSELEEN (N)
Cupples & Leon Co.: 1909 (11-1/2 x 17", 58 pgs. in two colors)

nn - By Norman E. Jennett (strip-r New York Herald) 100.00 250.00 450.00

MOON MULLINS (N)
Cupples & Leon Co.: 1927 - 1933 (52 pgs., B&W daily strip-r)

Series 1 ('27)-By Willard 63.00 250.00 500.00
Series 2 ('28), Series 3 ('29), Series 4 ('30) 39.00 156.00 300.00
Series 5 ('31), 6 ('32), 7 ('33) 39.00 156.00 300.00
Big Book 1 ('30)-B&W (scarce) 100.00 400.00 750.00
w/dust jacket (rare) 183.00 732.00 1100.00

MOVING PICTURE FUNNIES
Saml Gabriel Sons & Company: 1918 (5-1/4 x 10-1/4", 52 pgs, B&W, illustrated hard-c)
nn 20.00 40.00 80.00
NOTE: *823 Comical illustrations that show a different scene when folded.*

MUTT & JEFF (...Cartoon, The) (N)
Ball Publications: 1911 - No. 5, 1916 (5-3/4 x 15-1/2", 72 pgs, B&W, hard-c)

1 (1910)(50¢) very common 71.00 286.00 500.00
2,3: 2 (1911)-Opium den panels; Jeff smokes opium (pipe dreams).
3 (1912) both very common 71.00 286.00 500.00
2-(1913) Reprint of 1911 edition with black ink cover 50.00 175.00 300.00
4 (1915) (50¢) (Scarce) 150.00 350.00 650.00
5 (1916) (Rare) -Photos of Fisher, 1st pg. (68 pages) 200.00 480.00 900.00
5-Scarce 84 page reprint edition 150.00 450.00 800.00
NOTE: *Mutt & Jeff first appeared in newspapers in 1907. Cover variations exist showing Mutt & Jeff reading various newspapers; i.e., The Oregon Journal, The American, and The Detroit News. Reprinting of each issue began soon after publication. No. 4 and 5 may not have been reprinted. Values listed include the reprints. Mutt & Jeff was the first successful American daily newspaper comic strip and as such remains one of the seminal strips of all time.*

MUTT & JEFF (N)
Cupples & Leon Co.: No. 6, 1919 - No. 22, 1934? (9-1/2x9-1/2", 52 pgs., B&W dailies, stiff-c)

6, 7 - By Bud Fisher (very common) 32.00 128.00 225.00
8-10 46.00 186.00 325.00
11-18 (Somewhat Scarcer) (#19-#22 do not exist) 60.00 â240.00 420.00
nn (1920) (Advs. of...) 11x16"; 44 pgs.; full color reprints of 1919 Sunday strips
93.00 372.00 650.00
Big Book nn (1926, 144 pgs., hardcovers) 114.00 456.00 800.00
w/dust jacket 193.00 772.00 1350.00
Big Book 1 (1928) - Thick book (hardcovers) 114.00 456.00 800.00
w/dust jacket (rare) 182.00 729.00 1275.00
Big Book 2 (1929) - Thick book (hardcovers) 114.00 456.00 800.00
w/dust jacket (rare) 182.00 729.00 1275.00
NOTE: *The Big Books contain three previous issues rebound.*

MUTT & JEFF (N)
Embee Publ. Co.: 1921 (9x15", color cardboard-c & interior)

nn - Sunday strips in color (Rare)- BY Bud Fisher 143.00 572.00 1000.00
NOTE: *Ties with The Trouble of Bringing Up Father (EmBee) and Jimmie Dugan & The Reg'lar Fellers (C&L) as the last of this size.*

MYSTERIOUS STRANGER AND OTHER CARTOONS, THE
McClure, Phillips & Co.: 1905 (12-3/8x9-3/4", 338 pgs, hardcover, B&W)

nn - By John McCutcheon 32.00 128.00 225.00

MY WAR - Szeged (Szuts)
Wm. Morrow Co.: 1932 (7x10-1/2", 210 pgs, hard-c, B&W)

nn - (All story panels, no words - powerful) 32.00 128.00 225.00

NAUGHTY ADVENTURES OF VIVACIOUS MR. JACK, THE
New York American & Journal: 1904 (15x10", color strips)

nn - By James Swinnerton; (Very Rare - 3 known copies) 900.00 1600.00 2100.00

GD2.0 FN6.0 VF8.0

NEBBS, THE (N)
Cupples & Leon Co.: 1928 (52 pgs., B&W daily strip-r)

nn - By Sol Hess; Carlson-a 40.00 160.00 280.00

NERVY NAT'S ADVENTURES (E)
Leslie-Judge Co.: 1911 (90 pgs, 85¢, 1903 strip reprints from **Judge**)

nn - By James Montgomery Flagg 75.00 263.00 450.00

THE NEWLYWEDS AND THEIR BABY (N)
Saalfield Publ. Co.: 1907 (13x10", 52 pgs., hardcover)

...& Their Baby' by McManus; daily strips 50% color 300.00 900.00 -
NOTE: *Strip ran Apr 10, 1904 thru Jan 14, 1906 and then May 19, 1907-Dec 5, 1916; was a huge success with Baby Snookums long before McManus invented Bringing Up Father; Snookums brought back as a topper strip over BUF Nov 19, 1944-Dec 30, 1956.*

THE NEWLYWEDS AND THEIR BABY'S COMIC PICTURES FOR PAINTING AND CRAYONING (N)
Saalfield Publishign Company: 1916 (10-1/4x14-3/4", 52 pgs. Cardboard-c)

nn - 44 B&W pages, covers, and one color wrap glued to B&W title page.
Color wrap: color title pg. & 3 pgs of color strips 83.00 290.00 500.00
nn - (1917, 10x14", 20 pgs, oblong, cardboard-c) partial reprint of 1916 edition
31.00 124.00 275.00

THE NEWLYWEDS AND THEIR BABY (N)
Saalfield Publishing Company: 1917 (10-1/8x13-9/16 ", 52 pgs, full color cardstock-c, some pages full color, others two color (orange, blue))

nn 83.00 290.00 450.00

NEW YORKER CARTOON ALBUM, THE (M)
Doubleday, Doran & Company Inc.: (1928-1931); **Harper & Brothers.:** (1931-1933); **Random House** (1935-1937), 12x9", various pg counts, hardcovers w/dust jackets)

1928: nn-114 pgs Arno, Held, Soglow, Williams, etc 20.00 60.00 120.00
1928: SECOND-114 pgs Arno, Bairnsfather, Gross, Held, Soglow, Williams
10.00 30.00 60.00
1930: THIRD-172 pgs Arno, Bairnsfather, Held, Soglow, Art Young
10.00 30.00 60.00
1931: FOURTH-154 pgs Arno, Held, Soglow, Steig, Thurber, Williams, Art Young, "Little King" by Soglow begins 10.00 30.00 60.00
1932: FIFTH-156 pgs Arno, Bairnsfather, Held, Hoff, Soglow, Steig, Thurber, Williams 10.00 30.00 60.00
1933: SIXTH-156 pgs same as above 10.00 30.00 60.00
1935: SEVENTH-164 pgs 10.00 30.00 60.00
1937: 168 pgs; Charles Addams plus same as above but no Little King, two page "Gone With The Wind" parody strip 10.00 30.00 60.00
NOTE: *Some sequential strips but mostly single panel cartoons.*

NIPPY'S POP (N)
The Saalfield Publishing Co.: 1917 (10-1/2x13-1/2", 36 pgs., B&W, Sunday strip-r)

nn - Charles M Payne (better known as S'Matter Pop) 43.00 152.00 260.00

OH, MAN (A Bully Collection of Those Inimitable Humor Cartoons) (S)
P.F. Volland & Co.: 1919 (8-1/2x13"; 136 pgs.)

nn - By Briggs 43.00 152.00 260.00
NOTE: *Originally came in illustrated box with Briggs art (box is Rare - worth 50% more with box).*

OH SKIN-NAY! (S)
P.F. Volland & Co.: 1913 (8-1/2x13", 136 pgs.)

nn - The Days Of Real Sport by Briggs 43.00 152.00 240.00
NOTE: *Originally came in illustrated box with Briggs art (box is Rare - worth 50% more with box).*

OLD GOLD THE SMOOTHER AND BETTER CIGARETTE...NOT A COUGH IN A CARLOAD (M,N,P) (see also BY BRIGGS)
Old Gold Cigarettes: nd (c1920's) (16 pgs, paper-c, color) (both Scarce)
nn- (4-1/4" x 3-7/8") cover strip is "Oh, Man!"; also contains: "Real Folks at Home", "Ain't It a Grand and Glorious Feelin?", "It Happens in the Best Regulated Families", and "Mr. and Mrs." (no known sales)
1440- (5-9/16" x 5-1/4") cover strip is "Frank and Ernest"; also contains: "That Guiltiest Feeling", "Real Folks at Home", "Oh, Man!", "When a Feller Needs a Friend". (no known sales)
NOTE: *Collection reprinting strip cartoons by Clare Briggs, advertising Old Gold Cigarettes. These strips originally appeared in various magazines, play program booklets, newspapers, etc. Some of the strips involve regular Briggs strip series. The two booklets contain a completely different set of comics.*

ON AND OFF MOUNT ARARAT (also see **Tigers**) (N)
Hearst's New York American & Journal: 1902, 86pgs. 10x15-1/4"

nn - Rare Noah's Ark satire by Jimmy Swinnerton (rare) 450.00 1500.00 -

ON THE LINKS (N)
Associated Feature Service: Dec, 1926 (9x10", 48 pgs.)

nn - Daily strip-r 25.00 100.00 175.00

ONE HUNDRED WAR CARTOONS (S)
Idaho Daily Statesman: 1918 (7-3/4x10", 102 pgs, paperback, B&W)

nn - By Villeneuve (WW I cartoons) 20.00 60.00 120.00

OUR ANTEDILUVIAN ANCESTORS (N,S)

Percy and Ferdie
1921 © Cupples & Leon

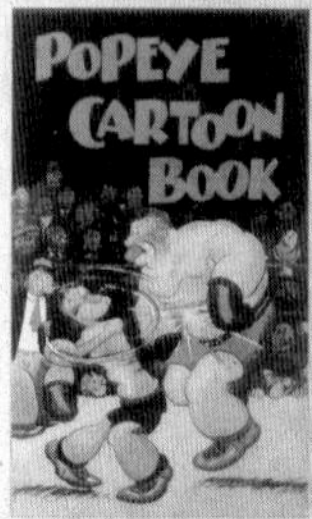

Popeye Cartoon Book
1934 © The Saalfield Co.

Roger Bean, R.G. #4
1917 © Indiana News Co., Distributors

New York Evening Journal, NY: 1903 (11-3/8x8-7/8", hardcover)

nn - By F Opper 75.00 200.00 400.00
NOTE: *There is a simultaneously published British edition, identical size and contents, from C. Arthur Pearson Ltd, London. A collection of single panel cartoons about cavemen. Similar to an earlier British cartoon book "Prehistoric Peeps from Punch", by E.T. Reed.*

OUTBURSTS OF EVERETT TRUE, THE (N)
Saalfield Publ. Co.(Werner Co.): 1907 (92 pgs, 9-7/16x5-1/4")

1907 (2-4 panel strips-r)-By Condo & Raper 125.00 350.00 675.00
1921-Full color-c; reprints 56 of 88 cartoons from 1907 ed. (10x10", 32 pgs B&W) 125.00 225.00 350.00

OVER THERE COMEDY FROM FRANCE
Observer House Printing: nd (WW 1 era) (6x14", 60 pgs, paper cover)

nn - Artist(s) unknown 15.00 53.00 90.00

OWN YOUR OWN HOME (I)
Bobbs-Merrill Company, Indianapolis: 1919 (7-7/16x5-1/4")

nn - By Fontaine Fox – – –

PECKS BAD BOY (N)
Charles C. Thompson Co, Chicago (by Walt McDougal): 1906-1908 (strip-r)

The Adventures of... (1906) 11-1/2x16-1/4", 68 pgs 100.00 400.00 800.00
...& His Country Cousin Cynthia (1907) 12x16-1/2," 34 pgs In color 100.00 400.00 800.00
Advs. of...And His Country Cousins (1907) 5-1/2x10 1/2", 18 pgs In color 50.00 175.00 300.00
Advs. of...And His Country Cousins (1907) 11-1/2x16-1/4", 36 pgs 50.00 175.00 300.00
...& Their Advs With The Teddy Bear (1907) 5-1/2x10-1/2", 18 pgs in color 50.00 175.00 300.00
...& Their Balloon Trip To the Country (1907) 5-1/2x 10-1/2, 18 pgs in color 50.00 175.00 300.00
...With the Teddy Bear Show (1907) 5-1/2x 10-1/2 50.00 175.00 300.00
...With The Billy Whiskers Goats (1907) 5-1/2 x 10-1/2, 18 pgs in color 50.00 175.00 300.00
...& His Chums (1908) - 11x16-3/8", 36 pgs. Stanton & Van Vliet Co 100.00 400.00 750.00
...& His Chums (1908)-Hardcover; full color;16 pgs. 100.00 350.00 600.00
Advs. of...in Pictures (1908) (11x17, 36 pgs)-In color; Stanton & Van V. Liet Co. 100.00 400.00 700.00

PERCY & FERDIE (N)
Cupples & Leon Co.: 1921 (10x10", 52 pgs., B&W dailies, cardboard-c)

nn - By H. A. MacGill (Rare) 61.00 244.00 450.00

PETER RABBIT (N)
John H. Eggers Co. The House of Little Books Publishers: 1922 - 1923

B1-B4-(Rare)-(Set of 4 books which came in a cardboard box)-Each book reprints half of a Sunday page per page and contains 8 B&W and 2 color pages; by Harrison Cady (9-1/4x6-1/4", paper-c) each.... 43.00 172.00 300.00
Box only 57.00 228.00 400.00

PHILATELIC CARTOONS (M)
Essex Publishing Company, Lynn, Mass.: 1916 (8-11/16" x 5-7/8", 40 pgs, light blue construction paper-c, B&W interior)

nn - By Leroy S. Bartlett 25.00 75.00 175.00
NOTE: *Comics reprinted from The New England Philatelist.*

PICTORIAL HISTORY OF THE DEPARTMENT OF COMMERCE UNDER HERBERT HOOVER (see Picture Life of a Great American) (O)
Hoover-Curtis Campaign Committee of New York State: no date, 1928 (3-1/4 x 5-1/4, 32 pgs, paper cover, B&W)

nn - By Satterfield (scarce) 50.00 140.00 260.00
NOTE: *1928 Presidential Campaign giveaway. Original material, contents completely different from Picture Life of a Great American.*

PICTURE LIFE OF A GREAT AMERICAN (see Pictorial History of the Department of Commerce under Herbert Hoover) (O)
Hoover-Curtis Campaign Committee of New York State: no date, 1928 (paper cover, B&W)

nn - (8-3/4 x 7, 20 pgs) Text cover, 2 page text introduction, 18 pgs of comics (scarcer first print) 43.00 129.00 260.00
nn - (9 x 6-3/4,24 pgs) Illustrated cover,5 page text introduction, 18 pgs of comics (scarce) 43.00 129.00 260.00
NOTE: *1928 Presidential Campaign giveaway. Unknown which above version was published first. Both contain the same original comics material by Satterfield.*

PINK LAFFIN (I)
Whitman Publishing Co.: 1922 (9x12")(Strip-r; some of these actually text joke books)

...the Lighter Side of Life, ...He Tells 'Em, ...and His Family, ...Knockouts; Ray Gleason-a (All rare) each... 26.00 104.00 185.00

POLLY (AND HER PALS) - (N)
Newspaper Feature Service: 1916 (3x2-1/2", color)

Altogether: Three Rahs and a Tiger! by Cliff Sterrett 21.00 63.00 130.00
There Is A Limit To Pa's Patience by Cliff Sterrett 21.00 63.00 130.00
Pa's Lil Book Has Some Uncut Pages by Sterrett 21.00 63.00 130.00
NOTE: *Single newsprint sheet printed in full color on both sides, unfolds to show 12 panel story.*

POPEYE PAINT BOOK (N)
McLaughlin Bros, Inc., Springfield, Mass.: 1932 (9-7/8x13", 28 pgs, color-c)

2052 - By E. C. Segar 90.00 300.00 600.00
NOTE: *Contains a full color panel above and the exact same art in below panel n B&W which one was to color in; strip-r panels.*

POPEYE CARTOON BOOK (N)
The Saalfield Co.: 1934 (8-1/2x13", 40 pgs, cardboard-c)

2095-(scarce)-1933 strip reprints in color by Segar. Each page contains a vertical half of a Sunday strip, so the continuity reads row by row completely across each double page spread. If each page is read by itself, the continuity makes no sense. Each double page spread reprints one complete Sunday page from 1933 300.00 900.00 2600.00
12 Page Version 100.00 300.00 900.00

POPEYE (See **Thimble Theatre** for earlier Popeye-r from Sonnett) (N)
David McKay Publications: 1935 (25¢; 52 pgs, B&W) (By Segar)

1-Daily strip reprints- "The Gold Mine Thieves" 200.00 400.00 800.00
2-Daily strip-r (scarce) 200.00 400.00 900.00
NOTE: *Ties with Henry & Little Annie Rooney (David McKay) as the last of the 10x10" size books.*

PORE LI'L MOSE (N)
New York Herald Publ. by Grand Union Tea
Cupples & Leon Co.: 1902 (10-1/2x15", 78 pgs., color)

nn - By R. F. Outcault; Earliest known C&L comic book (scarce in high grade - very high demand) 1500.00 4500.00 –
NOTE: *Black Americana one page newspaper strips; falls in between Yellow Kid & Buster Brown. Complete copies have become scarce. Some have cut this book apart thinking that reselling individual pages will bring them more money.*

PRETTY PICTURES (M)
Farrar & Rinehart: 1931 (12 x 8-7/8", 104 pgs, color hardcover w/dust jacket, B&W; reprints from New Yorker, Judge, Life, Collier's Weekly)

nn - By Otto Soglow (contains "The Little King") 33.00 134.00 235.00

QUAINT OLD NEW ENGLAND (S)
Triton Syndicate: 1936 (5-1/4x6-1/4", 100 pgs, soft-c squarebound, B&W)

nn - By Jack Withycomb 36.00 144.00 250.00
NOTE: *Comics about weird doings in Old New England.*

RED CARTOONS (S)
Daily Worker Publishing Company: 1926 (12 x 9", 68 pgs,cardboard cover, B&W)

nn - By Various (scarce) 40.00 160.00 280.00
NOTE: *Reprint of American Communist Party editorial cartoons, from The Daily Worker, The Workers Monthly, and the Liberator. Art by Fred Ellis, William Gropper, Clive Weed, Art Young.*

REG'LAR FELLERS (See All-American Comics, Jimmie Dugan & The..., Popular Comics & Treasure Box of Famous Comics) (N)
Cupples & Leon Co./MS Publishing Co.: 1921-1929

1 (1921)-52 pgs. B&W dailies (Cupples & Leon, 10x10") 43.00 171.00 300.00
1925, 48 pgs. B&W dailies (MS Publ.) 39.00 157.00 275.00
Hardcover (1929, 8-3/4x7-1/2"; 96 pgs.)-B&W-r 54.00 214.00 375.00

REG'LAR FELLERS STORY PAINT BOOK
Whitman, Racine, Wisc.: 1932 (8-3/4x12-1/8", 132 pgs, red soft-c)

By Gene Byrnes 25.00 75.00 150.00

ROGER BEAN, R. G. (Regular Guy) (N)
The Indiana News Co, Distributers.: 1915 - No. 2, 1915 (5-3/8x17", 68 pgs., B&W, hardcovers); #3-#5 published by **Chas. B. Jackson:** 1916-1919
(No. 1 2 4 & 5 bound on side, No. 3 bound at top)

1-By Chas B. Jackson (68pgs.)(Scarce) 60.00 210.00 360.00
2- 5-5/8x17-1/8", 66 pgs (says 1913 inside - an obvious printing error) (red or green binding) 60.00 210.00 360.00
3-Along the Firing Line... (1916; 68 pgs, 6x17") 60.00 210.00 360.00
3-Along the Firing Line side-bound version 60.00 210.00 360.00
4-Into the Trenches and Out Again with... (1917, 68 pgs) 60.00 210.00 360.00
5 ...And The Reconstruction Period (1919, 5-3/8x15-1/2", 84 pgs) (Scarce) (has $1 printed on cover) 60.00 210.00 360.00
Baby Grand Editions 1-5 (10x10", cardboard-c) 60.00 210.00 360.00
NOTE: *No. 1 & 2 of the Twin Baby Grands (nd) 8-1/4x10-7/8", 52 pgs. #3 & #4 9x10-7/8" Cardboard cover. B&W strip reprints. Cover also says "Politics Pickles People Police."*
nn - 9x11, 68 pgs 60.00 210.00 360.00
NOTE: Has picture of Chic Jackson and a posthumous dedication from his three children. strip-r 1931-32

ROGER BEAN PHILOSOPHER
Schnull & Co: 1917 (5-1/2x17", 36 pgs., B&W, brown & black paper-c, square binding)

nn - By Chic Jackson (no known sales)

ROOKIE FROM THE 13TH SQUAD, THAT (N) (also Between Shots; Always Belittlin';Skippy)
Harper & Brothers Publishers: Feb. 1918 (8x9-1/4", 72 pgs, hardcover, B&W)

nn - By Lieut. P(ercy) L. Crosby 75.00 225.00 400.00

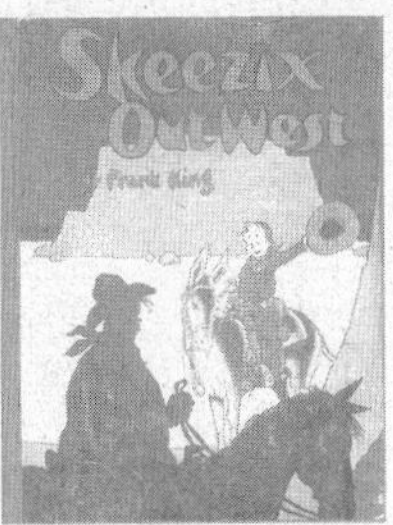

Skeezix Out West by Frank King
1928 © Reilly & Lee

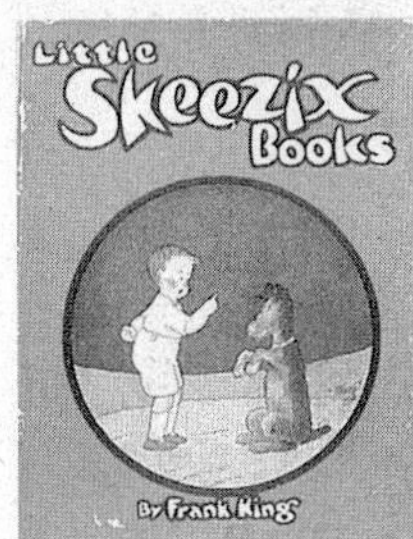

Little Skeezix Books by Frank King
1929 © Reilly & Lee

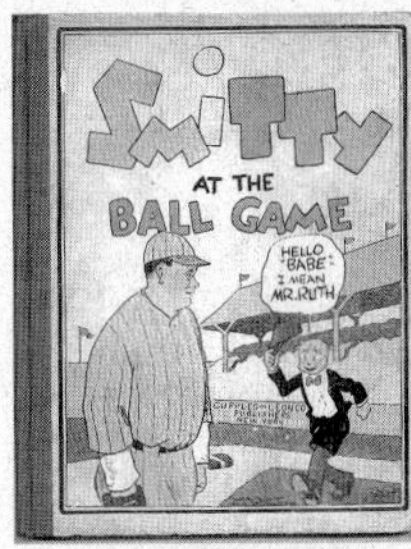

Smitty #2 By Walter Berndt
1929 © Cupples & Leon

GD2.0 FN6.0 VF8.0

NOTE: Strip began in 1917 at an Army base during basic training.

ROUND THE WORLD WITH THE DOO-DADS (see Doings of the Doo-Dads, Doo Dads)
Universal Feature And Specialty Co, Chicago: 1922 (12x10-1/2", 52 pgs, B&W, red & light blue-c, square binding)
nn - By Arch Dale newspaper strip-r 43.00 173.00 300.00
NOTE: Intermixed single panel and sequential comic strips with scenes from Scotland, Ireland, England, Holland, Italy, Spain, Egypt, Africa, and Lions & Elephants along the Nile River, China, Australia & back home.

RUBAIYKT OF THE EGG
The John C Winston Co, Philadelphia: 1905 (7x5/12", 64 pgs, purple-c, B&W)
nn - By Clare Victor Dwiggins 20.00 60.00 125.00
NOTE: Book is printed & cut into the shape of an egg.

RULING CLAWSS, THE (N,S)
The Daily Worker: 1935 (192 pgs, 10-1/4 x 7-3/8", hard-c, B&W)
nn - By Redfield 60.00 240.00 –
NOTE: Reprints cartoons from the American Communist Party newspaper The Daily Worker.

SAGARA'S ENGLISH CARTOONS AND CARTOON STORIES (N)
Bunkosha, Tokyo: nd (c1925) (6-5/8" x 4-1/4", 272 pgs, hard-c, B&W)
nn- (Scarce) – – –
NOTE: Published in Tokyo, Japan, with all strips in both English and Japanese, to facilitate learning English. Majority of book is Bringing Up Father by George McManus. Also contains Japanese strip Father Takes it Easy, by T. Sagara, reprinted from the Kokusai News Agency.

SAM AND HIS LAUGH (N)
Frederick A. Stokes: 1906 (10x15", cardboard-c, Sunday strip-r in color)
nn - By Jimmy Swinnerton (Extremely Rare) 800.00 1400.00 2800.00
NOTE: Strip ran July 24, 1904-Dec 26 1906; its ethnic humor might be considered racist by today's standards.

SCHOOL DAYS (N)
Harper & Bros.: 1919 (9x8", 104 pgs.)
nn - By Clare Victor Dwiggins 75.00 150.00 300.00

SEAMAN SI - A Book of Cartoons About the Funniest "Gob" in the Navy (N)
Pierce Publishing Co.: 1916 (4x8-1/2, 200 pgs, hardcover, B&W); 1918 (4-1/8x8-1/4, 104 pgs, hardcover, B&W)
nn - By Perce Pearce (1916) 50.00 150.00 300.00
nn - 1918 - (Reilly & Britton Co.) 30.00 125.00 200.00
NOTE: There exists two different covers for the 1918 reprints. The earlier edition was self published by the artist. The newspaper strip is sometimes also known as "The American Sailor."

SECRET AGENT X-9 (N)
David McKay Pbll.: 1934 (Book 1: 84 pgs; Book 2: 124 pgs.) (8x7-1/2")
Book 1-Contains reprints of the first 13 weeks of the strip by Dashiell Hammett & Alex Raymond, complete except for 2 dailies 100.00 300.00 700.00
Book 2-Contains reprints immediately following contents of Book 1, for 20 weeks by Dashiell Hammett & Alex Raymond; complete except for two dailies. Last 5 strips misdated from 6/34, continuity correct 100.00 300.00 700.00

SILK HAT HARRY'S DIVORCE SUIT (N)
M. A. Donoghue & Co.: 1912 (5-3/4x15-1/2", oblong, B&W)
nn - Newspaper-r by Tad (Thomas A. Dorgan) 33.00 117.00 400.00

SINBAD A DOG'S LIFE (M)
Coward - McCann, Inc.: 1930 (11x 8-3/4", 104 pgs., single-sided, illustrated hard-c, B&W
nn - By Edwina 11.00 33.00 100.00
Sinbad...Again (1932, 10-15/16x 8-9/16", 104 pgs.) 11.00 33.00 100.00
NOTE: Wordless comic strips from LIFE.

SIS HOPKINS OWN BOOK AND MAGAZINE OF FUN
Leslie-Judge Co.: 1899-July 1911 (36 pgs, color-c, B&W) (merged into Judge's Library, later titled Film Fun)
any issue - By various 11.00 33.00 100.00
NOTE: Zim, Flagg, Young, Newell, Adams, etc.

SKEEZIX (Also see Gasoline Alley & Little Skeezix Books listed below) (I)
Reilly & Lee Co.: 1925 - 1928 (Strip-r, soft covers) (pictures & text)
...and Uncle Walt (1924)-Origin 26.00 104.00 180.00
...and Pal (1925), ...at the Circus (1926) 21.00 84.00 160.00
...& Uncle Walt (1927) (does this actually exist? reprint? never seen one yet)
...Out West (1928) 30.00 100.00 200.00
Hardback Editions... 34.00 136.00 235.00

SKEEZIX BOOKS, LITTLE (Also see Skeezix, Gasoline Alley) (G)
Reilly & Lee Co.: No date (1928, 1929) (Boxed set of three Skeezix books)
nn - Box with 3 issues of Skeezix. Skeezix & Pal, Skeezix at the Circus, Skeezix & Uncle Walt known. 1928 Set... 60.00 180.00 360.00
nn - Box with 4 issues of (3) above Skeezix plus "Out West" 80.00 330.00 550.00

SKEEZIX COLOR BOOK (N)
McLaughlin Bros. Inc, Springfield, Mass: 1929 (9-1/2x10-1/4", 28 pgs, one third in full color, rest in B&W)
2023 - By Frank King; strip-r to color 20.00 75.00 135.00

SKIPPY (see also Life Presents Skippy, Always Belittlin', That Rookie From 13th Squad)
No publisher listed: Circa 1920s (10x8", 16 pgs., color/B&W cartoons)
nn - By Percy Crosby 20.00 84.00 150.00

SKIPPY, LIFE PRESENTS (M)
Life Publishing Company & Henry Holt, NY: nd 1924 (134 pgs, 10-13/16x8-3/4", color hard-c, B&W
nn - By Percy L Crosby 100.00 300.00 500.00
NOTE: Many sequential & single panel reprints from Skippy's earliest appearances in Life Magazine.

SKIPPY
Greenberg, Publisher, Inc, NY: 1925. (11-14x8-5/8, 72 pgs, hard-c, B&W and color
nn - By Percy L. Crosby 50.00 150.00 300.00
NOTE: Some but not all of these comics were also in Life Presents Skippy; issued with dust wrapper.

SKIPPY AND OTHER HUMOR
Greenberg: Publisher, NY: 1929 (11-1/4x8-1/2",72 pgs,tan hard-c, B&W and color)
nn - By Percy L. Crosby 25.00 75.00 150.00
NOTE: Came with a dust jacket.

SKIPPY (I)
Grossett & Dunlap: 1929 (7-3/8x6, 370 pgs, hardcover text with some art)
nn - By Percy Crosby (issued with a dust jacket) 23.00 92.00 160.00
NOTE: This is worth very little without the dust wrapper; very common without athe dust jacket.

SKIPPY
Greenberg Press: 1930 (soft cover, ca. 16 pp.,
nn - By Percy Crosby (scarce) 50.00 175.00 300.00
NOTE: Reprints from LIFE cartoons, color, b/w. Crosby told Greenberg to withdraw from the market as it cheapened the hard cover prior editions. Greenberg then stopped publishing per agreement, and sent Crosby all the copper & zinc bookplates, which were in Crosby estate until 1996.

SKIPPY CRAYON AND COLORING BOOK (N)
McLoughlin Bros, Inc., Springfield, MA: 1931 (13x9-3/4", 28 pgs, color-c, color & B&W)
2050 - By Percy Crosby 28.00 84.00 195.00
NOTE: This item says on the front cover: "Licensed by Percy Crosby" because he owned his creation. About half the pages have one panel pre-printed in full color with same one b&w below for person to copy the colors.

SKIPPY RAMBLES (I)
G.P. Putnam's Sons: 1932 (7 1/8 x 5 1/8, 202 pgs)
nn - By Percy Crosby 21.00 84.00 150.00
NOTE: Issued with a dustjacket. Has Skippy plates by Crosby every 4 or 5 pages.

SKUDDABUD STARRY STORY SERIES - FOLK FROM THE FUTURE (O,G)
no publisher listed: 1936 (9" x 11-7/8", 48 pgs, cardboard-c, B&W)
Book One (Rare) "Parachuting" 21.00 84.00 150.00
NOTE: By Columba Krebs. Top half of each page is a continuing strip story, while bottom half are different stories, in prose, about the same characters -- a race of aliens who have migrated to Earth, from their dying world.

S'MATTER POP? (N)
Saalfield Publ. Co.: 1917 (10x14", 44 pgs., B&W, cardboard-c,)
nn - By Charlie Payne; in full color; pages printed on one side 48.00 169.00 290.00

S'MATTER POP? (N) (25 ¢ cover price)
E.I. Company, New York: 1927 (8-15/16x7-1/8", 52 pgs, yellow soft-c perfect bound
nn - By C.M. Payne (scarce) 24.00 84.00 145.00
NOTE: First comic book published by Hugo Gernsback, noted for inventing Amazing Stories among other memorable science fiction pulps. The World Science Fiction Convention Award, The Hugo, is named for him.

SMITTY (See Treasure Box of Famous Comics) (N)
Cupples & Leon Co.: 1928 - 1933 (9x7", 96 pgs., B&W strip-r, hardcover)
1928-(96 pgs. 7x8-3/4") By Walter Berndt 43.00 172.00 300.00
1929-At the Ball Game (Babe Ruth on cover) 57.00 229.00 450.00
1930-The Flying Office Boy, 1931-The Jockey, 1932-In the North Woods each... 31.00 126.00 250.00
1933-At Military School 31.00 126.00 250.00
NOTE: Each hardbound was published with a dust jacket; worth 50% more with dust jacket. The 1929 edition is very popular with baseball collectors. Strip debuted Nov 27, 1922.

SMOKEY STOVER (See Dan Dunn & King of the Royal Mounted) (N)
Whitman Publishing: 1937 (5 1/2 x 7 1/4", 68pgs., color cardboard-c, B&W)
1010 36.00 144.00 250.00

SOCIAL COMEDY (M)
Life Publishing Company: 1902 (11-3/4 x 9-1/2", 128 pgs, B&W, illustrated hardcover)
nn - Artists include C.D. Gibson & Kemble. 20.00 70.00 120.00
NOTE: Reprints cartoons and a few sequential comics from LIFE. Came in unmarked slipcase.

SOCIAL HELL, THE (O)
Rich Hill: 1902
nn - By Ryan Walker 21.00 74.00 130.00
NOTE: "The conditions of workers and the corruption of a political system beholden to corporate interests have been a major focus of human rights concerns since the 19th century. This early graphic novel depicts the social evils of unreformed capitalism. Ryan Walker was a syndicate cartoonist for many mainstream newspapers as well as for the communist Daily Worker." This description comes from http://www.lib.uconn.edu/DoddCenter/ascexh3.html, where you can find also a reproduction of the cover. I add that Ryan Walker was the editor of "The Saint Louis Republic" comic section since its inception in 1897; the supplement published "Alma and Oliver", George McManus's first series.

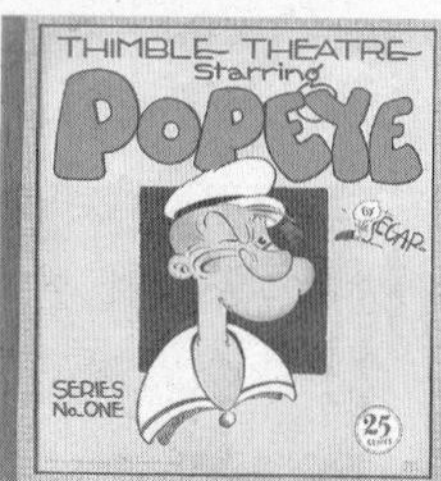

Thimble Theater #1 by E.C. Segar
1931 © Sonnet Publishing Co.

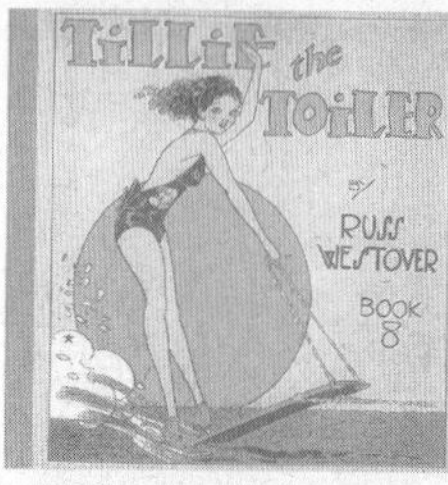

Tillie the Toiler #8 by Russ Westover
1933 © Cupples & Leon

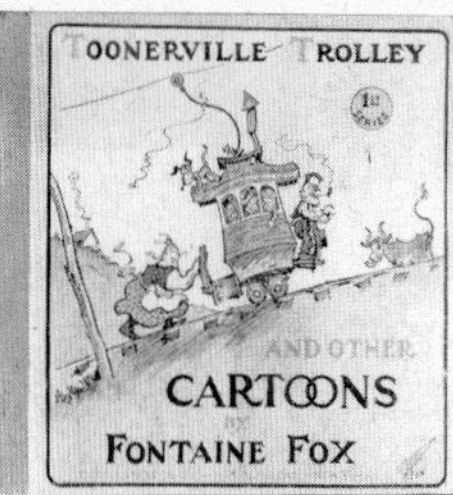

Toonerville Trolley And Other Cartoons
1921 © Cupples & Leon

GD2.0 FN6.0 VF8.0

SPORT AND THE KID (see The Umbrella Man) (N)
Lowman & Hanford Co.: 1913 (6-1/4x6-5/8",114 pgs, hardcover, B&W&orange)
nn - By J.R. "Dok" Hager 20.00 70.00 120.00

STORY OF CONNECTICUT (N)
The Hartford Times: Vol.1 1935 - Vol.3 1936 (10-1/2" x 7-3/8",304 pgs,color hard-c, B&W)
Vol.1 - 3 20.00 70.00 120.00
NOTE: *Collects a newspaper strip on Connecticut State history, which ran in the Hartford Times. Strip is in a similar format to "Texas History Movies". Also published in a plain, blue hardcover.*

STORY OF JAPAN IN CHINA, THE (N,S)
Trans-Pacific News Service, NYC: Vol. 3, No.1 March 10, 1938 (9" x 6", 36 pgs, construction paper-c, B&W)
Vol.3 No.1 21.00 64.00 150.00
NOTE: *Part of the "China Reference Series" of booklets, detailing the Japanese occupation and brutalization of China. Consists entirely of cartoons. The other booklets in the series have no cartoons. Art by: Ding, Fitzpatrick, Herblock, Herman, Rollin Kirby, Knox, Low, Manning, Orr, Shoemaker, Talburt.*

STRANGE AS IT SEEMS (S)
Blue-Star Publishing Co.: 1932 (64 pgs., B&W, square binding)
1-Newspaper-r (*Published with & without No. 1 and price on cover.*) 32.00 128.00 200.00
Ex-Lax giveaway (1936, B&W, 24 pgs., 5x7") - McNaught Synd.
13.00 52.00 90.00

SULLIVANT'S ABC ZOO (I)
The Old Wine Press: 1946 (11-3/4x9-3/8", hardcover)
nn - By T.S. Sullivant (Rare) – – –
NOTE: *Reprints Mitchell & Miller material 1895-1898 and Life Publishing 1898-1926.*

TAILSPIN TOMMY STORY & PICTURE BOOK (N)
McLoughlin Bros.: No. 266, 1931? (nd) (10x10-1/2", color strip-r)
266 - By Forrest 43.00 172.00 300.00

TAILSPIN TOMMY (Also see Famous Feature Stories & The Funnies)(N)
Cupples & Leon Co.: 1932 (100 pgs., hard-c) (B&W 1930 strip reprints)
nn - (Scarce)- by Hal Forrest & Glenn Chaffin 50.00 150.00 375.00

TALES OF DEMON DICK AND BUNKER BILL (O)
Whitman Publishing Co.: 1934 (5-1/4x10-1/2", 80 pgs, color hardcover, B&W)
793 - By Spencer 33.00 100.00 300.00

TARZAN BOOK (The Illustrated...) (N)
Grosset & Dunlap: 1929 (9x7", 80 pgs.)
1(Rare)-Contains 1st B&W Tarzan newspaper comics from 1929. By Hal Foster Cloth reinforced spine & dust jacket (50¢); Foster-c
With dust jacket... 86.00 344.00 630.00
Without dust jacket... 43.00 172.00 300.00
2nd Printing(1934, 25¢, 76 pgs.)-4 Foster pgs. dropped; paper spine, circle in lower right cover with 25¢ price. The 25¢ is barely visible on some copies
34.00 136.00 225.00
1967-House of Greystoke reprint-7x10", using the complete 300 illustrations/text from the 1929 edition minus the original indicia, foreword, etc. Initial version bound in gold paper & sold for $5.00. Officially titled **Burroughs Bibliophile #2**. A very few additional copies were bound in heavier blue paper. Gold binding... 2.25 6.75 20.00
Blue binding... 2.50 7.50 27.00

TARZAN OF THE APES TO COLOR (N)
Saalfield Publishing Co.: No. 988, 1933 (15-1/4x10-3/4", 24 pgs)
(Coloring book)
988-(Very Rare)-Contains 1929 daily reprints with some new art by Hal Foster. Two panels blown up large on each page with one at the top of opposing pages on every other double-page spread. Believed to be the only time these panels appeared in color. Most color panels are reproduced a second time in B&W to be colored
271.00 1084.00 2000.00

TARZAN OF THE APES The Big Little Cartoon Book (N)
Whitman Publishing Company: 1933 (4-1/2x3 5/8", 320 pgs, color-c, B&W)
744 - By Hal Foster (comic strips on every page) 60.00 175.00 325.00

TECK HASKINS AT OHIO STATE (S)
Lea-Mar Press: 1908 (7-1/4x5-3/8", 84 pgs, B&W hardcover)
nn - By W.A. Ireland; football cartoons-r from Columbus Ohio Evening Dispatch
28.00 99.00 170.00
NOTE: *Small blue & white patch of cover art pasted atop a color cloth quilt patter; pasted patch can easily peel off some copies.*

TECK 1909 (S)
Lea-Mar Press: 1909 (8-5/8 x 8-1/8", 124 pgs., B&W hardcover, 25¢)
nn - By W.A. Ireland; Ohio State University baseball cartoons-r from Columbus Evening Dispatch 28.00 99.00 170.00

TEDDY BEAR BOOKS, THE (M) (see also LITTLE JOHNNY AND THE TEDDY BEARS)
Reilly & Britton Co., Chicago: 1907 (7-1/16" x 5-3/8", 24 pgs, hard-c, color
The Teddy Bears Come to Life, The Teddy Bears at the Circus, The Teddy Bears in a Smashup, The Teddy Bears on a Lark, The Teddy Bears on a Toboggan, The Teddy Bears at School, The Teddy Bears Go Fishing, The Teddy Bears in Hot Water

GD2.0 FN6.0 VF8.0

21.00 63.00 130.00
NOTE: *Books are all unnumbered. C & A by J.R. Bray; s-Robert D. Towne. Reprints "Little Johnny & the Teddy Bears" strips, from Judge Magazine. Similar in format to the Buster Brown Nuggets series. All eight books debuted simultaneously.*

TEDDY BEARS IN FUN AND FROLIC (M) (see LITTLE JOHNNY & THE TEDDY BEARS)
Reilly & Britton Co., Chicago: 1908 (8-3/4" x 8-3/4", 50 pgs, cardboard-c, color)
nn - (Rare) by J.R. Bray-a; Robert D. Towne-s 100.00 400.00 700.00
NOTE: *Reprints "Little Johnny & the Teddy Bears" strips, from Judge Magazine. Unknown if there were any other "Teddy Bear" titles published in this format.*

THE TEENIE WEENIES
Reilly & Britton, Chicago: 1916 (16-3/8x10-1/2", 52 pgs, cardboard-c, full color)
nn - By Wm. Donahey (Chicago Tribune-r) 200.00 550.00 900.00

TERROR OF THE TINY TADS (see also UPSIDE DOWNS OF LITTLE LADY LOVEKINS AND OLD MAN MUFFAROO)
Cupples & Leon: 1909 (11x17, 26 Sunday strips in Black & Red, Stiff cardboard-c)
nn - By Gustave Verbeek (Very Rare) (no known sales)

TEXAS HISTORY MOVIES (N)
Various editions, 1928 to 1986 (B&W)
Book I -1928 Southwest Press (7-1/4 x 5-3/8, 56 pgs, cardboard cover) for the Magnolia Petroleum Company 50.00 125.00 250.00
nn - 1928 Southwest Press (12-3/8 x 9-1/4, 232 pgs, HC) 75.00 200.00 400.00
nn - 1935 Magnolia Petroleum Company (6 x 9, 132 pgs, paper cover)
21.00 63.00 130.00
NOTE: *Exists with either Wagon Train or Texas Flag & Lafitte/pirate covers.*
nn - 1943 Magnolia Petroleum Company (132 pgs, paper cover)
16.00 48.00 100.00
nn - 1963 Graphic Ideas Inc (11 x 8-1/2, softcover) 12.00 37.00 75.00
NOTE: *Reprints daily newspaper strips from the Dallas News, on Texas history. 1935 editions onward distributed within the Texas Public School System. Prior to that they appear to be giveaway comic books for the Magnolia Petroleum Company. There are many more editions than the ones pointed out above.*

THAT SON-IN-LAW OF PA'S! (N)
Newspaper Feature Service: 1914 (2-1/2 by 3", color)
nn - *Imprinted on back for THE LESTER SHOE STORE.* 15.00 25.00 50.00
NOTE: *Single sheet printed in full color on both sides, unfolds to show 12 panel story.*

THIMBLE THEATRE STARRING POPEYE (See also Popeye) (N)
Sonnet Publishing Co.: 1931 - No. 2, 1932 (25¢, B&W, 52 pgs.)(Rare)
1-Daily strip serial-r in both by Segar 157.00 650.00 1300.00
2 136.00 544.00 1100.00
NOTE: *The very first Popeye reprint book. The first Thimble Theatre Sunday page appeared Dec 19, 1919. Popeye first entered Thimble Theatre on Jan 17, 1929.*

THREE FUN MAKERS, THE (N)
Stokes and Company: 1908 (10x15", 64 pgs., color) (1904-06 Sunday strip-r)
nn - Maud, Katzenjammer Kids, Happy Hooligan 800.00 2000.00 –
NOTE: *This is the first comic book to compile more than one newspaper strip together.*

TIGERS (Also see On and Off Mount Ararat) (N)
Hearst's New York American & Journal: 1902, 86 pgs. 10x15-1/4"
nn - Funny animal strip-r by Jimmy Swinnerton 600.00 1600.00 –
NOTE: *The strip began as The Journal Tigers in The New York Journal Dec 12, 1897-Sept 28 1903*

TILLIE THE TOILER (N)
Cupples & Leon Co.: 1925 - No. 8, 1933 (52 pgs., B&W, daily strip-r)
nn (#1) By Russ Westover 54.00 216.00 425.00
2-8 50.00 175.00 360.00
NOTE: *First newspaper strip appearance was in January, 1921.*

TILLIE THE TOILER MAGIC DRAWING AND COLORING BOOK
Sam L Gabriel Sons And Company: 1931 (8-1/2 x 12", 36 pages, stiff-c)
838-By Russ Westover 39.00 156.00 275.00

TIMID SOUL, THE (N)
Simon & Schuster: 1931 (12-1/4x9", 136 pgs, B&W hardcover, dust jacket?)
nn - By H. T. Webster (newspaper strip-r) 40.00 120.00 260.00

TIM McCOY, POLICE CAR 17 (O)
Whitman Publishing Co.: 1934 (14-3/4x11", 32 pgs, stiff color covers)
674-1933 original material 100.00 350.00 625.00
NOTE: *Historically important as first movie adaptation in comic books.*

TOAST BOOK
John C. Winston Co: 1905 (7-1/4 x 6,104 pgs, skull-shaped book, feltcover, B&W)
nn - By Clare Dwiggins 50.00 175.00 300.00
NOTE: *Cartoon illustrations accompanying toasts/poems, most involving alcohol.*

TOM SAWYER & HUCK FINN (N)
Stoll & Edwards Co.:1925 (10x10-3/4", 52 pgs, stiff covers)
nn - By "Dwig" Dwiggins; 1923, 1924-r color Sunday strips 5000 200.00 350.00
NOTE: *By Permission of the Estate of Samuel L. Clemons and the Mark Twain Company.*

TOONERVILLE TROLLEY AND OTHER CARTOONS (N) (See Cartoons by Fontaine Fox)
Cupples & Leon Co.: 1921 (10 x10", 52 pgs., B&W, daily strip-r)

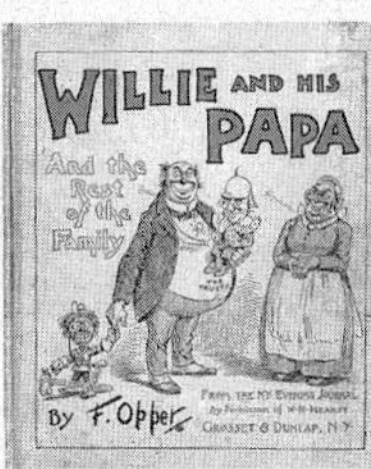

Willie and His Papa & the Rest of the Family by Opper
1901 © Grossett & Dunlap

Winnie Winkle by Branner
1932 © Cupples & Leon

The Yellow Kid #4 cover by Outcault
1897 © Howard Ainslee & Co.

GD2.0 FN6.0 VF8.0

	GD2.0	FN6.0	VF8.0
1 - By Fontaine Fox	100.00	350.00	600.00

TRAINING FOR THE TRENCHES (M)
Palmer Publishing Company: 1917 (5-3/8 x 7", 20 pgs., paper-c, 10¢)

nn - By Lieut. Alban B. Butler, Jr.	21.00	84.00	150.00

NOTE: *Subtitle: "A book of humorous cartoons on a serious subject." Single-panels about military training.*

TREASURE BOX OF FAMOUS COMICS (N) (see Wonder Chest of Famous Comics)
Cupples & Leon Co.: 1934 8-1/2x(6-7/8", 36 pgs, soft covers) (Boxed set of 5 books)

Little Orphan Annie (1926)	21.00	84.00	165.00
Reg'lar Fellers (1928)	19.00	76.00	145.00
Smitty (1928)	19.00	76.00	145.00
Harold Teen (1931)	19.00	76.00	145.00
How Dick Tracy & Dick Tracy Jr. Caught The Racketeers (1933)	26.00	104.00	205.00
Softcover set of five books in box	160.00	640.00	1250.00
Box only	57.00	228.00	450.00

NOTE: *Dates shown are copyright dates; all books actually came out in 1934 or later. The softcovers are abbreviated versions of the hardcover editions listed under each character.*

T.R. IN CARTOONS (N)
A.C. McClurg & Co., Chicago: June 13, 1910 (10-5/8" x 8", 104? pgs, paper-c, B&W)

nn - By McCutcheon about Teddy Roosevelt	-	-	-

TRUTH (See Victorian section for earlier issues including the first Yellow Kid appearances)
Truth Company, NY: 1886-1906? (13-11/16x10-5/16", 16 pgs, process color-c & center-folds, rest B&W)

1900-1906 issues	20.00	40.00	75.00

TRUTH SAVE IT FROM ABUSE & OVERWORK BEING THE EPISODE OF THE HIRED HAND & MRS. STIX PLASTER, CONCERTIST (N)
Radio Truth Society of WBAP: no date, 1924 (6-3/8 x 4-7/8, 40 pgs, paper cover, B&W)

nn - By V.T. Hamlin (Very Rare)	100.00	400.00	700.00

NOTE: *Radio station WBAP giveaway reprints strips from the Ft. Worth Texas Star-Telegram set at local radio station. 1st collected work by V.T. Hamlin, pre-Alley Oop.*

TWENTY FIVE YEARS AGO (see At The Bottom Of The Ladder) (M,S)
Coward-McCann: 1931 (5-3/4x8-1/4, 328 pgs, hardcover, B&W)

nn - By Camillus Kessler	32.00	128.00	225.00

NOTE: *Multi-image panel cartoons showing historical events for dates during the year.*

UMBRELLA MAN, THE (N) (See Sport And The Kid)
Lowman & Hanford Co.: 1911 (8-7/8x5-7/8",112 pgs, hard-c, B&W & orange)

nn - By J.R. "Dok" Hager (Seattle Times-r)	20.00	70.00	120.00

UNCLE REMUS AND BRER RABBIT (N)
Frederick A. Stokes Co.: 1907 (64 pgs, hardbound, color)

nn - By Joel C Harris & J.M. Conde	50.00	175.00	300.00

UPSIDE DOWNS OF LITTLE LADY LOVEKINS AND OLD MAN MUFFAROO
(see also TERROR OF THE TINY TADS)
New York Herald: 1905 (?) (N)

nn - By Gustav Verbeck	150.00	450.00	750.00

VAUDEVILLES AND OTHER THINGS (N)
Isaac H. Blandiard Co.: 1900 (13x10-1/2", 22 pgs., color) plus two reprints

nn - By Bunny (Scarce)	400.00	1200.00	-
nn - 2nd print "By the Creator of Foxy Grandpa" on-c but only has copyright info of 1900 (10-1/2x15 1/2, 28 pgs, color)	450.00	900.00	-
nn - 3rd print. "By the creator of Foxy Grandpa" on-c; has both 1900 and 1901 copyright info (11x13")	350.00	700.00	-

WALLY - HIS CARTOONS OF THE A.E.F. (N)
Stars & Stripes: 1917 (96 and 108 pgs, B&W)

nn - By Abian A "Wally" Wallgren (7x18; 96 pgs)	25.00	75.00	150.00
nn - another edition (108 pgs, 7x17-1/2)	25.00	75.00	150.00

NOTE: *World War One cartoons reprints from Stars & Stripes; sold to U.S. servicemen with profits to go to French War Orphans Fund. various editions from 1917-1920; there might be more than what we list here.*

WAR CARTOONS (S)
Dallas News: 1918 (11x9", 112 pgs, hardcover, B&W)

nn - By John Knott (WWOne cartoons)	20.00	70.00	125.00

WAR CARTOONS FROM THE CHICAGO DAILY NEWS (N,S)
Chicago Daily News: 1914 (10 cents, 7-3/4x10-3/4", 68 pgs, paper-c, B&W)

nn - By L.D. Bradley	20.00	70.00	125.00

WEBER & FIELD'S FUNNYISMS (S,M,O)
Arkell Comoany, NY: 1904 (10-7/8x8", 112 pgs, color-c, B&W)

1 - By various (only issue?)	20.00	70.00	150.00

NOTE: *Contains some sequential & many single panel strips by Outcault, George Luks, CA David, Houston, L Smith, Hy Mayer, Verbeck, Woolf, Sydney Adams, Frank "Chip" Bellew, Eugene "ZIM" Zimmerman, Phil May, FT Richards, Billy Marriner, Grosvenor and many others.*

WE'RE NOT HEROES (O,S)
E.C. Wells and J.W. Moss: 1933 (8-11/16" x 5-7/8", 52 pgs, B&W interior)

nn - By Eddie Wells; red & black paper-c	10.00	30.00	60.00

NOTE: *Amateurish cartoons about World War I vets in the Walter Reed Veteran's Hospital.*

GD2.0 FN6.0 VF8.0

WHEN A FELLER NEEDS A FRIEND (S)
P. F. Volland & Co.: 1914 (11-11/16x8-7/8)

nn - By Clare Briggs	37.00	131.00	225.00

NOTE: *Originally came in box with Briggs art (box is Rare); also numerous more modern reprints)*

WILD PILGRIMAGE (O)
Harrison Smith & Robert Haas: 1932 (9-7/8x7", 210 pgs, B&W hardcover w/dust jacket) (original wordless graphic novel in woodcuts)

nn - By Lynd Ward	50.00	175.00	300.00

WILLIE AND HIS PAPA AND THE REST OF THE FAMILY (I)
Grossett & Dunlap: 1901 (9-1/2x8", 200 pgs, hardcover from N.Y. Evening Journal by Permission of W. R. Hearst) (pictures & text)

nn - By Frederick Opper	100.00	260.00	450.00

NOTE: *Political satire series of single panel cartoons, involving whiny child Willie (President William McKinley), his rambunctious and uncontrollable cousin Teddy (Vice President Roosevelt), and Willie's Papa (trusts/monopolies) and their Maid (Senator) Hanna.*

WILLIE GREEN COMICS, THE (N) (see Adventures of Willie Green)
Frank M. Acton Co./Harris Brown: 1915 (8x15, 36 pgs); 1921 (6x10-1/8", 52 pgs, color paper cover, B&W interior, 25¢)

Book No. 1 By Harris Brown	45.00	158.00	270.00
Book 2 (#2 sold via mail order directly from the artist)(very rare)	45.00	172.00	300.00

NOTE: *Book No. 1 possible reprint of Adv. of Willie Green; definitely two different editions.*

WILLIE WESTINGHOUSE EDISON SMITH THE BOY INVENTOR (N)
William A. Stokes Co.: 1906 (10x16", 36 pgs. in color)

nn - By Frank Crane (Scarce)	350.00	850.00	1300.00

NOTE: *Comic strip began May 27, 1900 and ran thru 1914. Parody of inventors Westinghouse and Edison.*

WINNIE WINKLE (N)*Strip began as a daily Sept 20, 1920.*
Cupples & Leon Co.: 1930 - No. 4, 1933 (52 pgs., B&W daily strip-r)

1	43.00	172.00	400.00
2-4	29.00	116.00	300.00

WISDOM OF CHING CHOW, THE (see also The Gumps)
R. J. Jefferson Printing Co.: 1928 (4x3", 100 pgs, red & B&W cardboard cover) (newspaper strip-r The Chicago Tribune)

nn - By Sidney Smith (scarce)	30.00	90.00	150.00

WONDER CHEST OF FAMOUS COMICS (N) see Treasure Chest of Famous Comics)
Cupples & Leon Co.: 1935? 8-1/2x(6-7/8", 36 pgs, soft covers) (Boxed set of 5 books)

Little Orphan Annie #2 (1927) (Haunted House)	21.00	84.00	130.00
Little Orphan Annie #3 (1928) (in the Circus)	19.00	76.00	130.00
Smitty #2 (1929) (Babe Ruth app.)	19.00	76.00	130.00
Dolly Dimples and Bobby Bounce (1933) by Grace Drayton	19.00	76.00	130.00
How Dick Tracy & Dick Tracy Jr. Caught The Racketeers (1933)	26.00	104.00	185.00
Softcover set of five books in box	160.00	640.00	1125.00
Box only	57.00	228.00	400.00

NOTE: *Dates shown are original copyright dates of the first printings; all actually came out in 1934 or later. Extremely abbreviated versions of the hardcover editions listed under each character. It is suspected this came out the Christmas season following Teasure Chest of Famous Comics. which contains earlier editions.*

WORLD OF TROUBLE, A (S)
Minneapolis Journal: 1901 (10x8-3/4", 100 pgs, 40 pgs full color)

v3#1 - By Charles L. Bartholomew (editorial-r)	28.00	99.00	170.00

WRIGLEY'S "MOTHER GOOSE"
Wm. Wrigley Jr. Company, Chicago: 1915 (6" x 4", 28 pgs, full color)

nn - *Promotional comics for Wrigley's gum. Intro Wrigley's "Spearmen*	20.00	70.00	120.00
Book No. 2	20.00	70.00	120.00

YELLOW KID, THE (Magazine)(I) (becomes **The Yellow Book** #10 on)
Howard Ainslee & Co., N.Y.: Mar. 20, 1897 - #9, July 17, 1897
(5¢, B&W w/color covers, 52p., stapled) (not a comic book)

1-R.F. Outcault Yellow kid on-c only #1-6. The same Yellow Kid color ad app. on back-c #1-6 (advertising the New York Sunday Journal)	857.00	3500.00	-
2-6 (#2 4/3/97, #5 5/22/97, #6, 6/5/97)	743.00	2800.00	-
7-9 (Yellow Kid not on-c)	121.00	425.00	-

NOTE: *Richard Outcault's Yellow Kid from the Hearst New York American represents the very first successful newspaper comic strip in America. Listed here due to historical importance.*

YELLOW KID IN MCFADDEN'S FLATS, THE (N)
G. W. Dillingham Co., New York: 1897 (50¢, 7-1/2x5-1/2", 196 pgs., B&W, squarebound)

nn - The first "comic" book featuring The Yellow Kid; E. W. Townsend narrative w/R. F. Outcault Sunday comic page art-r & some original drawings (Prices vary widely. Rare.)	7000.00	14000.00	-

NOTE: *A Fair condition copy sold for $2,901 in August 2004.; restored app VF sold for $10,500 in 2005. A copy in Fine+ (spine intact) and loose bacl cover sold for $17,000 in 2006.*

YESTERDAYS (S)
The Reilly & Lee Co.: 1930 (8-3/4 x 7-1/2", 128 pgs, illustrated hard-c with dust jacket

nn - Text and cartoons about Victorian times by Frank Wing	20.00	40.00	80.00

Any addititions or corrections to this section are always welcome, very much encouraged and can be sent to **feedback@gemstonepub.com** to be processed for next year's Guide.

Golden Age & Beyond

The American Comic Book 1938–Present

by J.C. Vaughn & Gene Gonzales

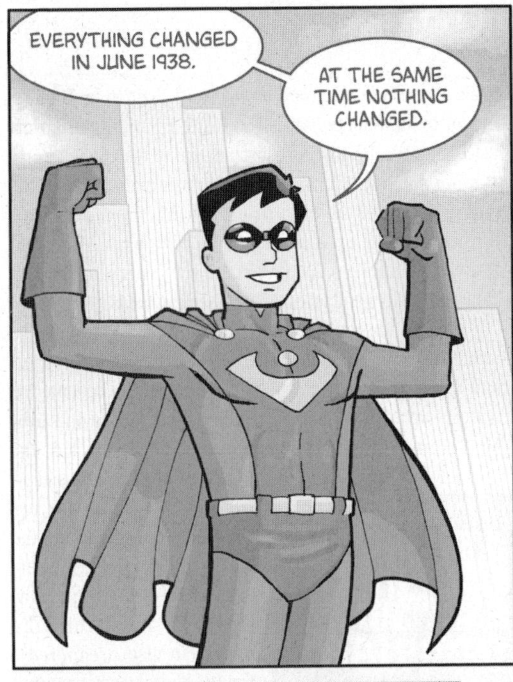
EVERYTHING CHANGED IN JUNE 1938.
AT THE SAME TIME NOTHING CHANGED.

THE ERA OF THE SUPERHEROES ARRIVED, SO THE CONTENT OF COMICS DEFINITELY CHANGED . . .
. . . BUT NOTHING FUNDAMENTALLY CHANGED IN THE METHOD OF DELIVERING SEQUENTIAL STORYTELLING TO THE MASSES.

STILL, IT'S HARD TO IGNORE WHAT FOLLOWED.

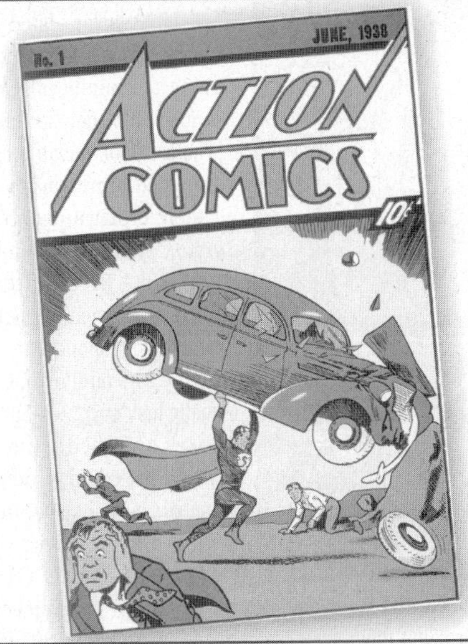
No. 1
JUNE, 1938
ACTION COMICS
10¢

AND IT'S HARD TO IGNORE THE VALUE ATTACHED TO SOME OF THE COMICS LISTED IN THIS SECTION.

FIRST, THOUGH, WE'LL TAKE A CLOSE-UP LOOK AT THE COMICS OF THE 1970S COURTESY OF *BACK ISSUE* EDITOR AND OVERSTREET ADVISOR MICHAEL EURY . . .
FOLLOWED BY OUR LARGEST PRICING SECTION.
TAKE IT AWAY, MICHAEL!

THE BRONZE AGE

GOING FOR THE BRONZE: LIFE AFTER THE SILVER AGE

by Michael Eury

It was 1970, and the Silver Age was over. The Silver Age's innovations, the Julie Schwartz-edited revamps of Golden Age favorites and the Lee/Kirby/et al.-constructed House of Ideas, had grown familiar, and in some cases, stale. The bottom had dropped out of the TV *Batman* superhero boom and the Big Two and its competitors, reeling from declining sales, scratched their heads and pondered, "What do we try next?"

Their answer: *Try everything!* The 1970s *was* the decade of excess, after all, when there was no such thing as "too much" and nothing we, as a culture, wouldn't try. Hair got longer, music got louder, lapels got wider, bras got burned, movies got bloodier, drugs got mainstreamed . . . and Mom wore pantsuits while Dad sprouted muttonchops. Marvel and DC also got "with it," trying new genres, new ideas, and new formats, all in a hungry pursuit of the one thing there could *never* be too much of: money.

Today, Mom's pantsuits may have elastic waistlines and Dad's muttonchops-and hair-may be a distant memory, but the decade we now call the Bronze Age-1970–1979-was, arguably, the most influential of all of comics' landmark eras. It could have been comics' last dance, but instead it became a decade of renaissance, when through trial and error inroads were made that paved the way for the innovations of the 1980s, the 1990s, and the comic book industry we know today.

In their quest to find the next big thing, the first place publishers looked was *outside* of comics. For a mere $200 licensing fee ($50 beyond tight-fisted publisher Martin Goodman's budgeted $150), Marvel Comics writer/editor Roy Thomas landed the publication rights to Robert E. Howard's famed swordsman Conan. And while Marvel's *Conan the Barbarian* #1, written by Thomas, drawn by newcomer Barry (Windsor-) Smith, and cover-dated October 1970, didn't instantly ignite the comics world (*Conan* didn't look or read like the other material available, and early issues suffered from distribution challenges), before long the series developed a growing audience, and proved to publishers that they could sell material other than caped crusaders and lovesick all-American teens.

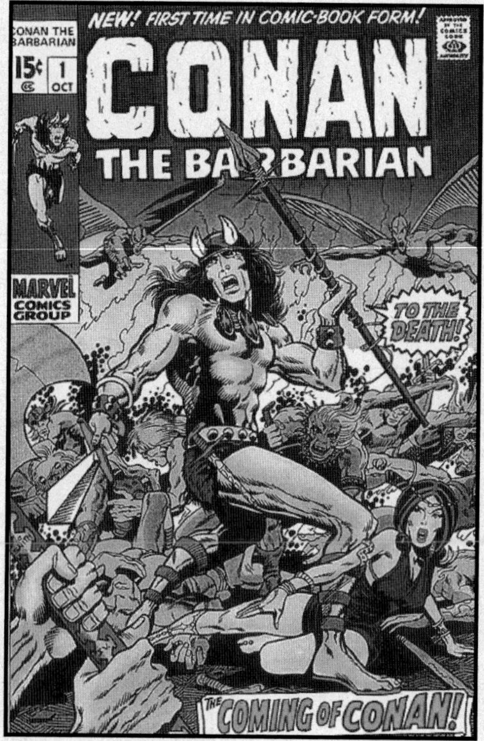

Sword-and-sorcery comics soon cut a swath through the stands, with licensed acquisitions Kull, Red Sonja, Thongor, and Solomon Kane joining Marvel's line, and DC countering with its acquisition of Fritz Leiber's Fafhrd and the Grey Mouser, in a 1973 series that made no attempt to hide the craze upon which it was capitalizing: *Sword and Sorcery* (original characters like the Warlord, Starfire, Stalker, Claw the Unconquered, IronJaw, and Wulf the Barbarian also premiered). Yet DC had already ventured into licensed terrain with its April 1972 cover–dated first issue of *Tarzan* (#207, continuing the numbering from previous publisher Gold Key). "[The estate of Tarzan creator Edgar Rice Burroughs] wanted their creative people on *Tarzan,*" Carmine Infantino, at the time DC's Editorial Director, revealed, a request to which he responded, "No, I want my guys on the book"—actually his "guy," Joe Kubert, whose heralded stint as writer/artist/editor produced some of, perhaps *the*, finest illustrated Tarzan stories ever.

Tomb of Dracula (*TOD*), first seen in (cover date) April 1972, was not a licensed property but might have been had Bram Stoker's 1897 vampire novel not fallen into public domain. *TOD* and *Werewolf by Night*, which preceded it into print by two months in

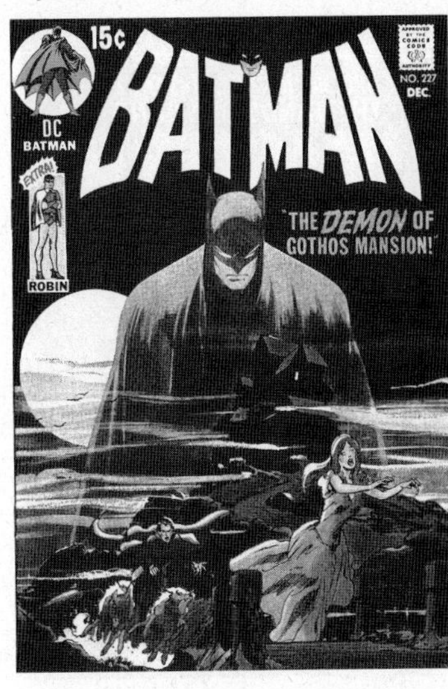

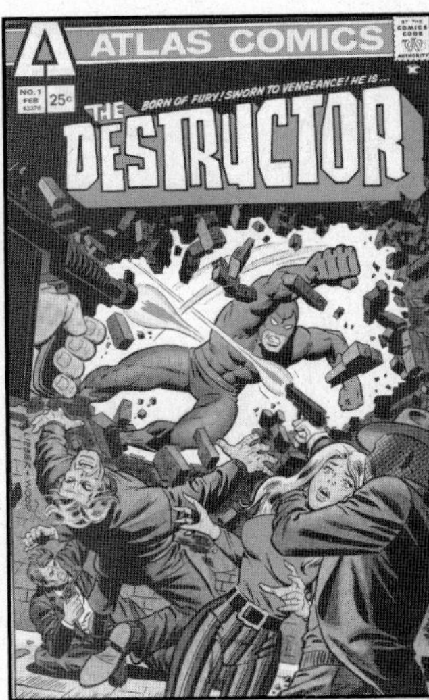

Marvel Spotlight #2, were Marvel's response to the 1971 lifting of the Comics Code Authority's prohibition against the depiction of vampires, werewolves, and the undead (although Morbius the Living Vampire, who debuted in October 1971's *Amazing Spider-Man* #101, was first out the gruesome gate), and spawned one of the decade's most popular trends. Frankenstein, Swamp Thing, Man-Thing, Bog Beast, Brother Voodoo, the Demon, and the Living Mummy were among the macabre protagonists in 1970s comics ("I pray that you will discontinue this corruption of impressionable young minds. . ." penned one concerned mother in response to Marvel's hellspawned super-hero, the Son of Satan). Some of them have resurfaced in the 2000s and have achieved acclaim beyond the four-color pages, including Ghost Rider, the star of a 2006 motion picture starring Nicolas Cage—who was weaned on Bronze Age comics (and chose his stage name from Marvel's own Hero for Hire, Luke Cage, another product of the 1970s).

Fu Manchu, the fictional "Yellow Peril" mastermind and subject of a series of novels by Sax Rohmer, brought his claw-fingered menace to comics in *Special Marvel Edition* #15 (December 1973), the first appearance of his created-for-comics son, Shang-Chi, better known as the Master of Kung Fu. Steve Englehart and Jim Starlin's response to the TV hit *Kung Fu* (1972–1975)—which itself was television's response to the trend of Hong Kong–born martial-arts movies and their patron saint, Bruce Lee—*Master of Kung Fu* became a long-running success for Marvel (most notably under Doug Moench and Paul Gulacy's tenure), and encouraged a gaggle of companions and imitators, including Sons of the Tiger, Iron Fist, Bronze Tiger, Lady Shiva, Karate Kid, and Richard Dragon, Kung Fu Fighter, as well as Seaboard/Atlas' 1975 copycat title *The Hands of the Dragon*.

Martial arts aside, Rohmer's Fu Manchu novels repre-

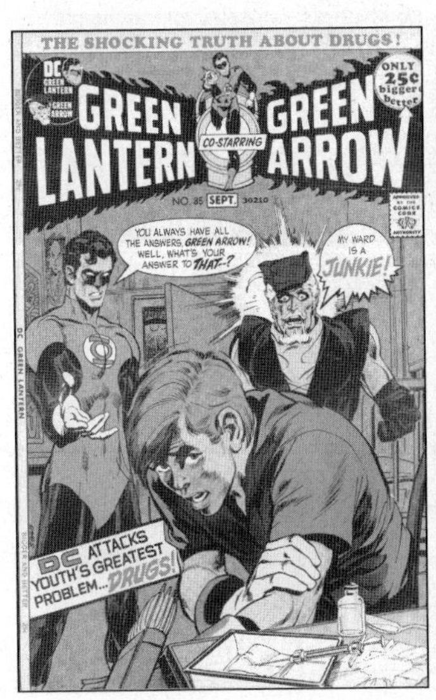

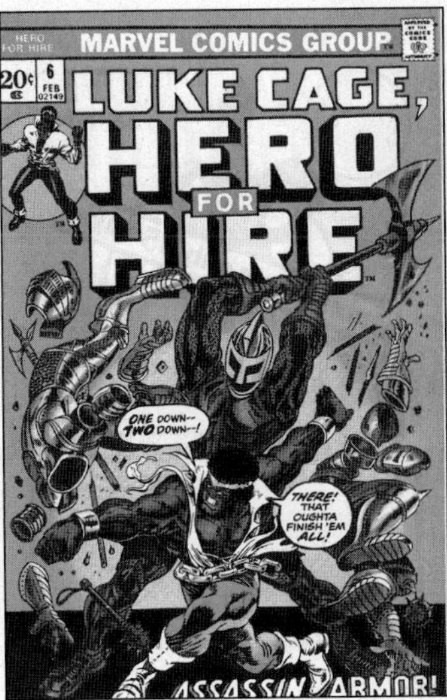

sented another 1970s' comics trend: pulp heroes. Doc Savage returned to spin racks in the form of a Marvel series in 1972. Dennis O'Neil and Michael Kaluta brought *The Shadow* to DC in 1973 (Jim Steranko, Alex Toth, and Bernie Wrightson were considered as the *Shadow* artist before then-newcomer Kaluta was signed). In 1975 DC also published four issues of *Justice, Inc.*, starring the chalk-skinned globe-trotter the Avenger, and Howard Chaykin's mid-1970s' Dominic Fortune (for Marvel) and the Scorpion (for Seaboard) mined this pulp vein.

Beyond the world of pop literature, Marvel found mass media a ripe market for exploitation. Rock stars KISS became super-heroes, even fighting Dr. Doom (premiering in a magazine-formatted comic featuring the audacious stunt of mixing the band's *blood* with the printer's ink!), and comics based upon popular sci-fi films *Logan's Run*, *Planet of the Apes*, *Godzilla*, and *2001: A Space Odyssey* invaded the racks. DC was less ambitious in adapting cinematic properties, although its "DC TV Comic" line, including *Welcome Back, Kotter*, is noteworthy if for no other reason than the utter strangeness of it all.

No 1970s' screen property was more popular as a comic book than *Star Wars*, which premiered a few months before the May 25, 1977 release of the film, an anticipation-building maneuver brainstormed by Jedi master George Lucas. Roy Thomas was at the writing helm, and as he told *BACK ISSUE* in 2005, Lucas "had in mind the idea of Howard Chaykin as the artist." *Star Wars*' success title paved the way for other popular late-1970s' Marvel titles based upon sci-fi and toy properties, such as *Battlestar Galactica*, *The Micronauts*, and *Rom*.

Chaykin as Lucas' go-to artist illustrates another hallmark of 1970s' comics: the emergence of young talent. Comics publishing houses had been the exclusive domain of

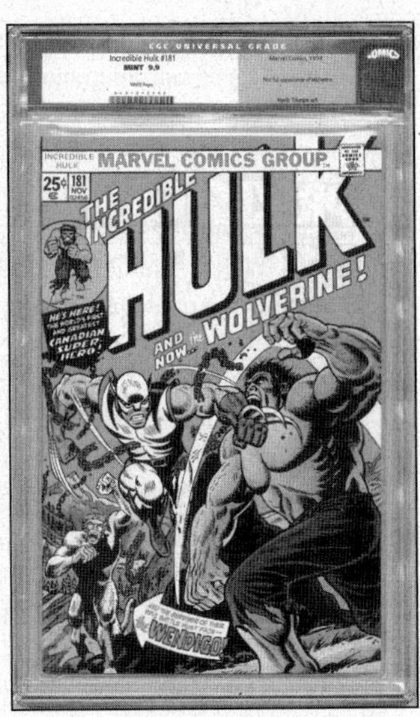

stuffed shirts in elbow-patched tweed jackets, but while looking outside of the field for new properties, the medium also looked *within* its fan base for the next talent wave. The transition, however, was not without its bumps in the road. As one of the "long-hairs" who broke the barrier, writer Denny O'Neil revealed, reflecting upon his visits to DC's headquarters, that "Steve Skeates and I were told by one of the functionaries not to walk past the Big Boss' office 'looking like that,' to take the long way around." "DC had been a closed shop," concurred Carmine Infantino, who "put aside a room for the freelance artists and writers, a place for them to go and discuss and enjoy each other's work." Another such site was Continuity Associates, the studio co-founded in 1971 by Neal Adams and Dick Giordano. Following the lead established in the late 1960s by visionaries Adams and his contemporary Steranko, who demonstrated that comics storytelling was not restricted to stodgy panel layouts or stereotypical dialogue, new artists and writers stormed the medium, daring to do things differently, Frank Brunner, John Byrne, Chris Claremont, Gerry Conway, Dave Cockrum, José Luis Garcia-Lopez, Steve Gerber, Michael Golden, Mike Grell, George Pérez, Mike Ploog, Frank Miller, Marshall Rogers, Bill Sienkiewicz, Walter Simonson, Len Wein, and Marv Wolfman, among their number.

Not to rest on their laurels, established talent became energized by this exciting new climate: John Buscema, Nick Cardy, Gene Colan, Gil Kane, Jack Kirby, Joe Kubert, Stan Lee, and John Romita, Sr. produced some of their best work in the 1970s, as did Curt Swan and Murphy Anderson with their "Swanderson" pairing on *Superman*. Marvel and DC took chances with traditional characters and with new characters existing within their universes. The coming of Kirby's Fourth World, *Green Lantern/Green Arrow*, Swamp Thing, Jonah Hex, the Punisher and Wolverine, Howard the Duck, Warlock, ethnic characters, and the new X-Men, plus the Joker's return to his homicidal roots and the deaths of Gwen

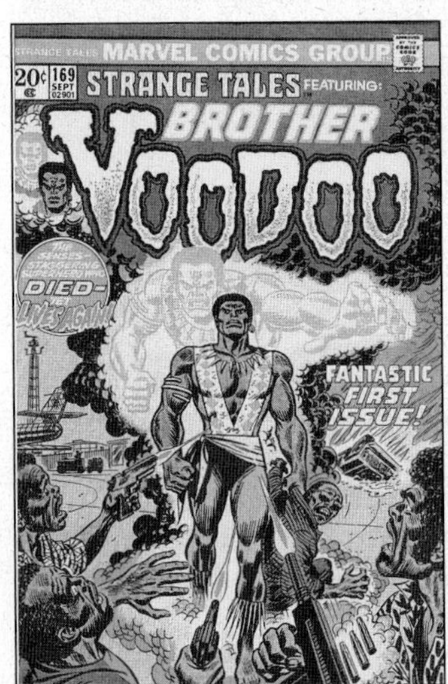

Stacy and the Green Goblin, suggest that the most significant innovation of the 1970s might have been a willingness to explore new directions with icons.

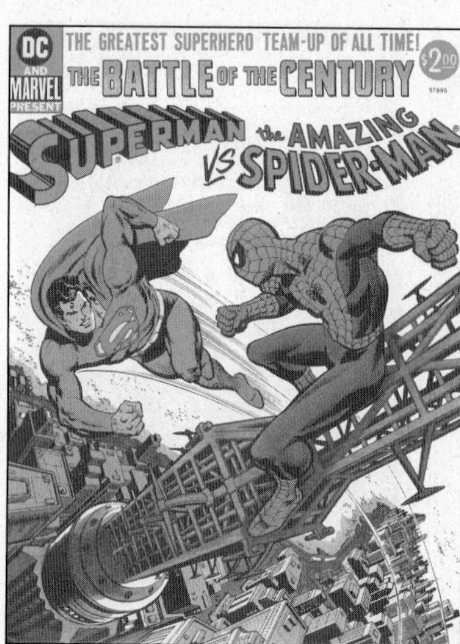

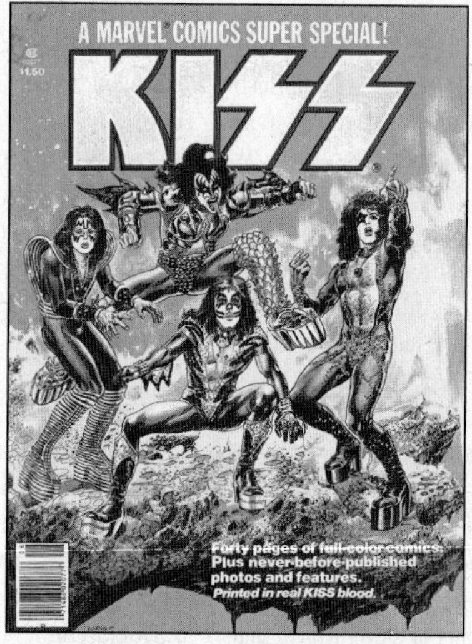

With new properties, new talent, and new characters bombarding the reader at a dizzying pace, little stability was to be found in the *shapes* of the comic books themselves. Publishers experimented with a variety of formats, in a move initially inspired by that perennial enemy of the long-time comic-book reader: the price increase.

Two years after jumping from a 12- to a 15-cent cover price, the 25-cent comic originated in the summer of 1971, as DC's titles, with their August cover dates, were now 48 pages (52 counting covers), hyped as "bigger and better" with roughly 22–25 new story pages backed up by 6–12 pages of Golden and Silver Age reprints. Marvel sucker-punched DC, delaying their price hike by one month (while blurbing their covers "Still 15¢"), then matching DC's price the next month, but trumping their original page count with 34–35 new story pages—and *then* undercutting their competitor by reverting to the standard 32–page format the following month, but at the cover price of 20 cents. DC, however, offered its readers something that Marvel's streamlined package could not: history. Newer readers sampled adventures of long-retired characters like Starman and Sandman, or more recently cancelled heroes including Deadman, keeping them alive in the fandom consciousness and inspiring budding writers and artists to, in later years, resuscitate them.

Is there any format that "says" the 1970s more than DC's 100-page Super Spectacular? In June and July 1971, DC published a trio of 100-pagers—*Weird Mystery Tales*, *Love Stories*, and *World's Greatest Super-Heroes*—each priced at 50 cents and reprinting material from the publisher's rich past. By 1973, 100-pagers returned as reprint specials, following in the footsteps of the Silver Age's beloved Annuals and 80-page giants. Before long several of DC's regular titles were converted to a bimonthly 100-page format, with new lead feature (or features) backed up by classics from yesteryear. (In December 1976 DC similarly converted some of its character-heavy titles like *Superman Family* into its new "Dollar Comic" format, featuring *all-new* stories in an 80-page [later a 64-page] package.)

Sharing the Super Spectacular's page count but at a much smaller size, the digest-sized comic (which began in the late 1960s at Gold Key) gained prominence in the 1970s in an attempt to broaden comics' availability. DC experimented with a 1972 *Tarzan* digest, announcing but never releasing a *Laurel and Hardy* digest (DC did, however, release a *Laurel and Hardy* one-shot comic). By decade's end, DC, Marvel, and Archie were publishing a host of reprint digests, aggressively fighting for rack space in supermarkets' highly visible checkouts. DC's and Marvel's digests were cancelled by the mid-1980s, but Archie's remain a durable fixture today, and the digest has morphed into a popular format for manga.

Comics reprints gained a bookstore presence throughout the 1970s, including Bonanza's trio of hardcovers, *Batman: From the 30's to the 70's*, *Superman: From the 30's to the 70's*, and *Shazam: From the 40's to the 70's*, the latter of which, not experiencing reprintings like the Batman and Superman editions, being quite scarce in today's collectibles market. Fireside's full-color trade paperback collections of Marvel and DC material were popular, particularly the Stan Lee–sanctioned line of super-hero trades beginning with *Origins of Marvel Comics* (1974). Near the end of the decade, Tempo Books' black-and-white paperback reprints of 1950s and 1960s DC material could be found in bookstores and K-Marts, as could Pocket Books' full-color line of reprints of early Marvels.

The *biggest* reprint format of the 1970s, bar none, was the tabloid, measuring approximately 10 1/4" x 13 1/4" and called "Treasury Editions" by Marvel and "Limited Collectors' Editions" by DC. Offering the added bonus of printing comics art close to full size (the standard dimensions of comics artboard of the day was 10" x 15"), these oversized comics soon housed all-new as well as classic material, and became the spotlight format for influential projects, including DC and Marvel's first super-hero team-up, *Superman vs. The Amazing Spider-Man* (1976).

Tabloids were envisioned as a doorway for comics to hop off the claustrophobic, kid-centric spin rack and be shelved alongside compatibly sized periodicals, but the black-and-white (B&W) comics magazine was most attrac-

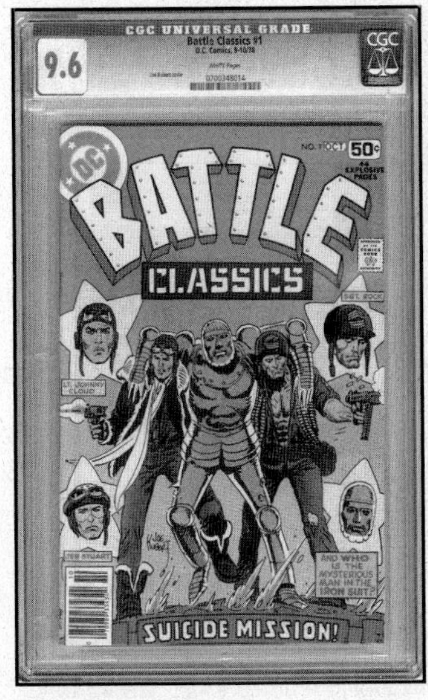

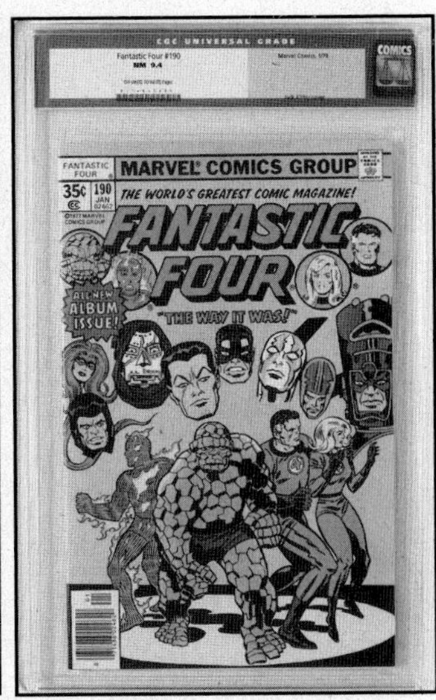

tive to publishers as a means of luring the older, more discerning reader to the comic-book art form. While the medium had previously dabbled in this arena, E.C.'s "Picto-Fiction" B&Ws of the 1950s being an early example, during the 1970s almost every comics house tried its hand at it, following the lead of publisher James Warren, the indisputable champ of black-and-whites since his 1964 launch of *Creepy*. Skywald's *Psycho*, Ross Andru and Mike Esposito's *Up Your Nose and Out Your Ear*, and Charlton's TV-licensed *The Six Million Dollar Man* were among 1970s' B&W comics magazine fare, but Marvel successfully milked this trend for several years, most notably with its long-running *Savage Sword of Conan*. A single issue each of Jack Kirby's ill-fated "Speak-Out" black-and-whites *In the Days of the Mob* and *Spirit World*, DC's 1971 attempt to stick an apprehensive toe in the B&W waters, was released under the banner of "Hampshire Distributor's Ltd." Always the trailblazer, Kirby had high hopes for finding a new audience with these magazines (he was developing two other titles, *True Divorce Cases* and *Soul Love*, but they were not produced), but spotty distribution of *Mob* and *Spirit* intimidated the publisher from releasing additional B&Ws.

The graphic novel was also born in the 1970s, thanks to Will Eisner's *A Contract with God* (1978). The biographical "comix" found in the undergrounds motivated Eisner to return to the fold after a hiatus, and at a time when he could have easily retired, Eisner essentially re-created the comics art form by producing this pioneering collection of intensely personal stories.

The final, but widest-reaching, breakthrough of the Bronze Age was merchandising. While popular comics stars had long been licensed for various products, comic-book characters became household names during the 1970s due to a ubiquitous barrage of Saturday-morning TV cartoons and primetime live-action dramas, action figures, records, coloring books, 7-11 Slurpee cups, lunchboxes, electric toothbrushes, Colorforms, clothing patches, View-Master reels, and Halloween costumes, culminating in *Superman: The Movie*'s elevation of the comic-book film to blockbuster status in 1978. While the innovations of 1970s publishing rebuilt the industry from within, the non-comics retailing of its characters cemented their statuses as cultural institutions.

Overstreet advisor Michael Eury is the Editor of TwoMorrows' *BACK ISSUE* magazine, the co-editor/co-author of *The Supervillain Book: The Ultimate Encyclopedia of Comic-Book and Hollywood Masterminds, Megalomaniacs, and Menaces* (Visible Ink Press, 2006), and the author of *The Justice League Companion* (2005), *Dick Giordano: Changing Comics, One Day at a Time* (2003), and *Captain Action: The Original Super-Hero Action Figure* (2002). A former editor for DC, Dark Horse, and Comico, Eury has written cartoons, comics, and copy for Nike, Toys R Us, Warner Bros., MSN, *Cracked*, and Bowen Designs. *Quotes for this article originally appeared in interviews in BACK ISSUE magazine and the book,* The Justice League Companion. *The author wishes to thank Dewey Cassell, Tom Field, Glenn Greenberg, Allan Harvey, Carmine Infantino, Dan Johnson, John Morrow, Dennis O'Neil, Diana Schutz, Tom Stewart, and Roy Thomas for their contributions.*

Abadazad #2 © DIS

Abbott and Costello #4 © STJ

Aces High #4 © WMG

	GD 2.0	VG 4.0	FN 6.0	VF 8.0	VF/NM 9.0	NM- 9.2

The correct title listing for each comic book can be determined by consulting the indicia (publication data) on the beginning interior pages of the comic. The official title is determined by those words of the title in capital letters only, and not by what is on the cover. Titles are listed in this book as if they were one word, ignoring spaces, hyphens, and apostrophes, to make finding titles easier. Exceptions are made in rare cases. Comic books listed should be assumed to be in color unless noted "B&W".

Comic publishers are invited to send us sample copies for possible inclusion in future guides.

PRICING IN THIS GUIDE: Prices for **GD 2.0** (Good), **VG 4.0** (Very Good), **FN 6.0** (Fine), **VF 8.0** (Very Fine), **VF/NM 9.0** (Very Fine/Near Mint),and **NM– 9.2** (Near Mint–) are listed in whole U.S. dollars except for prices below $7 which show dollars and cents. **The minimum price listed is $3.00**, the cover price for current new comics. Many books listed at this price can be found in $1.00 boxes at conventions and dealers stores.

A-1 (See A-One)

ABADAZAD
CrossGen (Code 6): Mar, 2004 - No. 3, May, 2004 ($2.95)

1-3-Ploog-a/c; DeMatteis-s 3.00
1-2nd printing with new cover 3.00

ABATTOIR
Radical Comics: Oct, 2010 - No. 6, Aug, 2011 ($3.99/$3.50, limited series)

1-($3.99) Cansino-a/Levin & Peteri-s 4.00
2-6-($3.50) 3.50

ABBIE AN' SLATS (...With Becky No. 1-4) (See Comics On Parade, Fight for Love, Giant Comics Edition 2, Giant Comics Editions #1, Sparkler Comics, Tip Topper, Treasury of Comics, & United Comics)
United Features Syndicate: 1940; March, 1948 - No. 4, Aug, 1948 (Reprints)

	GD	VG	FN	VF	VF/NM	NM-
Single Series 25 ('40)	39	78	117	236	388	540
Single Series 28	33	66	99	194	317	440
1 (1948)	17	34	51	98	154	210
2-4: 3-r/Sparkler #68-72	10	20	30	58	79	100

ABBOTT AND COSTELLO (...Comics)(See Giant Comics Editions #1 & Treasury of Comics)
St. John Publishing Co.: Feb, 1948 - No. 40, Sept, 1956 (Mort Drucker-a in most issues)

	GD	VG	FN	VF	VF/NM	NM-
1	65	130	195	416	708	1000
2	37	74	111	222	361	500
3-9 (#8, 8/49; #9, 2/50)	25	50	75	150	245	340
10-Son of Sinbad story by Kubert (new)	30	60	90	177	289	400
11,13-20 (#11, 10/50; #13, 8/51; #15, 12/52)	18	36	54	105	165	225
12-Movie issue	19	38	57	111	176	240
21-30: 28-r/#8. 29,30-Painted-c	14	28	42	80	115	150
31-40: 33,38-Reprints	11	22	33	60	83	105
3-D #1 (11/53, 25¢)-Infinity-c	32	64	96	188	307	425

ABBOTT AND COSTELLO (TV)
Charlton Comics: Feb, 1968 - No. 22, Aug, 1971 (Hanna-Barbera)

	GD	VG	FN	VF	VF/NM	NM-
1	8	16	24	53	89	125
2	4	8	12	28	44	60
3-10	4	8	12	22	34	45
11-22	3	6	9	18	27	35

ABC (See America's Best TV Comics)

ABC: A-Z (one-shots)
America's Best Comics: Nov, 2005 - July, 2006 ($3.99, one-shots)

... Greyshirt and Cobweb (1/06) character bios; Veitch-s/a; Gebbie-a; Dodson-c 4.00
... Terra Obscura and Splash Brannigan (3/06) character bios; Barta-a; Dodson-c 4.00
... Tom Strong and Jack B. Quick (11/05) character bios; Sprouse-a; Nowlan-a; Dodson-c 4.00
... Top Ten and Teams (7/06) character bios; Ha & Cannon-a; Veitch-a; Dodson-c 4.00

ABE SAPIEN... (Hellboy character)
Dark Horse Comics

...: Drums of the Dead (3/98, $2.95) 1-Thompson-a. Hellboy back-up; Mignola-s/a/c 4.00
...: The Abyssal Plain (6/10 - No. 2, 7/10, $3.50) 1,2-Mignola & Arcudi-s/Snejbjerg-a 3.50
...: The Devil Does Not Jest (9/11 - No. 2, 10/11, $3.50) Mignola & Arcudi-s. 1-Two covers by Johnson & Francavilla 3.50
...: The Drowning (2/08 - No. 5, 6/08, $2.99) 1-5-Mignola-s/c; Alexander-a 3.50
...: The Haunted Boy (10/09, $3.50) 1-Mignola & Arcudi-s/Reynolds-a/Johnson-c 3.50

A. BIZARRO
DC Comics: Jul, 1999 - No. 4, Oct, 1999 (2.50, limited series)

1-4-Gerber-s/Bright-a 3.00

	GD 2.0	VG 4.0	FN 6.0	VF 8.0	VF/NM 9.0	NM- 9.2

ABOMINATIONS (See Hulk)
Marvel Comics: Dec, 1996 - No. 3, Feb, 1997 (1.50, limited series)

1-3-Future Hulk storyline 3.00

ABRAHAM LINCOLN LIFE STORY (See Dell Giants)

ABRAHAM STONE
Marvel Comics (Epic): July, 1995 - No. 2, Aug, 1995 ($6.95, limited series)

1,2-Joe Kubert-s/a 7.00

ABSENT-MINDED PROFESSOR, THE
Dell Publishing Co.: Apr, 1961 (Disney)

	GD	VG	FN	VF	VF/NM	NM-
Four Color #1199-Movie, photo-c; variant edition has a "Fabulous Formula" strip on back-c	8	16	24	55	93	130

ABSOLUTE VERTIGO
DC Comics (Vertigo): Winter, 1995 (99¢, mature)

	GD	VG	FN	VF	VF/NM	NM-
nn-1st app. Preacher. Previews upcoming titles including Jonah Hex: Riders of the Worm, The Invisibles (King Mob), The Eaters, Ghostdancing & Preacher	1	2	3	5	7	9

ABYSS, THE (Movie)
Dark Horse Comics: June, 1989 - No. 2, July, 1989 ($2.25, limited series)

1,2-Adaptation of film; Kaluta & Moebius-a 3.00

ACCELERATE
DC Comics (Vertigo): Aug, 2000 - No. 4, Nov, 2000 ($2.95, limited series)

1-4-Pander Bros.-a/Kadrey-s 3.00

ACCLAIM ADVENTURE ZONE
Acclaim Books: 1997 ($4.50, digest size)

1-Short stories of Turok, Troublemakers, Ninjak and others 4.50

ACE COMICS
David McKay Publications: Apr, 1937 - No. 151, Oct-Nov, 1949 (All contain some newspaper strip reprints)

	GD	VG	FN	VF	VF/NM	NM-
1-Jungle Jim by Alex Raymond, Blondie, Ripley's Believe It Or Not, Krazy Kat begin (1st app. of each)	314	628	942	2198	3849	5500
2	92	184	276	538	982	1425
3-5	61	122	183	390	670	950
6-10	45	90	135	284	482	680
11-The Phantom begins (1st app., 2/38) (in brown costume)	87	174	261	553	952	1350
12-20	39	78	117	231	378	525
21-25,27-30	34	68	102	199	325	450
26-Origin & 1st app. Prince Valiant (5/39); begins series?	108	216	324	686	1181	1675
31-40: 37-Krazy Kat ends	24	48	72	142	234	325
41-60	19	38	57	109	172	235
61-64,66-76-(7/43; last 68 pgs.)	15	30	45	94	147	200
65-(8/42)-Flag-c	19	38	57	109	172	235
77-84 (3/44; all 60 pgs.)	14	28	42	80	115	150
85-99 (52 pgs.)	12	24	36	69	97	125
100 (7/45; last 52 pgs.)	14	28	42	80	115	150
101-134: 128-(11/47)-Brick Bradford begins. 134-Last Prince Valiant (all 36 pgs.)	10	20	30	56	76	95
135-151: 135-(6/48)-Lone Ranger begins	9	18	27	52	69	85

ACE KELLY (See Tops Comics & Tops In Humor)

ACE KING (See Adventures of Detective...)

ACES
Acme Press (Eclipse): Apr, 1988 - No. 5, Dec, 1988 ($2.95, B&W, magazine)

1-5 3.00

ACES HIGH
E.C. Comics: Mar-Apr, 1955 - No. 5, Nov-Dec, 1955

	GD	VG	FN	VF	VF/NM	NM-
1-Not approved by code	24	48	72	192	306	420
2	14	28	42	112	176	240
3-5	13	26	39	104	162	220

NOTE: *All have stories by* ***Davis, Evans, Krigstein,*** *and* ***Wood. Evans*** *c-1-5.*

ACES HIGH
Gemstone Publishing: Apr, 1999 - No. 5, Aug, 1999 ($2.50)

1-5-Reprints E.C. issues 3.00
Annual 1 ($13.50) r/#1-5 13.50

ACME NOVELTY LIBRARY, THE
Fantagraphics Books: Winter 1993-94 - Present (quarterly, various sizes)

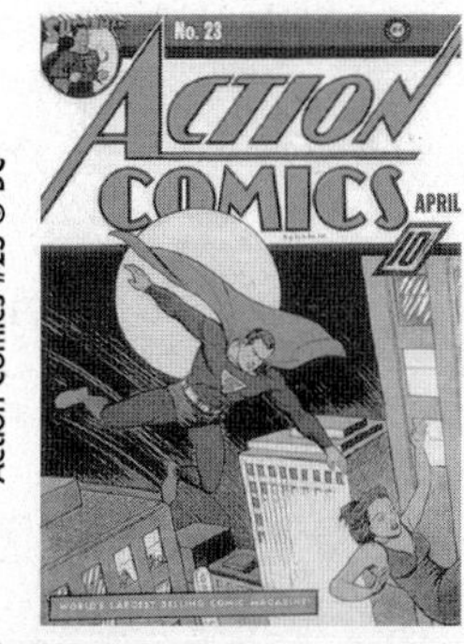

Action Comics #23 © DC

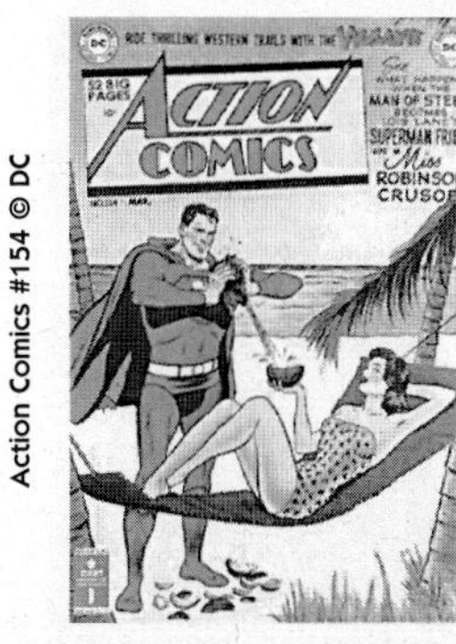

Action Comics #154 © DC

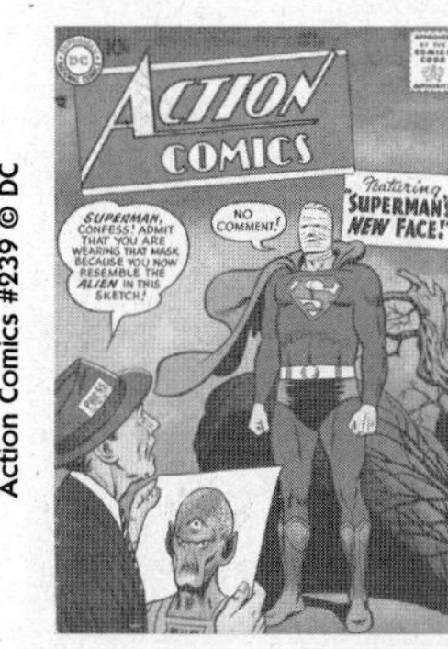

Action Comics #239 © DC

	GD 2.0	VG 4.0	FN 6.0	VF 8.0	VF/NM 9.0	NM- 9.2
1-Introduces Jimmy Corrigan; Chris Ware-s/a in all	1	3	4	6	8	10
1-2nd and later printings						4.00
2,3: 2-Quimby						6.00
4-Sparky's Best Comics & Stories	1	2	3	4	5	7
5-12: Jimmy Corrigan in all						5.00
13,15-($10.95-c)						11.00
14-($12.95-c) Concludes Jimmy Corrigan saga						13.00
16,19-($15.95, hardcover) Rusty Brown						16.00
17-($16.95, hardcover) Rusty Brown						17.00
18-($17.95, hardcover)						18.00
Jimmy Corrigan, The Smartest Kid on Earth (2000, Pantheon Books, Hardcover, $27.50, 380 pgs.) Collects Jimmy Corrigan stories; folded dust jacket						27.50
Jimmy Corrigan, The Smartest Kid on Earth (2003, Softcover, $17.95)						18.00

NOTE: *Multiple printings exist for most issues.*

ACROSS THE UNIVERSE: THE DC UNIVERSE STORIES OF ALAN MOORE (Also see DC Universe: The Stories of Alan Moore)
DC Comics: 2003 ($19.95, TPB)

	GD 2.0	VG 4.0	FN 6.0	VF 8.0	VF/NM 9.0	NM- 9.2
nn-Reprints selected Moore stories from '85-'87; Superman, Batman, Swamp Thing app.						20.00

ACTION ADVENTURE (War) (Formerly Real Adventure)
Gillmor Magazines: V1#2, June, 1955 - No. 4, Oct, 1955

	GD 2.0	VG 4.0	FN 6.0	VF 8.0	VF/NM 9.0	NM- 9.2
V1#2-4	6	12	18	31	38	45

ACTION COMICS (...Weekly #601-642) (Also see The Comics Magazine #1, More Fun #14-17 & Special Edition) (Also see Promotional Comics section)
National Periodical Publ./Detective Comics/DC Comics: 6/38 - No. 583, 9/86; No. 584, 1/87 - No. 904, Oct, 2011

	GD 2.0	VG 4.0	FN 6.0	VF 8.0	VF/NM 9.0	NM- 9.2
1-Origin & 1st app. Superman by Siegel & Shuster, Marco Polo, Tex Thompson, Pep Morgan, Chuck Dawson & Scoop Scanlon; 1st app. Zatara & Lois Lane; Superman story missing 4 pgs. which were included when reprinted in Superman #1; Clark Kent works for Daily Star; story continued in #2	110,000	220,000	330,000	850,000	1,300,000	1,750,000
1-Reprint, Oversize 13-1/2x10". **WARNING:** This comic is an exact reprint of the original except for its size. DC published it in 1974 with a second cover titling it as a Famous First Edition. There have been many reported cases of the outer cover being removed and the interior sold as the original edition. The reprint with the new outer cover removed is practically worthless. See Famous First Edition for value.						
2-O'Mealia non-Superman covers thru #6	6470	12,940	19,410	48,525	79,263	110,000
3 (Scarce)-Superman apps. in costume in only one panel	4118	8236	12,354	30,885	50,443	70,000
4-6: 6-1st Jimmy Olsen (called office boy)	2353	4706	7059	17,648	28,824	40,000
7-2nd Superman cover	9706	19,412	29,118	72,795	118,898	165,000
8,9	1588	3176	4764	11,910	19,455	27,000
10-3rd Superman cover by Shuster; splash panel used as cover art for Superman #1	5588	11,176	16,764	41,910	68,455	95,000
11,14: 1st X-Ray Vision? 14-Clip Carson begins, ends #41; Zatara-c	882	1764	2646	6615	10,808	15,000
12-Has 1 panel Batman ad for Det. #27 (5/39); Zatara sci-fi cover	1059	2118	3177	7943	12,972	18,000
13-Shuster Superman-c; last Scoop Scanlon; centerspread has a 2-page ad for Superman #1	2647	5294	7941	19,853	32,427	45,000
15-Guardineer Superman-c; has ad mentioning Detective Comics and Batman; full page ad for New York World's Fair 1939 with 25¢-c	1588	3176	4764	11,910	19,455	27,000
16-Has full page ad and 1 panel ad for New York World's Fair 1939 25¢ cover edition	559	1118	1677	4193	6847	9500
17-Superman cover; last Marco Polo; full page ad for New York World's Fair 1939 with 15¢-c	1294	2588	3882	9705	15,853	22,000
18-Origin 3 Aces; has a 1 panel ad for New York World's Fair 1939 at the end of the Superman story (ad also in #16,17,19)	559	1118	1677	4193	6847	9500
19-Superman covers begin	1206	2412	3618	9045	14,773	20,500
20-The 'S' left off Superman's chest; Clark Kent works at 'Daily Star'	1177	2354	3531	8828	14,414	20,000
21-Has 2 ads for More Fun #52 (1st Spectre)	423	846	1269	3000	5250	7500
22	459	918	1377	3350	5925	8500
23-1st app. Luthor (w/red hair) & Black Pirate; Black Pirate by Moldoff; 1st mention of The Daily Planet (4/40)-Has 1 panel ad for Spectre in More Fun	1050	2100	3150	7980	14,490	21,000
24,25: 24-Kent at Daily Planet. 25-Last app. Gargantua T. Potts, Tex Thompson's sidekick	432	864	1296	3154	5577	8000
26-28,30	400	800	1200	2800	4900	7000
29-1st Lois Lane-c (10/40)	423	846	1269	3067	5384	7700
31,32: 32-Intro/1st app. Krypto Ray Gun in Superman story by Burnley	277	554	831	1759	3030	4300
33-Origin Mr. America; Superman by Burnley; has half page ad for All Star Comics #3	284	568	852	1818	3109	4400
34,35,38,39	265	530	795	1694	2897	4100
36, 40: 36-Classic robot-c. 40-(9/41)-Intro/1st app. Star Spangled Kid & Stripesy; Jerry Siegel photo	277	554	831	1759	3030	4300
37-Origin Congo Bill	274	548	822	1740	2995	4250
41	232	464	696	1485	2543	3600
42-1st app./origin Vigilante; Bob Daley becomes Fat Man; origin Mr. America's magic flying carpet; The Queen Bee & Luthor app; Black Pirate ends; not in #41	258	516	774	1651	2826	4000
43-46,48-50: 44-Fat Man's i.d. revealed to Mr. America. 45-1st app. Stuff (Vigilante's oriental sidekick)	226	452	678	1446	2473	3500
47-1st Luthor cover in comics (4/42)	300	600	900	2010	3505	5000
51-1st app. The Prankster	226	452	678	1446	2473	3500
52-Fat Man & Mr. America become the Ameri-commandos; origin Vigilante retold; classic Superman and back-ups-c	271	542	813	1734	2967	4200
53-56,59,60: 56-Last Fat Man. 59-Kubert Vigilante begins?, ends #70. 60-First app. Lois Lane as Super-woman	181	362	543	1158	1979	2800
57-2nd Lois Lane-c in Action (3rd anywhere, 2/43)	194	388	582	1242	2121	3000
58-"Slap a Jap-c"	213	426	639	1363	2332	3300
61-Historic Atomic Radiation-c (6/43)	194	388	582	1242	2121	3000
62,63-Japan war-c: 63-Last 3 Aces	181	362	543	1158	1979	2800
64-Intro Toyman	174	348	522	1114	1907	2700
65-70	135	270	405	864	1482	2100
71-79: 74-Last Mr. America	107	214	321	680	1165	1650
80-2nd app. & 1st Mr. Mxyztplk-c (1/45)	135	270	405	864	1482	2100
81-88,90: 83-Intro Hocus & Pocus	100	200	300	635	1093	1550
89-Classic rainbow cover	103	206	309	659	1130	1600
91-99: 93-X-Mas-c. 99-1st small logo (8/46)	84	168	252	538	919	1300
100	119	238	357	762	1306	1850
101-Nuclear explosion-c (10/46)	168	336	504	1075	1838	2600
102-107,109-120: 102-Mxyztplk-c. 105,117-X-Mas-c	74	148	222	470	810	1150
108-Classic molten metal-c	82	164	246	528	902	1275
121,122,124-126,128-140: 135,136,138-Zatara by Kubert	71	142	213	454	777	1100
123-(8/48) 1st time Superman flies, not leaps	73	146	219	467	796	1125
127-Vigilante by Kubert; Tommy Tomorrow begins (12/48, see Real Fact #6)	73	146	219	467	796	1125
141-157,159-161: 151-Luthor/Mr. Mxyztplk/Prankster team-up. 156-Lois as Super Woman. 161- Last 52 pgs.	69	138	207	442	759	1075
158-Origin Superman retold	135	270	405	864	1482	2100
162-180: 168,176-Used in **POP**, pg. 90. 173-Robot-c	68	136	204	435	743	1050
181-201: 191-Intro. Janu in Congo Bill. 198-Last Vigilante. 201-Last pre-code issue	65	130	195	416	708	1000
202-220,232: 212-(1/56)-Includes 1956 Superman calendar that is part of story. 232-1st Curt Swan-c in Action	56	112	168	353	614	875
221-231,233-240: 221-1st S.A. issue. 224-1st Golden Gorilla story. 228-(5/57)-Kongorilla in Congo Bill story (Congorilla try-out)	47	94	141	296	511	725
241,243-251: 241-Batman x-over. 248-Origin/1st app. Congorilla; Congo Bill renamed Congorilla. 251-Last Tommy Tomorrow	40	80	120	246	423	600
242-Origin & 1st app. Brainiac (7/58); 1st mention of Shrunken City of Kandor	232	464	696	1950	4225	6500
252-Origin & 1st app. Supergirl (5/59); 1st app. Metallo	257	514	771	2159	4680	7200
253-2nd app. Supergirl	61	122	183	390	720	1050
254-1st meeting of Bizarro & Superman-c/story; 3rd app. Supergirl	43	86	129	271	486	700
255-1st Bizarro Lois Lane-c/story & both Bizarros leave Earth to make Bizarro World; 4th app. Supergirl	39	78	117	240	408	575
256-260: 259-Red Kryptonite used	28	56	84	165	283	400
261-1st X-Kryptonite which gave Streaky his powers; last Congorilla in Action; origin & 1st app. Streaky The Super Cat	31	62	93	186	318	450
262,264-266,268-270	24	48	72	140	245	350
263-Origin Bizarro World (continues in #264)	31	62	93	182	316	450
267(8/60)-3rd Legion app; 1st app. Chameleon Boy, Colossal Boy, & Invisible Kid, 1st app. of Supergirl as Superwoman.	55	110	165	352	614	875
271-275,277-282: 274-Lois Lane as Superwoman. 280-Brief origin of Superman & Supergirl retold; Brainiac-c. 282-Last 10¢ issue	21	42	63	122	211	300
276(5/61)-6th Legion app; 1st app. Brainiac 5, Phantom Girl, Triplicate Girl, Bouncing Boy, Sun Boy, & Shrinking Violet; Supergirl joins Legion	39	78	117	231	441	650
283(12/61)-Legion of Super-Villains app. 1st 12¢	13	26	39	87	186	285
284(1/62)-Mon-El app.	13	26	39	87	186	285
285(2/62)-12th Legion app; Brainiac 5 cameo; Supergirl's existence revealed to world; JFK & Jackie cameos	21	42	63	146	311	475
286-287,289-292,294-299: 286(3/62)-Legion of Super Villains app. 287(4/62)-15th Legion app. (cameo). 289(6/62)-16th Legion app. (Adult); Lightning Man & Saturn Woman's marriage 1st revealed. 290(7/62)-Legion app. (cameo); Phantom Girl app. 1st Supergirl emergency						

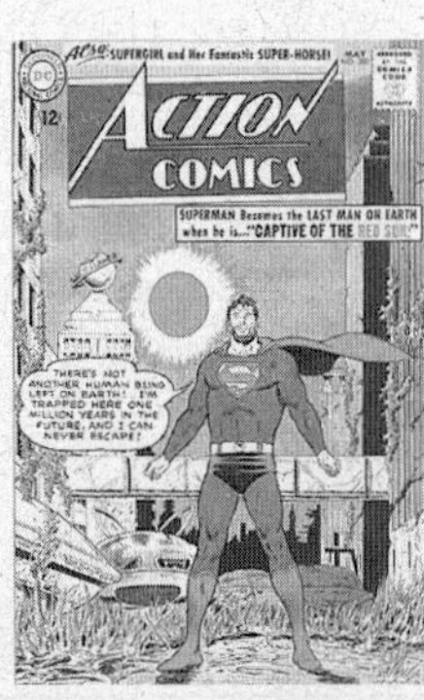

Action Comics #300 © DC

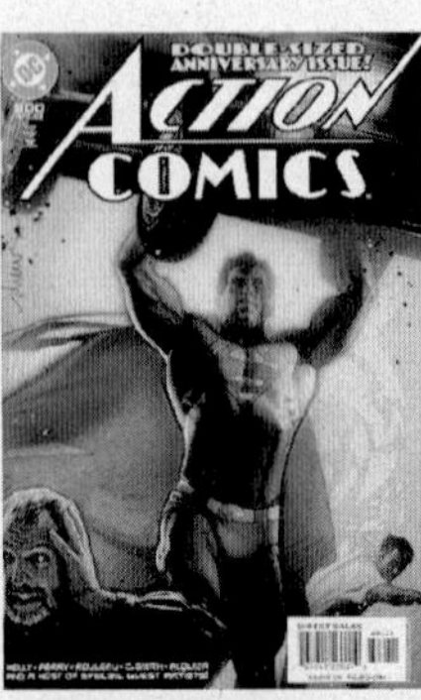

Action Comics #800 © DC

Action Comics #904 © DC

	GD 2.0	VG 4.0	FN 6.0	VF 8.0	VF/NM 9.0	NM- 9.2
squad. 291-1st meeting Supergirl & Mr. Mxyzptlk. 292-2nd app. Superhorse (see Adv.#293). 297-Mon-El app. 298-Legion cameo	12	24	36	79	160	240
288-Mon-El app.; r-origin Supergirl	12	24	36	81	166	250
293-Origin Comet (Superhorse)	13	26	39	88	189	290
300-(5/63)	13	26	39	85	180	275
301-303,305,307,308,310-312,315-320: 307-Saturn Girl app. 317-Death of Nor-Kan of Kandor. 319-Shrinking Violet app.	9	18	27	63	112	160
304,306,313: 304-Origin/1st app. Black Flame (9/63). 306-Brainiac 5, Mon-El app. 313-Batman app.	10	20	30	64	115	165
309-(2/64)-Legion app.; Batman & Robin-c & cameo; JFK app. (he died 11/22/63; on stands last week of Dec, 1963)	10	20	30	66	121	175
314-Retells origin Supergirl; J.L.A. x-over	10	20	30	64	115	165
321-333,335-339: 336-Origin Akvar (Flamebird)	8	16	24	53	89	125
334-Giant G-20; origin Supergirl, Streaky, Superhorse & Legion (all-r)	11	22	33	73	142	210
340-Origin, 1st app. of the Parasite; 2 pg. pin-up	8	16	24	56	96	135
341,344,350,358: 341-Batman app. in Supergirl back-up story. 344-Batman x-over. 350-Batman, Green Arrow & Green Lantern app. in Supergirl back-up story. 358-Superboy meets Supergirl	7	14	21	46	76	105
342,343,345,346,348,349,351-357,359: 342-UFO story. 345-Allen Funt/Candid Camera story.	7	14	21	44	72	100
347,360-Giant Supergirl G-33,G-45; 347-Origin Comet-r plus Bizarro story. 360-Legion app.-r; r/origin Supergirl	9	18	27	61	106	150
361-364,367-372,374-378: 361-2nd app. Parasite. 362-366-Leper/Death story. 370-New facts about Superman's origin. 376-Last Supergirl in Action; last 12¢-c. 377-Legion begins (thru #392)	6	12	18	37	59	80
365,366: 365-JLA & Legion app. 366-JLA app.	6	12	18	39	62	85
373-Giant Supergirl G-57; Legion-r	8	16	24	56	96	135
379-399,401: 388-Sgt. Rock app. 392-Batman-c/app.; last Legion in Action; Saturn Girl gets new costume. 393-401-All Superman issues	3	6	9	20	30	40
400	4	8	12	24	37	50
402-Last 15¢ issue; Superman vs. Supergirl duel	3	6	9	21	32	42
403-413: All 52 pg. issues. 411-Origin Eclipso-(r). 413-Metamorpho begins, ends #418	3	6	9	20	30	40
414-424: 419-Intro. Human Target. 421-Intro Capt. Strong; Green Arrow begins. 422,423-Origin Human Target	2	4	6	9	13	16
425-Neal Adams-a(p); The Atom begins	3	6	9	14	20	26
426-431,433-436,438,439	2	4	6	8	10	12
432-1st Bronze Age Toyman app. (2/74)	2	4	6	13	18	22
437,443-(100 pg. Giants)	4	8	12	28	44	60
440-1st Grell-a on Green Arrow	2	4	6	9	13	16
441,442,444-448: 441-Grell-a on Green Arrow continues	1	3	4	6	8	10
449-(68 pgs.)	2	4	6	10	14	18
450-465,467-483,486,489-499: 454-Last Atom. 456-Grell Jaws-c. 458-Last Green Arrow.	1	2	3	4	5	7
466,485,487,488: 466-Batman, Flash app. 485-Adams-c. 487,488-(44 pgs.). 487-Origin & 1st app. Microwave Man; origin Atom retold	1	2	3	5	7	9
481-483,485-492,495-499,501-505,507,508-Whitman variants (low print run; none show issue # on cover)	1	3	4	6	8	10
484-Earth II Superman & Lois Lane wed; 40th anniversary issue(6/78)	2	4	6	8	10	12
484-Variant includes 3-D Superman punchout doll in cello. pack; 4 different inserts; Canadian promo?)	3	6	9	16	22	28
500-($1.00, 68 pgs.)-Infinity-c; Superman life story retold; shows Legion statues in museum	2	4	6	8	10	12
501-543,545,547-551: 511-514-Airwave II solo stories. 513-The Atom begins. 517-Aquaman begins; ends #541. 521-1st app. The Vixen. 532,536-New Teen Titans cameo. 535,536-Omega Men app. 551-Starfire becomes Red-Star						5.00
504,505,507,508-Whitman variants (no cover price)	1	3	4	6	8	10
544-(6/83, Mando paper, 68 pgs.)-45th Anniversary issue; origins new Luthor & Brainiac; Omega Men cameo; Shuster-a (pin-up); article by Siegel	1	2	3	4	5	7
546-J.L.A., New Teen Titans app.	1	2	3	5	6	8
552,553-Animal Man-c & app. (2/84 & 3/84)						6.00
554-582						3.00
583-Alan Moore scripts; last Earth 1 Superman story (cont'd from Superman #423)	2	4	6	8	10	12
584-Byrne-a begins; New Teen Titans app.						6.00
585-599: 586-Legends x-over. 596-Millennium x-over; Spectre app. 598-1st Checkmate						3.00
600-($2.50, 84 pgs., 5/88)						6.00
601-610,619-642: (#601-642 are weekly issues) ($1.50, 52 pgs.) 601-Re-intro The Secret Six; death of Katma Tui						3.00
611-618: 611-614-Catwoman stories (new costume in #611). 613-618-Nightwing stories						3.00

	GD 2.0	VG 4.0	FN 6.0	VF 8.0	VF/NM 9.0	NM- 9.2
643-Superman & monthly issues begin again; Perez-c/a/scripts begin; swipes cover to Superman #1						4.00
644-649,651-661,663-666,668-673,675-683: 645-1st app. Maxima. 654-Part 3 of Batman storyline. 655-Free extra 8 pgs. 660-Death of Lex Luthor. 661-Begin $1.00-c. 675-Deathstroke cameo. 679-Last $1.00 issue. 683-Doomsday cameo						3.00
650,667: 650-($1.50, 52 pgs.)-Lobo cameo (last panel). 667-($1.75, 52 pgs.)						4.00
662-Clark Kent reveals i.d. to Lois Lane; story cont'd in Superman #53						4.00
674-Supergirl logo & c/story (reintro)						6.00
683-685-2nd & 3rd printings						3.00
684-Doomsday battle issue						4.00
685,686-Funeral for a Friend issues; Supergirl app.						4.00
687-($1.95)-Collector's Ed.w/die-cut-c						3.50
687-($1.50)-Newsstand Edition with mini-poster						3.00
688-699,701-703-($1.50): 688-Guy Gardner-c/story. 697-Bizarro-c/story. 703-(9/94)-Zero Hour						3.00
695-($2.50)-Collector's Edition w/embossed foil-c						4.00
700-($2.95, 68 pgs.)-Fall of Metropolis Pt 1, Guice-a; Pete Ross marries Lana Lang and Smallville flashbacks with Curt Swan art & Murphy Anderson inks						4.00
700-Platinum						15.00
700-Gold						18.00
0(10/94), 704(11/94)-719,721-731: 710-Begin $1.95-c. 714-Joker app. 719-Batman-c/app. 721-Mr. Mxyzptlk app. 723-Dave Johnson-c. 727-Final Night x-over.						3.00
720-Lois breaks off engagement w/Clark						4.00
720-2nd print.						3.00
732-749,751-767: 732-New powers. 733-New costume, Ray app. 738-Immonen-s/a(p) begins. 741-Legion app. 744-Millennium Giants x-over. 745-747-70's-style Superman vs. Prankster. 753-JLA-c/app. 757-Hawkman-c. 760-1st Encantadora. 761-Wonder Woman app. 765-Joker & Harley-c/app. 766-Batman-c/app.						3.00
750-($2.95)						4.00
768,769,771-774: 768-Begin $2.25-c; Marvel Family-c/app. 771-Nightwing-c/app. 772,773-Ra's al Ghul app. 774-Martian Manhunter-c/app.						3.00
770-($3.50) Conclusion of Emperor Joker x-over						4.00
775-($3.75) Bradstreet-c; intro. The Elite						4.00
776-799: 776-Farewell to Krypton; Rivoche-c. 780-782-Our Worlds at War x-over. 781-Hippolyta and Major Lane killed. 782-War ends. 784-Joker: Last Laugh; Batman & Green Lantern app. 793-Return to Krypton. 795-The Elite app. 798-Van Fleet-c						3.00
800-(4/03, $3.95) Struzan painted-c; guest artists include Ross, Jim Lee, Jurgens, Sale						4.00
801-811: 801-Raney-a. 809-The Creeper app. 811-Mr. Majestic app.						3.00
812-Godfall part 1; Turner-c; Caldwell-a(p)						4.00
812-2nd printing; B&W sketch-c by Turner						3.00
813-Godfall pt. 4; Turner-c; Caldwell-a(p)						4.00
814-824, 826-828,830-836: 814-Reis-a/Art Adams-c; Darkseid app.; begin $2.50-c. 815,816-Teen Titans-c/app. 820-Doomsday app. 826-Capt. Marvel app. 827-Byrne-c/a begin. 831-Villains United tie-in. 835-Livewire app. 836-Infinite Crisis; revised origin						3.00
825-($2.99, 40 pgs.) Doomsday app.						4.00
829-Omac Project x-over Sacrifice pt. 2						5.00
829-(2nd printing) red tone cover						4.00
837-843-One Year Later; powers return after Infinite Crisis; Johns & Busiek-s						3.00
844-Donner & Johns-s/Adam Kubert-a/c begin; brown-toned cover						4.00
844-Andy Kubert variant-c						5.00
844-2nd printing with red-toned Adam Kubert cover						3.00
845-849,851-857: 845-Bizarro-c/app.; re-intro. General Zod, Ursa & Non. 846-Jax-Ur app. 847-849-No Kubert-a. 851-Kubert-a/c. 855-857-Bizarro app.; Powell-a/c						3.00
850-($3.99) Supergirl and LSH app., origin re-told; Guedes-a/c						4.00
858-($3.50) Legion of Super-Heroes app.; 1st meeting re-told; Johns-s/Frank-a/c						4.00
858-Variant-c (Superman & giant Brainiac robot) by Frank						5.00
858-Second printing with regular cover with red background instead of yellow						3.00
858-Special Edition (7/10, $1.00) r/#858 with "What's Next?" cover logo						3.00
859-878: 859-863-Legion of Super-Heroes app.; var-c on each (859-Andy Kubert. 860-Lightle. 861-Grell. 862-Giffen. 863-Frank) 864-Batman and Lightning Lad app. 866-Brainiac returns 869-"Soda Pop" cover edition, 870-Pa Kent dies. 871-New Krypton; Ross-c						3.00
869-Initial printing recalled because of beer bottles on cover						8.00
879-896: 879-($3.99) Back-up Capt. Atom feature begins. 890-Luthor stories begin. 893-Comics debut of Chloe Sullivan (Smallville TV show) in regular DCU. 894-Death (Sandman) app. 896-Secret Six app.						4.00
897-899, 901-903-($2.99) 897-Joker app. 898-Larfleeze app. 899-Brainiac app.						3.00
900 (6/11, $5.99, 96 pgs.) Conclusion of Luthor Black Ring saga; Doomsday app.; bonus short stories by various; Superman renounces U.S. citizenship						6.00
904-(10/11) Last issue of first volume; Doomsday app.; Rocafort-c						3.00
904-Variant-c by Ordway						5.00
#1,000,000 (11/98) Gene Ha-c; 853rd Century x-over						3.00
Annual 1 ('87, $2.95) Art Adams-c/a(p); Batman app.						5.00
Annual 2-6 ('89-'94, $2.95)-2-Pérez-c/a(i). 3-Armageddon 2001. 4-Eclipso vs. Shazam. 5-Bloodlines; 1st app. Loose Cannon. 6-Elseworlds story						4.00

Action Comics (2nd series) #1 © DC

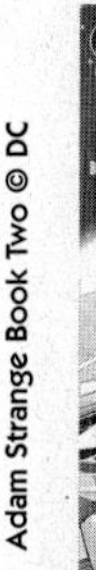

Adam Strange Book Two © DC

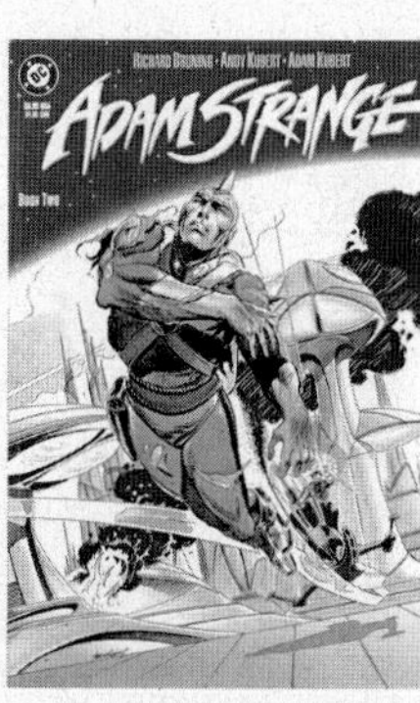

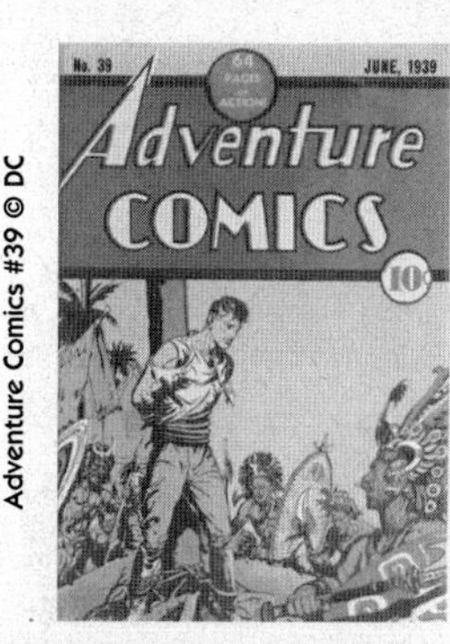

Adventure Comics #39 © DC

GD 2.0 | VG 4.0 | FN 6.0 | VF 8.0 | VF/NM 9.0 | NM- 9.2

Annual 7,9 ('95, '97, $3.95) 7-Year One story. 9-Pulp Heroes story 4.00
Annual 8 (1996, $2.95) Legends of the Dead Earth story 4.00
Annual 10 ('07, $3.99) Short stories by Johns & Donner and various incl. A. Adams, J. Kubert, Wight, Morales; origin of Phantom Zone, Mon-El; Metallo app.; Adam & Joe Kubert-c 4.00
Annual 11 (7/08, $4.99) Conclusion to General Zod story continued from #851; Kubert-a 5.00
Annual 12 (8/09, $4.99) Origin of Nightwing and Flamebird 5.00
Annual 13 (2/11, $4.99) 1st meeting of Luthor and Darkseid; Ra's al Ghul app. 5.00

NOTE:***Supergirl's*** *origin in 262, 280, 285, 291, 305, 309.* ***N. Adams*** *c-356, 358, 359, 361-364, 366, 367, 370-374, 377-379i, 398-400, 402, 404,405, 419p, 466, 468, 469, 473i, 485.* ***Aparo*** *a-642.* ***Austin*** *c/a-682i.* ***Baily*** *a-24, 25.* ***Boring*** *a-164, 194, 211, 223, 233, 241, 250, 261, 266-268, 346, 348, 352, 356, 357.* ***Burnley*** *a-28-33; c-48?, 53-55, 58, 59?, 60-63, 65, 66p, 67p, 70p, 71p, 79p, 82p, 84-86p, 90-92p, 93p?, 94p, 107p, 108p.* ***Byrne*** *a-584-598p, 599i, 600p; c-584-591, 596-600.* ***Ditko*** *a-642.* ***Giffen*** *a-560, 563, 565, 577, 579; c-539, 560, 563, 565, 577, 579.* ***Grell*** *a-440-442, 444-446, 450-452, 456-458; c-456.* ***Guardineer*** *a-24, 25; c-8, 11, 12, 14-16, 18. 25.* ***Guice*** *a(p)-676-681, 683-698, 700; c-683, 685, 686, 687(direct), 688-693i, 694-696, 697i, 698-700.* ***Infantino*** *a-642.* ***Kaluta*** *c-613.* ***Bob Kane's*** *Clip Carson-14-41.* ***Gil Kane*** *a-443r, 493r, 539-541, 544-546, 551-554, 601-605, 642; c-535p, 540, 541, 544p, 545-549, 551-554, 580, 627.* ***Kirby*** *c-638.* ***Meskin*** *a-42-121(most).* ***Mignola*** *a-600, Annual 2; c-c-614.* ***Moldoff*** *a-23-25, 443r.* ***Mooney*** *a-667p.* ***Mortimer*** *c-153, 154, 159-172, 174, 178-181, 184, 186-189, 191-193, 196, 200, 206.* ***Orlando*** *a-617p; c-621.* ***Perez*** *a-600i, 643-652p, Annual 2p; c-529p, 602, 643-651, Annual 2p.* ***Quesada*** *c-Annual 4p.* ***Fred Ray*** *c-34, 36-46, 50-52.* ***Siegel & Shuster*** *a-1-27.* ***Paul Smith*** *c-608.* ***Starlin*** *a-509; c-631.* ***Leonard Starr*** *a-597i(part),* ***Staton*** *a-525p, 526p, 531p, 535p, 536p.* ***Swan/Moldoff*** *c-281, 286, 287, 293, 298, 334.* ***Thibert*** *c-676, 677p, 678-681, 684.* ***Toth*** *a-406, 407, 413, 431; c-616.* ***Tuska*** *a-486p, 550.* ***Williamson*** *a-568i.* ***Zeck*** *c-Annual 5*

ACTION COMICS (2nd series)(DC New 52)
DC Comics: Nov, 2011 - Present ($3.99)

1-Grant Morrison-s/Rags Morales-a/c; re-introduces Superman 5.00
1-Variant-c by Jim Lee of Superman in new armor costume 10.00
1-(2nd - 5th printings) 4.00
2-8: 2-Morales & Brent Anderson-a; behind the scenes sketch art and commentary. 3-Gene Ha & Morales-a. 4-Re-intro. Steel. 5-Flashback to Krypton; Andy Kubert-a. 6-Legion of Super-Heroes app.; Andy Kubert-a. 7-Gets the new costume; intro. Steel 4.00
2-8-Variant covers. 2-Van Sciver. 3-Ha. 4-Choi. 5,6-Morales. 8-Frank 5.00

ACTION COMICS
DC Comics: (no date)

1-Ashcan comic, not distributed to newsstands, only for in-house use. Cover art is the rejected art to Detective Comics #2 and interior from Detective Comics #1. A CGC certified 9.0 copy sold for $17,825 in 2002 and for $29,000 in 2008.

ACTION FORCE (Also see G.I. Joe European Missions)
Marvel Comics Ltd. (British): Mar, 1987 - No. 50, 1988 ($1.00, weekly, magazine)

1,3: British G.I. Joe series. 3-w/poster insert 2 4 6 8 10 12
2,4 1 2 3 5 6 8
5-10 5.00
11-50 3.00
...Special 1 (7/87) Summer holiday special; Snake Eyes-c/app. 1 2 3 5 6 8
...Special 2 (10/87) Winter special; 5.00

ACTION FUNNIES
DC Comics: 1937/1938

nn - Ashcan comic, not distributed to newsstands, only for in house use. Cover art is Action Comics #3 and interior from Detective Comics #10. The Mallette/Brown copy in VG+ condition sold for $15,000 in 2005.

ACTION GIRL
Slave Labor Graphics: Oct, 1994 - No. 19 ($2.50/$2.75/$2.95, B&W)

1-19: 4-Begin $2.75-c. 19-Begin $2.95-c 3.00
1-6 ($2.75, 2nd printings): All read 2nd Print in indicia. 1-(2/96). 2-(10/95). 3-(2/96). 4-(7/96). 5-(2/97). 6-(9/97) 3.00
1-4 ($2.75, 3rd printings): All read 3rd Print in indicia. 3.00

ACTION PLANET COMICS
Action Planet: 1996 - No. 3, Sept, 1997 ($3.95, B&W, 44 pgs.)

1-3: 1-Intro Monster Man by Mike Manley & other stories 4.00
Giant Size Action Planet Halloween Special (1998, $5.95, oversized) 6.00

ACTUAL CONFESSIONS (Formerly Love Adventures)
Atlas Comics (MPI): No. 13, Oct, 1952 - No. 14, Dec, 1952

13,14 10 20 30 54 72 90

ACTUAL ROMANCES (Becomes True Secrets #3 on?)
Marvel Comics (IPS): Oct, 1949 - No. 2, Jan, 1950 (52 pgs.)

1 15 30 45 86 133 180
2-Photo-c 11 22 33 60 83 105

ADAM AND EVE
Spire Christian Comics (Fleming H. Revell Co.): 1975,1978 (35¢/39¢/49¢)

nn-By Al Hartley 2 4 6 9 13 16

ADAM: LEGEND OF THE BLUE MARVEL
Marvel Comics: Jan, 2009 - No. 5, May, 2009 ($3.99, limited series)

1-5-Grevioux-s/Broome-a; Avengers app. 4.00

ADAM STRANGE (Also see Green Lantern #132, Mystery In Space #53 & Showcase #17)
DC Comics: 1990 - No. 3, 1990 ($3.95, 52 pgs, limited series, squarebound)

Book One - Three: Andy & Adam Kubert-c/a 4.00
...: The Man of Two Worlds (2003, $19.95, TPB) r/#1-3; sketch pages by Andy Kubert 20.00

ADAM STRANGE (Leads into the Rann/Thanagar War mini-series)
DC Comics: Nov, 2004 - No. 8, June, 2005 ($2.95, limited series)

1-8-Andy Diggle-s/Pascal Ferry-a/c. 1-Superman app. 3.00
...: Planet Heist TPB (2005, $19.99) r/series; sketch pages 20.00
... Special (11/08, $3.50) Takes place durng Rann/Thanagar Holy War series; Starlin-s 4.00

ADAM-12 (TV)
Gold Key: Dec, 1973 - No. 10, Feb, 1976 (Photo-c)

1 6 12 18 42 69 95
2-10 4 8 12 22 34 45

ADDAMS FAMILY (TV cartoon)
Gold Key: Oct, 1974 - No. 3, Apr, 1975 (Hanna-Barbera)

1 8 16 24 53 89 125
2,3 6 12 18 37 59 80

ADLAI STEVENSON
Dell Publishing Co.: Dec, 1966

12-007-612-Life story; photo-c 4 8 12 22 34 45

ADOLESCENT RADIOACTIVE BLACK BELT HAMSTERS (See Clint)
Comic Castle/Eclipse Comics: 1986 - No. 9, Jan, 1988 ($1.50, B&W)

1-9: 1st & 2nd printings exist 3.00
1-Limited Edition 6.00
1-In 3-D (7/86), 2-4 ($2.50) 3.00
Massacre The Japanese Invasion #1 (8/89, $2.00) 3.00

ADOLESCENT RADIOACTIVE BLACK BELT HAMSTERS
Dynamite Entertainment: 2008 - No. 4, 2008 ($3.50, limited series)

1-4-Tom Nguyen-a/Keith Champagne-s; 2 covers by Nguyen and Oeming 3.50

ADRENALYNN (See The Tenth)
Image Comics: Aug, 1999 - No. 4, Feb, 2000 ($2.50)

1-4-Tony Daniel-s/Marty Egeland-a; origin of Adrenalynn 3.00

ADULT TALES OF TERROR ILLUSTRATED (See Terror Illustrated)

ADVANCED DUNGEONS & DRAGONS (Also see TSR Worlds)
DC Comics: Dec, 1988 - No. 36, Dec, 1991 (Newsstand #1 is Holiday, 1988-89) ($1.25-$1.75)

1-Based on TSR role playing game 4.00
2-36: 25-$1.75-c begins 3.00
Annual 1 (1990, $3.95, 68 pgs.) 4.00

ADVENTURE BOUND
Dell Publishing Co.: Aug, 1949

Four Color #239 6 12 18 39 62 85

ADVENTURE COMICS (Formerly New Adventure)(...Presents Dial H For Hero #479-490)
National Periodical Publications/DC Comics: No. 32, 11/38 - No. 490, 2/82; No. 491, 9/82 - No. 503, 9/83

32-Anchors Aweigh (ends #52), Barry O'Neil (ends #60, not in #33), Captain Desmo (ends #47), Dale Daring (ends #47), Federal Men (ends #70), The Golden Dragon (ends #36), Rusty & His Pals (ends #52) by Bob Kane, Todd Hunter (ends #38) and Tom Brent (ends #39) begin 430 860 1290 2450 3575 4700
33-38: 37-Cover used on Double Action #2 220 440 660 1250 1875 2500
39(6/39)- Jack Wood begins, ends #42; early mention of Marijuana in comics 220 440 660 1250 1875 2500
40-(Rare, 7/39, on stands 6/10/39)-The Sandman begins by Bert Christman (who died in WWII); believed to be 1st conceived story (see N.Y. World's Fair for 1st published app.); Socko Strong begins, ends #54 6333 12,667 19,000 47,000 86,000 125,000
41-O'Mealia shark-c 595 1190 1785 4350 7675 11,000
42,44-Sandman-c by Flessel. 44-Opium story 784 1568 2352 5723 10,112 14,500
43,45: 45-Full page ad for Flash Comics #1 400 800 1200 2800 4900 7000
46,47-Sandman covers by Flessel. 47-Steve Conrad Adventurer begins, ends #76 568 1136 1704 4146 7323 10,500
48-1st app. The Hourman by Bernard Baily; Baily-c (Hourman c-48,50,52-59) 2750 5500 8250 20,500 37,750 55,000
49,50: 50-Cotton Carver by Jack Lehti begins, ends #64 297 594 891 1888 3244 4600
51,60-Sandman-c: 51-Sandman-c by Flessel. 371 742 1113 2600 4550 6500

Adventure Comics #119 © DC

Adventure Comics #219 © DC

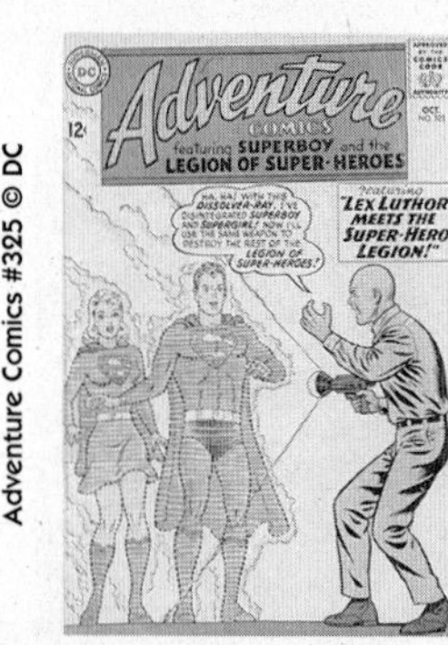

Adventure Comics #325 © DC

	GD 2.0	VG 4.0	FN 6.0	VF 8.0	VF/NM 9.0	NM- 9.2
52-59: 53-1st app. Jimmy "Minuteman" Martin & the Minutemen of America in Hourman; ends #78. 58-Paul Kirk Manhunter begins (1st app.), ends #72	258	516	774	1651	2826	4000
61-1st app. Starman by Jack Burnley (4/41); Starman c-61-72; Starman by Burnley in #61-80	1200	2400	3600	9000	16,500	24,000
62-65,67,68,70: 67-Origin & 1st app. The Mist; classic Burnley-c. 70-Last Federal Men	226	452	678	1446	2473	3500
66-Origin/1st app. Shining Knight (9/41)	271	542	813	1734	2967	4200
69-1st app. Sandy the Golden Boy (Sandman's sidekick) by Paul Norris (in a Bob Kane style); Sandman dons new costume	245	490	735	1568	2684	3800
71-Jimmy Martin becomes costumed aide to the Hourman; 1st app. Hourman's Miracle Ray machine	219	438	657	1402	2401	3400
72-1st Simon & Kirby Sandman (3/42, 1st DC work)	975	1950	2919	7100	12,550	18,000
73-Origin Manhunter by Simon & Kirby; begin new series; Manhunter-c (scarce)	1275	2550	3825	9550	17,275	25,000
74-78,80: 74-Thorndyke replaces Jimmy, Hourman's assistant; new Sandman-c begin by S&K. 75-Thor app. by Kirby; 1st Kirby Thor (see Tales of the Unexpected #16). 77-Origin Genius Jones; Mist story. 80-Last S&K Manhunter & Burnley Starman	194	388	582	1242	2121	3000
79-Classic Manhunter-c	277	554	831	1759	3030	4300
81-90: 83-Last Hourman. 84-Mike Gibbs begins, ends #102	123	246	369	787	1344	1900
91-Last Simon & Kirby Sandman	113	226	339	718	1234	1750
92-99,101,102: 92-Last Manhunter. 101-Shining Knight origin retold. 102-Last Starman, Sandman, & Genius Jones; most-S&K-c (Genius Jones cont'd in More Fun #108)	97	194	291	621	1061	1500
100-S&K-c	132	264	396	838	1444	2050
103-Aquaman, Green Arrow, Johnny Quick & Superboy all move over from More Fun Comics #107; 8th app. Superboy; Superboy-c begin; 1st small logo (4/46)	300	600	900	1950	3375	4800
104	110	220	330	704	1202	1700
105-110	77	154	231	493	847	1200
111-120: 113-X-Mas-c	70	140	210	445	765	1085
121,122-126,128-130: 128-1st meeting Superboy & Lois Lane	64	128	192	406	696	985
127-Brief origin Shining Knight retold	65	130	195	416	708	1000
131-141,143-149: 132-Shining Knight 1st return to King Arthur time; origin aide Sir Butch	54	108	162	348	594	840
142-Origin Shining Knight & Johnny Quick retold	57	114	171	362	624	885
150,151,153,155,157,159,161,163-All have 6 pg. Shining Knight stories by Frank Frazetta. 159-Origin Johnny Quick. 161-1st Lana Lang app. in this title	68	136	204	438	749	1060
152,154,156,158,160,162,164-169: 166-Last Shining Knight. 168-Last 52 pg. issue	50	100	150	315	533	750
170-180	47	94	141	297	504	710
181-199: 189-B&W and color illo in **POP**	46	92	138	290	488	685
200 (5/54)	58	116	174	371	636	900
201-208: 207-Last Johnny Quick (not in 205)	42	84	126	265	445	625
209-Last pre-code issue; origin Speedy	43	86	129	271	461	650
210-1st app. Krypto (Superdog)-c/story (3/55)	340	680	1020	2800	5400	8000
211-213,215-219	40	80	120	246	411	575
214-2nd app. Krypto	71	142	213	454	777	1100
220-Krypto-c/sty	45	90	135	284	480	675
221-246: 229-1st S.A. issue. 237-1st Intergalactic Vigilante Squadron (6/57). 239-Krypto-c	36	72	108	211	343	475
247(4/58)-1st Legion of Super Heroes app.; 1st app. Cosmic Boy, Saturn Girl & Lightning Boy (later Lightning Lad in #267) (origin)	575	1150	1725	5200	10,600	16,000
248-252,254,255-Green Arrow in all: 255-Intro. Red Kryptonite in Superboy (used in #252 but with no effect)	30	60	90	177	289	400
253-1st meeting of Superboy & Robin; Green Arrow by Kirby in #250-255 (also see World's Finest #96-99)	34	68	102	204	332	460
256-Origin Green Arrow by Kirby	68	136	204	435	743	1050
257-259: 258-Green Arrow x-over in Superboy	24	48	72	142	234	325
260-1st Silver-Age origin Aquaman (5/59)	76	152	228	486	831	1175
261-265,268,270: 262-Origin Speedy in Green Arrow. 270-Congorilla begins, ends #281,283	20	40	60	118	192	265
266-(11/59)-Origin & 1st app. Aquagirl (tryout, not same as later character)	21	42	63	122	199	275
267(12/59)-2nd Legion of Super Heroes; Lightning Boy now called Lightning Lad; new costumes for Legion	97	194	291	611	1306	2000
269-Intro. Aqualad (2/60); last Green Arrow (not in #206)	32	64	96	192	314	435
271-Origin Luthor retold	39	78	117	240	395	550
272-274,277-280: 279-Intro White Kryptonite in Superboy. 280-1st meeting Superboy & Lori Lemaris	19	38	57	111	176	240
275-Origin Superman-Batman team retold (see World's Finest #94)	25	50	75	147	241	335
276-(9/60) Robinson Crusoe-like story	20	40	60	114	182	250
281,284,287-289: 281-Last Congorilla. 284-Last Aquaman in Adv.; Mooney-a. 287,288-Intro Dev-Em, the Knave from Krypton. 287-1st Bizarro Perry White & Jimmy Olsen. 288-Bizarro-c. 289-Legion cameo (statues)	18	36	54	103	162	220
282(3/61)-5th Legion app; intro/origin Star Boy	39	78	117	231	378	525
283-Intro. The Phantom Zone	28	56	84	165	270	375
285-1st Tales of the Bizarro World-c/story (ends #299) in Adv. (see Action #255)	23	46	69	136	223	310
286-1st Bizarro Mxyzptlk; Bizarro-c	22	44	66	132	216	300
290(11/61)-9th Legion app; origin Sunboy in Legion (last 10¢ issue)	36	72	108	211	343	475
291,292,295-298: 291-1st 12¢ ish, (12/61). 292-1st Bizarro Lana Lang & Lucy Lane. 295-Bizarro-c; 1st Bizarro Titano	10	20	30	70	133	195
293(2/62)-13th Legion app; Mon-El & Legion of Super Pets (1st app./origin) app. (1st Superhorse). 1st Bizarro Luthor & Kandor	16	32	48	111	243	375
294-1st Bizarro Marilyn Monroe, Pres. Kennedy.	12	24	36	81	166	250
299-1st Gold Kryptonite (8/62)	11	22	33	75	138	200
300-Tales of the Legion of Super-Heroes series begins (9/62); Mon-El leaves Phantom Zone (temporarily), joins Legion	46	92	138	359	780	1200
301-Origin Bouncing Boy	14	28	42	97	211	325
302-305: 303-1st app. Matter-Eater Lad. 304-Death of Lightning Lad in Legion	12	24	36	81	166	250
306-310: 306-Intro. Legion of Substitute Heroes. 307-1st app. Element Lad in Legion. 308-1st app. Lightning Lass in Legion. 309-1st app. Legion of Super-Monsters	11	22	33	76	151	225
311-320: 312-Lightning Lad back in Legion. 315-Last new Superboy story; Colossal Boy app. 316-Origins & powers of Legion given. 317-Intro. Dream Girl in Legion; Lightning Lass becomes Light Lass; Hall of Fame series begins. 320-Dev-Em 2nd app.	10	20	30	66	121	175
321-Intro. Time Trapper	9	18	27	61	106	150
322-330: 327-Intro/1st app. Lone Wolf in Legion. 329-Intro The Bizarro Legionnaires; intro. Legion flight rings	8	16	24	56	96	135
331-340: 337-Chlorophyll Kid & Night Girl app. 340-Intro Computo in Legion	8	16	24	53	89	125
341-Triplicate Girl becomes Duo Damsel	7	14	21	48	79	110
342-345,347-351: 345-Last Hall of Fame; returns in 356,371. 348-Origin Sunboy; intro Dr. Regulus in Legion. 349-Intro Universo & Rond Vidar. 351-1st app. White Witch	7	14	21	46	76	105
346-1st app. Karate Kid, Princess Projectra, Ferro Lad, & Nemesis Kid.	9	18	27	61	106	150
352,354-360: 354,355-Superman meets the Adult Legion. 355-Insect Queen joins Legion (4/67)	6	12	18	41	66	90
353-Death of Ferro Lad in Legion	7	14	21	48	79	110
361-364,366,368-370: 369-Intro Mordru in Legion	6	12	18	37	59	80
365,367: 365-Intro Shadow Lass (memorial to Shadow Woman app. in #354's Adult Legion-s); lists origins & powers of L.S.H. 367-New Legion headquarters	6	12	18	39	62	85
371,372: 371-Intro. Chemical King (mentioned in #354's Adult Legion-s). 372-Timber Wolf & Chemical King join	6	12	18	39	62	85
373,374,376-380: 373-Intro. Tornado Twins (Barry Allen Flash descendants). 374-Article on comics fandom. 380-Last Legion in Adventure; last 12¢-c	5	10	15	35	55	75
375-Intro Quantum Queen & The Wanderers	6	12	18	39	62	85
381-Supergirl begins; 1st full length Supergirl story & her 1st solo book (6/69)	13	26	39	85	180	275
382-389	5	10	15	35	55	75
390-Giant Supergirl G-69	7	14	21	48	79	110
391-396,398	4	8	12	24	37	50
397-1st app. new Supergirl	5	10	15	35	55	75
399-Unpubbed G.A. Black Canary story	4	8	12	26	41	55
400-New costume for Supergirl (12/70)	5	10	15	35	55	75
401,402,404-408-(15¢-c)	3	6	9	18	27	35
403-68 pg. Giant G-81; Legion-r/#304,305,308,312	7	14	21	44	72	100
409-411,413-415,417-420-(52 pgs.): 413-Hawkman by Kubert r/B&B #44; G.A. Robotman-r/Det. #178; Zatanna by Morrow. 414-r-2nd Animal Man/Str. Advs. #184. 415-Animal Man-r/Str. Adv.#190 (origin recap). 417-Morrow Vigilante; Frazetta Shining Knight-r/Adv. #161; origin The Enchantress; no Zatanna. 418-Prev. unpub. Dr. Mid-Nite story from 1948; no Zatanna. 420-Animal Man-r/Str. Adv. #195	3	6	9	19	29	38
412-(52 pgs.) Reprints origin & 1st app. of Animal Man from Strange Adventures #180	3	6	9	19	29	38

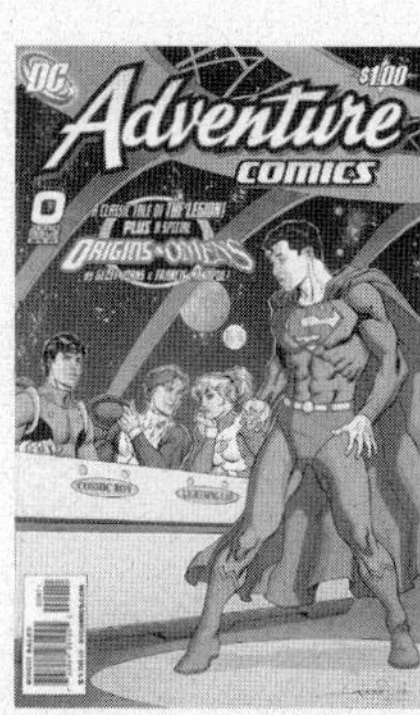

Adventure Comics (2009 series) #0 © DC

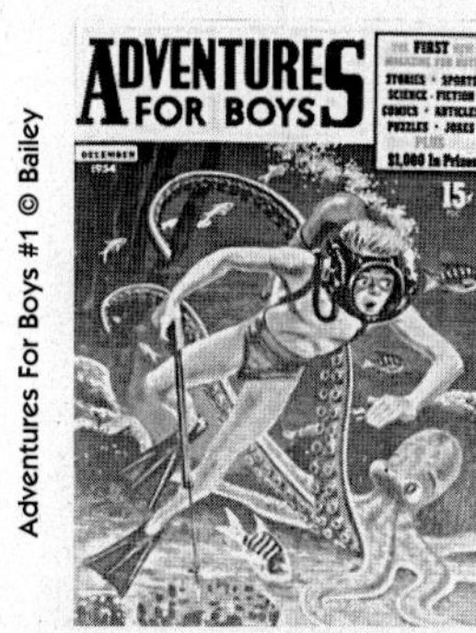

Adventures For Boys #1 © Bailey

Adventures Into Darkness #9 © STD

	GD 2.0	VG 4.0	FN 6.0	VF 8.0	VF/NM 9.0	NM- 9.2

416-Also listed as DC 100 Pg. Super Spectacular #10; Golden Age-r; r/1st app. Black Canary from Flash #86; no Zatanna 11 22 33 75 148 220
421-424: 424-Last Supergirl in Adventure 3 6 9 14 20 25
425-New look, content change to adventure; Kaluta-c; Toth-a, origin Capt. Fear 3 6 9 16 23 30
426,427: 426-1st Adventurers Club. 427-Last Vigilante 2 4 6 9 12 15
428-Origin/1st app. Black Orchid (c/story, 6-7/73) 6 12 18 37 59 80
429,430-Black Orchid-c/stories 3 6 9 21 32 42
431-Spectre by Aparo begins, ends #440. 6 12 18 41 66 90
432-439-Spectre app. 433-437-Cover title is Weird Adventure Comics. 436-Last 20¢ issue 4 8 12 22 34 45
440-New Spectre origin. 4 8 12 24 37 50
441-458: 441-452-Aquaman app. 443-Fisherman app. 445-447-The Creeper app. 446-Flag-c. 449-451-Martian Manhunter app. 450-Weather Wizard app. in Aquaman story. 453-458-Superboy app. 453-Intro. Mighty Girl. 457,458-Eclipso app. 1 3 4 6 8 10
459,460 (68 pgs.): 459-New Gods/Darkseid storyline concludes from New Gods #19 (#459 is dated 9-10/78) without missing a month. 459-Flash (ends #466), Deadman (ends #466), Wonder Woman (ends #464), Green Lantern (ends #460). 460-Aquaman (ends #478) 3 6 9 14 20 26
461,462 ($1.00, 68 pgs.): 461-Justice Society begins; ends 466. 461,462-Death Earth II Batman 4 8 12 26 41 55
463-466 ($1.00 size, 68 pgs.) 2 4 6 10 14 18
467-Starman by Ditko & Plastic Man begins; 1st app. Prince Gavyn (Starman). 2 4 6 8 11 14
468-490: 470-Origin Starman. 479-Dial 'H' For Hero begins, ends #490. 478-Last Starman & Plastic Man. 480-490: Dial 'H' For Hero 5.00
491-503: 491-100pg. Digest size begins; r/Legion of Super Heroes/Adv. #247, 267; Spectre, Aquaman, Superboy, S&K Sandman, Black Canary-r & new Shazam by Newton begin. 492,495,496,499-S&K Sandman-r/Adventure in all. 493-Challengers of the Unknown begins by Tuska w/brief origin. 493-495,497-499-G.A. Captain Marvel-r. 494-499-Spectre-r/Spectre 1-3, 5-7. 496-Capt. Marvel Jr. new-s, Cockrum-a. 498-Mary Marvel new-s; Plastic Man-r begin; origin Bouncing Boy-r/ #301. 500-Legion-r (Digest size, 148 pgs.). 501-503: G.A.-r 2 4 6 9 13 16
... 80 Page Giant (10/98, $4.95) Wonder Woman, Shazam, Superboy, Supergirl, Green Arrow, Legion, Bizarro World stories 5.00

NOTE: *Bizarro covers-285, 286, 288, 294, 295, 329. Vigilante app.-420, 426, 427.* ***N. Adams*** *a(r)-495i-498i; c-365-369, 371-373, 375-379, 381-383.* ***Aparo*** *a-431-433, 434i, 435, 436, 437i, 438i, 439-452, 503r; c-431-452.* ***Austin*** *a-449i 451i.* ***Bernard Baily*** *c-48, 50, 52-59.* ***Bolland*** *c-475.* ***Burnley*** *c-61-72, 116-120p.* ***Chaykin*** *a-438.* ***Ditko*** *a-467-478p; c-467p.* ***Creig Flessel*** *c-32, 33, 40, 42, 44, 46, 47, 51, 60.* ***Giffen*** *c-491p-494p, 500p.* ***Grell*** *a-435-437, 440.* ***Guardineer*** *c-34, 35, 45.* ***Infantino*** *a-416r.* ***Kaluta*** *c-425.* ***Bob Kane*** *a-38.* ***G. Kane*** *a-414r, 425; c-496-499, 537.* ***Kirby*** *a-250-256.* ***Kubert*** *a-413.* ***Meskin*** *a-81,127.* ***Moldoff*** *a-494i; c-49.* ***Morrow*** *a-413-415, 417, 422, 502r, 503r.* ***Netzer/Nasser*** *a-449-451.* ***Newton*** *a-459-461, 464-466, 491p, 492p.* ***Paul Norris*** *a-69.* ***Orlando*** *a-457p, 458p.* ***Perez*** *c-484-486, 490p.* ***Simon/Kirby*** *a-503r; c-73-97, 100-102.* ***Starlin*** *c-471.* ***Staton*** *a-445-447i, 456-458p, 459, 460, 461p-465p, 466,467p-478p, 502p(r); c-458, 461(back).* ***Toth*** *a-418, 419, 425, 431, 495p-497p.* ***Tuska*** *a-494p.*

ADVENTURE COMICS (Also see All Star Comics 1999 crossover titles)
DC Comics: May, 1999 ($1.99, one-shot)

1-Golden Age Starman and the Atom; Snejbjerg-a 3.00

ADVENTURE COMICS (See Final Crisis: Legion of Three Worlds)
DC Comics: No. 0, Apr, 2009 - No. 12, Aug, 2010; No. 516, Sept, 2010 - No. 529, Oct, 2011 ($1.00/$3.99)

0-($1.00) R/Adventure Comics #247; new Luthor & Brainiac back-up-s; Lopresti-c 3.00
1-7-($3.99) Superboy stories; Johns-s/Manapul-a; Legion back-up-s. 5-7-Blackest Night 4.00
1-12-Variant 7-panel covers by various numbered with original #504-#515 5.00
8-12: 8-11-New Krypton x-over. 11-Mon-El leaves 21st century. 12-Legion; Levitz-s 4.00
516-521: 516-(9/10, resumes original numbering) flashback to Legion formation; Atom back-ups. 521-Adult Legion resumes; Mon-El joins Green Lanterns 4.00
522-529-($2.99) Legion Academy. 523-527-Jimenez-a/c 3.00

ADVENTURE COMICS SPECIAL (See New Krypton issues in 2009 Superman titles)
DC Comics: Jan, 2009 ($2.99, one-shot)

... Featuring the Guardian - James Robinson-s/Pere Pérez-a; origin re-told; intro. Gwen 3.00

ADVENTURE INTO MYSTERY
Atlas Comics (BFP No. 1/OPI No. 2-8): May, 1956 - No. 8, July, 1957

1-Powell s/f-a; Forte-a; Everett-c 39 78 117 242 401 560
2-Flying Saucer story 22 44 66 132 216 300
3,6-Everett-c 20 40 60 118 192 265
4,5,7: 4-Williamson-a, 4 pgs; Powell-a. 5-Everett-c/a, Orlando-a. 7-Torres-a; Everett-c 21 42 63 126 206 285
8-Moreira, Sale, Torres, Woodbridge-a, Severin-c 20 40 60 118 192 265

ADVENTURE IS MY CAREER
U.S. Coast Guard Academy/Street & Smith: 1945 (44 pgs.)

nn-Simon, Milt Gross-a 22 44 66 128 209 290

	GD 2.0	VG 4.0	FN 6.0	VF 8.0	VF/NM 9.0	NM- 9.2

ADVENTURERS, THE
Aircel Comics/Adventure Publ.: Aug, 1986 - No. 10, 1987? ($1.50, B&W)
V2#1, 1987 - V2#9, 1988; V3#1, Oct, 1989 - V3#6, 1990

1-Peter Hsu-a 1 2 3 5 6 8
1-Cover variant, limited ed. 2 4 6 9 12 15
1-2nd print (1986); 1st app. Elf Warrior 3.00
2,3, 0 (#4, 12/86)-Origin, 5-10, Book II, reg. & Limited Ed. #1 3.50
Book II, #2,3,0,4-9 3.00
Book III, #1 (10/89, $2.25)-Reg. & limited-c, Book III, #2-6 3.00

ADVENTURES (No. 2 Spectacular... on cover)
St. John Publishing Co.: Nov, 1949 - No. 2, Feb, 1950 (No. 1 ...in Romance on cover) (Slightly larger size)

1(Scarce); Bolle, Starr-a(2) 28 56 84 165 270 375
2(Scarce)-Slave Girl; China Bombshell app.; Bolle, L. Starr-a 40 80 120 246 411 575

ADVENTURES FOR BOYS
Bailey Enterprises: Dec, 1954

nn-Comics, text, & photos 8 16 24 40 50 60

ADVENTURES IN PARADISE (TV)
Dell Publishing Co.: Feb-Apr, 1962

Four Color #1301 6 12 18 39 62 85

ADVENTURES IN ROMANCE (See Adventures)

ADVENTURES IN SCIENCE (See Classics Illustrated Special Issue)

ADVENTURES IN THE DC UNIVERSE
DC Comics: Apr, 1997 - No. 19, Oct, 1998 ($1.75/$1.95/$1.99)

1-Animated style in all: JLA-c/app 5.00
2-11,13-17,19: 2-Flash app. 3-Wonder Woman. 4-Green Lantern. 6-Aquaman. 7-Shazam Family. 8-Blue Beetle & Booster Gold. 9-Flash. 10-Legion. 11-Green Lantern & Wonder Woman. 13-Impulse & Martian Manhunter. 14-Superboy/Flash race 3.50
12,18-JLA-c/app 3.50
Annual 1(1997, $3.95)-Dr. Fate, Impulse, Rose & Thorn, Superboy, Mister Miracle app. 4.50

ADVENTURES IN THE RIFLE BRIGADE
DC Comics (Vertigo): Oct, 2000 - No. 3, Dec, 2000 ($2.50, limited series)

1-3-Ennis-s/Ezquerra-a/Bolland-c 3.00
TPB (2004, $14.95) r/series and Operation Bollock series 15.00

ADVENTURES IN THE RIFLE BRIGADE: OPERATION BOLLOCK
DC Comics (Vertigo): Oct, 2001 - No. 3, Jan, 2002 ($2.50, limited series)

1-3-Ennis-s/Ezquerra-a/Fabry-c 3.00

ADVENTURES IN 3-D (With glasses)
Harvey Publications: Nov, 1953 - No. 2, Jan, 1954 (25¢)

1-Nostrand, Powell-a, 2-Powell-a 14 28 42 80 115 150

ADVENTURES INTO DARKNESS (See Seduction of the Innocent 3-D)
Better-Standard Publications/Visual Editions: No. 5, Aug, 1952- No. 14, 1954

5-Katz-c/a; Toth-a(p) 44 88 132 277 469 660
6-Tuska, Katz-a 34 68 102 199 325 450
7-9: 7-Katz-c/a. 8,9-Toth-a(p) 34 68 102 199 325 450
10-12: 10,11-Jack Katz-a. 12-Toth-a; lingerie panel 30 60 90 177 289 400
13-Toth-a(p); Cannibalism story cited by T. E. Murphy articles 39 78 117 231 378 525
14 22 44 66 132 216 300

NOTE: ***Fawcette*** *a-13.* ***Moreira*** *a-5.* ***Sekowsky*** *a-10, 11, 13(2).*

ADVENTURES INTO TERROR (Formerly Joker Comics)
Marvel/Atlas Comics (CDS): No. 43, Nov, 1950 - No. 31, May, 1954

43(#1) 71 142 213 454 777 1100
44(#2, 2/51)-Sol Brodsky-c 42 84 126 265 445 625
3(4/51), 4 32 64 96 192 314 435
5-Wolverton-c panel/Mystic #6; Rico-c panel also; Atom Bomb story 36 72 108 216 351 485
6,8: 8-Wolverton text illo r-/Marvel Tales #104; prototype of Spider-Man villain The Lizard 31 62 93 182 296 410
7-Wolverton-a "Where Monsters Dwell", 6 pgs.; Tuska-c; Maneely-c panels 62 124 186 394 677 960
9,10,12-Krigstein-a. 9-Decapitation panels 28 56 84 165 270 375
11,13-20 23 46 69 136 223 310
21-24,26-31 21 42 63 126 206 285
25-Matt Fox-a 27 54 81 158 259 360

NOTE: ***Ayers*** *a-21.* ***Colan*** *a-3, 5, 14, 21, 24, 25, 28, 29; c-27.* ***Colletta*** *a-30.* ***Everett*** *c-13, 21, 25.* ***Fass*** *a-28, 29.* ***Forte*** *a-28.* ***Heath*** *a-43, 44, 4-6, 22, 24, 26; c-43, 9, 11.* ***Lazarus*** *a-7.* ***Maneely*** *a-7(3 pg.), 10, 11, 21., 22 c-15, 29.*

Adventures Into the Unknown #14 © AC

Adventures of Barry Ween, Boy Genius #1 © Judd Winick

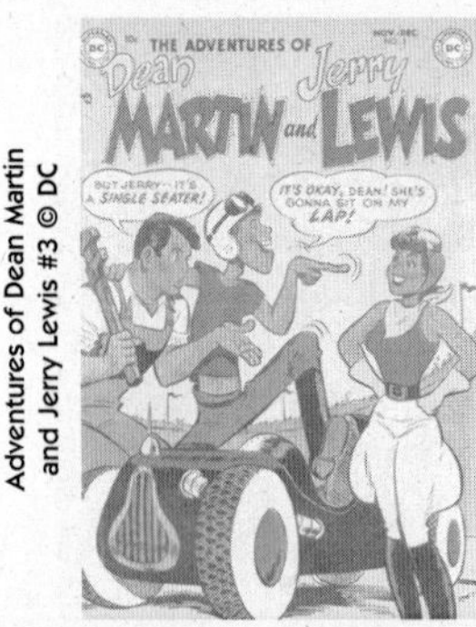

Adventures of Dean Martin and Jerry Lewis #3 © DC

	GD 2.0	VG 4.0	FN 6.0	VF 8.0	VF/NM 9.0	NM- 9.2

*Don Rico a-4, 5(3 pg.). **Sekowsky** a-43, 3, 4. **Sinnott** a-8, 9, 11, 24, 28. **Tuska** a-14; c-7.*

ADVENTURES INTO THE UNKNOWN
American Comics Group: Fall, 1948 - No. 174, Aug, 1967 (No. 1-33: 52 pgs.)
(1st continuous series Supernatural comic; see Eerie #1)

	GD 2.0	VG 4.0	FN 6.0	VF 8.0	VF/NM 9.0	NM- 9.2
1-Guardineer-a; adapt. of 'Castle of Otranto' by Horace Walpole	239	478	717	1530	2615	3700
2,3: 3-Feldstein-a (9 pgs)	82	164	246	528	902	1275
4,5: 5- 'Spirit Of Frankenstein' series begins, ends #12 (except #11)	43	86	129	271	461	650
6-10	36	72	108	216	351	485
11-16,18-20: 13-Starr-a. 15-Hitler app.	30	60	90	177	289	400
17-Story similar to movie 'The Thing'	34	68	102	204	335	465
21-26,28-30	26	52	78	154	252	350
27-Williamson/Krenkel-a (8 pgs.)	32	64	96	188	307	425
31-50: 38-Atom bomb panels; Devil-c	20	40	60	118	192	265
51-(1/54)-(3-D effect-c/story)-Only white cover	40	80	120	250	418	585
52-58: (3-D effect-c/stories with black covers). 52-E.C. swipe/Haunt Of Fear #14	39	78	117	234	385	535
59-3-D effect story only; new logo	30	60	90	177	289	400
60-Wood*esque*-a by Landau	15	30	45	88	137	185
61-Last pre-code issue (1-2/55)	15	30	45	88	137	185
62-70	8	16	24	53	89	125
71-90: 80-Hydrogen bomb panel	6	12	18	42	69	95
91,96(#95 on inside),107,116-All have Williamson-a	7	14	21	46	76	105
92-95,97-99,101-106,108-115,117-128: 109-113,118-Whitney painted-c. 128-Williamson/Krenkel/Torres-a(r)/Forbidden Worlds #63; last 10¢ issue	5	10	15	35	55	75
100	6	12	18	39	62	85
129-153,157: 153,157-Magic Agent app.	4	8	12	24	37	50
154-Nemesis series begins (origin), ends #170	5	10	15	30	48	65
155,156,158-167,170-174: 174-Flying saucer-c	4	8	12	23	36	48
168-Ditko-a(p)	4	8	12	28	44	60
169-Nemesis battles Hitler	4	8	12	28	44	60
Nemesis Archives: Vol. One (Dark Horse Books, 9/08, $59.95) r/#154-170; creator bios						60.00

NOTE: *"Spirit of Frankenstein" series in 5, 6, 8-10, 12, 16. **Buscema** a-100, 106, 108-110, 158r, 165r. **Cameron** a-34. **Craig** a-152, 160. **Goode** a-45, 47, 60. **Landau** a-51, 59-63. **Lazarus** a-34, 48, 51, 52, 56, 58, 79, 87; c-31-56, 58. **Reinman** a-102, 111, 112, 115-118, 124, 130, 137, 141, 145, 164. **Whitney** c-12-30, 57, 59-on (most.) **Torres/Williamson** a-116.*

ADVENTURES INTO WEIRD WORLDS
Marvel/Atlas Comics (ACI): Jan, 1952 - No. 30, June, 1954

	GD 2.0	VG 4.0	FN 6.0	VF 8.0	VF/NM 9.0	NM- 9.2
1-Atom bomb panels	87	174	261	553	952	1350
2-Sci/fic stories (2); one by Maneely	41	82	123	256	428	600
3-10: 7-Tongue ripped out. 10-Krigstein, Everett-a	31	62	93	182	296	410
11-20	24	48	72	140	230	320
21-Hitler in Hell story	30	60	90	177	289	400
22-26: 24-Man holds hypo & splits in two-c	22	44	66	128	209	290
27-Matt Fox end of world story-a; severed head-c	41	82	123	256	428	600
28-Atom bomb story; decapitation panels	24	48	72	140	230	320
29,30	20	40	60	114	182	250

NOTE: ***Ayers** a-8, 26. **Everett** a-4, 5; c-6, 8, 10-13, 18, 19, 22, 24, 25; a-4, 25. **Fass** a-7. **Forte** a-21, 24. **Al Hartley** a-2. **Heath** a-1, 4, 17, 22; c-7, 9, 20. **Maneely** a-2, 3, 11, 20, 22, 23, 25; c-1, 3, 22, 25-27, 29. **Reinman** a-24, 28. **Rico** a-13. **Robinson** a-13. **Sinnott** a-25, 30. **Tuska** a-1, 2, 12, 15. **Whitney** a-7. **Wildey** a-28. Bondage c-22.*

ADVENTURES IN WONDERLAND (Also see Uncle Charlies Fables)
Lev Gleason Publications: April, 1955 - No. 5, Feb, 1956 (Jr. Readers Guild)

	GD 2.0	VG 4.0	FN 6.0	VF 8.0	VF/NM 9.0	NM- 9.2
1-Maurer-a	11	22	33	62	86	110
2-4	7	14	21	37	46	55
5-Christmas issue	8	16	24	40	50	60

ADVENTURES OF ALAN LADD, THE
National Periodical Publ.: Oct-Nov, 1949 - No. 9, Feb-Mar, 1951 (All 52 pgs.)

	GD 2.0	VG 4.0	FN 6.0	VF 8.0	VF/NM 9.0	NM- 9.2
1-Photo-c	68	136	204	435	743	1050
2-Photo-c	37	74	111	222	361	500
3-6: Last photo-c	30	60	90	177	289	400
7-9	24	48	72	140	230	320

NOTE: ***Dan Barry** a-1. **Moreira** a-3-7.*

ADVENTURES OF ALICE (Also see Alice in Wonderland & ...at Monkey Island)
Civil Service Publ./Pentagon Publishing Co.: 1945

	GD 2.0	VG 4.0	FN 6.0	VF 8.0	VF/NM 9.0	NM- 9.2
1	15	30	45	83	124	165
2-Through the Magic Looking Glass	11	22	33	62	86	110

ADVENTURES OF BARON MUNCHAUSEN, THE
Now Comics: July, 1989 - No. 4, Oct, 1989 ($1.75, limited series)

	GD 2.0	VG 4.0	FN 6.0	VF 8.0	VF/NM 9.0	NM- 9.2
1-4: Movie adaptation						3.00

	GD 2.0	VG 4.0	FN 6.0	VF 8.0	VF/NM 9.0	NM- 9.2

ADVENTURES OF BARRY WEEN, BOY GENIUS, THE
Image Comics: Mar, 1999 - No. 3, May, 1999 ($2.95, B&W, limited series)

	GD 2.0	VG 4.0	FN 6.0	VF 8.0	VF/NM 9.0	NM- 9.2
1-3-Judd Winick-s/a						3.00
...: Secret Crisis Origin Files (Oni, 7/04, Free Comic Book Day giveaway) - Winick-s/a						3.00
TPB (Oni Press, 11/99, $8.95) r/#1-3						9.00

ADVENTURES OF BARRY WEEN, BOY GENIUS 2.0, THE
Oni Press: Feb, 2000 - No. 3, Apr, 2000 ($2.95, B&W, limited series)

	GD 2.0	VG 4.0	FN 6.0	VF 8.0	VF/NM 9.0	NM- 9.2
1-3-Judd Winick-s/a						3.00
TPB (2000, $8.95)						9.00

ADVENTURES OF BARRY WEEN, BOY GENIUS 3, THE : MONKEY TALES
Oni Press: Feb, 2001 - No. 6, Feb, 2002 ($2.95, B&W, limited series)

	GD 2.0	VG 4.0	FN 6.0	VF 8.0	VF/NM 9.0	NM- 9.2
1-6-Judd Winick-s/a						3.00
TPB (2001, $8.95) r/#1-3; intro. by Peter David						9.00
...4 TPB (5/02, $8.95) r/#4-6						9.00

ADVENTURES OF BAYOU BILLY, THE (Based on video game)
Archie Comics: Sept, 1989 - No. 5, June, 1990 ($1.00)

	GD 2.0	VG 4.0	FN 6.0	VF 8.0	VF/NM 9.0	NM- 9.2
1-5: Esposito-c/a(i). 5-Kelley Jones-c						3.00

ADVENTURES OF BOB HOPE, THE (Also see True Comics #59)
National Per. Publ.: Feb-Mar, 1950 - No. 109, Feb-Mar, 1968 (#1-10: 52pgs.)

	GD 2.0	VG 4.0	FN 6.0	VF 8.0	VF/NM 9.0	NM- 9.2
1-Photo-c	210	420	630	1334	2292	3250
2-Photo-c	87	174	261	553	952	1350
3,4-Photo-c. 4-Horror-c	54	108	162	343	574	825
5-10	40	80	120	246	411	575
11-20	28	56	84	165	270	375
21-31 (2-3/55; last precode)	20	40	60	114	182	250
32-40	10	20	30	66	121	175
41-50	9	18	27	60	103	145
51-70	7	14	21	49	82	115
71-93	6	12	18	37	59	80
94-Aquaman cameo	6	12	18	37	59	80
95-1st app. Super-Hip & 1st monster issue (11/65)	7	14	21	50	83	115
96-105: Super-Hip and monster stories in all. 103-Batman, Robin, Ringo Starr cameos	6	12	18	37	59	80
106-109-All monster-c/stories by N. Adams-c/a	8	16	24	51	86	120

NOTE: *Buzzy in #34. Kitty Karr of Hollywood in #15, 17-20, 23, 28. Liz in #26, 109. Miss Beverly Hills of Hollywood in #7, 8, 10, 13, 14. Miss Melody Lane of Broadway in #15. Rusty in #23, 25. Tommy in #24. No 2nd feature in #2-4, 6, 8, 11, 12, 28-108.*

ADVENTURES OF CAPTAIN AMERICA
Marvel Comics: Sept, 1991 - No. 4, Jan, 1992 ($4.95, 52 pgs., squarebound, limited series)

	GD 2.0	VG 4.0	FN 6.0	VF 8.0	VF/NM 9.0	NM- 9.2
1-4: 1-Origin in WW2; embossed-c; Nicieza scripts; Maguire-c/a(p) begins, ends #3. 2-4-Austin-c/a(i). 3,4-Red Skull app.						5.00

ADVENTURES OF CYCLOPS AND PHOENIX (Also See Askani'son & The Further Adventures of Cyclops And Phoenix)
Marvel Comics: May, 1994 - No. 4, Aug, 1994 ($2.95, limited series)

	GD 2.0	VG 4.0	FN 6.0	VF 8.0	VF/NM 9.0	NM- 9.2
1-4-Characters from X-Men; origin of Cable						4.00
Trade paperback ($14.95)-reprints #1-4						15.00

ADVENTURES OF DEAN MARTIN AND JERRY LEWIS, THE
(The Adventures of Jerry Lewis #41 on) (See Movie Love #12)
National Periodical Publications: July-Aug, 1952 - No. 40, Oct, 1957

	GD 2.0	VG 4.0	FN 6.0	VF 8.0	VF/NM 9.0	NM- 9.2
1	118	236	354	749	1287	1825
2-3 pg origin on how they became a team	53	106	159	334	567	800
3-10: 3- I Love Lucy text featurette	32	64	96	192	314	435
11-19: Last precode (2/55)	20	40	60	120	195	270
20-30	16	32	48	92	144	195
31-40	14	28	42	80	115	150

ADVENTURES OF DETECTIVE ACE KING, THE (Also see Bob Scully-- & Detective Dan)
Humor Publ. Corp.: No date (1933) (36 pgs., 9-1/2x12") (10¢, B&W, one-shot) (paper-c)

	GD 2.0	VG 4.0	FN 6.0	VF 8.0	VF/NM 9.0	NM- 9.2
Book 1-Along with Bob Scully & Detective Dan, the first comic w/original art & the first of a single theme.; Not reprints; Ace King by Martin Nadle (The American Sherlock Holmes). A Dick Tracy look-alike	425	850	1275	3400	-	-

ADVENTURES OF EVIL AND MALICE, THE
Image Comics: June, 1999 - No. 3, Nov, 1999 ($3.50/$3.95, limited series)

	GD 2.0	VG 4.0	FN 6.0	VF 8.0	VF/NM 9.0	NM- 9.2
1-3-Jimmie Robinson-s/a. 3-($3.95-c)						4.00

ADVENTURES OF FELIX THE CAT, THE
Harvey Comics: May, 1992 ($1.25)

	GD 2.0	VG 4.0	FN 6.0	VF 8.0	VF/NM 9.0	NM- 9.2
1-Messmer-r						5.00

ADVENTURES OF FORD FAIRLANE, THE

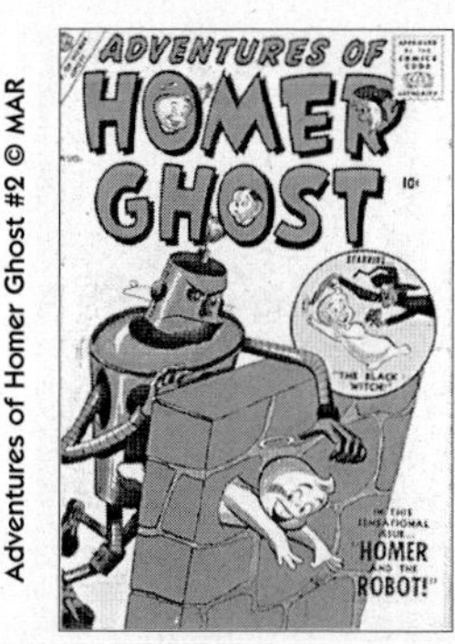

Adventures of Homer Ghost #2 © MAR

Adventures of Pinky Lee #2 © MAR

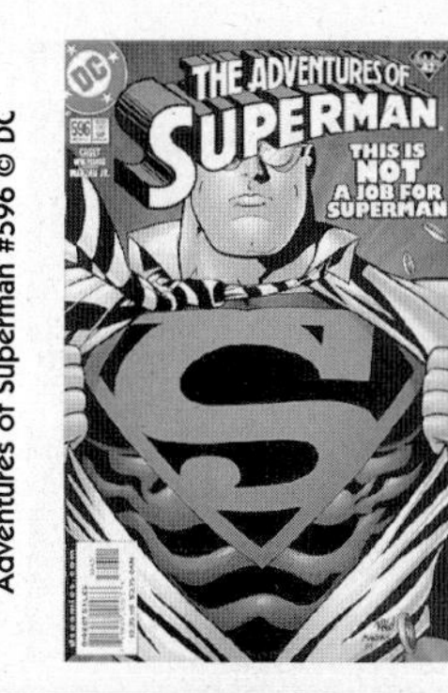

Adventures of Superman #596 © DC

DC Comics: May, 1990 - No. 4, Aug, 1990 ($1.50, limited series, mature)

	GD 2.0	VG 4.0	FN 6.0	VF 8.0	VF/NM 9.0	NM- 9.2
1-4: Andrew Dice Clay movie tie-in; Don Heck inks						3.00

ADVENTURES OF HOMER COBB, THE
Say/Bart Prod. : Sept, 1947 (Oversized) (Published in the U.S., but printed in Canada)

	GD 2.0	VG 4.0	FN 6.0	VF 8.0	VF/NM 9.0	NM- 9.2
1-(Scarce)-Feldstein-c/a	36	72	108	211	343	475

ADVENTURES OF HOMER GHOST (See Homer The Happy Ghost)
Atlas Comics: June, 1957 - No. 2, Aug, 1957

	GD 2.0	VG 4.0	FN 6.0	VF 8.0	VF/NM 9.0	NM- 9.2
V1#1,2: 2-Robot-c	12	24	36	69	97	125

ADVENTURES OF JERRY LEWIS, THE (Adventures of Dean Martin & Jerry Lewis No. 1-40) (See Super DC Giant)
National Periodical Publ.: No. 41, Nov, 1957 - No. 124, May-June, 1971

	GD 2.0	VG 4.0	FN 6.0	VF 8.0	VF/NM 9.0	NM- 9.2
41	10	20	30	64	115	165
42-60	8	16	24	51	86	120
61-67,69-73,75-80	6	12	18	42	69	95
68,74-Photo-c (movie)	9	18	27	63	112	160
81,82,85-87,90,91,94,96,98,99	6	12	18	37	59	80
83,84,88: 83-1st Monsters-c/s. 84-Jerry as a Super-hero-c/s. 88-1st Witch, Miss Kraft	6	12	18	42	69	95
89-Bob Hope app.; Wizard of Oz & Alfred E. Neuman in MAD parody	7	14	21	46	76	105
92-Superman cameo	7	14	21	46	76	105
93-Beatles parody as babies	6	12	18	42	69	95
95-1st Uncle Hal Wack-A-Boy Camp-c/s	6	12	18	42	69	95
97-Batman/Robin/Joker-c/story; Riddler & Penguin app; Dick Sprang-c.	9	18	27	62	109	155
100	7	14	21	44	72	100
101,103,104-Neal Adams-c/a	8	16	24	51	86	120
102-Beatles app.; Neal Adams c/a	9	18	27	63	112	160
105-Superman x-over	7	14	21	46	76	105
106-111,113-116	4	8	12	28	44	60
112,117: 112-Flash x-over. 117-W. Woman x-over	7	14	21	44	72	100
118-124	4	8	12	26	41	55

NOTE: *Monster-c/s-90,93,96,98,101. Wack-A-Buy Camp-c/s-96,99,102,107,108.*

ADVENTURES OF JO-JOY, THE (See Jo-Joy)

ADVENTURES OF LASSIE, THE (See Lassie)

ADVENTURES OF LUTHER ARKWRIGHT, THE
Valkyrie Press/Dark Horse Comics: Oct, 1987 - No. 9, Jan, 1989 ($2.00, B&W) V2, #1, Mar, 1990 - V2#9, 1990 ($1.95, B&W)

	GD 2.0	VG 4.0	FN 6.0	VF 8.0	VF/NM 9.0	NM- 9.2
1-9: 1-Alan Moore intro., V2#1-9 (Dark Horse): r-1st series; new-c						4.00
TPB (1997, $14.95) r/#1-9 w/Michael Moorcock intro.						15.00

ADVENTURES OF MIGHTY MOUSE (Mighty Mouse Adventures No. 1)
St. John Publishing Co.: No. 2, Jan, 1952 - No. 18, May, 1955

	GD 2.0	VG 4.0	FN 6.0	VF 8.0	VF/NM 9.0	NM- 9.2
2	26	52	78	154	252	350
3-5	15	30	45	85	130	175
6-18	11	22	33	64	90	115

ADVENTURES OF MIGHTY MOUSE (2nd Series) (Becomes Mighty Mouse #161 on) (Two No. 144's; formerly Paul Terry's Comics; No. 129-137 have nn's)
St. John/Pines/Dell/Gold Key: No. 126, Aug, 1955 - No. 160, Oct, 1963

	GD 2.0	VG 4.0	FN 6.0	VF 8.0	VF/NM 9.0	NM- 9.2
126(8/55), 127(10/55), 128(11/55)-St. John	10	20	30	56	76	95
nn(129, 4/56)-144(8/59)-Pines	5	10	15	32	51	70
144(10-12/59)-155(7-9/62) Dell	4	8	12	28	44	60
156(10/62)-160(10/63) Gold Key	4	8	12	28	44	60

NOTE: *Early issues titled "Paul Terry's Adventures of ...."*

ADVENTURES OF MIGHTY MOUSE (Formerly Mighty Mouse)
Gold Key: No. 166, Mar, 1979 - No. 172, Jan, 1980

	GD 2.0	VG 4.0	FN 6.0	VF 8.0	VF/NM 9.0	NM- 9.2
166-172	1	2	3	5	6	8

ADVS. OF MR. FROG & MISS MOUSE (See Dell Junior Treasury No. 4)

ADVENTURES OF OZZIE & HARRIET, THE (See Ozzie & Harriet)

ADVENTURES OF PATORUZU
Green Publishing Co.: Aug, 1946 - Winter, 1946

	GD 2.0	VG 4.0	FN 6.0	VF 8.0	VF/NM 9.0	NM- 9.2
nn's-Contains Animal Crackers reprints	6	12	18	28	34	40

ADVENTURES OF PINKY LEE, THE (TV)
Atlas Comics: July, 1955 - No. 5, Dec, 1955

	GD 2.0	VG 4.0	FN 6.0	VF 8.0	VF/NM 9.0	NM- 9.2
1	24	48	72	142	234	325
2-5	15	30	45	88	137	185

ADVENTURES OF PIPSQUEAK, THE (Formerly Pat the Brat)
Archie Publications (Radio Comics): No. 34, Sept, 1959 - No. 39, July, 1960

	GD 2.0	VG 4.0	FN 6.0	VF 8.0	VF/NM 9.0	NM- 9.2
34	4	8	12	22	34	45
35-39	3	6	9	18	27	35

ADVENTURES OF QUAKE & QUISP, THE (See Quaker Oats "Plenty of Glutton")

ADVENTURES OF REX THE WONDER DOG, THE (Rex...No. 1)
National Periodical Publ.: Jan-Feb, 1952 - No. 45, May-June, 1959; No. 46, Nov-Dec, 1959

	GD 2.0	VG 4.0	FN 6.0	VF 8.0	VF/NM 9.0	NM- 9.2
1-(Scarce)-Toth-c/a	155	310	465	992	1696	2400
2-(Scarce)-Toth-c/a	66	132	198	419	722	1025
3-(Scarce)-Toth-a	53	106	159	334	567	800
4,5	41	82	123	256	428	600
6-10	34	68	102	206	336	465
11-Atom bomb-c/story; dinosaur-c/sty	39	78	117	240	395	550
12-19: 19-Last precode (1-2/55)	22	44	66	132	216	300
20-46	16	32	48	94	147	200

NOTE: ***Infantino, Gil Kane*** *art in 5-19 (most)*

ADVENTURES OF ROBIN HOOD, THE (Formerly Robin Hood)
Magazine Enterprises (Sussex Publ. Co.): No. 7, 9/57 - No. 8, 11/57 (Based on Richard Greene TV Show)

	GD 2.0	VG 4.0	FN 6.0	VF 8.0	VF/NM 9.0	NM- 9.2
7,8-Richard Greene photo-c. 7-Powell-a	15	30	45	83	124	165

ADVENTURES OF ROBIN HOOD, THE
Gold Key: Mar, 1974 - No. 7, Jan, 1975 (Disney cartoon) (36 pgs.)

	GD 2.0	VG 4.0	FN 6.0	VF 8.0	VF/NM 9.0	NM- 9.2
1(90291-403)-Part-r of $1.50 editions	2	4	6	13	18	22
2-7: 1-7 are part-r	2	4	6	8	11	14

ADVENTURES OF SNAKE PLISSKEN
Marvel Comics: Jan, 1997 ($2.50, one-shot)

	GD 2.0	VG 4.0	FN 6.0	VF 8.0	VF/NM 9.0	NM- 9.2
1-Based on Escape From L.A. movie; Brereton-c						4.00

ADVENTURES OF SPAWN, THE
Image Comics (Todd McFarlane Prods.): Jan, 2007; Nov, 2008 ($5.99)

	GD 2.0	VG 4.0	FN 6.0	VF 8.0	VF/NM 9.0	NM- 9.2
1,2-Printed adaptation of the Spawn.com web comic; Khary Randolph-a						6.00

ADVENTURES OF SPIDER-MAN, THE (Based on animated TV series)
Marvel Comics: Apr, 1996 - No. 12, Mar, 1997 (99¢)

	GD 2.0	VG 4.0	FN 6.0	VF 8.0	VF/NM 9.0	NM- 9.2
1-12: 1-Punisher app. 2-Venom cameo. 3-X-Men. 6-Fantastic Four						3.00

ADVENTURES OF SUPERBOY, THE (See Superboy, 2nd Series)

ADVENTURES OF SUPERMAN (Formerly Superman)
DC Comics: No. 424, Jan, 1987 - No. 499, Feb, 1993; No. 500, Early June, 1993 - No. 649, Apr, 2006 (This title's numbering continues with Superman #650, May, 2006)

	GD 2.0	VG 4.0	FN 6.0	VF 8.0	VF/NM 9.0	NM- 9.2
424-Ordway-c/a/Wolfman-s begin following Byrne's Superman revamp						4.00
425-435,437-462: 426-Legends x-over. 432-1st app. Jose Delgado who becomes Gangbuster in #434. 437-Millennium x-over. 438-New Brainiac app. 440-Batman app. 449-Invasion						3.00
436-Byrne scripts begin; Millennium x-over						3.50
463-Superman/Flash race; cover swipe/Superman #199						5.00
464-Lobo-c & app. (pre-dates Lobo #1)						4.00
465-479,481-495: 467-Part 2 of Batman story. 473-Hal Jordan, Guy Gardner x-over. 477-Legion app. 491-Last $1.00-c. 495-Forever People-c/story; Darkseid app.						3.00
480,496,497: 480-($1.75, 52 pgs.). 496-Doomsday cameo. 497-Doomsday battle issue						4.00
496,497-2nd printings						3.00
498,499-Funeral for a Friend; Supergirl app.						4.00
498-2nd & 3rd printings						3.00
500-($2.95, 68 pgs.)-Collector's edition w/card						5.00
500-($2.50, 68 pgs.)-Regular edition w/different-c						4.00
500-Platinum edition						30.00
501-($1.95)-Collector's edition with die-cut-c						3.50
501-($1.50)-Regular edition w/mini-poster & diff.-c						3.00
502-516: 502-Supergirl-c/story. 508-Challengers of the Unknown app. 510-Bizarro-c/story. 516-(9/94)-Zero Hour						3.00
505-($2.50)-Holo-grafx foil-c edition						3.50
0,517-523: 0-(10/94). 517-(11/94)						3.00
524-549,551-580: 524-Begin $1.95-c. 527-Return of Alpha Centurion (Zero Hour). 533-Impulse-c/app. 535-Luthor-c/app. 536-Brainiac app. 537-Parasite app. 540-Final Night x-over. 541-Superboy-c/app.; Lois & Clark honeymoon. 545-New powers. 546-New costume. 555-Red & Blue Supermen battle. 557-Millennium Giants x-over. 558-560: Superman Silver Age-style story; Krypto app. 561-Begin $1.99-c. 565-JLA app.						3.00
550-($3.50)-Double sized						4.00
581-588: 581-Begin $2.25-c. 583-Emperor Joker. 588-Casey-s						3.00
589-595: 589-Return to Krypton; Rivoche-c. 591-Wolfman-s. 593-595-Our Worlds at War x-over. 593-New Suicide Squad formed. 594-Doomsday-c/app.						3.00
596-Aftermath of "War" x-over has panel showing damaged World Trade Center buildings; issue went on sale the day after the Sept. 11 attack						6.00
597-599,601-624: 597-Joker: Last Laugh. 604,605-Ultraman, Owlman, Superwoman app.						

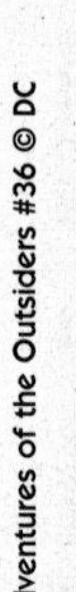
Adventures of Superman #626 © DC

Adventures of the Outsiders #36 © DC

Adventure Time #1 © Cartoon Network

	GD 2.0	VG 4.0	FN 6.0	VF 8.0	VF/NM 9.0	NM- 9.2
606-Return to Krypton. 612-616,619-623-Nowlan-c. 624-Mr. Majestic app.						3.00
600-($3.95) Wieringo-a; painted-c by Adel; pin-ups by various						4.00
625,626-Godfall parts 2,5; Turner-c; Caldwell-a(p)						4.00
627-641,643-648: 627-Begin $2.50-c, Rucka-s/Clark-a/Ha-c begin. 628-Wagner-c. 631-Bagged with Sky Captain CD; Lois shot. 634-Mxyzptlk visits DC offices. 639-Capt. Marvel & Eclipso app. 641-OMAC app. 643-Sacrifice aftermath; Batman & Wonder Woman app.						3.00
642-OMAC Project x-over Sacrifice pt. 3; JLA app.						5.00
642-(2nd printing) red tone cover						3.00
649-Last issue; Infinite Crisis x-over, Superman vs. Earth-2 Superman						4.00
#1,000,000 (11/98) Gene Ha-c; 853rd Century x-over						3.00
Annual 1 (1987, $1.25, 52 pgs.)-Starlin-c & scripts						4.00
Annual 2,3 (1990, 1991, $2.00, 68 pgs.): 2-Byrne-c/a(i); Legion '90 (Lobo) app. 3-Armageddon 2001 x-over						4.00
Annual 4-6 ('92-'94, $2.50, 68 pgs.): 4-Guy Gardner/Lobo-c/story; Eclipso storyline; Quesada-c(p). 5-Bloodlines storyline. 6-Elseworlds sty.						4.00
Annual 7,9('95, '97, $3.95)-7-Year One story. 9-Pulp Heroes sty						4.00
Annual 8 (1996, $2.95)-Legends of the Dead Earth story						4.00

NOTE: *Erik Larsen a-431.*

ADVENTURES OF THE DOVER BOYS
Archie Comics (Close-up): September, 1950 - No. 2, 1950 (No month given)

	GD 2.0	VG 4.0	FN 6.0	VF 8.0	VF/NM 9.0	NM- 9.2
1,2	9	18	27	52	69	85

ADVENTURES OF THE FLY (The Fly #1-6; Fly Man No. 32-39; See The Double Life of Private Strong, The Fly, Laugh Comics & Mighty Crusaders)
Archie Publications/Radio Comics: Aug, 1959 - No. 30, Oct, 1964; No. 31, May, 1965

	GD 2.0	VG 4.0	FN 6.0	VF 8.0	VF/NM 9.0	NM- 9.2
1-Shield app.; origin The Fly; S&K-c/a	48	96	144	389	845	1300
2-Williamson, S&K-a	26	52	78	182	391	600
3-Origin retold; Davis, Powell-a	21	42	63	150	318	485
4-Neal Adams-a(p)(1 panel); S&K-c; Powell-a; 2 pg. Shield story	14	28	42	96	208	320
5,6,9,10: 9-Shield app. 9-1st app. Cat Girl. 10-Black Hood app.	11	22	33	75	148	220
7,8: 7-1st S.A. app. Black Hood (7/60). 8-1st S.A. app. Shield (9/60)	12	24	36	81	166	250
11-13,15-20: 13-1st app. Fly Girl w/o costume. 16-Last 10¢ issue. 20-Origin Fly Girl retold	8	16	24	56	96	135
14-Origin & 1st app. Fly Girl in costume	9	18	27	62	109	155
21-30: 23-Jaguar cameo. 27-29-Black Hood 1 pg. strips. 30-Comet x-over (1st S.A. app.) in Fly Girl	7	14	21	44	72	100
31-Black Hood, Shield, Comet app.	7	14	21	46	76	105
Vol. 1 TPB ('04, $12.95) r/#1-4 & Double Life of Private Strong #1,2; foreward by Joe Simon						13.00

NOTE: ***Simon** c-2-4. **Tuska** a-1. Cover title to #31 is Flyman; Advs. of the Fly inside.*

ADVENTURES OF THE JAGUAR, THE (See Blue Ribbon Comics, Laugh Comics & Mighty Crusaders)
Archie Publications (Radio Comics): Sept, 1961 - No. 15, Nov, 1963

	GD 2.0	VG 4.0	FN 6.0	VF 8.0	VF/NM 9.0	NM- 9.2
1-Origin Jaguar (1st app?) by J. Rosenberger	21	42	63	142	304	465
2,3: 3-Last 10¢ issue	11	22	33	75	148	220
4-6-Catgirl app. (#4's-c is same as splash pg.)	9	18	27	62	109	155
7-10: 10-Dinosaur-c	8	16	24	53	89	125
11-15:13,14-Catgirl, Black Hood app. in both	7	14	21	46	76	105

ADVENTURES OF THE MASK (TV cartoon)
Dark Horse Comics: Jan, 1996 - No. 12, Dec, 1996 ($2.50)

	GD 2.0	VG 4.0	FN 6.0	VF 8.0	VF/NM 9.0	NM- 9.2
1-12: Based on animated series						3.00

ADVENTURES OF THE NEW MEN (Formerly Newmen #1-21)
Maximum Press: No. 22, Nov, 1996; No. 23, March, 1997 ($2.50)

	GD 2.0	VG 4.0	FN 6.0	VF 8.0	VF/NM 9.0	NM- 9.2
22,23-Sprouse-c/a						3.00

ADVENTURES OF THE OUTSIDERS, THE (Formerly Batman & The Outsiders; also see The Outsiders)
DC Comics: No. 33, May, 1986 - No. 46, June, 1987

	GD 2.0	VG 4.0	FN 6.0	VF 8.0	VF/NM 9.0	NM- 9.2
33-46: 39-45-r/Outsiders #1-7 by Aparo						3.00

ADVENTURES OF THE SUPER MARIO BROTHERS (See Super Mario Bros.)
Valiant: 1990 - No. 9, Oct, 1991 ($1.50)

	GD 2.0	VG 4.0	FN 6.0	VF 8.0	VF/NM 9.0	NM- 9.2
V2#1-9	1	2	3	5	6	8

ADVENTURES OF THE THING, THE (Also see The Thing)
Marvel Comics: Apr, 1992 - No. 4, July, 1992, ($1.25, limited series)

	GD 2.0	VG 4.0	FN 6.0	VF 8.0	VF/NM 9.0	NM- 9.2
1-4: 1-r/Marvel Two-In-One #50 by Byrne; Kieth-c. 2-4-r/Marvel Two-In-One #80,51 & 77; 2-Ghost Rider-c/story; Quesada-c. 3-Miller-r/Quesada-c; new Perez-a (4 pgs.)						3.00

ADVENTURES OF THE X-MEN, THE (Based on animated TV series)
Marvel Comics: Apr, 1996 - No. 12, Mar, 1997 (99¢)

	GD 2.0	VG 4.0	FN 6.0	VF 8.0	VF/NM 9.0	NM- 9.2
1-12: 1-Wolverine/Hulk battle. 3-Spider-Man-c. 5,6-Magneto-c/app.						3.00

ADVENTURES OF TINKER BELL (See Tinker Bell, 4-Color No. 896 & 982)

ADVENTURES OF TOM SAWYER (See Dell Junior Treasury No. 10)

ADVENTURES OF YOUNG DR. MASTERS, THE
Archie Comics (Radio Comics): Aug, 1964 - No. 2, Nov, 1964

	GD 2.0	VG 4.0	FN 6.0	VF 8.0	VF/NM 9.0	NM- 9.2
1	4	8	12	22	34	45
2	3	6	9	16	22	28

ADVENTURES ON OTHER WORLDS (See Showcase #17 & 18)

ADVENTURES ON THE PLANET OF THE APES (Also see Planet of the Apes)
Marvel Comics Group: Oct, 1975 - No. 11, Dec, 1976

	GD 2.0	VG 4.0	FN 6.0	VF 8.0	VF/NM 9.0	NM- 9.2
1-Planet of the Apes magazine-r in color; Starlin-c; adapts movie thru #6	3	6	9	18	27	35
2-5: 5-(25¢-c edition)	2	4	6	10	14	18
5-7-(30¢-c variants, limited distribution)	4	8	12	24	37	50
6-10: 6,7-(25¢-c edition). 7-Adapts 2nd movie (thru #11)	2	4	6	11	16	20
11-Last issue; concludes 2nd movie adaptation	3	6	9	14	20	26

NOTE: ***Alcala** a-6-11r. **Buckler** c-2p. **Nasser** c-7. **Ploog** a-1-9. **Starlin** c-6. **Tuska** a-1-5r.*

ADVENTURES WITH THE DC SUPER HEROES (Interior also inserted into some DC issues)
DC Comics/Geppi's Entertainment Museum: 2007 Free Comic Book Day giveaway

	GD 2.0	VG 4.0	FN 6.0	VF 8.0	VF/NM 9.0	NM- 9.2
"The Batman and Cal Ripken, Jr. Hall of Fame Edition "A Rare Catch" " in indicia						3.00

ADVENTURE TIME (With Finn & Jake) (Based on the Cartoon Network animated series)
Boom Entertainment (KaBOOM!): Feb, 2012 - Present ($3.99)

	GD 2.0	VG 4.0	FN 6.0	VF 8.0	VF/NM 9.0	NM- 9.2
1-Cover A						8.00
1-Covers B & C; interlocking image						10.00
1-Cover D variant by Jeffrey Brown						20.00
1-Cover E wraparound-c						30.00
1-Second & third printings						4.00
2-Four covers						4.00

AEON FLUX (Based on the 2005 movie which was based on the MTV animated series)
Dark Horse Comics: Oct, 2005 - No. 4, Jan, 2006 ($2.99, limited series)

	GD 2.0	VG 4.0	FN 6.0	VF 8.0	VF/NM 9.0	NM- 9.2
1-4-Timothy Green II-a/Mike Kennedy-s						3.00
TPB (5/06, $12.95) r/series; cover gallery						13.00

AFRICA
Magazine Enterprises: 1955

	GD 2.0	VG 4.0	FN 6.0	VF 8.0	VF/NM 9.0	NM- 9.2
1(A-1#137)-Cave Girl, Thun'da; Powell-c/a(4)	27	54	81	158	259	360

AFRICAN LION (Disney movie)
Dell Publishing Co.: Nov, 1955

	GD 2.0	VG 4.0	FN 6.0	VF 8.0	VF/NM 9.0	NM- 9.2
Four Color #665	6	12	18	37	59	80

AFTER DARK
Sterling Comics: No. 6, May, 1955 - No. 8, Sept, 1955

	GD 2.0	VG 4.0	FN 6.0	VF 8.0	VF/NM 9.0	NM- 9.2
6-8-Sekowsky-a in all	9	18	27	52	69	85

AFTER DARK (Co-created by Wesley Snipes)
Radical Comics: No. 0, Jun, 2010 - No. 3 ($1.00/$4.99, limited series)

	GD 2.0	VG 4.0	FN 6.0	VF 8.0	VF/NM 9.0	NM- 9.2
0-($1.00) Milligan-s/Nentrup & Mattina-a						3.00
1-3-($4.99) Milligan-s/Manco-a						5.00

AFTER THE CAPE
Image Comics (Shadowline): Mar, 2007 - No. 3, May, 2007 ($2.99, B&W, limited series)

	GD 2.0	VG 4.0	FN 6.0	VF 8.0	VF/NM 9.0	NM- 9.2
1-3-Jim Valentino-s/Marco Rudy-a						3.00
... Volume One TPB (9/07, $12.99) r/series; scripts, sketch pages, character profiles						13.00
...II (11/07 - No. 3, 1/08, $2.99) 1-3-Jim Valentino-s/Sergio Carrera-a						3.00

AGAINST BLACKSHARD 3-D (Also see SoulQuest)
Sirius Comics: August, 1986 ($2.25)

	GD 2.0	VG 4.0	FN 6.0	VF 8.0	VF/NM 9.0	NM- 9.2
1						3.00

AGENCY, THE
Image Comics (Top Cow): August, 2001 - No. 6, Mar, 2002 ($2.50/$2.95/$4.95)

	GD 2.0	VG 4.0	FN 6.0	VF 8.0	VF/NM 9.0	NM- 9.2
1-5: 1-Jenkins-s/Hotz-a; three covers by Hotz, Turner, Silvestri. 3-5-($2.95)						3.00
6-($4.95) Flip-c preview of Jeremiah TV series						5.00
Preview (2001, 16 pgs.) B&W pages, cover previews, sketch pages						3.00

AGENT LIBERTY SPECIAL (See Superman, 2nd Series)
DC Comics: 1992 ($2.00, 52 pgs, one-shot)

	GD 2.0	VG 4.0	FN 6.0	VF 8.0	VF/NM 9.0	NM- 9.2
1-1st solo adventure; Guice-c/a(i)						4.00

AGENTS, THE
Image Comics: Apr, 2003 - No. 6, Sept, 2003 ($2.95, B&W)

	GD 2.0	VG 4.0	FN 6.0	VF 8.0	VF/NM 9.0	NM- 9.2
1-5-Ben Dunn-c/a in all						3.00

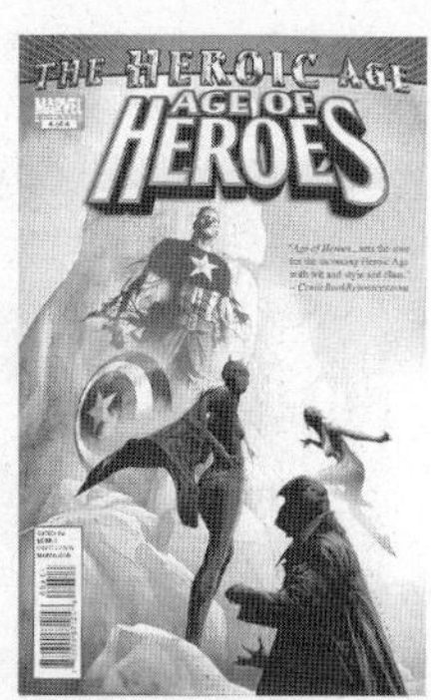

Age of Heroes #4 © MAR

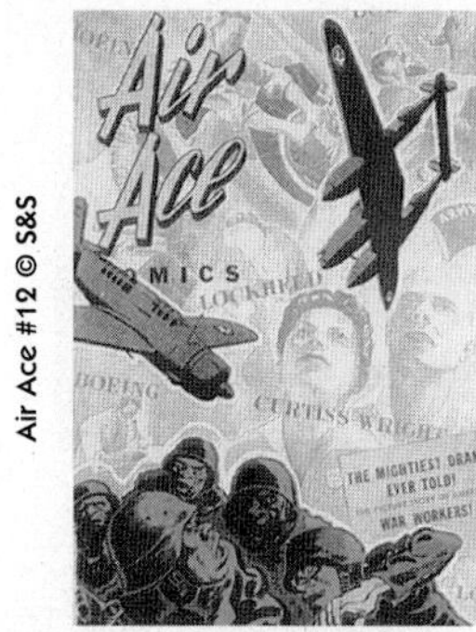

Air Ace #12 © S&S

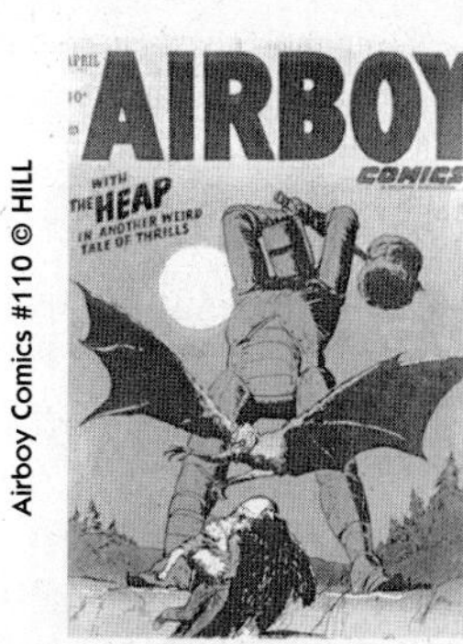

Airboy Comics #110 © HILL

	GD 2.0	VG 4.0	FN 6.0	VF 8.0	VF/NM 9.0	NM- 9.2
6-Five pg. preview of The Walking Dead #1	2	4	6	11	16	20

AGENTS OF ATLAS
Marvel Comics: Oct, 2006 - No. 6, Mar, 2007 ($2.99, limited series)

1-6: 1-Golden Age heroes Marvel Boy & Venus app.; Kirk-a 3.00
... MGC 1 (7/10, $1.00) r/#1 with "Marvel's Greatest Comics" logo on cover 3.00
HC (2007, $24.99, dustjacket) r/#1-6, What If? #9, agents' debuts in '40s-'50s Atlas comics, creator interviews, character design art 25.00

AGENTS OF ATLAS (Dark Reign)
Marvel Comics: Apr, 2009 - Present ($3.99)

1-11: 1-Pagulayan-a; 2 covers by Art Adams and McGuinness; back-up with Wolverine app. 5-New Avengers app. 8-Hulk app. 4.00

AGENTS OF LAW (Also see Comic's Greatest World)
Dark Horse Comics: Mar, 1995 - No. 6, Sept, 1995 ($2.50)

1-6: 5-Predator app. 6-Predator app.; death of Law 3.00

AGENT X (Continued from Deadpool)
Marvel Comics: Sept. 2002 - No. 15, Dec, 2003 ($2.99/$2.25)

1-($2.99) Simone-s/Udon Studios-a; Taskmaster app. 3.50
2-9-($2.25) 2-Punisher app. 3.00
10-15-($2.99) 10,11-Evan Dorkin-s. 12-Hotz-a 3.00

AGE OF APOCALYPSE (See Uncanny X-Force)
Marvel Comics: May, 2012 - Present ($2.99)

1-Lapham-s/De La Torre-a/Ramos-c 3.00

AGE OF APOCALYPSE: THE CHOSEN
Marvel Comics: Apr, 1995 ($2.50, one-shot)

1-Wraparound-c 3.00

AGE OF BRONZE
Image Comics: Nov, 1998 - Present ($2.95/$3.50, B&W)

1-6-Eric Shanower-c/s/a 3.50
7-31-($3.50) 3.50
...Behind the Scenes (5/02, $3.50) background info and creative process 3.50
Image Firsts: Age of Bronze #1 (4/10, $1.00) r/#1 with "Image Firsts" cover logo 3.00
...Special (6/99, $2.95) Story of Agamemnon and Menelaus 3.50
A Thousand Ships (7/01, $19.95, TPB) r/#1-9 20.00
Sacrifice (9/04, $19.95, TPB) r/#10-19 20.00

AGE OF HEROES, THE
Halloween Comics/Image Comics #3 on: 1996 - No. 5, 1999 ($2.95, B&W)

1-5: James Hudnall scripts; John Ridgway-c/a 3.00
...Special ($4.95) r/#1,2 5.00
...Special 2 ($6.95) r/#3,4 7.00
...Wex 1 ('98, $2.95) Hudnall-s/Angel Fernandez-a 3.00

AGE OF HEROES (The Heroic Age)
Marvel Comics: Jul, 2010 - No. 4, Oct, 2010 ($3.99, limited series)

1-4-Short stories of Avengers members by various. 4-Jae Lee-c 4.00

AGE OF INNOCENCE: THE REBIRTH OF IRON MAN
Marvel Comics: Feb, 1996 ($2.50, one-shot)

1-New origin of Tony Stark 3.00

AGE OF REPTILES
Dark Horse Comics: Nov, 1993 - No. 4, Feb, 1994 ($2.50, limited series)

1-4: Delgado-c/a/scripts in all 3.00
... The Hunt 1-5 (5/96 - No. 5, 9/96, $2.95) Delgado-c/a/scripts in all; wraparound-c 3.00
... The Journey 1-4 (11/09 - No. 4, 7/10 $3.50) Delgado-c/a/scripts in all; wraparound-c 3.50

AGE OF THE SENTRY, THE
Marvel Comics: Nov, 2008 - No. 6, Mar, 2010 ($2.99, limited series)

1-6-Silver Age style stories. 1-Origin retold; Bullock-c. 3-Coover-a 3.00

AGE OF X (X-Men titles crossover)
Marvel Comics: ($3.99, limited series)

... Alpha 1 (3/11, $3.99) Short stories by various; covers by Bachalo & Coipel 4.00
...: Universe 1,2 (5/11 - No. 2, 6/11, $3.99) Pham-a; Bianchi-c; Avengers & Spider-Man app. 4.00

AGGIE MACK
Four Star Comics Corp./Superior Comics Ltd.: Jan, 1948 - No. 8, Aug, 1949

	GD 2.0	VG 4.0	FN 6.0	VF 8.0	VF/NM 9.0	NM- 9.2
1-Feldstein-a, "Johnny Prep"	41	82	123	256	428	600
2,3-Kamen-c	23	46	69	136	223	310
4-Feldstein "Johnny Prep"; Kamen-c	31	62	93	182	296	410
5-8-Kamen-c/a	25	50	75	150	245	340

AGGIE MACK
Dell Publishing Co.: Apr - Jun, 1962

	GD 2.0	VG 4.0	FN 6.0	VF 8.0	VF/NM 9.0	NM- 9.2
Four Color #1335	5	10	15	30	48	65

AIR
DC Comics (Vertigo): Oct, 2008 - No. 24, Oct, 2010 ($2.99)

1-6,8-24-G. Willow Wilson-s/M.K. Perker-a 3.00
7-($1.00) Includes story re-cap 3.00
... A History of the Future TPB (2011, $14.99) r/#18-24 15.00
... Flying Machine TPB (2009, $12.99) r/#6-10; Wilson intro. 13.00
... Letters From Lost Countries TPB (2009, $9.99) r/#1-5; character sketch pages 10.00
... Pure Land TPB (2010, $14.99) r/#11-17 15.00

AIR ACE (Formerly Bill Barnes No. 1-12)
Street & Smith Publications: V2#1, Jan, 1944 - V3#8(No. 20), Feb-Mar, 1947

	GD 2.0	VG 4.0	FN 6.0	VF 8.0	VF/NM 9.0	NM- 9.2
V2#1-Nazi concentration camp-c	47	94	141	296	498	700
V2#2-Classic WWII-c	90	180	270	576	988	1400
V2#3-12: 7-Powell-a	16	32	48	94	147	200
V3#1-6: 2-Atomic explosion on-c	14	28	42	80	115	150
V3#7-Powell bondage-c/a; all atomic issue	23	46	69	136	223	310
V3#8 (V5#8 on-c)-Powell-c/a	15	30	45	84	127	170

AIRBOY (Also see Airmaidens, Skywolf, Target: Airboy & Valkyrie)
Eclipse Comics: July, 1986 - No. 50, Oct, 1989 (#1-8, 50¢, 20 pgs., bi-weekly; #9-on, 36 pgs.; #34-on monthly)

1-4: 2-1st Marisa; Skywolf gets new costume. 3-The Heap begins 4.00

	GD 2.0	VG 4.0	FN 6.0	VF 8.0	VF/NM 9.0	NM- 9.2
5-Valkyrie returns; Dave Stevens-c	1	2	3	5	6	8

6-49: 9-Begin $1.25-c; Skywolf begins. 11-Origin of G.A. Airboy & his plane Birdie. 28-Mr. Monster vs. The Heap. 33-Begin $1.75-c. 38-40-The Heap by Infantino. 41-r/1st app. Valkyrie from Air Fighters. 42-Begin $1.95-c. 46,47-part-r/Air Fighters. 48-Black Angel-r/A.F 3.00
50 ($4.95, 52 pgs.)-Kubert-c 5.00
NOTE: *Evans* c-21. *Gulacy* c-7, 20. *Spiegle* a-34, 35, 37. *Ken Steacy* painted c-17, 33.

AIRBOY COMICS (Air Fighters Comics No. 1-22)
Hillman Periodicals: V2#11, Dec, 1945 - V10#4, May, 1953 (No V3#3)

	GD 2.0	VG 4.0	FN 6.0	VF 8.0	VF/NM 9.0	NM- 9.2
V2#11	61	122	183	390	670	950
12-Valkyrie-c/app.	52	104	156	323	549	775
V3#1,2(no #3)	40	80	120	246	411	575
4-The Heap app. in Skywolf	37	74	111	222	361	500
5,7,8,10,11	33	66	99	194	317	440
6-Valkyrie-c/app.	36	72	108	216	351	485
9-Origin The Heap	37	74	111	222	361	500
12-Skywolf & Airboy x-over; Valkyrie-c/app.	39	78	117	240	395	550
V4#1-Iron Lady app.	33	66	99	194	317	440
2,3,12: 2-Rackman begins	25	50	75	147	241	335
4-Simon & Kirby-c	30	60	90	177	289	400
5-9,11-All S&K-a	28	56	84	165	270	375
10-Valkyrie-c/app.	31	62	93	182	296	410
V5#1-4,6-11: 4-Infantino Heap. 10-Origin The Heap	19	38	57	112	179	245
5-Skull-c.	21	42	63	126	206	285
12-Krigstein-a(p)	20	40	60	115	185	255
V6#1-3,5-12: 6,8-Origin The Heap	18	36	54	107	169	230
4-Origin retold	21	42	63	126	206	285
V7#1-12: 7,8,10-Origin The Heap	18	36	54	105	165	225
V8#1-3,5-12	16	32	48	96	151	205
4-Krigstein-a	17	34	51	100	158	215
V9#1,3,4,6-12: 7-One pg. Frazetta ad	15	30	45	84	127	170
2-Valkyrie app.	15	30	45	88	137	185
5(#100)	15	30	45	88	137	185
V10#1-4	14	28	42	81	118	155

NOTE: *Barry* a-V2#3, 7. *Bolle* a-V4#12. *McWilliams* a-V3#7, 9. *Powell* a-V7#2, 3, V8#1, 6. *Starr* a-V5#1, 12. *Dick Wood* a-V4#12. Bondage-c V5#8.

AIRBOY MEETS THE PROWLER
Eclipse Comics: Aug, 1987 ($1.95, one-shot)

1-John Snyder, III-c/a 3.00

AIRBOY-MR. MONSTER SPECIAL
Eclipse Comics: Aug, 1987 ($1.75, one-shot)

1 3.00

AIRBOY VERSUS THE AIR MAIDENS
Eclipse Comics: July, 1988 ($1.95)

1 3.00

AIR FIGHTERS CLASSICS
Eclipse Comics: Nov, 1987 - No. 6, May, 1989 ($3.95, 68 pgs., B&W)

Air Fighters Comics V2 #2 © HILL

Akiko #50 © Mark Crilley

Alarming Tales #2 © HARV

	GD 2.0	VG 4.0	FN 6.0	VF 8.0	VF/NM 9.0	NM- 9.2
1-6: Reprints G.A. Air Fighters #2-7. 1-Origin Airboy						4.00

AIR FIGHTERS COMICS (Airboy Comics #23 (V2#11) on)
Hillman Periodicals: Nov, 1941; No. 2, Nov, 1942 - V2#10; Fall, 1945

	GD 2.0	VG 4.0	FN 6.0	VF 8.0	VF/NM 9.0	NM- 9.2
V1#1-(Produced by Funnies, Inc.); No Airboy; Black Commander only app.	226	452	678	1446	2473	3500
2(11/42)-(Produced by Quality artists & Biro for Hillman); Origin & 1st app. Airboy & Iron Ace; Black Angel (1st app.), Flying Dutchman & Skywolf (1st app.) begin; Fuje-a; Biro-c/a	459	918	1377	3350	5925	8500
3-Origin/1st app. The Heap; origin Skywolf; 2nd Airboy app./c	200	400	600	1280	2190	3100
4-Japan war-c	168	336	504	1075	1838	2600
5-Japanese octopus War-c	142	284	426	909	1555	2200
6-Japanese soldiers as rats-c	174	348	522	1114	1907	2700
7-Classic Nazi swastika-c	168	336	504	1075	1838	2600
8-12: 8,10,11-War covers	87	174	261	553	952	1350
V2#1-Classic Nazi War-c	94	188	282	597	1024	1450
2-Skywolf by Giunta; Flying Dutchman by Fuje; 1st meeting Valkyrie & Airboy (she worked for the Nazis in beginning); 1st app. Valkyrie (11/43); Valkyrie-c	129	258	387	826	1413	2000
3,4,6,8,9	60	120	180	381	658	935
5,7: 5-Flag-c; Fuje-a. 7-Valkyrie app.	64	128	192	406	696	985
10-Origin The Heap & Skywolf	69	138	207	442	759	1075

NOTE: ***Fuje** a-V1#2, 5, 7, V2#2, 3, 5, 7-9. **Giunta** a-V2#2, 3, 7, 9.*

AIRFIGHTERS MEET SGT. STRIKE SPECIAL, THE
Eclipse Comics: Jan, 1988 ($1.95, one-shot, stiff-c)

	GD 2.0	VG 4.0	FN 6.0	VF 8.0	VF/NM 9.0	NM- 9.2
1-Airboy, Valkyrie, Skywolf app.						3.00

AIR FORCES (See American Air Forces)

AIRMAIDENS SPECIAL
Eclipse Comics: August, 1987 ($1.75, one-shot, Baxter paper)

	GD 2.0	VG 4.0	FN 6.0	VF 8.0	VF/NM 9.0	NM- 9.2
1-Marisa becomes La Lupina (origin)						3.00

AIR RAIDERS
Marvel Comics (Star Comics)/Marvel #3 on: Nov, 1987- No. 5, Mar, 1988 ($1.00)

	GD 2.0	VG 4.0	FN 6.0	VF 8.0	VF/NM 9.0	NM- 9.2
1,5: Kelley Jones-a in all						4.00
2-4: 2-Thunderhammer app.						3.00

AIRTIGHT GARAGE, THE (Also see Elsewhere Prince)
Marvel Comics (Epic Comics): July, 1993 - No. 4, Oct, 1993 ($2.50, lim. series, Baxter paper)

	GD 2.0	VG 4.0	FN 6.0	VF 8.0	VF/NM 9.0	NM- 9.2
1-4: Moebius-c/a/scripts						5.00

AIR WAR STORIES
Dell Publishing Co.: Sept-Nov, 1964 - No. 8, Aug, 1966

	GD 2.0	VG 4.0	FN 6.0	VF 8.0	VF/NM 9.0	NM- 9.2
1-Painted-c; Glanzman-c/a begins	4	8	12	28	44	60
2-8: 2,3-Painted-c	3	6	9	18	27	35

A.K.A. GOLDFISH
Caliber Comics: 1994 - 1995 (B&W, $3.50/$3.95)

	GD 2.0	VG 4.0	FN 6.0	VF 8.0	VF/NM 9.0	NM- 9.2
...:Ace; ...:Jack; ...:Queen; ...:Joker; ...:King -Brian Michael Bendis-s/a						4.00
TPB (1996, $17.95)						20.00
Goldfish: The Definitive Collection (Image, 2001, $19.95) r/series plus promo art and new prose story; intro. by Matt Wagner						20.00
10th Anniversary HC (Image, 2002, $49.95)						50.00

AKIKO
Sirius: Mar, 1996 - No. 52, Feb, 2004 ($2.50/$2.95, B&W)

	GD 2.0	VG 4.0	FN 6.0	VF 8.0	VF/NM 9.0	NM- 9.2
1-Crilley-c/a/scripts in all						5.00
2						4.00
3-39: 25-($2.95, 32 pgs.)-w/Asala back-up pages						3.00
40-49,51,52: 40-Begin $2.95-c						3.00
50-($3.50)						3.50
Flights of Fancy TPB (5/02, $12.95) r/various features, pin-ups and gags						13.00
TPB Volume 1,4 ('97, 2/00, $14.95) 1-r/#1-7. 4-r/#19-25						15.00
TPB Volume 2,3 ('98, '99, $11.95) 2-r/#8-13. 3- r/#14-18						12.00
TPB Volume 5 (12/01, $12.95) r/#26-31						13.00
TPB Volume 6,7 (6/03, 4/04, $14.95) 6-r/#32-38. 7-r/#40-47						15.00

AKIKO ON THE PLANET SMOO
Sirius: Dec, 1995 ($3.95, B&W)

	GD 2.0	VG 4.0	FN 6.0	VF 8.0	VF/NM 9.0	NM- 9.2
V1#1-($3.95)-Crilley-c/a/scripts; gatefold-c						5.00
Ashcan ('95, mail offer)						3.00
Hardcover V1#1 (12/95, $19.95, B&W, 40 pgs.)						20.00
The Color Edition(2/00,$4.95)						5.00

AKIRA
Marvel Comics (Epic): Sept, 1988 - No. 38, Dec, 1995 ($3.50/$3.95/$6.95, deluxe, 68 pgs.)

	GD 2.0	VG 4.0	FN 6.0	VF 8.0	VF/NM 9.0	NM- 9.2
1-Manga by Katsuhiro Otomo	3	6	9	16	23	30
1,2-2nd printings (1989, $3.95)						5.00
2	2	4	6	9	12	15
3-5	2	4	6	8	10	12
6-16	1	2	3	5	7	9
17-33: 17-$3.95-c begins						6.00
34-37: 34-(1994)-$6.95-c begins. 35-37: 35-(1995). 37-Texeira back-up, Gibbons, Williams pin-ups	2	4	6	8	10	12
38-Moebius, Allred, Pratt, Toth, Romita, Van Fleet, O'Neill, Madureira pin-ups	2	4	6	8	11	14

ALADDIN & HIS WONDERFUL LAMP (See Dell Jr Treasury #2)

ALAN LADD (See The Adventures of...)

ALAN MOORE'S AWESOME UNIVERSE HANDBOOK (Also see Across the Universe:...)
Awesome Entertainment: Apr, 1999 ($2.95, B&W)

	GD 2.0	VG 4.0	FN 6.0	VF 8.0	VF/NM 9.0	NM- 9.2
1-Alan Moore-text/ Alex Ross-sketch pages and 2 covers						5.00

ALAN MOORE...
DC Comics (WildStorm): TPB

	GD 2.0	VG 4.0	FN 6.0	VF 8.0	VF/NM 9.0	NM- 9.2
...'s Complete WildC.A.T.S. (2007, $29.99) r/#21-34,50; ...Homecoming & ...Gang War						30.00
...: Wild Worlds (2007, $24.99) r/various WildStorm one-shots and limited series						25.00

ALARMING ADVENTURES
Harvey Publications: Oct, 1962 - No. 3, Feb, 1963

	GD 2.0	VG 4.0	FN 6.0	VF 8.0	VF/NM 9.0	NM- 9.2
1-Crandall/Williamson-a	9	18	27	58	99	140
2-Williamson/Crandall-a	5	10	15	35	55	75
3-Torres-a	5	10	15	30	48	65

NOTE: ***Bailey** a-1, 3. **Crandall** a-1p, 2i. **Powell** a-2(2). **Severin** c-1-3. **Torres** a-2? **Tuska** a-1. **Williamson** a-1i, 2p.*

ALARMING TALES
Harvey Publications (Western Tales): Sept, 1957 - No. 6, Nov, 1958

	GD 2.0	VG 4.0	FN 6.0	VF 8.0	VF/NM 9.0	NM- 9.2
1-Kirby-c/a(4); Kamandi prototype story by Kirby	30	60	90	177	289	400
2-Kirby-a(4)	20	40	60	118	192	265
3,4-Kirby-a. 4-Powell, Wildey-a	16	32	48	94	147	200
5-Kirby/Williamson-a; Wildey-a; Severin-c	17	34	51	100	158	215
6-Williamson-a?; Severin-c	14	28	42	80	115	150

ALBEDO
Thoughts And Images: Apr, 1985 - No. 14, Spring, 1989 (B&W)
Antarctic Press: (Vol. 2) Jun, 1991 - No. 10 ($2.50)

	GD 2.0	VG 4.0	FN 6.0	VF 8.0	VF/NM 9.0	NM- 9.2
0-Yellow cover; 50 copies	13	26	39	90	195	300
0-White cover, 450 copies	8	16	24	53	89	125
0-Blue, 1st printing, 500 copies	7	14	21	48	79	110
0-Blue, 2nd printing, 1000 copies	4	8	12	26	41	55
0-3rd & 4th printing	3	6	9	14	19	24
1-Dark red - low print run	9	18	27	61	106	150
1-Bright red - low print run	6	12	18	39	62	85
2 -1st app. Usagi Yojimbo by Stan Sakai; 2000 copies - no 2nd printing	33	66	99	239	520	800
3	3	6	9	20	30	40
4-Usagi Yojimbo-c	4	8	12	26	41	55
5-14	1	2	3	5	7	9
(Vol. 2) 1-10, Color Special						4.00

ALBEDO ANTHROPOMORPHICS
Antarctic Press: (Vol. 3) Spring, 1994 - No. 4, Jan, 1996 ($2.95, color);
(Vol. 4) Dec, 1999 - No. 2, Jan, 1999 ($2.95/$2.99, B&W)

	GD 2.0	VG 4.0	FN 6.0	VF 8.0	VF/NM 9.0	NM- 9.2
V3#1-4-Steve Gallacci-c/a. V4#1,2						3.00

ALBERTO (See The Crusaders)

ALBERT THE ALLIGATOR & POGO POSSUM (See Pogo Possum)

ALBION (Inspired by 1960s IPC British comics characters)
DC Comics (WildStorm): Aug, 2005 - No. 6, Nov, 2006 ($2.99, limited series)

	GD 2.0	VG 4.0	FN 6.0	VF 8.0	VF/NM 9.0	NM- 9.2
1-6-Alan Moore, Leah Moore & John Reppion-s/Shane Oakley-a; Dave Gibbons-c						3.00
TPB (2007, $19.99) r/series; intro by Neil Gaiman; reprints from 1960s British comics						20.00

ALBUM OF CRIME (See Fox Giants)

ALBUM OF LOVE (See Fox Giants)

AL CAPP'S DOGPATCH (Also see Mammy Yokum)
Toby Press: No. 71, June, 1949 - No. 4, Dec, 1949

	GD 2.0	VG 4.0	FN 6.0	VF 8.0	VF/NM 9.0	NM- 9.2
71(#1)-Reprints from Tip Top #112-114	15	30	45	83	124	165
2-4: 4-Reprints from Li'l Abner #73	11	22	33	62	86	110

AL CAPP'S SHMOO (Also see Oxydol-Dreft & Washable Jones & Shmoo)
Toby Press: July, 1949 - No. 5, Apr, 1950 (None by Al Capp)

Alias #9 © MAR

Alien Legion #18 © MAR

Alien Resurrection #1 © 20th Cent. Fox

	GD 2.0	VG 4.0	FN 6.0	VF 8.0	VF/NM 9.0	NM- 9.2
1-1st app. Super-Shmoo	28	56	84	165	270	375
2-5: 3-Sci-fi trip to moon. 4-X-Mas-c	20	40	60	114	182	250
AL CAPP'S WOLF GAL						
Toby Press: 1951 - No. 2, 1952						
1,2-Edited-r from Li'l Abner #63,64	17	34	51	98	154	210
ALEISTER ARCANE						
IDW Publishing: Apr, 2004 - No. 3, June, 2004 ($3.99, limited series)						
1-3-Steve Niles-s/Breehn Burns-a						4.00
TPB (10/04, $17.99) r/series; sketch pages						18.00
ALEXANDER THE GREAT (Movie)						
Dell Publishing Co.: No. 688, May, 1956						
Four Color 688-Buscema-a; photo-c	7	14	21	48	79	110
ALF (TV) (See Star Comics Digest)						
Marvel Comics: Mar, 1988 - No. 50, Feb, 1992 ($1.00)						
1-Photo-c						5.00
1-2nd printing						3.00
2-19: 6-Photo-c						3.00
20-22: 20-Conan parody. 21-Marx Brothers. 22-X-Men parody						3.50
23-30: 24-Rhonda-c/app. 29-3-D cover						3.00
31-43,46,47,49:						3.00
44,45: 44-X-Men parody. 45-Wolverine, Punisher, Capt. America-c						4.00
48-(12/91) Risqué Alf with seal cover	2	4	6	8	10	12
50-($1.75, 52 pgs.)-Final issue; photo-c						4.00
Annual 1-3: 1-Rocky & Bullwinkle app. 2-Sienkiewicz-c. 3-TMNT parody						4.00
...Comics Digest 1,2: 1-(1988)-Reprints Alf #1,2	1	3	4	6	8	10
Holiday Special 1,2 ('88, Wint. '89, 68 pgs.): 2-X-Men parody-c						4.00
Spring Special 1 (Spr/89, $1.75, 68 pgs.) Invisible Man parody						4.00
TPB (68 pgs.) r/#1-3; photo-c						5.00
ALFRED HARVEY'S BLACK CAT						
Lorne-Harvey Productions: 1995 ($3.50, B&W/color)						
1-Origin by Mark Evanier & Murphy Anderson; contains history of Alfred Harvey & Harvey Publications; 5 pg. B&W Sad Sack story; Hildebrandts-c						6.00
ALGIE (LITTLE...)						
Timor Publ. Co.: Dec, 1953 - No. 3, 1954						
1-Teenage	8	16	24	40	50	60
1-Algie #1 cover w/Secret Mysteries #19 inside	9	18	27	50	65	80
2,3	5	10	15	24	30	35
Accepted Reprint #2(nd)	3	6	8	12	14	16
Super Reprint #15	2	4	6	8	11	14
ALIAS:						
Now Comics: July, 1990 - No. 5, Nov, 1990 ($1.75)						
1-5: 1-Sienkiewicz-c						3.00
ALIAS (Also see Jessica Jones apps. in New Avengers and The Pulse)						
Marvel Comics (MAX Comics): Nov, 2001 - No. 28, Jan, 2004 ($2.99)						
1-Bendis-s/Gaydos-a/Mack-c; intro Jessica Jones; Luke Cage app.	1	2	3	5	6	8
2-4						5.00
5-28: 7,8-Sienkiewicz-a (2 pgs.) 16-21-Spider-Woman app. 22,23-Jessica's origin. 24-28-Purple; Avengers app.; flashback-a by Bagley						3.00
... MGC 1 (6/10, $1.00) r/#1 with "Marvel's Greatest Comics" logo on cover						3.00
HC (2002, $29.99) r/#1-9; intro. by Jeph Loeb						30.00
Omnibus (2006, $69.99, hardcover with dustjacket) r/#1-28 and What If Jessica Jones Had Joined the Avengers?; original pitch, script and sketch pages						70.00
Vol. 1: TPB (2003, $19.99) r/#1-9						20.00
Vol. 2: Come Home TPB (2003, $13.99) r/#11-15						14.00
Vol. 3: The Underneath TPB (2003, $16.99) r/#10,16-21						17.00
ALICE (New Adventures in Wonderland)						
Ziff-Davis Publ. Co.: No. 10, 7-8/51 - No. 11(#2), 11-12/51						
10-Painted-c; Berg-a	26	52	78	154	252	350
11-(#2 on inside) Dave Berg-a	16	32	48	94	147	200
ALICE AT MONKEY ISLAND (See The Adventures of Alice)						
Pentagon Publ. Co. (Civil Service): No. 3, 1946						
3	10	20	30	54	72	90
ALICE IN WONDERLAND (Disney; see Advs. of Alice, Dell Jr. Treasury #1, The Dreamery, Movie Comics, Walt Disney Showcase #22, and World's Greatest Stories)						
Dell Publishing Co.: No. 24, 1940; No. 331, 1951; No. 341, July, 1951						
Single Series 24 (#1)(1940)	49	98	147	309	522	735

	GD 2.0	VG 4.0	FN 6.0	VF 8.0	VF/NM 9.0	NM- 9.2
Four Color 331, 341-"Unbirthday Party w/..."	13	26	39	88	189	290
1-(Whitman, 3/84, pre-pack only)-r/4-Color #331	2	4	6	11	16	20
ALIEN ENCOUNTERS (Replaces Alien Worlds)						
Eclipse Comics: June, 1985 - No. 14, Aug, 1987 ($1.75, Baxter paper, mature)						
1-10: Nudity, strong language in all. 9-Snyder-a						4.00
11-14-Low print run						5.00
ALIEN LEGION (See Epic & Marvel Graphic Novel #25)						
Marvel Comics (Epic Comics): Apr, 1984 - No. 20, Sept, 1987						
nn-With bound-in trading card; Austin-i						4.00
2-20: 2-$1.50-c. 7,8-Portacio-i						3.00
ALIEN LEGION (2nd Series)						
Marvel Comics (Epic): Aug, 1987(indicia)(10/87 on-c) - No. 18, Aug, 1990						
V2#1-18-Stroman-a in all. 7-18-Farmer-i						3.00
...: Force Nomad TPB (Checker Book Pub. Group, 2001, $24.95) r/#1-11						25.00
...: Piecemaker TPB (Checker Book Pub. Group, 2002, $19.95) r/#12-18						20.00
ALIEN LEGION: (Series of titles; all Marvel/Epic Comics)						
--BINARY DEEP, 1993 ($3.50, one-shot, 52 pgs.), nn-With bound-in trading card						4.00
--JUGGER GRIMROD, 8/92 ($5.95, one-shot, 52 pgs.) Book 1						6.00
--ONE PLANET AT A TIME, 5/93 - Book 3, 7/93 ($4.95, squarebound, 52 pgs.)						
Book 1-3: Hoang Nguyen-a						5.00
--ON THE EDGE (The... #2 & 3), 11/90 - No. 3, 1/91 ($4.50, 52 pgs.)						
1-3-Stroman & Farmer-a						4.50
--TENANTS OF HELL, '91 - No. 2, '91 ($4.50, squarebound, 52 pgs.)						
Book 1,2-Stroman-c/a(p)						4.50
ALIEN NATION (Movie)						
DC Comics: Dec, 1988 ($2.50; 68 pgs.)						
1-Adaptation of film; painted-c						4.00
ALIEN PIG FARM 3000						
Image Comics (RAW Studios): Apr, 2007 - No. 4, July, 2007 ($2.99, limited series)						
1-4-Steve Niles, Thomas Jane & Todd Farmer-s/Don Marquez-a						3.00
ALIEN RESURRECTION (Movie)						
Dark Horse Comics: Oct, 1997 - No. 2, Nov, 1997 ($2.50; limited series)						
1,2-Adaptation of film; Dave McKean-c						3.00
ALIENS, THE (Captain Johner and...)(Also see Magnus Robot Fighter...)						
Gold Key: Sept-Dec, 1967; No. 2, May, 1982						
1-Reprints from Magnus #1,3,4,6-10; Russ Manning-a in all	3	6	9	20	30	40
2-(Whitman) Same contents as #1	1	2	3	5	6	8
ALIENS (Movie) (See Alien: The Illustrated..., Dark Horse Comics & Dark Horse Presents #24)						
Dark Horse Comics: May, 1988 - No. 6, July, 1989 ($1.95, B&W, limited series)						
1-Based on movie sequel; 1st app. Aliens in comics	3	6	9	14	20	26
1-2nd - 6th printings; 4th w/new inside front-c						3.00
2	2	4	6	8	10	12
2-2nd & 3rd printing, 3-6-2nd printings						3.00
3	1	2	3	5	7	9
4-6						5.00
Mini Comic #1 (2/89, 4x6")-Was included with Aliens Portfolio						4.00
Collection 1 ($10.95,)-r/#1-6 plus Dark Horse Presents #24 plus new-a						12.00
Collection 1-2nd printing (1991, $11.95)-On higher quality paper than 1st print; Dorman painted-c						12.00
Hardcover ('90, $24.95, B&W)-r/1-6, DHP #24						30.00
... Omnibus Vol. 1 (7/07, $24.95, 9x6") r/1st & 2nd series and Aliens: Earth War						25.00
... Omnibus Vol. 2 (12/07, $24.95, 9x6") r/Genocide, Harvest and Colonial Marines series						25.00
... Omnibus Vol. 3 (3/08, $24.95, 9x6") r/Rogue, Salvation and Sacrifice, Labyrinth series						25.00
... Omnibus Vol. 4 (8/08, $24.95, 9x6") r/Music of the Spears, Stronghold, Berserker, Mondo Pest and Mondo Heat series and one-shots						25.00
... Omnibus Vol. 5 (11/08, $24.95, 9x6") r/Alchemy, Survival, Havoc series and various						25.00
... Omnibus Vol. 6 (2/09, $24.95, 9x6") r/Apocalypse GN, Xenogenesis & one-shots						25.00
... Outbreak (3rd printing, 8/96, $17.95)-Bolton-c						18.00
Platinum Edition - (See Dark Horse Presents: Aliens Platinum Edition)						-
ALIENS						
Dark Horse Comics: V2#1, Aug, 1989 - No. 4, 1990 ($2.25, limited series)						
V2#1-Painted art by Denis Beauvais						5.00
1-2nd printing (1990), 2-4						3.00
...: Nightmare Asylum TPB (12/96, $16.95) r/series; Bolton-c						17.00
ALIENS						

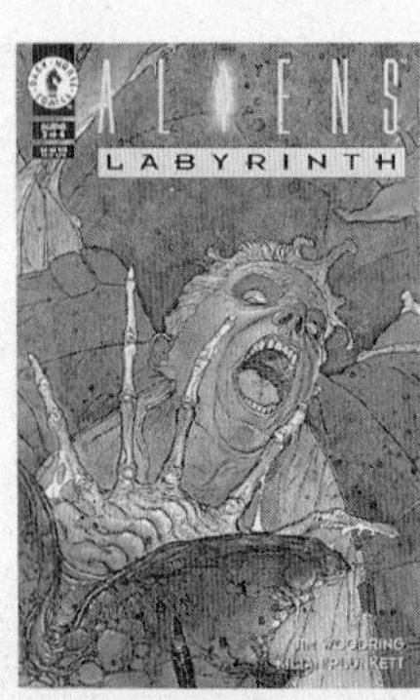

Aliens: Labyrinth #3 © 20th Cent. Fox

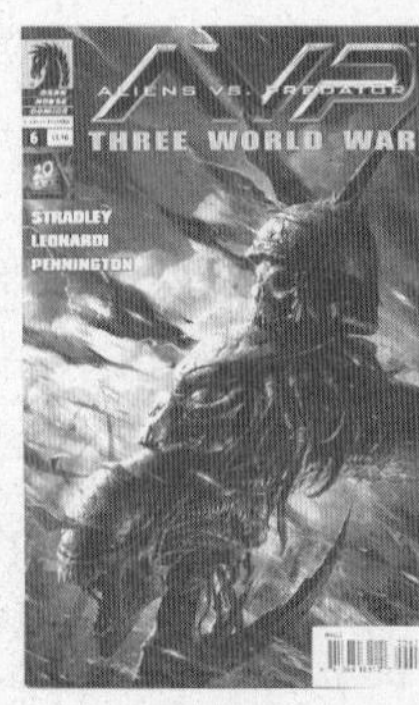

Alien vs. Predator: Three World War #6 © 20th Cent. Fox

All-American Comics #27 © DC

GD 2.0 | VG 4.0 | FN 6.0 | VF 8.0 | VF/NM 9.0 | NM- 9.2

Dark Horse Comics: May, 2009 - No. 4, Nov, 2009 ($3.50, limited series)
1-4-John Arcudi-s/Zach Howard-a. 1,2-Howard-c. 3,4-Swanland-c 3.50

ALIENS: (Series of titles, all Dark Horse)
--ALCHEMY, 10/97 - No. 3, 11/97 ($2.95),1-3-Corben-c/a, Arcudi-s 3.00
--APOCALYPSE - THE DESTROYING ANGELS, 1/99 - No. 4, 4/99 ($2.95)
1-4-Doug Wheatly-a/Schultz-s 3.00
--BERSERKERS, 1/95 - No. 4, 4/95 ($2.50) 1-4 3.00
--COLONIAL MARINES, 1/93 - No. 10, 7/94 ($2.50) 1-10 3.00
--EARTH ANGEL. 8/94 ($2.95) 1-Byrne-a/story; wraparound-c 3.00
--EARTH WAR, 6/90 - No. 4, 10/90 ($2.50) 1-All have Sam Kieth-a & Bolton painted-c 5.00
1-2nd printing, 3,4 3.00
2 4.00
--GENOCIDE, 11/91 - No. 4, 2/92 ($2.50) 1-4-Suydam painted-c. 4-Wraparound-c, poster 3.00
--GLASS CORRIDOR, 6/98 ($2.95) 1-David Lloyd-s/a 3.00
--HARVEST (See Aliens: Hive)
--HAVOC, 6/97 - No. 2, 7/97 ($2.95) 1,2: Schultz-s, Kent Williams-c, 40 artists including Art Adams, Kelley Jones, Duncan Fegredo, Kevin Nowlan 3.00
--HIVE, 2/92 - No. 4,5/92 ($2.50) 1-4: Kelley Jones-c/a in all 3.00
...Harvest TPB ('98, $16.95) r/series; Bolton-c 17.00
--KIDNAPPED, 12/97 - No. 3, 2/98 ($2.50) 1-3 3.00
--LABYRINTH, 9/93 - No. 4, 1/94 ($2.50)1-4: 1-Painted-c 3.00
--LOVESICK, 12/96 ($2.95) 1 3.00
--MONDO HEAT, 2/96 ($2.50) nn-Sequel to Mondo Pest 3.00
--MONDO PEST, 4/95 ($2.95, 44 pgs.)nn-r/Dark Horse Comics #22-24 3.00
--MUSIC OF THE SPEARS, 1/94 - No. 4, 4/94 ($2.50) 1-4 3.00
--NEWT'S TALE, 6/92 - No. 2, 7/92 ($4.95) 1,2-Bolton-c 5.00
--PIG, 3/97 ($2.95)1 3.00
--PREDATOR: THE DEADLIEST OF THE SPECIES, 7/93 - No. 12,8/95 ($2.50)
1-Bolton painted-c; Guice-a(p) 5.00
1-Embossed foil platinum edition 10.00
2-12: Bolton painted-c. 2,3-Guice-a(p) 3.00
--PURGE, 8/97 ($2.95) nn-Hester-a 3.00
--ROGUE, 4/93 - No. 4, 7/93 ($2.50)1-4: Painted-c 3.00
--SACRIFICE, 5/93 ($4.95, 52 pgs.) nn-P. Milligan scripts; painted-c/a 5.00
--SALVATION, 11/93 ($4.95, 52 pgs.) nn-Mignola-c/a(p); Gibbons script 5.00
--SPECIAL, 6/97 ($2.50) 1 3.00
--STALKER, 6/98 ($2.50)1-David Wenzel-s/a 3.00
--STRONGHOLD, 5/94 - No. 4, 9/94 ($2.50) 1-4 3.00
--SURVIVAL, 2/98 - No. 3, 4/98 ($2.95) 1-3-Tony Harris-c 3.00
--TRIBES, 1992 ($24.95, hardcover graphic novel) Bissette text-s with Dorman painted-a 25.00
...softcover ($9.95) 10.00

ALIENS VS. PREDATOR (See Dark Horse Presents #36)
Dark Horse Comics: June, 1990 - No. 4, Dec, 1990 ($2.50, limited series)
1-Painted-c 1 2 3 5 6 8
1-2nd printing 3.00
0-(7/90, $1.95, B&W)-r/Dark Horse Pres. #34-36 1 2 3 5 7 9
2,3 5.00
4-Dave Dorman painted-c 4.00
Annual (7/99, $4.95) Jae Lee-c 5.00
... : Booty (1/96, $2.50) painted-c 3.00
... Omnibus Vol. 1 (5/07, $24.95, 9x6") r/#1-4 & Annual; ...: War; ...: Eternal 25.00
... Omnibus Vol. 2 (10/07, $24.95, 9x6") r/...: Xenogenesis #1-4; ...: Deadliest of the Species; ...: Booty and stories from ... Annual 25.00
...: One For One (8/10, $1.00) r/#1 with red cover frame 3.00
... : Thrill of the Hunt (9/04, $6.95, digest-size TPB) Based on 2004 movie 7.00
... Wraith 1 (7/98, $2.95) Jay Stephens-s 3.00
--VS. PREDATOR: DUEL, 3/95 - No. 2, 4/95 ($2.50) 1,2 3.00
--VS. PREDATOR: ETERNAL, 6/98 - No. 4, 9/98 ($2.50)1-4: Edginton-s/Maleev-a; Fabry-c 3.00
--VS. PREDATOR: THREE WORLD WAR, 1/10 - No. 6, 9/10 ($3.50) 1-6-Leonardi-a 3.50
--VS. PREDATOR VS. THE TERMINATOR, 4/00 - No. 4, 7/00 ($2.95) 1-4: Ripley app. 3.00
--VS. PREDATOR: WAR, No. 0, 5/95 - No. 4, 8/95 ($2.50) 0-4: Corben painted-c 3.00
--VS. PREDATOR: XENOGENESIS, 12/99 - No. 4, 3/00 ($2.95) 1-4: Watson-s/Mel Rubi-a 3.00
--XENOGENESIS, 8/99 - No. 4, 11/99 ($2.95) 1-4: T&M Bierbaum-s 3.00

ALIEN TERROR (See 3-D Alien Terror)

ALIEN: THE ILLUSTRATED STORY (Also see Aliens)
Heavy Metal Books: 1980 ($3.95, soft-c, 8x11")
nn-Movie adaptation; Simonson-a 3 6 9 14 19 24

ALIEN^3 (Movie)
Dark Horse Comics: June, 1992 - No. 3, July, 1992 ($2.50, limited series)
1-3: Adapts 3rd movie; Suydam painted-c 3.00

ALIEN WORLDS (Also see Eclipse Graphic Album #22)
Pacific Comics/Eclipse: Dec, 1982 - No. 9, Jan, 1985
1,2,4: 2,4-Dave Stevens-c/a 6.00
3,5-7 4.00
8,9 1 2 3 4 5 7
3-D No. 1-Art Adams 1st published art 1 2 3 4 5 7

ALISON DARE, LITTLE MISS ADVENTURES (Also see Return of ...)
Oni Press: Sept, 2000 ($4.50, B&W, one-shot)
1-J. Torres-s/J.Bone-c/a 4.50

ALISON DARE & THE HEART OF THE MAIDEN
Oni Press: Jan, 2002 - No. 2, Feb, 2002 ($2.95, B&W, limited series)
1,2-J. Torres-s/J.Bone-c/a 3.00

ALISTER THE SLAYER
Midnight Press: Oct, 1995 ($2.50)
1-Boris-c 3.00

ALL-AMERICAN COMICS (...Western #103-126, ...Men of War #127 on; also see The Big All-American Comic Book)
All-American/National Periodical Publ.: April, 1939 - No. 102, Oct, 1948
1-Hop Harrigan (1st app.), Scribbly by Mayer (1st DC app.), Toonerville Folks, Ben Webster, Spot Savage, Mutt & Jeff, Red White & Blue (1st app.), Adventures in the Unknown, Tippie, Reg'lar Fellers, Skippy, Bobby Thatcher, Mystery Men of Mars, Daiseybelle, Wiley of West Point begin 575 1150 1725 4000 6500 9000
2-Ripley's Believe It or Not begins, ends #24 171 342 513 1086 1868 2650
3-5: 5-The American Way begins, ends #10 139 278 417 883 1517 2150
6,7: 6-Last Spot Savage; Popsicle Pete begins, ends #26, 28. 7-Last Bobby Thatcher 113 226 339 718 1234 1750
8-The Ultra Man begins & 1st-c app. 314 628 942 2198 3849 5500
9,10: 10-X-Mas-c 100 200 300 635 1093 1550
11,15: 11-Ultra Man-c. 15-Last Tippie & Reg'lar Fellars; Ultra Man-c 129 258 387 826 1413 2000
12-14: 12-Last Toonerville Folks 97 194 291 621 1061 1500
16-(Rare)-Origin/1st app. Green Lantern by Sheldon Moldoff (c/a)(7/40) & begin series; appears in costume on-c & only one panel inside; created by Martin Nodell. Inspired in 1940 by a switchman's green lantern that would give trains the go ahead to proceed. G.L. cover pose swiped from last panel of a Jan, 1939 Flash Gordon Sunday page. 18,333 36,667 55,000 140,000 310,000 480,000
17-2nd Green Lantern 1200 2400 3600 90000 17,000 25,000
18-N.Y. World's Fair-c/story (scarce); The Atom app. in one panel announcing debut in next issue 1167 2334 3500 8800 16,400 24,000
19-Origin/1st app. The Atom (10/40); last Ultra Man 1950 3900 5850 14,600 27,300 40,000
20-Atom dons costume; Ma Hunkle becomes Red Tornado (1st app.)(1st DC costumed heroine, before Wonder Woman, 11/40); Rescue on Mars begins, ends #25; 1 pg. origin Green Lantern 568 1136 1704 4146 7323 10,500
21-Last Wiley of West Point & Skippy; classic Moldoff-c 476 952 1428 3475 6138 8800
22,23: 23-Last Daiseybelle; 3 Idiots begin, end #82 354 708 1062 2478 4339 6200
24-Sisty & Dinky become the Cyclone Kids; Ben Webster ends; origin Dr. Mid-Nite & Sargon, The Sorcerer in text with app. 371 742 1113 2597 4549 6500
25-Origin & 1st story app. Dr. Mid-Nite by Stan Asch; Hop Harrigan becomes Guardian Angel; last Adventure in the Unknown (scarce) 1150 2300 3450 8625 15,813 23,000
26-Origin/1st story app. Sargon, the Sorcerer 389 778 1167 2723 4762 6800
27: #27-32 are misnumbered in indicia with correct No. appearing on-c. Intro. Doiby Dickles, Green Lantern's sidekick 400 800 1200 2800 4900 7000
28-Hop Harrigan gives up costumed i.d. 213 426 639 1363 2332 3300
29,30 213 426 639 1363 2332 3300
31-40: 35-Doiby learns Green Lantern's i.d. 168 336 504 1075 1838 2600
41-50: 50-Sargon ends 132 264 396 838 1444 2050
51-60: 59-Scribbly & the Red Tornado ends 113 226 339 718 1234 1750

All-American Men of War #5 © DC

Allegra #3 © WSP

Alley Oop #17 © STD

	GD 2.0	VG 4.0	FN 6.0	VF 8.0	VF/NM 9.0	NM- 9.2
61-Origin/1st app. Solomon Grundy (11/44)	919	1838	2757	6709	11,855	17,000
62-70: 70-Kubert Sargon; intro Sargon's helper, Maximillian O'Leary	94	188	282	597	1024	1450
71-88: 71-Last Red White & Blue. 72-Black Pirate begins (not in #74-82); last Atom. 73-Winky, Blinky & Noddy begins, ends #82. 79,83-Mutt & Jeff-c. 85-1st Sportsmaster; Hasen "Derby" cover	74	148	222	470	810	1150
89-Origin & 1st app. Harlequin	135	270	405	864	1482	2100
90-99: 90-Origin/1st app. Icicle. 99-Last Hop Harrigan	129	258	387	826	1413	2000
100-1st app. Johnny Thunder by Alex Toth (8/48); western theme begins (Scarce)	206	412	618	1318	2259	3200
101-Last Mutt & Jeff (Scarce)	142	284	426	909	1555	2200
102-Last Green Lantern, Black Pirate & Dr. Mid-Nite (Scarce)	271	542	813	1734	2967	4200

NOTE: *No Atom in 47, 62-69.* **Kinstler** *Black Pirate-89.* **Stan Aschmeier** *a (Dr. Mid-Nite) 25-84; c-7.* **Mayer** *c-1, 2(part), 6, 10.* **Moldoff** *c-16-23.* **Nodell** *c-31.* **Paul Reinman** *a (Green Lantern)-53-55p, 56-84, 87; (Black Pirate)-83-88, 90; c-52, 55-76, 78, 80, 81, 87.* **Toth** *a-88, 92, 96, 98-102; c(p)-92, 96-102. Scribbly by* **Mayer** *in #1-59. Ultra Man by* **Mayer** *in #8-19.*

ALL AMERICAN COMICS
DC Comics: April 1939

nn - Ashcan comic, not distributed to newsstands, only for in house use. Cover art is Advenure Comics #33 and interior from Detective Comics #23 (no known sales)

ALL-AMERICAN COMICS (Also see All Star Comics 1999 crossover titles)
DC Comics: May, 1999 ($1.99, one-shot)

	GD 2.0	VG 4.0	FN 6.0	VF 8.0	VF/NM 9.0	NM- 9.2
1-Golden Age Green Lantern and Johnny Thunder; Barreto-a						3.00

ALL-AMERICAN MEN OF WAR (Previously All-American Western)
National Periodical Publ.: No. 127, Aug-Sept, 1952 - No. 117, Sept-Oct, 1966

	GD 2.0	VG 4.0	FN 6.0	VF 8.0	VF/NM 9.0	NM- 9.2
127 (#1, 1952)	115	230	345	932	2016	3100
128 (1952)	54	108	162	437	944	1450
2(12-1/'52-53)-5	46	92	138	373	812	1250
6-Devil Dog story; Ghost Squadron story	38	76	114	285	618	950
7-10: 8-Sgt. Storm Cloud-s	38	76	114	285	618	950
11-16,18: 18-Last precode; 1st Kubert-c (2/55)	34	68	102	247	536	825
17-1st Frogman-s in this title	35	70	105	254	552	850
19,20,22-27	27	54	81	189	407	625
21-Easy Co. prototype	32	64	96	232	504	775
28 (12/55)-1st Sgt. Rock prototype; Kubert-a	46	92	138	373	812	1250
29,30,32-Wood-a	27	54	81	189	407	625
31,33,34,36-38,40: 34-Gunner prototype-s. 36-Little Sure Shot prototype-s. 38-1st S.A. issue	24	48	72	168	359	550
35-Greytone-c	27	54	81	196	423	650
39 (11/56)-2nd Sgt. Rock prototype; 1st Easy Co.?	35	70	105	254	552	850
41,43-47,49,50: 46-Tankbusters-c/s	21	42	63	146	311	475
42-Pre-Sgt. Rock Easy Co.-c/s	26	52	78	177	381	585
48-Easy Co.-c/s; Nick app.; Kubert-a	26	52	78	177	381	585
51-56,58-62,65,66: 61-Gunner-c/s	16	32	48	107	234	360
57(5/58),63,64 -Pre-Sgt. Rock Easy Co.-c/s	22	44	66	154	327	500
67-1st Gunner & Sarge by Andru & Esposito	44	88	132	330	715	1100
68,69: 68-2nd app. Gunner & Sarge. 69-1st Tank Killer-c/s	20	40	60	137	294	450
70	13	26	39	90	195	300
71-80: 71,72,76-Tank Killer-c/s. 74-Minute Commandos-c/s	12	24	36	81	166	250
81-Greytone-c	11	22	33	75	148	220
82-Johnny Cloud begins(1st app.), ends #117	22	44	66	154	327	500
83-2nd Johnny Cloud	13	26	39	87	186	285
84-88: 88-Last 10¢ issue	11	22	33	71	136	200
89-100: 89-Battle Aces of 3 Wars begins, ends #98	9	18	27	58	99	140
101-111,113-116: 111,114,115-Johnny Cloud	6	12	18	41	66	90
112-Balloon Buster series begins, ends #114,116	6	12	18	42	69	95
117-Johnny Cloud-c & 3-part story	6	12	18	42	69	95

NOTE: *Frogman stories in 17, 38, 44, 45, 50, 51, 53, 55-58, 63, 65, 66, 72, 76, 77.* **Colan** *a-112.* **Drucker** *a-47, 58, 61, 63, 65, 69, 71, 74, 77.* **Grandenetti** *c(p)-127, 128, 2-17(most).* **Heath** *a-14, 27, 32, 38, 41, 45, 47, 50, 51, 55-58, 62, 64, 71, 75, 76, 78, 95, 111-117; c-85, 91, 94-96, 100, 101, 110-112, others?* **Infantino** *a-8.* **Kirby** *a-29.* **Krigstein** *a-128('52), 2, 3, 5.* **Kubert** *a-22, 24, 28, 29, 33, 34, 36, 38, 39, 41-43, 47-50, 52, 53, 55, 56, 59, 60, 63-65, 69, 71-73, 76, 102, 103, 105, 106, 108, 114; c-41, 44, 52, 54, 55, 58, 64, 69, 76, 77, 79, 102-106, 108, 113-117, others? Tank Killer in 69, 71, 76 by* **Kubert**. **P. Reinman** *c-55, 57, 61, 62, 71, 72, 74-76, 80.* **J. Severin** *a-58.*

ALL AMERICAN MEN OF WAR
DC Comics: Aug/Sept. 1952

nn - Ashcan comic, not distributed to newsstands, only for in-house use. Cover art is All Star Western #58 and interior from Mr. District Attorney #21 (no known sales)

ALL-AMERICAN SPORTS
Charlton Comics: Oct, 1967

	GD 2.0	VG 4.0	FN 6.0	VF 8.0	VF/NM 9.0	NM- 9.2
1	3	6	9	20	30	40

ALL-AMERICAN WESTERN (Formerly All-American Comics; Becomes All-American Men of War)
National Periodical Publ.: No. 103, Nov, 1948 - No. 126, June-July, 1952 (103-121: 52 pgs.)

	GD 2.0	VG 4.0	FN 6.0	VF 8.0	VF/NM 9.0	NM- 9.2
103-Johnny Thunder & his horse Black Lightning continues by Toth, ends #126; Foley of The Fighting 5th, Minstrel Maverick, & Overland Coach begin; Captain Tootsie by Beck; mentioned in Love and Death	50	100	150	315	533	750
104-Kubert-a	36	72	108	216	351	485
105,107-Kubert-a	31	62	93	182	296	410
106,108-110,112: 112-Kurtzman's "Pot-Shot Pete" (1 pg.)	25	50	75	150	245	340
111,114-116-Kubert-a	26	52	78	156	256	355
113-Intro. Swift Deer, J. Thunder's new sidekick (4-5/50); classic Toth-c; Kubert-a	28	56	84	165	270	375
117-126: 121-Kubert-a; bondage-c	19	38	57	111	176	240

NOTE: ***G. Kane*** *c(p)-112, 119, 120, 123.* **Kubert** *a-103-105, 107, 111, 112(1 pg.), 113-116, 121.* **Toth** *a 103-125; c(p)-103-111,113-116, 121, 122, 124-126. Some copies of #125 have #12 on-c.*

ALL COMICS
Chicago Nite Life News: 1945

	GD 2.0	VG 4.0	FN 6.0	VF 8.0	VF/NM 9.0	NM- 9.2
1	15	30	45	83	124	165

ALLEGRA
Image Comics (WildStorm): Aug, 1996 - No. 4, Dec, 1996 ($2.50)

	GD 2.0	VG 4.0	FN 6.0	VF 8.0	VF/NM 9.0	NM- 9.2
1-4						3.00

ALLEY CAT (Alley Baggett)
Image Comics: July, 1999 - No. 6, Mar, 2000 ($2.50/$2.95)

	GD 2.0	VG 4.0	FN 6.0	VF 8.0	VF/NM 9.0	NM- 9.2
Preview Edition						6.00
Prelude						5.00
Prelude w/variant-c						6.00
1-Photo-c						3.00
1-Painted-c by Dorian						3.50
1-Another Universe Edition, 1-Wizard World Edition						7.00
2-4: 4-Twin towers on-c						3.00
5,6-($2.95)						3.00
Lingerie Edition (10/99, $4.95) Photos, pin-ups, cover gallery						5.00
...Vs. Lady Pendragon ('99, $3.00) Stinsman-c						3.00

ALLEY OOP (See The Comics, The Funnies, Red Ryder and Super Book #9)
Dell Publishing Co.: No. 3, 1942

	GD 2.0	VG 4.0	FN 6.0	VF 8.0	VF/NM 9.0	NM- 9.2
Four Color 3 (#1)	42	84	126	315	683	1050

ALLEY OOP
Argo Publ.: Nov, 1955 - No. 3, Mar, 1956 (Newspaper reprints)

	GD 2.0	VG 4.0	FN 6.0	VF 8.0	VF/NM 9.0	NM- 9.2
1	16	32	48	92	144	195
2,3	12	24	36	67	94	120

ALLEY OOP
Dell Publishing Co.: 12-2/62-63 - No. 2, 9-11/63

	GD 2.0	VG 4.0	FN 6.0	VF 8.0	VF/NM 9.0	NM- 9.2
1	6	12	18	41	66	90
2	5	10	15	34	55	75

ALLEY OOP
Standard Comics: No. 10, Sept, 1947 - No. 18, Oct, 1949

	GD 2.0	VG 4.0	FN 6.0	VF 8.0	VF/NM 9.0	NM- 9.2
10	24	48	72	140	230	320
11-18: 17,18-Schomburg-c	20	40	60	111	182	250

ALLEY OOP ADVENTURES
Antarctic Press: Aug, 1998 - No. 3, Dec, 1998 ($2.95)

	GD 2.0	VG 4.0	FN 6.0	VF 8.0	VF/NM 9.0	NM- 9.2
1-3-Jack Bender-s/a						3.00

ALLEY OOP ADVENTURES (Alley Oop Quarterly in indicia)
Antarctic Press: Sept, 1999 - No. 3, Mar, 2000 ($2.50/$2.99, B&W)

	GD 2.0	VG 4.0	FN 6.0	VF 8.0	VF/NM 9.0	NM- 9.2
1-3-Jack Bender-s/a						3.00

ALL-FAMOUS CRIME (2nd series - Formerly Law Against Crime #1-3; becomes All-Famous Police Cases #6 on)
Star Publications: No. 8, 5/51 - No. 10, 11/51; No. 4, 2/52 - No. 5, 5/52;

	GD 2.0	VG 4.0	FN 6.0	VF 8.0	VF/NM 9.0	NM- 9.2
8 (#1-1st series)	22	44	66	128	209	290
9 (#2)-Used in **SOTI**, illo- "The wish to hurt or kill couples in lovers' lanes is a not uncommon perversion;" L.B. Cole-c/a(r)/Law-Crime #3	37	74	111	222	361	500
10 (#3)	20	40	60	114	182	250
4 (#4-2nd series)-Formerly Law-Crime	19	38	57	109	172	235
5 (#5) Becomes All-Famous Police Cases #6	19	38	57	109	172	235

NOTE: *All have* ***L.B. Cole*** *covers.*

ALL FAMOUS CRIME STORIES (See Fox Giants)

ALL-FAMOUS POLICE CASES (Formerly All Famous Crime #5)

All-Flash #18 © DC

All Humor Comics #9 © QUA

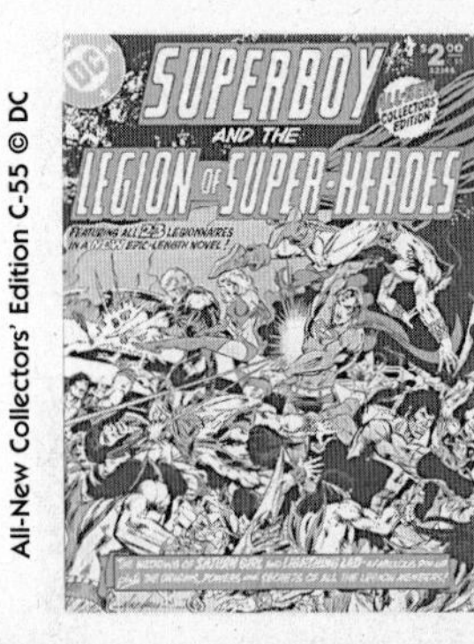

All-New Collectors' Edition C-55 © DC

	GD 2.0	VG 4.0	FN 6.0	VF 8.0	VF/NM 9.0	NM- 9.2

Star Publications: No. 6, Feb, 1952 - No. 16, Sept, 1954

6	19	38	57	112	176	240
7,8: 7-Baker story. 8-Marijuana story	18	36	54	105	165	225
9-16	16	32	48	94	147	200

NOTE: *L. B. Cole c-all; a-15, 1pg. Hollingsworth a-15.*

ALL-FLASH (...Quarterly No. 1-5)
National Per. Publ./All-American: Summer, 1941 - No. 32, Dec-Jan, 1947-48

1-Origin The Flash retold by E. E. Hibbard; Hibbard c-1-10,12-14,16,31p.	1400	2800	4200	10,500	18,250	26,000
2-Origin recap	314	628	942	2198	3849	5500
3,4	177	354	531	1124	1937	2750
5-Winky, Blinky & Noddy begins (1st app.), ends #32	129	258	387	826	1413	2000
6-10	106	212	318	673	1162	1650
11-13: 12-Origin/1st The Thinker. 13-The King app.	90	180	270	576	988	1400
14-Green Lantern cameo	106	212	318	673	1162	1650
15-20: 18-Mutt & Jeff begins, ends #22	82	164	246	528	902	1275
21-31	69	138	207	442	759	1075
32-Origin/1st app. The Fiddler; 1st Star Sapphire	139	278	417	883	1517	2150

NOTE: *Book length stories in 2-13, 16. Bondage c-31, 32. Martin Nodell c-15, 17-28.*

ALL FLASH (Leads into Flash [2nd series] #231)
DC Comics: Sept, 2007 ($2.99, one-shot)

1-Wally West hunts down Bart's killers; Waid-s; two covers by Middleton & Sienkiewicz 3.00

ALL FOR LOVE (Young Love V3#5-on)
Prize Publications: Apr-May, 1957 - V3#4, Dec-Jan, 1959-60

V1#1	9	18	27	58	99	140
2-6: 5-Orlando-c	5	10	15	32	51	70
V2#1-5(1/59), 5(3/59)	4	8	12	28	44	60
V3#1(5/59), 1(7/59)-4: 2-Powell-a	4	8	12	24	37	50

ALL FUNNY COMICS
Tilsam Publ./National Periodical Publications (Detective): Winter, 1943-44 - No. 23, May-June, 1948

1-Genius Jones (see Adventure #77 for debut), Buzzy (1st app., ends #4), Dover & Clover (see More Fun #93) begin; Bailey-a	47	94	141	296	498	700
2	22	44	66	132	216	300
3-10	15	30	45	83	124	165
11-13,15,18,19-Genius Jones app.	14	28	42	80	115	150
14,17,20-23	10	20	30	56	76	95
16-DC Super Heroes app.	31	62	93	182	296	410

ALL GOOD
St. John Publishing Co.: Oct, 1949 (50¢, 260 pgs.)

nn-(8 St. John comics bound together)	77	154	231	493	847	1200

NOTE: *Also see Li'l Audrey Yearbook & Treasury of Comics.*

ALL GOOD COMICS (See Fox Giants)
Fox Features Syndicate: No.1, Spring, 1946 (36 pgs.)

1-Joy Family, Dick Transom, Rick Evans, One Round Hogan	27	54	81	158	259	360

ALL GREAT
William H. Wise & Co.: nd (1945?) (132 pgs.)

nn-Capt. Jack Terry, Joan Mason, Girl Reporter, Baron Doomsday; Torture scenes	42	84	126	265	445	625

ALL GREAT COMICS (See Fox Giants)
Fox Feature Syndicate: 1946 (36 pgs.)

1-Crazy House, Bertie Benson Boy Detective, Gussie the Gob	27	54	81	158	259	360

ALL GREAT COMICS (Formerly Phantom Lady #13? Dagar, Desert Hawk No. 14 on)
Fox Features Syndicate: No. 14, Oct, 1947 - No. 13, Dec, 1947 (Newspaper strip reprints)

14(#12)-Brenda Starr & Texas Slim-r (Scarce)	57	114	171	362	621	880
13-Origin Dagar, Desert Hawk; Brenda Starr (all-r); Kamen-c; Dagar covers begin	65	130	195	416	708	1000

ALL-GREAT CONFESSIONS (See Fox Giants)

ALL GREAT CRIME STORIES (See Fox Giants)

ALL GREAT JUNGLE ADVENTURES (See Fox Giants)

ALL HALLOW'S EVE
Innovation Publishing: 1991 ($4.95, 52 pgs.)

1-Painted-c/a	1	2	3	4	5	7

ALL HERO COMICS
Fawcett Publications: Mar, 1943 (100 pgs., cardboard-c)

1-Capt. Marvel Jr., Capt. Midnight, Golden Arrow, Ibis the Invincible, Spy Smasher, Lance O'Casey; 1st Banshee O'Brien; Raboy-c	174	348	522	1114	1907	2700

ALL HUMOR COMICS
Quality Comics Group: Spring, 1946 - No. 17, December, 1949

1	21	42	63	122	199	275
2-Atomic Tot story; Gustavson-a	13	26	39	74	105	135
3-9: 3-Intro Kelly Poole who is cover feature #3 on. 5-1st app. Hickory? 8-Gustavson-a	9	18	27	47	61	75
10-17	8	16	24	42	54	65

ALLIANCE, THE
Image Comics (Shadowline Ink): Aug, 1995 - No. 3, Nov, 1995 ($2.50)

1-3: 2-(9/95) 3.00

ALL LOVE (...Romances No. 26)(Formerly Ernie Comics)
Ace Periodicals (Current Books): No. 26, May, 1949 - No. 32, May, 1950

26 (No. 1)-Ernie, Lily Belle app.	11	22	33	62	86	110
27-L. B. Cole-a	14	28	42	76	108	140
28-32	8	16	24	44	57	70

ALL-NEGRO COMICS
All-Negro Comics: June, 1947 (15¢)

1 (Rare)	1700	3400	5100	9200	12,100	15,000

NOTE: *Seldom found in fine or mint condition; many copies have brown pages.*

ALL-NEW ATOM, THE (See The Atom and DCU Brave New World)
DC Comics: Sept, 2006 - No. 25, Sept, 2008 ($2.99)

1-25: 1-18-Simone-s. 1-Intro Ryan Choi; Byrne-a thru #3. 4-11-Barrows-a. 12,13-Chronos app. 14,15-Countdown x-over. 17,18-Wonder Woman app. 3.00
...: Future/Past TPB (2007, $14.99) r/#7-11 15.00
...: My Life in Miniature TPB (2007, $14.99) r/#1-6 and app. in DCU Brave New World #1 15.00
...: Small Wonder TPB (2008, $17.99) r/#17,18,21-25 18.00
...: The Hunt For Ray Palmer TPB (2008, $14.99) r/#12-16 15.00

ALL-NEW BATMAN: BRAVE & THE BOLD (See Batman: The Brave and the Bold)

ALL-NEW COLLECTORS' EDITION (Formerly Limited Collectors' Edition: see for C-57, C-59)
DC Comics, Inc.: Jan, 1978 - Vol. 8, No. C-62, 1979 (No. 54-58: 76 pgs.)

C-53-Rudolph the Red-Nosed Reindeer	5	10	15	30	48	65
C-54-Superman Vs. Wonder Woman	4	8	12	26	41	55
C-55-Superboy & the Legion of Super-Heroes; Wedding of Lightning Lad & Saturn Girl; Grell-c/a	4	8	12	26	41	55
C-56-Superman Vs. Muhammad Ali: Wraparound Neal Adams-c/a; Adams & O'Neil-s (see "Superman Vs. Muhammad Ali" for reprint)	8	16	24	51	86	120
C-56-Superman Vs. Muhammad Ali (Whitman variant)-low print	9	18	27	63	112	160
C-57,C-59-(See Limited Collectors' Edition)						
C-58-Superman Vs. Shazam; Buckler-c/a	4	8	12	26	41	55
C-60-Rudolph's Summer Fun(8/78)	4	8	12	26	41	55
C-61-(See Famous First Edition-Superman #1)						
C-62-Superman the Movie (68 pgs.; 1979)-Photo-c from movie plus photos inside (also see DC Special Series #25)	3	6	9	16	22	28

ALL-NEW COMICS (...Short Story Comics No. 1-3)
Family Comics (Harvey Publications): Jan, 1943 - No. 14, Nov, 1946; No. 15, Mar-Apr, 1947 (10 x 13-1/2")

1-Steve Case, Crime Rover, Johnny Rebel, Kayo Kane, The Echo, Night Hawk, Ray O'Light, Detective Shane begin (all 1st app.?); Red Blazer on cover only; Sultan-a; Nazi WWII-c	300	600	900	1980	3440	4900
2-Origin Scarlet Phantom by Kubert	115	230	345	730	1253	1775
3-Nazi war-c	92	184	276	584	1005	1425
4	76	152	228	486	831	1175
5-11: 5-Schomburg-c thru #11. 5,9-11-Japanese WWII-c. 6-8 Nazi WWII-c. 6-The Boy Heroes & Red Blazer (text story) begin, end #12; Black Cat app.; intro. Sparky in Red Blazer. 7-Kubert, Powell-a; Black Cat & Zebra app. 8,9: 8-Shock Gibson app.; Kubert, Powell-a; Schomburg-c. 9-Black Cat app.; Kubert-a. 10-The Zebra app. (from Green Hornet Comics); Kubert-a(3). 11-Girl Commandos, Man In Black app.	94	188	282	597	1024	1450
12,13: 12-Kubert-a; Japanese WWII-c. 13-Stuntman by Simon & Kirby; Green Hornet, Joe Palooka, Flying Fool app.; Green Hornet-c	58	116	174	371	636	900
14-The Green Hornet & The Man in Black Called Fate by Powell, Joe Flying Fool app.; Flying Fool app.; J. Palooka-c by Ham Fisher	45	90	135	284	480	675
15-(Rare)-Small size (5-1/2x8-1/2"; B&W; 32 pgs.). Distributed to mail subscribers only. Black Cat and Joe Palooka app.	148	296	444	947	1624	2300

NOTE: *Also see Boy Explorers No. 2, Flash Gordon No. 5, and Stuntman No. 3. Powell a-11. Schomburg c-5-11.*

All Nighter #1 © David Haun

All Star Batman & Robin, The Boy Wonder #1 © DC

All Star Comics #8 © DC

GD VG FN VF VF/NM NM-
2.0 4.0 6.0 8.0 9.0 9.2

Captain Red Blazer & Spark on c-5-11 (w/Boy Heroes #12).

ALL-NEW OFFICIAL HANDBOOK OF THE MARVEL UNIVERSE A TO Z
Marvel Comics: 2006 - No. 12, 2006 ($3.99, limited series)

1-12-Profile pages of Marvel characters not covered in 2004-2005 Official Handbooks 4.00
...: Update 1-4 (2007, $3.99) Profile pages 4.00

ALL NIGHTER
Image Comics: Jun, 2011 - No. 5, Oct, 2011 ($2.99, B&W, limited series)

1-5-David Haun-s/a/c 3.00

ALL-OUT WAR
DC Comics: Sept-Oct, 1979 - No. 6, Aug, 1980 ($1.00, 68 pgs.)

1-The Viking Commando (origin), Force Three(origin), & Black Eagle Squadron begin
2 4 6 13 18 22
2-6 2 4 6 8 10 12
NOTE: ***Ayers** a(p)-1-6. **Elias** r-2. **Evans** a-1-6. **Kubert** c-16.*

ALL PICTURE ADVENTURE MAGAZINE
St. John Publishing Co.: Oct, 1952 - No. 2, Nov, 1952 (100 pg. Giants, 25¢, squarebound)

1-War comics 36 72 108 211 343 475
2-Horror-crime comics 50 100 150 315 533 750
NOTE: *Above books contain three St. John comics rebound; variations possible. **Baker** art known in both.*

ALL PICTURE ALL TRUE LOVE STORY
St. John Publishing Co.: Oct., 1952 - No. 2, Nov., 1952 (100 pgs., 25¢)

1-Canteen Kate by Matt Baker 54 108 162 343 574 825
2-Baker-c/a 39 78 117 240 395 550

ALL-PICTURE COMEDY CARNIVAL
St. John Publishing Co.: October, 1952 (100 pgs., 25¢)(Contains 4 rebound comics)

1-Contents can vary; Baker-a 43 86 129 271 461 650

ALL REAL CONFESSION MAGAZINE (See Fox Giants)

ALL ROMANCES (Mr. Risk No. 7 on)
A. A. Wyn (Ace Periodicals): Aug, 1949 - No. 6, June, 1950

1 14 28 42 81 118 155
2 9 18 27 50 65 80
3-6 8 16 24 44 57 70

ALL-SELECT COMICS (Blonde Phantom No. 12 on)
Timely Comics (Daring Comics): Fall, 1943 - No. 11, Fall, 1946

1-Capt. America (by Rico #1), Human Torch, Sub-Mariner begin; Black Widow story (4 pgs.); Classic Schomburg-c 1600 3200 4800 11,000 21,000 31,000
2-Red Skull app. 514 1028 1542 3750 6625 9500
3-The Whizzer begins 343 686 1029 2400 4200 6000
4,5-Last Sub-Mariner 297 594 891 1900 3250 4600
6-9: 6-The Destroyer app. 8-No Whizzer 232 464 696 1485 2543 3600
10-The Destroyer & Sub-Mariner app.; last Capt. America & Human Torch issue
232 464 696 1485 2543 3600
11-1st app. Blonde Phantom; Miss America app.; all Blonde Phantom-c by Shores
277 554 831 1773 3037 4350
NOTE: ***Schomburg** c-1-10. **Sekowsky** a-7. #7 & 8 show 1944 in indicia, but should be 1945.*

ALL SELECT COMICS 70th ANNIVERARY SPECIAL
Marvel Comics: Sept, 2009 ($3.99, one-shot)

1-New stories of Blonde Phantom and Marvex the Super Robot; r/Marvex G.A. app. 4.00

ALL SPORTS COMICS (Formerly Real Sports Comics; becomes All Time Sports Comics No. 4 on)
Hillman Periodicals: No. 2, Dec-Jan, 1948-49; No. 3, Feb-Mar, 1949

2-Krigstein-a(p), Powell, Starr-a 36 72 108 211 343 475
3-Mort Lawrence-a 22 44 66 132 216 300

ALL STAR BATMAN & ROBIN, THE BOY WONDER
DC Comics: Sept, 2005 - No. 10, Aug, 2008 ($2.99)

1-Two covers; retelling of Robin's origin; Frank Miller-s/Jim Lee-a/c 4.00
1-Diamond Retailer Summit Edition (9/05) sketch-c 60.00
2-10: 2-7-Two covers by Lee and Miller. 3-Black Canary app. 4-Six pg. Batcave gatefold. 10-Edition without profanity 3.00
8-10: 8,9-Variant cover by Neal Adams. 10-Variant-c by Quitely 5.00
10-Recalled edition with insufficiently covered profanity inside; Jim Lee-c 20.00
10-Recalled edition with variant Quitely-c 40.00
... Special Edition (2/06, $3.99) r/#1 with Lee pencil pages and Miller script; new Miller-c 4.00
Vol. 1 HC (2008, $24.99, dustjacket) r/#1-9; cover gallery, sketch pages; Schreck intro. 25.00
Vol. 1 SC (2009, $19.99) r/#1-9; cover gallery, sketch pages; Schreck intro. 20.00

ALL STAR COMICS
DC Comics: Spring 1940

1-Ashcan comic, not distributed to newsstands, only for in-house use. Cover art is Flash Comics #1 and interior from Detective Comics #37. A CGC certified 7.0 copy sold for $15,600 in 2002.

GD VG FN VF VF/NM NM-
2.0 4.0 6.0 8.0 9.0 9.2

ALL STAR COMICS (All Star Western No. 58 on)
National Periodical Publ./All-American/DC Comics: Sum, 1940 - No. 57, Feb-Mar, 1951; No. 58, Jan-Feb, 1976 - No. 74, Sept-Oct, 1978

1-The Flash (#1 by E.E. Hibbard), Hawkman (by Shelly), Hourman (by Bernard Baily), The Sandman (by Creig Flessel), The Spectre (by Baily), Biff Bronson, Red White & Blue (ends #2) begin; Ultra Man's only app. (#1-3 are quarterly; #4 begins bi-monthly issues)
1200 2400 3600 9000 16,500 24,000
2-Green Lantern (by Martin Nodell), Johnny Thunder begin; Green Lantern figure swipe from the cover of All-American Comics #16; Flash figure swipe from cover of Flash Comics #8; Moldoff/Bailey-c (cut & paste-c.) 514 1028 1542 3750 6625 9500
3-Origin & 1st app. The Justice Society of America (Win/40); Dr. Fate & The Atom begin, Red Tornado cameo 4800 9600 14,400 36,000 65,500 95,000
3-Reprint, Oversize 13-1/2x10". **WARNING:** This comic is an exact reprint of the original except for its size. DC published it in 1974 with a second cover titling it as a Famous First Edition. There have been many reported cases of the outer cover being removed and the interior sold as the original edition. The reprint with the new outer cover removed is practically worthless. See Famous First Edition for value.
4-1st adventure for J.S.A. 530 1060 1590 3869 6835 9800
5-1st app. Shiera Sanders as Hawkgirl (1st costumed super-heroine, 6-7/41)
459 918 1377 3350 5925 8500
6-Johnny Thunder joins JSA 300 600 900 1935 3343 4750
7-Batman, Superman, Flash cameo; last Hourman; Doiby Dickles app.
331 662 993 2317 4059 5800
8-Origin & 1st app. Wonder Woman (12-1/41-42)(added as 9 pgs. making book 76 pgs.; origin cont'd in Sensation #1; see W.W. #1 for more detailed origin); Dr. Fate dons new helmet; Hop Harrigan text stories & Starman begin; Shiera app.; Hop Harrigan JSA guest; Starman & Dr. Mid-Nite become members 4000 8000 12,000 30,000 55,000 80,000
9-11: 9-JSA's girlfriends cameo; Shiera app.; J. Edgar Hoover of FBI made associate member of JSA. 10-Flash, Green Lantern cameo; Sandman new costume. 11-Wonder Woman begins; Spectre cameo; Shiera app.; Moldoff Hawkman-c
300 600 900 1920 3310 4700
12-Wonder Woman becomes JSA Secretary 277 554 831 1773 3037 4300
13,15: Sandman w/Sandy in #14 & 15. 15-Origin & 1st app. Brain Wave; Shiera app.
252 504 756 1613 2757 3900
14-(12/42) Junior JSA Club begins; w/membership offer & premiums
258 516 774 1651 2826 4000
16-20: 19-Sandman w/Sandy. 20-Dr. Fate & Sandman cameo
213 426 639 1363 2332 3300
21-23: 21-Spectre & Atom cameo; Dr. Fate by Kubert; Dr. Fate, Sandman end. 22-Last Hop Harrigan; Flag-c. 23-Origin/1st app. Psycho Pirate; last Spectre & Starman 171 342 513 1086 1868 2650
24-Flash & Green Lantern cameo; Mr. Terrific only app.; Wildcat, JSA guest; Kubert Hawkman begins; Hitler-c 174 348 522 1114 1907 2700
25-27: 25-Flash & Green Lantern start again. 26-Robot-c. 27-Wildcat, JSA guest (#24-26: only All-American imprint) 148 296 444 947 1624 2300
28-32 126 252 378 806 1378 1950
33-Solomon Grundy & Doiby Dickles app; classic Solomon Grundy cover & last G.A. app.
354 708 1062 2478 4339 6200
34,35-Johnny Thunder cameo in both 123 246 369 787 1344 1900
36-Batman & Superman JSA guests 284 568 852 1818 3109 4400
37-Johnny Thunder cameo; origin & 1st app. Injustice Society; last Kubert Hawkman
161 322 483 1030 1765 2500
38-Black Canary begins; JSA Death issue 226 452 678 1446 2473 3500
39,40: 39-Last Johnny Thunder 119 238 357 762 1306 1850
41-Black Canary joins JSA; Injustice Society app. (2nd app.?)
119 238 357 762 1306 1850
42-Atom & the Hawkman don new costumes 119 238 357 762 1306 1850
43-49,51-56: 43-New logo; Robot-c. 55-Sci/Fi story. 56-Robot-c
119 238 357 762 1306 1850
50-Frazetta art, 3 pgs. 127 254 381 807 1391 1975
57-Kubert-a, 6 pgs. (Scarce); last app. G.A. Green Lantern, Flash & Dr. Mid-Nite
174 348 522 1114 1907 2700
V12 #58-(1976) JSA (Flash, Hawkman, Dr. Mid-Nite, Wildcat, Dr. Fate, Green Lantern, Robin & Star Spangled Kid) app.; intro. Power Girl 6 12 18 42 69 95
V12 #59,60: 59-Estrada & Wood-a 3 6 9 18 27 35
V12 #61-68: 62-65-Superman app. 64,65-Wood-c/a; Vandal Savage app. 66-Injustice Society app. 68-Psycho Pirate app. 3 6 9 18 27 35
V12 #69-1st Earth-2 Huntress (Helena Wayne) 5 10 15 30 48 65
V12 #70-73: 70-Full intro. of Huntress 3 6 9 18 27 35
V12 #74-(44 pgs.) Last issue, story continues in Adventure Comics #461 & 462 (death of Earth-2 Batman); Staton-c/a 4 8 12 28 44 60
(See Justice Society Vol. 1 TPB for reprints of V12 revival)

All-Star Squadron #47 © DC

All Star Western (2011 series) #1 © DC

All Top Comics #11 © FOX

GD VG FN VF VF/NM NM-
2.0 4.0 6.0 8.0 9.0 9.2

NOTE: *No Atom-27, 36; no Dr. Fate-13; no Flash-8, 9, 11-23; no Green Lantern-8, 9,11-23; Hawkman in 1-57 (only one to app. in all 57 issues); no Johnny Thunder-5, 36; no Wonder Woman-9, 10, 23. Book length stories in 4-9, 11-14, 18-22, 25, 26, 29, 30, 32-36, 40, 42, 43. Johnny Peril in #42-46, 48, 49, 51, 52,54-57.* ***Baily*** *a-1-10, 12, 13, 14i, 15-20.* ***Burnley*** *Starman-8-13; c-12, 13.* ***Grell*** *c-58.* ***E.E. Hibbard*** *c-3, 4, 6-10.* ***Infantino*** *c-40.* ***Kubert*** *Hawkman-24-30, 33-37.* ***Lampert/Baily/Flessel*** *c-1, 2.* ***Moldoff*** *Hawkman-3-23; c-11.* ***Mart Nodell*** *c-25i, 26i, 27-32.* ***Purcell*** *c-5.* ***Simon & Kirby*** *Sandman 14-17, 19.* ***Staton*** *a-66-74p. c-74p.* ***Toth*** *a-37(2), 38(2), 40, 41; c-38, 41.* ***Wood*** *a-58i-63i, 64, 65; c-63i, 64, 65. Issues 1-7, 9-16 are 68 pgs.; #8 is 76 pgs.; #17-19 are 60 pgs.; #20-57 are 52 pgs.*

ALL STAR COMICS (Also see crossover 1999 editions of Adventure, All-American, National, Sensation, Smash, Star Spangled and Thrilling Comics)
DC Comics: May, 1999 - No. 2, May, 1999 ($2.95, bookends for JSA x-over)

1,2-Justice Society in World War 2; Robinson-s/Johnson-c 3.00
1-RRP Edition (price will be based on future sales)
...80-Page Giant (9/99, $4.95) Phantom Lady app. 5.00

ALL STAR INDEX, THE
Independent Comics Group (Eclipse): Feb, 1987 ($2.00, Baxter paper)

1 1 2 3 5 6 8

ALL-STAR SQUADRON (See Justice League of America #193)
DC Comics: Sept, 1981 - No. 67, Mar, 1987

1-Original Atom, Hawkman, Dr. Mid-Nite, Robotman (origin), Plastic Man, Johnny Quick, Liberty Belle, Shining Knight begin 1 2 3 5 7 9
2-10: 3-Solomon Grundy app. 4,7-Spectre app. 8-Re-intro Steel, the Indestructable Man 5.00
11-46,48,49: 12-Origin G.A. Hawkman retold. 23-Origin/1st app. The Amazing Man. 24-Batman app. 25-1st app. Infinity, Inc. (9/83), 26-Origin Infinity, Inc.(2nd app.); Robin app. 27-Dr. Fate vs. The Spectre. 30-35-Spectre app. 33-Origin Freedom Fighters of Earth-X. 36,37-Superman vs. Capt. Marvel; Ordway-c. 41-Origin Starman 4.00
47-Origin Dr. Fate; McFarlane-a (1st full story)/part-c (7/85) 2 4 6 9 12 15
50-Double size; Crisis x-over 1 2 3 5 6 8
51-66: 51-56-Crisis x-over. 61-Origin Liberty Belle. 62-Origin The Shining Knight. 63-Origin Robotman. 65-Origin Johnny Quick. 66-Origin Tarantula 6.00
67-Last issue; retells first case of the Justice Society 1 2 3 5 6 8
Annual 1-3: 1(11/82)-Retells origin of G.A. Atom, Guardian & Wildcat; Jerry Ordway's 1st pencils for DC. (1st work was inking Carmine Infantino in Mystery in Space #117). 2(11/83)-Infinity, Inc. app. 3(9/84) 6.00

NOTE: ***Buckler*** *a-1-5; c-1, 3-5, 51.* ***Kubert*** *c-2, 7-18. JLA app. in 14, 15. JSA app. in 4, 14, 15, 19, 27, 28.*

ALL-STAR STORY OF THE DODGERS, THE
Stadium Communications: Apr, 1979 ($1.00)

1 2 4 6 9 13 16

ALL-STAR SUPERMAN (Also see FCBD edition in the Promotional Comics section)
DC Comics: Jan, 2006 - No. 12, Oct, 2008 ($2.99)

1-Grant Morrison-s/Frank Quitely-a/c 5.00
1-Variant-c by Neal Adams 20.00
1-Special Edition (2009, $1.00) r/#1 with "After Watchmen" cover logo frame 3.00
2-12: 3-Lois gets super powers. 7,8-Bizarro app. 3.00
Free Comic Book Day giveaway (6/08) reprints #1 3.00
Vol. 1 HC (2007, $19.99, dustjacket) r/#1-6; Bob Schreck intro. 20.00
Vol. 1 SC (2008, $12.99) r/#1-6; Schreck intro. 13.00
Vol. 2 HC (2009, $19.99, dustjacket) r/#7-12; Mark Waid intro. 20.00
Vol. 2 SC (2009, $12.99) r/#7-12; Mark Waid intro. 13.00

ALL STAR WESTERN (Formerly All Star Comics No. 1-57)
National Periodical Publ.: No. 58, Apr-May, 1951 - No. 119, June-July, 1961

58-Trigger Twins (ends #116), Strong Bow, The Roving Ranger & Don Caballero begin 45 90 135 284 480 675
59,60: Last 52 pgs. 27 54 81 158 259 360
61-66: 61-64-Toth-a 22 44 66 128 209 290
67-Johnny Thunder begins; Gil Kane-a 28 56 84 165 270 375
68-81: Last precode (2-3/55) 15 30 45 84 127 170
82-98: 97-1st S.A. issue 14 28 42 76 108 140
99-Frazetta-r/Jimmy Wakely #4 14 28 42 78 112 145
100 14 28 42 78 112 145
101-107,109-116,118,119 12 24 36 67 94 120
108-Origin J. Thunder; J. Thunder logo begins 22 44 66 128 209 290
117-Origin Super Chief 14 28 42 82 121 160

NOTE: ***Gil Kane*** *c(p)-58, 59, 61, 63, 64, 68, 69, 70-95(most), 97-199(most).* ***Infantino*** *art in most issues. Madame .44 app.- #117-119.*

ALL-STAR WESTERN (Weird Western Tales No. 12 on)
National Periodical Publications: Aug-Sept, 1970 - No. 11, Apr-May, 1972

1-Pow-Wow Smith-r; Infantino-a 5 10 15 35 55 75
2-Outlaw begins; El Diablo by Morrow begins; has cameos by Williamson, Torres, Kane, Giordano & Phil Seuling 5 10 15 32 51 70
3-Origin El Diablo 5 10 15 30 48 65
4-6: 5-Last Outlaw issue. 6-Billy the Kid begins, ends #8 3 6 9 21 32 42
7-9-(52 pgs.) 9-Frazetta-a, 3pgs.(r) 4 8 12 24 37 50
10-(52 pgs.) Jonah Hex begins (1st app., 2-3/72) 35 70 105 254 552 850
11-(52 pgs.) 2nd app. Jonah Hex; 1st cover 13 26 39 90 195 300

NOTE: ***Neal Adams*** *c-2-5;* ***Aparo*** *a-5.* ***G. Kane a****-3, 4, 6, 8.* ***Kubert*** *a-4r, 7-9r.* ***Morrow*** *a-2-4, 10, 11. No. 7-11 have 52 pgs.*

ALL STAR WESTERN (DC New 52)
DC Comics: Nov, 2011 - Present ($3.99)

1-7-Jonah Hex in 1880s Gotham City; Gray & Palmiotti-s/Moritat-a. 2,3-El Diablo back-up 4.00

ALL SURPRISE (Becomes Jeanie #13 on) (Funny animal)
Timely/Marvel (CPC): Fall, 1943 - No. 12, Winter, 1946-47

1-Super Rabbit, Gandy & Sourpuss begin 40 80 120 246 411 575
2 20 40 60 117 189 260
3-10,12 15 30 45 90 140 190
11-Kurtzman "Pigtales" art 16 32 48 94 147 200

ALL TEEN (Formerly All Winners; All Winners & Teen Comics No. 21 on)
Marvel Comics (WFP): No. 20, January, 1947

20-Georgie, Mitzi, Patsy Walker, Willie app.; Syd Shores-c 20 40 60 114 182 250

ALL-TIME SPORTS COMICS (Formerly All Sports Comics)
Hillman Per.: V2, No. 4, Apr-May, 1949 - V2, No. 7, Oct-Nov, 1949 (All 52 pgs.)

V2#4 23 46 69 136 223 310
5-7: 5-(V1#5 inside)-Powell-a; Ty Cobb sty. 7-Krigstein-p; Walter Johnson & Knute Rockne sty 18 36 54 105 165 225

ALL TOP
William H. Wise Co.: 1944 (132 pgs.)

nn-Capt. V, Merciless the Sorceress, Red Robbins, One Round Hogan, Mike the M.P., Snooky, Pussy Katnip app. 34 68 102 206 336 465

ALL TOP COMICS (My Experience No. 19 on)
Fox Features Synd./Green Publ./Norlen Mag.: 1945; No. 2, Sum, 1946 - No. 18, Mar, 1949; 1957 - 1959

1-Cosmo Cat & Flash Rabbit begin (1st app.) 28 56 84 165 270 375
2 (#1-7 are funny animal) 15 30 45 83 124 165
3-7: 7-Two diff. issues (7/47 & 9/47) 12 24 36 67 94 120
8-Blue Beetle, Phantom Lady, & Rulah, Jungle Goddess begin (11/47); Kamen-c 300 600 900 1920 3310 4700
9-Kamen-c 152 304 456 965 1658 2350
10-Kamen bondage-c 158 316 474 1003 1727 2450
11-13,15-17: 11,12-Rulah-c. 15-No Blue Beetle 124 248 372 787 1356 1925
14-No Blue Beetle; used in **SOTI**, illo- "Corpses of colored people strung up by their wrists" 187 374 561 1197 2049 2900
18-Dagar, Jo-Jo app; no Phantom Lady or Blue Beetle 81 162 243 518 884 1250
6(1957-Green Publ.)-Patoruzu the Indian; Cosmo Cat on cover only. 6(1958-Literary Ent.)-Muggy Doo; Cosmo Cat on cover only. 6(1959-Norlen)-Atomic Mouse; Cosmo Cat on-c only. 6(1959)-Little Eva. 6(Cornell)-Supermouse on-c 5 10 15 24 30 35

NOTE: *Jo-Jo by* ***Kamen****-12,18.*

ALL TRUE ALL PICTURE POLICE CASES
St. John Publishing Co.: Oct, 1952 - No. 2, Nov, 1952 (100 pgs.)

1-Three rebound St. John crime comics 45 90 135 284 480 675
2-Three comics rebound 34 68 102 199 325 450

NOTE: *Contents may vary.*

ALL-TRUE CRIME (...Cases No. 26-35; formerly Official True Crime Cases)
Marvel/Atlas Comics: No. 26, Feb, 1948 - No. 52, Sept, 1952
(OFI #26,27/CFI #28,29/LCC #30-46/LMC #47-52)

26(#1)-Syd Shores-c 34 68 102 199 325 450
27(4/48)-Electric chair-c 28 56 84 165 270 375
28-41,43-48,50-52: 35-37-Photo-c 14 28 42 78 112 145
42,49-Krigstein-a. 49-Used in **POP**, Pg 79 14 28 42 81 118 155

NOTE: ***Colan*** *a-46.* ***Keller*** *a-46.* ***Robinson*** *a-47, 50.* ***Sale*** *a-46.* ***Shores*** *c-26.* ***Tuska*** *a-48(3).*

ALL-TRUE DETECTIVE CASES (Kit Carson No. 5 on)
Avon Periodicals: #2, Apr-May, 1954 - No. 4, Aug-Sept, 1954

2(#1)-Wood-a 23 46 69 136 223 310
3-Kinstler-c 14 28 42 81 118 155
4-r/Gangsters And Gun Molls #2; Kamen-a 18 36 54 105 165 225
nn(100 pgs.)-7 pg. Kubert-a, Kinstler back-c 40 80 120 249 417 585

ALL TRUE ROMANCE (...Illustrated No. 3)
Artful Publ. #1-3/Harwell(Comic Media) #4-20?/Ajax-Farrell(Excellent Publ.)

All Western Winners #3 © MAR

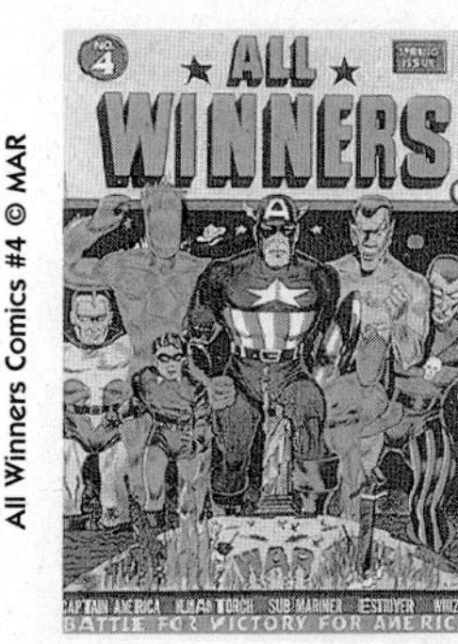

All Winners Comics #4 © MAR

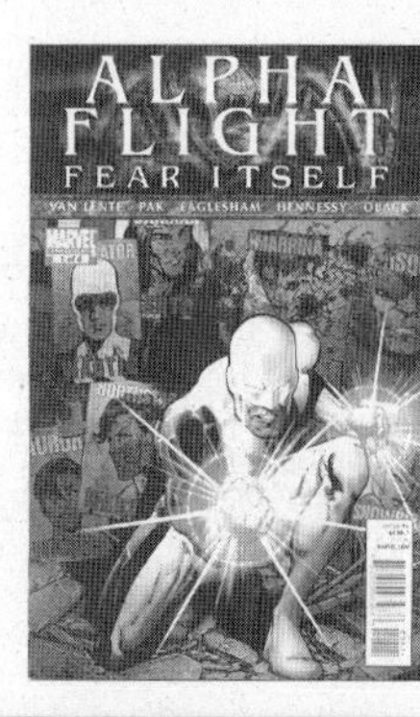

Alpha Flight (2011 series) #1 © MAR

GD 2.0 | VG 4.0 | FN 6.0 | VF 8.0 | VF/NM 9.0 | NM- 9.2

No. 22 on/Four Star Comic Corp.: 3/51 - No. 20, 12/54; No. 22, 3/55 - No. 30?, 7/57; No. 3(#31), 9/57;No. 4(#32), 11/57; No. 33, 2/58 - No. 34, 6/58

1 (3/51) 20 40 60 114 182 250
2 (10/51; 11/51 on-c) 12 24 36 69 97 125
3(12/51) - #5(5/52) 10 20 30 58 79 100
6-Wood-a, 9 pgs. (exceptional) 20 40 60 114 182 250
7-10 [two #7s: #7(11/52, 9/52 inside), #7(11/52, 11/52 inside)]. 10-Hollingsworth-c
10 20 30 54 72 90
11-13,16-19(9/54),20(12/54) (no #21): 11,13-Heck-a 8 16 24 44 57 70
14-Marijuana story 9 18 27 47 61 75
22: Last precode issue (1st Ajax, 3/55) 8 16 24 44 57 70
23-27,29,30(7/57): 29-Disbrow-a 8 16 24 40 50 60
28 (9/56)-L. B. Cole, Disbrow-a 11 22 33 64 90 115
3(#31, 9/57),4(#32, 11/57),33,34 (Farrell, '57- '58) 7 14 21 37 46 55

ALL WESTERN WINNERS (Formerly All Winners; becomes Western Winners with No. 5; see Two-Gun Kid No. 5)
Marvel Comics(CDS): No. 2, Winter, 1948-49 - No. 4, April, 1949

2-Black Rider (origin/1st app.) & his horse Satan, Kid Colt & his horse Steel, & Two-Gun Kid & his horse Cyclone begin; Shores c-2-4 74 148 222 470 810 1150
3-Anti-Wertham editorial 37 74 111 222 361 500
4-Black Rider i.d. revealed; Heath, Shores-a 37 74 111 222 361 500

ALL WINNERS COMICS (All Teen #20) (Also see Timely Presents: ...)
USA No. 1-7/WFP No. 10-19/YAI No. 21: Summer, 1941 - No. 19, Fall, 1946; No. 21, Winter, 1946-47; (No #20) (No. 21 continued from Young Allies No. 20)

1-The Angel & Black Marvel only app.; Capt. America by Simon & Kirby, Human Torch & Sub-Mariner begin (#1 was advertised as All Aces); 1st app. All-Winners Squad in text story by Stan Lee 1900 3800 5700 13,500 24,250 35,000
2-The Destroyer & The Whizzer begin; Simon & Kirby Captain America
530 1060 1590 3869 6835 9800
3 423 846 1269 3000 5250 7500
4-Classic War-c by Al Avison 443 886 1329 3234 5717 8200
5 300 600 900 2010 3505 5000
6-The Black Avenger only app.; no Whizzer story; Hitler, Hirohito & Mussolini-c
400 800 1200 2800 4900 7000
7-10 300 600 900 1950 3375 4800
11,13-18: 11-1st Atlas globe on-c (Winter, 1943-44; also see Human Torch #14). 14-16-No Human Torch 206 412 618 1318 2259 3200
12-Red Skull story; last Destroyer; no Whizzer story
284 568 852 1818 3109 4400
19-(Scarce)-1st story app. & origin All Winners Squad (Capt. America & Bucky, Human Torch & Toro, Sub-Mariner, Whizzer, & Miss America; r-in Fantasy Masterpieces #10
811 1622 2433 5920 10,460 15,000
21-(Scarce)-All Winners Squad; bondage-c 649 1298 1947 4738 8369 12,000
NOTE: *Everett Sub-Mariner-1, 3, 4; **Burgos** Torch-1, 3, 4. **Schomburg** c-1, 7-18. **Shores** c-19p, 21.*

(2nd Series - August, 1948, Marvel Comics (CDS))
(Becomes All Western Winners with No. 2)

1-The Blonde Phantom, Capt. America, Human Torch, & Sub-Mariner app.
300 600 900 1965 3408 4850

ALL WINNERS COMICS 70th ANNIVERARY SPECIAL
Marvel Comics: Oct, 2009 ($3.99, one-shot)

1-New story of All Winners Squad; r/G.A. Capt America app. from All Winners #12 5.00

ALL-WINNERS SQUAD: BAND OF HEROES
Marvel Comics: Aug, 2011 - No. 8 ($2.99, one-shot)

1-5-WWII story of the Young Avenger and Captain Flame; Jenkins-s/DiGiandomenico-a 3.00

ALL YOUR COMICS (See Fox Giants)
Fox Feature Syndicate (R. W. Voight): Spring, 1946 (36 pgs.)

1-Red Robbins, Merciless the Sorceress app. 22 44 66 128 209 290

ALMANAC OF CRIME (See Fox Giants)

AL OF FBI (See Little Al of the FBI)

ALONE IN THE DARK (Based on video game)
Image Comics: Feb, 2003 ($4.95)

1-Matt Haley-c/a; Jean-Marc & Randy Lofficier-s 5.00

ALPHA AND OMEGA
Spire Christian Comics (Fleming H. Revell): 1978 (49¢)

nn 2 4 6 9 12 15

ALPHA CENTURION (See Superman, 2nd Series & Zero Hour)
DC Comics: 1996 ($2.95, one-shot)

1 3.00

ALPHA FLIGHT (See X-Men #120,121 & X-Men/Alpha Flight)
Marvel Comics: Aug, 1983 - No. 130, Mar, 1994 (#52-on are direct sales only)

1-(52 pgs.) Byrne-a begins (thru #28) -Wolverine & Nightcrawler cameo 5.00
2-11,13-28: 2-Vindicator becomes Guardian; origin Marrina & Alpha Flight. 3-Concludes origin Alpha Flight. 6-Origin Shaman. 7-Origin Snowbird. 10,11-Origin Sasquatch. 13-Wolverine app. 16,17-Wolverine cameo. 17-X-Men x-over (mostly r-/X-Men #109). 20-New headquarters. 25-Return of Guardian. 28-Last Byrne issue 3.50
12-(52 pgs.)-Death of Guardian 4.00
29-32,35-49: 39-47,49-Portacio-a(i) 3.00
33,34-1st & 2nd app. Lady Deathstrike; Wolverine app. 34-Origin Wolverine 4.00
50-Double size; Portacio-a(i) 4.00
51-Jim Lee's 1st work at Marvel (10/87); Wolverine cameo; 1st Lee Wolverine; Portacio-a(i) 6.00
52,53-Wolverine app.; Lee-a on Wolverine; Portacio-a(i); 53-Lee/Portacio-a 4.00
54-73,76-86,91-99,101-105: 54,63,64-No Jim Lee-a. 54-Portacio-a(i). 55-62-Jim Lee-a(p). 71-Intro The Sorcerer (villain). 91-Dr. Doom app. 94-F.F. x-over. 99-Galactus, Avengers app. 102-Intro Weapon Omega 3.00
74,75,87-90,100: 74-Wolverine, Spider-Man & The Avengers app. 75-Double size ($1.95, 52 pgs.). 87-90-Wolverine. 4 part story w/Jim Lee-c. 89-Original Guardian returns. 100-($2.00, 52 pgs.)-Avengers & Galactus app. 4.00
106-Northstar revealed to be gay 3.50
106-2nd printing (direct sale only) 3.00
107-109,112-119,121-129: 107-X-Factor x-over. 112-Infinity War x-overs 3.00
110,111: Infinity War x-overs, Wolverine app. (brief). 111-Thanos cameo 3.00
120-($2.25)-Polybagged w/Paranormal Registration Act poster 4.00
130-($2.25, 52 pgs.) 4.00
Annual 1,2 (9/86, 12/87) 4.00
...Classics Vol. 1 TPB (2007, $24.99) r/#1-8; character profile pages; Byrne interview 25.00
Special V2#1(6/92, $2.50, 52 pgs.)-Wolverine-c/story 4.00
NOTE: ***Austin** c-1i, 2i, 53i. **Byrne** c-81, 82. **Guice** c-85, 91-99. **Jim Lee** a(p)-51, 53, 55-62, 64; c-53, 87-90. **Mignola** a-29-31p. **Whilce Portacio** a(i)-39-47, 49-54.*

ALPHA FLIGHT (2nd Series)
Marvel Comics: Aug, 1997 - No. 20, Mar, 1999 ($2.99/$1.99)

1-($2.99)-Wraparound cover 6.00
2,3: 2-Variant-c 4.00
4-11: 8,9-Wolverine-c/app. 3.00
12-($2.99) Death of Sasquatch; wraparound-c 4.00
13-20 3.00
.../Inhumans '98 Annual ($3.50) Raney-a 4.00

ALPHA FLIGHT (3rd Series)
Marvel Comics: May, 2004 - No. 12, April, 2005 ($2.99)

1-12: 1-6-Lobdell-s/Henry-c/a 3.00
... Vol. 1: You Gotta Be Kiddin' Me (2004, $14.99) r/#1-6 15.00

ALPHA FLIGHT (4th Series)
Marvel Comics: No. 0.1, Jul, 2011 - No. 8, Mar, 2012 ($2.99)

0.1-Pak & Van Lente-s/Oliver & Green-a; Kara Killgrave app. 3.00
1-(8/11, $3.99) Fear Itself tie-in; Eaglesham-a/Jimenez-c; bonus design sketch pages 4.00
2-8-($2.99) Fear Itself tie-ins. 2-Puck returns. 5-Taskmaster app. 7,8-Wolverine app. 3.00

ALPHA FLIGHT: IN THE BEGINNING
Marvel Comics: July, 1997 ($1.95, one-shot)

(-1)-Flashback w/Wolverine 3.00

ALPHA FLIGHT SPECIAL
Marvel Comics: July, 1991 - No. 4, Oct, 1991 ($1.50, limited series)

1-4: 1-3-r-A. Flight #97-99 w/covers. 4-r-A.Flight #100 3.00

ALPHA GIRL
Image Comics: Feb, 2012 - Present ($2.99)

1-Roenning & Bonjour-s/Love-a; intro. Judith Meyers 3.00

ALPHA KORPS
Diversity Comics: Sept, 1996 ($2.50)

1-Origin/1st app. Alpha Korps 3.00

ALTERED IMAGE
Image Comics: Apr, 1998 - No. 3, Sept, 1998 ($2.50, limited series)

1-3-Spawn, Witchblade, Savage Dragon; Valentino-s/a 3.00

ALTER EGO
First Comics: May, 1986 - No. 4, Nov, 1986 (Mini-series)

1-4 3.00

ALTER NATION
Image Comics: Feb, 2004 - No. 4, Jun, 2004 ($2.95, limited series)

1-4: 1-Two covers by Art Adams and Barberi; Barberi-a 3.00

Amazing Adult Fantasy #7 © MAR

Amazing Adventures #1 © Z-D

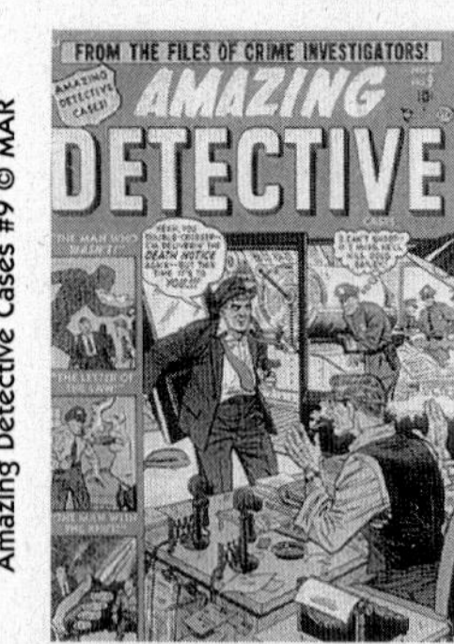

Amazing Detective Cases #9 © MAR

GD VG FN VF VF/NM NM-
2.0 4.0 6.0 8.0 9.0 9.2

ALVIN (TV) (See Four Color Comics No. 1042 or Three Chipmunks #1)
Dell Publishing Co.: Oct-Dec, 1962 - No. 28, Oct, 1973

12-021-212 (#1) 9 18 27 58 99 140
2 5 10 15 35 55 75
3-10 5 10 15 30 48 65
11-"Chipmunks sing the Beatles' Hits" 5 10 15 35 55 75
12-28 4 8 12 24 37 50
Alvin For President (10/64) 5 10 15 30 48 65
...& His Pals in Merry Christmas with Clyde Crashcup & Leonardo 1
(02-120-402)-(12-2/64) 7 14 21 49 82 115
Reprinted in 1966 (12-023-604) 4 8 12 24 37 50

ALVIN & THE CHIPMUNKS
Harvey Comics: July, 1992 - No. 5, May, 1994

1-5: 1-Richie Rich app. 5.00

AMALGAM AGE OF COMICS, THE: THE DC COMICS COLLECTION
DC Comics: 1996 ($12.95, trade paperback)

nn-r/Amazon, Assassins, Doctor Strangefate, JLX, Legends of the Dark Claw, & Super Soldier 13.00

AMANDA AND GUNN
Image Comics: Apr, 1997 - No. 4, Oct, 1997 ($2.95, B&W, limited series)

1-4 3.00

AMAZING ADULT FANTASY (Formerly Amazing Adventures #1-6; becomes Amazing Fantasy #15) (See Amazing Fantasy for Omnibus HC reprint of #1-15)
Marvel Comics Group (AMI): No. 7, Dec, 1961 - No. 14, July, 1962

7-Ditko-c/a begins, ends #14 46 92 138 345 748 1150
8-Last 10¢ issue 37 74 111 278 602 925
9-13: 12-1st app. Mailbag. 13-Anti-communist sty 36 72 108 270 585 900
13-2nd printing (1994) 2 4 6 8 10 12
14-Prototype issue (Professor X) 38 76 114 285 618 950

AMAZING ADVENTURE FUNNIES (Fantoman No. 2 on)
Centaur Publications: June, 1940 - No. 2, Sept. 1940

1-The Fantom of the Fair by Gustavson (r/Amaz. Mystery Funnies V2#7,V2#8), The Arrow, Skyrocket Steele From the Year X by Everett (r/AMF #2); Burgos-a 174 348 522 1114 1907 2700
2-Reprints; Published after Fantoman #2 114 228 342 724 1242 1760
NOTE: ***Burgos** a-1(2). **Everett** a-1(3). **Gustavson** a-1(5), 2(3). **Pinajian** a-2.*

AMAZING ADVENTURES (Also see Boy Cowboy & Science Comics)
Ziff-Davis Publ. Co.: 1950; No. 1, Nov, 1950 - No. 6, Fall, 1952 (Painted covers)

1950 (no month given) (8-1/2x11) (8 pgs.) Has the front & back cover plus Schomburg story used in Amazing Advs. #1 (Sent to subscribers of Z-D s/f magazines & ordered through mail for 10¢. Used to test market) 68 136 204 435 743 1050
1-Wood, Schomburg, Anderson, Whitney-a 87 174 261 553 952 1350
2-5: 2-Schomburg-a. 2,4,5-Anderson-a. 3,5-Starr-a 42 84 126 265 445 625
6-Krigstein-a 42 84 126 267 451 635

AMAZING ADVENTURES (Becomes Amazing Adult Fantasy #7 on) (See Amazing Fantasy for Omnibus HC reprint of #1-15)
Atlas Comics (AMI)/Marvel Comics No. 3 on: June, 1961 - No. 6, Nov, 1961

1-Origin Dr. Droom (1st Marvel-Age Superhero) by Kirby; Kirby/Ditko-a (5 pgs.) Ditko & Kirby-a in all; Kirby monster c-1-6 107 214 321 867 1884 2900
2 45 90 135 338 732 1125
3-6: 6-Last Dr. Droom 39 78 117 293 634 975

AMAZING ADVENTURES
Marvel Comics Group: Aug, 1970 - No. 39, Nov, 1976

1-Inhumans by Kirby(p) & Black Widow (1st app. in Tales of Suspense #52) double feature begins 7 14 21 46 76 105
2-4: 2-F.F. brief app. 4-Last Inhumans by Kirby 4 8 12 22 34 45
5-8: Adams-a(p); 8-Last Black Widow; last 15¢-c 5 10 15 32 51 70
9,10: Magneto app. 10-Last Inhumans (origin-r by Kirby) 4 8 12 22 34 45
11-New Beast begins(1st app. in mutated form; origin in flashback); X-Men cameo in flashback (#11-17 are X-Men tie-ins) 17 34 51 119 260 400
12-17: 12-Beast battles Iron Man. 13-Brotherhood of Evil Mutants x-over from X-Men. 15-X-Men app. 16-Rutland Vermont - Bald Mountain Halloween x-over; Juggernaut app. 17-Last Beast (origin); X-Men app. 8 16 24 55 93 130
18-War of the Worlds begins (5/73); 1st app. Killraven; Neal Adams-a(p) 3 6 9 20 30 40
19-35,38,39: 19-Chaykin-a. 25-Buckler-a. 35-Giffen's first published story (art), along with Deadly Hands of Kung-Fu #22 (3/76) 1 3 4 6 8 10
36,37-(Regular 25¢ edition)(7-8/76) 1 3 4 6 8 10
36,37-(30¢-c variants, limited distribution) 6 12 18 37 59 80
NOTE: ***N. Adams** c-6-8. **Buscema** a-1p, 2p. **Colan** a-3-5p, 26p. **Ditko** a-24r. **Everett** a(i)3-5, 7-9. **Giffen** a-35i, 38p. **G. Kane** c-11, 25p, 29p. **Ploog** a-12i. **Russell** a-27-32, 34-37, 39; c-28, 30-32, 33i, 34, 35, 37, 39i. **Starliing** a-17. **Starlin** c-15p, 16, 17, 27. **Sutton** a-11-15p.*

AMAZING ADVENTURES
Marvel Comics Group: Dec, 1979 - No. 14, Jan, 1981

V2#1-Reprints story/X-Men #1 & 38 (origins) 1 3 4 6 8 10
2-14: 2-6-Early X-Men-r. 7,8-Origin Iceman 1 2 3 4 5 7
NOTE: ***Byrne** c-6p, 9p. **Kirby** a-1-14r; c-7, 9. **Steranko** a-12r. **Tuska** a-7-9.*

AMAZING ADVENTURES
Marvel Comics: July, 1988 ($4.95, squarebound, one-shot, 80 pgs.)

1-Anthology; Austin, Golden-a 5.00

AMAZING ADVENTURES OF CAPTAIN CARVEL AND HIS CARVEL CRUSADERS, THE
(See Carvel Comics in the Promotional Comics section)

AMAZING CHAN & THE CHAN CLAN, THE (TV)
Gold Key: May, 1973 - No. 4, Feb, 1974 (Hanna-Barbera)

1-Warren Tufts-a in all 4 8 12 22 34 45
2-4 3 6 9 16 23 30

AMAZING COMICS (Complete Comics No. 2)
Timely Comics (EPC): Fall, 1944

1-The Destroyer, The Whizzer, The Young Allies (by Sekowsky), Sergeant Dix; Schomburg-c 271 542 813 1734 2967 4200

AMAZING DETECTIVE CASES (Formerly Suspense No. 2?)
Marvel/Atlas Comics (CCC): No. 3, Nov, 1950 - No. 14, Sept, 1952

3 30 60 90 177 289 400
4-6: 6-Jerry Robinson-a 18 36 54 103 162 220
7-10 16 32 48 92 144 195
11,12: 11-(3/52)-Horror format begins. 12-Krigstein-a 40 80 120 246 411 575
13-(Scarce)-Everett-a; electrocution-c/story 42 84 126 265 445 625
14 37 74 111 222 361 500
NOTE: ***Colan** a-9. **Maneely** c-13. **Sekowsky** a-12. **Sinnott** a-13. **Tuska** a-10.*

AMAZING FANTASY (Formerly Amazing Adult Fantasy #7-14)
Atlas Magazines/Marvel: #15, Aug, 1962 (Sept, 1962 shown in indicia); #16, Dec, 1995 - #18, Feb, 1996

15-Origin/1st app. of Spider-Man by Steve Ditko (11 pgs.); 1st app. Aunt May & Uncle Ben; Kirby/Ditko-c 3500 7000 15,000 50,000 100,000 150,000
16-18 ('95-'96, $3.95): Kurt Busiek scripts; painted-c/a by Paul Lee 4.00
Amazing Fantasy Omnibus HC ("Amazing Adult Fantasy" on-c) (2007, $75.00, dustjacket) r/Amazing Adventures #1-6, Amazing Adult Fantasy #7-14 and Amazing Fantasy #15 with letter pages; foreword by Bissette; cover gallery from '70s reprint titles 75.00

AMAZING FANTASY (Continues from #6 in Araña: The Heart of the Spider)
Marvel Comics: Aug, 2004 - No. 20, June, 2006 ($2.99)

1-Intro. Anya Corazon; Fiona Avery-s/Mark Brooks-c/a 4.00
2-14,16-20: 3,4-Roger Cruz-a. 7-Intro. new Scorpion; Kirk-a. 10-Intro. Vampire By Night 13,14-Back-up Captain Universe stories. 16-20-Death's Head 3.00
15-($3.99) Spider-Man app.; intro 6 new characters incl. Mastermind Excello seen in World War Hulk series; s/a by various 4.00
Death's Head 3.0: Unnatural Selection TPB (2006, $13.99) r/#16-20 14.00
Scorpion: Poison Tomorrow (2005, $7.99, digest) r/#7-13 8.00

AMAZING GHOST STORIES (Formerly Nightmare)
St. John Publishing Co.: No. 14, Oct, 1954 - No. 16, Feb, 1955

14-Pit & the Pendulum story by Kinstler; Baker-c 36 72 108 216 351 485
15-r/Weird Thrillers #5; Baker-c, Powell-a 27 54 81 158 259 360
16-Kubert reprints of Weird Thrillers #4; Baker-c; Roussos, Tuska-a; Kinstler-a (1 pg.) 27 54 81 160 263 365

AMAZING HIGH ADVENTURE
Marvel Comics: 8/84; No. 2, 10/85; No. 3, 10/86 - No. 5, 1986 ($2.00)

1-5: Painted-c on all. 3,4-Baxter paper. 4-Bolton-c/a. 5-Bolton-a 4.00
NOTE: ***Bissette** a-4. **Severin** a-1, 3. **Sienkiewicz** a-1,2. **Paul Smith** a-2. **Williamson** a-2i.*

AMAZING JOY BUZZARDS
Image Comics: 2005 - No. 4, 2005 ($2.95, B&W with pink spot color in #1)

1-4-Mark Andrew Smith-s/Dan Hipp-a. 1-Mahfood back-c. 2-Morse back-c 3.00
Vol. 1 TPB (2005, $11.95) r/#1-4; bonus art and character design sketches 12.00
TPB (2008, $19.99) r/#1-4 and Vol. 2 #1-5 20.00

AMAZING JOY BUZZARDS (Volume 2)
Image Comics: Oct, 2005 - No. 5, Aug, 2006 ($2.99, B&W)

1-5: 1-Mark Andrew Smith-s/Dan Hipp-a. 4-Mahfood-a; Crosland-a. 5-Holgate-a 3.00
Vol. 2 TPB (2006, $12.99) r/#1-4; bonus art, pin-ups and character sketches 13.00

Amazing-Man Comics #15 © CEN

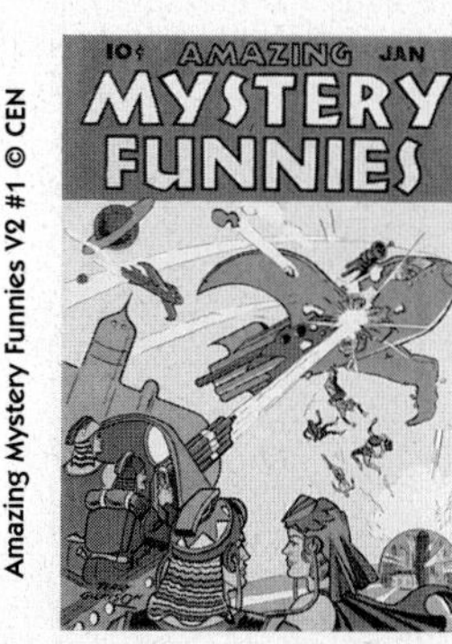

Amazing Mystery Funnies V2 #1 © CEN

Amazing Spider-Man #8 © MAR

GD VG FN VF VF/NM NM-
2.0 4.0 6.0 8.0 9.0 9.2

GD VG FN VF VF/NM NM-
2.0 4.0 6.0 8.0 9.0 9.2

AMAZING-MAN COMICS (Formerly Motion Picture Funnies Weekly?)
(Also see Stars And Stripes Comics)
Centaur Publications: No. 5, Sept, 1939 - No. 26, Jan, 1942

5(#1)(Rare)-Origin/1st app. A-Man the Amazing Man by Bill Everett; The Cat-Man by Tarpe Mills (also #8), Mighty Man by Filchock, Minimidget & sidekick Ritty, & The Iron Skull by Burgos begins 1633 3267 4900 12,200 22,100 32,000
6-Origin The Amazing Man retold; The Shark begins; Ivy Menace by Tarpe Mills app. 354 708 1062 2478 4339 6200
7-Magician From Mars begins; ends #11 265 530 795 1694 2897 4100
8-Cat-Man dresses as woman 200 400 600 1280 2190 3100
9-Magician From Mars battles the 'Elemental Monster,' swiped into The Spectre in More Fun #54 & 55. Ties w/Marvel Mystery #4 for 1st Nazi War-c on a comic (2/40) 213 426 639 1363 2332 3300
10,11: 11-Zardi, the Eternal Man begins; ends #16; Amazing Man dons costume; last Everett issue 148 296 444 947 1624 2300
12,13 139 278 417 883 1517 2150
14-Reef Kinkaid, Rocke Wayburn (ends #20), & Dr. Hypno (ends #21) begin; no Zardi or Chuck Hardy 113 226 339 718 1234 1750
15,17-20: 15-Zardi returns; no Rocke Wayburn. 17-Dr. Hypno returns; no Zardi 100 200 300 635 1093 1550
16-Mighty Man's powers of super strength & ability to shrink & grow explained; Rocke Wayburn returns; no Dr. Hypno; Al Avison (a character) begins, ends #18 (a tribute to the famed artist) 107 214 321 680 1165 1650
21-Origin Dash Dartwell (drug-use story); origin & only app. T.N.T. 116 232 348 742 1271 1800
22-Dash Dartwell, the Human Meteor & The Voice app; last Iron Skull & The Shark; Silver Streak app. (classic-c) 258 516 774 1651 2826 4000
23-Two Amazing Man stories; intro/origin Tommy the Amazing Kid; The Marksman only app. 90 180 270 576 988 1400
24-King of Darkness, Nightshade, & Blue Lady begin; end #26; 1st app. Super-Ann 90 180 270 576 988 1400
25,26 (Scarce): Meteor Martin by Wolverton in both; 26-Electric Ray app. 194 388 582 1242 2121 3000

NOTE: ***Everett*** *a-5-11; c-5-11.* ***Gilman*** *a-14-20.* ***Giunta/Mirando*** *a-7-10.* ***Sam Glanzman*** *a-14-16, 18-21, 23.* ***Louis Glanzman*** *a-6, 9-11, 14-21; c-13-19, 21.* ***Robert Golden*** *a-9.* ***Gustavson*** *a-6; c-22, 23.* ***Lubbers*** *a-14-21.* ***Simon*** *a-10.* ***Frank Thomas*** *a-6, 9-11, 14, 15, 17-21.*

AMAZING MYSTERIES (Formerly Sub-Mariner Comics No. 31)
Marvel Comics (CCC): No. 32, May, 1949 - No. 35, Jan, 1950 (1st Marvel Horror Comic)

32-The Witness app. 94 188 282 597 1024 1450
33-Horror format 42 84 126 265 445 625
34,35: Changes to Crime. 34,35-Photo-c 21 42 63 126 206 285

AMAZING MYSTERY FUNNIES
Centaur Publications: Aug, 1938 - No. 24, Sept, 1940 (All 52 pgs.)

V1#1-Everett-c(1st); Dick Kent Adv. story; Skyrocket Steele in the Year X on cover only 389 778 1167 2723 4762 6800
2-Everett 1st-a (Skyrocket Steele) 213 426 639 1363 2332 3300
3 116 232 348 742 1271 1800
3(#4, 12/38)-nn on cover, #3 on inside; bondage-c 107 214 321 680 1165 1650
V2#1-4,6: 2-Drug use story. 3-Air-Sub DX begins by Burgos. 4-Dan Hastings, Sand Hog begins (ends #5). 6-Last Skyrocket Steele 89 178 267 565 970 1375
5-Classic Everett-c 206 412 618 1318 2259 3200
7 (Scarce)-Intro. The Fantom of the Fair & begins; Everett, Gustavson, Burgos-a 371 742 1113 2600 4550 6500
8-Origin & 1st app. Speed Centaur 155 310 465 992 1696 2400
9-11: 11-Self portrait and biog. of Everett; Jon Linton begins; early Robot cover (11/39) 89 178 267 565 970 1375
12 (Scarce)-1st Space Patrol; Wolverton-a (12/39); new costume Phantom of the Fair 206 412 618 1318 2259 3200
V3#1(#17, 1/40)-Intro. Bullet; Tippy Taylor serial begins, ends #24 (continued in The Arrow #2) 87 174 261 553 952 1350
18,20: 18-Fantom of the Fair by Gustavson 84 168 252 538 919 1300
19,21-24: Space Patrol by Wolverton in all 100 200 300 635 1093 1550

NOTE: ***Burgos*** *a-V2#3-9.* ***Eisner*** *a-V1#2, 3(2).* ***Everett*** *a-V1#2-4, V2#1, 3-6; c-V1#1-4,V2#3, 5, 18.* ***Filchock*** *a-V2#9.* ***Flessel*** *a-V2#6.* ***Guardineer*** *a-V1#4, V2#4-6;* ***Gustavson*** *a-V2#4, 5, 9-12, V3#1, 18, 19; c-V2#7, 9, 12, V3#1, 21, 22;* ***McWilliams*** *a-V2#9, 10.* ***TarpeMills*** *a-V2#2, 4-6, 9-12, V3#1.* ***Leo Morey****(Pulp artist) c-V2#10; text illo-V2#11.* ***FrankThomas*** *a-6-V2#11.* ***Webster*** *a-V2#4.*

AMAZING SAINTS
Logos International: 1974 (39¢)

nn-True story of Phil Saint 2 4 6 9 13 16

AMAZING SCARLET SPIDER
Marvel Comics: Nov, 1995 - No. 2, Dec, 1995 ($1.95, limited series)

1,2: Replaces "Amazing Spider-Man" for two issues. 1-Venom/Carnage cameos. 2-Green Goblin & Joystick-c/app. 3.00

AMAZING SCREW-ON HEAD, THE
Dark Horse Comics (Maverick): May, 2002 ($2.99, one-shot)

1-Mike Mignola-s/a/c 3.00

AMAZING SPIDER-GIRL (Also see Spider-Girl and What If...? (2nd series) #105)
Marvel Comics: No. 0, 2006; No. 1, Dec, 2006 - No. 30, May, 2009 ($2.99)

0-($1.99) Recap of the Spider-Girl series and character profiles; A.F. #15 cover swipe 3.00
1-14,16-24,26-($2.99) Frenz & Buscema-a. 9-Carnage returns. 19-Has #17 on cover 3.00
15,25,30-($3.99) 15-10th Anniversary issue. 25-Three covers 4.00
... Vol. 1: What Ever Happened to the Daughter of Spider-Man? TPB (2007, $14.99) r/#0-6 15.00
... Vol. 2: Comes the Carnage! TPB (2007, $13.99) r/#7-12 14.00
... Vol. 3: Mind Games TPB (2008, $13.99) r/#13-18 14.00

AMAZING SPIDER-MAN, THE (See All Detergent Comics, Amazing Fantasy, America's Best TV Comics, Aurora, Deadly Foes of..., Fireside Book Series, Friendly Neighborhood..., Giant-Size..., Giant Size Super-Heroes Featuring..., Marvel Age..., Marvel Collectors Item Classics, Marvel Fanfare, Marvel Graphic Novel, Marvel Knoghts..., Marvel Spec. Ed., Marvel Tales, Marvel Team-Up, Marvel Treasury Ed., New Avengers, Nothing Can Stop the Juggernaut, Official Marvel Index To..., Peter Parker..., Power Record Comics, Spectacular..., Spider-Man, Spider-Man Digest, Spider-Man Saga, Spider-Man 2099, Spider-Man Vs. Wolverine, Spidey Super Stories, Strange Tales Annual #2, Superman Vs. ..., Try-Out Winner Book, Ultimate Marvel Team-Up, Ultimate Spider-Man, Web of Spider- Man & Within Our Reach)

AMAZING SPIDER-MAN, THE
Marvel Comics Group: March, 1963 - No. 441, Nov, 1998

1-Retells origin by Steve Ditko; 1st Fantastic Four x-over (ties with F.F. #12 as first Marvel x-over); intro. John Jameson & The Chameleon; Spider-Man's 2nd app.; Kirby/Ditko-c; Ditko-c/a #1-38 1733 3467 5200 15,200 36,100 57,000
1-Reprint from the Golden Record Comic set 17 34 51 119 260 400
With record (1966) 26 52 78 182 391 600
2-1st app. the Vulture & the Terrible Tinkerer 400 800 1200 3600 7550 11,500
3-1st app. Doc Octopus; 1st full-length story; Human Torch cameo; Spider-Man pin-up by Ditko 321 642 963 2793 6047 9300
4-Origin & 1st app. The Sandman (see Strange Tales #115 for 2nd app.); 1st monthly issue; intro. Betty Brant & Liz Allen 268 536 804 2250 4875 7500
5-Dr. Doom app. 214 428 642 1800 3900 6000
6-1st app. Lizard 179 358 537 1500 3250 5000
7-Vs. The Vulture 119 238 357 964 2082 3200
8-Fantastic Four app. in back-up story by Kirby & Ditko 93 186 279 753 1627 2500
9-Origin & 1st app. Electro (2/64) 120 240 360 972 2111 3250
10-1st app. Big Man & The Enforcers 100 200 300 81 1755 2700
11-1st app. Bennett Brant 104 208 312 842 1821 2800
12-Doc Octopus unmasks Spider-Man-c/story 82 164 246 664 1432 2200
13-1st app. Mysterio 119 238 357 964 2082 3200
14-(7/64)-1st app. The Green Goblin (c/story)(Norman Osborn); Hulk x-over 171 342 513 1436 3118 4800
15-1st app. Kraven the Hunter; 1st mention of Mary Jane Watson (not shown) 85 170 255 689 1495 2300
16-Spider-Man battles Daredevil (1st x-over 9/64); still in old yellow costume 74 148 222 600 1300 2000
17-2nd app. Green Goblin (c/story); Human Torch x-over (also in #18 & #21) 80 160 240 648 1399 2150
18-1st app. Ned Leeds who later becomes Hobgoblin; Fantastic Four cameo; 3rd app. Sandman 46 92 138 373 812 1250
19-Sandman app. 37 74 111 278 602 925
20-Origin & 1st app. The Scorpion 65 130 195 527 1139 1750
21-2nd app. The Beetle (see Strange Tales #123) 38 76 114 285 618 950
22-1st app. Princess Python 37 74 111 278 602 925
23-3rd app. The Green Goblin-c/story; Norman Osborn app.; Marvel Masterwork pin-up by Ditko; fan letter by Jim Shooter 46 92 138 359 780 1200
24 35 70 105 254 552 850
25-(6/65)-1st brief app. Mary Jane Watson (face not shown); 1st app. Spencer Smythe; Norman Osborn app. 38 76 114 285 618 950
26-4th app. The Green Goblin-c/story; 1st app. Crime Master; dies in #27 39 78 117 293 634 975
27-5th app. The Green Goblin-c/story; Norman Osborn app. 38 76 114 285 618 950
28-Origin & 1st app. Molten Man (9/65, scarcer in high grade) 85 170 255 689 1495 2300
29,30 27 54 81 196 423 650
31-1st app. Harry Osborn who later becomes 2nd Green Goblin, Gwen Stacy & Prof. Warren. 31 62 93 225 488 750
32-38: 34-4th app. Kraven the Hunter. 36-1st app. Looter. 37-Intro. Norman Osborn. 38-(7/66)-2nd brief app. Mary Jane Watson (face not shown); last Ditko issue

Amazing Spider-Man #42 © MAR

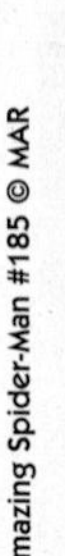
Amazing Spider-Man #185 © MAR

Amazing Spider-Man #276 © MAR

	GD 2.0	VG 4.0	FN 6.0	VF 8.0	VF/NM 9.0	NM- 9.2
	22	44	66	154	327	500
39-The Green Goblin-c/story; Green Goblin's i.d. revealed as Norman Osborn; Romita-a begins (8/66; see Daredevil #16 for 1st Romita-a on Spider-Man)	34	68	102	247	536	825
40-1st told origin The Green Goblin-c/story	36	72	108	270	585	900
41-1st app. Rhino	33	66	99	239	520	800
42-(11/66)-3rd app. Mary Jane Watson (cameo in last 2 panels); 1st time face is shown	21	42	63	142	304	465
43-49: 44,45-2nd & 3rd app. The Lizard. 46-Intro. Shocker. 47-M. J. Watson & Peter Parker 1st date. 47-Green Goblin cameo; Harry & Norman Osborn app. 47,49-5th & 6th app. Kraven the Hunter	16	32	48	107	234	360
50-1st app. Kingpin (7/67)	59	118	177	478	1039	1600
51-2nd app. Kingpin; Joe Robertson 1-panel cameo	21	42	63	146	311	475
52-58,60: 52-1st app. Joe Robertson & 3rd app. Kingpin. 56-1st app. Capt. George Stacy. 57,58-Ka-Zar app.	12	24	36	83	172	260
59-1st app. Brainwasher (alias Kingpin); 1st-c app. M. J. Watson	13	26	39	87	186	285
61-74: 61-1st Gwen Stacy cover app. 67-1st app. Randy Robertson. 69-Kingpin-c. 69,70-Kingpin app. 73-1st app. Silvermane. 74-Last 12¢ issue	10	20	30	69	130	190
75-83,87-89,91,92,95,99: 78,79-1st app. The Prowler. 83-1st app. Schemer & Vanessa (Kingpin's wife)	9	18	27	62	109	155
84-86,93: 84,85-Kingpin-c/story. 86-Re-intro & origin Black Widow in new costume. 93-1st app. Arthur Stacy	9	18	27	63	112	160
90-Death of Capt. Stacy	11	22	33	71	136	200
94-Origin retold	11	22	33	71	136	200
96-98-Green Goblin app. (97,98-Green Goblin-c); drug books not approved by CCA	11	22	33	73	142	210
100-Anniversary issue (9/71); Green Goblin cameo (2 pgs.)	13	26	39	90	195	300
101-1st app. Morbius the Living Vampire; Wizard cameo; last 15¢ issue (10/71)	17	34	51	114	250	385
101-Silver ink 2nd printing (9/92, $1.75)						3.00
102-Origin & 2nd app. Morbius (25¢, 52 pgs.)	12	24	36	81	166	250
103-118: 104,111-Kraven the Hunter-c/stories. 108-1st app. Sha-Shan. 109-Dr. Strange-c/story (6/72). 110-1st app. Gibbon. 113-1st app. Hammerhead. 116-118-reprints story from Spectacular Spider-Man Mag. in color with some changes	7	14	21	48	79	110
119,120-Spider-Man vs. Hulk (4 & 5/73)	10	20	30	64	115	165
121-Death of Gwen Stacy (6/73) (killed by Green Goblin) (reprinted in Marvel Tales #98 & 192)	20	40	60	137	294	450
122-Death of The Green Goblin-c/story (7/73) (reprinted in Marvel Tales #99 & 192)	20	40	60	137	294	450
123,126-128: 123-Cage app. 126-1st mention of Harry Osborn becoming Green Goblin	7	14	21	44	72	100
124-1st app. Man-Wolf (9/73)	7	14	21	49	82	115
125-Man-Wolf origin	7	14	21	46	76	105
129-1st app. The Punisher (2/74); 1st app. Jackal	38	76	114	285	618	950
130-133: 131-Last 20¢ issue	6	12	18	39	62	85
134-(7/74); 1st app. Tarantula; Harry Osborn discovers Spider-Man's ID; Punisher cameo	6	12	18	42	69	95
135-2nd full Punisher app. (8/74)	9	18	27	63	112	160
136-1st app. Harry Osborn Green Goblin in costume	8	16	24	56	96	135
137-Green Goblin-c/story (2nd Harry Osborn Goblin)	6	12	18	42	69	95
138-141: 139-1st Grizzly. 140-1st app. Glory Grant	4	8	12	24	37	50
142,143-Gwen Stacy clone cameos: 143-1st app. Cyclone	4	8	12	24	37	50
144-147: 144-Full app. of Gwen Stacy clone. 145,146-Gwen Stacy clone storyline continues. 147-Spider-Man learns Gwen Stacy is clone	4	8	12	24	37	50
148-Jackal revealed	4	8	12	26	41	55
149-Spider-Man clone story begins, clone dies (?); origin of Jackal	7	14	21	48	79	110
150-Spider-Man decides he is not the clone	4	8	12	26	41	55
151-Spider-Man disposes of clone body	4	8	12	26	41	55
152-160-(Regular 25¢ editions). 159-Last 25¢ issue(8/76)	3	6	9	20	30	40
155-159-(30¢-c variants, limited distribution)	7	14	21	48	79	110
161-Nightcrawler app. from X-Men; Punisher cameo; Wolverine & Colossus app.	4	8	12	24	37	50
162-Punisher, Nightcrawler app.; 1st Jigsaw	4	8	12	24	37	50
163-168: 167-1st app. Will O' The Wisp	3	6	9	16	23	30
169-173-(Regular 30¢ edition). 169-Clone story recapped; Stan Lee cameo. 171-Nova app.	3	6	9	16	23	30
169-173-(35¢-c variants, limited dist.)(6-10/77)	13	26	39	86	183	280

	GD 2.0	VG 4.0	FN 6.0	VF 8.0	VF/NM 9.0	NM- 9.2
174,175-Punisher app.	3	6	9	18	27	35
176-180-Green Goblin app.	3	6	9	19	29	38
181-188: 181-Origin retold; gives life history of Spidey; Punisher cameo in flashback (1 panel). 182-(7/78)-Peter's first proposal to Mary Jane, but she declines (in #183)	3	6	9	14	20	25
189,190-Byrne-a	3	6	9	16	23	30
191-193,196-199: 193-Peter & Mary Jane break up. 196-Faked death of Aunt May	2	4	6	11	16	20
NOTE: *Whitman 3-packs containing #192-194,196 exist.*						
194-1st app. Black Cat	5	10	15	35	55	75
195-2nd app. Black Cat	3	6	9	16	23	30
200-Giant origin issue (1/80)	4	8	12	22	34	45
201,202-Punisher app.	3	6	9	14	19	24
203-205,207,208,210-219: 203-3rd app. Dazzler (4/80). 210-1st app. Madame Web. 212-1st app. & origin of Hydro-Man	2	4	6	8	10	12
206-Byrne-a	2	4	6	9	12	15
209-Origin & 1st app. Calypso (10/80)	2	4	6	11	16	20
220-237: 225-(2/82)-Foolkiller II-c/story. 226,227-Black Cat returns. 234-Free 16 pg. insert "Marvel Guide to Collecting Comics". 235-Origin Will-'O-The-Wisp. 236-Tarantula dies	1	3	4	6	8	10
238-(3/83)-1st app. Hobgoblin (Ned Leeds); came with skin "Tattooz" decal.						
NOTE: The same decal appears in the more common Fantastic Four #252 which is being removed & placed in this issue as incentive to increase value						
(Value listed is with or without tattooz)	8	16	24	55	93	130
239-2nd app. Hobgoblin & 1st battle w/Spidey	4	8	12	28	44	60
240-243,246-248: 241-Origin The Vulture. 242-Mary Jane Watson cameo (last panel). 243-Reintro Mary Jane after 4 year absence	1	3	4	6	8	10
244-3rd app. Hobgoblin (cameo)	2	4	6	9	12	15
245-(10/83)-4th app. Hobgoblin (cameo); Lefty Donovan gains powers of Hobgoblin & battles Spider-Man	2	4	6	9	12	15
249-251: 3 part Hobgoblin/Spider-Man battle. 249-Retells origin & death of 1st Green Goblin. 251-Last old costume	2	4	6	9	13	16
252-Spider-Man dons new black costume (5/84); ties with Marvel Team-Up #141 & Spectacular Spider-Man #90 for 1st new costume in regular title (See Marvel Super-Heroes Secret Wars #8 (12/84) for acquisition of costume)	5	10	15	32	51	70
253-1st app. The Rose	2	4	6	9	12	15
254-258: 256-1st app. Puma. 257-Hobgoblin cameo; 2nd app. Puma; M.J. Watson reveals she knows Spidey's i.d. 258-Hobgoblin app.	1	3	4	6	8	10
259-Full Hobgoblin app.; Spidey back to old costume; origin Mary Jane Watson	2	4	6	9	12	15
260-Hobgoblin app.	2	4	6	8	10	12
261-Hobgoblin-c/story; painted-c by Vess	2	4	6	9	11	14
262-Spider-Man unmasked; photo-c	1	3	4	6	8	10
263,264,266-274,277-280,282,283: 274-Zarathos (The Spirit of Vengeance) app. 277-Vess back-up art. 279-Jack O'Lantern-c/story. 282-X-Factor x-over	1	2	3	5	6	8
265-1st app. Silver Sable (6/85)	2	4	6	9	13	16
265-Silver ink 2nd printing ($1.25)						3.00
275-($1.25, 52 pgs.)-Hobgoblin-c/story; origin-r by Ditko	3	6	9	14	20	25
276-Hobgoblin app.	1	3	4	6	8	10
281-Hobgoblin battles Jack O'Lantern	1	3	4	6	8	10
284,285: 284-Punisher cameo; Gang War story begins; Hobgoblin-c/story. 285-Punisher app.; minor Hobgoblin app.	1	3	4	6	8	10
286-288: 286-Hobgoblin-c & app. (minor). 287-Hobgoblin app. (minor). 288-Full Hobgoblin app.; last Gang War	1	3	4	6	8	10
289-(6/87, $1.25, 52 pgs.)-Hobgoblin's i.d. revealed as Ned Leeds; death of Ned Leeds; Macendale (Jack O'Lantern) becomes new Hobgoblin (1st app.)	3	6	9	14	20	25
290-292,295-297: 290-Peter proposes to Mary Jane. 292-She accepts; leads into wedding in Amazing Spider-Man Annual #21	1	2	3	5	6	8
293,294-Part 2 & 5 of Kraven story from Web of Spider-Man. 294-Death of Kraven	2	4	6	9	12	15
298-Todd McFarlane-c/a begins (3/88); 1st brief app. Eddie Brock who becomes Venom; (last pg.)	5	10	15	35	55	75
299-1st brief app. Venom with costume	4	8	12	22	34	45
300 ($1.50, 52 pgs.; 25th Anniversary)-1st full Venom app.; last black costume (5/88)	9	18	27	63	112	160
301-305: 301 ($1.00 issues begin). 304-1st bi-weekly issue	2	4	6	9	13	16
306-311,313,314: 306-Swipes-c from Action #1	2	4	6	8	11	14
312-Hobgoblin battles Green Goblin	2	4	6	11	16	20
315-317-Venom app.	3	6	9	14	19	24
318-323,325: 319-Bi-weekly begins again	1	2	3	5	7	9
324-Sabretooth app.; McFarlane cover only	1	2	3	5	7	9

Amazing Spider-Man #393 © MAR

Amazing Spider-Man Annual #28 © MAR

Amazing Spider-Man V2 #20 © MAR

GD 2.0 | VG 4.0 | FN 6.0 | VF 8.0 | VF/NM 9.0 | NM- 9.2

326,327,329: 327-Cosmic Spidey continues from Spectacular Spider-Man (no McFarlane-c/a) 5.00
328-Hulk x-over; last McFarlane issue 1 3 4 6 8 10
330,331-Punisher app. 331-Minor Venom app. 5.00
332,333-Venom-c/story 1 3 4 6 8 10
334-336,338-343: 341-Tarantula app. 4.00
337-Hobgoblin app. 5.00
344-(2/91) 1st app. Cletus Kasady (Carnage) 2 4 6 9 12 15
345-1st full app. Cletus Kasady; Venom cameo on last pg. 2 4 6 9 12 15
346,347-Venom app. 1 3 4 6 8 10
348,349,351-359: 348-Avengers x-over. 351,352-Nova of New Warriors app. 353-Darkhawk app.; brief Punisher app. 354-Punisher cameo & Nova, Night Thrasher (New Warriors), Darkhawk & Moon Knight app. 357,358-Punisher, Darkhawk, Moon Knight, Night Thrasher, Nova x-over. 358-3 part gatefold-c; last $1.00-c. 360-Carnage cameo 3.00
350-($1.50, 52pgs.)-Origin retold; Spidey vs. Dr. Doom; pin-ups; Uncle Ben app. 5.00
360-Carnage cameo 4.00
361-(4/92) Intro Carnage (the Spawn of Venom); begin 3 part story; recap of how Spidey's alien costume became Venom 2 4 6 9 12 15
361-($1.25)-2nd printing; silver-c 3.00
362,363-Carnage & Venom-c/story 1 2 3 5 7 9
362-2nd printing 3.00
364,366-374,376-387: 364-The Shocker app. (old villain). 366-Peter's parents-c/story. 369-Harry Osborn back-up (Gr. Goblin II). 373-Venom back-up. 374-Venom-c/story. 376-Cardiac app. 378-Maximum Carnage part 3. 381,382-Hulk app. 383-The Jury app. 384-Venom/carnage app. 387-New costume Vulture 3.00
365-($3.95, 84 pgs.)-30th anniversary issue w/silver hologram on-c; Spidey/Venom/Carnage pull-out poster; contains 5 pg. preview of Spider-Man 2099 (1st app.); Spidey's origin retold; Lizard app.; reintro Peter's parents in Stan Lee 3 pg. text w/illo (story continues thru #370) 5.00
375-($3.95, 68 pgs.)-Holo-grafx foil-c; vs. Venom story; ties into Venom: Lethal Protector #1; Pat Olliffe-a. 5.00
388-($2.25, 68 pgs.)-Newsstand edition; Venom back-up & Cardiac & chance back-up 4.00
388-($2.95, 68 pgs.)-Collector's edition w/foil-c 4.50
389-396,398,399,401-420: 389-$1.50-c begins; bound-in trading card sheet; Green Goblin app. 394-Power & Responsibility Pt. 2. 396-Daredevil-c & app. 403-Carnage app. 406-1st New Doc Octopus. 407-Human Torch, Silver Sable, Sandman app. 409-Kaine, Rhino app. 410-Carnage app. 414-The Rose app. 415-Onslaught story; Spidey vs. Sentinels. 416-Epilogue to Onslaught; Garney-a(p); Williamson-a(i) 3.00
390-($2.95)-Collector's edition polybagged w/16 pg. insert of new animated Spidey TV show plus animation cel 4.00
394-($2.95, 48 pgs.)-Deluxe edition; flip book w/Birth of a Spider-Man Pt. 2; silver foil both-c; Power & Responsibility Pt. 2 4.00
397-($2.25)-Flip book w/Ultimate Spider-Man 3.00
400-($2.95)-Death of Aunt May 4.00
400-($3.95)-Death of Aunt May; embossed double-c 6.00
400-Collector's Edition; white-c 1 3 4 6 8 10
408-($2.95) Polybagged version with TV theme song cassette 8.00
421-424,426,428,429,432,433: 426-Begin $1.99-c. 432-Spiderhunt pt. 2 3.00
425-($2.99)-48 pgs., wraparound-c 4.00
427-($2.25) Return of Dr. Octopus; double gatefold-c 3.00
430,431-Carnage & Silver Surfer app. 4.00
434-440: 434-Double-c with "Amazing Ricochet #1". 438-Daredevil app. 439-Avengers-c/app. 440-Byrne-s 3.00
441-Final issue; Byrne-s 5.00
#500-up (See Amazing Spider-Man Vol. 2; series resumed original numbering after Vol. 2 #58)
#(-1) Flashback issue (7/97, $1.95-c) 3.00
Annual 1 (1964, 72 pgs.)-Origin Spider-Man; 1st app. Sinister Six (Dr. Octopus, Electro, Kraven the Hunter, Mysterio, Sandman, Vulture) (new 41 pg. story); plus gallery of Spidey foes; early X-Men app. 87 174 261 705 1528 2350
Annual 2 (1965, 25¢, 72 pgs.)-Reprints from #1,2,5 plus new Doctor Strange story 34 68 102 247 536 825
Special 3 (11/66, 25¢, 72 pgs.)-New Avengers story & Hulk x-over; Doctor Octopus-r from #11,12; Romita-a 16 32 48 111 243 375
Special 4 (11/67, 25¢, 68 pgs.)-Spidey battles Human Torch (new 41 pg. story) 13 26 39 90 195 300
Special 5 (11/68, 25¢, 68 pgs.)-New 40 pg. Red Skull story; 1st app. Peter Parker's parents; last annual with new-a 12 24 36 79 160 240
Special 5-2nd printing (1994) 2 4 6 8 10 12
Special 6 (11/69, 25¢, 68 pgs.)-Reprints 41 pg. Sinister Six story from annual #1 plus 2 Kirby/Ditko stories (r) 6 12 18 39 62 85
Special 7 (12/70, 25¢, 68 pgs.)-All-r(#1,2) new Vulture-c 6 12 18 39 62 85
Special 8 (12/71)-All-r 6 12 18 39 62 85
King Size 9 ('73)-Reprints Spectacular Spider-Man (mag.) #2; 40 pg. Green Goblin-c/story (re-edited from 58 pgs.) 6 12 18 39 62 85
Annual 10 (1976)-Origin Human Fly (vs. Spidey); new-a begins 3 6 9 16 22 28
Annual 11-13 ('77-'79):12-Spidey vs. Hulk-r/#119,120. 13-New Byrne/Austin-a; Dr. Octopus x-over w/Spectacular S-M Ann. #1 2 4 6 10 14 18
Annual 14 (1980)-Miller-c/a(p); Dr. Strange app. 3 6 9 14 20 25
Annual 15 (1981)-Miller-c/a(p); Punisher app. 3 6 9 18 27 35
Annual 16-20:16 ('82)-Origin/1st app. new Capt. Marvel (female heroine). 17 ('83)-Kingpin app. 18 ('84)-Scorpion app.; JJJ weds. 19 ('85). 20 ('86)-Origin Iron Man of 2020 1 2 3 4 5 7
Annual 21 (1987)-Special wedding issue; newsstand & direct sale versions exist & are worth same 2 4 6 8 10 12
Annual 22 (1988, $1.75, 68 pgs.)-1st app. Speedball; Evolutionary War x-over; Daredevil app. 6.00
Annual 23 (1989, $2.00, 68 pgs.)-Atlantis Attacks; origin Spider-Man retold; She-Hulk app.; Byrne-c; Liefeld-a(p), 23 pgs. 5.00
Annual 24 (1990, $2.00, 68 pgs.)-Ant-Man app. 4.00
Annual 25 (1991, $2.00, 68 pgs.)-3 pg. origin recap; Iron Man app.; 1st Venom solo story; Ditko-a (6 pgs.) 5.00
Annual 26 (1992, $2.25, 68 pgs.)-New Warriors-c/story; Venom solo story cont'd in Spectacular Spider-Man Annual #12 5.00
Annual 27,28 ('93, '94, $2.95, 68 pgs.)-27-Bagged w/card; 1st app. Annex. 28-Carnage-c/story; Rhino & Cloak and Dagger back-ups 4.00
'96 Special-($2.95, 64 pgs.)-"Blast From The Past" 4.00
'97 Special-($2.99)-Wraparound-c,Sundown app. 4.00
Marvel Graphic Novel - Parallel Lives (3/89, $8.95) 2 4 6 8 10 12
Marvel Graphic Novel - Spirits of the Earth (1990, $18.95, HC) 3 6 9 16 22 28
Super Special 1 (4/95, $3.95)-Flip Book 4.00
...: Skating on Thin Ice 1(1990, $1.25, Canadian)-McFarlane-c; anti-drug issue; Electro app. 1 2 3 5 7 9
...: Skating on Thin Ice 1 (2/93, $1.50, American) 4.00
...: Double Trouble 2 (1990, $1.25, Canadian) 6.00
...: Double Trouble 2 (2/93, $1.50, American) 3.00
...: Hit and Run 3 (1990, $1.25, Canadian)-Ghost Rider-c/story 1 2 3 5 7 9
...: Hit and Run 3 (2/93. $1.50, American) 3.00
... : Carnage (6/93, $6.95)-r/ASM #344,345,359-363 1 2 3 4 5 7
...: Chaos in Calgary 4 (Canadian; part of 5 part series)-Turbine,Night Rider, Frightful app. 2 4 6 8 11 14
...: Chaos in Calgary 4 (2/93, $1.50, American) 3.00
...: Deadball 5 (1993, $1.60, Canadian)-Green Goblin-c/story; features Montreal Expos 2 4 6 10 14 18

Note: Prices listed above are for English Canadian editions. French editions are worth double.

...: Soul of the Hunter nn (8/92, $5.95, 52 pgs.)-Zeck-c/a(p) 6.00
Wizard #1 Ace Edition ($13.99) r/#1 w/ new Ramos acetate-c 14.00
Wizard #129 Ace Edition ($13.99) r/#129 w/ new Ramos acetate-c 14.00

NOTE: **Austin** *a(i)-248, 335, 337, Annual 13; c(i)-188, 241, 242, 248, 331, 334, 343, Annual 25.* **J. Buscema** *a(p)-72, 73, 76-81, 84, 85.* **Byrne** *a-189p, 190p, 206p, Annual 3r, 6r, 7r, 13p; c-189p, 268, 296, Annual 12.* **Ditko** *a-1-38, Annual 1, Special 3(r), 2, 24(2); c-1i, 2-38.* **Guice** *c/a-Annual 18i.* **Gil Kane** *a(p)-89-105, 120-124, 150, Annual 10, 12i, 24p; c-90p, 96, 98, 99, 101-105p, 129p, 131p, 132p, 137-140p, 143p, 148p, 149p, 151p, 153p, 160p, 161p, Annual 10p, 24.* **Kirby** *a-8.* **Erik Larsen** *a-324, 327, 329-350; c-327, 329-350, 354i, Annual 25.* **McFarlane** *a-298p, 299p, 300-303, 304-323p, 325p, 328; c-298-325, 328.* **Miller** *c-218, 219.* **Mooney** *a-65i, 67-82i, 84-88i, 173i, 178i, 189i, 190i, 192i, 193i, 196-202i, 207i, 211-219i, 221i, 222i, 226i, 227i, 229-233i, Annual 11i, 17i.* **Nasser** *c-228p.* **Nebres** *a-Annual 24i.* **Russell** *c-357i.* **Simonson** *c-222, 337i.* **Starlin** *a-113i, 114i, 187p.* **Williamson** *a-365i.*

AMAZING SPIDER-MAN (Volume 2) (Some issues reprinted in "Spider-Man, Best Of" hardcovers)
Marvel Comics: Jan, 1999 - Present ($2.99/$1.99/$2.25)

1-($2.99)-Byrne-a 6.00
1-Sunburst variant-c 1 2 3 5 6 8
1-($6.95) Dynamic Forces variant-c by the Romitas 1 3 4 6 8 10
1-Marvel Matrix sketch variant-c 1 3 4 6 8 10
2-($1.99) Two covers -by John Byrne and Andy Kubert 4.00
3-11: 4-Fantastic Four app. 5-Spider-Woman-c 3.00
12-($2.99) Sinister Six return (cont. in Peter Parker #12) 4.00
13-17: 13-Mary Jane's plane explodes 3.00
18,19,21-24,26-28: 18-Begin $2.25-c. 19-Venom-c. 24-Maximum Security 3.00
20-($2.99, 100 pgs.) Spider-Slayer issue; new story and reprints 4.00
25-($2.99) Regular cover; Peter Parker becomes the Green Goblin 3.00
25-($3.99) Holo-foil enhanced cover 4.00
29-Peter is reunited with Mary Jane 3.00
30-Straczynski-s/Campbell-c begin; intro. Ezekiel 6.00
31-35: Battles Morlun 4.00
36-Black cover; aftermath of the Sept. 11 tragedy in New York 12.00
37-49: 39-'Nuff Said issue 42-Dr. Strange app. 43-45-Doctor Octopus app. 46-48-Cho-c 3.00

Amazing Spider-Man #509 © MAR

Amazing Spider-Man #658 © MAR

Amazing World of DC Comics #3 © DC

GD 2.0 | VG 4.0 | FN 6.0 | VF 8.0 | VF/NM 9.0 | NM- 9.2

50-Peter and MJ reunite; Captain America & Dr. Doom app.; Campbell-c 4.00
51-58: 51,52-Campbell-c. 55,56-Avery scripts. 57,58-Avengers, FF, Cyclops app. 3.00
(After #58 [Nov, 2003] numbering reverts back to original Vol. 1 with #500, Dec, 2003)
500-($3.50) J. Scott Campbell-c; Romita Jr. & Sr.-a; Uncle Ben app. 4.00
501-524: 501-Harris-c. 503-504-Loki app. 506-508-Ezekiel app. 509-514-Sins Past; intro. Gabriel and Sarah Osborn; Deodato-a. 519-Moves into Avengers HQ. 521-Begin $2.50-c 524-Harris-c 3.00
525,526-Evolve or Die x-over. 525-David-s. 526-Hudlin-s; Spider-Man loses eye 4.00
525-528-2nd printings with variant-c. 525-Ben Reilly costume. 526-Six-Armed Spidey. 527-Spider-Man 2099. 528-Spider-Ham 5.00
527,528: Evolve or Die pt.9, 12 3.00
529-Debut of red and gold costume; Garney-a 10.00
529-2nd printing 5.00
529-3rd printing with Wieringo-c 3.00
530,531-Titanium Man app.; Kirkham-a. 531-Begin $2.99-c 6.00
532-538-Civil War tie-in. 538-Aunt May shot 5.00
539-543-Back in Black. 539-Peter wears the black costume 3.00
544-($3.99) "One More Day" pt. 1; Quesada-a/Straczynski-s 4.00
545-(12/08, $3.99) "One More Day" pt. 4; Quesada-a/Straczynski-s, Peter & MJ's marriage un-done; r/wedding from ASM Annual #21; 2 covers by Quesada and Djurdjevic 4.00
546-($3.99) Brand New Day begins; McNiven-a; Deodato, Winslade, Land, Romita Jr.-a; 1st app. Mr. Negative 5.00
546-Variant-c by Bryan Hitch 8.00
546-Second printing with new McNiven-c of Peter Parker 4.00
546-MGC (7/10, $1.00) r/#546 with "Marvel's Greatest Comics" logo on cover 3.00
547-567: 547,548-McNiven-a. 549-551-Larroca-a. 550-Intro. Menace. 555-557-Bachalo-a. 559-Intro. Screwball. 560,561-MJ app. 565-New Kraven intro. 566,567-Spidey in Daredevil costume 3.00
568-($3.99) Romita Jr.-a begins; two covers by Romita Jr. and Alex Ross 6.00
568-Variant-c by John Romita Sr. 20.00
568-2nd printing with Romita Jr. Anti-Venom costume cover 4.00
569-Debut of Anti-Venom; Norman Osborn and Thunderbolts app.;Romita Jr.-c 3.00
569-Variant Venom-c by Granov 5.00
570-572-Two covers on each 3.00
573-($3.99) New Ways to Die conclusion; Spidey meets Stephen Colbert back-up; Ollife-a; two covers by Romita Jr. and Maguire 5.00
573-Variant cover with Stephen Colbert; cover swipe of AF #15 by Quesada 10.00
574-582: 577-Punisher app. 3.00
583-($3.99) Spidey meets Obama back-up story; regular Romita Sr. "Cougars" cover 10.00
583-($3.99) Obama variant-c with Spidey on left; Spidey meets Obama back-up story 30.00
583-($3.99) Second printing Obama variant-c with Spidey on right and yellow bkgrd 8.00
583-($3.99) 3rd-5th printings Obama variant-c: 3rd-Blue bkgrd w/flag. 4th-White bkgrd w/flag. 5th-Lincoln Memorial bkgrd 5.00
584-587, 589-599: 585-Menace ID revealed. 590,591-Fantastic Four app. 594-Aunt May engaged. 595-599-American Son; Osborn Avengers app. app. 3.00
588-($3.99) Conclusion to "Character Assassination"; Romita Jr.-a 4.00
600-(9/09, $4.99) Aunt May's wedding; Romita Jr.-a; Doc Octopus, FF app.; Mary Jane cameo; back-up story by Stan Lee; back-up with Doran-a; 2 covers by Romita Jr. & Ross 5.00
600-Variant covers by Romita Sr. and Quesada 10.00
601-604,606-611,613-616,618-621,623-627: 601-Back-up w/Quesada-a. 606,607-Black Cat app.; Campbell-c. 611-Deadpool-c/app. 612-The Gauntlet begins; Waid-s. 615,616-Sandman app. 621-Black Cat app. 624-Peter Parker fired. 626-Gaydos-a 3.00
605,612,617,622,628-($3.99): 605-Mayhew-c. 613-Rhino back-up story. 617-New Rhino. 622-Bianchi-c; Morbius app. 628-Captain Universe app. 4.00
629-633-($2.99)-Bachalo-a; Lizard app. 3.00
634-641-($3.99) 634-637-Grim Hunt; Kaine app. 635-Kraven returns. 638-641-"One Moment in Time" wedding flashback/ret-con; Quesada-s 4.00
638-641-Variant covers by Quesada 10.00
642-646-($2.99) Waid-s/Azaceta-a; interlocking covers by Djurdjevic 3.00
647-($4.99) Short stories by various; Djurdjevic-c; cover gallery of Brand New Day issues 5.00
648-681-($3.99) 648-Big Time begins; Ramos-a; Hobgoblin app. 654-Flash Thompson becomes Venom; Marla Jameson killed. 655-Martin-a. 657-660-Fantastic Four app. 666-673-Spider Island. 667-672-Ramos-a; Avengers app. 677-X-over w/Daredevil #8 4.00
654.1-(4/11, $2.99) Flash Thompson as Venom; Ramos-a 3.00
679.1-(4/12, $2.99) Morbius the Living Vampire app. 3.00
1999, 2000 Annual (6/99, '00, $3.50) 1999-Buscema-a 4.00
2001 Annual ($2.99) Follows Peter Parker: S-M #29; last Mackie-s 4.00
Annual 1 (2008, $3.99) McKone-a; secret of Jackpot revealed; death of Jackpot 4.00
Annual 36 (9/09, $3.99) Debut of Raptor; Olliffe-a 4.00
Annual 37 (7/10, $3.99) Untold 1st meeting with Captain America; back-up w/Olliffe-a 4.00
Annual 38 (6/11, $3.99) Deadpool & Hulk app.; Garbett-a/McNiven-c 4.00
...: Big Time 1 (8/11, $5.99) r/#648-650 6.00
Collected Edition #30-32 ($3.95) reprints #30-32 w/cover #30 4.00
... 500 Covers HC (2004, $49.99) reprints covers for #1-500 & Annuals; yearly re-caps 50.00

Free Comic Book Day 2011 (Spider-Man) 1-Ramos-c/a; Spider-Woman & Shang-Chi app. 3.00
.../Ghost Rider: Motorstorm 1 ('11, $2.99) r/#558-560 3.00
...: Infested 1 (11/11, $3.99) Spider Island tie-in; short stories by various; Ramos-c 4.00
... Omnibus HC (2007, $99.99, dustjacket) r/Amazing Fantasy #15, Amazing Spider-Man #1-38, Annual #1,2, Strange Tales Annual #2 & Fantastic Four Annual #1; letter pages, bonus art, intro. by Stan Lee; bios, essays, Marvel Tales cover gallery 100.00
Spider-Man: Brand New Day - Extra!! #1 (9/08, $3.99) short stories; Bachalo,Olliffe-a 4.00
Spider-Man: Brand New Day Yearbook #1 (2008, $4.99) plot synopses; profile pages 5.00
... Spidey Sunday Spectacuar (7/11, $3.99) collects back-ups from ASM #634-645 4.00
...: Swing Shift (2007 FCBD Edition) Jimenez-c/a; Slott-s 4.00
...: Swing Shift Director's Cut (2008, $3.99) story from 2007 FCBD; Brand New Day info 4.00
The Many Loves of the Amazing Spider-Man (7/10, $3.99) short stories of Black Cat, Gwen & Carlie, and Mary Jane; s/a by various 4.00
...: The Short Halloween (7/09, $3.99) Bill Hader & Seth Meyers-s/Maguire-a 4.00
...: You're Hired 1 (5/11, $3.99) r/story from New York Daily News insert 4.00
...Vol. 1: Coming Home (2001, $15.95) r/#30-35; J. Scott Campbell-c 16.00
...Vol. 2: Revelations (2002, $8.99) r/#36-39; Kaare Andrews-c 9.00
...Vol. 3: Until the Stars Turn Cold (2002, $12.99) r/#40-45; Romita Jr.-c 13.00
...Vol. 4: The Life and Death of Spiders (2003, $11.99) r/#46-50; Campbell-c 12.00
...Vol. 5: Unintended Consequences (2003, $12.99) r/#51-56; Dodson-c 13.00
...Vol. 6: Happy Birthday (2003, $12.99) r/#57,58,500-502 13.00
...Vol. 7: The Book of Ezekiel (2004, $12.99) r/#503-508; Romita Jr.-c 13.00
...Vol. 8: Sins Past (2005, $12.99) r/#509-514; cover sketch gallery 13.00
...Vol. 9: Skin Deep (2005, $9.99) r/#515-518 10.00
...Vol. 10: New Avengers (2005, $14.99) r/#519-524 15.00
Brand New Day #1-3 (11/08-1/09, $3.99) reprints #546-551 4.00
Civil War: Amazing Spider-Man TPB (2007, $17.99) r/#532-538; variant covers 18.00

AMAZING SPIDER-MAN EXTRA! (Continued from Spider-Man: Brand New Day - Extra!! #1)
Marvel Comics: No. 2, Mar, 2009 - No. 3, May, 2009 ($3.99)

2,3: 2-Anti-Venom app.; Bachalo-a. 3-Ana Kraven app.; Jimenez-a 4.00

AMAZING SPIDER-MAN FAMILY (Also see Spider-Man Family)
Marvel Comics: Oct, 2008 - No. 8, Sept, 2009 ($4.99, anthology)

1-8-New tales and reprints. 1-Includes r/ASM #300; Granov-c. 2-Deodato-c. 5-Spider-Girl new story. 6-Origin of Jackpot 5.00

AMAZING SPIDER-MAN PRESENTS: AMERICAN SON
Marvel Comics: Jul, 2010 - No. 4, Oct, 2010 ($3.99, limited series)

1-4-Reed-s/Briones-a/Djurdjevic-c; Gabriel Stacy app. 4.00

AMAZING SPIDER-MAN PRESENTS: ANTI-VENOM - NEW WAYS TO LIVE
Marvel Comics: Nov, 2009 - No. 3, Feb, 2010 ($3.99, limited series)

1-3-Wells-s/Siqueira-a; Punisher app. 4.00

AMAZING SPIDER-MAN PRESENTS: JACKPOT
Marvel Comics: Mar, 2010 - No. 3, Jun, 2010 ($3.99, limited series)

1-3-Guggenheim-s/Melo-a; Boomerang and White Rabbit app. 4.00

AMAZING WILLIE MAYS, THE
Famous Funnies Publ.: No date (Sept, 1954)

nn 82 164 246 528 902 1275

AMAZING WORLD OF DC COMICS
DC Comics: Jul, 1974 - No. 17, 1978 ($1.50, B&W, mail-order DC Pro-zine)

1-Kubert interview; unpublished Kirby-a; Infantino-c 7 14 21 49 82 115
2-4: 3-Julie Schwartz profile. 4-Batman; Robinson-c 5 10 15 35 55 75
5-Sheldon Mayer 5 10 15 30 48 65
6,8,13: 6-Joe Orlando; EC-r; Wrightson pin-up. 8-Infantino; Batman-r from Pop Tart giveaway. 13-Humor; Aragonés-c; Wood/Ditko-a; photos from serials of Superman, Batman, Captain Marvel 4 8 12 23 36 48
7,10-12: 7-Superman; r/1955 Pep comic giveaway. 10-Behind the scenes at DC; Showcase article. 11-Super-Villains; unpubl. Secret Society of S.V. story. 12-Legion; Grell-c/interview; 4 8 12 24 37 50
9-Legion of Super-Heroes; lengthy bios and history; Cockrum-c 7 14 21 49 82 115
14-Justice League 4 8 12 26 41 55
15-Wonder Woman; Nasser-c 5 10 15 32 51 70
16-Golden Age heroes 5 10 15 30 48 65
17-Shazam; G.A., 70s, TV and Fawcett heroes 4 8 12 26 41 55
Special 1 (Digest size) 3 6 9 21 32 42

AMAZING WORLD OF SUPERMAN (See Superman)

AMAZING X-MEN
Marvel Comics: Mar, 1995 - No. 4, July, 1995 ($1.95, limited series)

1-Age of Apocalypse; Andy Kubert-c/a 4.00
2-4 3.00

America in Action #1 © Mayflower

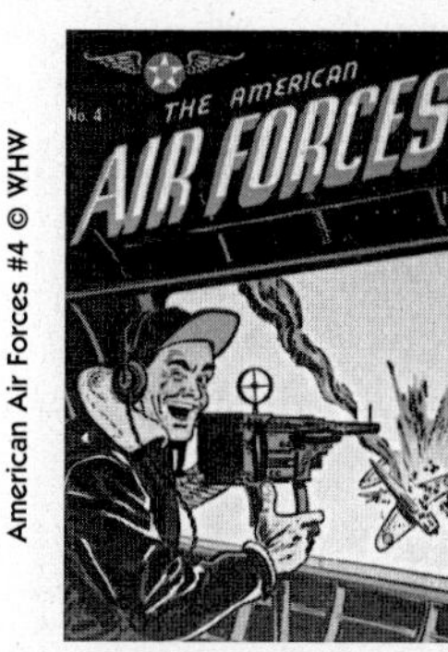

American Air Forces #4 © WHW

American Vampire #15 © Snyder & DC

	GD	VG	FN	VF	VF/NM	NM-
	2.0	4.0	6.0	8.0	9.0	9.2

AMAZON
Comico: Mar, 1989 - No. 3, May, 1989 ($1.95, limited series)

1-3: Ecological theme; Steven Seagle-s/Tim Sale-a 3.00
1-3-(Dark Horse, 3/09 - No. 3, 5/09, $3.50) recolored reprint with creator interviews 3.50

AMAZON (Also see Marvel Versus DC #3 & DC Versus Marvel #4)
DC Comics (Amalgam): Apr, 1996 ($1.95, one-shot)

1-John Byrne-c/a/scripts 3.00

AMAZON ATTACK 3-D
The 3-D Zone: Sept, 1990 ($3.95, 28 pgs.)

1-Chaykin-a 6.00

AMAZONS ATTACK (See Wonder Woman #8 - 2006 series)
DC Comics: Jun, 2007 - No. 6, Late Oct, 2007 ($2.99, limited series)

1-6-Queen Hippolyta and Amazons attacks Wash., DC; Pfeifer-s/Woods-a 3.00

AMAZON WOMAN (1st Series)
FantaCo: Summer, 1994 - No. 2, Fall, 1994 ($2.95, B&W, limited series, mature)

1,2: Tom Simonton-c/a/scripts 3.00

AMAZON WOMAN (2nd Series)
FantaCo: Feb, 1996 - No. 4, May, 1996 ($2.95, B&W, limited series, mature)

1-4: Tom Simonton-a/scripts 3.00
...: Invaders of Terror ('96, $5.95) Simonton-a/s 6.00

AMBUSH (See Zane Grey, Four Color 314)

AMBUSH BUG (Also see Son of...)
DC Comics: June, 1985 - No. 4, Sept, 1985 (75¢, limited series)

1-4: Giffen-c/a in all 4.00
Nothing Special 1 (9/92, $2.50, 68pg.)-Giffen-c/a 4.00
Stocking Stuffer (2/86, $1.25)-Giffen-c/a 4.00

AMBUSH BUG: YEAR NONE
DC Comics: Sept, 2008 - No. 5, Jan, 2009; No. 7, Dec, 2009 ($2.99, limited series, no #6)

1-5,7-Giffen-s/a; Jonni DC app. 4-Conner-c. 7-Baltazar & Franco-a; Giffen-a 3.00

AMERICA AT WAR - THE BEST OF DC WAR COMICS (See Fireside Book Series)

AMERICA IN ACTION
Dell (Imp. Publ. Co.)/ Mayflower House Publ.: 1942; Winter, 1945 (36 pgs.)

1942-Dell-(68 pgs.) 17 34 51 98 154 210
1-(1945)-Has 3 adaptations from American history; Kiefer, Schrotter & Webb-a
14 28 42 76 108 140

AMERICAN, THE
Dark Horse Comics: July, 1987 - No. 8, 1989 ($1.50/$1.75, B&W)

1-8: ($1.50) 3.00
Collection ($5.95, B&W)-Reprints 6.00
Special 1 (1990, $2.25, B&W) 3.00

AMERICAN AIR FORCES, THE (See A-1 Comics)
William H. Wise(Flying Cadet Publ. Co./Hasan(No.1)/Life's Romances/ Magazine Ent. No. 5 on): Sept-Oct, 1944-No. 4, 1945; No. 5, 1951-No. 12, 1954

1-Article by Zack Mosley, creator of Smilin' Jack; German war-c
34 68 102 199 325 450
2-Classic-Japan war-c 53 106 159 334 567 800
3,4-Japan war-c 18 36 54 105 165 225

NOTE: *All part comic, part magazine. Art by* ***Whitney, Chas. Quinlan, H. C. Kiefer,*** *and* ***Tony Dipreta.***

5(A-1 45)(Formerly Jet Powers), 6(A-1 54), 7(A-1 58), 8(A-1 65), 9(A-1 67), 10(A-1 74), 11(A-1 79), 12(A-1 91) 9 18 27 52 69 85

NOTE: ***Powell*** *c/a-5-12.*

AMERICAN CENTURY
DC Comics (Vertigo): May, 2001 - No. 27, Oct, 2003 ($2.50/$2.75)

1-Chaykin-s/painted-c; Tischman-a 4.00
2-27: 5-New story arc begins. 10-16,22-27-Orbik-c. 17-21-Silke-c. 18-$2.75-c begins 3.00
Hollywood Babylon (2002, $12.95, TPB) r/#5-9; w/sketch-to-art pages 13.00
Scars & Stripes (2001, $8.95, TPB) r/#1-4; Tischman intro. 9.00

AMERICAN DREAM (From the M2 Avengers)
Marvel Comics: Jul, 2008 - No. 5, Sept, 2008 ($2.99, limited series)

1-5-DeFalco-s/Nauck-a 3.00

AMERICAN FLAGG! (See First Comics Graphic Novel 3,9,12,21 & Howard Chaykin's..)
First Comics: Oct, 1983 - No. 50, Mar, 1988

1,21-27: 1-Chaykin-c/a begins. 21-27-Alan Moore scripts 4.00
2-20,28-49: 31-Origin Bob Violence 3.00
50-Last issue 4.00

Special 1 (11/86)-Introduces Chaykin's Time[2] 4.00
...: Hard Times TPB (6/85, $11.95) r/#1-7; intro. by Michael Moorcock; bonus materials 12.00
...: Definitive Collection Volume 1 HC (2008, $49.99) r/#1-14 and material from the...: Hard Times TPB; intro by Michael Chabon; afterword by Jim Lee 50.00

AMERICAN FREAK: A TALE OF THE UN-MEN
DC Comics (Vertigo): Feb, 1994 - No. 5, Jun, 1994 ($1.95, mini-series, mature)

1-5 3.00

AMERICAN GRAPHICS
Henry Stewart: No. 1, 1954; No. 2, 1957 (25¢)

1-The Maid of the Mist, The Last of the Eries (Indian Legends of Niagara) (sold at Niagara Falls) 11 22 33 60 83 105
2-Victory at Niagara & Laura Secord (Heroine of the War of 1812)
8 16 24 40 50 60

AMERICAN INDIAN, THE (See Picture Progress)

AMERICAN LIBRARY
David McKay Publ.: 1943 - No. 6, 1944 (15¢, 68 pgs., B&W, text & pictures)

nn (#1)-Thirty Seconds Over Tokyo (movie) 39 78 117 231 378 525
nn (#2)-Guadalcanal Diary; painted-c (only 10¢) 28 56 84 165 270 375
3-6: 3-Look to the Mountain. 4-Case of the Crooked Candle (Perry Mason). 5-Duel in the Sun. 6-Wingate's Raiders 15 30 45 88 137 185

AMERICAN: LOST IN AMERICA, THE
Dark Horse Comics: July, 1992 - No. 4, Oct, 1992 ($2.50, limited series)

1-4: 1-Dorman painted-c. 2-Phillips painted-c. 3-Mignola-c. 4-Jim Lee-c 3.00

AMERICAN SPLENDOR: (Series of titles)
Dark Horse Comics: Aug, 1996 - Apr, 2001 (B&W, all one-shots)

--**COMIC-CON COMICS** (8/96) 1-H. Pekar script. --**MUSIC COMICS** (11/97) nn-H. Pekar-s/ Sacco-a; r/Village Voice jazz strips. --**ODDS AND ENDS** (12/97) 1-Pekar-s. --**ON THE JOB** (5/97) 1-Pekar-s. --**A STEP OUT OF THE NEST** (8/94) 1-Pekar-s. --**TERMINAL** (9/99) 1-Pekar-s. --**TRANSATLANTIC** (7/98) 1-"American Splendour" on cover; Pekar-s 3.00
--**A PORTRAIT OF THE AUTHOR IN HIS DECLINING YEARS** (4/01, $3.99) 1-Photo-c. --**BEDTIME STORIES** (6/00, $3.95) 4.00

AMERICAN SPLENDOR
DC Comics: Nov, 2006 - No. 4, Feb, 2007 ($2.99, B&W)

1-4-Pekar-s/art by Haspiel and various. 1-Fabry-c 3.00
...: Another Day TPB (2007, $14.99) r/#1-4 15.00

AMERICAN SPLENDOR (Volume 2)
DC Comics (Vertigo): Jun, 2008 - No. 4, Sept, 2008 ($2.99, B&W)

1-4-Pekar-s/art by Haspiel and various. 1-Bond-c. 3-Cooke-c 3.00
...: Another Dollar TPB (2009, $14.99) r/#1-4 15.00

AMERICAN SPLENDOR: UNSUNG HERO
Dark Horse Comics: Aug, 2002 - No. 3, Oct, 2002 ($3.99, B&W, limited series)

1-3-Pekar script/Collier-a; biography of Robert McNeill 4.00
TPB (8/03, $11.95) r/#1-3 12.00

AMERICAN SPLENDOR: WINDFALL
Dark Horse Comics: Sept, 1995 - No. 2, Oct,1995 ($3.95, B&W, limited series)

1,2-Pekar script 4.00

AMERICAN TAIL: FIEVEL GOES WEST, AN
Marvel Comics: Early Jan, 1992 - No. 3, Early Feb, 1992 ($1.00, limited series)

1-3-Adapts Universal animated movie; Wildman-a 3.00
1-($2.95-c, 69 pgs.) Deluxe squarebound edition 5.00

AMERICAN VAMPIRE
DC Comics (Vertigo): May, 2010 - Present ($3.99/$2.99)

1-10: 1-9-Snyder-s/Albuquerque-a. 1-5-Back-up story by Stephen King 4.00
1-5-Variant-c: 1-Jim Lee. 2-Berni Wrightson. 3-Andy Kubert. 5-Paul Pope 6.00
11-25-($2.99) 11-Santolouco-a. 12-Zezelj-a. 19-21-Bernet-a 3.00
HC (2010, $24.99, d.j.) r/#1-5; intro. by Stephen King; script pages and sketch art 25.00
...Volume Two HC (2011, $24.99, d.j.) r/#6-11; cover design art 25.00

AMERICAN VAMPIRE: SURVIVAL OF THE FITTEST
DC Comics (Vertigo): Aug, 2011 - No. 5, Dec, 2011 ($2.99, limited series)

1-5-Set during WWII; Snyder-s/Murphy-a/c 3.00

AMERICAN VIRGIN
DC Comics (Vertigo): May, 2006 - No. 23, Mar, 2008 ($2.99)

1-23-Steven Seagle-s/Becky Cloonan-a in most. 1-3-Quitely-c. 4-14-Middleton-c 3.00
...: Head (2006, $9.99, TPB) r/#1-4; interviews with the creators and page development 10.00
...: Going Down (2007, $14.99, TPB) r/#5-9 15.00

America's Best Comics #28 © STD

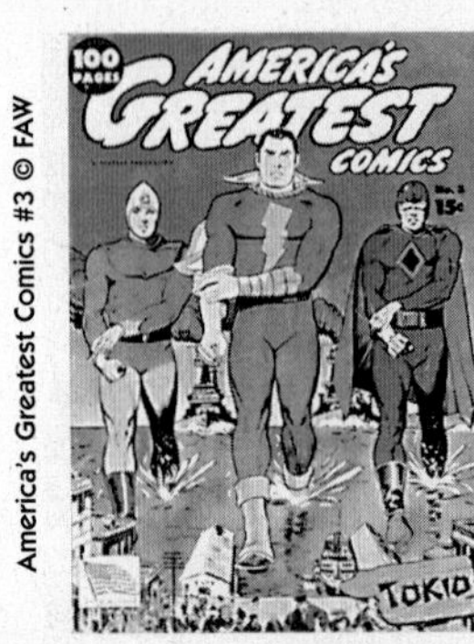

America's Greatest Comics #3 © FAW

Anarky #8 © DC

GD VG FN VF VF/NM NM-
2.0 4.0 6.0 8.0 9.0 9.2

...: Wet (2007, $12.99, TPB) r/#10-14 13.00
...: Around the World (Vol. 4) (2008, $17.99, TPB) r/#15-23 18.00

AMERICAN WAY, THE
DC Comics (WildStorm): Apr, 2006 - No. 8, Nov, 2006 ($2.99, limited series)

1-8-John Ridley-s/Georges Jeanty-a/c 3.00
TPB (2007, $19.99) r/series; covers; Jeanty sketch pages 20.00

AMERICA'S BEST COMICS
Nedor/Better/Standard Publications: Feb, 1942; No. 2, Sept, 1942 - No. 31, July, 1949 (New logo with #9)

1-The Woman in Red, Black Terror, Captain Future, Doc Strange, The Liberator, & Don Davis, Secret Ace begin 320 640 960 2240 3920 5600
2-Origin The American Eagle; The Woman in Red ends 123 246 369 787 1344 1900
3-Pyroman begins (11/42, 1st app.; also see Startling Comics #18, 12/42) 103 206 309 659 1130 1600
4-6: 5-Last Capt. Future (not in #4); Lone Eagle app. 6-American Crusader app. 81 162 243 518 884 1250
7-Hitler, Mussolini & Hirohito-c 194 388 582 1242 2121 3000
8-Last Liberator 77 154 231 493 847 1200
9-The Fighting Yank begins; The Ghost app. 84 168 252 538 919 1300
10-Flag-c 74 148 222 470 810 1150
11-Hirohito & Tojo-c. (10/44) 103 206 309 659 1130 1600
12-17: 14-American Eagle ends; Doc Strange vs. Hitler story 65 130 195 416 708 1000
18-Classic-c 82 164 246 528 902 1275
19-21: 21-Infinity-c 60 120 180 381 653 925
22-Capt. Future app. 52 104 156 328 557 785
23-Miss Masque begins; last Doc Strange 61 122 183 387 664 940
24-Miss Masque bondage-c 58 116 174 371 636 900
25-Last Fighting Yank; Sea Eagle app. 43 86 129 271 461 650
26-31: 26-The Phantom Detective & The Silver Knight app.; Frazetta text illo & some panels in Miss Masque. 27,28-Commando Cubs. 27-Doc Strange. 28-Tuska Black Terror. 29-Last Pyroman 42 84 126 265 445 625

NOTE: *American Eagle not in 3, 8, 9, 13. Fighting Yank not in 10, 12. Liberator not in 2, 6, 7. Pyroman not in 9, 11, 14-16, 23, 25-27.* ***Schomburg (Xela)*** *c-5, 7-31. Bondage c-18, 24.*

AMERICA'S BEST COMICS
America's Best Comics: 1999 - 2008

... Preview (1999, Wizard magazine supplement) - Previews Tom Strong, Top Ten, Promethea, Tomorrow Stories 3.00
... Primer (2008, $4.99, TPB) r/Tom Strong #1, Tom Strong's Terrific Tales, Top Ten #1, Promethea #1, Tomorrow Stories #1,6 5.00
... Sketchbook (2002, $5.95, square-bound)-Design sketches by Sprouse, Ross, Adams, Nowlan, Ha and others 6.00
Special 1 (2/01, $6.95)-Short stories of Alan Moore's characters; art by various; Ross-c 7.00
TPB (2004, $17.95) Reprints short stories and sketch pages from ABC titles 18.00

AMERICA'S BEST TV COMICS (TV)
American Broadcasting Co. (Prod. by Marvel Comics): 1967 (25¢, 68 pgs.)

1-Spider-Man, Fantastic Four (by Kirby/Ayers), Casper, King Kong, George of the Jungle, Journey to the Center of the Earth stories (promotes new TV cartoon show) 11 22 33 76 151 225

AMERICA'S BIGGEST COMICS BOOK
William H. Wise: 1944 (196 pgs., one-shot)

1-The Grim Reaper, The Silver Knight, Zudo, the Jungle Boy, Commando Cubs, Thunderhoof app. 41 82 123 256 428 600

AMERICA'S FUNNIEST COMICS
William H. Wise: 1944 - No. 2, 1944 (15¢, 80 pgs.)

nn(#1), 2 24 48 72 142 234 325

AMERICA'S GREATEST COMICS
Fawcett Publications: May?, 1941 - No. 8, Summer, 1943 (15¢, 100 pgs., soft cardboard-c)

1-Bulletman, Spy Smasher, Capt. Marvel, Minute Man & Mr. Scarlet begin; Classic Mac Raboy-c. 1st time that Fawcett's major super-heroes appear together as a group on a cover. Fawcett's 1st squarebound comic 343 686 1029 2400 4200 6000
2 145 290 435 921 1586 2250
3 107 214 321 680 1165 1650
4,5: 4-Commando Yank begins; Golden Arrow, Ibis the Invincible & Spy Smasher cameo in Captain Marvel 77 154 231 489 837 1185
6,7: 7-Balbo the Boy Magician app.; Captain Marvel, Bulletman cameo in Mr. Scarlet 68 136 204 435 743 1050
8-Capt. Marvel Jr. & Golden Arrow app.; Spy Smasher x-over in Capt. Midnight; no Minute Man or Commando Yank 68 136 204 435 743 1050

AMERICA'S SWEETHEART SUNNY (See Sunny, ...)

AMERICA VS. THE JUSTICE SOCIETY
DC Comics: Jan, 1985 - No. 4, Apr, 1985 ($1.00, limited series)

1-Double size; Alcala-a(i) in all 2 4 6 8 10 12
2-4: 3,4-Spectre cameo 1 2 3 5 7 9

AMERICOMICS
Americomics: April, 1983 - No. 6, Mar, 1984 ($2.00, Baxter paper/slick paper)

1-Intro/origin The Shade; Intro. The Slayer, Captain Freedom and The Liberty Corps; Perez-c 5.00
1,2-2nd printings ($2.00) 3.00
2-6: 2-Messenger app. & 1st app. Tara on Jungle Island. 3-New & old Blue Beetle battle. 4-Origin Dragonfly & Shade. 5-Origin Commando D. 6-Origin the Scarlet Scorpion 3.00
Special 1 (8/83, $2.00)-Sentinels of Justice (Blue Beetle, Captain Atom, Nightshade & The Question) 5.00

AMETHYST
DC Comics: Jan, 1985 - No. 16, Aug, 1986 (75¢)

1-16: 8-Fire Jade's i.d. revealed 3.00
Special 1 (10/86, $1.25), 1-4 (11/87 - 2/88)(Limited series) 4.00

AMETHYST, PRINCESS OF GEMWORLD (See Legion of Super-Heroes #298)
DC Comics: May, 1983 - No. 12, Apr, 1984 (Maxi-series)

1-(60¢) 3.00
1,2-(35¢): tested in Austin & Kansas City 3 6 9 20 30 40
2-12, Annual 1(9/84): 5-11-Pérez-c(p) 4.00

NOTE: *Issues #1 & 2 also have Canadian variants with a 75¢ cover price.*

AMORY WARS (Based on the Coheed and Cambria album The Second Stage Turbine Blade)
Image Comics: Jun, 2007 - No. 5, Jan, 2008 ($2.99, limited series)

1-5: 1-Claudio Sanchez-s/Gus Vasquez-a 3.00

AMORY WARS II
Image Comics: Jun, 2008 - No. 5, Oct, 2008 ($2.99, limited series)

1-5-Claudio Sanchez-s/Gabriel Guzman-a 3.00

AMORY WARS IN KEEPING SECRETS OF SILENT EARTH: 3
BOOM! Studios: May, 2010 - No. 12, Jun, 2011 ($3.99)

1-12: 1-Claudio Sanchez & Peter David-s/Chris Burnham-a. 1-Four covers 4.00

AMY RACECAR COLOR SPECIAL (See Stray Bullets)
El Capitán Books: July, 1997; Oct, 1999 ($2.95/$3.50)

1,2-David Lapham-a/scripts. 2-($3.50) 3.50

ANARCHO DICTATOR OF DEATH (See Comics Novel)

ANARKY (See Batman titles)
DC Comics: May, 1997 - No. 4, Aug, 1997 ($2.50, limited series)

1 3.50
2-4 3.00

ANARKY (See Batman titles)
DC Comics: May, 1999 - No. 8, Dec, 1999 ($2.50)

1-8: 1-JLA app.; Grant-s/Breyfogle-a. 3-Green Lantern app. 7-Day of Judgment; Haunted Tank app. 8-Joker-c/app. 3.00

ANCHORS ANDREWS (The Saltwater Daffy)
St. John Publishing Co.: Jan, 1953 - No. 4, July, 1953 (Anchors the Saltwater... No. 4)

1-Canteen Kate by Matt Baker (9 pgs.) 22 44 66 128 209 290
2-4 9 18 27 52 69 85

ANDY & WOODY (See March of Comics No. 40, 55, 76)

ANDY BURNETT (TV, Disney)
Dell Publishing Co.: Dec, 1957

Four Color 865-Photo-c 8 16 24 56 96 135

ANDY COMICS (Formerly Scream Comics; becomes Ernie Comics)
Current Publications (Ace Magazines): No. 20, June, 1948-No. 21, Aug, 1948

20,21: Archie-type comic 8 16 24 42 54 65

ANDY DEVINE WESTERN
Fawcett Publications: Dec, 1950 - No. 2, 1951

1 41 82 123 256 428 600
2-Photo-c 30 60 90 177 289 400

ANDY GRIFFITH SHOW, THE (TV)(1st show aired 10/3/60)
Dell Publishing Co.: #1252, Jan-Mar, 1962; #1341, Apr-Jun, 1962

Four Color 1252(#1) 33 66 99 239 512 785
Four Color 1341-Photo-c 31 62 93 225 480 735

A-Next #1 © MAR

Angel #40 © 20th Century Fox

Angel & Faith #1 © 20th Century Fox

	GD 2.0	VG 4.0	FN 6.0	VF 8.0	VF/NM 9.0	NM- 9.2

ANDY HARDY COMICS (See Movie Comics #3 by Fiction House)
Dell Publishing Co.: April, 1952 - No. 6, Sept-Nov, 1954

	GD	VG	FN	VF	VF/NM	NM-
Four Color 389(#1)	5	10	15	35	55	75
Four Color 447,480,515, #5,#6	4	8	12	26	41	55

ANDY PANDA (Also see Crackajack Funnies #39, The Funnies, New Funnies & Walter Lantz...)
Dell Publishing Co.: 1943 - No. 56, Nov-Jan, 1961-62 (Walter Lantz)

	GD	VG	FN	VF	VF/NM	NM-
Four Color 25(#1, 1943)	46	92	138	359	780	1200
Four Color 54(1944)	26	52	78	182	391	600
Four Color 85(1945)	15	30	45	102	221	340
Four Color 130(1946),154,198	11	22	33	74	145	215
Four Color 216,240,258,280,297	9	18	27	58	99	140
Four Color 326,345,358	7	14	21	44	72	100
Four Color 383,409	6	12	18	37	59	80
16(11-1/52-53) - 30	5	10	15	30	48	65
31-56	4	8	12	24	37	50

(See March of Comics #5, 22, 79, & Super Book #4, 15, 27.)

A-NEXT (See Avengers)
Marvel Comics: Oct, 1998 - No. 12, Sept, 1999 ($1.99)

1-12: 1-Next generation of Avengers; Frenz-a. 2-Two covers. 3-Defenders app. 3.00
Spider-Girl Presents Avengers Next Vol. 1: Second Coming (2006, $7.99, digest) r/#1-6 8.00

ANGEL
Dell Publishing Co.: Aug, 1954 - No. 16, Nov-Jan, 1958-59

	GD	VG	FN	VF	VF/NM	NM-
Four Color 576(#1, 8/54)	4	8	12	26	41	55
2(5-7/55) - 16	3	6	9	18	27	35

ANGEL (TV) (Also see Buffy the Vampire Slayer)
Dark Horse Comics: Nov, 1999 - No. 17, Apr, 2001 ($2.95/$2.99)

1-17: 1-3,5-7,10-14-Zanier-a. 1-4,7,10-Matsuda & photo-c. 16-Buffy-c/app. 3.00
...: Earthly Possessions TPB (4/01, $9.95) r/#5-7, photo-c 10.00
...: Surrogates TPB (12/00, $9.95) r/#1-3; photo-c 10.00

ANGEL (Buffy the Vampire Slayer)
Dark Horse Comics: Sept, 2001 - No. 4, May, 2002 ($2.99, limited series)

1-4-Joss Whedon & Matthews-s/Rubi-a; photo-c and Rubi-c on each 3.00

ANGEL (Buffy the Vampire Slayer) (Previously titled Angel: After the Fall)
IDW Publishing: No. 18, Feb, 2009 - No. 44, Apr, 2011 ($3.99)

18-44: Multiple covers on all. 25-Juliet Landau-s 4.00

ANGEL (one-shots) (Buffy the Vampire Slayer)
IDW Publishing: ($3.99/$7.49)

...: Connor (8/06, $3.99) Jay Faerber-s/Bob Gill-a; 4 covers + 1 retailer cover 4.00
...: Doyle (7/06, $3.99) Jeff Mariotte-s/David Messina-a; 4 covers + 1 retailer cover 4.00
...: Gunn (5/06, $3.99) Dan Jolley-s/Mark Pennington-a; 4 covers + 2 retailer covers 4.00
...: Illyria (4/06, $3.99) Peter David-s/Nicola Scott-a; 4 covers + 2 retailer covers 4.00
...: Masks (10/06, $7.49) short stories of Angel, Illyria, Cordilia & Lindsay; puppet Angel app. 8.00
... 100-Page Spectacular (4/11, $7.99) reprints of 4 issues; Runge-c 8.00
... Special • Lorne (3/10, $7.99) John Byrne-s/a; The Groosalugg app. 8.00
Team Angel 100-Page Spectacular (4/11, $7.99) reprints; Runge-c 8.00
...: Vs. Frankenstein (10/09, $3.99) John Byrne-s/a/c 4.00
...: Vs. Frankenstein II (10/10, $3.99) John Byrne-s/a/c 4.00
...: Wesley (6/06, $3.99) Scott Tipton-s/Mike Norton-a; 4 covers + 1 retailer cover 4.00
Spotlight TPB (12/06, $19.99) r/Connor, Doyle, Gunn, Illyria & Wesley one-shots 20.00
... Yearbook (5/11, $7.99) short stories by various; 3 covers 8.00

ANGELA
Image Comics (Todd McFarlane Prod.): Dec, 1994 - No. 3, Feb, 1995 ($2.95, lim. series)

	GD	VG	FN	VF	VF/NM	NM-
1-Gaiman scripts & Capullo-c/a in all; Spawn app.	1	2	3	5	6	8
2						6.00
3						5.00
Special Edition (1995)-Pirate Spawn-c	3	6	9	14	20	25
Special Edition (1995)-Angela-c	3	6	9	14	20	25
TPB ($9.95, 1995) reprints #1-3 & Special Ed. w/additional pin-ups						10.00

ANGEL: AFTER THE FALL (Buffy the Vampire Slayer) (Follows the last TV episode)
IDW Publishing: Nov, 2007 - No. 17, Feb, 2009 ($3.99)(Continues as Angel with #18)

1-Whedon & Lynch-s; multiple covers 5.00
2-17: Multiple covers on all 4.00

ANGELA/GLORY: RAGE OF ANGELS (See Glory/Angela: Rage of Angels)
Image Comics (Todd McFarlane Productions): Mar, 1996 ($2.50, one-shot)

1-Liefeld-c/Cruz-a(p); Darkchylde preview flip book 4.00
1-Variant-c 4.00

ANGEL: A HOLE IN THE WORLD (Adaptation of the 2-part TV episode)
IDW Publishing: Dec, 2009 - No. 5, Apr, 2010 ($3.99, limited series)

1-5-Fred becomes Illyria; Casagrande-a/c 4.00

ANGEL & FAITH (Follows Buffy the Vampire Slayer Season Eight)
Dark Horse Comics: Aug, 2011 - Present ($2.99)

1-Gage-s/Isaacs-a; two covers by Morris & Chen 3.00
2-7-Two covers by Morris & Isaacs. 5-Harmony & Clem app.; Noto-a. 7-Drusilla app. 3.00

ANGEL AND THE APE (Meet Angel No. 7) (See Limited Collector's Edition C-34 & Showcase No. 77)
National Periodical Publications: Nov-Dec, 1968 - No. 6, Sept-Oct, 1969

	GD	VG	FN	VF	VF/NM	NM-
1-(11-12/68)-Not Wood-a	5	10	15	30	48	65
2-5-Wood inks in all. 4-Last 12¢ issue	3	6	9	20	30	40
6-Wood inks	4	8	12	22	34	45

ANGEL AND THE APE (2nd Series)
DC Comics: Mar, 1991 - No. 4, June, 1991 ($1.00, limited series)

1-4 3.00

ANGEL AND THE APE (3rd Series)
DC Comics (Vertigo): Oct, 2001 - No. 4, Jan 2002 ($2.95, limited series)

1-4-Chaykin & Tischman-s/Bond-a/Art Adams-c 3.00

ANGEL: AULD LANG SYNE (Buffy the Vampire Slayer)
IDW Publishing: Nov, 2006 - No. 5, Mar, 2007 ($3.99, limited series)

1-5: 1-Three covers plus photo-c; Tipton-s/Messina-a 4.00

ANGEL: BARBARY COAST (Buffy the Vampire Slayer)
IDW Publishing: Apr, 2010 - No. 3, Jun, 2010 ($3.99, limited series)

1-3-Angel in 1906 San Francisco; Tischman-s/Urru-a; 2 covers on each 4.00

ANGEL: BLOOD & TRENCHES (Buffy the Vampire Slayer)
IDW Publishing: Mar, 2009 - No. 4, June, 2009 ($3.99, B&W&Red, limited series)

1-4-Angel in World War II Europe; John Byrne-s/a/c 4.00

ANGEL: ILLYRIA: HAUNTED (Buffy the Vampire Slayer)
IDW Publishing: Nov, 2010 - No. 4, Feb, 2011 ($3.99, limited series)

1-4-Tipton & Huehner-s/Casagrande-a; 2 covers 4.00

ANGEL LOVE
DC Comics: Aug, 1986 - No. 8, Mar, 1987 (75¢, limited series)

1-8, Special 1 (1987, $1.25, 52 pgs.) 4.00

ANGEL: NOT FADE AWAY (Buffy the Vampire Slayer)
IDW Publishing: May, 2009 - No. 3, July, 2009 ($3.99, limited series)

1-3-Adaptation of TV show's final episodes; Mooney-a 4.00

ANGEL OF LIGHT, THE (See The Crusaders)

ANGEL: OLD FRIENDS (Buffy the Vampire Slayer)
IDW Publishing: Nov, 2005 - No. 5, Mar, 2006 ($3.99, limited series)

1-5: Four covers plus photo-c on each; Mariotte-s/Messina-a; Gunn, Spike and Illyria app. 4.00
... Cover Gallery (6/06, $3.99) gallery of variant covers for the series 4.00
... Cover Gallery (12/06, $3.99) gallery of variant covers; preview of Angel: Auld Lang Syne 4.00
TPB (2006, $19.99) r/series; gallery of Messina covers 20.00

ANGEL: ONLY HUMAN (Buffy the Vampire Slayer)
IDW Publishing: Aug, 2009 - No. 5, Dec, 2009 ($3.99, limited series)

1-5-Lobdell-s/Messina-a; covers by Messina and Dave Dorman 4.00

ANGEL: REVELATIONS (X-Men character)
Marvel Comics: July, 2008 - No. 5, Nov, 2008 ($3.99, limited series)

1-5-Origin from childhood re-told; Adam Pollina-a/Aquirre-Sacasa-s 4.00

ANGEL: SMILE TIME (Buffy the Vampire Slayer)
IDW Publishing: Dec, 2008 - No. 3, Apr, 2009 ($3.99, limited series)

1-3-Adaptation of TV episode; Messina-a; Messina and photo covers for each 4.00

ANGEL: THE CURSE (Buffy the Vampire Slayer)
IDW Publishing: June, 2005 - No. 5, Oct, 2005 ($3.99, limited series)

1-5-Four covers on each; Mariotte-s/Messina-a 4.00
TPB (1/06, $19.99) r/#1-5; cover gallery of Messina covers 20.00

ANGELTOWN
DC Comics (Vertigo): Jan, 2005 - No. 5, May, 2005 ($2.95, limited series)

1-5-Gary Phillips-s/Shawn Martinbrough-a 3.00

ANGELUS
Image Comics (Top Cow): Dec, 2007; Dec, 2009 - Nov, 2010 ($2.99)

... Pilot Season 1-(12/07) Sejic-a/c; Edington-s; origin re-told 3.00

Animal Comics #15 © DELL

Animal Man (2011 series) #7 © DC

Animaniacs #51 © WB

	GD 2.0	VG 4.0	FN 6.0	VF 8.0	VF/NM 9.0	NM- 9.2

1-6-Marz-s/Sejic-a; multiple covers on each 3.00

ANGRY CHRIST COMIX (See Cry For Dawn)

ANIMA
DC Comics: Mar, 1994 - No. 15, July, 1995 ($1.75/$1.95/$2.25)

1-7,0,8-15: 7-(9/94)-Begin $1.95-c; Zero Hour x-over 3.00

ANIMAL ADVENTURES
Timor Publications/Accepted Publ. (reprints): Dec, 1953 - No. 3, May?, 1954

1-Funny animal	8	16	24	40	50	60
2,3: 2-Featuring Soopermutt (2/54)	6	12	18	28	34	40
1-3 (reprints, nd)	3	6	8	11	13	15

ANIMAL ANTICS
DC Comics: Feb, 1946

nn - Ashcan comic, not distributed to newsstands, only for in-house use. Cover art is Star Spangled Comics #49 and interior is Boy Commandos #12 ; a NM cover sold for $1000 in 2012, and FN/VF copy sold for $1553.50 in 2012.

ANIMAL ANTICS (Movietown... No. 24 on)
National Periodical Publ: Mar-Apr, 1946 - No. 23, Nov-Dec, 1949 (All 52 pgs.?)

1-Raccoon Kids begins by Otto Feuer; many-c by Grossman; Seaman Sy Wheeler by Kelly in some issues; Grossman-a in most issues	43	86	129	271	461	650
2	24	48	72	140	230	320
3-10: 10-Post-c/a	16	32	48	92	144	195
11-23: 14,15,18,19-Post-a	12	24	36	67	94	120

ANIMAL COMICS
Dell Publishing Co.: Dec-Jan, 1941-42 - No. 30, Dec-Jan, 1947-48

1-1st Pogo app. by Walt Kelly (Dan Noonan art in most issues)	107	214	321	680	1165	1650
2-Uncle Wiggily begins	53	106	159	334	567	800
3,5	27	54	81	197	399	600
4,6,7-No Pogo	15	30	45	106	216	325
8-10	18	36	54	131	266	400
11-15	12	24	36	87	164	240
16-20	9	18	27	63	107	150
21-30: 24-30- "Jigger" by John Stanley	8	16	24	52	86	120

NOTE: ***Dan Noonan** a-18-30. **Gollub** art in most later issues; c-29, 30. **Kelly** c-7-26, part #27-30.*

ANIMAL CRACKERS (Also see Adventures of Patoruzu)
Green Publ. Co./Norlen/Fox Feat.(Hero Books): 1946; No. 31, July, 1950; No. 9, 1959

1-Super Cat begins (1st app.)	19	38	57	111	176	240
2	10	20	30	58	79	100
31(Fox)-Formerly My Love Secret	8	16	24	42	54	65
9(1959-Norlen)-Infinity-c	5	10	14	20	24	28
nn, nd ('50s), no publ.; infinity-c	5	10	14	20	24	28

ANIMAL FABLES
E. C. Comics (Fables Publ. Co.): July-Aug, 1946 - No. 7, Nov-Dec, 1947

1-Freddy Firefly (clone of Human Torch), Korky Kangaroo, Petey Pig, Danny Demon begin	54	108	162	343	574	825
2-Aesop Fables begin	34	68	102	204	335	465
3-6	29	58	87	170	278	385
7-Origin Moon Girl	70	140	210	445	765	1085

ANIMAL FAIR (Fawcett's...)
Fawcett Publications: Mar, 1946 - No. 11, Feb, 1947

1	28	56	84	165	270	375
2	14	28	42	82	121	160
3-6	12	24	36	67	94	120
7-11	10	20	30	54	72	90

ANIMAL FUN
Premier Magazines: 1953 (25¢, came w/glasses)

1-(3-D)-Ziggy Pig, Silly Seal, Billy & Buggy Bear	36	72	108	216	351	485

ANIMAL MAN (See Action Comics #552, 553, DC Comics Presents #77, 78, Last Days of Animal Man, Secret Origins #39, Strange Adventures #180 & Wonder Woman #267, 268)
DC Comics (Vertigo imprint #57 on): Sept, 1988 - No. 89, Nov, 1995 ($1.25/$1.50/$1.75/$1.95/$2.25, mature)

1-Grant Morrison scripts begin, ends #26	2	4	6	8	10	12
2-10: 2-Superman cameo. 6-Invasion tie-in. 9-Manhunter-c/story. 10-Psycho Pirate app.	1	2	3	4	5	7
11-49,51-55,57-89: 23,24-Psycho Pirate app. 24-Arkham Asylum story; Bizarro Superman app. 25-Inferior Five app. 26-Morrison apps. in story; part photo-c (of Morrison?)						3.00
50-($2.95, 52 pgs.)-Last issue w/Veitch scripts						5.00
56-($3.50, 68 pgs.)						5.00
Annual 1 (1993, $3.95, 68 pgs.)-Bolland-c; Children's Crusade Pt. 3						6.00
...: Deus Ex Machina TPB (2003, $19.95) r/#18-26; Morrison-s; new Bolland-c						20.00
...: Origin of the Species TPB (2002, $19.95) r/#10-17 & Secret Origins #39						20.00

NOTE: ***Bolland** c-1-63. 71-**Sutton**-a(i)*

ANIMAL MAN (DC New 52)
DC Comics: Nov, 2011 - Present ($2.99)

1-Jeff Lemire-s/Travel Foreman-a/c; 1st printing with yellow cover background						10.00
1-Second printing (red cover background), Third printing (grey cover background)						3.00
2-8: 2-4 Foreman-a. 5-Huat-a						3.00

ANIMAL MYSTIC (See Dark One...)
Cry For Dawn/Sirius: 1993 - No. 4, 1995 ($2.95?/$3.50, B&W)

1	3	6	9	14	19	24
1-Alternate	4	8	12	22	34	45
1-2nd printing						5.00
2	2	4	6	10	14	18
2,3-2nd prints (Sirius)						3.50
3 ,4: 4-Color poster insert, Linsner-s	1	2	3	5	7	9
TPB ($14.95) r/series						18.00

ANIMAL MYSTIC WATER WARS
Sirius: 1996 - No. 6 ($2.95, limited series)

1-6-Dark One-c/a/scripts 5.00

ANIMAL WORLD, THE (Movie)
Dell Publishing Co.: No. 713, Aug, 1956

Four Color 713	4	8	12	26	41	55

ANIMANIACS (TV)
DC Comics: May, 1995 - No. 59, Apr, 2000 ($1.50/$1.75/$1.95/$1.99)

1	1	2	3	4	5	7
2-20: 13-Manga issue. 19-X-Files parody; Miran Kim-c; Adlard-a (4 pgs.)						4.00
21-59: 26-E.C. parody-c. 34-Xena parody. 43-Pinky & the Brain take over						3.00
A Christmas Special (12/94, $1.50, "1" on-c)						5.00

ANIMATED COMICS
E. C. Comics: No date given (Summer, 1947?)

1 (Rare)	87	174	261	553	952	1350

ANIMATED FUNNY COMIC TUNES (See Funny Tunes)

ANIMATED MOVIE-TUNES (Movie Tunes No. 3)
Margood Publishing Corp. (Timely): Fall, 1945 - No. 2, Sum, 1946

1,2-Super Rabbit, Ziggy Pig & Silly Seal	37	74	111	222	361	500

ANIMAX
Marvel Comics (Star Comics): Dec, 1986 - No. 4, June, 1987

1-4: Based on toys; Simonson-a 3.00

ANITA BLAKE (Circus of the Damned - The Charmer on cover)
Marvel Comics: July, 2010 - No. 5, Dec, 2010 ($3.99, limited series)

1-5-Laurell K. Hamilton & Jess Ruffner-s/Ron Lim-a/ Brett Booth-c						4.00
... - The Ingenue 1-5 (3/11 - No. 5, 10/11, $3.99) Hamilton & Ruffner-s/Lim-a/Booth-c						4.00
... - The Scoundrel 1-4 (11/11 - No. 5, $3.99) Hamilton & Ruffner-s/Lim-a/Booth-c						4.00

ANITA BLAKE: VAMPIRE HUNTER GUILTY PLEASURES
Marvel Comics (Dabel Brothers): Dec, 2006 - No. 12, Aug, 2008 ($2.99)

1-Laurell K. Hamilton-s/Brett Booth-a; blue cover						6.00
1-Variant-c by Greg Horn						20.00
1-Sketch cover						25.00
1-2nd printing with red cover						3.00
2-Two covers						5.00
3-12						3.00
...: Handbook (2007, $3.99) profile pages of characters; glossary						4.00
... Volume One HC (6/07, $19.99, dust jacket) r/#1-6; cover gallery						20.00

ANITA BLAKE: VAMPIRE HUNTER THE FIRST DEATH, (LAURELL K. HAMILTON'S...)
Marvel Comics (Dabel Brothers): July, 2007 - No. 2, Dec, 2007 ($3.99)

1,2-Laurell K. Hamilton & Jonathon Green-s/Wellington Alves-a. 2-Marvel Zombie var-c						4.00
... HC (2008, $19.99, dust jacket) r/#1,2 & Guilty Pleasures Handbook						20.00

ANITA BLAKE, VAMPIRE HUNTER: THE LAUGHING CORPSE
Marvel Comics: Dec, 2008 - No. 5, Apr, 2009 ($3.99)

... - Book One (12/08 - No. 5, 4/09) 1-5-Laurell K. Hamilton-s/Ron Lim-a/c						4.00
... - Necromancer 1-5 (6/09 - No. 5, 11/09, $3.99) Lim-a/c						4.00
Anita Blake (Executioner on-c) #11-15 (12/09 - No. 15, 5/10) numbering continued; Lim-a						4.00

Annie Oakley & Tagg #13 © DELL

Annihilators #4 © MAR

Anti-Hitler Comics #1 © NEC

GD VG FN VF VF/NM NM-
2.0 4.0 6.0 8.0 9.0 9.2

ANNE RICE'S INTERVIEW WITH THE VAMPIRE
Innovation Books: 1991 - No. 12, Jan, 1994 ($2.50, limited series)
1-12: Adapts novel; Moeller-a 3.00

ANNE RICE'S THE MASTER OF RAMPLING GATE
Innovation Books: 1991 ($6.95, one-shot)
1-Bolton painted-c; Colleen Doran painted-a 7.00

ANNE RICE'S THE MUMMY OR RAMSES THE DAMNED
Millennium Publications: Oct, 1990 - No. 12, Feb, 1992 ($2.50, limited series)
1-12: Adapts novel; Mooney-p in all 3.00

ANNE RICE'S THE WITCHING HOUR
Millennium Publ./Comico: 1992 - No. 13, Jan, 1993 ($2.50, limited series)
1-13 3.00

ANNETTE (Disney, TV)
Dell Publishing Co.: No. 905, May, 1958; No. 1100, May, 1960
(Mickey Mouse Club)
Four Color 905-Annette Funicello photo-c 22 44 66 154 327 500
Four Color 1100-...'s Life Story (Movie); A. Funicello photo-c
17 34 51 119 260 400

ANNEX (See Amazing Spider-Man Annual #27 for 1st app.)
Marvel Comics: Aug, 1994 - No. 4, Nov, 1994 ($1.75)
1-4: 1,4-Spider-Man app. 3.00

ANNIE
Marvel Comics Group: Oct, 1982 - No. 2, Nov, 1982 (60¢)
1,2-Movie adaptation 4.00
Treasury Edition ($2.00, tabloid size) 3 6 9 18 27 35

ANNIE OAKLEY (See Tessie The Typist #19, Two-Gun Kid & Wild Western)
Marvel/Atlas Comics(MPI No. 1-4/CDS No. 5 on): Spring, 1948 - No. 4, 11/48; No. 5, 6/55 - No. 11, 6/56
1 (1st Series, 1948)-Hedy Devine app. 48 96 144 302 514 725
2 (7/48, 52 pgs.)-Kurtzman-a, "Hey Look", 1 pg; Intro. Lana; Hedy Devine app; Captain Tootsie by Beck 28 56 84 165 270 375
3,4 23 46 69 136 223 310
5 (2nd Series, 1955)-Reinman-a ; Maneely-c 17 34 51 98 154 210
6-9: 6,8-Woodbridge-a. 9-Williamson-a (4 pgs.) 14 28 42 80 115 150
10,11: 11-Severin-c 13 26 39 74 105 135

ANNIE OAKLEY AND TAGG (TV)
Dell Publishing Co./Gold Key: 1953 - No. 18, Jan-Mar, 1959; July, 1965 (Gail Davis photo-c #3 on)
Four Color 438 (#1) 12 24 36 84 175 265
Four Color 481,575 (#2,3) 9 18 27 62 109 155
4(7-9/55)-10 8 16 24 53 89 125
11-18(1-3/59) 7 14 21 44 72 100
1(7/65-Gold Key)-Photo-c (c-r/#6) 4 8 12 28 44 60
NOTE: ***Manning** a-13. Photo back c-4, 9, 11.*

ANNIHILATION
Marvel Comics: May, 2006 - No. 6, Mar, 2007 ($3.99/$2.99, limited x-over series)
Prologue (5/06, $3.99, one-shot) Nova, Thanos and Silver Surfer app. 4.00
1-6: 1-(10/06) Giffen-s/DiVito-a; Annihilus app. 3.00
...: Heralds of Galactus 1,2 (4/07-5/07, $3.99) 2-Silver Surfer app. 4.00
...: Nova 1-4 (6/06-9/06, $2.99) Abnett & Lanning-s/Walker-a/Dell'Otto-c. 2,3-Quasar app. 3.00
...: Ronan 1-4 (6/06-9/06, $2.99) Furman-s/Lucas-a/Dell'Otto-c 3.00
... Saga (2007, $1.99) re-cap of the series; DiVito-c 3.00
...: Silver Surfer 1-4 (6/06-9/06, $2.99) Giffen-s/Arlem-a/Dell'Otto-c 3.00
...: Super-Skrull 1-4 (6/06-9/06, $2.99) Grillo-Marxuach-s/Titus-a/Dell'Otto-c 3.00
...: The Nova Corps Files (2006, $3.99) profile pages of characters and alien races 4.00
Annihilation Book 1 HC (2007, $29.99, dustjacket) r/Drax the Destroyer #1-4, Annihilation Prologue and Annihilation: Nova #1-4; sketch and layout pages 30.00
Annihilation Book 1 SC (2007, $24.99) same content as HC 25.00
Annihilation Book 2 HC (2007, $29.99, dustjacket) r/Annihilation: Silver Surfer #1-4, ...: Super Skrull #1-4 and ...: Ronan #1-4; sketch and layout pages 30.00
Annihilation Book 2 SC (2007, $24.99) same content as HC 25.00
Annihilation Book 3 HC (2007, $29.99, dustjacket) r/Annihilation #1-6, Annihilation: Heralds of Galactus #1,2 and Annihilation: Nova Corps Files; sketch pages 30.00
Annihilation Book 3 SC (2007, $24.99) same content as HC 25.00

ANNIHILATION: CONQUEST (Also see Nova 2007 series)
Marvel Comics: Jan, 2008 - No. 6, Jun, 2008 ($3.99/$2.99, limited x-over series)
Prologue (8/07, $3.99, one-shot) the new Quasar, Moondragon app.; Perkins-a 4.00
1-5-Raney-a; Ultron app. 3-Moondragon dies 3.00
6-($3.99) 4.00
... - Quasar 1-4 (9/07-No. 4, 12/07, $2.99) Gage-s/Lilly-a. 1-Super-Adaptoid app. 3.00
... - Starlord 1-4 (9/07-No. 4, 12/07, $2.99) Giffen-s/Green-a 3.00
... - Wraith 1-4 (9/07-No. 4, 12/07, $2.99) Hotz-a/Grillo-Marxuach-s 3.00
Annihilation: Conquest Book 1 HC (2008, $29.99, dustjacket) r/Prologue; ...Quasar #1-4, ...Star-Lord #1-4; Annihilation Saga; design pages 30.00

ANNIHILATORS
Marvel Comics: May, 2011 - No. 4, Aug, 2011 ($4.99, limited series)
1-4: Quasar, Silver Surfer, Beta-Ray Bill, Ronan, Gladiator app.; Huat-a 5.00

ANNIHILATORS: EARTHFALL
Marvel Comics: Nov, 2011 - No. 4, Feb, 2012 ($3.99, limited series)
1-4-Avengers app.; Abnett & Lanning-s/Huat-a/Christopher-c 4.00

ANOTHER WORLD (See Strange Stories From...)

ANT
Image Comics: Aug, 2005 - No. 11 ($2.99)
1-11: 1-Mario Gulley-s/a. 2-Savage Dragon & Spawn app. 3-Spawn-c/app. 3.00
Vol. 1: Reality Bites TPB (2006, $12.99) r/#1-4; sketch and concept art 13.00

ANTHRO (See Showcase #74)
National Periodical Publications: July-Aug, 1968 - No. 6, July-Aug, 1969
1-(7-8/68)-Howie Post-a in all 6 12 18 37 59 80
2-5: 5-Last 12¢ issue 4 8 12 22 34 45
6-Wood-c/a (inks) 4 8 12 24 37 50

ANTI-HITLER COMICS
New England Comics Press: Summer, 1992 ($2.75, B&W, one-shot)
1-Reprints Hitler as Devil stories from wartime comics 6.00

ANT-MAN (See Irredeemable Ant-Man, The)

ANT-MAN & WASP
Marvel Comics: Jan, 2011 - No. 3, Mar, 2011 ($3.99, limited series)
1-3-Tim Seeley-s/a; Espin-c; Tigra app. 4.00

ANT-MAN'S BIG CHRISTMAS
Marvel Comics: Feb, 2000 ($5.95, square-bound, one-shot)
1-Bob Gale-s/Phil Winslade-a; Avengers app. 6.00

ANTONY AND CLEOPATRA (See Ideal, a Classical Comic)

ANYTHING GOES
Fantagraphics Books: Oct, 1986 - No. 6, 1987 ($2.00, #1-5 color & B&W/#6 B&W, lim. series)
1-6: 1-Flaming Carrot app. (1st in color?); G. Kane-c. 2-6: 2-Miller-c(p); Alan Moore scripts; Kirby-a; early Sam Kieth-a (2 pgs.). 3-Capt. Jack, Cerebus app.; Cerebus-c by N. Adams. 4-Perez-c. 5-3rd color Teenage Mutant Ninja Turtles app. 3.50

A-1
Marvel Comics (Epic Comics): 1992 - No. 4, 1993 ($5.95, limited series, mature)
1-4: 1-Fabry-c/a, Russell-a, S. Hampton-a. 3-Bisley-c; Kent Williams-a. 4-McKean-a; Dorman-s/a 1 2 3 4 5 7

A-1 COMICS (A-1 appears on covers No. 1-17 only)(See individual title listings for #11-139) (1st two issues not numbered.)
Life's Romances Publ.-No. 1/Compix/Magazine Ent.: 1944 - No. 139, Sept-Oct, 1955 (No #2)
nn-(1944) (See Kerry Drake Detective Cases)
1-Dotty Dripple (1 pg.), Mr. Ex, Bush Berry, Rocky, Lew Loyal (20 pgs.)
16 32 48 94 147 200
3-8,10: Texas Slim & Dirty Dalton, The Corsair, Teddy Rich, Dotty Dripple, Inca Dinca, Tommy Tinker, Little Mexico & Tugboat Tim, The Masquerader & others. 7-Corsair-c/s. 8-Intro Rodeo Ryan 10 20 30 58 79 100
9-All Texas Slim 11 22 33 60 83 105

(See Individual Alphabetical listings for prices)

11-Teena; Ogden Whitney-c
13-Guns of Fact & Fiction (1948). Used in **SOTI**, pg. 19; Ingels & Johnny Craig-a
17-Tim Holt #2; photo-c; last issue to carry A-1 on cover (9-10/48)
19-Tim Holt #3; photo-c
22-Dick Powell (1949)-Photo-c
23-Cowboys and Indians #6; Doc Holiday-c/story
25-Fibber McGee & Molly (1949) (Radio)
26-Trail Colt #2-Ingels-c
12,15-Teena
14-Tim Holt Western Adventures #1
16-Vacation Comics; The Pixies, Tom Tom, Flying Fredd, & Koko & Kola
18,20-Jimmy Durante; photo covers on both
21-Joan of Arc (1949)-Movie adaptation; Ingrid Bergman photo-covers & interior photos; Whitney-a
24-Trail Colt #1-Frazetta-r in-Manhunt #13; Ingels-c; L. B. Cole-a
27-Ghost Rider #1(1950)-Origin

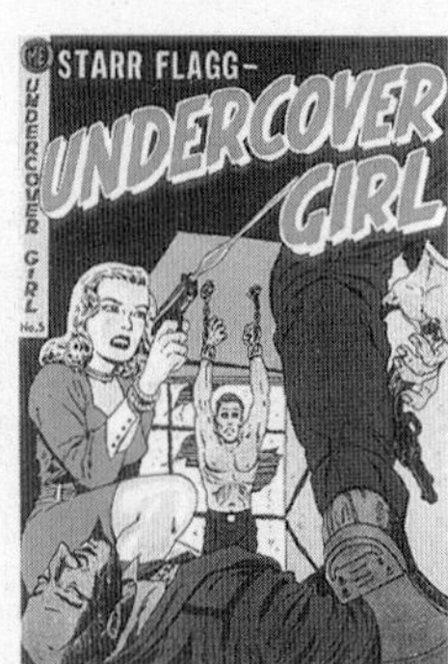

A-1 Comics #62 © ME

Apache Kid #14 © MAR

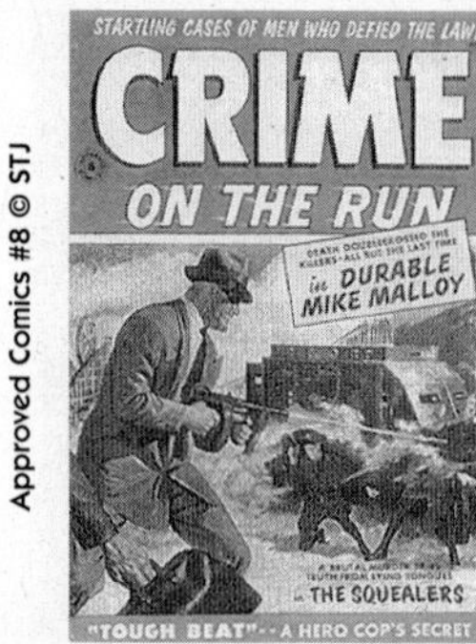

Approved Comics #8 © STJ

	GD	VG	FN	VF	VF/NM	NM-
	2.0	4.0	6.0	8.0	9.0	9.2

28-Christmas-(Koko & Kola #6) ('50)
29-Ghost Rider #2-Frazetta-c (1950)
30-Jet Powers #1-Powell-a
31-Ghost Rider #3-Frazetta-c & origin ('51)
32-Jet Powers #2
33-Muggsy Mouse #1('51)
34-Ghost Rider #4-Frazetta-c (1951)
35-Jet Powers #3-Williamson/Evans-a
36-Muggsy Mouse #2; Racist-c
37-Ghost Rider #5-Frazetta-c (1951)
38-Jet Powers #4-Williamson/Wood-a
39-Muggsy Mouse #3
40-Dogface Dooley #1('51)
41-Cowboys 'N' Indians #7 (1951)
42-Best of the West #1-Powell-a
43-Dogface Dooley #2
44-Ghost Rider #6
45-American Air Forces #5-Powell-c/a
46-Best of the West #2
47-Thun'da, King of the Congo #1-Frazetta-c/a('52)
48-Cowboys 'N' Indians #8
49-Dogface Dooley #3
50-Danger Is Their Business #11 ('52)-Powell-a
51-Ghost Rider #7 ('52)
52-Best of the West #3
53-Dogface Dooley #4
54-American Air Forces #6(8/52)-Powell-a
55-U.S. Marines #5-Powell-a
56-Thun'da #2-Powell-c/a
57-Ghost Rider #8
58-American Air Forces #7-Powell-a
59-Best of the West #4
60-The U.S. Marines #6-Powell-a
61-Space Ace #5('53)-Guardineer-a
62-Starr Flagg, Undercover Girl #5 (#1) reprinted from A-1 #24
63-Manhunt #13-Frazetta
64-Dogface Dooley #5
65-American Air Forces #8-Powell-a
66-Best of the West #5
67-American Air Forces #9-Powell-a
68-U.S. Marines #7-Powell-a
69-Ghost Rider #9(10/52)
70-Best of the West #6
71-Ghost Rider #10(12/52)-Vs. Frankenstein
72-U.S. Marines #8-Powell-a(3)
73-Thun'da #3-Powell-c/a
74-American Air Forces #10-Powell-a
75-Ghost Rider #11(3/52)
76-Best of the West #7
77-Manhunt #14
78-Thun'da #4-Powell-c/a
79-American Air Forces #11-Powell-a
80-Ghost Rider #12(6/52)-One-eyed Devil-c
81-Best of the West #8
82-Cave Girl #11(1953)-Powell-c/a; origin (#1)
83-Thun'da #5-Powell-c/a
84-Ghost Rider #13(7-8/53)
85-Best of the West #9
86-Thun'da #6-Powell-c/a
87-Best of the West #10(9-10/53)
88-Bobby Benson's B-Bar-B Riders #20
89-Home Run #3-Powell-a; Stan Musial photo-c
90-Red Hawk #11(1953)-Powell-c/a
91-American Air Forces #12-Powell-a
92-Dream Book of Romance #5-Photo-c; Guardineer-a
93-Great Western #8('54)-Origin The Ghost Rider; Powell-a
94-White Indian #11-Frazetta-a(r); Powell-c
95-Muggsy Mouse #4
96-Cave Girl #12, with Thun'da; Powell-c/a
97-Best of the West #11
98-Undercover Girl #6-Powell-c
99-Muggsy Mouse #5
100-Badmen of the West #1-Meskin-a(?)
101-White Indian #12-Frazetta-a(r)
101-Dream Book of Romance #6 (4-6/54); Marlon Brando photo-c; Powell, Bolle, Guardineer-a
103-Best of the West #12-Powell-a
104-White Indian #13-Frazetta-a(r) ('54)
105-Great Western #9-Ghost Rider app.; Powell-a, 6 pgs.; Bolle-c
106-Dream Book of Love #1 (6-7/54) -Powell, Bolle-a; Montgomery Clift, Donna Reed photo-c
107-Hot Dog #1
108-Red Fox #15 (1954)-L.B. Cole-c/a; Powell-a
109-Dream Book of Romance #7 (7-8/54). Powell-a; movie photo-c
110-Dream Book of Romance #8 (10/54)-Movie photo-c
111-I'm a Cop #1 ('54); drug mention story; Powell-a
112-Ghost Rider #14 ('54)
113-Great Western #10; Powell-a
114-Dream Book of Love #2- Guardineer, Bolle-a; Piper Laurie, Victor Mature photo-c
115-Hot Dog #3
116-Cave Girl #13-Powell-c/a
117-White Indian #14
118-Undercover Girl #7-Powell-c
119-Straight Arrow's Fury #1 (origin); Fred Meagher-c/a
120-Badmen of the West #2
121-Mysteries of Scotland Yard #1; reprinted from Manhunt (5 stories)
122-Black Phantom #1 (11/54)
123-Dream Book of Love #3 (10-11/54)-Movie photo-c
124-Dream Book of Romance #8 (10-11/54)
125-Cave Girl #14-Powell-c/a
126-I'm a Cop #2-Powell-a
127-Great Western #11('54)-Powell-a
128-I'm a Cop #3-Powell-a
129-The Avenger #1('55)-Powell-c
130-Strongman #1-Powell-a (2-3/55)
131-The Avenger #2('55)-Powell-c/a
132-Strongman #2
133-The Avenger #3-Powell-c/a
134-Strongman #3
135-White Indian #15
136-Hot Dog #4
137-Africa #1-Powell-c/a(4)
138-The Avenger #4-Powell-c/a
139-Strongman #4-Powell-a

NOTE: ***Bolle*** *a-110. Photo-c-17-22, 89, 92, 101, 106, 109, 110, 114, 123, 124.*

APACHE
Fiction House Magazines: 1951

	GD	VG	FN	VF	VF/NM	NM-
1	22	44	66	132	216	300
I.W. Reprint No. 1-r/#1 above	3	6	9	18	27	35

APACHE KID (Formerly Reno Browne; Western Gunfighters #20 on)
(Also see Two-Gun Western & Wild Western)
Marvel/Atlas Comics(MPC No. 53-10/CPS No. 11 on): No. 53, 12/50 - No. 10, 1/52; No. 11, 12/54 - No. 19, 4/56

53(#1)-Apache Kid & his horse Nightwind (origin), Red Hawkins by Syd Shores begins

	GD	VG	FN	VF	VF/NM	NM-
	34	68	102	199	325	450
2(2/51)	17	34	51	98	154	210
3-5	13	26	39	72	101	130
6-10 (1951-52): 7-Russ Heath-a	11	22	33	60	83	105
11-19 (1954-56)	9	18	27	50	65	80

NOTE: ***Heath*** *a-7. c-11, 13.* ***Maneely*** *a-53; c-53(#1), 12, 14-16.* ***Powell*** *a-14.* ***Severin*** *c-17.*

APACHE MASSACRE (See Chief Victorio's...)

APACHE SKIES
Marvel Comics: Sept, 2002 - No. 4, Dec, 2002 ($2.99, limited series)

1-4-Apache Kid app.; Ostrander-s/Manco-c/a — 3.00
TPB (2003, $12.99) r/#1-4 — 13.00

APACHE TRAIL
Steinway/America's Best: Sept, 1957 - No. 4, June, 1958

	GD	VG	FN	VF	VF/NM	NM-
1	11	22	33	62	86	110
2-4: 2-Tuska-a	8	16	24	40	50	60

APE (Magazine)
Dell Publishing Co.: 1961 (52 pgs., B&W)

	GD	VG	FN	VF	VF/NM	NM-
1-Comics and humor	4	8	12	28	44	60

APHRODITE IX
Image Comics (Top Cow): Sept, 2000 - No. 4, Mar, 2002 ($2.50)

1-3: 1-Four covers by Finch, Turner, Silvestri, Benitez — 4.00
1-Tower Record Ed.; Finch-c — 3.00
1-DF Chrome ($14.99) — 15.00
4-($4.95) Double-sized issue; Finch-c — 5.00
Convention Preview — 10.00
...: Time Out of Mind TPB (6/04, $14.99) r/#1-4, & #0; cover gallery — 15.00
Wizard #0 (4/00, bagged w/Tomb Raider magazine) Preview & sketchbook — 5.00
#0-(6/01, $2.95) r/Wizard #0 with cover gallery — 3.00

APOCALYPSE NERD
Dark Horse Comics: January, 2005 - No. 6, Oct, 2007 ($2.99, B&W)

1-6-Peter Bagge-s/a — 3.00

APPARITION
Caliber Comics: 1995 ($3.95, 52 pgs., B&W)

1 ($3.95) — 4.00
V2#1-6 ($2.95) — 3.00
Visitations — 4.00

APPLESEED
Eclipse Comics: Sept, 1988 - Book 4, Vol. 4, Aug, 1991 ($2.50/$2.75/$3.50, 52/68 pgs, B&W)

Book One, Vol. 1-5: 5-(1/89), Book Two, Vol. 1(2/89) -5(7/89): Art Adams-c, Book Three, Vol. 1(8/89) -4 ($2.75), Book Three, Vol. 5 ($3.50), Book Four, Vol. 1 (1/91) - 4 (8/91) ($3.50, 68 pgs.) — 6.00

APPLESEED DATABOOK
Dark Horse Comics: Apr, 1994 - No. 2, May, 1994 ($3.50, B&W, limited series)

1,2: 1-Flip book format — 3.50

APPROVED COMICS (Also see Blue Ribbon Comics)
St. John Publishing Co. (Most have no c-price): March, 1954 - No. 12, Aug, 1954 (Painted-c on #1-5,7,8,10)

	GD	VG	FN	VF	VF/NM	NM-
1-The Hawk #5-r	10	20	30	56	76	95
2-Invisible Boy (3/54)-Origin; Saunders-c	16	32	48	92	144	195
3-Wild Boy of the Congo #11-r (4/54)	10	20	30	56	76	95
4,5: 4-Kid Cowboy-r. 5-Fly Boy-r	10	20	30	56	76	95
6-Daring Adv.-r (5/54); Krigstein-a(2); Baker-c	14	28	42	76	108	140
7-The Hawk #6-r	10	20	30	56	76	95
8-Crime on the Run (6/54); Powell-a; Saunders-c	10	20	30	56	76	95
9-Western Bandit Trails #3-r, with new-c; Baker-c/a	14	28	42	76	108	140
10-Dinky Duck (Terrytoons)	6	12	18	31	38	45
11-Fightin' Marines #3-r (8/54); Canteen Kate app; Baker-c/a	14	28	42	76	108	140
12-Northwest Mounties #4-r(8/54); new Baker-c	14	28	42	76	108	140

AQUAMAN (See Adventure Comics #260, Brave & the Bold, DC Comics Presents #5, DC Special #28,

Aquaman (1991 series) #5 © DC

Aquaman (2011 series) #7 © DC

Archer & Armstrong #25 © VAL

	GD 2.0	VG 4.0	FN 6.0	VF 8.0	VF/NM 9.0	NM- 9.2

DC Special Series #1, DC Super Stars #7, Detective Comics, JLA, Justice League of America, More Fun #73, Showcase #30-33, Super DC Giant, Super Friends, and World's Finest Comics)

AQUAMAN (1st Series)
National Periodical Publications/DC Comics: Jan-Feb, 1962 - #56, Mar-Apr, 1971; #57, Aug-Sept,1977 - #63, Aug-Sept, 1978

	GD	VG	FN	VF	VF/NM	NM-
1-(1-2/62)-Intro. Quisp	93	186	279	753	1627	2500
2	32	64	96	232	504	775
3-5	19	38	57	132	284	435
6-10	13	26	39	85	180	275
11,18: 11-1st app. Mera. 18-Aquaman weds Mera; JLA cameo	11	22	33	73	142	210
12-17,19,20	11	22	33	71	136	200
21-32: 23-Birth of Aquababy. 26-Huntress app.(3-4/66). 29-1st app. Ocean Master, Aquaman's step-brother. 30-Batman & Superman-c & cameo	7	14	21	49	82	115
33-1st app. Aqua-Girl (see Adventure #266)	8	16	24	53	89	125
34-40: 35-1st app. Black Manta. 40-Jim Aparo's 1st DC work (8/68)	6	12	18	41	66	90
41-46,47,49: 45-Last 12¢-c	5	10	15	35	55	75
48-Origin reprinted	6	12	18	37	59	80
50-52-Deadman by Neal Adams	9	18	27	58	99	140
53-56('71): 56-1st app. Crusader; last 15¢-c	3	6	9	18	27	35
57('77)-63: 58-Origin retold	2	3	4	6	8	10
...: Death of a Prince TPB (2011, $29.99) r/#58-63 and Adventure #435-437,441-455						30.00

NOTE: *Aparo a-40-45, 46p, 47-59; c-58-63.* ***Nick Cardy*** *c-1-40.* ***Newton*** *a-60-63.*

AQUAMAN (1st limited series)
DC Comics: Feb, 1986 - No. 4, May, 1986 (75¢, limited series)

	GD	VG	FN	VF	VF/NM	NM-
1-New costume; 1st app. Nuada of Thierna Na Oge	1	2	3	4	5	7
2-4: 3-Retelling of Aquaman & Ocean Master's origins.						5.00
Special 1 (1988, $1.50, 52 pgs.)						4.00

NOTE: ***Craig Hamilton*** *c/a-1-4p.* ***Russell*** *c-2-4i.*

AQUAMAN (2nd limited series)
DC Comics: June, 1989 - No. 5, Oct, 1989 ($1.00, limited series)

1-5: Giffen plots/breakdowns; Swan-a(p). 4.00
Special 1 (Legend of..., $2.00, 1989, 52 pgs.)-Giffen plots/breakdowns; Swan-a(p) 4.00

AQUAMAN (2nd Series)
DC Comics: Dec, 1991 - No. 13, Dec, 1992 ($1.00/$1.25)

1-5 3.00
6-13: 6-Begin $1.25-c. 9-Sea Devils app. 3.00

AQUAMAN (3rd Series)(Also see Atlantis Chronicles)
DC Comics: Aug, 1994 - No. 75, Jan, 2001 ($1.50/$1.75/$1.95/$1.99/$2.50)

1-(8/94)-Peter David scripts begin; reintro Dolphin 6.00
2-(9/94)-Aquaman loses hand 6.50
0-(10/94)-Aquaman replaces lost hand with hook. 6.50
3-8: 3-(11/94)-Superboy-c/app. 4-Lobo app. 6-Deep Six app. 3.50
9-69: 9-Begin $1.75-c. 10-Green Lantern app. 11-Reintro Mera. 15-Re-intro Kordax. 16-vs. JLA. 18-Reintro Ocean Master & Atlan (Aquaman's father). 19-Reintro Garth (Aqualad). 23-1st app. Deep Blue (Neptune Perkins & Tsunami's daughter). 23,24-Neptune Perkins, Nuada, Tsunami, Arion, Power Girl, & The Sea Devils app. 26-Final Night. 28-Martian Manhunter-c/app. 29-Black Manta-c/app. 32-Swamp Thing-c/app. 37-Genesis x-over. 41-Maxima-c/app. 43-Millennium Giants x-over; Superman-c/app. 44-G.A. Flash & Sentinel app. 50-Larsen-s begins. 53-Superman app. 60-Tempest marries Dolphin; Teen Titans app. 63-Kaluta covers begin. 66-JLA app. 3.00
70-75: 70-Begin $2.50-c. 71-73-Warlord-c/app. 75-Final issue 3.00
#1,000,000 (11/98) 853rd Century x-over 3.00
Annual 1 (1995, $3.50)-Year One story 4.00
Annual 2 (1996, $2.95)-Legends of the Dead Earth story 4.00
Annual 3 (1997, $3.95)-Pulp Heroes story 4.00
Annual 4,5 ('98, '99, $2.95)-4-Ghosts; Wrightson-c. 5-JLApe 4.00
...Secret Files 1 (12/98, $4.95) Origin-s and pin-ups 5.00

NOTE: ***Art Adams****-c, Annual 5.* ***Mignola*** *c-6.* ***Simonson*** *c-15.*

AQUAMAN (4th Series)(Titled Aquaman: Sword of Atlantis #40-on) (Also see JLA #69-75)
DC Comics: Feb, 2003 - No. 57, Dec, 2007 ($2.50/$2.99)

1-Veitch-s/Guichet-a/Maleev-c 4.00
2-14: 2-Martian Manhunter app. 8-11-Black Manta app. 3.00
15-39: 15-San Diego flooded; Pfeifer-s/Davis-c begin. 23,24-Sea Devils app. 33-Mera returns. 39-Black Manta app. 3.00
40-Sword of Atlantis; One Year Later begins ($2.99-c) Guice-a ; two covers 4.00
41-49,51-57: 41-Two covers. 42-Sea Devils app. 44-Ocean Master app. 3.00
50-($3.99) Tempest app.; McManus-a 4.00
...Secret Files 2003 (5/03, $4.95) background on Aquaman's new powers; pin-ups 5.00
...: Once and Future TPB (2006, $12.99) r/#40-45 13.00
...: The Waterbearer TPB (2003, $12.95) r/#1-4, stories from Aquaman Secret Files and JLA/JSA Secret Files #1; JG Jones-c 13.00

AQUAMAN (DC New 52)
DC Comics: Nov, 2011 - Present ($2.99)

1-7: 1-Geoff Johns-s/Ivan Reis-a/c. 7-Black Manta app. 3.00

AQUAMAN: TIME & TIDE (3rd limited series) (Also see Atlantis Chronicles)
DC Comics: Dec, 1993 - No. 4, Mar, 1994 ($1.50, limited series)

1-4: Peter David scripts; origin retold. 3.00
Trade paperback ($9.95) 10.00

AQUANAUTS (TV)
Dell Publishing Co.: May - July, 1961

	GD	VG	FN	VF	VF/NM	NM-
Four Color 1197-Photo-c	7	14	21	46	76	105

ARABIAN NIGHTS (See Cinema Comics Herald)

ARACHNOPHOBIA (Movie)
Hollywood Comics (Disney Comics): 1990 ($5.95, 68 pg. graphic novel)

nn-Adaptation of film; Spiegle-a 6.00
Comic edition ($2.95, 68 pgs.) 4.00

ARAK/SON OF THUNDER (See Warlord #48)
DC Comics: Sept, 1981 - No. 50, Nov, 1985

1,24,50: 1-1st app. Angelica, Princess of White Cathay. 24,50-(52 pgs.) 4.00
2-23,25-49: 3-Intro Valda. 12-Origin Valda. 20-Origin Angelica 3.00
Annual 1(10/84) 4.00

ARAÑA THE HEART OF THE SPIDER (See Amazing Fantasy (2004) #1-6)
Marvel Comics: March, 2005 - No. 12, Feb, 2006 ($2.99)

1-12: 1-Avery-s/Cruz-a. 4-Spider-Man-c/app. 3.00
Vol. 1: Heart of the Spider (2005, $7.99, digest) r/Amazing Fantasy (2004) #1-6 8.00
Vol. 2: In the Beginning (2005, $7.99, digest) r/#1-6 8.00
Vol. 3: Night of the Hunter (2006, $7.99, digest) r/#7-12 8.00

ARCANA (Also see Books of Magic limited & ongoing series and Mister E)
DC Comics (Vertigo): 1994 ($3.95, 68 pgs., annual)

1-Bolton painted-c; Children's Crusade/Tim Hunter story 4.00

ARCANUM
Image Comics (Top Cow Productions): Apr, 1997 - No. 8, Feb, 1998 ($2.50)

1/2 Gold Edition 12.00
1-Brandon Peterson-s/a(p), 1-Variant-c, 4-American Ent. Ed. 3.50
2-8 3.00
3-Variant-c 4.00
...: Millennium's End TPB (2005, $16.99) r/#1-8 & #1/2; cover gallery and sketch pages 17.00

ARCHANGEL (See Uncanny X-Men, X-Factor & X-Men)
Marvel Comics: Feb, 1996 ($2.50, B&W, one-shot)

1-Milligan story 3.00

ARCHARD'S AGENTS (See Ruse)
CrossGeneration Comics: Jan, 2003; Nov, 2003; Apr, 2004 ($2.95)

1-Dixon-s/Perkins-a 3.00
...: The Case of the Puzzled Pugilist (11/03) Dixon-s/Perkins-a 3.00
Vol. 3 - Deadly Dare (4/04) Dixon-s/McNiven-a; preview of Lady Death: The Wild Hunt 3.00

ARCHENEMIES
Dark Horse Comics: Apr, 2006 - No. 4, July, 2006 ($2.99, limited series)

1-4-Melbourne-s/Guichet-a 3.00

ARCHER & ARMSTRONG
Valiant: July (June inside), 1992 - No. 26, Oct, 1994 ($2.50)

	GD	VG	FN	VF	VF/NM	NM-
0-(7/92)-B. Smith-c/a; Reese-i assists						4.00
0-(with Gold Valiant Logo)	2	4	6	8	10	12
1-7,9-26: 1-(8/92)-Origin & 1st app. Archer; Miller-c; B. Smith/Layton-a. 2-2nd app. Turok (c/story); Smith/Layton-a; Simonson-c. 3,4-Smith-c&a(p) & scripts. 10-2nd app. Ivar. 10,11-B. Smith-c. 21,22-Shadowman app. 22-w/bound-in trading card. 25-Eternal Warrior app. 26-Flip book w/Eternal Warrior #26						3.00
8-($4.50, 52 pgs.)-Combined with Eternal Warrior #8; B. Smith-c/a & scripts; 1st app. Ivar the Time Walker						4.50
...: First Impressions HC (2008, $24.95) recolored reprints #0-6; new "Formation of the Sect" story by Jim Shooter and Sal Velutto; Shooter commentary; new cover by Golden						25.00

ARCHIE (See Archie Comics) (Also see Christmas & Archie, Everything's..., Explorers of the Unknown, Jackpot, Little..., Oxydol-Dreft, Pep, Riverdale High, Teenage Mutant Ninja Turtles Adventures & To Riverdale and Back Again)

ARCHIE ALL CANADIAN DIGEST
Archie Publications: Aug, 1996 ($1.75, 96 pgs.)

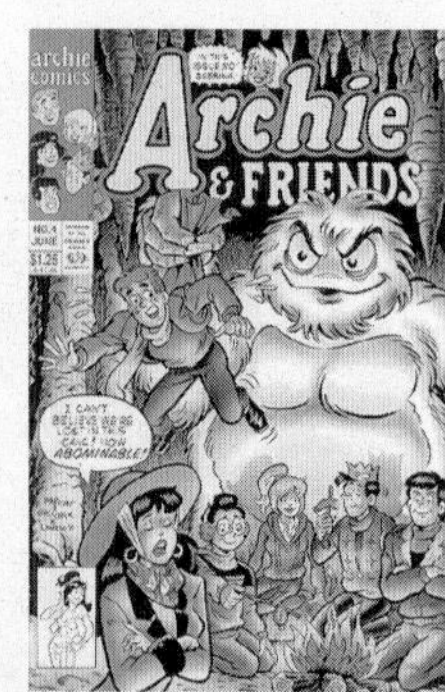

Archie & Friends #4 © AP

Archie Comics #8 © AP

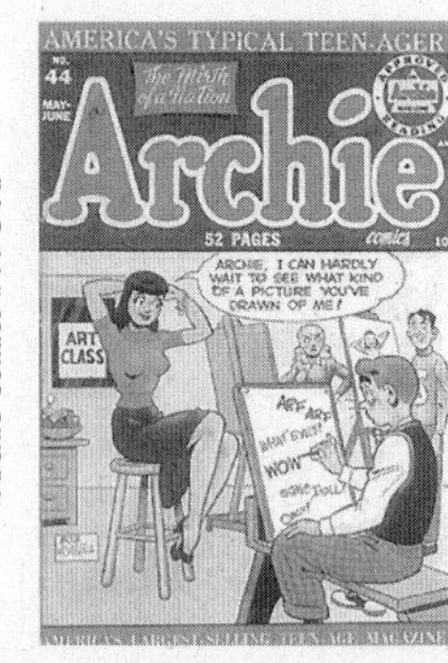

Archie Comics #44 © AP

	GD 2.0	VG 4.0	FN 6.0	VF 8.0	VF/NM 9.0	NM- 9.2
1	1	2	3	5	6	8

ARCHIE AMERICANA SERIES, BEST OF THE FORTIES
Archie Publications: 1991,2002 ($10.95, trade paperback)

	GD 2.0	VG 4.0	FN 6.0	VF 8.0	VF/NM 9.0	NM- 9.2
Vol. 1,2-r/early strips from 1940s 1-Intro. by Steven King. 2-Intro. by Paul Castiglia						12.00

ARCHIE AMERICANA SERIES, BEST OF THE FIFTIES
Archie Publications: 1991 ($8.95, trade paperback)

	GD 2.0	VG 4.0	FN 6.0	VF 8.0	VF/NM 9.0	NM- 9.2
Vol. 2-r/strips from 1950's;						12.00
2nd printing (1998, $9.95)						12.00
Book 2 (2003, $10.95)						12.00

ARCHIE AMERICANA SERIES, BEST OF THE SIXTIES
Archie Publications: 1995 ($9.95, trade paperback)

	GD 2.0	VG 4.0	FN 6.0	VF 8.0	VF/NM 9.0	NM- 9.2
Vol. 3-r/strips from 1960s; intro. by Frankie Avalon.						12.00

ARCHIE AMERICANA SERIES, BEST OF THE SEVENTIES
Archie Publications: 1997, 2008 ($9.95/$10.95, trade paperback)

	GD 2.0	VG 4.0	FN 6.0	VF 8.0	VF/NM 9.0	NM- 9.2
Vol. 4 (1997, $9.95)-r/strips from 1970s						12.00
Vol. 8 Book 2 (2008, $10.95)-r/other strips from 1970s						12.00

ARCHIE AMERICANA SERIES, BEST OF THE EIGHTIES
Archie Publications: 2001 ($10.95, trade paperback)

	GD 2.0	VG 4.0	FN 6.0	VF 8.0	VF/NM 9.0	NM- 9.2
Vol. 5-r/strips from 1980s; foreward by Steve Geppi						12.00

ARCHIE AMERICANA SERIES, BEST OF THE '90S
Archie Publications: 2008 ($11.95, trade paperback)

	GD 2.0	VG 4.0	FN 6.0	VF 8.0	VF/NM 9.0	NM- 9.2
Vol. 9-r/strips from 1990s; new Lindsey cover						12.00

ARCHIE AND BIG ETHEL
Spire Christian Comics (Fleming H. Revell Co.): 1982 (69¢)

	GD 2.0	VG 4.0	FN 6.0	VF 8.0	VF/NM 9.0	NM- 9.2
nn-(Low print run)	2	4	6	11	16	22

ARCHIE & FRIENDS
Archie Comics: Dec, 1992 - No. 159, Feb, 2012 ($1.25-$2.99)

	GD 2.0	VG 4.0	FN 6.0	VF 8.0	VF/NM 9.0	NM- 9.2
1						5.00
2,4,10-14,17,18,20-Sabrina app. 20-Archie's Band-c						4.00
3,5-9,16						3.00
15-Babewatch-s with Sabrina app.						6.00
19-Josie and the Pussycats app.; E.T. parody-c/s						5.00
21-46						3.00
47-All Josie and the Pussycats issue; movie and actress profiles/photos						4.00
48-142: 48-56,58,60,96-Josie and the Pussycats-c/s. 79-Cheryl Blossom returns. 100-The Veronicas-c/app. 101-Katy Keene begins. 129-Begin $2.50. 130,131-Josie and the Pussycats. 137-Cosmo, Super Duck, Pat the Brat and other old characters app.						3.00
143-159: 143-Begin $2.99-c. 145-Jersey Shore spoof. 146,147-Twilite. 154-Little Archie						3.00

ARCHIE & FRIENDS DOUBLE DIGEST MAGAZINE
Archie Comics: Feb, 2011 - Present ($3.99, digest-size)

	GD 2.0	VG 4.0	FN 6.0	VF 8.0	VF/NM 9.0	NM- 9.2
1-16: 1-Staton-a. 7-13-SuperTeens app.						4.00

ARCHIE AND ME (See Archie Giant Series Mag. #578, 591, 603, 616, 626)
Archie Publications: Oct, 1964 - No. 161, Feb, 1987

	GD 2.0	VG 4.0	FN 6.0	VF 8.0	VF/NM 9.0	NM- 9.2
1	14	28	42	93	202	310
2	9	18	27	62	109	155
3-5	7	14	21	44	72	100
6-10	5	10	15	30	48	65
11-20	3	6	9	21	32	42
21(6/68)-26,28-30: 21-UFO story. 26-X-Mas-c	3	6	9	17	25	32
27-Groovyman & Knowman superhero-s; UFO-sty	3	6	9	20	30	40
31-42: 37-Japan Expo '70-c/s	3	6	9	14	19	24
43-48,50-63-(All Giants): 43-(8/71) Mummy-s. 44-Mermaid-s. 62-Elvis cameo-c. 63-(2/74)	3	6	9	16	22	28
49-(Giant) Josie & the Pussycats-c/app.	3	6	9	21	32	42
64-66,68-99-(Regular size): 85-Bicentennial-s. 98-Collectors Comics	2	4	6	8	10	12
67-Sabrina app.(8/74)	2	4	6	10	14	18
100-(4/78)	2	4	6	8	11	14
101-120: 107-UFO-s	1	2	3	5	6	8
121(8/80)-159: 134-Riverdale 2001						6.00
160,161: 160-Origin Mr. Weatherbee. 161-Last issue	1	2	3	5	6	8

ARCHIE AND MR. WEATHERBEE
Spire Christian Comics (Fleming H. Revell Co.): 1980 (59¢)

	GD 2.0	VG 4.0	FN 6.0	VF 8.0	VF/NM 9.0	NM- 9.2
nn - (Low print run)	2	4	6	13	18	22

ARCHIE...ARCHIE ANDREWS, WHERE ARE YOU? (...Comics Digest #9, 10; ...Comics Digest Mag. No. 11 on)
Archie Publications: Feb, 1977 - No. 114, May, 1998 (Digest size, 160-128 pgs., quarterly)

	GD 2.0	VG 4.0	FN 6.0	VF 8.0	VF/NM 9.0	NM- 9.2
1	3	6	9	18	27	35
2,3,5,7-9-N. Adams-a; 8-r-/origin The Fly by S&K. 9-Steel Sterling-r	2	4	6	10	14	18
4,6,10 ($1.00/$1.50)	2	4	6	8	11	14
11-20: 17-Katy Keene story	2	3	4	6	8	10
21-50,100	1	2	3	5	6	8
51-70						4.00
71-99,101-114: 113-Begin $1.95-c						3.00

ARCHIE AS PUREHEART THE POWERFUL (Also see Archie Giant Series #142, Jughead as Captain Hero, Life With Archie & Little Archie)
Archie Publications (Radio Comics): Sept, 1966 - No. 6, Nov, 1967

	GD 2.0	VG 4.0	FN 6.0	VF 8.0	VF/NM 9.0	NM- 9.2
1-Super hero parody	11	22	33	73	142	210
2	7	14	21	46	76	105
3-6	6	12	18	41	66	90

NOTE: *Evilheart cameos in all. Title: Archie As Pureheart the Powerful #1-3; ...As Capt. Pureheart-#4-6.*

ARCHIE AT RIVERDALE HIGH (See Archie Giant Series Magazine #573, 586, 604 & Riverdale High)
Archie Publications: Aug, 1972 - No. 113, Feb, 1987

	GD 2.0	VG 4.0	FN 6.0	VF 8.0	VF/NM 9.0	NM- 9.2
1	6	12	18	41	66	90
2	4	8	12	22	34	45
3-5	3	6	9	16	23	30
6-10	2	4	6	11	16	20
11-30	2	4	6	8	10	12
31(12/75)-46,48-50(12/77)	1	3	4	6	8	10
47-Archie in drag-s; Betty mud wrestling-s	2	4	6	9	13	16
51-80,100 (12/84)	1	2	3	5	6	8
81(8/81)-88, 91,93-95,98						6.00
89,90-Early Cheryl Blossom app. 90-Archies Band app.	3	6	9	14	19	24
92,96,97,99-Cheryl Blossom app. 96-Anti-smoking issue	2	4	6	10	14	18
101,102,104-109,111,112: 102-Ghost-c						6.00
103-Archie dates Cheryl Blossom-s	2	4	6	10	14	18
110,113: 110-Godzilla-s. 113-Last issue	1	2	3	5	6	8

ARCHIE COMICS (See Pep Comics #22 [12/41] for Archie's debut) (1st Teen-age comic; Radio show first aired 6/2/45 by NBC)
MLJ Magazines No. 1-19/Archie Publ. No. 20 on: Winter, 1942-43 - No. 19, 3-4/46; No. 20, 5-6/46 - Present

	GD 2.0	VG 4.0	FN 6.0	VF 8.0	VF/NM 9.0	NM- 9.2
1 (Scarce)-Jughead, Veronica app.; 1st app. Mrs. Andrews	5333	10,667	16,000	40,000	65,000	90,000
2 (Scarce)	676	1352	2028	4935	8718	12,500
3 (60 pgs.)(scarce)	443	886	1329	3234	5717	8200
4,5: 4-Article about Archie radio series. 5-Halloween-c	300	600	900	2010	3505	5000
6,8-10: 6-X-Mas-c. 9-1st Miss Grundy cover	226	452	678	1446	2473	3500
7-1st definitive love triangle story	258	516	774	1651	2826	4000
11-15: 15-Dotty & Ditto by Woggon	145	290	435	921	1586	2250
16-20: 15,17,18-Dotty & Ditto by Woggon. 16,19-Woggon-a. 18-Halloween pumpkin-c.	135	270	405	864	1482	2100
21-30: 23-Betty & Veronica by Woggon. 25-Woggon-a. 30-Coach Piffle app., a Coach Kleats prototype. 34-Pre-Dilton try-out (named Dilbert)	81	162	243	518	884	1250
31-40	48	96	144	302	514	725
41-50	37	74	111	222	361	500
51-60	14	28	42	96	208	320
61-70 (1954): 65-70, Katy Keene app.	11	22	33	76	151	225
71-80: 72-74-Katy Keene app.	10	20	30	66	121	175
81-93,95-99	8	16	24	56	96	135
94-1st Coach Kleats in this title (see Pep #24)	9	18	27	62	109	155
100	10	20	30	64	115	165
101-122,126,128-130 (1962)	6	12	18	39	62	85
123-125,127-Horror/SF covers. 123-UFO-c/s	8	16	24	51	86	120
131,132,134-157,159,160: 137-1st Caveman Archie gang story	4	8	12	24	37	50
133 (12/62)-1st app. Cricket O'Dell	4	8	12	28	44	60
158-Archie in drag story	4	8	12	26	41	55
161(2/66)-184,186-188,190-195,197-199: 168-Superhero gag-c. 176,178-Twiggy-c 183-Caveman Archie gang story	3	6	9	18	27	35
185-1st "The Archies" Band story	4	8	12	26	41	55
189 (3/69)-Archie's band meets Don Kirshner who developed the Monkees	3	6	9	20	30	40
196 (12/69)-Early Cricket O'Dell app.	3	6	9	20	30	40
200 (6/70)	3	6	9	19	29	38

Archie Comics #606 © AP

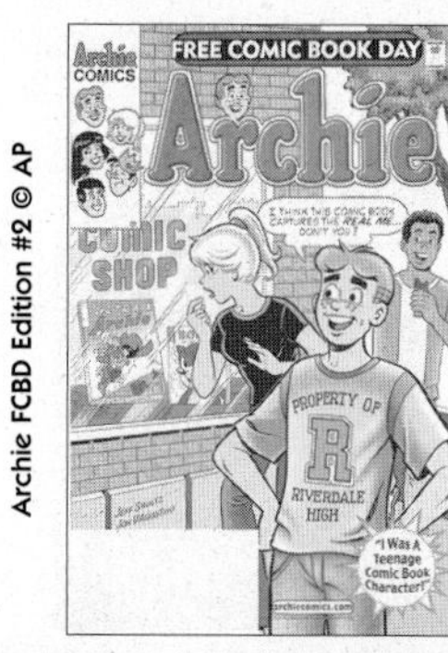

Archie FCBD Edition #2 © AP

Archie Giant Series Magazine #18 © AP

GD 2.0 | VG 4.0 | FN 6.0 | VF 8.0 | VF/NM 9.0 | NM- 9.2

201-230(11/73): 213-Sabrina/Josie-c cameos. 229-Lost Child issue
2 4 6 11 16 20
231-260(3/77): 253-Tarzan parody 2 4 6 8 11 14
261-282, 284-299 1 3 4 6 8 10
283(8/79)-Cover/story plugs "International Children's Appeal" which was a fraudulent charity, according to TV's 20/20 news program broadcast July 20, 1979
2 4 6 8 10 12
300(1/81)-Anniversary issue 2 4 6 8 11 14
301-321,323-325,327-335,337-350: 323-Cheryl Blossom pin-up. 325-Cheryl Blossom app. 6.00
322-E.T. story 1 2 3 5 6 8
326-Early Cheryl Blossom story 2 4 6 10 14 18
336-Michael Jackson/Boy George parody 2 4 6 8 10 12
351-399: 356-Calgary Olympics Special. 393-Infinity-c; 1st comic book printed on recycled paper 5.00
400 (6/92)-Shows 1st meeting of Little Archie and Veronica 6.00
401-428 4.00
429-Love Showdown part 1 5.00
430-599: 467- "A Storm Over Uniforms" x-over parts 3,4. 538-Comic-Con issue 3.00
600-602: 600-(10/09) Archie proposes to Veronica. 601-Marries Veronica. 602-Twins born 3.00
603-606: 603-(1/10) Archie proposes to Betty. 604-Marries Betty. 605-Twins born 3.00
607-626: 609-Begin $2.99-c. 610-613-Man From RIVERDALE. 616,617-Obama & Palin app.; two covers on each. 625-70th Anniversary. 626-Michael Strahan app. 3.00
627-630-Archie Meets KISS; 2 covers on each by Parent & Francavilla 3.00
631-633: 632-Archie marries Valerie from the Pussycats 3.00
Annual 1 ('50)-116 pgs. (Scarce) 258 516 774 1651 2826 4000
Annual 2 ('51) 110 220 330 704 1202 1700
Annual 3 ('52) 63 126 189 403 689 975
Annual 4,5 (1953-54) 44 88 132 277 469 660
Annual 6-10 (1955-59): 8,9-(100 pgs.). 10-(84 pgs.) Elvis record on-c
14 28 42 97 211 325
Annual 11-15 (1960-65): 12,13-(84 pgs.) 14,15-(68 pgs.)
10 20 30 64 115 165
Annual 16-20 (1966-70)(all 68 pgs.): 20-Archie's band-c
6 12 18 41 66 90
Annual 21,22,24-26 (1971-75): 21,22-(68 pgs.). 22-Archie's band-s. 24-26-(52 pgs.). 25-Cavemen-s 4 8 12 22 34 45
Annual 23-Archie's band-c/s; Josie/Sabrina-c 5 10 15 30 48 65
Annual Digest 27 ('75) 4 8 12 24 37 50
...28-30 3 6 9 14 20 25
...31-34 2 4 6 9 13 16
...35-40 (...Magazine #35 on) 1 3 4 6 8 10
...41-65 ('94) 5.00
...66-69 3.00
...All-Star Specials (Winter '75, $1.25)-6 remaindered Archie comics rebound in each; titles: "The World of Giant Comics", "Giant Grab Bag of Comics", "Triple Giant Comics" & "Giant Spec. Comics 5 10 15 30 48 65

NOTE: *Archies Band-s-185, 188-192, 197, 198, 201, 204, 205, 208, 209, 215, 329, 330; Band-c-191, 330. Cavemen Archie Gang-s-183, 192, 197, 208, 210, 220, 223, 282, 333, 335, 338, 340.* ***Al Fagly*** *c-17-35.* ***Bob Montana*** *c-38, 41-50, 58, Annual 1-4.* ***Bill Woggon*** *c-53, 54.*

ARCHIE COMICS DIGEST (...Magazine No. 37-95)
Archie Publications: Aug, 1973 - No. 267, Nov, 2010 (Digest-size, 160-128 pgs.)

1-1st Archie digest 9 18 27 63 112 160
2 5 10 15 32 51 70
3-5 4 8 12 24 37 50
6-10 3 6 9 16 23 30
11-33: 32,33-The Fly-r by S&K 2 4 6 10 14 18
34-60 1 3 4 6 8 10
61-80,100 1 2 3 5 6 8
81-99 5.00
101-140: 36-Katy Keene story 4.00
141-165 3.00
166-267: 194-Begin $2.39-c. 225-Begin $2.49-c. 236-65th Anniversary issue, r/1st app. in Pep #22 and entire Archie Comics #1 (1942) 3.00

NOTE: ***Neal Adams*** *a-1, 2, 4, 5, 19-21, 24, 25, 27, 29, 31, 33. X-mas c-88, 94, 100, 106.*

ARCHIE COMICS (Free Comic Book Day editions) (Also see Pep Comics)
Archie Publications: 2003 - Present

... Free Comic Book Day Edition 1,2: 1-(7/03). 2-(9/04) 3.00
Little Archie "The Legend of the Lost Lagoon" FCBD Edition (5/07) Bolling-s/a 3.00
... Presents the Mighty Archie Art Players ('09) Free Comic Book Day giveaway 3.00
...'s 65th Anniversary Bash ('06) Free Comic Book Day giveaway 3.00
...'s Summer Splash FCBD Edition (5/10) Parent-a; Cheryl Blossom app. 3.00

ARCHIE COMICS PRESENTS: THE LOVE SHOWDOWN COLLECTION
Archie Publications: 1994 ($4.95, squarebound)

nn-r/Archie #429, Betty #19, Betty & Veronica #82, & Veronica #39
1 2 3 5 6 8

ARCHIE DOUBLE DIGEST (See Archie's Double Digest Quarterly Magazine)

ARCHIE GETS A JOB
Spire Christian Comics (Fleming H. Revell Co.): 1977

nn 2 4 6 13 18 22

ARCHIE GIANT SERIES MAGAZINE
Archie Publications: 1954 - No. 632, July, 1992 (No #36-135, no #252-451)
(#1 not code approved) (#1-233 are Giants; #12-184 are 68 pgs.,#185-194,197-233 are 52 pgs.; #195,196 are 84 pgs.; #234-up are 36 pgs.)

1-Archie's Christmas Stocking 155 310 465 992 1696 2400
2-Archie's Christmas Stocking('55) 77 154 231 493 847 1200
3-6-Archie's Christmas Stocking('56- '59) 53 106 159 334 567 800
7-10: 7-Katy Keene Holiday Fun(9/60); Bill Woggon-c. 8-Betty & Veronica Summer Fun (10/60); baseball story w/Babe Ruth & Lou Gehrig. 9-The World of Jughead (12/60); Neal Adams-a. 10-Archie's Christmas Stocking(1/61) 39 78 117 240 395 550
11,13,16,18: 11-Betty & Veronica Spectacular (6/61). 13-Betty & Veronica Summer Fun (10/61). 16-Betty & Veronica Spectacular (6/62). 18-Betty & Veronica Summer Fun (10/62)
25 50 75 150 245 340
12,14,15,17,19,20: 12-Katy Keene Holiday Fun (9/61). 14-The World of Jughead (12/61); Vampire-s. 15-Archie's Christmas Stocking (1/62). 17-Archie's Jokes (9/62); Katy Keene app. 19-The World of Jughead (12/62). 20-Archie's Christmas Stocking (1/63)
19 38 57 112 179 245
21,23,28: 21-Betty & Veronica Spectacular (6/63). 23-Betty & Veronica Summer Fun (10/63). 28-Betty & Veronica Summer Fun (9/64) 10 20 30 66 121 175
22,24,25,27,29,30: 22-Archie's Jokes (9/63). 24-The World of Jughead (12/63). 25-Archie's Christmas Stocking (1/64). 27-Archie's Jokes (8/64). 29-Around the World with Archie (10/64); Doris Day-s. 30-The World of Jughead (12/64) 9 18 27 61 106 150
26-Betty & Veronica Spectacular (6/64); all pin-ups; DeCarlo-c/a
10 20 30 67 124 180
31,33-35: 31-Archie's Christmas Stocking (1/65). 33-Archie's Jokes (8/65). 34-Betty & Veronica Summer Fun (9/65). 35-Around the World with Archie (10/65).
7 14 21 44 72 100
32-Betty & Veronica Spectacular (6/65); all pin-ups; DeCarlo-c/a
8 16 24 53 89 125
36-135-**Do not exist**
136-141: 136-The World of Jughead (12/65). 137-Archie's Christmas Stocking (1/66). 138-Betty & Veronica Spect. (6/66). 139-Archie's Jokes (6/66). 140-Betty & Veronica Summer Fun (8/66). 141-Around the World with Archie (9/66) 7 14 21 44 72 100
142-Archie's Super-Hero Special (10/66)-Origin Capt. Pureheart, Capt. Hero, and Evilheart
8 16 24 56 96 135
143-The World of Jughead (12/66); Capt. Hero-c/s; Man From R.I.V.E.R.D.A.L.E., Pureheart, Superteen app. 7 14 21 44 72 100
144-160: 144-Archie's Christmas Stocking (1/67). 145-Betty & Veronica Spectacular (6/67). 146-Archie's Jokes (6/67). 147-Betty & Veronica Summer Fun (8/67) 148-World of Archie (9/67). 149-World of Jughead (10/67). 150-Archie's Christmas Stocking (1/68). 151-World of Archie (2/68). 152-World of Jughead (2/68). 153-Betty & Veronica Spectacular (6/68). 154-Archie Jokes (6/68). 155-Betty & Veronica Summer Fun (8/68). 156-World of Archie (10/68). 157-World of Jughead (12/68). 158-Archie's Christmas Stocking (1/69). 159-Betty & Veronica Christmas Spectacular (1/69). 160-World of Archie (2/69); Frankenstein-s each... 4 8 12 24 37 50
161-World of Jughead (2/69); Super-Jughead-s; 11 pg. early Cricket O'Dell-s
4 8 12 26 41 55
162-183: 162-Betty & Veronica Spectacular (6/69). 163-Archie's Jokes(8/69). 164-Betty & Veronica Summer Fun (9/69). 165-World of Archie (9/69). 166-World of Jughead (9/69). 167-Archie's Christmas Stocking (1/70). 168-Betty & Veronica Christmas Spect. (1/70). 169-Archie's Christmas Love-In (1/70). 170-Jughead's Eat-Out Comic Book Mag. (12/69). 171-World of Archie (2/70). 172-World of Jughead (2/70). 173-Betty & Veronica Spectacular (6/70). 174-Archie's Jokes (8/70). 175-Betty & Veronica Summer Fun (9/70). 176-Li'l Jinx Giant Laugh-Out (8/70). 177-World of Archie (9/70). 178-World of Jughead (9/70). 179-Archie's Christmas Stocking(1/71). 180-Betty & Veronica Christmas Spect. (1/71). 181-Archie's Christmas Love-In (1/71). 182-World of Archie (2/71). 183-World of Jughead (2/71)-Last squarebound each... 3 6 9 18 27 35
184-189,193,194,197-199 (52 pgs.): 184-Betty & Veronica Spectacular (6/71). 185-Li'l Jinx Giant Laugh-Out (6/71). 186-Archie's Jokes (8/71). 187-Betty & Veronica Summer Fun (9/71). 188-World of Archie (9/71). 189-World of Jughead (9/71). 193-World of Archie (3/72).194-World of Jughead (4/72). 197-Betty & Veronica Spectacular (6/72). 198-Archie's Jokes (8/72). 199-Betty & Veronica Summer Fun (9/72)
each... 3 6 9 16 22 28
190-Archie's Christmas Stocking (12/71); Sabrina-c 4 8 12 28 44 60
191-Betty & Veronica Christmas Spect.(2/72); Sabrina app.
4 8 12 24 37 50
192-Archie's Christmas Love-In (1/72); Archie Band-c/s

Archie Giant Series Magazine #187 © AP

Archie Giant Series Magazine #612 © AP

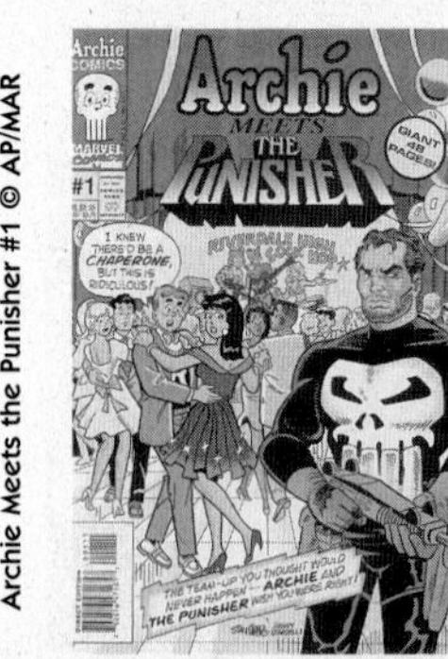

Archie Meets the Punisher #1 © AP/MAR

	GD 2.0	VG 4.0	FN 6.0	VF 8.0	VF/NM 9.0	NM- 9.2

3 6 9 21 32 42
195-(84 pgs.)-Li'l Jinx Christmas Bag (1/72). 4 8 12 22 34 45
196-(84 pgs.)-Sabrina's Christmas Magic (1/72) 6 12 18 37 59 80
200-(52 pgs.)-World of Archie (10/72) 3 6 9 21 32 42
201-206,208-219,221-230,232,233 (All 52 pgs.): 201-Betty & Veronica Spectacular (10/72). 202-World of Jughead (11/72). 203-Archie's Christmas Stocking (12/72). 204-Betty & Veronica Christmas Spectacular (2/73). 205-Archie's Christmas Love-In (1/73). 206-Li'l Jinx Christmas Bag (12/72). 208-World of Archie (3/73). 209-World of Jughead (4/73). 210-Betty & Veronica Spectacular (6/73). 211-Archie's Jokes (8/73). 212-Betty & Veronica Summer Fun (9/73). 213-World of Archie (10/73). 214-Betty & Veronica Spectacular (10/73). 215-World of Jughead (11/73). 216-Archie's Christmas Stocking (12/73). 217-Betty & Veronica Christmas Spectacular (2/74). 218-Archie's Christmas Love-In (1/74). 219-Li'l Jinx Christmas Bag (12/73). 221-Betty & Veronica Spectacular (Advertised as World of Archie) (6/74). 222-Archie's Jokes (advertised as World of Jughead) (8/74). 223-Li'l Jinx (8/74). 224-Betty & Veronica Summer Fun (9/74). 225-World of Archie (9/74). 226-Betty & Veronica Spectacular (10/74). 227-World of Jughead (10/74). 228-Archie's Christmas Stocking (12/74). 229-Betty & Veronica Christmas Spectacular (12/74). 230-Archie's Christmas Love-In (1/75). 232-World of Archie (3/75). 233-World of Jughead (4/75)
each... 2 4 6 11 16 20
207,220,231,243: Sabrina's Christmas Magic. 207-(12/72). 220-(12/73). 231-(1/75). 243-(1/76)
each... 3 6 9 17 25 32
234-242,244-251 (36 pgs.): 234-Betty & Veronica Spectacular (6/75). 235-Archie's Jokes (8/75). 236-Betty & Veronica Summer Fun (9/75). 237-World of Archie (9/75) 238-Betty & Veronica Spectacular (10/75). 239-World of Jughead (10/75). 240-Archie's Christmas Stocking (12/75). 241-Betty & Veronica Christmas Spectacular (12/75). 242-Archie's Christmas Love-In (1/76). 244-World of Archie (3/76). 245-World of Jughead (4/76). 246-Betty & Veronica Spectacular (6/76). 247-Archie's Jokes (8/76). 248-Betty & Veronica Summer Fun (9/76). 249-World of Archie (9/76). 250-Betty & Veronica Spectacular (10/76). 251-World of Jughead each.... 2 4 6 9 12 15
252-451-**Do not exist**
452-454,456-466,468-478, 480-490,492-499: 452-Archie's Christmas Stocking (12/76). 453-Betty & Veronica Christmas Spectacular (12/76). 454-Archie's Christmas Love-In (1/77). 456-World of Archie (3/77). 457-World of Jughead (4/77). 458-Betty & Veronica Spectacular (6/77). 459-Archie's Jokes (8/77)-Shows 8/76 in error. 460-Betty & Veronica Summer Fun (9/77). 461-World of Archie (9/77). 462-Betty & Veronica Spectacular (10/77). 463-World of Jughead (10/77). 464-Archie's Christmas Stocking (12/77). 465-Betty & Veronica Christmas Spectacular (12/77). 466-Archie's Christmas Love-In (1/78). 468-World of Archie (2/78). 469-World of Jughead (2/78). 470-Betty & Veronica Spectacular(6/78). 471-Archie's Jokes (8/78). 472-Betty & Veronica Summer Fun (9/78). 473-World of Archie (9/78). 474-Betty & Veronica Spectacular (10/78). 475-World of Jughead (10/78). 476-Archie's Christmas Stocking (12/78). 477-Betty & Veronica Christmas Spectacular (12/78). 478-Archie's Christmas Love-In (1/79). 480-The World of Archie (3/79). 481-World of Jughead (4/79). 482-Betty & Veronica Spectacular (6/79). 483-Archie's Jokes (8/79). 484-Betty & Veronica Summer Fun(9/79). 485-The World of Archie (9/79). 486-Betty & Veronica Spectacular (10/79). 487-The World of Jughead (10/79). 488-Archie's Christmas Stocking (12/79). 489-Betty & Veronica Christmas Spectacular (1/80). 490-Archie's Christmas Love-in (1/80). 492-The World of Archie (2/80). 493-The World of Jughead (4/80). 494-Betty & Veronica Spectacular (6/80). 495-Archie's Jokes (8/80). 496-Betty & Veronica Summer Fun (9/80). 497-The World of Archie (9/80). 498-Betty & Veronica Spectacular (10/80). 499-The World of Jughead (10/80) each... 2 4 6 8 10 12
455,467,479,491,503-Sabrina's Christmas Magic: 455-(1/77). 467-(1/78). 479-(1/79) Dracula/Werewolf-s. 491-(1/80), 503(1/81) 2 4 6 11 16 20
500-Archie's Christmas Stocking (12/80) 2 4 6 8 11 14
501-514,516-527,529-532,534-539,541-543,545-550: 501-Betty & Veronica Christmas Spectacular (12/80). 502-Archie's Christmas Love-in (1/81). 504-The World of Archie (3/81). 505-The World of Jughead (4/81). 506-Betty & Veronica Spectacular (6/81). 507-Archie's Jokes (8/81). 508-Betty & Veronica Summer Fun (9/81). 509-The World of Archie (9/81). 510-Betty & Vernonica Spectacular (9/81). 511-The World of Jughead (10/81). 512-Archie's Christmas Stocking (12/81). 513-Betty & Veronica Christmas Spectacular (12/81). 514-Archie's Christmas Love-in (1/82). 516-The World of Archie(3/82). 517-The World of Jughead (4/82). 518-Betty & Veronica Spectacular (6/82). 519-Archie's Jokes (8/82). 520-Betty & Veronica Summer Fun (9/82). 521-The World of Archie (9/82). 522-Betty & Veronica Spectacular (10/82). 523-The World of Jughead (10/82).524-Archie's Christmas Stocking (1/83). 525-Betty and Veronica Christmas Spectacular (1/83). 526-Betty and Veronica Spectacular (5/83). 527-Little Archie (8/83). 529-Betty and Veronica Summer Fun (8/83). 530-Betty and Veronica Spectacular (9/83). 531-The World of Jughead (9/83). 532-The World of Archie (10/83). 534-Little Archie (1/84). 535-Archie's Christmas Stocking (1/84). 536-Betty and Veronica Christmas Spectacular (1/84). 537-Betty and Veronica Spectacular (6/84). 538-Little Archie (8/84). 539-Betty and Veronica Summer Fun (8/84). 541-Betty and Veronica Spectacular (9/84). 542-The World of Jughead (9/84). 543-The World of Archie (10/84). 545-Little Archie (12/84). 546-Archie's Christmas Stocking (12/84). 547-Betty and Veronica Christmas Spectacular (12/84). 548-?. 549-Little Archie. 550-Betty and Veronica Summer Fun each... 1 2 3 5 7 9
515,528,533,540,544: 515-Sabrina's Christmas Magic (1/82). 528-Josie and the Pussycats (8/83). 533-Sabrina; Space Pirates by Frank Bolling (10/83). 540-Josie and the Pussycats (8/84). 544-Sabrina the Teen-Age Witch (10/84).
each... 2 4 6 10 14 18
551,562,571,584,597-Josie and the Pussycats 2 4 6 8 10 12
552-561,563-570,572-583,585-596,598-600: 552-Betty & Veronica Spectacular. 553-The World of Jughead. 554-The World of Archie. 555-Betty's Diary. 556-Little Archie (1/86). 557-Archie's Christmas Stocking (1/86). 558-Betty & Veronica Christmas Spectacular (1/86). 559-Betty & Veronica Spectacular. 560-Little Archie. 561-Betty & Veronica Summer Fun. 563-Betty & Veronica Spectacular. 564-World of Jughead. 565-World of Archie. 566-Little Archie. 567-Archie's Christmas Stocking. 568-Betty & Veronica Christmas Spectacular. 569-Betty & Veronica Spring Spectacular. 570-Little Archie. 571-Dracula-c/s. 572-Betty & Veronica Summer Fun. 573-Archie At Riverdale High. 574-World of Archie. 575-Betty & Veronica Spectacular. 576-Pep. 577-World of Jughead. 578-Archie And Me. 579-Archie's Christmas Stocking. 580-Betty and Veronica Christmas Spectacular. 581-Little Archie Christmas Special. 582-Betty & Veronica Spring Spectacular. 583-Little Archie. 585-Betty & Veronica Summer Fun. 586-Archie At Riverdale High. 587-The World of Archie (10/88); 1st app. Explorers of the Unknown. 588-Betty & Veronica Spectacular. 589-Pep (10/88). 590-The World of Jughead. 591-Archie & Me. 592-Archie's Christmas Stocking. 593-Betty & Veronica Christmas Spectacular. 594-Little Archie. 595-Betty & Veronica Spring Spectacular. 596-Little Archie. 598-Betty & Veronica Summer Fun. 599-The World of Archie (10/89); 2nd app. Explorers of the Unknown. 600-Betty and Veronica Spectacular
each.... 6.00
601,602,604-609,611-629: 601-Pep. 602-The World of Jughead. 604-Archie at Riverdale High. 605-Archie's Christmas Stocking. 606-Betty and Veronica Christmas Spectacular. 607-Little Archie. 608-Betty and Veronica Spectacular. 609-Little Archie. 611-Betty and Veronica Summer Fun. 612-The World of Archie. 613-Betty and Veronica Spectacular. 614-Pep (10/90). 615-Veronica's Summer Special. 616-Archie and Me. 617-Archie's Christmas Stocking. 618-Betty & Veronica Christmas Spectacular. 619-Little Archie. 620-Betty and Veronica Spectacular. 621-Betty and Veronica Summer Fun. 622-Josie & the Pussycats; not published. 623-Betty and Veronica Spectacular. 624-Pep Comics. 625-Veronica's Summer Special. 626-Archie and Me. 627-World of Archie. 628-Archie's Pals 'n' Gals Holiday Special. 629-Betty & Veronica Christmas Spectacular.
each.... 4.00
603-Archie and Me; Titanic app. 5.00
610-Josie and the Pussycats 1 2 3 4 5 7
630-631: 630-Archie's Christmas Stocking. 631-Archie's Pals 'n' Gals 4.00
632-Last issue; Betty & Veronica Spectacular 1 2 3 4 5 7
NOTE: *Archies Band-c-173,180,192; s-189,192. Archie Cavemen-165,225,232,244,249. Little Sabrina-527,534, 538,545,556,566. UFO-s-178,487,594.*

ARCHIE MEETS THE PUNISHER (Same contents as The Punisher Meets Archie)
Marvel Comics & Archie Comics Publ.: Aug, 1994 ($2.95, 52 pgs., one-shot)
1-Batton Lash story, John Buscema-a on Punisher, Stan Goldberg-a on Archie
1 2 3 4 5 7

ARCHIE'S ACTIVITY COMICS DIGEST MAGAZINE
Archie Enterprises: 1985 - No. 4 (Annual, 128 pgs., digest size)
1 (Most copies are marked) 2 4 6 9 13 16
2-4 1 2 3 5 7 9

ARCHIE'S CAR
Spire Christian Comics (Fleming H. Revell co.): 1979 (49¢)
nn 2 4 6 13 18 22

ARCHIE'S CHRISTMAS LOVE-IN (See Archie Giant Series Mag. No. 169, 181,192, 205, 218, 230, 242, 454, 466, 478, 490, 502, 514)

ARCHIE'S CHRISTMAS STOCKING (See Archie Giant Series Mag. No. 1-6,10, 15, 20, 25, 31, 137, 144, 150, 158, 167, 179, 190, 203, 216, 228, 240, 452, 464, 476, 488, 500, 512, 524, 535, 546, 557, 567, 579, 592, 605, 617, 630)

ARCHIE'S CHRISTMAS STOCKING
Archie Comics: 1993 - No. 7, 1999 ($2.00-$2.29, 52 pgs.)(Bound-in calendar poster in all)
1-Dan DeCarlo-c/a 5.00
2-5 4.00
6,7: 6-(1998, $2.25). 7-(1999, $2.29) 4.00

ARCHIE'S CIRCUS
Barbour Christian Comics: 1990 (69¢)
nn 2 4 6 10 14 18

ARCHIE'S CLASSIC CHRISTMAS STORIES
Archie Comics: 2002 ($10.95, TPB)
Volume 1 - Reprints stories from 1955-1964 Archie's Christmas Stocking issues 12.00

ARCHIE'S CLEAN SLATE
Spire Christian Comics (Fleming H. Revell Co.): 1973 (35/49¢)
1-(35¢-c edition)(Some issues have nn) 3 6 9 14 19 24
1-(49¢-c edition) 2 4 6 10 14 18

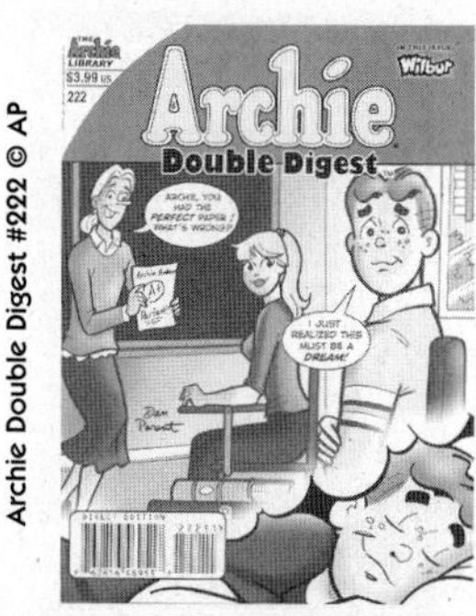

Archie Double Digest #222 © AP

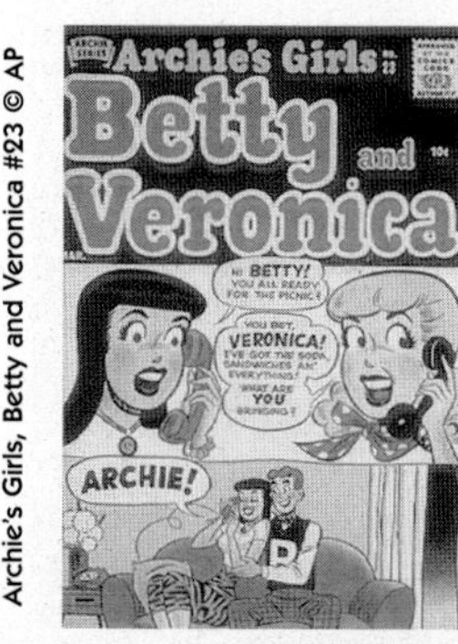

Archie's Girls, Betty and Veronica #23 © AP

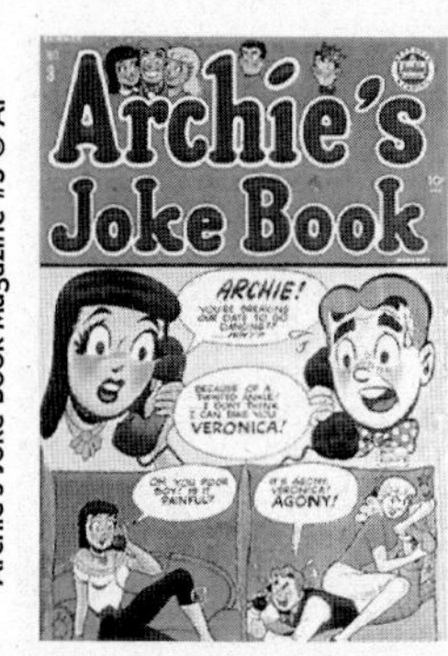

Archie's Joke Book Magazine #3 © AP

ARCHIE'S DATE BOOK
Spire Christian comics (Fleming H. Revell Co.): 1981

	GD 2.0	VG 4.0	FN 6.0	VF 8.0	VF/NM 9.0	NM- 9.2
nn-(Low print)	2	4	6	13	18	22

ARCHIE'S DOUBLE DIGEST QUARTERLY MAGAZINE
Archie Comics: 1981 - Present ($1.95-$3.99, 256 pgs.) (Archie's Double Digest Magazine No. 10 on)

	GD 2.0	VG 4.0	FN 6.0	VF 8.0	VF/NM 9.0	NM- 9.2
1	3	6	9	16	23	30
2-10; 6-Katy Keene story.	2	4	6	10	14	18
11-30: 29-Pureheart story	2	4	6	8	10	12
31-50	1	2	3	4	5	7
51-70,100						5.00
71-99						4.00
101-229: 115-Begin $3.19-c. 123-Begin $3.29-c. 170-Begin $3.69. 197-Begin $3.99-c.						4.00

ARCHIE'S FAMILY ALBUM
Spire Christian Comics (Fleming H. Revell Co.): 1978 (39¢/49¢, 36 pgs.)

	GD 2.0	VG 4.0	FN 6.0	VF 8.0	VF/NM 9.0	NM- 9.2
nn	2	4	6	13	18	22
nn (49¢-c edition)	2	4	6	9	13	16

ARCHIE'S FESTIVAL
Spire Christian Comics (Fleming H. Revell Co.): 1980 (49¢)

	GD 2.0	VG 4.0	FN 6.0	VF 8.0	VF/NM 9.0	NM- 9.2
nn	2	4	6	13	18	22

ARCHIE'S GIRLS, BETTY AND VERONICA (Becomes Betty & Veronica)(Also see Veronica)
Archie Publications (Close-Up): 1950 - No. 347, Apr, 1987

	GD 2.0	VG 4.0	FN 6.0	VF 8.0	VF/NM 9.0	NM- 9.2
1	300	600	900	1920	3310	4700
2	119	238	357	762	1306	1850
3-5: 3-Betty's 1st ponytail. 4-Dan DeCarlo's 1st Archie work	69	138	207	442	759	1075
6-10: 10-Katy Keene app. (2 pgs.)	54	108	162	343	574	825
11-20: 11,13,14,17-19-Katy Keene app. 17-Last pre-code issue (3/55). 20-Debbie's Diary (2 pgs.)	41	82	123	249	417	585
21-30: 27,30-Katy Keene app. 29-Tarzan	31	62	93	182	296	410
31-43,45-50: 41-Marilyn Monroe and Brigitte Bardot mentioned. 45-Fabian 1 pg. photo & bio. 46-Bobby Darin 1 pg. photo & bio	20	40	60	118	192	265
44-Elvis Presley 1 pg. photo & bio	23	46	69	136	223	310
51-55,57-74: 67-Jackie Kennedy homage. 73-Sci-fi-c	9	18	27	62	109	155
56-Elvis and Bobby Darin records parody	10	20	30	69	130	190
75-Betty & Veronica sell souls to Devil	16	32	48	111	243	375
76-99: 82-Bobby Rydell 1 pg. illustrated bio; Elvis mentioned on-c. 84-Connie Francis 1 pg. illustrated bio	6	12	18	42	69	95
100	7	14	21	48	79	110
101-104, 106-117,120 (12/65): 113-Monsters-s	5	10	15	30	48	65
105-Beatles wig parody (5 pg. story)(9/64)	5	10	15	32	51	70
118-(10/65) 1st app./origin Superteen (also see Betty & Me #3)	7	14	21	46	76	105
119-2nd app./last Superteen story	5	10	15	35	55	75
121,122,124-126,128-140 (8/67): 135,140-Mod-c. 136-Slave Girl-s	3	6	9	20	30	40
123-"Jingo"-Ringo parody-c	4	8	12	23	36	48
127-Beatles Fan Club-s	5	10	15	32	51	70
141-156,158-163,165-180 (12/70)	3	6	9	16	22	28
157,164-Archies Band	3	6	9	19	29	38
181-193,195-199	2	4	6	11	16	20
194-Sabrina-c/s	3	6	9	19	29	38
200-(8/72)	3	6	9	14	19	24
201-205,207,209,211-215,217-240	2	4	6	8	10	12
206,208,210, 216: 206,208,216-Sabrina c/app. 206-Josie-c. 210-Sabrina app.	3	6	9	16	22	28
241 (1/76)-270 (6/78)	1	3	4	6	8	10
271-299: 281-UFO-s	1	2	3	5	7	9
300 (12/80)-Anniversary issue	2	4	6	8	10	12
301-309	1	2	3	4	5	7
310-John Travolta parody story	1	3	4	6	8	10
311-319						6.00
320 (10/82)-Intro. of Cheryl Blossom on cover and inside story (she also appears, but not on the cover, in Jughead #325 with same 10/82 publication date)	8	16	24	56	96	135
321,322-Cheryl Blossom app. 322-Cheryl meets Archie for the 1st time	3	6	9	21	32	42
323,326,329,330,331,333-338: 333-Monsters-s						6.00
324,325-Crickett O'Dell app.	2	4	6	9	12	15
327,328-Cheryl Blossom app.	3	6	9	18	27	35
332,339: 332-Superhero costume party. 339-(12/85) Betty dressed as Madonna.	2	4	6	9	12	15
340-346 Low print	1	3	4	6	8	10
347 (4/87) Last issue; low print	2	4	6	8	10	12
Annual 1 (1953)	126	252	378	806	1378	1950
Annual 2 (1954)	49	98	147	309	522	735
Annual 3-5 (1955-1957)	39	78	117	236	388	540
Annual 6-8 (1958-1960)	27	54	81	158	259	360

ARCHIE'S HOLIDAY FUN DIGEST
Archie Comics: 1997 - Present ($1.75/$1.95/$1.99/$2.19/$2.39/$2.49, annual)

	GD 2.0	VG 4.0	FN 6.0	VF 8.0	VF/NM 9.0	NM- 9.2
1-12-Christmas stories						3.00

ARCHIE'S JOKEBOOK COMICS DIGEST ANNUAL (See Jokebook...)

ARCHIE'S JOKE BOOK MAGAZINE (See Joke Book ...)
Archie Publ: 1953 - No. 3, Sum, 1954; No. 15, Fall, 1954 - No. 288, 11/82 (subtitled...Laugh-In #127-140; ...Laugh-Out #141-194)

	GD 2.0	VG 4.0	FN 6.0	VF 8.0	VF/NM 9.0	NM- 9.2
1953-One Shot (#1)	116	232	348	742	1271	1800
2	52	104	156	322	549	775
3 (no #4-14)	41	82	123	249	417	585
15-20: 15-Formerly Archie's Rival Reggie #14; last pre-code issue (Fall/54). 15-17-Katy Keene app.	26	52	78	154	252	350
21-30	16	32	48	94	147	200
31-43: 42-Bio of Ed "Kookie" Byrnes. 43-story about guitarist Duane Eddy	14	28	42	76	108	140
44-1st professional comic work by Neal Adams, 4 pgs.	32	64	96	188	307	425
45-47-N. Adams-a in all, 2-6 pgs.	19	38	57	109	172	235
48-Four pgs. N. Adams-a	19	38	57	109	172	235
49,50	6	12	18	41	66	90
51-56,60 (1962)	4	8	12	28	44	60
57-Elvis mentioned; Marilyn Monroe cameo	6	12	18	41	66	90
58,59-Horror/Sci-Fi-c	6	12	18	42	69	95
61-80 (8/64): 66-(12¢ cover). 76-Robot-c	3	6	9	18	27	35
66-(15¢ cover variant)	4	8	12	22	34	45
81-89,91,92,94-99	3	6	9	14	20	25
90,93: 90-Beatles gag. 93-Beatles cameo	3	6	9	17	25	32
100 (5/66)	3	6	9	16	23	30
101,103-117,119-123,127,129,131-140 (9/69): 105-Superhero gag-c. 108-110-Archies Archers Band-s. 116-Beatles/Monkees/Bob Dylan cameos (posters)	2	4	6	11	16	20
102 (7/66) Archie Band prototype-c; Elvis parody panel, Rolling Stones mention	3	6	9	18	27	35
118,124,125,126,128,130: 118-Archie Band-c; Veronica & Groovers band-s. 124-Archies Band-c/app. 125-Beatles cameo (poster). 126,130-Monkees cameo. 128-Veronica/Archies Band app.	3	6	9	16	23	30
141-173,175-181,183-199	2	4	6	8	11	14
174-Sabrina-c. 182-Sabrina cameo	2	4	6	9	13	16
200 (9/74)	2	4	6	9	13	16
201-230 (3/77)	1	2	3	5	6	8
231-239,241-287						6.00
240-Elvis record-c	2	3	4	6	8	10
288-Last issue	1	2	3	4	5	7

NOTE: *Archies Band-c-118,124,147,172; 1 pg.-s-127,128,138,140,143,147,167; 2 pg.-s-124,131, 155. Sabrina app.-247,248,252-259,261,262,264,266-270,274,277,284-286.*

ARCHIE'S JOKES (See Archie Giant Series Mag. No. 17, 22, 27, 33, 139, 146, 154, 163, 174, 186, 198, 211, 222, 235, 247, 459, 471, 483, 495, 519)

ARCHIE'S LOVE SCENE
Spire Christian Comics (Fleming H. Revell Co.): 1973 (35¢/39¢/49¢/no price)

	GD 2.0	VG 4.0	FN 6.0	VF 8.0	VF/NM 9.0	NM- 9.2
1-(35¢ Edition)	3	6	9	14	19	24
1-(39¢/49¢ Edition/no price) (Some copies have nn)	2	4	6	10	14	18

ARCHIE'S LOVE SHOWDOWN SPECIAL
Archie Publications: 1994 ($2.00, one-shot)

	GD 2.0	VG 4.0	FN 6.0	VF 8.0	VF/NM 9.0	NM- 9.2
1-Concludes x-over from Archie #429, Betty #19, B&V #82, Veronica #39						4.00

ARCHIE'S MADHOUSE (Madhouse Ma-ad No. 67 on)
Archie Publications: Sept, 1959 - No. 66, Feb, 1969

	GD 2.0	VG 4.0	FN 6.0	VF 8.0	VF/NM 9.0	NM- 9.2
1-Archie begins	22	44	66	154	327	500
2	12	24	36	81	166	250
3-5	9	18	27	63	112	160
6-10	7	14	21	48	79	110
11-17 (Last w/regular characters)	6	12	18	41	66	90
18-21,23,29: 18-New format begins. 23-No Sabrina	5	10	15	35	55	75
22-1st app. Sabrina, the Teen-age Witch (10/62)	25	50	75	178	382	585
24-2nd app.Sabrina a	11	22	33	76	151	225

Archie's Pal, Jughead #57 © AP

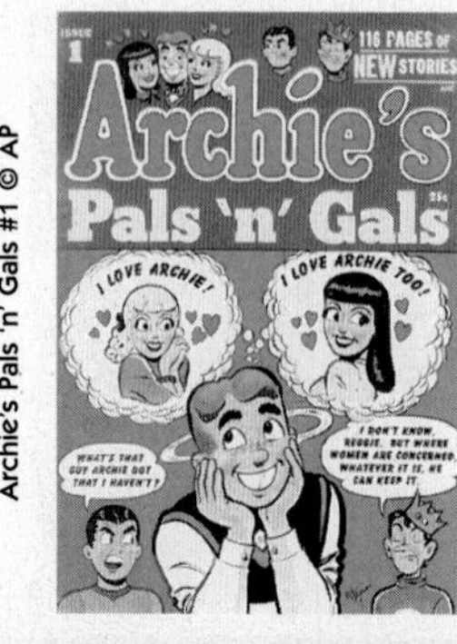

Archie's Pals 'n' Gals #1 © AP

Archie's Rival Reggie #6 © AP

	GD 2.0	VG 4.0	FN 6.0	VF 8.0	VF/NM 9.0	NM- 9.2
25,26,28-Sabrina app. 25-1st app. Captain Sprocket (4/63); 3rd app. Sabrina; sci-fi/horror-c	9	18	27	63	112	160
27-Sabrina-c; no story	8	16	24	51	86	120
30,34,38-40: No Sabrina. 34-Bordered-c begin.	4	8	12	22	34	45
31,33,37-Sabrina app.	7	14	21	49	82	115
32-Sabrina app.?	4	8	12	22	34	45
35-Beatles cameo. No Sabrina	4	8	12	26	41	55
36-1st Salem the Cat w/Sabrina story	10	20	30	66	121	175
41-48,51-57,60-62,64-66; No Sabrina 43-Mighty Crusaders cameo. 44-Swipes Mad #4 (Super-Duperman) in "Bird Monsters From Outer Space"	3	6	9	19	29	38
49,50,58,59,63-Sabrina stories	6	12	18	37	59	80
Annual 1 (1962-63) no Sabrina	8	16	24	53	89	125
Annual 2 (1964) no Sabrina	5	10	15	35	55	75
Annual 3 (1965)-Origin Sabrina the Teen-Age Witch	10	20	30	69	130	190
Annual 4,5('66-68)(Becomes Madhouse Ma-ad Annual #7 on); no Sabrina	4	8	12	26	41	55
Annual 6 (1969)-Sabrina the Teen-Age Witch-sty	6	12	18	42	69	95

NOTE: *Cover title to #61-65 is "Madhouse" and to #66 is "Madhouse Ma-ad Jokes". Sci-Fi/Horror covers 6, 8, 11, 13, 15-26, 29, 35, 36, 38, 42, 43, 48, 51, 58, 60.*

ARCHIE'S MECHANICS
Archie Publications: Sept, 1954 - No. 3, 1955

	GD	VG	FN	VF	VF/NM	NM-
1-(15¢; 52 pgs.)	94	188	282	597	1024	1450
2-(10¢)-Last pre-code issue	52	104	156	328	552	775
3-(10¢)	42	84	126	265	445	625

ARCHIE'S MYSTERIES (Continued from Archie's Weird Mysteries)
Archie Comics: No. 25, Feb, 2003 - No. 34, June, 2004 ($2.19)

	GD	VG	FN	VF	VF/NM	NM-
25-34- Archie and gang as "Teen Scene Investigators"						3.00

ARCHIE'S ONE WAY
Spire Christian Comics (Fleming H. Revell Co.): 1972 (35¢/39¢/49¢, 36 pgs.)

	GD	VG	FN	VF	VF/NM	NM-
nn-(35¢ Edition)	3	6	9	14	19	24
nn-(39¢, 49¢, no price editions)	2	4	6	10	14	18

ARCHIE'S PAL, JUGHEAD (Jughead No. 127 on)
Archie Publications: 1949 - No. 126, Nov, 1965

	GD	VG	FN	VF	VF/NM	NM-
1 (1949)-1st app. Moose (see Pep #33)	258	516	774	1651	2826	4000
2 (1950)	94	188	282	597	1024	1450
3-5	54	108	162	343	574	825
6-10: 7-Suzie app.	37	74	111	222	361	500
11-20: 20-Jughead as Sherlock Holmes parody	24	48	72	142	234	325
21-30: 23-25,28-30-Katy Keene app. 23-Early Dilton-s. 28-Debbie's Diary app.	17	34	51	98	154	210
31-50: 49-Archies Rock 'N' Rollers band-c	8	16	24	51	86	120
51-57,59-70: 59- Bio of Will Hutchins of TV's Sugarfoot. 67-Betty seducing Jughead-c. 68-Early Archie Gang Cavemen-s	6	12	18	37	59	80
58-Neal Adams-a	7	14	21	44	72	100
71-76,83,84,89-99: 72-Jughead dates Betty & Veronica. 83 (4/62) 1st mention of Secret Society of Jughead Hating Girls. 84-1st app. Big Ethyl (5/62). 95-2nd app. Cricket O'Dell	4	8	12	26	41	55
77,78,80-82,85,86,88-Horror/Sci-Fi-c. 86(7/62) 1st app. The Brain	7	14	21	44	72	100
79-Creature From the Black Lagoon-c	8	16	24	51	86	120
87-2nd app. of Big Ethyl; UGAJ (United Girls Against Jughead)-s	5	10	15	32	51	70
100	5	10	15	30	48	65
101-Return of Big Ethyl	4	8	12	28	44	60
102-126	3	6	9	20	30	40
Annual 1 (1953, 25¢)	82	164	246	528	902	1275
Annual 2 (1954, 25¢)-Last pre-code issue	41	82	123	256	428	600
Annual 3-5 (1955-57, 25¢)	31	62	93	182	296	410
Annual 6-8 (1958-60, 25¢)	20	40	60	117	189	260

ARCHIE'S PAL JUGHEAD COMICS (Formerly Jughead #1-45)
Archie Comic Publ.: No. 46, June, 1993 - Present ($1.25-$2.99)

	GD	VG	FN	VF	VF/NM	NM-
46-213: 100-"A Storm Over Uniforms" x-over part 1,2. 166-Three Geeks cameo. 200-Tom Root-s; Sabrina cameo. 201-Begin $2.99-c						3.00

ARCHIE'S PALS 'N' GALS (Also see Archie Giant Series Magazine #628)
Archie Publ: 1952-53 - No. 6, 1957-58; No. 7, 1958 - No. 224, Sept, 1991
(...All News Stories on-c #49-59)

	GD	VG	FN	VF	VF/NM	NM-
1-(116 pgs., 25¢)	100	200	300	635	1093	1550
2(Annual)('54, 25¢)	47	94	141	296	498	700
3-5(Annual, '55-57, 25¢): 3-Last pre-code issue	34	68	102	206	336	465
6-10('58-'60)	21	42	63	122	199	275
11,13,14,16,17,20-(84 pgs.): 17-B&V paper dolls	14	28	42	76	108	140
12,15-(84 pgs.) Neal Adams-a. 12-Harry Belafonte 2 pg. photos & bio.	15	30	45	85	130	175
18-(84 pgs.) Horror/Sci-Fi-c	15	30	45	83	124	165
19-Marilyn Monroe app.	19	38	57	109	172	235
21,22,24-28,30 (68 pgs.)	7	14	21	44	72	100
23-(Wint./62) 6 pg. Josie-s with Pepper and Melody (1st app.) by DeCarlo; Betty in towel pin-up	16	32	48	107	234	360
29-Beatles satire (68 pgs.)	10	20	30	64	115	165
31(Wint. 64/65)-39 -(68 pgs.)	6	12	18	37	59	80
40-Early Superteen-s; with Pureheart	7	14	21	48	79	110
41(8/67)-43,45-50(2/69) (68 pgs.)	4	8	12	26	41	55
44-Archies Band-s; WEB cameo	5	10	15	30	48	65
51(4/69),52,55-64(6/71): 62-Last squarebound	3	6	9	19	29	38
53-Archies Band-c/s	4	8	12	22	34	45
54-Satan meets Veronica-s	5	10	15	35	55	75
65(8/70),67-70,73,74,76-81,83(6/74) (52 pgs.)	3	6	9	14	20	25
66,82-Sabrina-c	4	8	12	22	34	45
71,72-Two part drug story (8/72,9/72)	4	8	12	22	34	45
75-Archies Band-s	3	6	9	17	25	32
84-99	2	4	6	8	10	12
100 (12/75)	2	4	6	9	13	16
101-130(3/79): 125,126-Riverdale 2001-s	1	2	3	5	6	8
131-160,162-170 (7/84)						6.00
161 (11/82) 3rd app./1st solo Cheryl Blossom-s and pin-up; 2nd Jason Blossom	4	8	12	23	36	48
171-173,175,177-197,199: 197-G. Colan-a						5.00
174,176,198: 174-New Archies Band-s. 176-Cyndi Lauper-c. 198-Archie gang on strike at Archie Ent. offices						6.00
200(9/88)-Illiteracy-s						6.00
201,203-223: Later issues $1.00 cover						4.00
202-Explains end of Archie's jalopy; Dezerland-c/s; James Dean cameo						6.00
224-Last issue						6.00

NOTE: *Archies Band-c-45,47,49,53,56; s-44,53,75,174. UFO-s-50,63,209,220.*

ARCHIE'S PALS 'N' GALS DOUBLE DIGEST MAGAZINE
Archie Comic Publications: Nov, 1992 - No. 146, Dec, 2010 ($2.50-$3.99)

	GD	VG	FN	VF	VF/NM	NM-
1-Capt. Hero story; Pureheart app.	2	4	6	8	10	12
2-10: 2-Superduck story; Little Jinx in all. 4-Begin $2.75-c	1	2	3	4	5	7
11-29						4.00
30-146: 40-Begin $2.99-c. 48-Begin $3.19-c. 56-Begin $3.29-c. 72-Begin $3.59-c. 100-Story uses screen captures from classic animated series. 102-Begin $3.69-c 125-128-"New Look" art; Moose and Midge break up. 130-Begin $3.99-c. 133-Reggie spotlight, also reprints early apps.						4.00

ARCHIE'S PARABLES
Spire Christian Comics (Fleming H. Revell Co.): 1973,1975 (39/49¢, 36 pgs.)

	GD	VG	FN	VF	VF/NM	NM-
nn-By Al Hartley; 39¢ Edition	3	6	9	14	19	24
49¢, no price editions	2	4	6	9	13	16

ARCHIE'S R/C RACERS (Radio controlled cars)
Archie Comics: Sept, 1989 - No. 10, Mar, 1991 (95¢/$1)

	GD	VG	FN	VF	VF/NM	NM-
1						6.00
2,5-7,10: 5-Elvis parody. 7-Supervillain-c/s. 10-UFO-c/s						4.00
3,4,8,9						3.00

ARCHIE'S RIVAL REGGIE (Reggie & Archie's Joke Book #15 on)
Archie Publications: 1949 - No. 14, Aug, 1954

	GD	VG	FN	VF	VF/NM	NM-
1-Reggie 1st app. in Jackpot Comics #5	90	180	270	576	988	1400
2	42	84	126	265	445	625
3-5	33	66	99	194	317	440
6-10	22	44	66	132	216	300
11-14: Katy Keene in No. 10-14, 1-2 pgs.	18	36	54	103	162	220

ARCHIE'S RIVERDALE HIGH (See Riverdale High)

ARCHIE'S ROLLER COASTER
Spire Christian Comics (Fleming H. Revell Co.): 1981 (69¢)

	GD	VG	FN	VF	VF/NM	NM-
nn-(Low print)	2	4	6	13	18	22

ARCHIE'S SOMETHING ELSE
Spire Christian Comics (Fleming H. Revell Co.): 1975 (39/49¢, 36 pgs.)

	GD	VG	FN	VF	VF/NM	NM-
nn-(39¢-c) Hell's Angels Biker on motorcycle-c	3	6	9	14	19	24
nn-(49¢-c)	2	4	6	10	14	18
Barbour Christian Comics Edition ('86, no price listed)	2	3	4	6	8	10

ARCHIE'S SONSHINE

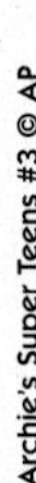
Archie's Super Teens #3 © AP

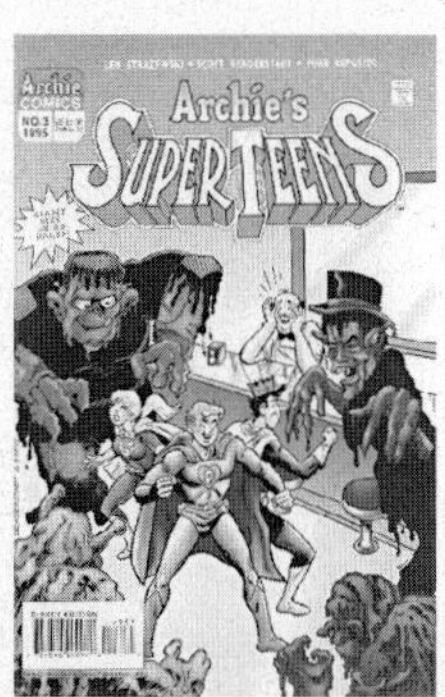

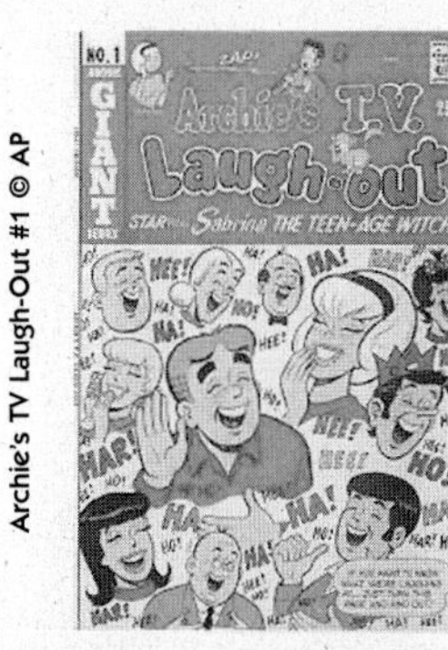

Archie's TV Laugh-Out #1 © AP

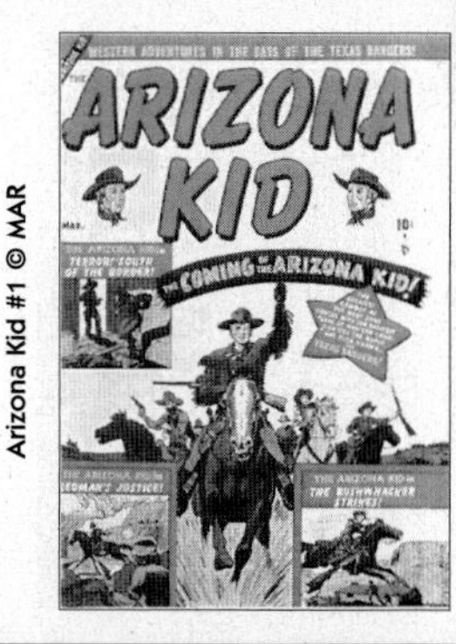

Arizona Kid #1 © MAR

GD 2.0 | VG 4.0 | FN 6.0 | VF 8.0 | VF/NM 9.0 | NM- 9.2

Spire Christian Comics (Fleming H. Revell Co.): 1973, 1974 (39/49¢, 36 pgs.)
39¢ Edition 3 6 9 14 19 24
49¢, no price editions 2 4 6 9 13 16

ARCHIE'S SPORTS SCENE
Spire Christian Comics (Fleming H. Revell Co.): 1983 (no cover price)
nn-(Low print) 2 4 6 13 18 22

ARCHIE'S SPRING BREAK
Archie Comics: 1996 - Present ($2.00, 48 pgs., annual)
1-4: 1,2-Dan DeCarlo-c 4.00

ARCHIE'S STORY & GAME COMICS DIGEST MAGAZINE
Archie Enterprises: Nov, 1986 - No. 39, Jan, 1998 ($1.25-$1.95, 128 pgs., digest-size)
1: Marked-up copies are common 2 4 6 11 16 20
2-10 2 4 6 8 10 12
11-20 1 2 3 4 5 7
21-39: 39-($1.95) 4.00

ARCHIE'S SUPER HERO SPECIAL (See Archie Giant Series Mag. No. 142)

ARCHIE'S SUPER HERO SPECIAL (...Comics Digest Mag. 2)
Archie Publications (Red Circle): Jan, 1979 - No. 2, Aug, 1979 (95¢, 148 pgs.)
1-Simon & Kirby r-/Double Life of Pvt. Strong #1,2; Black Hood, The Fly, Jaguar, The Web app. 2 4 6 11 16 20
2-Contains contents to the never published Black Hood #1; origin Black Hood; N. Adams, Wood, McWilliams, Morrow, S&K-a(r); N. Adams-c. The Shield, The Fly, Jaguar, Hangman, Steel Sterling, The Web, The Fox-r 2 4 6 11 16 20

ARCHIE'S SUPER TEENS
Archie Comic Publications, Inc.: 1994 - No. 4, 1996 ($2.00, 52 pgs.)
1-Staton/Esposito-c/a; pull-out poster 5.00
2-4: 2-Fred Hembeck script; Bret Blevins/Terry Austin-a 4.00

ARCHIE'S TV LAUGH-OUT ("...Starring Sabrina" on-c #1-50)
Archie Publications: Dec, 1969 - No. 105, Feb, 1986 (#1-7: 68 pgs.)
1-Sabrina begins, thru #106 10 20 30 68 127 185
2 (68 pgs.) 6 12 18 41 66 90
3-6 (68 pgs.) 5 10 15 32 51 70
7-Josie begins, thru #105; Archie's & Josie's Bands cover logos begin 7 14 21 49 82 115
8-23 (52 pgs.): 10-1st Josie on-c. 12-1st Josie and Pussycats on-c. 14-Beatles cameo on poster 4 8 12 26 41 55
24-40: 37,39,40-Bicenntennial-c 3 6 9 14 20 25
41,47,56: 41-Alexandra rejoins J&P band. 47-Fonz cameo; voodoo-s. 56-Fonz parody; B&V with Farrah hair-c 3 6 9 16 22 28
42-46,48-55,57-60 2 4 6 9 12 15
61-68,70-80: 63-UFO-s. 79-Mummy-s 1 3 4 6 8 10
69-Sherlock Holmes parody 1 3 4 6 8 10
81-90,94,95,97-99: 84 Voodoo-s 1 2 3 5 6 8
91-Early Cheryl Blossom-s; Sabrina/Archies Band-c 3 6 9 16 22 28
92-A-Team parody 1 3 4 6 8 10
93-(2/84) Archie in drag-s; Hill Street Blues-s; Groucho Marx parody; cameo parody app. of Batman, Spider-Man, Wonder Woman and others 2 4 6 9 12 15
96-MASH parody-s; Jughead in drag; Archies Band-c 1 3 4 6 8 10
100-(4/85) Michael Jackson parody-c/s; J&P band and Archie band on-c 2 4 6 10 14 18
101-104-Lower print run. 104-Miami Vice parody-c 1 2 3 5 7 9
105-Wrestling/Hulk Hogan parody-c; J&P band-s 2 4 6 9 12 15
NOTE: *Dan DeCarlo-a 78-up(most), c-89-up(most). Archies Band-s 2,7,9-11,15,20,25,37,64,65,67,68,70,73, 76,78,79,83,84,86,90,96,100,101; Archies Band-c 2,17,20,91,94,96,99-103. Josie-s 12,21,26,35,52,78,80,90. Josie-c 10,91,94. Josie and the Pussycats (as a band in costume)-s 7,9,10,37,38,41,42,66,84,99-101,105. Josie w/Pussycats member Valerie &/or Melody-s 17,20,22,25,27-29,31,33,36,39,40,43-51,53-65,67-77,79,81-83,85-89,92-94,102-104. Josie w/Pussycats band-c 12,14,17,18,22,24. Sabrina-s 1-9,11-86,88-106. Sabrina-c 1-18,21,23,27,49,91,94.*

ARCHIE'S VACATION SPECIAL
Archie Publications: Winter, 1994 - Present ($2.00/$2.25/$2.29/$2.49, annual)
1 4.00
2-8: 8-(2000, $2.49) 3.00

ARCHIE'S WEIRD MYSTERIES (Continues as Archie's Mysteries)
Archie Comics: Feb, 2000 - No. 24, Dec, 2002 ($1.79/$1.99)
1 3.50
2-24: 3-Mighty Crusaders app. 14-Super Teens-c/app.; Mighty Crusaders app. 3.00

ARCHIE'S WORLD
Spire Christian Comics (Fleming H. Revell Co.): 1973, 1976 (39/49¢)
39¢ Edition 3 6 9 14 19 24
49¢ Edition, no price editions 2 4 6 9 13 16

ARCHIE 3000
Archie Comics: May, 1989 - No. 16, July, 1991 (75¢/95¢/$1.00)
1,16: 16-Aliens-c/s 4.00
2-15: 6-Begin $1.00-c; X-Mas-c 3.00

ARCOMICS PREMIERE
Arcomics: July, 1993 ($2.95)
1-1st lenticular-c on a comic (flicker-c) 4.00

AREA 52
Image Comics: Jan, 2001 - No. 4, June, 2001 ($2.95)
1-4-Haberlin-s/Henry-a 3.00

ARES
Marvel Comics: Mar, 2006 - No. 5, July, 2006 ($2.99, limited series)
1-5-Oeming-s/Foreman-a 3.00
...: God of War TPB (2006, $13.99) r/series 14.00

ARGUS (See Flash, 2nd Series) (Also see Showcase '95 #1,2)
DC Comics: Apr, 1995 - No. 6, Oct, 1995 ($1.50, limited series)
1-6: 4-Begin $1.75-c 3.00

ARIA
Image Comics (Avalon Studios): Jan, 1999 - Present ($2.50)
Preview (11/98, $2.95) 5.00
1-Anacleto-c/a 1 2 3 5 6 8
1-Variant-c by Michael Turner 1 2 3 5 6 8
1-($10.00) Alternate-c by Turner 1 3 4 6 8 10
1,2-(Blanc & Noir) Black and white printing of pencil art 3.00
1-(Blanc & Noir) DF Edition 5.00
2-4: 2,4-Anacleto-c/a. 3-Martinez-a 3.00
4-($6.95) Glow in the Dark-c 1 3 4 6 8 10
Aria Angela 1 (2/00, $2.95) Anacleto-a; 4 covers by Anacleto, JG Jones, Portacio and Quesada 3.00
Aria Angela Blanc & Noir 1 (4/00, $2.95) Anacleto-c 3.00
Aria Angela European Ashcan 10.00
Aria Angela 2 (10/00, $2.95) Anacleto-a/c 3.00
...: A Midwinter's Dream 1 (1/02, $4.95, 7"x7") text-s w/Anacleto panels 5.00
...: The Enchanted Collection (5/04, $16.95) r/Summer's Spell & The Uses of Enchantment 17.00

ARIA: SUMMER'S SPELL
Image Comics (Avalon Studios): Mar, 2002 - No. 2, Jun, 2002 ($2.95)
1,2-Anacleto-c/Holguin-s/Pajarillo & Medina-a 3.00

ARIA: THE SOUL MARKET
Image Comics (Avalon Studios): Mar, 2001 - No. 6, Dec, 2001 ($2.95)
1-6-Anacleto-c/Holguin-s 3.00
HC (2002, $26.95, 8.25" x 12.25") oversized r/#1-6 27.00
SC (2004, $16.95, 8.25" x 12.25") oversized r/#1-6 17.00

ARIA: THE USES OF ENCHANTMENT
Image Comics (Avalon Studios): Feb, 2003 - No. 4, Sept, 2003 ($2.95)
1-4-Anacleto-c/Holguin-s/Medina-a 3.00

ARIANE AND BLUEBEARD (See Night Music #8)

ARIEL & SEBASTIAN (See Cartoon Tales & The Little Mermaid)

ARION, LORD OF ATLANTIS (Also see Warlord #55)
DC Comics: Nov, 1982 - No. 35, Sept, 1985
1-Story cont'd from Warlord #62 4.00
2-35 3.00
... Special #1 (11/85) 4.00

ARION THE IMMORTAL (Also see Showcase '95 #7)
DC Comics: July, 1992 - No. 6, Dec, 1992 ($1.50, limited series)
1-6: 4-Gustovich-a(i) 3.00

ARISTOCATS (See Movie Comics & Walt Disney Showcase No. 16)

ARISTOKITTENS, THE (...Meet Jiminy Cricket No. 1)(Disney)
Gold Key: Oct, 1971 - No. 9, Oct, 1975
1 3 6 9 20 30 40
2-5,7-9 3 6 9 14 19 24
6-(52 pgs.) 3 6 9 16 22 28

ARIZONA KID, THE (Also see The Comics & Wild Western)
Marvel/Atlas Comics(CSI): Mar, 1951 - No. 6, Jan, 1952

Armorines #4 © VAL

Army and Navy Comics #3 © CN

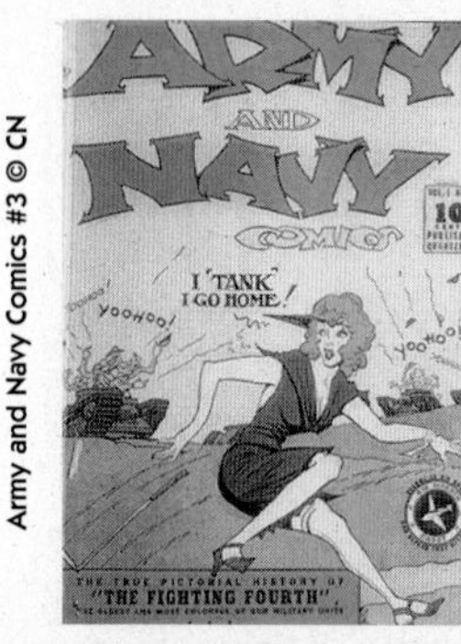

Army of Darkness V3 #1 © Raimi

	GD 2.0	VG 4.0	FN 6.0	VF 8.0	VF/NM 9.0	NM- 9.2
1	22	44	66	128	209	290
2-4: 2-Heath-a(3)	12	24	36	69	97	125
5,6	10	20	30	56	76	95

NOTE: *Heath a-1-3; c-1-3. **Maneely** c-4-6. **Morisi** a-4-6. **Sinnott** a-6.*

ARK, THE (See The Crusaders)

ARKAGA
Image Comics: Sept, 1997 ($2.95, one-shot)

1-Jorgensen-s/a 3.00

ARKANIUM
Dreamwave Productions: Sept, 2002 - No. 5 ($2.95)

1-5: 1-Gatefold wraparound-c 3.00

ARKHAM ASYLUM: LIVING HELL
DC Comics: July, 2003 - No. 6, Dec, 2003 ($2.50, limited series)

1-6-Ryan Sook-a; Batman app. 3-Batgirl-c/app. 3.00

ARKHAM ASYLUM: MADNESS
DC Comics: 2010 ($19.99, HC graphic novel, dustjacket)

HC-Sam Kieth-s/a/c; Joker, Two-Face, Harley and Ivy app. 20.00
SC-(2011, $14.99) Sam Kieth-s/a/c; Joker, Two-Face, Harley and Ivy app. 15.00

ARKHAM REBORN
DC Comics: Dec, 2009 - No. 3, Feb, 2010 ($2.99, limited series)

1-3-David Hine-s/Jeremy Haun-a 3.00
Batman: Arkham Reborn TPB (2010, $12.99) r/#1-3, Detective Comics #864,865 and Batman: Battle For the Cowl: Arkham Asylum #1 13.00

ARMAGEDDON
Chaos! Comics: Oct, 1999 - No. 4, Jan, 2000 ($2.95, limited series)

Preview 5.00
1-4-Lady Death, Evil Ernie, Purgatori app. 3.00

ARMAGEDDON: ALIEN AGENDA
DC Comics: Nov, 1991 - No. 4, Feb, 1992 ($1.00, limited series)

1-4 3.00

ARMAGEDDON FACTOR, THE
AC Comics: 1987 - No. 2, 1987; No. 3, 1990 ($1.95)

1,2: Sentinels of Justice, Dragonfly, Femforce 3.00
3-($3.95, color)-Almost all AC characters app. 4.00

ARMAGEDDON: INFERNO
DC Comics: Apr, 1992 - No. 4, July, 1992 ($1.00, limited series)

1-4: Many DC heroes app. 3-A. Adams/Austin-a 3.00

ARMAGEDDON 2001
DC Comics: May, 1991 - No. 2, Oct, 1991 ($2.00, squarebound, 68 pgs.)

1-Features many DC heroes; intro Waverider 5.00
1-2nd & 3rd printings; 3rd has silver ink-c 4.00
2 4.00

ARMED & DANGEROUS
Acclaim Comics (Armada): Apr, 1996 - No.4, July, 1996 ($2.95, B&W)

1-4-Bob Hall-c/a & scripts 3.00
Special 1 (8/96, $2.95, B&W)-Hall-c/a & scripts. 3.00

ARMED & DANGEROUS HELL'S SLAUGHTERHOUSE
Acclaim Comics (Armada): Oct, 1996 - No. 4, Jan, 1997 ($2.95, B&W)

1-4: Hall-c/a/scripts. 3.00

ARMOR (AND THE SILVER STREAK) (Revengers Featuring... in indicia for #1-3)
Continuity Comics: Sept, 1985 - No.13, Apr, 1992 ($2.00)

1-13: 1-Intro/origin Armor & the Silver Streak; Neal Adams-c/a. 7-Origin Armor; Nebres-i 3.50

ARMOR (DEATHWATCH 2000)
Continuity Comics: Apr, 1993 - No. 6, Nov, 1993 ($2.50)

1-6: 1-3-Deathwatch 2000 x-over 3.00

ARMORINES (See X-O Manowar #25 for 16 pg. bound-in Armorines #0)
Valiant: June, 1994 - No. 12, June, 1995 ($2.25)

0-Stand-alone edition with cardstock-c 25.00
0-Gold 15.00
1-12: 7-Wraparound-c. 12-Byrne-c/swipe (X-Men, 1st Series #138) 3.00

ARMORINES (Volume 2)
Acclaim Comics: Oct, 1999 - No. 4 ($3.95/$2.50, limited series)

1-($3.95) Calafiore & P. Palmiotti-a 4.00

2,3-($2.50) 3.00

ARMOR X
Image Comics: March, 2005 - No. 4, June, 2005 ($2.95, limited series)

1-Keith Champagne-s/Andy Smith-a; flip covers on #2-4 3.00

ARMY AND NAVY COMICS (Supersnipe No. 6 on)
Street & Smith Publications: May, 1941 - No. 5, July, 1942

	GD 2.0	VG 4.0	FN 6.0	VF 8.0	VF/NM 9.0	NM- 9.2
1-Cap Fury & Nick Carter	51	102	153	321	546	770
2-Cap Fury & Nick Carter	30	60	90	177	289	400
3,4: 4-Jack Farr-c/a	22	44	66	130	213	295
5-Supersnipe app.; see Shadow V2#3 for 1st app.; Story of Douglas MacArthur; George Marcoux-c/a	52	104	156	325	553	780

ARMY @ LOVE
DC Comics (Vertigo): May, 2007 - No. 12, Apr, 2008;
V2 #1, Oct, 2008 - No. 6, Mar, 2009 ($2.99)

1-12-Rick Veitch-s/a(p); Gary Erskine-a(i) 3.00
(Vol. 2) 1-6-Veitch-s/a(p); Erskine-a(i) 3.00
...: Generation Pwned TPB (2008, $12.99) r/#6-12 13.00
...: The Hot Zone Club TPB (2007, $9.99) r/#1-5; intro. by Peter Kuper 10.00

ARMY ATTACK
Charlton Comics: July, 1964 - No. 4, Feb, 1965; V2#38, July, 1965 - No. 47, Feb, 1967

	GD 2.0	VG 4.0	FN 6.0	VF 8.0	VF/NM 9.0	NM- 9.2
V1#1	5	10	15	30	48	65
2-4(2/65)	3	6	9	19	29	38
V2#38(7/65)-47 (formerly U.S. Air Force #1-37)	3	6	9	16	22	28

NOTE: ***Glanzman** a-1-3. **Montes/Bache** a-44.*

ARMY AT WAR (Also see Our Army at War & Cancelled Comic Cavalcade)
DC Comics: Oct-Nov, 1978

	GD 2.0	VG 4.0	FN 6.0	VF 8.0	VF/NM 9.0	NM- 9.2
1-Kubert-c; all new story and art	2	4	6	11	16	20

ARMY OF DARKNESS (Movie)
Dark Horse Comics: Nov, 1992 - No. 2, Dec, 1992; No. 3, Oct, 1993 ($2.50, limited series)

	GD 2.0	VG 4.0	FN 6.0	VF 8.0	VF/NM 9.0	NM- 9.2
1-3-Bolton painted-c/a	2	4	6	9	12	15

... Movie Adaptation TPB (2006, $14.99) r/#1-3; intro. by Busiek; Bruce Campbell interview 15.00

ARMY OF DARKNESS (Also see Marvel Zombies vs. Army of Darkness)
Dynamite Entertainment: 2005 - No. 13, 2007 ($2.99)

1-4 (Vs. Re-Animator):1,2-Four covers; Greene-a/Kuhoric-s. 3,4-Three covers 3.00
5-13: 5-7-Kuhoric-s/Sharpe-a; four covers. 8-11-Ash Vs. Dracula. 12,13-Death of Ash 3.00

ARMY OF DARKNESS: ...
Dynamite Entertainment: 2007 - No. 27, 2010 ($3.50/$3.99)

... From the Ashes 1-4-Kuhoric-s/Blanco-a; covers by Blanco & Suydam 3.50
5-8-(The Long Road Home); two covers on each 3.50
9-25: 9-12-(Home Sweet Hell), 13-King For a Day. 14-17-Hellbillies and Deadnecks 3.50
26,27-($3.99) Raicht-s/Cohn-a/c 4.00
...: Ash's Christmas Horror Special (2008, $4.99) Kuhoric-s/Simons-a; 2 covers 5.00

ARMY OF DARKNESS VOLUME 3
Dynamite Entertainment: 2012 - Present ($3.99)

1-Female Ash; Michaels-a 4.00

ARMY OF DARKNESS: ASHES 2 ASHES (Movie)
Devil's Due Publ.: July, 2004 - No. 4, 2004 ($2.99, limited series)

1-4-Four covers for each; Nick Bradshaw-a 3.00
1-Director's Cut (12/04, $4.99) r/#1, cover gallery, script and sketch pages 5.00
TPB (2005, $14.99) r/series; cover gallery; Bradshaw interview and sketch pages 15.00

ARMY OF DARKNESS: ASH SAVES OBAMA
Dynamite Entertainment: 2009 - No. 4, 2009 ($3.50, limited series)

1-4-Serrano-s/Padilla-a; covers by Parrillo and Nauck. 4-Obama app. 3.50

ARMY OF DARKNESS: SHOP TILL YOU DROP DEAD (Movie)
Devil's Due Publ.: Jan, 2005 - No. 4, July, 2005 ($2.99, limited series)

1-4:1-Five covers; Bradshaw-a/Kuhoric-s. 2-4: Two covers. 3-Greene-a 3.00

ARMY OF DARKNESS / XENA
Dynamite Entertainment: 2008 - No. 4, 2008 ($3.50, limited series)

1-4-Layman-s/Montenegro-a; two covers on each 3.50

ARMY SURPLUS KOMIKZ FEATURING CUTEY BUNNY
Army Surplus Komikz/Eclipse Comics: 1982 - No. 5, 1985 ($1.50, B&W)

	GD 2.0	VG 4.0	FN 6.0	VF 8.0	VF/NM 9.0	NM- 9.2
1-Cutey Bunny begins	2	4	6	8	10	12

2-5: 5-(Eclipse)-JLA/X-Men/Batman parody 4.50

ARMY WAR HEROES (Also see Iron Corporal)
Charlton Comics: Dec, 1963 - No. 38, June, 1970

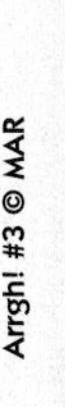
Arrgh! #3 © MAR

Artifacts #2 © TCOW

Ash: Cinder & Smoke #5 © Q&P

	GD 2.0	VG 4.0	FN 6.0	VF 8.0	VF/NM 9.0	NM- 9.2
1	5	10	15	35	55	75
2-10	3	6	9	19	29	38
11-21,23-30: 24-Intro. Archer & Corp. Jack series	3	6	9	16	22	28
22-Origin/1st app. Iron Corporal series by Glanzman	4	8	12	24	37	50
31-38	2	4	6	10	14	18
Modern Comics Reprint 36 ('78)						4.00

NOTE: ***Montes/Bache** a-1, 16, 17, 21, 23-25, 27-30.*

AROUND THE BLOCK WITH DUNC & LOO (See Dunc and Loo)

AROUND THE WORLD IN 80 DAYS (Movie) (See A Golden Picture Classic)
Dell Publishing Co.: Feb, 1957

Four Color 784-Photo-c 7 14 21 49 82 115

AROUND THE WORLD UNDER THE SEA (See Movie Classics)

AROUND THE WORLD WITH ARCHIE (See Archie Giant Series Mag. #29, 35, 141)

AROUND THE WORLD WITH HUCKLEBERRY & HIS FRIENDS (See Dell Giant No. 44)

ARRGH! (Satire)
Marvel Comics Group: Dec, 1974 - No. 5, Sept, 1975 (25¢)

1-Dracula story; Sekowsky-a(p) 3 6 9 18 27 35
2-5: 2-Frankenstein. 3-Mummy. 4-Nightstalker(TV); Dracula-c/app., Hunchback. 5-Invisible Man, Dracula 2 4 6 13 18 22

NOTE ***Alcala** a-2; c-3. **Everett** a-1r, 2r. **Grandenetti** a-4. **Maneely** a-4r. **Sutton** a-1-3.*

ARROW (See Protectors)
Malibu Comics: Oct, 1992 ($1.95, one-shot)

1-Moder-a(p) 3.00

ARROW, THE (See Funny Pages)
Centaur Publications: Oct, 1940 - No. 2, Nov, 1940; No. 3, Oct, 1941

1-The Arrow begins(r/Funny Pages) 326 652 978 2282 3991 5700
2,3: 2-Tippy Taylor serial continues from Amazing Mystery Funnies #24. 3-Origin Dash Dartwell, the Human Meteor; origin The Rainbow-r; bondage-c 148 296 444 947 1624 2300

NOTE: ***Gustavson** a-1, 2; c-3.*

ARROWHEAD (See Black Rider and Wild Western)
Atlas Comics (CPS): April, 1954 - No. 4, Nov, 1954

1-Arrowhead & his horse Eagle begin 15 30 45 88 137 185
2-4: 4-Forte-a 10 20 30 54 72 90

NOTE: ***Heath** c-3. **Jack Katz** a-3. **Maneely** c-2. **Pakula** a-2. **Sinnott** a-1-4; c-1.*

ARROWSMITH (Also see Astro City/Arrowsmith flip book)
DC Comics (Cliffhanger): Sept, 2003 - No. 6, May, 2004 ($2.95)

1-6-Pacheco-a/Busiek-s 3.00
...: So Smart in Their Fine Uniforms TPB (2004, $14.95) r/#1-6 15.00

ARSENAL (Teen Titans' Speedy)
DC Comics: Oct, 1998 - No. 4, Jan, 1999 ($2.50, limited series)

1-4: Grayson-s. 1-Black Canary app. 2-Green Arrow app. 3.00

ARSENAL SPECIAL (See New Titans, Showcase '94 #7 & Showcase '95 #8)
DC Comics: 1996 ($2.95, one-shot)

1 3.00

ARTBABE
Fantagraphics Books: May, 1996 - Apr, 1999 ($2.50/$2.95/$3.50, B&W)

V1 #5, V2 #1-3 3.00
#4-($3.50) 3.50

ARTEMIS: REQUIEM (Also see Wonder Woman, 2nd Series #90)
DC Comics: June, 1996 - No. 6, Nov, 1996 ($1.75, limited series)

1-6: Messner-Loebs scripts & Benes-c/a in all. 1,2-Wonder Woman app. 3.00

ARTIFACTS
Image Comics (Top Cow): Jul, 2010 - Present ($3.99, intended as a limited series)

0-(5/10, free) Free Comic Book Day edition; Sejic-a
1-15: 1-6-Marz-s/Broussard-a. 1-Multiple covers; back-up origin of Witchblade. 7,8-Portacio-a. 9-12-Haun-a. 10-Wraparound-c by Sejic. 13-Keown-a. 14,15-Sejic-a 4.00
...Origins (1/12, $3.99) Two-page spread origins of the 13 artifacts; wraparound-c 4.00

ART OF HOMAGE STUDIOS, THE
Image Comics: Dec, 1993 ($4.95, one-shot)

1-Short stories and pin-ups by Jim Lee, Silvestri, Williams, Portacio & Chiodo 5.00

ART OF ZEN INTERGALACTIC NINJA, THE
Entity Comics: 1994 - No. 2, 1994 ($2.95)

1,2 3.00

ARZACH (See Moebius...)

GD VG FN VF VF/NM NM- 2.0 4.0 6.0 8.0 9.0 9.2

Dark Horse Comics: 1996 ($6.95, one-shot)
nn-Moebius-c/a/scripts 1 2 3 4 5 7

ASCENSION
Image Comics (Top Cow Productions): Oct, 1997 - No. 22, Mar, 2000 ($2.50)

Preview 5.00
Preview Gold Edition 8.00
Preview San Diego Edition 2 4 6 8 10 12
0 4.00
1/2 6.00
1-David Finch-s/a(p)/Batt-s/a(i) 4.00
1-Variant-c w/Image logo at lower right 6.00
2-22 3.00
... Collected Edition 1,2 (1998 - No. 2, $4.95, squarebound) 1-r/#1,2. 2-r/#3,4 5.00
Fan Club Edition 5.00

ASH
Event Comics: Nov, 1994 - No. 6, Dec, 1995; No. 0, May, 1996 ($2.50/$3.00)

0-Present & Future (Both 5/96, $3.00, foil logo-c)-w/pin-ups 3.00
0-Blue Foil logo-c (Present and Future) (1000 each) 4.00
0-Silver Prism logo-c (Present and Future) (500 each) 10.00
0-Red Prism logo-c (Present and Future) (250 each) 20.00
0-Gold Hologram logo-c (Present and Future) (1000 each) 8.00
1-Quesada-p/story; Palmiotti-i/story: Barry Windsor-Smith pin-up 2 4 6 8 10 12
2-Mignola Hellboy pin-up 1 2 3 4 5 7
3,4: 3-Big Guy pin-up by Geoff Darrow. 4-Jim Lee pin-up 4.00
4-Fahrenheit Gold 7.00
4-6-Fahrenheit Red (5,6-1000) 8.00
4-6-Fahrenheit White 12.00
5, 6-Double-c w/Hildebrandt Bros.-a, Quesada & Palmiotti. 6-Texeira-c 3.00
5,6-Fahrenheit Gold (2000) 4.00
6-Fahrenheit White (500)-Texeira-c 12.00
Volume 1 (1996, $14.95, TPB)-r/#1-5, intro by James Robinson 15.00
Wizard Mini-Comic (1996, magazine supplement) 3.00
Wizard #1/2 (1997, mail order) 4.00

ASH: CINDER & SMOKE
Event Comics: May, 1997 - No. 6, Oct, 1997 ($2.95, limited series)

1-6: Ramos-a/Waid, Augustyn-s in all. 2-6-variant covers by Ramos and Quesada 3.00

ASH: FILES
Event Comics: Mar, 1997 ($2.95, one-shot)

1-Comics w/text 3.00

ASH: FIRE AND CROSSFIRE
Event Comics: Jan, 1999 - No. 5 ($2.95, limited series)

1,2-Robinson-s/Quesada & Palmiotti-c/a 3.00

ASH: FIRE WITHIN, THE
Event Comics: Sept, 1996 - No. 2, Jan, 1997 ($2.95, unfinished limited series)

1,2: Quesada & Palmiotti-c/s/a 3.00

ASH/ 22 BRIDES
Event Comics: Dec, 1996 - No. 2, Apr, 1997 ($2.95, limited series)

1,2: Nicieza-s/Ramos-c/a 3.00

ASKANI'SON (See Adventures of Cyclops & Phoenix limited series)
Marvel Comics: Jan, 1996 - No. 4, May, 1996 ($2.95, limited series)

1-4: Story cont'd from Advs. of Cyclops & Phoenix; Lobdell/Loeb story; Gene Ha-c/a(p) 3.00
TPB (1997, $12.99) r/#1-4; Gene Ha painted-c 13.00

ASPEN (MICHAEL TURNER PRESENTS:...) (Also see Fathom)
Aspen MLT, Inc.: July, 2003 - No. 3, Aug, 2003 ($2.99)

1-Fathom story; Turner-a/Johns-s; interviews w/Turner & Johns; two covers by Turner 3.00
2,3:2-Fathom story; Turner-a/Johns-s; two covers by Turner; pin-ups and interviews 3.00
... Seasons: Fall 2005 (12/05, $2.99) short stories by various; Turner-c 3.00
... Seasons: Spring 2005 (4/05, $2.99) short stories by various; Turner-c 3.00
... Seasons: Summer 2006 (10/06, $2.99) short stories by various; Turner-c 3.00
... Seasons: Winter 2009 (3/09, $2.99) short stories by various; Benitez-c 3.00
... Showcase: Aspen Matthews 1 (7/08, $2.99) Caldwell-a 3.00
... Showcase: Kiani 1 (10/09, $2.99) Scott Clark-a; covers by Clark and Caldwell 3.00
... Sketchbook 1 (2003, $2.99) sketch pages by Michael Turner and Talent Caldwell 3.00
... Splash: 2006 Swimsuit Spectacular 1 (3/06, $2.99) pin-up pages by various; Turner-c 3.00
... Splash: 2007 Swimsuit Spectacular 1 (8/07, $2.99) pin-up pages by various; Turner-c 3.00
... Splash: 2008 Swimsuit Spectacular 1 (7/08, $2.99) pin-up pages by various; Turner-c 3.00
... Splash: 2010 Swimsuit Spectacular 1 (8/10, $2.99) pin-up pages by various; 2 covers 3.00

Astonishing #5 © MAR

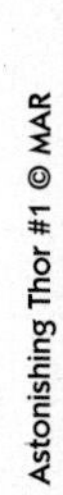

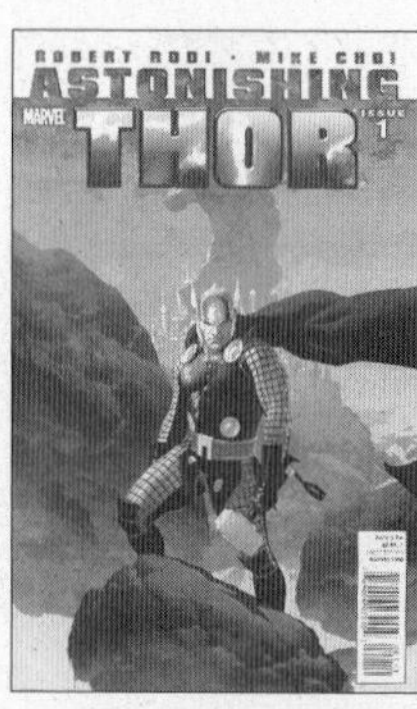

Astonishing Thor #1 © MAR

Astonishing X-Men #10 © MAR

GD VG FN VF VF/NM NM-
2.0 4.0 6.0 8.0 9.0 9.2

ASPEN SHOWCASE
Aspen MLT: Oct, 2008 ($2.99)

...: Benoist 1 (10/08) - Krul-s/Gunnell-a; two covers by Gunnell & Manapul 3.00
...: Ember 1 (2/09) - Randy Green-a; two covers by Gunnell & Green 3.00

ASSASSINS
DC Comics (Amalgam): Apr, 1996 ($1.95)

1 3.00

ASSASSIN'S CREED: THE FALL (Based on the Ubisoft Entertainment videogame)
DC Comics: Jan, 2011 - No. 3, Mar, 2011 ($3.99, limited series)

1-3-Cam Stewart & Karl Kerschl-s/a 4.00

ASSAULT ON NEW OLYMPUS PROLOGUE
Marvel Comics: Jan, 2010 ($3.99, one-shot)

1-Spider-Man, Hercules, Amadeus Cho app.; Granov-c; leads into Inc. Hercules #138 4.00

ASTONISHING (Formerly Marvel Boy No. 1, 2)
Marvel/Atlas Comics(20CC): No. 3, Apr, 1951 - No. 63, Aug, 1957

3-Marvel Boy continues; 3-5-Marvel Boy-c 98 196 294 622 1074 1525
4-6-Last Marvel Boy; 4-Stan Lee app. 69 138 207 442 759 1075
7-10: 7-Maneely s/f story. 10-Sinnott s/f story 37 74 111 222 361 500
11,12,15,17,20 33 66 99 194 317 440
13,14,16,18,19-Krigstein-a. 18-Jack The Ripper sty 34 68 102 199 325 450
21,22,24 28 56 84 165 270 375
23-E.C. swipe "The Hole In The Wall" from Vault Of Horror #16
29 58 87 170 278 385
25,29: 25-Crandall-a. 29-Decapitation-c 26 52 78 154 252 350
26-28 24 48 72 142 234 325
30-Tentacled eyeball-c/story; classic-c 49 98 147 309 522 735
31-37-Last pre-code issue 21 42 63 126 206 285
38-43,46,48-52,56,58,59,61 18 36 54 105 165 225
44,45,47,53-55,57,60: 44-Crandall swipe/Weird Fantasy #22. 45,47-Krigstein-a. 53-Ditko-a.
54-Torres-a, 55-Crandall, Torres-a. 57-Williamson/Krenkel-a (4 pgs.).
60-Williamson/Mayo-a (4 pgs.) 19 38 57 111 176 240
62,63: 62-Torres, Powell-a. 63-Woodbridge-a 19 38 57 109 172 235

NOTE: ***Ayers** a-16, 49. **Berg** a-36, 53, 56. **Cameron** a-50. **Gene Colan** a-12, 20, 29, 56. **Ditko** a-53. **Drucker** a-41, 62. **Everett** a-3-6(3), 6, 10, 12, 37, 47, 48, 58; c-3-5, 13,15, 16, 18, 29, 47, 49, 51, 53-55, 57, 59-63. **Fass** a-11, 34. **Forte** a-26, 48, 53, 58, 60. **Fuje** a-11. **Heath** a-8, 29; c-8, 9, 19, 22, 25, 26. **Kirby** a-56. **Lawrence** a-28, 37, 38, 42. **Maneely** a-7(2), 19; c-7, 31, 33, 34, 56. **Moldoff** a-33. **Morisi** a-10, 60. **Morrow** a-52, 61. **Orlando** a-47, 58, 61. **Pakula** a-10. **Powell** a-43, 44, 48. **Ravielli** a-26, 28. **Reinman** a-32, 34, 38. **Robinson** a-20. **J. Romita** a-7, 18, 24, 43, 57,61. **Roussos** a-55. **Sale** a-28, 38, 59; c-32. **Sekowsky** a-13. **Severin** c-46. **Shores** a-16, 60. **Sinnott** a-11, 30, 31. **Whitney** a-13. **Ed Win** a-20. Canadian reprints exist.*

ASTONISHING SPIDER-MAN AND WOLVERINE
Marvel Comics: Jul, 2010 - No. 6, Jul. 2011 ($3.99, limited series)

1-6-Adam Kubert-a/Jason Aaron-s. 1-Bonus pin-up gallery; wraparound-c 4.00
1-Director's Cut (10/10, $4.99) r/#1 with full script & B&W art 5.00
...: Another Fine Mess (6/11, $4.99) r/#1-3; wraparound-c 5.00

ASTONISHING TALES (See Ka-Zar)
Marvel Comics Group: Aug, 1970 - No. 36, July, 1976 (#1-7: 15¢; #8: 25¢)

1-Ka-Zar (by Kirby(p) #1,2; by B. Smith #3-6) & Dr. Doom (by Wood #1-4; by Tuska #5,6; by Colan #7,8; 1st Marvel villain solo series) double feature begins; Kraven the Hunter-c/story; Nixon cameo 7 14 21 44 72 100
2-Kraven the Hunter-c/story; Kirby, Wood-a 4 8 12 22 34 45
3-6: B. Smith-p; Wood-a-#3,4. 5,6-Red Skull 2-part story
4 8 12 24 37 50
7-Last 15¢ issue; Black Panther app. 3 6 9 16 23 30
8-(25¢, 52 pgs.)-Last Dr. Doom of series 4 8 12 22 34 45
9-All Ka-Zar issues begin; Lorna-r/Lorna #14 2 4 6 11 16 20
10-B. Smith/Sal Buscema-a. 3 6 9 14 20 25
11-Origin Ka-Zar & Zabu; death of Ka-Zar's father 2 4 6 13 18 22
12-2nd app.Man-Thing; by Neal Adams (see Savage Tales #1 for 1st app.)
4 8 12 28 44 60
13-3rd app.Man-Thing 3 6 9 21 32 42
14-20: 14-Jann of the Jungle-r (1950s); reprints censored Ka-Zar-s from Savage Tales #1. 17-S.H.I.E.L.D. begins. 19-Starlin-a(p). 20-Last Ka-Zar (continues into 1974 Ka-Zar series)
1 3 4 6 8 10
21-(12/73)-It! the Living Colossus begins, ends #24 (see Supernatural Thrillers #1)
4 8 12 24 37 50
22-24: 23,24-IT vs. Fin Fang Foom 3 6 9 18 27 35
25-1st app. Deathlok the Demolisher; full length stories begin, end #36; Perez's 1st work, 2 pgs. (8/74) 6 12 18 37 59 80
26-28,30 2 4 6 11 16 22
29-r/origin/1st app. Guardians of the Galaxy from Marvel Super-Heroes #18 plus-c w/4 pgs. omitted; no Deathlok story 1 3 4 6 8 10

GD VG FN VF VF/NM NM-
2.0 4.0 6.0 8.0 9.0 9.2

31-34: 31-Watcher-r/Silver Surfer #3 2 4 6 10 13 16
35,36-(Regular 25¢ edition)(5,7/76) 2 4 6 10 13 16
35,36-(30¢-c, low distribution) 5 10 15 32 51 70

NOTE: ***Buckler** a-13i, 16p, 25, 26p, 27p, 28, 29p-36p; c-13, 25p, 26-30, 32-35p, 36. **John Buscema** a-9, 12p-14p, 16p; c-4-6p, 12p. **Colan** a-7p, 8p. **Ditko** a-21r. **Everett** a-6i. **G. Kane** a-11p, 15p; c-9, 10p, 11p, 14, 15p, 21p. **McWilliams** a-30i. **Starlin** a-19p; c-16p. **Sutton & Trimpe** a-8. **Tuska** a-5p, 6p, 8p. **Wood** a-1-4. **Wrightson** c-31i.*

ASTONISHING TALES (Anthology)
Marvel Comics: Apr, 2009 - No. 6, Sept, 2009 ($3.99, limited series)

1-6-Wolverine, Punisher, Iron Man and Iron Man 2020 app. 1-Wraparound-c 4.00

ASTONISHING THOR
Marvel Comics: Jan, 2011 - No. 5, Sept, 2011 ($3.99, limited series)

1-5: 1-Robert Rodi-s/Mike Choi-a/Esad Ribic-c 4.00

ASTONISHING X-MEN
Marvel Comics: Mar, 1995 - No. 4, July, 1995 ($1.95, limited series)

1-Age of Apocalypse; Magneto-c 4.00
2-4 3.00

ASTONISHING X-MEN
Marvel Comics: Sept, 1999 - No.3, Nov, 1999 ($2.50, limited series)

1-3-New team, Cable & X-Man app.; Peterson-a 3.00
TPB (11/00, $15.95) r/#1-3, X-Men #92 & #95, Uncanny X-Men #375 16.00

ASTONISHING X-MEN (See Giant-Size Astonishing X-Men for story folllowing #24)
Marvel Comics: July, 2004 - Present ($2.99/$3.99)

1-Whedon-s/Cassaday-c/a; team of Cyclops, Beast, Wolverine, Emma Frost & Kitty Pryde 3.00
1-Director's Cut (2004, $3.99) different Cassaday partial sketch-c; cover gallery, sketch pages and script excerpt 4.00
1-Variant-c by Cassaday 10.00
1-Variant-c by Dell'Otto 5.00
2,3,5,6-X-Men battle Ord 3.00
4-Colossus returns 4.00
4-Variant Colossus cover by Cassaday 5.00
7-24: 7-Fantastic Four app. 9,10-X-Men vs. the Danger Room 3.00
7,9,10-12,19-24-Second printing variant covers 3.00
25-35: 25-Ellis-s/Bianchi-a begins; Bianchi wraparound-c. 31-Jimenez-a begins 3.00
36-47-($3.99): 36-Pearson wraparound-c; Way-s/Pearson-a. 44-47-McKone-a 4.00
.../Amazing Spider-Man: The Gauntlet Sketchbook ('09, giveaway) flip book preview 3.00
...: Ghost Boxes 1,2 (12/08-1/09, $3.99) Ellis-s/Davis & Granov-a; full Ellis script 4.00
... Saga (2006, $3.99) reprints highlights from #1-12; sketch pages and cover gallery 4.00
... Sketchbook Special ('08, $2.99) Costume sketches & blueprints by Bianchi & Larroca 3.00
...Vol. 1 HC (2006, $29.99, dust jacket) r/#1-12; interviews, sketch pages and covers 30.00
...Vol. 1: Gifted (2004, $14.99) r/#1-6; variant cover gallery 15.00
...Vol. 2: Dangerous (2005, $14.99) r/#7-12; variant cover gallery 15.00
...Vol. 3: Torn (2007, $14.99) r/#13-18; variant & sketch cover gallery 15.00

ASTONISHING X-MEN: XENOGENESIS
Marvel Comics: July, 2010 - No. 5, Apr, 2011 ($3.99, limited series)

1-5-Warren Ellis-s/Kaare Andrews-a/c. 1-Wraparound-c; script 4.00
1-Director's Cut (10/10, $4.99) r/#1 with full script & B&W art; cover sketches 5.00

ASTOUNDING SPACE THRILLS: THE COMIC BOOK
Image Comics: Apr, 2000 - No. 4, Dec, 2000 ($2.95, limited series)

1-4-Steve Conley-s/a. 2,3-Flip book w/Crater Kid 3.00
Galaxy-Sized Astounding Space Thrills 1 (10/01, $4.95) 5.00

ASTOUNDING WOLF-MAN
Image Comics: Jun, 2007 - No. 25, Nov, 2010 ($2.99)

1-Free Comic Boy Day issue; Kirkman-s/Howard-a; origin story 3.00
2-24: 11-Invincible x-over from Invincble #57 3.00
25-($4.99) Wraparound-c; Wolfcorps app. 5.00
Vol. 1 TPB (2008, $14.99) r/#1-7; sketch pages; Kirkman intro. 15.00

ASTRA
CPM Manga: 2001 - No. 8 ($2.95, B&W, limited series)

1-8: Created by Jerry Robinson; Tanaka-a. 1-Balent variant-c 3.00
TPB (2002, $15.95) r/#1-8; JH Williams III-c from #3 16.00

ASTRO BOY (TV) (See March of Comics #285 & The Original...)
Gold Key: August, 1965 (12¢)

1(10151-508)-Scarce; 1st app. Astro Boy in comics 25 50 75 175 375 575

ASTRO BOY THE MOVIE (Based on the 2009 CGI movie)
IDW Publishing: 2009 ($3.99, limited series)

...Official Movie Adaptation 1-4 (8/09 - No. 4, 9/09, $3.99) EJ Su-a 4.00
...Official Movie Prequel 1-4 (5/09 - No. 4, 8/09) Jourdan-a/c; Ashley Wood var-c on each 4.00

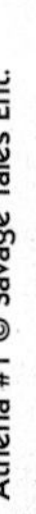

Athena #1 © Savage Tales Ent.

The Atom #7 © DC

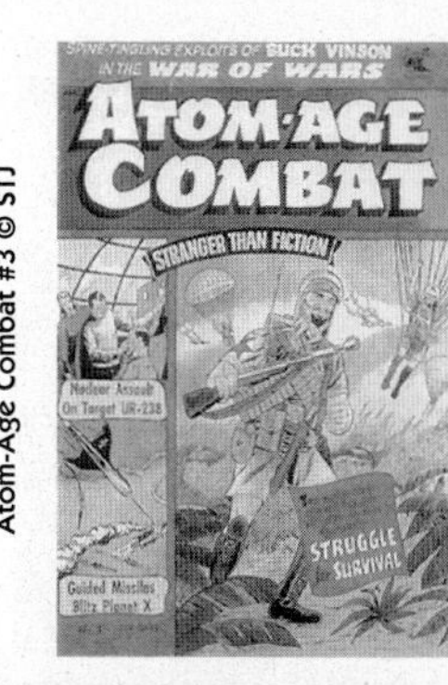

Atom-Age Combat #3 © STJ

	GD	VG	FN	VF	VF/NM	NM-
	2.0	4.0	6.0	8.0	9.0	9.2

GD VG FN VF VF/NM NM-
2.0 4.0 6.0 8.0 9.0 9.2

ASTRO CITY / ARROWSMITH (Flip book)
DC Comics (WildStorm Productions): Jun, 2004 ($2.95, one-shot flip book)

1-Intro. Black Badge; Ross-c; Arrowsmith a/c by Pacheco 3.00

ASTRO CITY (Also see Kurt Busiek's Astro City)
DC Comics (WildStorm Productions): Dec, 2004 - Dec, 2009 (one-shots)

...#1 Special Edition (8/10, $1.00) reprints first issue with "What's Next? cover logo 3.00
...: Astra Special 1,2 (11/09, 12/09, $3.99) Busiek-s/Anderson-a/Ross-c 4.00
... A Visitor's Guide (12/04, $5.95) short story, city guide and pin-ups by various; Ross-c 6.00
...: Beautie (4/08, $3.99) Busiek-s/Anderson-a/Ross-c; origin 4.00
...: Samaritan (9/06, $3.99) Busiek-s/Anderson-a/Ross-c; origin of Infidel 4.00
...: Shining Stars HC (2011, $24.99, d.j) r/...: Astra Special 1,2, ...: Beautie, ...: Samaritan, and ...: Silver Agent 1,2; bonus design art and Ross cover sketch art 25.00
...: Silver Agent 1,2 (8,9/10, $3.99) Busiek-s/Anderson-a/Ross-c 4.00

ASTRO CITY: DARK AGE
DC Comics (WildStorm Productions): Aug, 2005 - No. 4, Dec, 2005 ($2.95, limited series)

Book One 1-4-Busiek-s/Anderson-a/Ross-c; Silver Agent and The Blue Knight app. 3.00
Book Two #1-4 (1/07-11/07, $2.99) Busiek-s/Anderson-a/Ross-c 3.00
Book Three #1-4 (7/09-10/09, $3.99) Busiek-s/Anderson-a/Ross-c 4.00
Book Four #1-4 (3/10-6/10, $3.99) Busiek-s/Anderson-a/Ross-c 4.00
... 1: Brothers and Other Strangers HC (2008, $29.99, d.j.) r/Book One #1-4, Book Two #1-4, and story from Astro City/Arrowsmith #1; Marc Guggenheim intro.; new Ross-c 30.00
... 1: Brothers and Other Strangers SC (2009, $19.99) same contents as HC 20.00
... 2: Brothers in Arms HC ('10, $29.99, d.j.) r/Book Three #1-4, Book Four #1-4, Ross-c 30.00

ASTRO CITY: LOCAL HEROES
DC Comics (WildStorm Productions): Apr, 2003 - No. 5, Feb, 2004 ($2.95, limited series)

1-5-Busiek-s/Anderson-a/Ross-c 3.00
HC (2005, $24.95) r/series; Kurt Busiek's Astro City V2 #21,22; stories from Astro City/ Arrowsmith #1; and 9-11, The World's Finest... Vol. 2; Alex Ross sketch pages 25.00
SC (2005, $17.99) same contents as HC 18.00

ASYLUM
Millennium Publications: 1993 ($2.50)

1-3: 1-Bolton-c/a; Russell 2-pg. illos 3.00

ASYLUM
Maximum Press: Dec, 1995 - No. 11, Jan, 1997 ($2.95/$2.99, anthology)
(#1-6 are flip books)

1-11: 1-Warchild by Art Adams, Beanworld, Avengelyne, Battlestar Galactica. 2-Intro Mike Deodato's Deathkiss. 4-1st app.Christian; painted Battlestar Galactica story begins. 6-Intro Bionix (Six Million Dollar Man & the Bionic Woman). 7-Begin $2.99-c. 8-B&W-a. 9- Foot Soldiers & Kid Supreme. 10-Lady Supreme by Terry Moore-c/app. 4.00

ATARI FORCE (Also see Promotional comics section)
DC Comics: Jan, 1984 - No. 20, Aug, 1985 (Mando paper)

1-(1/84)-Intro Tempest, Packrat, Babe, Morphea, & Dart 4.00
2-20 3.00
Special 1 (4/86) 4.00
NOTE: ***Byrne*** *c-Special 1i.* ***Giffen*** *a-12p, 13i.* ***Rogers*** *a-18p, Special 1p.*

A-TEAM, THE (TV) (Also see Marvel Graphic Novel)
Marvel Comics Group: Mar, 1984 - No. 3, May, 1984 (limited series)

	GD 2.0	VG 4.0	FN 6.0	VF 8.0	VF/NM 9.0	NM- 9.2
1-3						6.00
1,2-(Whitman bagged set) w/75¢-c	2	4	6	8	10	12
3-(Whitman, no bag) w/75¢-c	1	2	3	5	6	8

A-TEAM: SHOTGUN WEDDING (Based on the 2010 movie)
IDW Publishing: Mar, 2010 - No. 4, Apr, 2010 ($3.99, limited series)

1-4-Co-plotted by Joe Carnahan; Stephen Mooney-a; Snyder III-c 4.00

A-TEAM: WAR STORIES (Based on the 2010 movie)
IDW Publishing: Mar, 2010 - Apr, 2010 ($3.99, series of one-shots)

...: B.A. (3/10) Dixon & Burnham-s/Maloney-a/Gaydos & photo-c 4.00
...: Face (4/10) Dixon & Burnham-s/Muriel-a/Gaydos & photo-c 4.00
...: Hannibal (3/10) Dixon & Burnham-s/Petrus-a/Gaydos & photo-c 4.00
...: Murdock (4/10) Dixon & Burnham-s/Vilanova-a/Gaydos & photo-c 4.00

ATHENA INC. THE MANHUNTER PROJECT
Image Comics: Dec, 2001; Apr, 2002 - No. 6 ($2.95/$4.95/$5.95)

...The Beginning (12/01, $5.95) Anacleto-c/a; Haberlin-s 6.00
1-5: 1-(4/02, $2.95) two covers by Anacleto 3.00
6-($4.95) 5.00
...: Agents Roster #1 (11/02, $5.95, 8 1/2 x 11") bios and sketch pages by Anacleto 6.00
Vol. 1 TPB (4/03, $19.95) r/#1-6 & Agents Roster; cover gallery 20.00

ATHENA
Dynamite Entertainment: 2009 - No. 4, 2010 ($3.50)

1-4-Murray-s/Neves-a; multiple covers on each. 1-Obama flip cover 3.50

ATLANTIS CHRONICLES, THE (Also see Aquaman, 3rd Series & Aquaman: Time & Tide)
DC Comics: Mar, 1990 - No. 7, Sept, 1990 ($2.95, limited series, 52 pgs.)

1-7: 1-Peter David scripts. 7-True origin of Aquaman; nudity panels 4.00

ATLANTIS, THE LOST CONTINENT
Dell Publishing Co.: May, 1961

	GD 2.0	VG 4.0	FN 6.0	VF 8.0	VF/NM 9.0	NM- 9.2
Four Color #1188-Movie, photo-c	10	20	30	65	118	170

ATLAS (See 1st Issue Special)

ATLAS
Dark Horse Comics: Feb, 1994 - No. 4, 1994 ($2.50, limited series)

1-4 3.00

ATLAS (Agents of Atlas)(The Heroic Age)
Marvel Comics: Jul, 2010 - No. 5, Nov, 2010 ($3.99/$2.99)

1-($3.99) Parker-s/Hardman-a/Dodson-c; 3-D Man app.; profile page 4.00
2-5-($2.99) 2,3,5-Pagulayan-c. 4-Jae Lee-c 3.00

ATLAS UNIFIED
Atlas Comics: Nov, 2011 - Present ($2.99, limited series)

1-Three covers; Peyer-s/Salgado-a; crossover of Grim Ghost, Wulf, Phoenix & others 3.00

ATMOSPHERICS
Avatar Press: June, 2002 ($5.95, B&W, one-shot graphic novel)

1-Warren Ellis-s/Ken Meyer Jr.-painted-a/c 6.00

ATOM, THE (See Action #425, All-American #19, Brave & the Bold, D.C. Special Series #1, Detective Comics, Flash Comics #80, Hawkman, Identity Crisis, JLA, Power Of The Atom, Showcase #34 -36, Super Friends, Sword of The Atom, Teen Titans & World's Finest)

ATOM, THE (...& the Hawkman No. 39 on)
National Periodical Publ.: June-July, 1962 - No. 38, Aug-Sept, 1968

	GD 2.0	VG 4.0	FN 6.0	VF 8.0	VF/NM 9.0	NM- 9.2
1-(6-7/62)-Intro Plant-Master; 1st app. Maya	93	186	279	753	1627	2500
2	32	64	96	232	499	765
3-1st Time Pool story; 1st app. Chronos (origin)	21	42	63	148	317	485
4,5: 4-Snapper Carr x-over	15	30	45	104	227	350
6,9,10	12	24	36	81	166	250
7-Hawkman x-over (6-7/63; 1st Atom & Hawkman team-up); 1st app. Hawkman since Brave & the Bold tryouts	24	48	72	168	359	550
8-Justice League, Dr. Light app.	12	24	36	83	172	260
11-15: 13-Chronos-c/story	10	20	30	67	124	180
16-20: 19-Zatanna x-over	8	16	24	53	89	125
21-28,30: 26-Two-page pin-up. 28-Chronos-c/story	7	14	21	48	79	110
29-1st solo Golden Age Atom x-over in S.A.	12	24	36	84	175	265
31-35,37,38: 31-Hawkman x-over. 37-Intro. Major Mynah; Hawkman cameo	6	12	18	41	66	90
36-G.A. Atom x-over	7	14	21	48	79	110

NOTE: ***Anderson*** *a-1-11i, 13i; c-inks-1-25, 31-35, 37.* ***Sid Greene*** *a-8i-37i.* ***Gil Kane*** *a-1p-37p; c-1p-28p, 29, 33p, 34; c-26i.* ***George Roussos*** *a-38i.* ***Mike Sekowsky*** *a-38p. Time Pool stories also in 6, 9,12, 17, 21, 27, 35.*

ATOM, THE (See All New Atom and Tangent Comics/ The Atom)

ATOM AGE (See Classics Illustrated Special Issue)

ATOM-AGE COMBAT
St. John Publishing Co.: June, 1952 - No. 5, Apr, 1953; Feb, 1958

	GD 2.0	VG 4.0	FN 6.0	VF 8.0	VF/NM 9.0	NM- 9.2
1-Buck Vinson in all	52	104	156	328	552	775
2-Flying saucer story	31	62	93	186	303	420
3,5: 3-Mayo-a (6 pgs.). 5-Flying saucer-c/story	27	54	81	162	266	370
4 (Scarce)	31	62	93	186	303	420
1(2/58-St. John)	23	46	69	136	223	310

ATOM-AGE COMBAT
Fago Magazines: No. 2, Jan, 1959 - No. 3, Mar, 1959

	GD 2.0	VG 4.0	FN 6.0	VF 8.0	VF/NM 9.0	NM- 9.2
2-A-Bomb explosion-c;	29	58	87	170	278	385
3	22	44	66	128	209	290

ATOMAN
Spark Publications: Feb, 1946 - No. 2, April, 1946

	GD 2.0	VG 4.0	FN 6.0	VF 8.0	VF/NM 9.0	NM- 9.2
1-Origin & 1st app. Atoman; Robinson/Meskin-a; Kidcrusaders, Wild Bill Hickok, Marvin the Great app.	66	132	198	419	722	1025
2-Robinson/Meskin-a; Robinson c-1,2	41	82	123	256	428	600

ATOM & HAWKMAN, THE (Formerly The Atom)
National Periodical Publ: No. 39, Oct-Nov, 1968 - No. 45, Oct-Nov, 1969; No. 46, Mar, 2010

	GD 2.0	VG 4.0	FN 6.0	VF 8.0	VF/NM 9.0	NM- 9.2
39-43: 40-41-Kubert/Anderson-a. 43-(7/69)-Last 12¢ issue; 1st S.A. app. Gentleman Ghost	6	12	18	39	62	85

Atomic Comics #4 © Green Pub.

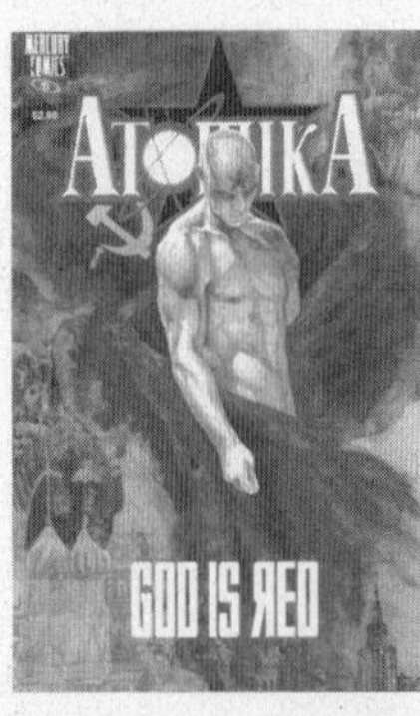

Atomika #5 © Sal Abbinanti

Attack #54 © CC

GD VG FN VF VF/NM NM-
2.0 4.0 6.0 8.0 9.0 9.2

44,45: 44-(9/69)-1st 15¢-c; origin Gentleman Ghost 6 12 18 39 62 85
46-(3/10, $2.99) Blackest Night crossover one-shot; Geoff Johns-s/Ryan Sook-a/c 3.00
NOTE: *M. Anderson a-39, 40i, 41i, 43, 44. Sid Greene a-40i-45i. Kubert a-40p, 41p; c-39-45.*

ATOM ANT (TV) (See Golden Comics Digest #2) (Hanna-Barbera)
Gold Key: January, 1966 (12¢)
1(10170-601)-1st app. Atom Ant, Precious Pup, and Hillbilly Bears
15 30 45 104 227 350

ATOM ANT & SECRET SQUIRREL (See Hanna-Barbera Presents)

ATOMIC AGE
Marvel Comics (Epic Comics): Nov, 1990 - No. 4, Feb, 1991 ($4.50, limited series, square-bound, 52 pgs.)
1-4: Williamson-a(i); sci-fi story set in 1957 4.50

ATOMIC ATTACK (True War Stories; formerly Attack, first series)
Youthful Magazines: No. 5, Jan, 1953 - No. 8, Oct, 1953 (1st story is sci/fi in all issues)
5-Atomic bomb-c; science fiction stories in all 40 80 120 246 411 575
6-8 27 54 81 158 259 360

ATOMIC BOMB
Jay Burtis Publications: 1945 (36 pgs.)
1-Superheroes Airmale & Stampy (scarce) 71 142 213 454 777 1100

ATOMIC BUNNY (Formerly Atomic Rabbit)
Charlton Comics: No. 12, Aug, 1958 - No. 19, Dec, 1959
12 12 24 36 69 97 125
13-19 8 16 24 42 54 65

ATOMIC COMICS
Daniels Publications (Canadian): Jan, 1946 (Reprints, one-shot)
1-Rocketman, Yankee Boy, Master Key app. 40 80 120 244 405 565

ATOMIC COMICS
Green Publishing Co.: Jan, 1946 - No. 4, July-Aug, 1946 (#1-4 were printed w/o cover gloss)
1-Radio Squad by Siegel & Shuster; Barry O'Neal app.; Fang Gow cover-r/ Detective Comics (Classic-c) 81 162 243 518 884 1250
2-Inspector Dayton; Kid Kane by Matt Baker; Lucky Wings, Congo King, Prop Powers (only app.) begin 55 110 165 352 601 850
3,4: 3-Zero Ghost Detective app.; Baker-a(2) each; 4-Baker-c
39 78 117 242 401 560

ATOMIC KNIGHTS (See Strange Adventures #117)
DC Comics: 2010 ($39.99, HC with dustjacket)
HC-Reprints the original 1960-64 run from debut in Strange Adventures #117 to S.A. #160; new intro. by Murphy Anderson 40.00

ATOMIC MOUSE (TV, Movies) (See Blue Bird, Funny Animals, Giant Comics Edition & Wotalife Comics)
Capitol Stories/Charlton Comics: 3/53 - No. 52, 2/63; No. 1, 12/84; V2#10, 9/85 - No. 12, 1/86
1-Origin & 1st app.; Al Fago-c/a in most 34 68 102 199 325 450
2 15 30 45 84 127 170
3-10: 5-Timmy The Timid Ghost app.; see Zoo Funnies
10 20 30 58 79 100
11-13,16-25 8 16 24 40 50 60
14,15-Hoppy The Marvel Bunny app. 9 18 27 50 65 80
26-(68 pgs.) 12 24 36 67 94 120
27-40: 36,37-Atom The Cat app. 6 12 18 29 36 42
41-52 5 10 15 22 26 30
1 (1984)-Low print run; rep/#7-c w/diff. stories 2 4 6 8 10 12
V2#10 (9/85) -12(1/86)-Low print run 1 3 4 6 8 10

ATOMIC RABBIT (Atomic Bunny #12 on; see Giant Comics #3 & Wotalife)
Charlton Comics: Aug, 1955 - No. 11, Mar, 1958
1-Origin & 1st app.; Al Fago-c/a in all? 30 60 90 177 289 400
2 14 28 42 80 115 150
3-10 10 20 30 56 76 95
11-(68 pgs.) 14 28 42 80 115 150

ATOMICS, THE
AAA Pop Comics: Jan, 2000 - No. 15, Nov, 2001 ($2.95)
1-11-Mike Allred-s/a; 1-Madman-c/app. 3.00
12-15-($3.50): 13-15-Savage Dragon-c/app. 15-Afterword by Alex Ross; colored reprint of 1st Frank Einstein story 3.50
...King-Size Giant Spectacular: Jigsaw (2000, $10.00) r/#1-4 10.00
...King-Size Giant Spectacular: Lessons in Light, Lava, & Lasers (2000, $8.95) r/#5-8 9.00
...King-Size Giant Spectacular: Running With the Dragon ('02, $8.95) r/#13-15 and r/1st Frank Einstein app. in color 9.00

GD VG FN VF VF/NM NM-
2.0 4.0 6.0 8.0 9.0 9.2

...King-Size Giant Spectacular: Worlds Within Worlds ('01, $8.95) r/#9-12 9.00
Madman and the Atomics, Vol. 1 TPB (2007, $24.99) r/#1-15, cover gallery, pin-ups, afterword by Alex Ross 25.00
...: Spaced Out & Grounded in Snap City TPB (10/03, $12.95) r/one-shots - It Girl, Mr. Gum, Spaceman and Crash Metro & the Star Squad; sketch pages 13.00

ATOMIC SPY CASES
Avon Periodicals: Mar-Apr, 1950 (Painted-c)
1-No Wood-a; A-bomb blast panels; Fass-a 36 72 108 216 351 485

ATOMIC THUNDERBOLT, THE
Regor Company: Feb, 1946 (one-shot) (scarce)
1-Intro. Atomic Thunderbolt & Mr. Murdo 63 126 189 403 689 975

ATOMIC TOYBOX
Image Comics: Dec, 1999 ($2.95)
1- Aaron Lopresti-c/s/a 3.00

ATOMIC WAR!
Ace Periodicals (Junior Books): Nov, 1952 - No. 4, Apr, 1953
1-Atomic bomb-c 142 284 426 909 1555 2200
2,3: 3-Atomic bomb-c 66 132 198 419 722 1025
4-Used in **POP**, pg. 96 & illo. 66 132 198 419 722 1025

ATOMIKA
Speakeasy Comics/Mercury Comics: Mar, 2005 - No. 6 ($2.99)
1-6: 1-Alex Ross-c/Sal Abbinanti-a/Dabb-s. 3-Fabry-c. 4-Four covers; Romita back-c 3.00
... God is Red TPB (5/06, $19.99) r/#1-6; cover gallery; Dabb foreword 20.00

ATOMIK ANGELS
Crusade Comics: May, 1996 - No. 4, Nov. 1996 ($2.50)
1-4: 1-Freefall from Gen 13 app. 3.00
1-Variant-c 4.00
Intrep-Edition (2/96, B&W, giveaway at launch party)-Previews Atomik Angels #1; includes Billy Tucci interview. 4.00

ATOM SPECIAL (See Atom & Justice League of America)
DC Comics: 1993/1995 ($2.50/$2.95)(68pgs.)
1,2: 1-Dillon-c/a. 2-McDonnell-a/Bolland-c/Peyer-s 4.00

ATOM THE CAT (Formerly Tom Cat; see Giant Comics #3)
Charlton Comics: No. 9, Oct, 1957 - No. 17, Aug, 1959
9 10 20 30 54 72 90
10,13-17 7 14 21 35 43 50
11,12: 11(64 pgs)-Atomic Mouse app. 12(100 pgs.) 11 22 33 62 86 110

ATTACK
Youthful Mag./Trojan No. 5 on: May, 1952 - No. 4, Nov, 1952; No. 5, Jan, 1953 - No. 5, Sept, 1953
1-(1st series)-Extreme violence 40 80 120 246 411 575
2,3-Both Harrison-c/a; bondage, whipping 22 44 66 132 216 300
4-Krenkel-a (7 pgs.); Harrison-a (becomes Atomic Attack #5 on)
22 44 66 132 216 300
5-(#1, Trojan, 2nd series) 15 30 45 90 140 190
6-8 (#2-4), 5 13 26 39 72 101 130

ATTACK
Charlton Comics: No. 54, 1958 - No. 60, Nov, 1959
54 (25¢, 100 pgs.) 12 24 36 69 97 125
55-60 7 14 21 35 43 50

ATTACK!
Charlton Comics: 1962 - No. 15, 3/75; No. 16, 8/79 - No. 48, 10/84
nn(#1)-('62) Special Edition 5 10 15 35 55 75
2('63), 3(Fall, '64) 3 6 9 21 32 42
V4#3(10/66), 4(10/67)-(Formerly Special War Series #2; becomes Attack At Sea V4#5):
3-Tokyo Rose story 3 6 9 17 25 32
1(9/71)-D-Day story 3 6 9 16 23 30
2-5: 2-Hitler app. 4-American Eagle app. 2 4 6 9 12 15
6-15(3/75): 8-Nixon app. 1 3 4 6 8 10
16(8/79) - 40 5.00
41-47 Low print run 7.00
48(10/84)-Wood-r; S&K-c (low print) 1 3 4 6 8 10
Modern Comics 13('78)-r 4.00
NOTE: *Sutton a-9,10,13.*

ATTACK!
Spire Christian Comics (Fleming H. Revell Co.): 1975 (39¢/49¢, 36 pgs.)

Authentic Police Cases #10 © STJ

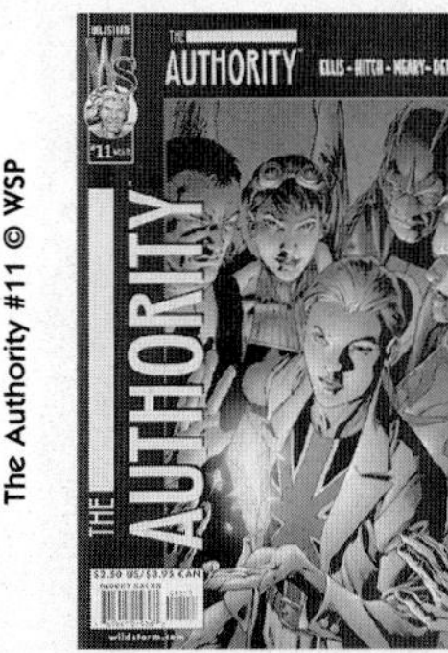

The Authority #11 © WSP

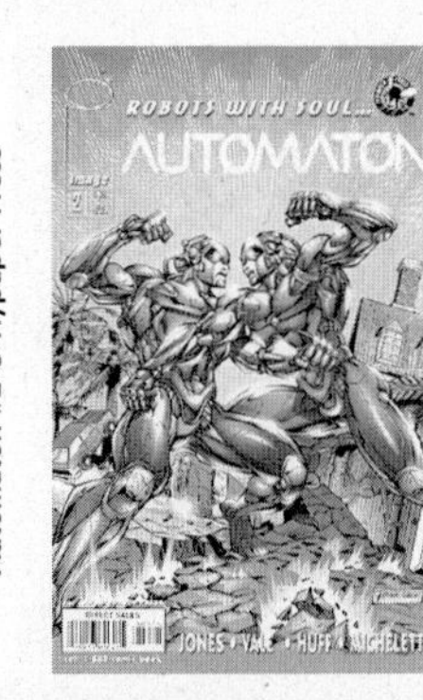

Automaton #2 © Flypaper Press

GD VG FN VF VF/NM NM-
2.0 4.0 6.0 8.0 9.0 9.2

nn 2 4 6 10 14 18

ATTACK AT SEA (Formerly Attack!, 1967)
Charlton Comics: V4#5, Oct, 1968 (one-shot)

V4#5 3 6 9 17 25 32

ATTACK ON PLANET MARS (See Strange Worlds #18)
Avon Periodicals: 1951

nn-Infantino, Fawcette, Kubert & Wood-a; adaptation of Tarrano the Conqueror by Ray Cummings 86 172 258 546 936 1325

ATTITUDE LAD
Slave Labor Graphics: Apr, 1994 - No. 3, Nov, 1994 ($2.95, B&W)

1-3 3.00

AUDREY & MELVIN (Formerly Little...)(See Little Audrey & Melvin)
Harvey Publications: No. 62, Sept, 1974

62 2 4 6 9 13 16

AUGIE DOGGIE (TV) (See Hanna-Barbera Band Wagon, Quick-Draw McGraw, Spotlight #2, Top Cat & Whitman Comic Books)
Gold Key: October, 1963 (12¢)

1-Hanna-Barbera character 15 30 45 102 221 340

AUTHENTIC POLICE CASES
St. John Publishing Co.: 2/48 - No. 6, 11/48; No. 7, 5/50 - No. 38, 3/55

1-Hale the Magician by Tuska begins 48 96 144 302 514 725
2-Lady Satan, Johnny Rebel app. 30 60 90 177 289 400
3-Veiled Avenger app.; blood drainage story plus 2 Lucky Coyne stories; used in **SOTI**, illo. from Red Seal #16 52 104 156 328 552 775
4,5: 4-Masked Black Jack app. 5-Late 1930s Jack Cole-a(r); transvestism story 30 60 90 177 289 400
6-Matt Baker-c; used in **SOTI**, illo- "An invitation to learning", r-in Fugitives From Justice #3; Jack Cole-a; also used by the N.Y. Legis. Comm. 58 116 174 371 636 900
7,8,10-14: 7-Jack Cole-a; Matt Baker-a begins #8, ends #?; Vic Flint in #10-14. 10-12-Baker-a(2 each) 32 64 96 188 307 425
9-No Vic Flint 28 56 84 165 270 375
15-Drug-c/story; Vic Flint app.; Baker-c 33 66 99 194 317 440
16,17,19,22-Baker-c 26 52 78 154 252 350
18,20,21,23: Baker-a(i) 21 42 63 122 199 275
24-28 (All 100 pgs.): 26-Transvestism 39 78 117 240 395 550
29,31,32-Baker-c 20 40 60 118 192 265
30 16 32 48 94 147 200
33-38: 33-Baker-c. 34-Baker-c; r/#9. 35-Baker-c/a(2); r/#10. 36-r/#11; Vic Flint strip-r; Baker-c/a(2) unsigned. 37-Baker-c; r/#17. 38- Baker-c/a; r/#18 21 42 63 122 199 275

NOTE: ***Matt Baker** c-6-16, 17, 19, 22, 27, 29, 31-38; a-13, 16. Bondage c-1, 3.*

AUTHORITY, THE (See Stormwatch and Jenny Sparks: The Secret History of...)
DC Comics (WildStorm): May, 1999 - No. 29, Jul, 2002 ($2.50)

1-Wraparound-c; Warren Ellis-s/Bryan Hitch and Paul Neary-a 2 4 6 8 11 14
1-Special Edition (7/10, $1.00) r/#1 with "What's Next?" logo on cover 3.00
2-4 1 3 4 6 8 10
5-12: 12-Death of Jenny Sparks; last Ellis-s 1 2 3 5 6 8
13-Mark Millar-s/Frank Quitely-c/a begins 2 4 6 8 10 12
14-16-Authority vs. Marvel-esque villains 1 2 3 4 5 7
17-22: 17,18-Weston-a. 19,20,22-Quitely-a. 21-McCrea-a 5.00
23-29: 23-26-Peyer-s/Nguyen-a; new Authority. 24-Preview of "The Establishment." 25,26-Jenny Sparks app. 27,28-Millar-s/Adams-a/c 4.00
Annual 2000 ($3.50) Devil's Night x-over; Hamner-a/Bermejo-c 1 2 3 4 5 7
Absolute Authority Slipcased Hardcover (2002, $49.95) oversized r/#1-12 plus script pages by Ellis and sketch pages by Hitch 50.00
...: Earth Inferno and Other Stories TPB (2002, $14.95) r/#17-20, Annual 2000, and Wildstorm Summer Special; new Quitely-c 15.00
...: Human on the Inside HC (2004, $24.95, dust jacket) Ridley-s/Oliver-a/c 25.00
...: Human on the Inside SC (2004, $17.99) Ridley-s/Oliver-a/c 18.00
...: Kev (10/02, $4.95) Ennis-s/Fabry-c/a 5.00
...: Relentless TPB (2000, $17.95) r/#1-8 18.00
...: Scorched Earth (2/03, $4.95) Robbie Morrison-s/Frazer Irving-a/Ashley Wood-c 5.00
...: Transfer of Power TPB (2002, $17.95) r/#22-29 18.00
...: Under New Management TPB (2000, $17.95) r/#9-16; new Quitely-c 18.00

AUTHORITY, THE (See previews in Sleeper, Stormwatch: Team Achilles and Wildcats Version 3.0)
DC Comics (WildStorm): Jul, 2003 - No. 14, Oct, 2004 ($2.95)

1-14: 1-Robbie Morrison-s/Dwayne Turner-a. 5-Huat-a. 14-Portacio-a 3.00
#0 (10/03, $2.95) r/preview back-up-s listed above; Turner sketch pages 3.00
...: Fractured Worlds TPB (2005, $17.95) r/#6-14; cover gallery 18.00
...: Harsh Realities TPB (2004, $14.95) r/#0-5; cover gallery 15.00
.../Lobo: Jingle Hell (2/04, $4.95) Bisley-c/a; Giffen & Grant-s 5.00
.../Lobo: Spring Break Massacre (8/05, $4.99) Bisley-c/a; Giffen & Grant-s 5.00

AUTHORITY, THE (Volume 4) (The Lost Year)
DC Comics (WildStorm): Dec, 2006 - No. 2, May 2007; No. 3, Jan, 2010 - No. 12, Oct, 2010 ($2.99)

1,2-Grant Morrison-s/Gene Ha-a/c 3.00
1-Variant cover by Art Adams 5.00
3-12: 3-(1/10) Morrison & Giffen-s/Robertson-a. 3-12-Ha-c. 12-Ordway-a 3.00
...Reader: The Lost Year (1/10, $2.99) r/#1,2 3.00
... Book One (2010, $17.99) r/#1-7; cover sketch art 18.00

AUTHORITY, THE (Volume 5) (World's End)
DC Comics (WildStorm): Oct, 2008 - No. 29, Jan, 2011 ($2.99)

1-29: 1-5-Simon Coleby-a/c; Lynch back-up story w/Hairsine-a/Gage-s. 21-Simonson-c 3.00
...: Rule Britannia TPB (2010, $19.99) r/#8-17 20.00
...: World's End TPB (2009, $17.99) r/#1-7 18.00

AUTHORITY, THE: MORE KEV
DC Comics (WildStorm): Jul, 2004 - No. 4, Dec, 2004 ($2.95, limited series)

1-4-Garth Ennis-s/Glenn Fabry-c/a 3.00
...: Kev TPB (2005, $14.99) r/Authority: Kev one-shot and Authority: More Kev series 15.00

AUTHORITY, THE: PRIME
DC Comics (WildStorm): Dec, 2007 - No. 6, May, 2008 ($2.99, limited series)

1-6-Gage-s/Robertson-c/a; Bendix app. 3.00
TPB (2008, $17.99) r/#1-6 18.00

AUTHORITY, THE: REVOLUTION
DC Comics (WildStorm): Dec, 2004 - No. 12, Dec, 2005 ($2.95/$2.99)

1-12-Brubaker-s/Nguyen-a. 5-Henry Bendix returns. 7-Jenny Sparks app. 3.00
...: Book One TPB (2005, $14.99) r/#1-6; cover gallery and Nguyen sketch pages 15.00
...: Book Two TPB (2006, $14.99) r/#7-12; cover gallery and Nguyen sketch pages 15.00

AUTHORITY, THE: THE MAGNIFICENT KEV
DC Comics (WildStorm): Nov, 2005 - No. 5, Feb, 2006 ($2.99, limited series)

1-5-Garth Ennis-s/Carlos Ezquerra-a/Glenn Fabry-c 3.00
TPB (2006, $14.99) r/#1-5 15.00

AUTOMATIC KAFKA
DC Comics (WildStorm): Sept, 2002 - No. 9, Jul, 2003 ($2.95)

1-9-Ashley Wood-c/a; Joe Casey-s 3.00

AUTOMATON
Image Comics (Flypaper Press): Sept, 1998 - No. 3, 1998 ($2.95, lim. series)

1-3-R.A. Jones-s/Peter Vale-a 3.00

AUTUMN
Caliber Comics: 1995 - No. 3, 1995 ($2.95, B&W)

1-3 3.00

AUTUMN ADVENTURES (Walt Disney's...)
Disney Comics: Autumn, 1990; No. 2, Autumn, 1991 ($2.95, 68 pgs.)

1-Donald Duck-r(2) by Barks, Pluto-r, & new-a 4.00
2-D. Duck-r by Barks; new Super Goof story 4.00

AVATAARS: COVENANT OF THE SHIELD
Marvel Comics: Sept, 2000 - No. 3, Nov, 2000 ($2.99, limited series)

1-3-Kaminski-s/Oscar Jimenez-a 3.00

AVATAR
DC Comics: Feb, 1991 - No. 3, Apr, 1991 ($5.95, limited series, 100 pgs.)

1-3: Based on TSR's Forgotten Realms 6.00

AVENGELYNE
Maximum Press: May, 1995 - No. 3, July, 1995 ($2.50/$3.50, limited series)

1/2 2 4 6 8 10 12
1/2 Platinum 15.00
1-Newstand ($2.50)-Photo-c; poster insert 6.00
1-Direct Market ($3.50)-Chromium-c; poster 1 2 3 4 5 7
1-Glossy edition 2 4 6 12 16 20
1-Gold 12.00
2-3: 2-Polybagged w/card 3.00
3-Variant-c; Deodato pin-up 5.00
...Bible (10/96, $3.50) 4.00
.../Glory (9/95, $3.95) 2 covers 4.00

Avengelyne V2 #7 © Rob Liefeld

The Avengers #23 © MAR

The Avengers #58 © MAR

GD 2.0 | VG 4.0 | FN 6.0 | VF 8.0 | VF/NM 9.0 | NM- 9.2

.../Glory Swimsuit Special (6/96, $2.95) photo and illos. covers 3.00
.../Glory: The Godyssey (9/96, $2.99) 2 covers (1 photo) 3.00
...Revelation One (Avatar, 1/01, $3.50) 3 covers by Haley, Rio, Shaw; Shaw-a 3.50
.../Shi (Avatar, 11/01, $3.50) Eight covers; Waller-a 3.50
...Swimsuit (8/95, $2.95)-Pin-ups/photos. 3-Variant-c exist (2 photo, 1 Liefeld-a) 4.00
...Swimsuit (1/96, $3.50, 2nd printing)-photo-c 4.00
Trade paperback (12/95, $9.95) 10.00
.../Warrior Nun Areala 1 (11/96, $2.99) also see Warrior Nun/Avengelyne 3.00

AVENGELYNE
Maximum Press: V2#1, Apr, 1996 - No. 14, Apr, 1997 ($2.95/$2.50)

V2#1-Four covers exist (2 photo-c). 4.00
V2#2-Three covers exist (1 photo-c); flip book w/Darkchylde 5.00
V2#0, 3-14: 0-(10/96).3-Flip book w/Priest preview. 5-Flip book w/Blindside 3.00

AVENGELYNE (Volume 3)
Awesome Comics: Mar, 1999 ($2.50)

1-Fraga & Liefeld-a 3.00

AVENGELYNE (4th series)
Image Comics: Jul, 2011 - Present ($2.99)

1-7-Liefeld & Poulson-s/Gieni-a. 1-Three covers by Liefeld, Gieni, and Benitez 3.00

AVENGELYNE: ARMAGEDDON
Maximum Press: Dec, 1996 - No. 3, Feb, 1997 ($2.99, limited series)

1-3-Scott Clark-a(p) 3.00

AVENGELYNE: DEADLY SINS
Maximum Press: Feb, 1996 - No. 2, Mar, 1996 ($2.95, limited series)

1,2: 1-Two-c exist (1 photo, 1 Liefeld-a). 2-Liefeld-c; Pop Mhan-a(p) 3.00

AVENGELYNE/POWER
Maximum Press: Nov, 1995 - No.3, Jan, 1996 ($2.95, limited series)

1-3: 1,2-Liefeld-c. 3-Three variant-c. exist (1 photo-c) 3.00

AVENGELYNE • PROPHET
Maximum Press: May, 1996; No. 2, Feb. 1997 ($2.95, unfinished lim. series)

1,2-Liefeld-c/a(p) 3.00

AVENGER, THE (See A-1 Comics)
Magazine Enterprises: Feb-Mar, 1955 - No. 4, Aug-Sept, 1955

1(A-1 #129)-Origin 39 78 117 240 395 550
2(A-1 #131), 3(A-1 #133) Robot-c, 4(A-1 #138) 27 54 81 158 259 360
IW Reprint #9('64)-Reprints #1 (new cover) 4 8 12 20 29 38
NOTE: *Powell a-2-4; c-1-4.*

AVENGERS, THE (TV)(Also see Steed and Mrs. Peel)
Gold Key: Nov, 1968 ("John Steed & Emma Peel" cover title) (15¢)

1-Photo-c 13 26 39 90 195 300
1-(Variant with photo back-c) 17 34 51 119 260 400

AVENGERS, THE (See Essential..., Giant-Size..., JLA/..., Kree/Skrull War Starring..., Marvel Graphic Novel #27, Marvel Super Action, Marvel Super Heroes('66), Marvel Treasury Ed., Marvel Triple Action, New Avengers, Solo Avengers, Tales Of Suspense #49, West Coast Avengers & X-Men Vs....)

AVENGERS, THE (The Mighty Avengers on cover only #63-69)
Marvel Comics Group: Sept, 1963 - No. 402, Sept, 1996

1-Origin & 1st app. The Avengers (Thor, Iron Man, Hulk, Ant-Man, Wasp); Loki app. 575 1150 2300 7000 16,000 25,000
2-Hulk leaves Avengers 111 222 333 900 1950 3000
3-2nd Sub-Mariner x-over outside the F.F. (see Strange Tales #107 for 1st); Sub-Mariner & Hulk team-up & battle Avengers; Spider-Man cameo (1/64) 74 148 222 600 1300 2000
4-Revival of Captain America who joins the Avengers; 1st Silver Age app. of Captain America & Bucky (3/64) 214 428 642 1800 3900 6000
4-Reprint from the Golden Record Comic set 13 26 39 86 183 280
With Record (1966) 18 36 54 126 273 420
5-Hulk app. 46 92 138 359 780 1200
6,8: 6-Intro/1st app. original Zemo & his Masters of Evil. 8-Intro Kang 34 68 102 247 536 825
7-Rick Jones app. in Bucky costume 36 72 108 270 585 900
9-Intro Wonder Man who dies in same story 48 96 144 389 845 1300
10-Intro/1st app. Immortus; early Hercules app. (11/64) 27 54 81 196 423 650
11-Spider-Man-c & x-over (12/64) 35 70 105 254 552 850
12-15: 15-Death of original Zemo 18 36 54 123 267 410
16-New Avengers line-up (Hawkeye, Quicksilver, Scarlet Witch join; Thor, Iron Man, Giant-Man, Wasp leave) 29 58 87 210 455 700
17,18 13 26 39 85 180 275
19-1st app. Swordsman; origin Hawkeye (8/65) 14 28 42 93 202 310
20-22: Wood inks 10 20 30 69 130 190
23,24,26-30: 23-Romita Sr. inks (1st Silver Age Marvel work). 28-Giant-Man becomes Goliath (5/66) 9 18 27 63 112 160
25-Dr. Doom-c/story 11 22 33 76 151 225
31-40 8 16 24 55 93 130
41-46,49-52,54,55: 43-1st app. Red Guardian (dies in #44) . 46-Ant-Man returns (re-intro, 11/67). 52-Black Panther joins; 1st app. The Grim Reaper. 54-1st app. new Masters of Evil. 7 14 21 48 79 110
47-Magneto-c/story 7 14 21 49 82 115
48-Origin/1st app. new Black Knight (1/68) 7 14 21 49 82 115
53-X-Men app. 10 20 30 65 118 170
56-Zemo app; story explains how Capt. America became imprisoned in ice during WWII, only to be rescued in Avengers #4 8 16 24 53 89 125
57-1st app. S.A. Vision (10/68) 19 38 57 128 277 425
58-Origin The Vision 10 20 30 69 130 190
59-65: 59-Intro. Yellowjacket. 60-Wasp & Yellowjacket wed. 63-Goliath becomes Yellowjacket; Hawkeye becomes the new Goliath. 65-Last 12¢ issue 6 12 18 41 66 90
66,67-B. Smith-a 6 12 18 42 69 95
68-70: 69-Nighthawk cameo. 70-1st full app. Nighthawk 6 12 18 39 62 85
71-1st app. The Invaders (12/69); Black Knight joins 8 16 24 56 96 135
72-79,81,82,84-86,89-91: 82-Daredevil app 5 10 15 35 55 75
80-Intro. Red Wolf (9/70) 6 12 18 37 59 80
83-Intro. The Liberators (Wasp, Valkyrie, Scarlet Witch, Medusa & the Black Widow) 6 12 18 41 66 90
87-Origin The Black Panther 6 12 18 39 62 85
88-Written by Harlan Ellison 6 12 18 37 59 80
88-2nd printing (1994) 2 4 6 8 10 12
92-Last 15¢ issue; Neal Adams-c 6 12 18 42 69 95
93-(52 pgs.)-Neal Adams-c/a 13 26 39 85 180 275
94-96-Neal Adams-c/a 8 16 24 55 93 130
97-G.A. Capt. America, Sub-Mariner, Human Torch, Patriot, Vision, Blazing Skull, Fin, Angel, & new Capt. Marvel x-over 6 12 18 41 66 90
98,99: 98-Goliath becomes Hawkeye; Smith c/a(i). 99-Smith-c, Smith/Sutton-a 5 10 15 35 55 75
100-(6/72)-Smith-c/a; featuring everyone who was an Avenger 10 20 30 65 118 170
101-Harlan Ellison scripts 4 8 12 24 37 50
102-106,108,109 4 8 12 22 34 45
107-Starlin-a(p) 4 8 12 24 37 50
110,111-X-Men app. 6 12 18 39 62 85
112-1st app. Mantis 5 10 15 30 48 65
113-115,119-124,126-130: 123-Origin Mantis 3 6 9 19 29 38
116-118-Defenders/Silver Surfer app. 6 12 18 37 59 80
125-Thanos-c & brief app. 4 8 12 24 37 50
131-133,136-140: 136-Ploog-r/Amazing Advs. #12 3 6 9 16 22 28
134,135-Origin of the Vision revised (also see Avengers Forever mini-series) 4 8 12 22 34 45
141-143,145,152-163 2 4 6 9 12 15
144-Origin & 1st app. Hellcat 3 6 9 14 20 25
146-149-(Reg.25¢ editions)(4-7/76) 2 4 6 9 12 15
146-149-(30¢-c variants, limited distribution) 4 8 12 22 34 45
150-Kirby-a(r); new line-up: Capt. America, Scarlet Witch, Iron Man, Wasp, Yellowjacket, Vision & The Beast 2 4 6 10 14 18
150-(30¢-c variant, limited distribution) 4 8 12 26 41 55
151-Wonder Man returns w/new costume 2 4 6 10 14 18
160-164-(35¢-c variants, limited dist.)(6-10/77) 7 14 21 46 76 105
164-166: Byrne-a 2 4 6 10 14 18
167-180: 168-Guardians of the Galaxy app. 174-Thanos cameo. 176-Starhawk app. 1 2 3 5 6 8
181-191-Byrne-a: 181-New line-up: Capt. America, Scarlet Witch, Iron Man, Wasp, Vision, Beast & The Falcon. 183-Ms. Marvel joins. 185-Origin Quicksilver & Scarlet Witch 2 4 6 8 10 12
192-194,197-199 6.00
195,196: 195-1st Taskmaster cameo. 196-1st Taskmaster full app. 1 3 4 6 8 10
200-(10/80, 52 pgs.)-Ms. Marvel leaves. 2 4 6 8 10 12
201-213,217-238: 211-New line-up: Capt. America, Iron Man, Tigra, Thor, Wasp & Yellowjacket. 213-Yellowjacket leaves. 217-Yellowjacket & Wasp return. 221-Hawkeye & She-Hulk join. 227-Capt. Marvel (female) joins; origins of Ant-Man, Wasp, Giant-Man, Goliath, Yellowjacket, & Avengers. 230-Yellowjacket quits. 231-Iron Man leaves. 232-Starfox (Eros) joins. 234-Origin Quicksilver, Scarlet Witch. 238-Origin Blackout 4.50

The Avengers #376 © MAR

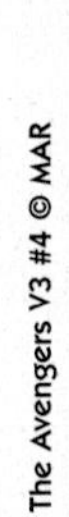

The Avengers V3 #4 © MAR

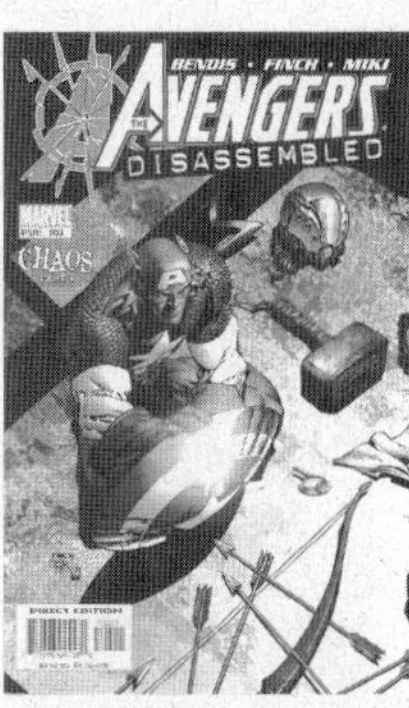

The Avengers #503 © MAR

	GD 2.0	VG 4.0	FN 6.0	VF 8.0	VF/NM 9.0	NM- 9.2

214-Ghost Rider-c/story 6.00
215,216,239,240,250: 215,216-Silver Surfer app. 216-Tigra leaves. 239-(1/84) Avengers app. on David Letterman show. 240-Spider-Woman revived. 250-($1.00, 52 pgs.) 5.00
241-249, 251-262 3.50
263-(1/86) Return of Jean Grey, leading into X-Factor #1(story continues in FF #286) 6.00
264-299: 272-Alpha Flight app. 291-$1.00 issues begin. 297-Black Knight, She-Hulk & Thor resign. 298-Inferno tie-in 3.00
300 (2/89, $1.75, 68 pgs.)-Thor joins; Simonson-a 4.00
301-304,306-313,319-325,327,329-343: 302-Re-intro Quasar. 320-324-Alpha Flight app. (320-cameo). 327-2nd app. Rage. 341,342-New Warriors app. 343-Last $1.00-c 3.00
305,314-318: 305-Byrne scripts begin. 314-318-Spider-Man x-over 3.50
326-1st app. Rage (11/90) 4.00
328,344-349,351-359,361,362,364,365,367: 328-Origin Rage. 365-Contains coupon for Hunt for Magneto contest 3.00
350-($2.50, 68 pgs.)-Double gatefold-c showing-c to #1; r/#53 w/cover in flip book format; vs. The Starjammers 4.00
360-($2.95, 52 pgs.)-Embossed all-foil-c; 30th ann. 4.00
363-($2.95, 52 pgs.)-All silver foil-c 4.00
366-($3.95, 68 pgs.)-Embossed all gold foil-c 4.00
368,370-374,376-399: 368-Bloodties part 1; Avengers/X-Men x-over. 374-bound-in trading card sheet. 380-Deodato-a. 390,391-"The Crossing." 395-Death of "old" Tony Stark; wraparound-c. 3.00
369-($2.95)-Foil embossed-c; Bloodties part 5 4.00
375-($2.00, 52 pgs.)-Regular ed.; Thunderstrike returns; leads into Malibu Comics' Black September. 4.00
375-($2.50, 52 pgs.)-Collector's ed. w/bound-in poster; leads into Malibu Comics' Black September. 4.50
400-402: Waid-s; 402-Deodato breakdowns; cont'd in X-Men #56 & Onslaught: Marvel Universe. 4.00
#500-503 (See Avengers Vol. 3; series resumed original numbering after Vol. 3 #84)
Special 1 (9/67, 25¢, 68 pgs.)-New-a; original & new Avengers team-up 11 22 33 77 154 230
Special 2 (9/68, 25¢, 68 pgs.)-New-a; original vs. new Avengers 8 16 24 55 93 130
Special 3 (9/69, 25¢, 68 pgs.)-r/Avengers #4 plus 3 Capt. America stories by Kirby (art); origin Red Skull 5 10 15 32 51 70
Special 4 (1/71, 25¢, 68 pgs.)-Kirby-r/Avengers #5,6 3 6 9 20 30 40
Special 5 (1/72, 52 pgs.)-Spider-Man x-over 3 6 9 20 30 40
Annual 6 (11/76) Pérez-a; Kirby-c 2 4 6 11 16 20
Annual 7 (11/77)-Starlin-c/a; Warlock dies; Thanos app. 5 10 15 35 55 75
Annual 8 (1978)-Dr. Strange, Ms. Marvel app. 2 4 6 8 11 14
Annual 9 (1979)-Newton-a(p) 2 3 4 6 8 10
Annual 10 (1981)-Golden-p; X-Men cameo; 1st app. Rogue & Madelyne Pryor 5 10 15 35 55 75
Annual 11-13: 11(1982)-Vs. The Defenders. 12('83), 13('84) 5.00
Annual 14-18: 14('85),15('86),16('87),17('88)-Evolutionary War x-over, 18('89)-Atlantis Attacks 4.00
Annual 19-23 (90-'94, 68 pgs.). 22-Bagged/card 4.00
...: Galactic Storm Vol. 1 ('06, $29.99, TPB) r/Kree-Shi'ar war from Avengers #345-346, Capt. America #398-399, Avengers West Coast #80-81, Quasar #32-33, Wonder Man #7-8, Iron Man #278 and Thor #445; new Epting-c 30.00
...: Galactic Storm Vol. 2 ('06, $29.99, TPB) r/Kree-Shi'ar war from Avengers #347, Capt. America #400-401, Avengers West Coast #82, Quasar #34-36, Wonder Man #9, Iron Man #279, Thor #446 and What If #55-56 30.00
...: Kang - Time and Time Again ('05, $19.99, TPB) r/Avengers #69-71 & 267-269, Thor #140 and Incredible Hulk #135 20.00
...Kree-Skrull War ('00, $24.95, TPB) new Neal Adams-c 25.00
...: Legends Vol. 3: George Perez ('03, $16.99)-r/#161,162,194-196,201, Ann. #6 & 8 17.00
Marvel Double Feature...Avengers/Giant-Man #379 ($2.50, 52 pgs.)-Same as Avengers #379 w/Giant-Man flip book 4.00
Marvel Graphic Novel - Deathtrap: The Vault (1991, $9.95) Venom-c/app. 2 4 6 8 10 12
The Korvac Saga TPB (2003, $19.95)-r/#167,168,170-177; Perez-c 20.00
The Serpent Crown TPB (2005, $15.99)-r/#141-144,147-149; Hellcat app. 16.00
The Yesterday Quest ($6.95)-r/#181,182,185-187 1 2 3 4 5 7
Under Siege ('98, $16.95, TPB) r/#270,271,273-277 17.00
...: Vision and the Scarlet Witch TPB (2005, $15.99) r/wedding from Giant-Size Avengers #4 and "Vision and the Scarlet Witch" mini-series #1-4 16.00
...: Visionaries ('99, $16.95)-r/early George Perez art 17.00

NOTE: ***Austin*** *c(i)-157, 167, 168, 170-177, 181, 183-188, 198-201, Annual 8.* ***John Buscema*** *a-41-44p, 46p, 47p, 49, 50, 51-62p, 74-77, 79-85, 87-91, 97, 105p, 121p, 124p,125p, 152, 153p, 255-279p, 281-302p; c-41-66, 68-71, 73-91, 97-99, 178, 256-259p, 261-279p, 281-302p.* ***Byrne*** *a-164-166p, 181-191p, 233p, Annual 13i, 14p; c-186-190p, 233p, 260, 305p; scripts-305-312.* ***Colan*** *a(p)-63-65, 111, 206-208, 210, 211; c(p)-65, 206-208, 210, 211.* ***Ditko*** *a-Annual 13.* ***Guice*** *a-Annual 12p.* ***Don Heck*** *a-9-15, 17-40, 157.* ***Kane*** *c-37p, 159p.* ***Kane/Everett*** *c-97.* ***Kirby*** *a-1-8p, Special 3r, 4r(p); c-1-30, 148, 151-158; layouts-14-16.* ***Ron Lim*** *c(p)-335-341.* ***Miller*** *c-193p.* ***Mooney*** *a-86i, 179p, 180p.* ***Nebres*** *a-178i; c-179i.* ***Newton*** *a-204p, Annual 9p.* ***Perez*** *a(p)-141, 143, 144, 148, 150, 154, 155, 160, 161, 162, 167,168, 170, 171, 194-196, 198-202, Annual 6, 8; c(p)-160-162, 164-166, 170-174, 181,183-185, 191, 192, 194-201, 379-382, Annual 8.* ***Starlin*** *c-121, 135.* ***Staton*** *a-127-134i.* ***Tuska*** *a-47i,48i, 51i, 53i, 54i, 106p, 107p, 135p, 137-140p, 163p. Guardians of the Galaxy app. in #167, 168, 170, 173, 175, 181.*

AVENGERS, THE (Volume Two)
Marvel Comics: V2#1, Nov, 1996 - No. 13, Nov, 1997 ($2.95/$1.95/$1.99) (Produced by Extreme Studios)

1-($2.95)-Heroes Reborn begins; intro new team (Captain America, Swordsman, Scarlet Witch, Vision, Thor, Hellcat & Hawkeye); 1st app. Avengers Island; Loki & Enchantress app.; Rob Liefeld-p & plot; Chap Yaep-p; Jim Valentino scripts; variant-c exists 5.00
1-($1.95)-Variant-c 6.00
2-13: 2,3-Jeph Loeb scripts begin, Kang app. 4-Hulk-c/app. 5-Thor/Hulk battle; 2 covers. 10,11,13-"World War 3"-pt. 2, x-over w/Image characters. 12-($2.99) "Heroes Reunited"-pt. 2 4.00
Heroes Reborn: Avengers (2006, $29.99, TPB) r/#1-12; pin-up and cover gallery 30.00

AVENGERS, THE (Volume Three)(See New Avengers for next series)
Marvel Comics: Feb, 1998 - No. 84, Aug, 2004; No. 500, Sept, 2004 - No. 503, Dec, 2004 ($2.99/$1.99/$2.25)

1-($2.99, 48 pgs.) Busiek-s/Pérez-a/wraparound-c; Avengers reassemble after Heroes Return 5.00
1-Variant Heroes Return cover 1 2 3 4 5 7
1-Rough Cut-Features original script and pencil pages 3.00
2-($1.99)Pérez-c, 2-Lago painted-c 4.00
3,4: 3-Wonder Man-c/app. 4-Final roster chosen; Perez poster 3.50
5-11: 5,6-Squadron Supreme-c/app. 8-Triathlon-c/app. 3.00
12-($2.99) Thunderbolts app. 4.00
12-Alternate-c of Avengers w/white background; no logo 15.00
13-24,26,28: 13-New Warriors app. 16-18-Ordway-s/a. 19-Ultron returns. 26-Immonen-a 3.00
16-Variant-c with purple background 5.00
25,27-($2.99) 25-vs. the Exemplars; Spider-Man app. 27-100 pgs. 4.00
29-33,35-47: 29-Begin $2.25-c. 35-Maximum Security x-over; Romita Jr.-a. 36-Epting-a; poster by Alan Davis. 38-Davis-a begins ($1.99-c) 3.00
34-($2.99) Last Pérez-a; Thunderbirds app. 4.00
48-($3.50, 100 pgs.) new story w/Dwyer-a & r/#98-100 4.00
49,51-59: 49-'Nuff Said story. 51-Anderson-a. 52-Reis-a. 57-Johns-s begin 3.00
50,60-($3.50): 50 Dwyer-a; Quasar app. 4.00
61-84: 61,62-Frank-a; new line-up. 63-Davis-a. 64-Reis-a. 65-70-Coipel-a. 75-Hulk app. 76-Jack of Hearts dies; Jae Lee-c. 77-(50¢-c) Coipel-a/Cassaday-c. 78,80,81-Coipel-a. 83,84-New Invaders app. 3.00
(After #84 [Aug, 2004], numbering reverted back to original Vol. 1 with #500, Sept, 2004)
500-($3.50) "Avengers Disassembled" begins; Bendis-s/Finch-a; Ant-Man (Scott Lang) killed, Vision destroyed 4.00
500-Director's Cut ($4.99) Cassaday foil variant-c plus interviews and galleries 5.00
501, 502-($2.25): 502-Hawkeye killed 3.00
503-($3.50) "Avengers Disassembled" ends; reprint pages from Avengers V1#16 4.00
#1 1/2 (12/99, $2.50) Timm-c/a/Stern-s; 1963-style issue 3.00
.../ Squadron Supreme '98 Annual ($2.99) 4.00
1999, 2000 Annual (7/99, '00, $3.50) 1999-Manco-a. 2000-Breyfogle-a 4.00
2001 Annual ($2.99) Reis-a; back-up-s art by Churchill 4.00
...: Above and Beyond TPB ('05, $24.99) r/#36-40,56, Annual 2001, & Avengers: The Ultron Imperative; Alan Davis-c 25.00
... Assemble HC ('04, $29.95, oversized) r/#1-11 & '98 Annual; Busiek intro.; Pérez pencil art and Busiek script from Avengers #1 30.00
... Assemble Vol. 2 HC ('05, $29.95, oversized) r/#12-22, #0 & Ann. 1999; Ordway intro. 30.00
... Assemble Vol. 3 HC ('06, $34.99, oversized) r/#23-34, #1 1/2 & Thunderbolts #42-44 35.00
... Assemble Vol. 4 HC ('07, $34.99, oversized) r/#35-40, Avengers 2000, Avengers 2001, Avengers: The Ultron Imperative, Maximum Security #1-3 & ...Dangerous Planet 35.00
... Assemble Vol. 5 HC ('07, $39.99, oversized) r/#41-56 and Avengers 2001 40.00
...: Clear and Present Dangers TPB ('01, $19.95) r/#8-15 20.00
...: Defenders War HC ('07, $19.99) r/#115-118 & Defenders #8-11; Englehart intro. 20.00
...: Disassembled HC ('06, $24.99) r/#500-503 & Avengers Finale; Director's Cut extras 25.00
...: Disassembled TPB ('05, $15.99) r/#500-503 & Avengers Finale; Director's Cut extras 16.00
...Finale 1 (1/05, $3.50) Epilogue to Avengers Disassembled; Neal Adams-c; art by various incl. Peréz, Maleev, Oeming, Powell, Mayhew, Mack, McNiven, Cheung, Frank 4.00
Free Comic Book Day (5/09, giveaway) New Avengers 1st battle vs. Dark Avengers 3.00
...: Living Legends TPB ('04, $19.99) r/#23-30; last Busiek/Pérez arc 20.00
...Supreme Justice TPB (4/01, $17.95) r/Squadron Supreme appearances in Avengers #5-7, '98 Annual, Iron Man #7, Capt. America #8, Quicksilver #10; Pérez-c 18.00
The Kang Dynasty TPB ('02, $29.99) r/#41-55 & 2001 Annual 30.00
The Morgan Conquest TPB ('00, $14.95) r/#1-4 15.00
.../Thunderbolts Vol. 1: The Nefaria Protocols (2004, $19.99) r/#31-34, 42-44 20.00
Ultron Unleashed TPB (8/99, $3.50) reprints early app. 4.00
Ultron Unlimited TPB (4/01, $14.95) r/#19-22 & #0 prelude 15.00

Avengers (2010 series) #12.1 © MAR

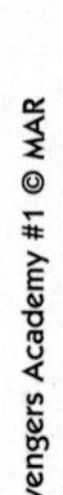

Avengers Academy #1 © MAR

Avengers Origins: Thor #1 © MAR

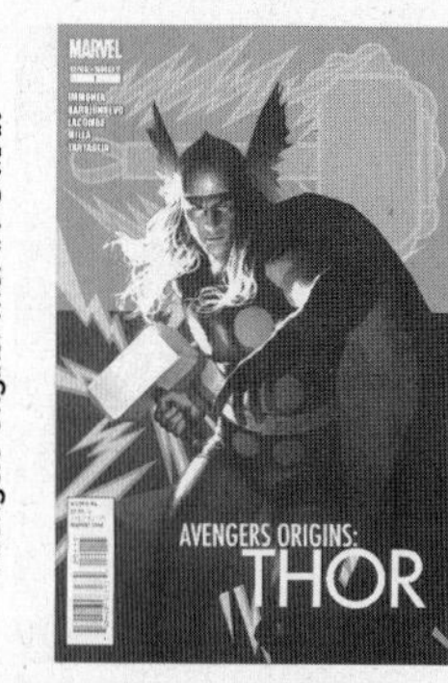

GD VG FN VF VF/NM NM-
2.0 4.0 6.0 8.0 9.0 9.2

Wizard #0-Ultron Unlimited prelude 3.00
Vol. 1: World Trust TPB ('03, $14.99) r/#57-62 & Marvel Double-Shot #2 15.00
Vol. 2: Red Zone TPB ('04, $14.99) r/#64-70 15.00
Vol. 3: The Search For She-Hulk TPB ('04, $12.99) r/#71-76 13.00
Vol. 4: The Lionheart of Avalon TPB ('04, $11.99) r/#77-81 12.00
Vol. 5: Once an Invader TPB ('04, $14.99) r/#82-84, V1 #71; Invaders #0 & Ann #1 ('77) 15.00

AVENGERS (The Heroic Age)
Marvel Comics: July, 2010 - Present ($3.99)

1-New team assembled; Bendis-s/Romita Jr.-a; Kang app.; back-up text Avengers history 4.00
1-Variant-c by Land 6.00
1-Variant covers by Djurdjevic and John Romita Sr. 10.00
1-3-Second printings 4.00
2-12: 2-Wonder Man app. 4-6-Ultron app. 7-Red Hulk app. 12-Red Hulk joins 4.00
12.1 -(6/11, $2.99) Hitch & Neary-c/a; The Wizard & The Intelligencia app.; Ultron returns 3.00
13-24: 13-17-Fear Itself tie-ins. 13,15-Bachalo-a. 17-New Avengers app. 18-20-Acuña-a. 19-Vision returns, Storm joins 4.00
... Annual 1 (3/12, $4.99) Bendis-s/Dell'Otto-c/a; Wonder Man app. 5.00
... Assemble 1 (7/10, $3.99) Handbook-style profiles of Avengers, enemies, allies 4.00
...: Infinity Quest 1 (8/11, $4.99) r/#7-9 with variant covers 5.00
... Spotlight (7/10, $3.99) Creator interviews, previews, history of the team; trivia 4.00

AVENGERS ACADEMY (The Heroic Age)
Marvel Comics: Aug, 2010 - Present ($3.99/$2.99)

1-($3.99) Gage-s/McKone-a/c; Intro. team of Veil, Hazmat, Striker, Mettle, Finesse, Reptil 4.00
1-Variant-c by Djurdjevic 8.00
2-14,14.1 -($2.99) 3,4-Juggernaut app. 5-Molina-a. 7-Absorbing Man app.; Raney-a. 3.00
15-27: 15-20-Fear Itself tie-in. 22-Magneto app. 27-Runaways app. 3.00
... Giant Size 1 (7/11, $7.99) Young Allies and Arcade app.; Tobin-s/Baldeon-a 8.00

AVENGERS AND POWER PACK ASSEMBLE!
Marvel Comics: June, 2006 - No. 4, Sept, 2006 ($2.99, limited series)

1-4-GuriHiru-a/Sumerak-s. 1-Capt. America app. 2-Iron Man. 3-Spider-Man, Kang app. 3.00
TPB (2006, $6.99, digest-size) r/#1-4 7.00

AVENGERS AND THE INFINITY GAUNTLET
Marvel Comics: Oct, 2010 - No. 4, Jan, 2011 ($2.99, limited series)

1-Clevinger-s/Churilla-a; Dr. Doom and Thanos app. 1-Ramos-c. 2-Lim-c 3.00

AVENGERS ASSEMBLE
Marvel Comics: May, 2012 - Present ($3.99)

1-Bendis-s/Bagley-a/c; movie roster in regular Marvel universe 4.00

AVENGERS: CELESTIAL QUEST
Marvel Comics: Nov, 2001 - No. 8, June, 2002 ($2.50/$3.50, limited series)

1-7-Englehart-s/Santamaría-a; Thanos app. 3.00
8-($3.50) 4.00

AVENGERS: CLASSIC
Marvel Comics: Aug, 2007 - No. 12, Juy, 2008 ($3.99/$2.99)

1,12-($3.99) 1-Reprints Avengers #1 ('63) with new stories about that era; Art Adams-c 4.00
2-11-($2.99) R/#2-11 with back-up w/art by Oeming and others 3.00

AVENGERS COLLECTOR'S EDITION, THE
Marvel Comics: 1993 (Ordered through mail w/candy wrapper, 20 pgs.)

1-Contains 4 bound-in trading cards 5.00

AVENGERS: EARTH'S MIGHTIEST HEROES
Marvel Comics: Jan, 2005 - No. 8, Apr, 2005 ($3.50, limited series)

1-8-Retells origin; Casey-s/Kolins-a 3.50
HC (2005, $24.99, 7 1/2" x 11" with dustjacket) r/#1-8 25.00

AVENGERS: EARTH'S MIGHTIEST HEROES (Based on the Disney animated series)
Marvel Comics: Jan, 2011 - No. 4, Apr, 2011 ($3.99)

1-4-Yost-s/Wegener-a. 1-Hero profile pages. 2-Villain profile pages 4.00

AVENGERS: EARTH'S MIGHTIEST HEROES II
Marvel Comics: Jan, 2007 - No. 8, May, 2007 ($3.99, limited series)

1-8-Retells time when the Vision joined; Casey-s/Rosado-a. 6-Hank & Janet's wedding 4.00
HC (2007, $24.99, 7 1/2" x 11" with dustjacket) r/#1-8; cover sketches 25.00

AVENGERS FAIRY TALES
Marvel Comics: May, 2008 - No. 4, Dec, 2008 ($2.99, limited series)

1-4: 1-Peter Pan-style tale; Cebulski-a/Lemos-a. 2-The Vision. 3-Miyazawa-a 3.00

AVENGERS FOREVER
Marvel Comics: Dec, 1998 - No. 12, Feb, 2000 ($2.99)

1-Busiek-s/Pacheco-a in all 4.00
2-12: 4-Four covers. 6-Two covers. 8-Vision origin revised. 12-Rick Jones becomes Capt. Marvel 3.00

GD VG FN VF VF/NM NM-
2.0 4.0 6.0 8.0 9.0 9.2

TPB (1/01, $24.95) r/#1-12; Busiek intro.; new Pacheco-c 25.00

AVENGERS INFINITY
Marvel Comics: Sept, 2000 - No. 4, Dec, 2000 ($2.99, limited series)

1-4-Stern-s/Chen-a 3.00

AVENGERS/ INVADERS
Marvel Comics: Jul, 2008 - No. 12, Aug, 2009 ($2.99, limited series)

1-Invaders journey to the present; Alex Ross-c/Sadowski-a; Thunderbolts app. 3.00
2-12: 2-New Avengers app.; Perkins variant-c. 3-12-Variant-c on each 3.00
... Sketchbook (2008, giveaway) Ross and Sadowski sketch art; Krueger commentary 3.00

AVENGERS/ JLA (See JLA/Avengers for #1 & #3)
DC Comics: No, 2, 2003; No. 4, 2003 ($5.95, limited series)

2-Busiek-s/Pérez-a; wraparound-c; Krona, Galactus app. 6.00
4-Busiek-s/Pérez-a; wraparound-c 6.00

AVENGERS LOG, THE
Marvel Comics: Feb, 1994 ($1.95)

1-Gives history of all members; Perez-c 3.00

AVENGERS NEXT (See A-Next and Spider-Girl)
Marvel Comics: Jan, 2007 - No. 5, Mar, 2007 ($2.99, limited series)

1-5-Lim-a/Wieringo-c; Spider-Girl app. 1-Avengers vs. zombies. 2-Thena app. 3.00
...: Rebirth TPB (2007, $13.99) r/#1-5 14.00

AVENGERS 1959
Marvel Comics: Dec, 2011 - No. 5, Mar, 2012 ($2.99, limited series)

1-5-Chaykin-s/a/c; Nick Fury, Kraven, Namora, Sabretooth, Dominic Fortune app. 3.00

AVENGERS ORIGINS (Series of one-shots)
Marvel Comics: Jan, 2012 - Present ($3.99, limited series)

...: Ant-Man & The Wasp 1 (1/12) Aguirre-Sacasa-s/Hans-a/Djurdjevic-c; origin of both 4.00
...: Luke Cage 1 (1/12) Glass & Benson-s/Talajic-a/Djurdjevic-c; 4.00
...: Scarlet Witch & Quicksilver 1 (1/12) McKeever-s/Pierfederici-a/Djurdjevic-c 4.00
...: Thor 1 (1/12) K. Immonen-s/Barrionuevo-a/Djurdjevic-c 4.00
...: Vision 1 (1/12) Higgins & Siegel-s/Perger-a/Djurdjevic-c; Ultron-5 app. 4.00

AVENGERS PRIME (The Heroic Age)
Marvel Comics: Aug, 2010 - No. 5, Mar, 2011 ($3.99, limited series)

1-5-Thor, Iron Man & Steve Rogers; Bendis-s/Davis-a; Enchantress app. 4.00
1-Variant-c by Djurdjevic 8.00

AVENGERS: SOLO
Marvel Comics: Dec, 2011 - No. 5, Apr, 2012 ($3.99, limited series)

1-5-Hawkeye; back-up Avengers Academy 4.00

AVENGERS SPOTLIGHT (Formerly Solo Avengers #1-20)
Marvel Comics: No. 21, Aug, 1989 - No. 40, Jan, 1991 (75¢/$1.00)

21-Byrne-c/a 3.50
22-40: 26-Acts of Vengeance story. 31-34-U.S. Agent series. 36-Heck-i. 37-Mortimer-i. 40-The Black Knight app. 3.00

AVENGERS STRIKEFILE
Marvel Comics: Jan, 1994 ($1.75, one-shot)

1 3.00

AVENGERS: THE CHILDREN'S CRUSADE
Marvel Comics: Sept, 2010 - No. 9, May, 2012 ($3.99, limited series)

1-9-Young Avengers search for Scarlet Witch; Heinberg-s/Cheung-a. 6-9-X-Men app. 4.00
1-4-Variant-c. 1-Jelena Djurdjevic. 2-Travis Charest. 3,4-Art Adams 6.00
... - Young Avengers (5/11, $3.99) Takes place between #4&5; Alan Davis-a/c 4.00

AVENGERS: THE CROSSING
Marvel Comics: July, 1995 ($4.95, one-shot)

1-Deodato-c/a; 1st app. Thor's new costume 5.00

AVENGERS: THE INITIATIVE (See Civil War and related titles)
Marvel Comics: Jun, 2007 - No. 35, Jun, 2010 ($2.99)

1-Caselli-a/Slott-s/Cheung-c; War Machine app. 4.00
2-35: 4,5-World War Hulk. 6-Uy-a. 14-19-Secret Invasion; 3-D Man app. 16-Skrull Kill Krew returns. 20-Tigra pregnancy revealed, 21-25-Ramos-a. 32-35-Siege 3.00
Annual 1 (1/08, $3.99) Secret Invasion tie-in; Cheung-c 4.00
... Featuring Reptil (5/09, $3.99) Gage-s/Uy-a 4.00
... Special 1 (1/09, $3.99) Slott & Gage-s/Uy-a 4.00
...: Vol. 1 - Basic Training HC (2007, $19.99, d.j.) r/#1-6 20.00
...: Vol. 1 - Basic Training SC (2008, $14.99) r/#1-6 15.00

AVENGERS: THE ORIGIN

Avengers United They Stand #4 © MAR

Avenging Spider-Man #1 © MAR

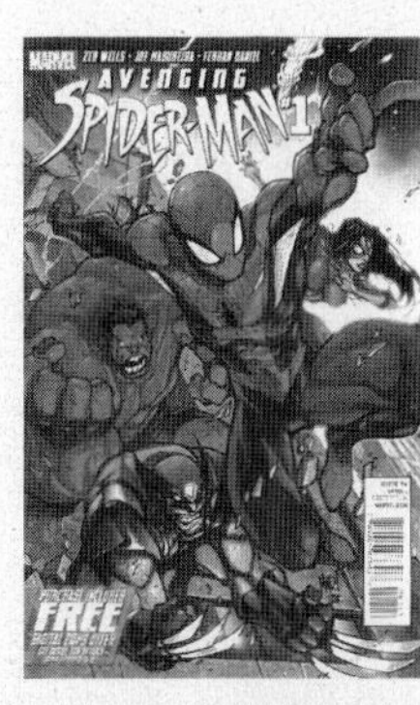

Azrael #60 © DC

GD VG FN VF VF/NM NM-
2.0 4.0 6.0 8.0 9.0 9.2

GD VG FN VF VF/NM NM-
2.0 4.0 6.0 8.0 9.0 9.2

Marvel Comics: Jun, 2010 - No. 5, Oct, 2010 ($3.99, limited series)
1-5-Casey-s/Noto-a/c; team origin (pre-Capt. America) re-told; Loki app. 4.00

AVENGERS: THE TERMINATRIX OBJECTIVE
Marvel Comics: Sept, 1993 - No. 4, Dec, 1993 ($1.25, limited series)
1 ($2.50)-Holo-grafx foil-c 4.00
2-4-Old vs. current Avengers 3.00

AVENGERS: THE ULTRON IMPERATIVE
Marvel Comics: Nov, 2001 ($5.99, one-shot)
1-Follow-up to the Ultron Unlimited ending in Avengers #42; BWS-c 6.00

AVENGERS, THOR & CAPTAIN AMERICA: OFFICIAL INDEX TO THE MARVEL UNIVERSE
Marvel Comics: Jun, 2010 - No. 15, 2001 ($3.99)
1-15-Each issue has chronological synopsies, creator credits, character lists for 30-40 issues of Avengers, Captain America and Journey Into Mystery starting with debuts 4.00

AVENGERS/THUNDERBOLTS
Marvel Comics: May, 2004 - No. 6, Sept, 2004 ($2.99, limited series)
1-6: Busiek & Nicieza-s/Kitson-c. 1,2-Kitson-a. 3-6-Grummett-a 3.00
Vol. 2: Best Intentions (2004, $14.99) r/#1-6 15.00

AVENGERS: TIMESLIDE
Marvel Comics: Feb, 1996 ($4.95, one-shot)
1-Foil-c 5.00

AVENGERS TWO: WONDER MAN & BEAST
Marvel Comics: May, 2000 - No. 3, July, 2000 ($2.99, limited series)
1-3: Stern-s/Bagley-c/a 3.00

AVENGERS/ULTRAFORCE (See Ultraforce/Avengers)
Marvel Comics: Oct, 1995 ($3.95, one-shot)
1-Wraparound foil-c by Pérez 4.00

AVENGERS UNITED THEY STAND
Marvel Comics: Nov, 1999 - No. 7, June, 2000 ($2.99/$1.99)
1-Based on the animated series 4.00
2-6-($1.99) 2-Avengers battle Hydra 3.00
7-($2.99) Devil Dinosaur-c/app.; reprints Avengers Action Figure Comic 4.00

AVENGERS UNIVERSE
Marvel Comics: Jun, 2000 - No. 3, Oct, 2000 ($3.99)
1-3-Reprints recent stories 4.00

AVENGERS UNPLUGGED
Marvel Comics: Oct, 1995 - No. 6, Aug, 1996 (99¢, bi-monthly)
1-6 3.00

AVENGERS VS. ATLAS (Leads into Atlas #1)
Marvel Comics: Mar, 2010 - No. 4, Jun, 2010 ($3.99, limited series)
1-4-Hardman-a; Ramos-c. 1-Back-up w/Miyazawa-a. 2-4-Original Avengers app. 4.00

AVENGERS VS. PET AVENGERS
Marvel Comics: Dec, 2010 - No. 4, Mar, 2011 ($2.99, limited series)
1-4-Eliopoulos-s/Guara-a; Fin Fang Foom app. 3.00

AVENGERS WEST COAST (Formerly West Coast Avengers)
Marvel Comics: No. 48, Sept, 1989 - No. 102, Jan, 1994 ($1.00/$1.25)
48,49: 48-Byrne-c/a & scripts continue thru #57 3.50
50-Re-intro original Human Torch 4.00
51-69,71-74,76-83,85,86,89-99: 54-Cover swipe/F.F. #1. 78-Last $1.00-c. 79-Dr. Strange x-over. 93-95-Darkhawk app. 3.00
70,75,84,87,88: 70-Spider-Woman app. 75 (52 pgs.)-Fantastic Four x-over. 84-Origin Spider-Woman retold; Spider-Man app. (also in #85,86). 87,88-Wolverine-c/story 4.00
100-($3.95, 68 pgs.)-Embossed all red foil-c 4.00
101,102: 101-X-Men x-over 5.00
Annual 5-8 ('90- '93, 68 pgs.)-5,6-West Coast Avengers in indicia. 7-Darkhawk app. 8-Polybagged w/card 4.00
...: Darker Than Scarlet TPB (2008, $24.99) r/#51-57,60-62; Byrne-s/a 25.00
...: Vision Quest TPB (2005, $24.99) r/#42-50; Byrne-s/a 25.00

AVENGERS: X-SANCTION
Marvel Comics: Feb, 2012 - No. 4, May, 2012 ($3.99, limited series)
1-4-Loeb-s/McGuinness-a/c; Cable battles the Avengers. 3,4-Wolverine & Spidey app. 4.00

AVENGING SPIDER-MAN (Spider-Man and Avengers member team-up)
Marvel Comics: Jan, 2012 - Present ($3.99)
1-3-Madureira-a/Wells-s; Madureira-c. 1-3-Red Hulk & Avengers app. 4-Hawkeye app. 4.00
1-Variant-c by Ramos 8.00
1-Variant-c by J. Scott Campbell 8.00

AVIATION ADVENTURES AND MODEL BUILDING (True Aviation Advs. ...No. 15)
Parents' Magazine Institute: No. 16, Dec, 1946 - No. 17, Feb, 1947
16,17-Half comics and half pictures 8 16 24 42 54 65

AVIATION CADETS
Street & Smith Publications: 1943
nn 19 37 57 109 172 235

A-V IN 3-D
Aardvark-Vanaheim: Dec, 1984 ($2.00, 28 pgs. w/glasses)
1-Cerebus, Flaming Carrot, Normalman & Ms. Tree 4.00

AWAKENING, THE
Image Comics: Oct, 1997 - No. 4, Apr, 1998 ($2.95, B&W, limited series)
1-4-Stephen Blue-s/c/a 3.00

AWESOME ADVENTURES
Awesome Entertainment: Aug, 1999 ($2.50)
1-Alan Moore-s/ Steve Skroce-a; Youngblood story 3.00

AWESOME HOLIDAY SPECIAL
Awesome Entertainment: Dec, 1997 ($2.50, one-shot)
1-Flip book w/covers of Fighting American & Coven. Holiday stories also featuring Kaboom and Shaft by regular creators. 3.00
1-Gold Edition 5.00

AWFUL OSCAR (Formerly & becomes Oscar Comics with No. 13)
Marvel Comics: No. 11, June, 1949 - No. 12, Aug, 1949
11,12 14 28 42 81 118 155

AWKWARD UNIVERSE
Slave Labor Graphics: 12/95 ($9.95, graphic novel)
nn 10.00

AXA
Eclipse Comics: Apr, 1987 - No. 2, Aug, 1987 ($1.75)
1,2 3.00

AXE COP: BAD GUY EARTH
Dark Horse Comics: Mar, 2011 - No. 3, May, 2011 ($3.50, limited series)
1-3-Malachai Nicolle-s/Ethan Nicolle-a 3.50

AXEL PRESSBUTTON (Pressbutton No. 5; see Laser Eraser &...)
Eclipse Comics: Nov, 1984 - No. 6, July, 1985 ($1.50/$1.75, Baxter paper)
1-6: Reprints Warrior (British mag.). 1-Bolland-c; origin Laser Eraser & Pressbutton 3.00

AXIS ALPHA
Axis Comics: Feb, 1994 ($2.50, one-shot)
V1-Previews Axis titles including, Tribe, Dethgrip, B.E.A.S.T.I.E.S. & more; Pitt app. in Tribe story. 3.00

AZRAEL (...Agent of the Bat #47 on)(Also see Batman: Sword of Azrael)
DC Comics: Feb, 1995 - No. 100, May, 2003 ($1.95/$2.25/$2.50/$2.95)
1-Dennis O'Neil scripts begin 5.00
2,3 3.50
4-46,48-62: 5,6-Ras Al Ghul app. 13-Nightwing-c/app. 15-Contagion Pt. 5 (Pt. 4 on-c). 16-Contagion Pt. 10. 22-Batman-c/app. 23,27-Batman app. 27,28-Joker app. 35-Hitman app. 36-39-Batman, Bane app. 50-New costume. 53-Joker-c/app. 56,57,60-New Batgirl app. 3.00
47-($3.95) Flip book with Batman: Shadow of the Bat #80 4.00
63-74,76-92: 63-Huntress-c/app.; Azrael returns to old costume. 67-Begin $2.50-c. 70-79-Harris-c. 83-Joker x-over. 91-Bruce Wayne: Fugitive pt. 15 3.00
75-($3.95) New costume; Harris-c 4.00
93-100: 93-Begin $2.95-c. 95,96-Two-Face app. 100-Last issue; Zeck-c 3.00
#1,000,000 (11/98) Giarrano-a 3.00
Annual 1 (1995, $3.95)-Year One story 4.00
Annual 2 (1996, $2.95)-Legends of the Dead Earth story 4.00
Annual 3 (1997, $3.95)-Pulp Heroes story; Orbik-c 4.00
.../Ash (1997, $4.95) O'Neil-s/Quesada, Palmiotti-a 5.00
Plus (12/96, $2.95)-Question-c/app. 4.00

AZRAEL
DC Comics: Dec, 2009 - No. 18, May, 2011 ($2.99)
1-18: 1-9-Nicieza-s/Bachs-a. 1-Covers by Jock & Irving. 2,3-Jock-c. 5-Ragman app. 3.00
...: Angel in the Dark TPB (2010, $17.99) r/#1-6; cover gallery 18.00

AZRAEL: DEATH'S DARK KNIGHT
DC Comics: May, 2009 - No. 3, Jul, 2009 ($2.99, limited series)

Babe #2 © PRIZE

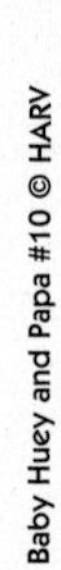
Baby Huey and Papa #10 © HARV

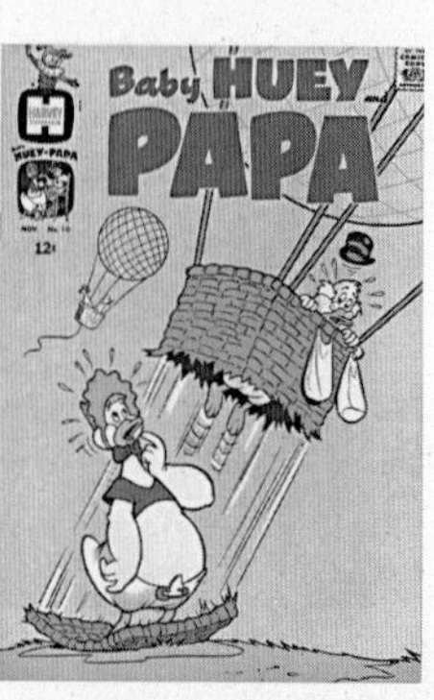

Backlash #7 © WSP

GD 2.0 | VG 4.0 | FN 6.0 | VF 8.0 | VF/NM 9.0 | NM- 9.2

1-Battle For the Cowl tie-in; Nicieza-s/Irving-a/March-c 3.00
TPB (2010, $14.99) r/#1-3, Batman Annual #27 and Detective Annual #11 15.00

AZTEC ACE
Eclipse Comics: Mar, 1984 - No. 15, Sept, 1985 ($2.25/$1.50/$1.75, Baxter paper)

1-$2.25-c (52 pgs.) 4.00
2-15: 2-Begin 36 pgs. 3.00
NOTE: *N. Redondo a-1i-8i, 10i. c-6-8i.*

AZTEK: THE ULTIMATE MAN
DC Comics: Aug, 1996 - No. 10, May 1997 ($1.75)

1-1st app. Aztek & Synth; Grant Morrison & Mark Millar scripts in all 6.00
2-9: 2-Green Lantern app. 3-1st app. Death-Doll. 4-Intro The Lizard King. 5-Origin. 6-Joker app.; Batman cameo. 7-Batman app. 8-Luthor app. 9-vs. Parasite-c/app. 4.00
10-JLA-c/app. 1 2 4 6 8 10
JLA Presents: Aztek the Ultimate Man TPB (2008, $19.99) r/#1-10 20.00
NOTE: *Breyfogle c-5p. N. Steven Harris a-1-5p. Porter c-1p. Wieringo c-2p.*

BABE (...Darling of the Hills, later issues)(See Big Shot and Sparky Watts)
Prize/Headline/Feature: June-July, 1948 - No. 11, Apr-May, 1950

1-Boody Rogers-a 29 58 87 170 278 385
2-Boody Rogers-a 17 34 51 98 154 210
3-11-All by Boody Rogers 15 30 45 86 133 180

BABE
Dark Horse Comics (Legend): July, 1994 - No. 4, Jan, 1994 ($2.50, lim. series)

1-4: John Byrne-c/a/scripts; ProtoTykes back-up story 3.00

BABE RUTH SPORTS COMICS (Becomes Rags Rabbit #11 on?)
Harvey Publications: April, 1949 - No. 11, Feb, 1951

1-Powell-a 40 80 120 246 411 575
2-Powell-a 27 54 81 158 259 360
3-11: Powell-a in most 22 44 66 130 213 295
NOTE: *Baseball c-2-4, 9. Basketball c-1, 6. Football c-5. Yogi Berra c/story-8. Joe DiMaggio c/story-3. Bob Feller c/story-4. Stan Musial c-9.*

BABES IN TOYLAND (Disney, Movie) (See Golden Pix Story Book ST-3)
Dell Publishing Co.: No. 1282, Feb-Apr, 1962

Four Color 1282-Annette Funicello photo-c 12 24 36 84 175 265

BABES OF BROADWAY
Broadway Comics: May, 1996 ($2.95, one-shot)

1-Pin-ups of Broadway Comics' female characters; Alan Davis, Michael Kaluta, J. G. Jones, Alan Weiss, Guy Davis & others-a; Giordano-c. 3.00

BABE 2
Dark Horse Comics (Legend): Mar, 1995 - No. 2, May, 1995 ($2.50, lim. series)

1,2: John Byrne-c/a/scripts 3.00

BABY HUEY
Harvey Comics: No. 1, Oct, 1991 - No. 9, June, 1994 ($1.00/$1.25/$1.50, quarterly)

1 ($1.00): 1-Cover says "Big Baby Huey" 5.00
2-9 ($1.25-$1.50) 3.00

BABY HUEY AND PAPA (See Paramount Animated...)
Harvey Publications: May, 1962 - No. 33, Jan, 1968 (Also see Casper The Friendly Ghost)

1 13 26 39 88 189 290
2 8 16 24 56 96 135
3-5 6 12 18 37 59 80
6-10 3 6 9 21 32 42
11-20 3 6 9 16 22 28
21-33 2 4 6 13 18 22

BABY HUEY DIGEST
Harvey Publications: June, 1992 (Digest-size, one-shot)

1-Reprints 1 3 4 6 8 10

BABY HUEY DUCKLAND
Harvey Publications: Nov, 1962 - No. 15, Nov, 1966 (25¢ Giants, 68 pgs.)

1 11 22 33 73 142 210
2-5 6 12 18 39 62 85
6-15 4 8 12 22 34 45

BABY HUEY, THE BABY GIANT (Also see Big Baby Huey, Casper, Harvey Hits #22, Harvey Comics Hits #60, & Paramount Animated Comics)
Harvey Publ: 9/56 - #97, 10/71; #98, 10/72; #99, 10/80; #100, 10/90; #101, 11/90

1-Infinity-c 46 92 138 373 812 1250
2 22 44 66 154 327 500
3-Baby Huey takes anti-pep pills 13 26 39 90 195 300
4,5 10 20 30 68 127 185
6-10 7 14 21 46 76 105
11-20 5 10 15 35 55 75
21-40 4 8 12 24 37 50
41-60 3 6 9 16 23 30
61-79 (12/67) 2 4 6 13 18 22
80(12/68) - 95-All 68 pg. Giants 3 6 9 17 25 32
96,97-Both 52 pg. Giants 3 6 9 14 19 24
98-Regular size 2 4 6 9 12 15
99-Regular size 1 2 3 5 6 8
100,101 ($1.00) 4.00

BABYLON 5 (TV)
DC Comics: Jan, 1995 - No. 11, Dec, 1995 ($1.95/$2.50)

1 2 4 6 8 11 14
2-5 1 2 3 5 7 9
6-11: 7-Begin $2.50-c 1 2 3 4 5 7
... The Price of Peace (1998, $9.95, TPB) r/#1-4,11 10.00

BABYLON 5: IN VALEN'S NAME
DC Comics: Mar, 1998 - No. 3, May, 1998 ($2.50, limited series)

1-3 4.00

BABY SNOOTS (Also see March of Comics #359,371,396,401,419,431,443,450,462,474,485)
Gold Key: Aug, 1970 - No. 22, Nov, 1975

1 3 6 9 20 30 40
2-11 2 4 6 11 16 20
12-22: 22-Titled Snoots, the Forgetful Elefink 2 4 6 8 10 12

BACCHUS (Also see Eddie Campbell's ...)
Harrier Comics (New Wave): 1988 - No. 2, Aug, 1988 ($1.95, B&W)

1,2: Eddie Campbell-c/a/scripts. 3.00

BACHELOR FATHER (TV)
Dell Publishing Co.: No. 1332, 4-6/62 - No. 2, Sept.-Nov., 1962

Four Color 1332 (#1), 2-Written by Stanley 7 14 21 49 82 115

BACHELOR'S DIARY
Avon Periodicals: 1949 (15¢)

1(Scarce)-King Features panel cartoons & text-r; pin-up, girl wrestling photos; similar to Sideshow 90 180 270 576 988 1400

BACK DOWN THE LINE
Eclipse Books: 1991 (Mature adults, 8-1/2 x 11", 52 pgs.)

nn (Soft-c, $8.95)-Bolton-c/a 9.00
nn (Limited Hard-c, $29.95) 30.00

BACKLASH (Also see The Kindred)
Image Comics (WildStorm Prod.): Nov,1994 - No. 32, May, 1997 ($1.95/$2.50)

1-Double-c; variant-double-c 4.00
2-7,9-32: 5-Intro Mindscape; 2 pinups. 19-Fire From Heaven Pt 2. 20-Fire From Heaven Pt 10. 31-WildC.A.T.S app. 3.00
8-($1.95, newsstand)-Wildstorm Rising Pt. 8 3.00
8-($2.50, direct market)-Wildstorm Rising Pt. 8 3.00
25-($3.95)-Double-size 4.00
...& Taboo's African Holiday (9/99, $5.95) Booth-s/a(p) 6.00

BACKLASH/SPIDER-MAN
Image Comics (WildStorm Productions): Aug, 1996 - No. 2, Sept, 1996 ($2.50, lim. series)

1,2: Pike (villain from WildC.A.T.S) & Venom app. 3.00

BACKPACK MARVELS (B&W backpack-sized reprint collections)
Marvel Comics: Nov, 2000 ($6.95, B&W, digest-size)

Avengers 1 -r/Avengers #181-189; profile pages 7.00
Spider-Man 1-r/ASM #234-240 7.00
X-Men 1-r/Uncanny X-Men #167-173 7.00
X-Men 2-r/Uncanny X-Men #174-179; new painted-c by Greg Horn 7.00

BACK TO THE FUTURE (Movie, TV cartoon)
Harvey Comics: Nov, 1991 - No. 4, June, 1992 ($1.25)

1-4: 1,2-Gil Kane-c; based on animated cartoon 3.00

BACK TO THE FUTURE: FORWARD TO THE FUTURE
Harvey Comics: Oct, 1992 - No. 3, Feb, 1993 ($1.50, limited series)

1-3 3.00

BAD BOY
Oni Press: Dec, 1997 ($4.95, one-shot)

1-Frank Miller-s/Simon Bisley-a/painted-c 5.00

Bad Planet #1 © Raw Studios

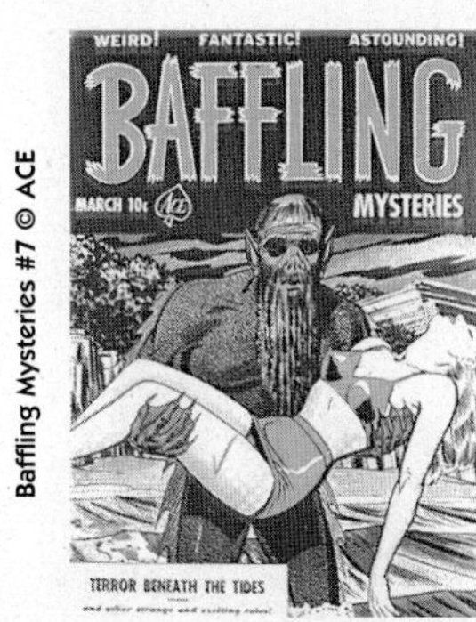

Baffling Mysteries #7 © ACE

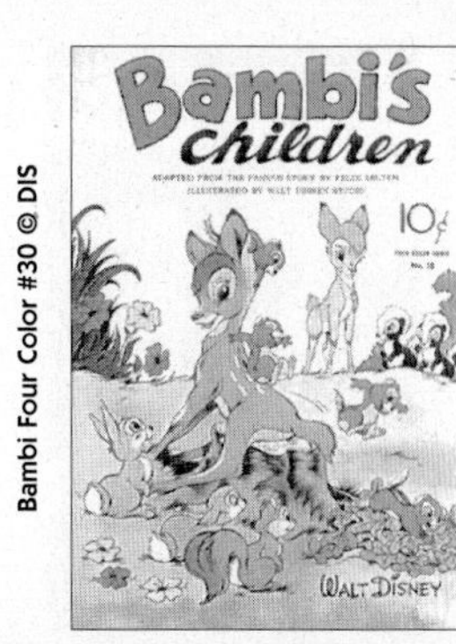

Bambi Four Color #30 © DIS

GD VG FN VF VF/NM NM-
2.0 4.0 6.0 8.0 9.0 9.2

BAD COMPANY
Quality Comics/Fleetway Quality #15 on: Aug, 1988 - No. 19?, 1990 ($1.50/$1.75, high quality paper)
1-19: 5,6-Guice-c 3.00

BADGE OF JUSTICE (Formerly Crime And Justice #21)
Charlton Comics: No. 22, Jan, 1955; No. 2, Apr, 1955 - No. 4, Oct, 1955
22(#1)-Giordano-c 10 20 30 58 79 100
2-4 7 14 21 35 43 50

BADGER, THE
Capital Comics(#1-4)/First Comics: Dec, 1983 - No. 70, Apr, 1991; V2#1, Spring, 1991
1 5.00
2-70: 52-54-Tim Vigil-c/a 3.00
50-($3.95, 52 pgs.) 4.00
V2#1 (Spring, 1991, $4.95) 5.00

BADGER, THE
Image Comics: V3#78, May, 1997 - V3#88 ($2.95, B&W)
78-Cover lists #1, Baron-s 3.00
79/#2, 80/#3, 81(indicia lists #80)/#4,82-88/#5-11 3.00

BADGER GOES BERSERK
First Comics: Sept, 1989 - No. 4, Dec, 1989 ($1.95, lim. series, Baxter paper)
1-4: 2-Paul Chadwick-c/a(2pgs.) 3.00

BADGER: SHATTERED MIRROR
Dark Horse Comics: July, 1994 - No. Oct, 1994 ($2.50, limited series)
1-4 3.00

BADGER: ZEN POP FUNNY-ANIMAL VERSION
Dark Horse Comics: July, 1994 - No. 2, Aug, 1994 ($2.50, limited series)
1,2 3.00

BAD GIRLS
DC Comics: Oct, 2003 - No. 5, Feb, 2004 ($2.50, limited series)
1-5-Steve Vance-s/Jennifer Graves-a/Darwyn Cooke-c 3.00
TPB (2009, $14.99) r/#1-5; Graves sketch pages 15.00

BAD IDEAS
Image Comics: Apr, 2004 - No. 2, July, 2004 ($5.95, B&W, limited series)
1,2-Chinsang-s/Mahfood & Crosland-a 6.00
..., Vol. 1: Collected! (2005, $12.99) r/#1,2 13.00

BADLANDS
Vortex Comics: May, 1990 ($3.00, glossy stock, mature)
1-Chaykin-c 3.00

BADLANDS
Dark Horse Comics: July, 1991 - No. 6, Dec, 1991 ($2.25, B&W, limited series)
1-6: 1-John F. Kennedy-c; reprints Vortex Comics issue 3.00

BADMEN OF THE WEST
Avon Periodicals: 1951 (Giant) (132 pgs., painted-c)
1-Contains rebound copies of Jesse James, King of the Bad Men of Deadwood, Badmen of Tombstone; other combinations possible.
Issues with Kubert-a... 40 80 120 244 405 565

BADMEN OF THE WEST! (See A-1 Comics)
Magazine Enterprises: 1953 - No. 3, 1954
1 (A-1 100)-Meskin-a? 22 44 66 132 216 300
2 (A-1 120), 3: 2-Larsen-a 15 30 45 85 130 175

BADMEN OF TOMBSTONE
Avon Periodicals: 1950
nn 15 30 45 94 147 200

BAD PLANET
Image Comics (Raw Studios): Dec, 2005 - No. 6, Nov, 2008 ($2.99)
1-6: 1-Thomas Jane & Steve Niles-s/Larosa & Bradstreet-a/c. 2-Wrightson-c. 3-3-D pages 3.00

BADROCK (Also see Youngblood)
Image Comics (Extreme Studios): Mar, 1995 - No. 2, Jan, 1996 ($1.75/$2.50)
1-Variant-c (3) 3.50
2-Liefeld-c/a & story; Savage Dragon app, flipbook w/Grifter/Badrock #2; variant-c exist 3.00
Annual 1(1995,$2.95)-Arthur Adams-c 4.00
Annual 1 Commemorative ($9.95)-3,000 printed 10.00
.../Wolverine (6/96, $4.95, squarebound)-Sauron app; pin-ups; variant-c exists 5.00
.../Wolverine (6/96)-Special Comicon Edition 5.00

BADROCK AND COMPANY (Also see Youngblood)
Image Comics (Extreme Studios): Sept, 1994 - No.6, Feb, 1995 ($2.50)
1-6 : 6-Indicia reads "October 1994"; story cont'd in Shadowhawk #17 3.00

BAFFLING MYSTERIES (Formerly Indian Braves No. 1-4; Heroes of the Wild Frontier No. 26-on)
Periodical House (Ace Magazines): No. 5, Nov, 1951 - No. 26, Oct, 1955
5 40 80 120 246 411 575
6-19,21-24: 8-Woodish-a by Cameron. 10-E.C. Crypt Keeper swipe on-c.
24-Last pre-code issue 26 52 78 154 252 350
20-Classic bondage-c 36 72 108 211 343 475
25-Reprints; surrealistic-c 19 38 57 111 176 240
26-Reprints 17 34 51 100 158 215
NOTE: ***Cameron** a-8, 10, 16-18, 20-22. **Colan** a-5, 11, 25r/5. **Sekowsky** a-5, 6, 22. Bondage c-20, 23. Reprints in 18(1), 19(1), 24(3).*

BALBO (See Master Comics #33 & Mighty Midget Comics)

BALDER THE BRAVE
Marvel Comics Group: Nov, 1985 - No. 4, 1986 (Limited series)
1-4: Simonson-c/a; character from Thor 3.00

BALLAD OF HALO JONES, THE
Quality Comics: Sept, 1987 - No. 12, Aug, 1988 ($1.25/$1.50)
1-12: Alan Moore scripts in all 3.00

BALL AND CHAIN
DC Comics (Homage): Nov, 1999 - No. 4, Feb, 2000 ($2.50, limited series)
1-4-Lobdell-s/Garza-a 3.00

BALLISTIC (Also See Cyberforce)
Image Comics (Top Cow Productions): Sept, 1995 - No. 3, Dec, 1995 ($2.50, limited series)
1-3: Wetworks app, Turner-c/a 3.00
... Action (5/96, $2.95) Pin-ups of Top Cow characters participating in outdoor sports 3.00
... Imagery (1/96, $2.50, anthology) Cyberforce app. 3.00
.../ Wolverine (2/97, $2.95) Devil's Reign pt. 4; Witchblade cameo (1 page) 4.00

BALOO & LITTLE BRITCHES (Disney)
Gold Key: Apr, 1968
1-From the Jungle Book 4 8 12 24 37 50

BALTIMORE: THE CURSE BELLS
Dark Horse Comics: Aug, 2011 - No. 5, Dec, 2011 ($3.50, limited series)
1-5-Mignola-s/c; Stenbeck-a. 1-Variant-c by Francavilla 3.50

BALTIMORE: THE PLAGUE SHIPS
Dark Horse Comics: Aug, 2010 - No. 5, Dec, 2010 ($3.50, limited series)
1-5-Mignola-s/c; Stenbeck-a; Lord Baltimore hunting vampires in 1916 Europe 3.50

BAMBI (Disney) (See Movie Classics, Movie Comics, and Walt Disney Showcase No. 31)
Dell Publishing Co.: No. 12, 1942; No. 30, 1943; No. 186, Apr, 1948; 1984
Four Color 12-Walt Disney's... 46 92 138 354 770 1185
Four Color 30-Bambi's Children (1943) 41 82 123 311 673 1035
Four Color 186-Walt Disney's...; reprinted as Movie Classic Bambi #3 (1956)
14 28 42 97 211 325
1-(Whitman, 1984; 60¢)-r/Four Color #186 (3-pack) 2 4 6 10 14 18

BAMBI (Disney)
Grosset & Dunlap: 1942 (50¢, 7"x8-1/2", 32pg, hard-c w/dust jacket)
nn-Given away w/a copy of Thumper for a $2.00, 2-yr. subscription to WDC&S
in 1942 (Xmas offer). Book only 22 44 66 132 216 300
w/dust jacket 39 78 117 240 395 550

BAMM BAMM & PEBBLES FLINTSTONE (TV)
Gold Key: Oct, 1964 (Hanna-Barbera)
1 9 18 27 58 99 140

BANANA SPLITS, THE (TV) (See Golden Comics Digest & March of Comics No. 364)
Gold Key: June, 1969 - No. 8, Oct, 1971 (Hanna-Barbera)
1-Photo-c on all 9 18 27 63 112 160
2-8 6 12 18 39 62 85

BANANA SUNDAY
Oni Press: July, 2005 - No. 4, Oct, 2005 ($2.99, B&W, limited series)
1-4-Root Nibot-s/Colleen Coover-a 3.00
TPB (3/06, $11.95) r/#1-4; sketch gallery 12.00

BAND WAGON (See Hanna-Barbera Band Wagon)

BANG! TANGO
DC Comics (Vertigo): Apr, 2009 - No. 6, Sept, 2009 ($2.99, limited series)

Barbie #16 © Mattel

The Barker #7 © QUA

Baseball Comics #1 © Will Eisner

	GD 2.0	VG 4.0	FN 6.0	VF 8.0	VF/NM 9.0	NM- 9.2

1-6-Kelly-s/Sibar-a/Chaykin-c 3.00

BANG-UP COMICS
Progressive Publishers: Dec, 1941 - No. 3, June, 1942

1-Cosmo Mann & Lady Fairplay begin; Buzz Balmer by Rick Yager in all (origin #1)
98 196 294 622 1074 1525
2,3 48 96 144 302 514 725

BANISHED KNIGHTS (See Warlands)
Image Comics: Dec, 2001 - No. 4, June, 2002 ($2.95)

1-4-Two covers (Alvin Lee, Pat Lee) 3.00

BANNER COMICS (Becomes Captain Courageous No. 6)
Ace Magazines: No. 3, Sept, 1941 - No. 5, Jan, 1942

3-Captain Courageous (1st app.) & Lone Warrior & Sidekick Dicky begin;
Jim Mooney-c 111 222 333 705 1215 1725
4,5: 4-Flag-c 69 138 207 442 759 1075

BARACK OBAMA (See Presidential Material: Barack Obama, Amazing Spider-Man #583, Savage Dragon #137)

BARACK THE BARBARIAN
Devil's Due Publishing: Jun, 2009 - No. 4, Oct, 2009 ($3.50/$3.99, limited series)

...Quest For The Treasure of Stimuli 1-3-($3.50) Conan spoof with Barack Obama; Hama-s 3.50
...Quest For The Treasure of Stimuli 4-($3.99) 4.00
...: The Red of Red Sarah 1 ($5.99, B&W) Sarah Palin satire; Hama-s 6.00

BARBARIANS, THE
Atlas Comics/Seaboard Periodicals: June, 1975

1-Origin, only app. Andrax; Iron Jaw app.; Marcos-a 2 4 6 11 16 20

BARBIE
Marvel Comics: Jan, 1991 - No. 63, Mar, 1996 ($1.00/$1.25/$1.50)

1-Polybagged w/doorknob hanger; Romita-c 2 4 6 9 12 15
2-49,51-62 1 2 3 5 7 9
50,63: 50-(Giant). 63-Last issue 2 4 6 8 10 12
... And Baby Sister Kelly (1995, 99¢-c, part of a Marvel 4-pack) scarce
3 6 9 14 20 25

BARBIE & KEN
Dell Publishing Co.: May-July, 1962 - No. 5, Nov-Jan, 1963-64

01-053-207(#1)-Based on Mattel toy dolls 36 72 108 261 561 860
2-4 27 54 81 189 407 625
5 (Last issue) 27 54 81 196 423 650

BARBIE FASHION
Marvel Comics: Jan, 1991 - No. 53, May, 1995 ($1.00/$1.25/$1.50)

1-Polybagged w/Barbie Pink Card 2 4 6 9 12 15
2-49,51,52: 4-Contains preview to Sweet XVI 1 2 3 5 7 9
50,53: 50-(Giant). 53-Last issue 2 4 6 8 10 12

BARB WIRE (See Comics' Greatest World)
Dark Horse Comics: Apr, 1994 - No. 9, Feb, 1995 ($2.00/$2.50)

1-9: 1-Foil logo 3.00
Trade paperback (1996, $8.95)-r/#2,3,5,6 w/Pamela Anderson bio 9.00

BARB WIRE: ACE OF SPADES
Dark Horse Comics: May, 1996 - No. 4, Sept, 1996 ($2.95, limited series)

1-4: Chris Warner-c/a(p)/scripts; Tim Bradstreet-c/a(i) in all 3.00

BARB WIRE COMICS MAGAZINE SPECIAL
Dark Horse Comics: May, 1996 ($3.50, B&W, magazine, one-shot)

nn-Adaptation of film; photo-c; poster insert. 3.50

BARB WIRE MOVIE SPECIAL
Dark Horse Comics: May, 1996 ($3.95, one-shot)

nn-Adaptation of film; photo-c; 1st app. new look 4.00

BARKER, THE (Also see National Comics #42)
Quality Comics Group/Comic Magazine: Autumn, 1946 - No. 15, Dec, 1949

1 24 48 72 142 234 325
2 14 28 42 82 121 160
3-10 12 24 36 67 94 120
11-14 10 20 30 54 72 90
15-Jack Cole-a(p) 10 20 30 56 76 95
NOTE: ***Jack Cole** art in some issues.*

BARNABY
Civil Service Publications Inc.: 1945 (25¢,102 pgs., digest size)

V1#1-r/Crocket Johnson strips from 1942 5 10 14 20 24 28

BARNEY AND BETTY RUBBLE (TV) (Flintstones' Neighbors)
Charlton Comics: Jan, 1973 - No. 23, Dec, 1976 (Hanna-Barbera)

1 4 8 12 24 37 50
2-11: 11(2/75)-1st Mike Zeck-a (illos) 3 6 9 14 20 25
12-23: 17-Columbo parody 2 4 6 10 14 18
Digest Annual (1972, B&W, 100 pgs.) (scarce) 4 8 12 26 41 55

BARNEY BAXTER (Also see Magic Comics)
David McKay/Dell Publishing Co./Argo: 1938 - No. 2, 1956

Feature Books 15(McKay-1938) 40 80 120 246 411 575
Four Color 20(1942) 23 46 69 161 343 525
1,2 (1956-Argo) 9 18 27 50 65 80

BARNEY BEAR ...
Spire Christian Comics (Fleming H. Revell Co.): 1977-1982

...Home Plate nn-(1979, 49¢), ...In Toyland nn-(1982, 49¢),...Lost and Found nn-(1979, 49¢), Out of The Woods nn-(1980, 49¢), Sunday School Picnic nn-(1981, 69¢), The Swamp Gang!-(1977, 39¢) 2 4 6 9 13 16

BARNEY GOOGLE & SNUFFY SMITH
Dell Publishing Co./Gold Key: 1942 - 1943; April, 1964

Four Color 19(1942) 47 94 141 296 498 700
Four Color 40(1944) 19 38 57 128 277 425
Large Feature Comic 11(1943) 38 76 114 225 368 510
1(10113-404)-Gold Key (4/64) 4 8 12 26 41 55

BARNEY GOOGLE & SNUFFY SMITH
Toby Press: June, 1951 - No. 4, Feb, 1952 (Reprints)

1 14 28 42 76 108 140
2,3 8 16 24 44 57 70
4-Kurtzman-a "Pot Shot Pete", 5 pgs.; reprints John Wayne #5
12 24 36 69 97 125

BARNEY GOOGLE AND SNUFFY SMITH
Charlton Comics: Mar, 1970 - No. 6, Jan, 1971

1 3 6 9 17 25 32
2-6 2 4 6 11 16 20

BARNUM!
DC Comics (Vertigo): 2003; 2005 ($29.95, $19.95)

Hardcover (2003, $29.95, with dust jacket)-Chaykin & Tischman-s/Henrichon-a 30.00
Softcover (2005, $19.95)-Chaykin & Tischman-s/Henrichon-a 20.00

BARNYARD COMICS (Dizzy Duck No. 32 on)
Nedor/Polo Mag./Standard(Animated Cartoons): June, 1944 - No. 31, Sept, 1950; No. 10, 1957

1 (nn, 52 pgs.)-Funny animal 20 40 60 120 195 270
2 (52 pgs.) 13 26 39 74 105 135
3-5 10 20 30 54 72 90
6-12,16 9 18 27 47 61 75
13-15,17,21,23,26,27,29-All contain Frazetta text illos
10 20 30 56 76 95
18-20,22,24,25-All contain Frazetta-a & text illos 13 26 39 72 101 130
28,30,31 8 16 24 40 50 60
10 (1957)(Exist?) 4 7 10 14 17 20

BARRY M. GOLDWATER
Dell Publishing Co.: Mar, 1965 (Complete life story)

12-055-503-Photo-c 4 8 12 24 37 50

BARRY WINDSOR-SMITH: STORYTELLER
Dark Horse Comics: Oct, 1996 - No. 9, July, 1997 ($4.95, oversize)

1-9: 1-Intro Young Gods, Paradox Man & the Freebooters; Barry Smith-c/a/scripts 5.00
Preview 4.00

BAR SINISTER (Also see Shaman's Tears)
Acclaim Comics (Windjammer): Jun, 1995 - No. 4, Sept, 1995 ($2.50, lim. series)

1-4: Mike Grell-c/a/scripts 3.00

BARTMAN (Also see Simpsons Comics & Radioactive Man)
Bongo Comics: 1993 - No. 6, 1994 ($1.95/$2.25)

1-($2.95)-Foil-c; bound-in jumbo Bartman poster 6.00
2-6: 3-w/trading card 4.00

BART SIMPSON (See Simpsons Comics Presents Bart Simpson)

BASEBALL COMICS
Will Eisner Productions: Spring, 1949 (Reprinted later as a Spirit section)

1-Will Eisner-c/a 70 140 210 445 765 1085

Basil #2 © STJ

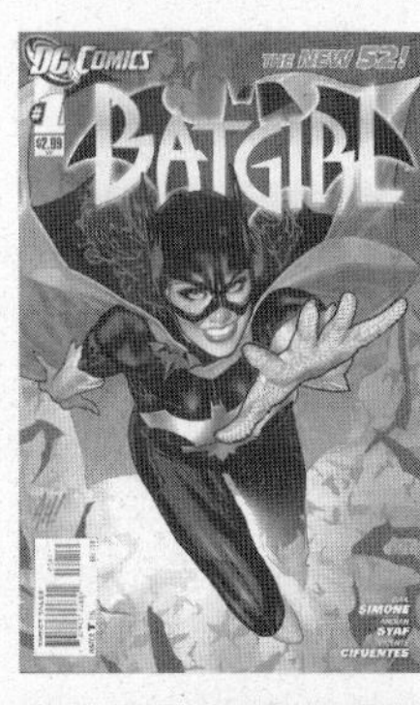

Batgirl (2011 series) #1 © DC

Batman #1 © DC

GD VG FN VF VF/NM NM-
2.0 4.0 6.0 8.0 9.0 9.2

BASEBALL COMICS
Kitchen Sink Press: 1991 ($3.95, coated stock)
1-r/1949 ish. by Eisner; contains trading cards 6.00

BASEBALL HEROES
Fawcett Publications: 1952 (one-shot)
nn (Scarce)-Babe Ruth photo-c; baseball's Hall of Fame biographies
83 166 249 527 906 1285

BASEBALL'S GREATEST HEROES
Magnum Comics: Dec, 1991 - No. 2, May, 1992 ($1.75)
1-Mickey Mantle #1; photo-c; Sinnott-a(p) 5.00
2-Brooks Robinson #1; photo-c; Sinnott-a(i) 4.00

BASEBALL THRILLS
Ziff-Davis Publ. Co.: No. 10, Sum, 1951 - No. 3, Sum, 1952 (Saunders painted-c No.1,2)
10(#1)-Bob Feller, Musial, Newcombe & Boudreau stories
44 88 132 277 469 660
2-Powell-a(2)(Late Sum, '51); Feller, Berra & Mathewson stories
32 64 96 188 307 425
3-Kinstler-c/a; Joe DiMaggio story 32 64 96 188 307 425

BASEBALL THRILLS 3-D
The 3-D Zone: May, 1990 ($2.95, w/glasses)
1-New L.B. Cole-c; life stories of Ty Cobb & Ted Williams 6.00

BASICALLY STRANGE (Magazine)
John C. Comics (Archie Comics Group): Dec, 1982 ($1.95, B&W)
1-(21,000 printed; all but 1,000 destroyed; pgs. out of sequence)
3 6 9 16 23 30
1-Wood, Toth-a; Corben-c; reprints & new art 2 4 6 13 18 22

BASIC HISTORY OF AMERICA ILLUSTRATED
Pendulum Press: 1976 (B&W) (Soft-c $1.50; Hard-c $4.50)
07-1999-America Becomes a World Power 1890-1920. 07-2251-The Industrial Era 1865-1915. 07-226x-Before the Civil War 1830-1860. 07-2278-Americans Move Westward 1800-1850. 07-2286-The Civil War 1850-1876; Redondo-a. 07-2294-The Fight for Freedom 1750-1783. 07-2308-The New World 1500-1750. 07-2316-Problems of the New Nation 1800-1830. 07-2324-Roaring Twenties and the Great Depression 1920-1940. 07-2332-The United States Emerges 1783-1800. 07-2340-America Today 1945-1976. 07-2359-World War II 1940-1945
Softcover editions each 1 2 3 4 5 7
Hardcover editions each 14.00

BASIL (...the Royal Cat)
St. John Publishing Co.: Jan, 1953 - No. 4, Sept, 1953
1-Funny animal 7 14 21 37 46 55
2-4 5 10 15 22 26 30
I.W. Reprint 1 2 4 6 9 12 15

BASIL WOLVERTON'S FANTASTIC FABLES
Dark Horse Comics: Oct, 1993 - No. 2, Dec, 1993 ($2.50, B&W, limited series)
1,2-Wolverton-c/a(r) 6.00

BASIL WOLVERTON'S GATEWAY TO HORROR
Dark Horse Comics: June, 1988 ($1.75, B&W, one-shot)
1-Wolverton-r 6.00

BASIL WOLVERTON'S PLANET OF TERROR
Dark Horse Comics: Oct, 1987 ($1.75, B&W, one-shot)
1-Wolverton-r; Alan Moore-c 6.00

BASTARD SAMURAI
Image Comics: Apr, 2002 - No. 3, Aug, 2002 ($2.95)
1-3-Oeming & Gunter-s; Shannon-a/Oeming-i 3.00
TPB (2003, $12.95) r/#1-3; plus sketch pages and pin-ups 13.00

BATGIRL (See Batman: No Man's Land stories)
DC Comics: Apr, 2000 - No. 73, Apr, 2006 ($2.50)
1-Scott & Campanella-a 6.00
1-(2nd printing) 3.00
2-10: 8-Lady Shiva app. 4.50
11-24: 12-"Officer Down" x-over. 15-Joker-c/app. 24-Bruce Wayne: Murderer pt. 2. 4.00
25-($3.25) Batgirl vs Lady Shiva 4.50
26-29: 27- Bruce Wayne: Fugitive pt. 5; Noto-a. 29-B.W.:F. pt. 13 3.50
30-49,51-73: 30-32-Connor Hawke app. 39-Intro. Black Wind. 41-Superboy-c/app. 53-Robin (Spoiler) app. 54-Bagged with Sky Captain CD. 55-57-War Games. 63,64-Deathstroke app. 67-Birds of Prey app. 73-Lady Shiva origin; Sale-c 3.00
50-($3.25) Batgirl vs Batman 4.00
Annual 1 ('00, $3.50) Planet DC; intro. Aruna 5.00
...: A Knight Alone (2001, $12.95, TPB) r/#7-11,13,14 13.00
...: Death Wish (2003, $14.95, TPB) r/#17-20,22,23,25 & Secret Files and Origins #1 15.00
...: Destruction's Daughter (2006, $19.99, TPB) r/#65-73 20.00
...: Fists of Fury (2004, $14.95, TPB) r/#15,16,21,26-28 15.00
...: Kicking Assassins (2005, $14.99, TPB) r/#60-64 15.00
... Secret Files and Origins (8/02, $4.95) origin-s Noto-a; profile pages and pin-ups 5.00
...: Silent Running (2001, $12.95, TPB) r/#1-6 13.00

BATGIRL (Cassandra Cain)
DC Comics: Sept, 2008 - No. 6, Feb, 2009 ($2.99)
1-6-Beechen-s/Calafiore-a 3.00

BATGIRL (Spoiler/Stephanie Brown)(Batman: Reborn)
DC Comics: Oct, 2009 - No. 24, Oct, 2011 ($2.99)
1-24: 1-7-Garbett-a/Noto-c. 3-New costume. 8-Caldwell-a. 9-14-Lau-c. 14-Supergirl app. 3.00
1-Variant-c by Hamner 5.00
...: Batgirl Rising TPB (2010, $17.99) r/#1-7 20.00
...: The Flood TPB (2011, $14.99) r/#9-14 15.00

BATGIRL (Barbara Gordon)(DC New 52)
DC Comics: Nov, 2011 - Present ($2.99)
1-Barbara Gordon back in costume; Simone-s/Syaf-a/Hughes-c 5.00
1-Second & Third printings 3.00
2-8: 2-6-Hughes-c. 3-Nightwing app. 7,8-Syaf-c 3.00

BATGIRL ADVENTURES (See Batman Adventures, The)
DC Comics: Feb, 1998 ($2.95, one-shot) (Based on animated series)
1-Harley Quinn and Poison Ivy app.; Timm-c 5.00

BATGIRL SPECIAL
DC Comics: 1988 ($1.50, one-shot, 52 pgs)
1-Kitson-a/Mignola-c 1 2 3 5 7 9

BATGIRL: YEAR ONE
DC Comics: Feb, 2003 - No. 9, Oct, 2003 ($2.95, limited series)
1-9-Barbara Gordon becomes Batgirl; Killer Moth app.; Beatty & Dixon-s 3.00
TPB (2003, $17.95) r/#1-9 18.00

BAT LASH (See DC Special Series #16, Showcase #76, Weird Western Tales)
National Periodical Publications: Oct-Nov, 1968 - No. 7, Oct-Nov, 1969
(All 12¢ issues)
1-(10-11/68)-2nd app. Bat Lash; classic Nick Cardy-c/a in all
7 14 21 44 72 100
2-7 4 8 12 28 44 60

BAT LASH
DC Comics: Feb, 2008 - No. 6, Jul, 2008 ($2.99, limited series)
1-6-Aragonés & Brandvold-s/John Severin-a. 1-Two covers by Severin and Simonson 3.00
...: Guns and Roses TPB (2008, $17.99) r/#1-6 18.00

BATMAN (See All Star Batman & Robin, Anarky, Aurora [in Promo. Comics section], Azrael, The Best of DC #2, Blind Justice, The Brave & the Bold, Cosmic Odyssey, DC 100-Page Super Spec. #14,20, DC Special, DC Special Series, Detective, Dynamic Classics, 80-Page Giants, Gotham By Gaslight, Gotham Nights, Greatest Batman Stories Ever Told, Greatest Joker Stories Ever Told, Heroes Against Hunger, JLA,The Joker, Justice League of America, Justice League Int., Legends of the Dark Knight, Limited Coll. Ed., Man-Bat, Nightwing, Power Record Comics, Real Fact #5, Robin, Saga of Ra's Al Ghul, Shadow of the..., Star Spangled, Super Friends, 3-D Batman, Untold Legend of..., Wanted... & World's Finest Comics)

BATMAN
National Per. Publ./Detective Comics/DC Comics: Spring, 1940 - No. 713, Oct, 2011
(#1-5 were quarterly)
1-Origin The Batman reprinted (2 pgs.) from Det. #33 w/splash from #34 by Bob Kane; see Detective #33 for 1st origin; 1st app. Joker (2 stories intended for 2 separate issues of Det. Comics which would have been 1st & 2nd app.); splash pg. to 2nd Joker story is similar to cover of Det. #40 (story intended for #40); 1st app. The Cat (Catwoman) (1st villainess in comics); has Batman story (w/Hugo Strange) without Robin originally planned for Det. #38; mentions location (Manhattan) where Batman lives (see Det. #31). This book was created entirely from the inventory of Det. Comics; 1st Batman/Robin pin-up on back-c; has text piece & photo of Bob Kane
17,000 34,000 51,000 120,000 235,000 350,000
1-Reprint, oversize 13-1/2x10". **WARNING**: This comic is an exact duplicate reprint of the original except for its size. DC published it in 1974 with a second cover titling it as a Famous First Edition. There have been many reported cases of the outer cover being removed and the interior sold as the original edition. The reprint with the new outer cover removed is practically worthless. See Famous First Edition for value.
2-2nd app. The Joker; 2nd app. Catwoman (out of costume) in Joker story; 1st time called Catwoman (NOTE: A 15¢-c for Canadian distr. exists.)
1800 3600 5400 13,500 25,750 38,000
3-3rd app Catwoman (1st in costume & 1st costumed villainess); 1st Puppet Master app.; classic Kane & Robinson-c 1050 2100 3150 7980 14,490 21,000

Batman #49 © DC

Batman #65 © DC

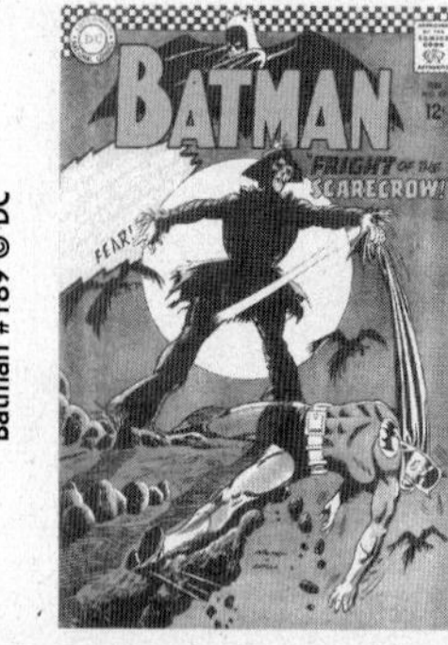

Batman #189 © DC

	GD 2.0	VG 4.0	FN 6.0	VF 8.0	VF/NM 9.0	NM- 9.2
4-4th app. The Joker (see Det. #45 for 3rd); 1st mention of Gotham City in a Batman comic (on newspaper)(Win/40)	865	1730	2595	6315	11,158	16,000
5-1st app. the Batmobile with its bat-head front	649	1298	1947	4738	8369	12,000
6,7: 7-Bullseye-c; Joker app.	530	1060	1590	3869	6835	9800
8-Infinity-c by Fred Ray; Joker app.	432	864	1296	3154	5577	8000
9-10:9-1st Batman x-mas story; Burnley-c. 10-Catwoman story (gets new costume)	423	846	1269	3000	5250	7500
11-Classic Joker-c by Ray/Robinson (3rd Joker-c, 6-7/42); Joker & Penguin app.	838	1676	2514	6117	10,809	15,500
12,15: 12-Joker app. 15-New costume Catwoman	320	640	960	2240	3920	5600
13-Jerry Siegel (Superman's co-creator) appears in a Batman story; Batman parachuting on black-c	343	686	1029	2400	4200	6000
14-2nd Penguin-c; Penguin app. (12-1/42-43)	331	662	993	2317	4059	5800
16-Intro/origin Alfred (4-5/43); cover is a reverse of #9 cover by Burnley; 1st small logo	611	1222	1833	4460	7880	11,300
17,20: 17-Classic war-c; Penguin app. 20-1st Batmobile-c (12-1/43-44); Joker app.	300	600	900	1920	3310	4700
18-Hitler, Hirohito, Mussolini-c.	366	732	1098	2562	4481	6400
19-Joker app.	213	426	639	1363	2332	3300
21,22,24,26,28-30: 21-1st skinny Alfred in Batman (2-3/44). 21,30-Penguin app. 22-1st Alfred solo-c/story (Alfred solo stories in 22-32,36); Catwoman & The Cavalier app. 28-Joker story	161	322	483	1030	1765	2500
23-Joker-c/story; classic black-c	300	600	900	1920	3310	4700
25-Only Joker/Penguin team-up; 1st team-up between two major villains	265	530	795	1694	2897	4100
27-Classic Burnley Christmas-c; Penguin app.	219	438	657	1402	2401	3400
31,32,34-36,39: 32-Origin Robin retold; Joker app. 35-Catwoman story (in new costume w/o cat head mask). 36-Penguin app.	123	246	369	787	1344	1900
33-Christmas-c	147	294	441	934	1605	2275
37,40,44-Joker-c/stories	194	388	582	1242	2121	3000
38-Penguin-c/story	148	296	444	947	1624	2300
41,45,46: 41-1st Sci-fi cover/story in Batman; Penguin app.(6-7/47). 45-Christmas-c/story; Catwoman story. 46-Joker app.	94	188	282	597	1024	1450
42-2nd Catwoman-c (1st in Batman)(8-9/47); Catwoman story also.	181	362	543	1158	1979	2800
43-Penguin-c/story	129	258	387	826	1413	2000
47-1st detailed origin The Batman (6-7/48); 1st Bat-signal-c this title (see Detective #108); Batman tracks down his parent's killer and reveals i.d. to him	411	822	1233	2877	5039	7200
48-1000 Secrets of the Batcave; r-in #203; Penguin story	123	246	369	787	1344	1900
49-Joker-c/story; 1st app. Mad Hatter; 1st app. Vicki Vale	213	426	639	1363	2332	3300
50-Two-Face impostor app.	113	226	339	718	1234	1750
51,54,56,57,59,60: 57-Centerfold is a 1950 calendar; Joker app. 59-1st app. Deadshot; Batman in the future-c/story	97	194	291	621	1061	1500
52-Joker-c/story	155	310	465	992	1696	2400
53-Joker story	100	200	300	635	1093	1550
55-Joker-c/stories	142	284	426	909	1555	2200
58,61: 58-Penguin-c. 61-Origin Batman Plane II	108	216	324	686	1181	1675
62-Origin Catwoman; Catwoman-c	168	336	504	1075	1838	2600
63,80-Joker stories. 63-1st app. Killer Moth; flying saucer story(2-3/51)	90	180	270	576	988	1400
64,70-72,74-77,79: 70-Robot-c. 72-Last 52 pg. issue. 74-Used in **POP**, Pg. 90. 76-Penguin story. 79-Vicki Vale in "The Bride of Batman"	77	154	231	493	847	1200
65,69-Catwoman-c/stories	123	246	369	787	1344	1900
66,73-Joker-c/stories. 66-Pre-2nd Batman & Robin team try-out. 73-Vicki Vale story	129	258	387	826	1413	2000
67-Joker story	90	180	270	576	988	1400
68,81-Two-Face-c/stories	100	200	300	635	1093	1550
78-(8-9/53)-Roh Kar, The Man Hunter from Mars story-the 1st lawman of Mars to come to Earth (green skinned)	94	188	282	597	1024	1450
82,83,87-89: 89-Last pre-code issue	74	148	222	470	810	1150
84-Catwoman-c/story; Two-Face app.	116	232	348	742	1271	1800
85,86-Joker story. 86-Intro Batmarine (Batman's submarine)	76	152	228	486	831	1175
90,91,93-96,98,99: 99-(4/56)-Last G.A. Penguin app.	68	136	204	435	743	1050
92-1st app. Bat-Hound-c/story	116	232	348	742	1271	1800
97-2nd app. Bat-Hound-c/story; Joker story	74	148	222	470	810	1150
100-(6/56)	300	600	900	1920	3310	4700
101-(8/56)-Clark Kent x-over who protects Batman's i.d. (3rd story)	68	136	204	432	746	1060
102-104,106-109: 103-1st S.A. issue; 3rd Bat-Hound-c/story	63	126	189	403	689	975
105-1st Batwoman in Batman (2nd anywhere)	110	220	330	704	1202	1700
110-Joker story	65	130	195	416	708	1000
111-120: 112-1st app. Signalman (super villain). 113-1st app. Fatman; Batman meets his counterpart on Planet X w/a chest plate similar to S.A. Batman's design (yellow oval w/black design inside).	54	108	162	343	574	825
121- Origin/1st app. of Mr. Zero (Mr. Freeze).	97	194	291	621	1061	1500
122,124-126,128,130: 122,126-Batwoman-c/story. 124-2nd app. Signal Man. 128-Batwoman cameo. 130-Lex Luthor app.	43	86	129	271	461	650
123,127: 123-Joker story; Bat-Hound app. 127-(10/59)-Batman vs. Thor the Thunder God c/story; Joker story; Superman cameo	45	90	135	284	480	675
129-Origin Robin retold; bondage-c; Batwoman-c/story (reprinted in Batman Family #8)	54	108	162	343	574	825
131-135,137-139,141-143: 131-Intro 2nd Batman & Robin series (see #66; also in #135,145, 154,159,163). 133-1st Bat-Mite in Batman (3rd app. anywhere). 134-Origin The Dummy (not Vigilante's villain). 139-Intro 1st original Bat-Girl; only app. Signalman as the Blue Bowman. 141-2nd app. original Bat-Girl. 143-(10/61)-Last 10¢ issue	39	78	117	240	395	550
136-Joker-c/story	43	86	129	271	461	650
140-Joker story, Batwoman-c/s; Superman cameo	40	80	120	246	411	575
144-(12/61)-1st 12¢ issue; Joker story	24	48	72	168	359	550
145,148-Joker-c/stories	26	52	78	182	391	600
146,147,149,150	19	38	57	133	287	440
151-154,156-158,160-162,164-168,170: 152-Joker story. 156-Ant-Man/Robin team-up(6/63). 164-New Batmobile(6/64) new look & Mystery Analysts series begins	15	30	45	104	227	350
155-1st S.A. app. The Penguin (5/63)	31	62	93	225	488	750
159,163-Joker-c/stories. 159-Bat-Girl app. 163-Last Bat-Girl app. until Teen Titans #50	19	38	57	133	287	440
169-2nd SA Penguin app.	17	34	51	119	260	400
171-1st Riddler app.(5/65) since Dec. 1948	44	88	132	330	715	1100
172-175,177,178,180,184	11	22	33	75	148	220
176-(80-Pg. Giant G-17); Joker-c/story; Penguin app. in strip-r; Catwoman reprint	12	24	36	84	177	270
179-2nd app. Silver Age Riddler	17	34	51	114	250	385
181-Batman & Robin poster insert; intro. Poison Ivy	26	52	78	182	391	600
182,187-(80 Pg. Giants G-24, G-30); Joker-c/stories	12	24	36	78	157	235
183-2nd app. Poison Ivy	14	28	42	93	202	310
185-(80 Pg. Giant G-27)	11	22	33	77	154	230
186-Joker-c/story	12	24	36	78	157	235
188,191,192,194-196,199	9	18	27	63	112	160
189-1st S.A. app. Scarecrow; retells origin of G.A. Scarecrow from World's Finest #3(1st app.)	17	34	51	114	250	385
190-Penguin-c/app.	11	22	33	77	154	230
193-(80-Pg. Giant G-37)	11	22	33	73	142	210
197-4th S.A. Catwoman app. cont'd from Det. #369; 1st new Batgirl app. in Batman (5th anywhere)	14	28	42	93	202	310
198-(80-Pg. Giant G-43); Joker-c/story-r/World's Finest #61; Catwoman-r/Det. #211; Penguin-r; origin-r/#47	11	22	33	75	148	220
200-(3/68)-Joker cameo; retells origin of Batman & Robin; 1st Neal Adams work this title (cover only)	12	24	36	83	172	260
201-Joker story	8	16	24	51	86	120
202,204-207,209-212: 210-Catwoman-c/app. 212-Last 12¢ issue	7	14	21	48	79	110
203-(80 Pg. Giant G-49); r/#48, 61, & Det. 185; Batcave Blueprints	9	18	27	61	106	150
208-(80 Pg. Giant G-55); New origin Batman by Gil Kane plus 3 G.A. Batman reprints w/Catwoman, Vicki Vale & Batwoman	9	18	27	61	106	150
213-(80-Pg. Giant G-61); 30th anniversary issue (7-8/69); origin Alfred (r/Batman #16), Joker(r/Det. #168), Clayface; new origin Robin with new facts	10	20	30	66	121	175
214-217: 214-Alfred given a new last name- "Pennyworth" (see Detective #96)	6	12	18	41	66	90
218-(80-Pg. Giant G-67)	8	16	24	51	86	120
219-Neal Adams-a	8	16	24	55	93	130
220,221,224-226,229-231	6	12	18	37	59	80
222-Beatles take-off; art lesson by Joe Kubert	7	14	21	48	79	110
223,228,233: 223,228-(80-Pg. Giants G-73,G-79). 233-G-85-(68 pgs., "64 pgs." on-c)	7	14	21	49	82	115
227-Neal Adams cover swipe of Detective #31	15	30	45	104	227	350
232-(6/71) Adams-a. Intro/1st app. Ra's al Ghul; origin Batman & Robin retold; last 15¢ issue (see Detective #411 (5/71) for Talia's debut)	17	34	51	114	250	385
234-(9/71)-1st modern app. of Harvey Dent/Two-Face; (see World's Finest #173 for Batman as						

Batman #245 © DC

Batman #575 © DC

Batman #615 © DC

GD 2.0 | VG 4.0 | FN 6.0 | VF 8.0 | VF/NM 9.0 | NM- 9.2

Two-Face; only S.A. mention of character); N. Adams-a; 52 pg. issues begin, end #242 17 34 51 119 260 400
235,236,239-242: 239-XMas-c. 241-Reprint/#5 6 12 18 41 66 90
237-N. Adams-a. 1st Rutland Vermont - Bald Mountain Halloween x-over. G.A. Batman-r/ Det. #37; 1st app. The Reaper; Wrightson/Ellison plots 13 26 39 87 186 285
238-Also listed as DC 100 Page Super Spectacular #8; Batman, Legion, Aquaman-r; G.A. Atom, Sargon (r/Sensation #57), Plastic Man (r/Police #14) stories; Doom Patrol origin-r; N. Adams wraparound-c 12 24 36 81 166 250
243-245-Neal Adams-a 9 18 27 58 99 140
246-250,252,253: 246-Scarecrow app. 253-Shadow-c & app. 6 12 18 37 59 80
251-(9/73)-N. Adams-c/a; Joker-c/story 10 20 30 68 127 185
254,256-259,261-All 100 pg. editions; part-r: 254-(2/74)-Man-Bat-c & app. 256-Catwoman app. 257-Joker & Penguin app. 258-First mention of Arkham (Hospital, renamed Arkham Asylum in #260). 259-Shadow-c/app. 7 14 21 48 79 110
255-(100 pgs.)-N. Adams-c/a; tells of Bruce Wayne's father who wore bat costume & fought crime (r/Det. #235); r/story Batman #22 8 16 24 55 93 130
260-(100 pgs.) Joker-c/story; 2nd Arkham Asylum (see #258 for 1st mention) 8 16 24 55 93 130
262 (68 pgs.) 5 10 15 35 55 75
263,264,266-285,287-290,292,293,295-299: 266-Catwoman back to old costume 3 6 9 14 20 25
265-Wrightson-a(i) 3 6 9 16 22 28
286,291,294: 294-Joker-c/stories 3 6 9 18 27 35
300-Double-size 3 6 9 20 30 40
301-(7/78)-310,312-315,317-320,325-331,333-352: 304-(44 pgs.). 306-3rd app. Black Spider. 308-Mr. Freeze app. 310-1st modern app. The Gentleman Ghost in Batman; Kubert-c. 312,314,346-Two-Face-c/stories. 313-2nd app. Calendar Man. 318-Intro Firebug. 319-2nd modern age app. The Gentleman Ghost; Kubert-c. 344-Poison Ivy app. 345-1st app. new Dr. Death. 345,346,351-Catwoman back-ups 2 4 6 9 12 15
306-308,311-320,323,324,326-(Whitman variants; low print run; none show issue # on cover) 2 4 6 13 18 22
311,316,322-324: 311-Batgirl-c/story; Batgirl reteams w/Batman. 316-Robin returns. 322-324-Catwoman (Selina Kyle) app. 322,323-Cat-Man cameos (1st in Batman, 1 panel each). 323-1st meeting Catwoman & Cat-Man. 324-1st full app. Cat-Man this title 2 4 6 10 14 18
321,353,359-Joker-c/stories 3 6 9 14 20 25
332-Catwoman's 1st solo 2 4 6 11 16 20
354-356,358,360-365,369,370: 361-1st app Harvey Bullock 1 3 4 6 8 10
357-1st app. Jason Todd (3/83); see Det. #524; 1st brief app. Croc 2 4 6 9 13 16
366-Jason Todd 1st in Robin costume; Joker-c/story 2 4 6 13 18 22
367-Jason in red & green costume (not as Robin) 2 4 6 8 10 12
368-1st new Robin in costume (Jason Todd) 2 4 6 10 14 18
371-399,401-403: 371-Cat-Man-c/story; brief origin Cat-Man (cont'd in Det. #538). 386,387-Intro Black Mask (villain). 380-391-Catwoman app. 398-Catwoman & Two-Face app. 401-2nd app. Magpie (see Man of Steel #3 for 1st). 403-Joker cameo 1 2 3 5 6 8

NOTE: *Issues 397-399, 401-403, 408-416, 421-425, 430-432 all have 2nd printings in 1989; some with up to 8 printings. Some are not identified as reprints but have newer ads copyrighted after cover dates. All reprints are scarcer than 1st prints and have same value to variant collectors.*

400 ($1.50, 68pgs.)-Dark Knight special; intro by Stephen King; Art Adams/Austin-a 3 6 9 17 25 32
404-Miller scripts begin (end 407); Year 1; 1st modern app. Catwoman (2/87) 3 6 9 16 23 30
405-407: 407-Year 1 ends (See Detective Comics #575-578 for Year 2) 3 6 9 14 19 24
408-410: New Origin Jason Todd (Robin) 2 4 6 13 18 22
411-416,421-425: 411-Two-face app. 412-Origin/1st app. Mime. 414-Starlin scripts begin, end #429. 416-Nightwing-c/story. 423-McFarlane-c 6.00
417-420: "Ten Nights of the Beast" storyline 2 4 6 8 10 12
426-($1.50, 52 pgs.)- "A Death In The Family" storyline begins, ends #429 2 4 6 13 18 22
427- "A Death In The Family" part 2. 2 4 6 9 12 15
428-Death of Robin (Jason Todd) 2 4 6 13 18 22
429-Joker-c/story; Superman app. 2 4 6 8 10 12
430-432 4.00
433-435-Many Deaths of the Batman story by John Byrne-c/scripts 4.00
436-Year 3 begins (ends #439); origin original Robin retold by Nightwing (Dick Grayson); 1st app. Timothy Drake (8/89) 5.00
436-441: 436-2nd printing. 437-Origin Robin cont. 440,441: "A Lonely Place of Dying" Parts 1 & 3 4.00
442-1st app. Timothy Drake in Robin costume 5.00
443-456,458,459,462-464: 445-447-Batman goes to Russia. 448,449-The Penguin Affair Pts 1 & 3. 450-Origin Joker. 450,451-Joker-c/stories. 452-454-Dark Knight Dark City storyline; Riddler app. 455-Alan Grant scripts begin, ends #466, 470. 464-Last solo Batman story; free 16 pg. preview of Impact Comics line 4.00
457-Timothy Drake officially becomes Robin & dons new costume 6.00
457-Direct sale edition (has #000 in indicia) 6.00
460,461,465-487: 460,461-Two part Catwoman story. 465-Robin returns to action with Batman. 470-War of the Gods x-over. 475-1st app. Renee Montoya. 475,476-Return of Scarface. 476-Last $1.00-c. 477,478-Photo-c 4.00
488-Cont'd from Batman: Sword of Azrael #4; Azrael-c & app. 1 2 3 5 6 8
489-Bane-c/story; 1st app. Azrael in Bat-costume 5.00
490-Riddler-c/story; Azrael & Bane app. 6.00
491,492: 491-Knightfall lead-in; Joker-c/story; Azrael & Bane app.; Kelley Jones-c begin. 492-Knightfall part 1; Bane app. 5.00
492-Platinum edition (promo copy) 10.00
493-496: 493-Knightfall Pt. 3. 494-Knightfall Pt. 5; Joker-c & app. 495-Knightfall Pt. 7; brief Bane & Joker apps. 496-Knightfall Pt. 9, Joker-c/story; Bane cameo 4.00
497-(Late 7/93)-Knightfall Pt. 11; Bane breaks Batman's back; B&W outer-c; Aparo-a(p); Giordano-a(i) 6.00
497-499: 497-2nd printing. 497-Newsstand edition w/o outer cover. 498-Knightfall part 15; Bane & Catwoman-c & app. (see Showcase 93 #7 & 8) 499-Knightfall Pt. 17; Bane app. 4.00
500-($2.50, 68 pgs.)-Knightfall Pt. 19; Azrael in new Bat-costume; Bane-c/story 4.00
500-($3.95, 68 pgs.)-Collector's Edition w/die-cut double-c w/foil by Joe Quesada & 2 bound-in post cards 6.00
501-508,510,511: 501-Begin $1.50-c. 501-508-Knightquest. 503,504-Catwoman app. 507-Ballistic app.; Jim Balent-a(p). 510-KnightsEnd Pt. 7. 511-(9/94)-Zero Hour; Batgirl-c/story 3.00
509-($2.50, 52 pgs.)-KnightsEnd Pt. 1 4.00
512-514,516-518: 512-(11/94)-Dick Grayson assumes Batman role 3.00
515-Special Ed.($2.50)-Kelley Jones-a begins; all black embossed-c; Troika Pt. 1 4.00
515-Regular Edition 3.00
519-534,536-549: 519-Begin $1.95-c. 521-Return of Alfred, 522-Swamp Thing app. 525-Mr. Freeze app. 527,528-Two Face app. 529-Contagion Pt. 6. 530-532-Deadman app. 533-Legacy prelude. 534-Legacy Pt. 5. 536-Final Night x-over; Man-Bat-c/app. 540,541-Spectre-c-app. 544-546-Joker & The Demon. 548,549-Penguin-c/app. 3.00
530-532 ($2.50)-Enhanced edition; glow-in-the-dark-c. 4.00
535-(10/96, $2.95)-1st app. The Ogre 4.00
535-(10/96, $3.95)-1st app. The Ogre; variant, cardboard, foldout-c 5.00
550-($3.50)-Collector's Ed., includes 4 collector cards; intro. Chase, return of Clayface; Kelley Jones-c 5.00
550-($2.95)-Standard Ed.; Williams & Gray-c 4.00
551,552,554-562: 551,552-Ragman c/app. 554-Cataclysm pt. 12. 3.00
553-Cataclysm pt.3 4.00
563-No Man's Land; Joker-c by Campbell; Bob Gale-s 5.00
564-574: 569-New Batgirl-c/app. 572-Joker and Harley app. 3.00
575-579: 575-New look Batman begins; McDaniel-a 3.00
580-598: 580-Begin $2.25-c. 587-Gordon shot. 591,592-Deadshot-c/app. 3.00
599-Bruce Wayne: Murderer pt. 7 3.50
600-($3.95) Bruce Wayne: Fugitive pt. 1; back-up homage stories in '50s, 60's, & 70s styles; by Aragonés, Gaudiano, Shanower and others 5.00
600-(2nd printing) 4.00
601-604, 606,607: 601,603-Bruce Wayne: Fugitive pt.3,13. 606,607-Deadshot-c/app. 3.00
605-($2.95) Conclusion to Bruce Wayne: Fugitive x-over; Noto-c 4.00
608-(12/02) Jim Lee-a/c & Jeph Loeb-s begin; Poison Ivy & Catwoman app. 8.00
608-2nd printing; has different cover with Batman standing on gargoyle 12.00
608-Special Edition; has different cover; 200 printed; used for promotional purposes (a CGC certified 9.2 copy sold for $700, and a CGC certified 9.8 copy sold for $2,100)
608-Special Edition (9/09, $1.00) printing has new "After Watchmen" logo cover frame 3.00
609-Huntress app. 9.00
610,611: 610-Killer Croc-c/app.; Batman & Catwoman kiss 8.00
612-Batman vs. Superman; 1st printing with full color cover 9.00
612-2nd printing with B&W sketch cover 15.00
613,614: 614-Joker-c/app. 7.00
615-617: 615-Reveals ID to Catwoman. 616-Ra's al Ghul app. 617-Scarecrow app. 5.00
618-Batman vs. "Jason Todd" 4.00
619-Newsstand cover; Hush story concludes; Riddler app. 5.00
619-Two variant tri-fold covers; one Heroes group, one Villains group 5.00
619-2nd printing with Riddler chess cover 5.00
620-Broken City pt. 1; Azzarello-s/Risso-a/c begin; Killer Croc app. 4.00
621-633: 621-625-Azzarello-s/Risso-a/c. 626-630-Winick-s/Nguyen-a/Wagner-c; Penguin & Scarecrow app. 631-633-War Games. 633-Conclusion to War Games x-over 3.00
634-638-Winick-s/Nguyen-a/Wagner-c; Red Hood app. 637-Amazo app. 638-Red Hood

Batman #713 © DC

Batman (2011 series) #1 © DC

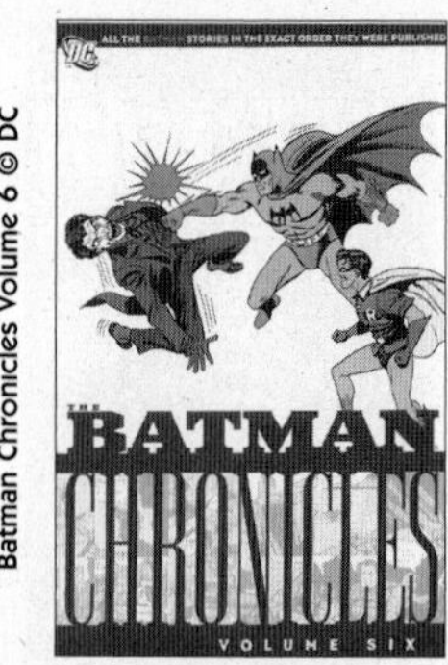

Batman Chronicles Volume 6 © DC

	GD 2.0	VG 4.0	FN 6.0	VF 8.0	VF/NM 9.0	NM- 9.2
unmasked as Jason Todd						3.00
639-650: 640-Superman app. 641-Begin $2.50-c. 643,644-War Crimes; Joker app. 650-Infinite Crisis; Joker and Jason Todd app.						3.00
651-654-One Year Later; Bianchi-c						3.50
655-Begin Grant Morrison-s/Andy Kubert-a; Kubert-c w/red background						5.00
655-Variant cover by Adam Kubert, brown-toned image						15.00
656-665: 656-Intro. Damien, son of Talia and Batman (see Batman: Son of the Demon). 657-Damien in Robin costume. 659-662-Mandrake-a. 663-Van Fleet-a. 664-Bane app.						3.00
666-675: 666-Future story of adult Damien; Andy Kubert-a. 667-669-Williams III-a. 670,671-Resurrection of Ra's al Ghul; Daniel-a. 671-2nd printing						3.00
676-Batman R.I.P. begins; Morrison-s/Daniel-a/Alex Ross-c						4.00
676-Variant-c by Tony Daniel						12.00
676-Second (red-tinted Daniel-c) & third (B&W Daniel-c) printings						3.00
677-680,682-685: Batman R.I.P.; Alex Ross-c. 678-Bat-Mite app. 682-685-Last Rites						3.00
677-Variant-c with Red Hood by Tony Daniel						10.00
677-Second printing with B&W&red-tinted Daniel-c						3.00
681-($3.99) Batman R.I.P. conclusion						4.00
686-($3.99) Gaiman-s/Andy Kubert-a; continues in Detective #853; Kubert sketch pgs.; covers by Kubert and Ross; 2nd & 3rd printings exist						4.00
687-($3.99) Batman: Reborn begins; Dick Grayson becomes Batman; Winick-s/Benes-a						4.00
688-699: 688-691-Bagley-a. 692-697,699-Tony Daniel-s/a. 692-Catwoman app.						3.00
700-(8/10, $4.99) Morrison-s; art by Daniel, Quitely, Finch & Andy Kubert; Finch-c						5.00
700-Variant-c by Mignola						10.00
701-712: 701,702-Morrison-s; R.I.P story. 704-Batman Inc. begins; Daniel-s/a						3.00
713-(10/11) Last issue of first volume; Nicieza-s; Robin flashbacks						3.00
#0 (10/94)-Zero Hour issue released between #511 & #512; Origin retold						3.00
#1,000,000 (11/98) 853rd Century x-over						3.00
Annual 1 (8-10/61)-Swan-c	54	108	162	437	944	1450
Annual 2	25	50	75	175	375	575
Annual 3 (Summer, '62)-Joker-c/story	26	52	78	182	391	600
Annual 4,5	13	26	39	87	186	285
Annual 6,7 (7/64, 25¢, 80 pgs.)	11	22	33	76	151	225
Annual V5#8 (1982)-Painted-c	1	3	4	6	8	10
Annual 9,10,12: 9(7/85). 10(1986). 12(1988, $1.50)	1	2	3	4	5	7
Annual 11 (1987, $1.25)-Penguin-c/story; Moore-s	1	2	3	5	7	9
Annual 13 (1989, $1.75, 68 pgs.)-Gives history of Bruce Wayne, Dick Grayson, Jason Todd, Alfred, Comm. Gordon, Barbara Gordon (Batgirl) & Vicki Vale; Morrow-i						6.00
Annual 14-17 ('90-'93, 68 pgs.)-14-Origin Two-Face. 15-Armageddon 2001 x-over; Joker app. 15 (2nd printing). 16-Joker-c/s; Kieth-c. 17 (1993, $2.50, 68 pgs.)-Azrael in Bat-costume; intro Ballistic						4.00
Annual 18 (1994, $2.95)						4.00
Annual 19 (1995, $3.95)-Year One story; retells Scarecrow's origin						4.00
Annual 20 (1996, $2.95)-Legends of the Dead Earth story; Giarrano-a						4.00
Annual 21 (1997, $3.95)-Pulp Heroes story						4.00
Annual 22,23 ('98, '99, $2.95)-22-Ghosts; Wrightson-c. 23-JLApe; Art Adams-c						4.00
Annual 24 ('00, $3.50) Planet DC; intro. The Boggart; Aparo-a						4.00
Annual 25 ('06, $4.99) Infinite Crisis-revised story of Jason Todd; unused Aparo page						6.00
Annual 26 ('07, $3.99) Origin of Ra's al Ghul; Damien app.						4.00
Annual 27 ('09, $4.99) Azrael app.; Calafiore-a; back-up story w/Kelley Jones-a						5.00
Annual 28 (2/11, $4.99) The Question, Nightrunner and Veil app.; Lau-c						5.00

NOTE: ***Art Adams*** *a-400p.* ***Neal Adams*** *c-200, 203, 210, 217, 219-222, 224-227, 229, 230, 232, 234, 236-241, 243-246, 251, 255, Annual 14.* ***Aparo*** *a-414-420, 426-435, 440-448, 450, 451, 480-483, 486-491, 494-500; c-414-416, 481, 482, 463i, 486, 487i.* ***Bolland*** *a-400; c-445-447.* ***Burnley*** *a-10, 12-18, 20, 22, 25, 27; c-9, 15, 16, 27, 28p, 40p, 42p.* ***Byrne*** *c-401, 433-435, 533-535, Annual 11.* ***Travis Charest*** *c-488-490p.* ***Colan*** *a-340p, 343-345p, 348-351p, 373p, 383p; c-343p, 345p, 350p.* ***J. Cole*** *a-238r.* ***Cowan*** *a-Annual 10p.* ***Golden*** *a-295p, 303p, 484, 485.* ***Alan Grant*** *scripts-455-466, 470, 474-476, 479, 480, Annual 16(part).* ***Grell*** *a-287, 288p, 289p, 290; c-287-290.* ***Infantino/Anderson*** *c-167, 173, 175, 181, 186, 191, 192, 194, 195, 198, 199.* ***Infantino/Giella*** *c-190.* ***Kelley Jones*** *a-513-519, 521-525, 527; c-491-499, 500(newsstand), 501-510, 513.* ***Kaluta*** *c-242, 248, 253, Annual 12.* ***G. Kane/Anderson*** *c-178-180.* ***Bob Kane*** *a-1, 2, 5; c-1-5, 7, 17.* ***G. Kane*** *a-(r)-254, 255, 259, 261, 353i.* ***Kubert*** *a-238r, 400; c-310, 319p, 327, 328, 344.* ***McFarlane*** *c-423.* ***Mignola*** *c-426-429, 452-454, Annual 18.* ***Moldoff*** *c-101-140.* ***Moldoff/Giella*** *a-164-175, 177-181, 183, 184, 186.* ***Moldoff/Greene*** *a-169, 172-174, 177-179, 181, 184.* ***Mooney*** *a-255r.* ***Morrow*** *a-Annual 13i.* ***Newton*** *a-305, 306, 328p, 331p, 332p, 337p, 338p, 346p, 352-357p, 360-372p, 374-378p; c-374p, 378p.* ***Nino*** *a-Annual 9.* ***Irv Novick*** *c-201, 202.* ***Perez*** *a-400; c-436-442.* ***Fred Ray*** *c-8, 10; w/****Robinson****-11.* ***Robinson/Roussos*** *a-12-17, 20, 22, 24, 25, 27, 28, 31, 33, 37.* ***Robinson*** *a-12, 14, 18, 22-32,34, 36, 37, 255r, 260r, 261r; c-6, 10, 12-14, 18, 21, 24, 26, 30, 37, 39.* ***Simonson*** *a-300p, 312p, 321p; c-300p, 312p, 366, 413i.* ***P. Smith*** *a-Annual 9.* ***Dick Sprang*** *c-19, 20, 22, 23, 25, 29, 31-36, 38, 51, 55, 66, 73, 76.* ***Starlin*** *c/a-402.* ***Staton*** *a-334.* ***Sutton*** *a-400.* ***Wrightson*** *a-265i, 400; c-320r. Bat-Hound app. in 92, 97, 103, 123, 125, 133, 156, 158. Bat-Mite app. in 133, 136, 144, 146, 158, 161. Batwoman app. in 105, 116, 122, 125, 128, 129, 131, 133, 139, 140, 141, 144, 145, 150, 151, 153, 154, 157, 159, 162, 163.* ***Zeck*** *c-417-420. Catwoman back-ups in 332, 345, 346, 348-351. Joker app. in 1, 2, 4, 5, 7-9, 11-13, 19, 20, 23, 25, 28, 32 & many more. Robin solo back-up stories in 337-339, 341-343.*

BATMAN (DC New 52)
DC Comics: Nov, 2011 - Present ($2.99)

	NM- 9.2
1-Snyder-s/Capullo-a/c	5.00
1-Variant-c by Van Sciver	8.00
1-2nd-4th printings	3.00
2-4	3.00
2-5-Variant covers 2. Jim Lee. 3-Ivan Reis. 4-Mike Choi, 5-Burnham. 6-Frank	5.00
5-7-Court of Owls	3.00
5-7 Combo Pack ($3.99) polybagged with digital download code	4.00

BATMAN (Hardcover books and trade paperbacks)

	NM- 9.2
...: ABSOLUTION (2002, $24.95)-Hard-c.; DeMatteis-s/Ashmore painted-a	25.00
...: ABSOLUTION (2003, $17.95)-Soft-c.; DeMatteis-s/Ashmore painted-a	18.00
...: A LONELY PLACE OF DYING (1990, $3.95, 132 pgs.)-r/Batman #440-442 & New Titans #60,61; Perez-c	4.00
...: ANARKY TPB (1999, $12.95) r/early appearances	13.00
...AND DRACULA: RED RAIN nn (1991, $24.95)-Hard-c.; Elseworlds storyline	32.00
...AND DRACULA: RED RAIN nn (1992, $9.95)-SC	12.00
...AND SON HC (2007, $24.99, dustjacket) r/Batman #655-658,663-666	25.00
...AND SON SC (2008, $14.99) r/Batman #655-658,663-666	15.00
...ANNUALS (See DC Comics Classics Library for reprints of early Annuals)	
ARKHAM ASYLUM Hard-c; Morrison-s/McKean-a (1989, $24.95)	30.00
ARKHAM ASYLUM Soft-c ($14.95)	15.00
ARKHAM ASYLUM 15TH ANNIVERSARY EDITION Hard-c (2004, $29.95) reprint with Morrison's script and annotations, original page layouts; Karen Berger afterword	30.00
ARKHAM ASYLUM 15TH ANNIVERSARY EDITION Soft-c (2005, $17.99)	18.00
...: AS THE CROW FLIES-(2004, $12.95) r/#626-630; Nguyen sketch pages	13.00
BIRTH OF THE DEMON Hard-c (1992, $24.95)-Origin of Ra's al Ghul	25.00
BIRTH OF THE DEMON Soft-c (1993, $12.95)	13.00
BLIND JUSTICE nn (1992, $7.50)-r/Det. #598-600	7.50
BLOODSTORM (1994, $24.95,HC) Kelley Jones-c/a	28.00
BRIDE OF THE DEMON Hard-c (1990, $19.95)	20.00
BRIDE OF THE DEMON Soft-c ($12.95)	13.00
...: BROKEN CITY HC-(2004, $24.95) r/#620-625; new Johnson-c; intro by Schreck	25.00
...: BROKEN CITY SC-(2004, $14.99) r/#620-625; new Johnson-c; intro by Schreck	15.00
...: BRUCE WAYNE: FUGITIVE Vol. 1 ('02, $12.95)-r/ story arc	13.00
...: BRUCE WAYNE: FUGITIVE Vol. 2 ('03, $12.95)-r/ story arc	13.00
...: BRUCE WAYNE: FUGITIVE Vol. 3 ('03, $12.95)-r/ story arc	13.00
...: BRUCE WAYNE-MURDERER? ('02, $19.95)-r/ story arc	20.00
...: BRUCE WAYNE - THE ROAD HOME HC ('11, $24.99) r/Bruce Wayne: The Road Home one-shots	25.00
...: CASTLE OF THE BAT ($5.95)-Elseworlds story	6.00
...: CATACLYSM ('99, $17.95)-r/ story arc	18.00
...: CHILD OF DREAMS (2003, $24.95, B&W, HC) Reprint of Japanese manga with Kia Asamiya-s/a/c; English adaptation by Max Allan Collins; Asamiya interview	25.00
...: CHILD OF DREAMS (2003, $19.95, B&W, SC)	20.00
...CHRONICLES VOL. 1 (2005, $14.99)-r/apps. in Detective Comics #27-38; Batman #1	15.00
...CHRONICLES VOL. 2 (2006, $14.99)-r/apps. in Detective Comics #39-45 and NY World's Fair 1940; Batman #2,3	15.00
...CHRONICLES VOL. 3 (2007, $14.99)-r/apps. in Detective Comics #46-50 and World's Best Comics #1; Batman #4,5	15.00
...CHRONICLES VOL. 4 (2007, $14.99)-r/apps. in Detective Comics #51-56 and World's Finest Comics #2,3; Batman #6,7	15.00
...CHRONICLES VOL. 5 (2008, $14.99)-r/apps. in Detective Comics #57-61 and World's Finest Comics #4; Batman #8,9	15.00
...CHRONICLES VOL. 6 (2008, $14.99)-r/apps. in Detective Comics #62-65 and World's Finest Comics #5,6; Batman #10,11	15.00
...CHRONICLES VOL. 7 (2009, $14.99)-r/apps. in Detective Comics #66-70 and World's Finest Comics #7; Batman #12,13	15.00
...CHRONICLES VOL. 8 (2009, $14.99)-r/apps. in Detective Comics #71-74 and World's Finest Comics #8,9; Batman #14,15	15.00
...CHRONICLES VOL. 9 (2010, $14.99)-r/apps. in Detective Comics #75-77 and World's Finest Comics #10; Batman #16,17	15.00
...CHRONICLES VOL. 10 (2010, $14.99)-r/apps. in Detective Comics #78-81 and World's Finest Comics #11; Batman #18,19	15.00
...: CITY OF CRIME (2006, $19.99) r/Detective Comics #800-808,811-814; Lapham-s	20.00
...: COLLECTED LEGENDS OF THE DARK KNIGHT nn (1994, $12.95)-r/Legends of the Dark Knight #32-34,38,42,43	13.00
...: CRIMSON MIST (1999, $24.95,HC)-Vampire Batman Elseworlds story Doug Moench-s/Kelley Jones-c/a	25.00
...: CRIMSON MIST (2001, $14.95,SC)	15.00
...: DARK JOKER-THE WILD (1993, $24.95,HC)-Elseworlds story; Moench-s/Jones-c/a	25.00
...: DARK JOKER-THE WILD (1993, $9.95,SC)	10.00
...DARK KNIGHT DYNASTY nn (1997, $24.95)-Hard-c.; 3 Elseworlds stories; Barr-s/ S. Hampton painted-a, Gary Frank, McDaniel-a(p)	25.00
...DARK KNIGHT DYNASTY Softcover (2000, $14.95) Hampton-c	15.00
...DEADMAN: DEATH AND GLORY nn (1996, $24.95)-Hard-c.; Robinson-s/ Estes-c/a	25.00
...DEADMAN: DEATH AND GLORY ($12.95)-SC	13.00
DEATH AND THE CITY (2007, $14.99, TPB)-r/Detective #827-834	15.00
DEATH IN THE FAMILY (1988, $3.95, trade paperback)-r/Batman #426-429 by Aparo	5.00
DEATH IN THE FAMILY: (2nd - 5th printings)	4.00

Batman: Going Sane © DC

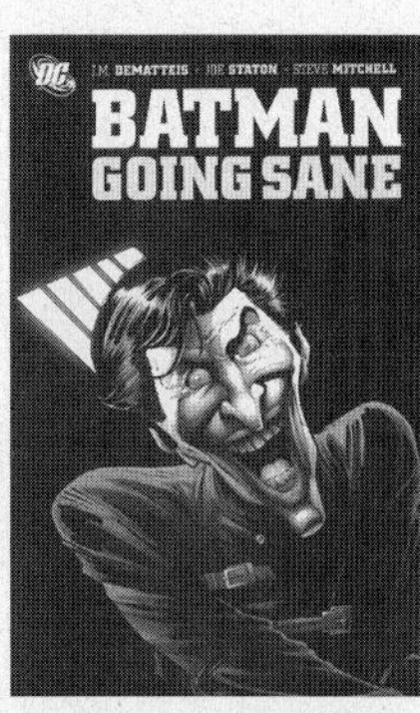

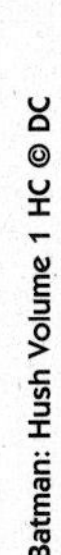
Batman: Hush Volume 1 HC © DC

Batman International TPB © DC

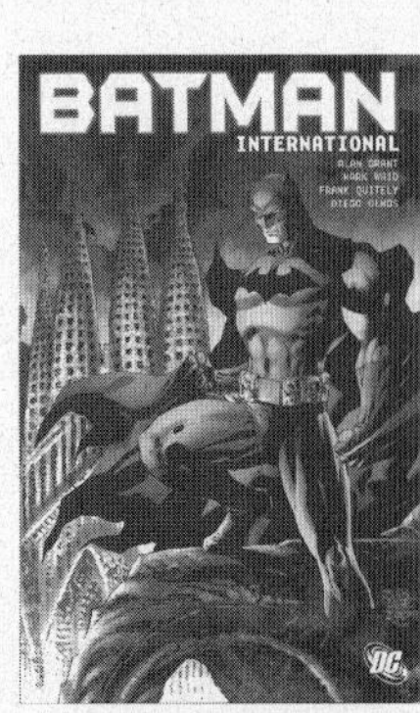

GD 2.0 | VG 4.0 | FN 6.0 | VF 8.0 | VF/NM 9.0 | NM- 9.2

...: DETECTIVE (2007, $14.99, SC)-r/Detective Comics #821-826 15.00
...: DETECTIVE #27 HC (2003, $19.95)-Elseworlds; Uslan-s/Snejbjerg-a 20.00
...: DETECTIVE #27 SC (2004, $12.95)-Elseworlds; Uslan-s/Snejbjerg-a 13.00
DIGITAL JUSTICE nn (1990, $24.95, Hard-c.)-Computer generated art 25.00
... : EGO AND OTHER TALES HC (2007, $24.99)-r/Batman: Ego, Catwoman: Selina's Big Score, and stories from Batman Black and White and Solo; Darwyn Cooke-s/a 25.00
... : EGO AND OTHER TALES SC (2008, $17.99) same contents as HC 18.00
... :EVOLUTION (2001, $12.95, SC)-r/Detective Comics #743-750 13.00
... FACES (1995, $9.95, TPB) r/Legends of the Dark Knight #28-30 10.00
... FACES (2008, $12.99, TPB) Second printing 13.00
...: FACE THE FACE (2006, $14.99, TPB)-r/Batman #651-654, Detective #817-820 15.00
...: FALSE FACES HC (2008, $19.99)-r/Batman #588-590, Wonder Woman #160,161; Batman: Gotham City Secret Files #1 and Detective #787; Brian K. Vaughn intro. 20.00
...: FALSE FACES SC (2008, $14.99)-r/Batman #588-590, Wonder Woman #160,161; Batman: Gotham City Secret Files #1 and Detective #787; Brian K. Vaughn intro. 15.00
...: FORTUNATE SON HC (1999, $24.95) Gene Ha-a 25.00
...: FORTUNATE SON SC (2000, $14.95) Gene Ha-a 15.00
FOUR OF A KIND TPB (1998, $14.95)-r/1995 Year One Annuals featuring Poison Ivy, Riddler, Scarecrow, & Man-Bat 15.00
... GOING SANE (2008, $14.95, TPB) r/Legends of the Dark Knight #65-68,200 15.00
...: GOTHAM BY GASLIGHT (2006, $12.99, TPB) r/Gotham By Gaslight & Master of the Future one-shots; Elseworlds Batman vs. Jack the Ripper 13.00
...GOTHIC (1992, $12.95, TPB)-r/Legends of the Dark Knight #6-10 13.00
...GOTHIC (2007, $14.99, TPB)-r/Legends of the Dark Knight #6-10 15.00
...: HARVEST BREED-(2000, $24.95) George Pratt-s/painted-a 25.00
...: HARVEST BREED-(2003, $17.95) George Pratt-s/painted-a 18.00
...: HAUNTED KNIGHT-(1997, $12.95) r/ Halloween specials 13.00
...: HEART OF HUSH HC-(2009, $19.99) r/#Detective #846-850; pin-ups 20.00
...: HEART OF HUSH SC-(2010, $14.99) r/#Detective #846-850; pin-ups 15.00
...: HONG KONG HC (2003, $24.95, with dustjacket) Doug Moench-s/Tony Wong-a 25.00
...: HONG KONG SC (2004, $17.95) Doug Moench-s/Tony Wong-a 18.00
...: HUSH DOUBLE FEATURE-(2003, $3.95) r/#608,609(1st 2 Jim Lee-a issues) 4.00
...: HUSH SC-(2009, $24.99) r/#608-619; Wizard 0; variant cover gallery; Loeb intro 25.00
...: HUSH UNWRAPPED-(2011, $39.99, HC) r/#608-619's original Jin Lee pencil art 40.00
...: HUSH VOLUME 1 HC-(2003, $19.95) r/#608-612; & new 2 pg. origin w/Lee-a 20.00
...: HUSH VOLUME 1 SC-(2004, $12.95) r/#608-612; includes CD of DC GN art 13.00
...: HUSH VOLUME 2 HC-(2003, $19.95) r/#613-619; Lee intro & sketchpages 20.00
...: HUSH VOLUME 2 SC-(2004, $12.95) r/#613-619; Lee intro & sketchpages 13.00
...: ILLUSTRATED BY NEAL ADAMS VOLUME 1 HC-(2003, $49.95) r/Batman, Brave and the Bold, and Detective Comics stories and covers 50.00
...: ILLUSTRATED BY NEAL ADAMS VOLUME 2 HC-(2004, $49.95) r/Adams' Batman art from 1969-71; intro. by Dick Giordano 50.00
...: ILLUSTRATED BY NEAL ADAMS VOLUME 3 HC-(2006, $49.99) r/Adams' Batman art from 1971-74; covers, pin-ups and design art; intro. by Denny O'Neil 50.00
... IMPOSTERS TPB (2011, $14.99) r/Detective Comics #867-870 15.00
... INTERNATIONAL TPB (2010, $17.99) R/Batman: Scottish Connection, Batman in Barcelona: Dragon's Knight and Batman: Legends of the DK #52,53; Jim Lee-c 18.00
... IN THE FORTIES TPB ($19.95) Intro. by Bill Schelly 20.00
... IN THE FIFTIES TPB ($19.95) Intro. by Michael Uslan 20.00
... IN THE SIXTIES TPB ($19.95) Intro. by Adam West 20.00
... IN THE SEVENTIES TPB ($19.95) Intro. by Dennis O'Neil 20.00
... IN THE EIGHTIES TPB ($19.95) Intro. by John Wells 20.00
.../ JUDGE DREDD FILES (2004, $14.95) reprints cross-overs 15.00
... :KING TUT'S TOMB TPB (2010, $14.99) r/Batman Confidential #26-28, Batman #353 and Brave and the Bold #164,171 15.00
... LEGACY-(1996, $17.95) reprints Legacy 18.00
...: LIFE AFTER DEATH HC-(2010, $19.99, dustjacket) r/#Batman #692-699 20.00
...: LONG SHADOWS HC-(2010, $19.99, dustjacket) r/#Batman #687-691 20.00
...: LONG SHADOWS SC-(2011, $14.99) r/#Batman #687-691 15.00
...: LOVERS & MADMEN-(See Batman Confidential)
...: MAD LOVE AND OTHER STORIES HC (2009, $19.99) r/Batman Adventures: Mad Love, Batman Advs. Holiday Special and other Dini/Timm collaborations; commentary 20.00
...: THE MANY DEATHS OF THE BATMAN (1992, $3.95, 84 pgs.)-r/Batman #433-435 w/new Byrne-c 4.00
...: MONSTERS (2009, $19.99, TPB)-r/Legends of the Dark Knight #71-73,83,84,89,90 20.00
...: THE MOVIES (1997, $19.95)-r/movie adaptations of Batman, Batman Returns, Batman Forever, Batman and Robin 20.00
...: NINE LIVES HC (2002, $24.95, sideways format) Motter-s/Lark-a 25.00
...: NINE LIVES SC (2003, $17.95, sideways format) Motter-s/Lark-a 18.00
...: OFFICER DOWN (2001, $12.95)-r/Commissioner shot x-over; Talon-c 13.00
.../ PLANETARY DELUXE HC (2011, $22.99)-r/Planetary/Batman: Night on Earth; script 23.00
...: PREY (1992, $12.95)-Gulacy/Austin-a 13.00
...: PRIVATE CASEBOOK HC (2008, $19.99)-r/Detective Comics #840-845 and story from DC Infinite Halloween Special #1 20.00
...: PRODIGAL (1997, $14.95)-Gulacy/Austin-a 15.00
...: R.I.P.: THE DELUXE EDITION HC (2009, $24.99)-r/Batman #676-683 and story from DC Universe #0 25.00
...: R.I.P.: SC (2010, $14.99)-r/Batman #676-683 and story from DC Universe #0 15.00
... SCARECROW TALES (2005, $19.99, TPB) r/Scarecrow stories & pin-ups from World's Finest #3 to present 20.00
...: SECRETS OF THE BATCAVE (2007, $17.99, TPB) r/Batcave stories 18.00
SHAMAN (1993, $12.95)-r/Legends/D.K. #1-5 13.00
...: SNOW (2007, $14.99, TPB)-r/Legends of the Dark Knight #192-196; Fisher-a 15.00
...: SON OF THE DEMON Hard-c (9/87, $14.95) (see Batman #655-658) 30.00
...: SON OF THE DEMON limited signed & numbered Hard-c (1,700) 45.00
...: SON OF THE DEMON Soft-c w/new-c ($8.95) 10.00
...: SON OF THE DEMON Soft-c (1989, $9.95, 2nd printing - 5th printing) 10.00
... : STRANGE APPARITIONS ($12.95) r/'77-'78 Englehart/Rogers stories from Detective #469-479; also Simonson-a 13.00
...: TALES OF THE DEMON (1991, $17.95, 212 pgs.)-Intro by Sam Hamm; reprints by Neal Adams(3) & Golden; contains Saga of Ra's al Ghul #1 18.00
TALES OF THE MULTIVERSE: BATMAN - VAMPIRE (2007, $19.99) r/Batman & Dracula: Red Rain, Batman: Bloodstorm and Batman: Crimson Mist; Van Lustbader foreword 20.00
...: TEN NIGHTS OF THE BEAST (1994, $5.95)-r/Batman #417-420 6.00
...: TERROR (2003, $12.95, TPB)-r/Legends of the Dark Knight #137-141; Gulacy-c 13.00
...: THE BLACK GLOVE (2009, $17.99, TPB) r/Batman #667-669,672-675 18.00
...: THE CHALICE (HC, '99, $24.95) Van Fleet painted-a 25.00
...: THE CHALICE (SC, '00, $14.95) Van Fleet painted-a 15.00
...: THE GREATEST STORIES EVER TOLD (2005, $19.99, TPB) Les Daniels intro. 20.00
...: THE GREATEST STORIES EVER TOLD VOLUME TWO (2007, $19.99, TPB) 20.00
...: THE JOKER'S LAST LAUGH ('08, $17.99) r/Joker's Last Laugh series #1-6 18.00
...: THE LAST ANGEL (1994, $12.95, TPB) Lustbader-s 13.00
...: THE RESURRECTION OF RA'S AL GHUL (2008, $29.99, HC w/DJ) r/x-over 30.00
...: THE RESURRECTION OF RA'S AL GHUL (2009, $19.99, SC) r/x-over 20.00
...: THE RING, THE ARROW AND THE BAT (2003, $19.95, TPB) r/Legends of the DCU #7-9 & Batman: Legends of the Dark Knight #127-131; Green Lantern & Green Arrow app. 20.00
...: THE STRANGE DEATHS OF BATMAN ('09, $19.99) r/Batman #291-294, Det. #347, World's Finest #184,269, Brave & the Bold #115, Nightwing #52; Aparo-c 20.00
...: THE WRATH ('09, $17.99) r/Batman Special #1 and Batman Confidential #13-16 18.00
...: THRILLKILLER (1998, $12.95, TPB)-r/series & Thrillkiller '62 13.00
...: TIME AND THE BATMAN HC ('11, $19.99) r/Batman #700-703; cover gallery 20.00
...: TWO-FACE AND SCARECROW YEAR ONE (2009, $19.99, TPB)-r/Year One: Batman Scarecrow #1,2 and Two Face: Year One #1,2 20.00
...: UNDER THE COWL (2010, $17.99, TPB)-r/app. Dick Grayson, Tim Drake, Damien Wayne, Jean Paul Valley and Terry McGinnis as Batman 18.00
...: UNDER THE HOOD (2005, $9.99, TPB)-r/Batman #635-641 10.00
...: UNDER THE HOOD Vol. 2 (2006, $9.99, TPB)-r/Batman #645-650 & Annual #25 10.00
...: UNDER THE RED HOOD (2011, $29.99, TPB)-r/Batman #635-641,645-650, Ann. #25 30.00
...: VENOM (1993, $9.95, TPB)-r/Legends of the Dark Knight #16-20; embossed-c 10.00
... VS. TWO-FACE (2008, $19.99, TPB) r/initial (Det. #80) & classic battles; Bianchi-c 20.00
...: WAR CRIMES (2006, $12.99, TPB) r/x-over; James Jean-c 13.00
... WAR DRUMS (2004, $17.95) r/Detective #790-796 & Robin #126-128 18.00
...: WAR GAMES ACT 1,2,3 (2005, $14.95/$14.99, TPB) r/x-over; James Jean-c; each.. 15.00
...: WHATEVER HAPPENED TO THE CAPED CRUSADER? HC-(2009, $24.99, d.j.) r/Batman #686, Detective #853 and other Gaiman Batman stories; Gaiman intro.; Andy Kubert sketch pages; new Kubert cover 25.00
...: WHATEVER HAPPENED TO THE CAPED CRUSADER? SC-(2010, $14.99) 15.00
YEAR ONE Hard-c (1988, $12.95) r/Batman #404-407 18.00
YEAR ONE (1988, $9.95, TPB)-r/Batman #404-407 by Miller; intro by Miller 10.00
YEAR ONE (TPB, 2nd & 3rd printings) 10.00
YEAR ONE Deluxe HC (2005, $19.99, die-cut d.j.) new intro. by Miller and developmental material from Mazzucchelli; script pages and sketches 20.00
YEAR ONE (Deluxe) SC (2007, $14.99) r/story plus bonus material from 2005 HC 15.00
YEAR TWO (1990, $9.95, TPB)-r/Det. 575-578 by McFarlane; wraparound-c 10.00

BATMAN (one-shots)
... ABDUCTION, THE (1998, $5.95) 6.00
... ALLIES SECRET FILES AND ORIGINS 2005 (8/05, $4.99) stories/pin-ups by various 5.00
... & ROBIN (1997, $5.95)-Movie adaptation 6.00
...: ARKHAM ASYLUM - TALES OF MADNESS (5/98, $2.95) Cataclysm x-over pt. 16 4.00
... : BANE (1997, $4.95)-Dixon-s/Burchett-a; Stelfreeze-c; cover art interlocks w/Batman:(Batgirl, Mr. Freeze, Poison Ivy) 5.00
... : BATGIRL (1997, $4.95)-Puckett-s/Haley,Kesel-a; Stelfreeze-c; cover art interlocks w/Batman:(Bane, Mr. Freeze, Poison Ivy) 5.00
... : BATGIRL (6/98, $1.95)-Girlfrenzy; Balent-a 3.00
... : BLACKGATE (1/97, $3.95) Dixon-s 4.00
... : BLACKGATE - ISLE OF MEN (4/98, $2.95) Cataclysm x-over pt. 8; Moench-s/Aparo-a 3.00
... BOOK OF SHADOWS, THE (1999, $5.95) 6.00
BROTHERHOOD OF THE BAT (1995, $5.95)-Elseworlds-s 6.00

Batman: The Man Who Laughs GN © DC

Batman: The 10-Cent Adventure © DC

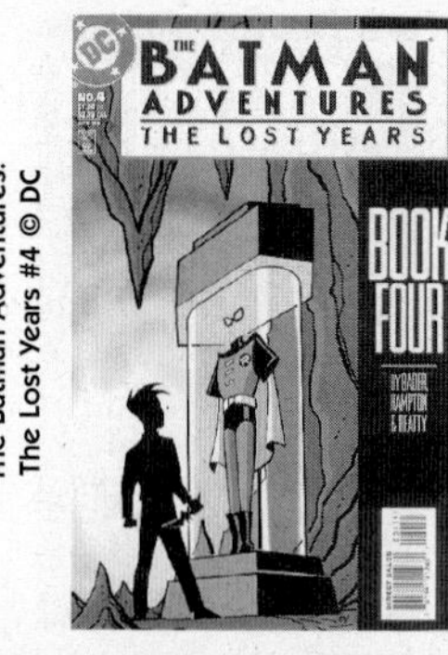

The Batman Adventures: The Lost Years #4 © DC

	GD 2.0	VG 4.0	FN 6.0	VF 8.0	VF/NM 9.0	NM- 9.2

... BULLOCK'S LAW (8/99, $4.95) Dixon-s 5.00
.../CAPTAIN AMERICA (1996, $5.95, DC/Marvel) Elseworlds story; Byrne-c/s/a 6.00
... : CATWOMAN DEFIANT nn (1992, $4.95, prestige format)-Milligan scripts; cover art interlocks w/Batman: Penguin Triumphant; special foil logo 5.00
.../CATWOMAN: FOLLOW THE MONEY (1/11, $4.99) Chaykin-c/s/a 5.00
... /DANGER GIRL (2/05, $4.95)-Leinil Yu-a/c; Joker, Harley Quinn & Catwoman app. 5.00
... /DAREDEVIL (2000, $5.95)-Barreto-a 6.00
...: DARK ALLEGIANCES (1996, $5.95)-Elseworlds story, Chaykin-c/a 6.00
...: DARK KNIGHT GALLERY (1/96, $3.50)-Pin-ups by Pratt, Balent, & others 4.00
...:DAY OF JUDGMENT (11/99, $3.95) 4.00
...:DEATH OF INNOCENTS (12/96, $3.95)-O'Neil-s/ Staton-a(p) 4.00
.../DEMON (1996, $4.95)-Alan Grant scripts 5.00
.../DEMON: A TRAGEDY (2000, $5.95)-Grant-s/Murray painted-a 6.00
...:D.O.A. (1999, $6.95)-Bob Hall-s/a 7.00
...:/DOC SAVAGE SPECIAL (2010, $4.99)-Azzarello-s/Noto-a/covers by JG Jones & Morales; preview of First Wave line (Batman, Doc Savage, The Spirit, Blackhawks) 5.00
...:DREAMLAND (2000, $5.95)-Grant-s/Breyfogle-a 6.00
... : EGO (2000, $6.95)-Darwyn Cooke-s/a 7.00
... 80-PAGE GIANT (8/98, $4.95) Stelfreeze-c 6.00
... 80-PAGE GIANT 1 (2/10, $5.99) Andy Kubert-c; Catwoman, Poison Ivy app. 6.00
... 80-PAGE GIANT 2 (10/99, $4.95) Luck of the Draw 6.00
... 80-PAGE GIANT 3 (7/00, $5.95) Calendar Man 6.00
... 80-PAGE GIANT 2011 (2/11, $5.95) Nguyen-c; short stories of villains by various 6.00
... 80-PAGE GIANT 2011 (10/11, $5.99) Nguyen-c; art by Naifeh & others 6.00
... FOREVER (1995, $5.95, direct market) 6.00
... FOREVER (1995, $3.95, newsstand) 4.00
FULL CIRCLE nn (1991, $5.95, 68 pgs.)-Sequel to Batman: Year Two 6.00
...GALLERY, The 1 (1992, $2.95)-Pin-ups by Miller, N. Adams & others 4.00
...GOLDEN STREETS OF GOTHAM (2003, $6.95) Elseworlds in early 1900s 7.00
...GOTHAM BY GASLIGHT (1989, $3.95) Elseworlds; Mignola-a/Augustyn-s 4.00
...GOTHAM CITY SECRET FILES 1 (4/00, $4.95) Batgirl app. 5.00
...: GOTHAM NOIR (2001, $6.95)-Elseworlds; Brubaker-s/Phillips-c/a 7.00
.../GREEN ARROW: THE POISON TOMORROW nn (1992, $5.95, square-bound, 68 pgs.) Netzer-c/a 6.00
...: HIDDEN TREASURES 1 (12/10, $4.99) unpubl. story Wrightson-a; r/Swamp Thing #7 5.00
HOLY TERROR nn (1991, $4.95, 52 pgs.)-Elseworlds story 5.00
.../HOUDINI: THE DEVIL'S WORKSHOP (1993, $5.95) 6.00
... :HUNTRESS/SPOILER - BLUNT TRAUMA (5/98, $2.95) Cataclysm pt. 13; Dixon-s/Barreto & Sienkiewicz-a 4.00
...: I, JOKER nn (1998, $4.95)-Elseworlds story; Bob Hall-s/a 5.00
...: IN BARCELONA: DRAGON'S KNIGHT 1 (7/09, $3.99) Waid-s/Olmos-a/Jim Lee-c 4.00
...: IN DARKEST KNIGHT nn (1994, $4.95, 52 pgs.)-Elseworlds story; Batman w/Green Lantern's ring. 5.00
...:JOKER'S APPRENTICE (5/99, $3.95) Von Eeden-a 4.00
.../ JOKER: SWITCH (2003, $6.95)-Bolton-a/Grayson-s 7.00
...:JUDGE DREDD: JUDGEMENT ON GOTHAM nn (1991, $5.95, 68 pgs.) Simon Bisley-c/a; Grant/Wagner scripts 6.00
...:JUDGE DREDD: JUDGEMENT ON GOTHAM nn (2nd printing) 6.00
...:JUDGE DREDD: THE ULTIMATE RIDDLE (1995, $4.95) 5.00
...:JUDGE DREDD: VENDETTA IN GOTHAM (1993, $5.95) 6.00
...: KNIGHTGALLERY (1995, $3.50)-Elseworlds sketchbook. 4.00
.../ LOBO (2000, $5.95)-Elseworlds; Joker app.; Bisley-a 6.00
...: MASK OF THE PHANTASM (1994, $2.95)-Movie adapt. 4.00
...: MASK OF THE PHANTASM (1994, $4.95)-Movie adapt. 5.00
...: MASQUE (1997, $6.95)-Elseworlds; Grell-c/s/a 7.00
...: MASTER OF THE FUTURE nn (1991, $5.95, 68 pgs.)-Elseworlds; sequel to Gotham By Gaslight; Barreto-a; embossed-c 6.00
...: MITEFALL (1995, $4.95)-Alan Grant script, Kevin O'Neill-a 5.00
... : MR. FREEZE (1997, $4.95)-Dini-s/Buckingham-a; Stelfreeze-c; cover art interlocks w/Batman:(Bane, Batgirl, Poison Ivy) 5.00
... /NIGHTWING: BLOODBORNE (2002, $5.95) Cypress-a; McKeever-c 6.00
...: NOEL (2011, $22.99, HC graphic novel with dustjacket) Lee Bermejo-s/a; Jim Lee intro.; Catwoman, Superman & The Joker app.; bonus sketch & layout art pages 23.00
...: NOSFERATU (1999, $5.95) McKeever-a 6.00
...: OF ARKHAM (2000, $5.95)-Elseworlds; Grant-s/Alcatena-a 6.00
...: OUR WORLDS AT WAR (8/01, $2.95)-Jae Lee-c 3.00
...: PENGUIN TRIUMPHANT nn (1992, $4.95)-Staton-a(p); foil logo 5.00
...·PHANTOM STRANGER nn (1997, $4.95) nn-Grant-s/Ransom-a 5.00
... : PLUS (2/97, $2.95) Arsenal-c/app. 4.00
... : POISON IVY (1997, $4.95)-J.F. Moore-s/Apthorp-a; Stelfreeze-c; cover art interlocks w/Batman:(Bane, Batgirl, Mr. Freeze) 5.00
.../POISON IVY: CAST SHADOWS (2004, $6.95) Van Fleet-c/a; Nocenti-s 7.00
.../PUNISHER: LAKE OF FIRE (1994, $4.95, DC/Marvel) 5.00
... :REIGN OF TERROR ('99, $4.95) Elseworlds 5.00
...RETURNS MOVIE SPECIAL (1992, $3.95) 4.00
...RETURNS MOVIE PRESTIGE (1992, $5.95, squarebound)-Dorman painted-c 6.00
...:RIDDLER-THE RIDDLE FACTORY (1995, $4.95)-Wagner script 5.00
...: ROOM FULL OF STRANGERS (2004, $5.95) Scott Morse-s/c/a 6.00
...: SCARECROW 3-D (12/98, $3.95) w/glasses 4.00
.../ SCARFACE: A PSYCHODRAMA (2001, $5.95)-Adlard-a/Sienkiewicz-c 6.00
...: SCAR OF THE BAT nn (1996, $4.95)-Elseworlds; Max Allan Collins script; Barreto-a 5.00
... :SCOTTISH CONNECTION (1998, $5.95) Quitely-a 6.00
... :SEDUCTION OF THE GUN nn (1992, $2.50, 68 pgs.) 4.00
.../SPAWN: WAR DEVIL nn (1994, $4.95, 52 pgs.) 5.00
... SPECIAL 1 (4/84)-Mike W. Barr story; Golden-c/a 1 2 3 5 6 8
.../SPIDER-MAN (1997, $4.95) Dematteis-s/Nolan & Kesel-a 5.00
... : THE ABDUCTION ('98, $5.95) 6.00
...: THE BLUE, THE GREY, & THE BAT (1992, $5.95)-Weiss/Lopez-a 6.00
... :THE HILL (5/00, $2.95)-Priest-s/Martinbrough-a 3.00
... :THE KILLING JOKE (1988, deluxe 52 pgs., mature readers)-Bolland-c/a; Alan Moore scripts; Joker cripples Barbara Gordon 2 4 6 11 16 20
...: THE KILLING JOKE (2nd thru 12th printings) 2 4 6 8 10 12
...: THE KILLING JOKE : THE DELUXE EDITION (2008, $17.99, HC) re-colored version along with Bolland-s/a from Batman Black and White #4; sketch pages; Tim Sale intro. 18.00
...: THE MAN WHO LAUGHS (2005, $6.95)-Retells 1st meeting with the Joker; Mahnke-a 7.00
...: THE OFFICIAL COMIC ADAPTATION OF THE WARNER BROS. MOTION PICTURE (1989, $2.50, regular format, 68 pgs.)-Ordway-c 4.00
...: THE OFFICIAL COMIC ADAPTATION OF THE WARNER BROS. MOTION PICTURE (1989, $4.95, prestige format, 68 pgs.)-same interiors but different-c 5.00
...: THE ORDER OF BEASTS (2004, $5.95)-Elseworlds; Eddie Campbell-a 6.00
...: THE SPIRIT (1/07, $4.99)-Loeb-s/Cooke-a; P'Gell & Commissioner Dolan app. 5.00
...: THE 10-CENT ADVENTURE (3/02, 10¢) intro. to the "Bruce Wayne: Murderer" x-over; Rucka-s/Burchett & Janson-a/Dave Johnson-c 3.00

NOTE: (Also see Promotional Comics section for alternate copies with special outer half-covers promoting local comic shops)

...: THE 12-CENT ADVENTURE (10/04, 12¢) intro. to the "War Games" x-over; Grayson-s/Bachs-a; Catwoman & Spoiler app. 3.00
...: TWO-FACE-CRIME AND PUNISHMENT-(1995, $4.95)-McDaniel-a 5.00
... : TWO FACES (11/98, $4.95) Elseworlds 5.00
...Vs. THE INCREDIBLE HULK (1995, $3.95)-r/DC Special Series #27 4.00
...: VILLAINS SECRET FILES (10/98, $4.95) Origin-s 5.00
... VILLAINS SECRET FILES AND ORIGINS 2005 (7/05, $4.99) Clayface origin w/ Mignola-a; Black Mask story, pin-up of villains by various; Barrionuevo-c 5.00

BATMAN ADVENTURES, THE (Based on animated series)
DC Comics: Oct, 1992 - No. 36, Oct, 1995 ($1.25/$1.50)

1-Penguin-c/story 5.00
1 ($1.95, Silver Edition)-2nd printing 3.00
2-6,8-11,13-19: 2,12-Catwoman-c/story. 3-Joker-c/story. 5-Scarecrow-c/story. 10-Riddler-c/story. 11-Man-Bat-c/story. 16-Joker-c/story; begin $1.50-c. 18-Batgirl-c/story. 19-Scarecrow-c/story. 3.50
7-Special edition polybagged with Man-Bat trading card 6.00
12-(9/93) 1st Harley Quinn app. in comics; 1st animated-version Batgirl app. in title 3 6 9 16 23 30
20-24,26-32: 26-Batgirl app. 3.00
25-($2.50, 52 pgs.)-Superman app. 4.00
33-36: 33-Begin $1.75-c 3.00
Annual 1,2 ('94, '95): 2-Demon-c/story; Ra's al Ghul app. 4.00
...: Dangerous Dames & Demons (2003, $14.95, TPB) r/Annual 1,2, Mad Love & Adventures in the DC Universe #3; Bruce Timm painted-c 30.00
Holiday Special 1 (1995, $2.95) 5.00
The Collected Adventures Vol. 1,2 ('93, '95, $5.95) 6.00
TPB ('98, $7.95) r/#1-6; painted wraparound-c 8.00

BATMAN ADVENTURES (Based on animated series)
DC Comics: Jun, 2003 - No. 17, Oct, 2004 ($2.25)

1-Timm-c 3.00
1-Free Comic Book Day edition (6/03) Timm-c 3.00
2-17: 3,16-Joker-c/app. 4-Ra's al Ghul app. 6-8-Phantasm app. 14-Grey Ghost app. 3.00
Vol. 1: Rogues Gallery (2004, $6.95, digest size) r/#1-4 & Batman: Gotham Advs. #50 7.00
Vol. 2: Shadows & Masks (2004, $6.95, digest size) r/#5-9 7.00

BATMAN ADVENTURES, THE: MAD LOVE
DC Comics: Feb, 1994 ($3.95/$4.95)

1-Origin of Harley Quinn; Dini-s/Timm-c/a 3 6 9 14 19 24
1-($4.95, Prestige format) new Timm painted-c 2 3 4 6 8 10

BATMAN ADVENTURES, THE: THE LOST YEARS (TV)
DC Comics: Jan, 1998 - No. 5, May, 1998 ($1.95) (Based on animated series)

1-5-Leads into Fall '97's new animated episodes. 4-Tim Drake becomes Robin.

Batman and Robin #16 © DC

Batman: Battle For the Cowl #1 © DC

Batman Beyond #3 © DC

	GD 2.0	VG 4.0	FN 6.0	VF 8.0	VF/NM 9.0	NM- 9.2

5-Dick becomes Nightwing 3.00
TPB-(1999, $9.95) r/series 10.00

BATMAN/ALIENS
DC Comics/Dark Horse: Mar, 1997 - No. 2, Apr, 1997 ($4.95, limited series)
1,2: Wrightson-c/a. 5.00
TPB-(1997, $14.95) w/prequel from DHP #101,102 15.00

BATMAN/ALIENS II
DC Comics/Dark Horse: 2003 - No. 3, 2003 ($5.95, limited series)
1-3-Edginton-s/Staz Johnson-a 6.00
TPB-(2003, $14.95) r/#1-3 15.00

BATMAN AND ROBIN (See Batman R.I.P. and Batman: Battle For The Cowl series)
DC Comics: Aug, 2009 - No. 26, Oct, 2011 ($2.99)
1-Grant Morrison-s/Frank Quitely-a/c; Dick Grayson & Damian Wayne team 5.00
1-Variant cover by J.G. Jones 20.00
1-Second thru Fourth printings - recolored Quitely covers 3.00
2-16-Quitely-c. 2-Three printings. 4-6-Tan-a. 7-9-Stewart-a; Batwoman & Squire app. 13-15-Joker app.; Irving-a. 16-Bruce Wayne returns; Batman Inc. announced 3.00
2-Variant-c by Adam Kubert 10.00
17-26: 17-McDaniel-a/March-c. 21,22-Gleason-a. 23-25-Red Hood app. 3.00
... #1 Special Edition (6/10, $1.00) r/#1 with "What's Next?" cover logo 3.00
...: Batman and Robin Must Die - The Deluxe Edition HC (2011, $24.99) r/#13-16; cover and costume design sketch art 25.00
...: Batman Reborn - The Deluxe Edition HC (2010, $24.99) r/#1-6; design sketch art 25.00
...: Batman Reborn SC (2011, $14.99) r/#1-6; cover and character design sketch art 15.00
...: Batman vs. Robin - The Deluxe Edition HC (2010, $24.99) r/#7-12; cover sketch art 25.00

BATMAN AND ROBIN (DC New 52)
DC Comics: Nov, 2011 - Present ($2.99)
1-Bruce and Damien Wayne in costume; Tomasi-s/Gleason-a 3.00
2-8: 5,6-Ducard flashback 3.00

BATMAN AND ROBIN ADVENTURES (TV)
DC Comics: Nov, 1995 - No. 25, Dec, 1997 ($1.75) (Based on animated series)
1-Dini-s. 4.00
2-24: 2-4-Dini script. 4-Penguin-c/story. 5-Joker-c/story; Poison Ivy, Harley Quinn-c/app. 9-Batgirl & Talia-c/story. 10-Ra's al Ghul-c/story. 11-Man-Bat app. 12-Bane-c/app. 13-Scarecrow-c/app. 15 Deadman-c/app. 16-Catwoman-c/app. 18-Joker-c/app. 24-Poison Ivy app. 3.00
25-($2.95, 48 pgs.) 4.00
Annual 1,2 (11/96, 11/97): 1-Phantasm-c/app. 2-Zatara & Zatanna-c/app. 4.00
...: Sub-Zero(1998, $3.95) Adaptation of animated video 4.00

BATMAN AND SUPERMAN ADVENTURES: WORLD'S FINEST
DC Comics: 1997 ($6.95, square-bound, one-shot) (Based on animated series)
1-Adaptation of animated crossover episode; Dini-s/Timm-c. 7.00

BATMAN AND SUPERMAN: WORLD'S FINEST
DC Comics: Apr, 1999 - No. 10, Jan, 2000 ($4.95/$1.99, limited series)
1,10-($4.95, squarebound) Taylor-a 5.00
2-9-($1.99) 5-Batgirl app. 8-Catwoman-c/app. 3.00
TPB (2003, $19.95) r/#1-10 20.00

BATMAN AND THE OUTSIDERS (The Adventures of the Outsiders #33 on)
(Also see Brave & The Bold #200 & The Outsiders) (Replaces The Brave and the Bold)
DC Comics: Aug, 1983 - No. 32, Apr, 1986 (Mando paper #5 on)
1-Batman, Halo, Geo-Force, Katana, Metamorpho & Black Lightning begin 5.00
2-32: 5-New Teen Titans x-over. 9-Halo begins. 11,12-Origin Katana. 18-More info on Metamorpho's origin. 28-31-Lookers origin. 32-Team disbands 3.00
Annual 1,2 (9/84, 9/85): 2-Metamorpho & Sapphire Stagg wed 4.00
NOTE: ***Aparo** a-1-9, 11-13p, 16-20; c-1-4, 5i, 6-21, Annual 1, 2.* ***B. Kane** a-3r.* ***Layton** a-19i, 20i.* ***Lopez** a-3p.* ***Miller** c-Annual 1.* ***Perez** c-5p.* ***B. Willingham** a-14p.*

BATMAN AND THE OUTSIDERS (Continues as The Outsiders for #15-39)
DC Comics: Dec, 2007 - No. 14, Feb, 2009; No. 40, Jul, 2011 ($2.99)
1-14: 1-Batman, Catwoman, Martian Manhunter, Katana, Metamorpho, Thunder & Grace begin. 4-Batgirl joins. 11-13-Batman R.I.P. 3.00
40 (7/11) Final issue; Didio-s/Tan-a; history of the team 3.00
... Special (3/09, $3.99) Alfred assembles a new team; Andy Kubert-a; two covers 4.00
...: The Chrysalis TPB (2008, $14.99) r/#1-5 15.00
...: The Snare TPB (2008, $14.99) r/#6-10 15.00

BATMAN: ARKHAM CITY (Prequel to the video game)
DC Comics: Early Jul, 2011 - No. 5, Oct, 2011 ($2.99, limited series)
1-5-Dini-s/D'Anda-a; Joker app. 3.00

BATMAN: ARKHAM UNHINGED (Based on the Batman: Arkham City video game)
DC Comics: Jun, 2012 - Present ($2.99)
1-Wilkins-c; Catwoman, Two-Face & Hugo Strange app. 3.00

BATMAN: BANE OF THE DEMON
DC Comics: Mar, 1998 - No. 4, June, 1998 ($1.95, limited series)
1-4-Dixon-s/Nolan-a; prelude to Legacy x-over 3.00

BATMAN: BATTLE FOR THE COWL (Follows Batman R.I.P. storyline)
DC Comics: May, 2009 - No. 3, Jul, 2009 ($3.99, limited series)
1-3-Tony Daniel-s/a/c; 2 covers on each 4.00
...: Arkham Asylum (6/09, $2.99) Hine-s/Haun-a/Ladronn-c 3.00
...: Commissioner Gordon (5/09, $2.99) Mandrake-a/Ladronn-c; Mr. Freeze app. 3.00
...: Man-Bat (6/09, $2.99) Harris-s/Calafiore-a/Ladronn-c; Dr. Phosphorus app. 3.00
...: The Network (7/09, $2.99) Nicieza-s/Calafiore & Kramer-a/Ladronn-c 3.00
...: The Underground (6/09, $2.99) Yost-s/Raimondi-a/Ladronn-c 3.00
Companion SC (2009, $14.99) r/ five one-shots 15.00
HC (2009, $19.99) r/#1-3 & Gotham Gazette: Batman Dead & Gotham Gazette: Batman Alive; gallery of variant covers and sketch art 20.00
SC (2010, $14.99) same contents as HC 15.00

BATMAN BEYOND (Based on animated series)
DC Comics: Mar, 1999 - No. 6, Aug, 1999 ($1.99, limited series)
1-6: 1,2-Adaptation of pilot episode, Timm-c 3.00
TPB (1999, $9.95) r/#1-6 10.00

BATMAN BEYOND (Based on animated series)(Continuing series)
DC Comics: Nov, 1999 - No. 24, Oct, 2001 ($1.99)
1-24: 1-Rousseau-a; Batman vs. Batman. 14-Demon-c/app. 21,22-Justice League Unlimited-c/app. 3.00
...: Return of the Joker (2/01, $2.95) adaptation of video release 4.00

BATMAN BEYOND (Animated series)(See Superman/Batman Annual #4)
DC Comics: Aug, 2010 - No. 6, Jan, 2011 ($2.99, limited series)
1-6: 1-Benjamin-a; Nguyen-c; return of Hush 3.00
1-Variant-c by J.H. Williams III 6.00
...: Hush Beyond TPB (2011, $14.99) r/#1-6 15.00

BATMAN BEYOND
DC Comics: Mar, 2011 - No. 8, Oct, 2011 ($2.99)
1-8: 1-3-Justice League app.; Beechen-s/Benjamin-a/Nguyen-c. 8-Inque app. 3.00
1-Variant-c by Darwyn Cooke 4.00

BATMAN BEYOND UNLIMITED
DC Comics: Apr, 2012- Present ($3.99)
1,2-Beechen-s/Breyfogle-a; Justice League back-ups; Nguyen-a/Nguyen-c 4.00

BATMAN: BLACK & WHITE
DC Comics: June, 1996 - No. 4, Sept, 1996 ($2.95, B&W, limited series)
1-Stories by McKeever, Timm, Kubert, Chaykin, Goodwin; Jim Lee-c; Allred inside front-c; Moebius inside back-c 4.00
2-4: 2-Stories by Simonson, Corben, Bisley & Gaiman; Miller-c. 3-Stories by M. Wagner, Janson, Sienkiewicz, O'Neil & Kristiansen; B. Smith-c; Russell inside front-c; Silvestri inside back-c. 4-Stories by Bolland, Goodwin & Gianni, Strnad & Nowlan, O'Neil & Stelfreeze; Toth-c; pin-ups by Neal Adams & Alex Ross 3.00
Hardcover ('97, $39.95) r/series w/new art & cover plate 40.00
Softcover ('00, $19.95) r/series 20.00
Volume 2 HC ('02, $39.95, 7 3/4"x12") r/B&W back-up-s from Batman: Gotham Knights #1-16; stories and art by various incl. Ross, Buscema, Byrne, Ellison, Sale; Mignola-c 40.00
Volume 2 SC ('03, $19.95, 7 3/4"x12") same contents as HC 20.00
Volume 2 SC ('08, $19.99, reg. size) same contents as HC 20.00
Volume 3 HC ('07, $24.99, reg. size) r/B&W back-up-s from Batman: Gotham Knights #17-49; stories and art by various incl. Davis, DeCarlo, Morse, Schwartz, Thompson; Miller-c 25.00

BATMAN: BOOK OF THE DEAD
DC Comics: Jun, 1999 - No. 2, July, 1999 ($4.95, limited series, prestige format)
1,2-Elseworlds; Kitson-a 5.00

BATMAN CACOPHONY
DC Comics: Jan, 2009 - No. 3, Mar, 2009 ($3.99, limited series)
1-3-Kevin Smith-s/Walt Flanagan-a; Joker and Onomatoapoeia app.; Adam Kubert-c 4.00
1-3-Variant-c by Sienkiewicz 10.00
HC (2009, $19.99, d.j.) r/#1-3; Kevin Smith intro.; script for #3, cover gallery 20.00
SC (2010, $14.99) r/#1-3; Kevin Smith intro.; script for #3, cover gallery 15.00

BATMAN: CATWOMAN DEFIANT (See Batman one-shots)

BATMAN/ CATWOMAN: TRAIL OF THE GUN
DC Comics: 2004 - No. 2, 2004 ($5.95, limited series, prestige format)

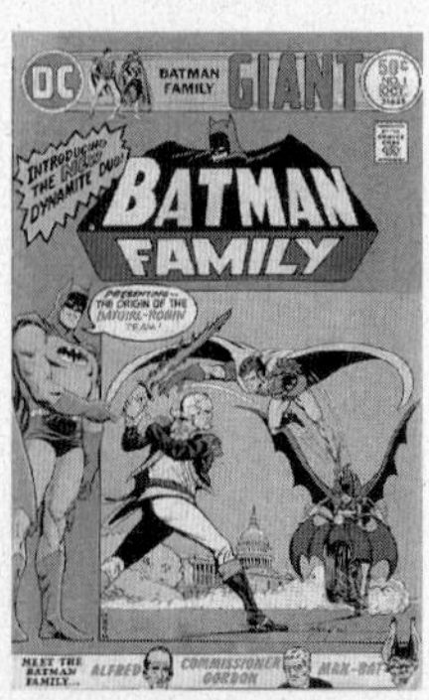

Batman Family #1 © DC

Batman: Gotham Adventures #3 © DC

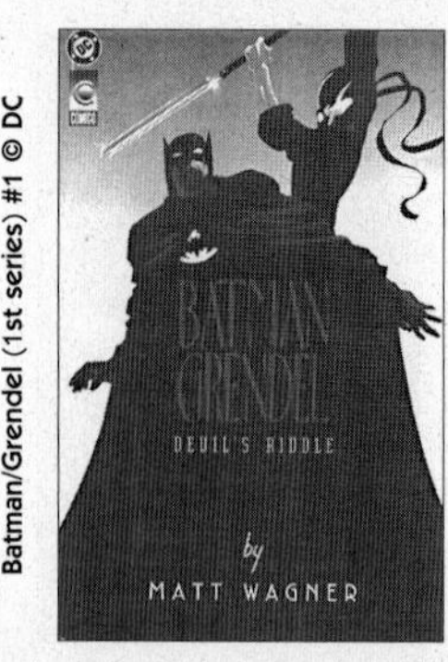

Batman/Grendel (1st series) #1 © DC

GD	VG	FN	VF	VF/NM	NM-
2.0	4.0	6.0	8.0	9.0	9.2

1,2-Elseworlds; Van Sciver-a/Nocenti-s 6.00

BATMAN CHRONICLES, THE (See the Batman TPB listings for the Golden Age reprint series that shares this title)
DC Comics: Summer, 1995 - No. 23, Winter, 2001 ($2.95, quarterly)

1-3,5-19: 1-Dixon/Grant/Moench script. 3-Bolland-c. 5-Oracle Year One story, Richard Dragon app.,Chaykin-c. 6-Kaluta-c; Ra's al Ghul story. 7-Superman-c/app.11-Paul Pope-s/a. 12-Cataclysm pt. 10. 18-No Man's Land 3.50
4-Hitman story by Ennis, Contagion tie-in; Balent-c 2 4 6 8 10 12
20-23: 20-Catwoman and Relative Heroes-c/app. 21-Pander Bros.-a 3.00
...Gallery (3/97, $3.50) Pin-ups 4.00
...Gauntlet, The (1997, $4.95, one-shot) 5.00

BATMAN: CITY OF LIGHT
DC Comics: Dec, 2003 - No. 8, July, 2004 ($2.95, limited series)

1-8-Pander Brothers-a/s; Paniccia-s 3.00

BATMAN CONFIDENTIAL
DC Comics: Feb, 2007 - Present ($2.99)

1-49,51-54: 1-6-Diggle-s/Portacio-a/c. 7-12-Cowan-a; Joker's origin. 13-16-Morales-a. 17-21-Batgirl vs. Catwoman; Maguire-a. 22-25-McDaniel-a; Joker app. 26-28-King Tut app.; Garcia-Lopez-a. 40-43-Kieth-s/a. 44-48-Mandrake-a/c 3.00
50-($4.99) Bingham-a; back-up Silver Age-style JLA story 5.00
...: Dead to Rights SC (2010, $14.99) r/#22-25,29,30 15.00
...: Lovers and Madmen HC (2008, $24.99, dustjacket) r/#7-12; Brad Meltzer intro. 25.00
...: Lovers and Madmen SC (2009, $14.99) r/#7-12; Brad Meltzer intro. 15.00
...: Rules of Engagement HC (2007, $24.99, dustjacket) r/#1-6 25.00
...: The Bat and the Beast SC (2010, $12.99) r/#31-35 13.00
...: The Cat and the Bat SC (2009, $12.99) r/#17-21 13.00
...: Vs. The Undead SC (2010, $14.99) r/#44-48 15.00

BATMAN: DARK DETECTIVE
DC Comics: Early July, 2005 - No. 6, Late September, 2005 ($2.99, limited series)

1-6-Englehart-s/Rogers & Austin-a; Silver St. Cloud and The Joker app. 3.00

BATMAN: DARK KNIGHT OF THE ROUND TABLE
DC Comics: 1999 - No. 2, 1999 ($4.95, limited series, prestige format)

1,2-Elseworlds; Giordano-a 5.00

BATMAN: DARK VICTORY
DC Comics: 1999 - No. 13, 2000 ($4.95/$2.95, limited series)

Wizard #0 Preview 3.00
1-($4.95) Loeb-s/Sale-c/a 5.00
2-12-($2.95) 3.00
13-($4.95) 5.00
Hardcover (2001, $29.95) with dust jacket; r/#0,1-13 30.00
Softcover (2002, $19.95) r/#0,1-13 20.00

BATMAN: DEATH AND THE MAIDENS
DC Comics: Oct, 2003 - No. 9, Aug, 2004 ($2.95, limited series)

1-Ra's al Ghul app.; Rucka-s/Janson-a 4.00
2-9: 9-Ra's al Ghul dies 3.00
TPB (2004, $19.95) r/#1-9 & Detective #783 20.00

BATMAN/ DEATHBLOW: AFTER THE FIRE
DC Comics/WildStorm: 2002 - No. 3, 2002 ($5.95, limited series)

1-3-Azzarello-s/Bermejo & Bradstreet-a 6.00
TPB (2003, $12.95) r/#1-3; plus concept art 13.00

BATMAN: DEATH MASK
DC Comics/CMX: Jun, 2008 - No. 4, Sept, 2008 ($2.99, B&W, limited series, right-to-left manga style)

1-4-Yoshinori Natsume-s/a 3.00
TPB (2008, $9.99, digest size) r/#1-4; interview with Yoshinori Natsume 10.00

BATMAN FAMILY, THE
National Periodical Pub./DC Comics: Sept-Oct, 1975 - No. 20, Oct-Nov, 1978 (#1-4, 17-on: 68 pgs.) (Combined with Detective Comics with No. 481)

1-Origin/2nd app. Batgirl-Robin team-up (The Dynamite Duo); reprints plus one new story begins; N. Adams-a(r); r/1st app. Man-Bat from Det. #400
4 8 12 26 41 55
2-5: 2-r/Det. #369. 3-Batgirl & Robin learn each's i.d.; r/Batwoman app. from Batman #105. 4-r/1st Fatman app. from Batman #113. 5-r/1st Bat-Hound app. from Batman #92
3 6 9 16 23 30
6,9-Joker's daughter on cover (1st app?) 3 6 9 17 25 32
7,8,14-16: 8-r/Batwoman app.14-Batwoman app. 15-3rd app. Killer Moth. 16-Bat-Girl cameo (last app. in costume until New Teen Titans #47) 2 4 6 13 18 22
10-1st revival Batwoman; Cavalier app.; Killer Moth app.
3 6 9 19 29 38
11-13,17-20: 11-13-Rogers-a(p): 11-New stories begin; Man-Bat begins. 13-Batwoman cameo. 17-($1.00 size)-Batman, Huntress begin; Batwoman & Catwoman 1st meet. 18-20: Huntress by Staton in all. 20-Origin Ragman retold
3 6 9 18 27 35

NOTE: ***Aparo*** *a-17; c-11-16.* ***Austin*** *a-12i.* ***Chaykin*** *a-14p.* ***Michael Golden*** *a-15-17,18-20p.* ***Grell*** *a-1; c-1.* ***Gil Kane*** *a-2r.* ***Kaluta*** *c-17, 19.* ***Newton*** *a-13.* ***Robinson*** *a-1r, 3i(r), 9r.* ***Russell*** *a-18i, 19i.* ***Starlin*** *a-17; c-18, 20.*

BATMAN: FAMILY
DC Comics: Dec, 2002 - No. 8, Feb, 2003 ($2.95/$2.25, weekly limited series)

1,8-($2.95): 1-John Francis Moore-s/Hoberg & Gaudiano-a 4.00
2-7-($2.25): 3-Orpheus & Black Canary app. 3.00

BATMAN: GATES OF GOTHAM
DC Comics: Jul, 2011 - No. 5, Late Oct, 2011 ($2.99, limited series)

1-5-Flashbacks to 1880s Gotham City; Snyder-s/Higgins-a 3.00

BATMAN: GCPD
DC Comics: Aug, 1996 - No. 4, Nov, 1996 ($2.25, limited series)

1-4: Features Jim Gordon; Aparo/Sienkiewicz-a 3.00

BATMAN: GORDON OF GOTHAM
DC Comics: June, 1998 - No. 4, Sept, 1998 ($1.95, limited series)

1-4: Gordon's early days in Chicago 3.00

BATMAN: GORDON'S LAW
DC Comics: Dec, 1996 - No. 4, Mar, 1997 ($1.95, limited series)

1-4: Dixon-s/Janson-c/a 3.00

BATMAN: GOTHAM ADVENTURES (TV)
DC Comics: June, 1998 - No. 60, May, 2003 ($2.95/$1.95/$1.99/$2.25)

1-($2.95) Based on Kids WB Batman animated series 4.00
2-3-($1.95): 2-Two-Face-c/app. 3.00
4-22: 4-Begin $1.99-c. 5-Deadman-c. 13-MAD #1 cover swipe 3.00
23-60: 31,60-Joker-c/app. 50-Catwoman-c/app. 53-Begin $2.25-c. 58-Creeper-c/app. 3.00
TPB (2000, $9.95) r/#1-6 10.00

BATMAN: GOTHAM AFTER MIDNIGHT
DC Comics: July, 2008 - No. 12, Jun, 2009 ($2.99, limited series)

1-12-Steve Niles-s/Kelley Jones-a/c. 1-Scarecrow app. 2-Man-Bat app. 5,6-Joker app. 3.00
TPB (2009, $19.99) r/#1-12; John Carpenter intro.; Jones sketch pages 20.00

BATMAN: GOTHAM COUNTY LINE
DC Comics: 2005 - No. 3, 2005 ($5.99, square-bound, limited series)

1-3-Steve Niles-s/Scott Hampton-a. 2,3-Deadman app. 6.00
TPB (2006, $17.99) r/#1-3 18.00

BATMAN: GOTHAM KNIGHTS
DC Comics: Mar, 2000 - No. 74, Apr, 2006 ($2.50/$2.75)

1-Grayson-s; B&W back-up by Warren Ellis & Jim Lee 4.00
2-10-Grayson-s; B&W back-ups by various 3.00
11-($3.25) Bolland-c; Kyle Baker back-up story 4.00
12-24: 13-Officer Down x-over; Ellison back-up-s. 15-Colan back-up. 20-Superman-c/app. 3.00
25,26-Bruce Wayne: Murderer pt. 4,10 3.50
27-31: 28,30,31-Bruce Wayne: Fugitive pt. 7,14,17 3.00
32-49: 32-Begin $2.75-c; Kaluta-a back-up. 33,34-Bane-c/app. 35-Mahfood-a back-up. 38-Bolton-a back-up. 43-Jason Todd & Batgirl app. 44-Jason Todd flashback 3.00
50-54-Hush returns-Barrionuevo-a/Bermejo-c. 53,54-Green Arrow app. 4.00
55-($3.75) Batman vs. Hush; Joker & Riddler app. 4.00
56-74: 56-58-War Games; Jae Lee-c. 60-65-Hush app. 66-Villains United tie-in; Talia app. 3.00
Batman: Hush Returns TPB (2006, $12.99) r/#50-55,66; cover gallery 13.00

BATMAN: GOTHAM NIGHTS II (First series listed under Gotham Nights)
DC Comics: Mar, 1995 - No. 4, June, 1995 ($1.95, limited series)

1-4 3.00

BATMAN/GRENDEL (1st limited series)
DC Comics: 1993 - No. 2, 1993 ($4.95, limited series, squarebound; 52 pgs.)

1,2: Batman vs. Hunter Rose. 1-Devil's Riddle; Matt Wagner-c/a/scripts. 2-Devil's Masque; Matt Wagner-c/a/scripts 6.00

BATMAN/GRENDEL (2nd limited series)
DC Comics: June, 1996 - No. 2, July, 1996 ($4.95, limited series, squarebound)

1,2: Batman vs. Grendel Prime. 1-Devil's Bones. 2-Devil's Dance; Wagner-c/a/s 5.00

BATMAN: HARLEY & IVY
DC Comics: Jun, 2004 - No. 3, Aug, 2004 ($2.50, limited series)

1-3-Paul Dini-s/Bruce Timm-c/a 3.00
TPB (2007, $14.99) r/series; newly colored story from Batman: Gotham Knights #14 and

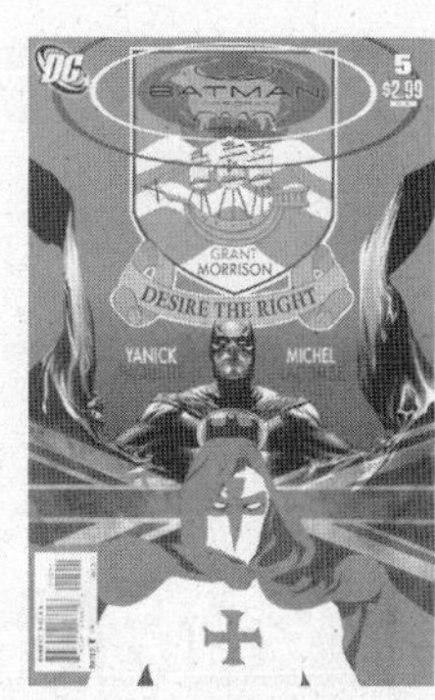

Batman Incorporated #5 © DC

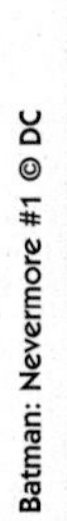

Batman: Nevermore #1 © DC

Batman: Odyssey #1 © DC

GD 2.0 | VG 4.0 | FN 6.0 | VF 8.0 | VF/NM 9.0 | NM- 9.2

Harley and Ivy: Love on the Lam series 15.00

BATMAN: HARLEY QUINN
DC Comics: 1999 ($5.95, prestige format)

1-Intro. of Harley Quinn into regular DC continuity; Dini-s/Alex Ross-c 3 6 9 14 19 24
1-(2nd printing) 6.00

BATMAN: HAUNTED GOTHAM
DC Comics: 2000 - No. 4, 2000 ($4.95, limited series, squarebound)

1-4-Doug Moench-s/Kelley Jones-c/a 5.00
TPB (2009, $19.99) r/#1-4 20.00

BATMAN/ HELLBOY/STARMAN
DC Comics/Dark Horse: Jan, 1999 - No. 2, Feb, 1999 ($2.50, limited series)

1,2: Robinson-s/Mignola-a. 2-Harris-c 3.00

BATMAN: HOLLYWOOD KNIGHT
DC Comics: Apr, 2001 - No. 3, Jun, 2001 ($2.50, limited series)

1-3-Elseworlds Batman as a 1940's movie star; Giordano-a/Layton-s 3.00

BATMAN/ HUNTRESS: CRY FOR BLOOD
DC Comics: Jun, 2000 - No. 6, Nov, 2000 ($2.50, limited series)

1-6: Rucka-s/Burchett-a; The Question app. 3.00
TPB (2002, $12.95) r/#1-6 13.00

BATMAN, INC.
DC Comics: Jan, 2011 - No. 8, Aug, 2011 ($3.99/$2.99)

1-3-Morrison-s/Paquette-a; covers by Paquette & Williams 4.00
4-8-($2.99) 4-Burnham-a, original Batwoman (Kathy Kane) app. 3.00
...: Leviathan Strikes (2/12, $6.99) Morrison-s/Burnham & Stewart-a; cover gallery 7.00

BATMAN: JEKYLL & HYDE
DC Comics: June, 2005 - No. 6, Nov, 2005 ($2.99, limited series)

1-6-Paul Jenkins-s; Two-Face app. 1-3-Jae Lee-a. 4-6-Sean Phillips-a 3.00
TPB (2008, $14.99) r/#1-6 15.00

BATMAN: JOKER TIME (...: It's Joker Time! on cover)
DC Comics: 2000 - No. 3 ($4.95, limited series, squarebound)

1-3-Bob Hall-s/a 5.00

BATMAN: JOURNEY INTO KNGHT
DC Comics: Oct, 2005 - No. 12, Nov, 2006 ($2.50/$2.99, limited series)

1-9-Andrew Helfer-s/Tan Eng Huat-a/Pat Lee-c 3.00
10-12-($2.99) Joker app. 3.00

BATMAN/ JUDGE DREDD "DIE LAUGHING"
DC Comics: 1998 - No. 2, 1999 ($4.95, limited series, squarebound)

1,2: 1-Fabry-c/a. 2-Jim Murray-c/a 5.00

BATMAN: KNIGHTGALLERY (See Batman one-shots)

BATMAN: LEAGUE OF BATMEN
DC Comics: 2001 - No. 2, 2001 ($5.95, limited series, squarebound)

1,2-Elseworlds; Moench-s/Bright & Tanghal-a/Van Fleet-c 6.00

BATMAN: LEGENDS OF THE DARK KNIGHT (Legends of the Dark...#1-36)
DC Comics: Nov, 1989 - No. 214, Mar, 2007 ($1.50/$1.75/$1.95/$1.99/$2.25/$2.50/$2.99)

1- "Shaman" begins, ends #5; outer cover has four different color variations, all worth same 4.00
2-10: 6-10- "Gothic" by Grant Morrison (scripts) 3.00
11-15: 11-15-Gulacy/Austin-a. 13-Catwoman app. 3.00
16-Intro drug Bane uses; begin Venom story 5.00
17-20 4.00
21-49,51-63: 38-Bat-Mite-c/story. 46-49-Catwoman app. w/Heath-c/a. 51-Ragman app.; Joe Kubert-c. 59,60,61-Knightquest x-over. 62,63-KnightsEnd Pt. 4 & 10 3.00
50-($3.95, 68 pgs.)-Bolland embossed gold foil-c; Joker-c/story; pin-ups by Chaykin, Simonson, Williamson, Kaluta, Russell, others 5.00
64-99: 64-(9/94)-Begin $1.95-c. 71-73-James Robinson-s,Watkiss-c/a. 74,75-McKeever-c/a/s. 76-78-Scott Hampton-c/a/s. 81-Card insert. 83,84-Ellis-s. 85-Robinson-s. 91-93-Ennis-s. 94-Michael T. Gilbert-s/a. 3.00
100-($3.95) Alex Ross painted-c; gallery by various 5.00
101-115: 101-Ezquerra-a. 102-104-Robinson-s 3.00
116-No Man's Land stories begin; Huntress-c 4.00
117-119,121-126: 122-Harris-c 3.00
120-ID of new Batgirl revealed 4.00
127-131: Return to Legends stories; Green Arrow app. 3.00
132-199, 201-204: 132-136 ($2.25-c) Archie Goodwin-s/Rogers-a. 137-141-Gulacy-a. 142-145-Joker and Ra's al Ghul app. 146-148-Kitson-a. 158-Begin $2.50-c 169-171-Tony Harris-c/a. 182-184-War Games. 182-Bagged with Sky Captain CD 3.00
200-($4.99) Joker-c/app. 5.00
205-214: 205-Begin $2.99-c. 207,208-Olivetti-a. 214-Deadshot app. 3.00
#0-(10/94)-Zero Hour; Quesada/Palmiotti-c; released between #64&65 3.00
Annual 1-7 ('91-'97, $3.50-$3.95, 68 pgs.): 1-Joker app. 2-Netzer-c/a. 3-New Batman (Azrael) app. 4-Elseworlds story. 5-Year One; Man-Bat app. 6-Legend of the Dead Earth story. 7-Pulp Heroes story 4.00
Halloween Special 1 (12/93, $6.95, 84 pgs.)-Embossed & foil stamped-c 1 2 3 4 5 7
Batman Madness-...Halloween Special (1994, $4.95) 5.00
Batman Ghosts-...Halloween Special (1995, $4.95) 5.00

NOTE: ***Aparo*** *a-Annual 1.* ***Chaykin*** *scripts-24-26.* ***Giffen*** *a-Annual 1.* ***Golden*** *a-Annual 1.* ***Alan Grant*** *scripts-38, 52, 53.* ***Gil Kane*** *c/a-24-26.* ***Mignola*** *a-54; c-54, 62.* ***Morrow*** *a-Annual 3i.* ***Quesada*** *a-Annual 1.* ***James Robinson*** *scripts- 71-73.* ***Russell*** *c/a-42, 43.* ***Sears*** *a-21, 23; c-21, 23.* ***Zeck*** *a-69, 70; c-69, 70.*

BATMAN-LEGENDS OF THE DARK KNIGHT: JAZZ
DC Comics: Apr, 1995 - No. 3, June, 1995 ($2.50, limited series)

1-3 3.00

BATMAN/LOBO
DC Comics: Oct, 2007 - No. 2, Nov, 2007 ($5.99, squarebound, limited series)

1,2-Sam Kieth-s/a 6.00

BATMAN: MANBAT
DC Comics: Oct, 1995 - No. 3, Dec, 1995 ($4.95, limited series)

1-3-Elseworlds-Delano-script; Bolton-a 5.00
TPB-(1997, $14.95) r/#1-3 15.00

BATMAN: MITEFALL (See Batman one-shots)

BATMAN MINIATURE (See Batman Kellogg's)

BATMAN: NEVERMORE
DC Comics: June, 2003 - No. 5, Oct, 2003 ($2.50, limited series)

1-5-Elseworlds Batman & Edgar Allan Poe; Wrightson-c/Guy Davis-a/Len Wein-s 3.00

BATMAN: NO MAN'S LAND (Also see 1999 Batman titles)
DC Comics: (one shots)

nn (3/99, $2.95) Alex Ross-c; Bob Gale-s; begins year-long story arc 3.00
Collector's Ed. (3/99, $3.95) Ross lenticular-c 5.00
#0 (: Ground Zero on cover) (12/99, $4.95) Orbik-c 5.00
...: Gallery (7/99, $3.95) Jim Lee-c 4.00
...: Secret Files (12/99, $4.95) Maleev-c 5.00
TPB ('99, $12.95) r/early No Man's Land stories; new Batgirl early app. 13.00
No Law and a New Order TPB(1999, $5.95) Ross-c 6.00
Volume 2 ('00, $12.95) r/later No Man's Land stories; Batgirl(Huntress) app.; Deodato-c 13.00
Volume 3-5 ('00,'01 $12.95) 3-Intro. new Batgirl. 4-('00). 5-('01) Land-c 13.00

BATMAN: ODYSSEY
DC Comics: Sept, 2010 - No. 6, Feb, 2011 ($3.99, limited series)

1-6-Neal Adams-s/a/c. 1-Man-Bat app.; bonus sketch pages. 5,6-Joker app. 4.00
1-6-Variant B&W-version cover 5.00
Vol. 2 (12/11 - No. 7) 1-6-Neal Adams-s/a/c 4.00

BATMAN: ORPHANS
DC Comics: Early Feb, 2011 - No. 2, Late Feb, 2011 ($3.99, limited series)

1,2-Berganza-s/Barberi-a/c 4.00

BATMAN: ORPHEUS RISING
DC Comics: Oct, 2001 - No. 5, Feb, 2002 ($2.50, limited series)

1-5-Intro. Orpheus; Simmons-s/Turner & Miki-a 3.00

BATMAN: OUTLAWS
DC Comics: 2000 - No. 3, 2000 ($4.95, limited series)

1-3-Moench-s/Gulacy-a 5.00

BATMAN: PENGUIN TRIUMPHANT (See Batman one-shots)

BATMAN/PREDATOR III: BLOOD TIES
DC Comics/Dark Horse Comics: Nov, 1997 - No. 4, Feb, 1998 ($1.95, lim. series)

1-4: Dixon-s/Damaggio-c/a 3.00
TPB-(1998, $7.95) r/#1-4 8.00

BATMAN/RA'S AL GHUL (See Year One:...)

BATMAN RETURNS MOVIE SPECIAL (See Batman one-shots)

BATMAN: RIDDLER-THE RIDDLE FACTORY (See Batman one-shots)

BATMAN: RUN, RIDDLER, RUN
DC Comics: 1992 - Book 3, 1992 ($4.95, limited series)

Book 1-3: Mark Badger-a & plot 5.00

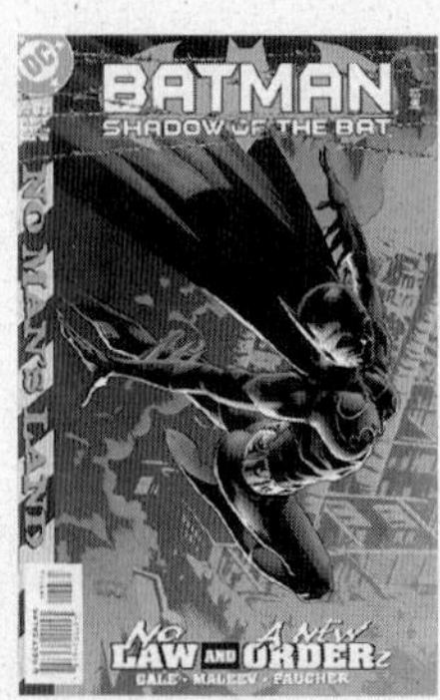

Batman: Shadow of the Bat #83 © DC

Batman: Streets of Gotham #1 © DC

Batman: The Dark Knight #1 © DC

	GD	VG	FN	VF	VF/NM	NM-
	2.0	4.0	6.0	8.0	9.0	9.2

	GD	VG	FN	VF	VF/NM	NM-
	2.0	4.0	6.0	8.0	9.0	9.2

BATMAN SCARECROW (See Year One:...)

BATMAN: SECRET FILES
DC Comics: Oct, 1997 ($4.95)

1-New origin-s and profiles 5.00

BATMAN: SECRETS
DC Comics: May, 2006 - No. 5, Sept, 2006 ($2.99, limited series)

1-5-Sam Kieth-s/a/c; Joker app. 3.00
TPB (2007, $12.99) r/series 13.00

BATMAN: SHADOW OF THE BAT
DC Comics: June, 1992 - No. 94, Feb, 2000 ($1.50/$1.75/$1.95/$1.99)

1-The Last Arkham-c/story begins; Alan Grant scripts in all 4.00
1-($2.50)-Deluxe edition polybagged w/poster, pop-up & book mark 5.00
2-7: 4-The Last Arkham ends. 7-Last $1.50-c 3.00
8-28: 14,15-Staton-a(p). 16-18-Knightfall tie-ins. 19-28-Knightquest tie-ins w/Azrael as Batman. 25-Silver ink-c; anniversary issue 3.00
29-($2.95, 52 pgs.)-KnightsEnd Pt. 2 4.00
30-72: 30-KnightsEnd Pt. 8. 31-(9/94)-Begin $1.95-c; Zero Hour. 32-(11/94). 33-Robin-c. 35-Troika-Pt.2. 43,44-Cat-Man & Catwoman-c. 48-Contagion Pt. 1; card insert. 49-Contagion Pt.7. 56,57,58-Poison Ivy-c/app. 62-Two-Face app. 69,70-Fate app. 3.00
35-($2.95)-Variant embossed-c 4.00
73,74,76-78: Cataclysm x-over pts. 1,9. 76-78-Orbik-c 3.00
75-($2.95) Mr. Freeze & Clayface app.; Orbik-c 4.00
79,81,82: 79-Begin $1.99-c; Orbik-c 3.00
80-($3.95) Flip book with Azrael #47 4.00
83-No Man's Land; intro. new Batgirl (Huntress) 12.00
84,85-No Man's Land 4.00
86-94: 87-Deodato-a. 90-Harris-c. 92-Superman app. 93-Joker and Harley app. 94-No Man's Land ends 3.00
#0 (10/94) Zero Hour; released between #31&32 3.00
#1,000,000 (11/98) 853rd Century x-over; Orbik-c 3.00
Annual 1-5 ('93-'97 $2.95-$3.95, 68 pgs.): 3-Year One story; Poison Ivy app. 4-Legends of the Dead Earth story; Starman cameo. 5-Pulp Heroes story; Poison Ivy app. 4.00

BATMAN: SON OF THE DEMON (Also see Batman #655-658 and Batman Hardcovers)
DC Comics: 2006 ($5.99, reprints the 1987 HC in comic book format)

nn-Talia has Batman's son; Mike W. Barr-s/Jerry Bingham-a; new Andy Kubert-c 6.00

BATMAN-SPAWN: WAR DEVIL (See Batman one-shots)

BATMAN SPECTACULAR (See DC Special Series No. 15)

BATMAN: STREETS OF GOTHAM (Follows Batman: Battle For The Cowl series)
DC Comics: Aug, 2009 - No. 21, May, 2011 ($3.99$2.99)

1-18: 1-Dini-s/Nguyen-a; back-up Manhunter feature; Jeanty-a. 10,11-Zsasz app. 4.00
19-21-($2.99) 19-Joker app. 3.00
...- Hush Money HC (2010, $19.99) r/#1-4, Detective #852 and Batman #685 20.00
...- Hush Money SC (2011, $14.99) r/#1-4, Detective #852 and Batman #685 15.00
...- Leviathan HC (2010, $19.99) r/#5-11 20.00
...- The House of Hush HC (2011, $22.99) r/#12-14,16-21 23.00

BATMAN STRIKES!, THE (Based on the 2004 animated series)
DC Comics: Nov, 2004 - No. 50, Dec, 2008 ($2.25)

1,2,4-50: 1,11-Penguin app. 2-Man-Bat app. 4-Bane app. 9-Joker app. 18-Batgirl debut. 29-Robin debuts. 32,33-Cal Ripken 8-pg. insert. 44-Superman app. 3.00
1-Free Comic Book Day edition (6/05) Penguin app. 3.00
3-($2.95) Joker-c/app.; Catwoman & Wonder Woman-r from Advs. in the DCU 4.00
Jam Packed Action (2005, $7.99, digest) adaptations of two TV episodes 8.00
... Vol. 1: Crime Time (2005, $6.99, digest) r/#1-5 7.00
... Vol. 2: In Darkest Knight (2005, $6.99, digest) r/#6-10 7.00

BATMAN/ SUPERMAN/WONDER WOMAN: TRINITY
DC Comics: 2003 - No. 3, 2003 ($6.95, limited series, squarebound)

1-3-Matt Wagner-s/a/c. 1-Ra's al Ghul & Bizarro app. 7.00
HC (2004, $24.95, with dust-jacket) r/series; intro. by Brad Meltzer 30.00
SC (2004, $17.99) r/series; intro. by Brad Meltzer 18.00

BATMAN: SWORD OF AZRAEL (Also see Azrael & Batman #488,489)
DC Comics: Oct, 1992 - No. 4, Jan, 1993 ($1.75, limited series)

	GD	VG	FN	VF	VF/NM	NM-
1-Wraparound gatefold-c; Quesada-c/a(p) in all; 1st app. Azrael	2	4	6	8	10	12
2-4: 4-Cont'd in Batman #488	1	2	3	5	6	8

Silver Edition 1-4 (1993, $1.95)-Reprints #1-4 3.00
Trade Paperback (1993, $9.95)-Reprints #1-4 10.00
Trade Paperback Gold Edition 15.00

BATMAN/ TARZAN: CLAWS OF THE CAT-WOMAN
Dark Horse Comics/DC Comics: Sept, 1999 - No. 4, Dec, 1999 ($2.95, limited series)

1-4: Marz-s/Kordey-a 3.00

BATMAN: TENSES
DC Comics: 2003 - No. 2, 2003 ($6.95, limited series)

1,2-Joe Casey-s/Cully Hamner-a; Bruce Wayne's first year back in Gotham 7.00

BATMAN: THE ANKH
DC Comics: 2002 - No. 2, 2002 ($5.95, limited series)

1,2-Dixon-s/Van Fleet-a 6.00

BATMAN: THE BRAVE AND THE BOLD (Based on the 2008 animated series)
DC Comics: Mar, 2009 - No. 22, Dec, 2010 ($2.50/$2.99)

1-18: 1-Power Girl app. 4-Sugar & Spike cameo. 7-Doom Patrol app. 9-Catman app. 3.00
19-22-($2.99) Cyborg Superman and the Green Lantern Corps app. 22-Aquaman app. 3.00
TPB (2009, $12.99) r/#1-6 13.00
...: Emerald Knight TPB (2011, $12.99) r/#13,14,16,18,19,21 13.00
...: The Fearsome Fangs Strike Again TPB (2010, $12.99) r/#7-12 13.00

BATMAN: THE BRAVE AND THE BOLD (Titled "All New Batman: Brave & the Bold" for #1-13)
DC Comics: Jan, 2011 - No. 16, Apr, 2012 ($2.99)

1-16: 1-Superman. 4-Wonder Woman app. 8-Aquaman app. 9-Hawkman app. 3.00

BATMAN: THE CULT
DC Comics: 1988 - No. 4, Nov, 1988 ($3.50, deluxe limited series)

1-Wrightson-a/painted-c in all 6.00
2-4 5.00
Trade Paperback (1991, $14.95)-New Wrightson-c; Starlin intro. 15.00
Trade Paperback (2009, $19.99) 20.00

BATMAN: THE DARK KNIGHT
DC Comics: Jan, 2011 - No. 5, Oct, 2011 ($3.99/$2.99)

1-David Finch-s/a; Penguin & Killer Croc app.; covers by Finch and Clarke 4.00
2-5-($2.99) Demon app. 3.00

BATMAN: THE DARK KNIGHT (DC New 52)
DC Comics: Nov, 2011 - Present ($2.99)

1-7: 1-Jenkins & Finch-s/Finch-a/c; White Rabbit debut. 3-Flash app. 5,6-Superman app. 6,7-Bane app. 3.00

BATMAN: THE DARK KNIGHT RETURNS (Also see Dark Knight Strikes Again)
DC Comics: Mar, 1986 - No. 4, 1986 ($2.95, squarebound, limited series)

	GD	VG	FN	VF	VF/NM	NM-
1-Miller story & c/a(p); set in the future	5	10	15	30	48	65
1,2-2nd & 3rd printings, 3-2nd printing						6.00
2-Carrie Kelly becomes 1st female Robin	3	6	9	16	23	30
3-Death of Joker; Superman app.	3	6	9	14	20	25
4-Death of Alfred; Superman app.	2	4	6	11	16	20
Hardcover, signed & numbered edition ($40.00)(4000 copies)						250.00
Hardcover, trade edition						50.00
Softcover, trade edition (1st printing only)	2	4	6	9	12	15
Softcover, trade edition (2nd thru 8th printings)	1	2	3	4	5	7
10th Anniv. Slipcase set ('96, $100.00): Signed & numbered hard-c edition (10,000 copies), sketchbook, copy of script for #1, 2 color prints						100.00
10th Anniv. Hardcover ('96, $45.00)						45.00
10th Anniv. Softcover ('97, $14.95)						15.00
Hardcover 2nd printing ('02, $24.95) with 3 1/4" tall partial dustjacket						25.00

NOTE: *The #2 second printings can be identified by matching the grey background colors on the inside front cover and facing page. The inside front cover of the second printing has a dark grey background which does not match the lighter grey of the facing page. On the true 1st printings, the backgrounds are both light grey. All other issues are clearly marked.*

BATMAN: THE DOOM THAT CAME TO GOTHAM
DC Comics: 2000 - No. 3, 2001 ($4.95, limited series)

1-3-Elseworlds; Mignola-c/s; Nixey-a; Etrigan app. 5.00

BATMAN: THE KILLING JOKE (See Batman one-shots)

BATMAN: THE LONG HALLOWEEN
DC Comics: Oct, 1996 - No. 13, Oct, 1997 ($2.95/$4.95, limited series)

	GD	VG	FN	VF	VF/NM	NM-
1-($4.95)-Loeb-s/Sale-c/a in all	1	2	3	5	6	8
2-5($2.95): 2-Solomon Grundy-c/app. 3-Joker-c/app., Catwoman, Poison Ivy app.						6.00
6-10: 6-Poison Ivy-c. 7-Riddler-c/app.						5.00
11,12						4.00
13-($4.95, 48 pgs.)-Killer revelations						5.00
Absolute Batman: The Long Halloween (2007, $75.00, oversized HC) r/series; interviews with the creators; Sale sketch pages; action figure line; unpubbed 4-page sequence						75.00
HC-($29.95) r/series						30.00
SC-($19.95)						20.00

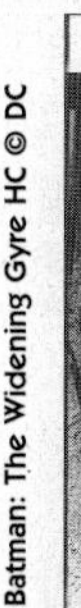
Batman: The Widening Gyre HC © DC

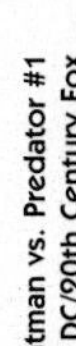
Batman vs. Predator #1 © DC/20th Century Fox

Battle #4 © MAR

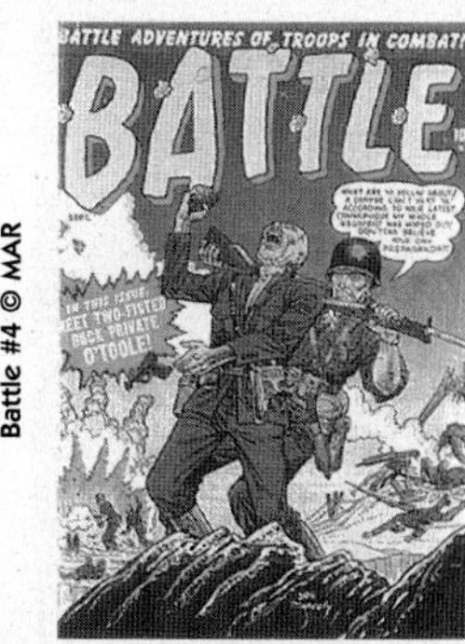

	GD 2.0	VG 4.0	FN 6.0	VF 8.0	VF/NM 9.0	NM- 9.2

BATMAN: THE MAD MONK ("Batman & the Mad Monk" on cover)
DC Comics: Oct, 2006 - No. 6, ($3.50, limited series)
1-5-Matt Wagner-s/a/c. 1-Catwoman app. 3.50
TPB (2007, $14.99) r/#1-6 15.00

BATMAN: THE MONSTER MEN ("Batman & the Monster Men" on cover)
DC Comics: Jan, 2006 - No. 6, June, 2006 ($2.99, limited series)
1-6-Matt Wagner-s/a/c 3.00
TPB (2006, $14.99) r/#1-6 15.00

BATMAN: THE OFFICIAL COMIC ADAPTATION OF THE WARNER BROS. MOTION PICTURE
(See Batman one-shots)

BATMAN: THE RETURN
DC Comics: Jan, 2011 ($4.99, one-shot)
1-Morrison-s/Finch-a; covers by Finch & Ha; costume design sketch art; script pages 5.00

BATMAN: THE RETURN OF BRUCE WAYNE (Follows Batman's "death" in Final Crisis #6)
DC Comics: Early Jul, 2010 - No. 6, Dec, 2010 ($3.99, limited series)
1-6-Bruce Wayne's time travels; Morrison-s/Andy Kubert-c. 1-Sprouse-a. 4-Jeanty-a 4.00
1-Second & third printings; 4.00
1-6-Variant covers: 1-Sprouse. 2-Irving. 3-Paquette. 4-Jeanty. 5-Sook. 6-Garbett 8.00
... - The Deluxe Edition HC (2011, $29.99) r/#1-6; sketch pages 30.00

BATMAN: THE ULTIMATE EVIL
DC Comics: 1995 ($5.95, limited series, prestige format)
1,2-Barrett, Jr. adaptation of Vachss novel. 6.00

BATMAN: THE WIDENING GYRE
DC Comics: Oct, 2009 - No. 6, Sept, 2010 ($3.99/$2.99/$4.99, limited series)
1-($3.99) Kevin Smith-s/Walt Flanagan-a; debut Baphomet; Demon app.; Sienkiewicz-c 4.00
1-5-Variant covers by Gene Ha 8.00
2-5-($2.99) 2-Silver St. Cloud returns. 5-Catwoman app. 3.00
6-($4.99) Joker, Deadshot & Catwoman app. 5.00
6-Variant cover by Gene Ha 10.00
HC (2010, $19.99, dj) r/#1-6; variant covers; afterword by Kevin Smith 20.00

BATMAN 3-D (Also see 3-D Batman)
DC Comics: 1990 ($9.95, w/glasses, 8-1/8x10-3/4")
nn-Byrne-a/scripts; Riddler, Joker, Penguin & Two-Face app. plus r/1953 3-D Batman; pin-ups by many artists 2 4 6 8 10 12

BATMAN: TOYMAN
DC Comics: Nov, 1998 - No. 4, Feb, 1999 ($2.25, limited series)
1-4-Hama-s 3.00

BATMAN: TURNING POINTS
DC Comics: Jan, 2001 - No. 5, Jan, 2001 ($2.50, weekly limited series)
1-5: 2-Giella-a. 3-Kubert-c/Giordano-a. 4-Chaykin-c/Brent Anderson-a. 5-Pope-c/a 3.00
TPB (2007, $14.99) r/#1-5 15.00

BATMAN: TWO-FACE-CRIME AND PUNISHMENT (See Batman one-shots)

BATMAN: TWO-FACE STRIKES TWICE
DC Comics: 1993 - No. 2, 1993 ($4.95, 52 pgs.)
1,2-Flip book format w/Staton-a (G.A. side) 5.00

BATMAN UNSEEN
DC Comics: Early Dec, 2009 - No. 5, Feb, 2010 ($2.99, limited series)
1-5-Doug Moench-s/Kelley Jones-a/c. Black Mask app. 3.00
SC (2010, $14.99) r/#1-5 15.00

BATMAN: VENGEANCE OF BANE (Also see Batman #491)
DC Comics: Jan, 1993; 1995 ($2.50, 68 pgs.)
... Special 1 - Origin & 1st app. Bane; Dixon-s/Nolan & Barreto-a/Fabry-c 3 6 9 16 23 30
... Special 1 (2nd printing) 4.00
.... II nn (1995, $3.95)-sequel; Dixon-s/Nolan & Barreto-a/Fabry-c 4.00

BATMAN VERSUS PREDATOR
DC Comics/Dark Horse Comics: 1991 - No. 3, 1992 ($4.95/$1.95, limited series)
(1st DC/Dark Horse x-over)
1 (Prestige format, $4.95)-1 & 3 contain 8 Batman/Predator trading cards; Andy & Adam Kubert-a; Suydam painted-c 6.00
1-3 (Regular format, $1.95)-No trading cards 3.00
2,3-(Prestige)-2-Extra pin-ups inside; Suydam-c 5.00
TPB (1993, $5.95, 132 pgs.)-r/#1-3 w/new introductions & forward plus new wraparound-c by Dave Gibbons 6.00

BATMAN VERSUS PREDATOR II: BLOODMATCH
DC Comics: Late 1994 - No. 4, 1995 ($2.50, limited series)
1-4-Huntress app.; Moench scripts; Gulacy-a 3.00
TPB (1995, $6.95)-r/#1-4 7.00

BATMAN VS. THE INCREDIBLE HULK (See DC Special Series No. 27)

BATMAN: WAR ON CRIME
DC Comics: Nov, 1999 ($9.95, treasury size, one-shot)
nn-Painted art by Alex Ross; story by Alex Ross and Paul Dini 10.00

BATMAN/ WILDCAT
DC Comics: Apr, 1997 - No. 3, June, 1997 ($2.25, mini-series)
1-3: Dixon/Smith-s: 1-Killer Croc app. 3.00

BATMAN: YEAR 100
DC Comics: 2006 - No. 4, 2006 ($5.99, squarebound, limited series)
1-4-Paul Pope-s/a/c 6.00
TPB (2007, $19.99) r/series 20.00

BAT MASTERSON (TV) (Also see Tim Holt #28)
Dell Publishing Co.: Aug-Oct, 1959; Feb-Apr, 1960 - No. 9, Nov-Jan, 1961-62
Four Color 1013 (#1) (8-10/59) 11 22 33 71 136 200
2-9: Gene Barry photo-c on all. 2,3,6-Two different back-c exist; variants have a comic strip on the back-c 7 14 21 44 72 100

BATS (See Tales Calculated to Drive You Bats)

BATS, CATS & CADILLACS
Now Comics: Oct, 1990 - No. 2, Nov, 1990 ($1.75)
1,2: 1-Gustovich-a(i); Snyder-c 3.00

BAT-THING
DC Comics (Amalgam): June, 1997 ($1.95, one-shot)
1-Hama-s/Damaggio & Sienkiewicz-a 3.00

BATTLE
Marvel/Atlas Comics(FPI #1-62/ Male #63 on): Mar, 1951 - No. 70, Jun, 1960

	GD 2.0	VG 4.0	FN 6.0	VF 8.0	VF/NM 9.0	NM- 9.2
1	37	74	111	222	361	500
2	20	40	60	114	182	250
3-10: 4-1st Buck Pvt. O'Toole. 10-Pakula-a	15	30	45	86	133	180
11-20: 11-Check-a	14	28	42	76	108	140
21,23-Krigstein-a	14	28	42	80	115	150
22,24-36: 32-Tuska-a. 36-Everett-a	12	24	36	67	94	120
37-Kubert-a (Last precode, 2/55)	13	26	39	72	101	130
38-40,42-48	11	22	33	60	83	105
41,49: 41-Kubert/Moskowitz-a. 49-Davis-a	11	22	33	64	90	115
50-54,56-58: 56-Colan-a; Ayers-a	10	20	30	58	79	100
55-Williamson-a (5 pgs.)	11	22	33	64	90	115
59-Torres-a	11	22	33	60	83	105
60-62: 60,62-Combat Kelly app. 61-Combat Casey app.	10	20	30	58	79	100
63-Ditko-a	15	30	45	88	137	185
64-66-Kirby-a. 66-Davis-a; has story of Fidel Castro in pre-Communism days (an admiring profile)	18	36	54	103	162	220
67,68: 67-Williamson/Crandall-a (4 pgs.); Kirby, Davis-a. 68-Kirby/Williamson-a (4 pgs.); Kirby/Ditko-a	18	36	54	105	165	225
69,70: 69-Kirby-a. 70-Kirby/Ditko-a	18	36	54	103	162	220

NOTE: *Andru a-37. Berg a-38, 14, 60-62. Colan a-19, 33, 55. Everett a-36, 50, 70; c-56, 57. Heath a-6, 9, 13, 31, 69; c-6, 9, 12, 26, 35, 37. Kirby c-64-69. Maneely a-4, 6, 31, 61; c-4, 22, 33, 48, 59, 61. Orlando a-47. Powell a-53, 55. Reinman a-4, 8-10, 14, 26, 32, 48. Robinson a-9, 39. Romita a-14, 26. Severin a-28, 32-34, 66-69; c-36, 50, 55. Sinnott a-33, 37, 63, 66. Whitney s-10. Woodbridge a-52, 55.*

BATTLE ACTION
Atlas Comics (NPI): Feb, 1952 - No. 12, 5/53; No. 13, 10/54 - No. 30, 8/57

	GD 2.0	VG 4.0	FN 6.0	VF 8.0	VF/NM 9.0	NM- 9.2
1-Pakula-a	29	58	87	170	278	385
2	15	30	45	90	140	190
3,4,6,7,9,10: 6-Robinson-c/a. 7-Partial nudity	12	24	36	67	94	120
5-Used in **POP**, pg. 93,94	12	24	36	69	97	125
8-Krigstein-a	13	26	39	72	101	130
11-15 (Last precode, 2/55)	11	22	33	64	90	115
16-30: 20-Romita-a. 22-Pakula-a. 27,30-Torres-a	10	20	30	58	79	100

NOTE: *Battle Brady app. 5-7, 10-12. Berg a-3. Check a-11. Everett a-7; c-13, 25. Heath a-3, 8, 18; c-3,15, 18, 21. Maneely a-1; c-5. Reinman a-1, 2, 20. Robinson a-6, 7; c-6. Shores a-7(2), 12, 20; c-11. Sinnott a-3, 27. Woodbridge a-28, 30.*

BATTLE ATTACK
Stanmor Publications: Oct, 1952 - No. 8, Dec, 1955

	GD 2.0	VG 4.0	FN 6.0	VF 8.0	VF/NM 9.0	NM- 9.2
1	14	28	42	81	118	155
2	9	18	27	47	61	75

Battle Chasers #1 © Joe Madureira

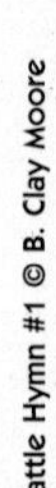
Battle Hymn #1 © B. Clay Moore

Battle of the Planets #7 © WHIT

	GD 2.0	VG 4.0	FN 6.0	VF 8.0	VF/NM 9.0	NM- 9.2
3-8: 3-Hollingsworth-a	8	16	24	42	54	65

BATTLEAXES
DC Comics (Vertigo): May, 2000 - No. 4, Aug, 2000 ($2.50, limited series)

	GD	VG	FN	VF	VF/NM	NM-
1-4: Terry LaBan-s/Alex Horley-a						3.00

BATTLE BEASTS
Blackthorne Publishing: Feb, 1988 - No. 4, 1988 ($1.50/$1.75, B&W/color)

	GD	VG	FN	VF	VF/NM	NM-
1-4: 1-3- (B&W)-Based on Hasbro toys. 4-Color						3.00

BATTLE BRADY (Formerly Men in Action No. 1-9; see 3-D Action)
Atlas Comics (IPC): No. 10, Jan, 1953 - No. 14, June, 1953

	GD	VG	FN	VF	VF/NM	NM-
10: 10-12-Syd Shores-c	18	36	54	103	162	220
11-Used in **POP**, pg. 95 plus B&W & color illos	12	24	36	69	97	125
12-14	11	22	33	60	83	105

BATTLE CHASERS
Image Comics (Cliffhanger): Apr, 1998 - No. 4, Dec, 1998;
DC Comics (Cliffhanger): No. 5, May, 1999 - No. 8, May, 2001 ($2.50)
Image Comics: No. 9, Sept, 2001 ($3.50)

	GD	VG	FN	VF	VF/NM	NM-
Prelude (2/98)	1	3	4	6	8	10
Prelude Gold Ed.	1	3	4	6	8	10
1-Madureira & Sharrieff-s/Madureira-a(p)/Charest-c	1	2	3	5	7	9
1-American Ent. Ed. w/"racy" cover	1	3	4	6	8	10
1-Gold Edition						9.00
1-Chromium cover						40.00
1-2nd printing						3.00
2						5.00
2-Dynamic Forces BattleChrome cover	2	4	6	8	10	12
3-Red Monika cover by Madureira						4.00
4-8: 4-Four covers. 6-Back-up by Adam Warren-s/a. 7-Three covers (Madureira, Ramos, Campbell)						3.00
9-($3.50, Image) Flip cover/story by Adam Warren						4.00
...: A Gathering of Heroes HC ('99, $24.95) r/#1-5, Prelude, Frank Frazetta Fantasy Ill.; cover gallery						25.00
...: A Gathering of Heroes SC ('99, $14.95)						15.00
...Collected Edition 1,2 (11/98, 5/99, $5.95) 1-r/#1,2. 2-r/#3,4						6.00

BATTLE CLASSICS (See Cancelled Comic Cavalcade)
DC Comics: Sept-Oct, 1978 (44 pgs.)

	GD	VG	FN	VF	VF/NM	NM-
1-Kubert-r; new Kubert-c	2	4	6	8	10	12

BATTLE CRY
Stanmor Publications: 1952 (May) - No. 20, Sept, 1955

	GD	VG	FN	VF	VF/NM	NM-
1	17	34	51	98	154	210
2	11	22	33	60	83	105
3,5-10: 8-Pvt. Ike begins, ends #13,17	9	18	27	50	65	80
4-Classic E.C. swipe	10	20	30	56	76	95
11-20	8	16	24	44	57	70

NOTE: ***Hollingsworth** a-9; c-20.*

BATTLEFIELD (War Adventures on the...)
Atlas Comics (ACI): April, 1952 - No. 11, May, 1953

	GD	VG	FN	VF	VF/NM	NM-
1-Pakula, Reinman-a	23	46	69	136	223	310
2-5: 2-Heath, Maneely, Pakula, Reinman-a	14	28	42	81	118	155
6-11	11	22	33	62	86	110

NOTE: ***Colan** a-11. **Everett** a-8. **Heath** a-1, 2, 5p,7; c-2, 8, 9, 11. **Ravielli** a-11.*

BATTLEFIELD ACTION (Formerly Foreign Intrigues)
Charlton Comics: No. 16, Nov, 1957 - No. 62, 2-3/66; No. 63, 7/80 - No. 89, 11/84

	GD	VG	FN	VF	VF/NM	NM-
V2#16	8	16	24	44	57	70
17,20-30: 29-D-Day story	6	12	18	27	33	38
18,19-Check-a (2 stories in #18)	3	6	9	21	32	42
31-34,36-62(1966): 55,61-Hitler app.	3	6	9	16	22	28
35-Hitler-c	3	6	9	18	27	35
63-80(1983-84)						5.00
81-83,85-89 (Low print run)	1	2	3	4	5	7
84-Kirby reprints; 3 stories	1	3	4	6	8	10

NOTE: ***Montes/Bache** a-43, 55, 62. **Glanzman** a-87r.*

BATTLEFIELDS
Dynamite Entertainment: 2008 - No. 9, 2010 ($3.50, limited series then numbered issues)

	GD	VG	FN	VF	VF/NM	NM-
...: Dear Billy 1-3 ('09 - No. 3, '09, $3.50) Ennis-s/Snejbjerg-a/Cassaday-c.1-Leach var-c						3.50
...: Happy Valley 1-3 ('09 - No. 3, '09, $3.50) Ennis-s/Holden-a/Leach-c						3.50
...: The Night Witches 1-3 ('08 - No. 3, '09, $3.50) Ennis-s/Braun-a/Cassaday-c; Russian female pilots in WW2. 1-Leach var-c						3.50
...: The Tankies 1-3 ('09 - No. 3, '09, $3.50) Ennis-s/Ezquerra-a/Cassaday-c.1-Leach var-c						3.50
4-9: 4-6-Ezquerra-a/Leach-c. 7-9-Sequel to "The Night Witches"; Braun-a						3.50

BATTLE FIRE
Aragon Magazine/Stanmor Publications: Apr, 1955 - No. 7, 1955

	GD	VG	FN	VF	VF/NM	NM-
1	13	26	39	74	105	135
2	8	16	24	44	57	70
3-7	8	16	24	40	50	60

BATTLE FOR A THREE DIMENSIONAL WORLD
3D Cosmic Publications: May, 1983 (20 pgs., slick paper w/stiff-c, $3.00)

	GD	VG	FN	VF	VF/NM	NM-
nn-Kirby c/a in 3-D; shows history of 3-D	2	4	6	8	11	14

BATTLEFORCE
Blackthorne Publishing: Nov, 1987 - No. 2, 1988 ($1.75, color/B&W)

	GD	VG	FN	VF	VF/NM	NM-
1,2: Based on game. 1-In color. 2-B&W						3.00

BATTLE FOR INDEPENDENTS, THE (Also See Cyblade/Shi & Shi/Cyblade: The Battle For Independents)
Image Comics (Top Cow Productions)/Crusade Comics: 1995 ($29.95)

	GD	VG	FN	VF	VF/NM	NM-
nn-Boxed set of all editions of Shi/Cyblade & Cyblade/Shi plus new variant	3	6	9	20	30	40

BATTLE FOR THE PLANET OF THE APES (See Power Record Comics)

BATTLEFRONT
Atlas Comics (PPI): June, 1952 - No. 48, Aug, 1957

	GD	VG	FN	VF	VF/NM	NM-
1-Heath-c	32	64	96	192	314	435
2-Robinson-a(4)	17	34	51	98	154	210
3-5-Robinson-a	15	30	45	83	124	165
6-10: Combat Kelly in No. 6-10. 6-Romita-a	13	26	39	74	105	135
11-22,24-28: 14,16-Battle Brady app. 22-Teddy Roosevelt & His Rough Riders story. 28-Last pre-code (2/55)	11	22	33	64	90	115
23,43-Check-a	12	24	36	67	94	120
29-39,41,44-47	10	20	30	58	79	100
40,42-Williamson-a	12	24	36	67	94	120
48-Crandall-a	11	22	33	62	86	110

NOTE: ***Ayers** a-19, 32, 35. **Berg** a-44. **Colan** a-21, 22, 32, 33, 35, 38, 40, 42. **Drucker** a-28, 29. **Everett** a-44. **Heath** c-23, 26, 27, 29, 32. **Maneely** a-22, 23, 26; c-2, 7, 13, 22, 34, 35, 41. **Morisi** a-42. **Morrow** a-41.**Orlando** a-47. **Powell** a-19, 21, 25, 29, 32, 40, 47. **Robinson** a-1-3, 4&5(4); c-4, 5. **Robert Sale** a-19. **Severin** a-32; c-40, 42, 45. **Sinnott** a-26; 48. **Woodbridge** a-45, 46.*

BATTLEFRONT
Standard Comics: No. 5, June, 1952

	GD	VG	FN	VF	VF/NM	NM-
5-Toth-a	15	30	45	83	124	165

BATTLE GODS: WARRIORS OF THE CHAAK
Dark Horse Comics: Apr, 2000 - No. 4, July, 2000 ($2.95)

	GD	VG	FN	VF	VF/NM	NM-
1-4-Francisco Ruiz Velasco-s/a						3.00

BATTLE GROUND
Atlas Comics (OMC): Sept, 1954 - No. 20, Aug, 1957

	GD	VG	FN	VF	VF/NM	NM-
1	23	46	69	136	223	310
2-Jack Katz-a	14	28	42	81	118	155
3,4: 3-Jack Katz-a. 4-Last precode (3/55)	12	24	36	67	94	120
5-8,10	11	22	33	60	83	105
9,11,13,18: 9-Krigstein-a. 11,13,18-Williamson-a in each	12	24	36	69	97	125
12,15-17,19,20	10	20	30	56	76	95
14-Kirby-a	14	28	42	80	115	150

NOTE: ***Ayers** a-4, 13, 16. **Colan** a-3, 11, 13. **Drucker** a-7, 12, 13, 20. **Heath** c-2, 3, 5, 7, 13. **Maneely** a-3, 14, 19; c-1, 18, 19. **Orlando** a-17. **Pakula** a-11. **Reinman** a-2. **Severin** a-4, 5, 12, 19. c-20. **Sinnott** a-7, 16. **Tuska** a-11.*

BATTLE HEROES
Stanley Publications: Sept, 1966 - No. 2, Nov, 1966 (25¢, squarebound giants)

	GD	VG	FN	VF	VF/NM	NM-
1	4	8	12	23	36	48
2	3	6	9	17	25	32

BATTLE HYMN
Image Comics: Jan, 2005 - No. 5, Oct, 2005 ($2.95/$2.99, limited series)

	GD	VG	FN	VF	VF/NM	NM-
1-5-WW2 super team; B. Clay Moore-s/Jeremy Haun-a; flip cover on #1-4						3.00

BATTLE OF THE BULGE (See Movie Classics)

BATTLE OF THE PLANETS (Based on syndicated cartoon by Sandy Frank)
Gold Key/Whitman No. 6 on: 6/79 - No. 10, 12/80

	GD	VG	FN	VF	VF/NM	NM-
1: Mortimer a-1-4,7-10	5	10	15	30	48	65
2-6,10	3	6	9	20	30	40
7-Low print run	6	12	18	37	59	80
8,9-Low print run: 8(11/80). 9-(3-pack only?)	5	10	15	32	51	70

BATTLE OF THE PLANETS (Also see Thundercats/...)
Image Comics (Top Cow): Aug, 2002 - No. 12, Sept, 2003 ($2.95/$2.99)

Battle Report #1 © AJAX

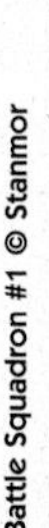
Battle Squadron #1 © Stanmor

Battlestar Galactica #4 © MAR

	GD 2.0	VG 4.0	FN 6.0	VF 8.0	VF/NM 9.0	NM- 9.2

1-($2.95) Alex Ross-c & art director; Tortosa-a(p); re-intro. G-Force 3.00
1-($5.95) Holofoil-c by Ross 6.00
2-11-($2.99) Ross-c on all 3.00
12-($4.99) 5.00
#1/2 (7/03, $2.99) Benitez-c; Alex Ross sketch pages 3.00
... Battle Book 1 (5/03, $4.99) background info on characters, equipment, stories 5.00
... : Jason 1 (7/03, $4.99) Ross-c; Erwin David-a; preview of Tomb Raider: Epiphany 5.00
... : Mark 1 (5/03, $4.99) Ross-c; Erwin David-a; preview of BotP: Jason 5.00
.../Thundercats 1 (Image/WildStorm, 5/03, $4.99) 2 covers by Ross & Campbell 5.00
.../Witchblade 1 (2/03, $5.95) Ross-c; Christina and Jo Chen-a 6.00
Vol. 1: Trial By Fire (2003, $7.99) r/#1-3 8.00
Vol. 2: Blood Red Sky (9/03, $16.95) r/#4-9 17.00
Vol. 3: Destroy All Monsters (11/03, $19.95) r/#10-12, ...: Jason, ...: Mark, .../Witchblade 20.00
Vol. 1: Digest (1/04, $9.99, 7-3/8x5", B&W) r/#1-9 & ...: Mark 10.00
Vol. 2: Digest (8/04, $9.99, B&W) r/#10-12, ...: Jason, ...: Manga #1-3, .../Witchblade 10.00

BATTLE OF THE PLANETS: MANGA
Image Comics (Top Cow): Nov, 2003 - No. 3, Jan, 2004 ($2.99, B&W)

1-3-Edwin David-a/David Wohl-s; previews for Wanted & Tomb Raider #35 3.00

BATTLE OF THE PLANETS: PRINCESS
Image Comics (Top Cow): Nov, 2004 - No. 6, May, 2005 ($2.99, B&W, limited series)

1-6-Tortosa-a/Wohl-s. 1-Ross-c. 2-Tortosa-c 3.00

BATTLE POPE
Image Comics: June, 2005 - No. 14, Apr, 2007 ($2.99/$3.50, reprints 2000 B&W series in color)

1-5-Kirkman-s/Moore-a 3.00
6-10,12-14-($3.50) 14-Wedding 3.50
11-($4.99) Christmas issue 5.00
... Vol. 1: Genesis TPB (2006, $12.95) r/#1-4; sketch pages 13.00
... Vol. 2: Mayhem TPB (2006, $12.99) r/#5-8; sketch pages 13.00
... Vol. 3: Pillow Talk TPB (2007, $12.99) r/#9-11; sketch pages 13.00

BATTLER BRITTON (British comics character who debuted in 1956)
DC Comics (WildStorm): Sept, 2006 - No. 5, Jan, 2007 ($2.99, limited series)

1-5-WWII fighter pilots; Garth Ennis-s/Colin Wilson-a 3.00
TPB (2007, $19.99) r/#1-5; background of the character's British origins in the 1950s 20.00

BATTLE REPORT
Ajax/Farrell Publications: Aug, 1952 - No. 6, June, 1953

	GD	VG	FN	VF	VF/NM	NM-
1	12	24	36	69	97	125
2-6	8	16	24	40	50	60

BATTLE SCARS
Marvel Comics: Jan, 2012 - No. 6 ($2.99, limited series)

1-5: 1-Intro. Marcus Johnson; Eaton-a/Pagulayan-c. 4-Deadpool app. 5-Nick Fury app. 3.00

BATTLE SQUADRON
Stanmor Publications: April, 1955 - No. 5, Dec, 1955

	GD	VG	FN	VF	VF/NM	NM-
1	11	22	33	62	86	110
2-5: 3-Iwo Jima & flag-c	7	14	21	37	46	55

BATTLESTAR GALACTICA (TV) (Also see Marvel Comics Super Special #8)
Marvel Comics Group: Mar, 1979 - No. 23, Jan, 1981

	GD	VG	FN	VF	VF/NM	NM-
1: 1-5 adapt TV episodes	2	4	6	9	12	15
2-23: 1-3-Partial-r	1	3	4	6	8	10

NOTE: *Austin c-9i, 10i. Golden c-18. Simonson a(p)-4, 5, 11-13, 15-20, 22, 23; c(p)-4, 5,11-17, 19, 20, 22, 23.*

BATTLESTAR GALACTICA (TV) (Also see Asylum)
Maximum Press: July, 1995 - No. 4, Nov, 1995 ($2.50, limited series)

1-4: Continuation of 1978 TV series 4.00
Trade paperback (12/95, $12.95)-reprints series 13.00

BATTLESTAR GALACTICA (1978 TV series)
Realm Press: Dec, 1997 - No. 5, July, 1998 ($2.99)

1-5-Chris Scalf-s/painted-a/c 3.00
...Search For Sanctuary (9/98, $2.99) Scalf & Kuhoric-s 3.00
...Search For Sanctuary Special (4/00, $3.99) Kuhoric-s/Scalf & Scott-a 4.00

BATTLESTAR GALACTICA (2003-2009 TV series)
Dynamite Entertainment: No. 0, 2006 - No. 12, 2007 (25¢/$2.99)

0-(25¢-c) Two covers; Pak-s/Raynor-a 3.00
1-($2.99) Covers by Turner, Tan, Raynor & photo-c; Pak-s/Raynor-a 3.00
2-12-Four covers on each 3.00
... Pegasus (2007, $4.99) story of Battlestar Pegasus & Admiral Cain; 2 covers 5.00
... Volume 1 HC (2007, $19.99) r/#0-4; cover gallery; Raynor sketch pages; commentary 20.00
... Volume 1 TPB (2007, $14.99) r/#0-4; cover gallery; Raynor sketch pages; commentary 15.00
... Volume 2 HC (2007, $19.99) r/#5-8; cover gallery; Raynor sketch pages 20.00
... Volume 2 TPB (2007, $14.99) r/#5-8; cover gallery; Raynor sketch pages 15.00

BATTLESTAR GALACTICA, (Classic...) (1978 TV series characters)
Dynamite Entertainment: 2006 - No. 5 ($2.99)

1-5: 1-Two covers by Dorman & Caldwell; Rafael-a. 2-Two covers 3.00

BATTLESTAR GALACTICA: APOLLO'S JOURNEY (1978 TV series)
Maximum Press: Apr, 1996 - No. 3, June, 1996 ($2.95, limited series)

1-3: Richard Hatch scripts 4.00

BATTLESTAR GALACTICA: CYLON APOCALYPSE (1978 TV series characters)
Dynamite Entertainment: 2007 - No. 4, 2007 ($2.99, limited series)

1-4-Carlos Rafael-a; 4 covers on each 3.00
TPB (2007, $14.99) r/series with cover gallery 15.00

BATTLESTAR GALACTICA: CYLON WAR (2003-2009 TV series)
Dynamite Entertainment: 2009 - No. 4, 2010 ($3.99, limited series)

1-3-First cylon war 40 years before the Caprica attack; Raynor-a; 2 covers 4.00

BATTLESTAR GALACTICA: GHOSTS (2003-2009 TV series)
Dynamite Entertainment: 2008 - No. 4, 2009 ($4.99, 40 pgs., limited series)

1-4-Intro. of the Ghost Squadron; Jerwa-s/Lau-a/Calero-c 5.00

BATTLESTAR GALACTICA: JOURNEY'S END (1978 TV series)
Maximum Press: Aug, 1996 - No. 4, Nov, 1996 ($2.99, limited series)

1-4-Continuation of the T.V. series 4.00

BATTLESTAR GALACTICA: ORIGINS (2003-2009 TV series)
Dynamite Entertainment: 2007 - No. 11, 2008 ($3.50)

1-11: 1-4-Baltar's origin; multiple covers. 5-8-Adama's origin. 9-11-Starbuck & Helo 3.50

BATTLESTAR GALACTICA: SEASON III
Realm Press: June/July, 1999 - No. 3, Sept, 1999 ($2.99)

1-3: 1-Kuhoric-s/Scalf & Scott-a; two covers by Scalf & Jae Lee. 2,3-Two covers 3.00
Gallery (4/00, $3.99) short story and pin-ups 4.00
1999 Tour Book (5/99, $2.99) 3.00
1999 Tour Book Convention Edition (6.99) 7.00
...Special: Centurion Prime (12/99, $3.99) Kuhoric-s 4.00

BATTLESTAR GALACTICA: SEASON ZERO (2003-2009 TV series)
Dynamite Entertainment: 2007 - No. 12, 2008 ($2.99)

1-12-Set 2 years before the Cylon attack; multiple covers 3.00
.../The Lone Ranger 2007 Free Comic Book Day Edition; flip book with Cassaday Lone Ranger-c 3.00

BATTLESTAR GALACTICA: SPECIAL EDITION (TV)
Maximum Press: Jan, 1997 ($2.99, one-shot)

1-Fully painted; Scalf-c/s/a; r/Asylum 3.00

BATTLESTAR GALACTICA: STARBUCK (TV)
Maximum Press: Dec, 1995 - No. 3, Mar, 1996 ($2.50, limited series)

1-3 4.00

BATTLESTAR GALACTICA: THE COMPENDIUM (TV)
Maximum Press: Feb, 1997 ($2.99, one-shot)

1 3.00

BATTLESTAR GALACTICA: THE ENEMY WITHIN (TV)
Maximum Press: Nov, 1995 - No. 3, Feb, 1996 ($2.50, limited series)

1-3: 3-Indicia reads Feb, 1995 in error. 4.00

BATTLESTAR GALACTICA: THE FINAL FIVE (2003 series)
Dynamite Entertainment: 2009 - No. 4, 2009 ($3.99, limited series)

1-4-Raynor-a; 2 covers on each 4.00

BATTLESTAR GALACTICA ZAREK (2003 series)
Dynamite Entertainment: 2007 - No. 4, 2007 ($3.50, limited series)

1-4-Origin story of political activist Tom Zarek; 2 covers on each 3.50

BATTLE STORIES (See XMas Comics)
Fawcett Publications: Jan, 1952 - No. 11, Sept, 1953

	GD	VG	FN	VF	VF/NM	NM-
1-Evans-a	16	32	48	92	144	195
2	10	20	30	56	76	95
3-11	9	18	27	47	61	75

BATTLE STORIES
Super Comics: 1963 - 1964

	GD	VG	FN	VF	VF/NM	NM-
Reprints #10-13,15-18: 10-r/U.S Tank Commandos #? 11-r/? 11, 12,17-r/Monty Hall #?; 13-Kintsler-a (1pg).15-r/American Air Forces #7 by Powell; Bolle-r. 18-U.S. Fighting Air Force #?	2	4	6	9	13	16

Batwoman #6 © DC

Beast #1 © MAR

Beavis and Butthead #21 © MTV

	GD	VG	FN	VF	VF/NM	NM-
	2.0	4.0	6.0	8.0	9.0	9.2

GD VG FN VF VF/NM NM-
2.0 4.0 6.0 8.0 9.0 9.2

BATTLETECH (See Blackthorne 3-D Series #41 for 3-D issue)
Blackthorne Publishing: Oct, 1987 - No. 6, 1988 ($1.75/$2.00)

1-6: Based on game. 1-Color. 2-Begin B&W 3.00
Annual 1 ($4.50, B&W) 5.00

BATTLETECH
Malibu Comics: Feb, 1995 ($2.95)

0 3.00

BATTLETECH FALLOUT
Malibu Comics: Dec, 1994 - No. 4, Mar, 1995 ($2.95)

1-4-Two edi. exist #1; normal logo 3.00
1-Gold version w/foil logo stamped "Gold Limited Edition 8.00
1-Full-c holographic limited edition 6.00

BATTLETIDE (Death's Head II & Killpower...)
Marvel Comics UK, Ltd.: Dec, 1992 - No. 4, Mar, 1993 ($1.75, mini-series)

1-4: Wolverine, Psylocke, Dark Angel app. 3.00

BATTLETIDE II (Death's Head II & Killpower...)
Marvel Comics UK, Ltd.: Aug, 1993 - No. 4, Nov, 1993 ($1.75, mini-series)

1-($2.95)-Foil embossed logo 4.00
2-4: 2-Hulk-c/story 3.00

BATWING (DC New 52)
DC Comics: Nov, 2011 - Present ($2.99)

1-8: 1-3,5-Judd Winick-s/Ben Oliver-a. 4-Origin; Chriscross-a 3.00

BATWOMAN (See 52 #9 & 11 for debut and Detective Comics #854-860)
DC Comics: No. 0, Jan, 2011; No. 1, Nov, 2011 - Present ($2.99)

0-Williams III-s; art by Williams III and Reeder; Williams III-c 3.00
0-Variant-c by Reeder 5.00
1-New DC 52; Williams III-a; Williams III & Blackman-s; Bette Kane app. 5.00
2-8-Cameron Chase app. 6-8-Reeder-a/c 3.00
... Elegy The Deluxe Edition HC (2010, $24.99, d.j.) r/Detective #854-860; gallery of variant covers, sketch art and script pages; intro. by Rachel Maddow 25.00
... Elegy SC (2011, $17.99) same contents as Deluxe HC 18.00

BAY CITY JIVE
DC Comics (WildStorm): Jul, 2001 - No. 3, Sept, 2001 ($2.95, limited series)

1-3: Intro Sugah Rollins in 1970s San Francisco; Layman-s/Johnson-a 3.00

BAYWATCH COMIC STORIES (TV) (Magazine)
Acclaim Comics (Armada): May, 1996 - No. 4, 1997 ($4.95) (Photo-c on all)

1-4: Photo comics based on TV show 5.00

BEACH BLANKET BINGO (See Movie Classics)

BEAGLE BOYS, THE (Walt Disney)(See The Phantom Blot)
Gold Key: 11/64; No. 2, 11/65; No. 3, 8/66 - No. 47, 2/79 (See WDC&S #134)

	GD	VG	FN	VF	VF/NM	NM-
1	5	10	15	32	51	70
2-5	3	6	9	18	27	35
6-10	3	6	9	16	22	28
11-20: 11,14,19-r	2	4	6	11	16	20
21-30: 27-r	2	4	6	8	11	14
31-47	1	3	4	6	8	10

BEAGLE BOYS VERSUS UNCLE SCROOGE
Gold Key: Mar, 1979 - No. 12, Feb, 1980

	GD	VG	FN	VF	VF/NM	NM-
1	2	4	6	9	13	16
2-12: 9-r	1	2	3	5	6	8

BEANBAGS
Ziff-Davis Publ. Co. (Approved Comics): Winter, 1951 - No. 2, Spring, 1952

	GD	VG	FN	VF	VF/NM	NM-
1,2	13	26	39	72	101	130

BEANIE THE MEANIE
Fago Publications: No. 3, May, 1959

	GD	VG	FN	VF	VF/NM	NM-
3	5	10	15	24	30	35

BEANY AND CECIL (TV) (Bob Clampett's...)
Dell Publishing Co.: Jan, 1952 - 1955; July-Sept, 1962 - No. 5, July-Sept, 1963

	GD	VG	FN	VF	VF/NM	NM-
Four Color 368	21	42	63	146	311	475
Four Color 414,448,477,530,570,635(1/55)	13	26	39	85	180	275
01-057-209 (#1)	12	24	36	82	169	255
2-5	10	20	30	65	118	170

BEAR COUNTRY (Disney)
Dell Publishing Co.: No. 758, Dec, 1956

	GD	VG	FN	VF	VF/NM	NM-
Four Color 758-Movie	5	10	15	35	55	75

BEAST (See X-Men)
Marvel Comics: May, 1997 - No. 3, 1997 ($2.50, mini-series)

1-3-Giffen-s/Nocon-a 3.00

BEAST BOY (See Titans)
DC Comics: Jan, 2000 - No. 4, Apr, 2000 ($2.95, mini-series)

1-4-Justiano-c/a; Raab & Johns-s 3.00

B.E.A.S.T.I.E.S. (Also see Axis Alpha)
Axis Comics: Apr, 1994 ($1.95)

1-Javier Saltares-c/a/scripts 3.00

BEASTS OF BURDEN (See Dark Horse Book of Hauntings, ...Monsters, ...The Dead, ...Witchcraft)
Dark Horse Comics: Sept, 2009 - No. 4, Dec, 2009 ($2.99, limited series)

1-4-Evan Dorkin-s/Jill Thompson-a/c 3.00
Volume 1: Animal Rites HC (6/10, $19.99) r/#1-4 & short stories from Dark Horse Books 20.00

BEATLES, THE (See Girls' Romances #109, Go-Go, Heart Throbs #101, Herbie #5, Howard the Duck Mag. #4, Laugh #166, Marvel Comics Super Special #4, My Little Margie #54, Not Brand Echh, Strange Tales #130, Summer Love, Superman's Pal Jimmy Olsen #79, Teen Confessions #37, Tippy's Friends & Tippy Teen)

BEATLES, THE (Life Story)
Dell Publishing Co.: Sept-Nov, 1964 (35¢)

	GD	VG	FN	VF	VF/NM	NM-
1-(Scarce)-Stories with color photo pin-ups; Paul S. Newman-s	42	84	126	315	683	1050

BEATLES EXPERIENCE, THE
Revolutionary Comics: Mar, 1991 - No. 8, 1991 ($2.50, B&W, limited series)

1-8: 1-Gold logo 5.00

BEATLES YELLOW SUBMARINE (See Movie Comics under Yellow...)

BEAUTIFUL KILLER
Black Bull Comics: Sept., 2002 - No. 3, Jan, 2003 ($2.99, limited series)

...Limited Preview Edition (5/02, $5.00) preview pgs. & creator interviews 5.00
1-Noto-a/Palmiotti-s; Hughes-c; intro Brigit Cole 3.00
2,3: 2-Jusko-c. 3-Noto-c 3.00
TPB (5/03, $9.99) r/#1-3; cover gallery and Adam Hughes sketch pages 10.00

BEAUTIFUL PEOPLE
Slave Labor Graphics: Apr, 1994 ($4.95, 8-1/2x11", one-shot)

nn 5.00

BEAUTIFUL STORIES FOR UGLY CHILDREN
DC Comics (Piranha Press): 1989 - No. 30, 1991 ($2.00/$2.50, B&W, mature)

Vol. 1-20: 12-$2.50-c begins 4.00
21-25 5.00

	GD	VG	FN	VF	VF/NM	NM-
26-30-(Lower print run)	1	2	3	4	5	7

A Cotton Candy Autopsy ($12.95, B&W)-Reprints 1st two volumes 13.00

BEAUTY AND THE BEAST, THE
Marvel Comics Group: Jan, 1985 - No. 4, Apr, 1985 (limited series)

1-4: Dazzler & the Beast from X-Men; Sienkiewicz-c on all 3.00

BEAUTY AND THE BEAST (Graphic novel)(Also see Cartoon Tales & Disney's New Adventures of...)
Disney Comics: 1992

nn-($4.95, prestige edition)-Adapts animated film 7.00
nn-($2.50, newsstand edition) 4.00

BEAUTY AND THE BEAST
Disney Comics: Sept., 1992 - No. 2, 1992 ($1.50, limited series)

1,2 3.00

BEAUTY AND THE BEAST: PORTRAIT OF LOVE (TV)
First Comics: May, 1989 - No. 2, Mar, 1990 ($5.95, 60 pgs., squarebound)

1,2: 1-Based on TV show, Wendy Pini-a/scripts. 2-...: Night of Beauty; by Wendy Pini 6.00

BEAVER VALLEY (Movie)(Disney)
Dell Publishing Co.: No. 625, Apr, 1955

	GD	VG	FN	VF	VF/NM	NM-
Four Color 625	6	12	18	41	66	90

BEAVIS AND BUTTHEAD (MTV's...)(TV cartoon)
Marvel Comics: Mar, 1994 - No. 28, June, 1996 ($1.95)

	GD	VG	FN	VF	VF/NM	NM-
1-Silver ink-c. 1, 2-Punisher & Devil Dinosaur app.	1	2	3	4	5	7

1-2nd printing 3.00
2,3: 2-Wolverine app. 3-Man-Thing, Spider-Man, Venom, Carnage, Mary Jane & Stan Lee cameos; John Romita, Sr. art (2 pgs.) 5.00
4-28: 5-War Machine, Thor, Loki, Hulk, Captain America & Rhino cameos. 6-Psylocke,

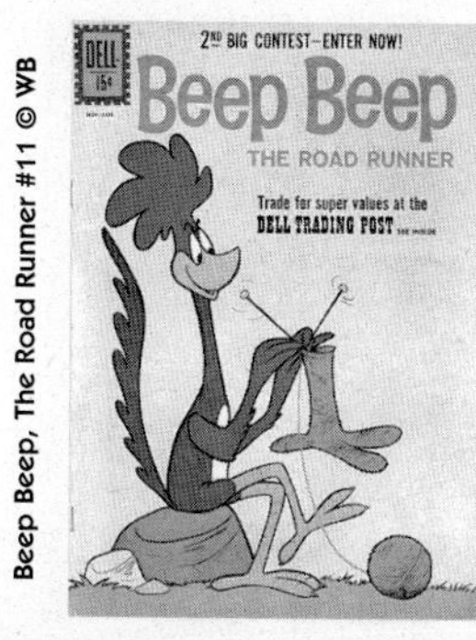

Beep Beep, The Road Runner #11 © WB

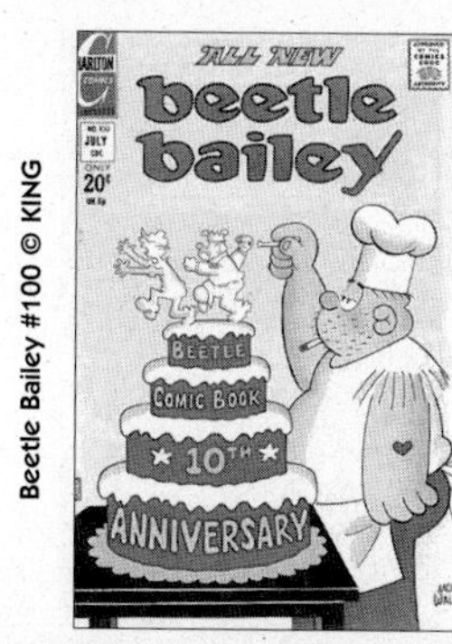

Beetle Bailey #100 © KING

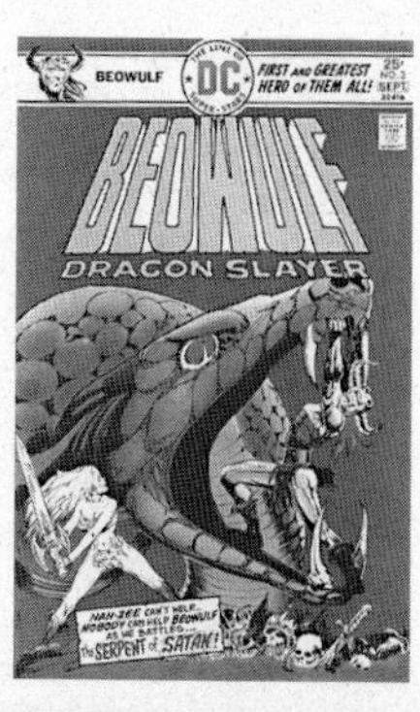

Beowulf #3 © DC

	GD 2.0	VG 4.0	FN 6.0	VF 8.0	VF/NM 9.0	NM- 9.2
Polaris, Daredevil & Bullseye app. 7-Ghost Rider & Sub-Mariner app. 8-Quasar & Eon app. 9-Prowler & Nightwatch app. 11-Black Widow app. 12-Thunderstrike & Bloodaxe app. 13-Night Thrasher app. 14-Spider-Man 2099 app. 15-Warlock app. 16-X-Factor app. 25-Juggernaut app.						4.00

BECK & CAUL INVESTIGATIONS
Gauntlet Comics (Caliber): Jan, 1994 - No. 5, 1995? ($2.95, B&W)

1-5						3.00
Special 1 ($4.95)						5.00

BEDKNOBS AND BROOMSTICKS (See Walt Disney Showcase No. 6 & 50)

BEDLAM!
Eclipse Comics: Sept, 1985 - No. 2, Sept, 1985 (B&W-r in color)

1,2: Bissette-a						3.00

BEDTIME STORIES FOR IMPRESSIONABLE CHILDREN
Moonstone Books: Nov, 2010 ($3.99, B&W)

1-Short story anthology; Vaughn, Kuhoric & Tinnell-s; 3 covers						4.00

BEDTIME STORY (See Cinema Comics Herald)

BEELZELVIS
Slave Labor Graphics: Feb, 1994 ($2.95, B&W, one-shot)

1						3.00

BEEP BEEP, THE ROAD RUNNER (TV) (See Dell Giant Comics Bugs Bunny Vacation Funnies #8 for 1st app.) (Also see Daffy & Kite Fun Book)
Dell Publishing Co./Gold Key No. 1-88/Whitman No. 89 on: July, 1958 - No. 14, Aug-Oct, 1962; Oct, 1966 - No. 105, 1984

	GD	VG	FN	VF	VF/NM	NM-
Four Color 918 (#1, 7/58)	11	22	33	76	151	225
Four Color 1008,1046 (11-1/59-60)	7	14	21	48	79	110
4(2-4/60)-14(Dell)	6	12	18	43	69	95
1(10/66, Gold Key)	7	14	21	44	72	100
2-5	4	8	12	28	44	60
6-14	3	6	9	20	30	40
15-18,20-40	3	6	9	16	23	30
19-With pull-out poster	4	8	12	26	41	55
41-50	3	6	9	14	19	24
51-70	2	4	6	9	13	16
71-88	2	3	4	6	8	10
89,90,94-101: 100(3/82), 101(4/82)	2	4	6	8	10	12
91(8/80), 92(9/80), 93 (3-pack?) (low printing)	4	8	12	24	37	50
102-105 (All #90189 on-c; nd or date code; pre-pack) 102(6/83), 103(7/83), 104(5/84), 105(6/84)	3	6	9	16	22	28
#63-2970 (Now Age Books/Pendulum Pub. Comic Digest, 1971, 75¢, 100 pages, B&W) collection of one-page gags	4	8	12	28	44	60

NOTE: *See March of Comics #351, 353, 375, 387, 397, 416, 430, 442, 455. #5, 8-10, 35, 53, 59-62, 68-r; 96-102, 104 are 1/3-r.*

BEETLE BAILEY (See Giant Comic Album, Sarge Snorkel; also Comics Reading Libraries in the Promotional Comics section)
Dell Publishing Co./Gold Key #39-53/King #54-66/Charlton #67-119/Gold Key #120-131/ Whitman #132: #459, 5/53 - #38, 5-7/62; #39, 11/62 - #53, 5/66; #54, 8/66 - #65, 12/67;#67, 2/69 - #119, 11/76; #120, 4/78 - #132, 4/80

	GD	VG	FN	VF	VF/NM	NM-
Four Color 469 (#1)-By Mort Walker	11	22	33	76	151	225
Four Color 521,552,622	7	14	21	48	79	110
5(2-4/56)-10(5-7/57)	6	12	18	41	66	90
11-20(4-5/59)	5	10	15	30	48	65
21-38(5-7/62)	3	6	9	21	32	42
39-53(5/66)	3	6	9	18	27	35
54-65 (No. 66 publ. overseas only?)	3	6	9	16	23	30
67-69: 69-Last 12¢ issue	3	6	9	14	20	25
70-99	2	4	6	9	13	16
100	2	4	6	11	16	20
101-111,114-119	1	3	4	6	8	10
112,113-Byrne illos. (4 each)	2	4	6	9	12	18
120-132	1	2	3	4	5	7

BEETLE BAILEY
Harvey Comics: V2#1, Sept, 1992 - V2#9, Aug, 1994 ($1.25/$1.50)

V2#1						5.00
2-9-($1.50)						3.50
Big Book 1(11/92),2(5/93)(Both $1.95, 52 pgs.)						4.00
Giant Size V2#1(10/92),2(3/93)(Both $2.25,68 pgs.)						4.00

BEETLEJUICE (TV)
Harvey Comics: Oct, 1991 ($1.25)

1						4.00

BEETLEJUICE CRIMEBUSTERS ON THE HAUNT
Harvey Comics: Sept, 1992 - No. 3, Jan, 1993 ($1.50, limited series)

1-3						4.00

BEE 29, THE BOMBARDIER
Neal Publications: Feb, 1945

	GD	VG	FN	VF	VF/NM	NM-
1-(Funny animal)	34	68	102	206	336	465

BEFORE THE FANTASTIC FOUR: BEN GRIMM AND LOGAN
Marvel Comics: July, 2000 - No. 3, Sept, 2000 ($2.99, limited series)

1-3-The Thing and Wolverine app.; Hama-s						3.00

BEFORE THE FANTASTIC FOUR: REED RICHARDS
Marvel Comics: Sept, 2000 - No. 3, Dec, 2000 ($2.99, limited series)

1-3-Peter David-s/Duncan Fegredo-c/a						3.00

BEFORE THE FANTASTIC FOUR: THE STORMS
Marvel Comics: Dec, 2000 - No. 3, Feb, 2001 ($2.99, limited series)

1-3-Adlard-a						3.00

BEHIND PRISON BARS
Realistic Comics (Avon): 1952

	GD	VG	FN	VF	VF/NM	NM-
1-Kinstler-c	33	66	99	194	317	440

BEHOLD THE HANDMAID
George Pflaum: 1954 (Religious) (25¢ with a 20¢ sticker price)

	GD	VG	FN	VF	VF/NM	NM-
nn	6	12	18	31	38	45

BELIEVE IT OR NOT (See Ripley's...)

BEN AND ME (Disney)
Dell Publishing Co.: No. 539, Mar, 1954

	GD	VG	FN	VF	VF/NM	NM-
Four Color 539	4	8	12	26	41	55

BEN BOWIE AND HIS MOUNTAIN MEN
Dell Publishing Co.: 1952 - No. 17, Nov-Jan, 1958-59

	GD	VG	FN	VF	VF/NM	NM-
Four Color 443 (#1)	9	18	27	58	99	140
Four Color 513,557,599,626,657	5	10	15	32	51	70
7(5-7/56)-11: 11-Intro/origin Yellow Hair	4	8	12	26	41	55
12-17	4	8	12	24	37	50

BEN CASEY (TV)
Dell Publishing Co.: June-July, 1962 - No. 10, June-Aug, 1965 (Photo-c)

	GD	VG	FN	VF	VF/NM	NM-
12-063-207 (#1)	6	12	18	41	66	90
2(10/62),3,5-10	4	8	12	24	37	50
4-Marijuana & heroin use story	4	8	12	28	44	60

BEN CASEY FILM STORIES (TV)
Gold Key: Nov, 1962 (25¢) (Photo-c)

	GD	VG	FN	VF	VF/NM	NM-
30009-211-All photos	7	14	21	44	72	100

BENEATH THE PLANET OF THE APES (See Movie Comics & Power Record Comics)

BEN FRANKLIN (See Kite Fun Book)

BEN HUR
Dell Publishing Co.: No. 1052, Nov, 1959

	GD	VG	FN	VF	VF/NM	NM-
Four Color 1052-Movie, Manning-a	10	20	30	64	115	165

BEN ISRAEL
Logos International: 1974 (39¢)

	GD	VG	FN	VF	VF/NM	NM-
nn-Christian religious	2	4	6	10	14	18

BEOWULF (Also see First Comics Graphic Novel #1)
National Periodical Publications: Apr-May, 1975 - No. 6, Feb-Mar, 1976

	GD	VG	FN	VF	VF/NM	NM-
1	2	4	6	8	11	14
2,3,5,6: 5-Flying saucer-c/story	1	2	3	5	6	8
4-Dracula-c/s	1	2	3	5	7	9

BERNI WRIGHTSON, MASTER OF THE MACABRE
Pacific Comics/Eclipse Comics No. 5: July, 1983 - No. 5, Nov, 1984 ($1.50, Baxter paper)

1-5: Wrightson-c/a(r). 4-Jeff Jones-r (11 pgs.)						6.00

BERRYS, THE (Also see Funny World)
Argo Publ.: May, 1956

	GD	VG	FN	VF	VF/NM	NM-
1-Reprints daily & Sunday strips & daily Animal Antics by Ed Nofziger	6	12	18	29	36	42

BERZERKER (Milo Ventimiglia Presents...)
Image Comics (Top Cow): No. 0, Feb, 2009 - No. 6, Jun, 2010 ($2.99/$3.99)

0-3-Jeremy Haun-a/Rick Loverd-s/Dale Keown-c. 0-Creator interviews						3.00

Best Love #34 © MAR

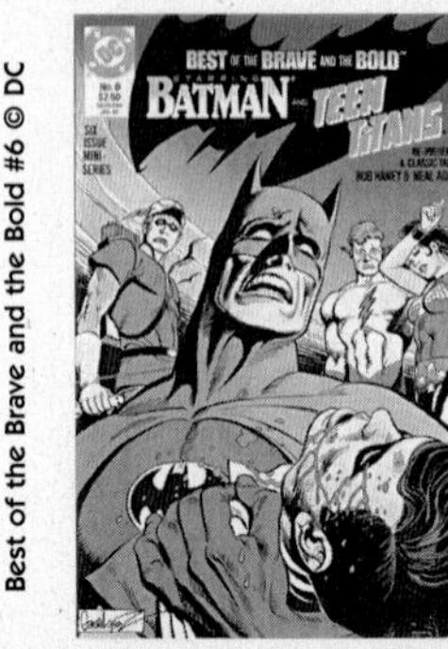

Best of the Brave and the Bold #6 © DC

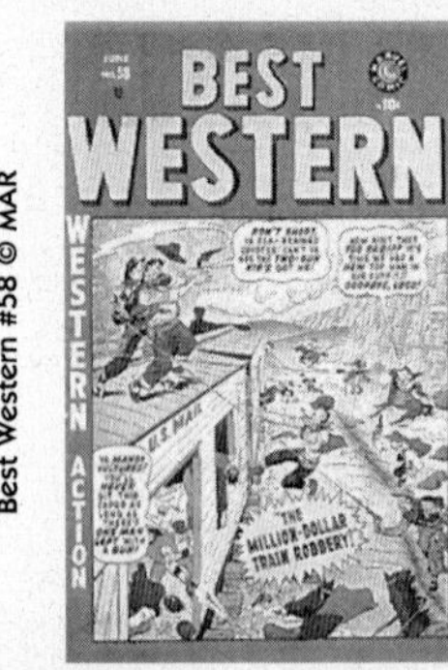

Best Western #58 © MAR

GD VG FN VF VF/NM NM-
2.0 4.0 6.0 8.0 9.0 9.2

4-6-($3.99) Covers by Haun & Keown 4.00

BERZERKERS (See Youngblood V1#2)
Image Comics (Extreme Studios): Aug, 1995 - No. 3, Oct, 1995 ($2.50, limited series)

1-3: Beau Smith scripts, Fraga-a 3.00

BEST COMICS
Better Publications: Nov, 1939 - No. 4, Feb, 1940(10-11/16" wide x 8" tall, reads sideways)

1-(Scarce)-Red Mask begins(1st app.) & c/s-all 97 194 291 621 1061 1500
2-4: 4-Cannibalism story 53 106 159 334 567 800

BEST FROM BOY'S LIFE, THE
Gilberton Company: Oct, 1957 - No. 5, Oct, 1958 (35¢)

1-Space Conquerors & Kam of the Ancient Ones begin, end #5; Bob Cousy photo/story 13 26 39 72 101 130
2,3,5 8 16 24 42 54 65
4-L.B. Cole-a 8 16 24 44 57 70

BEST LOVE (Formerly Sub-Mariner Comics No. 32)
Marvel Comics (MPI): No. 33, Aug, 1949 - No. 36, April, 1950 (Photo-c 33-36)

33-Kubert-a 14 28 42 82 121 160
34 10 20 30 56 76 95
35,36-Everett-a 11 22 33 62 86 110

BEST OF ARCHIE, THE
Perigee Books: 1980 ($7.95, softcover TPB)

nn-Intro by Michael Uslan & Jeffrey Mendel 6 12 18 39 62 85

BEST OF BUGS BUNNY, THE
Gold Key: Oct, 1966 - No. 2, Oct, 1968

1,2-Giants 4 8 12 28 44 60

BEST OF DC, THE (Blue Ribbon Digest) (See Limited Coll. Ed. C-52)
DC Comics: Sept-Oct, 1979 - No. 71, Apr, 1986 (100-148 pgs; mostly reprints)

1-Superman, w/"Death of Superman"-r 2 4 6 11 16 20
2,5-9: 2-Batman 40th Ann. Special. 5-Best of 1979. 6,8-Superman. 7-Superboy. 9-Batman, Creeper app. 2 4 6 8 10 12
3-Superfriends 2 4 6 9 12 15
4-Rudolph the Red Nosed Reindeer 2 4 6 9 13 16
10-Secret Origins of Super Villains; 1st ever Penguin origin-s 3 6 9 16 22 28
11-16,18-20: 11-The Year's Best Stories. 12-Superman Time and Space Stories.13-Best of DC Comics Presents. 14-New origin stories of Batman villains. 15-Superboy. 16-Superman Anniv. 18-Teen Titans new-s., Adams, Kane-a; Perez-c. 19-Superman. 20-World's Finest 1 2 3 5 7 9
17-Supergirl 2 4 6 8 10 12
21,22: 21-Justice Society. 22-Christmas; unpublished Sandman story w/Kirby-a 2 4 6 10 14 18
23-27: 23-(148 pgs.)-Best of 1981. 24 Legion, new story and 16 pgs. new costumes. 25-Superman. 26-Brave & Bold. 27-Superman vs. Luthor 2 4 6 9 12 15
28,29: 28-Binky, Sugar & Spike app. 29-Sugar & Spike, 3 new stories; new Stanley & his Monster story 2 4 6 9 13 16
30,32-36,38,40: 30-Detective Comics. 32-Superman. 33-Secret origins of Legion Heroes and Villains. 34-Metal Men; has #497 on-c from Adv. Comics. 35-The Year's Best Comics Stories (148 pgs.). 36-Superman vs. Kryptonite. 38-Superman. 40-World of Krypton 2 4 6 9 12 15
31-JLA 2 4 6 10 14 18
37,39: 37-"Funny Stuff", Mayer-a. 39-Binky 2 4 6 10 14 18
41,43,45,47,49,53,55,58,60,63,65,68,70: 41-Sugar & Spike new stories with Mayer-a. 43,49,55-Funny Stuff. 45,53,70-Binky. 47,65,68-Sugar & Spike. 58-Super Jrs. Holiday Special; Sugar & Spike. 60-Plop!; Wood-c(r) & Aragonés-r (5/85). 63-Plop!; Wrightson-a(r) 3 6 9 14 19 24
42,44,46,48,50-52,54,56,57,59,61,62,64,66,67,69,71: 42,56-Superman vs. Aliens. 44,57,67-Superboy & LSH. 46-Jimmy Olsen. 48-Superman Team-ups. 50-Year's best Superman. 51-Batman Family. 52 Best of 1984. 54,56,59-Superman. 61-(148 pgs.)Year's best. 62-Best of Batman 1985. 69-Year's best Team stories. 71-Year's best 2 4 6 10 14 18

NOTE: ***N. Adams*** *a-2r, 14r, 18r, 26, 51.* ***Aparo*** *a-9, 14, 26, 30; c-9, 14, 26.* ***Austin*** *a-51i.* ***Buckler*** *a-40p; c-16, 22.* ***Giffen*** *a-50, 52; c-33p.* ***Grell*** *a-33p.* ***Grossman*** *a-37.* ***Heath*** *a-26.* ***Infantino*** *a-10r, 18.* ***Kaluta*** *a-40.* ***G. Kane*** *a-10r, 18r; c-40, 44.* ***Kubert*** *a-10r, 21, 26.* ***Layton*** *a-21.* ***S. Mayer*** *c-29, 37, 41, 43, 47; a-28, 29, 37, 41, 43, 47, 58, 65, 68.* ***Moldoff*** *c-64p.* ***Morrow*** *a-40; c-40.* ***W. Mortimer*** *a-39p.* ***Newton*** *a-5, 51.* ***Perez*** *a-24, 50p; c-18, 21, 23.* ***Rogers*** *a-14, 51p.* ***Simonson*** *a-11r.* ***Spiegle*** *a-52.* ***Starlin*** *a-51.* ***Staton*** *a-5, 21.* ***Tuska*** *a-24.* ***Wolverton*** *a-60.* ***Wood*** *a-60, 63; c-60, 63.* ***Wrightson*** *a-60. New art in #14, 18, 24.*

BEST OF DENNIS THE MENACE, THE
Hallden/Fawcett Publications: Summer, 1959 - No. 5, Spring, 1961 (100 pgs.)

1-All reprints; Wiseman-a 7 14 21 44 72 100
2-5 4 8 12 28 44 60

BEST OF DONALD DUCK, THE
Gold Key: Nov, 1965 (12¢, 36 pgs.)(Lists 2nd printing in indicia)

1-Reprints Four Color #223 by Barks 8 16 24 53 89 125

BEST OF DONALD DUCK & UNCLE SCROOGE, THE
Gold Key: Nov, 1964 - No. 2, Sept, 1967 (25¢ Giants)

1(30022-411)('64)-Reprints 4-Color #189 & 408 by Carl Barks; cover of F.C. #189 redrawn by Barks 9 18 27 61 106 150
2(30022-709)('67)-Reprints 4-Color #256 & "Seven Cities of Cibola" & U.S. #8 by Barks 8 16 24 51 86 120

BEST OF HORROR AND SCIENCE FICTION COMICS
Bruce Webster: 1987 ($2.00)

1-Wolverton, Frazetta, Powell, Ditko-r 5.00

BEST OF JOSIE AND THE PUSSYCATS
Archie Comics: 2001 ($10.95, TPB)

1-Reprints 1st app. and noteworthy stories 12.00

BEST OF MARMADUKE, THE
Charlton Comics: 1960

1-Brad Anderson's strip reprints 3 6 9 20 30 40

BEST OF MS. TREE, THE
Pyramid Comics: 1987 - No. 4, 1988 ($2.00, B&W, limited series)

1-4 3.00

BEST OF RAY BRADBURY, THE
ibooks: 2003 ($18.95, TPB)

The Graphic Novel - Reprints from Ray Bradbury Comics; adaptations by various 19.00

BEST OF THE BRAVE AND THE BOLD, THE (See Super DC Giant)
DC Comics: Oct, 1988 - No. 6, Jan, 1989 ($2.50, limited series)

1-6: Neal Adams-r, Kubert-r & Heath-r in all 4.00

BEST OF THE SPIRIT, THE
DC Comics: 2005 ($14.99, TPB)

nn-Reprints 1st app. and noteworthy stories; intro by Neil Gaiman; Eisner bio. 15.00

BEST OF THE WEST (See A-1 Comics)
Magazine Enterprises: 1951 - No. 12, April-June, 1954

1(A-1 42)-Ghost Rider, Durango Kid, Straight Arrow, Bobby Benson begin 41 82 123 256 428 600
2(A-1 46) 22 44 66 128 209 290
3(A-1 52), 4(A-1 59), 5(A-1 66) 18 36 54 105 165 225
6(A-1 70), 7(A-1 76), 8(A-1 81), 9(A-1 85), 10(A-1 87), 11(A-1 97), 12(A-1 103) 15 30 45 84 127 170

NOTE: ***Bolle*** *a-9.* ***Borth*** *a-12.* ***Guardineer*** *a-5, 12.* ***Powell*** *a-1, 12.*

BEST OF UNCLE SCROOGE & DONALD DUCK, THE
Gold Key: Nov, 1966 (25¢)

1(30030-611)-Reprints part 4-Color #159 & 456 & Uncle Scrooge #6,7 by Carl Barks 8 16 24 52 86 120

BEST OF WALT DISNEY COMICS, THE
Western Publishing Co.: 1974 ($1.50, 52 pgs.) (Walt Disney)
(8-1/2x11" cardboard covers; 32,000 printed of each)

96170-Reprints 1st two stories less 1 pg. each from 4-Color #62 6 12 18 42 69 95
96171-Reprints Mickey Mouse and the Bat Bandit of Inferno Gulch from 1934 (strips) by Gottfredson 6 12 18 42 69 95
96172-r/Uncle Scrooge #386 & two other stories 6 12 18 42 69 95
96173-Reprints "Ghost of the Grotto" (from 4-Color #159) & "Christmas on Bear Mountain" (from 4-Color #178) 6 12 18 42 69 95

BEST ROMANCE
Standard Comics (Visual Editions): No. 5, Feb-Mar, 1952 - No. 7, Aug, 1952

5-Toth-a; photo-c 15 30 45 84 127 170
6,7-Photo-c 9 18 27 52 69 85

BEST SELLER COMICS (See Tailspin Tommy)

BEST WESTERN (Formerly Terry Toons? or Miss America Magazine
Marvel Comics (IPC): V7#24(#57)?; Western Outlaws & Sheriffs No. 60 on)
No. 58, June, 1949 - No. 59, Aug, 1949

58,59-Black Rider, Kid Colt, Two-Gun Kid app.; both have Syd Shores-c 20 40 60 115 185 255

Betrayal of the Planet of the Apes #1 © 20th Century Fox

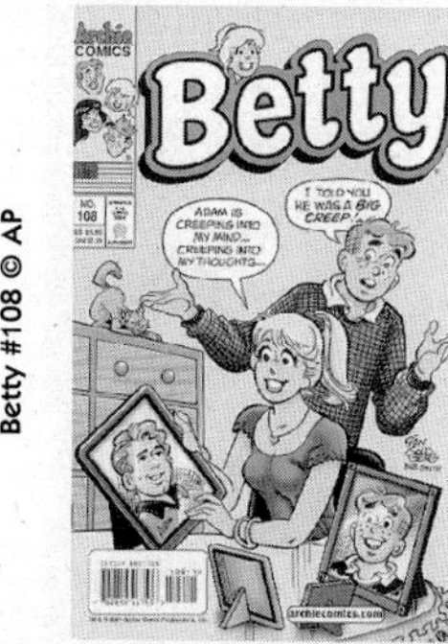

Betty #108 © AP

Beverly Hillbillies #16 © Filmway

GD 2.0 | VG 4.0 | FN 6.0 | VF 8.0 | VF/NM 9.0 | NM- 9.2

BETA RAY BILL: GODHUNTER
Marvel Comics: Aug, 2009 - No. 3, Oct, 2009 ($3.99, limited series)
1-3-Kano-a; Thor and Galactus app.; reprints form Thor #337-339. 2,3-Silver Surfer app. 4.00

BETRAYAL OF THE PLANET OF THE APES (Set 20 years before the first movie)
BOOM! Studios: Nov, 2011 - No. 4, Feb, 2012 ($3.99, limited series)
1-4-Dr. Zaius app.; Bechko-s/Hardman-a. 1-Three covers. 2-Two covers 4.00

BETTIE PAGE COMICS
Dark Horse Comics: Mar, 1996 ($3.95)
1-Dave Stevens-c; Blevins & Heath-a; Jaime Hernandez pin-up
2 4 6 9 12 15

BETTIE PAGE COMICS: QUEEN OF THE NILE
Dark Horse Comics: Dec, 1999 - No. 3, Apr, 2000 ($2.95, limited series)
1-3-Silke-s/a; Stevens-c 1 3 4 6 8 10

BETTIE PAGE COMICS: SPICY ADVENTURE
Dark Horse Comics: Jan, 1997 ($2.95, one-shot, mature)
nn-Silke-c/s/a 1 3 4 6 8 10

BETTY (See Pep Comics #22 for 1st app.)
Archie Comics: Sept, 1992 - No. 195, Jan, 2012 ($1.25-$2.99)
1 6.00
2-18,20-24: 20-1st Super Sleuther-s 4.00
19-Love Showdown part 2 5.00
25-Pin-up page of Betty as Marilyn Monroe, Madonna, Lady Di 5.00
26-50 3.00
51-195: 57- "A Storm Over Uniforms" x-over part 5,6. 186-Begin $2.99-c 3.00

BETTY AND HER STEADY (Going Steady with Betty No. 1)
Avon Periodicals: No. 2, Mar-Apr, 1950
2 10 20 30 56 76 95

BETTY AND ME
Archie Publications: Aug, 1965 - No. 200, Aug, 1992
1 10 20 30 69 130 190
2,3: 3-Origin Superteen 6 12 18 42 69 95
4-8: Superteen in new costume #4-7; dons new helmet in #5, ends #8. 5 10 15 32 51 70
9,10: Girl from R.I.V.E.R.D.A.L.E. 9-UFO-s 4 8 12 26 41 55
11-15,17-20(4/69) 3 6 9 20 30 40
16-Classic cover; w/risqué cover dialogue 5 10 15 32 51 70
21,24-35: 33-Paper doll page 3 6 9 16 23 30
22-Archies Band-s 3 6 9 17 25 32
23-I Dream of Jeannie parody 3 6 9 20 30 40
36(8/71),37,41-55 (52 pgs.): 42-Betty as vamp-s 3 6 9 16 23 30
38-Sabrina app. 4 8 12 24 37 50
39-Josie and Sabrina cover cameos 3 6 9 20 30 40
40-Archie & Betty share a cabin 3 6 9 18 27 35
56(4/71)-80(12/76): 79 Betty Cooper mysteries thru #86. 79-81-Drago the Vampire-s
2 4 6 9 13 16
81-99: 83-Harem-c. 84-Jekyll & Hyde-c/s 2 4 6 8 10 12
100(3/79) 2 4 6 9 12 15
101,118: 101-Elvis mentioned. 118-Tarzan mentioned 1 2 3 5 7 9
102-117,119-130(9/82): 103,104-Space-s. 124-DeCarlo-c begins 7.00
131-138,140,142-147,149-154,156-158: 135,136-Jason Blossom app. 136-Cheryl Blossom cameo. 137-Space-s. 138-Tarzan parody 5.00
139,141,148: 139-Katy Keene collecting-s; Archie in drag-s. 141-Tarzan parody-s. 148-Cyndi Lauper parody-s 6.00
155,159,160(8/87): 155-Archie in drag-s. 159-Superhero gag-c. 160-Wheel of Fortune parody 6.00
161-169,171-199 4.00
170,200: 170-New Archie Superhero-s 6.00

BETTY AND VERONICA (Also see Archie's Girls...)
Archie Enterprises: June, 1987 - Present (75¢-$2.99)
1 2 3 4 6 8 10
2-10 6.00
11-30 4.00
31-50 3.00
51-81 3.00
82-Love Showdown part 3 5.00
83-259: 242-Begin $2.50-c. 247-Begin $2.99-c 3.00
... Free Comic Book Day Edition #1 (6/05) Katy Keene-c/app.; Cheryl Blossom app. 3.00

BETTY & VERONICA ANNUAL DIGEST (...Digest Magazine #1-4, 44 on; ...Comics Digest Mag. #5-43)(Continues as Betty & Veronica Friends Double Digest #209-on)
Archie Publications: Nov, 1980 - No. 208, Nov, 2010 ($1.00/-$2.69, digest size)
1 3 6 9 16 22 28
2-10: 2(11/81-Katy Keene story), 3(8/82) 2 4 6 9 13 16
11-30 1 3 4 6 8 10
31-50 1 2 3 4 5 7
51-70 4.00
71-191: 110-Begin $2.19-c. 135-Begin $2.39-c. 165-Begin $2.49. 185-Includes reprint of Archie's Girls B&V #1 (1950) and new story where 1950 & 2008 B&V meet 3.00
192-208: 192-Begin $2.69-c 3.00

BETTY & VERONICA ANNUAL DIGEST MAGAZINE
Archie Comics: Sept, 1989 - No. 16, Aug, 1997 ($1.50/$1.75/$1.79, 128 pgs.)
1 1 2 3 5 7 9
2-10: 9-Neon ink logo 5.00
11-16: 16-Begin $1.79-c 3.00

BETTY & VERONICA CHRISTMAS SPECTACULAR (See Archie Giant Series Magazine #159, 168, 180, 191, 204, 217, 229, 241, 453, 465, 477, 489, 501, 513, 525, 536, 547, 558, 568, 580, 593, 606, 618)

BETTY & VERONICA DOUBLE DIGEST MAGAZINE
Archie Enterprises: 1987 - Present ($2.25-$3.99, digest size, 256 pgs.)(...Digest #12 on)
1 2 4 6 8 10 12
2-10 1 2 3 4 5 7
11-25: 5,17-Xmas-c. 16-Capt. Hero story 5.00
26-50 4.00
51-150: 87-Begin $3.19-c. 95-Begin $3.29-c. 114-Begin $3.59-c. 142-Begin $3.69-c 4.00
151-202: 151-(7/07)-Realistic style Betty & Veronica debuts (thru #154). 160-Cheryl Blossom spotlight. 170-173-Realistic style 4.00
Betty & Veronica: in Bad Boy Trouble Vol.1 TPB (2007, $7.49) r/new style from #151-154 8.00

BETTY & VERONICA FRIENDS DOUBLE DIGEST (Continues from B&V Digest Mag. #208)
Archie Publications: No. 209, Jan, 2011 - Present ($3.99, digest size)
209-225: 209-Cheryl Blossom app. 4.00

BETTY & VERONICA SPECTACULAR (See Archie Giant Series Mag. #11, 16, 21, 26, 32, 138, 145, 153, 162, 173, 184, 197, 201, 210, 214, 221, 226, 234, 238, 246, 250, 458, 462, 470, 482, 486, 494, 498, 506, 510, 518, 522, 526, 530, 537, 552, 559, 563, 569, 575, 582, 588, 600, 608, 613, 620, 623, and Betty & Veronica)

BETTY AND VERONICA SPECTACULAR
Archie Comics: Oct, 1992 - No. 90, Sept, 2009 ($1.25/$1.50/$1.75/$1.99/$2.19/$2.25/$2.50)
1-Dan DeCarlo-c/a 5.00
2-90: 48-Cheryl Blossom leaves Riverdale. 64-Cheryl Blossom returns 3.00

BETTY & VERONICA SPRING SPECTACULAR (See Archie Giant Series Magazine #569, 582, 595)

BETTY & VERONICA SUMMER FUN (See Archie Giant Series Mag. #8, 13, 18, 23, 28, 34, 140, 147, 155, 164, 175, 187, 199, 212, 224, 236, 248, 460, 484, 496, 508, 520, 529, 539, 550, 561, 572, 585, 598, 611, 621)
Archie Comics: 1994 - Present ($2.00/$2.25/$2.29)
1-($2.00, 52 pgs. plus poster) 4.00
2-6: 5-($2.25-c). 6-($2.29-c) 3.00
Vol. 1 (2003, $10.95) reprints stories from Archie Giant Series editions 12.00

BETTY BOOP'S BIG BREAK
First Publishing: 1990 ($5.95, 52 pgs.)
nn-By Joshua Quagmire; 60th anniversary ish. 6.00

BETTY PAGE 3-D COMICS
The 3-D Zone: 1991 ($3.95, "7-1/2x10-1/4," 28 pgs., no glasses)
1-Photo inside covers; back-c nudity 2 4 6 8 10 12

BETTY'S DIARY (See Archie Giant Series Magazine No. 555)
Archie Enterprises: April, 1986 - No. 40, Apr, 1991 (#1:65¢; 75¢/95¢)
1 1 2 3 4 5 7
2-10 4.00
11-40 3.00

BETTY'S DIGEST
Archie Enterprises: Nov, 1996 - No. 2 ($1.75/$1.79)
1,2 3.00

BEVERLY HILLBILLIES (TV)
Dell Publishing Co.: 4-6/63 - No. 18, 8/67; No. 19, 10/69; No. 20, 10/70; No. 21, Oct, 1971
1-Photo-c 13 26 39 86 183 280
2-Photo-c 9 18 27 58 99 140
3-9: All have photo covers 7 14 21 46 76 105
10: No photo cover 5 10 15 32 51 70
11-21: All have photo covers. 18-Last 12¢ issue. 19-21-Reprint #1-3 (covers and insides)
6 12 18 37 59 80
NOTE: *#1-9, 11-21 are photo covers.*

Beyond the Fringe #1 © WB

The Big Book of Fun Comics #1 © DC

GD VG FN VF VF/NM NM-
2.0 4.0 6.0 8.0 9.0 9.2

GD VG FN VF VF/NM NM-
2.0 4.0 6.0 8.0 9.0 9.2

BEWARE (Formerly Fantastic; Chilling Tales No. 13 on)
Youthful Magazines: No. 10, June, 1952 - No. 12, Oct, 1952

10-E.A. Poe's Pit & the Pendulum adaptation by Wildey; Harrison/Bache-a; atom bomb and shrunken head-c 61 122 183 390 670 950
11-Harrison-a; Ambrose Bierce adapt. 40 80 120 246 411 575
12-Used in **SOTI**, pg. 388; Harrison-a 40 80 120 246 411 575

BEWARE
Trojan Magazines/Merit Publ. No. ?: No. 13, 1/53 - No. 16, 7/53; No. 5, 9/53 - No. 15, 5/55

13(#1)-Harrison-a 60 120 180 381 653 925
14(#2, 3/53)-Krenkel/Harrison-c; dismemberment, severed head panels 40 80 120 246 411 575
15,16(#3, 5/53; #4, 7/53)-Harrison-a 38 76 114 228 369 510
5,9,12,13 37 74 111 222 361 500
6-Ill. in **SOTI**- "Children are first shocked and then desensitized by all this brutality." Corpse on cover swipe/V.O.H. #26; girl on cover swipe/Advs. Into Darkness #10 66 132 198 419 722 1025
7,8-Check-a 38 76 114 228 369 510
10-Frazetta/Check-c; Disbrow, Check-a 77 154 231 493 847 1200
11-Disbrow-a; heart torn out, blood drainage 40 80 120 246 411 575
14,15: 14-Myron Fass-c. 15-Harrison-a 32 64 96 188 307 425

NOTE: ***Fass** a-5, 6, 8; c-6, 11, 14. **Forte** a-8. **Hollingsworth** a-15(#3), 16(#4), 9; c-16(#4), 8, 9. **Kiefer** a-16(#4), 5, 6, 10.*

BEWARE (Becomes Tomb of Darkness No. 9 on)
Marvel Comics Group: Mar, 1973 - No. 8, May, 1974 (All reprints)

1-Everett-c; Kirby & Sinnott-r ('54) 3 6 9 20 30 40
2-8: 2-Forte, Colan-r. 6-Tuska-a. 7-Torres-r/Mystical Tales #7 3 6 9 14 19 24

NOTE: ***Infantino** a-4r. **Gil Kane** c-4. **Wildey** a-7r.*

BEWARE TERROR TALES
Fawcett Publications: May, 1952 - No. 8, July, 1953

1-E.C. art swipe/Haunt of Fear #5 & Vault of Horror #26 49 98 147 309 522 735
2 33 66 99 194 317 440
3-5,7 27 54 81 160 263 365
6-Classic skeleton-c 30 60 90 177 289 400
8-Tothish-a; people being cooked-c 34 68 102 199 325 450

NOTE: ***Andru** a-2. **Bernard Bailey** a-1; c-1-5. **Powell** a-1, 2, 8. **Sekowsky** a-2.*

BEWARE THE CREEPER (See Adventure, Best of the Brave & the Bold, Brave & the Bold, 1st Issue Special, Flash #318-323, Showcase #73, World's Finest Comics #249)
National Periodical Publications: May-June, 1968 - No. 6, Mar-Apr, 1969 (All 12¢ issues)

1-(5-6/68)-Classic Ditko-c; Ditko-a in all 9 18 27 61 106 150
2-6: 2-5-Ditko-c. 2-Intro. Proteus. 6-Gil Kane-c 5 10 15 35 55 75

BEWARE THE CREEPER
DC Comics (Vertigo): June, 2003 - No. 5, Oct, 2003 ($2.95, limited series)

1-5-Female vigilante in 1920s Paris; Jason Hall-s/Cliff Chiang-a 3.00

BEWITCHED (TV)
Dell Publishing Co.: 4-6/65 - No. 11, 10/67; No. 12, 10/68 - No. 13, 1/69; No. 14, 10/69

1-Photo-c 13 26 39 87 186 285
2-No photo-c 8 16 24 53 89 125
3-13-All have photo-c. 12-Rep. #1. 13-Last 12¢-c 7 14 21 46 76 105
14-No photo-c; reprints #2 5 10 15 35 55 75

BEYOND!
Marvel Comics: Sept, 2006 - No. 6, Feb, 2007 ($2.99, limited series)

1-6-McDuffie-s/Kolins-a; Spider-Man, Venom, Gravity, Wasp app. 6-Gravity dies 3.00
HC (2007, $19.99, dustjacket) r/series; cover sketches and sketch design pages 20.00
SC (2008, $14.99) r/series; cover sketches and sketch design pages 15.00

BEYOND, THE
Ace Magazines: Nov, 1950 - No. 30, Jan, 1955

1-Bakerish-a(p) 45 90 135 284 480 675
2-Bakerish-a(p) 30 60 90 177 289 400
3-10: 10-Woodish-a by Cameron 21 42 63 124 202 280
11-20: 18-Used in **POP**, pgs. 81,82 18 36 54 105 165 225
21-26,28-30 17 34 51 100 158 215
27-Used in **SOTI**, pg. 111 18 36 54 105 165 225

NOTE: ***Cameron** a-10, 11p, 12p, 15, 16, 21-27, 30; c-20. **Colan** a-6, 13, 17. **Sekowsky** a-2, 3, 5, 7, 11, 14, 27r. No. 1 was to appear as Challenge of the Unknown No. 7.*

BEYOND THE FRINGE (Based on the TV series Fringe)
DC Comics: May, 2012 ($3.99, one-shot)

1-Joshua Jackson-s/Jorge Jimenez-a/Drew Johnson-c 4.00

BEYOND THE GRAVE
Charlton Comics: July, 1975 - No. 6, June, 1976; No. 7, Jan, 1983 - No. 17, Oct, 1984

1-Ditko-a (6 pgs.); Sutton painted-c 3 6 9 20 30 40
2-6: 2-5-Ditko-a; Ditko c-2,3,6 2 4 6 13 18 22
7-17: ('83-'84) Reprints. 8,11,16-Ditko-a. 11-Staton-a. 13-Aparo-c(r). 15-Sutton-c (low print run). 16-Palais-a 1 2 3 4 5 7
Modern Comics Reprint 2('78) 5.00

NOTE: ***Howard** a-4. **Kim** a-1. **Larson** a-4, 6.*

BIBLE, THE: EDEN
IDW Publishing: 2003 ($21.99, hardcover graphic novel)

HC-Scott Hampton painted-a; adaptation of Genesis by Dave Elliot and Keith Giffen 22.00

BIBLE TALES FOR YOUNG FOLK (...Young People No. 3-5)
Atlas Comics (OMC): Aug, 1953 - No. 5, Mar, 1954

1 27 54 81 158 259 360
2-Everett, Krigstein-a; Robinson-c 18 36 54 105 165 225
3-5: 4,5-Robinson-c 15 30 45 88 137 185

BIG (Movie)
Hit Comics (Dark Horse Comics): Mar, 1989 ($2.00)

1-Adaptation of film; Paul Chadwick-c 3.00

BIG ALL-AMERICAN COMIC BOOK, THE (See All-American Comics)
All-American/National Per. Publ.: 1944 (132 pgs., one-shot) (Early DC Annual)

1-Wonder Woman, Green Lantern, Flash, The Atom, Wildcat, Scribbly, The Whip, Ghost Patrol, Hawkman by Kubert (1st on Hawkman), Hop Harrigan, Johnny Thunder, Little Boy Blue, Mr. Terrific, Mutt & Jeff app.; Sargon on cover only; cover by Kubert/Hibbard/Mayer and others 649 1298 1947 4738 8369 12,000

BIG BABY HUEY (See Baby Huey)

BIG BANG COMICS (Becomes Big Bang #4)
Caliber Press: Spring, 1994 - No. 4, Feb, 1995; No. 0, May, 1995 ($1.95, lim. series)

1-4-($1.95-c) 3.00
0-(5/95, $2.95) Alex Ross-c; color and B&W pages 3.00
Your Big Book of Big Bang Comics TPB ('98, $11.00) r/#0-2 11.00

BIG BANG COMICS (Volume 2)
Image Comics (Highbrow Ent.): V2#1, May, 1996 - No. 35, Jan, 2001 ($1.95-$3.95)

1-23,26: 1-Mighty Man app. 2-4-S.A. Shadowhawk app. 5-Begin $2.95-c. 6-Curt Swan/Murphy Anderson-c. 7-Begin B&W. 12-Savage Dragon-c/app. 16,17,21-Shadow Lady 3.00
24,25,27-35-($3.95): 35-Big Bang vs. Alan Moore's "1963" characters 4.00
...Presents the Ultiman Family (2/05, $3.50) 3.50
...Round Table of America (2/04, $3.95) Don Thomas-a 4.00
...Summer Special (8/03, $4.95) World's Nastiest Nazis app. 5.00

BIG BANG PRESENTS (Volume 3)
Big Bang Comics: July, 2006 - No. 5 ($2.95/$3.95, B&W)

1,2: 1-Protoplasman (Plastic Man homage) 3.00
3-5-($3.95) 3-Origin of Protoplasman. 4-Flip book 4.00

BIG BLACK KISS
Vortex Comics: Sep, 1989 - No, 3, Nov, 1989 ($3.75, B&W, lim. series, mature)

1-3-Chaykin-s/a 4.00

BIG BLOWN BABY (Also see Dark Horse Presents)
Dark Horse Comics: Aug, 1996 - No. 4, Nov, 1996 ($2.95, lim. series, mature)

1-4: Bill Wray-c/a/scripts 3.00

BIG BOOK OF ..., THE
DC Comics (Paradox Press): 1994 - 1999 (B&W)($12.95 - $14.95)

nn-...**BAD**,1998 ($14.95),...**CONSPIRACIES**, 1995 ($12.95), ...**DEATH**,1994 ($12.95), ...**FREAKS**, 1996 ($14.95), ...**GRIMM**, 1999 ($14.95), ...**HOAXES**, 1996 ($14.95), ...**LITTLE CRIMINALS**, 1996 ($14.95), ...**LOSERS**,1997 ($14.95), **MARTYRS**, 1997 ($14.95), ...**SCANDAL**,1997 ($14.95), ...**THE WEIRD WILD WEST**,1998 ($14.95), ...**THUGS**, 1997 ($14.95), ...**UNEXPLAINED**, 1997 ($14.95), ...**URBAN LEGENDS**, 1994 ($12.95), ...**VICE**, 1999 ($14.95), ...**WEIRDOS**, 1995 ($12.95) cover price

BIG BOOK OF FUN COMICS (See New Book of Comics)
National Periodical Publications: Spring, 1936 (Large size, 52 pgs.)
(1st comic book annual & DC annual)

1 (Very rare)-r/New Fun #1-5 2300 4600 6900 15,000 - -

BIG BOOK ROMANCES
Fawcett Publications: Feb, 1950 (no date given) (148 pgs.)

1-Contains remaindered Fawcett romance comics - several combinations possible 47 94 141 296 498 700

Big Chief Wahoo #2 © EAS

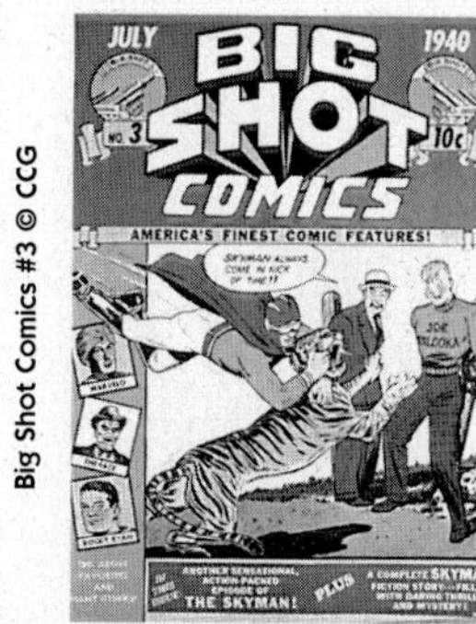

Big Shot Comics #3 © CCG

Big-3 #6 © FOX

GD 2.0 | VG 4.0 | FN 6.0 | VF 8.0 | VF/NM 9.0 | NM- 9.2

BIG CHIEF WAHOO
Eastern Color Printing/George Dougherty (distr. by Fawcett): July, 1942 - No. 7, Wint., 1943/44?(no year given)(Quarterly)

1-Newspaper-r (on sale 6/15/42) 42 84 126 265 445 625
2-Steve Roper app. 23 46 69 136 223 310
3-5: 4-Chief is holding a Katy Keene comic 18 36 54 105 165 225
6-7 14 28 42 82 121 160
NOTE: *Kerry Drake in some issues.*

BIG CIRCUS, THE (Movie)
Dell Publishing Co.: No. 1036, Sept-Nov, 1959
Four Color 1036-Photo-c 6 12 18 42 69 95

BIG COUNTRY, THE (Movie)
Dell Publishing Co.: No. 946, Oct, 1958
Four Color 946-Photo-c 7 14 21 46 76 105

BIG DADDY DANGER
DC Comics: Oct, 2002 - No. 9, June, 2003 ($2.95, limited series)
1-9-Adam Pollina-s/a/c 3.00

BIG DADDY ROTH (Magazine)
Millar Publications: Oct-Nov, 1964 - No. 4, Apr-May, 1965 (35¢)
1-Toth-a 16 32 48 107 234 360
2-4-Toth-a 11 22 33 75 148 220

BIGFOOT
IDW Publishing: Feb, 2005 - No. 4, May, 2005 ($3.99, limited series)
1-4-Steve Niles & Rob Zombie-s/Richard Corben-a/c 4.00

BIGG TIME
DC Comics (Vertigo): 2002 ($14.95, B&W, graphic novel)
nn-Ty Templeton-s/c/a 15.00

BIG GUY AND RUSTY THE BOY ROBOT, THE (Also See Madman Comics #6,7 & Martha Washington Stranded In Space)
Dark Horse (Legend): July, 1995 - No. 2, Aug, 1995 ($4.95, oversize, limited series)
1,2-Frank Miller scripts & Geoff Darrow-c/a 1 2 3 4 5 7
Trade paperback (10/96, $14.95)-r/1,2 w/cover gallery 15.00

BIG HAIR PRODUCTIONS
Image Comics: Feb, 2000 - No. 2, Mar, 2000 ($3.50, B&W)
1,2 3.50

BIG HERO ADVENTURES (See Jigsaw)

BIG HERO 6 (Also see Sunfire & Big Hero Six)
Marvel Comics: Nov, 2008 - No. 5, Mar, 2009 ($3.99, limited series)
1-5-Claremont-s/Nakayama-a; 1-Character design pages & Handbook entries 4.00

BIG JON & SPARKIE (Radio)(Formerly Sparkie, Radio Pixie)
Ziff-Davis Publ. Co.: No. 4, Sept-Oct, 1952 (Painted-c)
4-Based on children's radio program 18 36 54 107 169 230

BIG LAND, THE (Movie)
Dell Publishing Co.: No. 812, July, 1957
Four Color 812-Alan Ladd photo-c 9 18 27 58 99 140

BIG LIE, THE
Image Comics: Sept, 2011 ($3.99, one-shot)
1-Revisits the 9-11 attacks; Rick Veitch-s/a(p); Thomas Yeates-c 4.00

BIG RED (See Movie Comics)

BIG SHOT COMICS
Columbia Comics Group: May, 1940 - No. 104, Aug, 1949
1-Intro. Skyman; The Face (1st app.; Tony Trent), The Cloak (Spy Master), Marvelo, Monarch of Magicians, Joe Palooka, Charlie Chan, Tom Kerry, Dixie Dugan, Rocky Ryan begin; Charlie Chan moves over from Feature Comics #31 (4/40)
271 542 813 1734 2967 4200
2 92 184 276 584 1005 1425
3-The Cloak called Spy Chief; Skyman-c 82 164 246 528 902 1275
4,5 60 120 180 381 653 925
6-10: 8-Christmas-c 48 96 144 302 514 725
11-13 45 90 135 284 480 675
14-Origin & 1st app. Sparky Watts (6/41) 48 96 144 302 514 725
15-Origin The Cloak 53 106 159 334 567 800
16-20 39 78 117 231 378 525
21-23,27,30: 30-X-Mas-c 32 64 96 192 314 435
24-Classic Tojo-c. 74 148 222 470 810 1150
25-Hitler-c 58 116 174 371 636 900
26,29-Japanese WWII-c. 29-Intro. Capt. Yank; Bo (a dog) newspaper strip-r by Frank Beck begin, ends #104. 37 74 111 222 361 500
28-Hitler, Tojo & Mussolini-c 81 162 243 518 884 1250
31,33-40 24 48 72 140 230 320
32-Vic Jordan newspaper strip reprints begin, ends #52; Hitler, Tojo & Mussolini-c
71 142 213 454 777 1100
41,42,44,45,47-50: 42-No Skyman. 50-Origin The Face retold
20 40 60 120 195 270
43-Hitler-c 68 136 204 435 743 1050
46-Hitler, Tojo-c (6/44) 65 130 195 416 708 1000
51-Tojo Japanese war-c 34 68 102 199 325 450
52-56,58-60: 18 36 54 103 162 220
57-Hitler, Tojo Halloween mask-c 39 78 117 240 395 550
61-70: 63 on-Tony Trent, the Face 14 28 42 82 121 160
71-80: 73-The Face cameo. 74-(2/47)-Mickey Finn begins. 74,80-The Face app. in Tony Trent. 78-Last Charlie Chan strip-r 14 28 42 76 108 140
81-90: 85-Tony Trent marries Babs Walsh. 86-Valentines-c
11 22 33 62 86 110
91-99,101-104: 69-94-Skyman in Outer Space. 96-Xmas-c
10 20 30 56 76 95
100 11 22 33 64 90 115
NOTE: ***Mart Bailey** art on "The Face" No. 1-104. **Guardineer** a-5. Sparky Watts by **Boody Rogers**-No. 14-42, 77-104, (by others No. 43-76). Others than Tony Trent wear "The Face" mask in No. 46-63, 93. Skyman by **Ogden Whitney**-No. 1, 2, 4, 12-37, 49, 70-101. Skyman covers-No. 1, 3, 7-12, 14, 16, 20, 27, 89, 95, 100.*

BIG SMASH BARGAIN COMICS
No publisher listed: Early 1950s (25¢, 160pgs., Canadian reprints)
1-4: Contains 4 comics from various companies bundled with new cover (scarce)
31 62 93 186 303 420

BIG TEX
Toby Press: June, 1953
1-Contains (3) John Wayne stories-r with name changed to Big Tex
10 20 30 58 79 100

BIG-3
Fox Features Syndicate: Fall, 1940 - No. 7, Jan, 1942
1-Blue Beetle, The Flame, & Samson begin 226 452 678 1446 2473 3500
2 84 168 252 538 919 1300
3-5 60 120 180 381 653 925
6,7: 6-Last Samson. 7-V-Man app. 45 90 135 284 480 675

BIG TOP COMICS, THE (TV's Great Circus Show)
Toby Press: 1951 - No. 2, 1951 (No month)
1 10 20 30 58 79 100
2 9 18 27 47 61 75

BIG TOWN (Radio/TV) (Also see Movie Comics, 1946)
National Periodical Publ: Jan, 1951 - No. 50, Mar-Apr, 1958 (No. 1-9: 52pgs.)
1-Dan Barry-a begins 68 136 204 438 749 1060
2 36 72 108 216 351 485
3-10 21 42 63 126 206 285
11-20 16 32 48 92 144 195
21-31: Last pre-code (1-2/55) 13 26 39 74 105 135
32-50: 46-Grey tone cover 10 20 30 56 76 95

BIG VALLEY, THE (TV)
Dell Publishing Co.: June, 1966 - No. 5, Oct, 1967; No. 6, Oct, 1969
1: Photo-c #1-5 5 10 15 35 55 75
2-6: 6-Reprints #1 4 8 12 22 34 45

BIKER MICE FROM MARS (TV)
Marvel Comics: Nov, 1993 - No. 3, Jan, 1994 ($1.50, limited series)
1-3: 1-Intro Vinnie, Modo & Throttle. 2-Origin 4.00

BILL & TED'S BOGUS JOURNEY
Marvel Comics: Sept, 1991 ($2.95, squarebound, 84 pgs.)
1-Adapts movie sequel 4.00

BILL & TED'S EXCELLENT COMIC BOOK (Movie)
Marvel Comics: Dec, 1991 - No. 12, 1992 ($1.00/$1.25)
1-12: 3-Begin $1.25-c 3.00

BILL BARNES COMICS (...America's Air Ace Comics No. 2 on) (Becomes Air Ace V2#1 on; also see Shadow Comics)
Street & Smith Publications: Oct, 1940(No. month given) - No. 12, Oct, 1943
1-23 pgs.-comics; Rocket Rooney begins 90 180 270 576 988 1400

Bill Battle, The One Man Army #1 © FAW

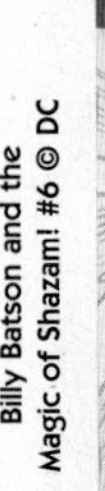
Billy Batson and the Magic of Shazam! #6 © DC

KING OF THE OLD WEST!! BILLY THE KID ADVENTURE MAGAZINE — THRILL TO THE HAUNTED CAVE

Billy the Kid #8 © TOBY

	GD 2.0	VG 4.0	FN 6.0	VF 8.0	VF/NM 9.0	NM- 9.2
2-Barnes as The Phantom Flyer app.; Tuska-a	46	92	138	290	488	685
3-5	40	80	120	246	411	575
6,8,10,12	36	72	108	211	343	475
7-(1942) Story about dropping atomic bomb on Japan	41	82	123	256	428	600
9-Classic WWII cover	43	86	129	271	461	650
11-Japanese WWII Gremlin cover	37	74	111	222	361	500

BILL BATTLE, THE ONE MAN ARMY (Also see Master Comics No. 133)
Fawcett Publications: Oct, 1952 - No. 4, Apr, 1953 (All photo-c)

	GD 2.0	VG 4.0	FN 6.0	VF 8.0	VF/NM 9.0	NM- 9.2
1	14	28	42	76	108	140
2	8	16	24	44	57	70
3,4	8	16	24	40	50	60

BILL BLACK'S FUN COMICS
Paragon #1-3/Americomics #4: Dec, 1982 - No. 4, Mar, 1983 ($1.75/$2.00, Baxter paper) (1st AC comic)

	GD 2.0	VG 4.0	FN 6.0	VF 8.0	VF/NM 9.0	NM- 9.2
1-(B&W fanzine; 7x8-1/2"; low print) Intro. Capt. Paragon, Phantom Lady & Commando D	2	4	6	13	18	22
2-4: 2,3-(B&W fanzines; 8-1/2x11"). 3-Kirby-c. 4-($2.00, color)-Origin Nightfall (formerly Phantom Lady); Nightveil app.; Kirby-a	1	3	4	6	8	10

BILL BOYD WESTERN (Movie star; see Hopalong Cassidy & Western Hero)
Fawcett Publ: Feb, 1950 - No. 23, June, 1952 (1-3,7,11,14-on: 36 pgs.)

	GD 2.0	VG 4.0	FN 6.0	VF 8.0	VF/NM 9.0	NM- 9.2
1-Bill Boyd & his horse Midnite begin; photo front/back-c	30	60	90	177	289	400
2-Painted-c	16	32	48	94	147	200
3-Photo-c begin, end #23; last photo back-c	14	28	42	80	115	150
4-6(52 pgs.)	12	24	36	69	97	125
7,11(36 pgs.)	10	20	30	56	76	95
8-10,12,13(52 pgs.)	10	20	30	58	79	100
14-22	9	18	27	52	69	85
23-Last issue	10	20	30	56	76	95

BILL BUMLIN (See Treasury of Comics No. 3)

BILL ELLIOTT (See Wild Bill Elliott)

BILLI 99
Dark Horse Comics: Sept, 1991 - No. 4, 1991 ($3.50, B&W, lim. series, 52 pgs.)

	GD 2.0	VG 4.0	FN 6.0	VF 8.0	VF/NM 9.0	NM- 9.2
1-4: Tim Sale-c/a						4.00

BILL STERN'S SPORTS BOOK
Ziff-Davis Publ. Co.(Approved Comics): Spring-Sum, 1951 - V2#2, Win, 1952

	GD 2.0	VG 4.0	FN 6.0	VF 8.0	VF/NM 9.0	NM- 9.2
V1#10-(1951) Whitney painted-c	21	42	63	122	199	275
2-(Sum/52; reg. size)	16	32	48	94	147	200
V2#2-(1952, 96 pgs.)-Krigstein, Kinstler-a	21	42	63	126	206	285

BILL THE BULL: ONE SHOT, ONE BOURBON, ONE BEER
Boneyard Press: Dec, 1994 ($2.95, B&W, mature)

	GD 2.0	VG 4.0	FN 6.0	VF 8.0	VF/NM 9.0	NM- 9.2
1						3.00

BILLY AND BUGGY BEAR (See Animal Fun)
I.W. Enterprises/Super: 1958; 1964

	GD 2.0	VG 4.0	FN 6.0	VF 8.0	VF/NM 9.0	NM- 9.2
I.W. Reprint #1, #7('58)-All Surprise Comics #?(Same issue-r for both)	2	4	6	10	14	18
Super Reprint #10(1964)	2	4	6	8	11	14

BILLY BATSON AND THE MAGIC OF SHAZAM! (Follows Shazam: The Monster Society of Evil mini-series)
DC Comics: Sept, 2008 - No. 21, Dec, 2010 ($2.25/$2.50, all ages title)

	GD 2.0	VG 4.0	FN 6.0	VF 8.0	VF/NM 9.0	NM- 9.2
1-17: 1-4-Mike Kunkel-s/a/c; Theo (Black) Adam app. 5-DeStefano-a. 13-16-Black Adam						3.00
1-Variant B&W sketch cover						3.50
18-21 ($2.99) 21-Justice League cameo						3.00
TPB (2010, $12.99) r/#1-6; cover and haracter sketches						13.00
...: Mr. Mind Over Matter TPB (2011, $12.99) r/#7-12						13.00

BILLY BUCKSKIN WESTERN (2-Gun Western No. 4)
Atlas Comics (IMC No. 1/MgPC No. 2,3): Nov, 1955 - No. 3, Mar, 1956

	GD 2.0	VG 4.0	FN 6.0	VF 8.0	VF/NM 9.0	NM- 9.2
1-Mort Drucker-a; Maneely-c/a	16	32	48	88	137	185
2-Mort Drucker-a	10	20	30	56	76	95
3-Williamson, Drucker-a	12	24	36	67	94	120

BILLY BUNNY (Black Cobra No. 6 on)
Excellent Publications: Feb-Mar, 1954 - No. 5, Oct-Nov, 1954

	GD 2.0	VG 4.0	FN 6.0	VF 8.0	VF/NM 9.0	NM- 9.2
1	9	18	27	50	65	80
2	6	12	18	28	34	40
3-5	5	10	15	24	30	35

BILLY BUNNY'S CHRISTMAS FROLICS
Farrell Publications: 1952 (25¢ Giant, 100 pgs.)

	GD 2.0	VG 4.0	FN 6.0	VF 8.0	VF/NM 9.0	NM- 9.2
1	20	40	60	118	192	265

BILLY MAKE BELIEVE
United Features Syndicate: No. 14, 1939

	GD 2.0	VG 4.0	FN 6.0	VF 8.0	VF/NM 9.0	NM- 9.2
Single Series 14	30	60	90	177	289	400

BILLY NGUYEN, PRIVATE EYE
Caliber Press: V2#1, 1990 ($2.50)

	GD 2.0	VG 4.0	FN 6.0	VF 8.0	VF/NM 9.0	NM- 9.2
V2#1						3.00

BILLY THE KID (Formerly The Masked Raider; also see Doc Savage Comics & Return of the Outlaw)
Charlton Publ. Co.: No. 9, Nov, 1957 - No. 121, Dec, 1976; No. 122, Sept, 1977 - No. 123, Oct, 1977; No. 124, Feb, 1978 - No. 153, Mar, 1983

	GD 2.0	VG 4.0	FN 6.0	VF 8.0	VF/NM 9.0	NM- 9.2
9	10	20	30	58	79	100
10,12,14,17-19: 12-2 pg Check-sty	8	16	24	40	50	60
11-(68 pgs.)-Origin & 1st app. The Ghost Train	9	18	27	50	65	80
13-Williamson/Torres-a	8	16	24	44	57	70
15-Origin; 2 pgs. Williamson-a	8	16	24	44	57	70
16-Williamson-a, 2 pgs.	8	16	24	42	54	65
20-26-Severin-a(3-4 each)	8	16	24	44	57	70
27-30: 30-Masked Rider app.	3	6	9	19	29	38
31-40	3	6	9	16	22	28
41-60	2	4	6	13	18	22
61-65	2	4	6	10	14	18
66-Bounty Hunter series begins.	3	6	9	14	20	25
67-80: Bounty Hunter series; not in #79,82,84-86	2	4	6	10	14	18
81-84,86-90: 87-Last Bounty Hunter. 88-1st app. Mr. Young of the Boothill Gazette	2	4	6	8	10	12
85-Early Kaluta-a (4 pgs.)	2	4	6	9	13	16
91-123: 110-Mr. Young of Boothill app. 111-Origin The Ghost Train. 117-Gunsmith & Co., The Cheyenne Kid app.	1	2	3	5	6	8
124(2/78)-153						6.00
Modern Comics 109 (1977 reprint)						4.00

NOTE: ***Boyette*** *a-88-110.* ***Kim*** *a-73.* ***Morsi*** *a-12,14.* ***Sattler*** *a-118-123.* ***Severin*** *a(r)-121-129, 134; c-23, 25.* ***Sutton*** *a-111.*

BILLY THE KID ADVENTURE MAGAZINE
Toby Press: Oct, 1950 - No. 29, 1955

	GD 2.0	VG 4.0	FN 6.0	VF 8.0	VF/NM 9.0	NM- 9.2
1-Williamson/Frazetta-a (2 pgs) r/from John Wayne Adventure Comics #2; photo-c	31	62	93	182	296	410
2-Photo-c	12	24	36	69	97	125
3-Williamson/Frazetta "The Claws of Death", 4 pgs. plus Williamson art	34	68	102	199	325	450
4,5,7,8,10: 4,7-Photo-c	9	18	27	52	69	85
6-Frazetta assist on "Nightmare"; photo-c	15	30	45	83	124	165
9-Kurtzman Pot-Shot Pete; photo-c	11	22	33	64	90	115
11,12,15-20: 11-Photo-c	8	16	24	42	54	65
13-Kurtzman-r/John Wayne #12 (Genius)	9	18	27	47	61	75
14-Williamson/Frazetta; r-of #1 (2 pgs.)	10	20	30	56	76	95
21,23-29	7	14	21	37	46	55
22-Williamson/Frazetta-r(1pg.)/#1; photo-c	8	16	24	42	54	65

BILLY THE KID AND OSCAR (Also see Fawcett's Funny Animals)
Fawcett Publications: Winter, 1945 - No. 3, Fall, 1946 (Funny animal)

	GD 2.0	VG 4.0	FN 6.0	VF 8.0	VF/NM 9.0	NM- 9.2
1	15	30	45	84	127	170
2,3	10	20	30	56	76	95

BILLY THE KID'S OLD TIMEY ODDITIES
Dark Horse Comics: Apr, 2005 - No. 4, July, 2005 ($2.99, limited series)

	GD 2.0	VG 4.0	FN 6.0	VF 8.0	VF/NM 9.0	NM- 9.2
1-4-Eric Powell-s/c; Kyle Hotz-a						3.00
TPB (2005, $13.95) r/series						14.00
... and the Ghostly Fiend of London (9/10 - No. 4, 12/10, $3.99) 1-3-Powell-s/c; Kyle Hotz-a; Goon back-up; Powell-s/a						4.00

BILLY WEST (Bill West No. 9,10)
Standard Comics (Visual Editions): 1949-No. 9, Feb, 1951; No. 10, Feb, 1952

	GD 2.0	VG 4.0	FN 6.0	VF 8.0	VF/NM 9.0	NM- 9.2
1	15	30	45	86	133	180
2	10	20	30	54	72	90
3-6,9,10	9	18	27	47	61	75
7,8-Schomburg-c	10	20	30	54	72	90

NOTE: ***Celardo*** *a-1-6, 9; c-1-3.* ***Moreira*** *a-3.* ***Roussos*** *a-2.*

BING CROSBY (See Feature Films)

BINGO (...Comics) (H. C. Blackerby)
Howard Publ.: 1945 (Reprints National material)

The Bionic Man #4 © Universal

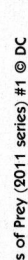

Birds of Prey (2011 series) #1 © DC

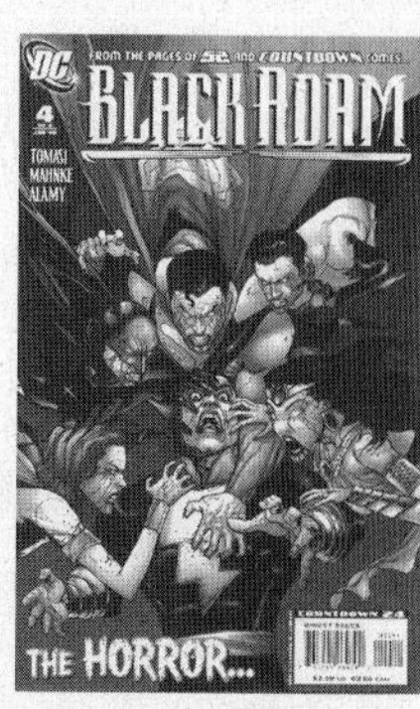

Black Adam #4 © DC

	GD 2.0	VG 4.0	FN 6.0	VF 8.0	VF/NM 9.0	NM- 9.2

1-L. B. Cole opium-c; blank back-c 36 72 108 211 343 475

BINGO, THE MONKEY DOODLE BOY
St. John Publishing Co.: Aug, 1951; Oct, 1953

1(8/51)-By Eric Peters 8 16 24 42 54 65
1(10/53) 6 12 18 31 38 45

BINKY (Formerly Leave It to...)
National Periodical Publ./DC Comics: No. 72, 4-5/70 - No. 81, 10-11/71; No. 82, Summer/77

72-76 4 8 12 26 41 55
77-79: (68 pgs.). 77-Bobby Sherman 1pg. story w/photo. 78-1 pg. sty on Barry Williams of Brady Bunch. 79-Osmonds 1pg. story 6 12 18 41 66 90
80,81 (52 pgs.)-Sweat Pain story 5 10 15 35 55 75
82 (1977, one-shot) 4 8 12 28 44 60

BINKY'S BUDDIES
National Periodical Publications: Jan-Feb, 1969 - No. 12, Nov-Dec, 1970

1 8 16 24 51 86 120
2-12: 3-Last 12¢ issue 4 8 12 28 44 60

BIONIC MAN (TV)
Dynamite Entertainment: 2011 - Present ($3.99)

1-7-Kevin Smith & Phil Hester-s; Jonathan Lau-a; multiple covers on each 4.00

BIONIC WOMAN, THE (TV)
Charlton Publications: Oct, 1977 - No. 5, June, 1978

1 4 8 12 23 36 48
2-5 3 6 9 17 25 32

BIRDS OF PREY (Also see Black Canary/Oracle: Birds of Prey)
DC Comics: Jan, 1999 - No. 127, Apr, 2009 ($1.99/$2.50/$2.99)

1-Dixon-s/Land-c/a 1 3 4 6 8 10
2-4 6.00
5-7,9-15: 15-Guice-a begins. 4.00
8-Nightwing-c/app.; Barbara & Dick's circus date 2 4 6 9 12 15
16-38: 23-Grodd-c/app. 26-Bane app. 32-Noto-c begin 3.00
39,40-Bruce Wayne: Murderer pt. 5,12 3.50
41-Bruce Wayne: Fugitive pt. 2 4.00
42-46: 42-Fabry-a. 45-Deathstroke-c/app. 3.00
47-74,76-91: 47-49-Terry Moore-s/Conner & Palmiotti-a; Noto-c. 50-Gilbert Hernandez-s begin. 52,54-Metamorpho app. 56-Simone-s/Benes-a begin. 65,67,68,70-Land-c. 76-Debut of Black Alice (from Day of Vengeance). 86-Timm-a (7 pgs.) 3.00
75-($2.95) Pearson-c; back-up story of Lady Blackhawk 4.00
92-99,101-127: 92-One Year Later. 94-Begin $2.99-c; Prometheus app. 96,97-Black Alice app. 98,99-New Batgirl app. 99-Black Canary leaves the team. 104-107-Secret Six app. 3.00
100-($3.99) new team recruited; Black Canary origin re-told 4.00
TPB (1999, $17.95) r/ previous series and one-shots 18.00
...: Batgirl 1 (2/98, $2.95) Dixon-s/Frank-c 5.00
...: Batgirl/Catwoman 1 ('03, $5.95) Robertson-a; cont'd in BOP: Catwoman/Oracle 1 6.00
...: Between Dark & Dawn TPB (2006, $14.99) r/#69-75 15.00
...: Blood and Circuits TPB (2007, $17.99) r/#96-103 18.00
...: Catwoman/Oracle 1 ('03, $5.95) Cont'd from BOP: Batgirl/Catwoman 1; David Ross-a 6.00
...: Club Kids TPB (2008, $17.99) r/#109-112,118 18.00
...: Dead of Winter TPB (2008, $17.99) r/#104-108 18.00
...: Metropolis or Dust TPB (2008, $17.99) r/#113-117 18.00
...: Of Like Minds TPB (2004, $14.95) r/#55-61 15.00
...: Old Friends, New Enemies TPB (2003, $17.95) r/#1-6, ...: Batgirl, ...: Wolves 18.00
...: Perfect Pitch TPB (2007, $17.99) r/#86-90,92-95 18.00
...: Platinum Flats TPB (2009, $17.99) r/#119-124 18.00
...: Revolution 1 (1997, $2.95) Frank-c/Dixon-s 5.00
... Secret Files 2003 (8/03, $4.95) Short stories, pin-ups and profile pages; Noto-c 5.00
...: Sensei and Student TPB (2005, $17.95) r/#62-68 18.00
...: The Battle Within TPB (2006, $17.99) r/#76-85 18.00
...: The Ravens 1 (6/98, $1.95)-Dixon-s; Girlfrenzy issue 4.00
...: Wolves 1 (10/97, $2.95) Dixon-s/Giordano & Faucher-a 5.00

BIRDS OF PREY (Brightest Day)
DC Comics: Jul, 2010 - No. 15, Oct, 2011 ($2.99)

1-Simone-s/Benes-a/c; Hawk and Dove join team, Penguin app. 3.00
1-Variant cover by Chiang 5.00
2-15: 2-4-Penguin app. 7-10-"Death of Oracle". 11-Catman app. 14,15-Tucci-a 3.00
... End Run HC (2011, $22.99, d.j.) r/#1-6 23.00

BIRDS OF PREY (DC New 52)
DC Comics: Nov, 2011 - Present ($2.99)

1-7: 1-Swierczynski-s/Saiz-a; intro. Starling. 2-Katana & Poison Ivy join. 4-7-Batgirl app. 3.00

BIRDS OF PREY: MANHUNT
DC Comics: Sept, 1996 - No. 4, Dec, 1996 ($1.95, limited series)

1-Features Black Canary, Oracle, Huntress, & Catwoman; Chuck Dixon scripts; Gary Frank-c on all. 1-Catwoman cameo only 1 2 3 5 6 8
2-4 6.00

NOTE: ***Gary Frank*** *c-1-4.* ***Matt Haley*** *a-1-4p.* ***Wade Von Grawbadger*** *a-1i.*

BIRTH CAUL, THE
Eddie Campbell Comics: 1999 ($5.95, B&W, one-shot)

1-Alan Moore-s/Eddie Campbell-a 6.00

BIRTH OF THE DEFIANT UNIVERSE, THE
Defiant Comics: May, 1993

nn-Contains promotional artwork & text; limited print run of 1000 copies. 2 4 6 8 10 12

BISHOP (See Uncanny X-Men & X-Men)
Marvel Comics: Dec, 1994 - No.4, Mar, 1995 ($2.95, limited series)

1-4: Foil-c; Shard & Mountjoy in all. 1-Storm app. 4.00

BISHOP THE LAST X-MAN
Marvel Comics: Oct, 1999 - No. 16, Jan, 2001 ($2.99/$1.99/$2.25)

1-($2.99)-Jeanty-a 4.00
2-8-($1.99): 2-Two covers 3.00
9-11,13-16: 9-Begin $2.25-c. 15-Maximum Security x-over; Xavier app. 3.00
12-($2.99) 4.00

BISHOP: XAVIER SECURITY ENFORCER
Marvel Comics: Jan, 1998 - No.3, Mar, 1998 ($2.50, limited series)

1-3: Ostrander-s 3.00

BITE CLUB
DC Comics (Vertigo): Jun, 2004 - No. 6, Nov, 2004 ($2.95, limited series)

1-6-Chaykin-s/Tischman-a/Quitely-c 3.00
TPB Digest (2005, $9.99) r/#1-6; cover gallery 10.00
The Complete Bite Club TPB (2007, $19.99) r/#1-6 and ...: Vampire Crime Unit #1-5 20.00

BITE CLUB: VAMPIRE CRIME UNIT
DC Comics (Vertigo): Jun, 2006 - No. 5 ($2.99, limited series)

1-5:1-Chaykin & Tischman-s/Hahn-a/Quitely-c. 4-Chaykin-c 3.00

BIZARRE ADVENTURES (Formerly Marvel Preview)
Marvel Comics Group: No. 25, 3/81 - No. 34, 2/83 (#25-33: Magazine-$1.50)

25,26: 25-Lethal Ladies. 26-King Kull; Bolton-c/a 2 4 6 8 10 12
27,28: 27-Phoenix, Iceman & Nightcrawler app. 28-The Unlikely Heroes; Elektra by Miller; Neal Adams-a 2 4 6 10 14 18
29,30,32,33: 29-Stephen King's Lawnmower Man. 30-Tomorrow; 1st app. Silhouette. 32-Gods; Thor-c/s. 33-Horror; Dracula app.; photo-c 2 3 4 6 8 10
31-After The Violence Stops; new Hangman story; Miller-a 2 4 6 8 10 12
34 ($2.00, Baxter paper, comic size)-Son of Santa; Christmas special; Howard the Duck by Paul Smith 1 2 3 5 7 9

NOTE: ***Alcala*** *a-27i.* ***Austin*** *a-25i, 28i.* ***Bolton*** *a-26, 32.* ***J. Buscema*** *a-27p, 29, 30p; c-26.* ***Byrne*** *a-31 (2 pg.).* ***Golden*** *a-25p, 28p.* ***Perez*** *a-27p.* ***Rogers*** *a-25p.* ***Simonson*** *a-29; c-29.* ***Paul Smith*** *a-34.*

BIZARRO COMICS!
DC Comics: 2001 ($29.95, hardcover, one-shot)

HC-Short stories of DC heroes by various alternative cartoonists including Dorkin, Pope, Haspiel, Kidd, Kochalka, Millionaire, Stephens, Wray; includes "Superman's Babysitter" by Kyle Baker from Elseworlds 80-Page Giant recalled by DC; Groening-c 30.00
Softcover (2003, $19.95) 20.00

BIZARRO WORLD
DC Comics: 2005 ($29.95, hardcover, one-shot)

HC-Short stories by various alternative cartoonists including Bagge, Baker, Dorkin, Dunn, Kupperman, Morse, Oswalt, Pekar, Simpson, Stewart; Jaime Hernandez-c 30.00
Softcover (2006, $19.99) 20.00

BLACK ADAM (See 52 and Countdown)
DC Comics: Oct, 2007 - No. 6, Mar, 2008 ($2.99, limited series)

1-6: 1-Mahnke-a/c; Isis returns; Felix Faust app. 3.00
...: The Dark Age TPB (2008, $17.99) r/#1-6; Alex Ross-c 18.00

BLACK AND WHITE (See Large Feature Comic, Series I)

BLACK & WHITE (Also see Codename: Black & White)
Image Comics (Extreme): Oct, 1994 - No. 3, Jan, 1995 ($1.95, limited series)

1-3: Thibert-c/story 3.00

BLACK & WHITE MAGIC

Black Cat Comics #4 © HARV

Black Cobra #6 (#2) © Farrell

Blackest Night #8 © DC

	GD 2.0	VG 4.0	FN 6.0	VF 8.0	VF/NM 9.0	NM- 9.2

Innovation Publishing: 1991 ($2.95, 98 pgs., B&W w/30 pgs. color, squarebound)
1-Contains rebound comics w/covers removed; contents may vary 4.00

BLACK AXE
Marvel Comics (UK): Apr, 1993 - No. 7, Oct, 1993 ($1.75)
1-4: 1-Romita Jr.-c. 2-Sunfire-c/s 3.00
5-7: 5-Janson-c; Black Panther app. 6,7-Black Panther-c/s 3.00

BLACKBALL COMICS
Blackball Comics: Mar, 1994 ($3.00)
1-Trencher-c/story by Giffen; John Pain by O'Neill 3.00

BLACKBEARD'S GHOST (See Movie Comics)

BLACK BEAUTY (See Son of Black Beauty)
Dell Publishing Co.: No. 440, Dec, 1952
Four Color 440 5 10 15 30 48 65

BLACKBURNE COVENANT, THE
Dark Horse Comics: Apr, 2003 - No. 4, July, 2003 ($2.99, limited series)
1-4-Nicieza-s/Raffaele-a 3.00
TPB (2003, $12.95) r/#1-4 13.00

BLACK CANARY (See All Star Comics #38, Flash Comics #86, Justice League of America #75 & World's Finest #244)
DC Comics: Nov, 1991 - No. 4, Feb, 1992 ($1.75, limited series)
1-4 3.00

BLACK CANARY
DC Comics: Jan, 1993 - No. 12, Dec, 1993 ($1.75)
1-7 3.00
8-12: 8-The Ray-c/story. 9,10-Huntress-c/story 3.00

BLACK CANARY (Follows Oliver Queen's marriage proposal in Green Arrow #75)
DC Comics: Early Sept, 2007 - No. 4, Late Oct, 2007 ($2.99, bi-weekly limited series)
1-4-Bedard-s/Siqueira-a 3.00
... Wedding Planner 1 (11/07, $2.99) Roux-c/Ferguson & Norrie-a 3.00

BLACK CANARY/ORACLE: BIRDS OF PREY (Also see Showcase '96 #3)
DC Comics: 1996 ($3.95, one-shot)
1-Chuck Dixon scripts & Gary Frank-c/a. 1 2 3 5 7 9

BLACK CAT (AMAZING SPIDER-MAN PRESENTS...)
Marvel Comics: Aug, 2010 - No. 4, Dec, 2010 ($3.99, limited series)
1-4-Van Meter-s/Pulido-a/Conner-c; Spider-Man & Ana Kraven app. 4.00

BLACK CAT COMICS (...Western #16-19; ...Mystery #30 on)
(See All-New #7,9, The Original Black Cat, Pocket & Speed Comics)
Harvey Publications (Home Comics): June-July, 1946 - No. 29, June, 1951
1-Kubert-a; Joe Simon c-1,2 77 154 231 489 837 1185
2-Kubert-a 40 80 120 242 401 560
3,4: 4-The Red Demons begin (The Demon #4 & 5)
33 66 99 194 317 440
5,6,7: 5,6-The Scarlet Arrow app. in ea. by Powell; S&K-a in both. 6-Origin Red Demon.
7-Vagabond Prince by S&K plus 1 more story 39 78 117 240 395 550
8-S&K-a; Kerry Drake begins, ends #13 35 70 105 208 339 470
9-Origin Stuntman (r/Stuntman #1) 38 76 114 226 368 510
10-20: 14,15,17-Mary Worth app. plus Invisible Scarlet O'Neil-#15,20,24
26 52 78 154 252 350
21-26 21 42 63 124 202 280
27,28: 27-Used in **SOTI**, pg. 193; X-Mas-c; 2 pg. John Wayne story. 28-Intro.
Kit, Black Cat's new sidekick 23 46 69 134 220 305
29-Black Cat bondage-c; Black Cat stories 22 44 66 128 209 290

BLACK CAT MYSTERY (Formerly Black Cat; ...Western Mystery #54; ...Western #55,56; ...Mystery #57; ...Mystic #58-62; Black Cat #63-65)
Harvey Publications: No. 30, Aug, 1951 - No. 65, Apr, 1963
30-Black Cat on cover and splash page only 33 66 99 194 317 440
31,32,34,37,38,40 27 54 81 158 259 360
33-Used in **POP**, pg. 89; electrocution-c 30 60 90 177 289 400
35-Atomic disaster cover/story 34 68 102 199 325 450
36,39-Used in **SOTI**: #36-Pgs. 270,271; #39-Pgs. 386-388
32 64 96 188 307 425
41-43 26 52 78 154 252 350
44-Eyes, ears, tongue cut out; Nostrand-a 29 58 87 170 278 385
45-Classic "Colorama" by Powell; Nostrand-a 53 106 159 334 567 800
46-49,51-Nostrand-a in all. 51-Story has blank panel covering censored art (post-Code)
27 54 81 158 259 360
50-Check-a; classic Warren Kremer-c showing a man's face & hands burning away
129 258 387 826 1413 2000
52,53 (r/#34 & 35) 17 34 51 100 158 215
54-Two Black Cat stories (2/55, last pre-code) 19 38 57 111 176 240
55,56-Black Cat app. 17 34 51 100 158 215
57(7/56)-Kirby-c 19 38 57 111 176 240
58-60-Kirby-a(4). 58,59-Kirby-c. 60,61-Simon-c 22 44 66 132 216 300
61-Nostrand-a; "Colorama" r/#45 20 40 60 117 189 260
62 (3/58)-E.C. story swipe 17 34 51 100 158 215
63-65: Giants(10/62,1/63, 4/63); Reprints; Black Cat app. 63-origin Black Kitten.
65-1 pg. Powell-a 20 40 60 115 185 255
NOTE: ***Kremer** a-37, 39, 43; c-36, 37, 47. **Meskin** a-51. **Palais** a-30, 31(2), 32(2), 33-35, 37-40. **Powell** a-32-35, 36(2), 40, 41, 43-53, 57. **Simon** c-63-65. **Sparling** a-44. Bondage c-32, 34, 43.*

BLACK COBRA (Bride's Diary No. 4 on) (See Captain Flight #8)
Ajax/Farrell Publications(Excellent Publ.): No. 1, 10-11/54; No. 6(No. 2), 12-1/54-55; No. 3, 2-3/55
1-Re-intro Black Cobra & The Cobra Kid (costumed heroes)
36 72 108 216 351 485
6(#2)-Formerly Billy Bunny 19 38 57 111 176 240
3-(Pre-code)-Torpedoman app. 18 36 54 105 165 225

BLACK CONDOR (Also see Crack Comics, Freedom Fighters & Showcase '94 #10,11)
DC Comics: June, 1992 - No. 12, May, 1993 ($1.25)
1-8-Heath-c 3.00
9-12: 9,10,12-Heath-c. 9,10-The Ray app. 12-Batman-c/app. 3.00

BLACK CROSS SPECIAL (See Dark Horse Presents)
Dark Horse Comics: Jan, 1988 ($1.75, B&W, one-shot)(Reprints & new-a)
1-1st printing 3.00
1-(2nd printing) has 2 pgs. new-a 3.00

BLACK CROSS: DIRTY WORK (See Dark Horse Presents)
Dark Horse Comics: Apr, 1997 ($2.95, one-shot)
1-Chris Warner-c/s/a 3.00

BLACK DIAMOND
Americomics: May, 1983 - No. 5, 1984 (no month)($2.00-$1.75, Baxter paper)
1-3-Movie adapt.; 1-Colt back-up begins 4.00
4,5 3.00
NOTE: ***Bill Black** a-1i; c-1. **Gulacy** c-2-5. Sybil Danning photo back-c-1.*

BLACK DIAMOND WESTERN (Formerly Desperado No. 1-8)
Lev Gleason Publ: No. 9, Mar, 1949 - No. 60, Feb, 1956 (No. 9-28: 52 pgs.)
9-Black Diamond & his horse Reliapon begin; origin & 1st app. Black Diamond
21 42 63 122 199 275
10 12 24 36 69 97 125
11-15 10 20 30 54 72 90
16-28(11/49-11/51)-Wolverton's Bingbang Buster 14 28 42 76 108 140
29-40: 31-One pg. Frazetta anti-drug ad 9 18 27 47 61 75
41-50,53-59 8 16 24 40 50 60
51-3-D effect-c/story 15 30 45 85 130 175
52-3-D effect story 14 28 42 81 118 155
60-Last issue 8 16 24 44 57 70
NOTE: ***Biro** c-9-35?. **Cooper** a-12. **Myron Foss** a-54-58, c-54-56, 58. **Guardineer** a-9, 12, 15, 18. **Jack Keller** a-12. **Kida** a-9. **Maurer** a-10. **Ed Moore** a-16. **Morisi** a-55. **William Overgard** a-9-23. **Tuska** a-10, 48. **Bill Walton** a-57.*

BLACK DRAGON, THE
Marvel Comics (Epic Comics): 5/85 - No. 6, 10/85 (Baxter paper, mature)
1-6: 1-Chris Claremont story & John Bolton painted-c/a in all 3.00
TPB (Dark Horse, 4/96, $17.95, B&W, trade paperback) r/#1-6; intro by Anne McCaffrey 18.00

BLACKEST NIGHT (2009 Green Lantern & DC crossover) (Leads into Brightest Day series)
DC Comics: No. 0, Jun, 2009 - No. 8, May, 2010 ($3.99, limited series)
0-Free Comic Book Day edition; Johns-s/Reis-a; profile pages of different corps 3.00
1-8: 1-($3.99) Black Lantern Corps arises; Johns-s/Reis-c/a; Hawkman & Hawkgirl killed.
4-Nekron rises. 8-Dead heroes return 4.00
1-Variant cover by Van Sciver 15.00
1-3,5: 2nd-4th printings 4.00
2-8: 2-Cascioli variant-c. 3-Van Sciver variant-c. 4-7-Migliari variant-c. 8-Mahnke var-c 8.00
... Director's Cut (6/10, $5.99) Commentary with story panels; cover gallery, script pgs. 6.00
HC (2010, $29.99, d.j.) r/#0-8 & Blackest Night Director's Cut; variant cover gallery 30.00
SC (2011, $19.99) r/#0-8 & Blackest Night Director's Cut; variant cover gallery 20.00
...: Black Lantern Corps Vol. 1 HC (2010, $24.99, d.j.) r/BN: Batman, BN: Superman, and BN: Titans series; cover gallery and character sketch designs 25.00
...: Black Lantern Corps Vol. 1 SC (2011, $19.99) same contents as HC edition 20.00
...: Black Lantern Corps Vol. 2 HC (2010, $24.99, d.j.) r/BN: The Flash, BN: JSA, and

Blackest Night: Wonder Woman #3 © DC

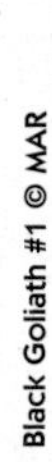
Black Goliath #1 © MAR

Blackhawk #253 © DC

GD VG FN VF VF/NM NM-
2.0 4.0 6.0 8.0 9.0 9.2

BN: Wonder Woman series; cover gallery and character sketch designs 25.00
...: Rise of the Black Lanterns HC (2010, $24.99) r/one-shots Atom and Hawkman #46, Catwoman #83, Phantom Stranger #42, Power of Shazam #48, The Question #37, Starman #81, Weird Western Tales #71, Green Arrow #30 & Adventure Comics #7; sketch art 25.00
...: Rise of the Black Lanterns SC (2011, $19.99) same contents as HC edition 20.00

BLACKEST NIGHT: BATMAN (2009 Green Lantern & DC crossover)
DC Comics: Oct, 2009 - No. 3, Dec, 2009 ($2.99, limited series)

1-3: 1-Bat-parents rise as Black Lanterns; Deadman app.; Syaf-a/Andy Kubert-c; 2 printings. 3-Flying Graysons return 3.00
1-3-Variant-c by Sienkiewicz 5.00

BLACKEST NIGHT: JSA (2009 Green Lantern & DC crossover)
DC Comics: Feb, 2010 - No. 3, Apr, 2010 ($2.99, limited series)

1-3-Original Sandman, Dr. Midnite and Mr. Terrific rise; Barrows-a/c 3.00
1-3-Variant-c by Gene Ha 5.00

BLACKEST NIGHT: SUPERMAN (2009 Green Lantern & DC crossover)
DC Comics: Oct, 2009 - No. 3, Dec, 2009 ($2.99, limited series)

1-3-Earth-2 Superman and Lois become Black Lanterns; Barrows-a/c; 2 printings 3.00
1-3-Variant-c by Shane Davis 5.00

BLACKEST NIGHT: TALES OF THE CORPS (2009 Green Lantern & DC crossover)
DC Comics: Sept, 2009 - No. 3, Sept, 2009 ($3.99, weekly limited series)

1-3-Short stories by various; interlocking cover images. 3-Commentary on B.N. #0 4.00
HC (2010, $24.99) r/#1-3 & Adventure Comics #4,5 & Green Lantern #49; sketch art 25.00
SC (2011, $19.99) r/#1-3 & Adventure Comics #4,5 & Green Lantern #49; sketch art 20.00

BLACKEST NIGHT: THE FLASH (2009 Green Lantern & DC crossover)
DC Comics: Feb, 2010 - No. 3, Apr, 2010 ($2.99, limited series)

1-3-Rogues vs. Dead Rogues; Johns-s/Kolins-a 3.00
1-3-Variant-c by Manapul 5.00

BLACKEST NIGHT: TITANS (2009 Green Lantern & DC crossover)
DC Comics: Oct, 2009 - No. 3, Dec, 2009 ($2.99, limited series)

1-3-Terra and the original Hawk return; Benes-a/c 3.00
1-3-Variant-c by Brian Haberlin 5.00

BLACKEST NIGHT: WONDER WOMAN (2009 Green Lantern & DC crossover)
DC Comics: Feb, 2010 - No. 3, Apr, 2010 ($2.99, limited series)

1-3-Maxwell Lord returns; Rucka-s/Scott-a/Horn-c. 2,3-Mera app.; Star Sapphire 3.00
1-3-Variant-c by Ryan Sook 5.00

BLACK FLAG (See Asylum #5)
Maximum Press: Jan, 1995 - No.4, 1995; No. 0, July, 1995 ($2.50, B&W) (No. 0 in color)

Preview Edition (6/94, $1.95, B&W)-Fraga/McFarlane-c. 3.00
0-4: 0-(7/95)-Liefeld/Fraga-c. 1-(1/95). 3.00
1-Variant cover 5.00
2,4-Variant covers 3.00
NOTE: *Fraga a-0-4, Preview Edition; c-1-4.* ***Liefeld/Fraga*** *c-0.* ***McFarlane/Fraga*** *c-Preview Edition.*

BLACK FURY (Becomes Wild West No. 58) (See Blue Bird)
Charlton Comics Group: May, 1955 - No. 57, Mar-Apr, 1966 (Horse stories)

	GD 2.0	VG 4.0	FN 6.0	VF 8.0	VF/NM 9.0	NM- 9.2
1	12	24	36	67	94	120
2	7	14	21	37	46	55
3-10	6	12	18	28	34	40
11-15,19,20	4	8	10	18	22	25
16-18-Ditko-a	12	24	36	67	94	120
21-30	4	7	10	14	17	20
31-57	3	6	8	12	14	16

BLACK GOLIATH (See Avengers #32-35,41,54 and Civil War #4)
Marvel Comics Group: Feb, 1976 - No. 5, Nov, 1976

	GD 2.0	VG 4.0	FN 6.0	VF 8.0	VF/NM 9.0	NM- 9.2
1-Tuska-a(p) thru #3	3	6	9	14	20	25
2-5: 2-4-(Regular 25¢ editions). 4-Kirby-c/Buckler-a	2	4	6	9	13	16
2-4-(30¢-c variants, limited distribution)(4,6,8/76)	4	8	12	24	37	50

BLACKHAWK (Formerly Uncle Sam #1-8; see Military Comics & Modern Comics)
Comic Magazines(Quality)No. 9-107(12/56); National Periodical Publications No. 108 (1/57) -250; DC Comics No. 251 on: No. 9, Winter, 1944 - No. 243, 10-11/68; No. 244, 1-2/76 - No. 250, 1-2/77; No. 251, 10/82 - No. 273, 11/84

	GD 2.0	VG 4.0	FN 6.0	VF 8.0	VF/NM 9.0	NM- 9.2
9 (1944)	258	516	774	1651	2826	4000
10 (1946)	103	206	309	659	1130	1600
11-15: 14-Ward-a; 13,14-Fear app.	71	142	213	454	777	1100
16-19	61	122	183	390	670	950
20-Classic Crandall bondage-c; Ward Blackhawk	94	188	282	597	1024	1450
21-30 (1950)	47	94	141	296	498	700
31-40: 31-Chop Chop by Jack Cole	39	78	117	235	385	535
41-49,51-60: 42-Robot-c	32	64	96	192	314	435
50-1st Killer Shark; origin in text	36	72	108	216	351	485
61,62: 61-Used in **POP**, pg. 91. 62-Used in **POP**, pg. 92 & color illo	29	58	87	170	278	385
63-70,72-80: 65-H-Bomb explosion panel. 66-B&W & color illos **POP**. 67-Hitler-s. 70-Return of Killer Shark; atomic explosion panel. 75-Intro. Blackie the Hawk	27	54	81	160	263	365
71-Origin retold; flying saucer-c; A-Bomb panels	31	62	93	186	303	420
81-86: Last precode (3/55)	24	48	72	142	234	325
87-92,94-99,101-107: 91-Robot-c. 105-1st S.A.	20	40	60	117	189	260
93-Origin in text	20	40	60	118	192	265
100	24	48	72	142	234	325
108-1st DC issue (1/57); re-intro. Blackie, the Hawk, their mascot; not in #115	36	72	108	270	585	900
109-117: 117-(10/57)-Mr. Freeze app.	13	26	39	90	195	300
118-(11/57)-Frazetta-r/Jimmy Wakely #4 (3 pgs.)	14	28	42	93	202	310
119-130 (11/58): 120-Robot-c	11	22	33	76	151	225
131-140 (9/59): 133-Intro. Lady Blackhawk	10	20	30	67	124	180
141-150,152-163,165,166: 141-Cat-Man returns-c/s. 143-Kurtzman-r/Jimmy Wakely #4. 150-(7/60)-King Condor returns. 166-Last 10¢ issue	8	16	24	56	96	135
151-Lady Blackhawk receives & loses super powers	9	18	27	60	103	145
164-Origin retold	9	18	27	60	103	145
167-180	6	12	18	41	66	90
181-190	5	10	15	35	55	75
191-196,199: 196-Combat Diary series begins	4	8	12	28	44	60
197,198,200: 197-New look for Blackhawks. 198-Origin retold	5	10	15	30	48	65
201,202,204-210	4	8	12	22	34	45
203-Origin Chop Chop (12/64)	4	8	12	26	41	55
211-227,229-243(1968): 230-Blackhawks become superheroes; JLA cameo 242-Return to old costumes	3	6	9	18	27	35
228-Batman, Green Lantern, Superman, The Flash cameos.	3	6	9	20	30	40
244 ('76) -250: 250-Chuck dies	1	2	3	5	6	8

251-273: 251-Origin retold; Black Knights return. 252-Intro Domino. 253-Part origin Hendrickson. 258-Blackhawk's Island destroyed. 259-Part origin Chop-Chop. 265-273 (75¢ cover price) 4.00
NOTE: ***Chaykin*** *a-260; c-257-260, 262.* ***Crandall*** *a-10, 11, 13, 16?, 18-20, 22-26, 30-33, 35p, 36(2), 37, 38?, 39-44, 46-50, 52-58, 60, 63, 64, 66, 67; c-14-20, 22-63(most except #28-33, 36, 37, 39).* ***Evans*** *a-244, 245,246i, 248-250i.* ***G. Kane*** *c-263, 264.* ***Kubert c****-244, 245.* ***Newton*** *a-266p.* ***Severin*** *a-257.* ***Spiegle*** *a-261-267, 269-273; c-265-272.* ***Toth*** *a-260p.* ***Ward*** *a-16-27(Chop Chop, 8pgs. ea.); pencilled stories-No. 17-63(approx.).* ***Wildey*** *a-268. Chop Chop solo stories in #10-95?*

BLACKHAWK
DC Comics: Mar, 1988 - No. 3, May, 1988 ($2.95, limited series, mature)

1-3: Chaykin painted-c/a/scripts 4.00

BLACKHAWK (Also see Action Comics #601)
DC Comics: Mar, 1989 - No. 16, Aug, 1990 ($1.50, mature)

1 4.00
2-6,8-16: 16-Crandall-c swipe 3.00
7-($2.50, 52 pgs.)-Story-r/Military #1 4.00
Annual 1 (1989, $2.95, 68 pgs.)-Recaps origin of Blackhawk, Lady Blackhawk, and others 4.00
Special 1 (1992, $3.50, 68 pgs.)-Mature readers 4.00

BLACKHAWK INDIAN TOMAHAWK WAR, THE
Avon Periodicals: 1951 (Also see Fighting Indians of the Wild West)

nn-Kinstler-c; Kit West story 20 40 60 114 182 250

BLACKHAWKS (DC New 52)
DC Comics: Nov, 2011 - No. 8, Jun, 2012 ($2.99)

1-8: 1-Costa-s/Nolan & Lashley-a 3.00

BLACK HEART ASSASSIN
Iguana Comics: Jan, 1994 ($2.95)

1 3.00

BLACK HOLE (See Walt Disney Showcase #54) (Disney, movie)
Whitman Publishing Co.: Mar, 1980 - No. 4, Sept, 1980

	GD 2.0	VG 4.0	FN 6.0	VF 8.0	VF/NM 9.0	NM- 9.2
11295(#1) (1979, Golden, $1.50-c, 52 pgs., graphic novel; 8 1/2x11") Photo-c; Spiegle-a.	3	6	9	14	19	24
1-3: 1,2-Movie adaptation. 2,3-Spiegle-a. 3-McWilliams-a; photo-c. 3-New stories	2	4	6	9	12	15
4-Sold only in pre-packs; new story; Spiegle-a	8	16	24	51	86	120

BLACK HOOD, THE (See Blue Ribbon, Flyman & Mighty Comics)
Red Circle Comics (Archie): June, 1983 - No. 3, Oct, 1983 (Mandell paper)

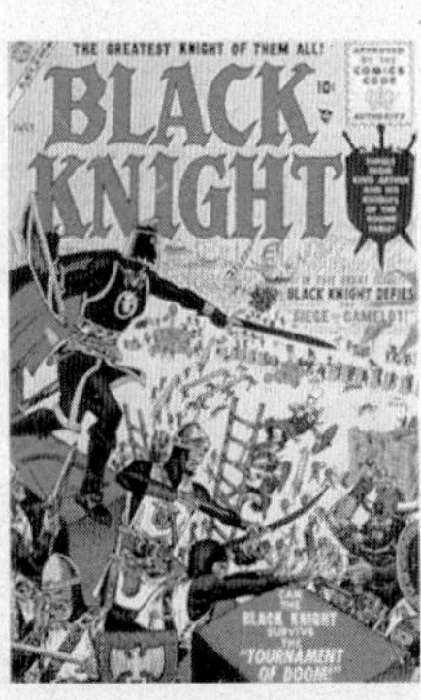

Black Knight #2 © MAR

Black Magic V2 #1 © Headline

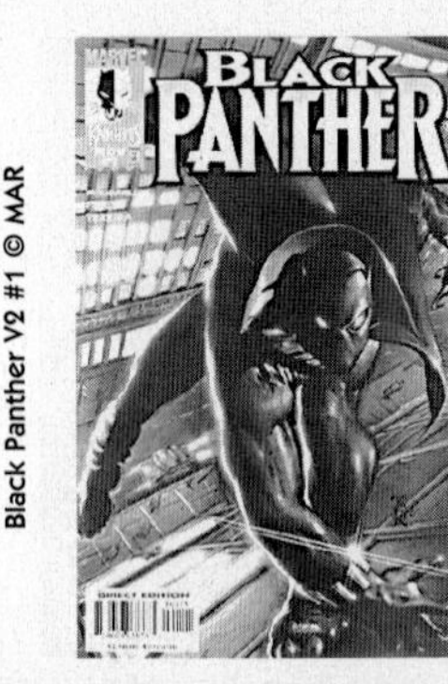

Black Panther V2 #1 © MAR

	GD 2.0	VG 4.0	FN 6.0	VF 8.0	VF/NM 9.0	NM- 9.2
1-Morrow, McWilliams, Wildey-a; Toth-c						6.00
2,3: The Fox by Toth-c/a; Boyette-a. 3-Morrow-a; Toth wraparound-c						4.00

NOTE: *Also see Archie's Super-Hero Special Digest #2*

BLACK HOOD
DC Comics (Impact Comics): Dec, 1991 - No. 12, Dec, 1992 ($1.00)

	GD 2.0	VG 4.0	FN 6.0	VF 8.0	VF/NM 9.0	NM- 9.2
1						4.00
2-12: 11-Intro The Fox. 12-Origin Black Hood						3.00
Annual 1 (1992, $2.50, 68 pgs.)-w/Trading card						4.00

BLACK HOOD COMICS (Formerly Hangman #2-8; Laugh Comics #20 on; also see Black Swan, Jackpot, Roly Poly & Top-Notch #9)
MLJ Magazines: No. 9, Wint., 1943-44 - No. 19, Sum., 1946 (on radio in 1943)

	GD 2.0	VG 4.0	FN 6.0	VF 8.0	VF/NM 9.0	NM- 9.2
9-The Hangman & The Boy Buddies cont'd	113	226	339	718	1234	1750
10-Hangman & Dusty, the Boy Detective app.	64	128	192	406	696	985
11-Dusty app.; no Hangman	50	100	150	315	533	750
12-18: 14-Kinstler blood-c. 17-Hal Foster swipe from Prince Valiant; 1st issue with "An Archie Magazine" on-c	44	88	132	277	469	660
19-I.D. exposed; last issue	52	104	156	328	557	785

NOTE: *Hangman by* ***Fuje*** *in 9, 10.* ***Kinstler*** *a-15, c-14-16.*

BLACK JACK (Rocky Lane's...; formerly Jim Bowie)
Charlton Comics: No. 20, Nov, 1957 - No. 30, Nov, 1959

	GD 2.0	VG 4.0	FN 6.0	VF 8.0	VF/NM 9.0	NM- 9.2
20	9	18	27	52	69	85
21,27,29,30	6	12	18	31	38	45
22,23: 22-(68 pgs.). 23-Williamson/Torres-a	8	16	24	42	54	65
24-26,28-Ditko-a	10	20	30	56	76	95

BLACK KNIGHT, THE
Toby Press: May, 1953; 1963

	GD 2.0	VG 4.0	FN 6.0	VF 8.0	VF/NM 9.0	NM- 9.2
1-Bondage-c	31	62	93	182	296	410
Super Reprint No. 11 (1963)-Reprints 1953 issue	3	6	9	19	25	32

BLACK KNIGHT, THE
Atlas Comics (MgPC): May, 1955 - No. 5, April, 1956

	GD 2.0	VG 4.0	FN 6.0	VF 8.0	VF/NM 9.0	NM- 9.2
1-Origin Crusader; Maneely-c/a	94	188	282	597	1024	1450
2-Maneely-c/a(4)	63	126	189	403	689	975
3-5: 4-Maneely-c/a. 5-Maneely-c, Shores-a	49	98	147	309	522	735

BLACK KNIGHT (See The Avengers #48, Marvel Super Heroes & Tales To Astonish #52)
Marvel Comics: June, 1990 - No. 4, Sept, 1990 ($1.50, limited series)

	GD 2.0	VG 4.0	FN 6.0	VF 8.0	VF/NM 9.0	NM- 9.2
1-4: 1-Original Black Knight returns. 3,4-Dr. Strange app.						3.00
... (MDCU) 1 (01/10, $3.99) Origin re-told; Frenz-a; originally from Marvel Digital Comics						4.00

NOTE: ***Buckler*** *c-1-4p*

BLACK KNIGHT: EXODUS
Marvel Comics: Dec, 1996 ($2.50, one-shot)

	GD 2.0	VG 4.0	FN 6.0	VF 8.0	VF/NM 9.0	NM- 9.2
1-Raab-s; Apocalypse-c/app.						3.00

BLACK LAMB, THE
DC Comics (Helix): Nov, 1996 - No. 6, Apr, 1997 ($2.50, limited series)

	GD 2.0	VG 4.0	FN 6.0	VF 8.0	VF/NM 9.0	NM- 9.2
1-6: Tim Truman-c/a/scripts						3.00

BLACKLIGHT (From ShadowHawk)
Image Comics: June, 2005 - No. 2, Jul, 2005 ($2.99)

	GD 2.0	VG 4.0	FN 6.0	VF 8.0	VF/NM 9.0	NM- 9.2
1,2-Toledo & Deering-a/Wherle-s						3.00

BLACK LIGHTNING (See The Brave & The Bold, Cancelled Comic Cavalcade, DC Comics Presents #16, Detective #490 and World's Finest #257)
National Periodical Publ./DC Comics: Apr, 1977 - No. 11, Sept-Oct, 1978

	GD 2.0	VG 4.0	FN 6.0	VF 8.0	VF/NM 9.0	NM- 9.2
1-Origin Black Lightning	2	4	6	9	13	16
2,3,6-10	1	2	3	5	6	8
4,5-Superman-c/s. 4-Intro Cyclotronic Man	1	3	4	6	8	10
11-The Ray new solo story	2	4	6	8	10	12

NOTE: ***Buckler*** *c-1-3p, 6-11p. #11 is 44 pgs.*

BLACK LIGHTNING (2nd Series)
DC Comics: Feb, 1995 - No. 13, Feb, 1996 ($1.95/$2.25)

	GD 2.0	VG 4.0	FN 6.0	VF 8.0	VF/NM 9.0	NM- 9.2
1-5-Tony Isabella scripts begin, ends #8						3.00
6-13: 6-Begin $2.25-c. 13-Batman-c/app.						3.00

BLACK LIGHTNING: YEAR ONE
DC Comics: Mar, 2009 - No. 6, May, 2009 ($2.99, bi-weekly limited series)

	GD 2.0	VG 4.0	FN 6.0	VF 8.0	VF/NM 9.0	NM- 9.2
1-6-Van Meter-s/Hamner-a. 1-Two printings (white and yellow cover title logos)						3.00
TPB (2009, $17.99) r/#1-6						18.00

BLACK MAGIC (...Magazine) (Becomes Cool Cat V8#6 on)
Crestwood Publ. V1#1-4,V6#1-V7#5/Headline V1#5-V5#3,V7#6-V8#5: 10-11/50 - V4#1, 6-7/53: V4#2, 9-10/53 - V5#3, 11-12/54; V6#1, 9-10/57 - V7#2, 11-12/58: V7#3, 7-8/60 - V8#5, 11-12/61 (V1#1-5, 52pgs.; V1#6-V3#3, 44pgs.)

	GD 2.0	VG 4.0	FN 6.0	VF 8.0	VF/NM 9.0	NM- 9.2
V1#1-S&K-a, 10 pgs.; Meskin-a(2)	155	310	465	992	1696	2400
2-S&K-a, 17 pgs.; Meskin-a	66	132	198	419	722	1025
3-6(8-9/51)-S&K, Roussos, Meskin-a	56	112	168	356	608	860
V2#1(10-11/51),4,5,7(#13),9(#15),12(#18)-S&K-a	39	78	117	236	388	540
2,3,6,8,10,11(#17)	31	62	93	182	296	410
V3#1(#19, 12/52) - 6(#24, 5/53)-S&K-a	31	62	93	186	303	420
V4#1(#25, 6-7/53), 2(#26, 9-10/53)-S&K-a(3-4)	32	64	96	192	314	435
3(#27, 11-12/53)-S&K-a; Ditko-a (2nd published-a); also see Captain 3-D, Daring Love #1, Strange Fantasy #9, & Fantastic Fears #5 (Fant. Fears was 1st drawn, but not 1st publ.)	58	116	174	371	636	900
4(#28)-Eyes ripped out/story-S&K, Ditko-a	43	86	129	271	461	650
5(#29, 3-4/54)-S&K, Ditko-a	34	68	102	206	336	465
6(#30, 5-6/54)-S&K, Powell?-a	27	54	81	160	263	365
V5#1(#31, 7-8/54 - 3(#33, 11-12/54)-S&K-a	20	40	60	114	182	250
V6#1(#34, 9-10/57), 2(#35, 11-12/57)	12	24	36	67	94	120
3(1-2/58) - 6(7-8/58)	12	24	36	67	94	120
V7#1(9-10/58) - 3(7-8/60), 4(9-10/60)	10	20	30	56	76	95
5(11-12/60)-Hitler-c; Torres-a	16	32	48	94	147	200
6(1-2/61)-Powell-a(2)	10	20	30	56	76	95
V8#1(3-4/61)-Powell-c/a	10	20	30	56	76	95
2(5-6/61)-E.C. story swipe/W.F. #22; Ditko, Powell-a	11	22	33	60	83	105
3(7-8/61)-E.C. story swipe/W.F. #22; Powell-a(2)	11	22	33	60	83	105
4(9-10/61)-Powell-a(5)	10	20	30	56	76	95
5-E.C. story swipe/W.S.F. #28; Powell-a(3)	11	22	33	60	83	105

NOTE: ***Bernard Baily*** *a-V4#6?, V5#3(2).* ***Grandenetti*** *a-V2#3, 11.* ***Kirby*** *c-V1#1-6, V2#1-12, V3#1-6, V4#1, 2, 4-6, V5#1-3.* ***McWilliams*** *a-V3#2i.* ***Meskin*** *a-V1#1(2), 2, 3, 4(2), 5(2), 6, V2/1, 2, 3(2), 4(3), 5, 6(2), 7-9, 11, 12i, V3#1(2), 5, 6, V5#1(2), 2.* ***Orlando*** *a-V6#1, 4, V7#2; c-V6/1-6.* ***Powell*** *a-V5#1?.* ***Roussos*** *a-V1#3-5, 6(2), V2#3(2), 4, 5(2), 6, 8, 9, 10(2), 11, 12p, V3#1(2), 2i, 5, V5#2.* ***Simon*** *a-V2#12, V3#2, V7#5? c-V4#3?, V7#3?, 4, 5?, 6?, V8#1-5.* ***Simon & Kirby*** *a-V1#1, 2(2), 3-6, V2#1, 4, 5, 7, 9, 12, V3#1-6, V4#1(3), 2(4), 3(2), 4(2), 5, 6, V5#1-3; c-V2#1.* ***Leonard Starr*** *a-V1#1.* ***Tuska*** *a-V6#3, 4.* ***Woodbridge*** *a-V7#4.*

BLACK MAGIC
National Periodical Publications: Oct-Nov, 1973 - No. 9, Apr-May, 1975

	GD 2.0	VG 4.0	FN 6.0	VF 8.0	VF/NM 9.0	NM- 9.2
1-S&K reprints	3	6	9	17	25	32
2-8-S&K reprints	2	4	6	10	14	18
9-S&K reprints	2	4	6	11	16	20

BLACKMAIL TERROR (See Harvey Comics Library)

BLACK MASK
DC Comics: 1993 - No. 3, 1994 ($4.95, limited series, 52 pgs.)

	GD 2.0	VG 4.0	FN 6.0	VF 8.0	VF/NM 9.0	NM- 9.2
1-3						5.00

BLACK OPS
Image Comics (WildStorm): Jan, 1996 - No. 5, May, 1996 ($2.50, lim. series)

	GD 2.0	VG 4.0	FN 6.0	VF 8.0	VF/NM 9.0	NM- 9.2
1-5						3.00

BLACK ORCHID (See Adventure Comics #428 & Phantom Stranger)
DC Comics: Holiday, 1988-89 - No. 3, 1989 ($3.50, lim. series, prestige format)

	GD 2.0	VG 4.0	FN 6.0	VF 8.0	VF/NM 9.0	NM- 9.2
Book 1,3: Gaiman scripts & McKean painted-a in all						6.00
Book 2-Arkham Asylum story; Batman app.	1	2	3	5	6	8
TPB (1991, $19.95) r/#1-3; new McKean-c						20.00

BLACK ORCHID
DC Comics: Sept, 1993 - No. 22, June, 1995 ($1.95/$2.25)

	GD 2.0	VG 4.0	FN 6.0	VF 8.0	VF/NM 9.0	NM- 9.2
1-22: Dave McKean-c all issues						3.00
1-Platinum Edition						12.00
Annual 1 (1993, $3.95, 68 pgs.)-Children's Crusade						4.00

BLACKOUTS (See Broadway Hollywood...)

BLACK PANTHER, THE (Also see Avengers #52, Fantastic Four #52, Jungle Action & Marvel Premiere #51-53)
Marvel Comics Group: Jan, 1977 - No. 15, May, 1979

	GD 2.0	VG 4.0	FN 6.0	VF 8.0	VF/NM 9.0	NM- 9.2
1-Jack Kirby-s/a thru #12	4	8	12	22	34	45
2-13: 4,5-(Regular 30¢ editions). 8-Origin	2	4	6	10	14	18
4,5-(35¢-c variants, limited dist.)(7,9/77)	6	12	18	39	62	85
14,15-Avengers x-over. 14-Origin	3	6	9	14	20	26
...By Jack Kirby Vol. 1 TPB (2005, $19.99) r/#1-7; unused covers and sketch pages						20.00
...By Jack Kirby Vol. 2 TPB (2006, $19.99) r/#8-12 by Kirby and #13 non-Kirby						20.00

NOTE: ***J. Buscema*** *c-15p.* ***Layton*** *c-13i.*

BLACK PANTHER
Marvel Comics Group: July, 1988 - No. 4, Oct, 1988 ($1.25)

	GD 2.0	VG 4.0	FN 6.0	VF 8.0	VF/NM 9.0	NM- 9.2
1-4-Gillis-s/Cowan & Delarosa-a						3.00

BLACK PANTHER (Marvel Knights)
Marvel Comics: Nov, 1998 - No. 62, Sept, 2003 ($2.50)

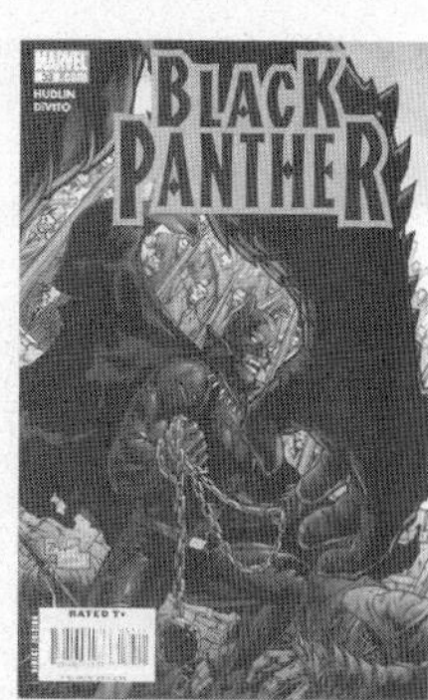

Black Panther (2005 series) #33 © MAR

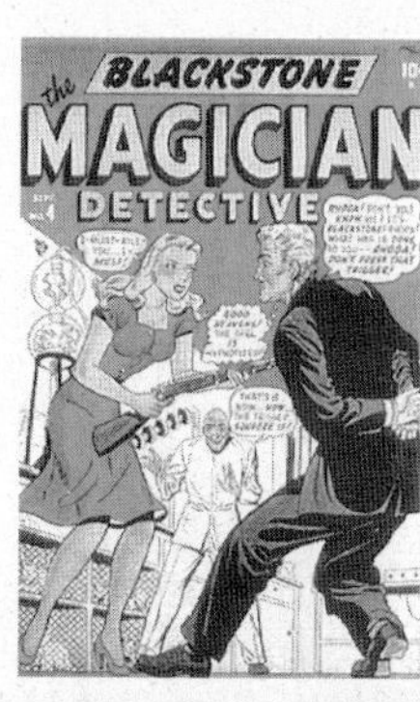

Blackstone, The Magician #4 © MAR

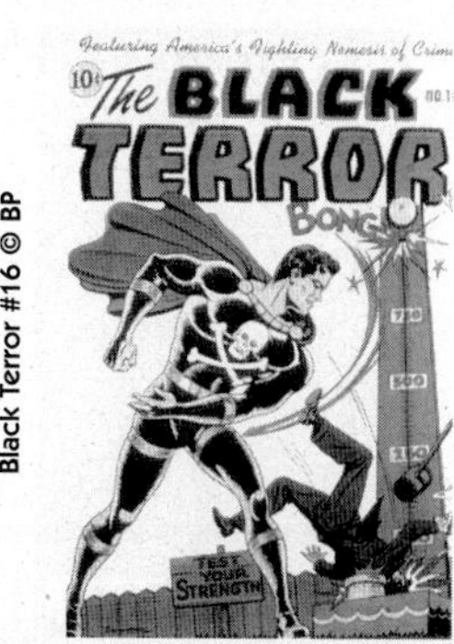

Black Terror #16 © BP

GD VG FN VF VF/NM NM-
2.0 4.0 6.0 8.0 9.0 9.2

1-Texeira-a/c; Priest-s 6.00
1-($6.95) DF edition w/Quesada & Palmiotti-c 1 2 3 5 6 8
2-4: 2-Two covers by Texeira and Timm. 3-Fantastic Four app. 4.00
5-35,37-40: 5-Evans-a. 6-8-Jusko-a. 8-Avengers-c/app. 15-Hulk app. 22-Moon Knight app. 23-Avengers app. 25-Maximum Security x-over. 26-Storm-c/app. 28-Magneto & Sub-Mariner-c/app. 29-WWII flashback meeting w/Captain America. 35-Defenders-c/app. 37-Luke Cage and Falcon-c/app. 3.00
36-($3.50, 100 pgs.) 35th Anniversary issue incl. r/1st app. in FF #52 4.00
41-56: 41-44-Wolverine app. 47-Thor app. 48,49-Magneto app. 3.00
57-62: 57-Begin $2.99-c. 59-Falcon app. 3.00
...: The Client (6/01, $14.95, TPB) r/#1-5 15.00
... 2099 #1 (11/04, $2.99) Kirkman-s/Hotz-a/Pat Lee-c 3.00

BLACK PANTHER (Marvel Knights)
Marvel Comics: Apr, 2005 - No. 41, Nov, 2008 ($2.99)

1-Reginald Hudlin-s/John Romita Jr. & Klaus Janson-a; covers by Romita & Ribic 5.00
1-2nd printing; variant-c by Ribic 3.00
2-7,9-15,17-20: 7-House of M; Hairsine-a. 10-14-Luke Cage app. 12,13-Blade app. 17-Linsner-c. 19-Doctor Doom app. 3.00
8-Cho-c; X-Men app. 4.00
8-2nd printing variant-c 3.00
16-($3.99) Wedding of T'Challa and Storm; wraparound Cho-c; Hudlin-s/Eaton-a 4.00
21-Civil War x-over; Namor app. 8.00
21-2nd printing with new cover and Civil War logo 3.00
22-25-Civil War: 23-25-Turner-c 4.00
26-41: 26-30-T'Challa and Storm join the Fantastic Four. 27-30-Marvel Zombies app. 28-30-Suydam-c. 39-41-Secret Invasion 3.00
Annual 1 (4/08, $3.99) Hudlin-s/Stroman & Lashley-a; alternate future; Uatu app. 4.00
...: Bad Mutha TPB (2006, $10.99) r/#10-13 11.00
...: Civil War TPB (2007, $17.99) r/#19-25 18.00
...: Four the Hard Way TPB (2007, $13.99) r/#26-30; page layouts and character designs 14.00
...: Little Green Men TPB (2008, $10.99) r/#31-34 11.00
...: The Bride TPB (2006, $14.99) r/#14-18; interview with the dress designer 15.00
...: Who Is The Black Panther HC (2005, $21.99) r/#1-6; Hudlin afterword; cover gallery 22.00
...: Who Is The Black Panther SC (2006, $14.99) r/#1-6; Hudlin afterword; cover gallery 15.00

BLACK PANTHER
Marvel Comics: Apr, 2009 - No. 12, Mar, 2010 ($3.99/$2.99)

1-($3.99) Hudlin-s/Lashley-a; covers by Campbell & Lashley; Dr. Doom app. 4.00
2-12-($2.99) 2-6-Campbell-c. 6-Shuri becomes female Black Panther 3.00

BLACK PANTHER/CAPTAIN AMERICA: FLAGS OF OUR FATHERS
Marvel Comics: Jun, 2010 - No. 4, Sept, 2010 ($3.99, limited series)

1-4-Hudlin-s/Cowan-a; WW2 story; Howling Commandos & Red Skull app. 4.00

BLACK PANTHER: PANTHER'S PREY
Marvel Comics: May, 1991 - No. 4, Oct, 1991 ($4.95, squarebound, lim. series, 52 pgs.)

1-4: McGregor-s/Turner-a 5.00

BLACK PANTHER: THE MAN WITHOUT FEAR (Continues from Daredevil #512)
Marvel Comics: No. 513, Feb, 2011 - No. 523, Nov, 2011 ($2.99)

513-523: 513-Shadowland aftermath; Liss-s/Francavilla-a/Bianchi-c. 521-523-Fear Itself 3.00
513-Variant-c by Francavilla 5.00

BLACK PANTHER: THE MOST DANGEROUS MAN ALIVE
Marvel Comics: No. 523.1, Nov, 2011 - No. 529, Apr, 2012 ($2.99)

523.1, 524-529: 523.1-Palo-a/Zircher-c. 524-Spider Island tie-in; Lady Bullseye app. 3.00

BLACK PEARL, THE
Dark Horse Comics: Sept, 1996 - No. 5, Jan, 1997 ($2.95, limited series)

1-5: Mark Hamill scripts 3.00

BLACK PHANTOM (See Tim Holt #25, 38)
Magazine Enterprises: Nov, 1954 (one-shot) (Female outlaw)

1 (A-1 #122)-The Ghost Rider story plus 3 Black Phantom stories; Headlight-c/a 36 72 108 216 351 485

BLACK PHANTOM
AC Comics: 1989 - No. 3, 1990 ($2.50, B&W; #2 color)(Reprints & new-a)

1-3: 1-Ayers-r, Bolle-r/B.P. #1-3-Redmask-r 3.00

BLACK PHANTOM, RETURN OF THE (See Wisco)

BLACK RIDER (Western Winners #1-7; Western Tales of Black Rider #28-31; Gunsmoke Western #32 on)(See All Western Winners, Best Western, Kid Colt, Outlaw Kid, Rex Hart, Two-Gun Kid, Two-Gun Western, Western Gunfighters, Western Winners, & Wild Western)
Marvel/Atlas Comics(CDS No. 8-17/CPS No. 19 on): No. 8, 3/50 - No. 18, 1/52; No. 19, 11/53 - No. 27, 3/55

GD VG FN VF VF/NM NM-
2.0 4.0 6.0 8.0 9.0 9.2

8 (#1)-Black Rider & his horse Satan begin; 36 pgs; Stan Lee photo-c as Black Rider) 42 84 126 265 445 625
9-52 pgs. begin, end #14 22 44 66 132 216 300
10-Origin Black Rider 27 54 81 158 259 360
11-14: 14-Last 52pgs. 17 34 51 98 154 210
15-19: 19-Two-Gun Kid app. 15 30 45 85 130 175
20-Classic-c; Two-Gun Kid app. 16 32 48 92 144 195
21-27: 21-23-Two-Gun Kid app. 24,25-Arrowhead app. 26-Kid Colt app. 27-Last issue; last precode. Kid Colt app. The Spider (a villain) burns to death 14 28 42 81 118 155

NOTE: ***Ayers*** *c-22.* ***Jack Keller*** *a-15, 26, 27.* ***Maneely*** *a-14; c-16, 17, 25, 27.* ***Syd Shores*** *a-19, 21, 22, 23(3), 24(3), 25-27; c-19, 21, 23.* ***Sinnott*** *a-24, 25.* ***Tuska*** *a-12, 19-21.*

BLACK RIDER RIDES AGAIN!, THE
Atlas Comics (CPS): Sept, 1957

1-Kirby-a(3); Powell-a; Severin-c 25 50 75 147 241 335

BLACK SEPTEMBER (Also see Avengers/Ultraforce, Ultraforce (1st series) #10 & Ultraforce/Avengers)
Malibu Comics (Ultraverse): 1995 ($1.50, one-shot)

Infinity-Intro to the new Ultraverse; variant-c exists. 3.00

BLACKSTONE (See Super Magician Comics & Wisco Giveaways)

BLACKSTONE, MASTER MAGICIAN COMICS
Vital Publ./Street & Smith Publ.: Mar-Apr, 1946 - No. 3, July-Aug, 1946

1 36 72 108 211 343 475
2,3 20 40 60 118 192 265

BLACKSTONE, THE MAGICIAN (...Detective on cover only #3 & 4)
Marvel Comics (CnPC): No. 2, May, 1948 - No. 4, Sept, 1948 (No #1) (Cont'd from E.C. #1?)

2-The Blonde Phantom begins, ends #4 77 154 231 493 847 1200
3,4: 3-Blonde Phantom by Sekowsky 45 90 135 284 480 675

BLACKSTONE, THE MAGICIAN DETECTIVE FIGHTS CRIME
E. C. Comics: Fall, 1947

1-1st app. Happy Houlihans 54 108 162 343 574 825

BLACK SUN (X-Men Black Sun on cover)
Marvel Comics: Nov, 2000 - No. 5, Nov, 2000 ($2.99, weekly limited series)

1-(...: X-Men), 2-(...: Storm), 3-(...: Banshee and Sunfire), 4-(...: Colossus and Nightcrawler), 5-(...: Wolverine and Thunderbird); Claremont-s in all; Evans interlocking painted covers; Magik returns 3.00

BLACK SUN
DC Comics (WildStorm): Nov, 2002 - No. 6, Jun, 2003 ($2.95, limited series)

1-6-Andreyko-s/Scott-a 3.00

BLACK SWAN COMICS
MLJ Magazines (Pershing Square Publ. Co.): 1945

1-The Black Hood reprints from Black Hood No. 14; Bill Woggon-a; Suzie app. Caribbean Pirates-c 21 42 63 122 199 275

BLACK TARANTULA (See Feature Presentations No. 5)

BLACK TERROR (See America's Best Comics & Exciting Comics)
Better Publications/Standard: Winter, 1942-43 - No. 27, June, 1949

1-Black Terror, Crime Crusader begin 343 686 1029 2400 4200 6000
2 135 270 405 864 1482 2100
3 97 194 291 621 1061 1500
4,5 81 162 243 518 884 1250
6-10: 7-The Ghost app. 69 138 207 442 759 1075
11-20: 20-The Scarab app. 55 110 165 352 601 850
21-Miss Masque app. 57 114 171 362 619 875
22-Part Frazetta-a on one Black Terror story 54 108 162 343 574 825
23,25-27 48 96 144 302 514 725
24-Frazetta-a (1/4 pg.) 49 98 147 309 522 735

NOTE: ***Schomburg (Xela)*** *c-2-27; bondage c-2, 17, 24.* ***Meskin*** *a-27.* ***Moreira*** *a-27.* ***Robinson/Meskin*** *a-23, 24(3), 25, 26.* ***Roussos/Mayo*** *a-24.* ***Tuska*** *a-26, 27.*

BLACK TERROR, THE (Also see Total Eclipse)
Eclipse Comics: Oct, 1989 - No. 3, June, 1990 ($4.95, 52 pgs., squarebound, limited series)

1-3: Beau Smith & Chuck Dixon scripts; Dan Brereton painted-c/a 5.00

BLACK TERROR (Also see Project Superpowers)
Dynamite Entertainment: 2008 - No. 14, 2011 ($3.50/$3.99)

1-14-Golden Age hero. 1-Alex Ross-c/Mike Lilly-a; various variant-c exist 4.00

BLACKTHORNE 3-D SERIES
Blackthorne Publishing Co.: May, 1985 - No. 80, 1989 ($2.25/$2.50)

Black Widow (2010 series) #4 © MAR

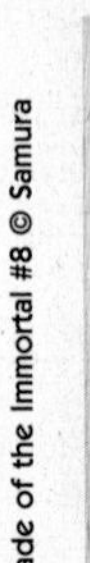

Blade of the Immortal #8 © Samura

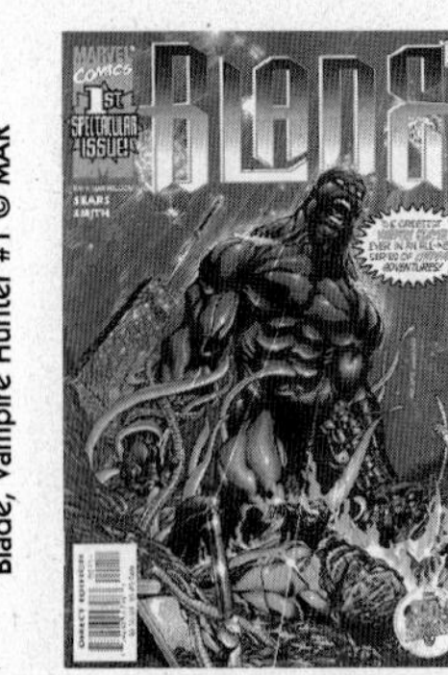

Blade, Vampire Hunter #1 © MAR

	GD	VG	FN	VF	VF/NM	NM-
	2.0	4.0	6.0	8.0	9.0	9.2

1-Sheena in 3-D #1. D. Stevens-c/retouched-a 1 2 3 5 6 8

2-10: 2-MerlinRealm in 3-D #1. 3-3-D Heroes #1. Goldyn in 3-D #1. 5-Bizarre 3-D Zone #1. 6-Salimba in 3-D #1. 7-Twisted Tales in 3-D #1. 8-Dick Tracy in 3-D #1. 9-Salimba in 3-D #2. 10-Gumby in 3-D #1 6.00

11-19: 11-Betty Boop in 3-D #1. 12-Hamster Vice in 3-D #1. 13-Little Nemo in 3-D #1. 14-Gumby in 3-D #2. 15-Hamster Vice #6 in 3-D. 16-Laffin' Gas #6 in 3-D. 17-Gumby in 3-D #3. 18-Bullwinkle and Rocky in 3-D #1. 19-The Flintstones in 3-D #1 6.00

20(#1),26(#2),35(#3),39(#4),52(#5),62,71(#6)-G.I. Joe in 3-D. 62-G.I. Joe Annual 2 4 6 8 11 14

21-24,27-28: 21-Gumby in 3-D #4. 22-The Flintstones in 3-D #2. 23-Laurel & Hardy in 3-D #1. 24-Bozo the Clown in 3-D #1. 27-Bravestarr in 3-D #1. 28- Gumby in 3-D #5 6.00

25,29,37-The Transformers in 3-D 2 4 6 10 14 18

30-Star Wars in 3-D #1 3 6 9 14 19 24

31-34,36,38,40: 31-The California Raisins in 3-D #1. 32-Richie Rich & Casper in 3-D #1. 33-Gumby in 3-D #6. 34-Laurel & Hardy in 3-D #2. 36-The Flintstones in 3-D #3. 38-Gumby in 3-D #7. 40-Bravestarr in 3-D #2 6.00

41-46,49,50: 41-Battletech in 3-D #1. 42-The Flintstones in 3-D #4. 43-Underdog in 3-D #1 44-The California Raisins in 3-D #2. 45-Red Heat in 3-D #1 (movie adapt.). 46-The California Raisins in 3-D #3. 49-Rambo in 3-D #1. 49-Sad Sack in 3-D #1. 50-Bullwinkle For President in 3-D #1 6.00

47,48-Star Wars in 3-D #2,3 2 4 6 9 13 16

51,53-60: 51-Kull in 3-D #1. 53-Red Sonja in 3-D #1. 54-Bozo in 3-D #2. 55-Waxwork in 3-D #1 (movie adapt.). 57-Casper in 3-D #1. 58-Baby Huey in 3-D #1. 59-Little Dot in 3-D #1. 60-Solomon Kane in 3-D #1 6.00

61,63-70,72-80: 61-Werewolf in 3-D #1. 63-The California Raisins in 3-D #4. 64-To Die For in 3-D #1. 65-Capt. Holo in 3-D #1. 66-Playful Little Audrey in 3-D #1. 67-Kull in 3-D #2. 69-The California Raisins in 3-D #5. 70-Wendy in 3-D #1. 72-Sports Hall of Shame #1. 74-The Noid in 3-D #1. 75-Moonwalker in 3-D #1 (Michael Jackson movie adapt.). 76-79. 80-The Noid in 3-D #2 1 2 3 4 5 7

BLACK WIDOW (Marvel Knights) (Also see Marvel Graphic Novel)
Marvel Comics: May, 1999 - No. 3, Aug, 1999 ($2.99, limited series)

1-(June on-c) Devin Grayson-s/J.G. Jones-c/a; Daredevil app. 5.00
1-Variant-c by J.G. Jones 6.00
2,3 4.00
...Web of Intrigue (6/99, $3.50) r/origin & early appearances 4.00
TPB (7/01, $15.95) r/Vol. 1 & 2; Jones-c 16.00

BLACK WIDOW (Marvel Knights) (Volume 2)
Marvel Comics: Jan, 2001 - No. 3, May, 2001 ($2.99, limited series)

1-3-Grayson & Rucka-s/Scott Hampton-c/a; Daredevil app. 3.00

BLACK WIDOW (Marvel Knights)
Marvel Comics: Nov, 2004 - No. 6, Apr, 2005 ($2.99, limited series)

1-6-Sienkiewicz-a/Land-c 3.00

BLACK WIDOW (Continues in Widowmaker #1)
Marvel Comics: Jun, 2010 - No. 8, Jan, 2011 ($3.99/$2.99)

1-($3.99) Liu-s/Acuña-a; Wolverine app.; back-up history text 4.00
1-Variant photo-c of Scarlett Johansson from Iron Man 2 movie 8.00
2-8-($2.99) 2-5-Acuña-a. 2,3-Elektra app. 3.00

BLACK WIDOW & THE MARVEL GIRLS
Marvel Comics: Feb, 2010 - No. 4, Apr, 2010 ($2.99, limited series)

1-4-Tobin-s. 1-Enchantress app. 2-Avengers app. 4-Storm app.; Miyazawa-a 3.00

BLACK WIDOW: DEADLY ORIGIN
Marvel Comics: Jan, 2010 - No. 4, Apr, 2010 ($3.99, limited series)

1-4-Granov-c; origin retold. 1-Wolverine and Bucky app. 3-Daredevil app. 4.00

BLACK WIDOW: PALE LITTLE SPIDER (Marvel Knights) (Volume 3)
Marvel Comics: Jun, 2002 - No. 3, Aug, 2002 ($2.99, limited series)

1-3-Rucka-s/Kordey-a/Horn-c 3.00

BLACK WIDOW 2 (THE THINGS THEY SAY ABOUT HER) (Marvel Knights)
Marvel Comics: Nov, 2005 - No. 6, Apr, 2006 ($2.99, limited series)

1-6-Phillips & Sienkiewicz-a/Morgan-s; Daredevil app. 3.00
TPB (2006, $15.99) r/#1-6 16.00

BLACKWULF
Marvel Comics: June, 1994 - No. 10, Mar, 1995 ($1.50)

1-($2.50)-Embossed-c; Angel Medina-a 3.50
2-10 3.00

BLADE (The Vampire Hunter)
Marvel Comics

1-(3/98, $3.50) Colan-a(p)/Christopher Golden-s 4.00
... Black & White TPB (2004, $15.99, B&W) reprints from magazines Vampire Tales #8,9; Marvel Preview #3,6; Crescent City Blues #1 and Marvel Shadow and Light #1 16.00
San Diego Con Promo (6/97) Wesley Snipes photo-c 3.00
...Sins of the Father (10/98, $5.99) Sears-a; movie adaption 6.00
Blade 2: Movie Adaptation (5/02, $5.95) Ponticelli-a/Bradstreet-c 6.00

BLADE (The Vampire Hunter)
Marvel Comics: Nov, 1998 - No. 3, Jan, 1999 ($3.50/$2.99)

1-($3.50) Contains Movie insider pages; McKean-a 3.50
2,3-($2.99): 2-Two covers 3.00

BLADE (Volume 2)
Marvel Comics (MAX): May, 2002 -No. 6, Oct, 2002 ($2.99)

1-6-Bradstreet-c/Hinz-s. 1-5-Pugh-a. 6-Homs-a 3.00

BLADE
Marvel Comics: Nov, 2006 - No. 12, Oct, 2007 ($2.99)

1-12: 1-Chaykin-a/Guggenheim-s; origin retold; Spider-Man app. 2-Dr. Doom-c/app. 5-Civil War tie-in; Wolverine app. 6-Blade loses a hand. 10-Spider-Man app. 3.00
...: Sins of the Father TPB (2007, $14.99) r/#7-12; afterword by Guggenheim 15.00
...: Undead Again TPB (2007, $14.99) r/#1-6; letters pages from #1&2 15.00

BLADE OF THE IMMORTAL (Manga)
Dark Horse Comics: June, 1996 - No. 131, Nov, 2007 ($2.95/$2.99/$3.95, B&W)

1-Hiroaki Samura-s/a in all 1 3 4 6 8 10
2-5: 2-#1 on cover in error 6.00
6-10 5.00
11,19,20,34-($3.95, 48 pgs.): 34-Food one-shot 4.00
12-18,21-33,35-41,43-105,107-131: 12-20-Dreamsong. 21-28-On Silent Wings. 29-33-Dark Shadow. 35-42-Heart of Darkness. 43-57-The Gathering 3.00
42-($3.50) Ends Heart of Darkness 3.50
106-($3.99) 4.00

BLADE RUNNER (Movie)
Marvel Comics Group: Oct, 1982 - No. 2, Nov, 1982

1,2-r/Marvel Super Special #22; 1-Williamson-c/a. 2-Williamson-a 3.50

BLADE: THE VAMPIRE-HUNTER
Marvel Comics: July, 1994 - No. 10, Apr, 1995 ($1.95)

1-($2.95)-Foil-c; Dracula returns; Wheatley-c/a 4.00
2-10: 2,3,10-Dracula-c/app. 8-Morbius app. 3.00

BLADE: VAMPIRE-HUNTER
Marvel Comics: Dec, 1999 - No. 6, May, 2000 ($3.50/$2.50)

1-($3.50)-Bart Sears-s; Sears and Smith-a 3.50
2-6-($2.50): 2-Regular & Wesley Snipes photo-c 3.00

BLAIR WITCH CHRONICLES, THE
Oni Press: Mar, 2000 - No. 4, July, 2000 ($2.95, B&W, limited series)

1-4-Van Meter-s.1-Guy Davis-a. 2-Mireault-a 3.00
1-DF Alternate-c by John Estes 4.00
TPB (9/00, $15.95) r/#1-4 & Blair Witch Project one-shot 16.00

BLAIR WITCH: DARK TESTAMENTS
Image Comics: Oct, 2000 ($2.95, one-shot)

1-Edington-s/Adlard-a; story of murderer Rustin Parr 3.00

BLAIR WITCH PROJECT, THE (Movie companion, not adaptation)
Oni Press: July, 1999 ($2.95, B&W, one-shot)

1-(1st printing) History of the Blair Witch, art by Edwards, Mireault, and Davis; Van Meter-s; only the stick figure is red on the cover 5.00
1-(2nd printing) Stick figure and title lettering are red on cover 4.00
1-(3rd printing) Stick figure, title, and creator credits are red on cover 3.00
DF Glow in the Dark variant-c ($10.00) 10.00

BLAST (Satire Magazine)
G & D Publications: Feb, 1971 - No. 2, May, 1971

1-Wrightson & Kaluta-a/Everette-c 8 16 24 55 93 130
2-Kaluta-c/a 6 12 18 41 66 90

BLAST CORPS
Dark Horse Comics: Oct, 1998 ($2.50, one-shot, based on Nintendo game)

1-Reprints from Nintendo Power magazine; Mahn-a 3.00

BLASTERS SPECIAL
DC Comics: 1989 ($2.00, one-shot)

1-Peter David scripts; Invasion spin-off 4.00

BLAST-OFF (Three Rocketeers)
Harvey Publications (Fun Day Funnies): Oct, 1965 (12¢)

Blaze of Glory #1 © MAR

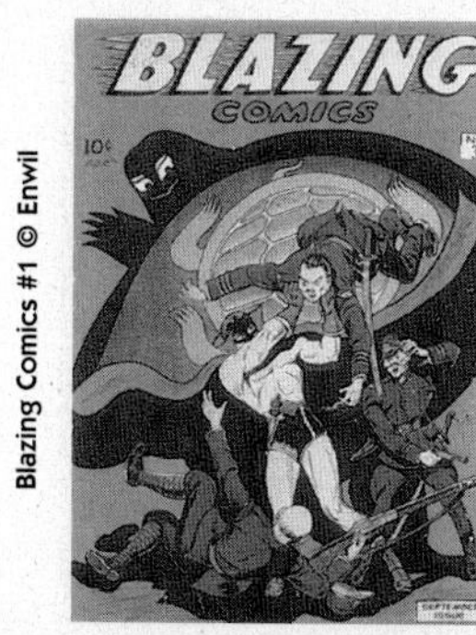

Blazing Comics #1 © Enwil

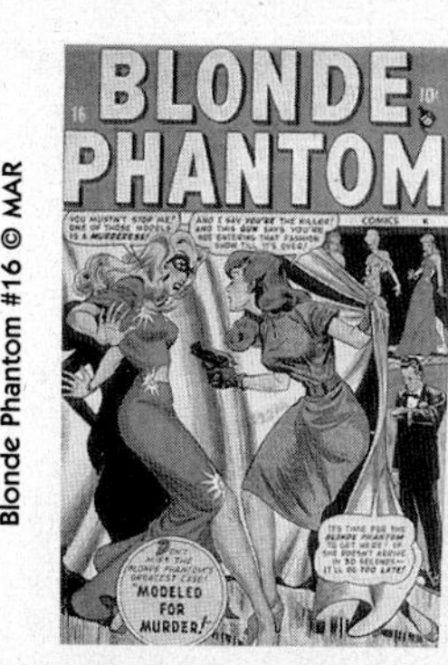

Blonde Phantom #16 © MAR

GD VG FN VF VF/NM NM-
2.0 4.0 6.0 8.0 9.0 9.2

1-Kirby/Williamson-a(2); Williamson/Crandall-a; Williamson/Torres/Krenkel-a; Kirby/Simon-c 7 14 21 48 79 110

BLAZE
Marvel Comics: Aug, 1994 - No. 12, July, 1995 ($1.95)
1-($2.95)-Foil embossed-c 4.00
2-12: 2-Man-Thing-c/story. 11,12-Punisher app. 3.00

BLAZE CARSON (Rex Hart #6 on)(See Kid Colt, Tex Taylor, Wild Western, Wisco)
Marvel Comics (USA): Sept, 1948 - No. 5, June, 1949
1: 1,2-Shores-c 27 54 81 158 259 360
2,4,5: 4-Two-Gun Kid app. 5-Tex Taylor app. 18 36 54 105 165 225
3-Used by N.Y. State Legis. Comm. (injury to eye splash); Tex Morgan app. 19 38 57 111 176 240

BLAZE: LEGACY OF BLOOD (See Ghost Rider & Ghost Rider/Blaze)
Marvel Comics (Midnight Sons imprint): Dec, 1993 - No. 4, Mar, 1994 ($1.75, limited series)
1-4 3.00

BLAZE OF GLORY
Marvel Comics: Feb, 2000 - No. 4, Mar, 2000 ($2.99, limited series)
1-4-Ostrander-s/Manco-a; Two-Gun Kid, Rawhide Kid, Red Wolf and Ghost Rider app. 3.00
TPB (7/02, $9.99) r/#1-4 10.00

BLAZE THE WONDER COLLIE (Formerly Molly Manton's Romances #1?)
Marvel Comics(SePI): No. 2, Oct, 1949 - No. 3, Feb, 1950 (Both have photo-c)
2(#1), 3-(Scarce) 24 48 72 142 234 325

BLAZING BATTLE TALES
Seaboard Periodicals (Atlas): July, 1975
1-Intro. Sgt. Hawk & the Sky Demon; Severin, McWilliams, Sparling-a; Nazi-c by Thorne 2 4 6 11 16 20

BLAZING COMBAT (Magazine)
Warren Publishing Co.: Oct, 1965 - No. 4, July, 1966 (35¢, B&W)
1-Frazetta painted-c on all 24 48 72 168 359 550
2 8 16 24 53 89 125
3,4: 4-Frazetta half pg. ad 7 14 21 48 79 110
nn-Anthology (reprints from No. 1-4) (low print) 8 16 24 55 93 130
NOTE: *Adkins a-4. Colan a-3,4,nn. Crandall a-all. Evans a-1,4. Heath a-4,nn. Morrow a-1-3,nn. Orlando a-1-3,nn. J. Severin a-all. Torres a-1-4. Toth a-all. Williamson a-2. and Wood a-3,4,nn.*

BLAZING COMBAT: WORLD WAR I AND WORLD WAR II
Apple Press: Mar, 1994 ($3.75, B&W)
1,2: 1-r/Colan, Toth, Goodwin, Severin, Wood-a. 2-r/Crandall, Evans, Severin, Torres, Williamson-a 4.00

BLAZING COMICS (Also see Blue Circle Comics and Red Circle Comics)
Enwil Associates/Rural Home: 6/44 - #3, 9/44; #4, 2/45; #5, 3/45; #5(V2#2), 3/55 - #6(V2#3), 1955?
1-The Green Turtle, Red Hawk, Black Buccaneer begin; origin Jun-Gal; classic Japanese WWII splash 53 106 159 334 567 800
2-5: 3-Briefer-a. 5-(V2#2 inside) 36 72 108 216 351 485
5(3/55, V2#2-inside)-Black Buccaneer-c, 6(V2#3-inside, 1955)-Indian/Japanese-c; cover is from Apr. 1945 20 40 60 117 189 260
NOTE: *No. 5 & 6 contain remaindered comics rebound and the contents can vary. Cloak & Daggar, Will Rogers, Superman 64, Star Spangled 130, Kaanga known. Value would be half of contents.*

BLAZING SIXGUNS
Avon Periodicals: Dec, 1952
1-Kinstler-c/a; Larsen/Alascia-a(2), Tuska?-a; Jesse James, Kit Carson, Wild Bill Hickok app. 18 36 54 103 162 220

BLAZING SIXGUNS
I.W./Super Comics: 1964
I.W. Reprint #1,8,9: 1-r/Wild Bill Hickok #26, Western True Crime #? & Blazing Sixguns #1 by Avon; Kinstler-c. 8-r/Blazing Western #?; Kinstler-c. 9-r/Blazing Western #1; Ditko-r; Kintsler-c reprinted from Dalton Boys #1 2 4 6 10 14 18
Super Reprint #10,11,15-17: 10,11-r/The Rider #2,1. 15-r/Silver Kid Western #?. 16-r/Buffalo Bill #?; Wildey-r; Severin-c. 17(1964)-r/Western True Crime #? 2 4 6 10 14 18
12-Reprints Bullseye #3; S&K-a 4 8 12 19 29 38
18-r/Straight Arrow #? by Powell; Severin-c 2 4 6 10 14 18

BLAZING SIX-GUNS (Also see Sundance Kid)
Skywald Comics: Feb, 1971 - No. 2, Apr, 1971 (52 pgs.)
1-The Red Mask (3-D effect, not true 3-D), Sundance Kid begin (new-s), Avon's Geronimo reprint by Kinstler; Wyatt Earp app. 3 6 9 14 20 25
2-Wild Bill Hickok, Jesse James, Kit Carson-r plus M.E. Red Mask-r (3-D effect) 2 4 6 10 14 18

BLAZING WEST (The Hooded Horseman #21 on)
American Comics Group (B&I Publ./Michel Publ.): Fall, 1948 - No. 20, Nov-Dec, 1951
1-Origin & 1st app. Injun Jones, Tenderfoot & Buffalo Belle; Texas Tim & Ranger begins, ends #13 20 40 60 114 182 250
2,3 (1-2/49) 11 22 33 62 86 110
4-Origin & 1st app. Little Lobo; Starr-a (3-4/49) 10 20 30 56 76 95
5-10: 5-Starr-a 9 18 27 50 65 80
11-13 8 16 24 42 54 65
14(11-12/50)-Origin/1st app. The Hooded Horseman 13 26 39 74 105 135
15-20: 15,16,18,19-Starr-a 9 18 27 50 65 80

BLAZING WESTERN
Timor Publications: Jan, 1954 - No. 5, Sept, 1954
1-Ditko-a (1st Western-a?); text story by Bruce Hamilton 19 38 57 109 172 235
2-4 9 18 27 50 65 80
5-Disbrow-a; L.B. Cole-c 9 18 27 52 69 85

BLINDSIDE
Image Comics (Extreme Studios): Aug, 1996 ($2.50)
1-Variant-c exists 3.00

BLINK (See X-Men Age of Apocalypse storyline)
Marvel Comics: March, 2001 - No. 4, June, 2001 ($2.99, limited series)
1-4-Adam Kubert-c/Lobdell-s/Winick-script; leads into Exiles #1 3.00

BLIP
Marvel Comics Group: 2/1983 - 1983 (Video game mag. in comic format)
1-1st app. Donkey Kong & Mario Bros. in comics, 6pgs. comics; photo-c 2 3 4 6 8 10
2-Spider-Man photo-c; 6pgs. Spider-Man comics w/Green Goblin 2 4 6 8 10 12
3,4,6 6.00
5-E.T., Indiana Jones; Rocky-c 1 2 3 4 5 7
7-6pgs. Hulk comics; Pac-Man & Donkey Kong Jr. Hints 1 2 3 5 6 8

BLISS ALLEY
Image Comics: July, 1997 - No. 2, Sept, 1997 ($2.95, B&W)
1,2-Messner-Loebs-s/a 3.00

BLITZKRIEG
National Periodical Publications: Jan-Feb, 1976 - No. 5, Sept-Oct, 1976
1-Kubert-c on all 4 8 12 26 41 55
2-5 3 6 9 17 25 32

BLOCKBUSTERS OF THE MARVEL UNIVERSE
Marvel Comics: March, 2011 ($4.99, one-shot)
1-Handbook-style summaries of Marvel crossover events like Civil War & Heroes Reborn 5.00

BLONDE PHANTOM (Formerly All-Select #1-11; Lovers #23 on)(Also see Blackstone, Marvel Mystery, Millie The Model #2, Sub-Mariner Comics #25 & Sun Girl)
Marvel Comics (MPC): No. 12, Winter, 1946-47 - No. 22, Mar, 1949
12-Miss America begins, ends #14 181 362 543 1158 1979 2800
13-Sub-Mariner begins (not in #16) 105 210 315 667 1146 1625
14,15: 15-Kurtzman's "Hey Look" 98 196 294 622 1074 1525
16-Captain America with Bucky story by Rico(p), 6 pgs.; Kurtzman's "Hey Look" (1 pg.) 129 258 387 826 1413 2000
17-22: 22-Anti Wertham editorial 84 168 252 538 919 1300
NOTE: *Shores c-12-18.*

BLONDIE (See Ace Comics, Comics Reading Libraries (Promotional Comics section), Dagwood, Daisy & Her Pups, Eat Right to Work..., King & Magic Comics)
David McKay Publications: 1942 - 1946
Feature Books 12 (Rare) 82 164 246 528 902 1275
Feature Books 27-29,31,34(1940) 21 42 63 122 199 275
Feature Books 36,38,40,42,43,45,47 20 40 60 114 182 250
...1944 (Hard-c, 1938, B&W, 128 pgs.)-1944 daily strip-r 16 32 48 94 147 200

BLONDIE & DAGWOOD FAMILY
Harvey Publ. (King Features Synd.): Oct, 1963 - No. 4, Dec, 1965 (68 pgs.)
1 5 10 15 32 51 70
2-4 3 6 9 20 30 40

BLONDIE COMICS (...Monthly No. 16-141)
David McKay #1-15/Harvey #16-163/King #164-175/Charlton #177 on:
Spring, 1947 - No. 163, Nov, 1965; No. 164, Aug, 1966 - No. 175, Dec, 1967; No. 177,

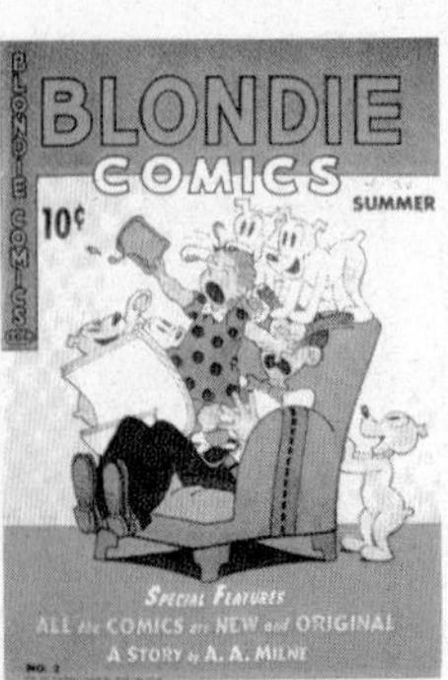
Blondie Comics #2 © HARV

Blood Red Dragon #0 © POW Ent.

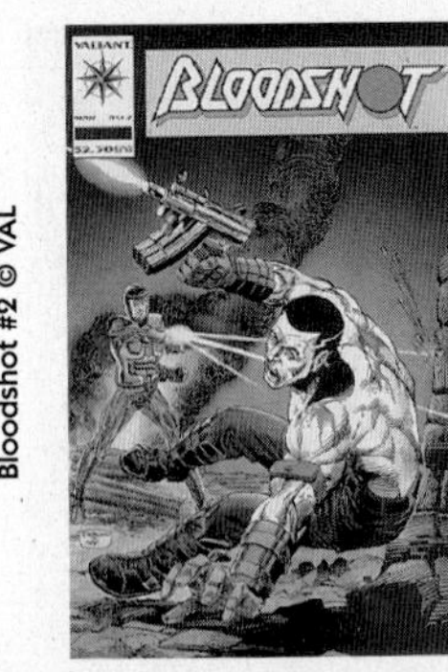
Bloodshot #2 © VAL

	GD 2.0	VG 4.0	FN 6.0	VF 8.0	VF/NM 9.0	NM- 9.2
Feb, 1969 - No. 222, Nov, 1976						
1	34	68	102	199	325	450
2	17	34	51	100	158	215
3-5	15	30	45	83	124	165
6-10	13	26	39	74	105	135
11-15	10	20	30	54	72	90
16-(3/50; 1st Harvey issue)	11	22	33	62	86	110
17-20: 20-(3/51)-Becomes Daisy & Her Pups #21 & Chamber of Chills #21	6	12	18	39	62	85
21-30	5	10	15	35	55	75
31-50	4	8	12	28	44	60
51-80	4	8	12	24	37	50
81-99	4	8	12	22	34	45
100	4	8	12	26	41	55
101-124,126-130	3	6	9	18	27	35
125 (80 pgs.)	4	8	12	28	44	60
131-136,138,139	3	6	9	17	25	32
137,140-(80 pgs.)	4	8	12	26	41	55
141-147,149-154,156,160,164-167	3	6	9	16	23	30
148,155,157-159,161-163 are 68 pgs.	4	8	12	22	34	45
168-175	2	4	6	11	16	20
177-199 (no #176)-Moon landing-c/s	2	4	6	9	13	16
200-Anniversary issue; highlights of the Bumsteads	2	4	6	10	14	18
201-210,213-222	2	4	6	8	10	12
211,212-1st & 2nd app. Super Dagwood	2	4	6	9	13	16
Blondie, Dagwood & Daisy by Chic Young #1(Harvey, 1953, 100 pg. squarebound giant) new stories; Popeye (1 pg.) and Felix (1pg.) app.	30	60	90	177	289	400

BLOOD
Marvel Comics (Epic Comics): Feb, 1988 - No. 4, Apr, 1988 ($3.25, mature)
1-4: DeMatteis scripts & Kent Williams-c/a 4.00

BLOOD AND GLORY (Punisher & Captain America)
Marvel Comics: Oct, 1992 - No. 3, Dec, 1992 ($5.95, limited series)
1-3: 1-Embossed wraparound-c by Janson; Chichester & Clarke-s 6.00

BLOOD & ROSES: FUTURE PAST TENSE (Bob Hickey's...)
Sky Comics: Dec, 1993 ($2.25)
1-Silver ink logo 3.00

BLOOD & ROSES: SEARCH FOR THE TIME-STONE (Bob Hickey's...)
Sky Comics: Apr, 1994 ($2.50)
1 3.00

BLOOD AND SHADOWS
DC Comics (Vertigo): 1996 - Book 4, 1996 ($5.95, squarebound, mature)
Books 1-4: Joe R. Lansdale scripts; Mark A. Nelson-c/a. 6.00

BLOOD AND WATER
DC Comics (Vertigo): May, 2003 - No. 5, Sept, 2003 ($2.95, limited series)
1-5-Judd Winick-s/Tomm Coker-a/Brian Bolland-c 3.00
TPB (2009, $14.99) r/#1-5 15.00

BLOOD: A TALE
DC Comics (Vertigo): Nov, 1996 - No. 4, Feb, 1997 ($2.95, limited series)
1-4: Reprints Epic series w/new-c; DeMatteis scripts; Kent Williams-c/a 3.00
TPB (2004, $19.95) r/#1-4 20.00

BLOODBATH
DC Comics: Early Dec, 1993 - No. 2, Late Dec, 1993 ($3.50, 68 pgs.)
1-Neon ink-c; Superman app.; new Batman-c /app. 4.00
2-Hitman 2nd app. 1 2 3 4 5 7

BLOODHOUND
DC Comics: Sept, 2004 - No. 10, June, 2005 ($2.95)
1-10: 1-Jolley-s/Kirk-a/Johnson-c. 5-Firestorm app. (cont. from Firestorm #7) 3.00

BLOOD LEGACY
Image Comics (Top Cow): May, 2000 - No. 4, Nov, 2000; Apr, 2003 ($2.50/$4.99)
...: The Story of Ryan 1-4-Kerri Hawkins-s. 1-Andy Park-a(p); 3 covers 3.00
...: The Young Ones 1 (4/03, $4.99, one-shot) Basaldua-c/a 5.00
Preview Special ('00, $4.95) B&W flip-book w/The Magdalena Preview 5.00

BLOODLINES: A TALE FROM THE HEART OF AFRICA (See Tales From the Heart of Africa)
Marvel Comics (Epic Comics): 1992 ($5.95, 52 pgs.)
1-Story cont'd from Tales From... 6.00

BLOOD OF DRACULA
Apple Comics: Nov, 1987 - No. 20?, 1990 ($1.75/$1.95, B&W)($2.25 #14,16 on)
1-3,5-14,20: 1-10-Chadwick-c 4.00
4,16-19-Lost Frankenstein pgs. by Wrightson 1 2 3 4 5 7
15-Contains stereo flexidisc ($3.75) 5.00

BLOOD OF THE DEMON (Etrigan the Demon)
DC Comics: May, 2005 - No. 17, Sept, 2006 ($2.50/$2.99)
1-14-Byrne-a(p) & plot/Pfeifer-script. 3,4-Batman app. 13-One Year Later 3.00
15-17-($2.99) 3.00

BLOOD OF THE INNOCENT (See Warp Graphics Annual)
WaRP Graphics: 1/7/86 - No. 4, 1/28/86 (Weekly mini-series, mature)
1-4 3.00

BLOODPACK
DC Comics: Mar, 1995 - No. 4, June,1995 ($1.50, limited series)
1-4 3.00

BLOODPOOL
Image Comics (Extreme): Aug, 1995 - No. 4, Nov, 1995 ($2.50, limited series)
1-4: Jo Duffy scripts in all 3.00
Special (3/96, $2.50)-Jo Duffy scripts 3.00
Trade Paperback (1996, $12.95)-r/#1-4 13.00

BLOOD RED DRAGON (Stan Lee and Yoshiki's...)
Image Comics: No. 0, Aug, 2011 - No. 3, Nov, 2011 ($3.99)
0-3-Goff-s/Soriano-a 4.00

BLOODSCENT
Comico: Oct, 1988 ($2.00, one-shot, Baxter paper)
1-Colan-p 3.00

BLOODSEED
Marvel Comics (Frontier Comics): Oct, 1993 - No. 2, Nov, 1993 ($1.95)
1,2: Sharp/Cam Smith-a 3.00

BLOODSHOT (See Eternal Warrior #4 & Rai #0)
Valiant/Acclaim Comics (Valiant): Feb, 1993 - No. 51, Aug, 1996 ($2.25/$2.50)
0-(3/94, $3.50)-Wraparound chromium-c by Quesada(p); origin 4.00
0-Gold variant; no cover price 10.00
Note: There is a "Platinum variant" ; press run error of Gold ed. (25 copies exist)
(A CGC certified 9.8 copy sold for $2,067 in 2004)
1-($3.50)-Chromium embossed-c by B. Smith w/poster 4.00
2-5,8-14: 3-$2.25-c begins; cont'd in Hard Corps #5. 4-Eternal Warrior-c/story. 5-Rai & Eternal Warrior app. 14-(3/94)-Reese-c(i) 3.00
6,7: 6-1st app. Ninjak (out of costume). 7-In costume 3.00
15(4/94)-51: 16-w/bound-in trading card. 51-Bloodshot dies? 3.00
Yearbook 1 (1994, $3.95) 4.00
Special 1 (3/94, $5.95)-Zeck-c/a(p); Last Stand 6.00

BLOODSHOT (Volume Two)
Acclaim Comics (Valiant): July, 1997 - No. 16, Oct, 1998 ($2.50)
1-16: 1-Two covers. 5-Copycat-c. X-O Manowar-c/app 3.00

BLOODSTONE
Marvel Comics: Dec, 2001 - No. 4, Mar, 2002 ($2.99)
1-4-Intro. Elsa Bloodstone; Abnett & Lanning-s/Lopez-a 3.00

BLOODSTREAM
Image Comics: Jan, 2004 - No. 4, Dec, 2004 ($2.95)
1-4-Adam Shaw painted-a 3.00

BLOODSTRIKE (See Supreme V2#3)
Image Comics (Extreme Studios): 1993 - No. 22, May, 1995; No. 25, May, 1994 ($1.95/$2.50)
1-22, 25: Liefeld layouts in early issues. 1-Blood Brothers prelude. 2-1st app. Lethal. 5-1st app. Noble. 9-Black and White part 6 by Art Thibert; Liefeld pin-up. 9,10-Have coupon #3 & 7 for Extreme Prejudice #0. 10-(4/94). 11-(7/94). 16:Platt-c; Prophet app. 17-19-polybagged w/card . 25-(5/94)-Liefeld/Fraga-c 3.00
NOTE: *Giffen story/layouts-4-6. **Jae Lee** c-7, 8. **Rob Liefeld** layouts-1-3. **Art Thibert** c-6i.*

BLOODSTRIKE
Image Comics: No. 26, Mar, 2012 - Present ($2.99)
26,27: 26-Two covers by Seeley & Liefeld; Seeley-s/Gaston-a 3.00

BLOODSTRIKE ASSASSIN
Image Comics (Extreme Studios): June, 1995 - No. 3, Aug, 1995; No. 0, Oct, 1995 ($2.50, limited series)
0-3: 3-(8/95)-Quesada-c. 0-(10/95)-Battlestone app. 3.00

BLOOD SWORD, THE

Blue Beetle #5 © FOX

Blue Beetle (1986 series) #10 © DC

Blue Beetle (2011 series) #2 © DC

GD VG FN VF VF/NM NM-
2.0 4.0 6.0 8.0 9.0 9.2

Jademan Comics: Aug, 1988 - No. 53, Dec, 1992 ($1.50/$1.95, 68 pgs.)
1-53-Kung Fu stories in all 4.00

BLOOD SWORD DYNASTY
Jademan Comics: 1989 -No. 41, Jan, 1993 ($1.25, 36 pgs.)
1-Ties into Blood Sword 3.00
2-41: Ties into Blood Sword 3.00

BLOOD SYNDICATE
DC Comics (Milestone): Apr, 1993 - No. 35, Feb, 1996 ($1.50/-$3.50)
1-($2.95)-Collector's Edition; polybagged with poster, trading card, & acid-free backing board (direct sale only) 4.00
1-9,11-24,26,27,29,33-34: 8-Intro Kwai. 15-Byrne-c. 16-Worlds Collide Pt. 6; Superman-c/app. 17-Worlds Collide Pt. 13. 29-(99¢); Long Hot Summer x-over 3.00
10,28,30-32: 10-Simonson-c. 30-Long Hot Summer x-over 3.00
25-($2.95, 52 pgs.) 4.00
35-Kwai disappears; last issue 4.00

BLOODWULF
Image Comics (Extreme): Feb, 1995 - No. 4, May, 1995 ($2.50, limited series)
1-4: 1-Liefeld-c w/4 diferent captions & alternate-c. 3.00
Summer Special (8/95, $2.50)-Jeff Johnson-c/a; Supreme app; story takes place between Legend of Supreme #3 & Supreme #23. 3.00

BLOODY MARY
DC Comics (Helix): Oct, 1996 - No. 4, Jan, 1997 ($2.25, limited series)
1-4: Garth Ennis scripts; Ezquerra-c/a in all 3.50
TPB (2005, $19.99) r/#1-4 and Bloody Mary: Lady Liberty #1-4 20.00

BLOODY MARY: LADY LIBERTY
DC Comics (Helix): Sept, 1997 - No. 4, Dec, 1997 ($2.50, limited series)
1-4: Garth Ennis scripts; Ezquerra-c/a in all 3.00

BLUE
Image Comics (Action Toys): Aug, 1999 - No. 2, Apr, 2000 ($2.50)
1,2-Aronowitz-s/Struzan-c 3.00

BLUEBEARD
Slave Labor Graphics: Nov, 1993 - No. 3, Mar, 1994 ($2.95, B&W, lim. series)
1-3: James Robinson scripts. 2-(12/93) 3.00
Trade paperback (6/94, $9.95) 13.00
Trade paperback (2nd printing, 7/96, $12.95)-New-c 13.00

BLUE BEETLE, THE (Also see All Top, Big-3, Mystery Men & Weekly Comic Magazine)
Fox Publ. No. 1-11, 31-60; Holyoke No. 12-30: Winter, 1939-40 - No. 57, 7/48; No. 58, 4/50 - No. 60, 8/50

1-Reprints from Mystery Men #1-5; Blue Beetle origin; Yarko the Great-r/from Wonder Comics /Wonderworld #2-5 all by Eisner; Master Magician app.; (Blue Beetle in 4 different costumes) 459 918 1377 3350 5925 8500
2-K-51-r by Powell/Wonderworld #8,9 171 342 513 1086 1868 2650
3-Simon-c 126 252 378 806 1378 1950
4-Marijuana drug mention story 84 168 252 538 919 1300
5-Zanzibar The Magician by Tuska 73 146 219 467 796 1125
6-Dynamite Thor begins (1st); origin Blue Beetle 69 138 207 438 752 1065
7,8-Dynamo app. in both. 8-Last Thor 62 124 186 394 680 965
9-12: 9,10-The Blackbird & The Gorilla app. in both. 10-Bondage/hypo-c. 11(2/42)-The Gladiator app. 12(6/42)-The Black Fury app. 55 110 165 352 601 850
13-V-Man begins (1st app.), ends #19; Kubert-a; centerfold spread 65 130 195 416 708 1000
14,15-Kubert-a in both. 14-Intro. side-kick (c/text only), Sparky (called Spunky #17-19); BB vs. The Red Robe (Red Skull swipe) 56 112 168 356 611 865
16-18: 17-Brodsky-c 47 94 141 296 498 700
19-Kubert-a 48 96 144 302 514 725
20-Origin/1st app. Tiger Squadron; Arabian Nights begin 51 102 153 320 543 765
21-26: 24-Intro. & only app. The Halo. 26-General Patton story & photo 39 78 117 240 395 550
27-Tamaa, Jungle Prince app. 37 74 111 222 361 500
28-30(2/44) 34 68 102 199 325 450
31(6/44), 33,34,36-40: 34-38-"The Threat from Saturn" serial. 31 62 93 182 296 410
32-Hitler-c 68 136 204 435 743 1050
35-Extreme violence 37 74 111 222 361 500
41-45 (#43 exist?) 30 60 90 177 289 400
46-The Puppeteer app. 33 66 99 194 317 440
47-Kamen & Baker-a begin 155 310 465 992 1696 2400
48-50 113 226 339 718 1234 1750
51,53 97 194 291 621 1061 1500
52-Kamen bondage-c; true crime stories begin 142 284 426 909 1555 2200
54-Used in **SOTI**. Illo, "Children call these 'headlights' comics"; classic-c 290 580 870 1856 3178 4500
55-57: 56-Used in **SOTI**, pg. 145. 57(7/48)-Last Kamen issue; becomes Western Killers? 94 188 282 597 1024 1450
58(4/50)-60-No Kamen-a 20 40 60 118 192 265
NOTE: *Kamen a-47-51, 53, 55-57; c-47, 49-52.* **Powell** *a-4(2). Bondage-c 9-12, 46, 52.*

BLUE BEETLE (Formerly The Thing; becomes Mr. Muscles No. 22 on) (See Charlton Bullseye & Space Adventures)
Charlton Comics: No. 18, Feb, 1955 - No. 21, Aug, 1955
18,19-(Pre-1944-r). 18-Last pre-code issue. 19-Bouncer, Rocket Kelly-r 21 42 63 122 199 275
20-Joan Mason by Kamen 26 52 78 154 252 350
21-New material 20 40 60 118 192 265

BLUE BEETLE (Unusual Tales #1-49; Ghostly Tales #55 on)(See Captain Atom #83 & Charlton Bullseye)
Charlton Comics: V2#1, June, 1964 - V2#5, Mar-Apr, 1965; V3#50, July, 1965 - V3#54, Feb-Mar, 1966; #1, June, 1967 - #5, Nov, 1968
V2#1-Origin/1st S.A. app. Dan Garrett-Blue Beetle 9 18 27 60 103 145
2-5: 5-Weiss illo; 1st published-a? 6 12 18 37 59 80
V3#50-54-Formerly Unusual Tales 5 10 15 34 55 75
1(1967)-Question series begins by Ditko 10 20 30 67 124 180
2-Origin Ted Kord-Blue Beetle (see Capt. Atom #83 for 1st Ted Kord Blue Beetle); Dan Garrett x-over 6 12 18 41 66 90
3-5 (All Ditko-c/a in #1-5) 6 12 18 37 59 80
1,3(Modern Comics-1977)-Reprints 1 2 3 5 6 8
NOTE: *#6 only appeared in the fanzine 'The Charlton Portfolio.'*

BLUE BEETLE (Also see Americomics, Crisis On Infinite Earths, Justice League & Showcase '94 #2-4)
DC Comics: June, 1986 - No. 24, May, 1988
1-Origin retold; intro. Firefist 4.00
2-10,15-19,21-24: 2-Origin Firefist. 5-7-The Question app. 21-Millennium tie-in 3.00
11-14-New Teen Titans x-over 3.50
20-Justice League app.; Millennium tie-in 3.50

BLUE BEETLE (See Infinite Crisis, Teen Titans, and Booster Gold #21)
DC Comics: May, 2006 - No. 36, Apr, 2009 ($2.99)
1-Hamner-a/Giffen & Rogers-s; Guy Gardner app. 4.00
1-2nd & 3rd printings 3.00
2-36: 2-2nd printing exists. 2-4-Oracle app. 5-Phantom Stranger app. 16-Eclipso app. 18,33-Teen Titans app. 20-Sinestro Corps. 21-Spectre app. 26-Spanish issue 3.00
...: Black and Blue TPB (2010, $17.99) r/#27,28,35,36 & Booster Gold #21-25,28,29 18.00
...: Boundaries TPB (2009, $14.99) r/#29-34 15.00
...: End Game TPB (2008, $14.99) r/#20-26; English script for #26 15.00
...: Reach For the Stars TPB (2008, $14.99) r/#13-19 15.00
...: Road Trip TPB (2007, $12.99) r/#7-12 13.00
...: Shellshocked TPB (2006, $12.99) r/#1-6 13.00

BLUE BEETLE (DC New 52)
DC Comics: Nov, 2011 - Present ($2.99)
1-7: 1-Tony Bedard-s/Ig Guara-a; new origin 3.00

BLUEBERRY (See Lt. Blueberry & Marshal Blueberry)
Marvel Comics (Epic Comics): 1989 - No. 5, 1990 ($12.95/$14.95, graphic novel)
1,3,4,5-($12.95)-Moebius-a in all 3 6 9 14 19 24
2-($14.95) 3 6 9 14 20 26

BLUE BOLT
Funnies, Inc. No. 1/Novelty Press/Premium Group of Comics: June, 1940 - No. 101 (V10#2), Sept-Oct, 1949
V1#1-Origin Blue Bolt by Joe Simon, Sub-Zero Man, White Rider & Super Horse, Dick Cole, Wonder Boy & Sgt. Spook (1st app. of each) 320 640 960 2240 3920 5600
2-Simon & Kirby's 1st art & 1st super-hero (Blue Bolt) 184 368 552 1168 2009 2850
3-1 pg. Space Hawk by Wolverton; 2nd S&K-a on Blue Bolt (same cover date as Red Raven #1); Simon-c 161 322 483 1030 1765 2500
4-S&K-a; classic Everett shark-c 155 310 465 992 1696 2400
5-S&K-a; Everett-a begins on Sub-Zero; 1st time S&K names app. in a comic 135 270 405 864 1482 2100
6,8-10-S&K-a 123 246 369 787 1344 1900
7-S&K-c/a 145 290 435 921 1586 2250
11,12: 11-Robot-c 116 232 348 742 1271 1800
V2#1-Origin Dick Cole & The Twister; Twister x-over in Dick Cole, Sub-Zero, & Blue Bolt;

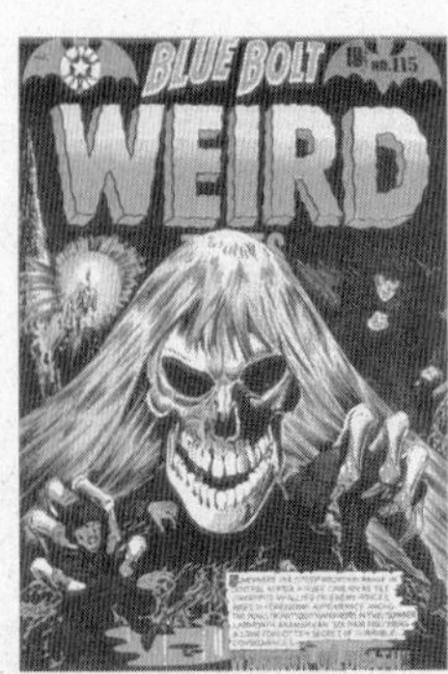

Blue Bolt #115 © STAR

Blue Monday: Nobody's Fool © Chynna Clugston

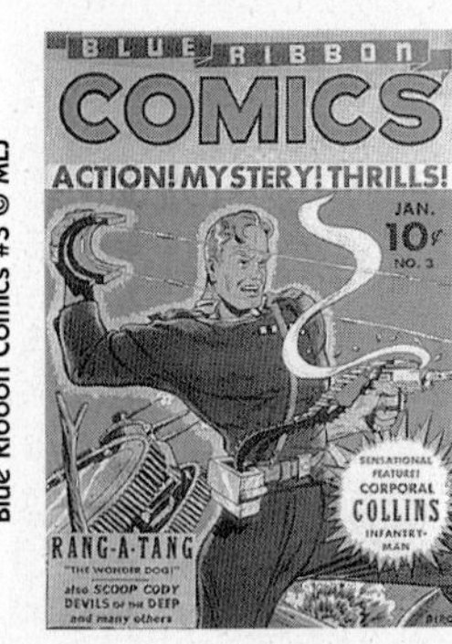

Blue Ribbon Comics #3 © MLJ

GD 2.0 | VG 4.0 | FN 6.0 | VF 8.0 | VF/NM 9.0 | NM- 9.2

GD 2.0 | VG 4.0 | FN 6.0 | VF 8.0 | VF/NM 9.0 | NM- 9.2

origin Simba Karno who battles Dick Cole thru V2#5 & becomes main supporting
character V2#6 on; battle-c 41 82 123 249 417 585
2-Origin The Twister retold in text 34 68 102 204 332 460
3-5: 5-Intro. Freezum 30 60 90 177 289 400
6-Origin Sgt. Spook retold 26 52 78 154 252 350
7-12: 7-Lois Blake becomes Blue Bolt's costume aide; last Twister. 12-Text-sty
by Mickey Spillaine 22 44 66 128 209 290
V3#1-3 18 36 54 107 169 230
4-12: 4-Blue Bolt abandons costume 15 30 45 86 133 180
V4#1-Hitler, Tojo, Mussolini-c 55 110 165 352 601 850
V4#2-12: 3-Shows V4#3 on-c, V4#4 inside (9-10/43). 5-Infinity-c. 8-Last Sub-Zero
13 26 39 72 101 130
V5#1-8, V6#1-3,5-10, V7#1-12 11 22 33 64 90 115
V6#4-Racist cover 21 42 63 126 206 285
V8#1-6,8-12, V9#1-4,7,8, V10#1(#100),V10#2(#101)-Last Dick Cole, Blue Bolt
10 20 30 56 76 95
V8#7,V9#6,9-L. B. Cole-c 22 44 66 128 209 290
V9#5-Classic fish in the face-c 22 44 66 128 209 290

NOTE: ***Everett** c-V1#4, 11, V2#1, 2. **Gustavson** a-V1#1-12, V2#1-7. **Kiefer** c-V3#1. **Rico** a-V6#10, V7#4. Blue Bolt not in V9#8.*

BLUE BOLT (Becomes Ghostly Weird Stories #120 on; continuation of Novelty Blue Bolt)
(...Weird Tales of Terror #111,112,...Weird Tales #113-119)
Star Publications: No. 102, Nov-Dec, 1949 - No. 119, May-June, 1953

102-The Chameleon, & Target app. 39 78 117 240 395 550
103,104-The Chameleon app. 104-Last Target 39 78 117 231 378 525
105-Origin Blue Bolt (from #1) retold by Simon; Chameleon & Target app.; opium den story
58 116 174 371 636 900
106-Blue Bolt by S&K begins; Spacehawk reprints from Target by Wolverton begin, ends #110;
Sub-Zero begins; ends #109 56 112 168 356 608 860
107-110: 108-Last S&K Blue Bolt reprint. 109-Wolverton-c(r)/inside Spacehawk splash.
110-Target app. 54 108 162 346 591 835
111,112: 111-Red Rocket & The Mask-r; last Blue Bolt; 1pg. L. B. Cole-a.
112-Last Torpedo Man app. 52 104 156 328 552 775
113-Wolverton's Spacehawk-r/Target V3#7 53 106 159 334 567 800
114,116: 116-Jungle Jo-r 52 104 156 328 552 775
115-Sgt. Spook app. 53 106 159 334 567 800
117-Jo-Jo & Blue Bolt-r 52 104 156 328 557 785
118-"White Spirit" by Wood 53 106 159 334 567 800
119-Disbrow/Cole-c; Jungle Jo-r 52 104 156 328 557 785
Accepted Reprint #103(1957?, nd) 14 28 42 80 115 150

NOTE: ***L. B. Cole** c-102-108, 110 on. **Disbrow** a-112(2), 113(3), 114(2), 115(2), 116-118. **Hollingsworth** a-117. **Palais** a-112r. Sci/Fi c-105-110. Horror c-111.*

BLUE BULLETEER, THE (Also see Femforce Special)
AC Comics: 1989 ($2.25, B&W, one-shot)

1-Origin by Bill Black; Bill Ward-a 4.00

BLUE BULLETEER (Also see Femforce Special)
AC Comics: 1996 ($5.95, B&W, one-shot)

1-Photo-c 6.00

BLUE CIRCLE COMICS (Also see Red Circle Comics, Blazing Comics & Roly Poly Comic Book)
Enwil Associates/Rural Home: June, 1944 - No. 6, Apr, 1945

1-The Blue Circle begins (1st app.); origin & 1st app. Steel Fist
34 68 102 206 336 465
2 20 40 60 118 192 265
3-Hitler parody-c 39 78 117 240 395 550
4-6: 5-Last Steel Fist. 19 38 57 111 176 240
6-(Dated 4/45, Vol. 2#3 inside)-Leftover covers to #6 were later restapled over early 1950's
coverless comics; variations of the coverless comics exist.
Colossal Features known. 19 38 57 111 176 240

BLUE DEVIL (See Fury of Firestorm #24, Underworld Unleashed, Starman (2nd) #38, Infinite Crisis and Shadowpact)
DC Comics: June, 1984 - No. 31, Dec, 1986 (75¢/$1.25)

1 4.00
2-16,19-31: 4-Origin Nebiros. 7-Gil Kane-a. 8-Giffen-a 3.00
17,18-Crisis x-over 3.50
Annual 1 (11/85)-Team-ups w/Black Orchid, Creeper, Demon, Madame Xanadu,
Man-Bat & Phantom Stranger 4.00

BLUE MONDAY: ... (one-shots)
Oni Press: Feb, 2002 - Present (B&W, Chynna Clugston-Major-s/a/c in all)

Dead Man's Party (10/02, $2.95) Dan Brereton painted back-c 3.00
Inbetween Days (9/03, $9.95, 8" x 5-1/2") r/Dead Man's Party, Lovecats, & Nobody's Fool 10.00
Lovecats (2/02, $2.95) Valentine's Day themed 3.00
Nobody's Fool (2/03, $2.95) April Fool's Day themed 3.00
Thieves Like Us (12/08, $3.50) Part 1 of an unfinished 5-part series 3.50

BLUE MONDAY: ABSOLUTE BEGINNERS
Oni Press: Feb, 2001 - No. 4, Sept, 2001 ($2.95, B&W, limited series)

1-4-Chynna Clugston-Major-s/a/c 3.00
TPB (12/01, $11.95, 8" x 6") r/series 12.00

BLUE MONDAY: PAINTED MOON
Oni Press: Feb, 2004 - No. 4, Mar, 2005 ($2.99, B&W, limited series)

1-4-Chynna Clugston-Major-s/a/c 3.00
TPB (4/05, $11.95, digest-sized) r/series; sketch pages 12.00

BLUE MONDAY: THE KIDS ARE ALRIGHT
Oni Press: Feb, 2000 - No. 3, May, 2000 ($2.95, B&W, limited series)

1-3-Chynna Clugston-Major-s/a/c. 1-Variant-c by Warren. 2-Dorkin-c 3.00
3-Variant cover by J. Scott Campbell 4.00
TPB (12/00, $10.95, digest-sized) r/#1-3 & earlier short stories 11.00

BLUE PHANTOM, THE
Dell Publishing Co.: June-Aug, 1962

1(01-066-208)-by Fred Fredericks 3 6 9 21 32 42

BLUE RIBBON COMICS (...Mystery Comics No. 9-18)
MLJ Magazines: Nov, 1939 - No. 22, Mar, 1942 (1st MLJ series)

1-Dan Hastings, Richy the Amazing Boy, Rang-A-Tang the Wonder Dog begin
(1st app. of each); Little Nemo app. (not by W. McCay); Jack Cole-a(3)
(1st MLJ comic) 245 490 735 1568 2684 3800
2-Bob Phantom, Silver Fox (both in #3), Rang-A-Tang Club & Cpl. Collins begin
(1st app. of each); Jack Cole-a 119 238 357 762 1306 1850
3-J. Cole-a 79 158 237 502 864 1225
4-Doc Strong, The Green Falcon, & Hercules begin (1st app. each); origin & 1st app.
The Fox & Ty-Gor, Son of the Tiger 87 174 261 553 952 1350
5-8: 8-Last Hercules; 6,7-Biro, Meskin-a. 7-Fox app. on-c
64 128 192 406 696 985
9-(Scarce)-Origin & 1st app. Mr. Justice (2/41) 300 600 900 2070 3635 5200
10-13: 12-Last Doc Strong. 13-Inferno, the Flame Breather begins, ends #19; Devil-c
108 216 324 686 1181 1675
14,15,17,18: 15-Last Green Falcon 92 184 276 584 1005 1425
16-Origin & 1st app. Captain Flag (9/41) 161 322 483 1030 1765 2500
19-22: 20-Last Ty-Gor. 22-Origin Mr. Justice retold 92 184 276 584 1005 1425

NOTE: ***Biro** c-3-5; a-2 (Cpl. Collins & Scoop Cody). **S. Cooper** c-9-17. 20-22 contain "Tales From the Witch's Cauldron" (same strip as "Stories of the Black Witch" in Zip Comics). Mr. Justice c-9-18. Captain Flag c-16-18 (w/Mr. Justice), 19-22.*

BLUE RIBBON COMICS (Becomes Teen-Age Diary Secrets #4)
(Also see Approved Comics, Blue Ribbon Comics and Heckle & Jeckle)
Blue Ribbon (St. John): Feb, 1949 - No. 6, Aug, 1949

1-Heckle & Jeckle (Terrytoons) 15 30 45 83 124 165
2(4/49)-Diary Secrets; Baker-c 40 80 120 246 411 575
3-Heckle & Jeckle (Terrytoons) 11 22 33 62 86 110
4(6/49)-Teen-Age Diary Secrets; Baker c/a(2) 40 80 120 246 411 575
5(8/49)-Teen-Age Diary Secrets; Oversize; photo-c; Baker-a(2)- Continues
as Teen-Age Diary Secrets 47 94 141 296 498 700
6-Dinky Duck(8/49)(Terrytoons) 8 16 24 42 54 65

BLUE RIBBON COMICS
Red Circle Prod./Archie Ent. No. 5 on: Nov, 1983 - No. 14, Dec, 1984

1-S&K-r/Advs. of the Fly #1,2; Williamson/Torres-r/Fly #2; Ditko-c
1 2 3 5 6 8
2-7,9,10: 3-Origin Steel Sterling. 5-S&K Shield-r; new Kirby-c. 6,7-The Fox app. 6.00
8-Toth centerspread; Black Hood app.; Neal Adams-a(r)
1 2 3 4 5 7
11,13,14: 11-Black Hood. 13-Thunder Bunny. 14-Web & Jaguar 6.00
12-Thunder Agents; Noman new Ditko-a 1 2 3 5 6 8

NOTE: ***N. Adams** a(r)-8. **Buckler** a-4i. **Nino** a-2i. **McWilliams** a-8. **Morrow** a-8.*

BLUE STREAK (See Holyoke One-Shot No. 8)

BLUNTMAN AND CHRONIC TPB(Also see Jay and Silent Bob, Clerks, and Oni Double Feature)
Image Comics: Dec, 2001 ($14.95, TPB)

nn-Tie-in for "Jay & Silent Bob Strike Back" movie; new Kevin Smith-s/Michael Oeming-a;
r/app. from Oni Double Feature #12 in color; Ben Affleck & Jason Lee afterwords 15.00

BLYTHE (Marge's)
Dell Publishing Co.: No. 1072, Jan-Mar, 1960

Four Color 1072 6 12 18 37 59 80

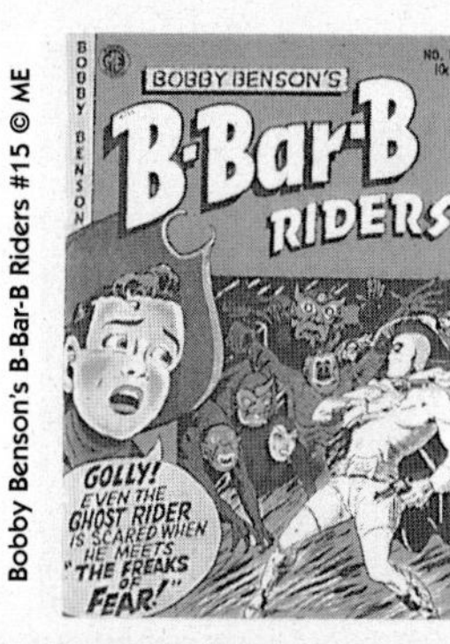

Bobby Benson's B-Bar-B Riders #15 © ME

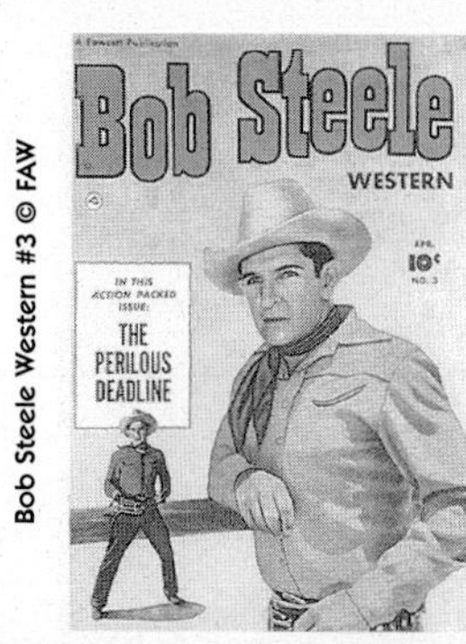

Bob Steele Western #3 © FAW

Body Doubles #4 © DC

GD VG FN VF VF/NM NM-
2.0 4.0 6.0 8.0 9.0 9.2

B-MAN (See Double-Dare Adventures)

BO (Tom Cat #4 on) (Also see Big Shot #29 & Dixie Dugan)
Charlton Comics Group: June, 1955 - No. 3, Oct, 1955 (A dog)
1-3: Newspaper reprints by Frank Beck; Noodnik the Eskimo app. 8 16 24 40 50 60

BOATNIKS, THE (See Walt Disney Showcase No. 1)

BOB BURDEN'S ORIGINAL MYSTERYMEN PRESENTS
Dark Horse Comics: 1999 - No. 4 ($2.95/$3.50)
1-3-Bob Burden-s/Sadowski-a(p) 3.50
4-($3.50) All Villain issue 3.50

BOBBY BENSON'S B-BAR-B RIDERS (Radio) (See Best of The West, The Lemonade Kid & Model Fun)
Magazine Enterprises/AC Comics: May-June, 1950 - No. 20, May-June, 1953
1-The Lemonade Kid begins; Powell-a (Scarce) 41 82 123 256 428 600
2 17 34 51 98 154 210
3-5: 4,5-Lemonade Kid-c (#4-Spider-c) 14 28 42 76 108 140
6-8,10 13 26 39 72 101 130
9,11,13-Frazetta-c; Ghost Rider in #13-15 by Ayers-a. 13-Ghost Rider-c 37 74 111 222 361 500
12,17-20: 20-(A-1 #88) 11 22 33 64 90 115
14-Decapitation/Bondage-c & story; classic horror-c 29 58 87 170 278 385
15-Ghost Rider-c 22 44 66 132 216 300
16-Photo-c 14 28 42 80 115 150
1 (1990, $2.75, B&W)-Reprints; photo-c & inside covers 3.00
NOTE: *Ayers a-13-15, 20. Powell a-1-12(4 ea.), 13(3), 14-16(Red Hawk only); c-1-8,1 0, 12. Lemonade Kid in most 1-13.*

BOBBY COMICS
Universal Phoenix Features: May, 1946
1-By S. M. Iger 9 18 27 47 61 75

BOBBY SHERMAN (TV)
Charlton Comics: Feb, 1972 - No. 7, Oct, 1972
1-Based on TV show "Getting Together" 6 12 18 37 59 80
2-7: Photo-c on all. 7-Bobby Sherman for President 4 8 12 24 37 50

BOB COLT (Movie star)(See XMas Comics)
Fawcett Publications: Nov, 1950 - No. 10, May, 1952
1-Bob Colt, his horse Buckskin & sidekick Pablo begin; photo front/back-c begin 24 48 72 142 234 325
2 14 28 42 80 115 150
3-5 12 24 36 67 94 120
6-Flying Saucer story 10 20 30 58 79 100
7-10: 9-Last photo back-c 9 18 27 52 69 85

BOB HOPE (See Adventures of... & Calling All Boys #12)

BOB MARLEY, TALE OF THE TUFF GONG (Music star)
Marvel Comics: Aug, 1994 - No, 3, Nov, 1994 ($5.95, limited series)
1-3 6.00

BOB POWELL'S TIMELESS TALES
Eclipse Comics: March, 1989 ($2.00, B&W)
1-Powell-r/Black Cat #5 (Scarlet Arrow), 9 & Race for the Moon #1 3.00

BOB SCULLY, THE TWO-FISTED HICK DETECTIVE (Also see Advs. of Detective Ace King and Detective Dan)
Humor Publ. Co.: No date (1933) (36 pgs., 9-1/2x11", B&W, paper-c; 10¢-c)
nn-By Howard Dell; not reprints; along with Advs. of Det. Ace King and Detective Dan, the first comic w/original art & the first of a single theme; has a blue 2-tone cover 425 850 1275 3400 - -

BOB SON OF BATTLE
Dell Publishing Co.: No. 729, Nov, 1956
Four Color 729 4 8 12 24 37 50

BOB STEELE WESTERN (Movie star)
Fawcett Publications/AC Comics: Dec, 1950 - No. 10, June, 1952; 1990
1-Bob Steele & his horse Bullet begin; photo front/back-c begin 37 74 111 222 361 500
2 19 38 57 109 172 235
3-5: 4-Last photo back-c 14 28 42 82 121 160
6-10: 10-Last photo-c 13 26 39 72 101 130
1 (1990, $2.75, B&W)-Bob Steele & Rocky Lane reprints; photo-c & inside covers 3.00

BOB SWIFT (Boy Sportsman)
Fawcett Publications: May, 1951 - No. 5, Jan, 1952
1 10 20 30 58 79 100
2-5: Saunders painted-c #1-5 7 14 21 35 43 50

BOB, THE GALACTIC BUM
DC Comics: Feb, 1995 - No. 4, June, 1995 ($1.95, limited series)
1-4: 1-Lobo app. 3.00

BODY BAGS
Dark Horse Comics (Blanc Noir): Sept, 1996 - No. 4, Jan, 1997 ($2.95, mini-series, mature) (1st Blanc Noir series)
1-Jason Pearson-c/a/scripts in all. 1-Intro Clownface & Panda. 1 2 3 5 6 8
2 1 3 4 6 8 10
3,4 6.00
Body Bags 1 (Image Comics, 7/05, $5.99) r/#1&2 6.00
Body Bags 2 (Image Comics, 8/05, $5.99) r/#3&4 6.00
...: 3 The Hard Way (Image, 2/06, $5.99) new story & r/Dark Horse Presents Annual 1997 and Dark Horse Maverick 2000; Pearson-c 6.00
...: One Shot (Image, 11/08, $5.99) wraparound-c; Pearson-c/a/s 6.00

BODYCOUNT (Also see Casey Jones & Raphael)
Image Comics (Highbrow Entertainment): Mar, 1996 - No. 4, July, 1996 ($2.50, lim. series)
1-4: Kevin Eastman-a(p)/scripts; Simon Bisley-c/a(i); Turtles app. 3.00

BODY DOUBLES (See Resurrection Man)
DC Comics: Oct, 1999 - No. 4, Jan, 2000 ($2.50, limited series)
1-4-Lanning & Abnett-s. 2-Black Canary app. 4-Wonder Woman app. 3.00
...(Villains) (2/98, $1.95, one-shot) 1-Pearson-c; Deadshot app. 3.00

BOFFO LAFFS
Paragraphics: 1986 - No. 5 ($2.50/$1.95)
1-($2.50) First comic cover with hologram 4.00
2-5 3.00

BOLD ADVENTURES
Pacific Comics: Oct, 1983 - No. 3, June, 1984 ($1.50)
1-Time Force, Anaconda, & The Weirdling begin 3.00
2,3: 2-Soldiers of Fortune begins. 3-Spitfire 3.00
NOTE: *Kaluta c-3. Nebres a-1-3. Nino a-2, 3. Severin a-3.*

BOLD STORIES (Also see Candid Tales & It Rhymes With Lust)
Kirby Publishing Co.: Mar, 1950 - July, 1950 (Digest size, 144 pgs.)
March issue (Very Rare) - Contains "The Ogre of Paris" by Wood 194 388 582 1242 2121 3000
May issue (Very Rare) - Contains "The Cobra's Kiss" by Graham Ingels (21 pgs.) 161 322 483 1030 1765 2500
July issue (Very Rare) - Contains "The Ogre of Paris" by Wood 148 296 444 947 1624 2300

BOLT AND STAR FORCE SIX
Americomics: 1984 ($1.75)
1-Origin Bolt & Star Force Six 3.00
Special 1 (1984, $2.00, 52pgs., B&W) 4.00

BOMBARDIER (See Bee 29, the Bombardier & Cinema Comics Herald)

BOMBAST
Topps Comics: 1993 ($2.95, one-shot) (Created by Jack Kirby)
1-Polybagged w/Kirbychrome trading card; Savage Dragon app.; Kirby-c; has coupon for Amberchrome Secret City Saga #0 3.00

BOMBA THE JUNGLE BOY (TV)
National Periodical Publ.: Sept-Oct, 1967 - No. 7, Sept-Oct, 1968 (12¢)
1-Intro. Bomba; Infantino/Anderson-c 4 8 12 24 37 50
2-7 3 6 9 16 23 30

BOMBER COMICS
Elliot Publ. Co./Melverne Herald/Farrell/Sunrise Times: Mar, 1944 - No. 4, Winter, 1944-45
1-Wonder Boy, & Kismet, Man of Fate begin 87 174 261 553 952 1350
2-Hitler-c and 8 pg. story 110 220 330 704 1202 1700
3: 2-4-Have Classics Comics ad to HRN 20 48 96 144 302 514 725
4-Hitler, Tojo & Mussolini-c; Sensation Comics #13-c/swipe; has Classics Comics ad to HRN 20. 103 206 309 659 1130 1600

BOMB QUEEN
Image Comics (Shadowline): Feb, 2006 - No. 4, May, 2006 ($3.50, mature)
1-4-Jimmie Robinson-s/a 3.50
... Vs. Blacklight One Shot #1 (8/06, $3.50) Robinson-a; Shadowhawk app. 3.50

Bonanza #21 © GK

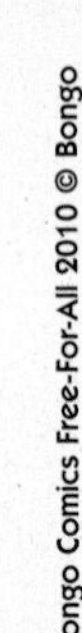
Bongo Comics Free-For-All 2010 © Bongo

Book of Night #1 © DH

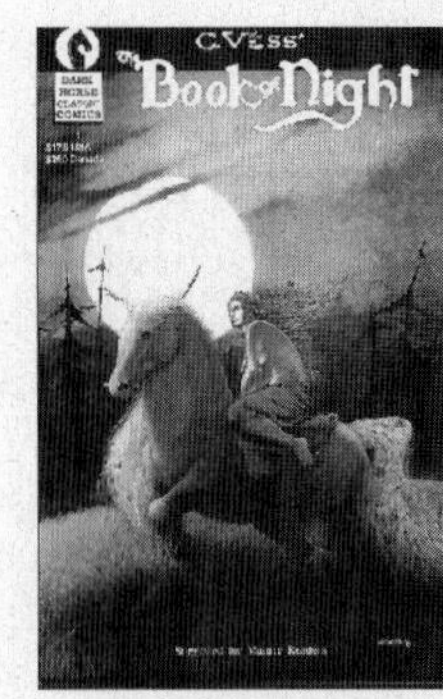

	GD 2.0	VG 4.0	FN 6.0	VF 8.0	VF/NM 9.0	NM- 9.2
..., Vol. 1: WMD: Woman of Mass Destruction TPB (7/06, $12.99) r/#1-4; bonus art						13.00

BOMB QUEEN II
Image Comics (Shadowline): Oct, 2006 - No. 3, Dec, 2006 ($3.50, mature)

	GD 2.0	VG 4.0	FN 6.0	VF 8.0	VF/NM 9.0	NM- 9.2
1-3-Jimmie Robinson-s/a; intro. The Four Queens						3.50
..., Vol. 2: Dirty Bomb - Queen of Hearts TPB (7/07, $14.99) r/#1-3 & Blacklight One Shot; bonus art; Robinson interview						15.00

BOMB QUEEN III THE GOOD, THE BAD & THE LOVELY
Image Comics (Shadowline): Mar, 2007 - No. 4, Jun, 2007 ($3.50, mature)

	GD 2.0	VG 4.0	FN 6.0	VF 8.0	VF/NM 9.0	NM- 9.2
1-4-Jimmie Robinson-a/Jim Valentino-s; Blacklight & Rebound app. 1-Linsner-c						3.50

BOMB QUEEN IV SUICIDE BOMBER
Image Comics (Shadowline): Aug, 2007 - No. 4, Dec, 2007 ($3.50, mature)

	GD 2.0	VG 4.0	FN 6.0	VF 8.0	VF/NM 9.0	NM- 9.2
1-4-Jim Robinson-s/a. 3-She-Spawn app.						3.50

BOMB QUEEN (Volume 5)
Image Comics (Shadowline): May, 2008 - No. 6, Mar, 2009 ($3.50, mature)

	GD 2.0	VG 4.0	FN 6.0	VF 8.0	VF/NM 9.0	NM- 9.2
Vol. 5 #1-6-Jim Robinson-s/a						3.50
Vol. 6 #1-4: 1-(9/09 - No. 4, 1/11, $3.50) Obama satire						3.50
Vol. 7 #1,2 (12/11 - No. 4) Bomb Queen returns in 2112						3.50
... Presents: All Girl Comics (5/09, $3.50) Dee Rail, Blacklight, Rebound, Tempest app.						3.50
... Presents: All Girl Special (7/11, $3.50) President Palin app.						3.50
... vs. Hack/Slash (2/11, $3.50) Cassie and Vlad app.; Robinson-s/a						3.50

BONANZA (TV)
Dell/Gold Key: June-Aug, 1960 - No. 37, Aug, 1970 (All Photo-c)

	GD 2.0	VG 4.0	FN 6.0	VF 8.0	VF/NM 9.0	NM- 9.2
Four Color 1110 (6-8/60)	28	56	84	203	439	675
Four Color 1221,1283, & #01070-207, 01070-210	15	30	45	102	221	340
1(12/62-Gold Key)	16	32	48	109	237	365
2	10	20	30	65	118	170
3-10	8	16	24	52	86	120
11-20	6	12	18	39	62	85
21-37: 29-Reprints	5	10	15	32	51	70

BONE
Cartoon Books #1-20, 28 on/Image Comics #21-27: Jul, 1991 - No. 55, Jun, 2004 ($2.95, B&W)

	GD 2.0	VG 4.0	FN 6.0	VF 8.0	VF/NM 9.0	NM- 9.2
1-Jeff Smith-c/a in all	22	44	66	154	327	500
1-2nd printing	2	4	6	9	12	15
1-3rd thru 5th printings						4.00
2-1st printing	7	14	21	49	80	110
2-2nd & 3rd printings						4.00
3-1st printing	6	12	18	39	62	85
3-2nd thru 4th printings						4.00
4,5	4	8	12	26	41	55
6-10	2	4	6	13	18	22
11-20						6.00
13 1/2 (1/95, Wizard)	2	4	6	8	10	12
13 1/2 (Gold)	2	4	6	9	12	15
21-37: 21-1st Image issue						5.00
38-($4.95) Three covers by Miller, Ross, Smith	1	2	3	4	5	7
39-55-($2.95)						4.00
1-27-($2.95): 1-Image reprints begin w/new-c. 2-Allred pin-up.						3.00
... Holiday Special (1993, giveaway)	2	3	4	6	8	10
... Reader -($9.95) Behind the scenes info						10.00
... Sourcebook-San Diego Edition						3.00
...10th Anniversary Edition (8/01, $5.95) r/#1 in color; came with figure						6.00
Complete Bone Adventures Vol 1,2 ('93, '94, $12.95, r/#1-6 & #7-12)						13.00
...: One Volume Edition (2004, $39.95, 1300 pgs.) r/#1-54; extra material						40.00
Volume 1-($19.95, hard-c)-"Out From Boneville"						20.00
Volume 1-($12.95, soft-c)						13.00
Volume 2,5-($22.95, hard-c)-"The Great Cow Race" & "Rock Jaw"						23.00
Volume 2,5-($14.95, soft-c)						15.00
Volume 3,4-($24.95, hard-c)-"Eyes of the Storm" & "The Dragonslayer"						25.00
Volume 3,4,7-($16.95, soft-c)						17.00
Volume 6-($15.95, soft-c)-"Old Man's Cave"						16.00
Volume 7-($24.95, hard-c)-"Ghost Circles"						25.00
Volume 8-($23.95, hard-c)-"Treasure Hunters"						24.00

NOTE: *Printings not listed sell for cover price.*

BONGO (See Story Hour Series)

BONGO & LUMPJAW (Disney, see Walt Disney Showcase #3)
Dell Publishing Co.: No. 706, June, 1956; No. 886, Mar, 1958

	GD 2.0	VG 4.0	FN 6.0	VF 8.0	VF/NM 9.0	NM- 9.2
Four Color 706 (#1)	6	12	18	37	59	80
Four Color 886	5	10	15	30	48	65

BONGO COMICS ...
Bongo Comics: 2005 - 2011 (Free Comic Book Day giveaways)

	GD 2.0	VG 4.0	FN 6.0	VF 8.0	VF/NM 9.0	NM- 9.2
Gimme Gimme Giveaway! (2005) - Short stories from Simpsons Comics, Futurama Comics and Radioactive Man						3.00
Free-For-All! (2006, 2007, 2008, 2009, 2010, 2011) - Short stories in each						3.00

BONGO COMICS PRESENTS RADIOACTIVE MAN (See Radioactive Man)

BON VOYAGE (See Movie Classics)

BOOF
Image Comics (Todd McFarlane Prod.): July, 1994 - No. 6, Dec, 1994 ($1.95)

	GD 2.0	VG 4.0	FN 6.0	VF 8.0	VF/NM 9.0	NM- 9.2
1-6						3.00

BOOF AND THE BRUISE CREW
Image Comics (Todd McFarlane Prod.): July, 1994 - No. 6, Dec, 1994 ($1.95)

	GD 2.0	VG 4.0	FN 6.0	VF 8.0	VF/NM 9.0	NM- 9.2
1-6						3.00

BOOK AND RECORD SET (See Power Record Comics)

BOOK OF ALL COMICS
William H. Wise: 1945 (196 pgs.)(Inside f/c has Green Publ. blacked out)

	GD 2.0	VG 4.0	FN 6.0	VF 8.0	VF/NM 9.0	NM- 9.2
nn-Green Mask, Puppeteer & The Bouncer	47	94	141	296	498	700

BOOK OF ANTS, THE
Artisan Entertainment: 1998 ($2.95, B&W)

	GD 2.0	VG 4.0	FN 6.0	VF 8.0	VF/NM 9.0	NM- 9.2
1-Based on the movie Pi; Aronofsky-s						3.00

BOOK OF BALLADS AND SAGAS, THE
Green Man Press: Oct, 1995 - No. 4 ($2.95/$3.50/$3.25, B&W)

	GD 2.0	VG 4.0	FN 6.0	VF 8.0	VF/NM 9.0	NM- 9.2
1-4: 1-Vess-c/a; Gaiman story.						3.50

BOOK OF COMICS, THE
William H. Wise: No date (1944) (25¢, 132 pgs.)

	GD 2.0	VG 4.0	FN 6.0	VF 8.0	VF/NM 9.0	NM- 9.2
nn-Captain V app.	42	84	126	265	450	635

BOOK OF FATE, THE (See Fate)
DC Comics: Feb, 1997 - No. 12, Jan, 1998 ($2.25/$2.50)

	GD 2.0	VG 4.0	FN 6.0	VF 8.0	VF/NM 9.0	NM- 9.2
1-12: 4-Two-Face-c/app. 6-Convergence. 11-Sentinel app.						3.00

BOOK OF LOST SOULS, THE
Marvel Comics (Icon): Dec, 2005 - No. 6, June, 2006 ($2.99)

	GD 2.0	VG 4.0	FN 6.0	VF 8.0	VF/NM 9.0	NM- 9.2
1-6-Colleen Doran-a/c; J. Michael Straczynski-s						3.00
... Vol. 1: Introductions All Around (2006, $16.99, TPB) r/series						17.00

BOOK OF LOVE (See Fox Giants)

BOOK OF NIGHT, THE
Dark Horse Comics: July, 1987 - No. 3, 1987 ($1.75, B&W)

	GD 2.0	VG 4.0	FN 6.0	VF 8.0	VF/NM 9.0	NM- 9.2
1-3: Reprints from Epic Illustrated; Vess-a						3.00
TPB-r/#1-3						15.00
Hardcover-Black-c with red crest						100.00
Hardcover w/slipcase (1991) signed and numbered						50.00

BOOK OF THE DEAD
Marvel Comics: Dec, 1993 - No. 4, Mar, 1994 ($1.75, limited series, 52 pgs.)

	GD 2.0	VG 4.0	FN 6.0	VF 8.0	VF/NM 9.0	NM- 9.2
1-4: 1-Ploog Frankenstein & Morrow Man-Thing-r begin; Wrightson-r/Chamber of Darkness #7. 2-Morrow new painted-c; Chaykin/Morrow Man-Thing; Krigstein-r/Uncanny Tales #54; r/Fear #10. 3-r/Astonishing Tales #10 & Starlin Man-Thing. 3,4-Painted-c	1	2	3	5	6	8

BOOKS OF DOOM (Dr. Doom from Fantastic Four)
Marvel Comics: Jan, 2006 - No. 6, June, 2006 ($2.99, limited series)

	GD 2.0	VG 4.0	FN 6.0	VF 8.0	VF/NM 9.0	NM- 9.2
1-6-Life story/origin of Dr. Doom; Brubaker-s/Raimondi-a/Rivera-c						3.00
Fantastic Four: Books of Doom HC (2006, $19.99) r/#1-6						20.00
Fantastic Four: Books of Doom SC (2007, $14.99) r/#1-6						15.00

BOOKS OF FAERIE, THE
DC Comics (Vertigo): Mar, 1997 - No. 3, May, 1997 ($2.50, limited series)

	GD 2.0	VG 4.0	FN 6.0	VF 8.0	VF/NM 9.0	NM- 9.2
1-3-Gross-a						3.00
TPB (1998, $14.95) r/#1-3 & Arcana Annual #1						15.00

BOOKS OF FAERIE, THE : AUBERON'S TALE
DC Comics (Vertigo): Aug, 1998 - No. 3, Oct, 1998 ($2.50, limited series)

	GD 2.0	VG 4.0	FN 6.0	VF 8.0	VF/NM 9.0	NM- 9.2
1-3-Gross-a						3.00

BOOKS OF FAERIE, THE : MOLLY'S STORY
DC Comics (Vertigo): Sept, 1999 - No. 4, Dec, 1999 ($2.50, limited series)

	GD 2.0	VG 4.0	FN 6.0	VF 8.0	VF/NM 9.0	NM- 9.2
1-4-Ney Rieber-s/Mejia-a						3.00

BOOKS OF MAGIC

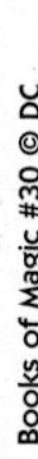
Books of Magic #30 © DC

Booster Gold (2007 series) #1 © DC

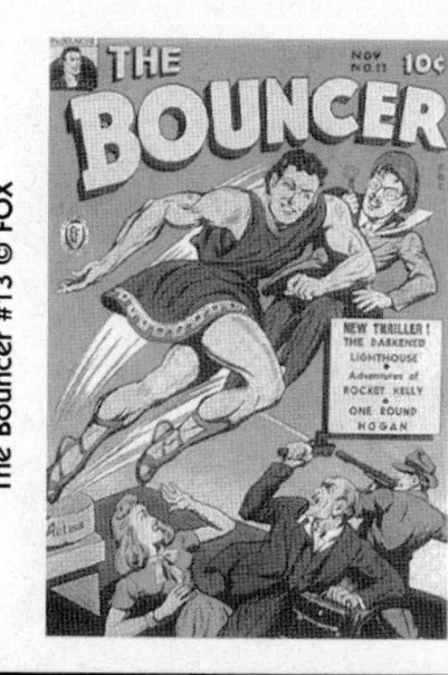

The Bouncer #13 © FOX

	GD 2.0	VG 4.0	FN 6.0	VF 8.0	VF/NM 9.0	NM- 9.2

DC Comics: 1990 - No. 4, 1991 ($3.95, 52 pgs., limited series, mature)

1-Bolton painted-c/a; Phantom Stranger app.; Gaiman scripts in all	1	3	4	6	8	10
2,3: 2-John Constantine, Dr. Fate, Spectre, Deadman app. 3-Dr. Occult app.; minor Sandman app.	1	2	3	4	5	7
4-Early Death-c/app. (early 1991)	1	2	3	5	6	8
Trade paperback-($19.95)-Reprints limited series						20.00

BOOKS OF MAGIC (Also see Hunter: The Age of Magic and Names of Magic)
DC Comics (Vertigo): May, 1994 - No. 75, Aug, 2000 ($1.95/$2.50, mature)

1-Charles Vess-c	2	4	6	8	10	12
1-Platinum	2	4	6	13	18	22
2-4: 4-Death app.	1	2	3	4	5	7
5-14; Charles Vess-c						4.00
15-75: 15-$2.50-c begins. 22-Kaluta-c. 25-Death-c/app; Bachalo-c. 51-Peter Gross-s/a begins. 55-Medley-a						3.00
Annual 1-3 (2/97, 2/98, '99, $3.95)						4.00
Bindings (1995, $12.95, TPB)-r/#1-4						13.00
Death After Death (2001, $19.95, TPB)-r/#42-50						20.00
Girl in the Box (1999, $14.95, TPB)-r/#26-32						15.00
Reckonings (1997, $12.95, TPB)-r/#14-20						13.00
Summonings (1996, $17.50, TPB)-r/#5-13, Vertigo Rave #1						17.50
The Burning Girl (2000, $17.95, TPB)-r/#33-41						18.00
Transformations (1998, $12.95, TPB)-r/#21-25						13.00

BOOKS OF MAGICK, THE : LIFE DURING WARTIME (See Books of Magic)
DC Comics (Vertigo): Sept, 2004 - No. 15, Dec, 2005 ($2.50/$2.75)

1-15: 1-Spencer-s/Ormston-a/Quitely-c; Constantine app. 2-Bagged with Sky Captain CD 6-Fegredo-a. 7-Constantine & Zatanna-c						3.00
... Book One TPB (2005, $9.95) r/#1-5						10.00

BOONDOCK SAINTS (Based on the movie)
12-Gauge Comics: May, 2010 - No. 2, Jun, 2010 ($3.99, limited series)

...: In Nomine Patris 1,2-Troy Duffy-s/Guus Floor-a						4.00
...: In Nomine Patris Vol. 2 (10/10 - No. 2, 11/10): 1,2-Duffy-s/Floor-a						4.00
...: In Nomine Patris Vol. 3 (3/11 - No. 2, 4/11): 1,2-Duffy-s/Floor-a						4.00

BOOSTER GOLD (See Justice League #4)
DC Comics: Feb, 1986 - No. 25, Feb, 1988 (75¢)

1-Dan Jurgens-s/a(p)						4.00
2-25: 4-Rose & Thorn app. 6-Origin. 6,7,23-Superman app. 8,9-LSH app. 22-JLI app. 24,25-Millennium tie-ins						3.00

NOTE: ***Austin** c-22i. **Byrne** c-23i.*

BOOSTER GOLD (See DC's weekly series 52)
DC Comics: Oct, 2007 - No. 47, Oct, 2011 ($3.50/$2.99/$3.99)

1-Geoff Johns-s/Dan Jurgens-a(p); covers by Jurgens and Art Adams; Rip Hunter app.						5.00
2-20: 3-Jonah Hex app. 4-Barry Allen app. 5-Joker and Batgirl app. 8-Superman app.						3.00
21-29-($3.99) 21-Blue Beetle back-ups begin. 22-New Teen Titans app. 23-Photo-c. 26,27-Blackest Night; Ted Kord rises. 29-Cyborg Superman app.						4.00
30-47-($2.99): 32-34-Giffen & DeMatteis-s. 32-Emerald Empress app. 40-Origin retold. 43-Legion of S.H. app. 44-47-Flashpoint tie-in; Doomsday app.						3.00
#0-(4/08) Blue Beetle (Ted Cord) returns; takes place between #6&7						3.00
#1,000,000-(9/08) Michelle Carter returns; takes place between #10&11						3.00
...: Blue and Gold (2008, $24.99, HC w/d.j.) r/#0,7-10,#1,000,000; cover sketches						25.00
...: Day of Death (2010, $14.99, SC) r/#20-25 and Brave and the Bold #23						15.00
...: 52 Pick-Up (2008, $24.99, HC w/d.j.) r/#1-6, original design sketches from Jurgens						25.00
...: Past Imperfect (2011, $17.99, SC) r/#32-38						18.00
...: Reality Lost (2009, $14.99, SC) r/#11,12,15-19						15.00
...: The Tomorrow Memory (2010, $17.99, SC) r/#26-31						18.00

BOOTS AND HER BUDDIES
Standard Comics/Visual Editions/Argo (NEA Service):
No. 5, 9/48 - No. 9, 9/49; 12/55 - No. 3, 1956

5-Strip-r	16	32	48	94	147	200
6,8	11	22	33	64	90	115
7-(Scarce)	14	28	42	80	115	150
9-(Scarce)-Frazetta-a (2 pgs.)	26	52	78	154	252	350
1-3(Argo-1955-56)-Reprints	6	12	18	31	38	45

BOOTS & SADDLES (TV)
Dell Publ. Co.: No. 919, July, 1958; No. 1029, Sept, 1959; No. 1116, Aug, 1960

Four Color 919 (#1)-Photo-c	7	14	21	49	82	115
Four Color 1029, 1116-Photo-c	5	10	15	34	55	75

BORDERLINE
Friction Press: June, 1992 ($2.25, B&W)

0-Ashcan edition; 1st app. of Cliff Broadway						3.00
1-Painted-c						3.00
1-Special Edition (bagged w/ photo, S&N)						4.00

BORDER PATROL
P. L. Publishing Co.: May-June, 1951 - No. 3, Sept-Oct, 1951

1	14	28	42	80	115	150
2,3	10	20	30	54	72	90

BORDER WORLDS (Also see Megaton Man)
Kitchen Sink Press: 7/86 - No. 7, 1987; V2#1, 1990 - No. 4, 1990 ($1.95-$2.00, B&W, mature)

1-7, V2#1-4: Donald Simpson-c/a/scripts						3.00

BORIS KARLOFF TALES OF MYSTERY (TV) (...Thriller No. 1,2)
Gold Key: No. 3, April, 1963 - No. 97, Feb, 1980

3-5-(Two #5's, 10/63,11/63): 5-(10/63)-11 pgs. Toth-a.	5	10	15	35	55	75
6-8,10: 10-Orlando-a	4	8	12	26	41	55
9-Wood-a	4	8	12	28	44	60
11-Williamson-a, 8 pgs.; Orlando-a, 5 pgs.	4	8	12	28	44	60
12-Torres, McWilliams-a; Orlando-a(2)	4	8	12	22	34	45
13,14,16-20	3	6	9	19	29	38
15-Crandall	3	6	9	20	30	40
21-Jeff Jones-a(3 pgs.) "The Screaming Skull"	3	6	9	20	30	40
22-Last 12¢ issue	3	6	9	16	23	30
23-30: 23-Reprint; photo-c	3	6	9	16	22	28
31-50: 36-Weiss-a	3	6	9	14	19	24
51-74: 74-Origin & 1st app. Taurus	2	4	6	10	14	18
75-79,87-97: 90-r/Torres, McWilliams-a/#12; Morrow-c	2	4	6	9	12	15
80-86-(52 pgs.)	2	4	6	10	14	18
Story Digest 1(7/70-Gold Key)-All text/illos.; 148 pp.	5	10	15	34	55	75

(See Mystery Comics Digest No. 2, 5, 8, 11, 14, 17, 20, 23, 26)
NOTE: ***Bolle** a-51-54, 56, 58, 59. **McWilliams** a-12, 14, 18, 19, 72, 80, 81, 93. **Orlando** a-11-15, 21. Reprints: 78, 81-86, 88, 90, 92, 95, 97.*

BORIS KARLOFF THRILLER (TV) (Becomes Boris Karloff Tales...)
Gold Key: Oct, 1962 - No. 2, Jan, 1963 (84 pgs.)

1-Photo-c	10	20	30	69	130	190
2	7	14	21	47	76	105

BORIS THE BEAR
Dark Horse Comics/Nicotat Comics #13 on: Aug, 1986 - No. 34, 1990 ($1.50/$1.75/$1.95, B&W)

1, 8, Annual 1 (1988, $2.50): 8-(44 pgs.)						4.00
1 (2nd printing),2,3,4A,4B,5-12, 14-34						3.00
13-1st Nicotat Comics issue						3.00

BORIS THE BEAR INSTANT COLOR CLASSICS
Dark Horse Comics: July, 1987 - No. 3, 1987 ($1.75/$1.95)

1-3						3.00

BORN
Marvel Comics: 2003 - No. 4, 2003 ($3.50, limited series)

1-4-Frank Castle (the Punisher) in 1971 Vietnam; Ennis-s/Robertson-a						3.50
HC (2004, $17.99) oversized reprint of series; proposal, layout pages						18.00
Punisher: Born SC (2004, $13.99) r/series; proposal, layout pages						14.00

BORN AGAIN
Spire Christian Comics (Fleming H. Revell Co.): 1978 (39¢)

nn-Watergate, Nixon, etc.	2	4	6	13	18	22

BOUNCER, THE (Formerly Green Mask #9)
Fox Features Syndicate: 1944 - No. 14, Jan, 1945

nn(1944, #10?)	31	62	93	182	296	410
11 (9/44)-Origin; Rocket Kelly, One Round Hogan app.	23	46	69	136	223	310
12-14: 14-Reprints no # issue	19	38	57	111	176	240

BOUNTY GUNS (See Luke Short's..., Four Color 739)

BOX OFFICE POISON
Antarctic Press: 1996 - No. 21, Sept, 2000 ($2.95, B&W)

1-Alex Robinson-s/a in all	1	2	3	4	5	7
2-5						4.00
6-21, ...Kolor Karnival 1 (5/99, $2.99)						3.00
...Super Special 0 (5/97, $4.95)						5.00
Sherman's March: Collected BOP Vol. 1 (9/98, $14.95) r/#0-4						15.00
TPB (2002, $29.95, 608 pgs.) r/entire series						30.00

Boy Comics #8 © LEV

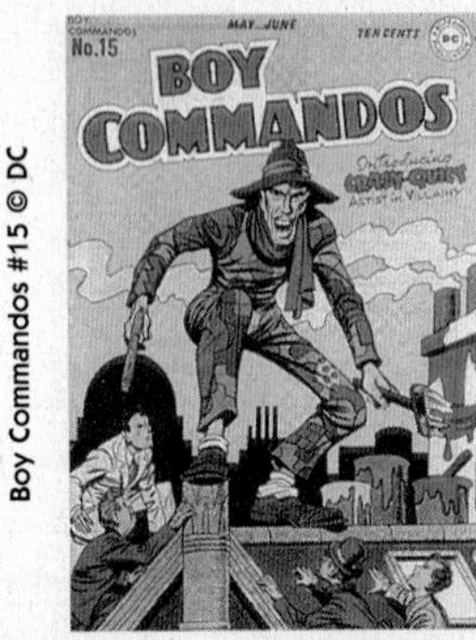

Boy Commandos #15 © DC

Boy Loves Girl #30 © LEV

BOY AND HIS 'BOT, A
Now Comics: Jan, 1987 ($1.95)

	GD 2.0	VG 4.0	FN 6.0	VF 8.0	VF/NM 9.0	NM- 9.2
1-A Holiday Special						3.00

BOY AND THE PIRATES, THE (Movie)
Dell Publishing Co.: No. 1117, Aug, 1960

	GD 2.0	VG 4.0	FN 6.0	VF 8.0	VF/NM 9.0	NM- 9.2
Four Color 1117-Photo-c	6	12	18	43	69	95

BOY COMICS (Captain Battle No. 1 & 2; Boy Illustories No. 43-108) (Stories by Charles Biro)
(Also see Squeeks)
Lev Gleason Publ. (Comic House): No. 3, Apr, 1942 - No. 119, Mar, 1956

	GD 2.0	VG 4.0	FN 6.0	VF 8.0	VF/NM 9.0	NM- 9.2
3 (No.1)-1st app. & origin Crimebuster (ends #110), Bombshell (ends #8) Young Robin Hood (ends # 32), Yankee Longago (ends #28), Hero of the Month (ends #31), Case 1001-1005, 1006-1009 (ends #10); Swoop Storm begins (ends #32); Pepper Casey only app.; 1st app. Iron Jaw; Crimebuster's pet monkey Squeeks begins	320	640	960	2240	3920	5600
4-Hitler, Tojo Mussolini-c; Iron Jaw app. Little Wise Guys (prototype of later version) begins, ends #5	155	310	465	992	1696	2400
5-Japanese war-c	107	214	321	680	1165	1650
6-Origin Iron Jaw; origin & death of Iron Jaw's son killed by his father; Hitler app.; Little Dynamite begins, ends #39; 1st Iron Jaw-c	320	640	960	2240	3920	5600
7-Flag & Hitler, Tojo, Mussolini-c; Dickey Dean app.	123	246	369	787	1344	1900
8-Death of Iron Jaw; Iron Jaw-c & spash pg.	103	206	309	659	1130	1600
9-Iron Jaw sty/classic-c	135	270	405	864	1482	2100
10-Return of Iron Jaw; classic Biro Iron Jaw/Nazi-c	161	322	483	1030	1765	2500
11-Iron Jaw sty/classic-c	103	206	309	659	1130	1600
12,13: 12-Japanese torture-c. 13-Nazi firing squad-c	68	136	204	435	743	1050
14-Iron Jaw-c	77	154	231	493	847	1200
15-Death of Iron Jaw, killed by The Rodent	86	172	258	546	936	1325
16,18,20 (2/45)	45	90	135	284	480	675
17-(8/44)-Flag-c; The Moth app.	47	94	141	296	498	700
19-One of the greatest all-time stories	53	106	159	334	567	800
21-24: 24-Concentration camp story	32	64	96	188	307	425
25-Devil-c; hanging story (52 pgs.)	39	78	117	231	378	525
26-Bondage, torture-c/story (68 pgs.)	41	82	123	256	428	600
27-29,31,32-(All 68 pgs.). 28-Yankee Longago ends. 32-Swoop Storm & Young Robin Hood end	34	68	102	199	325	450
30-(10/46, 68 pgs.)-Origin Crimebuster retold from #3 w/Iron Jaw; Nazi work camp story	39	78	117	231	378	525
33-40: 34-Crimebuster story (2); suicide-c/story	22	44	66	132	216	300
41-50-41-Daredevil illus. text story	19	38	57	111	176	240
51-59: 57(9/50)-Dilly Duncan begins, ends #71	16	32	48	94	147	200
60-(12/50)-Iron Jaw returns c/sty	18	36	54	103	162	220
61-Origin Crimebuster & Iron Jaw retold c/sty	19	38	57	112	179	245
62-(2/51)-Death of Iron Jaw explained w/Iron Jaw-c	19	38	57	109	172	235
63-67,69-72: 63-McWilliams-a	14	28	42	76	108	140
68,73-Iron Jaw c/sty; 73-Frazetta 1 pg. ad	14	28	42	80	115	150
74,78,81-Iron Jaw c/sty (2-3)	12	24	36	67	94	120
75-77,84	11	22	33	62	86	110
79,80-Iron Jaw sty: 80(8/52)-1st app. Rocky X of the Rocketeers; becomes "Rocky X" #101; Iron Jaw, Sniffer & the Deadly Dozen in #80-118	11	22	33	64	90	115
82-Iron Jaw-c only	11	22	33	62	86	110
83,85-88-Iron Jaw c/sty. 87-The Deadly Dozen begins; becomes Iron Jaw #88 (4/53)	11	22	33	64	90	115
89(5/53)-92-The Claw serial app. in Rocky X (also see Silver Streak & Daredevil); on-c. 89-"Iron Jaw" becomes "Sniffrer & Iron Jaw" (ends #118); Iron Jaw c/story in all	12	24	36	67	94	120
93-Claw cameo & last app.; Woodesque-a on Rocky X by Sid Check; Iron Jaw-c/sty	11	22	33	64	90	115
94-97-Iron Jaw-c/sty in all	11	22	33	60	83	105
98,100:(4/54): 98-Rocky X by Sid Check	11	22	33	62	86	110
99,101-107,109,111,119: 101-Rocky X becomes spy strip. 106-Robin Hood app. 111-Crimebuster becomes Chuck Chandler, ends #119	10	20	30	54	72	90
108-(2/55)-Kubert & Ditko-a (Crimebuster, 8 pgs.)	11	22	33	62	86	110
110,112-118-Kubert-a	10	20	30	58	79	100

(See Giant Boy Book of Comics)

NOTE: *Boy Movies in 3-5,40,41. Iron Jaw app. 3,4,6,8,10,11,13-15; returns-60,62, 68, 69, 72-79, 81-118; c-60-62, 73, 74, 78, 81-83, 85-97.* ***Biro*** *c-all.* ***Jack Alderman*** *a-26.* ***Dan Barry*** *a-31,32, 35-38.* ***Al Borth*** *a- 51.* ***Dick Briefer*** *a-3-28, 124.* ***Sid Check*** a-93, 98. ***Ditko*** a-108. ***Bob Fujitani (Fuje)*** *a-55, 18pgs.* ***Jerry Gandenetti*** *a-52.* ***R. W. Hall*** *a-19-22.* ***Hubbell*** *a-30, 106, 108, 110, 111.* ***Joe Kubert*** *a-108, 110, 112-118.* ***Kenneth Landau*** *a-92.* ***George Mandel*** *a-3-30.* ***Norman Maurer*** *a-4-9, 12, 13, 31, 32, 35, 41, 43, 46, 51, 57, 61, 73, 74, 78-83.* ***Bob Montana*** *a-4, 16, 19.* ***Pete Morisi*** *a-111.* ***William Overgard*** *a-68, 71, 74, 86, 88.* ***Palais*** *a-14, 16, 17, 19, 20, 25, 26. among others.* ***Tuska*** *a-30.* ***Bob Wood*** *a-8-13.*

BOY COMMANDOS (See Detective #64 & World's Finest Comics #8)
National Periodical Publications: Winter, 1942-43 - No. 36, Nov-Dec, 1949

	GD 2.0	VG 4.0	FN 6.0	VF 8.0	VF/NM 9.0	NM- 9.2
1-Origin Liberty Belle; The Sandman & The Newsboy Legion x-over in Boy Commandos; S&K-a, 48 pgs.; S&K cameo? (classic WWII-c)	400	800	1200	2800	4900	7000
2-Last Liberty Belle; Hitler-c; S&K-a, 46 pgs.; WWII-c	239	478	717	1530	2615	3700
3-S&K-a, 45 pgs.; WWII-c	135	270	405	864	1482	2100
4-6: All WWII-c. 6-S&K-a	84	168	252	538	919	1300
7-10: All WWII-c	53	106	159	334	567	800
11-13: All WWII-c. 11-Infinity-c	39	78	117	240	395	550
14,16,18-19-All have S&K-a. 18-2nd Crazy Quilt-c	32	64	96	188	307	425
15-1st app. Crazy Quilt, their arch nemesis	40	80	120	246	411	575
17,20-Sci/fi-c/stories	39	78	117	231	378	525
21,22,25: 22-3rd Crazy Quilt-c; Judy Canova x-over	25	50	75	150	245	340
23-S&K-c/a(all)	34	68	102	204	332	460
24-1st costumed superhero satire-c (11-12/47).	30	60	90	177	289	400
26-Flying Saucer story (3-4/48)-4th of this theme; see The Spirit 9/28/47(1st), Shadow Comics V7#10 (2nd, 1/48) & Captain Midnight #60 (3rd, 2/48)	31	62	93	182	296	410
27,28,30: 30-Cleveland Indians story	24	48	72	144	237	330
29-S&K story (1)	26	52	78	154	252	350
31-35: 32-Dale Evans app. on-c & in story. 33-Last Crazy Quilt-c. 34-Intro. Wolf, their mascot	22	44	66	128	209	290
36-Intro The Atomobile c/sci-fi story (Scarce)	40	80	120	246	411	575
The Boy Commandos by Joe Simon & Jack Kirby Volume One HC (2010, $49.99) reprints apps. in Detective #64-72, World's Finest #8,9 & Boy Commandos #1,2; Buhle intro.						50.00

NOTE: *Most issues signed by* ***Simon & Kirby*** *are not by them.* ***S&K*** *c-1-9, 13, 14, 17, 21, 23, 24, 30-32.* ***Feller*** *c-30.*

BOY COMMANDOS
National Per. Publ.: Sept-Oct, 1973 - No. 2, Nov-Dec, 1973 (G.A. S&K reprints)

	GD 2.0	VG 4.0	FN 6.0	VF 8.0	VF/NM 9.0	NM- 9.2
1,2: 1-Reprints story from Boy Commandos #1 plus-c & Detective #66 by S&K. 2-Infantino/Orlando-c	2	4	6	10	14	18

BOY COMMANDOS COMICS
DC Comics: Sept/Oct. 1942

1-Ashcan comic, not distributed to newsstands, only for in-house use. Cover art is the splash page from the Boy Commandos story in Detective Comics #68 interior is from an unidentified issue of Detective Comics (no known sales)

nn - (9-10/42) Ashcan comic, not distributed to newsstands, only for in-house use. Cover art is the splash page from the Boy Commandos story in Detective Comics #68 interior is from Detective Comics #68 (no known sales)

BOY COWBOY (Also see Amazing Adventures & Science Comics)
Ziff-Davis Publ. Co.: 1950 (8 pgs. in color)

	GD 2.0	VG 4.0	FN 6.0	VF 8.0	VF/NM 9.0	NM- 9.2
nn-Sent to subscribers of Ziff-Davis mags. & ordered through mail for 10¢; used to test market for Kid Cowboy	32	64	96	188	307	425

BOY DETECTIVE
Avon Periodicals: May-June, 1951 - No. 4, May, 1952

	GD 2.0	VG 4.0	FN 6.0	VF 8.0	VF/NM 9.0	NM- 9.2
1	20	40	60	114	182	250
2-4: 3,4-Kinstler-c	14	28	42	80	115	150

BOY EXPLORERS COMICS (Terry and The Pirates No. 3 on)
Family Comics (Harvey Publ.): May-June, 1946 - No. 2, Sept-Oct, 1946

	GD 2.0	VG 4.0	FN 6.0	VF 8.0	VF/NM 9.0	NM- 9.2
1-Intro The Explorers, Duke of Broadway, Calamity Jane & Danny Dixon...Cadet; S&K-c/a, 24 pgs.	74	148	222	470	810	1150
2-(Rare)-Small size (5-1/2x8-1/2"; B&W; 32 pgs.) Distributed to mail subscribers only; S&K-a	194	388	582	1242	2121	3000

(Also see All New No. 15, Flash Gordon No. 5, and Stuntman No. 3)

BOY ILLUSTORIES (See Boy Comics)

BOY LOVES GIRL (Boy Meets Girl No. 1-24)
Lev Gleason Publications: No. 25, July, 1952 - No. 57, June, 1956

	GD 2.0	VG 4.0	FN 6.0	VF 8.0	VF/NM 9.0	NM- 9.2
25(#1)	12	24	36	67	94	120
26,27,29-33: 30-33-Serial, 'Loves of My Life	9	18	27	47	61	75
34-42: 39-Lingerie panels	8	16	24	44	57	70
28-Drug propaganda story	9	18	27	47	61	75
43-Toth-a	9	18	27	50	65	80
44-50: 47-Toth-a? 50-Last pre-code (2/55)	8	16	24	42	54	65
51-57: 57-Ann Brewster-a	7	14	21	37	46	55

BOY MEETS GIRL (Boy Loves Girl No. 25 on)
Lev Gleason Publications: Feb, 1950 - No. 24, June, 1952 (No. 1-17: 52 pgs.)

	GD 2.0	VG 4.0	FN 6.0	VF 8.0	VF/NM 9.0	NM- 9.2
1-Guardineer-a	18	36	54	103	162	220
2	11	22	33	62	86	110
3-10	10	20	30	58	79	100
11-24	10	20	30	54	72	90

NOTE: ***Briefer*** *a-24.* ***Fuje*** *c-3,7. Painted-c 1-17. Photo-c 19-21, 23.*

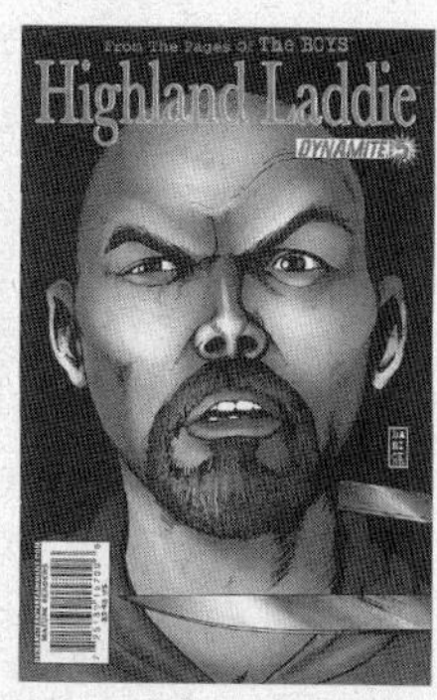

The Boys: Highland Laddie #5 © Spitfire & D. Robertson

The Bradleys #5 © Peter Bagge

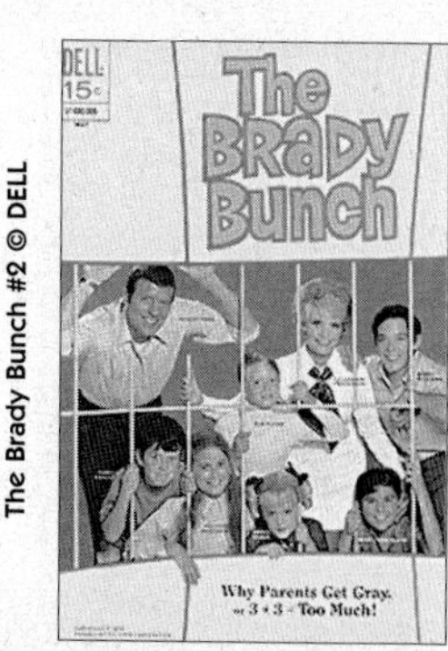

The Brady Bunch #2 © DELL

	GD 2.0	VG 4.0	FN 6.0	VF 8.0	VF/NM 9.0	NM- 9.2

BOYS, THE
DC Comics (WildStorm)/Dynamite Ent. #7 on: Oct, 2006 - Present ($2.99/$3.99, mature)

1-Garth Ennis-s/Darick Robertson-a 6.00
2-6 4.00
7-42-(Dynamite Ent.,). 19-Origin of the Homelander. 23-Variant-c by Cassaday 3.00
43-64-($3.99) Russ Braun-a in most. 54,55-McCrea-a 4.00
#1: Dynamite Edition (2009, $1.00) r/#1; flip book with Battlefields Night Witches 3.00
...: Herogasm 1-6 (2009 - No. 6, 2009, $2.99) Ennis-s/McCrea-a 3.00
... Volume 1: The Name of the Game TPB (2007, $14.99) r/#1-6; intro. by Simon Pegg 15.00
... Volume 2: Get Some TPB (2008, $19.99) r/#7-14 20.00
... Volume 3: Good For The Soul TPB (2008, $19.99) r/#15-22 20.00
... Volume 4: We Gotta Go Now TPB (2009, $19.99) r/#23-30; cover gallery 20.00

BOYS, THE: BUTCHER, BAKER, CANDLESTICKMAKER
Dynamite Entertainment: 2011 - No. 6, 2011 ($3.99, mature)

1-6-Garth Ennis-s/Darick Robertson-a; Billy Butcher's early years 4.00

BOYS, THE: HIGHLAND LADDIE
Dynamite Entertainment: 2010 - No. 6, 2011 ($3.99, mature)

1-6-Garth Ennis-s/John McCrea-a 4.00

BOYS' AND GIRLS' MARCH OF COMICS (See March of Comics)

BOYS' RANCH (Also see Western Tales & Witches' Western Tales)
Harvey Publ.: Oct, 1950 - No. 6, Aug, 1951 (No.1-3, 52 pgs.; No. 4-6, 36 pgs.)

	GD	VG	FN	VF	VF/NM	NM-
1-S&K-c/a(3)	58	116	174	371	636	900
2-S&K-c/a(3)	40	80	120	246	411	575
3-S&K-c/a(2); Meskin-a	39	78	117	231	378	525
4-S&K-c/a, 5 pgs.	34	68	102	199	325	450
5,6-S&K-c, splashes & centerspread only; Meskin-a	20	40	60	114	182	250

BOZO (Larry Harmon's Bozo, the World's Most Famous Clown)
Innovation Publishing: 1992 ($6.95, 68 pgs.)

	GD	VG	FN	VF	VF/NM	NM-
1-Reprints Four Color #285(#1)	1	2	3	4	5	7

BOZO THE CLOWN (TV) (Bozo No. 7 on)
Dell Publishing Co.: July, 1950 - No. 4, Oct-Dec, 1963

	GD	VG	FN	VF	VF/NM	NM-
Four Color 285(#1)	16	32	48	112	246	380
2(7-9/51)-7(10-12/52)	10	20	30	70	133	195
Four Color 464,508,551,594(10/54)	10	20	30	64	115	165
1(nn, 5-7/62)	8	16	24	51	86	120
2 - 4(1963)	6	12	18	41	66	90

BOZZ CHRONICLES, THE
Marvel Comics (Epic Comics): Dec, 1985 - No. 6, 1986 (Lim. series, mature)

1-6-Logan/Wolverine look alike in 19th century. 1,3,5-Blevins-a 3.00

B.P.R.D. (Bureau of Paranormal Research and Defense) (Also see Hellboy titles)
Dark Horse Comics: (one-shots)

... Dark Waters (7/03, $2.99) Guy Davis-c/a; Augustyn-s 3.00
... Night Train (9/03, $2.99) Johns & Kolins-s; Kolins & Stewart-a 3.00
... The Ectoplasmic Man (6/08, $2.99) Stenbeck-a/Mignola-c; origin of Johann Kraus 3.00
... There's Something Under My Bed (11/03, $2.99) Pollina-a/c 3.00
... The Soul of Venice (5/03, $2.99) Oeming-a/c; Gunter & Oeming-s 3.00
... The Soul of Venice and Other Stories TPB (8/04, $17.95) r/one-shots & new story by Mignola and Cam Stewart; sketch pages by various 18.00
... War on Frogs (6/08,12/08, 6/09, 12/09, $2.99) 1-Trimpe-a/Mignola-c; Abe Sapien app. 2-Severin-a. 3-Moline-a. 4-Snejbjerg 3.00

B.P.R.D.: GARDEN OF SOULS
Dark Horse Comics: Mar, 2007 - No. 5, July, 2007 ($2.99, limited series)

1-5-Mignola & Arcudi-s/Guy Davis-a/Mignola-c 3.00

B.P.R.D.: HELL ON EARTH
Dark Horse Comics: ($3.50, limited series)

... Gods (1/11 - No. 3, 3/11) 1-Mignola & Arcudi-s/Guy Davis-a; Ryan Sook-c 3.50
... Monsters (7/11 - No. 2, 8/11) 1,2-Mignola & Arcudi-s. 1-Sook & Francavilla covers 3.50
... New World (8/10 - No. 5, 12/10) 1-5-Mignola & Arcudi-s/Guy Davis-a/c 3.50
... Russia (9/11 - No. 5, 1/12) 1-5-Mignola & Arcudi-s/Crook-a 3.50
... The Long Death (2/12 - No. 3) 1,2-Mignola & Arcudi-s/Harren-a/Fegredo-c 3.50

B.P.R.D.: HOLLOW EARTH (Mike Mignola's...)
Dark Horse Comics: Jan, 2002 - No. 3, June, 2002 ($2.99, limited series)

1-3-Mignola, Golden & Sniegoski-s/Sook-a/Mignola-c; Hellboy and Abe Sapien app. 3.00
... and Other Stories TPB (1/03; 7/04, $17.95) r/#1-3, Hellboy: Box Full of Evil, Abe Sapien: Drums of the Dead, and Dark Horse Extra; plus sketch pages 18.00

B.P.R.D.: KILLING GROUND
Dark Horse Comics: Aug, 2007 - No. 5, Dec, 2007 ($2.99, limited series)

1-5-Mignola & Arcudi-s/Guy Davis-a/c 3.00

B.P.R.D.: KING OF FEAR
Dark Horse Comics: Jan, 2010 - No. 5, May, 2010 ($2.99, limited series)

1,2-Mignola & Arcudi-s/Guy Davis-a; Mignola-c 3.00

B.P.R.D.: 1946
Dark Horse Comics: Jan, 2008 - No. 5, May, 2008 ($2.99, limited series)

1-5-Mignola & Dysart-s/Azaceta-a; Mignola/c 3.00

B.P.R.D.: 1947
Dark Horse Comics: Jul, 2009 - No. 5, Nov, 2009 ($2.99, limited series)

1-5-Mignola & Dysart-s/Bá & Moon-a; Mignola/c 3.00

B.P.R.D.: PLAGUE OF FROGS
Dark Horse Comics: Mar, 2004 - No. 5, July, 2004 ($2.99, limited series)

1-5-Mignola-s/Guy Davis-c/a 3.00
TPB (1/05, $17.95) r/series; sketchbook pages & afterword by Davis & Mignola 18.00

B.P.R.D.: THE BLACK FLAME
Dark Horse Comics: Sept, 2005 - No. 6, Jan, 2006 ($2.99, limited series)

1-6-Mignola & Arcudi-s/Guy Davis-a/ Mignola-c 3.00
TPB (7/06, $17.95) r/series; sketchbook pages & afterword by Davis & Mignola 18.00

B.P.R.D.: THE BLACK GODDESS
Dark Horse Comics: Jan, 2009 - No. 5, May, 2009 ($2.99, limited series)

1-5-Mignola & Arcudi-s/Guy Davis-a/Nowlan-c 3.00

B.P.R.D.: THE DEAD
Dark Horse Comics: Nov, 2004 - No. 5, Mar, 2005 ($2.99, limited series)

1-5-Mignola-s/Guy Davis-c/a 3.00

B.P.R.D.: THE DEAD REMEMBERED
Dark Horse Comics: Apr, 2011 - No. 3, Jun, 2011 ($3.50, limited series)

1-3-Mignola-s; Moline-a; Jo Chen-c. 1-Variant-c by Moline 3.50

B.P.R.D.: THE UNIVERSAL MACHINE
Dark Horse Comics: Apr, 2006 - No. 5, Aug, 2006 ($2.99, limited series)

1-5-Mignola & Arcudi-s/Guy Davis-a/Mignola-c. 5-Mignola-a (5 pgs.) 3.00
TPB (1/07, $17.95) r/series; sketchbook pages by Davis; Mignola afterword 18.00

B.P.R.D.: THE WARNING
Dark Horse Comics: July, 2008 - No. 5, Nov, 2008 ($2.99, limited series)

1-5-Mignola & Arcudi-s/Guy Davis-c/a 3.00

BRADLEYS, THE (Also see Hate)
Fantagraphics Books: Apr, 1999 - No. 6, Jan, 2000 ($2.95, B&W, limited series)

1-6-Reprints Peter Bagge's-s/a 3.00

BRADY BUNCH, THE (TV)(See Kite Fun Book and Binky #78)
Dell Publishing Co.: Feb, 1970 - No. 2, May, 1970

	GD	VG	FN	VF	VF/NM	NM-
1	11	22	33	73	142	210
2	9	18	27	58	99	140

BRAIN, THE
Sussex Publ. Co./Magazine Enterprises: Sept, 1956 - No. 7, 1958

	GD	VG	FN	VF	VF/NM	NM-
1-Dan DeCarlo-a in all including reprints	13	26	39	72	101	130
2,3	8	16	24	44	57	70
4-7	4	8	12	26	41	55
I.W. Reprints #1-4,8-10('63),14: 2-Reprints Sussex #2 with new cover added	2	4	6	9	13	16
Super Reprint #17,18(nd)	2	4	6	9	13	16

BRAINBANX
DC Comics (Helix): Mar, 1997 - No. 6, Aug, 1997 ($2.50, limited series)

1-6: Elaine Lee-s/Temujin-a 3.00

BRAIN BOY
Dell Publishing Co.: Apr-June, 1962 - No. 6, Sept-Nov, 1963 (Painted c-#1-6)

	GD	VG	FN	VF	VF/NM	NM-
Four Color 1330(#1)-Gil Kane-a; origin	11	22	33	71	136	200
2(7-9/62),3-6: 4-Origin retold	7	14	21	48	79	110

BRAM STOKER'S BURIAL OF THE RATS (Movie)
Roger Corman's Cosmic Comics: Apr, 1995 - No.3, June, 1995 ($2.50)

1-3: Adaptation of film; Jerry Prosser scripts 3.00

BRAM STOKER'S DRACULA (Movie)(Also see Dracula: Vlad the Impaler)
Topps Comics: Oct, 1992 - No. 4, Jan, 1993 ($2.95, limited series, polybagged)

1-(1st & 2nd printing)-Adaptation of film begins; Mignola-c/a in all; 4 trading cards & poster;

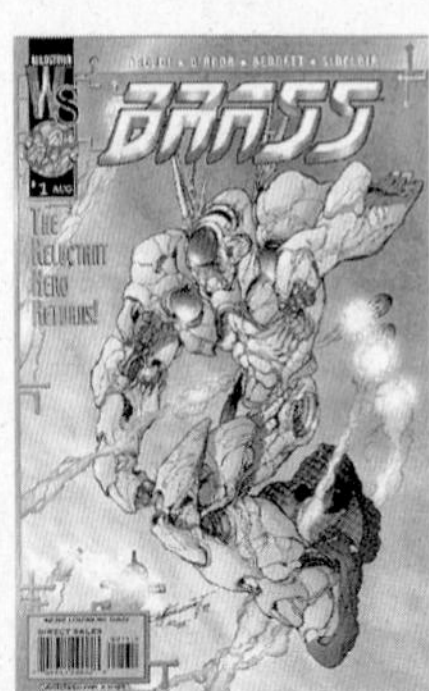
Brass (2000 series) #1 © WSP

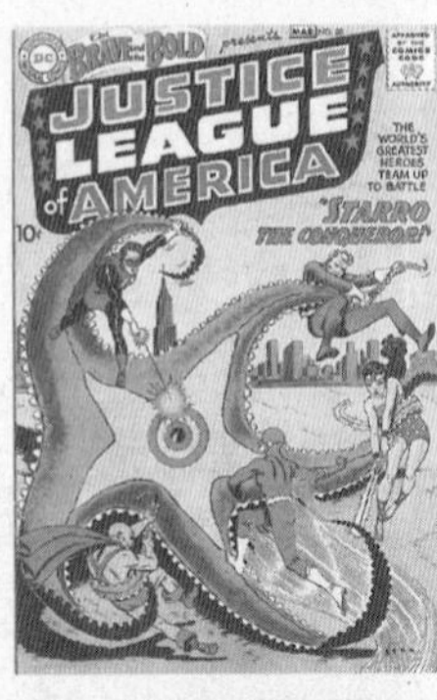

Brave and the Bold #28 © DC

Brave and the Bold #76 © DC

	GD	VG	FN	VF	VF/NM	NM-
	2.0	4.0	6.0	8.0	9.0	9.2

photo scenes of movie 3.00
1-Crimson foil edition (limited to 500) 8.00
2-4: 2-Bound-in poster & cards. 4 trading cards in both. 3-Contains coupon to win 1 of 500 crimson foil-c edition of #1. 4-Contains coupon to win 1 of 500 uncut sheets of all 16 trading cards 3.00

BRAND ECHH (See Not Brand Echh)

BRAND OF EMPIRE (See Luke Short's...Four Color 771)

BRASS
Image Comics (WildStorm Productions): Aug, 1996 - No. 3, May, 1997 ($2.50, lim. series)
1-($4.50) Folio Ed.; oversized 4.50
1-3: Wiesenfeld-s/Bennett-a. 3-Grunge & Roxy(Gen 13) cameo 3.00

BRASS
DC Comics (WildStorm): Aug, 2000 - No. 6, Jan, 2001 ($2.50, limited series)
1-6-Arcudi-s 3.00

BRATH
CrossGeneration Comics: Feb, 2003 - No. 14, June, 2004 ($2.95)
Prequel-Dixon-s/Di Vito-a 3.00
1-14: 1-(3/03)-Dixon-s/Di Vito-a 3.00
Vol. 1: Hammer of Vengeance (2003, $9.95) Digest-sized reprint of Prequel & #1-6 10.00

BRATPACK/MAXIMORTAL SUPER SPECIAL
King Hell Press: 1996 ($2.95, B&W, limited series)
1,2: Veitch-s/a 3.00

BRATS BIZARRE
Marvel Comics (Epic/Heavy Hitters): 1994 - No. 4, 1994 ($2.50, limited series)
1-4: All w/bound-in trading cards 3.00

BRAVADOS, THE (See Wild Western Action)
Skywald Publ. Corp.: Aug, 1971 (52 pgs., one-shot)
1-Red Mask, The Durango Kid, Billy Nevada-r; Bolle-a; 3-D effect story 3 6 9 14 19 24

BRAVE AND THE BOLD, THE (See Best Of... & Super DC Giant) (Replaced by Batman & The Outsiders)
National Periodical Publ./DC Comics: Aug-Sept, 1955 - No. 200, July, 1983
1-Viking Prince by Kubert, Silent Knight, Golden Gladiator begin; part Kubert-c 286 572 858 2488 5394 8300
2 119 238 357 964 2082 3200
3,4 63 126 189 510 1105 1700
5-Robin Hood begins (4-5/56, 1st DC app.), ends #15; see Robin Hood Tales #7 65 130 195 527 1139 1750
6-10: 6-Robin Hood by Kubert; last Golden Gladiator app.; Silent Knight; no Viking Prince. 8-1st S.A. issue 45 90 135 338 732 1125
11-22,24: 12,14-Robin Hood-c. 18,21-23-Grey tone-c. 22-Last Silent Knight. 24-Last Viking Prince by Kubert (2nd solo book) 36 72 108 261 568 875
23-Viking Prince origin by Kubert; 1st B&B single theme issue & 1st Viking Prince solo book 45 90 135 338 732 1125
25-1st app. Suicide Squad (8-9/59) 59 118 177 478 1039 1600
26,27-Suicide Squad 29 58 87 210 448 685
28-(2-3/60)-Justice League intro./1st app.; origin/1st app. Snapper Carr 633 1267 1900 7000 15,000 23,000
29-Justice League (4-5/60)-2nd app. battle the Weapons Master; robot-c 207 414 621 1739 3770 5800
30-Justice League (6-7/60)-3rd app.; vs. Amazo 164 328 492 1378 2989 4600
31-1st app. Cave Carson (8-9/60); scarce in high grade; 1st try-out series 37 74 111 278 602 925
32,33-Cave Carson 22 44 66 154 327 500
34-Origin/1st app. Silver-Age Hawkman, Hawkgirl & Byth (2-3/61); Gardner Fox story, Kubert-c/a ; 1st S.A. Hawkman tryout series; 2nd in #42-44; both series predate Hawkman #1 (4-5/64) 171 342 513 1436 3118 4800
35-Hawkman by Kubert (4-5/61)-2nd app. 41 82 123 308 667 1025
36-Hawkman by Kubert; origin & 1st app. Shadow Thief (6-7/61)-3rd app. 36 72 108 261 568 875
37-Suicide Squad (2nd tryout series) 19 38 57 132 284 435
38,39-Suicide Squad. 38-Last 10¢ issue 16 32 48 111 243 375
40,41-Cave Carson Inside Earth (2nd try-out series). 40-Kubert-a. 41-Meskin-a 13 26 39 87 186 285
42-Hawkman by Kubert (2nd tryout series); Hawkman earns helmet wings; Byth app. 24 48 72 168 359 550
43-Hawkman by Kubert; more detailed origin 28 56 84 203 439 675
44-Hawkman by Kubert; grey-tone-c 23 46 69 161 343 525
45-49-Strange Sports Stories by Infantino 9 18 27 63 112 160

	GD	VG	FN	VF	VF/NM	NM-
	2.0	4.0	6.0	8.0	9.0	9.2

50-The Green Arrow & Manhunter From Mars (10-11/63); 1st Manhunter x-over outside of Detective Comics (pre-dates House of Mystery #143); team-ups begin 17 34 51 114 250 385
51-Aquaman & Hawkman (12-1/63-64); pre-dates Hawkman #1 19 38 57 128 277 425
52-(2-3/64)-3 Battle Stars; Sgt. Rock, Haunted Tank, Johnny Cloud, & Mlle. Marie team-up for 1st time by Kubert (c/a) 22 44 66 154 327 500
53-Atom & The Flash by Toth 10 20 30 66 121 175
54-Kid Flash, Robin & Aqualad; 1st app./origin Teen Titans (6-7/64) 33 66 99 239 520 800
55-Metal Men & The Atom 9 18 27 61 106 150
56-The Flash & Manhunter From Mars 9 18 27 61 106 150
57-Origin & 1st app. Metamorpho (12-1/64-65) 16 32 48 109 237 365
58-2nd app. Metamorpho by Fradon 10 20 30 68 127 185
59-Batman & Green Lantern; 1st Batman team-up in Brave and the Bold 12 24 36 79 160 240
60-Teen Titans (2nd app.)-1st app. new Wonder Girl (Donna Troy), who joins Titans (6-7/65) 16 32 48 111 243 375
61-Origin Starman & Black Canary by Anderson 12 24 36 79 160 240
62-Origin Starman & Black Canary cont'd. 62-1st S.A. app. Wildcat (10-11/65); 1st S.A. app. of G.A. Huntress (W.W. villain) 11 22 33 73 142 210
63-Supergirl & Wonder Woman 9 18 27 58 99 140
64-Batman Versus Eclipso (see H.O.S. #61) 8 16 24 56 96 135
65-Flash & Doom Patrol (4-5/66) 6 12 18 43 69 95
66-Metamorpho & Metal Men (6-7/66) 6 12 18 43 69 95
67-Batman & The Flash by Infantino; Batman team-ups begin, end #200 (8-9/66) 7 14 21 49 82 115
68-Batman/Metamorpho/Joker/Riddler/Penguin-c/story; Batman as Bat-Hulk (Hulk parody) 9 18 27 58 99 140
69-Batman & Green Lantern 7 14 21 44 72 100
70-Batman & Hawkman; Craig-a(p) 7 14 21 44 72 100
71-Batman & Green Arrow 7 14 21 44 72 100
72-Spectre & Flash (6-7/67); 4th app. The Spectre; predates Spectre #1 7 14 21 46 76 105
73-Aquaman & The Atom 6 12 18 42 69 95
74-Batman & Metal Men 6 12 18 42 69 95
75-Batman & The Spectre (12-1/67-68); 6th app. Spectre; came out between Spectre #1 & #2 7 14 21 44 72 100
76-Batman & Plastic Man (2-3/68); came out between Plastic Man #8 & #9 6 12 18 42 69 95
77-Batman & The Atom 6 12 18 42 69 95
78-Batman, Wonder Woman & Batgirl 6 12 18 42 69 95
79-Batman & Deadman by Neal Adams (8-9/68); early Deadman app. 10 20 30 66 121 175
80-Batman & Creeper (10-11/68); N. Adams-a; early app. The Creeper; came out between Creeper #3 & #4 9 18 27 58 99 140
81-Batman & Flash; N. Adams-a 9 18 27 58 99 140
82-Batman & Aquaman; N. Adams-a; origin Ocean Master retold (2-3/69) 9 18 27 58 99 140
83-Batman & Teen Titans; N. Adams-a (4-5/69) 9 18 27 58 99 140
84-Batman (G.A., 1st S.A. app.) & Sgt. Rock; N. Adams-a; last 12¢ issue (6-7/69) 9 18 27 58 99 140
85-Batman & Green Arrow; 1st new costume for Green Arrow by Neal Adams (8-9/69) 10 20 30 66 121 175
86-Batman & Deadman (10-11/69); N. Adams-a; story concludes from Strange Adventures #216 (1-2/69) 9 18 27 58 99 140
87-Batman & Wonder Woman 4 8 12 28 44 60
88-Batman & Wildcat 4 8 12 28 44 60
89-Batman & Phantom Stranger (4-5/70); early Phantom Stranger app. (came out between Phantom Stranger #6 & 7 4 8 12 26 41 55
90-Batman & Adam Strange 4 8 12 26 41 55
91-Batman & Black Canary (8-9/70) 4 8 12 26 41 55
92-Batman; intro the Bat Squad 4 8 12 26 41 55
93-Batman-House of Mystery; N. Adams-a 8 16 24 51 86 120
94-Batman-Teen Titans 4 8 12 24 37 50
95-Batman & Plastic Man 3 6 9 21 32 42
96-Batman & Sgt. Rock; last 15¢ issue 4 8 12 22 34 45
97-Batman & Wildcat; 52 pg. issues begin, end #102; reprints origin & 1st app. Deadman from Strange Advs. #205 4 8 12 22 34 45
98-Batman & Phantom Stranger; 1st Jim Aparo Batman-a? 4 8 12 22 34 45
99-Batman & Flash 4 8 12 22 34 45
100-(2-3/72, 25¢, 52 pgs.)-Batman-Green Lantern-Green Arrow-Black Canary-Robin; Deadman-r by Adams/Str. Advs. #210 6 12 18 41 66 90

Brave and the Bold #158 © DC

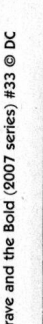

Brave and the Bold (2007 series) #33 © DC

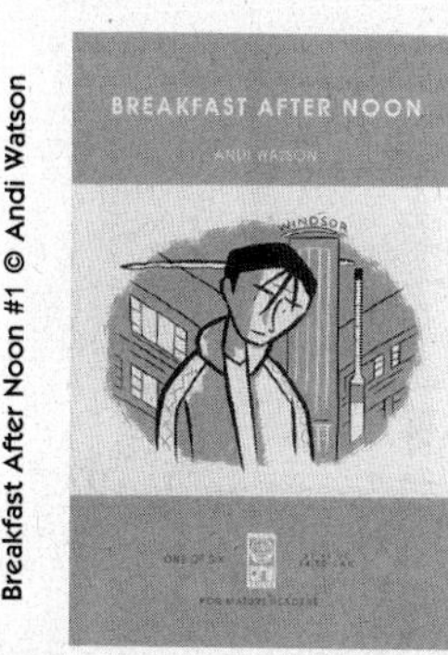
Breakfast After Noon #1 © Andi Watson

GD VG FN VF VF/NM NM-
2.0 4.0 6.0 8.0 9.0 9.2

101-Batman & Metamorpho; Kubert Viking Prince 3 6 9 21 32 42
102-Batman-Teen Titans; N. Adams-a(p) 5 10 15 32 51 70
103-107,109,110: Batman team-ups: 103-Metal Men. 104-Deadman. 105-Wonder Woman. 106-Green Arrow. 107-Black Canary. 109-Demon. 110-Wildcat
3 6 9 14 20 26
108-Sgt. Rock 3 6 9 16 22 28
111-Batman/Joker-c/story 3 6 9 19 29 38
112-117: All 100 pgs.; Batman team-ups: 112-Mr. Miracle. 113-Metal Men; reprints origin/1st Hawkman from Brave and the Bold #34; r/origin Multi-Man/Challengers #14. 114-Aquaman. 115-Atom; r/origin Viking Prince from #23; r/Dr. Fate/Hourman/Solomon Grundy/Green Lantern from Showcase #55. 116-Spectre. 117-Sgt. Rock; last 100 pg. issue
5 10 15 32 51 70
118-Batman/Wildcat/Joker-c/story 3 6 9 17 25 32
119,121-123,125-128,132-140: Batman team-ups: 119-Man-Bat. 121-Metal Men. 122-Swamp Thing. 123-Plastic Man/Metamorpho. 125-Flash. 126-Aquaman. 127-Wildcat. 128-Mr. Miracle. 132-Kung-Fu Fighter. 133-Deadman. 134-Green Lantern. 135-Metal Men. 136-Metal Men/Green Arrow. 137-Demon. 138-Mr. Miracle. 139-Hawkman. 140-Wonder Woman 2 4 6 8 10 12
120-Kamandi (68 pgs.) 3 6 9 14 19 24
124-Sgt. Rock 2 4 6 9 12 15
129,130-Batman/Green Arrow/Atom parts 1 & 2; Joker & Two Face-c/stories
2 4 6 13 18 22
131-Batman & Wonder Woman vs. Catwoman-c/sty 2 4 6 10 14 18
141-Batman/Black Canary vs. Joker-c/story 2 4 6 13 18 22
142-160: Batman team-ups: 142-Aquaman. 143-Creeper; origin Human Target (44 pgs.). 144-Green Arrow; origin Human Target part 2 (44 pgs.). 145-Phantom Stranger. 146-G.A. Batman/Unknown Soldier. 147-Supergirl. 148-Plastic Man; X-Mas-c. 149-Teen Titans. 150-Anniversary issue; Superman. 151-Flash. 152-Atom. 153-Red Tornado. 154-Metamorpho. 155-Green Lantern. 156-Dr. Fate. 157-Batman vs. Kamandi (ties into Kamandi #59). 158-Wonder Woman. 159-Ra's Al Ghul. 160-Supergirl.
1 3 4 6 8 10
145(11/79)-147,150-159,165(8/80)-(Whitman variants; low print run; none show issue # on cover) 2 4 6 9 13 16
161-181,183-190,192-195,198,199: Batman team-ups: 161-Adam Strange. 162-G.A. Batman/Sgt. Rock. 163-Black Lightning. 164-Hawkman. 165-Man-Bat. 166-Black Canary; Nemesis (intro) back-up story begins, ends #192; Penguin-c/story. 167-G.A. Batman/Blackhawk; origin Nemesis. 168-Green Arrow. 169-Zatanna. 170-Nemesis. 171-Scalphunter. 172-Firestorm. 173-Guardians of the Universe. 174-Green Lantern. 175-Lois Lane. 176-Swamp Thing. 177-Elongated Man. 178-Creeper. 179-Legion. 180-Spectre. 181-Hawk & Dove. 183-Riddler. 184-Huntress & Earth II Batman. 185-Green Arrow. 186-Hawkman. 187-Metal Men. 188,189-Rose & the Thorn. 190-Adam Strange. 192-Superboy vs. Mr. I.Q. 194-Flash. 195-I...Vampire. 198-Karate Kid. 199-Batman vs. The Spectre 6.00
182-G.A. Robin; G.A. Starman app.; 1st modern app. G.A. Batwoman
2 4 6 8 10 12
191-Batman/Joker-c/story; Nemesis app. 2 4 6 8 11 14
196-Ragman; origin Ragman retold. 1 2 3 5 6 8
197-Catwoman; Earth II Batman & Catwoman marry; 2nd modern app. of G.A. Batwoman; Scarecrow story in Golden Age style 2 4 6 11 16 20
200-Double-sized (64 pgs.); printed on Mando paper; Earth One & Earth Two Batman app. in separate stories; intro/1st app. Batman & The Outsiders
2 4 6 8 10 12

NOTE: ***Neal Adams*** *a-79-86, 93, 100r, 102; c-75, 76, 79-86, 88-90, 93, 95, 99, 100r.* ***M. Anderson*** *a-115r; c-72i, 96i.* ***Andru/Esposito*** *c-25-27.* ***Aparo*** *a-98, 100-102, 104-125, 126i, 127-136, 138-145, 147, 148i, 149-152, 154, 155, 157-162, 168-170, 173-178, 180-182, 184, 186i-189i, 191i-193i, 195, 196, 200; c-105-109, 111-136, 137i, 138-175, 177, 180-184, 186-200.* ***Austin*** *a-166i.* ***Bernard Baily*** *c-32, 33, 58.* ***Buckler*** *a-185, 186p; c-137, 178p, 185p, 186p.* ***Giordano*** *a-143, 144.* ***Infantino*** *a-67p, 72p, 97r, 98r, 115r, 172p, 183p, 190p, 194p; c-45-49, 67p, 69p, 70p, 72p, 96p, 98r.* ***Kaluta*** *c-176.* ***Kane*** *a-115r; c-59, 64.* ***Kubert*** *&/or* ***Heath*** *a-1-24; reprints-101, 113, 115, 117.* ***Kubert*** *a-99r; c-22-24, 34-36, 40, 42-44, 52.* ***Mooney*** *a-114r.* ***Mortimer*** *a-64, 69.* ***Newton*** *a-153p, 156p, 165p.* ***Irv Novick*** *c-1(part), 2-21.* ***Fred Ray*** *a-78r.* ***Roussos*** *a-50, 76i, 114r.* ***Staton*** *148p. 52 pgs.-97, 100; 68 pgs.-120; 100 pgs.-112-117.*

BRAVE AND THE BOLD, THE
DC Comics: Dec, 1991 - No. 6, June, 1992 ($1.75, limited series)

1-6: Green Arrow, The Butcher, The Question in all; Grell scripts in all 3.00
NOTE: ***Grell*** *c-3, 4-6.*

BRAVE AND THE BOLD, THE
DC Comics: Apr, 2007 - No. 35, Aug, 2010 ($2.99)

1-Batman & Green Lantern team-up; Roulette app.; Waid-s/Peréz-c/a; 2 covers 4.00
2-32,34,35: 2-GL & Supergirl. 3-Batman & Blue Beetle vs. Fatal Five; Lobo app. 4-6-LSH app. 12-Megistus conclusion; Ordway-a. 14-Kolins-a. 16-Superman & Catwoman. 28-Blackhawks app. 29-Batman/Brother Power the Geek. 31-Atom/Joker 3.00
33-Batgirl, Zatanna & W.W.; prelude to Killing Joke 2 4 6 11 16 20
...: Demons and Dragons HC (2009, $24.99, dustjacket) r/#13-16; Brave & the Bold V1 #181, Flash V3 #107 and Impulse #17; Mark Waid commentary 25.00
...: Demons and Dragons SC (2010, $17.99) same contents as HC 18.00
...: Milestone SC (2010, $17.99) r/#24-26 and Static #12, Hardware #16, Xombi #6 18.00

GD VG FN VF VF/NM NM-
2.0 4.0 6.0 8.0 9.0 9.2

Team-ups of the Brave and the Bold HC (2010, $24.99) r/#27-33 25.00
...: The Book of Destiny HC (2008, $24.99, dustjacket) r/#7-12; Ordway sketch pages 25.00
...: The Book of Destiny SC (2009, $17.99) r/#7-12; Ordway sketch pages 18.00
...: The Lords of Luck HC (2007, $24.99, dustjacket) r/#1-6 with Waid intro & annotations 25.00
...: The Lords of Luck SC (2008, $17.99) r/#1-6 with Waid intro & annotations 18.00
...: Without Sin SC (2009, $17.99) r/#17-22 18.00

BRAVE AND THE BOLD ANNUAL NO. 1 1969 ISSUE, THE
DC Comics: 2001 ($5.95, one-shot)

1-Reprints Silver Age team-ups in 1960s-style 80 pg. Giant format 6.00

BRAVE AND THE BOLD SPECIAL, THE (See DC Special Series No. 8)

BRAVE EAGLE (TV)
Dell Publishing Co.: No. 705, June, 1956 - No. 929, July, 1958

Four Color 705 (#1)-Photo-c 6 12 18 43 69 95
Four Color 770, 816, 879 (2/58), 929-All photo-c 4 8 12 26 41 55

BRAVE NEW WORLD (See DCU Brave New World)

BRAVE OLD WORLD (V2K)
DC Comics (Vertigo): Feb, 2000 - No. 4, May, 2000 ($2.50, mini-series)

1-4-Messner-Loeb-s/Guy Davis & Phil Hester-a 3.00

BRAVE ONE, THE (Movie)
Dell Publishing Co.: No. 773, Mar, 1957

Four Color 773-Photo-c 5 10 15 34 55 75

BRAVURA
Malibu Comics (Bravura): 1995 (mail-in offer)

0-wraparound holographic-c; short stories and promo pin-ups of Chaykin's Power & Glory, Gil Kane's & Steven Grant's Edge, Starlin's Breed, & Simonson's Star Slammers 5.00
1 1/2 7.00

BREACH
DC Comics: Mar, 2005 - No. 11, Jan, 2006 ($2.95/$2.50)

1-11: 1-Marcos Martin-a/Bob Harras-s; origin. 4-JLA-c/app. 3.00

BREAKDOWN
Devil's Due Publ.: Oct, 2004 - No. 6, Apr, 2005 ($2.95)

1-6: 1-Two covers by Dave Ross and Leinil Yu; Dixon-s/Ross-a 3.00

BREAKFAST AFTER NOON
Oni Press: May, 2000 - No. 6, Jan, 2001 ($2.95, B&W, limited series)

1-6-Andi Watson-s/a 3.00
TPB (2001, $19.95) r/series 20.00

BREAKING INTO COMICS THE MARVEL WAY
Marvel Comics: May, 2010 - No. 2, May, 2010 ($3.99, limited series)

1,2-Short stories by various newcomer artists; artist profiles 4.00

BREAKNECK BLVD.
MotioN Comics/Slave Labor Graphics Vol. 2: No. 0, Feb, 1994 - No. 2, Nov, 1994; Vol. 2#1, Jul, 1995 - #6, Dec., 1996 ($2.50/$2.95, B&W)

0-2, V2#1-6: 0-Perez/Giordano-c 3.00

BREAK-THRU (Also see Exiles V1#4)
Malibu Comics (Ultraverse): Dec, 1993 - No. 2, Jan, 1994 ($2.50, 44 pgs.)

1,2-Perez-c/a(p); has x-overs in Ultraverse titles 4.00

BREATHTAKER
DC Comics: 1990 - No. 4, 1990 ($4.95, 52 pgs., prestige format, mature)

Book 1-4: Mark Wheatley-painted-c/a & scripts; Marc Hempel-a 5.00
TPB (1994, $14.95) r/#1-4; intro by Neil Gaiman 15.00

'BREED
Malibu Comics (Bravura): Jan, 1994 - No. 6, 1994 ($2.50, limited series)

1-(48 pgs.)-Origin/1st app. of 'Breed by Starlin; contains Bravura stamps; spot varnish-c 4.00
2-6: 2-5-contains Bravura stamps. 6-Death of Rachel 3.00
...:Book of Genesis (1994, $12.95)-reprints #1-6 13.00

'BREED II
Malibu Comics (Bravura): Nov, 1994 - No. 6, Apr, 1995 ($2.95, limited series)

1-6: Starlin-c/a/scripts in all. 1-Gold edition 3.00

'BREED III
Image Comics: May, 2011 - No. 7, Dec, 2011 ($2.99)

1-7: Starlin-c/a/scripts in all 3.00

BREEZE LAWSON, SKY SHERIFF (See Sky Sheriff)

BRENDA LEE'S LIFE STORY

Brenda Starr #5 © SUPR

Brightest Day #16 © DC

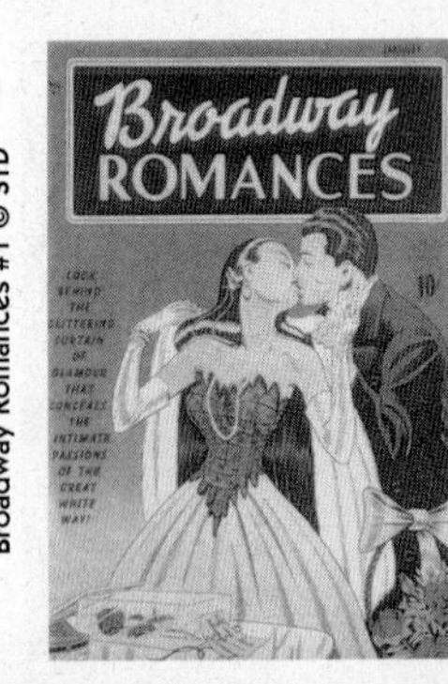

Broadway Romances #1 © STD

Dell Publishing Co.: July-Sept., 1962

	GD 2.0	VG 4.0	FN 6.0	VF 8.0	VF/NM 9.0	NM- 9.2
01-078-209	8	16	24	51	86	120

BRENDA STARR (Also see All Great)
Four Star Comics Corp./Superior Comics Ltd.: No. 13, 9/47; No. 14, 3/48; V2#3, 6/48 - V2#12, 12/49

	GD 2.0	VG 4.0	FN 6.0	VF 8.0	VF/NM 9.0	NM- 9.2
V1#13-By Dale Messick	90	180	270	576	988	1400
14-Classic Kamen bondage-c	181	362	543	1158	1979	2800
V2#3-Baker-a?	71	142	213	454	777	1100
4-Used in **SOTI**, pg. 21; Kamen-c	86	172	258	546	936	1325
5-10	68	136	204	435	743	1050
11,12 (Scarce)	71	142	213	454	777	1100

NOTE: *Newspaper reprints plus original material through #6. All original #7 on.*

BRENDA STARR (...Reporter)(Young Lovers No. 16 on?)
Charlton Comics: No. 13, June, 1955 - No. 15, Oct, 1955

	GD 2.0	VG 4.0	FN 6.0	VF 8.0	VF/NM 9.0	NM- 9.2
13-15-Newspaper-r	32	64	96	188	307	425

BRENDA STARR REPORTER
Dell Publishing Co.: Oct, 1963

	GD 2.0	VG 4.0	FN 6.0	VF 8.0	VF/NM 9.0	NM- 9.2
1	11	22	33	75	148	220

BRER RABBIT (See Kite Fun Book, Walt Disney Showcase #28 and Wheaties)
Dell Publishing Co.: No. 129, 1946; No. 208, Jan, 1949; No. 693, 1956 (Disney)

	GD 2.0	VG 4.0	FN 6.0	VF 8.0	VF/NM 9.0	NM- 9.2
Four Color 129 (#1)-Adapted from Disney movie "Song of the South"	23	46	69	161	343	525
Four Color 208 (1/49)	11	22	33	71	136	200
Four Color 693-Part-r #129	8	16	24	55	93	130

BRIAN BOLLAND'S BLACK BOOK
Eclipse Comics: July, 1985 (one-shot)

	GD 2.0	VG 4.0	FN 6.0	VF 8.0	VF/NM 9.0	NM- 9.2
1-British B&W-r in color						3.00

BRIAN PULIDO'S LADY DEATH... (See Lady Death)

BRICK BRADFORD (Also see Ace Comics & King Comics)
King Features Syndicate/Standard: No. 5, July, 1948 - No. 8, July, 1949 (Ritt & Grey reprints)

	GD 2.0	VG 4.0	FN 6.0	VF 8.0	VF/NM 9.0	NM- 9.2
5	19	38	57	112	176	240
6-Robot-c (by Schomburg?).	37	74	111	222	361	500
7-Schomburg-c. 8-Says #7 inside, #8 on-c	15	30	45	94	147	200

BRIDE'S DIARY (Formerly Black Cobra No. 3)
Ajax/Farrell Publ.: No. 4, May, 1955 - No. 10, Aug, 1956

	GD 2.0	VG 4.0	FN 6.0	VF 8.0	VF/NM 9.0	NM- 9.2
4 (#1)	10	20	30	56	76	95
5-8	8	16	24	40	50	60
9,10-Disbrow-a	9	18	27	50	65	80

BRIDES IN LOVE (Hollywood Romances & Summer Love No. 46 on)
Charlton Comics: Aug, 1956 - No. 45, Feb, 1965

	GD 2.0	VG 4.0	FN 6.0	VF 8.0	VF/NM 9.0	NM- 9.2
1	12	24	36	69	97	125
2	8	16	24	40	50	60
3-6,8-10	4	8	12	22	34	45
7-(68 pgs.)	4	8	12	28	44	60
11-20	3	6	9	16	23	30
21-45	2	4	6	11	16	20

BRIDES ROMANCES
Quality Comics Group: Nov, 1953 - No. 23, Dec, 1956

	GD 2.0	VG 4.0	FN 6.0	VF 8.0	VF/NM 9.0	NM- 9.2
1	16	32	48	94	147	200
2	10	20	30	56	76	95
3-10: Last precode (3/55)	9	18	27	52	69	85
11-17,19-22: 15-Baker-a(p)?; Colan-a	9	18	27	47	61	75
18-Baker-a	10	20	30	58	79	100
23-Baker-c/a	14	28	42	81	118	155

BRIDE'S SECRETS
Ajax/Farrell(Excellent Publ.)/Four-Star: Apr-May, 1954 - No. 19, May, 1958

	GD 2.0	VG 4.0	FN 6.0	VF 8.0	VF/NM 9.0	NM- 9.2
1	14	28	42	80	115	150
2	9	18	27	47	61	75
3-6: Last precode (3/55)	8	16	24	40	50	60
7-11,13-19: 18-Hollingsworth-a	7	14	21	37	46	55
12-Disbrow-a	8	16	24	42	54	65

BRIDE-TO-BE ROMANCES (See True...)

BRIGADE
Image Comics (Extreme Studios): Aug, 1992 - No. 4, 1993 ($1.95, lim. series)

	GD 2.0	VG 4.0	FN 6.0	VF 8.0	VF/NM 9.0	NM- 9.2
1-Liefeld part plots/scripts in all, Liefeld-c(p); contains 2 Brigade trading cards						3.00
1-Gold foil stamped logo edition						8.00
2-Contains coupon for Image Comics #0 & 2 trading cards						3.00
2-With coupon missing						2.00
3,4: 3-Contains 2 trading cards; 1st Birds of Prey. 4-Flip book featuring Youngblood #5						3.00

BRIGADE
Image Comics (Extreme): V2#1, May, 1993 - V2#22, July, 1995, V2#25, May, 1996 ($1.95/$2.50)

	GD 2.0	VG 4.0	FN 6.0	VF 8.0	VF/NM 9.0	NM- 9.2
V2#1-22,25: 1-Gatefold-c; Liefeld co-plots; Blood Brothers part 1; Bloodstrike app. 2-(6/93, V2#1 on inside)-Foil merricote-c (newsstand ed. w/out foil-c exists). 3-Perez-c(i); Liefeld scripts. 8,9-Coupons #2 & 6 for Extreme Prejudice #0 bound-in. 11-(8/94, $2.50) WildC.A.T.S app. 16-Polybagged w/ trading card. 22-"Supreme Apocalypse" Pt. 4; w/ trading card						3.00
0-(9/93)-Liefeld scripts; 1st app. Warcry; Youngblood & Wildcats app.;						3.00
20-Variant-c. by Quesada & Palmiotti						3.00
Sourcebook 1 (8/94, $2.95)						3.00
1-(Awesome Ent., 7/00, $2.99) Flip book w/Century preview						4.00
1-(6/10, $3.99) Liefeld-s/Mychaels-a; covers by Liefeld & Mychaels						4.00

BRIGAND, THE (See Fawcett Movie Comics No. 18)

BRIGHTEST DAY (Also see Blackest Night and Green Lantern)
DC Comics: No. 0, Jun, 2010 - No. 24, Late Jun, 2011 ($3.99/$2.99)

	GD 2.0	VG 4.0	FN 6.0	VF 8.0	VF/NM 9.0	NM- 9.2
0-($3.99) Johns & Tomasi-s/Pasarin-a/Finch-c						4.00
0-Variant-c by Reis						8.00
1-23-($2.99) 1-Black Manta returns. 4-Intro. Jackson (new Aqualad) 16-Aqualad origin. 18-Hawkman & Hawkgirl killed. 20-Aquaman killed						3.00
1-23: Variant covers. 1-6,9-18,20-23-by Reis, 7,8 White Lantern by Sook. 19-by Frank						6.00
24-($4.99) Swamp Thing and John Constantine return to DC universe						5.00
24-($4.99) Variant cover by Reis						8.00
...: The Atom Special (9/10, $2.99) Lemire-s/Asrar-a/Frank-c						3.00
... Volume 1 HC (2010, $29.99) r/#0-7; cover gallery						30.00
... Volume 2 HC (2011, $29.99) r/#8-16; cover gallery						30.00

BRIGHTEST DAY AFTERMATH: THE SEARCH FOR SWAMP THING
DC Comics: Aug, 2011 - No. 3, Oct, 2011 ($2.99, limited series)

	GD 2.0	VG 4.0	FN 6.0	VF 8.0	VF/NM 9.0	NM- 9.2
1-3-Vankin-s/Castiello-a; covers by Syaf & Jones; John Constantine & Zatanna app.						3.00

BRILLIANT
Marvel Comics (Icon): Jul, 2011 - Present ($3.95)

	GD 2.0	VG 4.0	FN 6.0	VF 8.0	VF/NM 9.0	NM- 9.2
1,2-Bendis-s/Bagley-a/c						4.00

BRING BACK THE BAD GUYS (Also see Fireside Book Series)
Marvel Comics: 1998 ($24.95, TPB)

	GD 2.0	VG 4.0	FN 6.0	VF 8.0	VF/NM 9.0	NM- 9.2
1-Reprints stories of Marvel villains' secrets						25.00

BRINGING UP FATHER
Dell Publishing Co.: No. 9, 1942 - No. 37, 1944

	GD 2.0	VG 4.0	FN 6.0	VF 8.0	VF/NM 9.0	NM- 9.2
Large Feature Comic 9	30	60	90	177	289	400
Four Color 37	17	34	51	114	250	385

BRING ON THE BAD GUYS (See Fireside Book Series)

BRING THE THUNDER
Dynamite Entertainment: 2010 - No. 4, 2011 ($3.99)

	GD 2.0	VG 4.0	FN 6.0	VF 8.0	VF/NM 9.0	NM- 9.2
1-4-Alex Ross-c/Ross & Nitz-s/Tortosa-a						4.00

BROADWAY HOLLYWOOD BLACKOUTS
Stanhall: Mar-Apr, 1954 - No. 3, July-Aug, 1954

	GD 2.0	VG 4.0	FN 6.0	VF 8.0	VF/NM 9.0	NM- 9.2
1	15	30	45	83	124	165
2,3	10	20	30	58	79	100

BROADWAY ROMANCES
Quality Comics Group: January, 1950 - No. 5, Sept, 1950

	GD 2.0	VG 4.0	FN 6.0	VF 8.0	VF/NM 9.0	NM- 9.2
1-Ward-c/a (9 pgs.); Gustavson-a	39	78	117	231	378	525
2-Ward-a (9 pgs.); photo-c	26	52	78	154	252	350
3-5: All-Photo-c	15	30	45	85	130	175

BROKEN ARROW (TV)
Dell Publishing Co.: No. 855, Oct, 1957 - No. 947, Nov, 1958

	GD 2.0	VG 4.0	FN 6.0	VF 8.0	VF/NM 9.0	NM- 9.2
Four Color 855 (#1)-Photo-c	6	12	18	37	59	80
Four Color 947-Photo-c	5	10	15	32	51	70

BROKEN CROSS, THE (See The Crusaders)

BROKEN PIECES
Aspen MLT: No. 0, Sept, 2011; Oct, 2011 - No. 5 ($2.50/$3.50, limited series)

	GD 2.0	VG 4.0	FN 6.0	VF 8.0	VF/NM 9.0	NM- 9.2
0-($2.50)-Roslan-s/Kaneshiro-a; three covers						2.50
1,2: 1-($3.50)-Roslan-s/Kaneshiro-a; three covers						3.50

BROKEN TRINITY
Image Comics (Top Cow): July, 2008 - No. 3, Nov, 2008 ($2.99, limited series)

Broken Trinity: Pandora's Box #6 © TCOW

The Brute #2 © Nemesis

Buccaneers #25 © QUA

	GD	VG	FN	VF	VF/NM	NM-
	2.0	4.0	6.0	8.0	9.0	9.2

1-3-Witchblade, Darkness & Angelus app.; Marz-s/Sejic & Hester-a; two covers 3.00
...: Aftermath 1 (4/09, $2.99) Marz & Hill-s/Lucas & Kirkham-a 3.00
...: Angelus 1 (12/08, $2.99) Marz-s/Stelfreeze-a; two covers 3.00
...: Pandora's Box 1-6 (2/10 - No. 6, 4/11 $3.99) Tommy Lee Edwards-c 4.00
...: The Darkness 1 (8/08, $2.99) Hester-s/Lucas-a; two covers 3.00
...: Witchblade 1 (12/08, $2.99) Marz-s/Blake-a; two covers 3.00

BRONCHO BILL (See Comics On Parade, Sparkler & Tip Top Comics)
United Features Syndicate/Standard(Visual Editions) No. 5-on: 1939 - 1940; No. 5, 1?/48 - No. 16, 8?/50

Single Series 2 ('39) 52 104 156 328 552 775
Single Series 19 ('40)(#2 on cvr) 42 84 126 265 445 625
5 15 30 45 84 127 170
6(4/48)-10(4/49) 10 20 30 54 72 90
11(6/49)-16 9 18 27 47 61 75
NOTE: *Schomburg c-6, 7, 9-13, 15, 16.*

BROOKS ROBINSON (See Baseball's Greatest Heroes #2)

BROTHER BILLY THE PAIN FROM PLAINS
Marvel Comics Group: 1979 (68pgs.)

1-B&W comics, satire, Jimmy Carter-c & x-over w/Brother Billy peanut jokes. Joey Adams-a (scarce) 4 8 12 24 37 50

BROTHERHOOD, THE (Also see X-Men titles)
Marvel Comics: July, 2001 - No. 9, Mar, 2002 ($2.25)

1-Intro. Orwell & the Brotherhood; Ribic-a/X-s/Sienkiewicz-c 3.00
2-9: 2-Two covers (JG Jones & Sienkiewicz). 4-6-Fabry-c. 7-9-Phillips-c/a 3.00

BROTHER POWER, THE GEEK (See Saga of Swamp Thing Annual & Vertigo Visions)
National Periodical Publications: Sept-Oct, 1968 - No. 2, Nov-Dec, 1968

1-Origin; Simon-c(i?) 5 10 15 34 55 75
2 3 6 9 20 30 40

BROTHERS, HANG IN THERE, THE
Spire Christian Comics (Fleming H. Revell Co.): 1979 (49¢)

nn 2 4 6 11 16 20

BROTHERS IN ARMS (Based on the World War II military video game)
Dynamite Entertainment: 2008 - No. 4, 2008 ($3.99/$3.50)

1-($3.99) Fabbri-a; two covers by Fabbri & Sejic 4.00
2-4-($3.50) Two covers by Fabbri & Sejic on each 3.50

BROTHERS OF THE SPEAR (Also see Tarzan)
Gold Key/Whitman No. 18: June, 1972 - No. 17, Feb, 1976; No. 18, May, 1982

1 5 10 15 35 55 75
2-Painted-c begin, end #17 3 6 9 19 29 38
3-10 3 6 9 16 22 28
11-18: 12-Line drawn-c. 13-17-Spiegle-a. 18(5/82)-r/#2; Leopard Girl-r 2 4 6 11 16 20

BROTHERS, THE CULT ESCAPE, THE
Spire Christian Comics (Fleming H. Revell Co.): 1980 (49¢)

nn 2 4 6 13 18 22

BROWNIES (See New Funnies)
Dell Publishing Co.: No. 192, July, 1948 - No. 605, Dec, 1954

Four Color 192(#1)-Kelly-a 12 24 36 82 169 255
Four Color 244(9/49), 293 (9/50)-Last Kelly c/a 10 20 30 65 118 170
Four Color 337(7-8/51), 365(12-1/51-52), 398(5/52) 6 12 18 37 59 80
Four Color 436(11/52), 482(7/53), 522(12/53), 605 5 10 15 34 55 75

BRUCE GENTRY
Better/Standard/Four Star Publ./Superior No. 3: Jan, 1948 - No. 8, Jul, 1949

1-Ray Bailey strip reprints begin, end #3; E. C. emblem appears as a monogram on stationery in story; negligee panels 61 122 183 390 670 950
2,3 39 78 117 231 378 525
4-8 26 52 78 154 252 350
NOTE: *Kamenish a-2-7; c-1-8.*

BRUCE JONES' OUTER EDGE
Innovation: 1993 ($2.50, B&W, one-shot)

1-Bruce Jones-c/a/script 3.00

BRUCE LEE (Also see Deadly Hands of Kung Fu)
Malibu Comics: July, 1994 - No. 6, Dec, 1994 ($2.95, 36 pgs.)

1-6: 1-(44 pgs.)-Mortal Kombat prev., 1st app. in comics. 2,6-(36 pgs.) 5.00

BRUCE WAYNE: AGENT OF S.H.I.E.L.D. (Also see Marvel Vs. DC #3 & DC Vs. Marvel #4)
Marvel Comics (Amalgam): Apr, 1996 ($1.95, one-shot)

1-Chuck Dixon scripts & Cary Nord-c/a. 3.00

BRUCE WAYNE: THE ROAD HOME (See Batman: The Return of Bruce Wayne)
(See Batman: Bruce Wayne - The Road Home HC for reprints)
DC Comics: Dec, 2010 ($2.99, series of one-shots with interlocking covers)

...: Batgirl 1 - Bryan Miller-s/Pere Pérez-a 3.00
...: Batman and Robin 1 - Nicieza-s/Richards-a; Vicki Vale app. 3.00
...: Catwoman 1 - Fridolfs-s/Nguyen-a; Harley & Ivy app. 3.00
...: Commissioner Gordon 1 - Beechen-s/Kudranski-a; Penguin app. 3.00
...: Oracle 1 - Andreyko-s/Padilla-a; Man-Bat & Manhunter app. 3.00
...: Outsiders 1 - Barr-s/Saltares-a 3.00
...: Ra's al Ghul 1 - Nicieza-s/McDaniel-a 3.00
...: Red Robin 1 - Nicieza-s/Bachs-a; Ra's al Ghul app. 3.00

BRUISER
Anthem Publications: Feb, 1994 ($2.45)

1 3.00

BRUTE, THE
Seaboard Publ. (Atlas): Feb, 1975 - No. 3, July, 1975

1-Origin & 1st app; Sekowsky-a(p) 2 4 6 13 18 22
2-Sekowsky-a(p); Fleisher-s 2 4 6 9 12 15
3-Brunner/Starlin/Weiss-a(p) 2 4 6 10 14 18

BRUTE & BABE
Ominous Press: July, 1994 - No. 2, Aug, 1994

1-($3.95, 8 tablets plus-c)-"...It Begins..."; tablet format 4.00
2-($2.50, 36 pgs.)-"Mael's Rage", 2-(40 pgs.)-Stiff additional variant-c 3.00

BRUTE FORCE
Marvel Comics: Aug, 1990 - No. 4, Nov, 1990 ($1.00, limited series)

1-4: Animal super-heroes; Delbo & DeCarlo-a 3.00

B-SIDES (The Craptacular...)
Marvel Comics: Nov, 2002 - No. 3, Jan, 2003 ($2.99, limited series)

1-3-Kieth-c/Weldele-a. 2-Dorkin-a (1 pg.) 2-FF cameo. 3-FF app. 3.00

BUBBLEGUM CRISIS: GRAND MAL
Dark Horse Comics: Mar, 1994 - No. 4, June, 1994 ($2.50, limited series)

1-4-Japanese manga 3.00

BUCCANEER
I. W. Enterprises: No date (1963)

I.W. Reprint #1(r-/Quality #20), #8(r-/#23): Crandall-a in each 3 6 9 16 23 30

BUCCANEERS (Formerly Kid Eternity)
Quality Comics: No. 19, Jan, 1950 - No. 27, May, 1951 (No. 24-27: 52 pgs.)

19-Captain Daring, Black Roger, Eric Falcon & Spanish Main begin; Crandall-a 48 96 144 302 514 725
20,23-Crandall-a 36 72 108 215 350 485
21-Crandall-c/a 39 78 117 236 388 540
22-Bondage-c 28 56 84 165 270 375
24-26: 24-Adam Peril, U.S.N. begins. 25-Origin & 1st app. Corsair Queen. 26-last Spanish Main 24 48 72 142 234 325
27-Crandall-c/a 34 68 102 205 335 465
Super Reprint #12 (1964)-Crandall-r/#21 3 6 9 16 23 30

BUCCANEERS, THE (TV)
Dell Publishing Co.: No. 800, 1957

Four Color 800-Photo-c 7 14 21 46 76 105

BUCKAROO BANZAI (Movie)
Marvel Comics Group: Dec, 1984 - No. 2, Feb, 1985

1,2-Movie adaptation; r/Marvel Super Special #33; Texiera-c/a 3.00

BUCKAROO BANZAI: RETURN OF THE SCREW
Moonstone: 2006 - No. 3, 2006 ($3.50, limited series)

1-3: 1-Three covers by Haley, Stribling, Beck; Thompson-a 3.50
Preview (2006, 50¢) B&W preview; history of movie and spin-off projects 3.00

BUCK DUCK
Atlas Comics (ANC): June, 1953 - No. 4, Dec, 1953

1-Funny animal stories in all 16 32 48 94 147 200
2-4: 2-Ed Win-a(5) 10 20 30 58 79 100

BUCK JONES (Also see Crackajack Funnies, Famous Feature Stories, Master Comics #7 & Wow Comics #1, 1936)
Dell Publishing Co.: No. 299, Oct, 1950 - No. 850, Oct, 1957 (All Painted-c)

Buck Rogers (2009 series) #2 © Dille family

Bucky O'Hare #4 © Continuity

Buffy the Vampire Slayer (2007 series) #8 © 20th Century Fox

	GD 2.0	VG 4.0	FN 6.0	VF 8.0	VF/NM 9.0	NM- 9.2
Four Color 299(#1)-Buck Jones & his horse Silver-B begin; painted back-c begins, ends #5	12	24	36	79	160	240
2(4-6/51)	8	16	24	51	86	120
3-8(10-12/52)	6	12	18	42	69	95
Four Color 460,500,546,589	6	12	18	41	66	90
Four Color 652,733,850	5	10	15	32	51	70

BUCK ROGERS (Also see Famous Funnies, Pure Oil Comics, Salerno Carnival of Comics, 24 Pages of Comics, & Vicks Comics)
Famous Funnies: Winter, 1940-41 - No. 6, Sept, 1943
NOTE: Buck Rogers first appeared in the pulp magazine Amazing Stories Vol. 3 #5 in Aug, 1928.

	GD	VG	FN	VF	VF/NM	NM-
1-Sunday strip reprints by Rick Yager; begins with strip #190; Calkins-c	320	640	960	2240	3920	5600
2 (7/41)-Calkins-c	135	270	405	864	1482	2100
3 (12/41), 4 (7/42)	116	232	348	742	1271	1800
5,6: 5-Story continues with Famous Funnies No. 80; Buck Rogers, Sky Roads. 6-Reprints of 1939 dailies; contains B.R. story "Crater of Doom" (2 pgs.) by Calkins not-r from Famous Funnies	97	194	291	621	1061	1500

BUCK ROGERS
Toby Press: No. 100, Jan, 1951 - No. 9, May-June, 1951

	GD	VG	FN	VF	VF/NM	NM-
100(#7)-All strip-r begin; Anderson, Chatton-a	31	62	93	182	296	410
101(#8), 9-All Anderson-a(1947-49-r/dailies)	23	46	69	136	223	310

BUCK ROGERS (...in the 25th Century No. 5 on) (TV)
Gold Key/Whitman No. 7 on: Oct, 1964; No. 2, July, 1979 - No. 16, May, 1982 (No #10; story was written but never released. #17 exists only as a press proof without covers and was never published)

	GD	VG	FN	VF	VF/NM	NM-
1(10128-410, 12¢)-1st S.A. app. Buck Rogers & 1st new B. R. in comics since 1933 giveaway; painted-c; back-c pin-up	10	20	30	69	130	190
2(7/79)-6: 3,4,6-Movie adaptation; painted-c	2	4	6	9	12	15
7,11 (Whitman)	2	4	6	11	16	20
8,9 (prepack)(scarce)	3	6	9	20	30	40
12-16: 14(2/82), 15(3/82), 16(5/82)	2	4	6	8	10	12
Giant Movie Edition 11296(64pp, Whitman, $1.50), reprints GK #2-4 minus cover; tabloid size; photo-c (See Marvel Treasury)	3	6	9	18	27	35
Giant Movie Edition 02489(Western/Marvel, $1.50), reprints GK #2-4 minus cover	3	6	9	17	25	32

NOTE: ***Bolle*** *a-2p,3p, Movie Ed.(p).* ***McWilliams*** *a-2i,3i, 5-11, Movie Ed.(i). Painted c-1-9,11-13.*

BUCK ROGERS (Comics Module)
TSR, Inc.: 1990 - No. 10, 1991 ($2.95, 44 pgs.)

1-10 (1990): 1-Begin origin in 3 parts. 2-Indicia says #1. 2,3-Black Barney back-up story. 4-All Black Barney issue; B. B.-c. 5-Indicia says #6; Black Barney-c & lead story; Buck Rogers back-up story. 10-Flip book (72pgs.)	4.00

BUCK ROGERS
Dynamite Entertainment: No. 0, 2009 - No. 12, 2010 (25¢/$3.50)

0-(25¢) Beatty-s/Rafael-a/Cassaday-c	3.00
1-12: 1-($3.50) Three covers by Cassaday, Ross and Wagner; origin re-told	3.50
Annual 1 (2011, $4.99) Rafael-a; covers by Rafael & Sadowski	5.00

BUCKSKIN (TV)
Dell Publishing Co.: No. 1011, July, 1959 - No. 1107, June-Aug, 1960

	GD	VG	FN	VF	VF/NM	NM-
Four Color 1011 (#1)-Photo-c	7	14	21	46	76	105
Four Color 1107-Photo-c	6	12	18	42	69	95

BUCKY O'HARE (Funny Animal)
Continuity Comics: 1988 ($5.95, graphic novel)

	GD	VG	FN	VF	VF/NM	NM-
1-Golden-c/a(r); r/serial-Echo of Futurepast #1-6	1	2	3	4	5	7
Deluxe Hardcover ($40.00, 52 pg., 8 x 11")						40.00

BUCKY O'HARE
Continuity Comics: Jan, 1991 - No. 5, 1991 ($2.00)

1-6: 1-Michael Golden-c/a	3.00

BUDDIES IN THE U.S. ARMY
Avon Periodicals: Nov, 1952 - No. 2, 1953

	GD	VG	FN	VF	VF/NM	NM-
1-Lawrence-c	14	28	42	80	115	150
2-Mort Lawrence-c/a	10	20	30	54	72	90

BUFFALO BEE (TV)
Dell Publishing Co.: No. 957, Nov, 1958 - No. 1061, Dec-Feb, 1959-60

	GD	VG	FN	VF	VF/NM	NM-
Four Color 957 (#1)	8	16	24	56	96	135
Four Color 1002 (8-10/59), 1061	7	14	21	44	72	100

BUFFALO BILL (See Frontier Fighters, Super Western Comics & Western Action Thrillers)
Youthful Magazines: No. 2, Oct, 1950 - No. 9, Dec, 1951

	GD	VG	FN	VF	VF/NM	NM-
2-Annie Oakley story	14	28	42	80	115	150
3-9: 2-4-Walter Johnson-c/a. 9-Wildey-a	10	20	30	54	72	90

BUFFALO BILL CODY (See Cody of the Pony Express)

BUFFALO BILL, JR. (TV) (See Western Roundup)
Dell/Gold Key: Jan, 1956 - No. 13, Aug-Oct, 1959; 1965 (All photo-c)

	GD	VG	FN	VF	VF/NM	NM-
Four Color 673 (#1)	9	18	27	58	99	140
Four Color 742,766,798,828,856(11/57)	6	12	18	39	62	85
7(2-4/58)-13	5	10	15	34	55	75
1(6/65, Gold Key)-Photo-c(r/F.C. #798); photo-b/c	4	8	12	24	37	50

BUFFALO BILL PICTURE STORIES
Street & Smith Publications: June-July, 1949 - No. 2, Aug-Sept, 1949

	GD	VG	FN	VF	VF/NM	NM-
1,2-Wildey, Powell-a in each	14	28	42	78	112	145

BUFFY THE VAMPIRE SLAYER (Based on the TV series)(Also see Tales of the Vampires)
Dark Horse Comics: 1998 - No. 63, Nov, 2003 ($2.95/$2.99)

	GD	VG	FN	VF	VF/NM	NM-
1-Bennett-a/Watson-s; Art Adams-c	1	2	3	5	7	9
1-Variant photo-c	1	2	3	5	7	9
1-Gold foil logo Art Adams-c						15.00
1-Gold foil logo photo-c						20.00
2-15-Regular and photo-c. 4-7-Gomez-a. 5,8-Green-c						5.00
16-48: 29,30-Angel x-over. 43-45-Death of Buffy. 47-Lobdell-s begin. 48-Pike returns						3.00
50-($3.50) Scooby gang battles Adam; back-up story by Watson						4.00
51-63: 51-54-Viva Las Buffy; pre-Sunnydale Buffy & Pike in Vegas						3.00
Annual '99 ($4.95)-Two stories and pin-ups	1	2	3	4	5	7
...: A Stake to the Heart TPB (3/04, $12.95) r/#60-63						13.00
...: Chaos Bleeds (6/03, $2.99) Based on the video game; photo & Campbell-c						3.00
...: Creatures of Habit (3/02, $17.95) text with Horton & Paul Lee-a						18.00
...: Jonathan 1 (1/01, $2.99) two covers; Richards-a						3.00
...: Lost and Found 1 (3/02, $2.99) aftermath of Buffy's death; Richards-a						3.00
... Lovers Walk (2/01, $2.99) short stories by various; Richards & photo-c						3.00
...: Note From the Underground (3/03, $12.95) r/#47-50						13.00
...: Omnibus Vol. 1 (7/07, $24.95, 9x6") r/Spike & Dru #3, Origin #1-3 and Buffy #51-59						25.00
...: Omnibus Vol. 2 (9/07, $24.95, 9x6") r/Buffy #60-63 and various one-shots & specials						25.00
...: Omnibus Vol. 3 (1/08, $24.95, 9x6") r/Buffy #1-8,12,16, Annual '99						25.00
...: Omnibus Vol. 4 (5/08, $24.95, 9x6") r/Buffy #9-11,13-15,17-20,50 and various						25.00
...: Omnibus Vol. 5 (9/08, $24.95, 9x6") r/Buffy #21-28 and various one-shots & specials						25.00
...: Omnibus Vol. 6 (2/09, $24.95, 9x6") r/Buffy #29-38 and various one-shots & specials						25.00
...: One For One (9/10, $1.00) r/#1 with red cover frame						3.00
...: Reunion (6/02, $3.50) Buffy & Angel's; Espenson-s; art by various						3.50
...: Slayer Interrupted TPB (2003, $14.95) r/#56-59						15.00
...: Tales of the Slayers (10/02, $3.50) art by Matsuda and Colan; art & photo-c						3.50
...: The Death of Buffy TPB (8/02, $15.95) r/#43-46						16.00
...: Viva Las Buffy TPB (7/03, $12.95) r/#51-54						13.00
Wizard #1/2	1	2	3	6	8	9

BUFFY THE VAMPIRE SLAYER ("Season Eight" of the TV series)
Dark Horse Comics: Mar, 2007 - No. 40, Jan, 2011 ($2.99)

1-Joss Whedon-s/Georges Jeanty-a/Jo Chen-c	6.00
1-Variant cover by Jeanty	6.00
1-RRP with B&W Jeanty cover (edition of 1000)	70.00
1-4: 1-2nd thru 5th printings. 2-2nd-4th printings. 3,4-2nd & 3rd printings	3.00
2-5-Jeanty-a; covers by Chen & Jeanty	4.00
6-13,16-19-Two covers by Chen & Jeanty. 6-9-Faith app.; Vaughan-s. 10,11-Whedon-s. 12-15-Goddard-s; Dracula app. 16-19-Fray app.; Whedon-s/Moline-a	3.00
20-40: 20-28,31-40-Two covers by Chen and Jeanty. 20-Animation style flashback. 21,26-30-Espenson-s. 30-Hughes-c. 31-Whedon-s. 32-35-Meltzer-s. 36-40-Whedon-s	3.00
...: Riley (8/10, $3.50) Espensen-s/Moline-a; Riley Finn and Sam; Angel app.	3.50
... Tales of the Vampires (6/09, $2.99) Cloonan-s/Lolos-a; covers by Chen & Bá/Moon	3.00
...: Willow (12/09, $3.50) Whedon-s/Moline-a; Willow meets the Snake Guide	3.50
...: Volume One: The Long Way Home TPB (11/07, $15.95) r/#1-5 and variant covers	16.00
...: Volume Two: No Future for You TPB (6/08, $15.95) r/#6-10 and variant covers	16.00
...: Volume Three: Wolves at the Gate TPB (11/08, $15.95) r/#11-15 and variant covers	16.00
...: Volume Four: Time of Your Life TPB (5/09, $15.95) r/#16-20 and variant covers	16.00
...: Volume Five: Predators and Prey TPB (9/09, $15.95) r/#21-25 and variant covers	16.00
...: Volume Six: Retreat TPB (3/10, $15.99) r/#26-30 and stories from MySpace DHP	16.00
...: Volume Seven: Twilight TPB (10/10, $16.99) r/#31-35 and Willow one-shot	17.00
...: Volume Eight: Last Gleaming TPB (6/11, $16.99) r/#36-40 and Riley one-shot	17.00

NOTE: *Later printings have Jo Chen cover art with different credit graphics.*

BUFFY THE VAMPIRE SLAYER ("Season Nine" of the TV series)
Dark Horse Comics: Sept, 2011 - Present ($2.99)

1-6: 1-Whedon-s/Jeanty-a; covers by Morris & Chen. 2-5-Chambliss-s; two covers by Morris & Jeanty. 6,7-Two covers by Jeanty & Noto	3.00

Buffy the Vampire Slayer: The Origin #1 © 20th Century Fox

Bugs Bunny #62 © WB

Bulletman #6 © FAW

BUFFY THE VAMPIRE SLAYER: ANGEL
Dark Horse Comics: May, 1999 - No. 3, July, 1999 ($2.95, limited series)

	GD 2.0	VG 4.0	FN 6.0	VF 8.0	VF/NM 9.0	NM- 9.2
1-3-Gomez-a; Matsuda-c & photo-c for each						3.00

BUFFY THE VAMPIRE SLAYER: GILES
Dark Horse Comics: Oct, 2000 ($2.95, one-shot)

	GD 2.0	VG 4.0	FN 6.0	VF 8.0	VF/NM 9.0	NM- 9.2
1-Eric Powell-a; Powell & photo-c						3.00

BUFFY THE VAMPIRE SLAYER: HAUNTED
Dark Horse Comics: Dec, 2001 - No. 4, Mar, 2002 ($2.99, limited series)

	GD 2.0	VG 4.0	FN 6.0	VF 8.0	VF/NM 9.0	NM- 9.2
1-4-Faith and the Mayor app.; Espenson-s/Richards-a						3.00
TPB (9/02, $12.95) r/series; photo-c						13.00

BUFFY THE VAMPIRE SLAYER: OZ
Dark Horse Comics: July, 2001 - No. 3, Sept, 2001 ($2.99, limited series)

	GD 2.0	VG 4.0	FN 6.0	VF 8.0	VF/NM 9.0	NM- 9.2
1-3-Totleben & photo-c; Golden-s						3.00

BUFFY THE VAMPIRE SLAYER: SPIKE AND DRU
Dark Horse Comics: Apr, 1999; No. 2, Oct, 1999; No. 3, Dec, 2000 ($2.95)

	GD 2.0	VG 4.0	FN 6.0	VF 8.0	VF/NM 9.0	NM- 9.2
1-3: 1,2-Photo-c. 3-Two covers (photo & Sook)						3.00

BUFFY THE VAMPIRE SLAYER: THE ORIGIN (Adapts movie screenplay)
Dark Horse Comics: Jan, 1999 - No. 3, Mar, 1999 ($2.95, limited series)

	GD 2.0	VG 4.0	FN 6.0	VF 8.0	VF/NM 9.0	NM- 9.2
1-3-Brereton-s/Bennett-a; reg & photo-c for each						3.00

BUFFY THE VAMPIRE SLAYER: WILLOW & TARA
Dark Horse Comics: Apr, 2001 ($2.99, one-shot)

	GD 2.0	VG 4.0	FN 6.0	VF 8.0	VF/NM 9.0	NM- 9.2
1-Terry Moore-a/Chris Golden & Amber Benson-s; Moore-c & photo-c						3.00
TPB (4/03, $9.95) r/#1 & W&T - Wilderness; photo-c						10.00

BUFFY THE VAMPIRE SLAYER: WILLOW & TARA - WILDERNESS
Dark Horse Comics: Jul, 2002 - No. 2, Sept, 2002 ($2.99, limited series)

	GD 2.0	VG 4.0	FN 6.0	VF 8.0	VF/NM 9.0	NM- 9.2
1,2-Chris Golden & Amber Benson-s; Jothikaumar-c & photo-c						3.00

BUG
Marvel Comics: Mar, 1997 ($2.99, one-shot)

	GD 2.0	VG 4.0	FN 6.0	VF 8.0	VF/NM 9.0	NM- 9.2
1-Micronauts character						3.00

BUGALOOS (Sid & Marty Krofft TV show)
Charlton Comics: Sept, 1971 - No. 4, Feb, 1972

	GD 2.0	VG 4.0	FN 6.0	VF 8.0	VF/NM 9.0	NM- 9.2
1	5	10	15	32	51	70
2-4	3	6	9	20	30	40

NOTE: *No. 3(1/72) went on sale late in 1972 (after No. 4) with the 1/73 issues.*

BUGHOUSE (Satire)
Ajax/Farrell (Excellent Publ.): Mar-Apr, 1954 - No. 4, Sept-Oct, 1954

	GD 2.0	VG 4.0	FN 6.0	VF 8.0	VF/NM 9.0	NM- 9.2
V1#1	22	44	66	128	209	290
2-4	14	28	42	80	115	150

BUGS BUNNY (See The Best of..., Camp Comics, Comic Album #2, 6, 10, 14, Dell Giant #28, 32, 46, Dynabrite, Golden Comics Digest #1, 3, 5, 6, 8, 10, 14, 15, 17, 21, 26, 30, 34, 39, 42, 47, Kite Fun Book, Large Feature Comic #8, Looney Tunes and Merry Melodies, March of Comics #44, 59, 75, 83, 97, 115, 132, 149, 160, 179, 188, 201, 220, 231, 245, 259, 273, 287, 301, 315, 329, 343, 363, 367, 380, 392, 403, 415, 428, 440, 452, 464, 476, 487, Porky Pig, Puffed Wheat, Story Hour Series #802, Super Book #14, 26 and Whitman Comic Books)

BUGS BUNNY (See Dell Giants for annuals)
Dell Publishing Co./Gold Key No. 86-218/Whitman No. 219 on: 1942 - No. 245, April, 1984

	GD 2.0	VG 4.0	FN 6.0	VF 8.0	VF/NM 9.0	NM- 9.2
Large Feature Comic 8(1942)-(Rarely found in fine-mint condition)	226	452	678	1446	2473	3500
Four Color 33 ('43)	96	192	288	778	1689	2600
Four Color 51	32	64	96	232	504	775
Four Color 88	21	42	63	148	317	485
Four Color 123('46),142,164	14	28	42	97	211	325
Four Color 187,200,217,233	11	22	33	77	154	230
Four Color 250-Used in **SOTI**, pg. 309	12	24	36	79	160	240
Four Color 266,274,281,289,298('50)	10	20	30	66	121	175
Four Color 307,317(#1),327(#2),338,347,355,366,376,393	9	18	27	60	103	145
Four Color 407,420,432(10/52)	8	16	24	51	86	120
Four Color 498(9/53),585(9/54), 647(9/55)	6	12	18	41	66	90
Four Color 724(9/56),838(9/57),1064(12/59)	5	10	15	35	55	75
28(12-1/52-53)-30	6	12	18	39	62	85
31-50	5	10	15	30	48	65
51-85(7-9/62)	4	8	12	24	37	50
86(10/62)-88-Bugs Bunny's Showtime-(25¢, 80pgs.)	6	12	18	41	66	90
89-99	3	6	9	17	25	32
100	3	6	9	18	27	35
101-118: 108-1st Honey Bunny. 118-Last 12¢ issue	3	6	9	14	19	24
119-140	2	4	6	11	16	20
141-170	2	4	6	9	12	15
171-218: 218-Publ. by Whitman only?	2	4	6	8	10	12
219,220,225-237(5/82): 229-Swipe of Barks story/WDC&S #223. 233(2/82)	2	4	6	8	10	12
221(9/80),222(11/80)-Pre-pack? (Scarce)	4	8	12	22	34	45
223 (1/81, 50¢-c), 224 (3/81)-Low distr.	2	4	6	11	16	20
223 (1/81, 40¢-c) Cover price error variant	3	6	9	16	22	28
238-245 (#90070 on-c, nd, nd code; pre-pack): 238(5/83), 239(6/83), 240(7/83), 241(7/83), 242(8/83), 243(8/83), 244(3/84), 245(4/84)	3	6	9	14	19	24

NOTE: *Reprints-100,102-104,110,115,123,143,144,147,167,173,175-177,179-185,187,190.*

	GD 2.0	VG 4.0	FN 6.0	VF 8.0	VF/NM 9.0	NM- 9.2
nn (Xerox Pub. Comic Digest, 1971, 100 pages, B&W) collection of one-page gags	4	8	12	24	37	50
...Comic-Go-Round 11196-(224 pgs.)($1.95)(Golden Press, 1979)	4	8	12	26	41	55
...Winter Fun 1(12/67-Gold Key)-Giant	5	10	15	32	51	70

BUGS BUNNY
DC Comics: June, 1990 - No. 3, Aug, 1990 ($1.00, limited series)

	GD 2.0	VG 4.0	FN 6.0	VF 8.0	VF/NM 9.0	NM- 9.2
1-3: Daffy Duck, Elmer Fudd, others app.						4.00

BUGS BUNNY (...Monthly on-c)
DC Comics: 1993 - No. 3, 1994? ($1.95)

	GD 2.0	VG 4.0	FN 6.0	VF 8.0	VF/NM 9.0	NM- 9.2
1-3-Bugs, Porky Pig, Daffy, Road Runner						3.50

BUGS BUNNY (Digest-size reprints from Looney Tunes)
DC Comics: 2005 - Present ($6.99, digest)

	GD 2.0	VG 4.0	FN 6.0	VF 8.0	VF/NM 9.0	NM- 9.2
Vol. 1: What's Up Doc? - Reprints from Looney Tunes #37,41,43-45,48,52,55,57-59,63						7.00

BUGS BUNNY & PORKY PIG
Gold Key: Sept, 1965 (Paper-c, giant, 100 pgs.)

	GD 2.0	VG 4.0	FN 6.0	VF 8.0	VF/NM 9.0	NM- 9.2
1(30025-509)	7	14	21	45	73	100

BUGS BUNNY'S ALBUM (See Bugs Bunny, Four Color No. 498,585,647,724)

BUGS BUNNY LIFE STORY ALBUM (See Bugs Bunny, Four Color No. 838)

BUGS BUNNY MERRY CHRISTMAS (See Bugs Bunny, Four Color No. 1064)

BUILDING, THE
Kitchen Sink Press: 1987; 2000 (8 1/2" x 11" sepia toned graphic novel)

	GD 2.0	VG 4.0	FN 6.0	VF 8.0	VF/NM 9.0	NM- 9.2
nn-Will Eisner-s/c/a						10.00
nn-(DC Comics, 9/00, $9.95) reprints 1987 edition						10.00

BULLET CROW, FOWL OF FORTUNE
Eclipse Comics: Mar, 1987 - No. 2, Apr, 1987 ($2.00, B&W, limited series)

	GD 2.0	VG 4.0	FN 6.0	VF 8.0	VF/NM 9.0	NM- 9.2
1,2-The Comic Reader-r & new-a						3.00

BULLETMAN (See Fawcett Miniatures, Master Comics, Mighty Midget Comics, Nickel Comics & XMas Comics)
Fawcett Publications: Sum, 1941 - #12, 2/12/43; #14, Spr, 1946 - #16, Fall, 1946 (No #13)

	GD 2.0	VG 4.0	FN 6.0	VF 8.0	VF/NM 9.0	NM- 9.2
1-Silver metallic-c	389	778	1167	2723	4762	6800
2-Raboy-c	171	342	513	1086	1868	2650
3,5-Raboy-c each	139	278	417	883	1517	2150
4	97	194	291	621	1061	1500
6,8-10: 10-Intro. Bulletdog	82	164	246	528	902	1275
7-Ghost Stories told by night watchman of cemetery begins; Eisnerish-a; hidden message "Chic Stone is a jerk".	92	184	276	584	1005	1425
11,12,14-16 (nn 13): 12-Robot-c	60	120	180	381	653	925

NOTE: ***Mac Raboy** c-1-3, 5, 6, 10. "Bulletman the Flying Detective" on cover #8 on.*

BULLET POINTS
Marvel Comics: Jan, 2007 - No. 5, May, 2007 ($2.99, limited series)

	GD 2.0	VG 4.0	FN 6.0	VF 8.0	VF/NM 9.0	NM- 9.2
1-5: 1-Steve Rogers becomes Iron Man; Straczynski-s/Edwards-a. 4,5-Galactus app.						3.00
TPB (2007, $13.99) r/#1-5; layout pages by Edwards						14.00

BULLETPROOF MONK (Inspired the 2003 film)
Image Comics (Flypaper Press): 1998 - No. 3, 1999 ($2.95, limited series)

	GD 2.0	VG 4.0	FN 6.0	VF 8.0	VF/NM 9.0	NM- 9.2
1-3-Oeming-a						3.00
...: Tales of the BPM (3/03, $2.95) Flip book; 2 covers by Sale; art by Sale, Oeming, Dave Johnson; Seann William Scott afterword						3.00
TPB (2002, $9.95) r/#1-3; foreword by John Woo						10.00

BULLETS AND BRACELETS (Also see Marvel Versus DC #3 & DC Versus Marvel #4)
Marvel Comics (Amalgam): Apr, 1996 ($1.95)

	GD 2.0	VG 4.0	FN 6.0	VF 8.0	VF/NM 9.0	NM- 9.2
1-John Ostrander script & Gary Frank-c/a						3.00

BULLS-EYE (Cody of The Pony Express No. 8 on)
Mainline No. 1-5/Charlton No. 6,7: 7-8/54-No. 5, 3-4/55; No. 6, 6/55; No. 7, 8/55

	GD 2.0	VG 4.0	FN 6.0	VF 8.0	VF/NM 9.0	NM- 9.2
1-S&K-c, 2 pgs.-a	65	130	195	416	708	1000

Bullseye: Greatest Hits #1 © MAR

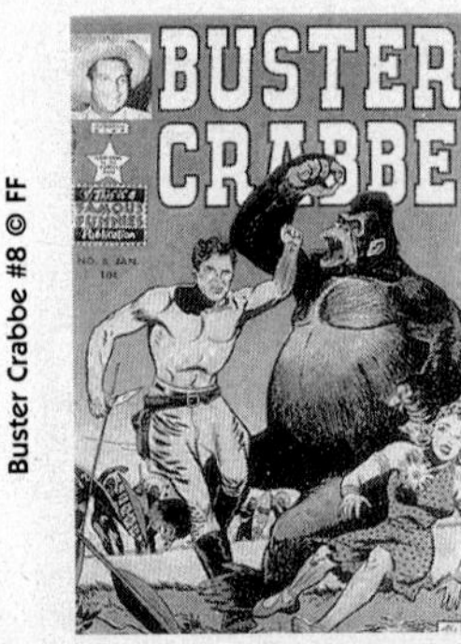

Buster Crabbe #8 © FF

Buzzy #49 © DC

GD VG FN VF VF/NM NM-
2.0 4.0 6.0 8.0 9.0 9.2

2-S&K-c/a 52 104 156 322 549 775
3-5-S&K-c/a(2 each). 4-Last pre-code issue (1-2/55). 5-Censored issue with tomahawks removed in battle scene 42 84 126 265 445 625
6-S&K-c/a 39 78 117 231 378 525
7-S&K-c/a(3) 42 84 126 265 445 625

BULLS-EYE COMICS (Formerly Komik Pages #10; becomes Kayo #12)
Harry 'A' Chesler: No. 11, 1944
11-Origin K-9, Green Knight's sidekick, Lance; The Green Knight, Lady Satan, Yankee Doodle Jones app. 47 94 141 296 498 700

BULLSEYE: GREATEST HITS (Daredevil villain)
Marvel Comics: Nov, 2004 - No. 5, Mar, 2005 ($2.99, limted series)
1-5-Origin of Bullseye; Steve Dillon-a/Deodato-c. 3-Punisher app. 3.00
TPB (2005, $13.99) r/#1-5 14.00

BULLSEYE: PERFECT GAME (Daredevil villain)
Marvel Comics: Jan, 2011 - No. 2, Feb, 2011 ($3.99, limited series)
1,2-Huston-s/Martinbrough-a; Bullseye as baseball pitcher 4.00

BULLWHIP GRIFFIN (See Movie Comics)

BULLWINKLE (...and Rocky No. 22 on; See March of Comics #233 and Rocky & Bullwinkle) (TV) (Jay Ward)
Dell/Gold Key: 3-5/62 - #11, 4/74; #12, 6/76 - #19, 3/78; #20, 4/79 - #25, 2/80
Four Color 1270 (3-5/62) 16 32 48 111 243 375
01-090-209 (Dell, 7-9/62) 13 26 39 88 189 290
1(11/62, Gold Key) 12 24 36 84 175 265
2(2/63) 9 18 27 61 106 150
3(4/72)-11(4/74-Gold Key) 5 10 15 34 55 75
12-14: 12(6/76)-Reprints. 13(9/76), 14-New stories 3 6 9 18 27 35
15-25 2 4 6 11 16 20
Mother Moose Nursery Pomes 01-530-207 (5-7/62, Dell) 15 30 45 102 221 340
NOTE: *Reprints: 6, 7, 20-24.*

BULLWINKLE AND ROCKY (TV)
Charlton Comics: July, 1970 - No. 7, July, 1971
1-Has 1 pg. pin-up 7 14 21 46 76 105
2-7: 3-Snidely Whiplash app. 5 10 15 32 51 70

BULLWINKLE AND ROCKY
Star Comics/Marvel Comics No. 3 on: Nov, 1987 - No. 9, Mar, 1989
1-9: Boris & Natasha in all. 3,5,8-Dudley Do-Right app. 4-Reagan-c 4.50
Marvel Moosterworks (1/92, $4.95) 2 4 6 8 10 12

BUMMER
Fantagraphics Books: June, 1995 ($3.50, B&W, mature)
1 3.50

BUNNY (Also see Harvey Pop Comics and Fruitman Special)
Harvey Publications: Dec, 1966 - No. 20, Dec, 1971; No. 21, Nov, 1976
1-68 pg. Giants begin 8 16 24 56 96 135
2-10: 2-1st app. Fruitman 5 10 15 30 48 65
11-18: 18-Last 68 pg. Giant 4 8 12 28 44 60
19-21-52 pg. Giants: 21-Fruitman app. 4 8 12 26 41 55

BURKE'S LAW (TV)
Dell Publ.: 1-3/64; No. 2, 5-7/64; No. 3, 3-5/65 (All have Gene Barry photo-c)
1-Photo-c 5 10 15 34 55 75
2,3-Photo-c 4 8 12 24 37 50

BURNING ROMANCES (See Fox Giants)

BUSTER BEAR
Quality Comics Group (Arnold Publ.): Dec, 1953 - No. 10, June, 1955
1-Funny animal 11 22 33 60 83 105
2 7 14 21 35 43 50
3-10 6 12 18 28 34 40
I.W. Reprint #9,10 (Super on inside) 2 4 6 9 13 16

BUSTER BROWN COMICS (See Promotional Comics section)

BUSTER BUNNY
Standard Comics(Animated Cartoons)/Pines: Nov, 1949 - No. 16, Oct, 1953
1-Frazetta 1 pg. text illo. 11 22 33 60 83 105
2 7 14 21 35 43 50
3-14,16 6 12 18 28 34 40
15-Racist-c 10 20 30 54 72 90

BUSTER CRABBE (TV)
Famous Funnies Publ.: Nov, 1951 - No. 12, 1953
1-1st app.(?) Frazetta anti-drug ad; text story about Buster Crabbe & Billy the Kid 39 78 117 235 385 535
2-Williamson/Evans-c; text story about Wild Bill Hickok & Pecos Bill 37 74 111 218 354 490
3-Williamson/Evans-c/a 39 78 117 231 378 525
4-Frazetta-c/a, 1pg.; bondage-c 47 94 141 296 498 700
5-Frazetta-c; Williamson/Krenkel/Orlando-a, 11pgs. (per Mr. Williamson) 124 248 372 787 1356 1925
6,8 19 38 57 109 172 235
7-Frazetta one pg. ad 19 38 57 111 176 240
9-One pg. Frazetta Boy Scouts ad (1st?) 15 30 45 94 147 200
10-12 12 24 36 69 97 125
NOTE: Eastern Color sold 3 dozen each NM file copies of #s 9-12 a few years ago.

BUSTER CRABBE (The Amazing Adventures of...)(Movie star)
Lev Gleason Publications: Dec, 1953 - No. 4, June, 1954
1,4: 1-Photo-c. 4-Flash Gordon-c 21 42 63 122 199 275
2,3-Toth-a 19 38 57 111 176 240

BUTCH CASSIDY
Skywald Comics: June, 1971 - No. 3, Oct, 1971 (52 pgs.)
1-Pre-code reprints and new material; Red Mask reprint, retitled Maverick; Bolle-a; Sutton-a 3 6 9 16 22 28
2,3: 2-Whip Wilson-r. 3-Dead Canyon Days reprint/Crack Western No. 63; Sundance Kid app.; Crandall-a 2 4 6 10 14 18

BUTCH CASSIDY (...& the Wild Bunch)
Avon Periodicals: 1951
1-Kinstler-c/a 19 38 57 111 176 240
NOTE: *Reinman story; Issue number on inside spine.*

BUTCH CASSIDY (See Fun-In No. 11 & Western Adventure Comics)

BUTCHER, THE (Also see Brave and the Bold, 2nd Series)
DC Comics: May, 1990 - No. 5, Sept, 1990 ($1.50, mature)
1-5: 1-No indicia inside 3.00

BUTCHER KNIGHT
Image Comics (Top Cow): Jan, 2001 - No. 4, June, 2001 ($2.95, limited series)
Preview (B&W, 16 pgs.) Dwayne Turner-c/a 3.00
1-4-Dwayne Turner-c/a 3.00

BUZ SAWYER (Sweeney No. 4 on)
Standard Comics: June, 1948 - No. 3, 1949
1-Roy Crane-a 28 56 84 165 270 375
2-Intro his pal Sweeney 15 30 45 88 137 185
3 12 24 36 69 97 125

BUZ SAWYER'S PAL, ROSCOE SWEENEY (See Sweeney)

BUZZ, THE (Also see Spider-Girl)
Marvel Comics: July, 2000 - No. 3, Sept, 2000 ($2.99, limited series)
1-3-Buscema-a/DeFalco & Frenz-s 3.00

BUZZARD (See The Goon)
Dark Horse Comics: Jun, 2010 - No. 3, Aug, 2010 ($3.50, limited series)
1-3-Eric Powell-c; Buzzard story w/Powell-s/a; Billy The Kid back-up; Powell-s/Hotz-a 3.50

BUZZ BUZZ COMICS MAGAZINE
Horse Press: May, 1996 ($4.95, B&W, over-sized magazine)
1-Paul Pope-c/a/scripts; Moebius-a 5.00

BUZZY (See All Funny Comics)
National Periodical Publications/Detective Comics: Winter, 1944-45 - No. 75, 1-2/57; No. 76, 10/57; No. 77, 10/58
1 (52 pgs. begin); "America's favorite teenster" 34 68 102 204 332 460
2 (Spr, 1945) 18 36 54 103 162 220
3-5 14 28 42 80 115 150
6-10 11 22 33 62 86 110
11-20 10 20 30 56 76 95
21-30 9 18 27 50 65 80
31,35-38 9 18 27 47 61 75
32-34,39-Last 52 pgs. Scribbly story by Mayer in each (these four stories were done for Scribbly #14 which was delayed for a year) 9 18 27 52 69 85
40-77: 62-Last precode (2/55) 8 16 24 44 57 70

BUZZY THE CROW (See Harvey Comics Hits #60 & 62, Harvey Hits #18 & Paramount Animated Comics #1)

BY BIZARRE HANDS

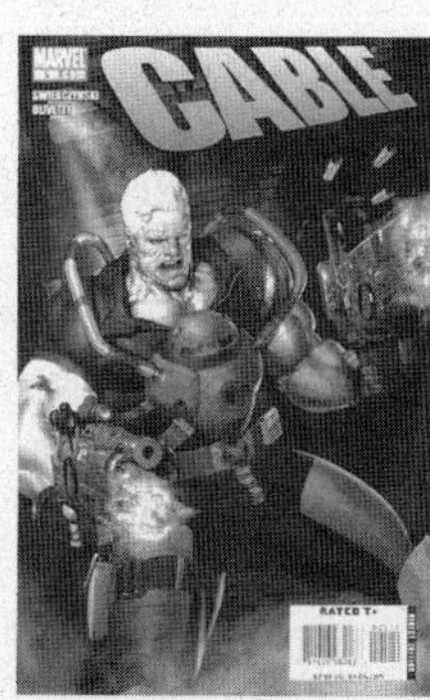

Cable (2008 series) #5 © MAR

Cage #11 © MAR

Calling All Boys #14 © PMI

GD VG FN VF VF/NM NM-
2.0 4.0 6.0 8.0 9.0 9.2

GD VG FN VF VF/NM NM-
2.0 4.0 6.0 8.0 9.0 9.2

Dark Horse Comics: Apr, 1994 - No. 3, June, 1994 ($2.50, B&W, mature)
1-3: Lansdale stories 3.00

CABBOT: BLOODHUNTER (Also see Bloodstrike & Bloodstrike: Assassin)
Maximum Press: Jan, 1997 ($2.50, one-shot)
1-Rick Veitch-a/script; Platt-c; Thor, Chapel & Prophet cameos 3.00

CABLE (See Ghost Rider &..., & New Mutants #87) (Title becomes Soldier X)
Marvel Comics: May, 1993 - No. 107, Sept, 2002 ($3.50/$1.95/$1.50-$2.25)
1-($3.50, 52 pgs.)-Gold foil & embossed-c; Thibert a-1-4p; c-1-3 5.00
2-15: 3-Extra 16 pg. X-Men/Avengers ann. preview. 4-Liefeld-a assist; last Thibert-a(p). 6-8-Reveals that Baby Nathan is Cable; gives background on Stryfe. 9-Omega Red-c/story. 11-Bound-in trading card sheet 3.50
16-Newsstand edition 3.00
16-Enhanced edition 5.00
17-20-($1.95)-Deluxe edition, 20-w/bound in '95 Fleer Ultra cards 3.50
17-20-($1.50)-Standard edition 3.00
21-24, 26-44, -1(7/97): 21-Begin $1.95-c; return from Age of Apocalyse. 24-Grizzly dies. 28-vs. Sugarman; Mr. Sinister app. 30-X-Man-c/app.; Exodus app. 31-vs. X-Man. 32-Post app. 33-Post-c/app; Mandarin app (flashback); includes "Onslaught Update". 34-Onslaught x-over; Hulk-c/app; Apocalypse app. (cont'd in Hulk #444). 35-Onslaught x-over; Apocalypse vs. Cable. 36-w/card insert. 38-Weapon X-c/app; Psycho Man & Micronauts app. 40-Scott Clark-a(p). 41-Bishop-c/app. 3.00
25 ($3.95)-Foil gatefold-c 4.00
45-49,51-74: 45-Operation Zero Tolerance. 51-1st Casey-s. 54-Black Panther. 55-Domino-c/app. 62-Nick Fury-c/app.63-Stryfe-c/app. 67,68-Avengers-c/app. 71,73-Liefeld-a 3.00
50-($2.99) Double sized w/wraparound-c 4.00
75 -($2.99) Liefeld-c/a; Apocalypse: The Twelve x-over 4.00
76-79: 76-Apocalypse: The Twelve x-over 3.00
80-96: 80-Begin $2.25-c. 87-Mystique-c/app. 3.00
97-99,101-107: 97-Tischman-s/Kordey-a/c begin 3.00
100-($3.99) Dialogue-free 'Nuff Said back-up story 4.00
... Classic Vol. 1 TPB (2008, $29.99) r/#1-4, New Mutants #87, Cable: Blood & Metal #1,2 30.00
.../Machine Man '98 Annual ($2.99) Wraparound-c 4.00
.../X-Force '96 Annual ($2.95) Wraparound-c 4.00
...'99 Annual ($3.50) vs. Sinister; computer photo-c 4.00
...Second Genesis 1 (9/99, $3.99) r/New Mutants #99, 100 and X-Force #1; Liefeld-c 4.00
...: The End (2002, $14.99, TPB) r/#101-107 15.00

CABLE
Marvel Comics: May, 2008 - No. 25, Jun, 2010 ($2.99/$3.99)
1-23: 1-10-Olivetti-c/a. 1-Liefeld var-c. 2-Finch var-c. 3-Romita Jr. var-c. 4-Bishop app.; Djurdjevic var-c. 5-Silvestri var-c. 6-Liefeld var-c. 13-15-Messiah War x-over; Deadpool app. 16,17-Gulacy-a 3.00
24,25-($3.99) 24-Bishop app. 25-Deadpool app.; Medina-a 4.00

CABLE - BLOOD AND METAL (Also see New Mutants #87 & X-Force #8)
Marvel Comics: Oct, 1992 - No. 2, Nov, 1992 ($2.50, limited series, 52 pgs.)
1-Fabian Nicieza scripts; John Romita, Jr.-c/a in both; Cable vs. Stryfe; 2nd app. of The Wild Pack (becomes The Six Pack); wraparound-c 4.00
2-Prelude to X-Cutioner's Song 4.00

CABLE/DEADPOOL ("Cable & Deadpool" on cover)
Marvel Comics: May, 2004 - No. 50, Apr, 2008 ($2.99)
1-49: 1-Nicieza-s/Liefeld-c. 7-9-X-Men app. 17-House of M. 21-Heroes For Hire app. 30,31-Civil War. 30-Great Lakes Avengers app. 33-Liefeld-c. 43,44-Wolverine app. 3.00
50-($3.99) Final issue; Spider-Man and the Avengers app. 4.00
Cable & Deadpool MCG 1 (7/11, $1.00) r/#1 with "Marvel's Greatest Comics" cover logo 3.00
... Vol. 1: If Looks Could Kill TPB (2004, $14.99) r/#1-6 15.00
... Vol. 2: The Burnt Offering TPB (2005, $14.99) r/#7-12 15.00
... Vol. 3: The Human Race TPB (2005, $14.99) r/#13-18 15.00
... Vol. 4: Bosom Buddies TPB (2006, $14.99) r/#19-24 15.00
... Vol. 5: Living Legends TPB (2006, $13.99) r/#25-29 14.00
... Vol. 6: Paved With Good Intentions TPB (2007, $14.99) r/#30-35 15.00
... Vol. 7: Separation Anxiety TPB (2007, $17.99) r/#36-42; sketch pages 18.00
Deadpool Vs. The Marvel Universe TPB (2008, $24.99) r/#43-50 25.00

CADET GRAY OF WEST POINT (See Dell Giants)

CADILLACS & DINOSAURS (TV)
Marvel Comics (Epic Comics): Nov, 1990 - No. 6, Apr, 1991 ($2.50, limited series)
1-6: r/Xenozoic Tales in color w/new-c 3.00
...In 3-D #1 (7/92, $3.95, Kitchen Sink)-With glasses 6.00

CADILLACS AND DINOSAURS (TV)
Topps Comics: V2#1, Feb, 1994 - V2#9, 1995 ($2.50, limited series)
V2#1-($2.95)-Collector's edition w/Stout-c & bound-in poster; Buckler-a; foil stamped logo; Giordano-a in all 6.00
V2#1-9: 1-Newsstand edition w/Giordano-c. 2,3-Collector's editions w/Stout-c & posters. 2,3-Newsstand ed. w/Giordano-c; w/o posters. 4-6-Collectors & Newsstand editions; Kieth-c. 7-9-Linsner-c 3.00

CAGE (Also see Hero for Hire, Power Man & Punisher)
Marvel Comics: Apr, 1992 - No. 20, Nov, 1993 ($1.25)
1,3,10,12: 3-Punisher-c & minor app. 10-Rhino & Hulk-c/app. 12-(52 pgs.)-Iron Fist app. 4.00
2,4-9,11,13-20: 9-Rhino-c/story; Hulk cameo 3.00

CAGE (Volume 3)
Marvel Comics (MAX): Mar, 2002 - No. 5, Sept, 2002 ($2.99, mature)
1-5-Corben-c/a; Azzarello-s 3.00
HC (2002, $19.99, with dustjacket) r/#1-5; intro. by Darius James; sketch pages 20.00
SC (2003, $13.99) r/#1-5; intro. by Darius James 14.00

CAGED HEAT 3000 (Movie)
Roger Corman's Cosmic Comics: Nov, 1995 - No. 3, Jan, 1996 ($2.50)
1-3: Adaptation of film 3.00

CAGES
Tundra Publ.: 1991 - No. 10, May, 1996 ($3.50/$3.95/$4.95, limited series)

	GD	VG	FN	VF	VF/NM	NM-
1-Dave McKean-c/a in all	2	4	6	8	10	12
2-Misprint exists	1	2	3	5	6	8
3-9: 5-$3.95-c begins						4.00
10-($4.95)						5.00

CAIN'S HUNDRED (TV)
Dell Publishing Co.: May-July, 1962 - No. 2, Sept-Nov, 1962

	GD	VG	FN	VF	VF/NM	NM-
nn(01-094-207)	3	6	9	20	30	40
2	3	6	9	16	22	28

CAIN/VAMPIRELLA FLIP BOOK
Harris Comics: Oct, 1994 ($6.95, one-shot, squarebound)

	GD	VG	FN	VF	VF/NM	NM-
nn-contains Cain #3 & #4; flip book is r/Vampirella story from 1993 Creepy Fearbook	1	2	3	5	7	9

CALIBER PRESENTS
Caliber Press: Jan, 1989 - No. 24, 1991 ($1.95/$2.50, B&W, 52 pgs.)

	GD	VG	FN	VF	VF/NM	NM-
1-Anthology; 1st app. The Crow; Tim Vigil-c/a	6	12	18	41	66	90
2-Deadworld story; Tim Vigil-a	2	4	6	10	14	18
3-24: 15-24 ($3.50, 68 pgs.)						4.00

CALIBER PRESENTS: CINDERELLA ON FIRE
Caliber Press: 1994 ($2.95, B&W, mature)
1 3.00

CALIBER SPOTLIGHT
Caliber Press: May, 1995 ($2.95, B&W)
1-Kabuki app 3.50

CALIFORNIA GIRLS
Eclipse Comics: June, 1987 - No. 8, May, 1988 ($2.00, 40 pgs, B&W)
1-8: All contain color paper dolls 4.00

CALL, THE
Marvel Comics: June, 2003 - No. 4, Sept, 2003 ($2.25)
1-4-Austen-s/Olliffe-a 3.00

CALLING ALL BOYS (Tex Granger No. 18 on)
Parents' Magazine Institute: Jan, 1946 - No. 17, May, 1948 (Photo c-1-5,7,8)

	GD	VG	FN	VF	VF/NM	NM-
1	15	30	45	84	127	170
2-Contains Roy Rogers article	9	18	27	52	69	85
3-7,9,11,14-17: 6-Painted-c. 11-Rin Tin Tin photo on-c; Tex Granger begins. 14-J. Edgar Hoover photo on-c. 15-Tex Granger-c begin	8	16	24	40	50	60
8-Milton Caniff story	10	20	30	54	72	90
10-Gary Cooper photo on-c	10	20	30	54	72	90
12-Bob Hope photo on-c	14	28	42	81	118	155
13-Bing Crosby photo on-c	13	26	39	72	101	130

CALLING ALL GIRLS
Parents' Magazine Institute: Sept, 1941 - No. 89, Sept, 1949 (Part magazine, part comic)

	GD	VG	FN	VF	VF/NM	NM-
1	21	42	63	122	199	275
2-Photo-c	12	24	36	67	94	120
3-Shirley Temple photo-c	15	30	45	88	134	185
4-10: 4,5,7,9-Photo-c. 9-Flag-c	10	20	30	58	79	100
11-Tina Thayer photo-c; Mickey Rooney photo-b/c; B&W photo inside of Gary Cooper as Lou Gehrig in "Pride of Yankees"	12	24	36	69	97	125
12-20	9	18	27	47	61	75

The Call of Duty: The Precinct #1 © MAR

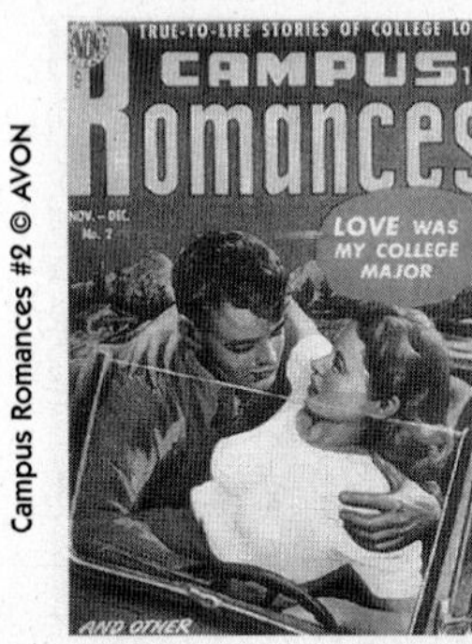

Campus Romances #2 © AVON

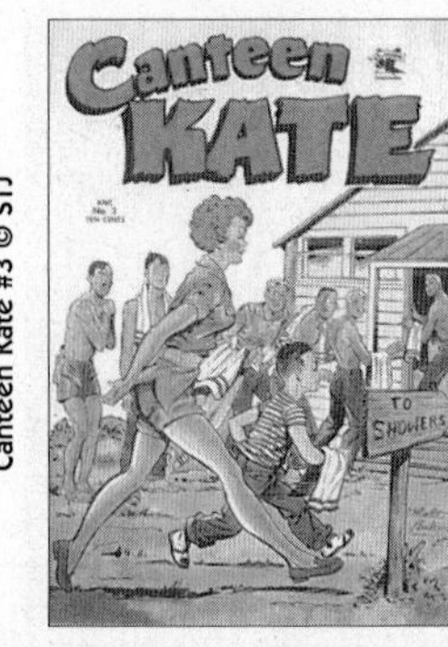

Canteen Kate #3 © STJ

	GD 2.0	VG 4.0	FN 6.0	VF 8.0	VF/NM 9.0	NM- 9.2
21-39,41-43(10-11/45)-Last issue with comics	8	16	24	44	57	70
40-Liz Taylor photo-c	22	44	66	132	216	300
44-51(7/46)-Last comic book size issue	8	16	24	40	50	60
52-89	7	14	21	35	43	50
NOTE: *Jack Sparling art in many issues; becomes a girls' magazine "Senior Prom" with #90.*						
CALLING ALL KIDS (Also see True Comics)						
Parents' Magazine Institute: Dec-Jan, 1945-46 - No. 26, Aug, 1949						
1-Funny animal	15	30	45	84	127	170
2	9	18	27	50	65	80
3-10	8	16	24	40	50	60
11-26	7	14	21	37	46	55
CALL OF DUTY, THE : THE BROTHERHOOD						
Marvel Comics: Aug, 2002 - No. 6, Jan, 2003 ($2.25)						
1-Exploits of NYC Fire Dept.; Finch-c/a; Austen & Bruce Jones-s						4.00
2-6-Austen-s						3.00
...Vol 1: The Brotherhood & The Wagon TPB (2002, $14.99) r/#1-6 & ...The Wagon #1-4						15.00
CALL OF DUTY, THE : THE PRECINCT						
Marvel Comics: Sept, 2002 - No. 5, Jan, 2003 ($2.25, limited series)						
1-Exploits of NYC Police Dept.; Finch-c; Bruce Jones-s/Mandrake-a						3.00
2-4						3.00
...Vol 2: The Precinct TPB (2003, $9.99) r/#1-4						10.00
CALL OF DUTY, THE : THE WAGON						
Marvel Comics: Oct, 2002 - No. 4, Jan, 2003 ($2.25, limited series)						
1-4-Exploits of NYC EMS Dept.; Finch-c; Austen-s/Zelzej-a						3.00
CALVIN (See Li'l Kids)						
CALVIN & THE COLONEL (TV)						
Dell Publishing Co.: No. 1354, Apr-June, 1962 - No. 2, July-Sept, 1962						
Four Color 1354(#1) (The last Four Color issue)	8	16	24	55	93	130
2	6	12	18	39	62	85
CAMELOT 3000						
DC Comics: Dec, 1982 - No. 11, July, 1984; No. 12, Apr, 1985 (Direct sales, maxi series, Mando paper)						
1-12: 1-Mike Barr scripts & Brian Bolland-c/a begin. 5-Intro Knights of New Camelot						4.00
TPB (1988, $12.95) r/#1-12						15.00
...: The Deluxe Edition (2008, $34.99, HC) r/#1-12; oversized & recolored; Barr intro.; design and promotional art; original proposal page						35.00
NOTE: *Austin a-7i-12i. Bolland a-1-12p; c-1-12.*						
CAMERA COMICS						
U.S. Camera Publishing Corp./ME: July, 1944 - No. 9, Summer, 1946						
nn (7/44)	26	52	78	154	252	350
nn (9/44)	20	40	60	114	182	250
1(10/44)-The Grey Comet (slightly smaller page size than subsequent issues)	20	40	60	117	189	260
2-16 pgs. of photos with 32 pgs. of comics	15	30	45	83	124	165
3-Nazi WW II-c; photos	16	32	48	94	147	200
4-9: All 1/3 photos	14	28	42	76	108	140
CAMP CANDY (TV)						
Marvel Comics: May, 1990 - No. 6, Oct, 1990 ($1.00, limited series)						
1-6: Post-c/a(p); featuring John Candy						4.00
CAMP COMICS						
Dell Publishing Co.: Feb, 1942 - No. 3, April, 1942 (All have photo-c)						
1- "Seaman Sy Wheeler" by Kelly, 7 pgs.; Bugs Bunny app.; Mark Twain adaptation (scarce)	81	162	243	518	884	1250
2-Kelly-a, 12 pgs.; Bugs Bunny app.; classic-c	81	162	243	518	884	1250
3-(Scarce)-Dave Berg & Walt Kelly-a	61	122	183	390	670	950
CAMP RUNAMUCK (TV)						
Dell Publishing Co.: Apr, 1966						
1-Photo-c	4	8	12	22	34	45
CAMPUS LOVES						
Quality Comics Group (Comic Magazines): Dec, 1949 - No. 5, Aug, 1950						
1-Ward-c/a (9 pgs.)	35	70	105	208	339	470
2-Ward-c/a	26	52	78	154	252	350
3-5	15	30	45	83	124	165
NOTE: *Gustavson a-1-5. Photo c-3-5.*						
CAMPUS ROMANCE (...Romances on cover)						
Avon Periodicals/Realistic: Sept-Oct, 1949 - No. 3, Feb-Mar, 1950						

	GD 2.0	VG 4.0	FN 6.0	VF 8.0	VF/NM 9.0	NM- 9.2
1-Walter Johnson-a; c-/Avon paperback #348	33	66	99	194	317	440
2-Grandenetti-a; c-/Avon paperback #151	22	44	66	132	216	300
3-c-/Avon paperback #201	22	44	66	132	216	300
Realistic reprint	15	30	45	83	124	165
CANADA DRY PREMIUMS (See Swamp Fox, The & Terry & The Pirates in the Promotional Comics section)						
CANCELLED COMIC CAVALCADE (See the Promotional Comics section)						
CANDID TALES (Also see Bold Stories & It Rhymes With Lust)						
Kirby Publ. Co.: April, 1950; June, 1950 (Digest size) (144 pgs.) (Full color)						
nn-(Scarce) Contains Wood female pirate story, 15 pgs., and 14 pgs. in June issue; Powell-a	142	284	426	909	1555	2200
NOTE: *Another version exists with Dr. Kilmore by Wood; no female pirate story.*						
CANDY (Teen-age)(Also see Police Comics #37)						
Quality Comics Group (Comic Magazines): Autumn, 1947 - No. 64, Jul, 1956						
1-Gustavson-a	24	48	72	144	237	330
2-Gustavson-a	15	30	45	83	124	165
3-10	10	20	30	58	79	100
11-30	8	16	24	44	57	70
31-64: 64-Ward-c(p)?	8	16	24	40	50	60
Super Reprint No. 2,10,12,16,17,18('63- '64):17-Candy #12	2	4	6	10	14	18
NOTE: *Jack Cole 1-2 pg. art in many issues.*						
CANDY COMICS						
William H. Wise & Co.: Fall, 1944 - No. 3, Spring, 1945						
1-Two Scoop Scuttle stories by Wolverton	39	78	117	240	395	550
2,3-Scoop Scuttle by Wolverton, 2-4 pgs.	26	52	78	154	252	350
CANNON (See Heroes, Inc. Presents Cannon)						
CANNON: DAWN OF WAR (Michael Turner's...)						
Aspen MLT, Inc.: Nov, 2004 ($2.99)						
1-Turnbull-a; two covers by Turnbull and Turner						3.00
CANNONBALL COMICS						
Rural Home Publishing Co.: Feb, 1945 - No. 2, Mar, 1945						
1-The Crash Kid, Thunderbrand, The Captive Prince & Crime Crusader begin; skull-c	110	220	330	704	1202	1700
2-Devil-c	84	168	252	538	919	1300
CANTEEN KATE (See All Picture All True Love Story & Fightin' Marines)						
St. John Publishing Co.: June, 1952 - No. 3, Nov, 1952						
1-Matt Baker-c/a	76	152	228	486	831	1175
2-Matt Baker-c/a	48	96	144	302	514	725
3-(Rare)-Used in **POP**, pg. 75; Baker-c/a	55	110	165	352	601	850
CAPE, THE						
IDW Publishing: Dec, 2010; Jul, 2011 - Present ($3.99)						
1-(12/10) Zach Howard-c/a; Jason Ciaramella-s						4.00
1,2: 1-(7/11) Story continues from 12/10 issue						4.00
...: Legacy Edition (6/11, $5.99) r/#1 (12/10) with Joe Hill's original short story						6.00
CAPER						
DC Comics: Dec, 2003 - No. 12, Nov, 2004 ($2.95, limited series)						
1-12: 1-4-Judd Winick-s/Farel Dalrymple-a. 5-8-John Severin-a. 9-12-Fowler-a						3.00
CAPES						
Image Comics: Sept, 2003 - No. 3, Nov, 2003 ($3.50)						
1-3-Robert Kirkman-s/Mark Englert-a/c						3.50
CAP'N QUICK & A FOOZLE (Also see Eclipse Mag. & Monthly)						
Eclipse Comics: July, 1984 - No. 3, Nov, 1985 ($1.50, color, Baxter paper)						
1-3-Rogers-c/a						3.00
CAPTAIN ACTION (Toy)						
National Periodical Publications: Oct-Nov, 1968 - No. 5, June-July, 1969 (Based on Ideal toy)						
1-Origin; Wally Wood-a; Superman-c app.	7	14	21	44	72	100
2,3,5-Gil Kane/Wally Wood-a	5	10	15	35	55	75
4- Gil Kane-c	4	8	12	28	44	60
CAPTAIN ACTION COMICS (Toy)						
Moonstone: No. 0, 2008 - Present (Based on the Ideal toy)						
0-($1.99) Origin re-told; Sparacio-a; three covers; character history by Michael Eury						3.00
1-5: 1-($3.99) Sparacio-a; intro. by Jim Shooter						4.00
... Comics Special 1 (2010, $5.99) 3 covers by Barreto, Ordway & Spiegle						6.00
...: First Mission, Last Day (2008, $3.99) origin story re-told; Nicieza-s/Procopio-a						4.00
... King Size Special 1 (2011, $6.99) 1-Covers by Byrne, Wheatley & M. Benes						7.00
... Season 2 (2010, $3.99) 1-3: 1-Covers by Allred & Texiera; Obama app.						4.00

Captain Aero Comics V2 #1 © HOKE

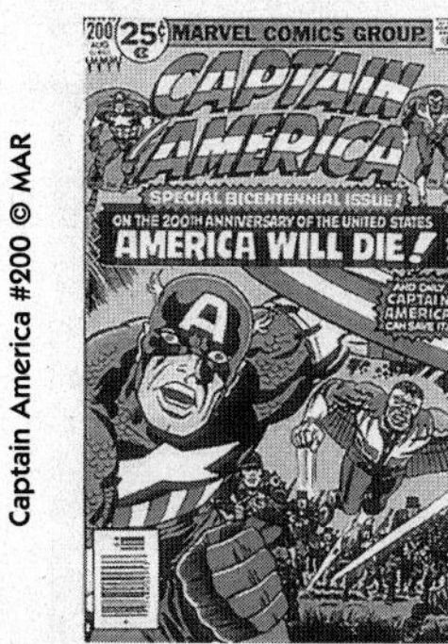

Captain America #200 © MAR

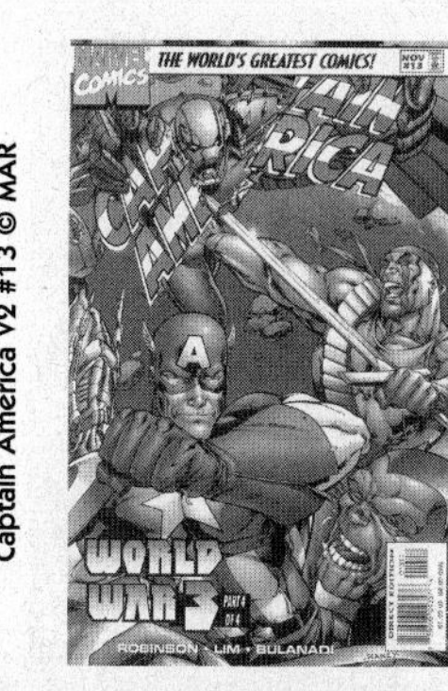

Captain America V2 #13 © MAR

	GD 2.0	VG 4.0	FN 6.0	VF 8.0	VF/NM 9.0	NM- 9.2

... Winter Special (2011, $4.99) Green Hornet & Kato on-c & text story 5.00

CAPTAIN AERO COMICS (Samson No. 1-6; also see Veri Best Sure Fire & Veri Best Sure Shot Comics)
Holyoke Publishing Co.: V1#7(#1), Dec, 1941 - V2#4(#10), Jan, 1943; V3#9(#11), Sept, 1943 -V4#3(#17), Oct, 1944; #21, Dec, 1944 - #26, Aug, 1946 (No #18-20)

V1#7(#1)-Flag-Man & Solar, Master of Magic, Captain Aero, Cap Stone, Adventurer begin; Nazi WWII-c 187 374 561 1197 2049 2900
8,10: 8(#2)-Pals of Freedom app. 10(#4)-Origin The Gargoyle; Kubert-a 94 188 282 597 1024 1450
9(#3)-Hitler-sty; Catman back-c; Alias X begins; Pals of Freedom app. 106 212 318 673 1162 1650
11,12(#5,6)-Kubert-a; Miss Victory in #6 74 148 222 470 810 1150
V2#1,2(#7,8): 8-Origin The Red Cross; Miss Victory app.; Brodsky-c(i) 48 96 144 302 514 725
3(#9)-Miss Victory app. 53 106 159 334 567 800
4(#10)-Miss Victory app.; Japanese WWII-c 43 86 129 271 461 650
V3#9 - V3#12(#11-14): All Quinlan Japanese WWII-c. 9-Miss Victory app. 40 80 120 246 411 575
V3#13(#15),V4#2(#16): Schomburg Japanese WWII-c. 13-Miss Victory app. 45 90 135 284 480 675
V4#3(#17), 21-24-L. B. Cole Japanese WWII covers. 22-Intro/origin Mighty Mite. 53 106 159 334 567 800
25-L. B. Cole SciFi-c 57 114 171 362 619 875
26-L. B. Cole SciFi-c; Palais-a(2) (scarce) 155 310 465 992 1696 2400

NOTE: ***L.B. Cole** c-17, 21-26. **Hollingsworth** a-23. **Infantino** a-23, 26. **Schomburg** c-15, 16.*

CAPTAIN AMERICA (See Adventures of..., All-Select, All Winners, Aurora, Avengers #4, Blood and Glory, Captain Britain 16-20, Giant-Size..., The Invaders, Marvel Double Feature, Marvel Fanfare, Marvel Mystery, Marvel Super-Action, Marvel Super Heroes V2#3, Marvel Team-Up, Marvel Treasury Special, Power Record Comics, Ultimates, USA Comics, Young Allies & Young Men)

CAPTAIN AMERICA (Formerly Tales of Suspense #1-99) (Captain America and the Falcon #134-223 & Steve Rogers: Captain America #444-454 appears on cover only)
Marvel Comics Group: No. 100, Apr, 1968 - No. 454, Aug, 1996

100-Flashback on Cap's revival with Avengers & Sub-Mariner; story continued from Tales of Suspense #99; Kirby-c/a begins 28 56 84 203 439 675
101-The Sleeper-c/story; Red Skull app. 9 18 27 63 112 160
102-104: 102-Sleeper-c/s. 103,104-Red Skull-c/sty 8 16 24 51 86 120
105-108: 107-Red Skull & Hitler-c 6 12 18 42 69 95
109-Origin Capt. America retold in detail 9 18 27 58 99 140
109-2nd printing (1994) 2 4 6 8 10 12
110-Rick Jones dons Bucky's costume & becomes Cap's partner; Hulk x-over; Steranko-a Classic Steranko-c 10 20 30 68 127 185
111,113-Classic Steranko-c/a: 111-Death of Steve Rogers. 113-Cap's funeral; Avengers app. 9 18 27 63 112 160
112-S.A. recovery retold; last Kirby-c/a 6 12 18 39 62 85
114-116,119,120: 115-Last 12¢ issue 4 8 12 28 44 60
117-1st app. The Falcon (9/69) 12 24 36 81 166 250
118-2nd app. The Falcon 7 14 21 44 72 100
121-136,139,140: 121-Retells origin. 133-The Falcon becomes Cap's partner; origin Modok. 140-Origin Grey Gargoyle retold 3 6 9 20 30 40
137,138-Spider-Man x-over 4 8 12 24 37 50
141,142: 142-Last 15¢ issue 3 6 9 16 23 30
143-(52 pgs). 3 6 9 20 30 40
144-153: 144-New costume Falcon. 153-1st brief app. Jack Monroe 2 4 6 13 18 22
154-1st full app. Jack Monroe (Nomad)(10/72) 3 6 9 14 19 24
155-Origin re-told; origin Jack Monroe 3 6 9 14 19 24
156-171,176-179: 155-158-Cap's strength increased. 160-1st app. Solarr. 164-1st app. Nightshade. 176-End of Capt. America. 2 4 6 8 11 14
172-175: X-Men x-over 2 4 6 13 18 22
180-Intro/origin of Nomad (Steve Rogers) 3 6 9 14 19 24
181-Intro/origin new Cap. 2 4 6 11 16 20
182,184-192: 186-True origin The Falcon 2 3 4 6 8 10
183-Death of new Cap; Nomad becomes Cap 2 4 6 9 12 15
193-Kirby-c/a begins 2 4 6 13 18 22
194-199-(Regular 25¢ edition)(4-7/76) 2 4 6 10 14 18
196-199-(30¢-c variants, limited distribution) 5 10 15 32 51 70
200-(Regular 25¢ edition)(8/76) 2 4 6 11 16 20
200-(30¢-c variant, limited distribution) 6 12 18 37 59 80
201-214-Kirby-c/a 2 4 6 8 11 14
210-214-(35¢-c variants, limited dist.)(6-10/77) 7 14 21 44 72 100
215,216,218-229,231-234,236-240,242-246: 215-Retells Cap's origin. 216-r/story from Strange Tales #114. 229-Marvel Man app. 233-Death of Sharon Carter. 234-Daredevil x-over. 244,245-Miller-c 6.00
217,230,235: 217-1st app. Marvel Man (later Quasar). 230-Battles Hulk-c/story cont'd in Hulk #232. 235-(7/79) Daredevil x-over; Miller-a(p) 1 2 3 4 5 7
241-Punisher app.; Miller-c. 3 6 9 19 29 38
241-2nd print 3.00
247-255-Byrne-a. 255-Origin; Miller-c. 1 2 3 5 7 9
256-281,284,285,289-322,324-326,328-331: 264-Old X-Men cameo in flashback. 265,266-Nick Fury & Spider-Man app. 267-1st app. Everyman. 269-1st Team America. 279-(3/83)-Contains Tattooz skin decals. 281-1950s Bucky returns. 284-Patriot (Jack Mace) app. 285-Death of Patriot. 298-Origin Red Skull. 328-Origin & 1st app. D-Man 3.00
282-Bucky becomes new Nomad (Jack Monroe) 5.00
282-Silver ink 2nd print ($1.75) w/original date (6/83) 3.00
283,327,333-340: 283-2nd app. Nomad. 327-Capt. Amer. battles Super Patriot. 333-Intro & origin new Captain (Super Patriot). 339-Fall of the Mutants tie-in 4.00
286-288-Deathlok app. 4.00
323-1st app. new Super Patriot (see Nick Fury) 4.00
332-Old Cap resigns 1 2 3 5 6 8
341-343,345-349 3.00
344-($1.50, 52 pgs.)-Ronald Reagan cameo 4.00
350-($1.75, 68 pgs.)-Return of Steve Rogers (original Cap) to original costume 4.00
351-382,384-396: 351-Nick Fury app. 354-1st app. U.S. Agent (6/89, see Avengers West Coast). 360-1st app. Crossbones. 375-Daredevil app. 386-U.S. Agent app. 387-389-Red Skull back-up stories. 396-Last $1.00-c. 396,397-1st app. all new Jack O'Lantern 3.00
383-($2.00, 68 pgs.)-50th anniversary issue; Red Skull story; Jim Lee-c(i) 4.00
397-399,401-424,425: 402-Begin 6 part Man-Wolf story w/Wolverine in #403-407. 405-410-New Jack O'Lantern app. in back-up story. 406-Cable & Shatterstar cameo. 407-Capwolf vs. Cable-c/story. 408-Infinity War x-over; Falcon solo back-up. 423-Vs. Namor-c/story 3.00
400-($2.25, 84 pgs.)-Flip book format w/double gatefold-c; r/Avengers #4 plus-c; contains cover pin-ups. 4.00
425-($2.95, 52 pgs.)-Embossed Foil-c ed.n; Fighting Chance Pt. 1 4.00
426-443,446,447,449-453: 427-Begin $1.50-c; bound-in trading card sheet. 449-Thor app. 450-"Man Without A Country" storyline begins, ends #453; Bill Clinton app; variant-c exists. 451-1st app.Cap's new costume. 453-Cap gets old costume back; Bill Clinton app. 3.00
444-Mark Waid scripts & Ron Garney-c/a(p) begins, ends #454; Avengers app. 5.00
445,454: 445-Sharon Carter & Red Skull return. 4.00
448-($2.95, double-sized issue)-Waid script & Garney-c/a; Red Skull "dies" 5.00
#600-up (See Captain America 2005 series, resumed original numbering after #50)
Special 1(1/71)-Origin retold 6 12 18 37 59 80
Special 2(1/72, 52 pgs.)-Colan-r/Not Brand Echh; all-r 4 8 12 22 34 45
Annual 3('76, 52 pgs.)-Kirby-c/a(new) 3 6 9 16 23 30
Annual 4('77, 34 pgs.)-Magneto-c/story 3 6 9 16 23 30
Annual 5-7: (52 pgs.)('81-'83) 5.00
Annual 8(9/86)-Wolverine-c/story 3 6 9 20 30 40
Annual 9-13('90-'94, 68 pgs.)-9-Nomad back-up. 10-Origin retold (2 pgs.). 11-Falcon solo story. 12-Bagged w/card. 13-Red Skull-c/story 4.00
...Ashcan Edition ('95, 75¢) 3.00
... and the Falcon: Madbomb TPB (2004, $16.99) r/#193-200; Kirby-s/a 17.00
... and the Falcon: Nomad TPB (2006, $24.99) r/#177-186; Cap becomes Nomad 25.00
... and the Falcon: Secret Empire TPB (2005, $19.99) r/#169-176 20.00
... and the Falcon: The Swine TPB (2006, $29.99) r/#206-214 & Annual #3,4 30.00
... By Jack Kirby: Bicentennial Battles TPB (2005, $19.99) r/#201-205 & Marvel Treasury Special Featuring Captain America's Bicentennial Battles; Kirby-s/a 20.00
...: Deathlok Lives! nn(10/93, $4.95)-r/#286-288 5.00
...Drug War 1-(1994, $2.00, 52 pgs.)-New Warriors app. 4.00
...Man Without a Country(1998, $12.99, TPB)-r/#450-453 13.00
...Medusa Effect 1 (1994, $2.95, 68 pgs.)-Origin Baron Zemo 4.00
...Operation Rebirth (1996, $9.95)-r/#445-448 10.00
... 65th Anniversary Special (5/06, $3.99) WWII flashback with Bucky; Brubaker-s 4.00
...Streets of Poison ($15.95)-r/#372-378 16.00
...: The Movie Special nn (5/92, $3.50, 52 pgs.)-Adapts movie; printed on coated stock; The Red Skull app. 4.00

NOTE: ***Austin** c-225i, 239i, 246i. **Buscema** a-115p, 217p; c-136p, 217, 297. **Byrne** c-223(part), 238, 239, 247p-254p, 290, 291, 313p; a-247-254p, 255, 313p, 350. **Colan** a(p)-116-137, 256, Annual 5; c(p)-116-123, 126, 129. **Everett** a-136i, 137i; c-126i. **Garney** a(p)-444-454. **Gil Kane** a-145p; c-147p, 149p, 150p, 170p, 172-174, 180, 181p, 183-190p, 215, 216, 220, 221. **Kirby** a(p)-100-109, 112, 193-214, 216, Special 1, 2(layouts), Annual 3, 4; c-100-109, 112, 126p, 193-214. **Ron Lim** a(p)-366, 368-378, 380-386; c-366p, 368-378p, 379, 380-393p. **Miller** c-241p, 244p, 245p, 255p, Annual 5. **Mooney** a-149i. **Morrow** a-144. **Perez** c-243p, 246p. **Robbins** c(p)-183-187, 189-192, 225. **Roussos** a-140i, 168i. **Shores** a-102i, 107i, 109i. **Starlin/Sinnott** c-162. **Sutton** a-244i. **Tuska** a-112i, 215p, Special 2. **Waid** scripts-444-454. **Williamson** a-313i. **Wood** a-127i. **Zeck** a-263-289; c-300.*

CAPTAIN AMERICA (Volume Two)
Marvel Comics: V2#1, Nov, 1996 - No. 13, Nov, 1997($2.95/$1.95/$1.99)
(Produced by Extreme Studios)

1-($2.95)-Heroes Reborn begins; Liefeld-c/a; Loeb scripts; reintro Nick Fury 6.00
1-($2.95)-(Variant-c)-Liefeld-c/a 6.00
1-(7/96, $2.95)-(Exclusive Comicon Ed.)-Liefeld-c/a. 1 2 3 5 6 8

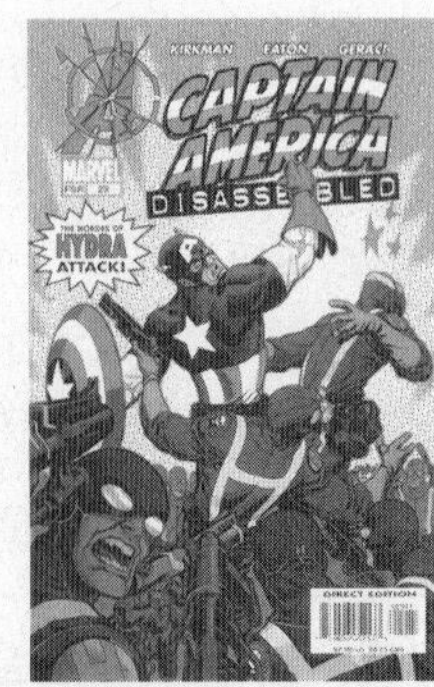

Captain America V4 #29 © MAR

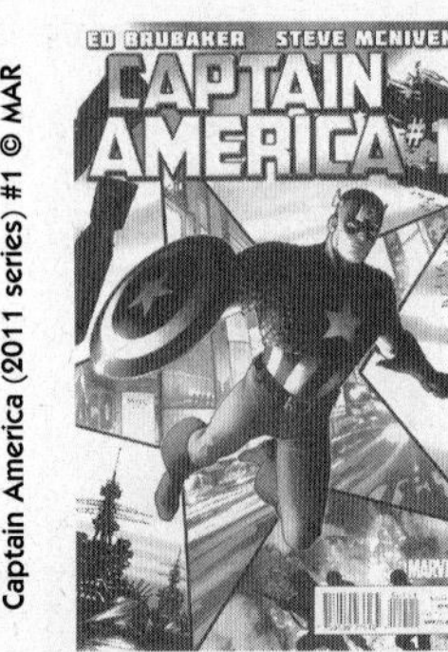

Captain America (2011 series) #1 © MAR

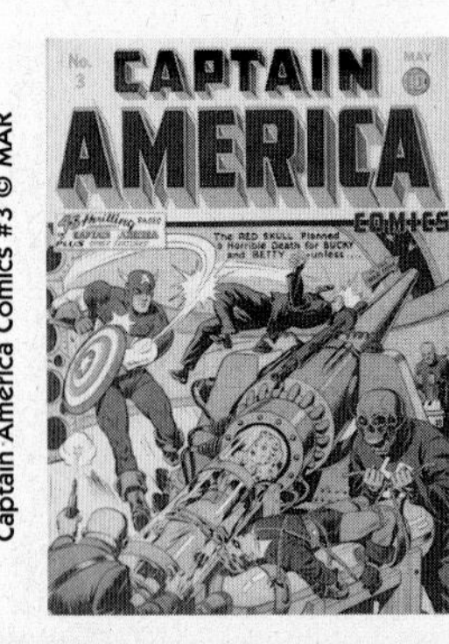

Captain America Comics #3 © MAR

GD 2.0 | VG 4.0 | FN 6.0 | VF 8.0 | VF/NM 9.0 | NM- 9.2

2-11,13: 5-Two-c. 6-Cable-c/app. 13-"World War 3"-pt. 4, x-over w/Image 3.00
12-($2.99) "Heroes Reunited"-pt. 4 4.00
Heroes Reborn: Captain America (2006, $29.99, TPB) r/#1-12 & Heroes Reborn #1/2 30.00

CAPTAIN AMERICA (Vol. Three) (Also see Capt. America: Sentinel of Liberty)
Marvel Comics: Jan, 1998 - No. 50, Feb, 2002 ($2.99/$1.99/$2.25)

1-($2.99) Mark Waid-s/Ron Garney-a 4.00
1-Variant cover 6.00
2-($1.99): 2-Two covers 3.00
3-11: 3-Returns to old shield. 4-Hawkeye app. 5-Thor-c/app. 7-Andy Kubert-c/a begin. 9-New shield 3.00
12-($2.99) Battles Nightmare; Red Skull back-up story 4.00
13-17,19-Red Skull returns 3.00
18-($2.99) Cap vs. Korvac in the Future 4.00
20-24,26-29: 20,21-Sgt. Fury back-up story painted by Evans 3.00
25-($2.99) Cap & Falcon vs. Hatemonger 4.00
30-49: 30-Begin $2.25-c. 32-Ordway-a. 33-Jurgens-s/a begins; U.S. Agent app. 36-Maximum Security x-over. 41,46-Red Skull app. 3.00
50-($5.95) Stories by various incl. Jurgens, Quitely, Immonen; Ha-c 6.00
.../Citizen V '98 Annual ($3.50) Busiek & Kesel-s 4.00
1999 Annual ($3.50) Flag Smasher app. 4.00
2000 Annual ($3.50) Continued from #35 vs. Protocide; Jurgens-s 4.00
2001 Annual ($2.99) Golden Age flashback; Invaders app. 4.00
...: To Serve and Protect TPB (2/02, $17.95) r/Vol. 3 #1-7 18.00

CAPTAIN AMERICA (Volume 4)
Marvel Comics: Jun, 2002 - No. 32, Dec, 2004 ($3.99/$2.99)

1-Ney Rieber-s/Cassaday-c/a 4.00
2-9-($2.99) 3-Cap reveals Steve Rogers ID. 7-9-Hairsine-a 3.00
10-32: 10-16-Jae Lee-a. 17-20-Gibbons-s/Weeks-a. 21-26-Bachalo-a. 26-Bucky flashback. 27,28-Eddie Campbell-a. 29-32-Red Skull app. 3.00
...Vol. 1: The New Deal HC (2003, $22.99) r/#1-6; foreward by Max Allan Collins 23.00
...Vol. 2: The Extremists TPB (2003, $13.99) r/#7-11; Cassaday-c 14.00
...Vol. 3: Ice TPB (2003, $12.99) r/#12-16; Jae Lee-a; Cassaday-c 13.00
...Vol. 4: Cap Lives TPB (2004, $12.99) r/#17-22 & Tales of Suspense #66 13.00
Avengers Disassembled: Captain America TPB (2004, $17.99) r/#29-32 and Captain America and the Falcon #5-7 18.00

CAPTAIN AMERICA
Marvel Comics: Jan, 2005 - No. 619, Aug, 2011 ($2.99/$3.99)

1-Brubaker-s/Epting-c/a; Red Skull app. 4.00
2-24: 10-House of M. 11-Origin of the Winter Soldier. 13-Iron Man app. 24-Civil War 3.00
6,8-Retailer variant covers 6.00
25-($3.99) Captain America shot dead; handcuffed red glove cover by Epting 10.00
25-($3.99) Variant edition with running Cap cover by McGuinness 8.00
25-($3.99) 2nd printing with "The Death of The Dream" cover by Epting 4.00
25-Director's Cut-($4.99) w/script with Brubaker commentary; pencil pages, variant and un-used covers gallery; article on media hype 5.00
26-33-Falcon & Winter Soldier app. 3.00
34-(3/08) Bucky becomes the new Captain America; Alex Ross-c 3.00
34-Variant-c by Steve Epting 3.00
34-($3.99) Director's Cut; includes script; pencil art, costume designs, cover gallery 4.00
34-DF Edition with Alex Ross portrait cover; signed by Ross 25.00
35-49-Bucky as Captain America. 43-45-Batroc app. 46,47-Sub-Mariner app. 3.00
50-(7/09, $3.99) Bucky's birthday flashbacks; Captain America's life synopsis; Martin-a 4.00
(After #50, numbering reverts to original with #600, Aug, 2009)
600-(8/09, $4.99) Covers by Ross and Epting; leads into Captain America: Reborn series; art by Guice, Chaykin, Ross, Eaglesham; commentary by Joe Simon; cover gallery 5.00
601-615,617-619-($3.99) 601-Gene Colan-a; 3 covers. 602-Nomad back-up feature begins. 606-Baron Zemo returns. 611-615-Trial of Captain America 4.00
615.1 (5/11, $2.99) Brubaker-s/Breitweiser-a/Acuña-c 3.00
616-(5/11, $4.99) 70th Anniversary Issue; short stories by Brubaker, Chaykin, Deodato, McGuinness, Grist and others, Charest-c 5.00
616-Variant-c by Epting 8.00
...: America's Avenger (8/11, $4.99) Handbook format profiles of friends and foes 5.00
... and Batroc (5/11, $3.99) Gillen-s/Arlem-a; Bucky vs. Batroc in Paris 4.00
... and Crossbones (5/11, $3.99) Harms-s/Shalvey-a/Tocchini-c 4.00
... and Falcon (5/11, $3.99) Williams-s/Isaacs-a/Tocchini-c 4.00
... and the First Thirteen (5/11, $3.99) Peggy Carter in WWII France 1943 4.00
... and the Secret Avengers (5/11, $3.99) DeConnick-s/Tocchini-a/c; Black Widow app. 4.00
... and Thor: Avengers 1 (9/11, $4.99) Movie version Cap; prequel to Thor movie; Lim-c 5.00
... By Ed Brubaker Omnibus Vol. 1 HC (2007, $74.99, dustjacket) r/#1-25; Capt. America 65th Anniv. Spec. and Winter Soldier: Winter Kills; Brubaker intro.; bonus material 75.00
Civil War: Captain America TPB (2007, $11.99) r/#22-24 & Winter Soldier: Winter Kills 12.00
...: Fighting Avenger (6/11, $4.99) 1st WWII mission; Gurihiru-a/c; Kitson var-c 5.00
...MGC #1 (5/10, $1.00) r/#1 with "Marvel's Greatest Comics" cover logo 3.00
...: Rebirth 1 (8/11, $4.99) r/origin & Red Skull apps. from Tales of Suspense #63,65-68 5.00
...: Red Menace Vol. 1 SC (2006, $11.99) r/#15-17 and 65th Anniversary Special 12.00
...: Red Menace Vol. 2 SC (2006, $10.99) r/#18-21; Brubaker interview 11.00
... Spotlight (7/11, $3.99) creator interviews; features on the movie and The Invaders 4.00
... Theater of War: America First! (2/09, $4.99) 1950s era tale; Chaykin-s/a; reprints 5.00
... Theater of War: America the Beautiful (3/09, $4.99) WW2 tale; Jenkins-s/Erskine-a 5.00
... Theater of War: Operation Zero-Point (12/08, $3.99) WW2 tale; Breitweiser-a 4.00
...: The Death of Captan America Vol. 1 HC (2007, $19.99) r/#25-30; variant covers 20.00
...: The Death of Captan America Vol. 2 HC (2008, $19.99) r/#31-36; variant covers 20.00
...Vol. 1: Winter Soldier HC (2005, $21.99) r/#1-7; concept sketches 22.00
...Vol. 1: Winter Soldier SC (2006, $16.99) r/#1-7; concept sketches 17.00
...: Who Won't Wield the Shield (6/10, $3.99) Deadpool & Forbush Man app. 4.00
...: Winter Soldier Vol. 2 HC (2006, $19.99) r/#8,9,11-14 20.00
...: Winter Soldier Vol. 2 SC (2006, $14.99) r/#8,9,11-14 15.00

CAPTAIN AMERICA
Marvel Comics: Sept, 2011 - Present ($3.99)

1-9: 1-5-Brubaker-s/McNiven-c/a. 1-Nick Fury & Baron Zemo app. 6-9-Davis-a/c 4.00
1-Variant-c by John Romita Sr. 8.00
1-Movie photo variant-c of Chris Evans in costume 5.00

CAPTAIN AMERICA AND BUCKY (Numbering continues from Captain America #619)
Marvel Comics: No. 620, Sept, 2011 - Present ($2.99)

620-624-Brubaker & Andreyko-s/Samnee-a/McGuinness-c. 620-Bucky's early WWII days 3.00
625-627-Francavilla-c/a 3.00

CAPTAIN AMERICA AND THE FALCON
Marvel Comics: May, 2004 - No. 14, June, 2005 ($2.99, limited series)

1-4-Priest-s/Sears-a 3.00
5-14: 5-8-Avengers Disassembled x-over. 6,7-Scarlet Witch app. 8-12-Modok app. 3.00
... Vol. 1: Two Americas (2005, $9.99) r/#1-4 10.00
... Vol. 2: Brothers and Keepers (2005, $17.99) r/#8-14 18.00

CAPTAIN AMERICA & THE KORVAC SAGA
Marvel Comics: Feb, 2011 - No. 4, May, 2011 ($2.99, limited series)

1-4-McCool-s/Rousseau-a/c. 4-Galactus app. 3.00

CAPTAIN AMERICA/BLACK PANTHER (See Black Panther/Captain America: Flags of Our Fathers)

CAPTAIN AMERICA COMICS
Timely/Marvel Comics (TCI 1-20/CmPS 21-68/MjMC 69-75/Atlas Comics (PrPI 76-78): Mar, 1941 - No. 75, Feb, 1950; No. 76, 5/54 - No. 78, 9/54
(No. 74 & 75 titled Capt. America's Weird Tales)

	GD 2.0	VG 4.0	FN 6.0	VF 8.0	VF/NM 9.0	NM- 9.2
1-Origin & 1st app. Captain America & Bucky by S&K; Hurricane, Tuk the Caveboy begin by S&K; 1st app. Red Skull; Hitler-c (by Simon?); intro of the "Capt. America Sentinels of Liberty Club" (advertised on inside front-c.); indicia reads Vol. 2, Number 1	11,000	22,000	33,000	77,000	154,000	275,000
2-S&K Hurricane; Tuk by Avison (Kirby splash); classic Hitler-c	1950	3900	5850	14,235	28,118	42,000
3-Classic Red Skull-c & app; Stan Lee's 1st text (1st work for Marvel)	1567	3134	4700	11,600	22,300	33,000
4-Early use of full pg. panel in comic; back-c pin-up of Captain America and Bucky	1000	2000	3000	7300	12,900	18,500
5	919	1838	2757	6709	11,855	17,000
6-Origin Father Time; Tuk the Caveboy ends	811	1622	2433	5920	10,460	15,000
7-Red Skull app.; classic-c	892	1784	2676	6512	11,506	16,500
8-10-Last S&K issue, (S&K centerfold #6-10)	676	1352	2028	4935	8718	12,500
11-Last Hurricane, Headline Hunter; Al Avison Captain America begins, ends #20; Avison-c(p)	486	972	1458	3550	6275	9000
12-The Imp begins, ends #16; last Father Time	476	952	1428	3475	6138	8800
13-Origin The Secret Stamp; classic-c	622	1244	1866	4541	8021	11,500
14,15	476	952	1428	3475	6138	8800
16-Red Skull unmasks Cap; Red Skull-c	649	1298	1947	4738	8369	12,000
17-The Fighting Fool only app.	423	846	1269	3067	5384	7700
18-Classic-c	443	886	1329	3234	5717	8200
19-Human Torch begins #19	389	778	1167	2723	4762	6800
20-Sub-Mariner app.; no Human Torch	383	766	1149	2681	4691	6700
21-25: 25-Cap drinks liquid opium	371	742	1113	2600	4550	6500
26-30: 27-Last Secret Stamp; last 68 pg. issue. 28-60 pg. issues begin.	360	720	1080	2520	4410	6300
31-35,38-40: 34-Centerfold poster of Cap	314	628	942	2198	3849	5500
36-Classic Hitler-c	432	864	1296	3154	5577	8000
37-Red Skull app.	371	742	1113	2600	4550	6500
41-Last Japan War-c	290	580	870	1856	3178	4500
42-45	258	516	774	1651	2826	4000
46-German Holocaust-c; classic	486	972	1458	3550	6275	9000

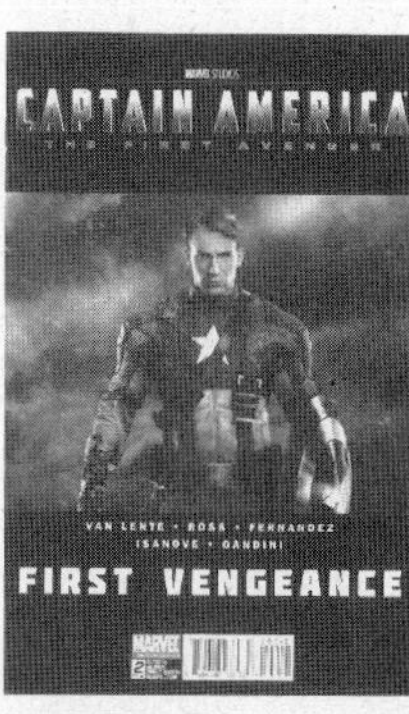
Captain America: First Vengeance #2 © MAR

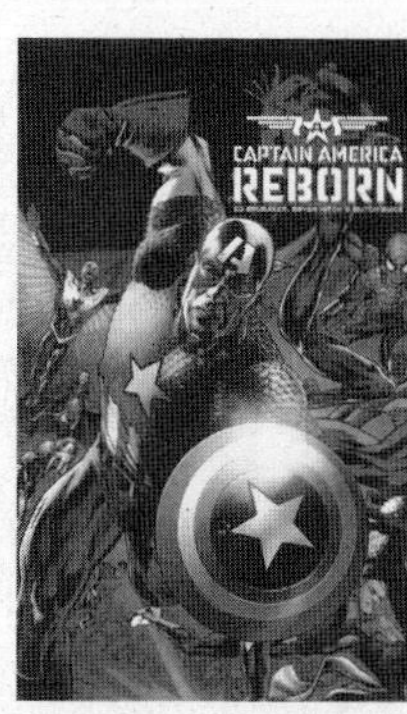
Captain America: Reborn #6 © MAR

Captain America: White #0 © MAR

	GD 2.0	VG 4.0	FN 6.0	VF 8.0	VF/NM 9.0	NM- 9.2
47-Last German War-c	284	568	852	1818	3109	4400
48-58,60	181	362	543	1158	1979	2800
59-Origin retold	331	662	993	2317	4059	5800
61-Red Skull-c/story	354	708	1062	2478	4339	6200
62,64,65: 65-Kurtzman's "Hey Look"	226	452	678	1446	2473	3500
63-Intro/origin Asbestos Lady	232	464	696	1485	2543	3600
66-Bucky is shot; Golden Girl teams up with Captain America & learns his i.d; origin Golden Girl	300	600	900	1950	3375	4800
67-69: 67-Captain America/Golden Girl team-up; Mxyztplk swipe; last Toro in Human Torch. 68-Sub-Mariner/Namora, and Captain America/Golden Girl team-up. 69-Human Torch/ Sun Girl team-up.	300	600	900	1920	3310	4700
70-73: 70-Sub-Mariner/Namora, and Captain America/Golden Girl team-up. 70-SciFi-c/story. 71-Anti Wertham editorial; The Witness, Bucky app.	303	606	909	2121	3711	5300
74-(Scarce)(10/49)-Titled "Captain America's Weird Tales"; Red Skull-c & app.; classic-c	1000	2000	3000	7400	13,200	19,000
75(2/50)-Titled "C.A.'s Weird Tales"; no C.A. app.; horror cover/stories	303	606	909	2121	3711	5300
76-78(1954): Human Torch/Toro stories; all have communist-c/stories	174	348	522	1114	1907	2700
132-Pg. Issue (B&W-1942)(Canadian)-Very rare. Has blank inside-c and back-c; contains Marvel Mystery #33 & Captain America #18 w/cover from Captain America #22; same contents as one version of the Marvel Mystery annuals	6000	12,000	18,000	36,000	-	-

NOTE: *Crandall a-2i, 3i, 9i, 10i.* ***Kirby*** *c-1, 2, 5-8p.* ***Rico*** *c-69-71.* ***Romita*** *c-77, 78.* ***Schomburg*** *c-3, 4, 26-29, 31, 33, 37-39, 41, 42, 45-54, 58.* ***Sekowsky*** *c-55, 56.* ***Shores*** *c-1i, 2i, 5-7i, 11i, 20-25, 30, 32, 34, 35, 40, 57, 59-67.* ***S&K*** *c-9, 10. Bondage c-3, 7, 15, 16, 34, 38.*

CAPTAIN AMERICA COMICS #1 70TH ANNIVERSARY EDITION
Marvel Comics: May, 2011 ($4.99, one-shot)

1-Recolored reprint of entire 1941 issue including Hurricane & Tuk stories; Ching-c 5.00

CAPTAIN AMERICA COMICS 70TH ANNIVERSARY SPECIAL
Marvel Comics: June, 2009 ($3.99, one-shot)

1-WWII flashback; Marcos Martin-a; Marcos-2 covers; r/Capt. America Comics #7 5.00

CAPTAIN AMERICA CORPS
Marvel Comics: Aug, 2011 - No. 5, Dec, 2011 ($2.99, limited series)

1-5-Stern-s/Briones-a/Jimenez-a; various versions of Captain America team-up 3.00

CAPTAIN AMERICA: DEAD MEN RUNNING
Marvel Comics: Mar, 2002 - No. 3, May, 2002 ($2.99, limited series)

1-3-Macan-s/Zezelj-a 3.00

CAPTAIN AMERICA: FIRST VENGEANCE (Based on the 2011 movie version)
Marvel Comics: Jul, 2011 - No. 4, Aug, 2011 ($2.99, limited series)

1-4-Van Lente-s; art by Luke Ross & others. 2-Movie photo-c 3.00

CAPTAIN AMERICA: FOREVER ALLIES
Marvel Comics: Oct, 2010 - No. 4, Jan, 2011 ($3.99, limited series)

1-4-Stern-s/Dragotta-a; Bucky in present & WW2 flashbacks; Young Allies app. 4.00

CAPTAIN AMERICA: HAIL HYDRA
Marvel Comics: Mar, 2011 - No. 5, Jul, 2011 ($2.99, limited series)

1-5-Cap vs. Hydra; Granov-c. 1-WWII flashback. 2-Kirby-style art by Scioli. 4-Hotz-a 3.00

CAPTAIN AMERICA: MAN OUT OF TIME
Marvel Comics: Jan, 2011 - No. 5, May, 2011 ($3.99, limited series)

1-5-Waid-s/Molina-a/Hitch-c; Cap's unfreezing in modern times re-told 4.00

CAPTAIN AMERICA/NICK FURY: BLOOD TRUCE
Marvel Comics: Feb, 1995 ($5.95, one-shot, squarebound)

nn-Chaykin story 6.00

CAPTAIN AMERICA/NICK FURY: THE OTHERWORLD WAR
Marvel Comics: Oct, 2001 ($6.95, one-shot, squarebound)

nn-Manco-a; Bucky and Red Skull app. 7.00

CAPTAIN AMERICA: PATRIOT
Marvel Comics: Nov, 2010 - No. 4, Feb, 2011 ($3.99, limited series)

1-4-Kesel-s/Breitweiser-a; 1-WW2 story; Patriot & the Liberty Legion app. 4.00

CAPTAIN AMERICA: REBORN (Titled Reborn in #1-3)
Marvel Comics: Sept, 2009 - No. 6, Mar, 2010 ($3.99, limited series)

1-6-Steve Rogers returns from the dead; Brubaker-s/Hitch & Guice-a. 1-Covers by Hitch, Ross & Quesada. 2-Origin re-told. 4-Joe Kubert var-c. 5-Cassaday var-c 4.00
1-4-Variant-c by Cassaday. 2-Variant-c by Sale. 5-Finch var-c 10.00
... MGC #1 (5/11, $1.00) r/#1 with "Marvel's Greatest Comics" logo on cover 3.00
...: Who Will Wield the Shield? (2/10, $3.99) Aftermath of series; Guice & Luke Ross-a 4.00

CAPTAIN AMERICA: RED, WHITE & BLUE
Marvel Comics: Sept, 2002 ($29.99, one-shot, hardcover with dustjacket)

nn-Reprints from Lee & Kirby, Steranko, Miller and others; and new short stories and pin-ups by various incl. Ross, Dini, Timm, Waid, Dorkin, Sienkiewicz, Miller, Bruce Jones, Collins, Piers-Rayner, Pope, Deodato, Quitely, Nino; Stelfreeze-c 30.00
TPB (2007, $19.99) 20.00

CAPTAIN AMERICA, SENTINEL OF LIBERTY (See Fireside Book Series)

CAPTAIN AMERICA: SENTINEL OF LIBERTY
Marvel Comics: Sept, 1998 - No. 12, Aug, 1999 ($1.99)

1-Waid-s/Garney-a 3.00
1-Rough Cut ($2.99) Features original script and pencil pages 3.00
2-5: 2-Two-c; Invaders WW2 story 3.00
6-($2.99) Iron Man-c/app. 4.00
7-11: 8-Falcon-c/app. 9-Falcon poses as Cap 3.00
12-($2.99) Final issue; Bucky-c/app. 4.00

CAPTAIN AMERICA SPECIAL EDITION
Marvel Comics Group: Feb, 1984 - No. 2, Mar, 1984 ($2.00, Baxter paper)

1-Steranko-c/a(r) in both; r/ Captain America #110,111 6.00

	GD 2.0	VG 4.0	FN 6.0	VF 8.0	VF/NM 9.0	NM- 9.2
2-Reprints the scarce Our Love Story #5, and C.A. #113	1	2	3	5	6	8

CAPTAIN AMERICA THEATER OF WAR
Marvel Comics: 2009 - 2010 ($3.99, series of one-shots)

...: A Brother in Arms (6/09) Jenkins-s/McCrea-a; WWII story 4.00
...: Ghosts of My Country (12/09) Jenkins-s/Bonetti-a/Guice-c 4.00
...: Prisoners of Duty (2/10) Higgins & Siegel-s/Padilla-a; WWII story 4.00
...: To Soldier On (10/09) Jenkins-s/Blanco-a/Noto-c; Captain America in Iraq 4.00

CAPTAIN AMERICA: THE CHOSEN
Marvel Comics: Nov, 2007 - No. 6, Mar, 2008 ($3.99, limited series)

1-6-Breitweiser-a/Morrell-s 4.00

CAPTAIN AMERICA: THE CLASSIC YEARS
Marvel Comics: Jun, 1998 -No. 2 (trade paperbacks)

1-($19.95) Reprints Captain America Comics #1-5 25.00
2-($24.95) Reprints Captain America Comics #6-10 25.00

CAPTAIN AMERICA: THE LEGEND
Marvel Comics: Sept, 1996 ($3.95, one-shot)

1-Tribute issue; wraparound-c 4.00

CAPTAIN AMERICA: THE 1940S NEWSPAPER STRIP
Marvel Comics: Aug, 2010 - No. 3, Oct, 2010 ($3.99, limited series)

1-3-Karl Kesel-s/a; new stories set in WW2, formatted like 1940s newspaper comics 4.00

CAPTAIN AMERICA: WHAT PRICE GLORY
Marvel Comics: May, 2003 - No. 4, May, 2003 ($2.99, weekly limited series)

1-4-Bruce Jones-s/Steve Rude & Mike Royer-a 3.00

CAPTAIN AMERICA: WHITE
Marvel Comics: No. 0, Sept, 2008 ($2.99, unfinished limited series)

0-Bucky's origin retold; Loeb-s/Sale-a; interviews with creators; Sale sketch art 3.00

CAPTAIN AND THE KIDS, THE (See Famous Comics Cartoon Books)

CAPTAIN AND THE KIDS, THE (See Comics on Parade, Katzenjammer Kids, Okay Comics & Sparkler Comics)
United Features Syndicate/Dell Publ. Co.: 1938 -12/39; Sum, 1947 - No. 32, 1955; Four Color No. 881, Feb, 1958

	GD 2.0	VG 4.0	FN 6.0	VF 8.0	VF/NM 9.0	NM- 9.2
Single Series 1(1938)	107	214	321	680	1165	1650
Single Series 1(Reprint)(12/39- "Reprint" on-c)	48	96	144	302	514	725
1(Summer, 1947-UFS)-Katzenjammer Kids	17	34	51	98	154	210
2	11	22	33	60	83	105
3-10	9	18	27	52	69	85
11-20	8	16	24	42	54	65
21-32 (1955)	8	16	24	40	50	60
50th Anniversary issue-(1948)-Contains a 2 pg. history of the strip, including an account of the famous Supreme Court decision allowing both Pulitzer & Hearst to run the same strip under different names	15	30	45	94	147	200
Special Summer issue, Fall issue (1948)	11	22	33	60	83	105
Four Color 881 (Dell)	4	8	12	28	44	60

CAPTAIN ATOM
Nationwide Publishers: 1950 - No. 7, 1951 (5¢, 5x7-1/4", 52 pgs.)

	GD 2.0	VG 4.0	FN 6.0	VF 8.0	VF/NM 9.0	NM- 9.2
1-Science fiction	42	84	126	265	445	625
2-7	23	46	69	136	223	310

Captain Atom (2011 series) #1 © DC

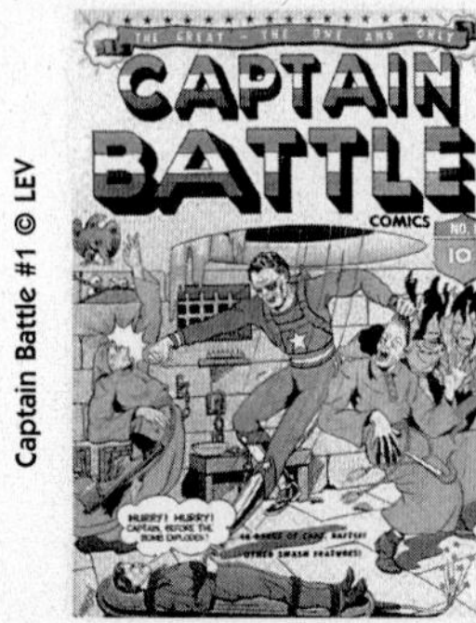

Captain Battle #1 © LEV

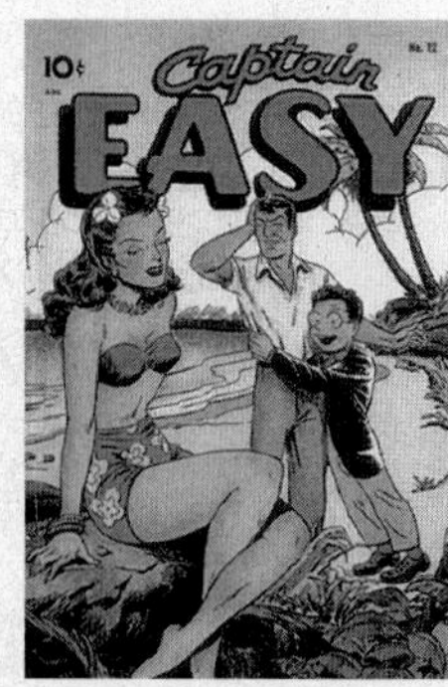

Captain Easy #12 © NEA

GD VG FN VF VF/NM NM-
2.0 4.0 6.0 8.0 9.0 9.2

CAPTAIN ATOM (Formerly Strange Suspense Stories #77)(Also see Space Adventures and Thunderbolt)
Charlton Comics: V2#78, Dec, 1965 - V2#89, Dec, 1967

V2#78-Origin retold; Bache-a (3 pgs.) 8 16 24 55 93 130
79-82: 79-1st app. Dr. Spectro; 3 pg. Ditko cut & paste /Space Adventures #24. 82-Intro. Nightshade (9/66) 6 12 18 37 59 80
83-86: Ted Kord Blue Beetle in all. 83-(11/66)-1st app. Ted Kord. 84-1st app. new Captain Atom 5 10 15 32 51 70
87-89: Nightshade by Aparo in all 5 10 15 32 51 70
83-85(Modern Comics-1977)-reprints 1 2 3 4 5 7
NOTE: *Aparo a-87-89.* ***Ditko*** *c/a(p) 78-89. #90 only published in fanzine 'The Charlton Bullseye' #1, 2.*

CAPTAIN ATOM (Also see Americomics & Crisis On Infinite Earths)
DC Comics: Mar, 1987 - No. 57, Sept, 1991 (Direct sales only #35 on)

1-(44 pgs.)-Origin/1st app. with new costume 4.00
2-49: 5-Firestorm x-over. 6-Intro. new Dr. Spectro. 11-Millennium tie-in. 14-Nightshade app. 16-Justice League app. 17-$1.00-c begins; Swamp Thing app. 20-Blue Beetle x-over. 24,25-Invasion tie-in 3.00
50-($2.00, 52 pgs.) 4.00
51-57: 57-War of the Gods x-over 3.00
Annual 1,2 ('88, '89)-1-Intro Major Force 4.00

CAPTAIN ATOM (DC New 52)
DC Comics: Nov, 2011 - Present ($2.99)

1-7-J.T. Krul-s/Freddie Williams II-a. 3-Flash app. 3.00

CAPTAIN ATOM: ARMAGEDDON (Restarts the WildStorm Universe)
DC Comics (WildStorm): Dec, 2005 - No. 9, Aug, 2006 ($2.99, limited series)

1-9-Captain Atom appears in WildStorm Universe; Pfeifer-s/Camuncoli-a. 1-Lee-c 3.00
TPB (2007, $19.99) r/series 20.00

CAPTAIN BATTLE (Boy Comics #3 on) (See Silver Streak Comics)
New Friday Publ./Comic House: Summer, 1941 - No. 2, Fall, 1941

1-Origin Blackout by Rico; Captain Battle begins (1st appeared in Silver Streak #10, 5/41) 145 290 435 921 1586 2250
2 81 162 243 518 884 1250

CAPTAIN BATTLE (2nd Series)
Magazine Press/Picture Scoop No. 5: No. 3, Wint, 1942-43; No. 5, Sum, 1943 (No #4)

3-Origin Silver Streak-r/SS#3; origin Lance Hale-r/Silver Streak; Simon-a(r) (52 pgs., nd) 71 142 213 454 777 1100
5-Origin Blackout retold (68 pgs.) 53 106 159 324 567 800

CAPTAIN BATTLE, JR.
Comic House (Lev Gleason): Fall, 1943 - No. 2, Winter, 1943-44

1-Nazi WWII-c by Rico. Hitler/Claw sty; The Claw vs. The Ghost 135 270 405 864 1482 2100
2-Wolverton's Scoop Scuttle; Don Rico-c/a; The Green Claw story is reprinted from Silver Streak #6; bondage/torture-c 81 162 243 518 884 1250

CAPTAIN BEN DIX (See Promotional Comics section)

CAPTAIN BRITAIN (Also see Marvel Team-Up No. 65, 66)
Marvel Comics International: Oct. 13, 1976 - No. 39, July 6, 1977 (Weekly)

1-Origin; with Capt. Britain's face mask inside 2 4 6 13 18 22
2-Origin, part II; Capt. Britain's Boomerang inside 2 4 6 9 13 16
3-7,9-11: 3-Vs. Bank Robbers. 4-7-Vs. Hurricane. 9-11- Battles Dr. Synne 1 2 3 5 6 8
8-(12/76) 1st app. Betsy Braddock, the sister of Capt. Britain (Brian Braddock) who later becomes Psylocke (X-Men); 1st app. Dr. Synne 2 4 6 10 14 18
12-23,25-27: (scarce)-12,13-Vs. Dr. Synne. 14,15-Vs. Mastermind. 16-23,25,26-With Captain America. 17-Misprinted & color section reprinted in #18. 27-Origin retold 2 4 6 10 14 18
24-With C.B.'s Jet Plane inside 3 6 9 14 19 24
28-32,36-39: 28-32-Vs. Lord Hawk. 37-39-Vs. Highwayman & Munipulator 5.00
33-35-More on origin 6.00
Annual (1978, Hardback, 64 pgs.)-Reprints #1-7 with pin-ups of Marvel characters 2 4 6 11 16 20
Summer Special (1980, 52 pgs.)-Reprints 1 2 3 4 5 7
NOTE: *No. 1, 2, & 24 are rarer in mint due to inserts. Distributed in Great Britain only. Nick Fury-r by* ***Steranko*** *in 1-20, 24-31, 35-37. Fantastic Four-r by* ***J. Buscema*** *in all. New* ***Buscema****-a in 24-30. Story from No. 39 continues in Super Spider-Man (British weekly) No. 231-247. Following cancellation of his series, new Captain Britain stories appeared in "Super Spider-Man" (British weekly) No. 231-247. Captain Britain stories which appear in Super-Spider-Man No 248-253 are reprints of Marvel Team-Up No. 65&66. Capt. Britain strips also appeared in Hulk Comic (weekly) 1, 3-30, 42-55, 57-60, in Marvel Superheroes (monthly) 377-388, in Daredevils (monthly) 1-11, Mighty World of Marvel (monthly) 7-16 & Captain Britain (monthly) 1-14. Issues 1-23 have B&W & color, paper-c, & are 32 pgs. Issues 24 on are all B&W w/glossy-c & are 36 pgs.*

CAPTAIN BRITAIN AND MI: 13 (Also see Secret Invasion x-over titles)

GD VG FN VF VF/NM NM-
2.0 4.0 6.0 8.0 9.0 9.2

Marvel Comics: Jul, 2008 - No. 15, Sept, 2009 ($2.99)

1-Skrull invasion; Black Knight app.; Kirk-a 4.00
1-2nd printing with Kirk variant-c; 3rd printing with B&W cover 3.00
2-15: 5-Blade app. 9,10-Dracula app. 3.00
... Annual 1 (8/09, $3.99) Land-c; Meggan in Hell; Dr. Doom cameo; Collins-a 4.00

CAPTAIN CANUCK
Comely Comix (Canada)(All distr. in U. S.): 7/75 - No. 4, 7/77; No. 4, 7-8/79 - No. 14, 3-4/81

1-1st app. Bluefox 5.00
2,3(5-7/76)-2-1st app. Dr. Walker, Redcoat & Kebec. 3-1st app. Heather 4.00
4(1st printing-2/77)-10x14-1/2"; (5.00); B&W; 300 copies serially numbered and signed with one certificate of authenticity 7 14 21 49 82 115
4(2nd printing-7/77)-11x17", B&W; only 15 copies printed; signed by creator Richard Comely, serially #'d and two certificates of authenticity inserted; orange cardboard covers (Very Rare) 10 20 30 69 130 190
4-14: 4(7-8/79)-1st app. Tom Evans & Mr. Gold; origin The Catman. 5-Origin Capt. Canuck's powers; 1st app. Earth Patrol & Chaos Corps. 8-Jonn 'The Final Chapter'. 9-1st World Beyond. 11-1st 'Chariots of Fire' story 4.00
15-(8/04, $15.00) Limited edition of unpublished issue from 1981; serially #'d edition of 150; signed by creator Richard Comely 5 10 15 30 48 65
... Legacy 1 (9-10/06) Comely-s/a 3.00
... Legacy Special Edition ($7.95, 52 pgs., limited ed. of 1000) Comely-s/a 1 2 3 5 6 8
Special Collectors Pack (polybagged) 1 3 4 6 8 10
Summer Special 1(7-9/80, 95¢, 64 pgs.) 4.00
NOTE: *30,000 copies of No. 2 were destroyed in Winnipeg.*

CAPTAIN CANUCK: UNHOLY WAR
Comely Comix: Oct, 2004 - No. 3 ($2.50, limited series)

1-Riel Langlois-s/Drue Langlois-a 3.00

CAPTAIN CARROT AND HIS AMAZING ZOO CREW (Also see New Teen Titans & Oz-Wonderland War)
DC Comics: Mar, 1982 - No. 20, Nov, 1983

1-20: 1-Superman app. 3-Re-intro Dodo & The Frog. 9-Re-intro Three Mouseketeers, the Terrific Whatzit. 10,11-Pig Iron reverts back to Peter Porkchops. 20-Changeling app. 3.00

CAPTAIN CARROT AND THE FINAL ARK (DC Countdown tie-in)
DC Comics: Dec, 2007 - No. 3, Feb, 2008 ($2.99, limited series)

1-3-Bill Morrison-s/Scott Shaw!-a. 3-Batman, Red Arrow, Hawkgirl & Zatanna app. 3.00
TPB (2008, $19.99) r/#1-3; Captain Carrot and His Amazing Zoo Crew #1,14,15; New Teen Titans #16 and stories from Teen Titans (2003 series) #30,31; cover gallery 20.00

CAPTAIN CARVEL AND HIS CARVEL CRUSADERS (See Carvel Comics)

CAPTAIN CONFEDERACY
Marvel Comics (Epic Comics): Nov, 1991 - No. 4, Feb, 1992 ($1.95)

1-4: All new stories 3.00

CAPTAIN COURAGEOUS COMICS (Banner #3-5; see Four Favorites #5)
Periodical House (Ace Magazines): No. 6, March, 1942

6-Origin & 1st app. The Sword; Lone Warrior, Capt. Courageous app.; Capt. moves to Four Favorites #5 in May 79 158 237 502 864 1225

CAPT'N CRUNCH COMICS (See Cap'n...)

CAPTAIN DAVY JONES
Dell Publishing Co.: No. 598, Nov, 1954

Four Color 598 5 10 15 30 48 65

CAPTAIN EASY (See The Funnies & Red Ryder #3-32)
Hawley/Dell Publ./Standard(Visual Editions)/Argo: 1939 - No. 17, Sept, 1949; April, 1956

nn-Hawley(1939)-Contains reprints from The Funnies & 1938 Sunday strips by Roy Crane 89 178 267 565 970 1375
Four Color 24 (1943) 50 100 150 315 533 750
Four Color 111(6/46) 12 24 36 81 166 250
10(Standard-10/47) 13 26 39 72 101 130
11,12,14,15,17: 11-17 all contain 1930s & '40s strip-r 10 20 30 54 72 90
13,16: Schomburg-c 11 22 33 62 86 110
Argo 1(4/56)-Reprints 7 14 21 37 46 55

CAPTAIN EASY & WASH TUBBS (See Famous Comics Cartoon Books)

CAPTAIN ELECTRON
Brick Computer Science Institute: Aug, 1986 ($2.25)

1-Disbrow-a 3.00

CAPTAIN EO 3-D (Michael Jackson Disney theme parks movie)
Eclipse Comics: July, 1987 (Eclipse 3-D Special #18, $3.50, Baxter)

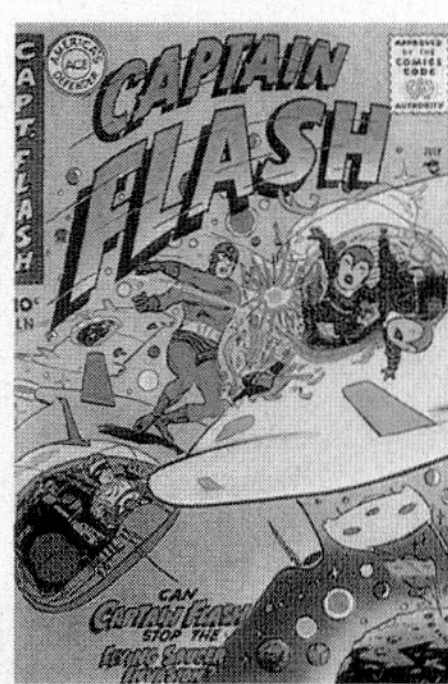

Captain Flash #4 © Sterling

Captain Jet #4 © Farrell

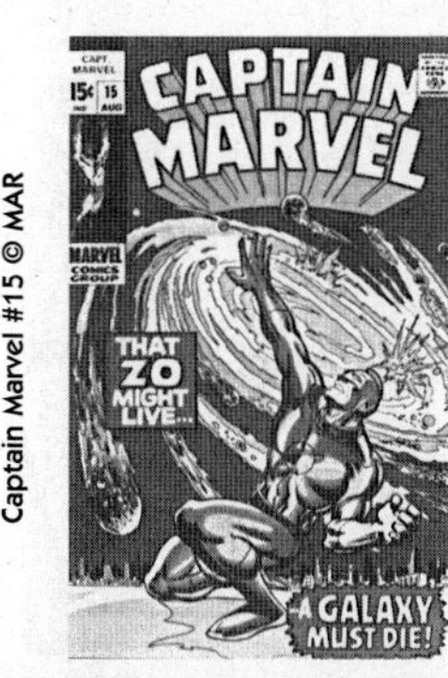

Captain Marvel #15 © MAR

GD 2.0 | VG 4.0 | FN 6.0 | VF 8.0 | VF/NM 9.0 | NM- 9.2

1-Adapts 3-D movie; Michael Jackson-c/app. 6.00
1-2-D limited edition 2 4 6 9 12 15
1-Large size (11x17", 8/87)-Sold only at Disney Theme parks ($6.95) 3 6 9 14 20 25

CAPTAIN FEARLESS COMICS (Also see Holyoke One-Shot #6, Old Glory Comics & Silver Streak #1)
Helnit Publishing Co. (Holyoke Publ. Co.): Aug, 1941 - No. 2, Sept, 1941

1-Origin Mr. Miracle, Alias X, Captain Fearless, Citizen Smith Son of the Unknown Soldier; Miss Victory (1st app.) begins (1st patriotic heroine? before Wonder Woman) 84 168 252 538 919 1300
2-Grit Grady, Captain Stone app. 50 100 150 315 533 750

CAPTAIN FLAG (See Blue Ribbon Comics #16)

CAPTAIN FLASH
Sterling Comics: Nov, 1954 - No. 4, July, 1955

1-Origin; Sekowsky-a; Tomboy (female super hero) begins; only pre-code issue; atomic rocket-c 40 80 120 246 411 575
2-4: 4-Flying saucer invasion-c 22 44 66 132 216 300

CAPTAIN FLEET (Action Packed Tales of the Sea)
Ziff-Davis Publishing Co.: Fall, 1952

1-Painted-c 16 32 48 92 144 195

CAPTAIN FLIGHT COMICS
Four Star Publications: May, 1944 - No. 10, Dec, 1945; No. 11, Feb-Mar, 1947

nn-Captain Flight begins 46 92 138 290 488 685
2-4: 4-Rock Raymond begins, ends #7 27 54 81 158 259 360
5-Bondage, classic torture-c; Red Rocket begins; the Grenade app. (scarce) 123 246 369 787 1344 1900
6 25 50 75 150 245 340
7-10: 7-L. B. Cole covers begin, end #11. 8-Yankee Girl begins; intro. Black Cobra & Cobra Kid & begins. 9-Torpedoman app.; last Yankee Girl; Kinstler-a. 10-Deep Sea Dawson, Zoom of the Jungle, Rock Raymond, Red Rocket, & Black Cobra app; bondage-c 52 104 156 328 557 785
11-Torpedoman, Blue Flame (Human Torch clone) app.; last Black Cobra, Red Rocket; classic L. B. Cole sci-fi robot-c (scarce) 181 362 543 1158 1979 2800

CAPTAIN GALLANT (...of the Foreign Legion) (TV) (Texas Rangers in Action No. 5 on?)
Charlton Comics: 1955; No. 2, Jan, 1956 - No. 4, Sept, 1956

Non-Heinz version (#1)-Buster Crabbe photo on-c; full page Buster Crabbe photo inside front-c 8 16 24 44 57 70
(Heinz version is listed in the Promotional Comics section)
2-4: Buster Crabbe in all. 2-Crabbe photo back-c 6 12 18 31 38 45

CAPTAIN GLORY
Topps Comics: Apr, 1993 ($2.95) (Created by Jack Kirby)

1-Polybagged w/Kirbychrome trading card; Ditko-a & Kirby-c; has coupon for Amberchrome Secret City Saga #0 3.00

CAPTAIN HERO (See Jughead as...)

CAPTAIN HERO COMICS DIGEST MAGAZINE
Archie Publications: Sept, 1981

1-Reprints of Jughead as Super-Guy 2 4 6 10 14 18

CAPTAIN HOBBY COMICS
Export Publication Ent. Ltd. (Dist. in U.S. by Kable News Co.): Feb, 1948 (Canadian)

1 8 16 24 40 50 60

CAPT. HOLO IN 3-D (See Blackthorne 3-D Series #65)

CAPTAIN HOOK & PETER PAN (Movie)(Disney)
Dell Publishing Co.: No. 446, Jan, 1953

Four Color 446 9 18 27 58 99 140

CAPTAIN JET (Fantastic Fears No. 7 on)
Four Star Publ./Farrell/Comic Media: May, 1952 - No. 5, Jan, 1953

1-Bakerish-a 23 46 69 136 223 310
2 14 28 42 82 121 160
3-5,6(?) 12 24 36 69 97 125

CAPTAIN JOHNER & THE ALIENS
Valiant: May, 1995 - No. 2, May, 1995 ($2.95, shipped in same month)

1,2: Reprints Magnus Robot Fighter 4000 A.D. back-up stories; new Paul Smith-c 3.00

CAPTAIN JUSTICE (TV)
Marvel Comics: Mar, 1988 - No. 2, Apr, 1988 (limited series)

1,2-Based on the 1987 "Once a Hero" television series 3.00

CAPTAIN KANGAROO (TV)
Dell Publishing Co.: No. 721, Aug, 1956 - No. 872, Jan, 1958

Four Color 721 (#1)-Photo-c 13 26 39 88 189 290
Four Color 780, 872-Photo-c 12 24 36 78 157 235

CAPTAIN KIDD (Formerly Dagar; My Secret Story #26 on)(Also see Comic Comics & Fantastic Comics)
Fox Feature Syndicate: No. 24, June, 1949 - No. 25, Aug, 1949

24,25: 24-Features Blackbeard the Pirate 15 30 45 83 124 165

CAPTAIN MARVEL (See All Hero, All-New Collectors' Ed., America's Greatest, Fawcett Miniature, Gift, JSA, Kingdom Come, Legends, Limited Collectors' Ed., Marvel Family, Master No. 21, Mighty Midget Comics, Power of Shazam!, Shazam, Special Edition Comics, Whiz, Wisco (in Promotional Comics section), World's Finest #253 and XMas Comics)

CAPTAIN MARVEL (Becomes ...Presents the Terrible 5 No. 5)
M. F. Enterprises: April, 1966 - No. 4, Nov, 1966 (25¢ Giants)

nn-(#1 on pg. 5)-Origin; created by Carl Burgos 5 10 15 35 55 75
2-4: 3-(#3 on pg. 4)-Fights the Bat 4 8 12 22 34 45

CAPTAIN MARVEL (Marvel's Space-Born Super-Hero! Captain Marvel #1-6; see Giant-Size..., Life Of..., Marvel Graphic Novel #1, Marvel Spotlight V2#1 & Marvel Super-Heroes #12)
Marvel Comics Group: May, 1968 - No. 19, Dec, 1969; No. 20, June, 1970 - No. 21, Aug, 1970; No. 22, Sept, 1972 - No. 62, May, 1979

1 14 28 42 97 211 325
2-Super Skrull-c/story 8 16 24 56 96 135
3-5: 4-Captain Marvel battles Sub-Mariner 7 14 21 44 72 100
6-11: 11-Capt. Marvel given great power by Zo the Ruler; Smith/Trimpe-c; Death of Una 4 8 12 26 41 55
12,13,15-20: 16,17-New costume 3 6 9 17 25 32
14,21: 14-Capt. Marvel vs. Iron Man; last 12¢ issue. 21-Capt. Marvel battles Hulk; last 15¢ issue 4 8 12 24 37 50
22-24 3 6 9 14 20 26
25,26: 25-Starlin-c/a begins; Starlin's 1st Thanos saga begins (3/73), ends #34; Thanos cameo (5 panels). 26-Minor Thanos app. (see Iron Man #55); 1st Thanos-c 5 10 15 35 55 75
27,28-2nd & 3rd app. Thanos. 28-Thanos-c/s 4 8 12 28 44 60
29,30-Thanos cameos. 29-C.M. gains more powers 3 6 9 19 29 38
31,32: Thanos app. 31-Last 20¢ issue. 32-Thanos-c 3 6 9 20 30 40
33-Thanos-c & app.; Capt. Marvel battles Thanos; Thanos origin re-told 4 8 12 28 44 60
34-1st app. Nitro; C.M. contracts cancer which eventually kills him; last Starlin-c/a 3 6 9 19 29 38
35,37-40,42,46-48,50,53-56,58-62: 39-Origin Watcher. 58-Thanos cameo 2 4 6 8 10 12
36,41,43,49: 36-R-origin/1st app. Capt. Marvel from Marvel Super-Heroes #12. 41,43-Wrightson part inks; #43-c(i). 49-Starlin & Weiss-p assists 2 4 6 8 11 14
44,45-(Regular 25¢ editions)(5,7/76) 2 4 6 8 10 12
44,45-(30¢-c variants, limited distribution) 4 8 12 28 44 60
51,52-(Regular 30¢ editions)(7,9/77) 2 4 6 8 10 12
51,52-(35¢-c variants, limited distribution) 5 10 15 32 51 70
57-Thanos appears in flashback 2 4 6 9 12 15

NOTE: ***Alcala*** *a-35.* ***Austin*** *a-46i, 49-53i; c-52i.* ***Buscema*** *a-18p-21p.* ***Colan*** *a(p)-1-4; c(p)-1-4, 8, 9.* ***Heck*** *a-5-10p, 16p.* ***Gil Kane*** *a-17-21p; c-17-24p, 37p, 53.* ***Starlin*** *a-36.* ***McWilliams*** *a-40i. #25-34 were reprinted in The Life of Captain Marvel.*

CAPTAIN MARVEL
Marvel Comics: Nov, 1989 ($1.50, one-shot, 52 pgs.)

1-Super-hero from Avengers; new powers 4.00

CAPTAIN MARVEL
Marvel Comics: Feb, 1994 ($1.75, 52 pgs.)

1-(Indicia reads Vol 2 #2)-Minor Captain America app. 4.00

CAPTAIN MARVEL
Marvel Comics: Dec, 1995 - No. 6, May, 1996 ($2.95/$1.95)

1 ($2.95)-Advs. of Mar-Vell's son begins; Fabian Nicieza scripts; foil-c 4.00
2-6: 2-Begin $1.95-c 3.00

CAPTAIN MARVEL (Vol. 3) (See Avengers Forever)
Marvel Comics: Jan, 2000 - No. 35, Oct, 2002 ($2.50)

1-Peter David-s in all; two covers 4.00
2-10: 2-Two covers; Hulk app. 9-Silver Surfer app. 3.00
11-35: 12-Maximum Security x-over. 17,18-Starlin-a. 27-30-Spider-Man 2099 app. 3.00
Wizard #0-Preview and history of Rick Jones 4.00
...: First Contact (8/01, $16.95, TPB) r/#0,1-6 17.00

CAPTAIN MARVEL (Vol. 4) (See Avengers Forever)

Captain Marvel Adventures #16 © FAW

Captain Marvel, Jr. #2 © FAW

Captain Midnight #23 © FAW

	GD 2.0	VG 4.0	FN 6.0	VF 8.0	VF/NM 9.0	NM- 9.2

Marvel Comics: Nov, 2002 - No. 25, Sept, 2004 ($2.25/$2.99)

Issue	GD	VG	FN	VF	VF/NM	NM-
1-Peter David-s/Chriscross-a ; 3 covers by Ross, Jusko & Chriscross						4.00
2-7: 2,3-Punisher app. 3-Alex Ross-c; new costume debuts. 4-Noto-c. 7-Thor app.						3.00
3-Sketchbook Edition-($3.50) includes Ross' concept design pages for new costume						4.00
8-25: 8-Begin $2.99-c; Thor app.; Manco-c. 10-Spider-Man-c/app. 15-Neal Adams-c						3.00
Vol. 1: Nothing To Lose (2003, $14.99, TPB) r/#1-6						15.00
Vol. 2: Coven (2003, $14.99, TPB) r/#7-12						15.00
Vol. 3: Crazy Like a Fox (2004, $14.99, TPB) r/#13-18						15.00
Vol. 4: Odyssey (2004, $16.99, TPB) r/#19-25						17.00

CAPTAIN MARVEL (Vol. 5) (See Secret Invasion x-over titles)
Marvel Comics: Jan, 2008 - No. 5, Jun, 2008 ($2.99)

Issue	GD	VG	FN	VF	VF/NM	NM-
1-5-Mar-Vell "from the past in the present"; McGuinness-c/Weeks-a						3.00
3,4-Skrull variant-c						4.00

CAPTAIN MARVEL ADVENTURES (See Special Edition Comics for pre #1)
Fawcett Publications: 1941 (March) - No. 150, Nov, 1953 (#1 on stands 1/16/41)

Issue	GD	VG	FN	VF	VF/NM	NM-
nn(#1)-Captain Marvel & Sivana by Jack Kirby. The cover was printed on unstable paper stock and is rarely found in Fine or Mint condition; blank back inside-c	3000	6000	9000	22,500	41,250	60,000
2-(Advertised as #3, which was counting Special Edition Comics as the real #1); Tuska-a	423	846	1269	3088	5444	7800
3-Metallic silver-c	309	618	927	2163	3782	5400
4-Three Lt. Marvels app.	213	426	639	1363	2332	3300
5	168	336	504	1075	1838	2600
6-10: 9-1st Otto Binder scripts on Capt. Marvel	126	252	378	806	1378	1950
11-15: 12-Capt. Marvel joins the Army. 13-Two pg. Capt. Marvel pin-up. 15-Comic cards on back-c begin, end #26	103	206	309	659	1130	1600
16,17: 17-Painted-c	94	188	282	597	1024	1450
18-Origin & 1st app. Mary Marvel & Marvel Family (12/11/42); painted-c; Mary Marvel by Marcus Swayze	277	554	831	1759	3030	4300
19-Mary Marvel x-over; Christmas-c	81	162	243	518	884	1250
20,21,23-Attached to the cover, each has a miniature comic just like the Mighty Midget Comics #11, except that each has a full color promo ad on the back cover. Most copies were circulated without the miniature comic. These issues with miniatures attached are very rare, and should not be mistaken for copies with the similar Mighty Midget glued in its place. The Mighty Midgets had blank back covers except for a small victory stamp seal. Only the Capt. Marvel, Captain Marvel Jr. and Golden Arrow No. 11 miniatures have been positively documented as having been affixed to these covers. Each miniature was only partially glued by its back cover to the Captain Marvel comic making it easy to see if it's the genuine miniature rather than a Mighty Midget. with comic attached....	389	778	1167	2723	4762	6800
20,23-Without miniature	71	142	213	454	777	1100
21-Without miniature; Hitler-c	123	246	369	787	1344	1900
22-Mr. Mind serial begins; Mr. Mind first heard	97	194	291	621	1061	1500
24,25	68	136	204	432	746	1060
26-28,30: 26-Flag-c; subtle Mr. Mind 2-panel cameo. 27-1st full Mr. Mind app. (his voice was only heard over the radio before now) (9/43)	57	114	171	362	619	875
29-1st Mr. Mind-c (11/43)	60	120	180	381	653	925
31-35: 35-Origin Radar (5/44, see Master #50)	51	102	153	318	539	760
36-40: 37-Mary Marvel x-over	47	94	141	296	498	700
41-46: 42-Christmas-c. 43-Capt. Marvel 1st meets Uncle Marvel; Mary Batson cameo. 46-Mr. Mind serial ends	39	78	117	240	395	550
47-50	37	74	111	222	361	500
51-53,55-60: 51-63-Bi-weekly issues. 52-Origin & 1st app. Sivana Jr.; Capt. Marvel Jr. x-over	33	66	99	194	317	440
54-Special oversize 68 pg. issue	34	68	102	199	325	450
61-The Cult of the Curse serial begins	36	72	108	211	343	475
62-65-Serial cont.; Mary Marvel x-over in #65	33	66	99	194	317	440
66-Serial ends; Atomic War-c	37	74	111	222	361	500
67-77,79: 69-Billy Batson's Christmas; Uncle Marvel, Mary Marvel, Capt. Marvel Jr. x-over. 71-Three Lt. Marvels app. 79-Origin Mr. Tawny	30	60	90	177	289	400
78-Origin Mr. Atom	33	66	99	194	317	440
80-Origin Capt. Marvel retold	71	142	213	454	777	1100
81-84,86-90: 81,90-Mr. Atom app. 82-Infinity-c. 82,86,88,90-Mr. Tawny app.	29	58	87	170	278	385
85-Freedom Train issue	33	66	99	194	317	440
91-99: 92-Mr. Tawny app. 96-Gets 1st name "Tawky"	28	56	84	165	270	375
100-Origin retold; silver metallic-c	47	94	141	296	498	700
101-115,117-120	27	54	81	162	266	370
116-Flying Saucer issue (1/51)	31	62	93	186	303	420
121-Origin retold	36	72	108	214	347	480
122-137,139,140	27	54	81	162	266	370
138-Flying Saucer issue (11/52)	31	62	93	186	303	420
141-Pre-code horror story "The Hideous Head-Hunter"	30	60	90	177	289	400
142-149: 142-used in **POP**, pgs. 92,96	29	58	87	170	278	385
150-(Low distribution)	52	104	156	328	552	775

NOTE: *Swayze a-12, 14, 15, 18, 19, 40; c-12, 15, 19.*

CAPTAIN MARVEL AND THE GOOD HUMOR MAN (Movie)
Fawcett Publications: 1950

Issue	GD	VG	FN	VF	VF/NM	NM-
nn-Partial photo-c w/Jack Carson & the Captain Marvel Club Boys	47	94	141	296	498	700

CAPTAIN MARVEL COMIC STORY PAINT BOOK (See Comic Story...)

CAPTAIN MARVEL, JR. (See Fawcett Miniatures, Marvel Family, Master Comics, Mighty Midget Comics, Shazam & Whiz Comics)

CAPTAIN MARVEL, JR.
Fawcett Publications: Nov, 1942 - No. 119, June, 1953 (No #34)

Issue	GD	VG	FN	VF	VF/NM	NM-
1-Origin Capt. Marvel Jr. retold (Whiz #25); Capt. Nazi app. Classic Raboy-c	568	1136	1704	4146	7323	10,500
2-Vs. Capt. Nazi; origin Capt. Nippon	203	406	609	1289	2220	3150
3	115	230	345	730	1253	1775
4-Classic Raboy-c	121	242	363	768	1322	1875
5-Vs. Capt. Nazi	97	194	291	621	1061	1500
6-8: 8-Vs. Capt. Nazi	81	162	243	518	884	1250
9-Classic flag-c	90	180	270	576	988	1400
10-Hitler-c	142	284	426	909	1555	2200
11,12,15-Capt. Nazi app.	68	136	204	435	743	1050
13-Classic Hitler, Tojo and Mussolini football-c	142	284	426	909	1555	2200
14,16-20: 14-X-Mas-c. 16-Capt. Marvel & Sivana x-over. 19-Capt. Nazi & Capt. Nippon app.	57	114	171	362	619	875
21-30: 25-Flag-c	45	90	135	284	480	675
31-33,36-40: 37-Infinity-c	33	66	99	194	317	440
35-#34 on inside; cover shows origin of Sivana Jr. which is not on inside. Evidently the cover to #35 was printed out of sequence and bound with contents to #34	33	66	99	194	317	440
41-70: 42-Robot-c. 53-Atomic Bomb-c/story	27	54	81	160	263	365
71-99,101-104: 87-Robot-c. 104-Used in **POP**, pg. 89	22	44	66	132	216	300
100	26	52	78	154	252	350
105-114,116-118: 116-Vampira, Queen of Terror app.	24	48	72	140	230	320
115-Classic injury to eye-c; Eyeball story w/injury-to-eye panels	81	162	243	518	884	1250
119-Electric chair-c (scarce)	68	136	204	435	743	1050

NOTE: *Mac Raboy c-1-28, 30-32, 57, 59 among others.*

CAPTAIN MARVEL PRESENTS THE TERRIBLE FIVE
M. F. Enterprises: Aug, 1966; V2#5, Sept, 1967 (No #2-4) (25¢)

Issue	GD	VG	FN	VF	VF/NM	NM-
1	5	10	15	32	51	70
V2#5-(Formerly Captain Marvel)	3	6	9	20	30	40

CAPTAIN MARVEL'S FUN BOOK
Samuel Lowe Co.: 1944 (1/2" thick) (cardboard covers)(25¢)

Issue	GD	VG	FN	VF	VF/NM	NM-
nn-Puzzles, games, magic, etc.; infinity-c	39	78	117	231	378	525

CAPTAIN MARVEL SPECIAL EDITION (See Special Edition)

CAPTAIN MARVEL STORY BOOK
Fawcett Publications: Summer, 1946 - No. 4, Summer?, 1948

Issue	GD	VG	FN	VF	VF/NM	NM-
1-Half text	54	108	162	343	574	825
2-4	39	78	117	240	395	550

CAPTAIN MARVEL THRILL BOOK (Large-Size)
Fawcett Publications: 1941 (B&W w/color-c)

Issue	GD	VG	FN	VF	VF/NM	NM-
1-Reprints from Whiz #8,10, & Special Edition #1 (Rare)	310	620	930	3100	-	-

NOTE: *Rarely found in Fine or Mint condition.*

CAPTAIN MIDNIGHT (TV, radio, films) (See The Funnies, Popular Comics & Super Book of Comics)(Becomes Sweethearts No. 68 on)
Fawcett Publications: Sept, 1942 - No. 67, Fall, 1948 (#1-14: 68 pgs.)

Issue	GD	VG	FN	VF	VF/NM	NM-
1-Origin Captain Midnight, star of radio and movies; Captain Marvel cameo on cover	303	606	909	2121	3711	5300
2-Smashes the Jap Juggarnaut	142	284	426	909	1555	2200
3-Classic Nazi war-c	129	258	387	826	1413	2000
4,5: 4-Grapples the Gremlins	107	214	321	680	1165	1650
6-8	65	130	195	416	708	1000
9-Raboy-c	67	134	201	426	731	1035
10-Raboy Flag-c	68	136	204	432	746	1060
11-20: 11,17,18-Raboy-c. 16 (1/44)	48	96	144	302	514	725
21-Classic WWII-c	54	108	162	343	574	825
22,25-30: 22-War savings stamp-c	40	80	120	246	411	575

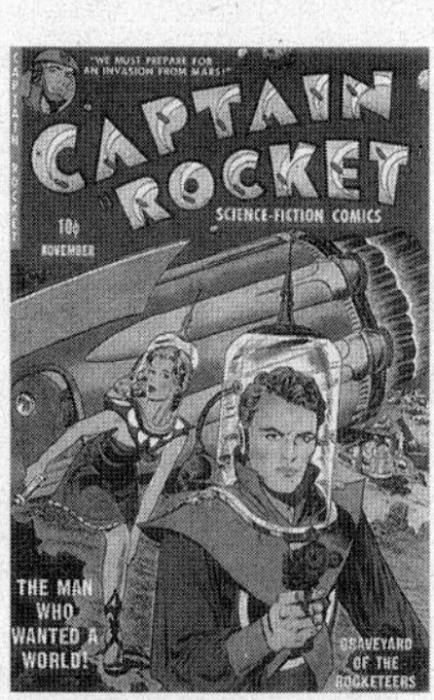

Captain Rocket #1 © P.L. Publ.

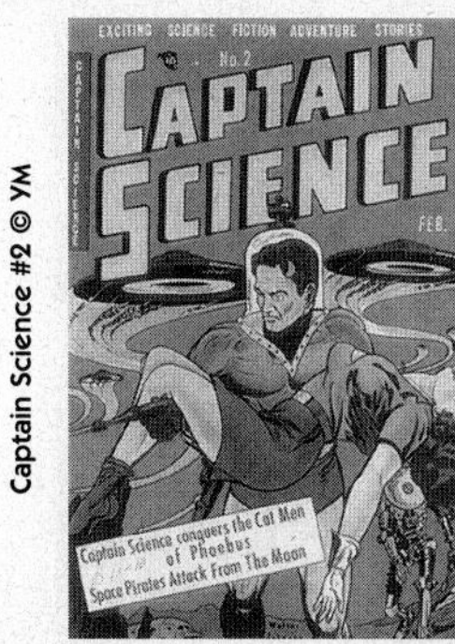

Captain Science #2 © YM

Captain Video #6 © FAW

	GD 2.0	VG 4.0	FN 6.0	VF 8.0	VF/NM 9.0	NM- 9.2
23-WWII Concentration Camp-c	50	100	150	315	533	750
24-Japan flag sunburst-c	55	110	165	352	601	850
31-40	31	62	93	182	296	410
41-59,61-67: 50-Sci/fi theme begins?	23	46	69	136	223	310
60-Flying Saucer issue (2/48)-3rd of this theme; see The Spirit 9/28/47(1st), Shadow Comics V7#10 (2nd, 1/48) & Boy Commandos #26 (4th, 3-4/48)	36	72	108	211	343	475

CAPTAIN NICE (TV)
Gold Key: Nov, 1967 (one-shot)

1(10211-711)-Photo-c 6 12 18 42 69 95

CAPTAIN N: THE GAME MASTER (TV)
Valiant Comics: 1990 - No. 6? ($1.95, thick stock, coated-c)

1-6: 4-6-Layton-c 4.00

CAPTAIN PARAGON (See Bill Black's Fun Comics)
Americomics: Dec, 1983 - No. 4, 1985

1-Intro/1st app. Ms. Victory 4.00
2-4 3.00

CAPTAIN PARAGON AND THE SENTINELS OF JUSTICE
AC Comics: April, 1985 - No. 6, 1986 ($1.75)

1-6: 1-Capt. Paragon, Commando D., Nightveil, Scarlet Scorpion, Stardust & Atoman 3.00

CAPTAIN PLANET AND THE PLANETEERS (TV cartoon)
Marvel Comics: Oct, 1991 - No. 12, Oct, 1992 ($1.00/$1.25)

1-N. Adams painted-c 4.00
2-12: 3-Romita-c 3.00

CAPTAIN POWER AND THE SOLDIERS OF THE FUTURE (TV)
Continuity Comics: Aug, 1988 - No. 2, 1988 ($2.00)

1,2: 1-Neal Adams-c/layouts/inks; variant-c exists. 3.00

CAPTAIN PUREHEART (See Archie as...)

CAPTAIN ROCKET
P. L. Publ. (Canada): Nov, 1951

1 46 92 138 290 488 685

CAPT. SAVAGE AND HIS LEATHERNECK RAIDERS (...And His Battlefield Raiders #9 on)
Marvel Comics Group (Animated Timely Features): Jan, 1968 - No. 19, Mar, 1970
(See Sgt. Fury No. 10)

	GD	VG	FN	VF	VF/NM	NM-
1-Sgt. Fury & Howlers cameo	6	12	18	37	59	80
2,7,11: 2,4-Origin Hydra. 7-Pre-"Thing" Ben Grimm story. 11-Sgt. Fury app.	3	6	9	18	27	35
3-6,8-10,12-14: 14-Last 12¢ issue	3	6	9	16	23	30
15-19	3	6	9	14	19	24

NOTE: *Ayres/Shores a-1-8,11. Ayres/Severin a-9,10,17-19. Heck/Shores a-12-15.*

CAPTAIN SCIENCE (Fantastic No. 8 on)
Youthful Magazines: Nov, 1950; No. 2, Feb, 1951 - No. 7, Dec, 1951

	GD	VG	FN	VF	VF/NM	NM-
1-Wood-a; origin; 2 pg. text w/ photos of George Pal's "Destination Moon."	94	188	282	597	1024	1450
2-Flying saucer-c swipes Weird Science #13(#2)-c	52	104	156	328	552	775
3,6,7; 3,6-Bondage c-swipes/Wings #94,91	43	86	129	271	461	650
4,5-Wood/Orlando-c/a(2) each	86	172	258	546	936	1325

NOTE: *Fass a-4. Bondage c-3, 6, 7.*

CAPTAIN SILVER'S LOG OF SEA HOUND (See Sea Hound)

CAPTAIN SINBAD (Movie Adaptation) (See Fantastic Voyages of... & Movie Comics)

CAPTAIN STERNN: RUNNING OUT OF TIME
Kitchen Sink Press: Sept, 1993 - No. 5, 1994 ($4.95, limited series, coated stock, 52 pgs.)

1-5: Berni Wrightson-c/a/scripts 6.00
1-Gold ink variant 10.00

CAPTAIN STEVE SAVAGE (...& His Jet Fighters, No. 2-13)
Avon Periodicals: 1950 - No. 8, 1/53; No. 5, 9-10/54 - No. 13, 5-6/56

	GD	VG	FN	VF	VF/NM	NM-
nn(1st series)-Harrison/Wood art, 22 pgs. (titled "...Over Korea")	40	80	120	246	411	575
1(4/51)-Reprints nn issue (Canadian)	19	38	57	109	172	235
2-Kamen-a	15	30	45	84	127	170
3-11 (#6, 11-12/54, last precode)	12	24	36	67	94	120
12-Wood-a (6 pgs.)	15	30	45	85	130	175
13-Check, Lawrence-a	12	24	36	69	97	125

NOTE: *Kinstler c-2-5, 7-9, 11. Lawrence a-8. Ravielli a-5, 9.*

	GD	VG	FN	VF	VF/NM	NM-
5(9-10/54-2nd series)(Formerly Sensational Police Cases)	10	20	30	58	79	100
6-Reprints nn issue; Harrison/Wood-a	11	22	33	60	83	105
7-13: 9,10-Kinstler-c. 10-r/cover #2 (1st series). 13-r/cover #8 (1st series)	9	18	27	47	61	75

CAPTAIN STONE (See Holyoke One-Shot No. 10)

CAPT. STORM (Also see G. I. Combat #138)
National Periodical Publications: May-June, 1964 - No. 18, Mar-Apr, 1967

	GD	VG	FN	VF	VF/NM	NM-
1-Origin	10	20	30	68	127	185
2-7,9-18: 3,6,13-Kubert-a. 4-Colan-a. 12-Kubert-c	7	14	21	46	76	105
8-Grey-tone-c	8	16	24	56	96	135

CAPTAIN 3-D (Super hero)
Harvey Publications: December, 1953 (25¢, came with 2 pairs of glasses)

1-Kirby/Ditko-a (Ditko's 3rd published work tied with Strange Fantasy #9, see also Daring Love #1 & Black Magic V4 #3); shows cover in 3-D on inside; Kirby/Meskin-c 12 24 36 69 97 125
NOTE: *Half price without glasses*

CAPTAIN THUNDER AND BLUE BOLT
Hero Comics: Sept, 1987 - No. 10, 1988 ($1.95)

1-10: 1-Origin Blue Bolt. 3-Origin Capt. Thunder. 6-1st app. Wicket. 8-Champions x-over 3.00

CAPTAIN TOOTSIE & THE SECRET LEGION (Advs. of...)(Also see Monte Hale #30,39 & Real Western Hero)
Toby Press: Oct, 1950 - No. 2, Dec, 1950

	GD	VG	FN	VF	VF/NM	NM-
1-Not Beck-a; both have sci/fi covers	32	64	96	188	307	425
2-The Rocketeer Patrol app.; not Beck-a	20	40	60	114	182	250

CAPTAIN TRIUMPH (See Crack Comics #27)

CAPTAIN UNIVERSE... (5-part x-over)
Marvel Comics: 2005; Jan, 2006

.../ Daredevil 1 (1/06, $2.99) Part 2; Faerber-s/Santacruz-a 3.00
.../ Hulk 1 (1/06, $2.99) Part 1; Faerber-s/Magno-a 3.00
.../ Invisible Woman 1 (1/06, $2.99) Part 4; Faerber-s/Raiz-a; Gladiator app. 3.00
.../ Silver Surfer 1 (1/06, $2.99) Part 5; Faerber-s/Magno-a 3.00
.../ X-23 1 (1/06, $2.99) Part 3; Faerber-s/Portella-a; Scorpion app. 3.00
...: Power Unimaginable TPB (2005, $19.99)-Reprints from Marvel Spotlight #9-11, Incredible Hulk Ann. #10, Marvel Fanfare #25, Web of Spider-Man Ann. #5&6, Marvel Comics Presents #148, Cosmic Power Unlimited #5 20.00
...: Universal Heroes TPB (2005, $13.99) reprints .../Hulk, .../Daredevil, ...X-23 and back-up stories from Amazing Fantasy (2005) #13,14 14.00

CAPTAIN VENTURE & THE LAND BENEATH THE SEA (See Space Family Robinson)
Gold Key: Oct, 1968 - No. 2, Oct, 1969

	GD	VG	FN	VF	VF/NM	NM-
1-r/Space Family Robinson serial; Spiegle-a	4	8	12	28	44	60
2-Spiegle-a	4	8	12	24	37	50

CAPTAIN VICTORY AND THE GALACTIC RANGERS (Also see Kirby: Genesis)
Pacific Comics: Nov, 1981 - No. 13, Jan, 1984 ($1.00, direct sales, 36-48 pgs.)
(Created by Jack Kirby)

1-1st app. Mr. Mind 4.00
2-13: 3-N. Adams-a 3.00
Special 1-(10/83)-Kirby c/a(p) 4.00
NOTE: *Conrad a-10, 11. Ditko a-6. Kirby a-1-3p; c-1-13.*

CAPTAIN VICTORY AND THE GALACTIC RANGERS
Jack Kirby Comics: July, 2000 - No. 2, Sept, 2000 ($2.95, B&W)

1,2-New Jeremy Kirby-s with reprinted Jack Kirby-a; Liefeld pin-up art 3.00

CAPTAIN VIDEO (TV) (See XMas Comics)
Fawcett Publications: Feb, 1951 - No. 6, Dec, 1951 (No. 1,5,6-36 pgs.; 2-4, 52 pgs.)

	GD	VG	FN	VF	VF/NM	NM-
1-George Evans-a(2); 1st TV hero comic	100	200	300	635	1093	1550
2-Used in **SOTI**, pg. 382	65	130	195	416	708	1000
3-6-All Evans-a except #5 mostly Evans	54	108	162	343	574	825

NOTE: *Minor Williamson assists on most issues. Photo c-1, 5, 6; painted c-2-4.*

CAPTAIN WILLIE SCHULTZ (Also see Fightin' Army)
Charlton Comics: No. 76, Oct, 1985 - No. 77, Jan, 1986

76,77-Low print run 1 2 3 5 6 8

CAPTAIN WIZARD COMICS (See Meteor, Red Band & Three Ring Comics)
Rural Home: 1946

1-Capt. Wizard dons new costume; Impossible Man, Race Wilkins app. 36 72 108 211 343 475

CAPTAIN WONDER
Image Comics: Feb, 2011 ($4.99, 3-D comic with glasses)

1-Haberlin-s/Tan-a; sketch pages, crossword puzzle, paper dolls 5.00

Carnage #4 © MAR

Cars 2 #1 © DIS & Pixar

Cartoon Network Block Party #59 © Cartoon Network

	GD 2.0	VG 4.0	FN 6.0	VF 8.0	VF/NM 9.0	NM- 9.2

CARBON GREY
Image Comics: Mar, 2011 - No. 3, May, 2011 ($2.99, limited series)

1-3-Khari Evans, Kinsun Loh & Hoang Nguyen-a; Nguyen-c 3.00
... Origins 1 (11/11, $3.99) Pop Mhan-a 4.00

CARE BEARS (TV, Movie)(See Star Comics Magazine)
Star Comics/Marvel Comics No. 15 on: Nov, 1985 - No. 20, Jan, 1989

1-20: Post-a begins. 11-$1.00-c begins. 13-Madballs app. 5.00

CAREER GIRL ROMANCES (Formerly Three Nurses)
Charlton Comics: June, 1964 - No. 78, Dec, 1973

V4#24-31 3 6 9 14 20 25
32-Elvis Presley, Herman's Hermits, Johnny Rivers line drawn-c 10 20 30 69 122 175
33-37,39-50: 39-Tiffany Sinn app. 2 4 6 13 18 22
38-(2/67) 1st app. Tiffany Sinn, C.I.A. Sweetheart, Undercover Agent (also see Secret Agent #10; Dominguel-a 3 6 9 17 25 32
51-78: 54-Jonnie Love anti-drup PSA. 67-Susan Dey pin-up. 70-David Cassidy pin-up 2 4 6 10 14 18

CAR 54, WHERE ARE YOU? (TV)
Dell Publishing Co.: Mar-May, 1962 - No. 7, Sept-Nov, 1963; 1964 - 1965 (All photo-c)

Four Color 1257(#1, 3-5/62) 8 16 24 55 93 130
2(6-8/62)-7 5 10 15 32 51 70
2,3(10-12/64), 4(1-3/65)-Reprints #2,3,&4 of 1st series 3 6 9 20 30 40

CARL BARKS LIBRARY OF WALT DISNEY'S GYRO GEARLOOSE COMICS AND FILLERS IN COLOR, THE
Gladstone: 1993 ($7.95, 8-1/2x11", limited series, 52 pgs.)

1-6: Carl Barks reprints 1 3 4 6 8 10

CARL BARKS LIBRARY OF WALT DISNEY'S COMICS AND STORIES IN COLOR, THE
Gladstone: Jan, 1992 - No. 51, Mar, 1996 ($8.95, 8-1/2x11", 60 pgs.)

1,2,6,8-51: 1-Barks Donald Duck-r/WDC&S #31-35; 2-r/#36,38-41; 6-r/#57-61; 8-r/#67-71; 9-r/#72-76; 10-r/#77-81; 11-r/#82-86; 12-r/#87-91; 13-r/#92-96; 14-r/#97-101; 15-r/#102-106; 16-r/#107-111; 17-r/#112,114,117,124,125; 18-r/#126-130; 19-r/#131,132(2),133,134; 20-r/#135-139; 21-r/#140-144; 22-r/#145-149; 23-r/#150-154; 24-r/#155-159; 25-r/#160-164; 26-r/#165-169; 27-r/#170-174;28-r/#175-179; 29-r/#180-184; 30-r/#185-189; 31-r/#190-194; 32-r/#195-199;33-r/#200-204; 34-r/#205-209; 35-r/#210-214; 36-r/#215-219; 37-r/#220-224; 38-r/#225-229; 39-r/#230-234; 40-r/#235-239; 41-r/#240-244; 42r/#245-249; 43-r/#250-254; 44-50; All contain one Heroes & Villains trading card each 2 4 6 9 12 15
3,4,7: 3-r/#42-46. 4-r/#47-51. 7-r/#62-66. 2 4 6 11 16 20
5-r/#52-56 3 6 9 16 23 30

CARL BARKS LIBRARY OF WALT DISNEY'S DONALD DUCK ADVENTURES IN COLOR, THE
Gladstone: Jan, 1994 - No. 25, Jan, 1996 ($7.95-$9.95, 44-68 pgs., 8-1/2"x11")
(all contain one Donald Duck trading card each)

1-5,7-25-Carl Barks-r: 1-r/FC #9; 2-r/FC #29; 3-r/FC #62; 4-r/FC #108; 5-r/FC #147 & #79(Mickey Mouse); 7-r/FC #159. 8-r/FC #178 & 189. 9-r/FC #199 & 203; 10-r/FC 223 & 238; 11-r/Christmas Parade #1 & 2; 12-r/FC #296; 13-r/FC #263; 14-r/MOC #20 & 41; 15-r/FC 275 & 282; 16-r/FC #291&300; 17-r/FC #308 & 318; 18-r/Vac. Parade #1 & Summer Fun #2; 19-r/FC #328 & 367 2 4 6 9 12 15
6-r/MOC #4, Cheerios "Atom Bomb," D.D. Tells About Kites 3 6 9 14 20 25

CARL BARKS LIBRARY OF WALT DISNEY'S DONALD DUCK CHRISTMAS STORIES IN COLOR, THE
Gladstone: 1992 ($7.95, 44pgs., one-shot)

nn-Reprints Firestone giveaways 1945-1949 2 4 6 10 14 18

CARL BARKS LIBRARY OF WALT DISNEY'S UNCLE SCROOGE COMICS ONE PAGERS IN COLOR, THE
Gladstone: 1992 - No. 2, 1993 ($8.95, limited series, 60 pgs., 8-1/2x11")

1-Carl Barks one pg. reprints 3 6 9 16 23 30
2-Carl Barks one pg. reprints 2 4 6 10 14 18

CARNAGE
Marvel Comics: Dec, 2010 - No. 5, Aug, 2011 ($3.99, limited series)

1-5-Spider-Man & Iron Man app.; Clayton Crain-a/c; Wells-s 4.00
...: It's a Wonderful Life (10/96, $1.95) David Quinn scripts 3.00
...: Mind Bomb (2/96, $2.95) Warren Ellis script; Kyle Hotz-a 3.00

CARNAGE, U.S.A.
Marvel Comics: Feb, 2012 - No. 5 ($3.99, limited series)

1-4-Clayton Crain-a/c; Wells-s; Spider-Man & Avengers app. 3,4-Venom app. 4.00

	GD 2.0	VG 4.0	FN 6.0	VF 8.0	VF/NM 9.0	NM- 9.2

CARNATION MALTED MILK GIVEAWAYS (See Wisco)

CARNEYS, THE
Archie Comics: Summer, 1994 ($2.00, 52 pgs)

1-Bound-in pull-out poster 4.00

CARNIVAL COMICS (Formerly Kayo #12; becomes Red Seal Comics #14)
Harry 'A' Chesler/Pershing Square Publ. Co.: 1945

nn (#13)-Guardineer-a 18 36 54 105 165 225

CAROLINE KENNEDY
Charlton Comics: 1961 (one-shot)

nn-Interior photo covers of Kennedy family 9 18 27 60 103 145

CAROUSEL COMICS
F. E. Howard, Toronto: V1#8, April, 1948

V1#8 8 16 24 42 54 65

CARS (Based on the 2006 Pixar movie)
Boom Entertainment: No. 0, Nov, 2009 - No. 7, Jun, 2010 ($2.99)

0-7: 0,1-Three covers on each. 2-7-Two covers on each 3.00
...: Adventures of Tow Mater 1-4 (7/10 - No. 4, 10/10, $2.99) 1-Two covers 3.00
...: Radiator Springs 1-4 (7/09 - No. 4, 10/09, $2.99) Two covers on each 3.00
...: The Rookie 1-4 (3/09 - No. 4, 6/09, $2.99) Origin of Lightning McQueen 3.00

CARS 2 (Based on the 2011 Pixar movie)
Marvel Worldwide (Disney Comics): Aug, 2011 - No. 2, Aug, 2011 ($3.99)

1,2-Movie adaptation; car profile pages 4.00

CARS, WORLD OF (Free Comic Book Day giveaway)
BOOM Kids!: May, 2009

1-Based on the Disney/Pixar movie 3.00

CARTOON CARTOONS (Anthology)
DC Comics: Mar, 2001 - No. 33, Oct, 2004 ($1.99/$2.25)

1-33-Short stories of Cartoon Network characters. 3,6,10,13,15-Space Ghost. 13-Begin $2.25-c. 17-Dexter's Laboratory begins 3.00

CARTOON KIDS
Atlas Comics (CPS): 1957 (no month)

1-Maneely-c/a; Dexter The Demon, Willie The Wise-Guy, Little Zelda app. 12 24 36 67 94 120

CARTOON NETWORK ACTION PACK (Anthology)
DC Comics: July, 2006 - Present ($2.25/$2.50/$2.99)

1-31-Short stories of Cartoon Network characters. 1,4,6-Rowdyruff Boys app. 3.00
32-67: 32-Begin $2.50-c. 50-Ben 10/Generator Rex team-up 3.00

CARTOON NETWORK BLOCK PARTY (Anthology)
DC Comics: Nov, 2004 - No. 59, Sept, 2009 ($2.25/$2.50)

1,2,4-51-Short stories of Cartoon Network characters 3.00
3-($2.95) Bonus pages 4.00
52-59: 52-Begin $2.50-c. 59-Last issue; Powerpuff Girls app. 3.00
Cartoon Network 2-in-1: Ben 10 Alien Force/The Secret Saturdays TPB (2010, $12.99) reprints stories from #26-42 13.00
Cartoon Network 2-in-1: Foster's Home For Imaginary Friends/Powerpuff Girls TPB (2010, $12.99) reprints stories from #19-21,23,25,26,28,30-32,34-38,41 13.00
... Vol. 1: Get Down! (2005, $6.99, digest) reprints from Dexter's Lab and Cartoon Cartoons 7.00
... Vol. 2: Read All About It! (2005, $6.99, digest) reprints 7.00
... Vol. 3: Can You Dig It?; ... Vol. 4: Blast Off! (2006, $6.99, digest) reprints 7.00

CARTOON NETWORK PRESENTS
DC Comics: Aug, 1997 - No. 24, Aug, 1999 ($1.75-$1.99, anthology)

1-Dexter's Lab 5.00
1-Platinum Edition 1 2 3 5 7 9
2-10: 2-Space Ghost 3.50
11-24: 12-Bizarro World 3.00

CARTOON NETWORK PRESENTS SPACE GHOST
Archie Comics: Mar, 1997 ($1.50)

1-Scott Rosema-p 6.00

CARTOON NETWORK STARRING... (Anthology)
DC Comics: Sept, 1999 - No. 18, Feb, 2001 ($1.99)

1-Powerpuff Girls 5.00
2-18: 2,8,11,14,17-Johnny Bravo. 12,15,18-Space Ghost 3.00

CARTOON TALES (Disney's...)
W.D. Publications (Disney): nd, nn (1992) ($2.95, 6-5/8x9-1/2", 52 pgs.)

Casey Jones #2 © Mirage

Casper and Nightmare #23 © Parmount

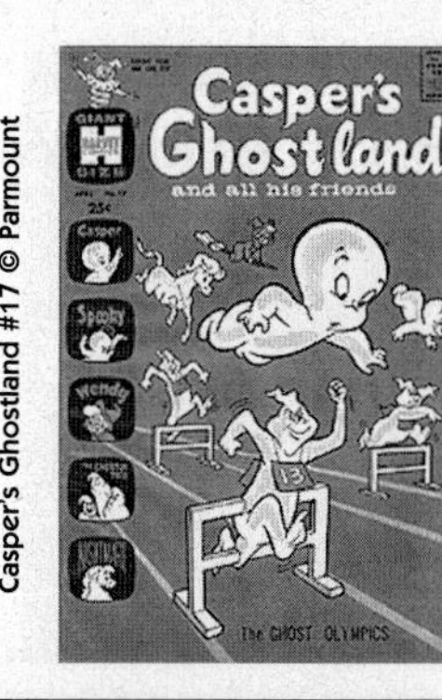

Casper's Ghostland #17 © Parmount

	GD 2.0	VG 4.0	FN 6.0	VF 8.0	VF/NM 9.0	NM- 9.2
nn-Ariel & Sebastian-Serpent Teen; Beauty and the Beast; A Tale of Enchantment; Darkwing Duck - Just Us Justice Ducks; 101 Dalmatians - Canine Classics; Tale Spin - Surprise in the Skies; Uncle Scrooge - Blast to the Past						4.00

CARVERS
Image Comics (Flypaper Press): 1998 - No. 3, 1999 ($2.95)

	GD	VG	FN	VF	VF/NM	NM-
1-3-Pander Bros.-a/Fleming-s						3.00

CAR WARRIORS
Marvel Comics (Epic): June, 1991 - No. 4, Sept, 1991 ($2.25, lim. series)

	GD	VG	FN	VF	VF/NM	NM-
1-4: 1-Says April in indicia						3.00

CASANOVA
Image Comics: June, 2006 - No. 14, May, 2008 ($1.99, B&W & olive green or blue)

	GD	VG	FN	VF	VF/NM	NM-
1-14: 1-7-Matt Fraction-s/Gabriel Bá-a/c. 8-14-Fabio Moon-a						3.00
...: Luxuria TPB (2008, $12.99) r/#1-7; sketch pages and cover gallery						13.00
1-4 (Marvel Comics, 10/10 - No. 4, 12/10, $3.99) Recolored reprints Image series #1-7						4.00
...: Gula (Marvel, 1/11 - No. 4, 4/11) r/Image series #8-14. 4-New story pages						4.00
...: Avaritia (III) 1 (Marvel, 11/11, $4.99) new story; Fraction-s/Bá-a						5.00

CASE FILES: SAM & TWITCH (Also see the Spawn titles)
Image Comics: May, 2003 - No. 25, July, 2006 ($2.50/$2.95, color #1-6/B&W #7-on)

	GD	VG	FN	VF	VF/NM	NM-
1-25: 1-5-Scott Morse-a/Marc Andreyko-s. 7-13-Paul Lee-a. 13-Niles-s						3.00

CASE OF THE SHOPLIFTER'S SHOE (See Perry Mason, Feature Book No.50)

CASE OF THE WINKING BUDDHA, THE
St. John Publ. Co.: 1950 (132 pgs.; 25¢; B&W; 5-1/2x7-5-1/2x8")

	GD	VG	FN	VF	VF/NM	NM-
nn-Charles Raab-a; reprinted in Authentic Police Cases No. 25	32	64	96	192	314	435

CASEY BLUE
DC Comics (WildStorm): Jul, 2008 - No. 6, Dec, 2008 ($2.99, limited series)

	GD	VG	FN	VF	VF/NM	NM-
1-6-B. Clay Moore-s/Carlos Barberi-a						3.00
...: Beyond Tomorrow TPB (2009, $19.99) r/#1-6; Barberi sketch pages						20.00

CASEY-CRIME PHOTOGRAPHER (Two-Gun Western No. 5 on)(Radio)
Marvel Comics (BFP): Aug, 1949 - No. 4, Feb, 1950

	GD	VG	FN	VF	VF/NM	NM-
1-Photo-c; 52 pgs.	25	50	75	150	245	340
2-4: Photo-c	18	36	54	105	165	225

CASEY JONES (TV)
Dell Publishing Co.: No. 915, July, 1958

	GD	VG	FN	VF	VF/NM	NM-
Four Color 915-Alan Hale photo-c	5	10	15	35	55	75

CASEY JONES & RAPHAEL (See Bodycount)
Mirage Studios: Oct, 1994 ($2.75, unfinished limited series)

	GD	VG	FN	VF	VF/NM	NM-
1-Bisley-c; Eastman story & pencils						3.00

CASEY JONES: NORTH BY DOWNEAST
Mirage Studios: May, 1994 - No. 2, July, 1994 ($2.75, limited series)

	GD	VG	FN	VF	VF/NM	NM-
1,2-Rick Veitch script & pencils; Kevin Eastman story & inks						3.00

CASPER ADVENTURE DIGEST
Harvey Comics: V2#1, Oct, 1992 - V2#8, Apr, 1994 ($1.75/$1.95, digest-size)

	GD	VG	FN	VF	VF/NM	NM-
V2#1: Casper, Richie Rich, Spooky, Wendy						5.00
2-8						3.50

CASPER AND...
Harvey Comics: Nov, 1987 - No. 12, June, 1990 (.75/$1.00, all reprints)

	GD	VG	FN	VF	VF/NM	NM-
1-Ghostly Trio						5.00
2-12: 2-Spooky; begin $1.00-c. 3-Wendy. 4-Nightmare. 5-Ghostly Trio. 6-Spooky. 7-Wendy. 8-Hot Stuff. 9-Baby Huey. 10-Wendy.11-Ghostly Trio. 12-Spooky						3.00

CASPER AND FRIENDS
Harvey Comics: Oct, 1991 - No. 5, July, 1992 ($1.00/$1.25)

	GD	VG	FN	VF	VF/NM	NM-
1-Nightmare, Ghostly Trio, Wendy, Spooky						4.00
2-5						3.00

CASPER AND FRIENDS MAGAZINE: Mar, 1997 - No. 3, July, 1997 ($3.99)

	GD	VG	FN	VF	VF/NM	NM-
1-3						4.00

CASPER AND NIGHTMARE (See Harvey Hits# 37, 45, 52, 56, 59, 62, 65, 68,71, 75)

CASPER AND NIGHTMARE (Nightmare & Casper No. 1-5)
Harvey Publications: No. 6, 11/64 - No. 44, 10/73; No. 45, 6/74 - No. 46, 8/74 (25¢)

	GD	VG	FN	VF	VF/NM	NM-
6: 68 pg. Giants begin, ends #32	5	10	15	35	55	75
7-10	4	8	12	22	34	45
11-20	3	6	9	18	27	35
21-37: 33-37-(52 pg. Giants)	3	6	9	14	20	26
38-46	2	4	6	10	14	18

NOTE: *Many issues contain reprints.*

CASPER AND SPOOKY (See Harvey Hits No. 20)
Harvey Publications: Oct, 1972 - No. 7, Oct, 1973

	GD	VG	FN	VF	VF/NM	NM-
1	3	6	9	18	27	35
2-7	2	4	6	10	14	18

CASPER AND THE GHOSTLY TRIO
Harvey Pub.: Nov, 1972 - No. 7, Nov, 1973; No. 8, Aug, 1990 - No. 10, Dec, 1990

	GD	VG	FN	VF	VF/NM	NM-
1	3	6	9	18	27	35
2-7	2	4	6	10	14	18
8-10						6.00

CASPER AND WENDY
Harvey Publications: Sept, 1972 - No. 8, Nov, 1973

	GD	VG	FN	VF	VF/NM	NM-
1: 52 pg. Giant	3	6	9	18	27	35
2-8	2	4	6	10	14	18

CASPER BIG BOOK
Harvey Comics: V2#1, Aug, 1992 - No. 3, May, 1993 ($1.95, 52 pgs.)

	GD	VG	FN	VF	VF/NM	NM-
V2#1-Spooky app.						4.00
2,3						4.00

CASPER CAT (See Dopey Duck)
I. W. Enterprises/Super: 1958; 1963

	GD	VG	FN	VF	VF/NM	NM-
1,7: 1-Wacky Duck #?.7-Reprint, Super No. 14('63)	2	4	6	9	13	16

CASPER DIGEST (...Magazine #?; ...Halloween Digest #8, 10)
Harvey Publications: Oct, 1986 - No. 18, Jan, 1991 ($1.25/$1.75, digest-size)

	GD	VG	FN	VF	VF/NM	NM-
1	1	3	4	6	8	10
2-18: 11-Valentine-c. 18-Halloween-c						6.00

CASPER DIGEST (...Magazine #? on)
Harvey Comics: V2#1, Sept, 1991 - V2#14, Nov, 1994 ($1.75/$1.95, digest-size)

	GD	VG	FN	VF	VF/NM	NM-
V2#1						5.00
2-14						3.50

CASPER DIGEST STORIES
Harvey Publications: Feb, 1980 - No. 4, Nov, 1980 (95¢, 132 pgs., digest size)

	GD	VG	FN	VF	VF/NM	NM-
1	2	4	6	9	13	16
2-4	1	2	3	5	7	9

CASPER DIGEST WINNERS
Harvey Publications: Apr, 1980 - No. 3, Sept, 1980 (95¢, 132 pgs., digest size)

	GD	VG	FN	VF	VF/NM	NM-
1	2	4	6	9	13	16
2,3	1	2	3	5	7	9

CASPER ENCHANTED TALES DIGEST
Harvey Comics: May, 1992 - No. 10, Oct, 1994 ($1.75, digest-size, 98 pgs.)

	GD	VG	FN	VF	VF/NM	NM-
1-Casper, Spooky, Wendy stories						5.00
2-10						4.00

CASPER GHOSTLAND
Harvey Comics: May, 1992 ($1.25)

	GD	VG	FN	VF	VF/NM	NM-
1						3.00

CASPER GIANT SIZE
Harvey Comics: Oct, 1992 - No. 4, Nov, 1993 ($2.25, 68 pgs.)

	GD	VG	FN	VF	VF/NM	NM-
V2#1-Casper, Wendy, Spooky stories						5.00
2-4						4.00

CASPER HALLOWEEN TRICK OR TREAT
Harvey Publications: Jan, 1976 (52 pgs.)

	GD	VG	FN	VF	VF/NM	NM-
1	3	6	9	18	27	35

CASPER IN SPACE (Formerly Casper Spaceship)
Harvey Publications: No. 6, June, 1973 - No. 8, Oct, 1973

	GD	VG	FN	VF	VF/NM	NM-
6-8	2	4	6	10	14	18

CASPER'S GHOSTLAND
Harvey Publications: Winter, 1958-59 - No. 97, 12/77; No. 98, 12/79 (25¢)

	GD	VG	FN	VF	VF/NM	NM-
1-84 pgs. begin, ends #10	16	32	48	111	243	375
2	10	20	30	66	121	175
3-10	8	16	24	51	86	120
11-20: 11-68 pgs. begin, ends #61. 13-X-Mas-c	6	12	18	41	66	90
21-40	5	10	15	30	48	65
41-61	3	6	9	17	25	32
62-77: 62-52 pgs. begin	2	4	6	9	13	16
78-98: 94-X-Mas-c	2	4	6	8	10	12

NOTE: *Most issues contain reprints w/new stories.*

Casper, The Friendly Ghost #12 © Parmount

Castle: Richard Castle's Deadly Storm GN © ABC TV

Catman Comics #7 © HOKE

GD VG FN VF VF/NM NM-
2.0 4.0 6.0 8.0 9.0 9.2

CASPER SPACESHIP (Casper in Space No. 6 on)
Harvey Publications: Aug, 1972 - No. 5, April, 1973
1: 52 pg. Giant 3 6 9 19 29 38
2-5 2 4 6 11 16 20

CASPER'S SCARE SCHOOL
Ape Entertainment: 2011 - No. 4 ($3.99, limited series)
1-New short stories and classic reprints 4.00

CASPER STRANGE GHOST STORIES
Harvey Publications: October, 1974 - No. 14, Jan, 1977 (All 52 pgs.)
1 3 6 9 19 29 38
2-14 2 4 6 11 16 20

CASPER, THE FRIENDLY GHOST (See America's Best TV Comics, Famous TV Funday Funnies, The Friendly Ghost..., Nightmare &..., Richie Rich and..., Tastee-Freez, Treasury of Comics, Wendy the Good Little Witch & Wendy Witch World)

CASPER, THE FRIENDLY GHOST (Becomes Harvey Comics Hits No. 61 (No. 6), and then continued with Harvey issue No. 7)(1st Series)
St. John Publishing Co.: Sept, 1949 - No. 5, Aug, 1951
1(1949)-Origin & 1st app. Baby Huey & Herman the Mouse (1st comic app. of Casper and the 1st time the name Casper app. in any media, even films)
300 600 900 2010 3505 5000
2,3 (2/50 & 8/50) 103 206 309 659 1130 1600
4,5 (3/51 & 8/51) 74 148 222 470 810 1150

CASPER, THE FRIENDLY GHOST (Paramount Picture Star...)(2nd Series)
Harvey Publications (Family Comics): No. 7, Dec, 1952 - No. 70, July, 1958
Note: No. 6 is Harvey Comics Hits No. 61 (10/52)
7-Baby Huey begins, ends #9 31 62 93 221 478 735
8,9 19 38 57 128 277 425
10-Spooky begins (1st app., 6/53), ends #70? 25 50 75 178 382 585
11,12: 2nd & 3rd app. Spooky 13 26 39 87 186 285
13-18: Alfred Harvey app. in story 12 24 36 81 166 250
19-1st app. Nightmare (4/54) 21 42 63 142 304 465
20-Wendy the Witch begins (1st app., 5/54) 25 50 75 175 375 575
21-30: 24-Infinity-c 10 20 30 66 121 175
31-40: 38-Early Wendy app. 39-1st app. Samson Honeybun. 40-1st app. Dr. Brainstorm
8 16 24 53 89 125
41-1st Wendy app. on-c 9 18 27 60 103 145
42-50: 43-2nd Wendy-c. 46-1st app. Spooky's girl Pearl.
6 12 18 42 69 95
51-70 (Continues as Friendly Ghost... 8/58) 58-Early app. Bat Balfrey. 63-2nd app. Something the Baby Ghost. 66-1st app. Wildcat Witch 5 10 15 35 55 75
Harvey Comics Classics Vol. 1 TPB (Dark Horse Books, 6/07, $19.95) Reprints Casper's earliest appearances in this title, Little Audrey, and The Friendly Ghost Casper, mostly B&W with some color stories; history, early concept drawings and animation art 20.00
NOTE: *Baby Huey app. 7-9, 11, 121, 14, 16, 20. Buzzy app. 14, 16, 20. Nightmare app. 19, 27, 36, 37, 42, 46, 51, 53, 56, 70. Spooky app. 10-70. Wendy app. 20, 29-31, 35, 37, 38, 41-49, 51, 52, 54-58, 61, 64, 68.*

CASPER THE FRIENDLY GHOST (Formerly The Friendly Ghost...)(3rd Series)
Harvey Comics: No. 254, July, 1990 - No. 260, Jan, 1991 ($1.00)
254-260 3.00

CASPER THE FRIENDLY GHOST (4th Series)
Harvey Comics: Mar, 1991 - No. 28, Nov, 1994 ($1.00/$1.25/$1.50)
1-Casper becomes Mighty Ghost; Spooky & Wendy app. 5.00
2-28: 7,8-Post-a. 11-28-($1.50) 3.00

CASPER T.V. SHOWTIME
Harvey Comics: Jan, 1980 - No. 5, Oct, 1980
1 2 4 6 9 13 16
2-5 1 2 3 5 7 9

CASSETTE BOOKS (Classics Illustrated)
Cassette Book Co./I.P.S. Publ.: 1984 (48 pgs, b&w comic with cassette tape)
NOTE: *This series was illegal. The artwork was illegally obtained, and the Classics Illustrated copyright owner, Twin Circle Publ. sued to get an injunction to prevent the continued sale of this series. Many C.I. collectors obtained copies before the 1987 injunction, but now they are already scarce. Here again the market is just developing, but sealed mint copies of com ic and tape should be worth at least $25.*
1001 (CI#1-A2)New-PC 1002(CI#3-A2)CI-PC 1003(CI#13-A2)CI-PC
1004(CI#25)CI-LDC 1005(CI#10-A2)New-PC 1006(CI#64)CI-LDC

CASTILIAN (See Movie Classics)

CASTLE: RICHARD CASTLE'S DEADLY STORM (Based on the ABC TV series Castle)
Marvel Comics: 2011 ($19.99, hardcover graphic novel with dustjacket)
HC-An "adaptation" of the show's fictional Derrick Storm novel; Bendis & DeConnick-s 20.00

CASTLEVANIA: THE BELMONT LEGACY
IDW Publishing: March 2005 - No. 5, July, 2005 ($3.99, limited series)
1-5-Marc Andreyko-s/E.J. Su-a 4.00

CASTLE WAITING
Olio: 1997 - No. 7, 1999 ($2.95, B&W)
Cartoon Books: Vol. 2, Aug, 2000 - No. 16 ($2.95/$3.95, B&W)
Fantagraphics Books: Vol. 3, 2006 - Present ($5.95/$3.95, B&W)
1-Linda Medley-s/a in all 1 2 3 5 6 8
2 4.00
3-7 3.00
The Lucky Road TPB r/#1-7 17.00
Hiatus Issue (1999) Crilley-c; short stories and previews 3.00
Vol. 2 #1-6,14-16 (#5&6 also have #12&13 on cover, for series numbering) 3.00
Vol. 3 #1 ($5.95) r/#15,16 and new story 6.00
Vol. 3 #2-15 ($3.95) 4.00

CASUAL HEROES
Image Comics (Motown Machineworks): Apr, 1996 ($2.25, unfinished lim. series)
1-Steve Rude-c 3.00

CAT, T.H.E. (TV) (See T.H.E. Cat)

CAT, THE (See Movie Classics)

CAT, THE (Female hero)
Marvel Comics Group: Nov, 1972 - No. 4, June, 1973
1-Origin & 1st app. The Cat (who later becomes Tigra); Mooney-a(i); Wood-c(i)/a(i)
4 8 12 24 37 50
2,3: 2-Marie Severin/Mooney-a. 3-Everett inks 3 6 9 14 20 25
4-Starlin/Weiss-a(p) 3 6 9 16 22 28

CATALYST: AGENTS OF CHANGE (Also see Comics' Greatest World)
Dark Horse Comics: Feb, 1994 - No.7, Nov, 1994 ($2.00, limited series)
1-7: 1-Foil stamped logo 3.00

CAT & MOUSE
EF Graphics (Silverline): Dec, 1988 ($1.75, color w/part B&W)
1-1st printing (12/88, 32 pgs.), 1-2nd printing (5/89, 36 pgs.) 3.00

CAT FROM OUTER SPACE (See Walt Disney Showcase #46)

CATHOLIC COMICS (See Heroes All Catholic...)
Catholic Publications: June, 1946 - V3#10, July, 1949
1 30 60 90 177 289 400
2 16 32 48 94 147 200
3-13(7/47): 11-Hollingsworth-a 14 28 42 82 121 160
V2#1-10 11 22 33 62 86 110
V3#1-10: Reprints 10-part Treasure Island serial from Target V2#2-11 (see Key Comics #5)
11 22 33 64 90 115
NOTE: ***Orlando** c-V2#10, V3#5, 6, 8.*

CATHOLIC PICTORIAL
Catholic Guild: 1947
1-Toth-a(2) (Rare) 39 78 117 240 395 550

CATMAN COMICS (Formerly Crash Comics No. 1-5)
Holyoke Publishing Co./Continental Magazines V2#12, 7/44 on:
5/41 - No. 17, 1/43; No. 18, 7/43 - No. 22, 12/43; No. 23, 3/44 - No. 26, 11/44; No. 27, 4/45 - No. 30, 12/45; No. 31, 6/46 - No. 32, 8/46
1(V1#6)-Origin The Deacon & Sidekick Mickey, Dr. Diamond & Rag-Man; The Black Widow app.; The Catman by Chas. Quinlan & Blaze Baylor begin
417 834 1251 2919 5110 7300
2(V1#7) 194 388 582 1242 2121 3000
3(V1#8)-The Pied Piper begins; classic Hitler, Stalin & Mussolini-c
194 388 582 1242 2121 3000
4(V1#9) 126 252 378 806 1378 1950
5(V2#10), 6(V2#11), 7(V2#12): 5-1st app. Kitten; The Hood begins (c-redated)
116 232 348 742 1271 1800
8(V2#13,3/42)-Origin Little Leaders; Volton by Kubert begins (his 1st comic book work)
135 270 405 864 1482 2100
9 (V2#14)-Japanese WWII-c 110 220 330 704 1202 1700
10 (V2#15)-Origin Blackout; Phantom Falcon begins
103 206 309 659 1130 1600
11 (V3#1)-Kubert-a 103 206 309 659 1130 1600
12 (V3#2),15,17: 12-Volton by Brodsky, not Kubert 90 180 270 576 988 1400
13-(scarce) 155 310 465 992 1696 2400
14-World War II-c; Brodsky-a 103 206 309 659 1130 1600
16 (V3#5)-Hitler, Tojo, Mussolini, Goehring-c 181 362 543 1158 1979 2800
18 (V3#8, 7/43)-(scarce) 110 220 330 704 1202 1700

Catwoman #12 © DC

Catwoman (2002 series) #45 © DC

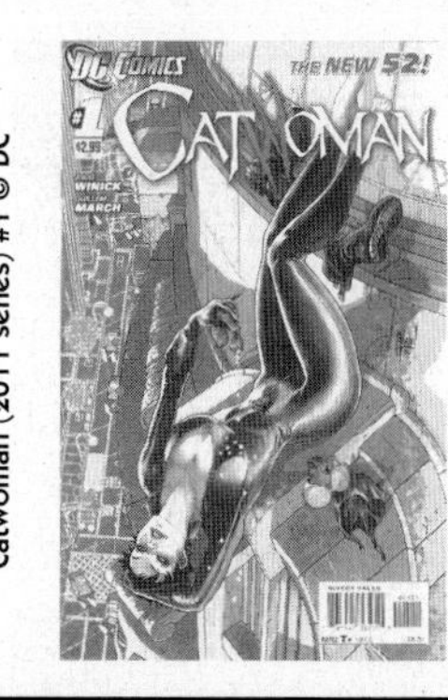

Catwoman (2011 series) #1 © DC

GD 2.0 | VG 4.0 | FN 6.0 | VF 8.0 | VF/NM 9.0 | NM- 9.2

19 (V2#6)-Hitler, Tojo, Mussolini-c 181 362 543 1158 1979 2800
20 (V2#7)-Classic Hitler-c 226 452 678 1446 2473 3500
21,22 (V2#8, V2#9) 87 174 261 553 952 1350
23 (V2#10, 3/44) World War II-c 94 188 282 597 1024 1450
nn(V3#13, 5/44) Rico-a; Schomburg Japanese WWII bondage-c (Rare)
129 258 387 826 1413 2000
nn(V2#12, 7/44) 84 168 252 538 919 1300
nn(V3#1, 9/44)-Origin The Golden Archer; Leatherface app.
90 180 270 576 988 1400
nn(V3#2, 11/44)-L. B. Cole-c 116 232 348 742 1271 1800
27-Origins Catman & Kitten retold; L. B. Cole Flag-c; Infantino-a
135 270 405 864 1482 2100
28-Dr. Macabre app.; L. B. Cole-c/a 161 322 483 1030 1765 2500
29-32-L. B. Cole-c; bondage-#30 129 258 387 826 1413 2000
NOTE: *Fuje a-11, 27, 28(2), 29(3), 30. **Palais** a-11, 16, 27, 28, 29(2), 30(2), 32; c-25(7/44). **Rico** a-11(2), 23, 27, 28.*

CAT TALES (3-D)
Eternity Comics: Apr, 1989 ($2.95)
1-Felix the Cat-r in 3-D 5.00

CATWOMAN (Also see Action Comics Weekly #611, Batman #404-407, Detective Comics, & Superman's Girlfriend Lois Lane #70, 71)
DC Comics: Feb, 1989 - No. 4, May, 1989 ($1.50, limited series, mature)
1 1 3 4 6 8 10
2-4: 3-Batman cameo. 4-Batman app. 1 2 3 5 7 9
Her Sister's Keeper (1991, $9.95, trade paperback)-r/#1-4 10.00

CATWOMAN (Also see Showcase '93, Showcase '95 #4, & Batman #404-407)
DC Comics: Aug, 1993 - No. 94, Jul, 2001 ($1.50-$2.25)
0-(10/94)-Zero Hour; origin retold. Released between #14&15 3.00
1-($1.95)-Embossed-c; Bane app.; Balent c-1-10; a-1-10p 5.00
2-20: 3-Bane flashback cameo. 4-Brief Bane app. 6,7-Knightquest tie-ins; Batman (Azrael) app. 8-1st app. Zephyr. 12-KnightsEnd pt. 6. 13-new Knights End Aftermath.
14-(9/94)-Zero Hour 3.50
21-24, 26-30, 33-49: 21-$1.95-c begins. 28,29-Penguin cameo app. 36-Legacy pt. 2. 38-40-Year Two; Batman, Joker, Penguin & Two-Face app. 46-Two-Face app. 3.00
25,31,32: 25-($2.95)-Robin app. 31,32-Contagion pt. 4 (Reads pt. 5 on-c) & pt. 9. 4.00
50-($2.95, 48 pgs.)-New armored costume 4.00
50-($2.95, 48 pgs.)-Collector's Ed.w/metallic ink-c 4.00
51-77: 51-Huntress-c/app. 54-Grayson-s begins. 56-Cataclysm pt.6. 57-Poison Ivy-c/app. 63-65-Joker-c/app. 72-No Man's Land; Ostrander-s begins 3.00
78-82: 80-Catwoman goes to jail 3.00
83-94: 83-Begin $2.25-c. 83,84,89-Harley Quinn-c/app. 3.00
#1,000,000 (11/98) 853rd Century x-over 3.00
Annual 1 (1994, $2.95, 68 pgs.)-Elseworlds story; Batman app.; no Balent-a 4.00
Annual 2,4 ('95, '97, $3.95) 2-Year One story. 4-Pulp Heroes 4.00
Annual 3 (1996, $2.95)-Legends of the Dead Earth story 4.00
...Plus 1 (11/97, $2.95) Screamqueen (Scare Tactics) app. 4.00
TPB ($9.95) r/#15-19, Balent-c 10.00

CATWOMAN (Also see Detective Comics #759-762)
DC Comics: Jan, 2002 - No. 82, Oct, 2008; No. 83, Mar, 2010 ($2.50/$2.99)
1-Darwyn Cooke & Mike Allred-a; Ed Brubaker-s 6.00
2-4 3.00
5-54: 5-9-Rader-a/Paul Pope-c. 10-Morse-c. 16-JG Jones-c. 22-Batman-c/app. 34-36-War Games. 43-Killer Croc app. 44-Hughes-c begin. 50-Zatanna app. 52-Catwoman kills Black Mask. 53-One Year Later; Helena born 3.00
55-82: 55-Begin $2.99-c. 56-58-Wildcat app. 74-Zatanna app. 75-78-Salvation Run 3.00
83-(3/10, $2.99) Blackest Night one-shot; Black Mask app.; Hughes-c 3.00
...: Catwoman Dies TPB (2008, $14.99) r/#66-72; Hughes cover gallery 15.00
...: Crime Pays TPB (2008, $14.99) r/#73-77 15.00
...: Crooked Little Town TPB (2003, $14.95) r/#5-10 & Secret Files; Oeming-c 15.00
...: It's Only a Movie TPB (2007, $19.99) r/#59-65 20.00
...: Relentless TPB (2005, $19.95) r/#12-19 & Secret Files 20.00
... Secret Files and Origins (10/02, $4.95) origin-s Oeming-a; profiles and pin-ups 5.00
...Selina's Big Score HC (2002, $24.95) Cooke-s/a; pin-ups by various 25.00
...Selina's Big Score SC (2003, $17.95) Cooke-s/a; pin-ups by various 18.00
...: The Dark End of the Street TPB (2002, $12.95) r/#1-4 & Slam Bradley back-up stories from Detective Comics #759-762 13.00
...: The Long Road Home TPB (2009, $17.99) r/#78-82 18.00
...: The Replacements TPB (2007, $14.99) r/#53-58 15.00
...: Wild Ride TPB (2005, $14.99) r/#20-24 & Secret Files #1 15.00

CATWOMAN (DC New 52)
DC Comics: Nov, 2011 - Present ($2.99)
1-Winick-s/March-a; Batman app. 5.00
2-7: 2-6-March-a. 7-Melo-a 3.00

CATWOMAN/ GUARDIAN OF GOTHAM
DC Comics: 1999 - No. 2, 1999 ($5.95, limited series)
1,2-Elseworlds; Moench-s/Balent-a 6.00

CATWOMAN: NINE LIVES OF A FELINE FATALE
DC Comics: 2004 ($14.95, TPB)
nn-Reprints notable stories from Batman #1 to the present; pin-ups by various; Bolland-c 15.00

CATWOMAN: THE MOVIE (2004 Halle Berry movie)
DC Comics: 2004 ($4.95/$9.95)
1-($4.95) Movie adaptation; Jim Lee-c and sketch pages; Derenick-a 5.00
... & Other Cat Tales TPB (2004, $9.95)-r/Movie adaptation; Jim Lee sketch pages, r/Catwoman #0, Catwoman (2nd series) #11 & 25; photo-c 10.00

CATWOMAN/VAMPIRELLA: THE FURIES
DC Comics/Harris Publ.: Feb, 1997 ($4.95, squarebound, 46 pgs.) (1st DC/Harris x-over)
nn-Reintro Pantha; Chuck Dixon scripts; Jim Balent-c/a 5.00

CATWOMAN: WHEN IN ROME
DC Comics: Nov, 2004 - No. 6, Aug, 2005 ($3.50, limited series)
1-6-Jeph Loeb-s/Tim Sale-a/c; Riddler app. 3.50
HC (2005, $19.99, dustjacket) r/series; intro by Mark Chiarello; sketch pages 20.00
SC (2007, $12.99) r/series; intro by Mark Chiarello; sketch pages 13.00

CATWOMAN/WILDCAT
DC Comics: Aug, 1998 - No. 4, Nov, 1998 ($2.50, limited series)
1-4-Chuck Dixon & Beau Smith-s; Stelfreeze-c 3.00

CAUGHT
Atlas Comics (VPI): Aug, 1956 - No. 5, Apr, 1957
1 22 44 66 132 216 300
2-4: 3-Maneely, Pakula, Torres-a. 4-Maneely-a 14 28 42 76 108 140
5-Crandall, Krigstein-a 14 28 42 80 115 150
NOTE: ***Drucker** a-2. **Heck** a-4. **Severin** c-1, 2, 4, 5. **Shores** a-4.*

CAVALIER COMICS
A. W. Nugent Publ. Co.: 1945; 1952 (Early DC reprints)
2(1945)-Speed Saunders, Fang Gow 20 40 60 117 189 260
2(1952) 12 24 36 67 94 120

CAVE GIRL (Also see Africa)
Magazine Enterprises: No. 11, 1953 - No. 14, 1954
11(A-1 82)-Origin; all Cave Girl stories 48 96 144 302 514 725
12(A-1 96), 13(A-1 116), 14(A-1 125)-Thunda by Powell in each
38 76 114 226 368 510
NOTE: ***Powell** c/a in all.*

CAVE GIRL
AC Comics: 1988 ($2.95, 44 pgs.) (16 pgs. of color, rest B&W)
1-Powell-r/Cave Girl #11; Nyoka photo back-c from movie; Powell/Bill Black-c; Special Limited Edition on-c 4.00

CAVE KIDS (TV) (See Comic Album #16)
Gold Key: Feb, 1963 - No. 16, Mar, 1967 (Hanna-Barbera)
1 7 14 21 44 72 100
2-5 4 8 12 24 37 50
6-16: 7,12-Pebbles & Bamm Bamm app. 16-1st Space Kidettes
3 6 9 20 30 40

CAVEWOMAN
Basement Comics: Jan, 1994 - No. 6, 1995 ($2.95)
1 3 6 9 20 30 40
2 2 4 6 9 12 15
3-6 1 2 3 5 6 8
...: Meets Explorers ('97, $2.95) 3.00
...: One-Shot Special (7/00, $2.95) Massey-s/a 3.00

CBLDF (Comic Book Legal Defense Fund) (See Liberty Comics)

CELESTINE (See Violator Vs. Badrock #1)
Image Comics (Extreme): May, 1996 - No. 2, June, 1996 ($2.50, limited series)
1,2: Warren Ellis scripts 3.00

CENTURION OF ANCIENT ROME, THE
Zondervan Publishing House: 1958 (no month listed) (B&W, 36 pgs.)
(Rare) All by Jay Disbrow 81 162 243 518 884 1250

CENTURIONS (TV)

Cerebus #2 © Sim & Gerhard

Challengers of the Unknown #4 © DC

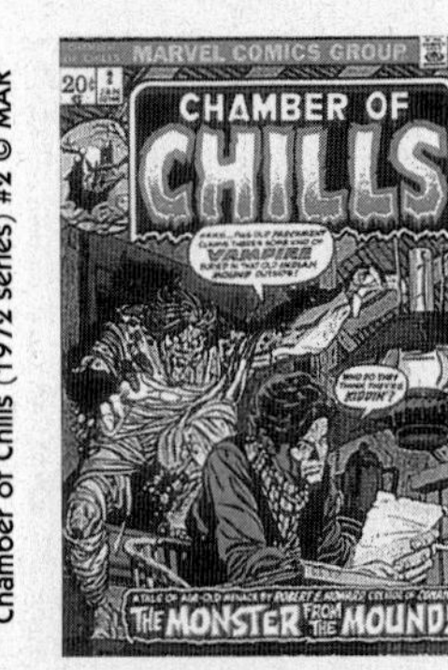

Chamber of Chills (1972 series) #2 © MAR

GD VG FN VF VF/NM NM-
2.0 4.0 6.0 8.0 9.0 9.2

DC Comics: June, 1987 - No. 4, Sept, 1987 (75¢, limited series)
1-4 4.00

CENTURY: DISTANT SONS
Marvel Comics: Feb, 1996 ($2.95, one-shot)
1-Wraparound-c 4.00

CENTURY OF COMICS (See Promotional Comics section)

CEREBUS BI-WEEKLY
Aardvark-Vanaheim: Dec. 2, 1988 - No. 27, Nov. 24, 1989 ($1.25, B&W)
Reprints Cerebus The Aardvark #1-27
1-16, 18, 19, 21-27: 3.00
17-Hepcats app. 2 4 6 8 10 12
20-Milk & Cheese app. 2 4 6 10 12 15

CEREBUS: CHURCH & STATE
Aardvark-Vanaheim: Feb, 1991 - No. 30, Apr, 1992 ($2.00, B&W, bi-weekly)
1-30: r/Cerebus #51-80 3.00

CEREBUS: HIGH SOCIETY
Aardvark-Vanaheim: Feb, 1990 - No. 25, 1991 ($1.70, B&W)
1-25: r/Cerebus #26-50 3.00

CEREBUS JAM
Aardvark-Vanaheim: Apr, 1985
1-Eisner, Austin, Dave Sim-a (Cerebus vs. Spirit) 6.00

CEREBUS THE AARDVARK (See A-V in 3-D, Nucleus, Power Comics)
Aardvark-Vanaheim: Dec, 1977 - No. 300, March, 2004 ($1.70/$2.00/$2.25, B&W)
0 3.00
0-Gold 20.00
1-1st app. Cerebus; 2000 print run; most copies poorly printed
56 112 168 454 977 1500
Note: *There is a counterfeit version known to exist. It can be distinguished from the original in the following ways: inside cover is glossy instead of flat, black background on the front cover is blotted or spotty. Reports show that a counterfeit #2 also exists.*
2-Dave Sim art in all 13 26 39 87 186 285
3-Origin Red Sophia 11 22 33 76 151 225
4-Origin Elrod the Albino 10 20 30 66 121 175
5,6 8 16 24 56 96 135
7-10 6 12 18 43 69 95
11,12: 11-Origin The Cockroach 5 10 15 35 55 75
13-15: 14-Origin Lord Julius 5 10 15 30 48 65
16-20 4 8 12 22 34 45
21-B. Smith letter in letter column 6 12 18 41 66 90
22-Low distribution; no cover price 4 8 12 26 41 55
23-30: 23-Preview of Wandering Star by Teri S. Wood. 26-High Society begins, ends #50
3 6 9 16 23 30
31-Origin Moonroach 3 6 9 17 25 32
32-40, 53-Intro. Wolveroach (brief app.) 2 4 6 8 10 12
41-50,52: 52-Church & State begins, ends #111; Cutey Bunny app.
1 2 3 5 7 9
51,54: 51-Cutey Bunny app. 54-1st full Wolveroach story
2 4 6 8 11 14
55,56-Wolveroach app.; Normalman back-ups by Valentino
1 3 4 6 8 10
57-100: 61,62: Flaming Carrot app. 65-Gerhard begins 4.00
101-160: 104-Flaming Carrot app. 112/113-Double issue. 114-Jaka's Story begins, ends #136. 139-Melmoth begins, ends #150. 151-Mothers & Daughters begins, ends #200 3.00
161-Bone app. 1 3 4 6 8 10
162-231: 175-($2.25, 44 pgs). 186-Strangers in Paradise cameo. 201-Guys storyline begins; Eddie Campbell's Bacchus app. 220-231-Rick's Story 3.00
232-265-Going Home 3.00
266-288,291-299-Latter Days: 267-Five-Bar Gate. 276-Spore (Spawn spoof) 3.00
289&290 ($4.50) Two issues combined 5.00
300-Final issue 3.00
Free Cerebus (Giveaway, 1991-92?, 36 pgs.)-All-r 4.00

CHAIN GANG WAR
DC Comics: July, 1993 - No. 12, June, 1994 ($1.75)
1-($2.50)-Embossed silver foil-c, Dave Johnson-c/a 4.00
2-4,6-12: 3-Deathstroke app. 4-Brief Deathstroke app. 6-New Batman (Azrael) cameo. 11-New Batman-c/story. 12-New Batman app. 3.00
5-($2.50)-Foil-c; Deathstroke app; new Batman cameo (1 panel) 4.00

CHAINS OF CHAOS
Harris Comics: Nov, 1994 - No. 3, Jan, 1995 ($2.95, limited series)
1-3-Re-Intro of The Rook w/ Vampirella 3.00

CHALLENGE OF THE UNKNOWN (Formerly Love Experiences)
Ace Magazines: No. 6, Sept, 1950 (See Web Of Mystery No. 19)
6- "Villa of the Vampire" used in N.Y. Joint Legislative Comm. Publ; Sekowsky-a
39 78 117 240 395 550

CHALLENGER, THE
Interfaith Publications/T.C. Comics: 1945 - No. 4, Oct-Dec, 1946
nn; nd; 32 pgs.; Origin the Challenger Club; Anti-Fascist with funny animal filler
58 116 174 371 636 900
2-4: Kubert-a; 4-Fuje-a 47 94 141 296 498 700

CHALLENGERS OF THE FANTASTIC
Marvel Comics (Amalgam): June 1997 ($1.95, one-shot)
1-Karl Kesel-s/Tom Grummett-a 3.00

CHALLENGERS OF THE UNKNOWN (See Showcase #6, 7, 11, 12, Super DC Giant, and Super Team Family) (See Showcase Presents for B&W reprints)
National Per. Publ./DC Comics: 4-5/58 - No. 77, 12-1/70-71; No. 78, 2/73 - No. 80, 6-7/73; No. 81, 6-7/77 - No. 87, 6-7/78
1-(4-5/58)-Kirby/Stein-a(2); Kirby-c 214 428 642 1800 3900 6000
2-Kirby/Stein-a(2) 65 130 195 527 1139 1750
3-Kirby/Stein-a(2); Rocky returns from space with powers similar to the Fantastic Four (9/58)
55 110 165 446 961 1475
4-8-Kirby/Wood-a plus cover to #8 43 86 129 323 699 1075
9,10 25 50 75 175 375 575
11-Grey tone-c 25 50 75 178 382 585
12-15: 14-Origin/1st app. Multi-Man (villain) 17 34 51 119 260 400
16-22: 18-Intro. Cosmo, the Challengers Spacepet. 22-Last 10¢ issue
12 24 36 84 175 265
23-30 9 18 27 62 109 155
31-Retells origin of the Challengers 9 18 27 63 112 160
32-40 7 14 21 48 79 110
41-47,49,50,52-60: 43-New look begins. 47-1st Sponge-Man. 49-Intro. Challenger Corps. 55-Death of Red Ryan. 60-Red Ryan returns 5 10 15 35 55 75
48,51: 48-Doom Patrol app. 51-Sea Devils app. 6 12 18 37 59 80
61-68: 64,65-Kirby origin-r, parts 1 & 2. 66-New logo. 68-Last 12¢ issue.
4 8 12 24 37 50
69-73,75-80: 69-1st app. Corinna. 77-Last 15¢ issue 3 6 9 16 23 30
74-Deadman by Tuska/Adams; 1 pg. Wrightson-a 6 12 18 41 66 90
81,83-87: 81-(6-7/77). 83-87-Swamp Thing app. 84-87-Deadman app.
2 4 6 8 10 12
82-Swamp Thing begins (thru #87, c/s 2 4 6 9 12 15
NOTE: ***N. Adams** c-67, 68, 70, 72, 74i, 81i. **Buckler** c-83-86p. **Giffen** a-83-87p. **Kirby** a-75-80r; c-75, 77, 78. **Kubert** c-64, 66, 69, 76, 79. **Nasser** c/a-81p, 82p. **Tuska** a-73. **Wood** r-76.*

CHALLENGERS OF THE UNKNOWN
DC Comics: Mar, 1991 - No. 8, Oct, 1991 ($1.75, limited series)
1-Jeph Loeb scripts & Tim Sale-a in all (1st work together); Bolland-c 3.50
2-8: 2-Superman app. 3-Dr. Fate app. 6-G. Kane-c(p). 7-Steranko-c/swipe by Art Adams 3.00
... Must Die! (2004, $19.95, TPB) r/series; intro by Bendis; Sale sketch pages 20.00
NOTE: ***Art Adams** c-7. **Hempel** c-5. **Gil Kane** c-6p. **Sale** a-1-8; c-3, 8. **Wagner** c-4.*

CHALLENGERS OF THE UNKNOWN
DC Comics: Feb, 1997 - No. 18, July, 1998 ($2.25)
1-18: 1-Intro new team; Leon-c/a(p) begins. 4-Origin of new team. 11,12-Batman app. 15-Millennium Giants x-over; Superman-c/app. 3.00

CHALLENGERS OF THE UNKNOWN
DC Comics: Aug, 2004 - No. 6, Jan, 2005 ($2.95, limited series)
1-6-Intro. new team; Howard Chaykin-s/a 3.00

CHALLENGE TO THE WORLD
Catechetical Guild: 1951 (10¢, 36 pgs.)
nn 6 12 18 31 38 45

CHAMBER (See Generation X and Uncanny X-Men)
Marvel Comics: Oct, 2002 - No. 4, Jan, 2003 ($2.99, limited series)
1-4-Bachalo-c/Vaughan-s/Ferguson-a. 1-Cyclops app. 3.00

CHAMBER OF CHILLS (Formerly Blondie Comics #20; ...of Clues No. 27 on)
Harvey Publications/Witches Tales: No. 21, June, 1951 - No. 26, Dec, 1954
21 (#1) 50 100 150 315 533 750
22,24 (#2,4) 37 74 111 222 361 500
23 (#3)-Excessive violence; eyes torn out 39 78 117 231 378 525
5(2/52)-Decapitation, acid in face scene 39 78 117 231 378 525
6-Woman melted alive 37 74 111 222 361 500

Champion Comics #4 © HARV

Channel Zero #1 © Brian Wood

Chapel #2 © Rob Liefeld

	GD 2.0	VG 4.0	FN 6.0	VF 8.0	VF/NM 9.0	NM- 9.2
7-Used in **SOTI**, pg. 389; decapitation/severed head panels	36	72	108	211	343	475
8-10: 8-Decapitation panels	30	60	90	177	289	400
11,12,14: 14-Spider-Man precursor (11/52)	24	48	72	142	234	325
13,15-24-Nostrand-a in all. 13,21-Decapitation panels. 18-Atom bomb panels. 20-Nostrand-c	29	58	87	170	278	385
25,26	20	40	60	114	182	250

NOTE: *About half the issues contain bondage, torture, sadism, perversion, gore, cannabalism, eyes ripped out, acid in face, etc.* ***Elias*** *c-4-11, 14-19, 21-26.* ***Kremer*** *a-12, 17.* ***Palais*** *a-21(1), 23.* ***Nostrand/Powell*** *a-13, 15, 16.* ***Powell*** *a-21, 23, 24('51), 5-8, 11, 13, 18-21, 23-25. Bondage-c-21, 24('51), 7. 25-r/#5; 26-r/#9.*

CHAMBER OF CHILLS
Marvel Comics Group: Nov, 1972 - No. 25, Nov, 1976

	GD	VG	FN	VF	VF/NM	NM-
1-Harlan Ellison adaptation	4	8	12	26	41	55
2-5: 2-1st app. John Jakes' Brak the Barbarian	3	6	9	16	22	28
6-25: 22,23-(Regular 25¢ editions)	2	4	6	13	18	22
22,23-(30¢-c variants, limited distribution)(5,7/76)	4	8	12	26	41	55

NOTE: ***Adkins*** *a-1i, 2i.* ***Brunner*** *a-2-4; c-4.* ***Chaykin*** *a-4.* ***Ditko*** *r-14, 16, 19, 23, 24.* ***Everett*** *a-3i, 11r,21r.* ***Heath*** *a-1r.* ***Gil Kane*** *c-2p.* ***Kirby*** *r-11, 18, 19, 22.* ***Powell*** *a-13r.* ***Russell*** *a-1p, 2p.* ***Shores*** *a-5 .* ***Williamson/Mayo*** *a-13r.* ***Robert E. Howard*** *horror story adaptation-2, 3.*

CHAMBER OF CLUES (Formerly Chamber of Chills)
Harvey Publications: No. 27, Feb, 1955 - No. 28, April, 1955

	GD	VG	FN	VF	VF/NM	NM-
27-Kerry Drake-r/#19; Powell-a; last pre-code	7	14	21	35	43	50
28-Kerry Drake	6	12	18	28	34	40

CHAMBER OF DARKNESS (Monsters on the Prowl #9 on)
Marvel Comics Group: Oct, 1969 - No. 8, Dec, 1970

	GD	VG	FN	VF	VF/NM	NM-
1-Buscema-a(p)	8	16	24	55	93	130
2,3: 2-Neal Adams scripts. 3-Smith, Buscema-a	5	10	15	30	48	65
4-A Conan-esque tryout by Smith (4/70); reprinted in Conan #16; Marie Severin/Everett-c	9	18	27	63	112	160
5,8: 5-H.P. Lovecraft adaptation. 8-Wrightson-c	4	8	12	26	41	55
6	4	8	12	22	34	45
7-Wrightson-c/a, 7pgs. (his 1st work at Marvel); Wrightson draws himself in 1st & last panels; Kirby/Ditko-r; last 15¢-c	6	12	18	41	66	90
1-(1/72; 25¢ Special, 52 pgs.)	4	8	12	26	41	55

NOTE: ***Adkins/Everett*** *a-8.* ***Buscema*** *a-Special 1r.* ***Craig*** *a-5.* ***Ditko*** *a-6-8r.* ***Heck*** *a-1, 2, 8, Special 1r.* ***Kirby*** *a(p)-4, 5, 7r.* ***Kirby/Everett*** *c-5.* ***Severin/Everett*** *c-6.* ***Shores*** *a-2, 3i, Special 1r.* ***Sutton*** *a-1, 2i, 4, 7, Special 1r.* ***Wrightson*** *c-7, 8.*

CHAMP COMICS (Formerly Champion No. 1-10)
Worth Publ. Co./Champ Publ./Family Comics(Harvey Publ.): No. 11, Oct, 1940 - No. 24, Dec, 1942; No. 25, April, 1943

	GD	VG	FN	VF	VF/NM	NM-
11-Human Meteor cont'd. from Champion	97	194	291	621	1061	1500
12-17,20: 14,15-Crandall-c. 20-The Green Ghost app.	76	152	228	486	831	1175
18,19-Simon-c. 19-The Wasp app.	97	194	291	621	1061	1500
21-23,25: 22-The White Mask app. 23-Flag-c	55	110	165	352	601	850
24-Hitler, Tojo & Mussolini-c	84	168	252	538	919	1300

CHAMPION (See Gene Autry's...)

CHAMPION COMICS
Worth Publ. Co.: Oct, 1939 (ashcan)

nn-Ashcan comic, not distributed to newsstands, only for in house use. A FN/VF copy sold for $2,261.76 in 2010.

CHAMPION COMICS (Formerly Speed Comics #1?; Champ Comics No. 11 on)
Worth Publ. Co.(Harvey Publications): No. 2, Dec, 1939 - No. 10, Aug, 1940 (no No.1)

	GD	VG	FN	VF	VF/NM	NM-
2-The Champ, The Blazing Scarab, Neptina, Liberty Lads, Jungleman, Bill Handy, Swingtime Sweetie begin	129	258	387	826	1413	2000
3-7: 7-The Human Meteor begins?	79	158	237	502	864	1225
8-10: 8-Simon-c. 9-1st S&K-c (1st collaboration together). 10-Bondage-c by Kirby	181	362	543	1158	1979	2800

CHAMPIONS, THE
Marvel Comics Group: Oct, 1975 - No. 17, Jan, 1978

	GD	VG	FN	VF	VF/NM	NM-
1-Origin & 1st app. The Champions (The Angel, Black Widow, Ghost Rider, Hercules, Iceman); Venus x-over	4	8	12	24	37	50
2-4,8-10,16: 2,3-Venus x-over	2	4	6	11	16	20
5-7-(Regular 25¢ edition)(4-8/76) 6-Kirby-c	2	4	6	11	16	20
5-7-(30¢-c variants, limited distribution)	5	10	15	30	48	65
11-14,17-Byrne-a. 14-(Regular 30¢ edition)	2	4	6	13	18	22
14,15-(35¢-c variant, limited distribution)	6	12	18	37	59	80
15-(Regular 30¢ edition)(9/77)-Byrne-a	2	4	6	13	18	22
... Classic Vol. 1 TPB (2006, $19.99) r/#1-11; unused cover to #7						20.00
... Classic Vol. 2 TPB (2007, $19.99) r/#12-17, Iron Man Ann. #4, Avengers #163, Super-Villain Team-Up #14 and Peter Parker, The Spectacular Spider-Man #17-18						20.00

NOTE: ***Buckler/Adkins*** *c-3.* ***Byrne*** *a-11-15, 17.* ***Kane/Adkins*** *c-1.* ***Kane/Layton*** *c-11.* ***Tuska*** *a-3p, 4p, 6p, 7p. Ghost Rider c-1-4, 7, 8, 10, 14, 16, 17 (4, 10, 14 are more prominent).*

CHAMPIONS (Game)
Eclipse Comics: June, 1986 - No. 6, Feb, 1987 (limited series)

1-6: 1-Intro Flare; based on game. 5-Origin Flare — 3.00

CHAMPIONS (Also see The League of Champions)
Hero Comics: Sept, 1987 - No. 12, 1989 ($1.95)

1-12: 1-Intro The Marksman & The Rose. 14-Origin Malice — 3.00
Annual 1(1988, $2.75, 52 pgs.)-Origin of Giant — 4.00

CHAMPION SPORTS
National Periodical Publications: Oct-Nov, 1973 - No. 3, Feb-Mar, 1974

	GD	VG	FN	VF	VF/NM	NM-
1	3	6	9	16	23	30
2,3	2	4	6	9	12	15

CHANNEL ZERO
Image Comics: Feb, 1998 - No. 5 ($2.95, B&W, limited series)

1-5, ...Dupe (1/99) -Brian Wood-s/a — 3.00

CHAOS (See The Crusaders)

CHAOS! BIBLE
Chaos! Comics: Nov, 1995 ($3.30, one-shot)

1-Profiles of characters & creators — 3.50

CHAOS! CHRONICLES
Chaos! Comics: Feb, 2000 ($3.50, one-shot)

1-Profiles of characters, checklist of Chaos! comics and products — 3.50

CHAOS EFFECT, THE
Valiant: 1994

Alpha (Giveaway w/trading card checklist) — 3.00
Alpha-Gold variant, Alpha-Red variant, Omega-Gold variant — 5.00
Omega (11/94, $2.25); Epilogue Pt. 1, 2 (12/94, 1/95; $2.95) — 3.00

CHAOS! GALLERY
Chaos! Comics: Aug, 1997 ($2.95, one-shot)

1-Pin-ups of characters — 3.00

CHAOS! QUARTERLY
Chaos! Comics: Oct, 1995 -No. 3, May, 1996 ($4.95, quarterly)

1-3: 1-anthology; Lady Death-c by Julie Bell. 2-Boris "Lady Demon"-c — 5.00
1-Premium Edition (7,500) — 25.00

CHAOS WAR
Marvel Comics: Dec, 2010 - No. 4, Mr, 2011 ($3.99, limited series)

1-5-Hercules, Thor and others vs. Chaos King; Pham-a. 3-5-Galactus app. — 4.00
...: Alpha Flight 1 (1/11, $3.99) McCann-s/Brown-a — 4.00
...: Ares 1 (2/11, $3.99) Oeming-s/Segovia-a — 4.00
...: Chaos King 1 (1/11, $3.99) Kaluta-a/c; Monclair-s — 4.00
...: Dead Avengers 1-3 (1/11 - No. 3, 3/11, $3.99) Grummett-a; Capt. Marvel app. — 4.00
...: God Squad 1 (2/11, $3.99) Sumerak-s/Panosian-a — 4.00
...: Thor 1,2 (1/11 - No. 2, 2/11, $3.99) DeMatteis-s/Ching-a — 4.00
...: X-Men 1,2 (2/11 - No. 2, 3/11, $3.99) Braithwaite-a; Thunderbird, Banshee app. — 4.00

CHAPEL (Also see Youngblood & Youngblood Strikefile #1-3)
Image Comics (Extreme Studios): No. 1 Feb, 1995 - No. 2, Mar, 1995 ($2.50, limited series)

1,2 — 3.00

CHAPEL (Also see Youngblood & Youngblood Strikefile #1-3)
Image Comics (Extreme Studios): V2 #1, Aug, 1995 - No. 7, Apr, 1996 ($2.50)

V2#1-7: 4-Babewatch x-over. 5-vs. Spawn. 7-Shadowhawk-c/app; Shadowhunt x-over — 3.00
#1-Quesada & Palmiotti variant-c — 3.00

CHAPEL (Also see Youngblood & Youngblood Strikefile #1-3)
Awesome Entertainment: Sept, 1997 ($2.99, one-shot)

1 (Reg. & alternate covers) — 3.00

CHARISMAGIC
Aspen MLT: No. 0, Mar, 2011 - No. 6 ($1.99/$2.99/$3.50)

0-($1.99) Khary Randolph-a/ Vince Hernandez-s; 3 covers — 3.00
1-4-($2.99) 1-4-Four covers on each — 3.00
5-($3.50) Three covers — 3.50

CHARLEMAGNE (Also see War Dancer)
Defiant Comics: Mar, 1994 - No. 5, July, 1994 ($2.50)

1/2 (Hero Illustrated giveaway)-Adam Pollina-c/a — 3.00
1-(3/94, $3.50, 52 pgs.)-Adam Pollina-c/a. — 4.00

Charlie Chan #4 © Prize

Chase #4 © DC

Chastity: Rocked #1 © Chaos!

	GD 2.0	VG 4.0	FN 6.0	VF 8.0	VF/NM 9.0	NM- 9.2
2,3,5: Adam Pollina-c/a. 2-War Dancer app. 5-Pre-Schism issue.						3.00
4-($3.25, 52 pgs.)						4.00

CHARLIE CHAN (See Big Shot Comics, Columbia Comics, Feature Comics & The New Advs. of...)

CHARLIE CHAN (The Adventures of...) (Zaza The Mystic No. 10 on) (TV)
Crestwood(Prize) No. 1-5; Charlton No. 6(6/55) on: 6-7/48 - No. 5, 2-3/49; No.6, 6/55 - No. 9, 3/56

	GD 2.0	VG 4.0	FN 6.0	VF 8.0	VF/NM 9.0	NM- 9.2
1-S&K-c, 2 pgs.; Infantino-a	87	174	261	553	952	1350
2-5-S&K-c: 3-S&K-c/a	50	100	150	315	533	750
6 (6/55-Charlton)-S&K-c	37	74	111	222	361	500
7-9	20	40	60	118	192	265

CHARLIE CHAN
Dell Publishing Co.: Oct-Dec, 1965 - No. 2, Mar, 1966

	GD 2.0	VG 4.0	FN 6.0	VF 8.0	VF/NM 9.0	NM- 9.2
1-Springer-a/c	5	10	15	35	55	75
2-Springer-a/c	4	8	12	22	34	45

CHARLIE McCARTHY (See Edgar Bergen Presents...)
Dell Publishing Co.: No. 171, Nov, 1947 - No. 571, July, 1954 (See True Comics #14)

	GD 2.0	VG 4.0	FN 6.0	VF 8.0	VF/NM 9.0	NM- 9.2
Four Color 171	22	44	66	154	327	500
Four Color 196-Part photo-c; photo back-c	13	26	39	90	195	300
1(3-5/49)-Part photo-c; photo back-c	12	24	36	84	177	270
2-9(7/52; #5,6-52 pgs.)	8	16	24	55	93	130
Four Color 445,478,527,571	6	12	18	39	62	85

CHARLTON ACTION: FEATURING "STATIC" (Also see Eclipse Monthly)
Charlton Comics: No, 11, Oct, 1985 - No. 12, Dec, 1985

	GD 2.0	VG 4.0	FN 6.0	VF 8.0	VF/NM 9.0	NM- 9.2
11,12-Ditko-c/a; low print run						6.00

CHARLTON BULLSEYE
CPL/Gang Publications: 1975 - No. 5, 1976 ($1.50, B&W, bi-monthly, magazine format)

	GD 2.0	VG 4.0	FN 6.0	VF 8.0	VF/NM 9.0	NM- 9.2
1: 1 & 2 are last Capt. Atom by Ditko/Byrne intended for the never published Capt. Atom #90; Nightshade app.; Jeff Jones-a	5	10	15	30	48	65
2-Part 2 Capt. Atom story by Ditko/Byrne	3	6	9	21	32	42
3-Wrong Country by Sanho Kim	2	4	6	13	18	22
4-Doomsday + 1 by John Byrne	3	6	9	17	25	32
5-Doomsday + 1 by Byrne, The Question by Toth; Neal Adams back-c; Toth-c	4	8	12	24	37	50

CHARLTON BULLSEYE
Charlton Publications: June, 1981 - No. 10, Dec, 1982; Nov, 1986

	GD 2.0	VG 4.0	FN 6.0	VF 8.0	VF/NM 9.0	NM- 9.2
1-1st Blue Beetle app. since '74, 1st app. The Question since '75; 1st app. Rocket Rabbit; Neil The Horse shown on preview page	1	2	3	5	7	9
2-5: 2-Charlton debut of Neil The Horse; Rocket Rabbit app. 4-Vanguards						6.00
6-10: Low print run. 6-Origin & 1st app. Thunderbunny. 7-1st apps. of Captain Atom & Nightshade since '75. 9-1st app. Bludd.	1	2	3	5	7	9

NOTE: *Material intended for issue #11-up was published in **Scary Tales** #37-up.*

CHARLTON CLASSICS
Charlton Comics: Apr, 1980 - No. 9, Aug, 1981

	GD 2.0	VG 4.0	FN 6.0	VF 8.0	VF/NM 9.0	NM- 9.2
1-Hercules-r by Glanzman in all						6.00
2-9						5.00

CHARLTON CLASSICS LIBRARY (1776)
Charlton Comics: V10 No.1, Mar, 1973 (one-shot)

	GD 2.0	VG 4.0	FN 6.0	VF 8.0	VF/NM 9.0	NM- 9.2
1776 (title) - Adaptation of the film musical "1776"; given away at movie theatres; also a newsstand version	3	6	9	14	19	24

CHARLTON PREMIERE (Formerly Marine War Heroes)
Charlton Comics: V1#19, July, 1967; V2#1, Sept, 1967 - No. 4, May, 1968

	GD 2.0	VG 4.0	FN 6.0	VF 8.0	VF/NM 9.0	NM- 9.2
V1#19, V2#1,2,4: V1#19-Marine War Heroes. V2#1-Trio; intro. Shape, Tyro Team & Spookman. 2-Children of Doom; Boyette classic-a. 4-Unlikely Tales; Aparo, Ditko-a	3	6	9	16	22	28
V2#3-Sinistro Boy Fiend; Blue Beetle & Peacemaker x-over	3	6	9	18	27	35

CHARLTON SPORT LIBRARY - PROFESSIONAL FOOTBALL
Charlton Comics: Winter, 1969-70 (Jan. on cover) (68 pgs.)

	GD 2.0	VG 4.0	FN 6.0	VF 8.0	VF/NM 9.0	NM- 9.2
1	3	6	9	20	30	40

CHARMED (TV)
Zenescope Entertainment: No. 0, Jun, 2010 - Present ($3.50)

	GD 2.0	VG 4.0	FN 6.0	VF 8.0	VF/NM 9.0	NM- 9.2
0-19-Multiple covers on most						3.50

CHASE (See Batman #550 for 1st app.)(Also see Batwoman)
DC Comics: Feb, 1998 - No. 9, Oct, 1998; #1,000,000 Nov, 1998 ($2.50)

	GD 2.0	VG 4.0	FN 6.0	VF 8.0	VF/NM 9.0	NM- 9.2
1-9: Williams III & Gray-a. 1-Includes 4 Chase cards. 4-Teen Titans app. 7,8-Batman app. 9-GL Hal Jordan-c/app.						3.00
#1,000,000 (11/98) Final issue; 853rd Century x-over						3.00

CHASING DOGMA (See Jay and Silent Bob)

CHASSIS
Millenium Publications: 1996 - No. 3 ($2.95)

	GD 2.0	VG 4.0	FN 6.0	VF 8.0	VF/NM 9.0	NM- 9.2
1-3: 1-Adam Hughes-c. 2-Conner var-c.						3.00

CHASSIS
Hurricane Entertainment: 1998 - No. 3 ($2.95)

	GD 2.0	VG 4.0	FN 6.0	VF 8.0	VF/NM 9.0	NM- 9.2
0,1-3: 1-Adam Hughes-c. 0-Green var-c.						3.00

CHASSIS (Vol. 3)
Image Comics: Nov, 1999 - No. 4 ($2.95, limited series)

	GD 2.0	VG 4.0	FN 6.0	VF 8.0	VF/NM 9.0	NM- 9.2
1-4: 1-Two covers by O'Neil and Green. 2-Busch var-c.						3.00
1-($6.95) DF Edition alternate-c by Wieringo						7.00

CHASTITY
Chaos! Comics: (one-shots)

	GD 2.0	VG 4.0	FN 6.0	VF 8.0	VF/NM 9.0	NM- 9.2
#1/2 (1/01, $2.95) Batista-a						3.00
Heartbreaker (3/02, $2.99) Adrian-a/Molenaar-c						3.00
Love Bites (3/01, $2.99) Vale-a/Romano-c						3.00
Reign of Terror 1 (10/00, $2.95) Grant-s/Ross-a/Rio-c						3.00
Re-Imagined 1 (7/02, $2.99) Conner-c; Toledo-a						3.00

CHASTITY: CRAZYTOWN
Chaos! Comics: Apr, 2002 - No. 3, June, 2002 ($2.99, limited series)

	GD 2.0	VG 4.0	FN 6.0	VF 8.0	VF/NM 9.0	NM- 9.2
1-3-Nicieza-s/Batista-c/a						3.00

CHASTITY: LUST FOR LIFE
Chaos! Comics: May, 1999 - No. 3, July, 1999 ($2.95, limited series)

	GD 2.0	VG 4.0	FN 6.0	VF 8.0	VF/NM 9.0	NM- 9.2
1-3-Nutman-s/Benes-c/a						3.00

CHASTITY: ROCKED
Chaos! Comics: Nov, 1998 - No. 4, Feb, 1999 ($2.95, limited series)

	GD 2.0	VG 4.0	FN 6.0	VF 8.0	VF/NM 9.0	NM- 9.2
1-4-Nutman-s/Justiniano-c/a						3.00

CHASTITY: SHATTERED
Chaos! Comics: Jun, 2001 - No. 3, Sept, 2001 ($2.99, limited series)

	GD 2.0	VG 4.0	FN 6.0	VF 8.0	VF/NM 9.0	NM- 9.2
1-3-Kaminski & Pulido-s/Batista-c/a						3.00

CHASTITY: THEATER OF PAIN
Chaos! Comics: Feb, 1997 - No. 3, June, 1997 ($2.95, limited series)

	GD 2.0	VG 4.0	FN 6.0	VF 8.0	VF/NM 9.0	NM- 9.2
1-3-Pulido-s/Justiniano-c/a						3.00
TPB (1997, $9.95) r/#1-3						10.00

CHECKMATE (TV)
Gold Key: Oct, 1962 - No. 2, Dec, 1962

	GD 2.0	VG 4.0	FN 6.0	VF 8.0	VF/NM 9.0	NM- 9.2
1-Photo-c on both	6	12	18	37	59	80
2	5	10	15	32	51	70

CHECKMATE! (See Action Comics #598 and The OMAC Project)
DC Comics: Apr, 1988 - No. 33, Jan, 1991 ($1.25)

	GD 2.0	VG 4.0	FN 6.0	VF 8.0	VF/NM 9.0	NM- 9.2
1-33: 13: New format begins						3.00

NOTE: ***Gil Kane** c-2, 4, 7, 8, 10, 11, 15-19.*

CHECKMATE (See Infinite Crisis and The OMAC Project)
DC Comics: Jun, 2006 - No. 31, Dec, 2008 ($2.99)

	GD 2.0	VG 4.0	FN 6.0	VF 8.0	VF/NM 9.0	NM- 9.2
1-Rucka-s/Saiz-a/Bermejo-c; Alan Scott, Mr. Terrific, Sasha Bordeaux app.						4.00
1-2nd printing with B&W cover						3.00
2-31: 2,3-Kobra, King Faraday, Amanda Waller, Fire app. 13-15-Outsiders app. 26-Chimera origin						3.00
...: A King's GameTPB (2007, $14.99) r/#1-7						15.00
...: Chimera TPB (2009, $17.99) r/#26-31						18.00
...: Fall of the Wall TPB (2008, $14.99) r/#16-22						15.00
...: Pawn Breaks TPB (2007, $14.99) r/#8-12						15.00

CHERYL BLOSSOM (See Archie's Girls, Betty and Veronica #320 for 1st app.)
Archie Publications: Sept, 1995 - No. 3, Nov, 1995 ($1.50, limited series)

	GD 2.0	VG 4.0	FN 6.0	VF 8.0	VF/NM 9.0	NM- 9.2
1	1	3	4	6	8	10
2,3	1	2	3	5	6	8
Special 1-4 ('95, '96, $2.00)	1	2	3	5	6	8

CHERYL BLOSSOM (Cheryl's Summer Job)
Archie Publications: July, 1996 - No. 3, Sept, 1996 ($1.50, limited series)

	GD 2.0	VG 4.0	FN 6.0	VF 8.0	VF/NM 9.0	NM- 9.2
1-3	1	2	3	4	5	7

CHERYL BLOSSOM (...Goes Hollywood)
Archie Publications: Dec, 1996 - No. 3, Feb, 1997 ($1.50, limited series)

	GD 2.0	VG 4.0	FN 6.0	VF 8.0	VF/NM 9.0	NM- 9.2
1-3	1	2	3	4	5	7

Chew #19 © John Layman

A Child is Born © Apostle Arts

Chilling Tales of Horror V2 #2 © Stanley

GD 2.0 | VG 4.0 | FN 6.0 | VF 8.0 | VF/NM 9.0 | NM- 9.2

CHERYL BLOSSOM
Archie Publications: Apr, 1997 - No. 37, Mar, 2001 ($1.50/$1.75/$1.79/$1.99)

1-Dan DeCarlo-c/a 1 3 4 6 8 10
2-10: 2-7-Dan DeCarlo-c/a 6.00
11-37: 32-Begin $1.99-c. 34-Sabrina app. 4.00

CHESTY SANCHEZ
Antarctic Press: Nov, 1995 - No. 2, Mar, 1996 ($2.95, B&W)

1,2 3.00
...Super Special (2/99, $5.99) 6.00

CHEVAL NOIR
Dark Horse Comics: 1989 - No. 48, Nov, 1993 ($3.50, B&W, 68 pgs.)

1-8,10 ($3.50): 6-Moebius poster insert 4.00
9,11,13,15,17,20,22 ($4.50, 84 pgs.) 4.50
12,18,19,21,23 ($3.95): 12-Geary-a; Mignola-c 4.00
14 ($4.95, 76 pgs.)(7 pgs. color) 5.00
16,24 ($3.75): 16-19-Contain trading cards 4.00
25,26 ($3.95): 26-Moebius-a begins 4.00
27-48 ($2.95): 33-Snyder III-c 3.00

NOTE: ***Bolland** a-2, 6, 7, 13, 14. **Bolton** a-2, 4, 45; c-4, 20. **Chadwick** c-13. **Dorman** painted c-16. **Geary** a-13, 14. **Kelley Jones** c-27. **Kaluta** a-6; c-6, 18. **Moebius** c-5, 9, 26. **Dave Stevens** c-1, 7. **Sutton** painted c-36.*

CHEW (See Walking Dead #61 for preview)
Image Comics: Jun, 2009 - Present ($2.99)

1-Layman-s/Guillory-a 5 10 15 35 55 75
1-2nd-4th printings 3.00
2-1st printing 3 6 9 14 20 25
2-(2nd printing), 3-5: Multiple printings exist 3.00
6-24: 15-Gatefold wraparound-c. 19-Neon green cover ink 3.00
27-(5/11) Future issue released between #18 & #19 3.00
Image Firsts: Chew #1 (4/10, $1.00) r/#1 with "Image Firsts" cover logo 3.00

CHEYENNE (TV)
Dell Publishing Co.: No. 734, Oct, 1956 - No. 25, Dec-Jan, 1961-62

Four Color 734(#1)-Clint Walker photo-c 13 26 39 87 186 285
Four Color 772,803: Clint Walker photo-c 9 18 27 58 99 140
4(8-10/57) - 20: 4-9,13-20-Clint Walker photo-c. 10-12-Ty Hardin photo-c
6 12 18 42 69 95
21-25-Clint Walker photo-c on all 7 14 21 44 72 100

CHEYENNE AUTUMN (See Movie Classics)

CHEYENNE KID (Formerly Wild Frontier No. 1-7)
Charlton Comics: No. 8, July, 1957 - No. 99, Nov, 1973

8 (#1) 8 16 24 42 54 65
9,15-19 6 12 18 29 36 42
10-Williamson/Torres-a(3); Ditko-c 11 22 33 60 83 105
11-(68 pgs.)-Cheyenne Kid meets Geronimo 10 20 30 58 79 100
12-Williamson/Torres-a(2) 10 20 30 58 79 100
13-Williamson/Torres-a (5 pgs.) 8 16 24 44 57 70
14-Williamson-a (5 pgs.?) 8 16 24 42 54 65
20-22,24,25-Severin c/a(3) each 4 8 12 22 34 45
23,27-29 3 6 9 16 22 28
26,30-Severin-a 3 6 9 18 27 35
31-59 2 4 6 10 14 18
60-65,67-80 2 4 6 8 11 14
66-Wander by Aparo begins, ends #87 2 4 6 10 14 18
81-99: Apache Red begins #88, origin in #89 2 4 6 8 11 14
Modern Comics Reprint 87,89(1978) 4.00

CHIAROSCURO (THE PRIVATE LIVES OF LEONARDO DA VINCI)
DC Comics (Vertigo): July, 1995 - No. 10, Apr, 1996 ($2.50/$2.95, limited series, mature)

1-9: McGreal and Rawson-s/Truog & Kayanan-a 3.00
10-($2.95) 3.00
TPB (2005, $24.99) r/series; intro. by Alisa Kwitney, afterword by Pat McGreal 25.00

CHICAGO MAIL ORDER (See C-M-O Comics)

CHIEF, THE (Indian Chief No. 3 on)
Dell Publishing Co.: No. 290, Aug, 1950 - No. 2, Apr-June, 1951

Four Color 290(#1) 8 16 24 51 86 120
2 6 12 18 41 66 90

CHIEF CRAZY HORSE (See Wild Bill Hickok #21)
Avon Periodicals: 1950 (Also see Fighting Indians of the Wild West!)

nn-Fawcette-c 21 42 63 126 206 285

CHIEF VICTORIO'S APACHE MASSACRE (See Fight Indians of/Wild West!)
Avon Periodicals: 1951

nn-Williamson/Frazetta-a (7 pgs.); Larsen-a; Kinstler-c
47 94 141 296 498 700

CHILD IS BORN, A
Apostle Arts: Nov, 2011 ($5.99, one-shot)

nn-Story of the birth of Jesus; Billy Tucci-s/a; cover by Tucci & Sparacio 6.00

CHILDREN OF FIRE
Fantagor Press: Nov, 1987 - No. 3, 1988 ($2.00, limited series)

1-3: by Richard Corben 4.00

CHILDREN OF THE VOYAGER (See Marvel Frontier Comics Unlimited)
Marvel Frontier Comics: Sept, 1993 - No. 4, Dec, 1993 ($1.95, limited series)

1-($2.95)-Embossed glow-in-the-dark-c; Paul Johnson-c/a 4.00
2-4 3.00

CHILDREN'S BIG BOOK
Dorene Publ. Co.: 1945 (25¢, stiff-c, 68 pgs.)

nn-Comics & fairy tales; David Icove-a 15 30 45 83 124 165

CHILDREN'S CRUSADE, THE
DC Comics (Vertigo): Dec, 1993 - No. 2, Jan, 1994 ($3.95, limited series)

1,2-Gaiman scripts & Bachalo-a; framing issues for Children's Crusade x-over 4.00

CHILD'S PLAY: THE SERIES (Movie)
Innovation Publishing: May, 1991 - #3, 1991 ($2.50, 28pgs.)

1-3 3.00

CHILD'S PLAY 2 THE OFFICIAL MOVIE ADAPTATION (Movie)
Innovation Publishing: 1990 - No. 3, 1990 ($2.50, bi-weekly limited series)

1-3: Adapts movie sequel 3.00

CHILI (Millie's Rival)
Marvel Comics Group: 5/69 - No. 17, 9/70; No. 18, 8/72 - No. 26, 12/73

1 10 20 30 65 118 170
2,4,5 6 12 18 39 62 85
3-Millie & Chili visit Marvel and meet Stan Lee & Stan Goldberg (6 pgs.)
6 12 18 42 69 95
6-17 5 10 15 32 51 70
18-26 4 8 12 28 44 60
Special 1(12/71, 52 pgs.) 6 12 18 41 66 90

CHILLER
Marvel Comics (Epic): Nov, 1993 - No. 2, Dec, 1993 ($7.95, lim. series)

1,2-(68 pgs.) 1 2 3 5 6 8

CHILLING ADVENTURES IN SORCERY (...as Told by Sabrina #1, 2)
(Red Circle Sorcery No. 6 on)
Archie Publications (Red Circle Prods.): 9/72 - No. 2, 10/72; No. 3, 10/73 - No. 5, 2/74

1-Sabrina cameo as narrator 5 10 15 32 51 70
2-Sabrina cameo as narrator 3 6 9 18 27 35
3-5: Morrow-c/a, all. 4,5-Alcazar-a 2 4 6 11 16 20

CHILLING TALES (Formerly Beware)
Youthful Magazines: No. 13, Dec, 1952 - No. 17, Oct, 1953

13(No.1)-Harrison-a; Matt Fox-c/a 73 146 219 467 796 1125
14-Harrison-a 48 96 114 302 514 725
15-Matt Fox-c; Harrison-a 55 110 165 352 601 850
16-Poe adapt.-'Metzengerstein'; Rudyard Kipling adapt.- 'Mark of the Beast,'
by Kiefer; bondage-c 42 84 126 265 445 625
17-Matt Fox-c; Sir Walter Scott & Poe adapt. 48 96 144 302 514 725

CHILLING TALES OF HORROR (Magazine)
Stanley Publications: V1#1, 6/69 - V1#7, 12/70; V2#2, 2/71 - V2#6, 10/71(50¢, B&W, 52 pgs.)

V1#1 8 16 24 53 89 125
2-4,(no #5),6,7: 7-Cameron-a 5 10 15 35 55 75
V2#2-6: 2-Two different #2 issues exist (2/71 & 4/71). 2-(2/71) Spirit of Frankenstein -r/Adventures into the Unknown #16. 4-(8/71) different from other V2#4(6/71)
5 10 15 32 51 70
V2#4-(6/71) r/9 pg. Feldstein-a from Adventures into the Unknown #3
5 10 15 35 55 75

NOTE: *Two issues of V2#2 exist, Feb, 1971 and April, 1971. Two issues of V2#4 exist, Jun, 1971 and Aug, 1971.*

CHILLY WILLY (Also see New Funnies #211)
Dell Publ. Co.: No. 740, Oct, 1956 - No. 1281, Apr-June, 1962 (Walter Lantz)

Four Color 740 (#1) 7 14 21 48 79 110
Four Color 852 (2/58),967 (2/59),1017 (9/59),1074 (2-4/60),1122 (8/60),

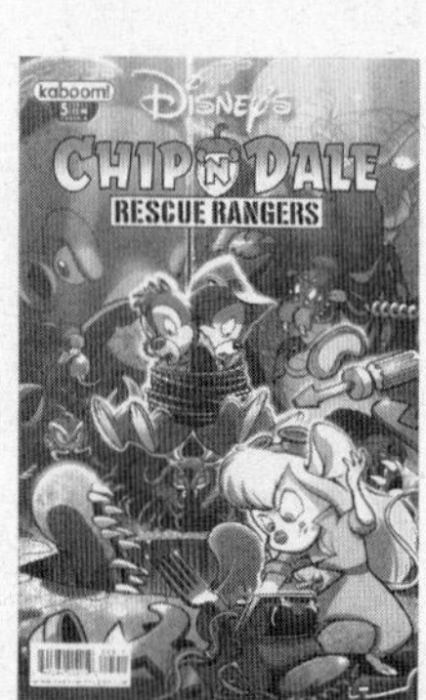

Chip 'n' Dale Rescue Rangers #5 © DIS

Choice Comics #3 © GP

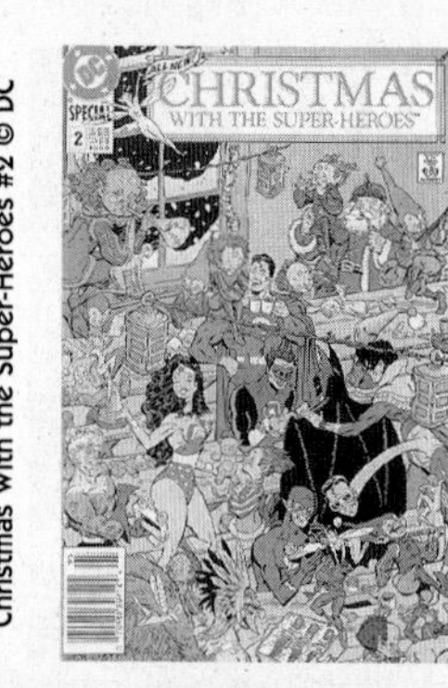

Christmas With the Super-Heroes #2 © DC

GD VG FN VF VF/NM NM-
2.0 4.0 6.0 8.0 9.0 9.2

1177 (4-6/61), 1212 (7-9/61), 1281 — 5 10 15 30 48 65

CHIMERA
CrossGeneration Comics: Mar, 2003 - No. 4, July, 2003 ($2.95, limited series)
1-4-Marz-s/Peterson-c/a — 3.00
Vol. 1 TPB (2003, $15.95) r/#1-4 plus sketch pages, 3-D models, how-to guides — 16.00

CHIMICHANGA
Albatross Exploding Funny Books: 2010 ($3.00, B&W)
1-3-Eric Powell-s/a/c — 3.00

CHINA BOY (See Wisco in the Promotional Comics section)

CHIP 'N' DALE (Walt Disney)(See Walt Disney's C&S #204)
Dell Publishing Co./Gold Key/Whitman No. 65 on: Nov, 1953 - No. 30, June-Aug, 1962; Sept, 1967 - No. 83, July, 1984
Four Color 517(#1) — 11 22 33 71 136 200
Four Color 581,636 — 6 12 18 42 69 95
4(12/55-2/56)-10 — 6 12 18 37 59 80
11-30 — 5 10 15 30 48 65
1(Gold Key, 1967)-Reprints — 3 6 9 20 30 40
2-10 — 2 4 6 13 18 22
11-20 — 2 4 6 9 12 15
21-40 — 2 4 6 8 10 12
41-64,70-77: 75(2/82), 76(2-3/82), 77(3/82) — 1 2 3 5 7 9
65,66 (Whitman) — 2 4 6 8 11 14
67-69 (3-pack? 1980): 67(8/80), 68(10/80) (scarce) — 4 8 12 24 37 50
78-83 (All #90214; 3-pack, nd, nd code): 78(4/83), 79(5/83), 80(7/83), 81(8/83), 82(5/84), 83(7/84) — 3 6 9 16 22 28
NOTE: *All Gold Key/Whitman issues have reprints except No. 32-35, 38-41, 45-47. No. 23-28, 30-42, 45-47, 49 have new covers.*

CHIP 'N DALE RESCUE RANGERS
Disney Comics: June, 1990 - No. 19, Dec, 1991 ($1.50)
1-New stories; origin begins — 3.50
2-19: 2-Origin continued — 3.00

CHIP 'N DALE RESCUE RANGERS
BOOM! Studios: Dec, 2010 - No. 8, Jul, 2011 ($3.99)
1-8: 1-Brill-s/Castellani-a; 3 covers — 4.00
... Free Comic Book Day Edition (5/11) Flip book with Darkwing Duck — 3.00

CHITTY CHITTY BANG BANG (See Movie Comics)

C.H.I.X.
Image Comics (Studiosaurus): Jan, 1998 ($2.50)
1-Dodson, Haley, Lopresti, Randall, and Warren-s/c/a — 3.00
1-($5.00) "X-Ray Variant" cover — 5.00
C.H.I.X. That Time Forgot 1 (8/98, $2.95) — 3.00

CHOICE COMICS
Great Publications: Dec, 1941 - No. 3, Feb, 1942
1-Origin Secret Circle; Atlas the Mighty app.; Zomba, Jungle Fight, Kangaroo Man, & Fire Eater begin — 155 310 465 992 1696 2400
2 — 77 154 231 493 847 1200
3-Double feature; Features movie "The Lost City" (classic cover); continued from Great Comics #3 — 161 322 483 1030 1765 2500

CHOLLY AND FLYTRAP (Arthur Suydam's...)
Image Comics: Nov, 2004 - No. 4, June, 2005 ($4.95/$5.95, limited series)
1-($4.95) Arthur Suydam-s/a/c — 6.00
2-4-($5.95) — 6.00

CHOO CHOO CHARLIE
Gold Key: Dec, 1969
1-John Stanley-a — 6 12 18 41 66 90

CHOSEN
Dark Horse Comics: Jan, 2004 - No. 3, Aug, 2004 ($2.99, limited series)
1-Story of the second coming; Mark Millar-s/Peter Gross-a — 4.00
2,3 — 3.00

CHRISTIAN (See Asylum)
Maximum Press: Jan, 1996 ($2.99, one-shot)
1-Pop Mhan-a — 3.00

CHRISTIAN HEROES OF TODAY
David C. Cook: 1964 (36 pgs.)
nn — 3 6 9 18 27 35

CHRISTMAS (Also see A-1 Comics)
Magazine Enterprises: No. 28, 1950
A-1 28 — 8 16 24 44 57 70

CHRISTMAS ADVENTURE, A (See Classics Comics Giveaways, 12/69)

CHRISTMAS ALBUM (See March of Comics No. 312)

CHRISTMAS ANNUAL
Golden Special: 1975 ($1.95, 100 pgs., stiff-c)
nn-Reprints Mother Goose stories with Walt Kelly-a — 4 8 12 22 34 45

CHRISTMAS & ARCHIE
Archie Comics: Jan, 1975 ($1.00, 68 pgs., 10-1/4x13-1/4" treasury-sized)
1-(scarce) — 6 12 18 39 62 85

CHRISTMAS BELLS (See March of Comics No. 297)

CHRISTMAS CARNIVAL
Ziff-Davis Publ. Co./St. John Publ. Co. No. 2: 1952 (25¢, one-shot, 100 pgs.)
nn — 36 72 108 214 347 480
2-Reprints Ziff-Davis issue plus-c — 17 34 51 98 154 210

CHRISTMAS CAROL, A (See March of Comics No. 33)

CHRISTMAS EVE, A (See March of Comics No. 212)

CHRISTMAS IN DISNEYLAND (See Dell Giants)

CHRISTMAS PARADE (See Dell Giant No. 26, Dell Giants, March of Comics No. 284, Walt Disney Christmas Parade & Walt Disney's...)

CHRISTMAS PARADE (Walt Disney's)
Gold Key: 1962 (no month listed) - No. 9, Jan, 1972 (#1,5: 80 pgs.; #2-4,7-9: 36 pgs.)
1 (30018-301)-Giant — 9 18 27 58 99 140
2-6: 2-r/F.C. #367 by Barks. 3-r/F.C. #178 by Barks. 4-r/F.C. #203 by Barks. 5-r/Christmas Parade #1 (Dell) by Barks; giant. 6-r/Christmas Parade #2 (Dell) by Barks (64 pgs.); giant — 6 12 18 41 66 90
7-Pull-out poster (half price w/o poster) — 5 10 15 32 51 70
8-r/F.C. #367 by Barks; pull-out poster — 6 12 18 41 66 90
9 — 4 8 12 26 41 55

CHRISTMAS PARTY (See March of Comics No. 256)

CHRISTMAS STORIES (See Little People No. 959, 1062)

CHRISTMAS STORY (See March of Comics No. 326 in the Promotional Comics section)

CHRISTMAS STORY BOOK (See Woolworth's Christmas Story Book)

CHRISTMAS TREASURY, A (See Dell Giants & March of Comics No. 227)

CHRISTMAS WITH ARCHIE
Spire Christian Comics (Fleming H. Revell Co.): 1973, 1974 (49¢, 52 pgs.)
nn-Low print run — 3 6 9 14 19 24

CHRISTMAS WITH MOTHER GOOSE
Dell Publishing Co.: No. 90, Nov, 1945 - No. 253, Nov, 1949
Four Color 90 (#1)-Kelly-a — 15 30 45 104 227 350
Four Color 126 ('46), 172 (11/47)-By Walt Kelly — 12 24 36 81 166 250
Four Color 201 (10/48), 253-By Walt Kelly — 11 22 33 71 136 200

CHRISTMAS WITH SANTA (See March of Comics No. 92)

CHRISTMAS WITH THE SUPER-HEROES (See Limited Collectors' Edition)
DC Comics: 1988; No. 2, 1989 ($2.95)
1,2: 1-(100 pgs.)-All reprints; N. Adams-r, Byrne-c; Batman, Superman, JLA, LSH Christmas stories; r-Miller's 1st Batman/DC Special Series #21. 2-(68 pgs.)-Superman by Chadwick; Batman, Wonder Woman, Deadman, Green Lantern, Flash app.; Morrow-a; Enemy Ace by Byrne; all new-a — 5.00

CHROMA-TICK, THE (...Special Edition, #1,2) (Also see The Tick)
New England Comics Press: Feb, 1992 - No. 8, Nov, 1993 ($3.95/$3.50, 44 pgs.)
1,2-Includes serially numbered trading card set — 5.00
3-8 ($3.50, 36 pgs.): 6-Bound-in card — 4.00

CHROME
Hot Comics: 1986 - No. 3, 1986 ($1.50, limited series)
1-3 — 3.00

CHROMIUM MAN, THE
Triumphant Comics: Aug, 1993 - No.10, May, 1994 ($2.50)
1-1st app. Mr. Death; all serially numbered — 3.00
2-10: 2-1st app. Prince Vandal. 3-1st app. Candi, Breaker & Coil. 4,5-Triumphant Unleashed x-over. 8,9-(3/94). 10-(5/94) — 3.00
0-(4/94)-Four color-c, 0-All pink-c & all blue-c; no cover price — 3.00

CHROMIUM MAN: VIOLENT PAST, THE

Chronos #4 © DC

Cinderella: From Fabletown With Love #6 © DC & Bill Willingham

The Cisco Kid #2 © DELL

	GD 2.0	VG 4.0	FN 6.0	VF 8.0	VF/NM 9.0	NM- 9.2

Triumphant Comics: Jan, 1994 - No. 2, Jan, 1994 ($2.50, limited series)
1,2-Serially numbered to 22,000 each 3.00

CHRONICLES OF CONAN, THE (See Conan the Barbarian)

CHRONICLES OF CORUM, THE (Also see Corum...)
First Comics: Jan, 1987 - No. 12, Nov, 1988 ($1.75/$1.95, deluxe series)
1-12: Adapts Michael Moorcock's novel 3.00

CHRONOS
DC Comics: Mar, 1998 - No. 11, Feb. 1999 ($2.50)
1-11-J.F. Moore-s/Guinan-a 3.00
#1,000,000 (11/98) 853rd Century x-over 3.00

CHUCK (Based on the NBC TV series)
DC Comics (WildStorm): Aug, 2008 - No. 6, Jan, 2009 ($2.99, limited series)
1-6-Jeremy Haun-a/Kristian Donaldson-c; Noto back-up-a 3.00
TPB (2009, $19.99) r/#1-6; photo-c 20.00

CHUCKLE, THE GIGGLY BOOK OF COMIC ANIMALS
R. B. Leffingwell Co.: 1945 (132 pgs., one-shot)
1-Funny animal 22 44 66 132 216 300

CHUCK NORRIS (TV)
Marvel Comics (Star Comics): Jan, 1987 - No. 4, July, 1987
1-3: Ditko-a 3.50
4-No Ditko-a (low print run) 5.00

CHUCK WAGON (See Sheriff Bob Dixon's...)

CHUCKY (Based on the 1988 killer doll movie Child's Play)
Devil's Due Publishing: Apr, 2007 - No. 4, Nov, 2007 ($3.50/$5.50)
1-3-Pulido-s/Medors-a; art & photo covers 5.00
4-($5.50) 1 2 3 4 5 7
TPB (2007, $18.99) r/series; gallery of variant covers; 4 pages of script and sketch art 19.00

CHYNA (WWF Wrestling)
Chaos! Comics: Sept, 2000; July, 2001 ($2.95/$2.99, one-shots)
1-Grant-s/Barrows-a; photo-c 3.00
1-($9.95) Premium Edition; Cleavenger-c 10.00
II -(7/01, $2.99) Deodato-a; photo-c 3.00

CICERO'S CAT
Dell Publishing Co.: July-Aug, 1959 - No. 2, Sept-Oct, 1959
1-Cat from Mutt & Jeff 5 10 15 30 48 65
2 4 8 12 26 41 55

CIMARRON STRIP (TV)
Dell Publishing Co.: Jan, 1968
1-Stuart Whitman photo-c 4 8 12 24 37 50

CINDER AND ASHE
DC Comics: May, 1988 - No. 4, Aug, 1988 ($1.75, limited series)
1-4: Mature readers 3.00

CINDERELLA (Disney) (See Movie Comics)
Dell Publishing Co.: No. 272, Apr, 1950 - No. 786, Apr, 1957
Four Color 272 12 24 36 78 157 235
Four Color 786-Partial-r #272 7 14 21 44 72 100

CINDERELLA
Whitman Publishing Co.: Apr, 1982
nn-Reprints 4-Color #272 1 2 3 4 5 7

CINDERELLA: FABLES ARE FOREVER (See Fables)
DC Comics (Vertigo): Apr, 2011 - No. 6, Sept, 2011 ($2.99, limited series)
1-6-Roberson-s/McManus-a/Zullo-c; Dorothy Gale app. 3.00

CINDERELLA: FROM FABLETOWN WITH LOVE (See Fables)
DC Comics (Vertigo): Jan, 2010 - No. 6, Jun, 2010 ($2.99, limited series)
1-6: Roberson-s/McManus-a/Zullo-c 3.00
TPB (2010, $14.99) r/#1-6 15.00

CINDERELLA LOVE
Ziff-Davis/St. John Publ. Co. No. 12 on: No. 10, 1950; No. 11, 4-5/51; No. 12, 9/51; No. 4, 10-11/51 - No. 11, Fall, 1952; No. 12, 10/53 - No. 15, 8/54; No. 25, 12/54 - No. 29, 10/55 (No #16-24)
10(#1)(1st Series, 1950)-Painted-c 19 38 57 111 176 240
11(#2, 4-5/51)-Crandall-a; Saunders painted-c 14 28 42 76 108 140
12(#3, 9/51)-Photo-c 12 24 36 67 94 120
4-8: 4,6,7-Photo-c 11 22 33 62 86 110
9-Kinstler-a; photo-c 12 24 36 69 97 125
10,11(Fall/'52): 10,11-Photo-c 11 22 33 62 86 110
12(St. John-10/53)-#13:13-Painted-c. 11 22 33 60 83 105
14-Baker-a 14 28 42 76 108 140
15(8/54)-Matt Baker-c 15 30 45 85 130 175
25(2nd Series)(Formerly Romantic Marriage) Baker-c 15 30 45 85 130 175
26-Baker-c; last precode (2/55) 15 30 45 85 130 175
27,29: Both Matt Baker-c 15 30 45 85 130 175
28 10 20 30 56 76 95

CINDY COMICS (...Smith No. 39, 40; Crime Can't Win No. 41 on)(Formerly Krazy Komics) (See Junior Miss & Teen Comics)
Timely Comics: No. 27, Fall, 1947 - No. 40, July, 1950
27-Kurtzman-a, 3 pgs: Margie, Oscar begin 24 48 72 142 234 325
28-31-Kurtzman-a 15 30 45 86 133 180
32-40: 33-Georgie story; anti-Wertham editorial 13 26 39 72 101 130
NOTE: *Kurtzman's "Hey Look"-#27(3), 29(2), 30(2), 31; "Giggles 'n' Grins"-28.*

CINNAMON: EL CICLO
DC Comics: Oct, 2003 - No. 5, Feb, 2004 ($2.50, limited series)
1-5-Van Meter-s/Chaykin-c/Paronzini-a 3.00

CIRCUS (...the Comic Riot)
Globe Syndicate: June, 1938 - No. 3, Aug, 1938
1-(Scarce)-Spacehawks (2 pgs.), & Disk Eyes by Wolverton (2 pgs.), Pewee Throttle by Cole (2nd comic book work; see Star Comics V1#11), Beau Gus, Ken Craig & The Lords of Crillon, Jack Hinton by Eisner, Van Bragger by Kane 500 1000 1500 3600 6300 9000
2,3-(Scarce)-Eisner, Cole, Wolverton, Bob Kane-a in each 280 560 840 1764 2982 4200

CIRCUS BOY (TV) (See Movie Classics)
Dell Publishing Co.: No. 759, Dec, 1956 - No. 813, July, 1957
Four Color 759 (#1)-The Monkees' Mickey Dolenz photo-c 11 22 33 76 151 225
Four Color 785 (4/57), 813-Mickey Dolenz photo-c 10 20 30 66 121 175

CIRCUS COMICS
Farm Women's Pub. Co./D. S. Publ.: 1945 - No. 2, Jun, 1945; Wint., 1948-49
1-Funny animal 14 28 42 80 115 150
2 9 18 27 50 65 80
1(1948)-D.S. Publ.; 2 pgs. Frazetta 24 48 72 140 230 320

CIRCUS OF FUN COMICS
A. W. Nugent Publ. Co.: 1945 - No. 3, Dec, 1947 (A book of games & puzzles)
1 15 30 45 84 127 170
2,3 10 20 30 54 72 90

CISCO KID, THE (TV)
Dell Publishing Co.: July, 1950 - No. 41, Oct-Dec, 1958
Four Color 292(#1)-Cisco Kid, his horse Diablo, & sidekick Pancho & his horse Loco begin; painted-c begin 20 40 60 137 294 450
2(1/51) 11 22 33 71 136 200
3-5 10 20 30 66 121 175
6-10 9 18 27 58 99 140
11-20 8 16 24 51 86 120
21-36-Last painted-c 6 12 18 42 69 95
37-41: All photo-c 8 16 24 53 89 125
NOTE: ***Buscema** a-40. **Ernest Nordli** painted c-5-16, 20, 35.*

CISCO KID COMICS
Bernard Bailey/Swappers Quarterly: Winter, 1944 (one-shot)
1-Illustrated Stories of the Operas: Faust; Funnyman by Giunta; Cisco Kid (1st app.) & Superbaby begin; Giunta-c 43 86 129 271 461 650

CITIZEN SMITH (See Holyoke One-Shot No. 9)

CITIZEN V AND THE V-BATTALION (See Thunderbolts)
Marvel Comics: June, 2001 - No. 3, Aug, 2001 ($2.99, limited series)
1-3-Nicieza-a; Michael Ryan-c/a 3.00
...: The Everlasting 1-4 (3/02 - No. 4, 7/02) Nicieza-s/LaRosa-a(p) 3.00

CITY OF HEROES (Online game)
Dark Horse Comics/Blue King Studios: Sept, 2002; May, 2004 - No. 7 ($2.95)
1-(no cover price) Dakan-s/Zombo-a 3.00
1-7-($2.95) 3.00

CITY OF HEROES (Online game)
Image Comics: June, 2005 - No. 20, Aug, 2007 ($2.99)

City of the Living Dead nn © AVON

Civil War: The Initiative #1 © MAR

Clandestine #2 © MAR

GD VG FN VF VF/NM NM-
2.0 4.0 6.0 8.0 9.0 9.2

1-20: 1-Waid-s; Pérez-c. 6-Flp-c with City of Villains. 7-9-Jurgens-s 3.00

CITY OF OTHERS
Dark Horse Comics: Apr, 2007 - No. 4, Aug, 2007 ($2.99, limited series)

1-4-Bernie Wrightson-a/c; Steve Niles & Wrightson-s 3.00
TPB (2/08, $14.95) r/#1-4; Wrightson sketch pages 15.00

CITY OF SILENCE
Image Comics: May, 2000 - No. 3, July, 2000 ($2.50)

1-3-Ellis-s/Erskine-a 3.00
TPB (6/04, $9.95) r/#1-3; pin-up gallery 10.00

CITY OF THE LIVING DEAD (See Fantastic Tales No. 1)
Avon Periodicals: 1952

nn-Hollingsworth-c/a 52 104 156 322 549 775

CITY OF TOMORROW
DC Comics (WildStorm): June, 2005 - No. 6, Nov, 2005 ($2.99, limited series)

1-6-Howard Chaykin-s/a 3.00
TPB (2006, $19.99) r/#1-6 20.00

CITY PEOPLE NOTEBOOK
Kitchen Sink Press: 1989 ($9.95, B&W, magazine sized)

nn-Will Eisner-s/a 10.00
nn-(DC Comics, 2000) Reprint 10.00

CITY SURGEON (Blake Harper...)
Gold Key: August, 1963

1(10075-308)-Painted-c 4 8 12 24 37 50

CIVIL WAR (Also see Amazing Spider-Man for TPB)
Marvel Comics: July, 2006 - No. 7, Jan, 2007 ($3.99/$2.99, limited series)

1-($3.99) Millar-s/McNiven-a & wraparound-c 1 2 3 5 6 8
1-Variant cover by Michael Turner 2 4 6 9 12 15
1-Aspen Comics Variant cover by Turner 2 4 6 9 12 15
1-Director's Cut (2006, $4.99) r/#1 plus promo art, variant covers, sketches and script 5.00
2-($2.99) Spider-Man unmasks 1 2 3 4 5 7
2-Turner variant cover 5.00
2-B&W sketch variant cover 20.00
2-2nd printing 4.00
3-7: 3-Thor returns. 4-Goliath killed 4.00
3-7-Turner variant covers 5.00
3-7-B&W sketch variant covers 15.00
TPB (2007, $24.99) r/#1-7; gallery of variant covers 25.00
...: Battle Damage Report (2007, $3.99) Post-Civil War character profiles; McGuinness-c 4.00
...: Choosing Sides (2/07, $3.99) Colan-c; Howard the Duck app.; 2 covers by Yu & Colan 4.00
... Companion TPB (2007, $13.99) r/Civil War Files, ...:Battle Damage Report, Marvel Spotlight: Millar/McNiven, Marvel Spotlight: Civil War Aftermath and Daily Bugle CW 14.00
Daily Bugle Civil War Newspaper Special #1 (9/06, 50¢, newsprint) Daily Bugle "newspaper" overview of the crossover; Mayhew-a 3.00
...Files (2006, $3.99) profile pages of major Civil War characters; McNiven-c 4.00
...: Marvel Universe TPB (2007, $11.99) r/Civil War: Choosing Sides, CW: The Return, She-Hulk #8, CW: The Initiative; She-Hulk sketch page; variant cover gallery 12.00
...: MGC #1 (6/10, $1.00) r/#1 with "Marvel's Greatest Comics" cover logo 3.00
...: The Confession (5/07, $2.99) Maleev-c/a; Bendis-s 3.00
...: The Initiative (4/07, $4.99) Silvestri-c/a; previews of post-Civil War series 5.00
...: The Return (3/07, $2.99) Captain Marvel returns; The Sentry app.; Raney-a 3.00
...: The Road to Civil War TPB (2007, $14.99) r/New Avengers: Illuminati, Fantastic Four #536 & 537, Amazing Spider-Man #529-531; Spider-Man costume sketches by Bachalo 15.00
... War Crimes (2/07, $3.99) Kingpin in prison; Tieri-s/Staz Johnson-a 4.00
... War Crimes TPB (2007, $17.99) r/Civil War: War Crimes one-shot and Underworld #1-5 18.00
... X-Men Universe TPB (2007, $13.99) r/Cable & Deadpool #30-32; X-Factor #8,9 14.00

CIVIL WAR CHRONICLES (Reprints of Civil War and related Marvel issues)
Marvel Comics: Oct, 2007 - No. 12, Sept, 2008 ($4.99, limited series)

1-12: Reprints Civil War, Civil War: Frontline and x-over issues 5.00

CIVIL WAR: FRONTLINE (Tie-in to Civil War and related Marvel issues)
Marvel Comics: Aug, 2006 - No. 11, Apr, 2007 ($2.99, limited series)

1-Jenkins-s/Bachs-a/Watson-c; back-up stories by various 4.00
2-11: 3-Green Goblin app. 11-Aftermath of Civil War #7 3.00
... Book 1 TPB (2007, $14.99) r/#1-6 15.00
... Book 2 TPB (2007, $14.99) r/#7-11 15.00

CIVIL WAR: HOUSE OF M
Marvel Comics: Nov, 2008 - No. 5, Mar, 2009 ($2.99, limited series)

1-5-Gage-s/DiVito-a 3.00

CIVIL WAR MUSKET, THE (Kadets of America Handbook)
Custom Comics, Inc.: 1960 (25¢, half-size, 36 pgs.)

nn 3 6 9 16 22 28

CIVIL WAR: X-MEN (Tie-in to Civil War)
Marvel Comics: Sept, 2006 - No. 4, Dec, 2006 ($2.99, limited series)

1-4-Paquette-a/Hine-s; Bishop app. 3.00
1-Variant cover by Michael Turner 10.00
TPB (2007, $11.99) r/#1-4, profile pages of minor characters 12.00

CIVIL WAR: YOUNG AVENGERS & RUNAWAYS (Tie-in to Civil War)
Marvel Comics: Sept, 2006 - No. 4, Dec, 2006 ($2.99, limited series)

1-4-Caselli-a/Wells-s/Cheung-c 3.00
TPB (2007, $11.99) r/#1-4, profile pages of characters 12.00

CLAIRE VOYANT (Also see Keen Teens)
Leader Publ./Standard/Pentagon Publ.: 1946 - No. 4, 1947 (Sparling strip reprints)

nn 71 142 213 454 777 1100
2,4: 2-Kamen-c. 4-Kamen bondage-c 53 106 159 334 567 800
3-Kamen bridal-c; contents mentioned in Love and Death, a book by Gershom Legman(1949) referenced by Dr. Wertham in **SOTI** 68 136 204 435 743 1050

CLANDESTINE (Also see Marvel Comics Presents & X-Men: ClanDestine)
Marvel Comics: Oct, 1994 - No.12, Sept, 1995 ($2.95/$2.50)

1-($2.95)-Alan Davis-c/a(p)/scripts & Mark Farmer-c/a(i) begin, ends #8; Modok app.; Silver Surfer cameo; gold foil-c 3.50
2-12: 2-Wraparound-c. 2,3-Silver Surfer app. 5-Origin of ClanDestine. 6-Capt. America, Hulk, Spider-Man, Thing & Thor-c; Spider-Man cameo. 7-Spider-Man-c/app; Punisher cameo. 8-Invaders & Dr. Strange app. 10-Captain Britain-c/app. 11-Sub-Mariner app. 3.00
Preview (10/94, $1.50) 3.00
... Classic HC (2008, $29.99, DJ) r/#1-8, Marvel Comics Presents #158, X-Men and Clandestine #1&2, sketch pages and cover gallery; Alan Davis afterword 30.00

CLANDESTINE
Marvel Comics: Apr, 2008 - No. 5, Aug, 2008 ($2.99, limited series)

1-5: 1-Alan Davis-c/a(p)/scripts & Mark Farmer-c/a(i). 2-5-Excalibur app. 3.00

CLASH
DC Comics: 1991 - No. 3, 1991 ($4.95, limited series, 52 pgs.)

Book One - Three: Adam Kubert-c/a 5.00

CLASSIC BATTLESTAR GALACTICA (See Battlestar Galactica, Classic...)

CLASSIC COMICS/ILLUSTRATED - INTRODUCTION
by Dan Malan

Since the first publication of this special introduction to the **Classics** section, a number of revisions have been made to further clarify the listings. **Classics** reprint editions prior to 1963 had either incorrect dates or no dates listed. Those reprint editions should be identified only by the highest number on the reorder list (HRN). Past *Guides* listed what were calculated to be approximately correct dates, but many people found it confusing for the *Guide* to list a date not listed in the comic itself.

We have also attempted to clear up confusion about edition variations, such as color, printer, etc. Such variations are identified by letters. Editions are determined by three categories. Original edition variations are designated as Edition 1A, 1B, etc. All reprint editions prior to 1963 are identified by HRN only. All reprint editions from 9/63 on are identified by the correct date listed in the comic.

Information is also included on four reprintings of **Classics**. From 1968-1976, Twin Circle, the Catholic newspaper, serialized over 100 **Classics** titles. That list can be found under non-series items at the end of this section. In 1972, twelve **Classics** were reissued as **Now Age Books Illustrated**. They are listed under **Pendulum Illustrated Classics**. In 1982, 20 **Classics** were reissued, adapted for teaching English as a second language. They are listed under **Regents Illustrated Classics**. Then in 1984, six **Classics** were reissued with cassette tapes. See the listing under **Cassette Books**.

UNDERSTANDING CLASSICS ILLUSTRATED
by Dan Malan

Since **Classics Illustrated** is the most complicated comic book series, with all its reprint editions and variations, changes in covers and artwork, a variety of means of identifying editions, and the most extensive worldwide distribution of any comic-book series, this introductory section is provided to assist you in gaining expertise about this series.

THE HISTORY OF CLASSICS
The **Classics** series was the brain child of Albert L. Kanter, who saw in the new comic-book medium a means of introducing children to the great classics of literature. In October of 1941 his Gilberton Co. began the **Classic Comics** series with **The Three Musketeers**, with 64 pages of storyline. In those early years, the struggling series saw irregular schedules and

Classic Comics #1 © GIL

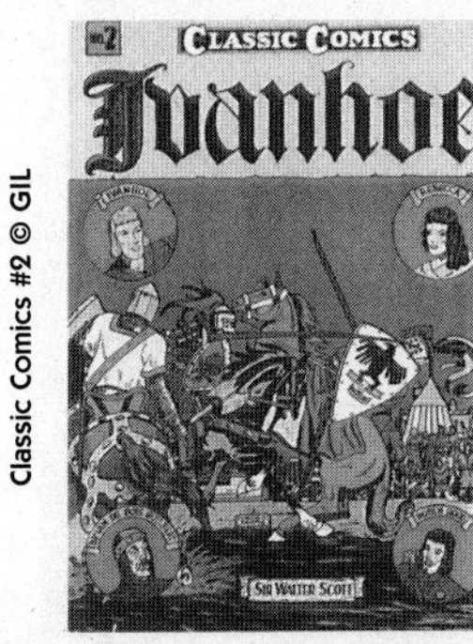

Classic Comics #2 © GIL

Classic Comics #3 © GIL

GD 2.0	VG 4.0	FN 6.0	VF 8.0	VF/NM 9.0	NM- 9.2

numerous printers, not to mention variable art quality and liberal story adaptations. With No.13 the page total was reduced to 56 (except for No. 33, originally scheduled to be No. 9), and with No. 15 the coming-next ad on the outside back cover moved inside. In 1945 the Jerry Iger Shop began producing all new CC titles, beginning with No. 23. In 1947 the search for a classier logo resulted in **Classics Illustrated**, beginning with No. 35, **Last Days of Pompeii**. With No. 45 the page total dropped again to 48, which was to become the standard.

Two new developments in 1951 had a profound effect upon the success of the series. One was the introduction of painted covers, instead of the old line drawn covers, beginning with No. 81, **The Odyssey**. The second was the switch to the major national distributor Curtis. They raised the cover price from 10 to 15 cents, making it the highest priced comic-book, but it did not slow the growth of the series, because they were marketed as books, not comics. Because of this higher quality image, **Classics** flourished during the fifties while other comic series were reeling from outside attacks. They diversified with their new **Juniors**, **Specials**, and **World Around Us** series.

Classics artwork can be divided into three distinct periods. The pre-Iger era (1941-44) was mentioned above for its variable art quality. The Iger era (1945-53) was a major improvement in art quality and adaptations. It came to be dominated by artists Henry Kiefer and Alex Blum, together accounting for some 50 titles. Their styles gave the first real personality to the series. The EC era (1954-62) resulted from the demise of the EC horror series, when many of their artists made the major switch to classical art.

But several factors brought the production of new CI titles to a complete halt in 1962. Gilberton lost its 2nd class mailing permit. External factors like television, cheap paperback books, and Cliff Notes were all eating away at their market. Production halted with No.167, **Faust**, even though many more titles were already in the works. Many of those found their way into foreign series, and are very desirable to collectors. In 1967, **Classics Illustrated** was sold to Patrick Frawley and his Catholic publication, Twin Circle. They issued two new titles in 1969 as part of an attempted revival, but succumbed to major distribution problems in 1971. In 1988, First Publishing acquired the rights to use the old CI series art, logo, and name from the Frawley Group, and released a short-lived series featuring contributions of modern creators. Acclaim Books and Twin Circles issued a series of **Classics** reprints from 1997-1998.

One of the unique aspects of the **Classics Illustrated** (CI) series was the proliferation of reprint variations. Some titles had as many as 25 editions. Reprinting began in 1943. Some **Classic Comics** (CC) reprints (r) had the logo format revised to a banner logo, and added a motto under the banner. In 1947 CC titles changed to the CI logo, but kept their line drawn covers (LDC). In 1948, Nos. 13, 18, 29 and 41 received second covers (LDC2), replacing covers considered too violent, and reprints of Nos. 13-44 had pages reduced to 48, except for No. 26, which had 48 pages to begin with.

Starting in the mid-1950s, 70 of the 80 LDC titles were reissued with new painted covers (PC). Thirty of them also received new interior artwork (A2). The new artwork was generally higher quality with larger art panels and more faithful but abbreviated storylines. Later on, there were 29 second painted covers (PC2), mostly by Twin Circle. Altogether there were 199 interior art variations (169 (O)s and 30 A2 editions) and 272 different covers (169 (O)s, four LDC2s, 70 new PCs of LDC (O)s, and 29 PC2s). It is mildly astounding to realize that there are nearly 1400 different editions in the U.S. CI series.

FOREIGN CLASSICS ILLUSTRATED

If U.S. Classics variations are mildly astounding, the veritable plethora of foreign CI variations will boggle your imagination. While we still anticipate additional discoveries, we presently know about series in 25 languages and 27 countries. There were 250 new CI titles in foreign series, and nearly 400 new foreign covers of U.S. titles. The 1400 U.S. CI editions pale in comparison to the 4000 plus foreign editions. The very nature of CI lent itself to flourishing as an international series. Worldwide, they published over one billion copies! The first foreign CI series consisted of six Canadian Classic Comic reprints in 1946.

The following chart shows when CI series first began in each country:
1946: Canada. 1947: Australia. 1948: Brazil/The Netherlands. 1950: Italy. 1951: Greece/Japan/Hong Kong(?)/England/Argentina/Mexico. 1952: West Germany. 1954: Norway. 1955: New Zealand/South Africa. 1956: Denmark/Sweden/Iceland. 1957: Finland/France. 1962: Singapore(?). 1964: India (8 languages). 1971: Ireland (Gaelic). 1973: Belgium(?)/Philippines(?) & Malaysia(?).

Significant among the early series were Brazil and Greece. In 1950, Brazil was the first country to begin doing its own new titles. They issued nearly 80 new CI titles by Brazilian authors. In Greece in 1951 they actually had debates in parliament about the effects of Classics Illustrated on Greek culture, leading to the inclusion of 88 new Greek History & Mythology titles in the CI series.

But by far the most important foreign CI development was the joint European series which began in 1956 in 10 countries simultaneously. By 1960, CI had the largest European distribution of any American publication, not just comics! So when all the problems came up with U.S. distribution, they literally moved the CI operation to Europe in 1962, and continued producing new titles in all four CI series. Many of them were adapted and drawn in the U.S., the most famous of which was the British CI #158A. Dr. No, drawn by Norman Nodel. Unfortunately, the British CI series ended in late 1963, which limited the European CI titles available in English to 15. Altogether there were 82 new CI art titles in the joint European series, which ran until 1976.

IDENTIFYING CLASSICS EDITIONS

HRN: This is the highest number on the reorder list. It should be listed in ( ) after the title number. It is crucial to understanding various CI editions.

ORIGINALS (O): This is the all-important First Edition. To determine (O)s,there is one primary rule and two secondary rules (with exceptions):

Rule No. 1: All (O)s and only (O)s have coming-next ads for the next number. **Exceptions**: No. 14(15) (reprint) has an ad on the last inside text page only. No. 14(0) also has a full-page outside back cover ad (also rule 2). Nos.55(75) and 57(75) have coming-next ads. (Rules 2 and 3 apply here). Nos. 168(0) and 169(0) do not have coming-next ads. No.168 was never reprinted; No. 169(0) has HRN (166). No. 169(169) is the only reprint.

Rule No. 2: On nos.1-80, all (O)s and only (O)s list 10c on the front cover. **Exceptions**: Reprint variations of Nos. 37(62), 39(71), and 46(62) list 10c on the front cover. (Rules 1 and 3 apply here.)

Rule No. 3: All (O)s have HRN close to that title No. **Exceptions**: Some reprints also have HRNs close to that title number: a few CC(r)s, 58(62), 60(62), 149(149), 152(149) 153(149), and title nos. in the 160's. (Rules 1 and 2 apply here.)

DATES: Many reprint editions list either an incorrect date or no date. Since Gilberton apparently kept track of CI editions by HRN, they often left the (O) date on reprints. Often, someone with a CI collection for sale will swear that all their copies are originals. That is why we are so detailed in pointing out how to identify original editions. Except for original editions, which should have a coming-next ad, etc., all CI dates prior to 1963 are incorrect! So you want to go by HRN only if it is (165) or below, and go by listed date if it is 1963 or later. There are a few (167) editions with incorrect dates. They could be listed either as (167) or (62/3), which is meant to indicate that they were issued sometime between late 1962 and early 1963.

COVERS: A change from CC to LDC indicates a logo change, not a cover change; while a change from LDC to LDC2, LDC to PC, or from PC to PC2 does indicate a new cover. New PCs can be identified by HRN, and PC2s can be identified by HRN and date. Several covers had color changes, particularly from purple to blue.

Notes: If you see 15 cents in Canada on a front cover, it does not necessarily indicate a Canadian edition. Editions with an HRN between 44 and 75, with 15 cents on the cover are Canadian. Check the publisher's address. An HRN listing two numbers with a / between them indicates that there are two different reorder lists in the front and back covers. Official Twin Circle editions have a full-page back cover ad for their TC magazine, with no CI reorder list. Any CI with just a Twin Circle sticker on the front is not an official TC edition.

TIPS ON LISTING CLASSICS FOR SALE

It may be easy to just list Edition 17, but Classics collectors keep track of CI editions in terms of HRN and/or date, (O) or (r), CC or LDC, PC or PC2, A1 or A2, soft or stiff cover, etc. Try to help them out. For originals, just list (0), unless there are variations such as color (Nos. 10 and 61), printer (Nos. 18-22), HRN (Nos. 95, 108, 160), etc. For reprints, just list HRN if it's (165) or below. Above that, list HRN and date. Also, please list type of logo/cover/art for the convenience of buyers. They will appreciate it.

CLASSIC COMICS (Also see Best from Boys Life, Cassette Books, Famous Stories, Fast Fiction, Golden Picture Classics, King Classics, Marvel Classics Comics, Pendulum Illustrated Classics, Picture Parade, Picture Progress, Regents Ill. Classics, Spitfire, Stories by Famous Authors, Superior Stories, and World Around Us.)

CLASSIC COMICS (Classics Illustrated No. 35 on)
Elliot Publishing #1-3 (1941-1942)/Gilberton Publications #4-167 (1942-1967) /Twin Circle Pub. (Frawley) #168-169 (1968-1971):
10/41 - No. 34, 2/47; No. 35, 3/47 - No. 169, Spring 1969
(Reprint Editions of almost all titles 5/43 - Spring 1971)
(Painted Covers (0)s No. 81 on, and (r)s of most Nos. 1-80)

Abbreviations:
A–Art; C or c–Cover; CC–Classic Comics; CI–Classics Ill.; Ed–Edition; LDC–Line Drawn Cover; PC–Painted Cover; r–Reprint

1. The Three Musketeers

Ed	HRN	Date	Details	A	C	GD 2.0	VG 4.0	FN 6.0	VF 8.0	VF/NM 9.0	NM- 9.2
1	–	10/41	Date listed-1941; Elliot Pub; 68 pgs.	1	1	465	930	1395	3395	6000	8600
2	10	–	10¢ price removed on all (r)s; Elliot Pub; CC-r	1	1	34	68	102	206	336	465
3	15	–	Long Isl. Ind. Ed.; CC-r	1	1	25	50	75	150	245	340
4	18/20	–	Sunrise Times Ed.; CC-r	1	1	19	38	57	109	172	235
5	21	–	Richmond Courier Ed.; CC-r	1	1	17	34	51	98	154	210
6	28	1946	CC-r	1	1	14	28	42	80	115	150
7	36	–	LDC-r	1	1	8	16	24	42	54	65
8	60	–	LDC-r	1	1	6	12	18	27	33	38
9	64	–	LDC-r	1	1	5	10	15	22	26	30
10	78	–	C-price 15¢;LDC-r	1	1	4	9	13	18	22	26

Classic Comics #4 © GIL

Classic Comics #5 © GIL

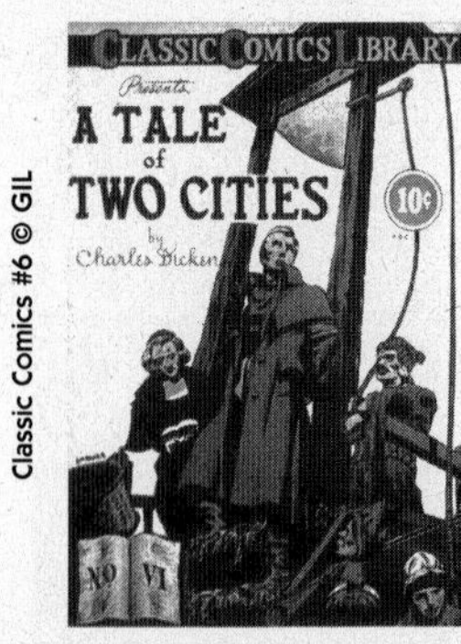

Classic Comics #6 © GIL

Ed	HRN	Date	Details	A	C	GD 2.0	VG 4.0	FN 6.0	VF 8.0	VF/NM 9.0	NM- 9.2
11	93	–	LDC-r	1	1	4	9	13	18	22	26
12	114	–	Last LDC-r	1	1	4	8	11	16	19	22
13	134	–	New-c; old-a; 64 pg. PC-r	1	2	3	6	9	19	29	38
14	143	–	Old-a; PC-r; 64 pg.	1	2	2	4	6	11	16	20
15	150	–	New-a; PC-r; Evans/Crandall-a	2	2	3	6	9	17	25	32
16	149	–	PC-r	2	2	2	4	6	8	11	14
17	167	–	PC-r	2	2	2	4	6	8	11	14
18	167	4/64	PC-r	2	2	2	4	6	8	11	14
19	167	1/65	PC-r	2	2	2	4	6	8	11	14
20	167	3/66	PC-r	2	2	2	4	6	8	11	14
21	166	11/67	PC-r	2	2	2	4	6	8	11	14
22	166	Spr/69	C-price 25¢ ; stiff-c; PC-r	2	2	2	4	6	8	11	14
23	169	Spr/71	PC-r; stiff-c	2	2	2	4	6	8	11	14

2. Ivanhoe

Ed	HRN	Date	Details	A	C	GD 2.0	VG 4.0	FN 6.0	VF 8.0	VF/NM 9.0	NM- 9.2
1	(O)	12/41?	Date listed-1941; Elliot Pub; 68 pgs.	1	1	232	464	696	1485	2543	3600
2	10	–	Price & 'Presents' removed; Elliot Pub; CC-r	1	1	31	62	93	186	303	420
3	15	–	Long Isl. Ind. ed.; CC-r	1	1	21	42	63	122	199	275
4	18/20	–	Sunrise Times ed.; CC-r	1	1	18	36	54	103	162	225
5	21	–	Richmond Courier ed.; CC-r	1	1	16	32	48	94	147	200
6	28	1946	Last 'Comics'-r	1	1	14	28	42	80	115	150
7	36	–	1st LDC-r	1	1	9	18	27	47	61	75
8	60	–	LDC-r	1	1	6	12	18	27	33	38
9	64	–	LDC-r	1	1	5	10	15	22	26	30
10	78	–	C-price 15¢; LDC-r	1	1	4	9	13	18	22	26
11	89	–	LDC-r	1	1	4	8	12	17	21	24
12	106	–	LDC-r	1	1	4	7	10	14	17	20
13	121	–	Last LDC-r	1	1	4	7	10	14	17	20
14	136	–	New-c&a; PC-r	2	2	5	10	15	25	31	36
15	142	–	PC-r	2	2	2	4	6	9	13	16
16	153	–	PC-r	2	2	2	4	6	9	13	16
17	149	–	PC-r	2	2	2	4	6	9	13	16
18	167	–	PC-r	2	2	2	4	6	8	11	14
19	167	5/64	PC-r	2	2	2	4	6	8	11	14
20	167	1/65	PC-r	2	2	2	4	6	8	11	14
21	167	3/66	PC-r	2	2	2	4	6	8	11	14
22A	166	9/67	PC-r	2	2	2	4	6	8	11	14
22B	166	–	Center ad for Children's Digest & Young Miss; rare; PC-r	2	2	7	14	21	46	76	105
23	166	R/68	C-Price 25¢; PC-r	2	2	2	4	6	8	11	14
24	169	Win/69	Stiff-c	2	2	2	4	6	8	11	14
25	169	Win/71	PC-r; stiff-c	2	2	2	4	6	8	11	14

3. The Count of Monte Cristo

Ed	HRN	Date	Details	A	C	GD 2.0	VG 4.0	FN 6.0	VF 8.0	VF/NM 9.0	NM- 9.2
1	(O)	3/42	Elliot Pub; 68 pgs.	1	1	152	304	456	965	1658	2350
2	10	–	Conray Prods; CC-r	1	1	26	52	78	154	252	350
3	15	–	Long Isl. Ind. ed.; CC-r	1	1	20	40	60	117	189	260
4	18/20	–	Sunrise Times ed.; CC-r	1	1	18	36	54	107	169	230
5	20	–	Sunrise Times ed.; CC-r	1	1	17	34	51	98	154	210
6	21	–	Richmond Courier ed.; CC-r	1	1	16	32	48	94	147	200
7	28	1946	CC-r; new Banner logo	1	1	14	28	42	80	115	150
8	36	–	1st LDC-r	1	1	9	18	27	47	61	75
9	60	–	LDC-r	1	1	6	12	18	27	33	38
10	62	–	LDC-r	1	1	6	12	18	29	36	42
11	71	–	LDC-r	1	1	5	10	14	20	24	28
12	87	–	C-price 15¢; LDC-r	1	1	4	9	13	18	22	26
13	113	–	LDC-r	1	1	4	7	10	14	17	20
14	135	–	New-c&a; PC-r; Cameron-a	2	2	3	6	9	18	27	35
15	143	–	PC-r	2	2	2	4	6	8	13	16
16	153	–	PC-r	2	2	2	4	6	8	13	16
17	161	–	PC-r	2	2	2	4	6	8	13	16
18	167	–	PC-r	2	2	2	4	6	8	11	14
19	167	7/64	PC-r	2	2	2	4	6	8	11	14
20	167	7/65	PC-r	2	2	2	4	6	8	11	14
21	167	7/66	PC-r	2	2	2	4	6	8	11	14
22	166	R/68	C-price 25¢; PC-r	2	2	2	4	6	8	11	14
23	169	Win/69	Stiff-c; PC-r	2	2	2	4	6	8	11	14

4. The Last of the Mohicans

Ed	HRN	Date	Details	A	C	GD 2.0	VG 4.0	FN 6.0	VF 8.0	VF/NM 9.0	NM- 9.2
1	(O)	8/42	Date listed-1942; Gilberton #4(0) on; 68 pgs.	1	1	129	258	387	826	1413	2000
2	12	–	Elliot Pub; CC-r	1	1	26	52	78	154	252	350
3	15	–	Long Isl. Ind. ed.; CC-r	1	1	20	40	60	117	189	260
4	20	–	Long Isl. Ind. ed.; CC-r; banner logo	1	1	18	36	54	105	165	225
5	21	–	Queens Home News ed.; CC-r	1	1	16	32	48	94	147	200
6	28	1946	Last CC-r; new	1	1	14	28	42	80	115	150
7	36	–	1st LDC-r	1	1	9	18	27	47	61	75
8	60	–	LDC-r	1	1	6	12	18	27	33	38
9	64	–	LDC-r	1	1	5	10	14	20	24	28
10	78	–	C-price 15¢; LDC-r	1	1	4	9	13	18	22	26
11	89	–	LDC-r	1	1	4	8	12	17	21	24
12	117	–	Last LDC-r	1	1	4	7	10	14	17	20
13	135	–	New-c; PC-r	1	2	5	10	15	24	30	35
14	141	–	PC-r	1	2	4	7	9	14	16	18
15	150	–	New-a; PC-r; Severin, L.B. Cole-a	2	2	6	12	18	27	33	38
16	161	–	PC-r	2	2	2	4	6	8	11	14
17	167	–	PC-r	2	2	2	4	6	8	11	14
18	167	6/64	PC-r	2	2	2	4	6	8	11	14
19	167	8/65	PC-r	2	2	2	4	6	8	11	14
20	167	8/66	PC-r	2	2	2	4	6	8	11	14
21	166	R/67	C-price 25¢; PC-r	2	2	2	4	6	8	11	14
22	169	Spr/69	Stiff-c; PC-r	2	2	2	4	6	8	11	14

5. Moby Dick

Ed	HRN	Date	Details	A	C	GD 2.0	VG 4.0	FN 6.0	VF 8.0	VF/NM 9.0	NM- 9.2
1A	(O)	9/42	Date listed-1942; Gilberton; 68 pgs.	1	1	152	304	456	965	1658	2350
1B			inside-c, rare free promo			232	464	696	1485	2543	3600
2	10	–	Conray Prods; Pg. 64 changed from 105 title list to letter from Editor; CC-r	1	1	28	56	84	165	270	375
3	15	–	Long Isl. Ind. ed.; Pg. 64 changed from Letter to the Editor to Ill. poem-Concord Hymn; CC-r	1	1	23	46	69	136	223	310
4	18/20	–	Sunrise Times ed.; CC-r	1	1	19	38	57	109	172	235
5	20	–	Sunrise Times ed.; CC-r	1	1	18	36	54	105	165	225
6	21	–	Sunrise Times ed.; CC-r	1	1	16	32	48	94	147	200
7	28	1946	CC-r; new banner logo	1	1	14	28	42	81	118	155
8	36	–	1st LDC-r	1	1	9	18	27	47	61	75
9	60	–	LDC-r	1	1	6	12	18	27	33	38
10	62	–	LDC-r	1	1	6	12	18	29	36	42
11	71	–	LDC-r	1	1	5	10	15	22	26	30
12	87	–	C-price 15¢; LDC-r	1	1	5	10	14	20	24	28
13	118	–	LDC-r	1	1	4	8	12	17	21	24
14	131	–	New c&a; PC-r	2	2	5	10	15	25	31	36
15	138	–	PC-r	2	2	2	4	6	9	12	16
16	148	–	PC-r	2	2	2	4	6	9	12	16

Classic Comics #7 © GIL

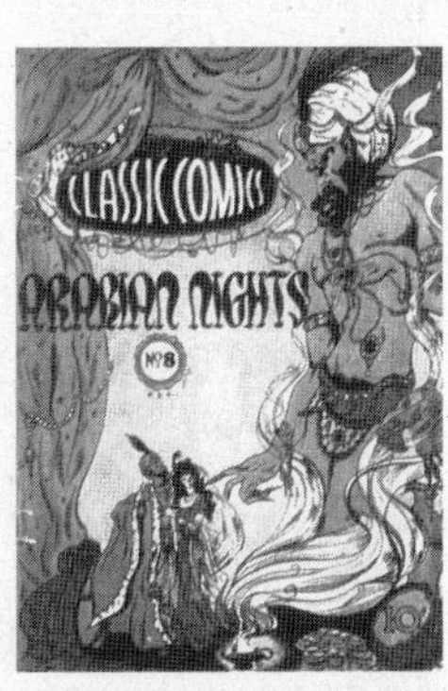

Classic Comics #8 © GIL

Classic Comics #10 © GIL

Ed	HRN	Date	Details	A	C	GD 2.0	VG 4.0	FN 6.0	VF 8.0	VF/NM 9.0	NM- 9.2
17	158	–	PC-r	2	2	2	4	6	9	12	16
18	167	–	PC-r	2	2	2	4	6	8	11	14
19	167	6/64	PC-r	2	2	2	4	6	8	11	14
20	167	7/65	PC-r	2	2	2	4	6	8	11	14
21	167	3/66	PC-r	2	2	2	4	6	8	11	14
22	166	9/67	PC-r	2	2	2	4	6	8	11	14
23	166	Win/69	New-c & c-price 25¢; Stiff-c; PC-r	2	3	3	6	9	16	23	30
24	169	Win/71	PC-r	2	3	3	6	9	14	19	24

6. A Tale of Two Cities

Ed	HRN	Date	Details	A	C	GD 2.0	VG 4.0	FN 6.0	VF 8.0	VF/NM 9.0	NM- 9.2
1	(O)	10/42	Date listed-1942; 68 pgs. Zeckerberg c/a	1	1	126	252	378	806	1378	1950
2	14	–	Elliot Pub; CC-r	1	1	24	48	72	142	234	325
3	18	–	Long Isl. Ind. ed.; CC-r	1	1	20	40	60	114	182	250
4	20	–	Sunrise Times ed.; CC-r	1	1	18	36	54	105	165	225
5	28	1946	Last CC-r; new banner logo	1	1	14	28	42	80	115	150
6	51	–	1st LDC-r	1	1	8	16	24	42	54	65
7	64	–	LDC-r	1	1	5	10	15	23	28	32
8	78	–	C-price 15¢; LDC-r	1	1	5	10	14	20	24	28
9	89	–	LDC-r	1	1	4	7	10	14	17	20
10	117	–	LDC-r	1	1	4	7	10	14	17	20
11	132	–	New-c&a; PC-r; Joe Orlando-a	2	2	5	10	15	25	31	36
12	140	–	PC-r	2	2	2	4	6	8	11	14
13	147	–	PC-r	2	2	2	4	6	8	11	14
14	152	–	PC-r; very rare	2	2	17	34	51	98	154	210
15	153	–	PC-r	2	2	2	4	6	9	13	16
16	149	–	PC-r	2	2	2	4	6	9	13	16
17	167	–	PC-r	2	2	2	4	6	8	11	14
18	167	6/64	PC-r	2	2	2	4	6	8	11	14
19	167	8/65	PC-r	2	2	2	4	6	8	11	14
20	166	5/67	PC-r	2	2	2	4	6	8	11	14
21	166	Fall/68	New-c & 25¢; PC-r	2	3	3	6	9	17	25	32
22	169	Sum/70	Stiff-c; PC-r	2	3	2	4	6	13	18	22

7. Robin Hood

Ed	HRN	Date	Details	A	C	GD 2.0	VG 4.0	FN 6.0	VF 8.0	VF/NM 9.0	NM- 9.2
1	(O)	12/42	Date listed-1942; first Gift Box ad-bc; 68 pgs.	1	1	97	194	291	621	1061	1500
2	12	–	Elliot Pub; CC-r	1	1	23	46	69	136	223	310
3	18	–	Long Isl. Ind. ed.; CC-r	1	1	19	38	57	111	176	240
4	20	–	Nassau Bulletin ed.; CC-r	1	1	18	36	54	103	162	220
5	22	–	Queens Cty. Times ed.; CC-r	1	1	16	32	48	94	147	200
6	28	–	CC-r	1	1	14	28	42	81	118	155
7	51	–	LDC-r	1	1	8	16	24	42	54	65
8	64	–	LDC-r	1	1	5	10	15	24	30	35
9	78	–	LDC-r	1	1	4	9	13	18	22	26
10	97	–	LDC-r	1	1	4	8	12	17	21	24
11	106	–	LDC-r	1	1	4	7	10	14	17	20
12	121	–	LDC-r	1	1	4	7	10	14	17	20
13	129	–	New-c; PC-r	1	2	5	10	15	25	31	36
14	136	–	New-a; PC-r	2	2	5	10	15	24	29	34
15	143	–	PC-r	2	2	2	4	6	9	13	16
16	153	–	PC-r	2	2	2	4	6	9	13	16
17	164	–	PC-r	2	2	2	4	6	8	11	14
18	167	–	PC-r	2	2	2	4	6	8	11	14
19	167	6/64	PC-r	2	2	2	4	6	8	11	14
20	167	5/65	PC-r	2	2	2	4	6	8	11	14
21	167	7/66	PC-r	2	2	2	4	6	8	11	14
22	166	12/67	PC-r	2	2	2	4	6	8	11	14
23	169	Sum/69	Stiff-c; c-price 25¢; PC-r	2	2	2	4	6	8	11	14

8. Arabian Nights

Ed	HRN	Date	Details	A	C	GD 2.0	VG 4.0	FN 6.0	VF 8.0	VF/NM 9.0	NM- 9.2
1	(O)	2/43	Original; 68 pgs. Lilian Chestney-c/a	1	1	150	300	450	953	1639	2325
2	17	–	Long Isl. ed.; pg. 64 changed from Gift Box ad to Letter from British Medical Worker; CC-r	1	1	52	104	156	323	549	775
3	20	–	Nassau Bulletin; Pg. 64 changed from letter to article-Three Men Named Smith; CC-r	1	1	42	84	126	265	445	625
4A	28	1946	CC-r; new banner logo, slick-c	1	1	31	62	93	182	296	410
4B	28	1946	Same, but w/stiff-c	1	1	31	62	93	182	296	410
5	51	–	LDC-r	1	1	22	44	66	128	209	290
6	64	–	LDC-r	1	1	19	38	57	111	176	240
7	78	–	LDC-r	1	1	18	36	54	105	165	225
8	164	–	New-c&a; PC-r	2	2	15	30	45	90	140	190

9. Les Miserables

Ed	HRN	Date	Details	A	C	GD 2.0	VG 4.0	FN 6.0	VF 8.0	VF/NM 9.0	NM- 9.2
1A	(O)	3/43	Original; slick paper cover; 68 pgs.	1	1	94	188	282	597	1024	1450
1B	(O)	3/43	Original; rough, pulp type-c; 68 pgs.	1	1	110	220	330	704	1202	1700
2	14	–	Elliot Pub; CC-r	1	1	26	52	78	154	252	350
3	18	3/44	Nassau Bul. Pg. 64 changed from Gift Box ad to Bill of Rights article; CC-r	1	1	22	44	66	128	209	290
4	20	–	Richmond Courier ed.; CC-r	1	1	19	38	57	111	176	240
5	28	1946	Gilberton; pgs. 60-64 rearranged/ illos added; CC-r	1	1	14	28	42	81	118	155
6	51	–	LDC-r	1	1	9	18	27	47	61	75
7	71	–	LDC-r	1	1	6	12	18	29	36	42
8	87	–	C-price 15¢; LDC-r	1	1	6	12	18	27	33	38
9	161	–	New-c&a; PC-r	2	2	7	14	21	37	46	55
10	167	9/63	PC-r	2	2	2	4	6	11	16	20
11	167	12/65	PC-r	2	2	2	4	6	11	16	20
12	166	R/1968	New-c & price 25¢; PC-r	2	3	3	6	9	18	27	35

10. Robinson Crusoe (Used in **SOTI**, pg. 142)

Ed	HRN	Date	Details	A	C	GD 2.0	VG 4.0	FN 6.0	VF 8.0	VF/NM 9.0	NM- 9.2
1A	(O)	4/43	Original; Violet-c; 68 pgs; Zuckerberg c/a	1	1	84	168	252	538	919	1300
1B	(O)	4/43	Original; blue-grey-c, 68 pgs.	1	1	92	184	276	584	1005	1425
2A	14	–	Elliot Pub; violet-c; 68 pgs; CC-r	1	1	29	58	87	170	278	385
2B	14	–	Elliot Pub; blue-grey-c; CC-r	1	1	25	50	75	147	241	335
3	18	–	Nassau Bul. Pg. 64 changed from Gift Box ad to Bill of Rights article; CC-r	1	1	19	38	57	111	176	240
4	20	–	Queens Home News ed.; CC-r	1	1	16	32	48	94	147	200
5	28	1946	Gilberton; pg. 64 changes from Bill of Rights to WWII article-One Leg Shot Away; last CC-r	1	1	14	28	42	80	115	150
6	51	–	LDC-r	1	1	8	16	24	42	54	65
7	64	–	LDC-r	1	1	6	12	18	27	33	38
8	78	–	C-price 15¢; LDC-r	1	1	5	10	14	20	24	28
9	97	–	LDC-r	1	1	4	9	13	18	22	26
10	114	–	LDC-r	1	1	4	7	10	14	17	20
11	130	–	New-c; PC-r	1	2	5	10	15	25	31	36
12	140	–	New-a; PC-r	2	2	5	10	15	24	29	34
13	153	–	PC-r	2	2	2	4	6	8	11	14
14	164	–	PC-r	2	2	2	4	6	8	11	14
15	167	–	PC-r	2	2	2	4	6	8	11	14
16	167	7/64	PC-r	2	2	2	4	6	10	14	18
17	167	5/65	PC-r	2	2	2	4	6	10	14	18

Classic Comics #12 © GIL

Classic Comics #13 © GIL

Classic Comics #15 © GIL

Ed	HRN	Date	Details	A	C	GD 2.0	VG 4.0	FN 6.0	VF 8.0	VF/NM 9.0	NM- 9.2
18	167	6/66	PC-r	2	2	2	4	6	8	11	14
19	166	Fall/68	C-price 25¢; PC-r	2	2	2	4	6	8	11	14
20	166	R/68	(No Twin Circle ad)	2	2	2	4	6	9	13	16
21	169	Sm/70	Stiff-c; PC-r	2	2	2	4	6	9	13	16

11. Don Quixote

Ed	HRN	Date	Details	A	C	GD 2.0	VG 4.0	FN 6.0	VF 8.0	VF/NM 9.0	NM- 9.2
1	10	5/43	First (O) with HRN list; 68 pgs.	1	1	87	174	261	553	952	1350
2	18	–	Nassau Bulletin ed.; CC-r	1	1	23	46	69	136	223	310
3	21	–	Queens Home News ed.; CC-r	1	1	19	38	57	111	176	240
4	28	–	CC-r	1	1	14	28	42	81	118	155
5	110	–	New-PC; PC-r	1	2	7	14	21	35	43	50
6	156	–	Pgs. reduced 68 to 52; PC-r	1	2	4	7	10	14	17	20
7	165	–	PC-r	1	2	2	4	6	9	13	16
8	167	1/64	PC-r	1	2	2	4	6	9	13	16
9	167	11/65	PC-r	1	2	2	4	6	9	13	16
10	166	R/1968	New-c & price 25¢; PC-r	1	3	3	6	9	18	27	36

12. Rip Van Winkle and the Headless Horseman

Ed	HRN	Date	Details	A	C	GD 2.0	VG 4.0	FN 6.0	VF 8.0	VF/NM 9.0	NM- 9.2
1	11	6/43	Original; 68 pgs.	1	1	90	180	270	576	988	1400
2	15	–	Long Isl. Ind. ed.; CC-r	1	1	24	48	72	142	234	325
3	20	–	Long Isl. Ind. ed.;	1	1	20	40	60	114	182	250
4	22	–	Queens Cty. Times ed.; CC-r	1	1	16	32	48	94	147	200
5	28	–	CC-r	1	1	14	28	42	80	115	150
6	60	–	1st LDC-r	1	1	8	16	24	40	50	60
7	62	–	LDC-r	1	1	5	10	15	23	28	32
8	71	–	LDC-r	1	1	4	9	13	18	22	26
9	89	–	C-price 15¢; LDC-r	1	1	4	8	12	17	21	24
10	118	–	LDC-r	1	1	4	7	10	14	17	20
11	132	–	New-c; PC-r	1	2	5	10	15	25	31	36
12	150	–	New-a; PC-r	2	2	5	10	15	24	29	34
13	158	–	PC-r	2	2	2	4	6	9	13	16
14	167	–	PC-r	2	2	2	4	6	9	13	16
15	167	12/63	PC-r	2	2	2	4	6	8	11	14
16	167	4/65	PC-r	2	2	2	4	6	8	11	14
17	167	4/66	PC-r	2	2	2	4	6	8	11	14
18	166	R/1968	New-c&price 25¢; PC-r; stiff-c	2	3	3	6	9	14	20	26
19	169	Sm/70	PC-r; stiff-c	2	3	2	4	6	10	14	18

13. Dr. Jekyll and Mr. Hyde (Used in **SOTI**, pg. 143)(1st horror comic?)

Ed	HRN	Date	Details	A	C	GD 2.0	VG 4.0	FN 6.0	VF 8.0	VF/NM 9.0	NM- 9.2
1	12	8/43	Original 60 pgs.	1	1	135	270	405	864	1482	2100
2	15	–	Long Isl. Ind. ed.; CC-r	1	1	34	68	102	206	336	465
3	20	–	Long Isl. Ind. ed.; CC-r	1	1	24	48	72	140	230	320
4	28	–	No c-price; CC-r	1	1	18	36	54	105	165	225
5	60	–	New-c; Pgs. reduced from 60 to 52; H.C. Kiefer-c; LDC-r	1	2	9	18	27	47	61	75
6	62	–	LDC-r	1	2	6	12	18	28	34	40
7	71	–	LDC-r	1	2	5	10	15	23	28	32
8	87	–	Date returns (erroneous); LDC-r	1	2	5	10	15	22	26	30
9	112	–	New-c&a; PC-r; Cameron-a	2	3	7	14	21	35	43	50
10	153	–	PC-r	2	3	2	4	6	9	13	16
11	161	–	PC-r	2	3	2	4	6	9	13	16
12	167	–	PC-r	2	3	2	4	6	8	11	14
13	167	8/64	PC-r	2	3	2	4	6	8	11	14
14	167	11/65	PC-r	2	3	2	4	6	8	11	14
15	166	R/68	C-price 25¢; PC-r	2	3	2	4	6	8	11	14
16	169	Wn/69	PC-r; stiff-c	2	3	2	4	6	8	11	14

14. Westward Ho!

Ed	HRN	Date	Details	A	C	GD 2.0	VG 4.0	FN 6.0	VF 8.0	VF/NM 9.0	NM- 9.2
1	13	9/43	Original; last outside bc coming-next ad; 60 pgs.	1	1	194	388	582	1242	2121	3000
2	15	–	Long Isl. Ind. ed.; CC-r	1	1	58	116	174	371	636	900
3	21	–	Queens Home News; Pg. 56 changed from coming-next ad to Three Men Named Smith; CC-r	1	1	46	92	138	290	488	685
4	28	1946	Gilberton; Pg. 56 changed again to WWII article-Speaking for America; last CC-r	1	1	39	78	117	242	401	560
5	53	–	Pgs. reduced from 60 to 52; LDC-r	1	1	36	72	108	216	351	485

15. Uncle Tom's Cabin (Used in **SOTI**, pgs. 102, 103)

Ed	HRN	Date	Details	A	C	GD 2.0	VG 4.0	FN 6.0	VF 8.0	VF/NM 9.0	NM- 9.2
1	14	11/43	Original; Outside-bc ad: 2 Gift Boxes; 60 pgs.; color var. on-c; green trunk,root on left & brown trunk, root on left	1	1	81	162	243	518	884	1250
2	15	–	Long Isl. Ind. listed- bottom inside-fc; also Gilberton listed bottom-pg. 1; CC-r; green root vs. brown root var. occurs again	1	1	26	52	78	154	252	350
3	21	–	Nassau Bulletin ed.; CC-r	1	1	20	40	60	117	189	260
4	28	–	No c-price; CC-r	1	1	14	28	42	82	121	160
5	53	–	Pgs. reduced 60 to 52; LDC-r	1	1	8	16	24	42	54	65
6	71	–	LDC-r	1	1	6	12	18	27	33	38
7	89	–	C-price 15¢; LDC-r	1	1	5	10	15	24	30	35
8	117	–	New-c/lettering changes; PC-r	1	2	5	10	15	25	31	36
9	128	–	'Picture Progress' promo; PC-r	1	2	2	4	6	10	14	18
10	137	–	PC-r	1	2	2	4	6	9	13	16
11	146	–	PC-r	1	2	2	4	6	9	13	16
12	154	–	PC-r	1	2	2	4	6	9	13	16
13	161	–	PC-r	1	2	2	4	6	8	11	14
14	167	–	PC-r	1	2	2	4	6	8	11	14
15	167	6/64	PC-r	1	2	2	4	6	8	11	14
16	167	5/65	PC-r	1	2	2	4	6	8	11	14
17	166	5/67	PC-r	1	2	2	4	6	8	11	14
18	166	Wn/69	New-stiff-c; PC-r	1	3	3	6	9	16	22	28
19	169	Sm/70	PC-r; stiff-c	1	3	2	4	6	10	14	18

16. Gulliver's Travels

Ed	HRN	Date	Details	A	C	GD 2.0	VG 4.0	FN 6.0	VF 8.0	VF/NM 9.0	NM- 9.2
1	15	12/43	Original-Lilian Chestney c/a; 60 pgs.	1	1	77	154	231	489	837	1185
2	18/20	–	Price deleted; Queens Home News ed; CC-r	1	1	22	44	66	128	209	290
3	22	–	Queens Cty. Times ed.; CC-r	1	1	18	36	54	105	165	225
4	28	–	CC-r	1	1	14	28	42	80	115	150
5	60	–	Pgs. reduced to 48; LDC-r	1	1	6	12	18	31	38	45
6	62	–	LDC-r	1	1	5	10	15	23	28	32
7	78	–	C-price 15¢; LDC-r	1	1	5	10	14	20	24	28
8	89	–	LDC-r	1	1	4	8	12	17	21	24
9	155	–	New-c; PC-r	1	2	5	10	15	25	31	36
10	165	–	PC-r	1	2	2	4	6	8	11	14
11	167	5/64	PC-r	1	2	2	4	6	8	11	14
12	167	11/65	PC-r	1	2	2	4	6	8	11	14
13	166	R/1968	C-price 25¢; PC-r	1	2	2	4	6	8	11	14
14	169	Wn/69	PC-r; stiff-c	1	2	2	4	6	8	11	14

17. The Deerslayer

Ed	HRN	Date	Details	A	C

Classic Comics #17 © GIL

Classic Comics #20 © GIL

Classic Comics #21 © GIL

Ed	HRN	Date	Details	A	C	GD 2.0	VG 4.0	FN 6.0	VF 8.0	VF/NM 9.0	NM- 9.2
1	16	1/44	Original; Outside-bc ad: 3 Gift Boxes; 60 pgs.	1	1	65	130	195	416	708	1000
2A	18	–	Queens Cty Times (inside-fc); CC-r	1	1	23	46	69	136	223	310
2B	18	–	Gilberton (bottom-pg. 1); CC-r; Scarce	1	1	33	66	99	194	317	440
3	22	–	Queens Cty. Times ed.; CC-r	1	1	19	38	57	109	172	235
4	28	–	CC-r	1	1	14	28	42	81	118	155
5	60	–	Pgs.reduced to 52; LDC-r	1	1	7	14	21	37	46	55
6	64	–	LDC-r	1	1	5	10	15	22	26	30
7	85	–	C-price 15¢; LDC-r	1	1	4	8	12	17	21	24
8	118	–	LDC-r	1	1	4	7	10	14	17	20
9	132	–	LDC-r	1	1	4	7	10	14	17	20
10	167	11/66	Last LDC-r	1	1	2	4	6	11	16	20
11	166	R/1968	New-c & price 25¢; PC-r	1	2	3	6	9	18	27	35
12	169	Spr/71	Stiff-c; letters from parents & educators; PC-r	1	2	2	4	6	10	14	18

18. The Hunchback of Notre Dame

Ed	HRN	Date	Details	A	C	GD	VG	FN	VF	VF/NM	NM-
1A	17	3/44	Orig.; Gilberton ed; 60 pgs.	1	1	87	174	261	553	952	1350
1B	17	3/44	Orig.; Island Pub. Ed.; 60 pgs.	1	1	77	154	231	493	847	1200
2	18/20	–	Queens Home News ed.; CC-r	1	1	24	48	72	142	234	325
3	22	–	Queens Cty. Times ed.; CC-r	1	1	19	38	57	111	176	240
4	28	–	CC-r	1	1	16	32	48	94	147	200
5	60	–	New-c; 8pgs. deleted; Kiefer-c; LDC-r	1	2	9	18	27	47	61	75
6	62	–	LDC-r	1	2	5	10	15	22	26	30
7	78	–	C-price 15¢; LDC-r	1	2	5	10	14	20	24	28
8A	89	–	H.C.Kiefer on bottom right-fc; LDC-r	1	2	4	9	13	18	22	26
8B	89	–	Name omitted; LDC-r	1	2	5	10	15	24	30	35
9	118	–	LDC-r	1	2	4	8	12	17	21	24
10	140	–	New-c; PC-r	1	3	7	14	21	35	43	50
11	146	–	PC-r	1	3	4	9	13	18	22	26
12	158	–	New-c&a; PC-r; Evans/Crandall-a	2	4	5	10	15	25	31	36
13	165	–	PC-r	2	4	2	4	6	9	13	16
14	167	9/63	PC-r	2	4	2	4	6	9	13	16
15	167	10/64	PC-r	2	4	2	4	6	9	13	16
16	167	4/66	PC-r	2	4	2	4	6	8	11	14
17	166	R/1968	New price 25¢; PC-r	2	4	2	4	6	8	11	14
18	169	Sp/70	Stiff-c; PC-r	2	4	2	4	6	8	11	14

19. Huckleberry Finn

Ed	HRN	Date	Details	A	C	GD	VG	FN	VF	VF/NM	NM-
1A	18	4/44	Orig.; Gilberton ed.; 60 pgs.	1	1	53	106	159	334	567	800
1B	18	4/44	Orig.; Island Pub.; 60 pgs.	1	1	55	110	165	352	601	850
2	18	–	Nassau Bulletin ed.; fc-price 15¢-Canada; no coming-next ad; CC-r	1	1	23	46	69	136	223	310
3	22	–	Queens City Times ed.; CC-r	1	1	19	38	57	111	176	240
4	28	–	CC-r	1	1	14	28	42	80	115	150
5	60	–	Pgs. reduced to 48; LDC-r	1	1	6	12	18	31	38	45
6	62	–	LDC-r	1	1	5	10	15	23	28	32
7	78	–	LDC-r	1	1	4	9	13	18	22	26
8	89	–	LDC-r	1	1	4	8	12	17	21	24
9	117	–	LDC-r	1	1	4	7	10	14	17	20
10	131	–	New-c&a; PC-r	2	2	5	10	15	24	30	35
11	140	–	PC-r	2	2	2	4	6	9	13	16
12	150	–	PC-r	2	2	2	4	6	9	13	16
13	158	–	PC-r	2	2	2	4	6	9	13	16
14	165	–	PC-r (scarce)	2	2	3	6	9	14	19	24
15	167	–	PC-r	2	2	2	4	6	8	11	14
16	167	6/64	PC-r	2	2	2	4	6	8	11	14
17	167	6/65	PC-r	2	2	2	4	6	8	11	14
18	167	10/65	PC-r	2	2	2	4	6	8	11	14
19	166	9/67	PC-r	2	2	2	4	6	8	11	14
20	166	Win/69	C-price 25¢; PC-r; stiff-c	2	2	2	4	6	8	11	14
21	169	Sm/70	PC-r; stiff-c	2	2	2	4	6	8	11	14

20. The Corsican Brothers

Ed	HRN	Date	Details	A	C	GD	VG	FN	VF	VF/NM	NM-
1A	20	6/44	Orig.; Gilberton ed.; bc-ad: 4 Gift Boxes; 60 pgs.	1	1	47	94	141	296	498	700
1B	20	6/44	Orig.; Courier ed.; 60 pgs.	1	1	40	80	120	246	411	575
1C	20	6/44	Orig.; Long Island Ind. ed.; 60 pgs.	1	1	40	80	120	246	411	575
2	22	–	Queens Cty. Times ed.; white logo banner; CC-r	1	1	20	40	60	114	182	250
3	28	–	CC-r	1	1	19	38	57	109	172	235
4	60	–	CI logo; no price; 48 pgs.; LDC-r	1	1	15	30	45	90	140	190
5A	62	–	LDC-r; Classics Ill. logo at top of pgs.	1	1	15	30	45	83	124	165
5B	62	–	w/o logo at top of pg. (scarcer)	1	1	15	30	45	86	133	180
6	78	–	C-price 15¢; LDC-r	1	1	14	28	42	81	118	155
7	97	–	LDC-r	1	1	14	28	42	78	112	145

21. 3 Famous Mysteries ("The Sign of the 4", "The Murders in the Rue Morgue", "The Flayed Hand")

Ed	HRN	Date	Details	A	C	GD	VG	FN	VF	VF/NM	NM-
1A	21	7/44	Orig.; Gilberton ed.; 60 pgs.	1	1	97	194	291	621	1061	1500
1B	21	7/44	Orig. Island Pub. Co.; 60 pgs.	1	1	100	200	300	635	1093	1550
1C	21	7/44	Original; Courier Ed.; 60 pgs.	1	1	87	174	261	553	952	1350
2	22	–	Nassau Bulletin ed.; CC-r	1	1	39	78	117	240	395	550
3	30	–	CC-r	1	1	28	56	84	165	270	375
4	62	–	LDC-r; 8 pgs. deleted; LDC-r	1	1	22	44	66	128	209	290
5	70	–	LDC-r	1	1	20	40	60	117	189	260
6	85	–	C-price 15¢; LDC-r	1	1	18	36	54	107	169	230
7	114	–	New-c; PC-r	1	2	18	36	54	107	169	230

22. The Pathfinder

Ed	HRN	Date	Details	A	C	GD	VG	FN	VF	VF/NM	NM-
1A	22	10/44	Orig.; No printer listed; ownership statement inside fc lists Gilberton & date; 60 pgs.	1	1	45	90	135	284	480	675
1B	22	10/44	Orig.; Island Pub. ed.; 60 pgs.	1	1	40	80	120	246	411	575
1C	22	10/44	Orig.; Queens Cty Times ed. 60 pgs.	1	1	40	80	120	246	411	575
2	30	–	C-price removed; CC-r	1	1	15	30	45	85	130	175
3	60	–	Pgs. reduced to 52; LDC-r	1	1	6	12	18	27	33	38
4	70	–	LDC-r	1	1	5	10	15	22	26	30
5	85	–	C-price 15¢; LDC-r	1	1	4	9	13	18	22	26
6	118	–	LDC-r	1	1	4	8	12	17	21	24
7	132	–	LDC-r	1	1	4	7	10	14	17	20
8	146	–	LDC-r	1	1	4	7	10	14	17	20
9	167	11/63	New-c; PC-r	1	2	4	8	12	24	37	50
10	167	12/65	PC-r	1	2	2	4	6	11	16	20
11	166	8/67	PC-r	1	2	2	4	6	11	16	20

23. Oliver Twist (1st Classic produced by the Iger Shop)

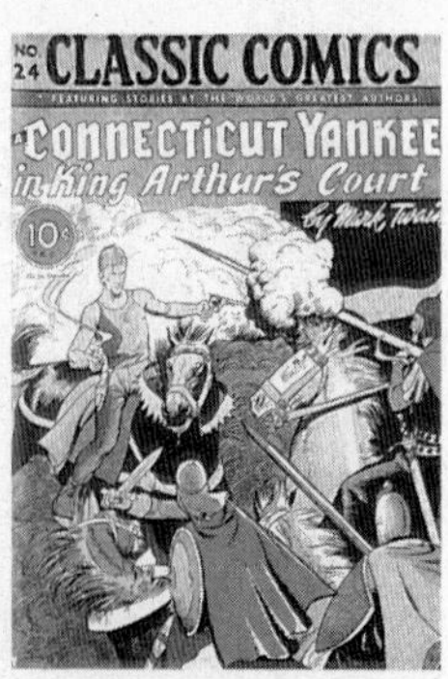

Classic Comics #24 © GIL

Classic Comics #26 © GIL

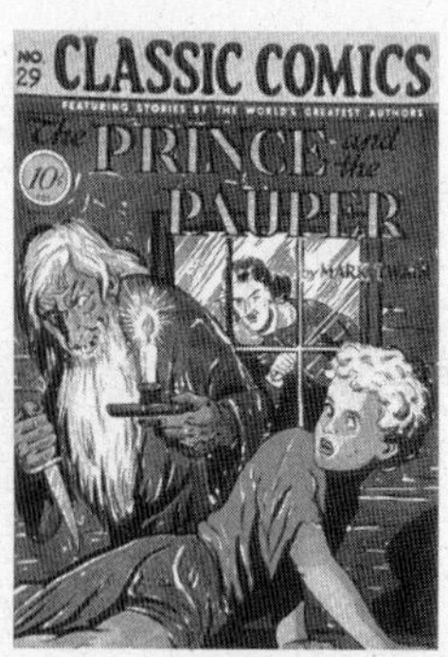

Classic Comics #29 © GIL

Ed	HRN	Date	Details	A	C	GD 2.0	VG 4.0	FN 6.0	VF 8.0	VF/NM 9.0	NM- 9.2
1	23	7/45	Original; 60 pgs.	1	1	46	92	138	290	488	685
2A	30	–	Printers Union logo on bottom left-fc same as 23(Orig.) (very rare); CC-r	1	1	30	60	90	177	289	400
2B	30	–	Union logo omitted; CC-r	1	1	15	30	45	84	127	170
3	60	–	Pgs. reduced to 48; LDC-r	1	1	6	12	18	29	36	42
4	62	–	LDC-r	1	1	5	10	15	23	28	32
5	71	–	LDC-r	1	1	5	10	14	20	24	28
6	85	–	C-price 15¢; LDC-r	1	1	4	9	13	18	22	26
7	94	–	LDC-r	1	1	4	7	10	14	17	20
8	118	–	LDC-r	1	1	4	7	10	14	17	20
9	136	–	New-PC, old-a; PC-r	1	2	5	10	15	24	30	35
10	150	–	Old-a; PC-r	1	2	4	7	10	14	17	20
11	164	–	Old-a; PC-r	1	2	4	8	11	16	19	22
12	164	–	New-a; PC-r; Evans/Crandall-a	2	2	4	8	12	24	37	50
13	167	–	PC-r	2	2	2	4	6	11	16	20
14	167	8/64	PC-r	2	2	2	4	6	8	11	14
15	167	12/65	PC-r	2	2	2	4	6	8	11	14
16	166	R/1968	New 25¢; PC-r	2	2	2	4	6	8	11	14
17	169	Win/69	Stiff-c; PC-r	2	2	2	4	6	8	11	14

24. A Connecticut Yankee in King Arthur's Court

Ed	HRN	Date	Details	A	C	GD 2.0	VG 4.0	FN 6.0	VF 8.0	VF/NM 9.0	NM- 9.2
1	–	9/45	Original	1	1	41	82	123	249	417	585
2	30	–	No price circle; CC-r	1	1	15	30	45	84	127	170
3	60	–	8 pgs. deleted; LDC-r	1	1	6	12	18	27	33	38
4	62	–	LDC-r	1	1	5	10	15	23	28	32
5	71	–	LDC-r	1	1	5	10	15	22	26	30
6	87	–	C-price 15¢; LDC-r	1	1	4	9	13	18	22	26
7	121	–	LDC-r	1	1	4	8	12	17	21	24
8	140	–	New-c&a; PC-r	2	2	5	10	15	25	31	36
9	153	–	PC-r	2	2	2	4	6	9	13	16
10	164	–	PC-r	2	2	2	4	6	8	11	14
11	167	–	PC-r	2	2	2	4	6	8	11	14
12	167	7/64	PC-r	2	2	2	4	6	8	11	14
13	167	6/66	PC-r	2	2	2	4	6	8	11	14
14	166	R/1968	C-price 25¢; PC-r	2	2	2	4	6	8	11	14
15	169	Spr/71	PC-r; stiff-c	2	2	2	4	6	8	11	14

25. Two Years Before the Mast

Ed	HRN	Date	Details	A	C	GD 2.0	VG 4.0	FN 6.0	VF 8.0	VF/NM 9.0	NM- 9.2
1	–	10/45	Original; Webb/Heames-a&c	1	1	41	82	123	249	417	585
2	30	–	Price circle blank; CC-r	1	1	15	30	45	84	127	170
3	60	–	8 pgs. deleted; LDC-r	1	1	6	12	18	27	33	38
4	62	–	LDC-r	1	1	5	10	15	23	28	32
5	71	–	LDC-r	1	1	4	9	13	18	22	26
6	85	–	C-price 15¢; LDC-r	1	1	4	8	12	17	21	24
7	114	–	LDC-r	1	1	4	7	10	14	17	20
8	156	–	3 pgs. replaced by fillers; new-c; PC-r	1	2	5	10	15	25	31	36
9	167	12/63	PC-r	1	2	2	4	6	8	11	14
10	167	12/65	PC-r	1	2	2	4	6	8	11	14
11	166	9/67	PC-r	1	2	2	4	6	8	11	14
12	169	Win/69	C-price 25¢; stiff-c PC-r	1	2	2	4	6	8	11	14

26. Frankenstein (2nd horror comic?)

Ed	HRN	Date	Details	A	C	GD 2.0	VG 4.0	FN 6.0	VF 8.0	VF/NM 9.0	NM- 9.2
1	26	12/45	Orig.; Webb/Brewster a&c; 52 pgs.	1	1	110	220	330	704	1202	1700
2A	30	–	Price circle blank; no indicia; CC-r	1	1	32	64	96	188	307	425
2B	30	–	With indicia; scarce; CC-r	1	1	36	72	108	216	351	485
3	60	–	LDC-r	1	1	17	34	51	98	154	210
4	62	–	LDC-r	1	1	15	30	45	88	137	185
5	71	–	LDC-r	1	1	8	16	24	42	54	65
6A	82	–	C-price 15¢; soft-c LDC-r	1	1	7	14	21	37	46	55
6B	82	–	Stiff-c; LDC-r	1	1	8	16	24	42	54	65
7	117	–	LDC-r	1	1	5	10	15	22	26	30
8	146	–	New Saunders-c; PC-r	1	2	6	12	18	31	38	45
9	152	–	Scarce; PC-r	1	2	8	16	24	42	54	65
10	153	–	PC-r	1	2	2	4	6	10	14	18
11	160	–	PC-r	1	2	2	4	6	10	14	18
12	165	–	PC-r	1	2	2	4	6	9	13	16
13	167	–	PC-r	1	2	2	4	6	9	13	16
14	167	6/64	PC-r	1	2	2	4	6	9	13	16
15	167	6/65	PC-r	1	2	2	4	6	9	13	16
16	167	10/65	PC-r	1	2	2	4	6	9	13	16
17	166	9/67	PC-r	1	2	2	4	6	9	13	16
18	169	Fall/69	C-price 25¢; stiff-c PC-r	1	2	2	4	6	9	13	16
19	169	Spr/71	PC-r; stiff-c	1	2	2	4	6	9	13	16

27. The Adventures of Marco Polo

Ed	HRN	Date	Details	A	C	GD 2.0	VG 4.0	FN 6.0	VF 8.0	VF/NM 9.0	NM- 9.2
1	–	4/46	Original	1	1	41	82	123	249	417	585
2	30	–	Last 'Comics' reprint; CC-r	1	1	15	30	45	84	127	170
3	70	–	8 pgs. deleted; no c-price; LDC-r	1	1	5	10	15	24	30	35
4	87	–	C-price 15¢; LDC-r	1	1	4	9	13	18	22	26
5	117	–	LDC-r	1	1	4	7	10	14	17	20
6	154	–	New-c; PC-r	1	2	5	10	15	24	30	35
7	165	–	PC-r	1	2	2	4	6	8	11	14
8	167	4/64	PC-r	1	2	2	4	6	8	11	14
9	167	6/66	PC-r	1	2	2	4	6	8	11	14
10	169	Spr/69	New price 25¢; stiff-c; PC-r	1	2	2	4	6	8	11	14

28. Michael Strogoff

Ed	HRN	Date	Details	A	C	GD 2.0	VG 4.0	FN 6.0	VF 8.0	VF/NM 9.0	NM- 9.2
1	–	6/46	Original	1	1	41	82	123	249	417	585
2	51	–	8 pgs. cut; LDC-r	1	1	15	30	45	84	127	170
3	115	–	New-c; PC-r	1	2	6	12	18	31	38	45
4	155	–	PC-r	1	2	4	7	10	14	17	20
5	167	11/63	PC-r	1	2	2	4	6	9	13	16
6	167	7/66	PC-r	1	2	2	4	6	9	13	16
7	169	Sm/69	C-price 25¢; stiff-c PC-r	1	3	3	6	9	15	21	26

29. The Prince and the Pauper

Ed	HRN	Date	Details	A	C	GD 2.0	VG 4.0	FN 6.0	VF 8.0	VF/NM 9.0	NM- 9.2
1	–	7/46	Orig.; "Horror"-c	1	1	58	116	174	371	636	900
2	60	–	8 pgs. cut; new-c by Kiefer; LDC-r	1	2	9	18	27	52	69	85
3	62	–	LDC-r	1	2	5	10	15	24	30	35
4	71	–	LDC-r	1	2	4	9	13	18	22	26
5	93	–	LDC-r	1	2	4	8	12	17	21	24
6	114	–	LDC-r	1	2	4	7	10	14	17	20
7	128	–	New-c; PC-r	1	3	5	10	15	24	30	35
8	138	–	PC-r	1	3	2	4	6	9	13	16
9	150	–	PC-r	1	3	2	4	6	9	13	16
10	164	–	PC-r	1	3	2	4	6	8	11	14
11	167	–	PC-r	1	3	2	4	6	8	11	14
12	167	7/64	PC-r	1	3	2	4	6	8	11	14
13	167	11/65	PC-r	1	3	2	4	6	8	11	14
14	166	R/68	C-price 25¢; PC-r	1	3	2	4	6	8	11	14
15	169	Sm/70	PC-r; stiff-c	1	3	2	4	6	8	11	14

30. The Moonstone

Ed	HRN	Date	Details	A	C	GD 2.0	VG 4.0	FN 6.0	VF 8.0	VF/NM 9.0	NM- 9.2
1	–	9/46	Original; Rico-c/a	1	1	41	82	123	256	428	600
2	60	–	LDC-r; 8pgs. cut	1	1	9	18	27	50	65	80
3	70	–	LDC-r	1	1	8	16	24	42	54	65
4	155	–	New L.B. Cole-c; PC-r	1	2	4	8	12	28	44	60
5	165	–	PC-r; L.B. Cole-c	1	2	3	6	9	16	23	30
6	167	1/64	PC-r; L.B. Cole-c	1	2	2	4	6	11	16	20
7	167	9/65	PC-r; L.B. Cole-c	1	2	2	4	6	10	14	18

Classic Comics #32 © GIL

Classics Illustrated #36 © GIL

Classics Illustrated #38 © GIL

Ed	HRN	Date	Details	A	C	GD 2.0	VG 4.0	FN 6.0	VF 8.0	VF/NM 9.0	NM- 9.2
8	166	R/1968	C-price 25¢; PC-r	1	2	2	4	6	9	13	16

31. The Black Arrow

Ed	HRN	Date	Details	A	C	GD 2.0	VG 4.0	FN 6.0	VF 8.0	VF/NM 9.0	NM- 9.2
1	30	10/46	Original	1	1	39	78	117	231	378	525
2	51	–	CI logo; LDC-r 8pgs. deleted	1	1	6	12	18	33	41	48
3	64	–	LDC-r	1	1	4	9	13	18	22	26
4	87	–	C-price 15¢; LDC-r	1	1	4	8	12	17	21	24
5	108	–	LDC-r	1	1	4	7	10	14	17	20
6	125	–	LDC-r	1	1	4	7	10	14	17	20
7	131	–	New-c; PC-r	1	2	5	10	15	24	30	35
8	140	–	PC-r	1	2	2	4	6	9	13	16
9	148	–	PC-r	1	2	2	4	6	9	13	16
10	161	–	PC-r	1	2	2	4	6	8	11	14
11	167	–	PC-r	1	2	2	4	6	8	11	14
12	167	7/64	PC-r	1	2	2	4	6	8	11	14
13	167	11/65	PC-r	1	2	2	4	6	8	11	14
14	166	R/1968	C-price 25¢; PC-r	1	2	2	4	6	8	11	14

32. Lorna Doone

Ed	HRN	Date	Details	A	C	GD 2.0	VG 4.0	FN 6.0	VF 8.0	VF/NM 9.0	NM- 9.2
1	–	12/46	Original; Matt Baker c&a	1	1	40	80	120	246	411	575
2	53/64	–	8 pgs. deleted; LDC-r	1	1	9	18	27	47	61	75
3	85	1951	C-price 15¢; LDC-r; Baker c&a	1	1	7	14	21	37	46	55
4	118	–	LDC-r	1	1	4	9	13	18	22	26
5	138	–	New-c; old-c becomes new title pg.; PC-r	1	2	6	12	18	28	34	40
6	150	–	PC-r	1	2	2	4	6	8	11	14
7	165	–	PC-r	1	2	2	4	6	8	11	14
8	167	1/64	PC-r	1	2	2	4	6	9	13	16
9	167	11/65	PC-r	1	2	2	4	6	9	13	16
10	166	R/1968	New-c; PC-r	1	3	3	6	9	17	25	32

33. The Adventures of Sherlock Holmes

Ed	HRN	Date	Details	A	C	GD 2.0	VG 4.0	FN 6.0	VF 8.0	VF/NM 9.0	NM- 9.2
1	33	1/47	Original; Kiefer-c; contains Study in Scarlet & Hound of the Baskervilles; 68 pgs.	1	1	126	252	378	806	1378	1950
2	53	–	"A Study in Scarlet" (17 pgs.) deleted; LDC-r	1	1	46	92	138	290	488	685
3	71	–	LDC-r	1	1	38	76	114	228	369	510
4A	89	–	C-price 15¢; LDC-r	1	1	30	60	90	117	289	400
4B	89	–	Kiefer's name omitted from-c	1	1	31	62	93	186	303	420

34. Mysterious Island (Last "Classic Comic")

Ed	HRN	Date	Details	A	C	GD 2.0	VG 4.0	FN 6.0	VF 8.0	VF/NM 9.0	NM- 9.2
1	35	2/47	Original; Webb/Heames-c/a	1	1	40	80	120	246	411	575
2	60	–	8 pgs. deleted; LDC-r	1	1	7	14	21	37	46	55
3	62	–	LDC-r	1	1	5	10	15	23	28	32
4	71	–	LDC-r	1	1	6	12	18	31	38	45
5	78	–	C-price 15¢ in circle; LDC-r	1	1	5	10	14	20	24	28
6	92	–	LDC-r	1	1	4	9	13	18	22	26
7	117	–	LDC-r	1	1	4	7	10	14	17	20
8	140	–	New-c; PC-r	1	2	5	10	15	24	30	35
9	156	–	PC-r	1	2	2	4	6	9	13	16
10	167	10/63	PC-r	1	2	2	4	6	8	11	14
11	167	5/64	PC-r	1	2	2	4	6	8	11	14
12	167	6/66	PC-r	1	2	2	4	6	8	11	14
13	166	R/1968	C-price 25¢; PC-r	1	2	2	4	6	8	11	14

35. Last Days of Pompeii (First "Classics Illustrated")

Ed	HRN	Date	Details	A	C	GD 2.0	VG 4.0	FN 6.0	VF 8.0	VF/NM 9.0	NM- 9.2
1	35	3/47	Original; LDC; Kiefer-c/a	1	1	40	80	120	246	411	575
2	161	–	New c&a; 15¢; PC-r; Kirby/Ayers-a	2	2	5	10	15	32	51	70
3	167	1/64	PC-r	2	2	3	6	9	16	22	28
4	167	7/66	PC-r	2	2	3	6	9	16	22	28
5	169	Spr/70	New price 25¢; stiff-c; PC-r	2	2	3	6	9	16	22	28

36. Typee

Ed	HRN	Date	Details	A	C	GD 2.0	VG 4.0	FN 6.0	VF 8.0	VF/NM 9.0	NM- 9.2
1	36	4/47	Original	1	1	28	56	84	165	270	375
2	64	–	No c-price; 8 pg. ed.; LDC-r	1	1	7	14	21	37	46	55
3	155	–	New-c; PC-r	1	2	5	10	15	24	30	35
4	167	9/63	PC-r	1	2	2	4	6	9	13	16
5	167	7/65	PC-r	1	2	2	4	6	9	13	16
6	169	Sm/69	C-price 25¢; stiff-c PC-r	1	2	2	4	6	9	13	16

37. The Pioneers

Ed	HRN	Date	Details	A	C	GD 2.0	VG 4.0	FN 6.0	VF 8.0	VF/NM 9.0	NM- 9.2
1	37	5/47	Original; Palais-c/a	1	1	26	52	78	154	252	350
2A	62	–	8 pgs. cut; LDC-r; price circle blank	1	1	6	12	18	28	34	40
2B	62	–	10¢; LDC-r;	1	1	28	56	84	165	270	375
3	70	–	LDC-r	1	1	4	8	12	17	21	24
4	92	–	15¢; LDC-r	1	1	4	8	11	16	19	22
5	118	–	LDC-r	1	1	4	7	10	14	17	20
6	131	–	LDC-r	1	1	4	7	10	14	17	20
7	132	–	LDC-r	1	1	4	7	10	14	17	20
8	153	–	LDC-r	1	1	4	7	10	14	17	20
9	167	5/64	LDC-r	1	1	2	4	6	9	13	16
10	167	6/66	LDC-r	1	1	2	4	6	9	13	16
11	166	R/1968	New-c; 25¢; PC-r	1	2	3	6	9	18	27	36

38. Adventures of Cellini

Ed	HRN	Date	Details	A	C	GD 2.0	VG 4.0	FN 6.0	VF 8.0	VF/NM 9.0	NM- 9.2
1	–	6/47	Original; Froehlich c/a	1	1	32	64	96	188	307	425
2	164	–	New-c&a; PC-r	2	2	3	6	9	18	27	36
3	167	12/63	PC-r	2	2	2	4	6	10	14	18
4	167	7/66	PC-r	2	2	2	4	6	10	14	18
5	169	Spr/70	Stiff-c; new price 25¢; PC-r	2	2	2	4	6	11	16	20

39. Jane Eyre

Ed	HRN	Date	Details	A	C	GD 2.0	VG 4.0	FN 6.0	VF 8.0	VF/NM 9.0	NM- 9.2
1	–	7/47	Original	1	1	31	62	93	182	296	410
2	60	–	No c-price; 8 pgs. cut; LDC-r	1	1	6	12	18	31	38	45
3	62	–	LDC-r	1	1	5	10	15	24	30	35
4	71	–	LDC-r; c-price 10¢	1	1	5	10	15	22	26	30
5	92	–	C-price 15¢; LDC-r	1	1	4	9	13	18	22	26
6	118	–	LDC-r	1	1	4	8	12	17	21	24
7	142	–	New-c; old-a; PC-r	1	2	6	12	18	28	34	40
8	154	–	Old-a; PC-r	1	2	4	8	12	17	21	24
9	165	–	New-a; PC-r	2	2	3	6	9	18	27	35
10	167	12/63	PC-r	2	2	3	6	9	14	19	24
11	167	4/65	PC-r	2	2	2	4	6	13	18	22
12	167	8/66	PC-r	2	2	2	4	6	13	18	22
13	166	R/1968	New-c; PC-r	2	3	5	10	15	34	55	75

40. Mysteries ("The Pit and the Pendulum", "The Advs. of Hans Pfall" & "The Fall of the House of Usher")

Ed	HRN	Date	Details	A	C	GD 2.0	VG 4.0	FN 6.0	VF 8.0	VF/NM 9.0	NM- 9.2
1	40	8/47	Original; Kiefer-c/a, Froehlich, Griffiths-a	1	1	58	116	174	371	636	900
2	62	–	LDC-r; 8pgs. cut	1	1	24	48	72	142	234	325
3	75	–	LDC-r	1	1	19	38	57	111	176	240
4	92	–	C-price 15¢; LDC-r	1	1	15	30	45	94	147	200

41. Twenty Years After

Ed	HRN	Date	Details	A	C	GD 2.0	VG 4.0	FN 6.0	VF 8.0	VF/NM 9.0	NM- 9.2
1	–	9/47	Original; 'horror'-c	1	1	39	78	117	231	378	525
2	62	–	New-c; no c-price 8 pgs. cut; LDC-r; Kiefer-c	1	2	7	14	21	37	46	55
3	78	–	C-price 15¢; LDC-r	1	2	5	10	15	23	28	32
4	156	–	New-c; PC-r	1	3	5	10	15	24	30	35
5	167	12/63	PC-r	1	3	2	4	6	8	11	14

Classics Illustrated #42 © GIL

Classics Illustrated #46 © GIL

Classics Illustrated #49 © GIL

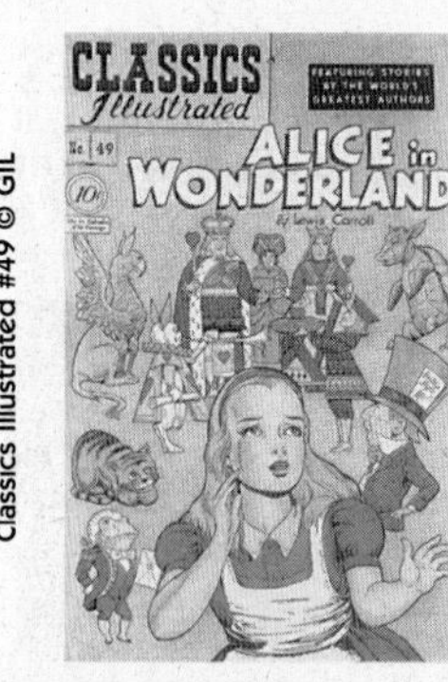

Ed	HRN	Date	Details	A	C	GD 2.0	VG 4.0	FN 6.0	VF 8.0	VF/NM 9.0	NM- 9.2
6	167	11/66	PC-r	1	3	2	4	6	8	11	14
7	169	Spr/70	New price 25¢; stiff-c; PC-r	1	3	2	4	6	8	11	14

42. Swiss Family Robinson

Ed	HRN	Date	Details	A	C	GD 2.0	VG 4.0	FN 6.0	VF 8.0	VF/NM 9.0	NM- 9.2
1	42	10/47	Orig.; Kiefer-c&a;	1	1	23	46	69	136	223	310
2A	62	–	8 pgs. cut; outside bc: Gift Box ad; LDC-r	1	1	6	12	18	31	38	45
2B	62	–	8 pgs. cut; outside-bc: Reorder list; scarce; LDC-r	1	1	10	20	30	58	79	100
3	75	–	LDC-r	1	1	5	10	14	20	24	28
4	93	–	LDC-r	1	1	5	10	14	20	24	28
5	117	–	LDC-r	1	1	3	6	9	14	19	24
6	131	–	New-c; old-a; PC-r	1	2	3	6	9	15	21	26
7	137	–	Old-a; PC-r	1	2	2	4	6	10	14	18
8	141	–	Old-a; PC-r	1	2	2	4	6	10	14	18
9	152	–	New-a; PC-r	2	2	3	6	9	16	23	30
10	158	–	PC-r	2	2	2	4	6	8	11	14
11	165	–	PC-r	2	2	3	6	9	17	25	32
12	167	12/63	PC-r	2	2	2	4	6	8	11	14
13	167	4/65	PC-r	2	2	2	4	6	8	11	14
14	167	5/66	PC-r	2	2	2	4	6	8	11	14
15	166	11/67	PC-r	2	2	2	4	6	8	11	14
16	169	Spr/69	PC-r; stiff-c	2	2	2	4	6	8	11	14

43. Great Expectations (Used in **SOTI**, pg. 311)

Ed	HRN	Date	Details	A	C	GD 2.0	VG 4.0	FN 6.0	VF 8.0	VF/NM 9.0	NM- 9.2
1	43	11/47	Original; Kiefer-a/c	1	1	90	180	270	576	988	1400
2	62	–	No c-price; 8 pgs. cut; LDC-r	1	1	57	114	171	362	624	885

44. Mysteries of Paris (Used in **SOTI**, pg. 323)

Ed	HRN	Date	Details	A	C	GD 2.0	VG 4.0	FN 6.0	VF 8.0	VF/NM 9.0	NM- 9.2
1A	44	12/47	Original; 56 pgs.; Kiefer-c/a	1	1	64	128	192	406	696	985
1B	44	12/47	Orig.; printed on white/heavier paper; (rare)	1	1	75	150	225	476	818	1160
2A	62	–	8 pgs. cut; outside-bc: Gift Box ad; LDC-r	1	1	30	60	90	177	289	400
2B	62	–	8 pgs. cut; outside-bc: reorder list; LDC-r	1	1	30	60	90	177	289	400
3	78	–	C-price 15¢; LDC-r	1	1	25	50	75	147	241	335

45. Tom Brown's School Days

Ed	HRN	Date	Details	A	C	GD 2.0	VG 4.0	FN 6.0	VF 8.0	VF/NM 9.0	NM- 9.2
1	44	1/48	Original; 1st 48pg. issue	1	1	19	38	57	111	176	240
2	64	–	No c-price; LDC-r	1	1	7	14	21	35	43	50
3	161	–	New-c&a; PC-r	2	2	3	6	9	17	25	32
4	167	2/64	PC-r	2	2	2	4	6	9	13	16
5	167	8/66	PC-r	2	2	2	4	6	9	13	16
6	166	R/1968	C-price 25¢; PC-r	2	2	2	4	6	9	13	16

46. Kidnapped

Ed	HRN	Date	Details	A	C	GD 2.0	VG 4.0	FN 6.0	VF 8.0	VF/NM 9.0	NM- 9.2
1	47	4/48	Original; Webb-c/a	1	1	19	38	57	111	176	240
2A	62	–	Price circle blank; LDC-r	1	1	7	14	21	35	43	50
2B	62	–	C-price 10¢; rare; LDC-r	1	1	30	60	90	177	289	400
3	78	–	C-price 15¢; LDC-r	1	1	5	10	14	20	24	28
4	87	–	LDC-r	1	1	4	9	13	18	22	26
5	118	–	LDC-r	1	1	4	7	10	14	17	20
6	131	–	New-c; PC-r	1	2	5	10	15	23	28	32
7	140	–	PC-r	1	2	2	4	6	9	13	16
8	150	–	PC-r	1	2	2	4	6	9	13	16
9	164	–	Reduced pg.width; PC-r	1	2	2	4	6	8	11	14
10	167	–	PC-r	1	2	2	4	6	8	11	14
11	167	3/64	PC-r	1	2	2	4	6	8	11	14
12	167	6/65	PC-r	1	2	2	4	6	8	11	14
13	167	12/65	PC-r	1	2	2	4	6	8	11	14
14	166	9/67	PC-r	1	2	2	4	6	8	11	14
15	166	Win/69	New price 25¢; PC-r; stiff-c	1	2	2	4	6	8	11	14
16	169	Sm/70	PC-r; stiff-c	1	2	2	4	6	8	11	14

47. Twenty Thousand Leagues Under the Sea

Ed	HRN	Date	Details	A	C	GD 2.0	VG 4.0	FN 6.0	VF 8.0	VF/NM 9.0	NM- 9.2
1	47	5/48	Orig.; Kiefer-a&c;	1	1	20	40	60	117	189	260
2	64	–	No c-price; LDC-r	1	1	6	12	18	28	34	40
3	78	–	C-price 15¢; LDC-r	1	1	4	9	13	18	22	26
4	94	–	LDC-r	1	1	4	8	12	17	21	24
5	118	–	LDC-r	1	1	4	7	10	14	17	20
6	128	–	New-c; PC-r	1	2	5	10	15	24	30	35
7	133	–	PC-r	1	2	2	4	6	10	14	18
8	140	–	PC-r	1	2	2	4	6	9	13	16
9	148	–	PC-r	1	2	2	4	6	9	13	16
10	156	–	PC-r	1	2	2	4	6	9	13	16
11	165	–	PC-r	1	2	2	4	6	9	13	16
12	167	–	PC-r	1	2	2	4	6	9	13	16
13	167	3/64	PC-r	1	2	2	4	6	9	13	16
14	167	8/65	PC-r	1	2	2	4	6	9	13	16
15	167	10/66	PC-r	1	2	2	4	6	9	13	16
16	166	R/1968	C-price 25¢; new-c PC-r	1	3	3	6	9	16	22	28
17	169	Spr/70	Stiff-c; PC-r	1	3	2	4	6	13	18	22

48. David Copperfield

Ed	HRN	Date	Details	A	C	GD 2.0	VG 4.0	FN 6.0	VF 8.0	VF/NM 9.0	NM- 9.2
1	47	6/48	Original; Kiefer-c/a	1	1	19	38	57	111	176	240
2	64	–	Price circle replaced by motif of boy reading; LDC-r	1	1	6	12	18	28	34	40
3	87	–	C-price 15¢; LDC-r	1	1	4	8	12	17	21	24
4	121	–	New-c; PC-r	1	2	5	10	15	22	26	30
5	130	–	PC-r	1	2	2	4	6	9	13	16
6	140	–	PC-r	1	2	2	4	6	9	13	16
7	148	–	PC-r	1	2	2	4	6	9	13	16
8	156	–	PC-r	1	2	2	4	6	9	13	16
9	167	–	PC-r	1	2	2	4	6	8	11	14
10	167	4/64	PC-r	1	2	2	4	6	8	11	14
11	167	6/65	PC-r	1	2	2	4	6	8	11	14
12	166	5/67	PC-r	1	2	2	4	6	8	11	14
13	166	R/67	PC-r; C-price 25¢	1	2	2	4	6	10	14	18
14	166	Spr/69	C-price 25¢; stiff-c PC-r	1	2	2	4	6	8	11	14
15	169	Win/69	Stiff-c; PC-r	1	2	2	4	6	8	11	14

49. Alice in Wonderland

Ed	HRN	Date	Details	A	C	GD 2.0	VG 4.0	FN 6.0	VF 8.0	VF/NM 9.0	NM- 9.2
1	47	7/48	Original; 1st Blum a & c	1	1	21	42	63	126	206	285
2	64	–	No c-price; LDC-r	1	1	8	16	24	42	54	65
3A	85	–	C-price 15¢; soft-c LDC-r	1	1	7	14	21	37	46	55
3B	85	–	Stiff-c; LDC-r	1	1	8	16	24	40	50	60
4	155	–	New PC, similar to orig.; PC-r	1	2	4	8	12	26	41	55
5	165	–	PC-r	1	2	3	6	9	18	27	35
6	167	3/64	PC-r	1	2	3	6	9	16	23	30
7	167	6/66	PC-r	1	2	3	6	9	16	23	60
8A	166	Fall/68	New-c; soft-c; 25¢ c-price; PC-r	1	3	4	8	12	26	41	55
8B	166	Fall/68	New-c; stiff-c; 25¢ c-price; PC-r	1	3	7	14	21	45	73	100

50. Adventures of Tom Sawyer (Used in **SOTI**, pg. 37)

Ed	HRN	Date	Details	A	C	GD 2.0	VG 4.0	FN 6.0	VF 8.0	VF/NM 9.0	NM- 9.2
1A	51	8/48	Orig.; Aldo Rubano a&c	1	1	19	38	57	111	176	240
1B	51	9/48	Orig.; Rubano c&a	1	1	19	38	57	111	176	240
1C	51	9/48	Orig.; outside-bc: blue & yellow only; rare	1	1	24	48	72	142	234	325
2	64	–	No c-price; LDC-r	1	1	5	10	15	23	28	32
3	78	–	C-price 15¢; LDC-r	1	1	4	8	12	17	21	24
4	94	–	LDC-r	1	1	4	7	10	14	17	20
5	117	–	LDC-r	1	1	2	4	6	10	14	18

Classics Illustrated #55 © GIL

Classics Illustrated #56 © GIL

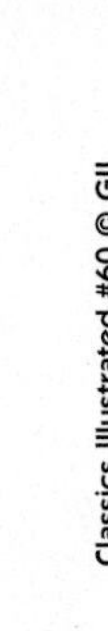

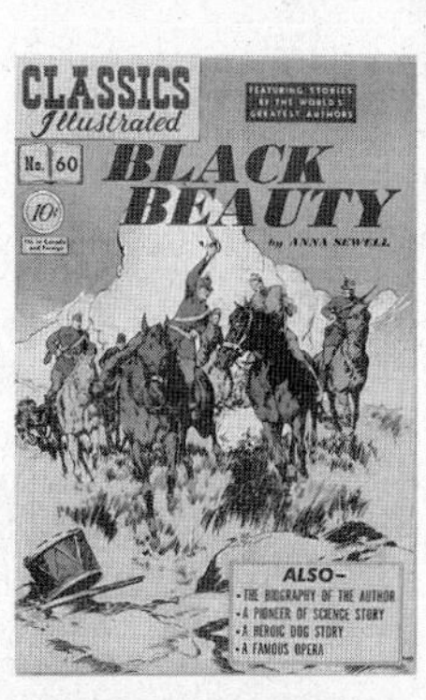

Ed	HRN	Date	Details	A	C	GD 2.0	VG 4.0	FN 6.0	VF 8.0	VF/NM 9.0	NM- 9.2
6	132	–	LDC-r	1	1	2	4	6	10	14	18
7	140	–	New-c; PC-r	1	2	3	6	9	18	27	35
8	150	–	PC-r	1	2	2	4	6	9	13	16
9	164	–	New-a; PC-r	2	2	3	6	9	18	27	35
10	167	–	PC-r	2	2	2	4	6	9	13	16
11	167	1/65	PC-r	2	2	2	4	6	8	11	14
12	167	5/66	PC-r	2	2	2	4	6	8	11	14
13	166	12/67	PC-r	2	2	2	4	6	8	11	14
14	169	Fall/69	C-price 25¢; stiff-c; PC-r	2	2	2	4	6	8	11	14
15	169	Win/71	PC-r	2	2	2	4	6	8	11	14

51. The Spy

Ed	HRN	Date	Details	A	C	GD 2.0	VG 4.0	FN 6.0	VF 8.0	VF/NM 9.0	NM- 9.2
1A	51	9/48	Original; inside-bc illo: Christmas Carol	1	1	18	36	54	105	165	225
1B	51	9/48	Original; inside-bc illo: Man in Iron Mask	1	1	18	36	54	105	165	225
1C	51	8/48	Original; outside-bc: full color	1	1	18	36	54	105	165	225
1D	51	8/48	Original; outside-bc: blue & yellow only; scarce	1	1	19	38	57	112	179	245
2	89	–	C-price 15¢; LDC-r	1	1	5	10	14	20	24	28
3	121	–	LDC-r	1	1	4	8	12	17	21	24
4	139	–	New-c; PC-r	1	2	3	6	9	18	27	35
5	156	–	PC-r	1	2	2	4	6	9	13	16
6	167	11/63	PC-r	1	2	2	4	6	8	11	14
7	167	7/66	PC-r	1	2	2	4	6	8	11	14
8A	166	Win/69	C-price 25¢; soft-c; scarce; PC-r	1	2	3	6	9	15	21	26
8B	166	Win/69	C-price 25¢; stiff-c; PC-r	1	2	2	4	6	8	11	14

52. The House of the Seven Gables

Ed	HRN	Date	Details	A	C	GD 2.0	VG 4.0	FN 6.0	VF 8.0	VF/NM 9.0	NM- 9.2
1	53	10/48	Orig.; Griffiths a&c	1	1	18	36	54	105	165	225
2	89	–	C-price 15¢; LDC-r	1	1	5	10	14	20	24	28
3	121	–	LDC-r	1	1	4	8	12	17	21	24
4	142	–	New-c&a; PC-r; Woodbridge-a	2	2	5	10	15	25	31	36
5	156	–	PC-r	2	2	2	4	6	9	13	16
6	165	–	PC-r	2	2	2	4	6	8	11	14
7	167	5/64	PC-r	2	2	2	4	6	9	13	16
8	167	3/66	PC-r	2	2	2	4	6	8	11	14
9	166	R/1968	C-price 25¢; PC-r	2	2	2	4	6	8	11	14
10	169	Spr/70	Stiff-c; PC-r	2	2	2	4	6	8	11	14

53. A Christmas Carol

Ed	HRN	Date	Details	A	C	GD 2.0	VG 4.0	FN 6.0	VF 8.0	VF/NM 9.0	NM- 9.2
1	53	11/48	Original & only ed; Kiefer-c/a	1	1	24	48	72	140	230	320

54. Man in the Iron Mask

Ed	HRN	Date	Details	A	C	GD 2.0	VG 4.0	FN 6.0	VF 8.0	VF/NM 9.0	NM- 9.2
1	55	12/48	Original; Froehlich-a, Kiefer-c	1	1	18	36	54	105	165	225
2	93	–	C-price 15¢; LDC-r	1	1	5	10	15	23	28	32
3A	111	–	(O) logo lettering; scarce; LDC-r	1	1	6	12	18	31	38	45
3B	111	–	New logo as PC; LDC-r	1	1	5	10	15	23	28	32
4	142	–	New-c&a; PC-r	2	2	5	10	15	24	30	35
5	154	–	PC-r	2	2	2	4	6	9	13	16
6	165	–	PC-r	2	2	2	4	6	8	11	14
7	167	5/64	PC-r	2	2	2	4	6	8	11	14
8	167	4/66	PC-r	2	2	2	4	6	8	11	14
9A	166	Win/69	C-price 25¢; soft-c PC-r	2	2	3	6	9	15	21	26
9B	166	Win/69	Stiff-c	2	2	2	4	6	8	11	14

55. Silas Marner (Used in **SOTI**, pgs. 311, 312)

Ed	HRN	Date	Details	A	C	GD 2.0	VG 4.0	FN 6.0	VF 8.0	VF/NM 9.0	NM- 9.2
1	55	1/49	Original-Kiefer-c	1	1	18	36	54	105	165	225
2	75	–	Price circle blank; 'Coming Next' ad; LDC-r	1	1	5	10	15	24	30	35
3	97	–	LDC-r	1	1	3	6	9	14	19	24
4	121	–	New-c; PC-r	1	2	3	6	9	18	27	35
5	130	–	PC-r	1	2	2	4	6	9	13	16
6	140	–	PC-r	1	2	2	4	6	9	13	16
7	154	–	PC-r	1	2	2	4	6	9	13	16
8	165	–	PC-r	1	2	2	4	6	8	11	14
9	167	2/64	PC-r	1	2	2	4	6	8	11	14
10	167	6/65	PC-r	1	2	2	4	6	8	11	14
11	166	5/67	PC-r	1	2	2	4	6	8	11	14
12A	166	Win/69	C-price 25¢; soft-c PC-r	1	2	3	6	9	15	21	26
12B	166	Win/69	C-price 25¢; stiff-c PC-r	1	2	2	4	6	8	11	14

56. The Toilers of the Sea

Ed	HRN	Date	Details	A	C	GD 2.0	VG 4.0	FN 6.0	VF 8.0	VF/NM 9.0	NM- 9.2
1	55	2/49	Original; A.M. Froehlich-c/a	1	1	24	48	72	140	230	320
2	165	–	New-c&a; PC-r; Angelo Torres-a	2	2	8	16	24	40	50	60
3	167	3/64	PC-r	2	2	3	6	9	16	23	30
4	167	10/66	PC-r	2	2	3	6	9	16	23	30

57. The Song of Hiawatha

Ed	HRN	Date	Details	A	C	GD 2.0	VG 4.0	FN 6.0	VF 8.0	VF/NM 9.0	NM- 9.2
1	55	3/49	Original; Alex Blum-c/a	1	1	17	34	51	98	154	210
2	75	–	No c-price w/15¢ sticker; 'Coming Next' ad; LDC-r	1	1	5	10	15	24	30	35
3	94	–	C-price 15¢; LDC-r	1	1	5	10	14	20	24	28
4	118	–	LDC-r	1	1	3	6	9	14	19	24
5	134	–	New-c; PC-r	1	2	3	6	9	18	27	35
6	139	–	PC-r	1	2	2	4	6	9	13	16
7	154	–	PC-r	1	2	2	4	6	9	13	16
8	167	–	Has orig.date; PC-r	1	2	2	4	6	8	11	14
9	167	9/64	PC-r	1	2	2	4	6	8	11	14
10	167	10/65	PC-r	1	2	2	4	6	8	11	14
11	166	F/1968	C-price 25¢; PC-r	1	2	2	4	6	8	11	14

58. The Prairie

Ed	HRN	Date	Details	A	C	GD 2.0	VG 4.0	FN 6.0	VF 8.0	VF/NM 9.0	NM- 9.2
1	60	4/49	Original; Palais c/a	1	1	16	32	48	94	147	200
2A	62	–	No c-price; no coming-next ad; LDC-r	1	1	9	18	27	47	61	75
2B	62		10¢ (rare)	1	1	19	38	57	109	172	235
3	78	–	C-price 15¢ in dbl. circle; LDC-r	1	1	5	10	15	22	26	30
4	114	–	LDC-r	1	1	4	8	12	17	21	24
5	131	–	LDC-r	1	1	4	7	10	14	17	20
6	132	–	LDC-r	1	1	4	7	10	14	17	20
7	146	–	New-c; PC-r	1	2	5	10	15	23	28	32
8	155	–	PC-r	1	2	2	4	6	9	13	16
9	167	5/64	PC-r	1	2	2	4	6	8	11	14
10	167	4/66	PC-r	1	2	2	4	6	8	11	14
11	169	Sm/69	New price 25¢; stiff-c; PC-r	1	2	2	4	6	8	11	14

59. Wuthering Heights

Ed	HRN	Date	Details	A	C	GD 2.0	VG 4.0	FN 6.0	VF 8.0	VF/NM 9.0	NM- 9.2
1	60	5/49	Original; Kiefer-c/a	1	1	18	36	54	105	165	225
2	85	–	C-price 15¢; LDC-r	1	1	6	12	18	28	34	40
3	156	–	New-c; PC-r	1	2	5	10	15	25	31	36
4	167	1/64	PC-r	1	2	2	4	6	9	13	16
5	167	10/66	PC-r	1	2	2	4	6	9	13	16
6	169	Sm/69	C-price 25¢; stiff-c; PC-r	1	2	2	4	6	9	13	16

60. Black Beauty

Ed	HRN	Date	Details	A	C	GD 2.0	VG 4.0	FN 6.0	VF 8.0	VF/NM 9.0	NM- 9.2
1	62	6/49	Original; Froehlich-c/a	1	1	17	34	51	98	154	210
2	62	–	No c-price; no coming-next ad; LDC-r (rare)	1	1	19	38	57	111	176	240
3	85	–	C-price 15¢; LDC-r	1	1	5	10	15	23	28	32
4	158	–	New L.B. Cole-	2	2	7	14	21	35	43	50

Classics Illustrated #61 © GIL

Classics Illustrated #65 © GIL

Classics Illustrated #69 © GIL

Ed	HRN	Date	Details	A	C	GD 2.0	VG 4.0	FN 6.0	VF 8.0	VF/NM 9.0	NM- 9.2
			c/a; PC-r								
5	167	2/64	PC-r	2	2	2	4	6	11	16	20
6	167	3/66	PC-r	2	2	2	4	6	11	16	20
7	166	R/1968	New-c&price, 25¢; PC-r	2	3	5	10	15	32	51	70

61. The Woman in White

Ed	HRN	Date	Details	A	C	GD 2.0	VG 4.0	FN 6.0	VF 8.0	VF/NM 9.0	NM- 9.2
1A	62	7/49	Original; Blum-c/a fc-purple; bc: top illos light blue	1	1	18	36	54	105	165	225
1B	62	7/49	Original; Blum-c/a fc-pink; bc: top illos light violet	1	1	18	36	54	105	165	225
2	156	–	New-c; PC-r	1	2	6	12	18	28	34	40
3	167	1/64	PC-r	1	2	2	4	6	11	16	20
4	166	R/1968	C-price 25¢; PC-r	1	2	2	4	6	11	16	20

62. Western Stories ("The Luck of Roaring Camp" and "The Outcasts of Poker Flat")

Ed	HRN	Date	Details	A	C	GD 2.0	VG 4.0	FN 6.0	VF 8.0	VF/NM 9.0	NM- 9.2
1	62	8/49	Original; Kiefer-c/a	1	1	16	32	48	94	147	200
2	89	–	C-price 15¢; LDC-r	1	1	5	10	15	23	28	32
3	121	–	LDC-r	1	1	3	6	9	15	21	26
4	137	–	New-c; PC-r	1	2	3	6	9	18	27	35
5	152	–	PC-r	1	2	2	4	6	8	11	14
6	167	10/63	PC-r	1	2	2	4	6	8	11	14
7	167	6/64	PC-r	1	2	2	4	6	8	11	14
8	167	11/66	PC-r	1	2	2	4	6	8	11	14
9	166	R/1968	New-c&price 25¢; PC-r	1	3	3	6	9	17	25	32

63. The Man Without a Country

Ed	HRN	Date	Details	A	C	GD 2.0	VG 4.0	FN 6.0	VF 8.0	VF/NM 9.0	NM- 9.2
1	62	9/49	Original; Kiefer-c/a	1	1	17	34	51	98	154	210
2	78	–	C-price 15¢ in double circle; LDC-r	1	1	5	10	15	23	28	32
3	156	–	New-c, old-a; PC-r	1	2	6	12	18	28	34	40
4	165	–	New-a & text pgs.; PC-r; A. Torres-a	2	2	5	10	15	23	28	32
5	167	3/64	PC-r	2	2	2	4	6	8	11	14
6	167	8/66	PC-r	2	2	2	4	6	8	11	14
7	169	Sm/69	New price 25¢; stiff-c; PC-r	2	2	2	4	6	8	11	14

64. Treasure Island

Ed	HRN	Date	Details	A	C	GD 2.0	VG 4.0	FN 6.0	VF 8.0	VF/NM 9.0	NM- 9.2
1	62	10/49	Original; Blum-c/a	1	1	18	36	54	105	165	225
2A	82	–	C-price 15¢; soft-c LDC-r	1	1	5	10	15	22	26	30
2B	82	–	Stiff-c; LDC-r	1	1	5	10	15	23	28	32
3	117	–	LDC-r	1	1	3	6	9	15	21	26
4	131	–	New-c; PC-r	1	2	3	6	9	18	27	35
5	138	–	PC-r	1	2	2	4	6	9	13	16
6	146	–	PC-r	1	2	2	4	6	9	13	16
7	158	–	PC-r	1	2	2	4	6	9	13	16
8	165	–	PC-r	1	2	2	4	6	8	11	14
9	167	–	PC-r	1	2	2	4	6	8	11	14
10	167	6/64	PC-r	1	2	2	4	6	8	11	14
11	167	12/65	PC-r	1	2	2	4	6	8	11	14
12A	166	10/67	PC-r	1	2	2	4	6	8	11	14
12B	166	10/67	w/Grit ad stapled in book	1	2	11	22	33	73	142	210
13	169	Spr/69	New price 25¢; stiff-c; PC-r	1	2	2	4	6	9	13	16
14	–	1989	Long John Silver's Seafood Shoppes; $1.95, First/Berkley Publ.; Blum-r	1	2						5.00

65. Benjamin Franklin

Ed	HRN	Date	Details	A	C	GD 2.0	VG 4.0	FN 6.0	VF 8.0	VF/NM 9.0	NM- 9.2
1	64	11/49	Original; Kiefer-c; Iger Shop-a	1	1	11	22	33	73	142	210
2	131	–	New-c; PC-r	1	2	5	10	15	24	30	35
3	154	–	PC-r	1	2	2	4	6	9	13	16
4	167	2/64	PC-r	1	2	2	4	6	9	13	16
5	167	4/66	PC-r	1	2	2	4	6	9	13	16
6	169	Fall/69	New price 25¢; stiff-c; PC-r	1	2	2	4	6	9	13	16

66. The Cloister and the Hearth

Ed	HRN	Date	Details	A	C	GD 2.0	VG 4.0	FN 6.0	VF 8.0	VF/NM 9.0	NM- 9.2
1	67	12/49	Original & only ed; Kiefer-a & c	1	1	32	64	96	188	307	425

67. The Scottish Chiefs

Ed	HRN	Date	Details	A	C	GD 2.0	VG 4.0	FN 6.0	VF 8.0	VF/NM 9.0	NM- 9.2
1	67	1/50	Original; Blum-a&c	1	1	15	30	45	88	137	185
2	85	–	C-price 15¢; LDC-r	1	1	5	10	15	23	28	32
3	118	–	LDC-r	1	1	3	6	9	15	21	26
4	136	–	New-c; PC-r	1	2	3	6	9	18	27	36
5	154	–	PC-r	1	2	2	4	6	9	13	16
6	167	11/63	PC-r	1	2	2	4	6	10	14	18
7	167	8/65	PC-r	1	2	2	4	6	9	13	16

68. Julius Caesar (Used in **SOTI**, pgs. 36, 37)

Ed	HRN	Date	Details	A	C	GD 2.0	VG 4.0	FN 6.0	VF 8.0	VF/NM 9.0	NM- 9.2
1	70	2/50	Original; Kiefer-c/a	1	1	15	30	45	88	137	185
2	85	–	C-price 15¢; LDC-r	1	1	5	10	15	22	26	30
3	108	–	LDC-r	1	1	4	9	13	18	22	26
4	156	–	New L.B. Cole-c; PC-r	1	2	6	12	18	28	34	40
5	165	–	New-a by Evans, Crandall; PC-r	2	2	5	10	15	24	30	35
6	167	2/64	PC-r	2	2	2	4	6	8	11	14
7	167	10/65	Tarzan books inside cover; PC-r	2	2	2	4	6	8	11	14
8	166	R/1967	PC-r	2	2	2	4	6	8	11	14
9	169	Win/69	PC-r; stiff-c	2	2	2	4	6	8	11	14

69. Around the World in 80 Days

Ed	HRN	Date	Details	A	C	GD 2.0	VG 4.0	FN 6.0	VF 8.0	VF/NM 9.0	NM- 9.2
1	70	3/50	Original; Kiefer-c/a	1	1	15	30	45	88	137	185
2	87	–	C-price 15¢; LDC-r	1	1	5	10	15	22	26	30
3	125	–	LDC-r	1	1	4	9	13	18	22	26
4	136	–	New-c; PC-r	1	2	5	10	15	25	31	36
5	146	–	PC-r	1	2	2	4	6	9	13	16
6	152	–	PC-r	1	2	2	4	6	9	13	16
7	164	–	PC-r	1	2	2	4	6	8	11	14
8	167	–	PC-r	1	2	2	4	6	8	11	14
9	167	7/64	PC-r	1	2	2	4	6	8	11	14
10	167	11/65	PC-r	1	2	2	4	6	8	11	14
11	166	7/67	PC-r	1	2	2	4	6	8	11	14
12	169	Spr/69	C-price 25¢; stiff-c; PC-r	1	2	2	4	6	8	11	14

70. The Pilot

Ed	HRN	Date	Details	A	C	GD 2.0	VG 4.0	FN 6.0	VF 8.0	VF/NM 9.0	NM- 9.2
1	71	4/50	Original; Blum-c/a	1	1	14	28	42	80	115	150
2	92	–	C-price 15¢; LDC-r	1	1	5	10	15	23	28	32
3	125	–	LDC-r	1	1	4	9	13	18	22	26
4	156	–	New-c; PC-r	1	2	6	12	18	28	34	40
5	167	2/64	PC-r	1	2	2	4	6	11	16	20
6	167	5/66	PC-r	1	2	2	4	6	9	13	16

71. The Man Who Laughs

Ed	HRN	Date	Details	A	C	GD 2.0	VG 4.0	FN 6.0	VF 8.0	VF/NM 9.0	NM- 9.2
1	71	5/50	Original; Blum-c/a	1	1	19	38	57	111	176	240
2	165	–	New-c&a; PC-r	2	2	14	28	42	80	115	155
3	167	4/64	PC-r	2	2	11	22	33	62	86	115

72. The Oregon Trail

Ed	HRN	Date	Details	A	C	GD 2.0	VG 4.0	FN 6.0	VF 8.0	VF/NM 9.0	NM- 9.2
1	73	6/50	Original; Kiefer-c/a	1	1	14	28	42	80	115	150
2	89	–	C-price 15¢; LDC-r	1	1	5	10	15	23	28	32
3	121	–	LDC-r	1	1	4	9	13	18	22	26
4	131	–	New-c; PC-r	1	2	5	10	15	25	31	36
5	140	–	PC-r	1	2	2	4	6	9	13	16
6	150	–	PC-r	1	2	2	4	6	9	13	16
7	164	–	PC-r	1	2	2	4	6	8	11	14
8	167	–	PC-r	1	2	2	4	6	8	11	14
9	167	8/64	PC-r	1	2	2	4	6	8	11	14
10	167	10/65	PC-r	1	2	2	4	6	8	11	14
11	166	R/1968	C-price 25¢; PC-r	1	2	2	4	6	8	11	14

73. The Black Tulip

Ed	HRN	Date	Details	A	C

Classics Illustrated #75 © GIL

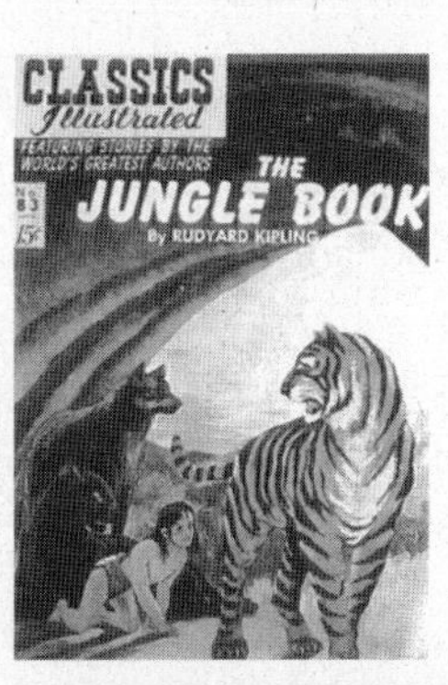

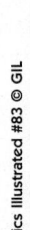

Classics Illustrated #83 © GIL

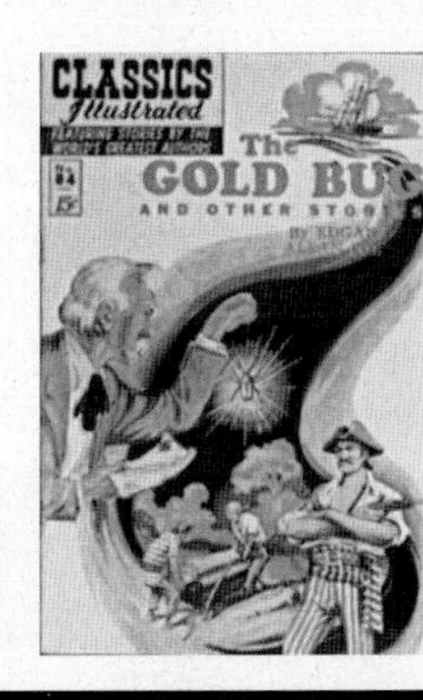

Classics Illustrated #84 © GIL

Ed	HRN	Date	Details	A	C	GD 2.0	VG 4.0	FN 6.0	VF 8.0	VF/NM 9.0	NM- 9.2
1	75	7/50	1st & only ed.; Alex Blum-c/a	1	1	37	74	111	222	361	500

74. Mr. Midshipman Easy

Ed	HRN	Date	Details	A	C	GD 2.0	VG 4.0	FN 6.0	VF 8.0	VF/NM 9.0	NM- 9.2
1	75	8/50	1st & only edition	1	1	37	74	111	222	361	500

75. The Lady of the Lake

Ed	HRN	Date	Details	A	C	GD 2.0	VG 4.0	FN 6.0	VF 8.0	VF/NM 9.0	NM- 9.2
1	75	9/50	Original; Kiefer-c/a	1	1	14	28	42	80	115	150
2	85	–	C-price 15¢; LDC-r	1	1	5	10	15	24	30	35
3	118	–	LDC-r	1	1	5	10	14	20	24	28
4	139	–	New-c; PC-r	1	2	5	10	15	25	31	36
5	154	–	PC-r	1	2	2	4	6	9	13	16
6	165	–	PC-r	1	2	2	4	6	8	11	14
7	167	4/64	PC-r	1	2	2	4	6	8	11	14
8	167	5/66	PC-r	1	2	2	4	6	8	11	14
9	169	Spr/69	New price 25¢; stiff-c; PC-r	1	2	2	4	6	8	11	14

76. The Prisoner of Zenda

Ed	HRN	Date	Details	A	C	GD 2.0	VG 4.0	FN 6.0	VF 8.0	VF/NM 9.0	NM- 9.2
1	75	10/50	Original; Kiefer-c/a	1	1	14	28	42	80	115	150
2	85	–	C-price 15¢; LDC-r	1	1	5	10	15	23	28	32
3	111	–	LDC-r	1	1	3	6	9	16	21	26
4	128	–	New-c; PC-r	1	2	3	6	9	18	27	35
5	152	–	PC-r	1	2	2	4	6	9	13	16
6	165	–	PC-r	1	2	2	4	6	8	11	14
7	167	4/64	PC-r	1	2	2	4	6	8	11	14
8	167	9/66	PC-r	1	2	2	4	6	8	11	14
9	169	Fall/69	New price 25¢; stiff-c; PC-r	1	2	2	4	6	8	11	14

77. The Iliad

Ed	HRN	Date	Details	A	C	GD 2.0	VG 4.0	FN 6.0	VF 8.0	VF/NM 9.0	NM- 9.2
1	78	11/50	Original; Blum-c/a	1	1	14	28	42	80	115	150
2	87	–	C-price 15¢; LDC-r	1	1	5	10	15	24	30	35
3	121	–	LDC-r	1	1	3	6	9	15	21	26
4	139	–	New-c; PC-r	1	2	3	6	9	17	25	32
5	150	–	PC-r	1	2	2	4	6	9	13	16
6	165	–	PC-r	1	2	2	4	6	8	11	14
7	167	10/63	PC-r	1	2	2	4	6	8	11	14
8	167	7/64	PC-r	1	2	2	4	6	8	11	14
9	167	5/66	PC-r	1	2	2	4	6	8	11	14
10	166	R/1968	C-price 25¢; PC-r	1	2	2	4	6	8	11	14

78. Joan of Arc

Ed	HRN	Date	Details	A	C	GD 2.0	VG 4.0	FN 6.0	VF 8.0	VF/NM 9.0	NM- 9.2
1	78	12/50	Original; Kiefer-c/a	1	1	14	28	42	80	115	150
2	87	–	C-price 15¢; LDC-r	1	1	5	10	15	23	28	32
3	113	–	LDC-r	1	1	3	6	9	15	21	26
4	128	–	New-c; PC-r	1	2	3	6	9	18	27	35
5	140	–	PC-r	1	2	2	4	6	9	13	16
6	150	–	PC-r	1	2	2	4	6	9	13	16
7	159	–	PC-r	1	2	2	4	6	9	13	16
8	167	–	PC-r	1	2	2	4	6	8	11	14
9	167	12/63	PC-r	1	2	2	4	6	8	11	14
10	167	6/65	PC-r	1	2	2	4	6	8	11	14
11	166	6/67	PC-r	1	2	2	4	6	8	11	14
12	166	Win/69	New-c&price, 25¢; PC-r; stiff-c	1	3	3	6	9	17	25	32

79. Cyrano de Bergerac

Ed	HRN	Date	Details	A	C	GD 2.0	VG 4.0	FN 6.0	VF 8.0	VF/NM 9.0	NM- 9.2
1	78	1/51	Orig.; movie promo inside front-c; Blum-c/a	1	1	14	28	42	80	115	150
2	85	–	C-price 15¢; LDC-r	1	1	5	10	15	23	28	32
3	118	–	LDC-r	1	1	3	6	9	17	23	28
4	133	–	New-c; PC-r	1	2	3	6	9	17	25	32
5	156	–	PC-r	1	2	2	4	6	11	16	20
6	167	8/64	PC-r	1	2	2	4	6	11	16	20

80. White Fang (Last line drawn cover)

Ed	HRN	Date	Details	A	C	GD 2.0	VG 4.0	FN 6.0	VF 8.0	VF/NM 9.0	NM- 9.2
1	79	2/51	Orig.; Blum-c/a	1	1	14	28	42	80	115	150
2	87	–	C-price 15¢; LDC-r	1	1	5	10	15	24	30	35
3	125	–	LDC-r	1	1	3	6	9	15	21	26
4	132	–	New-c; PC-r	1	2	3	6	9	17	25	32
5	140	–	PC-r	1	2	2	4	6	9	13	16
6	153	–	PC-r	1	2	2	4	6	9	13	16
7	167	–	PC-r	1	2	2	4	6	8	11	14
8	167	9/64	PC-r	1	2	2	4	6	8	11	14
9	167	7/65	PC-r	1	2	2	4	6	8	11	14
10	166	6/67	PC-r	1	2	2	4	6	8	11	14
11	169	Fall/69	New price 25¢; PC-r; stiff-c	1	2	2	4	6	8	11	14

81. The Odyssey (1st painted cover)

Ed	HRN	Date	Details	A	C	GD 2.0	VG 4.0	FN 6.0	VF 8.0	VF/NM 9.0	NM- 9.2
1	82	3/51	First 15¢ Original; Blum-c	1	1	14	28	42	80	115	150
2	167	8/64	PC-r	1	1	2	4	6	11	16	20
3	167	10/66	PC-r	1	1	2	4	6	11	16	20
4	169	Spr/69	New, stiff-c; PC-r	1	2	3	6	9	18	27	36

82. The Master of Ballantrae

Ed	HRN	Date	Details	A	C	GD 2.0	VG 4.0	FN 6.0	VF 8.0	VF/NM 9.0	NM- 9.2
1	82	4/51	Original; Blum-c	1	1	12	24	36	69	97	125
2	167	8/64	PC-r	1	1	3	6	9	14	19	24
3	166	Fall/68	New, stiff-c; PC-r	1	2	3	6	9	18	27	36

83. The Jungle Book

Ed	HRN	Date	Details	A	C	GD 2.0	VG 4.0	FN 6.0	VF 8.0	VF/NM 9.0	NM- 9.2
1	85	5/51	Original; Blum-c Bossert/Blum-a	1	1	12	24	36	69	97	125
2	110	–	PC-r	1	1	2	4	6	10	14	18
3	125	–	PC-r	1	1	2	4	6	9	13	16
4	134	–	PC-r	1	1	2	4	6	9	13	16
5	142	–	PC-r	1	1	2	4	6	9	13	16
6	150	–	PC-r	1	1	2	4	6	9	13	16
7	159	–	PC-r	1	1	2	4	6	9	13	16
8	167	–	PC-r	1	1	2	4	6	8	11	14
9	167	3/65	PC-r	1	1	2	4	6	8	11	14
10	167	11/65	PC-r	1	1	2	4	6	8	11	14
11	167	5/66	PC-r	1	1	2	4	6	8	11	14
12	166	R/1968	New c&a; stiff-c; PC-r	2	2	3	6	9	19	29	38

84. The Gold Bug and Other Stories ("The Gold Bug", "The Tell-Tale Heart", "The Cask of Amontillado")

Ed	HRN	Date	Details	A	C	GD 2.0	VG 4.0	FN 6.0	VF 8.0	VF/NM 9.0	NM- 9.2
1	85	6/51	Original; Blum-c/a; Palais, Laverly-a	1	1	15	30	45	83	124	165
2	167	7/64	PC-r	1	1	11	22	33	62	86	110

85. The Sea Wolf

Ed	HRN	Date	Details	A	C	GD 2.0	VG 4.0	FN 6.0	VF 8.0	VF/NM 9.0	NM- 9.2
1	85	7/51	Original; Blum-c/a	1	1	11	22	33	62	86	110
2	121	–	PC-r	1	1	2	4	6	9	13	16
3	132	–	PC-r	1	1	2	4	6	9	13	16
4	141	–	PC-r	1	1	2	4	6	9	13	16
5	161	–	PC-r	1	1	2	4	6	8	11	14
6	167	2/64	PC-r	1	1	2	4	6	8	11	14
7	167	11/65	PC-r	1	1	2	4	6	8	11	14
8	169	Fall/69	New price 25¢; stiff-c; PC-r	1	1	2	4	6	8	11	14

86. Under Two Flags

Ed	HRN	Date	Details	A	C	GD 2.0	VG 4.0	FN 6.0	VF 8.0	VF/NM 9.0	NM- 9.2
1	87	8/51	Original; first delBourgo-a	1	1	11	22	33	62	86	110
2	117	–	PC-r	1	1	2	4	6	10	14	18
3	139	–	PC-r	1	1	2	4	6	9	13	16
4	158	–	PC-r	1	1	2	4	6	9	13	16
5	167	2/64	PC-r	1	1	2	4	6	8	11	14
6	167	8/66	PC-r	1	1	2	4	6	8	11	14
7	169	Sm/69	New price 25¢; stiff-c; PC-r	1	1	2	4	6	8	11	14

87. A Midsummer Nights Dream

Ed	HRN	Date	Details	A	C	GD 2.0	VG 4.0	FN 6.0	VF 8.0	VF/NM 9.0	NM- 9.2
1	87	9/51	Original; Blum c/a	1	1	11	22	33	62	86	110
2	161	–	PC-r	1	1	2	4	6	9	13	16
3	167	4/64	PC-r	1	1	2	4	6	8	11	14
4	167	5/66	PC-r	1	1	2	4	6	8	11	14
5	169	Sm/69	New price 25¢; stiff-c; PC-r	1	1	2	4	6	8	11	14

Classics Illustrated #89 © GIL

Classics Illustrated #91 © GIL

Classics Illustrated #96 © GIL

88. Men of Iron

Ed	HRN	Date	Details	A	C	GD 2.0	VG 4.0	FN 6.0	VF 8.0	VF/NM 9.0	NM- 9.2
1	89	10/51	Original	1	1	11	22	33	62	86	110
2	154	–	PC-r	1	1	2	4	6	9	13	16
3	167	1/64	PC-r	1	1	2	4	6	8	11	14
4	166	R/1968	C-price 25¢; PC-r	1	1	2	4	6	8	11	14

89. Crime and Punishment (Cover illo. in **POP**)

Ed	HRN	Date	Details	A	C	GD 2.0	VG 4.0	FN 6.0	VF 8.0	VF/NM 9.0	NM- 9.2
1	89	11/51	Original; Palais-a	1	1	12	24	36	69	97	125
2	152	–	PC-r	1	1	2	4	6	9	13	16
3	167	4/64	PC-r	1	1	2	4	6	8	11	14
4	167	5/66	PC-r	1	1	2	4	6	8	11	14
5	169	Fall/69	New price 25¢ stiff-c; PC-r	1	1	2	4	6	8	11	14

90. Green Mansions

Ed	HRN	Date	Details	A	C	GD 2.0	VG 4.0	FN 6.0	VF 8.0	VF/NM 9.0	NM- 9.2
1	89	12/51	Original; Blum-c/a	1	1	11	22	33	62	86	110
2	148	–	New L.B. Cole-c; PC-r	1	2	5	10	15	22	26	30
3	165	–	PC-r	1	2	2	4	6	8	11	14
4	167	4/64	PC-r	1	2	2	4	6	8	11	14
5	167	9/66	PC-r	1	2	2	4	6	8	11	14
6	169	Sm/69	New price 25¢; stiff-c; PC-r	1	2	2	4	6	8	11	14

91. The Call of the Wild

Ed	HRN	Date	Details	A	C	GD 2.0	VG 4.0	FN 6.0	VF 8.0	VF/NM 9.0	NM- 9.2
1	92	1/52	Orig.; delBourgo-a	1	1	11	22	33	62	86	110
2	112	–	PC-r	1	1	2	4	6	9	13	16
3	125	–	'Picture Progress' on back-c; PC-r	1	1	2	4	6	9	13	16
4	134	–	PC-r	1	1	2	4	6	9	13	16
5	143	–	PC-r	1	1	2	4	6	9	13	16
6	165	–	PC-r	1	1	2	4	6	9	13	16
7	167	–	PC-r	1	1	2	4	6	8	11	14
8	167	4/65	PC-r	1	1	2	4	6	8	11	14
9	167	3/66	PC-r	1	1	2	4	6	8	11	14
10	166	11/67	PC-r	1	1	2	4	6	8	11	14
11	169	Spr/70	New price 25¢; stiff-c; PC-r	1	1	2	4	6	8	11	14

92. The Courtship of Miles Standish

Ed	HRN	Date	Details	A	C	GD 2.0	VG 4.0	FN 6.0	VF 8.0	VF/NM 9.0	NM- 9.2
1	92	2/52	Original; Blum-c/a	1	1	11	22	33	62	86	110
2	165	–	PC-r	1	1	2	4	6	9	13	16
3	167	3/64	PC-r	1	1	2	4	6	9	13	16
4	166	5/67	PC-r	1	1	2	4	6	9	13	16
5	169	Win/69	New price 25¢ stiff-c; PC-r	1	1	2	4	6	9	13	16

93. Pudd'nhead Wilson

Ed	HRN	Date	Details	A	C	GD 2.0	VG 4.0	FN 6.0	VF 8.0	VF/NM 9.0	NM- 9.2
1	94	3/52	Orig.; Kiefer-c/a;	1	1	11	22	33	62	86	110
2	165	–	New-c; PC-r	1	2	2	4	6	11	16	25
3	167	3/64	PC-r	1	2	2	4	6	9	13	16
4	166	R/1968	New price 25¢; soft-c; PC-r	1	2	2	4	6	9	13	16

94. David Balfour

Ed	HRN	Date	Details	A	C	GD 2.0	VG 4.0	FN 6.0	VF 8.0	VF/NM 9.0	NM- 9.2
1	94	4/52	Original; Palais-a	1	1	11	22	33	62	86	110
2	167	5/64	PC-r	1	1	2	4	6	11	16	20
3	166	R/1968	C-price 25¢; PC-r	1	1	2	4	6	13	18	22

95. All Quiet on the Western Front

Ed	HRN	Date	Details	A	C	GD 2.0	VG 4.0	FN 6.0	VF 8.0	VF/NM 9.0	NM- 9.2
1A	96	5/52	Orig.; del Bourgo-a	1	1	14	28	42	80	115	150
1B	99	5/52	Orig.; del Bourgo-a	1	1	12	24	36	69	97	125
2	167	10/64	PC-r	1	1	3	6	9	16	22	28
3	167	11/66	PC-r	1	1	3	6	9	16	22	28

96. Daniel Boone

Ed	HRN	Date	Details	A	C	GD 2.0	VG 4.0	FN 6.0	VF 8.0	VF/NM 9.0	NM- 9.2
1	97	6/52	Original; Blum-a	1	1	11	22	33	60	83	105
2	117	–	PC-r	1	1	2	4	6	9	13	16
3	128	–	PC-r	1	1	2	4	6	9	13	16
4	132	–	PC-r	1	1	2	4	6	9	13	16
5	134	–	"Story of Jesus" on back-c; PC-r	1	1	2	4	6	9	13	16
6	158	–	PC-r	1	1	2	4	6	9	13	16
7	167	1/64	PC-r	1	1	2	4	6	8	11	14
8	167	5/65	PC-r	1	1	2	4	6	8	11	14
9	167	11/66	PC-r	1	1	2	4	6	8	11	14
10	166	Win/69	New-c; price 25¢; PC-r; stiff-c	1	2	3	6	9	16	22	28

97. King Solomon's Mines

Ed	HRN	Date	Details	A	C	GD 2.0	VG 4.0	FN 6.0	VF 8.0	VF/NM 9.0	NM- 9.2
1	96	7/52	Orig.; Kiefer-a	1	1	11	22	33	60	83	105
2	118	–	PC-r	1	1	2	4	6	9	13	16
3	131	–	PC-r	1	1	2	4	6	9	13	16
4	141	–	PC-r	1	1	2	4	6	9	13	16
5	158	–	PC-r	1	1	2	4	6	9	13	16
6	167	2/64	PC-r	1	1	2	4	6	8	11	14
7	167	9/65	PC-r	1	1	2	4	6	8	11	14
8	169	Sm/69	New price 25¢; stiff-c; PC-r	1	1	2	4	6	8	11	14

98. The Red Badge of Courage

Ed	HRN	Date	Details	A	C	GD 2.0	VG 4.0	FN 6.0	VF 8.0	VF/NM 9.0	NM- 9.2
1	98	8/52	Original	1	1	11	22	33	60	83	105
2	118	–	PC-r	1	1	2	4	6	9	13	16
3	132	–	PC-r	1	1	2	4	6	9	13	16
4	142	–	PC-r	1	1	2	4	6	9	13	16
5	152	–	PC-r	1	1	2	4	6	9	13	16
6	161	–	PC-r	1	1	2	4	6	9	13	16
7	167	–	Has orig.date; PC-r	1	1	2	4	6	9	13	16
8	167	9/64	PC-r	1	1	2	4	6	9	13	16
9	167	10/65	PC-r	1	1	2	4	6	9	13	16
10	166	R/1968	New-c&price 25¢; PC-r; stiff-c	1	2	3	6	9	16	23	30

99. Hamlet (Used in **POP**, pg. 102)

Ed	HRN	Date	Details	A	C	GD 2.0	VG 4.0	FN 6.0	VF 8.0	VF/NM 9.0	NM- 9.2
1	98	9/52	Original; Blum-a	1	1	11	22	33	62	86	110
2	121	–	PC-r	1	1	2	4	6	9	13	16
3	141	–	PC-r	1	1	2	4	6	9	13	16
4	158	–	PC-r	1	1	2	4	6	9	13	16
5	167	–	Has orig.date; PC-r	1	1	2	4	6	8	11	14
6	167	7/65	PC-r	1	1	2	4	6	8	11	14
7	166	4/67	PC-r	1	1	2	4	6	8	11	14
8	169	Spr/69	New-c&price 25¢; PC-r; stiff-c	1	2	3	6	9	16	23	30

100. Mutiny on the Bounty

Ed	HRN	Date	Details	A	C	GD 2.0	VG 4.0	FN 6.0	VF 8.0	VF/NM 9.0	NM- 9.2
1	100	10/52	Original	1	1	11	22	33	60	83	105
2	117	–	PC-r	1	1	2	4	6	9	13	16
3	132	–	PC-r	1	1	2	4	6	9	13	16
4	142	–	PC-r	1	1	2	4	6	9	13	16
5	155	–	PC-r	1	1	2	4	6	9	13	16
6	167	–	Has orig. date;PC-r	1	1	2	4	6	8	11	14
7	167	5/64	PC-r	1	1	2	4	6	8	11	14
8	167	3/66	PC-r	1	1	2	4	6	8	11	14
9	169	Spr/70	PC-r; stiff-c	1	1	2	4	6	8	11	14

101. William Tell

Ed	HRN	Date	Details	A	C	GD 2.0	VG 4.0	FN 6.0	VF 8.0	VF/NM 9.0	NM- 9.2
1	101	11/52	Original; Kiefer-c delBourgo-a	1	1	11	22	33	60	83	105
2	118	–	PC-r	1	1	2	4	6	9	13	16
3	141	–	PC-r	1	1	2	4	6	9	13	16
4	158	–	PC-r	1	1	2	4	6	9	13	16
5	167	–	Has orig.date; PC-r	1	1	2	4	6	8	11	14
6	167	11/64	PC-r	1	1	2	4	6	8	11	14
7	166	4/67	PC-r	1	1	2	4	6	8	11	14
8	169	Win/69	New price 25¢; stiff-c; PC-r	1	1	2	4	6	8	11	14

102. The White Company

Ed	HRN	Date	Details	A	C	GD 2.0	VG 4.0	FN 6.0	VF 8.0	VF/NM 9.0	NM- 9.2
1	101	12/52	Original; Blum-a	1	1	13	26	39	74	105	135
2	165	–	PC-r	1	1	3	6	9	16	23	30
3	167	4/64	PC-r	1	1	3	6	9	16	23	30

103. Men Against the Sea

Ed	HRN	Date	Details	A	C

Classics Illustrated #106 © GIL

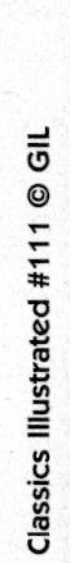

Classics Illustrated #111 © GIL

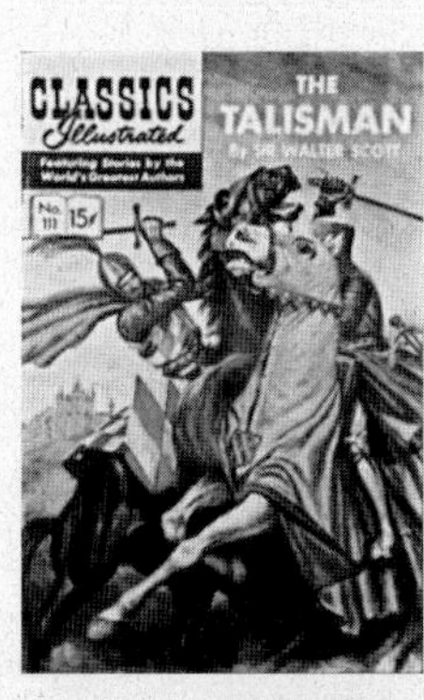

Classics Illustrated #118 © GIL

Ed	HRN	Date	Details	A	C	GD 2.0	VG 4.0	FN 6.0	VF 8.0	VF/NM 9.0	NM- 9.2
1	104	1/53	Original; Kiefer-c; Palais-a	1	1	11	22	33	62	86	110
2	114	–	PC-r	1	1	4	8	11	16	19	22
3	131	–	New-c; PC-r	1	2	5	10	15	24	30	35
4	158	–	PC-r	1	2	4	7	10	14	17	20
5	149	–	White reorder list; came after HRN-158; PC-r	1	2	5	10	15	22	26	30
6	167	3/64	PC-r	1	2	2	4	6	9	13	16

104. Bring 'Em Back Alive

Ed	HRN	Date	Details	A	C	GD 2.0	VG 4.0	FN 6.0	VF 8.0	VF/NM 9.0	NM- 9.2
1	105	2/53	Original; Kiefer-c/a	1	1	11	22	33	60	83	105
2	118	–	PC-r	1	1	2	4	6	9	13	16
3	133	–	PC-r	1	1	2	4	6	9	13	16
4	150	–	PC-r	1	1	2	4	6	9	13	16
5	158	–	PC-r	1	1	2	4	6	9	13	16
6	167	10/63	PC-r	1	1	2	4	6	8	11	14
7	167	9/65	PC-r	1	1	2	4	6	8	11	14
8	169	Win/69	New price 25¢; stiff-c; PC-r	1	1	2	4	6	8	11	14

105. From the Earth to the Moon

Ed	HRN	Date	Details	A	C	GD 2.0	VG 4.0	FN 6.0	VF 8.0	VF/NM 9.0	NM- 9.2
1	106	3/53	Original; Blum-a	1	1	11	22	33	60	83	105
2	118	–	PC-r	1	1	2	4	6	9	13	16
3	132	–	PC-r	1	1	2	4	6	9	13	16
4	141	–	PC-r	1	1	2	4	6	9	13	16
5	146	–	PC-r	1	1	2	4	6	9	13	16
6	156	–	PC-r	1	1	2	4	6	9	13	16
7	167	–	Has orig. date; PC-r	1	1	2	4	6	8	11	14
8	167	5/64	PC-r	1	1	2	4	6	8	11	14
9	167	5/65	PC-r	1	1	2	4	6	8	11	14
10A	166	10/67	PC-r	1	1	2	4	6	8	11	14
10B	166	10/67	w/Grit ad stapled in book	1	1	15	30	45	85	130	175
11	169	Sm/69	New price 25¢; stiff-c; PC-r	1	1	2	4	6	8	11	14
12	169	Spr/71	PC-r	1	1	2	4	6	8	11	14

106. Buffalo Bill

Ed	HRN	Date	Details	A	C	GD 2.0	VG 4.0	FN 6.0	VF 8.0	VF/NM 9.0	NM- 9.2
1	107	4/53	Orig.; delBourgo-a	1	1	10	20	30	58	79	100
2	118	–	PC-r	1	1	2	4	6	9	13	16
3	132	–	PC-r	1	1	2	4	6	9	13	16
4	142	–	PC-r	1	1	2	4	6	9	13	16
5	161	–	PC-r	1	1	2	4	6	8	11	14
6	167	3/64	PC-r	1	1	2	4	6	8	11	14
7	166	7/67	PC-r	1	1	2	4	6	8	11	14
8	169	Fall/69	PC-r; stiff-c	1	1	2	4	6	8	11	14

107. King of the Khyber Rifles

Ed	HRN	Date	Details	A	C	GD 2.0	VG 4.0	FN 6.0	VF 8.0	VF/NM 9.0	NM- 9.2
1	108	5/53	Original	1	1	10	20	30	58	79	100
2	118	–	PC-r	1	1	2	4	6	9	13	16
3	146	–	PC-r	1	1	2	4	6	9	13	16
4	158	–	PC-r	1	1	2	4	6	9	13	16
5	167	–	Has orig.date; PC-r	1	1	2	4	6	8	11	14
6	167	10/66	PC-r	1	1	2	4	6	8	11	14

108. Knights of the Round Table

Ed	HRN	Date	Details	A	C	GD 2.0	VG 4.0	FN 6.0	VF 8.0	VF/NM 9.0	NM- 9.2
1A	108	6/53	Original; Blum-a	1	1	11	22	33	62	86	110
1B	109	6/53	Original; scarce	1	1	11	22	33	64	90	115
2	117	–	PC-r	1	1	2	4	6	9	13	16
3	165	–	PC-r	1	1	2	4	6	8	11	14
4	167	4/64	PC-r	1	1	2	4	6	8	11	14
5	166	4/67	PC-r	1	1	2	4	6	8	11	14
6	169	Sm/69	New price 25¢; stiff-c; PC-r	1	1	2	4	6	8	11	14

109. Pitcairn's Island

Ed	HRN	Date	Details	A	C	GD 2.0	VG 4.0	FN 6.0	VF 8.0	VF/NM 9.0	NM- 9.2
1	110	7/53	Original; Palais-a	1	1	11	22	33	62	86	110
2	165	–	PC-r	1	1	2	4	6	9	13	16
3	167	3/64	PC-r	1	1	2	4	6	9	13	16
4	166	6/67	PC-r	1	1	2	4	6	9	13	16

110. A Study in Scarlet

Ed	HRN	Date	Details	A	C	GD 2.0	VG 4.0	FN 6.0	VF 8.0	VF/NM 9.0	NM- 9.2
1	111	8/53	Original	1	1	15	30	45	83	124	165
2	165	–	PC-r	1	1	11	22	33	62	86	110

111. The Talisman

Ed	HRN	Date	Details	A	C	GD 2.0	VG 4.0	FN 6.0	VF 8.0	VF/NM 9.0	NM- 9.2
1	112	9/53	Original; last H.C. Kiefer-a	1	1	11	22	33	62	86	110
2	165	–	PC-r	1	1	2	4	6	9	13	16
3	167	5/64	PC-r	1	1	2	4	6	9	13	16
4	166	Fall/68	C-price 25¢; PC-r	1	1	2	4	6	9	13	16

112. Adventures of Kit Carson

Ed	HRN	Date	Details	A	C	GD 2.0	VG 4.0	FN 6.0	VF 8.0	VF/NM 9.0	NM- 9.2
1	113	10/53	Original; Palais-a	1	1	11	22	33	60	83	105
2	129	–	PC-r	1	1	2	4	6	9	13	16
3	141	–	PC-r	1	1	2	4	6	9	13	16
4	152	–	PC-r	1	1	2	4	6	9	13	16
5	161	–	PC-r	1	1	2	4	6	8	11	14
6	167	–	PC-r	1	1	2	4	6	8	11	14
7	167	2/65	PC-r	1	1	2	4	6	8	11	14
8	167	5/66	PC-r	1	1	2	4	6	8	11	14
9	166	Win/69	New-c&price 25¢; PC-r; stiff-c	1	2	3	6	9	14	20	25

113. The Forty-Five Guardsmen

Ed	HRN	Date	Details	A	C	GD 2.0	VG 4.0	FN 6.0	VF 8.0	VF/NM 9.0	NM- 9.2
1	114	11/53	Orig.; delBourgo-a	1	1	13	26	39	74	105	135
2	166	7/67	PC-r	1	1	4	8	12	22	34	45

114. The Red Rover

Ed	HRN	Date	Details	A	C	GD 2.0	VG 4.0	FN 6.0	VF 8.0	VF/NM 9.0	NM- 9.2
1	115	12/53	Original	1	1	13	26	39	74	105	135
2	166	7/67	PC-r	1	1	4	8	12	22	23	45

115. How I Found Livingstone

Ed	HRN	Date	Details	A	C	GD 2.0	VG 4.0	FN 6.0	VF 8.0	VF/NM 9.0	NM- 9.2
1	116	1/54	Original	1	1	14	28	42	78	112	145
2	167	1/67	PC-r	1	1	4	8	12	28	44	60

116. The Bottle Imp

Ed	HRN	Date	Details	A	C	GD 2.0	VG 4.0	FN 6.0	VF 8.0	VF/NM 9.0	NM- 9.2
1	117	2/54	Orig.; Cameron-a	1	1	14	28	42	78	112	145
2	167	1/67	PC-r	1	1	4	8	12	28	44	60

117. Captains Courageous

Ed	HRN	Date	Details	A	C	GD 2.0	VG 4.0	FN 6.0	VF 8.0	VF/NM 9.0	NM- 9.2
1	118	3/54	Orig.; Costanza-a	1	1	13	26	39	72	101	130
2	167	2/67	PC-r	1	1	3	6	9	14	20	26
3	169	Fall/69	New price 25¢; stiff-c; PC-r	1	1	3	6	9	14	20	26

118. Rob Roy

Ed	HRN	Date	Details	A	C	GD 2.0	VG 4.0	FN 6.0	VF 8.0	VF/NM 9.0	NM- 9.2
1	119	4/54	Original; Rudy & Walter Palais-a	1	1	14	28	42	78	112	145
2	167	2/67	PC-r	1	1	4	8	12	28	44	60

119. Soldiers of Fortune

Ed	HRN	Date	Details	A	C	GD 2.0	VG 4.0	FN 6.0	VF 8.0	VF/NM 9.0	NM- 9.2
1	120	5/54	Schaffenberger-a	1	1	12	24	36	69	97	125
2	166	3/67	PC-r	1	1	3	6	9	14	20	26
3	169	Spr/70	New price 25¢; stiff-c; PC-r	1	1	3	6	9	14	20	26

120. The Hurricane

Ed	HRN	Date	Details	A	C	GD 2.0	VG 4.0	FN 6.0	VF 8.0	VF/NM 9.0	NM- 9.2
1	121	6/54	Orig.; Cameron-a	1	1	12	24	36	69	97	125
2	166	3/67	PC-r	1	1	4	8	12	22	34	45

121. Wild Bill Hickok

Ed	HRN	Date	Details	A	C	GD 2.0	VG 4.0	FN 6.0	VF 8.0	VF/NM 9.0	NM- 9.2
1	122	7/54	Original	1	1	10	20	30	58	79	100
2	132	–	PC-r	1	1	2	4	6	9	13	16
3	141	–	PC-r	1	1	2	4	6	9	13	16
4	154	–	PC-r	1	1	2	4	6	9	13	16
5	167	–	PC-r	1	1	2	4	6	8	11	14
6	167	8/64	PC-r	1	1	2	4	6	8	11	14
7	166	4/67	PC-r	1	1	2	4	6	8	11	14

Classics Illustrated #124 © GIL

Classics Illustrated #127 © GIL

Classics Illustrated #132 © GIL

Ed	HRN	Date	Details	A	C	GD 2.0	VG 4.0	FN 6.0	VF 8.0	VF/NM 9.0	NM- 9.2
8	169	Win/69	PC-r; stiff-c	1	1	2	4	6	8	11	14
122. The Mutineers											
Ed	HRN	Date	Details	A	C						
1	123	9/54	Original	1	1	11	22	33	62	86	110
2	136	–	PC-r	1	1	2	4	6	9	13	16
3	146	–	PC-r	1	1	2	4	6	9	13	16
4	158	–	PC-r	1	1	2	4	6	9	13	16
5	167	11/63	PC-r	1	1	2	4	6	8	11	14
6	167	3/65	PC-r	1	1	2	4	6	8	11	14
7	166	8/67	PC-r	1	1	2	4	6	8	11	14
123. Fang and Claw											
Ed	HRN	Date	Details	A	C						
1	124	11/54	Original	1	1	11	22	33	62	86	110
2	133	–	PC-r	1	1	2	4	6	9	13	16
3	143	–	PC-r	1	1	2	4	6	9	13	16
4	154	–	PC-r	1	1	2	4	6	9	13	16
5	167	–	Has orig.date; PC-r	1	1	2	4	6	8	11	14
6	167	9/65	PC-r	1	1	2	4	6	8	11	14
124. The War of the Worlds											
Ed	HRN	Date	Details	A	C						
1	125	1/55	Original; Cameron-c/a	1	1	14	28	42	78	112	145
2	131	–	PC-r	1	1	2	4	6	10	14	18
3	141	–	PC-r	1	1	2	4	6	10	14	18
4	148	–	PC-r	1	1	2	4	6	10	14	18
5	156	–	PC-r	1	1	2	4	6	10	14	18
6	165	–	PC-r	1	1	2	4	6	13	18	22
7	167	–	PC-r	1	1	2	4	6	9	13	16
8	167	11/64	PC-r	1	1	2	4	6	10	14	18
9	167	11/65	PC-r	1	1	2	4	6	9	13	16
10	166	R/1968	C-price 25¢; PC-r	1	1	2	4	6	9	13	16
11	169	Sm/70	PC-r; stiff-c	1	1	2	4	6	9	13	16
125. The Ox Bow Incident											
Ed	HRN	Date	Details	A	C						
1	–	3/55	Original; Picture Progress replaces reorder list	1	1	10	20	30	58	79	100
2	143	–	PC-r	1	1	2	4	6	9	13	16
3	152	–	PC-r	1	1	2	4	6	9	13	16
4	149	–	PC-r	1	1	2	4	6	9	13	16
5	167	–	PC-r	1	1	2	4	6	8	11	14
6	167	11/64	PC-r	1	1	2	4	6	8	11	14
7	166	4/67	PC-r	1	1	2	4	6	8	11	14
8	169	Win/69	New price 25¢; stiff-c; PC-r	1	1	2	4	6	8	11	14
126. The Downfall											
Ed	HRN	Date	Details	A	C						
1	5/55	–	Orig.; 'Picture Progress' replaces reorder list; Cameron-c/a	1	1	11	22	33	62	86	110
2	167	8/64	PC-r	1	1	2	4	6	13	18	22
3	166	R/1968	C-price 25¢; PC-r	1	1	2	4	6	13	18	22
127. The King of the Mountains											
Ed	HRN	Date	Details	A	C						
1	128	7/55	Original	1	1	11	22	33	62	86	110
2	167	6/64	PC-r	1	1	2	4	6	11	16	20
3	166	F/1968	C-price 25¢; PC-r	1	1	2	4	6	11	16	20
128. Macbeth (Used in **POP**, pg. 102)											
Ed	HRN	Date	Details	A	C						
1	128	9/55	Orig.; last Blum-a	1	1	11	22	33	62	86	110
2	143	–	PC-r	1	1	2	4	6	9	13	16
3	158	–	PC-r	1	1	2	4	6	9	13	16
4	167	–	PC-r	1	1	2	4	6	8	11	14
5	167	6/64	PC-r	1	1	2	4	6	8	11	14
6	166	4/67	PC-r	1	1	2	4	6	8	11	14
7	166	R/1968	C-Price 25¢; PC-r	1	1	2	4	6	8	11	14
8	169	Spr/70	Stiff-c; PC-r	1	1	2	4	6	8	11	14
129. Davy Crockett											
Ed	HRN	Date	Details	AC							
1	129	11/55	Orig.; Cameron-a	1	1	14	28	42	81	118	155
2	167	9/66	PC-r	1	1	11	22	33	62	86	110
130. Caesar's Conquests											
Ed	HRN	Date	Details	A	C						
1	130	1/56	Original; Orlando-a	1	1	11	22	33	62	86	110
2	142	–	PC-r	1	1	2	4	6	9	13	16
3	152	–	PC-r	1	1	2	4	6	9	13	16
4	149	–	PC-r	1	1	2	4	6	9	13	16
5	167	–	PC-r	1	1	2	4	6	8	11	14
6	167	10/64	PC-r	1	1	2	4	6	8	11	14
7	167	4/66	PC-r	1	1	2	4	6	8	11	14
131. The Covered Wagon											
Ed	HRN	Date	Details	A	C						
1	131	3/56	Original	1	1	7	14	21	44	72	100
2	143	–	PC-r	1	1	2	4	6	9	13	16
3	152	–	PC-r	1	1	2	4	6	9	13	16
4	158	–	PC-r	1	1	2	4	6	9	13	16
5	167	–	PC-r	1	1	2	4	6	8	11	14
6	167	11/64	PC-r	1	1	2	4	6	8	11	14
7	167	4/66	PC-r	1	1	2	4	6	8	11	14
8	169	Win/69	New price 25¢; stiff-c; PC-r	1	1	2	4	6	8	11	14
132. The Dark Frigate											
Ed	HRN	Date	Details	A	C						
1	132	5/56	Original	1	1	11	22	33	62	86	110
2	150	–	PC-r	1	1	2	4	6	9	13	16
3	167	1/64	PC-r	1	1	2	4	6	9	13	16
4	166	5/67	PC-r	1	1	2	4	6	9	13	16
133. The Time Machine											
Ed	HRN	Date	Details	A	C						
1	132	7/56	Orig.; Cameron-a	1	1	8	16	24	51	86	120
2	142	–	PC-r	1	1	2	4	6	10	14	18
3	152	–	PC-r	1	1	2	4	6	10	14	18
4	158	–	PC-r	1	1	2	4	6	9	13	16
5	167	–	PC-r	1	1	2	4	6	9	13	16
6	167	6/64	PC-r	1	1	2	4	6	10	14	18
7	167	3/66	PC-r	1	1	2	4	6	9	13	16
8	166	12/67	PC-r	1	1	2	4	6	9	13	16
9	169	Win/71	New price 25¢; stiff-c; PC-r	1	1	2	4	6	9	13	16
134. Romeo and Juliet											
Ed	HRN	Date	Details	A	C						
1	134	9/56	Original; Evans-a	1	1	7	14	21	48	79	110
2	161	–	PC-r	1	1	2	4	6	9	13	16
3	167	9/63	PC-r	1	1	2	4	6	8	11	14
4	167	5/65	PC-r	1	1	2	4	6	8	11	14
5	166	6/67	PC-r	1	1	2	4	6	8	11	14
6	166	Win/69	New c&price 25¢; stiff-c; PC-r	1	2	3	6	9	17	25	32
135. Waterloo											
Ed	HRN	Date	Details	A	C						
1	135	11/56	Orig.; G. Ingels-a	1	1	7	14	21	48	79	110
2	153	–	PC-r	1	1	2	4	6	9	13	16
3	167	–	PC-r	1	1	2	4	6	8	11	14
4	167	9/64	PC-r	1	1	2	4	6	8	11	14
5	166	R/1968	C-price 25¢; PC-r	1	1	2	4	6	8	11	14
136. Lord Jim											
Ed	HRN	Date	Details	A	C						
1	136	1/57	Original; Evans-a	1	1	7	14	21	48	79	110
2	165	–	PC-r	1	1	2	4	6	8	11	14
3	167	3/64	PC-r	1	1	2	4	6	8	11	14
4	167	9/66	PC-r	1	1	2	4	6	8	11	14
5	169	Sm/69	New price 25 ¢; stiff-c; PC-r	1	1	2	4	6	8	11	14
137. The Little Savage											
Ed	HRN	Date	Details	A	C						
1	136	3/57	Original; Evans-a	1	1	7	14	21	48	79	110
2	148	–	PC-r	1	1	2	4	6	9	13	16
3	156	–	PC-r	1	1	2	4	6	9	13	16
4	167	–	PC-r	1	1	2	4	6	8	11	14
5	167	10/64	PC-r	1	1	2	4	6	8	11	14
6	166	8/67	PC-r	1	1	2	4	6	8	11	14
7	169	Spr/70	New price 25¢; stiff-c; PC-r	1	1	2	4	6	8	11	14

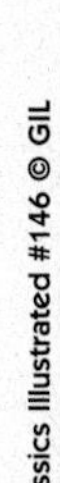
Classics Illustrated #140 © GIL

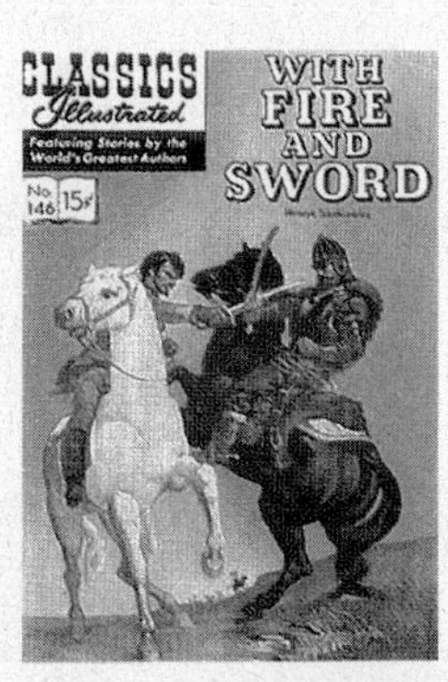

Classics Illustrated #146 © GIL

Classics Illustrated #150 © GIL

138. A Journey to the Center of the Earth

Ed	HRN	Date	Details	A	C	GD 2.0	VG 4.0	FN 6.0	VF 8.0	VF/NM 9.0	NM- 9.2
1	136	5/57	Original	1	1	8	16	24	56	96	135
2	146	–	PC-r	1	1	2	4	6	11	16	20
3	156	–	PC-r	1	1	2	4	6	11	16	20
4	158	–	PC-r	1	1	2	4	6	9	13	16
5	167	–	PC-r	1	1	2	4	6	8	11	14
6	167	6/64	PC-r	1	1	2	4	6	13	18	22
7	167	4/66	PC-r	1	1	2	4	6	13	18	22
8	166	R/68	C-price 25¢; PC-r	1	1	2	4	6	10	14	18

139. In the Reign of Terror

Ed	HRN	Date	Details	A	C	GD 2.0	VG 4.0	FN 6.0	VF 8.0	VF/NM 9.0	NM- 9.2
1	139	7/57	Original; Evans-a	1	1	7	14	21	44	72	100
2	154	–	PC-r	1	1	2	4	6	9	13	16
3	167	–	Has orig.date; PC-r	1	1	2	4	6	8	11	14
4	167	7/64	PC-r	1	1	2	4	6	8	11	14
5	166	R/1968	C-price 25¢; PC-r	1	1	2	4	6	8	11	14

140. On Jungle Trails

Ed	HRN	Date	Details	A	C	GD 2.0	VG 4.0	FN 6.0	VF 8.0	VF/NM 9.0	NM- 9.2
1	140	9/57	Original	1	1	7	14	21	44	72	100
2	150	–	PC-r	1	1	2	4	6	9	13	16
3	160	–	PC-r	1	1	2	4	6	9	13	16
4	167	9/63	PC-r	1	1	2	4	6	8	11	14
5	167	9/65	PC-r	1	1	2	4	6	8	11	14

141. Castle Dangerous

Ed	HRN	Date	Details	A	C	GD 2.0	VG 4.0	FN 6.0	VF 8.0	VF/NM 9.0	NM- 9.2
1	141	11/57	Original	1	1	7	14	21	49	82	115
2	152	–	PC-r	1	1	2	4	6	9	13	16
3	167	–	PC-r	1	1	2	4	6	9	13	16
4	166	7/67	PC-r	1	1	2	4	6	9	13	16

142. Abraham Lincoln

Ed	HRN	Date	Details	A	C	GD 2.0	VG 4.0	FN 6.0	VF 8.0	VF/NM 9.0	NM- 9.2
1	142	1/58	Original	1	1	7	14	21	48	79	110
2	154	–	PC-r	1	1	2	4	6	9	13	16
3	158	–	PC-r	1	1	2	4	6	9	13	16
4	167	10/63	PC-r	1	1	2	4	6	8	11	14
5	167	7/65	PC-r	1	1	2	4	6	8	11	14
6	166	11/67	PC-r	1	1	2	4	6	8	11	14
7	169	Fall/69	New price 25¢; stiff-c; PC-r	1	1	2	4	6	8	11	14

143. Kim

Ed	HRN	Date	Details	A	C	GD 2.0	VG 4.0	FN 6.0	VF 8.0	VF/NM 9.0	NM- 9.2
1	143	3/58	Original; Orlando-a	1	1	7	14	21	44	72	100
2	165	–	PC-r	1	1	2	4	6	8	11	14
3	167	11/63	PC-r	1	1	2	4	6	8	11	14
4	167	8/65	PC-r	1	1	2	4	6	8	11	14
5	169	Win/69	New price 25¢; stiff-c; PC-r	1	1	2	4	6	8	11	14

144. The First Men in the Moon

Ed	HRN	Date	Details	A	C	GD 2.0	VG 4.0	FN 6.0	VF 8.0	VF/NM 9.0	NM- 9.2
1	143	5/58	Original; Woodbridge/Williamson/Torres-a	1	1	8	16	24	51	86	120
2	152	–	(Rare)-PC-r	1	1	8	16	24	56	96	135
3	153	–	PC-r	1	1	2	4	6	9	13	16
4	161	–	PC-r	1	1	2	4	6	8	11	14
5	167	–	PC-r	1	1	2	4	6	8	11	14
6	167	12/65	PC-r	1	1	2	4	6	8	11	14
7	166	Fall/68	New-c&price 25¢; PC-r; stiff-c	1	2	3	6	9	16	23	30
8	169	Win/69	Stiff-c; PC-r	1	2	2	4	6	10	16	20

145. The Crisis

Ed	HRN	Date	Details	A	C	GD 2.0	VG 4.0	FN 6.0	VF 8.0	VF/NM 9.0	NM- 9.2
1	143	7/58	Original; Evans-a	1	1	7	14	21	48	79	110
2	156	–	PC-r	1	1	2	4	6	9	13	16
3	167	10/63	PC-r	1	1	2	4	6	8	11	14
4	167	3/65	PC-r	1	1	2	4	6	8	11	14
5	166	R/68	C-price 25¢; PC-r	1	1	2	4	6	8	11	14

146. With Fire and Sword

Ed	HRN	Date	Details	A	C	GD 2.0	VG 4.0	FN 6.0	VF 8.0	VF/NM 9.0	NM- 9.2
1	143	9/58	Original; Woodbridge-a	1	1	7	14	21	48	79	110
2	156	–	PC-r	1	1	2	4	6	10	14	18
3	167	11/63	PC-r	1	1	2	4	6	9	13	16
4	167	3/65	PC-r	1	1	2	4	6	9	13	16

147. Ben-Hur

Ed	HRN	Date	Details	A	C	GD 2.0	VG 4.0	FN 6.0	VF 8.0	VF/NM 9.0	NM- 9.2
1	147	11/58	Original; Orlando-a	1	1	7	14	21	46	76	105
2	152	–	Scarce; PC-r	1	1	7	14	21	48	79	110
3	153	–	PC-r	1	1	2	4	6	9	13	16
4	158	–	PC-r	1	1	2	4	6	9	13	16
5	167	–	Orig.date; but PC-r	1	1	2	4	6	8	11	14
6	167	2/65	PC-r	1	1	2	4	6	8	11	14
7	167	9/66	PC-r	1	1	2	4	6	8	11	14
8A	166	Fall/68	New-c&price 25¢; PC-r; soft-c	1	2	3	6	9	17	25	32
8B	166	Fall/68	New-c&price 25¢; PC-r; stiff-c; scarce	1	2	4	8	12	22	34	45

148. The Buccaneer

Ed	HRN	Date	Details	A	C	GD 2.0	VG 4.0	FN 6.0	VF 8.0	VF/NM 9.0	NM- 9.2
1	148	1/59	Orig.; Evans/Jenny-a; Saunders-c	1	1	7	14	21	44	72	100
2	568	–	Juniors list only PC-r	1	1	2	4	6	9	13	16
3	167	–	PC-r	1	1	2	4	6	8	11	14
4	167	9/65	PC-r	1	1	2	4	6	8	11	14
5	169	Sm/69	New price 25¢; PC-r; stiff-c	1	1	2	4	6	8	11	14

149. Off on a Comet

Ed	HRN	Date	Details	A	C	GD 2.0	VG 4.0	FN 6.0	VF 8.0	VF/NM 9.0	NM- 9.2
1	149	3/59	Orig.;G.McCann-a; blue reorder list	1	1	7	14	21	48	79	110
2	155	–	PC-r	1	1	2	4	6	9	13	16
3	149	–	PC-r; white reorder list; no coming-next ad	1	1	2	4	6	9	13	16
4	167	12/63	PC-r	1	1	2	4	6	8	11	14
5	167	2/65	PC-r	1	1	2	4	6	8	11	14
6	167	10/66	PC-r	1	1	2	4	6	8	11	14
7	166	Fall/68	New-c & price 25¢; PC-r	1	2	3	6	9	16	23	30

150. The Virginian

Ed	HRN	Date	Details	A	C	GD 2.0	VG 4.0	FN 6.0	VF 8.0	VF/NM 9.0	NM- 9.2
1	150	5/59	Original	1	1	7	14	21	49	82	115
2	164	–	PC-r	1	1	2	4	6	11	16	20
3	167	10/63	PC-r	1	1	3	6	9	15	21	26
4	167	12/65	PC-r	1	1	2	4	6	11	16	20

151. Won By the Sword

Ed	HRN	Date	Details	A	C	GD 2.0	VG 4.0	FN 6.0	VF 8.0	VF/NM 9.0	NM- 9.2
1	150	7/59	Original	1	1	7	14	21	48	79	110
2	164	–	PC-r	1	1	2	4	6	10	14	18
3	167	10/63	PC-r	1	1	2	4	6	10	14	18
4	166	7/67	PC-r	1	1	2	4	6	10	14	18

152. Wild Animals I Have Known

Ed	HRN	Date	Details	A	C	GD 2.0	VG 4.0	FN 6.0	VF 8.0	VF/NM 9.0	NM- 9.2
1	152	9/59	Orig.; L.B. Cole c/a	1	1	8	16	24	51	86	120
2A	149	–	PC-r; white reorder list; no coming-next ad; IBC: Jr. list #572	1	1	2	4	6	9	13	16
2B	149	–	PC-r; inside-bc: Jr. list to #555	1	1	2	4	6	9	13	16
2C	149	–	PC-r; inside-bc: has World Around Us ad; scarce	1	1	3	6	9	15	21	26
3	167	9/63	PC-r	1	1	2	4	6	8	11	14
4	167	8/65	PC-r	1	1	2	4	6	8	11	14
5	169	Fall/69	New price 25¢; stiff-c; PC-r	1	1	2	4	6	8	11	14

153. The Invisible Man

Ed	HRN	Date	Details	A	C	GD 2.0	VG 4.0	FN 6.0	VF 8.0	VF/NM 9.0	NM- 9.2
1	153	11/59	Original	1	1	8	16	24	55	93	130
2A	149	–	PC-r; white reorder list; no coming-next ad; inside-bc: Jr.	1	1	2	4	6	11	16	20

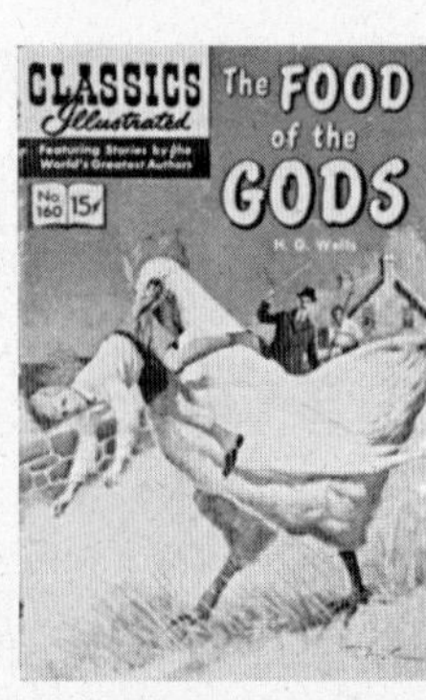

Classics Illustrated #160 © GIL

Classics Illustrated #164 © GIL

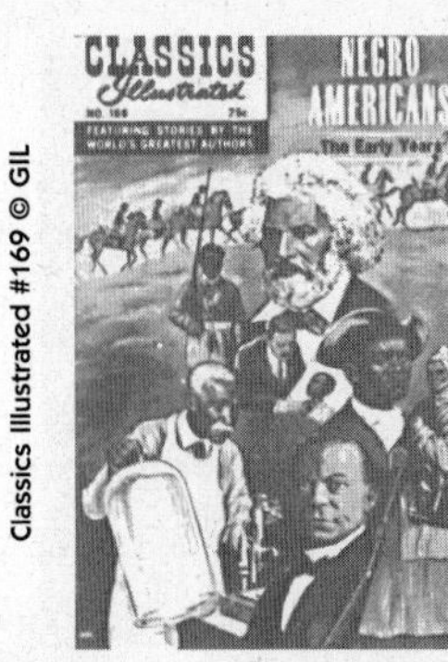

Classics Illustrated #169 © GIL

Ed	HRN	Date	Details	A	C	GD 2.0	VG 4.0	FN 6.0	VF 8.0	VF/NM 9.0	NM- 9.2
			list to #572								
2B	149	–	PC-r; inside-bc: Jr. list to #555	1	1	2	4	6	13	18	22
3	167	–	PC-r	1	1	2	4	6	9	13	16
4	167	2/65	PC-r	1	1	2	4	6	9	13	16
5	167	9/66	PC-r	1	1	2	4	6	9	13	16
6	166	Win/69	New price 25¢; PC-r; stiff-c	1	1	2	4	6	9	13	16
7	169	Spr/71	Stiff-c; letters spelling 'Invisible Man' are 'solid' not 'invisible;' PC-r	1	1	2	4	6	9	13	16

154. The Conspiracy of Pontiac

Ed	HRN	Date	Details	A	C	GD 2.0	VG 4.0	FN 6.0	VF 8.0	VF/NM 9.0	NM- 9.2
1	154	1/60	Original	1	1	7	14	21	49	82	115
2	167	11/63	PC-r	1	1	2	4	6	13	18	22
3	167	7/64	PC-r	1	1	2	4	6	13	18	22
4	166	12/67	PC-r	1	1	2	4	6	13	18	22

155. The Lion of the North

Ed	HRN	Date	Details	A	C	GD 2.0	VG 4.0	FN 6.0	VF 8.0	VF/NM 9.0	NM- 9.2
1	154	3/60	Original	1	1	7	14	21	48	79	110
2	167	1/64	PC-r	1	1	2	4	6	11	16	20
3	166	R/1967	C-price 25¢; PC-r	1	1	2	4	6	10	14	18

156. The Conquest of Mexico

Ed	HRN	Date	Details	A	C	GD 2.0	VG 4.0	FN 6.0	VF 8.0	VF/NM 9.0	NM- 9.2
1	156	5/60	Orig.; Bruno Premiani-c/a	1	1	7	14	21	48	79	110
2	167	1/64	PC-r	1	1	2	4	6	10	14	18
3	166	8/67	PC-r	1	1	2	4	6	10	14	18
4	169	Spr/70	New price 25¢; stiff-c; PC-r	1	1	2	4	6	9	13	16

157. Lives of the Hunted

Ed	HRN	Date	Details	A	C	GD 2.0	VG 4.0	FN 6.0	VF 8.0	VF/NM 9.0	NM- 9.2
1	156	7/60	Orig.; L.B. Cole-c	1	1	7	14	21	49	82	115
2	167	2/64	PC-r	1	1	2	4	6	13	18	22
3	166	10/67	PC-r	1	1	2	4	6	13	18	22

158. The Conspirators

Ed	HRN	Date	Details	A	C	GD 2.0	VG 4.0	FN 6.0	VF 8.0	VF/NM 9.0	NM- 9.2
1	156	9/60	Original	1	1	7	14	21	49	82	115
2	167	7/64	PC-r	1	1	2	4	6	13	18	22
3	166	10/67	PC-r	1	1	2	4	6	13	18	22

159. The Octopus

Ed	HRN	Date	Details	A	C	GD 2.0	VG 4.0	FN 6.0	VF 8.0	VF/NM 9.0	NM- 9.2
1	159	11/60	Orig.; Gray Morrow-a; L.B. Cole-c	1	1	7	14	21	49	82	115
2	167	2/64	PC-r	1	1	2	4	6	13	18	22
3	166	R/1967	C-price 25¢; PC-r	1	1	2	4	6	13	18	22

160. The Food of the Gods

Ed	HRN	Date	Details	A	C	GD 2.0	VG 4.0	FN 6.0	VF 8.0	VF/NM 9.0	NM- 9.2
1A	159	1/61	Original	1	1	8	16	24	51	86	120
1B	160	1/61	Original; same, except for HRN	1	1	7	14	21	49	82	115
2	167	1/64	PC-r	1	1	2	4	6	13	18	22
3	166	6/67	PC-r	1	1	2	4	6	13	18	22

161. Cleopatra

Ed	HRN	Date	Details	A	C	GD 2.0	VG 4.0	FN 6.0	VF 8.0	VF/NM 9.0	NM- 9.2
1	161	3/61	Original	1	1	7	14	21	49	82	115
2	167	1/64	PC-r	1	1	3	6	9	14	19	24
3	166	8/67	PC-r	1	1	3	6	9	14	19	24

162. Robur the Conqueror

Ed	HRN	Date	Details	A	C	GD 2.0	VG 4.0	FN 6.0	VF 8.0	VF/NM 9.0	NM- 9.2
1	162	5/61	Original	1	1	7	14	21	49	82	115
2	167	7/64	PC-r	1	1	3	6	9	14	19	24
3	166	8/67	PC-r	1	1	3	6	9	14	19	24

163. Master of the World

Ed	HRN	Date	Details	A	C	GD 2.0	VG 4.0	FN 6.0	VF 8.0	VF/NM 9.0	NM- 9.2
1	163	7/61	Original; Gray Morrow-a	1	1	7	14	21	49	82	115
2	167	1/65	PC-r	1	1	2	4	6	13	18	22
3	166	R/1968	C-price 25¢; PC-r	1	1	2	4	6	13	18	22

164. The Cossack Chief

Ed	HRN	Date	Details	A	C	GD 2.0	VG 4.0	FN 6.0	VF 8.0	VF/NM 9.0	NM- 9.2
1	164	(1961)	Orig.; nd(10/61?)	1	1	7	14	21	46	76	105
2	167	4/65	PC-r	1	1	2	4	6	13	18	22
3	166	Fall/68	C-price 25¢; PC-r	1	1	2	4	6	13	18	22

165. The Queen's Necklace

Ed	HRN	Date	Details	A	C	GD 2.0	VG 4.0	FN 6.0	VF 8.0	VF/NM 9.0	NM- 9.2
1	164	1/62	Original; Morrow-a	1	1	7	14	21	49	82	115
2	167	4/65	PC-r	1	1	2	4	6	13	18	22
3	166	Fall/68	C-price 25¢; PC-r	1	1	2	4	6	13	18	22

166. Tigers and Traitors

Ed	HRN	Date	Details	A	C	GD 2.0	VG 4.0	FN 6.0	VF 8.0	VF/NM 9.0	NM- 9.2
1	165	5/62	Original	1	1	9	18	27	61	106	150
2	167	2/64	PC-r	1	1	4	8	12	22	34	45
3	167	11/66	PC-r	1	1	4	8	12	22	34	45

167. Faust

Ed	HRN	Date	Details	A	C	GD 2.0	VG 4.0	FN 6.0	VF 8.0	VF/NM 9.0	NM- 9.2
1	165	8/62	Original	1	1	12	24	36	79	160	240
2	167	2/64	PC-r	1	1	6	12	18	39	62	85
3	166	6/67	PC-r	1	1	6	12	18	39	62	85

168. In Freedom's Cause

Ed	HRN	Date	Details	A	C	GD 2.0	VG 4.0	FN 6.0	VF 8.0	VF/NM 9.0	NM- 9.2
1	169	Win/69	Original; Evans/ Crandall-a; stiff-c; 25¢; no coming-next ad;	1	1	13	26	39	87	186	285

169. Negro Americans The Early Years

Ed	HRN	Date	Details	A	C	GD 2.0	VG 4.0	FN 6.0	VF 8.0	VF/NM 9.0	NM- 9.2
1	166	Spr/69	Orig. & last issue; 25¢; Stiff-c; no coming-next ad; other sources indicate publication date of 5/69	1	1	12	24	36	83	172	260
2	169	Spr/69	Stiff-c	1	1	8	16	24	51	86	120

NOTE: *Many other titles were prepared or planned but were only issued in British/European series.*

CLASSIC PUNISHER (Also see Punisher)
Marvel Comics: Dec, 1989 ($4.95, B&W, deluxe format, 68 pgs.)

1-Reprints Marvel Super Action #1 & Marvel Preview #2 plus new story 5.00

CLASSIC RED SONJA
Dynamite Entertainment: 2010 - No. 4, 2010 ($3.99)

1-4-Newly colored reprints of stories from Savage Sword of Conan magazine 4.00

CLASSICS ILLUSTRATED
First Publishing/Berkley Publishing: Feb, 1990 - No. 27, July, 1991 ($3.75/$3.95, 52 pgs.)

1-27: 1-Gahan Wilson-c/a. 4-Sienkiewicz painted-c/a. 6-Russell scripts/layouts. 7-Spiegle-a. 9-Ploog-c/a. 16-Staton-a. 18-Gahan Wilson-c/a; 20-Geary-a. 26-Aesop's Fables (6/91). 26,27-Direct sale only 5.00

CLASSICS ILLUSTRATED
Acclaim Books/Twin Circle PublishingCo.: Feb, 1997 - Jan, 1998 ($4.99, digest-size) (Each book contains study notes)

A Christmas Carol-(12/97), A Connecticut Yankee in King Arthur's Court-(5/97), All Quiet on the Western Front-(1/98), A Midsummer's Night Dream-(4/97) Around the World in 80 Days-(1/98), A Tale of Two Cities-(2/97)Joe Orlando-r, Captains Courageous-(11/97), Crime and Punishment-(3/97), Dr. Jekyll and Mr. Hyde-(10/97), Don Quixote-(12/97), Frankenstein-(10/97), Great Expectations-(4/97), Hamlet-(3/97), Huckleberry Finn-(3/97), Jane Eyre-(2/97), Kidnapped-(1/98), Les Miserables-(5/97), Lord Jim-(9/97), Macbeth-(5/97), Moby Dick-(4/97), Oliver Twist-(5/97), Robinson Crusoe-(9/97), Romeo & Juliet-(2/97), Silas Marner-(11/97), The Call of the Wild-(9/97), The Count of Monte Cristo-(1/98), The House of the Seven Gables-(9/97), The Iliad-(12/97), The Invisible Man-(10/97), The Last of the Mohicans-(12/97), The Master of Ballantrae-(11/97), The Odyssey-(3/97), The Prince and the Pauper-(4/97), The Red Badge Of Courage-(9/97), Tom Sawyer-(2/97) Wuthering Heights-(11/97) 5.00

NOTE: *Stories reprinted from the original Gilberton Classic Comics and Classics Illustrated.*

CLASSICS ILLUSTRATED GIANTS
Gilberton Publications: Oct, 1949 (One-Shots - "OS")

These Giant Editions, all with new front and back covers, were advertised from 10/49 to 2/52. They were 50¢ on the newsstand and 60¢ by mail. They are actually four Classics in one volume. All the stories are reprints of the Classics Illustrated Series.

NOTE: There were also British hardback Adventure & Indian Giants in 1952, with the same covers but different contents: Adventure - 2, 7, 10; Indian - 17, 22, 37, 58. They are also rare.

Classics Illustrated Junior #504 © GIL

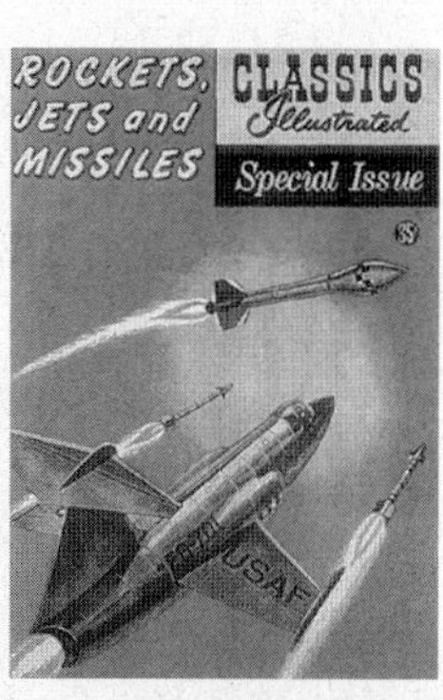

Classics Illustrated Special Issue #159A © GIL

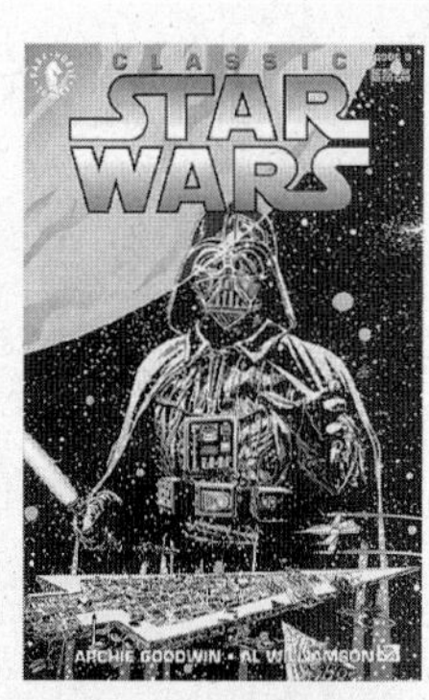

Classic Star Wars #3 © Lucasfilm

	GD 2.0	VG 4.0	FN 6.0	VF 8.0	VF/NM 9.0	NM- 9.2

"An Illustrated Library of Great Adventure Stories" - reprints of No. 6,7,8,10 (Rare); Kiefer-c 152 304 456 965 1658 2350
"An Illustrated Library of Exciting Mystery Stories" - reprints of No. 30,21,40, 13 (Rare); Blum-c 161 322 483 1030 1765 2500
"An Illustrated Library of Great Indian Stories" - reprints of No. 4,17,22,37 (Rare); Blum-c 152 304 456 965 1658 2350

INTRODUCTION TO CLASSICS ILLUSTRATED JUNIOR

Collectors of Juniors can be put into one of two categories: those who want any copy of each title, and those who want all the originals. Those seeking every original and reprint edition are a limited group, primarily because Juniors have no changes in art or covers to spark interest, and because reprints are so low in value it is difficult to get dealers to look for specific reprint editions.

In recent years it has become apparent that most serious Classics collectors seek Junior originals. Those seeking reprints seek them for low cost. This has made the previous note about the comparative market value of reprints inadequate. Three particular reprint editions are worth even more. For the 535-Twin Circle edition, see Giveaways. There are also reprint editions of 501 and 503 which have a full-page bc ad for the very rare Junior record. Those may sell as high as $10-$15 in mint. Original editions of 557 and 558 also have that ad.

There are no reprint editions of 577. The only edition, from 1969, is a 25 cent stiff-cover edition with no ad for the next issue. All other original editions have coming-next ad. But 577, like C.I. #168, was prepared in 1962 but not issued. Copies of 577 can be found in 1963 British/European series, which then continued with dozens of additional new Junior titles.

PRICES LISTED BELOW ARE FOR ORIGINAL EDITIONS, WHICH HAVE AN AD FOR THE NEXT ISSUE.

NOTE: *Non HRN 576 copies- many are written on or colored. Reprints with 576 HRN are worth about 1/3 original prices. All other HRN #'s are 1/2 original price*

CLASSICS ILLUSTRATED JUNIOR
Famous Authors Ltd. (Gilberton Publications): Oct, 1953 - Spring, 1971

501-Snow White & the Seven Dwarfs; Alex Blum-a 12 24 36 69 97 125
502-The Ugly Duckling 9 18 27 47 61 75
503-Cinderella 8 16 24 40 50 60
504-512: 504-The Pied Piper. 505-The Sleeping Beauty. 506-The Three Little Pigs. 507-Jack & the Beanstalk. 508-Goldilocks & the Three Bears. 509-Beauty and the Beast. 510-Little Red Riding Hood. 511-Puss-N Boots. 512-Rumpelstiltskin 6 12 18 27 33 38
513-Pinocchio 7 14 21 37 46 55
514-The Steadfast Tin Soldier 8 16 24 44 57 70
515-Johnny Appleseed 6 12 18 27 33 38
516-Aladdin and His Lamp 6 12 18 29 36 42
517-519: 517-The Emperor's New Clothes. 518-The Golden Goose. 519-Paul Bunyan 6 12 18 27 33 38
520-Thumbelina 6 12 18 29 36 42
521-King of the Golden River 6 12 18 27 33 38
522,523,530: 522-The Nightingale. 523-The Gallant Tailor. 530-The Golden Bird 5 10 15 24 30 35
524-The Wild Swans 6 12 18 29 36 42
525,526: 525-The Little Mermaid. 526-The Frog Prince 6 12 18 29 36 42
527-The Golden-Haired Giant 6 12 18 27 33 38
528-The Penny Prince 6 12 18 27 33 38
529-The Magic Servants 6 12 18 27 33 38
531-Rapunzel 6 12 18 27 33 38
532-534: 532-The Dancing Princesses. 533-The Magic Fountain. 534-The Golden Touch 5 10 15 23 28 32
535-The Wizard of Oz 8 16 24 44 57 70
536-The Chimney Sweep 6 12 18 27 33 38
537-The Three Fairies 6 12 18 28 34 40
538-Silly Hans 5 10 15 23 28 32
539-The Enchanted Fish 6 12 18 31 38 45
540-The Tinder-Box 6 12 18 31 38 45
541-Snow White & Rose Red 5 10 15 24 30 35
542-The Donkey's Tale 5 10 15 24 30 35
543-The House in the Woods 6 12 18 27 33 38
544-The Golden Fleece 6 12 18 31 38 45
545-The Glass Mountain 5 10 15 24 30 35
546-The Elves & the Shoemaker 5 10 15 24 30 35
547-The Wishing Table 6 12 18 27 33 38
548-551: 548-The Magic Pitcher. 549-Simple Kate. 550-The Singing Donkey. 551-The Queen Bee 5 10 15 23 28 32
552-The Three Little Dwarfs 6 12 18 27 33 38
553,556: 553-King Thrushbeard. 556-The Elf Mound 5 10 15 23 28 32
554-The Enchanted Deer 6 12 18 29 36 42
555-The Three Golden Apples 5 10 15 24 30 35
557-Silly Willy 6 12 18 28 34 40
558-The Magic Dish; L.B. Cole-c; soft and stiff-c exist on original 7 14 21 35 43 50
559-The Japanese Lantern; 1 pg. Ingels-a; L.B. Cole-c 7 14 21 35 43 50
560-The Doll Princess; L.B. Cole-c 7 14 21 35 43 50
561-Hans Humdrum; L.B. Cole-c 6 12 18 29 36 42
562-The Enchanted Pony; L.B. Cole-c 7 14 21 35 43 50
563,565-568,570: 563-The Wishing Well; L.B. Cole-c. 565-The Silly Princess; L.B. Cole-c. 566-Clumsy Hans; L.B. Cole-c. 567-The Bearskin Soldier; L.B. Cole-c. 570-The Pearl Princess 6 12 18 27 33 38
564-The Salt Mountain; L.B.Cole-c. 568-The Happy Hedgehog; L.B. Cole-c. 6 12 18 28 34 40
569,573: 569-The Three Giants.573-The Crystal Ball 5 10 15 23 28 32
571,572: 571-How Fire Came to the Indians. 572-The Drummer Boy 6 12 18 29 36 42
574-Brightboots 5 10 15 24 30 35
575-The Fearless Prince 6 12 18 28 34 40
576-The Princess Who Saw Everything 7 14 21 35 43 50
577-The Runaway Dumpling 8 16 24 44 57 70

NOTE: *Prices are for original editions. Last reprint - Spring, 1971.* **Costanza & Schaffenberger** *art in many issues.*

CLASSICS ILLUSTRATED SPECIAL ISSUE
Gilberton Co.: (Came out semi-annually) Dec, 1955 - Jul, 1962 (35¢, 100 pgs.)

129-The Story of Jesus (titled ...Special Edition) "Jesus on Mountain" cover 16 32 48 94 147 200
"Three Camels" cover (12/58) 17 34 51 98 154 210
"Mountain" cover (no date)-Has checklist on inside b/c to HRN #161 & different testimonial on back-c 13 26 39 72 101 130
"Mountain" cover (1968 re-issue; has white 50¢ circle)10 20 30 54 72 90
132A-The Story of America (6/56); Cameron-a 11 22 33 64 90 115
135A-The Ten Commandments(12/56) 11 22 33 62 86 110
138A-Adventures in Science(6/57); HRN to 137 10 20 30 58 79 100
138A-(6/57)-2nd version w/HRN to 149 7 14 21 35 43 50
138A-(12/61)-3rd version w/HRN to 149 7 14 21 35 43 50
141A-The Rough Rider (Teddy Roosevelt)(12/57); Evans-a 11 22 33 60 83 105
144A-Blazing the Trails West(6/58)- 73 pgs. of Crandall/Evans plus Severin-a 11 22 33 62 86 110
147A-Crossing the Rockies(12/58)-Crandall/Evans-a 11 22 33 60 83 105
150A-Royal Canadian Police(6/59)-Ingels, Sid Check-a 11 22 33 60 83 105
153A-Men, Guns & Cattle(12/59)-Evans-a (26 pgs.); Kinstler-a 11 22 33 60 83 105
156A-The Atomic Age(6/60)-Crandall/Evans, Torres-a 11 22 33 60 83 105
159A-Rockets, Jets and Missiles(12/60)-Evans, Morrow-a 11 22 33 60 83 105
162A-War Between the States(6/61)-Kirby & Crandall/Evans-a; Ingels-a 17 34 51 98 154 210
165A-To the Stars(12/61)-Torres, Crandall/Evans, Kirby-a 13 26 39 74 105 135
166A-World War II('62)-Torres, Crandall/Evans, Kirby-a 14 28 42 82 121 160
167A-Prehistoric World(7/62)-Torres & Crandall/Evans-a; two versions exist (HRN to 165 & HRN to 167) 14 28 42 80 115 150
nn Special Issue-The United Nations (1964; 50¢; scarce); this is actually part of the European Special Series, which cont'd on after the U.S. series stopped issuing new titles in 1962. This English edition was prepared specifically for sale at the U.N. It was printed in Norway 50 100 150 315 533 750

NOTE: *There was another U.S. Special Issue prepared in 1962 with artwork by* **Torres** *entitled World War I. Unfortunately, it was never issued in any English-language edition. It was issued in 1964 in West Germany, The Netherlands, and some Scandanavian countries, with another edition in 1974 with a new cover.*

CLASSICS LIBRARY (See King Classics)

CLASSIC STAR WARS (Also see Star Wars)
Dark Horse Comics: Aug, 1992 - No. 20, June, 1994 ($2.50)

1-Begin Star Wars strip-r by Williamson; Williamson redrew portions of the panels to fit comic book format 6.00
2-10: 8-Polybagged w/Star Wars Galaxy trading card. 8-M. Schultz-c 4.00
11-19: 13-Yeates-c. 17-M. Schultz-c. 19-Evans-c 3.00
20-($3.50, 52 pgs.)-Polybagged w/trading card 4.00
Escape To Hoth TPB ($16.95) r/#15-20 17.00
The Rebel Storm TPB - r/#8-14 17.00
Trade paperback ($29.95, slip-cased)-Reprints all movie adaptations 30.00

NOTE: *Williamson c-1-5,7,9,10,14,15,20.*

CLASSIC STAR WARS: (Title series). **Dark Horse Comics**

Claw the Unconquered #10 © DC

Clive Barker's Hellraiser #11 © Clive Barker

Cloak and Dagger #3 © MAR

	GD 2.0	VG 4.0	FN 6.0	VF 8.0	VF/NM 9.0	NM- 9.2

--A NEW HOPE, 6/94 - No. 2, 7/94 ($3.95)
1,2: 1-r/Star Wars #1-3, 7-9 publ; 2-r/Star Wars #4-6, 10-12 publ. by Marvel Comics 4.00

--DEVILWORLDS, 8/96 - No.2, 9/96 ($2.50s)1,2: r/Alan Moore-s 3.00

--HAN SOLO AT STARS' END, 3/97 - No. 3, 5/97 ($2.95)
1-3: r/strips by Alfredo Alcala 3.00

--RETURN OF THE JEDI, 10/94 - No.2, 11/94 ($3.50)
1,2: 1-r/1983-84 Marvel series; polybagged with w/trading card 3.50

--THE EARLY ADVENTURES, 8/94 - No. 9, 4/95 ($2.50)1-9 3.00

--THE EMPIRE STRIKES BACK, 8/94 - No. 2, 9/94 ($3.95)
1-r/Star Wars #39-44 published by Marvel Comics 4.00

CLASSIC X-MEN (Becomes X-Men Classic #46 on)
Marvel Comics Group: Sept, 1986 - No. 45, Mar, 1990

1-Begins-r of New X-Men 5.00
2-10: 10-Sabretooth app. 4.00
11-42,44,45: 11-1st origin of Magneto in back-up story. 17-Wolverine-c. 27-r/X-Men #121. 26-r/X-Men #120; Wolverine-c/app. 35-r/X-Men #129. 39-New Jim Lee back-up story (2nd-a on X-Men) 3.00
43-Byrne-c/a(r); ($1.75, double-size) 4.00
NOTE: ***Art Adams*** *c(p)-1-10, 12-16, 18-23.* ***Austin*** *c-10,15-21,24-28i.* ***Bolton*** *back up stories in 1-28,30-35.* ***Williamson*** *c-12-14i.*

CLAW (See Capt. Battle, Jr., Daredevil Comics & Silver Streak Comics)

CLAWS (See Wolverine & Black Cat: Claws 2 for sequel)
Marvel Comics: Oct, 2006 - No. 3, Dec, 2006 ($3.99, limited series)

1-3-Wolverine and Black Cat team-up; Linsner-a/c 4.00
Wolverine & Black Cat: Claws HC (2007, $17.99, dustjacket) r/#1-3 & bonus Linsner art 18.00

CLAW THE UNCONQUERED (See Cancelled Comic Cavalcade)
National Periodical Publications/DC Comics: 5-6/75 - No. 9, 9-10/76; No. 10, 4-5/78 - No. 12, 8-9/78

1-1st app. Claw 2 4 6 8 10 12
2-12: 3-Nudity panel. 9-Origin 1 2 3 4 5 7
NOTE: ***Giffen*** *a-8-12p.* ***Kubert*** *c-10-12.* ***Layton*** *a-9i, 12i.*

CLAW THE UNCONQUERED (See Red Sonja/Claw: The Devil's Hands)
DC Comics: Aug, 2006 - No. 6, Jan, 2007 ($2.99)

1-6: 1,2-Chuck Dixon-s/Andy Smith; two covers by Smith & Van Sciver 3.00
TPB (2007, $17.99) r/#1-6; cover gallery 18.00

CLAY CODY, GUNSLINGER
Pines Comics: Fall, 1957

1-Painted-c 6 12 18 31 38 45

CLEAN FUN, STARRING "SHOOGAFOOTS JONES"
Specialty Book Co.: 1944 (10¢, B&W, oversized covers, 24 pgs.)

nn-Humorous situations involving Negroes in the Deep South
White cover issue... 19 38 57 111 176 240
Dark grey cover issue... 20 40 60 114 182 250

CLEMENTINA THE FLYING PIG (See Dell Jr. Treasury)

CLEOPATRA (See Ideal, a Classical Comic No. 1)

CLERKS: THE COMIC BOOK (Also see Tales From the Clerks and Oni Double Feature #1)
Oni Press: Feb, 1998 ($2.95, B&W, one-shot)

1-Kevin Smith-s 2 4 6 8 10 12
1-Second printing 4.00
...Holiday Special (12/98, $2.95) Smith-s 5.00
...The Lost Scene (12/99, $2.95) Smith-s/Hester-a 5.00

CLIFFHANGER (See Battle Chasers, Crimson, and Danger Girl)
WildStorm Prod./Wizard Press: 1997 (Wizard supplement)

0-Sketchbook preview of Cliffhanger titles 6.00

CLIMAX! (Mystery)
Gillmor Magazines: July, 1955 - No. 2, Sept, 1955

1 16 32 48 94 147 200
2 14 28 42 76 108 140

CLINT (Also see Adolescent Radioactive Black Belt Hamsters)
Eclipse Comics: Sept, 1986 - No. 2, Jan, 1987 ($1.50, B&W)

1,2 3.00

CLINT & MAC (TV, Disney)
Dell Publishing Co.: No. 889, Mar, 1958

Four Color 889-Alex Toth-a, photo-c 11 22 33 71 136 200

	GD 2.0	VG 4.0	FN 6.0	VF 8.0	VF/NM 9.0	NM- 9.2

CLIVE BARKER'S BOOK OF THE DAMNED: A HELLRAISER COMPANION
Marvel Comics (Epic): Oct, 1991 - No. 3, Nov, 1992 ($4.95, semi-annual)

Volume 1-3-(52 pgs.): 1-Simon Bisley-c. 2-(4/92). 3-(11/92)-McKean-a (1 pg.) 5.00

CLIVE BARKER'S HELLRAISER (Also see Epic, Hellraiser Nightbreed –Jihad, Revelations, Son of Celluloid, Tapping the Vein & Weaveworld)
Marvel Comics (Epic Comics): 1989 - No. 20, 1993 ($4.50-6.95, mature, quarterly, 68 pgs.)

Book 1-4,10-16,18,19: Based on Hellraiser & Hellbound movies; Bolton-c/a; Spiegle & Wrightson-a (graphic album). 10-Foil-c. 12-Sam Kieth-a 6.00
Book 5-9 ($5.95): 7-Bolton-a. 8-Morrow-a 6.00
Book 17-Alex Ross-a, 34 pgs. 2 4 6 8 10 12
Book 20-By Gaiman/McKean 1 2 3 5 6 8
...Collected Best (Checker Books, '02, $21.95)-r/by various incl. Ross, Gaiman, Mignola 22.00
...Collected Best II ('03, $19.95)-r/by various incl. Bolton, L. Wachowski, Dorman 20.00
...Collected Best III ('04, $26.95)-r/by various incl. Bolton, L. Wachowski, Wrightson 27.00
...Dark Holiday Special ('92, $4.95)-Conrad-a 6.00
...Spring Slaughter 1 ('94, $6.95, 52 pgs.)-Painted-c 7.00
...Summer Special 1 ('92, $5.95, 68 pgs.) 6.00

CLIVE BARKER'S HELLRAISER
BOOM! Studios: Mar, 2011 - Present ($3.99)

1-11: 1-Barker & Monfette-s/Manco-a; preview of Hellraiser Masterpieces; 3 covers 4.00
... Masterpieces 1-9 (11/11, $3.99) reps from Marvel series. 1-Wrightson-a; Brereton-c 4.00

CLIVE BARKER'S NIGHTBREED (Also see Epic)
Marvel Comics (Epic Comics): Apr, 1990 - No. 25, Mar, 1993 ($1.95/$2.25/$2.50, mature)

1-25: 1-4-Adapt horror movie. 5-New stories; Guice-a(p) 3.00

CLIVE BARKER'S THE HARROWERS
Marvel Comics (Epic Comics): Dec, 1993 - No. 6, May, 1994 ($2.50)

1-($2.95)-Glow-in-the-dark-c; Colan-c/a in all 3.50
2-6 3.00
NOTE: ***Colan*** *a(p)-1-6; c-1-3, 4p, 5p.* ***Williamson*** *a(i)-2, 4, 5(part).*

CLOAK AND DAGGER
Ziff-Davis Publishing Co.: Fall, 1952

1-Saunders painted-c 29 58 87 172 281 390

CLOAK AND DAGGER (Also see Marvel Fanfare and Spectacular Spider-Man #64)
Marvel Comics Group: Oct, 1983 - No. 4, Jan, 1984 (Mini-series)

1-4-Austin-c/a(i) in all. 4-Origin 3.00

CLOAK AND DAGGER (2nd Series)(Also see Marvel Graphic Novel #34 & Strange Tales)
Marvel Comics Group: July, 1985 - No. 11, Jan, 1987

1-11: 9-Art Adams-p 3.00
...And Power Pack (1990, $7.95, 68 pgs.) 8.00
NOTE: ***Mignola*** *c-7, 8.*

CLOAK AND DAGGER (3rd Series listed as Mutant Misadventures Of...)

CLOAK AND DAGGER
Marvel Comics: May, 2010 ($3.99, one-shot)

1-Stuart Moore-s/Mark Brooks-a; X-Men app. 4.00

CLOBBERIN' TIME
Marvel Comics: Sept, 1995 ($1.95) (Based on card game)

nn-Overpower game guide; Ben Grimm story 3.00

CLOCK MAKER, THE
Image Comics: Jan, 2003 - No. 4, May, 2003 ($2.50, comic unfolds to 10"x13" pages)

1-4-Krueger-s 3.00
... Act Two (4/04, $4.95, standard format) Krueger-s/Matt Smith-c 5.00

CLONEZONE SPECIAL
Dark Horse Comics/First Comics: 1989 ($2.00, B&W)

1-Back-up series from Badger & Nexus 3.00

CLOSE ENCOUNTERS (See Marvel Comics Super Special & Marvel Special Edition)

CLOSE SHAVES OF PAULINE PERIL, THE (TV cartoon)
Gold Key: June, 1970 - No. 4, March, 1971

1 4 8 12 22 34 45
2-4 3 6 9 16 23 30

CLOWN COMICS (No. 1 titled Clown Comic Book)
Clown Comics/Home Comics/Harvey Publ.: 1945 - No. 3, Win, 1946

nn (#1) 13 26 39 74 105 135
2,3 9 18 27 47 61 75

CLOUDBURST

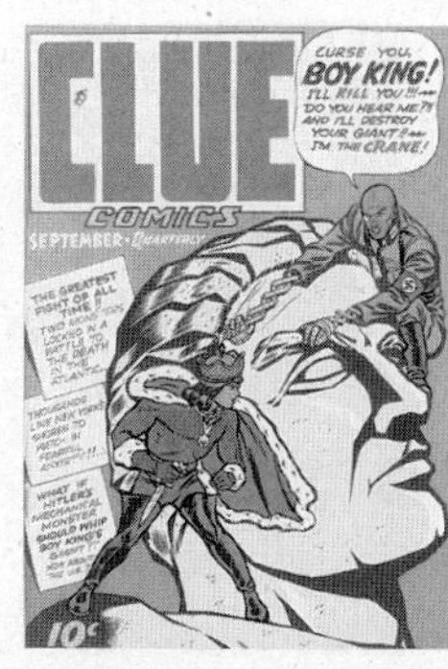

Clue Comics #5 © HP

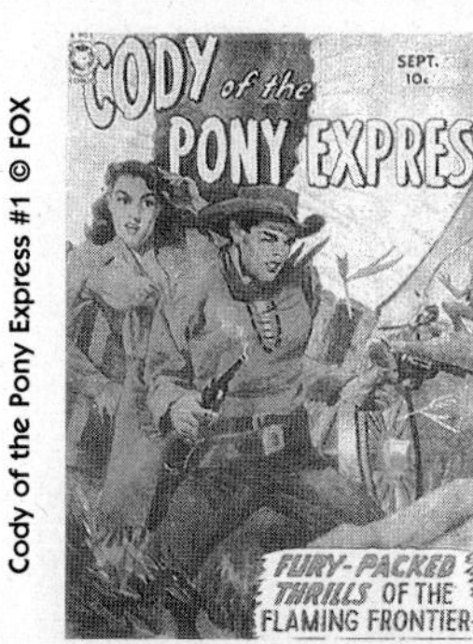

Cody of the Pony Express #1 © FOX

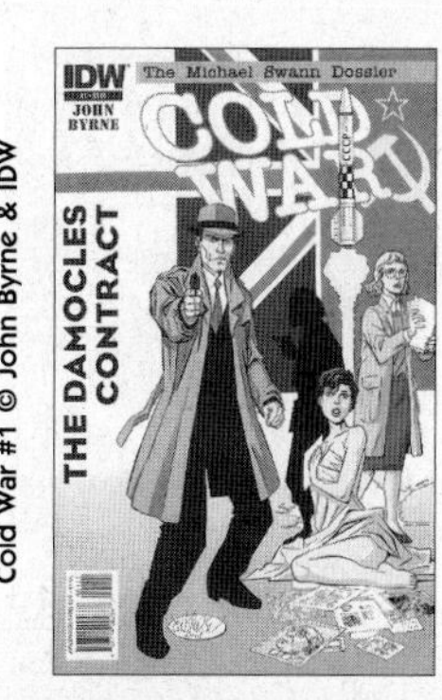

Cold War #1 © John Byrne & IDW

	GD	VG	FN	VF	VF/NM	NM-
	2.0	4.0	6.0	8.0	9.0	9.2

GD VG FN VF VF/NM NM- 2.0 4.0 6.0 8.0 9.0 9.2

Image Comics: June, 2004 ($7.95, squarebound)
1-Gray & Palmiotti-s/Shy & Gouveia-a 8.00

CLOUDFALL
Image Comics: Nov, 2003 ($4.95, B&W, squarebound)
1-Kirkman-s/Su-a/c 5.00

CLOWNS, THE (I Pagliacci)
Dark Horse Comics: 1998 ($2.95, B&W, one-shot)
1-Adaption of the opera; P. Craig Russell-script 3.00

CLUBHOUSE RASCALS (#1 titled ...Presents?) (Also see Three Rascals)
Sussex Publ. Co. (Magazine Enterprises): June, 1956 - No. 2, Oct, 1956
1-The Brain app. in both; DeCarlo-a 8 16 24 44 57 70
2 7 14 21 35 43 50

CLUB "16"
Famous Funnies: June, 1948 - No. 4, Dec, 1948
1-Teen-age humor 14 28 42 76 108 140
2-4 8 16 24 44 57 70

CLUE COMICS (Real Clue Crime V2#4 on)
Hillman Periodicals: Jan, 1943 - No. 15(V2#3), May, 1947
1-Origin The Boy King, Nightmare, Micro-Face, Twilight, & Zippo
181 362 543 1158 1979 2800
2 (scarce) 84 168 252 538 919 1300
3-5 (9/43) 45 90 135 284 480 675
6,8,9: 8-Palais-c/a(2) 34 68 102 206 336 465
7-Classic concentration camp torture-c (3/44) 71 142 213 454 777 1100
10-Origin/1st app. The Gun Master & begin series; content changes to crime
(10/46) 36 72 108 216 351 486
11 (12/46) 25 50 75 150 245 340
12-Origin Rackman; McWilliams-a, Guardineer-a(2) 31 62 93 182 296 410
V2#1-Nightmare new origin; Iron Lady app.; Simon & Kirby-a (3/47)
54 108 162 343 574 825
V2#2-S&K-a(2)-Bondage/torture-c; man attacks & kills people with electric iron.
Infantino-a 70 140 210 445 765 1085
V2#3-S&K-a(3) 55 110 165 352 601 850

CLUELESS SPRING SPECIAL (TV)
Marvel Comics: May, 1997 ($3.99, magazine sized, one-shot)
1-Photo-c from TV show 4.00

CLUTCHING HAND, THE
American Comics Group: July-Aug, 1954
1 40 80 120 246 411 575

CLYDE BEATTY COMICS (Also see Crackajack Funnies)
Commodore Productions & Artists, Inc.: October, 1953 (84 pgs.)
1-Photo front/back-c; movie scenes and comics 22 44 66 132 216 300

CLYDE CRASHCUP (TV)
Dell Publishing Co.: Aug-Oct, 1963 - No. 5, Sept-Nov, 1964
1-All written by John Stanley 7 14 21 48 79 110
2-5 4 8 12 28 44 60

COBALT BLUE (Also see Power Comics)
Innovation Publishing: Sept, 1989 - No. 2, Oct, 1989 ($1.95, 28 pgs.)
1,2-Gustovich-c/a/scripts 3.00
The Graphic Novel ($6.95, color, 52 pgs.)-r/1,2 7.00

COBB
IDW Publishing: May, 2006 - No. 3, July, 2007 ($3.99, B&W)
1-3-Beau Smith-s/Eduardo Barreto-a/c; regular and retailer incentive covers 4.00

COBRA (G.I. Joe)
IDW Publishing
... Annual 2012: The Origin of Cobra Commander (1/12, $7.99) Dixon-s 8.00

CODE NAME: ASSASSIN (See 1st Issue Special)

CODENAME: DANGER
Lodestone Publishing: Aug, 1985 - No. 4, May, 1986 ($1.50)
1-4 3.00

CODENAME: FIREARM (Also see Firearm)
Malibu Comics (Ultraverse): June, 1995 - No. 5, Sept, 1995 ($2.95, bimonthly limited series)
0-5: 0-2-Alec Swan back-up story by James Robinson 3.00
NOTE: *Perez c-0.*

CODENAME: GENETIX
Marvel Comics UK: Jan, 1993 - No. 4, May, 1993 ($1.75, limited series)
1-4: Wolverine in all 3.00

CODENAME: KNOCKOUT
DC Comics (Vertigo): No. 0, Jun, 2001 - No. 23, June, 2003 ($2.50/$2.75)
0-15: Rodi-s in all. 0-5-Small Jr. -a. 1-Two covers by Chiodo & Cho. 7,8,10,11,12-Paquette-a. 6,9,13,14-Conner-a 3.00
16-23: 16-Begin $2.75-c. 23-Last issue; JG Jones-c 3.00
...: The Devil You Say TPB (2010, $19.99) r/#0-6; intro. by Rodi 20.00

CODENAME SPITFIRE (Formerly Spitfire And The Troubleshooters)
Marvel Comics Group: No. 10, July, 1987 - No. 13, Oct, 1987
10-13: 10-Rogers-c/a (low printing) 3.50

CODENAME: STRYKE FORCE (Also See Cyberforce V1#4 & Cyberforce/Stryke Force: Opposing Forces
Image Comics (Top Cow Productions): Jan, 1994 - No. 14, Sept, 1995 ($1.95-$2.25)
0,1-14: 1-12-Silvestri stories, Peterson-a. 4-Stormwatch app. 14-Story continues in Cyberforce/Stryke Force: Opposing Forces; Turner-a 3.00
1-Gold, 1-Blue 4.00

CODE NAME: TOMAHAWK
Fantasy General Comics: Sept, 1986 ($1.75, high quality paper)
1-Sci/fi 3.00

CODE OF HONOR
Marvel Comics: Feb, 1997 - No. 4, May, 1997 ($5.95, limited series)
1-4-Fully painted by various; Dixon-s 6.00

CODY OF THE PONY EXPRESS (See Colossal Features Magazine)
Fox Features Syndicate: Sept, 1950 (See Women Outlaws)(One shot)
1-Painted-c 14 28 42 82 121 160

CODY OF THE PONY EXPRESS (Buffalo Bill...) (Outlaws of the West #11 on; Formerly Bullseye)
Charlton Comics: No. 8, Oct, 1955; No. 9, Jan, 1956; No. 10, June, 1956
8-Bullseye on splash pg; not S&K-a 8 16 24 44 57 70
9,10: Buffalo Bill app. in all 6 12 18 29 36 42

CODY STARBUCK (1st app. in Star Reach #1)
Star Reach Productions: July, 1978
nn-Howard Chaykin-c/a 3 6 9 14 20 25
2nd printing 2 4 6 8 10 12
NOTE: *Both printings say First Printing. True first printing is on lower-grade paper, somewhat off-register, and snow in snow sequence has green tint.*

CO-ED ROMANCES
P. L. Publishing Co.: November, 1951
1 9 18 27 52 69 85

COFFEE WORLD
World Comics: Oct, 1995 ($1.50, B&W, anthology)
1-Shannon Wheeler's Too Much Coffee Man story 3.00

COFFIN, THE
Oni Press: Sept, 2000 - No. 4, May, 2001 ($2.95, B&W, limited series)
1-4-Hester-s/Huddleston-a 3.00
TPB (8/01, $11.95, TPB) r/#1-4 12.00

COLD WAR
IDW Publishing: Oct, 2011 - Present ($3.99, limited series)
1-3-John Byrne-s/a/c; two covers on each 4.00

COLLECTORS DRACULA, THE
Millennium Publications: 1994 - No. 2, 1994 ($3.95, color/B&W, 52 pgs., limited series)
1,2-Bolton-a (7 pgs.) 4.00

COLLECTORS ITEM CLASSICS (See Marvel Collectors Item Classics)

COLORS IN BLACK
Dark Horse Comics: Mar, 1995 - No. 4, June, 1995 ($2.95, limited series)
1-4 3.00

COLOSSAL FEATURES MAGAZINE (Formerly I Loved) (See Cody of the Pony Express)
Fox Features Syndicate: No. 33, 5/50 - No. 34, 7/50; No. 3, 9/50 (Based on Columbia serial)
33,34: Cody of the Pony Express begins. 33-Painted-c. 34-Photo-c
14 28 42 81 118 155
3-Authentic criminal cases 14 28 42 81 118 155

COLOSSAL SHOW, THE (TV cartoon)

Combat #1 © MAR

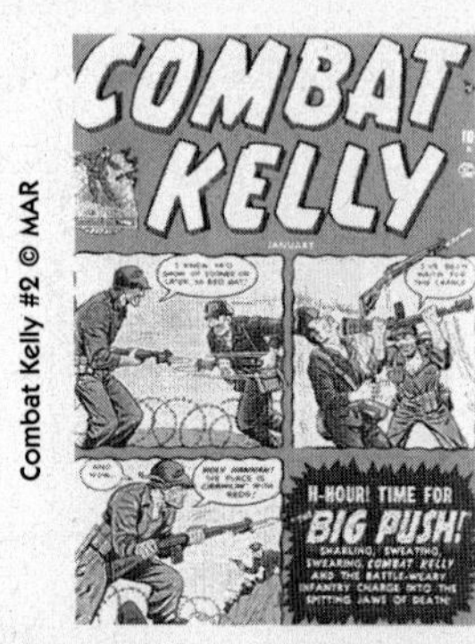

Combat Kelly #2 © MAR

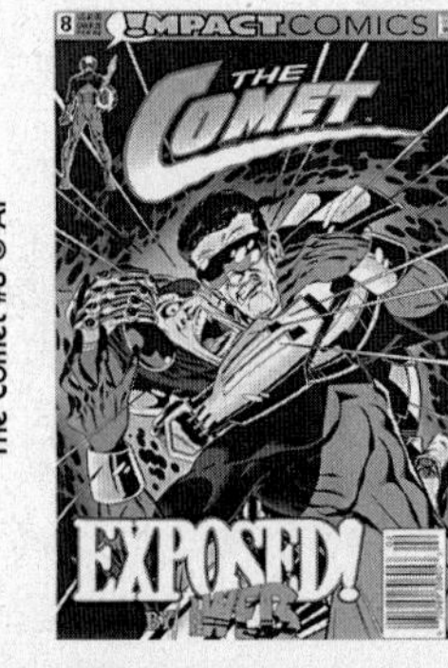

The Comet #8 © AP

Gold Key: Oct, 1969

	GD 2.0	VG 4.0	FN 6.0	VF 8.0	VF/NM 9.0	NM- 9.2
1	5	10	15	32	51	70

COLOSSUS (See X-Men)
Marvel Comics: Oct, 1997 ($2.99, 48 pgs., one-shot)

	GD 2.0	VG 4.0	FN 6.0	VF 8.0	VF/NM 9.0	NM- 9.2
1-Raab-s/Hitch & Neary-a, wraparound-c						4.00

COLOSSUS COMICS (See Green Giant & Motion Picture Funnies Weekly)
Sun Publications (Funnies, Inc.?): March, 1940

	GD 2.0	VG 4.0	FN 6.0	VF 8.0	VF/NM 9.0	NM- 9.2
1-(Scarce)-Tulpa of Tsang(hero); Colossus app.	811	1622	2433	5920	10,460	15,000

NOTE: *Cover by artist that drew Colossus in Green Giant Comics.*

COLOUR OF MAGIC, THE (Terry Pratchett's...)
Innovation Publishing: 1991 - No. 4, 1991 ($2.50, limited series)

	GD 2.0	VG 4.0	FN 6.0	VF 8.0	VF/NM 9.0	NM- 9.2
1-4: Adapts 1st novel of the Discworld series						3.00

COLT .45 (TV)
Dell Publishing Co.: No. 924, 8/58 - No. 1058, 11-1/59-60; No. 4, 2-4/60 - No. 9, 5-7/61

	GD 2.0	VG 4.0	FN 6.0	VF 8.0	VF/NM 9.0	NM- 9.2
Four Color 924(#1)-Wayde Preston photo-c on all	10	20	30	66	121	175
Four Color 1004,1058: 1004-Photo-b/c	8	16	24	55	93	130
4,5,7-9	8	16	24	55	93	130
6-Toth-a	9	18	27	58	99	140

COLUMBIA COMICS
William H. Wise Co.: 1943

	GD 2.0	VG 4.0	FN 6.0	VF 8.0	VF/NM 9.0	NM- 9.2
1-Joe Palooka, Charlie Chan, Capt. Yank, Sparky Watts, Dixie Dugan app.	27	54	81	160	263	365

COMANCHE
Dell Publishing Co.: No. 1350, Apr-Jun, 1962

	GD 2.0	VG 4.0	FN 6.0	VF 8.0	VF/NM 9.0	NM- 9.2
Four Color 1350-Disney movie; reprints FC #966 with title change from "Tonka" to "Comanche"; Sal Mineo photo-c	5	10	15	35	55	75

COMANCHEROS, THE
Dell Publishing Co.: No. 1300, Mar-May, 1962

	GD 2.0	VG 4.0	FN 6.0	VF 8.0	VF/NM 9.0	NM- 9.2
Four Color 1300-Movie, John Wayne photo-c	13	26	39	86	183	280

COMBAT
Atlas Comics (ANC): June, 1952 - No. 11, April, 1953

	GD 2.0	VG 4.0	FN 6.0	VF 8.0	VF/NM 9.0	NM- 9.2
1	27	54	81	160	263	365
2-Heath-c/a	15	30	45	86	133	180
3,5-9,11: 3-Romita-a. 6-Robinson-c; Romita-a	12	24	36	69	97	125
4-Krigstein-a	13	26	39	72	101	130
10-B&W and color illos. in **POP**; Sale-a, Forte-a	13	26	39	74	105	135

NOTE: *Combat Casey in 7-11.* ***Heath** a-2, 3; c-1, 2, 5, 9.* ***Maneely** a-1; c-3, 10.* ***Pakula** a-1.* ***Reinman** a-1.*

COMBAT
Dell Publishing Co.: Oct-Nov, 1961 - No. 40, Oct, 1973 (No #9)

	GD 2.0	VG 4.0	FN 6.0	VF 8.0	VF/NM 9.0	NM- 9.2
1	7	14	21	45	73	100
2,3,5	4	8	12	26	41	55
4-John F. Kennedy c/story (P.T. 109)	5	10	15	34	55	75
6,7,8(4-6/63), 8(7-9/63)	4	8	12	24	37	50
10-26: 26-Last 12¢ issue	3	6	9	20	30	40
27-40(reprints #1-14). 30-r/#4	3	6	9	14	19	24

COMBAT CASEY (Formerly War Combat)
Atlas Comics (SAI): No. 6, Jan, 1953 - No. 34, July, 1957

	GD 2.0	VG 4.0	FN 6.0	VF 8.0	VF/NM 9.0	NM- 9.2
6 (Indicia shows 1/52 in error)	19	36	57	111	176	240
7-R.Q. Sale-a	12	24	36	67	94	120
8-Used in **POP**, pg. 94	11	22	33	62	86	110
9,10,13-19-Violent art by R.Q. Sale; Battle Brady x-over #10	14	28	42	80	115	150
11,12,20-Last Precode (2/55)	10	20	30	56	76	95
21-34: 22,25-R.Q. Sale-a	9	18	27	52	69	85

NOTE: ***Everett** a-6.* ***Heath** c-10, 17, 19, 23, 30.* ***Maneely** c-6, 8, 15.* ***Powell** a-29(5), 30(5), 34.* ***Severin** c-26, 33, 34.*

COMBAT KELLY
Atlas Comics (SPI): Nov, 1951 - No. 44, Aug, 1957

	GD 2.0	VG 4.0	FN 6.0	VF 8.0	VF/NM 9.0	NM- 9.2
1-1st app. Combat Kelly; Heath-a	32	64	96	192	314	435
2	17	34	51	98	154	210
3-10	14	28	42	80	115	150
11-Used in **POP**, pgs. 94,95 plus color illo.	14	28	42	78	112	145
12-Color illo. in **POP**	13	26	39	74	105	135
13-16	11	22	33	62	86	110
17-Violent art by R. Q. Sale; Combat Casey app.	14	28	42	82	121	160
18-20,22-44: 18-Battle Brady app. 28-Last precode (1/55). 38-Green Berets story (8/56)	10	20	30	56	76	95
21-Transvestism-c	10	20	30	58	79	100

NOTE: ***Berg** a-8, 12-14, 15-17, 19-23, 25, 26, 28, 31-37, 39, 41-44; c-2.* ***Colan** a-42.* ***Heath** a-4, 18; c-31.* ***Lawrence** a-23.* ***Maneely** a-4(2), 6, 7(3), 8; c-4, 5, 7, 8, 10, 25, 29, 39.* ***R.Q. Sale** a-17, 25.* ***Severin** c-41, 42.* ***Whitney** a-5.*

COMBAT KELLY (...and the Deadly Dozen)
Marvel Comics Group: June, 1972 - No. 9, Oct, 1973

	GD 2.0	VG 4.0	FN 6.0	VF 8.0	VF/NM 9.0	NM- 9.2
1-Intro & origin new Combat Kelly; Ayers/Mooney-a; Severin-c (20¢)	3	6	9	20	30	40
2,5-8	2	4	6	11	16	20
3,4: 3-Origin. 4-Sgt. Fury-c/s	3	6	9	14	19	24
9-Death of the Deadly Dozen	3	6	9	16	23	30

COMBAT ZONE: TRUE TALES OF GIS IN IRAQ
Marvel Comics: 2005 ($19.99, squarebound)

	GD 2.0	VG 4.0	FN 6.0	VF 8.0	VF/NM 9.0	NM- 9.2
Vol. 1-Karl Zinsmeister scripts adapted from his non-fiction books; Dan Jurgens-a						20.00

COMBINED OPERATIONS (See The Story of the Commandos)

COMEBACK (See Zane Grey 4-Color 357)

COMEDY CARNIVAL
St. John Publishing Co.: no date (1950's) (100 pgs.)

	GD 2.0	VG 4.0	FN 6.0	VF 8.0	VF/NM 9.0	NM- 9.2
nn-Contains rebound St. John comics	36	72	108	211	343	475

COMEDY COMICS (1st Series) (Daring Mystery #1-8) (Becomes Margie Comics #35 on)
Timely Comics (TCI 9,10): No. 9, April, 1942 - No. 34, Fall, 1946

	GD 2.0	VG 4.0	FN 6.0	VF 8.0	VF/NM 9.0	NM- 9.2
9-(Scarce)-The Fin by Everett, Capt. Dash, Citizen V, & The Silver Scorpion app.; Wolverton-a; 1st app. Comedy Kid; satire on Hitler & Stalin; The Fin, Citizen V & Silver Scorpion cont. from Daring Mystery	300	600	900	1965	3408	4850
10-(Scarce)-Origin The Fourth Musketeer, Victory Boys; Monstro, the Mighty app.	216	432	648	1372	2361	3350
11-Vagabond, Stuporman app.	55	110	165	352	601	850
12,13	20	40	60	114	182	250
14-Origin/1st app. Super Rabbit (3/43) plus-c	60	120	180	381	653	925
15-19	19	38	57	109	172	235
20-Hitler parody-c	29	58	87	170	278	385
21-Tojo-c	21	42	63	122	199	275
22-Hitler parody-c	26	52	78	154	252	350
23-32	14	28	42	81	118	155
33-Kurtzman-a (5 pgs.)	15	30	45	86	133	180
34-Intro Margie; Wolverton-a (5 pgs.)	25	50	75	150	245	340

COMEDY COMICS (2nd Series)
Marvel Comics (ACI): May, 1948 - No. 10, Jan, 1950

	GD 2.0	VG 4.0	FN 6.0	VF 8.0	VF/NM 9.0	NM- 9.2
1-Hedy, Tessie, Millie begin; Kurtzman's "Hey Look" (he draws himself)	40	80	120	246	411	575
2	19	38	57	109	172	235
3,4-Kurtzman's "Hey Look" (?&3)	19	38	57	112	179	245
5-10	13	26	39	74	105	135

COMET, THE (See The Mighty Crusaders & Pep Comics #1)
Red Circle Comics (Archie): Oct, 1983 - No. 2, Dec, 1983

	GD 2.0	VG 4.0	FN 6.0	VF 8.0	VF/NM 9.0	NM- 9.2
1-Re-intro & origin The Comet; The American Shield begins. Nino & Infantino art in both. Hangman in both						6.00
2-Origin continues.						5.00

COMET, THE
DC Comics (Impact Comics): July, 1991 - No. 18, Dec, 1992 ($1.00/$1.25)

	GD 2.0	VG 4.0	FN 6.0	VF 8.0	VF/NM 9.0	NM- 9.2
1						4.00
2-18: 4-Black Hood app. 6-Re-intro Hangman. 8-Web x-over. 10-Contains Crusaders trading card. 4-Origin. Netzer(Nasser) c(p)-11,14-17						3.00
Annual 1 (1992, $2.50, 68 pgs.)-Contains Impact trading card; Shield back-up story						4.00

COMET MAN, THE (Movie)
Marvel Comics Group: Feb, 1987 - No. 6, July, 1987 (limited series)

	GD 2.0	VG 4.0	FN 6.0	VF 8.0	VF/NM 9.0	NM- 9.2
1-6: 3-Hulk app. 4-She-Hulk shower scene-c/s. Fantastic 4 app. 5-Fantastic 4 app.						3.00

NOTE: ***Kelley Jones** a-1-6p.*

COMIC ALBUM (Also see Disney Comic Album)
Dell Publishing Co.: Mar-May, 1958 - No. 18, June-Aug, 1962

	GD 2.0	VG 4.0	FN 6.0	VF 8.0	VF/NM 9.0	NM- 9.2
1-Donald Duck	9	18	27	58	99	140
2-Bugs Bunny	5	10	15	32	51	70
3-Donald Duck	7	14	21	46	76	105
4-6,8-10: 4-Tom & Jerry. 5-Woody Woodpecker. 6,10-Bugs Bunny. 8-Tom & Jerry. 9-Woody Woodpecker	4	8	12	28	44	60
7,11,15: Popeye. 11-(9-11/60)	6	12	18	33	49	65
12-14: 12-Tom & Jerry. 13-Woody Woodpecker. 14-Bugs Bunny	5	10	15	30	48	60
16-Flintstones (12-2/61-62)-3rd app. Early Cave Kids app.	8	16	24	53	89	125

Comic Cavalcade #5 © DC

The Comics #2 © DELL

Comics' Greatest World #1: X © DH

	GD 2.0	VG 4.0	FN 6.0	VF 8.0	VF/NM 9.0	NM- 9.2
17-Space Mouse (3rd app.)	5	10	15	32	51	70
18-Three Stooges; photo-c	8	16	24	53	89	125

COMIC BOOK
Marvel Comics-#1/Dark Horse Comics-#2: 1995 ($5.95, oversize)

	GD 2.0	VG 4.0	FN 6.0	VF 8.0	VF/NM 9.0	NM- 9.2
1-Spumco characters by John K.	1	2	3	4	5	7
2-(Dark Horse)						6.00

COMIC BOOK GUY: THE COMIC BOOK (BONGO COMICS PRESENTS...) (Simpsons)
Bongo Comics: 2010 - No. 5, 2010 ($3.99/$2.99, limited series)

	GD 2.0	VG 4.0	FN 6.0	VF 8.0	VF/NM 9.0	NM- 9.2
1-($3.99) Four-layer cover w/classic swipes incl. FF#1; intro Graphic Novel Kid						4.00
2-($2.99) 2-Stan Lee cameo. 3-Includes Little Lulu spoof. 4-CBG origin						3.00

COMIC CAPERS
Red Circle Mag./Marvel Comics: Fall, 1944 - No. 6, Fall, 1946

	GD 2.0	VG 4.0	FN 6.0	VF 8.0	VF/NM 9.0	NM- 9.2
1-Super Rabbit, The Creeper, Silly Seal, Ziggy Pig, Sharpy Fox begin	32	64	96	188	307	425
2	17	34	51	98	154	210
3-6: 4-(Summer 1945)	15	30	45	83	124	165

COMIC CAVALCADE
All-American/National Periodical Publications: Winter, 1942-43 - No. 63, June-July, 1954 (Contents change with No. 30, Dec-Jan, 1948-49 on)

	GD 2.0	VG 4.0	FN 6.0	VF 8.0	VF/NM 9.0	NM- 9.2
1-The Flash, Green Lantern, Wonder Woman, Wildcat, The Black Pirate by Moldoff (also #2), Ghost Patrol, and Red White & Blue begin; Scribbly app.; Minute Movie	865	1730	2595	6315	11,158	16,000
2-Mutt & Jeff begin; last Ghost Patrol & Black Pirate; Minute Movies	245	490	735	1568	2684	3800
3-Hop Harrigan & Sargon, the Sorcerer begin; The King app.	161	322	483	1030	1765	2500
4,5: 4-The Gay Ghost, The King, Scribbly, & Red Tornado app. 5-Christmas-c. 5-Prints ad for Jr. JSA membership kit that includes "The Minute Man Answers The Call"	145	290	435	921	1586	2250
6-10: 7-Red Tornado & Black Pirate app.; last Scribbly. 9-Fat & Slat app.; X-Mas-c	116	232	348	742	1271	1800
11,12,14: 12-Last Red White & Blue	97	194	291	621	1061	1500
13-Solomon Grundy app.; X-Mas-c	181	362	543	1158	1979	2800
15-Just a Story begins	98	196	294	622	1074	1525
16-20: 19-Christmas-c	90	180	270	576	988	1400
21-23: 22-Johnny Peril begins. 23-Harry Lampert-c (Toth swipes)	86	172	258	546	936	1325
24-Solomon Grundy x-over in Green Lantern	116	232	348	742	1271	1800
25-28: 25-Black Canary app.; X-Mas-c. 26-28-Johnny Peril app. 28-Last Mutt & Jeff	77	154	231	493	847	1200
29-(10-11/48)-Last Flash, Wonder Woman, Green Lantern & Johnny Peril; Wonder Woman invents "Thinking Machine"; 2nd computer in comics (after Flash Comics #52); Leave It to Binky story (early app.)	90	180	270	576	988	1400
30-(12-1/48-49)-The Fox & the Crow, Dodo & the Frog & Nutsy Squirrel begin	41	82	123	256	428	600
31-35	23	46	69	136	223	310
36-49: 41-Last squarebound issue	17	34	51	100	158	215
50-62(Scarce)	21	42	63	122	199	275
63(Rare)	34	68	102	204	332	460

NOTE: *Grossman a-30-63.* ***E.E. Hibbard*** *c-(Flash only)-1-4, 7-14, 16-19, 21.* ***Sheldon Mayer*** *a(2-3)-40-63.* ***Moulson*** *c(G.L.)-7, 15.* ***Nodell*** *c(G.L.)-9.* ***H.G. Peter*** *c(W. Woman only)-1, 3-21, 24.* ***Post*** *a-31, 36.* ***Purcell*** *c(G.L.)-2-5, 10.* ***Reinman*** *a(Green Lantern)-4-6, 8, 9, 13, 15-21; c(Gr. Lantern)-6, 8, 19.* ***Toth*** *a(Green Lantern)-26-28; c-27. Atom app.-22, 23.*

COMIC COMICS
Fawcett Publications: Apr, 1946 - No. 10, Feb, 1947

	GD 2.0	VG 4.0	FN 6.0	VF 8.0	VF/NM 9.0	NM- 9.2
1-Captain Kid; Nutty Comics #1 in indicia	15	30	45	85	130	175
2-10-Wolverton-a, 4 pgs. each. 5-Captain Kidd app. Mystic Moot by Wolverton in #2-10?	15	30	45	84	127	170

COMIC LAND
Fact and Fiction Publ.: March, 1946

	GD 2.0	VG 4.0	FN 6.0	VF 8.0	VF/NM 9.0	NM- 9.2
1-Sandusky & the Senator, Sam Stupor, Sleuth, Marvin the Great, Sir Passer, Phineas Gruff app.; Irv Tirman & Perry Williams art	15	30	45	85	130	175

COMICO CHRISTMAS SPECIAL
Comico: Dec, 1988 ($2.50, 44 pgs.)

	GD 2.0	VG 4.0	FN 6.0	VF 8.0	VF/NM 9.0	NM- 9.2
1-Rude/Williamson-a; Dave Stevens-c						4.00

COMICO COLLECTION (Also see Grendel)
Comico: 1987 ($9.95, slipcased collection)

	GD 2.0	VG 4.0	FN 6.0	VF 8.0	VF/NM 9.0	NM- 9.2
nn-Contains exclusive Grendel: Devil's Vagary, 9 random Comico comics, a poster and newsletter in black slipcase w/silver ink						25.00

COMICO PRIMER (See Primer)

COMIC PAGES (Formerly Funny Picture Stories)
Centaur Publications: V3#4, July, 1939 - V3#6, Dec, 1939

	GD 2.0	VG 4.0	FN 6.0	VF 8.0	VF/NM 9.0	NM- 9.2
V3#4-Bob Wood-a	55	110	165	352	601	850
5,6: 6-Schwab-c	48	96	144	302	514	725

COMICS (See All Good)

COMICS, THE
Dell Publ. Co.: Mar, 1937 - No. 11, Nov, 1938 (Newspaper strip-r; bi-monthly)

	GD 2.0	VG 4.0	FN 6.0	VF 8.0	VF/NM 9.0	NM- 9.2
1-1st app. Tom Mix in comics; Wash Tubbs, Tom Beatty, Myra North, Arizona Kid, Erik Noble & International Spy w/Doctor Doom begin	187	374	561	1197	2049	2900
2	82	164	246	528	902	1275
3-11: 3-Alley Oop begins	66	132	198	419	722	1025

COMICS AND STORIES (See Walt Disney's Comics and Stories)

COMICS & STORIES (Also see Wolf & Red)
Dark Horse Comics: Apr, 1996 - No. 4, July, 1996 ($2.95, lim. series) (Created by Tex Avery)

	GD 2.0	VG 4.0	FN 6.0	VF 8.0	VF/NM 9.0	NM- 9.2
1-4: Wolf & Red app; reads Comics and Stories on-c. 1-Terry Moore-a. 2-Reed Waller-a						3.00

COMICS CALENDAR, THE (The 1946...)
True Comics Press (ordered through the mail): 1946 (25¢, 116 pgs.) (Stapled at top)

	GD 2.0	VG 4.0	FN 6.0	VF 8.0	VF/NM 9.0	NM- 9.2
nn-(Rare) Has a "strip" story for every day of the year in color	40	80	120	242	401	560

COMICS DIGEST (Pocket size)
Parents' Magazine Institute: Winter, 1942-43 (B&W, 100 pgs)

	GD 2.0	VG 4.0	FN 6.0	VF 8.0	VF/NM 9.0	NM- 9.2
1-Reprints from True Comics (non-fiction World War II stories)	10	20	30	54	72	90

COMICS EXPRESS
Eclipse Comics: Nov, 1989 - No. 2, Jan, 1990 ($2.95, B&W, 68pgs.)

	GD 2.0	VG 4.0	FN 6.0	VF 8.0	VF/NM 9.0	NM- 9.2
1,2: Collection of strip-r; 2(12/89-c, 1/90 inside)						4.00

COMICS FOR KIDS
London Publ. Co./Timely: 1945 (no month); No. 2, Sum, 1945 (Funny animal)

	GD 2.0	VG 4.0	FN 6.0	VF 8.0	VF/NM 9.0	NM- 9.2
1,2-Puffy Pig, Sharpy Fox	19	38	57	111	176	240

COMICS' GREATEST WORLD
Dark Horse Comics: Jun, 1993 - V4#4, Sept, 1993 ($1.00, weekly, lim. series)

	GD 2.0	VG 4.0	FN 6.0	VF 8.0	VF/NM 9.0	NM- 9.2
Arcadia (Wk 1): V1#1,2,4: 1-X: Frank Miller-c. 2-Pit Bulls. 4-Monster.						3.00
1-B&W Press Proof Edition (1500 copies)	1	3	4	6	8	10
1-Silver-c; distr. retailer bonus w/print & cards	1	2	3	5	6	8
3-Ghost, Dorman-c; Hughes-a						4.00
Retailer's Prem. Emb. Silver Foil Logo-r/V1#1-4	1	3	4	6	8	10
Golden City (Wk 2: V2#1-4: 1-Rebel; Ordway-c. 2-Mecha; Dave Johnson-c. 3-Titan; Walt Simonson-c. 4-Catalyst; Perez-c.						3.00
1-Gold-c; distr. retailer bonus w/print & cards.						6.00
Retailer's Prem. Embos. Gold Foil Logo-r/V2#1-4	1	2	3	5	6	8
Steel Harbor (Week 3): V3#1-Barb Wire; Dorman-c; Gulacy-a(p)						4.00
2-4: 2-The Machine. 3-Wolfgang. 4-Motorhead						3.00
1-Silver-c; distr. retailer bonus w/print & cards	1	2	3	5	6	8
Retailer's Prem. Emb. Red Foil Logo-r/V3#1-4.	1	3	4	6	8	10
Vortex (Week 4): V4#1-4: 1-Division 13; Dorman-c. 2-Hero Zero; Art Adams-c. 3-King Tiger; Chadwick-a(p); Darrow-c. 4-Vortex; Miller-c.						3.00
1-Gold-c; distr. retailer bonus w/print & cards.						6.00
Retailer's Prem. Emb. Blue Foil Logo-r/V4#1-4.	1	2	3	5	6	8

COMICS' GREATEST WORLD: OUT OF THE VORTEX (See Out of The Vortex)

COMICS HITS (See Harvey Comics Hits)

COMICS MAGAZINE, THE (...Funny Pages #3)(Funny Pages #6 on)
Comics Magazine Co. (1st Comics Mag./Centaur Publ.): May, 1936 - No. 5, Sept, 1936 (Paper covers)

	GD 2.0	VG 4.0	FN 6.0	VF 8.0	VF/NM 9.0	NM- 9.2
1-1st app. Dr. Mystic (a.k.a. Dr. Occult) by Siegel & Shuster (the 1st app. of a Superman prototype in comics). Dr. Mystic is not in costume but later appears in costume as a more pronounced prototype in More Fun #14-17. (1st episode of "The Koth and the Seven"; continues in More Fun #14; originally scheduled for publication at DC). 1 pg. Kelly-a; Sheldon Mayer-a	3600	7200	10,800	21,000	-	-
2-Federal Agent (a.k.a. Federal Men) by Siegel & Shuster; 1 pg. Kelly-a	370	740	1110	2220	2960	3700
3-5	320	640	960	1920	2560	3200

COMICS NOVEL (Anarcho, Dictator of Death)
Fawcett Publications: 1947

	GD 2.0	VG 4.0	FN 6.0	VF 8.0	VF/NM 9.0	NM- 9.2
1-All Radar; 51 pg anti-fascism story	33	66	99	194	317	440

Comics on Parade #23 © UFS

Commander Battle and the Atomic Sub #3 © ACG

Complete Love Magazine V32 #2 © ACE

COMICS ON PARADE (No. 30 on are a continuation of Single Series)
United Features Syndicate: Apr, 1938 - No. 104, Feb, 1955

	GD 2.0	VG 4.0	FN 6.0	VF 8.0	VF/NM 9.0	NM- 9.2
1-Tarzan by Foster; Captain & the Kids, Little Mary Mixup, Abbie & Slats, Ella Cinders, Broncho Bill, Li'l Abner begin	371	742	1113	2600	4550	6500
2 (Tarzan & others app. on-c of #1-3,17)	129	258	387	826	1413	2000
3	97	194	291	621	1061	1500
4,5	77	154	231	493	847	1200
6-10	53	106	159	334	567	800
11-16,18-20	42	84	126	265	445	625
17-Tarzan-c	52	104	156	322	549	775
21-29: 22-Son of Tarzan begins. 22,24,28-Tailspin Tommy-c. 29-Last Tarzan issue	36	72	108	216	351	485
30-Li'l Abner	20	40	60	114	182	250
31-The Captain & the Kids	15	30	45	85	130	175
32-Nancy & Fritzi Ritz	14	28	42	78	112	145
33,36,39,42-Li'l Abner	16	32	48	94	147	200
34,37,40-The Captain & the Kids (10/41,6/42,3/43)	15	30	45	83	124	165
35,38-Nancy & Fritzi Ritz. 38-Infinity-c	14	28	42	76	108	140
41-Nancy & Fritzi Ritz	11	22	33	60	83	105
43-The Captain & the Kids	15	30	45	83	124	165
44 (3/44),47,50: Nancy & Fritzi Ritz	11	22	33	60	83	105
45-Li'l Abner	15	30	45	84	127	170
46,49-The Captain & the Kids	13	26	39	74	105	135
48-Li'l Abner (3/45)	15	30	45	84	127	170
51,54-Li'l Abner	14	28	42	76	108	140
52-The Captain & the Kids (3/46)	10	20	30	56	76	95
53,55,57-Nancy & Fritzi Ritz	10	20	30	56	76	95
56-The Captain & the Kids (r/Sparkler)	10	20	30	56	76	95
58-Li'l Abner; continues as Li'l Abner #61?	14	28	42	76	108	140
59-The Captain & the Kids	9	18	27	47	61	75
60-70-Nancy & Fritzi Ritz	8	16	24	44	57	70
71-99,101-104-Nancy & Sluggo: 71-76-Nancy only	8	16	24	42	54	65
100-Nancy & Sluggo	14	28	42	76	108	140
Special Issue, 7/46; Summer, 1948 - The Captain & the Kids app.	14	28	42	76	108	140
NOTE: Bound Volume (Very Rare) includes No. 1-12; bound by publisher in pictorial comic boards & distributed at the 1939 World's Fair and through mail order from ads in comic books (also see Tip Top)	297	594	891	1901	3251	4600

NOTE: *Li'l Abner reprinted from Tip Top.*

COMICS READING LIBRARIES (See the Promotional Comics section)

COMICS REVUE
St. John Publ. Co. (United Features Synd.): June, 1947 - No. 5, Jan, 1948

	GD 2.0	VG 4.0	FN 6.0	VF 8.0	VF/NM 9.0	NM- 9.2
1-Ella Cinders & Blackie	12	24	36	67	94	120
2,4: 2-Hap Hopper (7/47). 4-Ella Cinders (9/47)	9	18	27	47	61	75
3,5: 3-Iron Vic (8/47). 5-Gordo No. 1 (1/48)	8	16	24	44	57	70

COMIC STORY PAINT BOOK
Samuel Lowe Co.: 1943 (Large size, 68 pgs.)

	GD 2.0	VG 4.0	FN 6.0	VF 8.0	VF/NM 9.0	NM- 9.2
1055-Captain Marvel & a Captain Marvel Jr. story to read & color; 3 panels in color per pg. (reprints)	77	154	231	493	847	1200

COMIX BOOK
Marvel Comics Group/Krupp Comics Works No. 4,5: 1974 - No. 5, 1976 ($1.00, B&W, magazine) (#1-3 newsstand; #4,5 were direct distribution only)

	GD 2.0	VG 4.0	FN 6.0	VF 8.0	VF/NM 9.0	NM- 9.2
1-Underground comic artists; 2 pgs. Wolverton-a	3	6	9	16	22	28
2,3: 2-Wolverton-a (1 pg.)	3	6	9	14	19	24
4(2/76), 4(5/76), 5 (Low distribution)	3	6	9	16	23	30

NOTE: *Print run No. 1-3: 200-250M; No. 4&5: 10M each.*

COMIX INTERNATIONAL
Warren Magazines: Jul, 1974 - No. 5, Spring, 1977 (Full color, stiff-c, mail only)

	GD 2.0	VG 4.0	FN 6.0	VF 8.0	VF/NM 9.0	NM- 9.2
1-Low distribution; all Corben story remainders from Warren; Corben-c on all	9	18	27	65	113	165
2,4: 2-Two Dracula stories; Wood, Wrightson-r; Crandall-a; Maroto-a. 4-Printing w/ 3 Corben sty	6	12	18	37	59	80
3-5: 3-Dax story. 4-(printing without Corben story). 4-Crandall-a. 4,5-Vampirella stories. 5-Spirit story; Eisner-a	5	10	15	30	48	65

NOTE: *No. 4 had two printings with extra* ***Corben*** *story in one. No. 3 may also have a variation. No. 3 has two Jeff Jones reprints from Vampirella.*

COMMANDER BATTLE AND THE ATOMIC SUB
Amer. Comics Group (Titan Publ. Co.): Jul-Aug, 1954 - No. 7, Aug-Sep, 1955

	GD 2.0	VG 4.0	FN 6.0	VF 8.0	VF/NM 9.0	NM- 9.2
1 (3-D effect)-Moldoff flying saucer-c	49	98	147	309	522	735
2,4-7: 2-Moldoff-c. 4-(1-2/55)-Last pre-code; Landau-a. 5-3-D effect story (2 pgs.). 6,7-Landau-a. 7-Flying saucer-c	32	64	96	188	307	425
3-H-Bomb-c; Atomic Sub becomes Atomic Spaceship	33	66	99	194	317	440

COMMANDO ADVENTURES
Atlas Comics (MMC): June, 1957 - No. 2, Aug, 1957

	GD 2.0	VG 4.0	FN 6.0	VF 8.0	VF/NM 9.0	NM- 9.2
1-Severin-c	14	28	42	78	112	145
2-Severin-c; Reinman & Romita-a; Drucker-a?	10	20	30	54	72	90

COMMANDOS
DC Comics: Oct. 1942

1-Ashcan comic, not distributed to newsstands, only for in-house use. Cover art is Boy Commandos #1 with interior being a Boy Commandos story from an unidentified issue of Detective Comics (no known sales)

COMMANDO YANK (See The Mighty Midget Comics & Wow Comics)

COMMON GROUNDS
Image Comics (Top Cow): Feb, 2004 - No. 6, July, 2004 ($2.99)

	NM- 9.2
1-6: 1-Two covers; art by Jurgens and Oeming. 3-Bachalo, Jurgens-a. 4-Peréz-a	3.00
...: Baker's Dozen TPB (12/04, $14.99) r/#1-6; cover gallery; Holey Crullers pages	15.00

COMPLETE ALICE IN WONDERLAND (Adaptation of Carroll's original story)
Dynamite Entertainment: 2009 - Present ($4.99, limited series)

	NM- 9.2
1-4-Leah Moore & John Reppion-s/Erica Awano-a/John Cassaday-c	5.00

COMPLETE BOOK OF COMICS AND FUNNIES
William H. Wise & Co.: 1944 (25¢, one-shot, 196 pgs.)

	GD 2.0	VG 4.0	FN 6.0	VF 8.0	VF/NM 9.0	NM- 9.2
1-Origin Brad Spencer, Wonderman; The Magnet, The Silver Knight by Kinstler, & Zudo the Jungle Boy app.	46	92	138	290	488	685

COMPLETE BOOK OF TRUE CRIME COMICS
William H. Wise & Co.: No date (Mid 1940's) (25¢, 132 pgs.)

	GD 2.0	VG 4.0	FN 6.0	VF 8.0	VF/NM 9.0	NM- 9.2
nn-Contains Crime Does Not Pay rebound (includes #22)	148	296	444	947	1624	2300

COMPLETE COMICS (Formerly Amazing Comics No. 1)
Timely Comics (EPC): No. 2, Winter, 1944-45

	GD 2.0	VG 4.0	FN 6.0	VF 8.0	VF/NM 9.0	NM- 9.2
2-The Destroyer, The Whizzer, The Young Allies & Sergeant Dix; Schomburg-c	168	336	504	1075	1838	2600

COMPLETE DRACULA (Adaptation of Stoker's original story)
Dynamite Entertainment: 2009 - No. 5, 2009 ($4.99, limited series)

	NM- 9.2
1-5-Leah Moore & John Reppion-s/Colton Worley-a/John Cassaday-c	5.00

COMPLETE FRANK MILLER BATMAN, THE
Longmeadow Press: 1989 ($29.95, hardcover, silver gilded pages)

	NM- 9.2
HC-Reprints Batman: Year One, Wanted: Santa Claus--Dead or Alive, and The Dark Knight Returns	30.00

COMPLETE GUIDE TO THE DEADLY ARTS OF KUNG FU AND KARATE
Marvel Comics: 1974 (68 pgs., B&W magazine)

	GD 2.0	VG 4.0	FN 6.0	VF 8.0	VF/NM 9.0	NM- 9.2
V1#1-Bruce Lee-c and 5 pg. story (scarce)	7	14	21	44	72	100

COMPLETE LOVE MAGAZINE (Formerly a pulp with same title)
Ace Periodicals (Periodical House): V26#2, May-June, 1951 - V32#4(#191), Sept, 1956

	GD 2.0	VG 4.0	FN 6.0	VF 8.0	VF/NM 9.0	NM- 9.2
V26#2-Painted-c (52 pgs.)	12	24	36	67	94	120
V26#3-6(2/52), V27#1(4/52)-6(1/53)	9	18	27	52	69	85
V28#1(3/53), V28#2(5/53), V29#3(7/53)-6(12/53)	9	18	27	50	65	80
V30#1(2/54), V30#1(#176, 4/54),2,4-6(#181, 1/55)	9	18	27	50	65	80
V30#3(#178)-Rock Hudson photo-c	9	18	27	52	69	85
V31#1(#182, 3/55)-Last precode	9	18	27	47	61	75
V31#2(5/55)-6(#187, 1/56)	8	16	24	44	57	70
V32#1(#188, 3/56)-4(#191, 9/56)	8	16	24	44	57	70

NOTE: *(34 total issues). Photo-c V27#5-on. Painted-c V26#3.*

COMPLETE MYSTERY (True Complete Mystery No. 5 on)
Marvel Comics (PrPl): Aug, 1948 - No. 4, Feb, 1949 (Full length stories)

	GD 2.0	VG 4.0	FN 6.0	VF 8.0	VF/NM 9.0	NM- 9.2
1-Seven Dead Men	47	94	141	296	498	700
2-4: 2-Jigsaw of Doom!; Shores-a. 3-Fear in the Night; Burgos-c/a (28 pgs.). 4-A Squealer Dies Fast	39	78	117	231	378	525

COMPLETE ROMANCE
Avon Periodicals: 1949

	GD 2.0	VG 4.0	FN 6.0	VF 8.0	VF/NM 9.0	NM- 9.2
1-(Scarce)-Reprinted as Women to Love	43	86	129	271	461	650

CONAN (See Chamber of Darkness #4, Giant-Size..., Handbook of..., King Conan, Marvel Graphic Novel #19, 28, Marvel Treasury Ed., Power Record Comics, Robert E. Howard's.., Savage Sword of Conan, and Savage Tales)

CONAN
Dark Horse Comics: Feb, 2004 - No. 50, May, 2008 ($2.99)

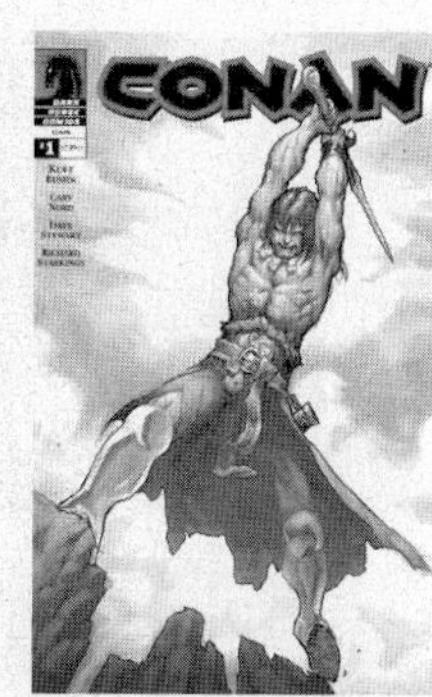

Conan #1 (3rd printing) © Conan Props. Inc.

Conan Saga #32 © Conan Props. Inc.

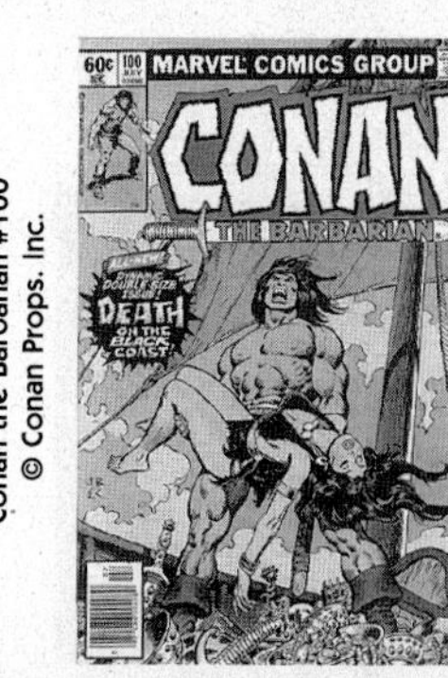

Conan the Barbarian #100 © Conan Props. Inc.

GD VG FN VF VF/NM NM-
2.0 4.0 6.0 8.0 9.0 9.2

0-(11/03, 25¢-c) Busiek-s/Nord-a 3.00
1-($2.99) Linsner-c/Busiek-s/Nord-a 5.00
1-(2nd printing) J. Scott Campell-c 3.00
1-(3rd printing) Nord-c 3.00
2-49: 18-Severin & Timm-a. 22-Kaluta-a (6 pgs.) 24-Harris-c. 29-31-Mignola-s 3.00
24-Variant-c with nude woman (also see Conan and the Demons of Khitai #3 for ad) 20.00
50-($4.99) Harris-c; new story and reprint from Conan the Barbarian #30 5.00
... and the Daughters of Midora (10/04, $4.99) Texiera-a/c 5.00
...: Born on the Battlefield TPB (6/08, $17.95) r/#0,8,15,23,32,45,46; Ruth sketch pages 18.00
...: FCBD 2006 Special (5/06) Paul Lee-a; flip book with Star Wars FCBD 2006 Special 3.00
...: One For One (8/10, $1.00) r/#1 with red cover frame 3.00
...: The Blood-Stained Crown and Other Stories TPB (1/08, $14.95) r/#18,26-28,39 15.00
...: The Weight of the Crown (1/10, $3.50) Darick Robertson-s/a; 2 covers by Robertson 3.50
HC Vol. 1: The Frost Giant's Daughter and Other Stories (2005, $24.95) r/#1-6, partial #7; signed by Busiek; Nord sketch pages 25.00
Vol. 1: The Frost Giant's Daughter and Other Stories (2005, $15.95) r/#1-6, partial #7 16.00
Vol. 2: The God in the Bowl and Other Stories HC (2005, $24.95) r/#9-14 25.00
Vol. 2: The God in the Bowl and Other Stories SC (2006, $15.95) r/#9-14 16.00
Vol. 3: The Tower of the Elephant and Other Stories HC (5/06, $24.95) r/#0,16,17,19-22 25.00
Vol. 3: The Tower of the Elephant and Other Stories SC (6/06, $15.95) r/#0,16,17,19-22 16.00
Vol. 4: The Hall of the Dead and Other Stories HC (5/07, $24.95) r/#0,24,25,29-31,33,34 25.00
Vol. 4: The Hall of the Dead and Other Stories SC (6/07, $17.95) r/#0,24,25,29-31,33,34 18.00
Vol. 5: Rogues in the House and Other Stories SC (3/08, $17.95) r/#0,37,38,41-44 18.00
Vol. 6: The Hand of Nergal HC (10/08, $24.95) r/#0,47-50; sketch pages 25.00

CONAN AND THE DEMONS OF KHITAI
Dark Horse Comics: Oct, 2005 - No. 4, Jan, 2006 ($2.99, limited series)

1,2,4-Paul Lee-a/Akira Yoshida-s/Pat Lee-c 3.00
3-1st printing with red cover logo; letters page has image of Conan #24 nude variant-c 5.00
3-2nd printing with black cover logo; letters page has image of Conan #24 regular-c 3.00
TPB (7/06, $12.95) r/series 13.00

CONAN AND THE JEWELS OF GWAHLUR
Dark Horse Comics: Apr, 2005 - No. 3, June, 2005 ($2.99, limited series)

1-3-P. Craig Russell-s/a/c 3.00
HC (12/05, $13.95) r/series; P. Craig Russell interview and sketch pages 14.00

CONAN AND THE MIDNIGHT GOD
Dark Horse Comics: Dec, 2006 - No. 5, May, 2007 ($2.99, limited series)

1-5-Dysart-s/Conrad-a/Alexander-c 3.00
TPB (10/07, $14.95) r/#1-5 and Age of Conan: Hyborian Adventures one-shot 15.00

CONAN AND THE SONGS OF THE DEAD
Dark Horse Comics: July, 2006 - No. 5, Nov, 2006 ($2.99, limited series)

1-5-Timothy Truman-a/c; Joe Lansdale-s 3.00
TPB (4/07, $14.95) r/series; Truman sketch pages 15.00

CONAN: (Title Series): Marvel Comics

CONAN, 8/95 - No. 11, 6/96 ($2.95), 1-11: 4-Malibu Comic's Rune app. 3.00
...CLASSIC, 6/94 - No. 11, 4/95 ($1.50), 1-11: 1-r/Conan #1 by B. Smith, r/covers w/changes. 2-11-r/Conan #2-11 by Smith. 2-Bound w/cover to Conan The Adventurer #2 by mistake 3.00
...DEATH COVERED IN GOLD, 9/99 - No. 3, 11/99 ($2.99), 1-3-Roy Thomas-s/ John Buscema-a 3.00
...FLAME AND THE FIEND, 8/00 - No. 3, 10/00 ($2.99), 1-3-Thomas-s 3.00
...RETURN OF STYRM, 9/98 - No. 3, 11/98 ($2.99), 1-3-Parente & Soresina-a; painted-c 3.00
...RIVER OF BLOOD, 6/98 - No. 3, 8/98 ($2.50), 1-3 3.00
...SCARLET SWORD, 12/98 - No. 3, 2/99 ($2.99), 1-3-Thomas-s/Raffaele-a 3.00

CONAN: ISLAND OF NO RETURN
Dark Horse Comics: Jun, 2011 - No. 2, Jul, 2011 ($3.50, limited series)

1,2-Marz-s/Sears-a 3.50

CONAN: ROAD OF KINGS
Dark Horse Comics: Dec, 2010 - No. 12, Jan, 2012 ($3.50)

1-12: 1-Roy Thomas-s/Mike Hawthorne-a; covers by Wheatley & Keown 3.50

CONAN SAGA, THE
Marvel Comics: June, 1987 - No. 97, Apr, 1995 ($2.00/$2.25, B&W, magazine)

1-Barry Smith-r; new Smith-c 1 2 3 5 6 8
2-27: 2-9,11-new Barry Smith-c. 13,15-Boris-c. 17-Adams-r.18,25-Chaykin-r. 22-r/Giant-Size Conan 1,2 4.00
28-90: 28-Begin $2.25-c. 31-Red Sonja-r by N. Adams/SSOC #1; 1 pg. Jeff Jones-r. 32-Newspaper strip-r begin by Buscema. 33-Smith/Conrad-a. 39-r/Kull #1('71) by Andru & Wood. 44-Swipes-c/Savage Tales #1. 57-Brunner-r/SSOC #30. 66-r/Conan Annual #2 by Buscema. 79-r/Conan #43-45 w/Red Sonja. 85-Based on Conan #57-63 3.00
91-96 4.50
97-Last issue 1 2 3 4 5 7

NOTE: ***J. Buscema** r-32-on; c-86. **Chaykin** r-34. **Chiodo** painted c-63, 65, 66, 82. **G. Colan** a-47p. **Jusko** painted c-64, 83. **Kaluta** c-84. **Nino** a-37. **Ploog** a-50. **N. Redondo** painted c-48, 50, 51, 53, 57, 62. **Simonson** r-50-54, 56. **B. Smith** r-51. **Starlin** c-34. **Williamson** r-50i.*

CONAN THE ADVENTURER
Marvel Comics: June, 1994 - No. 14, July, 1995 ($1.50)

1-($2.50)-Embossed foil-c; Kayaran-a 3.50
2-14 3.00
2-Contents are Conan Classics #2 by mistake 3.00

CONAN THE BARBARIAN
Marvel Comics: Oct, 1970 - No. 275, Dec, 1993

1-Origin/1st app. Conan (in comics) by Barry Smith; 1st brief app. Kull; #1-9 are 15¢ issues 21 42 63 148 317 485
2 10 20 30 67 116 165
3-(Low distribution in some areas) 14 28 42 96 191 285
4,5 8 16 24 58 97 135
6-9: 8-Hidden panel message, pg. 14. 9-Last 15¢-c 6 12 18 43 69 95
10,11 (25¢ 52 pg. giants): 10-Black Knight-r; Kull story by Severin 7 14 21 50 83 115
12,13: 12-Wrightson-c(i) 6 12 18 39 62 85
14,15-Elric app. 7 14 21 45 73 100
16,19,20: 16-Conan-r/Savage Tales #1 6 12 18 37 59 80
17,18-No Barry Smith-a 4 8 12 28 44 60
21,22: 22-Has reprint from #1 5 10 15 30 48 65
23-1st app. Red Sonja (2/73) 7 14 21 46 76 105
24-1st full Red Sonja story; last Smith-a 7 14 21 44 72 100
25-John Buscema-c/a begins 3 6 9 16 23 30
26-30 2 4 6 13 18 22
31-36,38-40 2 4 6 9 12 15
37-Neal Adams-c/a; last 20¢ issue; contains pull-out subscription form 3 6 9 17 25 32
41-43,46-50: 48-Origin retold 2 4 6 8 10 12
44,45-N. Adams-i(Crusty Bunkers). 45-Adams-c 2 4 6 9 12 15
51-57,59,60: 59-Origin Belit 1 2 3 5 6 8
58-2nd Belit app. (see Giant-Size Conan #1) 2 4 6 8 11 14
61-65-(Regular 25¢ editions)(4-8/76) 1 2 3 4 5 7
61-65-(30¢-c variants, limited distribution) 5 10 15 32 51 70
66-99: 68-Red Sonja story cont'd from Marvel Feature #7. 75-79-(Reg. 30¢-c). 84-Intro. Zula. 85-Origin Zula. 87-r/Savage Sword of Conan #3 in color 6.00
75-79-(35¢-c variants, limited distribution) 4 8 12 28 44 60
100-(52 pg. Giant)-Death of Belit 1 3 4 6 8 10
101-114 4.00
115-Double size 5.00
116-199,201-231,233-249: 116-r/Power Record Comic PR31. 244-Zula returns 4.00
200,232: 200-(52 pgs.). 232-Young Conan storyline begins; Conan is born 5.00
250-(60 pgs.) 5.00
251-270: 262-Adapted from R.E. Howard story 4.00
271-274 6.00
275-($2.50, 68 pgs.)-Final issue; painted-c (low print) 2 4 6 11 16 20
King Size 1(1973, 35¢)-Smith-r/#2,4; Smith-c 3 6 9 20 30 40
Annual 2(1976, 50¢)-New full length story 2 4 6 10 14 18
Annual 3,4: 3('78)-Chaykin/N. Adams-r/SSOC #2. 4('78)-New full length story 2 4 6 8 10 12
Annual 5,6: 5(1979)-New full length Buscema story & part-c, 6(1981)-Kane-c/a 6.00
Annual 7-12: 7('82)-Based on novel "Conan of the Isles" (new-a). 8(1984). 9(1984). 10(1986). 11(1986). 12(1987) 4.00
Special Edition 1 (Red Nails) 4.00
The Chronicles of Conan Vol. 1: Tower of the Elephant and Other Stories (Dark Horse, 2003, $15.95) r/#1-8; afterword by Roy Thomas 16.00
The Chronicles of Conan Vol. 2: Rogues in the House and Other Stories (Dark Horse, 2003, $15.95) r/#9-13,16; afterword by Roy Thomas 16.00
The Chronicles of Conan Vol. 3: The Monster of the Monoliths and Other Stories (Dark Horse, 2003, $15.95) r/#14,15,17-21; afterword by Roy Thomas 16.00
The Chronicles of Conan Vol. 4: The Song of Red Sonja and Other Stories (Dark Horse, 2004, $15.95) r/#23-26 & "Red Nails" from Savage Tales; afterword by Roy Thomas 16.00
The Chronicles of Conan Vol. 5: The Shadow in the Tomb and Other Stories (Dark Horse, 2004, $15.95) r/#27-34; afterword by Roy Thomas 16.00
The Chronicles of Conan Vol. 6: The Curse of the Skull and Other Stories (Dark Horse, 2004, $15.95) r/#35-42; afterword by Roy Thomas 16.00
The Chronicles of Conan Vol. 7: The Dweller in the Pool and Other Stories (Dark Horse, 2005, $15.95) r/#43-51; afterword by Roy Thomas 16.00

Conan the Barbarian: Queen of the Black Coast #1 © Conan Props. Inc.

Concrete - Strange Armor #1 © P. Chadwick

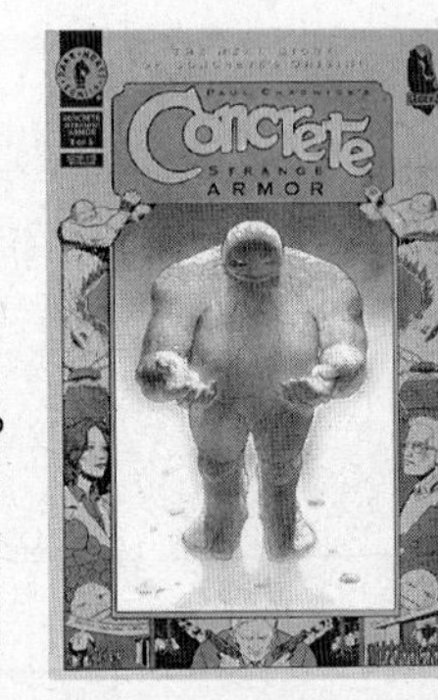

Confessions of Love #5 © STAR

GD 2.0 | VG 4.0 | FN 6.0 | VF 8.0 | VF/NM 9.0 | NM- 9.2

GD 2.0 | VG 4.0 | FN 6.0 | VF 8.0 | VF/NM 9.0 | NM- 9.2

The Chronicles of Conan Vol. 8: Brothers of the Blade and Other Stories (Dark Horse, 2005, $16.95) r/#52-59; afterword by Roy Thomas 17.00
The Chronicles of Conan Vol. 9: Riders of the River-Dragons and Other Stories (Dark Horse, 11/05, $16.95) r/#60-63,65,69-71; afterword by Roy Thomas 17.00
The Chronicles of Conan Vol. 10: When Giants Walk the Earth and Other Stories (Dark Horse, 3/06, $16.95) r/#72-77,79-82; afterword by Roy Thomas 17.00
The Chronicles of Conan Vol. 11: The Dance of the Skull and Other Stories (Dark Horse, 2/07, $16.95) r/#82-86,88-90; afterword by Roy Thomas 17.00
The Chronicles of Conan Vol. 12: The King Beast of Abombi and Other Stories (Dark Horse, 7/07, $16.95) r/#91,93-100; afterword by Roy Thomas 17.00
The Chronicles of Conan Vol. 13: Whispering Shadows and Other Stories (Dark Horse, 12/07, $16.95) r/#92,100-107; afterword by Roy Thomas 17.00
The Chronicles of Conan Vol. 14: Shadow of the Beast and Other Stories (Dark Horse, 3/08, $16.95) r/#92,108-115; afterword by Roy Thomas 17.00
The Chronicles of Conan Vol. 15: The Corridor of Mullah-Kajar and Other Stories (Dark Horse, 7/08, $16.95) r/#116-121 & Annual #2; afterword by Roy Thomas 17.00

NOTE: ***Arthur Adams*** *c-248, 249.* ***Neal Adams*** *a-116r(i); c-49i.* ***Austin*** *a-125, 126; c-125i, 126i.* ***Brunner*** *c-17i. c-40.* ***Buscema*** *a-25-36p, 38, 39, 41-56p, 58-63p, 65-67p, 68, 70-78p, 84-86p, 88-91p, 93-126p, 136p, 140, 141-144p, 146-158p, 159, 161, 162, 163p, 165-185p, 187-190p, Annual 2(3pgs.). 3-5p, 7p; c(p)-26, 36, 44, 46, 52, 56, 58, 59, 64, 65, 72, 78-80, 83-91, 93-103, 105-126, 136-151, 155-159, 161, 162, 168, 169, 171, 172, 174, 175, 178-185, 188, 189, Annual 4, 5, 7.* ***Chaykin*** *a-79-83.* ***Golden*** *c-152.* ***Kaluta*** *c-167.* ***Gil Kane*** *a-12p, 17p, 18p, 127-130, 131-134p; c-12p, 17p, 18p, 23, 25, 27-32, 34, 35, 38, 39, 41-43, 45-51, 53-55, 57, 60-63, 65-71, 73p, 76p, 127-134.* ***Jim Lee*** *c-242.* ***McFarlane*** *c-241p.* ***Ploog*** *a-57.* ***Russell*** *a-21; c-251i.* ***Simonson*** *c-135.* ***B. Smith*** *a-1-11p, 12, 13-15p, 16, 19-21, 23, 24; c-1-11, 13-16, 19-24p.* ***Starlin*** *a-64.* ***Wood*** *a-47r. Issue Nos. 3-5, 7-9, 11, 16-18, 21, 23, 25, 27-30, 35, 37, 38, 42, 45, 52, 57, 58, 65, 69-71, 73, 79-83, 99, 100, 104, 114, Annual 2 have original Robert E. Howard stories adapted. Issues #32-34 adapted from Norvell Page's novel* ***Flame Winds****.*

CONAN THE BARBARIAN (Volume 2)
Marvel Comics: July, 1997 - No. 3, Oct, 1997 ($2.50, limited series)
1-3-Castellini-a 3.00

CONAN THE BARBARIAN MOVIE SPECIAL (Movie)
Marvel Comics Group: Oct, 1982 - No. 2, Nov, 1982
1,2-Movie adaptation; Buscema-a 3.50

CONAN THE BARBARIAN: QUEEN OF THE BLACK COAST
Dark Horse Comics: Feb, 2012 - Present ($3.50)
1,2: 1-Brian Wood-s/Becky Cloonan-a. 1-Two covers by Carnevale & Cloonan 3.50

CONAN THE BARBARIAN: THE MASK OF ACHERON (Based on the 2011 movie)
Dark Horse Comics: Jul, 2011 ($6.99, one-shot)
1-Stuart Moore-s/Gabriel Guzman-a/c 7.00

CONAN THE BARBARIAN: THE USURPER
Marvel Comics: Dec, 1997 - No. 3, Feb, 1998 ($2.50, limited series)
1-3-Dixon-s 3.00

CONAN: THE BOOK OF THOTH
Dark Horse Comics: Mar, 2006 - No. 4, June, 2006 ($4.99, limited series)
1-4-Origin of Thoth-amon; Len Wein & Kurt Busiek-s/Kelley Jones-a/c 5.00
TPB (12/06, $17.95) r/#1-4 18.00

CONAN THE CIMMERIAN
Dark Horse Comics: No. 0, Jun, 2008 - No. 25, Nov, 2010 (99¢/$2.99)
0-Follows Conan #50; Truman-s/Giorello-a/c 3.00
1-(7/08, $2.99) Two covers by Joe Kubert and Cho; Giorello & Corben-a 3.00
2-25: 2-7-Cho-c; Giorello & Corben-a. 8-18-Linsner-c. 14-Joe Kubert-a (7 pgs.) 3.00

CONAN THE DESTROYER (Movie)
Marvel Comics Group: Jan, 1985 - No. 2, Mar, 1985
1,2-r/Marvel Super Special 3.00

CONAN THE FRAZETTA COVER SERIES
Dark Horse Comics: Dec, 2007 - No. 8 ($3.50/$5.99/$6.99)
1-($3.50) Reprints from Dark Horse series with Frazetta covers 3.50
2,3-($5.99) 6.00
4-8-($6.99) 7.00

CONAN THE KING (Formerly King Conan)
Marvel Comics Group: No. 20, Jan, 1984 - No. 55, Nov, 1989
20-49 4.00
50-54 5.00
55-Last issue 1 2 3 5 6 8
NOTE: ***Kaluta*** *c-20-23, 24i, 26, 27, 30, 50, 52.* ***Williamson*** *a-37i; c-37i, 38i.*

CONAN: THE LEGEND (See Conan 2004 series)

CONAN: THE LORD OF THE SPIDERS
Marvel Comics: Mar, 1998 - No. 3, May, 1998 ($2.50, limited series)
1-3-Roy Thomas-s/Raffaele-a 3.00

CONAN THE SAVAGE
Marvel Comics: Aug, 1995 - No. 10, May, 1996 ($2.95, B&W, Magazine)
1-10: 1-Bisley-c. 4-vs. Malibu Comics' Rune. 5,10-Brereton-c 4.00

CONAN VS. RUNE (Also See Conan #4)
Marvel Comics: Nov, 1995 ($2.95, one-shot)
1-Barry Smith-c/a/scripts 4.00

CONCRETE (Also see Dark Horse Presents & Within Our Reach)
Dark Horse Comics: March, 1987 - No. 10, Nov, 1988 ($1.50, B&W)
1-Paul Chadwick-c/a in all 1 3 4 6 8 10
1-2nd print 3.00
2 6.00
3-Origin 5.00
4-10 4.00
A New Life 1 (1989, $2.95, B&W)-r/#3,4 plus new-a (11 pgs.) 4.00
Celebrates Earth Day 1990 ($3.50, 52 pgs.) 6.00
Color Special 1 (2/89, $2.95, 44 pgs.)-r/1st two Concrete apps. from Dark Horse Presents #1,2 plus new-a 6.00
Depths TPB (7/05, $12.95)-r/#1-5, stories from DHP #1,8,10,150; other short stories 13.00
Land And Sea 1 (2/89, $2.95, B&W)-r/#1,2 6.00
Odd Jobs 1 (7/90, $3.50)-r/5,6 plus new-a 4.00
...Vol. 1: Depths ('05, $12.95, 9"x6") r/#1-5 & short stories 13.00
...Vol. 2: Heights ('05, $12.95, 9"x6") r/#6-10 & short stories 13.00
...Vol. 3: Fragile Creatures (1/06, $12.95, 9"x6") r/mini-series & short stories from DHP 13.00
...Vol. 4: Killer Smile (3/06, $12.95, 9"x6") r/mini-series & short stories from various 13.00
...Vol. 5: Think Like a Mountain (5/06, $12.95, 9"x6") r/mini-series & short stories 13.00
...Vol. 6: Strange Armor (7/06, $12.95, 9"x6") r/mini-series & short stories 13.00
...Vol. 7: The Human Dilemma (4/06, $12.95, 9"x6") r/mini-series 13.00

CONCRETE: (Title series), **Dark Horse Comics**
--ECLECTICA, 4/93 - No. 2, 5/93 ($2.95) 1,2 4.00
--FRAGILE CREATURE, 6/91 - No. 4, 2/92 ($2.50) 1-4 3.00
--KILLER SMILE, (Legend), 7/94 - No. 4, 10/94 ($2.95) 1-4 3.00
--STRANGE ARMOR, 12/97 - No. 5, 5/98 ($2.95, color) 1-5-Chadwick-s/c/a; retells origin 3.00
--THE HUMAN DILEMMA, 12/04 - No. 6, 5/05 ($3.50)
1-6: Chadwick-a/c & scripts; Concrete has a child 3.50
--THINK LIKE A MOUNTAIN, (Legend), 3/96 - No. 6, 8/96 ($2.95)
1-6: Chadwick-a/scripts & Darrow-c in all 3.00

CONDORMAN (Walt Disney)
Whitman Publishing: Oct, 1981 - No. 3, Jan, 1982
1-3: 1,2-Movie adaptation; photo-c 1 3 4 6 8 10

CONEHEADS
Marvel Comics: June, 1994 - No. 4, 1994 ($1.75, limited series)
1-4 3.00

CONFESSIONS ILLUSTRATED (Magazine)
E. C. Comics: Jan-Feb, 1956 - No. 2, Spring, 1956
1-Craig, Kamen, Wood, Orlando-a 29 58 87 172 281 390
2-Craig, Crandall, Kamen, Orlando-a 21 42 63 126 206 285

CONFESSIONS OF LOVE
Artful Publ.: Apr, 1950 - No. 2, July, 1950 (25¢, 7-1/4x5-1/4", 132 pgs.)
1-Bakerish-a 41 82 123 256 428 600
2-Art & text; Bakerish-a 26 52 78 154 252 350

CONFESSIONS OF LOVE (Formerly Startling Terror Tales #10; becomes Confessions of Romance No. 7 on)
Star Publications: No. 11, 7/52 - No. 14, 1/53; No. 4, 3/53- No. 6, 8/53
11-13: 12,13-Disbrow-a 15 30 45 90 140 190
14,5,6 14 28 42 78 112 145
4-Disbrow-a 14 28 42 81 118 155
NOTE: *All have* ***L. B. Cole*** *covers.*

CONFESSIONS OF ROMANCE (Formerly Confessions of Love)
Star Publications: No. 7, Nov, 1953 - No. 11, Nov, 1954
7 15 30 45 90 140 190
8 14 28 42 78 112 145
9-Wood-a 15 30 45 84 127 170
10,11-Disbrow-a 14 28 42 81 118 155
NOTE: *All have* ***L. B. Cole*** *covers.*

CONFESSIONS OF THE LOVELORN (Formerly Lovelorn)
American Comics Group (Regis Publ./Best Synd. Features): No. 52, Aug, 1954 - No. 114,

Congo Bill #3 © DC

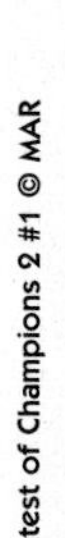
Contest of Champions 2 #1 © MAR

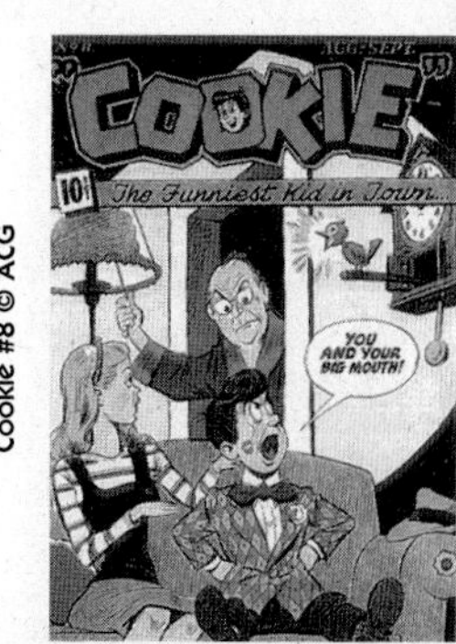

Cookie #8 © ACG

GD 2.0 | VG 4.0 | FN 6.0 | VF 8.0 | VF/NM 9.0 | NM- 9.2

June-July, 1960
52 (3-D effect) 30 60 90 177 289 400
53,55 12 24 36 67 94 120
54 (3-D effect) 30 60 90 177 289 400
56-Anti-communist propaganda story, 10 pgs; last pre-code (2/55)
15 30 45 84 127 170
57-90,100 9 18 27 50 65 80
91-Williamson-a 10 20 30 56 76 95
92-99,101-114 8 16 24 40 50 60
NOTE: ***Whitney** a-most issues; c-52, 53. Painted c-106, 107.*

CONFIDENTIAL DIARY (Formerly High School Confidential Diary; Three Nurses #18 on)
Charlton Comics: No. 12, May, 1962 - No. 17, Mar, 1963
12-17 3 6 9 15 21 26

CONGO BILL (See Action Comics & More Fun Comics #56)
National Periodical Publication: Aug-Sept, 1954 - No. 7, Aug-Sept, 1955
1 (Scarce) 200 400 600 1600 - -
2,7 (Scarce) 125 250 375 1000 - -
3-6 (Scarce). 4-Last pre-code issue 100 200 300 800 - -
NOTE: *(Rarely found in fine to mint condition.)* ***Nick Cardy** c-1-7.*

CONGO BILL
DC Comics (Vertigo): Oct, 1999 - No. 4, Jan, 2000 ($2.95, limited series)
1-4-Corben-c 3.00

CONGORILLA (Also see Actions Comics #224)
DC Comics: Nov, 1992 - No. 4, Feb, 1993 ($1.75, limited series)
1-4: 1,2-Brian Bolland-c 3.00

CONJURORS
DC Comics: Apr, 1999 - No. 3, Jun, 1999 ($2.95, limited series)
1-3-Elseworlds; Phantom Stranger app.; Barreto-c/a 3.00

CONNECTICUT YANKEE, A (See King Classics)

CONNOR HAWKE: DRAGON'S BLOOD (Also see Green Arrow titles)
DC Comics: Jan, 2007 - No. 6, Jun, 2007 ($2.99, limited series)
1-6-Chuck Dixon-s/Derec Donovan-a/c 3.00
SC (2008, $19.99) r/#1-6 20.00

CONQUEROR, THE
Dell Publishing Co.: No., 690, Mar, 1956
Four Color 690-Movie, John Wayne photo-c 14 28 42 99 200 300

CONQUEROR COMICS
Albrecht Publishing Co.: Winter, 1945
nn 22 44 66 128 209 290

CONQUEROR OF THE BARREN EARTH (See The Warlord #63)
DC Comics: Feb, 1985 - No. 4, May, 1985 (Limited series)
1-4: Back-up series from Warlord 3.00

CONQUEST
Store Comics: 1953 (6¢)
1-Richard the Lion Hearted, Beowulf, Swamp Fox 7 14 21 35 43 50

CONQUEST
Famous Funnies: Spring, 1955
1-Crandall-a, 1 pg.; contains contents of 1953 ish. 5 10 15 22 26 30

CONSPIRACY
Marvel Comics: Feb, 1998 - No. 2, Mar, 1998 ($2.99, limited series)
1,2-Painted art by Korday/Abnett-s 3.00

CONSTANTINE (Also see Hellblazer)
DC Comics (Vertigo): 2005 (Based on the 2005 Keanu Reeves movie)
...: The Hellblazer Collection (2005, $14.95) Movie adaptation and r/#1, 27, 41; photo-c 15.00
...: The Official Movie Adaptation (2005, $6.95) Seagle-s/Randall-a/photo-c 7.00

CONSTRUCT
Caliber (New Worlds): 1996 - No. 6, 1997 ($2.95, B&W, limited series)
1-6: Paul Jenkins scripts 3.00

CONSUMED
Platinum Studios: July, 2007 - No. 4, Oct, 2007 ($2.99, limited series)
1-4-Linsner-c/Budd-a/Shumskas-Tait-s 3.00

CONTACT COMICS
Aviation Press: July, 1944 - No. 12, May, 1946
nn-Black Venus, Flamingo, Golden Eagle, Tommy Tomahawk begin
54 108 162 348 594 840
2-5: 3-Last Flamingo. 3,4-Black Venus by L. B. Cole. 5-The Phantom Flyer app.
40 80 120 243 402 560
6,11-Kurtzman's Black Venus; 11-Last Golden Eagle, last Tommy Tomahawk;
Feldstein-a 47 94 141 296 498 700
7-10 39 78 117 240 395 550
12-Sky Rangers, Air Kids, Ace Diamond app.; L.B. Cole sci-fi cover
129 258 387 826 1413 2000
NOTE: ***L. B. Cole** a-3, 9; c-1-12. **Giunta** a-3. **Hollingsworth** a-5, 7, 10. **Palais** a-11, 12.*

CONTEMPORARY MOTIVATORS
Pendelum Press: 1977 - 1978 ($1.45, 5-3/8x8", 31 pgs., B&W)
14-3002 The Caine Mutiny; 14-3010 Banner in the Sky; 14-3029 God Is My Co-Pilot; 14-3037 Guadalcanal Diary; 14-3045 Hiroshima; 14-3053 Hot Rod; 14-3061 Just Dial a Number; 14-3088 The Diary of Anne Frank; 14-3096 Lost Horizon
2 4 6 8 10 12
NOTE: *Also see Pendulum Illustrated Classics. Above may have been distributed the same.*

CONTEST OF CHAMPIONS (See Marvel Super-Hero...)

CONTEST OF CHAMPIONS II
Marvel Comics: Sept, 1999 - No. 5 ($2.50, limited series)
1-5-Claremont-s/Jimenez-a 3.00

CONTRACTORS
Eclipse Comics: June, 1987 ($2.00, B&W, one-shot)
1-Funny animal 3.00

CONTRACT WITH GOD, A
Baronet Publishing Co./Kitchen Sink Press: 1978 ($4.95/$7.95, B&W, graphic novel)
nn-Will Eisner-s/a 3 6 9 14 20 25
Reprint (DC Comics, 2000, $12.95) 13.00

CONVOCATIONS: A MAGIC THE GATHERING GALLERY
Acclaim Comics (Armada): Jan, 1996 ($2.50, one-shot)
1-pin-ups by various artists including Kaluta, Vess, and Dringenberg 3.00

COO COO COMICS (...the Bird Brain No. 57 on)
Nedor Publ. Co./Standard (Animated Cartoons): Oct, 1942 - No. 62, Apr, 1952
1-Origin/1st app. Super Mouse & begin series (cloned from Superman); the first funny animal super hero series (see Looney Tunes #5 for 1st funny animal super hero)
33 66 99 194 317 440
2 16 32 48 92 144 195
3-10: 10-(3/44) 12 24 36 67 94 120
11-33: 33-1 pg. Ingels-a 10 20 30 54 72 90
34-40,43-46,48-Text illos by Frazetta in all. 36-Super Mouse covers begin
12 24 36 69 97 125
41-Frazetta-a (6-pg. story & 3 text illos) 22 44 66 128 209 290
42,47-Frazetta-a & text illos. 15 30 45 88 137 185
49-(1/50)-3-D effect story; Frazetta text illo 14 28 42 81 118 155
50,51-3-D effect-c only. 50-Frazetta text illo 14 28 42 76 108 140
52-62: 56-58,61-Super Mouse app. 9 18 27 47 61 75

"COOKIE" (Also see Topsy-Turvy)
Michel Publ./American Comics Group(Regis Publ.): Apr, 1946 - No. 55, Aug-Sept, 1955
1-Teen-age humor 26 52 78 154 252 350
2-1st app. Tee-Pee Tim who takes over Ha Ha Comics later
15 30 45 84 127 170
3-10: 8-Bing Crosby app. 12 24 36 69 97 125
11-20: 12-Hedy Lamarr app. 13-Jackie Robinson mentioned. 15-Gregory Peck app. 16-Ub Iwerks (a creator of Mickey Mouse) name used. 18-Jane Russell-type Jane Bustle. 19-Cookie takes a dog to see Lassie movie 11 22 33 60 83 105
21-23,26,28-30: 26-Milt Gross & Starlett O'Hara stories. 28,30-Starlett O'Hara stories
9 18 27 50 65 80
24,25,27-Starlett O'Hara stories 9 18 27 52 69 85
31-34,37-48,50,52-55 8 16 24 42 54 65
35,36-Starlett O'Hara stories 9 18 27 47 61 75
49,51: 49-(6-7/54)-3-D effect-c/s. 51-(10-11/54) 8pg. TrueVision 3-D effect story
13 26 39 74 105 135

COOL CAT (What's Cookin' With...) (Formerly Black Magic)
Prize Publications: V8#6, Mar-Apr, 1962 - V9#2, July-Aug, 1962
V8#6, nn(V9#1, 5-6/62), V9#2 3 6 9 18 27 35

COOL WORLD (Movie by Ralph Bakshi)
DC Comics: Apr, 1992 - No. 4, Sept, 1992 ($1.75, limited series)
1-4: Prequel to animated/live action movie. 1-Bakshi-c. Bill Wray inks in all 3.00

Cops: The Job #1 © MAR

Countdown #1 © DC

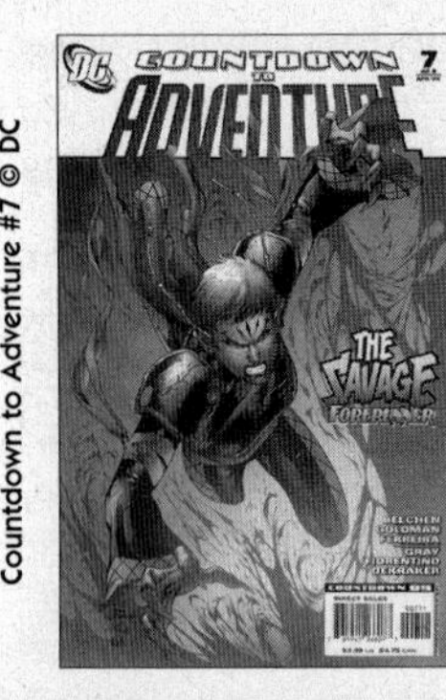

Countdown to Adventure #7 © DC

	GD 2.0	VG 4.0	FN 6.0	VF 8.0	VF/NM 9.0	NM- 9.2
Movie Adaptation nn ('92, $3.50, 68pg.)-Bakshi-c						4.00

COPPER CANYON (See Fawcett Movie Comics)

COPS (TV)
DC Comics: Aug, 1988 - No. 15, Aug, 1989 ($1.00)

	GD 2.0	VG 4.0	FN 6.0	VF 8.0	VF/NM 9.0	NM- 9.2
1 ($1.50, 52 pgs.)-Based on Hasbro Toys						4.00
2-15: 14-Orlando-c(p)						3.00

COPS: THE JOB
Marvel Comics: June, 1992 - No. 4, Sept, 1992 ($1.25, limited series)

	GD 2.0	VG 4.0	FN 6.0	VF 8.0	VF/NM 9.0	NM- 9.2
1-4: All have Jusko scripts & Golden-c						3.00

CORBEN SPECIAL, A
Pacific Comics: May, 1984 (one-shot)

	GD 2.0	VG 4.0	FN 6.0	VF 8.0	VF/NM 9.0	NM- 9.2
1-Corben-c/a; E.A. Poe adaptation						5.00

CORE, THE
Image Comics: July, 2008 ($3.99)

	GD 2.0	VG 4.0	FN 6.0	VF 8.0	VF/NM 9.0	NM- 9.2
Pilot Season - Hickman-s/Rocafort-a						4.00

CORKY & WHITE SHADOW (Disney, TV)
Dell Publishing Co.: No. 707, May, 1956 (Mickey Mouse Club)

	GD 2.0	VG 4.0	FN 6.0	VF 8.0	VF/NM 9.0	NM- 9.2
Four Color 707-Photo-c	7	14	21	46	76	105

CORLISS ARCHER (See Meet Corliss Archer)

CORMAC MAC ART (Robert E. Howard's...)
Dark Horse Comics: 1990 - No. 4, 1990 ($1.95, B&W, mini-series)

	GD 2.0	VG 4.0	FN 6.0	VF 8.0	VF/NM 9.0	NM- 9.2
1-4: All have Bolton painted-c; Howard adapts.						3.00

CORNY'S FETISH
Dark Horse Comics: Apr, 1998 ($4.95, B&W, one-shot)

	GD 2.0	VG 4.0	FN 6.0	VF 8.0	VF/NM 9.0	NM- 9.2
1-Renée French-s/a; Bolland-c						5.00

CORPORAL RUSTY DUGAN (See Holyoke One-Shot #2)

CORPSES OF DR. SACOTTI, THE (See Ideal a Classical Comic)

CORSAIR, THE (See A-1 Comics No. 5, 7, 10 under Texas Slim)

CORTEZ AND THE FALL OF THE AZTECS
Tome Press: 1993 ($2.95, B&W, limited series)

	GD 2.0	VG 4.0	FN 6.0	VF 8.0	VF/NM 9.0	NM- 9.2
1,2						3.00

CORUM: THE BULL AND THE SPEAR (See Chronicles Of Corum)
First Comics: Jan, 1989 - No. 4, July, 1989 ($1.95)

	GD 2.0	VG 4.0	FN 6.0	VF 8.0	VF/NM 9.0	NM- 9.2
1-4: Adapts Michael Moorcock's novel						3.00

COSMIC BOOK, THE
Ace Comics: Dec, 1986 - No. 1, 1987 ($1.95)

	GD 2.0	VG 4.0	FN 6.0	VF 8.0	VF/NM 9.0	NM- 9.2
1,2: 1-(44pgs.)-Wood, Toth-a. 2-(B&W)						4.00

COSMIC BOY (Also see The Legion of Super-Heroes)
DC Comics: Dec, 1986 - No. 4, Mar, 1987 (limited series)

	GD 2.0	VG 4.0	FN 6.0	VF 8.0	VF/NM 9.0	NM- 9.2
1-4: Legends tie-ins all issues						3.00

COSMIC GUARD
Devil's Due Publ.: Aug, 2004 - No. 6, Dec, 2005 ($2.99)

	GD 2.0	VG 4.0	FN 6.0	VF 8.0	VF/NM 9.0	NM- 9.2
1-6-Jim Starlin-s/a						3.00

COSMIC HEROES
Eternity/Malibu Graphics: Oct, 1988 - No. 11, Dec, 1989 ($1.95, B&W)

	GD 2.0	VG 4.0	FN 6.0	VF 8.0	VF/NM 9.0	NM- 9.2
1-11: Reprints 1934-1936's Buck Rogers newspaper strips #1-728						3.00

COSMIC ODYSSEY
DC Comics: 1988 - No. 4, 1988 ($3.50, limited series, squarebound)

	GD 2.0	VG 4.0	FN 6.0	VF 8.0	VF/NM 9.0	NM- 9.2
1-4: Reintro. New Gods into DC continuity; Superman, Batman, Green Lantern (John Stewart) app; Starlin scripts, Mignola-c/a in all. 2-Darkseid merges Demon & Jason Blood (separated in Demon limited series #4)						5.00
TPB (1992,2009, $19.99) r/#1-4; Robert Greenberger intro.						20.00

COSMIC POWERS
Marvel Comics: Mar, 1994 - No. 6, Aug, 1994 ($2.50, limited series)

	GD 2.0	VG 4.0	FN 6.0	VF 8.0	VF/NM 9.0	NM- 9.2
1-6: 1-Ron Lim-c/a(p). 1,2-Thanos app. 2-Terrax. 3-Ganymede & Jack of Hearts app.						3.00

COSMIC POWERS UNLIMITED
Marvel Comics: May, 1995 - No. 5, May, 1996 ($3.95, quarterly)

	GD 2.0	VG 4.0	FN 6.0	VF 8.0	VF/NM 9.0	NM- 9.2
1-5						4.00

COSMIC RAY
Image Comics: June, 1999 - No. 2 ($2.95, B&W)

	GD 2.0	VG 4.0	FN 6.0	VF 8.0	VF/NM 9.0	NM- 9.2
1,2-Steven Blue-s/a						3.00

COSMIC SLAM
Ultimate Sports Entertainment: 1999 ($3.95, one-shot)

	GD 2.0	VG 4.0	FN 6.0	VF 8.0	VF/NM 9.0	NM- 9.2
1-McGwire, Sosa, Bagwell, Justice battle aliens; Sienkiewicz-c						4.00

COSMO CAT (Becomes Sunny #11 on; also see All Top & Wotalife Comics)
Fox Publications/Green Publ. Co./Norlen Mag.: July-Aug, 1946 - No. 10, Oct, 1947; 1957; 1959

	GD 2.0	VG 4.0	FN 6.0	VF 8.0	VF/NM 9.0	NM- 9.2
1	26	52	78	152	249	345
2	15	30	45	84	127	170
3-Origin (11-12/46)	18	36	54	107	169	230
4-Robot-c	14	28	42	76	108	140
5-10	11	22	33	60	83	105
2-4(1957-Green Publ. Co.)	6	12	18	27	33	38
2-4(1959-Norlen Mag.)	5	10	15	23	28	32
I.W. Reprint #1	2	4	6	11	16	20

COSMO THE MERRY MARTIAN
Archie Publications (Radio Comics): Sept, 1958 - No. 6, Oct, 1959

	GD 2.0	VG 4.0	FN 6.0	VF 8.0	VF/NM 9.0	NM- 9.2
1-Bob White-a in all	15	30	45	86	133	180
2-6	11	22	33	60	83	105

COTTON WOODS
Dell Publishing Co.: No. 837, Sept, 1957

	GD 2.0	VG 4.0	FN 6.0	VF 8.0	VF/NM 9.0	NM- 9.2
Four Color 837	4	8	12	24	37	50

COUGAR, THE (Cougar No. 2)
Seaboard Periodicals (Atlas): April, 1975 - No. 2, July, 1975

	GD 2.0	VG 4.0	FN 6.0	VF 8.0	VF/NM 9.0	NM- 9.2
1,2: 1-Vampire; Adkins-a(p). 2-Cougar origin; werewolf-s; Buckler-c(p)	2	4	6	9	13	16

COUNTDOWN (See Movie Classics)

COUNTDOWN
DC Comics (WildStorm): June, 2000 - No. 8, Jan, 2001 ($2.95)

	GD 2.0	VG 4.0	FN 6.0	VF 8.0	VF/NM 9.0	NM- 9.2
1-8-Mariotte-s/Lopresti-a						3.00

COUNTDOWN (Continued from 52 weekly series)
DC Comics: No. 51, July, 2007 - No. 1, June, 2008 ($2.99, weekly, limited series)
(issue #s go in reverse)

	GD 2.0	VG 4.0	FN 6.0	VF 8.0	VF/NM 9.0	NM- 9.2
51-Gatefold wraparound-c by Andy Kubert; Duela Dent killed; the Monitors app.						3.00
50-1: 50-Joker-c. 48-Lightray dies. 47-Mary Marvel gains Black Adam's powers. 46-Intro. Forerunner. 43-Funeral for Bart Allen. 39-Karate Kid-c						3.00
Countdown to Final Crisis Vol. 1 TPB (2008, $19.99) r/#51-39						20.00
Countdown to Final Crisis Vol. 2 TPB (2008, $19.99) r/#38-26						20.00
Countdown to Final Crisis Vol. 3 TPB (2008, $19.99) r/#25-13						20.00
Countdown to Final Crisis Vol. 4 TPB (2008, $19.99) r/#12-1						20.00

COUNTDOWN: ARENA (Takes place during Countdown #21-18)
DC Comics: Feb, 2008 - No. 4, Feb, 2008 ($3.99, weekly, limited series)

	GD 2.0	VG 4.0	FN 6.0	VF 8.0	VF/NM 9.0	NM- 9.2
1-4-Battles between alternate Earth heroes; McDaniel-a; Andy Kubert variant-c on each						4.00
TPB (2008, $17.99) r/#1-4; variant covers						18.00

COUNTDOWN PRESENTS: LORD HAVOK & THE EXTREMISTS
DC Comics: Dec, 2007 - No. 8 ($2.99, limited series)

	GD 2.0	VG 4.0	FN 6.0	VF 8.0	VF/NM 9.0	NM- 9.2
1-6: 1-Tieri-s/Sharp-a/c; Challengers From Beyond app.						3.00
TPB (2008, $17.99) r/#1-6						18.00

COUNTDOWN PRESENTS THE SEARCH FOR RAY PALMER (Leads into Countdown #18)
DC Comics: Nov, 2007 - Feb, 2008 ($2.99, series of one-shots)

	GD 2.0	VG 4.0	FN 6.0	VF 8.0	VF/NM 9.0	NM- 9.2
...: Wildstorm (11/07) Part 1; The Authority app.; Art Adams-c/Unzueta-a						3.00
...: Crime Society (12/07) Earth-3 Owlman & Jokester app.; Igle-a						3.00
...: Red Rain (1/08) Vampire Batman app.; Kelley Jones-c; Jones, Battle & Unzueta-a						3.00
...: Gotham By Gaslight (1/08) Victorian Batman app.; Tocchini-a/Nguyen-c						3.00
...: Red Son (2/08) Soviet Superman app.; Foreman-a						3.00
...: Superwoman/Batwoman (2/08) Conclusion; gender-reversed heroes; Sook-c						3.00
TPB (2008, $17.99) r/one-shots						18.00

COUNTDOWN SPECIAL
DC Comics: Dec, 2007 - Jun, 2008 ($4.99, collection of reprints related to Countdown)

	GD 2.0	VG 4.0	FN 6.0	VF 8.0	VF/NM 9.0	NM- 9.2
...: Eclipso (5/08) r/Eclipso #10 & Spectre #17,18 (1994); Sook-c						5.00
...: Jimmy Olsen (1/08) r/Superman's Pal, Jimmy Olsen #136,147,148; Kirby-s/a; Sook-c						5.00
...: Kamandi (6/08) r/Kamandi: The Last Boy on Earth #1,10,29; Kirby-s/a; Sook-c						5.00
...: New Gods (3/08) r/Forever People #1, Mr. Miracle #1, New Gods #7; Kirby-s/a; Sook-c						5.00
...: Omac (4/08) r/Omac (1974) #1, Warlord #37-39, DC Comics Presents #61; Sook-c						5.00
...: The Atom 1,2 (2/08) r/stories from Super-Team Family #11-14; Sook-c on both						5.00
...: The Flash (12/07) r/Rogues Gallery in Flash (1st series) #106,113,155,174; Sook-c						5.00

COUNTDOWN TO ADVENTURE
DC Comics: Oct, 2007 - No. 8, May, 2008 ($3.99, limited series)

Countdown to Mystery #1 © DC

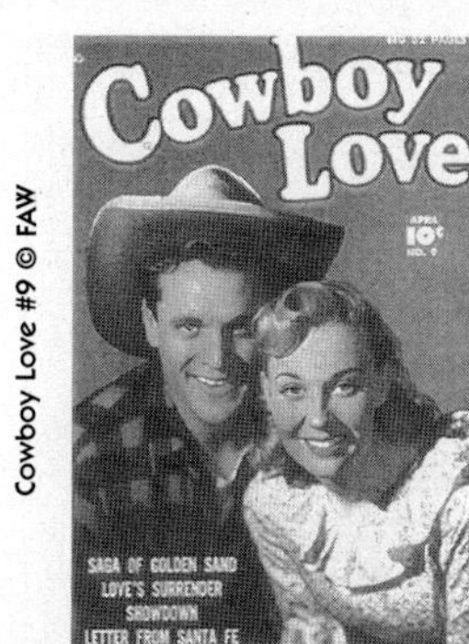

Cowboy Love #9 © FAW

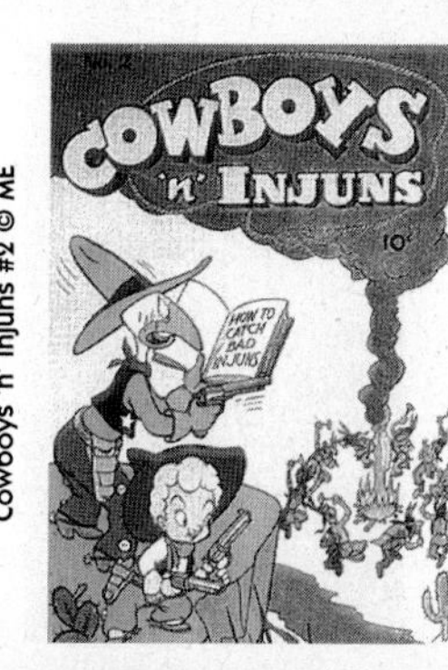

Cowboys 'n' Injuns #2 © ME

GD 2.0 | VG 4.0 | FN 6.0 | VF 8.0 | VF/NM 9.0 | NM- 9.2

1-8: 1-Adam Strange, Animal Man and Starfire app.; origin of Forerunner 4.00
TPB (2008, $17.99) r/#1-8 18.00

COUNTDOWN TO INFINITE CRISIS (See DC Countdown)

COUNTDOWN TO MYSTERY (See Eclipso: The Music of the Spheres TPB for reprint)
DC Comics: Nov, 2007 - No. 8, Jun, 2008 ($3.99, limited series)

1-8: 1-Doctor Fate, Eclipso, The Spectre and Plastic Man app. 4.00
TPB (2008, $17.99) r/#1-8 18.00

COUNT DUCKULA (TV)
Marvel Comics: Nov, 1988 - No. 15, Jan, 1991 ($1.00)

1,8: 1-Dangermouse back-up. 8-Geraldo Rivera photo-c/& app.; Sienkiewicz-a(i) 5.00
2-7,9-15: Dangermouse back-ups in all 4.00

COUNT OF MONTE CRISTO, THE
Dell Publishing Co.: No. 794, May, 1957

Four Color 794-Movie, Buscema-a 8 16 24 55 93 130

COUP D'ETAT (Oneshots)
DC Comics (WildStorm): April, 2004 ($2.95, weekly limited series)

...: Sleeper 1 (part 1 of 4) Jim Lee-a; 2 covers by Lee and Bermejo 3.00
...: Stormwatch 1 (part 2 of 4) D'Anda-a; 2 covers by D'Anda and Bermejo 3.00
...: Wildcats Version 3.0 1 (part 3 of 4) Garza-a; 2 covers by Garza and Bermejo 3.00
...: The Authority 1 (part 4 of 4) Portacio-a; 2 covers by Portacio and Bermejo 3.00
...: Afterword 1 (5/04) Profile pages and prelude stories for Sleeper & Wetworks 3.00
TPB (2004, $12.95) r/series and profile pages from Afterword 13.00

COURAGE COMICS
J. Edward Slavin: 1945

1,2,77 14 28 42 82 121 160

COURTNEY CRUMRIN...
Oni Press: July, 2005; July 2007; Dec, 2008 ($5.95, B&W, series of one-shots)

... And The Fire Thief's Tale (7/07) Naifeh-s/a 6.00
... And The Prince of Nowhere (12/08) Naifeh-s/a 6.00
... Tales (5/11) sequel to Tales Portrait of the Warlock...; Naifeh-s/a 6.00
... Tales Portrait of the Warlock as a Young Man (7/05) origin Uncle Aloysius; Naifeh-s/a 6.00

COURTNEY CRUMRIN & THE COVEN OF MYSTICS
Oni Press: Dec, 2002 - No. 4, March, 2003 ($2.95, B&W, limited series)

1-4-Ted Naifeh-s/a 3.00
TPB (9/03, $11.95, 8" x 5-1/2") r/#1-4 12.00

COURTNEY CRUMRIN & THE NIGHT THINGS
Oni Press: Mar, 2002 - No. 4, June, 2002 ($2.95, B&W, limited series)

1-4-Ted Naifeh-s/a 3.00
Free Comic Book Day Edition (5/03) Naifeh-s/a 3.00
TPB (12/02, $11.95) r/#1-4 12.00

COURTNEY CRUMRIN IN THE TWILIGHT KINGDOM
Oni Press: Dec, 2003 - No. 4, May, 2004 ($2.99, B&W, limited series)

1-4-Ted Naifeh-s/a 3.00
TPB (9/04, $11.95, digest-size) r/#1-4 12.00

COURTSHIP OF EDDIE'S FATHER (TV)
Dell Publishing Co.: Jan, 1970 - No. 2, May, 1970

1-Bill Bixby photo-c on both 6 12 18 37 59 80
2 4 8 12 24 37 50

COVEN
Awesome Entertainment: Aug, 1997 - No. 5, Mar, 1998 ($2.50)

Preview 1 2 3 5 6 8
1-Loeb-s/Churchill-a; three covers by Churchill, Liefeld, Pollina
1 2 3 5 6 8
1-Fan Appreciation Ed.(3/98); new Churchill-c 3.00
1+ :Includes B&W art from Kaboom 1 3 4 6 8 10
2-Regular-c w/leaping Fantom 6.00
2-Variant-c w/circle of candles 1 2 3 5 6 8
3-6-Contains flip book preview of ReGex 3.00
3-White variant-c 1 2 3 4 5 7
3,4: 3-Halloween wraparound-c. 4-Purple variant-c 3.00
...Black & White (9/98) Short stories 3.00
...Fantom Special (2/98) w/sketch pages 5.00

COVEN
Awesome Entertainment: Jan, 1999 - No. 3, June, 1999 ($2.50)

1-3: 1-Loeb-s/Churchill-a; 6 covers by various. 2-Supreme-c/app. 3-Flip book w/Kaboom preview 3.00

GD 2.0 | VG 4.0 | FN 6.0 | VF 8.0 | VF/NM 9.0 | NM- 9.2

... Dark Origins (7/99, 2.50) w/Lionheart gallery 3.00

COVENANT, THE
Image Comics (Top Cow): 2005 ($9.99, squarebound, one-shot)

nn-Tone Rodriguez-a/Aron Coleite-s 10.00

COVERED WAGONS, HO (Disney, TV)
Dell Publishing Co.: No. 814, June, 1957 (Donald Duck)

Four Color 814-Mickey Mouse app. 5 10 15 35 55 75

COWBOY ACTION (Formerly Western Thrillers No. 1-4; Becomes Quick-Trigger Western No. 12 on)
Atlas Comics (ACI): No. 5, March, 1955 - No. 11, March, 1956

5 14 28 42 76 108 140
6-10: 6-8-Heath-c 10 20 30 54 72 90
11-Williamson-a (4 pgs.); Baker-a 11 22 33 62 86 110
NOTE: *Ayers a-8. Drucker a-6. Maneely c/a-5, 6. Severin c-10. Shores a-7.*

COWBOY COMICS (Star Ranger #12, Stories #14)(Star Ranger Funnies #15)
Centaur Publishing Co.: No. 13, July, 1938 - No. 14, Aug, 1938

13-(Rare)-Ace and Deuce, Lyin Lou, Air Patrol, Aces High, Lee Trent, Trouble Hunters begin
139 278 417 883 1517 2150
14-Filchock-c 92 184 276 584 1005 1425
NOTE: *Guardineer a-13, 14. Gustavson a-13, 14.*

COWBOY IN AFRICA (TV)
Gold Key: Mar, 1968

1(10219-803)-Chuck Connors photo-c 4 8 12 26 41 55

COWBOY LOVE (Becomes Range Busters?)
Fawcett Publications/Charlton Comics No. 28 on: 7/49 - V2#10, 6/50; No. 11, 1951; No. 28, 2/55 - No. 31, 8/55

V1#1-Rocky Lane photo back-c 15 30 45 88 137 185
2 8 16 24 44 57 70
V1#3,4,6 (12/49) 8 16 24 40 50 60
5-Bill Boyd photo back-c (11/49) 9 18 27 47 61 75
V2#7-Williamson/Evans-a 10 20 30 54 72 90
V2#8-11 7 14 21 35 43 50
V1#28 (Charlton)-Last precode (2/55) (Formerly Romantic Story?)
6 12 18 31 38 45
V1#29-31 (Charlton; becomes Sweetheart Diary #32 on)
6 12 18 28 34 40
NOTE: *Powell a-10. Marcus Swayze a-2, 3. Photo c-1-11. No. 1-3, 5-7, 9, 10 are 52 pgs.*

COWBOY ROMANCES (Young Men No. 4 on)
Marvel Comics (IPC): Oct, 1949 - No. 3, Mar, 1950 (All photo-c & 52 pgs.)

1-Photo-c 22 44 66 132 216 300
2-William Holden, Mona Freeman "Streets of Laredo" photo-c
16 32 48 94 147 200
3-Photo-c 15 30 45 84 127 170

COWBOYS 'N' INJUNS (...and Indians No. 6 on)
Compix No. 1-5/Magazine Enterprises No. 6 on: 1946 - No. 5, 1947; No. 6, 1949 - No. 8, 1952

1-Funny animal western 14 28 42 82 121 160
2-5-All funny animal western 10 20 30 54 72 90
6(A-1 23)-Half violent, half funny; Ayers-a 14 28 42 76 108 140
7(A-1 41, 1950), 8(A-1 48)-All funny 9 18 27 47 61 75
I.W. Reprint No. 1,7,10 (Reprinted in Canada by Superior, No. 7), 10('63)
2 4 6 11 16 20

COWBOY WESTERN COMICS (TV)(Formerly Jack In The Box; Becomes Space Western No. 40-45 & Wild Bill Hickok & Jingles No. 68 on; title:Cowboy Western Heroes No. 47 & 48; Cowboy Western No. 49 on)
Charlton (Capitol Stories): No. 17, 7/48 - No. 39, 8/52; No. 46, 10/53; No. 47, 12/53; No. 48, Spr, '54; No. 49, 5-6/54 - No. 67, 3/58 (nn 40-45)

17-Jesse James, Annie Oakley, Wild Bill Hickok begin; Texas Rangers app.
16 32 48 94 147 200
18,19-Orlando-c/a. 18-Paul Bunyan begins. 19-Wyatt Earp story
10 20 30 58 79 100
20-25: 21-Buffalo Bill story. 22-Texas Rangers-c/story. 24-Joel McCrea photo-c & adaptation from movie "Three Faces West". 25-James Craig photo-c & adaptation from movie "Northwest Stampede" 9 18 27 52 69 85
26-George Montgomery photo-c and adaptation from movie "Indian Scout"; 1 pg. bio on Will Rogers 10 20 30 58 79 100
27-Sunset Carson photo-c & adapts movie "Sunset Carson Rides Again" plus 1 other Sunset Carson story 39 78 117 240 395 550
28-Sunset Carson line drawn-c; adapts movies "Battling Marshal" & "Fighting Mustangs"

Cowgirl Romances #7 © FH

Crackajack Funnies #32 © DELL

Crack Comics #51 © QUA

	GD 2.0	VG 4.0	FN 6.0	VF 8.0	VF/NM 9.0	NM- 9.2
starring Sunset Carson	20	40	60	114	182	250
29-Sunset Carson line drawn-c; adapts movies "Rio Grande" with Sunset Carson & "Winchester '73" w/James Stewart plus 5 pg. life history of Sunset Carson featuring Tom Mix	20	40	60	114	182	250
30-Sunset Carson photo-c; adapts movie "Deadline" starring Sunset Carson plus 1 other Sunset Carson story	39	78	117	240	395	550
31-34,38,39,47-50 (no #40-45): 50-Golden Arrow, Rocky Lane & Blackjack (r?) stories	9	18	27	47	61	75
35,36-Sunset Carson-c/stories (2 in each). 35-Inside front-c photo of Sunset Carson plus photo on-c	20	40	60	120	195	270
37-Sunset Carson stories (2)	15	30	45	94	147	200
46-(Formerly Space Western)-Space western story	15	30	45	94	147	200
51-57,59-66: 51-Golden Arrow(r?) & Monte Hale-r renamed Rusty Hall. 53,54-Tom Mix-r. 55-Monte Hale story(r?). 66-Young Eagle story. 67-Wild Bill Hickok and Jingles-c/story	7	14	21	35	43	50
58-(1/56, 15¢, 68 pgs.)-Wild Bill Hickok, Annie Oakley & Jesse James stories; Forgione-a	8	16	24	44	57	70
67-(15¢, 68 pgs.)-Williamson/Torres-a, 5 pgs.	9	18	27	50	65	80

NOTE: *Many issues trimmed 1" shorter.* ***Maneely*** *a-67(5). Inside front/back photo c-29.*

COWGIRL ROMANCES
Marvel Comics (CCC): No. 28, Jan, 1950 (52 pgs.)

	GD 2.0	VG 4.0	FN 6.0	VF 8.0	VF/NM 9.0	NM- 9.2
28(#1)-Photo-c	22	44	66	128	209	290

COWGIRL ROMANCES
Fiction House Magazines: 1950 - No. 12, Winter, 1952-53 (No. 1-3: 52 pgs.)

	GD 2.0	VG 4.0	FN 6.0	VF 8.0	VF/NM 9.0	NM- 9.2
1-Kamen-a	42	84	126	265	445	625
2	22	44	66	128	209	290
3-5: 5-12-Whitman-c (most)	20	40	60	114	182	250
6-9,11,12	19	38	57	111	176	240
10-Frazetta?/Williamson?-a; Kamen?/Baker-a; r/Mitzi story from Movie Comics #4 w/all new dialogue	32	64	96	188	307	425

COW PUNCHER (...Comics)
Avon Periodicals: Jan, 1947; No. 2, Sept, 1947 - No. 7, 1949

	GD 2.0	VG 4.0	FN 6.0	VF 8.0	VF/NM 9.0	NM- 9.2
1-Clint Cortland, Texas Ranger, Kit West, Pioneer Queen begin; Kubert-a; Alabam stories begin	45	90	135	284	480	675
2-Kubert, Kamen/Feldstein-a; Kamen-c	39	78	117	231	378	525
3-5,7: 3-Kiefer story	28	56	84	165	270	375
6-Opium drug mention story; bondage, headlight-c; Reinman-a	37	74	111	222	361	500

COWPUNCHER
Realistic Publications: 1953 (nn) (Reprints Avon's No. 2)

	GD 2.0	VG 4.0	FN 6.0	VF 8.0	VF/NM 9.0	NM- 9.2
nn-Kubert-a	12	24	36	69	97	125

COWSILLS, THE (See Harvey Pop Comics)

COW SPECIAL, THE
Image Comics (Top Cow): Spring-Summer 2000; 2001 ($2.95)

	GD 2.0	VG 4.0	FN 6.0	VF 8.0	VF/NM 9.0	NM- 9.2
1-Previews upcoming Top Cow projects; Yancy Butler photo-c						3.00
Vol. 2 #1-Witchblade-c; previews and interviews						3.00

COYOTE
Marvel Comics (Epic Comics): June, 1983 - No. 16, Mar, 1986

	GD 2.0	VG 4.0	FN 6.0	VF 8.0	VF/NM 9.0	NM- 9.2
1-10,15: 7-10-Ditko-a						3.00
11-1st McFarlane-a.	1	2	3	4	5	7
12-14,16: 12-14-McFarlane-a. 14-Badger x-over. 16-Reagan c/app.						5.00
Coyote Collection Vol. 1 (2005, $14.99) reprints from Coyote #1-7 & Scorpio Rose #1,2 plus Rogers layout pages for unpublished #3; Englehart intro.						15.00
Coyote Collection Vol. 2 (2005, $12.99) reprints from Coyote #1-4						13.00
Coyote Collection Vol. 3 (2006, $12.99) reprints from Coyote #5-8						13.00
Coyote Collection Vol. 4 (2007, $14.99) reprints from Coyote #9-12						15.00
Coyote Collection Vol. 5 (2007, $12.99) reprints from Coyote #13-16						13.00

CRACKAJACK FUNNIES (Also see The Owl)
Dell Publishing Co.: June, 1938 - No. 43, Jan, 1942

	GD 2.0	VG 4.0	FN 6.0	VF 8.0	VF/NM 9.0	NM- 9.2
1-Dan Dunn, Freckles, Myra North, Wash Tubbs, Apple Mary, The Nebbs, Don Winslow, Tom Mix, Buck Jones, Major Hoople, Clyde Beatty, Boots begin	181	362	543	1158	1979	2800
2	71	142	213	454	777	1100
3	53	106	159	334	567	800
4	42	84	126	265	445	625
5-Nude woman on cover	43	86	129	271	461	650
6-8,10: 8-Speed Bolton begins (1st app.)	39	78	117	231	378	525
9-(3/39)-Red Ryder strip-r begin by Harman; 1st app. in comics & 1st cover app.	161	322	483	1030	1765	2500
11-14	34	68	102	199	325	450
15-Tarzan text feature begins by Burroughs (9/39); not in #26,35	37	74	111	222	361	500
16-24: 18-Stratosphere Jim begins (1st app., 12/39). 23-Ellery Queen begins plus-c (1st comic book app., 5/40)	27	54	81	158	259	360
25-The Owl begins (1st app., 7/40); in new costume #26 by Frank Thomas (also see Popular Comics #72)	71	142	213	454	777	1100
26-30: 28-Part Owl-c	48	96	144	302	509	715
31-Owl covers begin, end #42	48	96	144	302	514	725
32-Origin Owl Girl	54	108	162	343	574	825
33-38: 36-Last Tarzan issue. 37-Cyclone & Midge begin (1st app.)	47	94	141	296	503	710
39-Andy Panda begins (intro/1st app., 9/41)	57	114	171	362	619	875
40-42: 42-Last Owl-c.	37	74	111	222	361	500
43-Terry & the Pirates-r	22	44	66	132	216	300

NOTE: ***McWilliams*** *art in most issues.*

CRACK COMICS (Crack Western No. 63 on)
Quality Comics Group: May, 1940 - No. 62, Sept, 1949

	GD 2.0	VG 4.0	FN 6.0	VF 8.0	VF/NM 9.0	NM- 9.2
1-Origin & 1st app. The Black Condor by Lou Fine, Madame Fatal, Red Torpedo, Rock Bradden & The Space Legion; The Clock, Alias the Spider (by Gustavson), Wizard Wells, & Ned Brant begin; Powell-a; Note: Madame Fatal is a man dressed as a woman	465	930	1395	3395	5998	8600
2	219	438	657	1402	2401	3400
3	152	304	456	965	1658	2350
4	123	246	369	787	1344	1900
5-10: 5-Molly The Model begins. 10-Tor, the Magic Master begins	92	184	276	584	1005	1425
11-20: 13-1 pg. J. Cole-a. 15-1st app. Spitfire	81	162	243	514	887	1260
21-24: 23-Pen Miller begins; continued from National Comics #22. 24-Last Fine Black Condor	64	128	192	406	696	985
25,26: 26-Flag-c	48	96	144	302	514	725
27-(1/43)-Intro & origin Captain Triumph by Alfred Andriola (Kerry Drake artist) & begin series	90	180	270	576	988	1400
28-30	41	82	123	256	428	600
31-39: 31-Last Black Condor	24	48	72	142	234	325
40-46	17	34	51	100	158	215
47-57,59,60-Capt. Triumph by Crandall	18	36	54	107	169	230
58,61,62-Last Captain Triumph	15	30	45	85	130	175

NOTE: *Black Condor by* ***Fine****: No. 1, 2, 5, 6, 8, 10-24; by* ***Sultan****: No. 3, 7; by* ***Fugitani****: No. 9.* ***Cole*** *a-34.* ***Crandall*** *a-61(unsigned); c-48, 49, 51-61.* ***Guardineer*** *a-17.* ***Gustavson*** *a-1, 2, 4, 7, 13, 17, 23.* ***McWilliams*** *a-15-27. Black Condor c-2, 4, 6, 8, 10, 12, 14, 16, 18, 20-26. Capt. Triumph c-27-62. The Clock c-1, 3, 5, 7, 9, 11, 13, 15, 17, 19.*

CRACK COMICS (Next Issue Project)
Image Comics: No. 63, Oct, 2011 ($4.99, one-shot)

	GD 2.0	VG 4.0	FN 6.0	VF 8.0	VF/NM 9.0	NM- 9.2
63-Mimics style & format of a 1949 issue; Weiss-c; s/a by various; Capt Triumph app.						5.00

CRACK COMICS
Quality Comics: May 1940

1-Ashcan comic, not distributed to newsstands, only for in-house use. Cover art is the same as published version of Crack Comics #1with exception of text panel on bottom left of cover. A CGC certified 4.0 copy sold for $1,495 in 2005.

CRACKED (Magazine) (Satire) (Also see The 3-D Zone #19)
Major Magazines(#1-212)/Globe Communications(#213-346/American Media #347 on): Feb-Mar, 1958 - No. 365, Nov, 2004

	GD 2.0	VG 4.0	FN 6.0	VF 8.0	VF/NM 9.0	NM- 9.2
1-One pg. Williamson-a; Everett-c; Gunsmoke-s	16	32	48	110	240	370
2-1st Shut-Ups & Bonus Cut-Outs; Superman parody-c by Severin (his 1st cover on the title) Frankenstein-s	10	20	30	66	121	175
3-5	8	16	24	53	89	125
6-10: 7-Reprints 1st 6 covers on-c. 8-Frankenstein-c. 10-Wolverton-a	6	12	18	41	66	90
11-12, 13(nn,3/60),	5	10	15	34	55	75
14-Kirby-a	6	12	18	41	66	90
15-17, 18(nn,2/61), 19,20	5	10	15	32	51	70
21-27(11/62), 27(No.28, 2/63; mis-#d), 29(5/63)	4	8	12	28	44	60
30-40(11/64): 37-Beatles and Superman cameos	4	8	12	24	37	50
41-45,47-56,59,60: 47,49,52-Munsters. 51-Beatles inside-c. 59-Laurel and Hardy photos	3	6	9	20	30	40
46,57,58: 46,58-Man From U.N.C.L.E. 46-Beatles. 57-Rolling Stones	4	8	12	22	34	45
61-80: 62-Beatles cameo. 69-Batman, Superman app. 70-(8/68) Elvis cameo. 71-Garrison's Gorillas; W.C. Fields photos	3	6	9	16	22	28
81-99: 99-Alfred E. Neuman on-c	3	6	9	14	19	24
100	3	6	9	18	27	35
101-119: 104-Godfather-c/s. 108-Archie Bunker-s. 112,119-Kung Fu (TV). 113-Tarzan-s.						

Cracked #125 © Globe CC

Cracked #226 © Globe CC

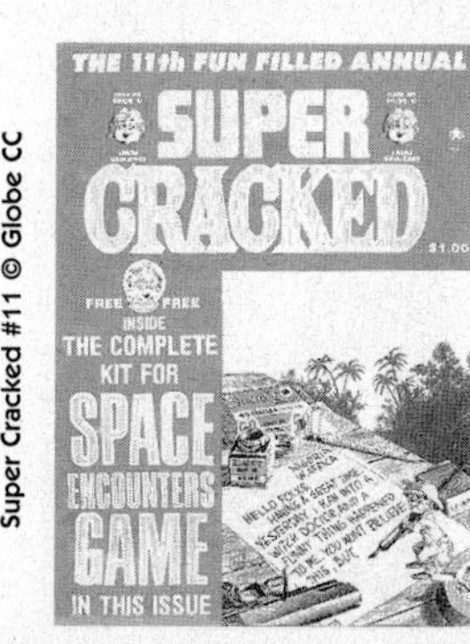

Super Cracked #11 © Globe CC

	GD 2.0	VG 4.0	FN 6.0	VF 8.0	VF/NM 9.0	NM- 9.2
115-MASH. 117-Cannon. 118-The Sting-c/s	2	4	6	10	14	18
120(12/74) Six Million Dollar Man-c/s; Ward-a	2	4	6	13	18	22
121,122,124-126,128-133,136-140: 121-American Graffiti. 122-Korak-c/s. 124,131-Godfather-c/s. 128-Capone-c. 129,131-Jaws. 132-Baretta-c/s. 133-Space 1999. 136-Laverne and Shirley/Fonz-c. 137-Travolta/Kotter-c/s. 138-Travolta/Laverne and Shirley/ Fonz-c. 139-Barney Miller-c/s. 140-King Kong-c/s; Fonz-s	2	4	6	10	14	18
123-Planet of the Apes-c/s; Six Million Dollar Man	2	4	6	13	18	22
127,134,135: 127-Star Trek-c/s; Ward-a. 134-Fonz-c/s; Starsky and Hutch. 135-Bionic Woman-c/s; Ward-a	2	4	6	11	16	20
141,151-Charlie's Angels-c/s. 151-Frankenstein	2	4	6	11	16	20
142,143,150,152-155,157: 142-MASH-c/s. 143-Rocky-c/s; King Kong-s. 150-(5/78) Close Encounters-c/s. 152-Close Enc./Star Wars-c/s. 153-Close Enc./Fonz-c/s. 154-Jaws II-c/s; Star Wars-s. 155-Star Wars/Fonz-c	2	4	6	9	13	16
144,149,156,158-160: 144-Fonz/Happy Days-c. 149-Star Wars/Six Mil.$ Man-c/s. 156-Grease/Travolta-c. 158-Mork & Mindy. 159-Battlestar Galactica-c/s; MASH-s. 160-Superman-c/s	2	4	6	11	16	20
145,147-Both have insert postcards: 145-Fonz/Rocky/L&S-c/s. 147-Star Wars-s; Farrah photo page (missing postcards-1/2 price)	3	6	9	14	20	26
146,148: 46-Star Wars-c/s with stickers insert (missing stickers-1/2 price). 148-Star Wars-c/s with inside-c color poster	3	6	9	16	23	30
161,170-Ward-a: 161-Mork & Mindy-c/s. 170-Dukes of Hazzard-c/s	2	4	6	8	11	14
162,165-168,171,172,175-178,180-Ward-a: 162-Sherlock Holmes-s. 165-Dracula-c/s. 167-Mork-c/s. 168,175-MASH-c/s. 168-Mork-s. 172-Dukes of Hazzard/CHiPs-c/s. 176-Barney Miller-c/s	2	4	6	8	10	12
163,179:163-Postcard insert; Mork & Mindy-c/s. 179-Insult cards insert; Popeye, Dukes of Hazzard-c/s	3	6	9	14	19	24
164,169,173,174: 164-Alien movie-c/s; Mork & Mindy-s. 169-Star Trek. 173,174-Star Wars-Empire Strikes Back. 173-SW poster	2	4	6	9	13	16
181,182,185-191,193,194,196-198-most Ward-a: 182-MASH-c/s. 185-Dukes of Hazzard-c/s; Jefferson-s. 187-Love Boat. 188-Fall Guy-s. 189-Fonz/Happy Days-c. 190,194-MASH-c/s. 191-Magnum P.I./Rocky-c; Magnum-s. 193-Knight Rider-s. 196-Dukes of Hazzard/Knight Rider-c/s. 198-Jaws III-c/s; Fall Guy-s	1	2	3	5	7	9
183,184,192,195,199,200-Ward-a in all: 183-Superman-c/s. 184-Star Trek-c/s. 192-E.T.-c/s; Rocky-s. 195-E.T.-c/s. 199-Jabba-c; Star Wars-s. 200-(12/83)	1	3	4	6	8	10
201,203,210-A-Team-c/s						6.00
202,204-206,211-224,226,227,230-233: 202-Knight Rider-s. 204-Magnum P.I.; A-Team-s. 206-Michael Jackson/Mr. T-c/s. 212-Prince-s; Cosby-s. 213-Monsters issue-c/s. 215-Hulk Hogan/Mr. T-c/s. 216-Miami Vice-s; James Bond-s. 217-Rambo-s; Cosby-s; A-Team-s. 218-Rocky-c/s. 219-Arnold/Commando-c/s; Rocky-s; Godzilla. 220-Rocky-c/s. 221-Stephen King app. 223-Miami Vice-s. 224-Cosby-s. 226-29th Anniv.; Tarzan-s; Aliens-s; Family Ties-s. 227-Cosby, Family Ties, Miami Vice-s. 230-Monkees-c/s; Elvis on-c; 232-Alf, Cheers, StarTrek-s. 233-Superman/James Bond-c/s; Robocop, Predator-s						5.00
207-209,225,234: 207-Michael Jackson-c/s. 208-Indiana Jones-c/s. 209-MichaelJackson/ Gremlins-c/s; Star Trek III-s. 225-Schwarzenegger/Stallone/G.I. Joe-c/s. 234-Don Martin-a begins; Batman/Robocop/Clint Eastwood-c/s						6.00
228,229: 228-Star Trek-c/s; Alf, Pee Wee Herman-s. 229-Monsters issue-c/s; centerfold with many superheroes						6.00
235,239,243,249: 235-1st Martin-c; Star Trek:TNG-s; Alf-s. 239-Beetlejuice-c/s; Mike Tyson-s. 243-X-Men and other heroes app. 249-Batman/Indiana Jones/Ghostbusters-c/s						6.00
236,244,245,248: 236-Madonna/Stallone-c/s; Twilight Zone-s. 244-Elvis-c/s; Martin-c. 245-Roger Rabbit-c/s. 248-Batman issue						6.00
237,238,240-242,246,247,250: 237-Robocop-s. 238-Rambo-c/s; Star Trek-s. 242-Dirty Harry-s, Ward-a. 246-Alf-s; Star Trek-s., Ward-a. 247-Star Trek-s. 250-Batman/Ghostbusters-s						4.00
251-253,255,256,259,261-265,275-278,281,284,286-297,299: 252-Star Trek-s. 253-Back to the Future-c/s. 255-TMNT-c/s. 256-TMNT-c/s; Batman, Bart Simpson on-c. 259-Die Hard II, Robocop-s. 261-TMNT, Twin Peaks-s. 262-Rocky-c/s; Rocky Horror-s. 265-TMNT-s. 276-Aliens III, Batman-s. 277-Clinton-c. 284-Bart Simpson-c; 90210-s. 297-Van Damme-s/photo-c. 299-Dumb & Dumber-c/s						4.00
254,257,266,267,272,280,282,285,298,300: 254-Back to the Future, Punisher-s; Wolverton-a, Batman-s, Ward-a. 257-Batman, Simpsons-s; Spider-Man and other heroes app. 266-Terminator-c/s. 267-Toons-c/s. 272-Star Trek VI-s. 280-Swimsuit issue. 282-Cheers-c/s. 285-Jurassic Park-c/s. 298-Swimsuit issue; Martin-c. 300-(8/95) Brady Bunch-c/s						5.00
258,260,274,279,283: 258-Simpsons-c/s; Back to the Future-s. 260-Spider-Man-c/s; Simpsons-s. 274-Batman-c/s. 279-Madonna-c/s. 283-Jurassic Park-c/s; Wolverine app. inside back-c						5.00
301-305,307-365: 365-Freas-c						3.00
306-Toy Story-c/s						4.00
Biggest... (Winter, 1977)	2	4	6	13	18	22
Biggest, Greatest... nn('65)	5	10	15	30	48	65
Biggest, Greatest... 2('66/67) - #5('69/70)	3	6	9	20	30	40
Biggest, Greatest... 6('70) - #12(Wint. '77)	3	6	9	14	19	24
Biggest, Greatest...13(Fall '78) - #21(Fall/Wint. '86)	2	4	6	8	11	14
...Blockbuster 1(Sum '87), 2('88), 3(Sum. '89)	1	3	4	6	8	10
...Blockbuster 4 - 6(Sum. '92)						6.00
...Collectors' Edition 4 ('73; formerly ...Special)	2	4	6	13	18	22
5-9,10(10/75)	2	4	6	11	16	20
11-19,20(11/17)	2	4	6	8	11	14
21,22,23(5/78): 23-Ward-a (#24-62,64 not numbered)	2	4	6	8	11	14
1978 (nn; July, Sept, Nov, Dec) (#24-27)	2	4	6	8	11	14
1979 (nn; May, July, Sept, Nov, Dec) (#28-33)	2	4	6	8	11	14
1980 (nn; Feb, May, July, Sept, Nov, Dec) (#34-39)	1	3	4	6	8	10
1981 (nn; Feb, May, July, Sept, Nov, Dec) (#40-45)	1	3	4	6	8	10
1982 (nn; Feb, May, July, Sept, Nov, Dec) (#46-51)	1	3	4	6	8	10
1983 (nn; Feb, May, Sept, Nov, Dec) (#52-56)	1	3	4	6	8	10
1984 (nn; Feb, May, July, Nov) (#57-60)	1	2	3	4	5	7
1985 (nn; Feb) (#61)	1	2	3	4	5	7
62(9/85), nn(#63,11/85), 64(12/85), 65-69, 70(4/87)	1	2	3	4	5	7
71,72,73(100 pgs., 1/88), 74-79, 80(9/89)						5.00
81-96, 97(two diff. issues), 98-115: 83-Elvis, Batman parodies						5.00
116('98)-Last issue?						6.00
...Digest 1(Fall, '86, 148 pgs.), 2(1/87)	1	2	3	6	8	10
...Digest 3-5	1	2	3	4	5	7
...Party Pack 1,2('88) - 4('90)						4.00
...Shut-Ups 1(2/72)	3	6	9	18	27	35
...Shut-Ups 2('72) becomes Cracked Spec. #3	3	6	9	14	19	24
...Special 3('73; formerly Cracked Shut-Ups; ...Collectors' Edition#4 on)	2	4	6	13	18	22
... Summer Special 1(Sum. '91), 2(Sum. '92)-Don Martin-a						4.00
... Summer Special 3(Sum. '93) - 8(Sum. '98)						3.00
... Super (Vol. 2, formerly Super Cracked) 5(Wint. '91/92) - 14(Wint.'97/98)						3.00
Extra Special... 1(Spr. '76)	2	4	6	11	16	20
Extra Special... 2(Spr./Sum. '77)	2	4	6	10	14	18
Extra Special... 3(Wint. '79) - 9(Wint. '86)	1	2	3	4	5	7
Giant... nn('65)	6	12	18	37	59	80
Giant... 2('66) - 5('69)	4	8	12	22	34	45
Giant...6('70) - 12('76)	3	6	9	17	25	32
Giant...nn(9/77, #13), nn(1/78, #14), nn(3/78, #15), nn(5/78, #16), nn(7/78, #17), nn(11/78, #18), nn(3/79, #19), nn(7/79, #20), nn(10/79, #21), nn(12/79, #22), nn(3/80, #23), nn(7/80, #24)	2	4	6	11	16	20
Giant...nn(10/80, #25), nn(12/80, #26), nn(3/81, #27), nn(7/81, #28), nn(10/81, #29), nn(12/81, #30), nn(7/82, #31), nn(10/82, #32), nn(12/82, #33), nn(7/83, #34),	2	4	6	8	11	14
Giant...nn(10/83, #35), nn(12/83, #36), nn(3/84, #37), nn(7/84, #38), nn(10/84, #39), nn(3/85, #40), nn(7/85, #41), nn(10/85, #42)	1	2	3	5	7	9
Giant...43(3/86) - 46(1/87), 47(Wint. '88), 48(Wint. '89)	1	2	3	4	5	7
King Sized... 1('67)	4	8	12	26	41	55
King Sized... 2('68) - 5('71)	3	6	9	18	27	35
King Sized... 6('72) - 11('77)	3	6	9	14	20	26
King Sized... 12(Fall '78) - 17(Sum. '83)	2	4	6	8	11	14
King Sized... 18-20 (Sum/'86) (#21,22 exist?)	1	3	4	6	8	10
Spaced Out... 1-4 ('93 - '94)						5.00
Super... 1('68)	4	8	12	26	41	55
Super... 2('69) - 6('73)	3	6	9	20	30	40
Super... 7('74), 8(Spr. '75) - 10(Spr. '77)	3	6	9	16	22	28
Super... 11(Sum. '78) - 16(Fall '81)	2	4	6	11	16	20
Super... 17(Spr. '82) - 22(Fall '83)	2	4	6	8	11	14
Super... 23(Sum. '84, mis-numbered as #24)	2	4	6	8	11	14
Super... 24(Fall '84, correctly numbered)	2	4	6	8	11	14
Super... 25(Wint. '85) - 32(Fall '86)	2	4	6	8	10	12
Super... (Vol. 2) 1('87, 100 pgs.)-Severin & Elder-a	1	3	4	6	8	10
Super... (Vol. 2) 2(Sum. '88), 3(Wint. '89), 4(exist?)(Becomes Cracked Super)						6.00

NOTE: ***Burgos** a-1-10. **Colan** a-257. **Davis** a-5, 11-17, 24, 40, 80; c-12-14, 16. **Elder** a-5, 6, 10-13; c-10. **Everett** a-1-10, 23-25, 61; c-1. **Heath** a-1-3, 6, 13, 14, 17, 110; c-6. **Jaffee** a-5, 6. **Don Martin** c-235, 244, 247, 259, 261, 264. **Morrow** a-8-10. **Reinman** a-1-4. **Severin** c/a-in most all issues. **Shores** a-3-7. **Torres** a-7-10. **Ward** a-22-24, 27, 35, 40, 120-193, 195, 197-205, 242, 244, 246, 247, 250, 252-257. **Williamson** a-1 (1 pg.). **Wolverton** a-10 (2 pgs.), Giant nn('65). **Wood** a-27, 35, 40. Alfred E. Neuman c-177, 200, 202. Batman c-234, 248, 249, 256, 274. Captain America c-256. Christmas c-234, 243. Spider-Man c-260. Star Trek c-127, 169, 207, 228. Star Wars c-145, 146, 148, 149, 152, 155, 173, 174, 199. Superman c-183, 233. #144, 146 have free full-color pre-glued stickers. #145, 147, 155, 163 have free full-color postcards. #123, 137, 154, 157 have free iron-ons.*

CRACKED MONSTER PARTY
Globe Communications: July, 1988 - No. 27, Wint. 1999/2000

	GD 2.0	VG 4.0	FN 6.0	VF 8.0	VF/NM 9.0	NM- 9.2
1	2	4	6	10	14	18
2-10	2	4	6	8	10	12
11-26	1	2	3	4	5	7
27-Interview with a Vampire-c/s	2	4	6	8	10	12

Crack Western #65 © QUA

Crash Ryan #1 © MAR

Crazy Magazine #52 © MAR

GD 2.0 | VG 4.0 | FN 6.0 | VF 8.0 | VF/NM 9.0 | NM- 9.2

GD 2.0 | VG 4.0 | FN 6.0 | VF 8.0 | VF/NM 9.0 | NM- 9.2

CRACKED'S FOR MONSTERS ONLY
Major Magazines: Sept, 1969 - No. 9, Sept, 1969; June, 1972

1 5 10 15 30 48 65
2-9, nn(6/72) 3 6 9 20 30 40

CRACK WESTERN (Formerly Crack Comics; Jonesy No. 85 on)
Quality Comics Group: No. 63, Nov, 1949 - No. 84, May, 1953 (36 pgs., 63-68,74-on)

63(#1)-Ward-c; Two-Gun Lil (origin & 1st app.)(ends #84), Arizona Ames, his horse Thunder (with sidekick Spurs & his horse Calico), Frontier Marshal (ends #70), & Dead Canyon Days (ends #69) begin; Crandall-a 18 36 54 107 169 230
64,65: 64-Ward-c. Crandall-a in both. 15 30 45 83 124 165
66,68-Photo-c. 66-Arizona Ames becomes A. Raines (ends #84) 13 26 39 72 101 130
67-Randolph Scott photo-c; Crandall-a 14 28 42 80 115 150
69(52pgs.)-Crandall-a 13 26 39 72 101 130
70(52pgs.)-The Whip (origin & 1st app.) & his horse Diablo begin (ends #84); Crandall-a 13 26 39 72 101 130
71(52pgs.)-Frontier Marshal becomes Bob Allen F. Marshal (ends #84); Crandall-c/a 14 28 42 80 115 150
72(52pgs.)-Tim Holt photo-c 12 24 36 67 94 120
73(52pgs.)-Photo-c 10 20 30 58 79 100
74-76,78,79,81,83-Crandall-c. 83-Crandall-a(p) 11 22 33 62 86 110
77,80,82 8 16 24 44 57 70
84-Crandall-c/a 12 24 36 67 94 120

NOTE: ***Crandall** c-71p, 74-81, 83p(w/**Cuidera**-i).*

CRASH COMICS (Catman Comics No. 6 on)
Tem Publishing Co.: May, 1940 - No. 5, Nov, 1940

1-The Blue Streak, Strongman (origin), The Perfect Human, Shangra begin (1st app. of each); Kirby-a 331 662 993 2317 4059 5800
2-Simon & Kirby-a 171 342 513 1086 1868 2650
3,5-Simon & Kirby-a 145 290 435 921 1586 2250
4-Origin & 1st app. The Catman; S&K-a 354 708 1062 2248 4224 6200

NOTE: *Solar Legion by **Kirby** No. 1-5 (5 pgs. each). Strongman c-1-4. Catman c-5.*

CRASH DIVE (See Cinema Comics Herald)

CRASH METRO AND THE STAR SQUAD
Oni Press: May, 1999 ($2.95, B&W, one-shot)

1-Allred-s/Ontiveros-a 3.00

CRASH RYAN (Also see Dark Horse Presents #44)
Marvel Comics (Epic): Oct, 1984 - No. 4, Jan, 1985 (Baxter paper, lim. series)

1-4 3.00

CRAZY (Also see This Magazine is Crazy)
Atlas Comics (CSI): Dec, 1953 - No. 7, July, 1954

1-Everett-c/a 32 64 96 188 307 425
2 21 42 63 124 202 280
3-7: 4-I Love Lucy satire. 5-Satire on censorship 18 36 54 107 169 230

NOTE: ***Ayers** a-5. **Berg** a-1, 2. **Burgos** c-5, 6. **Drucker** a-6. **Everett** a-1-4. **Al Hartley** a-4. **Heath** a-3, 7; c-7. **Maneely** a-1-7, c-3, 4. **Post** a-3-6. Funny monster c-1-4.*

CRAZY (Satire)
Marvel Comics Group: Feb, 1973 - No. 3, June, 1973

1-Not Brand Echh-r; Beatles cameo (r) 3 6 9 16 23 30
2,3-Not Brand Echh-r; Kirby-a 2 4 6 10 16 20

CRAZY MAGAZINE (Satire)
Oct, 1973 - No. 94, Apr, 1983 (40-90¢, B&W magazine)
Marvel Comics: (#1, 44 pgs; #2-90, reg. issues, 52 pgs; #92-95, 68 pgs)'

1-Wolverton(1 pg.), Bode-a; 3 pg. photo story of Neal Adams & Dick Giordano; Harlan Ellison story; TV Kung Fu sty. 5 10 15 30 48 65
2-"Live & Let Die" c/s; 8pgs; Adams/Buscema-a; McCloud w5 pgs. Adams-a; Kurtzman's "Hey Look" 2 pg.-r 3 6 9 20 30 40
3-5: 3-"High Plains Drifter" w/Clint Eastwood c/s; Waltons app; Drucker, Reese-a. 4-Shaft-c/s; Ploog-a; Nixon 3 pg. app; Freas-a. 5-Michael Crichton's "Westworld" c/s; Nixon app. 3 6 9 17 25 32
6,7,18: 6-Exorcist c/s; Nixon app. 7-TV's Kung Fu c/s; Nixon app.; Ploog & Freas-a. 18-Six Million Dollar Man/Bionic Woman c/s; Welcome Back Kotter story 3 6 9 16 22 28
8-10: 8-Serpico c/s; Casper parody; TV's Police Story. 9-Joker cameo; Chinatown story; Eisner s/a begins; Has 1st 8 covers on-c. 10-Playboy Bunny-c; M. Severin-a; Lee Marrs-a begins; "Deathwish" story 3 6 9 14 20 26
11-17,19: 11-Towering Inferno. 12-Rhoda. 13-"Tommy" the Who Rock Opera. 14-Mandingo. 15-Jaws story. 16-Santa/Xmas-c; "Good Times" TV story; Jaws. 17-Bicentennial issue; Baretta; Woody Allen. 19-King Kong c/s; Reagan, J. Carter, Howard the Duck cameos, "Laverne & Shirley" 2 4 6 11 16 20
20,24,27: 20-Bicentennial-c; Space 1999 sty; Superheroes song sheet, 4pgs. 24-Charlie's Angels. 27-Charlie's Angels/Travolta/Fonz-c; Bionic Woman sty 3 6 9 14 19 24
21-23,25,26,28-30: 21-Starsky & Hutch. 22-Mount Rushmore/J. Carter-c; TV's Barney Miller; Superheroes spoof. 23-Santa/Xmas-c; "Happy Days" sty; "Omen" sty. 25-J. Carter-c/s; Grandenetti-a begins; TV's Alice; Logan's Run. 26-TV Stars-c; Mary Hartman, King Kong. 28-Donny & Marie Osmond-c/s; Marathon Man. 29-Travolta/Kotter-c; "One Day at a Time", Gong Show. 30-1977, 84 pgs. w/bonus; Jaws, Baretta, King Kong, Happy Days 2 4 6 9 12 15
31,33-35,38,40: 31-"Rocky"-c/s; TV game shows. 33-Peter Benchley's "Deep". 34-J. Carter-c; TV's "Fish". 35-Xmas-c with Fonz/Six Million Dollar Man/Wonder Woman/Darth Vader/ Travolta, TV's "Mash" & "Family Matters". 38-Close Encounters of the Third Kind-c/s. 40-"Three's Company-c/s 1 3 4 6 8 11
32-Star Wars/Darth Vader-c/s; "Black Sunday" 3 6 9 14 19 24
36,42,47,49: 36-Farrah Fawcett/Six Million Dollar Man-c; TV's Nancy Drew & Hardy Boys; 1st app. Howard The Duck in Crazy, 2 pgs. 42-84 pgs. w/bonus; TV Hulk/Spider-Man-c; Mash, Gong Show, One Day at a Time, Disco, Alice. 47-Battlestar Galactica xmas-c; movie "Foul Play". 49-1979, 84 pgs. w/bonus; Mork & Mindy-c; Jaws, Saturday Night Fever, Three's Company 2 4 6 9 12 15
37-1978, 84 pgs. w/bonus. Darth Vader-c; Barney Miller, Laverne & Shirley, Good Times, Rocky, Donny & Marie Osmond, Bionic Woman 2 4 6 13 18 22
39,44: 39-Saturday Night Fever-c/s. 44-"Grease"-c w/Travolta/O. Newton-John 2 4 6 11 16 20
41-Kiss-c & 1pg. photos; Disaster movies, TV's "Family", Annie Hall 4 8 12 28 44 60
43,45,46,48,51: 43-Jaws-c; Saturday Night Fever. 43-E.C. swipe from Mad #131. 45-Travolta/O. Newton-John/J. Carter-c; Eight is Enough. 46-TV Hulk-c/s; Punk Rock. 48-"Wiz"-c, Battlestar Galactica-s. 51-Grease/Mork & Mindy/D&M Osmond-c, Mork & Mindy-sty. "Boys from Brazil" 1 3 4 6 8 11
50,58: 50-Superman movie-c/sty, Playboy Mag., TV Hulk, Fonz; Howard the Duck, 1 pg. 58-1980, 84 pgs. w/32 pg. color comic bonus insert-Full reprint of Crazy Comic #1, Battlestar Galactica, Charlie's Angels, Starsky & Hutch 2 4 6 11 16 20
52,59,60,64: 52-1979, 84 pgs. w/bonus. Marlon Brando-c; TV Hulk, Grease. Kiss, 1 pg. photos. 59-Santa Ptd-c by Larkin; "Alien", "Moonraker", Rocky-2, Howard the Duck, 1 pg. 60-Star Trek w/Muppets-c; Star Trek sty; 1st app/origin Teen Hulk; Severin-a. 64-84 pgs. w/bonus Monopoly game satire. "Empire Strikes Back", 8 pgs., One Day at a Time 2 4 6 11 16 20
53,54,65,67-70: 53-"Animal House"-c/sty; TV's "Vegas", Howard the Duck, 1 pg. 54-Love at First Bite-c/sty, Fantasy Island sty, Howard the Duck 1 pg. 65-(Has #66 on-c, Aug/'80). "Black Hole" w/Janson-a; Kirby,Wood/Severin-a(r), 5 pgs. Howard the Duck, 3 pgs.; Broderick-a; Buck Rogers, Mr. Rogers. 67-84 pgs. w/bonus; TV's Kung Fu, Exorcist; Ploog-a(r). 68-American Gigolo, Dukes of Hazzard, Teen Hulk; Howard the Duck, 3 pgs. Broderick-a; Monster sty/5 pg. Ditko-a(r). 69-Obnoxio the Clown-c/sty; Stephen King's "Shining", Teen Hulk, Richie Rich, Howard the Duck, 3pgs; Broderick-a. 70-84 pgs. Towering Inferno, Daytime TV; Trina Robbins-a 1 3 4 6 8 10
55-57,61,63: 55-84 pgs. w/bonus; Love Boat, Mork & Mindy, Fonz, TV Hulk. 56-Mork/Rocky/ J. Carter-c; China Syndrome. 57-TV Hulk with Miss Piggy-c, Dracula, Taxi, Muppets. 61-1980, 84 pgs. Adams-a(r), McCloud, Pro wrestling, Casper, TV's Police Story. 63-Apocalypse Now-Coppola's cult movie; 3rd app. Teen Hulk, Howard the Duck, 3 pgs. 2 4 6 8 11 14
62-Kiss-c & 2 pg. app; Quincy, 2nd app. Teen Hulk 4 8 12 24 37 50
66-Sept/'80, Empire Strikes Back-c/sty; Teen Hulk by Severin, Howard the Duck, 3pgs. by Broderick 2 4 6 10 14 18
71,72,75-77,79: 71-Blues Brothers parody, Teen Hulk, Superheroes parody, WKRP in Cincinnati, Howard the Duck, 3pgs. by Broderick. 72-Jackie Gleason/Smokey & the Bandit II-c/sty, Shogun, Teen Hulk. Howard the Duck, 3pgs. by Broderick. 75-Flash Gordon movie c/sty; Teen Hulk, Cat in the Hat, Howard the Duck 3pgs. by Broderick. 76-84 pgs. w/bonus; Monster-sty w/ Crandall-a(r), Monster-stys(2) w/Kirby-a(r), 5pgs. ea; Mash, TV Hulk, Chinatown. 77-Popeye movie/R. Williams-c/sty; Teen Hulk, Love Boat, Howard the Duck 3 pgs. 79-84 pgs. w/bonus color stickers; has new material; "9 to 5" w/Dolly Parton, Teen Hulk, Magnum P.I., Monster-sty w/5pgs, Ditko-a(r), "Rat" w/Sutton-a(r), Everett-a, 4 pgs.(r) 1 3 4 6 8 10
73,74,78,80: 73-84 pgs. w/bonus Hulk/Spiderman Finger Puppets-c & bonus; "Live & Let Die, Jaws, Fantasy Island. 74-Dallas/"Who Shot J.R."-c/sty; Elephant Man, Howard the Duck 3pgs. by Broderick. 78-Clint Eastwood-c/sty; Teen Hulk, Superheroes parody, Lou Grant. 80-Star Wars, 2 pg. app; "Howling", TV's "Greatest American Hero" 2 4 6 8 11 14
81,84,86,87,89: 81-.Superman Movie II-c/sty; Wolverine cameo, Mash, Teen Hulk. 84-American Werewolf in London, Johnny Carson app; Teen Hulk. 86-Time Bandits-c/sty; Private Benjamin. 87-Rubix Cube-c; Hill Street Blues, "Ragtime", Origin Obnoxio the Clown; Teen Hulk. 89-Burt Reynolds "Sharkey's Machine", Teen Hulk 1 3 4 6 8 10
82-X-Men-c w/new Byrne-a, 84 pgs. w/new material; Fantasy Island, Teen Hulk, "For Your

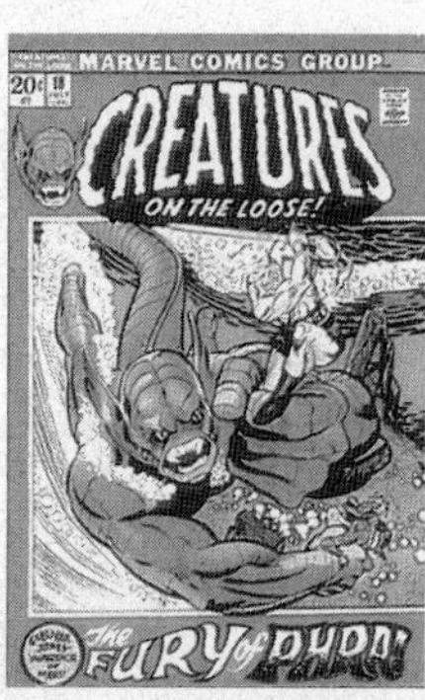

Creatures on the Loose #18 © MAR

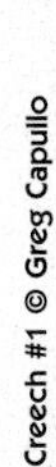
Creech #1 © Greg Capullo

Creepy #4 © WP

	GD	VG	FN	VF	VF/NM	NM-
	2.0	4.0	6.0	8.0	9.0	9.2

Eyes Only", Spiderman/Human Torch-r by Kirby/Ditko; Sutton-a(r); Rogers-a; Hunchback of Notre Dame, 5 pgs. 2 4 6 11 16 20
83-Raiders of the Lost Ark-c/sty; Hart to Hart; Reese-a; Teen Hulk 2 4 6 9 13 20
85,88: 85-84 pgs; Escape from New York, Teen Hulk; Kirby-a(r), 5 pgs, Poseidon Adventure, Flintstones, Sesame Street. 88-84 pgs. w/bonus Dr. Strange Game; some new material; Jeffersons, X-Men/Wolverine, 10 pgs.; Byrne-a; Apocalypse Now, Teen Hulk 1 3 4 6 8 11
90-94: 90-Conan-c/sty; M. Severin-a; Teen Hulk. 91-84 pgs, some new material; Bladerunner-c/sty, "Deathwish-II, Teen Hulk, Black Knight, 10 pgs.-'50s-r w/Maneely-a. 92-Wrath of Khan Star Trek-c/sty; Joanie & Chachi, Teen Hulk. 93-"E.T."-c/sty, Teen Hulk, Archie Bunkers Place, Dr. Doom Game. 94-Poltergeist, Smurfs, Teen Hulk, Casper, Avengers parody-8pgs. Adams-a 2 4 6 10 14 18
Crazy Summer Special #1 (Sum, '75, 100 pgs.)-Nixon, TV Kung Fu, Babe Ruth, Joe Namath, Waltons, McCloud, Chariots of the Gods 3 6 9 14 19 24

NOTE: ***N. Adams*** *a-2, 61r, 94p.* ***Austin*** *a-82i.* ***Buscema*** *a-2, 82.* ***Byrne*** *c-82p.* ***Nick Cardy*** *c-7, 8, 10, 12-16, Super Special 1.* ***Crandall*** *a-76r.* ***Ditko*** *a-68r, 79r, 82r.* ***Drucker*** *a-3.* ***Eisner*** *a-9-16.* ***Kelly Freas*** *c-1-6, 9, 11; a-7.* ***Kirby/Wood*** *a-66r.* ***Ploog*** *a-1, 4, 7, 67r, 73r.* ***Rogers*** *a-82.* ***Sparling*** *a-92.* ***Wood*** *a-65r. Howard the Duck in 36, 50, 51, 53, 54, 59, 63, 65, 66, 68, 69, 71, 72, 74, 75, 77. Hulk in 46, c-42, 46, 57, 73. Star Wars in 32, 66; c-37.*

CRAZYMAN
Continuity Comics: Apr, 1992 - No. 3, 1992 ($2.50, high quality paper)
1-($3.95, 52 pgs.)-Embossed-c; N. Adams part-i 4.00
2,3 ($2.50): 2-N. Adams/Bolland-c 3.00

CRAZYMAN
Continuity Comics: V2#1, 5/93 - No. 4, 1/94 ($2.50, high quality paper)
V2#1-4: 1-Entire book is die-cut. 2-(12/93)-Adams-c(p) & part scripts. 3-(12/93). 4-Indicia says #3, Jan. 1993 3.00

CRAZY, MAN, CRAZY (Magazine) (Becomes This Magazine is...?) (Formerly From Here to Insanity)
Humor Magazines (Charlton): V2#1, Dec, 1955 - V2#2, June, 1956
V2#1,V2#2-Satire; Wolverton-a, 3 pgs. 15 30 45 86 133 180

CREATURE, THE (See Movie Classics)

CREATURE COMMANDOS (See Weird War Tales #93 for 1st app.)
DC Comics: May, 2000 - No. 8, Dec, 2000 ($2.50, limited series)
1-8: Truman-s/Eaton-a 3.00

CREATURES OF THE ID
Caliber Press: 1990 ($2.95, B&W)
1-Frank Einstein (Madman) app.; Allred-a 3 6 9 16 23 30

CREATURES OF THE NIGHT
Dark Horse Books: Nov, 2004 ($12.95, hardcover graphic novel)
HC-Neil Gaiman-s/Michael Zulli-a/c 13.00

CREATURES ON THE LOOSE (Formerly Tower of Shadows No. 1-9)(See Kull)
Marvel Comics: No. 10, March, 1971 - No. 37, Sept, 1975 (New-a & reprints)
10-(15¢)-1st full app. King Kull; see Kull the Conqueror; Wrightson-a 8 16 24 53 89 125
11-15: 13-Last 15¢ issue 3 6 9 19 29 38
16-Origin Warrior of Mars (begins, ends #21) 3 6 9 14 20 26
17-20 2 4 6 9 13 16
21-Steranko-c 3 6 9 17 25 32
22-Steranko-c; Thongor stories begin 3 6 9 18 27 35
23-29-Thongor-c/stories 1 3 4 6 8 10
30-Manwolf begins 3 6 9 19 29 38
31-33 2 4 6 9 13 16
34-37 2 4 6 8 10 12

NOTE: ***Crandall*** *a-13.* ***Ditko*** *r-15, 17, 18, 20, 22, 24, 27, 28.* ***Everett*** *a-16i(new).* ***Matt Fox*** *r-21i.* ***Howard*** *a-26i.* ***Gil Kane*** *a-16p, 17p, 19i; c-16, 17, 19, 20, 25, 29, 33p, 35p, 36p.* ***Kirby*** *a-10-15r, 16(2)r, 17r, 19r.* ***Morrow*** *a-20, 21.* ***Perez*** *a-33-37; c-34p.* ***Shores*** *a-11.* ***innott*** *r-21.* ***Sutton*** *c-10.* ***Tuska*** *a-30-32p.*

CREECH, THE
Image Comics: Oct, 1997 - No. 3, Dec, 1997 ($1.95/$2.50, limited series)
1-3: 1-Capullo-s/c/a(p) 3.00
TPB (1999, $9.95) r/#1-3, McFarlane intro. 10.00
Out for Blood 1-3 (7/01 - No. 3, 11/01; $4.95) Capullo-s/c/a 5.00

CREED
Hall of Heroes Comics: Dec, 1994 - No. 2, Jan, 1995 ($2.50, B&W)
1 2 4 6 9 12 15
2 2 4 6 8 10 12

CREED
Lightning Comics: June, 1995 - No. 3 ($2.75/$3.00, B&W/color)
1-($2.75) 4.00
1-($3.00, color) 5.00
1-($9.95)-Commemorative Edition 10.00
1-TwinVariant Edition (1250? print run) 10.00
1-Special Edition; polybagged w/certificate 4.00
1 Gold Collectors Edition; polybagged w/certificate 3.00
2,3-($3.00, color)-Butt Naked Edition & regular-c 3.00
3-($9.95)-Commemorative Edition; polybagged w/certificate & card 10.00

CREED: CRANIAL DISORDER
Lightning Comics: Oct, 1996 ($3.00, limited series)
1-3-Two covers 3.00
1-($5.95)-Platinum Edition 6.00
2,3-($9.95)Ltd. Edition 10.00

CREED/TEENAGE MUTANT NINJA TURTLES
Lightning Comics: May, 1996 ($3.00, one-shot)
1-Kaniuga-a(p)/scripts; Laird-c; variant-c exists 3.00
1-($9.95)-Platinum Edition 10.00
1-Special Edition; polybagged w/certificate 5.00

CREEPER BY STEVE DITKO, THE
DC Comics: 2010 ($39.99, hardcover with dustjacket)
HC-Reprints Showcase #73, Beware the Creeper #1-6, First Issue Special #7 and apps. in World's Finest #249-255 and Cancelled Comic Cavalcade #2; intro. by Steve Niles 40.00

CREEPER, THE (See Beware... , Showcase #73 & 1st Issue Special #7)
DC Comics: Dec, 1997 - No. 11; #1,000,000 Nov, 1998 ($2.50)
1-11-Kaminski-s/Martinbrough-a(p). 7,8-Joker-c/app. 3.00
#1,000,000 (11/98) 853rd Century x-over 3.00

CREEPER, THE (See DCU Brave New World)
DC Comics: Oct, 2006 - No. 6, Mar, 2007 ($2.99, limited series)
1-6-Niles-s/Justiniano-a/c; Jack Ryder becomes the Creeper. 2-6-Batman app. 3.00
... - Welcome to Creepsville TPB ('07, $19.99) r/#1-6 & story from DCU Brave New World 20.00

CREEPS
Image Comics: Oct, 2001 - No. 4, May, 2002 ($2.95)
1-4-Mandrake-a/Mishkin-s 3.00

CREEPSHOW
Plume/New American Library Pub.: July, 1982 (softcover graphic novel)
1st edition-nn-(68 pgs.) Kamen-c/Wrightson-a; screenplay by Stephen King for the George Romero movie 4 8 12 28 44 60
2nd-7th printings 3 6 9 18 27 35

CREEPSVILLE
Laughing Reindeer Press: V2#1, Winter, 1995 ($4.95)
V2#1-Comics w/text 5.00

CREEPY (See Warren Presents)
Warren Publishing Co./Harris Publ. #146: 1964 - No. 145, Feb, 1983; No. 146, 1985 (B&W, magazine)
1-Frazetta-a (his last story in comics?); Jack Davis-c; 1st Warren all comics magazine; 1st app. Uncle Creepy 12 24 36 79 160 240
2-Frazetta-c & 1 pg. strip 8 16 24 53 89 125
3-8,11-13,15-17: 3-7,9-11,15-17-Frazetta-c. 7-Frazetta 1 pg. strip. 15,16-Adams-a. 16-Jeff Jones-a 6 12 18 37 59 80
9-Creepy fan club sketch by Wrightson (1st published-a); has 1/2 pg. anti-smoking strip by Frazetta; Frazetta-c; 1st Wood and Ditko art on this title; Toth-a (low print) 8 16 24 51 86 120
10-Brunner fan club sketch (1st published work) 6 12 18 39 62 85
14-Neal Adams 1st Warren work 6 12 18 39 62 85
18-28,30,31: 27-Frazetta-c 4 8 12 28 44 60
29,34: 29-Jones-a 5 10 15 30 48 65
32-(scarce) Frazetta-c; Harlan Ellison sty 7 14 21 44 72 100
33,35,37,39,40,42-47,49: 35-Hitler/Nazi-s. 39-1st Uncle Creepy solo-s, Cousin Eerie app.; early Brunner-a. 42-1st San Julian-c. 44-1st Ploog-a. 46-Corben-a 4 8 12 23 36 48
36-(11/70)1st Corben art at Warren 5 10 15 30 48 65
38,41-(scarce): 38-1st Kelly-c. 41-Corben-a 5 10 15 35 55 75
48,55,65-(1972, 1973, 1974 Annuals) #55 & 65 contain an 8 pg. slick comic insert. 48-(84 pgs.). 55-Color poster bonus (1/2 price if missing). 65-(100 pgs.) Summer Giant 5 10 15 30 48 65
50-Vampirella/Eerie/Creepy-c 5 10 15 35 55 75
51,54,56-61,64: All contain an 8 pg. slick comic insert in middle. 59-Xmas horror. 54,64-Chaykin-a 4 8 12 26 41 55

The Crew #1 © MAR

Crime and Punishment #10 © LEV

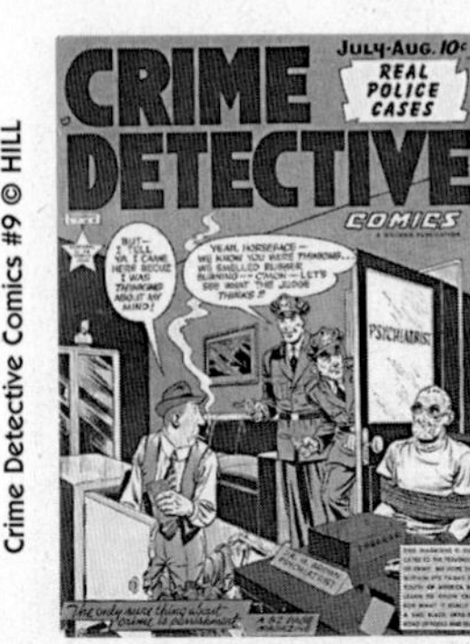

Crime Detective Comics #9 © HILL

GD 2.0 | VG 4.0 | FN 6.0 | VF 8.0 | VF/NM 9.0 | NM- 9.2

52,53,66,71,72,75,76,78-80: 71-All Bermejo-a; Space & Time issue. 72-Gual-a. 78-Fantasy issue. 79,80-Monsters issue 3 6 9 19 29 38
62,63-1st & 2nd full Wrightson story art; Corben-a; 8 pg. color comic insert
4 8 12 26 41 55
67,68,73 3 6 9 21 32 42
69,70-Edgar Allan Poe issues; Corben-a 3 6 9 20 40 60
74,77: 74-All Crandell-a. 77-Xmas Horror issue; Corben-a,Wrightson-a
4 8 12 23 36 48
81,84,85,88-90,92-94,96-99,102,104-112,114-118,120,122-130: 84,93-Sports issue. 85,97,102-Monster issue. 89-All war issue; Nino-a. 94-Weird Children issue. 96,109-Aliens issue. 99-Disasters. 103-Corben-a. 104-Robots issue. 106-Sword & Sorcery.107-Sci-fi. 116-End of Man. 125-Xmas Horror 2 4 6 10 14 18
82,100,101: 82-All Maroto issue. 100-(8/78) Anniversary. 101-Corben-a
3 6 9 14 20 26
83,95-Wrightson-a. 83-Corben-a. 95-Gorilla/Apes. 2 4 6 13 18 22
86,87,91,103-Wrightson-a. 86-Xmas Horror 2 4 6 13 18 22
113-All Wrightson-r issue 3 6 9 19 29 38
119,121: 119-All Nino issue.121-All Severin-r issue 2 4 6 13 18 22
131,133-136,138,140: 135-Xmas issue 2 4 6 13 18 22
132,137,139: 132-Corben. 137-All Williamson-r issue. 139-All Toth-r issue
3 6 9 14 20 26
141,143,144 (low dist.): 144-Giant, $2.25; Frazetta-c 3 6 9 16 23 30
142,145 (low dist.): 142-(10/82, 100 pgs.) All Torres issue. 145-(2/83) last Warren issue
3 6 9 18 27 35
146 ($2.95)-1st from Harris; resurrection issue 7 14 21 44 72 100
Year Book '68-'70: '70-Neal Adams, Ditko-a(r) 5 10 15 35 55 75
Annual 1971,1972 5 10 15 32 51 70
1993 Fearbook ($3.95)-Harris Publ.; Brereton-c; Vampirella by Busiek-s/Art Adams-a; David-s; Paquette-a 4 8 12 26 41 55
...:The Classic Years TPB (Harris/Dark Horse, '91, $12.95) Kaluta-c; art by Frazetta,Torres, Crandall, Ditko, Morrow, Williamson, Wrightson 25.00

NOTE: *All issues contain many good artists works:* ***Neal Adams, Brunner, Corben, Craig (Taycee), Crandall, Ditko, Evans, Frazetta, Heath, Jeff Jones, Krenkel, McWilliams, Morrow, Nino, Orlando, Ploog, Severin, Torres, Toth, Williamson, Wood, & Wrightson****; covers by* ***Crandall, Davis, Frazetta, Morrow, San Julian, Todd/Bode****; Otto Binder's "Adam Link" stories in No. 2, 4, 6, 8, 9, 12, 13, 15 with* ***Orlando*** *art.* ***Frazetta*** *c-2-7, 9-11, 15-17, 27, 32, 83r, 89r, 91r.* ***E.A. Poe*** *adaptations in 66, 69, 70.*

CREEPY (Mini-series)
Harris Comics/Dark Horse: 1992 - Book 4, 1992 (48 pgs, B&W, squarebound)

Book 1-4: Brereton painted-c on all. Stories and art by various incl. David (all), Busiek(2), Infantino(2), Guice(3), Colan(1) 2 4 6 8 10 12

CREEPY
Dark Horse Comics: July, 2009 - Present ($4.99, 48 pgs, B&W, quarterly)

1-7: 1-Powell-c; art by Wrightson, Toth, Alexander 5.00

CREEPY THINGS
Charlton Comics: July, 1975 - No. 6, June, 1976

1-Sutton-c/a 3 6 9 14 19 24
2-6: Ditko-a in 3,5. Sutton c-3,4. 6-Zeck-c 2 4 6 8 10 12
Modern Comics Reprint 2-6(1977) 5.00

NOTE: ***Larson*** *a-2,6.* ***Sutton*** *a-1,2,4,6.* ***Zeck*** *a-2.*

CREW, THE
Marvel Comics: July, 2003 - No. 7, Jan, 2004 ($2.50)

1-7-Priest-s/Bennett-a; James Rhodes (War Machine) app. 3.00

CRIME AND JUSTICE (Badge Of Justice #22 on; Rookie Cop? No. 27 on)
Capitol Stories/Charlton Comics: March, 1951 - No. 21, Nov, 1954; No. 23, Mar, 1955 - No. 26, Sept, 1955 (No #22)

1 36 72 108 216 351 485
2 16 32 48 94 147 200
3-8,10-13: 6-Negligee panels 15 30 45 84 127 170
9-Classic story "Comics Vs. Crime" 28 56 84 165 270 375
14-Color illos in **POP**; gory story of man who beheads women
23 46 69 136 223 310
15-17,19-21,23,24: 15-Negligee panels. 23-Rookie Cop (1st app.)
11 22 33 64 90 115
18-Ditko-a 27 54 81 158 259 360
25,26: (scarce) 15 30 45 90 140 190

NOTE: ***Alascia*** *c-20.* ***Ayers*** *a-17.* ***Shuster*** *a-19-21; c-19. Bondage c-11, 12.*

CRIME AND PUNISHMENT (Title inspired by 1935 film)
Lev Gleason Publications: April, 1948 - No. 74, Aug, 1955

1-Mr. Crime app. on-c 39 78 117 236 388 540
2-Narrator, Officer Common Sense (a ghost) begins, ends #27? (see Crime Does Not Pay #41) 20 40 60 117 189 260

GD 2.0 | VG 4.0 | FN 6.0 | VF 8.0 | VF/NM 9.0 | NM- 9.2

3-(6/48)-Used in **SOTI**, pg. 112; contains Biro & Gleason self censorship code of 12 listed restrictions 22 44 66 128 209 290
4,5 15 30 45 90 140 190
6-10 14 28 42 80 115 150
11-20 12 24 36 69 97 125
21-30 11 22 33 60 83 105
31-38,40-44,46: 46-One pg. Frazetta-a 10 20 30 54 72 90
39-Drug mention story "The Five Dopes" 15 30 45 84 127 170
45- "Hophead Killer" drug story 15 30 45 84 127 170
47-55,57,60-65,70-74: 9 18 27 52 69 85
56-Classic dagger/torture-c 11 22 33 60 83 105
58-Used in **POP**, pg. 79 11 22 33 60 83 105
59-Used in **SOTI**, illo "What comic-book America stands for"
34 68 102 199 325 450
66-Toth-c/a(4); 3-D effect issue (3/54); 1st "Deep Dimension" process
40 80 120 246 411 575
67- "Monkey on His Back" heroin story; 3-D effect issue
39 78 117 231 378 525
68-3-D effect issue; Toth-c (7/54) 32 64 96 188 307 425
69- "The Hot Rod Gang" dope crazy kids 15 30 45 84 127 170

NOTE: ***Belfi*** *a- 2, 3, 5.* ***Biro*** *c-most.* ***Al Borth*** *a-9, 35.* ***Cooper*** *a-9.* ***Joe Certa*** *a-8.* ***Tony Dipreta*** *a-3, 5, 15, 34.* ***Everett*** *a-31.* ***Bob Fujitani (Fuje)*** *a-2-20, 26, 27.* ***Joseph Gaguardi*** *a-15, 18, 20.* ***Fred Guardineer*** *a-2-5, 10-12, 14, 15, 17, 18, 20, 26-28, 32, 34, 35, 38-44, 51, 54.* ***Jack Keller*** *a-18.* ***Kinstler*** *c-69.* ***Martinott*** *a-13.* ***Al McWilliams*** *a-36, 41, 48, 49.* ***William Overgard*** *a-36.* ***Dick Rockwell*** *a-35, 51.* ***Robert Q. Sale*** *a-43.* ***George Tuska*** *a-28, 30, 51, 64, 70. Painted-c-31.*

CRIME AND PUNISHMENT: MARSHALL LAW TAKES MANHATTAN
Marvel Comics (Epic Comics): 1989 ($4.95, 52 pgs., direct sales only, mature)

nn-Graphic album featuring Marshall Law 5.00

CRIME BIBLE: THE FIVE LESSONS (Aftermath of DC's 52 series)
DC Comics: Dec, 2007 - No. 5, Apr, 2008 ($2.99, limited series)

1-5-Rucka-s; The Question (Renee Montoya) app. 3-Batwoman app. 3.00
The Question: The Five Books of Blood HC (2008, $19.99) r/#1-5 20.00
The Question: The Five Books of Blood SC (2009, $14.99) r/#1-5 15.00

CRIME CAN'T WIN (Formerly Cindy Smith)
Marvel/Atlas Comics (TCI 41/CCC 42,43,4-12): No. 41, 9/50 - No. 43, 2/51; No. 4, 4/51 - No. 12, 9/53

41(#1) 26 52 78 154 252 350
42(#2) 15 30 45 86 133 180
43(#3)-Horror story 18 36 54 107 169 230
4(4/51),5-12: 10-Possible use in **SOTI**, pg. 161 14 28 42 78 112 145

NOTE: ***Robinson*** *a-9-11.* ***Tuska*** *a-43.*

CRIME CASES COMICS (Formerly Willie Comics)
Marvel/Atlas Comics(CnPC No.24-8/MJMC No.9-12): No. 24, 8/50 - No. 27, 3/51; No. 5, 5/51 - No. 12, 7/52

24 (#1, 52 pgs.)-True police cases 20 40 60 114 182 250
25-27(#2-4): 27-Morisi-a 15 30 45 83 124 165
5-12: 11-Robinson-a. 12-Tuska-a 14 28 42 76 108 140

CRIME CLINIC
Ziff-Davis Publishing Co.: No. 10, July-Aug, 1951 - No. 5, Summer, 1952

10(#1)-Painted-c; origin Dr. Tom Rogers 28 56 84 165 270 375
11(#2),4,5: 4,5-Painted-c 19 38 57 111 176 240
3-Used in **SOTI**, pg. 18 20 40 60 114 182 250

NOTE: *All have painted covers by* ***Saunders. Starr*** *a-10.*

CRIME CLINIC
Slave Labor Graphics: May, 1995 - No. 2, Oct, 1995 ($2.95, B&W, limited series)

1,2 3.00

CRIME DETECTIVE COMICS
Hillman Periodicals: Mar-Apr, 1948 - V3#8, May-June, 1953

V1#1-The Invisible 6, costumed villains app; Fuje-c/a, 15 pgs.
31 62 93 186 303 420
2,5: 5-Krigstein-a 15 30 45 88 137 185
3,4,6,7,10-12: 6-McWilliams-a 14 28 42 78 112 145
8-Kirbyish-a by McCann 14 28 42 78 112 145
9-Used in **SOTI**, pg. 16 & "Caricature of the author in a position comic book publishers wish he were in permanently" illo. 39 78 117 234 385 535
V2#1,4,7-Krigstein-a: 1-Tuska-a 13 26 39 72 101 130
2,3,5,6,8-12 (1-2/52) 11 22 33 62 86 110
V3#1-Drug use-c 12 24 36 67 94 120
2-8 9 18 27 52 69 85

NOTE: ***Briefer*** *a-11, V3#1.* ***Kinstlerish****-a by* ***McCann****-V2#7, V3#2.* ***Powell*** *a-10, 11.* ***Starr*** *a-10.*

CRIME DETECTOR

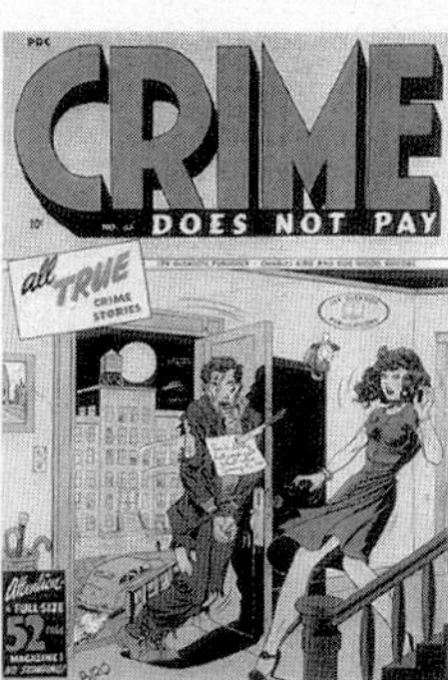

Crime Does Not Pay #43 © LEV

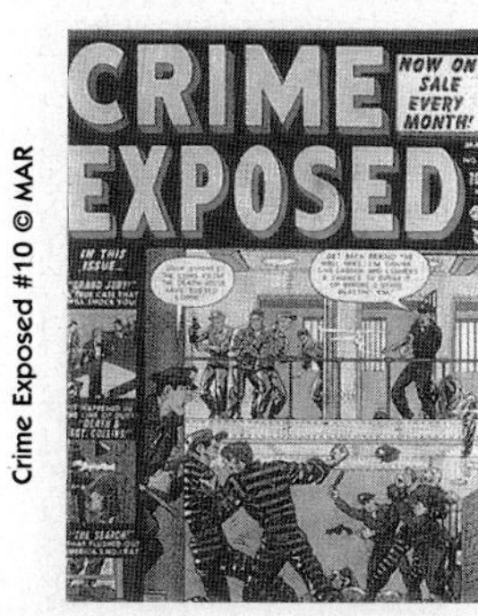

Crime Exposed #10 © MAR

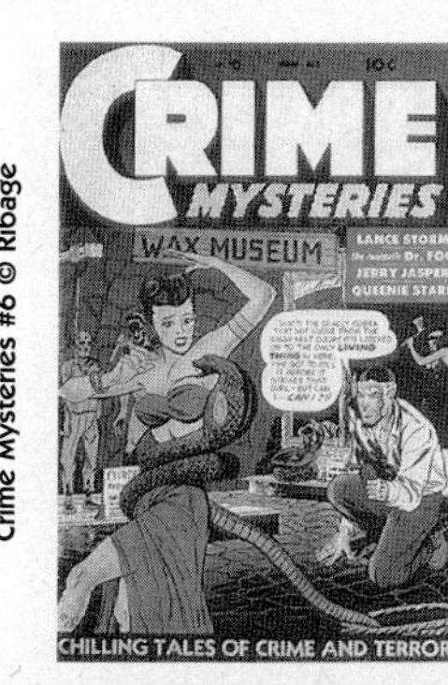

Crime Mysteries #6 © Ribage

Timor Publications: Jan, 1954 - No. 5, Sept, 1954

	GD 2.0	VG 4.0	FN 6.0	VF 8.0	VF/NM 9.0	NM- 9.2
1	22	44	66	128	209	290
2	14	28	42	78	112	145
3,4	12	24	36	67	94	120
5-Disbrow-a (classic)	22	44	66	132	216	300

CRIME DOES NOT PAY (Formerly Silver Streak Comics No. 1-21)
Comic House/Lev Gleason/Golfing: No. 22, June, 1942 - No. 147, July, 1955 (1st crime comic)(Title inspired by film)

	GD 2.0	VG 4.0	FN 6.0	VF 8.0	VF/NM 9.0	NM- 9.2
22 (23 on cover, 22 on indicia)-Origin The War Eagle & only app.; Chip Gardner begins; #22 was rebound in Complete Book of True Crime (Scarce)	486	972	1458	3550	6275	9000
23-(7/42) (Scarce)	258	516	774	1651	2826	4000
24-(11/42) Intro. & 1st app. Mr. Crime; classic Biro-c showing woman's head on fire being pushed onto hot stovetop burner	600	1200	1800	3000	5000	7000
25-(1/43) 2nd app. Mr. Crime; classic '40s crime-c	110	220	330	704	1202	1700
26-(3/43) 3rd app. Mr. Crime	90	180	270	576	988	1400
27-Classic Biro-c pushing man into hot oven	103	206	309	659	1130	1600
28-30: 30-Wood and Biro app.	74	148	222	470	810	1150
31,32,34-40	42	84	126	265	445	625
33-(5/44) Classic Biro hanging & hatchet-c	103	206	309	659	1130	1600
41-(9/45) Origin & 1st app. Officer Common Sense	36	72	108	216	351	485
42-(11/45) Classic electrocution-c	48	96	144	302	514	725
43-46,48-50: 44-50 are 68 pg. issues. 44-"Legs" Diamond story. 50-(3/47)-1st issue to advertise 5 million readers on front-c. 58-(12/47)-shows 6 million readers (these ads believed to have influenced the crime comic wave of 1948)	25	50	75	150	245	340
47-(9/46)-Electric chair-c	40	80	120	242	401	560
51-70: 58(12/47)-Thomas Dun, killer of thousands (1565) story. 63,64-Possible use in **SOTI**, pg. 306. 63-Contains Biro & Gleason self censorship code of 12 listed restrictions (5/48)	20	40	60	114	182	250
71-99: 87-Chip Gardner begins, ends #100	15	30	45	90	140	190
100	17	34	51	100	158	215
101-104,107-110: 102-Chip Gardner app	14	28	42	78	112	145
105-Used in **POP**, pg. 84	15	30	45	83	124	165
106,114-Frazetta-a, 1 pg.	14	28	42	80	115	150
111-Used in **POP**, pgs. 80 & 81; injury-to-eye sty illo	15	30	45	88	137	185
112,113,115-130	11	22	33	62	86	110
131-140	10	20	30	56	76	95
141,142-Last pre-code issue; Kubert-a(1)	11	22	33	64	90	115
143-Kubert-a in one story	11	22	33	64	90	115
144-146	10	20	30	56	76	95
147-Last issue (scarce); Kubert-a	15	30	45	90	140	190
1(Golfing-1945)	9	18	27	52	69	85
The Best of...(1944, 128 pgs.)-Series contains 4 rebound issues	97	194	291	621	1061	1500
...1945 issue	68	136	204	435	743	1050
...1946-48 issues	50	100	150	315	533	750
...1949-50 issues	42	84	126	265	445	625
...1951-53 issues (25¢)	37	74	111	222	361	500

NOTE: *Many issues contain violent covers and stories. Who Dunit by* ***Guardineer****-39-42, 44-105, 108-110; Chip Gardner by* ***Bob Jujitani (Fuge)****-88-103.* ***Alderman*** *a-29, 41-44, 49.* ***Dan Barry*** *a-67, 75.* ***Charles Biro*** *c-1-76, 122, 142.* ***Dick Briefer*** *a-29(2), 30, 31, 33, 37, 39.* ***G. Colan*** *a-105.* ***Tony Dipreta*** *a-79, 90, 92.* ***Fuje*** *c-88, 89, 91-94, 96, 98, 99, 102, 103.* ***Fred Guardineer*** *a-51, 57, 58(2), 66-68, 71, 74, 79, 81, 90, 92.* ***Joe Kubert*** *c-143.* ***Landau*** *a-118.* ***Al Mandell*** *a-37.* ***Norman Maurer*** *a-29, 39, 41, 42.* ***McWilliams*** *a-91, 93, 95, 100-103.* ***Rudy Palais*** *a-30, 33,* ***Bob Powell*** *a-146, 147.* ***George Tuska*** *a-48-50(2ea.), 51, 52 56, 57(2), 58, 60-64, 66-68, 71, 74, 81. Painted c-87-103. Bondage c-43, 62, 98.*

CRIME EXPOSED
Marvel Comics (PPI)/Marvel Atlas Comics (PrPI): June, 1948; Dec, 1950 - No. 14, June, 1952

	GD 2.0	VG 4.0	FN 6.0	VF 8.0	VF/NM 9.0	NM- 9.2
1(6/48)	34	68	102	204	332	460
1(12/50)	21	42	63	126	206	285
2	15	30	45	84	127	170
3-9,11,14	14	28	42	76	108	140
10-Used in **POP**, pg. 81	14	28	42	80	115	150
12-Krigstein & Robinson-a	14	28	42	80	115	150
13-Used in **POP**, pg. 81; Krigstein-a	14	28	42	81	118	155

NOTE: ***Keller*** *a-8, 10.* ***Maneely*** *c-8.* ***Robinson*** *a-11, 12.* ***Sale*** *a-4.* ***Tuska*** *a-3, 4.*

CRIMEFIGHTERS
Marvel Comics (CmPS 1-3/CCC 4-10): Apr, 1948 - No. 10, Nov, 1949

	GD 2.0	VG 4.0	FN 6.0	VF 8.0	VF/NM 9.0	NM- 9.2
1-Some copies are undated & could be reprints	26	52	78	154	252	350
2,3: 3-Morphine addict story	15	30	45	85	130	175
4-10: 4-Early John Buscema-a. 6-Anti-Wertham editorial. 9,10-Photo-c	14	28	42	78	112	145

CRIME FIGHTERS (...Always Win)
Atlas Comics (CnPC): No. 11, Sept, 1954 - No. 13, Jan, 1955

	GD 2.0	VG 4.0	FN 6.0	VF 8.0	VF/NM 9.0	NM- 9.2
11-13: 11-Maneely-a,13-Pakula, Reinman, Severin-a	12	24	36	69	97	125

CRIME-FIGHTING DETECTIVE (Shock Detective Cases No. 20 on; formerly Criminals on the Run)
Star Publications: No. 11, Apr-May, 1950 - No. 19, June, 1952 (Based on true crime cases)

	GD 2.0	VG 4.0	FN 6.0	VF 8.0	VF/NM 9.0	NM- 9.2
11-L. B. Cole-c/a (2 pgs.); L. B. Cole-c on all	18	36	54	107	169	230
12,13,15-19: 17-Young King Cole & Dr. Doom app.	15	30	45	83	124	165
14-L. B. Cole-c/a, r/Law-Crime #2	15	30	45	90	140	190

CRIME FILES
Standard Comics: No. 5, Sept, 1952 - No. 6, Nov, 1952

	GD 2.0	VG 4.0	FN 6.0	VF 8.0	VF/NM 9.0	NM- 9.2
5-1pg. Alex Toth-a; used in **SOTI**, pg. 4 (text)	23	46	69	136	223	310
6-Sekowsky-a	14	28	42	80	115	150

CRIME ILLUSTRATED (Magazine)
E. C. Comics: Nov-Dec, 1955 - No. 2, Spring, 1956 (25¢, Adult Suspense Stories on-c)

	GD 2.0	VG 4.0	FN 6.0	VF 8.0	VF/NM 9.0	NM- 9.2
1-Ingels & Crandall-a	18	36	54	105	165	225
2-Ingels & Crandall-a	14	28	42	82	121	160

NOTE: ***Craig*** *a-2.* ***Crandall*** *a-1, 2; c-2.* ***Evans*** *a-1.* ***Davis*** *a-2.* ***Ingels*** *a-1, 2.* ***Krigstein/Crandall*** *a-1.* ***Orlando*** *a-1, 2; c-1.*

CRIME INCORPORATED (Formerly Crimes Incorporated)
Fox Features Syndicate: No. 2, Aug, 1950; No. 3, Aug, 1951

	GD 2.0	VG 4.0	FN 6.0	VF 8.0	VF/NM 9.0	NM- 9.2
2	26	52	78	154	252	350
3(1951)-Hollingsworth-a	18	36	54	105	165	225

CRIME MACHINE (Magazine reprints pre-code crime and gangster comics)
Skywald Publications: Feb, 1971 - No. 2, May, 1971 (B&W, 68 pgs., roundbound)

	GD 2.0	VG 4.0	FN 6.0	VF 8.0	VF/NM 9.0	NM- 9.2
1-Kubert-a(2)(r)(Avon); bikini girl in cake-c	6	12	18	41	66	90
2-Torres, Wildey-a; violent-c/a	4	8	12	28	44	60

CRIME MUST LOSE! (Formerly Sports Action?)
Sports Action (Atlas Comics): No. 4, Oct, 1950 - No. 12, April, 1952

	GD 2.0	VG 4.0	FN 6.0	VF 8.0	VF/NM 9.0	NM- 9.2
4-Ann Brewster-a in all; c-used in N.Y. Legis. Comm. documents	19	38	57	111	176	240
5-10,12: 9-Robinson-a	14	28	42	80	115	150
11-Used in **POP**, pg 89	14	28	42	82	121	160

CRIME MUST PAY THE PENALTY (Formerly Four Favorites; Penalty #47, 48)
Ace Magazines (Current Books): No. 33, Feb, 1948; No. 2, Jun, 1948 - No. 48, Jan, 1956

	GD 2.0	VG 4.0	FN 6.0	VF 8.0	VF/NM 9.0	NM- 9.2
33(#1, 2/48)-Becomes Four Teeners #34?	39	78	117	234	385	535
2(6/48)-Extreme violence; Palais-a?	24	48	72	142	234	325
3,4,8: 3- "Frisco Mary" story used in Senate Investigation report, pg. 7. 4,8-Transvestism stories	19	38	57	111	176	240
5-7,9,10	14	28	42	82	121	160
11-19	14	28	42	78	112	145
20-Drug story "Dealers in White Death"	20	40	60	117	189	260
21-32,34-40,42-48: 44-Last pre-code	11	22	33	62	86	110
33(7/53)- "Dell Fabry-Junk King" drug story; mentioned in Love and Death	16	32	48	94	147	200
41-reprints "Dealers in White Death"	12	24	36	67	94	120

NOTE: ***Cameron*** *a-29-31, 34, 35, 39-41.* ***Colan*** *a-20, 31.* ***Kremer*** *a-3, 37r.* ***Larsen*** *a-32.* ***Palais*** *a-5?,37.*

CRIME MUST STOP
Hillman Periodicals: October, 1952 (52 pgs.)

	GD 2.0	VG 4.0	FN 6.0	VF 8.0	VF/NM 9.0	NM- 9.2
V1#1(Scarce)-Similar to Monster Crime; Mort Lawrence, Krigstein-a	100	200	300	635	1093	1550

CRIME MYSTERIES (Secret Mysteries #16 on; combined with Crime Smashers #7 on)
Ribage Publ. Corp. (Trojan Magazines): May, 1952 - No. 15, Sept, 1954

	GD 2.0	VG 4.0	FN 6.0	VF 8.0	VF/NM 9.0	NM- 9.2
1-Transvestism story; crime & terror stories begin	65	130	195	416	708	1000
2-Marijuana story (7/52)	42	84	126	265	445	625
3-One pg. Frazetta-a	39	78	117	240	395	550
4-Cover shows girl in bondage having her blood drained; 1 pg. Frazetta-a	68	136	204	435	743	1050
5-10	34	68	102	206	336	465
11,12,14	32	64	96	192	314	435
13-(5/54)-Angelo Torres 1st comic work (inks over Check's pencils); Check-a	39	78	117	231	378	525
15-Acid in face-c	48	96	144	302	514	725

NOTE: ***Fass*** *a-13; c-4, 6, 10.* ***Hollingsworth*** *a-10-13, 15; c-2, 12, 13, 15.* ***Kiefer*** *a-4.* ***Woodbridge*** *a-13? Bondage-c-1, 8, 12.*

CRIME ON THE RUN (See Approved Comics #8)

CRIME ON THE WATERFRONT (Formerly Famous Gangsters)

Crime Reporter #1 © STJ

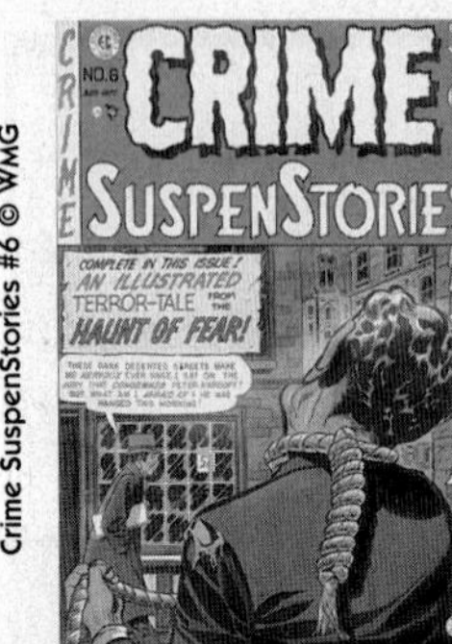

Crime SuspenStories #6 © WMG

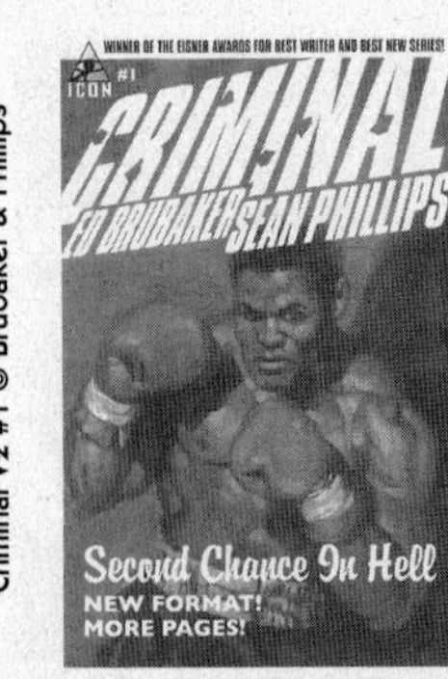

Criminal V2 #1 © Brubaker & Phillips

GD 2.0 VG 4.0 FN 6.0 VF 8.0 VF/NM 9.0 NM- 9.2

Realistic Publications: No. 4, May, 1952 (Painted cover)
4 28 56 84 165 270 375

CRIME PATROL (Formerly International #1-5; International Crime Patrol #6; becomes Crypt of Terror #17 on)
E. C. Comics: No. 7, Summer, 1948 - No. 16, Feb-Mar, 1950
7-Intro. Captain Crime 77 154 231 493 847 1200
8-14: 12-Ingels-a 69 138 207 442 759 1075
15-Intro. of Crypt Keeper (inspired by Witches Tales radio show) & Crypt of Terror (see Tales From the Crypt #33 for origin); used by N.Y. Legis. Comm.; last pg. Feldstein-a
269 538 807 2152 3426 4700
16-2nd Crypt Keeper app.; Roussos-a 171 342 513 1368 2184 3000
NOTE: ***Craig** c/a in most issues. **Feldstein** a-9-16. **Kiefer** a-8, 10, 11. **Moldoff** a-7.*

CRIME PATROL
Gemstone Publishing: Apr, 2000 - No. 10, Jan, 2001 ($2.50)
1-10: E.C. reprints 3.00
Volume 1,2 (2000, $13.50) 1-r/#1-5. 2-r/#6-10 14.00

CRIME PHOTOGRAPHER (See Casey...)

CRIME REPORTER
St. John Publ. Co.: Aug, 1948 - No. 3, Dec, 1948 (Indicia shows Oct.)
1-Drug club story 60 120 180 381 653 925
2-Used in **SOTI**: illo- "Children told me what the man was going to do with the red-hot poker;" r/Dynamic #17 with editing; Baker-c; Tuska-a 90 180 270 576 988 1400
3-Baker-c; Tuska-a 46 92 138 290 488 685

CRIMES BY WOMEN
Fox Features Syndicate: June, 1948 - No. 15, Aug, 1951; 1954 (True crime cases)
1-True story of Bonnie Parker 129 258 387 826 1413 2000
2,3: 3-Used in **SOTI**, pg. 234 68 136 204 435 743 1050
4,5,7-9,11-15: 8-Used in **POP**. 14-Bondage-c 61 122 183 390 670 950
6-Classic girl fight-c; acid-in-face panel 73 146 219 467 796 1125
10-Used in **SOTI**, pg. 72; girl fight-c 65 130 195 416 708 1000
54(M.S. Publ.-'54)-Reprint; (formerly My Love Secret)
24 48 72 140 230 320

CRIMES INCORPORATED (Formerly My Past)
Fox Features Syndicate: No. 12, June, 1950 (Crime Incorporated No. 2 on)
12 26 52 78 154 252 350

CRIMES INCORPORATED (See Fox Giants)

CRIME SMASHER (See Whiz #76)
Fawcett Publications: Summer, 1948 (one-shot)
1-Formerly Spy Smasher 41 82 123 256 428 600

CRIME SMASHERS (Becomes Secret Mysteries No. 16 on)
Ribage Publishing Corp.(Trojan Magazines): Oct, 1950 - No. 15, Mar, 1953
1-Used in **SOTI**, pg. 19,20, & illo "A girl raped and murdered;" Sally the Sleuth begins
90 180 270 576 988 1400
2-Kubert-c 48 96 144 302 514 725
3,4 39 78 117 240 395 550
5-Wood-a 47 94 141 296 498 700
6,8-11: 8-Lingerie panel 32 64 96 188 307 425
7-Female heroin junkie story 36 72 108 211 343 475
12-Injury to eye panel; 1 pg. Frazetta-a 34 68 102 204 332 460
13-Used in **POP**, pgs. 79,80; 1 pg. Frazetta-a 34 68 102 204 332 460
14,15 26 52 78 154 252 350
NOTE: ***Hollingsworth** a-14. **Kiefer** a-15. Bondage c-7, 9.*

CRIME SUSPENSTORIES (Formerly Vault of Horror No. 12-14)
E. C. Comics: No. 15, Oct-Nov, 1950 - No. 27, Feb-Mar, 1955
15-Identical to #1 in content; #1 printed on outside front cover. #15 (formerly "The Vault of Horror") printed and blackened out on inside front cover with Vol. 1, No. 1 printed over it. Evidently, several of No. 15 were printed before a decision was made not to drop the Vault of Horror and Haunt of Fear series. The print run was stopped on No. 15 and continued on No. 1. All of the No. 15 issues were changed as described above.
163 326 489 1304 2077 2850
1 129 258 387 1032 1641 2250
2 66 132 198 528 839 1150
3-5: 3-Poe adaptation. 3-Old Witch stories begin 45 90 135 360 573 785
6-10: 9-Craig bio. 39 78 117 312 499 685
11,12,14,15: 15-The Old Witch guest stars 31 62 93 248 392 535
13,16-Williamson-a 33 66 99 264 420 575
17-Williamson/Frazetta-a (6 pgs.) Williamson bio. 40 80 120 320 510 700
18,19: 19-Used in **SOTI**, pg. 235 27 54 81 216 346 475
20-Cover used in **SOTI**, illo "Cover of a children's comic book"
37 74 111 296 473 650

GD 2.0 VG 4.0 FN 6.0 VF 8.0 VF/NM 9.0 NM- 9.2

21,24-26: 24- "Food For Thought" similar to "Cave In" in Amazing Detective Cases #13 (1952)
20 40 60 160 255 350
22-Used in Senate investigation on juvenile delinquency; Ax decapitation-c
97 194 291 776 1238 1700
23-Used in Senate investigation on juvenile delinquency
27 54 81 216 346 475
27-Last issue (Low distribution) 25 50 75 200 318 435
NOTE: ***Craig** a-1-21; c-1-18, 20-22. **Crandall** a-18-26. **Davis** a-4, 5, 7, 9-12, 20. **Elder** a-17,18. **Evans** a-15, 19, 21, 23, 25, 27; c-23, 24. **Feldstein** c-19. **Ingels** a-1-12, 14, 15, 27. **Kamen** a-2, 4-18, 20-27; c-25-27. **Krigstein** a-22, 24, 25, 27. **Kurtzman** a-1, 3. **Orlando** a-16, 22, 24, 26. **Wood** a-1, 3. Issues No. 1-3 were printed in Canada as "Weird Suspenstories." Issues No. 11-15 have E. C. "quickie" stories. No. 25 contains the famous "Are You a Red Dupe?" editorial. Ray Bradbury adaptations-15, 17.*

CRIME SUSPENSTORIES
Russ Cochran/Gemstone Publ.: Nov, 1992 - No. 27, May, 1999 ($1.50/$2.00/$2.50)
1-27: Reprints Crime SuspenStories series 3.00

CRIMINAL (Also see Criminal: The Sinners)
Marvel Comics (Icon): Oct, 2006 - No. 10, Oct, 2007 ($2.99)
Volume 2: Feb, 2008 - No. 7, Nov, 2008 ($3.50)
1-10-Ed Brubaker-s/Sean Phillips-a/c 3.00
Volume 2: 1-7-Brubaker-s/Phillips-a 3.50
... Vol. 1: Coward TPB (2007, $14.99) r/#1-5; intro. by Tom Fontana 15.00
... Vol. 2: Lawless TPB (2007, $14.99) r/#6-10; intro. by Frank Miller 15.00
... Vol. 3: The Dead and the Dying TPB (2008, $11.99) r/V2#1-4; intro. by John Singleton 12.00

CRIMINAL MACABRE: A CAL MCDONALD MYSTERY (Also see Last Train to Deadsville)
Dark Horse Comics: May, 2003 - No. 5, Sept, 2003 ($2.99)
1-5-Niles-s/Templesmith-a 3.00

CRIMINAL MACABRE: (limited series and one-shots)
Dark Horse Comics: ($2.99)
...: Cellblock 666 (9/08 - No. 4, 5/09)(#25-28 in series) 1-4-Niles-s/Stakal-a/Bradstreet-c 3.00
...: Feat of Clay (6/06, $2.99) Niles-s/Hotz-a/c 3.00
Free Comic Book Day: Criminal Macabre - Call Me Monster (5/11) flip book w/Baltimore 3.00
...: My Demon Baby (9/07 - No. 4, 4/08)(#21-24 in the series) 1-4-Niles-s/Stakal-a 3.00
...: No Peace For Dead Men (9/11, $3.99) Niles-s/Mitten-a/Staples-c 4.00
...: The Goon (7/11, $3.99) Niles-s/Mitten-a; covers by Powell & Staples 4.00
...: Two Red Eyes (12/06 - No. 4, 3/07) 1-4-Niles-s/Hotz-a/Bradstreet-c 3.00

CRIMINALS ON THE RUN (Formerly Young King Cole) (Crime Fighting Detective No. 11 on)
Premium Group (Novelty Press): V4#1, Aug-Sep, 1948-#10, Dec-Jan, 1949-50
V4#1-Young King Cole continues 26 52 78 154 252 350
2-6: 6-Dr. Doom app. 22 44 66 132 216 300
7-Classic "Fish in the Face" c by L. B. Cole 52 104 156 322 549 775
V5#1,2 (#8,9),10: 9,10-L. B. Cole-c 20 40 60 118 192 265
NOTE: *Most issues have **L. B. Cole** covers. **McWilliams** a-V4#6, 7, V5#2; c-V4#5.*

CRIMINAL: THE LAST OF THE INNOCENT
Marvel Comics (Icon): Jun, 2011 - No. 4, Sept, 2011 ($3.50)
1-4-Ed Brubaker-s/Sean Phillips-a/c 3.50

CRIMINAL: THE SINNERS
Marvel Comics (Icon): Sept, 2009 - No. 5, Mar, 2010 ($3.50)
1-5-Ed Brubaker-s/Sean Phillips-a/c 3.50

CRIMSON (Also see Cliffhanger #0)
Image Comics (Cliffhanger Productions): May, 1998 - No. 7, Dec, 1998;
DC Comics (Cliffhanger Prod.): No. 8, Mar, 1999 - No. 24, Apr, 2001 ($2.50)
1-Humberto Ramos-a/Augustyn-s 5.00
1-Variant-c by Warren 8.00
1-Chromium-c 20.00
2-Ramos-c with street crowd, 2-Variant-c by Art Adams 4.00
2-Dynamic Forces CrimsonChrome cover 15.00
3-7: 3-Ramos Moon background-c. 7-Three covers by Ramos, Madureira, & Campbell 3.50
8-23: 8-First DC issue 3.00
24-($3.50) Final issue; wraparound-c 4.00
DF Premiere Ed. 1998 ($6.95) covers by Ramos and Jae Lee 7.00
Crimson: Scarlet X Blood on the Moon (10/99, $3.95) 4.00
Crimson Sourcebook (11/99, $2.95) Pin-ups and info 3.00
Earth Angel TPB (2001, $14.95) r/#13-18 15.00
Heaven and Earth TPB (1/00, $14.95) r/#7-12 15.00
Loyalty and Loss TPB ('99, $12.95) r/#1-6 13.00
Redemption TPB ('01, $14.95) r/#19-24 15.00

CRIMSON AVENGER, THE (See Detective Comics #20 for 1st app.)(Also see Leading Comics #1 & World's Best/Finest Comics)
DC Comics: June, 1988 - No. 4, Sept, 1988 ($1.00, limited series)

Crisis on Infinite Earths #4 © DC

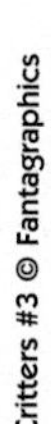
Critters #3 © Fantagraphics

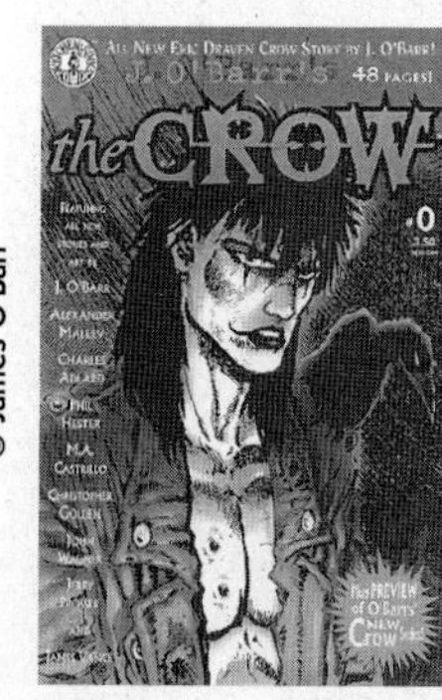

The Crow #0 - A Cycle of Shattered Lives © James O'Barr

	GD 2.0	VG 4.0	FN 6.0	VF 8.0	VF/NM 9.0	NM- 9.2

1-4 3.00

CRIMSON DYNAMO
Marvel Comics (Epic): Oct, 2003 - No. 6, Apr, 2004 ($2.50/$2.99)
1-4,6: 1-John Jackson Miller-s/Steve Ellis-a/c 3.00
5-($2.99) Iron Man-c/app. 4.00

CRIMSON PLAGUE
Event Comics: June, 1997 ($2.95, unfinished mini-series)
1-George Perez-a 3.00

CRIMSON PLAGUE (George Pérez's...)
Image Comics (Gorilla): June, 2000 - No. 2, Aug, 2000 ($2.95, mini-series)
1-George Perez-a; reprints 6/97 issue with 16 new pages 3.00
2-($2.50) 3.00

CRISIS AFTERMATH: THE BATTLE FOR BLUDHAVEN (Also see Infinite Crisis)
DC Comics: Jun, 2006 - No. 6, Sept, 2006 ($2.99, limited series)
1-Atomic Knights return; Teen Titans app.; Jurgens-a/Acuna-c 4.00
1-2nd printing with pencil cover 3.00
2-6: 2-Intro S.H.A.D.E. (new Freedom Fighters) 3.00
TPB (2007, $12.99) r/#1-6 13.00

CRISIS AFTERMATH: THE SPECTRE (Also see Infinite Crisis, Gotham Central and Tales of the Unexpected)
DC Comics: Jul, 2006 - No. 3, Sept, 2006 ($2.99, limited series)
1-3-Crispus Allen becomes the Spectre; Pfeifer-s/Chiang-a/c 3.00
TPB (2007, $12.99) r/#1-3 and Tales of the Unexpected #1-3 13.00

CRISIS ON INFINITE EARTHS (Also see Official... Index and Legends of the DC Universe)
DC Comics: Apr, 1985 - No. 12, Mar, 1986 (maxi-series)
1-1st DC app. Blue Beetle & Detective Karp from Charlton; Pérez-c on all
2 4 6 9 13 16
2-6: 6-Intro Charlton's Capt. Atom, Nightshade, Question, Judomaster, Peacemaker & Thunderbolt into DC Universe 1 3 4 6 8 10
7-Double size; death of Supergirl 2 4 6 13 16 22
8-Death of the Flash (Barry Allen) 2 4 6 11 16 20
9-11: 9-Intro. Charlton's Ghost into DC Universe. 10-Intro. Charlton's Banshee, Dr. Spectro, Image, Punch & Jewellee into DC Universe; Starman (Prince Gavyn) dies
1 3 4 6 8 10
12-(52 pgs.)-Deaths of Dove, Kole, Lori Lemaris, Sunburst, G.A. Robin & Huntress; Kid Flash becomes new Flash; 3rd & final DC app. of the 3 Lt. Marvels; Green Fury gets new look (becomes Green Flame in Infinity, Inc. #32) 2 4 6 8 11 14
Slipcased Hardcover (1998, $99.95) Wraparound dust-jacket cover by Pérez and Alex Ross; sketch pages by Pérez; intro by Wolfman 125.00
TPB (2000, $29.95) Wraparound-c by Pérez and Ross 30.00
NOTE: *Crossover issues: All Star Squadron 50-56,60; Amethyst 13; Blue Devil 17,18; DC Comics Presents 78,86-88,95; Detective Comics 558; Fury of Firestorm 41,42; G.I. Combat 274; Green Lantern 194-196,198; Infinity, Inc. 18-25 & Annual 1, Justice League of America 244,245 & Annual 3; Legion of Super-Heroes 16,18; Losers Special 1; New Teen Titans 13,14; Omega Men 31,33; Superman 413-415; Swamp Thing 44,46; Wonder Woman 327-329.*

CRISIS ON MULTIPLE EARTHS
DC Comics: 2002 - 2010 ($14.95, trade paperbacks)
TPB-(2003) Reprints 1st 4 Silver Age JLA/JSA crossovers from J.L.ofA. #21,22; 29,30; 37,38; 46,47; new painted-c by Alex Ross; intro. by Mark Waid 15.00
Volume 2 (2003, $14.95) r/J.L.ofA. #55,56; 64,65; 73,74; 82,83; new Ordway-c 15.00
Volume 3 (2004, $14.95) r/J.L.ofA. #91,92; 100-102; 107,108; 113; Wein intro., Ross-c 15.00
Volume 4 (2006, $14.99) r/J.L.ofA. #123-124 (Earth-Prime),135-137 (Fawcett's Shazam characters), 147-148 (Legion of Super-Heroes); Ross-c 15.00
Volume 5 (2010, $19.99) r/J.L.ofA. #159-160 (Jonah Hex, Enemy Ace),171-172 (Murder of Mr. Terrific), 183-185 (New Gods & Darkseid); Pérez-c 20.00
... The Team-Ups Volume 1 (2005, $14.99) r/Flash #123,129,137,151; Showcase #55,56; Green Lantern #40, Brave and the Bold #61 and Spectre #7; new Ordway-c 15.00

CRITICAL MASS (See A Shadowline Saga: Critical Mass)

CRITTERS (Also see Usagi Yojimbo Summer Special)
Fantagraphics Books: 1986 - No. 50, 1990 ($1.70/$2.00, B&W)
1-Cutey Bunny, Usagi Yojimbo app. 1 3 4 6 8 10
2,4,5,8,9 6.00
3,6,7,10-Usagi Yojimbo app. 1 2 3 4 5 7
11,14-Usagi Yojimbo app. 11-Christmas Special (68 pgs.) 4.00
12,13,15-22,24-37,39,40: 22-Watchmen parody; two diff. covers exist 3.00
23-With Alan Moore Flexi-disc ($3.95) 5.00
38-($2.75-c) Usagi Yojimbo app. 4.00
41-49 4.00
50 ($4.95, 84 pgs.)-Neil the Horse, Capt. Jack, Sam & Max & Usagi Yojimbo app.; Quagmire, Shaw-a 1 2 3 4 5 7

Special 1 (1/88, $2.00) 4.00

CROSS
Dark Horse Comics: No. 0, Oct, 1995 - No. 6, Apr, 1995 ($2.95, limited series, mature)
0-6: Darrow-c & Vachss scripts in all 3.00

CROSS AND THE SWITCHBLADE, THE
Spire Christian Comics (Fleming H. Revell Co.): 1972 (35-49¢)
1-Some issues have nn 3 6 9 14 19 24

CROSS BRONX, THE
Image Comics: Sept, 2006 - No. 4, Dec, 2006 ($2.99, limited series)
1-4: 1-Oeming-a/c; Oeming & Brandon-s; Ribic var-c. 2-Johnson var-c. 4-Mack var-c 3.00

CROSSFIRE
Spire Christian Comics (Fleming H. Revell Co.): 1973 (39/49¢)
nn 2 4 6 11 16 20

CROSSFIRE (Also see DNAgents)
Eclipse Comics: 5/84 - No. 17, 3/86; No. 18, 1/87 - No. 26, 2/88 ($1.50, Baxter paper) (#18-26 are B&W)
1-11,14-26: 1-DNAgents x-over; Spiegle-c/a begins 3.00
12-Death of Marilyn Monroe; Dave Stevens-c 1 2 3 4 5 7
13-Death of Marilyn Monroe 5.00

CROSSFIRE AND RAINBOW (Also see DNAgents)
Eclipse Comics: June, 1986 - No. 4, Sept, 1986 ($1.25, deluxe format)
1-3: Spiegle-a. 4-Dave Stevens-c 3.00

CROSSGEN...
CrossGeneration Comics
CrossGenesis (1/00) Previews CrossGen universe; cover gallery 3.00
...Primer (1/00) Wizard supplement; intro. to the CrossGen universe 3.00
...Sampler (2/00) Retailer preview book 3.00

CROSSGEN CHRONICLES
CrossGeneration Comics: June, 2000 - No. 8 ($3.95)
1-Intro. to CrossGen characters & company 4.00
1-(no cover price) same contents, customer preview 4.00
2-8: 2-(3/01) George Pérez-c/a. 3-5-Pérez-a/Waid-s. 6,7-Nebres-c/a 4.00

CROSSING MIDNIGHT
DC Comics (Vertigo): Jan, 2007 - No. 19, Jul, 2008 ($2.99)
1-19: 1-Carey-s/Fern-a/Williams III-c. 10-12-Nguyen-a 3.00
...: Cut Here TPB (2007, $9.99) r/#1-5 10.00
...: A Map of Midnight TPB (2008, $14.99) r/#6-12; afterword by Carey 15.00
...: The Sword in the Soul TPB (2008, $14.99) r/#13-19 15.00

CROSSING THE ROCKIES (See Classics Illustrated Special Issue)

CROSSOVERS, THE
CrossGeneration Comics: Feb, 2003 - No. 12 ($2.95)
1-12-Robert Rodi-s. 1-6-Mauricet & Ernie Colon-a. 7-Staton-a begins 3.00
Vol. 1: Cross Currents (2003, $9.95) digest-sized reprints #1-6 10.00

CROW, THE (Also see Caliber Presents)
Caliber Press: Feb, 1989 - No. 4, 1989 ($1.95, B&W, limited series)
1-James O'Barr-c/a/scripts 6 12 18 37 59 80
1-3-2nd printing 6.00
2-4 4 8 12 22 34 45
2-3rd printing 4.00

CROW, THE
Tundra Publishing, Ltd.: Jan, 1992 - No. 3, 1992 ($4.95, B&W, 68 pgs.)
1-3: 1-r/#1,2 of Caliber series. 2-r/#3 of Caliber series w/new material. 3-All new material
1 2 3 5 6 8

CROW, THE
Kitchen Sink Press: 1/96 - No. 3, 3/96 ($2.95, B&W)
1-3: James O'Barr-c/scripts 5.00
#0-A Cycle of Shattered Lives (12/98, $3.50) new story by O'Barr 4.00

CROW, THE
Image Comics (Todd McFarlane Prod.): Feb, 1999 - No. 10, Nov, 1999 ($2.50)
1-10: 1-Two covers by McFarlane and Kent Williams; Muth-s in all. 2-6,10-Paul Lee-a 3.00
Book 1 - Vengeance (2000, $10.95, TPB) r/#1-3,5,6 11.00
Book 2 - Evil Beyond Reach (2000, $10.95, TPB) r/#4,7-10 11.00
Todd McFarlane Presents The Crow Magazine 1 (3/00, $4.95) 5.00

CROW, THE: CITY OF ANGELS (Movie)

The Crow: Wild Justice #2 © James O'Barr

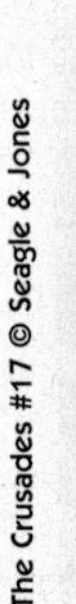
The Crusades #17 © Seagle & Jones

Crypt of Terror #19 © WMG

	GD 2.0	VG 4.0	FN 6.0	VF 8.0	VF/NM 9.0	NM- 9.2

Kitchen Sink Press: July, 1996 - No. 3, Sept, 1996 ($2.95, limited series)

1-3: Adaptation of film; two-c (photo & illos.). 1-Vincent Perez interview 3.00

CROW, THE: FLESH AND BLOOD
Kitchen Sink Press: May, 1996 - No. 3, July, 1996 ($2.95, limited series)

1-3: O'Barr-c 3.00

CROW, THE: RAZOR - KILL THE PAIN
London Night Studios: Apr, 1998 - No. 3, July, 1998 ($2.95, B&W, lim. series)

1-3-Hartsoe-s/O'Barr-painted-c 3.00
0(10/98) Dorien painted-c, Finale (2/99) 3.00
The Lost Chapter (2/99, $4.95), Tour Book-(12/97) pin-ups; 4 diff.-c 5.00

CROW, THE: WAKING NIGHTMARES
Kitchen Sink Press: Jan, 1997 - No. 4, 1998 ($2.95, B&W, limited series)

1-4-Miran Kim-c 5.00

CROW, THE: WILD JUSTICE
Kitchen Sink Press: Oct, 1996 - No. 3, Dec, 1996 ($2.95, B&W, limited series)

1-3-Prosser-s/Adlard-a 3.00

CROWN COMICS (Also see Vooda)
Golfing/McCombs Publ.: Wint, 1944-45; No. 2, Sum, 1945 - No. 19, July, 1949

	GD	VG	FN	VF	VF/NM	NM-
1- "The Oblong Box" E.A. Poe adaptation	43	86	129	271	461	650
2,3-Baker-a; 3-Voodah by Baker	32	64	96	188	307	425
4-6-Baker-c/a; Voodah app. #4,5	34	68	102	199	325	450
7-Feldstein, Baker, Kamen-a; Baker-c	36	72	108	211	343	475
8-Baker-a; Voodah app.	27	54	81	158	259	360
9-11,13-19: Voodah in #10-19. 13-New logo	18	36	54	107	169	230
12-Master Marvin by Feldstein, Starr-a; Voodah-c	19	38	57	111	176	240

NOTE: *Bolle a-11, 13-16, 18, 19; c-11p, 15.* ***Powell*** *a-19.* ***Starr*** *a-11-13; c-11i.*

CRUCIBLE
DC Comics (Impact): Feb, 1993 - No. 6, July, 1993 ($1.25, limited series)

1-6: 1-(99¢)-Neon ink-c. 1,2-Quesada-c(p). 1-4-Quesada layouts 3.00

CRUEL AND UNUSUAL
DC Comics (Vertigo): June, 1999 - No. 4, Sept, 1999 ($2.95, limited series)

1-4-Delano & Peyer-s/McCrea-c/a 3.00

CRUSADER FROM MARS (See Tops in Adventure)
Ziff-Davis Publ. Co.: Jan-Mar, 1952 - No. 2, Fall, 1952 (Painted-c)

	GD	VG	FN	VF	VF/NM	NM-
1-Cover is dated Spring	77	154	231	489	837	1185
2-Bondage-c	53	106	159	334	567	800

CRUSADER RABBIT (TV)
Dell Publishing Co.: No. 735, Oct, 1956 - No. 805, May, 1957

	GD	VG	FN	VF	VF/NM	NM-
Four Color 735 (#1)	22	44	66	154	327	500
Four Color 805	16	32	48	112	246	380

CRUSADERS, THE (Religious)
Chick Publications: 1974 - Vol. 17, 1988 (39/69¢, 36 pgs.)

	GD	VG	FN	VF	VF/NM	NM-
Vol.1-Operation Bucharest ('74). Vol.2-The Broken Cross ('74). Vol.3-Scarface ('74). Vol.4-Exorcists ('75). Vol.5-Chaos ('75)	3	6	9	16	22	28
Vol.6-Primal Man? ('76)-(Disputes evolution theory). Vol.7-The Ark-(claims proof of existence, destroyed by Bolsheviks). Vol.8-The Gift-(Life story of Christ). Vol.9-Angel of Light-(Story of the Devil). Vol.10-Spellbound?-(Tells how rock music is Satanic & produced by witches). 11-Sabotage?. 12-Alberto. 13-Double Cross. 14-The Godfathers. (No. 6-14 low in distribution; loaded with religious propaganda.). 15-The Force. 16-The Four Horsemen	3	6	9	16	22	28
Vol. 17-The Prophet (low print run)	3	6	9	17	25	32

CRUSADERS (Southern Knights No. 2 on)
Guild Publications: 1982 (B&W, magazine size)

	GD	VG	FN	VF	VF/NM	NM-
1-1st app. Southern Knights	2	4	6	9	12	16

CRUSADERS, THE (Also see Black Hood, The Jaguar, The Comet, The Fly, Legend of the Shield, The Mighty... & The Web)
DC Comics (Impact): May, 1992 - No. 8, Dec, 1992 ($1.00/$1.25)

1-8-Contains 3 Impact trading cards 3.00

CRUSADES, THE
DC Comics (Vertigo): 2001 - No. 20, Dec, 2002 ($3.95/$2.50)

...: Urban Decree ('01, $3.95) Intro. the Knight; Seagle-s/Kelley Jones-c/a 4.00
1-(5/01, $2.50) Sienkiewicz-c 3.00
2-20: 2-Moeller-c. 18-Begin $2.95-c 3.00

CRUSH
Dark Horse Comics: Oct, 2003 - No. 4, Jan, 2004 ($2.99, limited series)

1-4-Jason Hall-s/Sean Murphy-a 3.00

CRUSH, THE
Image Comics (Motown Machineworks): Jan, 1996 - No. 5, July, 1996 ($2.25, limited series)

1-5: Baron scripts 3.00

CRUX
CrossGeneration Comics: May, 2001 - No. 33, Feb, 2004 ($2.95)

1-33: 1-Waid-s/Epting & Magyar-a/c. 6-Pelletier-a. 13-Dixon-s begin. 25-Cover has fake creases and other aging 3.00
Atlantis Rising Vol. 1 TPB (2002, $15.95) r/#1-6 16.00
Test of Time Vol. 2 TPB (12/02, $15.95) r/#7-12 16.00
Vol. 3: Strangers in Atlantis (2003, $15.95) r/#13-18 16.00
Vol. 4: Chaos Reborn (2003, $15.95) r/#19-24 16.00

CRY FOR DAWN
Cry For Dawn Pub.: 1989 - No. 9 ($2.25, B&W, mature)

	GD	VG	FN	VF	VF/NM	NM-
1	8	16	24	52	86	120
1-2nd printing	3	6	9	18	27	35
1-3rd printing	3	6	9	14	20	25
2	5	10	15	32	51	70
2-2nd printing	2	4	6	11	16	20
3	4	8	12	24	37	50
3a-HorrorCon Edition (1990, less than 400 printed, signed inside-c)						200.00
4-6	3	6	9	14	19	24
5-2nd printing	1	2	3	5	6	8
7-9	2	4	6	10	14	18
4-9-Signed & numbered editions	3	6	9	14	20	25
Angry Christ Comix HC (4/03, $29.99) reprints various stories; and 30 pgs. new material						30.00
...Calendar (1993)						35.00

CRYIN' LION COMICS
William H. Wise Co.: Fall, 1944 - No. 3, Spring, 1945

	GD	VG	FN	VF	VF/NM	NM-
1-Funny animal	15	30	45	88	137	185
2-Hitler and Tojo app.	14	28	42	76	108	140
3	10	20	30	56	76	95

CRYPT
Image Comics (Extreme): Aug, 1995 - No.2, Oct. 1995 ($2.50, limited series)

1,2-Prophet app. 3.00

CRYPTIC WRITINGS OF MEGADETH
Chaos! Comics: Sept, 1997 - No. 4, Jun, 1998 ($2.95, quarterly)

1-4-Stories based on song lyrics by Dave Mustaine 3.00

CRYPT OF DAWN (see Dawn)
Sirius: 1996 ($2.95, B&W, limited series)

1-Linsner-c/s; anthology. 5.00
2, 3 (2/98) 4.00
4,5: 4- (6/98), 5-(11/98) 3.00
Ltd. Edition 20.00

CRYPT OF SHADOWS
Marvel Comics Group: Jan, 1973 - No. 21, Nov, 1975 (#1-9 are 20¢)

	GD	VG	FN	VF	VF/NM	NM-
1-Wolverton-r/Advs. Into Terror #7	4	8	12	22	34	45
2-10: 2-Starlin/Everett-c	3	6	9	14	20	26
11-21: 18,20-Kirby-a	2	4	6	13	18	22

NOTE: ***Briefer*** *a-2r.* ***Ditko*** *a-13r, 18-20r.* ***Everett*** *a-6, 14r; c-2i.* ***Heath*** *a-1r.* ***Gil Kane*** *c-1, 6.* ***Mort Lawrence*** *a-1r, 8r.* ***Maneely*** *a-2r.* ***Moldoff*** *a-8.* ***Powell*** *a-12r, 14r.* ***Tuska*** *a-2r.*

CRYPT OF TERROR (Formerly Crime Patrol; Tales From the Crypt No. 20 on)
(Also see EC Archives • Tales From the Crypt)
E. C. Comics: No. 17, Apr-May, 1950 - No. 19, Aug-Sept, 1950

	GD	VG	FN	VF	VF/NM	NM-
17-1st New Trend to hit stands	297	594	891	2376	3788	5200
18,19	166	332	498	1328	2114	2900

NOTE: ***Craig*** *c/a-17-19.* ***Feldstein*** *a-17-19.* ***Ingels*** *a-19.* ***Kurtzman*** *a-18.* ***Wood*** *a-18. Canadian reprints known; see Table of Contents.*

CRYSIS (Based on the EA videogame)
IDW Publishing: Jun, 2011 - No. 6, Oct, 2011 ($3.99, limited series)

1-6: 1-Richard K. Moran-s/Peter Bergting-a; two covers 4.00

CSI: CRIME SCENE INVESTIGATION (Based on TV series)
IDW Publishing: Jan, 2003 - No. 5, May, 2003 ($3.99, limited series)

1-Two covers (photo & Ashley Wood); Max Allan Collins-s 4.00
2-5 4.00
Free Comic Book Day edition (7/04) Previews CSI: Bad Rap; The Shield: Spotlight; 24: One Shot; and 30 Days of Night 3.00
...: Case Files Vol. 1 TPB (8/06, $19.99) B&W rep/Serial TPB, CSI - Bad Rap and

CSI: Crime Scene Investigation #5 © CBS

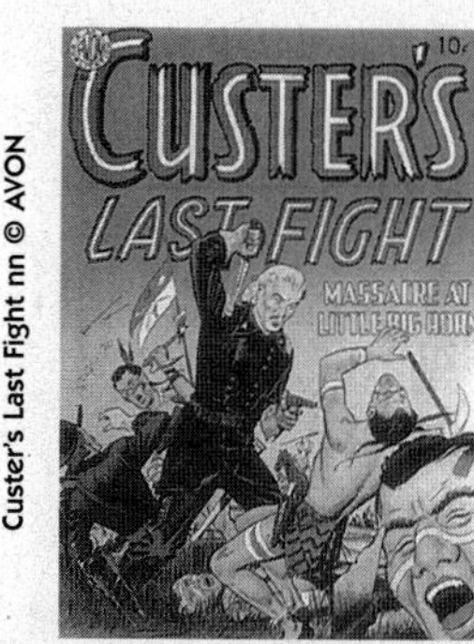

Custer's Last Fight nn © AVON

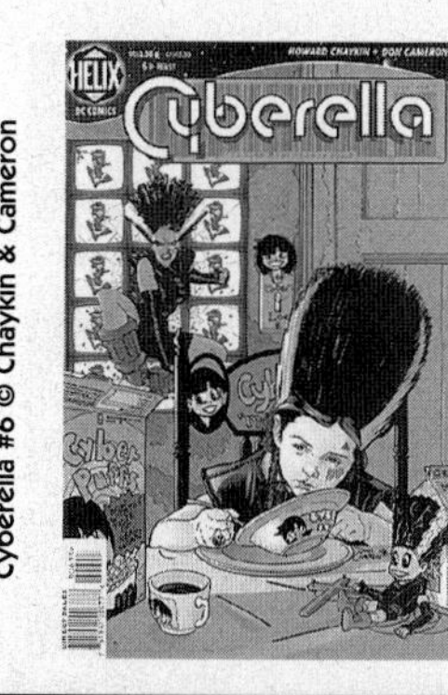

Cyberella #6 © Chaykin & Cameron

GD 2.0 VG 4.0 FN 6.0 VF 8.0 VF/NM 9.0 NM- 9.2

CSI - Demon House limited series 20.00
...: Serial TPB (2003, $19.99) r/#1-5; bonus short story by Collins/Wood 20.00
...: Thicker Than Blood (7/03, $6.99) Mariotte-s/Rodriguez-a 7.00

CSI: CRIME SCENE INVESTIGATION - BAD RAP
IDW Publishing: Aug, 2003 - No. 5, Dec, 2003 ($3.99, limited series)

1-5-Two photo covers; Max Allan Collins-s/Rodriguez-a 4.00
TPB (3/04, $19.99) r/#1-5 20.00

CSI: CRIME SCENE INVESTIGATION - DEMON HOUSE
IDW Publishing: Feb, 2004 - No. 5, Jun, 2004 ($3.99, limited series)

1-5-Photo covers on all; Max Allan Collins-s/Rodriguez-a 4.00
TPB (10/04, $19.99) r/#1-5 20.00

CSI: CRIME SCENE INVESTIGATION - DOMINOS
IDW Publishing: Aug, 2004 - No. 5, Dec, 2004 ($3.99, limited series)

1-5-Photo covers on all; Oprisko-s/Rodriguez-a 4.00

CSI: CRIME SCENE INVESTIGATION - DYING IN THE GUTTERS
IDW Publishing: Aug, 2006 - No. 5, Dec, 2006 ($3.99, limited series)

1-5-"Rich Johnston" murdered; comic creators (Quesada, Rucka, David, Brubaker, Silvestri and others) appear as suspects; Stephen Mooney-a; photo-c 4.00

CSI: CRIME SCENE INVESTIGATION - SECRET IDENTITY
IDW Publishing: Feb, 2005 - No. 5, Jun, 2005 ($3.99, limited series)

1-5-Photo covers on all; Steven Grant-s/Gabriel Rodriguez-a 4.00

CSI: MIAMI
IDW Publishing: Oct, 2003; Apr, 2004 ($6.99, one-shots)

... - Blood Money (9/04)-Oprisko-s/Guedes & Perkins-a 7.00
... - Smoking Gun (10/03)-Mariotte-s/Avilés & Wood-a 7.00
... - Thou Shalt Not... (4/04)-Oprisko-s/Guedes & Wood-a 7.00
TPB (2/05, $19.99) reprints one-shots 20.00

CSI: NY - BLOODY MURDER
IDW Publishing: July, 2005 - No. 5, Nov, 2005 ($3.99, limited series)

1-5-Photo covers on all; Collins-s/Woodward-a 4.00

C-23 (Jim Lee's...) (Based on Wizards of the Coast card game)
Image Comics: Apr, 1998 - No. 8, Nov, 1998 ($2.50)

1-8: 1,2-Choi & Mariotte-s/ Charest-c. 2-Variant-c by Jim Lee. 4-Ryan Benjamin-c. 5,8-Corben var-c. 6-Flip book with Planetary preview; Corben-c 3.00

CUD
Fantagraphics Books: 8/92 - No. 8, 12/94 ($2.25-$2.75, B&W, mature)

1-8: Terry LaBan scripts & art in all. 6-1st Eno & Plum 3.00

CUD COMICS
Dark Horse Comics: Jan, 1995 - No. 8, Sept, 1997 ($2.95, B&W)

1-8: Terry LaBan-c/a/scripts. 5-Nudity; marijuana story 3.00
Eno and Plum TPB (1997, $12.95) r/#1-4, DHP #93-95 13.00

CUPID
Marvel Comics (U.S.A.): Dec, 1949 - No. 2, Mar, 1950

1-Photo-c 19 38 57 111 176 240
2-Bettie Page ('50s pin-up queen) photo-c; Powell-a (see My Love #4) 55 110 165 352 601 850

CURIO
Harry 'A' Chesler: 1930's(?) (Tabloid size, 16-20 pgs.)

nn 19 38 57 109 172 235

CURLY KAYOE COMICS (Boxing)
United Features Syndicate/Dell Publ. Co.: 1946 - No. 8, 1950; Jan, 1958

1 (1946)-Strip-r (Fritzi Ritz); biography of Sam Leff, Kayoe's artist 18 36 54 107 169 230
2 11 22 33 64 90 115
3-8 10 20 30 56 76 95
United Presents...(Fall, 1948) 10 20 30 56 76 95
Four Color 871 (Dell, 1/58) 4 8 12 24 37 50

CURSED
Image Comics (Top Cow): Oct, 2003 - No. 4, Feb, 2004 ($2.99)

1-4-Avery & Blevins-s/Molenaar-a 3.00

CURSE OF DRACULA, THE
Dark Horse Comics: July, 1998 - No. 3, Sept, 1998 ($2.95, limited series)

1-3-Marv Wolfman-s/Gene Colan-a 3.00
TPB (2005, $9.95) r/series; intro. by Marv Wolfman 10.00

CURSE OF DREADWOLF
Lightning Comics: Sept, 1994 ($2.75, B&W)

1 3.00

CURSE OF RUNE (Becomes Rune, 2nd Series)
Malibu Comics (Ultraverse): May, 1995 - No. 4, Aug, 1995 ($2.50, lim. series)

1-4: 1-Two covers form one image 3.00

CURSE OF THE SPAWN
Image Comics (Todd McFarlane Prod.): Sept, 1996 - No. 29, Mar, 1999 ($1.95)

1-Dwayne Turner-a(p) 6.00
1-B&W Edition 2 4 6 9 13 16
2-3 4.00
4-29: 12-Movie photo-c of Melinda Clarke (Priest) 3.00
Blood and Sutures ('99, $9.95, TPB) r/#5-8 10.00
Lost Values ('00, $10.95, TPB) r/#12-14,22; Ashley Wood-c 11.00
Sacrifice of the Soul ('99, $9.95, TPB) r/#1-4 10.00
Shades of Gray ('00, $9.95, TPB) r/#9-11,29 10.00
The Best of the Curse of the Spawn (6/06, $16.99, TPB) B&W r/#1-8,12-16,20-29 17.00

CURSE OF THE WEIRD
Marvel Comics: Dec, 1993 - No. 4, Mar, 1994 ($1.25, limited series)
(Pre-code horror-r)

1-4: 1,3,4-Wolverton-r(1-Eye of Doom; 3-Where Monsters Dwell; 4-The End of the World). 2-Orlando-r. 4-Zombie-r by Everett; painted-c 1 2 3 5 6 8
NOTE: ***Briefer** r-2. **Davis** a-4r. **Ditko** a-1r, 2r, 4r; c-1r. **Everett** r-1. **Heath** r-1-3. **Kubert** r-3. **Wolverton** a-1r, 3r, 4r.*

CUSTER'S LAST FIGHT
Avon Periodicals: 1950

nn-Partial reprint of Cowpuncher #1 15 30 45 88 137 185

CUTEY BUNNY (See Army Surplus Komikz Featuring...)

CUTIE PIE
Junior Reader's Guild (Lev Gleason): May, 1955 - No. 3, Dec, 1955; No. 4, Feb, 1956; No. 5, Aug, 1956

1 9 18 27 47 61 75
2-5: 4-Misdated 2/55 6 12 18 31 38 45

CUTTING EDGE
Marvel Comics: Dec, 1995 ($2.95)

1-Hulk-c/story; Messner-Loebs scripts 3.00

CVO: COVERT VAMPIRIC OPERATIONS
IDW Publishing: June, 2003 ($5.99, one-shot)

1-Alex Garner-s/Mindy Lee-a(p) 6.00
... - Human Touch 1 (8/04, $3.99, one-shot) Hernandez & Garner-a 4.00
... - 100-Page Spactacular (4/11, $7.99) r/#1, African Blood #2 Rogue State #5 8.00
TPB (9/04, $19.99) r/#1 and ... - Artifact #1-3; intro. by Garner 20.00

CVO: COVERT VAMPIRIC OPERATIONS - AFRICAN BLOOD
IDW Publishing: Sept, 2006 - No. 4, May, 2007 ($3.99, limited series)

1-4-El Torres-s/Luis Czerniawski-a 4.00

CVO: COVERT VAMPIRIC OPERATIONS - ARTIFACT
IDW Publishing: Oct, 2003 - No. 3, Dec, 2003 ($3.99, limited series)

1-3-Jeff Mariotte-s/Gabriel Hernandez-a/Alex Garner-c 4.00

CVO: COVERT VAMPIRIC OPERATIONS - ROGUE STATE
IDW Publishing: Nov, 2004 - No. 5, Mar, 2005 ($3.99, limited series)

1-5-Jeff Mariotte-s/Vazquez-a 4.00
TPB (7/05, $19.99) r/#1-5; cover gallery 20.00

CYBERELLA
DC Comics (Helix): Sept, 1996 - No. 12, Aug, 1997 ($2.25/$2.50)(1st Helix series)

1-12: 1-5-Chaykin & Cameron-a. 1,2-Chaykin-c. 3-5-Cameron-c 3.00

CYBERFORCE
Image Comics (Top Cow Productions): Oct, 1992 - No. 4, 1993; No. 0, Sept, 1993 ($1.95, limited series)

1-Silvestri-c/a in all; coupon for Image Comics #0; 1st Top Cow Productions title 6.00
1-With coupon missing 2.50
2-4,0: 2-(3/93). 3-Pitt-c/story. 4-Codename: Stryke Force back-up (1st app.); foil-c. 0-(9/93)-Walt Simonson-c/a/scripts 3.00

CYBERFORCE
Image Comics (Top Cow Productions)/Top Cow Comics No. 28 on:
V2#1, Nov, 1993 - No. 35, Sept. 1997 ($1.95)

V2#1-24: 1-7-Marc Silvestri/Keith Williams-c/a. 8-McFarlane-c/a. 10-Painted variant-c exists.

Cyberforce V2 #23 © TCOW

Cyclone Comics #4 © Bilbara

Daffy Duck #63 © WB

	GD	VG	FN	VF	VF/NM	NM-
	2.0	4.0	6.0	8.0	9.0	9.2

18-Variant-c exists. 23-Velocity-c. 3.00
1-3: 1-Gold Logo-c. 2-Silver embossed-c. 3-Gold embossed-c 10.00
1-(99¢, 3/96, 2nd printing) 3.00
25-($3.95)-Wraparound, foil-c 4.00
26-35: 28-(11/96)-1st Top Cow Comics iss. Quesada & Palmiotti's Gabriel app. 27-Quesada & Palmiotti's Ash app. 3.00
Annual 1,2 (3/95, 8/96, $2.50, $2.95) 4.00
NOTE: *Annuals read Volume One in the indica.*

CYBERFORCE (Volume 3)
Image Comics (Top Cow): Apr, 2006 - No. 6, Nov, 2006 ($2.99)
1-6: 1-Pat Lee-a/Ron Marz-s; three covers by Pat Lee, Marc Silvestri and Dave Finch 3.00
#0-(6/06, $2.99) reprints origin story from Image Comics Hardcover Vol. 1 3.00
.../X-Men 1 (1/07, $3.99) Pat Lee-a/Ron Marz-s; 2 covers by Lee and Silvestri 4.00
Vol. 1 TPB (12/06, $14.99) r/#1-6, #0 & story from The Cow Quarterly; cover gallery 15.00

CYBERFORCE/HUNTER-KILLER
Image Comics (Top Cow Productions): July, 2009 - No. 5, Mar, 2010 ($2.99)
1-5-Waid-s/Rocafort-a; multiple covers on each 3.00

CYBERFORCE ORIGINS
Image Comics (Top Cow Productions): Jan, 1995 - No. 3, Nov, 1995 ($2.50)
1-Cyblade (1/95) 5.00
1-Cyblade (3/96, 99¢, 2nd printing) 3.00
1A-Exclusive Ed.; Tucci-c 4.00
2,3: 2-Stryker (2/95)-1st Mike Turner-a. 3-Impact 3.00
(#4) Misery (12/95, $2.95) 3.00

CYBERFORCE/STRYKEFORCE: OPPOSING FORCES (See Codename: Stryke Force #15)
Image Comics (Top Cow Productions): Sept, 1995 - No. 2, Oct, 1995 ($2.50, limited series)
1,2: 2-Stryker disbands Strykeforce. 3.00

CYBERFORCE UNIVERSE SOURCEBOOK
Image Comics (Top Cow Productions): Aug, 1994/Feb, 1995 ($2.50)
1,2-Silvestri-c 3.00

CYBERFROG
Hall of Heroes: June, 1994 - No. 2, Dec, 1994 ($2.50, B&W, limited series)
1,2 3.00

CYBERFROG
Harris Comics: Feb, 1996 - No. 3, Apr, 1996 ($2.95)
0-3: Van Sciver-c/a/scripts. 2-Variant-c exists 5.00

CYBERFROG: (Title series), **Harris Comics**
--RESERVOIR FROG, 9/96 - No. 2, 10/96 ($2.95) 1,2: Van Sciver-c/a/scripts; wraparound-c 3.00
--3RD ANNIVERSARY SPECIAL, 1/97 - #2, ($2.50, B&W) 1,2 3.00
--VS. CREED, 7/97 ($2.95, B&W)1 3.00

CYBERNARY (See Deathblow #1)
Image Comics (WildStorm Productions): Nov, 1995 - No.5, Mar, 1996 ($2.50)
1-5 3.00

CYBERNARY 2.0
DC Comics (WildStorm): Sept, 2001 - No. 6, Apr, 2002 ($2.95, limited series)
1-6: Joe Harris-s/Eric Canete-a. 6-The Authority app. 3.00

CYBERPUNK
Innovation Publishing: Sept, 1989 - No. 2, Oct, 1989 ($1.95, 28 pgs.) Book 2, #1, May, 1990 - No. 2, 1990 ($2.25, 28 pgs.)
1,2, Book 2 #1,2:1,2-Ken Steacy painted-covers (Adults) 3.00

CYBERPUNK: THE SERAPHIM FILES
Innovation Publishing: Nov, 1990 - No. 2, Dec, 1990 ($2.50, 28 pgs., mature)
1,2: 1-Painted-c; story cont'd from Seraphim 3.00

CYBERPUNX
Image Comics (Extreme Studios): Mar, 1996 ($2.50)
1 3.00

CYBERRAD
Continuity Comics: 1991 - No. 7, 1992 ($2.00)(Direct sale & newsstand-c variations) V2#1, 1993 ($2.50)
1-7: 5-Glow-in-the-dark-c by N. Adams (direct sale only). 6-Contains 4 pg. fold-out poster; N. Adams layouts 3.00
V2#1-($2.95, direct sale ed.)-Die-cut-c w/B&W hologram on-c; Neal Adams sketches 4.00
V2#1-($2.50, newsstand ed.)-Without sketches 3.00

	GD	VG	FN	VF	VF/NM	NM-
	2.0	4.0	6.0	8.0	9.0	9.2

CYBERRAD DEATHWATCH 2000 (Becomes CyberRad w/#2, 7/93)
Continuity Comics: Apr, 1993 - No. 2, 1993 ($2.50)
1,2: 1-Bagged w/2 cards; Adams-c & layouts & plots. 2-Bagged w/card; Adams scripts 3.00

CYBER 7
Eclipse Comics: Mar, 1989 - #7, Sept, 1989; V2#1, Oct, 1989 - #10, 1990 ($2.00, B&W)
1-7, Book 2 #1-10: Stories translated from Japanese 3.00

CYBLADE
Image Comics (Top Cow Productions): Oct, 2008 - No. 4, Mar, 2009 ($2.99)
1-4: 1,2-Mays-a/Fialkov-s. 1-Two covers. 3,4-Ferguson-a 3.00
.../ Ghost Rider 1 (Marvel/Top Cow, 1/97, $2.95) Devil's Reign pt. 2 4.00
...: Pilot Season 1 (9/07, $2.99) Rick Mays-a 3.00

CYBLADE/SHI (Also see Battle For The Independents & Shi/Cyblade: The Battle For The Independents)
Image Comics (Top Cow Productions): 1995 ($2.95, one-shot)

	GD	VG	FN	VF	VF/NM	NM-
San Diego Preview	3	6	9	16	20	25
1-($2.95)-1st app. Witchblade	2	4	6	12	16	20
1-($2.95)-variant-c; Tucci-a	2	4	6	10	12	15

CYBRID
Maximum Press: July, 1995; No. 0, Jan, 1997 ($2.95/$3.50)
1-(7/95) 3.50
0-(1/97)-Liefeld-a/script; story cont'd in Avengelyne #4 3.50

CYCLONE COMICS (Also see Whirlwind Comics)
Bilbara Publishing Co.: June, 1940 - No. 5, Nov, 1940

	GD	VG	FN	VF	VF/NM	NM-
1-Origin Tornado Tom; Volton (the human generator), Tornado Tom, Kingdom of the Moon, Mister Q begin (1st app. of each)	90	180	270	576	988	1400
2	47	94	141	296	498	700
3-Classic-c (scarce)	103	206	309	659	1130	1600
4	47	94	141	296	498	700
5-(Scarce)	65	130	195	416	708	1000

Ashcan - (5/40) Not distributed to newsstands, only for in house use. Cover produced on green stock paper. A CGC certified FN (6.0) copy sold for $2,000 in 2006.

CYCLOPS (X-Men)
Marvel Comics: Oct, 2001 - No. 4, Jan, 2002 ($2.50, limited series)
1-4-Texeira-c/a. 1,2-Black Tom and Juggernaut app. 3.00
1-(5/11, $2.99, one-shot) Haspiel-a; Batroc and the Circus of Crime app. 3.00

CYCLOPS: RETRIBUTION
Marvel Comics: 1994 ($5.95, trade paperback)
nn-r/Marvel Comics Presents #17-24 6.00

CY-GOR (See Spawn #38 for 1st app.)
Image Comics (Todd McFarlane Prod.): July, 1999 - No. 6, Dec, 1999 ($2.50)
1-6-Veitch-s 3.00

CYNTHIA DOYLE, NURSE IN LOVE (Formerly Sweetheart Diary)
Charlton Publications: No. 66, Oct, 1962 - No. 74, Feb, 1964

	GD	VG	FN	VF	VF/NM	NM-
66-74	3	6	9	14	19	24

DAFFODIL
Marvel Comics (Soleil): 2010 - No. 3, 2010 ($5.99, limited series)
1-3-English version of French comic; Brrémaud-s/Rigano-a 6.00

DAFFY (Daffy Duck No. 18 on)(See Looney Tunes)
Dell Publishing Co./Gold Key No. 31-127/Whitman No. 128 on: #457, 3/53 - #30, 7-9/62; #31, 10-12/62 - #145, 6/84 (No #132,133)

	GD	VG	FN	VF	VF/NM	NM-
Four Color 457(#1)-Elmer Fudd x-overs begin	11	22	33	71	136	200
Four Color 536,615('55)	7	14	21	44	72	100
4(1-3/56)-11('57)	6	12	18	37	59	80
12-19(1958-59)	5	10	15	30	48	65
20-40(1960-64)	3	6	9	21	32	42
41-60(1964-68)	3	6	9	16	23	30
61-90(1969-74)-Road Runner in most. 76-82-"Daffy Duck and the Road Runner" on-c	2	4	6	11	16	20
91-110	2	4	6	8	11	14
111-127	1	3	4	6	8	10
128,134-141: 139(2/82), 140(2-3/82), 141(4/82)	2	4	6	8	10	12
129(8/80),130,131 (pre-pack?) (scarce). 129-Sherlock Holmes parody-s	4	8	12	22	34	45
142-145(#90029 on-c; nd, nd code, pre-pack): 142(6/83), 143(8/83), 144(3/84), 145(6/84)	3	6	9	16	23	30
Mini-Comic 1 (1976; 3-1/4x6-1/2")	1	3	4	6	8	10

NOTE: *Reprint issues-No.41-46, 48, 50, 53-55, 58, 59, 65, 67, 69, 73, 81, 96, 103-108; 136-142, 144, 145(1/3-2/3-*

Dagar, Desert Fox #23 © FOX

Daken: Dark Wolverine #9.1 © MAR

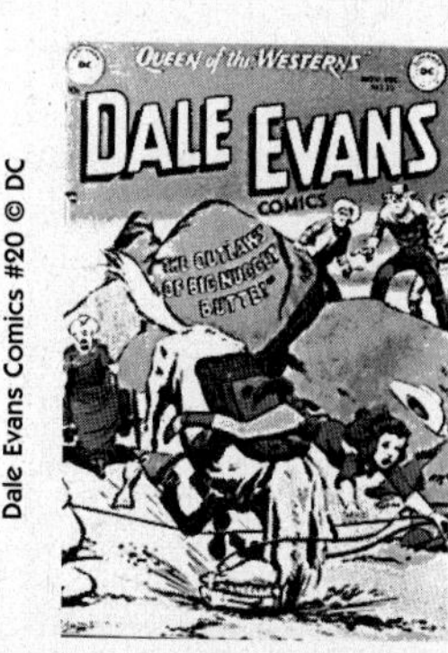

Dale Evans Comics #20 © DC

GD VG FN VF VF/NM NM-
2.0 4.0 6.0 8.0 9.0 9.2

r). (See March of Comics No. 277, 288, 303, 313, 331, 347, 357,375, 387, 397, 402, 413, 425, 437, 460).

DAFFY DUCK (Digest-size reprints from Looney Tunes)
DC Comics: 2005 ($6.99, digest)

Vol. 1: You're Despicable! - Reprints from Looney Tunes #38,43,45,47,51,53,54,58,61,62,66,70 7.00

DAFFY TUNES COMICS
Four-Star Publications: June, 1947; No. 12, Aug, 1947

nn 10 20 30 54 72 90
12-Al Fago-c/a; funny animal 9 18 27 50 65 80

DAGAR, DESERT HAWK (Captain Kidd No. 24 on; formerly All Great)
Fox Features Syndicate: No. 14, Feb, 1948 - No. 23, Apr, 1949 (No #17,18)

14-Tangi & Safari Cary begin; Good bondage-c/a 97 194 291 621 1061 1500
15,16-E. Good-a; 15-Bondage-c 54 108 162 343 574 825
19,20,22: 19-Used in **SOTI**, pg. 180 (Tangi) 50 100 150 315 533 750
21,23: 21-Bondage-c; "Bombs & Bums Away" panel in "Flood of Death" story used in **SOTI.** 23-Bondage-c 53 106 159 334 567 800
*NOTE: Tangi by **Kamen**-14-16, 19, 20; c-20, 21.*

DAGAR THE INVINCIBLE (Tales of Sword & Sorcery...) (Also see Dan Curtis Giveaways & Gold Key Spotlight)
Gold Key: Oct, 1972 - No. 18, Dec, 1976; No. 19, Apr, 1982

1-Origin; intro. Villains Olstellon & Scor 4 8 12 24 37 50
2-5: 3-Intro. Graylin, Dagar's woman; Jarn x-over 3 6 9 14 19 24
6-1st Dark Gods story 2 4 6 9 13 16
7-10: 9-Intro. Torgus. 10-1st Three Witches story 2 4 6 9 13 16
11-18: 13-Durak & Torgus x-over; story continues in Dr. Spektor #15. 14-Dagar's origin retold. 18-Origin retold 2 4 6 8 10 12
19(4/82)-Origin-r/#18 6.00
NOTE: Durak app. in 7, 12, 13. Tragg app. in 5, 11.

DAGWOOD (Chic Young's) (Also see Blondie Comics)
Harvey Publications: Sept, 1950 - No. 140, Nov, 1965

1 13 26 39 90 195 300
2 9 18 27 61 106 150
3-10 8 16 24 51 86 120
11-20 6 12 18 41 66 90
21-30 5 10 15 35 55 75
31-50 5 10 15 30 48 65
51-70 4 8 12 22 34 45
71-100 3 6 9 18 27 35
101-121,123-128,130,135 3 6 9 16 23 30
122,129,131-134,136-140-All are 68-pg. issues 4 8 12 22 34 45
NOTE: Popeye and other one page strips appeared in early issues.

DAI KAMIKAZE!
Now Comics: June, 1987 - No. 12, Aug, 1988 ($1.75)

1-1st app. Speed Racer 5.00
1-Second printing 3.00
2-12 3.00

DAILY BUGLE (See Spider-Man)
Marvel Comics: Dec, 1996 - No. 3, Feb, 1997 ($2.50, B&W, limited series)

1-3-Paul Grist-s 3.00

DAISY AND DONALD (See Walt Disney Showcase No. 8)
Gold Key/Whitman No. 42 on: May, 1973 - No. 59, July, 1984 (no No. 48)

1-Barks-r/WDC&S #280,308 3 6 9 20 30 40
2-5: 4-Barks-r/WDC&S #224 2 4 6 11 16 20
6-10 2 4 6 9 12 15
11-20 1 3 4 6 8 10
21-41: 32-r/WDC&S #308 1 2 3 5 6 8
42-44 (Whitman) 2 4 6 8 11 14
45 (8/80),46-(pre-pack?)(scarce) 4 8 12 22 34 45
47-(12/80)-Only distr. in Whitman 3-pack (scarce) 5 10 15 35 55 75
48(3/81)-50(8/81): 50-r/#3 2 4 6 10 14 18
51-54: 51-Barks-r/4-Color #1150. 52-r/#2. 53(2/82), 54(4/82) 2 4 6 9 13 16
55-59-(all #90284 on-c, nd, nd code, pre-pack): 55(5/83), 56(7/83), 57(8/83), 58(8/83), 59(7/84) 3 6 9 14 19 24

DAISY & HER PUPS (Dagwood & Blondie's Dogs)(Formerly Blondie Comics #20)
Harvey Publications: No. 21, 7/51 - No. 27, 7/52; No. 8, 9/52 - No. 18, 5/54

21 (#1)-Blondie's dog Daisy and her 5 pups led by Elmer begin. Rags Rabbit app. 6 12 18 41 66 90
22-27 (#2-7): 26 has No. 6 on cover but No. 26 on inside. 23,25-The Little King app. 24-Bringing Up Father by McManus app. 25-27-Rags Rabbit app. 4 8 12 28 44 60
8-18: 8,9-Rags Rabbit app. 8,17-The Little King app. 11-The Flop Family Swan begins. 22-Cookie app. 11-Felix The Cat app. by 17,18-Popeye app. 4 8 12 26 41 55

DAISY DUCK & UNCLE SCROOGE PICNIC TIME (See Dell Giant #33)

DAISY DUCK & UNCLE SCROOGE SHOW BOAT (See Dell Giant #55)

DAISY DUCK'S DIARY (See Dynabrite Comics, & Walt Disney's C&S #298)
Dell Publishing Co.: No. 600, Nov, 1954 - No. 1247, Dec-Fef, 1961-62 (Disney)

Four Color 600 (#1) 7 14 21 46 76 105
Four Color 659, 743 (11/56) 6 12 18 37 59 80
Four Color 858 (11/57), 948 (11/58), 1247 (12-2/61-62) 5 10 15 32 51 70
Four Color 1055 (11-1/59-60), 1150 (12-1/60-61)-By Carl Barks) 9 18 27 58 99 140

DAISY HANDBOOK
Daisy Manufacturing Co.: 1946; No. 2, 1948 (10¢, pocket-size, 132 pgs.)

1-Buck Rogers, Red Ryder; Wolverton-a (2 pgs.) 21 42 63 122 199 275
2-Captain Marvel & Ibis the Invincible, Red Ryder, Boy Commandos & Robotman; Wolverton-a (2 pgs.); contains 8 pg. color catalog 21 42 63 122 199 275

DAISY MAE (See Oxydol-Dreft)

DAISY'S RED RYDER GUN BOOK
Daisy Manufacturing Co.: 1955 (25¢, pocket-size, 132 pgs.)

nn-Boy Commandos, Red Ryder; 1pg. Wolverton-a 15 30 45 85 130 175

DAKEN: DARK WOLVERINE
Marvel Comics: Nov, 2010 - No. 23, May, 2012 ($3.99/$2.99)

1-Camuncoli-a/c; Way & Liu-s; back-up history of the character 4.00
2-9, 9.1, 10-23-($2.99) 3,4-Fantastic Four app. 7-9-Crossover with X-23 #8,9; Gambit app. 9.1-Avengers app. 13-16-Moon Knight app. 17-19-Runaways app. 3.00

DAKKON BLACKBLADE ON THE WORLD OF MAGIC: THE GATHERING
Acclaim Comics (Armada): June, 1996 ($5.95, one-shot)

1-Jerry Prosser scripts; Rags Morales-c/a. 6.00

DAKOTA LIL (See Fawcett Movie Comics)

DAKTARI (Ivan Tors) (TV)
Dell Publishing Co.: July, 1967 - No. 3, Oct, 1968; No. 4, Oct, 1969

1-Marshall Thompson photo-c on all 4 8 12 24 37 50
2-4 3 6 9 18 27 35

DALE EVANS COMICS (Also see Queen of the West...)(See Boy Commandos #32)
National Periodical Publications: Sept-Oct, 1948 - No. 24, Jul-Aug, 1952 (No. 1-19: 52 pgs.)

1-Dale Evans & her horse Buttermilk begin; Sierra Smith begins by Alex Toth 58 116 174 371 636 900
2-Alex Toth-a 30 60 90 177 289 400
3-11-Alex Toth-a 20 40 60 114 182 250
12-20: 12-Target-c 14 28 42 80 115 150
21-24 14 28 42 82 121 160
NOTE: Photo-c-1, 2, 4-14.

DALGODA
Fantagraphics Books: Aug, 1984 - No. 8, Feb, 1986 (High quality paper)

1,8: 1- Fujitake-c/a in all. 8-Alan Moore story 4.00
2-7: 2,3-Debut Grimwood's Daughter. 3.00

DALTON BOYS, THE
Avon Periodicals: 1951

1-(Number on spine)-Kinstler-c 17 34 51 100 158 215

DAMAGE
DC Comics: Apr, 1994 - No. 20, Jan, 1996 ($1.75/$1.95/$2.25)

1-20: 6-(9/94)-Zero Hour. 0-(10/94). 7-(11/94). 14-Ray app. 3.00

DAMAGE CONTROL (See Marvel Comics Presents #19)
Marvel Comics: 5/89 - No. 4, 8/89; V2#1, 12/89 - No. 4, 2/90 ($1.00)
V3#1, 6/91 - No. 4, 9/91 ($1.25, all are limited series)

V1#1-4,V2#1-4,V3#1-4: V1#4-Wolverine app. V2#2,4-Punisher app. 1-Spider-Man app. 2-New Warriors app. 3,4-Silver Surfer app. 4-Infinity Gauntlet parody 3.00

DAMAGED
Radical Comics: Jul, 2011 - No. 6 ($3.99/$3.50, limited series)

1-($3.99) Lapham-s/Manco-a; covers by Maleev & Manco 4.00
2-4-($3.50) Maleev-c 3.50

DAMNED

Dandy Comics #5 © WMG

Danger Girl: Revolver #1 © JSC

Danger Trail #1 © DC

GD VG FN VF VF/NM NM-
2.0 4.0 6.0 8.0 9.0 9.2

GD VG FN VF VF/NM NM-
2.0 4.0 6.0 8.0 9.0 9.2

Image Comics (Homage Comics): June, 1997 - No. 4, Sept, 1997 ($2.50, limited series)
1-4-Steven Grant-s/Mike Zeck-c/a in all 3.00

DAMN NATION
Dark Horse Comics: Feb, 2005 - No. 3, Apr, 2005 ($2.99, limited series)
1-3-J. Alexander-a/Andrew Cosby-s 3.00

DANCES WITH DEMONS (See Marvel Frontier Comics Unlimited)
Marvel Frontier Comics: Sept, 1993 - No. 4, Dec, 1993 ($1.95, limited series)
1-($2.95)-Foil embossed-c; Charlie Adlard & Rod Ramos-a 4.00
2-4 3.00

DAN DARE
Virgin Comics: Nov, 2007 - No. 7, July, 2008 ($2.99/$5.99)
1-6-Ennis-s/Erskine-a. 1-Two covers by Talbot and Horn. 2-6-Two covers on each 3.00
7-($5.99) Double sized finale with wraparound Erskine-c; Gibbons variant-c 6.00

DANDEE: Four Star Publications: 1947 (Advertised, not published)

DAN DUNN (See Crackajack Funnies, Detective Dan, Famous Feature Stories & Red Ryder)

DANDY COMICS (Also see Happy Jack Howard)
E. C. Comics: Spring, 1947 - No. 7, Spring, 1948
1-Funny animal; Vince Fago-a in all; Dandy in all 41 82 123 249 417 585
2 29 58 87 170 278 385
3-7: 3-Intro Handy Andy who is c-feature #3 on 23 46 69 136 223 310

DANGER
Comic Media/Allen Hardy Assoc.: Jan, 1953 - No. 11, Aug, 1954
1-Heck-c/a 31 62 93 186 303 420
2,3,5,7,9-11: 17 34 51 98 154 210
4-Marijuana cover/story 20 40 60 117 189 260
6- "Narcotics" story; begin spy theme 19 38 57 109 172 235
8-Bondage/torture/headlights panels 21 42 63 122 199 275
NOTE: *Morisi a-2, 5, 6(3), 10; c-2. Contains some reprints from Danger & Dynamite.*

DANGER (Formerly Comic Media title)
Charlton Comics Group: No. 12, June, 1955 - No. 14, Oct, 1955
12(#1) 14 28 42 76 108 140
13,14: 14-r/#12 11 22 33 60 83 105

DANGER
Super Comics: 1964
Super Reprint #10-12 (Black Dwarf; #10-r/Great Comics #1 by Novack. #11-r/Johnny Danger #1. #12-r/Red Seal #14), #15-r/Spy Cases #26. #16-Unpublished Chesler material (Yankee Girl), #17-r/Scoop #8 (Capt. Courage & Enchanted Dagger), #18(nd)-r/Guns Against Gangsters #5 (Gun-Master, Annie Oakley, The Chameleon; L.B. Cole-r)
2 4 6 11 16 20

DANGER AND ADVENTURE (Formerly This Magazine Is Haunted; Robin Hood and His Merry Men No. 28 on)
Charlton Comics: No. 22, Feb, 1955 - No. 27, Feb, 1956
22-Ibis the Invincible-c/story (last G.A. app.); Nyoka app.; last pre-code issue
11 22 33 62 86 110
23-Lance O'Casey-c/sty; Nyoka app.; Ditko-a thru #27
13 26 39 72 101 130
24-27: 24-Mike Danger & Johnny Adventure begin 9 18 27 50 65 80

DANGER GIRL (Also see Cliffhanger #0)
Image Comics (Cliffhanger Productions): Mar, 1998 - No. 4, Dec, 1998;
DC Comics (Cliffhanger Prod.): No. 5, July, 1999 - No. 7, Feb, 2001
Preview-Bagged in DV8 #14 Voyager Pack 4.00
Preview Gold Edition 8.00
1-($2.95) Hartnell & Campbell-s/Campbell/Garner-a 1 2 3 5 6 8
1-($4.95) Chromium cover 45.00
1-American Entertainment Ed. 8.00
1-American Entertainment Gold Ed., 1-Tourbook edition 10.00
1-"Danger-sized" ed.; over-sized format 3 6 9 16 23 30
2-($2.50) 4.00
2-Smoking Gun variant cover, 2-Platinum Ed., 2-Dynamic Forces Omnichrome variant-c 2 4 6 9 13 16
2-Gold foil cover 9.00
2-Ruby red foil cover 90.00
3,4: 3-c by Campbell, Charest and Adam Hughes. 4-Big knife variant-c 3.00
3,5: 3-Gold foil cover. 5-DF Bikini variant-c 5.00
4-6 3.00
7-($5.95) Wraparound gatefold-c; Last issue 6.00
...: Danger-Sized Treasury Edition #1 (IDW, 1/12, $9.99, 13" x 8-1/2") r/#1,2 & Preview 10.00
...: Hawaiian Punch (5/03, $4.95) Campbell-c; Phil Noto-a 5.00
...: Odd Jobs TPB (2004, $14.95) r/one-shots Hawaiian Punch, Viva Las Danger & Special; Campbell-c 15.00
San Diego Preview (8/98, B&W) flip book w/Wildcats preview 5.00
Sketchbook (2001, $6.95) Campbell-a; sketches for comics, toys, games 7.00
...Special (2/00, $3.50) art by Campbell, Chiodo, and Art Adams 3.50
... 3-D #1 (4/03, $4.95, bagged with 3-D glasses) r/ Preview & #1 in 3-D 5.00
...: Viva Las Danger (1/04, $4.95) Noto-a/Campbell-c 5.00
... :The Dangerous Collection nn (8/98; r-#1) 6.00
... :The Dangerous Collection 2,3: 2-(11/98, $5.95) r/#2,3. 3-('99) r/#4,5 6.00
... :The Dangerous Collection nn, 2-($10.00) Gold foil logo 10.00
... :The Ultimate Collection HC ($29.95) r/#1-7; intro by Bruce Campbell 30.00
... :The Ultimate Collection SC ($19.95) r/#1-7; intro by Bruce Campbell 20.00

DANGER GIRL AND THE ARMY OF DARKNESS
Dynamite Entertainment/ IDW Publ.: 2011 - No. 4, 2011 ($3.99, limited series)
1-4-Hartnell-s/Bolson-a. 1,2 Covers by Campbell, Bradshaw & Renaud 4.00

DANGER GIRL: BACK IN BLACK
DC Comics (Cliffhanger): Jan, 2006 - No. 4, Apr, 2006 ($2.99, limited series)
1-4-Hartnell-s/Bradshaw-a. 1-Campbell-c 3.00
TPB (2007, $12.99) r/series & covers 13.00

DANGER GIRL: BODY SHOTS
DC Comics (WildStorm): Jun, 2007 - No. 4, Sept, 2007 ($2.99, limited series)
1-4-Hartnell-s/Bradshaw-a 3.00
TPB (2007, $12.99) r/series & covers 13.00

DANGER GIRL KAMIKAZE
DC Comics (Cliffhanger): Nov, 2001 - No. 2, Dec., 2001 ($2.95, lim. series)
1,2-Tommy Yune-s/a 3.00

DANGER GIRL: REVOLVER
IDW Publishing: Jan, 2012 - Present ($3.99, limited series)
1-Hartnell-s/Madden-a; covers by Campbell & Madden 4.00

DANGER IS OUR BUSINESS!
Toby Press: 1953(Dec.) - No. 10, June, 1955
1-Captain Comet by Williamson/Frazetta-a, 6 pgs. (science fiction)
45 90 135 284 480 675
2 14 28 42 80 115 150
3-10 12 24 36 67 94 120
I.W. Reprint #9('64)-Williamson/Frazetta-r/#1; Kinstler-c
8 16 24 51 86 120

DANGER IS THEIR BUSINESS (Also see A-1 Comic)
Magazine Enterprises: No. 50, 1952
A-1 50-Powell-a 14 28 42 80 115 150

DANGER MAN (TV)
Dell Publishing Co.: No. 1231, Sept-Nov, 1961
Four Color 1231-Patrick McGoohan photo-c 10 20 30 67 124 180

DANGER TRAIL (Also see Showcase #50, 51)
National Periodical Publ.: July-Aug, 1950 - No. 5, Mar-Apr, 1951 (52 pgs.)
1-King Faraday begins, ends #4; Toth-a in all 129 258 387 826 1413 2000
2 89 178 267 565 970 1375
3-(Rare) one of the rarest early '50s DCs 139 278 417 883 1517 2150
4,5: 5-Johnny Peril-c/story (moves to Sensation Comics #107); new logo (also see Comic Cavalcade #15-29) 68 136 204 432 746 1060

DANGER TRAIL
DC Comics: Apr, 1993 - No. 4, July, 1993 ($1.50, limited series)
1-4: Gulacy-c on all 3.00

DANGER UNLIMITED (See San Diego Comic Con Comics #2 & Torch of Liberty Special)
Dark Horse (Legend): Feb, 1994 - No. 4, May, 1994 ($2.00, limited series)
1-4: Byrne-c/a/scripts in all; origin stories of both original team (Doc Danger, Thermal, Miss Mirage, & Hunk) & future team (Thermal, Belebet, & Caucus). 1-Intro Torch of Liberty & Golgotha (cameo) in back-up story. 4-Hellboy & Torch of Liberty cameo in lead story 3.00
TPB (1995, $14.95)-r/#1-4; includes last pg. originally cut from #4 15.00

DAN HASTINGS (See Syndicate Features)

DANIEL BOONE (See The Exploits of..., Fighting... Frontier Scout...,The Legends of... & March of Comics No. 306)
Dell Publishing Co.: No. 1163, Mar-May, 1961
Four Color 1163-Marsh-a 5 10 15 35 55 75

Dante's Inferno #4 © EA

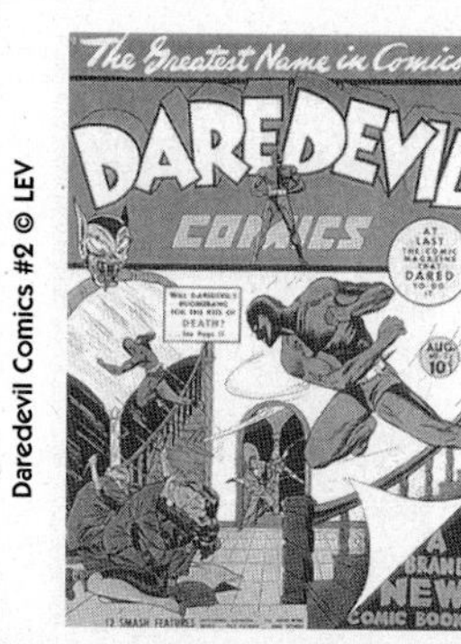

Daredevil Comics #2 © LEV

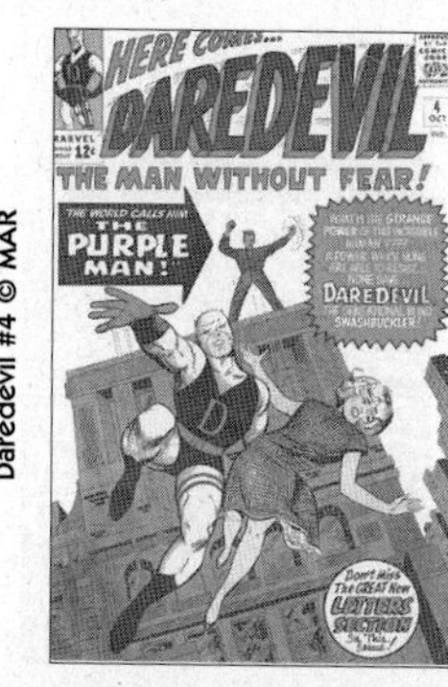

Daredevil #4 © MAR

GD VG FN VF VF/NM NM-
2.0 4.0 6.0 8.0 9.0 9.2

DANIEL BOONE (TV) (See March of Comics No. 306)
Gold Key: Jan, 1965 - No. 15, Apr, 1969 (All have Fess Parker photo-c)

1-Back-c and last eight pages fold in half to form "Official Handbook Fess Parker as Daniel Boone Trail Blazers Club" 8 16 24 55 93 130
2-Back-c pin-up 5 10 15 32 51 70
3-5-Back-c pin-ups 4 8 12 26 41 55
6-15: 7,8-Back-c pin-up 3 6 9 20 30 40

DAN'L BOONE
Sussex Publ. Co.: Sept, 1955 - No. 8, Sept, 1957

1 14 28 42 80 115 150
2 10 20 30 54 72 90
3-8 8 16 24 40 50 60

DANNY BLAZE (...Firefighter) (Nature Boy No. 3 on)
Charlton Comics: Aug, 1955 - No. 2, Oct, 1955

1-Authentic stories of fire fighting 13 26 39 74 105 135
2 9 18 27 50 65 80

DANNY DINGLE (See Sparkler Comics)
United Features Syndicate: No. 17, 1940

Single Series 17 26 52 78 154 252 350

DANNY THOMAS SHOW, THE (TV)
Dell Publishing Co.: No. 1180, Apr-June, 1961 - No. 1249, Dec-Feb, 1961-62

Four Color 1180-Toth-a, photo-c 13 26 39 88 189 290
Four Color 1249-Manning-a, photo-c 12 24 36 84 175 265

DANTE'S INFERNO (Based on the video game)
DC Comics (WildStorm): Feb, 2010 - No. 6, Jul, 2010 ($3.99, limited series)

1-6-Christos Gage-s/Diego Latorre-a 4.00
TPB (2010, $19.99) r/#1-6 20.00

DAOMU (Based on a novel series from China)
Image Comics: Feb, 2011 - Present ($2.99)

1-8-Kennedy Xu-s/Ken Chou-a 3.00

DARBY O'GILL & THE LITTLE PEOPLE (Movie)(See Movie Comics)
Dell Publishing Co.: 1959 (Disney)

Four Color 1024-Toth-a; photo-c. 9 18 27 63 112 160

DAREDEVIL ("Daredevil Comics" on cover of #2) (See Silver Streak Comics)
Lev Gleason Publications (Funnies, Inc. No. 1): July, 1941 - No. 134, Sept, 1956
(52 pgs. #52-80; 64 pgs. #35-41)(Charles Biro stories)

1-No. 1 titled "Dardedevil Battles Hitler," Classic battle issue as Daredevil teams up in each strip - The Silver Streak, Lance Hale, Cloud Curtis, Dickey Dean & Pirate Prince to battle Hitler; The Claw unites with Hitler and Japanese and battles Daredevil; Origin of Hitler feature story "The Man of Hate." Classic Hitler photo app. on-c 1275 2550 3825 9500 16,500 23,500
2-London (by Jerry Robinson), Pat Patriot (by Reed Crandall), Nightro, Real American No. 1 (by Briefer #2-11), Dash Dillon, Whirlwind begin; Dickie Dean, Pirate Prince end; intro. & only app. Pioneer, Champion of America & Times Square. The Claw continues #2-4 343 686 1029 2400 4200 6000
3-Intro./origin of 13. Newspaper editor has name "Roussos." Daredevil battles the Claw ill. text story 252 504 756 1613 2757 3900
4-The Claw captured and taken to New York Central Park Zoo. Whirlwind, the Blond Bomber begins, ends #6 194 388 582 1242 2121 3000
5-Ghost vs. Claw begins by Bob Wood, ends #20; 13 & Jinx begin; origin 13 retold in text; intro./origin Jinx, 13's sidekick; intro. Sniffer in Daredevil 142 284 426 909 1555 2200
6-(12/41)-Daredevil battles wolf with human brain. Dash Dillon ends 123 246 369 787 1344 1900
7,9: 7-(2/42), shows #6 on cover; delayed one month due to Pearl Harbor attack. 9-Daredevil vs. Daredevil-c; Sniffer strip begins, ends #69 100 200 300 635 1093 1550
8-Nazi WWII war-c. Nightro ends. Sniffer/Daredevil fight Nazi insurgents; 107 214 321 680 1165 1650
10-(5-42), "Remember Pearl Harbor" Japanese WWII-c; classic splash page w/American flag. Daredevil joins Air Corps. to fight Japanese. Ghost Battles Claw & Japanese. Last Whirlwind 119 238 357 762 1306 1850
11-Classic Quasimodo (hunchback of Notre Dame) bondage/torture-c/sty. London, Pat Patriot, Real America #1 end 350 700 1050 2300 3400 4500
12-Origin of The Claw; Scoop Scuttle by Wolverton begins (2-4 pgs.), ends #22, not in #21. Charles Biro biography. Dickey Dean, Pirate Prince return (both end #32) 139 278 417 883 1517 2150
13-Intro of Little Wise Guys (10/42)(also see Boy #4); Daredevil fights Nazi hooded cult; Ghost battles Claw, Hitler & Nazis in Britain; Bob Wood biography 107 214 321 680 1165 1650
14-Classic Daredevil facial portrait-c; Hitler app.; "Slap the Jap" game included 74 148 222 470 810 1150
15-Death of Meatball 100 200 300 635 1093 1550
16,17: 16-WWII-c w/freighter hit by German torpedo. Meatball is buried & Curly joins Little Wise Guys team. 17-Japanese WWII-c 68 136 204 435 743 1050
18-New origin of Daredevil (not same as Silver Streak #6). Hitler, Mussolini Tojo and Mickey Mouse app. on-c at carnival 119 238 357 762 1306 1850
19,20: Last Ghost vs. Claw 61 122 183 390 670 950
21-Reprints cover of Silver Streak #6 (on inside) plus intro. of The Claw from Silver Streak #1. The Claw strip begins by Bob Q. Siege, ends #31 84 168 252 538 919 1300
22,23: 22-Daredevil fights the Tramp. 23-Dickie Dean by Bob Montana 45 90 135 284 480 675
24-Bloody puppet show-c 52 104 156 328 557 785
25-1st Little Wise Guys-c without Daredevil 36 72 108 216 351 485
26,28-30 41 82 123 256 428 600
27-Bondage/torture-c 57 114 171 362 619 875
31-Death of The Claw 82 164 246 528 902 1275
32-34: 32,33-Egbert app. 33-Roger Wilco begins, ends #35 34 68 102 199 325 450
35-37,39-41: 35-Two Daredevil stories begin, end #68; Chauncey app. 37-39-Go Along Gallagher app. (#35-41 are 64 pgs.); 41-Dickie Dean ends 35 70 105 208 339 470
38-Origin Daredevil retold from #18 45 90 135 284 480 675
42-Intro. Kilroy in Daredevil who unveils Daredevil's I.D.-c/sty 29 58 87 172 281 390
43-45,47,48-All Daredevil-c. 43-Daredevil in costume on-c & 1 panel only inside; 44-DD back in costume; i.d. revealed on-c. 27 54 81 160 263 365
46,50: DD not on-c 22 44 66 132 216 300
49-Wise Guys fight secret hooded group c/sty. DD not on-c 27 54 81 158 263 365
51,52,56-60,63-66,68,69-Last Daredevil & Sniffer (12/50). 56-Wise Guys start their own circus. DD not on-c 19 38 57 111 176 240
53-Daredevil/Wise Guys find lost palace of Zanzarah, an underground Egyptian tomb w/mummy & treasure; classic c/story. DD-c 21 42 63 122 199 275
54,55-Daredevil-c 20 40 60 118 192 265
61-Daredevil & Wise Guys in haunted house classic c/story. Daredevil/Wise Guys fly rocket into stratosphere. DD not on-c 21 42 63 122 199 275
62-Wise Guys in medieval times, a dream by Peewee locked in a medieval museum; classic c/story. DD not on-c 21 42 63 122 199 275
67-Last Daredevil-c 20 40 60 118 192 265
70-Little Wise Guys take over book without Daredevil. Daredevil removed from-c & logo; Air Devils w/Hot Rock Flanagan begins, ends #80 14 28 42 76 108 140
71-78,81: 81-Dilly Duncan begins, ends #134 10 20 30 56 76 95
79,80: 79-(10/51)-Daredevil returns; Wise Guys go to Africa. 80-Daredevil & Wise Guys blast into space & land on Mars; last Daredevil app. in title 11 22 33 62 86 110
82,90: One pg. Frazetta ad in both 10 20 30 56 76 95
83-89,91-99,101-134 9 18 27 52 69 85
100-(7/53) 11 22 33 62 86 110

NOTE: **Biro** *a-1-22, 38; c-1-134; script-1-134.* **Dan Barry** *a(Daredevil) 40-48;* **Roy Belft**-*a (Daredevil) 49-55.* **Bolle** *a-125.* **Al Borth**-*a(Daredevil) #57-59.* **Briefer** *a-1-11 (Real American #1); Pirate Prince-#1, 2, 12-31.* **Tony Dipreta**-*a(Wise Guys) #108-110, 112-134.* **R.W. Hall** *a-22.* **Carl Hubbell** *a-9-21, 23-26, 27(Daredevil), 28-32.* **Al Mandel** *a-13.* **Hy Mankin**-*a(Wise Guys)-#80, 81.* **Maurer**-*a(Daredevil)-23, 31, 37, 38, 41, 43-51, 53-67, 69; (Little Wise Guys)-70-89.* **McWilliams** *a-70, 73-80.* **Bob Montana** *a-12, 23, 27, 28, 31-33.* **Wm. Overgard**-*a(Daredevil) #67, (Wise Guys) 74-79, 83-85, 87.* **Jerry Robinson** *a(London) #2-8.* **Roussos** *a(Nightro)-2-8.* **Bob Q. Siege**-*a(Claw) 27-31; (Daredevil)-#35.* **Wolverton** *a-12-22.* **Bob Wood**-*a(The Claw)-1-20; (The Ghost)-5-20.* **Dick Wood** *sty-2-10, 13-22, 27-32.* **Daredevil** *not on-c #46,49-52,56-66,68-134.*

DAREDEVIL (...& the Black Widow #92-107 on-c only; see Giant-Size...,Marvel Advs., Marvel Graphic Novel #24, Marvel Super Heroes, '66 & Spider-Man &...)
Marvel Comics Group: Apr, 1964 - No. 380, Oct, 1998

1-Origin/1st app. Daredevil; intro Foggy Nelson & Karen Page; death of Battling Murdock; Bill Everett-c/a; reprinted in Marvel Super Heroes #1 (1966) 310 620 930 2700 5850 9000
2-Fantastic Four cameo; 2nd app. Electro (Spidey villain); Thing guest star 67 134 201 545 1173 1800
3-Origin & 1st app. The Owl (villain) 41 82 123 328 664 1000
4-Origin & 1st app. The Purple Man 35 70 105 254 552 850
5-Minor costume change; Wood-a begins 27 54 81 196 423 650
6-Mr. Fear app. 19 38 57 128 277 425
7-Daredevil battles Sub-Mariner & dons red costume for 1st time (4/65) 67 134 201 545 1173 1800
8-10: 8-Origin/1st app. Stilt-Man 14 28 42 93 202 310
11-15: 12-1st app. Plunderer; Ka-Zar app. 13-Facts about Ka-Zar's origin; Kirby-a 11 22 33 73 142 210

GD VG FN VF VF/NM NM-
2.0 4.0 6.0 8.0 9.0 9.2

Daredevil #50 © MAR

Daredevil #241 © MAR

Daredevil V2 #2 © MAR

GD 2.0 | VG 4.0 | FN 6.0 | VF 8.0 | VF/NM 9.0 | NM- 9.2

16,17-Spider-Man x-over. 16-1st Romita-a on Spider-Man (5/66) 17 34 51 114 250 385
18-Origin & 1st app. Gladiator 11 22 33 71 136 200
19,20 9 18 27 61 106 150
21-26,28-30: 24-Ka-Zar app. 7 14 21 46 76 105
27-Spider-Man x-over 8 16 24 51 86 120
31-40: 38-Fantastic Four x-over; cont'd in F.F. #73. 39-1st Exterminator (later becomes Death-Stalker) 6 12 18 41 66 90
41,42,44-49: 41-Death Mike Murdock. 42-1st app. Jester. 45-Statue of Liberty photo-c 6 12 18 37 59 80
43-Daredevil battles Captain America; origin partially retold 7 14 21 48 79 110
50-53: 50-52-B. Smith-a. 53-Origin retold; last 12¢ issue 6 12 18 39 62 85
54-56,58-60: 54-Spider-Man cameo. 56-1st app. Death's Head (9/69); story cont'd in #57 (not same as new Death's Head) 4 8 12 26 41 55
57-Reveals i.d. to Karen Page; Death's Head app. 5 10 15 30 48 65
61-76,78-80: 79-Stan Lee cameo. 80-Last 15¢ issue 4 8 12 22 34 45
77-Spider-Man x-over 4 8 12 28 44 60
81-(52 pgs.) Black Widow begins (11/71). 5 10 15 35 55 75
82,84-99: 87-Electro-c/story 3 6 9 18 27 35
83-B. Smith layouts/Weiss-p 3 6 9 20 30 40
100-Origin retold 4 8 12 26 41 55
101-104,106-120: 107-Starlin-c; Thanos cameo. 113-1st brief app. Deathstalker. 114-1st full app. Deathstalker 3 6 9 16 23 30
105-Origin Moondragon by Starlin (12/73); Thanos cameo in flashback (early app.) 3 6 9 18 27 35
121-130,137: 124-1st app. Copperhead; Black Widow leaves. 126-1st new Torpedo 3 6 9 14 20 25
131-Origin/1st app. new Bullseye (see Nick Fury #15) 9 18 27 63 112 160
132-2nd app. new Bullseye (Regular 25¢ edition) 6 12 18 39 62 85
132-(30¢-c variant, limited distribution)(4/76) 10 20 30 65 118 170
133-136-(Regular 25¢ editions). 133-Uri Geller app. 3 6 9 14 20 25
133-136-(30¢-c variants, limited distribution)(5-8/76) 4 8 12 24 37 50
138-Ghost Rider-c/story; Death's Head is reincarnated; Byrne-a 3 6 9 20 30 40
139,140,142-145,147-157: 142-Nova cameo. 147,148-(Reg. 30¢-c). 150-1st app. Paladin. 151-Reveals i.d. to Heather Glenn. 155-Black Widow returns. 156-The '60s Daredevil app. 2 4 6 13 18 22
141,146-Bullseye app. 4 8 12 22 34 45
146-(35¢-c variant, limited distribution) 7 14 21 44 72 100
147,148-(35¢-c variants, limited distribution) 5 10 15 32 51 70
158-Frank Miller art begins (5/79); origin/death of Deathstalker (see Captain America #235 & Spectacular Spider-Man #27 9 18 27 60 103 145
159 5 10 15 32 51 70
160,161-Bullseye app. 4 8 12 26 41 55
162-Ditko-a; no Miller-a 3 6 9 14 20 25
163,164: 163-Hulk cameo. 164-Origin retold 3 6 9 19 29 38
165-167,170 3 6 9 17 25 32
168-Origin/1st app. Elektra; 1st Miller scripts 11 22 33 71 136 200
169-2nd Elektra app. 5 10 15 35 55 75
171-173 3 6 9 16 23 30
174,175-Elektra app. 3 6 9 18 27 35
176-180-Elektra app. 178-Cage app. 179-Anti-smoking issue mentioned in the Congressional Record 3 6 9 17 25 32
181-(52 pgs.)-Death of Elektra; Punisher cameo out of costume 4 8 12 26 41 55
182-184-Punisher app. by Miller (drug issues) 3 6 9 14 20 26
185-191: 187-New Black Widow. 189-Death of Stick. 190-($1.00, 52 pgs.)-Elektra returns, part origin; 2 pin-ups. 191-Last Miller Daredevil 2 4 6 8 10 12
192-195,198,199,201-207,209-218,220-226,234-237: 226-Frank Miller plots begin 4.00
196-Wolverine-c/app. 2 4 6 9 13 16
197-Bullseye-c/app.; 1st app. Yuriko Oyama (who becomes Lady Deathstrike) 5.00
200,238: 200-Bullseye app. 238-Mutant Massacre; Sabretooth app. 6.00
208,219,228-233: 208-Harlan Ellison scripts borrowed from Avengers TV episode "House that Jack Built". 219-Miller-c/script. 228-233-Last Miller scripts 5.00
227-Miller scripts begin 6.00
239,240,242-247 3.00
241-Todd McFarlane-a(p) 5.00
248,249-Wolverine app. 6.00
250,251,253,258: 250-1st app. Bullet. 258-Intro The Bengal (a villain) 3.00
252,260 (52 pgs.): 252-Fall of the Mutants. 260-Typhoid Mary app. 5.00
254-Origin & 1st app. Typhoid Mary (5/88) 1 2 3 4 5 8
255,256,258: 255,256-2nd/3rd app. Typhoid Mary. 259-Typhoid Mary app. 5.00
257-Punisher app. (x-over w/Punisher #10) 1 3 4 6 8 10
261-281,283-294,296-299,301-304,307-318: 270-1st app. Black Heart. 272-Intro Shotgun (villain). 281-Silver Surfer cameo. 283-Capt. America app. 297-Typhoid Mary app.; Kingpin storyline begins. 292-D.G. Chichester scripts begin. 293-Punisher app. 303-Re-intro the Owl. 304-Garney-c/a. 309-Punisher-c.; Terror app. 310-Calypso-c 3.00
282,295,300,305,306: 282-Silver Surfer app. 295-Ghost Rider app. 300-($2.00, 52 pgs.) Kingpin story ends. 305,306-Spider-Man-c 4.00
319-Prologue to Fall From Grace; Elektra returns 6.00
319-2nd printing w/black-c 3.00
320-Fall From Grace Pt 1 5.00
321-Fall From Grace regular ed.; Pt 2; new costume; Venom app. 3.00
321-($2.00)-Wraparound Glow-in-the-dark-c ed. 5.00
322-Fall From Grace Pt 3; Eddie Brock app. 4.00
323,324-Fall From Grace Pt. 4 & 5: 323-Vs. Venom-c/story. 324-Morbius-c/story 4.00
325-($2.50, 52 pgs.)-Fall From Grace ends; contains bound-in poster 4.00
326-349,351-353: 326-New logo. 328-Bound-in trading card sheet. 330-Gambit app. 348-1st Cary Nord art in DD (1/96);"Dec" on-c. 353-Karl Kesel scripts; Nord-c/a begins; Mr. Hyde-c/app. 3.00
350-($2.95)-Double-sized 4.00
350-($3.50)-Double-sized; gold ink-c 5.00
354-374,376-379: Kesel scripts, Nord-c/a in all. 354-$1.50-c begins. 355-Larry Hama layouts; Pyro app. 358-Mysterio-c/app. 359-Absorbing Man cameo. 360-Absorbing Man-c/app. 361-Black Widow-c/app. 363,366-370-Gene Colan-a(p). 368-Omega Red-c/app. 372-Ghost Rider-c/app. 376-379-"Flying Blind", DD goes undercover for S.H.I.E.L.D. 3.00
375-($2.99) Wraparound-c; Mr. Fear-c/app. 4.00
380-($2.99) Final issue; flashback story 5.00
Special 1(9/67, 25¢, 68 pgs.)-New art/story 7 14 21 48 79 110
Special 2,3: 2(2/71, 25¢, 52 pgs.)-Entire book has Powell/Wood-r; Wood-c. 3(1/72, 52 pgs.)-Reprints 3 6 9 20 30 40
Annual 4(10/76) 2 4 6 11 16 20
Annual 4(#5)-10: ('89-94 68 pgs.)-5-Atlantis Attacks. 6-Sutton-a. 7-Guice-a (7 pgs.). 8-Deathlok-c/story. 9-Polybagged w/card 4.00
... :Born Again TPB ($17.95)-r/#227-233; Miller-s/Mazzucchelli-a & new-c 20.00
... By Frank Miller and Klaus Janson Omnibus HC (2007, $99.99, dustjacket) r/#158-161, 163-191 and What If...? #28; intros by Miller and Janson; interviews, bonus art 100.00
... By Frank Miller and Klaus Janson Omnibus Companion HC (2007, $59.99, die-cut d.j.) r/#219,226-233, Daredevil: The Man Without Fear #1-5, Daredevil: Love and War, and Peter Parker, the Spect. Spider-Man #27-28; bonus materials 60.00
.../Deadpool- (Annual '97, $2.99)-Wraparound-c 4.00
...:Fall From Grace TPB ($19.95)-r/#319-325 20.00
... :Gang War TPB ($15.95)-r/#169-172,180; Miller-s/a(p) 16.00
...:Legends: (Vol. 4) Typhoid Mary TPB (2003, $19.95) r/#254-257,259-263 20.00
... :Love's Labors Lost TPB ($19.99)-r/#215-217,219-222,225,226; Mazzucchelli-c 20.00
.../Punisher TPB (1988, $4.95)-r/D.D. #182-184 (all printings) 5.00
...Visionaries: Frank Miller Vol. 1 TPB ($17.95) r/#158-161,163-167 18.00
...Visionaries: Frank Miller Vol. 2 TPB ($24.95) r/#168-182; new Miller-c 25.00
...Visionaries: Frank Miller Vol. 3 TPB ($24.95) r/#183-191, What If? #28,35 & Bizarre Adventures #28; new Miller-c 25.00
... Vs. Bullseye Vol. 1 TPB (2004, $15.99) r/#131-132,146,169,181,191 16.00
Wizard Ace Edition: Daredevil (Vol. 1) #1 (4/03, $13.99) Acetate Campbell-c 14.00

NOTE: ***Art Adams*** *c-238p, 239.* ***Austin*** *a-191i; c-151i, 200i.* ***John Buscema*** *a-136, 137p, 234p, 235p; c-86p, 136i, 137p, 142, 219.* ***Byrne*** *c-200p, 201, 203, 223.* ***Capullo*** *a-286p.* ***Colan*** *a(p)-20-49, 53-82, 84-98, 100, 110, 112, 124, 153, 154, 156, 157, 363, 366-370, Spec. 1p; c(p)-20-42, 44-49, 53-60, 71, 92, 98, 138, 153, 154, 156, 157, Annual 1.* ***Craig*** *a-50i, 52i.* ***Ditko*** *a-162, 234p, 235p, 264p; c-162.* ***Everett*** *c/a-1; inks-21, 83.* ***Garney*** *c/a-304.* ***Gil Kane*** *a-141p, 146-148p, 151p; c(p)-85, 90, 91, 93, 94, 115, 116, 119, 120, 125-128, 133, 139, 147, 152.* ***Kirby*** *c-2-4, 5p, 12p, 13p, 43, 136p.* ***Layton*** *c-202.* ***Miller*** *scripts-168-182, 183(part), 184-191, 219, 227-233; a-158-161p, 163-184p, 191p; c-158-161p, 163-184p, 185-189, 190p, 191.* ***Orlando*** *a-2-4p.* ***Powell*** *a-9p, 11p, Special 1r, 2r.* ***Simonson*** *c-199, 236p.* ***B. Smith*** *a-236p; c-51p, 52p, 217.* ***Starlin*** *a-105p.* ***Steranko*** *c-44i.* ***Tuska*** *a-39i, 145p.* ***Williamson*** *a(i)-237, 239, 240, 243, 248-257, 259-282, 283(part), 284, 285, 287, 288(part), 289(part), 293-300; c(i)-237, 243, 244, 248-257, 259-263, 265-278, 280-289, Annual 8.* ***Wood*** *a-5-8, 9i, 10, 11i, Spec. 2i; c-5i, 6-11, 164i.*

DAREDEVIL (Volume 2)(Marvel Knights)(Becomes Black Panther: The Man Without Fear #513)
Marvel Comics: Nov, 1998 - No. 512, Feb, 2011 ($2.50/$2.99)

1-Kevin Smith-s/Quesada & Palmiotti-a 12.00
1-($6.95) DF Edition w/Quesada & Palmiotti var.-c 15.00
1-($6.00) DF Sketch Ed. w/B&W-c 10.00
2-Two covers by Campbell and Quesada/Palmiotti 9.00
3-8: 4,5-Bullseye app. 5-Variant-c exists. 8-Spider-Man-c/app.; last Smith-s 6.00
9-15: 9-11-David Mack-s; intro Echo. 12-Begin $2.99-c; Haynes-a. 13,14-Quesada-a 4.00
16-19-Direct editions; Bendis-s/Mack-c/painted-a 4.00
18,19,21,22-Newsstand editions with variant cover logo "Marvel Unlimited Featuring... 4.00
20-($3.50) Gale-s/Winslade-a; back-up by Stan Lee-s/Colan-a; Mack-c 5.00
21-40: 21-25-Gale-s. 26-38-Bendis-s/Maleev-a. 32-Daredevil's ID revealed. 35-Spider-Man-c/app. 38-Iron Fist & Luke Cage app. 40-Dodson-a 3.50
41-(25¢-c) Begins "Lowlife" arc; Maleev-a; intro Milla Donovan 3.00
41-(Newsstand edition with 2.99¢-c) 3.00

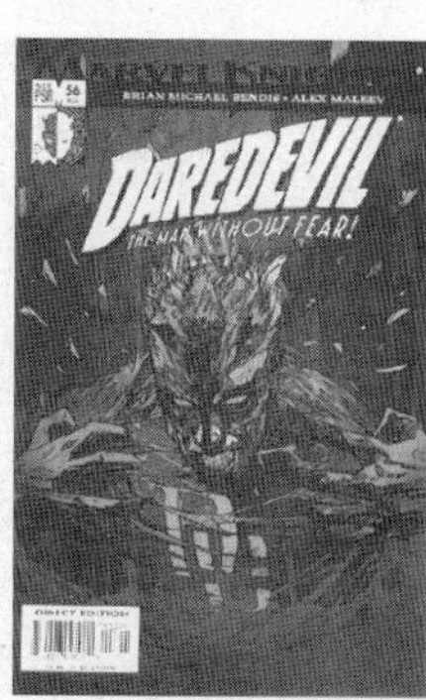

Daredevil V2 #56 © MAR

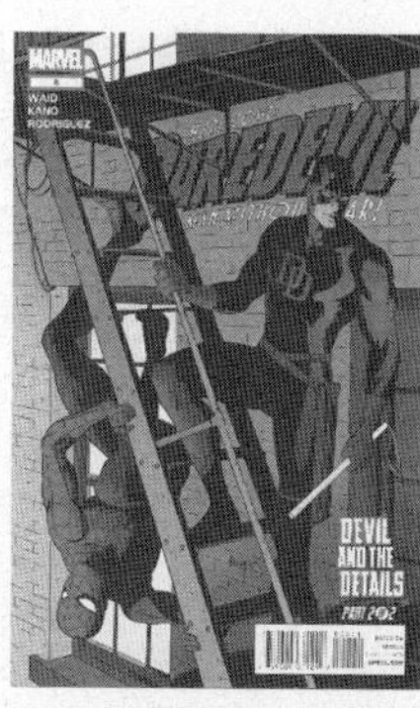

Daredevil V3 #8 © MAR

Daredevil: The Target #1 © MAR

	GD 2.0	VG 4.0	FN 6.0	VF 8.0	VF/NM 9.0	NM- 9.2

42-45-"Lowlife" arc; Maleev-a 3.00
46-50-($2.99). 46-Typhoid Mary returns. 49-Bullseye app. 50-Art panels by various incl. Romita, Colan, Mack, Janson, Oeming, Quesada 3.00
51-64,66-74,76-81: 51-55-Mack-s/a; Echo app. 54-Wolverine-c/app. 61-64-Black Widow app. 71-Decalogue begins. 76-81-The Murdock Papers. 81-Last Bendis-s/Maleev-a 3.00
65-($3.99) 40th Anniversary issue; Land-c; art by Maleev, Horn, Bachalo and others 4.00
75-($3.99) Decalogue ends; Jester app. 4.00
82-99,101-119: 82-Brubaker-s/Lark-a begin; Foggy "killed". 84-86-Punisher app. 87-Other Daredevil ID revealed. 94-Romita-c. 111-Lady Bullseye debut 3.00
82-Variant-c by McNiven 4.00
100-($3.99) Three covers (Djurdjevic, Bermejo and Turner); art by Romita Sr., Colan, Lark, Sienkiewicz, Maleev, Bermejo & Djurdjevic; sketch art gallery; r/Daredevil #90 (1972) 4.00

(After Vol. 2 #119, Aug, 2009, numbering reverts to original Vol. 1 with #500)

500-(10/09, $4.99) Kingpin, Lady Bullseye app.; back-up stories, pin-up & cover galleries; r/#191; five covers by Djurdjevic, Darrow, Dell'Otto, Ross and Zircher 5.00
501-512: 501-Daredevil takes over The Hand; Diggle-s begins; Ribic-c. 508-Shadowland begins. 512-Black Panther app. 3.00
Annual #1 (12/07, $3.99) Brubaker-s/Fernandez-a/Djurdjevic-c; Black Tarantula app. 4.00
... & Captain America: Dead on Arrival (2008, $4.99) English version of Italian story 5.00
... Black & White 1 (10/10, $3.99) B&W short stories by various; Aja-c 4.00
... Blood of the Tarantula (6/08, $3.99) Parks & Brubaker-s/Samnee-a/Djurdjevic-c 4.00
... By Brian Michael Bendis Omnibus Vol. 1 HC (2008, $99.99) oversized r/#16-19,26-50, and 56-60 100.00
... By Ed Brubaker Saga (2008, giveaway) synopsis of issues #82-110, preview of #111 3.00
... Cage Match 1 (7/10, $2.99) flashback early Luke Cage team-up; Chen-a 3.00
... MGC #26 (8/10, $1.00) r/#26 with "Marvel's Greatest Comics" logo on cover 3.00
...2099 #1 (11/04, $2.99) Kirkman-s/Moline-a 3.00
TPB ($9.95) r/#1-3 10.00
...Vol. 1 HC (2001, $29.99, with dustjacket) r/#1-11,13-15 30.00
...Vol. 1 HC (2003, $29.99, with dustjacket) r/#1-11,13-15; larger page size 30.00
...Vol. 2 HC (2002, $29.99, with dustjacket) r/#26-37; afterword by Bendis 30.00
...Vol. 3 HC (2004, $29.99, with dustjacket) r/#38-50; Maleev sketch pages 30.00
...Vol. 4 HC (2005, $29.99, with dustjacket) r/#56-65; Vol. 1 #81 (1971) Black Widow 30.00
...Vol. 5 HC (2006, $29.99, with dustjacket) r/#66-75 30.00
...Vol. 6 HC (2006, $34.99, with dustjacket) r/#76-81 & What If Karen Page Had Lived? 35.00
(Vol. 1) Visionaries TPB ($19.95) r/#1-8; Ben Affleck intro. 20.00
(Vol. 2) Parts of a Hole TPB (1/02, $17.95) r/#9-15; David Mack intro. 18.00
(Vol. 3) Wake Up TPB (7/02, $9.99) r/#16-19 10.00
...Vol. 4: Underboss TPB (8/02, $14.99) r/#26-31 15.00
...Vol. 5: Out TPB (2003, $19.99) r/#32-40 20.00
...Vol. 6: Lowlife TPB (2003, $13.99) r/#41-45 14.00
...Vol. 7: Hardcore TPB (2003, $13.99) r/#46-50 14.00
...Vol. 8: Echo - Vision Quest TPB (2004, $13.99) r/#51-55; David Mack-s/a 14.00
...Vol. 9: King of Hell's Kitchen TPB (2004, $13.99) r/#56-60 14.00
...Vol. 10: The Widow TPB (2004, $16.99) r/#61-65 & Vol. 1 #81 17.00
...Vol. 11: Golden Age TPB (2005, $13.99) r/#66-70 14.00
...Vol. 12: Decalogue TPB (2005, $14.99) r/#71-75 15.00
...Vol. 13: The Murdock Papers TPB (2006, $14.99) r/#76-81 15.00
...: The Devil Inside and Out Vol. 1 (2006, $14.99) r/#82-87; Brubaker & Lark interview 15.00
...: The Devil Inside and Out Vol. 2 (2007, $14.99) r/#88-93; Bermejo cover sketches 15.00
...: Hell To Pay Vol. 1 TPB (2007, $14.99) r/#94-99; Djurdjevic cover sketches 15.00
...: Hell To Pay Vol. 2 TPB (2008, $15.99) r/#100-105 16.00

DAREDEVIL (Volume 3)
Marvel Comics: Sept, 2011 - Present ($3.99/$2.99)

1-($3.99) Mark Waid-s/Paolo Rivera-a; back-up tale with Marcos Martin-a 4.00
1-Variant-c by Marcos Martin 8.00
1-Variant-c by Neal Adams 10.00
2-9-($2.99) 2-Capt. America app. 3-Klaw returns. 4-6-Marcos Martin-a. 8-X-over w/Amazing Spider-Man #677; Spider-Man and Black Cat app. 3.00

DAREDEVIL/ BATMAN (Also see Batman/Daredevil)
Marvel Comics/ DC Comics: 1997 ($5.99, one-shot)

nn-McDaniel-c/a 6.00

DAREDEVIL BATTLES HITLER (See Daredevil #1[1941 series])

DAREDEVIL: BATTLIN' JACK MURDOCK
Marvel Comics: Aug, 2007 - No. 4, Nov, 2007 ($3.99, limited series)

1-4-Wells-s/DiGiandomenico-a; flashback to the fixed fight 4.00
TPB (2007, $12.99) r/#1-4; page layouts and cover inks 13.00

DAREDEVIL COMICS (Golden Age title) (See Daredevil)

DAREDEVIL/ ELEKTRA: LOVE AND WAR
Marvel Comics: 2003 ($29.99, hardcover with dust jacket)

HC-Larger-size reprints of Daredevil: Love and War (Marvel Graphic Novel #24) & Elektra: Assassin; Frank Miller-s; Bill Sienkiewicz-a 30.00

DAREDEVIL: FATHER
Marvel Comics: June, 2004 - No. 6, Feb, 2007 ($3.50/$2.99, limited series)

1-Quesada-s/a; Isanove-painted color 3.50
1-Director's Cut ($2.99) cover and page development art; partial sketch-c 3.00
2-6: 2-($2.99,10/05). 3-Santerians app. 3.00
HC (2006, $24.99) r/series; Lindelof intro.; sketch pages, cover pencils and bonus art 25.00

DAREDEVIL: NINJA
Marvel Comics: Dec, 2000 - No. 3, Feb, 2001 ($2.99, limited series)

1-3: Bendis-s/Haynes-a 3.00
1-Dynamic Forces foil-c 10.00
TPB (7/01, $12.95) r/#1-3 with cover and sketch gallery 13.00

DAREDEVIL NOIR
Marvel Comics: June, 2009 - No. 4, Sept, 2009 ($3.99, limited series)

1-4-Irvine-s/Coker-a; covers by Coker and Calero 4.00

DAREDEVIL: REBORN (Follows Shadowland x-over)
Marvel Comics: Mar, 2011 - No. 4, Jul, 2011 ($3.99, limited series)

1-4-Diggle-s/Gianfelice-a 4.00

DAREDEVIL: REDEMPTION
Marvel Comics: Apr, 2005 - No. 6, Aug, 2005 ($2.99, limited series)

1-6-Hine-s/Gaydos-a/Sienkiewicz-c 3.00
TPB (2005, $14.99) r/#1-6 15.00

DAREDEVIL/ SHI (See Shi/ Daredevil)
Marvel Comics/ Crusade Comics: Feb,1997 ($2.95, one-shot)

1 3.00

DAREDEVIL/ SPIDER-MAN
Marvel Comics: Jan, 2001 - No. 4, Apr, 2001 ($2.99, limited series)

1-4-Jenkins-s/Winslade-a/Alex Ross-c; Stilt Man app. 3.00
TPB (8/01, $12.95) r/#1-4; Ross-c 13.00

DAREDEVIL THE MAN WITHOUT FEAR
Marvel Comics: Oct, 1993 - No. 5, Feb, 1994 ($2.95, limited series) (foil embossed covers)

1-Miller scripts; Romita, Jr./Williamson-c/a 6.00
2-5 5.00
Hardcover 100.00
Trade paperback 20.00

DAREDEVIL: THE MOVIE (2003 movie adaptation)
Marvel Comics: March, 2003 ($3.50/$12.95, one-shot)

1-Photo-c of Ben Affleck; Bruce Jones-s/Manuel Garcia-a 3.50
TPB ($12.95) r/movie adaptation; Daredevil #32; Ultimate Daredevil & Elektra #1 and Spider-Man's Tangled Web #4; photo-c of Ben Affleck 13.00

DAREDEVIL: THE TARGET (Daredevil Bullseye on cover)
Marvel Comics: Jan, 2003 ($3.50, unfinished limited series)

1-Kevin Smith-s/Glenn Fabry-c/a 3.50

DAREDEVIL VS. PUNISHER
Marvel Comics: Sept, 2005 - No. 6, Jan, 2006 ($2.99, limited series)

1-5-David Lapham-s/a 3.00
TPB (2005, $15.99) r/#1-6 16.00

DAREDEVIL: YELLOW
Marvel Comics: Aug, 2001 - No. 6, Jan, 2002 ($3.50, limited series)

1-6-Jeph Loeb-s/Tim Sale-a/c; origin & yellow costume days retold 3.50
HC (5/02, $29.95) r/#1-6 with dustjacket; intro by Stan Lee; sketch pages 30.00
Daredevil Legends Vol. 1: Daredevil Yellow (2002, $14.99, TPB) r/#1-6 15.00

DARING ADVENTURES (Also see Approved Comics)
St. John Publishing Co.: Nov, 1953 (25¢, 3-D, came w/glasses)

	GD	VG	FN	VF	VF/NM	NM-
1 (3-D)-Reprints lead story from Son of Sinbad #1 by Kubert	26	52	78	154	252	350

DARING ADVENTURES
I.W. Enterprises/Super Comics: 1963 - 1964

	GD	VG	FN	VF	VF/NM	NM-
I. W. Reprint #8-r/Fight Comics #53; Matt Baker-a	5	10	15	30	48	65
I.W. Reprint #9-r/Blue Bolt #115; Disbrow-a(3)	5	10	15	32	51	70
Super Reprint #10,11('63)-r/Dynamic #24,16; 11-Marijuana story; Yankee Boy app.; Mac Raboy-a	4	8	12	22	34	45
Super Reprint #12('64)-Phantom Lady from Fox (r/#14 only? w/splash pg. omitted); Matt Baker-a	10	20	30	64	115	165
Super Reprint #15('64)-r/Hooded Menace #1	6	12	18	42	69	95

Daring Comics #11 © TCI

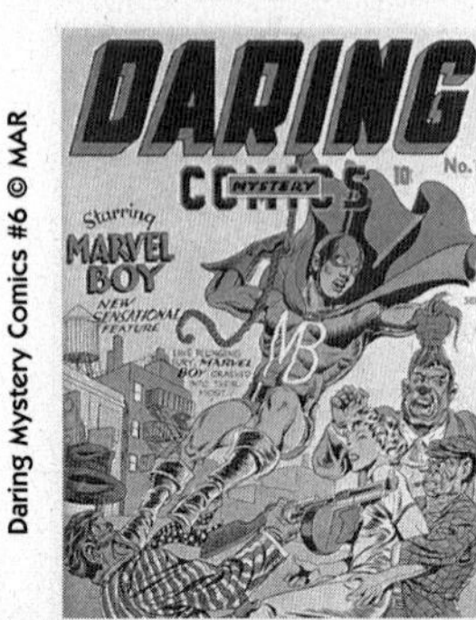

Daring Mystery Comics #6 © MAR

Dark Claw Adventures #1 © DC & MAR

	GD 2.0	VG 4.0	FN 6.0	VF 8.0	VF/NM 9.0	NM- 9.2

Super Reprint #16('64)-r/Dynamic #12 3 6 9 20 30 40
Super Reprint #17('64)-r/Green Lama #3 by Raboy 4 8 12 26 41 55
Super Reprint #18-Origin Atlas from unpublished Atlas Comics #1
4 8 12 24 37 50

DARING COMICS (Formerly Daring Mystery) (Jeanie Comics No. 13 on)
Timely Comics (HPC): No. 9, Fall, 1944 - No. 12, Fall, 1945

9-Human Torch, Toro & Sub-Mariner begin 145 290 435 921 1586 2250
10-12: 10-The Angel only app. 11,12-The Destroyer app.
119 238 357 762 1306 1850

NOTE: ***Schomburg** c-9-11. **Sekowsky** c-12? Human Torch, Toro & Sub-Mariner c-9-12.*

DARING CONFESSIONS (Formerly Youthful Hearts)
Youthful Magazines: No. 4, 11/52 - No. 7, 5/53; No. 8, 10/53

4-Doug Wildey-a; Tony Curtis story 17 34 51 100 158 215
5-8: 5-Ray Anthony photo on-c. 6,8-Wildey-a 14 28 42 78 112 145

DARING ESCAPES
Image Comics: Sept, 1998 - No. 4, Mar, 1999 ($2.95/$2.50, mini-series)

1-Houdini; following app. in Spawn #19,20 3.00
2-4-($2.50) 3.00

DARING LOVE (Radiant Love No. 2 on)
Gilmor Magazines: Sept-Oct, 1953

1–Steve Ditko's 1st published work (1st drawn was Fantastic Fears #5)(Also see Black Magic #27)(scarce) 107 214 321 680 1165 1650

DARING LOVE (Formerly Youthful Romances)
Ribage/Pix: No. 15, 12/52; No. 16, 2/53-c, 4/53-Indicia; No. 17-4/53-c & indicia

15 14 28 42 76 108 140
16,17: 17-Photo-c 12 24 36 67 94 120

NOTE: ***Colletta** a-15. **Wildey** a-17.*

DARING LOVE STORIES (See Fox Giants)

DARING MYSTERY COMICS (Comedy Comics No. 9 on; title changed to Daring Comics with No. 9)
Timely Comics (TPI 1-6/TCI 7,8): 1/40 - No. 5, 6/40; No. 6, 9/40; No. 7, 4/41 - No. 8, 1/42

1-Origin The Fiery Mask (1st app.) by Joe Simon; Monako, Prince of Magic (1st app.), John Steele, Soldier of Fortune (1st app.), Doc Denton (1st app.) begin; Flash Foster & Barney Mullen, Sea Rover only app; bondage-c
1950 3900 5850 14,625 26,312 38,000
2-(Rare)-Origin The Phantom Bullet (1st & only app.); The Laughing Mask & Mr. E only app.; Trojak the Tiger Man begins, ends #6; Zephyr Jones & K-4 & His Sky Devils app., also #4
1100 2200 3300 8400 15,200 22,000
3-The Phantom Reporter, Dale of FBI, Captain Strong only app.; Breeze Barton, Marvex the Super-Robot, The Purple Mask begin 541 1082 1623 3950 6975 10,000
4,5: 4-Last Purple Mask; Whirlwind Carter begins; Dan Gorman, G-Man app. 5-The Falcon begins (1st app.); The Fiery Mask, Little Hercules app. by Sagendorf in the Segar style; bondage-c 400 800 1200 2800 4900 7000
6-Origin & only app. Marvel Boy by S&K; Flying Flame, Dynaman, & Stuporman only app.; The Fiery Mask by S&K; S&K-c 470 940 1410 3431 6066 8700
7-Origin and 1st app. The Blue Diamond, Captain Daring by S&K, The Fin by Everett, The Challenger, The Silver Scorpion & The Thunderer by Burgos; Mr. Millions app
383 766 1149 2681 4691 6700
8-Origin Citizen V; Last Fin, Silver Scorpion, Capt. Daring by Borth, Blue Diamond & The Thunderer; Kirby & part solo Simon-c; Rudy the Robot only app.; Citizen V, Fin & Silver Scorpion continue in Comedy #9 309 618 927 2163 3782 5400

NOTE: ***Schomburg** c-1-4, 7. **Simon** a-2, 3, 5. Cover features: 1-Fiery Mask; 2-Phantom Bullet; 3-Purple Mask; 4-G-Man; 5-The Falcon; 6-Marvel Boy; 7, 8-Multiple characters.*

DARING MYSTERY COMICS 70th ANNIVERARY SPECIAL
Marvel Comics: Nov, 2009 ($3.99, one-shot)

1-New story of The Phantom Reporter; r/app. in Daring Mystery #3 (1940); 2 covers 4.00

DARING NEW ADVENTURES OF SUPERGIRL, THE
DC Comics: Nov, 1982 - No. 13, Nov, 1983 (Supergirl No. 14 on)

1-Origin retold; Lois Lane back-ups in #2-12 1 2 3 5 6 8
2-13: 8,9-Doom Patrol app. 13-New costume; flag-c 4.00

NOTE: ***Buckler** c-1p, 2p. **Giffen** c-3p, 4p. **Gil Kane** c-6,8, 9, 11-13.*

DARK, THE
Continum Comics: Nov, 1990 - No. 4, Feb, 1993; V2#1, May, 1993 - V2#7, Apr?, 1994 ($1.95)

1-4: 1-Bright-p; Panosian, Hanna-i; Stroman-c. 2-(1/92)-Stroman-c/a(p). 4-Perez-c & part-i 3.00
V2#1,V2#2-6: V2#1-Red foil Bart Sears-c. V2#1-Red non-foil variant-c. V2#1-2nd printing w/blue foil Bart Sears-c. V2#2-Stroman/Bryant-a. 3-Perez-c(i). 3-6-Foil-c. 4-Perez-c & part-i; bound-in trading cards. 5,6-(2,3/94)-Perez-c(i). 7-(B&W)-Perez-c(i) 3.00
Convention Book 1 ,2(Fall/94, 10/94)-Perez-c 3.00

DARK ANGEL (Formerly Hell's Angel)
Marvel Comics UK, Ltd.: No. 6, Dec, 1992 - No. 16, Dec, 1993 ($1.75)

6-8,13-16: 6-Excalibur-c/story. 8-Psylocke app. 3.00
9-12-Wolverine/X-Men app. 3.50

DARK ANGEL: PHOENIX RESURRECTION (Kia Asamiya's...)
Image Comics: May, 2000 - No. 4, Oct, 2001 ($2.95)

1-4-Kia Asamiya-s/a. 3-Van Fleet variant-c 3.00

DARK AVENGERS (See Secret Invasion and Dark Reign titles)
Marvel Comics: Mar, 2009 - No. 16, Jul, 2010 ($3.99)

1-Norman Osborn assembles his Avengers; Bendis-s/Deodato-a/c 4.00
1-Variant Iron Patriot armor cover by Djurdjevic 8.00
2-16: 2-6-Bendis-s/Deodato-a/c. 2-4 Dr. Doom app. 7,8-Utopia x-over; X-Men app. 9-Nick Fury app. 11,12-Deodato & Horn-a. 13-16-Siege. 13-Sentry origin 4.00
Annual 1 (2/10, $4.99) Bendis-s/Bachalo-a; Marvel Boy new costume; Siege preview 5.00
,,,/ Uncanny X-Men: Exodus (11/09, $3.99) Conclusion of x-over; Deodato & Dodson-a 4.00
,,,/ Uncanny X-Men: Utopia (8/09, $3.99) Part 1 of x-over w/Uncanny X-Men #513,514 4.00

DARK AVENGERS: ARES
Marvel Comics: Dec, 2009 - No. 3, Feb, 2010 ($3.99, limited series)

1-3-Garcia-a/Gillen-s. 1-Nord-c. 2-Tan-c. 3-McGuinness-c 4.00

DARKCHYLDE (Also see Dreams of the Darkchylde)
Maximum Press #1-3/ Image Comics #4 on: June, 1996 - No. 5, Sept, 1997 ($2.95/ $2.50)

1-Randy Queen-c/a/scripts; "Roses" cover 6.00
1-American Entertainment Edition-wraparound-c 6.00
1-"Fashion magazine-style" variant-c 1 2 3 4 5 7
1-Special Comicon Edition (contents of #1) Winged devil variant-c 5.00
1-($2.50)-Remastered Ed.-wraparound-c 4.00
2(Reg-c),2-Spiderweb and Moon variant-c 6.00
3(Reg-c),3-"Kalvin Clein" variant-c by Drew 4.00
4,5(Reg-c), 4-Variant-c 4.00
5-B&W Edition, 5-Dynamic Forces Gold Ed. 8.00
0-(3/98, $2.50) 3.00
0-Remastered (1/01, $2.95) includes Darkchylde: Redemption preview 3.00
1/2-WIzard offer 4.00
1/2 Variant-c 6.00
... The Descent TPB ('98, $19.95) r/#1-5; bagged with Darkchylde The Legacy Preview Special 1998; listed price is for TPB only 20.00

DARKCHYLDE LAST ISSUE SPECIAL
Darkchylde Entertainment: June, 2002 ($3.95)

1-Wraparound-c; cover gallery 4.00

DARKCHYLDE REDEMPTION
Darkchylde Entertainment: Feb, 2001 - No. 2, Dec, 2001 ($2.95)

1,2: 1-Wraparound-c 3.00
1-Dynamic Forces alternate-c 6.00
1-Dynamic Forces chrome-c 16.00

DARKCHYLDE SKETCH BOOK
Image Comics (Dynamic Forces): 1998

1-Regular-c 8.00
1-DarkChrome cover 16.00

DARKCHYLDE SUMMER SWIMSUIT SPECTACULAR
DC Comics (WildStorm): Aug, 1999 ($3.95, one-shot)

1-Pin-up art by various 4.00

DARKCHYLDE SWIMSUIT ILLUSTRATED
Image Comics: 1998 ($2.50, one-shot)

1-Pin-up art by various 3.00
1-(6.95) Variant cover 7.00
1-Chromium cover 15.00

DARKCHYLDE THE DIARY
Image Comics: June, 1997 ($2.50, one-shot)

1-Queen-c/s/ art by various 3.00
1-Variant-c 5.00
1-Holochrome variant-c 8.00

DARKCHYLDE THE LEGACY
Image Comics/DC (WildStorm) #3 on: Aug, 1998 - No. 3, June, 1999 ($2.50)

1-3: 1-Queen-c. 2-Two covers by Queen and Art Adams 3.00

DARK CLAW ADVENTURES
DC Comics (Amalgam): June, 1997 ($1.95, one-shot)

Dark Days #2 © Niles & Templesmith

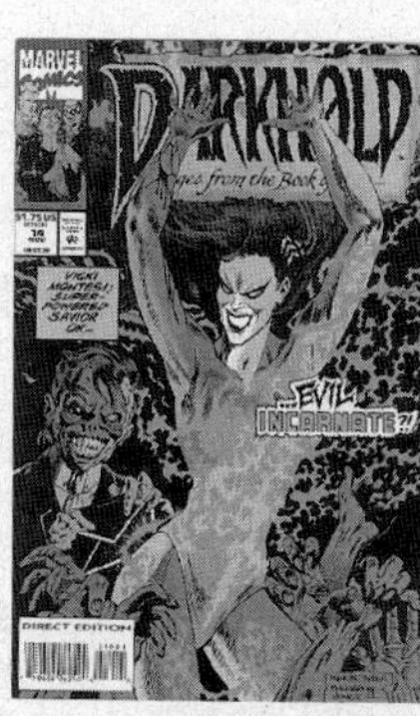

Darkhold #14 © MAR

Dark Horse Presents #89 © DH

GD 2.0 | VG 4.0 | FN 6.0 | VF 8.0 | VF/NM 9.0 | NM- 9.2

1-Templeton-c/s/a & Burchett-a 3.00

DARK CROSSINGS: DARK CLOUDS RISING
Image Comics (Top Cow): June, 2000; Oct, 2000 ($5.95, limited series)
1-Witchblade, Darkness, Tomb Raider crossover; Dwayne Turner-a 6.00
1-(Dark Clouds Overhead) 6.00

DARK CRYSTAL, THE (Movie)
Marvel Comics Group: April, 1983 - No. 2, May, 1983
1,2-Adaptation of film 3.00

DARK DAYS (See 30 Days of Night)
IDW Publishing: June, 2003 - No. 6, Dec, 2003 ($3.99, limited series)
1-6-Sequel to 30 Days of Night; Niles-s/Templesmith-a 4.00
1-Retailer variant (Diamond/Alliance Fort Wayne 5/03 summit) 15.00
TPB (2004, $19.99) r/#1-6; cover gallery; intro. by Eric Red 20.00

DARKDEVIL (See Spider-Girl)
Marvel Comics: Nov, 2000 - No. 3, Jan, 2001 ($2.99, limited series)
1-3: 1-Origin of Darkdevil; Kingpin-c/app. 3.00

DARK DOMINION
Defiant: Oct, 1993 - No. 10, July, 1994 ($2.50)
1-10-Len Wein scripts begin. 4-Free extra 16 pgs. 7-9-J.G. Jones-c/a. 10-Pre-Schism issue; Shooter/Wein script; John Ridgway-a 3.00

DARKER IMAGE (Also see Deathblow, The Maxx, & Bloodwulf)
Image Comics: Mar, 1993 ($1.95, one-shot)
1-The Maxx by Sam Kieth begins; Bloodwulf by Rob Liefeld & Deathblow by Jim Lee begin (both 1st app.); polybagged w/1 of 3 cards by Kieth, Lee or Liefeld 3.00
1-B&W interior pgs. w/silver foil logo 6.00

DARKEWOOD
Aircel Publishing: 1987 - No. 5, 1988 ($2.00, 28pgs, limited series)
1-5 3.00

DARK FANTASIES
Dark Fantasy: 1994 - No. 8, 1995 ($2.95)
1-Test print Run (3,000)-Linsner-c 1 2 3 5 6 8
1-Linsner-c 5.00
2-8: 2-4 (Deluxe), 2-4 (Regular), 5-8 (Deluxe; $3.95) 4.00
5-8 (Regular; $3.50) 3.50

DARK GUARD
Marvel Comics UK: Oct, 1993 - No. 4, Jan, 1994 ($1.75)
1-($2.95)-Foil stamped-c 3.50
2-4 3.00

DARKHAWK (Also see War of Kings)
Marvel Comics: Mar, 1991 - No. 50, Apr, 1995 ($1.00/$1.25/$1.50)
1-Origin/1st app. Darkhawk; Hobgoblin cameo 4.00
2,3,13,14: 2-Spider-Man & Hobgoblin app. 3-Spider-Man & Hobgoblin app. 13,14-Venom-c/story 3.50
4-12,15-24,26-49: 6-Capt. America & Daredevil x-over. 9-Punisher app. 11,12-Tombstone app. 19-Spider-Man & Brotherhood of Evil Mutants-c/story. 20-Spider-Man app. 22-Ghost Rider-c/story. 23-Origin begins, ends #25. 27-New Warriors-c/story. 35-Begin 3 part Venom story. 39-Bound-in trading card sheet 3.00
25,50: (52 pgs.)-Red holo-grafx foil-c w/double gatefold poster; origin of Darkhawk armor 4.00
Annual 1-3 ('92-'94,68 pgs.)-1-Vs. Iron Man. 2 -Polybagged w/card 4.00

DARKHOLD: PAGES FROM THE BOOK OF SINS (See Midnight Sons Unlimited)
Marvel Comics (Midnight Sons imprint #15 on): Oct, 1992 - No. 16, Jan, 1994
1-($2.75, 52 pgs.)-Polybagged w/poster by Andy & Adam Kubert; part 4 of Rise of the Midnight Sons storyline 4.00
2-10,12-16: 3-Reintro Modred the Mystic (see Marvel Chillers #1). 4-Sabertooth-c/sty. 5-Punisher & Ghost Rider app. 15-Spot varnish-c. 15,16-Siege of Darkness pt. 4&12 3.00
11-($2.25)-Outer-c is a Darkhold envelope made of black parchment w/gold ink 4.00

DARK HORSE BOOK OF..., THE
Dark Horse Comics: Aug, 2003 - Nov, 2006 ($14.95/$15.95, HC, 9 1/4" x 6 1/4")
... Hauntings (8/03, $14.95)-Short stories by various incl. Mignola (Hellboy), Thompson, Dorkin, Russell; Gianni-c 15.00
... Monsters (11/06, $15.95)-Short-s by Mignola, Thompson, Dorkin, Giffen, Busiek; Gianni-c 16.00
... The Dead (6/05, $14.95)-Short-s by Mignola, Thompson, Dorkin, Powell; Gianni-c 15.00
... Witchcraft (6/04, $14.95)-Short-s by Mignola, Thompson, Dorkin, Millionaire; Gianni-c 15.00

DARK HORSE CLASSICS (Title series), **Dark Horse Comics**
1992 ($3.95, B&W, 52 pgs. nn's): The Last of the Mohicans. 20,000 Leagues Under the Sea 4.00

GD 2.0 | VG 4.0 | FN 6.0 | VF 8.0 | VF/NM 9.0 | NM- 9.2

DARK HORSE CLASSICS, 5/96 ($2.95) 1-r/Predator: Jungle Tales 3.00
--ALIENS VERSUS PREDATOR, 2/97 - No. 6, 7/97 ($2.95,) 1-6: r/Aliens Versus Predator 3.00
--GODZILLA: KING OF THE MONSTERS, 4/98 ($2.95) 1-6: 1-r/Godzilla: Color Special; Art Adams-a 3.00
--STAR WARS: DARK EMPIRE, 3/97 - No. 6, 8/97 ($2.95) 1-6: r/Star Wars: Dark Empire 3.00
--TERROR OF GODZILLA, 8/98 - No. 6, 1/99 ($2.95) 1-6-r/manga Godzilla in color; Art Adams-c 3.00

DARK HORSE COMICS
Dark Horse Comics: Aug, 1992 - No. 25, Sept, 1994 ($2.50)
1-Dorman double gategold painted-c; Predator, Robocop, Timecop (3-part) & Renegade stories begin 4.00
2-6,11-25: 2-Mignola-c. 3-Begin 3-part Aliens story; Aliens-c. 4-Predator-c. 6-Begin 4 part Robocop story. 12-Begin 2-part Aliens & 3-part Predator stories. 13-Thing From Another World begins w/Nino-a(i). 15-Begin 2-part Aliens: Cargo story. 16-Begin 3-part Predator story. 17-Begin 3-part Star Wars: Droids story & 3-part Aliens: Alien story; Droids-c. 19-Begin 2-part X story; X cover 3.00
7-Begin Star Wars: Tales of the Jedi 3-part story 1 2 3 4 5 7
8-1st app. X and begins; begin 4-part James Bond 6.00
9,10: 9-Star Wars ends. 10-X ends; Begin 3-part Predator & Godzilla stories 4.00
NOTE: *Art Adams c-11.*

DARK HORSE DOWN UNDER
Dark Horse Comics: June, 1994 - No. 3, Oct, 1994 ($2.50, B&W, limited series)
1-3 3.00

DARK HORSE MAVERICK
Dark Horse Comics: July, 2000; July, 2001; Sept, 2002 (B&W, annual)
2000-($3.95) Short stories by Miller, Chadwick, Sakai, Pearson 4.00
2001-($4.99) Short stories by Sakai, Wagner and others; Miller-c 5.00
...: Happy Endings (9/02, $9.95) Short stories by Bendis, Oeming, Mahfood, Mignola, Miller, Kieth and others; Miller-c 10.00

DARK HORSE MONSTERS
Dark Horse Comics: Feb, 1997 ($2.95, one-shot)
1-Reprints 3.00

DARK HORSE PRESENTS
Dark Horse Comics: July, 1986 - No. 157, Sept, 2000 ($1.50-$2.95, B&W)
1-1st app. Concrete by Paul Chadwick 2 4 6 8 11 14
1-2nd printing (1988, $1.50) 3.00
1-Silver ink 3rd printing (1992, $2.25)-Says 2nd printing inside 3.00
2-9: 2-6,9-Concrete app. 6.00
10-1st app. The Mask; Concrete app. 2 4 6 9 12 15
11-19,21-23: 11-19,21-Mask stories. 12,14,16,18,22-Concrete app. 15(2/88). 17-All Roachmill issue 6.00
20-(68 pgs.)-Concrete, Flaming Carrot, Mask 1 3 4 6 8 10
24-Origin Aliens-c/story (11/88); Mr. Monster app. 2 4 6 10 14 18
25-27,29-31,37-39,41,44,45,47-49: 38-Concrete. 44-Crash Ryan. 48,49-Contain 2 trading cards 3.00
28,33,40: 28-(52 pgs.)-Concrete app.; Mr. Monster story (homage to Graham Ingels). 33-(44 pgs.). 40-(52 pgs.)-1st Argosy story 4.00
32,34,35: 32-(68 pgs.)-Annual; Concrete, American. 34-Aliens-c/story. 35-Predator-c/app. 4.00
36-1st Aliens Vs. Predator story; painted-c, 36-Variant line drawn-c 5.00
42,43,46: 42,43-Aliens-c/stories. 46-Prequel to new Predator II mini-series 3.00
50-S/F story by Perez; contains 2 trading cards 4.00
51-53-Sin City by Frank Miller, parts 2-4; 51,53-Miller-c (see D.H.P. Fifth Anniversary Special for pt. 1) 1 2 3 4 6 8
54-61: 54-(9/91) The Next Men begins (1st app.) by Byrne; Miller-a/Morrow-c. Homocide by Morrow (also in #55). 55-2nd app. The Next Men; parts 5 & 6 of Sin City by Miller; Miller-c. 56-(68 pg. annual)-part 7 of Sin City by Miller; part prologue to Aliens: Genocide; Next Men by Byrne. 57-(52 pgs.)-Part 8 of Sin City by Miller; Next Men by Byrne; Byrne & Miller-c; Alien Fire story; swipes cover to Daredevil #1. 58,59-Alien Fire stories. 58-61- Part 9-12 Sin City by Miller 5.00
62-Last Sin City (entire book by Miller, c/a; 52 pgs.) 1 3 4 6 8 10
63-66,68-79,81-84-($2.25): 64-Dr. Giggles begins (1st app.), ends #66; Boris the Bear story. 66-New Concrete-c/story by Chadwick. 71-Begin 3 part Dominque story by Jim Balent; Balent-c. 72-(3/93)-Begin 3-part Eudaemon (1st app.) story by Nelson 3.00
67-($3.95, 68 pgs.)-Begin 3-part prelude to Predator: Race War mini-series; Oscar Wilde adapt. by Russell 4.00
80-Art Adams-c/a (Monkeyman & O'Brien) 4.00
85-87,92-99: 85-Begin $2.50-c. 92, 93, 95-Too Much Coffee Man 3.00
88-91-Hellboy by Mignola. 6.00
NOTE: *There are 5 different Dark Horse Presents #100 issues*
100-1-Intro Lance Blastoff by Miller; Milk & Cheese by Evan Dorkin 4.00

Dark Horse Presents (2011 series) #7 © DH

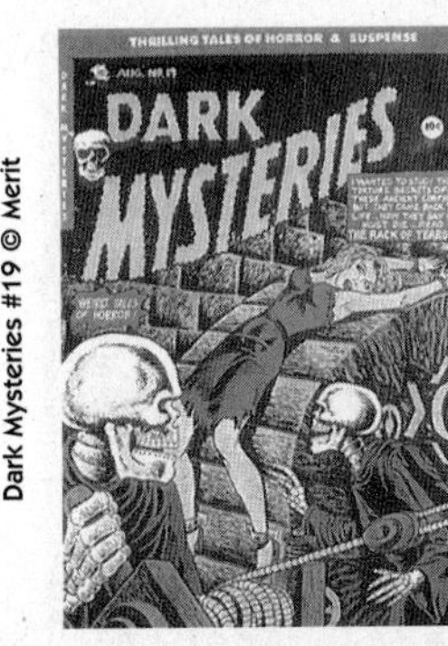

Dark Mysteries #19 © Merit

The Darkness #9 © TCOW

GD 2.0 | VG 4.0 | FN 6.0 | VF 8.0 | VF/NM 9.0 | NM- 9.2

100-2-Hellboy-c by Wrightson; Hellboy story by Mignola; includes Roberta Gregory & Paul Pope stories 6.00
100-3-100-5: 100-3-Darrow-c, Concrete by Chadwick; Pekar story. 100-4-Gibbons-c: Miller story, Geary story/a. 100-5-Allred-c, Adams, Dorkin, Pope 3.00
101-125: 101-Aliens c/a by Wrightson, story by Pope. 103-Kirby gatefold-c. 106-Big Blown Baby by Bill Wray. 107-Mignola-c/a. 109-Begin $2.95-c; Paul Pope-c. 110-Ed Brubaker-a/s. 114-Flip books begin; Lance Blastoff by Miller; Star Slammers by Simonson. 115-Miller-c. 117-Aliens-c/app. 118-Evan Dorkin-c/a. 119-Monkeyman & O'Brien. 124-Predator. 125-Nocturnals 3.00
126-($3.95, 48 pgs.)-Flip book: Nocturnals, Starship Troopers 4.00
127-134,136-140: 127-Nocturnals. 129-The Hammer. 132-134-Warren-a 3.00
135-($3.50) The Mark 3.50
141-All Buffy the Vampire Slayer issue 4.00
142-149: 142-Mignola-c. 143-Tarzan. 146,147-Aliens vs. Predator. 148-Xena 3.00
150-($4.50) Buffy-c by Green; Buffy, Concrete, Fish Police app. 4.50
151-157: 151-Hellboy-c/app. 153-155-Angel flip-c. 156,157-Witch's Son 3.00
Annual 1997 ($4.95, 64 pgs.)-Flip book; Body Bags, Aliens. Pearson-c; stories by Allred & Stephens, Pope, Smith & Morrow 1 2 3 5 6 8
Annual 1998 ($4.95, 64 pgs.) 1st Buffy the Vampire Slayer comic app.; Hellboy story and cover by Mignola 1 2 3 4 5 7
Annual 1999 (7/99, $4.95) Stories of Xena, Hellboy, Ghost, Luke Skywalker, Groo, Concrete, the Mask and Usagi Yojimbo in their youth. 5.00
Annual 2000 ($4.95) Girl sidekicks; Chiodo-c and flip photo Buffy-c 5.00
...Aliens Platinum Edition (1992)-r/DHP #24,43,43,56 & Special 11.00
...Fifth Anniversary Special nn (4/91, $9.95)-Part 1 of Sin City by Frank Miller (c/a); Aliens, Aliens vs. Predator, Concrete, Roachmill, Give Me Liberty & The American stories 25.00
The One Trick Rip-off (1997, $12.95, TPB)-r/stories from #101-112 13.00
NOTE: ***Geary*** *a-59, 60.* ***Miller*** *a-Special, 51-53, 55-62; c-59-62, 100-1; c-51, 53, 55, 59-62, 100-1.* ***Moebius*** *a-63; c-63, 70.* ***Vess*** *a-78; c-75, 78.*

DARK HORSE PRESENTS
Dark Horse Comics: Apr, 2011 - Present ($7.99, anthology)
1-10: 1-Frank Miller-c & Xerxes preview; Neal Adams-s/a. 1-3-Concrete by Chadwick. 1-8-Chaykin-s/a. 2,3,9-Corben-a. 3-Steranko interview. 7-Hellboy app. 10-Milk & Cheese 8.00

DARK HORSE TWENTY YEARS
Dark Horse Comics: 2006 (25¢, one-shot)
nn-Pin-ups by Dark Horse artists of other artists' Dark Horse characters; Mignola-c 3.00

DARK IVORY
Image Comics: Mar, 2008 - No. 4, Jan, 2009 ($2.99, limited series)
1-4-Eva Hopkins & Joseph Michael Linsner-s/Linsner-a/c 3.00

DARK KNIGHT (See Batman: The Dark Knight Returns & Legends of the...)

DARK KNIGHT STRIKES AGAIN, THE (Also see Batman: The Dark Knight Returns)
DC Comics: 2001 - No. 3, 2002 ($7.95, prestige format, limited series)
1-Frank Miller-s/a/c; sequel set 3 years after Dark Knight Returns; 2 covers 8.00
2,3 8.00
HC (2002, $29.95) intro. by Miller; sketch pages and exclusive artwork; cover has 3 1/4" tall partial dustjacket 30.00
SC (2002, $19.95) intro. by Miller; sketch pages 20.00

DARKLON THE MYSTIC (Also see Eerie Magazine #79,80)
Pacific Comics: Oct, 1983 (one-shot)
1-Starlin-c/a(r) 4.00

DARKMAN (Movie)
Marvel Comics: Sept, 1990; Oct, 1990 - No. 3, Dec, 1990 ($1.50)
1 (9/90, $2.25, B&W mag., 68 pgs.)-Adaptation of film 4.00
1-3: Reprints B&W magazine 3.00

DARKMAN
Marvel Comics: V2#1, Apr, 1993 -No. 6, Sept, 1993 ($2.95, limited series)
V2#1 ($3.95, 52 pgs.) 4.00
2-6 3.00

DARKMAN VS. THE ARMY OF DARKNESS (Movie crossover)
Dynamite Entertanment: 2006 - No. 4, 2007 ($3.50)
1-4: 1-Busiek & Stern-s/Fry-a; photo-c and Perez and Bradshaw covers 3.50

DARK MANSION OF FORBIDDEN LOVE, THE (Becomes Forbidden Tales of Dark Mansion No. 5 on)
National Periodical Publ.: Sept-Oct, 1971 - No. 4, Mar-Apr, 1972 (52 pgs.)
1 17 34 51 119 260 400
2-4: 2-Adams-c. 3-Jeff Jones-c 10 20 30 66 121 175

DARKMINDS
Image Comics (Dreamwave Prod.): July, 1998 - No. 8, Apr, 1999 ($2.50)
1-Manga; Pat Lee-s/a; 2 covers 1 3 4 6 8 10
1-2nd printing 3.00
2, 0-(1/99, $5.00) Story and sketch pages 5.00
3-8, 1/2-(5/99, $2.50) Story and sketch pages 3.00
... Collected 1,2 (1/99,3/99; $7.95) 1-r/#1-3. 2-r/#4-6 8.00
... Collected 3 (5/99; $5.95) r/#7,8 6.00

DARKMINDS (Volume 2)
Image Comics (Dreamwave Prod.): Feb, 2000 - No. 10, Apr, 2001 ($2.50)
1-10-Pat Lee-c 3.00
0-(7/00) Origin of Mai Murasaki; sketchbook 3.00

DARKMINDS: MACROPOLIS
Image Comics (Dreamwave Prod.): Jan, 2002 - No. 4, Dec, 2002 ($2.95)
Preview (8/01) Flip book w/Banished Knights preview 3.00
1-4-Jo Chen-a 3.00

DARKMINDS: MACROPOLIS (Volume 2)
Dreamwave Prod.: Sept, 2003 - No. 4, Jul, 2004 ($2.95)
1-4-Chris Sarracini-s/Kwang Mook Lim-a 3.00

DARKMINDS / WITCHBLADE (Also see Witchblade/Dark Minds)
Image Comics (Top Cow/Dreamwave Prod.): Aug, 2000 ($5.95, one-shot)
1-Wohl-s/Pat Lee-a; two covers by Silvestri and Lee 6.00

DARK MYSTERIES (Thrilling Tales of Horror & Suspense)
"Master" - "Merit" Publications: June-July, 1951 - No. 24, July, 1955
1-Wood-c/a (8 pgs.) 135 270 405 864 1482 2100
2-Classic skull-c; Wood/Harrison-c/a (8 pgs.) 94 188 282 597 1024 1450
3-9: 7-Dismemberment, hypo blood drainage stys 50 100 150 315 533 750
10-Cannibalism story; witch burning-c 54 108 162 343 574 825
11-13,15-18: 11-Severed head panels. 13-Dismemberment-c/story. 17-The Old Gravedigger host 43 86 129 271 461 650
14-Several E.C. Craig swipes 44 88 132 277 469 660
19-Injury-to-eye panel; E.C. swipe; torture-c 77 154 231 493 847 1200
20-Female bondage, blood drainage story 50 100 150 315 533 750
21,22: 21-Devil-c. 22-Last pre-code issue, misdated 3/54 instead of 3/55 36 72 108 211 343 475
23,24 23 46 69 136 223 310
NOTE: ***Cameron*** *a-1, 2.* ***Myron Fass*** *c/a-21.* ***Harrison*** *a-3, 7; c-3.* ***Hollingsworth*** *a-7-17, 20, 21, 23.* ***Wildey*** *a-5. Woodish art by* ***Fleishman****-9; c-10, 14-17. Bondage c-10, 18, 19.*

DARK NEMESIS (VILLAINS) (See Teen Titans)
DC Comics: Feb, 1998 ($1.95, one-shot)
1-Jurgens-s/Pearson-c 3.00

DARKNESS, THE (See Witchblade #10)
Image Comics (Top Cow Productions): Dec, 1996 - No. 40, Aug, 2001 ($2.50)
Special Preview Edition-(7/96, B&W)-Ennis script; Silvestri-a(p) 2 4 6 9 13 16
0 2 4 6 8 10 12
0-Gold Edition 16.00
1/2 1 3 4 6 8 10
1/2-Christmas-c 3 6 9 14 19 24
1/2-(3/01, $2.95) r/#1/2 w/new 6 pg. story & Silvestri-c 3.00
1-Ennis-s/Silvestri-a, 1-Black variant-c 2 4 6 9 12 15
1-Platinum variant-c 20.00
1-DF Green variant-c 12.00
1,2: 1-Fan Club Ed. 1 3 4 6 8 10
3-5 6.00
6-10: 9,10-Witchblade "Family Ties" x-over pt. 2,3 4.00
7-Variant-c w/concubine 1 2 3 5 7 9
8-American Entertainment 6.00
8-10-American Entertainment Gold Ed. 7.00
11-Regular Ed.; Ennis-s/Silverstri & D-Tron-c 3.00
11-Nine (non-chromium) variant-c (Benitez, Cabrera, the Hildebrandts, Finch, Keown, Peterson, Portacio, Tan, Turner 4.50
11-Chromium-c by Silvestri & Batt 20.00
12-19: 13-Begin Benitez-a(p) 3.00
20-24,26-40: 34-Ripclaw app. 3.00
25-($3.99) Two covers (Benitez, Silvestri) 4.00
25-Chromium-c variant by Silvestri 8.00
.../ Batman (8/99, $5.95) Silvestri, Finch, Lansing-a(p) 6.00
...Collected Editions #1-4 ($4.95,TPB) 1-r/#1,2. 2-r/#3,4. 3- r/#5,6. 4- r/#7,8 6.00
...Collected Editions #5,6 ($5.95, TPB)5- r/#11,12. 6-r/#13,14 6.00
Deluxe Collected Editions #1 (12/98, $14.95, TPB) r/#1-6 & Preview 15.00
...: Heart of Darkness (2001, $14.95, TPB) r/ #7,8, 11-14 15.00

Darkness #92 © TCOW

Dark Reign: Hawkeye #3 © MAR

Dark Shadows (2011 series) #1 © Dan Curtis

	GD 2.0	VG 4.0	FN 6.0	VF 8.0	VF/NM 9.0	NM- 9.2

Holiday Pin-up-American Entertainment 5.00
Holiday Pin-up Gold Ed.-American Entertainment 7.00
Image Firsts: Darkness #1 (9/10, $1.00) r/#1 with "Image Firsts" logo on cover 3.00
Infinity #1 (8/99, $3.50) Lobdell-s 3.50
Prelude-American Entertainment 4.00
Prelude Gold Ed.-American Entertainment 9.00
Volume 1 Compendium (2006, $59.99) r/#1-40, V2 #1, Tales of the Darkness #1-4; #1/2, Darkness/Witchblade #1/2, Darkness: Wanted Dead; cover and sketch gallery 60.00
...: Wanted Dead 1 (8/03, $2.99) Texiera-a/Tieri-s 3.00
Wizard ACE Ed.- Reprints #1 2 4 6 8 10 12

DARKNESS (Volume 2)
Image Comics (Top Cow Productions): Dec, 2002 - No. 24, Oct, 2004 ($2.99)

1-24: 1-6-Jenkins-s/Keown-a. 17-20-Lapham-s. 23,24-Magdalena app. 3.00
... Black Sails (3/05, $2.99) Marz-s/Cha-a; Hunter-Killer preview 3.00
... and Tomb Raider (4/05, $2.99) r/Darkness Prelude & Tomb Raider/Darkness Special 3.00
...: Resurrection TPB (2/04, $16.99) r/#1-6 & Vol. 1 #40 17.00
.../ The Incredible Hulk (7/04, $2.99) Keown-a/Jenkins-s 3.00
.../ Vampirella (7/05, $2.99) Terry Moore-s; two covers by Basaldua and Moore 3.00
... Vol. 5 TPB (2006, $19.99) r/#7-16 & The Darkness: Wanted Dead #1; cover gallery 20.00
... vs. Mr Hyde Monster War 2005 (9/05, $2.99) x-over w/Witchblade, Tomb Raider and Magdalena; two covers 3.00
.../ Wolverine (2006, $2.99) Kirkham-a/Tieri-s 3.00

DARKNESS (Volume 3) (Numbering jumps from #10 to #75)
Image Comics (Top Cow Productions): Dec, 2007 - Present ($2.99)

1-10: 1-Hester-s/Broussard-a. 1-Three covers. 7-9-Lucas-a. 8-Aphrodite IV app. 3.00
75 (2/09, $4.99) Four covers; Hester-s/art by various 5.00
76-99-($2.99) Multiple covers on each 3.00
100 (2/12, $4.99) Four covers; Hester-s/art by various; cover gallery; series timeline 5.00
...: Butcher (4/08, $3.99) Story of Butcher Joyce; Levin-s/Broussard-a/c 4.00
...: Confession (5/11) Free Comic Boy Day giveaway; Broussard & Molnar-a 3.00
... / Darkchylde: Kingdom Pain 1 (5/10, $4.99) Randy Queen-s/a 5.00
... First Look (11/07, 99¢) Previews series; sketch pages 3.00
...: Lodbrok's Hand (12/08, $2.99) Hester-s/Oeming-a/c; variant-c by Carnevale 3.00
...: Shadows and Flame 1 (1/10, $2.99) Lucas-c/a 3.00

DARKNESS: FOUR HORSEMEN
Image Comics (Top Cow): Aug, 2010 - No. 4, May, 2011 ($3.99, limited series)

1-4-Hine-s/Wamester-a 4.00

DARKNESS: LEVEL...
Image Comics (Top Cow): No. 0, Dec, 2006 - No. 5, Aug, 2007 ($2.99, limited series)

0-5: 0-Origin of The Darkness in WW1; Jenkins-s. 1-Jackie's origin retold; Sejic-a 3.00

DARKNESS/ PITT
Image Comics (Top Cow): Dec, 2006; Aug, 2009 - No. 3, Nov, 2009 ($2.99)

...: First Look (12/06) Jenkins script pages with Keown B&W and color art 3.00
1-3: 1-(8/09) Jenkins-s/Keown-a; covers by Keown and Sejic. 2,3-Two covers 3.00

DARKNESS/ SUPERMAN
Image Comics (Top Cow Productions): Jan, 2005 - No. 2, Feb, 2005 ($2.99, limited series)

1,2-Marz-s/Kirkham & Banning-a/Silvestri-c 3.00

DARKNESS VS. EVA: DAUGHTER OF DRACULA
Dynamite Entertainment: 2008 - No. 4, 2008 ($3.50, limited series)

1-4-Leah Moore & John Reppion-s/Salazar-a; three covers on each 3.50

DARK REIGN (Follows Secret Invasion crossover)
Marvel Comics: 2009 ($3.99/$4.99, one-shots)

...: Files 1 (2009, $4.99) profile pages of villains tied in to Dark Reign x-over 5.00
...: Made Men 1 (11/09, $3.99) short stories by various incl. Pham, Leon, Oliver 4.00
...: New Nation 1 (2/09, $3.99) previews of various series tied in to Dark Reign x-over 4.00
...: The Cabal 1 (6/09, $3.99) Cabal members stories by various incl. Granov, Acuña 4.00
...: The Goblin Legacy 1 (2009, $3.99) r/ASM #39,40; Osborn history; Mayhew-a 4.00

DARK REIGN: ELEKTRA
Marvel Comics: May, 2009 - No. 5, Oct, 2009 ($3.99, limited series)

1-5-Mann-a/Bermejo-c; Elektra after the Skrull replacement. 2,3-Bullseye app. 4.00

DARK REIGN: FANTASTIC FOUR
Marvel Comics: May, 2009 - No. 5, Sept, 2009 ($2.99, limited series)

1-5-Chen-a 3.00

DARK REIGN: HAWKEYE
Marvel Comics: June, 2009 - No. 5, Mar, 2010 ($3.99, limited series)

1-5-Bullseye in the Dark Avengers; Raney-a/Langley-c. 5-Guinaldo-a 4.00

DARK REIGN: LETHAL LEGION
Marvel Comics: Aug, 2009 - No. 3, Nov, 2009 ($3.99, limited series)

1-3-Santolouco-a/Edwards-c; Grim Reaper and Wonder Man app. 4.00

DARK REIGN: MR. NEGATIVE (Also see Amazing Spider-Man #546)
Marvel Comics: Aug, 2009 - No. 3, Oct, 2009 ($3.99, limited series)

1-3-Jae Lee-c/Gugliotta-a; Spider-Man app. 4.00

DARK REIGN: SINISTER SPIDER-MAN
Marvel Comics: Aug, 2009 - No. 4, Nov, 2009 ($3.99, limited series)

1-4-Bachalo-c/a; Venom/Scorpion as Dark Avenger Spider-Man 4.00

DARK REIGN: THE HOOD
Marvel Comics: Jul, 2009 - No. 5, Nov, 2009 ($3.99, limited series)

1-5-Hotz-a/Djurdjevic-c 4.00

DARK REIGN: THE LIST
Marvel Comics: 2009 - 2010 ($3.99, one-shots)

... - Amazing Spider-Man (1/10, $3.99) Adam Kubert-c/a; back-up r/Pulse #5 4.00
... - Avengers (11/09, $3.99) Bendis-s/Djurdjevic-c/a; Ronin (Hawkeye) app. 4.00
... - Daredevil (11/09, $3.99) Diggle-s/Tan-c/a; Bullseye app.; leads into Daredevil #501 4.00
... - Hulk (12/09, $3.99) Pak-s/Oliver-a; Skaar app.; back-up r/Amaz. Spider-Man #14 4.00
... - Punisher (12/09, $3.99) Romita Jr.-a/c; Castle killed by Daken; preview of Franken-Castle in Punisher #11 6.00
... - Secret Warriors (12/09, $3.99) McGuinness-a/c; Nick Fury; back-up r/Steranko-a 4.00
... - Wolverine (12/09, $3.99) Ribic-a/c; Marvel Boy and Fantomex app. 4.00
... - X-Men (11/09, $3.99) Alan Davis-a/c; Namor app.; back-up r/Kieth-a 4.00

DARK REIGN: YOUNG AVENGERS
Marvel Comics: Jul, 2009 - No. 5, Dec, 2009 ($3.99, limited series)

1-5-Brooks-a; Osborn's Young Avengers vs. original Young Avengers 4.00

DARK REIGN: ZODIAC
Marvel Comics: Aug, 2009 - No. 3, Nov, 2009 ($3.99, limited series)

1-3-Casey-s/Fox-a. 1-Human Torch app. 4.00

DARKSEID (VILLAINS) (See Jack Kirby's New Gods and New Gods)
DC Comics: Feb, 1998 ($1.95, one-shot)

1-Byrne-s/Pearson-c 3.00

DARKSEID VS. GALACTUS: THE HUNGER
DC Comics: 1995 ($4.95, one-shot) (1st DC/Marvel x-over by John Byrne)

nn-John Byrne-c/a/script 5.00

DARK SHADOWS
Steinway Comic Publ. (Ajax)(America's Best): Oct, 1957 - No. 3, May, 1958

1 28 56 84 165 270 375
2,3 20 40 60 114 182 250

DARK SHADOWS (TV) (See Dan Curtis Giveaways)
Gold Key: Mar, 1969 - No. 35, Feb, 1976 (Photo-c: 1-7)

1(30039-903)-With pull-out poster (25¢) 20 40 60 137 294 450
1-With poster missing 8 16 24 55 93 130
2 9 18 27 61 106 150
3-With pull-out poster 10 20 30 67 124 180
3-With poster missing 6 12 18 41 66 90
4-7: 7-Last photo-c 7 14 21 44 72 100
8-10 5 10 15 32 51 70
11-20 4 8 12 28 44 60
21-35: 30-Last painted-c 4 8 12 24 37 50
Story Digest 1 (6/70, 148pp.)-Photo-c (low print) 8 16 24 53 89 125

DARK SHADOWS (TV) (See Nightmare on Elm Street)
Innovation Publishing: June, 1992 - No. 4, Spring, 1993 ($2.50, limited series, coated stock)

1-Based on 1991 NBC TV mini-series; painted-c 5.00
2-4 4.00

DARK SHADOWS: BOOK TWO
Innovation Publishing: 1993 - No. 4, July, 1993 ($2.50, limited series)

1-4-Painted-c. 4-Maggie Thompson scripts 4.00

DARK SHADOWS: BOOK THREE
Innovation Publishing: Nov, 1993 ($2.50)

1-(Whole #9) 4.00

DARK SHADOWS, VOLUME 1
Dynamite Entertainment: 2011 - Present ($3.99)

1-4-Set in 1971; Aaron Campbell-a; covers by Campbell & Francavilla 4.00

DARKSTAR AND THE WINTER GUARD

Darkstars #12 © DC

Dark Tower: Treachery #6 © Stephen King

Darkwing Duck (2010 series) #8 © DIS

GD VG FN VF VF/NM NM-
2.0 4.0 6.0 8.0 9.0 9.2

Marvel Comics: Aug, 2010 - No. 3, Oct, 2010 ($3.99, limited series)

1-3-Gallaher-s/Ellis-a/Henry-c; back-up reprint from X-Men Unlimited #28 4.00

DARKSTARS, THE
DC Comics: Oct, 1992 - No. 38, Jan, 1996 ($1.75/$1.95)

1-1st app. The Darkstars 3.00
2-24,0,25-38: 5-Hawkman & Hawkwoman app. 18-20-Flash app. 24-(9/94)-Zero Hour. 0-(10/94). 25-(11/94). 30-Green Lantern app. 31-...vs. Darkseid. 32-Green Lantern app. 3.00
NOTE: ***Travis Charest*** *a(p)-4-7; c(p)-2-5; c-6-11.* ***Stroman*** *a-1-3; c-1.*

DARK TOWER: THE BATTLE OF JERICHO HILL (Based on Stephen King's Dark Tower)
Marvel Comics: Feb, 2010 - No. 5, Jun, 2010 ($3.99, limited series)

1-5-Peter David & Robin Furth-s/Jae Lee & Richard Isanove-a/c; variant-c for each 4.00

DARK TOWER: THE FALL OF GILEAD (Based on Stephen King's Dark Tower)
Marvel Comics: July, 2009 - No. 6, Jan, 2010 ($3.99, limited series)

1-6-Peter David & Robin Furth-s/Richard Isanove-a/Jae Lee-c; variant-c for each 4.00
Dark Tower: Guide to Gilead (2009, $3.99) profile pages of people and places 4.00

DARK TOWER: THE GUNSLINGER BORN (Based on Stephen King's Dark Tower series)
Marvel Comics: Apr, 2007 - No. 7, Oct, 2007 ($3.99, limited series)

1-Peter David & Robin Furth-s/Jae Lee & Richard Isanove-a; boyhood of Roland Deschain; afterword by Ralph Macchio; map of New Canaan 6.00
1-Variant cover by Quesada 8.00
1-Second printing with variant-c by Quesada 5.00
1-Sketch cover variant by Jae Lee 40.00
2-6-Jae Lee-c 4.00
2-Second printing with variant-c by Immonen 4.00
2-7-Variant covers. 2-Finch-c. 3-Yu-c. 4-McNiven-c. 5-Land-c. 6-Campbell. 7-Coipel 6.00
2-7-B&W sketch-c by Jae Lee 20.00
... MGC #1 (5/11, $1.00) r/#1 with "Marvel's Greatest Comics" logo on cover 3.00
... Sketchbook (2006, no cover price) pencil art and designs by Lee; coloring process 5.00
Dark Tower: Gunslinger's Guidebook (2007, $3.99) profile pages with Jae Lee-a 4.00
HC (2007, $24.99) r/#1-7; variant covers and sketch pages; Macchio intro. 25.00

DARK TOWER: THE GUNSLINGER - THE BATTLE OF TULL (Stephen King's Dark Tower)
Marvel Comics: Aug, 2011 - No. 5, Dec, 2011 ($3.99, limited series)

1-5-Peter David & Robin Furth-s/Michael Lark-a/c 4.00

DARK TOWER: THE GUNSLINGER - THE JOURNEY BEGINS (Stephen King's Dark Tower)
Marvel Comics: Jul, 2010 - No. 5, Nov, 2010 ($3.99, limited series)

1-Peter David & Robin Furth-s/Sean Phillips-a/c 4.00
1-Variant cover by Jae Lee 5.00

DARK TOWER: THE GUNSLINGER - THE LITTLE SISTERS OF ELURIA (Stephen King)
Marvel Comics: Feb, 2011 - No. 5, Jun, 2011 ($3.99, limited series)

1-5: 1-Peter David & Robin Furth-s/Luke Ross-a/c 4.00

DARK TOWER: THE GUNSLINGER - THE WAY STATION (Stephen King)
Marvel Comics: Feb, 2012 - No. 5 ($3.99, limited series)

1-3-Peter David & Robin Furth-s/Laurence Campbell-a/c 4.00

DARK TOWER: THE LONG ROAD HOME (Based on Stephen King's Dark Tower series)
Marvel Comics: May, 2008 - No. 5, Sept, 2008 ($3.99, limited series)

1-Peter David & Robin Furth-s/Jae Lee & Richard Isanove-a 4.00
1-Variant cover by Deodato 6.00
1-Sketch cover variant by Jae Lee 40.00
2-5-Jae Lee-c 4.00
2-5: 2-Variant-c by Quesada. 3-Djurdjevic var-c. 4-Garney var-c. 5-Bermejo var-c 6.00
2-5-B&W sketch-c by Jae Lee 20.00
2-Second printing with variant-c by Lee 4.00
Dark Tower: End-World Almanac (2008, $3.99) guide to locations and inhabitants 4.00

DARK TOWER: THE SORCEROR (Based on Stephen King's Dark Tower)
Marvel Comics: June, 2009 ($3.99, one-shot)

1-Robin Furth-s/Richard Isanove-a/c; the story of Marten Broadcloak 4.00

DARK TOWER: TREACHERY (Based on Stephen King's Dark Tower series)
Marvel Comics: Nov, 2008 - No. 6, Apr, 2009 ($3.99, limited series)

1-6-Peter David & Robin Furth-s/Jae Lee & Richard Isanove-a 4.00
1-Variant cover by Dell'otto 10.00

DARKWING DUCK (TV cartoon) (Also see Cartoon Tales)
Disney Comics: Nov, 1991 - No. 4, Feb, 1992 ($1.50, limited series)

1-4: Adapts hour-long premiere TV episode 3.00

DARKWING DUCK (TV cartoon)
BOOM! Studios (KABOOM!): Jun, 2010 - No. 18, Nov, 2011 ($3.99)

1-Brill-s/Silvani-a; Launchpad McQuack app.; 3 covers 5.00
2-18-Multiple covers on all. 7-Batman #1 cover swipe. 8-Detective #31 cover swipe 4.00
Annual 1 (3/11, $4.99) Three covers; Quackerjack app. 5.00
... Free Comic Book Day Edition (5/11) Flip book with Chip 'N' Dale Rescue Rangers 3.00

DARK WOLVERINE (See Wolverine 2003 series)

DARK X-MEN (See Dark Avengers and the Dark Reign mini-series)
Marvel Comics: Jan, 2010 - No. 5, May, 2010 ($3.99, limited series)

1-5-Cornell-s/Kirk-a. 1-3-Bianchi-c. 1-Nate Grey returns 4.00
...: The Confession (11/09, $3.99) Cansino-a; Paquette-c 4.00

DARK X-MEN: THE BEGINNING (See Dark Avengers and the Dark Reign mini-series)
Marvel Comics: Sept, 2009 - No. 3, Oct, 2009 ($3.99, limited series)

1-3: 1-Cornell-s/Kirk-a; Jae Lee-c on all. 2-Daken app. 3-Mystique app.; Jock-a 4.00

DARLING LOVE
Close Up/Archie Publ. (A Darling Magazine): Oct-Nov, 1949 - No. 11, 1952 (no month) (52 pgs.)(Most photo-c)

	GD 2.0	VG 4.0	FN 6.0	VF 8.0	VF/NM 9.0	NM- 9.2
1-Photo-c	21	42	63	126	206	285
2-Photo-c	14	28	42	76	108	140
3-8,10,11: 3-6-photo-c	11	22	33	62	86	110
9-Krigstein-a	12	24	36	67	94	120

DARLING ROMANCE
Close Up (MLJ Publications): Sept-Oct, 1949 - No. 7, 1951 (All photo-c)

	GD 2.0	VG 4.0	FN 6.0	VF 8.0	VF/NM 9.0	NM- 9.2
1-(52 pgs.)-Photo-c	23	46	69	136	223	310
2	14	28	42	76	108	140
3-7	11	22	33	62	86	110

DARQUE PASSAGES (See Master Darque)
Acclaim (Valiant): April, 1998 ($2.50)

1-Christina Z.-s/Manco-c/a 3.00

DART (Also see Freak Force & Savage Dragon)
Image Comics (Highbrow Entertainment): Feb, 1996 - No. 3, May, 1996 ($2.50, lim. series)

1-3 3.00

DASTARDLY & MUTTLEY (See Fun-In No. 1-4, 6 and Kite Fun Book)

DATE WITH DANGER
Standard Comics: No. 5, Dec, 1952 - No. 6, Feb, 1953

	GD 2.0	VG 4.0	FN 6.0	VF 8.0	VF/NM 9.0	NM- 9.2
5,6-Secret agent stories: 6-Atom bomb story	9	18	27	52	69	85

DATE WITH DEBBI (Also see Debbi's Dates)
National Periodical Publ.: Jan-Feb, 1969 - No. 17, Sept-Oct, 1971; No. 18, Oct-Nov, 1972

	GD 2.0	VG 4.0	FN 6.0	VF 8.0	VF/NM 9.0	NM- 9.2
1-Teenage	6	12	18	41	66	90
2-5,17-(52 pgs) James Taylor sty.	4	8	12	22	34	45
6-12,18-Last issue	3	6	9	20	30	40
13-16-(68 pgs.): 14-1 pg. story on Jack Wild. 15-Marlo Thomas/"That Girl" story	4	8	12	24	37	50

DATE WITH JUDY, A (Radio/TV, and 1948 movie)
National Periodical Publications: Oct-Nov, 1947 - No. 79, Oct-Nov, 1960 (No. 1-25: 52 pgs.)

	GD 2.0	VG 4.0	FN 6.0	VF 8.0	VF/NM 9.0	NM- 9.2
1-Teenage	29	58	87	172	281	390
2	15	30	45	84	127	170
3-10	13	26	39	72	101	130
11-20	10	20	30	54	72	90
21-40	9	18	27	50	65	80
41-45: 45-Last pre-code (2-3/55)	8	16	24	44	57	70
46-79: 79-Drucker-c/a	8	16	24	42	54	65

DATE WITH MILLIE, A (Life With Millie No. 8 on)(Teenage)
Atlas/Marvel Comics (MPC): Oct, 1956 - No. 7, Aug, 1957; Oct, 1959 - No. 7, Oct, 1960

	GD 2.0	VG 4.0	FN 6.0	VF 8.0	VF/NM 9.0	NM- 9.2
1(10/56)-(1st Series)-Dan DeCarlo-a in #1-7	30	60	90	177	289	400
2	16	32	48	94	147	200
3-7	14	28	42	80	115	150
1(10/59)-(2nd Series)	16	32	48	94	147	200
2-7	11	22	33	64	90	115

DATE WITH PATSY, A (Also see Patsy Walker)
Atlas Comics: Sept, 1957 (One-shot)

	GD 2.0	VG 4.0	FN 6.0	VF 8.0	VF/NM 9.0	NM- 9.2
1-Starring Patsy Walker	14	28	42	76	108	140

DAUGHTERS OF THE DRAGON (See Heroes For Hire)
Marvel Comics: 2005; Mar, 2006 - No. 6, Aug, 2006 ($2.99, limited series)

1-6-Palmiotti & Gray-s/Evans-a. 1-Rhino app. 5,6-Iron Fist app. 3.00
... Deadly Hands Special (2005, $3.99) reprints app. from Deadly Hands of Kung Fu #32,33 & Bizarre Adventures #25; Claremont-s/Rogers-a; new Rogers-c & interview 4.00

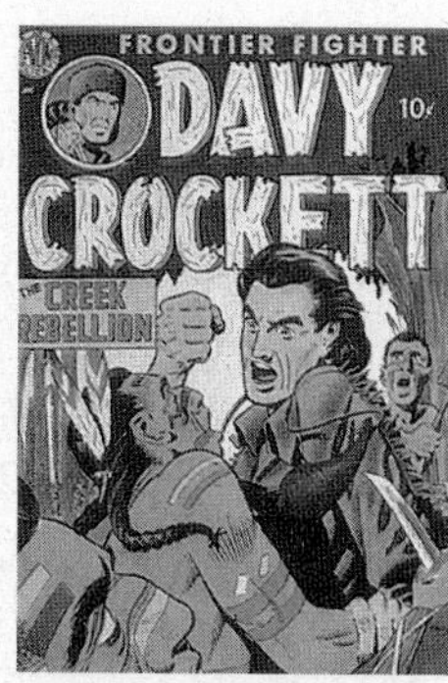

Davy Crockett nn © AVON

Dazzler (2010) #1 © MAR

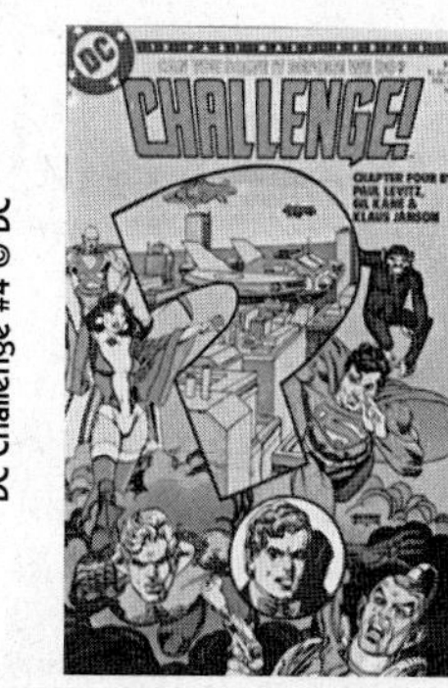

DC Challenge #4 © DC

	GD 2.0	VG 4.0	FN 6.0	VF 8.0	VF/NM 9.0	NM- 9.2
...: Samurai Bullets TPB (2006, $15.99) r/#1-6						16.00

DAVID AND GOLIATH (Movie)
Dell Publishing Co.: No. 1205, July, 1961

	GD	VG	FN	VF	VF/NM	NM-
Four Color 1205-Photo-c	6	12	18	42	69	95

DAVID BORING (See Eightball)
Pantheon Books: 2000 ($24.95, hardcover w/dust jacket)

	GD	VG	FN	VF	VF/NM	NM-
Hardcover - reprints David Boring stories from Eightball; Clowes-s/a						25.00

DAVID CASSIDY (TV)(See Partridge Family, Swing With Scooter #33 & Time For Love #30)
Charlton Comics: Feb, 1972 - No. 14, Sept, 1973

	GD	VG	FN	VF	VF/NM	NM-
1-Most have photo covers	7	14	21	44	72	100
2-5	4	8	12	26	41	55
6-14	4	8	12	24	37	50

DAVID LADD'S LIFE STORY (See Movie Classics)

DAVY CROCKETT (See Dell Giants, Fightin..., Frontier Fighters, It's Game Time, Power Record Comics, Western Tales & Wild Frontier)

DAVY CROCKETT (Frontier Fighter...)
Avon Periodicals: 1951

	GD	VG	FN	VF	VF/NM	NM-
nn-Tuska?, Reinman-a; Fawcette-c	18	36	54	105	165	225

DAVY CROCKETT (...King of the Wild Frontier No. 1,2)(TV)
Dell Publishing Co./Gold Key: 5/55 - No. 671, 12/55; No. 1, 12/63; No. 2, 11/69 (Walt Disney)

	GD	VG	FN	VF	VF/NM	NM-
Four Color 631(#1)-Fess Parker photo-c	14	28	42	97	211	325
Four Color 639-Photo-c	12	24	36	83	172	260
Four Color 664,671(Marsh-a)-Photo-c	12	24	36	80	163	245
1(12/63-Gold Key)-Fess Parker photo-c; reprints	8	16	24	53	89	125
2(11/69)-Fess Parker photo-c; reprints	4	8	12	28	44	60

DAVY CROCKETT (...Frontier Fighter #1,2; Kid Montana #9 on)
Charlton Comics: Aug, 1955 - No. 8, Jan, 1957

	GD	VG	FN	VF	VF/NM	NM-
1	10	20	30	58	79	100
2	7	14	21	37	46	55
3-8	6	12	18	28	34	40

DAWN
Sirius Entertainment/Image Comics: June, 1995 - No. 6, 1996 ($2.95)

	GD	VG	FN	VF	VF/NM	NM-
1/2-w/certificate	1	2	3	5	6	8
1/2-Variant-c	2	4	6	10	14	18
1-Linsner-c/a	1	2	3	5	6	8
1-Black Light Edition	2	4	6	9	13	16
1-White Trash Edition	3	6	9	16	23	30
1-Look Sharp Edition	3	6	9	19	29	38
2-4: Linsner-c/a						4.50
2-Variant-c, 3-Limited Edition	2	4	6	13	18	22
4-6-Vibrato-c						3.50
4, 5-Limited Edition	2	4	6	8	10	12
6-Limited Edition	2	4	6	8	10	12
...Convention Sketchbook (Image Comics, 2002, $2.95) pin-ups						3.00
...2003 Convention Sketchbook (Image Comics, 3/03, $2.95) pin-ups						3.00
...2004 Convention Sketchbook (Image Comics, 4/04, $2.95) pin-ups						3.00
...2005 Convention Sketchbook (Image Comics, 5/05, $2.95) pin-ups						3.00
Genesis Edition ('99, Wizard supplement) previews Return of the Goddess						3.00
Lucifer's Halo TPB (11/97, $19.95) r/Drama, Dawn #1-6 plus 12 pages of new artwork						20.00
...: Not to Touch The Earth (9/10, $5.99) Linsner-s/c/a; pin-ups by various incl. Turner						6.00
...: Tenth Anniversary Special (9/99, $2.95) Interviews						3.00
The Portable Dawn ($9.95, 5"x4", 64 pgs.) Pocket-sized cover gallery						10.00

DAWN OF THE DEAD (George A. Romaro's...)
IDW Publishing: Apr, 2004 - No. 3, Jun, 2004 ($3.99, limited series)

	GD	VG	FN	VF	VF/NM	NM-
1-3-Adaptation of the 2004 movie; Niles-s						4.00
TPB (9/04, $17.99) r/#1-3; intro. by George A. Romero						18.00

DAWN: THE RETURN OF THE GODDESS
Sirius Entertainment: Apr, 1999 - No. 4, July, 2000 ($2.95, limited series)

	GD	VG	FN	VF	VF/NM	NM-
1-4-Linsner-s/a						3.00
TPB (4/02, $12.95) r/#1-4; intro. by Linsner						13.00

DAWN: THREE TIERS
Image Comics: Jun, 2003 - No. 6, Aug, 2005 ($2.95, limited series)

	GD	VG	FN	VF	VF/NM	NM-
1-6-Linsner-s/a. 2-Preview of Vampire's Christmas						3.00

DAYDREAMERS (See Generation X)
Marvel Comics: Aug, 1997 - No. 3, Oct, 1997 ($2.50, limited series)

	GD	VG	FN	VF	VF/NM	NM-
1-3-Franklin Richards, Howard the Duck, Man-Thing app.						3.00

DAY OF JUDGMENT
DC Comics: Nov, 1999 - No. 5, Nov, 1999 ($2.95/$2.50, limited series)

	GD	VG	FN	VF	VF/NM	NM-
1-($2.95) Spectre possessed; Matt Smith-a						3.00
2-5: Parallax returns. 5-Hal Jordan becomes the Spectre						3.00
...Secret Files 1 (11/99, $4.95) Harris-c						5.00

DAY OF VENGEANCE (Prelude to Infinite Crisis)(Also see Birds of Prey #76 for 1st app. of Black Alice)
DC Comics: June, 2005 - No. 6, Nov, 2005 ($2.50, limited series)

	GD	VG	FN	VF	VF/NM	NM-
1-6: 1-Jean Loring becomes Eclipso; Spectre, Ragman, Enchantress, Detective Chimp, Shazam app.; Justiniano-a. 2,3-Capt. Marvel app. 4-6-Black Alice app.						3.00
...: Infinite Crisis Special 1 (3/06, $4.99) Justiniano-a/Simonson-c						5.00
TPB (2005, $12.99) r/series & Action #826, Advs. of Superman #639, Superman #216						13.00

DAYS OF THE DEFENDERS (See Defenders, The)
Marvel Comics: Mar, 2001 ($3.50, one-shot)

	GD	VG	FN	VF	VF/NM	NM-
1-Reprints early team-ups of members, incl. Marvel Feature #1; Larsen-c						3.50

DAYS OF THE MOB (See In the Days of the Mob)

DAYTRIPPER
DC Comics (Vertigo): Feb, 2010 - No. 10, Nov, 2010 ($2.99, limited series)

	GD	VG	FN	VF	VF/NM	NM-
1-10-Gabriel Bá & Fábio Moon-s/a						3.00
TPB (2010, $19.99) r/#1-10; sketch art pages						20.00

DAZEY'S DIARY
Dell Publishing Co.: June-Aug, 1962

	GD	VG	FN	VF	VF/NM	NM-
01-174-208: Bill Woggon-c/a	4	8	12	28	44	60

DAZZLER, THE (Also see Marvel Graphic Novel & X-Men #130)
Marvel Comics Group: Mar, 1981 - No. 42, Mar, 1986

	GD	VG	FN	VF	VF/NM	NM-
1,21,22,24,27,28,38,42: 1-X-Men app. 21-Double size; photo-c. 22 (12/82)-vs. Rogue Battle-c/sty. 24-Full app. Rogue w/Powerman (Iron Fist). 27-Rogue app. 28-Full app. Rogue; Mystique app. 38-Wolverine-c/app.; X-Men app. 42-Beast-c/app.						4.00
2-20,23,25,26,29-32,34-37,39-41: 2-X-Men app. 10,11-Galactus app. 23-Rogue/Mystique 1 pg. app. 26-Jusko-c. 40-Secret Wars II						3.00
33-Michael Jackson "Thriller" swipe-c/sty						4.00
One-shot (7/10, $3.99) Andrasofszky-a/c; Arcade app.						4.00

NOTE: *No. 1 distributed only through comic shops.* ***Alcala*** *a-1i, 2i.* ***Chadwick*** *a-38-42p; c(p)-39, 41, 42.* ***Guice*** *a-38i, 42i; c-38, 40.*

DC CHALLENGE (Most DC superheroes appear)
DC Comics: Nov, 1985 - No. 12, Oct, 1986 ($1.25/$2.00, maxi-series)

	GD	VG	FN	VF	VF/NM	NM-
1-11: 1-Colan-a. 2,8-Batman-c/app. 4-Gil Kane-c/a						3.00
12-($2.00-c) Giant; low print						4.00

NOTE: *Batman app. in 1-4, 6-12. Joker app. in 7.* ***Infantino*** *a-3.* ***Ordway*** *c-12.* ***Swan/Austin*** *c-10.*

DC COMICS CLASSICS LIBRARY (Hardcover collections of classic DC stories)
DC Comics: 2009 - Present ($39.99, hardcover with dustjacket)

	GD	VG	FN	VF	VF/NM	NM-
Batman: A Death in the Family ('09)- r/Batman #426-429, 440-442, New Titans #60,61						40.00
Batman Annuals ('09)- r/Batman Annual #1-3; afterword by Richard Bruning						40.00
Batman Annuals Volume 2 ('10)- r/Batman Annual #4-7; intro. by Michael Uslan						40.00
Flash of Two Worlds ('09)- r/Flash #123,129,137,151,170&173 team-ups with G.A. Flash						40.00
Justice League of America by George Pérez ('09) r/J.L.of A. #184-186, 192-194						40.00
Justice League of America by George Pérez Vol. 2 ('10) r/J.L.of A. #195-197,200						40.00
Legion of Super-Heroes: The Life and Death of Ferro Lad ('09) - r/Adventure Comics # 346, 347,352-355,357; intro. by Paul Levitz; afterword by Jim Shooter						40.00
Roots of the Swamp Thing ('09)- r/House of Secrets #92 & Swamp Thing #1-13; Wein intro.						40.00
Superman: Kryptonite Nevermore ('09)- r/Superman #233-238,240-242; afterword by Denny O'Neil						40.00

DC COMICS MEGA SAMPLER
DC Comics: 2009; Jul, 2010 (6-1/4" x 9-1/2", FCBD giveaways)

	GD	VG	FN	VF	VF/NM	NM-
1, 2010- Short stories of kid-friendly titles; Tiny Titans, Billy Batson, Super Friends app.						3.00

DC COMICS PRESENTS
DC Comics: July-Aug, 1978 - No. 97, Sept, 1986 (Superman team-ups in all)

	GD	VG	FN	VF	VF/NM	NM-
1-4th Superman/Flash race	5	10	15	30	48	65
1-(Whitman variant)	5	10	15	35	55	75
2-Part 2 of Superman/Flash race	3	6	9	16	22	28
2-(Whitman variant)	3	6	9	17	25	32
3,4,9-12,14-16,19,21,22-(Whitman variants, low print run, none have issue # on cover)	3	6	9	14	20	25
3-10: 4-Metal Men. 6-Green Lantern. 8-Swamp Thing. 9-Wonder Woman	2	4	6	8	10	12
11-25,27-40: 13-Legion of Super-Heroes. 19-Batgirl. 31-Robin. 35-Man-Bat						6.00

26-(10/80)-Green Lantern; intro Cyborg, Starfire, Raven (1st app. New Teen Titans in 16 pg.

DC Comics Presents: Hawkman © DC

DC First: Flash/Superman #1 © DC

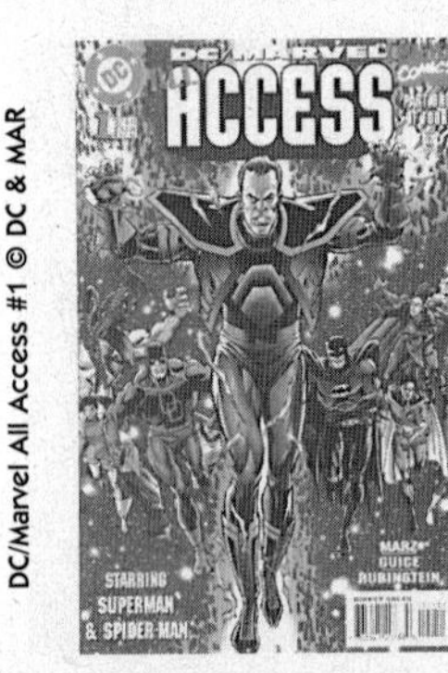

DC/Marvel All Access #1 © DC & MAR

	GD 2.0	VG 4.0	FN 6.0	VF 8.0	VF/NM 9.0	NM- 9.2

preview); Starlin-c/a; Sargon the Sorcerer back-up 6 12 18 37 59 80

41,72,77,78,97: 41-Superman/Joker-c/story. 72-Joker/Phantom Stranger-c/story. 77,78-Animal Man app. (77-c also). 97-Phantom Zone 6.00

42-46,48-50,52-71,73-76,79-83: 42-Sandman. 43,80-Legion of Super-Heroes. 52-Doom Patrol; 1st app. Ambush Bug. 58-Robin. 82-Adam Strange. 83-Batman & Outsiders 4.00

47-He-Man-c/s (1st app. in comics) 2 4 6 11 16 20

51-Preview insert (16 pgs.) of He-Man (2nd app.) 1 3 4 6 8 10

84-Challengers of the Unknown; Kirby-c/s. 6.00

85-Swamp Thing; Alan Moore scripts 6.00

86,88-96: 86-88-Crisis x-over. 88-Creeper 4.00

87-Origin/1st app. Superboy of Earth Prime 1 3 4 6 8 10

Annual 1,4: 1(9/82)-G.A. Superman; 1st app. Alexander Luthor. 4(10/85)-Superwoman 4.00

Annual 2,3: 2(7/83)-Intro/origin Superwoman. 3(9/84)-Shazam 4.00

NOTE: ***Adkins** a-2, 54; c-2. **Buckler** a-33, 34; c-30, 33, 34. **Giffen** a-39; c-59. **Gil Kane** a-28, 35, Annual 3; c-48p, 56, 58, 60, 62, 64, 68, Annual 2, 3. **Kirby** c/a-84. **Kubert** c/a-66. **Morrow** c/a-65. **Newton** c/a-54p. **Orlando** c-53i. **Perez** a-26p, 61p; c-38, 61, 94. **Starlin** a-26-29p, 36p, 37p; c-26-29, 36, 37, 93. **Toth** a-84. **Williamson** i-79, 85, 87.*

DC COMICS PRESENTS: ...(Julie Schwartz tribute series of one-shots based on classic covers)
DC Comics: Sept, 2004 - Oct, 2004 ($2.50)

The Atom -(Based on cover of Atom #10) Gibbons-s/Oliffe-a; Waid-s/Jurgens-a; Bolland-c 3.00
Batman -(Batman #183) Johns-s/Infantino-a; Wein-s/Kuhn-a; Hughes-c 3.00
The Flash -(Flash #163) Loeb-s/McGuinness-a; O'Neil-s/Mahnke-a; Ross-c 3.00
Green Lantern -(Green Lantern #31) Azzarello-s/Breyfogle-a; Pasko-s/McDaniel-a; Bolland-c 3.00
Hawkman -(Hawkman #6) Bates-s/Byrne-a; Busiek-s/Simonson-a; Garcia-Lopez-c 3.00
Justice League of America -(J.L. of A. #53) Ellison & David-s/Giella-a; Wolfman-s/Nguyen-a; Garcia-Lopez-c 3.00
Mystery in Space -(M.I.S. #82) Maggin-s/Williams-a; Morrison-s/Ordway-a; Ross-c 3.00
Superman -(Superman #264) Stan Lee-s/Cooke-a; Levitz-s/Giffen-a; Hughes-c 3.00

DC COMICS PRESENTS: ...
DC Comics: Dec, 2010 - Present ($7.99, squarebound, one-shot reprints)

The Atom 1 (3/11) r/Legends of the DC Universe #28,29,40,41; Gil Kane-a 8.00
Batman 1 (12/10) r/Batman #582-585,600 8.00
Batman 2 (1/11) r/Batman #591-594 8.00
Batman 3 (2/11) r/Batman #595-598 8.00
Batman: Arkham 1 (6/11) r/Batman Chronicles #6, Batman; Arkham Asylum - Tales of Madness #1, Batman Villains Secret Files #1 & Justice Leagues: J.L. of Arkham #1 8.00
Batman - Bad 1 (1/12) r/Batman: Legends of the D.K. #146-148 8.00
Batman Beyond 1 (2/11) r/Batman Beyond #13,14,21,22 8.00
Batman: Blaze of Glory 1 (2/12) r/Batman: Legends of the D.K. #197-199,212 8.00
Batman - Blink 1 (12/11) r/Batman: Legends of the D.K. #156-158 8.00
Batman/Catwoman 1 (12/10) r/Batman and Catwoman: Trail of the Gun 8.00
Batman - Conspiracy 1 (4/11) r/Batman: Legends of the D.K. #86-88; Detective #821 8.00
Batman - Dark Knight, Dark City 1 (7/11) r/Batman #452-454; Detective #633 8.00
Batman - Don't Blink 1 (1/12) r/Batman: Legends of the D.K. #164-167 8.00
Batman: Gotham Noir 1 (9/11) r/Batman: Gotham Noir #1 & Batman #604 8.00
Batman - Irresistible 1 (5/11) r/Batman: Legends of the D.K. #169-171; Hourman #22 8.00
Batman - The Demon Laughs 1 (12/11) r/Batman: Legends of the D.K. #142-145; Aparo-a 8.00
Batman: The Secret City 1 (2/12) r/Batman: Legends of the D.K. #180,181,190,191 8.00
Batman: Urban Legends 1 (2/12) r/Batman: Legends of the D.K. #168,177-179 8.00
Brightest Day 1 (12/10) r/Strange Advs. #205, Hawkman #27,34,36, Solo #8, DC Hol. '09 8.00
Brightest Day 2 (1/11) r/Firestorm #11-13 & Martian Manhunter #11,24 8.00
Brightest Day 3 (2/11) r/Legends of the DC Univ. #25-27 & Teen Titans #27,28 8.00
Captain Atom 1 (2/12) r/back-up stories from Action Comics #879-889 8.00
Catwoman - Guardian of Gotham 1 (12/11) r/Catwoman: Guardian of Gotham #1,2 8.00
Chase 1 (1/11) r/Chase #1,6-8 8.00
Elseworlds 80-Page Giant 1 (1/12) r/Elseworlds 80-Page Giant (pulled from distribution) 8.00
Flash 1 (7/11) r/Showcase #4,14 and Flash #125,130,139 8.00
Flash/Green Lantern: Faster Friends (1/11) r/G.L./Flash: Faster Friends & Flash/G.L. : FF 8.00
Green Lantern 1 (12/10) r/Green Lantern #137-140 (2001) 8.00
Green Lantern - Fear Itself 1 (4/11) r/Green Lantern: Fear Itself GN 8.00
Green Lantern - Willworld 1 (7/11) r/Green Lantern: Willworld GN 8.00
Impulse 1 (8/11) r/Impulse #50-53 8.00
Jack Kirby Omnibus Sampler 1 (12/11) r/Kirby art stories from 1957,1958 8.00
JLA 1 (2/11) r/JLA #90-93 8.00
JLA - Age of Wonder 1 (12/11) r/JLA: Age of Wonder 8.00
JLA: Black Baptism 1 (8/11) r/JLA: Black Baptism #1-4 8.00
JLA Heaven's Ladder 1 (10/11) comic-sized reprint; and r/Green Lantern #1,000,000 8.00
Legion of Super-Heroes 1 (6/11) r/Legion of Super-Heroes #122,123 & Legionnaires 79,80 8.00
Legion of Super-Heroes 2 (2/12) r/Adv. #247 and recent Legion short stories 8.00
Lobo 1 (3/11) r/Lobo #63,64 & DC First: Superman/Lobo #1 8.00
Metal Men 1 (4/11) r/Doom Patrol ('09) #1-7 and Silver Age: The Brave and the Bold #1 8.00
Night Force 1 (4/11) r/Night Force #1-4; Gene Colan-a 8.00
Ninja Boy 1 (6/11) r/Ninja Boy #1-4 8.00
Shazam! 1,2 (9/11,10/11) 1-r/Power of Shazam #38-41. 2-r/ #42-46 8.00
Son of Superman 1 (7/11) r/Son of Superman GN 8.00
Superboy's Legion 1 (12/11) r/Superboy's Legion #1,2 (Elseworlds) 8.00
Superman 1 (12/10) r/Superman: The Man of Steel #121 & Superman #179,180,185 8.00
Superman 2 (1/11) r/Action #798, Superman: The Man of Steel #133, Superman #189 & Advs. of Superman #611 8.00
Superman 3 (2/11) r/Superman #177,178,181,182 8.00
Superman 4 (9/11) r/Action #768,771-773 8.00
Superman/Doomsday 1 (5/11) r/Doomsday Annual #1 & Superman #175 8.00
Superman - Infestation 1 (8/11) r/Action #778, Advs. of Superman #591, Superman #169 and Superman: The Man of Steel #113 8.00
Superman - Secret Identity 1 (12/11) r/Superman: Secret Identity #1,2 8.00
Superman - Secret Identity 2 (1/12) r/Superman: Secret Identity #3,4 8.00
Superman - Sole Survivor 1 (3/11) r/Legends of the DC Universe #1-3,39 8.00
Superman - The Kents 1,2 (1/12, 2/12) 1-r/The Kents #1-4. 2-The Kents #5-8 8.00
Teen Titans 1 (10/11) Teen Titans Lost Annual #1 and Solo #7; Allred-a 8.00
The Life Story of the Flash 1 (1/12) r/The Life Story of the Flash GN 8.00
T.H.U.N.D.E.R. Agents 1 (2/11) r/T.H.U.N.D.E.R. Agents #1,2,7 (1966) 8.00
Wonder Woman 1 (4/11) r/Wonder Woman #139-142 (1998) 8.00
Young Justice 1 (12/10) r/JLA World Without Grownups #1,2 8.00
Young Justice 2 (1/11) r/Y.J: The Secret, Y.J. Secret Files #1, Y.J. In No Man's Land 8.00
Young Justice 3 (2/11) r/Young Justice #7 & Y.J Secret Origins 80-Page Giant #1 8.00

DC COMICS THE NEW 52 PRESENTS: ...
DC Comics: Mar, 2012 - Present ($7.99, squarebound, one-shot reprints)

The Dark 1 (3/12) r/Animal Man #1, Swamp Thing #1, I, Vampire #1, and J.L. Dark #1 8.00

DC COUNTDOWN (To Infinite Crisis)
DC Comics: May, 2005 ($1.00, 80 pages, one-shot)

1-Death of Blue Beetle; prelude to OMAC Project, Day of Vengeance, Rann/Thanagar War and Villains United mini-series; s/a by various; Jim Lee/Alex Ross-c 4.00

DC FIRST: ...(series of one-shots)
DC Comics: July, 2002 ($3.50)

Batgirl/Joker 1-Sienkiewicz & Terry Moore-a; Nowlan-c 3.50
Green Lantern/Green Lantern 1-Alan Scott & Hal Jordan vs. Krona 3.50
Flash/Superman 1-Superman races Jay Garrick; Abra Kadabra app. 3.50
Superman/Lobo 1-Giffen-s; Nowlan-c 3.50

DC GOES APE
DC Comics: 2008 ($19.99, trade paperback)

Vol. 1 - Reprints app. of Grodd, Beppo, Titano and other monkey tales; Art Adams-c 20.00

DC GRAPHIC NOVEL (Also see DC Science Fiction...)
DC Comics: Nov, 1983 - No. 7, 1986 ($5.95, 68 pgs.)

1-3,5,7: 1-Star Raiders. 2-Warlords; not from regular Warlord series. 3-The Medusa Chain; Ernie Colon story/a. 5-Me and Joe Priest; Chaykin-c. 7-Space Clusters; Nino-c/a 2 4 6 9 12 15
4-The Hunger Dogs by Kirby; Darkseid kills Himon from Mister Miracle & destroys New Genesis 5 10 15 35 55 75
6-Metalzoic; Sienkiewicz-c ($6.95) 2 4 6 9 12 15

DC HOLIDAY SPECIAL '09
DC Comics: Feb, 2010 ($5.99, one-shot)

1-Christmas short stories by various incl. Dragotta, Tucci, Chaykin; Dustin Nguyen-c 6.00

DC INFINITE HALLOWEEN SPECIAL
DC Comics: Dec, 2007 ($5.99, one-shot)

1-Halloween short stories by various incl. Dini, Waid, Hairsine, Kelley Jones; Gene Ha-c 6.00

DC KIDS MEGA SAMPLER
DC Comics: June, 2009 (Free Comic Book Day giveaway, one-shot)

1-Tiny Titans, Batman: The Brave and the Bold, Billy Batson/Shazam short stories 3.00

DC/MARVEL: ALL ACCESS (Also see DC Versus Marvel & Marvel Versus DC)
DC Comics: 1996 - No. 4, 1997 ($2.95, limited series)

1-4: 1-Superman & Spider-Man app. 2-Robin & Jubilee app. 3-Dr. Strange & Batman-c/app., X-Men, JLA app. 4-X-Men vs. JLA-c/app. rebirth of Amalgam 3.00

DC/MARVEL: CROSSOVER CLASSICS
DC Comics: 1998; 2003 ($14.95, TPB)

Vol. II-Reprints Batman/Punisher: Lake of Fire, Punisher/Batman: Deadly Knights, Silver Surfer/Superman, Batman & Capt. America 15.00
Vol. 4 (2003, $14.95) Reprints Green Lantern/Silver Surfer: Unholy Alliances, Darkseid/ Galactus: The Hunger, Batman & Spider-Man, and Superman/Fantastic Four 15.00

DC 100 PAGE SUPER SPECTACULAR
(Title is 100 Page... No. 14 on)(Square bound) (Reprints, 50¢)
National Periodical Publications: No. 4, Summer, 1971 - No. 13, 6/72; No. 14, 2/73 - No. 22,

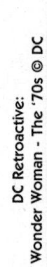

DC 100 Page Super Spectacular #17 © DC

DC Retroactive: Wonder Woman - The '70s © DC

DC Special #29 © DC

GD 2.0 VG 4.0 FN 6.0 VF 8.0 VF/NM 9.0 NM- 9.2

11/73 (No #1-3)

4-Weird Mystery Tales; Johnny Peril & Phantom Stranger; cover & splashes by Wrightson; origin Jungle Boy of Jupiter 20 40 60 137 294 450
5-Love Stories; Wood inks (7 pgs.)(scarcer) 46 92 138 345 748 1150
6- "World's Greatest Super-Heroes"; JLA, JSA, Spectre, Johnny Quick, Vigilante & Hawkman; contains unpublished Wildcat story; N. Adams wrap-around-c; r/JLA #21,22 17 34 51 119 260 400
6-Replica Edition (2004, $6.95) complete reprint w/wraparound-c 7.00
7-(Also listed as Superman #245) Air Wave, Kid Eternity, Hawkman-r; Atom-r/Atom #3 10 20 30 67 124 180
8-(Also listed as Batman #238) Batman, Legion, Aquaman-r; G.A. Atom, Sargon (r/Sensation #57), Plastic Man (r/Police #14) stories; Doom Patrol origin-r; Neal Adams wraparound-c 12 24 36 81 166 250
9-(Also listed as Our Army at War #242) Kubert-c 10 20 30 65 118 170
10-(Also listed as Adventure Comics #416) Golden Age-reprints; r/1st app. Black Canary from Flash #86; no Zatanna 11 22 33 75 148 220
11-(Also listed as Flash #214) origin Metal Men-r/Showcase #37; never before published G.A. Flash story. 9 18 27 61 106 150
12,14: 12-(Also listed as Superboy #185) Legion-c/story; Teen Titans, Kid Eternity (r/Hit #46), Star Spangled Kid-r(S.S. #55). 14-Batman-r/Detective #31,32,156; Atom-r/Showcase #34 8 16 24 53 89 125
13-(Also listed as Superman #252) Ray(r/Smash #17), Black Condor, (r/Crack #18), Hawkman(r/Flash #24); Starman-r/Adv. #67; Dr. Fate & Spectre-r/More Fun #57; Neal Adams-c 11 22 33 73 142 210
15,16,18,19,21,22: 15-r/2nd Boy Commandos/Det. #64. 16-Sgt. Rock. 18-Superman. 21-Superboy; r/Brave & the Bold #54. 22-r/All-Flash #13 6 12 18 42 69 95
17,20: 17-JSA-r/All Star #37 (10-11/47, 38 pgs.), Sandman-r/Adv. #65 (8/41), JLA #23 (11/63) & JLA #43 (3/66). 20-Batman-r/Det. #66,68, Spectre; origin Two-Face 7 14 21 44 72 100
... : Love Stories Replica Edition (2000, $6.95) reprints #5 7.00

NOTE: ***Anderson*** *r-11, 14, 18i, 22.* ***B. Baily*** *r-18, 20.* ***Burnley*** *r-18, 20.* ***Crandall*** *r-14p, 20.* ***Drucker*** *r-4.* ***Grandenetti*** *a-22(2)r.* ***Heath*** *a-22r.* ***Infantino*** *r-17, 20, 22.* ***G. Kane*** *r-18.* ***Kirby*** *r-15.* ***Kubert*** *r-6, 7, 16, 17; c-16, 19.* ***Manning*** *a-19r.* ***Meskin*** *r-4, 22.* ***Mooney*** *r-15, 21.* ***Toth*** *r-17, 20.*

DC ONE MILLION (Also see crossover #1,000,000 issues and JLA One Million TPB)
DC Comics: Nov, 1998 - No. 4, Nov, 1998 ($2.95/$1.99, weekly lim. series)

1-($2.95) JLA travels to the 853rd century; Morrison-s 4.00
2-4-($1.99) 3.00
... Eighty-Page Giant (8/99, $4.95) 5.00
TPB ('99, $14.95) r/#1-4 and several x-over stories 15.00

DC RETROACTIVE (New stories done in old style plus reprint from decade)
DC Comics: Sept, 2011 - Oct, 2011 ($4.99, series of one-shots)

...: Batman - The '70s (9/11, $4.99) Len Wein-s/Tom Mandrake-a; r/Batman #307 5.00
...: Batman - The '80s (10/11, $4.99) Mike Barr-s/Jerry Bingham-a; The Reaper app. 5.00
...: Batman - The '90s (10/11, $4.99) Grant-s/Breyfogle-a; Scarface & Ventriloquist app. 5.00
...: Flash - The '70s (9/11, $4.99) Bates-s/Gallego-a; r/DC Comics Presents #1,2 5.00
...: Flash - The '80s (10/11, $4.99) Messner-Loebs-s/LaRocque-a; r/Flash v2 #18 5.00
...: Flash - The '90s (10/11, $4.99) Augustyn-s/Bowden-a; r/Flash v2 #142 5.00
...: Green Lantern - The '70s (9/11, $4.99) O'Neil-s/Grell-a; r/Green Lantern #76 5.00
...: Green Lantern - The '80s (10/11, $4.99) Wein-s/Staton-a; r/Green Lantern #172 5.00
...: Green Lantern - The '90s (10/11, $4.99) Marz-s/Banks-a; r/Green Lantern v3 #78 5.00
...: JLA - The '70s (9/11, $4.99) Bates-s; Adam Strange app.; r/J.L. of A. #123 5.00
...: JLA - The '80s (10/11, $4.99) Conway-s/Randall-a; Felix Faust app.; r/J.L.of A. #239 5.00
...: JLA - The '90s (10/11, $4.99) Giffen & DeMatteis-s/Maguire-a; r/J.L.A. #6 5.00
...: Superman - The '70s (9/11, $4.99) Pasko-s/Barreto-a; r/Action Comics #484 5.00
...: Superman - The '80s (10/11, $4.99) Wolfman-s/Cariello-a; r/Superman #352 5.00
...: Superman - The '90s (10/11, $4.99) L. Simonson-s/Bogdanove-a; Guardian app. 5.00
...: Wonder Woman - The '70s (9/11, $4.99) O'Neil-s/J. Bone-a; r/Wonder Woman #201 5.00
...: Wonder Woman - The '80s (10/11, $4.99) Thomas-s/Buckler-a; r/W.W. #288 5.00
...: Wonder Woman - The '90s (10/11, $4.99) Messner-Loebs-s/Moder-a; r/W.W. v2 #66 5.00

DC SCIENCE FICTION GRAPHIC NOVEL
DC Comics: 1985 - No. 7, 1987 ($5.95)

SF1-SF7: SF1-Hell on Earth by Robert Bloch; Giffen-p. SF2-Nightwings by Robert Silverberg; G. Colan-p. SF3-Frost & Fire by Bradbury. SF4-Merchants of Venus. SF5-Demon With A Glass Hand by Ellison; M. Rogers-a. SF6-The Magic Goes Away by Niven. SF7-Sandkings by George R.R. Martin 2 4 6 8 11 14

DC SILVER AGE CLASSICS
DC Comics: 1992 ($1.00, all reprints)

...Action Comics #252-r/1st Supergirl. Adventure Comics #247-r/1st Legion of Super-Heroes. The Brave and the Bold #28-r/1st JLA. Detective Comics #225-r/1st Martian Manhunter. Detective Comics #327-r/1st new look Batman. Green Lantern #76-r/1st Green Lantern/ Green Arrow. House of Secrets #92-r/1st Swamp Thing. Showcase #4-r/1st S.A. Flash. Showcase #22-r/1st S.A. Green Lantern 3.00
...Sugar and Spike #99; includes 2 unpublished stories 4.00

GD 2.0 VG 4.0 FN 6.0 VF 8.0 VF/NM 9.0 NM- 9.2

DC SPECIAL (Also see Super DC Giant)
National Per. Publ.: 10-12/68 - No. 15, 11-12/71; No. 16, Spr/75 - No. 29, 8-9/77

1-All Infantino issue; Flash, Batman, Adam Strange-r; begin 68 pg. issues, end #21 9 18 27 61 106 150
2-Teen humor; Binky, Buzzy, Harvey app. 10 20 30 69 130 190
3-All-Girl issue; unpubl. GA Wonder Woman story 9 18 27 63 112 160
4,11: 4-Horror (1st Abel, brief). 11-Monsters 6 12 18 37 59 80
5-10,12-15: 5-All Kubert issue; Viking Prince, Sgt. Rock-r. 6-Western. 7,9,13-Strangest Sports. 12-Viking Prince; Kubert-c/a (r/B&B almost entirely). 15-G.A. Plastic Man origin-r/Police #1; origin Woozy by Cole; 14,15-(52 pgs.) 4 8 12 28 44 60
16-27: 16-Super Heroes Battle Super Gorillas; r/Capt. Storm #1, 1st Johnny Cloud/All-Amer. Men of War #82. 17-Early S.A. Green Lantern-r. 22-Origin Robin Hood. 26-Enemy Ace. 27-Captain Comet story 3 6 9 16 23 30
28-Earth Shattering Disaster Stories; Legion of Super-Heroes story 3 6 9 17 25 32
29-New "The Untold Origin of the Justice Society"; Staton-a/Neal Adams-c; Hitler app. in story and on cover 5 10 15 35 55 75

NOTE: ***N. Adams*** *c-3, 4, 6, 11, 29.* ***Grell*** *a-20; c-17, 20.* ***Heath*** *a-12r.* ***G. Kane*** *a-6p, 13r, 17r, 19-21r.* ***Kirby*** *a-4,11.* ***Kubert*** *a-6r, 12r, 22.* ***Meskin*** *a-10.* ***Moreira*** *a-10.* ***Staton*** *a-29p.* ***Toth*** *a-13, 20r. #1-15: 25¢; 16-27: 50¢; 28, 29: 60¢. #1-13, 16-21: 68 pgs.; 14, 15: 52 pgs.; 25-27: oversized.*

DC SPECIAL BLUE RIBBON DIGEST
DC Comics: Mar-Apr, 1980 - No. 24, Aug, 1982

1,2,4,5: 1-Legion reprints. 2-Flash. 4-Green Lantern. 5-Secret Origins; new Zatara and Zatanna 2 4 6 8 11 14
3-Justice Society 2 4 6 10 14 18
6,8-10: 6-Ghosts. 8-Legion. 9-Secret Origins. 10-Warlord-"The Deimos Saga"-Grell-s/c/a 2 4 6 8 11 14
7-Sgt. Rock's Prize Battle Tales 2 4 6 13 18 22
11,16: 11-Justice League. 16-Green Lantern/Green Arrow-r; all Adams-a 2 4 6 11 16 20
12-Haunted Tank; reprints 1st app. 2 4 6 13 18 22
13-15,17-19: 13-Strange Sports Stories. 14-UFO Invaders; Adam Strange app. 15-Secret Origins of Super Villains; JLA app. 17-Ghosts. 18-Sgt. Rock; Kubert front & back-c. 19-Doom Patrol; new Perez-c 2 4 6 9 13 16
20-Dark Mansion of Forbidden Love (scarce) 5 10 15 30 48 65
21-Our Army at War 3 6 9 16 22 28
22-24: 22-Secret Origins. 23-Green Arrow, w/new 7 pg. story. 24-House of Mystery; new Kubert wraparound-c 2 4 6 13 18 22

NOTE: ***N. Adams*** *a-16(6)r, 17r, 23r; c-16.* ***Aparo*** *a-6r, 24r; c-23.* ***Grell*** *a-8, 10; c-10.* ***Heath*** *a-14.* ***Infantino*** *a-15r.* ***Kaluta*** *a-17r.* ***Gil Kane*** *a-15r, 22r.* ***Kirby*** *a-5, 9, 23r.* ***Kubert*** *a-3, 18r, 21r; c-7, 12, 14, 17, 18, 21, 24.* ***Morrow*** *a-24r.* ***Orlando*** *a-17r, 22r; c-1, 20.* ***Toth*** *a-21r, 24r.* ***Wood*** *a-3, 17r, 24r.* ***Wrightson*** *a-16r, 17r, 24r.*

DC SPECIAL: CYBORG (From Teen Titans) (See Teen Titans 2003 series for TPB collection)
DC Comics: Jul, 2008 - No. 6, Dec, 2008 ($2.99, limited series)

1-6: 1-Sable-s/Lashley-a; origin re-told. 3-6-Magno-a 3.00

DC SPECIAL: RAVEN (From Teen Titans) (See Teen Titans 2003 series for TPB collection)
DC Comics: May, 2008 - No. 5, Sept, 2008 ($2.99, limited series)

1-5-Marv Wolfman-s/Damion Scott-a 3.00

DC SPECIAL SERIES
National Periodical Publications/DC Comics: 9/77 - No. 16, Fall, 1978; No. 17, 8/79 - No. 27, Fall, 1981 (No. 18, 19, 23, 24 - digest size, 100 pgs.; No. 25-27 - Treasury sized)

1-"5-Star Super-Hero Spectacular 1977"; Batman, Atom, Flash, Green Lantern, Aquaman, in solo stories, Kobra app.; N. Adams-c 4 8 12 26 41 55
2(#1)-"The Original Swamp Thing Saga 1977"-r/Swamp Thing #1&2 by Wrightson; new Wrightson wraparound-c. 2 4 6 11 16 20
3,4,6-8: 3-Sgt Rock. 4-Unexpected. 6-Secret Society of Super Villains, Jones-a. 7-Ghosts Special. 8-Brave and Bold w/ new Batman, Deadman & Sgt Rock team-up 2 4 6 13 18 22
5-"Superman Spectacular 1977"-(84 pg, $1.00)-Superman vs. Brainiac & Lex Luthor, new 63 pg. story 3 6 9 16 22 28
9-Wonder Woman; Ditko-a (11 pgs.) 3 6 9 16 22 28
10-"Secret Origins of Superheroes Special 1978"-(52 pgs.)-Dr. Fate, Lightray & Black Canary on-c/new origin stories; Staton, Newton-a 3 6 9 14 20 26
11-"Flash Spectacular 1978"-(84 pgs.) Flash, Kid Flash, GA Flash & Johnny Quick vs. Grodd; Wood-i on Kid Flash chapter 2 4 6 13 18 22
12-"Secrets of Haunted House Special Spring 1978" 2 4 6 13 18 22
13-"Sgt. Rock Special Spring 1978", 50 pg new story 3 6 9 14 19 24
14,17,20-"Original Swamp Thing Saga", Wrightson-a: 14-Sum '78, r/#3,4. 17-Sum '79 r/#5-7. 20-Jan/Feb '80, r/#8-10 2 4 6 9 13 16
15-"Batman Spectacular Summer 1978", Ra's Al Ghul-app.; Golden-a. Rogers-a/front & back-c

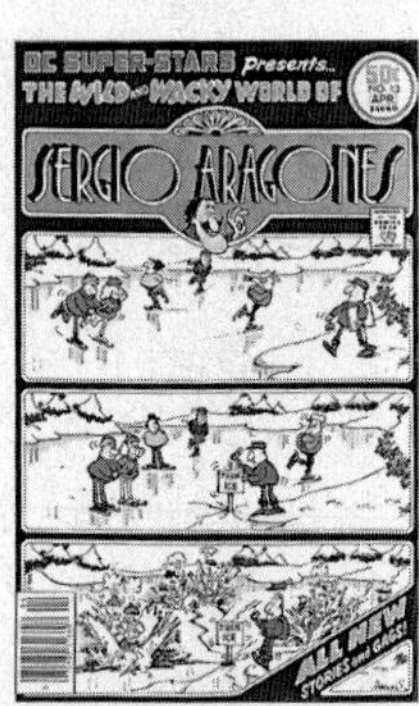

DC Super-Stars #13 © DC

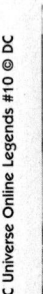

DC Universe Online Legends #10 © DC

DC Universe Presents #1 © DC

GD VG FN VF VF/NM NM-
2.0 4.0 6.0 8.0 9.0 9.2

3 6 9 21 32 42
16-"Jonah Hex Spectacular Fall 1978"; death of Jonah Hex, Heath-a; Bat Lash and Scalphunter stories 6 12 18 43 69 95
18,19-Digest size: 18-"Sgt. Rock's Prize Battle Tales Fall 1979". 19-"Secret Origins of Super-Heroes Fall 1979"; origins Wonder Woman (new-a),r/Robin, Batman-Superman team, Aquaman, Hawkman and others 2 4 6 13 18 22
21-"Super-Star Holiday Special Spring 1980", Frank Miller-a in "Batman--Wanted Dead or Alive" (1st Batman story); Jonah Hex, Sgt. Rock, Superboy & LSH and House of Mystery/ Witching Hour-c/stories 4 8 12 26 41 55
22-"G.I. Combat Sept. 1980", Kubert-c. Haunted Tank-s 3 6 9 14 19 24
23,24-Digest size: 23-World's Finest-r. 24-Flash 2 4 6 11 16 20
V5#25-($2.95)-"Superman II, the Adventure Continues Summer 1981"; photos from movie & photo-c (see All-New Coll. Ed. C-62) 3 6 9 14 19 24
26-($2.50)-"Superman and His Incredible Fortress of Solitude Summer 1981"
3 6 9 14 19 24
27-($2.50)-"Batman vs. The Incredible Hulk Fall 1981" 4 8 12 24 37 50
NOTE: ***Aparo*** *c-8.* ***Heath*** *a-12i, 16.* ***Infantino*** *a-19r.* ***Kirby*** *a-23, 19r.* ***Kubert*** *c-13, 19r.* ***Nasser/Netzer*** *a-1, 10i, 15.* ***Newton*** *a-10.* ***Nino*** *a-4, 7.* ***Starlin*** *c-12.* ***Staton*** *a-1.* ***Tuska*** *a-19r. #25 & 26. were advertised as All-New Collectors' Edition C-63, C-64. #26 was originally planned as All-New Collectors' Ed. C-30?; has C-630 & A.N.C.E. on cover.*

DC SPECIAL: THE RETURN OF DONNA TROY
DC Comics: Aug, 2005 - No. 4, Late Oct, 2005 ($2.99, limited series)
1-4-Jimenez-s/Garcia-Lopez-a(p)/Pérez-i 3.00

DC SUPER-STARS
National Periodical Publications/DC Comics: March, 1976 - No. 18, Winter, 1978 (No. 3-18: 52 pgs.)
1-(68 pgs.)-Re-intro Teen Titans (predates T. T. #44 (11/76); tryout iss.) plus r/Teen Titans; W.W. as girl was original Wonder Girl 3 6 9 20 30 40
2-7,9,11,12,16: 2,4,6,8-Adam Strange; 2-(68 pgs.)-r/1st Adam Strange/Hawkman team-up from Mystery in Space #90 plus Atomic Knights origin-r. 3-Legion issue. 4-r/Tales/Unexpected #45 2 4 6 8 11 14
8-r/1st Space Ranger from Showcase #15, Adam Strange-r/Mystery in Space #89 & Star Rovers-r/M.I.S. #80 2 4 6 9 13 16
10-Strange Sports Stories; Batman/Joker-c/story 2 4 6 10 14 18
13-Sergio Aragonés Special 3 6 9 16 22 28
14,15,18: 15-Sgt. Rock 2 4 6 9 13 16
17-Secret Origins of Super-Heroes (origin of The Huntress); origin Green Arrow by Grell; Legion app.; Earth II Batman & Catwoman marry (1st revealed; also see B&B #197 & Superman Family #211) 5 10 15 35 55 75
NOTE: ***M. Anderson*** *r-2, 4, 6.* ***Aparo*** *c-7, 14, 18.* ***Austin*** *a-11i.* ***Buckler*** *a-14p; c-10.* ***Grell*** *a-17.* ***G. Kane*** *a-1r, 10r.* ***Kubert*** *c-15.* ***Layton*** *c/a-16i, 17i.* ***Mooney*** *a-4r, 6r.* ***Morrow*** *c/a-11r.* ***Nasser*** *a-11.* ***Newton*** *c/a-16p.* ***Staton*** *a-17; c-17. No. 10, 12-18 contain all new material; the rest are reprints. #1 contains new and reprint material.*

DC: THE NEW FRONTIER (Also see Justice League: The New Frontier Special)
DC Comics: Mar, 2004 - No. 6, Nov, 2004 ($6.95, limited series)
1-6-DCU in the 1940s-60s; Darwyn Cooke-c/s/a in all. 1-Hal Jordan and The Losers app. 2-Origin Martian Manhunter; Barry Allen app. 3-Challengers of the Unknown 7.00
...Volume One (2004, $19.95, TPB) r/#1-3; cover gallery & intro. by Paul Levitz 20.00
...Volume Two (2005, $19.99, TPB) r/#4-6; cover gallery & afterword by Cooke 20.00

DC TOP COW CROSSOVERS
DC Comics/Top Cow Productions: 2007 ($14.99, TPB)
SC-r/The Darkness/Batman; JLA/Witchblade; The Darkness/Superman; JLA/Cyberforce 15.00

DC 2000
DC Comics: 2000 - No. 2, 2000 ($6.95, limited series)
1,2-JLA visit 1941 JSA; Semeiks-a 7.00

DCU BRAVE NEW WORLD (See Infinite Crisis and tie-ins)
DC Comics: Aug, 2006 ($1.00, 80 pgs., one-shot)
1-Previews 2006 series Martian Manhunter, OMAC, The Creeper, The All-New Atom, The Trials of Shazam, and Uncle Sam and the Freedom Fighters; the Monitor app. 4.00

DCU (Halloween and Christmas one-shot anthologies)
DC Comics
... Halloween Special '09 (12/09, $5.99) Ha-c; art from Bagley, Tucci, K. Jones, Nguyen 6.00
... Halloween Special 2010 (12/10, $4.99) Ha-c; art from Tucci, Garbett; I...Vampire app. 5.00
... Holiday Special (2/09, $5.99) Christmas by various incl. Dini, Maguire, Reis; Quitely-c 6.00
... Holiday Special 2010 (2/11, $4.99) Jonah Hex, Spectre, Legion of S.H., Anthro app. 5.00
... Infinite Halloween Special (12/08, $5.99) Ralph & Sue Dibny app.; Gene Ha-c 6.00
... Infinite Holiday Special (2/07, $4.99) by various; Batwoman app.; Porter-c 5.00

DCU HEROES SECRET FILES
DC Comics: Feb, 1999 ($4.95, one-shot)
1-Origin-s and pin-ups; new Star Spangled Kid app. 5.00

DCU: LEGACIES
DC Comics: Jul, 2010 - No. 10, Apr, 2011 ($3.99, limited series)

GD VG FN VF VF/NM NM-
2.0 4.0 6.0 8.0 9.0 9.2

1-10: 1,2-Andy Kubert-c; JSA app.; two covers on each. 3-JLA app.; Garcia-Lopez-a. 4-Sgt. Rock back-up; Joe Kubert-a. 5-Pérez-a. 8-Back-up Quitely-a 4.00

DC UNIVERSE CHRISTMAS, A
DC Comics: 2000 ($19.95)
TPB-Reprints DC Christmas stories by various 20.00

DC UNIVERSE: DECISIONS
DC Comics: Early Nov, 2008 - No. 4, Late Dec, 2008 ($2.99, limited series)
1-4-Assassination plot in the Presidential election; Winick & Willingham-s/Porter-a 3.00

DC UNIVERSE HOLIDAY BASH
DC Comics: 1997- 1999 ($3.95)
I,II-(X-mas '96,'97) Christmas stories by various 5.00
III (1999, for Christmas '98, $4.95) 5.00

DC UNIVERSE ILLUSTRATED BY NEAL ADAMS (Also see Batman Illustrated by Neal Adams HC Vol. 1-3)
DC Comics: 2008 ($39.99, hardcover with dustjacket)
Vol. 1 - Reprints Adams' non-Batman/non-Green Lantern work from 1967-1972; incl. Teen Titans, DC war, Enemy Ace, Superman and PSAs; promo art; Levitz foreword 40.00

DC UNIVERSE: LAST WILL AND TESTAMENT
DC Comics: Oct, 2008 ($3.99, one-shot)
1-Geo-Force vs. Deathstroke; DC heroes prepare for Final Crisis; Brad Meltzer-s; Adam Kubert & Joe Kubert-a; two covers 4.00

DC UNIVERSE ONLINE LEGENDS (Based on the online game)
DC Comics: Early Apr. 2011 - Late May, 2012 ($2.99)
1-26: 1-Wolfman & Bedard-s/Porter-a; DC heroes & Luthor vs. Brainiac. 1-Wraparound-c 3.00

DC UNIVERSE: ORIGINS
DC Comics: 2009 ($14.99, TPB)
nn-Reprints 2-page origins of DC characters from back-ups in 52, Countdown and Justice League: Cry For Justice #1-3; s/a by various; Alex Ross-c 15.00

DC UNIVERSE PRESENTS (DC New 52)
DC Comics: Nov, 2011 - Present ($2.99)
1-5-Deadman. 1-Deadman origin re-told; Jenkins-s/Chang-a/Sook-c 3.00
6,7-Challengers of the Unknown; DiDio-s/Ordway-a/Sook-c 3.00

DC UNIVERSE SPECIAL
DC Comics: July, 2008 - Aug, 2008 ($4.99, collection of reprints related to Final Crisis)
...: Justice League of America (7/08) r/J.L. of A. #111,166-168 & Detective #274; Sook-c 5.00
...: Reign in Hell (8/08) r/Blaze/Satanus War x-over; Sook-c 5.00
...: Superman (7/08) r/Mongul app. in Superman #32, Showcase '95 #7,8, Flash #102 5.00

DC UNIVERSE: THE STORIES OF ALAN MOORE (Also see Across the Universe:...)
DC Comics: 2006 ($19.99)
TPB-Reprints Batman: The Killing Joke, "Whatever Happened to the Man of Tomorrow", "For The Man Who Has Everything, and other classic Moore DC stories; Bolland-c 20.00

DC UNIVERSE: TRINITY
DC Comics: Aug, 1993 - No. 2, Sept, 1993 ($2.95, 52 pgs, limited series)
1,2-Foil-c; Green Lantern, Darkstars, Legion app. 4.00

DCU VILLAINS SECRET FILES
DC Comics: Apr, 1999 ($4.95, one-shot)
1-Origin-s and profile pages 5.00

DC VERSUS MARVEL (See Marvel Versus DC) (Also see Amazon, Assassins, Bruce Wayne: Agent of S.H.I. E. L.D., Bullets & Bracelets, Doctor Strangefate, JLX, Legend of the Dark Claw, Magneto & The Magnetic Men, Speed Demon, Spider-Boy, Super Soldier, X-Patrol)
DC Comics: No. 1, 1996, No. 4, 1996 ($3.95, limited series)
1,4: 1-Marz script, Jurgens-a(p); 1st app. of Access. 4.00
.../Marvel Versus DC ($12.95, trade paperback) r/1-4 13.00

DC/WILDSTORM DREAMWAR
DC Comics: Jun, 2008 - No. 6, Nov, 2008 ($2.99, limited series)
1-6-Giffen-s; Silver Age JLA, Teen Titans, JSA, Legion app. on WildStorm Earth 3.00
1-Variant-c of Superman & Midnighter by Garbett 6.00
TPB (2009, $19.99) r/series 20.00

DC: WORLD WAR III (See 52/WWIII)

D-DAY (Also see Special War Series)
Charlton Comics (no No. 3): Sum/63; No. 2, Fall/64; No. 4, 9/66; No. 5, 10/67; No. 6, 11/68
1,2: 1(1963)-Montes/Bache-c. 2(Fall '64)-Wood-a(4) 4 8 12 22 34 45
4-6('66-'68)-Montes/Bache-a #5 3 6 9 14 20 25

DEAD AIR

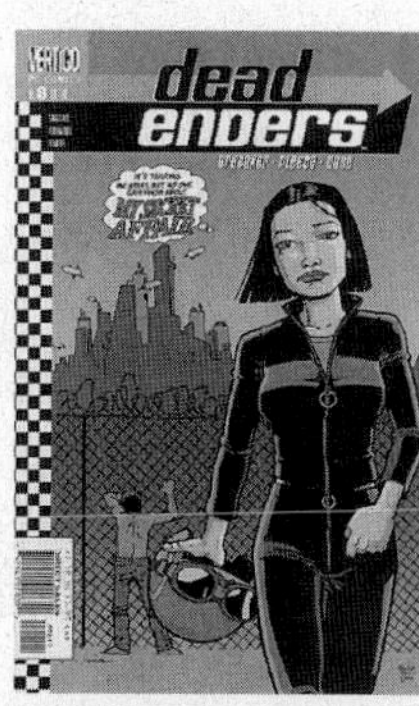
Dead Enders #8 © Brubaker & Pleece

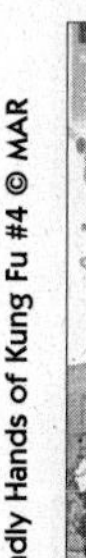
Deadly Hands of Kung Fu #4 © MAR

Deadman Book One TPB © DC

GD 2.0 | VG 4.0 | FN 6.0 | VF 8.0 | VF/NM 9.0 | NM- 9.2

Slave Labor Graphics: July, 1989 ($5.95, graphic novel)
nn-Mike Allred's 1st published work 6.00

DEAD CORPSE
DC Comics (Helix): Sept, 1998 - No. 4, Dec, 1998 ($2.50, limited series)
1-4-Pugh-a/Hinz-s 3.00

DEAD END CRIME STORIES
Kirby Publishing Co.: April, 1949 (52 pgs.)
nn-(Scarce)-Powell, Roussos-a; painted-c 53 106 159 334 567 800

DEAD ENDERS
DC Comics (Vertigo): Mar, 2000 - No. 16, June, 2001 ($2.50)
1-16-Brubaker-s/Pleece & Case-a 3.00
Stealing the Sun (2000, $9.95, TPB) r/#1-4, Vertigo Winter's Edge #3 10.00

DEAD-EYE WESTERN COMICS
Hillman Periodicals: Nov-Dec, 1948 - V3#1, Apr-May, 1953
V1#1-(52 pgs.)-Krigstein, Roussos-a 20 40 60 114 182 250
V1#2,3-(52 pgs.) 12 24 36 69 97 125
V1#4-12-(52 pgs.) 9 18 27 47 61 75
V2#1,2,5-8,10-12: 1-7-(52 pgs.) 8 16 24 40 50 60
3,4-Krigstein-a 8 16 24 44 57 70
9-One pg. Frazetta ad 8 16 24 40 50 60
V3#1 8 16 24 40 50 60
NOTE: *Briefer a-V1#8. Kinstleresque stories by* ***McCann****-12, V2#1, 2, V3#1.* ***McWilliams*** *a-V1#5.* ***Ed Moore*** *a-V1#4.*

DEADFACE: DOING THE ISLANDS WITH BACCHUS
Dark Horse Comics: July, 1991 - No. 3, Sept, 1991 ($2.95, B&W, lim. series)
1-3: By Eddie Campbell 3.00

DEADFACE: EARTH, WATER, AIR, AND FIRE
Dark Horse Comics: July, 1992 - No. 4, Oct, 1992 ($2.50, B&W, limited series; British-r)
1-4: By Eddie Campbell 3.00

DEAD IN THE WEST
Dark Horse Comics: Oct, 1993 - No. 2, Mar, 1994 ($3.95, B&W, 52 pgs.)
1,2-Timothy Truman-c 4.00

DEAD IRONS
Dynamite Entertainment: 2009 - No. 4, 2009 ($3.99)
1-4-Kuhoric-s/Alexander-a/Jae Lee-c 4.00

DEADLANDER (Becomes Dead Rider for #2)
Dark Horse Comics: Oct, 2007 - No. 4, ($2.99, limited series)
1-2-Kevin Ferrara-s/a 3.00

DEADLANDS (Old West role playing game)
Image Comics: Jul, 2011; Aug, 2011; Jan, 2012 ($2.99, one-shots)
...: Black Water (1/12) Mariotte-s/Brook Turner-a 3.00
...: Death Was Silent (8/11) Marz-s/Sears-a/c 3.00
...: Massacre at Red Wing (7/11) Palmiotti & Gray-s/Moder-a/c 3.00

DEADLIEST HEROES OF KUNG FU (Magazine)
Marvel Comics Group: Summer, 1975 (B&W)(76 pgs.)
1-Bruce Lee vs. Carradine painted-c; TV Kung Fu, 4pgs. photos/article; Enter the Dragon, 24 pgs. photos/article w/ Bruce Lee; Bruce Lee photo pinup 4 8 12 28 44 60

DEADLINE
Marvel Comics: June, 2002 - No. 4, Sept, 2002 ($2.99, limited series)
1-4: 1-Intro. Kat Farrell; Bill Rosemann-s/Guy Davis-a; Horn painted-c 3.00
TPB (2002. $9.99) r/#1-4 10.00

DEADLY DUO, THE
Image Comics (Highbrow Entertainment): Nov, 1994 - No. 3, Jan, 1995 ($2.50, lim. series)
1-3: 1-1st app. of Kill Cat 3.00

DEADLY DUO, THE
Image Comics (Highbrow Entertainment): June, 1995 - No. 4, Oct, 1995 ($2.50, lim. series)
1-4: 1-Spawn app. 2-Savage Dragon app. 3-Gen 13 app. 3.00

DEADLY FOES OF SPIDER-MAN (See Lethal Foes of...)
Marvel Comics: May, 1991 - No. 4, Aug, 1991 ($1.00, limited series)
1-4: 1-Punisher, Kingpin, Rhino app. 3.00

DEADLY HANDS OF KUNG FU, THE (See Master of Kung Fu)
Marvel Comics Group: April, 1974 - No. 33, Feb, 1977 (75¢) (B&W, magazine)
1(V1#4 listed in error)-Origin Sons of the Tiger; Shang-Chi, Master of Kung Fu begins (ties w/Master of Kung Fu #17 as 3rd app. Shang-Chi); Bruce Lee painted-c by Neal Adams; 2pg. memorial photo pinup w/8 pgs. photos/articles; TV Kung Fu, 9 pgs. photos/articles; 15 pgs. Starlin-a 6 12 18 37 59 80
2-Adams painted-c; 1st time origin of Shang-Chi, 34 pgs. by Starlin. TV Kung Fu, 6 pgs. photos & article w/2 pg. pinup. Bruce Lee, 11 pgs. ph/a 4 8 12 28 44 60
3,4,7,10: 3-Adams painted-c; Gulacy-a. Enter the Dragon, photos/articles, 8 pgs. 4-TV Kung Fu painted-c by Neal Adams; TV Kung Fu 7 pg. article/art; Fu Manchu; Enter the Dragon, 10 pg. photos/article w/Bruce Lee. 7-Bruce Lee painted-c & 9 pgs. photos/articles-Return of Dragon plus 1 pg. photo pinup. 10-(3/75)-Iron Fist painted-c & 34 pg. sty-Early app. 3 6 9 20 30 40
5,6: 5-1st app. Manchurian, 6 pgs. Gulacy-a. TV Kung Fu, 4 pg. article; reprints books w/Barry Smith-a. Capt. America-sty, 10 pgs. Kirby-a(r). 6-Bruce Lee photos/article, 6 pgs.; 15 pgs. early Perez-a 3 6 9 19 29 38
8,9,11: 9-Iron Fist, 2 pg. Preview pinup; Nebres-a. 11-Billy Jack painted-c by Adams; 17 pgs. photos/article 3 6 9 18 27 35
12,13: 12-James Bond painted-c by Adams; 14 pg. photos/article. 13-16 pgs. early Perez-a; Piers Anthony, 7 pgs. photos/article 3 6 9 17 25 32
14-Classic Bruce Lee painted-c by Adams. Lee pinup by Chaykin. Lee 16 pg. photos/article w/2 pgs. Green Hornet TV 6 12 18 42 69 95
15,19: 15-Sum, '75 Giant Annual #1. 20pgs. Starlin-a. Bruce Lee photo pinup & 3 pg. photos/article re book; Man-Thing app. Iron Fist-c/sty; Gulacy-a 18pgs. 19-Iron Fist painted-c & series begins; 1st White Tiger 3 6 9 18 27 35
16,18,20: 16-1st app. Corpse Rider, a Samurai w/Sanho Kim-a. 20-Chuck Norris painted-c & 16 pgs. interview w/photos/article; Bruce Lee vs. C. Norris pinup by Ken Barr. Origin The White Tiger, Perez-a 3 6 9 16 23 30
17-Bruce Lee painted-c by Adams; interview w/R. Clouse, director Enter Dragon 7 pgs. w/B. Lee app. 1st Giffen-a (1pg. 11/75) 4 8 12 28 44 60
21-Bruce Lee 1pg. photos/article 3 6 9 16 23 30
22,30-32: 22-1st brief app. Jack of Hearts. 1st Giffen sty-a (along w/Amazing Adv. #35, 3/76). 30-Swordquest-c/sty & conclusion; Jack of Hearts app. 31-Jack of Hearts app; Staton-a. 32-1st Daughters of the Dragon-c/sty, 21 pgs. M. Rogers-a/Claremont-sty; Iron Fist pinup 3 6 9 16 22 28
23-26,29: 23-1st full app. Jack of Hearts. 24-Iron Fist-c & centerfold pinup. early Zeck-a; Shang Chi pinup; 6 pgs. Piers Anthony text sty w/Perez/Austin-a; Jack of Hearts app. early Giffen-a. 25-1st app. Shimuru, "Samurai", 20 pgs. Mantlo-sty/Broderick-a; "Swordquest"-c & begins 17 pg. sty by Sanho Kim; 11 pg. photos/article; partly Bruce Lee. 26-Bruce Lee painted-c & pinup; 16 pgs. interviews w/Kwon & Clouse; talk about Bruce Lee re-filming of Lee legend. 29-Ironfist vs. Shang Chi battle-c/sty; Jack of Hearts app. 3 6 9 18 27 35
27 3 6 9 14 20 26
28-All Bruce Lee Special Issue; (1st time in comics). Bruce Lee painted-c by Ken Barr & pinup. 36 pgs. comics chronicaling Bruce Lee's life; 15 pgs. B. Lee photos/article (Rare in high grade) 8 16 24 51 86 120
33-Shang Chi-c/sty; Classic Daughters of the Dragon, 21 pgs. M. Rogers-a/Claremont-story with nudity; Bob Wall interview, photos/article, 14 pgs. 3 6 9 20 30 40
...Special Album Edition 1(Summer, '74)-Iron Fist-c/story (early app., 3rd?); 10 pgs. Adams-i; Shang Chi/Fu Manchu, 10 pgs.; Sons of Tiger, 11 pgs.; TV Kung Fu, 6 pgs. photos/article 4 8 12 22 34 45
NOTE: ***Bruce Lee:*** *1-7, 14, 15, 17, 25, 26, 28.* ***Kung Fu (TV):*** *1, 2, 4.* ***Jack of Hearts:*** *22, 23, 29-33.* ***Shang Chi Master of Kung Fu:*** *1-9, 11-18, 29, 31, 33.* ***Sons of Tiger:*** *1, 3, 4, 6-14, 16-19.* ***Swordquest:*** *25-27, 29-33.* ***White Tiger:*** *19-24, 26, 27, 29-33.* ***N. Adams*** *a-1i(part), 27i; c-1, 2-4, 11, 12, 14, 17.* ***Giffen*** *a-22p, 24p.* ***G. Kane*** *a-23p.* ***Kirby*** *a-5r.* ***Nasser*** *a-27p, 28.* ***Perez*** *a(p)-6-14, 16, 17, 19, 21.* ***Rogers*** *a-26, 32, 33.* ***Starlin*** *a-1, 2r, 15r.* ***Staton*** *a-28p, 31, 32.*

DEADMAN (See The Brave and the Bold & Phantom Stranger #39)
DC Comics: May, 1985 - No. 7, Nov, 1985 ($1.75, Baxter paper)
1-7: 1-Deadman-r by Infantino, N. Adams in all. 5-Batman-c/story-r/Strange Adventures. 7-Batman-r 3.00
... Book One TPB (2011, $19.99) r/apps. in Strange Adventures #205-213 20.00

DEADMAN
DC Comics: Mar, 1986 - No. 4, June, 1986 (75¢, limited series)
1-4: Lopez-c/a. 4-Byrne-c(p) 3.00

DEADMAN
DC Comics: Feb, 2002 - No. 9, Oct, 2002 ($2.50)
1-9: 1-4-Vance-s/Beroy-a. 3,4-Mignola-c. 5,6-Garcia-Lopez-a 3.00

DEADMAN
DC Comics (Vertigo): Oct, 2006 - No. 13, Oct, 2007 ($2.99)
1-13: 1-Bruce Jones-s/John Watkiss-a/c; intro Brandon Cayce 3.00
...: Deadman Walking TPB (2007, $9.99) r/#1-5 10.00

DEADMAN: DEAD AGAIN (Leads into 2002 series)
DC Comics: Oct, 2001 - No. 5, Oct, 2001 ($2.50, weekly limited series)

Deadpool #55 © MAR

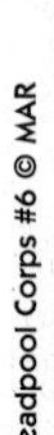
Deadpool Corps #6 © MAR

Deadshot #2 © DC

	GD 2.0	VG 4.0	FN 6.0	VF 8.0	VF/NM 9.0	NM- 9.2

1-5: Deadman at the deaths of the Flash, Robin, Superman, Hal Jordan 3.00

DEADMAN: EXORCISM
DC Comics: 1992 - No. 2, 1992 ($4.95, limited series, 52 pgs.)

1,2: Kelley Jones-c/a in both 5.00

DEADMAN: LOVE AFTER DEATH
DC Comics: 1989 - No. 2, 1990 ($3.95, 52 pgs., limited series, mature)

Book One, Two: Kelley Jones-c/a in both. 1-contains nudity 4.00

DEAD MAN'S RUN
Aspen MLT: No. 0, Dec, 2011 - Present ($2.50/$3.50)

0-($2.50) Greg Pak-s/Tony Parker-a; 3 covers; bonus design sketch art 2.50
1-(2/12, $3.50) Greg Pak-s/Tony Parker-a; 2 covers 3.50

DEAD OF NIGHT
Marvel Comics Group: Dec, 1973 - No. 11, Aug, 1975

	GD	VG	FN	VF	VF/NM	NM-
1-Horror reprints	3	6	9	20	30	40
2-10: 10-Kirby-a. 6-Jack the Ripper-c/s	3	6	9	14	20	25
11-Intro Scarecrow; Kane/Wrightson-c	4	8	12	22	34	45

NOTE: *Ditko r-7, 10. Everett c-2. Sinnott r-1.*

DEAD OF NIGHT FEATURING DEVIL-SLAYER
Marvel Comics (MAX): Nov, 2008 - No. 4, Feb, 2009 ($3.99, limited series)

1-4-Keene-s/Samnee-a/Andrews-c 4.00

DEAD OF NIGHT FEATURING MAN-THING
Marvel Comics (MAX): Apr, 2008 - No. 4, July, 2008 ($3.99, limited series)

1-4: 1-Man-Thing origin re-told; Kano-a. 2-4-Jennifer Kale app. 4.00

DEAD OF NIGHT FEATURING WEREWOLF BY NIGHT
Marvel Comics (MAX): Mar, 2009 - No. 4, Jun, 2009 ($3.99, limited series)

1-4: 1-Werewolf By Night origin re-told; Swierczynski-s/Suayan-a 4.00

DEAD OR ALIVE - A CYBERPUNK WESTERN
Image Comics (Shok Studio): Apr, 1998 - No. 4, July, 1998 ($2.50, limited series)

1-4 3.00

DEADPOOL (See New Mutants #98 for 1st app.)
Marvel Comics: Aug, 1994 - No. 4, Nov, 1994 ($2.50, limited series)

1-4: Mark Waid's 1st Marvel work; Ian Churchill-c/a 4.00

DEADPOOL (... : Agent of Weapon X on cover #57-60) (title becomes Agent X)
Marvel Comics: Jan, 1997 - No. 69, Sept, 2002 ($2.95/$1.95/$1.99)

	GD	VG	FN	VF	VF/NM	NM-
1-($2.95)-Wraparound-c	1	2	3	4	5	7

2-Begin-$1.95-c. 5.00
3-10,12-22,24: 4-Hulk-c/app. 12-Variant-c. 14-Begin McDaniel-a. 22-Cable app. 5.00
11-($3.99)-Deadpool replaces Spider-Man from Amazing Spider-Man #47; Kraven, Gwen Stacy app. 6.00
23,25-($2.99); 23-Dead Reckoning pt. 1; wraparound-c 4.00
26-40: 27-Wolverine-c/app. 37-Thor app. 3.00
41-53,56-60: 41-Begin $2.25-c. 44-Black Panther-c/app. 46-49-Chadwick-a 51-Cover swipe of Detective #38. 57-60-BWS-c 3.00
54,55-Punisher-c/app. 54-Dillon-c. 55-Bradstreet-c 3.00
61-69: 61-64-Funeral For a Freak on cover. 65-69-Udon Studios-a. 67-Dazzler-c/app. 3.00
#(-1) Flashback (7/97) Lopresti-a; Wade Wilson's early days 3.00
.../Death '98 Annual ($2.99) Kelly-s, ... Team-Up (12/98, $2.99) Widdle Wade-c/app., Baby's First Deadpool Book (12/98, $2.99), Encyclopædia Deadpoolica (12/98, $2.99) Synopses 4.00
.../GLI - Summer Fun Spectacular #1 (9/07, $3.99) short stories; Pelletier-c 4.00
... Classic Vol. 1 TPB (2008, $29.99) r/#1, New Mutants #98, Deadpool: The Circle Chase #1-4 and Deadpool (1994 series) #1-4 30.00
Mission Improbable TPB (9/98, $14.95) r/#1-5 15.00
Wizard #0 ('98, bagged with Wizard #87) 3.00

DEADPOOL
Marvel Comics: Nov, 2008 - Present ($3.99/$2.99)

1-($3.99) Medina-a; Secret Invasion x-over; 2 covers by Crain & Liefeld 4.00
2-24,26-33, 33.1,34-49-($2.99) Variant covers for most. 4-20-Pearson-c. 8,9-Thunderbolts x-over. 10-Dark Reign. 16-18-X-Men app. 19-21-Spider-Man & Hit-Monkey app. 26-Ghost Rider app. 27-29-Secret Avengers app. 30,31-Curse of the Mutants. 37-39-Hulk app. 3.00
25-($3.99) 3-D cover, fake 3-D glasses on back-c; back-up story w/Bond-a 4.00
49.1, 51-($2.99) 49-McCrea-a. 51-Garza-a 3.00
50-($3.99) Uncanny X-Force & Kingpin app.; Barberi-a 4.00
900-(12/09, $4.99) Stories by various incl. Liefeld, Baker; wraparound-c by Johnson 5.00
1000-(10/10, $4.99) Stories by various; gallery of variant covers; Johnson-c 5.00
Annual 1 (7/11, $3.99) "Identity Wars" crossover; Spider-Man & Hulk app. 4.00
... & Cable #26 (4/11, $3.99) Swierczynski-s/Fernandez-a 4.00
... Family 1 (6/11, $3.99) short stories by various; Pearson-c 4.00
...: Games of Death 1 (5/09, $3.99) Benson-s/Crystal-a/Land-c 4.00
... MCG (7/10, $1.00) r/#1 with "Marvel's Greatest Comics" logo on cover 3.00

DEADPOOL CORPS (Continues from Prelude to Deadpool Corps series)
Marvel Comics: Jun, 2010 - No. 12, May, 2011 ($3.99/$2.99)

1-($3.99) Liefeld-a/c; Gischler-s; 2 covers by Liefeld 4.00
2-12-($2.99) 2-5,7,9-Liefeld-a. 6-Mychaels-a 3.00
...: Rank and Foul 1 (5/10, $3.99) Handbook-style profile pages of allies and enemies 4.00

DEADPOOL MAX
Marvel Comics (MAX): Dec, 2010 - No. 12, Nov, 2011 ($3.99)

1-12: 1-8,10-12-David Lapham-s/Kyle Baker-a/c. 6,7-Domino app. 9-Crystal-a 4.00
... X-Mas Special 1 (2/12, $4.99) Lapham-s; art by Lapham, Baker & Crystal; Baker-c 5.00

DEADPOOL MAX 2
Marvel Comics (MAX): Dec, 2011 - Present ($3.99)

1-5: 1,2-David Lapham-s/Kyle Baker-a/c. 3-Crystal-a 4.00

DEADPOOL: MERC WITH A MOUTH
Marvel Comics: Sept, 2009 - No. 13, Sept, 2010 ($3.99/$2.99)

1-($3.99) Suydam-c/Dazo-a; Zombie-head Deadpool & Ka-Zar app.; r/Deadpool #4 ('97) 4.00
2-6,8-12-($2.99) Suydam-c on all. 8-Deadpool goes to Zombie dimension 3.00
7-13-($3.99) 7-Covers by Suydam & Liefeld; art by Liefeld, Baker, Pastoras, Dazo 4.00

DEADPOOL PULP
Marvel Comics: Nov, 2010 - No. 4, Feb, 2011 ($3.99, limited series)

1-4-Alternate Deadpool in 1955; Glass & Benson-s/Laurence Campbell-a/Jae Lee-c 4.00

DEADPOOL: SUICIDE KINGS
Marvel Comics: Jun, 2009 - No. 5, Oct, 2009 ($3.99, limited series)

1-5-Barberi-a; Punisher, Daredevil, & Spider-Man app. 4.00

DEADPOOL TEAM-UP
Marvel Comics: No. 899, Jan, 2010 - No. 883, May, 2011 ($2.99, numbering runs in reverse)

899-883: 899-Hercules app.; Ramos-c. 897-Ghost Rider app. 894-Franken-Castle app. 887-Thor app. 883-Galactus & Silver Surfer app. 3.00

DEADPOOL: THE CIRCLE CHASE (See New Mutants #98)
Marvel Comics: Aug, 1993 - No. 4, Nov, 1993 ($2.00, limited series)

1-($2.50)-Embossed-c 6.00
2-4 4.00

DEADPOOL: WADE WILSON'S WAR
Marvel Comics: Aug, 2010 - No. 4, Nov, 2010 ($3.99, limited series)

1-4-Swierczynski-s/Pearson-a/c; Bullseye, Domino & Silver Sable app. 4.00

DEAD RIDER (See Deadlander)

DEAD RISING: ROAD TO FORTUNE (Based on the CAPCOM videogame)
IDW Publishing: Oct, 2011 - Present ($3.99, limited series)

1-2-Tom Waltz-s/Kenneth Loh-a 3.00

DEAD ROMEO
DC Comics: June, 2009 - No. 6, Nov, 2009 ($2.99, limited series)

1-6-Ryan Benjamin-a/Jesse Snider-s 3.00
TPB (2010, $19.99) r/#1-6; cover gallery 20.00

DEAD, SHE SAID
IDW Publishing: May, 2008 - No. 3, Sept, 2008 ($3.99, limited series)

1-3-Bernie Wrightson-a/Steve Niles-s 4.00

DEADSHOT (See Batman #59, Detective Comics #474, & Showcase '93 #8)
DC Comics: Nov, 1988 - No. 4, Feb, 1989 ($1.00, limited series)

1-4 3.00

DEADSHOT
DC Comics: Feb, 2005 - No. 5, June 2005 ($2.95, limited series)

1-5-Zeck-c/Gage-s/Cummings-a. 3-Green Arrow app. 3.00

DEAD SPACE (Based on the Electronics Arts videogame)
Image Comics: Mar, 2008 - No. 6, Sept, 2008 ($2.99, limited series)

1-6-Templesmith-a/Johnston-s 3.00
... Extraction (9/09, $3.50) Templesmith-a/Johnston-s 3.50

DEAD WHO WALK, THE (See Strange Mysteries, Super Reprint #15, 16)
Realistic Comics: 1952 (one-shot)

	GD	VG	FN	VF	VF/NM	NM-
nn	55	110	165	348	594	840

DEADWORLD (Also see The Realm)
Arrow Comics/Caliber Comics: Dec, 1986 - No. 26 ($1.50/$1.95/#15-28: $2.50, B&W)

Deathblow #7 © WSP

Death Jr. #1 © Backbone Ent.

Deathlok (1999 series) #1 © MAR

	GD 2.0	VG 4.0	FN 6.0	VF 8.0	VF/NM 9.0	NM- 9.2
1-4						4.00
5-26-Graphic cover version						4.00
5-26-Tame cover version						3.00
...Archives 1-3 (1992, $2.50)						3.00

DEAN MARTIN & JERRY LEWIS (See Adventures of...)

DEAR BEATRICE FAIRFAX
Best/Standard Comics (King Features): No. 5, Nov, 1950 - No. 9, Sept, 1951 (Vern Greene art)

	GD 2.0	VG 4.0	FN 6.0	VF 8.0	VF/NM 9.0	NM- 9.2
5-All have Schomburg air brush-c	14	28	42	80	115	150
6-9	10	20	30	58	79	100

DEAR HEART (Formerly Lonely Heart)
Ajax: No. 15, July, 1956 - No. 16, Sept, 1956

	GD 2.0	VG 4.0	FN 6.0	VF 8.0	VF/NM 9.0	NM- 9.2
15,16	8	16	24	42	54	65

DEAR LONELY HEART (...Illustrated No. 1-6)
Artful Publications: Mar, 1951; No. 2, Oct, 1951 - No. 8, Oct, 1952

	GD 2.0	VG 4.0	FN 6.0	VF 8.0	VF/NM 9.0	NM- 9.2
1	18	36	54	103	162	220
2	10	20	30	56	76	95
3-Matt Baker Jungle Girl story	20	40	60	117	189	260
4-8	9	18	27	52	69	85

DEAR LONELY HEARTS (Lonely Heart #9 on)
Harwell Publ./Mystery Publ. Co. (Comic Media): Aug, 1953 -No. 8, Oct, 1954

	GD 2.0	VG 4.0	FN 6.0	VF 8.0	VF/NM 9.0	NM- 9.2
1	14	28	42	80	115	150
2-8	10	20	30	58	79	100

DEARLY BELOVED
Ziff-Davis Publishing Co.: Fall, 1952

	GD 2.0	VG 4.0	FN 6.0	VF 8.0	VF/NM 9.0	NM- 9.2
1-Photo-c	18	36	54	105	165	225

DEAR NANCY PARKER
Gold Key: June, 1963 - No. 2, Sept, 1963

	GD 2.0	VG 4.0	FN 6.0	VF 8.0	VF/NM 9.0	NM- 9.2
1-Painted-c on both	4	8	12	23	36	48
2	3	6	9	17	25	32

DEATH, THE ABSOLUTE... (From Neil Gaiman's Sandman titles)
DC Comics (Vertigo): 2009 ($99.99, oversized hardcover in slipcase)

nn-Reprints 1st app. in Sandman #8, Sandman #20, Death: The High Cost of Living #1-3, Death: the Time of Your Life #1-3, Death Talks About Life; short stories and pin-ups; merchandise pics; script and sketch art for Sandman #8; Gaiman afterword 100.00

DEATH: AT DEATH'S DOOR (See Sandman: The Season of Mists)
DC Comics (Vertigo): 2003 ($9.95, graphic novel one-shot, B&W, 7-1/2" x 5")

1-Jill Thompson-s/a/c; manga-style; Morpheus and the Endless app. 10.00

DEATHBLOW (Also see Batman/Deathblow and Darker Image)
Image Comics (WildStorm Productions): May (Apr. inside), 1993 - No. 29, Aug, 1996 ($1.75/$1.95/$2.50)

0-(8/96, $2.95, 32 pgs.)-r/Darker Image w/new story & art; Jim Lee & Trevor Scott-a; new Jim Lee-c 3.00
1-($2.50)-Red foil stamped logo on black varnish-c; Jim Lee-c/a; flip-book side has Cybernary -c/story (#2 also) 4.00
1-($1.95)-Newsstand version w/o foil-c & varnish 3.00
2-29: 2-(8/93)-Lee-a; with bound-in poster. 2-($1.75)-Newsstand version w/o poster. 4-Jim Lee-c/Tim Sale-a begin. 13-W/pinup poster by Tim Sale & Jim Lee. 16-($1.95 Newsstand & $2.50 Direct Market editions)-Wildstorm Rising Pt. 6. 17-Variant "Chicago Comicon" edition exists. 20,21-Gen 13 app. 23-Backlash-c/app. 24,25-Grifter-c/app; Gen 13 & Dane from Wetworks app. 28-Deathblow dies. 29-Memorial issue 3.00
5-Alternate Portacio-c (Forms larger picture when combined with alternate-c for Gen 13 #5, Kindred #3, Stormwatch #10, Team 7 #1, Union #0, Wetworks #2 & WildC.A.T.S #11) 6.00
...:Sinners and Saints TPB ('99, $19.95) r/#1-12; Sale-c 20.00

DEATHBLOW (Volume 2)
DC Comics (WildStorm): Dec, 2006 - No. 9, Apr, 2008 ($2.99)

1-9: 1-Azzarello-s/D'Anda-a; two covers by D'Anda & Platt 3.00
...: And Then You Live! TPB (2008, $19.99) r/#1-9 20.00

DEATHBLOW BY BLOWS
DC Comics (WildStorm): Nov, 1999 - No. 3, Jan, 2000 ($2.95, limited series)

1-3-Alan Moore-s/Jim Baikie-a 3.00

DEATHBLOW/WOLVERINE
Image Comics (WildStorm Productions)/ Marvel Comics: Sept, 1996 - No. 2, Feb, 1997 ($2.50, limited series)

1,2: Wiesenfeld-s/Bennett-a 3.00

TPB (1997, $8.95) r/#1,2 9.00

DEATHDEALER (Also see Frank Frazetta's...)
Verotik: July, 1995 - No. 4, July, 1997 ($5.95)

	GD 2.0	VG 4.0	FN 6.0	VF 8.0	VF/NM 9.0	NM- 9.2
1-Frazetta-c; Bisley-a	1	2	3	5	6	8
1-2nd print, 2-4-($6.95)-Frazetta-c; embossed logo	1	2	3	4	5	7

DEATH-DEFYING 'DEVIL, THE (Also see Project Superpowers)
Dynamite Entertainment: 2008 - No. 4, 2009 ($3.50, limited series)

1-4-Casey & Ross-s/Salazar-a; multiple covers; the Dragon app. 3.50

DEATH, JR.
Image Comics: Apr, 2005 - No. 3, Aug, 2005 ($4.99, squarebound, limited series)

1-3-Gary Whitta-s/Ted Naifeh-a 5.00
Vol. 1 TPB (2005, $14.99) r/series; concept and promotional art 15.00

DEATH, JR. (Volume 2)
Image Comics: Jul, 2006 - No. 3, May, 2007 ($4.99, squarebound, limited series)

1-3-Gary Whitta-s/Ted Naifeh-a. 1-Dan Brereton-c 5.00
Vol. 2 TPB (2007, $14.99) r/series; Halloween story w/Guy Davis-a; promotional art 15.00

DEATHLOK (Also see Astonishing Tales #25)
Marvel Comics: July, 1990 - No. 4, Oct, 1990 ($3.95, limited series, 52 pgs.)

1-4: 1,2-Guice-a(p). 3,4-Denys Cowan-a, c-4 4.00

DEATHLOK
Marvel Comics: July, 1991 - No. 34, Apr, 1994 ($1.75)

1-Silver ink cover; Denys Cowan-c/a(p) begins 3.50
2-18,20-24,26-34: 2-Forge (X-Men) app. 3-Vs. Dr. Doom. 5-X-Men & F.F. x-over. 6,7-Punisher x-over. 9,10-Ghost Rider-c/story. 16-Infinity War x-over. 17-Jae Lee-c. 22-Black Panther app. 27-Siege app. 3.00
19-($2.25)-Foil-c 4.00
25-($2.95, 52 pgs.)-Holo-grafx foil-c 4.00
Annual 1 (1992, $2.25, 68 pgs.)-Guice-p; Quesada-c(p) 4.00
Annual 2 (1993, $2.95, 68 pgs.)-Bagged w/card; intro Tracer 4.00
NOTE: ***Denys Cowan** a(p)-9-13, 15, Annual 1; c-9-12, 13p, 14. **Guice/Cowan** c-8.*

DEATHLOK
Marvel Comics: Sept, 1999 - No. 11, June, 2000 ($1.99)

1-11: 1-Casey-s/Manco-a. 2-Two covers. 4-Canete-a 3.00

DEATHLOK (... The Demolisher on cover)
Marvel Comics: Jan, 2010 - No. 7, Jul, 2010 ($3.99, limited series)

1-7-Huston-s/Medina-a/Peterson-c 4.00

DEATHLOK SPECIAL
Marvel Comics: May, 1991 - No. 4, June, 1991 ($2.00, bi-weekly lim. series)

1-4: r/1-4(1990) w/new Guice-c #1,2; Cowan c-3,4 3.00
1-2nd printing w/white-c 3.00

DEATHMASK
Future Comics: Mar, 2003 - No. 3, June, 2003 ($2.99)

1-3-Giordano-a(p)/Michelinie & Layton-s 3.00

DEATHMATE
Valiant (Prologue/Yellow/Blue)/Image Comics (Black/Red/Epilogue): Sept, 1993 - Epilogue (#6), Feb, 1994 ($2.95/$4.95, limited series)

Preview-(7/93, 8 pgs.) 3.00
Prologue (#1)–Silver foil; Jim Lee/Layton-c; B. Smith/Lee-a; Liefeld-a(p) 3.00
Prologue–Special gold foil ed. of silver ed. 4.00
Black (#2)-(9/93, $4.95, 52 pgs.)-Silvestri/Jim Lee-c; pencils by Peterson/Silvestri/Capullo/Jim Lee/Portacio; 1st story app. Gen 13 telling their rebellion against the Troika (see WildC.A.T.S. Trilogy) 6.00
Black-Special gold foil edition 7.00
Yellow (#3)-(10/93, $4.95, 52 pgs)-Yellow foil-c; Indicia says Prologue Sept 1993 by mistake; 3rd app. Ninjak; Thibert-c(i) 5.00
Yellow-Special gold foil edition 6.00
Blue (#4)-(10/93, $4.95, 52 pgs.)-Thibert blue foil-c(i); Reese-a(i) 5.00
Blue-Special gold foil edition 6.00
Red (#5), Epilogue (#6)-(2/94, $2.95)-Silver foil Quesada/Silvestri-c; Silvestri-a(p) 3.00

DEATH METAL
Marvel Comics UK: Jan, 1994 - No. 4, Apr, 1994 ($1.95, limited series)

1-4: 1-Silver ink-c. Alpha Flight app. 3.00

DEATH METAL VS. GENETIX
Marvel Comics UK: Dec, 1993 - No. 2, Jan, 1994 (Limited series)

1-($2.95)-Polybagged w/2 trading cards 3.00
2-($2.50)-Polybagged w/2 trading cards 3.00

Deathstroke #1 © DC

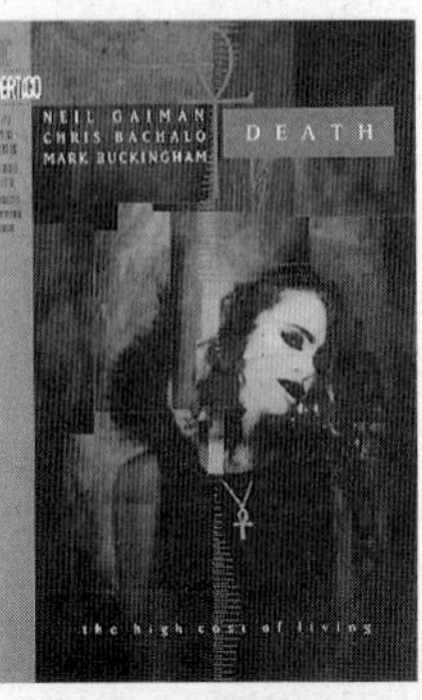

Death: The High Cost of Living #2 © DC

Death Valley #2 © Comic Media

	GD 2.0	VG 4.0	FN 6.0	VF 8.0	VF/NM 9.0	NM- 9.2

DEATH OF CAPTAIN MARVEL (See Marvel Graphic Novel #1)

DEATH OF DRACULA
Marvel Comics: Aug, 2010 ($3.99, one shot)

1-Gischler-s/Camuncoli-a/c 4.00

DEATH OF MR. MONSTER, THE (See Mr. Monster #8)

DEATH OF SUPERMAN (See Superman, 2nd Series)

DEATH OF THE NEW GODS (Tie-in to the Countdown series)
DC Comics: Early Dec, 2007 - No. 8, Jun, 2008 ($3.50, limited series)

1-8-Jim Starlin-s/a/c. 1-Barda killed. 6-Orion dies. 7-Scott Free and Metron die 3.50
TPB (2009, $19.99) r/#1-8; Starlin intro.; cover gallery 20.00

DEATH RACE 2020
Roger Corman's Cosmic Comics: Apr, 1995 - No. 8, Nov, 1995 ($2.50)

1-8: Sequel to the Movie 3.00

DEATH RATTLE (Formerly an Underground)
Kitchen Sink Press: V2#1, 10/85 - No. 18, 1988, 1994 ($1.95, Baxter paper, mature); V3#1, 11/95 - No. 5, 6/96 ($2.95, B&W)

V2#1-7,9-18: 1-Corben-c. 2-Unpubbed Spirit story by Eisner. 5-Robot Woman-r by Wolverton. 6-B&W issues begin. 10-Savage World-r by by Williamson/Torres/ Krenkel/Frazetta from Witzend #1. 16-Wolverton Spacehawk-r 5.00
8-(12/86)-1st app. Mark Schultz's Xenozoic Tales/Cadillacs & Dinosaurs 2 4 6 8 10 12
8-(1994)-r plus interview w/Mark Schultz 3.50
V3#1-5 ($2.95-c) 3.50

DEATH'S HEAD (See Daredevil #56, Dragon's Claws #5 & Incomplete...)(See Amazing Fantasy (2004) for Death's Head 3.0)
Marvel Comics: Dec, 1988 - No. 10, Sept, 1989 ($1.75)

1-Dragon's Claws spin-off 3.00
2-Fantastic Four app.; Dragon's Claws x-over 3.00
3-10: 8-Dr. Who app. 9-F. F. x-over; Simonson-c(p) 3.00

DEATH'S HEAD II (Also see Battletide)
Marvel Comics UK, Ltd.: Mar, 1992 - No. 4, June (May inside), 1992 ($1.75, color, lim. series)

1-4: 2-Fantastic Four app. 4-Punisher, Spider-Man, Daredevil, Dr. Strange, Capt. America & Wolverine in the year 2020 3.00
1,2-Silver ink 2nd printiings 3.00

DEATH'S HEAD II (Also see Battletide)
Marvel Comics UK, Ltd.: Dec, 1992 - No. 16, Mar, 1994 ($1.75/$1.95)

V2#1-13,15,16: 1-Gatefold-c. 1-4-X-Men app.15-Capt. America & Wolverine app. 3.00
14-($2.95)-Foil flip-c w/Death's Head II Gold #0 3.00
...Gold 1 (1/94, $3.95, 68 pgs.)-Gold foil-c 4.00

DEATH'S HEAD II & THE ORIGIN OF DIE CUT
Marvel Comics UK, Ltd.: Aug, 1993 - No. 2, Sept, 1993 (limited series)

1-($2.95)-Embossed-c 4.00
2 ($1.75) 3.00

DEATHSTROKE (DC New 52)
DC Comics: Nov, 2011 - Present ($2.99)

1-8: 1-Higgins-s/Bennett-a/Bisley-c. 4-Blackhawks app. 3.00

DEATHSTROKE: THE TERMINATOR (Deathstroke: The Hunted #0-47; Deathstroke #48-60) (Also see Marvel & DC Present, New Teen Titans #2, New Titans, Showcase '93 #7,9 & Tales of the Teen Titans #42-44)
DC Comics: Aug, 1991 - No. 60, June, 1996 ($1.75-$2.25)

1-New Titans spin-off; Mike Zeck c-1-28 4.00
1-Gold ink 2nd printing ($1.75) 3.00
2 3.00
3-40,0(10/94),41(11/94)-49,51-60: 6,8-Batman cameo. 7,9-Batman-c/story. 9-1st brief app. new Vigilante (female). 10-1st full app. new Vigilante; Perez-i. 13-Vs. Justice League; Team Titans cameo on last pg. 14-Total Chaos, part 1; Team Titans-c/story cont'd in New Titans #90. 40-(9/94). 0-(10/94)-Begin Deathstroke, The Hunted, ends #47. 3.00
50 ($3.50) 4.00
Annual 1-4 ('92-'95, 68 pgs.): 1-Nightwing & Vigilante app.; minor Eclipso app. 2-Bloodlines Deathstorm; 1st app. Gunfire. 3-Elseworlds story. 4-Year One story 4.00
NOTE: *Golden a-12. Perez a-11i. Zeck c-Annual 1, 2.*

DEATH: THE HIGH COST OF LIVING (See Sandman #8) (Also see the Books of Magic limited & ongoing series)
DC Comics (Vertigo): Mar, 1993 - No. 3, May, 1993 ($1.95, limited series)

1-Bachalo/Buckingham-a; Dave McKean-c; Neil Gaiman scripts in all 6.00
1-Platinum edition 40.00
2 3.50
3-Pgs. 19 & 20 had wrong placement 3.00
3-Corrected version w/pgs. 19 & 20 facing each other; has no-c & ads for Sebastion O & The Geek added 4.00
Death Talks About Life-giveaway about AIDS prevention 5.00
Hardcover (1994, $19.95)-r/#1-3 & Death Talks About Life; intro. by Tori Amos 20.00
Trade paperback (6/94, $12.95, Titan Books)-r/#1-3 & Death Talks About Life; prism-c 13.00

DEATH: THE TIME OF YOUR LIFE (See Sandman #8)
DC Comics (Vertigo): Apr, 1996 - No. 3, July, 1996 ($2.95, limited series)

1-3: Neil Gaiman story & Bachalo/Buckingham-a; Dave McKean-c. 2-(5/96) 3.00
Hardcover (1997, $19.95)-r/#1-3 w/3 new pages & gallery art by various 20.00
TPB (1997, $12.95)-r/#1-3 & Visions of Death gallery; Intro. by Claire Danes 13.00

DEATH 3
Marvel Comics UK: Sept, 1993 - No. 4, Dec, 1993 ($1.75, limited series)

1-($2.95)-Embossed-c 4.00
2-4 3.00

DEATH VALLEY (Cowboys and Indians)
Comic Media: Oct, 1953 - No. 6, Aug, 1954

1-Billy the Kid; Morisi-a; Andru/Esposito-c/a 20 40 60 117 189 260
2-Don Heck-c 13 26 39 74 105 135
3-6: 3,5-Morisi-a. 5-Discount-a 12 24 36 69 97 125

DEATH VALLEY (Becomes Frontier Scout, Daniel Boone No.10-13)
Charlton Comics: No. 7, 6/55 - No. 9, 10/55 (Cont'd from Comic Media series)

7-9: 8-Wolverton-a (half pg.) 10 20 30 56 76 95

DEATHWISH
DC Comics (Milestone Media): Dec, 1994 - No. 4, Mar, 1995 (2.50, lim. series)

1-4 3.00

DEATH WRECK
Marvel Comics UK: Jan, 1994 - No. 4, Apr, 1994 ($1.95, limited series)

1-4: 1-Metallic ink logo; Death's Head II app. 3.00

DEBBIE DEAN, CAREER GIRL
Civil Service Publ.: April, 1945 - No. 2, July, 1945

1,2-Newspaper reprints by Bert Whitman 14 28 42 76 108 140

DEBBI'S DATES (Also see Date With Debbi)
National Periodical Publications: Apr-May, 1969 - No. 11, Dec-Jan, 1970-71

1 6 12 18 41 66 90
2,3,5,7-11: 2-Last 12¢ issue 4 8 12 22 34 45
4-Neal Adams text illo 4 8 12 26 41 55
6-Superman cameo 6 12 18 39 62 85

DECADE OF DARK HORSE, A
Dark Horse Comics: Jul, 1996 - No. 4, Oct, 1996 ($2.95, B&W/color, lim. series)

1-4: 1-Sin City-c/story by Miller; Grendel by Wagner; Predator. 2-Star Wars wraparound-c. 3-Aliens-c/story; Nexus, Mask stories 3.00

DECAPITATOR (Randy Bowen's...)
Dark Horse Comics: Jun, 1998 - No. 4, ($2.95)

1-4-Bowen-s/art by various. 1-Mahnke-c. 3-Jones-c 4.00

DECEPTION, THE
Image Comics (Flypaper Press): 1999 - No. 3, 1999 ($2.95, B&W, mini-series)

1-3-Horley painted-c 3.00

DECIMATION: THE HOUSE OF M
Marvel Comics: Jan, 2006 ($3.99)

... - The Day After (one-shot) Claremont-s/Green-a 4.00

DECISION 2012 (Biographies of the main 2012 presidential candidates)
BOOM! Studios: Nov, 2011 - Present ($3.99, series of one-shots)

...: Barack Obama 1 (11/11, $3.99) biography; Damian Couceiro-a; 2 covers 4.00
...: Michelle Bachman 1 (11/11) biography; Aaron McConnell-a; 2 covers 4.00
...: Ron Paul 1 (11/11) biography; Dean Kotz-a; 2 covers 4.00
...: Sarah Palin 1 (11/11) biography; Damian Couceiro-a; 2 covers 4.00

DEEP, THE (Movie)
Marvel Comics Group: Nov, 1977 (Giant)

1-Infantino-c/a 1 3 4 6 8 10

DEEP SLEEPER
Oni Press/Image Comics: Feb, 2004 - No. 4, Sept, 2004 ($3.50/$2.95, B&W, limited series)

1,2-(Oni Press, $3.50)-Hester-s/Huddleston-a 3.50

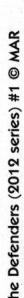

The Defenders (2012 series) #1 © MAR

Delirium's Party HC © DC

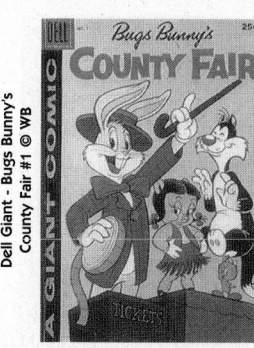

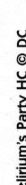

Dell Giant - Bugs Bunny's County Fair #1 © WB

GD 2.0 | VG 4.0 | FN 6.0 | VF 8.0 | VF/NM 9.0 | NM- 9.2

3,4-(Image Comics, $2.95) 3.00
... Omnibus (Image, 8/04, $5.95) r/#1,2 6.00
... Vol. 1 TPB (2005, $12.95) r/#1-4; cover gallery 13.00

DEFCON 4
Image Comics (WildStorm Productions): Feb, 1996 - No. 4, Sept, 1996 ($2.50, lim. series)

1/2 1 2 3 5 7 9
1/2 Gold-(1000 printed) 14.00
1-Main Cover by Mat Broome & Edwin Rosell 3.00
1-Hordes of Cymulants variant-c by Michael Golden 5.00
1-Backs to the Wall variant-c by Humberto Ramos & Alex Garner 5.00
1-Defcon 4-Way variant-c by Jim Lee 1 2 3 4 5 7
2-4 3.00

DEFENDERS, THE (TV)
Dell Publishing Co.: Sept-Nov, 1962 - No. 2, Feb-Apr, 1963

12-176-211(#1) 4 8 12 26 41 55
12-176-304(#2) 3 6 9 21 32 42

DEFENDERS, THE (Also see Giant-Size..., Marvel Feature, Marvel Treasury Edition, Secret Defenders & Sub-Mariner #34, 35; The New...#140-on)
Marvel Comics Group: Aug, 1972 - No. 152, Feb, 1986

1-The Hulk, Doctor Strange, Sub-Mariner begin 12 24 36 79 160 240
2-Silver Surfer x-over 7 14 21 48 79 110
3-5: 3-Silver Surfer x-over. 4-Valkyrie joins 5 10 15 32 51 70
6,7: 6-Silver Surfer x-over 4 8 12 22 34 45
8,9,11: 8-11-Defenders vs. the Avengers (Crossover with Avengers #115-118)
8,11-Silver Surfer x-over 4 8 12 28 44 60
10-Hulk vs. Thor battle 8 16 24 56 96 135
12-14: 12-Last 20¢ issue 3 6 9 14 19 24
15,16-Magneto & Brotherhood of Evil Mutants app. from X-Men
3 6 9 16 22 28
17-20: 17-Power Man x-over (11/74) 2 4 6 8 11 14
21-25: 24,25-Son of Satan app. 1 2 3 5 7 9
26-29-Guardians of the Galaxy app. (#26 is 8/75; pre-dates Marvel Presents #3): 28-1st full app. Starhawk (1st brief app. #27). 29-Starhawk joins Guardians
2 4 6 8 10 12
30-33,39-50: 31,32-Origin Nighthawk. 44-Hellcat joins. 45-Dr. Strange leaves. 47-49-Early Moon Knight app. (5/77). 48-50-(Reg. 30¢-c) 6.00
34-38-(Regular 25¢ editions): 35-Intro New Red Guardian 6.00
34-38-(30¢-c variants, limited distribution)(4-8/76) 3 6 9 20 30 40
48-52-(35¢-c variants, limited distribution)(6-10/77) 4 8 12 28 44 60
51-60: 51,52-(Reg. 30¢-c). 53-1st brief app. Lunatik (Lobo lookalike). 55-Origin Red Guardian; Lunatik cameo. 56-1st full Lunatik story 5.00
61-75: 61-Lunatik & Spider-Man app. 70-73-Lunatik (origin #71). 73-75-Foolkiller II app. (Greg Salinger). 74-Nighthawk resigns 4.00
76-93,95,97-99,102-119,123,124,126-149,151: 77-Origin Omega. 78-Original Defenders return thru #101. 104-The Beast joins. 105-Son of Satan joins. 106-Death of Nighthawk. 129-New Mutants cameo (3/84, early x-over) 3.00
94,101,120-122: 94-1st Gargoyle. 101-Silver Surfer-c & app. 120,121-Son of Satan-c/stories. 122-Final app. Son of Satan (2 pgs.) 4.00
96-Ghost Rider app. 4.00
100-(52 pgs.)-Hellcat (Patsy Walker) revealed as Satan's daughter 5.00
125,150: 125-(52 pgs.)-Intro new Defenders. 150-(52 pgs.)-Origin Cloud 4.00
152-(52 pgs.)-Ties in with X-Factor & Secret Wars II 4.00
Annual 1 (1976, 52 pgs.)-New book-length story 3 6 9 18 27 40

NOTE: ***Art Adams** c-142p. **Austin** a-53i; c-65i, 119i, 145i. **Frank Bolle** a-7i, 10i, 11i. **Buckler** c(p)-34, 38, 76, 77, 79-86, 90, 91. **J. Buscema** c-66. **Giffen** a-42-49p, 50, 51-54p. **Golden** a-53p, 54p; c-94, 96. **Guice** c-129. **G. Kane** c(p)-13, 16, 18, 19, 21-26, 31-33, 35-37, 40, 41, 52, 55. **Kirby** c-42-45. **Mooney** a-3i, 31-34i, 62i, 63i, 85i. **Nasser** c-88p. **Perez** c(p)-51, 53, 54. **Rogers** c-98. **Starlin** c-110. **Tuska** a-57p. Silver Surfer in No. 2, 3, 6, 8-11, 92, 98-101, 107, 112-115, 122-125.*

DEFENDERS, THE (Volume 2) (Continues in The Order)
Marvel Comics: Mar, 2001 - No. 12, Feb, 2002 ($2.99/$2.25)

1-Busiek & Larsen-s/Larsen & Janson-a/c 3.00
2-11: 2-Two covers by Larsen & Art Adams; Valkyrie app. 4-Frenz-a 3.00
12-($3.50) 'Nuff Said issue; back-up-s Reis-a 4.00
...: From the Vault (9/11, $2.99) Previously unpublished story; Bagley-a 3.00

DEFENDERS, THE
Marvel Comics: Sept, 2005 - No. 5, Jan, 2006 ($2.99, limited series)

1-5-Giffen & DeMatteis-s/Maguire-a. 2-Dormammu app. 3.00
...: Indefensible HC (2006, $19.99, dust jacket) r/#1-5; Giffen & Maguire sketch page 20.00
...: Indefensible SC (2007, $13.99) r/#1-5; Giffen & Maguire sketch page 14.00

DEFENDERS, THE
Marvel Comics: Feb, 2012 - Present ($3.99)

1-4-Dr. Strange, Namor, Silver Surfer, Red She-Hulk, Iron Fist team; Dodson-a 4.00
...: Strange Heroes 1 (2/12, $4.99) Handbook-style profiles of team members and foes 5.00
...: The Coming of the Defenders 1 (2/12, $5.99) r/Marvel Feature #1-3; recolored-c of #1 6.00
...: Tournament of Heroes 1 (3/12, $5.99) r/Defenders #62-65 (1978); recolored-c of #62 6.00

DEFENDERS OF DYNATRON CITY
Marvel Comics: Feb, 1992 - No. 6, July, 1992 ($1.25, limited series)

1-6-Lucasarts characters. 2-Origin 3.00

DEFENDERS OF THE EARTH (TV)
Marvel Comics (Star Comics): Jan, 1987 - No. 4, July, 1987

1-4: The Phantom, Mandrake The Magician, Flash Gordon begin. 3-Origin Phantom. 4-Origin Mandrake 4.00

DEFEX
Devil's Due Publ.: Oct, 2004 - No. 6, Apr, 2005 ($2.95)

1-6: 1-Wolfman-s/Caselli-a. 6-Pérez-c 3.00

DEFIANCE
Image Comics: Feb, 2002 - No. 8, Jun, 2003 ($2.95)

Preview Edition (12/01) 3.00
1-8-Barré-s/Kang & Suh-a 3.00

DEFINITIVE DIRECTORY OF THE DC UNIVERSE, THE (See Who's Who...)

DELECTA OF THE PLANETS (See Don Fortune & Fawcett Miniatures)

DELICATE CREATURES
Image Comics (Top Cow): 2001 ($16.95, hardcover with dust jacket)

nn-Fairy tale storybook; J. Michael Straczynski-s; Michael Zulli-a 17.00

DELIRIUM'S PARTY: A LITTLE ENDLESS STORYBOOK (Characters from The Sandman titles and The Little Endless Storybook)
DC Comics: 2011 ($14.99, hardcover, one-shot)

HC-Jill Thompson-s/painted-a/c; Little Delirium throws a party; watercolor page process 15.00

DELLA VISION (...The Television Queen) (Patty Powers #4 on)
Atlas Comics: April, 1955 - No. 3, Aug, 1955

1-Al Hartley-c 16 32 48 94 147 200
2,3 11 22 33 64 90 115
110

DELLEC
Aspen MLT.: Aug, 2009 - No. 6, Oct, 2011 ($2.50)

1-6-Gunnell-a/c 3.00

DELL GIANT COMICS

Dell Publishing began to release square bound comics in 1949 with a 132-page issue called Christmas Parade #1. The covers were of a heavier stock to accommodate the increased number of pages. The books proved profitable at 25 cents, but the average number of pages was quickly reduced to 100. Ten years later they were converted to a numbering system similar to the Four Color Comics, for greater ease in distribution and the page counts cut back to mostly 84 pages. The label "Dell Giant" began to appear on the covers in 1954. Because of the size of the books and the heavier, less pliant cover stock, they are rarely found in high grade condition, and with the exception of a small quantity of copies released from Western Publishing's warehouse–are almost never found in near mint.

Abraham Lincoln Life Story 1(3/58) 8 16 24 64 107 150
Bugs Bunny Christmas Funnies 1(11/50, 116pp) 19 38 57 152 269 385
...Christmas Funnies 2(11/51, 116pp) 12 24 36 96 166 235
...Christmas Funnies 3-5(11/52-11/54,)-Becomes Christmas Party #6
10 20 30 80 140 200
...Christmas Funnies 7-9(12/56-12/58) 9 18 27 72 124 175
...Christmas Party 6(11/55)-Formerly Bugs Bunny Christmas Funnies
9 18 27 72 124 175
...County Fair 1(9/57) 11 22 33 88 149 210
...Halloween Parade 1(10/53) 12 24 36 96 166 235
...Halloween Parade 2(10/54)-Trick 'N' Treat Halloween Fun #3 on
10 20 30 80 135 190
...Trick 'N' Treat Halloween Fun 3,4(10/55-10/56)-Formerly Halloween Parade #2
9 18 27 72 129 185
...Vacation Funnies 1(7/51, 112pp) 19 38 57 152 264 375
...Vacation Funnies 2('52) 13 26 39 104 180 255
...Vacation Funnies 3-5('53-'55) 10 20 30 80 138 195
...Vacation Funnies 6,7,9('56-'59) 9 18 27 72 124 175
...Vacation Funnies 8('58) 1st app. Beep Beep the Road Runner, Wile E. Coyote (1st meeting), Mathilda (Mrs. Beep Beep) and their 3 children who hatch from eggs; one month before Four Color #918 11 22 33 88 154 220
Cadet Gray of West Point 1(4/58)-Williamson-a, 10pgs.; Buscema-a; photo-c
8 16 24 64 107 150

Dell Giant - Christmas Parade #7 © DIS

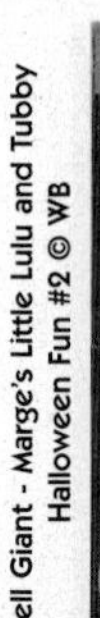
Dell Giant - Marge's Little Lulu and Tubby Halloween Fun #2 © WB

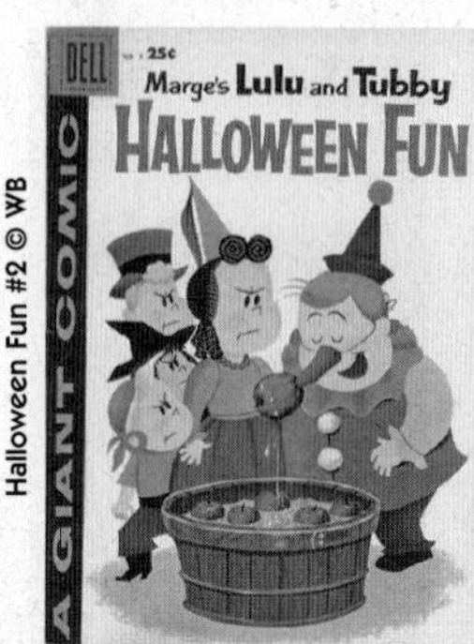

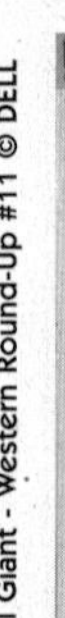
Dell Giant - Western Round-Up #11 © DELL

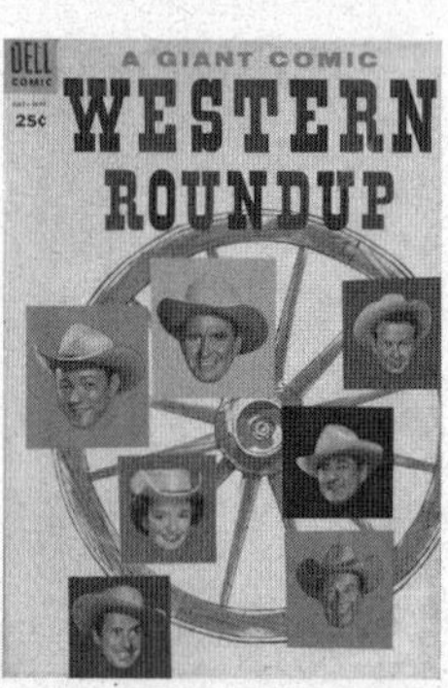

	GD 2.0	VG 4.0	FN 6.0	VF 8.0	VF/NM 9.0	NM- 9.2
Christmas In Disneyland 1(12/57)-Barks-a, 18 pgs.	25	50	75	200	350	500
Christmas Parade 1(11/49)(132 pgs.)(1st Dell Giant)-Donald Duck (25 pgs. by Barks, r-in G.K. Christmas Parade #5); Mickey Mouse & other film oriented stories; Cinderella (prior to movie), 7 Dwarfs, Bambi & Thumper, So Dear To My Heart, Flying Mouse, Dumbo, Cookieland & others	63	126	189	504	877	1250
Christmas Parade 2('50)-Donald Duck (132 pgs.)(25 pgs. by Barks, r-in Gold Key's Christmas Parade #6). Mickey, Pluto, Chip & Dale, etc. Contents shift to a holiday expansion of W.D. C&S type format	42	84	126	336	588	840
Christmas Parade 3-7('51-'55, #3-116pgs; #4-7, 100 pgs.)	14	28	42	112	196	280
Christmas Parade 8(12/56)-Barks-a, 8 pgs.	22	44	66	176	306	435
Christmas Parade 9(12/58)-Barks-a, 20 pgs.	25	50	75	200	350	500
Christmas Treasury, A 1(11/54)	9	18	27	72	126	180
Davy Crockett, King Of The Wild Frontier 1(9/55)-Fess Parker photo-c; Marsh-a	19	38	57	152	269	385
Disneyland Birthday Party 1(10/58)-Barks-a, 16 pgs. r-by Gladstone	25	50	75	200	350	500
Donald and Mickey In Disneyland 1(5/58)	11	22	33	88	157	225
Donald Duck Beach Party 1(7/54)-Has an Uncle Scrooge story (not by Barks) that prefigures the later rivalry with Flintheart Glomgold and tells of Scrooge's wild rivalry with another millionaire	16	32	48	128	224	320
...Beach Party 2(1955)-Lady & Tramp	11	22	33	88	157	225
...Beach Party 3-5(1956-58)	11	22	33	88	152	215
...Beach Party 6(8/59, 84pp)-Stapled	8	16	24	64	115	165
Donald Duck Fun Book 1,2 (1953 & 10/54)-Games, puzzles, comics & cut-outs (very rare in unused condition)(most copies commonly have defaced interior pgs.)	63	126	189	504	877	1250
Donald Duck In Disneyland 1(9/55)-1st Disneyland Dell Giant	15	30	45	120	210	300
Golden West Rodeo Treasury 1(10/57)	10	20	30	80	135	190
Huey, Dewey and Louie Back To School 1(9/58)	9	18	27	72	126	180
Lady and The Tramp 1(6/55)	17	34	51	136	233	330
Life Stories of American Presidents 1(11/57)-Buscema-a	8	16	24	64	107	150
Lone Ranger Golden West 3(8/55)-Formerly Lone Ranger Western Treasury	18	36	54	144	255	365
Lone Ranger Movie Story nn(3/56)-Origin Lone Ranger in text; Clayton Moore photo-c	36	72	108	288	507	725
...Western Treasury 1(9/53)-Origin Lone Ranger, Silver, & Tonto; painted cover	23	46	69	184	325	465
...Western Treasury 2(8/54)-Becomes Lone Ranger Golden West #3	18	36	54	144	255	365
Marge's Little Lulu & Alvin Story Telling Time 1(3/59)-r/#2,5,3,11,30,10,21,17,8, 14,16; Stanley-a	14	28	42	112	196	280
...& Her Friends 4(3/56)-Tripp-a	14	28	42	112	191	270
...& Her Special Friends 3(3/55)-Tripp-a	15	30	45	120	210	300
...& Tubby At Summer Camp 5,2: 5(10/57)-Tripp-a. 2(10/58)-Tripp-a	13	26	39	104	182	260
...& Tubby Halloween Fun 6,2: 6(10/57)-Tripp-a. 2(10/58)-Tripp-a	13	26	39	104	182	260
...& Tubby In Alaska 1(7/59)-Tripp-a	13	26	39	104	177	250
...On Vacation 1(7/54)-r/4C-110,14,4C-146,5,4C-97,4,4C-158,3,1;Stanley-a	25	50	75	200	350	500
...& Tubby Annual 1(3/53)-r/4C-165,4C-74,4C-146,4C-97,4C-158, 4C-139, 4C-131; Stanley-a (1st Lulu Dell Giant)	30	60	90	240	420	600
...& Tubby Annual 2('54)-r/4C-139,6,4C-115,4C-74,5,4C-97,3,4C-146,18; Stanley-a	25	50	75	200	350	500
Marge's Tubby & His Clubhouse Pals 1(10/56)-1st app. Gran'pa Feeb;1st app. Janie; written by Stanley; Tripp-a	15	30	45	120	210	300
Mickey Mouse Almanac 1(12/57)-Barks-a, 8pgs.	27	54	81	216	378	540
...Birthday Party 1(9/53)-r/entire 48pgs. of Gottfredson's "Mickey Mouse in Love Trouble" from WDC&S 36-39. Quality equal to original. Also reprints one story each from Four Color 27, 79, & 181 plus 6 panels of highlights in the career of Mickey Mouse	31	62	93	248	434	620
...Club Parade 1(12/55)-r/4-Color 16 with some death trap scenes redrawn by Paul Murry & recolored with night turned into day; quality less than original	22	44	66	176	308	440
...In Fantasy Land 1(5/57)	13	26	39	104	180	255
...In Frontier Land 1(5/56)-Mickey Mouse Club iss.	13	26	39	104	180	255
...Summer Fun 1(8/58)-Mobile cut-outs on back-c; becomes Summer Fun with #2; Canadian version exists with 30¢-c price	13	26	39	104	180	255
Moses & The Ten Commandments 1(8/57)-Not based on movie; Dell's adaptation; Sekowsky-a; variant version has "Gods of Egypt" comic back-c	8	16	24	64	107	150
Nancy & Sluggo Travel Time 1(9/58)	8	16	24	64	115	165

	GD 2.0	VG 4.0	FN 6.0	VF 8.0	VF/NM 9.0	NM- 9.2
Peter Pan Treasure Chest 1(1/53, 212pp)-Disney; contains 54-page movie adaptation & other Peter Pan stories; plus Donald & Mickey stories w/P. Pan; a 32-page retelling of "D. Duck Finds Pirate Gold" with yellow beak, called "Capt. Hook & the Buried Treasure"	130	260	390	1040	1820	2600
Picnic Party 6,7(7/55-6/56)(Formerly Vacation Parade)-Uncle Scrooge, Mickey & Donald	12	24	36	96	166	235
Picnic Party 8(7/57)-Barks-a, 6pgs	21	42	63	168	289	410
Pogo Parade 1(9/53)-Kelly-a(r-/Pogo from Animal Comics in this order: #11,13,21,14,27,16,23,9,18,15,17)	25	50	75	200	350	500
Raggedy Ann & Andy 1(2/55)	16	32	48	128	224	320
Santa Claus Funnies 1(11/52)-Dan Noonan -A Christmas Carol adaptation	9	18	27	72	126	180
Silly Symphonies 1(9/52)-Redrawing of Gotfredson's Mickey Mouse strip of "The Brave Little Tailor;" 2 Good Housekeeping pages (from 1943); Lady and the Two Siamese Cats, three years before "Lady & the Tramp;" a retelling of Donald Duck's first app. in "The Wise Little Hen" & other stories based on 1930's Silly Symphony cartoons	31	62	93	248	437	625
Silly Symphonies 2(9/53)-M. Mouse in "The Sorcerer's Apprentice", 2 Good Housekeeping pages (from 1944); The Pelican & the Snipe, Elmer Elephant, Peculiar Penguins, Little Hiawatha, & others	24	48	72	192	339	485
Silly Symphonies 3(2/54)-r/Mickey & The Beanstalk (4-Color #157, 39pgs.), Little Minnehaha, Pablo, The Flying Gauchito, Pluto, & Bongo, & 2 Good Housekeeping pages (1944)	20	40	60	160	275	390
Silly Symphonies 4(8/54)-r/Dumbo (4-Color 234), Morris The Midget Moose, The Country Cousin, Bongo, & Clara Cluck	20	40	60	160	275	390
Silly Symphonies 5-8: 5(2/55)-r/Cinderella (4-Color 272), Bucky Bug, Pluto, Little Hiawatha, The 7 Dwarfs & Dumbo, Pinocchio. 6(8/55)-r/Pinocchio (WDC&S 63), The 7 Dwarfs & Thumper (WDC&S 45), M. Mouse "Adventures With Robin Hood" (40 pgs.), Johnny Appleseed, Pluto & Peter Pan, & Bucky Bug; Cut-out on back-c. 7(2/57)-r/Reluctant Dragon, Ugly Duckling, M. Mouse & Peter Pan, Jiminy Cricket, Peter & The Wolf, Brer Rabbit, Bucky Bug; Cut-out on back-c. 8(2/58)-r/Thumper Meets The 7 Dwarfs (4-Color #19), Jiminy Cricket, Niok, Brer Rabbit; Cut-out on back-c	16	32	48	128	224	320
Silly Symphonies 9(2/59)-r/Paul Bunyan, Humphrey Bear, Jiminy Cricket, The Social Lion, Goliath II; cut-out on back-c	15	30	45	120	210	300
Sleeping Beauty 1(4/59)	25	50	75	200	350	500
Summer Fun 2(8/59, 84pp, stapled binding)(Formerly Mickey Mouse...)-Barks-a(2), 24 pgs.	24	48	72	192	336	480
Tarzan's Jungle Annual 1(8/52)-Lex Barker photo on-c of #1,2	15	30	45	120	210	300
...Annual 2(8/53)	11	22	33	88	152	215
...Annual 3-7('54-9/58)(two No. 5s)-Manning-a-No. 3,5-7; Marsh-a in No. 1-7 plus painted-c 1-7	9	18	27	72	124	175
Tom And Jerry Back To School 1(9/56) 2 different back-c, variant has "Apple for the Teacher" cut-out	12	24	36	96	168	240
...Picnic Time 1(7/58)	10	20	30	80	135	190
...Summer Fun 1(7/54)-Droopy written by Barks	15	30	45	120	205	290
...Summer Fun 2-4(7/55-7/57)	8	16	24	64	107	150
...Toy Fair 1(6/58)	9	18	27	72	126	180
...Winter Carnival 1(12/52)-Droopy written by Barks	20	40	60	160	280	400
...Winter Carnival 2(12/53)-Droopy written by Barks	16	32	48	128	224	320
...Winter Fun 3(12/54)	8	16	24	64	115	165
...Winter Fun 4-7(12/55-11/58)	7	14	21	56	101	145
Treasury of Dogs, A 1(10/56)	7	14	21	56	101	145
Treasury of Horses, A (9/55)	7	14	21	56	101	145
Uncle Scrooge Goes To Disneyland 1(8/57p)-Barks-a, 20 pgs. r-by Gladstone; 2 different back-c; variant shows 6 snapshots of Scrooge	26	52	78	208	359	510
Vacation In Disneyland 1(8/58)	11	22	33	88	157	225
Vacation Parade 1(7/50, 132pp)-Donald Duck & Mickey Mouse; Barks-a, 55 pgs.	95	190	285	760	1330	1900
Vacation Parade 2(7/51,116pp)	25	50	75	200	350	500
Vacation Parade 3-5(7/52-7/54)-Becomes Picnic Party No. 6 on. #4-Robin Hood Advs.	14	28	42	112	194	275
Western Roundup 1(6/52)-Photo-c; Gene Autry, Roy Rogers, Johnny Mack Brown, Rex Allen, & Bill Elliott begin; photo back-c begin, end No. 14,16,18	25	50	75	200	350	500
Western Roundup 2(2/53)-Photo-c	14	28	42	112	196	280
Western Roundup 3-5(7-9/53 - 1-3/54)-Photo-c	11	22	33	88	157	225
Western Roundup 6-10(4-6/54 - 4-6/55)-Photo-c	11	22	33	88	149	210
Western Roundup 11-17,25: 11-17-Photo-c; 11-13,16,17-Manning-a. 11-Flying A's Range Rider, Dale Evans begin	9	18	27	72	129	185
Western Roundup 18-Toth-a; last photo-c; Gene Autry ends	11	22	33	88	149	210
Western Roundup 19-24-Manning-a. 19-Buffalo Bill Jr. begins (7-9/57; early app.).						

Dell Giant #33 © DIS

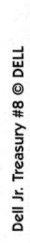

Dell Jr. Treasury #8 © DELL

Demon Knights #1 © DC

GD VG FN VF VF/NM NM-
2.0 4.0 6.0 8.0 9.0 9.2

19,20,22-Toth-a. 21-Rex Allen, Johnny Mack Brown end. 22-Jace Pearson's Texas Rangers, Rin Tin Tin, Tales of Wells Fargo (2nd app., 4-6/58) & Wagon Train (2nd app.) begin 9 18 27 72 129 185
Woody Woodpecker Back To School 1(10/52) 10 20 30 80 140 200
...Back To School 2-4,6('53-10/57)-County Fair No. 5 8 16 24 64 112 160
...County Fair 5(9/56)-Formerly Back To School 8 16 24 64 112 160
...County Fair 2(11/58) 7 14 21 56 101 145

DELL GIANTS (Consecutive numbering)
Dell Publishing Co.: No. 21, Sept, 1959 - No. 55, Sept, 1961 (Most 84 pgs., 25¢)

21-(#1)-M.G.M.'s Tom & Jerry Picnic Time (84pp, stapled binding)-Painted-c 11 22 33 88 157 225
22-Huey, Dewey & Louie Back to School (Disney; 10/59, 84pp, square binding begins) 9 18 27 72 129 185
23-Marge's Little Lulu & Tubby Halloween Fun (10/59)-Tripp-a 12 24 36 96 168 240
24-Woody Woodpecker's Family Fun (11/59)(Walter Lantz) 8 16 24 64 112 160
25-Tarzan's Jungle World(11/59)-Marsh-a; painted-c 11 22 33 88 152 215
26-Christmas Parade(Disney; 12/59)-Barks-a, 16pgs.; Barks draws himself on wanted poster on pg. 13 21 42 63 168 289 410
27-Walt Disney's Man in Space (10/59) r-/4-Color 716,866, & 954 (100 pgs., 35¢)(TV) 9 18 27 72 129 185
28-Bugs Bunny's Winter Fun (2/60) 9 18 27 72 126 180
29-Marge's Little Lulu & Tubby in Hawaii (4/60)-Tripp-a 12 24 36 96 166 235
30-Disneyland USA(Disney; 6/60) 9 18 27 72 124 175
31-Huckleberry Hound Summer Fun (7/60)(TV)(HannaBarbera)-Yogi Bear & Pixie & Dixie app. 12 24 36 96 173 250
32-Bugs Bunny Beach Party 7 14 21 56 101 145
33-Daisy Duck & Uncle Scrooge Picnic Time (Disney; 9/60) 9 18 27 72 124 175
34-Nancy & Sluggo Summer Camp (8/60) 7 14 21 56 101 145
35-Huey, Dewey & Louie Back to School (Disney; 10/60)-1st app. Daisy Duck's Nieces, April, May & June 12 24 36 96 163 230
36-Marge's Little Lulu & Witch Hazel Halloween Fun (10/60)-Tripp-a 11 22 33 88 157 225
37-Tarzan, King of the Jungle (11/60)-Marsh-a; painted-c 9 18 27 72 129 185
38-Uncle Donald & His Nephews Family Fun (Disney; 11/60)-Cover painting based on a pencil sketch by Barks 12 24 36 96 173 250
39-Walt Disney's Merry Christmas (Disney; 12/60)-Cover painting based on a pencil sketch by Barks 12 24 36 96 173 250
40-Woody Woodpecker Christmas Parade (12/60)(Walter Lantz) 6 12 18 48 87 125
41-Yogi Bear's Winter Sports (12/60)(TV)(Hanna-Barbera)-Huckleberry Hound, Pixie & Dixie, Augie Doggie app. 12 24 36 96 173 250
42-Marge's Little Lulu & Tubby in Australia (4/61) 11 22 33 88 157 225
43-Mighty Mouse in Outer Space (5/61) 18 36 54 144 252 360
44-Around the World with Huckleberry and His Friends (7/61)(TV)(Hanna-Barbera)-Yogi Bear, Pixie & Dixie, Quick Draw McGraw, Augie Doggie app.; 1st app. Yakky Doodle 13 26 39 104 182 260
45-Nancy & Sluggo Summer Camp (8/61) 7 14 21 56 96 135
46-Bugs Bunny Beach Party (8/61) 7 14 21 56 96 135
47-Mickey & Donald in Vacationland (Disney; 8/61) 8 16 24 64 115 165
48-The Flintstones (No. 1)(Bedrock Bedlam)(7/61)(TV)(Hanna-Barbera) 1st app. in comics 19 38 57 152 269 385
49-Huey, Dewey & Louie Back to School (Disney; 9/61) 9 18 27 72 124 175
50-Marge's Little Lulu & Witch Hazel Trick 'N' Treat (10/61) 11 22 33 88 157 225
51-Tarzan, King of the Jungle by Jesse Marsh (11/61)-Painted-c 8 16 24 64 110 155
52-Uncle Donald & His Nephews Dude Ranch (Disney; 11/61) 8 16 24 64 115 165
53-Donald Duck Merry Christmas (Disney; 12/61) 8 16 24 64 112 160
54-Woody Woodpecker's Christmas Party (12/61)-Issued after No. 55 7 14 21 56 98 140
55-Daisy Duck & Uncle Scrooge Showboat (Disney; 9/61) 8 16 24 64 117 170
NOTE: All issues printed with & without ad on back cover.

DELL JUNIOR TREASURY
Dell Publishing Co.: June, 1955 - No. 10, Oct, 1957 (15¢) (All painted-c)

1-Alice in Wonderland; r/4-Color #331 (52 pgs.) 9 18 27 61 106 150
2-Aladdin & the Wonderful Lamp 7 14 21 48 79 110
3-Gulliver's Travels (1/56) 6 12 18 42 69 95
4-Adventures of Mr. Frog & Miss Mouse 7 14 21 44 72 100
5-The Wizard of Oz (7/56) 7 14 21 48 79 110
6-10: 6-Heidi (10/56). 7-Santa and the Angel. 8-Raggedy Ann and the Camel with the Wrinkled Knees. 9-Clementina the Flying Pig. 10-Adventures of Tom Sawyer 6 12 18 42 69 95

DEMOLITION MAN
DC Comics: Nov, 1993 - No. 4, Feb, 1994 ($1.75, color, limited series)

1-4-Movie adaptation 3.00

DEMON, THE (See Detective Comics No. 482-485)
National Periodical Publications: Aug-Sept, 1972 - V3#16, Jan, 1974

1-Origin; Kirby-c/a in all 8 16 24 51 86 120
2-5 4 8 12 28 44 60
6-16 3 6 9 20 30 40

DEMON, THE (1st limited series)(Also see Cosmic Odyssey #2)
DC Comics: Nov, 1986 - No. 4, Feb, 1987 (75¢, limited series)(#2 has #4 of 4 on-c)

1-4: Matt Wagner-a(p) & scripts in all. 4-Demon & Jason Blood become separate entities. 3.00

DEMON, THE (2nd Series)
DC Comics: July, 1990 - No. 58, May, 1995 ($1.50/$1.75/$1.95)

1-Grant scripts begin, ends #39: 1-4-Painted-c 5.00
2-18,20-27,29-39,41,42: 3,8-Batman app. (cameo #4). 12-Bisley painted-c. 12-15,21-Lobo app. (1 pg. cameo #11). 23-Robin app. 29-Superman app. 31,33-39-Lobo app. 3.00
19-($2.50, 44 pgs.)-Lobo poster stapled inside 5.00
28,40: 28-Superman-c/story; begin $1.75-c. 40-Garth Ennis scripts begin 4.00
43-45-Hitman app. 1 2 3 5 7 9
46-48 Return of The Haunted Tank-c/s. 48-Begin $1.95-c. 5.00
49,51,0-(10/94),55-58: 51-(9/94) 3.00
50 ($2.95, 52 pgs.) 4.00
52-54-Hitman-s 5.00
Annual 1 (1992, $3.00, 68 pgs.)-Eclipso-c/story 4.00
Annual 2 (1993, $3.50, 68 pgs.)-1st app. of Hitman 2 4 6 9 13 16
NOTE: *Alan Grant scripts in #1-16, 20, 21, 23-25, 30-39, Annual 1.* ***Wagner*** *a/scripts-22.*

DEMON DREAMS
Pacific Comics: Feb, 1984 - No. 2, May, 1984

1,2-Mostly r-/Heavy Metal 3.00

DEMON: DRIVEN OUT
DC Comics: Nov, 2003 - No. 6, Apr, 2004 ($2.50, limited series)

1-6-Dysart-s/Mhan-a 3.00

DEMON-HUNTER
Seaboard Periodicals (Atlas): Sept, 1975

1-Origin/1st app. Demon-Hunter; Buckler-c/a 2 4 6 9 13 16

DEMON KNIGHT: A GRIMJACK GRAPHIC NOVEL
First Publishing: 1990 ($8.95, 52 pgs.)

nn-Flint Henry-a 9.00

DEMON KNIGHTS (New DC 52) (Set in the Dark Ages)
DC Comics: Nov, 2011 - Present ($2.99)

1-8: 1-Cornell-s/Neves-a/Daniel-c; Etrigan, Madame Xanadu & The Shining Knight app. 3.00

DEMONWARS (R.A. Salvatore's...) ("The Demon Awakens" on cover)
Devil's Due Publishing: Jan, 2007 - No. 3, May, 2007 ($4.99/$5.50, limited series)

1-Daab-s/Seeley-a 5.50
2,3-($5.50) 5.50
Volume 2 (The Demon Spirit) (3/08, $5.50, B&W) 1-Balan-a 5.50

DEMONWARS: EYE FOR AN EYE (R.A. Salvatore's...)
CrossGeneration Comics (Code 6 Comics): Jun, 2003 - No. 5, Nov, 2003 ($2.95, lim. series)

1-5-Ciencin-s/Tocchini-a 3.00

DEMONWARS: TRIAL BY FIRE (R.A. Salvatore's...)
CrossGeneration Comics (Code 6 Comics): Jan, 2003 - No. 5, May, 2003 ($2.95, lim. series)

1-5-Ciencin-s/Wagner-a 3.00
TPB (2003, $9.95) r/#1-5; new short story by Salvatore 10.00

DENNIS THE MENACE (TV with 1959 issues) (Becomes ...Fun Fest Series; See The Best of... & The Very Best of...)(...Fun Fest on-c only to #156-166)
Standard Comics/Pines No.15-31/Hallden (Fawcett) No.32 on: 8/53 - #14, 1/56; #15, 3/56 - #31, 11/58; #32, 1/59 - #166, 11/79

1-1st app. Dennis, Mr. & Mrs. Wilson, Ruff & Dennis' mom & dad; Wiseman-a,

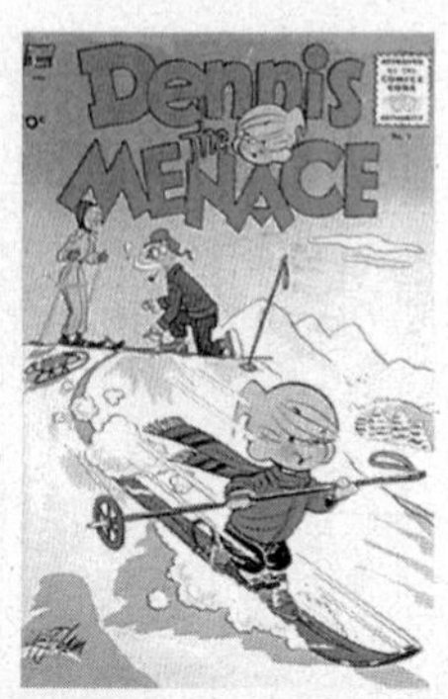

Dennis the Menace #9 © FAW

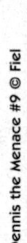

Dennis the Menace #9 © Fiel

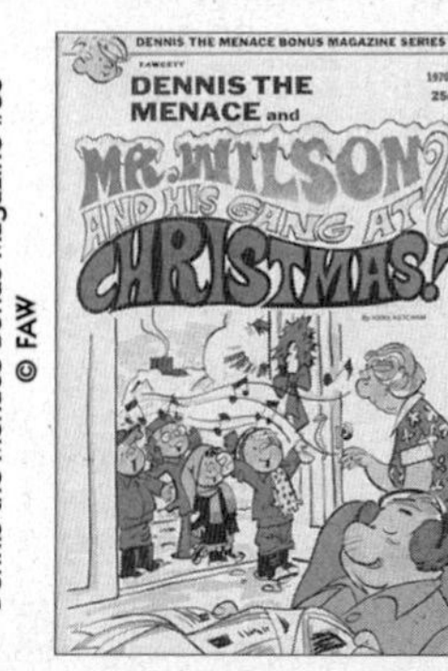

Dennis the Menace Bonus Magazine #86 © FAW

	GD 2.0	VG 4.0	FN 6.0	VF 8.0	VF/NM 9.0	NM- 9.2
written by Fred Toole-most issues	116	232	348	742	1271	1800
2	41	82	123	256	428	600
3-10: 8-Last pre-code issue	22	44	66	132	216	300
11-20	15	30	45	88	137	185
21,23-30	12	24	36	67	94	120
22-1st app. Margaret w/blonde hair	14	28	42	82	121	160
31-1st app. Joey	14	28	42	82	121	160
32-38,40(1/60): 37-A-Bomb blast panel	9	18	27	47	61	75
39-1st app. Gina (11/59)	10	20	30	54	72	90
41-60(7/62)	4	8	12	22	34	45
61-80(9/65),100(1/69)	3	6	9	14	20	25
81-99	2	4	6	11	16	20
101-117: 102-Last 12¢ issue	2	4	6	9	12	15
118(1/72)-131 (All 52 pages)	2	4	6	10	14	18
132(1/74)-142,144-160	1	2	3	5	7	9
143(3/76) Olympic-c/s; low print	2	4	6	10	14	18
161-166	1	3	4	6	8	10

NOTE: ***Wiseman** c/a-1-46, 53, 68, 69.*

DENNIS THE MENACE (Giants) (No. 1 titled Giant Vacation Special; becomes Dennis the Menace Bonus Magazine No. 76 on)
(#1-8,18,23,25,30,38: 100 pgs.; rest to #41: 84 pgs.; #42-75: 68 pgs.)
Standard/Pines/Hallden(Fawcett): Summer, 1955 - No. 75, Dec, 1969

	GD 2.0	VG 4.0	FN 6.0	VF 8.0	VF/NM 9.0	NM- 9.2
nn-Giant Vacation Special(Summ/55-Standard)	18	36	54	103	162	220
nn-Christmas issue (Winter '55)	15	30	45	88	137	185
2-Giant Vacation Special (Summer '56-Pines)	14	28	42	78	112	145
3-Giant Christmas issue (Winter '56-Pines)	13	26	39	72	101	130
4-Giant Vacation Special (Summer '57-Pines)	12	24	36	67	94	120
5-Giant Christmas issue (Winter '57-Pines)	12	24	36	67	94	120
6-In Hawaii (Giant Vacation Special)(Summer '58-Pines)	11	22	33	62	86	110
6-In Hawaii (Summer '59-Hallden)-2nd printing; says 3rd large printing on-c						
6-In Hawaii (Summer '60)-3rd printing; says 4th large printing on-c						
6-In Hawaii (Summer '62)-4th printing; says 5th large printing on-c each....	8	16	24	42	54	65
6-Giant Christmas issue (Winter '58)	11	22	33	62	86	110
7-In Hollywood (Winter '59-Hallden)	5	10	15	32	51	70
7-In Hollywood (Summer '61)-2nd printing	3	6	9	21	32	42
8-In Mexico (Winter '60, 100 pgs.-Hallden/Fawcett)	5	10	15	32	51	70
8-In Mexico (Summer '62, 2nd printing)	3	6	9	21	32	42
9-Goes to Camp (Summer '61, 84 pgs.)-1st CCA approved issue	5	10	15	32	51	70
9-Goes to Camp (Summer '62)-2nd printing	3	6	9	21	32	42
10-12: 10-X-Mas issue (Winter '61), 11-Giant Christmas issue (Winter '62), 12-Triple Feature (Winter '62)	6	12	18	37	59	80
13-17: 13-Best of Dennis the Menace (Spring '63)-Reprints, 14-And His Dog Ruff (Summer '63), 15-In Washington, D.C. (Summer '63), 16-Goes to Camp (Summer '63)-Reprints No. 9, 17-& His Pal Joey (Winter '63)	4	8	12	24	37	50
18-In Hawaii (Reprints No. 6)	3	6	9	20	30	40
19-Giant Christmas issue (Winter '63)	4	8	12	24	37	50
20-Spring Special (Spring '64)	4	8	12	24	37	50
21-40 (Summer '66): 30-r/#6. #35-Xmas spec.Wint,'65	3	6	9	18	27	35
41-60 (Fall '68)	3	6	9	14	19	24
61-75 (12/69): 68-Partial-r/#6	2	4	6	11	16	20

NOTE: ***Wiseman** c/a-1-8, 12, 14, 15, 17, 20, 22, 27, 28, 31, 35, 36, 41, 49.*

DENNIS THE MENACE
Marvel Comics Group: Nov, 1981 - No. 13, Nov, 1982

	GD 2.0	VG 4.0	FN 6.0	VF 8.0	VF/NM 9.0	NM- 9.2
1-New-a	2	4	6	8	10	12
2-13: 2-New art. 3-Part-r. 4,5-r. 5-X-Mas-c & issue, 7-Spider Kid-c/sty	1	2	3	4	5	7

NOTE: ***Hank Ketcham** c-most; a-3, 12. **Wiseman** a-4, 5.*

DENNIS THE MENACE AND HIS DOG RUFF
Hallden/Fawcett: Summer, 1961

	GD 2.0	VG 4.0	FN 6.0	VF 8.0	VF/NM 9.0	NM- 9.2
1-Wiseman-c/a	5	10	15	35	55	75

DENNIS THE MENACE AND HIS FRIENDS
Fawcett Publ.: 1969; No. 5, Jan, 1970 - No. 46, April, 1980 (All reprints)

	GD 2.0	VG 4.0	FN 6.0	VF 8.0	VF/NM 9.0	NM- 9.2
Dennis the Menace & Joey No. 2 (7/69)	2	4	6	13	18	22
Dennis the Menace & Ruff No. 2 (9/69)	2	4	6	13	18	22
Dennis the Menace & Mr. Wilson No. 1 (10/69)	3	6	9	16	22	28
Dennis & Margaret No. 1 (Winter '69)	3	6	9	16	22	28
5-12: 5-Dennis the Menace & Margaret. 6-...& Joey. 7-...& Ruff. 8-...& Mr. Wilson	2	4	6	8	11	14
13-21-(52 pg Giants): 13-(1/72). 21-(1/74)	2	4	6	10	14	18
22-37	1	3	4	6	8	10
38-46 (Digest size, 148 pgs., 4/78, 95¢)	2	4	6	8	11	14

NOTE: *Titles rotate every four issues, beginning with No. 5. Joey issues: #2(7/69),6,10,14,18,22,26,30,34. Ruff issues: #2(9/69), 7,11,15,19,23,27,31,35. Mr. Wilson issues: #1(10/69),8,12,16,20,24,28,32,36. Margaret issues: #1(Wint./69),5,9,13,17,21,25,29,33,37.*

DENNIS THE MENACE AND HIS PAL JOEY
Fawcett Publ.: Summer, 1961 (10¢) (See Dennis the Menace Giants No. 45)

	GD 2.0	VG 4.0	FN 6.0	VF 8.0	VF/NM 9.0	NM- 9.2
1-Wiseman-c/a	5	10	15	35	55	75

DENNIS THE MENACE AND THE BIBLE KIDS
Word Books: 1977 (36 pgs.)

	GD 2.0	VG 4.0	FN 6.0	VF 8.0	VF/NM 9.0	NM- 9.2
1-6: 1-Jesus. 2-Joseph. 3-David. 4-The Bible Girls. 5-Moses. 6-More About Jesus	2	4	6	9	12	15
7-9-Low print run: 7-The Lord's Prayer. 8-Stories Jesus told. 9-Paul, God's Traveller	3	6	9	20	30	40
10-Low print run; In the Beginning	6	12	18	37	59	80

NOTE: ***Ketcham** c/a in all.*

DENNIS THE MENACE BIG BONUS SERIES
Fawcett Publications: No. 10, Feb, 1980 - No. 11, Apr, 1980

	GD 2.0	VG 4.0	FN 6.0	VF 8.0	VF/NM 9.0	NM- 9.2
10,11	1	2	3	5	6	8

DENNIS THE MENACE BONUS MAGAZINE (Formerly Dennis the Menace Giants Nos. 1-75)
(...Big Bonus Series on-c for #174-194)
Fawcett Publications: No. 76, 1/70 - No. 95, 7/71; No. 95, 7/71; No. 97, '71; No. 194, 10/79;
(No. 76-124: 68 pgs.; No. 125-163: 52 pgs.; No. 164 on: 36 pgs.)

	GD 2.0	VG 4.0	FN 6.0	VF 8.0	VF/NM 9.0	NM- 9.2
76-90(3/71)	2	4	6	10	14	18
91-95, 97-110(10/72): Two #95's with same date(7/71) A-Summer Games, and B-That's Our Boy. No #96	2	4	6	9	13	16
111-124	2	4	6	8	10	12
125-163-(52 pgs.)	2	4	6	8	10	12
164-194: 166-Indicia printed backwards	1	2	3	4	5	7

DENNIS THE MENACE COMICS DIGEST
Marvel Comics Group: April, 1982 - No. 3, Aug, 1982 ($1.25, digest-size)

	GD 2.0	VG 4.0	FN 6.0	VF 8.0	VF/NM 9.0	NM- 9.2
1-3-Reprints	1	3	4	6	8	10
1-Mistakenly printed with DC emblem on cover	2	4	6	10	12	15

NOTE: ***Ketcham** c-all. **Wiseman** a-all. A few thousand #1's were published with a DC emblem on cover.*

DENNIS THE MENACE FUN BOOK
Fawcett Publications/Standard Comics: 1960 (100 pgs.)

	GD 2.0	VG 4.0	FN 6.0	VF 8.0	VF/NM 9.0	NM- 9.2
1-Part Wiseman-a	6	12	18	41	66	90

DENNIS THE MENACE FUN FEST SERIES (Formerly Dennis the Menace #166)
Hallden (Fawcett): No. 16, Jan, 1980 - No. 17, Mar, 1980 (40¢)

	GD 2.0	VG 4.0	FN 6.0	VF 8.0	VF/NM 9.0	NM- 9.2
16,17-By Hank Ketcham	1	2	3	4	5	7

DENNIS THE MENACE POCKET FULL OF FUN!
Fawcett Publications (Hallden): Spring, 1969 - No. 50, March, 1980 (196 pgs.) (Digest size)

	GD 2.0	VG 4.0	FN 6.0	VF 8.0	VF/NM 9.0	NM- 9.2
1-Reprints in all issues	6	12	18	37	59	80
2-10	4	8	12	24	37	50
11-20	3	6	9	16	22	28
21-28	2	4	6	11	16	20
29-50: 35,40,46-Sunday strip-r	2	4	6	8	11	14

NOTE: *No. 1-28 are 196 pgs.; No. 29-36: 164 pgs.; No. 37: 148 pgs.; No. 38 on: 132 pgs. No. 8, 11, 15, 21, 25, 29 all contain strip reprints.*

DENNIS THE MENACE TELEVISION SPECIAL
Fawcett Publ. (Hallden Div.): Summer, 1961 - No. 2, Spring, 1962 (Giant)

	GD 2.0	VG 4.0	FN 6.0	VF 8.0	VF/NM 9.0	NM- 9.2
1	6	12	18	39	62	85
2	4	8	12	22	34	45

DENNIS THE MENACE TRIPLE FEATURE
Fawcett Publications: Winter, 1961 (Giant)

	GD 2.0	VG 4.0	FN 6.0	VF 8.0	VF/NM 9.0	NM- 9.2
1-Wiseman-c/a	6	12	18	39	62	85

DEPUTY, THE (TV)
Dell Publishing Co.: No. 1077, Feb-Apr, 1960 - No. 1225, Oct-Dec, 1961
(all-Henry Fonda photo-c)

	GD 2.0	VG 4.0	FN 6.0	VF 8.0	VF/NM 9.0	NM- 9.2
Four Color 1077 (#1)-Buscema-a	11	22	33	71	136	200
Four Color 1130 (9-11/60)-Buscema-a,1225	9	18	27	61	106	150

DEPUTY DAWG (TV) (Also see New Terrytoons)
Dell Publishing Co./Gold Key: Oct-Dec, 1961 - No. 1299, 1962; No. 1, Aug, 1965

	GD 2.0	VG 4.0	FN 6.0	VF 8.0	VF/NM 9.0	NM- 9.2
Four Color 1238,1299	10	20	30	69	130	190
1(10164-508)(8/65)-Gold Key	10	20	30	69	130	190

DEPUTY DAWG PRESENTS DINKY DUCK AND HASHIMOTO-SAN (TV)

Desperadoes #4 © Aegis

The Destructor #4 © Seaboard

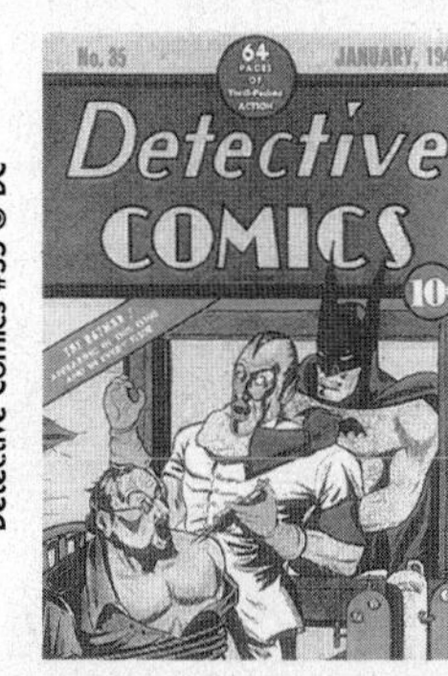

Detective Comics #35 © DC

GD VG FN VF VF/NM NM-
2.0 4.0 6.0 8.0 9.0 9.2

GD VG FN VF VF/NM NM-
2.0 4.0 6.0 8.0 9.0 9.2

Gold Key: August, 1965

1(10159-508) 9 18 27 63 112 160

DESERT GOLD (See Zane Grey 4-Color 467)

DESIGN FOR SURVIVAL (Gen. Thomas S. Power's...)
American Security Council Press: 1968 (36 pgs. in color) (25¢)

nn-Propaganda against the Threat of Communism-Aircraft cover; H-Bomb panel
3 6 9 18 27 35
Twin Circle Edition-Cover shows panels from inside 2 4 6 13 18 22

DESOLATION JONES
DC Comics (WildStorm): July, 2005 - Present ($2.95/$2.99)

1-8: 1-6-Warren Ellis-s/J.H. Williams-a. 7,8-Zezelj-a 3.00
...: Made in England TPB (2006, $14.99) r/series; cover gallery 15.00

DESPERADO (Becomes Black Diamond Western No. 9 on)
Lev Gleason Publications: June, 1948 - No. 8, Feb, 1949 (All 52 pgs.)

1-Biro-c on all; contains inside photo-c of Charles Biro, Lev Gleason & Bob Wood
15 30 45 90 140 190
2 10 20 30 56 76 95
3-Story with over 20 killings 10 20 30 58 79 100
4-8 8 16 24 44 57 70
NOTE: ***Barry** a-2. **Fuje** a-4, 8. **Guardineer** a-5-7. **Kida** a-3-7. **Ed Moore** a-4, 6.*

DESPERADO PRIMER
Image Comics (Desperado): Apr, 2005 ($1.99, one-shot)

1-Previews of Roundeye, World Traveler, A Mirror To The Soul; Bolland-c 3.00

DESPERADOES
Image Comics (Homage): Sept, 1997 - No. 5, June, 1998 ($2.50/$2.95)

1-5-Mariotte-s/Cassaday-c/a: 1-($2.50-c). 2-5-($2.95) 3.00
...: A Moment's Sunlight TPB ('98, $16.95) r/#1-5 17.00
...: Epidemic! (11/99, $5.95) Mariotte-s 6.00

DESPERADOES: BANNERS OF GOLD
IDW Publishing: Dec, 2004 - No. 5, Apr, 2005 ($3.99, limited series)

1-5: Mariotte-s/Haun-a. 1-Cassaday-c 4.00

DESPERADOES: BUFFALO DREAMS
IDW Publishing: Jan, 2007 - No. 4, Apr, 2007 ($3.99, limited series)

1-4: Mariotte-s/Dose-a/c 4.00

DESPERADOES: QUIET OF THE GRAVE
DC Comics (Homage): Jul, 2001 - No. 5, Nov, 2001 ($2.95)

1-5-Jeff Mariotte-s/John Severin-c/a 3.00
TPB (2002, $14.95) r/#1-5; intro. by Brian Keene 15.00

DESPERATE TIMES (See Savage Dragon)
Image Comics: Jun, 1998 - No. 4, Dec, 1998; Nov, 2000 - No. 4, July, 2001 ($2.95, B&W)

1-4-Chris Eliopoulos-s/a 3.00
(Vol. 2) 1-4 3.00
(Vol. 3) 0-(1/04, $3.50) Pages read sideways 3.50
(Vol. 3) 1-Pages read sideways 3.00

DESTINATION MOON (See Fawcett Movie Comics, Space Adventures #20, 23, & Strange Adventures #1)

DESTINY: A CHRONICLE OF DEATHS FORETOLD (See Sandman)
DC Comics (Vertigo): 1997 - No.3, 1998 ($5.95, limited series)

1-3-Alisa Kwitney-s in all: 1-Kent Williams & Michael Zulli-a, Williams painted-c. 2-Williams & Scott Hampton-painted-c/a. 3-Williams & Guay-a 6.00
TPB (2000, $14.95) r/series 15.00

DESTROY!!
Eclipse Comics: 1986 ($4.95, B&W, magazine-size, one-shot)

1 5.00
3-D Special 1-r-/#1 ($2.50) 5.00

DESTROYER
Marvel Comics: June, 2009 - No. 5, Oct, 2009 ($3.99, limited series)

1-5-Kirkman-s/Walker-a/Pearson-c 4.00

DESTROYER, THE
Marvel Comics (MAX): Nov, 1989 - No. 9, Jun, 1990 ($2.25, B&W, magazine, 52 pgs.)

1-Based on Remo Williams movie, paperbacks 6.00
2-9: 2-Williamson part inks. 4-Ditko-a 4.00

DESTROYER, THE
Marvel Comics: V2#1, March, 1991 ($1.95, 52 pgs.)
V3#1, Dec, 1991 - No. 4, Mar, 1992 ($1.95, mini-series)

V2#1,V3#1-4: Based on Remo Williams paperbacks. V3#1-4-Simonson-c. 3-Morrow-a 4.00

DESTROYER, THE (Also see Solar, Man of the Atom)
Valiant: Apr, 1995 ($2.95, color, one-shot)

0-Indicia indicates #1 3.00

DESTROYER DUCK
Eclipse Comics: Feb, 1982 - No. 7, May, 1984 (#2-7: Baxter paper) ($1.50)

1-Origin Destroyer Duck; 1st app. Groo; Kirby-c/a(p) 1 3 4 6 8 10
2-5: 2-Starling back-up begins; Kirby-c/a(p) thru #5 5.00
6,7 4.00
NOTE: ***Neal Adams** c-1i. **Kirby** c/a-1-5p. **Miller** c-7.*

DESTRUCTOR, THE
Atlas/Seaboard: February, 1975 - No. 4, Aug, 1975

1-Origin/1st app.; Ditko/Wood-a; Wood-c(i) 2 4 6 9 12 15
2-4: 2-Ditko/Wood-a. 3,4-Ditko-a(p) 2 4 6 8 10 12

DETECTIVE COMICS (Also see other Batman titles)
National Periodical Publications/DC Comics: Mar, 1937 - No. 881, Oct, 2011

1-(Scarce)-Slam Bradley & Spy by Siegel & Shuster, Speed Saunders by Stoner and Flessel, Cosmo, the Phantom of Disguise, Buck Marshall, Bruce Nelson begin; Chin Lung in 'Claws of the Red Dragon' serial begins; Vincent Sullivan-c
12,500 25,000 37,500 88,000 - -
2 (Rare)-Creig Flessel-c begin; new logo 4000 8000 12,000 28,000 - -
3 (Rare) 3000 6000 9000 12,000 - -
4,5: 5-Larry Steele begins 1450 2900 4350 7975 11,238 14,500
6,7,9,10 1000 2000 3000 5500 7750 10,000
8-Mister Chang-c; classic-c 1500 3000 4500 8250 11,625 15,000
11-17,19: 15,16-Have interior ad for Action Comics #1. 17-1st app. Fu Manchu in Detective
800 1600 2400 4400 6200 8000
18-Fu Manchu-c; last Flessel-c 1350 2700 4050 7425 10,463 13,500
20-The Crimson Avenger begins (1st app.) 1080 2160 3240 5940 8370 10,800
21,23-25 650 1300 1950 3575 5038 6500
22-1st Crimson Avenger-c by Chambers (12/38) 820 1640 246 4510 6355 8200
26 670 1340 2010 3685 5193 6700
27-The Bat-Man & Commissioner Gordon begin (1st app.), created by Bill Finger & Bob Kane (5/39); Batman-c (1st)(by Kane). Bat-Man's secret identity revealed as Bruce Wayne in six pg. story. Signed Rob't Kane (also see Det. PIcture Stories #5 & Funny Pages V3#1)
84,000 168,000 252,000 630,000 990,000 1,350,000
27-Reprint, Oversize 13-1/2x10". WARNING: This comic is an exact duplicate reprint of the original except for its size. DC published it in 1974 with a second cover titling it as Famous First Edition. There have been many reported cases of the outer cover being removed and the interior sold as the original edition. The reprint with the new outer cover removed is practically worthless; see Famous First Edition for value.
28-2nd app. The Batman (6 pg. story); non-Bat-Man-c; signed Rob't Kane
3500 7000 10,500 26,500 45,625 65,000
29-1st app. Doctor Death-c/story, Batman's 1st name villain. 1st 2 part story (10 pgs.). 2nd Batman-c by Kane 6000 12,000 18,000 45,000 77,500 110,000
30-Dr. Death app. Story concludes from issue #29. Classic Batman splash panel by Kane.
1200 2400 3600 9000 16,000 23,000
31-Classic Batman over castle cover; 1st app. The Monk & 1st Julie Madison (Bruce Wayne's 1st love interest); 1st Batplane (Bat-Gyro) and Batarang; 2nd 2-part Batman adventure. Gardner Fox takes over script from Bill Finger. 1st mention of locale (New York City) where Batman lives 7000 14,000 21,000 52,500 88,750 125,000
32-Batman story concludes from issue #31. 1st app. Dala (Monk's assistant). Batman uses gun for 1st time to slay The Monk and Dala. This was the 1st time a costumed hero used a gun in comic books. 1st Batman head logo on cover
1000 2000 3000 7400 13,200 19,000
33-Origin The Batman (2 pgs.)(1st told origin); Batman gun holster-c; Batman w/smoking gun panel at end of story. Batman story now 12 pgs. Classic Batman-c
6267 12,534 18,800 47,000 81,000 115,000
34-2nd Crimson Avenger-c by Creig Flessel and last non Batman-c. Story from issue #32 x-over as Bruce Wayne sees Julie Madison off to America from Paris. Classic Batman splash panel used later in Batman #1 for origin story. Steve Malone begins
757 1514 2271 5526 9763 14,000
35-Classic Batman hypodermic needle-c that reflects story in issue #34. Classic Batman with smoking .45 automatic splash panel. Batman-c begin
3267 6534 9800 24,500 42,250 60,000
36-Batman-c that reflects adventure in issue #35. Origin/1st app. of Dr. Hugo Strange (1st major villain, 2/40). 1st finned-gloves worn by Batman
1467 2934 4400 11,000 19,000 27,000
37-Last solo Golden-Age Batman adventure in Detective Comics. Panel at end of story reflects solo Batman adventure in Batman #1 that was originally planned for Detective #38. Cliff Crosby begins 1200 2400 3600 9000 16,000 23,000
38-Origin/1st app. Robin the Boy Wonder (4/40); Batman and Robin-c begin; cover by Kane
5000 10,000 15,000 37,500 63,750 90,000

Detective Comics #122 © DC

Detective Comics #168 © DC

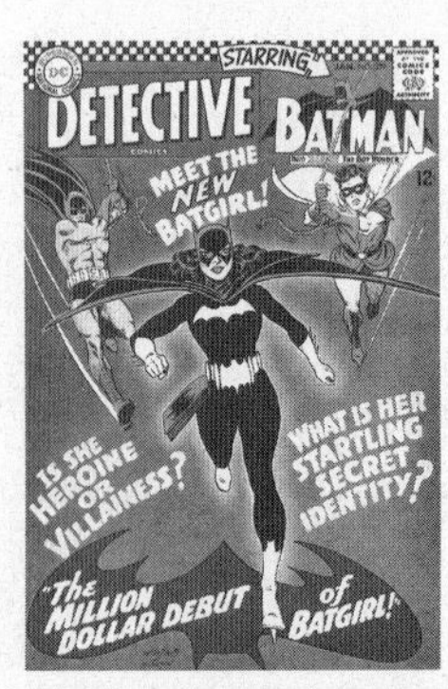

Detective Comics #359 © DC

	GD 2.0	VG 4.0	FN 6.0	VF 8.0	VF/NM 9.0	NM- 9.2
39-Opium story; Clayface app. in 1 panel ad at the end of the Batman story	784	1568	2352	5723	10,112	14,500
40-Origin & 1st app. Clayface (Basil Karlo); 1st Joker cover app. (6/40); Joker story intended for this issue was used in Batman #1 instead; cover is similar to splash page in 2nd Joker story in Batman #1	946	1892	2838	6906	12,203	17,500
41-Robin's 1st solo	423	846	1269	3000	5250	7500
42-44: 44-Crimson Avenger-new costume	320	640	960	2240	3920	5600
45-1st Joker story in Det. (3rd book app. & 4th story app. over all, 11/40)	432	864	1296	3154	5577	8000
46-50: 46-Death of Hugo Strange. 48-1st time car called Batmobile (2/41); Gotham City 1st mention in Detective (1st mentioned in Wow #1; also see Batman #4). 49-Last Clay Face	300	600	900	2070	3635	5200
51-57	226	452	678	1446	2473	3500
58-1st Penguin app. (12/41); last Speed Saunders; Fred Ray-c	524	1048	1572	3825	6763	9700
59,60: 59-Last Steve Malone; 2nd Penguin; Wing becomes Crimson Avenger's aide. 60-Intro. Air Wave; Joker app. (2nd in Det.)	232	464	696	1485	2543	3600
61,63: 63-Last Cliff Crosby; 1st app. Mr. Baffle	206	412	618	1318	2259	3200
62-Joker-c/story (2nd Joker-c, 4/42)	371	742	1113	2600	4550	6500
64-Origin & 1st app. Boy Commandos by Simon & Kirby (6/42); Joker app.	411	822	1233	2877	5039	7200
65-1st Boy Commandos-c (S&K-a on Boy Commandos & Ray/Robinson-a on Batman & Robin on-c; 4 artists on one-c)	300	600	900	2010	3505	5000
66-Origin & 1st app. Two-Face	541	1082	1623	3950	6975	10,000
67-1st Penguin-c (9/42)	309	618	927	2163	3782	5400
68-Two-Face-c/story; 1st Two-Face-c	284	568	852	1818	3109	4400
69-Joker-c/story	300	600	900	2010	3505	5000
70	181	362	543	1158	1979	2800
71-Joker-c/story	297	594	891	1901	3251	4600
72,74,75: 74-1st Tweedledum & Tweedledee plus-c; S&K-a	155	310	465	992	1696	2400
73-Scarecrow-c/story (1st Scarecrow-c)	226	452	678	1446	2473	3500
76-Newsboy Legion & The Sandman x-over in Boy Commandos; S&K-a; Joker-c/story	239	478	717	1530	2615	3700
77-79: All S&K-a	139	278	417	883	1517	2150
80-Two-Face app.; S&K-a	168	336	504	1075	1838	2600
81,82,84,86-90: 81-1st Cavalier-c & app. 89-Last Crimson Avenger; 2nd Cavalier-c & app.	110	220	330	704	1202	1700
83-1st "skinny" Alfred (1/44)(see Batman #21; last S&K Boy Commandos (also #92,128); most issues #84 on signed S&K are not by them	116	232	348	742	1271	1800
85-Joker-c/story; last Spy; Kirby/Klech Boy Commandos	187	374	561	1197	2049	2900
91,102,109-Joker-c/stories	174	348	522	1114	1907	2700
92-98: 96-Alfred's last name 'Beagle' revealed, later changed to 'Pennyworth' in #214	90	180	270	576	988	1400
99-Penguin-c/story	148	296	444	947	1624	2300
100 (6/45)	129	258	387	826	1413	2000
101,103-108,110-113,115-117,119: 108-1st Bat-signal-c (2/46)	82	164	246	528	902	1275
114,118-Joker-c/stories. 114-1st small logo (8/46)	158	316	474	1003	1727	2450
120-Penguin-c/story	152	304	456	965	1658	2350
121,123,125,127,129,130	79	158	237	502	864	1225
122-1st Catwoman-c (4/47)	213	426	639	1363	2332	3300
124,128-Joker-c/stories	142	284	426	909	1555	2200
126-Penguin-c	129	258	387	826	1413	2000
131-134,136,139	74	148	223	470	810	1150
135-Frankenstein-c/story	92	184	276	584	1005	1425
137-Joker-c/story; last Air Wave	123	246	369	787	1344	1900
138-Origin Robotman (see Star Spangled #7 for 1st app.); series ends #202	116	232	348	742	1271	1800
140-The Riddler-c/story (1st app., 10/48)	595	1190	1785	4350	7675	11,000
141,143-148,150: 150-Last Boy Commandos	74	148	222	470	810	1150
142-2nd Riddler-c/story	161	322	483	1030	1765	2500
149-Joker-c/story	116	232	348	742	1271	1800
151-Origin & 1st app. Pow Wow Smith, Indian lawman (9/49) & begins series	84	168	252	538	919	1300
152,154,155,157-160: 152-Last Slam Bradley	74	148	222	470	810	1150
153-1st app. Roy Raymond TV Detective (11/49); origin The Human Fly	77	154	231	493	847	1200
156(2/50)-The new classic Batmobile	107	214	321	680	1165	1650
161-167,169,170,172-176: Last 52 pg. issue	71	142	213	454	777	1100
168-Origin the Joker	459	918	1377	3350	5925	8500
171-Penguin-c	100	200	300	635	1093	1550
177-179,181-186,188,189,191,192,194-199,201,202,204,206-210,212,214-216: 184-1st app. Fire Fly. 185-Secret of Batman's utility belt. 187-Two-Face app. 202-Last Robotman & Pow Wow Smith. 215-1st app. of Batmen of all Nations. 216-Last precode (2/55)	68	136	204	435	743	1050
180,193-Joker-c/story	97	194	291	621	1061	1500
187-Two-Face-c/story	81	162	243	518	884	1250
190-Origin Batman retold	90	180	270	576	988	1400
200(10/53), 205: 205-Origin Batcave	84	168	252	538	919	1300
203,211-Catwoman-c/stories	89	178	267	565	970	1375
213-Origin & 1st app. Mirror Man	79	158	237	502	864	1225
217-224: 218-Batman Jr. & Robin Sr. app.	58	116	174	371	636	900
225-(11/55)-1st app. Martian Manhunter (J'onn J'onzz); origin begins; also see Batman #78	410	820	1230	3700	7600	11,500
226-Origin Martian Manhunter cont'd (2nd app.)	152	304	456	965	1733	2500
227-229: Martian Manhunter stories in all	61	122	183	390	720	1050
230-1st app. Mad Hatter; brief recap origin of Martian Manhunter	68	136	204	435	793	1150
231-Brief origin recap Martian Manhunter	50	100	150	315	558	800
232,234,237-240: 239-Early DC grey tone-c	47	94	141	296	523	750
233-Origin & 1st app. Batwoman (7/56)	194	388	582	1242	2221	3200
235-Origin Batman & his costume; tells how Bruce Wayne's father (Thomas Wayne) wore Bat costume & fought crime (reprinted in Batman #255)	76	152	228	486	856	1225
236-1st S.A. issue; J'onn J'onzz talks to parents and Mars-1st since being stranded on Earth; 1st app. Bat-Tank?	48	96	144	302	539	775
241-260: 246-Intro. Diane Meade, John Jones' girl. 249-Batwoman-c/app. 253-1st app. The Terrible Trio. 254-Bat-Hound-c/story. 257-Intro. & 1st app. Whirly Bats. 259-1st app. The Calendar Man	40	80	120	242	414	585
261-264,266,268-271: 261-J. Jones tie-in to sci/fi movie "Incredible Shrinking Man"; 1st app. Dr. Double X. 262-Origin Jackal. 268,271-Manhunter origin recap	33	66	99	194	322	450
265-Batman's origin retold with new facts	43	86	129	271	473	675
267-Origin & 1st app. Bat-Mite (5/59)	50	100	150	315	583	850
272,274,275,277-280	28	56	84	165	275	385
273-J'onn J'onzz i.d. revealed for 1st time	29	58	87	170	285	400
276-2nd app. Bat-Mite	34	68	102	199	342	485
281-292, 294-297: 286,292-Batwoman-c/app. 287-Origin J'onn J'onzz retold. 289-Bat-Mite-c/story. 292-Last Roy Raymond. 297-Last 10¢ issue (11/61)	22	44	66	132	221	310
293-(7/61)-Aquaman begins (pre #1); ends #300	23	46	69	136	228	320
298-(12/61)-1st modern Clayface (Matt Hagen)	26	52	78	186	381	575
299, 300-(2/62)-Aquaman ends	13	26	39	94	190	285
301-(3/62)-J'onn J'onzz returns to Mars (1st time since stranded on Earth six years before)	11	22	33	77	144	210
302-317,319-321,323,324,326,329,330: 302,307-Batwoman-c/app. 311-Intro. Zook in John Jones; 1st app. Cat-Man. 321-2nd Terrible Trio. 326-Last J'onn J'onzz, story cont'd in House of Mystery #143; intro. Idol-Head of Diabolu	10	20	30	69	125	180
318,322,325: 318,325-Cat-Man-c/story (2nd & 3rd app.); also 1st & 2nd app. Batwoman as the Cat-Woman. 322-Bat-Girl's 1st/only app. in Det. (6th in all); Batman cameo in J'onn J'onzz (only hero to app. in series)	10	20	30	70	128	185
327-(5/64)-Elongated Man begins, ends #383; 1st new look Batman with new costume; Infantino/Giella new look-a begins; Batman with gun	13	26	39	91	178	265
328-Death of Alfred; Bob Kane biog, 2 pgs.	12	24	36	87	166	245
331,333-340: 334-1st app. The Outsider	9	18	27	60	100	140
332,341,365-Joker-c/stories	10	20	30	70	128	185
342-358,360,361,366-368: 345-Intro Block Buster. 347-"What If" theme story (1/66). 350-Elongated Man new costume. 355-Zatanna x-over in Elongated Man. 356-Alfred brought back in Batman, early SA app.	8	16	24	53	86	120
359-Intro/origin Batgirl (Barbara Gordon)-c/story (1/67); 1st Silver Age app. Killer Moth	24	48	72	175	463	750
362,364-S.A. Riddler app. (early)	9	18	27	63	112	160
363-2nd app. new Batgirl	11	22	33	75	143	210
369(11/67)-N. Adams-a (Elongated Man); 3rd app. S.A. Catwoman (cameo; leads into Batman #197); 4th app. new Batgirl	11	22	33	80	160	240
370-1st Neal Adams-a on Batman (cover only, 12/67)	9	18	27	63	107	150
371-(1/68) 1st new Batmobile from TV show; classic Batgirl-c	11	22	33	75	143	210
372-376,378-386,389,390: 375-New Batmobile-c	6	12	18	43	69	95
377-S.A. Riddler-c/sty	8	16	24	52	86	120
387-r/1st Batman story from #27 (30th anniversary, 5/69); Joker-c; last 12¢ issue	9	18	27	65	113	160
388-Joker-c/story	9	18	27	61	106	150

Detective Comics #432 © DC

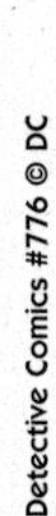

Detective Comics #776 © DC

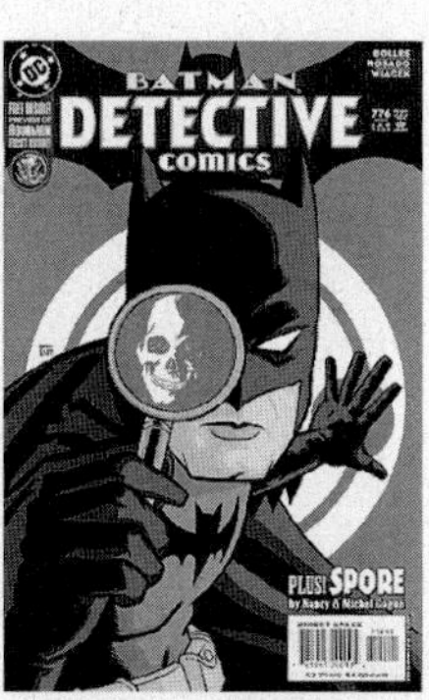

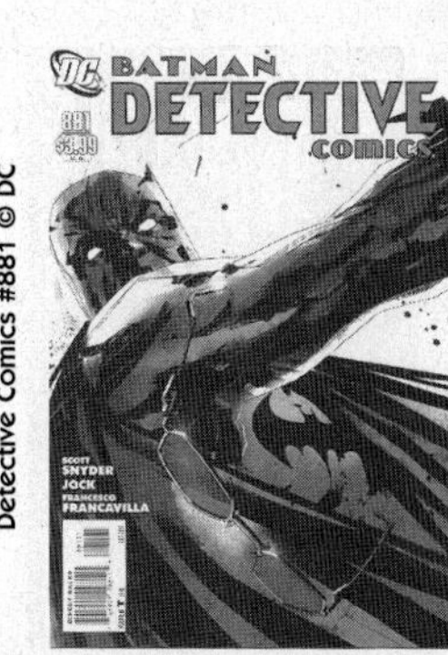

Detective Comics #881 © DC

	GD 2.0	VG 4.0	FN 6.0	VF 8.0	VF/NM 9.0	NM- 9.2
391-394,396,398,399,401,403,405,406,409: 392-1st app. Jason Bard. 401-2nd Batgirl/Robin team-up. 405-Debut League of Assassins	6	12	18	37	59	80
395,397,402,404,407,408,410-Neal Adams-a. 404-Tribute to Enemy Ace	9	18	27	65	120	175
400-(6/70)-Origin & 1st app. Man-Bat; 1st Batgirl/Robin team-up (cont'd in #401); Neal Adams-a	18	36	54	131	291	450
411-(5/71) Intro. Talia, daughter of Ra's al Ghul (Ra's mentioned, but doesn't appear until Batman #232 (6/71); Bob Brown-a	6	12	18	41	71	100
412-413: 413-Last 15¢ issue	5	10	15	30	53	75
414-424: All-25¢, 52 pgs. 418-Creeper x-over. 424-Last Batgirl.	5	10	15	32	56	80
425-436: 426,430,436-Elongated Man app. 428,434-Hawkman begins, ends #467	5	10	15	30	48	65
437-New Manhunter begins (10-11/73, 1st app.) by Simonson, ends #443	6	12	18	37	59	80
438-445 (All 100 Page Super Spectaculars): 438-Kubert Hawkman-r. 439-Origin Manhunter. 440-G.A. Manhunter(Adv. #79) by S&K, Hawkman, Dollman, Green Lantern; Toth-a. 441-G.A. Plastic Man, Batman, Ibis-r. 442-G.A. Newsboy Legion, Black Canary, Elongated Man, Dr. Fate-r. 443-Origin The Creeper-r; death of Manhunter; G.A. Green Lantern, Spectre-r; Batman-r/Batman #18. 444-G.A. Kid Eternity-r. 445-G.A. Dr. Midnite-r	7	14	21	44	72	100
446-460: 457-Origin retold & updated	3	6	9	17	25	32
461-465,470,480: 480-(44 pgs.). 463-1st app. Black Spider. 464-2nd app. Black Spider 470-Intro. Silver St. Cloud.	3	6	9	16	22	28
466-468,471-474,478,479-Rogers-a in all: 466-1st app. Signalman since Batman #139. 470,471-1st modern app. Hugo Strange. 474-1st app. new Deadshot. 478-1st app. 3rd Clayface (Preston Payne). 479-(44 pgs.)	4	8	12	26	41	55
469-Intro/origin Dr. Phosphorous; Simonson-a	4	8	12	24	37	50
475,476-Joker-c/stories; Rogers-a	8	16	24	52	89	125
477-Neal Adams-a(r); Rogers-a (3 pgs.)	4	8	12	24	37	50
481-(Combined with Batman Family, 12-1/78-79, begin $1.00, 68 pg. issues, ends #495); 481-495-Batgirl, Robin solo stories	3	6	9	17	25	32
482-Starlin/Russell, Golden-a; The Demon begins (origin-r), ends #485 (by Ditko #483-485)	3	6	9	14	19	24
483-40th Anniversary issue; origin retold; Newton Batman begins	3	6	9	16	22	28
484-495 (68 pgs): 484-Origin Robin. 485-Death of Batwoman. 486-Killer Moth app. 487-The Odd Man by Ditko. 489-Robin/Batgirl team-up. 490-Black Lightning begins. 491-(#492 on inside). 493-Intro. The Swashbuckler	2	4	6	9	13	16
496-499: 496-Clayface app.	2	4	6	8	10	12
500-($1.50, 52 pgs.)-Batman/Deadman team-up with Infantino-a; new Hawkman story by Joe Kubert; incorrectly says 500th Anniv. of Det.	2	4	6	13	18	22
501-503,505-523: 509-Catman-c. 510-Mad Hatter-c. 512-2nd app. new Dr. Death. 519-Last Batgirl. 521-Green Arrow series begins. 523-Solomon Grundy app.	1	2	3	5	6	8
504-Joker-c/story	2	4	6	9	13	16
524-2nd app. Jason Todd (cameo)(3/83)	1	3	4	6	8	10
525-3rd app. Jason Todd (See Batman #357)	1	3	4	6	8	10
526-Batman's 500th app. in Detective Comics ($1.50, 68 pgs.); Death of Jason Todd's parents, Joker-c/story (55 pgs.); Bob Kane pin-up	3	6	9	14	19	24
527-531,533,534,536-568,571,573: 538-Cat-Man-c/story cont'd from Batman #371. 542-Jason Todd quits as Robin (becomes Robin again #547). 549,550-Alan Moore scripts (Green Arrow). 554-1st new Black Canary (9/85). 566-Batman villains profiled. 567-Harlan Ellison scripts.						6.00
532,569,570-Joker-c/stories	2	4	6	9	13	16
535-Intro new Robin (JasonTodd)-1st appeared in Batman	1	3	4	6	8	10
572-(3/87, $1.25, 60 pgs.)-50th Anniv. of Det. Comics	1	2	3	5	6	8
574-Origin Batman & Jason Todd retold	1	3	4	6	8	10
575-Year 2 begins, ends #578	3	6	9	16	22	28
576-578: McFarlane-c/a; The Reaper app.	3	6	9	16	22	28
579-597,599,601-610: 579-New bat wing logo. 583-1st app. villains Scarface & Ventriloquist. 589-595-(52 pgs.)-Each contain free 16 pg. Batman stories. 604-607-Mudpack storyline; 604,607-Contain Batman mini-posters. 610-Faked death of Penguin; artists names app. on tombstone on-c						4.00
598-($2.95, 84 pgs.)- "Blind Justice" storyline begins by Batman movie writer Sam Hamm, ends #600						5.00
600-(5/89, $2.95, 84 pgs.)-50th Anniv. of Batman in Det.; 1 pg. Neal Adams pin-up, among other artists						5.00
611-626,628-658: 612-1st new look Cat-Man; Catwoman app. 615- "The Penguin Affair" part 2 (See Batman #448,449). 617-Joker-c/story. 624-1st new Catwoman (w/death) & 1st new Batwoman. 626-Batman's 600th app. in Detective. 642-Return of Scarface, part 2. 644-Last $1.00-c. 652,653-Huntress-c/story w/new costume plus Charest-c on both						4.00
627-($2.95, 84 pgs.)-Batman's 601st app. in Det.; reprints 1st story/#27 plus 3 versions (2 new) of same story						5.00

	GD 2.0	VG 4.0	FN 6.0	VF 8.0	VF/NM 9.0	NM- 9.2
659-664: 659-Knightfall part 2; Kelley Jones-c. 660-Knightfall part 4; Bane-c by Sam Kieth. 661-Knightfall part 6; brief Joker & Riddler app. 662-Knightfall part 8; Riddler app.; Sam Kieth-c. 663-Knightfall part 10; Kelley Jones-c. 664-Knightfall part 12; Bane-c/story; Joker app.; continued in Showcase 93 #7 & 8; Jones-c						4.00
665-675: 665,666-Knightfall parts 16 & 18; 666-Bane-c/story. 667-Knightquest: The Crusade & new Batman begins (1st app. in Batman #500). 669-Begin $1.50-c; Knightquest, cont'd in Robin #1. 671,673-Joker app.						3.00
675-($2.95)-Collectors edition w/foil-c						4.00
676-($2.50, 52 pgs.)-KnightsEnd pt. 3						4.00
677,678: 677-KnightsEnd pt. 9. 678-(9/94)-Zero Hour tie-in.						3.00
679-685: 679-(11/94). 682-Troika pt. 3						3.00
682-($2.50) Embossed-c Troika pt. 3						4.00
686-699,701-719: 686-Begin $1.95-c. 693,694-Poison Ivy-c/app. 695-Contagion pt. 2; Catwoman, Penguin app. 696-Contagion pt. 8. 698-Two-Face-c/app. 701-Legacy pt. 6; Batman vs. Bane-c/app. 702-Legacy Epilogue. 703-Final Night x-over. 705-707-Riddler-app. 714,715-Martian Manhunter-app.						3.00
700-($4.95, Collectors Edition)-Legacy pt. 1; Ra's Al Ghul-c/app; Talia & Bane app; book displayed at shops in envelope						6.00
700-($2.95, Regular Edition)-Different-c						4.00
720-740: 720,721-Cataclysm pts. 5,14. 723-Green Arrow app. 730-740-No Man's Land stories						3.00
741-($2.50) Endgame; Joker-c/app.						4.00
742-749,751-765: 742-New look Batman begins; 1st app. Crispus Allen (who later becomes the Spectre). 751,752-Poison Ivy app. 756-Superman-c/app. 759-762-Catwoman back-up						3.00
750-($4.95, 64 pgs.) Ra's al Ghul-c						6.00
766-772: 766,767-Bruce Wayne: Murderer pt. 1,8. 769-772-Bruce Wayne: Fugitive pts. 4,8,12,16						3.00
773,774,776-799: 773-Begin $2.75-c; Sienkiewicz-c. 777-784-Sale-c. 784-786-Alan Scott app. 787-Mad Hatter app. 793-Begin $2.95-c. 797-799-War Games						3.00
775-($3.50) Sienkiewicz-c						4.00
800-($3.50) Jock-c; aftermath of War Games; back-up by Lapham						4.00
801-816: 801-814-Lapham-s. 804-Mr. Freeze app. 809-War Crimes						3.00
817-849,851,852: 817-820: One Year Later 8-part x-over with Batman #651-654; Robinson-s/Bianchi-c. 819-Begin $2.99-c. 820-Dini-s/Williams III-a. 825-Doctor Phosphorus app. 827-Debut of new Scarface. 831-Harley app.; Dini-s. 833,834-Zatanna & Joker app. 838,839-Resurrection of Ra's al Ghul x-over. 846-847-Batman R.I.P. x-over						3.00
817,818,838,839-2nd printings. 817-Combo-c of #817̳ cover images. 818-Combo-c of #818 and Batman #653 cover images. 838-Andy Kubert variant-c. 839-Red bkgd-c						3.00
850-($3.99) Batman vs. Hush; Dini-s/Nguyen-a						4.00
853-($3.99) Gaiman-s/Andy Kubert-a; continued from Batman #686; Kubert sketch pgs.						4.00
853-Variant-c with red background by Andy Kubert						12.00
854-872-($3.99) 854-Batwoman features begin; Rucka-a/J.H. Williams-a/c; The Question back-ups begin. 858-860-Batwoman origin						4.00
854,858,859,860-Variant-c: 854-JG Jones. 858-Hughes. 859-Jock. 860-Alex Ross						6.00
854-Special Edition (8/10, $1.00) reprints issue with "What's Next?" logo on cover						3.00
873-880-($2.99) 874,875,879-Francavilla-a. 880-Jock-a						3.00
881-(10/11) Last issue of first volume; Snyder-s/Jock & Francavilla-a						3.00
#0-(10/94) Zero Hour tie-in, released between #678 & 679						3.00
#1,000,000 (11/98) 853rd Century x-over						3.00
Annual 1 (1988, $1.50)						5.00
Annual 2-7,9 ('89-'94, '96, 68 pgs.)-4-Painted-c. 5-Joker-c/story (54 pgs.) continued in Robin Annual #1; Sam Kieth-c; Eclipso app. 6-Azrael as Batman in new costume; intro Geist the Twilight Man; Bloodlines storyline. 7-Elseworlds story. 9-Legends of the Dead Earth story						5.00
Annual 8 (1995, $3.95, 68 pgs.)-Year One story						5.00
Annual 10 (1997, $3.95)-Pulp Heroes story						5.00
Annual 11 (12/09, $4.99)-Azrael & The Question app.; continued from Batman Ann. #27						5.00
Annual 12 (2/11, $4.99)-Nightrunner & The Question app.; continued in Batman Ann. #28						5.00

NOTE: **Neal Adams** *c-370, 372, 385, 389, 391, 392, 394-422, 439.* **Aparo** *a-437, 438, 444-446, 500, 625-632p, 638-643p; c-430, 437, 440-446, 448, 468-470, 480, 484(back), 492-502,508, 509, 515, 518-522, 641, 716, 719, 722, 724.* **Austin** *a(i)-450, 451, 463-468, 471-476; c(i)-474-476, 478.* **Baily** *a-443r.* **Buckler** *a-434, 446p, 479p; c(p)-467, 482, 505-507, 511, 513-516, 518.* **Burnley** *a(Batman)-65, 75, 78, 83, 100, 103, 125; c-62i, 63i, 64, 73i, 78, 83p, 96p, 103p, 105p, 106, 108, 121p, 123p, 125p.* **Chaykin** *a-441.* **Colan** *a(p)-510, 512, 517, 523, 528-538, 540-546, 555-567; c(p)-510, 512, 528, 530-535, 537, 538, 540, 541, 543-545, 556-558, 560-564.* **J. Craig** *a-488.* **Ditko** *a-443r, 483-485, 487.* **Golden** *a-482p; c-625, 626, 628-631, 633, 644-646.* **Alan Grant** *scripts-584-597, 601-621, 641, 642, Annual 5.* **Grell** *a-445, 455, 463p, 464p; c-455.* **Guardineer** *c-23, 24, 26, 28, 30, 32.* **Gustavson** *a-441r.* **Infantino** *a-354, 442(2)r, 500, 572.* **Infantino/Anderson** *c-333, 337-340, 343, 344, 347, 351, 352, 359, 361-368, 371.* **Kelley Jones** *c-651, 657i, 658i, 659, 661, 663-675.* **Kaluta** *c-423, 424, 426-428, 431, 434, 438, 484, 486, 572.* **Bob Kane** *a-Most early issues #27 on, 297r, 356r, 438-440r, 442r, 443r.* **Kane/Robinson** *c-33.* **Gil Kane** *a(p)-368, 370-374, 384, 385, 388-407, 438r, 439r, 520.* **Kane/Anderson** *c-369.* **Sam Kieth** *c-654-656 (657, 658 w/***Kelley Jones***), 660, 662, Annual #5.* **Kubert** *a-438r, 439r, 500; c-348, 350.* **McFarlane** *c/a(p)-576-578.* **Meskin** *a-420r.* **Mignola** *c-583.* **Moldoff** *c-233-354, 259, 266, 267, 275, 287, 289, 290, 297, 300.* **Moldoff/Giella** *a-328, 330, 332, 334, 336, 338, 340, 342, 344, 346, 348, 350, 352, 354, 356.* **Mooney** *a-444r.* **Moreira** *a-153-300, 419r, 444r, 445r.* **Nasser/Netzer** *a-654, 655, 657, 658.* **Newton** *a(p)-480, 481, 483-499, 501-509, 511, 513-516, 518-520, 524, 526, 539; c-526p.* **Irv Novick** *c-375-377, 383.* **Robbins** *a-426p, 429p.* **Robinson** *a-part: 66, 68, 71-73; all: 74-76, 79, 80; c-62, 64, 66, 68-74, 76, 79, 82, 86, 88, 442r, 443r.* **Rogers** *a-466-468, 471-479p, 481p; c-471p, 472p, 473, 474-479p.* **Roussos**

Detective Comics (2011 series) #1 © DC

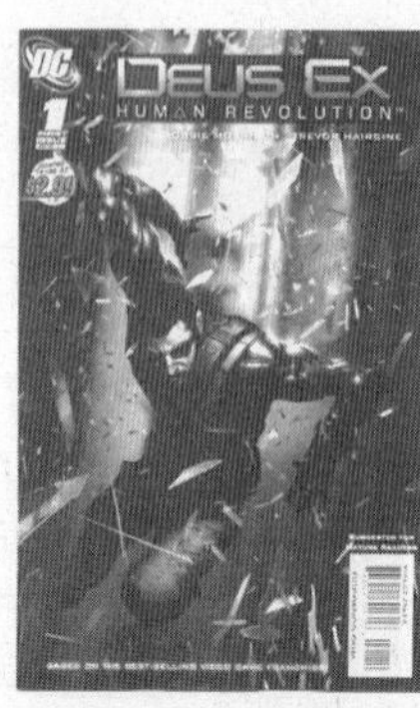
Deus Ex #1 © Square Enix

Devil Dinosaur #8 © MAR

GD VG FN VF VF/NM NM-
2.0 4.0 6.0 8.0 9.0 9.2

Airwave-76-105(most); c(i)-71, 72, 74-76, 79, 107. ***Russell*** *a-481i, 482i.* ***Simon/Kirby*** *a-440r, 442r.* ***Simonson*** *a-437-443, 450, 469, 470, 500.* ***Dick Sprang*** *c-77, 82, 84, 85, 87, 89-93, 95-100, 102, 103i, 104i, 106, 108, 114, 117, 118, 122, 123, 128, 129, 131, 133, 135, 141, 148, 149, 168, 622-624.* ***Starlin*** *a-481p, 482p; c-503, 504, 567p.* ***Starr*** *a-444r.* ***Toth*** *a-442; r-414, 416, 418, 424, 440-441, 443, 444.* ***Tuska*** *a-486p, 490p.* ***Matt Wagner*** *c-647-649.* ***Wrightson*** *c-425.*

DETECTIVE COMICS (DC New 52)
DC Comics: Nov, 2011 - Present ($2.99)

1-Joker app.; Tony Daniel-s/a/c 5.00
2-7: 2-Intro of The Dollmaker. 5-7-Penguin app. 3.00
8-($3.99) Catwoman & Scarecrow app.; back-up Two-Face story 4.00

DETECTIVE DAN, SECRET OP. 48 (Also see Adventures of Detective Ace King and Bob Scully, The Two-Fisted Hick Detective)
Humor Publ. Co. (Norman Marsh): 1933 (10¢, 10x13", 36 pgs., B&W, one-shot) (3 color, cardboard-c)

nn-By Norman Marsh, 1st comic w/ original-a; 1st newsstand-c; Dick Tracy look-alike; forerunner of Dan Dunn. (Title and Wu Fang character inspired Detective Comics #1 four years later.) (1st comic of a single theme) 1667 3334 5000 10,000 - -

DETECTIVE EYE (See Keen Detective Funnies)
Centaur Publications: Nov, 1940 - No. 2, Dec, 1940

1-Air Man (see Keen Detective) & The Eye Sees begins; The Masked Marvel & Dean Denton app. 239 478 717 1530 2615 3700
2-Origin Don Rance and the Mysticape; Binder-a; Frank Thomas-c 126 252 378 806 1378 1950

DETECTIVE PICTURE STORIES (Keen Detective Funnies No. 8 on?)
Comics Magazine Company: Dec, 1936 - No. 5, Apr, 1937

1 (All issues are very scarce) 580 1160 1740 3132 4566 6000
2-The Clock app. (1/37, early app.) 250 500 750 1350 2000 2650
3,4: 4-Eisner-a 170 340 510 918 1384 1850
5-The Clock-c/story (4/37); 1st detective/adventure art by Bob Kane; Bruce Wayne prototype app.(see Funny Pages V3/1) 195 390 585 1053 1577 2100

DETECTIVES, THE (TV)
Dell Publishing Co.: No. 1168, Mar-May, 1961 - No. 1240, Oct-Dec, 1961

Four Color 1168 (#1)-Robert Taylor photo-c 9 18 27 63 112 160
Four Color 1219-Robert Taylor, Adam West photo-c 9 18 27 58 99 140
Four Color 1240-Tufts-a; Robert Taylor photo-c; 2 different back-c 8 16 24 55 93 130

DETECTIVES, INC. (See Eclipse Graphic Album Series)
Eclipse Comics: Apr, 1985 - No. 2, Apr, 1985 ($1.75, both w/April dates)

1,2: 2-Nudity 3.00

DETECTIVES, INC.: A TERROR OF DYING DREAMS
Eclipse Comics: Jun, 1987 - No. 3, Dec, 1987 ($1.75, B&W& sepia)

1-3: Colan-a 3.00
TPB ('99, $19.95) r/series 20.00

DETENTION COMICS
DC Comics: Oct, 1996 ($3.50, 56 pgs., one-shot)

1-Robin story by Dennis O'Neil & Norm Breyfogle; Superboy story by Ron Marz & Ron Lim; Warrior story by Ruben Diaz & Joe Phillips; Phillips-c 5.00

DETHKLOK (Based on the animated series Metalocalypse)
Dark Horse Comics: Oct, 2010 - No. 3, Feb, 2011 ($3.99, limited series)

1-3-Small & Schnepp-s; covers by Schnepp & Eric Powell 4.00
...: Versus the Goon 1-(7/09, $3.50) Powell-s/a/c; Dethklok visits the Goon universe 3.50
...: Versus the Goon 1-Variant cover by Jon Schnepp 5.00
HC (7/11, $19.99) r/#1-3 & Dethklok: Versus the Goon 20.00

DETONATOR (Mike Baron's...)
Image Comics: Nov, 2004 - No. 4 ($2.50/$2.95)

1-4-Mike Baron-s/Mel Rubi-a 3.00

DEUS EX (Based on the Square Enix videogame)
DC Comics: Apr, 2011 - No. 6, Sept, 2011 ($2.99, limited series)

1-6-Robbie Morrison-s/Trevor Hairsine-a 3.00

DEVASTATOR
Image Comics/Halloween: 1998 - No. 3 ($2.95, B&W, limited series)

1,2-Hudnall-s/Horn-c/a 3.00

DEVI (Shekhar Kapur's...)
Virgin Comics: July, 2006 - No. 20, Jun, 2008 ($2.99)

1-20: 1-Mukesh Singh-a/Siddharth Kotian-s. 2-Greg Horn-c 3.00
.../Witchblade (4/08, $2.99) Singh-a/Land-c; continued from Witchblade/Devi 3.00

GD VG FN VF VF/NM NM-
2.0 4.0 6.0 8.0 9.0 9.2

... Vol. 1 TPB (5/07, $14.99) r/#1-5 and Story from Virgin Comics Preview #0 15.00
... Vol. 2 TPB (9/07, $14.99) r/#6-10; character and cover sketches 15.00

DEVIL CHEF
Dark Horse Comics: July, 1994 ($2.50, B&W, one-shot)

nn 3.00

DEVIL DINOSAUR
Marvel Comics Group: Apr, 1978 - No. 9, Dec, 1978

1-Kirby/Royer-a in all; all have Kirby-c 3 6 9 16 23 30
2-9: 4-7-UFO/sci. fic. 8-Dinoriders-c/sty 2 4 6 9 13 16
... By Jack Kirby Omnibus HC (2007, $29.99, dustjacket) r/#1-9; intro. by Brevoort 30.00

DEVIL DINOSAUR SPRING FLING
Marvel Comics: June, 1997 ($2.99. one-shot)

1-(48 pgs.) Moon-Boy-c/app. 4.00

DEVIL-DOG DUGAN (Tales of the Marines No. 4 on)
Atlas Comics (OPI): July, 1956 - No. 3, Nov, 1956

1-Severin-c 14 28 42 82 121 160
2-Iron Mike McGraw x-over; Severin-c 9 18 27 52 69 85
3 9 18 27 47 61 75

DEVIL DOGS
Street & Smith Publishers: 1942

1-Boy Rangers, U.S. Marines 30 60 90 177 289 400

DEVILINA (Magazine)
Atlas/Seaboard: Feb, 1975 - No. 2, May, 1975 (B&W)

1-Art by Reese, Marcos; "The Tempest" adapt. 4 8 12 24 37 50
2 (Low printing) 4 8 12 26 41 55

DEVIL KIDS STARRING HOT STUFF
Harvey Publications (Illustrated Humor): July, 1962 - No. 107, Oct, 1981 (Giant-Size #41-55)

1 (12¢ cover price #1-#41-9/69) 23 46 69 161 343 525
2 11 22 33 76 151 225
3-10 (1/64) 9 18 27 58 99 140
11-20 6 12 18 37 59 80
21-30 4 8 12 26 41 55
31-40: 40-(6/69) 3 6 9 20 30 40
41-50: All 68 pg. Giants 4 8 12 22 34 45
51-55: All 52 pg. Giants 3 6 9 20 30 40
56-70 2 4 6 11 16 20
71-90 2 4 6 8 11 14
91-107 1 2 3 5 6 8

DEVIL'S DUE FREE COMIC BOOK DAY
Devil's Due Publ.: May, 2005 (Free Comic Book Day giveaway)

nn-Short stories of G.I. Joe, Defex and Darkstalkers; Darkstalkers flip cover 3.00

DEVIL'S FOOTPRINTS, THE
Dark Horse Comics: March, 2003 - No. 4, June, 2003 ($2.99, limited series)

1-4-Paul Lee-c/a; Scott Allie-s 3.00

DEXTER COMICS
Dearfield Publ.: Summer, 1948 - No. 5, July, 1949

1-Teen-age humor 12 24 36 69 97 125
2-Junie Prom app. 9 18 27 47 61 75
3-5 8 16 24 40 50 60

DEXTER'S LABORATORY (Cartoon Network)
DC Comics: Sept, 1999 - No. 34, Apr, 2003 ($1.99/$2.25)

1 4.00
2-10: 2-McCracken-s 3.00
11-24, 26-34: 31-Begin $2.25-c. 32-34-Wray-c 3.00
25-(50¢-c) Tartakovsky-s/a; Action Hank-c/app. 3.00

DEXTER THE DEMON (Formerly Melvin The Monster)(See Cartoon Kids & Peter the Little Pest)
Atlas Comics (HPC): No. 7, Sept, 1957

7 9 18 27 47 61 75

DHAMPIRE: STILLBORN
DC Comics (Vertigo): 1996 ($5.95, one-shot, mature)

1-Nancy Collins script; Paul Lee-c/a 6.00

DIABLO
DC Comics: Jan, 2012 - No. 5 ($2.99, limited series)

1-3-Aaron Williams-s/Joseph Lacroix-a/c 3.00

DIARY CONFESSIONS (Formerly Ideal Romance)

Diary Loves #10 © QUA

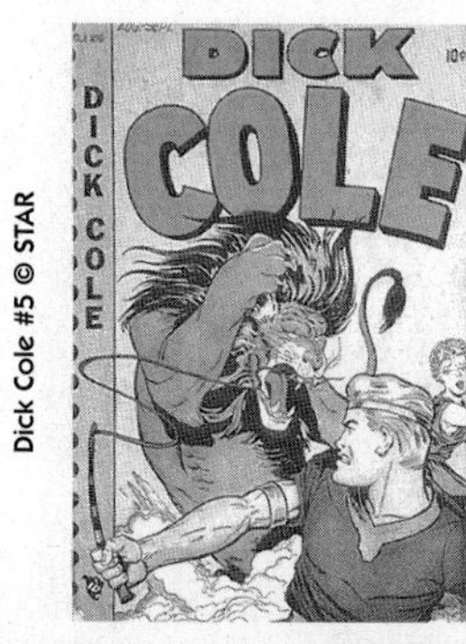

Dick Cole #5 © STAR

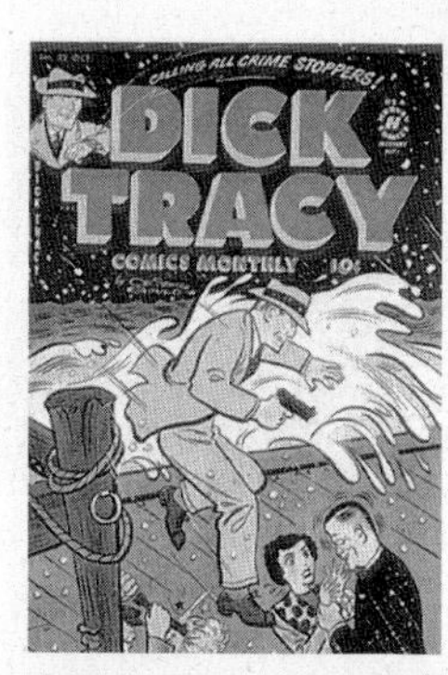

Dick Tracy #32 © NYNS

	GD 2.0	VG 4.0	FN 6.0	VF 8.0	VF/NM 9.0	NM- 9.2

Stanmor/Key Publ.(Medal Comics): No. 9, May, 1955 - No. 14, Apr, 1955

9 — 9 18 27 50 65 80
10-14 — 8 16 24 40 50 60

DIARY LOVES (Formerly Love Diary #1; G. I. Sweethearts #32 on)
Quality Comics Group: No. 2, Nov, 1949 - No. 31, April, 1953

2-Ward-c/a, 9 pgs. — 19 38 57 111 176 240
3 (1/50)-Photo-c begin, end #27? — 11 22 33 60 83 105
4-Crandall-a — 12 24 36 67 94 120
5-7,10 — 10 20 30 54 72 90
8,9-Ward-a 6,8 pgs. 8-Gustavson-a; Esther Williams photo-c — 14 28 42 81 118 155
11,13,14,17-20 — 9 18 27 52 69 85
12,15,16-Ward-a 9,7,8 pgs. — 14 28 42 76 108 140
21-Ward-a, 7 pgs. — 12 24 36 69 97 125
22-31: 31-Whitney-a — 9 18 27 50 65 80
NOTE: *Photo c-3-10, 12-27.*

DIARY OF HORROR
Avon Periodicals: December, 1952

1-Hollingsworth-c/a; bondage-c — 46 92 138 290 488 685

DIARY SECRETS (Formerly Teen-Age Diary Secrets)(See Giant Comics Ed.)
St. John Publishing Co.: No. 10, Feb, 1952 - No. 30, Sept, 1955

10-Baker-c/a most issues — 30 60 90 177 289 400
11-16,18,19 — 22 44 66 132 216 300
17,20: Kubert-r/Hollywood Confessions #1. 17-r/Teen Age Romances #9 — 22 44 66 132 216 300
21-30: 22,27-Signed stories by Estrada. 28-Last precode (3/55) — 17 34 51 98 154 210
nn-(25¢ giant, nd (1950?)-Baker-c & rebound St. John comics — 84 168 252 538 919 1300

DICK COLE (Sport Thrills No. 11 on)(See Blue Bolt & Four Most #1)
Curtis Publ./Star Publications: Dec-Jan, 1948-49 - No. 10, June-July, 1950

1-Sgt. Spook; L. B. Cole-c; McWilliams-a; Curt Swan's 1st work — 34 68 102 199 325 450
2,5 — 15 30 45 92 144 195
3,4,6-10: All-L.B. Cole-c. 10-Joe Louis story — 22 44 66 130 213 295
Accepted Reprint #7(V1#6 on-c)(1950's)-Reprints #7; L.B. Cole-c — 9 18 27 47 61 75
Accepted Reprint #9(nd)-(Reprints #9 & #8-c) — 9 18 27 47 61 75
NOTE: ***L. B. Cole** c-1, 3, 4, 6-10. **Al McWilliams** a-6. Dick Cole in 1-9. Baseball c-10. Basketball c-9. Football c-8.*

DICKIE DARE
Eastern Color Printing Co.: 1941 - No. 4, 1942 (#3 on sale 6/15/42)

1-Caniff-a, bondage-c by Everett — 62 124 186 394 677 960
2 — 29 58 87 170 278 385
3,4-Half Scorchy Smith by Noel Sickles who was very influential in Milton Caniff's development — 31 62 93 182 296 410

DICK POWELL (Also see A-1 Comics)
Magazine Enterprises: No. 22, 1949 (one shot)

A-1 22-Photo-c — 22 44 66 132 216 300

DICK QUICK, ACE REPORTER (See Picture News #10)

DICKS
Caliber Comics: 1997 - No. 4, 1998 ($2.95, B&W)

1-4-Ennis-s/McCrea-c/a; r/Fleetway — 3.00
TPB ('98, $12.95) r/series — 13.00

DICK'S ADVENTURES
Dell Publishing Co.: No. 245, Sept, 1949

Four Color 245 — 6 12 18 41 66 90

DICK TRACY (See Famous Feature Stories, Harvey Comics Library, Limited Collectors' Ed., Mammoth Comics, Merry Christmas, The Original..., Popular Comics, Super Book No. 1, 7, 13, 25, Super Comics & Tastee-Freez)

DICK TRACY
David McKay Publications: May, 1937 - Jan, 1938

Feature Books nn - 100 pgs., partially reprinted as 4-Color No. 1 (appeared before Large Feature Comics, 1st Dick Tracy comic book) (Very Rare-five known copies; two incomplete) — 1100 2200 3300 8400 15,200 22,000
Feature Books 4 - Reprints nn issue w/new-c — 139 278 417 883 1517 2150
Feature Books 6,9 — 98 196 294 622 1074 1525

DICK TRACY (...Monthly #1-24)
Dell Publishing Co.: 1939 - No. 24, Dec, 1949

	GD 2.0	VG 4.0	FN 6.0	VF 8.0	VF/NM 9.0	NM- 9.2

Large Feature Comic 1 (1939) -Dick Tracy Meets The Blank — 194 388 582 1242 2121 3000
Large Feature Comic 4,8 — 100 200 300 635 1093 1550
Large Feature Comic 11,13,15 — 87 174 261 553 952 1350
Four Color 1(1939)('35-r) — 1000 2000 3000 7600 13,800 20,000
Four Color 6(1940)('37-r)-(Scarce) — 226 452 678 1446 2473 3500
Four Color 8(1940)('38-'39-r) — 113 226 339 718 1234 1750
Large Feature Comic 3(1941, Series II) — 87 174 261 553 952 1350
Four Color 21('41)('38-r) — 82 164 246 528 902 1275
Four Color 34('43)('39-'40-r) — 37 74 111 278 602 925
Four Color 56('44)('40-r) — 33 66 99 239 520 800
Four Color 96('46)('40-r) — 22 44 66 154 327 500
Four Color 133('47)('40-'41-r) — 17 34 51 114 250 385
Four Color 163('47)('41-r) — 15 30 45 102 221 340
Four Color 215('48)-Titled "Sparkle Plenty", Dick Tracy-r — 11 22 33 73 142 210
1(1/48)('34-r) — 34 68 102 247 536 825
2,3 — 17 34 51 119 260 400
4-10 — 15 30 45 102 221 340
11-18: 13-Bondage-c — 12 24 36 81 166 250
19-1st app. Sparkle Plenty, B.O. Plenty & Gravel Gertie in a 3-pg. strip not by Gould — 12 34 36 84 175 265
20-1st app. Sam Catchem; c/a not by Gould — 12 24 36 79 160 240
21-24-Only 2 pg. Gould-a in each — 11 22 33 77 154 230
NOTE: *No. 19-24 have a 2 pg. biography of a famous villain illustrated by **Gould**: 19-Little Face; 20-Flattop; 21-Breathless Mahoney; 22-Measles; 23-Itchy; 24-The Brow.*

DICK TRACY (Continued from Dell series)(...Comics Monthly #25-140)
Harvey Publications: No. 25, Mar, 1950 - No. 145, April, 1961

25-Flat Top-c/story (also #26,27) — 12 24 36 81 166 250
26-28,30: 28-Bondage-c. 28,29-The Brow-c/stories — 10 20 30 68 127 185
29-1st app. Gravel Gertie in a Gould-r — 11 22 33 76 151 225
31,32,34,35,37-40: 40-Intro/origin 2-way wrist radio (6/51) — 9 18 27 60 103 145
33- "Measles the Teen-Age Dope Pusher" — 10 20 30 68 127 185
36-1st app. B.O. Plenty in a Gould-r — 10 20 30 68 127 185
41-50 — 8 16 24 53 89 125
51-56,58-80: 51-2pgs Powell-a — 7 14 21 46 76 105
57-1st app. Sam Catchem in a Gould-r — 8 16 24 53 89 125
81-99,101-140: 99-109-Painted-c — 6 12 18 42 69 95
100, 141-145 (25¢)(titled "Dick Tracy") — 7 14 21 46 76 105
NOTE: ***Powell** a(1-2pgs.)-43, 44, 104, 108, 109, 145. No. 110-120, 141-145 are all reprints from earlier issues.*

DICK TRACY ("Reuben Award" series)
Blackthorne Publishing: 12/84 - No. 24, 6/89 (1-12: $5.95; 13-24: $6.95, B&W, 76 pgs.)

1-8-1st printings; hard-c ed. ($14.95) — 20.00
1-3-2nd printings, 1986; hard-c ed. — 20.00
1-12-1st & 2nd printings; squarebound. thick-c — 12.00
13-24 ($6.95): 21,22-Regular-c & stapled — 14.00
NOTE: ***Gould** daily & Sunday strip-r in all. 1-12 r-12/31/45-4/5/49; 13-24 r-7/13/41-2/20/44.*

DICK TRACY (Disney)
WD Publications: 1990 - No. 3, 1990 (color) (Book 3 adapts 1990 movie)

Book One ($3.95, 52pgs.)-Kyle Baker-c/a — 6.00
Book Two, Three ($5.95, 68pgs.)-Direct sale — 6.00
Book Two, Three ($2.95, 68pgs.)-Newsstand — 4.00

DICK TRACY ADVENTURES
Gladstone Publishing: May, 1991 ($4.95, 76 pgs.)

1-Reprints strips 2/1/42-4/18/42 — 5.00

DICK TRACY, EXPLOITS OF
Rosdon Books, Inc.: 1946 ($1.00, hard-c strip reprints)

1-Reprints the near complete case of "The Brow" from 6/12/44 to 9/24/44 (story starts a few weeks late) — 25 50 75 147 241 335
with dust jacket... — 39 78 117 240 395 550

DICK TRACY MONTHLY/WEEKLY
Blackthorne Publishing: May, 1986 - No. 99, 1989 ($2.00, B&W)
(Becomes Weekly #26 on)

1-60: Gould-r. 30,31-Mr. Crime app. — 4.00
61-90 — 4.00
91-95 — 6.00
96-99-Low print — 1 2 3 5 7 9
NOTE: *#1-10 reprint strips 3/10/40-7/13/41; #10(pg.8)-51 reprint strips 4/6/49-12/31/55; #52-99 reprint strips 12/26/56-4/26/64.*

DICK TRACY SPECIAL

Die Cut #4 © MAR

Ding Dong #3 © ME

Dirty Pair #1 © Studio Proteus

	GD 2.0	VG 4.0	FN 6.0	VF 8.0	VF/NM 9.0	NM- 9.2

Blackthorne Publ.: Jan, 1988 - No. 3, Aug. (no month), 1989 ($2.95, B&W)
1-3: 1-Origin D. Tracy; 4/strips 10/12/31-3/30/32 3.00

DICK TRACY: THE EARLY YEARS
Blackthorne Publishing: Aug, 1987 - No. 4, Aug (no month) 1989 ($6.95, B&W, 76 pgs.)

	GD	VG	FN	VF	VF/NM	NM-
1-3: 1-4-r/strips 10/12/31(1st daily)-8/31/32 & Sunday strips 6/12/32-8/28/32; Big Boy apps. in #1-3	1	2	3	4	5	7
4 ($2.95, 52pgs.)						4.00

DICK TRACY UNPRINTED STORIES
Blackthorne Publishing: Sept, 1987 - No. 4, June, 1988 ($2.95, B&W)
1-4: Reprints strips 1/1/56-12/25/56 3.00

DICK TURPIN (See Legend of Young...)

DIE-CUT
Marvel Comics UK, Ltd: Nov, 1993 - No. 4, Feb, 1994 ($1.75, limited series)
1-4: 1-Die-cut-c; The Beast app. 3.00

DIE-CUT VS. G-FORCE
Marvel Comics UK, Ltd: Nov, 1993 - No. 2, Dec, 1993 ($2.75, limited series)
1,2-($2.75)-Gold foil-c on both 3.00

DIE HARD: YEAR ONE (Based on the John McClane character)
BOOM! Studios: Aug, 2009 - No. 8, Mar, 2010 ($3.99, limited series)
1-8-Chaykin-s; Officier McClane in 1976 NYC; multiple covers on each 4.00

DIE, MONSTER, DIE (See Movie Classics)

DIGIMON DIGITAL MONSTERS (TV)
Dark Horse Comics: May, 2000 - No. 12, Nov, 2000 ($2.95/$2.99)
1-12 3.00

DIGITEK
Marvel UK, Ltd: Dec, 1992 - No. 4, Mar, 1993 ($1.95/$2.25, mini-series)
1-4: 3-Deathlock-c/story 3.00

DILLY (Dilly Duncan from Daredevil Comics; see Boy Comics #57)
Lev Gleason Publications: May, 1953 - No. 3, Sept, 1953

	GD	VG	FN	VF	VF/NM	NM-
1-Teenage; Biro-c	7	14	21	37	46	55
2,3-Biro-c	5	10	15	24	30	35

DILTON'S STRANGE SCIENCE (See Pep Comics #78)
Archie Comics: May, 1989 - No. 5, May, 1990 (75¢/$1.00)
1-5 3.00

DIME COMICS
Newsbook Publ. Corp.: 1945; 1951

	GD	VG	FN	VF	VF/NM	NM-
1-Silver Streak/Green Dragon-c/sty; Japanese WWII-c by L. B. Cole (Rare)	155	310	465	992	1696	2400
1(1951)	15	30	45	85	130	175

DINGBATS (See 1st Issue Special)

DING DONG
Compix/Magazine Enterprises: Summer?, 1946 - No. 5, 1947 (52 pgs.)

	GD	VG	FN	VF	VF/NM	NM-
1-Funny animal	29	58	87	170	278	385
2 (9/46)	15	30	45	84	127	170
3 (Wint '46-'47) - 5	13	26	39	72	101	130

DINKY DUCK (Paul Terry's...) (See Approved Comics, Blue Ribbon, Giant Comics Edition #5A & New Terrytoons)
St. John Publishing Co./Pines No. 16 on: Nov, 1951 - No. 16, Sept, 1955; No. 16, Fall, 1956; No. 17, May, 1957 - No. 19, Summer, 1958

	GD	VG	FN	VF	VF/NM	NM-
1-Funny animal	13	26	39	72	101	130
2	8	16	24	42	54	65
3-10	6	12	18	29	36	42
11-16(9/55)	6	12	18	27	33	38
16 (Fall, '56) - 19	5	10	15	22	26	30

DINKY DUCK & HASHIMOTO-SAN (See Deputy Dawg Presents...)

DINO (TV)(The Flintstones)
Charlton Publications: Aug, 1973 - No. 20, Jan, 1977 (Hanna-Barbera)

	GD	VG	FN	VF	VF/NM	NM-
1	3	6	9	18	27	35
2-10	2	4	6	10	14	18
11-20	2	4	6	8	10	12
Digest nn (w/Xerox Pub., 1974) (low print run)	2	4	6	11	16	20

DINO ISLAND
Mirage Studios: Feb, 1994 - No. 2, Mar, 1994 ($2.75, limited series)
1,2-By Jim Lawson 3.00

DINO RIDERS
Marvel Comics: Feb, 1989 - No. 3, 1989 ($1.00)
1-3: Based on toys 3.00

DINOSAUR REX
Upshot Graphics (Fantagraphics): 1986 - No. 3, 1986 ($2.00, limited series)
1-3 3.00

DINOSAURS, A CELEBRATION
Marvel Comics (Epic): Oct, 1992 - No. 4, Oct, 1992 ($4.95, lim. series, 52 pgs.)
1-4: 2-Bolton painted-c 5.00

DINOSAURS ATTACK! THE GRAPHIC NOVEL
Eclipse Comics: 1991 ($3.95, coated stock, stiff-c)
Book One- Based on Topps trading cards 4.00

DINOSAURS FOR HIRE
Malibu Comics: Feb, 1993 - No. 12, Feb, 1994 ($1.95/$2.50)
1-12: 1,10-Flip bk. 8-Bagged w/Skycap; Staton-c. 10-Flip book 3.00

DINOSAURS GRAPHIC NOVEL (TV)
Disney Comics: 1992 - No. 2, 1993 ($2.95, 52 pgs.)
1,2-Staton-a; based on Dinosaurs TV show 4.00

DINOSAURUS
Dell Publishing Co.: No. 1120, Aug, 1960

	GD	VG	FN	VF	VF/NM	NM-
Four Color 1120-Movie, painted-c	8	16	24	55	93	130

DIPPY DUCK
Atlas Comics (OPI): October, 1957

	GD	VG	FN	VF	VF/NM	NM-
1-Maneely-a; code approved	10	20	30	58	79	100

DIRECTORY TO A NONEXISTENT UNIVERSE
Eclipse Comics: Dec, 1987 ($2.00, B&W)
1 3.00

DIRTY DOZEN (See Movie Classics)

DIRTY PAIR (Manga)
Eclipse Comics: Dec, 1988 - No. 4, Apr, 1989 ($2.00, B&W, limited series)
1-4: Japanese manga with original stories 3.00
...: Start the Violence (Dark Horse, 9/99, $2.95) r/B&W stories in color from Dark Horse Presents #132-134; covers by Warren & Pearson 3.00

DIRTY PAIR: FATAL BUT NOT SERIOUS (Manga)
Dark Horse Comics: July, 1995 - No. 5, Nov, 1995 ($2.95, limited series)
1-5 3.00

DIRTY PAIR: RUN FROM THE FUTURE (Manga)
Dark Horse Comics: Jan, 2000 - No. 4, Mar, 2000 ($2.95, limited series)
1-4-Warren-s/c/a. Var.-c by Hughes(1), Stelfreeze(2), Timm(3), Ramos(4) 3.00

DIRTY PAIR: SIM HELL (Manga)
Dark Horse Comics: May, 1993 - No. 4, Aug, 1993 ($2.50, B&W, limited series)
1-4 3.00
...Remastered #1-4 (5/01 - 8/01) reprints in color, with pin-up gallery 3.00

DIRTY PAIR II (Manga)
Eclipse Comics: June, 1989 - No. 5, Mar, 1990 ($2.00, B&W, limited series)
1-5: 3-Cover is misnumbered as #1 3.00

DIRTY PAIR III, THE (A Plague of Angels) (Manga)
Eclipse Comics: Aug, 1990 - No. 5, Aug, 1991 ($2.00/$2.25, B&W, lim. series)
1-5 3.00

DISHMAN
Eclipse Comics: Sept, 1988 ($2.50, B&W, 52 pgs.)
1 4.00

DISNEY AFTERNOON, THE (TV)
Marvel Comics: Nov, 1994 - No. 10?, Aug, 1995 ($1.50)
1-10: 3-w/bound-in Power Ranger Barcode Card 3.00

DISNEY COMIC ALBUM
Disney Comics: 1990(no month, year) - No. 8, 1991 ($6.95/$7.95)
1,2 ($6.95): 1-Donald Duck and Gyro Gearloose by Barks(r). 2-Uncle Scrooge by Barks(r); Jr. Woodchucks app. 9.00
3-8: 3-Donald Duck-r/F.C. 308 by Barks; begin $7.95-c. 4-Mickey Mouse Meets the Phantom Blot; r/M.M Club Parade (censored 1956 version of story). 5-Chip 'n' Dale Rescue Rangers;

Disney's Aladdin #4 © DIS

Disney's Hero Squad #8 © DIS

Divine Right #2 © DC

GD VG FN VF VF/NM NM-
2.0 4.0 6.0 8.0 9.0 9.2

new-a. 6-Uncle Scrooge. 7-Donald Duck in Too Many Pets; Barks-r(4) including F.C. #29. 8-Super Goof; r/S.G. #1, D.D. #102 9.00

DISNEY COMIC HITS
Marvel Comics: Oct, 1995 - No. 16, Jan, 1997 ($1.50/$2.50)

1-16: 4-Toy Story. 6-Aladdin. 7-Pocahontas. 10-The Hunchback of Notre Dame (Same story in Disney's The Hunchback of Notre Dame). 13-Aladdin and the Forty Thieves 4.00

DISNEY COMICS
Disney Comics: June, 1990

Boxed set of #1 issues includes Donald Duck Advs., Ducktales, Chip 'n Dale Rescue Rangers, Roger Rabbit, Mickey Mouse Advs. & Goofy Advs.; limited to 10,000 sets 2 4 6 11 16 20

DISNEYLAND BIRTHDAY PARTY (Also see Dell Giants)
Gladstone Publishing Co.: Aug, 1985 ($2.50)

1-Reprints Dell Giant with new-photo-c 2 4 6 8 10 12
...Comics Digest #1-(Digest) 2 4 6 8 11 14

DISNEYLAND MAGAZINE
Fawcett Publications: Feb. 15, 1972 - ? (10-1/4"x12-5/8", 20 pgs, weekly)

1-One or two page painted art features on Dumbo, Snow White, Lady & the Tramp, the Aristocats, Brer Rabbit, Peter Pan, Cinderella, Jungle Book, Alice & Pinocchio. Most standard characters app. 3 6 9 16 23 30

DISNEYLAND, USA (See Dell Giant No. 30)

DISNEY MOVIE BOOK
Walt Disney Productions (Gladstone): 1990 ($7.95, 8-1/2"x11", 52 pgs.) (w/pull-out poster)

1-Roger Rabbit in Tummy Trouble; from the cartoon film strips adapted to the comic format. Ron Dias-c 2 4 6 8 10 12

DISNEY'S ACTION CLUB
Acclaim Books: 1997 - No. 4 ($4.50, digest size)

1-4: 1-Hercules. 4-Mighty Ducks 4.50

DISNEY'S ALADDIN (Movie)
Marvel Comics: Oct, 1994 - No. 11, 1995 ($1.50)

1-11 3.00

DISNEY'S BEAUTY AND THE BEAST (Movie)
Marvel Comics: Sept, 1994 - No. 13, 1995 ($1.50)

1-13 3.00

DISNEY'S BEAUTY AND THE BEAST HOLIDAY SPECIAL
Acclaim Books: 1997 ($4.50, digest size, one-shot)

1-Based on The Enchanted Christmas video 4.50

DISNEY'S COLOSSAL COMICS COLLECTION
Disney Comics: 1991 - No. 10, 1993 ($1.95, digest-size, 96/132 pgs.)

1-10: Ducktales, Talespin, Chip 'n Dale's Rescue Rangers. 4-r/Darkwing Duck #1-4. 6-Goofy begins. 8-Little Mermaid 5.00

DISNEY'S COMICS IN 3-D
Disney Comics: 1992 ($2.95, w/glasses, polybagged)

1-Infinity-c; Barks, Rosa, Gottfredson-r 5.00

DISNEY'S ENCHANTING STORIES
Acclaim Books: 1997 - No. 5 ($4.50, digest size)

1-5: 1-Hercules. 2-Pocahontas 4.50

DISNEY'S HERO SQUAD
BOOM! Studios: Jan, 2010 - No. 8, Aug, 2010 ($2.99)

1-8: 1-3-Phantom Blot app. 1-Back-up reprint of Super Goof #1 3.00

DISNEY'S NEW ADVENTURES OF BEAUTY AND THE BEAST (Also see Beauty and the Beast & Disney's Beauty and the Beast)
Disney Comics: 1992 - No. 2, 1992 ($1.50, limited series)

1,2-New stories based on movie 3.00

DISNEY'S POCAHONTAS (Movie)
Marvel Comics: 1995 ($4.95, one-shot)

1-Movie adaptation 1 2 3 4 5 7

DISNEY'S TALESPIN LIMITED SERIES: "TAKE OFF" (TV) (See Talespin)
W. D. Publications (Disney Comics): Jan, 1991 - No. 4, Apr, 1991 ($1.50, lim. series, 52 pgs.)

1-4: Based on animated series; 4 part origin 4.00

DISNEY'S TARZAN (Movie)
Dark Horse Comics: June, 1999 - No. 2, July, 1999 ($2.95, limited series)

1,2: Movie adaptation 3.00

GD VG FN VF VF/NM NM-
2.0 4.0 6.0 8.0 9.0 9.2

DISNEY'S THE LION KING (Movie)
Marvel Comics: July, 1994 - No. 2, July, 1994 ($1.50, limited series)

1,2: 2-part movie adaptation 3.00
1-($2.50, 52 pgs.)-Complete story 5.00

DISNEY'S THE LITTLE MERMAID (Movie)
Marvel Comics: Sept, 1994 - No. 12, 1995 ($1.50)

1-12 4.00

DISNEY'S THE LITTLE MERMAID LIMITED SERIES (Movie)
Disney Comics: Feb, 1992 - No. 4, May, 1992 ($1.50, limited series)

1-4: Peter David scripts 3.00

DISNEY'S THE LITTLE MERMAID: UNDERWATER ENGAGEMENTS
Acclaim Books: 1997 ($4.50, digest size)

1-Flip book 4.50

DISNEY'S THE HUNCHBACK OF NOTRE DAME (Movie)(See Disney's Comic Hits #10)
Marvel Comics: July, 1996 ($4.95, squarebound, one-shot)

1-Movie adaptation. 1 2 3 4 5 7
NOTE: *A different edition of this series was sold at Wal-Mart stores with new covers depicting scenes from the 1989 feature film. Inside contents and price were identical.*

DISNEY'S THE THREE MUSKETEERS (Movie)
Marvel Comics: Jan, 1994 - No. 2, Feb, 1994 ($1.50, limited series)

1,2-Morrow-c; Spiegle-a; Movie adaptation 3.00

DISNEY'S TOY STORY (Movie)
Marvel Comics: Dec, 1995 ($4.95, one-shot)

nn-Adaptation of film 1 2 3 4 5 7

DISTANT SOIL, A (1st Series)
WaRP Graphics: Dec, 1983 - No. 9, Mar 1986 ($1.50, B&W)

1-Magazine size 4.00
2-9: 2-4 are magazine size 3.00
NOTE: *Second printings exist of #1, 2, 3 & 6.*

DISTANT SOIL, A
Donning (Star Blaze): Mar, 1989 ($12.95, trade paperback)

nn-new material 13.00

DISTANT SOIL, A (2nd Series)
Aria Press/Image Comics (Highbrow Entertainment) #15 on: June, 1991 - Present ($1.75/$2.50/$2.95/$3.95, B&W)

1-27: 13-$2.95-c begins. 14-Sketchbook. 15-(8/96)-1st Image issue 4.00
29-33,35,37-($3.95) 4.00
34-($4.95, 64 pages) includes sketchbook pages 5.00
36,38-($4.50) 36-Back-up story by Darnall & Doran. 38-Includes sketch pages 4.50
The Aria ('01, $16.95,TPB) r/#26-31 17.00
The Ascendant ('98, $18.95,TPB) r/#13-25 19.00
The Gathering ('97, $18.95,TPB) r/#1-13; intro. Neil Gaiman 19.00
Vol. 4: Coda (2005, $17.99, TPB) r/#32-38 18.00
NOTE: *Four separate printings exist for #1 and are clearly marked. Second printings exist of #2-4 and are also clearly marked.*

DISTANT SOIL, A: IMMIGRANT SONG
Donning (Star Blaze): Aug, 1987 ($6.95, trade paperback)

nn-new material 7.00

DISTRICT X (Also see X-Men titles) (Also see Mutopia X)
Marvel Comics: July, 2004 - No. 14, Aug, 2005 ($2.99)

1-14: 1-3-Bishop app.; Yardin-a/Hine-s 3.00
...Vol. 1: Mr. M (2005, $14.99) r/#1-6; sketch page by Yardin 15.00
...Vol. 2: Underground (2005, $19.99) r/#7-14; prologue from X-Men Unlimited #2 20.00

DIVER DAN (TV)
Dell Publishing Co.: Feb-Apr, 1962 - No. 2, June-Aug, 1962

Four Color 1254(#1), 2 5 10 15 35 55 75

DIVINE RIGHT
Image Comics (WildStorm Prod.): Sept, 1997 - No. 12, Nov, 1999 ($2.50)

Preview 5.00
1,2: 1-Jim Lee-s/a(p)/c, 1-Variant-c by Charest 4.00
1-($3.50)-Voyager Pack w/Stormwatch preview 3.50
1-American Entertainment Ed. 6.00
2-Variant-c of Exotica & Blaze 5.00
3-Chromium-c by Jim Lee 5.00
3-12: 3-5-Fairchild & Lynch app. 4-American Entertainment Ed. 8-Two covers. 9-1st DC issue. 11,12-Divine Intervention pt. 1,4 3.00

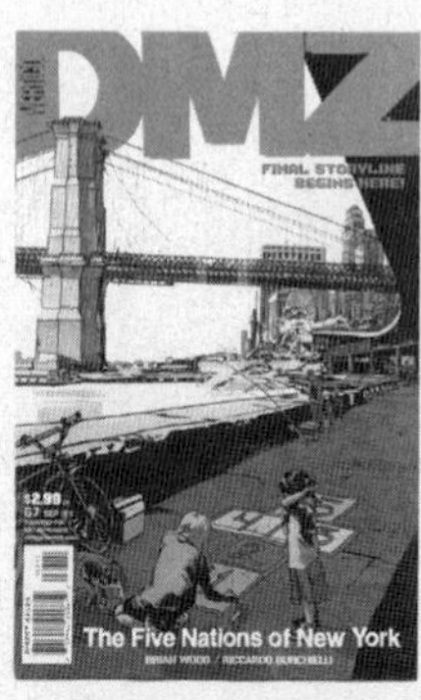

DMZ #67 © Wood & Burchielli

Doc Macabre #1 © Niles & Wrightson

Doc Savage Comics #10 © CN

	GD 2.0	VG 4.0	FN 6.0	VF 8.0	VF/NM 9.0	NM- 9.2

GD VG FN VF VF/NM NM- 2.0 4.0 6.0 8.0 9.0 9.2

5-Pacific Comicon Ed. 6.00
6-Glow in the dark variant-c, European Tour Edition 20.00
...Book One TPB (2002, $17.95) r/#1-7 18.00
...Book Two TPB (2002, $17.95) r/#8-12 & Divine Intervention Gen13, ...Wildcats 18.00
...Collected Edition #1-3 ($5.95, TPB) 1-r/#1,2. 2-r/#3,4. 3-r/#5,6 6.00
Divine Intervention/Gen 13 (11/99, $2.50) Part 3; D'Anda-a 3.00
Divine Intervention/Wildcats (11/99, $2.50) Part 2; D'Anda-a 3.00

DIVISION 13 (See Comic's Greatest World)
Dark Horse Comics: Sept, 1994 - Jan, 1995 ($2.50, color)

1-4: Giffen story in all. 1-Art Adams-c 3.00

DIXIE DUGAN (See Big Shot, Columbia Comics & Feature Funnies)
McNaught Syndicate/Columbia/Publication Ent.: July, 1942 - No. 13, 1949
(Strip reprints in all)

	GD	VG	FN	VF	VF/NM	NM-
1-Joe Palooka x-over by Ham Fisher	27	54	81	160	263	365
2	15	30	45	86	133	180
3	12	24	36	69	97	125
4,5(1945-46)-Bo strip-r	10	20	30	54	72	90
6-13(1/47-49): 6-Paperdoll cut-outs	9	18	27	47	61	75

DIXIE DUGAN
Prize Publications (Headline): V3#1, Nov, 1951 - V4#4, Feb, 1954

	GD	VG	FN	VF	VF/NM	NM-
V3#1	10	20	30	54	72	90
2-4	7	14	21	35	43	50
V4#1-4(#5-8)	6	12	18	28	34	40

DIZZY DAMES
American Comics Group (B&M Distr. Co.): Sept-Oct, 1952 - No. 6, Jul-Aug, 1953

	GD	VG	FN	VF	VF/NM	NM-
1-Whitney-c	18	36	54	107	169	230
2	11	22	33	64	90	115
3-6	10	20	30	54	72	90

DIZZY DON COMICS
F. E. Howard Publications/Dizzy Don Ent. Ltd (Canada): 1942 - No. 22, Oct, 1946; No. 3, Apr, 1947 - No. 4, Sept./Oct., 1947 (Most B&W)

	GD	VG	FN	VF	VF/NM	NM-
1 (B&W)	24	48	72	140	230	320
2 (B&W)	14	28	42	80	115	150
4-21 (B&W)	12	24	36	67	94	120
22-Full color, 52 pgs.	24	48	72	140	230	320
3 (4/47), 4 (9-10/47)-Full color, 52 pgs.	24	48	72	140	230	320

DIZZY DUCK (Formerly Barnyard Comics)
Standard Comics: No. 32, Nov, 1950 - No. 39, Mar, 1952

	GD	VG	FN	VF	VF/NM	NM-
32-Funny animal	10	20	30	54	72	90
33-39	6	12	18	31	38	45

DMZ
DC Comics (Vertigo): Jan, 2006 - No. 72, Feb, 2012 ($2.99)

1-Brian Wood-s/Riccardo Burchielli-a 4.00
1-(2008, no cover price) Convention Exclusive promotional edition 3.00
2-49,51-72: 2-10-Brian Wood-s/Riccardo Burchielli-a. 11-Donaldson-a. 12-Wood-s/a 3.00
50-($3.99) Short stories by various incl. Risso, Moon, Gibbons, Bermejo, Jim Lee 4.00
...: Blood in the Game TPB (2009, $12.99) r/#29-34; intro. by Greg Palast 13.00
...: Body of a Journalist TPB (2007, $12.99) r/#6-12; intro. by D. Randall Blythe 13.00
...: Collective Punishment TPB (2011, $14.99) r/#55-59 15.00
...: Friendly Fire TPB (2008, $12.99) r/#18-22; intro. by Sgt. John G. Ford 13.00
...: Hearts and Minds TPB (2010, $16.99) r/#42-49; intro. by Morgan Spurlock 17.00
...: M.I.A. TPB (2011, $14.99) r/#50-54 15.00
...: On the Ground TPB (2006, $9.99) r/#1-5; intro. by Brian Azzarello 10.00
...: Public Works TPB (2007, $12.99) r/#13-17; intro. by Cory Doctorow 13.00
...: The Hidden War TPB (2008, $12.99) r/#23-28 13.00
...: War Powers TPB (2009, $14.99) r/#35-41 15.00

DNAGENTS (The New DNAgents V2/1 on)(Also see Surge)
Eclipse Comics: March, 1983 - No. 24, July, 1985 ($1.50, Baxter paper)

1,24: 1-Origin. 4-Amber app. 24-Dave Stevens-c 3.50
2-23: 8-Infinity-c 3.00
... Industrial Strength Edition TPB (Image, 2008, $24.99) B&W r/#1-14; Evanier intro. 25.00

DOBERMAN (See Sgt. Bilko's Private...)

DOBIE GILLIS (See The Many Loves of...)

DOC CHAOS: THE STRANGE ATTRACTOR
Vortex Comics: Apr, 1990 - No. 3, 1990 ($3.00, 32 pgs.)

1-3: The Lust For Order 3.00

DOC FRANKENSTEIN

Burlyman Entertainment: Nov, 2004 - No. 6 ($3.50)

1-6-Wachowski brothers-s/Skroce-a 3.50

DOCK WALLOPER (Ed Burns' ...)
Virgin Comics: Nov, 2007 - No. 5, Jun, 2008 ($2.99)

1-5-Burns & Palmiotti-s/Siju Thomas-a; Prohibition time 3.00

DOC MACABRE
IDW Publishing: Dec, 2010 - No. 3, Feb, 2011 ($3.99)

1-3-Steve Niles-s/Bernie Wrightson-a/c 4.00

DOC SAMSON (Also see Incredible Hulk)
Marvel Comics: Jan, 1996 - No. 4, Apr, 1996 ($1.95, limited series)

1-4: 1-Hulk c/app. 2-She-Hulk-c/app. 3-Punisher-c/app. 4-Polaris-c/app. 3.00

DOC SAMSON (Incredible Hulk)
Marvel Comics: Mar, 2006 - No. 5, July, 2006 ($2.99, limited series)

1-5: 1-DiFilippo-s/Fiorentino-a. 3-Conner-c 3.00

DOC SAVAGE
Gold Key: Nov, 1966

	GD	VG	FN	VF	VF/NM	NM-
1-Adaptation of the Thousand-Headed Man; James Bama c-r/1964 Doc Savage paperback	11	22	33	73	142	210

DOC SAVAGE (Also see Giant-Size...)
Marvel Comics Group: Oct, 1972 - No. 8, Jan, 1974

	GD	VG	FN	VF	VF/NM	NM-
1	3	6	9	21	32	42
2,3-Steranko-c	3	6	9	16	22	28
4-8	2	4	6	9	13	16
...: The Man of Bronze TPB (DC Comics, 2010, $17.99) r/#1-8						18.00

NOTE: ***Gil Kane*** *c-5, 6.* ***Mooney*** *a-1i. No. 1, 2 adapts pulp story "The Man of Bronze"; No. 3, 4 adapts "Death in Silver"; No. 5, 6 adapts "The Monsters"; No. 7, 8 adapts "The Brand of The Werewolf".*

DOC SAVAGE (Magazine) (See Showcase Presents for reprint)
Marvel Comics Group: Aug, 1975 - No. 8, Spring, 1977 ($1.00, B&W)

	GD	VG	FN	VF	VF/NM	NM-
1-Cover from movie poster; Ron Ely photo-c	3	6	9	16	22	28
2-5: 3-Buscema-a. 5-Adams-a(1 pg.), Rogers-a(1 pg)	2	4	6	9	13	16
6-8	2	4	6	10	14	18

DOC SAVAGE
DC Comics: Nov, 1987 - No. 4, Feb, 1988 ($1.75, limited series)

1-4: Dennis O'Neil-s/Adam & Andy Kubert-a/c in all 3.00
...: The Silver Pyramid TPB (2009, $19.99) r/#1-4 20.00

DOC SAVAGE
DC Comics: Nov, 1988 - No. 24, Oct, 1990 ($1.75/$2.00: #13-24)

1-16,19-24 3.00
17,18-Shadow x-over 4.00
Annual 1 (1989, $3.50, 68 pgs.) 4.00

DOC SAVAGE (First Wave)
DC Comics: Jun, 2010 - No. 18, Nov, 2011 ($3.99/$2.99)

1-9: 1-4-Malmont-s/Porter-a/J.G. Jones-c. Justice Inc. back-up; S. Hampton-a 4.00
1-6-Variant covers by Cassaday 5.00
10-17-($2.99) 10,16,17-Winslade-a 3.00

DOC SAVAGE COMICS (Also see Shadow Comics)
Street & Smith Publ.: May, 1940 - No. 20, Oct, 1943 (1st app. in Doc Savage pulp, 3/33)

	GD	VG	FN	VF	VF/NM	NM-
1-Doc Savage, Cap Fury, Danny Garrett, Mark Mallory, The Whisperer, Captain Death, Billy the Kid, Sheriff Pete & Treasure Island begin; Norgil, the Magician app.	503	1006	1509	3672	6486	9300
2-Origin & 1st app. Ajax, the Sun Man; Danny Garrett, The Whisperer end; classic sci-fi cover	206	412	618	1318	2259	3200
3	132	264	396	838	1444	2050
4-Treasure Island ends; Tuska-a	105	210	315	667	1146	1625
5-Origin & 1st app. Astron, the Crocodile Queen, not in #9 & 11; Norgi the Magician app.; classic-c	94	188	282	597	1024	1450
6-10: 6-Cap Fury ends; origin & only app. Red Falcon in Astron story. 8-Mark Mallory ends; Charlie McCarthy app. on-c plus true life story. 9-Supersnipe app. 10-Origin & only app. The Thunderbolt	61	122	183	390	670	950
11,12	52	104	156	328	557	785
V2#1-6,8(#13-18,20): 15-Origin of Ajax the Sun Man; Jack Benny on-c; Hitler app. 16-The Pulp Hero, The Avenger app.; Fanny Brice story. 17-Sun Man ends; Nick Carter begins; Duffy's Tavern part photo-c & story. 18-Huckleberry Finn part-c/story. 19-Henny Youngman part photo-c & life story. 20-Only all funny-c w/Huckleberry Finn	47	94	141	296	498	700
V2#7-Classic Devil-c	52	104	156	328	557	785

DOC SAVAGE: CURSE OF THE FIRE GOD

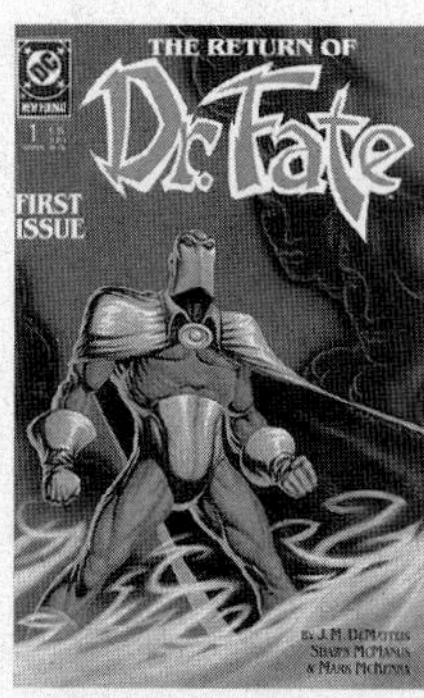

Doctor Fate #1 © DC

Doctor Solar #14 © GK

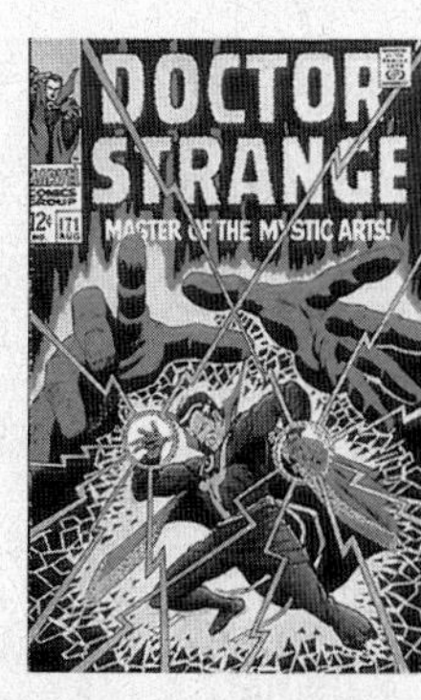

Doctor Strange #171 © MAR

GD VG FN VF VF/NM NM-
2.0 4.0 6.0 8.0 9.0 9.2

Dark Horse Comics: Sept, 1995 - No, 4, Dec, 1995 ($2.95, limited series)
1-4 3.00

DOC SAVAGE: THE MAN OF BRONZE
Skylark Pub: Mar, 1979, 68pgs. (B&W comic digest, 5-1/4x7-5/8")(low print)
15406-0: Whitman-a, 60 pgs., new comics 4 8 12 24 37 50

DOC SAVAGE: THE MAN OF BRONZE
Millennium Publications: 1991 - No. 4, 1991 ($2.50, limited series)
1-4: 1-Bronze logo 3.00
...: The Manual of Bronze 1 ($2.50, B&W, color, one-shot)-Unpublished proposed Doc Savage strip in color, B&W strip-r 3.00

DOC SAVAGE: THE MAN OF BRONZE, DOOM DYNASTY
Millennium Publ.: 1992 (Says 1991) - No. 2, 1992 ($2.50, limited series)
1,2 3.00

DOC SAVAGE: THE MAN OF BRONZE - REPEL
Innovation Publishing: 1992 ($2.50)
1-Dave Dorman painted-c 3.00

DOC SAVAGE: THE MAN OF BRONZE THE DEVIL'S THOUGHTS
Millennium Publ.: 1992 (Says 1991) - No. 3, 1992 ($2.50, limited series)
1-3 3.00

DOC STEARN...MR. MONSTER (See Mr. Monster)

DR. ANTHONY KING, HOLLYWOOD LOVE DOCTOR
Minoan Publishing Corp./Harvey Publications No. 4: 1952(Jan) - No. 3, May, 1953; No. 4, May, 1954
1 15 30 45 85 130 175
2-4: 4-Powell-a 10 20 30 54 72 90

DR. ANTHONY'S LOVE CLINIC (See Mr. Anthony's...)

DR. BOBBS
Dell Publishing Co.: No. 212, Jan, 1949
Four Color 212 6 12 18 37 59 80

DOCTOR CYBORG
Attention! Publishing: 1996 - No. 5 ($2.95, B&W)
1-5 3.00
The Clone Conspiracy TPB (1998, $14.95) r/#1-5 15.00

DOCTOR DOOM AND THE MASTERS OF EVIL (All ages title)
Marvel Comics: Mar, 2009 - No. 4, Jun, 2009 ($2.99)
1-4: 1-Sinister Six app. 4-Magneto app. 3.00

DR. DOOM'S REVENGE
Marvel Comics: 1989 (Came w/computer game from Paragon Software)
V1#1-Spider-Man & Captain America fight Dr. Doom 3.00

DR. FATE (See 1st Issue Special, The Immortal..., Justice League, More Fun #55, & Showcase)

DOCTOR FATE
DC Comics: July, 1987 - No. 4, Oct, 1987 ($1.50, limited series, Baxter paper)
1-4: Giffen-c/a in all 3.00

DOCTOR FATE
DC Comics: Winter, 1988-`89 - No. 41, June, 1992 ($1.25/$1.50 #5 on)
1,15: 15-Justice League app. 3.50
2-14 3.00
16-41: 25-1st new Dr. Fate. 36-Original Dr. Fate returns 3.00
Annual 1(1989, $2.95, 68 pgs.)-Sutton-a 4.00

DOCTOR FATE
DC Comics: Oct, 2003 - No. 5, Feb, 2004 ($2.50, limited series)
1-5-Golden-s/Kramer-a 3.00

DR. FU MANCHU (See The Mask of...)
I.W. Enterprises: 1964
1-r/Avon's "Mask of Dr. Fu Manchu"; Wood-a 7 14 21 48 79 110

DR. GIGGLES (See Dark Horse Presents #64-66)
Dark Horse Comics: Oct, 1992 - No. 2, Oct, 1992 ($2.50, limited series)
1,2-Based on movie 3.00

DOCTOR GRAVES (Formerly The Many Ghosts of...)
Charlton Comics: No. 73, Sept, 1985 - No. 75, Jan, 1986
73-75-Low print run 1 2 3 5 6 8
... Magic Book nn (Charlton Press/Xerox Education, 1977, 68 pgs., digest) Ditko-c/a; Staton-a
4 8 12 24 37 50

DR. HORRIBLE (Based on Joss Whedon's internet feature)
Dark Horse Comics: Nov, 2009 ($3.50, one-shot)
1-Zack Whedon-s/Joëlle Jones-a; Captain Hammer pin-up by Gene Ha; 3 covers 3.50
... and other Horrible Stories TPB (9/10, $9.99) r/#1 and 3 stories from MySpace DHP 10.00

DR. JEKYLL AND MR. HYDE (See A Star Presentation & Supernatural Thrillers #4)

DR. KILDARE (TV)
Dell Publishing Co.: No. 1337, 4-6/62 - No. 9, 4-6/65 (All Richard Chamberlain photo-c)
Four Color 1337(#1, 1962) 8 16 24 56 96 135
2-9 6 12 18 42 69 95

DR. MASTERS (See The Adventures of Young...)

DOCTOR MID-NITE (Also see All-American #25)
DC Comics: 1999 - No. 3, 1999 ($5.95, square-bound, limited series)
1-3-Matt Wagner-s/John K. Snyder III-painted art 6.00
TPB (2000, $19.95) r/series 20.00

DOCTOR OCTOPUS: NEGATIVE EXPOSURE
Marvel Comics: Dec, 2003 - No. 5, Apr, 2004 ($2.99, limited series)
1-5-Vaughan-s/Staz Johnson-a; Spider-Man app. 3.00
Spider-Man/Doctor Octopus: Negative Exposure TPB (2004, $13.99) r/series 14.00

DR. ROBOT SPECIAL
Dark Horse Comics: Apr, 2000 ($2.95, one-shot)
1-Bernie Mireault-s/a; some reprints from Madman Comics #12-15 3.00

DOCTOR SOLAR, MAN OF THE ATOM (See The Occult Files of Dr. Spektor #14 & Solar)
Gold Key/Whitman No. 28 on: 10/62 - No. 27, 4/69; No. 28, 4/81 - No. 31, 3/82 (1-27 have painted-c)
1-(#10000-210)-Origin/1st app. Dr. Solar (1st original Gold Key character)
19 38 57 128 277 425
2-Prof. Harbinger begins 10 20 30 65 118 170
3,4 7 14 21 44 72 100
5-Intro. Man of the Atom in costume 7 14 21 46 76 105
6-10 5 10 15 35 55 75
11-14,16-20 4 8 12 26 41 55
15-Origin retold 4 8 12 28 44 60
21-23: 23-Last 12¢ issue 4 8 12 22 34 45
24-27 3 6 9 20 30 40
28-31: 29-Magnus Robot Fighter begins. 31-(3/82)The Sentinel app.
2 4 6 13 18 22
Hardcover Volume One (Dark Horse Books, 2004, $49.95) r/#1-7; creator bios 50.00
Hardcover Volume Two (Dark Horse Books, 6/05, $49.95) r/#8-14; Jim Shooter foreword 50.00
Hardcover Volume Three (Dark Horse Books, 9/05, $49.95) r/#15-22; Mike Baron foreword 50.00
Hardcover Volume Four (Dark Horse Books, 11/07, $49.95) r/#23-31 and The Occult Files of Dr. Spektor #14; Batton Lash foreword 50.00
NOTE: ***Frank Bolle** a-6-19, 29-31; c-29i, 30i. **Bob Fugitani** a-1-5. **Spiegle** a-29-31. **Al McWilliams** a-20-23.*

DOCTOR SOLAR, MAN OF THE ATOM
Valiant Comics: 1990 - No. 2, 1991 ($7.95, card stock-c, high quality, 96 pgs.)
1,2: Reprints Gold Key series 1 2 3 5 6 8

DOCTOR SOLAR, MAN OF THE ATOM
Dark Horse Comics: Jul, 2010 - No. 8, Sept, 2011 ($3.50)
1-(48 pgs.) Shooter-s/Calero-a; back-up reprint of origin/1st app. in D.S. #1 (1962) 3.50
2-8: 2-7-Roger Robinson-a 3.50
Free Comic Book Day Doctor Solar, Man of the Atom & Magnus, Robot Fighter (5/10, free) short story re-intros of Solar & Magnus; Shooter-s/Swanland-c; Calero & Reinhold-a 3.00

DOCTOR SPECTRUM (See Supreme Power)
Marvel Comics: Oct, 2004 - No. 6, Mar, 2005 ($2.99, limited series)
1-6-Origin; Sara Barnes-s/Travel Foreman-a 3.00
TPB (2005, $16.99) r/#1-6 17.00

DOCTOR SPEKTOR (See The Occult Files of..., & Spine-Tingling Tales)

DOCTOR STRANGE (Formerly Strange Tales #1-168) (Also see The Defenders, Giant-Size..., Marvel Fanfare, Marvel Graphic Novel, Marvel Premiere, Marvel Treasury Edition, Strange & Strange Tales, 2nd Series)
Marvel Comics Group: No. 169, 6/68 - No. 183, 11/69; 6/74 - No. 81, 2/87
169(#1)-Origin retold; panel swipe/M.D. #1-c 13 26 39 86 183 280
170-177: 177-New costume 5 10 15 35 55 75
178-183: 178-Black Knight app. 179-Spider-Man story-r. 180-Photo montage-c. 181-Brunner-c(part-i), last 12¢ issue 5 10 15 32 51 70
1(6/74, 2nd series)-Brunner-c/a 9 18 27 58 99 140
2 5 10 15 32 51 70

Doctor Strange, Sorcerer Supreme #42 © MAR

Doctor Tomorrow #6 © Acclaim

Doctor Who (2011 series) #6 © BBC

	GD 2.0	VG 4.0	FN 6.0	VF 8.0	VF/NM 9.0	NM- 9.2
3-5	3	6	9	18	27	35
6-10	2	4	6	10	14	18
11-13,15-20: 13,15-17-(Regular 25¢ editions)	1	3	4	6	8	10
13,15-17-(30¢-c variants, limited distribution)	4	8	12	22	34	45
14-(5/76) Dracula app.; (regular 25¢ edition)	2	4	6	10	14	18
14-(30¢-c variant, limited distribution)	5	10	15	32	51	70

21-40: 21-Origin-r/Doctor Strange #169. 23-25-(Regular 30¢ editions). 31-Sub-Mariner-c/story 6.00

	GD	VG	FN	VF	VF/NM	NM-
23-25-(35¢-c variants, limited distribution)(6,8,10/77)	2	4	6	8	10	12

41-57,63-77,79-81: 56-Origin retold 4.00
58-62: 58-Re-intro Hannibal King (cameo). 59-Hannibal King full app. 59-62-Dracula app. (Darkhold storyline). 61,62-Doctor Strange, Blade, Hannibal King & Frank Drake team-up to battle. Dracula. 62-Death of Dracula & Lilith 6.00
78-New costume 5.00

	GD	VG	FN	VF	VF/NM	NM-
Annual 1(1976, 52 pgs.)-New Russell-a (35 pgs.)	3	6	9	14	20	25

....: From the Marvel Vault (4/11, $2.99) Stern-s/Vokes-a 3.00
.../Silver Dagger Special Edition 1 (3/83, $2.50)-r/#1,2,4,5; Wrightson-c 4.00
... Vs. Dracula TPB (2006, $19.99) r/#14,58-62 and Tomb of Dracula #44 20.00
...What Is It That Disturbs You, Stephen? #1 (10/97, $5.99, 48 pgs.) Russell-a/Andreyko & Russell-s, retelling of Annual #1 story 6.00

NOTE: **Adkins** *a-169, 170, 171i; c-169-171, 172i, 173.* **Adams** *a-4i.* **Austin** *a(i)-48-60, 66, 68, 70, 73; c(i)-38, 47-53, 55, 58-60, 70.* **Brunner** *a-1-5p; c-1-6, 22, 28-30, 33.* **Colan** *a(p)-172-178, 180-183, 6-18, 36-45, 47; c(p)-172, 174-183, 11-21, 23, 27, 35, 36, 47.* **Ditko** *a-179r, 3r.* **Everett** *c-183i.* **Golden** *a-46p, 55p; c-42-44, 46, 55p.* **G. Kane** *c(p)-8-10.* **Miller** *c-46p.* **Nebres** *a-20, 22, 23, 24i, 26i, 32i; c-32i, 34.* **Rogers** *a-48-53p; c-47p-53p.* **Russell** *a-34i, 46i, Annual 1.* **B. Smith** *c-179.* **Paul Smith** *a-54p, 56p, 65, 66p, 68p, 69, 71-73; c-56, 65, 66, 68, 71.* **Starlin** *a-23p, 26; c-25, 26.* **Sutton** *a-27-29p, 31i, 33, 34p. Painted c-62, 63.*

DOCTOR STRANGE (Volume 2)
Marvel Comics: Feb, 1999 - No. 4, May, 1999 ($2.99, limited series)

1-4: 1,2-Tony Harris-a/painted cover. 3,4-Chadwick-a 3.00

DOCTOR STRANGE CLASSICS
Marvel Comics Group: Mar, 1984 - No. 4, June, 1984 ($1.50, Baxter paper)

1-4: Ditko-r; Byrne-c. 4-New Golden pin-up 3.00
NOTE: **Byrne** *c-1i, 2-4.*

DOCTOR STRANGEFATE (See Marvel Versus DC #3 & DC Versus Marvel #4)
DC Comics (Amalgam): Apr, 1996 ($1.95)

1-Ron Marz script w/Jose Garcia-Lopez-(p) & Kevin Nowlan-(i). Access & Charles Xavier app. 3.00

DOCTOR STRANGE MASTER OF THE MYSTIC ARTS (See Fireside Book Series)

DOCTOR STRANGE, SORCERER SUPREME
Marvel Comics (Midnight Sons imprint #60 on): Nov, 1988 - No. 90, June, 1996 ($1.25/$1.50/$1.75/$1.95, direct sales only, Mando paper)

1 ($1.25) 5.00
2-9,12-14,16-25,27,29-40,42-49,51-64: 3-New Defenders app. 5-Guice-c/a begins. 14-18-Morbius story line. 31-36-Infinity Gauntlet x-overs. 31-Silver Surfer app. 33-Thanos-c & cameo. 36-Warlock app. 37-Silver Surfer app. 40-Daredevil x-over. 41-Wolverine-c/story. 42-47-Infinity War x-overs. 47-Gamora app. 52,53-Morbius-c/stories. 60,61-Siege of Darkness pt. 7 & 15. 60-Spot varnish-c. 61-New Doctor Strange begins (cameo, 1st app.). 62-Dr. Doom & Morbius app. 3.00
10,11,26,28,41: 10-Re-intro Morbius w/new costume (11/89). 11-Hobgoblin app. 26-Werewolf by Night app. 28-Ghost Rider-s cont'd from G.R. #12; published at same time as Doctor Strange/Ghost Rider Special #1(4/91) 4.00
15-Unauthorized Amy Grant photo-c 5.00
50-($2.95, 52 pgs.)-Holo-grafx foil-c; Hulk, Ghost Rider & Silver Surfer app.; leads into new Secret Defenders series 4.00
65-74, 76-90: 65-Begin $1.95-c; bound-in card sheet. 72-Silver ink-c. 80-82- Ellis-s. 84-DeMatteis story begins. 87-Death of Baron Mordo 3.00
75 ($2.50) 4.00
75 ($3.50)-Foil-c 5.00
Annual 2-4 ('92-'94, 68 pgs.)-2-Defenders app. 3-Polybagged w/card 4.00
Ashcan (1995, 75¢) 3.00
.../Ghost Rider Special 1 (4/91, $1.50)-Same book as D.S.S.S. #28 3.00
...Vs. Dracula 1 (3/94, $1.75, 52 pgs.)-r/Tomb of Dracula #44 & Dr. Strange #14 4.00
NOTE: **Colan** *c/a-19.* **Golden** *c-28.* **Guice** *a-5-16, 18, 20-24; c-5-12, 20-24. See 1st series for Annual #1.*

DOCTOR STRANGE: THE OATH
Marvel Comics: Dec, 2006 - No. 5, Apr, 2007 ($2.99, limited series)

1-5-Vaughan-s/Martin-a; Night Nurse app. 3.00
TPB (2007, $13.99) r/#1-5; sketch pages and promotional art 14.00

DR. TOM BRENT, YOUNG INTERN
Charlton Publications: Feb, 1963 - No. 5, Oct, 1963

	GD	VG	FN	VF	VF/NM	NM-
1	3	6	9	16	23	30
2-5	2	4	6	11	16	20

DR. TOMORROW
Acclaim Comics (Valiant): Sept, 1997 - No. 12 ($2.50)

1-12: 1-Mignola-c 3.00

DR. VOLTZ (See Mighty Midget Comics)

DOCTOR VOODOO: AVENGER OF THE SUPERNATURAL
Marvel Comics: Dec, 2009 - No. 5, Apr, 2010 ($2.99, limited series)

1-5-Dr. Doom, Son of Satan & Ghost Rider app.; Palo-a 3.00
Doctor Voodoo: The Origin of Jericho Drumm (1/10, $4.99) r/Strange Tales #169,170 5.00

DR. WEIRD
Big Bang Comics: Oct, 1994 - No. 2, May, 1995 ($2.95, B&W)

1,2: 1-Frank Brunner-c 4.00

DR. WEIRD SPECIAL
Big Bang Comics: Feb, 1994 ($3.95, B&W, 68 pgs.)

1-Origin-r by Starlin; Starlin-c. 4.00

DOCTOR WHO (Also see Marvel Premiere #57-60)
Marvel Comics Group: Oct, 1984 - No. 23, Aug, 1986 ($1.50, direct sales, Baxter paper)

1-15-British-r 4.00
16-23 5.00
Graphic Novel Voyager (1985, $8.95) color reprints of B&W comic pages from Doctor Who Magazine #88-99; Colin Baker afterword 12.00

DOCTOR WHO (Based on the 2005 TV series with David Tennant)
IDW Publishing: Jan, 2008 - No. 6, Jun, 2008 ($3.99)

1-6: 1-Nick Roche-a/Gary Russell-s; two covers 4.00

DOCTOR WHO (Based on the 2005 TV series with David Tennant)
IDW Publishing: Jul, 2009 - No. 16, Oct, 2010 ($3.99)

1-16-Grist-c on all. 3-5,13-16-Art by Matt Smith (not the actor) 4.00
... Annual 2010 (7/10, $7.99) short stories by various; Yates-c; cameo by 11th Doctor 8.00
...: Autopia (6/09, $3.99) Ostrander-s; Yates-a/c; variant photo-c 4.00
...: Black Death White Life (9/09, $3.99) Mandrake-a; Guy Davis- c; variant photo-c 4.00
...: Cold-Blooded War (8/09, $3.99) Salmon-a/c; variant photo-c 4.00
...: Room With a Déjà View (6/09, $3.99) Eric J-a; Mandrake-c; variant photo-c 4.00
...: The Whispering Gallery (2/09, $3.99) Moore & Reppion-s; Templesmith-a/2 covers 4.00
...: Time Machination (5/09, $3.99) Paul Grist-a/c; variant photo-c 4.00

DOCTOR WHO (Based on the 2010 TV series with Matt Smith)
IDW Publishing: Jan, 2011 - Present ($3.99)

1-13: 1-Edwards & photo-c; Currie-a. 5-Buckingham-a. 12-Grist-a 4.00
Annual 2011 (8/11, $7.99) short stories by Fialkov, Shedd, Smith, McDaid and others 8.00
... Convention Special (7/11, no cover price, BBC America Shop Exclusive) The Doctor, Amy, and Rory at the San Diego Comic-Con; Matthew Dow Smith-s/Domingues-a 15.00

DOCTOR WHO: A FAIRYTALE LIFE (Based on the 2010 TV series with Matt Smith)
IDW Publishing: Apr, 2011 - No. 4, Jul, 2011 ($3.99, limited series)

1-4: 1-Sturges-s/Yeates-a; covers by Buckingham & Mebberson. 3-Shearer-a 4.00

DR. WHO & THE DALEKS (See Movie Classics)

DOCTOR WHO CLASSICS
IDW Publishing: Nov, 2005 - Present ($3.99)

1-10: Reprints from Doctor Who Weekly (1979); art by Gibbons, Neary and others 4.00
Series 2 (12/08 - No. 12, 11/09, $3.99) 1-12 4.00
Series 3 (3/10 - No. 6, 8/10, $3.99) 1-6 4.00
...: The Seventh Doctor (2/11, $3.99) 1-5: 1-Furman-s/Ridgway-a; Sylvester McCoy-era 4.00

DOCTOR WHO: THE FORGOTTEN (Based on the 2005 TV series with David Tennant)
IDW Publishing: Aug, 2008 - No. 6, Jan, 2009 ($3.99)

1-6: 1,2-Pia Guerra-a/Tony Lee-s; two covers 4.00

DR. WONDER
Old Town Publishing: June, 1996 - No. 5 ($2.95, B&W)

1-5: 1-Intro & origin of Dr. Wonder; Dick Ayers-c/a; Irwin Hasen-a 3.00

DOCTOR ZERO
Marvel Comics (Epic Comics): Apr, 1988 - No. 8, Aug, 1989 ($1.25/$1.50)

1-8: 1-Sienkiewicz-c. 6,7-Spiegle-a 3.00
NOTE: **Sienkiewicz** *a-3i, 4i; c-1.* **Spiegle** *a-6, 7.*

DO-DO (Funny Animal Circus Stories)
Nation-Wide Publishers: 1950 - No. 7, 1951 (5¢, 5x7-1/4" Miniature)

	GD	VG	FN	VF	VF/NM	NM-
1 (52 pgs.)	27	54	81	158	259	360
2-7	15	30	45	88	137	185

DODO & THE FROG, THE (Formerly Funny Stuff; also see It's Game Time #2)

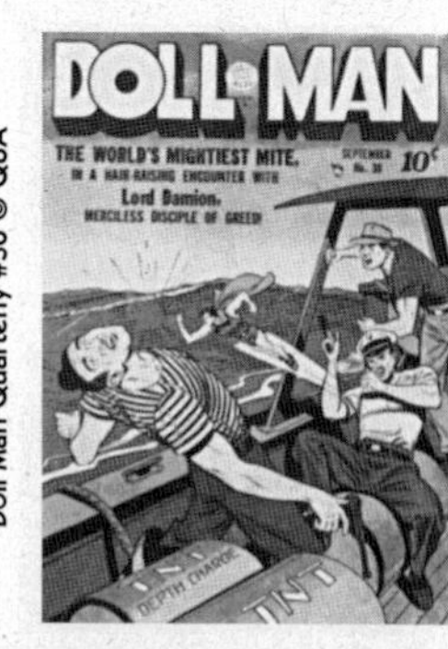

Doll Man Quarterly #30 © QUA

Dollz #1 © Randy Queen

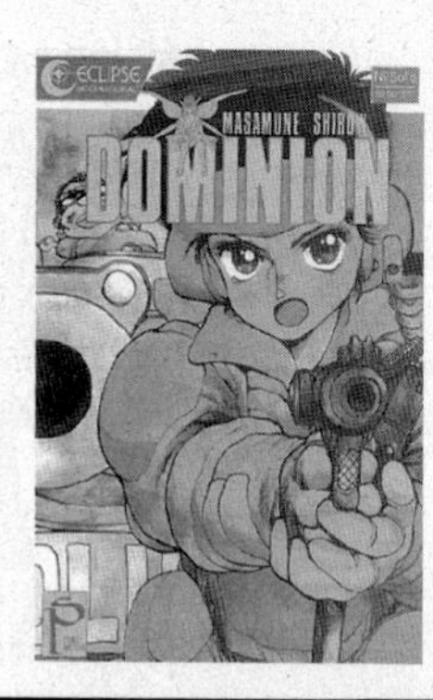

Dominion #5 © Masamune Shirow

GD VG FN VF VF/NM NM-
2.0 4.0 6.0 8.0 9.0 9.2

National Periodical Publications: No. 80, 9-10/54 - No. 88, 1-2/56; No. 89, 8-9/56; No. 90, 10-11/56; No. 91, 9/57; No. 92, 11/57 (See Comic Cavalcade and Captain Carrot)
80-1st app. Doodles Duck by Sheldon Mayer 20 40 60 114 182 250
81-91: Doodles Duck by Mayer in #81,83-90 14 28 42 76 108 140
92-(Scarce)-Doodles Duck by S. Mayer 18 36 54 105 165 225

DOGFACE DOOLEY
Magazine Enterprises: 1951 - No. 5, 1953
1(A-1 40) 8 16 24 40 50 60
2(A-1 43), 3(A-1 49), 4(A-1 53), 5(A-1 64) 6 12 18 28 34 40
I.W. Reprint #1('64), Super Reprint #17 2 4 6 9 13 16

DOG MOON
DC Comics (Vertigo): 1996 ($6.95, one-shot)
1-Robert Hunter-scripts; Tim Truman-c/a. 7.00

DOG OF FLANDERS, A
Dell Publishing Co.: No. 1088, Mar, 1960
Four Color 1088-Movie, photo-c 5 10 15 30 48 65

DOGPATCH (See Al Capp's... & Mammy Yokum)

DOGS OF WAR (Also see Warriors of Plasm)
Defiant: Apr, 1994 - No. 5, Aug, 1994 ($2.50)
1-5 3.00

DOGS-O-WAR
Crusade Comics: June, 1996 - No. 3, Jan, 1997 ($2.95, B&W, limited series)
1-3: 1,2-Photo-c 3.00

DOLLFACE & HER GANG (Betty Betz'...)
Dell Publishing Co.: No. 309, Jan, 1951
Four Color 309 5 10 15 35 55 75

DOLLHOUSE
Dark Horse Comics: Mar, 2011; Jul, 2011 - No. 5, Nov, 2011 ($3.50, limited series)
1-5-Richards-a; two covers on each 3.50
...: Epitaphs (3/11, $3.50) reprints story from DVD collection; covers by Noto & Morris 3.50

DOLLMAN (Movie)
Eternity Comics: Sept, 1991 - No. 4, Dec, 1991 ($2.50, limited series)
1-4: Adaptation of film 3.00

DOLL MAN QUARTERLY, THE (Doll Man #17 on; also see Feature Comics #27 & Freedom Fighters)
Quality Comics: Fall, 1941 - No. 7, Fall, '43; No. 8, Spr, '46 - No. 47, Oct, 1953
1-Dollman (by Cassone), Justin Wright begin 331 662 993 2317 4059 5800
2-The Dragon begins; Crandall-a(5) 145 290 435 921 1586 2250
3,4 89 178 267 565 970 1375
5-Crandall-a 86 172 258 546 936 1325
6,7(1943) 54 108 162 343 574 825
8(1946)-1st app. Torchy by Bill Ward 165 330 495 1048 1799 2550
9 53 106 159 334 567 800
10-20 41 82 123 256 428 600
21-30: 28-Vs. The Flame 36 72 108 216 351 485
31-36,38,40: 31-(12/50)-Intro Elmo, the wonder dog (Dollman's faithful dog).
32-34-Jeb Rivers app.; 34 by Crandall(p) 34 68 102 206 336 465
37-Origin & 1st app. Dollgirl; Dollgirl bondage-c 48 96 144 302 514 725
39- "Narcotics...the Death Drug" c-/story 39 78 117 231 378 525
41-47 24 48 72 142 234 325
Super Reprint #11('64, r/#20),15(r/#23),17(r/#28): 15,17-Torchy app.; Andru/Esposito-c
3 6 9 20 30 40

NOTE: ***Ward** Torchy in 8, 9, 11, 12, 14-24, 27; by Fox-#26, 30, 35-47. **Crandall** a-2, 5, 10, 13 & Super #11, 17, 18. **Crandall/Cuidera** c-40-42. **Guardineer** a-3. Bondage c-27, 37, 38, 39.*

DOLLY
Ziff-Davis Publ. Co.: No. 10, July-Aug, 1951 (Funny animal)
10-Painted-c 9 18 27 47 61 75

DOLLY DILL
Marvel Comics/Newsstand Publ.: 1945
1 19 38 57 109 172 235

DOLLZ, THE
Image Comics: Apr, 2001 - No. 2, June, 2001 ($2.95)
1,2: 1-Four covers; Sniegoski & Green-s/Green-a 3.00

DOMINATION FACTOR
Marvel Comics: Nov, 1999 - 4.8, Feb, 2000 ($2.50, interconnected mini- series)

GD VG FN VF VF/NM NM-
2.0 4.0 6.0 8.0 9.0 9.2

1.1, 2.3, 3.5, 4.7-Fantastic Four; Jurgens-s/a 3.00
1.2, 2.4, 3.6, 4.8-Avengers; Ordway-s/a 3.00

DOMINIC FORTUNE
Marvel Comics (MAX): Oct, 2009 - No. 4, Jan, 2010 ($3.99, limited series)
1-4-Howard Chaykin-s/a/c 4.00

DOMINION
Image Comics: Jan, 2003 - No. 2 ($2.95)
1,2-Keith Giffen-s/a 3.00

DOMINION (Manga)
Eclipse Comics: Dec, 1990 - No. 6., July, 1990 ($2.00, B&W, limited series)
1-6 3.00

DOMINION: CONFLICT 1 (Manga)
Dark Horse Comics: Mar, 1996 - No. 6, Aug, 1996 ($2.95, B&W, limited series)
1-6: Shirow-c/a/scripts 3.00

DOMINIQUE LAVEAU: VOODOO CHILD
DC Comics (Vertigo): May, 2012 - Present ($2.99)
1-Selwyn Seyfu Hinds-s/Denys Cowan-a 3.00

DOMINO (See X-Force)
Marvel Comics: Jan, 1997 - No. 3, Mar, 1997 ($1.95, limited series)
1-3: 2-Deathstrike-c/app. 3.00

DOMINO (See X-Force)
Marvel Comics: June, 2003 - No. 4, Aug, 2003 ($2.50, limited series)
1-4-Stelfreeze-c/a; Pruett-s. 3.00

DOMINO CHANCE
Chance Enterprises: May-June, 1982 - No. 9, May, 1985 (B&W)
1-9: 7-1st app. Gizmo, 2 pgs. 8-1st full Gizmo story. 1-Reprint, May, 1985 3.00

DONALD AND MICKEY IN DISNEYLAND (See Dell Giants)

DONALD AND SCROOGE
Disney Comics: 1992 ($8.95, squarebound, 100 pgs.)
nn-Don Rosa reprint special; r/U.S., D.D. Advs. 1 3 4 6 8 10
1-3 (1992, $1.50)-r/D.D. Advs. (Disney) #1,22,24 & U.S. #261-263,269 3.00

DONALD AND THE WHEEL (Disney)
Dell Publishing Co.: No. 1190, Nov, 1961
Four Color 1190-Movie, Barks-c 8 16 24 53 89 125

DONALD DUCK (See Adventures of Mickey Mouse, Cheerios, Donald & Mickey, Ducktales, Dynabrite Comics, Gladstone Comic Album, Mickey & Donald, Mickey Mouse Mag., Story Hour Series, Uncle Scrooge, Walt Disney's Comics & Stories, W. D.'s Donald Duck, Wheaties & Whitman Comic Books, Wise Little Hen, The)

DONALD DUCK
Whitman Publishing Co./Grosset & Dunlap/K.K.: 1935, 1936 (All pages on heavy linen-like finish cover stock in color;1st book ever devoted to Donald Duck; see Advs. of Mickey Mouse for 1st app.) (9-1/2x13")
978(1935)-16 pgs.; Illustrated text story book 206 412 618 1318 2259 3200
nn(1936)-36 pgs.plus hard cover & dust jacket. Story completely rewritten with B&W illos added. Mickey appears and his nephews are named Morty & Monty
Book only 194 388 582 1242 2121 3000
Dust jacket only.... 39 78 117 240 395 550

DONALD DUCK (Walt Disney's) (10¢)
Whitman/K.K. Publications: 1938 (8-1/2x11-1/2", B&W, cardboard-c)
(Has D. Duck with bubble pipe on-c)
nn-The first Donald Duck & Walt Disney comic book; 1936 & 1937 Sunday strip-r(in B&W); same format as the Feature Books; 1st strips with Huey, Dewey & Louie from 10/17/37
258 516 774 1651 2826 4000

DONALD DUCK (Walt Disney's...#262 on; see 4-Color listings for titles & Four Color No. 1109 for origin story)
Dell Publ. Co./Gold Key #85-216/Whitman #217-245/Gladstone #246 on: 1940 - No. 84, Sept-Nov, 1962; No. 85, Dec, 1962 - No. 245, July, 1984; No. 246, Oct, 1986 - No. 279, May, 1990; No. 280, Sept, 1993 - No. 307, Mar,1998
Four Color 4(1940)-Daily 1939 strip-r by Al Taliaferro
1800 3600 5400 13,500 20,750 28,000
Large Feature Comic 16(1/41?)-1940 Sunday strips-r in B&W
676 1352 2028 4935 8718 12,500
Large Feature Comic 20('41)-Comic Paint Book, r-single panels from Large Feature #16 at top of each pg. to color; daily strip-r across bottom of each pg. (Rare)
703 1406 2109 5132 9066 13,000
Four Color 9('42)- "Finds Pirate Gold"; 64 pgs. by Carl Barks & Jack Hannah (pgs. 1,2,5,12-40

Donald Duck Four Color #29 © DIS

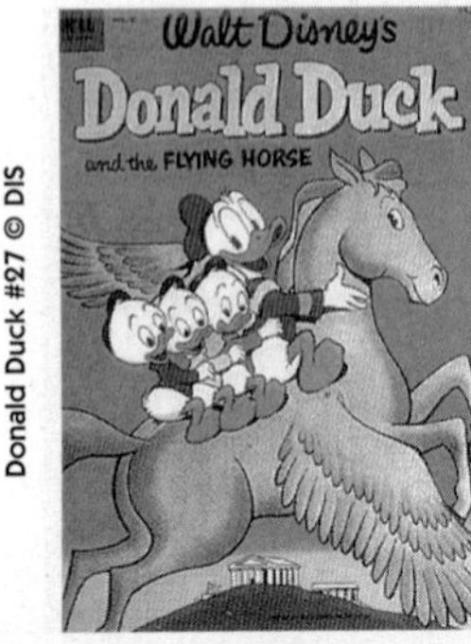

Donald Duck #27 © DIS

Donald Duck #366 © DIS

	GD 2.0	VG 4.0	FN 6.0	VF 8.0	VF/NM 9.0	NM- 9.2
are by Barks, his 1st Donald Duck comic book art work; © 8/17/42)	1000	2000	3000	7600	13,800	20,000
Four Color 29(9/43)- "Mummy's Ring" by Barks; reprinted in Uncle Scrooge & Donald Duck #1('65), W. D. Comics Digest #44('73) & Donald Duck Advs. #14	773	1546	2319	5643	9972	14,300
Four Color 62(1/45)- "Frozen Gold"; 52 pgs. by Barks, reprinted in The Best of W.D. Comics & Donald Duck Advs. #4	207	414	621	1739	3770	5800
Four Color 108(1946)- "Terror of the River"; 52 pgs. by Carl Barks; reprinted in Gladstone Comic Album #2	146	292	438	1226	2663	4100
Four Color 147(5/47)-in "Volcano Valley" by Barks	102	204	306	826	1788	2750
Four Color 159(8/47)-in "The Ghost of the Grotto";52 pgs. by Carl Barks; reprinted in Best of Uncle Scrooge & Donald Duck #1 ('66) & The Best of W.D. Comics & D.D. Advs. #9; two Barks stories	87	174	261	705	1528	2350
Four Color 178(12/47)-1st app. Uncle Scrooge by Carl Barks; reprinted in Gold Key Christmas Parade #3 & The Best of Walt Disney Comics	117	234	351	948	2049	3150
Four Color 189(6/48)-by Carl Barks; reprinted in Best of Donald Duck & Uncle Scrooge #1('64) & D.D. Advs. #19	72	144	216	583	1267	1950
Four Color 199(10/48)-by Carl Barks; mentioned in Love and Death; r/in Gladstone Comic Album #5	78	156	234	632	1366	2100
Four Color 203(12/48)-by Barks; reprinted as Gold Key Christmas Parade #4	55	110	165	446	961	1475
Four Color 223(4/49)-by Barks; reprinted as Best of Donald Duck #1 & Donald Duck Advs. #3	71	142	213	575	1250	1925
Four Color 238(8/49)-in "Voodoo Hoodoo" by Barks	55	110	165	446	961	1475
Four Color 256(12/49)-by Barks; reprinted in Best of Donald Duck & Uncle Scrooge #2('67), Gladstone Comic Album #16 & W.D. Comics Digest 44('73)	46	92	138	352	764	1175
Four Color 263(2/50)-Two Barks stories; r-in D.D. #278	46	92	138	345	748	1150
Four Color 275(5/50), 282(7/50), 291(9/50), 300(11/50)-All by Carl Barks; 275, 282 reprinted in W.D. Comics Digest #44('73). #275 r/in Gladstone Comic Album #10. #291 r/in D. Duck Advs. #16	45	90	135	338	732	1125
Four Color 308(1/51), 318(3/51)-by Barks; #318-reprinted in W.D. Comics Digest #34 & D.D. Advs. #2,19	42	86	126	315	683	1050
Four Color 328(5/51)-by Carl Barks	41	82	123	308	667	1025
Four Color 339(7-8/51), 379-2nd Uncle Scrooge-c; art not by Barks.	12	24	36	83	172	260
Four Color 348(9-10/51), 356,394-Barks-c only	20	40	60	137	294	450
Four Color 367(1-2/52)-by Barks; reprinted as Gold Key Christmas Parade #2 & #8	33	66	99	235	510	785
Four Color 408(7-8/52), 422(9-10/52)-All by Carl Barks. #408-r-in Best of Donald Duck & Uncle Scrooge #1('64) & Gladstone Comic Album #13	33	66	99	235	510	785
26(11-12/52)-In "Trick or Treat" (Barks-a, 36pgs.) 1st story r-in Walt Disney Digest #16 & Gladstone C.A. #23	33	66	99	235	510	785
27-30-Barks-c only	12	24	36	83	172	260
31-44,47-50	8	16	24	53	89	125
45-Barks-a (6 pgs.)	13	26	39	88	189	290
46- "Secret of Hondorica" by Barks, 24 pgs.; reprinted in Donald Duck #98 & 154	18	36	54	123	267	410
51-Barks-a,1/2 pg.	8	16	24	53	89	125
52- "Lost Peg-Leg Mine" by Barks, 10 pgs.	13	26	39	89	192	295
53,55-59	7	14	21	44	72	100
54- "Forbidden Valley" by Barks, 26 pgs. (10¢ & 15¢ versions exist)	15	30	45	100	218	335
60- "Donald Duck & the Titanic Ants" by Barks, 20 pgs. plus 6 more pgs.	15	30	45	100	218	335
61-67,69,70	6	12	18	39	62	85
68-Barks-a, 5 pgs.	10	20	30	69	130	190
71-Barks-r, 1/2 pg.	6	12	18	39	62	85
72-78,80,82-97,99,100: 96-Donald Duck Album	6	12	18	37	59	80
79,81-Barks-a, 1pg.	6	12	18	39	62	85
98-Reprints #46 (Barks)	6	12	18	39	62	85
101,103-111,113-135: 120-Last 12¢ issue. 134-Barks-r/#52 & WDC&S 194. 135-Barks-r/WDC&S 198, 19 pgs.	4	8	12	23	36	48
102-Super Goof. 112-1st Moby Duck	4	8	12	24	37	50
136-153,155,156,158: 149-20¢-c begin	3	6	9	14	20	26
154-Barks-r(#46)	3	6	9	17	25	32
157,159,160,164: 157-Barks-r(#45); 25¢-c begin. 159-Reprints/WDC&S #192 (10 pgs.). 160-Barks-r(#26). 164-Barks-r(#79)	3	6	9	14	20	26
161-163,165-173,175-187,189-191: 175-30¢-c begin. 187-Barks r/#68.	2	4	6	13	18	22
174,188: 174-r/4-Color #394.	3	6	9	14	19	24
192-Barks-r(40 pgs.) from Donald Duck #60 & WDC&S #226,234 (52 pgs.)	3	6	9	16	22	28
193-200,202-207,209-211,213-216	2	4	6	9	13	16
201,208,212: 201-Barks-r/Christmas Parade #26, 16pgs. 208-Barks-r/#60 (6 pgs.). 212-Barks-r/WDC&S #130	2	4	6	9	13	16
217-219: 217 has 216 on-c. 219-Barks-r/WDC&S #106,107, 10 pgs. ea.	2	4	6	10	14	18
220,225-228: 228-Barks-r/F.C. #275	2	4	6	13	18	22
221,223,224: Scarce; only sold in pre-packs. 221(8/80), 223(11/80), 224(12/80)	6	12	18	39	62	85
222-(9-10/80)-(Very low distribution)	15	30	45	102	221	340
229-240: 229-Barks-r/F.C. #282. 230-Barks-r/ #52 & WDC&S #194. 236(2/82), 237(2-3/82), 238(3/82), 239(4/82), 240(5/82)	2	4	6	9	13	16
241-245: 241(4/83), 242(5/83), 243(3/84), 244(4/84), 245(7/84)(low print)	3	6	9	14	19	24
246-(1st Gladstone issue)-Barks-r/FC #422	3	6	9	15	21	26
247-249,251: 248,249-Barks-r/DD #54 & 26. 251-Barks-r/1945 Firestone	2	4	6	9	13	16
250-($1.50, 68 pgs.)-Barks-r/4-Color #9	2	4	6	10	14	18
252-277,280: 254-Barks-r/FC #328. 256-Barks-r/FC #147. 257-($1.50, 52 pgs.)-Barks-r/ Vacation Parade #1. 261-Barks-r/FC #300. 275-Kelly-r/FC #92. 280 (#1, 2nd Series)	1	2	3	5	6	8
278,279,286: 278,279 ($1.95, 68 pgs.): 278-Rosa-a; Barks-r/FC #263. 279-Rosa-c; Barks-r/MOC #4. 286-Rosa-a	1	2	3	5	7	9
281,282,284	1	2	3	4	5	7
283-Don Rosa-a, part-c & scripts	1	2	3	5	6	8
285,287-307						5.00
286 ($2.95, 68 pgs.)-Happy Birthday, Donald						6.00
Mini-Comic #1(1976)-(3-1/4x6-1/2"); r/D.D. #150	2	4	6	8	11	14

NOTE: ***Carl Barks*** *wrote all issues he illustrated, but #117, 126, 138 contain his script only. Issues 4-Color #189, 199, 203, 223, 238, 256, 263, 275, 282, 308, 348, 356, 367, 394, 408, 422, 26-30, 35, 44, 46, 52, 55, 57, 60, 65, 70-73, 77-80, 83, 101, 103, 105, 106, 111, 126, 246r, 266r, 268r, 271r, 275r, 278r(F.C. 263) all have* ***Barks*** *covers.* ***Barks*** *r-263-267, 269-278-282, 284, 285. #96 titled "Comic Album", #99-"Christmas Album". New art issues (not reprints)-106-46, 148-63, 167, 169, 170, 172, 173, 175, 178, 179, 196, 209, 223, 225, 236.* ***Taliaferro*** *daily newspaper strips #258-260, 264, 284, 285; Sunday strips #247, 280-283.*

DONALD DUCK (Numbering continues from Donald Duck and Friends #362)
BOOM! Studios (Kaboom!): No. 363, Feb, 2011 - No. 367, Jun, 2011 ($3.99)

	GD 2.0	VG 4.0	FN 6.0	VF 8.0	VF/NM 9.0	NM- 9.2
363-367: 363-Barks reprints incl. "Mystery of the Loch". 364-Rosa-c						4.00

DONALD DUCK ADVENTURES (See Walt Disney's Donald Duck Adventures)

DONALD DUCK ALBUM (See Comic Album No. 1,3 & Duck Album)
Dell Publishing Co./Gold Key: 5-7/59 - F.C. No. 1239, 10-12/61; 1962; 8/63 - No. 2, Oct, 1963

	GD 2.0	VG 4.0	FN 6.0	VF 8.0	VF/NM 9.0	NM- 9.2
Four Color 995 (#1)	6	12	18	42	69	95
Four Color 1099,1140,1239-Barks-c	7	14	21	44	72	100
Four Color 1182, 01204-207 (1962-Dell)	5	10	15	32	51	70
1(8/63-Gold Key)-Barks-c	6	12	18	39	62	85
2(10/63)	5	10	15	30	48	65

DONALD DUCK AND FRIENDS (Numbering continues from Walt Disney's ...)
BOOM! Studios: No. 347, Oct, 2009 - No. 362, Jan, 2011 ($2.99)

	GD 2.0	VG 4.0	FN 6.0	VF 8.0	VF/NM 9.0	NM- 9.2
347-362: Two covers on most. Retitled "Donald Duck" with #363						3.00

DONALD DUCK AND THE BOYS (Also see Story Hour Series)
Whitman Publishing Co.: 1948 (5-1/4x5-1/2", 100pgs., hard-c; art & text)

	GD 2.0	VG 4.0	FN 6.0	VF 8.0	VF/NM 9.0	NM- 9.2
845-(49) new illos by Barks based on his Donald Duck 10-pager in WDC&S #74, Expanded text not written by Barks; Cover not by Barks	50	100	150	350	600	850

(Prices vary widely on this book)

DONALD DUCK AND THE CHRISTMAS CAROL
Whitman Publishing Co.: 1960 (A Little Golden Book, 6-3/8"x7-5/8", 28 pgs.)

	GD 2.0	VG 4.0	FN 6.0	VF 8.0	VF/NM 9.0	NM- 9.2
nn-Story book pencilled by Carl Barks with the intended title "Uncle Scrooge's Christmas Carol." Finished art adapted by Norman McGary. (Rare)-Reprinted in Uncle Scrooge in Color.	20	40	60	100	185	270

DONALD DUCK BEACH PARTY (Also see Dell Giants)
Gold Key: Sept, 1965 (12¢)

	GD 2.0	VG 4.0	FN 6.0	VF 8.0	VF/NM 9.0	NM- 9.2
1(#10158-509)-Barks-r/WDC&S #45; painted-c	6	12	18	42	69	95

DONALD DUCK BOOK (See Story Hour Series)

DONALD DUCK COMICS DIGEST
Gladstone Publishing: Nov, 1986 - No. 5, July, 1987 ($1.25/$1.50, 96 pgs.)

	GD 2.0	VG 4.0	FN 6.0	VF 8.0	VF/NM 9.0	NM- 9.2
1,3: 1-Barks-c/a-r	1	3	4	6	8	10
2,4,5: 4,5-$1.50-c						6.00

DONALD DUCK FUN BOOK (See Dell Giants)

Don Rosa's Comics & Stories #1 © Don Rosa

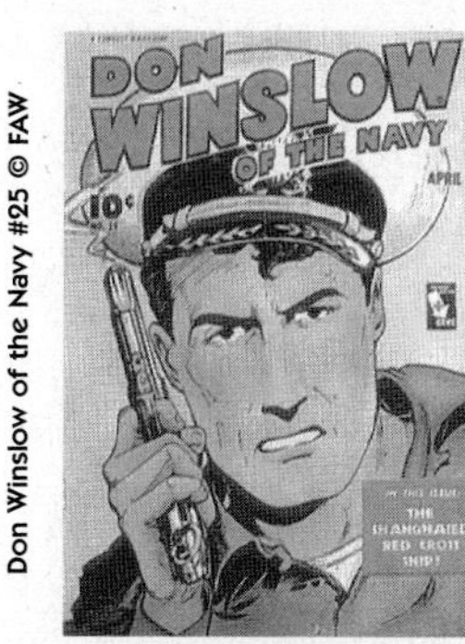

Don Winslow of the Navy #25 © FAW

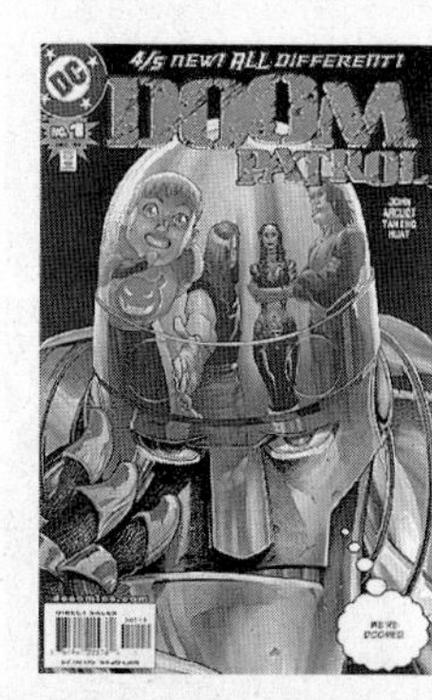

Doom Patrol (2001 series) #1 © DC

DONALD DUCK IN DISNEYLAND (See Dell Giants)

DONALD DUCK MARCH OF COMICS (See March of Comics #4,20,41,56,69,263)

DONALD DUCK MERRY CHRISTMAS (See Dell Giant No. 53)

DONALD DUCK PICNIC PARTY (See Picnic Party listed under Dell Giants)

DONALD DUCK TELLS ABOUT KITES (See Kite Fun Book)

DONALD DUCK, THIS IS YOUR LIFE (Disney, TV)
Dell Publishing Co.: No. 1109, Aug-Oct, 1960

	GD 2.0	VG 4.0	FN 6.0	VF 8.0	VF/NM 9.0	NM- 9.2
Four Color 1109-Gyro flashback to WDC&S #141; origin Donald Duck (1st told)	12	24	36	83	172	260

DONALD DUCK XMAS ALBUM (See regular Donald Duck No. 99)

DONALD IN MATHMAGIC LAND (Disney)
Dell Publishing Co.: No. 1051, Oct-Dec, 1959 - No. 1198, May-July, 1961

	GD 2.0	VG 4.0	FN 6.0	VF 8.0	VF/NM 9.0	NM- 9.2
Four Color 1051 (#1)-Movie	9	18	27	61	106	150
Four Color 1198-Reprint of above	6	12	18	42	69	95

DONATELLO, TEENAGE MUTANT NINJA TURTLE
Mirage Studios: Aug, 1986 ($1.50, B&W, one-shot, 44 pgs.)

	GD 2.0	VG 4.0	FN 6.0	VF 8.0	VF/NM 9.0	NM- 9.2
1	1	2	3	5	7	9

DONDI
Dell Publishing Co.: No. 1176, Mar-May, 1961 - No. 1276, Dec, 1961

	GD 2.0	VG 4.0	FN 6.0	VF 8.0	VF/NM 9.0	NM- 9.2
Four Color 1176 (#1)-Movie; origin, photo-c	5	10	15	35	55	75
Four Color 1276	4	8	12	22	34	45

DON FORTUNE MAGAZINE
Don Fortune Publishing Co.: Aug, 1946 - No. 6, Feb, 1947

	GD 2.0	VG 4.0	FN 6.0	VF 8.0	VF/NM 9.0	NM- 9.2
1-Delecta of the Planets by C.C. Beck in all	27	54	81	160	263	365
2	15	30	45	85	130	175
3-6: 3-Bondage-c	14	28	42	76	108	140

DONG XOAI, VIETNAM 1965
DC Comics: 2010 ($19.95, B&W graphic novel)

	GD 2.0	VG 4.0	FN 6.0	VF 8.0	VF/NM 9.0	NM- 9.2
SC-Joe Kubert-s/a/c; includes report of actual events that inspired the story						20.00

DONKEY KONG (See Blip #1)

DONNA MATRIX
Reactor, Inc.: Aug, 1993 ($2.95, 52 pgs.)

	GD 2.0	VG 4.0	FN 6.0	VF 8.0	VF/NM 9.0	NM- 9.2
1-Computer generated-c/a by Mike Saenz; 3-D effects						4.00

DON NEWCOMBE
Fawcett Publications: 1950 (Baseball)

	GD 2.0	VG 4.0	FN 6.0	VF 8.0	VF/NM 9.0	NM- 9.2
nn-Photo-c	46	92	138	290	488	685

DON ROSA'S COMICS AND STORIES
Fantagraphics Books (CX Comics): 1983 ($2.95)

	GD 2.0	VG 4.0	FN 6.0	VF 8.0	VF/NM 9.0	NM- 9.2
1,2: 1-(68 pgs.) Reprints Rosa's The Pertwillaby Papers episodes #128-133. 2-(60 pgs.) Reprints episodes #134-138	2	4	6	11	16	20

DON SIMPSON'S BIZARRE HEROES (Also see Megaton Man)
Fiasco Comics: May, 1990 - No. 17, Sept, 1996 ($2.50/$2.95, B&W)

	GD 2.0	VG 4.0	FN 6.0	VF 8.0	VF/NM 9.0	NM- 9.2
1-10,0,11-17: 0-Begin $2.95-c; r/Bizarre Heroes #1. 17-(9/96)-Indicia also reads Megaton Man #0; intro Megaton Man and the Fiascoverse to new readers						3.00

DON'T GIVE UP THE SHIP
Dell Publishing Co.: No. 1049, Aug, 1959

	GD 2.0	VG 4.0	FN 6.0	VF 8.0	VF/NM 9.0	NM- 9.2
Four Color 1049-Movie, Jerry Lewis photo-c	9	18	27	61	106	150

DON WINSLOW OF THE NAVY
Merwil Publishing Co.: Apr, 1937 - No. 2, May, 1937 (96 pgs.)(A pulp/comic book cross; stapled spine)

	GD 2.0	VG 4.0	FN 6.0	VF 8.0	VF/NM 9.0	NM- 9.2
V1#1-Has 16 pgs. comics in color. Captain Colorful & Jupiter Jones by Sheldon Mayer; complete Don Winslow novel	653	1306	1959	4900	-	-
2-Sheldon Mayer-a	177	354	531	1325	-	-

DON WINSLOW OF THE NAVY (See Crackajack Funnies, Famous Feature Stories, Popular Comics & Super Book #5,6)
Dell Publishing Co.: No. 2, Nov, 1939 - No. 22, 1941

	GD 2.0	VG 4.0	FN 6.0	VF 8.0	VF/NM 9.0	NM- 9.2
Four Color 2 (#1)-Rare	200	400	600	1280	2190	3100
Four Color 22	48	96	144	302	514	725

DON WINSLOW OF THE NAVY (See TV Teens; Movie, Radio, TV) (Fightin' Navy No. 74 on)
Fawcett Publications/Charlton No. 70 on: 2/43 - #64, 12/48; #65, 1/51 - #69, 9/51; #70, 3/55 - #73, 9/55

	GD 2.0	VG 4.0	FN 6.0	VF 8.0	VF/NM 9.0	NM- 9.2
1-(68 pgs.)-Captain Marvel on cover	110	220	330	704	1202	1700
2	42	84	126	265	445	625
3	34	68	102	199	325	450
4-6: 6-Flag-c	26	52	78	154	252	350
7-10: 8-Last 68 pg. issue?	20	40	60	114	182	250
11-20	15	30	45	90	140	190
21-40	14	28	42	80	115	150
41-43,45-64: 51,60-Singapore Sal (villain) app. 64-(12/48)	13	26	39	74	105	135
44-Classic spider-c	30	60	90	177	289	400
65(1/51)-Flying Saucer attack; photo-c	20	40	60	117	189	260
66 - 69(9/51): All photo-c. 66-sci-fi story	14	28	42	80	115	150
70(3/55)-73: 70-73 r-/#26,58 & 59	9	18	27	50	65	80

DOOM
Marvel Comics: Oct, 2000 - No. 3, Dec, 2000 ($2.99, limited series)

	GD 2.0	VG 4.0	FN 6.0	VF 8.0	VF/NM 9.0	NM- 9.2
1-3-Dr. Doom; Dixon-s/Manco-a						3.00

DOOM FORCE SPECIAL
DC Comics: July, 1992 ($2.95, 68 pgs., one-shot, mature) (X-Force parody)

	GD 2.0	VG 4.0	FN 6.0	VF 8.0	VF/NM 9.0	NM- 9.2
1-Morrison scripts; Simonson, Steacy, & others-a; Giffen/Mignola-c						4.00

DOOM PATROL, THE (Formerly My Greatest Adventure No. 1-85; see Brave and the Bold, DC Special Blue Ribbon Digest 19, Official... Index & Showcase No. 94-96)
National Periodical Publ.: No. 86, 3/64 - No. 121, 9-10/68; No. 122, 2/73 - No. 124, 6-7/73

	GD 2.0	VG 4.0	FN 6.0	VF 8.0	VF/NM 9.0	NM- 9.2
86-1 pg. origin (#86-121 are 12¢ issues)	11	22	33	71	136	200
87-98: 88-Origin The Chief. 91-Intro. Mento	8	16	24	56	96	135
99-Intro. Beast Boy (later becomes the Changeling in New Teen Titans)	10	20	30	65	118	170
100-Origin Beast Boy; Robot-Maniac series begins (12/65)	10	20	30	65	118	170
101-110: 102-Challengers of the Unknown app. 105-Robot-Maniac series ends. 106-Negative Man begins (origin)	6	12	18	42	69	95
111-120	5	10	15	35	55	75
121-Death of Doom Patrol; Orlando-c.	10	20	30	68	127	185
122-124: All reprints	2	4	6	8	11	14

DOOM PATROL
DC Comics (Vertigo imprint #64 on): Oct, 1987 - No, 87, Feb, 1995 (75¢-$1.95, new format)

	GD 2.0	VG 4.0	FN 6.0	VF 8.0	VF/NM 9.0	NM- 9.2
1-Wraparound-c; Lightle-a						6.00
2-18: 3-1st app. Lodestone. 4-1st app. Karma. 8,15,16-Art Adams-c(i). 18-Invasion tie-in						4.00
19-(2/89)-Grant Morrison scripts begin, ends #63; 1st app Crazy Jane; $1.50-c & new format begins.	1	2	3	5	6	8
20-30: 29-Superman app. 30-Night Breed fold-out						5.00
31-34,37-41,45-49,51-56,58-60: 39-World Without End preview						3.00
35-1st brief app. of Flex Mentallo						5.00
36-1st full app. of Flex Mentallo						6.00
42-44-Origin of Flex Mentallo						4.00
50,57 ($2.50, 52 pgs.)						4.00
61-87: 61,70-Photo-c. 73-Death cameo (2 panels)						3.00
...And Suicide Squad 1 (3/88, $1.50, 52 pgs.)-Wraparound-c						4.00
Annual 1 (1988, $1.50, 52 pgs.)						4.00
Annual 2 (1994, $3.95, 68 pgs.)-Children's Crusade tie-in.						4.00
...: Crawling From the Wreckage TPB (2004, $19.95) r/#19-25; Morrison-s						20.00
...: Down Paradise Way TPB (2005, $19.99) r/#35-41; Morrison-s						20.00
...: Magic Bus TPB (2007, $19.99) r/#51-57; Morrison-s; new Bolland-c						20.00
...: Musclebound TPB (2006, $19.99) r/#42-50; Morrison-s; new Bolland-c						20.00
...: Planet Love TPB (2008, $19.99) r/#58-63 & Doom Force Special #1; Morrison-s						20.00
...: The Painting That Ate Paris TPB (2004, $19.95) r/#26-34; Morrison-s						20.00

NOTE: ***Bisley** painted c-26-48, 55-58. **Bolland** c-64, 75. **Dringenberg** a-42(p). **Steacy** a-53.*

DOOM PATROL
DC Comics: Dec, 2001 - No. 22, Sept, 2003 ($2.50)

	GD 2.0	VG 4.0	FN 6.0	VF 8.0	VF/NM 9.0	NM- 9.2
1-Intro. new team with Robotman; Tan Eng Huat-c/a; John Arcudi-s						3.50
2-22: 4,5-Metamorpho & Elongated Man app. 13,14-Fisher-a. 20-Geary-a						3.00

DOOM PATROL (see JLA #94-99)
DC Comics: Aug, 2004 - No. 18, Jan, 2006 ($2.50)

	GD 2.0	VG 4.0	FN 6.0	VF 8.0	VF/NM 9.0	NM- 9.2
1-18-John Byrne-s/a. 1-Green Lantern, Batman app.						3.00

DOOM PATROL
DC Comics: Oct, 2009 - No. 22, Jul, 2011 ($3.99/$2.99)

	GD 2.0	VG 4.0	FN 6.0	VF 8.0	VF/NM 9.0	NM- 9.2
1-7: 1-Giffen-s/Clark-a; back-up Metal Men feature w/Maguire-a. 1-Two covers. 4-5-Blackest Night. 6-Negative Man origin re-told						4.00
8-22-($2.99) 11,12-Ambush Bug app. 16-Giffen-a. 21-Robotman origin retold						3.00
...: Brotherhood TPB (2011, $17.99) r/#7-13						18.00
...: We Who Are About to Die TPB (2010, $14.99) r/#1-6; cover gallery; design art						15.00

DOOM PATROL (See Tangent Comics/ Doom Patrol)

Doomwar #5 © MAR

Dorothy and the Wizard in Oz #1 © MAR

Double Comics 1941 © EP

GD 2.0 VG 4.0 FN 6.0 VF 8.0 VF/NM 9.0 NM- 9.2

DOOMSDAY
DC Comics: 1995 ($3.95, one-shot)

1-Year One story by Jurgens, L. Simonson, Ordway, and Gil Kane; Superman app. 4.00

DOOMSDAY + 1 (Also see Charlton Bullseye)
Charlton Comics: July, 1975 - No. 6, June, 1976; No. 7, June, 1978 - No. 12, May, 1979

1: #1-5 are 25¢ issues 3 6 9 16 22 28
2-6: 4-Intro Lor. 5-Ditko-a(1 pg.) 6-Begin 30¢-c 2 4 6 10 14 18
V3#7-12 (reprints #1-6) 6.00
5 (Modern Comics reprint, 1977) 6.00
NOTE: *Byrne c/a-1-12; Painted covers-2-7.*

DOOMSDAY SQUAD, THE
Fantagraphics Books: Aug, 1986 - No. 7, 1987 ($2.00)

1,2,4-7: Byrne-a in all. 1,2-New Byrne-c. 4-Neal Adams-c. 5-7-Gil Kane-c 4.00
3-Usagi Yojimbo app. (1st in color); new Byrne-c 6.00

DOOM'S IV
Image Comics (Extreme): July, 1994 - No.4, Oct, 1994 ($2.50, limited series)

1-4-Liefeld story 3.00
1,2-Two alternate Liefeld-c each, 4 covers form 1 picture 5.00

DOOM: THE EMPEROR RETURNS
Marvel Comics: Jan, 2002 - No. 3, Mar, 2002 ($2.50, limited series)

1-3-Dixon-s/Manco-a; Franklin Richards app. 3.00

DOOM 2099 (See Marvel Comics Presents #118 & 2099: World of Tomorrow)
Marvel Comics: Jan, 1993 - No. 44, Aug, 1996 ($1.25/$1.50/$1.95)

1-24,26-44: 1-Metallic foil stamped-c. 4-Ron Lim-c(p). 17-bound-in trading card sheet. 40-Namor & Doctor Strange app. 41-Daredevil app., Namor-c/app. 44-Intro The Emissary; story contin'd in 2099: World of Tomorrow 3.00
1-2nd printing 3.00
18-Variant polybagged with Sega Sub-Terrania poster 4.00
25 ($2.25, 52 pgs.) 4.00
25 ($2.95, 52pgs.) Foil embossed cover 5.00
29 ($3.50)-acetate-c. 4.00

DOOMWAR
Marvel Comics: Apr, 2010 - No. 6, Sept, 2010 ($3.99, limited series)

1-6-Doctor Doom invades Wakanda; Black Panther & X-Men app.; Romita Jr.-c/Eaton-a 4.00

DOORWAY TO NIGHTMARE (See Cancelled Comic Cavalcade and Madame Xanadu)
DC Comics: Jan-Feb, 1978 - No. 5, Sept-Oct, 1978

1-Madame Xanadu in all 2 4 6 11 16 20
2-5: 4-Craig-a 2 4 6 8 11 14
NOTE: *Kaluta covers on all. Merged into The Unexpected with No. 190.*

DOPEY DUCK COMICS (Wacky Duck No. 3) (See Super Funnies)
Timely Comics (NPP): Fall, 1945 - No. 2, Apr, 1946

1,2-Casper Cat, Krazy Krow 26 52 81 158 259 350

DORK
Slave Labor: June, 1993 - Present ($2.50-$3.50, B&W, mature)

1-7,9-11: Evan Dorkin-c/a/scripts in all. 1(8/95),2(1/96)-(2nd printings). 1(3/97) (3rd printing). 1-Milk & Cheese app. 3-Eltingville Club starts. 6-Reprints 1st Eltingville Club app. from Instant Piano #1 3.00
8-($3.50) 4.00
Who's Laughing Now? TPB (2001, $11.95) reprints most of #1-5 12.00
The Collected Dork, Vol. 2: Circling the Drain (6/03, $13.95) r/most of #7-10 & other-s 14.00

DOROTHY & THE WIZARD IN OZ (Adaptation of the original 1908 L. Frank Baum book) (Also see Wonderful Wizard of Oz, Marvelous Land of Oz, and Ozma of Oz)
Marvel Comics: Nov, 2011 - No. 8 ($3.99, limited series)

1-5-Eric Shanower-a/Skottie Young-a/c 4.00

DOROTHY LAMOUR (Formerly Jungle Lil)(Stage, screen, radio)
Fox Features Syndicate: No. 2, June, 1950 - No. 3, Aug, 1950

2,3-Wood-a(3) each, photo-c 27 54 81 160 263 365

DOT DOTLAND (Formerly Little Dot Dotland)
Harvey Publications: No. 62, Sept, 1974 - No. 63, Nov, 1974

62,63 2 4 6 9 12 15

DOTTY (...& Her Boy Friends)(Formerly Four Teeners; Glamorous Romances No. 41 on)
Ace Magazines (A. A. Wyn): No. 35, June, 1948 - No. 40, May, 1949

35-Teen-age 9 18 27 50 65 80
36-40: 37-Transvestism story 7 14 21 35 43 50

DOTTY DRIPPLE (Horace & Dotty Dripple No. 25 on)
Magazine Ent.(Life's Romances)/Harvey No. 3 on: 1946 - No. 24, June, 1952 (Also see A-1 No. 1, 3-8, 10)

1 (nd) (10¢) 12 24 36 67 94 120
2 8 16 24 40 50 60
3-10: 3,4-Powell-a 6 12 18 31 38 45
11-24 6 12 18 27 33 38

DOTTY DRIPPLE AND TAFFY
Dell Publishing Co.: No. 646, Sept, 1955 - No. 903, May, 1958

Four Color 646 (#1) 5 10 15 32 51 70
Four Color 691,718,746,801,903 4 8 12 22 34 45

DOUBLE ACTION COMICS
National Periodical Publications: No. 2, Jan, 1940 (68 pgs., B&W)

2-Contains original stories(?); pre-hero DC contents; same cover as Adventure No. 37. (seven known copies, five in high grade) (not an ashcan)
2100 4200 6300 12,600 16,800 21,000
NOTE: *The cover to this book was probably reprinted from Adventure #37. #1 exists as an ash can copy with B&W cover; contains a coverless comic on inside with 1st & last page missing. There is proof of at least limited newsstand distribution. #2 cover proof only sold in 2005 for $4,000.*

DOUBLE COMICS
Elliot Publications: 1940 - 1944 (132 pgs.)

1940 issues; Masked Marvel-c & The Mad Mong vs. The White Flash covers known
271 542 813 1734 2967 4200
1941 issues; Tornado Tim-c, Nordac-c, & Green Light covers known
174 348 522 1114 1907 2700
1942 issues 126 252 378 806 1378 1950
1943,1944 issues 103 206 309 659 1130 1600
NOTE: *Double Comics consisted of an almost endless combination of pairs of remaindered, unsold issues of comics representing most publishers and usually mixed publishers in the same book; e.g., a Captain America with a Silver Streak, or a Feature with a Detective, etc., could appear inside the same cover. The actual contents would have to determine its price. Prices listed are for average contents. Any containing rare origin or first issues are worth much more. Covers also vary in same year. Value would be approximately 50 percent of contents.*

DOUBLE-CROSS (See The Crusaders)

DOUBLE-DARE ADVENTURES
Harvey Publications: Dec, 1966 - No. 2, Mar, 1967 (35¢/25¢, 68 pgs.)

1-Origin Bee-Man, Glowing Gladiator, & Magic-Master; Simon/Kirby-a (last S&K art as a team?) 6 12 18 42 69 95
2-Torres-a; r/Alarming Adv. #3('63) 5 10 15 30 48 65
NOTE: *Powell a-1. Simon/Sparling c-1, 2.*

DOUBLE DRAGON
Marvel Comics: July, 1991 - No. 6, Dec, 1991 ($1.00, limited series)

1-6: Based on video game. 2-Art Adams-c 3.00

DOUBLE EDGE
Marvel Comics: Alpha, 1995; Omega, 1995 ($4.95, limited series)

Alpha ($4.95)- Punisher story, Nick Fury app. 5.00
Omega ($4.95)-Punisher, Daredevil, Ghost Rider app. Death of Nick Fury 5.00

DOUBLE IMAGE
Image Comics: Feb, 2001 - No. 5, July, 2001 ($2.95)

1-5: 1-Flip covers of Codeflesh (Casey-s/Adlard-a) and The Bod (Young-s). 2-Two covers. 5-"Trust in Me" begins; Chaudhary-a 3.00

DOUBLE LIFE OF PRIVATE STRONG, THE
Archie Publications/Radio Comics: June, 1959 - No. 2, Aug, 1959

1-Origin & re-intro The Shield; Simon & Kirby-c/a, their re-entry into the super-hero genre; intro./1st app. The Fly; 1st S.A. super-hero for Archie Publ.
31 62 93 225 488 750
2-S&K-c/a; Tuska-a; The Fly app. (2nd or 3rd?) 19 38 57 128 277 425

DOUBLE TROUBLE
St. John Publishing Co.: Nov, 1957 - No. 2, Jan-Feb, 1958

1,2: Tuffy & Snuffy by Frank Johnson; dubbed "World's Funniest Kids"
6 12 18 31 38 45

DOUBLE TROUBLE WITH GOOBER
Dell Publishing Co.: No. 417, Aug, 1952 - No. 556, May, 1954

Four Color 417 4 8 12 28 44 60
Four Color 471,516,556 4 8 12 22 34 45

DOUBLE UP
Elliott Publications: 1941 (Pocket size, 200 pgs.)

1-Contains rebound copies of digest sized issues of Pocket Comics, Speed Comics, & Spitfire Comics 87 174 261 553 952 1350

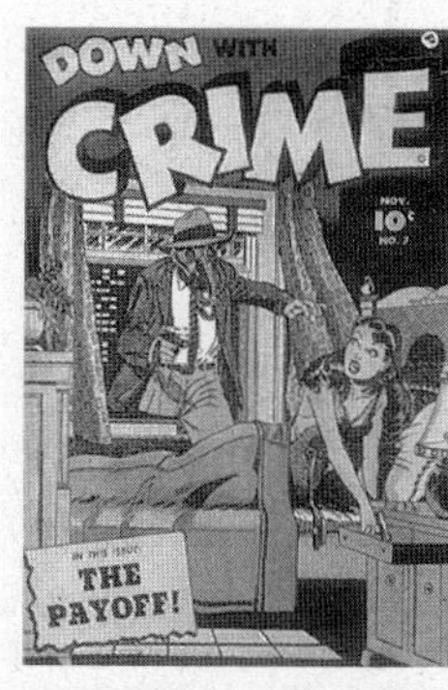

Down With Crime #7 © FAW

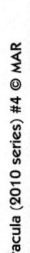

Dracula (2010 series) #4 © MAR

The Dragon #2 © Erik Larsen

	GD 2.0	VG 4.0	FN 6.0	VF 8.0	VF/NM 9.0	NM- 9.2

DOVER & CLOVER (See All Funny & More Fun Comics #93)

DOVER BOYS (See Adventures of the...)

DOVER THE BIRD
Famous Funnies Publishing Co.: Spring, 1955

	GD	VG	FN	VF	VF/NM	NM-
1-Funny animal; code approved	7	14	21	35	43	50

DOWN
Image Comics (Top Cow): Dec, 2005 - No. 4, Mar, 2006 ($2.99)

	GD	VG	FN	VF	VF/NM	NM-
1-4-Warren Ellis-s. 1-Tony Harris-a/c. 2-4-Cully Hamner-a						3.00
Down & Top Cow's Best of Warren Ellis TPB (6/06, $15.99) r/#1-4 & Tales of the Witchblade #3,4; Ellis-s; script for Down #1 with Harris sketch pages						16.00

DOWN WITH CRIME
Fawcett Publications: Nov, 1952 - No. 7, Nov, 1953

	GD	VG	FN	VF	VF/NM	NM-
1	37	74	111	222	361	500
2,4,5: 2,4-Powell-a in each. 5-Bondage-c	19	38	57	111	176	240
3-Used in **POP**, pg. 106; "H is for Heroin" drug story	21	42	63	126	206	285
6,7: 6-Used in **POP**, pg. 80	16	32	48	94	147	200

DO YOU BELIEVE IN NIGHTMARES?
St. John Publishing Co.: Nov, 1957 - No. 2, Jan, 1958

	GD	VG	FN	VF	VF/NM	NM-
1-Mostly Ditko-c/a	53	106	159	334	567	800
2-Ayers-a	30	60	90	177	289	400

D.P. 7
Marvel Comics Group (New Universe): Nov, 1986 - No. 32, June, 1989

	GD	VG	FN	VF	VF/NM	NM-
1-20, Annual #1 (11/87)-Intro. The Witness						3.00
21-32-Low print						4.00
... Classic Vol. 1 TPB (2007, $24.99) r/#1-9; Mark Gruenwald-s/Paul Ryan-a in all						25.00

NOTE: ***Williamson** a-9i, 11i; c-9i.*

DRACULA (See Bram Stoker's Dracula, Giant-Size..., Little Dracula, Marvel Graphic Novel, Requiem for Dracula, Spider-Man Vs...., Stoker's..., Tomb of... & Wedding of...; also see Movie Classics under Universal Presents as well as Dracula)

DRACULA (See Movie Classics for #1)(Also see Frankenstein & Werewolf)
Dell Publ. Co.: No. 2, 11/66 - No. 4, 3/67; No. 6, 7/72 - No. 8, 7/73 (No #5)

	GD	VG	FN	VF	VF/NM	NM-
2-Origin & 1st app. Dracula (11/66) (super hero)	5	10	15	30	48	65
3,4: 4-Intro. Fleeta ('67)	3	6	9	20	30	40
6-('72)-r/#2 w/origin	3	6	9	15	21	26
7,8-r/#3, #4	2	4	6	11	16	20

DRACULA (Magazine)
Warren Publishing Co.: 1979 (120 pgs., full color)

	GD	VG	FN	VF	VF/NM	NM-
Book 1-Maroto art; Spanish material translated into English (mail order only)	6	12	18	41	66	90

DRACULA
Marvel Comics: Jul, 2010 - No. 4, Sept, 2010 ($3.99, limited series)

	GD	VG	FN	VF	VF/NM	NM-
1-4-Colored reprint of Bram Stoker's Classic Dracula adapt. from Dracula Lives!, Legion of Monsters and Stoker's Dracula; Thomas-s/Giordano-a; J. Djurdjevic-c						4.00

DRACULA CHRONICLES
Topps Comics: Apr, 1995 - No. 3, June, 1995 ($2.50, limited series)

	GD	VG	FN	VF	VF/NM	NM-
1-3-Linsner-c						3.00

DRACULA LIVES! (Magazine)(Also see Tomb of Dracula) (Reprinted in Stoker's Dracula)
Marvel Comics Group: 1973(no month) - No. 13, July, 1975 (75¢, B&W) (76 pgs.)

	GD	VG	FN	VF	VF/NM	NM-
1-Boris painted-c	8	16	24	53	89	125
2 (7/73)-1st time origin Dracula; Adams, Starlin-a	5	10	15	35	55	75
3-1st app. Robert E. Howard's Soloman Kane; Adams-c/a	5	10	15	35	55	75
4,5: 4-Ploog-a. 5(V2#1)-Bram Stoker's Classic Dracula adapt. begins	4	8	12	24	37	50
6-9: 6-8-Bram Stoker adapt. 9-Bondage-c	4	8	12	24	37	50
10 (1/75)-16 pg. Lilith solo (1st?)	4	8	12	28	44	60
11-13: 11-21 pg. Lilith solo sty. 12-31 pg. Dracula sty	4	8	12	24	37	50
Annual 1(Summer, 1975, $1.25, 92 pgs.)-Morrow painted-c; 6 Dracula stys. 25 pgs. Adams-a(r)	4	8	12	26	41	55

NOTE: ***N. Adams** a-2, 3i, 10i, Annual 1r(2, 3i). **Alcala** a-9. **Buscema** a-3p, 6p, Annual 1p. **Colan** a(p)-1, 2, 5, 6, 8. **Evans** a-7. **Gulacy** a-9. **Heath** a-1r, 13. **Pakula** a-6r. Sutton a-13. **Weiss** r-Annual 1p. 4 **Dracula** stories each in 1, 609; 3 **Dracula** stories each in 2, 4, 5,, 13.*

DRACULA: LORD OF THE UNDEAD
Marvel Comics: Dec, 1998 - No. 3, Dec, 1998 ($2.99, limited series)

	GD	VG	FN	VF	VF/NM	NM-
1-3-Olliffe & Palmer-a						3.00

DRACULA: RETURN OF THE IMPALER
Slave Labor Graphics: July, 1993 - No. 4, Oct, 1994 ($2.95, limited series)

	GD	VG	FN	VF	VF/NM	NM-
1-4						3.00

DRACULA'S REVENGE
IDW Publishing: Apr, 2004 - No. 3 ($3.99, limited series)

	GD	VG	FN	VF	VF/NM	NM-
1,2-Forbeck-s/Kudranski-a						4.00

DRACULA: THE COMPANY OF MONSTERS
BOOM! Studios: Aug, 2010 - No. 12, Jul, 2011 ($3.99)

	GD	VG	FN	VF	VF/NM	NM-
1-12: 1-5-Busiek & Gregory-s/Godlewski-a. 1-Two covers by Brereton and Salas						4.00

DRACULA VERSUS ZORRO
Topps Comics: Oct, 1993 - No. 2, Nov, 1993 ($2.95, limited series)

	GD	VG	FN	VF	VF/NM	NM-
1,2: 1-Spot varnish & red foil-c. 2-Polybagged w/16 pg. Zorro #0						3.00

DRACULA VERSUS ZORRO
Dark Horse Comics: Sept, 1998 - No. 2, Oct, 1998 ($2.95, limited series)

	GD	VG	FN	VF	VF/NM	NM-
1,2						3.00

DRACULA: VLAD THE IMPALER (Also see Bram Stoker's Dracula)
Topps Comics: Feb, 1993 - No. 3, Apr, 1993 ($2.95, limited series)

	GD	VG	FN	VF	VF/NM	NM-
1-3-Polybagged with 3 trading cards each; Maroto-c/a						3.00

DRAFT, THE
Marvel Comics: 1988 ($3.50, one-shot, squarebound)

	GD	VG	FN	VF	VF/NM	NM-
1-Sequel to "The Pitt"						4.00

DRAFTED: ONE HUNDRED DAYS
Devil's Due Publishing: June, 2009 ($5.99, one-shot)

	GD	VG	FN	VF	VF/NM	NM-
1-Barack Obama on a post-galactic-war Earth; Powers-s						6.00

DRAG 'N' WHEELS (Formerly Top Eliminator)
Charlton Comics: No. 30, Sept, 1968 - No. 59, May, 1973

	GD	VG	FN	VF	VF/NM	NM-
30	4	8	12	28	44	60
31-40-Scot Jackson begins	3	6	9	19	29	38
41-50	3	6	9	17	25	32
51-59: Scot Jackson	2	4	6	13	18	22
Modern Comics Reprint 58('78)						5.00

DRAGON, THE (Also see The Savage Dragon)
Image Comics (Highbrow Ent.): Mar, 1996 - No. 5, July, 1996 (99¢, lim. series)

	GD	VG	FN	VF	VF/NM	NM-
1-5: Reprints Savage Dragon limited series w/new story & art. 5-Youngblood app; includes 5 pg. Savage Dragon story from 1984						3.00

DRAGON AGE (Based on the EA videogame)
IDW Publishing (EA Comics): Mar, 2010 - No. 6, Nov, 2010 ($3.99)

	GD	VG	FN	VF	VF/NM	NM-
1-6-Orson Scott Card & Aaron Johnston-s; Ramos-c						4.00

DRAGON ARCHIVES, THE (Also see The Savage Dragon)
Image Comics: Jun, 1998 - No. 4, Jan, 1999 ($2.95, B&W)

	GD	VG	FN	VF	VF/NM	NM-
1-4: Reprints early Savage Dragon app.						3.00

DRAGON BALL
Viz Comics: Mar, 1998 - Part 6: #2, Feb, 2003($2.95, B&W, Manga reprints read right to left)

	GD	VG	FN	VF	VF/NM	NM-
Part 1: 1-Akira Toriyama-s/a	2	4	6	8	10	12
2-12						6.00
1-12 (2nd & 3rd printings)						3.00
Part 2: 1-15: 15-($3.50-c)						5.00
Part 3: 1-14						4.00
Part 4: 1-10						4.00
Part 5: 1-7						4.00
Part 6: 1,2						4.00

DRAGON BALL Z
Viz Comics: Mar, 1998 - Part 5: #10, Oct, 2002 ($2.95, B&W, Manga reprints read right to left)

	GD	VG	FN	VF	VF/NM	NM-
Part 1: 1-Akira Toriyama-s/a	2	4	6	8	10	12
2-9						6.00
1-9 (2nd & 3rd printings)						3.00
Part 2: 1-14						5.00
Part 3: 1-10						4.00
Part 4: 1-15						4.00
Part 5: 1-10						4.00

DRAGON, THE: BLOOD & GUTS (Also see The Savage Dragon)
Image Comics (Highbrow Entertainment): Mar, 1995 - No. 3, May, 1995 ($2.50, lim. series)

	GD	VG	FN	VF	VF/NM	NM-
1-3: Jason Pearson-c/a/scripts						3.00

DRAGON CHIANG
Eclipse Books: 1991 ($3.95, B&W, squarebound, 52 pgs.)

Dragonheart #2 © Universal

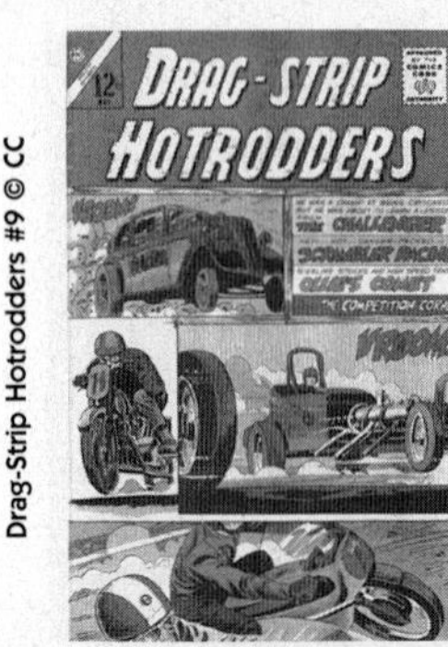

Drag-Strip Hotrodders #9 © CC

Dreadstar #14 © MAR

	GD 2.0	VG 4.0	FN 6.0	VF 8.0	VF/NM 9.0	NM- 9.2

nn-Timothy Truman-c/a(p) 4.00

DRAGONFLIGHT
Eclipse Books: Feb, 1991 - No. 3, 1991 ($4.95, 52 pgs.)
Book One - Three: Adapts 1968 novel 5.00

DRAGONFLY (See Americomics #4)
Americomics: Sum, 1985 - No. 8, 1986 ($1.75/$1.95)
1 4.00
2-8 3.00

DRAGONFORCE
Aircel Publishing: 1988 - No. 13, 1989 ($2.00)
1-Dale Keown-c/a/scripts in #1-12 3.50
2-13: 13-No Keown-a 3.00
...Chronicles Book 1-5 ($2.95, B&W, 60 pgs.): Dale Keown-r/Dragonring & Dragonforce 4.00

DRAGONHEART (Movie)
Topps Comics: May, 1996 - No. 2, June, 1996 ($2.95/$4.95, limited series)
1-($2.95, 24 pgs.)-Adaptation of the film; Hildebrandt Bros-c; Lim-a. 3.00
2-($4.95, 64 pgs.) 5.00

DRAGONLANCE (Also see TSR Worlds)
DC Comics: Dec, 1988 - No. 34, Sept, 1991 ($1.25/$1.50, Mando paper)
1-Based on TSR game 4.00
2-34: Based on TSR game. 30-32-Kaluta-c 3.00

DRAGONLANCE: CHRONICLES
Devil's Due Publ.: Aug, 2005 - No. 8, Mar, 2006 ($2.95)
1-8-Dabb-s/Kurth-a 3.00
...: Dragons of Autumn Twilight TPB (2006, $17.95) r/#1-8 18.00

DRAGONLANCE: CHRONICLES (Volume 2)
Devil's Due Publ.: July, 2006 - No. 4, Jan, 2007 ($4.95/$4.99, 48 pgs.)
1-4-Dragons of Winter Night; Dabb-s/Kurth-a 5.00
...: Dragons of Winter Night TPB (3/07, $18.99) r/#1-4; cover gallery 19.00

DRAGONLANCE: CHRONICLES (Volume 3)
Devil's Due Publ.: Mar, 2007 - No. 12, ($3.50)
1-11-Dragons of Spring Dawning; Dabb-s/Cope-a 3.50

DRAGONLANCE: THE LEGEND OF HUMA
Devil's Due Publ.: Jan, 2004 - No. 6, Oct, 2005 ($2.95)
1-6-Mike Miller & Rael-a 3.00

DRAGON LINES
Marvel Comics (Epic Comics/Heavy Hitters): May, 1993 - No. 4, Aug, 1993 ($1.95, limited series)
1-($2.50)-Embossed-c; Ron Lim-c/a in all 3.50
2-4 3.00

DRAGON LINES: WAY OF THE WARRIOR
Marvel Comics (Epic Comics/ Heavy Hitters): Nov, 1993 - No. 2, Jan, 1994 ($2.25, limited series)
1,2-Ron Lim-c/a(p) 3.00

DRAGON PRINCE
Image Comics (Top Cow): Sept, 2008 - No. 4, Jan, 2009 ($2.99)
1-4-Marz-s/Moder-a; two covers 3.00

DRAGONQUEST
Silverwolf Comics: Dec, 1986 - No. 2, 1987 ($1.50, B&W, 28 pgs.)
1,2-Tim Vigil-c/a in all 5.00

DRAGONRING
Aircel Publishing: 1986 - V2#15, 1988 ($1.70/$2.00, B&W/color)
1-6: 6-Last B&W issue, V2#1-15($2.00, color) 3.00

DRAGON'S CLAWS
Marvel UK, Ltd.: July, 1988 - No. 10, Apr, 1989 ($1.25/$1.50/$1.75, British)
1-10: 3-Death's Head 1 pg. strip on back-c (1st app.). 4-Silhouette of Death's Head on last pg. 5-1st full app. new Death's Head 3.00

DRAGON'S LAIR: SINGE'S REVENGE (Based on the Don Bluth video game)
CrossGen Comics: Sept, 2003 - No. 3 ($2.95, limited series)
1-3-Mangels-s/Laguna-a 3.00

DRAGONSLAYER (Movie)
Marvel Comics Group: October, 1981 - No. 2, Nov, 1981
1,2-Paramount Disney movie adaptation 3.00

DRAGOON WELLS MASSACRE
Dell Publishing Co.: No. 815, June, 1957
Four Color 815-Movie, photo-c 7 14 21 49 82 115

DRAGSTRIP HOTRODDERS (World of Wheels No. 17 on)
Charlton Comics: Sum, 1963; No. 2, Jan, 1965 - No. 16, Aug, 1967
1 7 14 21 48 79 110
2-5 4 8 12 26 41 55
6-16 4 8 12 22 34 45

DRAIN
Image Comics: Nov, 2006 - No. 6, Mar, 2008 ($2.99)
1-6: 1-Cebulski-s/Takeda-a; two covers by Takeda and Finch 3.00
Vol. 1 TPB (2008, $16.99) r/#1-6; cover gallery and Takeda sketch art gallery 17.00

DRAKUUN
Dark Horse Comics: Feb, 1997 - No. 25, Mar, 1999 ($2.95, B&W, manga)
1-25; 1-6- Johji Manabe-s/a in all. Rise of the Dragon Princess series. 7-12-Revenge of Gustav. 13-18-Shadow of the Warlock. 19-25-The Hidden War 3.00

DRAMA
Sirius: June, 1994 ($2.95, mature)
1-1st full color Dawn app. in comics 2 4 6 11 16 20
1-Limited edition (1400 copies); signed & numbered; fingerprint authenticity 4 8 12 24 37 50
NOTE: *Dawn's 1st full color app. was a pin-up in Amazing Heroes' Swimsuit Special #5.*

DRAMA OF AMERICA, THE
Action Text: 1973 ($1.95, 224 pgs.)
1- "Students' Supplement to History" 1 3 4 6 8 10

DRAWING ON YOUR NIGHTMARES
Dark Horse Comics: Oct, 2003 ($2.99, one-shot)
1-Short stories; The Goon, Criminal Macabre, Tales of the Vampires; Templesmith-c 3.00

DRAX THE DESTROYER
Marvel Comics: Nov, 2005 - No. 4, Feb, 2006 ($2.99, limited series)
1-4-Giffen-s/Breitweiser-a 3.00
...: Earthfall TPB (2006, $10.99) r/#1-4; character design page 11.00

DREADLANDS (Also see Epic)
Marvel Comics (Epic Comics): 1992 - No. 4, 1992 ($3.95, lim. series, 52 pgs.)
1-4: Stiff-c 4.00

DREADSTAR (See Epic Illustrated #3 for 1st app. and Eclipse Graphic Album Series #5)
Marvel Comics (Epic Comics)/First Comics No. 27 on: Nov, 1982 - No. 64, Mar, 1991
1 4.00
2-5,8-49 3.00
6,7,51-64: 6,7-1st app. Interstellar Toybox; 8pgs. ea.; Wrightson-a. 51-64-Lower print run 4.00
50 5.00
Annual 1 (12/83)-r/The Price (Eclipse Graphic Album Series #5) 4.00

DREADSTAR
Malibu Comics (Bravura): Apr, 1994 - No. 6, Jan, 1995 ($2.50, limited series)
1-6-Peter David scripts: 1,2-Starlin-c 3.00
NOTE: *Issues 1-6 contain Bravura stamps.*

DREADSTAR AND COMPANY
Marvel Comics (Epic Comics): July, 1985 - No. 6, Dec, 1985
1-6: 1,3,6-New Starlin-a: 2-New Wrightson-c; reprints of Dreadstar series 3.00

DREAM BOOK OF LOVE (Also see A-1 Comics)
Magazine Enterprises: No. 106, June-July, 1954 - No. 123, Oct-Nov, 1954
A-1 106 (#1)-Powell, Bolle-a; Montgomery Clift, Donna Reed photo-c 15 30 45 83 124 165
A-1-114 (#2)-Guardineer, Bolle-a; Piper Laurie, Victor Mature photo-c 11 22 33 62 86 110
A-1 123 (#3)-Movie photo-c 11 22 33 60 83 105

DREAM BOOK OF ROMANCE (Also see A-1 Comics)
Magazine Enterprises: No. 92, 1954 - No. 124, Oct-Nov, 1954
A-1 92 (#5)-Guardineer-a; photo-c 14 28 42 81 118 155
A-1 101 (#6)(4-6/54)-Marlon Brando photo-c; Powell, Bolle, Guardineer-a 23 46 69 136 223 310
A-1 109,110,124: 109 (#7)(7-8/54)-Powell-a; movie photo-c. 110 (#8)(1/54)-Movie photo-c. 124 (#8)(10-11/54) 11 22 33 60 83 105

DREAMER, THE
Kitchen Sink Press: 1986 ($6.95, B&W, graphic novel)

The Dreaming #56 © DC

Duck Album Four Color #450 © DIS

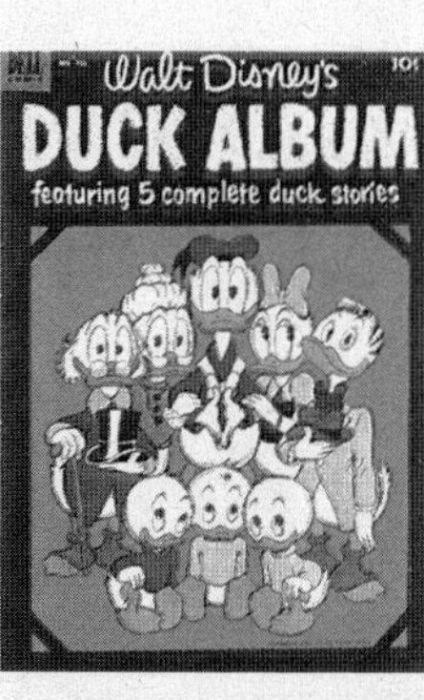

Ducktales (2011 series) #1 © DIS

GD 2.0 | VG 4.0 | FN 6.0 | VF 8.0 | VF/NM 9.0 | NM- 9.2

nn-Will Eisner-s/a 12.00
DC Comics Reprint ($7.95, 6/00) 8.00

DREAMERY, THE
Eclipse Comics: Dec, 1986 - No. 14, Feb, 1989 ($2.00, B&W, Baxter paper)
1-14: 2-7-Alice In Wonderland adapt. 3.00

DREAMING, THE (See Sandman, 2nd Series)
DC Comics (Vertigo): June, 1996 - No. 60, May, 2001 ($2.50)
1-McKean-c on all.; LaBan scripts & Snejbjerg-a 4.00
2-30,32-60: 2,3-LaBan scripts & Snejbjerg-a. 4-7-Hogan scripts; Parkhouse-a. 8-Zulli-a. 9-11-Talbot-s/Taylor-a(p). 41-Previews Sandman: The Dream Hunters. 50-Hempel, Fegredo, McManus, Totleben-a 3.00
31-($3.95) Art by various 4.00
...Beyond The Shores of Night TPB ('97, $19.95) r/#1-8 20.00
...Special (7/98, $5.95, one-shot) Trial of Cain 6.00
...Through The Gates of Horn and Ivory TPB ('99, $19.95) r/#15-19,22-25 20.00

DREAM OF LOVE
I. W. Enterprises: 1958 (Reprints)
1,2,8: 1-r/Dream Book of Love #1; Bob Powell-a. 2-r/Great Lover's Romances #10. 8-Great Lover's Romances #1; also contains 2 Jon Juan stories by Siegel & Schomburg; Kinstler-c. 2 4 6 10 14 18
9-Kinstler-c; 1pg. John Wayne interview & Frazetta illo from John Wayne Adv. Comics #2 2 4 6 10 14 18

DREAM POLICE
Marvel Comics (Icon): Aug, 2005 ($3.99)
1-Straczynski-s/Deodato-a/c 4.00

DREAMS OF THE DARKCHYLDE
Darkchylde Entertainment: Oct, 2000 - No. 6, Sept, 2001 ($2.95)
1-6-Randy Queen-s in all. 1-Brandon Peterson-c/a 3.00

DREAM TEAM (See Battlezones: Dream Team 2)
Malibu Comics (Ultraverse): July, 1995 ($4.95, one-shot)
1-Pin-ups teaming up Marvel & Ultraverse characters by various artists including Allred, Romita, Darrow, Balent, Quesada & Palmiotti 5.00

DREAMWAVE PRODUCTIONS PREVIEW
Dreamwave Productions: May, 2002 ($1.00, one-shot)
nn-Previews Arkanium, Transformers: The War Within and other series 3.00

DRESDEN FILES (See Jim Butcher's...)

DRIFT FENCE (See Zane Grey 4-Color 270)

DRIFT MARLO
Dell Publishing Co.: May-July, 1962 - No. 2, Oct-Dec, 1962
01-232-207 (#1) 5 10 15 32 51 70
2 (12-232-212) 4 8 12 28 44 60

DRISCOLL'S BOOK OF PIRATES
David McKay Publ. (Not reprints): 1934 (B&W, hardcover; 124 pgs, 7x9")
nn-By Montford Amory 23 46 69 136 223 310

DRIVER: CROSSING THE LINE (Based on the Ubisoft videogame)
DC Comics: Oct, 2011 ($2.99, one-shot)
1-David Lapham-s/Greg Scott-a/ Jock-c; bonus character design art 3.00

DROIDS (Based on Saturday morning cartoon) (Also see Dark Horse Comics)
Marvel Comics (Star Comics): April, 1986 - No. 8, June, 1987
1-R2D2 & C-3PO from Star Wars app. in all 2 4 6 11 16 20
2-8: 2,5,7,8-Williamson-a(i) 2 4 6 8 10 12
NOTE: *Romita a-3p. Sinnott a-3i.*

DROOPY (see Tom & Jerry #60)

DROOPY (Tex Avery's...)
Dark Horse Comics: Oct, 1995 - No. 3, Dec, 1995 ($2.50, limited series)
1-3: Characters created by Tex Avery; painted-c 3.00

DROPSIE AVENUE: THE NEIGHBORHOOD
Kitchen Sink Press: June, 1995 ($15.95/$24.95, B&W)
nn-Will Eisner (softcover) 16.00
nn-Will Eisner (hardcover) 25.00

DROWNED GIRL, THE
DC Comics (Piranha Press): 1990 ($5.95, 52 pgs, mature)
nn 6.00

DRUG WARS
Pioneer Comics: 1989 ($1.95)
1-Grell-c 3.00

DRUID
Marvel Comics: May, 1995 - No. 4, Aug, 1995 ($2.50, limited series)
1-4: Warren Ellis scripts. 3.00

DRUM BEAT
Dell Publishing Co.: No. 610, Jan, 1955
Four Color 610-Movie, Alan Ladd photo-c 8 16 24 55 93 130

DRUMS OF DOOM
United Features Syndicate: 1937 (25¢)(Indian)(Text w/color illos.)
nn-By Lt. F.A. Methot; Golden Thunder app.; Tip Top Comics ad in comic; nice-c 37 74 111 222 361 500

DRUNKEN FIST
Jademan Comics: Aug, 1988 - No. 54, Jan, 1993 ($1.50/$1.95, 68 pgs.)
1 5.00
2-50 4.00
51-54 4.00

DUCK ALBUM (See Donald Duck Album)
Dell Publishing Co.: No. 353, Oct, 1951 - No. 840, Sept, 1957
Four Color 353 (#1)-Barks-c; 1st Uncle Scrooge-c (also appears on back-c). 10 20 30 66 121 175
Four Color 450-Barks-c 7 14 21 48 79 110
Four Color 492,531,560,586,611,649,686, 6 12 18 41 66 90
Four Color 726,782,840 5 10 15 35 55 75

DUCKMAN
Dark Horse Comics: Sept, 1990 ($1.95, B&W, one-shot)
1-Story & art by Everett Peck 4.00

DUCKMAN
Topps Comics: Nov, 1994 - No. 5, May, 1995; No. 0, Feb, 1996 ($2.50)
0 (2/96, $2.95, B&W)-r/Duckman #1 from Dark Horse Comics 4.00
1-5: 1-w/ coupon #A for Duckman trading card. 2-w/Duckman 1st season episode guide 3.00

DUCKMAN: THE MOB FROG SAGA
Topps Comics: Nov, 1994 - No. 3, Feb, 1995 ($2.50, limited series)
1-3: 1-w/coupon #B for Duckman trading card, S. Shaw!-c 3.00

DUCKTALES
Gladstone Publ.: Oct, 1988 - No. 13, May, 1990 (1,2,9-11: $1.50; 3-8: 95¢)
1-Barks-r 6.00
2-11: 2-7,9-11-Barks-r 4.00
12,13 ($1.95, 68 pgs.)-Barks-r; 12-r/F.C. #495 5.00
Disney Presents Carl Barks' Greatest DuckTales Stories Vol. 1 (Gemstone Publ., 2006, $10.95) r/stories adapted for the animated TV series including "Back to the Klondike" 11.00
Disney Presents Carl Barks' Greatest DuckTales Stories Vol. 2 (Gemstone Publ., 2006, $10.95) r/stories adapted for the animated TV series; "Robot Robbers" app. 11.00

DUCKTALES (TV)
Disney Comics: June, 1990 - No. 18, Nov, 1991 ($1.50)
1-All new stories; Marv Wolfman-s 3.50
2-18 3.00
Disney's DuckTales by Marv Wolfman: Scrooge's Quest TPB (Gemstone, 9/07, $15.99) r/#1-7; intro. by Wolfman 16.00
Disney's DuckTales: The Gold Odyssey TPB (Gemstone, 10/08, $15.99) 16.00
The Movie nn (1990, $7.95, 68 pgs.)-Graphic novel adapting animated movie 8.00

DUCKTALES (TV)
Boom Entertainment (KABOOM!): May, 2011 - No. 4, Aug, 2011 ($3.99)
1-6: 1-4-Three covers on each; Spector-s/Massaroli-a. 5,6-Two covers; Crossover with Darkwing Duck #17,18 4.00

DUDLEY (Teen-age)
Feature/Prize Publications: Nov-Dec, 1949 - No. 3, Mar-Apr, 1950
1-By Boody Rogers 15 30 45 85 130 175
2,3 10 20 30 56 76 95

DUDLEY DO-RIGHT (TV)
Charlton Comics: Aug, 1970 - No. 7, Aug, 1971 (Jay Ward)
1 9 18 27 60 103 145
2-7 6 12 18 42 69 95

DUEL MASTERS (Based on a trading card game) (Also see Free Comic Book Day Edition in the Promotional Comics section)

Dungeons & Dragons #1 © WOTC

DV8 #14 © DC

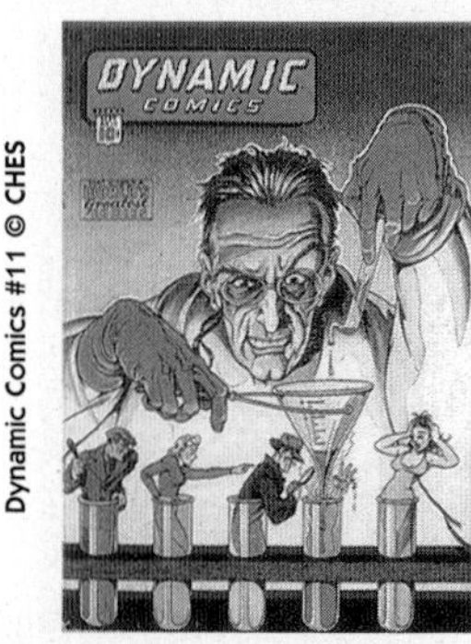

Dynamic Comics #11 © CHES

GD VG FN VF VF/NM NM-
2.0 4.0 6.0 8.0 9.0 9.2

Dreamwave Productions: Nov, 2003 - No. 8, Sept, 2004 ($2.95)

1-8: 1-Bagged with card; Augustyn-s 3.00

DUKE NUKEM: GLORIOUS BASTARD (Based on the video game)
IDW Publishing: Jul, 2011 - Present ($3.99)

1-3: 1-Three covers; Waltz-s/Xermanico-a 4.00

DUKE OF THE K-9 PATROL
Gold Key: Apr, 1963

1 (10052-304) 4 8 12 24 37 50

DUMBO (Disney; see Movie Comics, & Walt Disney Showcase #12)
Dell Publishing Co.: No. 17, 1941 - No. 668, Jan, 1958

Four Color 17 (#1)-Mickey Mouse, Donald Duck, Pluto app.
265 530 795 1694 2897 4100
Large Feature Comic 19 ('41)-Part-r 4-Color 17 297 594 891 1888 3244 4600
Four Color 234 ('49) 12 24 36 84 177 270
Four Color 668 (12/55)-1st of two printings. Dumbo on-c with starry sky. Same-c as #234
10 20 30 67 124 180
Four Color 668 (1/58)-2nd printing. Same cover altered with Timothy Mouse added. Same contents 7 14 21 44 72 100

DUMBO COMIC PAINT BOOK (See Dumbo, Large Feature Comic No. 19)

DUNC AND LOO (#1-3 titled "Around the Block with Dunc and Loo")
Dell Publishing Co.: Oct-Dec, 1961 - No. 8, Oct-Dec, 1963

1 8 16 24 51 86 120
2 6 12 18 37 59 80
3-8 4 8 12 28 44 60

NOTE: *Written by* ***John Stanley; Bill Williams*** *art.*

DUNE (Movie)
Marvel Comics: Apr, 1985 - No. 3, June, 1985

1-3-r/Marvel Super Special; movie adaptation 3.00

DUNGEONS & DRAGONS
IDW Publishing: No. 0, Aug, 2010 - Present ($1.00/$3.99)

0-(8/10, $1.00) Five covers; previews D&D series and Dark Sun mini-series 3.00
1-11: 1-(11/10, $3.99) Di Vito-a/Rogers-s; two covers. 2-Two covers 4.00

DUNGEONS & DRAGONS: THE LEGEND OF DRIZZT: NEVERWINTER TALES
IDW Publishing: Aug, 2011 - Present ($3.99)

1,2-R.A. & Geno Salvatore-s/Agustin Padilla-a 4.00

DURANGO KID, THE (Also see Best of the West, Great Western & White Indian)
(Charles Starrett starred in Columbia's Durango Kid movies)
Magazine Enterprises: Oct-Nov, 1949 - No. 41, Oct-Nov, 1955 (All 36 pgs.)

1-Charles Starrett photo-c; Durango Kid & his horse Raider begin; Dan Brand & Tipi (origin) begin by Frazetta & continue through #16 71 142 213 454 777 1100
2-Starrett photo-c. 34 68 102 199 325 450
3-5-All have Starrett photo-c. 29 58 87 172 281 390
6-10: 7-Atomic weapon-c/story 16 32 48 94 147 200
11-16-Last Frazetta issue 14 28 42 80 115 150
17-Origin Durango Kid 16 32 48 94 147 200
18-30: 18-Fred Meagher-a on Dan Brand begins.19-Guardineer-c/a(3) begins, end #41. 23-Intro. The Red Scorpion 10 20 30 54 72 90
31-Red Scorpion returns 9 18 27 52 69 85
32-41-Bolle/Frazetta*ish*-a (Dan Brand; true in later issues?)
9 18 27 50 65 80

NOTE: *#6, 8, 14, 15 contain* ***Frazetta*** *art not reprinted in White Indian.* ***Ayers*** *c-18.* ***Guardineer*** *a(3)-19-41; c-19-41.* ***Fred Meagher*** *a-18-29 at least.*

DURANGO KID, THE
AC Comics: 1990 - #2, 1990 ($2.50,$2.75, half-color)

1,2: 1-Starrett photo front/back-c; Guardineer-r. 2-B&W)-Starrett photo-c; White Indian-r by Frazetta; Guardineer-r (50th anniversary of films) 3.00

DUSTCOVERS: THE COLLECTED SANDMAN COVERS 1989-1997
DC Comics (Vertigo): 1997 ($39.95, Hardcover)

Reprints Dave McKean's Sandman covers with Gaiman text 40.00
Softcover (1998, $24.95) 25.00

DUSTY STAR
Image Comics (Desperado Studios): No. 0, Apr, 1997 - No. 1 ($2.95, B&W)

0,1-Pruett-s/Robinson-a 3.00

DUSTY STAR
Image Comics (Desperado Publishing): June, 2006 ($3.50)

1-Pruett-s/Robinson-s/a 3.50

GD VG FN VF VF/NM NM-
2.0 4.0 6.0 8.0 9.0 9.2

DV8 (See Gen 13)
Image Comics (WildStorm Productions): Aug, 1996 - No. 25, Dec, 1998;
DC Comics (WildStorm Prod.): No. 0, Apr, 1999 - No. 32, Nov, 1999 ($2.50)

1/2 6.00
1-Warren Ellis scripts & Humberto Ramos-c/a(p) 4.00
1-(7-variant covers, w/1 by Jim Lee) ...each 4.00
2-4: 3-No Ramos-a 3.00
5-32: 14-Regular-c, 14-Variant-c by Charest. 26-(5/99)-McGuinness-c 3.00
14-($3.50) Voyager Pack w/Danger Girl preview 5.00
0-(4/99, $2.95) Two covers (Rio and McGuinness) 3.00
Annual 1 (1/98, $2.95) 4.00
Annual 1999 ($3.50) Slipstream x-over with Gen13 4.00
Rave-(7/96, $1.75)-Ramos-c; pinups & interviews 3.00
...: Neighborhood Threat TPB (2002, $14.95) r/#1-6 & #1/2; Ellis intro.; Ramos-c 15.00

DV8: GODS AND MONSTERS
DC Comics (WildStorm): June, 2010 - No. 8, Jan, 2011 ($2.99, limited series)

1-8-Wood-s/Issacs-a 3.00
TPB (2011, $17.99) r/#1-8 18.00

DV8 VS. BLACK OPS
Image Comics (WildStorm): Oct, 1997 - No. 3, Dec, 1997 ($2.50, limited series)

1-3-Bury-s/Norton-a 3.00

DWIGHT D. EISENHOWER
Dell Publishing Co.: December, 1969

01-237-912 - Life story 5 10 15 30 48 65

DYNABRITE COMICS
Whitman Publishing Co.: 1978 - 1979 (69¢, 10x7-1/8", 48 pgs., cardboard-c)
(Blank inside covers)

11350 - Walt Disney's Mickey Mouse & the Beanstalk (4-C 157). 11350-1 - Mickey Mouse Album (4-C 1057, 1151,1246). 11351 - Mickey Mouse & His Sky Adventure (4-C 214, 343). 11354 - Goofy: A Gaggle of Giggles. 11354-1 - Super Goof Meets Super Thief. 11356 - (?). 11359 - Bugs Bunny-r. 11360 - Winnie the Pooh Fun and Fantasy (Disney-r).
each.... 2 4 6 9 12 15

11352 - Donald Duck (4-C 408, Donald Duck 45,52)-Barks-a. 11352-1 - Donald Duck (4-C 318, 10 pg. Barks/WDC&S 125,128)-Barks-c(r). 11353 - Daisy Duck's Diary (4-C 1055,1150) Barks-a. 11355 - Uncle Scrooge (Barks-a/U.S. 12,33). 11355-1 - Uncle Scrooge (Barks-a/U.S. 13,16) - Barks-c(r). 11357 - Star Trek (r/-Star Trek 33,41). 11358 - Star Trek (r/-Star Trek 34,36). 11361 - Gyro Gearloose & the Disney Ducks (r/4-C 1047,1184)-Barks-c(r)
each.... 2 4 6 10 14 18

DYNAMIC ADVENTURES
I. W. Enterprises: No. 8, 1964 - No. 9, 1964

8-Kayo Kirby-r by Baker?/Fight Comics 53. 3 6 9 14 20 25
9-Reprints Avon's "Escape From Devil's Island"; Kinstler-c
3 6 9 16 23 30
nn (no date)-Reprints Risks Unlimited with Rip Carson, Senorita Rio; r/Fight #53
3 6 9 16 22 28

DYNAMIC CLASSICS (See Cancelled Comic Cavalcade)
DC Comics: Sept-Oct, 1978 (44 pgs.)

1-Neal Adams Batman, Simonson Manhunter-r 2 4 6 8 10 12

DYNAMIC COMICS (No #4-7)
Harry 'A' Chesler: Oct, 1941 - No. 3, Feb, 1942; No. 8, Mar, 1944 - No. 25, May, 1948

1-Origin Major Victory by Charles Sultan (reprinted in Major Victory #1), Dynamic Man & Hale the Magician; The Black Cobra only app.; Major Victory & Dynamic Man begin
219 438 657 1402 2401 3400
2-Origin Dynamic Boy & Lady Satan; intro. The Green Knight & sidekick Lance Cooper
100 200 300 635 1093 1550
3-1st small logo, resumes with #10 97 194 291 621 1061 1500
8-Classic-c; Dan Hastings, The Echo, The Master Key, Yankee Boy begin; Yankee Doodle Jones app.; hypo story 129 258 387 826 1413 2000
9-Mr. E begins; Mac Raboy-c 82 164 246 528 902 1275
10-Small logo begins 65 130 195 416 708 1000
11-16: 15-The Sky Chief app. 16-Marijuana story 55 110 165 352 601 850
17(1/46)-Illustrated in **SOTI**, "The children told me what the man was going to do with the hot poker," but Wertham saw this in Crime Reporter #2
71 142 213 454 777 1100
18-Classic Airplanehead monster-c 58 116 174 371 636 900
19-Classic puppeteer-c by Gattuso 58 116 174 371 636 900
20-Bare-breasted woman-c 90 180 270 576 988 1400
21,22,25: 21-Dinosaur-c; new logo 43 86 129 271 461 650
23,24-(68 pgs.): 23-Yankee Girl app. 42 84 126 265 445 625
I.W. Reprint #1,8('64): 1-r/#23. 8-Exist? 3 7 10 18 27 35

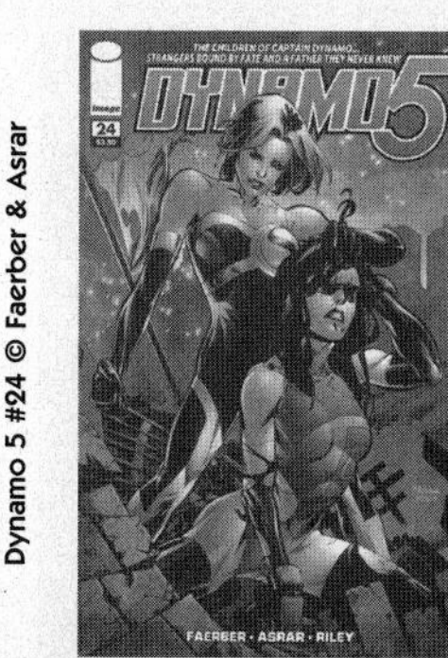

Dynamo 5 #24 © Faerber & Asrar

Earth X #5 © MAR

Echo #24 © Terry Moore

	GD 2.0	VG 4.0	FN 6.0	VF 8.0	VF/NM 9.0	NM- 9.2

NOTE: *Kinstler c-IW #1. Tuska art in many issues, #3, 9, 11, 12, 16, 19. Bondage c-16.*

DYNAMITE (Becomes Johnny Dynamite No. 10 on)
Comic Media/Allen Hardy Publ.: May, 1953 - No. 9, Sept, 1954

	GD	VG	FN	VF	VF/NM	NM-
1-Pete Morisi-a; Don Heck-c; r-as Danger #6	39	78	117	231	378	525
2	20	40	60	117	189	260
3-Marijuana story; Johnny Dynamite (1st app.) begins by Pete Morisi(c/a); Heck text-a; man shot in face at close range	25	50	75	150	245	340
4-Injury-to-eye, prostitution; Morisi-c/a	23	46	69	136	223	310
5-9-Morisi-c/a in all. 7-Prostitute story & reprints	19	38	57	112	179	245

DYNAMO (Also see Tales of Thunder & T.H.U.N.D.E.R. Agents)
Tower Comics: Aug, 1966 - No. 4, June, 1967 (25¢)

	GD	VG	FN	VF	VF/NM	NM-
1-Crandall/Wood, Ditko/Wood-a; Weed series begins; NoMan & Lightning cameos; Wood-c/a	9	18	27	61	106	150
2-4: Wood-c/a in all	6	12	18	39	62	85

NOTE: *Adkins/Wood a-2. Ditko a-4?. Tuska a-2, 3.*

DYNAMO 5 (See Noble Causes: Extended Family #2 for debut of Captain Dynamo)
Image Comics: Jan, 2007 - No. 25, Oct, 2009 ($3.50/$2.99)

1-Intro. the offspring of Captain Dynamo; Faerber-s/Asrar-a 8.00
2 5.00
3-7,11-24 : 5-Intro. Synergy. 13-Origin of Myriad. 21-Firebird app. 3.50
8-10-($2.99) 3.50
25-($4.99) Back-up short stories of team members 5.00
Annual #1 (4/08, $5.99) r/Captain Dynamo app. in Nobel Causes: Extended Family #2 and three new stories by Faerber & various; pin-up gallery 6.00
#0 (2/09, 99¢) short story leading into #20; text synopsis of story so far 3.00
...: Holiday Special 2010 (12/10, $3.99) Faerber-s/Takara-a 4.00
... Vol. 1: Post-Nuclear Family TPB (2007, $9.99) r/#1-7; Kirkman intro. 10.00
... Vol. 2: Moments of Truth TPB (2008, $14.99) r/#8-13 15.00

DYNAMO 5: SINS OF THE FATHER
Image Comics: Jun, 2010 - No. 5, Oct, 2010 ($3.99, limited series)

1-5-Faerber-s/Brilha-a. 2-4-Invincible app. 4.00

DYNAMO JOE (Also see First Adventures & Mars)
First Comics: May, 1986 - No. 15, Jan, 1988 (#12-15: $1.75)

1-15: 4-Cargonauts begin, Special 1(1/87)-Mostly-r/Mars 3.00

DYNOMUTT (TV)(See Scooby-Doo (3rd series))
Marvel Comics Group: Nov, 1977 - No. 6, Sept, 1978 (Hanna-Barbera)

	GD	VG	FN	VF	VF/NM	NM-
1-The Blue Falcon, Scooby Doo in all	4	8	12	26	41	55
2-6-All newsstand only	3	6	9	18	27	35

EAGLE, THE (1st Series) (See Science Comics & Weird Comics #8)
Fox Features Syndicate: July, 1941 - No. 4, Jan, 1942

	GD	VG	FN	VF	VF/NM	NM-
1-The Eagle begins; Rex Dexter of Mars app. by Briefer; all issues feature German war covers	184	368	552	1168	2009	2850
2-The Spider Queen begins (origin)	87	174	261	553	952	1350
3,4: 3-Joe Spook begins (origin)	68	136	204	435	743	1050

EAGLE (2nd Series)
Rural Home Publ.: Feb-Mar, 1945 - No. 2, Apr-May, 1945

	GD	VG	FN	VF	VF/NM	NM-
1-Aviation stories	50	100	150	315	533	750
2-Lucky Aces	27	54	81	158	259	360

NOTE: *L. B. Cole c/a in each.*

EAGLE
Crystal Comics/Apple Comics #17 on: Sept, 1986 - No. 23, 1989 ($1.50/1.75/1.95, B&W)

1-23: 12-Double size origin issue ($2.50) 3.00
1-Signed and limited 4.00

EARTH 4 (Also see Urth 4)
Continuity Comics: Dec, 1993 - No. 4, Jan, 1994 ($2.50)

1-4: 1-3 all listed as Dec, 1993 in indicia 3.00

EARTH 4 DEATHWATCH 2000
Continuity Comics: Apr, 1993 - No. 3, Aug, 1993 ($2.50)

1-3 3.00

EARTH MAN ON VENUS (An...) (Also see Strange Planets)
Avon Periodicals: 1951

	GD	VG	FN	VF	VF/NM	NM-
nn-Wood-a (26 pgs.); Fawcette-c	145	290	435	921	1586	2250

EARTHWORM JIM (TV, cartoon)
Marvel Comics: Dec, 1995 - No. 3, Feb, 1996 ($2.25)

1-3: Based on video game and toys 3.00

EARTH X
Marvel Comics: No. 0, Mar, 1999 - No. 12, Apr, 2000 ($3.99/$2.99, lim. series)

nn- (Wizard supplement) Alex Ross sketchbook; painted-c 6.00
Sketchbook (2/99) New sketches and previews 6.00

	GD	VG	FN	VF	VF/NM	NM-
0-(3/99)-Prelude; Leon-a(p)/Ross-c	1	2	3	4	5	7
1-(4/99)-Leon-a(p)/Ross-c	1	2	3	4	5	7

1-2nd printing 3.00
2-12 3.50
#1/2 (Wizard) Nick Fury on cover; Reinhold-a 6.00
#X (6/00, $3.99) 4.00
... Trilogy Companion TPB (2008, $29.99) r/#1/2; artwork and content from the Earth X, Paradise X and Universe X series; gallery of variant covers and promotional art 30.00
HC (2005, $49.99) r/#0,1-12, #1/2, X; foreward by Joss Whedon; Ross sketch pages 50.00
TPB (12/00, $24.95) r/#0,1-12, X; foreward by Joss Whedon 25.00

EASTER BONNET SHOP (See March of Comics No. 29)

EASTER WITH MOTHER GOOSE
Dell Publishing Co.: No. 103, 1946 - No. 220, Mar, 1949

	GD	VG	FN	VF	VF/NM	NM-
Four Color 103 (#1)-Walt Kelly-a	15	30	45	104	227	350
Four Color 140 ('47)-Kelly-a	13	26	39	85	180	275
Four Color 185 ('48), 220-Kelly-a	12	24	36	80	163	245

EAST MEETS WEST
Innovation Publishing: Apr, 1990 - No. 2, 1990 ($2.50, limited series, mature)

1,2: 1-Stevens part-i; Redondo-c(i). 2-Stevens-c(i); 1st app. Cheech & Chong in comics 3.00

EC ARCHIVES (Also see EC Sampler in the Promotional Comics section)
Gemstone Publishing: 2006 - Present ($49.95, hardcover with dustjacket)

Crime SuspenStories Vol. 1 - Recolored reprints of #1-6; foreward by Max Allan Collins 50.00
Frontline Combat Vol. 1 - Recolored reprints of #1-6; foreward by Henry G. Franke III 50.00
Shock SuspenStories Vol. 1 - Recolored reprints of #1-6; foreward by Steven Spielberg 50.00
Shock SuspenStories Vol. 2 - Recolored reprints of #7-12; foreward by Dean Kamen 50.00
Tales From the Crypt Vol. 1 - Recolored reprints of Crypt of Terror #17-19 and Tales From the Crypt #20-22; foreward by John Carpenter; Al Feldstein behind-the-scenes info 50.00
Tales From the Crypt Vol. 2 - Recolored reprints of #23-28; foreward by Joe Dante 50.00
Tales From the Crypt Vol. 3 - Recolored reprints of #29-34; foreward by Bob Overstreet 50.00
Two-Fisted Tales Vol. 1 - Recolored reprints of #18-23; foreward by Stephen Geppi 50.00
Two-Fisted Tales Vol. 2 - Recolored reprints of #24-29; foreward by Rocco Versaci, Ph.D. 50.00
Vault of Horror Vol. 1 - Recolored reprints of #12-17; foreward by R.L. Stine 50.00
Weird Science Vol. 1 - Recolored reprints of #1-6; foreward by George Lucas 50.00
Weird Science Vol. 2 - Recolored reprints of #7-12; foreward by Paul Levitz 50.00
Weird Science Vol. 3 - Recolored reprints of #13-18; foreward by Jerry Weist 50.00

E. C. CLASSIC REPRINTS
East Coast Comix Co.: May, 1973 - No. 12, 1976 (E. C. Comics reprinted in color minus ads)

	GD	VG	FN	VF	VF/NM	NM-
1-The Crypt of Terror #1 (Tales from the Crypt #46)	2	4	6	11	16	20
2-12: 2-Weird Science #15('52). 3-Shock SuspenStories #12. 4-Haunt of Fear #12. 5-Weird Fantasy #13('52). 6-Crime SuspenStories #25. 7-Vault of Horror #26. 8-Shock SuspenStories #6. 9-Two-Fisted Tales #34. 10-Haunt of Fear #23. 11-Weird Science 12(#1). 12-Shock SuspenStories #2	2	4	6	8	11	14

EC CLASSICS
Russ Cochran: Aug, 1985 - No. 12, 1986? (High quality paper; each-r 8 stories in color) (#2-12 were resolicited in 1990)($4.95, 56 pgs., 8x11")

	GD	VG	FN	VF	VF/NM	NM-
1-12: 1-Tales From the Crypt. 2-Weird Science. 3-Two-Fisted Tales (r/31); Frontline Combat (r/9). 4-Shock SuspenStories. 5-Weird Fantasy. 6-Vault of Horror. 7-Weird Science-Fantasy (r/23,24). 8-Crime SuspenStories (r/17,18). 9-Haunt of Fear (r/14,15). 10-Panic (r/1,2). 11-Tales From the Crypt (r/23,24). 12-Weird Science (r/20,22)	1	2	3	4	5	7

ECHO
Image Comics (Dreamwave Prod.): Mar, 2000 - No. 5, Sept, 2000 ($2.50)

1-5: 1-3-Pat Lee-c 3.00
0-(7/00) 3.00

ECHO
Abstract Studio: Mar, 2008 - No. 30, May, 2011 ($3.50)

1-Terry Moore-s/a/c 8.00
2-30 3.50
Terry Moore's Echo: Moon Lake TPB (2008, $15.95) r/#1-5; Moore sketch pages 16.00

ECHO OF FUTUREPAST
Pacific Comics/Continuity Com.: May, 1984 - No. 9, Jan, 1986 ($2.95, 52 pgs.)

1-9: Neal Adams-c/a in all? 6.00
NOTE: *N. Adams a-1-6,7i,9i; c-1-3, 5p,7i,8,9i. Golden a-1-6 (Bucky O'Hare); c-6. Toth a-6,7.*

ECLIPSE GRAPHIC ALBUM SERIES
Eclipse Comics: Oct, 1978 - 1989 (8-1/2x11") (B&W #1-5)

Eclipse Monthly #9 © ECL

Eclipso #4 © DC

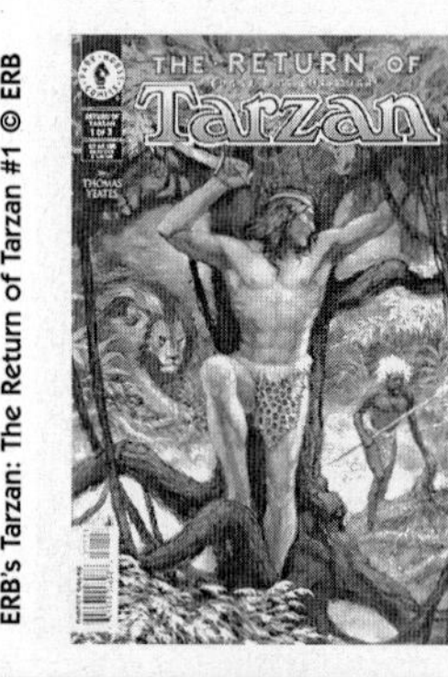

ERB's Tarzan: The Return of Tarzan #1 © ERB

1-Sabre (10/78, B&W, 1st print.); Gulacy-a; 1st direct sale graphic novel 16.00
1-Sabre (2nd printing, 1/79) 8.00
1-Sabre (3rd printing, $5.95) 6.00
1-Sabre 30th Anniversary Edition (2008, $14.99, 9x6" HC) new McGregor & Gulacy intros. original script with sketch art 15.00
2,6,7: 2-Night Music (11/79, B&W)-Russell-a. 6-I Am Coyote (11/84, color)-Rogers-c/a. 7-The Rocketeer (2nd print, $7.95). 7-The Rocketeer (3rd print, 1991, $8.95) 10.00
3,4: 3-Detectives, Inc. (5/80, B&W, $6.95)-Rogers-a. 4-Stewart The Rat (1980, B&W) -G. Colan-a 10.00
5-The Price (10/81, B&W)-Starlin-a 16.00
7-The Rocketeer (9/85, color)-Dave Stevens-a (r/chapters 1-5)(see Pacific Presents & Starslayer); has 7 pgs. new-a 14.00
7-The Rocketeer, signed & limited HC 60.00
7-The Rocketeer, hardcover (1986, $19.95) 20.00
7-The Rocketeer, unsigned HC (3rd, $32.95) 33.00
8-Zorro In Old California ('86, color) 14.00
8,12-Hardcover 18.00
9,10: 9-Sacred And The Profane ('86)-Steacy-a. 10-Somerset Holmes ('86, $15.95)-Adults, soft-c 16.00
9,10,12-Hardcover ($24.95). 12-signed & #'d 25.00
11-Floyd Farland, Citizen of the Future ('87, $2.95, B&W) Chris Ware-s/a 7.00
12,28,31,35: 12-Silverheels ('87, $7.95, color). 28-Miracleman Book I ($5.95). 31-Pigeons From Hell by R. E. Howard (11/88). 35-Rael: Into The Shadow of the Sun ('88, $7.95) 10.00
13-The Sisterhood of Steel ('87, $8.95, color) 10.00
14,16,18,20,23,24: 14-Samurai, Son of Death ('87, $4.95, B&W). 16,18,20,23-See Airfighters Classics #1-4. 24-Heartbreak ($4.95, B&W) 7.00
14 (2nd pr.),17,21: 14-Samurai, Son of Death ($3.95, 2nd printing). 17-Valkyrie, Prisoner of the Past SC ('88, $3.95, color). 21-XYR-Multiple ending comic ('88, $3.95, B&W) 6.00
15,22,27: 15-Twisted Tales (11/87, color)-Dave Stevens-c. 22-Alien Worlds #1 (5/88, $3.95, 52 pgs.)-Nudity. 27-Fast Fiction (She) ($5.95, B&W) 8.00
17-Valkyrie, Prisoner of the Past S&N Hardcover ('88, $19.95) 20.00
19-Scout: The Four Monsters ('88, $14.95, color)-r/Scout #1-7; soft-c 15.00
25,30,32-34: 25-Alex Toth's Zorro Vol. 1 ,2($10.95, B&W). 30-Brought To Light; Alan Moore scripts ('89). 32-Teenaged Dope Slaves and Reform School Girls. 33-Bogie. 34-Air Fighters Classics #5 12.00
29-Real Love: Best of Simon & Kirby Romance Comics(10/88, $12.95) 15.00
30,31: Limited hardcover ed. ($29.95). 31-signed 30.00
36-Dr. Watchstop: Adventures in Time and Space ('89, $8.95) 10.00

ECLIPSE MAGAZINE (Becomes Eclipse Monthly)
Eclipse Publishing: May, 1981 - No. 8, Jan, 1983 ($2.95, B&W, magazine)

1-8: 1-1st app. Cap'n Quick and a Foozle by Rogers, Ms. Tree by Beatty, and Dope by Trina Robbins. 2-1st app. I Am Coyote by Rogers. 7-1st app. Masked Man by Boyer 3.00

NOTE: *Colan a-3, 5, 8.* ***Golden*** *c/a-2.* ***Gulacy*** *a-6, c-1, 6.* ***Kaluta*** *c/a-5.* ***Mayerik*** *a-2, 3.* ***Rogers*** *a-1-8.* ***Starlin*** *a-1.* ***Sutton*** *a-6.*

ECLIPSE MONTHLY
Eclipse Comics: Aug, 1983 - No. 10, Jul, 1984 (Baxter paper, $2.00/$1.50/$1.75)

1-10: ($2.00, 52 pgs.)-Cap'n Quick and a Foozle by Rogers, Static by Ditko, Dope by Trina Robbins, Rio by Wildey, The Masked Man by Boyer begin. 3-Ragamuffins begins 4.00

NOTE: ***Boyer*** *c-6.* ***Ditko*** *a-1-3.* ***Rogers*** *a-1-4; c-2, 4, 7.* ***Wildey*** *a-1, 2, 5, 9, 10; c-5, 10.*

ECLIPSO (See Brave and the Bold #64, House of Secrets #61 & Phantom Stranger, 1987)
DC Comics: Nov, 1992 - No. 18, Apr, 1994 ($1.25)

1-18: 1-Giffen plots/breakdowns begin. 10-Darkseid app. Creeper in #3-6,9,11-13. 18-Spectre-c/s 3.00
Annual 1 (1993, $2.50, 68 pgs.)-Intro Prism 4.00
...: The Music of the Spheres TPB (2009, $19.99) r/stories from Countdown to Mystery #1-8 20.00

ECLIPSO: THE DARKNESS WITHIN
DC Comics: July, 1992 - No. 2, Oct, 1992 ($2.50, 68 pgs.)

1,2: 1-With purple gem attached to-c, 1-Without gem; Superman, Creeper app., 2-Concludes Eclipso storyline from annuals 4.00

EC SAMPLER - FREE COMIC BOOK DAY
Gemstone Publishing: May, 2008

Reprinted stories with restored color from Weird Science #6, Two-Fisted Tales #22, Crypt of Terror #17, Shock Suspenstories #6 3.00

E. C. 3-D CLASSICS (See Three Dimensional...)

ECTOKID (See Razorline)
Marvel Comics: Sept, 1993 - No. 9, May, 1994 ($1.75/$1.95)

1-($2.50)-Foil embossed-c; created by C. Barker 4.00
2-9: 2-Origin. 5-Saint Sinner x-over 3.00
...: Unleashed! 1 (10/94, $2.95, 52 pgs.) 4.00

ED "BIG DADDY" ROTH'S RATFINK COMIX (Also see Ratfink)
World of Fandom/ Ed Roth: 1991 - No. 3, 1991 ($2.50)

1-3: Regular Ed., 1-Limited double cover 1 3 4 6 8 10

EDDIE CAMPBELL'S BACCHUS
Eddie Campbell Comics: May, 1995 - No. 60, May, 2001 ($2.95, B&W)

1-Cerebus app. 1 2 3 5 6 8
1-2nd printing (5/97) 3.00
2-10: 9-Alex Ross back-c 5.00
11-60 3.00
Doing The Islands With Bacchus ('97, $17.95) 18.00
Earth, Water, Air & Fire ('98, $9.95) 10.00
King Bacchus ('99, $12.95) 13.00
The Eyeball Kid ('98, $8.50) 8.50

EDDIE STANKY (Baseball Hero)
Fawcett Publications: 1951 (New York Giants)

nn-Photo-c 34 68 102 206 336 465

EDEN'S TRAIL
Marvel Comics: Jan, 2003 - No. 6 ($2.99, limited series, Marvelscope-printed sideways)

1-5-Chuck Austen-s/Steve Uy-a 3.00

EDGAR ALLAN POE'S - THE FALL OF THE HOUSE OF USHER AND OTHER TALES OF HORROR
Catlan Communications Pub.: Sept. 1985 (hardcover graphic novel)

nn-Reprints of Poe story issues from Warren comic mags; all Richard Corben-a; numbered edition of 350 signed by Corben; 60 pgs. 130.00
nn-Softcover edition 60.00

EDGAR BERGEN PRESENTS CHARLIE McCARTHY
Whitman Publishing Co. (Charlie McCarthy Co.): No. 764, 1938 (36 pgs.; 15x10-1/2"; color)

764 77 154 231 489 837 1185

EDGAR RICE BURROUGHS' TARZAN: A TALE OF MUGAMBI
Dark Horse Comics: 1995 ($2.95, one-shot)

1 3.00

EDGAR RICE BURROUGHS' TARZAN: IN THE LAND THAT TIME FORGOT AND THE POOL OF TIME
Dark Horse Comics: 1996 ($12.95, trade paperback)

nn-r/Russ Manning-a 13.00

EDGAR RICE BURROUGHS' TARZAN OF THE APES
Dark Horse Comics: May, 1999 ($12.95, trade paperback)

nn-reprints 13.00

EDGAR RICE BURROUGHS' TARZAN: THE LOST ADVENTURE
Dark Horse Comics: Jan, 1995 - No. 4, Apr, 1995 ($2.95, B&W, limited series)

1-4: ERB's last Tarzan story, adapted by Joe Lansdale 3.00
Hardcover (12/95, $19.95) 20.00
Limited Edition Hardcover ($99.95)-signed & numbered 100.00

EDGAR RICE BURROUGHS' TARZAN: THE RETURN OF TARZAN
Dark Horse Comics: May, 1997 - No. 3, July, 1997 ($2.95, limited series)

1-3 3.00

EDGAR RICE BURROUGHS' TARZAN: THE RIVERS OF BLOOD
Dark Horse Comics: Nov, 1999 - No. 4, Feb, 2000 ($2.95, limited series)

1-4-Kordey-c/a 3.00

EDGE
Malibu Comics (Bravura): July, 1994 - No. 3, Apr, 1995 ($2.50/$2.95, unfinished lim.series)

1,2-S. Grant-story & Gil Kane-c/a; w/Bravura stamp 3.00
3-($2.95-c) 3.00

EDGE (Re-titled as Vector starting with #13)
CrossGeneration Comics: May, 2002 - No. 12, Apr, 2003 ($9.95/$11.95/$7.95, TPB)

1-3: Reprints from various CrossGen titles 10.00
4-8-($11.95) 12.00
9-12-($7.95, 8-1/4" x 5-1/2") digest-sized reprints 8.00

EDGE OF CHAOS
Pacific Comics: July, 1983 - No. 3, Jan, 1984 (Limited series)

1-3-Morrow c/a; all contain nudity 3.00

EDGE OF DOOM (Horror anthology)
IDW Publishing: Oct, 2010 - No. 4, Mar, 2011 ($3.99)

1-5-Steve Niles-s/Kelley Jones-a 4.00

Eerie #10 © AVON

Eerie #16 © WP

Egypt #7 © Milligan & Dillon

GD VG FN VF VF/NM NM-
2.0 4.0 6.0 8.0 9.0 9.2

GD VG FN VF VF/NM NM-
2.0 4.0 6.0 8.0 9.0 9.2

ED WHEELAN'S JOKE BOOK STARRING FAT & SLAT (See Fat & Slat)

EERIE (Strange Worlds No. 18 on)
Avon Per.: No. 1, Jan, 1947; No. 1, May-June, 1951 - No. 17, Aug-Sept, 1954

1(1947)-1st supernatural comic; Kubert, Fugitani-a; bondage-c 486 972 1458 3550 6275 9000
1(1951)-Reprints story from 1947 #1 81 162 243 518 884 1250
2-Wood-c/a; bondage-c 82 164 246 528 902 1275
3-Wood-c; Kubert, Wood/Orlando-a 82 164 246 528 902 1275
4,5-Wood-c 63 126 189 403 689 975
6,8,13,14: 8-Kinstler-a; bondage-c; Phantom Witch Doctor story 37 74 111 222 361 500
7-Wood/Orlando-c; Kubert-a 48 96 144 302 514 725
9-Kubert-a; Check-c 39 78 117 240 395 550
10,11: 10-Kinstler-a. 11-Kinstlerish-a by McCann 37 74 111 222 361 500
12-Dracula story from novel, 25 pgs. 40 80 120 246 411 575
15-Reprints No. 1('51) minus-c(bondage) 24 48 72 142 234 325
16-Wood-a r-/No. 2 24 48 72 142 234 325
17-Wood/Orlando & Kubert-a; reprints #3 minus inside & outside Wood-c 24 48 72 142 234 325

NOTE: ***Hollingsworth** a-9-11; c-10, 11.*

EERIE
I. W. Enterprises: 1964

I.W. Reprint #1('64)-Wood-c(r); r-story/Spook #1 4 8 12 22 34 45
I.W. Reprint #2,6,8: 8-Dr. Drew by Grandenetti from Ghost #9 3 6 9 20 30 40
I.W. Reprint #9-r/Tales of Terror #1(Toby); Wood-c 4 8 12 24 37 50

EERIE (Magazine)(See Warren Presents)
Warren Publ. Co.: No. 1, Sept, 1965; No. 2, Mar, 1966 - No. 139, Feb, 1983

1-24 pgs., black & white, small size (5-1/4x7-1/4"), low distribution; cover from inside back cover of Creepy No. 2; stories reprinted from Creepy No. 7, 8. At least three different versions exist.
First Printing - B&W, 5-1/4" wide x 7-1/4" high, evenly trimmed. On page 18, panel 5, in the upper left-hand corner, the large rear view of a bald headed man blends into solid black and is unrecognizable. Overall printing quality is poor. 43 86 129 323 699 1075
Second Printing - B&W, 5-1/4x7-1/4", with uneven, untrimmed edges (if one of these were trimmed evenly, the size would be less than as indicated). The figure of the bald headed man on page 18, panel 5 is clear and discernible. The staples have a 1/4" blue stripe. 14 28 42 97 211 325
Other unauthorized reproductions for comparison's sake would be practically worthless. One known version was probably shot off a first printing copy with some loss of detail; the finer lines tend to disappear in this version which can be determined by looking at the lower right-hand corner of page one, first story. The roof of the house is shaded with straight lines. These lines are sharp and distinct on original, but broken on this version.

NOTE: ***The Overstreet Comic Book Price Guide** recommends that, before buying a 1st issue, you consult an expert.*

2-Frazetta-c; Toth-a; 1st app. host Cousin Eerie 11 22 33 71 136 200
3-Frazetta-c & half pg. ad (rerun in #4); Toth, Williamson, Ditko-a 9 18 27 61 106 150
4-7: 4-Frazetta-a (1/2 pg. ad). 5,7-Frazetta-c. Ditko-a in all. 6 12 18 41 66 90
8-Frazetta-c; Ditko-a 7 14 21 44 72 100
9-11,25: 9,10-Neal Adams-a, Ditko-a. 11-Karloff Mummy adapt.-Wood-s/a. 25-Steranko-c 6 12 18 42 69 95
12-16,18-22,24,32-35,40,45: 12,13,20-Poe-s. 12-Bloch-s. 12,15-Jones-a. 13-Lovecraft-s. 14,16-Toth-a. 16,19,24-Stoker-s. 16,32,33,43-Corben-a. 34-Early Boris-c. 35-Early Brunner-a. 35,40-Early Ploog-a. 40-Frankenstein; Ploog-a (6/72, 6 months before Marvel's series) 4 8 12 28 44 60
17-(low distribution) 16 32 48 107 234 360
23-Frazetta-c; Adams-a(reprint) 7 14 21 46 76 105
26-31,36-38,43,44 4 8 12 24 37 50
39,41: 39-1st Dax the Warrior; Maroto-a. 41-(low distribution) 5 10 15 30 48 65
42,51: 42-('73 Annual, 84 pgs.) Spooktacular; Williamson-a. 51-('74 Annual, 76 pgs.) Color poster insert; Toth-a 4 8 12 28 44 60
46,48: 46-Dracula series by Sutton begins; 2pgs. Vampirella. 48-Begin "Mummy Walks" and "Curse of the Werewolf" series (both continue in #49,50,52,53) 4 8 12 24 37 50
47,49,50,52,53: 47-Lilith. 49-Marvin the Dead Thing. 50-Satanna, Daughter of Satan. 52-Hunter by Neary begins. 53-Adams-a 4 8 12 22 34 45
54,55-Color insert Spirit story by Eisner, reprints sections 12/21/47 & 6/16/46 54-Dr. Archaeus series begins 3 6 9 20 30 40
56,57,59,63,69,77,78: All have 8 pg. slick color insert. 56,57,77-Corben-a. 59-(100 pgs.) Summer Special, all Dax issue. 69-Summer Special, all Hunter issue, Neary-a. 78-All Mummy issue 3 6 9 20 30 40
58,60,62,68,72,: 8 pg. slick color insert & Wrightson-a in all. 58,60,62-Corben-a. 60-Summer Giant (9/74, $1.25) 1st Exterminator One; Wood-a. 62-Mummies Walk. 68-Summer Special (84 pgs.) 4 8 12 22 34 45
61,64-67,71: 61-Mummies Walk-s, Wood-a. 64-Corben-a. 64,65,67-Toth-a. 65,66-El Cid. 67-Hunter II. 71-Goblin-c/1st app. 3 6 9 18 27 35
70,73-75 3 6 9 14 20 26
76-1st app. Darklon the Mystic by Starlin-s/a 3 6 9 21 32 42
79,80-Origin Darklon the Mystic by Starlin 3 6 9 18 27 35
81,86,97: 81-Frazetta-c, King Kong; Corben-a. 86-(92 pgs.) All Corben issue. 97-Time Travel/Dinosaur issue; Corben,Adams-a 3 6 9 16 23 30
82-Origin/1st app. The Rook 3 6 9 19 29 38
83,85,88,89,91-93,98,99: 98-Rook (31 pgs.). 99-1st Horizon Seekers. 2 4 6 10 14 18
84,87,90,96,100: 84,100-Starlin-a. 87-Hunter 3; Nino-a. 87,90-Corben-a. 96-Summer Special (92 pgs.). 100-(92 pgs.) Anniversary issue; Rook (30 pgs.) 2 4 6 13 18 22
94,95-The Rook & Vampirella team-up. 95-Vampirella-c; 1st MacTavish 3 6 9 17 25 32
101,106,112,115,118,120,121,128: 101-Return of Hunter II, Starlin-a. 106-Hard John Nuclear Hit Parade Special, Corben-a. 112-All Maroto issue, Luana-s. 115-All José Ortiz issues. 118-1st Haggarth. 120-1st Zud Kamish. 121-Hunter/Darklon. 128-Starlin-a, Hsu-a 2 4 6 10 14 18
102-105,107-111,113,114,116,117,119,122-124,126,127,129: 103-105,109-111-Gulacy-a. 104-Beast World. 2 4 6 9 13 16
125-(10/81, 84 pgs.) all Neal Adams issue 3 6 9 14 19 24
130-(76 pgs.) Vampirella-c/sty (54 pgs.); Pantha, Van Helsing, Huntress, Dax, Schreck, Hunter, Exterminator One, Rook app. 3 6 9 16 23 30
131-(Lower distr.); all Wood issue 3 6 9 14 20 26
132-134,136: 132-Rook returns. 133-All Ramon Torrents-a issue. 134,136-Color comic insert 2 4 6 10 14 18
135-(Lower distr., 10/82, 100 pgs.) All Ditko issue 3 6 9 14 20 26
137-139 (lower distr.):137-All Super-Hero issue. 138-Sherlock Holmes. 138,139-Color comic insert 2 4 6 13 18 22
Yearbook '70-Frazetta-c 6 12 18 37 59 80
Annual '71, '72-Reprints in both 4 8 12 26 41 55
... Archives - Volume One HC (Dark Horse, 3/09, $49.95, dustjacket) r/#1-5 50.00
... Archives - Volume Two HC (Dark Horse, 9/09, $49.95, dustjacket) r/#6-10; interview with Frank Frazetta from 1985 50.00

NOTE: *The above books contain art by many good artists: **N. Adams, Brunner, Corben, Craig (Taycee), Crandall, Ditko, Eisner, Evans, Jeff Jones, Krenkel, McWilliams, Morrow, Orlando, Ploog, Severin, Starlin, Torres, Toth, Williamson, Wood,** and **Wrightson**; covers by **Bode', Corben, Davis, Frazetta, Morrow,** and **Orlando**. **Frazetta** c-2, 3, 7, 8, 23. Annuals from 1973-on are included in regular numbering. 1970-74 Annuals are complete reprints. Annuals from 1975-on are in the format of the regular issues.*

EERIE ADVENTURES (Also see Weird Adventures)
Ziff-Davis Publ. Co.: Winter, 1951 (Painted-c)

1-Powell-a(2), McCann-a; used in **SOTI;** bondage-c; Krigstein back-c 55 110 165 352 601 850

NOTE: *Title dropped due to similarity to Avon's Eerie & legal action.*

EERIE TALES (Magazine)
Hastings Associates: 1959 (Black & White)

1-Williamson, Torres, Tuska-a, Powell(2), & Morrow(2)-a 16 32 48 92 144 195

EERIE TALES
Super Comics: 1963-1964

Super Reprint No. 10,11,12,18: 10('63)-r/Spook #27. Purple Claw in #11,12 ('63); #12-r/Avon's Eerie #1('51)-Kida-r 3 6 9 17 25 32
15-Wolverton-a, Spacehawk-r/Blue Bolt Weird Tales #113; Disbrow-a 5 10 15 30 48 65

EGBERT
Arnold Publications/Quality Comics Group: Spring, 1946 - No. 20, 1950

1-Funny animal; intro Egbert & The Count 20 40 60 114 182 250
2 11 22 33 62 86 110
3-10 9 18 27 47 61 75
11-20 7 14 21 37 46 55

EGON
Dark Horse Comics: Jan, 1998 - No.2, Feb, 1998 ($2.95, limited series)

1,2-Horley-painted-c 3.00

EGYPT
DC Comics (Vertigo): Aug, 1995 - No.7, Feb, 1996 ($2.50, lim. series, mature)

1-7: Milligan scripts in all. 3.00

EH! (...Dig This Crazy Comic) (From Here to Insanity No. 8 on)
Charlton Comics: Dec, 1953 - No. 7, Nov-Dec, 1954 (Satire)

80 Page Giant #15 © DC

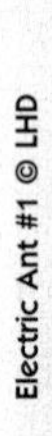

Electric Ant #1 © LHD

Elektra V2 #8 © MAR

	GD 2.0	VG 4.0	FN 6.0	VF 8.0	VF/NM 9.0	NM- 9.2
1-Davis-*ish*-c/a by Ayers, Wood-*ish*-a by Giordano; Atomic Mouse app.	39	78	117	231	378	525
2-Ayers-c/a	22	44	66	128	209	290
3,5,7	20	40	60	115	185	255
4,6: Sexual innuendo-c. 6-Ayers-a	20	40	60	120	195	270

EIGHTBALL (Also see David Boring)
Fantagraphics Books: Oct, 1989 - Present ($2.75/$2.95/$3.95, semi-annually, mature)

	GD 2.0	VG 4.0	FN 6.0	VF 8.0	VF/NM 9.0	NM- 9.2
1 (1st printing) Daniel Clowes-s/a in all	2	4	6	8	10	12
2,3	1	2	3	5	6	8
4-8						6.00
9-19: 17-(8/96)						4.00
20-($4.50)						4.50
21-($4.95) Concludes David Boring 3-parter						5.00
22-($5.95) 29 short stories						6.00
23-($7.00, 9" x 12") The Death Ray						7.00
Twentieth Century Eightball (2002, $19.00) r/Clowes strips						19.00

EIGHTH WONDER, THE
Dark Horse Comics: Nov, 1997 ($2.95, one-shot)

	NM- 9.2
nn-Reprints stories from Dark Horse Presents #85-87	3.00

EIGHT IS ENOUGH KITE FUN BOOK (See Kite Fun Book 1979 in the Promotional Comics section)

EIGHT LEGGED FREAKS
DC Comics (WildStorm): 2002 ($6.95, one-shot, squarebound)

	NM- 9.2
nn-Adaptation of 2002 mutant spider movie; Joe Phillips-a; intro by Dean Devlin	7.00

80 PAGE GIANT (...Magazine No. 2-15)
National Periodical Publications: 8/64 - No. 15, 10/65; No. 16, 11/65 - No. 89, 7/71 (25¢) (All reprints) (#1-56: 84 pgs.; #57-89: 68 pgs.)

	GD 2.0	VG 4.0	FN 6.0	VF 8.0	VF/NM 9.0	NM- 9.2
1-Superman Annual; originally planned as Superman Annual #9 (8/64)	35	70	105	254	547	840
2-Jimmy Olsen	19	38	57	128	277	425
3,4: 3-Lois Lane. 4-Flash-G.A.-r; Infantino-a	15	30	45	102	221	340
5-Batman; has Sunday newspaper strip; Catwoman-r; Batman's Life Story-r (25th anniversary special)	15	30	45	102	221	340
6-Superman	13	26	39	89	192	295
7-Sgt. Rock's Prize Battle Tales; Kubert-c/a	21	42	63	148	317	485
8-More Secret Origins-origins of JLA, Aquaman, Robin, Atom, & Superman; Infantino-a	27	54	81	189	407	625
9-15: 9-Flash (r/Flash #106,117,123 & Showcase #14); Infantino-a. 10-Superboy. 11-Superman; all Luthor issue. 12-Batman; has Sunday newspaper strip. 13-Jimmy Olsen. 14-Lois Lane. 15-Superman and Batman; Joker-c/story	13	26	39	85	180	275

Continued as part of regular series under each title in which that particular book came out, a Giant being published instead of the regular size. Issues No. 16 to No. 89 are listed for your information. See individual titles for prices. 16-JLA #39 (11/65), 17-Batman #176, 18-Superman #183, 19-Our Army at War #164, 20-Action #334, 21-Flash #160, 22-Superboy #129, 23-Superman #187, 24-Batman #182, 25-Jimmy Olsen #95, 26-Lois Lane #68, 27-Batman #185, 28-World's Finest #161, 29-JLA #48, 30-Batman #187, 31-Superman #193, 32-Our Army at War #177, 33-Action #347, 34-Flash #169, 35-Superboy #138, 36-Superman #197, 37-Batman #193, 38-Jimmy Olsen #104, 39-Lois Lane #77, 40-World's Finest #170, 41-JLA #58, 42-Superman #202, 43-Batman #198, 44-Our Army at War #190, 45-Action #360, 46-Flash #178, 47-Superboy #147, 48-Superman #207, 49-Batman #203, 50-Jimmy Olsen #113, 51-Lois Lane #86, 52-World's Finest #179, 53-JLA #67, 54-Superman #212, 55-Batman #208, 56-Our Army at War #203, 57-Action #373, 58-Flash #187, 59-Superboy #156, 60-Superman #217, 61-Batman #213, 62-Jimmy Olsen #122, 63-Lois Lane #95, 64-World's Finest #188, 65-JLA #76, 66-Superman #222, 67-Batman #218, 68-Our Army at War #216, 69-Adventure #390, 70-Flash #196, 71-Superboy #165, 72-Superman #227, 73-Batman #223, 74-Jimmy Olsen #131, 75-Lois Lane #104, 76-World's Finest #197, 77-JLA #85, 78-Superman #232, 79-Batman #228, 80-Our Army at War #229, 81-Adventure #403, 82-Flash #205, 83-Superboy #174, 84-Superman #239, 85-Batman #233, 86-Jimmy Olsen #140, 87-Lois Lane #113, 88-World's Finest #206, 89-JLA #93.

87TH PRECINCT (TV) (Based on the Ed McBain novels)
Dell Publishing Co.: Apr-June, 1962 - No. 2, July-Sept, 1962

	GD 2.0	VG 4.0	FN 6.0	VF 8.0	VF/NM 9.0	NM- 9.2
Four Color 1309(#1)-Krigstein-a	9	18	27	63	112	160
2	8	16	24	55	93	130

EL BOMBO COMICS
Standard Comics/Frances M. McQueeny: 1946

	GD 2.0	VG 4.0	FN 6.0	VF 8.0	VF/NM 9.0	NM- 9.2
nn(1946), 1(no date)	15	30	45	83	124	165

EL CAZADOR
CrossGen Comics: Oct, 2003 - No. 6, Jun, 2004 ($2.95)

	NM- 9.2
1-Dixon-s/Epting-a	5.00
2-6: 5-Lady Death preview	3.00
Collected Edition (2003, $5.95) r/#1-3	6.00
...: The Bloody Ballad of Blackjack Tom 1 (4/04, $2.95, one-shot) Cariello-a	3.00

EL CID
Dell Publishing Co.: No. 1259, 1961

	GD 2.0	VG 4.0	FN 6.0	VF 8.0	VF/NM 9.0	NM- 9.2
Four Color 1259-Movie, photo-c	7	14	21	46	76	105

EL DIABLO (See All-Star Western #2 & Weird Western Tales #12)
DC Comics: Aug, 1989 - No. 16, Jan, 1991 ($1.50-$1.75, color)

	NM- 9.2
1 ($2.50, 52pgs.)-Masked hero	4.00
2-16	3.00

EL DIABLO
DC Comics (Vertigo): Mar, 2001 - No. 4, Jun, 2001 ($2.50, limited series)

	NM- 9.2
1-4-Azzarello-s/Zezelj-a/Sale-c	3.00
TPB (2008, $12.99) r/#1-4	13.00

EL DIABLO
DC Comics: Nov, 2008 - No. 6, Apr, 2009 ($2.99, limited series)

	NM- 9.2
1-6-Nitz-s/Hester-a/c. 4,5-Freedom Fighters app.	3.00
...: The Haunted Horseman TPB (2009, $17.99) r/#1-6	18.00

EL DORADO (See Movie Classics)

ELECTRIC ANT
Marvel Comics: Jun, 2010 - No. 5, Oct, 201 ($3.99, Baxter paper)

	NM- 9.2
1-5-Based on a Philip K. Dick story; David Mack-s/Pascal Alixe-a; Paul Pope-c	4.00

ELECTRIC UNDERTOW (See Strikeforce Morituri: Electric Undertow)

ELECTRIC WARRIOR
DC Comics: May, 1986 - No. 18, Oct, 1987 ($1.50, Baxter paper)

	NM- 9.2
1-18	3.00

ELECTROPOLIS
Image Comics: May, 2001 - No. 4, Jan, 2003 ($2.95/$5.95)

	NM- 9.2
1-3-Dean Motter-s/a. 3-(12/01)	3.00
4-(1/03, $5.95, 72 pages) The Infernal Machine pts. 4-6	6.00

ELEKTRA (Also see Daredevil #319-325)
Marvel Comics: Mar, 1995 - No. 4, June, 1995 ($2.95, limited series)

	NM- 9.2
1-4-Embossed-c; Scott McDaniel-a	3.00

ELEKTRA (Also see Daredevil)
Marvel Comics: Nov, 1996 - No. 19, Jun, 1998 ($1.95)

	NM- 9.2
1-Peter Milligan scripts; Deodato-c/a	4.00
1-Variant-c	6.00
2-19: 4-Dr. Strange-c/app. 10-Logan-c/app.	3.00
#(-1) Flashback (7/97) Matt Murdock-c/app.; Deodato-c/a	3.00
.../Cyblade (Image, 3/97,$2.95) Devil's Reign pt. 7	3.00

ELEKTRA (Vol. 2) (Marvel Knights)
Marvel Comics: Sept, 2001 - No. 35, Jun, 2004 ($3.50/$2.99)

	NM- 9.2
1-Bendis-s/Austen-a/Horn-c	4.00
2-6: 2-Two covers (Sienkiewicz and Horn) 3,4-Silver Samurai app.	3.00
3-Initial printing with panel of nudity; most copies pulped	18.00
7-35: 7-Rucka-s begin. 9,10,17-Bennett-a. 19-Meglia-a. 23-25-Chen-a; Sienkiewicz-c	3.00
...Vol. 1: Introspect TPB (2002, $16.99) r/#10-15; Marvel Knights: Double Shot #3	17.00
...Vol. 2: Everything Old is New Again TPB (2003, $16.99) r/#16-22	17.00
...Vol. 3: Relentless TPB (2004, $14.99) r/#23-28	15.00
...Vol. 4: Frenzy TPB (2004, $17.99) r/#29-35	18.00

ELEKTRA & WOLVERINE: THE REDEEMER
Marvel Comics: Jan, 2002 - No. 3, Mar, 2002 ($5.95, square-bound, lim. series)

	NM- 9.2
1-3-Greg Rucka-s/Yoshitaka Amano-a/c	6.00
HC (5/02, $29.95, with dustjacket) r/#1-3, interview with Greg Rucka	30.00

ELEKTRA: ASSASSIN (Also see Daredevil)
Marvel Comics (Epic Comics): Aug, 1986 - No. 8, June, 1987 (Limited series, mature)

	NM- 9.2
1,8-Miller scripts in all; Sienkiewicz-c/a.	6.00
2-7	5.00
Signed & numbered hardcover (Graphitti Designs, $39.95, 2000 print run)- reprints 1-8	50.00
TPB (2000, $24.95)	25.00

ELEKTRA: GLIMPSE & ECHO
Marvel Comics: Sept, 2002 - No. 4, Dec, 2002 ($2.99, limited series)

	NM- 9.2
1-4-Scott Morse-s/painted-a	3.00

ELEKTRA LIVES AGAIN (Also see Daredevil)
Marvel Comics (Epic Comics): 1990 ($24.95, oversize, hardcover, 76 pgs.)(Produced by Graphitti Designs)

	NM- 9.2
nn-Frank Miller-c/a/scripts; Lynn Varley painted-a; Matt Murdock & Bullseye app.	35.00
2nd printing (9/02, $24.99)	25.00

ELEKTRA MEGAZINE
Marvel Comics: Nov, 1996 - No. 2, Dec, 1996 ($3.95, 96 pgs., reprints, limited series)

Elektra: The Movie #1 © MAR

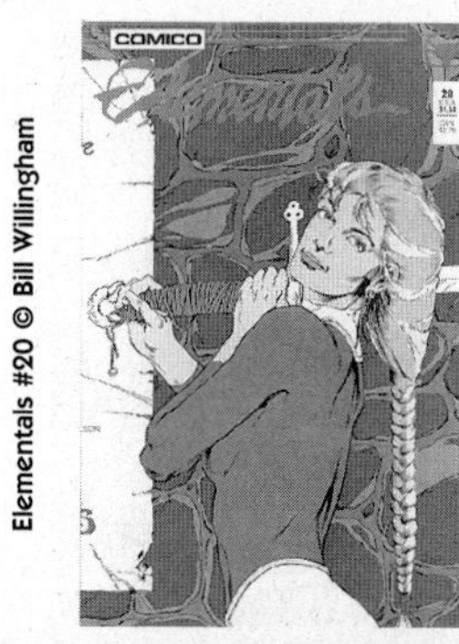

Elementals #20 © Bill Willingham

Elfquest V2 #18 © Warp

GD 2.0 VG 4.0 FN 6.0 VF 8.0 VF/NM 9.0 NM- 9.2

1,2: Reprints Frank Miller's Elektra stories in Daredevil 4.00

ELEKTRA SAGA, THE
Marvel Comics Group: Feb, 1984 - No. 4, June, 1984 ($2.00, limited series, Baxter paper)
1-4-r/Daredevil 168-190; Miller-c/a 4.00

ELEKTRA: THE HAND
Marvel Comics: Nov, 2004 - No. 5, Feb, 2005 ($2.99, limited series)
1-5-Gossett-a/Sienkiewicz-c/Yoshida-s; origin of the Hand in the 16th century 3.00
TPB (2005, $13.99) r/#1-5 14.00

ELEKTRA: THE MOVIE
Marvel Comics: Feb, 2005 ($5.99)
1-Movie adaptation; McKeever-s/Perkins-a; photo-c 6.00
TPB (2005, $12.95) r/movie adaptation, Daredevil #168, 181 & Elektra #(-1) 13.00

ELEMENTALS, THE (See The Justice Machine & Morningstar Spec.)
Comico The Comic Co. : June, 1984 - No. 29, Sept, 1988; V2#1, Mar, 1989 - No. 28, 1994? ($1.50/$2.50, Baxter paper); V3#1, Dec, 1995 - No. 3 ($2.95)
1-Willingham-c/a, 1-8 5.00
2-29, V2#1-28: 9-Bissette-a(p). 10-Photo-c. V2#6-1st app. Strike Force America. 18-Prelude to Avalon mini-series. 27-Prequel to Strike Force America series 3.00
V3#1-3: 1-Daniel-a(p), bagged w/gaming card 3.00
Lingerie (5/96, $2.95) 3.00
Special 1,2 (3/86, 1/89)-1-Willingham-a(p) 3.00

ELEMENTALS: (Title series), **Comico**
--GHOST OF A CHANCE, 12/95 ($5.95)-graphic novel, nn-Ross-c. 6.00
--HOW THE WAR WAS WON, 6/96 - No. 2, 8/96 ($2.95) 1,2-Tony Daniel-a, & 1-Variant-c; no logo 3.00
--SEX SPECIAL, 1991 - No. 4, Feb, 1993 ($2.95, color) 2 covers for each 3.00
--SEX SPECIAL, 5/97 - No. 2, 6/97 ($2.95, B&W) 1-Tony Daniel, Jeff Moy-a, 2-Robb Phipps, Adam McDaniel-a 3.00
--SWIMSUIT SPECTACULAR 1996, 6/96 ($2.95), 1-pin-ups, 1-Variant-c; no logo 3.00
--THE VAMPIRE'S REVENGE, 6/96 - No. 2 8/96 ($2.95) 1,2-Willingham-s, 1-Variant-c; no logo 3.00

ELEPHANTMEN
Image Comics: July, 2006 - Present ($2.99/$3.50) (Flip covers on most)
1-16: 1-Starkings-s/Moritat-a/Ladronn-c. 6-Campbell flip-c. 15-Sale flip-c 4.00
17-30-($3.50) 25-Flip book preview of Marineman 4.00
31-37-($3.99) 32-Conan/Sonja homage. 33-Shaky Kane-c/a 4.00
...: Man and Elephantman 1 (3/11, $3.99) Three covers 4.00
...: The Pilot (5/07, $2.99) short stories and pin-ups by various incl. Sale, Jim Lee, Jae Lee 4.00
...: War Toys (11/07 - No. 3, 4/08, $2.99) 1-3-Mappo war; Starkings-s/Moritat-a/Ladronn-c 4.00
... War Toys: Yvette (7/09, $3.50) Starkings-s/Moritat-a 4.00
Giant-Size Elephantmen 1 (10/11, $5.99) r/#31,32 & Man and Elephantman; Campbell-c 6.00

1111 (ELEVEN ELEVEN)
Crusade Entertainment: Oct, 1996 ($2.95, B&W, one-shot)
1-Wrightson-c/a 4.00

ELEVEN OR ONE
Sirius: Apr, 1995 ($2.95)
1-Linsner-c/a 1 3 4 6 8 10
1-(6/96) 2nd printing 3.50

ELFLORD
Nightwind Productions: Jun, 1980 - Vol. 2 #1, 1982 (B&W, magazine-size)
1-1st Barry Blair-s/c/a in comics; B&W-c; limited print run for all 11 22 33 71 136 200
2-5-B&W-c 5 10 15 35 55 75
6-14: 9-14-Color-c 4 8 12 28 44 60
Vol. 2 #1 (1982) 4 8 12 24 37 50

ELFLORD
Aircel Publ.: 1986 - No. 6, Oct, 1989 ($1.70, B&W); V2#1- V2#31, 1995 ($2.00)
1 4.00
2-4,V2#1-20,22-30: 4-6: Last B&W issue. V2#1-Color-a begin. 22-New cast. 25-Begin B&W 3.00
1,2-2nd printings 3.00
21-Double size ($4.95) 5.00

ELFLORD
Warp Graphics: Jan, 1997-No.4, Apr, 1997 ($2.95, B&W, mini-series)
1-4 3.00

ELFLORD (CUTS LOOSE) (Vol. 2)
Warp Graphics: Sept, 1997 - No. 7, Apr, 1998 ($2.95, B&W, mini-series)
1-7 3.00

ELFLORD: DRAGON'S EYE
Night Wynd Enterprises: 1993 ($2.50, B&W)
1 3.00

ELFLORD: THE RETURN
Mad Monkey Press: 1996 ($6.95, magazine size)
1 7.00

ELFQUEST (Also see Fantasy Quarterly & Warp Graphics Annual)
Warp Graphics, Inc.: No. 2, Aug, 1978 - No. 21, Feb, 1985 (All magazine size)
No. 1, Apr, 1979
NOTE: ***Elfquest*** was originally published as one of the stories in **Fantasy Quarterly** #1. When the publisher went out of business, the creative team, Wendy and Richard Pini, formed WaRP Graphics and continued the series, beginning with **Elfquest** #2. **Elfquest** #1, which reprinted the story from **Fantasy Quarterly**, was published about the same time **Elfquest** #4 was released. Thereafter, most issues were reprinted as demand warranted, until Marvel announced it would reprint the entire series under its Epic imprint (Aug., 1985).
1(4/79)-Reprints Elfquest story from Fantasy Quarterly No. 1
1st printing ($1.00-c) 4 8 12 24 37 50
2nd printing ($1.25-c) 1 3 4 6 8 10
3rd printings ($1.50-c) 4.00
4th printing; different-c ($1.50-c) 4.00
2(8/78) 1st printing ($1.00-c) 3 6 9 18 27 40
2nd printings ($1.25-c) 5.00
3rd & 4th printings ($1.50-c)(all 4th prints 1989) 4.00
3-5: 1st printings ($1.00-c) 3 6 9 16 23 30
6-9: 1st printings ($1.25-c) 2 4 6 10 14 18
2nd & 3rd printings ($1.50-c) 4.00
10-21: ($1.50-c); 16-8pg. preview of A Distant Soil 1 3 4 6 8 10
10-14: 2nd printings ($1.50) 4.00

ELFQUEST
Marvel Comics (Epic Comics): Aug, 1985 - No. 32, Mar, 1988
1-Reprints in color the Elfquest epic by Warp Graphics 4.00
2-32 3.00

ELFQUEST
DC Comics: 2003 - 2005
Archives Vol. 1 (2003, $49.95, HC) r/#1-5 50.00
Archives Vol. 2 (2005, $49.95, HC) r/#6-10 & Epic Illustrated #1 50.00
25th Anniversary Special (2003, $2.95) r/Elfquest #1 (Apr, 1979); interview w/Pinis 3.00

ELFQUEST (Title series), Warp Graphics
'89 - No. 4, '89 ($1.50, B&W) 1-4: R-original Elfquest series 3.00

ELFQUEST (Volume 2),**Warp Graphics:** V2#1, 5/96 - No. 33, 2/99 ($4.95/$2.95, B&W)
V2#1-31: 1,3,5,8,10,12,13,18,21,23,25-Wendy Pini-c 5.00
32,33-($2.95-c) 3.00
--BLOOD OF TEN CHIEFS, 7/93 - No. 20, 9/95 ($2.00/$2.50) 1-20-By Richard & Wendy Pini 3.00
--HIDDEN YEARS, 5/92 - No. 29, 3/96 ($2.00/$2.25)1-9,9 1/2, 10-29 3.00
--JINK, 11/94 - No. 12, 2/6 ($2.25/$2.50) 1-12-W. Pini/John Byrne-back-c 3.00
--KAHVI, 10/95 - No. 6,3/96 ($2.25, B&W) 1-6 3.00
--KINGS CROSS, 11/97 - No. 2, 12/97 ($2.95, B&W) 1,2 3.00
--KINGS OF THE BROKEN WHEEL, 6/90 - No. 9, 2/92 ($2.00, B&W) (3rd Elfquest saga) 1-9: By R. & W. Pini; 1-Color insert 3.00
1-2nd printing 3.00
--METAMORPHOSIS, 4/96 ($2.95, B&W) 1 3.00
--NEW BLOOD (...Summer Special on-c #1 only), 8/92 - No. 35, 1/96 ($2.00-$2.50, color/B&W) 1-($3.95, 68 pgs.,...Summer Special on-c)-Byrne-a/scripts (16 pgs.) 4.00
2-35: Barry Blair-a in all 3.00
1993 Summer Special ($3.95) Byrne-a/scripts 4.00
--SHARDS, 8/94 - No. 16, 3/96 ($2.25/$2.50) 1-16 3.00
--SIEGE AT BLUE MOUNTAIN, WaRP Graphics/Apple 3/87 - No. 8, 12/88 (1.75/ $1.95, B&W) 1-Staton-a(i) in all; 2nd Elfquest saga 4.00
1-3-2nd printing, 3-8 3.00
2 3.00
--THE REBELS, 11/94 - No. 12, 3/96 ($2.25/$2.50, B&W/color) 1-12 3.00
--TWO-SPEAR, 10/95 - No. 5, 2/96 ($2.25, B&W) 1-5 3.00
--WAVE DANCERS, 12/93 - No. 6, 3/96, 1-6: 1-Foil-c & poster 3.00

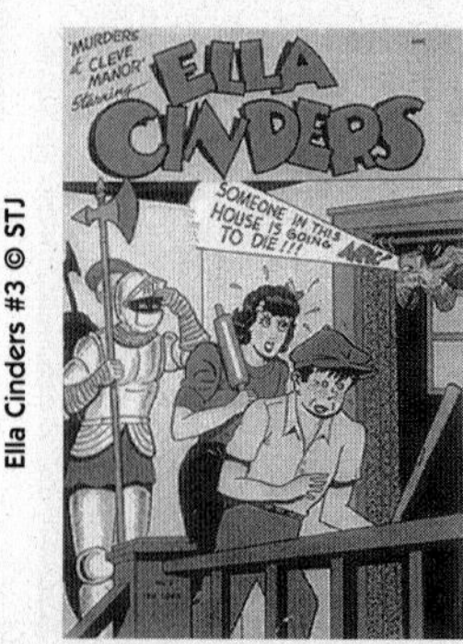

Ella Cinders #3 © STJ

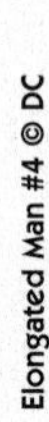
Elongated Man #4 © DC

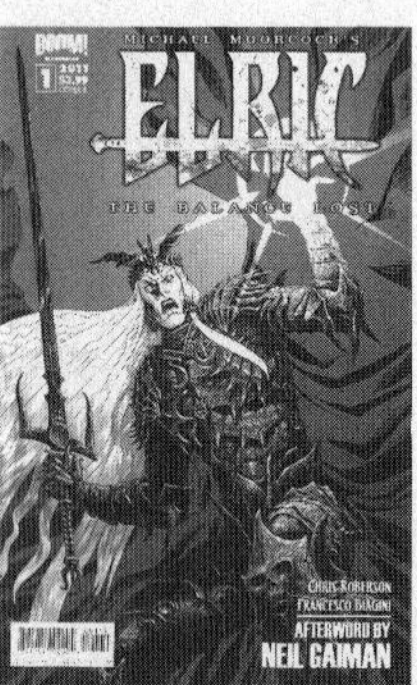

Elric: The Balance Lost #1 © Michael Moorcock

	GD 2.0	VG 4.0	FN 6.0	VF 8.0	VF/NM 9.0	NM- 9.2

Special 1 ($2.95) 3.00

--WORLDPOOL, 7/97 ($2.95, B&W) 1-Richard Pini-s/Barry Blair-a 3.00

ELFQUEST: THE DISCOVERY
DC Comics: March,2006 - No. 4, Sept, 2006 ($3.99, limited series)

1-4-Wendy Pini-a/Wendy & Richard Pini-s 4.00
TPB (2006, $14.99) r/#1-4 15.00

ELFQUEST: THE GRAND QUEST
DC Comics: 2004 - Present ($9.95/$9.99, B&W, digest-size)

Vol. 1-6 ('04)1-r/Elfquest #1-5; new W. Pini-c. 2-r/#5-8. 3-r/#8-11. 4-r/#11-15. 5-r/#15-18 6-r/#18-20 10.00
Vol. 7-9 ('05) 1-r/Siege At Blue Mountain #1-3. 8-r/SABM #3-5. 9-r/SABM #6-8 10.00
Vol. 10-14 ('05) 10-r/Kings of the Broken Wheel #1-3. 11-KotBW #5-7 & Frazetta Fant. Ill. 12-r/Kings of the Broken Wheel #8&9. 13-r/Elfquest V2 #4-18. 14-r/Hidden Years #4-9 1/2 10.00

ELFQUEST: THE SEARCHER AND THE SWORD
DC Comics: 2004 ($24.95/$14.99, graphic novel)

HC (2004, $24.95, with dust jacket)-Wendy and Richard Pini-s/a/c 25.00
SC (2004, $14.99) 15.00

ELFQUEST: WOLFRIDER
DC Comics: 2003 - Present ($9.95, digest-size)

Volume 1 ('03, $9.95, digest-size) r/Elfquest V2#19,21,23,25,27,29,31; Blood of Ten Chiefs #2; Hidden Years #5; New Blood Special #1; New Blood 1993 Special #1; new W. Pini-c 10.00
Volume 2 ('03, $9.95, digest-size) r/Elfquest V2#33; Blood of Ten Chiefs #10,11,19; Warp Graphics Annual #1 10.00

ELF-THING
Eclipse Comics: March, 1987 ($1.50, B&W, one-shot)

1 3.00

ELIMINATOR (Also see The Solution #16 & The Night Man #16)
Malibu Comics (Ultraverse): Apr, 1995 - No. 3, Jul, 1995 ($2.95/$2.50, lim. series)

0-Mike Zeck-a in all 3.00
1-3-($2.50): 1-1st app. Siren 3.00
1-($3.95)-Black cover edition 4.00

ELIMINATOR FULL COLOR SPECIAL
Eternity Comics: Oct, 1991 ($2.95, one-shot)

1-Dave Dorman painted-c 3.00

ELLA CINDERS (See Comics On Parade, Comics Revue #1,4, Famous Comics Cartoon Book, Giant Comics Editions, Sparkler Comics, Tip Top & Treasury of Comics)

ELLA CINDERS
United Features Syndicate: 1938 - 1940

	GD	VG	FN	VF	VF/NM	NM-
Single Series 3(1938)	40	80	120	246	411	575
Single Series 21(#2 on-c, #21 on inside), 28('40)	35	70	105	208	339	470

ELLA CINDERS
United Features Syndicate: Mar, 1948 - No. 5, Mar, 1949

	GD	VG	FN	VF	VF/NM	NM-
1-(#2 on cover)	14	28	42	80	115	150
2	10	20	30	54	72	90
3-5	8	16	24	40	50	60

ELLERY QUEEN
Superior Comics Ltd.: May, 1949 - No. 4, Nov, 1949

	GD	VG	FN	VF	VF/NM	NM-
1-Kamen-c; L.B. Cole-a; r-in Haunted Thrills	52	104	156	328	557	785
2-4: 3-Drug use stories(2)	39	78	117	240	395	550

NOTE: *Iger shop art in all issues.*

ELLERY QUEEN (TV)
Ziff-Davis Publishing Co.: 1-3/52 (Spring on-c) - No. 2, Summer/52 (Saunders painted-c)

	GD	VG	FN	VF	VF/NM	NM-
1-Saunders-c	47	94	141	296	498	700
2-Saunders bondage, torture-c	39	78	117	231	378	525

ELLERY QUEEN (Also see Crackajack Funnies No. 23)
Dell Publishing Co.: No. 1165, Mar-May, 1961 - No.1289, Apr, 1962

	GD	VG	FN	VF	VF/NM	NM-
Four Color 1165 (#1)	10	20	30	66	121	175
Four Color 1243 (11-1/61-61), 1289	8	16	24	55	93	130

ELMER FUDD (Also see Camp Comics, Daffy, Looney Tunes #1 & Super Book #10, 22)
Dell Publishing Co.: No. 470, May, 1953 - No. 1293, Mar-May, 1962

	GD	VG	FN	VF	VF/NM	NM-
Four Color 470 (#1)	9	18	27	61	106	150
Four Color 558,628,689('56)	5	10	15	35	55	75
Four Color 725,783,841,888,938,977,1032,1081,1131,1171,1222,1293('62)	4	8	12	28	44	60

ELMO COMICS
St. John Publishing Co.: Jan, 1948 (Daily strip-r)

	GD	VG	FN	VF	VF/NM	NM-
1-By Cecil Jensen	10	20	30	58	79	100

ELONGATED MAN (See Flash #112 & Justice League of America #105)
DC Comics: Jan, 1992 - No. 4, Apr, 1992 ($1.00, limited series)

1-4: 3-The Flash app. 3.00

ELRIC (Of Melnibone)(See First Comics Graphic Novel #6 & Marvel Graphic Novel #2)
Pacific Comics: Apr, 1983 - No. 6, Apr, 1984 ($1.50, Baxter paper)

1-6: Russell-c/a(i) in all 3.00

ELRIC
Topps Comics: 1996 ($2.95, one-shot)

0--One Life: Russell-c/a; adapts Neil Gaiman's short story "One Life--Furnished in Early Moorcock." 3.00

ELRIC, SAILOR ON THE SEAS OF FATE
First Comics: June, 1985 - No. 7, June, 1986 ($1.75, limited series)

1-7: Adapts Michael Moorcock's novel 3.00

ELRIC, STORMBRINGER
Dark Horse Comics/Topps Comics: 1997 - No. 7, 1997 ($2.95, limited series)

1-7: Russell-c/s/a; adapts Michael Moorcock's novel 3.00

ELRIC: THE BALANCE LOST
BOOM! Studios: Jul, 2011 - No. 12 ($3.99)

1-9: 1-Roberson-s/Biagini-a; four covers. 2-9-Three covers 4.00

ELRIC: THE BANE OF THE BLACK SWORD
First Comics: Aug, 1988 - No. 6, June, 1989 ($1.75/$1.95, limited series)

1-6: Adapts Michael Moorcock's novel 3.00

ELRIC: THE VANISHING TOWER
First Comics: Aug, 1987 - No. 6, June, 1988 ($1.75, limited series)

1-6: Adapts Michael Moorcock's novel 3.00

ELRIC: WEIRD OF THE WHITE WOLF
First Comics: Oct, 1986 - No. 5, June, 1987 ($1.75, limited series)

1-5: Adapts Michael Moorcock's novel 3.00

EL SALVADOR - A HOUSE DIVIDED
Eclipse Comics: March, 1989 ($2.50, B&W, Baxter paper, stiff-c, 52 pgs.)

1-Gives history of El Salvador 4.00

ELSEWHERE PRINCE, THE (Moebius' Airtight Garage)
Marvel Comics (Epic): May, 1990 - No. 6, Oct, 1990 ($1.95, limited series)

1-6: Moebius scripts & back-up-a in all 3.00

ELSEWORLDS 80-PAGE GIANT (See DC Comics Presents: ... for reprint)
DC Comics: Aug, 1999 ($5.95, one-shot)

	GD	VG	FN	VF	VF/NM	NM-
1-Most copies destroyed by DC over content of the "Superman's Babysitter" story; some UK shipments sold before recall	11	22	33	71	136	200

ELSEWORLD'S FINEST
DC Comics: 1997 - No. 2, 1997 ($4.95, limited series)

1,2: Elseworld's story-Superman & Batman in the 1920's 5.00

ELSEWORLD'S FINEST: SUPERGIRL & BATGIRL
DC Comics: 1998 ($5.95, one-shot)

1-Haley-a 6.00

ELSIE THE COW
D. S. Publishing Co.: Oct-Nov, 1949 - No. 3, July-Aug, 1950

	GD	VG	FN	VF	VF/NM	NM-
1-(36 pgs.)	25	50	75	150	245	340
2,3	18	36	54	105	165	225

ELSINORE
Alias Entertainment: Apr, 2005 - No. 5, Apr, 2006 (75¢/$2.99/$3.25)

1-5: 1-(75¢-c) Brian Denham-a/Kenneth Lillie-Paetz-s. 2-($2.99-c). 4-($3.25-c) 5-Sparacio-a 3.25

ELSON'S PRESENTS
DC Comics: 1981 (100 pgs., no cover price)

	GD	VG	FN	VF	VF/NM	NM-
Series 1-6: Repackaged 1981 DC comics; 1-DC Comics Presents #29, Flash #303, Batman #331. 2-Superman #335, Ghosts #96, Justice League of America #186. 3-New Teen Titans #3, Secrets of Haunted House #32, Wonder Woman #275. 4-Secrets of the LSH #1, Brave & the Bold #170, New Adv. of Superboy #13. 5-LSH #271, Green Lantern #136, Super Friends #40. 6-Action #515, Mystery in Space #115, Detective #498	2	4	6	11	16	20

E-Man #3 © FC

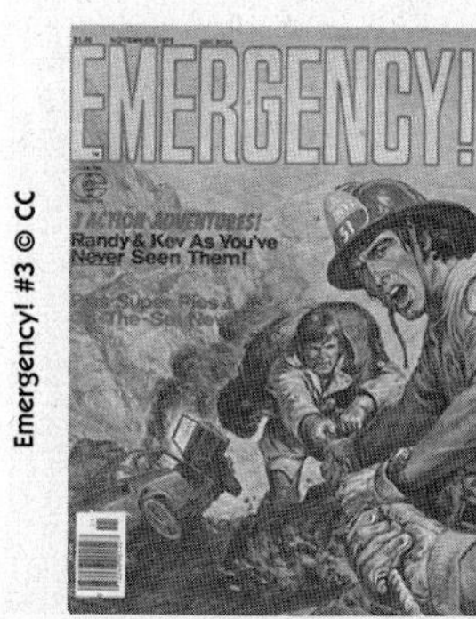

Emergency! #3 © CC

Emma #5 © MAR

	GD 2.0	VG 4.0	FN 6.0	VF 8.0	VF/NM 9.0	NM- 9.2

ELVEN (Also see Prime)
Malibu Comics (Ultraverse): Oct, 1994 - No. 4, Feb, 1995 ($2.50, lim. series)

0 ($2.95)-Prime app. 3.00
1-4: 2,4-Prime app. 3-Primevil app. 3.00
1-Limited Foil Edition- no price on cover 4.00

ELVIRA MISTRESS OF THE DARK
Marvel Comics: Oct, 1988 ($2.00, B&W, magazine size)

1-Movie adaptation 5.00

ELVIRA MISTRESS OF THE DARK
Claypool Comics (Eclipse): May, 1993 - No. 166, Feb, 2007 ($2.50, B&W)

1-Austin-a(i). Spiegle-a 6.00
2-6: Spiegle-a 4.00
7-99,101-166-Photo-c: 3.00
100-(8/01) Kurt Busiek back-up-s; art by DeCarlo and others 3.00
TPB ($12.95) 13.00

ELVIRA'S HOUSE OF MYSTERY
DC Comics: Jan, 1986 - No. 11, Jan, 1987

1,11: 11-Dave Stevens-c 6.00
2-10: 9-Photo-c, Special 1 (3/87, $1.25) 4.00

ELVIS MANDIBLE, THE
DC Comics (Piranha Press): 1990 ($3.50, 52 pgs., B&W, mature)

nn 4.00

ELVIS PRESLEY (See Career Girl Romances #32, Go-Go, Howard Chaykin's American Flagg #10, Humbug #8, I Love You #60 & Young Lovers #18)

EL ZOMBO FANTASMA
Dark Horse Comics (Rocket Comics): Apr, 2004 - No. 3, June, 2004 ($2.99)

1-3-Wilkins-s&a/Munroe-s 3.00

E-MAN
Charlton Comics: Oct, 1973 - No. 10, Sept, 1975 (Painted-c No. 7-10)

1-Origin & 1st app. E-Man; Staton c/a in all 3 6 9 16 23 30
2-5: 2,4,5-Ditko-a. 3-Howard-a. 5-Miss Liberty Belle app. by Ditko 2 4 6 9 12 15
6-10: 6,7,9,10-Early Byrne-a (#6 is 1/75). 6-Disney parody. 8-Full-length story; Nova begins as E-Man's partner 2 4 6 11 16 20
1-4,9,10 (Modern Comics reprints, '77) 5.00

NOTE: *Killjoy app.-No. 2, 4. Liberty Belle app.-No. 5. Rog 2000 app.-No. 6, 7, 9, 10. Travis app.-No. 3.* ***Sutton*** *a-1.*

E-MAN
Comico: Sept, 1989 ($2.75, one-shot, no ads, high quality paper)

1-Staton-c/a; Michael Mauser story 3.00

E-MAN
Comico: V4#1, Jan, 1990 - No. 3, Mar, 1990 ($2.50, limited series)

1-3: Staton-c/a 3.00

E-MAN
Alpha Productions: Oct, 1993 ($2.75)

V5#1-Staton-c/a; 20th anniversary issue 3.00

E-MAN COMICS (Also see Michael Mauser & The Original E-Man)
First Comics: Apr, 1983 - No. 25, Aug, 1985 ($1.00/$1.25, direct sales only)

1-25: 2-X-Men satire. 3-X-Men/Phoenix satire. 6-Origin retold. 8-Cutey Bunny app. 10-Origin Nova Kane. 24-Origin Michael Mauser 3.00

NOTE: ***Staton*** *a-1-5, 6-25p; c-1-25.*

E-MAN RETURNS
Alpha Productions: 1994 ($2.75, B&W)

1-Joe Staton-c/a(p) 3.00

EMERALD DAWN
DC Comics: 1991 ($4.95, trade paperback)

nn-Reprints Green Lantern: Emerald Dawn #1-6 5.00

EMERALD DAWN II (See Green Lantern...)

EMERGENCY (Magazine)
Charlton Comics: June, 1976 - No. 4, Jan, 1977 (B&W)

1-Neal Adams-c/a; Heath, Austin-a 4 8 12 24 37 50
2,3: 2-N. Adams-c. 3-N. Adams-a. 3 6 9 19 29 38
4-Alcala-a 3 6 9 14 20 25

EMERGENCY (TV)
Charlton Comics: June, 1976 - No. 4, Dec, 1976

1-Staton-c; early Byrne-a (22 pages) 3 6 9 20 30 40
2-4: 2-Staton-c. 2,3-Byrne text illos. 3 6 9 14 20 25

EMERGENCY DOCTOR
Charlton Comics: Summer, 1963 (one-shot)

1 3 6 9 19 29 38

EMIL & THE DETECTIVES (See Movie Comics)

EMISSARY (Jim Valentino's...)
Image Comics (Shadowline): May, 2006 - Present ($3.50)

1-6: 1-Rand-s/Ferreyra-a. 4-6-Long-s 3.50

EMMA (Adaptation of the Jane Austen novel)
Marvel Comics: May, 2011 - No. 5, Sept, 2011 ($3.99)

1-5-Nancy Butler-s/Janet K. Lee-a 4.00

EMMA FROST
Marvel Comics: Aug, 2003 - No. 18, Feb, 2005 ($2.50/$2.99)

1-7-Emma in high school; Bollers-s/Green-a/Horn-c 3.00
8-18-($2.99) 3.00
... Vol. 1: Higher Learning TPB (2004, $7.99, digest size) r/#1-6 8.00
... Vol. 2: Mind Games TPB (2005, $7.99, digest size) r/#7-12 8.00
... Vol. 3: Bloom TPB (2005, $7.99, digest size) r/#13-18 8.00

EMMA PEEL & JOHN STEED (See The Avengers)

EMPEROR'S NEW CLOTHES, THE
Dell Publishing Co.: 1950 (10¢, 68 pgs., 1/2 size, oblong)

nn - (Surprise Books series) 6 12 18 28 34 40

EMPIRE
Image Comics (Gorilla): May, 2000 - No. 2, Sept, 2000 ($2.50)
DC Comics: No. 0, Aug, 2003; Sept, 2003 - No. 6, Feb, 2004 ($4.95/$2.50, limited series)

1,2: 1 (5/00)-Waid-s/Kitson-a; w/Crimson Plague prologue 3.00
0-(8/03) reprints #1,2 5.00
1-6: 1-(9/03) new Waid-s/Kitson-a/c 3.00
TPB (DC, 2004, $14.95) r/series; Kitson sketch pages; Waid intro. 15.00

EMPIRE STRIKES BACK, THE (See Marvel Comics Super Special #16 & Marvel Special Edition)

EMPTY LOVE STORIES
Slave Labor #1 & 2/Funny Valentine Press: Nov, 1994 - Present ($2.95, B&W)

1,2: Steve Darnall scripts in all. 1-Alex Ross-c. 2-(8/96)-Mike Allred-c 4.00
1,2-2nd printing (Funny Valentine Press) 3.00
... 1999-Jeff Smith-c; Doran-a 3.00
..."Special" (2.95) Ty Templeton-c 3.00

ENCHANTED APPLES OF OZ, THE (See First Comics Graphic Novel #5)

ENCHANTER
Eclipse Comics: Apr, 1987 - No. 3, Aug. 1987 ($2.00, B&W, limited series)

1-3 3.00

ENCHANTING LOVE
Kirby Publishing Co.: Oct, 1949 - No. 6, July, 1950 (All 52 pgs.)

1-Photo-c 17 34 51 98 154 210
2-Photo-c; Powell-a 11 22 33 60 83 105
3,4,6: 3-Jimmy Stewart photo-c 10 20 30 58 79 100
5-Ingels-a, 9 pgs.; photo-c 17 34 51 98 154 210

ENCHANTMENT VISUALETTES (Magazine)
World Editions: Dec, 1949 - No. 5, Apr, 1950 (Painted c-1)

1-Contains two romance comic strips each 16 32 48 94 147 200
2 13 26 39 72 101 130
3-5 10 20 30 58 79 100

ENDER IN EXILE (ORSON SCOTT CARD'S...)
Marvel Comics: Aug, 2010 - No. 5, Dec, 2010 ($3.99, limited series)

1-5-Sequel to Ender's Game; Johnston-s/Mhan-a/Fiumara-c 4.00

ENDER'S GAME: BATTLE SCHOOL
Marvel Comics: Dec, 2008 - No. 5, Jun, 2009 ($3.99, limited series)

1-5-Adaptation of Orson Scott Card novel Ender's Game; Yost-s/Ferry-a. 1-Two covers 4.00
Ender's Game: Mazer in Prison Special (4/10, $3.99) Johnston-s/Mhan-a 4.00
Ender's Game: Recruiting Valentine (8/09, $3.99) Timothy Green-a 4.00
Ender's Game: The League War (6/10, $3.99) Aaron Johnston-s/Timothy Green-a 4.00
Ender's Game: War of Gifts Special (2/10, $4.99) Timothy Green-a 5.00

ENDER'S GAME: COMMAND SCHOOL
Marvel Comics: Nov, 2009 - No. 5, Apr, 2010 ($3.99, limited series)

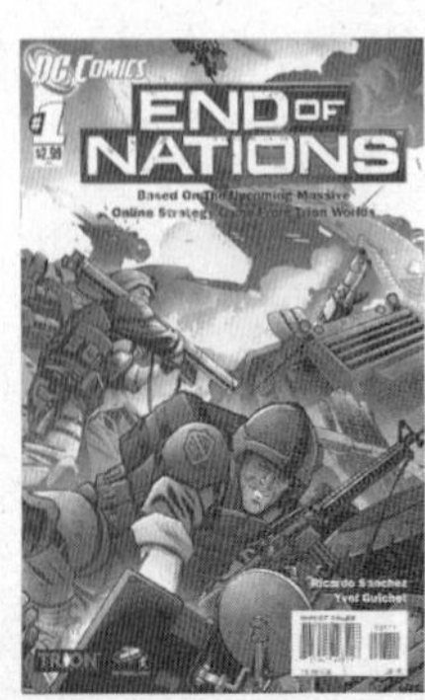

End of Nations #1 © Trion

Epic Illustrated #17 © MAR

Espers #6 © James Hudnall

1-5-Adaptation of Orson Scott Card novel Ender's Game; Yost-s/Ferry-a 4.00

ENDER'S SHADOW: BATTLE SCHOOL
Marvel Comics: Feb, 2009 - No. 5, Jun, 2009 ($3.99, limited series)

1-5-Adaptation of O.S. Card novel Ender's Shadow; Carey-s/Fiumara-a. 1-Two covers 4.00

ENDER'S SHADOW: COMMAND SCHOOL
Marvel Comics: Nov, 2009 - No. 5, Apr, 2010 ($3.99, limited series)

1-5-Adaptation of O.S. Card novel Ender's Shadow; Carey-s/Fiumara-a 4.00

END LEAGUE, THE
Dark Horse Comics: Dec, 2007 - No. 9, Nov, 2009 ($2.99/$3.99)

1-8: 1-Broome-c/a; Remender-s. 5,6-Canete-a 3.00
9-($3.99) MacDonald-a/Canete-c 4.00

END OF NATIONS
DC Comics: Jan, 2012 - No. 4, Apr, 2012 ($2.99, limited series)

1-4-Based on the Trion Worlds videogame; Sanchez-s/Guichet-a/Sprouse-c 3.00

ENEMY ACE SPECIAL (Also see Our Army at War #151, Showcase #57, 58 & Star Spangled War Stories #138)
DC Comics: 1990 ($1.00, one-shot)

1-Kubert-r/Our Army #151,153; c-r/Showcase 57 5.00

ENEMY ACE: WAR IDYLL
DC Comics: 1990 (Graphic novel)

Hardcover-George Pratt-s/painted-a/c 30.00
Softcover (1991, $14.95) 15.00

ENEMY ACE: WAR IN HEAVEN
DC Comics: 2001 - No. 2, 2001 ($5.95, squarebound, limited series)

1,2-Ennis-s; Von Hammer in WW2. 1-Weston & Alamy-a. 2-Heath-a 6.00
TPB (2003, $14.95) r/#1,2 & Star Spangled War Stories #139; Jim Dietz-painted-c 15.00

ENGINEHEAD
DC Comics: June, 2004 - No. 6, Nov, 2004 ($2.50, limited series)

1-6-Joe Kelly-s/Ted McKeever-a/c. 6-Metal Men app. 3.00

ENIGMA
DC Comics (Vertigo): Mar, 1993 - No. 8, Oct, 1993 ($2.50, limited series)

1-8: Milligan scripts 3.00
Trade paperback ($19.95)-reprints 20.00

ENO AND PLUM (Also see Cud Comics)
Oni Press: Mar, 1998 ($2.95, B&W)

1-Terry LaBan-s/c/a 3.00

ENSIGN O'TOOLE (TV)
Dell Publishing Co.: Aug-Oct, 1963

1 3 6 9 20 30 40

ENSIGN PULVER (See Movie Classics)

ENTER THE HEROIC AGE
Marvel Comics: July, 2010 ($3.99, one-shot)

1-Short stories of Avengers Academy, Atlas, Black Widow, Thunderbolts; Hitch-c 4.00

EPIC
Marvel Comics (Epic Comics): 1992 - Book 4, 1992 ($4.95, lim. series, 52 pgs.)

Book One-Four: 2-Dorman painted-c 5.00
NOTE: *Alien Legion in #3. Cholly & Flytrap by* ***Burden****(scripts) &* ***Suydam****(art) in 3, 4. Dinosaurs in #4. Dreadlands in #1. Hellraiser in #1. Nightbreed in #2. Sleeze Brothers in #2. Stalkers in #1-4. Wild Cards in #1-4.*

EPIC ANTHOLOGY
Marvel Comics (Epic Comics): Apr, 2004 ($5.99)

1-Short stories by various 6.00

EPIC ILLUSTRATED (Magazine)
Marvel Comics Group: Spring, 1980 - No. 34, Feb, 1986 ($2.00/$2.50, B&W/color, mature)

1-Frazetta-c; Silver Surfer/Galactus-sty; Wendy Pini-s/a; Suydam-s/a; Metamorphosis Odyssey begins (thru #9) Starlin-a 2 4 6 8 10 12
2-10: 2-Bissette/Veitch-a; Goodwin-s. 3-1st app. Dreadstar. 4-Ellison 15 pg. story w/Steacy-a; Hempel-s/a; Veitch-s/a. 5-Hildebrandts-c/interview; Jusko-a; Vess-s/a. 6-Ellison-s (26 pgs). 7-Adams-s/a(16 pgs.); BWS interview. 8-Suydam-s/a; Vess-s/a. 9-Conrad-c. 10-Marada the She-Wolf-c/sty(21 pgs.) by Claremont/Bolton 1 2 3 4 5 7
11-20: 11-Wood-a; Jusko-a. 12-Wolverton Spacehawk-r edited & recolored w/article on him; Muth-a. 13-Blade Runner preview by Williamson. 14-Elric of Melnibone by Russell; Revenge of the Jedi preview. 15-Vallejo-c & interview; 1st Dreadstar solo story (cont'd in Dreadstar #1). 16-B. Smith-c/a(2); Sim-s/a. 17-Starslammers preview. 18-Go Nagai; Williams-a. 19-Jabberwocky w/Hampton-a; Cheech Wizard-s. 20-The Sacred & the Profane begins by Ken Steacy; Elric by Gould; Williams-a 1 2 3 5 6 8
21-30: 21-Vess-s/a. 22-Frankenstein w/Wrightson-a. 26-Galactus series begins (thru #34); Cerebus the Aardvark story by Dave Sim. 27-Groo. 28-Cerebus. 29-1st Sheeva. 30-Cerebus; History of Dreadstar, Starlin-s/a; Williams-a; Vess-a 1 3 4 6 8 10
31-33: 31-Bolton-c/a. 32-Cerebus portfolio. 2 4 6 8 10 12
34-R.E.Howard tribute by Thomas-s/Plunkett-a; Moore-s/Veitch-a; Cerebus; Cholly & Flytrap w/Suydam-a; BWS-a 2 4 6 10 14 18
Sampler (early 1980 8 pg. preview giveaway) same cover as #1 with "Sampler" text 6.00
NOTE: ***N. Adams*** *a-7; c-6.* ***Austin*** *a-15-20i.* ***Bode*** *a-19, 23, 27r.* ***Bolton*** *a-7, 10-12, 15, 18, 22-25; c-10, 18, 22, 23.* ***Boris*** *c/a-15.* ***Brunner*** *c-12.* ***Buscema*** *a-1p, 9p, 11-13p.* ***Byrne/Austin*** *a-26-34.* ***Chaykin*** *a-2; c-8.* ***Conrad*** *a-2-5, 7-9, 25-34; c-17.* ***Corben*** *a-15; c-2.* ***Frazetta*** *c-1.* ***Golden*** *a-3r.* ***Gulacy*** *c/a-3.* ***Jeff Jones*** *c-25.* ***Kaluta*** *a-17r, 21, 24r, 26; c-4, 28.* ***Nebres*** *a-1.* ***Reese*** *a-12.* ***Russell*** *a-2-4, 9, 14, 33; c-14.* ***Simonson*** *a-17.* ***B. Smith*** *c/a-7, 16.* ***Starlin*** *a-1-9, 14, 15, 34.* ***Steranko*** *c-19.* ***Williamson*** *a-13, 27, 34.* ***Wrightson*** *a-13p, 22, 25, 27, 34; c-30.*

EPIC LITE
Marvel Comics (Epic Comics): Sept, 1991 ($3.95, 52 pgs., one-shot)

1-Bob the Alien, Normalman by Valentino 4.00

EPICURUS THE SAGE
DC Comics (Piranha Press): Vol. 1, 1991 - Vol. 2, 1991 ($9.95, 8-1/8x10-7/8")

Volume 1,2-Sam Kieth-c/a; Messner-Loebs-s 10.00
TPB (2003, $19.95) r/ #1,2, Fast Forward Rising the Sun; new story 20.00

EPILOGUE
IDW Publishing: Sept, 2008 - No. 4, Dec, 2008 ($3.99)

1-4-Steve Niles-s/Kyle Hotz-a/c 4.00

ERADICATOR
DC Comics: Aug, 1996 - No. 3, Oct, 1996 ($1.75, limited series)

1-3: Superman app. 3.00

ERNIE COMICS (Formerly Andy Comics #21; All Love Romances #26 on)
Current Books/Ace Periodicals: No. 22, Sept, 1948 - No. 25, Mar, 1949

nn (9/48,11/48; #22,23)-Teenage humor 8 16 24 42 54 65
24,25 6 12 18 31 38 45

ESCAPADE IN FLORENCE (See Movie Comics)

ESCAPE FROM DEVIL'S ISLAND
Avon Periodicals: 1952

1-Kinstler-c; r/as Dynamic Adventures #9 41 82 123 249 417 585

ESCAPE FROM THE PLANET OF THE APES (See Power Record Comics)

ESCAPE TO WITCH MOUNTAIN (See Walt Disney Showcase No. 29)

ESCAPISTS, THE (See Michael Chabon Presents The Amazing Adventures of the Escapist)
Dark Horse Comics: July, 2006 - No. 6, Dec, 2006 ($1.00/$2.99, limited series)

1-($1.00) Frank Miller-c; r/Vaughan story from Michael Chabon... #8 3.00
2-6($2.99) Vaughan-s/Rolston & Alexander-a. 2-James Jean-c. 3-Cassaday-c 3.00

ESPERS (Also see Interface)
Eclipse Comics: July, 1986 - No. 5, Apr, 1987 ($1.25/$1.75, Mando paper)

1-5-James Hudnall story & David Lloyd-a. 3.00

ESPERS
Halloween Comics: V2#1, 1996 - No. 6, 1997 ($2.95, B&W) (1st Halloween Comics series)

V2#1-6: James D. Hudnall scripts 3.00
Undertow TPB ('98, $14.95) r/#1-6 15.00

ESPERS
Image Comics: V3#1, 1997 - Present ($2.95, B&W, limited series)

V3#1-7: James D. Hudnall scripts 3.00
Black Magic TPB ('98, $14.95) r/#1-4 15.00

ESPIONAGE (TV)
Dell Publishing Co.: May-July, 1964

1 3 6 9 20 30 40

ESSENTIAL (Title series), **Marvel Comics**

--ANT-MAN, '02 (B&W- r) V1-Reprints app. from Tales To Astonish #27, #35-69; Kirby-c 15.00

--AVENGERS, '98 (B&W- r) V1-R-Avengers #1-24; new Immonen-c 15.00
V2(6/00)-Reprints Avengers #25-46, King-Size Special #1; Immonen-c 15.00
V3(3/01)-Reprints Avengers #47-68, Annual #2; Immonen-c 15.00
V4('04)-Reprints Avengers #69-97, Incredible Hulk #140; Neal Adams-c 17.00
V5('06)-Reprints Avengers #98-119, Daredevil #99, Defenders #8-11 17.00
V6('08)-Reprints Avengers #120-140, Giant Size #1-4, Capt. Marvel #33 & FF #150 17.00

--CAPTAIN AMERICA, '00 (B&W- r) V1-Reprints stories from Tales of Suspense #59-99, Captain America #100-102; new Romita & Milgrom-c 15.00

Essential Doctor Strange V2 © MAR

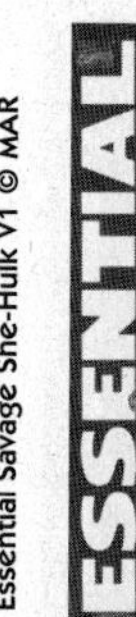

Essential Savage She-Hulk V1 © MAR

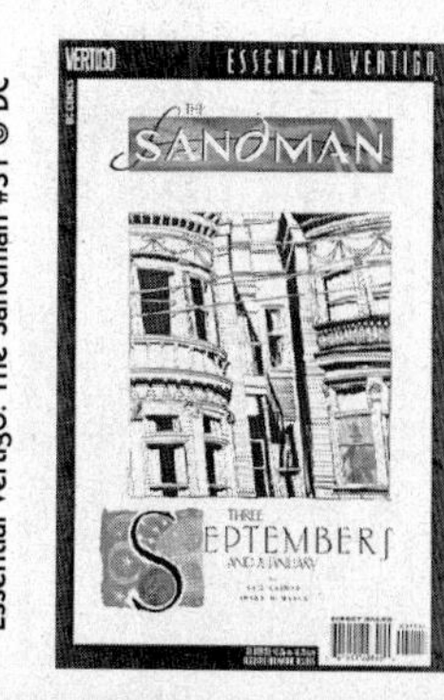

Essential Vertigo: The Sandman #31 © DC

GD 2.0 | VG 4.0 | FN 6.0 | VF 8.0 | VF/NM 9.0 | NM- 9.2

V2(1/02)-Reprints #103-126; Steranko-c 15.00
V3('06)-Reprints #127-153 17.00
V4('07)-Reprints #157-186 17.00

--CLASSIC X-MEN, '06 - Present (B&W- r) (See Essential Uncanny X-Men for V1)
V2-($16.99) R-X-Men #25-53 & Avengers #53; Gil Kane-c 17.00

--CONAN, '00 (B&W- r) V1-R-Conan the Barbarian#1-25; new Buscema-c 15.00

--DAREDEVIL, '02 - Present (B&W-r)
V1-R-Daredevil #1-25 15.00
V2-($16.99) R-Daredevil #26-48, Special #1, Fantastic Four #73 17.00
V3-($16.99) R-Daredevil #49-74, Iron Man #35-38 17.00
V4-($16.99) R-Daredevil #75-101, Avengers #111 17.00

--DAZZLER, '07 (B&W- r) V1-R/#1-21, X-Men #130-131, Amaz. Spider-Man #203 17.00

--DEFENDERS, '05 (B&W-r) V1-Reprints Doctor Strange #183, Sub-Mariner #22,34,35, Incredible Hulk #126, Marvel Feature #1-3, Defenders #1-14, Avengers #115-118 17.00
V2-($16.99) R- Defenders #15-30, Giant-Size Defenders #1-4, Marvel Two-In-One #6,7, Marvel Team-Up #33-35 and Marvel Treasury Edition #12 17.00
V3-($16.99) R- Defenders #31-60 and Annual #1 17.00

--DOCTOR STRANGE, '04 - Present (B&W-r)
V1-($15.95) Reprints Strange Tales #110,111,114-168 16.00
V1 (2nd printing)-(2006, $16.99) Reprints Strange Tales #110,111,114-168 17.00
V2-($16.99) R-Doctor Strange #169-178,180-183; Avengers #61, Sub-Mariner #22 Marvel Feature #1, Incredible Hulk #126 and Marvel Premiere #3-14 17.00
V3-($16.99) R-Doctor Strange #1-29 & Annual #1;Tomb of Dracula #44,45 17.00

--FANTASTIC FOUR, '98 - Present (B&W-r)
V1-Reprints FF #1-20, Annual #1; new Alan Davis-c; multiple printings exist 17.00
V2-Reprints FF #21-40, Annual #2; Davis and Farmer-c 15.00
V3-Reprints FF #41-63, Annual #3,4; Davis-c 15.00
V4-Reprints FF #64-83, Annual #5,6 17.00
V5-Reprints FF #84-110 17.00
V6-Reprints FF #111-137 17.00

--GHOST RIDER, '05 (B&W-r) V1-Reprints Marvel Spotlight #5-12, Ghost Rider #1-20 and Daredevil #138 17.00
V2-Reprints Ghost Rider #21-50 17.00

--GODZILLA, '06 (B&W-r) V1-Godzilla #1-24 20.00

--HOWARD THE DUCK, '02 (B&W- r) V1-Reprints #1-27, Annual #1; plus stories from Marvel Treasury Ed. #12, Man-Thing #1, Giant-Size Man-Thing #4,5, Fear #19; Bolland-c 15.00

--HULK, '99 (B&W-r) V1-R-Incred. Hulk #1-6, Tales To Astonish stories; new Timm-c 15.00
V2-Reprints Tales To Astonish #102-117, Annual #1 15.00
V3-Reprints Incredible Hulk #118-142, Capt. Marvel #20&21, Avengers #88 17.00
V4-Reprints Incredible Hulk #143-170 17.00
V5-Reprints Incredible Hulk #171-200, Annual #5 17.00

--HUMAN TORCH, '03 (B&W-r) V1-Strange Tales #101-134 & Ann. 2; Kirby-c 15.00

--IRON MAN, '00 - Present (B&W-r)
V1-Reprints Tales Of Suspense #39-72; new Timm-c and back-c 15.00
V2-Reprints Tales Of Suspense #73-99, Tales To Astonish #82 & Iron Man #1-11 17.00
V3-Reprints Iron Man #12-38 & Daredevil #73 17.00

--KILLRAVEN, '05 (B&W-r) V1-Reprints Amazing Adventures V2 #18-39, Marvel Team-Up #45, Marvel Graphic Novel #7, Killraven #1 (2001) 17.00

--LUKE CAGE, POWER MAN, '05 (B&W-r) V1-Hero For Hire #1-16 & Power Man #17-27 17.00
V2-Reprints Power Man #28-49 & Annual #1 17.00

--MAN-THING, '06 (B&W-r) V1-Reprints Savage Tales #1, Astonishing Tales #12-13, Adventure Into Fear #10-19, Man-Thing #1-14, Giant-Size Man-Thing #1-2 & Monsters Unleashed #5,8,9 17.00
V2-R/Man-Thing #15-22 & #1-11 ('79 series), Giant-Size Man-Thing #3-5, Rampaging Hulk #7, Marvel Team-Up #68, Marvel Two-In-One #43 & Doctor Strange #41 17.00

--MARVEL HORROR, '06 (B&W-r) V1-R/#Ghost Rider #1-2, Marvel Spotlight #12-24, Son of Satan #1-8, Marvel Two-In-One #14, Marvel Team-Up #32,80,81, Vampire Tales #2-3, Haunt of Horror #2,4,5, Marvel Premiere #27, & Marvel Preview #7 17.00

--MARVEL SAGA, '08 (B&W-r) V1-R/#1-12 17.00

--MARVEL TEAM-UP, '02 - Present (B&W-r) V1('02, '06)-R/#1-24 17.00
V2-R/#25-51 and Marvel Two-In-One #17 17.00

--MARVEL TWO-IN-ONE, '05 - Present (B&W-r)
V1-Reprints Marvel Feature #11&12, Marvel Two-In-One #1-20,22-25 & Annual #1, Marvel Team-Up #47 and Fantastic Four Ann. #11 17.00
V2-R/#26-52 & Annual #2,3 17.00

--MONSTER OF FRANKENSTEIN, '04 (B&W-r) V1-Reprints Monster of Frankenstein #1-5, Frankenstein Monster #6-18, Giant-Size Werewolf #2, Monsters Unleashed #2,4-10 & Legion of Monsters #1 17.00

--MOON KNIGHT, '06 (B&W-r) V1-Reprints Moon Knight #1-10 and early apps. 17.00
V2-R/#11-30 17.00

--MS. MARVEL, '07 (B&W-r) V1-Reprints Ms. Marvel #1-23, Marvel Super-Heroes Magazine #10,11, and Avengers Annual #10 17.00

--NOVA, '06 (B&W-r) V1-Reprints Nova #1-25, AS-M #175, Marvel Two-In-One Ann. #3 17.00

--OFFICIAL HANDBOOK OF THE MARVEL UNIVERSE, '06 (B&W-r) V1-Reprints #1-15 profiling Abomination through Zzzax; dead and inactive characters; weapons & hardware; wraparound-c by Byrne 17.00

--OFFICIAL HANDBOOK OF THE MARVEL UNIVERSE - DELUXE EDITION, '06 (B&W-r)
V1-Reprints #1-7 profiling Abomination through Magneto; wraparound-c by Byrne 17.00
V2-Reprints #8-14 profiling Magus through Wolverine; wraparound-c by Byrne 17.00
V3-Reprints #15-20 profiling Wonder Man through Zzzax & Book of the Dead 17.00

--OFFICIAL HANDBOOK OF THE MARVEL UNIVERSE - MASTER EDITION, '08 (B&W-r)
V1-Reprints profiling Abomination through Gargoyle 17.00
V2-Reprints profiles 17.00

--OFFICIAL HANDBOOK OF THE MARVEL UNIVERSE - UPDATE '89, '06 (B&W-r)
V1-Reprints #1-8; wraparound-c by Frenz 17.00

--PETER PARKER, THE SPECTACULAR SPIDER-MAN, '05 (B&W-r) V1-Reprints #1-31 17.00
V2-Reprints #32-53 & Annual #1,2; Amazing Spider-Man Annual #13 17.00
V3-Reprints #54-74 & Annual #3; Frank Miller-c 17.00

--POWER MAN AND IRON FIST, '07 (B&W-r) V1-R/#50-72,74-75 17.00

--PUNISHER, '04, '06 - Present (B&W-r) V1-Reprints early app. in Amazing Spider-Man, Captain America, Daredevil, Marvel Preview and Punisher #1-5 (2 printings) 17.00
V2-Punisher #1-20, Annual #1 and Daredevil #257 17.00
V3-Punisher #21-40, Annual #2,3 17.00

--RAMPAGING HULK, '08 (B&W-r) V1-R/#1-9, The Hulk! #10-15 & Incredible Hulk #269 17.00

--SAVAGE SHE-HULK, '06 (B&W-r) V1-R/#1-25 17.00

--SILVER SURFER, '98 - Present (B&W-r)
V1-R-material from SS#1-18 and Fantastic Four Ann. #5 15.00
V2-R-SS#1(1982), SS#1-18 & Ann#1(1987), Epic Illustrated #1, Marvel Fanfare #51 17.00

--SPIDER-MAN, '96 - Present (B&W-r)
V1-R-AF #15, Amaz. S-M #1-20, Ann. #1 (2 printings) 15.00
V2-R-Amaz. Spider-Man #21-43, Annual #2,3 15.00
V3-R-Amaz. Spider-Man #44-68 15.00
V4-R-Amaz. Spider-Man #69-89; Annual #4,5; new Timm-f&b-c 15.00
V5-R-Amaz. Spider-Man #90-113; new Romita-c 15.00
V6-R-Amaz. Spider-Man #114-137, Giant-Size Super-Heroes #1 G-S S-M #1,2 17.00
V7-R-Amaz. Spider-Man #138-160, Annual #10; Giant-Size Spider-Man #3-5 17.00
V8-R-Amaz. Spider-Man #161-185, Annual #11; G-S Spider-Man #6; Nova #12 17.00

--SPIDER-WOMAN, '05 (B&W-r) V1-Reprints Marvel Spotlight #32, Marvel Two-In-One #29-33, Spider-Woman #1-25 17.00
V2-R-Spider-Woman #26-50, Marvel Team-Up #97 & Uncanny X-Men #148 17.00

--SUPER-VILLAIN TEAM-UP, '04 (B&W-r) V1-r/S-V T-U #1-14 & 16-17, Giant-Size S-V T-U #1,2; Avengers #154-156; Champions #16, & Astonishing Tales #1-8 17.00

--TALES OF THE ZOMBIE, '06 (B&W-r) V1-($16.99) r/#1-10 & Dracula Lives #1,2 17.00

--THOR, '01 (B&W-r) V1-R-Journey Into Mystery #83-112 15.00
V2-($16.99) R-Thor #113-136 & Annual #1,2 17.00
V3-($16.99) R-Thor #137-166 17.00

--TOMB OF DRACULA, '03 - Present (B&W-r) V1-R-Tomb of Dracula #1-25, Werewolf By Night #15, Giant-Size Chillers #1 15.00
V2-($16.99) R-Tomb of Dracula #26-49, Giant-Size Dracula #2-5, Dr. Strange #14 17.00
V3-($16.99) R-Tomb of Dracula #50-70, Tomb of Dracula Magazine #1-4 17.00
V4-($16.99) R/Stories from Tomb of Dracula Magazine #2-6, Dracula Lives! #1-13, and Frankenstein Monster #7-9 17.00

--UNCANNY X-MEN, '99 - Present (B&W reprints) (See Essential Classic X-Men for V2)
V1-Reprints X-Men (1st series) #1-24; Timm-c 15.00

ESSENTIAL VERTIGO: THE SANDMAN
DC Comics (Vertigo): Aug, 1996 - No. 32, Mar, 1999 ($1.95/$2.25, reprints)
1-13,15-31: Reprints Sandman, 2nd series 3.00
14-($2.95) 3.50
32-($4.50) Reprints Sandman Special #1 4.50

ESSENTIAL VERTIGO: SWAMP THING
DC Comics: Nov, 1996 - No. 24, Oct, 1998 ($1.95/$2.25,B&W, reprints)
1-11,13-24: 1-9-Reprints Alan Moore's Swamp Thing stories 3.00
12-($3.50) r/Annual #2 4.00

The Eternals #17 © MAR

Eternal Warrior #11 © VAL

E.V.E. Protomecha #2 © Lichtner & Lusen

ESSENTIAL WEREWOLF BY NIGHT
Marvel Comics: 2005 - Present (B&W reprints)

V1-($16.99) r/Marvel Spotlight #2-4, Werewolf By Night 1-23, Marvel Team-Up #12, Tomb of Dracula #18, Giant-Size Creatures #1 17.00
V2-R/#22-43, Giant-Size Werewolf #2-5 and Marvel Premiere #28 17.00

ESSENTIAL WOLVERINE
Marvel Comics: 1999 - Present (B&W reprints)

V1-r/#1-23, V2-r/#24-47, V3-R/#48-69, V4-R/#70-90 17.00

ESSENTIAL X-FACTOR
Marvel Comics: 2005 - Present (B&W reprints)

V1-($16.99) r/X-Factor #1-16 & Annual #1, Avengers #262, Fantastic Four #286, Thor #373&374 and Power Pack #27 17.00
V2-Reprints X-Factor #17-35 & Annual #2, Thor #378 17.00

ESSENTIAL X-MEN
Marvel Comics: 1996 - Present (B&W reprints)

V1-V4: V1-R/Giant Size X-Men #1, X-Men #94-119. V2-R-X-Men #120-144. V3-R-Uncanny X-Men #145-161, Ann. #3-5. V4-Uncanny X-Men #162-179, Ann. #6 15.00
V5-($16.99) R/Uncanny X-Men #180-198, Ann. #7-8 17.00
V6-($16.99) R/Uncanny X-Men #199-213, Ann. #9, New Mutants Special Edition #1, X-Factor #9-11, New Mutants #46, Thor #373-374 and Power Pack #27 17.00
V7-($16.99) R/Uncanny X-Men #214-228, Ann. #10,11, and F.F. vs. The X-Men #1-4 17.00
V8-($16.99) R/Uncanny X-Men #229-243, Ann. #12 & X-Factor #36-39 17.00

ESTABLISHMENT, THE (Also see The Authority and The Monarchy)
DC Comics (WildStorm): Nov, 2001 - No. 13, Nov, 2002 ($2.50)

1-13-Edginton-s/Adlard-a 3.00

ETERNAL, THE
Marvel Comics (MAX): Aug, 2003 - No. 6, Jan, 2004 ($2.99, mature)

1-6-Austen-s/Walker-a 3.00

ETERNAL BIBLE, THE
Authentic Publications: 1946 (Large size) (16 pgs. in color)

	GD	VG	FN	VF	VF/NM	NM-
1	15	30	45	86	133	180

ETERNALS, THE
Marvel Comics Group: July, 1976 - No. 19, Jan, 1978

	GD	VG	FN	VF	VF/NM	NM-
1-(Regular 25¢ edition)-Origin & 1st app. Eternals	3	6	9	16	23	30
1-(30¢-c variant, limited distribution)	4	8	12	22	34	45
2-(Reg. 25¢ edition)-1st app. Ajak & The Celestials	2	4	6	9	12	15
2-(30¢-c variant, limited distribution)	2	4	6	13	18	25
3-19: 14,15-Cosmic powered Hulk-c/story	2	4	6	8	10	12
12-16-(35¢-c variants, limited distribution)	2	4	6	10	14	18
Annual 1(10/77)	2	4	6	9	12	15

Eternals by Jack Kirby HC (2006, $75.00, dust jacket) r/#1-19 & Annual #1; intro by Royer; letter pages from #1,2,Annual #1; afterwords by Robert Greenberger 75.00
NOTE: *Kirby c/a(p) in all.*

ETERNALS, THE
Marvel Comics: Oct, 1985 - No. 12, Sept, 1986 (Maxi-series, mando paper)

1,12 (52 pgs.): 12-Williamson-a(i) 4.00
2-11 3.00

ETERNALS
Marvel Comics: Aug, 2006 - No. 7, Mar, 2007 ($3.99, limited series)

1-7-Neil Gaiman-s/John Romita Jr.-a/Rick Berry-c 4.00
1-7-Variant covers by Romita Jr. 4.00
1-Variant cover by Coipel 4.00
... Sketchbook (2006, $1.99, B&W) character sketches and sketch pages from #1 3.00
HC (2007, $29.99, dustjacket) r/#1-7; gallery of variant covers; sketches, Gaiman interview, Gaiman's original proposal; background essay on Kirby's Eternals 30.00

ETERNALS
Marvel Comics: Aug, 2008 - No. 9, May, 2009 ($2.99)

1-9: 1-6-Acuña-a/c; Knauf-s. 2,4-Iron Man app. 7,8-Nguyen-a; X-Men app. 3.00
Annual 1 (1/09, $3.99) Alixe-a/McGuinness-c; & reprint from Eternals #7 ('77) Kirby-s/a 4.00

ETERNALS: THE HEROD FACTOR
Marvel Comics: Nov, 1991 ($2.50, 68 pgs.)

1 4.00

ETERNAL WARRIOR (See Solar #10 & 11)
Valiant/Acclaim Comics (Valiant): Aug, 1992 - No. 50, Mar, 1996 ($2.25/$2.50)

1-Unity x-over; Miller-c; origin Eternal Warrior & Aram (Armstrong) 4.00
1-($2.25-c) Gold logo 5.00
1-Gold foil logo on embossed cover; no cover price 6.00
2-8: 2-Unity x-over; Simonson-c. 3-Archer & Armstrong x-over. 4-1st brief app. Bloodshot (last pg.); see Rai #0 for 1st full app.; Cowan-c. 5-2nd full app. Bloodshot (12/92; see Rai #0). 6,7: 6-2nd app. Master Darque. 8-Flip book w/Archer & Armstrong #8 3.50
9-25,27-34: 9-1st Book of Geomancer. 14-16-Bloodshot app. 18-Doctor Mirage cameo. 19-Doctor Mirage app. 22-W/bound-in trading card. 25-Archer & Armstrong app.; cont'd from A&A #25 3.00
26-($2.75, 44 pgs.)-Flip book w/Archer & Armstrong 4.00
35-50: 35-Double-c; $2.50-c begins. 50-Geomancer app. 3.00
Special 1 (2/96, $2.50)-Wings of Justice; Art Holcomb script 3.00
Yearbook 1 (1993, $3.95), 2(1994, $3.95) 4.00

GD VG FN VF VF/NM NM-
2.0 4.0 6.0 8.0 9.0 9.2

ETERNAL WARRIORS: BLACKWORKS
Acclaim Comics (Valiant Heroes): Mar, 1998 ($3.50, one-shot)

1 3.50

ETERNAL WARRIORS: DIGITAL ALCHEMY
Acclaim Comics (Valiant Heroes): Vol. 2, Sep, 1997 ($3.95, one-shot, 64 pgs.)

Vol. 2-Holcomb-s/Eaglesham-a(p) 4.00

ETERNAL WARRIORS: FIST AND STEEL
Acclaim Comics (Valiant): May, 1996 - No. 2, June, 1996 ($2.50, lim. series)

1,2: Geomancer app. in both. 1-Indicia reads "June." 2-Bo Hampton-a 3.00

ETERNAL WARRIORS: TIME AND TREACHERY
Acclaim Comics (Valiant Heroes): Vol. 1, Jun, 1997 ($3.95, one-shot, 48 pgs.)

Vol. 1-Reintro Aram, Archer, Ivar the Timewalker, & Gilad the Warmaster; 1st app. Shalla Redburn; Art Holcomb script 4.00

ETERNITY SMITH
Renegade Press: Sept, 1986 - No. 5, May, 1987 ($1.25/$1.50, 36 pgs.)

1-5: 1st app. Eternity Smith. 5-Death of Jasmine 3.00

ETERNITY SMITH
Hero Comics: Sept, 1987 - No. 9, 1988 ($1.95)

V2#1-9: 8-Indigo begins 3.00

ETTA KETT
King Features Syndicate/Standard: No. 11, Dec, 1948 - No. 14, Sept, 1949

	GD	VG	FN	VF	VF/NM	NM-
11-Teenage	13	26	39	72	101	130
12-14	9	18	27	52	69	85

EVA: DAUGHTER OF THE DRAGON
Dynamite Entertainment: 2007 ($4.99, one-shot)

1-Two covers by Jo Chen and Edgar Salazar; Jerwa-s/Salazar-a 5.00

EVANGELINE (Also see Primer)
Comico/First Comics V2#1 on/Lodestone Publ.: 1984 - #2, 6/84; V2#1, 5/87 - V2#12, Mar, 1989 (Baxter paper)

1,2, V2#1 (5/87) - 12, Special #1 (1986, $2.00)-Lodestone Publ. 3.00

EVA THE IMP
Red Top Comic/Decker: 1957 - No. 2, Nov, 1957

	GD	VG	FN	VF	VF/NM	NM-
1,2	5	10	14	20	24	28

EVEN MORE FUND COMICS (Benefit book for the Comic Book Legal Defense Fund) (Also see More Fund Comics)
Sky Dog Press: Sept, 2004 ($10.00, B&W, trade paperback)

nn-Anthology of short stories and pin-ups by various; Spider-Man-c by Cho 10.00

E.V.E. PROTOMECHA
Image Comics (Top Cow): Mar, 2000 - No. 6, Sept, 2000 ($2.50)

	GD	VG	FN	VF	VF/NM	NM-
Preview ($5.95) Flip book w/Soul Saga preview	2	4	6	8	10	12

1-6: 1-Covers by Finch, Madureira, Garza. 2-Turner var-c 3.00
1-Another Universe variant-c 5.00
TPB (5/01, $17.95) r/#1-6 plus cover galley and sketch pages 18.00

EVERQUEST: ... (Based on online role-playing game)
DC Comics (WildStorm): 2002 ($5.95, one-shots)

The Ruins of Kunark - Jim Lee & Dan Norton-a; McQuaid & Lee-s; Lee-c 6.00
Transformations - Philip Tan-a; Devin Grayson-s; Portacio-c 6.00

EVERYBODY'S COMICS (See Fox Giants)

EVERYMAN, THE
Marvel Comics (Epic Comics): Nov, 1991 ($4.50, one-shot, 52 pgs.)

	GD	VG	FN	VF	VF/NM	NM-
1-Mike Allred-a	1	2	3	4	5	7

EVERYTHING HAPPENS TO HARVEY
National Periodical Publications: Sept-Oct, 1953 - No. 7, Sept-Oct, 1954

Everything Happens to Harvey #4 © DC

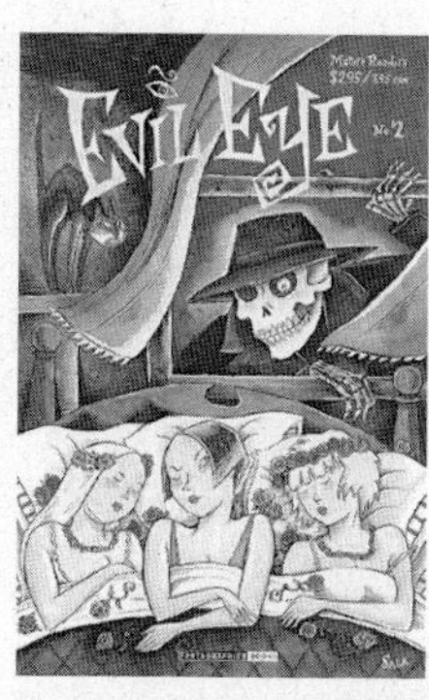

Evil Eye #2 © Richard Sala

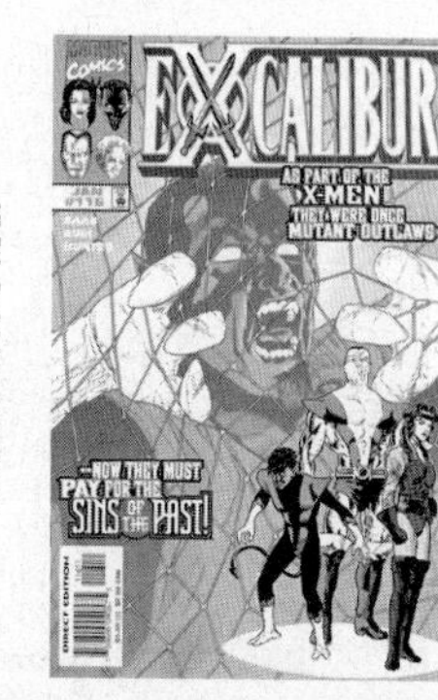

Excalibur #116 © MAR

	GD 2.0	VG 4.0	FN 6.0	VF 8.0	VF/NM 9.0	NM- 9.2
1	30	60	90	177	289	400
2	17	34	51	98	154	210
3-7	15	30	45	83	124	165

EVERYTHING'S ARCHIE
Archie Publications: May, 1969 - No. 157, Sept, 1991 (Giant issues No. 1-20)

	GD	VG	FN	VF	VF/NM	NM-
1-(68 pages)	8	16	24	56	96	135
2-(68 pages)	5	10	15	30	48	65
3-5-(68 pages)	4	8	12	26	41	55
6-13-(68 pages)	3	6	9	18	27	35
14-31-(52 pages)	2	4	6	13	18	22
32 (7/74)-50 (8/76)	2	4	6	8	10	12
51-80 (12/79),100 (4/82)	1	2	3	5	6	8
81-99						6.00
101-120						5.00
121-156: 142,148-Gene Colan-a						4.00
157-Last issue						5.00

EVERYTHING'S DUCKY (Movie)
Dell Publishing Co.: No. 1251, 1961

	GD	VG	FN	VF	VF/NM	NM-
Four Color 1251	5	10	15	30	48	65

EVIL DEAD, THE (Movie)
Dark Horse Comics: Jan, 2008 - No. 4, Apr, 2008 ($2.99, limited series)

	GD	VG	FN	VF	VF/NM	NM-
1-4-Adaptation of the Sam Raimi/Bruce Campbell movie; Bolton painted-a/c						3.00

EVIL ERNIE
Eternity Comics: Dec, 1991 - No. 5, 1992 ($2.50, B&W, limited series)

	GD	VG	FN	VF	VF/NM	NM-
1-1st app. Lady Death by Steven Hughes (12,000 print run); Lady Death app. in all issues	4	8	12	24	37	50
2,3: 2-1st Lady Death-c. 2,3-(7,000 print run)	3	6	9	14	20	25
4-(8,000 print run)	2	4	6	11	16	20
5	2	4	6	9	13	16
Special Edition 1	3	6	9	14	20	25
Youth Gone Wild! ($9.95, trade paperback)-r/#1-5	1	3	4	6	8	10
Youth Gone Wild! Director's Cut ($4.95)-Limited to 15,000, shows the making of the comic						5.00

EVIL ERNIE (Monthly series)
Chaos! Comics: July, 1998 - No. 10, Apr, 1999 ($2.95)

	GD	VG	FN	VF	VF/NM	NM-
1-10-Pulido & Nutman-s/Brewer-a						3.00
1-($10.00) Premium Ed.						10.00
... Baddest Battles (1/97, $1.50) Pin-ups; 2 covers						3.00
... Pieces of Me (11/00, $2.95, B&W) Flashback story; Pulido-s/Beck-a						3.00
... Relentless (5/02, $4.99, B&W) Pulido-s/Beck, Bonk, & Brewer-a						5.00
... Returns (10/01, $3.99, B&W) Pulido-s/Beck-a						4.00

EVIL ERNIE: DEPRAVED
Chaos! Comics: Jul, 1999 - No. 3, Sept, 1999 ($2.95, limited series)

	GD	VG	FN	VF	VF/NM	NM-
1-3-Pulido-s/Brewer-a						3.00

EVIL ERNIE: DESTROYER
Chaos! Comics: Oct, 1997 - No. 9, Jun, 1998 ($2.95, limited series)

	GD	VG	FN	VF	VF/NM	NM-
Preview ($2.50), 1-9-Flip cover						3.00

EVIL ERNIE: IN SANTA FE
Devil's Due Publ.: Sept, 2005 - Mar, 2006 ($2.95, limited series)

	GD	VG	FN	VF	VF/NM	NM-
1-4-Alan Grant-s/Tommy Castillo-a/Alex Horley-c						3.00

EVIL ERNIE: REVENGE
Chaos! Comics: Oct, 1994 - No. 4, Feb, 1995 ($2.95, limited series)

	GD	VG	FN	VF	VF/NM	NM-
1-Glow-in-the-dark-c; Lady Death app. 1-3-flip book w. Kilzone Preview (series of 3)						5.00
1-Commemorative-(4000 print run)	1	3	4	6	8	10
2-4						4.00
Trade paperback (10/95, $12.95)						13.00

EVIL ERNIE: STRAIGHT TO HELL
Chaos! Comics: Oct, 1995 - No. 5, May, 1996 ($2.95, limited series)

	GD	VG	FN	VF	VF/NM	NM-
1-5: 1-fold-out-c						3.00
1,3:1-($19.95) Chromium Ed. 3-Chastity Chase-c-(4000 printed)						20.00
Special Edition (10,000)						20.00

EVIL ERNIE: THE RESURRECTION
Chaos! Comics: 1993 - No. 4, 1994 (Limited series)

	GD	VG	FN	VF	VF/NM	NM-
0						5.00
1	2	4	6	8	10	12
1A-Gold	3	6	9	16	23	30
2-4	1	2	3	5	6	8

EVIL ERNIE VS. THE MOVIE MONSTERS
Chaos! Comics: Mar, 1997 ($2.95, one-shot)

	GD	VG	FN	VF	VF/NM	NM-
1						3.00
1-Variant-"Chaos-Scope•Terror Vision" card stock-c						5.00

EVIL ERNIE VS. THE SUPER HEROES
Chaos! Comics: Aug, 1995; Sept, 1998 ($2.95)

	GD	VG	FN	VF	VF/NM	NM-
1-Lady Death poster						3.00
1-Foil-c variant (limited to 10,000)	2	4	6	11	16	20
1-Limited Edition (1000)	2	4	6	11	16	20
2-(9/98) Ernie vs. JLA and Marvel parodies						3.00

EVIL ERNIE: WAR OF THE DEAD
Chaos! Comics: Nov, 1999 - No. 3, Jan, 2000 ($2.95, limited series)

	GD	VG	FN	VF	VF/NM	NM-
1-3-Pulido & Kaminski-s/Brewer-a. 3-End of Evil Ernie						3.00

EVIL EYE
Fantagraphics Books: June, 1998 - No. 12, Jun, 2004 ($2.95/$3.50/$3.95, B&W)

	GD	VG	FN	VF	VF/NM	NM-
1-7-Richard Sala-s/a						4.00
8-10-($3.50)						4.00
11,12-($3.95)						4.00

EVO (Crossover from Tomb Raider #25 & Witchblade #60)
Image Comics (Top Cow): Feb, 2003 ($2.99, one-shot)

	GD	VG	FN	VF	VF/NM	NM-
1-Silvestri-c/a(p); Endgame x-over pt. 3; Sara Pezzini & Lara Croft app.						3.00

EWOKS (Star Wars) (TV) (See Star Comics Magazine)
Marvel Comics (Star Comics): June, 1985 - No. 14, Jul, 1987 (75¢/$1.00)

	GD	VG	FN	VF	VF/NM	NM-
1,10: 10-Williamson-a (From Star Wars)	2	4	6	9	12	15
2-9	2	4	6	8	10	12
11-14: 14-($1.00-c)	2	4	6	8	11	14

EXCALIBUR (Also see Marvel Comics Presents #31)
Marvel Comics: Apr, 1988; Oct, 1988 - No. 125, Oct, 1998 ($1.50/$1.75/$1.99)

	GD	VG	FN	VF	VF/NM	NM-
Special Edition nn (The Sword is Drawn)(4/88, $3.25)-1st Excalibur comic						6.00
Special Edition nn (4/88)-no price on-c	1	3	4	6	8	10
Special Edition nn (2nd & print, 10/88, 12/89)						3.00
...The Sword is Drawn (Apr, 1992, $4.95)						5.00
1($1.50, 10/88)-X-Men spin-off; Nightcrawler, Shadowcat(Kitty Pryde), Capt. Britain, Phoenix & Meggan begin						6.00
2-4						5.00
5-10						4.00
11-49,51-70,72-74,76: 10,11-Rogers/Austin-a. 21-Intro Crusader X. 22-Iron Man x-over. 24-John Byrne app. in story. 26-Ron Lim-c/a. 27-B. Smith-a(p). 37-Dr. Doom & Iron Man app. 41-X-Men (Wolverine) app.; Cable cameo. 49-Neal Adams c-swipe. 52,57-X-Men (Cyclops, Wolverine) app. 53-Spider-Man-c/story. 58-X-Men (Wolverine, Gambit, Cyclops, etc.)-c/story. 61-Phoenix returns. 68-Starjammers-c/story						3.00
50-($2.75, 56 pgs.)-New logo						4.00
71-($3.95, 52 pgs.)-Hologram on-c; 30th anniversary						5.00
75-($3.50, 52 pgs.)-Holo-grafx foil-c						5.00
75-($2.25, 52 pgs.)-Regular edition						4.00
77-81,83-86: 77-Begin $1.95-c; bound-in trading card sheet. 83-86-Deluxe Editions and Standard Editions. 86-1st app. Pete Wisdom						3.00
82-($2.50)-Newsstand edition						4.00
82-($3.50)-Enhanced edition						5.00
87-89,91-99,101-110: 87-Return from Age of Apocalypse. 92-Colossus-c/app. 94-Days of Future Tense 95-X-Man-c/app. 96-Sebastian Shaw & the Hellfire Club app. 99-Onslaught app. 101-Onslaught tie-in. 102-w/card insert. 103-Last Warren Ellis scripts; Belasco app. 104,105-Hitch & Neary-c/a. 109-Spiral-c/app.						3.00
90,100-($2.95)-double-sized. 100-Onslaught tie-in; wraparound-c						4.00
111-124: 111-Begin $1.99-c, wraparound-c. 119-Calafiore-a						3.00
125-($2.99) Wedding of Capt. Britain and Meggan						4.00
Annual 1,2 ('93, '94, 68 pgs.)-1st app. Khaos. 2-X-Men & Psylocke app.						4.00
#(-1) Flashback (7/97)						3.00
...Air Apparent nn (12/91, $4.95)-Simonson-c						5.00
...Mojo Mayhem nn (12/89, $4.50)-Art Adams/Austin-c/a						5.00
...: The Possession nn (7/91, $2.95, 52 pgs.)						4.00
...: XX Crossing (7/92, 5/92-inside, $2.50)-vs. The X-Men						4.00
...Classic Vol. 1: The Sword is Drawn TPB (2005, $19.99) r/#1-5 & Special Edition nn (The Sword is Drawn)						20.00
...Classic Vol. 2: Two-Edged Sword TPB (2006, $24.99) r/#6-11						25.00
...Classic Vol. 3: Cross-Time Caper Book 1 TPB (2007, $24.99) r/#12-20						25.00
...Classic Vol. 4: Cross-Time Caper Book 2 TPB (2007, $24.99) r/#21-28						25.00
...Classic Vol. 5 TPB (2008, $24.99) r/#29-34 & Marvel GN Excalibur: Weird War III						25.00

EXCALIBUR
Marvel Comics: Feb, 2001 - No. 4, May, 2001 ($2.99)

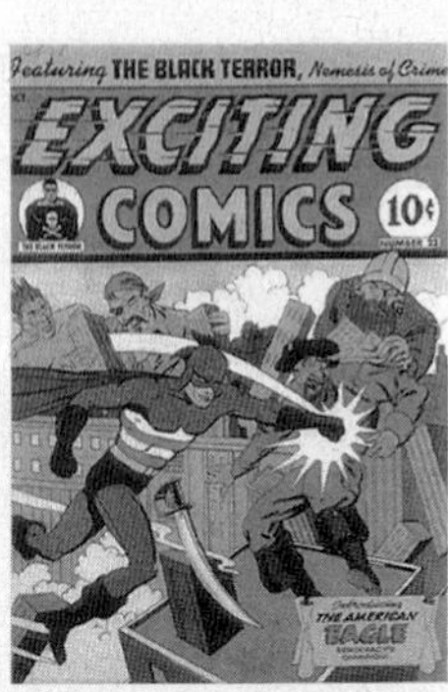

Exciting Comics #22 © STD

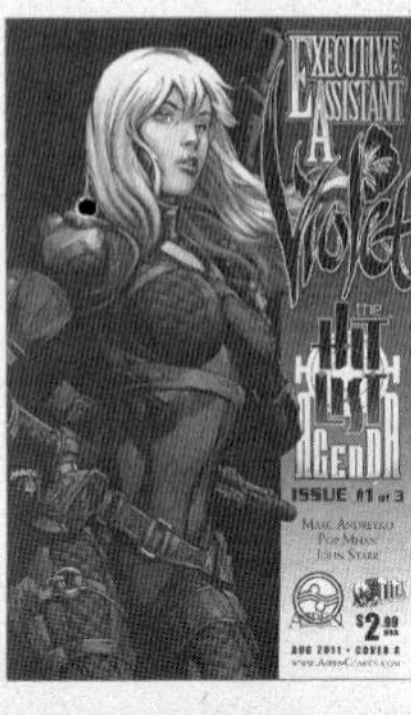

Executive Assistant: Violet #1 © MLT

Exiles #22 © MAR

	GD	VG	FN	VF	VF/NM	NM-
	2.0	4.0	6.0	8.0	9.0	9.2

1-4-Return of Captain Britain; Raimondi-a 3.00

EXCALIBUR (X-Men Reloaded title) (Leads into House of M series, then New Excalibur)
Marvel Comics: July, 2004 - No. 14, July, 2005 ($2.99)

1-14: 1-Claremont-s/Lopresti-a/Park-c; Magneto returns. 6-11-Beast app. 13,14-Prelude to House of M; Dr. Strange app. 3.00
House of M Prelude: Excalibur TPB (2005, $11.99) r/#11-14 12.00
... Vol. 1: Forging the Sword (2004, $9.99) r/#1-4 10.00
... Vol. 2: Saturday Night Fever (2005, $14.99) r/#5-10 15.00

EXCITING COMICS
Nedor/Better Publications/Standard Comics: Apr, 1940 - No. 69, Sept, 1949

1-Origin & 1st app. The Mask, Jim Hatfield, Sgt. Bill King, Dan Williams begin; early Robot-c (see Smash #1) 423 846 1269 3067 5384 7700
2-The Sphinx begins; The Masked Rider app.; Son of the Gods begins, ends #8 194 388 582 1242 2121 3000
3-Robot-c 142 284 426 909 1555 2200
4-6 87 174 261 553 952 1350
7,8 68 136 204 435 743 1050
9-Origin/1st app. of The Black Terror & sidekick Tim, begin series (5/41) (Black Terror c-9-21,23-52,54,55) 1050 2100 3150 7980 14,490 21,000
10-2nd app. Black Terror 320 640 960 2240 3920 5600
11 181 362 543 1158 1979 2800
12,13 123 246 369 787 1344 1900
14-Last Sphinx, Dan Williams 97 194 291 621 1061 1500
15-The Liberator begins (origin) 135 270 405 864 1482 2100
16-20: 20-The Mask ends 71 142 213 454 777 1100
21,23-25: 25-Robot-c 58 116 174 371 636 900
22-Origin The Eaglet; The American Eagle begins 71 142 213 454 777 1100
26-Schomburg-c begin 116 232 348 742 1271 1800
27,29,30 103 206 309 659 1130 1600
28-(Scarce) Crime Crusader begins, ends #58 206 412 618 1318 2259 3200
31-38: 35-Liberator ends, not in 31-33 81 162 243 518 884 1250
39-Nazis giving poison candy to kids on cover; origin Kara, Jungle Princess 194 388 582 1242 2121 3000
40,41-Last WWII covers in this title 77 154 231 493 847 1200
42-50: 42-The Scarab begins. 45-Schomburg Robot-c. 49-Last Kara, Jungle Princess. 50-Last American Eagle 66 132 198 419 722 1025
51-Miss Masque begins (1st app.) 71 142 213 454 777 1100
52-54: Miss Masque ends. 53-Miss Masque-c 58 116 174 371 636 900
55-58: 55-Judy of the Jungle begins (origin), ends #69; 1 pg. Ingels-a; Judy of the Jungle c-56-66. 57,58-Airbrush-c 58 116 174 371 636 900
59-Frazetta art in Caniff style; signed Frank Frazeta (one t), 9 pgs. 60 120 180 381 653 925
60-66: 60-Rick Howard, the Mystery Rider begins. 66-Robinson/Meskin-a 54 108 162 343 574 825
67-69-All western covers 21 42 63 122 199 275

NOTE: ***Schomburg (Xela)*** *c-26-68; airbrush c-57-66. Black Terror by* ***R. Moreira****-#65.* ***Roussos*** *a-62. Bondage-c 9, 12, 13, 20, 23, 25, 30, 59.*

EXCITING ROMANCES
Fawcett Publications: 1949 (nd); No. 2, Spring, 1950 - No. 5, 10/50; No. 6 (1951, nd); No. 7, 9/51 -No. 12, 1/53

1,3: 1(1949). 3-Wood-a 14 28 42 80 115 150
2,4,5-(1950) 10 20 30 54 72 90
6-12 9 18 27 47 61 75

NOTE: ***Powell*** *a-8-10.* ***Marcus Swayze*** *a-5, 6, 9. Photo c-1-7, 10-12.*

EXCITING ROMANCE STORIES (See Fox Giants)

EXCITING WAR (Korean War)
Standard Comics (Better Publ.): No. 5, Sept, 1952 - No. 8, May, 1953; No. 9, Nov, 1953

5 12 24 36 67 94 120
6-Flamethrower/burning body-c 14 28 42 82 121 160
7,9 9 18 27 50 65 80
8-Toth-a 10 20 30 56 76 95

EXCITING X-PATROL
Marvel Comics (Amalgam): June, 1997 ($1.95, one-shot)

1-Barbara Kesel-s/ Bryan Hitch-a 3.00

EXECUTIONER, THE (Don Pendleton's...)
IDW Publishing: Apr, 2008 - No. 5, Aug, 2008 ($3.99)

1-5-Mack Bolan origin re-told; Gallant-a/Wojtowicz-s 4.00

EXECUTIVE ASSISTANT: IRIS
Aspen MLT: No. 0, Apr, 2009 - No. 6, Nov, 2010 ($2.50/$2.99)

0-($2.50) Wohl-s/Francisco-a; 3 covers 3.00
1-6-($2.99) Multiple covers on each 3.00

EXECUTIVE ASSISTANT: IRIS (Volume 2) (The Hit List Agenda x-over)
Aspen MLT: No. 0, Jul, 2011 - No. 5, Dec, 2011 ($2.50/$2.99/$3.50)

0-($2.50) Wohl-s/Francisco-a; sketch page art; 3 covers 3.00
1-4-($2.99) Multiple covers on each. 1-Francisco-a. 2-4-Odagawa-a 3.00
5-($3.50) Odagawa-a 3.50

EXECUTIVE ASSISTANT: LOTUS (The Hit List Agenda x-over)
Aspen MLT: Aug, 2011 - No. 3, Oct, 2011 ($2.99, limited series)

1-3-Multiple covers on each. Hernandez-s/Nome-a 3.00

EXECUTIVE ASSISTANT: ORCHID (The Hit List Agenda x-over)
Aspen MLT: Aug, 2011 - No. 3, Oct, 2011 ($2.99, limited series)

1-3: 1-Lobdell-s/Gunnell-a; multiple covers 3.00

EXECUTIVE ASSISTANT: VIOLET (The Hit List Agenda x-over)
Aspen MLT: Aug, 2011 - No. 3, Oct, 2011 ($2.99, limited series)

1-3: 1-Andreyko-s/Mhan-a; multiple covers 3.00

EXILE ON THE PLANET OF THE APES
BOOM! Studios: Mar, 2012 - No. 4 ($3.99, limited series)

1-Bechko & Hardman-s/Laming-a 4.00

EXILES (Also see Break-Thru)
Malibu Comics (Ultraverse): Aug, 1993 - No. 4, Nov, 1993 ($1.95)

1,2,4: 1,2-Bagged copies of each exist. 4-Team dies; story cont'd in Break-Thru #1 3.00
3-($2.50, 40 pgs.)-Rune flip-c/story by B. Smith (3 pgs.) 4.00
1-Holographic-c edition 1 2 3 5 6 8

EXILES (All New, The) (2nd Series) (Also see Black September)
Malibu Comics (Ultraverse): Sept, 1995 - V2#11, Aug, 1996 ($1.50)

Infinity (9/95, $1.50)-Intro new team including Marvel's Juggernaut & Reaper 3.00
Infinity (2000 signed), V2#1 (2000 signed) 1 3 4 6 8 10
V2 #1-(10/95, 64 pgs.)-Reprint of Ultraforce V2#1 follows lead story 4.00
V2#2-4,6-11: 2-1st app. Hellblade. 8-Intro Maxis. 11-Vs. Maxis; Ripfire app.; cont'd in Ultraforce #12 3.00
V2#5-($2.50) Juggernaut returns to the Marvel Universe. 4.00

EXILES (Also see X-Men titles) (Leads into New Exiles series)
Marvel Comics: Aug, 2001 - No. 100, Feb, 2008 ($2.99/$2.25)

1-($2.99) Blink and parallel world X-Men; Winick-s/McKone & McKenna-a 1 2 3 4 5 7
2-10-($2.25) 2-Two covers (McKone & JH Williams III). 5-Alpha Flight app. 3.50
11-24: 22-Blink leaves; Magik joins. 23,24-Walker-a; alternate Weapon-X app. 3.00
25-99: 25-Begin $2.99-c; Inhumans app.; Walker-a. 26-30-Austen-s. 33-Wolverine app. 35-37-Fantastic Four app. 37-Sunfire dies, Blink returns. 38-40-Hyperion app. 69-71-House of M. 77,78-Squadron Supreme app. 85,86-Multiple Wolverines. 90-Claremont-s begin; Psylocke app. 97-Shadowcat joins 3.00
100-($3.99) Last issue; Blink leaves; continues in Exiles (Days of Then and Now); r/#1 4.00
Annual 1 (2/07, $3.99) Bedard-s/Raney-a/c 4.00
Exiles #1 (Days of Then and Now) (3/08, $3.99) short stories by various 4.00
TPB (3/02, $12.95) r/#1-4 13.00
...: A World Apart TPB (7/02, $14.99) r/#5-11 15.00
...: Vol. 3: Out of Time TPB (2003, $17.99) r/#12-19 18.00
...: Vol. 4: Legacy TPB (2003, $12.99) r/#20-25 13.00
...: Vol. 5: Unnatural Instinct TPB (2003, $14.99) r/#26-30 15.00
...: Vol. 6: Fantastic Voyage TPB (2004, $17.99) r/#31-37 18.00
...: Vol. 7: A Blink in Time TPB (2004, $19.99) r/#38-45 20.00
...: Vol. 8: Earn Your Wings TPB (2004, $14.99) r/#46-51 15.00
...: Vol. 9: Bump in the Night TPB (2005, $17.99) r/#52-58 18.00
...: Vol. 10: Age of Apocalypse TPB ('05, $12.99) r/#59-61 & Official Handbook:AoA 2005 13.00
...: Vol. 11: Time Breakers TPB (2006, $17.99) r/#62-68 18.00
...: Vol. 12: World Tour Book 1 TPB (2006, $16.99) r/#69-74 17.00
...: Vol. 13: World Tour Book 2 TPB (2006, $23.99) r/#75-83 24.00
...: Vol. 14: The New Exiles TPB (2007, $14.99) r/#84-89 and Annual #1 15.00
...: Vol. 15: Enemy of the Stars TPB (2007, $13.99) r/#90-94 14.00
...: Vol. 16: Starting Over TPB (2008, $14.99) r/#95-100 & ...: Days of Then and Now 15.00

EXILES
Marvel Comics: Jun, 2009 - No. 6, Nov, 2009 ($2.99/$3.99)

1,6-($3.99) Blink and parallel world Scarlet Witch, Beast and others; Bullock-c 4.00
2-5-($2.99) 3.00

EXILES VS. THE X-MEN
Malibu Comics (Ultraverse): Oct, 1995 (one-shot)

0-Limited Super Premium Edition; signed w/certificate; gold foil logo,
0-Limited Premium Edition 1 3 4 6 8 10

Ex Machina #42 © Vaughan & Harris

Exposed #9 © DS

Extreme Justice #17 © DC

GD VG FN VF VF/NM NM-
2.0 4.0 6.0 8.0 9.0 9.2

EX MACHINA
DC Comics: Aug, 2004 - No. 50, Sept, 2010 ($2.95/$2.99)
1-Intro. Mitchell Hundred; Vaughan-s/Harris-a/c 4.00
1-Special Edition (6/10, $1.00) Reprints #1 with "What's Next?" logo on cover 3.00
2-49: 12-Intro. Automaton. 33-Mitchell meets the Pope 3.00
50-($4.99) Wraparound-c 5.00
...: The Deluxe Edition Book One HC (2008, $29.99, dustjacket) r/#1-11; Vaughan's original proposal, Harris sketch pages; Brad Meltzer intro. 30.00
...: The Deluxe Edition Book Two HC (2009, $29.99, dustjacket) r/#12-20; Special #1,2; script and pencil art for #20; Wachowski Bros. intro. 30.00
...: The Deluxe Edition Book Three HC (2010, $29.99, dustjacket) r/#21-29; Special #3 and Ex Machina: Inside the Machine 30.00
...: The Deluxe Edition Book Four HC (2010, $29.99, dustjacket) r/#30-40; cover gallery 30.00
...: The Deluxe Edition Book Five HC (2011, $29.99, dustjacket) r/#41-50; Special #4 30.00
...: Inside the Machine (4/07, $2.99) script pages and Harris art and cover process 3.00
...: Masquerade Special (#3) (10/07, $3.50) John Paul Leon-a; Harris-c 3.50
... Special 1,2 (6/06 - No. 2, 8/06, $2.99) Sprouse-a; flashback to the Great Machine 3.00
... Special 4 (5/09, $3.99) Leon-a; Great Machine flashback; covers by Harris & Leon 4.00
...: Dirty Tricks TPB (2009, $12.99) r/#35-39 and Masquerade Special #3 13.00
...: Ex Cathedra TPB (2008, $12.99) r/#30-34 13.00
...: March To War TPB (2006, $12.99) r/#17-20 and Special #1,2 13.00
...: Power Down TPB (2008, $12.99) r/#26-29 & ...: Inside the Machine 13.00
...: Ring Out the Old TPB (2010, $14.99) r/#40-44 and Special #4 15.00
...: Smoke Smoke TPB (2007, $12.99) r/#21-25 13.00
...: The First Hundred Days TPB ('05, $9.95) r/#1-5; photo reference and sketch pages 10.00
...: Tag TPB (2005, $12.99) r/#6-10; Harris sketch pages 13.00
...: Term Limits TPB (2010, $14.99) r/#45-50 15.00

EX-MUTANTS
Malibu Comics: Nov, 1992 - No. 18, Apr, 1994 ($1.95/$2.25/$2.50)
1-18: 1-Polybagged w/Skycap; prismatic cover 3.00

EXORCISTS (See The Crusaders)

EXOSQUAD (TV)
Topps Comics: No. 0, Jan, 1994 ($1.25)
0-($1.00, 20 pgs.)-1st app.; Staton-a(p); wraparound-c 3.00

EXOTIC ROMANCES (Formerly True War Romances)
Quality Comics Group (Comic Magazines): No. 22, Oct, 1955-No. 31, Nov, 1956
22 14 28 42 76 108 140
23-26,29 9 18 27 50 65 80
27,31-Baker-c/a 16 32 48 94 147 200
28,30-Baker-a 14 28 42 78 112 145

EXPENDABLES, THE (Movie)
Dynamite Entertainment: 2010 - No. 4, 2010 ($3.99, limited series)
1-4-Chuck Dixon-s/Esteve Polls-a/Lucio Parrillo-c; prelude to the 2010 movie 4.00

EXPLOITS OF DANIEL BOONE
Quality Comics Group: Nov, 1955 - No. 6, Oct, 1956
1-All have Cuidera-c(i) 20 40 60 114 182 250
2 14 28 42 82 121 160
3-6 13 26 39 74 105 135

EXPLOITS OF DICK TRACY (See Dick Tracy)

EXPLORER JOE
Ziff-Davis Comic Group (Approved Comics): Win, 1951 - No. 2, Oct-Nov, 1952
1-2: Saunders painted covers; 2-Krigstein-a 14 28 42 76 108 140

EXPLORERS OF THE UNKNOWN (See Archie Giant Series #587, 599)
Archie Comics: June, 1990 - No. 6, Apr, 1991 ($1.00)
1-6: Featuring Archie and the gang 3.00

EXPOSED (...True Crime Cases; ...Cases in the Crusade Against Crime #5-9)
D. S. Publishing Co.: Mar-Apr, 1948 - No. 9, July-Aug, 1949
1 26 52 78 154 252 350
2-Giggling killer story with excessive blood; two injury-to-eye panels; electrocution panel 33 66 99 194 317 440
3,8,9 15 30 45 84 127 170
4-Orlando-a 15 30 45 86 133 180
5-Breeze Lawson, Sky Sheriff by E. Good 15 30 45 86 133 180
6,7: 6-Ingels-a; used in **SOTI**, illo. "How to prepare an alibi" 7-Illo. in **SOTI**, "Diagram for housebreakers;" used by N.Y. Legis. Committee 36 72 108 211 343 475

EXTERMINATORS, THE
DC Comics (Vertigo): Mar, 2006 - No. 30, Aug, 2008 ($2.99)

GD VG FN VF VF/NM NM-
2.0 4.0 6.0 8.0 9.0 9.2

1-30: Simon Oliver-s/Tony Moore-a in most. 11,12-Hawthorne-a 3.00
...: Bug Brothers TPB (2006, $9.99) r/#1-5; intro. by screenwriter Josh Olson 10.00
...: Bug Brothers Forever TPB (2008, $14.99) r/#24-30; intro. by Simon Oliver 15.00
...: Crossfire and Collateral TPB (2008, $14.99) r/#17-23 15.00
...: Insurgency TPB (2007, $12.99) r/#6-10 13.00
...: Lies of Our Fathers TPB (2007, $14.99) r/#11-16 15.00

EXTINCT!
New England Comics Press: Wint, 1991-92 - No. 2, Fall, 1992 ($3.50, B&W)
1,2-Reprints and background info of "perfectly awful" Golden Age stories 3.50

EXTINCTION EVENT
DC Comics (WildStorm): Sept, 2003 - No. 5, Jan, 2004 ($2.50, limited series)
1-5-Booth-a/Weinberg-s 3.00

EXTRA!
E. C. Comics: Mar-Apr, 1955 - No. 5, Nov-Dec, 1955
1-Not code approved 20 40 60 160 255 350
2-5 13 26 39 104 165 225
NOTE: *Craig, Crandall, Severin art in all.*

EXTRA!
Gemstone Publishing: Jan, 2000 - No. 5, May, 2000 ($2.50)
1-5-Reprints E.C. series 3.00

EXTRA COMICS
Magazine Enterprises: 1948 (25¢, 3 comics in one)
1-Giant; consisting of rebound ME comics. Two versions known; (1)-Funnyman by Siegel & Shuster, Space Ace, Undercover Girl, Red Fox by L.B. Cole, Trail Colt & (2)-All Funnyman 57 114 171 362 619 875

EXTREME
Image Comics (Extreme Studios): Aug, 1993 (Giveaway)
0 3.00

EXTREME DESTROYER
Image Comics (Extreme Studios): Jan, 1996 ($2.50)
Prologue 1-Polybagged w/card; Liefeld-c, Epilogue 1-Liefeld-c 3.00

EXTREME JUSTICE
DC Comics: No. 0, Jan, 1995 - No. 18, July, 1996 ($1.50/$1.75)
0-18 3.00

EXTREMELY YOUNGBLOOD
Image Comics (Extreme Studios): Sept, 1996 ($3.50, one-shot)
1 3.50

EXTREME SACRIFICE
Image Comics (Extreme Studios): Jan, 1995 ($2.50, limited series)
Prelude (#1)-Liefeld wraparound-c; polybagged w/ trading card 3.00
Epilogue (#2)-Liefeld wraparound-c; polybagged w/trading card 3.00
Trade paperback (6/95, $16.95)-Platt-a 17.00

EXTREME SUPER CHRISTMAS SPECIAL
Image Comics (Extreme Studios): Dec, 1994 ($2.95, one-shot)
1 3.00

EXTREMIST, THE
DC Comics (Vertigo): Sept, 1993 - No. 4, Dec, 1993 ($1.95, limited series)
1-4-Peter Milligan scripts; McKeever-c/a 3.00
1-Platinum Edition 5.00

EYE OF THE STORM
Rival Productions: Dec, 1994 - No. 7, June, 1995? ($2.95)
1-7: Computer generated comic 3.00

EYE OF THE STORM
DC Comics (WildStorm): Sept, 2003 ($4.95)
Annual 1-Short stories by various incl. Portacio, Johns, Coker, Pearson, Arcudi 5.00

FABLES
DC Comics (Vertigo): July, 2002 - Present ($2.50/$2.75/$2.99)
1-Willingham-s/Medina-a; two covers by Maleev & Jean 15.00
1: Special Edition (12/06, 25¢) r/#1 with preview of 1001 Nights of Snowfall 3.00
1: Special Edition (9/09, $1.00) r/#1 with preview of Peter & Max 3.00
1-Special Edition (8/10, $1.00) Reprints #1 with "What's Next?" logo on cover 3.00
2-Medina-a 5.00
3-5 4.00
6-37: 6-10-Buckingham-a. 11-Talbot-a. 18-Medley-a. 26-Preview of The Witching 3.00

Fables #70 © Bill Willingham & DC

Fairest #1 © Bill Willingham & DC

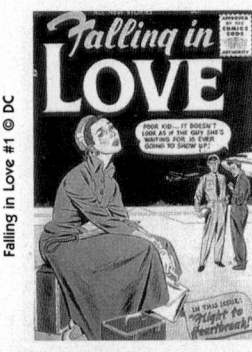

Falling in Love #1 © DC

	GD 2.0	VG 4.0	FN 6.0	VF 8.0	VF/NM 9.0	NM- 9.2

6-RRP Edition wraparound variant-c; promotional giveaway for retailers (200 printed) 50.00
38-49,51-74,76-99,101-115: 38-Begin $2.75-c. 49-Begin $2.99-c. 57,58,76-Allred-a. 83-85-X-over with Jack of Fables & The Literals. 101-Shanower-a. 107-Terry Moore-a 113-Back-up art by Russell, Cannon, Hughes 3.00
50-($3.99) Wedding of Snow White and Bigby Wolf; preview of Jack of Fables series 4.00
75-($4.99) Geppetto surrenders; pin-up gallery by Powell, Nowlan, Cooke & others 5.00
100-(1/11, $9.99, squarebound) Buckingham-a; short stories art by Hughes & others 10.00
Animal Farm (2003, $12.95, TPB) r/#6-10; sketch pages by Buckingham & Jean 13.00
...: Arabian Nights (And Days) (2006, $14.99, TPB) r/#42-47 15.00
...: Homelands (2005, $14.99, TPB) r/#34-41 15.00
Legends in Exile (2002, $9.95, TPB) r/#1-5; new short story Willingham-s/a 10.00
...: March of the Wooden Soldiers (2004, $17.95, TPB) r/#19-21 & ...: The Last Castle 18.00
...: 1001 Nights of Snowfall HC (2006, $19.99) short stories by Willingham with art by various incl. Bolton, Kaluta, Jean, McPherson, Thompson, Vess, Wheatley, Buckingham 20.00
...: 1001 Nights of Snowfall (2008, $14.99, TPB) short stories with art by various 15.00
...: Rose Red (2011, $17.99, TPB) r/#94-100; Buckingham design and sketch pages 18.00
...: Sons of Empire (2007, $17.99, TPB) r/#52-59 18.00
...: Storybook Love (2004, $14.95, TPB) r/#11-18 15.00
...: The Dark Ages (2009, $17.99, TPB) r/#76-82 18.00
...: The Deluxe Edition Book One HC (2009, $29.99, DJ) r/#1-10; character sketch-a 30.00
...: The Deluxe Edition Book Two HC (2010, $29.99, DJ) r/#11-18 & ...: The Last Castle 30.00
...: The Good Prince (2008, $17.99, TPB) r/#60-69 18.00
...: The Great Fables Crossover (2010, $17.99, TPB) r/#83-85, Jack of Fables #33-35 and The Literals #1-3; sneak preview of Peter & Max: A Fables Novel 18.00
...: The Last Castle (2003, $5.95) Hamilton-a/Willingham-s; prequel to title 6.00
...: The Mean Seasons (2005, $14.99, TPB) r/#22,28-33 15.00
...: War and Pieces (2008, $17.99, TPB) r/#70-75; sketch and pin-up pages 18.00
...: Witches (2010, $17.99, TPB) r/#86-93 18.00
...: Wolves (2006, $17.99, TPB) r/#48-51; script to #50 18.00

FACE, THE (Tony Trent, the Face No. 3 on) (See Big Shot Comics)
Columbia Comics Group: 1941 - No. 2, 1943

	GD	VG	FN	VF	VF/NM	NM-
1-The Face; Mart Bailey-c	90	180	270	576	988	1400
2-Bailey-c	51	102	153	321	543	765

FACES OF EVIL
DC Comics: Mar, 2009 ($2.99, series of one-shots)

...: Deathstroke 1 - Jeanty-a/Ladronn-c; Ravager app. 3.00
...: Kobra 1 - Jason Burr returns; Julian Lopez-a 3.00
...: Prometheus 1 - Gates-s/Dallacchio-a; origin re-told; Anima killed 3.00
...: Solomon Grundy 1 - Johns-s/Kolins-a; leads into Solomon Grundy mini-series 3.00

FACTOR X
Marvel Comics: Mar, 1995 - No. 4, July, 1995 ($1.95, limited series)

1-Age of Apocalypse 3.50
2-4 3.00

FACULTY FUNNIES
Archie Comics: June, 1989 - No. 5, May, 1990 (75¢/95¢ #2 on)

1-5: 1,2-The Awesome Four app. 3.00

FADE FROM GRACE
Beckett Comics: Aug, 2004 - No. 5, Mar, 2005 (99¢/$1.99)

1-(99¢) Jeff Amano-a/c; Gabriel Benson-s; origin of Fade 3.00
2-5-($1.99) 3.00
TPB (2005, $14.99) r/#1-5; cover gallery, afterword by David Mack 15.00

FAFHRD AND THE GREY MOUSER (Also see Sword of Sorcery & Wonder Woman #202)
Marvel Comics: Oct, 1990 - No. 4, 1991 ($4.50, 52 pgs., squarebound)

1-4: Mignola/Williamson-a; Chaykin scripts 4.50

FAGIN THE JAW
Doubleday: Oct, 2003 ($15.95, softcover graphic novel)

nn-Will Eisner-s/a; story of Fagin from Dickens' Oliver Twist 16.00

FAIREST (Characters from Fables)
DC Comics (Vertigo): May, 2012 - Present ($2.99)

1,2-Willingham-s/Jimenez-a. 1-Wraparound-c by Hughes and variant-c by Jimenez 3.00

FAIRY TALE PARADE (See Famous Fairy Tales)
Dell Publishing Co.: June-July, 1942 - No. 121, Oct, 1946 (Most by Walt Kelly)

	GD	VG	FN	VF	VF/NM	NM-
1-Kelly-a begins	89	178	267	721	1561	2400
2(8-9/42)	40	80	120	300	650	1000
3-5 (10-11/42 - 2-4/43)	29	58	87	206	446	685
6-9 (5-7/43 - 11-1/43-44)	23	46	69	161	343	525
Four Color 50('44),69('45), 87('45)	22	44	66	154	327	500
Four Color 104,114('46)-Last Kelly issue	17	34	51	114	250	385
Four Color 121('46)-Not by Kelly	11	22	33	76	151	225

*NOTE: #1-9, 4-Color #50, 69 have **Kelly** c/a; 4-Color #87, 104, 114-**Kelly** art only. #9 has a redrawn version of The Reluctant Dragon. This series contains all the classic fairy tales from Jack In The Beanstalk to Cinderella.*

FAIRY TALES
Ziff-Davis Publ. Co. (Approved Comics): No. 10, Apr-May, 1951 - No. 11, June-July, 1951

	GD	VG	FN	VF	VF/NM	NM-
10,11-Painted-c	20	40	60	118	192	265

FAITH
DC Comics (Vertigo): Nov, 1999 - No. 5, Mar, 2000 ($2.50, limited series)

1-5-Ted McKeever-s/c/a 3.00

FAITHFUL
Marvel Comics/Lovers' Magazine: Nov, 1949 - No. 2, Feb, 1950 (52 pgs.)

	GD	VG	FN	VF	VF/NM	NM-
1,2-Photo-c	13	26	39	72	101	130

FAKER
DC Comics (Vertigo): Sept, 2007 - No. 6, Feb, 2008 ($2.99, limited series)

1-6-Mike Carey-s/Jock-a/c 3.00
TPB (2008, $14.99) r/#1-6; Jock sketch pages 15.00

FALCON (See Marvel Premiere #49, Avengers #181 & Captain America #117 & 133)
Marvel Comics Group: Nov, 1983 - No. 4, Feb, 1984 (Mini-series)

1-4: 1-Paul Smith-c/a(p). 2-Paul Smith-c/Mark Bright-a. 3-Kupperberg-c 3.00

FALLEN ANGEL
DC Comics: Sept, 2003 - No. 20, July, 2005 ($2.50/$2.95)

1-9-Peter David-s/David Lopez-a/Stelfreeze-c; intro. Lee 3.00
10-20: 10-Begin $2.95-c. 13,17-Kaluta-c. 20-Last issue; Pérez-c 3.00
TPB (2004, $12.95) r/#1-6; intro. by Harlan Ellison 13.00
Down to Earth TPB (2007, $14.99) r/#7-12 15.00

FALLEN ANGEL
IDW Publ.: Dec, 2005 - No. 33, Dec, 2008 ($3.99)

1-33: 1-14-Peter David-s/J.K Woodward-a. Retailer variant-c for each. 15-Donaldson-a. 17-Flip cover with Shi story; Tucci-a. 25-Wraparound-c; character gallery 4.00
... Reborn 1-4 (7/09 - No. 4, 10/09, $3.99) David-s/Woodward-a; Illyria (from Angel) app. 4.00
... Return of the Son 1-4 (1/11 - No. 4, 4/11, $3.99) David-s/Woodward-a; 4.00
...: To Serve in Heaven TPB (8/06, $19.99) r/#1-5; gallery of reg & variant covers 20.00

FALLEN ANGEL ON THE WORLD OF MAGIC: THE GATHERING
Acclaim (Armada): May, 1996 ($5.95, one-shot)

1-Nancy Collins story 6.00

FALLEN ANGELS
Marvel Comics Group: April, 1987 - No. 8, Nov, 1987 (Limited series)

1-8 3.00

FALLEN SON: THE DEATH OF CAPTAIN AMERICA
Marvel Comics: June, 2007 - No. 5, Aug, 2007 ($2.99, limited series)

1-5: Loeb-s in all. 1-Wolverine; Yu-a/c. 2-Avengers; McGuinness-a/c. 3-Captain America; Romita Jr.-a/c; Hawkeye app. 4-Spider-Man; Finch-c/a. 5-Cassaday-c/a 3.00
1-5-Variant covers by Turner 3.00
HC (2007, $19.99, dustjacket) r/#1-5 20.00
TPB (2008, $13.99) r/#1-5 14.00

FALLING IN LOVE
Arleigh Pub. Co./National Per. Pub.: Sept-Oct, 1955 - No. 143, Oct-Nov, 1973

	GD	VG	FN	VF	VF/NM	NM-
1	40	80	120	246	411	575
2	21	42	63	126	206	285
3-10	15	30	45	83	124	165
11-20	13	26	39	72	101	130
21-40	10	20	30	58	79	100
41-47: 47-Last 10¢ issue	9	18	27	52	69	85
48-70	5	10	15	30	48	65
71-99,108: 108-Wood-a (4 pgs., 7/69)	3	6	9	20	30	40
100	4	8	12	26	41	55
101-107,109-124	3	6	9	16	22	28
134-143	3	6	9	14	19	24
125-133: 52 pgs.	4	8	12	22	34	45

NOTE: Colan c/a-75, 81. 52 pgs.-#125-133.

FALLING MAN, THE
Image Comics: Feb, 1998 ($2.95)

1-McCorkindale-s/Hester-a 3.00

FALL OF THE HOUSE OF USHER, THE (See A Corben Special & Spirit section 8/22/48)

FALL OF THE HULKS (Also see Hulk and Incredible Hulk)
Marvel Comics: Feb, 2010 - July, 2010 ($3.99, one-shots & limited series)

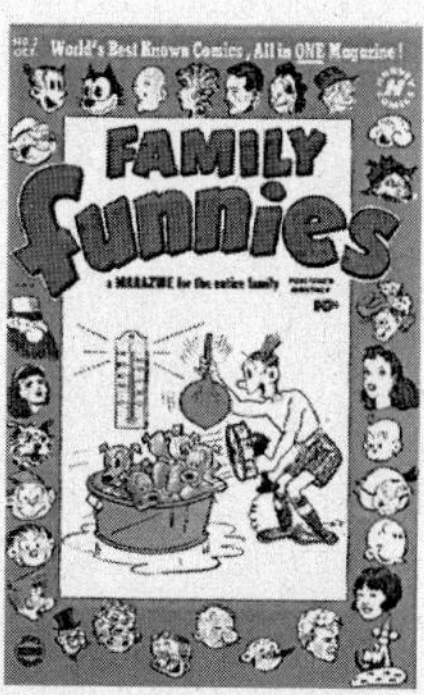

Family Funnies #2 © PMI

Famous First Edition F-4 © DC

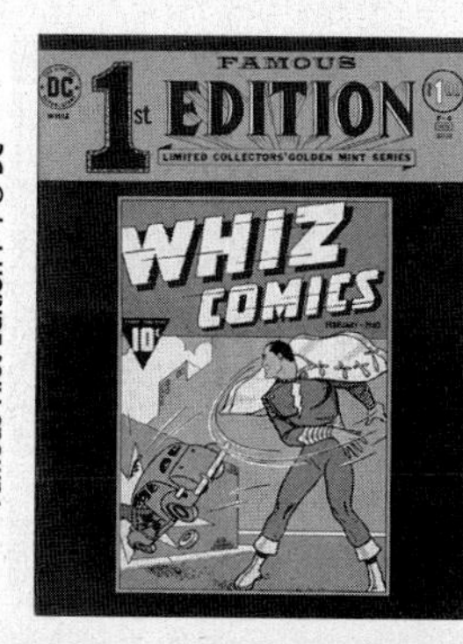

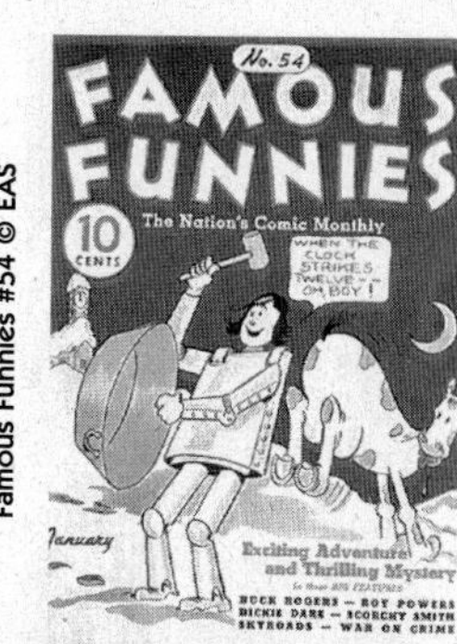

Famous Funnies #54 © EAS

	GD 2.0	VG 4.0	FN 6.0	VF 8.0	VF/NM 9.0	NM- 9.2

Alpha (2/10) Pelletier-a; The Leader, Dr. Doom, MODOK and The Thinker app. 4.00
Gamma (2/10) Romita Jr. -a; funeral for General Ross 4.00
Red Hulk (3/10 - No. 4, 6/10) 1-4: 1-A-Bomb app. 4.00
Savage She-Hulks (5/10 - No. 3, 7/10) 1-3: Cover tryptich by Campbell; Espin-a 4.00

FALL OF THE ROMAN EMPIRE (See Movie Comics)

FALL OUT TOY WORKS
Image Comics: Sept, 2009 - No. 5, Jun, 2010 ($3.99)
1-5-Co-created by Pete Wentz of the band Fall Out Boy; Basri-a. 5-Lau-c 4.00

FAMILY AFFAIR (TV)
Gold Key: Feb, 1970 - No. 4, Oct, 1970 (25¢)
1-With pull-out poster; photo-c 6 12 18 39 62 85
1-With poster missing 3 6 9 18 27 35
2-4-Photo-c 3 6 9 21 32 42

FAMILY DYNAMIC, THE
DC Comics: Oct, 2008 - No. 3, Dec, 2008 ($2.25)
1-3-J. Torres-s/Tim Levins-a 3.00

FAMILY FUNNIES
Parents' Magazine Institute: No. 9, Aug-Sept, 1946
9 6 12 18 28 34 40

FAMILY FUNNIES (Tiny Tot Funnies No. 9)
Harvey Publications: Sept, 1950 - No. 8, Apr, 1951
1-Mandrake (has over 30 King Feature strips) 10 20 30 58 79 100
2-Flash Gordon, 1 pg. 8 16 24 40 50 60
3-8: 4,5,7-Flash Gordon, 1 pg. 6 12 18 31 38 45

FAMILY GUY (TV)
Devil's Due Publ.: 2006 ($6.95)
nn-101 Ways to Kill Lois; 2-Peter Griffin's Guide to Parenting; 3-Books Don't Taste Very Good 7.00
... A Big Book o' Crap TPB (10/06, $16.95) r/nn,2,3 17.00

FAMILY MATTER
Kitchen Sink Press: 1998 ($24.95/$15.95, graphic novel)
Hardcover ($24.95) Will Eisner-s/a 25.00
Softcover ($15.95) 16.00

FAMOUS AUTHORS ILLUSTRATED (See Stories by...)

FAMOUS CRIMES
Fox Features Syndicate/M.S. Dist. No. 51,52: June, 1948 - No. 19, Sept, 1950; No. 20, Aug, 1951; No. 51, 52, 1953
1-Blue Beetle app. & crime story-r/Phantom Lady #16
54 108 162 343 574 825
2-Has woman dissolved in acid; lingerie-c/panels 42 84 126 268 452 635
3-Injury-to-eye story used in **SOTI**, pg. 112; has two electrocution stories
52 104 156 328 557 785
4-6 25 50 75 150 245 340
7- "Tarzan, the Wyoming Killer" (**SOTI**, pg. 44) 41 82 123 260 435 610
8-20: 17-Morisi-a. 20-Same cover as #15 20 40 60 114 182 250
51 (nd, 1953) 16 32 48 94 147 200
52 (Exist?) 16 32 48 94 147 200

FAMOUS FEATURE STORIES
Dell Publishing Co.: 1938 (7-1/2x11", 68 pgs.)
1-Tarzan, Terry & the Pirates, King of the Royal Mtd., Buck Jones, Dick Tracy, Smilin' Jack, Dan Dunn, Don Winslow, G-Man, Tailspin Tommy, Mutt & Jeff, Little Orphan Annie reprints - all illustrated text 63 126 189 400 688 975

FAMOUS FIRST EDITION (See Limited Collectors' Edition)
National Periodical Publications/DC Comics: ($1.00, 10x13-1/2", 72 pgs.) (No.6-8, 68 pgs.) 1974 - No. 8, Aug-Sept, 1975; C-61, 1979
(Hardbound editions with dust jackets are from Lyle Stuart, Inc.)
C-26-Action Comics #1; gold ink outer-c 6 12 18 41 66 90
C-26-Hardbound edition w/dust jacket 15 30 45 104 227 350
C-28-Detective #27; silver ink outer-c 6 12 18 41 66 90
C-28-Hardbound edition w/dust jacket 15 30 45 104 227 350
C-30-Sensation #1(1974); bronze ink outer-c 5 10 15 30 48 65
C-30-Hardbound edition w/dust jacket 13 26 39 88 189 290
F-4-Whiz Comics #2(#1)(10-11/74)-Cover not identical to original (dropped "Gangway for Captain Marvel" from cover); gold ink on outer-c 5 10 15 30 48 65
F-4-Hardbound edition w/dust jacket 13 26 39 88 189 290
F-5-Batman #1(F-6 inside); silver ink on outer-c 5 10 15 34 55 75
F-5-Hardbound edition w/dust jacket 13 26 39 88 189 290
V2#F-6-Wonder Woman #1 5 10 15 30 48 65
F-6-Wonder Woman #1 Hardbound w/dust jacket 13 26 39 88 189 290
F-7-All-Star Comics #3 5 10 15 30 48 65
F-8-Flash Comics #1(8-9/75) 5 10 15 30 48 65
V8#C-61-Superman #1(1979, $2.00) 4 8 12 26 41 55
V8#C-61 (Whitman variant) 4 8 12 28 44 60
V8#C-61 (SC in slipcase, edition of 250 copies) Each signed by Jerry Siegel and Joe Shuster 550.00

Warning: The above books are almost **exact** reprints of the originals that they represent except for the Giant-Size format. None of the originals are Giant-Size. The first five issues and C-61 were printed with two covers. Reprint information can be found on the outside cover, but not on the inside cover which was reprinted exactly like the original (inside and out).

FAMOUS FUNNIES
Eastern Color: 1934; July, 1934 - No. 218, July, 1955

A Carnival of Comics (See Promotional Comics section)
Series 1-(Very rare)(nd-early 1934)(68 pgs.) No publisher given (Eastern Color PrintingCo.); sold in chain stores for 10¢. 35,000 print run. Contains Sunday strip reprints of Mutt & Jeff, Reg'lar Fellers, Nipper, Hairbreadth Harry, Strange As It Seems, Joe Palooka, Dixie Dugan, The Nebbs, Keeping Up With the Jones, and others. Inside front and back covers and pages 1-16 of Famous Funnies Series 1, #s 49-64 reprinted from **Famous Funnies, A Carnival of Comics**, and most of pages 17-48 reprinted from **Funnies on Parade**.
4267 8534 12,800 32,000 - -
No. 1 (Rare)(7/34-on stands 5/34) - Eastern Color Printing Co. First monthly newsstand comic book. Contains Sunday strip reprints of Toonerville Folks, Mutt & Jeff, Hairbreadth Harry, S'Matter Pop, Nipper, Dixie Dugan, The Bungle Family, Connie, Ben Webster, Tailspin Tommy, The Nebbs, Joe Palooka, & others.
3200 6400 9600 24,000 - -
2 (Rare, 9/34) 720 1440 2160 5400 - -
3-Buck Rogers Sunday strip-r by Rick Yager begins, ends #218; not in #191-208; 1st comic book app. of Buck Rogers; the number of the 1st strip reprinted is pg. 190, Series No. 1
907 1814 2721 6800 - -
4 293 586 879 2200 - -
5-1st Christmas-c on a newsstand comic 320 640 960 2400 - -
6-10 193 386 579 1450 - -
11,12,18-Four pgs. of Buck Rogers in each issue, completes stories in Buck Rogers #1 which lacks these pages. 18-Two pgs. of Buck Rogers reprinted in Daisy Comics #1
102 204 306 612 1031 1450
13-17,19,20: 14-Has two Buck Rogers panels missing. 17-2nd Christmas-c on a newsstand comic (12/35) 79 158 237 474 812 1150
21,23-30: 27-(10/36)-War on Crime begins (4 pgs.); 1st true crime in comics (reprints); part photo-c. 29-X-Mas-c (12/36) 60 120 180 360 618 875
22-Four pgs. of Buck Rogers needed to complete stories in Buck Rogers #1
63 126 189 378 639 900
31,33,34,36,37,39,40: 33-Careers of Baby Face Nelson & John Dillinger traced
42 84 126 252 439 625
32-(3/37) 1st app. the Phantom Magician (costume hero) in Advs. of Patsy
46 92 138 276 479 675
35-Two pgs. Buck Rogers omitted in Buck Rogers #2
46 92 138 276 479 675
38-Full color portrait of Buck Rogers 44 88 132 264 457 650
41-60: 41,53-X-Mas-c. 55-Last bottom panel, pg. 4 in Buck Rogers redrawn in Buck Rogers #3 32 64 96 192 314 435
61,63,64,66,67,69,70 25 50 75 147 241 335
62,65,68,73-78-Two pgs. Kirby-a "Lightnin' & the Lone Rider". 65,77-X-Mas-c
27 54 81 158 259 360
71,79,80: 80-(3/41)-Buck Rogers story continues from Buck Rogers #5
20 40 60 117 189 260
72-Speed Spaulding begins by Marvin Bradley (artist), ends #88. This series was written by Edwin Balmer & Philip Wylie (later appeared as film & book "When Worlds Collide")
22 44 66 130 213 295
81-Origin & 1st app. Invisible Scarlet O'Neil (4/41); strip begins #82, ends #167; 1st non-funny-c (Scarlet O'Neil) 23 46 69 136 223 310
82-Buck Rogers-c 25 50 75 150 245 340
83-87,90: 86-Connie vs. Monsters on the Moon-c (sci/fi). 87 has last Buck Rogers full page-r. 90-Bondage-c 19 38 57 109 172 235
88,89: 88-Buck Rogers in "Moon's End" by Calkins, 2 pgs.(not reprints). Beginning with #88, all Buck Rogers pgs. have rearranged panels. 89-Origin & 1st app. Fearless Flint, the Flint Man 19 38 57 112 179 245
91-93,95,96,98-99,101,103-110: 105-Series 2 begins (Strip Page #1)
15 30 45 90 140 190
94-Buck Rogers in "Solar Holocaust" by Calkins, 3 pgs.(not reprints)
17 34 51 98 154 210
97-War Bond promotion, Buck Rogers by Calkins, 2 pgs.(not reprints)
17 34 51 98 154 210
100-1st comic to reach #100; 100th Anniversary cover features 11 major Famous Funnies characters, including Buck Rogers 21 42 63 122 199 275
102-Chief Wahoo vs. Hitler,Tojo & Mussolini-c (1/43) 74 148 222 470 810 1150

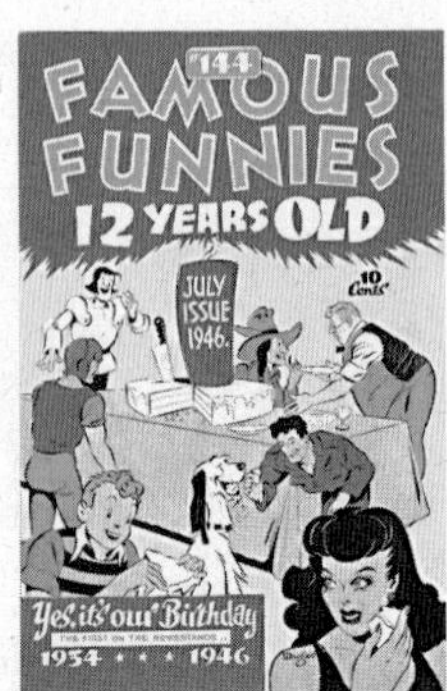

Famous Funnies #144 © EAS

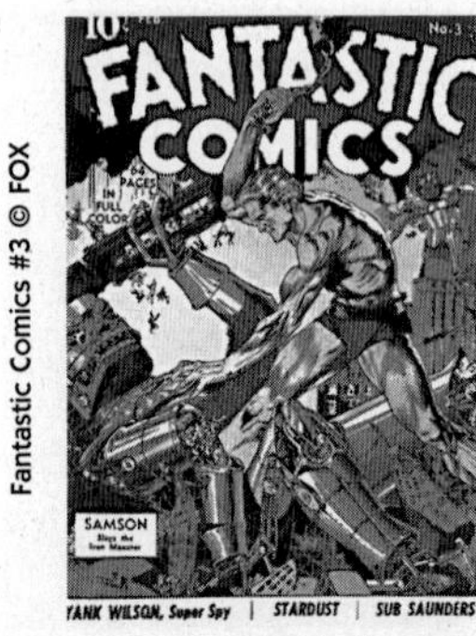

Fantastic Comics #3 © FOX

Fantastic Fears #8 © AJAX

	GD 2.0	VG 4.0	FN 6.0	VF 8.0	VF/NM 9.0	NM- 9.2

111-130 (5/45): 113-X-Mas-c 13 26 39 72 101 130
131-150 (1/47): 137-Strip page No. 110 omitted. 144-(7/46) 12th Anniversary cover 11 22 33 64 90 115
151-162,164-168 11 22 33 60 83 105
163-St. Valentine's Day-c 11 22 33 62 86 110
169,170-Two text illos. by Al Williamson, his 1st comic book work 14 28 42 76 108 140
171-190: 171-Strip pgs. 227,229,230, Series 2 omitted. 172-Strip Pg. 232 omitted. 190-Buck Rogers ends with start of strip pg. 302, Series 2; Oaky Doaks-c/story 10 20 30 56 76 95
191-197,199,201,203,206-208: No Buck Rogers. 191-Barney Carr, Space detective begins, ends #192. 10 20 30 54 72 90
198,200,202,205-One pg. Frazetta ads; no B. Rogers 10 20 30 56 76 95
204-Used in **POP**, pg. 79,99; war-c begin, end #208 10 20 30 58 79 100
209-216: Frazetta-c. 209-Buck Rogers begins (12/53) with strip pg. 480, Series 2; 211-Buck Rogers ads by Anderson begins, ends #217. #215-Contains B. Rogers strip pg. 515-518, series 2 followed by pgs.179-181, Series 3 129 258 387 826 1413 2000
217,218-B. Rogers ends with pg. 199, Series 3. 218-Wee Three-c/story 10 20 30 56 76 95

NOTE: ***Rick Yager*** *did the Buck Rogers Sunday strips reprinted in Famous Funnies. The Sundays were formerly done by Russ Keaton and Lt. Dick Calkins did the dailies, but would sometimes assist Yager on a panel or two from time to time. Strip No. 169 is Yager's first full Buck Rogers page. Yager did the strip until 1958 when* ***Murphy Anderson*** *took over.* ***Tuska*** *art from 4/26/59 - 1965. Virtually every panel was rewritten for Famous Funnies. Not identical to the original Sunday page. The Buck Rogers reprints run continuously through Famous Funnies issue No. 190 (Strip No. 302) with no break in story line. The story line has no continuity after No. 190. The Buck Rogers newspaper strips came out in four series: Series 1, 3/30/30 - 9/21/41 (No. 1 - 600); Series 2, 9/28/41 -10/21/51 (No. 1 -525)(Strip No. 110-1/2 (1/2 pg.) published in only a few newspapers); Series 3, 10/28/51 -2/9/58 (No. 100-428)(No No.1-99); Series 4, 2/16/58 - 6/13/65 (No numbers, dates only).* ***Everett*** *c-85, 86.* ***Moulton*** *a-100. Chief Wahoo c-93, 97, 102, 116, 136, 139, 151. Dickie Dare c-83, 88. Fearless Flint c-89. Invisible Scarlet O'Neil c-81, 87, 95, 121(part), 132. Scorchy Smith c-84, 90.*

FAMOUS FUNNIES
Super Comics: 1964

Super Reprint Nos. 15-18:17-r/Double Trouble #1. 18-Space Comics #? 2 4 6 9 12 15

FAMOUS GANGSTERS (Crime on the Waterfront No. 4)
Avon Periodicals/Realistic No. 3: Apr, 1951 - No. 3, Feb, 1952

1-3: 1-Capone, Dillinger; c-/Avon paperback #329. 2-Dillinger Machine Gun Killer; Wood-c/a (1 pg.); r/Saint #7 & retitled "Mike Strong". 3-Lucky Luciano & Murder, Inc; c-/Avon paperback #66 37 74 111 218 354 490

FAMOUS INDIAN TRIBES
Dell Publishing Co.: July-Sept, 1962; No. 2, July, 1972

12-264-209(#1) (The Sioux) 3 6 9 15 21 26
2(7/72)-Reprints above 1 3 4 6 8 10

FAMOUS STARS
Ziff-Davis Publ. Co.: Nov-Dec, 1950 - No. 6, Spring, 1952 (All have photo-c)

1-Shelley Winters, Susan Peters, Ava Gardner, Shirley Temple; Jimmy Stewart & Shelley Winters photo-c; Whitney-a 38 76 114 228 369 510
2-Betty Hutton, Bing Crosby, Colleen Townsend, Gloria Swanson; Betty Hutton photo-c; Everett-a(2) 24 48 72 142 234 325
3-Farley Granger, Judy Garland's ordeal (life story; she died 6/22/69 at the age of 47), Alan Ladd; Farley Granger photo-c; Whitney-a 31 62 93 182 296 410
4-Al Jolson, Bob Mitchum, Ella Raines, Richard Conte, Vic Damone; Jane Russell and Bob Mitchum photo-c; Crandall-a, 6pgs. 21 42 63 126 206 285
5-Liz Taylor, Betty Grable, Esther Williams, George Brent, Mario Lanza; Liz Taylor photo-c; Krigstein-a 47 94 141 296 498 700
6-Gene Kelly, Hedy Lamarr, June Allyson, William Boyd, Janet Leigh, Gary Cooper; Gene Kelly photo-c 20 40 60 114 182 250

FAMOUS STORIES (...Book No. 2)
Dell Publishing Co.: 1942 - No. 2, 1942

1,2: 1-Treasure Island. 2-Tom Sawyer 30 60 90 177 289 400

FAMOUS TV FUNDAY FUNNIES
Harvey Publications: Sept, 1961 (25¢ Giant)

1-Casper the Ghost, Baby Huey, Little Audrey 6 12 18 39 62 85

FAMOUS WESTERN BADMEN (Formerly Redskin)
Youthful Magazines: No. 13, Dec, 1952 - No. 15, Apr, 1953

13-Redskin story 14 28 42 82 121 160
14,15: 15-The Dalton Boys story 11 22 33 60 83 105

FAN BOY
DC Comics: Mar, 1999 - No. 6, Aug, 1999 ($2.50, limited series)

1-6: 1-Art by Aragonés and various in all. 2-Green Lantern-c/a by Gil Kane. 3-JLA. 4-Sgt. Rock art by Heath, Marie Severin. 5-Batman art by Sprang, Adams, Miller, Timm.
6-Wonder Woman; art by Rude, Grell 3.00
TPB (2001, $12.95) r/#1-6 13.00

FANTASTIC (Formerly Captain Science; Beware No. 10 on)
Youthful Magazines: No. 8, Feb, 1952 - No. 9, Apr, 1952

8-Capt. Science by Harrison 44 88 132 277 469 660
9-Harrison-a; decapitation, shrunken head panels 36 72 108 216 351 485

FANTASTIC ADVENTURES
Super Comics: 1963 - 1964 (Reprints)

9,10,12,15,16,18: 9-r/? 10-r/He-Man #2(Toby). 11-Disbrow-a. 12-Unpublished Chesler material? 15-r/Spook #23. 16-r/Dark Shadows #2(Steinway); Briefer-a.18-r/Superior Stories #1 3 6 9 18 27 35
11-Wood-a; r/Blue Bolt #118 4 8 12 24 37 50
17-Baker-a(2) r/Seven Seas #6 4 8 12 24 37 50

FANTASTIC COMICS
Fox Features Syndicate: Dec, 1939 - No. 23, Nov, 1941

1-Intro/origin Samson; Stardust, The Super Wizard, Sub Saunders (by Kiefer), Space Smith, Capt. Kidd begin 503 1006 1509 3672 6486 9300
2-Powell text illos 271 542 813 1734 2967 4200
3-Classic Lou Fine Robot-c; Powell text illos 1650 3300 4950 8250 12,375 16,500
4-Lou Fine-c 239 478 717 1530 2615 3700
5-Classic Lou Fine-c 271 542 813 1734 2967 4200
6,7-Simon-c 168 336 504 1075 1838 2600
8-10: 10-Intro/origin David, Samson's aide 103 206 309 659 1130 1600
11-17,19,20: 16-Stardust ends 82 164 246 528 902 1275
18,23: 18-1st app. Black Fury & sidekick Chuck; ends #23. 23-Origin The Gladiator 84 168 252 538 919 1300
21-The Banshee begins(origin); ends #23; Hitler-c 107 214 321 680 1165 1650
22-Hitler-c (likeness of Hitler as furnace on cover) 116 232 348 742 1271 1800

NOTE: ***Lou Fine*** *c-1-5.* ***Tuska*** *a-3-5, 8. Bondage c-6, 8, 9. Issue #11 has indicia to Mystery Men Comics #15. All issues feature Samson covers.*

FANTASTIC COMICS (Imagining of a 1941 issue by modern creators in Golden Age style)
Image Comics: No. 24, Jan, 2008 ($5.99, Golden Age sized, one-shot)

24-Samson, Yank Wilson, Stardust, Sub Saunders, Space Smith, Capt. Kidd app.; Larsen-c/a; art by Allred, Sienkiewicz, Yeates, Scioli, Hembeck, Ashley Wood & others 6.00

FANTASTIC COMICS (Fantastic Fears #1-9; Becomes Samson #12)
Ajax/Farrell Publ.: No. 10, Nov-Dec, 1954 - No. 11, Jan-Feb, 1955

10 (#1) 22 44 66 128 209 290
11-Robot-c 27 54 81 160 263 365

FANTASTIC FABLES
Silverwolf Comics: Feb, 1987 - No. 2, 1987 ($1.50, 28 pgs., B&W)

1,2: 1-Tim Vigil-a (6 pgs.). 2-Tim Vigil-a (7 pgs.) 4.00

FANTASTIC FEARS (Formerly Captain Jet) (Fantastic Comics #10 on)
Ajax/Farrell Publ.: No. 7, May, 1953 - No. 9, Sept-Oct, 1954

7(#1, 5/53)-Tales of Stalking Terror 52 104 156 327 556 785
8(#2, 7/53) 39 78 117 234 385 535
3,4 31 62 93 182 296 410
5-(1-2/54)-Ditko story (1st drawn) is written by Bruce Hamilton; r-in Weird V2#8 (1st pro work for Ditko but Daring Love #1 was published 1st) 116 232 348 742 1271 1800
6-Decapitation-girl's head w/paper cutter (classic) 71 142 213 454 777 1100
7(5-6/54), 9(9-10/54) 31 62 93 182 296 410
8(7-8/54)-Contains story intended for Jo-Jo; name changed to Kaza; decapitation story 31 62 93 186 303 420

FANTASTIC FIVE
Marvel Comics: Oct, 1999 - No. 5, Feb, 2000 ($1.99)

1-5: 1-M2 Universe; recaps origin; Ryan-a. 2-Two covers 3.00
Spider-Girl Presents Fantastic Five: In Search of Doom (2006, $7.99, digest) r/#1-5 8.00

FANTASTIC FIVE
Marvel Comics: Sept, 2007 - No. 5, Nov, 2007 ($2.99, limited series)

1-5-DeFalco-s/Lim-a; Dr. Doom returns vs. the future Fantastic Five 3.00
...: The Final Doom TPB (2007, $13.99) r/#1-5; cover sketches with inks 14.00

FANTASTIC FORCE
Marvel Comics: Nov, 1994 - No. 18, Apr, 1996 ($1.75)

1-($2.50)-Foil wraparound-c; intro Fantastic Force w/Huntara, Delvor, Psi-Lord & Vibraxas 4.00
2-18: 13-She-Hulk app. 3.00

FANTASTIC FORCE (See Fantastic Four #558, Nu-World heroes from 500 years in the future)
Marvel Comics: Jun, 2009 - No. 4, Sept, 2009 ($3.99/$2.99, limited series)

1-($3.99)-Ahearne-s/Kurth-a/Hitch-c; Fantastic Four app. 4.00

Fantastic Four #6 © MAR

Fantastic Four #221 © MAR

Fantastic Four #360 © MAR

	GD 2.0	VG 4.0	FN 6.0	VF 8.0	VF/NM 9.0	NM- 9.2
2-4-($2.99) 3,4-Ego the Living Planet app.						3.00

FANTASTIC FOUR (See America's Best TV..., Fireside Book Series, Giant-Size..., Giant Size Super-Stars, Marvel Age..., Marvel Collectors Item Classics, Marvel Knights 4, Marvel Milestone Edition, Marvel's Greatest, Marvel Treasury Edition, Marvel Triple Action, Official Marvel Index to..., Power Record Comics & Ultimate...)

FANTASTIC FOUR
Marvel Comics Group: Nov, 1961 - No. 416, Sept, 1996 (Created by Stan Lee & Jack Kirby)

	GD 2.0	VG 4.0	FN 6.0	VF 8.0	VF/NM 9.0	NM- 9.2
1-Origin & 1st app. The Fantastic Four (Reed Richards: Mr. Fantastic, Johnny Storm: The Human Torch, Sue Storm: The Invisible Girl, & Ben Grimm: The Thing–Marvel's 1st super-hero group since the G.A.; 1st app. S.A. Human Torch); origin/1st app. The Mole Man.	2000	4000	7500	26,000	58,000	90,000
1-Golden Record Comic Set Reprint (1966)-cover not identical to original	20	40	60	137	294	450
with Golden Record	28	56	84	203	439	675
2-Vs. The Skrulls (last 10¢ issue)	410	820	1230	3700	7850	12,000
3-Fantastic Four don costumes & establish Headquarters; brief 1pg. origin; intro. The Fantasti-Car; Human Torch drawn w/two left hands on-c	345	690	1035	3000	6500	10,000
4-1st S. A. Sub-Mariner app. (5/62)	357	714	1071	3213	7357	11,500
5-Origin & 1st app. Doctor Doom	520	1040	1820	5500	11,000	16,000
6-Sub-Mariner, Dr. Doom team up; 1st Marvel villain team-up (2nd S.A. Sub-Mariner app.	214	428	642	1800	3900	6000
7-10: 7-1st app. Kurrgo. 8-1st app. Puppet-Master & Alicia Masters. 9-3rd Sub-Mariner app. 10-Stan Lee & Jack Kirby app. in story	141	282	423	1142	2471	3800
11-Origin/1st app. The Impossible Man (2/63)	137	274	411	1110	2405	3700
12-Fantastic Four vs. The Hulk (1st meeting); 1st Hulk x-over & ties w/Amazing Spider-Man #1 as 1st Marvel x-over; (3/63)	357	714	1071	3213	7107	11,000
13-Intro. The Watcher; 1st app. The Red Ghost	93	186	279	753	1627	2500
14,15,17,19: 14-Sub-Mariner x-over. 15-1st app. Mad Thinker. 19-Intro. Rama-Tut; Stan Lee & Jack Kirby cameo	52	104	156	421	911	1400
16-1st Ant-Man x-over (7/63); Wasp cameo	75	150	225	608	1204	1800
18-Origin/1st app. The Super Skrull	80	160	240	648	1274	1900
20-Origin/1st app. The Molecule Man	56	112	168	454	977	1500
21-Intro. The Hate Monger; 1st Sgt. Fury x-over (12/63)	46	92	138	359	780	1200
22-24: 22-Sue Storm gains more powers	33	66	99	239	520	800
25,26-The Hulk vs. The Thing (their 1st battle). 25-3rd Avengers x-over (1st time w/Captain America)(cameo, 4/64); 2nd S.A. app. Cap (takes place between Avengers #4 & 5.) 26-4th Avengers x-over	61	122	183	494	1072	1650
27-1st Doctor Strange x-over (6/64)	37	74	111	278	602	925
28-Early X-Men x-over (7/64); same date as X-Men #6	46	92	138	373	812	1250
29,30: 30-Intro. Diablo	27	54	81	189	407	625
31-40: 31-Early Avengers x-over (10/64). 33-1st app. Attuma; part photo-c. 35-Intro/1st app. Dragon Man. 36-Intro/1st app. Madam Medusa & the Frightful Four (Sandman, Wizard, Paste Pot Pete). 39-Wood inks on Daredevil (early x-over)	21	42	63	148	317	485
41-44,47: 41-43-Frightful Four app. 44-Intro. Gorgon	13	26	39	90	195	300
45-Intro/1st app. The Inhumans (c/story, 12/65); also see Incredible Hulk Special #1 & Thor #146, & 147	25	50	75	175	375	575
46-1st Black Bolt-c (Kirby) & 1st full app.	15	30	45	104	227	350
48-Partial origin/1st app. The Silver Surfer & Galactus (3/66) by Lee & Kirby; Galactus brief app. in last panel; 1st of 3 part story	56	112	168	454	977	1500
49-2nd app./1st cover Silver Surfer & Galactus	37	74	111	278	602	925
50-Silver Surfer battles Galactus; full S.S.-c	41	82	123	308	667	1025
51-Classic "This Man...This Monster" story	19	38	57	128	277	425
52-1st app. The Black Panther (7/66)	29	58	87	210	455	700
53-Origin & 2nd app. The Black Panther	16	32	48	111	243	375
54-Inhumans cameo	12	24	36	79	160	240
55-Thing battles Silver Surfer; 4th app. Silver Surfer	20	40	60	137	294	450
56-Silver Surfer cameo	12	24	36	78	157	235
57-60: Dr. Doom steals Silver Surfer's powers (also see Silver Surfer: Loftier Than Mortals). 59,60-Inhumans cameo	11	22	33	71	136	200
61-65,68-71: 61-Silver Surfer cameo; Sandman-c/s	9	18	27	61	106	150
66-Begin 2 part origin of Him (Warlock); does not app. (9/67)	12	24	36	79	160	240
66,67-2nd printings (1994)	2	4	6	8	10	12
67-Origin/1st brief app. Him (Warlock); 1 page; see Thor #165,166 for 1st full app.	12	24	36	79	160	240
72-Silver Surfer-c/story (pre-dates Silver Surfer #1)	12	24	36	81	166	250
73-Spider-Man, D.D., Thor x-over; cont'd from Daredevil #38	11	22	33	75	148	220
74-77: Silver Surfer app.(#77 is same date/S.S. #1)	10	20	30	68	127	185
78-80	7	14	21	46	76	105

	GD 2.0	VG 4.0	FN 6.0	VF 8.0	VF/NM 9.0	NM- 9.2
81-88: 81-Crystal joins & dons costume. 82,83-Inhumans app. 84-87-Dr. Doom app. 88-Last 12¢ issue	6	12	18	42	69	95
89-99,101: 94-Intro. Agatha Harkness.	6	12	18	39	62	85
100 (7/70) F.F. vs Thinker and Puppet-Master	10	20	30	68	127	185
102-104: F.F. vs. Sub-Mariner. 104-Magneto-c/story	6	12	18	39	62	85
105-109,111: 108-Last Kirby issue (not in #103-107)	6	12	18	37	59	80
110-Initial version w/green Thing and blue faces and pink uniforms on-c	7	14	21	46	76	105
110-Corrected-c w/accurately colored faces and uniforms and orange Thing	6	12	18	39	62	85
112-Hulk Vs. Thing (7/71)	15	30	45	104	227	350
113-115: 115-Last 15¢ issue	5	10	15	30	48	65
116 (52 pgs.)	6	12	18	42	69	95
117-120	4	8	12	28	44	60
121-123-Silver Surfer-c/stories. 122,123-Galactus	5	10	15	32	51	70
124,125,127,129-140: 129-Intro. Thundra. 130-Sue leaves F.F. 131-Quicksilver app. 132-Medusa joins. 133-Thundra Vs. Thing	4	8	12	24	37	50
126-Origin F.F. retold; cover swipe of F.F. #1	4	8	12	26	41	55
128-Four pg. insert of F.F. Friends & Foes	4	8	12	26	41	55
141-149: 142-Kirbyish-a by Buckler begins. 143-Dr. Doom-c/story. 147-Sub-Mariner	4	8	12	22	34	45
150-Crystal & Quicksilver's wedding	4	8	12	26	41	55
151-154,158-160: 151-Origin Thundra. 159-Medusa leaves; Sue rejoins	3	6	9	16	22	28
155-157: Silver Surfer in all	3	6	9	20	30	40
161-165,168,174-180: 164-The Crusader (old Marvel Boy) revived (origin #165); 1st app. Frankie Raye. 168-170-Cage app. 176-Re-intro Impossible Man; Marvel artists app. 180-r/#101 by Kirby	2	4	6	10	14	18
166,167-vs. Hulk	3	6	9	17	25	32
169-173-(Regular 25¢ edition)(4-8/75)	2	4	6	10	14	18
169-173-(30¢-c, limited distribution)	3	6	9	18	27	36
181-199: 189-G.A. Human Torch app. & origin retold. 190,191-Fantastic Four break up	2	4	6	8	10	12
183-187-(35¢-c variants, limited dist.)(6-10/77)	4	8	12	24	37	50
200-(11/78, 52 pgs.)-F.F. re-united vs. Dr. Doom	2	4	6	10	14	18
201-208,219,222-231: 207-Human Torch vs. Spider-Man-c/story. 211-1st app. Terrax. 224-Contains unused alternate-c for FF #3 and pin-ups						6.00
209-216,218,220,221-Byrne-a. 209-1st Herbie the Robot. 220-Brief origin	1	2	3	5	6	8
217-Early app. Dazzler (4/80); by Byrne	1	2	3	5	6	8
232-Byrne-a begins	1	2	3	5	6	8
233-235,237-249,251-260: All Byrne-a. 238-Origin Frankie Raye. 244-Frankie Raye becomes Nova, Herald of Galactus. 252-Reads sideways; Annihilus app.; contains skin "Tattooz" decals						6.00
236-20th Anniversary issue(11/81, 68 pgs., $1.00)-Brief origin F.F.; Byrne-c(p)/a; new Kirby-a(p); Marvel Heroes and Stan Lee app. on cover	1	2	3	5	6	8
250-(52 pgs)-Spider-Man x-over; Byrne-a; Skrulls impersonate New X-Men	1	2	3	5	6	8
261-285: 261-Silver Surfer. 262-Origin Galactus; Byrne writes & draws himself into story. 264-Swipes-c of F.F. #1. 274-Spider-Man's alien costume app. (4th app., 1/85, 2 pgs.)						4.00
286-2nd app. X-Factor continued from Avengers #263; story continues in X-Factor #1						5.00
287-295: 291-Action Comics #1 cover swipe. 292-Nick Fury app. 293-Last Byrne-a						4.00
296-($1.50)-Barry Smith-c/a; Thing rejoins						5.00
297-318,321-330: 300-Johnny Storm & Alicia Masters wed. 306-New team begins (9/87). 311-Re-intro The Black Panther. 327-Mr. Fantastic & Invisible Girl return						3.00
319,320: 319-Double size. 320-Thing vs. Hulk						4.00
331-346,351-357,359,360: 334-Simonson-c/scripts begin. 337-Simonson-a begins. 342-Spider-Man cameo. 356-F.F. vs. The New Warriors; Paul Ryan-c/a begins. 360-Last $1.00-c						3.00
347-Ghost Rider, Wolverine, Spider-Man, Hulk-c/stories thru #349; Arthur Adams-c/a(p) in each						5.00
347,348-Gold 2nd printing						3.00
348-350: 350-($1.50, 52 pgs.)-Dr. Doom app.						4.00
358-(11/91, $2.25, 88 pgs.)-30th anniversary issue; gives history of F.F.; die cut-c; Art Adams back-up story-a						4.00
361-368,370,372-374,376-380,382-386: 362-Spider-Man app. 367-Wolverine app. (brief). 370-Infinity War x-over; Thanos & Magus app. 374-Secret Defenders (Ghost Rider, Hulk, Wolverine) x-over						3.00
369-Infinity War x-over; Thanos app.						3.00
371-All white embossed-c ($2.00)						4.00
371-All red 2nd printing ($2.00)						3.00
375-($2.95, 52 pgs.)-Holo-grafx foil-c; ann. issue						4.00
376-($2.95)-Variant polybagged w/Dirt Magazine #4 and music tape						5.00
381-Death of Reed Richards (Mister Fantastic) & Dr. Doom						4.00

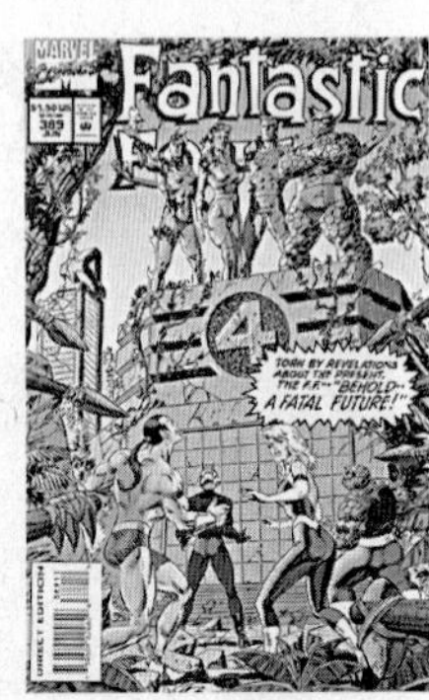

Fantastic Four #389 © MAR

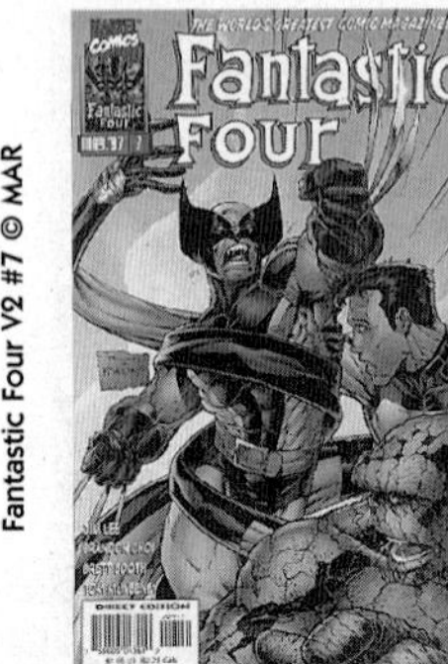

Fantastic Four V2 #7 © MAR

Fantastic Four #588 © MAR

GD VG FN VF VF/NM NM-
2.0 4.0 6.0 8.0 9.0 9.2

387-Newsstand ed. ($1.25) 3.00
387-($2.95)-Collector's Ed. w/Die-cut foil-c 4.00
388-393,395-397: 388-bound-in trading card sheet. 394-($1.50-c) 3.00
394,398,399: 394 ($2.95)-Collector's Edition-polybagged w/16 pg. Marvel Action Hour book and acetate print; pink logo. 398,399-Rainbow Foil-c 4.00
400-Rainbow-Foil-c 5.00
401-415: 401,402-Atlantis Rising. 407,408-Return of Reed Richards. 411-Inhumans app. 414-Galactus vs. Hyperstorm. 415-Onslaught tie-in; X-Men app. 3.00
416-($2.50)-Onslaught tie-in; Dr. Doom app.; wraparound-c 4.00
#500-up (See Fantastic Four Vol. 3; series resumed original numbering after Vol. 3 #70)
Annual 1('63)-Origin F.F.; Ditko-i; early Spidey app. 70 140 210 567 1234 1900
Annual 2('64)-Dr. Doom origin & c/story 36 72 108 270 585 900
Annual 3('65)-Reed & Sue wed; r/#6,11 19 38 57 128 277 425
Special 4(11/66)-G.A. Torch x-over (1st S.A. app.) & origin retold; r/#25,26 (Hulk vs. Thing); Torch vs. Torch battle 12 24 36 83 172 260
Special 5(11/67)-New art; Intro. Psycho-Man; early Black Panther, Inhumans & Silver Surfer (1st solo story) app. 12 24 36 84 177 270
Special 6(11/68)-Intro. Annihilus; birth of Franklin Richards; new 48 pg. movie length epic; last non-reprint annual 9 18 27 63 112 160
Special 7(11/69)-r/F.F. #1,2; Marvel staff photos 5 10 15 35 55 75
Special 8-10: All reprints. 8(12/70)-F.F. vs. Sub-Mariner plus gallery of F.F. foes. 9(12/71). 10('73) 3 6 9 21 32 42
Annual 11-14: 11(1976)-New art begins again. 12(1978). 13(1978). 14(1979) 2 4 6 8 10 12
Annual 15-17: 15('80, 68 pgs.). 17(1983)-Byrne-c/a 6.00
Annual 18-27: 21(1988)-Evolutionary War x-over. 22-Atlantis Attacks x-over; Sub-Mariner & The Avengers app.; Buckler-a. 23-Byrne-c; Guice-p. 24-2 pg. origin recap of Fantastic Four; Guardians of the Galaxy x-over. 25-Moondragon story. 26-Bagged w/card 4.00
Best of the Fantastic Four Vol. 1 HC (2005, $29.99) oversized reprints of classic stories from FF#1,39,40,51,100,116,176,236,267, Ann.2, V3#56,60 and more; Brevoort intro. 30.00
Maximum Fantastic Four HC (2005, $49.99, dust jacket) r/Fantastic Four #1 with super-sized art; historical background from Walter Mosley and Mark Evanier; dust jacket unfolds to a poster: giant FF#1 cover on one side, gallery of interior pages on other 50.00
...: Monsters Unleashed nn (1992, $5.95)-r/F.F. #347-349 w/new Arthur Adams-c 6.00
...: Nobody Gets Out Alive (1994, $15.95) TPB r/ #387-392 16.00
... Omnibus Vol. 1 HC (2005, $99.99) r/#1-30 & Annual 1 plus letter pages; 3 intros. and a 1974 essay by Stan Lee; original plot synopsis for FF #1; essays and Kirby art 100.00
... Omnibus Vol. 2 HC (2007, $99.99) r/#31-60, Annual 2-4 and Not Brand Echh #1 plus letter pages and essays by Stan Lee, Reginald Hudlin, Roy Thomas and others 100.00
Special Edition 1(5/84)-r/Annual #1; Byrne-c/a 4.00
...: The Lost Adventure (4/08, $4.99) Lee & Kirby story partially used in flashback in FF #108 completed with additional art by Frenz & Sinnott; plus reprint of FF #108 5.00
... Visionaries: George Pérez Vol. 1 (2005, $19.99) r/#164-167,170,176-178,184-186 20.00
... Visionaries: George Pérez Vol. 2 (2006, $19.99) r/#187-188,191-192, Annual #14-15, Marvel Two-In-One #60 and back-up story from Adventures of the Thing #3 20.00
... Visionaries (11/01, $19.95) r/#232-240 by John Byrne 20.00
... Visionaries Vol. 2 (2004, $24.99) r/#241-250 by John Byrne 25.00
... Visionaries John Byrne Vol. 3 (2004, $24.99) r/#251-257; Annual #17; Avengers #233 and Thing #2 25.00
... Visionaries John Byrne Vol. 4 (2005, $24.99) r/#258-267; Alpha Flight #4 & Thing #10 25.00
... Visionaries John Byrne Vol. 5 (2005, $24.99) r/#268-275; Annual #18 & Thing #19 25.00
... Visionaries John Byrne Vol. 6 ('06, $24.99) r/#276-284; Secret Wars II #2 & Thing #23 25.00
... Visionaries John Byrne Vol. 7 ('07, $24.99) r/#285,286, Ann. #19, Avengers #263 & Ann. #14, and X-Factor #1 25.00
... Visionaries John Byrne Vol. 8 ('07, $24.99) r/#287-295 25.00
... Visionaries: Walter Simonson Vol. 1 (2007, $19.99) r/#334-341 20.00

NOTE: ***Arthur Adams*** *c/a-347-349p.* ***Austin*** *c(i)-232-236, 238, 240-242, 250i, 286i.* ***Buckler*** *c-151, 168.* ***John Buscema*** *a(p)-107, 108(w/**Kirby, Sinnott** & **Romita**),109-130, 132, 134-141, 160, 173-175, 202, 296-309p, Annual 11, 13; c(p)-107-122, 124-129, 133-139, 202, Annual 12p, Special 10.* ***Byrne*** *a-209-218p, 220p, 221p, 232-265, 266i, 267-273, 274-293p, Annual 17, 19; c-211-214p, 220p, 232-236p, 237, 238p, 239, 240-242p, 243-249, 250p, 251-267, 269-277, 278-281p, 283p, 284, 285, 286p, 288-293, Annual 17, 18.* ***Ditko*** *a-13i, 14i(w/**Kirby**-p), Annual 16.* ***G. Kane*** *c-145p, 146p, 150p, 160p.* ***Kirby*** *a-1-102p, 108p, 180r, 189r, 236p, Special 1-10; c-1-101, 164, 167, 171-177, 180, 181, 190, 200, Annual 11, Special 1-7, 9.* ***Marcos*** *a-Annual 14i.* ***Mooney*** *a-118i, 152i.* ***Perez*** *a(p)-164-167, 170-172, 176-178, 184-188, 191p, 192p. Annual 14p, 15p; c(p)-183-188, 191, 192, 194-197.* ***Simonson*** *a-337-341, 343, 344p, 345p, 346, 350p, 352-354; c-212, 334-341, 342p, 343-346, 350, 353, 354.* ***Steranko*** *c-130-132p.* ***Williamson*** *c-357i.*

FANTASTIC FOUR (Volume Two)
Marvel Comics: V2#1, Nov, 1996 - No. 13, Nov, 1997 ($2.95/$1.95/$1.99) (Produced by WildStorm Productions)

1-($2.95)-Reintro Fantastic Four; Jim Lee-c/a; Brandon Choi scripts; Mole Man app. 5.00
1-($2.95)-Variant-c 1 2 3 4 5 7
2-9: 2-Namor-c/app. 3-Avengers-c/app. 4-Two covers; Dr. Doom cameo 3.00
10,11,13: All $1.99-c. 13-"World War 3"-pt. 1, x-over w/Image 3.00
12-($2.99) "Heroes Reunited"-pt. 1 4.00
...: Heroes Reborn (7/00, $17.95, TPB) r/#1-6 18.00
Heroes Reborn: Fantastic Four (2006, $29.99, TPB) r/#1-12; Jim Lee intro.; pin-ups 30.00

FANTASTIC FOUR (Volume Three)
Marvel Comics: V3#1, Jan, 1998 - No. 588, Apr, 2011 ($2.99/$1.99/$2.25)
No. 600, Jan, 2012 - Present (Issues #589-#599 do not exist, see FF series)

1-($2.99)-Heroes Return; Lobdell-s/Davis & Farmer-a 1 2 3 5 6 8
1-Alternate Heroes Return-c 1 3 4 6 8 10
2-4,12: 2-2-covers. 4-Claremont-s/Larroca-a begin; Silver Surfer c/app. 12-($2.99) Wraparound-c by Larroca 5.00
5-11: 6-Heroes For Hire app. 9-Spider-Man-c/app. 4.00
13-24: 13,14-Ronan-c/app. 3.00
25-($2.99) Dr. Doom returns 4.00
26-49: 27-Dr. Doom marries Sue. 30-Begin $2.25-c. 32,42-Namor-c/app. 35-Regular cover; Pacheco-s/a begins. 37-Super-Skrull-c/app. 38-New Baxter Building 3.00
35-($3.25) Variant foil enhanced-c; Pacheco-s/a begins 4.00
50-($3.99, 64 pgs.) BWS-c; Grummett, Pacheco, Rude, Udon-a 4.00
51-53,55-59: 51-53-Bagley-a(p)/Wieringo-c; Inhumans app. 55,56-Immonen-a 57-59-Warren-s/Grant-a 3.00
54-($3.50, 100 pgs.) Birth of Valeria; r/Annual #6 birth of Franklin 4.00
60-(9¢-c) Waid-s/Wieringo-a begin 3.00
60-($2.25 newsstand edition)(also see Promotional Comics section) 3.00
61-70: 62-64-FF vs. Modulus. 65,66-Buckingham-a. 68-70-Dr. Doom app. 3.00
(After #70 [Aug, 2003] numbering reverted back to original Vol. 1 with #500, Sept, 2003)
500-($3.50) Regular edition; concludes Dr. Doom app.; Dr. Strange app.; Rivera painted-c 4.00
500-($4.99) Director's Cut Edition; chromium-c by Wieringo; sketch and script pages 8.00
501-516: 501,502-Casey Jones-a. 503-508-Porter-a. 509-Wieringo-c/a resumes. 512,513-Spider-Man app. 514-516-Ha-c/Medina-a 3.00
517-537: 517-Begin $2.99-c. 519-523-Galactus app. 527-Straczynski-s begins. 537-Dr. Doom. 3.00
527-Variant Edition with different McKone-c 3.00
527-Wizard World Philadelphia Edition with B&W McKone sketch-c 3.00
536-Variant cover by Bryan Hitch 5.00
537-B&W variant cover 5.00
538-542-Civil War. 538-Don Blake reclaims Thor's hammer 4.00
543-45th Anniversary; Black Panther and Storm replace Reed and Sue; Granov-c 4.00
544-553: 544-546-Silver Surfer app.; Turner-c 3.00
554-568-Millar-s/Hitch-a/c. 558-561-Dr. Doom-c/app. 562-Funeral & proposal 3.00
554-Variant-c by Bianchi 6.00
554-Variant Skrull-c by Suydam 30.00
569-($3.99) Wraparound-c; Immonen-a; Dr. Doom app. 4.00
570-586: 570-572,575-578-Eaglesham-a. 574-Spider-Man app. 584-586-Galactus app. 3.00
587-(3/11, $3.99) Death of Human Torch; Epting-a; issue is in black polybag; Davis-c 4.00
587-Variant-c by Cassaday 10.00
588-($3.99) Last issue; Dragotta-a; preview of FF #1; back-up w/Spider-Man; Davis-c 4.00
589-599-**Do not exist**; story continues in FF series
600-(1/12, $7.99) Avengers app.; Human Torch returns, back-up short stories; Dell'Otto-c 8.00
600-Variant-c by John Romita, Jr. 10.00
600-Variant-c by Art Adams 15.00
601-603-Johnny Storm & Avengers app. 602,603-Galactus app. 3.00
...'98 Annual ($3.50) Immonen-a 4.00
...'99 Annual ($3.50) Ladronn-a 4.00
...'00 Annual ($3.50) Larocca-a; Marvel Girl back-up story 4.00
...'01 Annual ($2.99) Maguire-a; Thing back-up w/Yu-a 4.00
... Annual 32 (8/10, $4.99) Hitch-a/c 5.00
... : A Death in the Family (7/06, $3.99, one-shot) Weeks-a/c; and r/F.F. #245 4.00
... By J. Michael Straczynski Vol. 1 (2005, $19.99, HC) r/#527-532 20.00
Civil War: Fantastic Four TPB (2007, $17.99) r/#538-543; 45th Anniversary Toasts 18.00
... Cosmic-Size Special 1 (2/09, $4.99) Cary Bates-s/Bing Cansino-a; r/F.F. #237 5.00
Fantastic 4th Voyage of Sinbad (9/01, $5.95) Claremont-s/Ferry-a 6.00
Flesh and Stone (8/01, $12.95, TPB) r/#35-39 13.00
... Giant-Size Adventures 1 (8/09, $3.99) Cifuentes & Coover-a; Egghead app. 4.00
... In...Ataque del M.O.D.O.K.! (11/10, $3.99) English & Spanish editions; Beland-s/Doe-a 4.00
... /Inhumans TPB (2007, $19.99) r/#51-54 and Inhumans ('00) #1-4 20.00
...: Isla De La Muerte! (2/08, $3.99) English & Spanish editions; Beland-s/Doe-a 4.00
... MGC #570 (7/11, $1.00) r/#570 with "Marvel's Greatest Comics" cover banner 3.00
... Presents: Franklin Richards 1 (11/05, $2.99) r/back-up stories from Power Pack #1-4 plus new 5 pg. story; Sumerak-s/Eliopoulos-a (Also see Franklin Richards) 3.00
...Special (2/06, $2.99) McDuffie-s/Casey Jones-a; dinner with Dr. Doom 3.00
...Tales Vol. 1 (2005, $7.99, digest) r/Marvel Age: FF Tales #1, Tales of the Thing #1-3, and Spider-Man Team-Up Special 8.00
...: The Last Stand (8/11, $4.99) r/#574, 587 & 588 (death of Johnny Storm) 5.00
...: The New Fantastic Four HC (2007, $19.99) r/#544-550; variant covers & sketch pgs. 20.00
...: The New Fantastic Four SC (2008, $15.99) r/#544-550; variant covers & sketch pgs. 16.00
... : The Wedding Special 1 (1/06, $5.00) 40th Anniversary new story & r/FF Annual #3 5.00

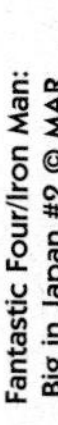
Fantastic Four/Iron Man: Big in Japan #2 © MAR

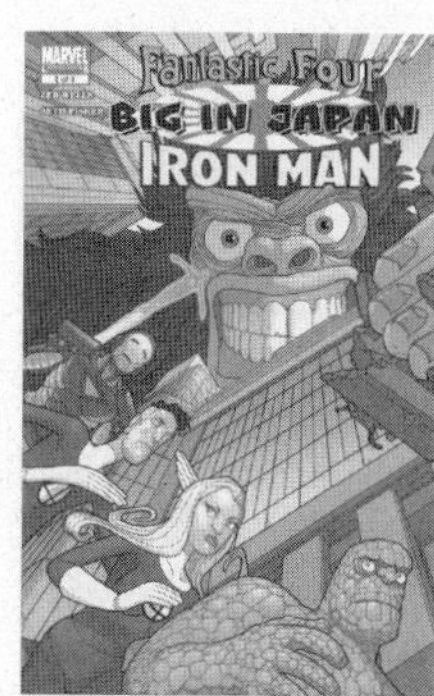

Fantastic Four: World's Greatest Comics Magazine #11 © MAR

Fantastic Worlds #6 © STD

GD VG FN VF VF/NM NM-
2.0 4.0 6.0 8.0 9.0 9.2

... Vol. 1 HC (2004, $29.99, dust jacket) oversized reprint /#60-70, 500-502; Mark Waid intro and series proposal; cover gallery 30.00
... Vol. 2 HC (2005, $29.99, d.j.) oversized r/#503-513; Waid intro.; deleted scenes 30.00
... Vol. 3 HC (2005, $29.99, d.j.) oversized r/#514-524; Waid commentaries; cover sketches 30.00
... Vol. 1: Imaginauts (2003, $17.99, TPB) r/#56,60-66; Mark Waid's series proposal 18.00
... Vol. 2: Unthinkable (2003, $17.99, TPB) r/#67-70,500-502; #500 Director's Cut extras 18.00
... Vol. 3: Authoritative Action (2004, $12.99, TPB) r/#503-508 13.00
... Vol. 4: Hereafter (2004, $11.99, TPB) r/#509-513 12.00
... Vol. 5: Disassembled (2004, $14.99, TPB) r/#514-519 15.00
... Vol. 6: Rising Storm (2005, $13.99, TPB) r/#520-524 14.00
...: The Beginning of the End TPB (2008, $14.99) r/#525,526,551-553 & Fantastic Four: Isla De La Muerte! one-shot 15.00
...: The Life Fantastic TPB (2006, $16.99) r/#533-535; The Wedding Special, Special (2/06) and A Death in the Family one-shots 17.00
Wizard #1/2 -Lim-a 10.00

FANTASTIC FOUR AND POWER PACK
Marvel Comics: Sept, 2007 - No. 4, Dec, 2007 ($2.99, limited series)
1-4-Gurihiru-a/Van Lente-s; the Wizard app. 3.00
...: Favorite Son TPB (2008, $7.99, digest size) r/#1-4 8.00

FANTASTIC FOUR: ATLANTIS RISING
Marvel Comics: June, 1995 - No. 2, July, 1995 ($3.95, limited series)
1,2: Acetate-c 5.00
Collector's Preview (5/95, $2.25, 52 pgs.) 4.00

FANTASTIC FOUR: BIG TOWN
Marvel Comics: Jan, 2001 - No. 4, Apr, 2001 ($2.99, limited series)
1-4:"What If?" story; McKone-a/Englehart-s 3.00

FANTASTIC FOUR: FIREWORKS
Marvel Comics: Jan, 1999 - No. 3, Mar, 1999 ($2.99, limited series)
1-3-Remix; Jeff Johnson-a 3.00

FANTASTIC FOUR: FIRST FAMILY
Marvel Comics: May, 2006 - No. 6, Oct, 2006 ($2.99, limited series)
1-6-Casey-s/Weston-a; flashback to the days after the accident 3.00
TPB (2006, $15.99) r/#1-6 16.00

FANTASTIC FOUR: FOES
Marvel Comics: Mar, 2005 - No. 6, Aug, 2005 ($2.99, limited series)
1-6-Kirkman-s/Rathburn-a. 1-Puppet Master app. 3-Super-Skrull app. 4-Mole Man app. 3.00
TPB (2005, $16.99) r/#1-6 17.00

FANTASTIC FOUR: HOUSE OF M (Reprinted in House of M: Fantastic Four/ Iron Man TPB)
Marvel Comics: Sept, 2005 - No. 3, Nov, 2005 ($2.99, limited series)
1-3: Fearsome Four, led by Doom; Scot Eaton-a 3.00

FANTASTIC FOUR INDEX (See Official...)

FANTASTIC FOUR/ IRON MAN: BIG IN JAPAN
Marvel Comics: Dec, 2005 - No. 4, Mar, 2006 ($3.50, limited series)
1-4-Seth Fisher-a/c; Zeb Wells-s; wraparound-c on each 3.50
TPB (2006, $12.99) r/#1-4 and Seth Fisher illustrated story from Spider-Man Unlimited #8 13.00

FANTASTIC FOUR: 1 2 3 4
Marvel Comics: Oct, 2001 - No. 4, Jan, 2002 ($2.99, limited series)
1-4-Morrison-s/Jae Lee-a. 2-4-Namor-c/app. 3.00
TPB (2002, $9.99) r/#1-4 10.00

FANTASTIC FOUR ROAST
Marvel Comics Group: May, 1982 (75¢, one-shot, direct sales)
1-Celebrates 20th anniversary of F.F.#1; X-Men, Ghost Rider & many others cameo; Golden, Miller, Buscema, Rogers, Byrne, Anderson art; Hembeck/Austin-c 4.00

FANTASTIC FOUR: THE END
Marvel Comics: Jan, 2007 - No. 6, May, 2007 ($2.99, limited series)
1-6-Alan Davis-s/a; last adventure of the future FF. 1-Dr. Doom-c/app. 3.00
Roughcut #1 ($3.99) B&W pencil art for full story and text script; B&W sketch cover 4.00
HC (2007, $19.99, dustjacket) r/#1-6 20.00
SC (2008, $14.99) r/#1-6 15.00

FANTASTIC FOUR: THE LEGEND
Marvel Comics: Oct, 1996 ($3.95, one-shot)
1-Tribute issue 4.00

FANTASTIC FOUR: THE MOVIE
Marvel Comics: Aug, 2005 ($4.99/$12.99, one-shot)
1-($4.99) Movie adaptation; Jurgens-a; behind the scenes feature; Doom origin; photo-c 5.00

GD VG FN VF VF/NM NM-
2.0 4.0 6.0 8.0 9.0 9.2

TPB-($12.99) Movie adaptation, r/Fantastic Four #5 & 190, and FF Vol. 3 #60, photo-c 13.00

FANTASTIC FOUR: TRUE STORY
Marvel Comics: Sept, 2008 - No. 4, Jan, 2009 ($2.99, limited series)
1-4-Cornell-s/Domingues-a/Henrichon-c 3.00

FANTASTIC FOUR 2099
Marvel Comics: Jan, 1996 - No. 8, Aug, 1996 ($3.95/$1.95)
1-($3.95)-Chromium-c; X-Nation preview 4.00
2-8: 4-Spider-Man 2099-c/app. 5-Doctor Strange app. 7-Thibert-c 3.00
NOTE: *Williamson a-1i; c-1i.*

FANTASTIC FOUR UNLIMITED
Marvel Comics: Mar, 1993 - No. 12, Dec, 1995 ($3.95, 68 pgs.)
1-12: 1-Black Panther app. 4-Thing vs. Hulk. 5-Vs. The Frightful Four. 6-Vs. Namor. 7, 9-12-Wraparound-c 4.00

FANTASTIC FOUR UNPLUGGED
Marvel Comics: Sept, 1995 - No. 6, Aug 1996 (99¢, bi-monthly)
1-6 3.00

FANTASTIC FOUR - UNSTABLE MOLECULES
(Indicia for #1 reads STARTLING STORIES: ... ; #2 reads UNSTABLE MOLECULES)
Marvel Comics: Mar, 2003 - No. 4, June, 2003 ($2.99, limited series)
1-4-Guy Davis-c/a 3.00
Fantastic Four Legends Vol. 1 TPB (2003, $13.99) r/#1-4, origin from FF #1 (1963) 14.00
TPB (2005, $13.99) r/#1-4 14.00

FANTASTIC FOUR VS. X-MEN
Marvel Comics: Feb, 1987 - No. 4, June, 1987 (Limited series)
1-4: 4-Austin-a(i) 4.00

FANTASTIC FOUR: WORLD'S GREATEST COMICS MAGAZINE
Marvel Comics: Feb, 2001 - No. 12 (Limited series)
1-12: Homage to Lee & Kirby era of F.F.; s/a by Larsen & various. 5-Hulk-c/app. 10-Thor app. 3.00

FANTASTIC GIANTS (Formerly Konga #1-23)
Charlton Comics: V2#24, Sept, 1966 (25¢, 68 pgs.)
V2#24-Special Ditko issue; origin Konga & Gorgo reprinted plus two new Ditko stories 7 14 21 45 73 100

FANTASTIC TALES
I. W. Enterprises: 1958 (no date) (Reprint, one-shot)
1-Reprints Avon's "City of the Living Dead" 3 6 9 20 30 40

FANTASTIC VOYAGE (See Movie Comics)
Gold Key: Aug, 1969 - No. 2, Dec, 1969
1 (TV) 4 8 12 28 44 60
2-Cover has the text "Civilian Miniaturized Defense Force" in yellow bar at top; back cover has painted art 3 6 9 20 30 40
2-Variant cover has text "In This Issue Sweepstakes..." along top; ad on back-c 4 8 12 24 37 50

FANTASTIC VOYAGES OF SINDBAD, THE
Gold Key: Oct, 1965 - No. 2, June, 1967
1-Painted-c on both 6 12 18 43 69 95
2 5 10 15 32 51 70

FANTASTIC WORLDS
Standard Comics: No. 5, Sept, 1952 - No. 7, Jan, 1953
5-Toth, Anderson-a 37 74 111 222 361 500
6-Toth-c/a 30 60 90 177 289 400
7 20 40 60 118 192 265

FANTASY FEATURES
Americomics: 1987 - No. 2, 1987 ($1.75)
1,2 3.00

FANTASY ILLUSTRATED
New Media Publ.: Spring 1982 ($2.95, B&W magazine)
1-P. Craig Russell-c/a; art by Ditko, Sekowsky, Sutton; Englehart-s 1 2 3 4 5 7

FANTASY MASTERPIECES (Marvel Super Heroes No. 12 on)
Marvel Comics Group: Feb, 1966 - No. 11, Oct, 1967; V2#1, Dec, 1979 - No. 14, Jan, 1981
1-Photo of Stan Lee (12¢-c #1,2) 9 18 27 58 99 140
2-r/1st Fin Fang Foom from Strange Tales #89 6 12 18 37 59 80
3-8: 3-G.A. Capt. America-r begin, end #11; 1st 25¢ Giant; Colan-r. 3-6-Kirby-c(p).

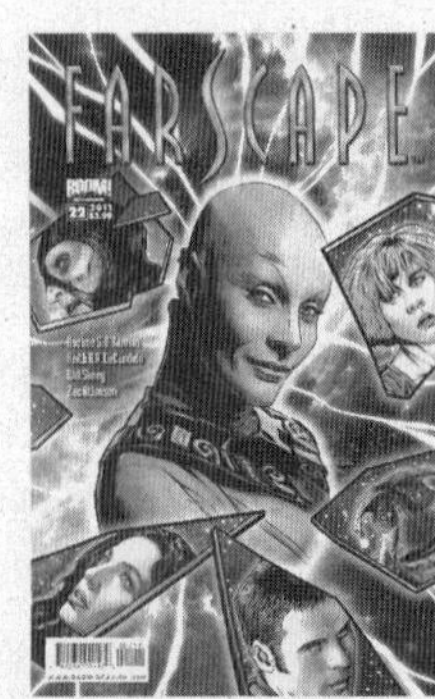

Farscape #22 © Henson Co.

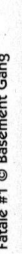

Fast Fiction #5 © Seaboard

Fatale #1 © Basement Gang

	GD 2.0	VG 4.0	FN 6.0	VF 8.0	VF/NM 9.0	NM- 9.2
4-Kirby-c(p)(i). 7-Begin G.A. Sub-Mariner, Torch-r/M. Mystery. 8-Torch battles the Sub-Mariner-r/Marvel Mystery #9	6	12	18	39	62	85
9-Origin Human Torch-r/Marvel Comics #1	6	12	18	41	66	90
10,11: 10-r/origin & 1st app. All Winners Squad from All Winners #19. 11-r/origin of Toro (H.T. #1) & Black Knight #1	6	12	18	37	59	80
V2#1(12/79, 75¢, 52 pgs.)-r/origin Silver Surfer from Silver Surfer #1 with editing plus reprints cover; J. Buscema-a	1	3	4	6	8	10
2-14-Reprints Silver Surfer #2-14 w/covers						6.00
NOTE: ***Buscema** c-V2#7-9(in part). **Ditko** r-1-3, 7, 9. **Everett** r-1,7-9. **Matt Fox** r-9i. **Kirby** r-1-11; c(p)-3, 4i, 5, 6. **Starlin** r-8-13. Some direct sale V2#14's had a 50¢ cover price. #3-11 contain Capt. America-r/Capt. America #3-10. #7-11 contain G.A.Human Torch & Sub-Mariner-r.*						
FANTASY QUARTERLY (Also see Elfquest)						
Independent Publishers Syndicate: Spring, 1978 (B&W)						
1-1st app. Elfquest; Dave Sim-a (6 pgs.)	8	16	24	56	96	135
FANTOMAN (Formerly Amazing Adventure Funnies)						
Centaur Publications: No. 2, Aug, 1940 - No. 4, Dec, 1940						
2-The Fantom of the Fair, The Arrow, Little Dynamite-r begin; origin The Ermine by Filchock; Fantoman app. in 2-4; Burgos, J. Cole, Ernst, Gustavson-a	110	220	330	704	1202	1700
3,4: Gustavson-r. 4-Red Blaze story	86	172	258	546	936	1325
FAREWELL MOONSHADOW (See Moonshadow)						
DC Comics (Vertigo): Jan, 1997 ($7.95, one-shot)						
nn-DeMatteis-s/Muth-c/a						8.00
FARGO KID (Formerly Justice Traps the Guilty)(See Feature Comics #47)						
Prize Publications: V11#3(#1), June-July, 1958 - V11#5, Oct-Nov, 1958						
V11#3(#1)-Origin Fargo Kid, Severin-c/a; Williamson-a(2); Heath-a	18	36	54	105	165	225
V11#4,5-Severin-c/a	13	26	39	74	105	135
FARMER'S DAUGHTER, THE						
Stanhall Publ./Trojan Magazines: Feb-Mar, 1954 - No. 3, June-July, 1954; No. 4, Oct, 1954						
1-Lingerie, nudity panel	50	100	150	315	533	750
2-4(Stanhall)	37	74	111	222	361	500
FARSCAPE (Based on TV series)						
BOOM! Studios: Nov, 2008 - No. 4, Feb, 2009 ($3.99)						
1-4-O'Bannon-s/Patterson-a; multiple covers						4.00
FARSCAPE (Based on TV series)						
BOOM! Studios: Nov, 2009 - No. 24, Oct, 2011 ($3.99)						
1-24-O'Bannon-s/Sliney-a; multiple covers						4.00
...: D'Argo's Lament 1-4 (4/09 - No. 4, 7/09, $3.99) Edwards-a; three covers on each						4.00
...: D'Argo's Quest 1-4 (12/09 - No. 4, 3/10, $3.99) Cleveland-a; three covers on each						4.00
...: D'Argo's Trial 1-4 (8/09 - No. 4, 11/09, $3.99) Cleveland-a; multiple covers on each						4.00
...: Gone and Back 1-4 (7/09 - No. 4, 10/09, $3.99) Patterson-a; multiple covers on each						4.00
...: Scorpius 0-7 (4/10 - Present, $3.99) 0-3-Ruiz-a; multiple-c. 4-7-Purcell-a						4.00
...: Strange Detractors 1-4 (3/09 - No. 4, 6/09, $3.99) Sliney-a; three covers on each						4.00
FARSCAPE: WAR TORN (Based on TV series)						
DC Comics (WildStorm): Apr, 2002 - No. 2, May, 2002 ($4.95, limited series)						
1,2-Teranishi-a/Wolfman-s; photo-c						5.00
FASHION IN ACTION						
Eclipse Comics: Aug, 1986 - Feb, 1987 (Baxter paper)						
Summer Special 1 , Winter Special 1, each Snyder III-c/a						3.00
FASTBALL EXPRESS (Major League Baseball)						
Ultimate Sports Force: 2000 ($3.95, one-shot)						
1-Polybagged with poster; Johnson, Maddux, Park, Nomo, Clemens app.						4.00
FASTEST GUN ALIVE, THE (Movie)						
Dell Publishing Co.: No. 741, Sept, 1956 (one-shot)						
Four Color 741-Photo-c	7	14	21	46	76	105
FAST FICTION (...Action) (Stories by Famous Authors Illustrated #6 on)						
Seaboard Publ./Famous Authors Ill.: Oct, 1949 - No. 5, Mar, 1950 (All have Kiefer-c)(48 pgs.)						
1-Scarlet Pimpernel; Jim Lavery-c/a	28	56	84	135	270	375
2-Captain Blood; H. C. Kiefer-c/a	24	48	72	142	234	325
3-She, by Rider Haggard; Vincent Napoli-a	30	60	90	177	289	400
4-(1/50, 52 pgs.)-The 39 Steps; Lavery-c/a	19	38	57	112	176	240
5-Beau Geste; Kiefer-c/a	19	38	57	112	176	240
NOTE: ***Kiefer** a-2, 5; c-2, 3,5. **Lavery** c/a-1, 4. **Napoli** a-3.*						
FAST FORWARD						
DC Comics (Piranha Press): 1992 - No. 3, 1993 ($4.95, 68 pgs.)						

	GD 2.0	VG 4.0	FN 6.0	VF 8.0	VF/NM 9.0	NM- 9.2
1-3: 1-Morrison scripts; McKean-c/a. 3-Sam Kieth-a						5.00
FAST WILLIE JACKSON						
Fitzgerald Periodicals, Inc.: Oct, 1976 - No. 7, 1977						
1	3	6	9	16	23	30
2-7	2	4	6	10	16	20
FAT ALBERT (...& the Cosby Kids) (TV)						
Gold Key: Mar, 1974 - No. 29, Feb, 1979						
1	4	8	12	24	37	50
2-10	3	6	9	14	20	26
11-29	2	4	6	10	14	18
FATALE (Also see Powers That Be #1 & Shadow State #1,2)						
Broadway Comics: Jan, 1996 - No. 6, Aug, 1996 ($2.50)						
1-6: J.G. Jones-c/a in all, Preview Edition 1 (11/95, B&W)						3.00
FATALE						
Image Comics: Jan, 2012 - Present ($3.50)						
1-3-Brubaker-s/Phillips-a/c						3.50
FAT AND SLAT (Ed Wheelan) (Becomes Gunfighter No. 5 on)						
E. C. Comics: Summer, 1947 - No. 4, Spring, 1948						
1-Intro/origin Voltage, Man of Lightning; "Comics" McCormick, the World's No. 1 Comic Book Fan begins, ends #4	39	78	117	231	378	525
2-4: 4-Comics McCormick-c feature	25	50	75	147	241	335
FAT AND SLAT JOKE BOOK						
All-American Comics (William H. Wise): Summer, 1944 (52 pgs., one-shot)						
nn-by Ed Wheelan	29	58	87	170	278	385
FATE (See Hand of Fate & Thrill-O-Rama)						
FATE						
DC Comics: Oct, 1994 - No. 22, Sept, 1996 ($1.95/$2.25)						
0,1-22: 8-Begin $2.25-c. 11-14-Alan Scott (Sentinel) app. 10,14-Zatanna app. 21-Phantom Stranger app. 22-Spectre app.						3.00
FATHOM						
Comico: May, 1987 - No. 3, July, 1987 ($1.50, limited series)						
1-3						3.00
FATHOM						
Image Comics (Top Cow Prod.): Aug, 1998 - No. 14, May, 2002 ($2.50)						
Preview						12.00
0-Wizard supplement						7.00
0-($6.95) DF Alternate						7.00
1/2 (Wizard) origin of Cannon; Turner-a						6.00
1/2 (3/03, $2.99) origin of Cannon						3.00
1-Turner-s/a; three covers; alternate story pages						6.00
1-Wizard World Ed.						9.00
2-14: 12-14-Witchblade app. 13,14-Tomb Raider app.						3.00
9-Green foil-c edition						15.00
9,12-Holofoil editions						18.00
12,13-DFE alternate-c						6.00
13,14-DFE Gold edition						8.00
14-DFE Blue						15.00
... Collected Edition 1 (3/99, $5.95) r/Preview & all three #1's						6.00
... Collected Edition 2-4 (3-12/99, $5.95) 2-r/#2,3. 3-r/#4,5. 4-r/#6,7						6.00
... Collected Edition 5 (4/00, $5.95) 5-r/#8,9						6.00
... Primer (6/11, $1.00) Comic style summary of Volume 1; text summaries of Vol. 2 & 3						3.00
... Swimsuit Special (5/99, $2.95) Pin-ups by various						3.00
... Swimsuit Special 2000 (12/00, $2.95) Pin-ups by various; Turner-c						3.00
Michael Turner's Fathom HC ('01, $39.95) r/#1-9, black-c w/silver foil						40.00
Michael Turner's Fathom SC ('01, $24.95) r/#1-9, new Turner-c						25.00
Michael Turner's Fathom The Definitive Edition ('08, $49.95) r/Preview, #0,1/2,1-14, Swimsuit Special 1999 & 2000; cover gallery; foreword by Geoff Johns						50.00
FATHOM (MICHAEL TURNER'S...) (Volume 2)						
Aspen MLT, Inc.: No. 0, Apr, 2005 - No. 11, Dec, 2006 ($2.50/$2.99)						
0-($2.50) Turnbull-a/Turner-c						3.00
1-11-($2.99) 1-Five covers. 2-Two covers. 4-Six covers						3.00
... Beginnings (2005, $1.99) Two covers; Turnbull-a						3.00
...: Killian's Vessel 1 (7/07, $2.99) 3 covers; Odagawa-a						3.00
... Prelude (6/05, $2.99) Seven covers; Garza-a						3.00
FATHOM (MICHAEL TURNER'S...) (Volume 3)						
Aspen MLT, Inc.: No. 0, Jun, 2008 - No. 10, Feb, 2010 ($2.50/$2.99)						
0-($2.50) Garza-a/c						3.00

Fathom V4 #1 © Aspen MLT

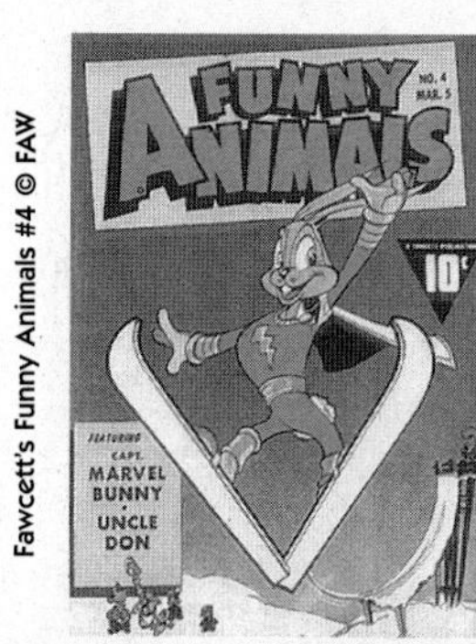

Fawcett's Funny Animals #4 © FAW

Fear #3 © MAR

GD 2.0 | VG 4.0 | FN 6.0 | VF 8.0 | VF/NM 9.0 | NM- 9.2

1-10-($2.99) Garza-a; multiple covers on each 3.00

FATHOM (MICHAEL TURNER'S...) (Volume 4)
Aspen MLT, Inc.: No. 0, Jun, 2011 - Present ($2.50/$2.99)

0-($2.50) Lobdell-s/Konat-a/c; interview with Lobdell; sketch art 3.00
1-4-($2.99) 1-Five covers 3.00

FATHOM: BLUE DESCENT (MICHAEL TURNER'S...)
Aspen MLT, Inc.: Jun, 2010 - No. 4, Feb, 2012 ($2.50/$2.99, limited series)

0-($2.50) Scott Clark-a; covers by Clark & Benitez 3.00
1-4-($2.99) Alex Sanchez-a. 1-Covers by Clark & Finch 3.00

FATHOM: CANNON HAWKE (MICHAEL TURNER'S...)
Aspen MLT, Inc.: Nov, 2005 - No. 5, Feb, 2006 ($2.99)

1-5-To-a/Turner-c 3.00
... Prelude (11/05, $2.50) Turner-c 3.00

FATHOM: DAWN OF WAR (MICHAEL TURNER'S...)
Aspen MLT, Inc.: Oct, 2004 - No. 3, Dec, 2004 ($2.99, limited series)

0-Caldwell-a 3.00
1-3-Caldwell-a 3.00
...: Cannon Hawke #0 ('04, $2.50) Turner-c 3.00
... The Complete Saga Vol. 1 (2005, $9.99) r/series with cover gallery 10.00

FATHOM: KIANI (MICHAEL TURNER'S...)
Aspen MLT, Inc.: No. 0, Feb, 2007 - No. 4, Dec, 2007 ($2.99, limited series)

0-4-Marcus To-a. 1-Six covers 3.00

FATHOM: KILLIAN'S TIDE
Image Comics (Top Cow Prod.): Apr, 2001 - No. 4, Nov, 2001 ($2.95)

1-4-Caldwell-a(p); two covers by Caldwell and Turner. 2-Flip-book preview of Universe 3.00
1-DFE Blue, 1-Holographic logo 12.00
4-Foil-c 12.00

FATIMA...CHALLENGE TO THE WORLD
Catechetical Guild: 1951, 36 pgs. (15¢)

nn (not same as 'Challenge to the World') 6 12 18 29 36 42

FATMAN, THE HUMAN FLYING SAUCER
Lightning Comics(Milson Publ. Co.): April, 1967 - No. 3, Aug-Sept, 1967 (68 pgs.) (Written by Otto Binder)

1-Origin/1st app. Fatman & Tinman by Beck 6 12 18 41 66 90
2-C. C. Beck-a 4 8 12 26 41 55
3-(Scarce)-Beck-a 6 12 18 42 69 95

FAULTLINES
DC Comics (Vertigo): May, 1997 - No. 6, Oct, 1997 ($2.50, limited series)

1-6-Lee Marrs-s/Bill Koeb-a in all 3.00

FAUNTLEROY COMICS (Super Duck Presents...)
Close-Up/Archie Publications: 1950; No. 2, 1951; No. 3, 1952

1-Super Duck-c/stories by Al Fagaly in all 9 18 27 52 69 85
2,3 6 12 18 31 38 45

FAUST
Northstar Publishing/Rebel Studios #7 on: 1989 - No 11, 1997 ($2.00/$2.25, B&W, mature themes)

1-Decapitation-c; Tim Vigil-c/a in all 3 6 9 14 19 24
1-2nd - 4th printings 3.00
2 2 4 6 8 10 12
2-2nd & 3rd printings, 3,5-2nd printing 3.00
3 1 3 4 6 8 10
4-10: 7-Begin Rebel Studios series 5.00
11-($2.25) 3.00

FAWCETT MOTION PICTURE COMICS (See Motion Picture Comics)

FAWCETT MOVIE COMIC
Fawcett Publications: 1949 - No. 20, Dec, 1952 (All photo-c)

nn- "Dakota Lil"; George Montgomery & Rod Cameron (1949)
20 40 60 114 182 250
nn- "Copper Canyon"; Ray Milland & Hedy Lamarr (1950)
15 30 45 86 133 180
nn- "Destination Moon" (1950) 61 122 183 390 670 950
nn- "Montana"; Errol Flynn & Alexis Smith (1950) 15 30 45 86 133 180
nn- "Pioneer Marshal"; Monte Hale (1950) 15 30 45 86 133 180
nn- "Powder River Rustlers"; Rocky Lane (1950) 20 40 60 114 182 250
nn- "Singing Guns"; Vaughn Monroe, Ella Raines & Walter Brennan (1950)
14 28 42 82 121 160
7- "Gunmen of Abilene"; Rocky Lane; Bob Powell-a (1950)
16 32 48 92 144 195
8- "King of the Bullwhip"; Lash LaRue; Bob Powell-a (1950)
21 42 63 126 206 285
9- "The Old Frontier"; Monte Hale; Bob Powell-a (2/51; mis-dated 2/50)
15 30 45 90 140 190
10- "The Missourians"; Monte Hale (4/51) 15 30 45 90 140 190
11- "The Thundering Trail"; Lash LaRue (6/51) 19 38 57 111 176 240
12- "Rustlers on Horseback"; Rocky Lane (8/51) 15 30 45 90 140 190
13- "Warpath"; Edmond O'Brien & Forrest Tucker (10/51)
14 28 42 80 115 150
14- "Last Outpost"; Ronald Reagan (12/51) 32 64 96 188 307 425
15-(Scarce)- "The Man From Planet X"; Robert Clark; Schaffenberger-a (2/52)
245 490 735 1568 2684 3800
16- "10 Tall Men"; Burt Lancaster 13 26 39 74 105 135
17- "Rose of Cimarron"; Jack Buetel & Mala Powers 10 20 30 58 79 100
18- "The Brigand"; Anthony Dexter & Anthony Quinn; Schaffenberger-a
10 20 30 58 79 100
19- "Carbine Williams"; James Stewart; Costanza-a; James Stewart photo-c
11 22 33 62 86 110
20- "Ivanhoe"; Robert Taylor & Liz Taylor photo-c 18 36 54 105 165 225

FAWCETT'S FUNNY ANIMALS (No. 1-26, 80-on titled "Funny Animals"; becomes Li'l Tomboy No. 92 on?)
Fawcett Publications/Charlton Comics No. 84 on: 12/42 - #79, 4/53; #80, 6/53 - #83, 12?/53; #84, 4/54 - #91, 2/56

1-Capt. Marvel on cover; intro. Hoppy The Captain Marvel Bunny, cloned from Capt. Marvel; Billy the Kid & Willie the Worm begin 58 116 174 371 636 900
2-Xmas-c 36 72 108 211 343 475
3-5: 3(2/43)-Spirit of '43-c 25 50 75 150 245 340
6,7,9,10 15 30 45 88 137 185
8-Flag-c 16 32 48 92 144 195
11-20: 14-Cover is a 1944 calendar 12 24 36 69 97 125
21-40: 25-Xmas-c. 26-St. Valentine's Day-c 10 20 30 54 72 90
41-86,90,91 9 18 27 47 61 75
87-89(10-54-2/55)-Merry Mailman ish (TV/Radio)-part photo-c
10 20 30 54 72 90

NOTE: *Marvel Bunny in all issues to at least No. 68 (not in 49-54).*

FAZE ONE FAZERS
AC Comics: 1986 - No. 4, Sept, 1986 (Limited series)

1-4 3.00

F.B.I., THE
Dell Publishing Co.: Apr-June, 1965

1-Sinnott-a 3 6 9 18 27 35

F.B.I. STORY, THE (Movie)
Dell Publishing Co.: No. 1069, Jan-Mar, 1960

Four Color 1069-Toth-a; James Stewart photo-c 9 18 27 61 106 150

FEAR (Adventure into...)
Marvel Comics Group: Nov, 1970 - No. 31, Dec, 1975

1-Fantasy & Sci-Fi-r in early issues; 68 pg. Giant size; Kirby-a(r)
6 12 18 41 66 90
2-6: 2-4-(68 pgs.). 5,6-(52 pgs.) Kirby-a(r) 4 8 12 24 37 50
7-9-Kirby-a(r) 3 6 9 16 22 28
10-Man-Thing begins (10/72, 4th app.), ends #19; see Savage Tales #1 for 1st app.; 1st solo series; Chaykin/Morrow-c/a; 5 10 15 32 51 70
11,12: 11-N. Adams-c. 12-Starlin/Buckler-a 3 6 9 16 22 28
13,14,16-18: 17-Origin/1st app. Wundarr 3 6 9 14 19 24
15-1st full-length Man-Thing story (8/73) 3 6 9 16 23 30
19-Intro. Howard the Duck; Val Mayerik-a (12/73) 5 10 15 32 51 70
20-Morbius, the Living Vampire begins, ends #31; has history recap of Morbius with X-Men & Spider-Man 5 10 15 32 51 70
21-23,25 3 6 9 14 19 24
24-Blade-c/sty 3 6 9 21 32 42
26-31 2 4 6 10 14 18

NOTE: ***Bolle** a-13i. **Brunner** c-15-17. **Buckler** a-11p, 12i. **Chaykin** a-10i. **Colan** a-23r. **Craig** a-10p. **Ditko** a-6-8r. **Evans** a-30. **Everett** a-9, 10i, 21r. **Gulacy** a-20p. **Heath** a-12r. **Heck** a-8r, 13r. **Gil Kane** a-21p; c(p)-20, 21, 23-28, 31. **Kirby** a-1-9r. **Maneely** a-24r. **Mooney** a-11i, 26r. **Morrow** a-11i. **Paul Reinman** a-14r. **Robbins** a(p)-25-27, 31. **Russell** a-23p, 24p. **Severin** c-8. **Starlin** c-12p.*

FEAR AGENT
Image Comics (#1-11)/Dark Horse Comics.: Oct, 2005 - No. 32, Nov, 2011 ($2.99/$3.50)

1-11: 1-Remender-s/Moore-a. 5-Opeña-a begins. 11-Francavilla-a 3.00
... The Last Goodbye 1-4 (Dark Horse, 6/07 - No. 4, 9/07) (#12-15) 3.00

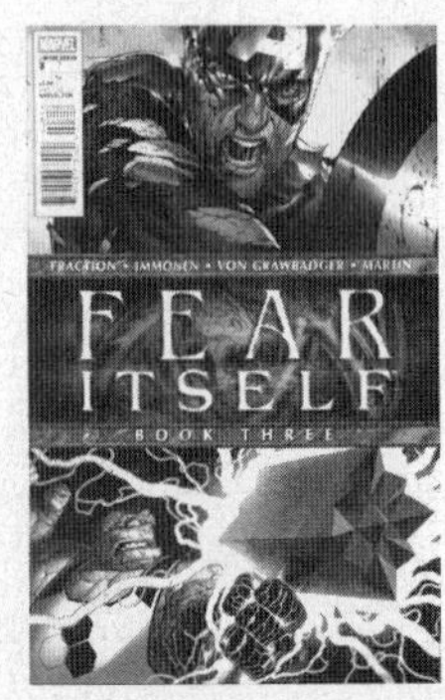

Fear Itself #3 © MAR

Feature Books #11 © KING

Feature Comics #37 © QUA

GD 2.0 | VG 4.0 | FN 6.0 | VF 8.0 | VF/NM 9.0 | NM- 9.2

Tales of the Fear Agent: Twelve Steps in One (#16), 17-27 3.00
28-32-($3.50) Hawthorne & Moore-a/Moore-c 3.50
... Vol 1.: Re-Ignition TPB (2006, $9.99) r/#1-4 10.00
... Vol 2.: My War TPB (Dark Horse Books, 2007, $14.95) r/#5-10; Opeña sketch pages 15.00

FEARBOOK
Eclipse Comics: April, 1986 ($1.75, one-shot, mature)

1-Scholastic Mag-r; Bissette-a 3.00

FEAR EFFECT (Based on the video game)
Image Comics (Top Cow): May, 2000; March, 2001 ($2.95)

Retro Helix 1 (3/01), Special 1 (5/00) 3.00

FEAR IN THE NIGHT (See Complete Mystery No. 3)

FEAR ITSELF
Marvel Comics: Jun, 2011 - No. 7, Dec, 2011 ($3.99/$4.99, limited series)

1-6-Fraction-s/Immonen-a/McNiven-c. 3-Bucky apparently killed 4.00
1-Blank cover 4.00
7-($4.99) Thor perishes; previews of ...: The Fearless, Incredible Hulk #1, Defenders #1 5.00
7.1 Captain America (1/12, $3.99) Brubaker-s/Guice-a; Bucky's fate 4.00
7.2 Thor (1/12, $3.99) Fraction-s/Adam Kubert-a/c; Thor's funeral; Tanarus returns 4.00
7.3 Iron Man (1/12, $3.99) Fraction-s/Larroca-a/c; Odin app. 4.00
...: Black Widow (8/11, $3.99) Peter Nguyen-a; Peregrine app. 4.00
...: Book of the Skull (5/11, $3.99) prequel to series; WWII flashback, Red Skull app. 4.00
...: Fellowship of Fear (10/11, $3.99) profiles of hammer-wielders and fear thrivers 4.00
...: FF (9/11, $2.99) Reed & Sue vs. Ben Grimm; Grummett-a/Dell'Otto-c 3.00
...: Sin's Past (6/11, $4.99) r/Captain America #355-357; Sisters of Sin app. 5.00
... Spotlight (6/11, $3.99) Interviews with Fraction and Immonen; feature articles 4.00
...: The Monkey King (11/11, $2.99) Joshua Fialkov-s/Juan Doe-a 3.00
...: The Worthy (9/11, $3.99) Origins of the hammer wielders; s/a by various 4.00

FEAR ITSELF: DEADPOOL
Marvel Comics: Aug, 2011 - No. 3, Oct, 2011 ($2.99, limited series)

1-3-Hastings-s/Dazo-a 3.00

FEAR ITSELF: FEARSOME FOUR
Marvel Comics: Aug, 2011 - No. 4, Nov, 2011 ($2.99, limited series)

1-4-Art by Bisley and others; Man-Thing, She-Hulk & Howard the Duck app. 3.00

FEAR ITSELF: HULK VS. DRACULA
Marvel Comics: Nov, 2011 - No. 3, Dec, 2011 ($2.99, limited series)

1-3-Gischler-s/Stegman-a; Dell'Otto-c 3.00

FEAR ITSELF: SPIDER-MAN
Marvel Comics: Jul, 2011 - No. 3, Sept, 2011 ($2.99, limited series)

1-3-Yost-s/McKone-a; Vermin app. 3.00

FEAR ITSELF: THE DEEP
Marvel Comics: Aug, 2011 - No. 4, Nov, 2011 ($2.99, limited series)

1-4-Bunn-s/Garbett-a; Sub-Mariner vs. Attuma; Doctor Strange & Silver Surfer app. 3.00

FEAR ITSELF: THE FEARLESS (Follows Fear Itself #7)
Marvel Comics: Dec, 2011 - No. 12 ($2.99, limited series)

1-10: 1-Fate of the Hammers; Bagley & Pelletier-a; Art Adams-c. 7-Wolverine app. 3.00

FEAR ITSELF: THE HOME FRONT
Marvel Comics: Jun, 2011 - No. 7, Dec, 2011 ($3.99, limited series)

1-7-Short story anthology; Speedball w/Mayhew-a in all; Chaykin-a; Djurdjevic-c 4.00

FEAR ITSELF: UNCANNY X-FORCE
Marvel Comics: Sept, 2011 - No. 3, Nov, 2011 ($2.99, limited series)

1-3-Bianchi-a/c 3.00

FEAR ITSELF: WOLVERINE
Marvel Comics: Sept, 2011 - No. 3, Nov, 2011 ($2.99, limited series)

1-3-Boschi-a; Wolverine vs. S.T.R.I.K.E. 1-Acuña-c. 2,3-Molina-c 3.00

FEAR ITSELF: YOUTH IN REVOLT
Marvel Comics: Jul, 2011 - No. 6, Dec, 2011 ($2.99, limited series)

1-6-Firestar and The Initiative app.; McKeever-s/Norton-a 3.00

FEARLESS FAGAN
Dell Publishing Co.: No. 441, Dec, 1952 (one-shot)

	GD 2.0	VG 4.0	FN 6.0	VF 8.0	VF/NM 9.0	NM- 9.2
Four Color 441	4	8	12	24	37	50

FEATURE BOOK (Dell) (See Large Feature Comic)

FEATURE BOOKS (Newspaper-r, early issues)
David McKay Publications: May, 1937 - No. 57, 1948 (B&W)
(Full color, 68 pgs. begin #26 on)

Note: See individual alphabetical listings for prices

nn-Popeye & the Jeep (#1, 100 pgs.); reprinted as Feature Books #3(Very Rare; only 3 known copies, 1-VF, 2-in low grade)
nn-Dick Tracy (#1)-Reprinted as Feature Book #4 (100 pgs.) & in part as 4-Color #1 (Rare, less than 10 known copies)

NOTE: *Above books were advertised together with different covers from Feat. Books #3 & 4.*

1-King of the Royal Mtd. (#1)
2-Popeye (6/37) by Segar same as nn issue but a new cover added
3-Popeye (7/37) by Segar;
4-Dick Tracy (8/37)-Same as nn issue but a new cover added
5-Popeye (9/37) by Segar
6-Dick Tracy (10/37)
7-Little Orphan Annie (#1, 11/37) (Rare)-Reprints strips from 12/31/34 to 7/17/35
8-Secret Agent X-9 (12/37) -Not by Raymond
9-Dick Tracy (1/38)
10-Popeye (2/38)
11-Little Annie Rooney (#1, 3/38)
12-Blondie (#1) (4/38) (Rare)
13-Inspector Wade (5/38)
14-Popeye (6/38) by Segar
15-Barney Baxter (#1) (7/38)
16-Red Eagle (8/38)
17-Gangbusters (#1, 9/38) (1st app.)
18,19-Mandrake
20-Phantom (#1, 12/38)
21-Lone Ranger
22-Phantom
23-Mandrake
24-Lone Ranger (1941)
25-Flash Gordon (#1)-Reprints not by Raymond
26-Prince Valiant (1941)-Hal Foster-c/a; newspaper strips reprinted, pgs. 1-28,30-63; color & 68 pg. issues begin; Foster cover is only original comic book artwork by him
27-29,31,34-Blondie
30-Katzenjammer Kids (#1, 1942)
32,35,41,44-Katzenjammer Kids
33(nn)-Romance of Flying; World War II photos
36('43),38,40('44),42,43, 45,47-Blondie
37-Katzenjammer Kids; has photo & biog. of Harold H. Knerr (1883-1949) who took over strip from Rudolph Dirks in 1914
39-Phantom
46-Mandrake in the Fire World-(58 pgs.)
48-Maltese Falcon by Dashiell Hammett('46)
49,50-Perry Mason; based on Gardner novels
51,54-Rip Kirby; Raymond-c/s; origin-#51
52,55-Mandrake
53,56,57-Phantom

NOTE: *All Feature Books through #25 are over-sized 8-1/2x11-3/8" comics with color covers and black and white interiors. The covers are rough, heavy stock. The page counts, including covers, are as follows: nn, #3, 4-100 pgs.; #1, 2-52 pgs.; #5-25 are all 76 pgs. #33 was found in bound set from publisher. Reprints from 1980s exist.*

FEATURE COMICS (Formerly Feature Funnies)
Quality Comics Group: No. 21, June, 1939 - No. 144, May, 1950

	GD 2.0	VG 4.0	FN 6.0	VF 8.0	VF/NM 9.0	NM- 9.2
21-The Clock, Jane Arden & Mickey Finn continue from Feature Funnies	54	108	162	343	574	825
22-26: 23-Charlie Chan begins (8/39, 1st app.)	40	80	120	242	401	560
26-(nn, nd)-Cover in one color, (10¢, 36 pgs.; issue No. blanked out. Two variations exist, each contain half of the regular #26)	40	80	120	242	401	560
27-(Rare)-Origin/1st app. Doll Man by Eisner (scripts) & Lou Fine (art); Doll Man begins, ends #139	541	1082	1623	3950	6975	10,000
28-(Rare)-2nd app. Doll Man by Lou Fine	206	412	618	1318	2259	3200
29	110	220	330	704	1202	1700
30-1st Doll Man-c	184	368	552	1168	2009	2850
31-Last Clock & Charlie Chan issue (4/40); Charlie Chan moves to Big Shot #1 following month (5/40)	74	148	222	470	810	1150
32,34,36: Dollman covers. 32-Rusty Ryan & Samar begin. 34-Captain Fortune app.	73	146	219	467	796	1125
33,35,37: 37-Last Fine Doll Man	48	96	144	302	514	725

NOTE: *A 15¢ Canadian version of Feature Comics #37, made in the US, exists.*

	GD 2.0	VG 4.0	FN 6.0	VF 8.0	VF/NM 9.0	NM- 9.2
38,40-Dollman covers. 38-Origin the Ace of Space. 40-Bruce Blackburn in costume	55	110	165	352	601	850
39,41: 39-Origin The Destroying Demon, ends #40; X-Mas-c.	40	80	120	242	401	560
42,46,48,50-Dollman covers. 42-USA, the Spirit of Old Glory begins. 46-Intro. Boyville Brigadiers in Rusty Ryan. 48-USA ends	42	84	126	265	445	625
43,45,47,49: 47-Fargo Kid begins	30	60	90	177	289	400
44-Doll Man by Crandall begins, ends #63; Crandall-a(2)	54	108	162	343	574	825
51,53,55,57,59: 57-Spider Widow begins	22	44	66	128	209	290
52,54,56,58,60-Dollman covers. 56-Marijuana story in Swing Sisson strip. 60-Raven begins, ends #71	31	62	93	186	303	420
61,63,65,67	20	40	60	114	182	250
62,64,66,68-Dollman covers. 68-(5/43)	27	54	81	160	263	365
69,71-Phantom Lady x-over in Spider Widow	22	44	66	128	209	290
70-Dollman-c; Phantom Lady x-over	30	60	90	177	289	400
72,74,77-80,100-Dollman covers. 72-Spider Widow ends	22	44	66	128	209	290

Feature Films #3 © DC

Felix the Cat #22 © KING

Femforce #90 © AC

	GD 2.0	VG 4.0	FN 6.0	VF 8.0	VF/NM 9.0	NM- 9.2
73,75,76	16	32	48	94	147	200
81-99-All Dollman covers	16	32	48	94	147	200
101-144: 139-Last Doll Man & last Doll Man cover. 140-Intro. Stuntman Stetson (Stuntman Stetson c-140-144)	14	28	42	82	121	160

NOTE: ***Celardo** a-37-43. **Crandall** a-44-60, 62, 63-on(most). **Gustavson** a-(Rusty Ryan)- 32-134. **Powell** a-34, 64-73. The Clock c-25, 28, 29. Doll Man c-30, 32, 34, 36, 38, 40, 42, 44, 46, 48, 50, 52, 54, 56, 58, 60, 62, 64, 66, 68, 70, 72, 74, 77-139. Joe Palooka c-21, 24, 27.*

FEATURE FILMS
National Periodical Publ.: Mar-Apr, 1950 - No. 4, Sept-Oct, 1950 (All photo-c)

	GD	VG	FN	VF	VF/NM	NM-
1- "Captain China" with John Payne, Gail Russell, Lon Chaney & Edgar Bergen	66	132	198	416	701	985
2- "Riding High" with Bing Crosby	69	138	207	435	735	1035
3- "The Eagle & the Hawk" with John Payne, Rhonda Fleming & D. O'Keefe	66	132	198	416	701	985
4- "Fancy Pants"; Bob Hope & Lucille Ball	72	144	216	454	770	1085

FEATURE FUNNIES (Feature Comics No. 21 on)
Harry 'A' Chesler: Oct, 1937 - No. 20, May, 1939

	GD	VG	FN	VF	VF/NM	NM-
1(V9#1-indicia)-Joe Palooka, Mickey Finn (1st app.), The Bungles, Jane Arden, Dixie Dugan (1st app.), Big Top, Ned Brant, Strange As It Seems, & Off the Record strip reprints begin	322	644	966	1770	2635	3500
2-The Hawk app. (11/37); Goldberg-c	150	300	450	825	1213	1600
3-Hawks of Seas begins by Eisner, ends #12; The Clock begins; Christmas-c	117	234	351	644	947	1250
4,5	86	172	258	473	699	925
6-12: 11-Archie O'Toole by Bud Thomas begins, ends #22	67	134	201	369	542	715
13-Espionage, Starring Black X begins by Eisner, ends #20	71	142	213	391	578	765
14-20	50	100	150	275	408	540

NOTE: *Joe Palooka covers 1, 6, 9, 12, 15, 18.*

FEATURE PRESENTATION, A (Feature Presentations Magazine #6)
(Formerly Women in Love) (Also see Startling Terror Tales #11)
Fox Features Syndicate: No. 5, April, 1950

	GD	VG	FN	VF	VF/NM	NM-
5(#1)-Black Tarantula (scarce)	55	110	165	352	601	850

FEATURE PRESENTATIONS MAGAZINE (Formerly A Feature Presentation #5; becomes Feature Stories Magazine #3 on)
Fox Features Syndicate: No. 6, July, 1950

	GD	VG	FN	VF	VF/NM	NM-
6(#2)-Moby Dick; Wood-c	34	68	102	199	325	450

FEATURE STORIES MAGAZINE (Formerly Feature Presentations Mag. #6)
Fox Features Syndicate: No. 3, Aug, 1950

	GD	VG	FN	VF	VF/NM	NM-
3-Jungle Lil, Zegra stories; bondage-c	39	78	117	240	395	550

FEDERAL MEN COMICS
DC Comics: 1936

nn-Ashcan comic, not distributed to newsstands, only for in house use (no known sales)

FEDERAL MEN COMICS (See Adventure Comics #32, The Comics Magazine, New Adventure Comics, New Book of Comics, New Comics & Star Spangled Comics #91)
Gerard Publ. Co.: No. 2, 1945 (DC reprints from 1930's)

	GD	VG	FN	VF	VF/NM	NM-
2-Siegel/Shuster-a; cover redrawn from Det. #9	37	74	111	218	354	490

FELICIA HARDY: THE BLACK CAT
Marvel Comics: July, 1994 - No. 4, Oct, 1994 ($1.50, limited series)

1-4: 1,4-Spider-Man app. 3.00

FELIX'S NEPHEWS INKY & DINKY
Harvey Publications: Sept, 1957 - No. 7, Oct, 1958

	GD	VG	FN	VF	VF/NM	NM-
1-Cover shows Inky's left eye with 2 pupils	10	20	30	58	79	100
2-7	7	14	21	37	46	55

NOTE: ***Messmer** art in 1-6. **Oriolo** a-1-7.*

FELIX THE CAT (See Cat Tales 3-D, The Funnies, March of Comics #24,36,51, New Funnies & Popular Comics)
Dell Publ. No. 1-19/Toby No. 20-61/Harvey No. 62-118/Dell No. 1-12:
1943 - No. 118, Nov, 1961; Sept-Nov, 1962 - No. 12, July-Sept, 1965

	GD	VG	FN	VF	VF/NM	NM-
Four Color 15	72	144	216	583	1267	1950
Four Color 46('44)	36	72	108	270	585	900
Four Color 77('45)	35	70	105	250	545	840
Four Color 119('46)-All new stories begin	30	60	90	214	462	710
Four Color 135('46)	21	42	63	146	311	475
Four Color 162(9/47)	15	30	45	104	227	350
1(2-3/48)(Dell)	24	48	72	168	359	550
2	12	24	36	81	166	250
3-5	10	20	30	68	127	185
6-19(2-3/51-Dell)	8	16	24	56	96	135
20-30,32,33,36,38-61(6/55)-All Messmer issues.(Toby): 28-(2/52)-Some copies have #29 on cover, #28 on inside (Rare in high grade)	14	28	42	95	205	315
31,34,35-No Messmer-a; Messmer-c only 31,34	8	16	24	56	96	135
37-(100 pgs., 25 ¢, 1/15/53, X-Mas-c, Toby; daily & Sunday-r (rare)	35	70	105	250	545	840
62(8/55)-80,100 (Harvey)	4	8	12	28	44	60
81-99	4	8	12	24	37	50
101-118(11/61): 101-117-Reprints. 118-All new-a	3	6	9	18	27	35
12-269-211(#1, 9-11/62)(Dell)-No Messmer	5	10	15	30	48	65
2-12(7-9/65)(Dell, TV)-No Messmer	4	8	12	24	37	50
3-D Comic Book 1(1953-One Shot, 25¢)-w/glasses	28	56	84	168	309	450
Summer Annual nn ('53, 25¢, 100 pgs., Toby)-Daily & Sunday-r	38	76	114	239	457	675
Winter Annual 2 ('54, 25¢, 100 pgs., Toby)-Daily & Sunday-r	35	70	105	221	423	625

(Special note: Despite the covers on Toby 37 and the Summer Annual above proclaiming "all new stories," they were actually reformatted newspaper strips)

NOTE: ***Otto Messmer** went to work for Universal Film as an animator in 1915 and then worked for the Pat Sullivan animation studio in 1916. He created a black cat in the cartoon short, Feline Follies in 1919 that became known as Felix in the early 1920s. The Felix Sunday strip began Aug. 14, 1923 and continued until Sept. 19, 1943 whjen **Messmer** took the character to Dell (Western Publishing) and began doing Felix comic books, first adapting strips to the comic format. The first all new Felix comic was Four Color #119 in 1946 (#4 in the Dell run). The daily Felix was begun on May 9, 1927 by another artist, but by the following year, **Messmer** did it too. King Features took the daily away from **Messmer** in 1954 and he began to do some of his most dynamic art for Toby Press. The daily was continued by **Joe Oriolo** who drew it until it was discontinued Jan. 9, 1967. **Oriolo** was **Messmer's** assistant for many years and inked some of **Messmer's** pencils through the Toby run, as well as doing some of the stories by himself. Though **Messmer** continued to work for Harvey, his contirubitons were limited, and no all **Messmer** stories appeared after the Toby run until some early Toby reprints were published in the 1990s Harvey revival of the title. 4-Color No. 15, 46, 77 and the Toby Annuals are all daily or Sunday newspaper reprints from the 1930's-1940's drawn by **Otto Messmer**. #101-r/#64; 102-r/#65; 103-r/#67; 104-117-r/#68-81. **Messmer**-a in all Dell/Toby/Harvey issues except #31, 34, 35, 97, 98, 100, 118. **Oriolo** a-20, 31-on.*

FELIX THE CAT (Also see The Nine Lives of...)
Harvey Comics/Gladstone: Sept, 1991 - No. 7, Jan, 1993 ($1.25/$1.50, bi-monthly)

1: 1950s-r/Toby issues by Messmer begins. 1-Inky and Dinky back-up story (produced by Gladstone) 4.00
2-7, Big Book, V2#1 (9/92, $1.95, 52 pgs.) 3.00

FELIX THE CAT AND FRIENDS
Felix Comics: 1992 - No. 5, 1993 ($1.95)

1-5: 1-Contains Felix trading cards 3.00

FELIX THE CAT & HIS FRIENDS (Pat Sullivan's...)
Toby Press: Dec, 1953 - No. 3, 1954 (Indicia title for #2&3 as listed)

	GD	VG	FN	VF	VF/NM	NM-
1 (Indicia title, "Felix and His Friends," #1 only)	29	58	87	170	278	385
2-3	18	36	54	105	165	225

FELIX THE CAT DIGEST MAGAZINE
Harvey Comics: July, 1992 ($1.75, digest-size, 98 pgs.)

1-Felix, Richie Rich stories 6.00

FELIX THE CAT KEEPS ON WALKIN'
Hamilton Comics: 1991 ($15.95, 8-1/2"x11", 132 pgs.)

nn-Reprints 15 Toby Press Felix the Cat and Felix and His Friends stories in new color 16.00

FELL
Image Comics: Sept, 2005 - No. 9, Jan, 2008 ($1.99)

1-9-Warren Ellis-s/Ben Templesmith-a 3.00
..., Vol. 1: Feral City TPB (2007, $14.99) r/#1-8 15.00

FELON
Image Comics (Minotaur Press): Nov, 2001 - No. 4, Apr, 2002 ($2.95, B&W)

1-4-Rucka-s/Clark-a/c 3.00

FEM FANTASTIQUE
AC Comics: Aug, 1988 ($1.95, B&W)

V2#1-By Bill Black; Betty Page pin-up 4.00

FEMFORCE (Also see Untold Origin of the Femforce)
Americomics: Apr, 1985 - No. 109 (1.75-/2.95, B&W #16-56)

	GD	VG	FN	VF	VF/NM	NM-
1-Black-a in most; Nightveil, Ms. Victory begin	1	3	4	6	8	10

2-10 4.00
11-43: 25-Origin/1st app. new Ms. Victory. 28-Colt leaves. 29,30-Camilla-r by Mayo from Jungle Comics. 36-(2.95, 52 pgs.) 4.00
44,64: 44-W/mini-comic, Catman & Kitten #0. 64-Re-intro Black Phantom 5.00
45-49,51-63,65-99: 51-Photo-c from movie. 57-Begin color issues. 95-Photo-c 3.00
50 ($2.95, 52 pgs.)-Contains flexi-disc; origin retold; most AC characters app. 4.00
100-($3.95) 5.00

FF #3 © MAR

50 Girls 50 #1 © Cho & Murray

Fight Against Crime #2 © Story

GD 2.0 | VG 4.0 | FN 6.0 | VF 8.0 | VF/NM 9.0 | NM- 9.2

100-($6.90)-Polybagged 1 2 3 5 6 8
101-109-($4.95) 5.00
Special 1 (Fall, '84)(B&W, 52pgs.)-1st app. Ms. Victory, She-Cat, Blue Bulleteer, Rio Rita & Lady Luger 4.00
Bad Girl Backlash-(12/95, $5.00) 5.00
Frightbook 1 ('92, $2.95, B&W)-Halloween special, In the House of Horror 1 ('89, 2.50, B&W), Night of the Demon 1 ('90, 2.75, B&W), Out of the Asylum Special 1 ('87, B&W, $1.95), Pin-Up Portfolio 4.00
Pin-Up Portfolio (5 issues) 4.00

FEMFORCE UP CLOSE
AC Comics: Apr, 1992 - No. 11, 1995 ($2.75, quarterly)
1-11: 1-Stars Nightveil; inside f/c photo from Femforce movie. 2-Stars Stardust. 3-Stars Dragonfly. 4-Stars She-Cat 3.50

FERDINAND THE BULL (See Mickey Mouse Magazine V4#3)
Dell Publishing Co.: 1938 (10¢, large size, some color w/rest B&W)
nn 20 40 60 114 182 250

FERRET
Malibu Comics: Sept, 1992; May, 1993 - No. 10, Feb, 1994 ($1.95)
1-(1992, one-shot) 3.00
1-10: 1-Die-cut-c. 2-4-Collector's Ed. w/poster. 5-Polybagged w/Skycap 3.00
2-4-($1.95)-Newsstand Edition w/different-c 3.00

FERRYMAN
DC Comics (WildStorm): Early Dec, 2008 - No. 5, Mar, 2009 ($3.50)
1-5-Andreyko-s/Wayshak-a 3.50

FF (Fantastic Four after Human Torch's death)
Marvel Comics: May, 2011 - Present ($3.99)
1-Hickman-s/Epting-a; Spider-Man joins 4.00
1-Blank variant cover 4.00
1-Variant-c by Daniel Acuña 8.00
1-Variant-c by Stan Goldberg 6.00
2-15-($2.99) 2-Dr. Doom joins. 4,5-Kitson-a. 5-7-Black Bolt returns. 10,11-Avengers app. 3.00
...: Fifty Fantastic Years 1 (11/11, $4.99) Handbook format profiles of heroes and foes 5.00

F5
Image Comics/Dark Horse: Jan, 2000 - No. 4, Oct, 2000 ($2.50/$2.95)
Preview (1/00, $2.50) Character bios and b&w pages; Daniel-s/a 3.00
1-($2.95, 48 pages) Tony Daniel-s/a 4.00
1-($20.00) Variant bikini-c 20.00
2-4-($2.50) 3.00
F5 Origin (Dark Horse Comics, 11/01, $2.99) w/cover gallery & sketches 3.00

FIBBER McGEE & MOLLY (Radio)(Also see A-1 Comics)
Magazine Enterprises: No. 25, 1949 (one-shot)
A-1 25 12 24 36 69 97 125

FICTION ILLUSTRATED
Byron Preiss Visual Publ./Pyramid: No. 1, Jan, 1975 - No. 4, Jan, 1977 ($1.00, #1,2 are digest size, 132 pgs.; #3,4 are graphic novels for mail order and specialty bookstores only)
1,2: 1-Schlomo Raven; Sutton-a. 2-Starfawn; Stephen Fabian-a. 2 4 6 13 18 22
3-($1.00-c, 4 3/4 x 6 1/2" digest size) Chandler; new Steranko-a 3 6 9 14 20 26
3-($4.95-c, 8 1/2 x 11" graphic novel; low print) same contents and indicia, but "Chandler" is the cover feature title 5 10 15 35 55 75
4-($4.95-c, 8 1/2 x 11" graphic novel; low print) Son of Sherlock Holmes; Reese-a 4 8 12 28 44 60

FIERCE
Dark Horse Comics (Rocket Comics): July, 2004 - No. 4, Dec, 2004 ($2.99, limited series)
1-4-Jeremy Love-s/Robert Love-a 3.00

15-LOVE
Marvel Comics: Aug, 2011 - No. 3, Oct, 2011 ($4.99, limited series)
1-3-Tennis academy story; Andi Watson-s/Tommy Ohtsuka-a/c; Sho Murase-c 5.00

50 GIRLS 50
Image Comics: Jun, 2011 - No. 4, Sept, 2011 ($2.99, limited series)
1-4-Frank Cho-c; Cho & Murray-s/Medellin-a 3.00

52 (Leads into Countdown series)
DC Comics: Week One, July, 2006 - Week Fifty-Two, Jul, 2007 ($2.50, weekly series)
1-Chronicles the year after Infinite Crisis; Johns, Morrison, Rucka & Waid-s; JG Jones-c 4.00
2-10: 2-History of the DC Universe back-up thru #11. 7-Intro. Kate Kane. 10-Supernova 3.00

GD 2.0 | VG 4.0 | FN 6.0 | VF 8.0 | VF/NM 9.0 | NM- 9.2

11-Batwoman debut (single panel cameo in #9) 4.00
12-52: 12-Isis gains powers; back-up 2 pg. origins begin. 15-Booster Gold killed. 17-Lobo returns. 30-Batman-c/Robin & Nightwing app. 37-Booster Gold returns. 38-The Question dies. 42-Ralph Dibny dies. 44-Isis dies. 48-Renee becomes The Question. 50-World War III. 51-Mister Mind evolves. 52-The Multiverse is re-formed; wraparound-c 3.00
...: The Companion TPB (2007, $19.99) r/solo stories of series' prominent characters 20.00
...: Volume One TPB (2007, $19.99) r/#1-13; sample of page development; cover gallery 20.00
...: Volume Two TPB (2007, $19.99) r/#14-26; creator notes and sketches; cover gallery 20.00
...: Volume Three TPB (2007, $19.99) r/#27-39; notes and sketches; cover gallery 20.00
...: Volume Four TPB (2007, $19.99) r/#40-52; creator commentary; cover gallery 20.00

52 AFTERMATH: THE FOUR HORSEMEN (Takes place during 52 Week Fifty)
DC Comics: Oct, 2007 - No. 6, Mar, 2008 ($2.99, limited series)
1-6-Giffen-s/Olliffe-a; Superman, Batman & Wonder Woman app. 2-4,6-Van Sciver-c 3.00
TPB (2008, $19.99) r/#1-6 20.00

52/WWIII (Takes place during 52 Week Fifty)
DC Comics: Part One, Jun, 2007 - Part Four, Jun, 2007 ($2.50, 4 issues came out same day)
Part One - Part Four: Van Sciver-c; heroes vs. Black Adam. 3-Terra dies 3.00
DC: World War III TPB (2007, $17.99) r/Part One - Four and 52 Week 50 18.00

55 DAYS AT PEKING (See Movie Comics)

FIGHT AGAINST CRIME (Fight Against the Guilty #22, 23)
Story Comics: May, 1951 - No. 21, Sept, 1954
1-True crime stories #1-4 41 82 123 260 435 610
2 23 46 69 136 223 310
3,5: 5-Frazetta-a, 1 pg.; content change to horror & suspense 20 40 60 118 192 265
4-Drug story "Hopped Up Killers" 22 44 66 128 209 290
6,7: 6-Used in **POP**, pgs. 83,84 19 38 57 111 176 240
8-Last crime format issue 18 36 54 105 165 225
NOTE: *No. 9-21 contain violent, gruesome stories with blood, dismemberment, decapitation, E.C. style plot twists and several E.C. swipes. Bondage c-4, 6, 18, 19.*
9-11,13 43 86 129 271 461 650
12-Morphine drug story "The Big Dope" 47 94 141 296 498 700
14-Tothish art by Ross Andru; electrocution-c 46 92 138 290 488 685
15-B&W & color illos in **POP** 45 90 135 284 480 675
16-E.C. story swipe/Haunt of Fear #19; Tothish-a by Ross Andru; bondage-c 47 94 141 296 498 700
17-Wildey E.C. swipe/Shock SuspenStories #9; knife through neck-c (1/54) 50 100 150 315 533 750
18,19: 19-Bondage/torture-c 42 84 126 268 452 635
20-Decapitation cover; contains hanging, ax murder, blood & violence 103 206 309 659 1130 1600
21-E.C. swipe 39 78 117 233 384 535
NOTE: ***Cameron** a-4, 5, 8. **Hollingsworth** a-3-7, 9, 10, 13. **Wildey** a-6, 15, 16.*

FIGHT AGAINST THE GUILTY (Formerly Fight Against Crime)
Story Comics: No. 22, Dec, 1954 - No. 23, Mar, 1955
22-Tothish-a by Ross Andru; Ditko-a; E.C. story swipe; electrocution-c (Last pre-code) 39 78 117 240 395 550
23-Hollingsworth-a 26 52 78 154 252 350

FIGHT COMICS
Fiction House Magazines: Jan, 1940 - No. 83, 11/52; No. 84, Wint, 1952-53; No. 85, Spring, 1953; No. 86, Summer, 1954
1-Origin Spy Fighter, Starring Saber; Jack Dempsey life story; Shark Brodie & Chip Collins begin; Fine-c; Eisner-a 354 708 1062 2478 4339 6200
2-Joe Louis life story; Fine/Eisner-c 126 252 378 806 1378 1950
3-Rip Regan, the Power Man begins (3/40) 116 232 348 742 1271 1800
4,5: 4-Fine-c 68 136 204 435 743 1050
6-10: 6,7-Powell-c 53 106 159 334 567 800
11-14: Rip Regan ends 50 100 150 315 533 750
15-1st app. Super American plus-c (10/41) 62 124 186 394 677 960
16-Captain Fight begins (12/41); Spy Fighter ends 62 124 186 394 677 960
17,18: Super American ends 48 96 144 302 514 725
19-Japanese WWII-c; Captain Fight ends; Senorita Rio begins (6/42, origin & 1st app.); Rip Carson, Chute Trooper begins 51 102 153 320 543 765
20 43 86 129 271 461 650
21-30: 22,23-Japanese WWII-c 40 80 120 246 411 575
31-Classic decapitation-c 129 258 387 826 1413 2000
32-Tiger Girl begins (6/44, 1st app.?) 41 82 123 256 428 600
33-50: 44-Capt. Fight returns. 48-Used in Love and Death by Legman. 49-Jungle-c begin, end #81 34 68 102 204 332 460
51-Origin Tiger Girl; Patsy Pin-Up app. 39 78 117 236 388 540
52-60,62-64-Last Baker issue 24 48 72 142 234 325

Fight Comics #74 © FH

Fighting Daniel Boone nn © AVON

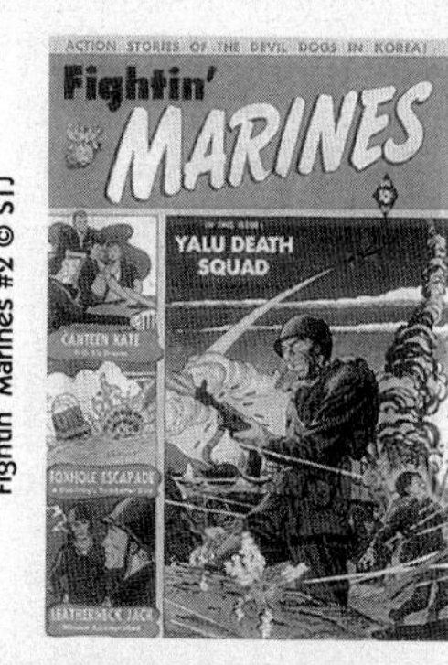

Fightin' Marines #2 © STJ

	GD 2.0	VG 4.0	FN 6.0	VF 8.0	VF/NM 9.0	NM- 9.2
61-Origin Tiger Girl retold	25	50	75	150	245	340
65-78: 78-Used in **POP**, pg. 99	20	40	60	117	189	260
79-The Space Rangers app.	20	40	60	120	195	270
80-85: 81-Last jungle-c. 82-85-War-c/stories	18	36	54	103	162	220
86-Two Tigerman stories by Evans-r/Rangers Comics #40,41; Moreira-r/Rangers Comics #45	18	36	54	103	162	220

NOTE: *Bondage covers, Lingerie, headlights panels are common. Captain Fight by* **Kamen**-*51-66. Kayo Kirby by* **Baker**-*#43-64, 67(not by Baker). Senorita Rio by* **Kamen**-*#57-64; by* **Grandenetti**-*#65, 66. Tiger Girl by* **Baker**-*#36-60, 62-64;* **Eisner** *c-1-3, 5, 10, 11.* **Kamen** *a-54?, 57?* **Tuska** *a-1, 5, 8, 10, 21, 29, 34.* **Whitman** *c-73-84.* **Zolnerwich** *c-16, 17, 22. Power Man c-5, 6, 9. Super American c-15-17. Tiger Girl c-49-81.*

FIGHT FOR LOVE
United Features Syndicate: 1952 (no month)

	GD 2.0	VG 4.0	FN 6.0	VF 8.0	VF/NM 9.0	NM- 9.2
nn-Abbie & Slats newspaper-r	9	18	27	47	61	75

FIGHT FOR TOMORROW
DC Comics (Vertigo): Nov, 2002 - No. 6, Apr, 2003 ($2.50, limited series)

	GD 2.0	VG 4.0	FN 6.0	VF 8.0	VF/NM 9.0	NM- 9.2
1-6-Denys Cowan-a/Brian Wood-s. 1-Jim Lee-c. 5-Jo Chen-c						3.00
TPB (2008, $14.99) r/#1-6						15.00

FIGHTING AIR FORCE (See United States Fighting Air Force)

FIGHTIN' AIR FORCE (Formerly Sherlock Holmes?; Never Again? War and Attack #54 on)
Charlton Comics: No. 3, Feb, 1956 - No. 53, Feb-Mar, 1966

	GD 2.0	VG 4.0	FN 6.0	VF 8.0	VF/NM 9.0	NM- 9.2
V1#3	9	18	27	50	65	80
4-10	7	14	21	35	43	50
11(3/58, 68 pgs.)	8	16	24	44	57	70
12 (100 pgs.)-U.S. Nukes Russia	12	24	36	69	97	125
13-30: 13,24-Glanzman-a. 24-Glanzman-c. 27-Area 51, UFO story	3	6	9	19	29	38
31-50: 50-American Eagle begins	3	6	9	14	20	26
51-53: 51-Hitler-c/story	2	4	6	13	18	22

FIGHTING AMERICAN
Headline Publ./Prize (Crestwood): Apr-May, 1954 - No. 7, Apr-May, 1955

	GD 2.0	VG 4.0	FN 6.0	VF 8.0	VF/NM 9.0	NM- 9.2
1-Origin & 1st app. Fighting American & Speedboy (Capt. America & Bucky clones); S&K-c/a(3); 1st super hero satire series	174	348	522	1114	1907	2700
2-S&K-a(3)	81	162	243	518	884	1250
3-5: 3,4-S&K-a(3). 5-S&K-a(2); Kirby/?-a	62	124	186	394	680	965
6-Origin-r (4 pgs.) plus 2 pgs. by S&K	59	118	177	375	643	910
7-Kirby-a	53	106	159	334	567	800

NOTE: **Simon & Kirby** *covers on all. 6 is last pre-code issue.*

FIGHTING AMERICAN
Harvey Publications: Oct, 1966 (25¢)

	GD 2.0	VG 4.0	FN 6.0	VF 8.0	VF/NM 9.0	NM- 9.2
1-Origin Fighting American & Speedboy by S&K-r; S&K-c/a(3); 1 pg. Neal Adams ad	6	12	18	37	59	80

FIGHTING AMERICAN
DC Comics: Feb, 1994 - No. 6, 1994 ($1.50, limited series)

	GD 2.0	VG 4.0	FN 6.0	VF 8.0	VF/NM 9.0	NM- 9.2
1-6						3.00

FIGHTING AMERICAN (Vol. 3)
Awesome Entertainment: Aug, 1997 - No. 2, Oct, 1997 ($2.50)

	GD 2.0	VG 4.0	FN 6.0	VF 8.0	VF/NM 9.0	NM- 9.2
Preview-Agent America (pre-lawsuit)	1	2	3	5	6	7
1-Four covers by Liefeld, Churchill, Platt, McGuinness						3.00
1-Platinum Edition, 1-Gold foil Edition						10.00
1-Comic Cavalcade Edition, 2-American Ent. Spice Ed.						4.00
2-Platt-c, 2-Liefeld variant-c						3.00

FIGHTING AMERICAN: DOGS OF WAR
Awesome-Hyperwerks: Sept, 1998 - No. 3, May, 1999 ($2.50)

	GD 2.0	VG 4.0	FN 6.0	VF 8.0	VF/NM 9.0	NM- 9.2
Limited Convention Special (7/98, B&W) Platt-a						3.00
1-3-Starlin-s/Platt-a/c						3.00

FIGHTING AMERICAN: RULES OF THE GAME
Awesome Entertainment: Nov, 1997 - No. 3, Mar, 1998 ($2.50, lim. series)

	GD 2.0	VG 4.0	FN 6.0	VF 8.0	VF/NM 9.0	NM- 9.2
1-3: 1-Loeb-s/McGuinness-a/c. 2-Flip book with Swat! preview						3.00
1-Liefeld SPICE variant-c, 1-Dynamic Forces Ed.; McGuinness-c						3.00
1-Liefeld Fighting American & cast variant-c						3.00

FIGHTIN' ARMY (Formerly Soldier and Marine Comics) (See Captain Willy Schultz)
Charlton Comics: No. 16, 1/56 - No. 127, 12/76; No. 128, 9/77 - No. 172, 11/84

	GD 2.0	VG 4.0	FN 6.0	VF 8.0	VF/NM 9.0	NM- 9.2
16	9	18	27	50	65	80
17-19,21-23,25-30	7	14	21	35	43	50
20-Ditko-a	9	18	27	50	65	80
24 (3/58, 68 pgs.)	8	16	24	42	54	65
31-45	3	6	9	19	28	38
46-60: 51-Hitler-c	3	6	9	16	23	30
61-75	3	6	9	14	19	24
76-1st The Lonely War of Willy Schultz	3	6	9	18	27	35
77-80: 77-92-The Lonely War of Willy Schultz. 79-Devil Brigade	3	6	9	14	19	24
81-88,91,93-99: 82,83-Devil Brigade	2	4	6	10	14	18
89,90,92-Ditko-a	3	6	9	14	20	26
100	2	4	6	13	18	22
101-127	2	4	6	8	11	14
128-140	1	2	3	5	7	9
141-165	1	2	3	4	5	7
166-172-Low print run	1	2	3	5	6	8
108 (Modern Comics-1977)-Reprint						5.00

NOTE: **Aparo** *c-154.* **Glanzman** *a-77-88.* **Montes/Bache** *a-48, 49, 51, 69, 75, 76, 170r.*

FIGHTING CARAVANS (See Zane Grey 4-Color 632)

FIGHTING DANIEL BOONE
Avon Periodicals: 1953

	GD 2.0	VG 4.0	FN 6.0	VF 8.0	VF/NM 9.0	NM- 9.2
nn-Kinstler-c/a, 22 pgs.	18	36	54	105	165	225
I.W. Reprint #1-Reprints #1 above; Kinstler-c/a; Lawrence/Alascia-a	3	6	9	14	19	24

FIGHTING DAVY CROCKETT (Formerly Kit Carson)
Avon Periodicals: No. 9, Oct-Nov, 1955

	GD 2.0	VG 4.0	FN 6.0	VF 8.0	VF/NM 9.0	NM- 9.2
9-Kinstler-c	10	20	30	54	72	90

FIGHTIN' FIVE, THE (Formerly Space War) (Also see The Peacemaker)
Charlton Comics: July, 1964 - No. 41, Jan, 1967; No. 42, Oct, 1981 - No. 49, Dec, 1982

	GD 2.0	VG 4.0	FN 6.0	VF 8.0	VF/NM 9.0	NM- 9.2
V2#28-Origin/1st app. Fightin' Five; Montes/Bache-a	6	12	18	41	66	90
29-39,41-Montes/Bache-a in all	4	8	12	22	34	45
40-Peacemaker begins (1st app.)	6	12	18	42	69	95
41-Peacemaker (2nd app.)	5	10	15	30	48	65
42-49: Reprints						5.00

FIGHTING FRONTS!
Harvey Publications: Aug, 1952 - No. 5, Jan, 1953

	GD 2.0	VG 4.0	FN 6.0	VF 8.0	VF/NM 9.0	NM- 9.2
1	10	20	30	54	72	90
2-Extreme violence; Nostrand/Powell-a	11	22	33	60	83	105
3-5: 3-Powell-a	7	14	21	37	46	55

FIGHTING INDIAN STORIES (See Midget Comics)

FIGHTING INDIANS OF THE WILD WEST!
Avon Periodicals: Mar, 1952 - No. 2, Nov, 1952

	GD 2.0	VG 4.0	FN 6.0	VF 8.0	VF/NM 9.0	NM- 9.2
1-Geronimo, Chief Crazy Horse, Chief Victorio, Black Hawk begin; Larsen-a; McCann-a(2)	17	34	51	98	154	210
2-Kinstler-c & inside-c only; Larsen, McCann-a	12	24	36	69	97	125
100 Pg. Annual (1952, 25¢)-Contains three comics rebound; Geronimo, Chief Crazy Horse, Chief Victorio; Kinstler-c	36	72	108	216	351	485

FIGHTING LEATHERNECKS
Toby Press: Feb, 1952 - No. 6, Dec, 1952

	GD 2.0	VG 4.0	FN 6.0	VF 8.0	VF/NM 9.0	NM- 9.2
1- "Duke's Diary"; full pg. pin-ups by Sparling	14	28	42	81	118	155
2-5: 2- "Duke's Diary" full pg. pin-ups. 3-5- "Gil's Gals"; full pg. pin-ups	10	20	30	54	72	90
6-(Same as No. 3-5?)	10	20	30	54	72	90

FIGHTING MAN, THE (War)
Ajax/Farrell Publications(Excellent Publ.): May, 1952 - No. 8, July, 1953

	GD 2.0	VG 4.0	FN 6.0	VF 8.0	VF/NM 9.0	NM- 9.2
1	14	28	42	81	118	155
2	9	18	27	47	61	75
3-8	8	16	24	40	50	60
Annual 1 (1952, 25¢, 100 pgs.)	25	50	75	150	245	340

FIGHTIN' MARINES (Formerly The Texan; also see Approved Comics)
St. John(Approved Comics)/Charlton Comics No. 14 on:
No. 15, 8/51 - No. 12, 3/53; No. 14, 5/55 - No. 132, 11/76; No. 133, 10/77 - No. 176, 9/84 (No #13?) (Korean War #1-3)

	GD 2.0	VG 4.0	FN 6.0	VF 8.0	VF/NM 9.0	NM- 9.2
15(#1)-Matt Baker c/a "Leatherneck Jack"; slightly large size; Fightin' Texan No. 16 & 17?	45	90	135	284	480	675
2-1st Canteen Kate by Baker; slightly large size; partial Baker-c	54	108	162	343	574	825
3-9,11-Canteen Kate by Baker; Baker c-#2,3,5-11; 4-Partial Baker-c	32	64	96	192	314	435
10-Matt Baker-c	15	30	45	88	137	185
12-No Baker-a; Last St. John issue?	9	18	27	52	69	85
14 (5/55; 1st Charlton issue; formerly?)-Canteen Kate by Baker; all stories reprinted from #2	19	38	57	109	172	235

Fighting Undersea Commndos #4 © AVON

The Filth #1 © Morrison & Weston

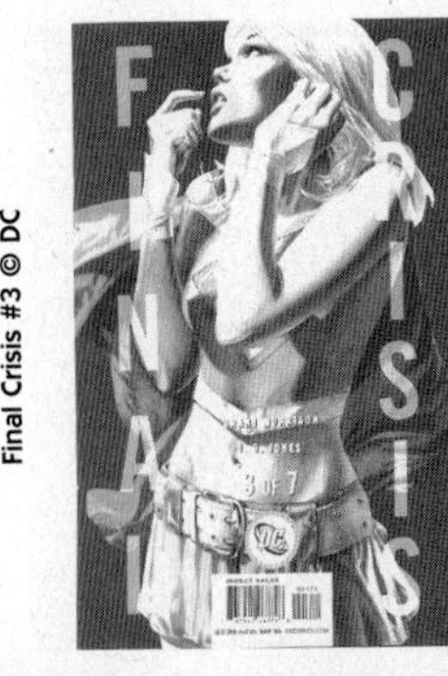

Final Crisis #3 © DC

	GD 2.0	VG 4.0	FN 6.0	VF 8.0	VF/NM 9.0	NM- 9.2
15-Baker-c	12	24	36	67	94	120
16,18-20-Not Baker-c	7	14	21	37	46	55
17-Canteen Kate by Baker	15	30	45	85	130	175
21-24	7	14	21	35	43	50
25-(68 pgs.)(3/58)-Check-a?	10	20	30	56	76	95
26-(100 pgs.)(8/58)-Check-a(5)	14	28	42	81	118	155
27-50	3	6	9	19	29	38
51-81: 78-Shotgun Harker & the Chicken series begin	3	6	9	16	22	28
82-85: 85-Last 12¢ issue	3	6	9	14	20	25
86-94: 94-Last 15¢ issue	2	4	6	10	14	18
95-100,122: 122-(1975) Pilot issue for "War" title (Fightin' Marines Presents War)	2	4	6	9	13	16
101-121	2	4	6	8	10	12
123-140	1	2	3	5	7	9
141-170						6.00
171-176-Low print run	1	2	3	5	6	8
120(Modern Comics reprint, 1977)						5.00

NOTE: *No. 14 & 16 (CC) reprint St. John issues; No. 16 reprints St. John insignia on cover.* **Colan** *a-3, 7.* **Glanzman** *c/a-92, 94.* **Montes/Bache** *a-48, 53, 55, 64, 65, 72-74, 77-83, 176r.*

FIGHTING MARSHAL OF THE WILD WEST (See The Hawk)

FIGHTIN' NAVY (Formerly Don Winslow)
Charlton Comics: No. 74, 1/56 - No. 125, 4-5/66; No. 126, 8/83 - No. 133, 10/84

	GD	VG	FN	VF	VF/NM	NM-
74	6	12	18	37	59	80
75-81	4	8	12	22	34	45
82-Sam Glanzman-a (68 pg. Giant)	5	10	15	32	51	70
83-(100 pgs.)	7	14	21	46	76	105
84-99,101: 101-UFO-c/story	3	6	9	17	25	32
100	3	6	9	18	27	35
102-105,106-125('66)	3	6	9	14	19	24
126-133 (1984)-Low print run	1	2	3	5	6	8

NOTE: **Montes/Bache** *a-109.* **Glanzman** *a-82, 92, 96, 98, 100, 131r.*

FIGHTING PRINCE OF DONEGAL, THE (See Movie Comics)

FIGHTIN' TEXAN (Formerly The Texan & Fightin' Marines?)
St. John Publishing Co.: No. 16, Sept, 1952 - No. 17, Dec, 1952

	GD	VG	FN	VF	VF/NM	NM-
16,17: Tuska-a each. 17-Cameron-c/a	9	18	27	47	61	75

FIGHTING UNDERSEA COMMANDOS (See Undersea Fighting...)
Avon Periodicals: May, 1952 - No. 5, April, 1953 (U.S. Navy frogmen)

	GD	VG	FN	VF	VF/NM	NM-
1-Cover title is Undersea Fighting... #1 only	15	30	45	85	130	175
2	10	20	30	56	76	95
3-5: 1,3-Ravielli-c. 4-Kinstler-c	9	18	27	50	65	80

FIGHTING WAR STORIES
Men's Publications/Story Comics: Aug, 1952 - No. 5, 1953

	GD	VG	FN	VF	VF/NM	NM-
1	12	24	36	69	97	125
2-5	8	16	24	42	54	65

FIGHTING YANK (See America's Best Comics & Startling Comics)
Nedor/Better Publ./Standard: Sept, 1942 - No. 29, Aug, 1949

	GD	VG	FN	VF	VF/NM	NM-
1-The Fighting Yank begins; Mystico, the Wonder Man app; bondage-c	300	600	900	2010	3505	5000
2	129	258	387	826	1413	2000
3,4: 4-Schomburg-c begin	97	194	291	621	1061	1500
5,6,8-10: 8,10-Bondage/torture-c	81	162	243	518	884	1250
7-Hitler special bomb-c; Grim Reaper app.	103	206	309	659	1130	1600
11,13-20: 11-The Oracle app. 15-Bondage/torture-c. 18-The American Eagle app.	55	100	165	352	601	850
12-Hirohito bondage-c	97	194	291	621	1061	1500
21,24: 21-Kara, Jungle Princess app.; lingerie-c. 24-Miss Masque app.	50	100	150	315	533	750
22-Miss Masque-c/story	55	110	165	352	601	850
23-Classic Schomburg hooded vigilante-c	82	164	246	528	902	1275
25-Robinson/Meskin-a; strangulation, lingerie panel; The Cavalier app.	54	108	162	343	574	825
26-29: All-Robinson/Meskin-a. 28-One pg. Williamson-a	43	86	129	271	461	650

NOTE: **Schomburg (Xela)** *c-4-29; airbrush-c 28, 29. Bondage c-1, 4, 8, 10, 11, 12, 15, 17.*

FIGHTMAN
Marvel Comics: June, 1993 ($2.00, one-shot, 52 pgs.)

	GD	VG	FN	VF	VF/NM	NM-
1						4.00

FIGHT THE ENEMY
Tower Comics: Aug, 1966 - No. 3, Mar, 1967 (25¢, 68 pgs.)

	GD 2.0	VG 4.0	FN 6.0	VF 8.0	VF/NM 9.0	NM- 9.2
1-Lucky 7 & Mike Manly begin	4	8	12	28	44	60
2-1st Boris Vallejo comic art; McWilliams-a	4	8	12	22	34	45
3-Wood-a (1/2 pg.); McWilliams, Bolle-a	4	8	12	22	34	45

FILM FUNNIES
Marvel Comics (CPC): Nov, 1949 - No. 2, Feb, 1950 (52 pgs.)

	GD	VG	FN	VF	VF/NM	NM-
1-Krazy Krow, Wacky Duck	20	40	60	117	189	260
2-Wacky Duck	15	30	45	84	127	170

FILM STARS ROMANCES
Star Publications: Jan-Feb, 1950 - No. 3, May-June, 1950 (True life stories of movie stars)

	GD	VG	FN	VF	VF/NM	NM-
1-Rudy Valentino & Gregory Peck stories; L. B. Cole-c; lingerie panels	44	88	132	277	469	660
2-Liz Taylor/Robert Taylor photo-c & true life story	58	116	174	371	636	900
3-Douglas Fairbanks story; photo-c	27	54	81	158	259	360

FILTH, THE
DC Comics (Vertigo): Aug, 2002 - No. 13, Oct, 2003 ($2.95, limited series)

	NM-
1-13-Morrison-s/Weston & Erskine-a	3.00
TPB (2004, $19.95) r/#1-13	20.00

FINAL CRISIS
DC Comics: July, 2008 - No. 7, Mar, 2009 ($3.99, limited series)

	NM-
1-Grant Morrison-s/J.G. Jones-a/c; Martian Manhunter killed; 2 covers	4.00
1-Director's Cut (10/08, $4.99) B&W printing of #1 with creator commentary	5.00
2-7: 2-Barry Allen-c/cameo; intro Big Science Action; two covers. 6-Batman zapped	4.00
SC (2010, $19.99) r/#1-7, FC: Superman Beyond #1,2, FC: Submit & FC Sketchbook	20.00
...: Rage of the Red Lanterns (12/08, $3.99) Atrocitus app.; intro. Blue Lantern; 3 covers	4.00
...: Requiem (9/08, $3.99) History, death and funeral of the Martian Manhunter; 2 covers	4.00
...: Resist (12/08, $3.99) Checkmate app; Rucka & Trautman-s/Sook-a; 2 covers	4.00
...: Secret Files (2/09, $3.99) origin of Libra; Wein-s/Shasteen-a; JG Jones sketch-a	4.00
... Sketchbook (7/08, $2.99) Jones development sketches with Morrison commentary	3.00
...: Submit (12/08, $3.99) Black Lightning & Tattooed Man team up; Morrison-s; 2 covers	4.00

FINAL CRISIS: DANCE (Final Crisis Aftermath)
DC Comics: Jul, 2009 - No. 6, Dec, 2009 ($2.99, limited series)

	NM-
1-6-Super Young Team; Joe Casey-s/Chriscross-a/Stanley Lau-c	3.00
TPB (2009, $17.99) r/#1-6	18.00

FINAL CRISIS: ESCAPE (Final Crisis Aftermath)
DC Comics: Jul, 2009 - No. 6, Dec, 2009 ($2.99, limited series)

	NM-
1-6-Nemesis & Cameron Chase app.; Ivan Brandon-s/Marco Rudy-a/Scott Hampton-c	3.00
TPB (2010, $17.99) r/#1-6	18.00

FINAL CRISIS: INK (Final Crisis Aftermath)
DC Comics: Jul, 2009 - No. 6, Dec, 2009 ($2.99, limited series)

	NM-
1-6-The Tattooed Man; Eric Wallace-s/Fabrizio Florentino-a/Brian Stelfreeze-c	3.00
TPB (2010, $17.99) r/#1-6	18.00

FINAL CRISIS: LEGION OF THREE WORLDS
DC Comics: Oct, 2008 - No. 5, Sept, 2009 ($3.99, limited series)

	NM-
1-Johns-s/Pérez-a; R.J. Brande killed; Time Trapper app.; two covers on each issue	5.00
2-5-Three Legions meet; two covers. 3-Bart Allen returns. 4-Superboy (Conner) returns	4.00
HC (2009, $19.99) r/#1-5; variant covers	20.00
SC (2010, $14.99) r/#1-5; variant covers	15.00

FINAL CRISIS: REVELATIONS
DC Comics: Oct, 2008 - No. 5, Feb, 2009 ($3.99, limited series)

	NM-
1-5-Spectre and The Question; 2 covers on each. 1-Dr. Light killed; Rucka-s/Tan-a	4.00
HC (2009, $19.99, d.j.) r/#1-5; variant covers	20.00
SC (2010, $14.99) r/#1-5; variant covers	15.00

FINAL CRISIS: ROGUE'S REVENGE
DC Comics: Sept, 2008 - No. 3, Nov, 2008 ($3.99, limited series)

	NM-
1-3-Johns-s/Kolins-a; Flash's Rogues, Zoom and Inertia app.	4.00
HC (2009, $19.99, d.j.) r/#1-3 & Flash #182,197; variant covers	20.00
SC (2010, $14.99) r/#1-3 & Flash #182,197; variant covers	15.00

FINAL CRISIS: RUN (Final Crisis Aftermath)
DC Comics: Jul, 2009 - No. 6, Dec, 2009 ($2.99, limited series)

	NM-
1-6-The Human Flame on the run; Sturges-s/Williams-a/Kako-c	3.00
TPB (2010, $17.99) r/#1-6	18.00

FINAL CRISIS: SUPERMAN BEYOND
DC Comics: Oct, 2008 - No. 2, Mar, 2009 ($4.50, limited series)

	NM-
1,2-Morrison-s/Mahnke-a; parallel-Earth Supermen app.; 3-D pages and glasses	4.50

FINAL NIGHT, THE (See DC related titles and Parallax: Emerald Night)
DC Comics: Nov, 1996 - No. 4, Nov, 1996 ($1.95, weekly limited series)

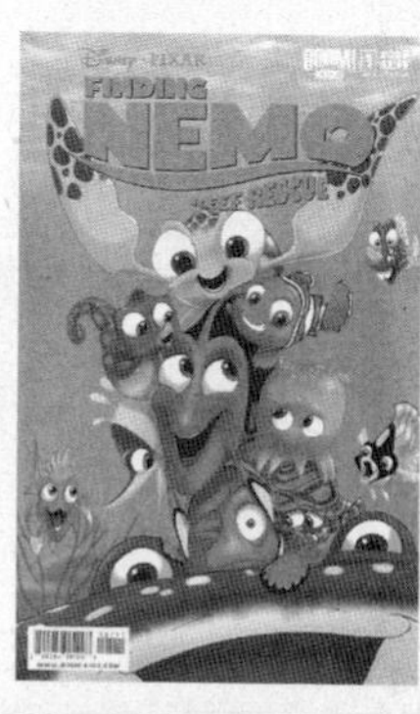

Finding Nemo: Reef Rescue #1 © DIS & Pixar

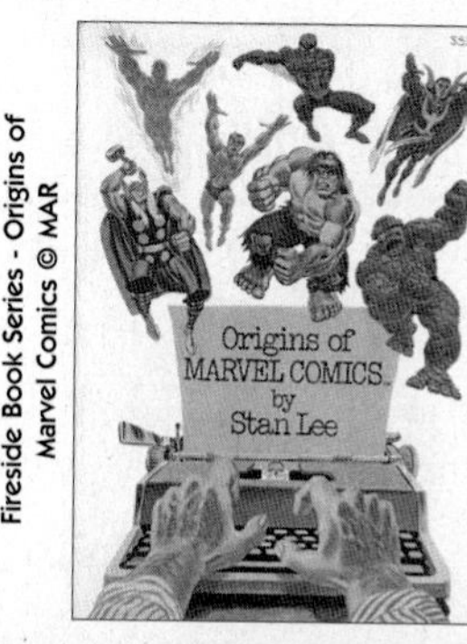

Fireside Book Series - Origins of Marvel Comics © MAR

Firestorm (2004 series) #6 © DC

	GD 2.0	VG 4.0	FN 6.0	VF 8.0	VF/NM 9.0	NM- 9.2

1-4: Kesel-s/Immonen-a(p) in all. 4-Parallax's final acts 3.50
Preview 3.00
TPB-(1998, $12.95) r/#1-4, Parallax: Emerald Night #1, and preview 13.00

FINALS (See Vertigo Resurrected:... for collected reprint)
DC Comics (Vertigo): Sept, 1999 - No. 4, Dec, 1999 ($2.95, limited series)

1-4-Will Pfeifer-s/Jill Thompson-a 3.00

FINDING NEMO (Based on the Pixar movie)
BOOM! Studios: Jul, 2010 - No. 4, Oct, 2010 ($2.99, limited series)

1-4-Michael Raicht & Brian Smith-s/Jake Myler-a.1-Three covers 3.00

FINDING NEMO: REEF RESCUE (Based on the Pixar movie)
BOOM! Studios: May, 2009 - No. 4, Aug, 2009 ($2.99, limited series)

1-4-Marie Croall-s/Erica Leigh Currey-a; 2 covers 3.00

FIN FANG FOUR RETURN!
Marvel Comics: Jul, 2009 ($3.99, one-shot)

1-Fin Fang Foom, Googam, Elektro, Gorgilla and Doc Samson app. 4.00

FIRE
Caliber Press: 1993 - No. 2, 1993 ($2.95, B&W, limited series, 52 pgs.)

1,2-Brian Michael Bendis-s/a 4.00
TPB (1999, 2001, $9.95) Restored reprints of series 10.00

FIREARM (Also see Codename: Firearm, Freex #15, Night Man #4 & Prime #10)
Malibu Comics (Ultraverse): Sept, 1993 - No. 18, Mar, 1995 ($1.95/$2.50)

0 ($14.95)-Came w/ video containing 1st half of story (comic contains 2nd half); 1st app. Duet 15.00
1,3-6: 1-James Robinson scripts begin; Cully Hamner-a; Chaykin-c; 1st app. Alec Swan. 3-Intro The Sportsmen; Chaykin-c. 4-Break-Thru x-over; Chaykin-c. 5-1st app. Ellen (Swan's girlfriend); 2 pg. origin of Prime. 6-Prime app. (story cont'd in Prime #10); Brereton-c 3.00
1-($2.50)-Newsstand edition polybagged w/card 3.50
1-Ultra Limited silver foil-c 5.00
2 ($2.50, 44 pgs.)-Hardcase app.;Chaykin-c; Rune flip-c/story by B. Smith (3 pgs.) 4.00
7-10,12-17: 12-The Rafferty Saga begins, ends #18; 1st app. Rafferty. 15-Night Man & Freex app. 17-Swan marries Ellen 3.00
11-($3.50, 68 pgs.)-Flip book w/Ultraverse Premiere #5 4.00
18-Death of Rafferty; Chaykin-c 4.00
NOTE: *Brereton c-6. Chaykin c-1-4, 14, 16, 18. Hamner a-1-4. Herrera a-12. James Robinson scripts-0-18.*

FIRE BALL XL5 (See Steve Zodiac & The ...)

FIREBIRDS (See Noble Causes)
Image Comics: Nov, 2004 ($5.95)

1-Faerber-s/Ponce-a/c; intro. Firebird 6.00

FIREBRAND (Also see Showcase '96 #4)
DC Comics: Feb, 1996 - No. 9, Oct, 1996 ($1.75)

1-9: Brian Augustyn scripts; Velluto-c/a in all. 9-Daredevil #319-c/swipe 3.00

FIREBREATHER
Image Comics: Jan, 2003 - No. 4, Apr, 2003 ($2.95)

1-4-Hester-s/Kuhn-a 3.00
...: The Iron Saint (12/04, $6.95, squarebound) Hester-s/Kuhn-a 7.00
TPB (7/04, $13.95) r/#1-4; foreword by Brad Meltzer; gallery and sketch pages 14.00

FIREBREATHER
Image Comics: Jun, 2008 - No. 4, Feb, 2009 ($2.99)

1-4-Hester-s/Kuhn-a 3.00

FIREBREATHER (Vol.3): HOLMGANG
Image Comics: Nov, 2010 - No. 4, ($3.99, limited series)

1,2-Hester-s/Kuhn-a 4.00

FIRE FROM HEAVEN
Image Comics (WildStorm Productions): Mar, 1996 ($2.50)

1,2-Moore-s 3.00

FIREHAIR COMICS (Formerly Pioneer West Romances #3-6; also see Rangers Comics)
Fiction House Magazines (Flying Stories): Winter/48-49; No. 2, Wint/49-50; No. 7, Spr/51 - No. 11, Spr/52

	GD	VG	FN	VF	VF/NM	NM-
1-Origin Firehair	34	68	102	199	325	450
2-Continues as Pioneer West Romances for #3-6	18	36	54	105	165	225
7-11	14	28	42	80	115	150
I.W. Reprint 8-(nd)-Kinstler-c; reprints Rangers #57; Dr. Drew story by Grandenetti	3	6	9	18	24	30

FIRESIDE BOOK SERIES (Hard and soft cover editions)
Simon and Schuster: 1974 - 1980 (130-260 pgs.), Square bound, color

		GD	VG	FN	VF	VF/NM	NM-
Amazing Spider-Man, The, 1979, 130 pgs., $3.95, Bob Larkin-c	HC	8	16	24	55	93	130
	SC	6	12	18	37	59	80
America At War–The Best of DC War Comics, 1979, $6.95, 260 pgs, Kubert-c	HC	11	22	33	71	136	200
	SC	7	14	21	49	82	115
Best of Spidey Super Stories (Electric Company) 1978, $3.95,	HC	10	20	30	64	115	165
	SC	6	12	18	42	69	95
Bring On The Bad Guys (Origins of the Marvel Comics Villains) 1976, $6.95, 260 pgs.; Romita-c	HC	8	16	24	53	89	125
	SC	5	10	15	34	55	75
Captain America, Sentinel of Liberty,1979, 130 pgs., $12.95, Cockrum-c	HC	8	16	24	55	93	130
	SC	6	12	18	37	59	80
Doctor Strange Master of the Mystic Arts, 1980, 130 pgs.	HC	8	16	24	55	93	130
	SC	6	12	18	37	59	80
Fantastic Four, The, 1979, 130 pgs.	HC	8	16	24	53	89	125
	SC	5	10	15	34	55	75
Heart Throbs–The Best of DC Romance Comics, 1979, 260 pgs., $6.95	HC	13	26	39	88	189	290
	SC	9	18	27	63	112	160
Incredible Hulk, The, 1978, 260 pgs. (8 1/4" x 11")	HC	8	16	24	53	89	125
	SC	5	10	15	34	55	75
Marvel's Greatest Superhero Battles, 1978, 260 pgs., $6.95, Romita-c	HC	10	20	30	64	115	165
	SC	6	12	18	42	69	95
Mysteries in Space, 1980, $7,95, Anderson-c. r-DC sci/fi stories	HC	9	18	27	60	103	145
	SC	6	12	18	39	62	85
Origins of Marvel Comics, 1974, 260 pgs., $5.95. r-covers & origins of Fantastic Four, Hulk, Spider-Man, Thor, & Doctor Strange	HC	8	16	24	53	89	125
	SC	5	10	15	34	55	75
Silver Surfer, The, 1978, 130 pgs., $4.95, Norem-c	HC	8	16	24	55	93	130
	SC	6	12	18	39	62	85
Son of Origins of Marvel Comics, 1975, 260 pgs., $6.95, Romita-c. Reprints covers & origins of X-Men, Iron Man, Avengers, Daredevil, Silver Surfer	HC	8	16	24	53	89	125
	SC	5	10	15	34	55	75
Superhero Women, The–Featuring the Fabulous Females of Marvel Comics, 1977, 260 pgs., $6.95, Romita-c	HC	10	20	30	64	115	165
	SC	6	12	18	42	69	95

Note: Prices listed are for 1st printings. Later printings have lesser value.

FIRESTAR
Marvel Comics Group: Mar, 1986 - No. 4, June, 1986 (75¢)(From Spider-Man TV series)

1,2: 1-X-Men & New Mutants app. 2-Wolverine-c (not real Wolverine?); Art Adams-a(p) 6.00
3,4: 3-Art Adams/Sienkiewicz-c. 4-B. Smith-c 4.00
X-Men: Firestar Digest (2006, $7.99, digest-size) r/#1-4; profile pages 8.00
1 (Jun, 2010, $3.99) Sean McKeever-s/Emma Rios-a 4.00

FIRESTONE (See Donald And Mickey Merry Christmas)

FIRESTORM (Also see The Fury of Firestorm, Cancelled Comic Cavalcade, DC Comics Presents, Flash #289, & Justice League of America #179)
DC Comics: March, 1978 - No. 5, Oct-Nov, 1978

	GD	VG	FN	VF	VF/NM	NM-
1,5: 1-Origin & 1st app.	2	4	6	9	12	15
2-4: 2-Origin Multiplex. 3-Origin & 1st app. Killer Frost. 4-1st app. Hyena	1	2	3	5	7	9

...: The Nuclear Man TPB (2011, $17.99) r/#1-5 and stories from Flash #289-293, plus story from Cancelled Comic Cavalcade (uncolored) 18.00

FIRESTORM
DC Comics: July, 2004 - No. 35, June, 2007 ($2.50/$2.99)

1-24: 1-Intro. Jason Rusch; Jolley-s/ChrisCross-a. 6-Identity Crisis tie-in. 7-Bloodhound x-over. 8-Killer Frost returns. 9-Ronnie Raymond returns. 17-Villains United tie-in. 21-Infinite Crisis. 24-One Year Later; Killer Frost app. 3.00
25-35: 25-Begin ($2.99-c; Mr. Freeze app. 33-35-Mister Miracle & Orion app. 3.00
...: Reborn TPB (2007, $14.99) r/#23-27 15.00

FIRESTORM, THE NUCLEAR MAN (Formerly Fury of Firestorm)
DC Comics: No. 65, Nov, 1987 - No. 100, Aug, 1990

65-99: 66-1st app. Zuggernaut; Firestorm vs. Green Lantern. 67,68-Millennium tie-ins. 71-Death of Capt. X. 83-1st new look 3.00
100-($2.95, 68 pgs.) 4.00
Annual 5 (10/87)-1st app. new Firestorm 4.00

FIRST, THE
CrossGeneration Comics: Jan, 2001 - No. 37, Jan, 2004 ($2.95)

First Adventures #4 © FC

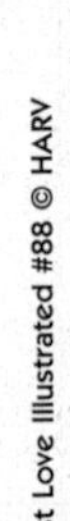
First Love Illustrated #88 © HARV

5 Ronin #1 © MAR

	GD 2.0	VG 4.0	FN 6.0	VF 8.0	VF/NM 9.0	NM- 9.2

1-3: 1-Barbara Kesel-s/Bart Sears & Andy Smith-a 5.00
4-10 4.00
11-37 3.00
Preview (11/00, free) 8 pg. intro 3.00
Two Houses Divided Vol. 1 TPB (11/01, $19.95) r/#1-7; new Moeller-c 20.00
Magnificent Tension Vol. 2 TPB (2002, $19.95) r/#8-13 20.00
Sinister Motives Vol. 3 TPB (2003, $15.95) r/#14-19 16.00
Vol. 4 Futile Endeavors (2003, $15.95) r/#20-25 16.00
Vol. 5 Liquid Alliances (2003, $15.95) r/#26-31 16.00
Vol. 6 Ragnarok (2004, $15.95) r/#32-37 16.00

FIRST ADVENTURES
First Comics: Dec, 1985 - No. 5, Apr, 1986 ($1.25)

1-5: Blaze Barlow, Whisper & Dynamo Joe in all 3.00

FIRST AMERICANS, THE
Dell Publishing Co.: No. 843, Sept, 1957

Four Color 843-Marsh-a 8 16 24 55 93 130

FIRST BORN (See Witchblade and Darkness titles)
Image Comics (Top Cow): Aug, 2007 - No. 3 ($2.99, limited series)

... First Look (6/07, 99¢) Preview; The Darkness app.; Sejic-a; 2 covers (color & B&W) 3.00
1-3-($2.99) Two covers; Marz-s/Sejic-a. 3-Sara's baby is born 3.00
1-B&W variant Sejic cover 5.00
...: Aftermath (5/08, $3.99) short stories; Magdalena app.; two covers by Sook & Sejic 4.00

FIRST CHRISTMAS, THE (3-D)
Fiction House Magazines (Real Adv. Publ. Co.): 1953 (25¢, 8-1/4x10-1/4", oversize)(Came w/glasses)

nn-(Scarce)-Kelly Freas painted-c; Biblical theme, birth of Christ; Nativity-c
33 66 99 194 317 440

FIRST COMICS GRAPHIC NOVEL
First Comics: Jan, 1984 - No. 21? (52 pgs./176 pgs., high quality paper)

1,2: 1-Beowulf ($5.95)(both printings). 2-Time Beavers 9.00
3($11.95, 100 pgs.)-American Flagg! Hard Times (2nd printing exists) 15.00
4-Nexus ($6.95)-r/B&W 1-3 12.00
5,7: 5-The Enchanted Apples of Oz ($7.95, 52 pgs.)-Intro by Harlan Ellison (1986). 7-The Secret Island Of Oz ($7.95) 10.00
6-Elric of Melnibone ($14.95, 176 pgs.)-Reprints with new color 18.00
8,10,14,18: Teenage Mutant Ninja Turtles Book I -IV ($9.95, 132 pgs.)-8-r/TMNT #1-3 in color w/12 pgs. new-a; origin. 10-r/TMNT #4-6 in color. 14-r/TMNT #7,8 in color plus new 12 pg. story. 18-r/TMNT #10,11 plus 3 pg. fold-out 11.00
9-Time 2: The Epiphany by Chaykin (11/86, $7.95, 52pgs. - indicia says #8) 10.00
11-Sailor On The Sea of Fate ($14.95) 16.00
nn-Time 2: The Satisfaction of Black Mariah (9/87) 10.00
12-American Flagg! Southern Comfort (10/87, $11.95) 14.00
13,16,17,21: 13-The Ice King Of Oz. 16-The Forgotten Forest of Oz ($8.95). 17-Mazinger (68 pgs., $8.95). 21-Elric, The Weird of the White Wolf; r/#1-5 10.00
15,19: 15-Hex Breaker: Badger ($7.95). 19-The Original Nexus Graphic Novel ($7.95, 104 pgs.)-Reprints First Comics Graphic Novel #4 12.00
20-American Flagg!: State of the Union ($11.95, 96 pgs.); r/A.F. #7-9 15.00
NOTE: *Most or all issues have been reprinted.*

1ST FOLIO (The Joe Kubert School Presents...)
Pacific Comics: Mar, 1984 ($1.50, one-shot)

1-Joe Kubert-c/a(2 pgs.); Adam & Andy Kubert-a 3.00

1ST ISSUE SPECIAL
National Periodical Publications: Apr, 1975 - No. 13, Apr, 1976 (Tryout series)

1,6: 1-Intro. Atlas; Kirby-c/a/script. 6-Dingbats 2 4 6 11 16 20
2,12: 2-Green Team (see Cancelled Comic Cavalcade). 12-Origin/1st app. "Blue" Starman (2nd app. in Starman, 2nd Series #3); Kubert-c 2 4 6 8 11 14
3-Metamorpho by Ramona Fradon 2 4 6 8 11 14
4,10,11: 4-Lady Cop. 10-The Outsiders. 11-Code Name: Assassin; Grell-c
1 3 4 6 8 10
5-Manhunter; Kirby-c/a/script 3 6 9 14 20 26
7,9: 7-The Creeper by Ditko (c/a). 9-Dr. Fate; Kubert-c/Simonson-a.
2 4 6 11 16 20
8-Origin/1st app. The Warlord; Grell-c/a (11/75) 5 10 15 32 51 70
13-Return of the New Gods; Darkseid app.; 1st new costume Orion; predates New Gods #12 by more than a year 3 6 9 20 30 40

FIRST KISS
Charlton Comics: Dec, 1957 - No. 40, Jan, 1965

V1#1 5 10 15 30 48 65
V1#2-10 3 6 9 19 29 38
11-40 3 6 9 14 19 24

FIRST LOVE ILLUSTRATED
Harvey Publications(Home Comics)(True Love): 2/49 - No. 9, 6/50; No. 10, 1/51 - No. 86, 3/58; No. 87, 9/58 - No. 88, 11/58; No. 89, 11/62, No. 90, 2/63

1-Powell-a(2) 19 38 57 111 176 240
2-Powell-a 12 24 36 67 94 120
3-"Was I Too Fat To Be Loved" story 14 28 42 82 121 160
4-10 9 18 27 50 65 80
11-30: 13-"I Joined a Teen-age Sex Club" story. 30-Lingerie panel
8 16 24 40 50 60
31-34,37,39-49: 49-Last pre-code (2/55) 7 14 21 35 43 50
35-Used in **SOTI**, illo "The title of this comic book is First Love"
20 40 60 114 182 250
36-Communism story, "Love Slaves" 12 24 36 67 94 120
38-Nostrand-a 8 16 24 44 57 70
50-66,71-90 6 12 18 28 34 40
67-70-Kirby-c 8 16 24 40 50 60
NOTE: ***Disbrow** a-13. **Orlando** c-87. **Powell** a-1, 3-5, 7, 10, 11, 13-17, 19-24, 26-29, 33,35-41, 43, 45, 46, 50, 54, 55, 57, 58, 61-63, 65, 71-73, 76, 79r, 82, 84, 88.*

FIRST MEN IN THE MOON (See Movie Comics)

FIRST ROMANCE MAGAZINE
Home Comics(Harvey Publ.)/True Love: 8/49 - #6, 6/50; #7, 6/51 - #50, 2/58; #51, 9/58 - #52, 11/58

1 17 34 51 98 154 210
2 11 22 33 60 83 105
3-5 9 18 27 50 65 80
6-10,28: 28-Nostrand-a(Powell swipe) 8 16 24 40 50 60
11-20 7 14 21 35 43 50
21-27,29-32: 32-Last pre-code issue (2/55) 6 12 18 31 38 45
33-40,44-52 6 12 18 28 34 40
41-43-Kirby-c 8 16 24 40 50 60
NOTE: ***Powell** a-1-5, 8-10, 14, 18, 20-22, 24, 25, 28, 36, 46, 48, 51.*

FIRST TRIP TO THE MOON (See Space Adventures No. 20)

FIRST WAVE (Based on Sci-Fi Channel TV series)
Andromeda Entertainment: Dec, 2000 - No. 4, Jun, 2001 ($2.99)

1-4-Kuhoric-s/Parsons-a/Busch-c 3.00

FIRST WAVE (Also see Batman/Doc Savage Special #1)
DC Comics: May, 2010 - No. 6, Mar, 2011 ($3.99, limited series)

1-6-Batman, Doc Savage and The Spirit app.; Azzarello-s/Morales-a/JG Jones-c 4.00
... Special 1 (6/11, $3.99) Winslade-a/Jones-c 4.00
HC (2011, $29.99, dustjacket) r/#1-6 & Batman/Doc Savage Special #1; sketch art 30.00

FISH POLICE (Inspector Gill of the...#2, 3)
Fishwrap Productions/Comico V2#5-17/Apple Comics #18 on:
Dec, 1985 - No. 11, Nov, 1987 ($1.50, B&W); V2#5, April, 1988 - V2#17, May, 1989 ($1.75, color) No. 18, Aug, 1989 - No. 26, Dec, 1990 ($2.25, B&W)

1-11, 1(5/86),2-2nd print, V2#5-17-(Color): V2#5-11. 12-17, new-a, 18-26 ($2.25-c, B&W). 18-Origin Inspector Gill 3.00
Special 1($2.50, 7/87, Comico) 3.00
Graphic Novel: Hairballs (1987, $9.95, TPB) r/#1-4 in color 10.00

FISH POLICE
Marvel Comics: V2#1, Oct, 1992 - No. 6, Mar, 1993 ($1.25)

V2#1-6: 1-Hairballs Saga begins; r/#1 (1985) 3.00

5 CENT COMICS (Also see Whiz Comics)
Fawcett Publ.: Feb, 1940 (8 pgs., reg. size, B&W)

nn - 1st app. Dan Dare. Ashcan comic, not distributed to newsstands, only for in-house use. A CGC certified 9.6 copy sold for $10,800 in 2003, and a CGC 9.4 sold for $11,500 in 2005.

5 RONIN (Marvel characters in Samurai setting)
Marvel Comics: May, 2011 - No. 5, May, 2011 ($2.99, weekly limited series)

1-Wolverine. 2-Hulk. 3-Punisher. 4-Psylocke; Mack-c. 5-Deadpool 3.00

5-STAR SUPER-HERO SPECTACULAR (See DC Special Series No. 1)

FLAME, THE (See Big 3 & Wonderworld Comics)
Fox Features Synd.: Sum, 1940 - No. 8, Jan, 1942 (#1,2: 68 pgs; #3-8: 44 pgs.)

1-Flame stories reprinted from Wonderworld #5-9; origin The Flame; Lou Fine-a (36 pgs.),
300 600 900 2070 3635 5200
2-Fine-a(2); Wing Turner by Tuska; r/Wonderworld #3,10
123 246 369 787 1344 1900
3-8: 3-Powell-a 81 162 243 518 884 1250

Flaming Carrot Comics #25 © Bob Burden

The Flash #129 © DC

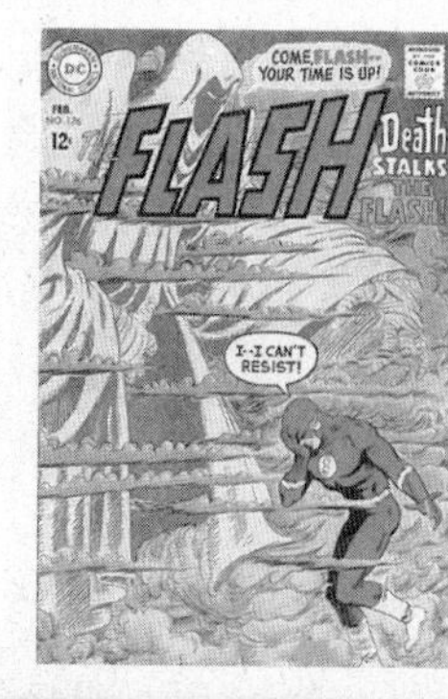

The Flash #176 © DC

	GD 2.0	VG 4.0	FN 6.0	VF 8.0	VF/NM 9.0	NM- 9.2

FLAME, THE (Formerly Lone Eagle)
Ajax/Farrell Publications (Excellent Publ.): No. 5, Dec-Jan, 1954-55 - No. 3, April-May, 1955

5(#1)-1st app. new Flame 48 96 144 302 514 725
2,3 30 60 90 177 289 400

FLAMING CARROT COMICS (Also see Junior Carrot Patrol)
Killian Barracks Press: Summer-Fall, 1981 ($1.95, one shot) (Lg size, 8-1/2x11")

1-Bob Burden-c/a/scripts; serially #'ed to 6500 5 10 15 34 55 75

FLAMING CARROT COMICS (See Anything Goes, Cerebus, Teenage Mutant Ninja Turtles/Flaming Carrot Crossover & Visions)
Aardvark-Vanaheim/Renegade Press #6-17/Dark Horse #18-31: May, 1984 - No. 5, Jan, 1985; No. 6, Mar, 1985 - No. 31, Oct, 1994 ($1.70/$2.00, B&W)

1-Bob Burden story/art 4 8 12 28 44 60
2 3 6 9 16 23 30
3 2 4 6 10 16 20
4-6 2 4 6 9 12 15
7-9 1 3 4 6 8 10
10-12 6.50
13-15 4.00
15-Variant without cover price 6.00
16-(6/87) 1st app. Mystery Men 1 2 3 5 6 8
17-20: 18-1st Dark Horse issue 4.00
21-23,25: 25-Contains trading cards; TMNT app. 3.00
24-(2.50, 52 pgs.)-10th anniversary issue 4.00
26-28: 26-Begin $2.25-c. 26,27-Teenage Mutant Ninja Turtles x-over. 27-McFarlane-c 3.00
29-31-(2.50-c) 3.00
Annual 1(1/97, $5.00) 5.00
... & Reid Fleming, World's Toughest Milkman (12/02, $3.99) listed as #32 in indicia 4.00
... :Fortune Favors the Bold (1998, $16.95, TPB) r/#19-24 17.00
... :Men of Mystery (7/97, $12.95, TPB) r/#1-3, + new material 13.00
... 's Greatest Hits (4/98, $17.95, TPB) r/#12-18, + new material 18.00
... :The Wild Shall Wild Remain (1997, $17.95, TPB) r/#4-11, + new s/a 18.00

FLAMING CARROT COMICS
Image Comics (Desperado): Dec, 2004 - 2006 ($2.95/$3.50, B&W)

1-3-Bob Burden story/art 3.00
4-($3.50-c) 3.50
... Special #1 (3/06, $3.50) All Photo comic 3.50
... Vol. 6 (2006, $14.99) r/1-4 & Special #1; intro. by Brian Bolland 15.00

FLAMING LOVE
Quality Comics Group (Comic Magazines): Dec, 1949 - No. 6, Oct, 1950 (Photo covers #2-6) (52 pgs.)

1-Ward-c/a (9 pgs.) 40 80 120 242 401 560
2 19 38 57 109 172 235
3-Ward-a (9 pgs.); Crandall-a 27 54 81 158 259 360
4-6: 4-Gustavson-a 15 30 45 90 140 190

FLAMING WESTERN ROMANCES (Formerly Target Western Romances)
Star Publications: No. 3, Mar-Apr, 1950

3-Robert Taylor, Arlene Dahl photo on-c with biographies inside; L. B. Cole-c 34 68 102 199 325 450

FLARE (Also see Champions for 1st app. & League of Champions)
Hero Comics/Hero Graphics Vol. 2 on: Nov, 1988 - No. 3, Jan, 1989 ($2.75, color, 52 pgs); V2#1, Nov, 1990 - No. 7, Nov, 1991 ($2.95/$3.50, color, mature, 52 pgs.);V2#8, Oct, 1992 - No. 16, Feb, 1994 ($3.50/$3.95, B&W, 36 pgs.)

V1#1-3, V2#1-16: 5-Eternity Smith returns. 6-Intro The Tigress 4.00
Annual 1(1992, $4.50, B&W, 52 pgs.)-Champions-r 4.50

FLARE ADVENTURES
Hero Graphics: Feb, 1992 - No. 12, 1993? ($3.50/$3.95)

1 (90¢, color, 20 pgs.) 4.00
2-12-Flip books w/Champions Classics 4.00

FLASH, THE (See Adventure Comics, The Brave and the Bold, Crisis On Infinite Earths, DC Comics Presents, DC Special, DC Special Series, DC Super-Stars, The Greatest Flash Stories Ever Told, Green Lantern, Impulse, JLA, Justice League of America, Showcase, Speed Force, Super Team Family, Titans & World's Finest)

FLASH, THE (1st Series)(Formerly Flash Comics)(See Showcase #4,8,13,14)
National Periodical Publ./DC: No. 105, Feb-Mar, 1959 - No. 350, Oct, 1985

105-(2-3/59)-Origin Flash(retold), & Mirror Master (1st app.) 500 1000 1750 6000 12,500 19,000
106-Origin Grodd & Pied Piper; Flash's 1st visit to Gorilla City; begin Grodd the Super Gorilla trilogy (Scarce) 196 392 588 1646 3573 5500
107-Grodd trilogy, part 2 111 222 333 900 1950 3000
108-Grodd trilogy ends 93 186 279 753 1627 2500
109-2nd app. Mirror Master 74 148 222 600 1300 2000
110-Intro/origin Kid Flash who later becomes Flash in Crisis On Infinite Earths #12; begin Kid Flash trilogy, ends #112 (also in #114,116,118); 1st app. & origin of The Weather Wizard 161 322 483 1352 2926 4500
111-2nd Kid Flash tryout; Cloud Creatures 52 104 156 421 911 1400
112-Origin & 1st app. Elongated Man (4-5/60); also apps. in #115,119,130 59 118 177 478 1039 1600
113-Origin & 1st app. Trickster 47 94 141 381 828 1275
114-Captain Cold app. (see Showcase #8) 40 80 120 300 650 1000
115,116,118-120: 119-Elongated Man marries Sue Dearborn. 120-Flash & Kid Flash team-up for 1st time 34 68 102 247 536 825
117-Origin & 1st app. Capt. Boomerang; 1st & only S.A. app. Winky Blinky & Noddy 36 72 108 270 585 900
121,122: 122-Origin & 1st app. The Top 27 54 81 189 407 625
123-(9/61)-Re-intro. Golden Age Flash; origins of both Flashes; 1st mention of an Earth II where DC G. A. heroes live 157 314 471 1319 2860 4400
124-Last 10¢ issue 22 44 66 154 327 500
125-128,130: 127-Return of Grodd-c/story. 128-Origin & 1st app. Abra Kadabra. 130-(7/62)-1st Gauntlet of Super-Villains (Mirror Master, Capt. Cold, The Top, Capt. Boomerang & Trickster) 21 42 63 142 304 465
129-2nd G.A. Flash x-over; J.S.A. cameo in flashback (1st S.A. app. G.A. Green Lantern, Hawkman, Atom, Black Canary & Dr. Mid-Nite. Wonder Woman (1st S.A. app.?) appears) 27 54 81 196 423 650
131-136,138,140: 131-Early Green Lantern x-over (9/62). 135-1st app. of Kid Flash's yellow costume (3/63). 136-1st Dexter Miles. 140-Origin & 1st app. Heat Wave 15 30 45 102 221 340
137-G.A. Flash x-over; J.S.A. cameo (1st S.A. app.)(1st real app. since 2-3/51); 1st S.A. app. Vandal Savage & Johnny Thunder; JSA team decides to re-form 36 72 108 261 568 875
139-Origin & 1st app. Prof. Zoom 16 32 48 109 237 365
141-150: 142-Trickster app. 147-2nd Prof. Zoom 12 24 36 81 166 250
151-Engagement of Barry Allen & Iris West; G.A. Flash vs. The Shade. 13 26 39 85 180 275
152-159: 159-Dr. Mid-Nite cameo 11 22 33 71 136 200
160-(80-Pg. Giant G-21); G.A. Flash & Johnny Quick-r 12 24 36 79 160 240
161-164,166,167: 167-New facts about Flash's origin 9 18 27 61 106 150
165-Barry Allen weds Iris West 9 18 27 63 112 160
168,170: 168-Green Lantern-c/app. 170-Dr. Mid-Nite, Dr. Fate, G.A. Flash x-over 9 18 27 61 106 150
169-(80-Pg. Giant G-34)-New facts about origin 10 20 30 64 115 165
171,172,174,176,177,179,180: 171-JLA, Green Lantern, Atom flashbacks. 174-Barry Allen reveals I.D. to wife. 179-(5/68)-Flash travels to Earth-Prime and meets DC editor Julie Schwartz; 1st unnamed app. Earth-Prime (See Justice League of America #123 for 1st named app. & 3rd app. overall) 8 16 24 53 89 125
173-G.A. Flash x-over 9 18 27 61 106 150
175-2nd Superman/Flash race (12/67) (See Superman #199 & World's Finest #198,199); JLA cameo; gold kryptonite used (on J'onn J'onzz impersonating Superman) 17 34 51 114 250 385
178-(80-Pg. Giant G-46) 9 18 27 60 103 145
181-186,188,189: 186-Re-intro. Sargon. 189-Last 12¢-c 6 12 18 39 62 85
187,196: (68-Pg. Giants G-58, G-70) 7 14 21 46 76 105
190-195,197-199 4 8 12 28 44 60
200 5 10 15 32 51 70
201-204,206,207: 201-New G.A. Flash story. 206-Elongated Man begins 207-Last 15¢ issue 4 8 12 22 34 45
205-(68-Pg. Giant G-82) 7 14 21 48 79 110
208-213-(52 pg.): 211-G.A. Flash origin-r/#104. 213-Reprints #137 4 8 12 26 41 55
214-DC 100 Page Super Spectacular DC-11; origin Metal Men-r/Showcase #37; never before published G.A. Flash story 9 18 27 61 106 150
215 (52 pgs.)-Flash-r/Showcase #4; G.A. Flash x-over, continued in #216 4 8 12 28 44 60
216,220: 220-1st app. Turtle since Showcase #4 3 6 9 18 27 35
217-219: Neal Adams-a in all. 217-Green Lantern/Green Arrow series begins (9/72); 2nd G.L. & G.A. team-up series (see Green Lantern #76). 219-Last Green Arrow 5 10 15 30 48 65
221-225,227,228,230,231,233: 222-G. Lantern x-over. 228-(7-8/74)-Flash writer Cary Bates travels to Earth-One & meets Flash, Iris Allen & Trickster; 2nd unnamed app. Earth-Prime (See Justice League of America #123 for 1st named app. & 3rd app. overall) 3 6 9 14 19 24
226-Neal Adams-p 3 6 9 17 25 32
229,232-(100 pg. issues)-G.A. Flash-r & new-a 5 10 15 30 48 65

The Flash #337 © DC

The Flash (2nd series) #215 © DC

The Flash (2011 series) #1 © DC

	GD 2.0	VG 4.0	FN 6.0	VF 8.0	VF/NM 9.0	NM- 9.2
234-250: 235-Green Lantern x-over. 243-Death of The Top. 245-Origin The Floronic Man in Green Lantern back-up, ends #246. 246-Last Green Lantern. 247-Jay Garrick app. 250-Intro Golden Glider	2	4	6	10	14	18
251-274: 256-Death of The Top retold. 265-267-(44 pgs.). 267-Origin of Flash's uniform. 270-Intro The Clown	2	4	6	8	10	12
268,273-276,278,283,286-(Whitman variants; low print run; no issue #s shown on covers	2	4	6	8	11	14
275,276-Iris Allen dies	2	4	6	9	12	15
277-288,290: 286-Intro/origin Rainbow Raider	1	2	3	5	6	8
289-1st Pérez DC art (Firestorm); new Firestorm back-up series begins (9/80), ends #304	2	3	4	6	8	10
291-299,301-305: 291-1st app. Saber-Tooth (villain). 295-Gorilla Grodd-c/story. 298-Intro & origin new Shade. 301-Atomic bomb-c. 303-The Top returns. 304-Intro/origin Colonel Computron; 305-G.A. Flash x-over						6.00
300-(8/81, 52 pgs.)-25th Anniversary issue; Flash's origin and life story retold; wraparound-c by Infantino; no ads	1	2	3	5	6	8
306-313-Dr. Fate by Giffen. 309-Origin Flash retold						6.00
314-340: 318-323-Creeper back-ups. 323,324-Two part Flash vs. Flash story. 324-Death of Reverse Flash (Professor Zoom). 328-Iris West Allen's death retold. 329-JLA app. 340-Trial of the Flash begins						5.00
341-349: 344-Origin Kid Flash						6.00
350-Double size ($1.25) Final issue	1	2	3	5	6	8
Annual 1 (10-12/63, 84 pgs.)-Origin Elongated Man & Kid Flash-r; origin Grodd; G.A. Flash-r	33	66	99	239	520	800
Annual 1 Replica Edition (2001, $6.95)-Reprints the entire 1963 Annual						7.00
...Chronicles SC Vol. 1 (2009, $14.99)-r/Showcase #4,8,13,14 and Flash #105,106						15.00
...Chronicles SC Vol. 2 (2010, $14.99)-r/Flash #107-112						15.00
The Flash Spectacular (See DC Special Series No. 11)						
The Flash vs. The Rogues TPB (2009, $14.99) r/1st app. of classic rogues in Showcase #8 and Flash #105,106,110,113,117,122,140,155; new Van Sciver-c						15.00
The Life Story of the Flash (1997, $19.95, Hardcover) "Iris Allen's" chronicle of Barry Allen's life; comic panels w/additional text; Waid & Augustyn-s/ Kane & Staton-a/Orbik painted-c						20.00
The Life Story of the Flash (1998, $12.95, Softcover) New Orbik-c						13.00

NOTE: **N. Adams** *c-194, 195, 203, 204, 206-208, 211, 213, 215, 226p, 246.* **M. Anderson** *c-165, a(i)-195, 200-204, 206-208.* **Austin** *a-233i, 234i, 246i.* **Buckler** *a-271p, 272p; c(p)-247-250, 252, 253p, 255, 256p, 258, 262, 265-267, 269-271.* **Giffen** *a-306-313p; c-310p, 315.* **Giordano** *a-226i.* **Sid Greene** *a-167-174i, 229i(r).* **Grell** *a-237p, 238p, 240-243p; c-236.* **Heck** *a-198p.* **Infantino/Anderson** *a-135. c-135, 170-174, 192, 200, 201, 328-330.* **Infantino/Giella** *c-105-112, 163, 164, 166-168.* **G. Kane** *a-195p, 197-199p, 229r, 232r; c-197-199, 312p.* **Kubert** *a-108p, 215i(r); c-189-191.* **Lopez** *c-272.* **Meskin** *a-229r, 232r.* **Perez** *a-289-293p; c-293.* **Starlin** *a-294-296p.* **Staton** *c-263p, 264p. Green Lantern x-over-131, 143, 168, 171, 191.*

FLASH (2nd Series)(See Crisis on Infinite Earths #12 and All Flash #1)
DC Comics: June, 1987 - No. 230, Mar, 2006; No. 231, Oct, 2007 - No. 247, Feb, 2009

	GD 2.0	VG 4.0	FN 6.0	VF 8.0	VF/NM 9.0	NM- 9.2
1-Guice-c/a begins; New Teen Titans app.	1	3	4	6	8	10
2-10: 3-Intro. Kilgore. 5-Intro. Speed McGee. 7-1st app. Blue Trinity. 8,9-Millennium tie-ins. 9-1st app. The Chunk						4.00
11-61: 12-Free extra 16 pg. Dr. Light story. 19-Free extra 16 pg. Flash story. 28-Capt. Cold app. 29-New Phantom Lady app. 40-Dr. Alchemy app. 50-($1.75, 52 pgs.)						4.00
62-78,80: 62-Flash: Year One begins, ends #65. 65-Last $1.00-c. 66-Aquaman app. 69,70-Green Lantern app. 70-Gorilla Grodd story ends. 73-Re-intro Barry Allen & begin saga ("Barry Allen's" true ID revealed in #78). 76-Re-intro of Max Mercury (Quality Comics' Quicksilver), not in uniform until #77. 80-($1.25-c) Regular Edition						4.00
79,80 ($2.50): 79-(68 pgs.) Barry Allen saga ends. 80-Foil-c						5.00
81-91,93,94,0,95-99,101: 81,82-Nightwing & Starfire app. 84-Razer app. 94-Zero Hour. 0-(10/94). 95-"Terminal Velocity" begins, ends #100. 96,98,99-Kobra app. 97-Origin Max Mercury; Chillblaine app.						4.00
92-1st Impulse	1	3	4	6	8	10
100 ($2.50)-Newstand edition; Kobra & JLA app.						4.00
100 ($3.50)-Foil-c edition; Kobra & JLA app.						5.00
102-131: 102-Mongul app.; begin-$1.75-c. 105-Mirror Master app. 107-Shazam app. 108-"Dead Heat" begins; 1st app. Savitar. 109-"Dead Heat" Pt. 2 (cont'd in Impulse #10). 110-"Dead Heat" Pt. 4 (cont'd in Impulse #11). 111-"Dead Heat" finale; Savitar disappears into the Speed Force; John Fox cameo (2nd app.). 112-"Race Against Time" begins, ends #118; re-intro John Fox. 113-Tornado Twins app. 119-Final Night x-over. 127-129-Rogue's Gallery & Neron. 128,129-JLA-app.130-Morrison & Millar-s begin						3.50
132-150: 135-GL & GA app. 142-Wally almost marries Linda; Waid-s return. 144-Cobalt Blue origin. 145-Chain Lightning begins.147-Professor Zoom app. 149-Barry Allen app. 150-($2.95) Final showdown with Cobalt Blue						3.00
151-162: 151-Casey-s. 152-New Flash-c. 154-New Flash ID revealed. 159-Wally marries Linda. 162-Last Waid-s.						3.00
163-187,189-196,198,199,201-206: 163-Begin $2.25-c. 164-186-Bolland-c. 183-New Trickster. 196-Winslade-a. 201-Dose-a begins. 205-Batman-c/app.						3.00
188-($2.95) Mirror Master, Weather Wizard, Trickster app.						4.00
197-Origin of Zoom (6/03)						6.00
200-($3.50) Flash vs. Zoom; Barry Allen & Hal Jordan app.; wraparound-c						4.00
207-230: 207-211-Turner-c/Porter-a. 209-JLA app. 210-Nightwing app. 212-Origin Mirror Master. 214-216-Identity Crisis x-over. 219-Wonder Woman app. 220-Rogue War 224-Zoom & Prof. Zoom app. 225-Twins born; Barry Allen app.; last Johns-s						3.00
231-247: 231-(10/07) Waid-s/Acuña-a. 240-Grodd app.; "Dark Side Club"						3.00
#1,000,000 (11/98) 853rd Century x-over						3.00
Annual 1-7,9: 2-('87-'94,'96, 68 pgs), 3-Gives history of G.A.,S.A., & Modern Age Flash in text. 4-Armaggedon 2001. 5-Eclipso-c/story. 7-Elseworlds story. 9-Legends of the Dead Earth story; J.H. Williams-a(p); Mick Gray-a(i)						4.00
Annual 8 (1995, $3.50)-Year One story						4.00
Annual 10 (1997, $3.95)-Pulp Heroes stories						4.00
Annual 11,12 ('98, '99)-11-Ghosts; Wrightson-c. 12-JLApe; Art Adams-c						4.00
Annual 13 ('00, $3.50) Planet DC; Alcatena-c/a						4.00
...: Blitz (2004, $19.95, TPB)-r/#192-200; Kolins-c						20.00
...: Blood Will Run (2002, 2008; $17.95, TPB)-r/#170-176, Secret Files #3, Iron Heights						18.00
...: Crossfire (2004, $17.95, TPB)-r/#183-191 & parts of Flash Secret Files #3						18.00
Dead Heat (2000, $14.95, TPB)-r/#108-111, Impulse #10,11						15.00
...80-Page Giant (8/98, $4.95) Flash family stories by Waid, Millar and others; Mhan-c						5.00
...80-Page Giant 2 (4/99, $4.95) Stories of Flash family, future Kid Flash, original Teen Titans and XS						5.00
...: Emergency Stop (2008, $12.99, TPB)-r/#130-135; Morrison & Millar-s						13.00
...: Ignition (2005, $14.95, TPB)-r/#201-206						15.00
...: Iron Heights (2001, $5.95)-Van Sciver-c/a; intro. Murmur						6.00
...: Mercury Falling (2009, $14.99, TPB)-r/Impulse #62-67						15.00
...: Our Worlds at War 1 (10/01, $2.95)-Jae Lee-c; Black Racer app.						3.00
...Plus 1 (1/1997, $2.95)-Nightwing-c/app.						3.00
Race Against Time (2001, $14.95, TPB)-r/#112-118						15.00
...: Rogues (2003, $14.95, TPB)-r/#177-182						15.00
...: Rogue War (2006, $17.99, TPB)-r/#1/2,212,218,220-225; cover gallery						18.00
...Secret Files 1 (11/97, $4.95) Origin-s & pin-ups						5.00
...Secret Files 2 (11/99, $4.95) Origin of Replicant						5.00
...Secret Files 3 (11/01; $4.95) Intro. Hunter Zolomon (who later becomes Zoom)						5.00
Special 1 (1990, $2.95, 84 pgs.)-50th anniversary issue; Kubert-c; 1st Flash story by Mark Waid; 1st app. John Fox (27th Century Flash)						4.00
Terminal Velocity (1996, $12.95, TPB)-r/#95-100.						13.00
...: The Greatest Stories Ever Told (2007, $19.99, TPB) reprints; Ross-c/Waid intro.						20.00
The Return of Barry Allen (1996, $12.95, TPB)-r/#74-79						13.00
The Secret of Barry Allen (2005, $19.99, TPB)-r/#207-211,213-217; Turner sketch page						20.00
...: The Wild Wests HC (2008, $24.99, dustjacket)-r/#231-237						25.00
...: Time Flies (2002, $5.95)-Seth Fisher-c/a; Rozum-s						6.00
TV Special 1 (1991, $3.95, 76 pgs.)-Photo-c plus behind the scenes photos of TV show; Saltares-a, Byrne scripts						4.00
Wizard #1/2 (2005) prelude to Rogue Wars; Justiano-a						10.00
...: Wonderland TPB (2007, $12.99, TPB)-r/#164-169						13.00

NOTE: **Guice** *a-1-9p, 11p, Annual 1p; c-1-9p, Annual 1p.* **Perez** *c-15-17, Annual 2i.* **Charest** *c/a-Annual 5p.*

FLASH, THE (Brightest Day)(Leads into Flashpoint series)
DC Comics: Jun, 2010 - No. 12, Jul, 2011 ($3.99/$2.99)

	NM- 9.2
1-($3.99) Barry Allen vs. the 25th Century Rogues; Johns-s/Manapul-a/c	4.00
1-Variant-c by Tony Harris	10.00
2-12-($2.99) Capt. Boomerang app. 8-Reverse Flash origin retold	3.00
2-12-Variant covers. 2-Sook. 3-Horn. 4-Kolins. 5-Sook. 6-Garza. 7-Cooke	5.00
...: Secret Files and Origins 1 (5/10, $3.99) Johns-s/Kolins-a; profiles of the Rogues	4.00
...: The Dastardly Death of the Rogues HC (2011, $19.99, dj) r/#1-7 & Secret Files	20.00

FLASH (New DC 52)
DC Comics: Nov, 2011 - Present ($2.99)

	NM- 9.2
1-7-Manapul & Buccellato-s/Manapul-a/c. 6,7-Captain Cold app.	3.00

FLASH: REBIRTH
DC Comics: Jun, 2009 - No. 6, Apr, 2010 ($3.99/$2.99, limited series)

	NM- 9.2
1-($3.99) Barry Allen's return; Johns-s/Van Sciver-a; Flash-c by Van Sciver	4.00
1-Variant Barry Allen-c by Van Sciver	10.00
1-Second thru fourth printings	4.00
1-Special Edition (8/10, $1.00) reprints #1 with "What's Next?" logo on cover	3.00
2-6-($2.99) 3-Max Mercury returns	3.00
2-6-Variant covers by Van Sciver	8.00
HC (2010, $19.99, dustjacket) r/#1-6; Johns original proposal; sketch art; cover gallery	20.00
SC (2011, $14.99) r/#1-6; Johns original proposal; sketch art; cover gallery	15.00

FLASH: THE FASTEST MAN ALIVE (3rd Series)(See Infinite Crisis)
DC Comics: Aug, 2006 - No. 13, Aug, 2007 ($2.99)

	NM- 9.2
1-Bart Allen becomes the Flash; Lashley-a/Bilson & Demeo-s	3.00
1-Variant-c by Joe and Andy Kubert	5.00
2-12: 5-Cyborg app. 7-Inertia returns. 10-Zoom app.	3.00
13-Bart Allen dies; 2 covers	3.00
13-DC Nation Edition from the 2007 San Diego Comic-Con	8.00

Flash Comics #9 © DC

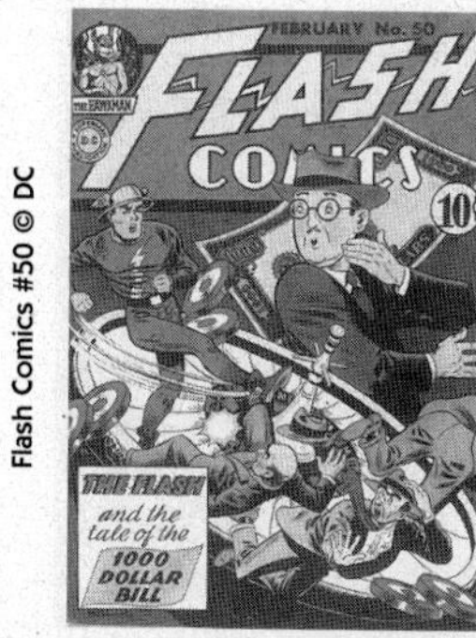

Flash Comics #50 © DC

Flash Gordon (DELL) #2 © KING

GD VG FN VF VF/NM NM-
2.0 4.0 6.0 8.0 9.0 9.2

...: Full Throttle TPB (2007, $12.99) r/#7-13, All-Flash #1, DCU Infinite Holiday Spec. story 13.00
...: Lightning in a Bottle TPB (2007, $12.99) r/#1-6 13.00

FLASH, THE (See Tangent Comics/ The Flash)

FLASH AND GREEN LANTERN: THE BRAVE AND THE BOLD
DC Comics: Oct, 1999 - No. 6, Mar, 2000 ($2.50, limited series)

1-6-Waid & Peyer-s/Kitson-a. 4-Green Arrow app.; Grindberg-a(p) 3.00
TPB (2001, $12.95) r/#1-6 13.00

FLASH COMICS
DC Comics:. Dec. 1939

1-Ashcan comic, not distributed to newsstands, only for in-house use. Cover art is Adventure Comics #41 and interior from All-American Comics #8. A CGC certified 9.6 sold for $11,500 in 2004. A CGC certified 9.4 sold for $6,572.50 in 2008.

FLASH COMICS (Whiz Comics No. 2 on)
Fawcett Publications: Jan, 1940 (12 pgs., B&W, regular size)
(Not distributed to newsstands; printed for in-house use)

NOTE: *Whiz Comics #2 was preceded by two books,* ***Flash Comics*** *and* ***Thrill Comics****, both dated Jan, 1940, (12 pgs, B&W, regular size) and were not distributed. These two books are identical except for the title, and were sent out to major distributors as ad copies to promote sales. It is believed that the complete 68 page issue of Fawcett's* ***Flash*** *and* ***Thrill Comics*** *#1 was finished and ready for publication with the January date. Since DC Comics was also about to publish a book with the same date and title, Fawcett hurriedly printed up the black and white version of* ***Flash Comics*** *to secure copyright before DC. The inside covers are blank, with the covers and inside pages printed on a high quality uncoated paper stock. The eight page origin story of Captain Thunder is composed of pages 1-7 and 13 of the Captain Marvel story essentially as they appeared in the first issue of* ***Whiz Comics****. The balloon dialogue on page thirteen was relettered to tie the story into the end of page seven in* ***Flash*** *and* ***Thrill Comics*** *to produce a shorter version of the origin story for copyright purposes. Obviously, DC acquired the copyright and Fawcett dropped* ***Flash*** *as well as* ***Thrill*** *and came out with* ***Whiz Comics*** *a month later. Fawcett never used the cover to* ***Flash*** *and* ***Thrill*** *#1, designing a new cover for* ***Whiz Comics****. Fawcett also must have discovered that Captain Thunder had already been used by another publisher (Captain Terry Thunder by Fiction House). All references to Captain Thunder were relettered to Captain Marvel before appearing in* ***Whiz****.*

1 (nn on-c, #1 on inside)-Origin & 1st app. Captain Thunder. Cover by C.C. Beck. Eight copies of Flash and three copies of Thrill exist. All 3 copies of Thrill sold in 1986 for between $4,000-$10,000 each. A NM copy of Thrill sold in 1987 for $12,000. A VG copy of Thrill sold in 1987 for $9000 cash. A VF(8.0) copy of Thrill sold in 2003 for $11,400. A CGC certified 9.0 copy of the Flash Comics version sold for $10,117.50 in 2006. A CGC certified 9.4 copy of the Flash Comics version sold for $14,340 in 2008. A CGC certified 9.0 copy of the Thrill Comics version sold for $8,000 in 2006. A CGC certified 9.0 copy of the Thrill Comics version sold for $20,315 in 2008.

FLASH COMICS (The Flash No. 105 on) (Also see All-Flash)
National Periodical Publ./All-American: Jan, 1940 - No. 104, Feb, 1949

1-The Flash (origin/1st app.) by Harry Lampert, Hawkman (origin/1st app.) by Gardner Fox, The Whip, & Johnny Thunder (origin/1st app.) by Stan Asch; Cliff Cornwall by Moldoff, Flash Picture Novelets (later Minute Movies w/#12) begin; Moldoff (Shelly) cover; 1st app. Shiera Sanders who later becomes Hawkgirl, #24; reprinted in Famous First Edition (on sale 11/10/39); The Flash-c 8250 16,500 24,750 62,000 113,500 165,000

1-Reprint, Oversize 13-1/2x10". **WARNING:** This comic is an exact reprint of the original except for its size. DC published it in 1974 with a second cover titling it as a Famous First Edition. There have been many reported cases of the outer cover being removed and the interior sold as the original edition. The reprint with the new outer cover removed is practically worthless. See Famous First Edition for value.

2-Rod Rian begins, ends #11; Hawkman-c 892 1784 2676 6512 11,506 16,500
3-King Standish begins (1st app.), ends #41 (called The King #16-37,39-41); E.E. Hibbard-a begins on Flash 541 1082 1623 3950 6975 10,000
4-Moldoff (Shelly) Hawkman begins; The Whip-c 371 742 1113 2600 4550 6500
5-The King-c 300 600 900 2010 3505 5000
6-2nd Flash-c (alternates w/Hawkman #6 on) 611 1222 1833 4460 7880 11,300
7-2nd Hawkman-c; 1st Moldoff Hawkman-c 568 1136 1704 4146 7323 10,500
8-New logo begins; classic Moldoff Flash-c 360 720 1080 2520 4410 6300
9,10: 9-Moldoff Hawkman-c; 10-Classic Moldoff Flash-c 371 742 1113 2600 4550 6500
11-13,15-20: 12-Les Watts begins; "Sparks" #16 on. 13-Has full page ad for All Star Comics #3. 17-Last Cliff Cornwall 239 478 717 1530 2615 3700
14-World War II cover 277 554 831 1759 3030 4300
21-Classic Hawkman-c 226 452 678 1446 2473 3500
22,23 200 400 600 1280 2190 3100
24-Shiera becomes Hawkgirl (12/41); see All-Star Comics #5 for 1st app. 242 484 726 1537 2644 3750
25-28,30: 28-Last Les Sparks. 135 270 405 864 1482 2100
29-Ghost Patrol begins (origin/1st app.), ends #104 139 278 417 883 1517 2150
31,33-Classic Hawkman-c. 33-Origin Shade 148 296 444 947 1624 2300
32,34-40: 36-1st app. Rag Doll 126 252 378 806 1378 1950
41-50 105 210 315 667 1146 1625
51-61: 52-1st computer in comics, c/s (4/44). 59-Last Minute Movies. 61-Last Moldoff Hawkman 92 184 276 584 1005 1425
62-Hawkman by Kubert begins 116 232 348 742 1271 1800
63-85: 66-68-Hop Harrigan in all. 70-Mutt & Jeff app. 80-Atom begins, ends #104 82 164 246 528 902 1275
86-Intro. The Black Canary in Johnny Thunder (8/47); see All-Star #38. 300 600 900 1980 3440 4900
87,88,90: 87-Intro. The Foil. 88-Origin Ghost. 129 258 387 826 1413 2000
89-Intro villain The Thorn (scarce) 213 426 639 1363 2332 3300
91,93-99: 98-Atom & Hawkman don new costumes 135 270 405 864 1482 2100
92-1st solo Black Canary plus-c; rare in Mint due to black ink smearing on white-c 360 720 1080 2520 4410 6300
100 (10/48),103(Scarce)-52 pgs. each 300 600 900 1950 3375 4800
101,102(Scarce) 265 530 795 1694 2897 4100
104-Origin The Flash retold (Scarce) 692 1384 2076 5052 8926 12,800

NOTE: ***Irwin Hasen*** *a-Wheaties Giveaway. c-97, Wheaties Giveaway.* ***E.E. Hibbard*** *c-6, 12, 20, 24, 26, 28, 30, 44, 46, 48, 50, 62, 66, 68, 69, 72, 74, 76, 78, 80, 82.* ***Infantino*** *a-86p, 90, 93-95, 99-104; c-90, 92, 93, 97, 99, 101, 103.* ***Kinstler*** *a-87, 89(Hawkman); c-87.* ***Chet Kozlak*** *c-77, 79, 81.* ***Krigstein*** *a-94.* ***Kubert*** *a-62-76, 83, 85, 86, 88-104; c-63, 65, 67, 70, 71, 73, 75, 83, 85, 86, 88, 89, 91, 94, 96, 98, 100, 104.* ***Moldoff*** *a-3; c-3, 7-11, 13-17, plus odd #'s 19-61.* ***Martin Naydell*** *c-52, 54, 56, 58, 60, 64, 84.*

FLASH DIGEST, THE (See DC Special Series #24)

FLASH GORDON (See Defenders Of The Earth, Eat Right to Work..., Giant Comic Album, King Classics, King Comics, March of Comics #118, 133, 142, The Phantom #18, Street Comix & Wow Comics, 1st series)

FLASH GORDON
Dell Publishing Co.: No. 25, 1941; No. 10, 1943 - No. 512, Nov, 1953

Feature Books 25 (#1)(1941))-r-not by Raymond 135 270 405 864 1482 2100
Four Color 10(1942)-by Alex Raymond; reprints "The Ice Kingdom" 82 164 246 664 1432 2200
Four Color 84(1945)-by Alex Raymond; reprints "The Fiery Desert" 40 80 120 300 650 1000
Four Color 173 18 36 54 123 267 410
Four Color 190-Bondage-c; "The Adventures of the Flying Saucers"; 5th Flying Saucer story (6/48)- see The Spirit 9/28/47(1st), Shadow Comics V7#10 (2nd, 1/48), Captain Midnight #60 (3rd, 2/48) & Boy Commandos #26 (4th, 3-4/48) 20 40 60 140 300 460
Four Color 204,247 14 28 42 93 202 310
Four Color 424-Painted-c 11 22 33 73 142 210
2(5-7/53-Dell)-Painted-c; Evans-a? 9 18 27 61 106 150
Four Color 512-Painted-c 9 18 27 61 106 150

FLASH GORDON (See Tiny Tot Funnies)
Harvey Publications: Oct, 1950 - No. 4, April, 1951

1-Alex Raymond-a; bondage-c; reprints strips from 7/14/40 to 12/8/40 39 78 117 231 378 525
2-Alex Raymond-a; r/strips 12/15/40-4/27/41 23 46 69 136 223 310
3,4-Alex Raymond-a; 3-bondage-c; r/strips 5/4/41-9/21/41. 4-r/strips 10/24/37-3/27/38 21 42 63 126 206 285
5-(Rare)-Small size-5-1/2x8-1/2"; B&W; 32 pgs.; Distributed to some mail subscribers only 81 162 243 518 884 1250
(Also see All-New No. 15, Boy Explorers No. 2, and Stuntman No. 3)

FLASH GORDON
Gold Key: June, 1965

1 (1947 reprint)-Painted-c 7 14 21 46 76 105

FLASH GORDON (Also see Comics Reading Libraries in the Promotional Comics section)
King #1-11/Charlton #12-18/Gold Key #19-23/Whitman #28 on:
9/66 - #11, 12/67; #12, 2/69 - #18, 1/70; #19, 9/78 - #37, 3/82 (Painted covers No. 19-30, 34)

1-1st S.A. app Flash Gordon; Williamson c/a(2); E.C. swipe/Incredible S.F. #32; Mandrake story 8 16 24 55 93 130
1-Army giveaway(1968)("Complimentary" on cover)(Same as regular #1 minus Mandrake story & back-c) 5 10 15 30 48 65
2-8: 2-Bolle, Gil Kane-c; Mandrake story. 3-Williamson-c. 4-Secret Agent X-9 begins, Williamson-c/a(3). 5-Williamson-c/a(2). 6,8-Crandall-a. 7-Raboy-a (last in comics?). 8-Secret Agent X-9-r 5 10 15 30 48 65
9-13: 9,10-Raymond-r. 10-Buckler's 1st pro work (11/67). 11-Crandall-a. 12-Crandall-c/a. 13-Jeff Jones-a (15 pgs.) 4 8 12 28 44 60
14,15: 15-Last 12¢ issue 3 6 9 20 30 40
16,17: 17-Brick Bradford story 3 6 9 17 25 32
18-Kaluta-a (3rd pro work?)(see Teen Confessions) 4 8 12 22 34 45
19(9/78, G.K.), 20-26 2 4 6 8 10 12
27-29,34-37: 34-37-Movie adaptation 2 4 6 8 11 14
30 (10/80) (scarce, from Whitman 3-pack only, 40¢-c) 3 6 9 20 30 40
30 (7/81; re-issue, 50¢-c), 31-33-single issues 2 4 6 8 11 14
31-33 (Bagged 3-pack): Movie adaptation; Williamson-a. 42.00

NOTE: ***Aparo*** *a-8.* ***Bolle*** *a-21, 22.* ***Boyette*** *a-14-18.* ***Briggs*** *c-10.* ***Buckler*** *a-10.* ***Crandall*** *c-6.* ***Estrada*** *a-3.* ***Gene Fawcette*** *a-29, 30, 34, 37.* ***McWilliams*** *a-31-33, 36.*

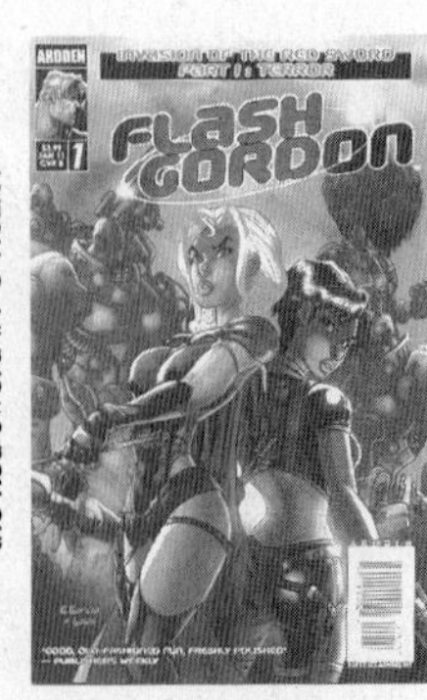

Flash Gordon: Invasion of the Red Sword #1 © Hearst

Flashpoint #5 © DC

Flintstones #20 © H-B

	GD 2.0	VG 4.0	FN 6.0	VF 8.0	VF/NM 9.0	NM- 9.2

FLASH GORDON
DC Comics: June, 1988 - No. 9, Holiday, 1988-'89 ($1.25, mini-series)

1-9: 1,5-Painted-c 3.00

FLASH GORDON
Marvel Comics: June, 1995 - No. 2, July, 1995 ($2.95, limited series)

1,2: Schultz scripts; Williamson-a 3.00

FLASH GORDON (The Mercy Wars)
Ardden Entertainment: Aug, 2008 - No. 6, Jul, 2009 ($3.99)

1-6: 1-Deneen-s/Green-a; two covers 4.00
...: The Mercy Wars #0 (4/09, $2.99) 3.00

FLASH GORDON: INVASION OF THE RED SWORD
Ardden Entertainment: Jan, 2011 - No. 6, Nov, 2011 ($3.99)

1-6-Deneen-s/Garcia-a. 1-Two covers 4.00

FLASH GORDON THE MOVIE
Western Publishing Co.: 1980 (8-1/4 x 11", $1.95, 68 pgs.)

11294-Williamson-c/a; adapts movie 2 4 6 10 14 18
13743-Hardback edition 3 6 9 15 21 26

FLASH GORDON: ZEITGEIST
Dynamite Entertainment: 2011 - Present ($1.00/$3.99)

1-($1.00) Flash, Dale and Zarkov head to Mongo; 4 covers by Ross, Renaud & others 3.00
2,3-($3.99) Three covers 4.00

FLASH/ GREEN LANTERN: FASTER FRIENDS (See Green Lantern/Flash...)
DC Comics: No. 2, 1997 ($4.95, continuation of Green Lantern/Flash: Faster Friends #1)

2-Waid/Augustyn-s 5.00

FLASHPOINT (Elseworlds Flash)
DC Comics: Dec, 1999 - No. 3, Feb, 2000 ($2.95, limited series)

1-3-Paralyzed Barry Allen; Breyfogle-a/McGreal-s 3.00

FLASHPOINT (Leads into DC New 52 relaunches)
DC Comics: Jul, 2011 - No. 5, Late Oct, 2011 ($3.99, limited series)

1-5-Johns-s/Andy Kubert-a; 2 covers on each. 2-4-Bonus design art. 5-New timeline 4.00
...: Abin Sur - The Green Lantern 1-3 (8/11 - No. 3, 10/11, $2.99) Massaferra-a/c 3.00
...: Batman Knight of Vengeance 1-3 (8/11 - No. 3, 10/11, $2.99) Risso-a/Johnson-c 3.00
...: Canterbury Cricket, The (8/11, $2.99, one-shot) Carlin-s/Morales-a 3.00
...: Citizen Cold 1-3 (8/11 - No. 3, 10/11, $2.99) Scott Kolins-s/a/c 3.00
...: Deadman and the Flying Grayson 1-3 (8/11 - No. 3, 10/11, $2.99) Chiang-c 3.00
...: Deathstroke & The Curse of the Ravager 1-3 (8/11 - No. 3, 10/11, $2.99) Bennett-a 3.00
...: Emperor Aquaman 1-3 (8/11 - No. 3, 10/11, $2.99) Bedard-s/Syaf-c 3.00
...: Frankenstein and the Creatures of the Unknown 1-3 (8/11 - No. 3, 10/11, $2.99) 3.00
...: Green Arrow Industries (8/11, $2.99, one-shot) Kalvachev-c 3.00
...: Grodd of War (8/11, $2.99, one-shot) Manapul-c 3.00
...: Hal Jordan 1-3 (8/11 - No. 3, 10/11, $2.99) 1-Oliver-a. 2,3-Richards-a 3.00
...: Kid Flash Lost 1-3 (8/11 - No. 3, 10/11, $2.99) Gates-s/Manapul-c; Brainiac app. 3.00
...: Legion of Doom 1-3 (8/11 - No. 3, 10/11, $2.99) Glass-s/Sepulveda-c 3.00
...: Lois Lane and the Resistance 1-3 (8/11 - No. 3, 10/11, $2.99) Abnett & Lanning-s 3.00
...: Outsider, The 1-3 (8/11 - No. 3, 10/11, $2.99) Robinson-s/Nowlan-c 3.00
...: Project Superman 1-3 (8/11 - No. 3, 10/11, $2.99) Gene Ha-c/a 3.00
...: Reverse Flash (8/11, $2.99, one-shot) Kolins-s/Gomez-a 3.00
...: Secret Seven 1-3 (8/11 - No. 3, 10/11, $2.99) Pérez-c on all. 1-Pérez-a. 3.00
...: Wonder Woman and The Furies 1-3 (8/11 - No. 3, 10/11, $2.99) Aquaman app. 3.00
...: World of Flashpoint 1-3 (8/11 - No. 3, 10/11, $2.99) Traci 13 app. 3.00

FLAT-TOP
Mazie Comics/Harvey Publ.(Magazine Publ.) No. 4 on: 11/53 - No. 3, 5/54; No. 4, 3/55 - No. 7, 9/55

1-Teenage; Flat-Top, Mazie, Mortie & Stevie begin 9 18 27 52 69 85
2,3 6 12 18 29 36 42
4-7 6 12 18 27 33 38

FLESH & BLOOD
Brainstorm Comics: Dec, 1995 ($2.95, B&W, mature)

1-Balent-c; foil-c. 3.00

FLESH AND BONES
Upshot Graphics (Fantagraphics Books): June, 1986 - No. 4, Dec, 1986 (Limited series)

1-4: Alan Moore scripts (r) & Dalgoda by Fujitake 3.00

FLESH CRAWLERS
Kitchen Sink Press: Aug, 1993 - No. 3, 1995 ($2.50, B&W, limited series, mature)

1-3 3.00

FLEX MENTALLO (Man of Muscle Mystery) (See Doom Patrol, 2nd Series)
DC Comics (Vertigo): Jun, 1996 - No. 4, Sept, 1996 ($2.50, lim. series, mature)

1-4: Grant Morrison scripts & Frank Quitely-c/a in all; banned from reprints due to Charles Atlas legal action 2 4 6 9 13 16

FLINCH (Horror anthology)
DC Comics (Vertigo): Jun, 1999 - No. 16, Jan, 2001 ($2.50)

1-16: 1-Art by Jim Lee, Quitely, and Corben. 5-Sale-c. 11-Timm-a 3.00

FLINTSTONE KIDS, THE (TV) (See Star Comics Digest)
Star Comics/Marvel Comics #5 on: Aug, 1987 - No. 11, Apr, 1989

1-11 4.50

FLINTSTONES, THE (TV)(See Dell Giant #48 for No. 1)
Dell Publ. Co./Gold Key No. 7 (10/62) on: No. 2, Nov-Dec, 1961 - No. 60, Sept, 1970 (Hanna-Barbera)

2-2nd app. (TV show debuted on 9/30/60); 1st app. of Cave Kids; 15¢-c thru #5
10 20 30 66 121 175
3-6(7-8/62): 3-Perry Gunnite begins. 6-1st 12¢-c 7 14 21 44 72 100
7 (10/62; 1st GK) 7 14 21 44 72 100
8-10 6 12 18 37 59 80
11-1st app. Pebbles (6/63) 8 16 24 56 96 135
12-15,17-20 5 10 15 30 48 65
16-1st app. Bamm-Bamm (1/64) 8 16 24 53 89 125
21-23,25-30,33: 26,27-2nd & 3rd app. The Grusomes. 30-1st app. Martian Mopheads (10/65). 33-Meet Frankenstein & Dracula 4 8 12 28 44 60
24-1st app. The Grusomes 6 12 18 39 62 85
31,32,35-40: 31-Xmas-c. 36-Adaptation of "the Man Called Flintstone" movie. 39-Reprints
4 8 12 24 37 50
34-1st app. The Great Gazoo 6 12 18 39 62 85
41-60: 45-Last 12¢ issue 3 6 9 21 32 42
At N. Y. World's Fair ('64)-J.W. Books (25¢)-1st printing; no date on-c (29¢ version exists, 2nd print?) Most H-B characters app.; including Yogi Bear, Top Cat, Snagglepuss and the Jetsons 5 10 15 34 55 75
At N. Y. World's Fair (1965 on-c; re-issue; Warren Pub.)
NOTE: Warehouse find in 1984 2 4 6 10 14 18
Bigger & Boulder 1(#30013-211) (Gold Key Giant, 11/62, 25¢, 84 pgs.)
8 16 24 53 89 125
Bigger & Boulder 2-(1966, 25¢)-Reprints B&B No. 1 4 8 12 24 37 50
...On the Rocks (9/61, $1.00, 6-1/4x9", cardboard-c, high quality paper,116 pgs.)
B&W new material 9 18 27 61 106 150
...With Pebbles & Bamm Bamm (100 pgs., G.K.)-30028-511 (paper-c, 25¢) (11/65)
7 14 21 44 72 100

NOTE: *(See Comic Album #16, Bamm-Bamm & Pebbles Flintstone, Dell Giant 48, Golden Comics Digest, March of Comics #229, 243, 271, 289, 299, 317, 327, 341, Pebbles Flintstone, Top Comics #2-4, and Whitman Comic Book.)*

FLINTSTONES, THE (TV)(...& Pebbles)
Charlton Comics: Nov, 1970 - No. 50, Feb, 1977 (Hanna-Barbera)

1 8 16 24 51 86 120
2 4 8 12 28 44 60
3-7,9,10 3 6 9 20 30 40
8- "Flintstones Summer Vacation" (Summer, 1971, 52 pgs.)
5 10 15 34 55 75
11-20,36: 36-Mike Zeck illos (early work) 3 6 9 16 23 30
21-35,38-41,43-45 3 6 9 14 19 24
37-Byrne text illos (early work; see Nightmare #20) 3 6 9 16 23 30
42-Byrne-a (2 pgs.) 3 6 9 16 23 30
46-50 2 4 6 13 18 22
Digest nn (1972, B&W, 100 pgs.) (low print run) 3 6 9 20 30 40
(Also see Barney & Betty Rubble, Dino, The Great Gazoo, & Pebbles & Bamm-Bamm)

FLINTSTONES, THE (TV)(See Yogi Bear, 3rd series) (Newsstand sales only)
Marvel Comics Group: October, 1977 - No. 9, Feb, 1979 (Hanna-Barbera)

1,7-9: 1-(30¢-c). 7-9-Yogi Bear app. 3 6 9 20 30 40
1-(35¢-c variant, limited distribution) 9 18 27 58 99 140
2,3,5,6: Yogi Bear app. 3 6 9 16 22 28
4-The Jetsons app. 3 6 9 17 25 32

FLINTSTONES, THE (TV)
Harvey Comics: Sept, 1992 - No. 13, Jun, 1994 ($1.25/$1.50) (Hanna-Barbera)

V2#1-13 4.00
...Big Book 1,2 (11/92, 3/93; both $1.95, 52 pgs.) 4.50
...Giant Size 1-3 (10/92, 4/93, 11/93; $2.25, 68 pgs.) 4.50

FLINTSTONES, THE (TV)
Archie Publications: Sept, 1995 - No. 22, June, 1997 ($1.50)

1-22 3.00

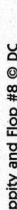

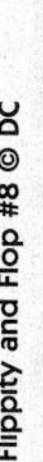
Flippity and Flop #8 © DC

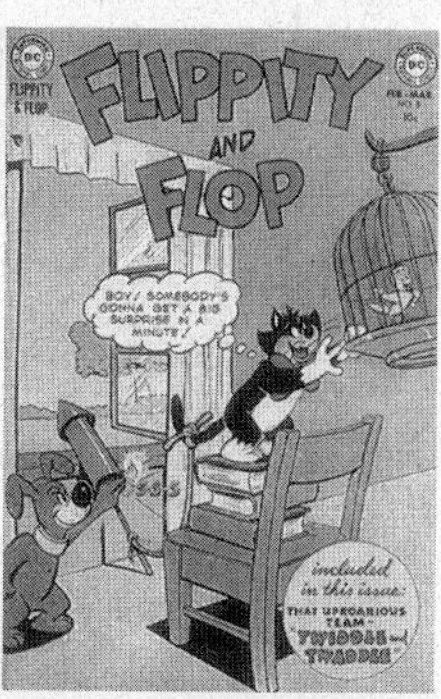

Flyin' Jenny #2 © Pentagon

Foolkiller #1 © MAR

FLINTSTONES AND THE JETSONS, THE (TV)
DC Comics: Aug, 1997 - No. 21, May, 1999 ($1.75/$1.95/$1.99)

	GD 2.0	VG 4.0	FN 6.0	VF 8.0	VF/NM 9.0	NM- 9.2
1						6.00
2-21: 19-Bizarro Elroy-c						3.00

FLINTSTONES CHRISTMAS PARTY, THE (See The Funtastic World of Hanna-Barbera No. 1)

FLIP
Harvey Publications: April, 1954 - No. 2, June, 1954 (Satire)

	GD 2.0	VG 4.0	FN 6.0	VF 8.0	VF/NM 9.0	NM- 9.2
1,2-Nostrand-a each. 2-Powell-a	22	44	66	128	209	290

FLIPPER (TV)
Gold Key: Apr, 1966 - No. 3, Nov, 1967 (All have photo-c)

	GD 2.0	VG 4.0	FN 6.0	VF 8.0	VF/NM 9.0	NM- 9.2
1	7	14	21	44	72	100
2,3	5	10	15	30	48	65

FLIPPITY & FLOP
National Per. Publ. (Signal Publ. Co.): 12-1/51-52 - No. 46, 8-10/59; No. 47, 9-11/60

	GD 2.0	VG 4.0	FN 6.0	VF 8.0	VF/NM 9.0	NM- 9.2
1-Sam dog & his pets Flippity The Bird and Flop The Cat begin; Twiddle and Twaddle begin	28	56	84	165	270	375
2	15	30	45	88	137	185
3-5	14	28	42	80	115	150
6-10	12	24	36	67	94	120
11-20: 20-Last precode (3/55)	10	20	30	58	79	100
21-47	9	18	27	52	69	85

FLOATERS
Dark Horse Comics: Sept, 1993 - No. 5, Jan, 1994 ($2.50, B&W, lim. series)

	GD 2.0	VG 4.0	FN 6.0	VF 8.0	VF/NM 9.0	NM- 9.2
1-5						3.00

FLOYD FARLAND (See Eclipse Graphic Album Series #11)

FLY, THE (Also see Adventures of..., Blue Ribbon Comics & Flyman)
Archie Enterprises, Inc.: May, 1983 - No. 9, Oct, 1984

	GD 2.0	VG 4.0	FN 6.0	VF 8.0	VF/NM 9.0	NM- 9.2
1,2: 1-Mr. Justice app; origin Shield; Kirby-a; Steranko-c. 2-Ditko-a; Flygirl app.						6.00
3-5: Ditko-a in all. 4,5-Ditko-c(p)						4.50
6-9: Ditko-a in all. 6-8-Ditko-c(p)						6.00

NOTE: ***Ayers** c-9. **Buckler** a-1, 2. **Kirby** a-1. **Nebres** c-3, 4, 5i, 6, 7i. **Steranko** c-1, 2.*

FLY, THE
Impact Comics (DC): Aug, 1991 - No. 17, Dec, 1992 ($1.00)

	GD 2.0	VG 4.0	FN 6.0	VF 8.0	VF/NM 9.0	NM- 9.2
1						3.50
2-17: 4-Vs. The Black Hood. 9-Trading card inside						3.00
Annual 1 ('92, $2.50, 68 pgs.)-Impact trading card						4.00

FLYBOY (Flying Cadets)(Also see Approved Comics #5)
Ziff-Davis Publ. Co. (Approved): Spring, 1952 - No. 2, Oct-Nov, 1952

	GD 2.0	VG 4.0	FN 6.0	VF 8.0	VF/NM 9.0	NM- 9.2
1-Saunders painted-c	20	40	60	114	182	250
2-(10-11/52)-Saunders painted-c	14	28	42	80	115	150

FLYING ACES (Aviation stories)
Key Publications: July, 1955 - No. 5, Mar, 1956

	GD 2.0	VG 4.0	FN 6.0	VF 8.0	VF/NM 9.0	NM- 9.2
1	9	18	27	47	61	75
2-5: 2-Trapani-a	6	12	18	27	33	38

FLYING A'S RANGE RIDER, THE (TV)(See Western Roundup under Dell Giants)
Dell Publishing Co.: #404, 6-7/52; #2, June-Aug, 1953 - #24, Aug, 1959 (All photo-c)

	GD 2.0	VG 4.0	FN 6.0	VF 8.0	VF/NM 9.0	NM- 9.2
Four Color 404(#1)-Titled "The Range Rider"	9	18	27	63	112	160
2	6	12	18	41	66	90
3-10	5	10	15	34	55	75
11-16,18-24	5	10	15	30	48	65
17-Toth-a	6	12	18	37	59	80

FLYING CADET (WW II Plane Photos)
Flying Cadet Publ. Co.; Jan, 1943 - V2#8, Nov, 1944 (Half photos, half comics)

	GD 2.0	VG 4.0	FN 6.0	VF 8.0	VF/NM 9.0	NM- 9.2
V1#1-Painted-c	15	30	45	90	140	190
2-Photo-c, P-47 Thunderbolt	10	20	30	56	76	95
3-9 (Two #6's, Sept. & Oct.): 4,5,6a,6b-Photo-c	9	18	27	52	69	85
V2#1-7 (1/44-9/44)(#10-16): 1,2,4-7-Photo-c	9	18	27	47	61	75
7 (#17 on cover)-Bare-breasted woman-c	20	40	60	114	182	250

FLYING COLORS 10th ANNIVERSARY SPECIAL
Flying Colors Comics: Fall 1998 ($2.95, one-shot)

	GD 2.0	VG 4.0	FN 6.0	VF 8.0	VF/NM 9.0	NM- 9.2
1-Dan Brereton-c; pin-ups by Jim Lee and Jeff Johnson						3.00

FLYIN' JENNY
Pentagon Publ. Co./Leader Enterprises #2: 1946 - No. 2, 1947 (1945 strip-r)

	GD 2.0	VG 4.0	FN 6.0	VF 8.0	VF/NM 9.0	NM- 9.2
nn-Marcus Swayze strip-r (entire insides)	15	30	45	85	130	175
2-Baker-c; Swayze strip reprints	18	36	54	103	162	220

FLYING MODELS
H-K Publ. (Health-Knowledge Publs.): V61#3, May, 1954 (5¢, 16 pgs.)

	GD 2.0	VG 4.0	FN 6.0	VF 8.0	VF/NM 9.0	NM- 9.2
V61#3 (Rare)	9	18	27	50	65	80

FLYING NUN (TV)
Dell Publishing Co.: Feb, 1968 - No. 4, Nov, 1968

	GD 2.0	VG 4.0	FN 6.0	VF 8.0	VF/NM 9.0	NM- 9.2
1-Sally Field photo-c	7	14	21	44	72	100
2-4: 2-Sally Field photo-c	4	8	12	28	44	60

FLYING NURSES (See Sue & Sally Smith...)

FLYING SAUCERS (See The Spirit 9/28/47(1st app.), Shadow Comics V7#10 (2nd, 1/48), Captain Midnight #60 (3rd, 2/48), Boy Commandos #26 (4th, 3-4/48) & Flash Gordon Four Color 190 (5th, 6/48))

FLYING SAUCERS (See Out of This World Adventures #2)
Avon Periodicals/Realistic: 1950; 1952; 1953

	GD 2.0	VG 4.0	FN 6.0	VF 8.0	VF/NM 9.0	NM- 9.2
1(1950)-Wood-a, 21 pgs.; Fawcette-c	87	174	261	553	952	1350
nn(1952)-Cover altered plus 2 pgs. of Wood-a not in original	47	94	141	296	498	700
nn(1953)-Reprints above (exist?)	36	72	108	211	343	475

FLYING SAUCERS (Comics)
Dell Publishing Co.: April, 1967 - No. 4, Nov, 1967; No. 5, Oct, 1969

	GD 2.0	VG 4.0	FN 6.0	VF 8.0	VF/NM 9.0	NM- 9.2
1-(12¢-c)	4	8	12	28	44	60
2-5: 5-Has same cover as #1, but with 15¢ price	3	6	9	20	30	40

FLY MAN (Formerly Adventures of The Fly; Mighty Comics #40 on)
Mighty Comics Group (Radio Comics) (Archie): No. 32, July, 1965 - No. 39, Sept, 1966 (Also see Mighty Crusaders)

	GD 2.0	VG 4.0	FN 6.0	VF 8.0	VF/NM 9.0	NM- 9.2
32,33-Comet, Shield, Black Hood, The Fly & Flygirl x-over. 33-Re-intro Wizard, Hangman (1st S.A. appearances)	6	12	18	39	62	85
34-39: 34-Shield begins. 35-Origin Black Hood. 36-Hangman x-over in Shield; re-intro. & origin of Web (1st S.A. app.). 37-Hangman, Wizard x-over in Flyman; last Shield issue. 38-Web story. 39-Steel Sterling (1st S.A. app.)	4	8	12	28	44	60

FOLLOW THE SUN (TV)
Dell Publishing Co.: May-July, 1962 - No. 2, Sept-Nov, 1962 (Photo-c)

	GD 2.0	VG 4.0	FN 6.0	VF 8.0	VF/NM 9.0	NM- 9.2
01-280-207(No.1)	5	10	15	32	51	70
12-280-211(No.2)	4	8	12	28	44	60

FOODANG
Continum Comics: July, 1994 ($1.95, B&W, bi-monthly)

	GD 2.0	VG 4.0	FN 6.0	VF 8.0	VF/NM 9.0	NM- 9.2
1						3.00

FOODINI (TV)(The Great...; see Jingle Dingle & Pinhead &...)
Continental Publ. (Holyoke): March, 1950 - No. 4, Aug, 1950 (All have 52 pgs.)

	GD 2.0	VG 4.0	FN 6.0	VF 8.0	VF/NM 9.0	NM- 9.2
1-Based on TV puppet show (very early TV comic)	22	44	66	132	216	300
2-Jingle Dingle begins	14	28	42	80	115	150
3,4	10	20	30	58	79	100

FOOEY (Magazine) (Satire)
Scoff Publishing Co.: Feb, 1961 - No. 4, May, 1961

	GD 2.0	VG 4.0	FN 6.0	VF 8.0	VF/NM 9.0	NM- 9.2
1	5	10	15	30	48	65
2-4	3	6	9	20	30	40

FOOFUR (TV)
Marvel Comics (Star Comics)/Marvel No. 5 on: Aug, 1987 - No. 6, Jun, 1988

	GD 2.0	VG 4.0	FN 6.0	VF 8.0	VF/NM 9.0	NM- 9.2
1-6						4.00

FOOLKILLER (Also see The Amazing Spider-Man #225, The Defenders #73, Man-Thing #3 & Omega the Unknown #8)
Marvel Comics: Oct, 1990 - No. 10, Oct, 1991 ($1.75, limited series)

	GD 2.0	VG 4.0	FN 6.0	VF 8.0	VF/NM 9.0	NM- 9.2
1-10: 1-Origin 3rd Foolkiller; Greg Salinger app; DeZuniga-a(i) in 1-4. 8-Spider-Man x-over						3.00

FOOLKILLER
Marvel Comics: Dec, 2007 - No. 5, Jul, 2008 ($3.99, limited series)

	GD 2.0	VG 4.0	FN 6.0	VF 8.0	VF/NM 9.0	NM- 9.2
1-5-Hurwitz-s/Medina-a. 2-Origin						4.00

FOOLKILLER: WHITE ANGELS
Marvel Comics: Sept, 2008 - No. 5, Jan, 2009 ($3.99, limited series)

	GD 2.0	VG 4.0	FN 6.0	VF 8.0	VF/NM 9.0	NM- 9.2
1-5-Hurwitz-s/Azaceta-a						4.00

FOOM (Friends Of Ol' Marvel)
Marvel Comics: 1973 - No. 22, 1979 (Marvel fan magazine)

	GD 2.0	VG 4.0	FN 6.0	VF 8.0	VF/NM 9.0	NM- 9.2
1	9	18	27	58	99	140
2-Hulk-c by Steranko	6	12	18	39	62	85
3,4	6	12	18	37	59	80
5-11: 11-Kirby-a and interview	5	10	15	32	51	70
12-15: 12-Vision-c. 13-Daredevil-c. 14-Conan. 15-Howard the Duck	5	10	15	32	51	70

Forbidden Worlds #12 © ACG

Force Works #3 © MAR

Forever People (2nd) #6 © DC

	GD 2.0	VG 4.0	FN 6.0	VF 8.0	VF/NM 9.0	NM- 9.2
16-20: 16-Marvel bullpen. 17-Stan Lee issue. 19-Defenders	4	8	12	28	44	60
21-Star Wars	5	10	15	30	48	65
22-Spider-Man-c; low print run final issue	6	12	18	42	69	95

FOOTBALL THRILLS (See Tops In Adventure)
Ziff-Davis Publ. Co.: Fall-Winter, 1951-52 - No. 2, Fall, 1952 (Edited by "Red" Grange)

	GD	VG	FN	VF	VF/NM	NM-
1-Powell a(2); Saunders painted-c; Red Grange, Jim Thorpe stories	27	54	81	158	259	360
2-Saunders painted-c	18	36	54	105	165	225

FOOT SOLDIERS, THE
Dark Horse Comics: Jan, 1996 - No. 4, Apr, 1996 ($2.95, limited series)

1-4: Krueger story & Avon Oeming-a. in all. 1-Alex Ross-c. 4-John K. Snyder, III-c 3.00

FOOT SOLDIERS, THE (Volume Two)
Image Comics: Sept, 1997 - No. 5, May, 1998 ($2.95, limited series)

1-5: 1-Yeowell-a. 2-McDaniel, Hester, Sienkiewicz, Giffen-a 3.00

FOR A NIGHT OF LOVE
Avon Periodicals: 1951

	GD	VG	FN	VF	VF/NM	NM-
nn-Two stories adapted from the works of Emile Zola; Astarita, Ravielli-a; Kinstler-c	32	64	96	192	314	435

FORBIDDEN KNOWLEDGE: ADVENTURE BEYOND THE DOORWAY TO SOULS WITH RADICAL DREAMER (Also see Radical Dreamer)
Mark's Giant Economy Size Comics: 1996 ($3.50, B&W, one-shot, 48 pgs.)

nn-Max Wrighter app.; Wheatley-c/a/script; painted infinity-c 4.00

FORBIDDEN LOVE
Quality Comics Group: Mar, 1950 - No. 4, Sept, 1950 (52 pgs.)

	GD	VG	FN	VF	VF/NM	NM-
1-(Scarce)-Classic photo-c; Crandall-a	81	162	243	518	884	1250
2-(Scarce)-Classic photo-c	66	132	198	419	722	1025
3-(Scarce)-Photo-c	41	82	123	260	435	610
4-(Scarce)-Ward/Cuidera-a; photo-c	42	84	126	265	445	625

FORBIDDEN LOVE (See Dark Mansion of...)

FORBIDDEN PLANET
Innovation Publishing: May, 1992 - No. 4, 1992 ($2.50, limited series)

1-4: Adapts movie; painted-c 3.00

FORBIDDEN TALES OF DARK MANSION (Formerly Dark Mansion of Forbidden Love #1-4)
National Periodical Publ.: No. 5, May-June, 1972 - No. 15, Feb-Mar, 1974

	GD	VG	FN	VF	VF/NM	NM-
5-(52 pgs.)	6	12	18	39	62	85
6-15: 13-Kane/Howard-a	3	6	9	18	27	35

NOTE: ***N. Adams*** *c-9.* ***Alcala*** *a-9-11, 13.* ***Chaykin*** *a-7,15.* ***Evans*** *a-14.* ***Heck*** *a-5.* ***Kaluta*** *a-7i, 8-12; c-7, 8, 13.* ***G. Kane*** *a-13.* ***Kirby*** *a-6.* ***Nino*** *a-8, 12, 15.* ***Redondo*** *a-14.*

FORBIDDEN WORLDS
American Comics Group: 7-8/51 - No. 34, 10-11/54; No. 35, 8/55 - No. 145, 8/67 (No. 1-5: 52 pgs.; No. 6-8: 44 pgs.)

	GD	VG	FN	VF	VF/NM	NM-
1-Williamson/Frazetta-a (10 pgs.)	165	330	495	1048	1799	2550
2	68	136	204	435	743	1050
3-Williamson/Wood-a (7 pgs.); Frazetta (1 panel)	69	138	207	438	752	1065
4	44	88	132	277	469	660
5-Krenkel/Williamson-a (8 pgs.)	54	108	162	343	574	825
6-Harrison/Williamson-a (8 pgs.)	48	96	144	302	514	725
7,8,10: 7-1st monthly issue	34	68	102	199	325	450
9-A-Bomb explosion story	37	74	111	222	361	500
11-20	22	44	66	132	216	300
21-33: 24-E.C. swipe by Landau	19	38	57	109	172	235
34(10-11/54)(Scarce)(becomes Young Heroes #35 on)-Last pre-code issue; A-Bomb explosion story	20	40	60	118	192	265
35(8/55)-Scarce	20	40	60	115	185	255
36-62	14	28	42	76	108	140
63,69,76,78-Williamson-a in all; w/Krenkel #69	14	28	42	78	112	145
64,66-68,70-72,74,75,77,79-85,87-90	10	20	30	56	76	95
65- "There's a New Moon Tonight" listed in #114 as holding 1st record fan mail response	14	28	42	78	112	145
73-1st app. Herbie by Ogden Whitney	43	86	129	271	461	650
86-Flying saucer-c by Schaffenberger	11	22	33	62	86	110
91-93,95-100	5	10	15	34	55	75
94-Herbie (2nd app.)	11	22	33	73	142	210
101-109,111-113,115,117-120	4	8	12	28	44	60
110,116-Herbie app. 116-Herbie goes to Hell	8	16	24	53	89	125
114-1st Herbie-c; contains list of editor's top 20 ACG stories	10	20	30	65	118	170
121-123	4	8	12	22	34	45
124,127-130: 124-Magic Agent app.	4	8	12	24	37	50
125-Magic Agent app.; intro. & origin Magicman series, ends #141; Herbie app.	5	10	15	34	55	75
126-Herbie app.	4	8	12	28	44	60
131-139: 133-Origin/1st app. Dragonia in Magicman (1-2/66); returns in #138. 136-Nemesis x-over in Magicman	4	8	12	22	34	45
140-Mark Midnight app. by Ditko	4	8	12	24	37	50
141-145	3	6	9	20	30	40

NOTE: ***Buscema*** *a-75, 79, 81, 82, 140r.* ***Cameron*** *a-5.* ***Disbrow*** *a-10.* ***Ditko*** *a-137p, 138, 140.* ***Landau*** *a-24, 27-29, 31-34, 48, 86r, 96, 143-45.* ***Lazarus*** *a-18, 23, 24, 57.* ***Moldoff*** *a-27, 31, 139r.* ***Reinman*** *a-93.* ***Whitney*** *a-70, 115, 116, 137; c-40, 46, 57, 60, 68, 70, 78, 79, 90, 93, 94, 100, 102, 103, 106-108, 114, 129.*

FORCE, THE (See The Crusaders)

FORCE MAJEURE: PRAIRIE BAY (Also see Wild Stars)
Little Rocket Publications: May, 2002 ($2.95, B&W)

1-Tierney-s/Gil-c/a 3.00

FORCE OF BUDDHA'S PALM THE
Jademan Comics: Aug, 1988 - No. 55, Feb, 1993 ($1.50/$1.95, 68 pgs.)

1,55-Kung Fu stories in all 5.00
2-54 4.00

FORCE WORKS
Marvel Comics: July, 1994 - No. 22, Apr, 1996 ($1.50)

1-($3.95)-Fold-out pop-up-c; Iron Man, Wonder Man, Spider-Woman, U.S. Agent & Scarlet Witch (new costume) 4.00
2-11, 13-22: 5-Blue logo & pink logo versions. 9-Intro Dreamguard. 13-Avengers app. 3.00
5-Pink logo ($2.95)-polybagged w/ 16pg. Marvel Action Hour Preview & acetate print 4.00
12 ($2.50)-Flip book w/War Machine. 4.00

FORD ROTUNDA CHRISTMAS BOOK (See Christmas at the Rotunda)

FOREIGN INTRIGUES (Formerly Johnny Dynamite; becomes Battlefield Action #16 on)
Charlton Comics: No. 14, 1956 - No. 15, Aug, 1956

	GD	VG	FN	VF	VF/NM	NM-
14,15-Johnny Dynamite continues	8	16	24	44	57	70

FOREMOST BOYS (See 4Most)

FOREVER AMBER
Image Comics: July, 1999 - Oct, 1999 ($2.95, B&W)

1-4-Don Hudson-s/a 3.00

FOREVER DARLING (Movie)
Dell Publishing Co.: No. 681, Feb, 1956

	GD	VG	FN	VF	VF/NM	NM-
Four Color 681-w/Lucille Ball & Desi Arnaz; photo-c	11	22	33	77	144	210

FOREVER MAELSTROM
DC Comics: Jan, 2003 - No. 6, Jun, 2003 ($2.95, limited series)

1-6-Chaykin & Tischman-s/Lucas & Barreto-a 3.00

FOREVER PEOPLE, THE
National Periodical Publications: Feb-Mar, 1971 - No. 11, Oct-Nov, 1972 (Fourth World) (#1-3, 10-11 are 36 pgs.; #4-9 are 52 pgs.)

	GD	VG	FN	VF	VF/NM	NM-
1-1st app. Forever People; Superman x-over; Kirby-c/a begins; 1st full app. Darkseid (3rd anywhere, 3 weeks before New Gods #1); Darkseid storyline begins, ends #8 (app. in 1-4,6,8; cameos in 5,11)	7	14	21	48	79	110
2-9: 4-G.A. reprints thru #9. 9,10-Deadman app.	4	8	12	26	41	55
10,11	3	6	9	20	30	40

Jack Kirby's Forever People TPB ('99, $14.95, B&W&Grey) r/#1-11 plus cover gallery 15.00

NOTE: ***Kirby*** *c/a(p)-1-11; #4-9 contain Sandman reprints from Adventure #85, 84, 75, 80, 77, 74 in that order.*

FOREVER PEOPLE
DC Comics: Feb, 1988 - No. 6, July, 1988 ($1.25, limited series)

1-6 3.00

FORGE
CrossGeneration Comics: Feb, 2002 - No. 13, May, 2003 ($9.95/$11.95/$7.95, TPB)

1-3: Reprints from various CrossGen titles 10.00
4-8-($11.95) 12.00
9-13-($7.95, 8-1/4" x 5-1/2") digest-sized reprints 8.00

FOR GIRLS ONLY
Bernard Baily Enterprises: 11/53 - No. 2, 6/54 (100 pgs., digest size, 25¢)

	GD	VG	FN	VF	VF/NM	NM-
1-25% comic book, 75% articles, illos, games	20	40	60	114	182	250
2-Eddie Fisher photo & story.	14	28	42	80	115	150

FORGOTTEN FOREST OF OZ, THE (See First Comics Graphic Novel #16)

FORGOTTEN REALMS (Also see Avatar & TSR Worlds)

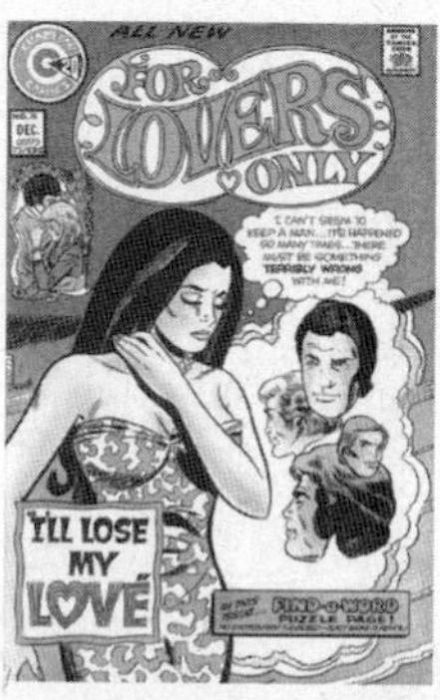

For Lovers Only #74 © CC

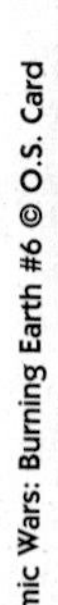

Formic Wars: Burning Earth #6 © O.S. Card

Four Color Comics Series 1 #8 © NYNS

GD VG FN VF VF/NM NM-
2.0 4.0 6.0 8.0 9.0 9.2

DC Comics: Sept, 1989 - No. 25, Sept, 1991 ($1.50/$1.75)
1, Annual 1 (1990, $2.95, 68 pgs.) 4.00
2-25: Based on TSR role-playing game. 18-Avatar story 3.00

FORGOTTEN REALMS (Based on Wizards of the Coast game)
Devil's Due Publ.: June, 2005 - No. 3, Aug, 2005 ($4.95)
1-3-Salvatore-s/Seeley-a 5.00
...Exile (11/05 - No. 3, 1/06, $4.95) 1-3-Daab-s/Seeley-a. 1-Flip cover 5.00
...: Legacy (2/08 - No. 3, 6/08, $5.50) 1-3-Daab-s/Atkins-a 5.50
The Legend of Drizzt Book II: Exile (2006, $14.95, TPB) r/#1-3 15.00
...Sojourn (3/06 - No. 3, 6/06, $4.95) 1-3-Daab-s/Seeley-a 5.00
...: Streams of Silver (12/06 - No. 3, $5.50) 1-3-Daab-s/Semeiks-a 5.50
...The Crystal Shard (8/06 - No. 3, 12/06, $4.95) 1-3-Daab-s/Semeiks-a 5.00
...The Halfling's Gem (8/07 - No. 3, 12/07, $5.50) 1-3-Daab-s/Seeley-a; two covers 5.50

FORLORN RIVER (See Zane Grey Four Color 395)

FOR LOVERS ONLY (Formerly Hollywood Romances)
Charlton Comics: No. 60, Aug, 1971 - No. 87, Nov, 1976
60 3 6 9 20 30 40
61-80,82-87: 67-Morisi-a 2 4 6 11 16 20
81-Psychedelic cover 3 6 9 16 23 30

FORMERLY KNOWN AS THE JUSTICE LEAGUE
DC Comics: Sept, 2003 - No. 6, Feb, 2004 ($2.50, limited series)
1-Giffen & DeMatteis-s/Maguire-a; Booster Gold, Blue Beetle, Captain Atom, Mary Marvel, Fire, and Elongated Man app. 3.50
2-6: 3,4-Roulette app. 6-JLA app. 3.00
TPB (2004, $12.95) r/#1-6 13.00

FORMIC WARS: BURNING EARTH
Marvel Comics: Apr, 2011 - No. 7, Sept, 2011 ($3.99, limited series)
1-7-Prequel to Orson Scott Card's novel Ender's Game. 1-Covers by Larroca & Hitch 4.00

FORMIC WARS: SILENT STRIKE (Follows Burning Earth limited series)
Marvel Comics: Feb, 2012 - No. 5 ($3.99, limited series)
1-3-Johnston-s/Caracuzzo-a/Camuncoli-c 4.00

FORT: PROPHET OF THE UNEXPLAINED
Dark Horse Comics: June, 2002 - No. 4, Sept, 2002 ($2.99, B&W, limited series)
1-4-Peter Lenkov-s/Frazer Irving-c/a 3.00
TPB (2003, $9.95) r/#1-4 10.00

FORTUNE AND GLORY
Oni Press: Dec, 1999 - No. 3, Apr, 2000 ($4.95, B&W, limited series)
1-3-Brian Michael Bendis in Hollywood 5.00
TPB ($14.95) 15.00

40 BIG PAGES OF MICKEY MOUSE
Whitman Publ. Co.: No. 945, Jan, 1936 (10-1/4x12-1/2", 44 pgs., cardboard-c)
945-Reprints Mickey Mouse Magazine #1, but with a different cover; ads were eliminated and some illustrated stories had expanded text. The book is 3/4" shorter than Mickey Mouse Mag. #1, but the reprints are same size (Rare) 164 328 492 1025 1663 2300

40 oz. COLLECTED
Image Comics: Nov, 2003 ($9.95, digest-size, B&W)
Vol. 1-Reprints Jim Mahfood's mini-comics plus 20 pgs. new material; Grrl Scouts app. 10.00

FOR YOUR EYES ONLY (See James Bond...)

FOUNTAIN, THE (Companion graphic novel to the Darren Aronofsky film)
DC Comics (Vertigo): 2005 ($39.99, hardcover with dust jacket)
1-Darren Aronofsky-s/Kent Williams-a 40.00

FOUR (Fantastic Four; See Marvel Knights 4 #28-30)

FOUR COLOR
Dell Publishing Co.: Sept?, 1939 - No. 1354, Apr-June, 1962
(Series I are all 68 pgs.)

NOTE: *Four Color only appears on issues #19-25, 1-99,101. Dell Publishing Co. filed these as Series I, #1-25, and Series II, #1-1354. Issues beginning with #710? were printed with and without ads on back cover. Issues without ads are worth more.*

SERIES I:
1(nn)-Dick Tracy 1000 2000 3000 7600 13,800 20,000
2(nn)-Don Winslow of the Navy (#1) (Rare) (11/39?)
200 400 600 1280 2190 3100
3(nn)-Myra North (1/40) 97 194 291 621 1061 1500
4-Donald Duck by Al Taliaferro (1940)(Disney)(3/40?)
1800 3600 5400 13,500 20,750 28,000
(Prices vary widely on this book)

GD VG FN VF VF/NM NM-
2.0 4.0 6.0 8.0 9.0 9.2

5-Smilin' Jack (#1) (5/40?) 74 148 222 470 810 1150
6-Dick Tracy (Scarce) 226 452 678 1446 2473 3500
7-Gang Busters 52 104 156 322 549 775
8-Dick Tracy 113 226 339 718 1234 1750
9-Terry and the Pirates-r/Super #9-29 68 136 204 435 743 1050
10-Smilin' Jack 62 124 186 394 680 965
11-Smitty (#1) 46 92 138 290 488 685
12-Little Orphan Annie; reprints strips from 12/19/37 to 6/4/38
58 116 174 371 636 900
13-Walt Disney's Reluctant Dragon('41)-Contains 2 pgs. of photos from film; 2 pg. foreword to Fantasia by Leopold Stokowski; Donald Duck, Goofy, Baby Weems & Mickey Mouse (as the Sorcerer's Apprentice) app. (Disney) 219 438 657 1402 2401 3400
14-Moon Mullins (#1) 45 90 135 284 480 675
15-Tillie the Toiler (#1) 45 90 135 284 480 675
16-Mickey Mouse (#1) (Disney) by Gottfredson 1250 2500 3750 16,500 - -
17-Walt Disney's Dumbo, the Flying Elephant (#1)(1941)-Mickey Mouse, Donald Duck, & Pluto app. (Disney) 265 530 795 1694 2897 4100
18-Jiggs and Maggie (#1)(1936-38-r) 48 96 144 302 514 725
19-Barney Google and Snuffy Smith (#1)-(1st issue with Four Color on the cover)
47 94 141 296 498 700
20-Tiny Tim 37 74 111 222 361 500
21-Dick Tracy 82 164 246 528 902 1275
22-Don Winslow 48 96 144 302 514 725
23-Gang Busters 41 82 123 249 417 585
24-Captain Easy 50 100 150 315 533 750
25-Popeye (1942) 89 178 267 565 970 1375

SERIES II:
1-Little Joe (1942) 52 104 156 421 911 1400
2-Harold Teen 27 54 81 191 413 635
3-Alley Oop (#1) 42 84 126 315 683 1050
4-Smilin' Jack 35 70 105 254 552 850
5-Raggedy Ann and Andy (#1) 43 86 129 323 704 1085
6-Smitty 19 38 57 132 284 435
7-Smokey Stover (#1) 25 50 75 175 375 575
8-Tillie the Toiler 21 42 63 142 304 465
9-Donald Duck Finds Pirate Gold, by Carl Barks & Jack Hannah (Disney) (© 8/17/42) 1000 2000 3000 7600 13,800 20,000
10-Flash Gordon by Alex Raymond; reprinted from "The Ice Kingdom"
82 164 246 664 1432 2200
11-Wash Tubbs 24 48 72 168 359 550
12-Walt Disney's Bambi (#1) 46 92 138 354 770 1185
13-Mr. District Attorney (#1)-See The Funnies #35 for 1st app.
25 50 75 171 366 560
14-Smilin' Jack 27 54 81 192 414 635
15-Felix the Cat (#1) 72 144 216 583 1267 1950
16-Porky Pig (#1)(1942)- "Secret of the Haunted House"
80 160 240 648 1399 2150
17-Popeye 40 80 120 300 650 1000
18-Little Orphan Annie's Junior Commandos; Flag-c; reprints strips from 6/14/42 to 11/21/42 31 62 93 225 488 750
19-Walt Disney's Thumper Meets the Seven Dwarfs (Disney); reprinted in Silly Symphonies
42 84 126 315 683 1050
20-Barney Baxter 23 46 69 161 343 525
21-Oswald the Rabbit (#1)(1943) 39 78 117 293 634 975
22-Tillie the Toiler 15 30 45 102 221 340
23-Raggedy Ann and Andy 31 62 93 225 488 750
24-Gang Busters 25 50 75 175 375 575
25-Andy Panda (#1) (Walter Lantz) 46 92 138 359 780 1200
26-Popeye 40 80 120 300 650 1000
27-Walt Disney's Mickey Mouse and the Seven Colored Terror
73 146 219 591 1283 1975
28-Wash Tubbs 16 32 48 109 237 365
29-Donald Duck and the Mummy's Ring, by Carl Barks (Disney) (9/43)
773 1546 2319 5643 9972 14,300
30-Bambi's Children (1943)-Disney 41 82 123 311 673 1035
31-Moon Mullins 15 30 45 102 221 340
32-Smitty 13 26 39 90 195 300
33-Bugs Bunny "Public Nuisance #1" 96 192 288 778 1689 2600
34-Dick Tracy 37 74 111 278 602 925
35-Smokey Stover 14 28 42 96 208 320
36-Smilin' Jack 20 40 60 137 294 450
37-Bringing Up Father 17 34 51 114 250 385
38-Roy Rogers (#1, © 4/44)-1st western comic with photo-c

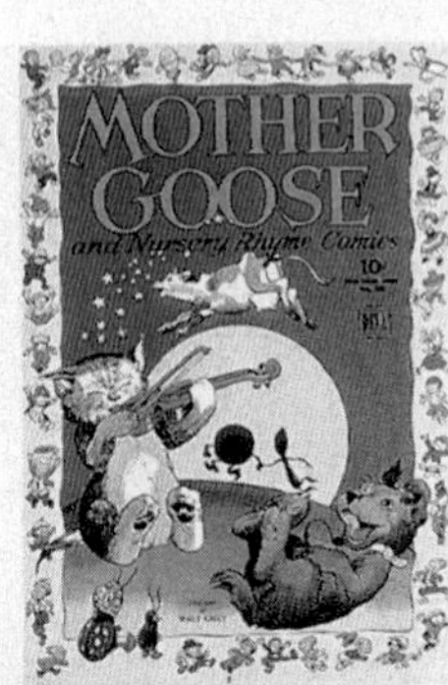

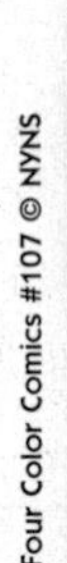
Four Color Comics #68 © Oskar Lebeck

Four Color Comics #107 © NYNS

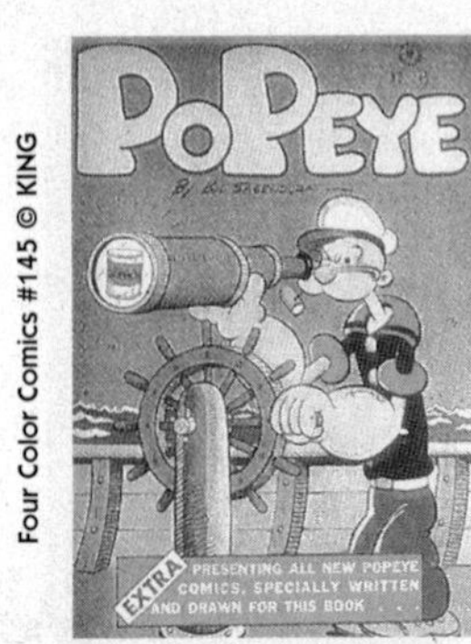

Four Color Comics #145 © KING

	GD 2.0	VG 4.0	FN 6.0	VF 8.0	VF/NM 9.0	NM- 9.2
(see Movie Comics #3)	146	292	438	1226	2663	4100
39-Oswald the Rabbit (1944)	26	52	78	182	391	600
40-Barney Google and Snuffy Smith	19	38	57	128	277	425
41-Mother Goose and Nursery Rhyme Comics (#1)-All by Walt Kelly	20	40	60	137	294	450
42-Tiny Tim (1934-r)	14	28	42	95	205	315
43-Popeye (1938-'42-r)	27	54	81	189	407	625
44-Terry and the Pirates (1938-r)	31	62	93	225	483	740
45-Raggedy Ann	26	52	78	182	391	600
46-Felix the Cat and the Haunted Castle	36	72	108	270	585	900
47-Gene Autry (copyright 6/16/44)	29	58	87	210	455	700
48-Porky Pig of the Mounties by Carl Barks (7/44)	83	166	249	672	1461	2250
49-Snow White and the Seven Dwarfs (Disney)	46	92	138	345	748	1150
50-Fairy Tale Parade-Walt Kelly art (1944)	22	44	66	154	327	500
51-Bugs Bunny Finds the Lost Treasure	32	64	96	232	504	775
52-Little Orphan Annie; reprints strips from 6/18/38 to 11/19/38	23	46	69	163	349	535
53-Wash Tubbs	12	24	36	83	172	260
54-Andy Panda	26	52	78	182	391	600
55-Tillie the Toiler	12	24	36	80	163	245
56-Dick Tracy	33	66	99	239	520	800
57-Gene Autry	27	54	81	196	423	650
58-Smilin' Jack	20	40	60	137	294	450
59-Mother Goose and Nursery Rhyme Comics-Kelly-c/a	16	32	48	109	237	365
60-Tiny Folks Funnies	13	26	39	88	189	290
61-Santa Claus Funnies(11/44)-Kelly art	21	42	63	146	311	475
62-Donald Duck in Frozen Gold, by Carl Barks (Disney) (1/45)	207	414	621	1739	3770	5800
63-Roy Rogers; color photo-all 4 covers	36	72	108	261	568	875
64-Smokey Stover	12	24	36	79	160	240
65-Smitty	12	24	36	78	157	235
66-Gene Autry	27	54	81	196	423	650
67-Oswald the Rabbit	15	30	45	102	221	340
68-Mother Goose and Nursery Rhyme Comics, by Walt Kelly	16	32	48	109	237	365
69-Fairy Tale Parade, by Walt Kelly	22	44	66	154	327	500
70-Popeye and Wimpy	20	40	60	137	294	450
71-Walt Disney's Three Caballeros, by Walt Kelly (© 4/45)-(Disney)	57	114	171	462	1006	1550
72-Raggedy Ann	21	42	63	148	317	485
73-The Gumps (#1)	11	22	33	75	148	220
74-Marge's Little Lulu (#1)	143	286	429	1200	2600	4000
75-Gene Autry and the Wildcat	22	44	66	154	327	500
76-Little Orphan Annie; reprints strips from 2/28/40 to 6/24/40	19	38	57	130	280	430
77-Felix the Cat	35	70	105	250	545	840
78-Porky Pig and the Bandit Twins	24	48	72	168	359	550
79-Walt Disney's Mickey Mouse in The Riddle of the Red Hat by Carl Barks (8/45)	89	178	267	721	1561	2400
80-Smilin' Jack	13	26	39	85	180	275
81-Moon Mullins	10	20	30	68	127	185
82-Lone Ranger	35	70	105	254	552	850
83-Gene Autry in Outlaw Trail	22	44	66	154	327	500
84-Flash Gordon by Alex Raymond-Reprints from "The Fiery Desert"	40	80	120	300	650	1000
85-Andy Panda and the Mad Dog Mystery	15	30	45	102	221	340
86-Roy Rogers; photo-c	26	52	78	182	391	600
87-Fairy Tale Parade by Walt Kelly; Dan Noonan-c	22	44	66	154	327	500
88-Bugs Bunny's Great Adventure (Sci/fi)	21	42	63	148	317	485
89-Tillie the Toiler	12	24	36	80	163	245
90-Christmas with Mother Goose by Walt Kelly (11/45)	15	30	45	104	227	350
91-Santa Claus Funnies by Walt Kelly (11/45)	15	30	45	104	227	350
92-Walt Disney's The Wonderful Adventures Of Pinocchio (1945); Donald Duck by Kelly, 16 pgs. (Disney)	46	92	138	345	748	1150
93-Gene Autry in The Bandit of Black Rock	19	38	57	128	277	425
94-Winnie Winkle (1945)	11	22	33	76	151	225
95-Roy Rogers Comics; photo-c	26	52	78	182	391	600
96-Dick Tracy	22	44	66	154	327	500
97-Marge's Little Lulu (1946)	56	112	168	454	977	1500
98-Lone Ranger, The	26	52	78	182	391	600
99-Smitty	10	20	30	68	127	185
100-Gene Autry Comics; 1st Gene Autry photo-c	21	42	63	150	320	490

	GD 2.0	VG 4.0	FN 6.0	VF 8.0	VF/NM 9.0	NM- 9.2
101-Terry and the Pirates	19	38	57	132	284	435

NOTE: *No. 101 is last issue to carry "Four Color" logo on cover; all issues beginning with No. 100 are marked "...O. S." (One Shot) which can be found in the bottom left-hand panel on the first page; the numbers following "O. S." relate to the year/month issued.*

	GD 2.0	VG 4.0	FN 6.0	VF 8.0	VF/NM 9.0	NM- 9.2
102-Oswald the Rabbit-Walt Kelly art, 1 pg.	13	26	39	85	180	275
103-Easter with Mother Goose by Walt Kelly	15	30	45	104	227	350
104-Fairy Tale Parade by Walt Kelly	17	34	51	114	250	385
105-Albert the Alligator and Pogo Possum (#1) by Kelly (4/46)	47	94	141	381	828	1275
106-Tillie the Toiler (5/46)	10	20	30	65	118	170
107-Little Orphan Annie; reprints strips from 11/16/42 to 3/24/43	16	32	48	110	240	370
108-Donald Duck in The Terror of the River, by Carl Barks (Disney) (© 4/16/46)	146	292	438	1226	2663	4100
109-Roy Rogers Comics; photo-c	20	40	60	137	294	450
110-Marge's Little Lulu	37	74	111	278	602	925
111-Captain Easy	12	24	36	81	166	250
112-Porky Pig's Adventure in Gopher Gulch	14	28	42	97	211	325
113-Popeye; all new Popeye stories begin	12	24	36	84	175	265
114-Fairy Tale Parade by Walt Kelly	17	34	51	114	250	385
115-Marge's Little Lulu	36	72	108	270	585	900
116-Mickey Mouse and the House of Many Mysteries (Disney)	24	48	72	168	359	550
117-Roy Rogers Comics; photo-c	16	32	48	107	234	360
118-Lone Ranger, The	26	52	78	182	391	600
119-Felix the Cat; all new Felix stories begin	30	60	90	214	462	710
120-Marge's Little Lulu	31	62	93	225	488	750
121-Fairy Tale Parade-(not Kelly)	11	22	33	76	151	225
122-Henry (#1) (10/46)	13	26	39	85	180	275
123-Bugs Bunny's Dangerous Venture	14	28	42	97	211	325
124-Roy Rogers Comics; photo-c	16	32	48	107	234	360
125-Lone Ranger, The	17	34	51	119	260	400
126-Christmas with Mother Goose by Walt Kelly (1946)	12	24	36	81	166	250
127-Popeye	12	24	36	84	175	265
128-Santa Claus Funnies- "Santa & the Angel" by Gollub; "A Mouse in the House" by Kelly	13	26	39	85	180	275
129-Walt Disney's Uncle Remus and His Tales of Brer Rabbit (#1) (1946)-Adapted from Disney movie "Song of the South"	23	46	69	161	343	525
130-Andy Panda (Walter Lantz)	11	22	33	74	145	215
131-Marge's Little Lulu	31	62	93	225	488	750
132-Tillie the Toiler (1947)	10	20	30	65	118	170
133-Dick Tracy	17	34	51	114	250	385
134-Tarzan and the Devil Ogre; Marsh-c/a	51	102	153	413	894	1375
135-Felix the Cat	21	42	63	146	311	475
136-Lone Ranger, The	17	34	51	119	260	400
137-Roy Rogers Comics; photo-c	16	32	48	107	234	360
138-Smitty	9	18	27	62	109	155
139-Marge's Little Lulu (1947)	30	60	90	218	472	725
140-Easter with Mother Goose by Walt Kelly	13	26	39	85	180	275
141-Mickey Mouse and the Submarine Pirates (Disney)	21	42	63	142	304	465
142-Bugs Bunny and the Haunted Mountain	14	28	42	97	211	325
143-Oswald the Rabbit & the Prehistoric Egg	9	18	27	61	106	150
144-Roy Rogers Comics (1947)-Photo-c	16	32	48	107	234	360
145-Popeye	12	24	36	84	175	265
146-Marge's Little Lulu	30	60	90	218	472	725
147-Donald Duck in Volcano Valley, by Carl Barks (Disney) (5/47)	102	204	306	826	1788	2750
148-Albert the Alligator and Pogo Possum by Walt Kelly (5/47)	38	76	114	285	618	950
149-Smilin' Jack	10	20	30	66	121	175
150-Tillie the Toiler (6/47)	9	18	27	61	106	150
151-Lone Ranger, The	15	30	45	102	221	340
152-Little Orphan Annie; reprints strips from 1/2/44 to 5/6/44	11	22	33	77	154	230
153-Roy Rogers Comics; photo-c	14	28	42	97	211	325
154-Walter Lantz Andy Panda	11	22	33	74	145	215
155-Henry (7/47)	10	20	30	65	118	170
156-Porky Pig and the Phantom	11	22	33	76	151	225
157-Mickey Mouse & the Beanstalk (Disney)	21	42	63	142	304	465
158-Marge's Little Lulu	30	60	90	218	472	725
159-Donald Duck in the Ghost of the Grotto, by Carl Barks (Disney) (8/47)	87	174	261	705	1528	2350

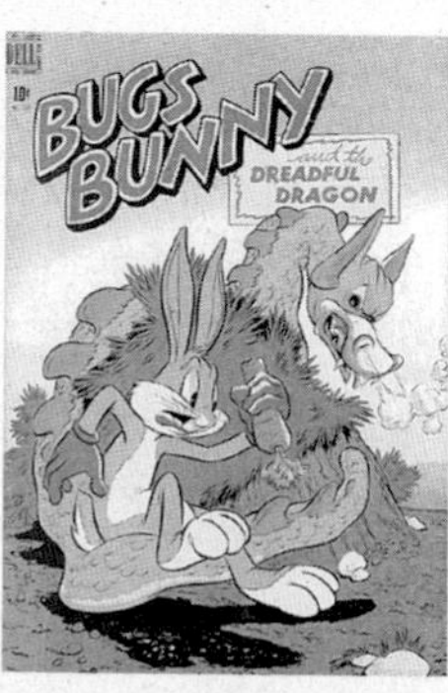

Four Color Comics #187 © WB

Four Color Comics #231 © DIS

Four Color Comics #252 © DIS

	GD 2.0	VG 4.0	FN 6.0	VF 8.0	VF/NM 9.0	NM- 9.2
160-Roy Rogers Comics; photo-c	14	28	42	97	211	325
161-Tarzan and the Fires Of Tohr; Marsh-c/a	44	88	132	330	715	1100
162-Felix the Cat (9/47)	15	30	45	104	227	350
163-Dick Tracy	15	30	45	102	221	340
164-Bugs Bunny Finds the Frozen Kingdom	14	28	42	97	211	325
165-Marge's Little Lulu	30	60	90	218	472	725
166-Roy Rogers Comics (52 pgs.)-Photo-c	14	28	42	97	211	325
167-Lone Ranger, The	15	30	45	102	221	340
168-Popeye (10/47)	12	24	36	84	175	265
169-Woody Woodpecker (#1)- "Manhunter in the North"; drug use story	15	30	45	104	227	350
170-Mickey Mouse on Spook's Island (11/47)(Disney)-reprinted in Mickey Mouse #103	17	34	51	119	260	400
171-Charlie McCarthy (#1) and the Twenty Thieves	22	44	66	154	327	500
172-Christmas with Mother Goose by Walt Kelly (11/47)	12	24	36	81	166	250
173-Flash Gordon	18	36	54	123	267	410
174-Winnie Winkle	8	16	24	56	96	135
175-Santa Claus Funnies by Walt Kelly (1947)	13	26	39	85	180	275
176-Tillie the Toiler (12/47)	9	18	27	61	106	150
177-Roy Rogers Comics-(36 pgs.); Photo-c	14	28	42	93	202	310
178-Donald Duck "Christmas on Bear Mountain" by Carl Barks; 1st app. Uncle Scrooge (Disney)(12/47)	117	234	351	948	2049	3150
179-Uncle Wiggily (#1)-Walt Kelly-c	13	26	39	88	189	290
180-Ozark Ike (#1)	10	20	30	64	115	165
181-Walt Disney's Mickey Mouse in Jungle Magic	17	34	51	119	260	400
182-Porky Pig in Never-Never Land (2/48)	11	22	33	76	151	225
183-Oswald the Rabbit (Lantz)	9	18	27	61	106	150
184-Tillie the Toiler	9	18	27	61	106	150
185-Easter with Mother Goose by Walt Kelly (1948)	12	24	36	80	163	245
186-Walt Disney's Bambi (4/48)-Reprinted as Movie Classic Bambi #3 (1956)	14	28	42	97	211	325
187-Bugs Bunny and the Dreadful Dragon	11	22	33	77	154	230
188-Woody Woodpecker (Lantz, 5/48)	11	22	33	71	136	200
189-Donald Duck in The Old Castle's Secret, by Carl Barks (Disney) (6/48)	72	144	216	583	1267	1950
190-Flash Gordon (6/48); bondage-c; "The Adventures of the Flying Saucers"; 5th Flying Saucer story- see The Spirit 9/28/47(1st), Shadow Comics V7#10 (2nd, 1/48),Captain Midnight #60 (3rd, 2/48) & Boy Commandos #26 (4th, 3-4/48)	20	40	60	140	300	460
191-Porky Pig to the Rescue	11	22	33	76	151	225
192-The Brownies (#1)-by Walt Kelly (7/48)	12	24	36	82	169	255
193-M.G.M. Presents Tom and Jerry (#1)(1948)	21	42	63	148	317	485
194-Mickey Mouse in The World Under the Sea (Disney)-Reprinted in Mickey Mouse #101	17	34	51	119	260	400
195-Tillie the Toiler	7	14	21	49	82	115
196-Charlie McCarthy in The Haunted Hide-Out; part photo-c	13	26	39	90	195	300
197-Spirit of the Border (#1) (Zane Grey) (1948)	11	22	33	71	136	200
198-Andy Panda	11	22	33	74	145	215
199-Donald Duck in Sheriff of Bullet Valley, by Carl Barks; Barks draws himself on wanted poster, last page; used in Love & Death (Disney) (10/48)	78	156	234	632	1366	2100
200-Bugs Bunny, Super Sleuth (10/48)	11	22	33	77	154	230
201-Christmas with Mother Goose by W. Kelly	11	22	33	71	136	200
202-Woody Woodpecker	8	16	24	56	96	135
203-Donald Duck in the Golden Christmas Tree, by Carl Barks (Disney) (12/48)	55	110	165	446	961	1475
204-Flash Gordon (12/48)	14	28	42	93	202	310
205-Santa Claus Funnies by Walt Kelly	12	24	36	79	160	240
206-Little Orphan Annie; reprints strips from 11/10/40 to 1/11/41	8	16	24	53	89	125
207-King of the Royal Mounted (#1) (12/48)	12	24	36	81	166	250
208-Brer Rabbit Does It Again (Disney) (1/49)	11	22	33	71	136	200
209-Harold Teen	6	12	18	39	62	85
210-Tippie and Cap Stubbs	5	10	15	32	51	70
211-Little Beaver (#1)	8	16	24	55	93	130
212-Dr. Bobbs	6	12	18	37	59	80
213-Tillie the Toiler	7	14	21	49	82	115
214-Mickey Mouse and His Sky Adventure (2/49)(Disney)-Reprinted in Mickey Mouse #105	13	26	39	90	195	300
215-Sparkle Plenty (Dick Tracy-r by Gould)	11	22	33	73	142	210
216-Andy Panda and the Police Pup (Lantz)	9	18	27	58	99	140
217-Bugs Bunny in Court Jester	11	22	33	77	154	230
218-Three Little Pigs and the Wonderful Magic Lamp (Disney) (3/49)(#1)	10	20	30	67	124	180
219-Swee'pea	8	16	24	56	93	130
220-Easter with Mother Goose by Walt Kelly	12	24	36	80	163	245
221-Uncle Wiggily-Walt Kelly cover in part	9	18	27	61	106	150
222-West of the Pecos (Zane Grey)	7	14	21	46	76	105
223-Donald Duck "Lost in the Andes" by Carl Barks (Disney-4/49) (square egg story)	71	142	213	575	1250	1925
224-Little Iodine (#1), by Hatlo (4/49)	11	22	33	76	151	225
225-Oswald the Rabbit (Lantz)	7	14	21	44	72	100
226-Porky Pig and Spoofy, the Spook	10	20	30	66	121	175
227-Seven Dwarfs (Disney)	9	18	27	63	112	160
228-Mark of Zorro, The (#1) (1949)	17	34	51	119	260	400
229-Smokey Stover	6	12	18	41	66	90
230-Sunset Pass (Zane Grey)	7	14	21	46	76	105
231-Mickey Mouse and the Rajah's Treasure (Disney)	13	26	39	90	195	300
232-Woody Woodpecker (Lantz, 6/49)	8	16	24	56	96	135
233-Bugs Bunny, Sleepwalking Sleuth	11	22	33	77	154	230
234-Dumbo in Sky Voyage (Disney)	12	24	36	84	177	270
235-Tiny Tim	6	12	18	37	59	80
236-Heritage of the Desert (Zane Grey) (1949)	7	14	21	46	76	105
237-Tillie the Toiler	7	14	21	49	82	115
238-Donald Duck in Voodoo Hoodoo, by Carl Barks (Disney) (8/49)	55	110	165	446	961	1475
239-Adventure Bound (8/49)	6	12	18	39	62	85
240-Andy Panda (Lantz)	9	18	27	58	99	140
241-Porky Pig, Mighty Hunter	10	20	30	66	121	175
242-Tippie and Cap Stubbs	4	8	12	26	41	55
243-Thumper Follows His Nose (Disney)	11	22	33	71	136	200
244-The Brownies by Walt Kelly	10	20	30	65	118	170
245-Dick's Adventures (9/49)	6	12	18	41	66	90
246-Thunder Mountain (Zane Grey)	5	10	15	32	51	70
247-Flash Gordon	14	28	42	93	202	310
248-Mickey Mouse and the Black Sorcerer (Disney)	13	26	39	90	195	300
249-Woody Woodpecker in the "Globetrotter" (10/49)	8	16	24	56	96	135
250-Bugs Bunny in Diamond Daze; used in **SOTI**, pg. 309	12	24	36	79	160	240
251-Hubert at Camp Moonbeam	8	16	24	51	86	120
252-Pinocchio (Disney)-not by Kelly; origin	10	20	30	68	127	185
253-Christmas with Mother Goose by W. Kelly	11	22	33	71	136	200
254-Santa Claus Funnies by Walt Kelly; Pogo & Albert story by Kelly (11/49)	12	24	36	79	160	240
255-The Ranger (Zane Grey) (1949)	5	10	15	32	51	70
256-Donald Duck in "Luck of the North" by Carl Barks (Disney) (12/49)-Shows #257 on inside	46	92	138	352	764	1175
257-Little Iodine	8	16	24	56	96	135
258-Andy Panda and the Balloon Race (Lantz)	9	18	27	58	99	140
259-Santa and the Angel (Gollub art-condensed from #128) & Santa at the Zoo (12/49) -two books in one	5	10	15	35	55	75
260-Porky Pig, Hero of the Wild West (12/49)	10	20	30	66	121	175
261-Mickey Mouse and the Missing Key (Disney)	13	26	39	90	195	300
262-Raggedy Ann and Andy	10	20	30	64	115	165
263-Donald Duck in "Land of the Totem Poles" by Carl Barks (Disney) (2/50)-Has two Barks stories	46	92	138	345	748	1150
264-Woody Woodpecker in the Magic Lantern (Lantz)	8	16	24	56	96	135
265-King of the Royal Mounted (Zane Grey)	8	16	24	56	96	135
266-Bugs Bunny on the "Isle of Hercules" (2/50)-Reprinted in Best of Bugs Bunny #1	10	20	30	66	121	175
267-Little Beaver; Harmon-c/a	5	10	15	35	55	75
268-Mickey Mouse's Surprise Visitor (1950)(Disney)	13	26	39	85	180	275
269-Johnny Mack Brown (#1)-Photo-c	19	38	57	128	277	425
270-Drift Fence (Zane Grey) (3/50)	5	10	15	32	51	70
271-Porky Pig in Phantom of the Plains	10	20	30	66	121	175
272-Cinderella (Disney) (4/50)	12	24	36	78	157	235
273-Oswald the Rabbit (Lantz)	7	14	21	44	72	100
274-Bugs Bunny, Hare-brained Reporter	10	20	30	66	121	175
275-Donald Duck in "Ancient Persia" by Carl Barks (Disney) (5/50)	45	90	135	338	732	1125
276-Uncle Wiggily	8	16	24	51	86	120
277-Porky Pig in Desert Adventure (5/50)	10	20	30	66	121	175
278-(Wild) Bill Elliott Comics (#1)-Photo-c	11	22	33	77	154	230
279-Mickey Mouse and Pluto Battle the Giant Ants (Disney); reprinted in						

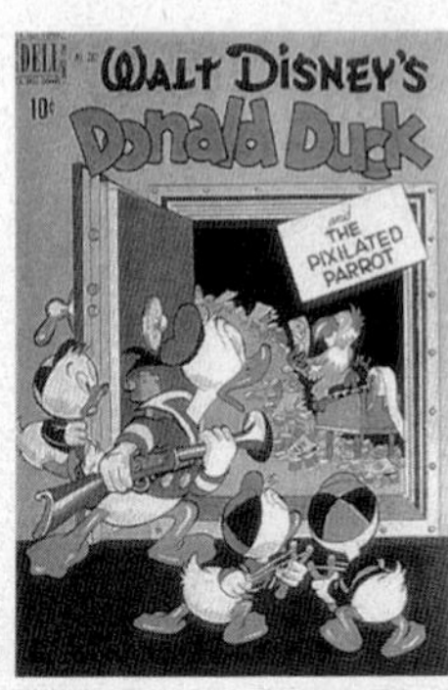
Four Color Comics #282 © DIS

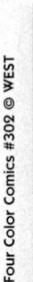

Four Color Comics #302 © WEST

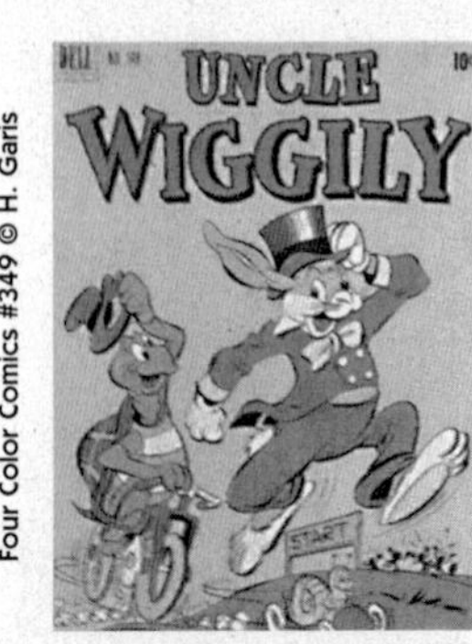
Four Color Comics #349 © H. Garis

	GD 2.0	VG 4.0	FN 6.0	VF 8.0	VF/NM 9.0	NM- 9.2
Mickey Mouse #102 & 245	11	22	33	73	142	210
280-Andy Panda in The Isle Of Mechanical Men (Lantz)	9	18	27	58	99	140
281-Bugs Bunny in The Great Circus Mystery	10	20	30	66	121	175
282-Donald Duck and the Pixilated Parrot by Carl Barks (Disney) (© 5/23/50)	45	90	135	338	732	1125
283-King of the Royal Mounted (7/50)	8	16	24	56	96	135
284-Porky Pig in The Kingdom of Nowhere	10	20	30	66	121	175
285-Bozo the Clown & His Minikin Circus (#1) (TV)	16	32	48	112	246	380
286-Mickey Mouse in The Uninvited Guest (Disney	11	22	33	73	142	210
287-Gene Autry's Champion in The Ghost Of Black Mountain; photo-c	11	22	33	71	136	200
288-Woody Woodpecker in Klondike Gold (Lantz)	8	16	24	56	96	135
289-Bugs Bunny in "Indian Trouble"	10	20	30	66	121	175
290-The Chief (#1) (8/50)	8	16	24	51	86	120
291-Donald Duck in "The Magic Hourglass" by Carl Barks (Disney) (9/50)	45	90	135	338	732	1125
292-The Cisco Kid Comics (#1)	20	40	60	137	294	450
293-The Brownies-Kelly-c/a	10	20	30	65	118	170
294-Little Beaver	5	10	15	35	55	75
295-Porky Pig in President Porky (9/50)	10	20	30	66	121	175
296-Mickey Mouse in Private Eye for Hire (Disney)	11	22	33	73	142	210
297-Andy Panda in The Haunted Inn (Lantz, 10/50)	9	18	27	58	99	140
298-Bugs Bunny in Sheik for a Day	10	20	30	66	121	175
299-Buck Jones & the Iron Horse Trail (#1)	12	24	36	79	160	240
300-Donald Duck in "Big-Top Bedlam" by Carl Barks (Disney) (11/50)	45	90	135	338	732	1125
301-The Mysterious Rider (Zane Grey)	5	10	15	32	51	70
302-Santa Claus Funnies (11/50)	7	14	21	44	72	100
303-Porky Pig in The Land of the Monstrous Flies	8	16	24	53	89	125
304-Mickey Mouse in Tom-Tom Island (Disney) (12/50)	10	20	30	68	127	185
305-Woody Woodpecker (Lantz)	6	12	18	41	66	90
306-Raggedy Ann	7	14	21	49	82	115
307-Bugs Bunny in Lumber Jack Rabbit	9	18	27	60	103	145
308-Donald Duck in "Dangerous Disguise" by Carl Barks (Disney) (1/51)	42	86	126	315	683	1050
309-Betty Betz' Dollface and Her Gang (1951)	5	10	15	35	55	75
310-King of the Royal Mounted (1/51)	6	12	18	42	69	95
311-Porky Pig in Midget Horses of Hidden Valley	8	16	24	53	89	125
312-Tonto (#1)	10	20	30	69	130	190
313-Mickey Mouse in The Mystery of the Double-Cross Ranch (#1) (Disney) (2/51)	10	20	30	68	127	185

Note: Beginning with the above comic in 1951 Dell/Western began adding #1 in small print on the covers of several long running titles with the evident intention of switching these titles to their own monthly numbers, but when the conversions were made, there was no connection. It is thought that the post office may have stepped in and decreed the sequences should commence as though the first four colors printed had each begun with number one, or the first issues sold by subscription. Since the regular series' numbers don't correctly match to the numbers of earlier issues published, it's not known whether or not the numbering was in error.

	GD 2.0	VG 4.0	FN 6.0	VF 8.0	VF/NM 9.0	NM- 9.2
314-Ambush (Zane Grey)	5	10	15	32	51	70
315-Oswald the Rabbit (Lantz)	6	12	18	39	62	85
316-Rex Allen (#1)-Photo-c; Marsh-a	12	24	36	84	175	265
317-Bugs Bunny in Hair Today Gone Tomorrow (#1)	9	18	27	60	103	145
318-Donald Duck in "No Such Varmint" by Carl Barks (#1)-Indicia shows #317 (Disney, © 1/23/51)	42	86	126	315	683	1050
319-Gene Autry's Champion; painted-c	6	12	18	41	66	90
320-Uncle Wiggily (#1)	8	16	24	51	86	120
321-Little Scouts (#1) (3/51)	5	10	15	30	48	65
322-Porky Pig in Roaring Rockets (#1 on-c)	8	16	24	53	89	125
323-Susie Q. Smith (#1) (3/51)	5	10	15	32	51	70
324-I Met a Handsome Cowboy (3/51)	8	16	24	55	93	130
325-Mickey Mouse in The Haunted Castle (#2) (Disney) (4/51)	10	20	30	68	127	185
326-Andy Panda (#1) (Lantz)	7	14	21	44	72	100
327-Bugs Bunny and the Rajah's Treasure (#2)	9	18	27	60	103	145
328-Donald Duck in Old California (#2) by Carl Barks-Peyote drug use issue (Disney) (5/51)	41	82	123	308	667	1025
329-Roy Roger's Trigger (#1)(5/51)-Painted-c	12	24	36	84	175	265
330-Porky Pig Meets the Bristled Bruiser (#2)	8	16	24	53	89	125
331-Alice in Wonderland (Disney) (1951)	13	26	39	88	189	290
332-Little Beaver	5	10	15	35	55	75
333-Wilderness Trek (Zane Grey) (5/51)	5	10	15	32	51	70
334-Mickey Mouse and Yukon Gold (Disney) (6/51)	10	20	30	68	127	185
335-Francis the Famous Talking Mule (#1, 6/51)-1st Dell non animated movie comic (all issues based on movie)	10	20	30	67	124	180
336-Woody Woodpecker (Lantz)	6	12	18	41	66	90
337-The Brownies-not by Walt Kelly	6	12	18	37	59	80
338-Bugs Bunny and the Rocking Horse Thieves	9	18	27	60	103	145
339-Donald Duck and the Magic Fountain-not by Carl Barks (Disney) (7-8/51)	12	24	36	83	172	260
340-King of the Royal Mounted (7/51)	6	12	18	42	69	95
341-Unbirthday Party with Alice in Wonderland (Disney) (7/51)	13	26	39	88	189	290
342-Porky Pig the Lucky Peppermint Mine; r/in Porky Pig #3	6	12	18	42	69	95
343-Mickey Mouse in The Ruby Eye of Homar-Guy-Am (Disney)-Reprinted in Mickey Mouse #104	9	18	27	61	106	150
344-Sergeant Preston from Challenge of The Yukon (#1) (TV)	11	22	33	73	142	210
345-Andy Panda in Scotland Yard (8-10/51) (Lantz)	7	14	21	44	72	100
346-Hideout (Zane Grey)	5	10	15	32	51	70
347-Bugs Bunny the Frigid Hare (8-9/51)	9	18	27	60	103	145
348-Donald Duck "The Crocodile Collector"; Barks-c only (Disney) (9-10/51)	20	40	60	137	294	450
349-Uncle Wiggily	6	12	18	42	69	95
350-Woody Woodpecker (Lantz)	6	12	18	41	66	90
351-Porky Pig & the Grand Canyon Giant (9-10/51)	6	12	18	42	69	95
352-Mickey Mouse in The Mystery of Painted Valley (Disney)	9	18	27	61	106	150
353-Duck Album (#1)-Barks-c (Disney)	10	20	30	66	121	175
354-Raggedy Ann & Andy	7	14	21	49	82	115
355-Bugs Bunny Hot-Rod Hare	9	18	27	60	103	145
356-Donald Duck in "Rags to Riches"; Barks-c only	20	40	60	137	294	450
357-Comeback (Zane Grey)	4	8	12	28	44	60
358-Andy Panda (Lantz) (11-1/52)	7	14	21	44	72	100
359-Frosty the Snowman (#1)	9	18	27	61	106	150
360-Porky Pig in Tree of Fortune (11-12/51)	6	12	18	42	69	95
361-Santa Claus Funnies	7	14	21	44	72	100
362-Mickey Mouse and the Smuggled Diamonds (Disney)	9	18	27	61	106	150
363-King of the Royal Mounted	6	12	18	39	62	85
364-Woody Woodpecker (Lantz)	5	10	15	35	55	75
365-The Brownies-not by Kelly	6	12	18	37	59	80
366-Bugs Bunny Uncle Buckskin Comes to Town (12-1/52)	9	18	27	60	103	145
367-Donald Duck in "A Christmas for Shacktown" by Carl Barks (Disney) (1-2/52)	33	66	99	235	510	785
368-Bob Clampett's Beany and Cecil (#1)	21	42	63	146	311	475
369-The Lone Ranger's Famous Horse Hi-Yo Silver (#1); Silver's origin	10	20	30	67	124	180
370-Porky Pig in Trouble in the Big Trees	6	12	18	42	69	95
371-Mickey Mouse in The Inca Idol Case (1952) (Disney)	9	18	27	61	106	150
372-Riders of the Purple Sage (Zane Grey)	4	8	12	28	44	60
373-Sergeant Preston (TV)	8	16	24	51	86	120
374-Woody Woodpecker (Lantz)	5	10	15	35	55	75
375-John Carter of Mars (E. R. Burroughs)-Jesse Marsh-a; origin	26	52	78	182	391	600
376-Bugs Bunny, "The Magic Sneeze"	9	18	27	60	103	145
377-Susie Q. Smith	4	8	12	26	41	55
378-Tom Corbett, Space Cadet (#1) (TV)-McWilliams-a	14	28	42	97	211	325
379-Donald Duck in "Southern Hospitality"; Not by Barks (Disney)	12	24	36	83	172	260
380-Raggedy Ann & Andy	7	14	21	49	82	115
381-Marge's Tubby (#1)	17	34	51	119	260	400
382-Snow White and the Seven Dwarfs (Disney)-origin; partial reprint of Four Color #49 (Movie)	9	18	27	63	112	160
383-Andy Panda (Lantz)	6	12	18	37	59	80
384-King of the Royal Mounted (3/52)(Zane Grey)	6	12	18	39	62	85
385-Porky Pig in The Isle of Missing Ships (3-4/52)	6	12	18	42	69	95
386-Uncle Scrooge (#1)-by Carl Barks (Disney) in "Only a Poor Old Man" (3/52)	186	372	558	1562	3381	5200
387-Mickey Mouse in High Tibet (Disney) (4-5/52)	9	18	27	61	106	150
388-Oswald the Rabbit (Lantz)	6	12	18	39	62	85
389-Andy Hardy Comics (#1)	5	10	15	35	55	75
390-Woody Woodpecker (Lantz)	5	10	15	35	55	75

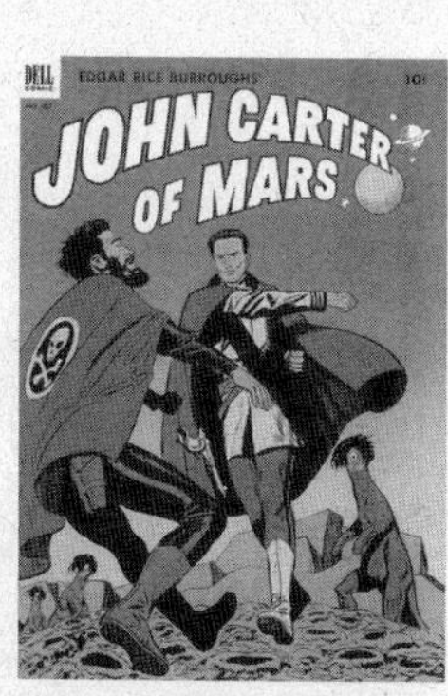

Four Color Comics #437 © ERB

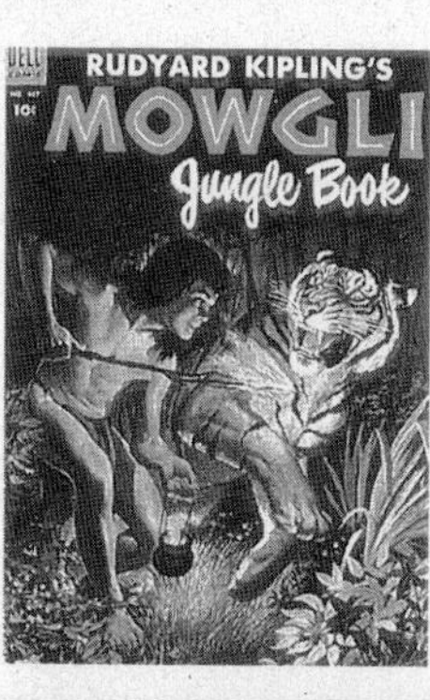

Four Color Comics #487 © WP

Four Color Comics #521 © KING

	GD 2.0	VG 4.0	FN 6.0	VF 8.0	VF/NM 9.0	NM- 9.2
391-Uncle Wiggily	6	12	18	42	69	95
392-Hi-Yo Silver	6	12	18	41	66	90
393-Bugs Bunny	9	18	27	60	103	145
394-Donald Duck in Malayalaya-Barks-c only (Disney)	20	40	60	137	294	450
395-Forlorn River(Zane Grey)-First Nevada (5/52)	4	8	12	28	44	60
396-Tales of the Texas Rangers(#1)(TV)-Photo-c	10	20	30	68	127	185
397-Sergeant Preston of the Yukon (TV) (5/52)	8	16	24	51	86	120
398-The Brownies-not by Kelly	6	12	18	37	59	80
399-Porky Pig in The Lost Gold Mine	6	12	18	42	69	95
400-Tom Corbett, Space Cadet (TV)-McWilliams-c/a	10	20	30	66	121	175
401-Mickey Mouse and Goofy's Mechanical Wizard (Disney) (6-7/52)	8	16	24	51	86	120
402-Mary Jane and Sniffles	7	14	21	49	82	115
403-Li'l Bad Wolf (Disney) (6/52)(#1)	7	14	21	46	76	105
404-The Range Rider (#1) (Flying A's...)(TV)-Photo-c	9	18	27	63	112	160
405-Woody Woodpecker (Lantz) (6-7/52)	5	10	15	35	55	75
406-Tweety and Sylvester (#1)	11	22	33	71	136	200
407-Bugs Bunny, Foreign-Legion Hare	8	16	24	51	86	120
408-Donald Duck and the Golden Helmet by Carl Barks (Disney) (7-8/52)	33	66	99	235	510	785
409-Andy Panda (7-9/52)	6	12	18	37	59	80
410-Porky Pig in The Water Wizard (7/52)	6	12	18	42	69	95
411-Mickey Mouse and the Old Sea Dog (Disney) (8-9/52)	8	16	24	51	86	120
412-Nevada (Zane Grey)	4	8	12	28	44	60
413-Robin Hood (Disney-Movie) (8/52)-Photo-c (1st Disney movie Four Color book)	9	18	27	63	112	160
414-Bob Clampett's Beany and Cecil (TV)	13	26	39	85	180	275
415-Rootie Kazootie (#1) (TV)	9	18	27	63	112	160
416-Woody Woodpecker (Lantz)	5	10	15	35	55	75
417-Double Trouble with Goober (#1) (8/52)	4	8	12	28	44	60
418-Rusty Riley, a Boy, a Horse, and a Dog (#1)-Frank Godwin-a (strip reprints) (8/52)	5	10	15	32	51	70
419-Sergeant Preston (TV)	8	16	24	51	86	120
420-Bugs Bunny in The Mysterious Buckaroo (8-9/52)	8	16	24	51	86	120
421-Tom Corbett, Space Cadet(TV)-McWilliams-a	10	20	30	66	121	175
422-Donald Duck and the Gilded Man, by Carl Barks (Disney) (9-10/52) (#423 on inside)	33	66	99	235	510	785
423-Rhubarb, Owner of the Brooklyn Ball Club (The Millionaire Cat) (#1)-Painted cover	6	12	18	39	62	85
424-Flash Gordon-Test Flight in Space (9/52)	11	22	33	73	142	210
425-Zorro, the Return of	11	22	33	73	142	210
426-Porky Pig in The Scalawag Leprechaun	6	12	18	42	69	95
427-Mickey Mouse and the Wonderful Whizzix (Disney) (10-11/52)-Reprinted in Mickey Mouse #100	8	16	24	51	86	120
428-Uncle Wiggily	5	10	15	35	55	75
429-Pluto in "Why Dogs Leave Home" (Disney) (10/52)(#1)	10	20	30	64	115	165
430-Marge's Tubby, the Shadow of a Man-Eater	11	22	33	75	148	220
431-Woody Woodpecker (10/52) (Lantz)	5	10	15	35	55	75
432-Bugs Bunny and the Rabbit Olympics	8	16	24	51	86	120
433-Wildfire (Zane Grey) (11-1/52-53)	4	8	12	28	44	60
434-Rin Tin Tin "In Dark Danger" (#1) (TV) (11/52)-Photo-c	13	26	39	85	180	275
435-Frosty the Snowman (11/52)	6	12	18	37	59	80
436-The Brownies-not by Kelly (11/52)	5	10	15	34	55	75
437-John Carter of Mars (E.R. Burroughs)-Marsh-a	14	28	42	97	211	325
438-Annie Oakley (#1) (TV)	12	24	36	84	175	265
439-Little Hiawatha (Disney) (12/52)j(#1)	6	12	18	39	62	85
440-Black Beauty (12/52)	5	10	15	30	48	65
441-Fearless Fagan	4	8	12	24	37	50
442-Peter Pan (Disney) (Movie)	10	20	30	66	121	175
443-Ben Bowie and His Mountain Men (#1)	9	18	27	58	99	140
444-Marge's Tubby	11	22	33	75	148	220
445-Charlie McCarthy	6	12	18	39	62	85
446-Captain Hook and Peter Pan (Disney)(Movie)(1/53)	9	18	27	58	99	140
447-Andy Hardy Comics	4	8	12	26	41	55
448-Bob Clampett's Beany and Cecil (TV)	13	26	39	85	180	275
449-Tappan's Burro (Zane Grey) (2-4/53)	4	8	12	28	44	60
450-Duck Album; Barks-c (Disney)	7	14	21	48	79	110
451-Rusty Riley-Frank Godwin-a (strip-r) (2/53)	4	8	12	26	41	50
452-Raggedy Ann & Andy (1953)	7	14	21	49	82	115

	GD 2.0	VG 4.0	FN 6.0	VF 8.0	VF/NM 9.0	NM- 9.2
453-Susie Q. Smith (2/53)	4	8	12	26	41	55
454-Krazy Kat Comics; not by Herriman	5	10	15	32	51	70
455-Johnny Mack Brown Comics(3/53)-Photo-c	7	14	21	46	76	105
456-Uncle Scrooge Back to the Klondike (#2) by Barks (3/53) (Disney)	91	182	273	737	1594	2450
457-Daffy (#1)	11	22	33	71	136	200
458-Oswald the Rabbit (Lantz)	5	10	15	32	51	70
459-Rootie Kazootie (TV)	7	14	21	46	76	105
460-Buck Jones (4/53)	6	12	18	41	66	90
461-Marge's Tubby	10	20	30	69	130	190
462-Little Scouts	4	8	12	24	37	50
463-Petunia (4/53)	4	8	12	28	44	60
464-Bozo (4/53)	10	20	30	64	115	165
465-Francis the Famous Talking Mule	6	12	18	41	66	90
466-Rhubarb, the Millionaire Cat; painted-c	5	10	15	35	55	75
467-Desert Gold (Zane Grey) (5-7/53)	4	8	12	28	44	60
468-Goofy (#1) (Disney)	11	22	33	73	142	210
469-Beetle Bailey (#1) (5/53	11	22	33	76	151	225
470-Elmer Fudd	9	18	27	61	106	150
471-Double Trouble with Goober	4	8	12	22	34	45
472-Wild Bill Elliott (6/53)-Photo-c	5	10	15	35	55	75
473-Li'l Bad Wolf (Disney) (6/53)(#2)	5	10	15	32	51	70
474-Mary Jane and Sniffles	7	14	21	46	76	105
475-M.G.M.'s The Two Mouseketeers (#1)	8	16	24	51	86	120
476-Rin Tin Tin (TV)-Photo-c	8	16	24	55	93	130
477-Bob Clampett's Beany and Cecil (TV)	13	26	39	85	180	275
478-Charlie McCarthy	6	12	18	39	62	85
479-Queen of the West Dale Evans (#1)-Photo-c	16	32	48	109	237	365
480-Andy Hardy Comics	4	8	12	26	41	55
481-Annie Oakley And Tagg (TV)	9	18	27	62	109	155
482-Brownies-not by Kelly	5	10	15	34	55	75
483-Little Beaver (7/53)	5	10	15	30	48	65
484-River Feud (Zane Grey) (8-10/53)	4	8	12	28	44	60
485-The Little People-Walt Scott (#1)	8	16	24	51	86	120
486-Rusty Riley-Frank Godwin strip-r	4	8	12	26	41	50
487-Mowgli, the Jungle Book (Rudyard Kipling's)	6	12	18	37	59	80
488-John Carter of Mars (Burroughs)-Marsh-a; painted-c	14	28	42	97	211	325
489-Tweety and Sylvester	7	14	21	44	72	100
490-Jungle Jim (#1)	7	14	21	48	79	110
491-Silvertip (#1) (Max Brand)-Kinstler-a (8/53)	8	16	24	51	86	120
492-Duck Album (Disney)	6	12	18	41	66	90
493-Johnny Mack Brown; photo-c	7	14	21	46	76	105
494-The Little King (#1)	9	18	27	58	99	140
495-Uncle Scrooge (#3) (Disney)-by Carl Barks (9/53)	61	122	183	494	1072	1650
496-The Green Hornet; painted-c	23	46	69	161	343	525
497-Zorro (Sword of...)-Kinstler-a	11	22	33	76	151	225
498-Bugs Bunny's Album (9/53)	6	12	18	41	66	90
499-M.G.M.'s Spike and Tyke (#1) (9/53)	7	14	21	44	72	100
500-Buck Jones	6	12	18	41	66	90
501-Francis the Famous Talking Mule	5	10	15	32	51	70
502-Rootie Kazootie (TV)	7	14	21	46	76	105
503-Uncle Wiggily (10/53)	5	10	15	35	55	75
504-Krazy Kat; not by Herriman	5	10	15	32	51	70
505-The Sword and the Rose (Disney) (10/53)(Movie)-Photo-c	8	16	24	55	93	130
506-The Little Scouts	4	8	12	24	37	50
507-Oswald the Rabbit (Lantz)	5	10	15	32	51	70
508-Bozo (10/53)	10	20	30	64	115	165
509-Pluto (Disney) (10/53)	6	12	18	41	66	90
510-Son of Black Beauty	4	8	12	26	41	55
511-Outlaw Trail (Zane Grey)-Kinstler-a	5	10	15	32	51	70
512-Flash Gordon (11/53)	9	18	27	61	106	150
513-Ben Bowie and His Mountain Men	5	10	15	32	51	70
514-Frosty the Snowman (11/53)	6	12	18	37	59	80
515-Andy Hardy	4	8	12	26	41	55
516-Double Trouble With Goober	4	8	12	22	34	45
517-Chip 'N' Dale (#1) (Disney)	11	22	33	71	136	200
518-Rivets (11/53)	4	8	12	24	37	50
519-Steve Canyon (#1)-Not by Milton Caniff	8	16	24	55	93	130
520-Wild Bill Elliott-Photo-c	5	10	15	35	55	75
521-Beetle Bailey (12/53)	7	14	21	48	79	110
522-The Brownies	5	10	15	34	55	75

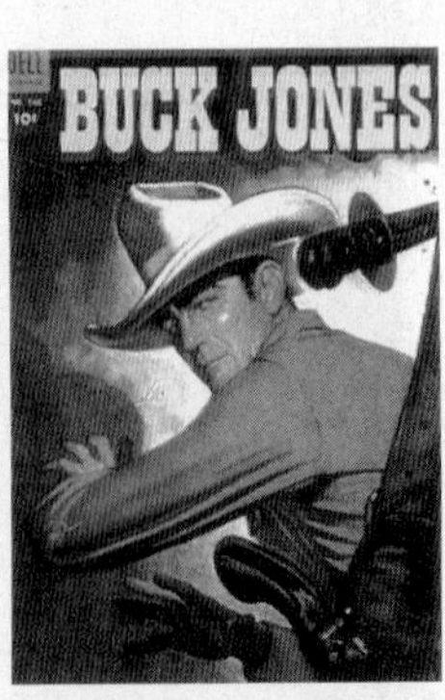

Four Color Comics #546 © DELL

Four Color Comics #602 © Columbia

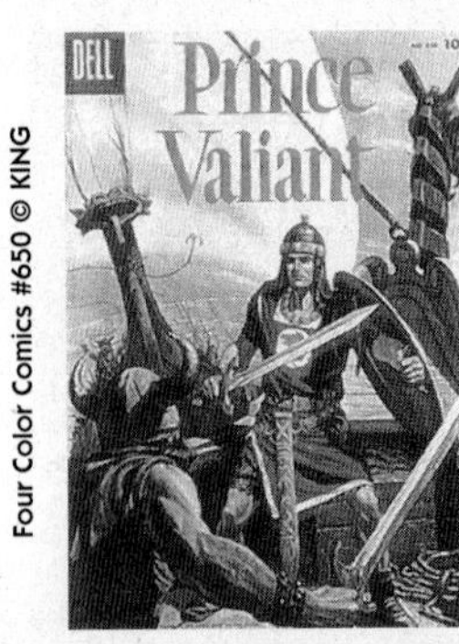

Four Color Comics #650 © KING

	GD 2.0	VG 4.0	FN 6.0	VF 8.0	VF/NM 9.0	NM- 9.2
523-Rin Tin Tin (TV)-Photo-c (12/53)	8	16	24	55	93	130
524-Tweety and Sylvester	7	14	21	44	72	100
525-Santa Claus Funnies	7	14	21	44	72	100
526-Napoleon	4	8	12	24	37	50
527-Charlie McCarthy	6	12	18	39	62	85
528-Queen of the West Dale Evans; photo-c	10	20	30	66	121	175
529-Little Beaver	5	10	15	30	48	65
530-Bob Clampett's Beany and Cecil (TV) (1/54)	13	26	39	85	180	275
531-Duck Album (Disney)	6	12	18	41	66	90
532-The Rustlers (Zane Grey) (2-4/54)	4	8	12	28	44	60
533-Raggedy Ann and Andy	7	14	21	49	82	115
534-Western Marshal(Ernest Haycox's)-Kinstler-a	6	12	18	39	62	85
535-I Love Lucy (#1) (TV) (2/54)-Photo-c	39	78	117	293	634	975
536-Daffy (3/54)	7	14	21	44	72	100
537-Stormy, the Thoroughbred... (Disney-Movie) on top 2/3 of each page; Pluto story on bottom 1/3 of each page (2/54)	5	10	15	30	48	65
538-The Mask of Zorro; Kinstler-a	11	22	33	76	151	225
539-Ben and Me (Disney) (3/54)	4	8	12	26	41	55
540-Knights of the Round Table (3/54) (Movie)-Photo-c	7	14	21	46	76	105
541-Johnny Mack Brown; photo-c	7	14	21	46	76	105
542-Super Circus Featuring Mary Hartline (TV) (3/54)	7	14	21	46	76	105
543-Uncle Wiggily (3/54)	5	10	15	35	55	75
544-Rob Roy (Disney-Movie)-Manning-a; photo-c	7	14	21	49	82	115
545-The Wonderful Adventures of Pinocchio-Partial reprint of Four Color #92 (Disney-Movie)	7	14	21	46	76	105
546-Buck Jones	6	12	18	41	66	90
547-Francis the Famous Talking Mule	5	10	15	32	51	70
548-Krazy Kat; not by Herriman (4/54)	5	10	15	30	48	65
549-Oswald the Rabbit (Lantz)	5	10	15	32	51	70
550-The Little Scouts	4	8	12	24	37	50
551-Bozo (4/54)	10	20	30	64	115	165
552-Beetle Bailey	7	14	21	48	79	110
553-Susie Q. Smith	4	8	12	26	41	55
554-Rusty Riley (Frank Godwin strip-r)	4	8	12	26	41	50
555-Range War (Zane Grey)	4	8	12	28	44	60
556-Double Trouble With Goober (5/54)	4	8	12	22	34	45
557-Ben Bowie and His Mountain Men	5	10	15	32	51	70
558-Elmer Fudd (5/54)	5	10	15	35	55	75
559-I Love Lucy (#2) (TV)-Photo-c	25	50	75	175	375	575
560-Duck Album (Disney) (5/54)	6	12	18	41	66	90
561-Mr. Magoo (5/54)	10	20	30	65	118	170
562-Goofy (Disney)(#2)	7	14	21	46	76	105
563-Rhubarb, the Millionaire Cat (6/54)	5	10	15	35	55	75
564-Li'l Bad Wolf (Disney)(#3)	5	10	15	32	51	70
565-Jungle Jim	5	10	15	30	48	65
566-Son of Black Beauty	4	8	12	26	41	55
567-Prince Valiant (#1)-By Bob Fuje (Movie)-Photo-c	10	20	30	68	127	185
568-Gypsy Colt (Movie) (6/54)	5	10	15	32	51	70
569-Priscilla's Pop	4	8	12	26	41	55
570-Bob Clampett's Beany and Cecil (TV)	13	26	39	85	180	275
571-Charlie McCarthy	6	12	18	39	62	85
572-Silvertip (Max Brand) (7/54); Kinstler-a	5	10	15	30	48	65
573-The Little People by Walt Scott	5	10	15	32	51	70
574-The Hand of Zorro; Kinstler-a	11	22	33	76	151	225
575-Annie Oakley and Tagg (TV)-Photo-c	9	18	27	62	109	155
576-Angel (#1) (8/54)	4	8	12	26	41	55
577-M.G.M.'s Spike and Tyke	5	10	15	30	48	65
578-Steve Canyon (8/54)	5	10	15	35	55	75
579-Francis the Famous Talking Mule	5	10	15	32	51	70
580-Six Gun Ranch (Luke Short-8/54)	4	8	12	28	44	60
581-Chip 'N' Dale (#2) (Disney)	6	12	18	42	69	95
582-Mowgli Jungle Book (Kipling) (8/54)	5	10	15	30	48	65
583-The Lost Wagon Train (Zane Grey)	4	8	12	28	44	60
584-Johnny Mack Brown-Photo-c	7	14	21	46	76	105
585-Bugs Bunny's Album	6	12	18	41	66	90
586-Duck Album (Disney)	6	12	18	41	66	90
587-The Little Scouts	4	8	12	24	37	50
588-King Richard and the Crusaders (Movie) (10/54) Matt Baker-a; photo-c	9	18	27	61	106	150
589-Buck Jones	6	12	18	41	66	90
590-Hansel and Gretel; partial photo-c	6	12	18	42	69	95

	GD 2.0	VG 4.0	FN 6.0	VF 8.0	VF/NM 9.0	NM- 9.2
591-Western Marshal(Ernest Haycox's)-Kinstler-a	5	10	15	35	55	75
592-Super Circus (TV)	6	12	18	42	69	95
593-Oswald the Rabbit (Lantz)	5	10	15	32	51	70
594-Bozo (10/54)	10	20	30	64	115	165
595-Pluto (Disney)	5	10	15	32	51	70
596-Turok, Son of Stone (#1)	54	108	162	437	944	1450
597-The Little King	5	10	15	35	55	75
598-Captain Davy Jones	5	10	15	30	48	65
599-Ben Bowie and His Mountain Men	5	10	15	32	51	70
600-Daisy Duck's Diary (#1) (Disney) (11/54)	7	14	21	46	76	105
601-Frosty the Snowman	6	12	18	37	59	80
602-Mr. Magoo and Gerald McBoing-Boing	10	20	30	65	118	170
603-M.G.M.'s The Two Mouseketeers	6	12	18	37	59	80
604-Shadow on the Trail (Zane Grey)	4	8	12	28	44	60
605-The Brownies-not by Kelly (12/54)	5	10	15	34	55	75
606-Sir Lancelot (not TV)	7	14	21	48	79	110
607-Santa Claus Funnies	7	14	21	44	72	100
608-Silvertip- "Valley of Vanishing Men" (Max Brand)-Kinstler-a	5	10	15	30	48	65
609-The Littlest Outlaw (Disney-Movie) (1/55)-Photo-c	6	12	18	42	69	95
610-Drum Beat (Movie); Alan Ladd photo-c	8	16	24	55	93	130
611-Duck Album (Disney)	6	12	18	41	66	90
612-Little Beaver (1/55)	5	10	15	30	48	65
613-Western Marshal (Ernest Haycox's) (2/55)-Kinstler-a	5	10	15	35	55	75
614-20,000 Leagues Under the Sea (Disney) (Movie) (2/55)-Painted-c	8	16	24	56	96	135
615-Daffy	7	14	21	44	72	100
616-To the Last Man (Zane Grey)	4	8	12	28	44	60
617-The Quest of Zorro	11	22	33	73	142	210
618-Johnny Mack Brown; photo-c	7	14	21	46	76	105
619-Krazy Kat; not by Herriman	5	10	15	30	48	65
620-Mowgli Jungle Book (Kipling)	5	10	15	30	48	65
621-Francis the Famous Talking Mule (4/55)	4	8	12	28	44	60
622-Beetle Bailey	7	14	21	48	79	110
623-Oswald the Rabbit (Lantz)	4	8	12	28	44	60
624-Treasure Island(Disney-Movie)(4/55)-Photo-c	8	16	24	53	89	125
625-Beaver Valley (Disney-Movie)	6	12	18	41	66	90
626-Ben Bowie and His Mountain Men	5	10	15	32	51	70
627-Goofy (Disney) (5/55)	7	14	21	46	76	105
628-Elmer Fudd	5	10	15	35	55	75
629-Lady and the Tramp with Jock (Disney)	7	14	21	46	76	105
630-Priscilla's Pop	4	8	12	26	41	55
631-Davy Crockett, Indian Fighter (#1) (Disney) (5/55) (TV)-Fess Parker photo-c	14	28	42	97	211	325
632-Fighting Caravans (Zane Grey)	4	8	12	28	44	60
633-The Little People by Walt Scott (6/55)	5	10	15	32	51	70
634-Lady and the Tramp Album (Disney) (6/55)	5	10	15	32	51	70
635-Bob Clampett's Beany and Cecil (TV)	13	26	39	85	180	275
636-Chip 'N' Dale (Disney)	6	12	18	42	69	95
637-Silvertip (Max Brand)-Kinstler-a	5	10	15	30	48	65
638-M.G.M.'s Spike and Tyke (8/55)	5	10	15	30	48	65
639-Davy Crockett at the Alamo (Disney) (7/55) (TV)-Fess Parker photo-c	12	24	36	83	172	260
640-Western Marshal(Ernest Haycox's)-Kinstler-a	5	10	15	35	55	75
641-Steve Canyon (1955)-by Caniff	5	10	15	35	55	75
642-M.G.M.'s The Two Mouseketeers	6	12	18	37	59	80
643-Wild Bill Elliott; photo-c	5	10	15	30	48	65
644-Sir Walter Raleigh (5/55)-Based on movie "The Virgin Queen"; photo-c	7	14	21	44	72	100
645-Johnny Mack Brown; photo-c	7	14	21	46	76	105
646-Dotty Dripple and Taffy (#1)	5	10	15	32	51	70
647-Bugs Bunny's Album (9/55)	6	12	18	41	66	90
648-Jace Pearson of the Texas Rangers (TV)-Photo-c	6	12	18	41	66	90
649-Duck Album (Disney)	6	12	18	41	66	90
650-Prince Valiant; by Bob Fuje	7	14	21	49	82	115
651-King Colt (Luke Short) (9/55)-Kinstler-a	4	8	12	28	44	60
652-Buck Jones	5	10	15	32	51	70
653-Smokey the Bear (#1) (10/55)	10	20	30	67	124	180
654-Pluto (Disney)	5	10	15	32	51	70
655-Francis the Famous Talking Mule	4	8	12	28	44	60
656-Turok, Son of Stone (#2) (10/55)	29	58	87	210	455	700

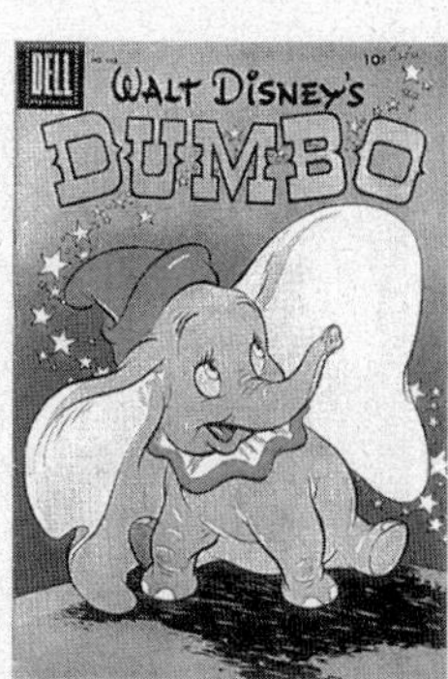

Four Color Comics #668 © DIS

Four Color Comics #721 © Bob Keeshan

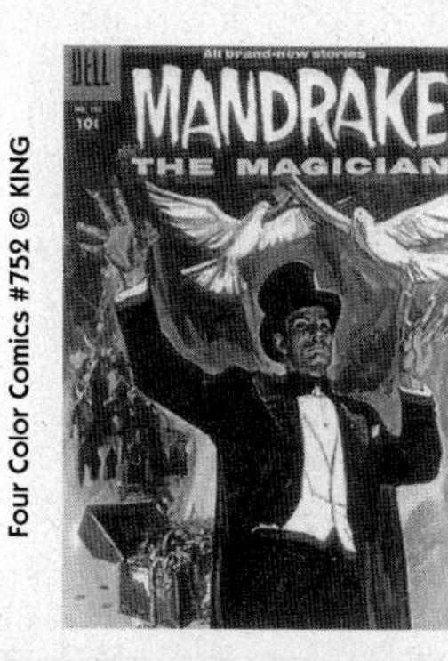

Four Color Comics #752 © KING

	GD 2.0	VG 4.0	FN 6.0	VF 8.0	VF/NM 9.0	NM- 9.2
657-Ben Bowie and His Mountain Men	5	10	15	32	51	70
658-Goofy (Disney)	7	14	21	46	76	105
659-Daisy Duck's Diary (Disney)(#2)	6	12	18	37	59	80
660-Little Beaver	5	10	15	30	48	65
661-Frosty the Snowman	6	12	18	37	59	80
662-Zoo Parade (TV)-Marlin Perkins (11/55)	5	10	15	32	51	70
663-Winky Dink (TV)	8	16	24	51	86	120
664-Davy Crockett in the Great Keelboat Race (TV) (Disney) (11/55)-Fess Parker photo-c	12	24	36	80	163	245
665-The African Lion (Disney-Movie) (11/55)	6	12	18	37	59	80
666-Santa Claus Funnies	7	14	21	44	72	100
667-Silvertip and the Stolen Stallion (Max Brand) (12/55)-Kinstler-a	5	10	15	30	48	65
668-Dumbo (Disney) (12/55)-First of two printings. Dumbo on cover with starry sky. Reprints 4-Color #234?; same-c as #234	10	20	30	67	124	180
668-Dumbo (Disney) (1/58)-Second printing. Same cover altered, with Timothy Mouse added. Same contents as above	7	14	21	44	72	100
669-Robin Hood (Disney-Movie) (12/55)-Reprints #413 plus-c; photo-c	6	12	18	37	59	80
670-M.G.M's Mouse Musketeers (#1) (1/56)-Formerly the Two Mouseketeers	5	10	15	35	55	75
671-Davy Crockett and the River Pirates (TV) (Disney) (12/55)-Jesse Marsh-a; Fess Parker photo-c	12	24	36	80	163	245
672-Quentin Durward (1/56) (Movie)-Photo-c	7	14	21	44	72	100
673-Buffalo Bill, Jr. (#1) (TV)-James Arness photo-c	9	18	27	58	99	140
674-The Little Rascals (#1) (TV)	9	18	27	58	99	140
675-Steve Donovan, Western Marshal (#1) (TV)-Kinstler-a; photo-c	8	16	24	51	86	120
676-Will-Yum!	4	8	12	26	41	55
677-Little King	5	10	15	35	55	75
678-The Last Hunt (Movie)-Photo-c	7	14	21	44	72	100
679-Gunsmoke (#1) (TV)-Photo-c	14	28	42	97	211	325
680-Out Our Way with the Worry Wart (2/56)	4	8	12	24	37	50
681-Forever Darling (Movie) with Lucille Ball & Desi Arnaz (2/56)-; photo-c	11	22	33	77	144	210
682-The Sword & the Rose (Disney-Movie)-Reprint of #505; Renamed When Knighthood Was in Flower for the novel; photo-c	7	14	21	46	76	105
683-Hi and Lois (3/56)	5	10	15	30	48	65
684-Helen of Troy (Movie)-Buscema-a; photo-c	9	18	27	63	112	160
685-Johnny Mack Brown; photo-c	7	14	21	46	76	105
686-Duck Album (Disney)	6	12	18	41	66	90
687-The Indian Fighter (Movie)-Kirk Douglas photo-c	7	14	21	49	82	115
688-Alexander the Great (Movie) (5/56)-Buscema-a; photo-c	7	14	21	48	79	110
689-Elmer Fudd (3/56)	5	10	15	35	55	75
690-The Conqueror (Movie) - John Wayne photo-c	14	28	42	99	200	300
691-Dotty Dripple and Taffy	4	8	12	22	34	45
692-The Little People-Walt Scott	5	10	15	32	51	70
693-Song of the South (Disney) (1956)-Partial reprint of #129	8	16	24	55	93	130
694-Super Circus (TV)-Photo-c	6	12	18	42	69	95
695-Little Beaver	5	10	15	30	48	65
696-Krazy Kat; not by Herriman (4/56)	5	10	15	30	48	65
697-Oswald the Rabbit (Lantz)	4	8	12	28	44	60
698-Francis the Famous Talking Mule (4/56)	4	8	12	28	44	60
699-Prince Valiant-by Bob Fuje	7	14	21	49	82	115
700-Water Birds and the Olympic Elk (Disney-Movie) (4/56)	5	10	15	35	55	75
701-Jiminy Cricket (#1) (Disney) (5/56)	8	16	24	55	93	130
702-The Goofy Success Story (Disney)	7	14	21	46	76	105
703-Scamp (#1) (Disney)	8	16	24	56	96	135
704-Priscilla's Pop (5/56)	4	8	12	26	41	55
705-Brave Eagle (#1) (TV)-Photo-c	6	12	18	43	69	95
706-Bongo and Lumpjaw (Disney) (6/56)	6	12	18	37	59	80
707-Corky and White Shadow (Disney) (5/56)-Mickey Mouse Club (TV); photo-c	7	14	21	46	76	105
708-Smokey the Bear	6	12	18	41	66	90
709-The Searchers (Movie) - John Wayne photo-c	20	40	60	137	294	450
710-Francis the Famous Talking Mule	4	8	12	28	44	60
711-M.G.M's Mouse Musketeers	4	8	12	26	41	55
712-The Great Locomotive Chase (Disney-Movie) (9/56)-Photo-c	7	14	21	46	76	105
713-The Animal World (Movie) (8/56)	4	8	12	26	41	55
714-Spin and Marty (#1) (TV) (Disney)-Mickey Mouse Club (6/56); photo-c	11	22	33	76	151	225
715-Timmy (8/56)	5	10	15	30	48	65
716-Man in Space (Disney)(A science feature from Tomorrowland)	8	16	24	55	93	130
717-Moby Dick (Movie)-Gregory Peck photo-c	8	16	24	55	93	130
718-Dotty Dripple and Taffy	4	8	12	22	34	45
719-Prince Valiant; by Bob Fuje (8/56)	7	14	21	49	82	115
720-Gunsmoke (TV)-James Arness photo-c	9	18	27	60	103	145
721-Captain Kangaroo (TV)-Photo-c	13	26	39	88	189	290
722-Johnny Mack Brown-Photo-c	7	14	21	46	76	105
723-Santiago (Movie)-Kinstler-a (9/56); Alan Ladd photo-c	9	18	27	61	106	150
724-Bugs Bunny's Album	5	10	15	35	55	75
725-Elmer Fudd (9/56)	4	8	12	28	44	60
726-Duck Album (Disney) (9/56)	5	10	15	35	55	75
727-The Nature of Things (TV) (Disney)-Jesse Marsh-a	5	10	15	35	55	75
728-M.G.M's Mouse Musketeers	4	8	12	26	41	55
729-Bob Son of Battle (11/56)	4	8	12	24	37	50
730-Smokey Stover	5	10	15	32	51	70
731-Silvertip and The Fighting Four (Max Brand)-Kinstler-a	5	10	15	30	48	65
732-Zorro, the Challenge of (10/56)	11	22	33	73	142	210
733-Buck Jones	5	10	15	32	51	70
734-Cheyenne (#1) (TV) (10/56)-Clint Walker photo-c	13	26	39	87	186	285
735-Crusader Rabbit (#1) (TV)	22	44	66	154	327	500
736-Pluto (Disney)	5	10	15	32	51	70
737-Steve Canyon-Caniff-a	5	10	15	35	55	75
738-Westward Ho, the Wagons (Disney-Movie)-Fess Parker photo-c	9	18	27	61	106	150
739-Bounty Guns (Luke Short)-Drucker-a	4	8	12	26	41	55
740-Chilly Willy (#1) (Walter Lantz)	7	14	21	48	79	110
741-The Fastest Gun Alive (Movie)(9/56)-Photo-c	7	14	21	46	76	105
742-Buffalo Bill, Jr. (TV)-Photo-c	6	12	18	39	62	85
743-Daisy Duck's Diary (Disney) (11/56)	6	12	18	37	59	80
744-Little Beaver	5	10	15	30	48	65
745-Francis the Famous Talking Mule	4	8	12	28	44	60
746-Dotty Dripple and Taffy	4	8	12	22	34	45
747-Goofy (Disney)	7	14	21	46	76	105
748-Frosty the Snowman (11/56)	5	10	15	32	51	70
749-Secrets of Life (Disney-Movie)-Photo-c	5	10	15	32	51	70
750-The Great Cat Family (Disney-TV/Movie)-Pinocchio & Alice app.	6	12	18	42	69	95
751-Our Miss Brooks (TV)-Photo-c	7	14	21	49	82	115
752-Mandrake, the Magician	10	20	30	66	121	175
753-Walt Scott's Little People (11/56)	5	10	15	32	51	70
754-Smokey the Bear	6	12	18	41	66	90
755-The Littlest Snowman (12/56)	5	10	15	32	51	70
756-Santa Claus Funnies	7	14	21	44	72	100
757-The True Story of Jesse James (Movie)-Photo-c	8	16	24	56	96	135
758-Bear Country (Disney-Movie)	5	10	15	35	55	75
759-Circus Boy (TV)-The Monkees' Mickey Dolenz photo-c (12/56)	11	22	33	76	151	225
760-The Hardy Boys (#1) (TV) (Disney)-Mickey Mouse Club; photo-c	10	20	30	66	121	175
761-Howdy Doody (TV) (1/57)	10	20	30	68	127	185
762-The Sharkfighters (Movie) (1/57); Buscema-a; photo-c	7	14	21	49	82	115
763-Grandma Duck's Farm Friends (#1) (Disney)	8	16	24	51	86	120
764-M.G.M's Mouse Musketeers	4	8	12	26	41	55
765-Will-Yum!	4	8	12	26	41	55
766-Buffalo Bill, Jr. (TV)-Photo-c	6	12	18	39	62	85
767-Spin and Marty (TV) (Disney)-Mickey Mouse Club (2/57)	9	18	27	61	106	150
768-Steve Donovan, Western Marshal (TV)-Kinstler-a; photo-c	6	12	18	42	69	95
769-Gunsmoke (TV)-James Arness photo-c	9	18	27	60	103	145
770-Brave Eagle (TV)-Photo-c	4	8	12	26	41	55
771-Brand of Empire (Luke Short)(3/57)-Drucker-a	4	8	12	26	41	55
772-Cheyenne (TV)-Clint Walker photo-c	9	18	27	58	99	140
773-The Brave One (Movie)-Photo-c	5	10	15	34	55	75
774-Hi and Lois (3/57)	4	8	12	24	37	50
775-Sir Lancelot and Brian (TV)-Buscema-a; photo-c	9	18	27	63	112	160

Four Color Comics #790 © MGM

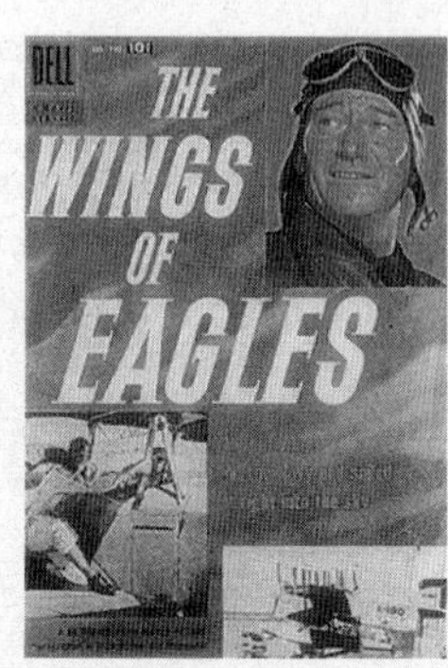

Four Color Comics #825 © DELL

Four Color Comics #845 © Universal

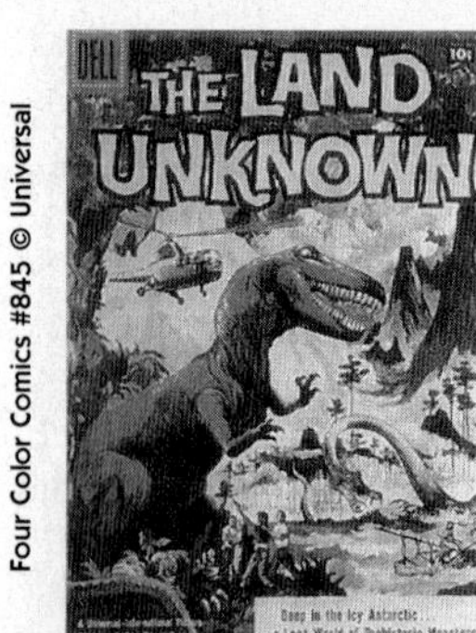

	GD 2.0	VG 4.0	FN 6.0	VF 8.0	VF/NM 9.0	NM- 9.2
776-Johnny Mack Brown; photo-c	7	14	21	46	76	105
777-Scamp (Disney) (3/57)	6	12	18	42	69	95
778-The Little Rascals (TV)	6	12	18	39	62	85
779-Lee Hunter, Indian Fighter (3/57)	5	10	15	35	55	75
780-Captain Kangaroo (TV)-Photo-c	12	24	36	78	157	235
781-Fury (#1) (TV) (3/57)-Photo-c	8	16	24	51	86	120
782-Duck Album (Disney)	5	10	15	35	55	75
783-Elmer Fudd	4	8	12	28	44	60
784-Around the World in 80 Days (Movie) (2/57)-Photo-c						
	7	14	21	49	82	115
785-Circus Boy (TV) (4/57)-The Monkees' Mickey Dolenz photo-c						
	10	20	30	66	121	175
786-Cinderella (Disney) (3/57)-Partial-r of #272	7	14	21	44	72	100
787-Little Hiawatha (Disney) (4/57)(#2)	5	10	15	30	48	65
788-Prince Valiant; by Bob Fuje	7	14	21	46	76	105
789-Silvertip-Valley Thieves (Max Brand) (4/57)-Kinstler-a						
	5	10	15	30	48	65
790-The Wings of Eagles (Movie) (John Wayne)-Toth-a; John Wayne photo-c;						
10¢ & 15¢ editions exist	12	24	36	82	169	255
791-The 77th Bengal Lancers (TV)-Photo-c	7	14	21	46	76	105
792-Oswald the Rabbit (Lantz)	4	8	12	28	44	60
793-Morty Meekle	4	8	12	24	37	50
794-The Count of Monte Cristo (5/57) (Movie)-Buscema-a						
	8	16	24	55	93	130
795-Jiminy Cricket (Disney)(#2)	6	12	18	42	69	95
796-Ludwig Bemelman's Madeleine and Genevieve	4	8	12	24	37	50
797-Gunsmoke (TV)-Photo-c	9	18	27	60	103	145
798-Buffalo Bill, Jr. (TV)-Photo-c	6	12	18	39	62	85
799-Priscilla's Pop	4	8	12	26	41	55
800-The Buccaneers (TV)-Photo-c	7	14	21	46	76	105
801-Dotty Dripple and Taffy	4	8	12	22	34	45
802-Goofy (Disney) (5/57)	7	14	21	46	76	105
803-Cheyenne (TV)-Clint Walker photo-c	9	18	27	58	99	140
804-Steve Canyon-Caniff-a (1957)	5	10	15	35	55	75
805-Crusader Rabbit (TV)	16	32	48	112	246	380
806-Scamp (Disney) (6/57)	6	12	18	42	69	95
807-Savage Range (Luke Short)-Drucker-a	4	8	12	26	41	55
808-Spin and Marty (TV)(Disney)-Mickey Mouse Club; photo-c						
	9	18	27	61	106	150
809-The Little People (Walt Scott)	5	10	15	32	51	70
810-Francis the Famous Talking Mule	4	8	12	26	41	55
811-Howdy Doody (TV) (7/57)	10	20	30	68	127	185
812-The Big Land (Movie); Alan Ladd photo-c	9	18	27	58	99	140
813-Circus Boy (TV)-The Monkees' Mickey Dolenz photo-c						
	10	20	30	66	121	175
814-Covered Wagons, Ho! (Disney)-Donald Duck (TV) (6/57); Mickey Mouse app.						
	5	10	15	35	55	75
815-Dragoon Wells Massacre (Movie)-photo-c	7	14	21	49	82	115
816-Brave Eagle (TV)-photo-c	4	8	12	26	41	55
817-Little Beaver	5	10	15	30	48	65
818-Smokey the Bear (6/57)	6	12	18	41	66	90
819-Mickey Mouse in Magicland (Disney) (7/57)	6	12	18	39	62	85
820-The Oklahoman (Movie)-Photo-c	8	16	24	56	96	135
821-Wringle Wrangle (Disney)-Based on movie "Westward Ho, the Wagons"; Marsh-a;						
Fess Parker photo-c	8	16	24	51	86	120
822-Paul Revere's Ride with Johnny Tremain (TV) (Disney)-Toth-a						
	8	16	24	56	96	135
823-Timmy	4	8	12	26	41	55
824-The Pride and the Passion (Movie) (8/57)-Frank Sinatra & Cary Grant photo-c						
	9	18	27	61	106	150
825-The Little Rascals (TV)	6	12	18	39	62	85
826-Spin and Marty and Annette (TV) (Disney)-Mickey Mouse Club; Annette Funicello						
photo-c	19	38	57	128	277	425
827-Smokey Stover (8/57)	5	10	15	32	51	70
828-Buffalo Bill, Jr. (TV)-Photo-c	6	12	18	39	62	85
829-Tales of the Pony Express (TV) (8/57)-Painted-c	5	10	15	30	48	65
830-The Hardy Boys (TV) (Disney)-Mickey Mouse Club (8/57); photo-c						
	9	18	27	58	99	140
831-No Sleep 'Til Dawn (Movie)-Karl Malden photo-c	6	12	18	42	69	95
832-Lolly and Pepper (#1)	5	10	15	30	48	65
833-Scamp (Disney) (9/57)	6	12	18	42	69	95
834-Johnny Mack Brown; photo-c	7	14	21	46	76	105
835-Silvertip-The False Rider (Max Brand)	5	10	15	30	48	65
836-Man in Flight (Disney) (TV) (9/57)	7	14	21	46	76	105

	GD 2.0	VG 4.0	FN 6.0	VF 8.0	VF/NM 9.0	NM- 9.2
837-Cotton Woods, (All-American Athlete...)	4	8	12	24	37	50
838-Bugs Bunny's Life Story Album (9/57)	5	10	15	35	55	75
839-The Vigilantes (Movie)	7	14	21	46	76	105
840-Duck Album (Disney) (9/57)	5	10	15	35	55	75
841-Elmer Fudd	4	8	12	28	44	60
842-The Nature of Things (Disney-Movie) ('57)-Jesse Marsh-a (TV series)						
	5	10	15	35	55	75
843-The First Americans (Disney) (TV)-Marsh-a	8	16	24	55	93	130
844-Gunsmoke (TV)-Photo-c	9	18	27	60	103	145
845-The Land Unknown (Movie)-Alex Toth-a	11	22	33	71	136	200
846-Gun Glory (Movie)-by Alex Toth; photo-c	8	16	24	56	96	135
847-Perri (squirrels) (Disney-Movie)-Two different covers published						
	5	10	15	35	55	75
848-Marauder's Moon (Luke Short)	4	8	12	26	41	55
849-Prince Valiant; by Bob Fuje	7	14	21	46	76	105
850-Buck Jones	5	10	15	32	51	70
851-The Story of Mankind (Movie) (1/58)-Hedy Lamarr & Vincent Price photo-c						
	7	14	21	46	76	105
852-Chilly Willy (2/58) (Lantz)	5	10	15	30	48	65
853-Pluto (Disney) (10/57)	5	10	15	32	51	70
854-The Hunchback of Notre Dame (Movie)-Photo-c	11	22	33	76	151	225
855-Broken Arrow (TV)-Photo-c	6	12	18	37	59	80
856-Buffalo Bill, Jr. (TV)-Photo-c	6	12	18	39	62	85
857-The Goofy Adventure Story (Disney) (11/57)	7	14	21	46	76	105
858-Daisy Duck's Diary (Disney) (11/57)	5	10	15	32	51	70
859-Topper and Neil (TV) (11/57)	5	10	15	30	48	65
860-Wyatt Earp (#1) (TV)-Manning-a; photo-c	9	18	27	63	112	160
861-Frosty the Snowman	5	10	15	32	51	70
862-The Truth About Mother Goose (Disney-Movie) (11/57)						
	7	14	21	48	79	110
863-Francis the Famous Talking Mule	4	8	12	26	41	55
864-The Littlest Snowman	5	10	15	32	51	70
865-Andy Burnett (TV) (Disney) (12/57)-Photo-c	8	16	24	56	96	135
866-Mars and Beyond (Disney-TV)(A science feature from Tomorrowland)						
	8	16	24	55	93	130
867-Santa Claus Funnies	7	14	21	44	72	100
868-The Little People (12/57)	5	10	15	32	51	70
869-Old Yeller (Disney-Movie)-Photo-c	5	10	15	35	55	75
870-Little Beaver (1/58)	5	10	15	30	48	65
871-Curly Kayoe	4	8	12	24	37	50
872-Captain Kangaroo (TV)-Photo-c	12	24	36	78	157	235
873-Grandma Duck's Farm Friends (Disney)	6	12	18	37	59	80
874-Old Ironsides (Disney-Movie with Johnny Tremain) (1/58)						
	6	12	18	42	69	95
875-Trumpets West (Luke Short) (2/58)	4	8	12	26	41	55
876-Tales of Wells Fargo (#1)(TV)(2/58)-Photo-c	9	18	27	58	99	140
877-Frontier Doctor with Rex Allen (TV)-Alex Toth-a; Rex Allen photo-c						
	9	18	27	61	106	150
878-Peanuts (#1)-Schulz-c only (2/58)	21	42	63	148	317	485
879-Brave Eagle (TV) (2/58)-Photo-c	4	8	12	26	41	55
880-Steve Donovan, Western Marshal-Drucker-a (TV)-Photo-c						
	5	10	15	30	48	65
881-The Captain and the Kids (2/58)	4	8	12	28	44	60
882-Zorro (Disney)-1st Disney issue; by Alex Toth (TV) (2/58); photo-c						
	13	26	39	87	186	285
883-The Little Rascals (TV)	6	12	18	37	59	80
884-Hawkeye and the Last of the Mohicans (TV) (3/58); photo-c						
	7	14	21	46	76	105
885-Fury (TV) (3/58)-Photo-c	6	12	18	41	66	90
886-Bongo and Lumpjaw (Disney) (3/58)	5	10	15	30	48	65
887-The Hardy Boys (Disney) (TV)-Mickey Mouse Club (1/58)-Photo-c						
	9	18	27	58	99	140
888-Elmer Fudd (3/58)	4	8	12	28	44	60
889-Clint and Mac (Disney) (TV) (3/58)-Alex Toth-a; photo-c						
	11	22	33	71	136	200
890-Wyatt Earp (TV)-by Russ Manning; photo-c	7	14	21	48	79	110
891-Light in the Forest (Disney-Movie) (3/58)-Fess Parker photo-c						
	7	14	21	49	82	115
892-Maverick (#1) (TV) (4/58)-James Garner photo-c						
	19	38	57	128	277	425
893-Jim Bowie (TV)-Photo-c	6	12	18	39	62	85
894-Oswald the Rabbit (Lantz)	4	8	12	28	44	60
895-Wagon Train (#1) (TV) (3/58)-Photo-c	10	20	30	67	124	180
896-The Adventures of Tinker Bell (Disney)	8	16	24	55	93	130

Four Color Comics #911 © CBS

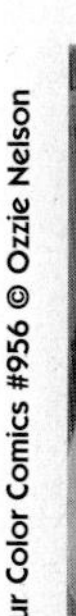
Four Color Comics #956 © Ozzie Nelson

Four Color Comics #1006 © Oscar Film

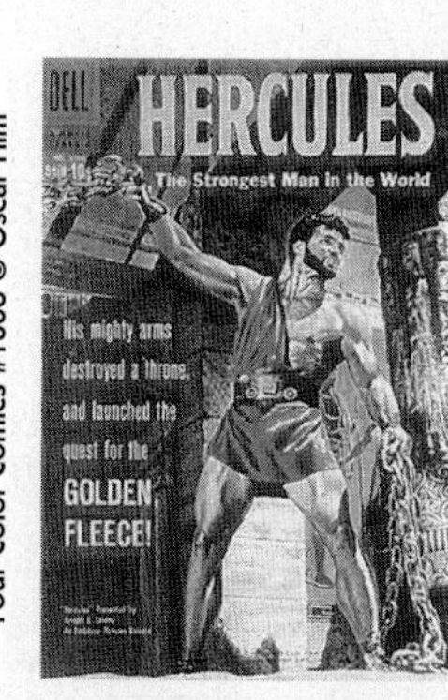

	GD 2.0	VG 4.0	FN 6.0	VF 8.0	VF/NM 9.0	NM- 9.2
897-Jiminy Cricket (Disney)	6	12	18	42	69	95
898-Silvertip (Max Brand)-Kinstler-a (5/58)	5	10	15	30	48	65
899-Goofy (Disney) (5/58)	5	10	15	32	51	70
900-Prince Valiant; by Bob Fuje	7	14	21	46	76	105
901-Little Hiawatha (Disney)	5	10	15	30	48	65
902-Will-Yum!	4	8	12	26	41	55
903-Dotty Dripple and Taffy	4	8	12	22	34	45
904-Lee Hunter, Indian Fighter	4	8	12	26	41	55
905-Annette (Disney) (TV) (5/58)-Mickey Mouse Club; Annette Funicello photo-c	22	44	66	154	327	500
906-Francis the Famous Talking Mule	4	8	12	26	41	55
907-Sugarfoot (#1) (TV)Toth-a; photo-c	11	22	33	74	145	215
908-The Little People and the Giant-Walt Scott (5/58)	5	10	15	32	51	70
909-Smitty	4	8	12	24	37	50
910-The Vikings (Movie)-Buscema-a; Kirk Douglas photo-c	8	16	24	53	89	125
911-The Gray Ghost (TV)-Photo-c	8	16	24	55	93	130
912-Leave It to Beaver (#1) (TV)-Photo-c	13	26	39	90	195	300
913-The Left-Handed Gun (Movie) (7/58); Paul Newman photo-c	9	18	27	61	106	150
914-No Time for Sergeants (Movie)-Andy Griffith photo-c; Toth-a	9	18	27	63	112	160
915-Casey Jones (TV)-Alan Hale photo-c	5	10	15	35	55	75
916-Red Ryder Ranch Comics (7/58)	5	10	15	30	48	65
917-The Life of Riley (TV)-Photo-c	10	20	30	66	121	175
918-Beep Beep, the Roadrunner (#1) (7/58)-Published with two different back covers	11	22	33	76	151	225
919-Boots and Saddles (#1) (TV)-Photo-c	7	14	21	49	82	115
920-Zorro (Disney) (TV) (6/58)Toth-a; photo-c	11	22	33	72	139	205
921-Wyatt Earp (TV)-Manning-a; photo-c	7	14	21	48	79	110
922-Johnny Mack Brown by Russ Manning; photo-c	7	14	21	48	79	110
923-Timmy	4	8	12	26	41	55
924-Colt .45 (#1) (TV) (8/58)-W. Preston photo-c	10	20	30	66	121	175
925-Last of the Fast Guns (Movie) (8/58)-Photo-c	6	12	18	432	69	95
926-Peter Pan (Disney)-Reprint of #442	4	8	12	28	44	60
927-Top Gun (Luke Short) Buscema-a	4	8	12	26	41	55
928-Sea Hunt (#1) (9/58) (TV)-Lloyd Bridges photo-c	11	22	33	71	136	200
929-Brave Eagle (TV)-Photo-c	4	8	12	26	41	55
930-Maverick (TV) (7/58)-James Garner photo-c	10	20	30	69	130	190
931-Have Gun, Will Travel (#1) (TV)-Photo-c	12	24	36	79	160	240
932-Smokey the Bear (His Life Story)	6	12	18	41	66	90
933-Zorro (Disney, 9/58) (TV)-Alex Toth-a; photo-c	11	22	33	72	139	205
934-Restless Gun (#1) (TV)-Photo-c	10	20	30	67	124	180
935-King of the Royal Mounted	4	8	12	28	44	60
936-The Little Rascals (TV)	6	12	18	37	59	80
937-Ruff and Reddy (#1) (9/58) (TV) (1st Hanna-Barbera comic book)	11	22	33	74	145	215
938-Elmer Fudd (9/58)	4	8	12	28	44	60
939-Steve Canyon - not by Caniff	5	10	15	35	55	75
940-Lolly and Pepper (10/58)	4	8	12	22	34	45
941-Pluto (Disney) (10/58)	4	8	12	28	44	60
942-Pony Express (Tales of the ...) (TV)	5	10	15	30	48	65
943-White Wilderness (Disney-Movie) (10/58)	6	12	18	42	69	95
944-The 7th Voyage of Sinbad (Movie) (9/58)-Buscema-a; photo-c	11	22	33	76	151	225
945-Maverick (TV)-James Garner/Jack Kelly photo-c	10	20	30	69	130	190
946-The Big Country (Movie)-Photo-c	7	14	21	46	76	105
947-Broken Arrow (TV)-Photo-c (11/58)	5	10	15	32	51	70
948-Daisy Duck's Diary (Disney) (11/58)	5	10	15	32	51	70
949-High Adventure(Lowell Thomas')(TV)-Photo-c	6	12	18	37	59	80
950-Frosty the Snowman	5	10	15	32	51	70
951-The Lennon Sisters Life Story (TV)-Toth-a, 32 pgs.; photo-c	12	24	36	79	160	240
952-Goofy (Disney) (11/58)	5	10	15	32	51	70
953-Francis the Famous Talking Mule	4	8	12	26	41	55
954-Man in Space-Satellites (TV)	7	14	21	46	76	105
955-Hi and Lois (11/58)	4	8	12	24	37	50
956-Ricky Nelson (#1) (TV)-Photo-c	15	30	45	102	221	340
957-Buffalo Bee (#1) (TV)	8	16	24	56	96	135
958-Santa Claus Funnies	6	12	18	41	66	90
959-Christmas Stories-(Walt Scott's Little People) (1951-56 strip reprints)	5	10	15	32	51	70
960-Zorro (Disney) (TV) (12/58)-Toth art; photo-c	11	22	33	72	139	205
961-Jace Pearson's Tales of the Texas Rangers (TV)-Spiegle-a; photo-c	6	12	18	37	59	80
962-Maverick (TV) (1/59)-James Garner/Jack Kelly photo-c	10	20	30	69	130	190
963-Johnny Mack Brown; photo-c	7	14	21	46	76	105
964-The Hardy Boys (TV) (Disney) (1/59)-Mickey Mouse Club; photo-c	9	18	27	58	99	140
965-Grandma Duck's Farm Friends (Disney)(1/59)	5	10	15	32	51	70
966-Tonka (starring Sal Mineo; Disney-Movie)-Photo-c	8	16	24	56	96	135
967-Chilly Willy (2/59) (Lantz)	5	10	15	30	48	65
968-Tales of Wells Fargo (TV)-Photo-c	8	16	24	55	93	130
969-Peanuts (2/59)	13	26	39	87	186	285
970-Lawman (#1) (TV)-Photo-c	11	22	33	76	151	225
971-Wagon Train (TV)-Photo-c	7	14	21	44	72	100
972-Tom Thumb (Movie)-George Pal (1/59)	8	16	24	56	96	135
973-Sleeping Beauty and the Prince(Disney)(5/59)	10	20	30	69	130	190
974-The Little Rascals (TV) (3/59)	6	12	18	37	59	80
975-Fury (TV)-Photo-c	6	12	18	41	66	90
976-Zorro (Disney) (TV)-Toth-a; photo-c	11	22	33	72	139	205
977-Elmer Fudd (3/59)	4	8	12	28	44	60
978-Lolly and Pepper	4	8	12	22	34	45
979-Oswald the Rabbit (Lantz)	4	8	12	28	44	60
980-Maverick (TV) (4-6/59)-James Garner/Jack Kelly photo-c	10	20	30	69	130	190
981-Ruff and Reddy (TV) (Hanna-Barbera)	8	16	24	51	86	120
982-The New Adventures of Tinker Bell (TV) (Disney)	8	16	24	51	86	120
983-Have Gun, Will Travel (TV) (4-6/59)-Photo-c	9	18	27	58	99	140
984-Sleeping Beauty's Fairy Godmothers (Disney)	9	18	27	60	103	145
985-Shaggy Dog (Disney-Movie)-Photo-all four covers; Annette on back-c(5/59)	7	14	21	49	82	115
986-Restless Gun (TV)-Photo-c	8	16	24	51	86	120
987-Goofy (Disney) (7/59)	5	10	15	32	51	70
988-Little Hiawatha (Disney)	5	10	15	30	48	65
989-Jiminy Cricket (Disney) (5-7/59)	6	12	18	42	69	95
990-Huckleberry Hound (#1)(TV)(Hanna-Barbera); 1st app. Huck, Yogi Bear, & Pixie & Dixie & Mr. Jinks	11	22	33	77	154	230
991-Francis the Famous Talking Mule	4	8	12	26	41	55
992-Sugarfoot (TV)-Toth-a; photo-c	10	20	30	70	133	195
993-Jim Bowie (TV)-Photo-c	5	10	15	35	55	75
994-Sea Hunt (TV)-Lloyd Bridges photo-c	8	16	24	53	89	125
995-Donald Duck Album (Disney) (5-7/59)(#1)	6	12	18	42	69	95
996-Nevada (Zane Grey)	4	8	12	28	44	60
997-Walt Disney Presents-Tales of Texas John Slaughter (#1) (TV) (Disney)-Photo-c; photo of W. Disney inside-c	7	14	21	48	79	110
998-Ricky Nelson (TV)-Photo-c	15	30	45	102	221	340
999-Leave It to Beaver (TV)-Photo-c	12	24	36	81	166	250
1000-The Gray Ghost (TV) (6-8/59)-Photo-c	8	16	24	55	93	130
1001-Lowell Thomas' High Adventure (TV) (8-10/59)-Photo-c	5	10	15	34	55	75
1002-Buffalo Bee (TV)	7	14	21	44	72	100
1003-Zorro (TV) (Disney)-Toth-a; photo-c	11	22	33	72	139	205
1004-Colt .45 (TV) (6-8/59)-Photo-c	8	16	24	55	93	130
1005-Maverick (TV)-James Garner/Jack Kelly photo-c	10	20	30	69	130	190
1006-Hercules (Movie)-Buscema-a; photo-c	9	18	27	58	99	140
1007-John Paul Jones (Movie)-Robert Stack photo-c	5	10	15	35	55	75
1008-Beep Beep, the Road Runner (7-9/59)	7	14	21	48	79	110
1009-The Rifleman (#1) (TV)-Photo-c	19	38	57	128	277	425
1010-Grandma Duck's Farm Friends (Disney)-by Carl Barks	11	22	33	76	151	225
1011-Buckskin (#1) (TV)-Photo-c	7	14	21	46	76	105
1012-Last Train from Gun Hill (Movie) (7/59)-Photo-c	8	16	24	55	93	130
1013-Bat Masterson (#1) (TV) (8/59)-Gene Barry photo-c	11	22	33	71	136	200
1014-The Lennon Sisters (TV)-Toth-a; photo-c	11	22	33	76	151	225
1015-Peanuts-Schulz-c	13	26	39	87	186	285
1016-Smokey the Bear Nature Stories	4	8	12	28	44	60
1017-Chilly Willy (Lantz)	5	10	15	30	48	65
1018-Rio Bravo (Movie)(6/59)-John Wayne; Toth-a; John Wayne, Dean Martin & Ricky Nelson photo-c	20	40	60	137	294	450
1019-Wagon Train (TV)-Photo-c	7	14	21	44	72	100
1020-Jungle Jim-McWilliams-a	4	8	12	26	41	55

Four Color Comics #1066 © WB

Four Color Comics #1099 © DIS

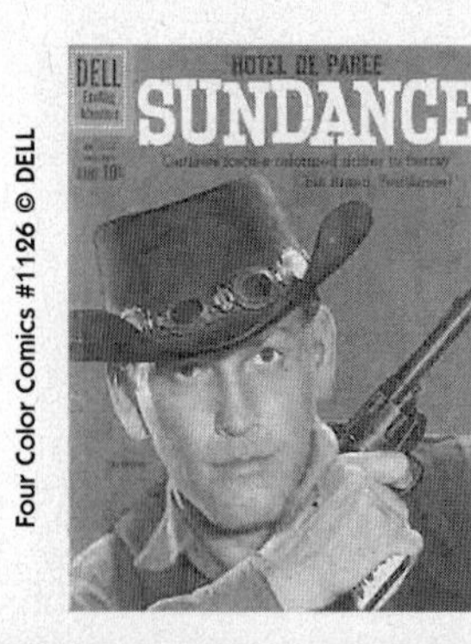

Four Color Comics #1126 © DELL

	GD 2.0	VG 4.0	FN 6.0	VF 8.0	VF/NM 9.0	NM- 9.2
1021-Jace Pearson's Tales of the Texas Rangers (TV)-Photo-c	6	12	18	37	59	80
1022-Timmy	4	8	12	26	41	55
1023-Tales of Wells Fargo (TV)-Photo-c	8	16	24	55	93	130
1024-Darby O'Gill and the Little People (Disney-Movie)-Toth-a; photo-c	9	18	27	63	112	160
1025-Vacation in Disneyland (8-10/59)-Carl Barks-a(24pgs.) (Disney)	14	28	42	95	205	315
1026-Spin and Marty (TV) (Disney) (9-11/59)-Mickey Mouse Club; photo-c	8	16	24	51	86	120
1027-The Texan (#1)(TV)-Photo-c	8	16	24	55	93	130
1028-Rawhide (#1) (TV) (9-11/59)-Clint Eastwood photo-c; Tufts-a	20	40	60	137	294	450
1029-Boots and Saddles (TV) (9/59)-Photo-c	5	10	15	34	55	75
1030-Spanky and Alfalfa, the Little Rascals (TV)	6	12	18	37	59	80
1031-Fury (TV)-Photo-c	6	12	18	41	66	90
1032-Elmer Fudd	4	8	12	28	44	60
1033-Steve Canyon-not by Caniff; photo-c	5	10	15	35	55	75
1034-Nancy and Sluggo Summer Camp (9-11/59)	5	10	15	32	51	70
1035-Lawman (TV)-Photo-c	8	16	24	53	89	125
1036-The Big Circus (Movie)-Photo-c	6	12	18	42	69	95
1037-Zorro (Disney) (TV)-Tufts-a; Annette Funicello photo-c	12	24	36	84	175	265
1038-Ruff and Reddy (TV)(Hanna-Barbera)(1959)	8	16	24	51	86	120
1039-Pluto (Disney) (11-1/60)	4	8	12	28	44	60
1040-Quick Draw McGraw (#1) (TV) (Hanna-Barbera) (12-2/60)	12	24	36	79	160	240
1041-Sea Hunt (TV) (10-12/59)-Toth-a; Lloyd Bridges photo-c	8	16	24	53	89	125
1042-The Three Chipmunks (Alvin, Simon & Theodore) (#1) (TV) (10-12/59)	9	18	27	58	99	140
1043-The Three Stooges (#1)-Photo-c	21	42	63	148	317	485
1044-Have Gun, Will Travel (TV)-Photo-c	9	18	27	58	99	140
1045-Restless Gun (TV)-Photo-c	8	16	24	51	86	120
1046-Beep Beep, the Road Runner (11-1/60)	7	14	21	48	79	110
1047-Gyro Gearloose (#1) (Disney)-All Barks-c/a	14	28	42	98	214	330
1048-The Horse Soldiers (Movie) (John Wayne)-Sekowsky-a; painted cover featuring John Wayne	12	24	36	79	160	240
1049-Don't Give Up the Ship (Movie) (8/59)-Jerry Lewis photo-c	9	18	27	61	106	150
1050-Huckleberry Hound (TV) (Hanna-Barbera) (10-12/59)	8	16	24	56	96	135
1051-Donald in Mathmagic Land (Disney-Movie)	9	18	27	61	106	150
1052-Ben-Hur (Movie) (11/59)-Manning-a	10	20	30	64	115	165
1053-Goofy (Disney) (11-1/60)	5	10	15	32	51	70
1054-Huckleberry Hound Winter Fun (TV) (Hanna-Barbera) (12/59)	8	16	24	56	96	135
1055-Daisy Duck's Diary (Disney)-by Carl Barks (11-1/60)	9	18	27	58	99	140
1056-Yellowstone Kelly (Movie)-Clint Walker photo-c	6	12	18	37	59	80
1057-Mickey Mouse Album (Disney)	5	10	15	35	55	75
1058-Colt .45 (TV)-Photo-c	8	16	24	55	93	130
1059-Sugarfoot (TV)-Photo-c	8	16	24	56	96	135
1060-Journey to the Center of the Earth (Movie)-Pat Boone & James Mason photo-c	10	20	30	71	128	185
1061-Buffalo Bee (TV)	7	14	21	44	72	100
1062-Christmas Stories (Walt Scott's Little People strip-r)	5	10	15	32	51	70
1063-Santa Claus Funnies	6	12	18	41	66	90
1064-Bugs Bunny's Merry Christmas (12/59)	5	10	15	35	55	75
1065-Frosty the Snowman	5	10	15	32	51	70
1066-77 Sunset Strip (#1) (TV)-Toth-a (1-3/60)-Efrem Zimbalist, Jr. & Edd "Kookie" Byrnes photo-c	10	20	30	67	124	180
1067-Yogi Bear (#1) (TV) (Hanna-Barbera)	11	22	33	73	142	210
1068-Francis the Famous Talking Mule	4	8	12	26	41	55
1069-The FBI Story (Movie)-Toth-a; James Stewart photo on-c	9	18	27	61	106	150
1070-Solomon and Sheba (Movie)-Sekowsky-a; photo-c	8	16	24	56	96	135
1071-The Real McCoys (#1) (TV) (1-3/60)-Toth-a; Walter Brennan photo-c	9	18	27	58	99	140
1072-Blythe (Marge's)	6	12	18	37	59	80
1073-Grandma Duck's Farm Friends-Barks-c/a (Disney)	11	22	33	76	151	225
1074-Chilly Willy (Lantz)	5	10	15	30	48	65
1075-Tales of Wells Fargo (TV)-Photo-c	8	16	24	55	93	130
1076-The Rebel (#1) (TV)-Sekowsky-a; photo-c	9	18	27	63	112	160
1077-The Deputy (#1) (TV)-Buscema-a; Henry Fonda photo-c	11	22	33	71	136	200
1078-The Three Stooges (2-4/60)-Photo-c	11	22	33	77	154	230
1079-The Little Rascals (TV) (Spanky & Alfalfa)	6	12	18	37	59	80
1080-Fury (TV) (2-4/60)-Photo-c	6	12	18	41	66	90
1081-Elmer Fudd	4	8	12	28	44	60
1082-Spin and Marty (Disney) (TV)-Photo-c	8	16	24	51	86	120
1083-Men into Space (TV)-Anderson-a; photo-c	5	10	15	35	55	75
1084-Speedy Gonzales	5	10	15	35	55	75
1085-The Time Machine (H.G. Wells) (Movie) (3/60)-Alex Toth-a; Rod Taylor photo-c	12	24	36	84	175	265
1086-Lolly and Pepper	4	8	12	22	34	45
1087-Peter Gunn (TV)-Photo-c	8	16	24	56	96	135
1088-A Dog of Flanders (Movie)-Photo-c	5	10	15	30	48	65
1089-Restless Gun (TV)-Photo-c	8	16	24	51	86	120
1090-Francis the Famous Talking Mule	4	8	12	26	41	55
1091-Jacky's Diary (4-6/60)	5	10	15	30	48	65
1092-Toby Tyler (Disney-Movie)-Photo-c	6	12	18	42	69	95
1093-MacKenzie's Raiders (Movie/TV)-Richard Carlson photo-c from TV show	6	12	18	42	69	95
1094-Goofy (Disney)	5	10	15	32	51	70
1095-Gyro Gearloose (Disney)-All Barks-c/a	10	20	30	64	115	165
1096-The Texan (TV)-Rory Calhoun photo-c	8	16	24	51	86	120
1097-Rawhide (TV)-Manning-a; Clint Eastwood photo-c	12	24	36	84	177	270
1098-Sugarfoot (TV)-Photo-c	8	16	24	56	96	135
1099-Donald Duck Album (Disney) (5-7/60)-Barks-c	7	14	21	44	72	100
1100-Annette's Life Story (Disney-Movie) (5/60)-Annette Funicello photo-c	17	34	51	119	260	400
1101-Robert Louis Stevenson's Kidnapped (Disney-Movie) (5/60); photo-c	6	12	18	42	69	95
1102-Wanted: Dead or Alive (#1) (TV) (5-7/60); Steve McQueen photo-c	11	22	33	76	151	225
1103-Leave It to Beaver (TV)-Photo-c	12	24	36	81	166	250
1104-Yogi Bear Goes to College (TV) (Hanna-Barbera) (6-8/60)	7	14	21	49	82	115
1105-Gale Storm (Oh! Susanna) (TV)-Toth-a; photo-c	10	20	30	70	133	195
1106-77 Sunset Strip(TV)(6-8/60)-Toth-a; photo-c	8	16	24	56	96	135
1107-Buckskin (TV)-Photo-c	6	12	18	42	69	95
1108-The Troubleshooters (TV)-Keenan Wynn photo-c	5	10	15	35	55	75
1109-This Is Your Life, Donald Duck (Disney) (TV) (8-10/60)-Gyro flashback to WDC&S #141; origin Donald Duck (1st told)	12	24	36	83	172	260
1110-Bonanza (#1) (TV) (6-8/60)-Photo-c	28	56	84	203	439	675
1111-Shotgun Slade (TV)-Photo-c	6	12	18	41	66	90
1112-Pixie and Dixie and Mr. Jinks (#1) (TV) (Hanna-Barbera) (7-9/60)	7	14	21	49	82	115
1113-Tales of Wells Fargo (TV)-Photo-c	8	16	24	55	93	130
1114-Huckleberry Finn (Movie) (7/60)-Photo-c	5	10	15	34	55	75
1115-Ricky Nelson (TV)-Manning-a; photo-c	12	24	36	84	175	265
1116-Boots and Saddles (TV) (8/60)-Photo-c	5	10	15	34	55	75
1117-Boy and the Pirates (Movie)-Photo-c	6	12	18	43	69	95
1118-The Sword and the Dragon (Movie) (6/60)-Photo-c	7	14	21	49	82	115
1119-Smokey the Bear Nature Stories	4	8	12	28	44	60
1120-Dinosaurus (Movie)-Painted-c	8	16	24	55	93	130
1121-Hercules Unchained (Movie) (8/60)-Crandall/Evans-a	9	18	27	58	99	140
1122-Chilly Willy (Lantz)	5	10	15	30	48	65
1123-Tombstone Territory (TV)-Photo-c	8	16	24	55	93	130
1124-Whirlybirds (#1) (TV)-Photo-c	8	16	24	55	93	130
1125-Laramie (#1) (TV)-Photo-c; G. Kane/Heath-a	8	16	24	56	96	135
1126-Hotel Deparee - Sundance (TV) (8-10/60)-Earl Holliman photo-c	6	12	18	42	69	95
1127-The Three Stooges-Photo-c (8-10/60)	11	22	33	77	154	230
1128-Rocky and His Friends (#1) (TV) (Jay Ward) (8-10/60)	26	52	78	182	391	600
1129-Pollyanna (Disney-Movie)-Hayley Mills photo-c	7	14	21	49	82	115
1130-The Deputy (TV)-Buscema-a; Henry Fonda photo-c	9	18	27	61	106	150

Four Color Comics #1141 © H-B

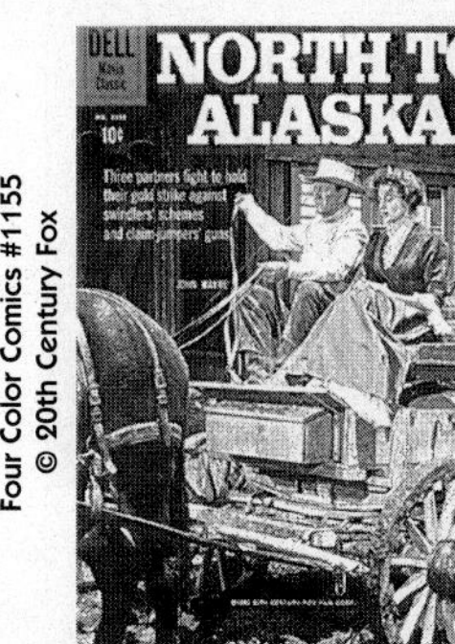

Four Color Comics #1155 © 20th Century Fox

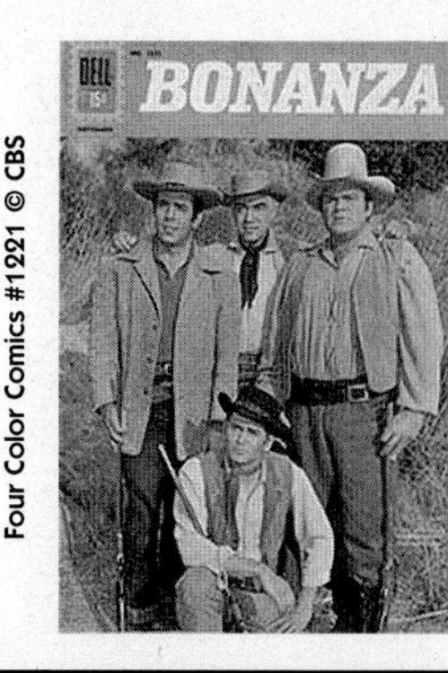

Four Color Comics #1221 © CBS

	GD 2.0	VG 4.0	FN 6.0	VF 8.0	VF/NM 9.0	NM- 9.2
1131-Elmer Fudd (9-11/60)	4	8	12	28	44	60
1132-Space Mouse (Lantz) (8-10/60)	4	8	12	28	44	60
1133-Fury (TV)-Photo-c	6	12	18	41	66	90
1134-Real McCoys (TV)-Toth-a; photo-c	9	18	27	58	99	140
1135-M.G.M.'s Mouse Musketeers (9-11/60)	4	8	12	24	37	50
1136-Jungle Cat (Disney-Movie)-Photo-c	6	12	18	42	69	95
1137-The Little Rascals (TV)	6	12	18	37	59	80
1138-The Rebel (TV)-Photo-c	8	16	24	55	93	130
1139-Spartacus (Movie) (11/60)-Buscema-a; Kirk Douglas photo-c	11	22	33	76	151	225
1140-Donald Duck Album (Disney)-Barks-c	7	14	21	44	72	100
1141-Huckleberry Hound for President (TV) (Hanna-Barbera) (10/60)	8	16	24	51	86	120
1142-Johnny Ringo (TV)-Photo-c	7	14	21	46	76	105
1143-Pluto (Disney) (11-1/61)	4	8	12	28	44	60
1144-The Story of Ruth (Movie)-Photo-c	8	16	24	56	96	135
1145-The Lost World (Movie)-Gil Kane-a; photo-c; 1 pg. Conan Doyle biography by Torres	9	18	27	62	109	155
1146-Restless Gun (TV)-Photo-c; Wildey-a	8	16	24	51	86	120
1147-Sugarfoot (TV)-Photo-c	8	16	24	56	96	135
1148-I Aim at the Stars-the Wernher Von Braun Story (Movie) (11-1/61)-Photo-c	7	14	21	46	76	105
1149-Goofy (Disney) (11-1/61)	5	10	15	32	51	70
1150-Daisy Duck's Diary (Disney) (12-1/61) by Carl Barks	9	18	27	58	99	140
1151-Mickey Mouse Album (Disney) (11-1/61)	5	10	15	35	55	75
1152-Rocky and His Friends (TV) (Jay Ward) (12-2/61)	16	32	48	109	237	365
1153-Frosty the Snowman	5	10	15	32	51	70
1154-Santa Claus Funnies	6	12	18	41	66	90
1155-North to Alaska (Movie)-John Wayne photo-c	14	28	42	95	205	315
1156-Walt Disney Swiss Family Robinson (Movie) (12/60)-Photo-c	7	14	21	48	79	110
1157-Master of the World (Movie) (7/61)	7	14	21	44	72	100
1158-Three Worlds of Gulliver (2 issues exist with different covers) (Movie)-Photo-c	7	14	21	44	72	100
1159-77 Sunset Strip (TV)-Toth-a; photo-c	8	16	24	56	96	135
1160-Rawhide (TV)-Clint Eastwood photo-c	12	24	36	84	177	270
1161-Grandma Duck's Farm Friends (Disney) by Carl Barks (2-4/61)	11	22	33	76	151	225
1162-Yogi Bear Joins the Marines (TV) (Hanna-Barbera) (5-7/61)	7	14	21	49	82	115
1163-Daniel Boone (3-5/61); Marsh-a	5	10	15	35	55	75
1164-Wanted: Dead or Alive (TV)-Steve McQueen photo-c	9	18	27	61	106	150
1165-Ellery Queen (#1) (3-5/61)	10	20	30	66	121	175
1166-Rocky and His Friends (TV) (Jay Ward)	16	32	48	109	237	365
1167-Tales of Wells Fargo (TV)-Photo-c	8	16	24	51	86	120
1168-The Detectives (TV)-Robert Taylor photo-c	9	18	27	63	112	160
1169-New Adventures of Sherlock Holmes	12	24	36	83	172	260
1170-The Three Stooges (3-5/61)-Photo-c	11	22	33	77	154	230
1171-Elmer Fudd	4	8	12	28	44	60
1172-Fury (TV)-Photo-c	6	12	18	41	66	90
1173-The Twilight Zone (#1) (TV) (5/61)-Crandall/Evans-c/a; Crandall tribute to Ingles	19	38	57	133	287	440
1174-The Little Rascals (TV)	5	10	15	30	48	65
1175-M.G.M.'s Mouse Musketeers (3-5/61)	4	8	12	24	37	50
1176-Dondi (Movie)-Origin; photo-c	5	10	15	35	55	75
1177-Chilly Willy (Lantz) (4-6/61)	5	10	15	30	48	65
1178-Ten Who Dared (Disney-Movie) (12/60)-Painted-c; cast member photo on back-c	7	14	21	48	79	110
1179-The Swamp Fox (TV) (Disney)-Leslie Nielsen photo-c	8	16	24	55	93	130
1180-The Danny Thomas Show (TV)-Toth-a; photo-c	13	26	39	88	189	290
1181-Texas John Slaughter (TV) (Walt Disney Presents...) (4-6/61)-Photo-c	6	12	18	39	62	85
1182-Donald Duck Album (Disney) (5-7/61)	5	10	15	32	51	70
1183-101 Dalmatians (Disney-Movie) (3/61)	10	20	30	65	118	170
1184-Gyro Gearloose; All Barks-c/a (Disney) (5-7/61) Two variations exist	10	20	30	64	115	165
1185-Sweetie Pie	5	10	15	30	48	65
1186-Yak Yak (#1) by Jack Davis (2 versions - one minus 3-pg. Davis-c/a)	8	16	24	56	96	135
1187-The Three Stooges (6-8/61)-Photo-c	11	22	33	77	154	230
1188-Atlantis, the Lost Continent (Movie) (5/61)-Photo-c	10	20	30	65	118	170
1189-Greyfriars Bobby (Disney-Movie) (11/61)-Photo-c (scarce)	7	14	21	46	76	105
1190-Donald and the Wheel (Disney-Movie) (11/61); Barks-c	8	16	24	53	89	125
1191-Leave It to Beaver (TV)-Photo-c	12	24	36	81	166	250
1192-Ricky Nelson (TV)-Manning-a; photo-c	12	24	36	84	175	265
1193-The Real McCoys (TV) (6-8/61)-Photo-c	8	16	24	55	93	130
1194-Pepe (Movie) (4/61)-Photo-c	4	8	12	24	37	50
1195-National Velvet (#1) (TV)-Photo-c	7	14	21	48	79	110
1196-Pixie and Dixie and Mr. Jinks (TV) (Hanna-Barbera) (7-9/61)	6	12	18	37	59	80
1197-The Aquanauts (TV) (5-7/61)-Photo-c	7	14	21	46	76	105
1198-Donald in Mathmagic Land (Disney-Movie)-Reprint of #1051	6	12	18	42	69	95
1199-The Absent-Minded Professor (Disney-Movie) (4/61)-Photo-c	8	16	24	55	93	130
1200-Hennessey (TV) (8-10/61)-Gil Kane-a; photo-c	7	14	21	46	76	105
1201-Goofy (Disney) (8-10/61)	5	10	15	32	51	70
1202-Rawhide (TV)-Clint Eastwood photo-c	12	24	36	84	177	270
1203-Pinocchio (Disney) (3/62)	5	10	15	35	55	75
1204-Scamp (Disney)	4	8	12	28	44	60
1205-David and Goliath (Movie) (7/61)-Photo-c	6	12	18	42	69	95
1206-Lolly and Pepper (9-11/61)	4	8	12	22	34	45
1207-The Rebel (TV)-Sekowsky-a; photo-c	8	16	24	55	93	130
1208-Rocky and His Friends (Jay Ward) (TV)	16	32	48	109	237	365
1209-Sugarfoot (TV)-Photo-c (10-12/61)	8	16	24	56	96	135
1210-The Parent Trap (Disney-Movie) (8/61)-Hayley Mills photo-c	9	18	27	58	99	140
1211-77 Sunset Strip (TV)-Manning-a; photo-c	8	16	24	53	89	125
1212-Chilly Willy (Lantz) (7-9/61)	5	10	15	30	48	65
1213-Mysterious Island (Movie)-Photo-c	8	16	24	55	93	130
1214-Smokey the Bear	4	8	12	28	44	60
1215-Tales of Wells Fargo (TV) (10-12/61)-Photo-c	8	16	24	51	86	120
1216-Whirlybirds (TV)-Photo-c	8	16	24	51	86	120
1218-Fury (TV)-Photo-c	6	12	18	41	66	90
1219-The Detectives (TV)-Robert Taylor & Adam West photo-c	9	18	27	58	99	140
1220-Gunslinger (TV)-Photo-c	8	16	24	55	93	130
1221-Bonanza (TV) (9-11/61)-Photo-c	15	30	45	102	221	340
1222-Elmer Fudd (9-11/61)	4	8	12	28	44	60
1223-Laramie (TV)-Gil Kane-a; photo-c	6	12	18	42	69	95
1224-The Little Rascals (TV) (10-12/61)	5	10	15	30	48	65
1225-The Deputy (TV)-Henry Fonda photo-c	9	18	27	61	106	150
1226-Nikki, Wild Dog of the North (Disney-Movie) (9/61)-Photo-c	5	10	15	35	55	75
1227-Morgan the Pirate (Movie)-Photo-c	7	14	21	49	82	115
1229-Thief of Baghdad (Movie)-Crandall/Evans-a; photo-c	7	14	21	44	72	100
1230-Voyage to the Bottom of the Sea (#1) (Movie)-Photo insert on-c	10	20	30	67	124	180
1231-Danger Man (TV) (9-11/61)-Patrick McGoohan photo-c	10	20	30	67	124	180
1232-On the Double (Movie)	5	10	15	30	48	65
1233-Tammy Tell Me True (Movie) (1961)	6	12	18	42	69	95
1234-The Phantom Planet (Movie) (1961)	7	14	21	46	76	105
1235-Mister Magoo (#1) (12-2/62)	8	16	24	55	93	130
1235-Mister Magoo (3-5/65) 2nd printing; reprint of 12-2/62 issue	6	12	18	41	66	90
1236-King of Kings (Movie)-Photo-c	7	14	21	49	82	115
1237-The Untouchables (#1) (TV)-Not by Toth; photo-c	17	34	51	116	253	390
1238-Deputy Dawg (TV)	10	20	30	69	130	190
1239-Donald Duck Album (Disney) (10-12/61)-Barks-c	7	14	21	44	72	100
1240-The Detectives (TV)-Tufts-a; Robert Taylor photo-c	8	16	24	55	93	130
1241-Sweetie Pie	4	8	12	24	37	50
1242-King Leonardo and His Short Subjects (#1) (TV) (11-1/62)	11	22	33	74	145	215
1243-Ellery Queen	8	16	24	55	93	130
1244-Space Mouse (Lantz) (11-1/62)	4	8	12	28	44	60

Four Color Comics #1268 © DIS

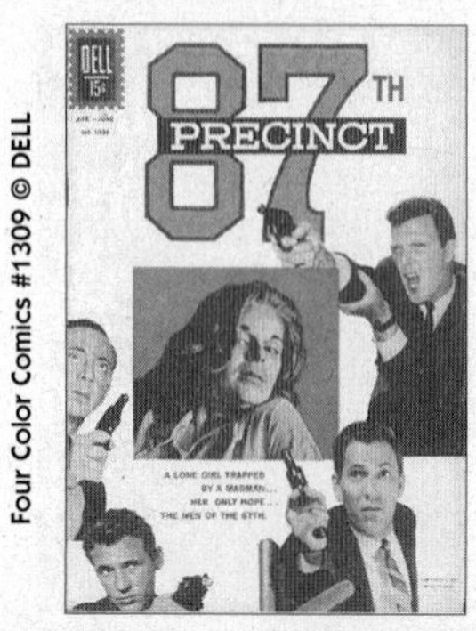

Four Color Comics #1309 © DELL

Four Favorites #14 © ACE

	GD 2.0	VG 4.0	FN 6.0	VF 8.0	VF/NM 9.0	NM- 9.2
1245-New Adventures of Sherlock Holmes	11	22	33	77	154	230
1246-Mickey Mouse Album (Disney)	5	10	15	35	55	75
1247-Daisy Duck's Diary (Disney) (12-2/62)	5	10	15	32	51	70
1248-Pluto (Disney)	4	8	12	28	44	60
1249-The Danny Thomas Show (TV)-Manning-a; photo-c	12	24	36	84	175	265
1250-The Four Horsemen of the Apocalypse (Movie)-Photo-c	6	12	18	42	69	95
1251-Everything's Ducky (Movie) (1961)	5	10	15	30	48	65
1252-The Andy Griffith Show (TV)-Photo-c; 1st show aired 10/3/60	33	66	99	239	512	785
1253-Space Man (#1) (1-3/62)	7	14	21	48	79	110
1254- "Diver Dan" (#1) (TV) (2-4/62)-Photo-c	5	10	15	35	55	75
1255-The Wonders of Aladdin (Movie) (1961)	6	12	18	42	69	95
1256-Kona, Monarch of Monster Isle (#1) (2-4/62)-Glanzman-a	9	18	27	63	112	160
1257-Car 54, Where Are You? (#1) (TV) (3-5/62)-Photo-c	8	16	24	55	93	130
1258-The Frogmen (#1)-Evans-a	8	16	24	51	86	120
1259-El Cid (Movie) (1961)-Photo-c	7	14	21	46	76	105
1260-The Horsemasters (TV, Movie) (Disney) (12-2/62)-Annette Funicello photo-c	11	22	33	76	151	225
1261-Rawhide (TV)-Clint Eastwood photo-c	12	24	36	84	177	270
1262-The Rebel (TV)-Photo-c	8	16	24	55	93	130
1263-77 Sunset Strip (TV) (12-2/62)-Manning-a; photo-c	8	16	24	53	89	125
1264-Pixie and Dixie and Mr. Jinks (TV) (Hanna-Barbera)	6	12	18	37	59	80
1265-The Real McCoys (TV)-Photo-c	8	16	24	55	93	130
1266-M.G.M.'s Spike and Tyke (12-2/62)	4	8	12	24	37	50
1267-Gyro Gearloose; Barks-c/a, 4 pgs. (Disney) (12-2/62)	8	16	24	53	89	125
1268-Oswald the Rabbit (Lantz)	4	8	12	28	44	60
1269-Rawhide (TV)-Clint Eastwood photo-c	12	24	36	84	177	270
1270-Bullwinkle and Rocky (#1) (TV) (Jay Ward) (3-5/62)	16	32	48	111	243	375
1271-Yogi Bear Birthday Party (TV) (Hanna-Barbera) (11/61) (Given away for 1 box top from Kellogg's Corn Flakes)	6	12	18	37	59	80
1272-Frosty the Snowman	5	10	15	32	51	70
1273-Hans Brinker (Disney-Movie)-Photo-c (2/62)	6	12	18	42	69	95
1274-Santa Claus Funnies (12/61)	6	12	18	41	66	90
1275-Rocky and His Friends (TV) (Jay Ward)	16	32	48	109	237	365
1276-Dondi	4	8	12	22	34	45
1278-King Leonardo and His Short Subjects (TV)	11	22	33	74	145	215
1279-Grandma Duck's Farm Friends (Disney)	5	10	15	32	51	70
1280-Hennesey (TV)-Photo-c	6	12	18	42	69	95
1281-Chilly Willy (Lantz) (4-6/62)	5	10	15	30	48	65
1282-Babes in Toyland (Disney-Movie) (1/62); Annette Funicello photo-c	12	24	36	84	175	265
1283-Bonanza (TV) (2-4/62)-Photo-c	15	30	45	102	221	340
1284-Laramie (TV)-Heath-a; photo-c	6	12	18	42	69	95
1285-Leave It to Beaver (TV)-Photo-c	12	24	36	81	166	250
1286-The Untouchables (TV)-Photo-c	12	24	36	84	175	265
1287-Man from Wells Fargo (TV)-Photo-c	6	12	18	37	59	80
1288-Twilight Zone (TV) (4/62)-Crandall/Evans-c/a	11	22	33	76	151	225
1289-Ellery Queen	8	16	24	55	93	130
1290-M.G.M.'s Mouse Musketeers	4	8	12	24	37	50
1291-77 Sunset Strip (TV)-Manning-a; photo-c	8	16	24	53	89	125
1293-Elmer Fudd (3-5/62)	4	8	12	28	44	60
1294-Ripcord (TV)	7	14	21	46	76	105
1295-Mister Ed, the Talking Horse (#1) (TV) (3-5/62)-Photo-c	11	22	33	76	151	225
1296-Fury (TV) (3-5/62)-Photo-c	6	12	18	41	66	90
1297-Spanky, Alfalfa and the Little Rascals (TV)	5	10	15	30	48	65
1298-The Hathaways (TV)-Photo-c	5	10	15	30	48	65
1299-Deputy Dawg (TV)	10	20	30	69	130	190
1300-The Comancheros (Movie) (1961)-John Wayne photo-c	13	26	39	86	183	280
1301-Adventures in Paradise (TV) (2-4/62)	6	12	18	39	62	85
1302-Johnny Jason, Teen Reporter (2-4/62)	4	8	12	24	37	50
1303-Lad: A Dog (Movie)-Photo-c	4	8	12	28	44	60
1304-Nellie the Nurse (3-5/62)-Stanley-a	7	14	21	46	76	105
1305-Mister Magoo (3-5/62)	8	16	24	55	93	130
1306-Target: The Corruptors (#1) (TV) (3-5/62)-Photo-c	6	12	18	37	59	80
1307-Margie (TV) (3-5/62)	6	12	18	37	59	80
1308-Tales of the Wizard of Oz (TV) (3-5/62)	11	22	33	71	136	200
1309-87th Precinct (#1) (TV) (4-6/62)-Krigstein-a; photo-c	9	18	27	63	112	160
1310-Huck and Yogi Winter Sports (TV) (Hanna-Barbera) (3/62)	8	16	24	55	93	130
1311-Rocky and His Friends (TV) (Jay Ward)	16	32	48	109	237	365
1312-National Velvet (TV)-Photo-c	4	8	12	28	44	60
1313-Moon Pilot (Disney-Movie)-Photo-c	7	14	21	46	76	105
1328-The Underwater City (Movie) (1961)-Evans-a; photo-c	7	14	21	46	76	105
1329-See Gyro Gearloose #01329-207						
1330-Brain Boy (#1)-Gil Kane-a	11	22	33	71	136	200
1332-Bachelor Father (TV)	7	14	21	49	82	115
1333-Short Ribs (4-6/62)	5	10	15	35	55	75
1335-Aggie Mack (4-6/62)	5	10	15	30	48	65
1336-On Stage; not by Leonard Starr	5	10	15	30	48	65
1337-Dr. Kildare (#1) (TV) (4-6/62)-Photo-c	8	16	24	56	96	135
1341-The Andy Griffith Show (TV) (4-6/62)-Photo-c	31	62	93	225	480	735
1348-Yak Yak (#2)-Jack Davis-c/a	8	16	24	51	86	120
1349-Yogi Bear Visits the U.N. (TV) (Hanna-Barbera) (1/62)-Photo-c	8	16	24	56	96	135
1350-Comanche (Disney-Movie)(1962)-Reprints 4-Color #966 (title change from "Tonka" to "Comanche") (4-6/62)-Sal Mineo photo-c	5	10	15	35	55	75
1354-Calvin & the Colonel (#1) (TV) (4-6/62)	8	16	24	55	93	130

NOTE: *Missing numbers probably do not exist.*

4-D MONKEY, THE (Adventures of... #? on)
Leung's Publications: 1988 - No. 11, 1990 ($1.80/$2.00, 52 pgs.)

1-11: 1-Karate Pig, Ninja Flounder & 4-D Monkey (48 pgs., centerfold is a Christmas card). 2-4 (52 pgs.) 4.00

FOUR FAVORITES (Crime Must Pay the Penalty No. 33 on)
Ace Magazines: Sept, 1941 - No. 32, Dec, 1947

	GD 2.0	VG 4.0	FN 6.0	VF 8.0	VF/NM 9.0	NM- 9.2
1-Vulcan, Lash Lightning (formerly Flash Lightning in Sure-Fire), Magno the Magnetic Man & The Raven begin; flag/Hitler-c	194	388	582	1242	2121	3000
2-The Black Ace only app.	68	136	204	435	743	1050
3-Last Vulcan	54	108	162	343	574	825
4,5: 4-The Raven & Vulcan end; Unknown Soldier begins (see Our Flag), ends #28. 5-Captain Courageous begins (5/42), ends #28 (moves over from Captain Courageous #6); not in #6	48	96	144	302	514	725
6-8: 6-The Flag app.; Mr. Risk begins (7/42)	45	90	135	284	480	675
9-Kurtzman-a (Lash Lightning); robot-c	50	100	150	315	533	750
10-Classic Kurtzman-c/a (Magno & Davey)	63	126	189	403	689	975
11-Kurtzman-a; Hitler, Mussolini, Hirohito-c; L.B. Cole-a; Unknown Soldier by Kurtzman	107	214	321	680	1165	1650
12-L.B. Cole-a	41	82	123	256	428	600
13-L.B. Cole-c (his first cover?)	71	142	213	454	777	1100
14-20: 18,20-Palais-c/a	39	78	117	231	378	525
21-No Unknown Soldier; The Unknown app.	27	54	81	160	263	365
22-26: 22-Captain Courageous drops costume. 23-Unknown Soldier drops costume. 25-29-Hap Hazard app. 26-Last Magno	27	54	81	160	263	365
27-29: Hap Hazard app. in all	21	42	63	126	206	285
30-32: 30-Funny-c begin (teen humor), end #32	15	30	45	85	130	175

NOTE: ***Dave Berg** c-5. **Jim Mooney** a-6; c-1-3. **Palais** a-18-20; c-18-25. Torture chamber c-5.*

FOUR HORSEMEN, THE (See The Crusaders)

FOUR HORSEMEN
DC Comics (Vertigo): Feb, 2000 - No. 4, May, 2000 ($2.50, limited series)

1-4-Essad Ribic-c/a; Robert Rodi-s 3.00

FOUR HORSEMEN OF THE APOCALYPSE, THE (Movie)
Dell Publishing Co.: No. 1250, Jan-Mar, 1962 (one-shot)

	GD 2.0	VG 4.0	FN 6.0	VF 8.0	VF/NM 9.0	NM- 9.2
Four Color 1250-Photo-c	6	12	18	42	69	95

4MOST (Foremost Boys No. 32-40; becomes Thrilling Crime Cases #41 on)
Novelty Publications/Star Publications No. 37-on:
Winter, 1941-42 - V8#5(#36), 9-10/49; #37, 11-12/49 - #40, 4-5/50

	GD 2.0	VG 4.0	FN 6.0	VF 8.0	VF/NM 9.0	NM- 9.2
V1#1-The Target by Sid Greene, The Cadet & Dick Cole begin with origins retold; produced by Funnies Inc.; quarterly issues begin, end V6#3; German WWII-c	152	304	456	965	1658	2350
2-Last Target (Spr/42); WWII cover	63	126	189	403	689	975
3-Dan'l Flannel begins; flag-c	47	94	141	296	498	700
4-1pg. Dr. Seuss (signed) (Aut/42); fish in the face-c						

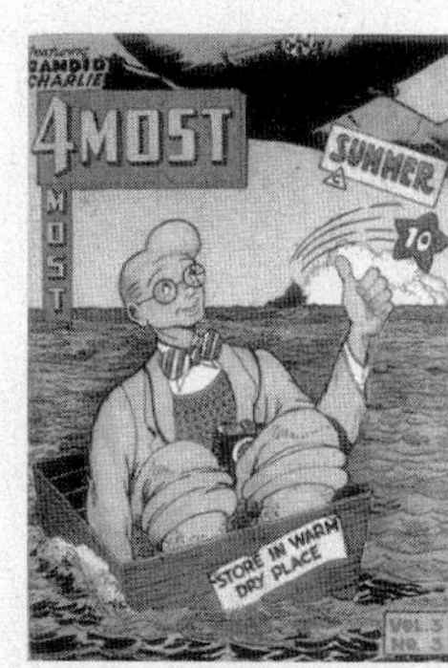

4Most V3 #3 © Prem. Serv.

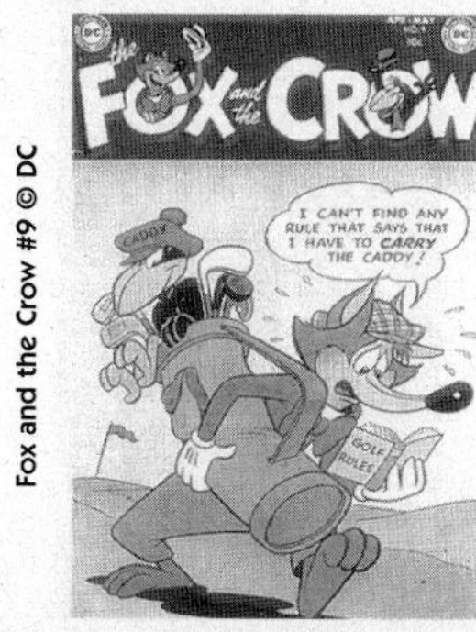

Fox and the Crow #9 © DC

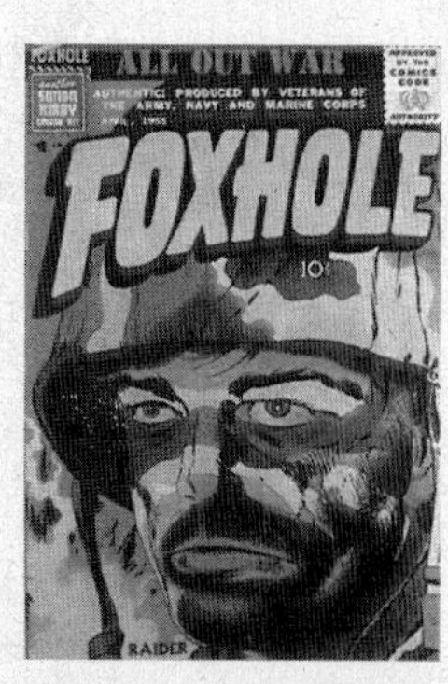

Foxhole #4 © Mainline

	GD 2.0	VG 4.0	FN 6.0	VF 8.0	VF/NM 9.0	NM- 9.2
	49	98	147	309	522	735
V2#1-3	20	40	60	114	182	250
4-Hitler, Tojo & Mussolini app. as pumpkins on-c	45	90	135	284	480	675
V3#1-4	15	30	45	88	137	185
V4#1-4: 2-Walter Johnson-c	13	26	39	74	105	135
V5#1-4: 1-The Target & Targeteers app.	11	22	33	64	90	115
V6#1-4	10	20	30	56	76	95
5-L. B. Cole-c	20	40	60	114	182	250
V7#1,3,5, V8#1, 37	10	20	30	56	76	95
2,4,6-L. B. Cole-c. 6-Last Dick Cole	20	40	60	114	182	250
V8#2,3,5-L. B. Cole-c/a	22	44	66	132	216	300
4-L. B. Cole-a	15	30	45	83	124	165
38-40: 38-Johnny Weismuller (Tarzan) life story & Jim Braddock (boxer) life story. 38-40-L.B. Cole-c. 40-Last White Rider	17	34	51	98	154	210
Accepted Reprint 38-40 (nd): 40-r/Johnny Weismuller life story; all have L.B. Cole-c	10	20	30	56	76	95

411
Marvel Comics: June, 2003 - No. 3 ($3.50, limited series)

1,2-Tributes to peacemakers; s/a by various. 1-Millar, Quitely, Mack, Winslade & others-s/a. 2-Harris, Phillips, Manco, Bruce Jones. 3.50

FOUR-STAR BATTLE TALES
National Periodical Publications: Feb-Mar, 1973 - No. 5, Nov-Dec, 1973

1-Reprints begin	3	6	9	17	25	32
2-5	2	4	6	11	16	20

NOTE: ***Drucker** r-1, 3-5. **Heath** r-2, 5; c-1. **Krigstein** r-5. **Kubert** r-4; c-2.*

FOUR STAR SPECTACULAR
National Periodical Publications: Mar-Apr, 1976 - No. 6, Jan-Feb, 1977

1-Includes G.A. Flash story with new art	2	4	6	11	16	20
2-6: Reprints in all. 2-Infinity cover	2	4	6	8	10	12

NOTE: *All contain DC Superhero reprints. #1 has 68 pgs.; #2-6, 52 pgs.. #1, 4-Hawkman app.; #2-Kid Flash app.; #3-Green Lantern app; #2, 4, 5-Wonder Woman, Superboy app; #5-Green Arrow, Vigilante app; #6-Blackhawk G.A.-r.*

FOUR TEENERS (Formerly Crime Must Pay The Penalty; Dotty No. 35 on)
A. A. Wyn: No. 34, April, 1948 (52 pgs.)

34-Teen-age comic; Dotty app.; Curly & Jerry continue from Four Favorites	11	22	33	60	83	105

FOURTH WORLD GALLERY, THE (Jack Kirby's...)
DC Comics: 1996 (9/96) ($3.50, one-shot)

nn-Pin-ups of Jack Kirby's Fourth World characters (New Gods, Forever People & Mister Miracle) by John Byrne, Rick Burchett, Dan Jurgens, Walt Simonson & others 3.50

FOUR WOMEN
DC Comics (Homage): Dec, 2001 - No. 5, Apr, 2002 ($2.95, limited series)

1-5-Sam Kieth-s/a 3.00
TPB (2002, $17.95) r/series; foreward by Kieth 18.00

FOX AND THE CROW (Stanley & His Monster No. 109 on) (See Comic Cavalcade & Real Screen Comics)
National Periodical Publications: Dec-Jan, 1951-52 - No. 108, Feb-Mar, 1968

1	123	246	369	787	1344	1900
2(Scarce)	55	110	165	352	601	850
3-5	37	74	111	222	361	500
6-10	26	52	78	154	252	350
11-20	20	40	60	114	182	250
21-30: 22-Last precode issue (2/55)	15	30	45	83	124	165
31-40	12	24	36	69	97	125
41-60	6	12	18	42	69	95
61-80	5	10	15	34	55	75
81-94: 94-(11/65)-The Brat Finks begin	4	8	12	26	41	55
95-Stanley & His Monster begins (origin & 1st app)	6	12	18	37	59	80
96-99,101-108	3	6	9	20	30	40
100 (10-11/66)	4	8	12	22	34	45

NOTE: *Many later covers by **Mort Drucker.***

FOX AND THE HOUND, THE (Disney)(Movie)
Whitman Publishing Co.: Aug, 1981 - No. 3, Oct, 1981

11292- Golden Press Graphic Novel	2	4	6	8	10	12
1-3-Based on animated movie	1	2	3	5	7	9

FOXFIRE (See The Phoenix Resurrection)
Malibu Comics (Ultraverse): Feb, 1996 - No. 4, May, 1996 ($1.50)

1-4: Sludge, Ultraforce app. 4-Punisher app. 3.00

FOX GIANTS (Also see Giant Comics Edition)
Fox Features Syndicate: 1944 - 1950 (25¢, 132 - 196 pgs.)

	GD 2.0	VG 4.0	FN 6.0	VF 8.0	VF/NM 9.0	NM- 9.2
Album of Crime nn(1949, 132p)	54	108	162	343	574	825
Album of Love nn(1949, 132p)	52	104	156	328	552	775
All Famous Crime Stories nn('49, 132p)	54	108	162	343	574	825
All Good Comics 1(1944, 132p)(R.W. Voigt)-The Bouncer, Purple Tigress, Rick Evans, Puppeteer, Green Mask; Infinity-c	57	114	171	362	619	875
All Great nn(1944, 132p)-Capt. Jack Terry, Rick Evans, Jaguar Man	43	86	129	271	461	650
All Great nn(Chicago Nite Life News)(1945, 132p)-Green Mask, Bouncer, Puppeteer, Rick Evans, Rocket Kelly	43	86	129	271	461	650
All-Great Confessions nn(1949, 132p)	50	100	150	315	533	750
All Great Crime Stories nn('49, 132p)	54	108	162	343	574	825
All Great Jungle Adventures nn('49, 132p)	58	116	174	371	636	900
All Real Confession Magazine 3 (3/49, 132p)	50	100	150	315	533	750
All Real Confession Magazine 4 (4/49, 132p)	50	100	150	315	533	750
All Your Comics 1(1944, 132p)-The Puppeteer, Red Robbins, & Merciless the Sorcerer	43	86	129	271	461	650
Almanac Of Crime nn(1948, 148p)-Phantom Lady	61	122	183	390	670	950
Almanac Of Crime 1(1950, 132p)	54	108	162	338	574	810
Book Of Love nn(1950, 132p)	48	96	144	302	514	725
Burning Romances 1(1949, 132p)	55	110	165	352	601	850
Crimes Incorporated nn(1950, 132p)	50	100	150	315	533	750
Daring Love Stories nn(1950, 132p)	48	96	144	302	514	725
Everybody's Comics 1(1944, 50¢, 196p)-The Green Mask, The Puppeteer, The Bouncer, Rocket Kelly, Rick Evans	52	104	156	328	552	775
Everybody's Comics 1(1946, 196p)-Green Lama, The Puppeteer	41	82	123	260	435	610
Everybody's Comics 1(1946, 196p)-Same as 1945 Ribtickler	34	68	102	199	325	450
Everybody's Comics nn(1947, 132p)-Jo-Jo, Purple Tigress, Cosmo Cat, Bronze Man	43	86	129	271	461	650
Exciting Romance Stories nn(1949, 132p)	52	104	156	328	552	775
Famous Love nn(1950, 132p)-Photo-c	48	96	144	302	514	725
Intimate Confessions nn(1950, 132p)	48	96	144	302	514	725
Journal Of Crime nn(1949, 132p)	54	108	162	343	574	825
Love Problems nn(1949, 132p)	50	100	150	315	533	750
Love Thrills nn(1950, 132p)	48	96	144	302	514	725
March of Crime nn('48, 132p)-Female w/rifle-c	54	108	162	343	574	825
March of Crime nn('49, 132p)-Cop w/pistol-c	52	104	156	328	552	775
March of Crime nn(1949, 132p)-Coffin & man w/machine-gun-c	52	104	156	328	552	775
Revealing Love Stories nn(1950, 132p)	48	96	144	302	514	725
Ribtickler nn(1945, 50¢, 196p)-Chicago Nite Life News; Marvel Mutt, Cosmo Cat, Flash Rabbit, The Nebbs app.	41	82	123	249	417	585
Romantic Thrills nn(1950, 132p)	48	96	144	302	514	725
Secret Love Stories nn(1949, 132p)	52	104	156	328	552	775
Strange Love nn(1950, 132p)-Photo-c	58	116	174	371	636	900
Sweetheart Scandals nn(1950, 132p)	48	96	144	302	514	725
Teen-Age Love nn(1950, 132p)	48	96	144	302	514	725
Throbbing Love nn(1950, 132p)-Photo-c; used in **POP**, pg. 107	61	122	183	390	670	950
Truth About Crime nn(1949, 132p)	54	108	162	343	574	825
Variety Comics 1(1946, 132p)-Blue Beetle, Jungle Jo	45	90	135	284	480	675
Variety Comics nn(1950, 132p)-Jungle Jo, My Secret Affair (w/Harrison/Wood-a), Crimes by Women & My Story	43	86	129	271	461	650
Western Roundup nn('50, 132p)-Hoot Gibson; Cody of the Pony Express app.	41	82	123	249	417	585

NOTE: *Each of the above usually contain four remaindered Fox books minus covers. Since these missing covers often had the first page of the first story, most Giants therefore are incomplete. Approximate values are listed. Books with appearances of Phantom Lady, Rulah, Jo-Jo, etc. could bring more.*

FOXHOLE (Becomes Never Again #8?)
Mainline/Charlton No. 5 on: 9-10/54 - No. 4, 3-4/55; No. 5, 7/55 - No. 7, 3/56

1-Classic Kirby-c	54	108	162	343	574	825
2-Kirby-c/a(2); Kirby scripts based on his war time experiences	39	78	117	231	378	525
3-5-Kirby-c only	24	48	72	142	234	325
6-Kirby-c/a(2)	34	68	102	199	325	450
7	14	28	42	80	115	150
Super Reprints #10,15-17: 10-r/? 15,16-r/United States Marines #5,8. 17-r/Monty Hall #?	2	4	6	11	16	20
11,12,18-r/Foxhole #1,2,3; Kirby-c	3	6	9	17	25	32

NOTE: ***Kirby** a(r)-Super #11, 12. **Powell** a(r)-Super #15, 16. Stories by actual veterans.*

FOXY FAGAN COMICS (Funny Animal)

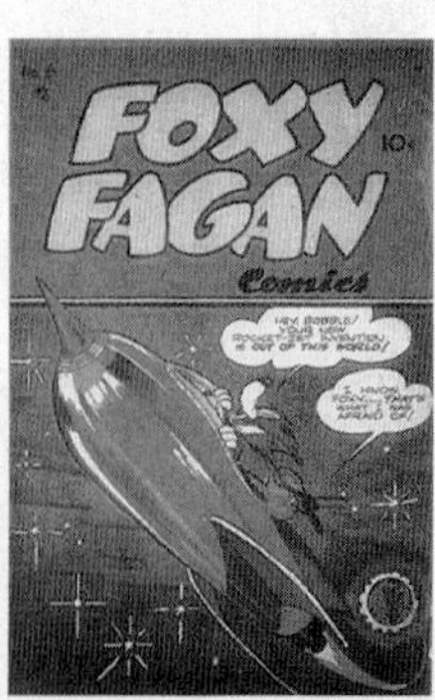

Foxy Fagan Comics #6 © Dearfield

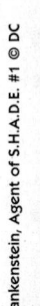

Frankenstein, Agent of S.H.A.D.E. #1 © DC

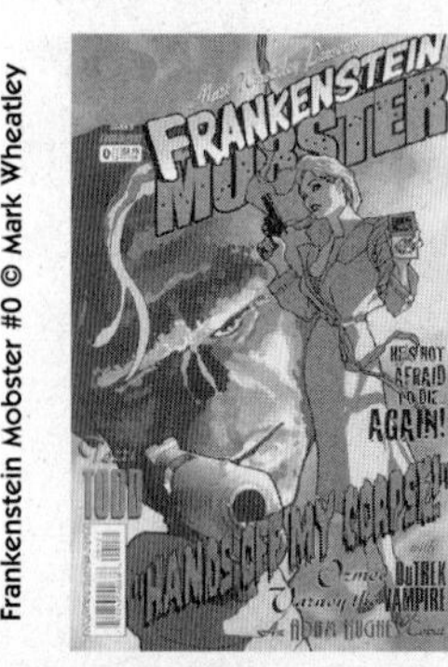

Frankenstein Mobster #0 © Mark Wheatley

GD 2.0 | VG 4.0 | FN 6.0 | VF 8.0 | VF/NM 9.0 | NM- 9.2

Dearfield Publishing Co.: Dec, 1946 - No. 7, Summer, 1948

1-Foxy Fagan & Little Buck begin 13 26 39 72 101 130
2 8 16 24 42 54 65
3-7: 6-Rocket ship-c 7 14 21 37 46 55

FRACTION
DC Comics (Focus): June, 2004 - No. 6, Nov, 2004 ($2.50, limited series)

1-6-David Tischman-s/Timothy Green II-a 3.00
SC (2011, $17.99) r/#1-6; cover gallery 18.00

FRACTURED FAIRY TALES (TV)
Gold Key: Oct, 1962 (Jay Ward)

1 (10022-210)-From Bullwinkle TV show 10 20 30 67 124 180

FRAGGLE ROCK (TV)
Marvel Comics (Star Comics)/Marvel V2#1 on: Apr, 1985 - No. 8, Sept, 1986; V2#1, Apr, 1988 - No. 5, Aug, 1988

1-6 (75¢-c) 5.00
7,8 6.00
V2#1-5-($1.00): Reprints 1st series 3.00

FRANCIS, BROTHER OF THE UNIVERSE
Marvel Comics Group: 1980 (75¢, 52 pgs., one-shot)

nn-John Buscema/Marie Severin-a; story of Francis Bernadone celebrating his 800th birthday in 1982 6.00

FRANCIS THE FAMOUS TALKING MULE (All based on movie)
Dell Publishing Co.: No. 335 (#1), June, 1951 - No. 1090, March, 1960

Four Color 335 (#1) 10 20 30 67 124 180
Four Color 465 6 12 18 41 66 90
Four Color 501,547,579 5 10 15 32 51 70
Four Color 621,655,698,710,745 4 8 12 28 44 60
Four Color 810,863,906,953,991,1068,1090 4 8 12 26 41 55

FRANK
Nemesis Comics (Harvey): Apr (Mar inside), 1994 - No. 4, 1994 ($1.75/$2.50, limited series)

1-4-($2.50, direct sale): 1-Foil-c Edition 3.50
1-4-($1.75)-Newsstand Editions; Cowan-a in all 3.00

FRANK
Fantagraphics Books: Sept, 1996 ($2.95, B&W)

1-Woodring-c/a/scripts 3.00

FRANK BUCK (Formerly My True Love)
Fox Features Syndicate: No. 70, May, 1950 - No. 3, Sept, 1950

70-Wood a(p)(3 stories)-Photo-c 32 64 96 188 307 425
71-Wood-a (9 pgs.); photo/painted-c 18 36 54 105 165 225
3: 3-Photo/painted-c 14 28 42 80 115 150
NOTE: *Based on "Bring 'Em Back Alive" TV show.*

FRANKEN-CASTLE (See The Punisher, 2009 series)

FRANKENSTEIN (See Dracula, Movie Classics & Werewolf)
Dell Publishing Co.: Aug-Oct, 1964; No. 2, Sept, 1966 - No. 4, Mar, 1967

1(12-283-410)(1964)(2nd printing; see Movie Classics for 1st printing)
5 10 15 34 55 75
2-Intro. & origin super-hero character (9/66) 4 8 12 28 44 60
3,4 3 6 9 20 30 40

FRANKENSTEIN (The Monster of...; also see Monsters Unleashed #2, Power Record Comics, Psycho & Silver Surfer #7)
Marvel Comics Group: Jan, 1973 - No. 18, Sept, 1975

1-Ploog-c/a begins, ends #6 8 16 24 53 89 125
2 4 8 12 28 44 60
3-5 4 8 12 22 34 45
6,7,10: 7-Dracula cameo 3 6 9 18 27 35
8,9-Dracula c/sty. 9-Death of Dracula 5 10 15 30 48 65
11-17 3 6 9 16 22 28
18-Wrightson-c(i) 3 6 9 17 25 32
NOTE: ***Adkins** c-17i. **Buscema** a-7-10p. **Ditko** a-12r. **G. Kane** c-15p. **Orlando** a-8r. **Ploog** a-1-3, 4p, 5p, 6; c-1-6. **Wrightson** c-18i.*

FRANKENSTEIN (Mary Wollstonecraft Shelley's...; A Marvel Illustrated Novel)
Marvel Pub.: 1983 ($8.95, B&W, 196 pgs., 8x11" TPB)

nn-Wrightson-a; 4 pg. intro. by Stephen King 5 10 15 32 51 70
Limited HC Edition 175.00

FRANKENSTEIN, AGENT OF S.H.A.D.E. (New DC 52)
DC Comics: Nov, 2011 - Present ($2.99)

1-8-Lemire-s/Ponticelli-a/J.G. Jones-c; Ray Palmer & The Creature Commandos app. 5-Crossover with OMAC #5 3.00

FRANKENSTEIN COMICS (Also See Prize Comics)
Prize Publ. (Crestwood/Feature): Sum, 1945 - V5#5(#33), Oct-Nov, 1954

1-Frankenstein begins by Dick Briefer (origin); Frank Sinatra parody
135 270 405 864 1482 2100
2 60 120 180 381 653 925
3-5 45 90 135 284 480 675
6-10: 7-S&K a(r)/Headline Comics. 8(7-8/47)-Superman satire
39 78 117 240 395 550
11-17(1-2/49)-11-Boris Karloff parody-c/story. 17-Last humor issue
36 72 108 211 343 475
18(3/52)-New origin, horror series begins 47 94 141 296 498 700
19,20(V3#4, 8-9/52) 31 62 93 182 296 410
21(V3#5), 22(V3#6), 23(V4#1) - #28(V4#6) 29 58 87 170 278 385
29(V5#1) - #33(V5#5) 28 56 84 165 270 375
NOTE: ***Briefer** c/a-all. **Meskin** a-21, 29.*

FRANKENSTEIN/DRACULA WAR, THE
Topps Comics: Feb, 1995 - No. 3, May, 1995 ($2.50, limited series)

1-3 3.00

FRANKENSTEIN, JR. (...& the Impossibles) (TV)
Gold Key: Jan, 1966 (Hanna-Barbera)

1-Super hero (scarce) 10 20 30 70 133 195

FRANKENSTEIN MOBSTER
Image Comics: No. 0, Oct, 2003 - No. 7, Dec, 2004 ($2.95)

0-7: 0-Two covers by Wheatley and Hughes; Wheatley-s/a. 1-Variant-c by Wieringo 3.00

FRANKENSTEIN: OR THE MODERN PROMETHEUS
Caliber Press: 1994 ($2.95, one-shot)

1 3.00

FRANK FRAZETTA FANTASY ILLUSTRATED (Magazine)
Quantum Cat Entertainment: Spring 1998 - No. 8 ($5.95, quarterly)

1-Anthology; art by Corben, Horley, Jusko 1 2 3 4 5 7
1-Linsner variant-c 10.00
2-Battle Chasers by Madureira; Harris-a 8.00
2-Madureira Battle Chasers variant-c 12.00
3-8-Frazetta-c 6.00
3-Tony Daniel variant-c 15.00
5,6-Portacio variant-c, 7,8-Alex Nino variant-c 10.00
8-Alex Ross Chicago Comicon variant-c 10.00

FRANK FRAZETTA'S DEATH DEALER
Image Comics: Mar, 2007 - No. 6, Jan, 2008 ($3.99)

1-6-Nat Jones-a; 3 covers (Frazetta, Jones, Jones sketch) 4.00

FRANK FRAZETTA'S...
Fantagraphics Books/Image Comics: one-shots

... Creatures 1 (Image Comics, 7/08, $3.99) Bergting-a; covers by Frazetta & Bergting 4.00
... Dark Kingdom 1-4 (Image, 4/08 - No. 4, 1/10, $3.99) Vigil-a; covers by Frazetta & Vigil 4.00
... Dracula Meets the Wolfman 1 (Image, 8/08, $3.99) Francavilla-a; 2 covers 4.00
... Moon Maid 1 (Image, 1/09, $3.99) Tim Vigil-a; covers by Frazetta & Vigil 4.00
... Neanderthal 1 (Image, 4/09, $3.99) Fotos & Vigil-a; covers by Frazetta & Fotos 4.00
... Sorcerer 1 (Image, 8/09, $3.99) Medors-a; covers by Frazetta & Medors 4.00
... Swamp Demon 1 (Image, 7/08, $3.99) Medors-a; covers by Frazetta & Medors 4.00
... Thun'da Tales 1 (Fantagraphics Books, 1987, $2.00) Frazetta-r 6.00
... Untamed Love 1 (Fantagraphics Books, 11/87, $2.00) r/1950's romance comics 6.00

FRANKIE COMICS (...& Lana No. 13-15) (Formerly Movie Tunes; becomes Frankie Fuddle No. 16 on)
Marvel Comics (MgPC): No. 4, Wint, 1946-47 - No. 15, June, 1949

4-Mitzi, Margie, Daisy app. 17 34 51 98 154 210
5-9 12 24 36 67 94 120
10-15: 13-Anti-Wertham editorial 11 22 33 60 83 105

FRANKIE DOODLE (See Sparkler, both series)
United Features Syndicate: No. 7, 1939

Single Series 7 33 66 99 194 317 440

FRANKIE FUDDLE (Formerly Frankie & Lana)
Marvel Comics: No. 16, Aug, 1949 - No. 17, Nov, 1949

16,17 11 22 33 60 83 105

FRANKLIN RICHARDS (Fantastic Four)
Marvel Comics: April, 2006 - Present ($2.99/$3.99, one-shots)

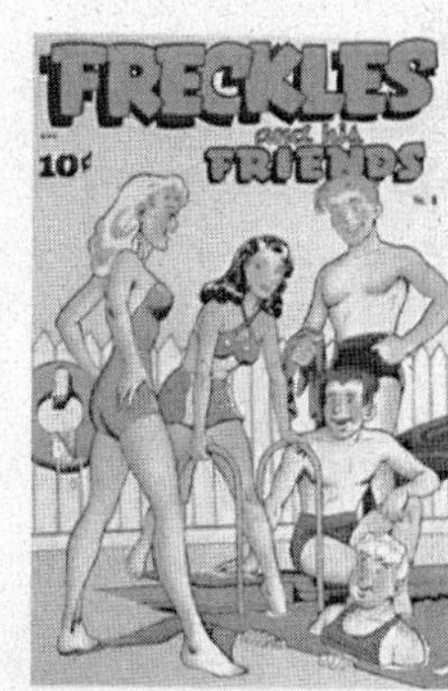

Freckles and His Friends #8 © STD

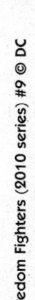

Freedom Fighters (2010 series) #9 © DC

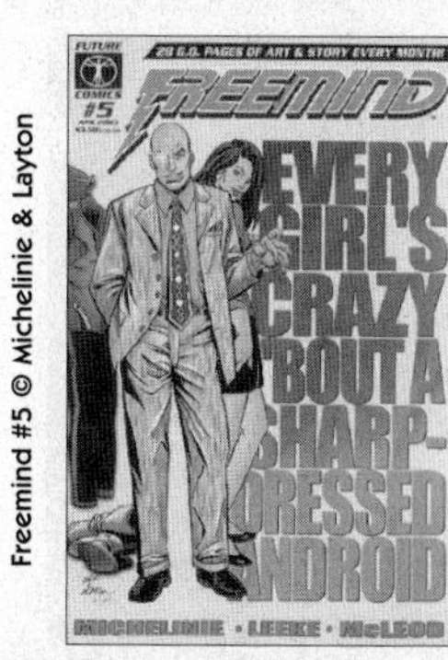

Freemind #5 © Michelinie & Layton

GD VG FN VF VF/NM NM-
2.0 4.0 6.0 8.0 9.0 9.2

...: April Fools (6/09, $3.99) Eliopoulos-s/a 4.00
...: Collected Chaos (2008, $8.99, digest) reprints various one-shots 9.00
...: Fall Football Fiasco (1/08, $2.99) Eliopoulos-a/Sumerak-s 3.00
...: Happy Franksgiving (1/07, $2.99) Thanksgiving stories by Eliopoulos-a/Sumerak-s 3.00
...: It's Dark Reigning Cats & Dogs (4/09, $3.99) Eliopoulos-s/a 4.00
...: Lab Brat (2007, $7.99, digest) reprints one-shots and Masked Marvel back-ups 8.00
...: March Madness (5/07, $2.99) More science gone wrong by Eliopoulos-a/Sumerak-s 3.00
...: Monster Mash (11/07, $2.99) Science mishaps by Eliopoulos-a/Sumerak-s 3.00
...: Not-So-Secret Invasion (7/08, $2.99) Skrull cover; The Wizard app. 3.00
... One Shot (4/06, $2.99) short stories by Eliopoulos-a/Sumerak-s 3.00
...: School's Out (4/09, $3.99) Eliopoulos-s/a; Katie Power app. 4.00
...: Sons of Geniuses (1/09, $3.99) parallel dimension alternate version hijinks 4.00
...: Spring Break (5/08, $2.99) short stories by Eliopoulos-a/Sumerak-s 3.00
...: Summer Smackdown (10/08, $2.99) short stories by Eliopoulos-a/Sumerak-s 3.00
...: Super Summer Spectacular (9/06, $2.99) short stories by Eliopoulos-a/Sumerak-s 3.00
...: World Be Warned (8/07, $2.99) short stories by Eliopoulos-a/Sumerak-s; Hulk app. 3.00

FRANK LUTHER'S SILLY PILLY COMICS (See Jingle Dingle...)
Children's Comics (Maltex Cereal): 1950 (10¢)

1-Characters from radio, records, & TV 9 18 27 47 61 75
NOTE: *Also printed as a promotional comic for Maltex cereal.*

FRANK MERRIWELL AT YALE (Speed Demons No. 5 on?)
Charlton Comics: June, 1955 - No. 4, Jan, 1956 (Also see Shadow Comics)

1 7 14 21 37 46 55
2-4 5 10 15 24 30 35

FRANTIC (Magazine) (See Ratfink & Zany)
Pierce Publishing Co.: Oct, 1958 - V2#2, Apr, 1959 (Satire)

V1#1 13 26 39 74 105 135
2 10 20 30 54 72 90
V2#1,2: 1-Burgos-a, Severin-c/a; Powell-a? 8 16 24 44 57 70

FRAY (Also see Buffy the Vampire Slayer "season eight" #16-19)
Dark Horse Comics: June, 2001 - No. 8, July, 2003 ($2.99, limited series)

1-Joss Whedon-s/Moline & Owens-a 1 2 3 5 6 8
1-DF Gold edition 2 4 6 9 12 15
2-8: 6-(3/02). 7-(4/03) 4.00
TPB (11/03, $19.95) r/#1-8; intros by Whedon & Loeb; Moline sketch pages 20.00

FREAK FORCE (Also see Savage Dragon)
Image Comics (Highbrow Ent.): Dec, 1993 - No. 18, July, 1995 ($1.95/$2.50)

1-18-Superpatriot & Mighty Man in all; Erik Larsen scripts in all. 4-Vanguard app. 8-Begin $2.50-c. 9-Cyberforce-c & app. 13-Variant-c 3.00

FREAK FORCE (Also see Savage Dragon)
Image Comics: Apr, 1997 - No. 3, July, 1997 ($2.95)

1-3-Larsen-s 3.00

FREAK OUT, USA (See On the Scene Presents...)

FREAK SHOW
Image Comics (Desperado): 2006 ($5.99, B&W, one-shot)

nn-Bruce Jones-s/Bernie Wrightson-c/a 6.00

FREAKS OF THE HEARTLAND
Dark Horse Comics: Jan, 2004 - No. 6, Nov, 2004 ($2.99)

1-6-Steve Niles-s/Greg Ruth-a 3.00

FRECKLES AND HIS FRIENDS (See Crackajack Funnies, Famous Comics Cartoon Book, Honeybee Birdwhistle... & Red Ryder)

FRECKLES AND HIS FRIENDS
Standard Comics/Argo: No. 5, 11/47 - No. 12, 8/49; 11/55 - No. 4, 6/56

5-Reprints 9 18 27 50 65 80
6-12-Reprints. 7-9-Airbrush-c (by Schomburg?). 11-Lingerie panels
7 14 21 35 43 50
NOTE: *Some copies of No. 8 & 9 contain a printing oddity. The negatives were elongated in the engraving process, probably to conform to page dimensions on the filler pages. Those pages only look normal when viewed at a 45 degree angle.*
1(Argo,'55)-Reprints (NEA Service) 6 12 18 28 34 40
2-4 4 8 12 18 22 25

FREDDY (Formerly My Little Margie's Boy Friends) (Also see Blue Bird)
Charlton Comics: V2#12, June, 1958 - No. 47, Feb, 1965

V2#12 4 8 12 22 34 45
13-15 3 6 9 16 22 28
16-47 2 4 6 11 16 20

FREDDY

GD VG FN VF VF/NM NM-
2.0 4.0 6.0 8.0 9.0 9.2

Dell Publishing Co.: May-July, 1963 - No. 3, Oct-Dec, 1964

1 3 6 9 19 29 38
2,3 3 6 9 14 20 26

FREDDY KRUEGER'S A NIGHTMARE ON ELM STREET
Marvel Comics: Oct, 1989 - No. 2, Dec, 1989 ($2.25, B&W, movie adaptation, magazine)

1,2: Origin Freddy Krueger; Buckler/Alcala-a 1 2 3 4 5 7

FREDDY'S DEAD: THE FINAL NIGHTMARE
Innovation Publishing: Oct, 1991 - No. 3, Dec 1991 ($2.50, color mini-series, adapts movie)

1-3: Dismukes (film poster artist) painted-c 3.00

FREDDY VS. JASON VS. ASH (Freddy Krueger, Friday the 13th, Army of Darkness)
DC Comics (WildStorm): Early Jan, 2008 - No. 6, May, 2008 ($2.99, limited series)

1-Three covers by J. Scott Campbell; Kuhoric-s/Craig-a 5.00
1-Second printing with 3 covers combined sideways 4.00
2-6: 2-4-Eric Powell-c. 5,6-Richard Friend-c 3.00
2-4-Second printings with B&W covers 3.00
TPB (2008, $17.99) r/#1-6; creators' interview afterword 18.00

FREDDY VS. JASON VS. ASH: THE NIGHTMARE WARRIORS
DC Comics (WildStorm): Aug, 2009 - No. 6, Jan, 2010 ($3.99, limited series)

1-6-Katz & Kuhoric-s/Craig-a. 1-Suydam-c 4.00
TPB (2010, $17.99) r/#1-6; cover gallery 18.00

FRED HEMBECK DESTROYS THE MARVEL UNIVERSE
Marvel Comics: July, 1989 ($1.50, one-shot)

1-Punisher app.; Staton-i (5 pgs.) 3.00

FRED HEMBECK SELLS THE MARVEL UNIVERSE
Marvel Comics: Oct, 1990 ($1.25, one-shot)

1-Punisher, Wolverine parodies; Hembeck/Austin-c 3.00

FREEDOM AGENT (Also see John Steele)
Gold Key: Apr, 1963 (12¢)

1 (10054-304)-Painted-c 4 8 12 26 41 55

FREEDOM FIGHTERS (See Justice League of America #107,108)
National Periodical Publ./DC Comics: Mar-Apr, 1976 - No. 15, July-Aug, 1978

1-Uncle Sam, The Ray, Black Condor, Doll Man, Human Bomb, & Phantom Lady begin (all former Quality characters) 3 6 9 14 19 24
2-9: 4,5-Wonder Woman x-over. 7-1st app. Crusaders 2 4 6 9 12 15
10-15: 10-Origin Doll Man; Cat-Man-c/story (4th app; 1st revival since Detective #325). 11-Origin The Ray. 12-Origin Firebrand. 13-Origin Black Condor. 14-Batgirl & Batwoman app. 15-Batgirl & Batwoman app.; origin Phantom Lady
2 4 6 9 13 16
NOTE: ***Buckler** c-5-11p, 13p, 14p.*

FREEDOM FIGHTERS (Also see "Uncle Sam and the Freedom Fighters")
DC Comics: Nov, 2010 - No. 9, Jul, 2011 ($2.99)

1-9-Travis Moore-a. 1-6-Dave Johnson-c 3.00

FREEDOM FORCE
Image Comics: Jan, 2005 - No. 6, June, 2005 ($2.95)

1-6-Eric Dieter-s/Tom Scioli-a 3.00

FREEMIND
Future Comics: No. 0, Aug, 2002; Nov, 2002 - No. 7, June, 2003 ($3.50)

0-($2.25) Giordano-c 3.00
0-($2.25) Variant-c by Layton 3.00
1-7 ($3.50) 1-Two covers by Giordano & Layton; Giordano-a thru #3. 4,5-Leeke-a 3.50

FREEREALMS
DC Comics (WildStorm): Sept, 2009 - No. 12, Oct, 2010 ($3.99, limited series)

1-12-Based on the online game; Jon Buran-a 4.00
... Book One TPB (2010, $19.99) r/#1-6 20.00
... Book Two TPB (2010, $19.99) r/#7-12 20.00

FREEX
Malibu Comics (Ultraverse): July, 1993 - No. 18, Mar, 1995 ($1.95)

1-3,5-14,16-18: 1-Polybagged w/trading card. 2-Some were polybagged w/card. 6-Nightman-c/story. 7-2 pg. origin Hardcase by Zeck. 17-Rune app. 3.00
1-Holographic-c edition 6.00
1-Ultra 5,000 limited silver ink-c 4.00
4-($2.50, 48 pgs.)-Rune flip-c/story by B. Smith (3 pgs.); 3 pg. Night Man preview 4.00
15 ($3.50)-w/Ultraverse Premiere #9 flip book; Alec Swan & Rafferty app. 4.00
Giant Size 1 (1994, $2.50)-Prime app. 4.00
NOTE: ***Simonson** c-1.*

Freshmen: Summer Vacation Special © TCOW

Friendly Ghost, Casper #155 © Paramount

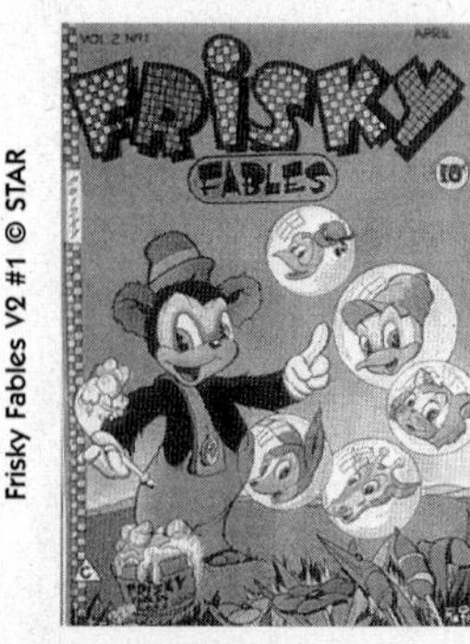

Frisky Fables V2 #1 © STAR

	GD 2.0	VG 4.0	FN 6.0	VF 8.0	VF/NM 9.0	NM- 9.2

FRENEMY OF THE STATE
Oni Press: May, 2010 - No. 5, Dec, 2011 ($3.99)

	GD	VG	FN	VF	VF/NM	NM-
1-5-Rashida Jones, Christina Weir & Nunzio DeFilippis-s						4.00

FRENZY (Magazine) (Satire)
Picture Magazine: Apr, 1958 - No. 6, Mar, 1959

	GD	VG	FN	VF	VF/NM	NM-
1	13	26	39	72	101	130
2-6	8	16	24	44	57	70

FRESHMEN
Image Comics: Jul, 2005 - No. 6, Mar, 2006 ($2.99)

	GD	VG	FN	VF	VF/NM	NM-
1-Sterbakov-s/Kirk-a; co-created by Seth Green; covers by Pérez, Migliari, Linsner						3.00
2-6-Migliari-c						3.00
... Yearbook (1/06, $2.99) profile pages of characters; art by various incl. Chaykin, Kirk						3.00
... Vol. 1 (3/06, $16.99, TPB) r/#1-6 & Yearbook; cover gallery with concept art						17.00

FRESHMEN (Volume 2)
Image Comics: Nov, 2006 - No. 6, Aug, 2007 ($2.99)

	GD	VG	FN	VF	VF/NM	NM-
1-6: 1-Sterbakov-s/Conrad-a; 4 covers						3.00
...: Summer Vacation Special (7/08, $4.99) Sterbakov-s; bonus pin-ups by various						5.00
... Vol. 2 Fundamentals of Fear (6/07, $16.99, TPB) r/#1-6; cover gallery, journals						17.00

FRIDAY FOSTER
Dell Publishing Co.: October, 1972

	GD	VG	FN	VF	VF/NM	NM-
1	4	8	12	24	37	50

FRIDAY THE 13TH (Based on the horror movie franchise)
DC Comics (WildStorm): Feb, 2007 - No. 6, July, 2007 ($2.99, mature)

	GD	VG	FN	VF	VF/NM	NM-
1-6: 1-Two covers by Sook and Bradstreet; Gray & Palmiotti-s						3.00
...: Abuser and The Abused (6/08, $3.50) Fialkov-s/Andy B. -a						3.50
...: Bad Land 1,2 (3/08 - No. 2, 4/08, $2.99) Marz-s/Huddleston-a/McKone-c						3.00
...: How I Spent My Summer Vacation 1,2 (11/07 - No. 2, 12/07, $2.99) Aaron-s/Archer-a						3.00
...: Pamela's Tale 1,2 (9/07 - No. 2, 10/07, $2.99) Andreyko-s/Moll-a/Nguyen-c						3.00

FRIENDLY GHOST, CASPER, THE (Becomes Casper... #254 on)
Harvey Publications: Aug, 1958 - No. 224, Oct, 1982; No. 225, Oct, 1986 - No. 253, June, 1990

	GD	VG	FN	VF	VF/NM	NM-
1-Infinity-c	36	72	108	270	585	900
2	16	32	48	111	243	375
3-10: 6-X-Mas-c	10	20	30	68	127	185
11-20: 18-X-Mas-c	8	16	24	53	89	125
21-30	5	10	15	34	55	75
31-50	4	8	12	24	37	50
51-70,100: 54-X-Mas-c	3	6	9	20	30	40
71-99	3	6	9	16	23	30
101-131: 131-Last 12¢ issue	3	6	9	14	20	26
132-159	2	4	6	11	16	20
160-163: All 52 pg. Giants	3	6	9	14	20	26
164-199: 173,179,185-Cub Scout Specials	2	4	6	8	10	12
200	2	4	6	8	11	14
201-224	1	2	3	5	7	9
225-237: 230-X-mas-c. 232-Valentine's-c						5.00
238-253: 238-Begin $1.00-c. 238,244-Halloween-c. 243-Last new material						4.00

FRIENDLY NEIGHBORHOOD SPIDER-MAN
Marvel Comics: Dec, 2005 - No. 24, Nov, 2007 ($2.99)

	GD	VG	FN	VF	VF/NM	NM-
1-Evolve or Die pt. 1; Peter David-s/Mike Wieringo-a; Morlun app.						4.00
1-Variant Wieringo-c with regular costume						5.00
2-4: 2-New Avengers app. 3-Spider-Man dies						3.00
2-4-var-c: 2-Bag-Head Fantastic Four costume. 3-Captain Universe. 4-Wrestler						5.00
5-10: 6-Red & gold costume. 8-10-Uncle Ben app.						3.00
11-23: 17-Black costume; Sandman app.						3.00
24-($3.99) "One More Day" part 2; Quesada-a; covers by Quesada & Djurdjevic						4.00
Annual 1 (7/07, $3.99) Origin of The Sandman; back-up w/Doran-a						4.00
... Vol. 1: Derailed (2006, $14.99) r/#5-10; Wieringo sketch pages						15.00
... Vol. 2: Mystery Date (2007, $13.99) r/#11-16						14.00

FRIENDS OF MAXX (Also see Maxx)
Image Comics (I Before E): Apr, 1996 - No. 3, Mar, 1997 ($2.95)

	GD	VG	FN	VF	VF/NM	NM-
1-3: Sam Kieth-c/a/scripts. 1-Featuring Dude Japan						3.00

FRIGHT
Atlas/Seaboard Periodicals: June, 1975 (Aug. on inside)

	GD	VG	FN	VF	VF/NM	NM-
1-Origin/1st app. The Son of Dracula; Frank Thorne-c/a	2	4	6	11	16	20

FRIGHT NIGHT
Now Comics: Oct, 1988 - No. 22, 1990 ($1.75)

	GD	VG	FN	VF	VF/NM	NM-
1-22: 1,2 Adapts movie. 8, 9-Evil Ed horror photo-c from movie						3.00

FRIGHT NIGHT II
Now Comics: 1989 ($3.95, 52 pgs.)

	GD	VG	FN	VF	VF/NM	NM-
1-Adapts movie sequel						4.00

FRINGE (Based on the 2008 FOX television series)
DC Comics (WildStorm): Oct, 2008 - No. 6, Aug, 2009 ($2.99, limited series)

	GD	VG	FN	VF	VF/NM	NM-
1-6-Anthology by various. 1-Mandrake & Coleby-a						3.00
TPB (2009, $19.99) r/#1-6; intro. by TV series co-creators Kurtzman & Orci						20.00

FRINGE: TALES FROM THE FRINGE (Based on the 2008 FOX television series)
DC Comics (WildStorm): Aug, 2010 - No. 6, Jan, 2011 ($3.99, limited series)

	GD	VG	FN	VF	VF/NM	NM-
1-6-Anthology by various; LaTorre-c. 1-Reg & photo-c						4.00
2-6-Variant covers from parallel world. 2-Death of Batman. 3-Superman/Dark Knight Returns. 4-Crisis #7 Supergirl holding dead Superman. 5-Justice League #1 w/Jonah Hex. 6-Red Lantern/Red Arrow #76						10.00
TPB (2011, $14.99) r/#1-6 with variant cover gallery and sketch art						15.00

FRISKY ANIMALS (Formerly Frisky Fables; Super Cat #56 on)
Star Publications: No. 44, Jan, 1951 - No. 55, Sept, 1953

	GD	VG	FN	VF	VF/NM	NM-
44-Super Cat; L.B. Cole	20	40	60	114	182	250
45-Classic L. B. Cole-c	28	56	84	165	270	375
46-51,53-55: Super Cat. 54-Super Cat-c begin	19	38	57	109	172	235
52-L. B. Cole-c/a, 3 1/2 pgs.; X-Mas-c	20	40	60	114	182	250

NOTE: *All have **L. B. Cole**-c. No. 47-No Super Cat. **Disbrow** a-49, 52. **Fago** a-51.*

FRISKY ANIMALS ON PARADE (Formerly Parade Comics; becomes Superspook)
Ajax-Farrell Publ. (Four Star Comic Corp.): Sept, 1957 - No. 3, Dec-Jan, 1957-1958

	GD	VG	FN	VF	VF/NM	NM-
1-L. B. Cole-c	17	34	51	98	154	210
2-No L. B. Cole-c	10	20	30	56	76	95
3-L. B. Cole-c	15	30	45	85	130	175

FRISKY FABLES (Frisky Animals No. 44 on)
Premium Group/Novelty Publ./Star Publ. V5#4 on: Spring, 1945 - No. 43, Oct, 1950

	GD	VG	FN	VF	VF/NM	NM-
V1#1-Funny animal; Al Fago-c/a #1-38	22	44	66	132	216	300
2,3(Fall & Winter, 1945)	14	28	42	76	108	140
V2#1(#4, 4/46) - 9,11,12(#15, 3/47): 4-Flag-c	10	20	30	58	79	100
10-Christmas-c. 12-Valentine's-c	11	22	33	60	83	105
V3#1(#16, 4/47) - 12(#27, 3/48): 4-Flag-c. 7,9-Infinity-c. 10-X-Mas-c. 12-Washington crossing the Delaware parody-c	9	18	27	50	65	80
V4#1(#28, 4/48) - 7(#34, 2-3/49)	9	18	27	47	61	75
V5#1(#35, 4-5/49) - 4(#38, 10-11/49)	9	18	27	47	61	75
39-43-L. B. Cole-c; 40-Xmas-c	20	40	60	114	182	250
Accepted Reprint No. 43 (nd); L.B. Cole-c	10	20	30	54	72	90

FRITZI RITZ (See Comics On Parade, Single Series #5, 1(reprint), Tip Top & United Comics)

FRITZI RITZ (United Comics No. 8-26) (Also see Tip Topper for early Peanuts by Schulz)
United Features Synd./St. John No. 37-55/Dell No. 56 on:
1939; Fall, 1948; No. 3, 1949 - No. 7, 1949; No. 27, 3-4/53 - No. 36, 9-10/54; No. 37 - No. 55, 9-11/57; No. 56, 12-2/57-58 - No. 59, 9-11/58

	GD	VG	FN	VF	VF/NM	NM-
Single Series #5 (1939)	34	68	102	199	325	450
nn(1948)-Special Fall issue; by Ernie Bushmiller	18	36	54	105	165	225
3(#1)	13	26	39	74	105	135
4-7(1949): 6-Abbie & Slats app.	10	20	30	54	72	90
27(1953)-33,37-50,57-59-Early Peanuts (1-4 pgs.) by Schulz. 29-Five pg. Abbie & Slats; 1 pg. Mamie by Russell Patterson. 38(9/55)-41(4/56)-Low print run	14	28	42	80	115	150
34-36,51-56: 36-1 pg. Mamie by Patterson	8	16	24	44	57	70

NOTE: *Abbie & Slats in #6,7, 27-31. Li'l Abner in #32-36.*

FROGMAN COMICS
Hillman Periodicals: Jan-Feb, 1952 - No. 11, May, 1953

	GD	VG	FN	VF	VF/NM	NM-
1	15	30	45	90	140	190
2	10	20	30	56	76	95
3,4,6-11: 4-Meskin-a	8	16	24	44	57	70
5-Krigstein-a	9	18	27	50	65	80

FROGMEN, THE
Dell Publishing Co.: No. 1258, Feb-Apr, 1962 - No. 11, Nov-Jan, 1964-65 (Painted-c)

	GD	VG	FN	VF	VF/NM	NM-
Four Color 1258(#1)-Evans-a	8	16	24	51	86	120
2,3-Evans-a; part Frazetta inks in #2,3	6	12	18	37	59	80
4,6-11	4	8	12	24	37	50
5-Toth-a	4	8	12	28	44	60

FROM BEYOND THE UNKNOWN
National Periodical Publications: 10-11/69 - No. 25, 11-12/73

	GD	VG	FN	VF	VF/NM	NM-
1	6	12	18	37	59	80

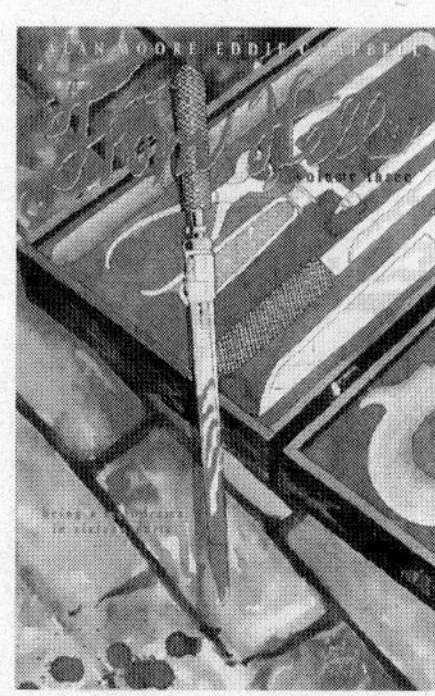
From Hell #3 © Moore & Campbell

Frontier Fighters #4 © DC

F-Troop #7 © WB

	GD 2.0	VG 4.0	FN 6.0	VF 8.0	VF/NM 9.0	NM- 9.2
2-6	3	6	9	20	30	40
7-11: (64 pgs.) 7-Intro Col. Glenn Merrit	4	8	12	22	34	45
12-17: (52 pgs.) 13-Wood-a(i)(r). 17-Pres. Nixon-c	3	6	9	18	27	35
18-25: Star Rovers-r begin #18,19. Space Museum in #23-25	2	4	6	13	18	22

NOTE: ***N. Adams** c-3, 6, 8, 9. **Anderson** c-2, 4, 5, 10, 11i, 15-17, 22; reprints-3, 4, 6-8, 10, 11, 13-16, 24, 25. **Infantino** r-1-5, 7-19, 23-25; c-11p. **Kaluta** c-18, 19. **Gil Kane** a-9r. **Kubert** c-1, 7, 12-14. **Toth** a-2r. **Wood** a-13i. Photo c-22.*

FROM DUSK TILL DAWN (Movie)
Big Entertainment: 1996 ($4.95, one-shot)

	GD 2.0	VG 4.0	FN 6.0	VF 8.0	VF/NM 9.0	NM- 9.2
nn-Adaptation of the film; Brereton-c						5.00
nn-($9.95)Deluxe Ed. w/ new material						10.00

FROM HELL
Mad Love/Tundra Publishing/Kitchen Sink: 1991 - No. 11, Sept, 1998 (B&W)

	GD 2.0	VG 4.0	FN 6.0	VF 8.0	VF/NM 9.0	NM- 9.2
1-Alan Moore and Eddie Campbell's Jack The Ripper story collected from the Taboo anthology series	2	4	6	11	16	20
1-(2nd printing)	2	4	6	8	10	12
1-(3rd printing)	1	2	3	4	5	7
2	1	2	3	5	6	8
2-(2nd printing)						6.00
2-(3rd printing)						4.00
3-1st Kitchen Sink Press issue	1	2	3	5	6	8
3-(2nd printing)						5.00
4-10: 10-(8/96)	1	2	3	4	5	7
11-Dance of the Gull Catchers (9/98, $4.95) Epilogue	2	4	6	9	12	15
Tundra Publishing reprintings 1-5 ('92)	1	2	3	4	5	7
HC						125.00
HC Ltd. Edition of 1,000 (signed and numbered)						225.00
TPB-1st printing (11/99)						60.00
TPB-2nd printing (3/00)						50.00
TPB-3rd printing (11/00)						40.00
TPB-4th printing (7/01) Regular and movie covers						35.00
TPB-5th printing - Regular and movie covers						35.00

FROM HERE TO INSANITY (Satire) (Formerly Eh! #1-7) (See Frantic & Frenzy)
Charlton Comics: No. 8, Feb, 1955 - V3#1, 1956

	GD 2.0	VG 4.0	FN 6.0	VF 8.0	VF/NM 9.0	NM- 9.2
8	19	38	57	111	176	240
9	17	34	51	100	158	215
10-Ditko-c/a (3 pgs.)	27	54	81	158	259	360
11,12-All Kirby except 4 pgs.	36	72	108	216	351	485
V3#1(1956)-Ward-c/a(2) (signed McCartney); 5 pgs. Wolverton-a; 3 pgs. Ditko-a; magazine format (cover says "Crazy, Man, Crazy" and becomes Crazy, Man, Crazy with V2#2)	42	84	126	265	445	625

FROM THE PIT
Fantagor Press: 1994 ($4.95, one-shot, mature)

	GD 2.0	VG 4.0	FN 6.0	VF 8.0	VF/NM 9.0	NM- 9.2
1-R. Corben-a; HP Lovecraft back-up story	1	2	3	5	6	8

FRONTIER DOCTOR (TV)
Dell Publishing Co.: No. 877, Feb, 1958 (one-shot)

	GD 2.0	VG 4.0	FN 6.0	VF 8.0	VF/NM 9.0	NM- 9.2
Four Color 877-Toth-a, Rex Allen photo-c	9	18	27	61	106	150

FRONTIER FIGHTERS
National Periodical Publications: Sept-Oct, 1955 - No. 8, Nov-Dec, 1956

	GD 2.0	VG 4.0	FN 6.0	VF 8.0	VF/NM 9.0	NM- 9.2
1-Davy Crockett, Buffalo Bill (by Kubert), Kit Carson begin (Scarce)	55	110	165	352	601	850
2	37	74	111	222	361	500
3-8	34	68	102	199	325	450

NOTE: *Buffalo Bill by **Kubert** in all.*

FRONTIER ROMANCES
Avon Periodicals/I. W.: Nov-Dec, 1949 - No. 2, Feb-Mar, 1950 (Painted-c)

	GD 2.0	VG 4.0	FN 6.0	VF 8.0	VF/NM 9.0	NM- 9.2
1-Used in **SOTI**, pg. 180 (General reference) & illo. "Erotic spanking in a western comic book"	52	104	156	327	556	785
2 (Scarce)-Woodish-a by Stallman	39	78	117	231	378	525
I.W. Reprint #1-Reprints Avon's #1	4	8	12	22	34	45
I.W. Reprint #9-Reprints ?	3	6	9	16	22	28

FRONTIER SCOUT: DAN'L BOONE (Formerly Death Valley; The Masked Raider No. 14 on)
Charlton Comics: No. 10, Jan, 1956 - No. 13, Aug, 1956; V2#14, Mar, 1965

	GD 2.0	VG 4.0	FN 6.0	VF 8.0	VF/NM 9.0	NM- 9.2
10	10	20	30	54	72	90
11-13(1956)	6	12	18	31	38	45
V2#14(3/65)	5	10	14	20	24	28

FRONTIER TRAIL (The Rider No. 1-5)
Ajax/Farrell Publ.: No. 6, May, 1958

	GD 2.0	VG 4.0	FN 6.0	VF 8.0	VF/NM 9.0	NM- 9.2
6	6	12	18	28	34	40

FRONTIER WESTERN
Atlas Comics (PrPI): Feb, 1956 - No. 10, Aug, 1957

	GD 2.0	VG 4.0	FN 6.0	VF 8.0	VF/NM 9.0	NM- 9.2
1	19	38	57	111	176	240
2,3,6-Williamson-a, 4 pgs. each	14	28	42	80	115	150
4,7,9,10: 10-Check-a	10	20	30	56	76	95
5-Crandall, Baker, Davis-a; Williamson text illos	14	28	42	76	108	140
8-Crandall, Morrow, & Wildey-a	10	20	30	58	79	100

NOTE: ***Baker** a-9. **Colan** a-2, 6. **Drucker** a-3, 4. **Heath** c-5. **Maneely** c/a-2, 7, 9. **Maurera** a-2. **Romita** a-7. **Severin** c-6, 8, 10. **Tuska** a-2. **Wildey** a-5, 8. Ringo Kid in No. 4.*

FRONTLINE COMBAT
E. C. Comics: July-Aug, 1951 - No. 15, Jan, 1954

	GD 2.0	VG 4.0	FN 6.0	VF 8.0	VF/NM 9.0	NM- 9.2
1-Severin/Kurtzman-a	73	146	219	584	930	1275
2	37	74	111	296	473	650
3	29	58	87	232	366	500
4-Used in **SOTI**, pg. 257; contains "Airburst" by Kurtzman which is his personal all-time favorite story	27	54	81	216	346	475
5-John Severin and Bill Elder bios.	23	46	69	184	292	400
6-10: 6-Kurtzman bio. 9-Civil War issue	20	40	60	160	255	350
11-15: 11-Civil War issue	15	30	45	120	193	265

NOTE: ***Davis** a-in all; c-11, 12. **Evans** a-10-15. **Heath** a-1. **Kubert** a-14. **Kurtzman** a-1-5; c-1-9. **Severin** a-5-7, 9, 13, 15. **Severin/Elder** a-2-11; c-10. **Toth** a-8, 12. **Wood** a-1-4, 6-10, 12-15; c-13-15. Special issues: No. 7 (Iwo Jima), No. 9 (Civil War), No. 12 (Air Force).*

(Canadian reprints known; see Table of Contents.)

FRONTLINE COMBAT
Russ Cochran/Gemstone Publishing: Aug, 1995 - No. 14 ($2.00/$2.50)

	GD 2.0	VG 4.0	FN 6.0	VF 8.0	VF/NM 9.0	NM- 9.2
1-14-E.C. reprints in all						3.00

FRONT PAGE COMIC BOOK
Front Page Comics (Harvey): 1945

	GD 2.0	VG 4.0	FN 6.0	VF 8.0	VF/NM 9.0	NM- 9.2
1-Kubert-a; intro. & 1st app. Man in Black by Powell; Fuje-c	41	82	123	249	417	585

FROST AND FIRE (See DC Science Fiction Graphic Novel)

FROSTY THE SNOWMAN
Dell Publishing Co.: No. 359, Nov, 1951 - No. 1272, Dec-Feb?/1961-62

	GD 2.0	VG 4.0	FN 6.0	VF 8.0	VF/NM 9.0	NM- 9.2
Four Color 359 (#1)	9	18	27	61	106	150
Four Color 435,514,601,661	6	12	18	37	59	80
Four Color 748,861,950,1065,1153,1272	5	10	15	32	51	70

FRUITMAN SPECIAL (See Bunny #2 for 1st app.)
Harvey Publications: Dec, 1969 (68 pgs.)

	GD 2.0	VG 4.0	FN 6.0	VF 8.0	VF/NM 9.0	NM- 9.2
1-Funny super hero	4	8	12	24	37	50

F-TROOP (TV)
Dell Publishing Co.: Aug, 1966 - No. 7, Aug, 1967 (All have photo-c)

	GD 2.0	VG 4.0	FN 6.0	VF 8.0	VF/NM 9.0	NM- 9.2
1	9	18	27	62	109	155
2-7	6	12	18	39	62	85

FUGITIVES FROM JUSTICE
St. John Publishing Co.: Feb, 1952 - No. 5, Oct, 1952

	GD 2.0	VG 4.0	FN 6.0	VF 8.0	VF/NM 9.0	NM- 9.2
1	22	44	66	132	216	300
2-Matt Baker-r/Northwest Mounties #2; Vic Flint strip reprints begin	22	44	66	128	209	290
3-Reprints panel from Authentic Police Cases that was used in **SOTI** with changes; Tuska-a	21	42	63	124	202	280
4	13	26	39	74	105	135
5-Last Vic Flint-r; bondage-c	14	28	42	81	118	155

FUGITOID
Mirage Studios: 1985 (B&W, magazine size, one-shot)

	GD 2.0	VG 4.0	FN 6.0	VF 8.0	VF/NM 9.0	NM- 9.2
1-Ties into Teenage Mutant Ninja Turtles #5	2	3	4	6	8	10

FULL OF FUN
Red Top (Decker Publ.)(Farrell)/I. W. Enterprises: Aug, 1957 - No. 2, Nov, 1957; 1964

	GD 2.0	VG 4.0	FN 6.0	VF 8.0	VF/NM 9.0	NM- 9.2
1(1957)-Funny animal; Dave Berg-a	7	14	21	37	46	55
2-Reprints Bingo, the Monkey Doodle Boy	5	10	15	22	26	30
8-I.W. Reprint('64)	2	4	6	9	12	15

FUN AT CHRISTMAS (See March of Comics No. 138)

FUN CLUB COMICS (See Interstate Theatres...)

FUN COMICS (Formerly Holiday Comics #1-8; Mighty Bear #13 on)
Star Publications: No. 9, Jan, 1953 - No. 12, Oct, 1953

	GD 2.0	VG 4.0	FN 6.0	VF 8.0	VF/NM 9.0	NM- 9.2
9-(25¢ Giant)-L. B. Cole X-Mas-c; X-Mas issue	22	44	66	132	216	300
10-12-L. B. Cole-c. 12-Mighty Bear-c/story	18	36	54	105	165	225

Fun-In #1 © H-B

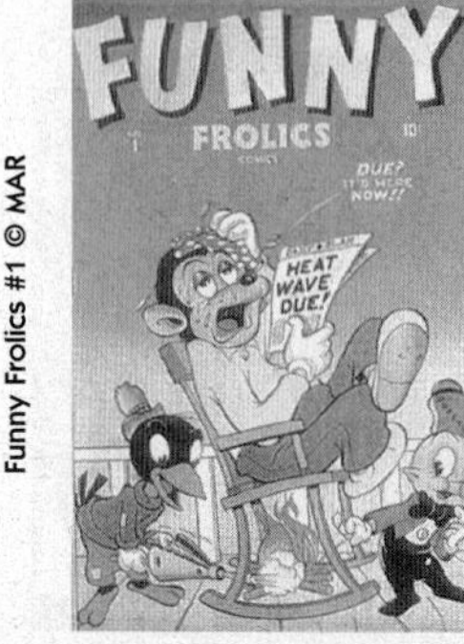

Funny Frolics #1 © MAR

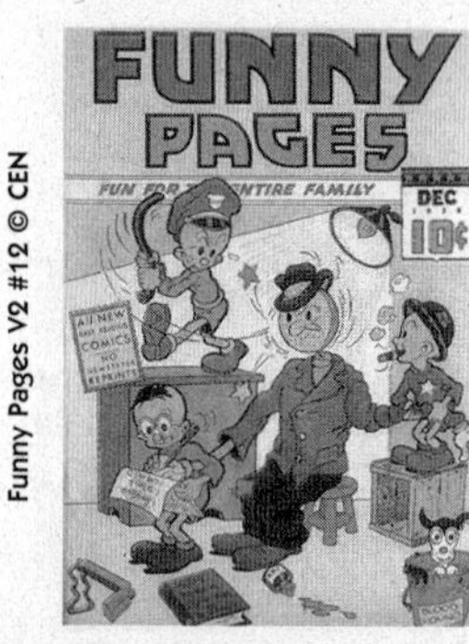

Funny Pages V2 #12 © CEN

FUNDAY FUNNIES (See Famous TV..., and Harvey Hits No. 35,40)

FUN-IN (TV)(Hanna-Barbera)
Gold Key: Feb, 1970 - No. 10, Jan, 1972; No. 11, 4/74 - No. 15, 12/74

	GD 2.0	VG 4.0	FN 6.0	VF 8.0	VF/NM 9.0	NM- 9.2
1-Dastardly & Muttley in Their Flying Machines; Perils of Penelope Pitstop in #1-4; It's the Wolf in all	7	14	21	48	79	110
2-4,6-Cattanooga Cats in 2-4	4	8	12	22	34	45
5,7-Motormouse & Autocat, Dastardly & Muttley in both; It's the Wolf in #7	4	8	12	24	37	50
8,10-The Harlem Globetrotters, Dastardly & Muttley in #10	4	8	12	24	37	50
9-Where's Huddles?, Dastardly & Muttley, Motormouse & Autocat app.	4	8	12	24	37	50
11-Butch Cassidy	3	6	9	20	30	40
12-15: 12,15-Speed Buggy. 13-Hair Bear Bunch. 14-Inch High Private Eye	3	6	9	20	30	40

FUNKY PHANTOM, THE (TV)
Gold Key: Mar, 1972 - No. 13, Mar, 1975 (Hanna-Barbera)

	GD 2.0	VG 4.0	FN 6.0	VF 8.0	VF/NM 9.0	NM- 9.2
1	5	10	15	32	51	75
2-5	3	6	9	18	27	38
6-13	3	6	9	15	21	28

FUNLAND
Ziff-Davis (Approved Comics): No date (1940s) (25¢)

	GD 2.0	VG 4.0	FN 6.0	VF 8.0	VF/NM 9.0	NM- 9.2
nn-Contains games, puzzles, cut-outs, etc.	19	38	57	111	176	240

FUNLAND COMICS
Croyden Publishers: 1945

	GD 2.0	VG 4.0	FN 6.0	VF 8.0	VF/NM 9.0	NM- 9.2
1-Funny animal	15	30	45	88	137	185

FUNNIES, THE (New Funnies No. 65 on)
Dell Publishing Co.: Oct, 1936 - No. 64, May, 1942

	GD 2.0	VG 4.0	FN 6.0	VF 8.0	VF/NM 9.0	NM- 9.2
1-Tailspin Tommy, Mutt & Jeff, Alley Oop (1st app?), Capt. Easy (1st app.), Don Dixon begin	400	800	1200	2300	3650	5000
2 (11/36)-Scribbly by Mayer begins (see Popular Comics #6 for 1st app.)	180	360	540	1035	1643	2250
3	124	248	372	713	1132	1550
4,5: 4(1/37)-Christmas-c	92	184	276	529	840	1150
6-10	70	140	210	403	639	875
11-20: 16-Christmas-c	65	130	195	374	597	820
21-29: 25-Crime Busters by McWilliams(4pgs.)	52	104	156	299	475	650
30-John Carter of Mars (origin/1st app.) begins by Edgar Rice Burroughs; Jim Gary-a Warner Bros.' Bosko-c (4/39)	155	310	465	992	1696	2400
31-34,36-44: 31,32-Gary-a. 33-John Coleman Burroughs art begins on John Carter. 34-Last funny-c	82	164	246	528	902	1275
35-(9/39)-Mr. District Attorney begins; based on radio show; 1st cover app. John Carter of Mars	94	188	282	597	1024	1450
45-Origin/1st app. Phantasmo, the Master of the World (Dell's 1st super-hero, 7/40) & his sidekick Whizzer McGee	94	188	282	597	1024	1450
46-50: 46-The Black Knight begins, ends #62	58	116	174	371	636	900
51-56-Last ERB John Carter of Mars	47	94	141	296	498	700
57-Intro. & origin Captain Midnight (7/41)	354	708	1062	2478	4339	6200
58-60: 58-Captain Midnight-c begin, end #63	87	174	261	553	952	1350
61-Andy Panda begins by Walter Lantz; WWII-c	105	210	315	667	1146	1625
62,63: 63-Last Captain Midnight-c; bondage-c	68	136	204	435	743	1050
64-Format change; Oswald the Rabbit, Felix the Cat, Li'l Eight Ball app.; origin & 1st app. Woody Woodpecker in Oswald; last Capt. Midnight; Oswald, Andy Panda, Li'l Eight Ball-c	155	310	465	992	1696	2400

NOTE: ***Mayer** c-26, 48. **McWilliams** art in many issues on "Rex King of the Deep". Alley Oop c-17, 20. Captain Midnight c-57(i/2), 58-63. John Carter c-35-37, 40. Phantasmo c-45-56, 57(1/2), 58-61(part). Rex King c-38, 39, 42. Tailspin Tommy c-41.*

FUNNIES ANNUAL, THE
Avon Periodicals: 1959 ($1.00, approx. 7x10", B&W; tabloid-size)

	GD 2.0	VG 4.0	FN 6.0	VF 8.0	VF/NM 9.0	NM- 9.2
1-(Rare)-Features the best newspaper comic strips of the year: Archie, Snuffy Smith, Beetle Bailey, Henry, Blondie, Steve Canyon, Buz Sawyer, The Little King, Hi & Lois, Popeye, & others. Also has a chronological history of the comics from 2000 B.C. to 1959.	45	90	135	284	480	675

FUNNIES ON PARADE (See Promotional Comics section)

FUNNY ANIMALS (See Fawcett's Funny Animals)
Charlton Comics: Sept, 1984 - No. 2, Nov, 1984

	GD 2.0	VG 4.0	FN 6.0	VF 8.0	VF/NM 9.0	NM- 9.2
1,2-Atomic Mouse-r; low print						6.00

FUNNYBONE (... The Laugh-Book of Comical Comics)
La Salle Publishing Co.: 1944 (25¢, 132 pgs.)

	GD 2.0	VG 4.0	FN 6.0	VF 8.0	VF/NM 9.0	NM- 9.2
nn	30	60	90	177	289	400

FUNNY BOOK (...Magazine for Young Folks) (Hocus Pocus No. 9)
Parents' Magazine Press (Funny Book Publishing Corp.):
Dec, 1942 - No. 9, Aug-Sept, 1946 (Comics, stories, puzzles, games)

	GD 2.0	VG 4.0	FN 6.0	VF 8.0	VF/NM 9.0	NM- 9.2
1-Funny animal; Alice In Wonderland app.	15	30	45	86	133	180
2-Gulliver in Giant-Land	10	20	30	56	76	95
3-9: 4-Advs. of Robin Hood. 9-Hocus-Pocus strip	9	18	27	47	61	75

FUNNY COMICS
Modern Store Publ.: 1955 (7¢, 5x7", 36 pgs.)

	GD 2.0	VG 4.0	FN 6.0	VF 8.0	VF/NM 9.0	NM- 9.2
1-Funny animal	4	8	12	22	34	45

FUNNY COMIC TUNES (See Funny Tunes)

FUNNY FABLES
Decker Publications (Red Top Comics): Aug, 1957 - V2#2, Nov, 1957

	GD 2.0	VG 4.0	FN 6.0	VF 8.0	VF/NM 9.0	NM- 9.2
V1#1	6	12	18	31	38	45
V1#2,V2#1,2: V1#2 (11/57)-Reissue of V1#1	5	10	14	20	24	28

FUNNY FILMS (Features funny animal characters from films)
American Comics Group(Michel Publ./Titan Publ.): Sept-Oct, 1949 - No. 29, May-June, 1954 (No. 1-4: 52 pgs.)

	GD 2.0	VG 4.0	FN 6.0	VF 8.0	VF/NM 9.0	NM- 9.2
1-Puss An' Boots, Blunderbunny begin	18	36	54	105	165	225
2	11	22	33	62	86	110
3-10: 3-X-Mas-c	9	18	27	47	61	75
11-20	7	14	21	35	43	50
21-29	6	12	18	28	34	40

FUNNY FOLKS
DC Comics: Feb, 1946

nn-Ashcan comic, not distributed to newsstands, only for in house use (no known sales)

FUNNY FOLKS (Hollywood... on cover only No. 16-26; becomes Hollywood Funny Folks No. 27 on)
National Periodical Publ.: April-May, 1946 - No. 26, June-July, 1950 (52 pgs., #15 on)

	GD 2.0	VG 4.0	FN 6.0	VF 8.0	VF/NM 9.0	NM- 9.2
1-Nutsy Squirrel begins (1st app.) by Rube Grossman; Grossman-a in most issues	39	78	117	240	395	550
2	20	40	60	114	182	250
3-5: 4-1st Nutsy Squirrel-c	15	30	45	84	127	170
6-10: 6,9-Nutsy Squirrel-c begin	11	22	33	62	86	110
11-26: 15-Begin 52 pg. issues (8-9/48)	10	20	30	54	72	90

NOTE: ***Sheldon Mayer** a-in some issues. **Post** a-18. Christmas c-12.*

FUNNY FROLICS
Timely/Marvel Comics (SPI): Summer, 1945 - No. 5, Dec, 1946

	GD 2.0	VG 4.0	FN 6.0	VF 8.0	VF/NM 9.0	NM- 9.2
1-Sharpy Fox, Puffy Pig, Krazy Krow	27	54	81	158	259	360
2	15	30	45	86	133	180
3,4	13	26	39	74	105	135
5-Kurtzman-a	14	28	42	80	115	150

FUNNY FUNNIES
Nedor Publishing Co.: April, 1943 (68 pgs.)

	GD 2.0	VG 4.0	FN 6.0	VF 8.0	VF/NM 9.0	NM- 9.2
1-Funny animals; Peter Porker app.	19	38	57	111	176	240

FUNNYMAN (Also see Cisco Kid Comics & Extra Comics)
Magazine Enterprises: Dec, 1947; No. 1, Jan, 1948 - No. 6, Aug, 1948

nn(12/47)-Prepublication B&W undistributed copy by Siegel & Shuster-(5-3/4x8"), 16 pgs.; Sold at auction in 1997 for $575.00

	GD 2.0	VG 4.0	FN 6.0	VF 8.0	VF/NM 9.0	NM- 9.2
1-Siegel & Shuster-a in all; Dick Ayers 1st pro work (as assistant) on 1st few issues	47	94	141	296	498	700
2	28	56	84	165	270	375
3-6	24	48	72	142	234	325

FUNNY MOVIES (See 3-D Funny Movies)

FUNNY PAGES (Formerly The Comics Magazine)
Comics Magazine Co./Ultem Publ.(Chesler)/Centaur Publications:
No. 6, Nov, 1936 - No. 42, Oct, 1940

	GD 2.0	VG 4.0	FN 6.0	VF 8.0	VF/NM 9.0	NM- 9.2
V1#6 (nn, nd)-The Clock begins (2 pgs., 1st app.), ends #11; The Clock is the 1st masked comic book hero	284	568	852	1818	3109	4400
7-11: 11-(6/37)	110	220	330	704	1202	1700
V2#1-V2#3: V2#1 (9/37)(V2#2 on-c; V2#1 in indicia). V2#2 (10/37)(V2#3 on-c; V2#2 in indicia). V2#3(11/37)-5	77	154	231	493	847	1200
6(1st Centaur, 3/38)	100	200	300	635	1093	1550
7-9	77	154	231	493	847	1200
10(Scarce, 9/38)-1st app. of The Arrow by Gustavson (Blue costume)	389	778	1167	2723	4762	6800
11,12	135	270	405	864	1482	2100

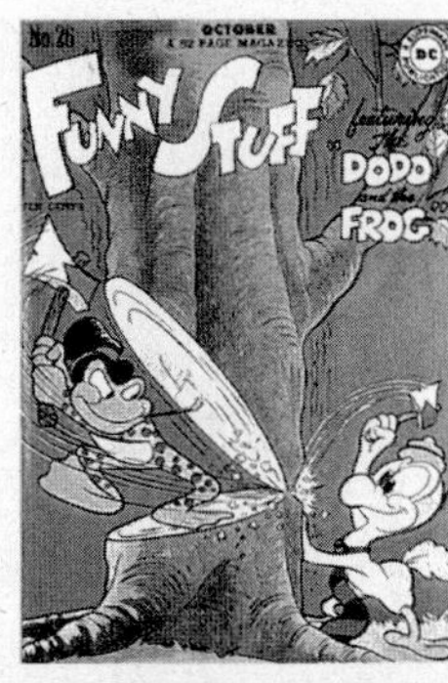

Funny Stuff #26 © DC

Fury / Agent 13 #1 © MAR

Fury of Firestorm: The Nuclear Men #1 © DC

GD VG FN VF VF/NM NM-
2.0 4.0 6.0 8.0 9.0 9.2

V3#1-Bruce Wayne prototype in "Case of the Missing Heir," by Bob Kane, 3 months before app. Batman (See Det. Pic. Stories #5) 148 296 444 947 1624 2300
2-6,8: 6,8-Last funny covers 119 238 357 762 1306 1850
7-1st Arrow-c (9/39) 326 652 978 2282 3991 5700
9-Tarpe Mills jungle-c 135 270 405 864 1482 2100
10-2nd Arrow-c 300 600 900 1950 3375 4800
V4#1(1/40, Arrow-c)-(Rare)-The Owl & The Phantom Rider app.; origin Mantoka, Maker of Magic by Jack Cole. Mad Ming begins, ends #42; Tarpe Mills-a
314 328 942 2198 3849 5500
35-Classic Arrow-c (Scarce) 314 328 942 2198 3849 5500
36-38-Mad Ming-c 135 270 405 864 1482 2100
39-41-Arrow-c 245 490 735 1568 2684 3800
42 (Scarce,10/40)-Last Arrow; Arrow-c 252 504 756 1613 2757 3900

NOTE: ***Biro*** *c-V2#9.* ***Burgos*** *c-V3#10.* ***Jack Cole*** *a-V2#3, 7, 8, 10, 11, V3#2, 6, 9, 10, V4#1, 37; c-V3#2, 4.* ***Eisner*** *a-V1#7, 8?, 10.* ***Ken Ernst*** *a-V1#7, 8.* ***Everett*** *a-V2#11 (illos).* ***Filchock*** *c-V2#10, V3#6.* ***Gill Fox*** *a-V2#11.* ***Sid Greene*** *a-39.* ***Guardineer*** *a-V2#2, 3, 5.* ***Gustavson*** *a-V2#5, 11, 12, V3#1-10, 35, 38-42; c-V3#7, 35, 39-42.* ***Bob Kane*** *a-V3#1.* ***McWilliams*** *a-V2#12, V3#1, 3-6.* ***Tarpe Mills*** *a-V3#8-10, V4#1; c-V3#9.* ***Ed Moore Jr.*** *a-V2#12.* ***Schwab*** *c-V3#1.* ***Bob Wood*** *a-V2#2, 3, 8, 11, V3#6, 9, 10; c-V2#6, 7. Arrow c-V3#7, 10, V4#1, 35, 40-42.*

FUNNY PICTURE STORIES (Comic Pages V3#4 on)
Comics Magazine Co./Centaur Publications: Nov, 1936 - V3#3, May, 1939

V1#1-The Clock begins (c-feature)(see Funny Pages for 1st app.)
377 754 1131 2639 4620 6600
2 142 284 426 909 1555 2200
3-6(4/37): 4-Eisner-a; X-Mas-c. 97 194 291 621 1061 1500
7-(6/37) (Rare) Racial humor-c 206 412 618 1318 2259 3200
V2#1 (9/37; V1#10 on-c; V2#1 in indicia)-Jack Strand begins
63 126 189 403 689 975
2 (10/37; V1#11 on-c; V2#2 in indicia) 63 126 189 403 689 975
3-5,7-11(11/38): 4-Xmas-c 57 114 171 362 619 875
6-(1st Centaur, 3/38) 84 168 252 538 919 1300
V3#1(1/39)-3 55 110 165 352 601 850

NOTE: ***Biro*** *c-V2#1, 8, 9, 11.* ***Guardineer*** *a-V1#11; c-V2#6, V3#5.* ***Bob Wood*** *c/a-V1#11, V2#2; c-V2#3, 5.*

FUNNY STUFF (Becomes The Dodo & the Frog No. 80)
All-American/National Periodical Publications No. 7 on: Summer, 1944 - No. 79, July-Aug, 1954 (#1-7 are quarterly)

1-The Three Mouseketeers (ends #28) & The "Terrific Whatzit" begin; Sheldon Mayer-a; Grossman-a in most issues 89 178 267 565 970 1375
2-Sheldon Mayer-a 42 84 126 265 445 625
3-5: 3-Flash parody. 5-All Mayer-a/scripts issue 30 60 90 177 289 400
6-10 10-(6/46) 20 40 60 114 182 250
11-17,19 15 30 45 90 140 190
18-The Dodo & the Frog (2/47, 1st app?) begin?; X-Mas-c
27 54 81 160 263 365
19-1st Dodo & the Frog-c (3/47) 18 36 54 105 165 225
20-2nd Dodo & the Frog-c (4/47) 14 28 42 80 115 150
21,23-30: 24-Infinity-c. 30-Christmas-c 11 22 33 62 86 110
22-Superman cameo 37 74 111 222 361 500
31-79: 70-1st Bo Bunny by Mayer & begins 10 20 30 56 76 95

NOTE: ***Mayer*** *a-1-8, 55, ,57, 58, 61, 62, 64, 65, 68, 70, 72, 74-79; c-2, 5, 6, 8.*

FUNNY STUFF STOCKING STUFFER
DC Comics: Mar, 1985 ($1.25, 52 pgs.)

1-Almost every DC funny animal featured 4.00

FUNNY 3-D
Harvey Publications: December, 1953 (25¢, came with 2 pair of glasses)

1-Shows cover in 3-D on inside 11 22 33 62 86 110

FUNNY TUNES (Animated Funny Comic Tunes No. 16-22; Funny Comic Tunes No. 23, on covers only; Oscar No. 24 on)
U.S.A. Comics Magazine Corp. (Timely): No. 16, Summer, 1944 - No. 23, Fall, 1946

16-Silly Seal, Ziggy Pig, Krazy Krow begin 19 38 57 111 176 240
17 (Fall/44)-Becomes Gay Comics #18 on? 15 30 45 84 127 170
18-22: 21-Super Rabbit app. 14 28 42 78 112 145
23-Kurtzman-a 14 28 42 82 121 160

FUNNY TUNES (Becomes Space Comics #4 on)
Avon Periodicals: July, 1953 - No. 3, Dec-Jan, 1953-54

1-Space Mouse, Peter Rabbit, Merry Mouse, Spotty the Pup, Cicero the Cat begin; all continue in Space Comics 11 22 33 60 83 105
2,3 8 16 24 44 57 70

FUNNY WORLD
Marbak Press: 1947 - No. 3, 1948

1-The Berrys, The Toodles & other strip-r begin 9 18 27 47 61 75

GD VG FN VF VF/NM NM-
2.0 4.0 6.0 8.0 9.0 9.2

2,3 6 12 18 31 38 45

FUNTASTIC WORLD OF HANNA-BARBERA, THE (TV)
Marvel Comics Group: Dec, 1977 - No. 3, June, 1978 ($1.25, oversized)

1-3: 1-The Flintstones Christmas Party(12/77). 2-Yogi Bear's Easter Parade(3/78). 3-Laff-a-lympics(6/78) 4 8 12 26 41 55

FUN TIME
Ace Periodicals: Spring, 1953; No. 2, Sum, 1953; No. 3(nn), Fall, 1953; No. 4, Wint, 1953-54

1-(25¢, 100 pgs.)-Funny animal 19 38 57 111 176 240
2-4 (All 25¢, 100 pgs.) 15 30 45 88 137 185

FUN WITH SANTA CLAUS (See March of Comics No. 11, 108, 325)

FURTHER ADVENTURES OF CYCLOPS AND PHOENIX (Also see Adventures of Cyclops and Phoenix, Uncanny X-Men & X-Men)
Marvel Comics: June, 1996 - No. 4, Sept, 1996 ($1.95, limited series)

1-4: Origin of Mr. Sinister; Milligan scripts; John Paul Leon-c/a(p). 2-4-Apocalypse app. 3.00
Trade Paperback (1997, $14.99) r/1-4 15.00

FURTHER ADVENTURES OF INDIANA JONES, THE (Movie) (Also see Indiana Jones and the Last Crusade & Indiana Jones and the Temple of Doom)
Marvel Comics Group: Jan, 1983 - No. 34, Mar, 1986

1-Byrne/Austin-a; Austin-c 6.00
2-34: 2-Byrne/Austin-c/a 4.00

NOTE: ***Austin*** *a-1i, 2i, 6i, 9i; c-1, 2i, 6i, 9i.* ***Byrne*** *a-1p, 2p; c-2p.* ***Chaykin*** *a-6p; c-6p, 8p-10p.* ***Ditko*** *a-21p, 25-28, 34.* ***Golden*** *c-24, 25.* ***Simonson*** *c-9. Painted c-14.*

FURTHER ADVENTURES OF NYOKA, THE JUNGLE GIRL, THE (See Nyoka)
AC Comics: 1988 - No. 5, 1989 ($1.95, color; $2.25/$2.50, B&W)

1-5 : 1,2-Bill Black-a plus reprints. 3-Photo-c. 5-(B&W)-Reprints plus movie photos 3.00

FURY (Straight Arrow's Horse...) (See A-1 No. 119)

FURY (TV) (See March Of Comics #200)
Dell Publishing Co./Gold Key: No. 781, Mar, 1957 - Nov, 1962 (All photo-c)

Four Color 781 8 16 24 51 86 120
Four Color 885,975,1031,1080,1133,1172,1218,1296 6 12 18 41 66 90
01292-208(#1-'62), 10020-211(11/62-G.K.) 6 12 18 37 59 80

FURY
Marvel Comics: May, 1994 ($2.95, one-shot)

1-Iron Man, Red Skull, FF, Hatemonger, Logan app.; Origin Nick Fury 3.00

FURY (Volume 3)
Marvel Comics (MAX): Nov, 2001 - No. 6, Apr, 2002 ($2.99, mature content)

1-6-Ennis-s/Robertson-a 3.00

FURY/ AGENT 13
Marvel Comics: June, 1998 - No. 2, July, 1998 ($2.99, limited series)

1,2-Nick Fury returns 3.00

FURY OF FIRESTORM, THE (Becomes Firestorm The Nuclear Man on cover with #50, in indicia with #65) (Also see Firestorm)
DC Comics: June, 1982 - No. 64, Oct, 1987 (75¢ on)

1-Intro The Black Bison; brief origin 6.00
2-40,43-64: 4-JLA x-over. 17-1st app. Firehawk. 21-Death of Killer Frost. 22-Origin. 23-Intro. Byte. 24-(6/84)-1st app. Blue Devil & Bug (origin); origin Byte. 34-1st app./origin Killer Frost II. 39-Weasel's ID revealed. 48-Intro. Moonbow. 53-Origin/1st app. Silver Shade. 55,56-Legends x-over. 58-1st app./origin new Parasite 3.00
41,42-Crisis x-over 3.50
61-Test cover variant; Superman logo 4 8 12 22 34 45
Annual 1-4: 1(1983), 2(1984), 3(1985), 4(1986) 4.00

NOTE: ***Colan*** *a-19p, Annual 4p.* ***Giffen*** *a-Annual 4p.* ***Gil Kane*** *c-30.* ***Nino*** *a-37.* ***Tuska*** *a-(p)-17, 18, 32, 45.*

FURY OF FIRESTORM: THE NUCLEAR MEN (New DC 52)
DC Comics: Nov, 2011 - Present ($2.99)

1-7: 1-Van Sciver & Simone-s/Cinar-a/Van Sciver-c. 7-Van Sciver-a 3.00

FURY OF SHIELD
Marvel Comics: Apr, 1995 - No. 4, July, 1995 ($2.50/$1.95, limited series)

1 ($2.50)-Foil-c 3.50
2-4: 4-Bagged w/ decoder 3.00

FURY: PEACEMAKER
Marvel Comics: Apr, 2006 - No. 6, Sept, 2006 ($3.50, limited series)

1-6-Flashback to WW2; Ennis-s/Robertson-a. 1-Deodato-c. 2-Texeira-c. 5-Dillon-c 3.50
TPB (2006, $17.99) r/#1-6 18.00

FUSED
Image Comics: Mar, 2002 - No. 4, Jan, 2003 ($2.95)

Fused #2 © Steve Niles

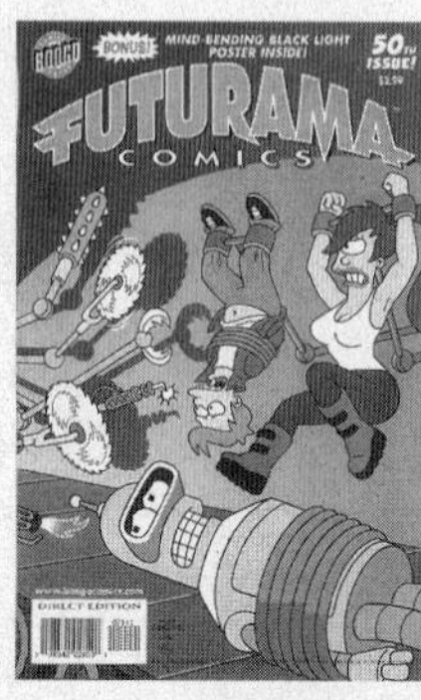

Futurama Comics #50 © Bongo

Galacta: Daughter of Galactus #1 © MAR

	GD 2.0	VG 4.0	FN 6.0	VF 8.0	VF/NM 9.0	NM- 9.2

1-4-Steve Niles-s. 1,2-Paul Lee-a. 3-Brad Rader-a. 4-Templesmith-a 3.00
Canned Heat TPB (Dark Horse, 6/04, $12.95) r/series; Dan Wickline intro. 13.00

FUSED
Dark Horse Comics: Dec, 2003 - No. 4, Mar, 2004 ($2.95)

1-4-Steve Niles-s/Josh Medors-a. 1-Powell-c 3.00

FUSION
Eclipse Comics: Jan, 1987 - No. 17, Oct, 1989 ($2.00, B&W, Baxter paper)

1-17: 11-The Weasel Patrol begins (1st app.?) 3.00

FUSION
Image Comics (Top Cow): May, 2009 - No. 3, Jul, 2009 ($2.99, limited series)

1-3-Avengers, Thunderbolts, Cyberforce and Hunter-Killer meet; Kirkham-a 3.00

FUTURAMA (TV)
Bongo Comics: 2000 - Present ($2.50/$2.99, bi-monthly)

1-Based on the FOX-TV animated series; Groening/Morrison-c 4.00
1-San Diego Comic-Con Premiere Edition 5.00
2-59: 8-CGC cover spoof; X-Men parody. 40-Santa app. 50-55-Poster included 3.00
Futurama Adventures TPB (2004, $14.95) r/#5-9 15.00
Futurama Conquers the Universe TPB (2007, $14.95) r/#10-13 15.00
Futurama-O-Rama TPB (2002, $12.95) r/#1-4; sketch pages of Fry's development 13.00
...: The Time Bender Trilogy TPB (2006, $14.95) r/#16-19; cover gallery 15.00

FUTURAMA/SIMPSONS INFINITELY SECRET CROSSOVER CRISIS (TV) (See Simpsons/Futurama Crossover Crisis II for sequel)
Bongo Comics: 2002 - No. 2, 2002 ($2.50, limited series)

1,2-Evil Brain Spawns put Futurama crew into the Simpsons' Springfield 3.00

FUTURE COMICS
David McKay Publications: June, 1940 - No. 4, Sept, 1940

	GD	VG	FN	VF	VF/NM	NM-
1-(6/40, 64 pgs.)-Origin The Phantom (1st in comics) (4 pgs.); The Lone Ranger (8 pgs.) & Saturn Against the Earth (4 pgs.) begin	300	600	900	1920	3310	4700
2	123	246	369	787	1344	1900
3,4	89	178	267	565	970	1375

FUTURE COP L.A.P.D. (Electronic Arts video game) (Also see Promotional Comics section)
DC Comics (WildStorm): Jan, 1999 ($4.95, magazine sized)

1-Stories & art by various 5.00

FUTURE SHOCK
Image Comics: 2006 (Free Comic Book Day giveaway)

...: FCBD 2006 Edition; Spawn, Invincible, Savage Dragon & others short stories 3.00

FUTURE WORLD COMICS
George W. Dougherty: Summer, 1946 - No. 2, Fall, 1946

	GD	VG	FN	VF	VF/NM	NM-
1,2: H. C. Kiefer-c; preview of the World of Tomorrow	29	58	87	170	278	385

FUTURE WORLD COMIX (Warren Presents...)
Warren Publications: Sept, 1978 (B&W magazine, 84 pgs.)

	GD	VG	FN	VF	VF/NM	NM-
1-Corben, Maroto, Morrow, Nino, Sutton-a; Todd-c/a; contains nudity panels	2	4	6	8	11	14

FUTURIANS, THE (See Marvel Graphic Novel #9)
Lodestone Publishing/Eternity Comics: Sept, 1985 - No. 3, 1985 ($1.50)

1-3: Indicia title "Dave Cockrum's..." 3.00
Graphic Novel 1 ($9.95, Eternity)-r/#1-3, plus never published #4 issue 10.00

FX
IDW Publishing: Mar, 2008 - No. 6, Aug, 2008 ($3.99)

1-6-John Byrne-a/c; Wayne Osborne-s 4.00

G-8 (Listed at G-Eight)

GABBY (Formerly Ken Shannon) (Teen humor)
Quality Comics Group: No. 11, Jul, 1953; No. 2, Sep, 1953 - No. 9, Sep, 1954

	GD	VG	FN	VF	VF/NM	NM-
11(#1)(7/53)	9	18	27	47	61	75
2	6	12	18	31	38	45
3-9	5	10	15	24	30	35

GABBY GOB (See Harvey Hits No. 85, 90, 94, 97, 100, 103, 106, 109)

GABBY HAYES ADVENTURE COMICS
Toby Press: Dec, 1953

	GD	VG	FN	VF	VF/NM	NM-
1-Photo-c	15	30	45	88	137	185

GABBY HAYES WESTERN (Movie star)(See Monte Hale, Real Western Hero & Western Hero)
Fawcett Publications/Charlton Comics No. 51 on: Nov, 1948 - No. 50, Jan, 1953; No. 51, Dec, 1954 - No. 59, Jan, 1957

	GD	VG	FN	VF	VF/NM	NM-
1-Gabby & his horse Corker begin; photo front/back-c begin	40	80	120	246	411	575
2	20	40	60	118	192	265
3-5	15	30	45	88	137	185
6-10: 9-Young Falcon begins	14	28	42	78	112	145
11-20: 19-Last photo back-c	11	22	33	64	90	115
21-49: 20,22,24,26,28,29-(52 pgs.)	9	18	27	52	69	85
50-(1/53)-Last Fawcett issue; last photo-c?	10	20	30	58	79	100
51-(12/54)-1st Charlton issue; photo-c	11	22	33	60	83	105
52-59(1955-57): 53,55-Photo-c. 58-Swayze-a	8	16	24	42	54	65

GAGS
United Features Synd./Triangle Publ. No. 9 on: Jul, 1937 - V3#10, Oct, 1944 (13-3/4x10-3/4")

	GD	VG	FN	VF	VF/NM	NM-
1(7/37)-52 pgs.; 20 pgs. Grin & Bear It, Fellow Citizen	12	24	36	67	94	120
V1#9 (36 pgs.) (7/42)	7	14	21	37	46	55
V3#10	7	14	21	35	43	50

GALACTA: DAUGHTER OF GALACTUS
Marvel Comics: July, 2010 ($3.99, one-shot)

1-Adam Warren-s/Hector Sevilla-a; Warren & Sevilla-c : Wolverine and the FF app. 4.00

GALACTICA 1980 (Based on the Battlestar Galactica TV series)
Dynamite Entertainment: 2009 - No. 4, 2009 ($3.50)

1-4-Guggenheim-s/Razek-a 3.50

GALACTICA: THE NEW MILLENNIUM
Realm Press: Sept, 1999 ($2.99)

1-Stories by Shooter, Braden, Kuhoric 3.00

GALACTIC GUARDIANS
Marvel Comics: July, 1994 - No. 4, Oct, 1994 ($1.50, limited series)

1-4 3.00

GALACTIC WARS COMIX (Warren Presents... on cover)
Warren Publications: Dec, 1978 (B&W magazine, 84 pgs.)

	GD	VG	FN	VF	VF/NM	NM-
nn-Wood, Williamson-r; Battlestar Galactica/Flash Gordon photo/text stories	2	4	6	8	11	14

GALACTUS THE DEVOURER
Marvel Comics: Sept, 1999 - No. 6, Mar, 2000 ($3.50/$2.50, limited series)

1-($3.50) L. Simonson-s/Muth & Sienkiewicz-a 4.00
2-5-($2.50) Buscema & Sienkiewicz-a 3.00
6-($3.50) Death of Galactus; Buscema & Sienkiewicz-a 4.00

GALAXIA (Magazine)
Astral Publ.: 1981 ($2.50, B&W, 52 pgs.)

	GD	VG	FN	VF	VF/NM	NM-
1-Buckler/Giordano-c; Texeira/Guice-a; 1st app. Astron, Sojourner, Bloodwing, Warlords; Buckler-s/a	2	4	6	9	13	16

GALAXY QUEST: GLOBAL WARNING! (Based on the 1999 movie)
IDW Publishing: Aug, 2008 - No. 5, Dec, 2008 ($3.99)

1-5-Lobdell-s/Kyriazis-a 4.00

GALLANT MEN, THE (TV)
Gold Key: Oct, 1963 (Photo-c)

	GD	VG	FN	VF	VF/NM	NM-
1(1008-310)-Manning-a	4	8	12	22	34	45

GALLEGHER, BOY REPORTER (Disney, TV)
Gold Key: May, 1965

	GD	VG	FN	VF	VF/NM	NM-
1(10149-505)-Photo-c	3	6	9	18	27	35

GAMBIT (See X-Men #266 & X-Men Annual #14)
Marvel Comics: Dec, 1993 - No. 4, Mar, 1994 ($2.00, limited series)

	GD	VG	FN	VF	VF/NM	NM-
1-($2.50)-Lee Weeks-c/a in all; gold foil stamped-c.						6.00
1 (Gold)	2	4	6	9	12	15
2-4						4.00

GAMBIT
Marvel Comics: Sept, 1997 - No. 4, Dec, 1997 ($2.50, limited series)

1-4-Janson-a/Mackie & Kavanagh-s 3.00

GAMBIT
Marvel Comics: Feb, 1999 - No. 25, Feb, 2001 ($2.99/$1.99)

1-($2.99) Five covers; Nicieza-a/Skroce-a 5.00
2-11,13-16-($1.99): 2-Two covers (Skroce & Adam Kubert) 3.00
12-($2.99) 4.00
17-24: 17-Begin $2.25-c. 21-Mystique-c/app. 3.00

A Game of Thrones #1 © G.R.R. Martin

Gangland #2 © DC

Gate Crasher #1 © Black Bull

	GD 2.0	VG 4.0	FN 6.0	VF 8.0	VF/NM 9.0	NM- 9.2
25-($2.99) Leads into "Gambit & Bishop"						4.00
...1999 Annual ($3.50) Nicieza-s/McDaniel-a						4.00
...2000 Annual ($3.50) Nicieza-s/Derenick & Smith-a						4.00

GAMBIT
Marvel Comics: Nov, 2004 - No. 12, Aug, 2005 ($2.99)

	GD 2.0	VG 4.0	FN 6.0	VF 8.0	VF/NM 9.0	NM- 9.2
1-12: 1-Jeanty-a/Land-c/Layman-s. 5-Wolverine-c/app. 9-Brother Voodoo-c/app.						3.00
... and the Champions: From the Marvel Vault 1 (10/11, $2.99) George Tuska's last art						3.00
...: Hath No Fury TPB (2005, $14.99) r/#7-12						15.00
...: House of Cards TPB (2005, $14.99) r/#1-6; Land cover sketches; unused covers						15.00

GAMBIT & BISHOP (... : Sons of the Atom on cover)
Marvel Comics: Feb, 2001 - No. 6, May, 2001 ($2.25, bi-weekly limited series)

	GD 2.0	VG 4.0	FN 6.0	VF 8.0	VF/NM 9.0	NM- 9.2
Alpha (2/01) Prelude to series; Nord-a						3.00
1-6-Jeanty-a/Williams-c						3.00
Genesis (3/01, $3.50) reprints their first apps. and first meeting						4.00

GAMBIT AND THE X-TERNALS
Marvel Comics: Mar, 1995 - No. 4, July, 1995 ($1.95, limited series)

	GD 2.0	VG 4.0	FN 6.0	VF 8.0	VF/NM 9.0	NM- 9.2
1-4-Age of Apocalypse						3.00

GAMEBOY (Super Mario covers on all)
Valiant: 1990 - No. 5 ($1.95, coated-c)

	GD 2.0	VG 4.0	FN 6.0	VF 8.0	VF/NM 9.0	NM- 9.2
1-5: 3,4-Layton-c. 4-Morrow-a. 5-Layton-c(i)						8.00

GAMEKEEPER (Guy Ritchie's...)
Virgin Comics: Mar, 2007 - No. 5, Sept, 2007; Mar, 2008 - No. 5, Jul, 2008 ($2.99)

	GD 2.0	VG 4.0	FN 6.0	VF 8.0	VF/NM 9.0	NM- 9.2
1-5-Andy Diggle-s/Mukesh Singh-a; 2 covers on each						3.00
1-Extended Edition (6/07, $2.99) r/#1 with script excerpt and sketch art						3.00
Series 2 (3/08 - No. 5, 7/08) 1-5-Parker-s/Randle-a						3.00
Vol. 1 TPB (10/07, $14.99) r/#1-5; script and sketch pages; Guy Ritchie intro.						15.00

GAME OF THRONES, A (George R.R. Martin's...) (Based on *A Song of Fire and Ice*)
Dynamite Entertainment: 2011 - Present ($3.99)

	GD 2.0	VG 4.0	FN 6.0	VF 8.0	VF/NM 9.0	NM- 9.2
1-6: 1,2-Covers by Alex Ross and Mike Miller						4.00

GAMERA
Dark Horse Comics: Aug, 1996 - No. 4, Nov, 1996 ($2.95, limited series)

	GD 2.0	VG 4.0	FN 6.0	VF 8.0	VF/NM 9.0	NM- 9.2
1-4						3.00

GAMMARAUDERS
DC Comics: Jan, 1989 - No. 10, Dec, 1989 ($1.25/$1.50/$2.00)

	GD 2.0	VG 4.0	FN 6.0	VF 8.0	VF/NM 9.0	NM- 9.2
1-10-Based on TSR game						3.00

GAMORRA SWIMSUIT SPECIAL
Image Comics (WildStorm Productions): June, 1996 ($2.50, one-shot)

	GD 2.0	VG 4.0	FN 6.0	VF 8.0	VF/NM 9.0	NM- 9.2
1-Campbell wraparound-c; pinups						3.00

GANDY GOOSE (Movies/TV)(See All Surprise, Giant Comics Edition #5A &10, Paul Terry's Comics & Terry-Toons)
St. John Publ. Co./Pines No. 5,6: Mar, 1953 - No. 5, Nov, 1953; No. 5, Fall, 1956 - No. 6, Sum/58

	GD 2.0	VG 4.0	FN 6.0	VF 8.0	VF/NM 9.0	NM- 9.2
1-All St. John issues are pre-code	10	20	30	58	79	100
2	7	14	21	35	43	50
3-5(1953)(St. John)	6	12	18	31	38	45
5,6(1956-58)(Pines)-CBS Television Presents...	5	10	15	24	30	35

GANG BUSTERS (See Popular Comics #38)
David McKay/Dell Publishing Co.: 1938 - 1943

	GD 2.0	VG 4.0	FN 6.0	VF 8.0	VF/NM 9.0	NM- 9.2
Feature Books 17(McKay)('38)-1st app.	69	138	207	442	759	1075
Large Feature Comic 10('39)-(Scarce)	69	138	207	442	759	1075
Large Feature Comic 17('41)	48	96	144	302	514	725
Four Color 7(1940)	52	104	156	322	549	775
Four Color 23('42)	41	82	123	249	417	585
Four Color 24('43)	25	50	75	175	375	575

GANG BUSTERS (Radio/TV)(Gangbusters #14 on)
National Periodical Publ.: Dec-Jan, 1947-48 - No. 67, Dec-Jan, 1958-59 (No. 1-23: 52 pgs.)

	GD 2.0	VG 4.0	FN 6.0	VF 8.0	VF/NM 9.0	NM- 9.2
1	84	168	252	538	919	1300
2	39	78	117	240	395	550
3-5	28	56	84	165	270	375
6-10: 9-Dan Barry-a. 9,10-Photo-c	21	42	63	122	199	275
11-13-Photo-c	17	34	51	100	158	215
14,17-Frazetta-a, 8 pgs. each. 14-Photo-c	36	72	108	211	343	475
15,16,18-20,26: 26-Kirby-a	15	30	45	85	130	175
21-25,27-30	14	28	42	76	108	140
31-44: 44-Last Pre-code (2-3/55)	12	24	36	67	94	120
45-67	10	20	30	54	72	90

NOTE: ***Barry** a-6, 8, 10. **Drucker** a-51. **Moreira** a-48, 50, 59. **Roussos** a-8.*

GANGLAND
DC Comics (Vertigo): Jun, 1998 - No. 4, Sept, 1998 ($2.95, limited series)

	GD 2.0	VG 4.0	FN 6.0	VF 8.0	VF/NM 9.0	NM- 9.2
1-4:Crime anthology by various. 2-Corben-a						3.00
TPB-(2000, $12.95) r/#1-4; Bradstreet-c						13.00

GANGSTERS AND GUN MOLLS
Avon Per./Realistic Comics: Sept, 1951 - No. 4, June, 1952 (Painted c-1-3)

	GD 2.0	VG 4.0	FN 6.0	VF 8.0	VF/NM 9.0	NM- 9.2
1-Wood-a, 1 pg; c-/Avon paperback #292	52	104	156	322	549	775
2-Check-a, 8 pgs.; Kamen-a; Bonnie Parker story	40	80	120	246	411	575
3-Marijuana mentioned; used in **POP**, pg. 84,85	39	78	117	236	388	540
4-Syd Shores-c	32	64	96	188	307	425

GANGSTERS CAN'T WIN
D. S. Publishing Co.: Feb-Mar, 1948 - No. 9, June-July, 1949 (All 52 pgs?)

	GD 2.0	VG 4.0	FN 6.0	VF 8.0	VF/NM 9.0	NM- 9.2
1-True crime stories	39	78	117	230	375	520
2-Skull-c	20	40	60	117	189	260
3,5,6	18	36	54	105	165	225
4-Acid in face story	23	46	69	136	223	310
7-9	15	30	45	85	130	175

NOTE: ***Ingles** a-5, 6. **McWilliams** a-5, 7, 8. **Reinman** c-6.*

GANG WORLD
Standard Comics: No. 5, Nov, 1952 - No. 6, Jan, 1953

	GD 2.0	VG 4.0	FN 6.0	VF 8.0	VF/NM 9.0	NM- 9.2
5-Bondage-c	19	38	57	109	172	235
6	15	30	45	83	124	165

GARGOYLE (See The Defenders #94)
Marvel Comics Group: June, 1985 - No. 4, Sept, 1985 (75¢, limited series)

	GD 2.0	VG 4.0	FN 6.0	VF 8.0	VF/NM 9.0	NM- 9.2
1-Wrightson-c; character from Defenders						4.00
2-4						3.00

GARGOYLES (TV cartoon)
Marvel Comics: Feb, 1995 - No. 11, Dec, 1995 ($2.50)

	GD 2.0	VG 4.0	FN 6.0	VF 8.0	VF/NM 9.0	NM- 9.2
1-11: Based on animated series						3.00

GARRISON
DC Comics (WildStorm): Jun, 2010 - No. 6, Nov, 2010 ($2.99)

	GD 2.0	VG 4.0	FN 6.0	VF 8.0	VF/NM 9.0	NM- 9.2
1-6-Mariotte-s/Francavilla-a/c						3.00

GARRISON'S GORILLAS (TV)
Dell Publishing Co.: Jan, 1968 - No. 4, Oct, 1968; No. 5, Oct, 1969 (Photo-c)

	GD 2.0	VG 4.0	FN 6.0	VF 8.0	VF/NM 9.0	NM- 9.2
1	5	10	15	30	48	65
2-5: 5-Reprints #1	3	6	9	20	30	40

GARY GIANNI'S THE MONSTERMEN
Dark Horse Comics: Aug, 1999 ($2.95, one-shot)

	GD 2.0	VG 4.0	FN 6.0	VF 8.0	VF/NM 9.0	NM- 9.2
1-Gianni-s/c/a; back-up Hellboy story by Mignola						3.00

GASM (Sci-Fi, Horror, Fantasy comics magazine)(Mature content)
Stories, Layouts & Press, Inc.: Nov, 1977 - nn (No. 5), Jun, 1978 (B&W/color)

	GD 2.0	VG 4.0	FN 6.0	VF 8.0	VF/NM 9.0	NM- 9.2
1-Mark Wheatley-s/a; Gene Day-s/a; Workman-a	3	6	9	14	19	24
2 (12/77) Wheatley-a; Winnick-s/a; Workman-a	2	4	6	11	16	20
nn(#3, 2/78) Day-s/a; Wheatley-a; Workman-a	2	4	6	10	14	18
nn(#4, 4/78) Day-s/a; Wheatley-a; Corben-a	3	6	9	14	20	26
nn(#5, 6/78) Hempel-a; Howarth-a; Corben-a	3	6	9	16	22	28

GASOLINE ALLEY (Top Love Stories No. 3 on?)
Star Publications: Sept-Oct, 1950 - No. 2, Dec, 1950 (Newspaper-r)

	GD 2.0	VG 4.0	FN 6.0	VF 8.0	VF/NM 9.0	NM- 9.2
1-Contains 1 pg. intro. history of the strip (The Life of Skeezix); reprints 15 scenes of highlights from 1921-1935, plus an adventure from 1935 and 1936 strips; a 2-pg. filler is included on the life of the creator Frank King, with photo of the cartoonist.	20	40	60	115	185	255
2-(1936-37 reprints)-L. B. Cole-c	22	44	66	128	209	290

(See Super Book No. 21)

GASP!
American Comics Group: Mar, 1967 - No. 4, Aug, 1967 (12¢)

	GD 2.0	VG 4.0	FN 6.0	VF 8.0	VF/NM 9.0	NM- 9.2
1	5	10	15	35	55	75
2-4	4	8	12	22	34	45

GATECRASHER
Black Bull Entertainment: Mar, 2000 - No. 4, Jun, 2000 ($2.50, limited series)

	GD 2.0	VG 4.0	FN 6.0	VF 8.0	VF/NM 9.0	NM- 9.2
1,2-Waid-s/Conner & Palmiotti-c/a; 1,2-variant-c by J.G. Jones						3.00
3,4: 3-Jusko var-c. 4-Linsner-c						3.00
... Ring of Fire TPB (11/00, $12.95) r/#1-4; Hughes-c; Ennis intro.						13.00

GATECRASHER (Regular series)
Black Bull Entertainment: Aug, 2000 - No. 6, Jan, 2001 ($2.50, limited series)

Gay Comics #26 © MAR

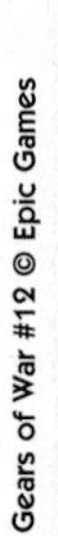
Gears of War #12 © Epic Games

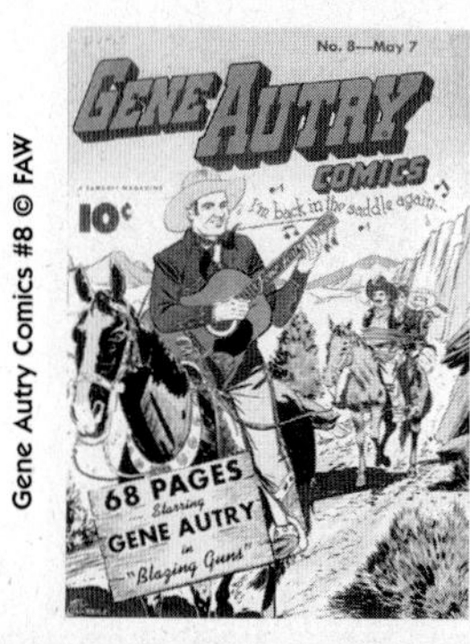
Gene Autry Comics #8 © FAW

	GD 2.0	VG 4.0	FN 6.0	VF 8.0	VF/NM 9.0	NM- 9.2

1-6-Waid-s/Conner & Palmiotti-c/a; 1-3-Variant-c by Fabry. 4-Hildebrandts variant-c. 5-Art Adams var-c. 6-Texeira var-c 3.00

GAY COMICS (Honeymoon No. 41)
Timely Comics/USA Comic Mag. Co. No. 18-24: Mar, 1944 (no month); No. 18, Fall, 1944 - No. 40, Oct, 1949

	GD	VG	FN	VF	VF/NM	NM-
1-Wolverton's Powerhouse Pepper; Tessie the Typist begins; 1st app. Willie (one shot)	58	116	174	371	636	900
18-(Formerly Funny Tunes #17?)-Wolverton-a	39	78	117	240	395	550
19-29: Wolverton-a in all. 21,24-6 pg., 7 pg. Powerhouse Pepper; additional 2 pg. story in 24). 23-7 pg Wolverton story & 2 two pg stories(total of 11pgs.). 24,29-Kurtzman-a (24-"Hey Look"(2))	37	74	111	222	361	500
30,33,36,37-Kurtzman's "Hey Look"	15	30	45	88	137	185
31-Kurtzman's "Hey Look" (1), Giggles 'N' Grins (1-1/2)	15	30	45	88	137	185
32,35,38-40: 35-Nellie The Nurse begins?	15	30	45	84	127	170
34-Three Kurtzman's "Hey Look"	16	32	48	92	144	195

GAY COMICS (Also see Smile, Tickle, & Whee Comics)
Modern Store Publ.: 1955 (7¢, 5x7-1/4", 52 pgs.)

	GD	VG	FN	VF	VF/NM	NM-
1	4	8	12	22	34	45

GAY PURR-EE (See Movie Comics)

GEARS OF WAR (Based on the video game)
DC Comics (WildStorm): Dec, 2008 - No. 17, Jun, 2011 ($3.99/$2.99)

1-15: 1-Liam Sharp-a/Joshua Ortega-s. 1-Two covers 4.00
16-22-($2.99) 16-Traviss-s/Gopez-a. 18-20-Mhan-a. 19-21-Prelude to Gears of War 3 3.00
... Reader (4/09, $3.99) r/#1 & 2 in flipbook 4.00
... Sourcebook (8/09, $3.99) character pin-ups by various; Platt-c 4.00
Book One HC (2009, $19.99, dustjacket) r/#1-6 & Sourcebook 20.00
Book One SC (2010, $14.99) r/#1-6 & Sourcebook 15.00
Book Two HC (2011, $24.99, dustjacket) r/#7-13 25.00

GEAR STATION, THE
Image Comics: Mar, 2000 - No. 5, Nov, 2000 ($2.50)

1-Four covers by Ross, Turner, Pat Lee, Fraga 3.00
1-($6.95) DF Cover 7.00
2-5: 2-Two covers by Fraga and Art Adams 3.00

GEEK, THE (See Brother Power... & Vertigo Visions)

GEEKSVILLE (Also see 3 Geeks, The)
3 Finger Prints/ Image: Aug, 1999 - No. 6, Mar, 2001 ($2.75/$2.95, B&W)

1,2,4-6-The 3 Geeks by Koslowski; Innocent Bystander by Sassaman 3.00
3-Includes "Babes & Blades" mini-comic 5.00
0-(3/00) First Image issue 3.00
(Vol. 2) 1-4-($2.95) 3-Mini-comic insert by the Geeks. 4-Steve Borock app. 3.00

G-8 AND HIS BATTLE ACES (Based on pulps)
Gold Key: Oct, 1966

	GD	VG	FN	VF	VF/NM	NM-
1 (10184-610)-Painted-c	4	8	12	26	41	55

G-8 AND HIS BATTLE ACES
Blazing Comics: 1991 ($1.50, one-shot)

1-Glanzman-a; Truman-c 3.00
NOTE: *Flip book format with "The Spider's Web" #1 on other side w/**Glanzman**-a, **Truman**-c.*

GEISHA (Also see Oni Press Summer Vacation Supercolor Fun Special)
Oni Press: Sept, 1998 - No. 4, Dec, 1998 ($2.95, limited series)

1-4-Andi Watson-s/a. 2-Adam Warren-c 3.00
...One Shot (5/00, $4.50) 4.50
The Complete Geisha TPB (5/03, $15.95, digest size) r/#1-4, One Shot & story from Oni Press Summer Vacation Supercolor Fun Special 16.00

GEM COMICS
Spotlight Publishers: Apr, 1945 (52 pgs)

	GD	VG	FN	VF	VF/NM	NM-
1-Little Mohee, Steve Strong app.; Jungle bondage-c	53	106	159	334	567	800

GEMINAR
Image Comics: July, 2000 ($4.95, B&W)

1-(72-Page Special) Terry Collins-s/Al Bigley-a 5.00

GEMINI BLOOD
DC Comics (Helix): Sept, 1996 - No. 9, May, 1997 ($2.25, limited series)

1-9: 5-Simonson-c 3.00

GEN ACTIVE
DC Comics (WildStorm): May, 2000 - No. 6, Aug, 2001 ($3.95)

1-6: 1-Covers by Campbell and Madureira; Gen 13 & DV8 app. 5-Mahfood-a; Quitely and Stelfreeze-c. 6-Portacio-a/c 4.00

GENE AUTRY (See March of Comics No. 25, 28, 39, 54, 78, 90, 104, 120, 135, 150 in the Promotional Comics section & Western Roundup under Dell Giants)

GENE AUTRY COMICS (Movie, Radio star; singing cowboy)
Fawcett Publications: Jan, 1942 (On sale 12/17/41) - No. 10, 1943 (68 pgs.)
(Dell takes over with No. 11)

	GD	VG	FN	VF	VF/NM	NM-
1 (Scarce)-Gene Autry & his horse Champion begin; photo back-c	423	846	1269	3000	5250	7500
2-(1942)	90	180	270	576	988	1400
3-5: 3-(11/1/42)	50	100	150	315	533	750
6-10	41	82	123	256	428	600

GENE AUTRY COMICS (...& Champion No. 102 on)
Dell Publishing Co.: No. 11, 1943 - No. 121, Jan-Mar, 1959 (TV - later issues)

	GD	VG	FN	VF	VF/NM	NM-
11 (1943, 60 pgs.)-Continuation of Fawcett series; photo back-c; first Dell issue	33	66	99	239	520	800
12 (2/44, 60 pgs.)	29	58	87	210	455	700
Four Color 47 (1944, 60 pgs.)	29	58	87	210	455	700
Four Color 57 (11/44),66('45)(52 pgs. each)	27	54	81	196	423	650
Four Color 75,83 ('45, 36 pgs. each)	22	44	66	154	327	500
Four Color 93 ('45, 36 pgs.)	19	38	57	128	277	425
Four Color 100 ('46, 36 pgs.) First Gene Autry photo-c	21	42	63	150	320	490
1 (5-6/46, 52 pgs.)	29	58	87	210	455	700
2 (7-8/46)-Photo-c begin, end #111	14	28	42	97	211	325
3-5: 4-Intro Flapjack Hobbs	12	24	36	81	166	250
6-10	11	22	33	71	136	200
11-20: 20-Panhandle Pete begins	10	20	30	67	124	180
21-29 (36 pgs.)	9	18	27	60	103	145
30-40 (52 pgs.)	8	16	24	51	86	120
41-56 (52 pgs.)	7	14	21	44	72	100
57-66 (36 pgs.): 58-X-mas-c	6	12	18	39	62	85
67-80 (52 pgs.): 70-X-mas-c	6	12	18	39	62	85
81-90 (52 pgs.): 82-X-mas-c. 87-Blank inside-c	5	10	15	34	55	75
91-99 (36 pgs. No. 91-on). 94-X-mas-c	5	10	15	30	48	65
100	5	10	15	32	51	70
101-111-Last Gene Autry photo-c	4	8	12	28	44	60
112-121-All Champion painted-c, most by Savitt	4	8	12	26	41	55

NOTE: *Photo back covers 4-18, 20-45, 48-65.* **Manning** *a-118.* ***Jesse Marsh*** *art: 4-Color No. 66, 75, 93, 100, No. 1-25, 27-37, 39, 40.*

GENE AUTRY'S CHAMPION (TV)
Dell Publ. Co.: No. 287, 8/50; No. 319, 2/51; No. 3, 8-10/51 - No. 19, 8-10/55

	GD	VG	FN	VF	VF/NM	NM-
Four Color 287(#1)('50, 52 pgs.)-Photo-c	11	22	33	71	136	200
Four Color 319(#2, '51), 3: 2-Painted-c begin, most by Sam Savitt	6	12	18	41	66	90
4-19: 19-Last painted-c	5	10	15	30	48	65

GENE COLAN TRIBUTE BOOK (Produced for The Hero Initiative)
Marvel Comics: 2008 ($9.99, one-shot)

1-Spotlighted stories from Tales of Suspense #89,90, Doctor Strange #174 and others 10.00

GENE DOGS
Marvel Comics UK: Oct, 1993 - No. 4, Jan, 1994 ($1.75, limited series)

1-($2.75)-Polybagged w/4 trading cards 3.50
2-4: 2-Vs. Genetix 3.00

GENE POOL
IDW Publishing: Oct, 2003 ($6.99, squarebound)

nn-Wein & Wolfman-s/Cummings-a 7.00

GENERAL DOUGLAS MACARTHUR
Fox Features Syndicate: 1951

	GD	VG	FN	VF	VF/NM	NM-
nn-True life story	20	40	60	114	182	250

GENERIC COMIC, THE
Marvel Comics Group: Apr, 1984 (one-shot)

1 3.00

GENERATION HEX
DC Comics (Amalgam): June, 1997 ($1.95, one-shot)

1-Milligan-s/ Pollina & Morales-a 3.00

GENERATION HOPE (See X-Men titles and Cable)
Marvel Comics: Jan, 2011 - No. 17, May, 2012 ($3.99/$2.99)

1-($3.99) Gillen-s/Espin-a; Coipel-c; back-up bio of Hope Summers 4.00

Generation Hope #4 © MAR

Generation X #45 © MAR

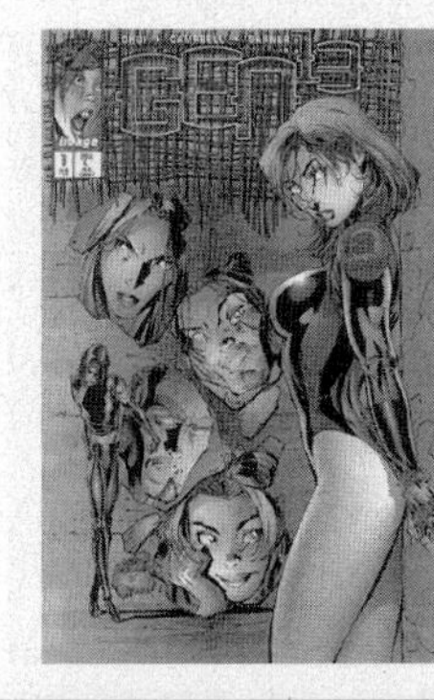
Gen 13 #8 © WSP

	GD 2.0	VG 4.0	FN 6.0	VF 8.0	VF/NM 9.0	NM- 9.2

1-Variant-c by Greg Land 8.00
2-17-($2.99) 5,9-McKelvie-a. 10,11-Seeley-a. 11-X-Men: Schism tie-in 3.00

GENERATION M (Follows House of M x-over)
Marvel Comics: Jan, 2006 - No. 5, May, 2006 ($2.99, limited series)

1-5-Jenkins-s/Bachs-a. 1-Chamber app. 2-Jubilee app. 3-Blob-c. 4-Angel-c 3.00
Decimation: Generation M TPB (2006, $13.99) r/#1-5 14.00

GENERATION NEXT
Marvel Comics: Mar, 1995 - No. 4, June, 1995 ($1.95, limited series)

1-4-Age of Apocalypse; Scott Lobdell scripts & Chris Bachalo-c/a 3.00

GENERATION X (See Gen 13/ Generation X)
Marvel Comics: Oct, 1994 - No. 75, June, 2001 ($1.50/$1.95/$1.99/$2.25)

Collectors Preview ($1.75), "Ashcan" Edition 3.00
-1(7/97) Flashback story 3.00
1/2 (San Diego giveaway) 2 4 6 8 10 12
1-($3.95)-Wraparound chromium-c; Scott Lobdell scripts & Chris Bachalo-a begins 6.00
2-($1.95)-Deluxe edition, Bachalo-a 4.00
3,4-($1.95)-Deluxe Edition; Bachalo-a 4.00
2-10: 2-4-Standard Edition. 5-Returns from "Age of Apocalypse," begin $1.95-c. 6-Bachalo-a(p) ends, returns #17. 7-Roger Cruz-a(p). 10-Omega Red-c/app. 3.00
11-24, 26-28: 13,14-Bishop-app. 17-Stan Lee app. (Stan Lee scripts own dialogue); Bachalo/Buckingham-a; Onslaught update. 18-Toad cameo. 20-Franklin Richards app; Howard the Duck cameo. 21-Howard the Duck app. 22-Nightmare app. 3.00
25-($2.99)-Wraparound-c. Black Tom, Howard the Duck app. 4.00
29-37: 29-Begin $1.99-c, "Operation Zero Tolerance". 33-Hama-s 3.00
38-49: 38-Dodson-a begins. 40-Penance ID revealed. 49-Maggott app. 3.00
50,57-($2.99): 50-Crossover w/X-Man #50 4.00
51-56, 58-62: 59-Avengers & Spider-Man app. 3.00
63-74: 63-Ellis-s begin. 64-Begin $2.25-c. 69-71-Art Adams-c 3.00
75-($2.99) Final issue; Chamber joins the X-Men; Lim-a 4.00
'95 Special-($3.95) 4.00
'96 Special-($2.95)-Wraparound-c; Jeff Johnson-c/a 4.00
'97 Special-($2.99)-Wraparound-c; 4.00
'98 Annual-($3.50)-vs. Dracula 4.00
'99 Annual-($3.50)-Monet leaves 4.00
75¢ Ashcan Edition 3.00
...Holiday Special 1 (2/99, $3.50) Pollina-a 4.00
...Underground Special 1 (5/98, $2.50, B&W) Mahfood-a 3.00

GENERATION X/ GEN 13 (Also see Gen 13/ Generation X)
Marvel Comics: 1997 ($3.99, one-shot)

1-Robinson-s/Larroca-a(p) 4.00

GENE RODDENBERRY'S LOST UNIVERSE
Tekno Comix: Apr, 1995 - No. 7, Oct, 1995 ($1.95)

1-7: 1-3-w/ bound-in game piece & trading card. 4-w/bound-in trading card 3.00

GENE RODDENBERRY'S XANDER IN LOST UNIVERSE
Tekno Comix: No. 0, Nov, 1995; No. 1, Dec, 1995 - No. 8, July, 1996 ($2.25)

0,1-8: 1-5-Jae Lee-c. 4-Polybagged. 8-Pt. 5 of The Big Bang x-over 3.00

GENESIS (See DC related titles)
DC Comics: Oct, 1997 - No. 4, Oct, 1997 ($1.95, weekly limited series)

1-4: Byrne-s/Wagner-a(p) in all. 3.00

GENESIS: THE #1 COLLECTION (WildStorm Archives)
WildStorm Productions: 1998 ($9.99, TPB, B&W)

nn-Reprints #1 issues of WildStorm titles and pin-ups 10.00

GENETIX
Marvel Comics UK: Oct, 1993 - No. 6, Mar, 1994 ($1.75, limited series)

1-($2.75)-Polybagged w/4 cards; Dark Guard app. 3.50
2-6: 2-Intro Tektos. 4-Vs. Gene Dogs 3.00

GENEXT (Next generation of X-Men)
Marvel Comics: July, 2008 - No. 5, Nov, 2008 ($3.99, limited series)

1-5: 1-Claremont-s/Scherberger-a; character profile pages 4.00

GENEXT: UNITED
Marvel Comics: July, 2009 - No. 5, Dec, 2009 ($3.99, limited series)

1-5: 1-Claremont-s/Meyers-a; Beast app. 4.00

GEN 12 (Also see Gen 13 and Team 7)
Image Comics (WildStorm Productions): Feb, 1998 - No. 5, June, 1998 ($2.50, lim. series)

1-5: 1-Team 7 & Gen 13 app.; wraparound-c 3.00

GEN 13 (Also see Wild C.A.T.S. #1 & Deathmate Black #2)
Image Comics (WildStorm Productions): Feb, 1994 - No. 5, July 1994 ($1.95, limited series)

0 (8/95, $2.50)-Ch. 1 w/Jim Lee-p; Ch. 4 w/Charest-p 3.00
1/2 1 2 3 4 5 7
1-($2.50)-Created by Jim Lee 1 3 4 6 8 10
1-2nd printing 3.00
1-"3-D" Edition (9/97, $4.95)-w/glasses 5.00
2-($2.50) 1 2 3 4 5 7
3-Pitt-c & story 4.00
4-Pitt-c & story; wraparound-c 4.00
5 4.00
5-Alternate Portacio-c; see Deathblow #5 6.00
...Collected Edition ('94, $12.95)-r/#1-5 13.00
...Rave ($1.50, 3/95)-wraparound-c 3.00
...: Who They Are And How They Came To Be... (2006, $14.99) r/#1-5; sketch gallery 15.00

NOTE: *Issues 1-4 contain coupons redeemable for the ashcan edition of Gen 13 #0. Price listed is for a complete book.*

GEN 13
Image Comics (WildStorm Productions): Mar, 1995 - No. 36, Dec, 1998;
DC Comics (WildStorm): No. 37, Mar, 1999 - No. 77, Jul, 2002 ($2.95/$2.50)

1-A (Charge)-Campbell/Garner-c 5.00
1-B (Thumbs Up)-Campbell/Garner-c 5.00
1-C-1-F,1-I-1-M: 1-C (Lil' GEN 13)-Art Adams-c. 1-D (Barbari-GEN)-Simon Bisley-c. 1-E (Your Friendly Neighborhood Grunge)-Cleary-c. 1-F (GEN 13 Goes Madison Ave.)-Golden-c. 1-I (That's the way we became GEN 13)-Campbell/Gibson-c. 1-J (All Dolled Up)-Campbell/McWeeney-c. 1-K (Verti-GEN)-Dunn-c. 1-L (Picto-Fiction). 1-M (Do it Yourself Cover) 1 2 3 4 5 7
1-G (Lin-GEN-re)-Michael Lopez-c 2 4 6 8 10 12
1-H (GEN-et Jackson)-Jason Pearson-c 2 4 6 8 10 12
1-Chromium-c by Campbell 4 8 12 28 44 60
1-Chromium-c by Jim Lee 6 12 18 37 59 80
1-"3-D" Edition (2/98, $4.95)-w/glasses 5.00
2 ($1.95, Newsstand)-WildStorm Rising Pt. 4; bound-in card 3.00
2-12: 2-($2.50, Direct Market)-WildStorm Rising Pt. 4, bound-in card. 6,7-Jim Lee-c/a(p). 9-Ramos-a. 10,11-Fire From Heaven Pt. 3. & Pt.9 4.00
11-($4.95)-Special European Tour Edition; chromium-c 2 4 6 10 14 18
13A,13B,13C-($1.30, 13 pgs.): 13A-Archie & Friends app. 13B-Bone-c/app.; Teenage Mutant Ninja Turtles, Madman, Spawn & Jim Lee app. 4.00
14-24: 20-Last Campbell-a 3.00
25-($3.50)-Two covers by Campbell and Charest 4.00
25-($3.50)-Voyager Pack w/Danger Girl preview 5.00
25-Foil-c 10.00
26-32,34: 26-Arcudi-s/Frank-a begins. 34-Back-up story by Art Adams 3.00
33-Flip book w/Planetary preview 4.00
35-49: 36,38,40-Two covers. 37-First DC issue. 41-Last Frank-a 3.00
50-($3.95) Two covers by Lee and Benes; art by various 4.00
51-76: 51-Moy-a; Fairchild loses her powers. 60-Warren-s/a. 66-Art by various incl. Campbell (3 pgs.). 70,75,76-Mays-a. 76-Original team dies 3.00
77-($3.50) Mays, Andrews, Warren-a 4.00
Annual 1 (1997, $2.95) Ellis-s/ Dillon-c/a. 4.00
Annual 1999 ($3.50, DC) Slipstream x-over w/ DV8 4.00
Annual 2000 ($3.50) Devil's Night x-over w/WildStorm titles; Bermejo-c 4.00
...: A Christmas Caper (1/00, $5.95, one-shot) McWeeney-s/a 6.00
... Archives (4/98, $12.99) B&W reprints of mini-series, #0,1/2,1-13ABC; includes cover gallery and sourcebook 13.00
...: Carny Folk (2/00, $3.50) Collect back-up stories 3.50
... European Vacation TPB ($6.95) r/#6,7 7.00
.../ Fantastic Four (2001, $5.95) Maguire-s/c/a(p) 6.00
...: Going West (6/99, $2.50, one-shot) Pruett-s 3.00
...: Grunge Saves the World (5/99, $5.95, one-shot) Altieri-c/a 6.00
... I Love New York TPB ($9.95) r/part #25, 26-29; Frank-c 10.00
... London, New York, Hell TPB ($6.95) r/Annual #1 & Bootleg Ann. #1 7.00
... Lost in Paradise TPB ($6.95) r/#3-5 7.00
.../ Maxx (12/95, $3.50, one-shot) Messner-Loebs-s, 1st Coker-c/a. 4.00
...: Meanwhile (2003, $17.95) r/#43,44,66-70; all Warren-s; art by various 18.00
...: Medicine Song (2001, $5.95) Brent Anderson-c/a(p)/Raab-s 6.00
... Science Friction (2001, $5.95) Haley & Lopresti-a 6.00
... Starting Over TPB ($14.95) r/#1-7 15.00
... Superhuman Like You TPB ($12.95) r/#60-65; Warren-c 13.00
... #13 A,B&C Collected Edition ($6.95, TPB) r/#13A,B&C 7.00
... 3-D Special (1997, $4.95, one-shot) Art Adams-s/a(p) 5.00
...: The Unreal World (7/96, $2.95, one-shot) Humberto Ramos-c/a 3.00
... We'll Take Manhattan TPB ($14.95) r/#45-50; new Benes-c 15.00
...: Wired (4/99, $2.50, one-shot) Richard Bennett-c/a 3.00

Gen 13 V4 #15 © WSP

Georgie Comics #4 © MAR

Ghost #2 © FH

GD VG FN VF VF/NM NM-
2.0 4.0 6.0 8.0 9.0 9.2

... Yearbook 1997 (6/97, $2.50) College-themed stories and pin-ups by various 3.00
...: 'Zine (12/96, $1.95, B&W, digest size) Campbell/Garner-c 3.00
Variant Collection-Four editions (all 13 variants w/Chromium variant-limited, signed) 100.00

GEN 13
DC Comics (WildStorm): No. 0, Sept, 2002 - No. 16, Feb, 2004 ($2.95)
0-(13¢-c) Intro. new team; includes previews of 21 Down & The Resistance 3.00
1-Claremont-s/Garza-c/a; Fairchild app. 3.00
2-16: 8-13-Bachs-a. 16-Original team returns 3.00
...: September Song TPB (2003, $19.95) r/#0-6; Garza sketch pages 20.00

GEN 13 (Volume 4)
DC Comics (WildStorm): Dec, 2006 - No. 39, Feb, 2011 ($2.99)
1-39: 1-Simone-s/Caldwell-a; re-intro the original team; Caldwell-c. 8-The Authority app. 3.00
1-Variant-c by J. Scott Campbell 5.00
...: Armageddon (1/08, $2.99) Gage-s/Meyers-a; future Gen13 app. 3.00
...: Best of a Bad Lot TPB (2007, $14.99) r/#1-6 15.00
...: 15 Minutes TPB (2008, $14.99) r/#14-20 15.00
...: Road Trip TPB (2008, $14.99) r/#7-13 15.00
...: World's End TPB (2009, $17.99) r/#21-26 18.00

GEN 13 BOOTLEG
Image Comics (WildStorm): Nov, 1996 - No. 20, Jul, 1998 ($2.50)
1-Alan Davis-a; alternate costumes-c 3.00
1-Team falling variant-c 3.50
2-7: 2-Alan Davis-a. 5,6-Terry Moore-s. 7-Robinson-s/Scott Hampton-a 3.00
8-10-Adam Warren-s/a 4.00
11-20: 11,12-Lopresti-s/a & Simonson-s. 13-Wieringo-s/a. 14-Mariotte-s/Phillips-a. 15,16-Strnad-s/Shaw-a. 18-Altieri-s/a(p)/c, 18-Variant-c by Bruce Timm 3.00
Annual 1 (2/98, $2.95) Ellis-s/Dillon-c/a 4.00
... Grunge: The Movie (12/97, $9.95) r/#8-10, Warren-c 10.00
...Vol. 1 TPB (10/98, $11.95) r/#1-4 12.00

GEN 13/ GENERATION X (Also see Generation X / Gen 13)
Image Comics (WildStorm Publications): July, 1997 ($2.95, one-shot)
1-Choi-s/ Art Adams-p/Garner-i. Variant covers by Adams/Garner and Campbell/McWeeney 3.00
1-($4.95) 3-D Edition w/glasses; Campbell-c 5.00

GEN 13 INTERACTIVE
Image Comics (WildStorm): Oct, 1997 - No. 3, Dec, 1997 ($2.50, lim. series)
1-3-Internet voting used to determine storyline 3.00
... Plus! (7/98, $11.95) r/series & 3-D Special (in 2-D) 12.00

GEN 13 : MAGICAL DRAMA QUEEN ROXY
Image Comics (WildStorm): Oct, 1998 - No. 3, Dec, 1998 ($3.50, lim. series)
1-3-Adam Warren-s/c/a; manga style, 2-Variant-c by Hiroyuki Utatane 3.50
1-($6.95) Dynamic Forces Ed. w/Variant Warren-c 7.00

GEN 13 /MONKEYMAN & O'BRIEN
Image Comics (WildStorm): Jun, 1998 - No. 2, July, 1998 ($2.50, lim. series)
1,2-Art Adams-s/a(p); 1-Two covers 3.00
1-($4.95) Chromium-c 5.00
1-($6.95) Dynamic Forces Ed. 7.00

GEN 13: ORDINARY HEROES
Image Comics (WildStorm Publications): Feb, 1996 - No. 2, July, 1996 ($2.50, lim. series)
1,2-Adam Hughes-c/a/scripts 3.00
TPB (2004, $14.95) r/series, Gen13 Bootleg #1&2 and Wildstorm Thunderbook; new Hughes-c and art pages 15.00

GENTLE BEN (TV)
Dell Publishing Co.: Feb, 1968 - No. 5, Oct, 1969 (All photo-c)
1 4 8 12 26 41 55
2-5: 5-Reprints #1 3 6 9 16 23 30

GEOMANCER (Also see Eternal Warrior: Fist & Steel)
Valiant: Nov, 1994 - No. 8, June, 1995 ($3.75/$2.25)
1 ($3.75)-Chromium wraparound-c; Eternal Warrior app. 4.00
2-8 3.00

GEORGE OF THE JUNGLE (TV)(See America's Best TV Comics)
Gold Key: Feb, 1969 - No. 2, Oct, 1969 (Jay Ward)
1 9 18 27 63 112 160
2 6 12 18 41 66 90

GEORGE PAL'S PUPPETOONS (Funny animal puppets)
Fawcett Publications: Dec, 1945 - No. 18, Dec, 1947; No. 19, 1950
1-Captain Marvel-c 42 84 126 265 445 625
2 23 46 69 136 223 310
3-10 15 30 45 86 133 180
11-19 13 26 39 74 105 135

GEORGIE COMICS (...& Judy Comics #20-35?; see All Teen & Teen Comics)
Timely Comics/GPI No. 1-34: Spr, 1945 - No. 39, Oct, 1952 (#1-3 are quarterly)
1-Dave Berg-a 33 66 99 194 317 440
2 18 36 54 103 162 220
3-5,7,8 15 30 45 90 140 190
6-Georgie visits Timely Comics 18 36 54 103 162 220
9,10-Kurtzman's "Hey Look" (1 & ?); Millie the Model & Margie app. 16 32 48 92 144 195
11,12: 11-Margie, Millie app. 13 26 39 74 105 135
13-Kurtzman's "Hey Look", 3 pgs. 14 28 42 78 112 145
14-Wolverton-a(1 pg.); Kurtzman's "Hey Look" 14 28 42 81 118 155
15,16,18-20 12 24 36 69 97 125
17,29-Kurtzman's "Hey Look", 1 pg. 13 26 39 74 105 135
21-24,27,28,30-39: 21-Anti-Wertham editorial. 33-38-Hy Rosen-c 11 22 33 64 90 115
25-Painted-c by classic pin-up artist Peter Driben 14 28 42 82 121 160
26-Logo design swipe from Archie Comics 12 24 36 67 94 120

GERALD McBOING-BOING AND THE NEARSIGHTED MR. MAGOO (TV)
(Mr. Magoo No. 6 on)
Dell Publishing Co.: Aug-Oct, 1952 - No. 5, Aug-Oct, 1953
1 10 20 30 69 130 190
2-5 9 18 27 61 106 150

GERONIMO (See Fighting Indians of the Wild West!)
Avon Periodicals: 1950 - No. 4, Feb, 1952
1-Indian Fighter; Maneely-a; Texas Rangers-r/Cowpuncher #1; Fawcette-c 19 38 57 111 176 240
2-On the Warpath; Kit West app.; Kinstler-c/a 14 28 42 76 108 140
3-And His Apache Murderers; Kinstler-c/a(2); Kit West-r/Cowpuncher #6 14 28 42 76 108 140
4-Savage Raids of; Kinstler-c & inside front-c; Kinstlerish-a by McCann(3) 13 26 39 72 101 130

GERONIMO JONES
Charlton Comics: Sept, 1971 - No. 9, Jan, 1973
1 2 4 6 13 18 22
2-9 2 4 6 8 10 12
Modern Comics Reprint #7('78) 5.00

GETALONG GANG, THE (TV)
Marvel Comics (Star Comics): May, 1985 - No. 6, Mar, 1986
1-6: Saturday morning TV stars 4.00

GET LOST
Mikeross Publications/New Comics: Feb-Mar, 1954 - No. 3, June-July, 1954 (Satire)
1-Andru/Esposito-a in all? 32 64 96 192 314 435
2-Andru/Esposito-c; has 4 pg. E.C. parody featuring "The Sewer Keeper" 22 44 66 128 209 290
3-John Wayne 'Hondo' parody 19 38 57 109 172 235
1,2 (10,12/87-New Comics)-B&W r-original 4.00

GET SMART (TV)
Dell Publ. Co.: June, 1966 - No. 8, Sept, 1967 (All have Don Adams photo-c)
1 10 20 30 66 121 175
2,3-Ditko-a 7 14 21 46 76 105
4-8: 8-Reprints #1 (cover and insides) 6 12 18 37 59 80

GHOST (...Comics #9)
Fiction House Magazines: 1951(Winter) - No. 11, Summer, 1954
1-Most covers by Whitman 84 168 252 538 919 1300
2-Ghost Gallery & Werewolf Hunter stories 43 86 129 271 461 650
3-9: 3,6,7,9-Bondage-c. 9-Abel, Discount-a 39 78 117 231 378 525
10,11-Dr. Drew by Grandenetti in each, reprinted from Rangers; 11-Evans-r/ Rangers #39; Grandenetti-r/Rangers #49 29 58 87 170 278 385

GHOST (See Comic's Greatest World)
Dark Horse Comics: Apr, 1995 - No. 36, Apr, 1998 ($2.50/$2.95)
1-Adam Hughes-a 1 2 3 5 6 8
2,3-Hughes-a 4.00
4-24: 4-Barb Wire app. 5,6-Hughes-c. 12-Ghost/Hellboy preview. 15,21-X app. 18,19-Barb Wire app. 3.00

Ghost Special #1 © DH

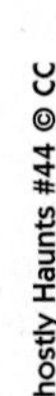
Ghostly Haunts #44 © CC

Ghost Manor #18 © CC

GD VG FN VF VF/NM NM-
2.0 4.0 6.0 8.0 9.0 9.2

25-($3.50)-48 pgs. special 4.00
26-36: 26-Begin $2.95-c. 29-Flip book w/Timecop. 33-36-Jade Cathedral; Harris painted-c 3.00
Special 1 (7/94, $3.95, 48 pgs.) 1 2 3 4 5 7
Special 2 (6/98, $3.95) Barb Wire app. 4.00
... Black October (1/99, $14.95, trade paperback)-r/#6-9,26,27 15.00
... Nocturnes (1996, $9.95, trade paperback)-r/#1-3 & 5 10.00
... Omnibus Vol. 1 (10/08, $24.95, 9x6") r/#1-12; Special 1 and Decade of Dark Horse #2 25.00
...Stories (1995, $9.95, trade paperback)-r/Early Ghost app. 10.00

GHOST (Volume 2)
Dark Horse Comics: Sept, 1998 - No. 22, Aug, 2000 ($2.95)

1-22: 1-4-Ryan Benjamin-c/Zanier-a 3.00
Handbook (8/99, $2.95) guide to issues and characters 3.00
Special 3 (12/98, $3.95) 4.00

GHOST AND THE SHADOW
Dark Horse Comics: Dec, 1995 ($2.95, one-shot)

1-Moench scripts 3.00

GHOST/BATGIRL
Dark Horse Comics: Aug, 2000 - No. 4, Dec, 2000 ($2.95, limited series)

1-4-New Batgirl; Oracle & Bruce Wayne app.; Benjamin-c/a 3.00

GHOST/HELLBOY
Dark Horse Comics: May, 1996 - No. 2, June, 1996 ($2.50, limited series)

1,2: Mike Mignola-c/scripts & breakdowns; Scott Benefiel finished-a 4.00

GHOST BREAKERS (Also see Racket Squad in Action, Red Dragon & (CC) Sherlock Holmes Comics)
Street & Smith Publications: Sept, 1948 - No. 2, Dec, 1948 (52 pgs.)

1-Powell-c/a(3); Dr. Neff (magician) app. 42 84 126 265 445 625
2-Powell-c/a(2); Maneely-a 34 68 102 206 336 465

GHOSTBUSTERS (TV) (Also, see Real...and Slimer)
First Comics: Feb, 1987 - No. 6, Aug, 1987 ($1.25)

1-6: Based on new animated TV series 3.00

GHOSTBUSTERS
IDW Publishing: Sept, 2011 - Present ($3.99)

1-3-Burnham-s/Schoening-a; multiple covers 4.00

GHOSTBUSTERS
IDW Publishing: (one-shots)

...: Con-Volution (6/10, $3.99) Josh Howard-a 4.00
...: Tainted Love (2/10, $3.99) Salgood Sam-a 4.00
...: What in Samhain Just Happened? (10/10, $3.99) Peter David-s/Dan Schoening-a 4.00

GHOSTBUSTERS: DISPLACED AGGRESSION
IDW Publishing: Sept, 2009 - No. 4, Dec, 2009 ($3.99)

1-3-Lobdell-s/Kyriazis-a 4.00
Hundred Penny Press: Ghostbusters: Displaced Aggression (3/11, $1.00) r/#1 3.00

GHOSTBUSTERS: INFESTATION (Zombie x-over with Star Trek, G.I. Joe & Transformers)
IDW Publishing: Mar, 2011 - No. 2, Mar, 2011 ($3.99, limited series)

1,2-Kyle Hotz-a; covers by Hotz and Snyder III 4.00

GHOSTBUSTERS: LEGION (Movie)
88 MPH Studios: Feb, 2004 - No. 4, May, 2004 ($2.95/$3.50)

1-4-Steve Kurth-a/Andrew Dabb-s 3.00
1-3-($3.50) Brereton variant-c 3.50

GHOSTBUSTERS: THE OTHER SIDE
IDW Publishing: Oct, 2008 - No. 4, Jan, 2009 ($3.99)

1-4-Champagne-s/Nguyen-a 4.00

GHOSTBUSTERS II
Now Comics: Oct, 1989 - No. 3, Dec, 1989 ($1.95, mini-series)

1-3: Movie Adaptation 3.00

GHOST CASTLE (See Tales of...)

GHOST IN THE SHELL (Manga)
Dark Horse: Mar, 1995 - No. 8, Oct, 1995 ($3.95, B&W/color, lim. series)

1,2 3 6 9 14 20 25
3 2 4 6 9 12 15
4-8 1 3 4 6 8 10

GHOST IN THE SHELL 2: MAN-MADE INTERFACE (Manga)
Dark Horse Comics: Jan, 2003 - No. 11, Dec, 2003 ($3.50, color/B&W, lim. series)

1-11-Masamune Shirow-s/a. 5-B&W 5.00

GHOSTLY HAUNTS (Formerly Ghost Manor)
Charlton Comics: #20, 9/71 - #53, 12/76; #54, 9/77 - #55, 10/77; #56, 1/78 - #58, 4/78

20 3 6 9 19 29 38
21 2 4 6 13 18 22
22-25,27,31-34,36,37-Ditko-c/a. 27-Dr. Graves x-over. 32-New logo. 33-Back to old logo 3 6 9 16 22 28
26,29,30,35-Ditko-c 2 4 6 13 18 22
28,38-40-Ditko-a. 39-Origin & 1st app. Destiny Fox 2 4 6 11 16 20
41,42: 41-Sutton-c; Ditko-a. 42-Newton-c/a 2 4 6 13 18 22
43-46,48,50,52-Ditko-a 2 4 6 10 14 18
47,54,56-Ditko-c/a. 56-Ditko-a(r). 3 6 9 14 19 24
49,51,53,55,57 2 4 6 8 10 12
58 (4/78) Last issue 3 6 9 14 19 24
40,41(Modern Comics-r, 1977, 1978) 6.00

NOTE: ***Ditko** a-22-25, 27, 28, 31-34, 36-41, 43-48, 50, 52, 54, 56r; c-22-27, 29, 30, 33-37, 47, 54, 56. **Glanzman** a-20. **Howard** a-27, 30, 35, 40-43, 48, 54, 57. **Kim** a-38, 41, 57. **Larson** a-48, 50. **Newton** c/a-42. **Staton** a-32, 35; c-28, 46. **Sutton** c-33, 37, 39, 41.*

GHOSTLY TALES (Formerly Blue Beetle No. 50-54)
Charlton Comics: No. 55, 4-5/66 - No. 124, 12/76; No. 125, 9/77 - No. 169, 10/84

55-Intro. & origin Dr. Graves; Ditko-a 8 16 24 55 93 130
56-58,60,61,70,71-Ditko-a. 70-Dr. Graves ends. 71-Last 12¢ issue 4 8 12 28 44 60
59,62-66,68 3 6 9 20 30 40
67,69-Ditko-c/a 5 10 15 32 51 70
72,75,76,79-82,85-Ditko-a 3 6 9 16 23 30
73,77,78,83,84,86-90,92-95,97,99-Ditko-c/a 3 6 9 21 32 42
74,91,98,119,123,124,127-130: 127,130-Sutton-a 2 4 6 11 16 20
96-Ditko-c 3 6 9 16 23 30
100-Ditko-c; Sutton-a 3 6 9 17 25 32
101,103-105-Ditko-a 2 4 6 13 18 22
102,109-Ditko-c/a 3 6 9 16 22 28
110,113-Sutton-c; Ditko-a 2 4 6 13 18 22
106-Ditko & Sutton-a; Sutton-c 2 4 6 13 18 22
107-Ditko, Wood, Sutton-a 3 6 9 14 19 24
108,116,117,126-Ditko-a 2 4 6 13 18 22
111,118,120-122,125-Ditko-c/a 3 6 9 16 22 28
112,114,115: 112,114-Ditko, Sutton-a. 114-Newton-a. 115-Newton, Ditko-a. 2 4 6 13 18 22
131-134,151,157,163-Ditko-c/a 2 4 6 11 16 20
135,142,145-150,153,154,156,158-160 1 2 3 5 7 9
136-141,143,144,152,155-Ditko-a 2 4 6 8 10 12
161,162,164-168-Lower print run. 162-Nudity panel 2 4 6 9 12 15
169 (10/84) Last issue; lower print run 2 4 6 11 16 20

NOTE: ***Aparo** a-65, 66, 68, 72, 137, 141r, 142r; c-71, 72, 74-76, 81, 146r, 149. **Ditko** a-55-58, 60, 61, 67, 69-73, 75-90, 92-95, 97, 99-118, 120-122, 125r, 126r, 131-141r, 143r, 144r, 146, 147, 149-152, 154-157, 159-161, 163; c-67, 69, 73, 77, 78, 83, 84, 86-90, 92-97, 99, 102, 109, 111, 118, 120-122, 125, 131-133, 147, 148, 151, 157-160, 163. **Glanzman** a-167. **Howard** a-95, 98, 99, 108, 117, 129, 131; c-98, 107, 120, 121, 161. **Larson** a-117, 119, 136, 159; c-136. **Morisi** a-83, 84, 86. **Newton** a-114; c-115(painted). **Palais** a-61. **Staton** a-161; c-117. **Sutton** a-106, 107, 111-114, 127, 130, 162; c-100, 106, 110, 113(painted). **Wood** a-107.*

GHOSTLY WEIRD STORIES (Formerly Blue Bolt Weird)
Star Publications: No. 120, Sept, 1953 - No. 124, Sept, 1954

120-Jo-Jo-r 41 82 123 256 428 600
121-124: 121-Jo-Jo-r. 122-The Mask-r/Capt. Flight #5; Rulah-r; has 1pg. story 'Death and the Devil Pills'-r/Western Outlaws #17. 123-Jo-Jo; Disbrow-a(2). 124-Torpedo Man 39 78 117 231 378 525

NOTE: ***Disbrow** a-120-124. **L. B. Cole** covers-all issues (#122 is a sci-fi cover).*

GHOST MANOR (Ghostly Haunts No. 20 on)
Charlton Comics: July, 1968 - No. 19, July, 1971

1 7 14 21 44 72 100
2-6: 6-Last 12¢ issue 4 8 12 24 37 50
7-12,17: 17-Morisi-a 3 6 9 18 27 35
13,14,16-Ditko-a 3 6 9 21 32 42
15,18,19-Ditko-c/a 4 8 12 26 41 55

GHOST MANOR (2nd Series)
Charlton Comics: Oct, 1971-No. 32, Dec, 1976; No. 33, Sept, 1977-No. 77, 11/84

1 5 10 15 32 51 70
2,3,5-7,9-Ditko-c 3 6 9 18 27 35
4,10-Ditko-c/a 4 8 12 22 34 45
8-Wood, Ditko-a; Sutton-c 3 6 9 20 30 40
11,14-Ditko-c/a 3 6 9 17 25 32
12,17,27,30 2 4 6 9 13 16
13,15,16,23-26,29: 13-Ditko-a. 15,16-Ditko-c. 23-Sutton-a. 24-26,29-Ditko-a. 26-Early Zeck-a; Boyette-c 2 4 6 13 18 22

Ghost Rider #30 © MAR

Ghost Rider V2 #52 © MAR

Ghost Rider (2006 series) #91 © MAR

	GD 2.0	VG 4.0	FN 6.0	VF 8.0	VF/NM 9.0	NM- 9.2
18-(3/74) Newton 1st pro art; Ditko-a; Sutton-c	3	6	9	16	22	28
19-21: 19-Newton, Sutton-a; nudity panels. 20-Ditko-a. 21-E-Man, Blue Beetle, Capt. Atom cameos; Ditko-a.	2	4	6	13	18	22
22-Newton-c/a; Ditko-a	3	6	9	14	19	24
25,28,31,37,38-Ditko-c/a: 28-Nudity panels	3	6	9	14	19	24
32-36,39,41,45,48-50,53: 34-Black Cat by Kim	2	4	6	8	10	12
40-Ditko-a; torture & drug use	2	4	6	13	18	22
42,43,46,47,51,52,60,62,69-Ditko-c/a	2	4	6	11	16	20
44,54,71-Ditko-a	2	4	6	8	11	14
55,56,58,59,61,63,65-68,70	1	2	3	5	7	9
57-Wood, Ditko, Howard-a	2	4	6	9	12	15
64-Ditko & Newton-a	2	4	6	8	11	14
71-76 (low print)	2	3	4	6	8	10
77-(11/84) Last issue Aparo-r/Space Adventures V3#60 (Paul Mann)	2	4	6	9	13	16
19 (Modern Comics reprint, 1977)						6.00

NOTE: ***Ditko*** *a-4, 8, 10, 11(2), 13, 14, 18, 20-22, 24-26, 28, 29, 31, 37r, 38r, 40r, 42-44r, 46r, 47, 51r, 52r, 54r, 57, 60, 62(4), 64r, 69, 71; c-2-7, 9-11, 14-16, 28, 31, 37, 38, 42, 43, 46, 47, 51, 52, 60, 62, 64.* ***Howard*** *a-4, 8, 12, 17, 19-21, 31, 41, 45, 57.* ***Newton*** *a-18-20, 22, 64; c-22.* ***Staton*** *a-13, 38, 44, 45.* ***Sutton*** *a-19, 23, 25, 45;c-8, 18.*

GHOST RIDER (See A-1 Comics, Best of the West, Black Phantom, Bobby Benson, Great Western, Red Mask & Tim Holt)
Magazine Enterprises: 1950 - No. 14, 1954

NOTE: *The character was inspired by Vaughn Monroe's "Ghost Riders in the Sky", and Disney's movie "The Headless Horseman".*

	GD 2.0	VG 4.0	FN 6.0	VF 8.0	VF/NM 9.0	NM- 9.2
1(A-1 #27)-Origin Ghost Rider	116	232	348	742	1271	1800
2-5: 2(A-1 #29), 3(A-1 #31), 4(A-1 #34), 5(A-1 #37)-All Frazetta-c only	77	154	231	493	847	1200
6,7: 6(A-1 #44)-Loco weed story, 7(A-1 #51)	34	68	102	206	336	465
8,9: 8(A-1 #57)-Drug use story, 9(A-1 #69)	30	60	90	177	289	400
10(A-1 #71)-Vs. Frankenstein	34	68	102	199	325	450
11-14: 11(A-1 #75). 12(A-1 #80)-Bondage-c; one-eyed Devil-c. 13(A-1 #84). 14(A-1 #112)	26	52	78	154	252	350

NOTE: ***Dick Ayers*** *art in all; c-1, 6-14.*

GHOST RIDER, THE (See Night Rider & Western Gunfighters)
Marvel Comics Group: Feb, 1967 - No. 7, Nov, 1967 (Western hero)(12¢)

	GD 2.0	VG 4.0	FN 6.0	VF 8.0	VF/NM 9.0	NM- 9.2
1-Origin & 1st app. Ghost Rider; Kid Colt-reprints begin	9	18	27	63	112	160
2	6	12	18	37	59	80
3-7: 6-Last Kid Colt-r; All Ayers-c/a(p)	5	10	15	32	51	70

GHOST RIDER (See The Champions, Marvel Spotlight #5, Marvel Team-Up #15, 58, Marvel Treasury Edition #18, Marvel Two-In-One #8, The Original Ghost Rider & The Original Ghost Rider Rides Again)
Marvel Comics Group: Sept, 1973 - No. 81, June, 1983 (Super-hero)

	GD 2.0	VG 4.0	FN 6.0	VF 8.0	VF/NM 9.0	NM- 9.2
1-Johnny Blaze, the Ghost Rider begins; 1st brief app. Daimon Hellstrom (Son of Satan)	15	30	45	102	221	340
2-1st full app. Daimon Hellstrom; gives glimpse of costume (1 panel); story continues in Marvel Spotlight #12	7	14	21	48	79	110
3-5: 3-Ghost Rider gains power to make cycle of fire; Son of Satan app.	5	10	15	32	51	70
6-10: 10-Hulk on cover; reprints origin/1st app. from Marvel Spotlight #5; Ploog-a	4	8	12	22	34	45
11-16: 11-Hulk app.	3	6	9	14	20	25
17,19-(Reg. 25¢ editions)(4,8/76)	3	6	9	14	20	25
17,19-(30¢-c variants, limited distribution)	4	8	12	28	44	60
18-(Reg. 25¢ edition)(6/76). Spider-Man-c & app.	3	6	9	16	22	28
18-(30¢-c variant, limited distribution)	5	10	15	32	51	70
20-Daredevil x-over; ties into D.D. #138; Byrne-a	3	6	9	18	27	35
21-30: 22-1st app. Enforcer. 29,30-Vs. Dr. Strange	2	4	6	9	12	15
24-26-(35¢-c variants, limited distribution)	4	8	12	26	41	55
31-34,36-49	2	3	4	6	8	10
35-Death Race classic; Starlin-c/a/sty	2	4	6	9	13	16
50-Double size	2	4	6	8	10	12
51-76: 68-Origin retold						6.00
77-80: 77-Origin retold. 80-Brief origin recap	1	2	3	5	6	8
81-Death of Ghost Rider (Demon leaves Blaze)	3	6	9	16	23	30
... Team Up TPB (2007, $15.99) r/#27, 50, Marvel Team-Up #91, Marvel Two-In-One #80, Avengers #214 and Marvel Premiere #28; Night Rider app.; cover gallery						16.00

NOTE: ***Anderson*** *c-64p.* ***Infantino*** *a(p)-43, 44, 51.* ***G. Kane*** *a-21p; c(p)-1, 2, 4, 5, 8, 9, 11-13, 19, 20, 24, 25.* ***Kirby*** *c-21-23.* ***Mooney*** *a-2-9p, 30i.* ***Nebres*** *c-26i.* ***Newton*** *a-23i.* ***Perez*** *c-26p.* ***Shores*** *a-2i. J.* ***Sparling*** *a-62p, 64p, 65p.* ***Starlin*** *a(p)-35.* ***Sutton*** *a-1p, 44i, 64i, 65i, 66, 67i.* ***Tuska*** *a-13p, 14p, 16p.*

GHOST RIDER (Volume 2) (Also see Doctor Strange/Ghost Rider Special, Marvel Comics Presents & Midnight Sons Unlimited)
Marvel Comics (Midnight Sons imprint #44 on): V2#1, May, 1990 - No. 93, Feb, 1998 ($1.50/$1.75/$1.95)

	GD 2.0	VG 4.0	FN 6.0	VF 8.0	VF/NM 9.0	NM- 9.2
1-($1.95, 52 pgs.)-Origin/1st app. new Ghost Rider; Kingpin app.	1	2	3	5	6	8
1-2nd printing (not gold)						3.00
2-5: 3-Kingpin app. 5-Punisher app.; Jim Lee-c						4.00
5-Gold background 2nd printing						3.00
6-14,16-24,29,30,32-39: 6-Punisher app. 6,17-Spider-Man/Hobgoblin-c/story. 9-X-Factor app. 10-Reintro Johnny Blaze on the last pg. 11-Stroman-c/a(p). 12,13-Dr. Strange x-over cont'd in D.S. #28. 13-Painted-c. 14-Johnny Blaze vs. Ghost Rider; origin recap 1st Ghost Rider (Blaze). 18-Painted-c by Nelson. 29-Wolverine-c/story. 32-Dr. Strange x-over; Johnny Blaze app. 34-Williamson-a(i). 36-Daredevil app. 37-Archangel app.						3.00
15-Glow in the dark-c						4.00
25-27: 25-($2.75)-Contains pop-up scene insert. 26,27-X-Men x-over; Lee/Williams-c on both						4.00
28,31-($2.50, 52 pgs.)-Polybagged w/poster; part 1 & part 6 of Rise of the Midnight Sons storyline (see Ghost Rider/Blaze #1)						4.00
40-Outer-c is Darkhold envelope made of black parchment w/gold ink; Midnight Massacre; Demogoblin app.						3.00
41-48: 41-Lilith & Centurious app.; begin $1.75-c. 41-43-Neon ink-c. 43-Has free extra 16 pg. insert on Siege of Darkness. 44,45-Siege of Darkness parts 2 & 10. 44-Spot varnish-c. 46-Intro new Ghost Rider. 48-Spider-Man app.						3.00
49,51-60,62-74: 49-Begin $1.95-c; bound-in trading card sheet; Hulk app. 55-Werewolf by Night app. 65-Punisher app. 67,68-Gambit app. 68-Wolverine app. 73,74-Blaze, Vengeance app.						3.00
50,61: 50-($2.50, 52 pgs.)-Regular edition						4.00
50-($2.95, 52 pgs.)-Collectors Ed. die cut foil-c						4.00
75-89: 76-Vs. Vengeance. 77,78-Dr. Strange-app. 78-New costume						3.00
90-92						6.00
93-($2.99)-Last issue; Saltares & Texeira-a	2	4	6	8	10	12
(#94, see Ghost Rider Finale for unpublished story)						
#(-1) Flashback (7/97) Saltares-a						3.00
Annual 1,2 ('93, '94, $2.95, 68 pgs.) 1-Bagged w/card						4.00
...And Cable 1 (9/92, $3.95, stiff-c, 68 pgs.)-Reprints Marvel Comics Presents #90-98 w/new Kieth-c						4.00
...:Crossroads (11/95, $3.95) Die cut cover; Nord-a						5.00
... Cycle of Vengeance 1 (3/12, $5.99) r/Marvel Spotlight #5, Ghost Rider (1990) #1 and Ghost Rider (2006) #1; Leinil Yu-c						6.00
... Finale (2007, $3.99) r/#93 and the story meant for the unpublished #94; Saltares-a						4.00
Highway to Hell (2001, $3.50) Reprints origin from Marvel Spotlight #5						3.50
...: Resurrected TPB (2001, $12.95) r/#1-7						13.00

NOTE: ***Andy & Joe Kubert*** *c/a-28-31.* ***Quesada*** *c-21.* ***Williamson*** *a(i)-33-35; c-33i.*

GHOST RIDER (Volume 3)
Marvel Comics: Aug, 2001 - No. 6, Jan, 2002 ($2.99, limited series)

	GD 2.0	VG 4.0	FN 6.0	VF 8.0	VF/NM 9.0	NM- 9.2
1-6-Grayson-s/Kaniuga-a/c						3.00
...: The Hammer Lane TPB (6/02, $15.95) r/#1-6						16.00

GHOST RIDER
Marvel Comics: Nov, 2005 - No. 6, Apr, 2006 ($2.99, limited series)

	GD 2.0	VG 4.0	FN 6.0	VF 8.0	VF/NM 9.0	NM- 9.2
1-6-Garth Ennis-s/Clayton Crain-a/c. 1-Origin retold						3.00
1 (Director's Cut) (2005, $3.99) r/#1 with Ennis pitch and script and Crain art process						4.00
...: Road to Damnation HC (2006, $19.99, dust jacket) r/#1-6; variant covers & concept-a						20.00
...: Road to Damnation SC (2007, $14.99) r/#1-6; variant covers & concept-a						15.00

GHOST RIDER
Marvel Comics: Sept, 2006 - No. 35, Jul, 2009 ($2.99)

	GD 2.0	VG 4.0	FN 6.0	VF 8.0	VF/NM 9.0	NM- 9.2
1-11: 1-Daniel Way-s/Saltares & Texeira-a. 2-4-Dr. Strange app. 6,7-Corben-a						3.00
12-27,29-35: 12,13-World War Hulk; Saltares-a/Dell'Otto-c. 23-Danny Ketch returns						3.00
28-($3.99) Silvestri-c/Huat-a; back-up history of Danny Ketch						4.00
Annual 1 (1/08, $3.99) Ben Oliver-a/c/Stuart Moore-s						4.00
Annual 2 (10/08, $3.99) Spurrier-s/Robinson-a; r/Ghost Rider #35 (1979)						4.00
... Vol. 1: Vicious Cycle TPB (2007, $13.99) r/#1-5						14.00
... Vol. 2: The Life and Death of Johnny Blaze TPB (2007, $13.99) r/#6-11						14.00
... Vol. 3: Apocalypse Soon TPB (2008, $10.99) r/#12,13 & Annual #1						11.00
... Vol. 4: Revelations TPB (2008, $14.99) r/#14-19						15.00

GHOST RIDER
Marvel Comics: No. 0.1, Aug, 2011 - No. 8, Mar, 2012 ($2.99/$3.99)

	GD 2.0	VG 4.0	FN 6.0	VF 8.0	VF/NM 9.0	NM- 9.2
0.1-($2.99) Johnny Blaze gets rid of the Spirit of Vengeance; Matthew Clark-a						3.00
1-($3.99) Adam Kubert-c; Fear Itself tie-in; new female Ghost Rider; Mephisto app.						4.00
2-8: 2-4-($2.99) Fear Itself tie-in. 5-Garbett-a. 7,8-Hawkeye app.						3.00

GHOST RIDER/BALLISTIC
Marvel Comics: Feb, 1997 ($2.95, one-shot)

	GD 2.0	VG 4.0	FN 6.0	VF 8.0	VF/NM 9.0	NM- 9.2
1-Devil's Reign pt. 3						3.00

Ghost Rider 2099 #4 © MAR

Ghosts #80 © DC

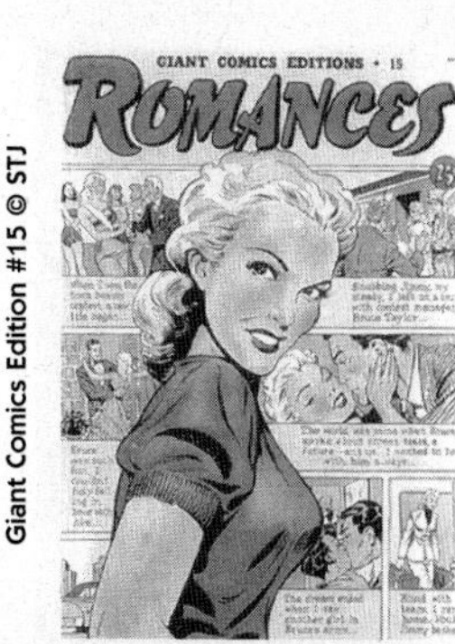

Giant Comics Edition #15 © STJ

GD VG FN VF VF/NM NM-
2.0 4.0 6.0 8.0 9.0 9.2

GHOST RIDER/BLAZE: SPIRITS OF VENGEANCE (Also see Blaze)
Marvel Comics (Midnight Sons imprint #17 on): Aug, 1992 - No. 23, June, 1994 ($1.75)
1-($2.75, 52 pgs.)-Polybagged w/poster; part 2 of Rise of the Midnight Sons storyline; Adam Kubert-c/a begins 4.00
2-11,14-21: 4-Art Adams & Joe Kubert-p. 5,6-Spirits of Venom parts 2 & 4 cont'd from Web of Spider-Man #95,96 w/Demogoblin. 14-17-Neon ink-c. 15-Intro Blaze's new costume & power. 17,18-Siege of Darkness parts 8 & 13. 17-Spot varnish-c 3.00
12-($2.95)-Glow-in-the-dark-c 4.00
13-($2.25)-Outer-c is Darkhold envelope made of black parchment w/gold ink; Midnight Massacre x-over 3.00
22,23: 22-Begin $1.95-c; bound-in trading card sheet 3.00
NOTE: *Adam & Joe Kubert c-7, 8. Adam Kubert/Steacy c-6. J. Kubert a-13p(6 pgs.)*

GHOST RIDER/CAPTAIN AMERICA: FEAR
Marvel Comics: Oct, 1992 ($5.95, 52 pgs.)
nn-Wraparound gatefold-c; Williamson inks 6.00

GHOST RIDER: DANNY KETCH
Marvel Comics: Dec, 2008 - No. 5, Apr, 2009 ($3.99, limited series)
1-5-Saltares-a 4.00

GHOST RIDER: HEAVEN'S ON FIRE
Marvel Comics: Oct, 2009 - No. 6, Mar, 2010 ($3.99, limited series)
1-6: 1-Jae Lee-c/Boschi-a/Aaron-s; Hellstorm app.; r/pages from Ghost Rider #1 ('73) 4.00

GHOST RIDER: TRAIL OF TEARS
Marvel Comics: Apr, 2007 - No. 6, Sept, 2007 ($2.99, limited series)
1-6-Garth Ennis-s/Clayton Crain-a/c; Civil War era tale 3.00
HC (2007, $19.99) r/series 20.00
SC (2008, $14.99) r/series 15.00

GHOST RIDER 2099
Marvel Comics: May, 1994 - No. 25, May, 1996 ($1.50/$1.95)
1 ($2.25)-Collector's Edition w/prismatic foil-c 4.00
1 ($1.50)-Regular Edition; bound-in trading card sheet 3.00
2-24: 7-Spider-Man 2099 app. 3.00
2-(Variant; polybagged with Sega Sub-Terrania poster) 5.00
25 ($2.95) 4.00

GHOST RIDER, WOLVERINE, PUNISHER: THE DARK DESIGN
Marvel Comics: Dec, 1994 ($5.95, one-shot)
nn-Gatefold-c 6.00

GHOST RIDER; WOLVERINE; PUNISHER: HEARTS OF DARKNESS
Marvel Comics: Dec, 1991 ($4.95, one-shot, 52 pgs.)
1-Double gatefold-c; John Romita, Jr.-c/a(p) 5.00

GHOSTS (Ghost No. 1)
National Periodical Publications/DC Comics: Sept-Oct, 1971 - No. 112, May, 1982 (No. 1-5: 52 pgs.)
1-Aparo-a 12 24 36 81 166 250
2-Wood-a(i) 8 16 24 51 86 120
3-5-(52 pgs.) 7 14 21 44 72 100
6-10 3 6 9 20 40 60
11-20 3 6 9 14 20 25
21-39 2 4 6 9 13 16
40-(68 pgs.) 3 6 9 16 23 30
41-60 2 4 6 8 10 12
61-96 1 2 3 5 6 8
97-99-The Spectre vs. Dr. 13 by Aparo. 97,98-Spectre-c by Aparo.
2 4 6 10 14 18
100-Infinity-c 2 3 4 6 8 10
101-112 1 2 3 5 6 8
NOTE: *B. Baily a-77. Buckler c-99, 100. J. Craig a-108. Ditko a-77, 111. Giffen a-104p, 106p, 111p. Glanzman a-2. Golden a-88. Infantino a-8. Kaluta c-7, 93, 101. Kubert a-8; c-89, 105-108, 111. Mayer a-111. McWilliams a-99. Win Mortimer a-89, 91, 94. Nasser/Netzer a-97. Newton a-92p, 94p. Nino a-35, 37, 57. Orlando a-74i; c-80. Redondo a-8, 13, 45. Sparling a(p)-90, 93, 94. Spiegle a-103, 105. Tuska a-2i. Dr. 13, the Ghostbreaker back-ups in 95-99, 101.*

GHOSTS SPECIAL (See DC Special Series No. 7)

GHOST STORIES (See Amazing Ghost Stories)

GHOST STORIES
Dell Publ. Co.: Sept-Nov, 1962; No. 2, Apr-June, 1963 - No. 37, Oct, 1973
12-295-211(#1)-Written by John Stanley 7 14 21 44 72 100
2 4 8 12 24 37 50
3-10: Two No. 6's exist with different c/a(12-295-406 & 12-295-503)
#12-295-503 is actually #9 with indicia to #6 3 6 9 20 30 40
11-21: 21-Last 12¢ issue 3 6 9 16 23 30
22-37 2 4 6 13 18 22
NOTE: *#21-34, 36, 37 all reprint earlier issues.*

GD VG FN VF VF/NM NM-
2.0 4.0 6.0 8.0 9.0 9.2

GHOST WHISPERER (Based on the CBS television series)
IDW Publishing: Mar, 2008 - No. 5, July, 2008 ($3.99)
1-5: 1-Two covers by Casagrande & Ho; Casagrande-a 4.00

GHOST WHISPERER: THE MUSE
IDW Publishing: Dec, 2008 - No. 4, Mar, 2009 ($3.99)
1-4-Two covers (photo & art) for each; Barbara Kesel-s/ Adriano Loyola-a 4.00

GHOUL, THE
IDW Publishing: Nov, 2009 - No. 3, Mar, 2010 ($3.99, limited series)
1-3-Niles-s/Wrightson-a 4.00

GHOUL TALES (Magazine)
Stanley Publications: Nov, 1970 - No. 5, July, 1971 (52 pgs.) (B&W)
1-Aragon pre-code reprints; Mr. Mystery as host; bondage-c
8 16 24 51 86 120
2,3: 2-(1/71)Reprint/Climax #1. 3-(3/71) 4 8 12 28 44 60
4-(5/71)Reprints story "The Way to a Man's Heart" used in **SOTI**
5 10 15 32 51 70
5-ACG reprints 4 8 12 22 34 45
NOTE: *No. 1-4 contain pre-code Aragon reprints.*

GIANT BOY BOOK OF COMICS (Also see Boy Comics)
Newsbook Publications (Gleason): 1945 (240 pgs., hard-c)
1-Crimebuster & Young Robin Hood; Biro-c 95 190 285 603 1039 1475

GIANT COMIC ALBUM
King Features Syndicate: 1972 (59¢, 11x14", 52 pgs., B&W, cardboard-c)
Newspaper reprints: Barney Google, Little Iodine, Katzenjammer Kids, Henry, Beetle Bailey, Blondie, & Snuffy Smith each... 3 6 9 20 30 40
Flash Gordon ('68-69 Dan Barry) 4 8 12 26 41 55
Mandrake the Magician ('59 Falk), Popeye 4 8 12 24 37 50

GIANT COMICS
Charlton Comics: Summer, 1957 - No. 3, Winter, 1957 (25¢, 96 pgs., not rebound material)
1-Atomic Mouse, Lil Genius, Lil Tomboy app. 22 44 66 128 209 290
2-(Fall '57) Romance 20 40 60 114 182 250
3-Christmas Book; Atomic Mouse, Atomic Rabbit, Li'l Genius, Li'l Tomboy & Atom the Cat stories 16 32 48 94 147 200

GIANT COMICS (See Wham-O Giant Comics)

GIANT COMICS EDITION (See Terry-Toons) (Also see Fox Giants)
St. John Publishing Co.: 1947 - No. 17, 1950 (25¢, 100-164 pgs.)
1-Mighty Mouse 52 104 156 328 557 785
2-Abbie & Slats 29 58 87 170 278 385
3-Terry-Toons Album; 100 pgs. 41 82 123 249 417 585
4-Crime comics; contains Red Seal No. 16, used & illo. in **SOTI**
58 116 174 371 636 900
5-Police Case Book (4/49, 132 pgs.)-Contents varies; contains remaindered St. John books - some volumes contain 5 copies rather than 4, with 160 pages; Matt Baker-c
60 120 180 381 653 925
5A-Terry-Toons Album (132 pgs.)-Mighty Mouse, Heckle & Jeckle, Gandy Goose & Dinky stories 37 74 111 222 361 500
6-Western Picture Stories; Baker-c/a(3); Tuska-a; The Sky Chief, Blue Monk, Ventrilo app., 132 pgs. 52 104 156 328 557 785
7-Contains a teen-age romance plus 3 Mopsy comics
36 72 108 216 351 485
8-The Adventures of Mighty Mouse (10/49) 37 74 111 222 361 500
9-Romance and Confession Stories; Kubert-a(4); Baker-a; photo-c (132 pgs.)
97 194 291 621 1061 1500
10-Terry-Toons Album (132 pgs.)-Mighty Mouse, Heckle & Jeckle, Gandy Goose stories
37 74 111 222 361 500
11-Western Picture Stories-Baker-c/a(4); The Sky Chief, Desperado, & Blue Monk app.; another version with Son of Sinbad by Kubert (132 pgs.)
52 104 156 328 557 785
12-Diary Secrets; Baker prostitute-c; 4 St. John romance comics; Baker-a
314 628 942 2198 3849 5500
13-Romances; Baker, Kubert-a 81 162 243 518 884 1250
14-Mighty Mouse Album (132 pgs.) 36 72 108 216 351 485
15-Romances (4 love comics)-Baker-c 90 180 270 576 988 1400
16-Little Audrey; Abbott & Costello, Casper 40 80 120 246 411 575
17(nn)-Mighty Mouse Album (nn, no date, but did follow No. 16); 100 pgs. on cover but has 148 pgs. 36 72 108 216 351 485

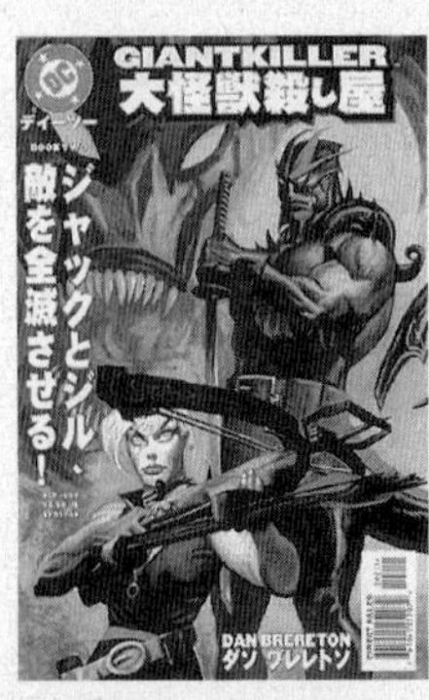

Giantkiller #2 © Dan Brereton

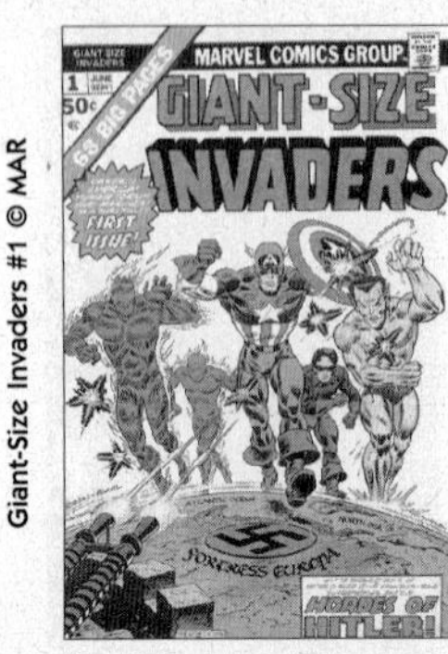

Giant-Size Invaders #1 © MAR

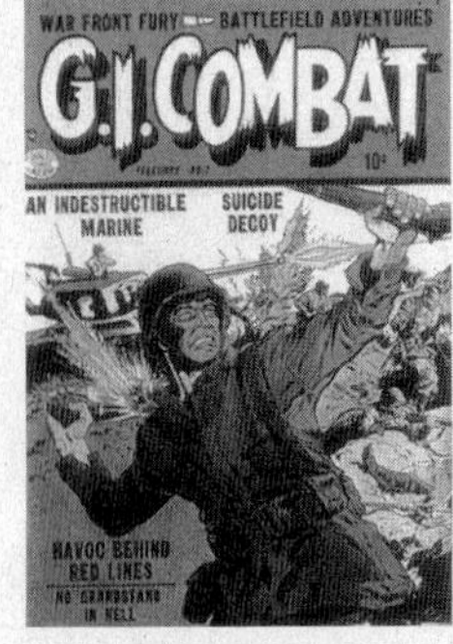

G.I. Combat #3 © QUA

	GD 2.0	VG 4.0	FN 6.0	VF 8.0	VF/NM 9.0	NM- 9.2

NOTE: *The above books contain remaindered comics and contents could vary with each issue. No. 11, 12 have part photo magazine insides.*

GIANT COMICS EDITIONS
United Features Syndicate: 1940's (132 pgs.)

1-Abbie & Slats, Abbott & Costello, Jim Hardy, Ella Cinders, Iron Vic, Gordo, & Bill Bumlin 39 78 117 240 395 550
2-Jim Hardy, Ella Cinders, Elmo & Gordo 27 54 81 158 259 360

NOTE: *Above books contain rebound copies; contents can vary.*

GIANT GRAB BAG OF COMICS (See Archie All-Star Specials under Archie Comics)

GIANTKILLER
DC Comics: Aug, 1999 - No. 6, Jan, 2000 ($2.50, limited series)

1-6-Story and painted art by Dan Brereton 3.00
...A to Z: A Field Guide to Big Monsters (8/99) 3.00
...Vol. 1 TPB (Image Comics, 2006, $14.99) r/#1-6 & A-Z; gallery of concept art 15.00

GIANTS (See Thrilling True Story of the Baseball...)

GIANT-SIZE ATOM
DC Comics: May, 2011 ($4.99, one-shot)

1-Gary Frank-c; Hawkman app.; Lemire-s/Asrar-a 5.00

GIANT-SIZE...
Marvel Comics Group: May, 1974 - Dec, 1975 (35/50¢, 52/68 pgs.)
(Some titles quarterly) (Scarce in strict NM or better due to defective cutting, gluing and binding; warping, splitting and off-center pages are common)

Avengers 1(8/74)-New-a plus G.A. H. Torch-r; 1st modern app. The Whizzer; 1st & only modern app. Miss America; 2nd app. Invaders; Kang, Rama-Tut, Mantis app. 6 12 18 42 69 95
Avengers 2,3,5: 2(11/74)-Death of the Swordsman; origin of Rama-Tut. 3(2/75). 5(12/75)-Reprints Avengers Special #1 4 8 12 26 41 55
Avengers 4 (6/75)-Vision marries Scarlet Witch. 5 10 15 32 51 70
Captain America 1(12/75)-r/stories T.O.S. 59-63 by Kirby (#63 reprints origin) 4 8 12 28 44 60
Captain Marvel 1(12/75)-r/Capt. Marvel #17, 20, 21 by Gil Kane (p) 4 8 12 23 36 48
Chillers 1(6/74, 52 pgs)-Curse of Dracula; origin/1st app. Lilith, Dracula's daughter; Heath-r, Colan-c/a(p); becomes Giant-Size Dracula #2 on 6 12 18 41 66 90
Chillers 1(2/75, 50¢, 68 pgs.)-Alcala-a 4 8 12 24 37 50
Chillers 2(5/75)-All-r; Everett-r from Advs. into Weird Worlds 3 6 9 19 29 38
Chillers 3(8/75)-Wrightson-c(new)/a(r); Colan, Kirby, Smith-r 4 8 12 24 37 50
Conan 1(9/74)-B. Smith-r/#3; start adaptation of Howard's "Hour of the Dragon" (ends #4); 1st app. Belit; new-a begins 4 8 12 23 36 48
Conan 2(12/74)-B. Smith-r/#5; Sutton-a(i)(#1 also); Buscema-c 3 6 9 19 29 38
Conan 3-5: 3(4/75)-B. Smith-r/#6; Sutton-a(i). 4(6/75)-B. Smith-r/#7. 5(1975)-B. Smith-r/#14,15; Kirby-c 3 6 9 17 25 32
Creatures 1(5/74, 52 pgs.)-Werewolf app; 1st app. Tigra (formerly Cat); Crandall-r; becomes Giant-Size Werewolf w/#2 5 10 15 30 48 65
Daredevil 1(1975)-Reprints Daredevil Annual #1 3 6 9 21 32 42
Defenders 1(7/74)-Silver Surfer app.; Starlin-a; Ditko, Everett & Kirby reprints 5 10 15 32 51 70
Defenders 2(10/74, 68 pgs.)-New G. Kane-c/a(p); Son of Satan app.; Sub-Mariner-r by Everett; Ditko-r/Strange Tales #119 (Dr. Strange); Maneely-r 4 8 12 23 36 48
Defenders 3-5: 3(1/75)-1st app. Korvac.; Newton, Starlin-a; Ditko, Everett-r. 4(4/75)-Ditko, Everett-r; G. Kane-c. 5-(7/75)-Guardians app. 3 6 9 21 32 42
Doc Savage 1(1975, 68 pgs.)-r/#1,2; Mooney-r 3 6 9 17 25 32
Doctor Strange 1(11/75)-Reprints stories from Strange Tales #164-168; Lawrence, Tuska-r 3 6 9 19 29 38
Dracula 2(9/74, 50¢)-Formerly Giant-Size Chillers 4 8 12 23 36 48
Dracula 3(12/74)-Fox-r/Uncanny Tales #6 3 6 9 21 32 42
Dracula 4(3/75)-Ditko-r(2) 3 6 9 21 32 42
Dracula 5(6/75)-1st Byrne art at Marvel 6 12 18 37 59 80
Fantastic Four 2-4: 2(8/74)-Formerly Giant-Size Super-Stars; Ditko-r. 2,4-Buscema-a. 3(11/74)-Buckler-a. 4(2/75)-1st Madrox. 4 8 12 26 41 55
Fantastic Four 5,6: 5(5/75)-All-r; Kirby, G. Kane-r. 6(10/75)-All-r; Kirby-r 3 6 9 21 32 42
Hulk 1(1975) r/Hulk Special #1 4 8 12 23 36 48
Invaders 1(6/75, 50¢, 68 pgs.)-Origin; G.A. Sub-Mariner-r/Sub-Mariner #1; intro Master Man 4 8 12 28 44 60
Iron Man 1(1975)-Ditko reprint 4 8 12 23 36 48
Kid Colt 1-3: 1(1/75). 2(4/75). 3(7/75)-new Ayers-a 8 16 24 55 93 130

	GD 2.0	VG 4.0	FN 6.0	VF 8.0	VF/NM 9.0	NM- 9.2

Man-Thing 1(8/74)-New Ploog-c/a (25 pgs.); Ditko-r/Amazing Adv. #11; Kirby-r/ Strange Tales Ann. #2 & T.O.S. #15; (#1-5 all have new Man-Thing stories, pre-hero-r & are 68 pgs.) 4 8 12 28 44 60
Man-Thing 2,3: 2(11/74)-Buscema-c/a(p); Kirby, Powell-r. 3(2/75)-Alcala-a; Ditko, Kirby, Sutton-r; Gil Kane-c 3 6 9 21 32 42
Man-Thing 4,5: 4(5/75)-Howard the Duck by Brunner-c/a; Ditko-r. 5(8/75)-Howard the Duck by Brunner (p); Dracula cameo in Howard the Duck; Buscema-a(p); Sutton-a(i); G. Kane-c 4 8 12 28 44 60
Marvel Triple Action 1,2: 1(5/75). 2(7/75) 3 6 9 17 25 32
Master of Kung Fu 1(9/74)-Russell-a; Yellow Claw-r in #1-4; Gulacy-a in #1,2 4 8 12 26 41 55
Master of Kung Fu 2-4: 2-(12/74)-r/Yellow Claw #1. 3(3/75)-Gulacy-a; Kirby-a. 4(6/75)-Kirby-a 3 6 9 21 32 42
Power Man 1(1975) 3 6 9 19 29 38
Spider-Man 1(7/74)-Spider-Man /Human Torch-r by Kirby/Ditko; Byrne-r plus new-a (Dracula-c/story) 7 14 21 46 76 105
Spider-Man 2,3: 2(10/74)-Shang-Chi-c/app. 3(1/75)-Doc Savage-c/app.; Daredevil/ Spider-Man-r w/Ditko-a 4 8 12 28 44 60
Spider-Man 4(4/75)-3rd Punisher app.; Byrne, Ditko-r 11 22 33 73 142 210
Spider-Man 5,6: 5(7/75)-Man-Thing/Lizard-c. 6(9/75) 4 8 12 24 37 50
Super-Heroes Featuring Spider-Man 1(6/74, 35¢, 52 pgs.)-Spider-Man vs. Man-Wolf; Morbius, the Living Vampire app.; Ditko-r; G. Kane-a(p); Spidey villains app. 6 12 18 42 69 95
Super-Stars 1(5/74, 35¢, 52 pgs.)-Fantastic Four; Thing vs. Hulk; Kirbyish-c/a by Buckler/Sinnott; F.F. villains profiled; becomes Giant-Size Fantastic Four #2 on 6 12 18 41 66 90
Super-Villain Team-Up 1(3/75, 68 pgs.)-Craig-r(i) (Also see Fantastic Four #6 for 1st super-villain team-up) 3 6 9 21 32 42
Super-Villain Team-Up 2(6/75, 68 pgs.)-Dr. Doom, Sub-Mariner app.; Spider-Man-r from Amazing Spider-Man #8 by Ditko; Sekowsky-a(p) 3 6 9 18 27 35
Thor 1(7/75) 4 8 12 26 41 55
Werewolf 2(10/74, 68 pgs.)-Formerly Giant-Size Creatures; Ditko-r; Frankenstein app. 3 6 9 20 30 40
Werewolf 3,5: 3(1/75, 68 pgs.). 5(7/75, 68 pgs.) 3 6 9 20 30 40
Werewolf 4(4/75, 68 pgs.)-Morbius the Living Vampire app. 4 8 12 22 34 45
X-Men 1(Summer, 1975, 50¢, 68 pgs.)-1st app. new X-Men; intro. Nightcrawler, Storm, Colossus & Thunderbird; 2nd full app. Wolverine after Incredible Hulk #181 48 96 144 389 845 1300
X-Men 2 (11/75)-N. Adams-r (51 pgs) 9 18 27 61 106 150
Giant Size Marvel TPB (2005, $24.99) reprints stories from Giant-Size Avengers #1, G-S Fantastic Four #4, G-S Defenders #4, G-S Super-Heroes #1, G-S Invaders #1, G-S X-Men #1 and Giant-Size Creatures #1 25.00

GIANT-SIZE...
Marvel Comics: 2005 - 2008 ($4.99/$3.99)

Astonishing X-Men 1 (7/08, $4.99) Concludes story from Astonishing X-Men #24; Whedon-s/ Cassaday-a/wraparound-c; Spider-Man, FF, Dr. Strange app.; variant cover gallery 5.00
Astonishing X-Men 1 (7/08, $4.99) Variant B&W cover 5.00
Avengers 1 (2/08, $4.99) new short stories and r/Avengers #58, 201; Hitch-c 5.00
Avengers/Invaders 1 ('08, $3.99) r/Avengers #71; Invaders #10, Ann. 1 & G-S #2 4.00
Hulk 1 (8/06, $4.99)-2 new stories; Planet Hulk (David-s/Santacruz-a) & Hulk vs. The Champions (Pak-s/Lopresti-a; r/Incredible Hulk: The End) 5.00
Incredible Hulk 1 (7/08, $3.99)-1 new story; r/Incredible Hulk Annual #7; Frank-c 4.00
Invaders 2 ('05, $4.99)-new Thomas-s/Weeks-a; r/Invaders #1&2 & All-Winners #1&2 5.00
Marvel Adventures The Avengers (9/07, $3.99) Agents of Atlas and Kang app.; Kirk-a: reprint of 1st Namora app. from Marvel Mystery Comics #82; reprint from Venus #1 4.00
Spider-Woman ('05, $4.99)-new Bendis-s/Mays-a; r/Marvel Spotlight #32 & S-W #1,37,38 5.00
Wolverine (12/06, $4.99)-new Lapham-s/Aja-a; r/X-Men #6,7 5.00
X-Men 3 ('05, $4.99)-new Whedon-s/N. Adams-a; r/team-ups; Cockrum & Cassaday-c 5.00

GIANT SPECTACULAR COMICS (See Archie All-Star Special under Archie Comics)

GIANT SUMMER FUN BOOK (See Terry-Toons...)

G. I. COMBAT
Quality Comics Group: Oct, 1952 - No. 43, Dec, 1956

1-Crandall-c; Cuidera a-1-43i 97 194 291 621 1061 1500
2 43 86 129 271 461 650
3-5,10-Crandall-c/a 40 80 120 242 401 560
6-Crandall-a 37 74 111 222 361 500
7-9 34 68 102 199 325 450
11-20 25 50 75 147 241 335
21-31,33,35-43: 41-1st S.A. issue 23 46 69 136 223 310
32-Nuclear attack-c/story "Atomic Rocket Assault" 26 52 78 154 252 350

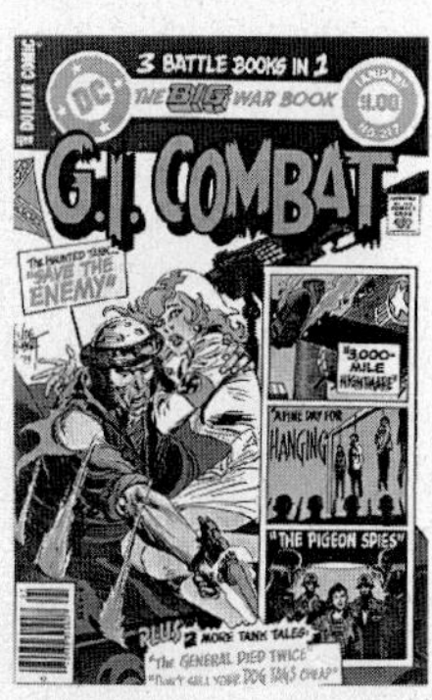

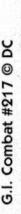

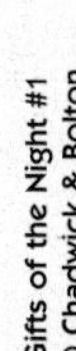
G.I. Combat #217 © DC

Gifts of the Night #1 © Chadwick & Bolton

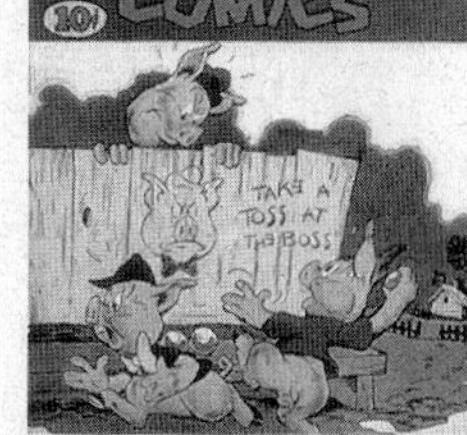

Giggle Comics #8 © ACG

	GD 2.0	VG 4.0	FN 6.0	VF 8.0	VF/NM 9.0	NM- 9.2
34-Crandall-a	24	48	72	142	234	325

G. I. COMBAT (See DC Special Series #22)
National Periodical Publ./DC Comics: No. 44, Jan, 1957 - No. 288, Mar, 1987

	GD 2.0	VG 4.0	FN 6.0	VF 8.0	VF/NM 9.0	NM- 9.2
44-Grey tone-c	70	140	210	567	1234	1900
45	34	68	102	247	536	825
46-50	29	58	87	210	455	700
51-Grey tone-c	37	74	111	278	602	925
52-54,59,60	27	54	81	189	407	625
55-Minor Sgt. Rock prototype by Finger	27	54	81	196	423	650
56-Sgt. Rock prototype by Kanigher/Kubert	35	70	105	254	552	850
57,58-Pre-Sgt. Rock Easy Co. stories	31	62	93	225	488	750
61-65,70-73	21	42	63	146	311	475
66-Pre-Sgt. Rock Easy Co. story	29	58	87	210	455	700
67-1st Tank Killer	36	72	108	270	585	900
68-(1/59) "The Rock" - Sgt. Rock prototype. Part of lead-up trio to 1st definitive Sgt. Rock. Character named Jimmy referred to as "The Rock" appears as a sergeant on the cover and as a private in the story. In reprint (Our Army at War #242) DC edits Jimmy's name out; also see Our Army at War #81-84	130	260	390	1053	2277	3500
69-Grey tone-c	35	70	105	254	552	850
74-American flag-c	23	46	69	161	343	525
75-80: 75-Grey tone-c begin, end #109	30	60	90	218	472	725
81,82,84-86-Grey tone-c	27	54	81	189	407	625
83-1st Big Al, Little Al, & Charlie Cigar; grey tone-c	33	66	99	239	520	800
87-(4-5/61) 1st Haunted Tank; series begins; classic Heath washtone-c	130	260	390	1053	2277	3500
88-(6-7/61) 2nd Haunted Tank; Grey tone-c	42	84	126	315	683	1050
89,90: 90-Last 10¢ issue; Grey tone-c	27	54	81	196	423	650
91-(12/61-1/62)1st Haunted Tank-c; Grey tone-c	52	104	156	421	911	1400
92-95,99-Grey tone-c	25	50	75	175	375	575
96-98-Grey tone-c	19	38	57	128	277	425
100,108: 100-(6-7/63). 108-1st Sgt. Rock x-over; Grey tone-c	21	42	63	146	311	475
101-103,105-107-Grey tone-c	15	30	45	104	227	350
104,109-Grey tone-c	20	40	60	137	294	450
110-112,115-118,120	12	24	36	84	175	265
113-Grey tone-c	16	32	48	109	237	365
114-Origin Haunted Tank	33	66	99	239	520	800
119-Grey tone-c	15	30	45	102	221	340
121-136: 121-1st app. Sgt. Rock's father. 125-Sgt. Rock app. 136-Last 12¢ issue	9	18	27	63	112	160
137,139,140	6	12	18	41	66	90
138-Intro. The Losers (Capt. Storm, Gunner/Sarge, Johnny Cloud) in Haunted Tank (10-11/69)	12	24	36	84	175	265
141-143	4	8	12	26	41	55
144-148 (68 pgs.)	5	10	15	32	51	70
149,151-154 (52 pgs.): 151-Capt. Storm story. 151,153-Medal of Honor series by Maurer	4	8	12	26	41	55
150- (52 pgs.) Ice Cream Soldier story (tells how he got his name); Death of Haunted Tank-c/s	5	10	15	32	51	70
155-167,169,170	3	6	9	14	20	25
168-Neal Adams-c	3	6	9	18	27	35
171-192,194-199: 195-Haunted Tank & War That Time Forgot	2	4	6	11	16	20
193-(10/76) Haunted Tank meets War That Time Forgot; Dinosaur-c/s; Kubert-a	3	6	9	14	20	25
200-(3/77) Haunted Tank-c/s; Sgt. Rock and the Losers app.; Kubert-c	3	6	9	16	23	30
201,202 ($1.00 size) Neal Adams-c	3	6	9	16	23	30
203-210 ($1.00 size)	3	6	9	14	20	25
211-230 ($1.00 size)	2	4	6	11	16	20
231-259 ($1.00 size).232-Origin Kana the Ninja. 244-Death of Slim Stryker; 1st app. The Mercenaries. 246-(76 pgs., $1.50)-30th Anniversary issue. 257-Intro. Stuart's Raiders	2	4	6	9	13	16
260-281: 260-Begin $1.25, 52 pg. issues, end #281. 264-Intro Sgt. Bullet; origin Kana. 269-Intro. The Bravos of Vietnam. 274-Cameo of Monitor from Crisis on Infinite Earths	2	4	6	8	10	12
282-288 (75¢): 282-New advs. begin	1	2	3	5	7	9

*NOTE: **N. Adams** c-168, 201, 202. **Check** a-168, 173. **Drucker** a-48, 61, 63, 66, 71, 72, 76, 134, 140, 141, 144, 147, 148, 153. **Evans** a-135, 138, 158, 164, 166, 201, 202, 204, 205, 215, 256. Giffen a-267. **Glanzman** a-most issues. **Kubert/Heath** a-most issues; **Kubert** covers most issues. **Morrow** a-159-161(2 pgs.). **Redondo** a-189, 240i, 243i. **Sekowsky** a-162p. **Severin** a-147, 152, 154. **Simonson** c-169. **Thorne** a-152, 156. **Wildey** a-153. Johnny Cloud app.-112, 115, 120. Mlle. Marie app.-123, 132, 200. Sgt. Rock app.-111-113, 115, 120, 125, 141, 146, 147, 149, 200. USS Stevens by **Glanzman**-145, 150-153, 157. **Grandenetti** c-44-48.*

G. I. COMBAT
DC Comics: Nov, 2010 ($3.99, one-shot)

	GD 2.0	VG 4.0	FN 6.0	VF 8.0	VF/NM 9.0	NM- 9.2
1-Haunted Tank and General J.E.B. Stuart app.; Sturges-s/Winslade-a/Darrow-c						4.00

GIDGET (TV)
Dell Publishing Co.: Apr, 1966 - No. 2, Dec, 1966

	GD 2.0	VG 4.0	FN 6.0	VF 8.0	VF/NM 9.0	NM- 9.2
1-Sally Field photo-c	9	18	27	58	99	140
2	6	12	18	42	69	95

GIFT COMICS
Fawcett Publications: 1942 - No. 4, 1949 (50¢/25¢, 324 pgs./152 pgs.)

	GD 2.0	VG 4.0	FN 6.0	VF 8.0	VF/NM 9.0	NM- 9.2
1-Captain Marvel, Bulletman, Golden Arrow, Ibis the Invincible, Mr. Scarlet, & Spy Smasher begin; not rebound, remaindered comics, printed at same time as originals; 50¢-c & 324 pgs. begin, end #3.	297	594	891	1901	3251	4600
2-Commando Yank, Phantom Eagle, others app.	174	348	522	1114	1907	2700
3-(50¢, 324 pgs.)	119	238	357	762	1306	1850
4-(25¢, 152 pgs.)-The Marvel Family, Captain Marvel, etc.; each issue can vary in contents	73	146	219	467	796	1125

GIFTS FROM SANTA (See March of Comics No. 137)

GIFTS OF THE NIGHT
DC Comics (Vertigo): Feb, 1999 - No. 4, May, 1999 ($2.95, limited series)

	GD 2.0	VG 4.0	FN 6.0	VF 8.0	VF/NM 9.0	NM- 9.2
1-4-Bolton-c/a; Chadwick-s						3.00

GIGANTIC
Dark Horse Comics: Nov, 2008 - No. 5, Jan, 2010 ($3.50, limited series)

	GD 2.0	VG 4.0	FN 6.0	VF 8.0	VF/NM 9.0	NM- 9.2
1-5-Remender-s/Nguyen-a; Earth as a reality show						3.50

GIGGLE COMICS (Spencer Spook No. 100) (Also see Ha Ha Comics)
Creston No.1-63/American Comics Group No. 64 on; Oct, 1943 - No. 99, Jan-Feb, 1955

	GD 2.0	VG 4.0	FN 6.0	VF 8.0	VF/NM 9.0	NM- 9.2
1-Funny animal	36	72	108	211	343	475
2	18	36	54	107	169	230
3-5: Ken Hultgren-a begins?	14	28	42	82	121	160
6-10: 9-1st Superkatt (6/44). 10-Superkatt shoots Japanese plane & fights Nazi robot	12	24	36	67	94	120
11-20	10	20	30	58	79	100
21-40: 22-Spencer Spook 2nd app. 32-Patriotic-c. 37-X-Mas-c	9	18	27	52	69	85
41-54,56-59,61-99: Spencer Spook app. in many. 44-Mussel-Man app. (Superman parody). 45-Witch Hazel 1st app. 46-Bob Hope & Bing Crosby app. 49,61,69-X-Mas-c. 61-Milt Gross-a	9	18	27	47	61	75
55,60-Milt Gross-a	10	20	30	58	79	100

G-I IN BATTLE (G-I No. 1 only)
Ajax-Farrell Publ./Four Star: Aug, 1952 - No. 9, July, 1953; Mar, 1957 - No. 6, May, 1958

	GD 2.0	VG 4.0	FN 6.0	VF 8.0	VF/NM 9.0	NM- 9.2
1	14	28	42	80	115	150
2	9	18	27	47	61	75
3-9	8	16	24	42	54	65
Annual 1(1952, 25¢, 100 pgs.)	27	54	81	158	259	360
1(1957-Ajax)	8	16	24	42	54	65
2-6	6	12	18	28	34	40

G. I. JANE
Stanhall/Merit No. 11: May, 1953 - No. 11, Mar, 1955 (Misdated 3/54)

	GD 2.0	VG 4.0	FN 6.0	VF 8.0	VF/NM 9.0	NM- 9.2
1-PX Pete begins; Bill Williams-c/a	15	30	45	86	133	180
2-7(5/54)	10	20	30	54	72	90
8-10(12/54, Stanhall)	9	18	27	50	65	80
11 (3/55, Merit)	9	18	27	47	61	75

G. I. JOE (Also see Advs. of..., Showcase #53, 54 & The Yardbirds)
Ziff-Davis Publ. Co. (Korean War): No. 10, 1950; No. 11, 4-5/51 - No. 51, 6/57(52pgs.: 10-14,6-17?)

	GD 2.0	VG 4.0	FN 6.0	VF 8.0	VF/NM 9.0	NM- 9.2
10(#1, 1950)-Saunders painted-c begin	17	34	51	98	154	210
11-14(#2-5, 10/51): 11-New logo. 12-New logo	12	24	36	67	94	120
V2#6(12/51)-17-(11/52; Last 52 pgs.?)	10	20	30	58	79	100
18-(25¢, 100 pg. Giant, 12-1/52-53)	25	50	75	147	241	335
19-30: 20-22,24,28-31-The Yardbirds app.	9	18	27	52	69	85
31-47,49-51	9	18	27	50	65	80
48-Atom bomb story	9	18	27	52	69	85

*NOTE: **Powell** a-V2#7, 8, 11. **Norman Saunders** painted c-10-14, V2#6-14, 26, 30, 31, 35, 38, 39. **Tuska** a-7. Bondage c-29, 35, 38.*

G. I. JOE (America's Movable Fighting Man)
Custom Comics: 1967 (5-1/8x8-3/8", 36 pgs.)

	GD 2.0	VG 4.0	FN 6.0	VF 8.0	VF/NM 9.0	NM- 9.2
nn-Schaffenberger-a; based on Hasbro toy	4	8	12	22	34	45

G.I. JOE
Dark Horse Comics: Dec, 1995 - No. 4, Apr, 1996 ($1.95, limited series)

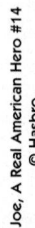

G.I. Joe (2001 series) #1 © Hasbro

G.I. Joe, A Real American Hero #14 © Hasbro

G.I. Joe, A Real American Hero #172 © Hasbro

GD VG FN VF VF/NM NM-
2.0 4.0 6.0 8.0 9.0 9.2

1-4: Mike W. Barr scripts. 1-Three Frank Miller covers with title logos in red, white and blue. 2-Breyfogle-c. 3-Simonson-c 3.00

G.I. JOE
Dark Horse Comics: V2#1, June, 1996 - V2#4, Sept, 1996 ($2.50)

V2#1-4: Mike W. Barr scripts. 4-Painted-c 3.00

G.I. JOE
Image Comics/Devil's Due Publishing: 2001 - No. 43, May, 2005 ($2.95)

1-Campbell-c; back-c painted by Beck; Blaylock-s 2 4 6 8 10 12
1-2nd printing with front & back covers switched 6.00
2,3 5.00
4-($3.50) 4.00
5-20,22-41: 6-SuperPatriot preview. 18-Brereton-c. 31-33-Wraith back-up; Caldwell-a 3.00
21-Silent issue; Zeck-a; two covers by Campbell and Zeck 3.00
42,43-($4.50)-Dawn of the Red Shadows; leads into G.I. Joe Vol. 2 4.50
...:Cobra Reborn (1/04, $4.95) Bradstreet-c/Jenkins-s 5.00
...:G.I. Joe Reborn (2/04, $4.95) Bradstreet-c/Bennett & Saltares-a 5.00
...: Malfunction (2003, $15.95) r/#11-15 16.00
... M. I. A. (2002, $4.95) r/#1&2; Beck back-c from #1 on cover 5.00
...: Players & Pawns (11/04, $12.95) r/#28-33; cover gallery 13.00
...: Reborn (2004, $9.95) r/Cobra Reborn & G.I. Joe Reborn 10.00
...: Reckonings (2002, $12.95) r/#6-9; Zeck-c 13.00
...: Reinstated (2002, $14.95) r/#1-4 15.00
...: The Return of Serpentor (9/04, $12.95) r/#16,22-25; cover gallery 13.00
...Vol. 8: The Rise of the Red Shadows (1/06, $14.95) r/#42,43 & prologue pgs. from #37-41 15.00

G.I. JOE (Volume 2) (Also see Snake Eyes: Declassified)
Devil's Due Publishing: No. 0, June, 2005 - No. 36, June, 2008 (25¢/$2.95/$3.50/$4.50)

0-(25¢-c) Casey-s/Caselli-a 3.00
1-4,7-19 ($2.95): 1-Four covers; Casey-s/Caselli-a. 4-R. Black-c 3.00
5,6-($4.50) 6-Wraparound-c 4.50
20-29,31-35-($3.50) 25-Wraparound-c World War III part 1 3.50
30,36-($5.50) 30-Double-sized World War III part 6. 36-Double-sized WW III part 12 5.50
...America's Elite Vol. 1: The Newest War TPB ('06, $14.95) r/#0-5; cover gallery 15.00
...America's Elite Vol. 2: The Ties That Bind TPB (8/06, $15.95) r/#6-12; cover gallery 16.00
...America's Elite Vol. 3: In Sheep's Clothing TPB (2007, $18.99) r/#13-18; cover gallery 19.00
...America's Elite Vol. 4: Truth and Consequences TPB (9/07, $18.99) r/#19-24; covers 19.00
... Data Desk Handbook (10/05, $2.95) character profile pages 3.00
... Data Desk Handbook A-M (10/07, $5.50) character profile pages 5.50
... Data Desk Handbook N-Z (11/07, $3.50) character profile pages 3.50
... :Scarlett: Declassified (7/06, $4.95) Scarlett's childhood and training; Noto-c/a 5.00
... Special Missions (2/06, $4.95) short stories and profile pages by various 5.00
... Special Missions Antarctica (12/06, $4.95) short stories and profile pages by various 5.00
... Special Missions Brazil (4/07, $5.50) short stories and profile pages by various 5.50
... Special Missions: The Enemy (9/07, $5.50) two stories and profile pages by various 5.50
... Special Missions Tokyo (9/06, $4.95) short stories and profile pages by various 5.00
...: The Hunt For Cobra Commander (5/06, 25¢) short story and character profiles 3.00

G.I. JOE
IDW Publishing: No. 0, Oct, 2008; No. 1, Jan, 2009 - No. 27, Feb, 2011 ($1.00/$3.99)

0-($1.00) Short stories by Dixon & Hama; creator interviews and character sketches 3.00
1-27-($3.99) 1-Dixon-s/Atkins-a; covers by Johnson, Atkins and Dell'Otto 4.00
...: Cobra Commander Tribute - 100-Page Spectacular 1 (4/11, $7.99) reprints 8.00
...: Special - Helix (8/09, $3.99) Reed-s/Suitor-a 4.00

G.I. JOE, VOLUME 2 (Prelude in G.I. Joe: Cobra Civil War #0)
IDW Publishing: May, 2011 - Present ($3.99)

1-9: 1-Dixon-s/Saltares-a; three covers by Howard. 9-Cobra Command Part 1 4.00

G.I. JOE AND THE TRANSFORMERS
Marvel Comics Group: Jan, 1987 - No. 4, Apr, 1987 (Limited series)

1-4 6.00

G.I. JOE, A REAL AMERICAN HERO (...Starring Snake-Eyes on-c #135 on)
Marvel Comics Group: June, 1982 - No. 155, Dec, 1994

1-Printed on Baxter paper; based on Hasbro toy 4 8 12 22 34 45
2-Printed on regular paper; 1st app. Kwinn 3 6 9 18 27 35
3-10: 6-1st app. Oktober Guard 3 6 9 14 20 25
11-20: 11-Intro Airborne. 13-1st Destro (cameo). 14-1st full app. Destro. 15-1st app. Major Blood. 16-1st app. Cover Girl and Trip-Wire 2 4 6 10 14 18
21-1st app. Storm Shadow; silent issue 4 8 12 28 44 60
22-1st app. Duke and Roadblock 2 4 6 10 14 18
23-25,28-30,60: 25-1st full app. Zartan, 1st app of Cutter, Deep Six, Mutt and Junkyard, and The Dreadnoks. 60-Todd McFarlane-a 2 3 4 6 8 10
26,27-Origin Snake-Eyes parts 1 & 2 3 6 9 14 19 24
31-50: 31-1st Spirit Iron-Knife. 32-1st Blowtorch, Lady J, Recondo, Ripcord. 33-New headquarters. 40-1st app. of Shipwreck, Barbecue. 48-1st app. Sgt. Slaughter. 49-1st app. of Lift-Ticket, Slipstream, Leatherneck, Serpentor 6.00
51-59,61-90 5.00
91,92,94-99: 94-96-Snake Eyes Trilogy 6.00
93-Snake-Eyes' face first revealed 2 4 6 11 16 20
100,135-138: 135-138-($1.75)-Bagged w/trading card. 138-Transformers app. 2 4 6 9 13 16
101-134: 101-New Oktober Guard app. 110-1st Garney-a. 117- Debut G.I. Joe Ninja Force 2 3 4 6 8 10
139-142-New Transformers app. 2 4 6 13 18 22
143,145-149: 145-Intro. G.I. Joe Star Brigade 2 4 6 9 13 16
144-Origin Snake-Eyes 3 6 9 14 19 24
150-Low print thru #155 3 6 9 20 30 40
151-154: 152-30th Anniversary (of doll) issue, original G.I. Joe General Joseph Colton app. (also app. in #151) 3 6 9 19 29 38
155-Last issue 6 12 18 37 59 80
All 2nd printings 4.00
Special #1 (2/95, $1.50) r/#60 w/McFarlane-a. Cover swipe from Spider-Man #1 4 8 12 26 41 55
Special Treasury Edition (1982)-r/#1 3 6 9 20 30 40
Volume 1 TPB (4/02, $24.95) r/#1-10; new cover by Michael Golden 25.00
Volume 2 TPB (6/02, $24.95) r/#11-20; new cover by J. Scott Campbell 25.00
Volume 3 TPB (2002, $24.99) r/#21-30; new cover by J. Scott Campbell 25.00
Volume 4 TPB (2002, $25.99) r/#31-40; new cover by J. Scott Campbell 26.00
Volume 5 TPB (2002, $24.99) r/#42-50; new cover by J. Scott Campbell 25.00
Yearbook 1-4: (3/85-3/88)-r/#1; Golden-c. 2-Golden-c/a 5.00
NOTE: ***Garney** a(p)-110. **Golden** c-23, 29, 34, 36. **Heath** a-24. **Rogers** a(p)-75, 77-82, 84, 86; c-77.*

G. I. JOE, A REAL AMERICAN HERO
IDW Publishing: No. 156, Jul, 2010 - Present ($3.99)

156-175-Continuation of story from Marvel series #155 (1994); Hama-s 4.00
Hundred Penny Press: G.I. Joe: Real American Hero #1 (3/11, $1.00) r/#1 (1982) 3.00

G.I. JOE: BATTLE FILES
Image Comics: 2002 - No. 3, 2002 ($5.95)

1-3-Profile pages of characters and history; Beck-c 6.00

G.I. JOE: COBRA (#5-on is continuation of G.I. Joe: Cobra II #4, not G.I. Joe: Cobra #4)
IDW Publishing: Mar, 2009 - No. 13, Feb, 2011 ($3.99)

1-4,5-13: 1-4-Gage & Costa-s/Fuso-a/covers by Chaykin & Fuso. 5-8-Carrera-a 4.00
Hundred Penny Press: G.I. Joe: Cobra #1 (4/11, $1.00) r/#1 with Chaykin-c 3.00
... Special (9/09, $3.99) Costa-s/Fuso-a 4.00
... Special 2 - Chameleon (9/10, $3.99) Costa-s/Fuso-a 4.00
... II (1/10 - No. 4, 4/10, $3.99) 1-4-Gage & Costa-s/Fuso-a/covers by Chaykin & Fuso 4.00

G.I. JOE: COBRA CIVIL WAR
IDW Publishing: No. 0, Apr, 2011 ($3.99)

0-Prelude to G.I. Joe, Cobra & Snake Eyes Civil War series; four covers 4.00
0-Muzzle Flash Edition (6/11, price not shown) r/#0 in B&W and partial color 4.00

G.I. JOE: COBRA VOLUME 2 (Prelude in G.I. Joe: Cobra Civil War #0)
IDW Publishing: May, 2011 - Present ($3.99)

1,2-Costa-s/Fuso-a 4.00

G. I. JOE COMICS MAGAZINE
Marvel Comics Group: Dec, 1986 - No. 13, 1988 ($1.50, digest-size)

1-13: G.I. Joe-r 2 4 6 8 10 12

G.I. JOE DECLASSIFIED
Devil's Due Publishing: June, 2006 - No. 3 ($4.95, bi-monthly)

1-3-New "early" adventures of the team; Hama-s; Quinn & DeLandro-a; var-c for each 5.00
TPB (1/07, $18.99) r/#1-3; cover gallery 19.00

G.I. JOE DREADNOKS: DECLASSIFIED
Devil's Due Publishing: Nov, 2006 - No. 3, Mar, 2007 ($4.95/$4.99/$5.50, bi-monthly)

1,2-Secret history of the team; Blaylock-s; var-c for each 5.00
3-($5.50) 5.50

G.I. JOE EUROPEAN MISSIONS (Action Force in indicia) (Series reprints Action Force)
Marvel Comics Ltd. (British): Jun, 1988 - No. 15, Dec, 1989 ($1.50/$1.75)

1,3-Snake Eyes & Storm Shadow-c/s 1 2 3 5 7 9
2,4-15 6.00

G.I. JOE: FRONT LINE
Image Comics: 2002 - No. 18, Dec, 2003 ($2.95)

1-18: 1-Jurgens-a/Hama-s. 1-Two covers by Dorman & Sharpe. 7,8-Harris-c 3.00
...Vol. 1 - The Mission That Never Was TPB (2003, $14.95) r/ #1-4; script pages 15.00
...Vol. 2 - Icebound TPB (3/04, $12.95) r/ #5-8 13.00

G.I. Joe: Infestation #2 © Hasbro

G.I. Joe: Reloaded #1 © Hasbro

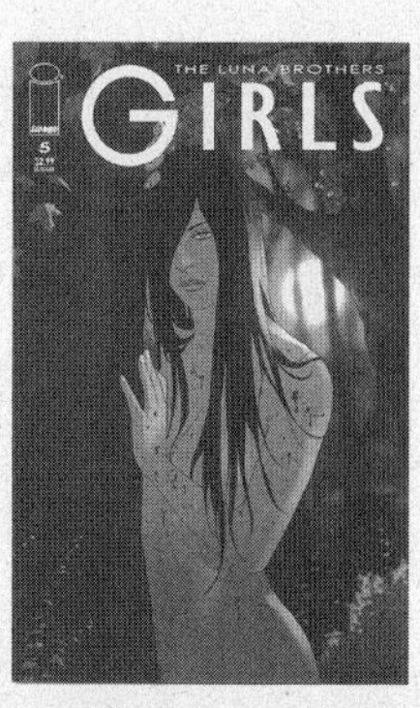

Girls #5 © Luna Brothers

	GD 2.0	VG 4.0	FN 6.0	VF 8.0	VF/NM 9.0	NM- 9.2

...Vol. 3 - History Repeating TPB (4/04, $9.95) r/#11-14 10.00
...Vol. 4 - One-Shots TPB (5/04, $15.95) r/#9,10,15-18 16.00

G.I. JOE: FUTURE NOIR SPECIAL
IDW Publishing: Nov, 2010 - No. 2, Dec, 2010 ($3.99, limited series, greytone art)
1,2-Schmidt-s/Bevilacqua-a 4.00

G. I. JOE: HEARTS & MINDS
IDW Publishing: May, 2010 - No. 5, Sept, 2010 ($3.99)
1-5: Short origin stories; Brooks-s; Chaykin & Fuso-a 4.00

G. I. JOE: INFESTATION (Zombie x-over with Star Trek, Ghostbusters & Transformers)
IDW Publishing: Mar, 2011 - No. 2, Mar, 2011 ($3.99, limited series)
1,2-Timpano-a; covers by Timpano and Snyder III 4.00

G.I. JOE: MASTER & APPRENTICE
Image Comics: May, 2004 - No. 4, Aug, 2004 ($2.95)
1-4-Caselli-a/Jerwa-s 3.00

G.I. JOE: MASTER & APPRENTICE 2
Image Comics: Feb, 2005 - No. 4, May, 2005 ($2.95, limited series)
1-4: Stevens & Vedder-a/Jerwa-s 3.00

G.I. JOE MOVIE PREQUEL...
IDW Publishing: Mar, 2009 - No. 4, June, 2009 ($3.99, limited series)
1-4-Two covers on each: 1-Duke. 2-Destro. 3-The Baroness. 4-SnakeEyes 4.00

G.I. JOE: OPERATION HISS
IDW Publishing: Feb, 2010 - No. 5, Jun, 2010 ($3.99, limited series)
1-5: 1-4-Reed-s/Padilla-a; covers by Corroney & Padilla. 5-Guglotta-a 4.00

G. I. JOE ORDER OF BATTLE, THE
Marvel Comics Group: Dec, 1986 - No. 4, Mar, 1987 (limited series)
1-4 6.00

G.I. JOE: ORIGINS
IDW Publishing: Feb, 2009 - No. 23, Jan, 2011 ($3.99)
1-23: 1-Origin of Snake Eyes; Hama-s. 12-Templesmith-a. 19-Benitez-a 4.00

G.I. JOE: RELOADED
Image Comics: Mar, 2004 -No. 14, Apr, 2005 ($2.95)
1-14: 1-3-Granov-c/Ney Rieber-s. 5,6-Rieber-s/Saltares-a. 8-Origin of the Baroness 3.00
Vol. 1 In the Name of Patriotism (11/04, $12.95) r/#1-6; cover gallery 13.00

G.I. JOE: RISE OF COBRA MOVIE ADAPTATION
IDW Publishing: July, 2009 - No. 4, July, 2009 ($3.99, weekly limited series)
1-4-Tipton-s/Maloney-a; two covers 4.00

G.I. JOE SIGMA 6 (Based on the cartoon TV series)
Devil's Due Publishing: Dec, 2005 - No. 6, May, 2006 ($2.95, limited series)
1-6-Andrew Daab-s 3.00
TPB Vol. 1 (10/06, $10.95, 8-1/4" x 5-3/4") r/#1-6; cover gallery 11.00

G.I. JOE: SNAKE EYES
IDW Publishing: Oct, 2009 - No. 4, Jan, 2010 ($3.99, limited series)
1-4-Ray Park & Kevin VanHook-s/Lee Ferguson-a; two covers 4.00

G.I. JOE: SNAKE EYES, VOLUME 2 (Prelude in G.I. Joe: Cobra Civil War #0)
IDW Publishing: May, 2011 - Present ($3.99, limited series)
1-6: 1-Dixon-s/Atkins & Padilla-a; two covers 4.00

G. I. JOE SPECIAL MISSIONS (Indicia title: Special Missions)
Marvel Comics Group: Oct, 1986 - No. 28, Dec, 1989 ($1.00)
1-20 4.00
21-28 5.00

G.I. JOE VS. THE TRANSFORMERS
Image Comics: Jun, 2003 - No. 6, Nov, 2003 ($2.95, limited series)
1-Blaylock-s/Mike Miller-a; three covers by Miller, Campbell & Andrews 3.00
1-2nd printing; black cover with logo; back-c by Campbell 3.00
2-6: 2-Two covers by Miller & Brooks 3.00
TPB (3/04, $15.95) r/series; sketch pages 16.00

G.I. JOE VS. THE TRANSFORMERS (Volume 2)
Devil's Due Publ.: Sept, 2004 - No. 4, Dec, 2004 ($4.95/$2.95, limited series)
1-($4.95) Three covers; Jolley-s/Su & Seeley-a 5.00
2-4-($2.95) Two covers by Su & Pollina 3.00
Vol. 2 TPB (4/05, $14.95) r/series; interview with creators; sketch pages and covers 15.00

G.I. JOE VS. THE TRANSFORMERS (Volume 3) THE ART OF WAR
Devil's Due Publ.: Mar, 2006 - No. 5, July, 2006 ($2.95, limited series)
1-5: 1-Three covers; Seeley-s/Ng-a 3.00
TPB (8/06, $14.95) r/series; cover gallery 15.00

G.I. JOE VS. THE TRANSFORMERS (Volume 4) BLACK HORIZON
Devil's Due Publ.: Jan, 2007 - No. 2, Feb, 2007 ($5.50, limited series)
1,2: 1-Three covers; Seeley-s/Wildman-a. 2-Two covers 5.50

G. I. JUNIORS (See Harvey Hits No. 86,91,95,98,101,104,107,110,112,114,116,118,120,122)

GILGAMESH II
DC Comics: 1989 - No. 4, 1989 ($3.95, limited series, prestige format, mature)
1-4: Starlin-c/a/scripts 4.00

GIL THORP
Dell Publishing Co.: May-July, 1963

	GD	VG	FN	VF	VF/NM	NM-
1-Caniff-*ish* art	4	8	12	24	37	50

GINGER
Archie Publications: 1951 - No. 10, Summer, 1954

	GD	VG	FN	VF	VF/NM	NM-
1-Teenage humor	15	30	45	85	130	175
2-(1952)	9	18	27	52	69	85
3-6: 6-(Sum/53)	8	16	24	44	57	70
7-10-Katy Keene app.	10	20	30	56	76	95

GINGER FOX (Also see The World of Ginger Fox)
Comico: Sept, 1988 - No. 4, Dec, 1988 ($1.75, limited series)
1-4: Part photo-c on all 3.00

G.I. R.A.M.B.O.T.
Wonder Color Comics/Pied Piper #2: Apr, 1987 - No. 2? ($1.95)
1,2: 2-Exist? 3.00

GIRL
DC Comics (Vertigo Verite): Jul, 1996 - No. 3, 1996 ($2.50, lim. series, mature)
1-3: Peter Milligan scripts; Fegredo-c/a 3.00

GIRL COMICS (Becomes Girl Confessions No. 13 on)
Marvel/Atlas Comics(CnPC): Oct, 1949 - No. 12, Jan, 1952 (#1-4: 52 pgs.)

	GD	VG	FN	VF	VF/NM	NM-
1-Photo-c	24	48	72	140	230	320
2-Kubert-a; photo-c	14	28	42	82	121	160
3-Everett-a; Liz Taylor photo-c	34	68	102	199	325	450
4-11: 4-Photo-c. 10-12-Sol Brodsky-c	12	24	36	69	97	125
12-Krigstein-a; Al Hartley-c	13	26	39	74	105	135

GIRL COMICS
Marvel Comics: May, 2010 - No. 3, Sept, 2010 ($4.99, limited series)
1-3-Anthology of short stories by women creators. 1-Conner-c. 2-Thompson-c. 3-Chen-c 5.00

GIRL CONFESSIONS (Formerly Girl Comics)
Atlas Comics (CnPC/ZPC): No. 13, Mar, 1952 - No. 35, Aug, 1954

	GD	VG	FN	VF	VF/NM	NM-
13-Everett-a	14	28	42	80	115	150
14,15,19,20	11	22	33	60	83	105
16-18-Everett-a	12	24	36	69	97	125
21-35: Robinson-a	9	18	27	52	69	85

GIRL CRAZY
Dark Horse Comics: May, 1996 - No. 3, July, 1996 ($2.95, B&W, limited series)
1-3: Gilbert Hernandez-a/scripts. 3.00

GIRL FROM U.N.C.L.E., THE (TV) (Also see The Man From...)
Gold Key: Jan, 1967 - No. 5, Oct, 1967

	GD	VG	FN	VF	VF/NM	NM-
1-McWilliams-a; Stephanie Powers photo front/back-c & pin-ups (no ads, 12¢)	8	16	24	53	89	125
2-5-Leonard Swift-Courier No. 5. 4-Back-c pin-up	6	12	18	37	59	80

GIRLS
Image Comics: May, 2005 - No. 24, Apr, 2007 ($2.95/$2.99)
1-Luna Brothers-s/a/c 4.00
2-24 3.00
Image Firsts: Girls #1 (4/10, $1.00) r/#1 with "Image Firsts" cover logo 3.00
... Vol. 1: Conception TPB (2005, $14.99) r/#1-6 15.00
... Vol. 2: Emergence TPB (2006, $14.99) r/#7-12 15.00
... Vol. 3: Survival TPB (2006, $14.99) r/#13-18 15.00
... Vol. 4: Extinction TPB (2007, $14.99) r/#19-24 15.00

GIRLS' FUN & FASHION MAGAZINE (Formerly Polly Pigtails)
Parents' Magazine Institute: V5#44, Jan, 1950 - V5#48, Sept., 1950

	GD	VG	FN	VF	VF/NM	NM-
V5#44	8	16	24	40	50	60
45-48	6	12	18	28	34	40

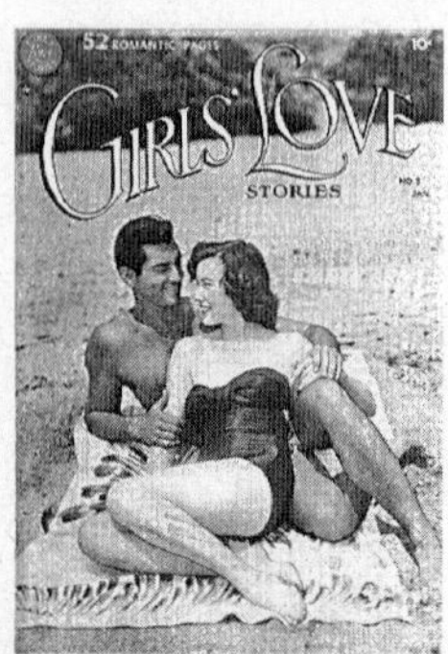

Girls' Love Stories #3 © DC

G.I. War Brides #1 © SUPR

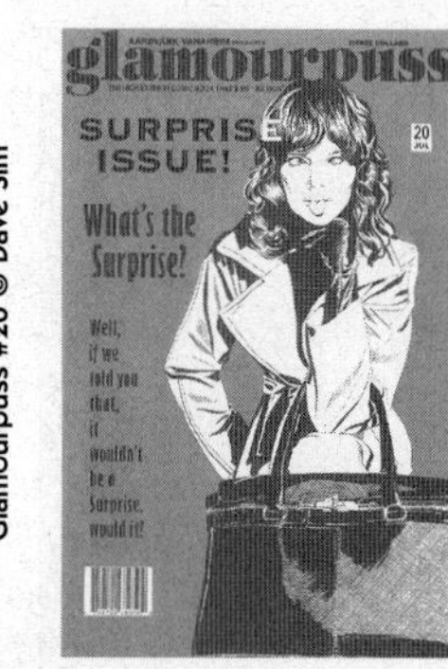

Glamourpuss #20 © Dave Sim

GIRLS IN LOVE
Fawcett Publications: May, 1950 - No. 2, July, 1950

	GD 2.0	VG 4.0	FN 6.0	VF 8.0	VF/NM 9.0	NM- 9.2
1-Photo-c	12	24	36	69	97	125
2-Photo-c	10	20	30	54	72	90

GIRLS IN LOVE (Formerly G. I. Sweethearts No. 45)
Quality Comics Group: No. 46, Sept, 1955 - No. 57, Dec, 1956

	GD 2.0	VG 4.0	FN 6.0	VF 8.0	VF/NM 9.0	NM- 9.2
46	10	20	30	54	72	90
47-53,55,56	8	16	24	40	50	60
54- 'Commie' story	9	18	27	52	69	85
57-Matt Baker-c/a	14	28	42	76	108	140

GIRLS IN WHITE (See Harvey Comics Hits No. 58)

GIRLS' LIFE (Patsy Walker's Own Magazine For Girls!)
Atlas Comics (BFP): Jan, 1954 - No. 6, Nov, 1954

	GD 2.0	VG 4.0	FN 6.0	VF 8.0	VF/NM 9.0	NM- 9.2
1	15	30	45	84	127	170
2-Al Hartley-c	9	18	27	52	69	85
3-6	9	18	27	47	61	75

GIRLS' LOVE STORIES
National Comics(Signal Publ. No. 9-65/Arleigh No. 83-117): Aug-Sept, 1949 - No. 180, Nov-Dec, 1973 (No. 1-13: 52 pgs.)

	GD 2.0	VG 4.0	FN 6.0	VF 8.0	VF/NM 9.0	NM- 9.2
1-Toth, Kinstler-a, 8 pgs. each; photo-c	56	112	168	350	595	840
2-Kinstler-a?	31	62	93	182	296	410
3-10: 1-9-Photo-c	21	42	63	122	199	275
11-20	16	32	48	94	147	200
21-33: 21-Kinstler-a. 33-Last pre-code (1-2/55)	13	26	39	72	101	130
34-50	11	22	33	60	83	105
51-70	10	20	30	54	72	90
71-99: 83-Last 10¢ issue	5	10	15	32	51	70
100	5	10	15	34	55	75
101-146: 113-117-April O'Day app.	3	6	9	20	30	40
147-151- "Confessions" serial. 150-Wood-a	3	6	9	21	32	42
152-160,171-179	3	6	9	16	22	28
161-170 (52 pgs.)	4	8	12	22	34	45
180 Last issue	3	6	9	20	30	40

Ashcan (8-9/49) not distributed to newsstands, only for in house use (no known sales)

GIRLS' ROMANCES
National Periodical Publ.(Signal Publ. No. 7-79/Arleigh No. 84): Feb-Mar, 1950 - No. 160, Oct, 1971 (No. 1-11: 52 pgs.)

	GD 2.0	VG 4.0	FN 6.0	VF 8.0	VF/NM 9.0	NM- 9.2
1-Photo-c	53	106	159	334	567	800
2-Photo-c; Toth-a	30	60	90	177	289	400
3-10: 3-6-Photo-c	21	42	63	122	199	275
11,12,14-20	15	30	45	86	133	180
13-Toth-c	15	30	45	90	140	190
21-31: 31-Last pre-code (2-3/55)	13	26	39	72	101	130
32-50	7	14	21	44	72	100
51-99: 80-Last 10¢ issue	5	10	15	32	51	70
100	5	10	15	34	55	75
101-108,110-120	3	6	9	20	30	40
109-Beatles-c/story	12	24	36	79	160	240
121-133,135-140	3	6	9	18	27	35
134-Neal Adams-c (splash pg. is same as-c)	5	10	15	34	55	75
141-158	3	6	9	16	22	28
159,160-52 pgs.	4	8	12	22	34	45

GIRL WHO WOULD BE DEATH, THE
DC Comics (Vertigo): Dec, 1998 - No. 4, March, 1999 ($2.50, lim. series)

	GD 2.0	VG 4.0	FN 6.0	VF 8.0	VF/NM 9.0	NM- 9.2
1-4-Kiernan-s/Ormston-a						3.00

G. I. SWEETHEARTS (Formerly Diary Loves; Girls In Love #46 on)
Quality Comics Group: No. 32, June, 1953 - No. 45, May, 1955

	GD 2.0	VG 4.0	FN 6.0	VF 8.0	VF/NM 9.0	NM- 9.2
32	10	20	30	58	79	100
33-45: 44-Last pre-code (3/55)	8	16	24	42	54	65

G.I. TALES (Formerly Sgt. Barney Barker No. 1-3)
Atlas Comics (MCI): No. 4, Feb, 1957 - No. 6, July, 1957

	GD 2.0	VG 4.0	FN 6.0	VF 8.0	VF/NM 9.0	NM- 9.2
4-Severin-a(4)	10	20	30	54	72	90
5	8	16	24	40	50	60
6-Orlando, Powell, & Woodbridge-a	8	16	24	42	54	65

GIVE ME LIBERTY (Also see Dark Horse Presents Fifth Anniversary Special, Dark Horse Presents #100-4, Happy Birthday Martha Washington, Martha Washington Goes to War, Martha Washington Stranded In Space & San Diego Comicon Comics #2)
Dark Horse Comics: June, 1990 - No. 4, 1991 ($4.95, limited series, 52 pgs.)

	GD 2.0	VG 4.0	FN 6.0	VF 8.0	VF/NM 9.0	NM- 9.2
1-4: 1st app. Martha Washington; Frank Miller scripts, Dave Gibbons-c/a in all						5.00

G. I. WAR BRIDES
Superior Publishers Ltd.: Apr, 1954 - No. 8, June, 1955

	GD 2.0	VG 4.0	FN 6.0	VF 8.0	VF/NM 9.0	NM- 9.2
1	11	22	33	60	83	105
2	8	16	24	42	54	65
3-8: 4-Kamen*esque*-a; lingerie panels	7	14	21	37	46	55

G. I. WAR TALES
National Periodical Publications: Mar-Apr, 1973 - No. 4, Oct-Nov, 1973

	GD 2.0	VG 4.0	FN 6.0	VF 8.0	VF/NM 9.0	NM- 9.2
1-Reprints in all; dinosaur-c/s	3	6	9	18	27	35
2-N. Adams-a(r)	2	4	6	13	18	22
3,4: 4-Krigstein-a(r)	2	4	6	11	16	20

NOTE: ***Drucker** a-3r, 4r. **Heath** a-4r. **Kubert** a-2, 3; c-4r.*

GIZMO (Also see Domino Chance)
Chance Ent.: May-June, 1985 (B&W, one-shot)

	GD 2.0	VG 4.0	FN 6.0	VF 8.0	VF/NM 9.0	NM- 9.2
1						6.00

GIZMO
Mirage Studios: 1986 - No. 6, July, 1987 ($1.50, B&W)

	GD 2.0	VG 4.0	FN 6.0	VF 8.0	VF/NM 9.0	NM- 9.2
1-6						3.00

G.L.A. (Great Lakes Avengers)(Also see GLX-Mas Special)
Marvel Comics: June, 2005 - No. 4, Sept, 2005 ($2.99, limited series)

	GD 2.0	VG 4.0	FN 6.0	VF 8.0	VF/NM 9.0	NM- 9.2
1-4-Slott-s/Pelletier-a						3.00
...: Misassembled TPB (2005, $14.99) r/#1-4, West Coast Avengers #46 (1st app.) and Marvel Super-Heroes #8 (1st app. Squirrel Girl; Ditko-a)						15.00

GLADSTONE COMIC ALBUM
Gladstone: 1987 - No. 28, 1990 ($5.95/$9.95, 8-1/2x11")(All Mickey Mouse albums are by Gottfredson)

	GD 2.0	VG 4.0	FN 6.0	VF 8.0	VF/NM 9.0	NM- 9.2
1-10: 1-Uncle Scrooge; Barks-r; Beck-c. 2-Donald Duck; r/F.C. #108 by Barks. 3-Mickey Mouse-r by Gottfredson. 4-Uncle Scrooge; r/F.C. #456 by Barks w/unedited story. 5-Donald Duck Advs.; r/F.C. #199. 6-Uncle Scrooge-r by Barks. 7-Donald Duck-r by Barks. 8-Mickey Mouse-r. 9-Bambi; r/F.C. #186? 10-Donald Duck Advs.; r/F.C. #275	1	3	4	6	8	10
11-20: 11-Uncle Scrooge; r/U.S. #4. 12-Donald And Daisy; r/F.C. #1055, WDC&S. 13-Donald Duck Advs.; r/F.C. #408. 14-Uncle Scrooge; Barks-r/U.S #21. 15-Donald And Gladstone; Barks-r. 16-Donald Duck Advs.; r/F.C. #238. 17-Mickey Mouse strip-r (The World of Tomorrow, The Pirate Ghost Ship). 18-Donald Duck and the Junior Woodchucks; Barks-r. 19-Uncle Scrooge; r/U.S. #12; Rosa-c. 20-Uncle Scrooge; r/F.C. #386; Barks-c/a(r)	1	3	4	6	8	10
21-25: 21-Donald Duck Family; Barks-c/a(r). 22-Mickey Mouse strip-r. 23-Donald Duck; Barks-r/D.D. #26 w/unedited story. 24-Uncle Scrooge; Barks-r; Rosa-c. 25-D. Duck; Barks-c/a-r/F.C. #367	1	3	4	6	8	10
26-28: All have $9.95-c. 26-Mickey & Donald; Gottfredson-c/a(r). 27-Donald Duck; r/WDC&S by Barks; Barks painted-c. 28-Uncle Scrooge & Donald Duck; Rosa-c/a (4 stories)	1	3	4	6	8	10
Special 1-7: 1 ('89-'90, $9.95/13.95)-1-Donald Duck Finds Pirate Gold; r/F.C. #9. 2 ('89, $8.95)-Uncle Scrooge and Donald Duck; Barks-r/Uncle Scrooge #5; Rosa-c. 3 ('89, $8.95)-Mickey Mouse strip-r. 4 ('89, $11.95)-Uncle Scrooge; Rosa-c/a-r/Son of the Sun from U.S. #219 plus Barks-r/U.S. 5 ('90, $11.95)-Donald Duck Advs.; Barks-r/F.C. #282 & 422 plus Barks painted-c. 6 ('90, $12.95)-Uncle Scrooge; Barks-c/a-r/Uncle Scrooge. 7 ('90, $13.95)-Mickey Mouse; Gottfredson strip-r	2	4	6	9	11	14

GLADSTONE COMIC ALBUM (2nd Series)(Also see The Original Dick Tracy)
Gladstone Publishing: 1990 ($5.95, 8-1/2 x 11," stiff-c, 52 pgs.)

	GD 2.0	VG 4.0	FN 6.0	VF 8.0	VF/NM 9.0	NM- 9.2
1,2-The Original Dick Tracy. 2-Origin of the 2-way wrist radio						6.00
3-D Tracy Meets the Mole-r by Gould ($6.95).	1	2	3	5	6	8

GLAMOROUS ROMANCES (Formerly Dotty)
Ace Magazines (A. A. Wyn): No. 41, July, 1949 - No. 90, Oct, 1956 (Photo-c 68-90)

	GD 2.0	VG 4.0	FN 6.0	VF 8.0	VF/NM 9.0	NM- 9.2
41-Dotty app.	12	24	36	69	97	125
42-72,74-80: 44-Begin 52 pg. issues. 45,50-61-Painted-c. 80-Last pre-code (2/55)	9	18	27	52	69	85
73-L.B. Cole-r/All Love #27	10	20	30	54	72	90
81-90	9	18	27	50	65	80

GLAMOURPUSS
Aardvark-Vanaheim Inc.: Apr, 2008 - Present ($3.00, B&W)

	GD 2.0	VG 4.0	FN 6.0	VF 8.0	VF/NM 9.0	NM- 9.2
1-23: 1-Two covers; Dave Sim-s/a/c. 9,10-Gene Colan-c. 11-Heath-c. 19-Allred-c						3.00
1-Comics Industry Preview Edition (Diamond Dateline supplement)						4.00

GLOBAL FREQUENCY
DC Comics (WildStorm): Dec, 2002 - No. 12, Aug, 2004 ($2.95, limited series)

	GD 2.0	VG 4.0	FN 6.0	VF 8.0	VF/NM 9.0	NM- 9.2
1-12-Warren Ellis-s. 1-Leach-a. 2-Fabry-a. 3-Dillon-a. 5-Muth-a. 7-Bisley-a. 12-Ha-a						3.00

Glory #4 © Rob Liefeld

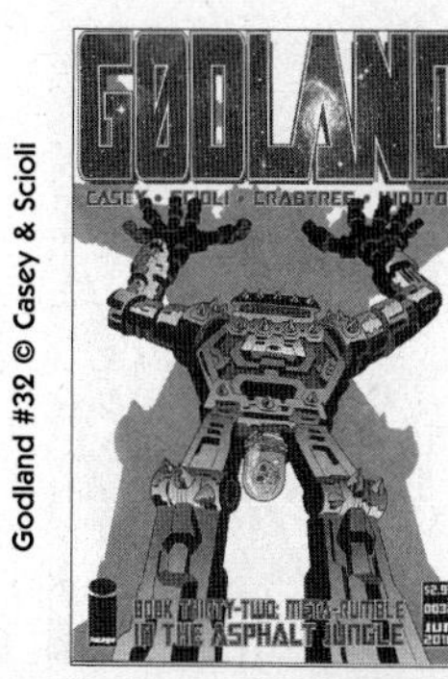

Godland #32 © Casey & Scioli

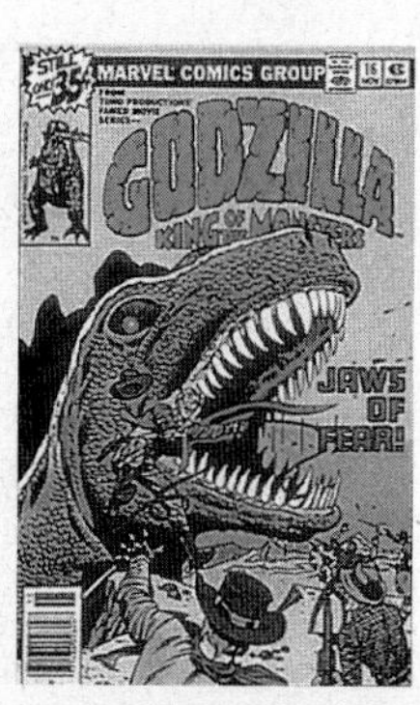

Godzilla #16 © MAR

GD 2.0 | VG 4.0 | FN 6.0 | VF 8.0 | VF/NM 9.0 | NM- 9.2

1-RRP Edition variant-c; promotional giveaway for retailers (200 printed) 10.00
...: Detonation Radio TPB (2005, $14.95) r/#7-12 15.00
...: Planet Ablaze TPB (2003, $14.95) r/#1-6 15.00

GLORY
Image Comics (Extreme Studios)/Maximum Press: Mar, 1995 - No. 22, Apr, 1997 ($2.50)

0-Deodato-c/a, 1-(3/95)-Deodato-a 3.00
1A-Variant-c 4.00
2-11,13-22: 4-Variant-c by Quesada & Palmiotti. 5-Bagged w/Youngblood gaming card. 7,8-Deodato-c/a(p). 8-Babewatch x-over. 9-Cruz-c; Extreme Destroyer Pt. 5; polybagged w/card. 10-Angela-c/app. 11-Deodato-c. 3.00
12-($3.50)-Photo-c 3.50
... & Friends Christmas Special (12/95, $2.50) Deodato-c 3.00
... & Friends Lingerie Special (9/95, $2.95) Pin-ups w/photos; photo-c; variant-c exists 3.00
... /Angela: Angels in Hell (4/96, $2.50) Flip book w/Darkchylde #1 3.00
... /Avengelyne (10/95, $3.95) 1-Chromium-c, 1-Regular-c 4.00
Trade Paperback (1995, $9.95)-r/#1-4 10.00

GLORY (Continues numbering from the 1995-1997 series)
Image Comics: Feb, 2012 - Present ($2.99)

23,24-Joe Keatinge-s/Ross Campbell-a. 23-Supreme app. 3.00

GLORY
Awesome Comics: Mar, 1999 ($2.50)

0-Liefeld-c; story and sketch pages 3.00

GLORY (ALAN MOORE'S...)
Avatar Press: Dec, 2001 - No. 2 ($3.50)

Preview-(9/01, $1.99) B&W pages and cover art; Alan Moore-s 3.00
0-Four regular covers 3.50
1,2: 1-Alan Moore-s/Mychaels & Gebbie-a; nine covers by various. 2-Five covers 3.50

GLORY & FRIENDS BIKINI FEST
Image Comics (Extreme): Sept, 1995 - No. 2, Oct, 1995 ($2.50, limited series)

1,2: 1-Photo-c; centerfold photo; pin-ups 3.00

GLORY/CELESTINE: DARK ANGEL
Image Comics/Maximum Press (Extreme Studios): Sept, 1996 - No. 3, Nov, 1996 ($2.50, limited series)

1-3 3.00

GLX-MAS SPECIAL (Great Lakes Avengers)
Marvel Comics: Feb, 2006 ($3.99, one-shot)

1-Christmas themed stories by various incl. Haley, Templeton, Grist, Wieringo 4.00

G-MAN: CAPE CRISIS
Image Comics: Aug, 2009 - No. 5, Jan, 2010 ($2.99, limited series)

1-5-Chris Giarrusso-s/a; back-up short strips by various 3.00

GNOME MOBILE, THE (See Movie Comics)

GOBBLEDYGOOK
Mirage Studios: 1984 - No. 2, 1984 (B&W)(1st Mirage comics, published at same time)

	GD	VG	FN	VF	VF/NM	NM-
1-(24 pgs.)-(distribution of approx. 50) Teenage Mutant Ninja Turtles app. on full page back-c ad; Teenage Mutant Ninja Turtles do not appear inside. 1st app of Fugitoid	196	392	588	1646	3573	5500
2-(24 pgs.)-Teenage Mutant Ninja Turtles on full page back-c ad	78	156	234	632	1366	2100

NOTE: Counterfeit copies exist. Originals feature both black & white covers and interiors. Signed and numbered copies do not exist.

GOBBLEDYGOOK
Mirage Studios: Dec, 1986 ($3.50, B&W, one-shot, 100 pgs.)

	GD	VG	FN	VF	VF/NM	NM-
1-New 8 pg. TMNT story plus a Donatello/Michaelangelo 7 pg. story & a Gizmo story; Corben-i(r)/TMNT #7	1	2	3	5	6	8

GOBLIN, THE
Warren Publishing Co.: June, 1982 - No. 3, Dec, 1982 ($2.25, B&W magazine with 8 pg. color insert comic in all)

	GD	VG	FN	VF	VF/NM	NM-
1-The Gremlin app. Philo Photon & the Troll Patrol, Micro-Buccaneers & Wizard Wormglow begin & app. in all. Tin Man app. Golden-a(p). Nebres-c/a in all	2	4	6	13	18	22
2,3: 2-1st Hobgoblin. 3-Tin Man app.	2	4	6	9	12	15

NOTE: ***Bermejo** a-1-3. **Elias** a-1-3. **Laxamana** a-1-3. **Nino** a-3.*

GOD COMPLEX
Image Comics: Dec, 2009 - No. 7, Jun, 2010 ($2.99)

1-7-Oeming & Berman-s/Broglia-a/Oeming-c 3.00

GODDESS
DC Comics (Vertigo): June, 1995 - No. 8, Jan, 1996 ($2.95, limited series)

1-Garth Ennis scripts; Phil Winslade-c/a in all 5.00
2-8 4.00
TPB (2002, $19.95) r/#1-8; foreword and sketch pages by Winslade 20.00

GODFATHERS, THE (See The Crusaders)

GOD IS
Spire Christian Comics (Fleming H. Revell Co.): 1973, 1975 (35-49¢)

	GD	VG	FN	VF	VF/NM	NM-
nn-(1973) By Al Hartley	2	4	6	11	16	20
nn-(1975)	2	4	6	8	11	14

GODLAND
Image Comics: July, 2005 - Present ($2.99)

1-15,17-35-Joe Casey-s; Kirby-esque art by Tom Scioli. 13-Var-c by Giffen & Larsen. 33-"Dogland" on cover 3.00
16-(60¢-c) Re-cap/origin issue 3.00
Image Firsts: Godland #1 (9/10, $1.00) r/#1 with "Image Firsts" cover logo 3.00
...: Celestial Edition One HC (2007, $34.99) r/#1-12 and story from Image Holiday Special; intro. by Grant Morrison; cover gallery, developmental art and original story pitches 35.00
... Vol. 1: Hello Cosmic! TPB (1/06, $14.99) r/#1-6; sketch development pages 15.00
... Vol. 2: Another Sunny Delight TPB (8/06, $14.99) r/#7-12; early Christmas story 15.00
... Vol. 3: Proto-Plastic Party TPB (2007, $14.99) r/#13-18 15.00
... Vol. 4: Amplified Now TPB (2008, $14.99) r/#19-24 15.00

GOD OF WAR (Based on the Sony videogame)
DC Comics (WildStorm): May, 2010 - No. 6, Mar, 2011 ($3.99/$2.99, limited series)

1-6-Wolfman-s/Sorrentino-a/Park-c. 6-($2.99) 4.00
TPB (2011, $14.99) r/#1-6; cover gallery 15.00

GOD SAVE THE QUEEN
DC Comics (Vertigo): 2007 ($19.99, hardcover with dustjacket, graphic novel)

HC-Mike Carey-s/John Bolton-painted art 20.00
SC-(2008, $12.99) Different painted-c by Bolton 13.00

GOD'S COUNTRY (Also see Marvel Comics Presents)
Marvel Comics: 1994 ($6.95)

nn-P. Craig Russell-a; Colossus story; r/Marvel Comics Presents #10-17 7.00

GOD'S HEROES IN AMERICA
Catechetical Guild Educational Society: 1956 (nn) (25¢/35¢, 68 pgs.)

	GD	VG	FN	VF	VF/NM	NM-
307	3	6	9	16	23	30

GOD'S SMUGGLER (Religious)
Spire Christian Comics/Fleming H. Revell Co.: 1972 (35¢/39¢/40¢)

	GD	VG	FN	VF	VF/NM	NM-
1-Three variations exist	2	4	6	11	16	20

GODWHEEL
Malibu Comics (Ultraverse): No. 0, Jan, 1995 - No. 3, Feb, 1995 ($2.50, limited series)

0-3: 0-Flip-c. 1-1st app. of Primevil; Thor cameo (1 panel). 3-Perez-a in Chapter 3, Thor app. 3.00

GODZILLA (Movie)
Marvel Comics : August, 1977 - No. 24, July, 1979 (Based on movie series)

	GD	VG	FN	VF	VF/NM	NM-
1-(Regular 30¢ edition)-Mooney-i	3	6	9	20	30	40
1-(35¢-c variant, limited distribution)	6	12	18	37	59	80
2-(Regular 30¢ edition)-Tuska-i.	2	4	6	9	13	16
2,3-(35¢-c variant, limited distribution)	3	6	9	20	30	40
3-(30¢-c) Champions app.(w/o Ghost Rider)	2	4	6	10	14	18
4-10: 4,5-Sutton-a	2	4	6	8	11	14
11-23: 14-Shield app. 20-F.F. app. 21,22-Devil Dinosaur app.	2	4	6	8	10	12
24-Last issue	2	4	6	9	13	16

GODZILLA (Movie)
Dark Horse Comics: May, 1988 - No. 6, 1988 ($1.95, B&W, limited series) (Based on movie series)

1 6.00
2-6 4.00
...Collection (1990, $10.95)-r/1-6 with new-c 11.00
...Color Special 1 (Sum, 1992, $3.50, color, 44 pgs.)-Arthur Adams wraparound-c/a & part scripts 5.00
...King Of The Monsters Special (8/87, $1.50)-Origin; Bissette-c/a 4.00
...Vs. Barkley nn (12/93, $2.95, color)-Dorman painted-c 4.00

GODZILLA (King of the Monsters) (Movie)
Dark Horse Comics: May, 1995 - No. 16, Sept, 1996 ($2.50) (Based on movies)

0-16: 0-r/Dark Horse Comics #10,11. 1-3-Kevin Maguire scripts. 3-8-Art Adams-c 4.00

Godzilla: Kingdom of Monsters #1 © Toho

Golden Arrow Western #6 © FAW

Golden Picture Classic CL-403 © WEST

GD VG FN VF VF/NM NM-
2.0 4.0 6.0 8.0 9.0 9.2

GD VG FN VF VF/NM NM-
2.0 4.0 6.0 8.0 9.0 9.2

...Vs. Hero Zero ($2.50) 3.00

GODZILLA: GANGSTERS AND GOLIATHS
IDW Publishing: Jun, 2011 - No. 5, Oct, 2011 ($3.99, limited series)
1-5-Layman-s/Ponticelli-a; Mothra app. 1-Darrow-c 4.00

GODZILLA: KINGDOM OF MONSTERS
IDW Publishing: Mar, 2011 - Present ($3.99)
1-9: 1-Hester-a; covers by Ross & Powell. 2,3-Covers by Hester & Powell 4.00
...: 100 Cover Charity Spectacular (8/11, $7.99) Variant covers for Japan Disaster Relief 8.00

GODZILLA LEGENDS (Spotlight on other monsters)
IDW Publishing: Nov, 2011 - No. 5, ($3.99, limited series)
1-3-Art Adams-c. 1-Anguirus. 2-Rodan. 3-Titanosaurus 4.00

GOG (VILLAINS) (See Kingdom Come)
DC Comics: Feb, 1998 ($1.95, one-shot)
1-Waid-s/Ordway-a(p)/Pearson-c 3.00

GO GIRL!
Image Comics: Aug, 2000 - No. 5 ($3.50, B&W, quarterly)
1-5-Trina Robbins-s/Anne Timmons-a; pin-up gallery 3.50

GO-GO
Charlton Comics: June, 1966 - No. 9, Oct, 1967
1-Miss Bikini Luv begins w/Jim Aparo's 1st published work; Rolling Stones, Beatles, Elvis, Sonny & Cher, Bob Dylan, Sinatra, parody; Herman's Hermits pin-ups; D'Agostino-c/a in #1-8 8 16 24 56 96 135
2-Ringo Starr, David McCallum & Beatles photos on cover; Beatles story and photos; Blooperman & parody of JLA heroes 8 16 24 56 96 135
3,4: 3-Blooperman, ends #6; 1 pg. Batman & Robin satire; full pg. photo pin-ups Lovin' Spoonful & The Byrds 5 10 15 35 55 75
5,7,9: 5 (2/67)-Super Hero & TV satire by Jim Aparo & Grass Green begins. 6-8-Aparo-a. 7-Photo of Brian Wilson of Beach Boys on-c & Beach Boys photo inside f/b-c. 9-Aparo-c/a 5 10 15 35 55 75
6-Parody of JLA & DC heroes vs. Marvel heroes; Aparo-a; Elvis parody; Petula Clark photo-c 6 12 18 39 62 85
8-Monkees photo on-c & photo inside f/b-c 6 12 18 42 69 95

GO-GO AND ANIMAL (See Tippy's Friends...)

GOING STEADY (Formerly Teen-Age Temptations)
St. John Publ. Co.: No. 10, Dec, 1954 - No. 13, June, 1955; No. 14, Oct, 1955
10(1954)-Matt Baker-c/a 31 62 93 186 303 420
11(2/55, last precode), 12(4/55)-Baker-c 19 38 57 112 179 245
13(6/55)-Baker-c/a 25 50 75 147 241 335
14(10/55)-Matt Baker-c/a, 25 pgs. 29 58 87 170 278 385

GOING STEADY (Formerly Personal Love)
Prize Publications/Headline: V3#3, Feb, 1960 - V3#6, Aug, 1960; V4#1, Sept-Oct, 1960
V3#3-6, V4#1 3 6 9 20 30 40

GOING STEADY WITH BETTY (Becomes Betty & Her Steady No. 2)
Avon Periodicals: Nov-Dec, 1949 (Teen-age)
1-Partial photo-c 17 34 51 98 154 210

GOLDEN AGE, THE (TPB also reprinted in 2005 as JSA: The Golden Age)
DC Comics (Elseworlds): 1993 - No. 4, 1994 ($4.95, limited series)
1-4: James Robinson scripts; Paul Smith-c/a; gold foil embossed-c 6.00
Trade Paperback (1995, $19.95) intro by Howard Chaykin 20.00

GOLDEN AGE SECRET FILES
DC Comics: Feb, 2001 ($4.95, one-shot)
1-Origins and profiles of JSA members and other G.A. heroes; Lark-c 5.00

GOLDEN ARROW (See Fawcett Miniatures, Mighty Midget & Whiz Comics)

GOLDEN ARROW (...Western No. 6)
Fawcett Publications: Spring, 1942 - No. 6, Spring, 1947 (68 pgs.)
1-Golden Arrow begins 47 94 141 296 498 700
2-(1943) 22 44 66 132 216 300
3-5: 3-(Win/45-46). 4-(Spr/46). 5-(Fall/46) 15 30 45 90 140 190
6-Krigstein-a 16 32 48 94 147 200
Ashcan (1942) not distributed to newsstands, only for in house use. A CGC certified 9.0 sold for $3,734.38 in 2008.

GOLDEN COMICS DIGEST
Gold Key: May, 1969 - No. 48, Jan, 1976
NOTE: *Whitman editions exist of many titles and are generally valued the same.*
1-Tom & Jerry, Woody Woodpecker, Bugs Bunny 6 12 18 37 59 80
2-Hanna-Barbera TV Fun Favorites; Space Ghost, Flintstones, Atom Ant, Jetsons, Yogi Bear, Banana Splits, others app. 7 14 21 48 79 110
3-Tom & Jerry, Woody Woodpecker 3 6 9 17 25 32
4-Tarzan; Manning & Marsh-a 5 10 15 30 48 65
5,8-Tom & Jerry, W. Woodpecker, Bugs Bunny 3 6 9 16 23 30
6-Bugs Bunny 3 6 9 16 23 30
7-Hanna-Barbera TV Fun Favorites 6 12 18 37 59 80
9-Tarzan 5 10 15 30 48 65
10,12-17: 10-Bugs Bunny. 12-Tom & Jerry, Bugs Bunny, W. Woodpecker Journey to the Sun. 13-Tom & Jerry. 14-Bugs Bunny Fun Packed Funnies. 15-Tom & Jerry, Woody Woodpecker, Bugs Bunny. 16-Woody Woodpecker Cartoon Special. 17-Bugs Bunny 3 6 9 16 23 30
11-Hanna-Barbera TV Fun Favorites 6 12 18 39 62 85
18-Tom & Jerry; Barney Bear-r by Barks 3 6 9 17 25 32
19-Little Lulu 4 8 12 26 41 55
20-22: 20-Woody Woodpecker Falltime Funtime. 21-Bugs Bunny Showtime. 22-Tom & Jerry Winter Wingding 3 6 9 16 23 30
23-Little Lulu & Tubby Fun Fling 4 8 12 26 41 55
24-26,28: 24-Woody Woodpecker Fun Festival. 25-Tom & Jerry. 26-Bugs Bunny Halloween Hulla-Boo-Loo; Dr. Spektor article, also #25. 28-Tom & Jerry 3 6 9 14 20 26
27-Little Lulu & Tubby in Hawaii 4 8 12 25 39 52
29-Little Lulu & Tubby 4 8 12 25 39 52
30-Bugs Bunny Vacation Funnies 3 6 9 14 20 26
31-Turok, Son of Stone; r/4-Color #596,656; c-r/#9 4 8 12 28 44 60
32-Woody Woodpecker Summer Fun 3 6 9 14 20 26
33,36: 33-Little Lulu & Tubby Halloween Fun; Dr. Spektor app. 36-Little Lulu & Her Friends 4 8 12 25 39 52
34,35,37-39: 34-Bugs Bunny Winter Funnies. 35-Tom & Jerry Snowtime Funtime. 37-Woody Woodpecker County Fair. 39-Bugs Bunny Summer Fun 3 6 9 14 20 26
38-The Pink Panther 3 6 9 17 25 32
40,43: 40-Little Lulu & Tubby Trick or Treat; all by Stanley. 43-Little Lulu in Paris 4 8 12 25 39 52
41,42,44,47: 41-Tom & Jerry Winter Carnival. 42-Bugs Bunny. 44-Woody Woodpecker Family Fun Festival. 47-Bugs Bunny 3 6 9 14 20 25
45-The Pink Panther 3 6 9 17 25 32
46-Little Lulu & Tubby 4 8 12 22 34 45
48-The Lone Ranger 3 6 9 18 27 35
NOTE: *#1-30, 164 pgs.; #31 on, 132 pgs..*

GOLDEN LAD
Spark/Fact & Fiction Publ.: July, 1945 - No. 5, June, 1946 (#4, 5: 52 pgs.)
1-Origin & 1st app. Golden Lad & Swift Arrow; Sandusky and the Senator begins 60 120 180 381 653 925
2-Mort Meskin-c/a 30 60 90 177 289 400
3,4-Mort Meskin-c/a 27 54 81 158 259 360
5-Origin & 1st app. Golden Girl; Shaman & Flame app. 30 60 90 177 289 400
NOTE: *All have* **Robinson,** *and* **Roussos** *art plus* **Meskin** *covers and art.*

GOLDEN LEGACY
Fitzgerald Publishing Co.: 1966 - 1972 (Black History) (25¢)
1-12,14-16: 1-Toussaint L'Ouverture (1966), 2-Harriet Tubman (1967), 3-Crispus Attucks & the Minutemen (1967), 4-Benjamin Banneker (1968), 5-Matthew Henson (1969), 6-Alexander Dumas & Family (1969), 7-Frederick Douglass, Part 1 (1969), 8-Frederick Douglass, Part 2 (1970), 9-Robert Smalls (1970), 10-J. Cinque & the Amistad Mutiny (1970), 11-Men in Action: White, Marshall J. Wilkins (1970), 12-Black Cowboys (1972), 14-The Life of Alexander Pushkin (1971), 15-Ancient African Kingdoms (1972), 16-Black Inventors (1972) each.... 4 8 12 22 34 45
13-The Life of Martin Luther King, Jr. (1972) 4 8 12 26 41 55
1-10,12,13,15,16(1976)-Reprints 2 4 6 8 11 14

GOLDEN LOVE STORIES (Formerly Golden West Love)
Kirby Publishing Co.: No. 4, April, 1950
4-Powell-a; Glenn Ford/Janet Leigh photo-c 17 34 51 98 154 210

GOLDEN PICTURE CLASSIC, A
Western Printing Co. (Simon & Shuster): 1956-1957 (Text stories w/illustrations in color; 100 pgs. each)
CL-401: Treasure Island 11 22 33 64 90 115
CL-402,403: 402: Tom Sawyer. 403: Black Beauty 10 20 30 54 72 90
CL-404, 405: CL-404: Little Women. CL-405: Heidi 10 20 30 54 72 90
CL-406: Ben Hur 8 16 24 44 57 70
CL-407: Around the World in 80 Days 8 16 24 44 57 70
CL-408: Sherlock Holmes 9 18 27 50 65 80

Gon on Safari © Kodansha Ltd.

Goofy FC #468 © DIS

Goofy Comics #9 © STD

	GD 2.0	VG 4.0	FN 6.0	VF 8.0	VF/NM 9.0	NM- 9.2
CL-409: The Three Musketeers	8	16	24	44	57	70
CL-410: The Merry Advs. of Robin Hood	8	16	24	44	57	70
CL-411,412: 411: Hans Brinker. 412: The Count of Monte Cristo	9	18	27	50	65	80

(Both soft & hardcover editions are valued the same)

NOTE: *Recent research has uncovered new information. Apparently #s 1-6 were issued in 1956 and #7-12 in 1957. But they can be found in five different series listings: CL-1 to CL-12 (softbound); CL-401 to CL-412 (also softbound); CL-101 to CL-112 (hardbound); plus two new series discoveries: A Golden Reading Adventure, publ. by Golden Press; edited down to 60 pages and reduced in size to 6x9"; only #s discovered so far are #381 (CL-4), #382 (CL-6) & #387 (CL-3). They have no reorder list and some have covers different from GPC. There have also been found British hardbound editions of GPC with dust jackets. Copies of all five listed series vary from scarce to very rare. Some editions of some series have not yet been found at all.*

GOLDEN PICTURE STORY BOOK
Racine Press (Western): Dec, 1961 (50¢, Treasury size, 52 pgs.) (All are scarce)

	GD	VG	FN	VF	VF/NM	NM-
ST-1-Huckleberry Hound (TV); Hokey Wolf, Pixie & Dixie, Quick Draw McGraw, Snooper and Blabber, Augie Doggie app.	15	30	45	104	227	350
ST-2-Yogi Bear (TV); Snagglepuss, Yakky Doodle, Quick Draw McGraw, Snooper and Blabber, Augie Doggie app.	15	30	45	104	227	350
ST-3-Babes in Toyland (Walt Disney's...)-Annette Funicello photo-c	20	40	60	137	294	450
ST-4-(...of Disney Ducks)-Walt Disney's Wonderful World of Ducks (Donald Duck, Uncle Scrooge, Donald's Nephews, Grandma Duck, Ludwig Von Drake, & Gyro Gearloose stories)	20	40	60	137	294	450

GOLDEN RECORD COMIC (See Amazing Spider-Man #1, Avengers #4, Fantastic Four #1, Journey Into Mystery #83)

GOLDEN STORY BOOKS
Western Printing Co. (Simon & Shuster): 1949-1950 (Heavy covers, digest size, 128 pgs.) (Illustrated text in color)

	GD	VG	FN	VF	VF/NM	NM-
7-Walt Disney's Mystery in Disneyville, a book-length adventure starring Donald and Nephews, Mickey and Nephews, and with Minnie, Daisy and Goofy. Art by Dick Moores & Manuel Gonzales (scarce)	30	60	90	177	289	400
10-Bugs Bunny's Treasure Hunt, a book-length adventure starring Bugs & Porky Pig, with Petunia Pig & Nephew, Cicero. Art by Tom McKimson (scarce)	21	42	63	122	199	275
11,12 ('50): 11-M-G-M's Tom & Jerry. 12-Walt Disney's "So Dear My Heart"	20	40	60	114	182	250

GOLDEN WEST LOVE (Golden Love Stories No. 4)
Kirby Publishing Co.: Sept-Oct, 1949 - No. 3, Feb, 1950 (All 52 pgs.)

	GD	VG	FN	VF	VF/NM	NM-
1-Powell-a in all; Roussos-a; painted-c	22	44	66	128	209	290
2,3: Photo-c	17	34	51	98	154	210

GOLDEN WEST RODEO TREASURY (See Dell Giants)

GOLDFISH (See A.K.A. Goldfish)

GOLDILOCKS (See March of Comics No. 1)

GOLD KEY CHAMPION
Gold Key: Mar, 1978 - No. 2, May, 1978 (50¢, 52pgs.)

	GD	VG	FN	VF	VF/NM	NM-
1,2: 1-Space Family Robinson; half-r. 2-Mighty Samson; half-r	1	3	4	6	8	10

GOLD KEY SPOTLIGHT
Gold Key: May, 1976 - No. 11, Feb, 1978

	GD	VG	FN	VF	VF/NM	NM-
1-Tom, Dick & Harriet	2	4	6	8	11	14
2-11: 2-Wacky Advs. of Cracky. 3-Wacky Witch. 4-Tom, Dick & Harriet. 5-Wacky Advs. of Cracky. 6-Dagar the Invincible; Santos-a; origin Demonomicon. 7-Wacky Witch & Greta Ghost. 8-The Occult Files of Dr. Spektor, Simbar, Lu-sai; Santos-a. 9-Tragg. 10-O. G. Whiz. 11-Tom, Dick & Harriet	2	4	6	8	10	12

GOLD MEDAL COMICS
Cambridge House: 1945 (25¢, one-shot, 132 pgs.)

	GD	VG	FN	VF	VF/NM	NM-
nn-Captain Truth by Fugitani as well as Stallman and Howie Post, Crime Detector, The Witch of Salem, Luckyman, others app.	32	64	96	192	314	435

GOMER PYLE (TV)
Gold Key: July, 1966 - No. 3, Oct, 1967

	GD	VG	FN	VF	VF/NM	NM-
1-Photo front/back-c	8	16	24	53	89	125
2,3	6	12	18	39	62	85

GON
DC Comics (Paradox Press): July, 1996 - No. 4, Oct, 1996; No. 5, 1997 ($5.95, B&W, digest-size, limited series)

	GD	VG	FN	VF	VF/NM	NM-
1-5: Misadventures of baby dinosaur; 1-Gon. 2-Gon Again. 3-Gon: Here Today, Gone Tomorrow. 4-Gon: Going, Going...Gon. 5-Gon Swimmin'. Tanaka-c/a/scripts in all	1	2	3	5	6	8

GON COLOR SPECTACULAR
DC Comics (Paradox Press): 1998 ($5.95, square-bound)

	GD	VG	FN	VF	VF/NM	NM-
nn-Tanaka-c/a/scripts	1	2	3	5	6	8

GON ON SAFARI
DC Comics (Paradox Press): 2000 ($7.95, B&W, digest-size)

	GD	VG	FN	VF	VF/NM	NM-
nn-Tanaka-c/a/scripts	1	2	3	5	6	8

GON UNDERGROUND
DC Comics (Paradox Press): 1999 ($7.95, B&W, digest-size)

	GD	VG	FN	VF	VF/NM	NM-
nn-Tanaka-c/a/scripts	1	2	3	5	6	8

GON WILD
DC Comics (Paradox Press): 1997 ($9.95, B&W, digest-size)

	GD	VG	FN	VF	VF/NM	NM-
nn-Tanaka-c/a/scripts in all. (Rep. Gon #3,4)	1	3	4	6	8	10

GOODBYE, MR. CHIPS (See Movie Comics)

GOOD GIRL ART QUARTERLY
AC Comics: Summer, 1990 - No. 15, Spring, 1994 (B&W/color, 52 pgs.)

	NM-
1,3-15 ($3.50)-All have one new story (often FemForce) & rest reprints by Baker, Ward & other "good girl" artists	4.00
2 ($3.95)	4.00

GOOD GIRL COMICS (Formerly Good Girl Art Quarterly)
AC Comics: No. 16, Summer, 1994 - No. 18, 1995 (B&W)

	NM-
16-18	4.00

GOOD GUYS, THE
Defiant: Nov, 1993 - No. 9, July, 1994 ($2.50/$3.25/$3.50)

	NM-
1-($3.50, 52 pgs.)-Glory x-over from Plasm	4.00
2,3,5-9: 9-Pre-Schism issue	3.00
4-($3.25, 52 pgs.)	4.00

GOOD, THE BAD AND THE UGLY, THE (Also see Man With No Name)
Dynamite Entertainment: 2009 - No. 8 ($3.50)

	NM-
1-8: 1-Character from the 1966 Clint Eastwood movie; Dixon-s/Polls-a; three covers	3.50

GOOD TRIUMPHS OVER EVIL! (Also see Narrative Illustration)
M.C. Gaines: 1943 (12 pgs., 7-1/4"x10", B&W) (not a comic book) (Rare)

	GD	VG	FN	VF	VF/NM	NM-
nn-A pamphlet, sequel to Narrative Illustration	116	232	348	742	1271	1800

NOTE: ***Print, A Quarterly Journal of the Graphic Arts*** *Vol. 3 No. 3 (64 pg. square bound) features 1st printing of Good Triumphs Over Evil! A VG copy sold for $350 in 2005.*

GOOFY (Disney)(See Dynabrite Comics, Mickey Mouse Magazine V4#7, Walt Disney Showcase #35 & Wheaties)
Dell Publishing Co.: No. 468, May, 1953 - Sept-Nov, 1962

	GD	VG	FN	VF	VF/NM	NM-
Four Color 468 (#1)	11	22	33	73	142	210
Four Color 562,627,658,702,747,802,857	7	14	21	46	76	105
Four Color 899,952,987,1053,1094,1149,1201	5	10	15	32	51	70
12-308-211(Dell, 9-11/62)	5	10	15	32	51	70

GOOFY ADVENTURES
Disney Comics: June, 1990 - No. 17, 1991 ($1.50)

	NM-
1-17: Most new stories. 2-Joshua Quagmire-a w/free poster. 7-WDC&S-r plus new-a. 9-Gottfredson-r. 14-Super Goof story. 15-All Super Goof issue. 17-Gene Colan-a(p)	3.00

GOOFY ADVENTURE STORY (See Goofy No. 857)

GOOFY COMICS (Companion to Happy Comics)(Not Disney)
Nedor Publ. Co. No. 1-14/Standard No. 14-48: June, 1943 - No. 48, 1953 (Animated Cartoons)

	GD	VG	FN	VF	VF/NM	NM-
1-Funny animal; Oriolo-c	31	62	93	186	303	420
2	17	34	51	98	154	210
3-10	14	28	42	81	118	155
11-19	11	22	33	62	86	110
20-35-Frazetta text illos in all	12	24	36	69	97	125
36-48	10	20	30	54	72	90

GOOFY SUCCESS STORY (See Goofy No. 702)

GOON, THE
Avatar Press: Mar, 1999 - No. 3, July, 1999 ($3.00, B&W)

	GD	VG	FN	VF	VF/NM	NM-
1-Eric Powell-s/a	4	8	12	22	34	45
2	3	6	9	14	20	25
3	2	4	6	9	12	15
...: Rough Stuff (Albatross, 1/03, $15.95) r/Avatar Press series #1-3						16.00
...: Rough Stuff (Dark Horse, 2/04, $12.95) r/Avatar Press series #1-3 newly colored						13.00

GOON, THE (2nd series)
Albatross Exploding Funny Books: Oct, 2002 - No. 4, Feb, 2003 ($2.95)

Gorgo #6 © CC

Gotham City Sirens #23 © DC

Graphique Musique #1 © SLG

GD VG FN VF VF/NM NM-
2.0 4.0 6.0 8.0 9.0 9.2

1-Eric Powell-s/a 2 4 6 9 12 15
2-4 1 2 3 5 6 8
...Color Special 1 (8/02) 2 4 6 9 12 15
...: Nothin' But Misery Vol. 1 (Dark Horse, 7/03, $15.95, TPB) - Reprints The Goon #1-4 (Albatross series), Color Special, and story from DHP #157 16.00

GOON, THE (3rd series) (Also see Dethklok Versus the Goon)
Dark Horse Comics: June, 2003 - Present ($2.99)

1-Eric Powell-s/a in all 1 2 3 5 6 8
2-4 5.00
5-31: 7-Hellboy-c/app; framing seq. by Mignola 14-Two covers 3.00
32-($3.99, 3/09) Tenth Anniversary issue; with sketch pages and pin-ups 4.00
33-38-($3.50) 33-Silent issue. 35-Dorkin-s 3.50
... 25¢ Edition (9/05, 25¢) 3.00
...: Chinatown and the Mystery of Mr. Wicker HC (11/07, $19.95) original GN; Powell-s/a 20.00
...: Fancy Pants Edition HC (10/05, $24.95, dust jacket) r/#1,2 of 2nd series & #1,3,5,9 of 3rd series; Powell intro.; sketch pages and cover gallery 25.00
...: Heaps of Ruination (5/05, $12.95, TPB) r/#5-8; intro. by Frank Darabont 13.00
...: My Murderous Childhood (And Other Grievous Yarns) (5/04, $13.95, TPB) r/#1-4 and short story from Drawing on Your Nightmares one-shot; intro. by Frank Cho 14.00
...: One For One (8/10, $1.00) r/#1 with red cover frame 3.00
...: Virtue and the Grim Consequences Thereof (2/06, $16.95) r/#9-13 17.00
...: Wicked Inclinations (12/06, $14.95) r/#14-18; intro. by Mike Allred 15.00

GOON NOIR, THE (Dwight T. Albatross's...)
Dark Horse Comics: Sept, 2006 - No. 3, Jan, 2007 ($2.99, B&W, limited series)

1-3-Anthology 1-Oswalt-s/Ploog-a; Sniegoski-s/Powell-a; Morrison-s/a; Niles-s/Sook-a. 2-Nowlan, Barta-a. 3-Ramos, Guy Davis-a; Nelson, Posehn, Thomas Lennon-s 3.00
TPB (7/07, $12.95) r/#1-3; sketch pages; intros by "Dwight" 13.00

GOOSE (Humor magazine)
Cousins Publ. (Fawcett): Sept, 1976 - No. 3, 1976 (75¢, 52 pgs., B&W)

1-Nudity in all 3 6 9 16 23 30
2,3: 2-(10/76) Fonz-c/s; Lone Ranger story. 3-Wonder Woman, King Kong, Six Million Dollar Man stories 2 4 6 11 16 20

GORDO (See Comics Revue No. 5 & Giant Comics Edition)

GORGO (Based on M.G.M. movie) (See Return of...)
Charlton Comics: May, 1961 - No. 23, Sept, 1965

1-Ditko-a, 22 pgs. 22 44 66 154 327 500
2,3-Ditko-c/a 12 24 36 83 172 260
4-Ditko-c 10 20 30 64 115 165
5-11,13-16: 11,13-16-Ditko-a. 11-Ditko-c 8 16 24 56 96 135
12,17-23: 12-Reptisaurus x-over. 17-23-Montes/Bache-a. 20-Giordano-c 6 12 18 39 62 85
Gorgo's Revenge('62)-Becomes Return of... 7 14 21 48 79 110

GORILLA MAN (From Agents of Atlas)
Marvel Comics: Sept, 2010 - No. 3, Nov, 2010 ($3.99, limited series)

1-3-Parker-s/Caracuzzo-a. 1-Johnson-c. 3-Dell'Otto-c 4.00

GOSPEL BLIMP, THE
Spire Christian Comics (Fleming H. Revell Co.): 1973,1975 (35¢/39¢, 36 pgs.)

nn-(1973) 2 4 6 13 18 22
nn-(1975) 2 4 6 8 11 14

GOTHAM BY GASLIGHT (A Tale of the Batman)(See Batman: Master of...)
DC Comics: 1989 ($3.95, one-shot, squarebound, 52 pgs.)

nn-Mignola/Russell-a; intro by Robert Bloch 4.00

GOTHAM CENTRAL
DC Comics: Early Feb, 2003 - No. 40, Apr, 2006 ($2.50)

1-40-Stories of Gotham City Police. 1-Brubaker & Rucka-s/Lark-c/a. 10-Two-Face app. 13,15-Joker-c. 18-Huntress app. 27-Catwoman-c. 32-Poison Ivy app. 34-Teen Titans-c/app. 38-Crispus Allen killed (becomes The Spectre in Infinite Crisis #5) 3.00
... Book One: In the Line of Duty HC (2008, $29.99, dustjacket) r/#1-10; sketch pages 70.00
... Book One: In the Line of Duty SC (2008, $19.99) r/#1-10; sketch pages 20.00
... Book Two: Jokers and Madmen HC (2009, $29.99, dustjacket) r/#11-22 30.00
... Book Two: Jokers and Madmen SC (2011, $19.99) r/#11-22 20.00
... Book Three: On the Freak Beat HC (2010, $29.99, dustjacket) r/#23-31 30.00
... Book Four: Corrigan HC (2011, $29.99, dustjacket) r/#32-40 30.00
...: Dead Robin (2007, $17.99, TPB) r/#33-40; cover gallery 18.00
...: Half a Life (2005, $14.99, TPB) r/#6-10, Batman Chronicles #16 and Detective #747 15.00
...: In The Line of Duty (2004, $9.95, TPB) r/#1-5, cover gallery & sketch pages 10.00
...: The Quick and the Dead TPB (2006, $14.99) r/#23-25,28-31 15.00
...: Unresolved Targets (2006, $14.99, TPB) r/#12-15,19-22, cover gallery 15.00

GD VG FN VF VF/NM NM-
2.0 4.0 6.0 8.0 9.0 9.2

GOTHAM CITY SIRENS (Batman:Reborn)
DC Comics: Aug, 2009 - No. 26, Oct, 2011 ($2.99)

1-26: 1-Catwoman, Harley Quinn and Poison Ivy; Dini-s/March-a/c 3.00
1-Variant-c by JG Jones 5,00
...: Song of the Sirens HC (2010, $19.99, dustjacket) r/#8-13 & Catwoman #83 20.00
...: Union HC (2010, $19.99, dustjacket) r/#1-7 20.00
...: Union SC (2011, $17.99) r/#1-7 18.00

GOTHAM GAZETTE (Battle For The Cowl crossover in Batman titles)
DC Comics: May, 2009; Jul, 2009 ($2.99, one-shots)

1-Short stories of Gotham without Batman; Nguyen, March, ChrisCross & others-a 3.00
...: Batman Alive? (7/09) Vicki Vale app.; Nguyen, March, ChrisCross & others-a 3.00

GOTHAM GIRLS
DC Comics: Oct, 2002 - No. 5, Feb, 2003 ($2.25, limited series)

1-5-Catwoman, Batgirl, Poison Ivy, Harley Quinn from animated series 3.00

GOTHAM NIGHTS (See Batman: Gotham Nights II)
DC Comics: Mar, 1992 - No. 4, June, 1992 ($1.25, limited series)

1-4: Featuring Batman 3.00

GOTHAM UNDERGROUND
DC Comics: Dec, 2007 - No. 9, Aug, 2008 ($2.99, limited series)

1-9-Nine covers interlock for single image; Tieri-s/Calafiore-a/c. 7,8-Vigilante app. 3.00
Batman: Gotham Underground TPB (2008, $19.99) r/#1-9; interlocked image cover 20.00

GOTHIC ROMANCES (Also see My Secrets)
Atlas/Seaboard Publ.: Dec, 1974 (75¢, B&W, magazine, 76 pgs.)

1-Text w/ illos by N. Adams, Chaykin, Heath (2 pgs. ea.); painted cover from Ravenwood Gothic paperback "The Conservatory"(scarce) 21 42 63 146 311 475

GOTHIC TALES OF LOVE (Magazine)
Marvel Comics: Apr, 1975 - No. 3, 1975 (B&W, 76 pgs.)

1-3-Painted-c/a (scarce) 24 48 72 168 359 550

GOVERNOR & J. J., THE (TV)
Gold Key: Feb, 1970 - No. 3, Aug, 1970 (Photo-c)

1 4 8 12 26 41 55
2,3 3 6 9 19 29 38

GRACKLE, THE
Acclaim Comics: Jan, 1997 - No. 4, Apr, 1997 ($2.95, B&W)

1-4: Mike Baron scripts & Paul Gulacy-c/a. 1-4-Doublecross 3.00

GRAFIK MUSIK
Caliber Press: Nov, 1990 - No. 4, Aug, 1991 ($3.50/$2.50)

1-($3.50, 48 pgs., color) Mike Allred-c/a/scripts-1st app. in color of Frank Einstein (Madman) 3 6 9 14 20 25
2-($2.50, 24 pgs., color) 2 4 6 9 12 15
3,4-($2.50, 24 pgs., B&W) 2 4 6 8 10 12

GRANDMA DUCK'S FARM FRIENDS(See Walt Disney's C&S 293 & Wheaties)
Dell Publishing Co.: No. 763, Jan, 1957 - No. 1279, Feb, 1962 (Disney)

Four Color 763 (#1) 8 16 24 51 86 120
Four Color 873 6 12 18 37 59 80
Four Color 965,1279 5 10 15 32 51 70
Four Color 1010,1073,1161-Barks-a; 1073,1161-Barks c/a 11 22 33 76 151 225

GRAND PRIX (Formerly Hot Rod Racers)
Charlton Comics: No. 16, Sept, 1967 - No. 31, May, 1970

16-Features Rick Roberts 4 8 12 22 34 45
17-20 3 6 9 18 27 35
21-31 3 6 9 16 23 30

GRAPHIQUE MUSIQUE
Slave Labor Graphics: Dec, 1989 - No. 3, May, 1990 ($2.95, 52 pgs.)

1-Mike Allred-c/a/scripts 3 6 9 20 30 40
2,3 3 6 9 16 23 30

GRAVESLINGER
Image Comics (Shadowline): Oct, 2007 - No. 4, Mar, 2008 ($3.50, limited series)

1-4-Denton & Mariotte-s/Cboins-a 3.50

GRAVE TALES
Hamilton Comics: Oct, 1991 - No. 3, Feb, 1992 ($3.95, B&W, mag., 52 pgs.)

1-Staton-c/a 2 3 4 6 8 10
2,3: 2-Staton-a; Morrow-c 1 2 3 5 6 8

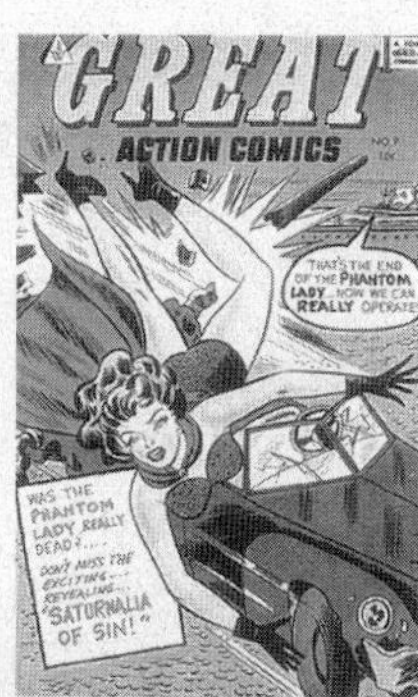

Great Action Comics #9 © I.W.

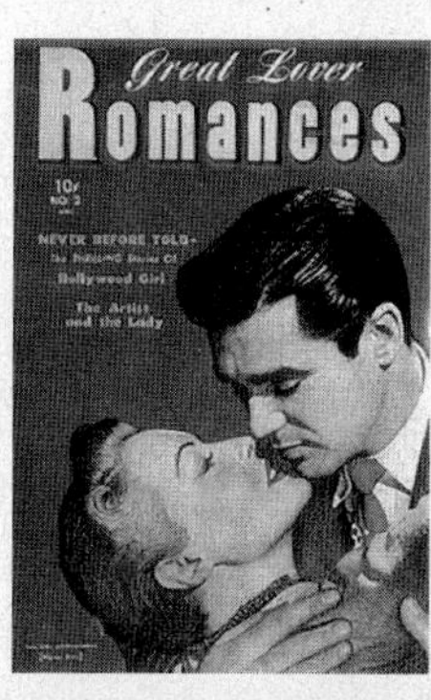

Great Lover Romances #2 © TOBY

The Great Ten #6 © DC

GD 2.0 | VG 4.0 | FN 6.0 | VF 8.0 | VF/NM 9.0 | NM- 9.2

GRAVITY (Also see Beyond! limited series)
Marvel Comics: Aug, 2005 - No. 5, Dec, 2005 ($2.99, limited series)

1-5: 1-Intro. Gravity; McKeever-s/Norton-a. 2-Rhino-c/app. 5-Spider-Man app. 3.00
...: Big-City Super Hero (2005, $7.99, digest) r/#1-5 8.00

GRAY AREA, THE
Image Comics: Jun, 2004 - No. 3, Oct, 2004 ($5.95/$3.95, limited series)

1,3-($5.95) Romita, Jr.-a/Brunswick-s; sketch pages and script pages. 3-Pin-up pages 6.00
2-($3.95) 4.00
...Vol. 1: All Of This Can Be Yours (2005, $14.95) r/series & sketch,script & pin-up pages 15.00

GRAY GHOST, THE
Dell Publishing Co.: No. 911, July, 1958; No. 1000, June-Aug, 1959

Four Color 911 (#1), 1000-Photo-c each 8 16 24 55 93 130

GREAT ACTION COMICS
I. W. Enterprises: 1958 (Reprints with new covers)

1-Captain Truth reprinted from Gold Medal #1 3 6 9 16 23 30
8,9-Reprints Phantom Lady #15 & 23 7 14 21 49 80 110

GREAT AMERICAN COMICS PRESENTS - THE SECRET VOICE
Peter George 4-Star Publ./American Features Syndicate: 1945 (10¢)

1-Anti-Nazi; "What Really Happened to Hitler" 42 84 126 265 445 625

GREAT AMERICAN WESTERN, THE
AC Comics: 1987 - No. 4, 1990? ($1.75/$2.95/$3.50, B&W with some color)

1-4: 1-Western-r plus Bill Black-a. 2-Tribute to ME comics; Durango Kid photo-c 3-Tribute to Tom Mix plus Roy Rogers, Durango Kid; Billy the Kid-r by Severin; photo-c. 4- ($3.50, 52 pgs., 16 pgs. color)-Tribute to Lash LaRue; photo-c & interior photos; Fawcett-r 4.00
...Presents 1 (1991, $5.00) New Sunset Carson; film history 5.00

GREAT CAT FAMILY, THE (Disney-TV/Movie)
Dell Publishing Co.: No. 750, Nov, 1956 (one-shot)

Four Color 750-Pinocchio & Alice app. 6 12 18 42 69 95

GREAT COMICS
Great Comics Publications: Nov, 1941 - No. 3, Jan, 1942

1-Origin/1st app. The Great Zarro; Madame Strange & Guy Gorham, Wizard of Science & The Great Zarro begin 135 270 405 864 1482 2100
2-Buck Johnson, Jungle Explorer app.; X-Mas-c 68 136 204 435 743 1050
3-Futuro Takes Hitler to Hell-c/s; "The Lost City" movie story (starring William Boyd); continues in Choice Comics #3 (scarce) 486 972 1458 3550 6275 9000

GREAT COMICS
Novack Publishing Co./Jubilee Comics/Knockout/Barrel O' Fun: 1945

1-(Four publ. variations: Barrel O-Fun, Jubilee, Knockout & Novack)-The Defenders, Capt. Power app.; L. B. Cole-c 32 64 96 188 307 425
1-(Jubilee)-Same cover; Boogey Man, Satanas, & The Sorcerer & His Apprentice 26 52 78 152 249 345
1-(Barrel O' Fun)-L. B. Cole-c; Barrel O' Fun overprinted in indicia; Li'l Cactus, Cuckoo Sheriff (humorous) 18 36 54 105 165 225

GREAT DOGPATCH MYSTERY (See Mammy Yokum & the...)

GREATEST AMERICAN HERO (Based on the 1981-1986 TV series)
Catastrophic Comics: Dec, 2008 - No. 3, May, 2009 ($3.50/$3.95)

1-3-Origin re-told; William Katt and others-s. 3-Obama-c/app. 4.00

GREATEST BATMAN STORIES EVER TOLD, THE
DC Comics

Hardcover ($24.95) 50.00
Softcover ($15.95) "Greatest DC Stories Vol. 2" on spine 20.00
Vol. 2 softcover (1992, $16.95) "Greatest DC Stories Vol. 7" on spine 20.00

GREATEST FLASH STORIES EVER TOLD, THE
DC Comics: 1991

nn-Hardcover ($29.95); Infantino-c 45.00
nn-Softcover ($14.95) 20.00

GREATEST GOLDEN AGE STORIES EVER TOLD, THE
DC Comics: 1990 ($24.95, hardcover)

nn-Ordway-c 60.00

GREATEST HITS
DC Comics (Vertigo): Dec, 2008 - No. 6, Apr, 2009 ($2.99, limited series)

1-6-Intro. The Mates superhero team in 1967 England; Tischman-s/Fabry-a/c 3.00

GREATEST JOKER STORIES EVER TOLD, THE (See Batman)
DC Comics: 1983

Hardcover ($19.95)-Kyle Baker painted-c 45.00
Softcover ($14.95) 20.00
Stacked Deck...Expanded Edition (1992, $29.95)-Longmeadow Press Publ. 32.00

GREATEST 1950s STORIES EVER TOLD, THE
DC Comics: 1990

Hardcover ($29.95)-Kubert-c 55.00
Softcover ($14.95) "Greatest DC Stories Vol. 5" on spine 22.00

GREATEST TEAM-UP STORIES EVER TOLD, THE
DC Comics: 1989

Hardcover ($24.95)-DeVries and Infantino painted-c 55.00
Softcover ($14.95) "Greatest DC Stories Vol. 4" on spine; Adams-c 22.00

GREATEST SUPERMAN STORIES EVER TOLD, THE
DC Comics: 1987

Hardcover ($24.95) 50.00
Softcover ($15.95) 22.00

GREAT EXPLOITS
Decker Publ./Red Top: Oct, 1957

1-Krigstein-a(2) (re-issue on cover); reprints Daring Advs. #6 by Approved Comics 6 12 18 31 38 45

GREAT FOODINI, THE (See Foodini)

GREAT GAZOO, THE (The Flintstones)(TV)
Charlton Comics: Aug, 1973 - No. 20, Jan, 1977 (Hanna-Barbera)

1 4 8 12 24 37 50
2-10 3 6 9 14 19 24
11-20 2 4 6 10 14 18

GREAT GRAPE APE, THE (TV)(See TV Stars #1)
Charlton Comics: Sept, 1976 - No. 2, Nov, 1976 (Hanna-Barbera)

1 4 8 12 22 34 45
2 3 6 9 14 20 25

GREAT LOCOMOTIVE CHASE, THE (Disney)
Dell Publishing Co.: No. 712, Sept, 1956 (one-shot)

Four Color 712-Movie, photo-c 7 14 21 46 76 105

GREAT LOVER ROMANCES (Young Lover Romances #4,5)
Toby Press: 3/51; #2, 1951(nd); #3, 1952 (nd); #6, Oct?, 1952 - No. 22, May, 1955 (Photo-c #1-5, 10 ,13, 15, 17) (no #4, 5)

1-Jon Juan story-r/Jon Juan #1 by Schomburg; Dr. Anthony King app. 20 40 60 114 182 250
2-Jon Juan, Dr. Anthony King app. 12 24 36 69 97 125
3,7,9-14,16-22: 10-Rita Hayworth photo-c. 17-Rita Hayworth & Aldo Ray photo-c 10 20 30 54 72 90
6-Kurtzman-a (10/52) 12 24 36 67 94 120
8-Five pgs. of "Pin-Up Pete" by Sparling 12 24 36 67 94 120
15-Liz Taylor photo-c (scarce) 42 84 126 265 445 625

GREAT RACE, THE (See Movie Classics)

GREAT SCOTT SHOE STORE (See Bulls-Eye)

GREAT SOCIETY COMIC BOOK, THE (Political parody)
Pocket Books Inc./Parallax Pub.: 1966 ($1.00, 36 pgs., 7"x10", one-shot)

nn-Super-LBJ-c/story; 60s politicians app. as super-heroes; Tallarico-a 3 6 9 18 27 35

GREAT TEN, THE (Characters from Final Crisis)
DC Comics: Jan, 2010 - No. 9, Sept, 2010 ($2.99, limited series)

1-9-Super team of China; Bedard-s/McDaniel-a/Stanley Lau-c 3.00

GREAT WEST (Magazine)
M. F. Enterprises: 1969 (B&W, 52 pgs.)

V1#1 2 4 6 10 14 18

GREAT WESTERN
Magazine Enterprises: No. 8, Jan-Mar, 1954 - No. 11, Oct-Dec, 1954

8(A-1 93)-Trail Colt by Guardineer; Powell Red Hawk-r/Straight Arrow begins, ends #11; Durango Kid story 18 36 54 103 162 220
9(A-1 105), 11(A-1 127)-Ghost Rider, Durango Kid app. in each. 9-Red Mask-c, but no app. 15 30 45 83 124 165
10(A-1 113)-The Calico Kid by Guardineer-r/Tim Holt #8; Straight Arrow, Durango Kid app. 12 24 36 69 97 125
I.W. Reprint #1,2 9: 1,2-r/Straight Arrow #36,42. 9-r/Straight Arrow #? 3 6 9 16 22 28

Greek Street #10 © Milligan & Gianfelice

Green Arrow (2001 series) #43 © DC

Green Arrow (2011 series) #1 © DC

	GD 2.0	VG 4.0	FN 6.0	VF 8.0	VF/NM 9.0	NM- 9.2

I.W. Reprint #8-Origin Ghost Rider(r/Tim Holt #11); Tim Holt app.; Bolle-a
3 6 9 17 25 32

NOTE: *Guardineer c-8.* ***Powell*** *a(r)-8-11 (from Straight Arrow).*

GREEK STREET
DC Comics (Vertigo): Sept, 2009 - No. 16, Dec, 2010 ($1.00/$2.99)

1-16: 1-($1.00) Milligan-s/Gianfelice-a. 2: Begin $2.99-c 3.00
...: Blood Calls For Blood SC (2010, $9.99) r/#1-5; Mike Carey intro.; sketch art 10.00
...: Cassandra Complex SC (2010, $14.99) r/#6-11 15.00

GREEN ARROW (See Action #440, Adventure, Brave & the Bold, DC Super Stars #17, Detective #521, Flash #217, Green Lantern #76, Justice League of America #4, Leading Comics, More Fun #73 (1st app.), Showcase '95 #9 & World's Finest Comics)

GREEN ARROW
DC Comics: May, 1983 - No. 4, Aug, 1983 (limited series)

1-Origin; Speedy cameo; Mike W. Barr scripts, Trevor Von Eeden-c/a 5.00
2-4 4.00

GREEN ARROW
DC Comics: Feb, 1988 - No. 137, Oct, 1998 ($1.00-$2.50) (Painted-c #1-3)

1-Mike Grell scripts begin, ends #80 6.00
2-49,51-74,76-86: 27,28-Warlord app. 35-38-Co-stars Black Canary; Bill Wray-i. 40-Grell-a. 47-Begin $1.50-c. 63-No longer has mature readers on-c. 63-66-Shado app. 81-Aparo-a begins, ends #100; Nuklon app. 82-Intro & death of Rival. 83-Huntress-c/story. 84, 85-Deathstroke app. 86-Catwoman-c/story w/Jim Balent layouts 3.00
50,75-($2.50, 52 pgs.): Anniversary issues. 75-Arsenal (Roy Harper) & Shado app. 4.00
0,87-96: 87-$1.95-c begins. 88-Guy Gardner, Martian Manhunter, & Wonder Woman-c/app.; Flash-c. 89-Anarky app. 90-(9/94)-Zero Hour tie-in. 0-(10/94)-1st app. Connor Hawke; Aparo-a(p). 91-(11/94). 93-1st app. Camorouge. 95-Hal Jordan cameo. 96-Intro new Force of July; Hal Jordan (Parallax) app; Oliver Queen learns that Connor Hawke is his son 3.00
97-99,102-109: 97-Begin $2.25-c; no Aparo-a. 97-99-Arsenal app. 102,103-Underworld Unleashed x-over. 104-GL(Kyle Rayner)-c/app. 105-Robin-c/app. 107-109-Thorn app. 109-Lois Lane cameo; Weeks-c. 3.00
100-($3.95)-Foil-c; Superman app. 1 3 4 6 8 10
101-Death of Oliver Queen; Superman app. 3 6 9 16 23 30
110,111-124: 110,111-GL x-over. 110-Intro Hatchet. 114-Final Night. 115-117-Black Canary & Oracle app. 3.00
125-($3.50, 48 pgs)-GL x-over cont. in GL #92 4.00
126-136: 126-Begin $2.50-c. 130-GL & Flash x-over. 132,133-JLA app. 134,135-Brotherhood of the Fist pts. 1,5. 136-Hal Jordan-c/app. 3.00
137-Last issue; Superman app.; last panel cameo of Oliver Queen
2 4 6 9 12 15
#1,000,000 (11/98) 853rd Century x-over 3.00
Annual 1-6 ('88-'94, 68 pgs.)-1-No Grell scripts. 2-No Grell scripts; recaps origin Green Arrow, Speedy, Black Canary & others. 3-Bill Wray-a. 4-50th anniversary issue. 5-Batman, Eclipso app. 6-Bloodlines; Hook app. 4.00
Annual 7-('95, $3.95)-Year One story 4.00

NOTE: ***Aparo*** *a-0, 81-85, 86 (partial),87p, 88p, 91-95, 96i, 98-100p, 109p; c-81,98-100p.* ***Austin*** *c-96i.* ***Balent*** *layouts-86.* ***Burchett*** *c-91-95.* ***Campanella*** *a-100-108i, 110-113i; c-99i, 101-108i,110-113i.* ***Denys Cowan*** *a-39p, 41-43p, 47p, 48p, 60p; c-41-43.* ***Damaggio*** *a(p)-97p, 100-108p, 110-112p; c-97-99p, 101-108p, 110-113p.* ***Mike Grell*** *c-1-4, 10p, 11, 39, 40, 44, 45, 47-80, Annual 4, 5.* ***Nasser/Netzer*** *a-89, 96.* ***Sienkiewicz*** *a-109i.* ***Springer*** *a-67, 68.* ***Weeks*** *c-109.*

GREEN ARROW
DC Comics: Apr, 2001 - No. 75, Aug, 2007 ($2.50/$2.99)

1-Oliver Queen returns; Kevin Smith-s/Hester-a/Wagner-painted-c
2 4 6 9 13 16
1-2nd-4th printings 3.00
2-Batman cameo 1 2 3 4 5 7
2-2nd printing 3.00
3-5: 4-JLA app. 5.00
6-15: 7-Barry Allen & Hal Jordan app. 9,10-Stanley & his Monster app. 10-Oliver regains his soul. 12-Hawkman-c/app. 3.00
16-25: 16-Brad Meltzer-s begin; The Shade app. 18-Solomon Grundy-c/app. 19-JLA app. 22-Beatty-s; Count Vertigo app. 23-25-Green Lantern app.; Raab-s/Adlard-a 3.00
26-49: 26-Winick-s begin. 35-37-Riddler app. 43-Mia learns she's HIV+. 45-Mia becomes the new Speedy. 46-Teen Titans app. 49-The Outsiders app. 3.00
50-($3.50) Green Arrow's team and the Outsiders vs. The Riddler and Drakon 4.00
51-59: 51-Anarky app. 52-Zatanna-c/app. 55-59-Dr. Light app. 3.00
60-74: 60-One Year Later starts. 62-Begin $2.99-c; Deathstroke app. 69-Batman app. 3.00
75-($3.50) Ollie proposes to Dinah (see Black Canary mini-series); JLA app. 4.00
...: City Walls SC (2005, $17.95) r/#32, 34-39 18.00
...: Crawling Through the Wreckage SC (2007, $12.99) r/#60-65 13.00
...: Heading Into the Light SC (2006, $12.99) r/#52,54-59 13.00
...: Moving Targets SC (2006, $17.99) r/#40-50 18.00
...: Quiver HC (2002, $24.95) r/#1-10; Smith intro. 25.00
...: Quiver SC (2003, $17.95) r/#1-10; Smith intro. 18.00

	GD 2.0	VG 4.0	FN 6.0	VF 8.0	VF/NM 9.0	NM- 9.2

...: Road to Jericho SC (2007, $17.99) r/#66-75 18.00
...Secret Files & Origins 1-(12/02, $4.95) Origin stories & profiles; Wagner-c 5.00
...: Sounds of Violence HC (2003, $19.95) r/#11-15; Hester intro. & sketch pages 20.00
...: Sounds of Violence SC (2003, $12.95) r/#11-15; Hester intro. & sketch pages 13.00
...: Straight Shooter SC (2004, $12.95) r/#26-31 13.00
...: The Archer's Quest HC (2003, $19.95) r/#16-21; pitch, script and sketch pages 20.00
...: The Archer's Quest SC (2004, $14.95) r/#16-21; pitch, script and sketch pages 15.00

GREEN ARROW (Brightest Day)
DC Comics: Aug, 2010 - No. 15, Oct, 2011 ($3.99/$2.99)

1-Oliver Queen in the Star City forest; Green Lantern app.; Neves-a/Cascioli-c 4.00
1-Variant-c by Van Sciver 8.00
2-15-($2.99) 2-Green Lantern app. 7-Mayhew-a. 8-11-The Demon app. 12-Swamp Thing 3.00
...: Into the Woods HC (2011, $22.99) r/#1-7; variant cover gallery 23.00

GREEN ARROW (DC New 52)
DC Comics: Nov, 2011 - Present ($2.99)

1-8: 1-Krul-s/Jurgens & Pérez-a/Wilkins-c. 4,5-Giffen-s 3.00

GREEN ARROW/BLACK CANARY (Titled Green Arrow for #30-32)
DC Comics: Dec, 2007 - No. 32, Jun, 2010 ($3.50/$2.99)

1-($3.50) Connor Hawke & Black Canary; follows Wedding Special; Winick-s/Chang-a 4.00
2-21-($2.99) 3-Two covers; Connor shot. 5-Dinah & Ollie's real wedding 3.00
22-30-($3.99) Back-up stories begin. 28-Origin of Cupid. 30-Blackest Night 4.00
30-Variant cover by Mike Grell 8.00
31-32-($2.99) Rise and Fall; Dallocchio-a 3.00
...: A League of Their Own TPB (2009, $17.99) r/#11-14 & G.A. Secret Files & Origins 18.00
...: Big Game TPB (2010, $19.99) r/#21-26 20.00
...: Enemies List TPB (2009, $17.99) r/#15-20 18.00
...: Family Business TPB (2008, $17.99) r/#5-10 18.00
...: Five Stages TPB (2010, $17.99) r/#27-30 18.00
...: Road To The Altar TPB (2008, $17.99) r/proposal pages from Green Arrow #75, Birds of Prey #109, Black Canary #1-4 and Black Canary Wedding Planner #1 18.00
...: The Wedding Album HC (2008, $19.99, dustjacket) r/#1-5 & Wedding Special #1 20.00
...: The Wedding Album SC (2009, $17.99) r/#1-5 & Wedding Special #1 18.00
... Wedding Special 1 (11/07, $3.99) Winick-s/Conner-a/c; Dinah & Ollie's "wedding" 4.00
... Wedding Special 1 (11/07, $3.99) 2nd printing with Ryan Sook variant-c 4.00

GREEN ARROW: THE LONG BOW HUNTERS
DC Comics: Aug, 1987 - No. 3, Oct, 1987 ($2.95, limited series, mature)

1-Grell-c/a in all 6.00
1,2-2nd printings 3.00
2,3 4.00
Trade paperback (1989, $12.95)-r/#1-3 13.00

GREEN ARROW: THE WONDER YEAR
DC Comics: Feb, 1993 - No. 4, May, 1993 ($1.75, limited series)

1-4: Mike Grell-a(p)/scripts & Gray Morrow-a(i) 3.00

GREEN ARROW: YEAR ONE
DC Comics: Early Sept, 2007 - No. 6, Late Nov, 2007 ($2.99, bi-weekly limited series)

1-6-Origin re-told; Diggle-s/Jock-a 3.00
HC (2008, $24.99) r/#1-6; intro. by Brian K. Vaughan; script and sketch pages 25.00
SC (2009, $14.99) r/#1-6; intro. by Brian K. Vaughan; script and sketch pages 15.00

GREEN BERET, THE (See Tales of...)

GREEN GIANT COMICS (Also see Colossus Comics)
Pelican Publ. (Funnies, Inc.): 1940 (No price on cover; distributed in New York City only)

1-Dr. Nerod, Green Giant, Black Arrow, Mundoo & Master Mystic app.; origin Colossus (Rare)
1200 2400 3600 9000 16,500 24,000

NOTE: *The idea for this book came from George Kapitan. Printed by Moreau Publ. of Orange, N.J. as an experiment to see if they could profitably use the idle time of their 40-page Hoe color press. The experiment failed due to the difficulty of obtaining good quality color registration and Mr. Moreau believes the book never reached the stands. The book has no price or date which lends credence to this. Contains five pages reprinted from Motion Picture Funnies Weekly.*

GREEN GOBLIN
Marvel Comics: Oct, 1995 - No. 13, Oct, 1996 ($2.95/$1.95)

1-($2.95)-Scott McDaniel-c/a begins, ends #7; foil-c 4.00
2-13: 2-Begin $1.95-c. 4-Hobgoblin-c/app; Thing app. 6-Daredevil-c/app. 8-Robertson-a; McDaniel-c. 12,13-Onslaught x-over. 13-Green Goblin quits; Spider-Man app. 3.00

GREENHAVEN
Aircel Publishing: 1988 - No. 3, 1988 ($2.00, limited series, 28 pgs.)

1-3 3.00

GREEN HORNET, THE (TV)
Dell Publishing Co./Gold Key: Sept, 1953; Feb, 1967 - No. 3, Aug, 1967

Green Hornet (2010 series) #17 © GH Inc.

Green Hornet Comics #32 © HARV

Green Lantern #31 © DC

GD VG FN VF VF/NM NM-
2.0 4.0 6.0 8.0 9.0 9.2

Four Color 496-Painted-c. 23 46 69 161 343 525
1-Bruce Lee photo-c and back-c pin-up 17 34 51 114 250 385
2,3-Bruce Lee photo-c 11 22 33 77 154 230

GREEN HORNET, THE (Also see Kato of the... & Tales of the...)
Now Comics: Nov, 1989 - No. 14, Feb, 1991 ($1.75)
V2#1, Sept, 1991 - V2#40, Jan, 1995 ($1.95)

1 ($2.95, double-size)-Steranko painted-c; G.A. Green Hornet 6.00
1,2: 1-2nd printing ('90, $3.95)-New Butler-c 4.00
3-14: 5-Death of original ('30s) Green Hornet. 6-Dave Dorman painted-c. 11-Snyder-c 4.00
V2#1-11,13-21,24-26,28-30,32-37: 1-Butler painted-c. 9-Mayerik-c 3.00
12-($2.50)-Color Green Hornet button polybagged inside 4.00
22,23-($2.95)-Bagged w/color hologravure card 4.00
27-($2.95)-Newsstand ed. polybagged w/multi-dimensional card (1993 Anniversary Special on cover), 27-($2.95)-Direct Sale ed. polybagged w/multi-dimensional card; cover variations 4.00
31,38: 31-($2.50)-Polybagged w/trading card 4.00
39,40-Low print run 6.00
1-($2.50)-Polybagged w/button (same as #12) 4.00
2,3-($1.95)-Same as #13 & 14 3.00
Annual 1 (12/92, $2.50), Annual 1994 (10/94, $2.95) 4.00

GREEN HORNET
Dynamite Entertainment: 2010 - Present ($3.99)

1-Kevin Smith-s/Jonathan Lau-a; multiple covers by Alex Ross, Cassaday, Campbell and Segovia 4.00
2-22-Multiple covers by Ross and others on each. 11-Hester-s begins 4.00
Annual 1 (2010, $5.99) Hester-s/Netzer & Rafael-a 6.00
Annual 2 (2012, $4.99) Hester-c/Rahner-s/Cliquet-a; back-up r/G.H. Comics #1 (1940) 5.00
... FCBD Edition; 5 previews of various new Green Hornet series; Cassaday-c 3.00

GREEN HORNET: AFTERMATH
Dynamite Entertainment: 2011 - No. 4, 2011 ($1.99/$3.99, limited series)

1-Nitz-s/Raynor-a; Green Hornet & Kato after the 2011 movie 3.00
2-4-($3.99) 4.00

GREEN HORNET: BLOOD TIES
Dynamite Entertainment: 2010 - No. 4, 2011 ($3.99)

1-4-Ande Parks-s/Johnny Desjardins-a; original Green Hornet & Kato 4.00

GREEN HORNET COMICS (...Racket Buster #44) (Radio, movies)
Helnit Publ. Co.(Holyoke) No. 1-6/Family Comics(Harvey) No. 7-on:
Dec, 1940 - No. 47, Sept, 1949 (See All New #13,14)(Early issues: 68 pgs.)

1-1st app. Green Hornet & Kato; origin of Green Hornet on inside front-c; intro the Black Beauty (Green Hornet's car); painted-c 595 1190 1785 4350 7675 11,000
2-Early issues based on radio adventures 239 478 717 1530 2615 3700
3 161 322 483 1030 1765 2500
4-6: 6-(8/41) 135 270 405 864 1482 2100
7 (6/42)-Origin The Zebra & begins; Robin Hood, Spirit of '76, Blonde Bomber & Mighty Midgets begin; new logo 110 220 330 704 1202 1700
8,10 94 188 282 597 1024 1450
9-Kirby-c 119 238 357 762 1306 1850
11,12-Mr. Q in both 90 180 270 576 988 1400
13-1st Nazi-c; shows Hitler poster on-c 116 232 348 742 1271 1800
14-19 74 148 222 470 810 1150
20-Classic-c 90 180 270 576 988 1400
21-23 54 108 162 343 574 825
24-Sci-Fi-c 57 114 171 362 619 875
25-30 47 94 141 296 498 700
31-The Man in Black Called Fate begins (11-12/45, early app.) 50 100 150 315 533 750
32-36 36 72 108 216 351 485
37,38: Shock Gibson app. by Powell. 37-S&K Kid Adonis reprinted from Stuntman #3. 38-Kid Adonis app. 36 72 108 211 343 475
39-Stuntman story by S&K 39 78 117 236 388 540
40-47: 42-47-Kerry Drake in all. 45-Boy Explorers on-c only. 46- "Case of the Marijuana Racket" cover/story; Kerry Drake app. 27 51 81 158 259 360

NOTE: ***Fuje*** *a-23, 24, 26.* ***Henkle*** *c-7-9.* ***Kubert*** *a-20, 30.* ***Powell*** *a-7-10, 12, 14, 16-21, 30, 31(2), 32(3), 33, 34(3), 35, 36, 37(2), 38.* ***Robinson*** *a-27.* ***Schomburg*** *c-15, 17-23. Kirbyish c-7, 15. Bondage c-8, 14, 18, 26, 36.*

GREEN HORNET: DARK TOMORROW
Now Comics: Jun, 1993 - No. 3, Aug, 1993 ($2.50, limited series)

1-3: Future Green Hornet 3.00

GREEN HORNET: GOLDEN AGE RE-MASTERED
Dynamite Entertainment: 2010 - No. 8, 2011 ($3.99)

1-8-Re-colored reprints of 1940's Green Hornet Comics; new Rubenstein-c 4.00

GD VG FN VF VF/NM NM-
2.0 4.0 6.0 8.0 9.0 9.2

GREEN HORNET: PARALLEL LIVES
Dynamite Entertainment: 2010 - No. 5, 2010 ($3.99, limited series)

1-5-Jai Nitz-s/Nigel Raynor-a; semi-prequel to the 2011 movie; Kato's origin 4.00

GREEN HORNET: SOLITARY SENTINEL, THE
Now Comics: Dec, 1992 - No. 3, 1993 ($2.50, limited series)

1-3 3.00

GREEN HORNET STRIKES!
Dynamite Entertainment: 2010 - No. 10, 2011 ($3.99, limited series)

1-9: 1-Matthews-s/Padilla-a/Cassaday-c; future Green Hornet 4.00

GREEN HORNET: YEAR ONE
Dynamite Entertainment: 2010 - No. 12, 2011 ($3.99, limited series)

1-12-Matt Wagner-s/Aaron Campbell-a; 1940s' Green Hornet & Kato. 1-5-Cassaday-c 4.00

GREEN JET COMICS, THE (See Comic Books, Series 1 in the Promotional Comics section)

GREEN LAMA (Also see Comic Books, Series 1, Daring Adventures #17 & Prize Comics #7)
Spark Publications/Prize No. 7 on: Dec, 1944 - No. 8, Mar, 1946

1-Intro. Lt. Hercules & The Boy Champions; Mac Raboy-c/a #1-8 118 236 354 749 1287 1825
2-Lt. Hercules borrows the Human Torch's powers for one panel 63 126 189 403 689 975
3-5,8: 4-Dick Tracy take-off in Lt. Hercules story by H. L. Gold (science fiction writer). 5-Lt. Hercules story; Little Orphan Annie, Smilin' Jack & Snuffy Smith take-off (5/45) 51 102 153 318 539 760
6-Classic Raboy swastika-c 54 108 162 343 574 825
7-X-mas-c; Raboy craft tint-c/a (note: a small quantity of NM copies surfaced) 34 68 102 199 325 450
... Archives Featuring the Art of Mac Raboy Vol. 1 HC (Dark Horse Books, 4/08, $49.95) r/#1-4 including back-up features; foreward by Chuck Rozanski 50.00
... Archives Featuring the Art of Mac Raboy Vol. 2 HC (Dark Horse Books, 1/09, $49.95) r/#5-8; foreward by Chuck Rozanski 50.00

NOTE: ***Robinson*** *a-3-5, 8.* ***Roussos*** *a-8. Formerly a pulp hero who began in 1940.*

GREEN LANTERN (1st Series) (See All-American, All Flash Quarterly, All Star Comics, The Big All-American & Comic Cavalcade)
National Periodical Publications/All-American: Fall, 1941 - No. 38, May-June, 1949 (#1-18 are quarterly)

1-Origin retold; classic Purcell-c 3000 6000 9000 22,000 38,000 64,000
2-1st book-length story 676 1352 2028 4935 8718 12,500
3-Classic German war-c by Mart Nodell 595 1190 1785 4350 7675 11,000
4-Green Lantern & Doiby Dickles join the Army 400 800 1200 2800 4900 7000
5-WWII-c 300 600 900 2070 3635 5200
6,8: 8-Hop Harrigan begins; classic-c 271 542 813 1734 2967 4200
7-Classic robot-c. 300 600 900 1920 3310 4700
9,10: 10-Origin/1st app. Vandal Savage 226 452 678 1446 2473 3500
11-15: 12-Origin/1st app. Gambler 161 322 483 1030 1765 2500
16-Classic jungle-c (scarce in high grade) 171 342 513 1086 1868 2650
17,19,20 135 270 405 864 1482 2100
18-Christmas-c 184 368 552 1168 2009 2850
21-26,28 126 252 378 806 1378 1950
27-Origin/1st app. Sky Pirate 148 296 444 947 1624 2300
29-All Harlequin issue; classic Harlequin-c 168 336 504 1075 1838 2600
30-Origin/1st app. Streak the Wonder Dog by Toth (2-3/48) (Rare) 309 618 927 2163 3782 5400
31-35: 35-Kubert-c. 35-38-New logo 115 230 345 730 1253 1775
36-38: 37-Sargon the Sorcerer app. 129 258 387 826 1413 2000

NOTE: *Book-length stories #2-7.* ***Mayer/Moldoff*** *c-9.* ***Mayer/Purcell*** *c-8.* ***Purcell*** *c-1.* ***Mart Nodell*** *c-2, 3, 7.* ***Paul Reinman*** *c-11, 12, 15-22.* ***Toth*** *a-28, 30, 31, 34-38; c-28, 30, 34p, 36-38p. Cover to #8 says Fall while the indicia says Summer Issue. Streak the Wonder Dog c-30 (w/Green Lantern), 34, 36, 38.*

GREEN LANTERN (See Action Comics Weekly, Adventure Comics, Brave & the Bold, Day of Judgment, DC Special, DC Special Series, Flash, Guy Gardner, Guy Gardner Reborn, JLA, JSA, Justice League of America, Parallax: Emerald Night, Showcase, Showcase '93 #12 & Tales of The...Corps)

GREEN LANTERN (2nd Series)(Green Lantern Corps #206 on) (See Showcase #22-24)
National Periodical Publ./DC Comics: Jul/Aug. 1960 - No. 89, Apr/May 1972;
No. 90, Aug/Sept. 1976 - No. 205, Oct, 1986

1-(7-8/60)-Origin retold; Gil Kane-c/a continues; 1st app. Guardians of the Universe 450 900 1350 4200 9100 14,000
2-1st Pieface 83 166 249 672 1461 2250
3-Contains readers poll 46 92 138 366 796 1225
4,5: 5-Origin/1st app. Hector Hammond 39 78 117 293 634 975
6-Intro Tomar-Re the alien G.L. 36 72 108 270 585 900
7-Origin/1st app. Sinestro (7-8/61); classic robot-c 52 104 156 421 911 1400
8-1st 5700 A.D. story; grey tone-c 33 66 99 239 520 800

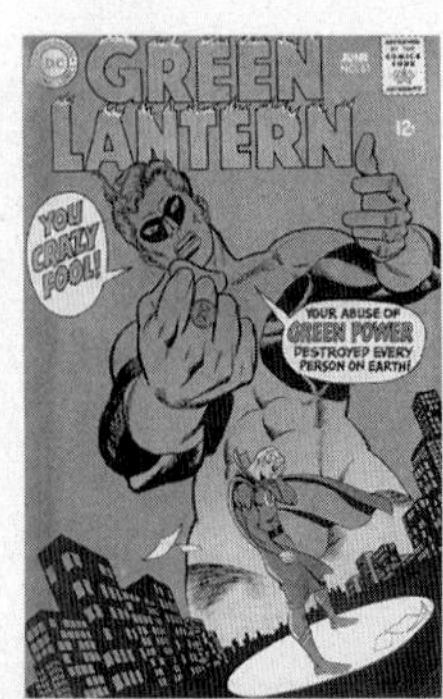

Green Lantern #61 © DC

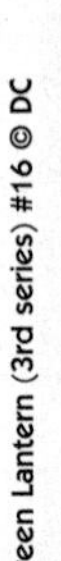
Green Lantern (3rd series) #16 © DC

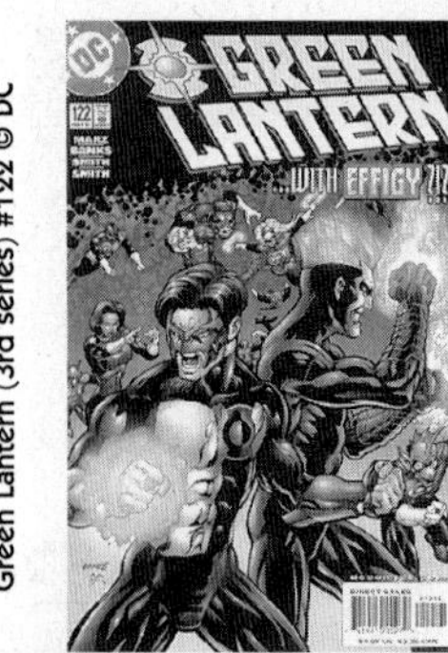

Green Lantern (3rd series) #122 © DC

GD VG FN VF VF/NM NM-
2.0 4.0 6.0 8.0 9.0 9.2

9-1st Sinestro-c; 1st Jordan Brothers; last 10¢-c 31 62 93 225 488 750
10 28 56 84 203 439 675
11,12 21 42 63 146 311 475
13-Flash x-over 32 64 96 232 504 775
14,15,17-20: 14-Origin/1st app. Sonar. 20-Flash x-over 17 34 51 114 250 385
16-Origin & 1st app. (Silver Age) Star Sapphire 26 52 78 182 391 600
21,22,24-28,30: 21-Origin & 1st app. Dr. Polaris. 24-Origin & 1st app. Shark 12 24 36 84 177 270
23-1st Tattooed Man 13 26 39 90 195 300
29-JLA cameo; 1st Blackhand 14 28 42 93 202 310
31-39: 37-1st app. Evil Star (villain) 12 24 36 82 154 225
40-Origin of Infinite Earths (10/65); 2nd solo G.A. Green Lantern in Silver Age (see Showcase #55); origin The Guardians; Doiby Dickles app. 46 92 138 352 764 1175
41-44,46-50: 42-Zatanna x-over. 43-Flash x-over 10 20 30 70 125 180
45-2nd S.A. app. G.A. Green Lantern in title (6/66) 14 28 42 93 202 310
51,53-58 9 18 27 60 100 140
52-G.A. Green Lantern x-over; Sinestro app. 10 20 30 69 130 190
59-1st app. Guy Gardner (3/68) 16 32 48 107 234 360
60,62-69: 69-Wood inks; last 12¢ issue 7 14 21 44 72 100
61-G.A. Green Lantern x-over 8 16 24 51 86 120
70-75 6 12 18 39 62 85
76-(4/70)-Begin Green Lantern/Green Arrow series (by Neal Adams #76-89) ends #122 (see Flash #217 for 2nd series) 96 192 288 778 1689 2600
77 12 24 36 81 166 250
78-80 11 22 33 73 142 210
81-84: 82-Wrightson-i(1 pg.). 83-G.L. reveals i.d. to Carol Ferris. 84-N. Adams/Wrightson-a (22 pgs.); last 15¢-c; partial photo-c 10 20 30 66 121 175
85,86-(52 pgs.)-Anti-drug issues. 86-G.A. Green Lantern-r; Toth-a 12 24 36 78 157 235
87-(52 pgs.): 2nd app. Guy Gardner (cameo); 1st app. John Stewart (12-1/71-72) (becomes 3rd Green Lantern in #182) 10 20 30 68 127 185
88-(2-3/72, 52 pgs.)-Unpubbed G.A. Green Lantern story; Green Lantern-r/Showcase #23. N. Adams-c/a (1 pg.) 7 14 21 49 82 115
89-(4-5/72, 52 pgs.)-G.A. Green Lantern-r; Green Lantern & Green Arrow move to Flash #217 (2nd team-up series) 9 18 27 62 109 155
90 (8-9/76)-Begin 3rd Green Lantern/Green Arrow team-up series; Mike Grell-c/a begins, ends #111 3 6 9 17 25 32
91-99 2 4 6 10 14 18
100-(1/78, Giant)-1st app. Air Wave II 3 6 9 16 22 28
101-107,111,113-115,117-119: 107-1st Tales of the G.L. Corps story 2 4 6 8 10 12
108-110-(44 pgs)-G.A. Green Lantern back-ups in each. 111-Origin retold; G.A. Green Lantern app. 2 4 6 9 12 15
112-G.A. Green Lantern origin retold 2 4 6 11 16 20
116-1st app. Guy Gardner as a G.L. (5/79) 4 8 12 28 44 60
116-Whitman variant; issue # on cover 5 10 15 35 55 75
117-119,121-(Whitman variants; low print run; none have issue # on cover) 2 4 6 10 14 18
120-122,124-150: 122-Last Green Lantern/Green Arrow team-up. 130-132-Tales of the G.L. Corps. 132-Adam Strange series begins, ends147. 136,137-1st app. Citadel; Space Ranger app. 141-1st app. Omega Men (6/81). 142,143-Omega Men app.;Perez-c. 144-Omega Men cameo. 148-Tales of the G.L. Corps begins, ends #173. 150-Anniversary issue, 52 pgs.; no G.L. Corps 1 2 3 5 7 9
123-Green Lantern back to solo action; 2nd app. Guy Gardner as Green Lantern 2 4 6 9 12 15
151-180,183,184,186,187: 159-Origin Evil Star. 160,161-Omega Men app. 6.00
181,182,185,188,191: 181-Hal Jordan resigns as G.L. 182-John Stewart becomes new G.L.; origin recap of Hal Jordan as G.L. 185-Origin new G.L. (John Stewart).188-I.D. revealed; Alan Moore back-up scripts. 191-Re-intro Star Sapphire (cameo) 1 2 3 5 6 8
189,190,193,196-199,201-205: 194,198-Crisis x-over. 199-Hal Jordan returns as a member of G.L. Corps (3 G.L.s now). 201-Green Lantern Corps begins (is cover title, says premiere issue); intro. Kilowog 5.00
192-Re-intro & origin of Star Sapphire (1st full app.) 2 4 6 9 13 16
194-Hal Jordan/Guy Gardner battle; Guardians choose Guy Gardner to become new Green Lantern 1 2 3 5 6 8
195-Guy Gardner becomes Green Lantern; Crisis on Infinite Earths x-over 2 4 6 9 13 16
200-Double-size 6.00
Annual 1 (Listed as Tales Of The Green Lantern Corps Annual 1)
Annual 2,3 (See Green Lantern Corps Annual #2,3) 5.00
Special 1 (1988), 2 (1989)-(Both $1.50, 52 pgs.) 4.00
... Chronicles TPB (2009, $14.99) r/Showcase #22-24 & Green Lantern #1-3 15.00
... Chronicles Vol. 2 TPB (2009, $14.99) r/Green Lantern #4-9 15.00
... Chronicles Vol. 3 TPB (2010, $14.99) r/Green Lantern #10-14 and Flash #131 15.00

NOTE: **N. Adams** *a-76, 77-87p, 89; c-63, 76-89.* **M. Anderson** *a-137i.* **Austin** *a-93i, 94i, 171i.* **Chaykin** *c-196.* **Greene** *a-39-49i, 58-63i; c-54-58i.* **Grell** *a-90-100, 106, 108-111; c-90-106, 108-112.* **Heck** *a-120-122p.* **Infantino** *a-137p, 145-147p, 151, 152p.* **Gil Kane** *a-1-49p, 50-57, 58-61p, 68-75p, 85p(r), 87p(r), 88p(r), 156, 177, 184p; c-1-52, 54-61p, 67-75, 123, 154, 156, 165-171, 177, 184.* **Newton** *a-148p, 149p, 181.* **Perez** *c-132p, 141-144.* **Sekowsky** *a-65p, 170p.* **Simonson** *c-200.* **Sparling** *a-63p.* **Starlin** *c-129, 133.* **Staton** *a-117p, 123-127p, 128, 129-131p, 132-139, 140p, 141-146, 147p, 148-150, 151-155p; c-107p, 117p, 135(i), 136p, 145p, 146, 147, 148-152p, 155p.* **Toth** *a-86r, 171p.* **Tuska** *a-166-168p, 170p.*

GREEN LANTERN (3rd Series)
DC Comics: June, 1990 - No. 181, Nov, 2004 ($1.00/$1.25/$1.50/$1.75/$1.95/$1.99/$2.25)

1-Hal Jordan, John Stewart & Guy Gardner return; Batman & JLA app. 6.00
2-18,20-26: 9-12-Guy Gardner solo story. 13-(52 pgs.). 18-Guy Gardner solo story. 25-($1.75, 52 pgs.)-Hal Jordan/Guy Gardner battle 4.00
19-($1.75, 52 pgs.)-50th anniversary issue; Mart Nodell (original G.A. artist) part-p on G.A. Green Lantern; G. Kane-c 5.00
27-45,47: 30,31-Gorilla Grodd-c/story(see Flash #69). 38,39-Adam Strange-c/story. 42-Deathstroke-c/s. 47-Green Arrow x-over 4.00
46,48,49,50: 46-Superman app. cont'd in Superman #82. 48-Emerald Twilight part 1. 50-($2.95, 52 pgs.)-Glow-in-the-dark-c 6.00
0, 51-62: 51-1st app. New Green Lantern (Kyle Rayner) with new costume. 53-Superman-c/story. 55-(9/94)-Zero Hour. 0-(10/94). 56-(11/94) 4.00
63,64-Kyle Rayner vs. Hal Jordan. 4.00
65-80,82-92: 63-Begin $1.75-c. 65-New Titans app. 66,67-Flash app. 71-Batman & Robin app. 72-Shazam!-c/app. 73-Wonder Woman-c/app. 73-75-Adam Strange app. 76,77-Green Arrow x-over. 80-Final Night. 87-JLA app. 91-Genesis x-over. 92-Green Arrow x-over 3.00
81-(Regular Ed.)-Memorial for Hal Jordan (Parallax); most DC heroes app. 5.00
81-($3.95, Deluxe Edition)-Embossed prism-c 6.00
93-99: 93-Begin $1.95-c; Deadman app. 94-Superboy app. 95-Starlin-a(p). 98,99-Legion of Super-Heroes-c/app. 3.00
100-($2.95) Two covers (Jordan & Rayner); vs. Sinestro 6.00
101-106: 101-106-Hal Jordan-c/app. 103-JLA-c/app. 104-Green Arrow app. 105,106-Parallax app. 3.00
107-126: 107-Jade becomes a Green Lantern. 119-Hal Jordan/Spectre app. 125-JLA app. 3.00
127-149: 127-Begin $2.25-c. 129-Winick-s begin. 134-136-JLA-c/app. 143-Joker: Last Laugh; Lee-c. 145-Kyle becomes The Ion. 149-Superman-c/app. 3.00
150-($3.50) Jim Lee-c; Kyle becomes Green Lantern again; new costume 4.00
151-181: 151-155-Jim Lee-c: 154-Terry attacked. 155-Spectre-c/app. 162-164-Crossover with Green Arrow #23-25. 165-Raab-s begin. 169-Kilowog returns 3.00
#1,000,000 (11/98) 853rd Century x-over; Hitch & Neary-a/c 3.00
Annual 1-3: ('92-'94, 68 pgs.)-1-Eclipso app. 2 -Intro Nightblade. 3-Elseworlds story 4.00
Annual 4 (1995, $3.50)-Year One story 4.00
Annual 5,7,8 ('96, '98, '99, $2.95): 5-Legends of the Dead Earth. 7-Ghosts; Wrightson-c. 8-JLApe; Art Adams-c 4.00
Annual 6 (1997, $3.95)-Pulp Heroes story 5.00
Annual 9 (2000, $3.50) Planet DC 4.00
...80 Page Giant (12/98, $4.95) Stories by various 5.00
...80 Page Giant 2 (6/99, $4.95) Team-ups 5.00
...80 Page Giant 3 (8/00, $5.95) Darkseid vs. the GL Corps 6.00
...: 1001 Emerald Nights (2001, $6.95) Elseworlds; Guay-a/c; LaBan-s 7.00
...3-D #1 (12/98, $3.95) Jeanty-a 4.00
...: A New Dawn TPB (1998, $9.95)-r/#50-55 10.00
...: Baptism of Fire TPB (1999, $12.95)-r/#59,66,67,70-75 13.00
...: Brother's Keeper (2003, $12.95)-r/#151-155; Green Lantern Secret Files #3 13.00
...: Emerald Allies TPB (2000, $14.95)-r/GL/GA team-ups 15.00
...: Emerald Knights TPB (1998, $12.95)-r/Hal Jordan's return 13.00
...: Emerald Twilight nn (1994, $5.95)-r/#48-50 6.00
...: Emerald Twilight/New Dawn TPB (2003, $19.95)-r/#48-55 20.00
...: Ganthet's Tale nn (1992, $5.95, 68 pgs.)-Silver foil logo; Niven scripts; Byrne-c/a 6.00
.../Green Arrow Vol. 1 (2004, $12.95) -r/GL #76-82; intro. by O'Neil 13.00
.../Green Arrow Vol. 2 (2004, $12.95) -r/GL #83-87,89 & Flash #217-219, 226; cover gallery with 1983-84 GL/GA covers #1-7; intro. by Giordano 13.00
.../Green Arrow Collection, Vol. 2-r/GL #84-87,89 & Flash #217-219 & GL/GA #5-7 by O'Neil/Adams/Wrightson 13.00
...: New Journey, Old Path TPB (2001, $12.95)-r/#129-136 13.00
... : Our Worlds at War (8/01, $2.95) Jae Lee-c; prelude to x-over 3.00
...: Passing The Torch (2004, $12.95, TPB) r/#156,158-161 & GL Secret Files #2 13.00
...Plus 1 (12/1996, $2.95)-The Ray & Polaris-c/app. 3.00
...Secret Files 1-3 (7/98-7/02, $4.95)1-Origin stories & profiles. 2-Grell-c 5.00
.../Superman: Legend of the Green Flame (2000, $5.95) 1988 unpub. Neil Gaiman story of Hal Jordan with new art by various; Frank Miller-c 6.00
...: The Power of Ion (2003, $14.95, TPB) r/#142-150 50.00
...The Road Back nn (1992, $8.95)-r/1-8 w/covers 9.00
...: Traitor TPB (2001, $12.95) r/Legends of the DCU #20,21,28,29,37,38 13.00
...: Willworld (2001, $24.95, HC) Seth Fisher-a/J.M. DeMatteis-s; Hal Jordan 25.00

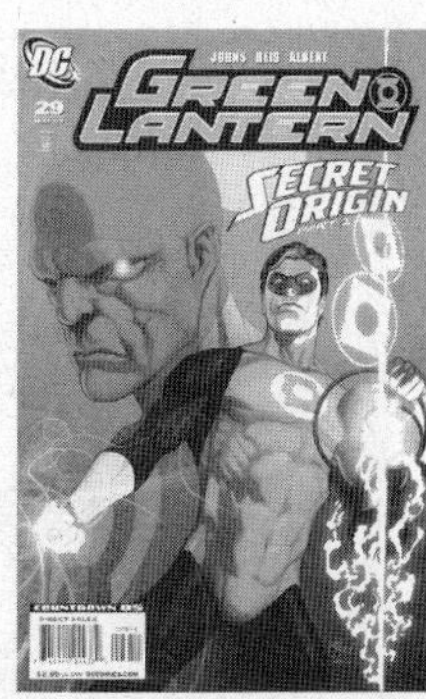

Green Lantern (2005 series) #29 © DC

Green Lantern (2011 series) #1 © DC

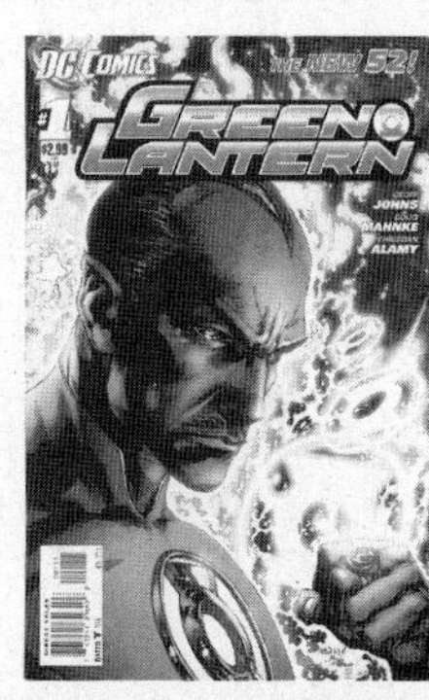

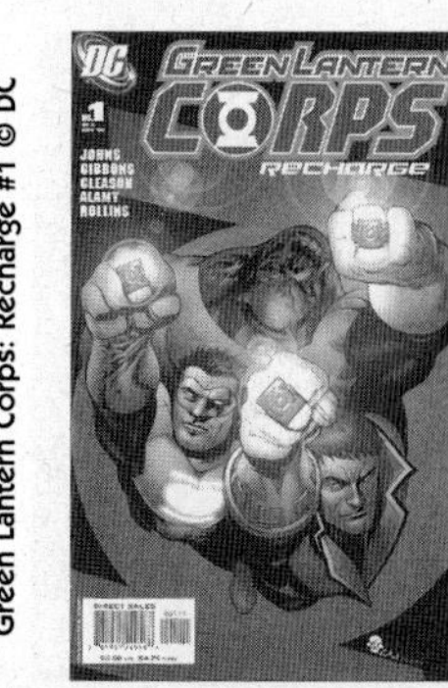

Green Lantern Corps: Recharge #1 © DC

GD 2.0 | VG 4.0 | FN 6.0 | VF 8.0 | VF/NM 9.0 | NM- 9.2

...: Willworld (2003, $17.95, SC) Seth Fisher-a/J.M. DeMatteis-s; Hal Jordan 18.00
NOTE: **Staton** *a(p)-9-12; c-9-12.*

GREEN LANTERN (See Tangent Comics/ Green Lantern)

GREEN LANTERN (4th Series) (Follows Hal Jordan's return in Green Lantern: Rebirth)
DC Comics: July, 2005 - No. 67, Aug, 2011 ($3.50/$2.99)

1-($3.50) Two covers by Pacheco and Ross; Johns-s/Van Sciver and Pacheco-a 5.00
2-20-($2.99) 2-4-Manhunters app. 6-Bianchi-a. 7,8-Green Arrow app. 8-Bianchi-c. 9-Batman app.; two covers by Bianchi and Van Sciver. 10,11-Reis-a. 17-19-Star Sapphire returns. 18-Acuna-a; Sinestro Corps back-ups begin 3.00
8-Variant-c by Neal Adams 8.00
21-Sinestro Corps War pt. 2 5.00
21-2nd printing with variant green hued background-c 3.00
22-24: 22-Sinestro Corps War pt. 4; green hued-c. 23-Part 6. 24-Part 8 4.00
22,23-2nd printings. 22-Yellow hued-c. 23-B&W Hal Jordan with colored rings 3.00
25-($4.99) Sinestro Corps War conclusion; Ivan Reis-c 6.00
25-($4.99) Variant cover by Gary Frank; Sinestro Corps War conclusion 8.00
26-43: 26-Alpha Lanterns. 29-35-Childhood & origin re-told; Sinestro app. 41-Origin Larfleeze. 43-Prologue to Blackest Night, origin of Black Hand; Mahnke-a 3.00
29-Special Edition (6/10, $1.00) reprints #29 with "What's Next?" logo on cover 1.00
29-Special Edition (2010 San Diego Comic-Con giveaway) reprints #29 with new Van Sciver cover and Geoff Johns intro on inside front cover 3.00
39-43-Variant covers: 39,40-Migliari. 41-42-Barrows 12.00
44-49,51,52-Blackest Night. 44-Flash app. 46-Sinestro vs. Mongul. 47-Black Lantern Abin Sur. 49-Art by Benes & Ordway; Atom and Mera app. 51-Nekron app. 3.00
44-49,51-Variant covers: 44-Tan. 45-Manapul. 46. Andy Kubert. 47-Benes. 48-Morales. 49-Migliari. 51-Horn. 52-Shane Davis 8.00
50-($3.99)-Black Lantern Spectre & Parallax app.; Mahnke-a/c 4.00
50-Variant-c by Jim Lee 12.00
53-67: 53-62-Brightest Day. 54,55-Lobo app. 58-60-Flash app. 60-Krona returns. 64-67-War of the Green Lanterns x-over. 67-Sinestro becomes a Green Lantern 3.00
FCBD 2011 Green Lantern Flashpoint Special Edition (6/11, giveaway) r/#30 and previews Flashpoint x-over; Andy Kubert-a 3.00
...: Larfleeze Christmas Special 1 (2/11, $3.99) Johns-s/Booth-a/Ha-c 4.00
.../Plastic Man: Weapons of Mass Deception (2/11, $4.99) Brent Anderson-a 5.00
...Secret Files and Origins 2005 (6/05, $4.99) Johns-s/Cooke & Van Sciver-a; profiles with art by various incl. Chaykin, Gibbons, Gleason, Igle; Pacheco-c 5.00
.../Sinestro Corps: Secret Files 1 (2/08, $4.99) Profiles of Green Lanterns and Corps info 5.00
...: Agent Orange HC (2009, $19.99) r/#38-42 & Blackest Night #0; sketch art 20.00
...: Agent Orange SC (2010, $14.99) r/#38-42 & Blackest Night #0; sketch art 15.00
Blackest Night: Green Lantern HC (2010, $24.99) r/#43-52; variant covers; sketch art 25.00
Blackest Night: Green Lantern SC (2011, $19.99) r/#43-52; variant covers; sketch art 20.00
...: Brightest Day HC (2011, $22.99) r/#53-62; variant cover gallery 23.00
...: In Brightest Day SC (2008, $19.99) r/stories selected by Geoff Johns w/commentary 20.00
...: No Fear HC (2006, $24.99) r/#1-6 & Secret Files and Origins 25.00
...: No Fear SC (2008, $12.99) r/#1-6 & Secret Files and Origins 13.00
...: Rage of the Red Lanterns HC (2009, $24.99) r/#26-28,36-38 & Final Crisis: Rage... 25.00
...: Rage of the Red Lanterns SC (2010, $14.99) r/#26-28,36-38 & Final Crisis: Rage... 15.00
...: Revenge of the Green Lanterns HC (2006, $19.99) r/#7-13; variant cover gallery 20.00
...: Revenge of the Green Lanterns SC (2008, $12.99) r/#7-13; variant cover gallery 13.00
...: Secret Origin HC (2008, $19.99) r/#29-35 20.00
...: Secret Origin (New Edition) HC (2010, $19.99) r/#29-35; intro. by Ryan Reynolds 20.00
...: Secret Origin SC (2008, $14.99) r/#29-35 15.00
...: Secret Origin (New Edition) SC (2011, $14.99) r/#29-35; intro. by Ryan Reynolds; photo-c of Reynolds from movie; movie preview photo gallery 15.00
... Super Spectacular (1/12, $7.99, magazine-size) r/Blackest Night #0,1, Green Lantern #76 from 1970 and Brave and the Bold #30 from 2009 8.00
...: Tales of the Sinestro Corps HC (2008, $29.99, d.j.) r/back-up stories from #18-20, Tales of the Sinestro Corps series, Green Lantern: Sinestro Corps Special and Sinestro Corps: Secret Files 30.00
...: Tales of the Sinestro Corps SC (2009, $14.99) same contents as HC 15.00
...: The Sinestro Corps War Vol. 1 HC (2008, $24.99, d.j.) r/#21-23, Green Lantern Corps #14-15 and Green Lantern: Sinestro Corps Special 25.00
...: The Sinestro Corps War Vol. 1 SC (2009, $14.99) same contents as HC 15.00
...: The Sinestro Corps War Vol. 2 HC (2008, $24.99, d.j.) r/#24,25, Green Lantern Corps #16-19; interview with the creators and sketch art 25.00
... - Wanted: Hal Jordan HC (2007, $19.99) r/#14-20 without Sinestro Corps back-ups 20.00
... - Wanted: Hal Jordan SC (2008, $14.99) r/#14-20 without Sinestro Corps back-ups 15.00

GREEN LANTERN (DC New 52)
DC Comics: Nov, 2011 - Present ($2.99)

1-8: 1-Sinestro as Green Lantern; Johns-s/Mahnke-a/Reis-c (1st & 2nd print). 6-Choi-a 3.00
1-8-Variant-c. 1-Capullo. 2-Finch. 3-Van Sciver. 4-Manapul. 5-Choi. 6-Reis. 8-Keown 4.00
8-Combo pack ($3.99) polybagged with digital code 4.00

GREEN LANTERN ANNUAL NO. 1, 1963
DC Comics: 1998 ($4.95, one-shot)

1-Reprints Golden Age & Silver Age stories in 1963-style 80 pg. Giant format; new Gil Kane sketch art 5.00

GREEN LANTERN: BRIGHTEST DAY; BLACKEST NIGHT
DC Comics: 2002 ($5.95, squarebound, one-shot)

nn-Alan Scott vs. Solomon Grundy in 1944; Snyder III-c/a; Seagle-s 1 2 3 5 6 8

GREEN LANTERN: CIRCLE OF FIRE
DC Comics: Early Oct, 2000 - No. 2, Late Oct, 2000 (limited series)

1-($4.95) Intro. other Green Lanterns 5.00
2-($3.75) 4.00
Green Lantern (x-overs)- .../Adam Strange; .../Atom; .../Firestorm; ... /Green Lantern, Winick-s; .../Power Girl (all $2.50-c) 3.00
TPB (2002, $17.95) r/#1,2 & x-overs 18.00

GREEN LANTERN CORPS, THE (Formerly Green Lantern; see Tales of...)
DC Comics: No. 206, Nov, 1986 - No. 224, May, 1988

206-223: 212-John Stewart marries Katma Tui. 220,221-Millennium tie-ins 4.00
224-Double-size last issue 5.00
...Corps Annual 2,3- (12/86,8/87) 1-Formerly Tales of ...Annual #1; Alan Moore scripts. 3-Indicia says Green Lantern Annual #3; Moore scripts; Byrne-a 4.00
NOTE: **Austin** *a-Annual 3i.* **Gil Kane** *a-223, 224p; c-223, 224, Annual 2.* **Russell** *a-Annual 3i.* **Staton** *a-207-213p, 217p, 221p, 222p, Annual 3; c-207-213p, 217p, 221p, 222p.* **Willingham** *a-213p, 219p, 220p, 218p, 219p, Annual 2, 3p; c-218p, 219p.*

GREEN LANTERN CORPS
DC Comics: Aug, 2006 - No. 63, Oct, 2011 ($2.99)

1,14-19: 1-Gibbons-s. 14-19-Sinestro Corps War pts. 3,5,7,9,10, Epilogue 4.00
2-13: 2-6,10,11-Gibbons-s. 9-Darkseid app. 3.00
20-38: 20-Mongul app. 3.00
20-Second printing with sketch-c 3.00
34-38: 34-37-Variant covers by Migliari. 38-Fabry var-c 10.00
39-45-Blackest Night. 43-45-Red Lantern Guy Gardner 3.00
39-45-Variant covers: 39-Jusko. 40-Tucci. 41,42,44-Horn. 43-Ladronn. 45 Bolland 8.00
46,47-($3.99) 46-Blackest Night. 47-Brightest Day 4.00
48-61-($2.99) 48-Migliari-c; Ganthet joins the Corps. 49-52-Cyborg Superman app. 58-60-War of the Green Lanterns x-over. 60-Mogo destroyed 3.00
Blackest Night: Green Lantern Corps HC (2010, $24.99, d.j.) r/#39-47, cover gallery 25.00
Blackest Night: Green Lantern Corps SC (2011, $19.99) r/#39-47, cover gallery 20.00
...: Emerald Eclipse HC (2009, $24.99) r/#33-39; gallery of variant covers 25.00
...: Emerald Eclipse SC (2010, $14.99) r/#33-39; gallery of variant covers 15.00
...: Revolt of the Alpha-Lanterns HC (2011, $22.99) r/#21,22,48-52 23.00
...: Ring Quest TPB (2008, $14.99) r/#19,20,23-26 15.00
...: The Dark Side of Green TPB (2007, $12.99) r/#7-13 13.00
...: To Be a Lantern TPB (2007, $12.99) r/#1-6 13.00

GREEN LANTERN CORPS (DC New 52)
DC Comics: Nov, 2011 - Present ($2.99)

1-7: 1-Tomasi-s/Pasarin-a/Mahnke-c; John Stewart & Guy Gardner. 4-6-Andy Kubert-c 3.00

GREEN LANTERN CORPS QUARTERLY
DC Comics: Summer, 1992 - No. 8, Spring, 1994 ($2.50/$2.95, 68 pgs.)

1-G.A. Green Lantern story; Staton-a(p) 5.00
2-8: 2-G.A. G.L.-c/story; Austin-c(i); Gulacy-a(p). 3-G.A. G.L. story. 4-Austin-i. 7-Painted-c; Tim Vigil-a. 8-Lobo-c/s 4.00

GREEN LANTERN CORPS: RECHARGE
DC Comics: Nov, 2005 - No. 5, Mar, 2006 ($3.50/$2.99, limited series)

1-($3.50) Kyle Rayner, Guy Gardner & Kilowog app.; Gleason-a 4.00
2-5-($2.99) 3.00
TPB (2006, $12.99) r/series 13.00

GREEN LANTERN: DRAGON LORD
DC Comics: 2001 - No. 3, 2001 ($4.95, squarebound, limited series)

1-3: A G.L. in ancient China; Moench-s/Gulacy-c/a 5.00

GREEN LANTERN: EMERALD DAWN (Also see Emerald Dawn)
DC Comics: Dec, 1989 - No. 6, May, 1990 ($1.00, limited series)

1-Origin retold; Giffen plots in all 6.00
2-6: 4-Re-intro. Tomar-Re 4.00

GREEN LANTERN: EMERALD DAWN II (Emerald Dawn II #1 & 2)
DC Comics: Apr, 1991 - No. 6, Sept, 1991 ($1.00, limited series)

1-6 3.00
TPB (2003, $12.95) r/#1-6; Alan Davis-c 13.00

Green Lantern Movie Prequel: Hal Jordan #1 © DC

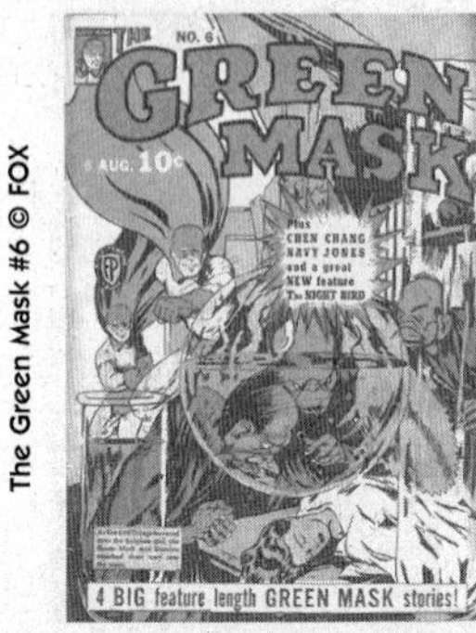

The Green Mask #6 © FOX

Grendel #3 © Matt Wagner

	GD 2.0	VG 4.0	FN 6.0	VF 8.0	VF/NM 9.0	NM- 9.2

GREEN LANTERN: EMERALD WARRIORS
DC Comics: Oct, 2010 - No. 13, Oct, 2011 ($3.99/$2.99)

1-5-($3.99) Guy Gardner's exploits; Migliari-c. 1-Bermejo variant-c. 2-5-Massaferra var-c 4.00
6-13-($2.99) 6,7-Covers by Migliari & Massaferra. 8-10-War of the Green Lanterns x-over 3.00

GREEN LANTERN: EVIL'S MIGHT (Elseworlds)
DC Comics: 2002 - No. 3 ($5.95, squarebound, limited series)

1-3-Kyle Rayner in 19th century NYC; Rogers-a; Chaykin & Tischman-s 6.00

GREEN LANTERN: FEAR ITSELF
DC Comics: 1999 (Graphic novel)

Hardcover ($24.95) Ron Marz-s/Brad Parker painted-a 25.00
Softcover ($14.95) 15.00

GREEN LANTERN/FLASH: FASTER FRIENDS (See Flash/Green Lantern...)
DC Comics: 1997 ($4.95, limited series)

1-Marz-s 5.00

GREEN LANTERN GALLERY
DC Comics: Dec, 1996 ($3.50, one-shot)

1-Wraparound-c; pin-ups by various 3.50

GREEN LANTERN/GREEN ARROW (Also see The Flash #217)
DC Comics: Oct, 1983 - No. 7, April, 1984 (52-60 pgs.)

1-7- r-Green Lantern #76-89 4.00
NOTE: ***Neal Adams** r-1-7; c-1-4. **Wrightson** r-4, 5.*

GREEN LANTERN · LEGACY: THE LAST WILL & TESTAMENT OF HAL JORDAN
DC Comics: 2002 ($24.95, hardcover graphic novel)

Hardcover-Anderson & Sienkiewicz-a/c; Kelly-s; Return of Oa 25.00
Softcover (2004, $17.95) 18.00

GREEN LANTERN: MOSAIC (Also see Cosmic Odyssey #2)
DC Comics: June, 1992 - No. 18, Nov, 1993 ($1.25)

1-18: Featuring John Stewart. 1-Painted-c by Cully Hamner 3.00

GREEN LANTERN MOVIE PREQUEL (2011 movie)
DC Comics: July, 2011; Oct, 2011 ($2.99, one-shots)

...: Abin Sur 1 - Green-s/Gleason-a; movie photo-c 3.00
...: Hal Jordan 1 - Johns & Berlanti-s/Ordway-a; movie photo-c; Sinestro & Tomar-Re app. 3.00
...: Kilowog 1 - Tomasi-s/Ferreira-a; movie photo-c 3.00
...: Sinestro 1 (10/11) - Johns-s/Tolibao, Richards & Ordway-a; movie photo-c 3.00
...: Tomar-Re 1 - Guggenheim-s/Richards-a; movie photo-c 3.00

GREEN LANTERN: NEW GUARDIANS (DC New 52)
DC Comics: Nov, 2011 - Present ($2.99)

1-7: 1-Bedard-s/Kirkham-a/c; Kyle origin flashback; Fatality app. 3-5,7-Larfleeze app. 3.00

GREEN LANTERN: REBIRTH
DC Comics: Dec, 2004 - No. 6, May, 2005 ($2.95, limited series)

1-Johns-s/Van Sciver-a; Hal Jordan as The Spectre on-c 8.00
1-2nd printing; Hal Jordan as Green Lantern on-c 4.00
1-3rd printing; B&W-c version of 1st printing 3.00
1 Special Edition (9/09, $1.00) r/#1 with "After Watchmen" cover frame 3.00
2-Guy Gardner becomes a Green Lantern again; JLA app. 5.00
2-2nd & 3rd printings 3.00
3-6: 3-Sinestro returns. 4-6-JLA & JSA app. 3.00
HC (2005, $24.99, dust jacket) r/series & Wizard preview; intro. by Brad Meltzer 25.00
SC (2007, 2010, $14.99) r/series & Wizard preview; intro. by Brad Meltzer 15.00

GREEN LANTERN/SENTINEL: HEART OF DARKNESS
DC Comics: Mar, 1998 - No. 3, May, 1998 ($1.95, limited series)

1-3-Marz-s/Pelletier-a 3.00

GREEN LANTERN/SILVER SURFER: UNHOLY ALLIANCES
DC Comics: 1995 ($4.95, one-shot)(Prelude to DC Versus Marvel)

nn-Hal Jordan app. 5.00

GREEN LANTERN SINESTRO CORPS SPECIAL (Continues in Green Lantern #21)
DC Comics: Aug, 2007 ($4.99, one-shot)

1-Kyle Rayner becomes Parallax; Cyborg Superman & Earth-Prime Superboy app.; Johns-s; Van Sciver-a/c; back-up story origin of Sinestro; Gibbons-a; Sinestro on cover 8.00
1-(2nd printing) Kyle Rayner as Parallax on cover 6.00
1-(3rd printing) Sinestro cover with muted colors 5.00

GREEN LANTERN: THE ANIMATED SERIES (Based on the Cartoon Network series)
DC Comics: No. 0, Jan, 2012 - Present ($2.99)

0,1: 0-Baltazar & Franco-s/Brizuela-a; Kilowog and Red Lanterns app. 3.00

GREEN LANTERN: THE GREATEST STORIES EVER TOLD
DC Comics: 2006 ($19.99, TPB)

SC-Reprints Showcase #22; G.L. #1,31,74,87,172; ('90 series) #3, and others; Ross-c 20.00

GREEN LANTERN: THE NEW CORPS
DC Comics: 1999 - No. 2, 1999 ($4.95, limited series)

1,2-Kyle recruits new GLs; Eaton-a 5.00

GREEN LANTERN VS. ALIENS
Dark Horse Comics: Sept, 2000 - No. 4, Dec, 2000 ($2.95, limited series)

1-4: 1-Hal Jordan and GL Corps vs. Aliens; Leonardi-p. 2-4-Kyle Rayner 3.00

GREEN MASK, THE (See Mystery Men)
Summer, 1940 - No. 9, 2/42; No. 10, 8/44 - No. 11, 11/44;
Fox Features Syndicate: V2#1, Spring, 1945 - No. 6, 10-11/46

	GD 2.0	VG 4.0	FN 6.0	VF 8.0	VF/NM 9.0	NM- 9.2
V1#1-Origin The Green Mask & Domino; reprints/Mystery Men #1-3,5-7; Lou Fine-c	300	600	900	1950	3375	4800
2-Zanzibar The Magician by Tuska	116	232	348	742	1271	1800
3-Powell-a; Marijuana story	84	168	252	538	919	1300
4-Navy Jones begins, ends #6	65	130	195	416	708	1000
5	53	106	159	334	567	800
6-The Nightbird begins, ends #9; bondage/torture-c	45	90	135	284	480	675
7-9: 9(2/42)-Becomes The Bouncer #10(nn) on? & Green Mask #10 on	39	78	117	231	378	525
10,11: 10-Origin One Round Hogan & Rocket Kelly	30	60	90	177	289	400
V2#1	23	46	69	136	223	310
2-6	19	38	57	112	179	245

GREEN PLANET, THE
Charlton Comics: 1962 (one-shot) (12¢)

	GD 2.0	VG 4.0	FN 6.0	VF 8.0	VF/NM 9.0	NM- 9.2
nn-Giordano-c; sci-fi	7	14	21	46	76	105

GREEN TEAM (See Cancelled Comic Cavalcade & 1st Issue Special)

GREEN WOMAN, THE
DC Comics (Vertigo): 2010 ($24.99, HC graphic novel)

HC-John Bolton-a/Peter Straub & Michael Easton-s 25.00

GREETINGS FROM SANTA (See March of Comics No. 48)

GRENDEL (Also see Primer #2, Mage and Comico Collection)
Comico: Mar, 1983 - No. 3, Feb, 1984 ($1.50, B&W)(#1 has indicia to Skrog #1)

	GD 2.0	VG 4.0	FN 6.0	VF 8.0	VF/NM 9.0	NM- 9.2
1-Origin Hunter Rose	10	20	30	69	130	190
2,3: 2-Origin Argent	8	16	24	53	89	125

GRENDEL
Comico: Oct, 1986 - No. 40, Feb, 1990 ($1.50/$1.95/$2.50, mature)

	GD 2.0	VG 4.0	FN 6.0	VF 8.0	VF/NM 9.0	NM- 9.2
1	1	2	3	5	7	9
1,2: 2nd printings						3.00
2,3,5-15: 13-15-Ken Steacy-c.						4.00
4,16: 4-Dave Stevens-c(i). 16-Re-intro Mage (series begins, ends #19)						6.00
17-40: 24-25,27-28,30-31-Snyder-c/a						3.00
Devil by the Deed (Graphic Novel, 10/86, $5.95, 52 pgs.)-r/Grendel back-ups/ Mage 6-14; Alan Moore intro.	1	2	3	4	5	7
Devil's Legacy ($14.95, 1988, Graphic Novel)	2	4	6	9	12	15
Devil's Vagary (10/87, B&W & red)-No price; included in Comico Collection	2	4	6	8	10	12

GRENDEL (Title series): **Dark Horse Comics**

--ARCHIVES, 5/07 ($14.95, HC) r/1st apps. in Primer #2 and Grendel #1-3; Wagner intro. 15.00

--BEHOLD THE DEVIL, No. 0, 7/07 - No. 8, 6/08 ($3.50/50¢, B&W&Red)
0-(50¢-c) Prelude to series; Matt Wagner-s/a; interview with Wagner 3.00
1-8-Matt Wagner-s/a/c in all 3.50

--BLACK, WHITE, AND RED, 11/98 - No. 4, 2/99 ($3.95, anthology)
1-Wagner-s in all. Art by Sale, Leon and others 5.00
2-4: 2-Mack, Chadwick-a. 3-Allred, Kristensen-a. 4-Pearson, Sprouse-a 4.00

--CLASSICS, 7/95 - 8/95 ($3.95, mature) 1,2-reprints; new Wagner-c 4.00

--CYCLE, 10/95 ($5.95) 1-nn-history of Grendel by M. Wagner & others 6.00

--DEVIL BY THE DEED, 7/93 ($3.95, varnish-c) 1-nn-M. Wagner-c/a/scripts; r/Grendel back-ups from Mage #6-14 4.00
Reprint (12/97, $3.95) w/pin-ups by various 4.00
Hardcover (2007, $12.95) reprint recolored to B&W&red; includes covers and intros from previously reprinted editions 13.00

--DEVIL CHILD, 6/99 - No. 2, 7/99 ($2.95, mature) 1,2-Sale & Kristiansen-a/Schutz-s 3.00

Grendel - Red, White & Black #1 © Matt Wagner

Grifter V2 #4 © WSP

Grimm Fairy Tales #55 © Zenescope

GD 2.0 | VG 4.0 | FN 6.0 | VF 8.0 | VF/NM 9.0 | NM- 9.2

--DEVIL QUEST, 11/95 ($4.95) 1-nn-Prequel to Batman/Grendel II; M. Wagner story & art; r/back-up story from Grendel Tales series. 5.00

--DEVILS AND DEATHS, 10/94 - 11/94 ($2.95, mature) 1,2 3.00

: DEVIL'S LEGACY, 3/00 - No. 12, 2/01 ($2.95, reprints 1986 series, recolored)
1-12-Wagner-s/c; Pander Bros.-a 3.00

: DEVIL'S REIGN, 5/04 - No. 7, 12/04 ($3.50, repr. 1989 series #34-40, recolored)
1-7-Sale-c/a. 3.50

: GOD AND THE DEVIL, No. 0, 1/03 - No. 10, 12/03 ($3.50/$4.99, repr. 1986 series, recolored)
0-9: 0-Sale-c/a; r/#23. 1-9-Snyder-c 3.50
10-($4.99) Double-sized; Snyder-c 5.00

--RED, WHITE & BLACK, 9/02 - No. 4, 12/02 ($4.99, anthology)
1-4-Wagner-s in all. 1-Art by Thompson, Sakai, Mahfood and others. 2-Kelley Jones, Watson, Brereton, Hester & Parks-a. 3-Oeming, Noto, Cannon, Ashley Wood, Huddleston-a 4-Chiang, Dalrymple, Robertson, Snyder III and Zulli-a 5.00
TPB (2005, $19.95) r/#1-4; cover gallery, artist bios 20.00

--TALES: DEVIL'S CHOICES, 3/95 - 6/95 ($2.95, mature) 1-4 3.00

--TALES: FOUR DEVILS, ONE HELL, 8/93 - 1/94 ($2.95, mature)
1-6-Wagner painted-c 3.00
TPB (12/94, $17.95) r/#1-6 18.00

--TALES: HOMECOMING, 12/94 - 2/95 ($2.95, mature) 1-3 3.00

--TALES: THE DEVIL IN OUR MIDST, 5/94 - 9/95 ($2.95, mature) 1-5-Wagner painted-c 3.00

--TALES: THE DEVIL MAY CARE, 12/95 - No. 6, 5/96 ($2.95, mature)
1-6-Terry LaBan scripts. 5-Batman/Grendel II preview 3.00

--TALES: THE DEVIL'S APPRENTICE, 9/97 - No. 3, 11/97 ($2.95, mature)
1-3 3.00

: THE DEVIL INSIDE, 9/01 - No. 3, 11/01 ($2.99)
1-3-r/#13-15 with new Wagner-c 3.00

: WAR CHILD, 8/92 - No. 10, 6/93 ($2.50, lim. series, mature)
1-9: 1-4-Bisley painted-c; Wagner-i & scripts in all 3.00
10-($3.50, 52 pgs.) Wagner-c 4.00
Limited Edition Hardcover ($99.95) 100.00

GREYFRIARS BOBBY (Disney)(Movie)
Dell Publishing Co.: No. 1189, Nov, 1961 (one-shot)
Four Color 1189-Photo-c (scarce) 7 14 21 46 76 105

GREYLORE
Sirius: 12/85 - No. 5, Sept, 1986 ($1.50/$1.75, high quality paper)
1-5: Bo Hampton-a in all 3.00

GREYSHIRT: INDIGO SUNSET (Also see Tomorrow Stories)
America's Best Comics: Dec, 2001 - No. 6, Aug, 2002 ($3.50, limited series)
1-6-Veitch-s/a. 4-Back-up w/John Severin-a. 6-Cho-a 3.50
TPB (2002, $19.95) r/#1-6; preface by Alan Moore 20.00

GRIDIRON GIANTS
Ultimate Sports Ent.: 2000 - No. 2 ($3.95, cardstock covers)
1,2-NFL players Sanders, Marino, Plummer, T. Davis battle evil 4.00

GRIFFIN, THE
DC Comics: 1991 - No. 6, 1991 ($4.95, limited series, 52 pgs.)
Book 1-6: Matt Wagner painted-c 5.00

GRIFTER (Also see Team 7 & WildC.A.T.S)
Image Comics (WildStorm Prod.): May, 1995 - No. 10, Mar, 1996 ($1.95)
1 ($1.95, Newsstand)-WildStorm Rising Pt. 5 3.00
1-10:1 ($2.50, Direct)-WildStorm Rising Pt. 5, bound-in trading card 3.00
...: One Shot (1/95, $4.95) Flip-c 5.00

GRIFTER
Image Comics (WildStorm Prod.): V2#1, July, 1996 - No. 14, Aug, 1997 ($2.50)
V2#1-14: Steven Grant scripts 3.00

GRIFTER (DC New 52)
DC Comics: Nov, 2011 - Present ($2.99)
1-8: 1-Grifter in the new DC universe; Edmonson-s/Cafu-a/c. 4-Green Arrow app. 3.00

GRIFTER & MIDNIGHTER
DC Comics (WildStorm Prod.): May, 2007 - No. 6, Oct, 2007 ($2.99, limited series)
1-6-Dixon-s/Benjamin-a/c. 1,3-The Authority app. 3.00
TPB (2008, $17.99) r/#1-6 18.00

GRIFTER AND THE MASK
Dark Horse Comics: Sept, 1996 - No. 2, Oct, 1996 ($2.50, limited series)
(1st Dark Horse Comics/Image x-over)
1,2: Steve Seagle scripts 3.00

GRIFTER/BADROCK (Also see WildC.A.T.S & Youngblood)
Image Comics (Extreme Studios): Oct, 1995 - No.2, Nov, 1995 ($2.50, unfinished lim. series)
1,2: 2-Flip book w/Badrock #2 3.00

GRIFTER/SHI
Image Comics (WildStorm Productions): Apr, 1996 - No. 2, May, 1996 ($2.95, limited series)
1,2: 1-Jim Lee-c/a(p); Travis Charest-a(p). 2-Billy Tucci-c/a(p); Travis Charest-a(p) 3.00

GRIM GHOST, THE
Atlas/Seaboard Publ.: Jan, 1975 - No. 3, July, 1975
1-3: Fleisher-s in all. 1-Origin. 2-Son of Satan; Colan-a. 3-Heath-c
2 4 6 9 13 16

GRIM GHOST
Ardden Entertainment (Atlas Comics): Mar, 2011 - Present ($2.99)
1-5-Isabella & Susco-s/Kelley Jones-a. 1-Re-intro. Matthew Dunsinane 3.00
... Issue Zero - NY Comicon Edtion (10/10, $2.99) Qing Ping Mui-a; prequel to #1 3.00

GRIMJACK (Also see Demon Knight & Starslayer)
First Comics: Aug, 1984 - No. 81, Apr, 1991 ($1.00/$1.95/$2.25)
1-John Ostrander scripts & Tim Truman-c/a begins. 4.00
2-25: 20-Sutton-c/a begins. 22-Bolland-a. 3.00
26-2nd color Teenage Mutant Ninja Turtles 6.00
27-74,76-81 (Later issues $1.95, $2.25): 30-Dynamo Joe x-over; 31-Mandrake-c/a begins. 73,74-Kelley Jones-a 3.00
75-($5.95, 52 pgs.)-Fold-out map; coated stock 6.00
The Legend of Grimjack Vol. 1 (IDW Publishing, 2004, $19.99) r/Starslayer #10-18; 8 new pages & art 20.00
The Legend of Grimjack Vol. 2 (IDW, 2005, $19.99) r/#1-7; unpublished art 20.00
The Legend of Grimjack Vol. 3 (IDW, 2005, $19.99) r/#8-14; cover gallery 20.00
The Legend of Grimjack Vol. 4 (IDW, 2005, $24.99) r/#15-21; cover gallery 25.00
The Legend of Grimjack Vol. 5 (IDW, 5/06, $24.99) r/#22-30; cover gallery 25.00
The Legend of Grimjack Vol. 6 (IDW, 1/07, $24.99) r/#31-37; cover gallery 25.00
The Legend of Grimjack Vol. 7 (IDW, 4/07, $24.99) r/#38-46; covers; "Rough Trade" 25.00
NOTE: ***Truman** c/a-1-17.*

GRIMJACK CASEFILES
First Comics: Nov, 1990 - No. 5, Mar, 1991 ($1.95, limited series)
1-5 Reprints 1st stories from Starslayer #10 on 3.00

GRIMJACK: KILLER INSTINCT
IDW Publ.: Jan, 2005 - No. 6, June, 2005 ($3.99, limited series)
1-6-Ostrander-s/Truman-a 4.00

GRIMJACK: THE MANX CAT
IDW Publ.: Aug, 2009 - No. 6, Jan, 2010 ($3.99, limited series)
1-6-Ostrander-s/Truman-a 4.00

GRIMM FAIRY TALES
Zenescope Entertainment: Jun, 2005 - Present ($2.99)
1-Al Rio-c; Little Red Riding Hood app.; multiple variant covers 30.00
2-Multiple variant covers 15.00
3-6-Multiple variant covers 8.00
7-12: Multiple covers on each 4.00
13-72: Multiple covers on each 3.00
... Halloween Special 1,2 (10/09, 10/10, $5.99) Multiple covers on each 6.00
... Presents Alice in Wonderland 1-5 (1/12 - Present, $2.99) Multiple covers on each 3.00

GRIMM FAIRY TALES MYTHS & LEGENDS
Zenescope Entertainment: Jan, 2011 - Present ($2.99)
1-14: 1-Campbell-c.; multiple variant covers 3.00

GRIMM'S GHOST STORIES (See Dan Curtis)
Gold Key/Whitman No. 55 on: Jan, 1972 - No. 60, June, 1982 (Painted-c #1-42,44,46-56)
1 4 8 12 22 34 45
2-5,8: 5,8-Williamson-a 2 4 6 13 18 22
6,7,9,10 2 4 6 11 16 20
11-20 2 4 6 8 11 14
21-42,45-54: 32,34-Reprints. 45-Photo-c 1 3 4 6 8 10
43,44,55-60: 43,44-(52 pgs.). 43-Photo-c. 58(2/82). 59(4/82)-Williamson-a(r/#8). 60(6/82)
2 4 6 8 11 14
Mini-Comic No. 1 (3-1/4x6-1/2", 1976) 1 3 4 6 8 10
NOTE: *Reprints-#32?, 34?, 39, 43, 44, 47?, 53; 56-60(1/3).* ***Bolle** a-8, 17, 22-25, 27, 29(2), 33, 35, 41, 43r, 45(2), 48(2), 50, 52, 57.* ***Celardo** a-17, 26, 28p, 30, 31, 43(2), 45.* ***Lopez** a-24, 25.* ***McWilliams** a-33, 44r, 48, 54(2), 57, 58.* ***Win Mortimer** a-31, 33, 49, 51, 55, 56, 58(2), 59, 60.* ***Roussos** a-25, 30.* ***Sparling** a-23, 24, 28, 30, 31, 33, 43r,*

Grip: The Strange World of Men #5 © Gilbert Hernandez

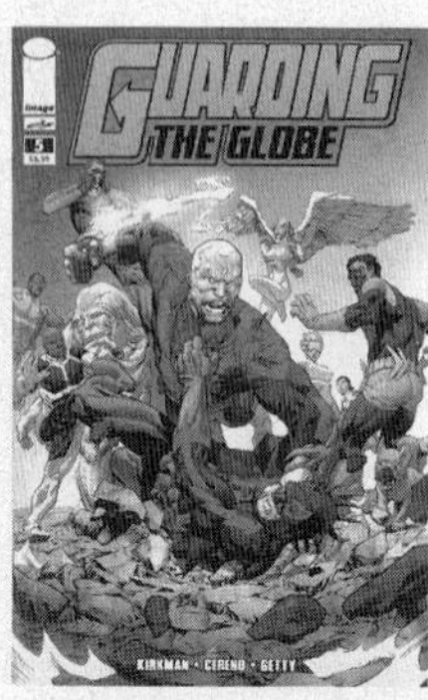

Guarding the Globe #5 © Robert Kirkman

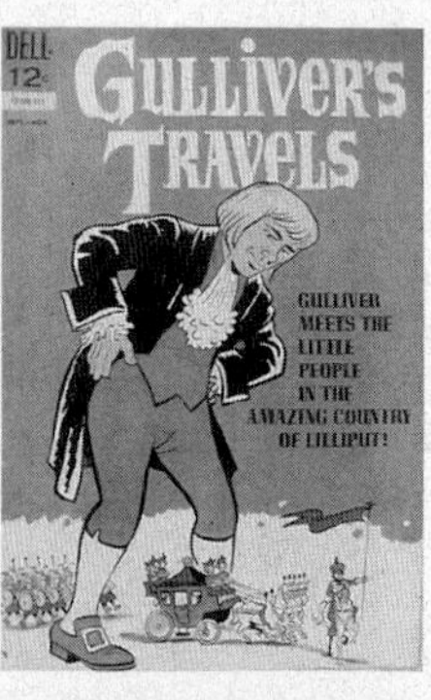

Gulliver's Travels #1 © DELL

*44, 45, 51(2), 52, 56-58, 59(2), 60. **Spiegle** a-44.*

GRIN (The American Funny Book) (Satire)
APAG House Pubs: Nov, 1972 - No. 3, April, 1973 (Magazine, 52 pgs.)

1-Parodies-Godfather, All in the Family 3 6 9 17 25 32
2,3 2 4 6 11 16 20

GRIN & BEAR IT (See Gags)
Dell Publishing Co.: No. 28, 1941

Large Feature Comic 28 16 32 48 94 147 200

GRIPS (Extreme violence)
Silverwolf Comics: Sept, 1986 - No. 4, Dec, 1986 ($1.50, B&W, mature)

1-Tim Vigil-c/a in all 6.00
2-4 4.00

GRIP: THE STRANGE WORLD OF MEN
DC Comics (Vertigo): Jan, 2002 - No. 5, May, 2002 ($2.50, limited series)

1-4-Gilbert Hernandez-s/a 3.00

GRIT GRADY (See Holyoke One-Shot No. 1)

GROO (Also see Sergio Aragonés' Groo...)

GROO (Sergio Aragonés'...)
Image Comics: Dec, 1994 - No. 12, Dec, 1995 ($1.95)

1-12: 2-Indicia reads #1, Jan, 1995; Aragonés-c/a in all 3.50

GROO (Sergio Aragonés'...)
Dark Horse Comics: Jan, 1998 - No. 4, Apr, 1998 ($2.95)

1-4: Aragonés-c/a in all 4.00
...: One For One (9/10, $1.00) reprints #1 with red cover frame 3.00

GROO CHRONICLES, THE (Sergio Aragonés)
Marvel Comics (Epic Comics): June, 1989 - No. 6, Feb, 1990 ($3.50)

Book 1-6: Reprints early Pacific issues 3.50

GROO SPECIAL
Eclipse Comics: Oct, 1984 ($2.00, 52 pgs., Baxter paper)

1-Aragonés-c/a 3 6 9 16 22 28

GROO THE WANDERER (See Destroyer Duck #1 & Starslayer #5)
Pacific Comics: Dec, 1982 - No. 8, Apr, 1984

1-Aragonés-c/a(p) in all; Aragonés bio., photo 2 4 6 13 18 22
2-5: 5-Deluxe paper (1.00-c) 2 4 6 9 12 15
6-8 2 4 6 10 14 18

GROO THE WANDERER (Sergio Aragonés'...) (See Marvel Graphic Novel #32)
Marvel Comics (Epic Comics): March, 1985 - No. 120, Jan, 1995

1-Aragonés-c/a in all 2 4 6 9 13 16
2-10 1 2 3 5 6 8
11-20,50-($1.50, double size) 5.00
21-49,51-99: 87-direct sale only, high quality paper 3.00
100-($2.95, 52 pgs.) 5.00
101-120 4.00
Groo Carnival, The (12/91, $8.95)-r/#9-12 11.00
Groo Garden, The (4/94, $10.95)-r/#25-28 11.00

GROOVY (Cartoon Comics - not CCA approved)
Marvel Comics Group: March, 1968 - No. 3, July, 1968

1-Monkees, Ringo Starr, Sonny & Cher, Mamas & Papas photos
9 18 27 58 99 140
2,3 6 12 18 41 66 90

GROSS POINT
DC Comics: Aug, 1997 - No. 14, Aug, 1998 ($2.50)

1-14: 1-Waid/Augustyn-s 3.00

GROUNDED
Image Comics: July, 2005 - No. 6, May, 2006 ($2.95/$2.99, limited series)

1-6-Mark Sable-s/Paul Azaceta-a. 1-Mike Oeming-c 3.00
Vol. 1: Powerless TPB (2006, $14.99) r/#1-6; sketch pages and creator bios 15.00

GRRL SCOUTS (Jim Mahfood's...) (Also see 40 oz. Collected)
Oni Press: Mar,1999 - No. 4, Dec, 1999 ($2.95, B&W, limited series)

1-4-Mahfood-s/c/a 3.00
TPB (2003, $12.95) r/#1-4; pin-ups by Warren, Winick, Allred, Fegredo and others 13.00

GRRL SCOUTS: WORK SUCKS
Image Comics: Feb, 2003 - No. 4, May, 2003 ($2.95, B&W, limited series)

1-4-Mahfood-s/c/a 3.00
TPB (2004, $12.95) r/#1-4; pin-ups by Oeming, Dwyer, Tennapel and others 13.00

GUADALCANAL DIARY (See American Library)

GUARDIAN ANGEL
Image Comics: May, 2002 - No. 2, July, 2002 ($2.95)

1,2-Peterson-s/Wiesenfeld-a 3.00

GUARDIANS
Marvel Comics: Sept, 2004 - No. 5, Dec, 2004 ($2.99, limited series)

1-5-Sumerak-s/Casey Jones-a 3.00

GUARDIANS OF METROPOLIS
DC Comics: Nov, 1995 - Feb, 1995 ($1.50, limited series)

1-4: 1-Superman & Granny Goodness app. 3.00

GUARDIANS OF THE GALAXY (Also see The Defenders #26, Marvel Presents #3, Marvel Super-Heroes #18, Marvel Two-In-One #5)
Marvel Comics: June, 1990 - No. 62, July, 1995 ($1.00/$1.25)

1-Valentino-c/a(p) begin. 4.00
2-15: 2-Zeck-c(i). 5-McFarlane-c(i). 7-Intro Malevolence (Mephisto's daughter); Perez-c(i). 8-Intro Rancor (descendant of Wolverine) in cameo. 9-1st full app. Rancor; Rob Liefeld-c(i). 10-Jim Lee-c(i). 13,14-1st app. Spirit of Vengeance (futuristic Ghost Rider). 14-Spirit of Vengeance vs. The Guardians. 15-Starlin-c(i) 3.00
16-($1.50, 52 pgs.)-Starlin-c(i) 4.00
17-24,26-38,40-47: 17-20-31st century Punishers storyline. 20-Last $1.00-c. 21-Rancor app. 22-Reintro Starhawk. 24-Silver Surfer-c/story; Ron Lim-c. 26-Origin retold. 27-28-Infinity War x-over; 27-Inhumans app. 43-Intro Wooden (son of Thor) 3.00
25-($2.50)-Prism foil-c; Silver Surfer/Galactus-c/s 4.00
25-($2.50)-Without foil-c; newsstand edition 3.00
39-($2.95, 52 pgs.)-Embossed & holo-grafx foil-c; Dr. Doom vs. Rancor 4.00
48,49,51-62: 48-bound-in trading card sheet 3.00
50-($2.00, 52 pgs.)-Newsstand edition 4.00
50-($2.95, 52 pgs.)-Collectors ed. w/foil embossed-c 5.00
Annual 1-4: ('91-'94, 68 pgs.)-1-Origin. 2-Spirit of Vengeance-c/story. 3,4-Bagged w/card 4.00

GUARDIANS OF THE GALAXY (See Annihilation series)
Marvel Comics: July, 2008 - No. 25, Jun, 2010 ($2.99)

1-25: 1-Pelletier-a/Abnett & Lanning-s; 2nd printing exists. 24-Thanos returns 3.00

GUARDING THE GLOBE (See Invincible)
Image Comics: Aug, 2010 - No. 6, Oct, 2011 ($3.50)

1-6-Kirkman & Cereno-s/Getty-a. 1-Back-c swipe of Avengers #4 w/Obama 3.50

GUERRILLA WAR (Formerly Jungle War Stories)
Dell Publishing Co.: No. 12, July-Sept, 1965 - No. 14, Mar, 1966

12-14 3 6 9 16 22 28

GUILD, THE (Based on the web-series)
Dark Horse Comics: Mar, 2010 - No. 3, May, 2010 ($3.50, limited series)

1-3-Felicia Day-s/Jim Rugg-a; two covers on each 3.50
... Bladezz 1 (6/11, $3.50) Currie-a/Kerschl-c; variant-c by Dalrymple 3.50
... Clara 1 (9/11, $3.50) Chan-a/Chaykin-c; variant-c by Aronowitz 3.50
... Tink 1 (3/11, $3.50) art by Donaldson, Warren, Seeley & others; variant-c by Bagge 3.50
... Vork 1 (12/10, $3.50) Robertson-a/c; variant-c by Hernandez 3.50
... Zaboo 1 (12/11, $3.50) Cloonan-a/Dorkin-c; variant-c by Jeanty 3.50

GUILTY (See Justice Traps the Guilty)

GULLIVER'S TRAVELS (See Dell Jr. Treasury No. 3)
Dell Publishing Co.: Sept-Nov, 1965

1 5 10 15 34 55 75

GUMBY
Wildcard Ink: July, 2006 - No. 3 ($3.99)

1-3-Bob Burden & Rick Geary-s&a 4.00

GUMBY'S SUMMER FUN SPECIAL
Comico: July, 1987 ($2.50)

1-Art Adams-c/a; B. Burden scripts 5.00

GUMBY'S WINTER FUN SPECIAL
Comico: Dec, 1988 ($2.50, 44 pgs.)

1-Art Adams-c/a 5.00

GUMPS, THE (See Merry Christmas..., Popular & Super Comics)
Dell Publ. Co./Bridgeport Herald Corp.: No. 73, 1945; Mar-Apr, 1947 - No. 5, Nov-Dec, 1947

Four Color 73 (Dell)(1945) 11 22 33 75 148 220
1 (3-4/47) 15 30 45 88 137 185

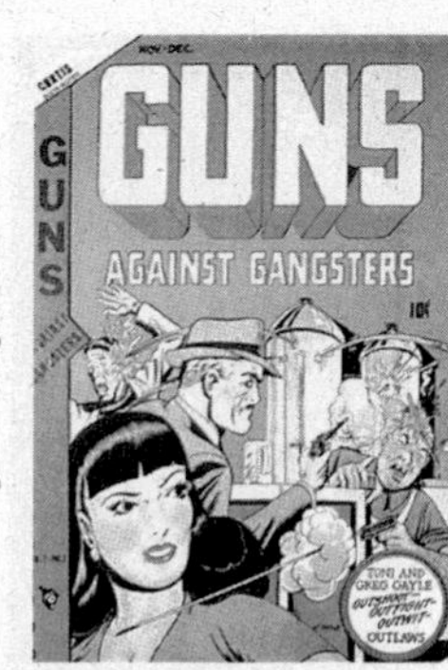

Guns Against Gangsters #2 © NOVP

Gunsmith Cats Mister V #1 © Kenichi Sonoda

Gunsmoke #2 © WEST

	GD 2.0	VG 4.0	FN 6.0	VF 8.0	VF/NM 9.0	NM- 9.2
2-5	11	22	33	60	83	105

GUN CANDY (Also see The Ride)
Image Comics: July, 2005 - Present ($5.99)

1,2-Stelfreeze-c/a; flip book with The Ride (1-Pearson-c. 2-Noto-c) 6.00

GUNFIGHTER (Fat & Slat #1-4) (Becomes Haunt of Fear #15 on)
E. C. Comics (Fables Publ. Co.): No. 5, Sum, 1948 - No. 14, Mar-Apr, 1950

	GD	VG	FN	VF	VF/NM	NM-
5,6-Moon Girl in each	54	108	162	343	574	825
7-14: 14-Bondage-c	40	80	120	246	411	575

NOTE: ***Craig & H. C. Kiefer*** *art in most issues.* ***Craig*** *c-5, 6, 13, 14.* ***Feldstein/Craig*** *a-10.* ***Feldstein*** *a-7-11.* ***Harrison/Wood*** *a-13, 14.* ***Ingels*** *a-5-14; c-7-12.*

GUNFIGHTERS, THE
Super Comics (Reprints): 1963 - 1964

10-12,15,16,18: 10,11-r/Billy the Kid #s? 12-r/The Rider #5(Swift Arrow). 15-r/Straight Arrow #42; Powell-r. 16-r/Billy the Kid #?(Toby). 18-r/The Rider #3; Severin-c
2 4 6 10 14 18

GUNFIGHTERS, THE (Formerly Kid Montana)
Charlton Comics: No. 51, 10/66 - No. 52, 10/67; No. 53, 6/79 - No. 85, 7/84

	GD	VG	FN	VF	VF/NM	NM-
51,52	2	4	6	11	16	20
53,54,56:53,54-Williamson/Torres-r/Six Gun Heroes #47,49. 56-Williamson/Severin-c; Severin-r/Sheriff of Tombstone #1	1	3	4	6	8	10
55,57-80						6.00
81-84-Lower print run	1	2	3	5	6	8
85-S&K-r/1955 Bullseye	1	3	4	6	8	10

GUNFIRE (See Deathstroke Annual #2 & Showcase 94 #1,2)
DC Comics: May, 1994 - No. 13, June, 1995 ($1.75/$2.25)

1-5,0,6-13: 2-Ricochet-c/story. 5-(9/94). 0-(10/94). 6-(11/94) 3.00

GUN GLORY (Movie)
Dell Publishing Co.: No. 846, Oct, 1957 (one-shot)

	GD	VG	FN	VF	VF/NM	NM-
Four Color 846-Toth-a, photo-c.	8	16	24	56	96	135

GUNHAWK, THE (Formerly Whip Wilson)(See Wild Western)
Marvel Comics/Atlas (MCI): No. 12, Nov, 1950 - No. 18, Dec, 1951
(Also see Two-Gun Western #5)

	GD	VG	FN	VF	VF/NM	NM-
12	18	36	54	105	165	225
13-18: 13-Tuska-a. 16-Colan-a. 18-Maneely-c	14	28	42	76	108	140

GUNHAWKS (Gunhawk No. 7)
Marvel Comics Group: Oct, 1972 - No. 7, October, 1973

	GD	VG	FN	VF	VF/NM	NM-
1,6: 1-Reno Jones, Kid Cassidy; Shores-c/a(p). 6-Kid Cassidy dies	3	6	9	16	23	30
2-5,7: 7-Reno Jones solo	2	4	6	11	16	20

GUNMASTER (Becomes Judo Master #89 on)
Charlton Comics: 9/64 - No. 4, 1965; No. 84, 7/65 - No. 88, 3-4/66; No. 89, 10/67

	GD	VG	FN	VF	VF/NM	NM-
V1#1	4	8	12	22	34	45
2,4, V5#84-86: 84-Formerly Six-Gun Heroes	3	6	9	16	22	28
V5#87-89	2	4	6	11	16	20

NOTE: *Vol. 5 was originally cancelled with #88 (3-4/66). #89 on, became Judo Master, then later in 1967, Charlton issued #89 as a Gunmaster one-shot.*

GUN RUNNER
Marvel Comics UK: Oct, 1993 - No. 6, Mar, 1994 ($1.75, limited series)

1-($2.75)-Polybagged w/4 trading cards; Spirits of Vengeance app. 4.00
2-6: 2-Ghost Rider & Blaze app. 3.00

GUNS AGAINST GANGSTERS (True-To-Life Romances #8 on)
Curtis Publications/Novelty Press: Sept-Oct, 1948 - No. 6, July-Aug, 1949; V2#1, Sept-Oct, 1949

	GD	VG	FN	VF	VF/NM	NM-
1-Toni & Greg Gayle begins by Schomburg; L.B. Cole-c	39	78	117	240	395	550
2-L.B. Cole-c	28	56	84	165	270	375
3-6, V2#1: 6-Toni Gayle-c by Cole	25	50	75	147	241	335

NOTE: ***L. B. Cole*** *c-1-6, V2#1, 2; a-1, 2, 3(2), 4-6.*

GUNSLINGER
Dell Publishing Co.: No. 1220, Oct-Dec, 1961 (one-shot)

	GD	VG	FN	VF	VF/NM	NM-
Four Color 1220-Photo-c	8	16	24	55	93	130

GUNSLINGER (Formerly Tex Dawson...)
Marvel Comics Group: No. 2, Apr, 1973 - No. 3, June, 1973

	GD	VG	FN	VF	VF/NM	NM-
2,3	2	4	6	13	18	22

GUNSLINGERS
Marvel Comics: Feb, 2000 ($2.99)

1-Reprints stories of Two-Gun Kid, Rawhide Kid and Caleb Hammer 3.00

GUNSMITH CATS: (Title series), **Dark Horse Comics**

--BAD TRIP (Manga), 6/98 - No. 6, 11/98 ($2.95, B&W) 1-6 3.00
--BEAN BANDIT (Manga), 1/99 - No. 9 ($2.95, B&W, limited series) 1-9 3.00
--GOLDIE VS. MISTY (Manga), 11/97 - No. 7, 5/98 ($2.95, B&W) 1-7 3.00
--KIDNAPPED (Manga), 11/99 - No. 10, 8/00 ($2.95, B&W) 1-10 3.00
--MISTER V (Manga), 10/00 - No. 11, 8/01 ($3.50/$2.99), B&W) 1-7,9-11 3.50
8-($2.99) 3.00
--THE RETURN OF GRAY (Manga), 8/96 - No. 7, 2/97 ($2.95, B&W) 1-7 3.00
--SHADES OF GRAY (Manga), 5/97 - No. 5, 9/97 ($2.95, B&W) 1-5 3.00
--SPECIAL (Manga) Nov, 2001 ($2.99, B&W, one-shot) 3.00

GUNSMOKE (Blazing Stories of the West)
Western Comics (Youthful Magazines): Apr-May, 1949 - No. 16, Jan, 1952

	GD	VG	FN	VF	VF/NM	NM-
1-Gunsmoke & Masked Marvel begin by Ingels; Ingels bondage-c	48	96	144	302	514	725
2-Ingels-c/a(2)	31	62	93	186	303	420
3-Ingels bondage-c/a	27	54	81	158	259	360
4-6: Ingels-c	21	42	63	124	202	280
7-10	14	28	42	82	121	160
11-16: 15,16-Western/horror stories	14	28	42	80	115	150

NOTE: ***Stallman*** *a-11, 14.* ***Wildey*** *a-15, 16.*

GUNSMOKE (TV)
Dell Publishing Co./Gold Key (All have James Arness photo-c): No. 679, Feb, 1956 - No. 27, Feb, 1969 - No. 6, Feb, 1970

	GD	VG	FN	VF	VF/NM	NM-
Four Color 679(#1)	14	28	42	97	211	325
Four Color 720,769,797,844 (#2-5),6(11-1/57-58)	9	18	27	60	103	145
7,8,9,11,12-Williamson-a in all, 4 pgs. each	9	18	27	61	106	150
10-Williamson/Crandall-a, 4 pgs.	9	18	27	61	106	150
13-27	8	16	24	51	86	120
1 (Gold Key)	6	12	18	41	66	90
2-6('69-70)	4	8	12	22	34	45

GUNSMOKE TRAIL
Ajax-Farrell Publ./Four Star Comic Corp.: June, 1957 - No. 4, Dec, 1957

	GD	VG	FN	VF	VF/NM	NM-
1	11	22	33	60	83	105
2-4	7	14	21	35	43	50

GUNSMOKE WESTERN (Formerly Western Tales of Black Rider)
Atlas Comics No. 32-35(CPS/NPI); Marvel No. 36 on: No. 32, Dec, 1955 - No. 77, July, 1963

	GD	VG	FN	VF	VF/NM	NM-
32-Baker & Drucker-a	18	36	54	105	165	225
33,35,36-Williamson-a in each: 5,6 & 4 pgs. plus Drucker-a #33. 33-Kinstler-a?	14	28	42	82	121	160
34-Baker-a, 4 pgs.; Severin-c	14	28	42	82	121	160
37-Davis-a(2); Williamson text illo	12	24	36	67	94	120
38,39: 39-Williamson text illo (unsigned)	10	20	30	54	72	90
40-Williamson/Mayo-a (4 pgs.)	10	20	30	58	79	100
41,42,45,46,48,49,52-54,57,58,60: 49,52-Kid from Texas story. 57-1st Two Gun Kid by Severin. 60-Sam Hawk app. in Kid Colt	8	16	24	44	57	70
43,44-Torres-a	8	16	24	44	57	70
47,51,59,61: 47,51,59-Kirby-a. 61-Crandall-a	9	18	27	52	69	85
50-Kirby, Crandall-a	10	20	30	58	79	100
55,56-Matt Baker-a	10	20	30	58	79	100
62-67,69,71-73,77-Kirby-a. 72-Origin Kid Colt	5	10	15	35	55	75
68,70,74-76: 68-(10¢-c)	4	8	12	28	44	60
68-(10¢ cover price blacked out, 12¢ printed on)	9	18	27	58	99	140

NOTE: ***Colan*** *a-35-37, 39, 72, 76.* ***Davis*** *a-37, 52, 54, 55; c-50, 54.* ***Ditko*** *a-66; c-56p.* ***Drucker*** *a-32-34.* ***Heath*** *c-33.* ***Jack Keller*** *a-34, 35, 40, 55, 56, 60, 61, 65, 68, 71, 72, 74, 75, 77; c-72.* ***Kirby*** *a-47, 50, 51, 59, 62(3), 63-67, 69, 71, 73, 77; c-56(w/****Ditko****), 57, 58, 60, 61(w/****Ayers****), 62, 63, 65, 66, 68, 69, 71-77.* ***Maleely*** *c-455.* ***Robinson*** *a-35.* ***Severin*** *a-35, 59-61; c-34, 35, 39, 42, 43.* ***Tuska*** *a-34.* ***Wildey*** *a-10, 37, 42, 56, 57. Kid Colt in all. Two-Gun Kid in No. 57, 59, 60-63. Wyatt Earp in No. 45, 48, 49, 52, 54, 55, 56, 58.*

GUNS OF FACT & FICTION (Also see A-1 Comics)
Magazine Enterprises: No. 13, 1948 (one-shot)

	GD	VG	FN	VF	VF/NM	NM-
A-1 13-Used in **SOTI**, pg. 19; Ingels & J. Craig-a	27	54	81	160	263	365

GUNS OF THE DRAGON
DC Comics: Oct, 1998 - No. 4, Jan, 1999 ($2.50, limited series)

1-4-DCU in the 1920's; Enemy Ace & Bat Lash app. 3.00

GUN THEORY
Marvel Comics (Epic): Oct, 2003 - No. 4 ($2.50, limited series)

1,2-Daniel Way-s/Jon Proctor-a 3.00

Guy Gardner Warrior #33 © DC

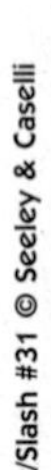
Hack/Slash #31 © Seeley & Caselli

Halo: Fall of Reach - Covenant #2 © Microsoft

	GD 2.0	VG 4.0	FN 6.0	VF 8.0	VF/NM 9.0	NM- 9.2

GUNWITCH, THE : OUTSKIRTS OF DOOM (See The Nocturnals)
Oni Press: June, 2001 - No. 3, Oct, 2001 ($2.95, B&W, limited series)

1-3-Brereton-s/painted-c/Naifeh-s 3.00

GUY GARDNER (Guy Gardner: Warrior #17 on)(Also see Green Lantern #59)
DC Comics: Oct, 1992 - No. 44, July, 1996 ($1.25/$1.50/$1.75)

1-Staton-c/a(p) begins 4.00
2-24,0,26-30: 6-Guy vs. Hal Jordan. 8-Vs. Lobo-c/story. 15-JLA x-over, begin $1.50-c. 18-Begin 4-part Emerald Fallout story; splash page x-over GL #50. 18-21-Vs. Hal Jordan. 24-(9/94)-Zero Hour. 0-(10/94) 3.00
25 (11/94, $2.50, 52 pgs.) 4.00
29 ($2.95)-Gatefold-c 4.00
29-Variant-c (Edward Hopper's Nighthawks) 3.00
31-44: 31-$1.75-c begins. 40-Gorilla Grodd-c/app. 44-Parallax-app. (1 pg.) 3.00
Annual 1 (1995, $3.50)-Year One story 4.00
Annual 2 (1996, $2.95)-Legends of the Dead Earth story 4.00

GUY GARDNER: COLLATERAL DAMAGE
DC Comics: 2006 - No. 2 ($5.99, square-bound, limited series)

1,2-Howard Chaykin-s/a 6.00

GUY GARDNER REBORN
DC Comics: 1992 - Book 3, 1992 ($4.95, limited series)

1-3: Staton-c/a(p). 1-Lobo-c/cameo. 2,3-Lobo-c/s 5.00

GYPSY COLT
Dell Publishing Co.: No. 568, June, 1954 (one-shot)

Four Color 568--Movie 5 10 15 32 51 70

GYRO GEARLOOSE (See Dynabrite Comics, Walt Disney's C&S #140 & Walt Disney Showcase #18)
Dell Publishing Co.: No. 1047, Nov-Jan/1959-60 - May-July, 1962 (Disney)

Four Color 1047 (No. 1)-All Barks-c/a 14 28 42 98 214 330
Four Color 1095,1184-All by Carl Barks 10 20 30 64 115 165
Four Color 1267-Barks c/a, 4 pgs. 8 16 24 53 89 125
01329-207 (#1, 5-7/62)-Barks-c only (intended as 4-Color 1329?) 6 12 18 41 66 90

HACKER FILES, THE
DC Comics: Aug, 1992 - No. 12, July, 1993 ($1.95)

1-12: 1-Sutton-a(p) begins; computer generated-c 3.00

HACK/SLASH
Devil's Due Publishing: Apr. 2004 - No. 32, Mar, 2010 ($3.25/$4.95)

1-Seeley-s/Caselli-a/c 5.00
...: (The Series) 1-24,26-32 (5/07-No. 32, 3/10, $3.50) Flashack to Cassie's childhood and origin. 12-Milk & Cheese cameo. 15-Re-Animator app. 3.50
25-($5.50) Double sized issue; Baugh-a; two covers 5.50
...: Comic Book Carnage (3/05) Manfredi-a/Seeley-s; Robert Kirkman & Steve Niles app. 5.00
...: First Cut TPB (10/05, $14.95) r/one-shots with sketch pages, designs, interviews 15.00
...: Girls Gone Dead (10/04, $4.95) Manfredi-a/Seeley-s 5.00
...: Land of Lost Toys 1-3 (11/05 - No. 3, 1/06, $3.25) Crossland-a/Seeley-s 3.25
...: New Reader Halloween Treat #1 (10/08, $3.50) origin retold; Cassie's diary pages 3.50
...: The Final Revenge of Evil Ernie (6/05, $4.95) Salman-a/Seeley-s; two covers 5.00
...: Trailers (2/05, $3.25) short stories by Seeley; art by various; three covers 3.25
...: Slice Hard (12/05, $4.95) Seeley-s 5.00
...: Slice Hard Pre-Sliced 25¢ Special (2/06, 25¢) origin story by Seeley; sketch pages 3.00
...: Vs Chucky (3/07, $5.50) Seeley-s/Merhoff-a; 3 covers 5.50
...: Vol. 2 Death By Sequel TPB (1/07, $18.99) r/Land of Lost Toys #1-3, Trailers, Slice Hard 19.00
...: Vol. 3 Friday the 31st TPB (10/07, $18.99) r/The Series #1-4 & ... Vs Chucky 19.00

HACK/SLASH
Image Comics: Jun, 2010 - Present ($3.50)

1-13: 1-(2/11, $3.50) Seeley-s/Leister-a. 5-Esquejo-c. 9-11-Bomb Queen app. 3.50
... Annual 2010: Murder Messiah (10/10, $5.99) Seeley-s/Morales-a 6.00
... Annual 2011: Hatchet/Slash (11/11, $5.99) 6.00
.../ Eva: Monster's Ball 1-4 (Dynamite Ent., 2011 - No. 4, 2011, $3.99) Jerwa-s/Razek-a 4.00
...: Me Without You (1/11, $3.50) Leister-a/Seeley-s; 2 covers 3.50
...: My First Maniac 1-4 (6/10- No. 4, 9/10) Leister-a/Seeley-s 3.50
...: Trailers #2 (11/10, $6.99) short stories; story & art by various; Seeley-c 7.00
Image Firsts: Hack/Slash #1 (10/10, $1.00) r/#1 (2004) with "Image Firsts" cover frame 3.00

HAGAR THE HORRIBLE (See Comics Reading Libraries in the Promotional Comics section)

HA HA COMICS (Teepee Tim No. 100 on; also see Giggle Comics)
Scope Mag.(Creston Publ.) No. 1-80/American Comics Group: Oct, 1943 - No. 99, Jan, 1955

1-Funny animal 36 72 108 211 343 475
2 18 36 54 107 169 230
3-5: Ken Hultgren-a begins? 14 28 42 80 115 150
6-10 12 24 36 67 94 120
11-20: 14-Infinity-c 10 20 30 58 79 100
21-40 9 18 27 50 65 80
41-43,45-94,97-99: 49,61-X-Mas-c 8 16 24 44 57 70
44-1st Tee-Pee Tim app.; begin series; Little Black Sambo app. 9 18 27 47 61 75
95,96-3-D effect-c/story 16 32 48 94 147 200

HAIR BEAR BUNCH, THE (TV) (See Fun-In No. 13)
Gold Key: Feb, 1972 - No. 9, Feb, 1974 (Hanna-Barbera)

1 4 8 12 24 37 50
2-9 3 6 9 17 25 32

HALCYON
Image Comics: Nov, 2010 - No. 5, May, 2011 ($2.99)

1-5-Guggenheim & Butters-s/Bodenheim-a 3.00

HALF DEAD
Marvel Comics (Dabel Brothers Prods.): March, 2007 ($10.99, softcover, graphic novel)

SC-Barb Lien-Cooper & Park Cooper-s/Jimmy Bott-a 11.00

HALLELUJAH TRAIL, THE (See Movie Classics)

HALL OF FAME FEATURING THE T.H.U.N.D.E.R. AGENTS
JC Productions(Archie Comics Group): May, 1983 - No. 3, Dec, 1983

1-3: Thunder Agents-r(Crandall, Kane, Tuska, Wood-a). 2-New Ditko-c 3.00

HALLOWEEN (Movie)
Chaos! Comics: Nov, 2000; Apr, 2001 ($2.95/$2.99, one-shots)

1-Brewer-a; Michael Myers childhood at the Sanitarium 3.00
...II: The Blackest Eyes (4/01, $2.99) Beck-a 3.00
...III: The Devil's Eyes (11/01, $2.99) Justiniano-a 3.00

HALLOWEEN (Halloween Nightdance on cover)(Movie)
Devils Due Publishing: Mar, 2008 - No. 4, May, 2008 ($3.50, limited series)

1-4-Seeley-a/Hutchinson-s; multiple covers on each 3.50
...: 30 Years of Terror (8/08, $5.50) short stories by various incl. Seeley 5.50

HALLOWEEN HORROR
Eclipse Comics: Oct, 1987 (Seduction of the Innocent #7)($1.75)

1-Pre-code horror-r 4.00

HALLOWEEN MEGAZINE
Marvel Comics: Dec, 1996 ($3.95, one-shot, 96 pgs.)

1-Reprints Tomb of Dracula 4.00

HALO GRAPHIC NOVEL (Based on video game)
Marvel Publishing Inc.: 2006 ($24.99, hardcover with dust jacket)

HC-Anthology set in the Halo universe; art by Bisley, Moebius and others; pin-up gallery by various incl. Darrow, Pratt, Williams and Van Fleet; Phil Hale painted-c 25.00

HALO: BLOOD LINE (Based on video game)
Marvel Comics: Feb, 2010 - No. 5, Jul, 2010 ($3.99, limited series)

1-5-Van Lente-s/Portela-a 4.00

HALO: FALL OF REACH - BOOT CAMP (Based on video game)
Marvel Comics: Nov, 2010 - No. 4, Apr, 2011 ($3.99, limited series)

1-4-Reed-s/Ruiz-a 4.00

HALO: FALL OF REACH - COVENANT (Based on video game)
Marvel Comics: Jun, 2011 - No. 4, Dec, 2011 ($3.99, limited series)

1-4-Reed-s/Ruiz-a 4.00

HALO: FALL OF REACH - INVASION (Based on video game)
Marvel Comics: Mar, 2012 - No. 4, ($3.99, limited series)

1,2-Reed-s/Ruiz-a 4.00

HALO: HELLJUMPER (Based on video game)
Marvel Comics: Sept, 2009 - No. 5, Jan, 2010 ($3.99, limited series)

1-5-Peter David-s/Eric Nguyen-a 4.00

HALO: UPRISING (Based on video game) (Also see Marvel Spotlight: Halo)
Marvel Comics: Oct, 2007 - No. 4, Jun, 2009 ($3.99, limited series)

1-4-Bendis-s/Maleev-a; takes place between the *Halo 2* and *Halo 3* video games 4.00

HALO JONES (See The Ballad of...)

HAMMER, THE
Dark Horse Comics: Oct, 1997 - No. 4, Jan, 1998 ($2.95, limited series)

Hammer: The Outsider #1 © Kelley Jones

Hangman Comics #2 © MLJ

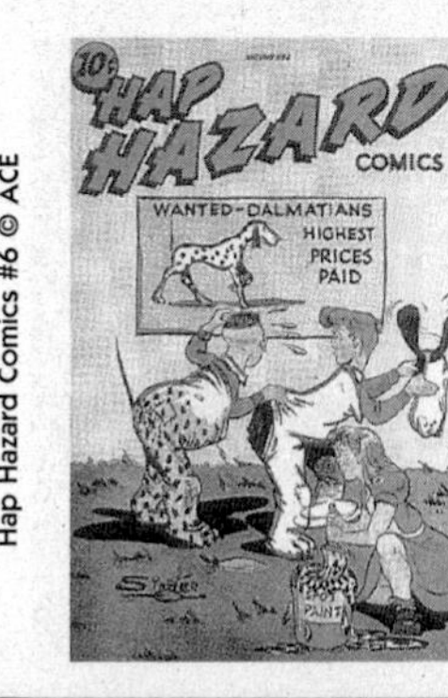

Hap Hazard Comics #6 © ACE

GD 2.0 | VG 4.0 | FN 6.0 | VF 8.0 | VF/NM 9.0 | NM- 9.2

1-4-Kelley Jones-s/c/a, ...: Uncle Alex (8/98, $2.95) 3.00

HAMMER, THE: THE OUTSIDER
Dark Horse Comics: Feb, 1999 - No. 3, Apr, 1999 ($2.95, limited series)
1-3-Kelley Jones-s/c/a 3.00

HAMMERLOCKE
DC Comics: Sept, 1992 - No. 9, May, 1993 ($1.75, limited series)
1-($2.50, 52 pgs.)-Chris Sprouse-c/a in all 4.00
2-9 3.00

HAMMER OF GOD (Also see Nexus)
First Comics: Feb, 1990 - No. 4, May, 1990 ($1.95, limited series)
1-4 3.00

HAMMER OF GOD: BUTCH
Dark Horse Comics: May, 1994 - No. 4, Aug, 1994 ($2.50, limited series)
1-3 3.00

HAMMER OF GOD: PENTATHLON
Dark Horse Comics: Jan, 1994 ($2.50, one shot)
1-Character from Nexus 3.00

HAMMER OF GOD: SWORD OF JUSTICE
First Comics: Feb 1991 - Mar 1991 ($4.95, lim. series, squarebound, 52 pgs.)
V2#1,2 5.00

HAMMER OF THE GODS
Insight Studio Groups: 2001 - No. 5, 2001 ($2.95, limited series)
1-Michael Oeming & Mark Wheatley-s/a; Frank Cho-c 6.00
1-(IDW, 7/11, $1.00) reprints #1 with "Hundred Penny Press" logo on Oeming cover 3.00
2-5: 3-Hughes-c. 5-Dave Johnson-c 3.00
The Color Saga (2002, $4.95) r/"Enemy of the Gods" internet strip 5.00
Mortal Enemy TPB (2002, $18.95) r/#1-5; intro. by Peter David; afterword by Raven 19.00

HAMMER OF THE GODS: HAMMER HITS CHINA
Image Comics: Feb, 2003 - No. 3, Sept, 2003 ($2.95, limited series)
1-3-Oeming & Wheatley-s/a; Oeming-c. 2-Frankenstein Mobster by Wheatley 3.00

HANDBOOK OF THE CONAN UNIVERSE, THE
Marvel Comics: June, 1985; Jan, 1986 ($1.25, one-shot)
1-(6/85) Kaluta-c (2 printings) 4.00
1-(1/86) Kaluta-c 6.00
nn-(no date, circa '87-88, B&W, 36 pgs.) reprints '86 with changes; new painted cover 1 2 3 5 6 8

HAND OF FATE (Formerly Men Against Crime)
Ace Magazines: No. 8, Dec, 1951 - No. 25, Dec, 1954 (Weird/horror stories) (Two #25's)
8-Surrealistic text story 45 90 135 284 480 675
9,10,21-Necronomicon sty; drug belladonna used 28 56 84 165 270 375
11-18,20,22,23 23 46 69 136 223 310
19-Bondage, hypo needle scenes 24 48 72 144 237 330
24-Electric chair-c 34 68 102 206 336 465
25a(11/54), 25b(12/54)-Both have Cameron-a 19 38 57 109 172 240
NOTE: ***Cameron*** *a-9, 10, 19-25a, 25b; c-13.* ***Sekowsky*** *a-8, 9, 13, 14.*

HAND OF FATE
Eclipse Comics: Feb, 1988 - No. 3, Apr, 1988 ($1.75/$2.00, Baxter paper)
1-3; 3-B&W 3.00

HANDS OF THE DRAGON
Seaboard Periodicals (Atlas): June, 1975
1-Origin/1st app.; Craig-a(p)/Mooney inks 2 4 6 9 13 16

HANGMAN COMICS (Special Comics No. 1; Black Hood No. 9 on)
(Also see Flyman, Mighty Comics, Mighty Crusaders & Pep Comics)
MLJ Magazines: No. 2, Spring, 1942 - No. 8, Fall, 1943
2-The Hangman, Boy Buddies begin 226 452 678 1446 2473 3500
3-Beheading splash pg.; 1st Nazi war-c 213 426 639 1363 2332 3300
4-Classic Nazi WWII hunchback torture-c 194 388 582 1242 2121 3000
5-1st Japan war-c 142 284 426 909 1555 2200
6-8: 8-2nd app. Super Duck (ties w/Jolly Jingles #11) 135 270 405 864 1482 2100
NOTE: ***Fuje*** *a-7(3), 8(3); c-3.* ***Reinman*** *c/a-3. Bondage c-3.* ***Sahle*** *c-6.*

HANK
Pentagon Publishing Co.: 1946
nn-Coulton Waugh's newspaper reprint 8 16 24 44 57 70

HANNA-BARBERA (See Golden Comics Digest No. 2, 7, 11)

HANNA-BARBERA ALL-STARS
Archie Publications: Oct, 1995 - No. 4, Apr, 1996 ($1.50, bi-monthly)
1-4 4.00

HANNA-BARBERA BANDWAGON (TV)
Gold Key: Oct, 1962 - No. 3, Apr, 1963
1-Giant, 84 pgs. 1-Augie Doggie app.; 1st app. Lippy the Lion, Touché Turtle & Dum Dum, Wally Gator, Loopy de Loop, 11 22 33 76 151 225
2-Giant, 84 pgs.; Mr. & Mrs. J. Evil Scientist (1st app.) in Snagglepuss story; Yakky Doodle, Ruff and Reddy and others app. 9 18 27 58 99 140
3-Regular size; Mr. & Mrs. J. Evil Scientist app. (pre-#1), Snagglepuss, Wally Gator and others app. 7 14 21 46 76 105

HANNA-BARBERA GIANT SIZE
Harvey Comics: Oct, 1992 - No. 3 ($2.25, 68 pgs.)
V2#1-3:Flintstones, Yogi Bear, Magilla Gorilla, Huckleberry Hound, Quick Draw McGraw, Yakky Doodle & Chopper, Jetsons & others 6.00

HANNA-BARBERA HI-ADVENTURE HEROES (See Hi-Adventure...)

HANNA-BARBERA PARADE (TV)
Charlton Comics: Sept, 1971 - No. 10, Dec, 1972
1 7 14 21 48 79 110
2,4-10 4 8 12 26 41 55
3-(52 pgs.)- "Summer Picnic" 6 12 18 37 59 80
NOTE: *No. 4 (1/72) went on sale late in 1972 with the January 1973 issues.*

HANNA-BARBERA PRESENTS
Archie Publications: Nov, 1995 - No. 8 ($1.50, bi-monthly)
1-8: 1-Atom Ant & Secret Squirrel. 2-Wacky Races. 3-Yogi Bear. 4-Quick Draw McGraw & Magilla Gorilla. 5-A Pup Named Scooby-Doo. 6-Superstar Olympics. 7-Wacky Races. 8-Frankenstein Jr. & the Impossibles 3.00

HANNA-BARBERA SPOTLIGHT (See Spotlight)

HANNA-BARBERA SUPER TV HEROES (TV)
Gold Key: Apr, 1968 - No. 7, Oct, 1969 (Hanna-Barbera)
1-The Birdman, The Herculoids (ends #6; not in #3), Moby Dick, Young Samson & Goliath (ends #2,4), and The Mighty Mightor begin; Spiegle-a in all 12 24 36 81 166 250
2-The Galaxy Trio app.; Shazzan begins; 12¢ & 15¢ versions exist 9 18 27 63 112 160
3,6,7-The Space Ghost app. 9 18 27 58 99 140
4,5 8 16 24 51 86 120
NOTE: *Birdman in #1,2,4,5. Herculoids in #2,4-7. Mighty Mightor in #1,2,4-7. Moby Dick in all. Shazzan in #2-5. Young Samson & Goliath in #1,3.*

HANNA-BARBERA TV FUN FAVORITES (See Golden Comics Digest #2,7,11)

HANNA-BARBERA (TV STARS) (See TV Stars)

HANS BRINKER (Disney)
Dell Publishing Co.: No. 1273, Feb, 1962 (one-shot)
Four Color 1273-Movie, photo-c 6 12 18 42 69 95

HANS CHRISTIAN ANDERSEN
Ziff-Davis Publ. Co.: 1953 (100 pgs., Special Issue)
nn-Danny Kaye (movie)-Photo-c; fairy tales 16 32 48 94 147 200

HANSEL & GRETEL
Dell Publishing Co.: No. 590, Oct, 1954 (one-shot)
Four Color 590-Partial photo-c 6 12 18 42 69 95

HANSI, THE GIRL WHO LOVED THE SWASTIKA
Spire Christian Comics (Fleming H. Revell Co.): 1973, 1976 (39¢/49¢)
1973 edition with 39¢-c 8 16 24 51 86 120
1976 edition with 49¢-c 6 12 18 37 59 80

HAP HAZARD COMICS (Real Love No. 25 on)
Ace Magazines (Readers' Research): Summer, 1944 - No. 24, Feb, 1949
(#1-6 are quarterly issues)
1 15 30 45 84 127 170
2 9 18 27 52 69 85
3-10 8 16 24 44 57 70
11-13,15-24 8 16 24 40 50 60
14-Feldstein-c (4/47) 10 20 30 56 76 95

HAP HOPPER (See Comics Revue No. 2)

HAPPIEST MILLIONAIRE, THE (See Movie Comics)

HAPPI TIM (See March of Comics No. 182)

Harbinger #5 © VAL

Hardcase #21 © MAL
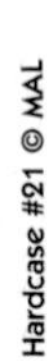

Harlem Globetrotters #10 © H-B

	GD 2.0	VG 4.0	FN 6.0	VF 8.0	VF/NM 9.0	NM- 9.2

HAPPY BIRTHDAY MARTHA WASHINGTON (Also see Give Me Liberty, Martha Washington Goes To War, & Martha Washington Stranded In Space)
Dark Horse Comics: Mar, 1995 ($2.95, one-shot)

1-Miller script; Gibbons-c/a 3.00

HAPPY COMICS (Happy Rabbit No. 41 on)
Nedor Publ./Standard Comics (Animated Cartoons): Aug, 1943 - No. 40, Dec, 1950 (Companion to Goofy Comics)

	GD	VG	FN	VF	VF/NM	NM-
1-Funny animal	27	54	81	158	259	360
2	15	30	45	86	133	180
3-10	12	24	36	67	94	120
11-19	10	20	30	54	72	90
20-31,34-37-Frazetta text illos in all (2 in #34&35, 3 in #27,28,30). 27-Al Fago-a	11	22	33	64	90	115
32-Frazetta-a, 7 pgs. plus 2 text illos; Roussos-a	20	40	60	120	195	270
33-Frazetta-a(2), 6 pgs. each (Scarce)	28	56	84	165	270	375
38-40	9	18	27	47	61	75

HAPPYDALE: DEVILS IN THE DESERT
DC Comics (Vertigo): 1999 - No. 2, 1999 ($6.95, limited series)

1,2-Andrew Dabb-s/Seth Fisher-a 7.00

HAPPY DAYS (TV)(See Kite Fun Book)
Gold Key: Mar, 1979 - No. 6, Feb, 1980

	GD	VG	FN	VF	VF/NM	NM-
1-Photo-c of TV cast; 35¢-c	3	6	9	16	23	30
2-6-(40¢-c)	2	4	6	9	12	15

HAPPY HOLIDAY (See March of Comics No. 181)

HAPPY HOULIHANS (Saddle Justice No. 3 on; see Blackstone, The Magician Detective)
E. C. Comics: Fall, 1947 - No. 2, Winter, 1947-48

	GD	VG	FN	VF	VF/NM	NM-
1-Origin Moon Girl (same date as Moon Girl #1)	57	114	171	362	619	875
2	32	64	96	192	314	435

HAPPY JACK
Red Top (Decker): Aug, 1957 - No. 2, Nov, 1957

	GD	VG	FN	VF	VF/NM	NM-
V1#1,2	5	10	15	22	26	30

HAPPY JACK HOWARD
Red Top (Farrell)/Decker: 1957

	GD	VG	FN	VF	VF/NM	NM-
nn-Reprints Handy Andy story from E. C. Dandy Comics #5, renamed "Happy Jack"	5	10	15	22	26	30

HAPPY RABBIT (Formerly Happy Comics)
Standard Comics (Animated Cartoons): No. 41, Feb, 1951 - No. 48, Apr, 1952

	GD	VG	FN	VF	VF/NM	NM-
41-Funny animal	8	16	24	44	57	70
42-48	7	14	21	35	43	50

HARBINGER (Also see Unity)
Valiant: Jan, 1992 - No. 41, June, 1995 ($1.95/$2.50)

	GD	VG	FN	VF	VF/NM	NM-
0-Prequel to the series; available by redeeming coupons in #1-6; cover image has pink sky; title logo is blue	4	8	12	24	37	50
0-(2nd printing) cover has blue sky & red logo						5.00
1-1st app.	2	4	6	8	10	12
2-4: 4-Low print run	1	2	3	5	7	9
5,6: 5-Solar app. 6-Torque dies	1	2	3	4	5	7
7-10: 8,9-Unity x-overs. 8-Miller-c. 9-Simonson-c. 10-1st app. H.A.R.D Corps (10/92)						5.00
11-24,26-41: 14-1st app. Stronghold. 18-Intro Screen. 19-1st app. Stunner. 22-Archer & Armstrong app. 24-Cover similar to #1. 26-Intro New Harbingers. 29-Bound-in trading card. 30-H.A.R.D. Corps app. 32-Eternal Warrior app. 33-Dr. Eclipse app.						3.00
25-($3.50, 52 pgs.)-Harada vs. Sting						4.00
...Files 1,2 (8/94,2/95 $2.50)						3.00
...: The Beginning HC (2007, $24.95) recolored reprints #0-7 and Story of Harada from coupons from #1-6; new "Origin of Harada" story by Shooter and Bob Hall						25.00
Trade paperback nn (11/92, $9.95)-Reprints #1-4 & comes polybagged with a copy of Harbinger #0 w/new-c. Price for TPB only						10.00

NOTE: *Issues 1-6 have coupons with origin of Harada and are redeemable for Harbinger #0.*

HARD BOILED
Dark Horse Comics: Sept, 1990 - No. 3, Mar, 1992 ($4.95/$5.95, 8 1/2x11", lim. series)

	GD	VG	FN	VF	VF/NM	NM-
1-3-Miller-s; Darrow-c/a; sexually explicit & violent	1	2	3	4	5	7
TPB (5/93, $15.95)						16.00
Big Damn Hard Boiled (12/97, $29.95, B&W) r/#1-3						30.00

HARDCASE (See Break Thru, Flood Relief & Ultraforce, 1st Series)
Malibu Comics (Ultraverse): June, 1993 - No. 26, Aug, 1995 ($1.95/$2.50)

	NM-
1-Intro Hardcase; Dave Gibbons-c; has coupon for Ultraverse Premiere #0; Jim Callahan-a(p) begin, ends #3	3.00
1-With coupon missing	2.00
1-Platinum Edition	4.00
1-Holographic Cover Edition; 1st full-c holograph tied w/Prime 1 & Strangers 1	7.00
1-Ultra Limited silver foil-c	4.00
2,3-Callahan-a, 2-($2.50)-Newsstand edition bagged w/trading card	3.00
4,6-15, 17-19: 4-Strangers app. 7-Break-Thru x-over. 8-Solution app. 9-Vs. Turf. 12-Silver foil logo, wraparound-c. 17-Prime app.	3.00
5-($2.50, 48 pgs.)-Rune flip-c/story by B. Smith (3 pgs.)	4.00
16 ($3.50, 68 pgs.)-Rune pin-up	4.00
20-26: 23-Loki app.	3.00

NOTE: *Perez a-8(2); c-20i.*

HARDCORE STATION
DC Comics: July, 1998 - No. 6, Dec, 1998 ($2.50, limited series)

1-6-Starlin-s/a(p). 3-Green Lantern-c/app. 5,6-JLA-c/app. 3.00

H.A.R.D. CORPS, THE (See Harbinger #10)
Valiant: Dec, 1992 - No. 30, Feb, 1995 ($2.25) (Harbinger spin-off)

	NM-
1-($2.50)-Gatefold-c by Jim Lee & Bob Layton	3.00
1-Gold variant	5.00
2-30: 5-Bloodshot-c/story cont'd from Bloodshot #3. 5-Variant edition; came w/Comic Defense System. 10-Turok app. 17-vs. Armorines. 18-Bound-in trading card. 20-Harbinger app.	3.00

HARD TIME
DC Comics (Focus): Apr, 2004 - No. 12, Mar, 2005 ($2.50)

	NM-
1-12-Gerber-s/Hurtt-a; 1-Includes previews of other DC Focus series	3.00
...: 50 to Life (2004, $9.95, TPB) r/#1-6; cover gallery with sketches	10.00

HARD TIME: SEASON TWO
DC Comics: Feb, 2006 - No. 7, Aug, 2006 ($2.50/$2.99)

	NM-
1-5-Gerber-s/Hurtt-a	3.00
6,7-($2.99) 7-Ethan paroled in 2053	3.00

HARDWARE
DC Comics (Milestone): Apr, 1993 - No. 50, Apr, 1997 ($1.50/$1.75/$2.50)

	NM-
1-($2.95)-Collector's Edition polybagged w/poster & trading card (direct sale only)	4.00
1-Platinum Edition	6.00
1-15,17-19: 11-Shadow War x-over. 11,14-Simonson-c. 12-Buckler-a(p). 17-Worlds Collide Pt. 2. 18-Simonson-c; Worlds Collide Pt. 9. 15-1st Humberto Ramos DC work	3.00
16,25: 16-($2.50, 52 pgs.)-Newsstand Ed. 25-($2.95, 52 pgs.)	4.00
16,50-($3.95, 52 pgs.)-16-Collector's Edition w/gatefold 2nd cover by Byrne; new armor; Icon app.	5.00
20-24,26-49: 49-Moebius-c	3.00
...: The Man in the Machine TPB (2010, $19.99) r/#1-8	20.00

HARDY BOYS, THE (Disney
Dell Publ. Co.: No. 760, Dec, 1956 - No. 964, Jan, 1959 (Mickey Mouse Club)

	GD	VG	FN	VF	VF/NM	NM-
Four Color 760 (#1)-Photo-c	10	20	30	66	121	175
Four Color 830(8/57), 887(1/58), 964-Photo-c	9	18	27	58	99	140

HARDY BOYS, THE (TV)
Gold Key: Apr, 1970 - No. 4, Jan, 1971

	GD	VG	FN	VF	VF/NM	NM-
1	4	8	12	28	44	60
2-4	3	6	9	18	27	35

HARLAN ELLISON'S DREAM CORRIDOR
Dark Horse Comics: Mar, 1995 - No. 5, July, 1995 ($2.95, anthology)

	NM-
1-5: Adaptation of Ellison stories. 1-4-Byrne-a.	3.00
Special (1/95, $4.95)	5.00
Trade paperback-(1996, $18.95, 192 pgs)-r/#1-5 & Special #1	19.00

HARLAN ELLISON'S DREAM CORRIDOR QUARTERLY
Dark Horse Comics: V2#1, Aug, 1996 ($5.95, anthology, squarebound)

	NM-
V2#1-Adaptations of Ellison's stories w/new material; Neal Adams-a	6.00
Volume 2 TPB (3/07, $19.95) r/V2#1 and unpublished material incl. last Swan-a	20.00

HARLEM GLOBETROTTERS (TV) (See Fun-In No. 8, 10)
Gold Key: Apr, 1972 - No. 12, Jan, 1975 (Hanna-Barbera)

	GD	VG	FN	VF	VF/NM	NM-
1	4	8	12	26	41	55
2-5	3	6	9	16	22	28
6-12	2	4	6	13	18	22

NOTE: *#4, 8, and 12 contain 16 extra pages of advertising.*

HARLEQUIN ROMANCE
Dark Horse Comics: Nov, 2001 ($10.95, hardcover, one-shot)

nn-Neil Gaiman-s; painted-a/c by John Bolton 11.00

HARLEY QUINN (Also see Gotham City Sirens)
DC Comics: Dec, 2000 - No. 38, Jan, 2004 ($2.95/$2.25/$2.50)

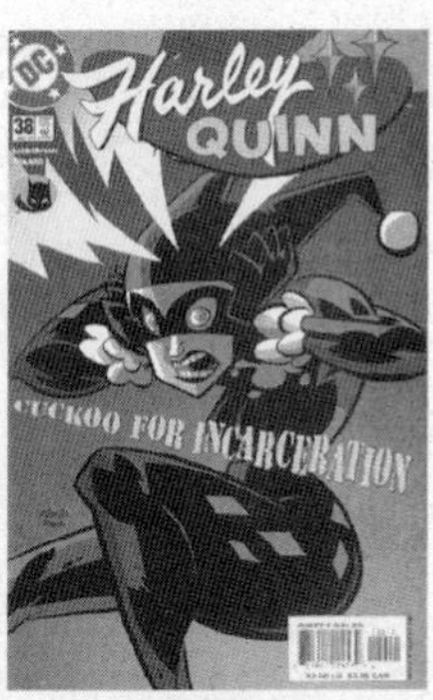
Harley Quinn #38 © DC

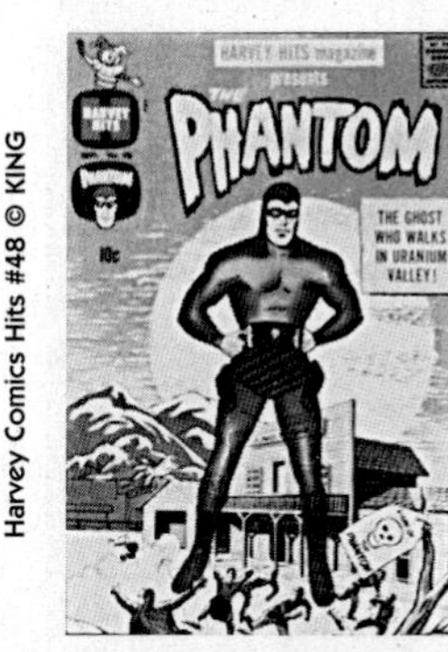

Harvey Comics Hits #48 © KING

Harvey Hits #14 © HARV

	GD 2.0	VG 4.0	FN 6.0	VF 8.0	VF/NM 9.0	NM- 9.2
1-Joker and Poison Ivy app.; Terry & Rachel Dodson-a/c						6.00
2-11-($2.25). 2-Two-Face-c/app. 3-Slumber party. 6,7-Riddler app.						3.00
12-($2.95) Batman app.						4.00
13-38: 13-Joker: Last Laugh. 17,18-Bizarro-c/app. 23-Begin $2.50-c. 23,24-Martian Manhunter app. 25,32-Joker-c/app.						3.00
Harley & Ivy: Love on the Lam (2001, $5.95) Winick-s/Chiodo-c/a						6.00
...: Our Worlds at War (10/01, $2.95) Jae Lee-c; art by various						3.00

HAROLD TEEN (See Popular Comics, & Super Comics)
Dell Publishing Co.: No. 2, 1942 - No. 209, Jan, 1949

	GD	VG	FN	VF	VF/NM	NM-
Four Color 2	27	54	81	191	413	635
Four Color 209	6	12	18	39	62	85

HARROWERS, THE (See Clive Barker's...)

HARSH REALM (Inspired 1999 TV series)
Harris Comics: 1993- No. 6, 1994 ($2.95, limited series)

	GD	VG	FN	VF	VF/NM	NM-
1-6: Painted-c. Hudnall-s/Paquette & Ridgway-a						3.50
TPB (2000, $14.95) r/series						15.00

HARVEY
Marvel Comics: Oct, 1970; No. 2, 12/70; No. 3, 6/72 - No. 6, 12/72

	GD	VG	FN	VF	VF/NM	NM-
1	10	20	30	67	124	180
2-6	7	14	21	46	76	105

HARVEY COLLECTORS COMICS (Titled Richie Rich Collectors Comics on cover of #6-on)
Harvey Publ.: Sept, 1975 - No. 15, Jan, 1978; No. 16, Oct, 1979 (52 pgs.)

	GD	VG	FN	VF	VF/NM	NM-
1-Reprints Richie Rich #1,2	2	4	6	13	18	22
2-10: 7-Splash pg. shows cover to Friendly Ghost Casper #1	2	4	6	8	11	14
11-16: 16-Sad Sack-r	1	2	3	5	7	9

NOTE: *All reprints: Casper-#2, 7, Richie Rich-#1, 3, 5, 6, 8-15, Sad Sack-#16. Wendy-#4.*

HARVEY COMICS HITS (Formerly Joe Palooka #50)
Harvey Publications: No. 51, Oct, 1951 - No. 62, Apr, 1953

	GD	VG	FN	VF	VF/NM	NM-
51-The Phantom	31	62	93	184	300	415
52-Steve Canyon's Air Power(Air Force sponsored)	13	26	39	72	101	130
53-Mandrake the Magician	20	40	60	114	182	250
54-Tim Tyler's Tales of Jungle Terror	13	26	39	74	105	135
55-Love Stories of Mary Worth	11	22	33	62	86	110
56-The Phantom; bondage-c	26	52	78	154	252	350
57-Rip Kirby Exposes the Kidnap Racket; entire book by Alex Raymond	15	30	45	85	130	175
58-Girls in White (nurses stories)	11	22	33	62	86	110
59-Tales of the Invisible featuring Scarlet O'Neil	12	24	36	67	94	120
60-Paramount Animated Comics #1 (9/52) (3rd app. Baby Huey); 2nd Harvey app. Baby Huey & Casper the Friendly Ghost (1st in Little Audrey #25 (8/52)); 1st app. Herman & Catnip (c/story) & Buzzy the Crow	46	92	138	290	488	685
61-Casper the Friendly Ghost #6 (3rd Harvey Casper, 10/52)-Casper-c	47	94	141	296	498	700
62-Paramount Animated Comics #2; Herman & Catnip, Baby Huey & Buzzy the Crow	17	34	51	98	154	210

HARVEY COMICS LIBRARY
Harvey Publications: Apr, 1952 - No. 2, 1952

	GD	VG	FN	VF	VF/NM	NM-
1-Teen-Age Dope Slaves as exposed by Rex Morgan, M.D.; drug propaganda story; used in **SOTI**, pg. 27	181	362	543	1158	1979	2800
2-Dick Tracy Presents Sparkle Plenty in "Blackmail Terror"	20	40	60	114	182	250

HARVEY COMICS SPOTLIGHT
Harvey Comics: Sept, 1987 - No. 4, Mar, 1988 (75¢/$1.00)

	GD	VG	FN	VF	VF/NM	NM-
1-New material; begin 75¢, ends #3; Sand Sack						5.00
2-4: 2,4-All new material. 2-Baby Huey. 3-Little Dot; contains reprints w/5 pg. new story. 4-$1.00-c; Little Audrey						4.00

NOTE: No. 5 was advertised but not published.

HARVEY HITS (Also see Tastee-Freez Comics in the Promotional Comics section)
Harvey Publications: Sept, 1957 - No. 122, Nov, 1967

	GD	VG	FN	VF	VF/NM	NM-
1-The Phantom	23	46	69	164	350	535
2-Rags Rabbit (10/57)	5	10	15	34	55	75
3-Richie Rich (11/57)-r/Little Dot; 1st book devoted to Richie Rich; see Little Dot for 1st app.	130	260	390	1053	2277	3500
4-Little Dot's Uncles (12/57)	14	28	42	97	211	325
5-Stevie Mazie's Boy Friend (1/58)	4	8	12	28	44	60
6-The Phantom (2/58); Kirby-c; 2pg. Powell-a	15	30	45	102	221	340
7-Wendy the Good Little Witch (3/58, pre-dates Wendy #1; 1st book devoted to Wendy)	27	54	81	189	407	625
8-Sad Sack's Army Life; George Baker-c	7	14	21	49	82	115
9-Richie Rich's Golden Deeds; (2nd book devoted to Richie Rich) reprints Richie Rich story from Tastee-Freez #1	52	104	156	421	911	1400
10-Little Lotta's Lunch Box	11	22	33	71	136	200
11-Little Audrey Summer Fun (7/58)	9	18	27	58	99	140
12-The Phantom; Kirby-c; 2pg. Powell-a (8/58)	13	26	39	85	180	275
13-Little Dot's Uncles (9/58); Richie Rich 1pg.	11	22	33	71	136	200
14-Herman & Katnip (10/58, TV/movies)	4	8	12	28	44	60
15-The Phantom (12/58)-1 pg. origin	13	26	39	85	180	275
16-Wendy the Good Little Witch (1/59); Casper app.	11	22	33	73	142	210
17-Sad Sack's Army Life (2/59)	6	12	18	39	62	85
18-Buzzy & the Crow	4	8	12	26	41	55
19-Little Audrey (4/59)	6	12	18	37	59	80
20-Casper & Spooky	8	16	24	51	86	120
21-Wendy the Witch	8	16	24	51	86	120
22-Sad Sack's Army Life	5	10	15	30	48	65
23-Wendy the Witch (8/59)	8	16	24	52	86	120
24-Little Dot's Uncles (9/59); Richie Rich 1pg.	9	18	27	58	99	140
25-Herman & Katnip (10/59)	4	8	12	22	34	45
26-The Phantom (11/59)	10	20	30	68	127	185
27-Wendy the Good Little Witch (12/59)	7	14	21	49	82	115
28-Sad Sack's Army Life (1/60)	4	8	12	26	41	55
29-Harvey-Toon (No.1)('60); Casper, Buzzy	5	10	15	34	55	75
30-Wendy the Witch (3/60)	7	14	21	49	82	115
31-Herman & Katnip (4/60)	3	6	9	20	30	40
32-Sad Sack's Army Life (5/60)	4	8	12	22	34	45
33-Wendy the Witch (6/60)	7	14	21	46	76	105
34-Harvey-Toon (7/60)	4	8	12	24	37	50
35-Funday Funnies (8/60)	3	6	9	20	30	40
36-The Phantom (1960)	10	20	30	65	118	170
37-Casper & Nightmare	6	12	18	37	59	80
38-Harvey-Toon	4	8	12	24	37	50
39-Sad Sack's Army Life (12/60)	3	6	9	21	32	42
40-Funday Funnies (1/61)	3	6	9	17	25	32
41-Herman & Katnip	3	6	9	17	25	32
42-Harvey-Toon (3/61)	3	6	9	19	29	38
43-Sad Sack's Army Life (4/61)	3	6	9	19	29	38
44-The Phantom (5/61)	9	18	27	63	112	160
45-Casper & Nightmare	5	10	15	30	48	65
46-Harvey-Toon (7/61)	3	6	9	17	25	32
47-Sad Sack's Army Life (8/61)	3	6	9	17	25	32
48-The Phantom (9/61)	9	18	27	63	112	160
49-Stumbo the Giant (1st app. in Hot Stuff)	9	18	27	63	112	160
50-Harvey-Toon (11/61)	3	6	9	16	23	30
51-Sad Sack's Army Life (12/61)	3	6	9	16	23	30
52-Casper & Nightmare	4	8	12	28	44	60
53-Harvey-Toons (2/62)	3	6	9	16	23	30
54-Stumbo the Giant	5	10	15	34	55	75
55-Sad Sack's Army Life (4/62)	3	6	9	16	23	30
56-Casper & Nightmare	4	8	12	26	41	55
57-Stumbo the Giant	5	10	15	34	55	75
58-Sad Sack's Army Life	3	6	9	16	23	30
59-Casper & Nightmare (7/62)	4	8	12	26	41	55
60-Stumbo the Giant (9/62)	5	10	15	34	55	75
61-Sad Sack's Army Life	3	6	9	16	22	28
62-Casper & Nightmare	4	8	12	23	36	48
63-Stumbo the Giant	4	8	12	28	44	60
64-Sad Sack's Army Life (1/63)	3	6	9	16	22	28
65-Casper & Nightmare	4	8	12	23	36	48
66-Stumbo The Giant (3/63)	4	8	12	28	44	60
67-Sad Sack's Army Life (4/63)	3	6	9	16	22	28
68-Casper & Nightmare	4	8	12	23	36	48
69-Stumbo the Giant (6/63)	4	8	12	28	44	60
70-Sad Sack's Army Life (7/63)	3	6	9	16	22	28
71-Casper & Nightmare (8/63)	3	6	9	21	32	42
72-Stumbo the Giant	4	8	12	28	44	60
73-Little Sad Sack (10/63)	3	6	9	16	22	28
74-Sad Sack's Muttsy... (11/63)	3	6	9	16	22	28
75-Casper & Nightmare	3	6	9	19	29	38
76-Little Sad Sack	3	6	9	16	22	28
77-Sad Sack's Muttsy...	3	6	9	16	22	28
78-Stumbo the Giant (3/64); JFK caricature	4	8	12	28	44	60

79-87: 79-Little Sad Sack (4/64). 80-Sad Sack's Muttsy... (5/64). 81-Little Sad Sack. 82-Sad Sack's Muttsy... 83-Little Sad Sack(8/64). 84-Sad Sack's Muttsy... 85-Gabby Gob (#1)

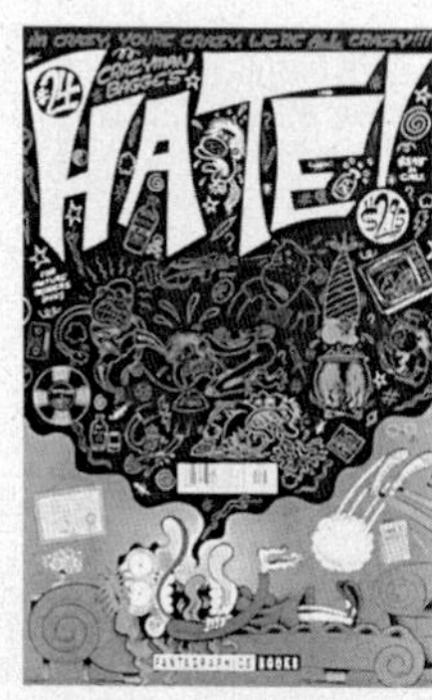

Hate #24 © Peter Bagge

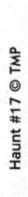

Haunt #17 © TMP

The Haunt of Fear #5 © WMG

GD VG FN VF VF/NM NM-
2.0 4.0 6.0 8.0 9.0 9.2

(10/64). 86-G. I. Juniors (#1)(11/64). 87-Sad Sack's Muttsy... (12/64)
3 6 9 16 22 28
88-Stumbo the Giant (1/65) 4 8 12 28 44 60
89-122: 89-Sad Sack's Muttsy... 90-Gabby Gob. 91-G. I. Juniors. 92-Sad Sack's Muttsy... (5/65). 93-Sadie Sack (6/65). 94-Gabby Gob. 95-G. I. Juniors (8/65). 96-Sad Sack's Muttsy... (9/65). 97-Gabby Gob (10/65). 98-G. I. Juniors (11/65). 99-Sad Sack's Muttsy... (12/65). 100-Gabby Gob(1/66). 101-G. I. Juniors (2/66). 102-Sad Sack's Muttsy... (3/66). 103-Gabby Gob. 104- G. I. Juniors. 105-Sad Sack's Muttsy... 106-Gabby Gob (7/66). 107-G. I. Juniors (8/66). 108-Sad Sack's Muttsy...109-Gabby Gob. 110-G. I. Juniors (11/66). 111-Sad Sack's Muttsy... (12/66). 112-G. I. Juniors. 113-Sad Sack's Muttsy... 114-G. I. Juniors. 115-Sad Sack's Muttsy... 116-G. I. Juniors (5/67). 117-Sad Sack's Muttsy... 118-G. I. Juniors. 119-Sad Sack's Muttsy... (8/67). 120-G. I. Juniors (9/67). 121-Sad Sack's Muttsy... (10/67). 122-G. I. Juniors (11/67) 2 4 6 10 14 18

HARVEY HITS COMICS
Harvey Publications: Nov, 1986 - No. 6, Oct, 1987
1-Little Lotta, Little Dot, Wendy & Baby Huey 1 2 3 4 5 7
2-6: 3-Xmas-c 4.50

HARVEY POP COMICS (Rock Happening) (Teen Humor)
Harvey Publications: Oct, 1968 - No. 2, Nov, 1969 (Both are 68 pg. Giants)
1-The Cowsills 6 12 18 39 62 85
2-Bunny 5 10 15 34 55 75

HARVEY 3-D HITS (See Sad Sack)

HARVEY-TOON (...S) (See Harvey Hits No. 29, 34, 38, 42, 46, 50, 53)

HARVEY WISEGUYS (...Digest #? on)
Harvey Comics: Nov, 1987; #2, Nov, 1988; #3, Apr, 1989 - No. 4, Nov, 1989 (98 pgs., digest-size, $1.25/$1.75)
1-Hot Stuff, Spooky, etc. 2 3 4 6 8 10
2-4: 2 (68 pgs.) 1 2 3 4 5 7

HATARI (See Movie Classics)

HATE
Fantagraphics Books: Spr, 1990 - No. 30, 1998 ($2.50/$2.95, B&W/color)
1 2 4 6 10 12 15
2-3 1 2 3 5 6 8
4-10 5.00
11-20: 16- color begins 4.00
21-29 3.00
30-($3.95) Last issue 4.00
Annual 1 (2/01, $3.95) Peter Bagge-s/a 5.00
Annual 2-9 (12/01-Present; $4.95) Peter Bagge-s/a 5.00
Buddy Bites the Bullet! (2001, $16.95) r/Buddy stories in color 17.00
Buddy Go Home! (1997, $16.95) r/Buddy stories in color 17.00
Hate-Ball Special Edition ($3.95, giveaway)-reprints 4.00
Hate Jamboree (10/98, $4.50) old & new cartoons 4.50

HATHAWAYS, THE (TV)
Dell Publishing Co.: No. 1298, Feb-Apr, 1962 (one-shot)
Four Color 1298-Photo-c 5 10 15 30 48 65

HAUNTED (See This Magazine Is Haunted)

HAUNT
Image Comics: Oct, 2009 - Present ($2.99)
1-McFarlane & Kirkman-s/Capullo & Ottley-a/McFarlane-a(i)/c; two variant-c 4.00
2-21: 2-Two covers. 13-($1.99). 19-21-Casey-s/Fox-a 3.00
Image Firsts: Haunt #1 (10/10, $1.00) r/#1 with "Image First" cover logo 3.00

HAUNTED (Baron Weirwulf's Haunted Library on-c #21 on)
Charlton Comics: 9/71 - No. 30, 11/76; No. 31, 9/77 - No. 75, 9/84
1-All Ditko issue 6 12 18 37 59 80
2-7-Ditko-c/a 3 6 9 20 30 40
8,12,28-Ditko-a 2 4 6 13 18 22
9,19 2 4 6 8 11 14
10,20,15,18: 10,20-Sutton-a. 15-Sutton-c 2 4 6 8 11 14
11,13,14,16-Ditko-c/a 3 6 9 16 22 28
17-Sutton-c/a; Newton-a 2 4 6 9 12 15
21-Newton-c/a; Sutton-a; 1st Baron Weirwulf 3 6 9 17 25 32
22-Newton-c/a; Sutton-a 2 4 6 9 13 16
23,24-Sutton-c; Ditko-a 2 4 6 9 13 16
25-27,29,32,33 1 3 4 6 8 10
30,41,47,49-52,60,74-Ditko-c/a: 51-Reprints #1 2 4 6 11 16 20
31,35,37,38-Sutton-a 1 3 4 6 8 10
34,36,39,40,42,57-Ditko-a 2 4 6 8 10 12

GD VG FN VF VF/NM NM-
2.0 4.0 6.0 8.0 9.0 9.2

43-46,48,53-56,58,59,61-73: 59-Newton-a. 64-Sutton-c. 71-73-Low print
1 2 3 5 6 8
75-(9/84) Last issue; low print 2 4 6 9 13 16
NOTE: *__Aparo__ c-45. __Ditko__ a-1-8, 11-16, 18, 23, 24, 28, 30, 34r, 36r, 39-42r, 47r, 49-52r, 57, 60, 74. c-1-7, 11, 13, 14, 16, 30, 41, 47, 49-52, 74. __Howard__ a-6, 9, 18, 22, 25, 32. __Kim__ a-9, 19. __Morisi__ a-13. __Newton__ a-17, 21, 59r; c-21, 22(painted). __Staton__ a-11, 12, 18, 21, 22, 30, 33, 35, 38; c-18, 33, 38. __Sutton__ a-10, 17, 20-22, 31, 35, 37, 38; c-15, 17, 18, 23(painted), 24(painted), 27, 64r. #49 reprints Tales of the Mysterious Traveler #4.*

HAUNTED, THE
Chaos! Comics: Jan, 2002 - No. 4, Apr, 2002 ($2.99, limited series)
1-4-Peter David-s/Nat Jones-a 3.00
...: Gray Matters (7/02, $2.99) David-s/Jones-a 3.00

HAUNTED CITY
Aspen MLT: No. 0, Aug, 2011 - Present ($2.50)
0-($2.50)-Taylor & Johnson-s/Michael Ryan-a; four covers 3.00
1,2-($3.50) 1-Taylor & Johnson-s/Michael Ryan-a; four covers 3.50

HAUNTED LOVE
Charlton Comics: Apr, 1973 - No. 11, Sept, 1975
1-Tom Sutton-a (16 pgs.) 6 12 18 37 59 80
2,3,6,7,10,11 3 6 9 18 27 35
4,5-Ditko-a 4 8 12 22 34 45
8,9-Newton-c 3 6 9 19 29 38
Modern Comics #1(1978) 2 3 4 6 8 10
NOTE: *__Howard__ a-8i. __Kim__ a-7-9. __Newton__ c-8, 9. __Staton__ a-1-6. __Sutton__ a-1, 3-5, 10, 11.*

HAUNTED TANK, THE
DC Comics (Vertigo): Feb, 2009 - No. 5, June, 2009 ($2.99, limited series)
1-5-Marraffino-s/Flint-a. 1-Two covers by Flint and Joe Kubert 3.00
TPB (2010, $14.99) r/#1-5 15.00

HAUNTED THRILLS (Tales of Horror and Terror)
Ajax/Farrell Publications: June, 1952 - No. 18, Nov-Dec, 1954
1-r/Ellery Queen #1 61 122 183 390 670 950
2-L. B. Cole-a r-/Ellery Queen #1 40 80 120 246 411 575
3,4: 3-Drug use story 37 74 111 222 361 500
5-Classic skull-c 39 78 117 231 378 525
6-10,12: 7-Hitler story. 33 66 99 194 317 440
11-Nazi death camp story 34 68 102 206 336 465
13-18: 18-Lingerie panels. 14-Jesus Christ apps. in story by Webb. 15-Jo-Jo-r
28 56 84 165 270 375
NOTE: *__Kamenish__ art in most issues. __Webb__ a-12.*

HAUNT OF FEAR (Formerly Gunfighter)
E. C. Comics: No. 15, May-June, 1950 - No. 28, Nov-Dec, 1954
15(#1, 1950)(Scarce) 291 582 873 2328 3714 5100
16-1st app. "The Witches Cauldron" & the Old Witch (by Kamen); begin series as hostess of Haunt of Fear 120 240 360 960 1530 2100
17-Origin of Crypt of Terror, Vault of Horror, & Haunt of Fear; used in **SOTI**, pg. 43; last pg. Ingels-a used by N.Y. Legis. Comm.; story "Monster Maker" based on Frankenstein. Old Witch by Feldstein 120 240 360 960 1530 2100
4-Ingels becomes regular artist for Old Witch. 1st Vault Keeper & Crypt Keeper app. in HOF; begin series 77 154 231 616 983 1350
5-Injury-to-eye panel, pg. 4 of Wood story 61 122 183 488 782 1075
6,7,9,10: 6-Crypt Keeper by Feldstein begins. 9-Crypt Keeper by Davis begins. 10-Ingels biog. 48 96 144 384 612 840
8-Classic Feldstein Shrunken Head-c 53 106 159 424 675 925
11,12: Classic Ingels-c; 11-Kamen biog. 12-Feldstein biog.
41 82 123 328 527 725
13,15,16,20: 16-Ray Bradbury adaptation. 20-Feldstein-r/Vault of Horror #12
39 78 117 312 494 675
14-Origin Old Witch by Ingels; classic-Ingels-c 50 100 150 400 638 875
17-Classic Ingels-c 41 82 123 328 527 725
18-Old Witch-c; Ray Bradbury adaptation & biography
41 82 123 328 519 710
19-Used in **SOTI**, ill. "A comic book baseball game" & Senate investigation on juvenile delinq. bondage/decapitation-c 47 94 141 376 601 825
21-27: 23-EC version of the Hansel and Gretel story; **SOTI**, pg. 241 discusses the original Grimm tale in relation to comics. 24-Used in Senate Investigative Report, pg.8. 26-Contains anti-censorship editorial, 'Are you a Red Dupe?' 27-Cannibalism story; Vault Keeper shown reading **SOTI** 28 56 84 224 355 485
28-Low distribution 36 72 108 288 457 625
NOTE: *(Canadian reprints known; see Table of Contents). __Craig__ a-15-17, 5, 7, 10, 12, 13; c-15-17, 5-7. __Crandall__ a-20, 21, 26, 27. __Davis__ a-4-26, 28. __Evans__ a-15-19, 22-25, 27. __Feldstein__ a-15-17, 20; c-4, 8-10. __Ingels__ a-16, 17, 4-28; c-11-28. __Kamen__ a-16, 4, 6, 7, 9-11, 13-19, 21-28. __Krigstein__ a-28. __Kurtzman__ a-15(#1), 17(#3). __Orlando__ a-9, 12. __Wood__ a-15, 16, 4-6.*

The Hawk #4 © Z-D

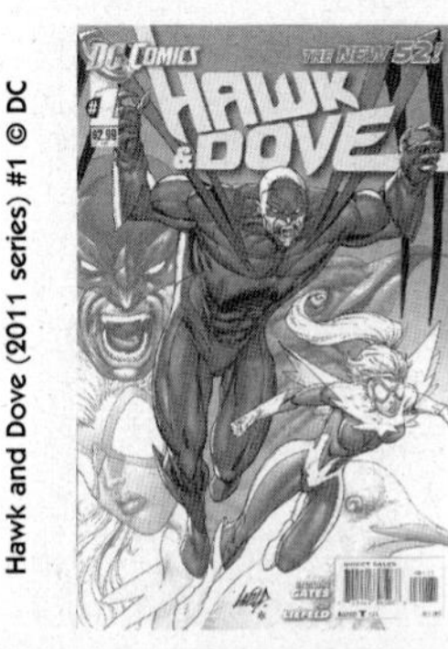

Hawk and Dove (2011 series) #1 © DC

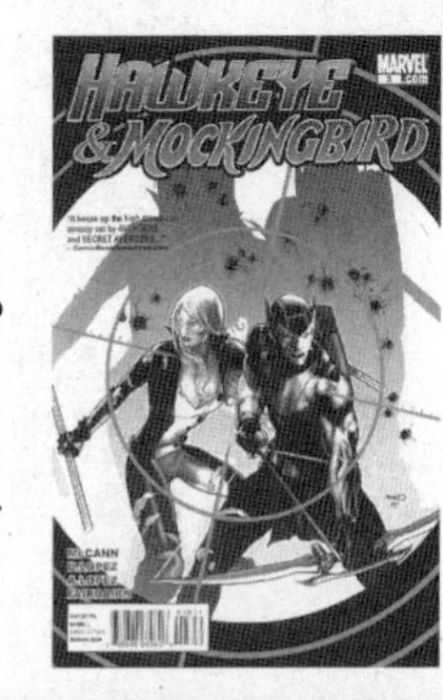

Hawkeye and Mockingbird #3 © MAR

	GD	VG	FN	VF	VF/NM	NM-
	2.0	4.0	6.0	8.0	9.0	9.2

HAUNT OF FEAR, THE
Gladstone Publishing: May, 1991 - No. 2, July, 1991 ($2.00, 68 pgs.)
1,2: 1-Ghastly Ingels-c(r); 2-Craig-c(r) 4.00

HAUNT OF FEAR
Russ Cochran/Gemstone Publ.: Sept, 1991 - No. 5, 1992 ($2.00, 68 pgs.); Nov, 1992 - No. 28, Aug, 1998 ($1.50/$2.00/$2.50)
1-28: 1-Ingels-c(r). 1-3-r/HOF #15-17 with original-c. 4,5-r/HOF #4,5 with original-c 4.00
Annual 1-5: 1- r/#1-5. 2- r/#6-10. 3- r/#11-15. 4- r/#16-20. 5- r/#21-25 14.00
Annual 6-r/#26-28 9.00

HAUNT OF HORROR, THE (Digest)
Marvel Comics: Jun, 1973 - No. 2, Aug, 1973 (164 pgs.; text and art)
1-Morrow painted skull-c; stories by Ellison, Howard, and Leiber; Brunner-a
4 8 12 24 37 50
2-Kelly Freas painted bondage-c; stories by McCaffrey, Goulart, Leiber, Ellison; art by Simonson, Brunner, and Buscema 3 6 9 17 25 32

HAUNT OF HORROR, THE (Magazine)
Cadence Comics Publ. (Marvel): May, 1974 - No. 5, Jan, 1975 (75¢) (B&W)
1,2: 2-Origin & 1st app. Gabriel the Devil Hunter; Satana begins
3 6 9 14 20 26
3-5: 4-Neal Adams-a. 5-Evans-a(2) 3 6 9 18 27 35
NOTE: ***Alcala*** *a-2.* ***Colan*** *a-2p.* ***Heath*** *r-1.* ***Krigstein*** *r-3.* ***Reese*** *a-1.* ***Simonson*** *a-1.*

HAUNT OF HORROR: EDGAR ALLAN POE
Marvel Comics (MAX): July, 2006 - No. 3, Sept, 2006 ($3.99, B&W, limited series)
1-3- Poe-inspired/adapted stories with Richard Corben-a 4.00
HC (2006, $19.99) r/series; cover sketches 20.00

HAUNT OF HORROR: LOVECRAFT
Marvel Comics (MAX): Aug, 2008 - No. 3, Oct, 2008 ($3.99, B&W, limited series)
1-3-Lovecraft-inspired/adapted stories with Richard Corben-a 4.00

HAVE GUN, WILL TRAVEL (TV)
Dell Publishing Co.: No. 931, 8/58 - No. 14, 7-9/62 (All Richard Boone photo-c)
Four Color 931 (#1) 12 24 36 79 160 240
Four Color 983,1044 (#2,3) 9 18 27 58 99 140
4 (1-3/60) - 10 8 16 24 53 89 125
11-14 8 16 24 51 86 120

HAVEN: THE BROKEN CITY (See JLA/Haven: Arrival and JLA/Haven: Anathema)
DC Comics: Feb, 2002 - No. 9, Oct, 2002 ($2.50, limited series)
1-9-Olivetti-c/a: 1- JLA app. Series concludes in JLA/Haven: Anathema 3.00

HAVOK & WOLVERINE - MELTDOWN (See Marvel Comics Presents #24)
Marvel Comics (Epic Comics): Mar, 1989 - No. 4, Oct, 1989 ($3.50, mini-series, squarebound, mature)
1-4: Art by Kent Williams & Jon J. Muth; story by Walt & Louise Simonson 4.00

HAWAIIAN DICK
Image Comics: Dec, 2002 - No. 3, Feb, 2003 ($2.95, limited series)
1-3-B. Clay Moore-s/Steven Griffin-a 3.00
...: Byrd of Paradise TPB (8/03, $14.95) r/#1-3, script & sketch pages 15.00

HAWAIIAN DICK: SCREAMING BLACK THUNDER
Image Comics: Nov, 2007 - No. 5, Oct, 2008 ($2.99, limited series)
1-5-B. Clay Moore-s/Scott Chantler-a 3.00

HAWAIIAN DICK: THE LAST RESORT
Image Comics: Aug, 2004 - No. 4, June, 2006 ($2.95/$2.99, limited series)
1-4-B. Clay Moore-s/Steven Griffin-a 3.00
Vol. 2 TPB (10/06, $14.99) r/#1-4 & the original series pitch 15.00

HAWAIIAN EYE (TV)
Gold Key: July, 1963 (Troy Donahue, Connie Stevens photo-c)
1 (10073-307) 5 10 15 34 55 75

HAWAIIAN ILLUSTRATED LEGENDS SERIES
Hogarth Press: 1975 (B&W)(Cover printed w/blue, yellow, and green)
1-Kalelealuaka, the Mysterious Warrior 5.00

HAWK, THE (Also see Approved Comics #1, 7 & Tops In Adventure)
Ziff-Davis/St. John Publ. Co. No. 4 on: Wint/51 - No. 3, 11-12/52; No. 4, 1-2/53; No. 8, 9/54 - No. 12, 5/55 (Painted c-1-4)(#5-7 don't exist)
1-Anderson-a 20 40 60 114 182 250
2 (Sum, '52)-Kubert, Infantino-a 12 24 36 69 97 125
3-4 10 20 30 56 76 95
8-12: 8(9/54)-Reprints #3 w/different-c by Baker. 9-Baker-c/a; Kubert-a(r)/#2. 10-Baker-c/a; r/one story from #2. 11-Baker-c; Buckskin Belle & The Texan app. 12-Baker-c/a; Buckskin Belle app. 15 30 45 85 130 175
3-D 1(11/53, 25¢)-Came w/glasses; Baker-c 32 64 96 188 307 425
NOTE: ***Baker*** *c-8-12.* ***Larsen*** *a-10.* ***Tuska*** *a-1, 9, 12. Painted c-1, 4, 7.*

HAWK AND THE DOVE, THE (See Showcase #75 & Teen Titans) (1st series)
National Periodical Publications: Aug-Sept, 1968 - No. 6, June-July, 1969
1-Ditko-c/a 8 16 24 53 89 125
2-6: 5-Teen Titans cameo 5 10 15 32 51 70
NOTE: ***Ditko*** *c/a-1, 2.* ***Gil Kane*** *a-3p, 4p, 5, 6p; c-3-6.*

HAWK AND DOVE (2nd Series)
DC Comics: Oct, 1988 - No. 5, Feb, 1989 ($1.00, limited series)
1-Rob Liefeld-c/a(p) in all 4.00
2-5 3.00
Trade paperback ('93, $9.95)-Reprints #1-5 10.00

HAWK AND DOVE
DC Comics: June, 1989 - No. 28, Oct, 1991 ($1.00)
1-28 3.00
Annual 1,2 ('90, '91; $2.00) 1-Liefeld pin-up. 2-Armageddon 2001 x-over 4.00

HAWK AND DOVE
DC Comics: Nov, 1997 - No. 5, Mar, 1998 ($2.50, limited series)
1-5-Baron-s/Zachary & Giordano-a 3.00

HAWK AND DOVE (DC New 52)
DC Comics: Nov, 2011 - No. 8, Jun, 2012 ($2.99)
1-8: 1-Gates-s/Liefeld-a/c; Deadman app. 6-Batman & Robin app.; Liefeld-s/a/c 3.00

HAWK AND WINDBLADE (See Elflord)
Warp Graphics: Aug, 1997 - No.2, Sept, 1997 ($2.95, limited series)
1,2-Blair-s/Chan-c/a 3.00

HAWKEYE (See The Avengers #16 & Tales Of Suspense #57)
Marvel Comics Group: Sept, 1983 - No. 4, Dec, 1983 (limited series)
1-4: Mark Gruenwald-a/scripts. 1-Origin Hawkeye. 3-Origin Mockingbird. 4-Hawkeye & Mockingbird elope 3.00

HAWKEYE
Marvel Comics: Jan, 1994 - No. 4, Apr, 1994 ($1.75, limited series)
1-4 3.00

HAWKEYE (Volume 2)
Marvel Comics: Dec, 2003 - No. 8, Aug, 2004 ($2.99)
1-8: 1-6-Nicieza-s/Raffaele-a. 7,8-Bennett-a; Black Widow app. 3.00

HAWKEYE AND MOCKINGBIRD (Avengers) (Leads into Widowmaker mini-series)
Marvel Comics: Aug, 2010 - No. 6, Jan, 2011 ($3.99/$2.99)
1-($3.99) Heroic Age; Jim McCann-s/David Lopez-a; history of the characters 4.00
2-6-($2.99) Phantom Rider, Dominic Fortune & Crossfire app. 3.00

HAWKEYE & THE LAST OF THE MOHICANS (TV)
Dell Publishing Co.: No. 884, Mar, 1958 (one-shot)
Four Color 884-Lon Chaney Jr. photo-c 7 14 21 46 76 105

HAWKEYE: BLINDSPOT (Avengers)
Marvel Comics: Apr, 2011 - No. 4, Jul, 2011 ($2.99, limited series)
1-4: 1-McCann-s/Diaz-a; Zemo app. 2-Diaz & Dragotta-a 3.00

HAWKEYE: EARTH'S MIGHTIEST MARKSMAN
Marvel Comics: Oct, 1998 ($2.99, one-shot)
1-Justice and Firestar app.; DeFalco-s 3.00

HAWKGIRL (Title continued from Hawkman #49, Apr, 2006)
DC Comics: No. 50, May, 2006 - No. 66, Sept, 2007 ($2.50/$2.99)
50-66: 50-Chaykin-a/Simonson-s begin; One Year Later. 52-Begin $2.99-c. 57,58-Bennett-a. 59-Blackfire app. 63-Batman app. 64-Superman app. 3.00
...: Hath-Set TPB (2008, $17.99) r/#61-66 18.00
...: Hawkman Returns TPB (2007, $17.99) r/#57-60 & JSA Classified #21,22 18.00
...: The Maw TPB (2007, $17.99) r/#50-56 18.00

HAWKMAN (See Atom & Hawkman, The Brave & the Bold, DC Comics Presents, Detective Comics, Flash Comics, Hawkworld, JSA, Justice League of America #31, Legend of the Hawkman, Mystery in Space, Savage Hawkman, Shadow War Of..., Showcase, & World's Finest #256)

HAWKMAN (1st Series) (Also see The Atom #7 & Brave & the Bold #34-36, 42-44, 51)
National Periodical Publications: Apr-May, 1964 - No. 27, Aug-Sept, 1968
1-(4-5/64)-Anderson-c/a begins, ends #21 53 106 159 429 927 1425
2 21 42 63 148 317 485
3,5: 5-2nd app. Shadow Thief 14 28 42 99 200 300

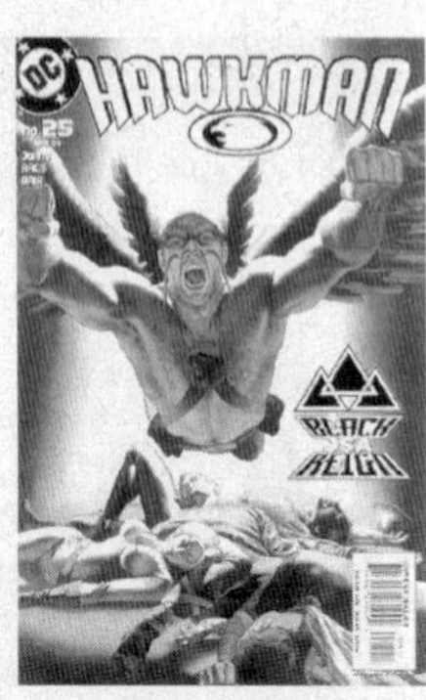

Hawkman (2002 series) #25 © DC

Headline Comics #29 © PRIZE

Heartland #1 © DC

GD VG FN VF VF/NM NM-
2.0 4.0 6.0 8.0 9.0 9.2

4-Origin & 1st app. Zatanna (10-11/64) 17 34 51 114 250 385
6 11 22 33 73 142 210
7 10 20 30 67 124 180
8-10: 9-Atom cameo; Hawkman & Atom learn each other's I.D.; 3rd app. Shadow Thief
9 18 27 61 106 150
11-15 7 14 21 46 76 105
16-27: 18-Adam Strange x-over (cameo #19). 25-G.A. Hawkman-r by Moldoff.
26-Kirby-a(r). 27-Kubert-c 6 12 18 37 59 80

HAWKMAN (2nd Series)
DC Comics: Aug, 1986 - No. 17, Dec, 1987
1-17: 10-Byrne-c, Special #1 (1986, $1.25) 3.00
Trade paperback (1989, $19.95)-r/Brave and the Bold #34-36,42-44 by Kubert; Kubert-c 20.00

HAWKMAN (4th Series)(See both Hawkworld limited & ongoing series)
DC Comics: Sept, 1993 - No. 33, July, 1996 ($1.75/$1.95/$2.25)
1-($2.50)-Gold foil embossed-c; storyline cont'd from Hawkworld ongoing series; new costume & powers. 4.00
2-13,0,14-33: 2-Green Lantern x-over. 3-Airstryke app. 4,6-Wonder Woman app. 13-(9/94)-Zero Hour. 0-(10/94). 14-(11/94). 15-Aquaman-c & app. 23-Wonder Woman app. 25-Kent Williams-c. 29,30-Chaykin-c. 32-Breyfogle-c 3.00
Annual 1 (1993, $2.50, 68 pgs.)-Bloodlines Earthplague 4.00
Annual 2 (1995, $3.95)-Year One story 4.00

HAWKMAN (Title continues as Hawkgirl #50-on) (See JSA #23 for return)
DC Comics: May, 2002 - No. 49, Apr, 2006 ($2.50)
1-Johns & Robinson-s/Morales-a 5.00
1-2nd printing 3.00
2-40: 2-4-Shadow Thief app. 5,6-Green Arrow-c/app. 8-Atom-c/app. 13-Van Sciver-a. 14-Gentleman Ghost app. 15-Hawkwoman app. 16-Byth returns. 23-25-Black Reign x-over with JSA #56-58. 26-Byrne-c/a. 29,30-Land-c. 37-Golden Eagle returns 3.00
41-49: 41-Hawkman killed. 43-Golden Eagle origin. 46-49-Adam Kubert-c 3.00
...: Allies & Enemies TPB (2004, $14.95) r/#7-14 & pages from Secret Files and Origins 15.00
...: Endless Flight TPB (2003, $12.95) r/#1-6 & Secret Files and Origins 13.00
...: Rise of the Golden Eagle TPB (2006, $17.99) r/#37-45 18.00
... Secret Files and Origins (10/02, $4.95) profiles and pin-ups by various 5.00
... Special 1 (10/08, $3.50) Tie-in to Rann-Thanagar Holy War series; Starlin-s/a(p) 3.50
...: Wings of Fury TPB (2005, $17.99) r/#15-22 18.00

HAWKMOON: THE JEWEL IN THE SKULL
First Comics: May, 1986 - No. 4, Nov, 1986 ($1.75, limited series, Baxter paper)
1-4: Adapts novel by Michael Moorcock 3.00

HAWKMOON: THE MAD GOD'S AMULET
First Comics: Jan, 1987 - No. 4, July, 1987 ($1.75, limited series, Baxter paper)
1-4: Adapts novel by Michael Moorcock 3.00

HAWKMOON: THE RUNESTAFF
First Comics: Jun, 1988 -No. 4, Dec, 1988 ($1.75-$1.95, lim. series, Baxter paper)
1-4: ($1.75) Adapts novel by Michael Moorcock. 3,4 ($1.95) 3.00

HAWKMOON: THE SWORD OF DAWN
First Comics: Sept, 1987 - No. 4, Mar, 1988 ($1.75, lim. series, Baxter paper)
1-4: Dorman painted-c; adapts Moorcock novel 3.00

HAWKS OF THE SEAS (WILL EISNER'S...)
Dark Horse Comics: July, 2003 ($19.95, B&W, hardcover)
nn-Reprints 1937-1939 weekly Pirate serial by Will Eisner; Williamson intro. 20.00

HAWKWORLD
DC Comics: 1989 - No. 3, 1989 ($3.95, prestige format, limited series)
Book 1-3: 1-Tim Truman story & art in all; Hawkman dons new costume; reintro Byth 4.00
TPB (1991, $16.95) r/#1-3 17.00

HAWKWORLD (3rd Series)
DC Comics: June, 1990 - No. 32, Mar, 1993 ($1.50/$1.75)
1-Hawkman spin-off; story cont'd from limited series. 4.00
2-32: 15,16-War of the Gods x-over. 22-J'onn J'onzz app. 3.00
Annual 1-3 ('90-'92, $2.95, 68 pgs.), 2-2nd printing with silver ink-c 4.00
NOTE: *Truman a-30-32; c-27-32, Annual 1.*

HAYWIRE
DC Comics: Oct, 1988 - No. 13, Sept, 1989 ($1.25, mature)
1-13 3.00

HAZARD
Image Comics (WildStorm Prod.): June, 1996 - No. 7, Nov, 1996 ($1.75)
1-7: 1-Intro Hazard; Jeff Mariotte scripts begin; Jim Lee-c(p) 3.00

GD VG FN VF VF/NM NM-
2.0 4.0 6.0 8.0 9.0 9.2

HEADHUNTERS
Image Comics: Apr, 1997 - No. 3, June, 1997 ($2.95, B&W)
1-3: Chris Marrinan-s/a 3.00

HEADLINE COMICS
DC Comics: Jan. 1942
nn - Ashcan comic, not distributed to newsstands, only for in-house use. Cover art is More Fun Comics #73 with interior being Star Spangled Comics #2 (no known sales)

HEADLINE COMICS (...For the American Boy) (...Crime No. 32-39)
Prize Publ./American Boys' Comics: Feb, 1943 - No. 22, Nov-Dec, 1946; No. 23, 1947 - No. 77, Oct, 1956
1-Junior Rangers-c/stories begin; Yank & Doodle x-over in Junior Rangers (Junior Rangers are Uncle Sam's nephews) 63 126 189 403 689 975
2 36 72 108 216 351 485
3-Used in **POP**, pg. 84 25 50 75 150 245 340
4-7,9,10: 4,9,10-Hitler stories in each 21 42 63 124 202 280
8-Classic Hitler-c 148 296 444 947 1624 2300
11,12 20 40 60 114 182 250
13-15-Blue Streak in all 20 40 60 117 189 260
16-Origin & 1st app. Atomic Man (11-12/45) 31 62 93 182 296 410
17,18,20,21: 21-Atomic Man ends (9-10/46) 18 36 54 103 162 220
19-S&K-a 32 64 96 192 314 435
22-Last Junior Rangers; Kiefer-c 15 30 45 85 130 175
23,24: (All S&K-a). 23-Valentine's Day Massacre story; content changes to true crime.
24-Dope-crazy killer story 32 64 96 192 314 435
25-35-S&K-c/a. 25-Powell-a 29 58 87 170 278 385
36-S&K-a; photo-c begin 21 42 63 124 202 280
37-1 pg. S&K, Severin-a; rare Kirby photo-c app. 22 44 66 128 209 290
38,40-Meskin-a 11 22 33 60 83 105
39,41-43,46-50,52-55: 41-J. Edgar Hoover 26th Anniversary Issue with photo on-c.
43,49-Meskin-a. 48-Meskin-c 9 18 27 52 69 85
44-S&K-c; Severin/Elder, Meskin-a 15 30 45 84 127 170
45-Kirby-a 13 26 39 72 101 130
51-Kirby-c 13 26 39 72 101 130
56-S&K-a 14 28 42 81 118 155
57-77: 72-Meskin-c/a(i) 8 16 24 44 57 70
NOTE: ***Hollingsworth** a-30. Photo c-36-43. **H. C. Kiefer** c-12-16, 22. Atomic Man c-17-19.*

HEADMAN
Innovation Publishing: 1990 ($2.50, mature)
1-Sci/fi 3.00

HEAP, THE
Skywald Publications: Sept, 1971 (52 pgs.)
1-Kinstler-r/Strange Worlds #8; new-s w/Sutton-a 4 8 12 26 41 55

HEART AND SOUL
Mikeross Publications: April-May, 1954 - No. 2, June-July, 1954
1,2 9 18 27 52 69 85

HEARTBREAKERS (Also see Dark Horse Presents)
Dark Horse Comics: Apr, 1996 - No. 4, July, 1996 ($2.95, limited series)
1-4: 1-W/paper doll & pin-up. 2-Alex Ross pin-up. 3-Evan Dorkin pin-ups. 4-Brereton-c; Matt Wagner pin-up 3.00
...Superdigest (7/98, $9.95, digest-size) new stories 10.00

HEARTLAND (See Hellblazer)
DC Comics (Vertigo): Mar, 1997 ($4.95, one-shot, mature)
1-Garth Ennis-s/Steve Dillon-c/a 5.00

HEART OF DARKNESS
Hardline Studios: 1994 ($2.95)
1-Brereton-c 3.00

HEART OF EMPIRE
Dark Horse Comics: Apr, 1999 - No. 9, Dec, 1999 ($2.95, limited series)
1-9-Bryan Talbot-s/a 3.00

HEART OF THE BEAST, THE
DC Comics (Vertigo): 1994 ($19.95, hardcover, mature)
1-Dean Motter scripts 20.00

HEARTS OF DARKNESS (See Ghost Rider; Wolverine; Punisher: Hearts of...)

HEART THROBS (Love Stories No. 147 on)
Quality Comics/National Periodical #47(4-5/57) on (Arleigh #48-101): 8/49 - No. 8, 10/50; No. 9, 3/52 - No. 146, Oct, 1972

Heart Throbs (1999 series) #1 © DC

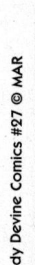

Hedy Devine Comics #27 © MAR

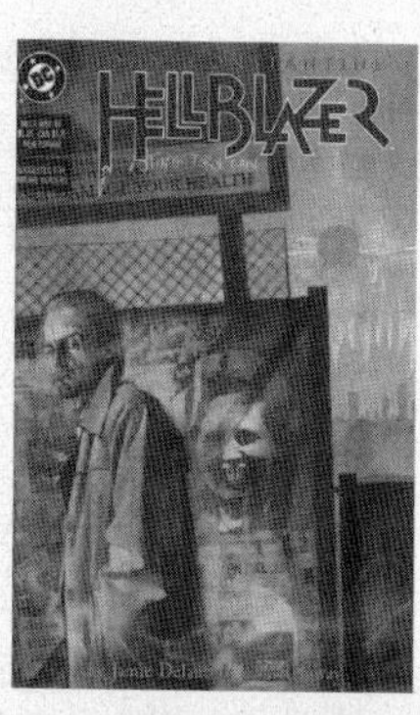

Hellblazer #3 © DC

	GD 2.0	VG 4.0	FN 6.0	VF 8.0	VF/NM 9.0	NM- 9.2
1-Classic Ward-c, Gustavson-a, 9 pgs.	43	86	129	271	461	650
2-Ward-c/a (9 pgs); Gustavson-a	27	54	81	158	259	360
3-Gustavson-a	14	28	42	80	115	150
4,6,8-Ward-a, 8-9 pgs.	17	34	51	98	154	210
5,7	12	24	36	67	94	120
9-Robert Mitchum, Jane Russell photo-c	14	28	42	82	121	160
10,15-Ward-a	14	28	42	82	121	160
11-14,16-20: 12 (7/52)	10	20	30	56	76	95
21-Ward-c	14	28	42	80	115	150
22,23-Ward-a(p)	11	22	33	60	83	105
24-33: 33-Last pre-code (3/55)	10	20	30	54	72	90
34-39,41-44,46 (12/56; last Quality issue)	9	18	27	52	69	85
40-Ward-a; r-7 pgs./#21	10	20	30	56	76	95
45-Baker-a	7	14	21	44	72	100
47-(4-5/57; 1st DC issue)	19	38	57	132	284	435
48-60, 100	9	18	27	63	112	160
61-70	7	14	21	46	76	105
71-99: 74-Last 10 cent issue	6	12	18	41	66	90
101-The Beatles app. on-c	12	24	36	84	177	270
102-120: 102-123-(Serial)-Three Girls, Their Lives, Their Loves	4	8	12	26	41	55
121-132,143-146	4	8	12	22	34	45
133-142-(52 pgs.)	4	8	12	28	44	60

NOTE: ***Gustavson** a-8. **Tuska** a-128. Photo c-4, 5, 8-10, 15, 17.*

HEART THROBS - THE BEST OF DC ROMANCE COMICS (See Fireside Book Series)

HEART THROBS
DC Comics (Vertigo): Jan, 1999 - No. 4, Apr, 1999 ($2.95, lim. series)

	GD 2.0	VG 4.0	FN 6.0	VF 8.0	VF/NM 9.0	NM- 9.2
1-4-Romance anthology. 1-Timm-c. 3-Corben-a						3.00

HEATHCLIFF (See Star Comics Magazine)
Marvel Comics (Star Comics)/Marvel Comics No. 23 on: Apr, 1985 - No. 56, Feb, 1991 (#16-on, $1.00)

	GD 2.0	VG 4.0	FN 6.0	VF 8.0	VF/NM 9.0	NM- 9.2
1-Post-a most issues	1	2	3	4	5	7
2-10,47: 47-Batman parody (Catman vs. the Soaker)						5.00
11-46,48-56: 43-X-Mas issue						4.00
Annual 1 ('87)						4.00

HEATHCLIFF'S FUNHOUSE
Marvel Comics (Star Comics)/Marvel No. 6 on: May, 1987 - No. 10, 1988

	GD 2.0	VG 4.0	FN 6.0	VF 8.0	VF/NM 9.0	NM- 9.2
1						5.00
2-10						4.00

HEAVEN'S DEVILS
Image Comics: Sept, 2003 - No. 4, July, 2004 ($2.95/$3.50, B&W, limited series)

	GD 2.0	VG 4.0	FN 6.0	VF 8.0	VF/NM 9.0	NM- 9.2
1-3-($2.95) Jai Nitz-s/Zach Howard-a						3.00
4-($3.50) Kevin Sharpe-a						3.50

HEAVY HITTERS
Marvel Comics (Epic Comics): 1993 ($3.75, 68 pgs.)

	GD 2.0	VG 4.0	FN 6.0	VF 8.0	VF/NM 9.0	NM- 9.2
1-Bound w/trading card; Lawdog, Feud, Alien Legion, Trouble With Girls, & Spyke						4.00

HEAVY LIQUID
DC Comics (Vertigo): Oct, 1999 - No. 5, Feb, 2000 ($5.95, limited series)

	GD 2.0	VG 4.0	FN 6.0	VF 8.0	VF/NM 9.0	NM- 9.2
1-5-Paul Pope-s/a; flip covers						6.00
TPB (2001, $29.95) r/#1-5						30.00
TPB (2009, $24.95) r/#1-5; development sketches and cover gallery; new cover						25.00
HC (2008, $39.99, dustjacket) r/#1-5; development sketches and cover gallery						40.00

HECKLE AND JECKLE (Paul Terry's...)(See Blue Ribbon, Giant Comics Edition #5A & 10, Paul Terry's, Terry-Toons Comics)
St. John Publ. Co. No. 1-24/Pines No. 25 on: No. 3, 2/52 - No. 24, 10/55; No. 25, Fall/56 - No. 34, 6/59

	GD 2.0	VG 4.0	FN 6.0	VF 8.0	VF/NM 9.0	NM- 9.2
3(#1)-Funny animal	24	48	72	140	230	320
4(6/52), 5	13	26	39	74	105	135
6-10(4/53)	9	18	27	50	65	80
11-20	8	16	24	40	50	60
21-34: 25-Begin CBS Television Presents on-c	7	14	21	35	43	50

HECKLE AND JECKLE (TV) (See New Terrytoons)
Gold Key/Dell Publ. Co.: 11/62 - No. 4, 8/63; 5/66; No. 2, 10/66; No. 3, 8/67

	GD 2.0	VG 4.0	FN 6.0	VF 8.0	VF/NM 9.0	NM- 9.2
1 (11/62; Gold Key)	6	12	18	42	69	95
2-4	4	8	12	22	34	45
1 (5/66; Dell)	4	8	12	26	41	55
2,3	3	6	9	19	29	38

(See March of Comics No. 379, 472, 484)

HECKLE AND JECKLE 3-D
Spotlight Comics: 1987 - No. 2?, 1987 ($2.50)

	GD 2.0	VG 4.0	FN 6.0	VF 8.0	VF/NM 9.0	NM- 9.2
1,2						5.00

HECKLER, THE
DC Comics: Sept, 1992 - No. 6, Feb, 1993 ($1.25)

	GD 2.0	VG 4.0	FN 6.0	VF 8.0	VF/NM 9.0	NM- 9.2
1-6-T&M Bierbaum-s/Keith Giffen-c/a						3.00

HECTIC PLANET
Slave Labor Graphics 1998 ($12.95/$14.95)

	GD 2.0	VG 4.0	FN 6.0	VF 8.0	VF/NM 9.0	NM- 9.2
Book 1,2-r-Dorkin-s/a from Pirate Corp$ Vol. 1 & 2						15.00

HECTOR COMICS (The Keenest Teen in Town)
Key Publications: Nov, 1953 - No. 3, 1954

	GD 2.0	VG 4.0	FN 6.0	VF 8.0	VF/NM 9.0	NM- 9.2
1-Teen humor	7	14	21	37	46	55
2,3	5	10	15	22	26	30

HECTOR HEATHCOTE (TV)
Gold Key: Mar, 1964

	GD 2.0	VG 4.0	FN 6.0	VF 8.0	VF/NM 9.0	NM- 9.2
1 (10111-403)	7	14	21	46	76	105

HECTOR THE INSPECTOR (See Top Flight Comics)

HEDGE KNIGHT, THE
Image Comics: Aug, 2003 - No. 6, Apr, 2004 ($2.95, limited series)

	GD 2.0	VG 4.0	FN 6.0	VF 8.0	VF/NM 9.0	NM- 9.2
1-6-George R.R. Martin-s/Mike S. Miller-a. 1-Two covers by Kaluta and Miller						3.00
George R.R. Martin's The Hedge Knight HC (Marvel, 2006, $19.99) r/series; 2 covers						20.00
George R.R. Martin's The Hedge Knight SC (Marvel, 2007, $14.99) r/series						15.00
TPB (2004, $14.95) r/series plus new short story						15.00

HEDGE KNIGHT II: SWORN SWORD
Marvel Comics (Dabel Brothers): Jun, 2007 - No. 6, Jun, 2008 ($2.99, limited series)

	GD 2.0	VG 4.0	FN 6.0	VF 8.0	VF/NM 9.0	NM- 9.2
1-6-George R.R. Martin-s/Mike Miller-a. 1-Two covers by Yu & Miller, plus Miller B&W-c						3.00
... HC (2008, $19.99) r/series; 2 covers						20.00

HEDY DEVINE COMICS (Formerly All Winners #21? or Teen #22?(6/47); Hedy of Hollywood #36 on; also see Annie Oakley, Comedy & Venus)
Marvel Comics (RCM)/Atlas #50: No. 22, Aug, 1947 - No. 50, Sept, 1952

	GD 2.0	VG 4.0	FN 6.0	VF 8.0	VF/NM 9.0	NM- 9.2
22-1st app. Hedy Devine (also see Joker #32)	36	72	108	211	343	475
23,24,27-30: 23-Wolverton-a, 1 pg; Kurtzman's "Hey Look", 2 pgs. 24,27-30- "Hey Look" by Kurtzman, 1-3 pgs.	21	42	63	122	199	275
25-Classic "Hey Look" by Kurtzman, "Optical Illusion"	22	44	66	132	216	300
26- "Giggles 'n' Grins" by Kurtzman	19	38	57	109	172	235
31-34,36-50: 32-Anti-Wertham editorial	14	28	42	78	112	145
35-Four pgs. "Rusty" by Kurtzman	17	34	51	98	154	210

HEDY-MILLIE-TESSIE COMEDY (See Comedy Comics)

HEDY WOLFE (Also see Patsy & Hedy & Miss America Magazine V1#2)
Atlas Publishing Co. (Emgee): Aug, 1957

	GD 2.0	VG 4.0	FN 6.0	VF 8.0	VF/NM 9.0	NM- 9.2
1-Patsy Walker's rival; Al Hartley-c	13	26	39	74	105	135

HEE HAW (TV)
Charlton Press: July, 1970 - No. 7, Aug, 1971

	GD 2.0	VG 4.0	FN 6.0	VF 8.0	VF/NM 9.0	NM- 9.2
1	4	8	12	28	44	60
2-7	3	6	9	19	29	38

HEIDI (See Dell Jr. Treasury No. 6)

HEIDI SAHA (AN ILLUSTRATED HISTORY OF...)
Warren Publishing: 1973 (500 printed)

nn-Photo-c; an early Vampirella model for Warren (a FN/VF copy sold in 2011 for $776.75)

HELEN OF TROY (Movie)
Dell Publishing Co.: No. 684, Mar, 1956 (one-shot)

	GD 2.0	VG 4.0	FN 6.0	VF 8.0	VF/NM 9.0	NM- 9.2
Four Color 684-Buscema-a, photo-c	9	18	27	63	112	160

HELL
Dark Horse Comics: July, 2003 - No. 4, Mar, 2004 ($2.99, limited series)

	GD 2.0	VG 4.0	FN 6.0	VF 8.0	VF/NM 9.0	NM- 9.2
1-4-Augustyn-s/Demong-a/Meglia-c						3.00

HELLBLAZER (John Constantine) (See Saga of Swamp Thing #37) (Also see Books of Magic limited series)
DC Comics (Vertigo #63 on): Jan, 1988 - Present ($1.25-$2.99)

	GD 2.0	VG 4.0	FN 6.0	VF 8.0	VF/NM 9.0	NM- 9.2
1-(44 pgs.)-John Constantine; McKean-c thru #21	2	4	6	9	12	15
1-Special Edition (7/10, $1.00) r/#1 with "What's Next?" cover logo						3.00
2-5	1	2	3	5	7	9
6-8,10: 10-Swamp Thing cameo						6.00
9,19: 9-X-over w/Swamp Thing #76. 19-Sandman app.						

Hellblazer #281 © DC

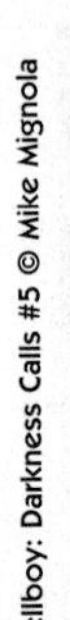

Hellboy: Darkness Calls #5 © Mike Mignola

Hellboy Premiere Edition © Mike Mignola

	GD 2.0	VG 4.0	FN 6.0	VF 8.0	VF/NM 9.0	NM- 9.2
	1	2	3	5	6	8
11-18,20						6.00
21-26,28-30: 22-Williams-c. 24-Contains bound-in Shocker movie poster. 25,26-Grant Morrison scripts.						5.00
27-Gaiman scripts; Dave McKean-a; low print run	2	4	6	10	12	15
31-39: 36-Preview of World Without End.						4.00
40-($2.25, 52 pgs.)-Dave McKean-a & colors; preview of Kid Eternity						5.00
41-Ennis scripts begin; ends #83						5.00
42-49,51-74,76-99,101-119: 44,45-Sutton-a(i). 52-Glenn Fabry painted-c begin. 62-Special Death insert by McKean. 63-Silver metallic ink on-c. 77-Totleben-c. 84-Sean Phillips-c/a begins; Delano story. 85-88-Eddie Campbell story. 89-Paul Jenkins scripts begin						3.50
50,75,100,120: 50-($3.00, 52 pgs.). 75-($2.95, 52 pgs.). 100,120 ($3.50,48 pgs.)						4.00
121-199, 201-249, 251-274,276-289: 129-Ennis-s. 141-Bradstreet-a. 146-150-Corben-a. 151-Azzarello-s begin. 175-Carey-s begin; Dillon-a. 176-Begin $2.75-c. 182,183-Bermejo-a. 216-Mina-s begins. 220-Begin $2.99-c. 229-Carey-s/Leon-a. 234-Initial printing (white title logo) has missing text; corrected printing has lt. blue title logo. 265,266,271-274-Bisley-a. 268-271-Shade the Changing Man app.						3.00
200-($4.50) Carey-s/Dillon, Frusin, Manco-a						4.50
250-($3.99) Short stories by various; art by Lloyd, Phillips, Milligan; Bermejo-c						4.00
275-($4.99) Constatine's wedding; Bisley-c						5.00
Annual 1 (1989, $2.95, 68 pgs.)-Bryan Talbot's 1st work in American comics						6.00
Annual 1 (Annual 2011 on cover, 2/12, $4.99)-Milligan-s/Bisley-a/c						5.00
Special 1 (1993, $3.95, 68 pgs.)-Ennis story; w/pin-ups.						4.00
...Black Flowers (2005, $14.99, TPB) r/#181-186						15.00
...Bloodlines (2007, $19.99, TPB) r/#47-50,52-55,59-61						20.00
...Damnation's Flame (1999, $16.95, TPB) r/#72-77						17.00
...Dangerous Habits (1997, $14.95, TPB) r/#41-46						15.00
...Fear and Loathing (1997, $14.95, TPB) r/#62-67						18.00
...Fear and Loathing (2nd printing, $17.95)						18.00
...: Freezes Over (2003, $14.95, TPB) r/#157-163						15.00
...Good Intentions (2002, $12.95, TPB) r/#151-156						13.00
...Hard Time (2001, $9.95, TPB) r/#146-150						10.00
...Haunting (2003, $12.95, TPB) r/#134-139						13.00
...Highwater (2004, $19.95, TPB) r/#164-174						20.00
John Constantine Hellblazer: All His Engines HC (2005, $24.95, with dustjacket) new graphic novel; Mike Carey-s/Leonardo Manco-a						25.00
John Constantine Hellblazer: All His Engines SC (2006, $14.99) new graphic novel						15.00
John Constantine Hellblazer: Bloody Carnations SC (2011, $19.99) r/#267-275						20.00
John Constantine Hellblazer: Empathy is the Enemy SC (2006, $14.99) r/#216-222						15.00
John Constantine Hellblazer: Hooked SC (2010, $14.99) r/#256-260						15.00
John Constantine Hellblazer: India SC (2010, $14.99) r/#261-266						15.00
John Constantine Hellblazer: Joyride SC (2008, $14.99) r/#230-237						15.00
John Constantine Hellblazer: Pandemonium HC (2010, $24.99,with dustjacket) new graphic novel; Jamie Delano-s/Jock-a						25.00
John Constantine Hellblazer: Pandemonium SC (2011, $7.99) new graphic novel						18.00
John Constantine Hellblazer: Scab SC (2009, $14.99) r/#250-255						15.00
John Constantine Hellblazer: The Devil You Know SC (2007, $19.99) r/#10-13, Annual #1 and The Horrorist miniseries #1,2						20.00
John Constantine Hellblazer: The Family Man SC (2008, $19.99, TPB) r/#23,24,28-33						20.00
John Constantine Hellblazer: The Fear Machine SC (2008, $19.99, TPB) r/#14-22						20.00
John Constantine Hellblazer: The Red Right Hand SC (2007, $14.99) r/#223-228						15.00
John Const. Hellblazer: The Roots of Coincidence SC ('09, $14.99) r/#243,244,247-249						15.00
...Original Sins (1993, $19.95, TPB) r/#1-9						20.00
...Original Sins (2011, $19.99, TPB) r/#1-9						20.00
...Rake at the Gates of Hell (2003, $19.95, TPB) r/#78-83; Heartland #1						20.00
...: Rare Cuts (2005, $14.95, TPB) r/#11,25,26,35,56,84 & Vertigo Secret Files: Hellblazer						15.00
...: Reasons To Be Cheerful (2007, $14.99, TPB) r/#201-206						15.00
...: Red Sepulchre (2005, $12.99, TPB) r/#175-180						13.00
...: Setting Sun (2004, $12.95, TPB) r/#140-143						13.00
...: Son of Man (2004, $12.95, TPB) r/#129-133						13.00
...: Stations of the Cross (2006, $14.99, TPB) r/#194-200						15.00
...: Staring At The Wall (2005, $14.99, TPB) r/#187-193						15.00
...Tainted Love (1998, $16.95, TPB) r/#68-71, Vertigo Jam #1 and Hellblazer Special #1						17.00

NOTE: ***Alcala** a-8i, 9i, 18-22i. **Gaiman** scripts-27. **McKean** a-27,40; c-1-21. **Sutton** a-44i, 45i. **Talbot** a-Annual 1.*

HELLBLAZER: CITY OF DEMONS
DC Comics (Vertigo): Early Dec, 2010 - No. 5, Feb, 2011 ($2.99, limited series)

1-5-Si Spencer-s/Sean Murphy-a/c		3.00
TPB (2011, $14.99) r/#1-5 & story from Vertigo Winter's Edge #3		15.00

HELLBLAZER SPECIAL: BAD BLOOD
DC Comics (Vertigo): Sept, 2000 - No. 4, Dec, 2000 ($2.95, limited series)

1-4-Delano-s/Bond-a; Constantine in 2025 London — 3.00

HELLBLAZER SPECIAL: CHAS
DC Comics (Vertigo): Sept, 2008 - No. 5, Jan, 2009 ($2.99, limited series)

	GD 2.0	VG 4.0	FN 6.0	VF 8.0	VF/NM 9.0	NM- 9.2
1-5-Story of Constantine's cab driver; Oliver-s/Sudzuka-a/Fabry-c						3.00
... - The Knowledge TPB (2009, $14.99) r/#1-5						15.00

HELLBLAZER SPECIAL: LADY CONSTANTINE
DC Comics (Vertigo): Feb, 2003 - No. 4, May, 2003 ($2.95, limited series)

1-4-Story of Johanna Constantine in 1785; Diggle-s/Sudzuka-a/Noto-c — 3.00

HELLBLAZER/THE BOOKS OF MAGIC
DC Comics (Vertigo): Dec, 1997 - No. 2, Jan, 1998 ($2.50, limited series)

1,2-John Constantine and Tim Hunter — 3.00

HELLBOY (Also see Batman/Hellboy/Starman, Danger Unlimited #4, Dark Horse Presents, Gen[13] #13B, Ghost/Hellboy, John Byrne's Next Men, San Diego Comic Con #2, & Savage Dragon)

HELLBOY
Dark Horse Comics: Apr, 2008

... : Free Comic Book Day; Three short stories; Mignola-c; art by Fegredo, Davis, Azaceta — 3.00

HELLBOY: ALMOST COLOSSUS
Dark Horse Comics (Legend): Jun, 1997 - No. 2, Jul, 1997 ($2.95, lim. series)

1,2-Mignola-s/a — 4.00

HELLBOY/BEASTS OF BURDEN
Dark Horse Comics: Oct, 2010 ($3.50, one-shot)

... Sacrifice - Evan Dorkin & Mignola-s/Jill Thompson-a — 3.50

HELLBOY: BEING HUMAN
Dark Horse Comics: May, 2011 ($3.50, one-shot)

nn-Mignola-s; Richard Corben-a/c; Roger app. — 3.50

HELLBOY: BOX FULL OF EVIL
Dark Horse Comics: Aug, 1999 - No. 2, Sept, 1999 ($2.95, lim. series)

1,2-Mignola-s/a; back-up story w/ Matt Smith-a — 4.00

HELLBOY: BUSTER OAKLEY GETS HIS WISH
Dark Horse Comics: Apr, 2011 ($3.50, one-shot)

nn-Mignola-s; Kevin Nowlan-a; two covers by Mignola & Nowlan — 3.50

HELLBOY CHRISTMAS SPECIAL
Dark Horse Comics: Dec, 1997 ($3.95, one-shot)

nn-Christmas stories by Mignola, Gianni, Darrow, Purcell — 5.00

HELLBOY: CONQUEROR WORM
Dark Horse Comics: May, 2001 - No. 4, Aug, 2001 ($2.99, lim. series)

1-4-Mignola-s/a/c — 4.00

HELLBOY: DARKNESS CALLS
Dark Horse Comics: Apr, 2007 - No. 6, Nov, 2007 ($2.99, lim. series)

1-6-Mignola-s/Fegredo-a — 3.00

HELLBOY: DOUBLE FEATURE OF EVIL
Dark Horse Comics: Nov, 2010 ($3.50, one-shot)

1-Mignola-s; Corben-a/c — 3.50

HELLBOY: HOUSE OF THE LIVING DEAD
Dark Horse Comics: Nov, 2011 ($14.99, hardcover graphic novel)

1-Mignola-s; Corben-a/c; Hellboy and Lucha Libre — 15.00

HELLBOY IN MEXICO
Dark Horse Comics: May, 2010 ($3.50, one-shot)

1-Mignola-s; Corben-a/c; Mexican wrestlers vs. monsters — 3.50

HELLBOY: IN THE CHAPEL OF MOLOCH
Dark Horse Comics: Oct, 2008 ($2.99, one-shot)

nn-Mignola-s/a/c — 3.00

HELLBOY, JR.
Dark Horse Comics: Oct, 1999 - No. 2, Nov, 1999 ($2.95, limited series)

1,2-Stories and art by various		4.00
TPB (1/04, $14.95) r/#1&2, Halloween; sketch pages; intro. by Steve Niles; Bill Wray-c		15.00

HELLBOY, JR., HALLOWEEN SPECIAL
Dark Horse Comics: Oct, 1997 ($3.95, one-shot)

nn-"Harvey" style renditions of Hellboy characters; Bill Wray, Mike Mignola & various-s/a; wraparound-c by Wray — 5.00

HELLBOY: MAKOMA, OR A TALE TOLD...
Dark Horse Comics: Feb, 2006 - No. 2, Mar, 2006 ($2.99, lim. series)

1,2-Mignola-s/c; Mignola & Corben-a — 3.00

HELLBOY PREMIERE EDITION
Dark Horse Comics (Wizard): 2004 (no price, one-shot)

Hellboy: Weird Tales #1 © Mike Mignola

Hello Pal Comics #3 © HARV

Hellshock #4 © Jae Lee

GD 2.0 | VG 4.0 | FN 6.0 | VF 8.0 | VF/NM 9.0 | NM- 9.2

nn- Two covers by Mignola & Davis; Mignola-s/a; BPRD story w/Arcudi-s/Davis-a 5.00
Wizard World Los Angeles-Movie photo-c; Mignola-s/a; BPRD story w/Arcudi-s/Davis-a 10.00

HELLBOY: SEED OF DESTRUCTION (First Hellboy series)
Dark Horse Comics (Legend): Mar, 1994 - No. 4, Jun, 1994 ($2.50, lim. series)

1-4-Mignola-c/a w/Byrne scripts; Monkeyman & O'Brien back-up story (origin) by Art Adams. 1 2 3 5 6 8
Hellboy: One for One (8/10, $1.00) r/#1 Hellboy story with red cover frame 3.00
Trade paperback (1994, $17.95)-collects all four issues plus r/Hellboy's 1st app. in San Diego Comic Con #2 & pin-ups 18.00
Limited edition hardcover (1995, $99.95)-includes everything in trade paperback plus additional material. 100.00

HELLBOY STRANGE PLACES
Dark Horse Books: Apr, 2006 ($17.95, TPB)

SC - Reprints Hellboy: The Third Wish #1,2 and Hellboy: The Island #1,2; sketch pages 18.00

HELLBOY: THE BRIDE OF HELL
Dark Horse Comics: Dec, 2009 ($3.50, one-shot)

1-Mignola-s/c; Corben-a; preview of The Marquis: Inferno 3.50

HELLBOY: THE CHAINED COFFIN AND OTHERS
Dark Horse Comics (Legend): Aug, 1998 ($17.95, TPB)

nn-Mignola-c/a/s; reprints out-of-print one shots; pin-up gallery 18.00

HELLBOY: THE COMPANION
Dark Horse Books: May, 2008 ($14.95, 9"x6", TPB)

nn-Overview of Hellboy history, characters, stories, mythology; text with Mignola panels 15.00

HELLBOY: THE CORPSE
Dark Horse Comics: Mar, 2004 (25¢, one-shot)

nn-Mignola-c/a/scripts; reprints "The Corpse" serial from Capitol City's Advance Comics catalog; development sketches and photos of the Corpse from the Hellboy movie 3.00

HELLBOY: THE CORPSE AND THE IRON SHOES
Dark Horse Comics (Legend): Jan, 1996 ($2.95, one-shot)

nn-Mignola-c/a/scripts; reprints "The Corpse" serial w/new story 4.00

HELLBOY: THE CROOKED MAN
Dark Horse Comics: Jul, 2008 - No. 3, Sept, 2008 ($2.99, lim. series)

1-3-Mignola-s/Corben-a/c 3.00

HELLBOY: THE FURY
Dark Horse Comics: Jun, 2011 - No. 3, Aug, 2011 ($2.99, lim. series)

1-3-Mignola-s/c; Fegredo-a. 1-Variant-c by Fegredo 3.00

HELLBOY: THE GOLDEN ARMY
Dark Horse Comics: Jan, 2008 (no cover price)

nn-Prelude to the 2008 movie; Del Toro & Mignola-s/Velasco-a; 3 photo covers 3.00

HELLBOY: THE ISLAND
Dark Horse Comics: June, 2005 - No. 2, July, 2005 ($2.99, lim. series)

1,2: Mignola-c/a & scripts 4.00

HELLBOY: THE RIGHT HAND OF DOOM
Dark Horse Comics (Legend): Apr, 2000 ($17.95, TPB)

nn-Mignola-c/a/s; reprints 18.00

HELLBOY: THE SLEEPING AND THE DEAD
Dark Horse Comics: Dec, 2010 - No. 2, Feb, 2011 ($3.50, lim. series)

1,2-Mignola-s/Scott Hampton-a 3.50

HELLBOY: THE STORM
Dark Horse Comics: Jul, 2010 - No. 3, Sept, 2010 ($2.99, lim. series)

1-3-Mignola-s/Fegredo-a 3.00

HELLBOY: THE THIRD WISH
Dark Horse Comics (Maverick): July, 2002 - No. 2, Aug, 2002 ($2.99, limited series)

1,2-Mignola-c/a/s 4.00

HELLBOY THE TROLL WITCH AND OTHERS
Dark Horse Books: Nov, 2007 ($17.95, TPB)

SC - Reprints Hellboy: Makoma, Hellboy Premiere Edition and stories from Dark Horse Book of Hauntings, DHB of Witchcraft, DHB of the Dead, DHB of Monsters 18.00

HELLBOY: THE WILD HUNT
Dark Horse Comics: Dec, 2008 - No. 8, Nov, 2009 ($2.99, lim. series)

1-8: Mignola-c/s; Fegredo-a 3.00

HELLBOY: THE WOLVES OF ST. AUGUST
Dark Horse Comics (Legend): 1995 ($4.95, squarebound, one-shot)

nn-Mignola--c/a/scripts; r/Dark Horse Presents #88-91 with additional story 5.00

HELLBOY: WAKE THE DEVIL (Sequel to Seed of Destruction)
Dark Horse Comics (Legend): Jun, 1996 - No. 5, Oct, 1996 ($2.95, lim. series)

1-5: Mignola-c/a & scripts; The Monstermen back-up story by Gary Gianni 5.00
TPB (1997, $17.95) r/#1-5 18.00

HELLBOY: WEIRD TALES
Dark Horse Comics: Feb, 2003 - No. 8, Apr, 2004 ($2.99, limited series, anthology)

1-8-Hellboy stories from other creators. 1-Cassaday-c/s/a; Watson-s/a. 6-Cho-c 4.00
... Vol. 1 (2004, 17.95) r/#1-4 18.00
... Vol. 2 (2004, 17.95) r/#5-8 and Lobster Johnson serial from #1-8 18.00

HELLCAT
Marvel Comics: Sept, 2000 - No. 3, Nov, 2000 ($2.99)

1-3-Englehart-s/Breyfogle-a; Hedy Wolfe app. 3.00

HELLCOP
Image Comics (Avalon Studios): Aug, 1998 - No. 4, Mar, 1999 ($2.50)

1-4: 1-(Oct. on-c) Casey-s 3.00

HELL ETERNAL
DC Comics (Vertigo Verité): 1998 ($6.95, squarebound, one-shot)

1-Delano-s/Phillips-a 7.00

HELLGATE: LONDON (Based on the video game)
Dark Horse Comics: No. 0, May 2006 - No. 3, Mar, 2007 ($2.99)

0-3-Edginton-s/Pugh-a/Briclot-c 3.00

HELLHOUNDS (...: Panzer Cops #3-6)
Dark Horse Comics: 1994 - No. 6, July, 1994 ($2.50, B&W, limited series)

1-6: 1-Hamner-c. 3-(4/94). 2-Joe Phillips-c 3.00

HELLHOUND, THE REDEMPTION QUEST
Marvel Comics (Epic Comics): Dec, 1993 - No. 4, Mar, 1994 ($2.25, lim. series, coated stock)

1-4 3.00

HELLO BUDDIES
Harvey Publications: 1953 (25¢, small size)

	GD 2.0	VG 4.0	FN 6.0	VF 8.0	VF/NM 9.0	NM- 9.2
1	3	6	9	14	20	25

HELLO, I'M JOHNNY CASH
Spire Christian Comics (Fleming H. Revell Co.): 1976 (39¢/49¢)

	GD 2.0	VG 4.0	FN 6.0	VF 8.0	VF/NM 9.0	NM- 9.2
nn-(39¢-c)	3	6	9	16	23	30
nn-(49¢-c)	2	4	6	11	16	20

HELL ON EARTH (See DC Science Fiction Graphic Novel)

HELLO PAL COMICS (Short Story Comics)
Harvey Publications: Jan, 1943 - No. 3, May, 1943 (Photo-c)

	GD 2.0	VG 4.0	FN 6.0	VF 8.0	VF/NM 9.0	NM- 9.2
1-Rocketman & Rocketgirl begin; Yankee Doodle Jones app.; Mickey Rooney photo-c	63	126	189	403	689	975
2-Charlie McCarthy photo-c (scarce)	56	112	168	349	595	840
3-Bob Hope photo-c (scarce)	60	120	180	384	660	935

HELLRAISER/NIGHTBREED – JIHAD (Also see Clive Barker's...)
Epic Comics (Marvel Comics): 1991 - Book 2, 1991 ($4.50, 52 pgs.)

Book 1,2 4.50

HELL-RIDER (Motorcycle themed magazine)
Skywald Publications: Aug, 1971 - No. 2, Oct, 1971 (B&W, 68 pgs.)

	GD 2.0	VG 4.0	FN 6.0	VF 8.0	VF/NM 9.0	NM- 9.2
1-Origin & 1st app.; Butterfly & the Wild Bunch begin; 1st Hell-Rider by Andru, Esposito and Friedrich	6	12	18	41	66	90
2-Andru, Ayers, Buckler, Shores-a	4	8	12	28	44	60

NOTE: *#3 advertised in Psycho #5 but did not come out.* **Buckler** *a-1, 2.* **Rosenbaum** *c-1,2.*

HELL'S ANGEL (Becomes Dark Angel #6 on)
Marvel Comics UK: July, 1992 - No. 5, Nov, 1993 ($1.75)

1-5: X-Men (Wolverine, Cyclops)-c/stories. 1-Origin. 3-Jim Lee cover swipe 3.00

HELLSHOCK
Image Comics: July, 1994 - No. 4, Nov, 1994 ($1.95, limited series)

1-4-Jae Lee-c/a & scripts. 4-Variant-c. 3.00

HELLSHOCK
Image Comics: Jan, 1997 - No. 3, Jan, 1998 ($2.95/$2.50, limited series)

1-($2.95)-Jae Lee-c/s/a, Villarrubia-painted-a 4.00
2-($2.50) 3.00
Book 3: The Science of Faith (1/98, $2.50) Jae Lee-c/s/a, Villarrubia-painted-a 3.00

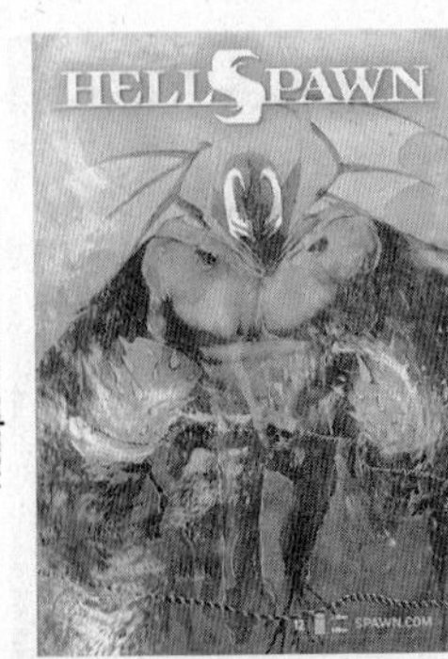

Hellspawn #12 © TMP

Heralds #4 © MAR

Herc #6 © MAR

GD VG FN VF VF/NM NM-
2.0 4.0 6.0 8.0 9.0 9.2

Vol. 1 HC (2006, $49.99) r/#1-3 re-colored, with unpublished 22 pg. conclusion; cover gallery and sketches; alternate opening art; intro. by Jim Lee 50.00

HELLSPAWN
Image Comics: Aug, 2000 - No. 16, Apr, 2003 ($2.50)

1-Bendis-s/Ashley Wood-c/a; Spawn and Clown app. 3.00
2-9: 6-Last Bendis-s; Mike Moran (Miracleman app.). 7-Niles-s 3.00
10-16-Templesmith-a 3.00
...: The Ashley Wood Collection Vol. 1 (4/06, $24.95, TPB) r/#1-10; sketch & cover gallery 25.00

HELLSTORM: PRINCE OF LIES (See Ghost Rider #1 & Marvel Spotlight #12)
Marvel Comics: Apr, 1993 - No. 21, Dec, 1994 ($2.00)

1-($2.95)-Parchment-c w/red thermographic ink 4.00
2-21: 14-Bound-in trading card sheet. 18-P. Craig Russell-c 3.00

HELLSTORM: SON OF SATAN
Marvel Comics (MAX): Dec, 2006 - No. 5, Apr, 2007 ($3.99, limited series)

1-5-Suydam-c/Irvine-s/Braun & Janson-a 4.00
... - Equinox TPB (2007, $17.99) r/#1-5; interviews with the creators 18.00

HELL YEAH
Image Comics: Mar, 2012 - Present ($2.99)

1-Joe Keatinge-s/Andre Szymanowicz-a 3.00

HELMET OF FATE, THE (Series of one-shots following Doctor Fate's helmet)
DC Comics: Mar, 2007 - May 2007 ($2.99, one-shots)

...: Black Alice (5/07) Simone-s/Rouleau-a/c 3.00
...: Detective Chimp (3/07) Willingham-s/McManus-a/Bolland-c 3.00
...: Ibis the Invincible (3/07) Williams-s/Winslade-a; the Ibistick returns 3.00
...: Sargon the Sorcerer (4/07) Niles-s/Scott Hampton-s; debut new Sargon 3.00
...: Zauriel (4/07) Gerber-s/Snejbjerg-a/Kaluta-c; leads into new Doctor Fate series 3.00
TPB (2007, $14.99) r/one-shots 15.00

HE-MAN (See Masters Of The Universe)

HE-MAN (Also see Tops In Adventure)
Ziff-Davis Publ. Co. (Approved Comics): Fall, 1952

1-Kinstler painted-c; Powell-a 16 32 48 94 147 200

HE-MAN
Toby Press: May, 1954 - No. 2, July, 1954 (Painted-c by B. Safran)

1 15 30 45 88 137 185
2-Shark-c 15 30 45 85 130 175

HENNESSEY (TV)
Dell Publishing Co.: No. 1200, Aug-Oct, 1961 - No. 1280, Mar-May, 1962

Four Color 1200-Gil Kane-a, photo-c 7 14 21 46 76 105
Four Color 1280-Photo-c 6 12 18 42 69 95

HENRY (Also see Little Annie Rooney)
David McKay Publications: 1935 (52 pgs.) (Daily B&W strip reprints)(10"x10" cardboard-c)

1-By Carl Anderson 39 78 117 240 395 550

HENRY (See King Comics & Magic Comics)
Dell Publishing Co.: No. 122, Oct, 1946 - No. 65, Apr-June, 1961

Four Color 122-All new stories begin 13 26 39 85 180 275
Four Color 155 (7/47), 1 (1-3/48)-All new stories 10 20 30 65 118 170
2 6 12 18 41 66 90
3-10 5 10 15 34 55 75
11-20: 20-Infinity-c 4 8 12 28 44 60
21-30 4 8 12 22 34 45
31-40 3 6 9 19 29 38
41-65 3 6 9 16 23 30

HENRY (See Giant Comic Album and March of Comics No. 43, 58, 84, 101, 112, 129, 147, 162, 178, 189)

HENRY ALDRICH COMICS (TV)
Dell Publishing Co.: Aug-Sept, 1950 - No. 22, Sept-Nov, 1954

1-Part series written by John Stanley; Bill Williams-a
9 18 27 63 112 160
2 6 12 18 37 59 80
3-5 5 10 15 30 48 65
6-10 4 8 12 26 41 55
11-22 4 8 12 22 34 45

HENRY BREWSTER
Country Wide (M.F. Ent.): Feb, 1966 - V2#7, Sept, 1967 (All 25¢ Giants)

1 3 6 9 19 29 38
2-6(12/66), V2#7-Powell-a in most 2 4 6 13 18 22

HEPCATS
Antarctic Press: Nov, 1996 - No. 12 ($2.95, B&W)

0-12-Martin Wagner-c/s/a: 0-color 3.00
0-($9.95) CD Edition 10.00

HERALDS
Marvel Comics: Aug, 2010 - No. 5, Aug, 2010 ($2.99, weelky limited series)

1-5-Kathryn Immonen-s/Zonjic & Harren-a; She-Hulk, Hellcat, Emma Frost, Photon app. 3.00

HERBIE (See Forbidden Worlds #73,94,110,114,116 & Unknown Worlds #20)
American Comics Group: April-May, 1964 - No. 23, Feb, 1967 (All 12¢)

1-Whitney-c/a in most issues 15 30 45 102 221 340
2-4 9 18 27 63 112 160
5-Beatles parody (10 pgs.), Dean Martin, Frank Sinatra app. (10-11/64)
10 20 30 68 127 185
6,7,9,10 8 16 24 55 93 130
8-Origin & 1st app. The Fat Fury 9 18 27 62 109 155
11-23: 14-Nemesis & Magicman app. 17-r/2nd Herbie from Forbidden Worlds #94. 23-r/1st Herbie from F.W. #73 6 12 18 42 69 95
... Archives Volume One HC (Dark Horse, 8/08, $49.95, dust jacket) r/earliest apps. in Forbidden Worlds, Unknown Worlds, and Herbie #1-5; Scott Shaw intro. 50.00

HERBIE
Dark Horse Comics: Oct, 1992 - No. 12, 1993 ($2.50, limited series)

1-Whitney-r plus new-c/a in all; Byrne-c/a & scripts 4.00
2-6: 3-Bob Burden-c/a. 4-Art Adams-c 3.00

HERBIE GOES TO MONTE CARLO, HERBIE RIDES AGAIN (See Walt Disney Showcase No. 24, 41)

HERC (Hercules from the Avengers)
Marvel Comics: Jun, 2011 - No. 10, Jan, 2012 ($2.99)

1-6, (6.1), 7-10: 1-Pak & Van Lente-s; Hobgoblin app. 3-6-Fear Itself tie-in. 6.1-Grell-a 7,8-Spider-Island tie-in; Herc gets Spider-powers. 10-Elektra app. 3.00

HERCULES (See Hit Comics #1-21, Journey Into Mystery Annual, Marvel Graphic Novel #37, Marvel Premiere #26 & The Mighty...)

HERCULES (See Charlton Classics)
Charlton Comics: Oct, 1967 - No. 13, Sept, 1969; Dec, 1968

1-Thane of Bagarth begins; Glanzman-a in all 4 8 12 26 41 55
2-13: 1-5,7-10-Aparo-a. 8-(12¢-c) 3 6 9 16 23 50
4-Magazine format (low distribution) 9 18 27 61 106 150
8-Magazine format (low distribution)(12/68, 35¢, B&W); new Hercules story plus-r story/#1; Thane-r/#1-3 6 12 18 37 59 80
Modern Comics reprint 10('77), 11('78) 6.00

HERCULES (Prince of Power) (Also see The Champions)
Marvel Comics Group: V1#1, Sept, 1982 - V1#4, Dec, 1982; V2#1, Mar, 1984 - V2#4, Jun, 1984 (color, both limited series)

1-4, V2#1-4: Layton-c/a. 4-Death of Zeus. 3.00
NOTE: *Layton a-1, 2, 3p, 4p, V2#1-4; c-1-4, V2#1-4.*

HERCULES
Marvel Comics: Jun, 2005 - No. 5, Sept, 2005 ($2.99, limited series)

1-5-Texeira-a/c; Tieri-s. 4-Capt. America, Wolverine and New Avengers app. 3.00
...: New Labors of Hercules TPB (2005, $13.99) r/#1-5 14.00

HERCULES: HEART OF CHAOS
Marvel Comics: Aug, 1997 - No. 3, Oct, 1997 ($2.50, limited series)

1-3-DeFalco-s, Frenz-a 3.00

HERCULES: OFFICIAL COMICS MOVIE ADAPTION
Acclaim Books: 1997 ($4.50, digest size)

nn-Adaption of the Disney animated movie 4.50

HERCULES: THE LEGENDARY JOURNEYS (TV)
Topps Comics: June, 1996 - No. 5, Oct, 1996 ($2.95)

1-2: 1-Golden-c. 3.00
3-Xena-c/app. 1 2 3 4 5 7
3-Variant-c 2 4 6 9 12 15
4,5: Xena-c/app. 5.00

HERCULES UNBOUND
National Periodical Publications: Oct-Nov, 1975 - No. 12, Aug-Sept, 1977

1-Wood-i begins 2 4 6 9 13 16
2-12: 7-Adams ad. 10-Atomic Knights x-over 2 3 4 6 8 10
NOTE: ***Buckler** c-7p. **Layton** inks-No. 9, 10. **Simonson** a-7-10p, 11, 12; c- 8p, 9-12. **Wood** a-1-8i; c-7i, 8i.*

HERCULES (...Unchained #1121) (Movie)
Dell Publishing Co.: No. 1006, June-Aug, 1959 - No.1121, Aug, 1960

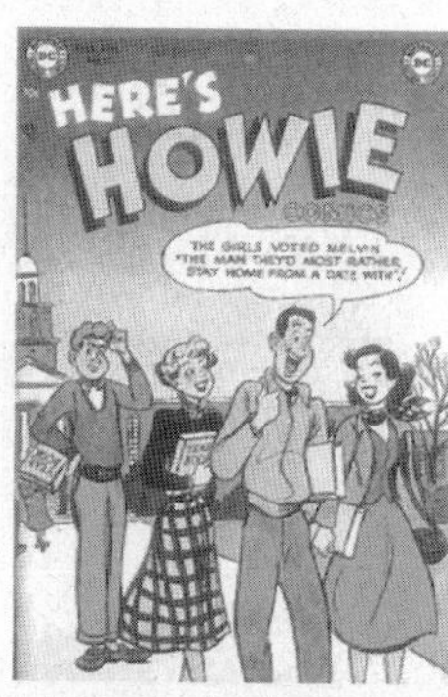

Here's Howie Comics #2 © DC

Hero Comics 2011 © IDW

Heroes For Hire (2006 series) #11 © MAR

	GD 2.0	VG 4.0	FN 6.0	VF 8.0	VF/NM 9.0	NM- 9.2
Four Color 1006-Buscema-a, photo-c	9	18	27	58	99	140
Four Color 1121-Crandall/Evans-a	9	18	27	58	99	140

HERCULES: FALL OF AN AVENGER (Continues in Heroic Age: Prince of Power)
Marvel Comics: May, 2010 - No. 2, June, 2010 ($3.99, limited series)

1,2-Follows Hercules' demise in Incredible Hercules #141; Olivetti-c/a 4.00

HERCULES: TWILIGHT OF A GOD
Marvel Comics: Aug, 2010 - No. 4, Nov, 2010 ($3.99, limited series)

1-4-Layton-s/a(i); Lim-a; Galactus app. 4.00

HERCULIAN
Image Comics: Mar, 2011 ($4.99, oversized, one-shot)

1-Golden Age style superhero stories and humor pages; Erik Larsen-s/a/c 5.00

HERE COMES SANTA (See March of Comics No. 30, 213, 340)

HERE'S HOWIE COMICS
National Periodical Publications: Jan-Feb, 1952 - No. 18, Nov-Dec, 1954

	GD 2.0	VG 4.0	FN 6.0	VF 8.0	VF/NM 9.0	NM- 9.2
1	29	58	87	170	278	385
2	15	30	45	90	140	190
3-5: 5-Howie in the Army issues begin (9-10/52)	14	28	42	78	112	145
6-10	12	24	36	67	94	120
11-18	11	22	33	62	86	110

Ashcan (1,2/51) not distributed to newsstands, only for in house use (no known sales)

HERETIC, THE
Dark Horse (Blanc Noir): Nov, 1996 - No. 4, Mar, 1997 ($2.95, lim. series)

1-4:-w/back-up story 3.00

HERITAGE OF THE DESERT (See Zane Grey, 4-Color 236)

HERMAN & KATNIP (See Harvey Comics Hits #60 & 62, Harvey Hits #14,25,31,41 & Paramount Animated Comics #1)

HERMES VS. THE EYEBALL KID
Dark Horse Comics: Dec, 1994 - No. 3,Feb, 1995 ($2.95, B&W, limited series)

1-3: Eddie Campbell-c/a/scripts 3.00

H-E-R-O (Dial H For HERO)
DC Comics: Apr, 2003 - No. 22, Jan, 2005 ($2.50)

1-Will Pfeiffer-s/Kano-a/Van Fleet-c 3.50
2-22: 2-6-Kano-a. 7,8-Gleason-a. 12-14-Kirk-a. 15-22-Robby Reed app. 3.00
...: Double Feature (6/03, $4.95) r/#1&2 5.00
...: Powers and Abilities (2003, $9.95) r/#1-6; intro. by Geoff Johns 10.00

HERO (Warrior of the Mystic Realms)
Marvel Comics: May, 1990 - No. 6, Oct, 1990 ($1.50, limited series)

1-6: 1-Portacio-i 3.00

HERO ALLIANCE, THE
Sirius Comics: Dec, 1985 - No. 2, Sept, 1986 (B&W)

1,2: 2-($1.50), Special Edition 1 (7/86, color) 3.00

HERO ALLIANCE
Wonder Color Comics: May, 1987 ($1.95)

1-Ron Lim-a 3.00

HERO ALLIANCE
Innovation Publishing: V2#1, Sept, 1989 - V2#17, Nov, 1991 ($1.95, 28 pgs.)

V2#1-17: 1,2-Ron Lim-a 3.00
Annual 1 (1990, $2.75, 36 pgs.)-Paul Smith-c/a 4.00
Special 1 (1992, $2.50, 32 pgs.)-Stuart Immonen-a (10 pgs.) 3.00

HERO ALLIANCE: END OF THE GOLDEN AGE
Innovation Publ.: July, 1989 - No. 3, Aug, 1989 ($1.75, bi-weekly lim. series)

1-3: Bart Sears & Ron Lim-c/a; reprints & new-a 3.00

HERO COMICS (Hero Initiative benefit book)
IDW Publishing: 2009, 2011 ($3.99)

1-Short story anthology by various incl. Colan, Chaykin; covers by Wagner & Campbell 4.00
2011-Covers by Campbell & Hughes; Gaiman-s/Kieth-a; Chew & Elephantmen app. 4.00

HEROES
Marvel Comics: Dec, 2001 ($3.50, magazine-size, one-shot)

1-Pin-up tributes to the rescue workers of the Sept. 11 tragedy; art and text by various; cover by Alex Ross 5.00
1-2nd and 3rd printings 3.50

HEROES (Also see Shadow Cabinet & Static)
DC Comics (Milestone): May, 1996 - No. 6, Nov, 1996 ($2.50, limited series)

1-6: 1-Intro Heroes (Iota, Donner, Blitzen, Starlight, Payback & Static) 3.00

HEROES (Based on the NBC TV series)
DC Comics (WildStorm): 2007; 2009 ($29.99, hardcover with dustjacket)

Vol. 1 - Collects 34 installments of the online graphic novel; art by various; two covers by Jim Lee and Alex Ross; intro. by Masi Oka; Jeph Loeb interview 30.00
Vol. 2 - (2009) Collects 46 installments of the online graphic novel; art by various incl. Gaydos, Grummett, Gunnell, Odagawa; two covers by Tim Sale and Gene Ha 30.00

HER-OES
Marvel Comics: Jun, 2010 - No. 4, Sept, 2010 ($2.99, limited series)

1-4-Randolph-s/Rousseau-a; Wasp, She-Hulk, Namora as teenagers 3.00

HEROES AGAINST HUNGER
DC Comics: 1986 ($1.50; one-shot for famine relief)

1-Superman, Batman app.; Neal Adams-c(p); includes many artists work; Jeff Jones assist (2 pg.) on B. Smith-a; Kirby-a 5.00

HEROES ALL CATHOLIC ACTION ILLUSTRATED
Heroes All Co.: 1943 - V6#5, Mar 10, 1948 (paper covers)

	GD 2.0	VG 4.0	FN 6.0	VF 8.0	VF/NM 9.0	NM- 9.2
V1#1-(16 pgs., 8x11")	24	48	72	142	234	325
V1#2-(16 pgs., 8x11")	19	38	57	111	176	240
V2#1(1/44)-3(3/44)-(16 pgs., 8x11")	15	30	45	94	147	200
V3#1(1/45)-10(12/45)-(16 pgs., 8x11")	15	30	45	85	130	175
V4#1-35 (12/20/46)-(16 pgs.)	14	28	42	80	115	150
V5#1(1/10/47)-8(2/28/47)-(16 pgs.), V5#9(3/7/47)-20(11/25/47)-(32 pgs.), V6#1(1/10/48)-5(3/10/48)-(32 pgs.)	12	24	36	69	97	125

HEROES ANONYMOUS
Bongo Comics: 2003 - No. 6, 2004 ($2.99, limited series)

1-6-($2.99)-Bill Morrison-c. 2-Guerra-a. 3-Pepoy-a 3.00

HEROES FOR HIRE
Marvel Comics: July, 1997 - No. 19, Jan, 1999 ($2.99/$1.99)

1-($2.99)-Wraparound cover 5.00
2-19: 2-Variant cover. 7-Thunderbolts app. 9-Punisher-c/app. 10,11-Deadpool-c/app. 18,19-Wolverine-c/app. 3.00
.../Quicksilver '98 Annual ($2.99) Siege of Wundagore pt.5 4.00

HEROES FOR HIRE
Marvel Comics: Oct, 2006 - No. 15, Dec, 2007 ($2.99)

1-5-Tucci-a/c; Black Cat, Shang-Chi, Tarantula, Humbug & Daughters of the Dragon app. 3.00
6-15: 6-8-Sparacio-c. 9,10-Golden-c. 11-13-World War Hulk x-over. 13-Takeda-c 3.00
... Vol. 1: Civil War (2007, $13.99) r/#1-5 14.00
... Vol. 2: Ahead of the Curve (2007, $13.99) r/#6-10 14.00
... Vol. 3: World War Hulk (2008, $13.99) r/#11-15 14.00

HEROES FOR HIRE
Marvel Comics: Feb, 2011 - Present ($3.99/$2.99)

1-($3.99) Abnett & Lanning-s/Walker-a; back-up history of the various teams 4.00
2-12-($2.99) 2-Silver Sable & Ghost Rider app. 5-Punisher app. 9-11-Fear Itself tie-in 3.00

HEROES FOR HOPE STARRING THE X-MEN
Marvel Comics Group: Dec, 1985 ($1.50, one-shot, 52 pgs., proceeds donated to famine relief)

1-Stephen King scripts; Byrne, Miller, Corben-a; Wrightson/J. Jones-a (3 pgs.); Art Adams-c; Starlin back-c 5.00

HEROES, INC. PRESENTS CANNON
Wally Wood/CPL/Gang Publ.:1969 - No. 2, 1976 (Sold at Army PXs)

	GD 2.0	VG 4.0	FN 6.0	VF 8.0	VF/NM 9.0	NM- 9.2
nn-Ditko, Wood-a; Wood-c; Reese-a(p)	2	4	6	9	12	15
2-Wood-c; Ditko, Byrne, Wood-a; 8-1/2x10-1/2"; B&W; $2.00	3	6	9	16	23	30

NOTE: *First issue not distributed by publisher; 1,800 copies were stored and 900 copies were stolen from warehouse. Many copies have surfaced in recent years.*

HEROES OF THE WILD FRONTIER (Formerly Baffling Mysteries)
Ace Periodicals: No. 27, Jan, 1956 - No. 2, Apr, 1956

	GD 2.0	VG 4.0	FN 6.0	VF 8.0	VF/NM 9.0	NM- 9.2
27(#1),2-Davy Crockett, Daniel Boone, Buffalo Bill	6	12	18	29	36	42

HEROES REBORN (one-shots)
Marvel Comics: Jan, 2000 ($1.99)

...:Ashema; ...:Doom; ...:Doomsday; ...:Masters of Evil; ...:Rebel; ...:Remnants; ...:Young Allies 3.00

HEROES REBORN: THE RETURN (Also see Avengers, Fantastic Four, Iron Man & Captain America titles for issues and TPBs)
Marvel Comics: Dec, 1997 - No. 4 ($2.50, weekly mini-series)

1-4-Avengers, Fantastic Four, Iron Man & Captain America rejoin regular Marvel Universe;

Hero For Hire #1 © MAR

Heroic Comics #16 © EAS

High Roads #2 © Leinil Yu

	GD 2.0	VG 4.0	FN 6.0	VF 8.0	VF/NM 9.0	NM- 9.2
Peter David-s/Larocca-c/a						4.00
1-4-Variant-c for each						6.00
Wizard 1/2	1	2	3	5	7	9
Return of the Heroes TPB ('98, $14.95) r/#1-4						15.00

HERO FOR HIRE (Power Man No. 17 on; also see Cage)
Marvel Comics Group: June, 1972 - No. 16, Dec, 1973

	GD 2.0	VG 4.0	FN 6.0	VF 8.0	VF/NM 9.0	NM- 9.2
1-Origin & 1st app. Luke Cage; Tuska-a(p)	13	26	39	85	180	275
2-Tuska-a(p)	7	14	21	44	72	100
3-5: 3-1st app. Mace. 4-1st app. Phil Fox of the Bugle	5	10	15	30	48	65
6-10: 8,9-Dr. Doom app. 9-F.F. app.	3	6	9	20	30	40
11-16: 14-Origin retold. 15-Everett Sub-Mariner-r('53). 16-Origin Stilletto; death of Rackham	3	6	9	16	23	30

HERO HOTLINE (1st app. in Action Comics Weekly #637)
DC Comics: April, 1989 - No. 6, Sept, 1989 ($1.75, limited series)

	GD 2.0	VG 4.0	FN 6.0	VF 8.0	VF/NM 9.0	NM- 9.2
1-6: Super-hero humor; Schaffenberger-i						3.00

HEROIC ADVENTURES (See Adventures)

HEROIC AGE
Marvel Comics: Nov, 2010 ($3.99, limited series)

	GD 2.0	VG 4.0	FN 6.0	VF 8.0	VF/NM 9.0	NM- 9.2
... Heroes 1 (11/10, $3.99) profile of heroes, bios, pros, cons, "power grid"; Raney-c						4.00
... Villains 1 (1/11, $3.99) profile of villains, bios, pros, cons, "power grid"; Jae Lee-c						4.00
... X-Men 1 (2/11, $3.99) profile of members in Steve Rogers journal entries,; Jae Lee-c						4.00

HEROIC AGE: PRINCE OF POWER (Continued from Hercules: Fall of an Avenger)
Marvel Comics: Jul, 2010 - No. 4, Oct, 2010 ($3.99, limited series)

	GD 2.0	VG 4.0	FN 6.0	VF 8.0	VF/NM 9.0	NM- 9.2
1-4-Van Lente & Pak-s; Thor app.; leads into Chaos War #1						4.00

HEROIC COMICS (Reg'lar Fellers...#1-15; New Heroic #41 on)
Eastern Color Printing Co./Famous Funnies (Funnies, Inc. No. 1):
Aug, 1940 - No. 97, June, 1955

	GD 2.0	VG 4.0	FN 6.0	VF 8.0	VF/NM 9.0	NM- 9.2
1-Hydroman (origin) by Bill Everett, The Purple Zombie (origin) & Mann of India by Tarpe Mills begins (all 1st apps.)	206	412	618	1318	2259	3200
2	84	168	252	538	919	1300
3,4	53	106	159	334	567	800
5,6	45	90	135	284	480	675
7-Origin & 1st app. Man O'Metal (1 pg.)	47	94	141	298	504	710
8-10: 10-Lingerie panels	36	72	108	216	351	485
11,13	34	68	102	199	325	450
12-Music Master (origin/1st app.) begins by Everett, ends No. 31; last Purple Zombie & Mann of India	38	76	114	226	368	510
14,15-Hydroman x-over in Rainbow Boy. 14-Origin & 1st app. Rainbow Boy (super hero). 15-1st app. Downbeat	36	72	108	216	351	485
16-20: 16-New logo. 17-Rainbow Boy x-over in Hydroman. 19-Rainbow Boy x-over in Hydroman & vice versa	25	50	75	147	241	335
21-30:25-Rainbow Boy x-over in Hydroman. 28-Last Man O'Metal. 29-Last Hydroman	19	38	57	111	176	240
31,34,38	9	18	27	50	65	80
32,36,37-Toth-a (3-4 pgs. each)	10	20	30	56	76	95
33,35-Toth-a (8 & 9 pgs.)	10	20	30	58	79	100
39-42-Toth, Ingels-a	10	20	30	58	79	100
43,46,47,49-Toth-a (2-4 pgs.). 47-Ingels-a	10	20	30	54	72	90
44,45,50-Toth-a (6-9 pgs.)	10	20	30	56	76	95
48,53,54	9	18	27	47	61	75
51-Williamson-a	10	20	30	56	76	95
52-Williamson-a (3 pg. story)	9	18	27	50	65	80
55-Toth-a	10	20	30	54	72	90
56-60: 60-Everett-a	9	18	27	50	65	80
61-Everett-a	9	18	27	47	61	75
62,64-Everett-c/a	10	20	30	54	72	90
63-Everett-c	9	18	27	52	69	85
65-Williamson/Frazetta-a; Evans-a (2 pgs.)	13	26	39	72	101	130
66,75,94-Frazetta-a (2 pgs. each)	9	18	27	52	69	85
67,73-Frazetta-a (4 pgs. each)	11	22	33	60	83	105
68,74,76-80,84,85,88-93,95-97: 95-Last pre-code	9	18	27	47	61	75
69,72-Frazetta-a (6 & 8 pgs. each); 1st (?) app. Frazetta Red Cross ad	13	26	39	72	101	130
70,71,86,87-Frazetta, 3-4 pgs. each; 1 pg. ad by Frazetta in #70	10	20	30	56	76	95
81,82-Frazetta art (1 pg. each): 81-1st (?) app. Frazetta Boy Scout ad (tied w/ Buster Crabbe #9	9	18	27	50	65	80
83-Frazetta-a (1/2 pg.)	9	18	27	50	65	80

NOTE: ***Evans*** *a-64, 65.* ***Everett*** *a-(Hydroman-c/a-No. 1-9), 44, 60-64; c-1-9, 62-64.* ***Harvey Fuller*** *c-28-35.* ***Sid Greene*** *a-38-43, 46.* ***Guardineer*** *a-42(3), 43, 44, 45(2), 49(3), 50, 60, 61(2), 65, 67(2) 70-72.* ***Ingels*** *c-41.* ***Kiefer*** *a-46, 48; c-19-22, 24, 44, 46, 48, 51-53, 65, 67-69, 71-74, 76, 77, 79, 80, 82, 85, 86, 88, 89, 94, 95.* ***Mort Lawrence*** *a-45.* ***Tarpe Mills*** *a-2(2), 3(2), 10.* ***Ed Moore*** *a-49, 52-54, 56-63, 65-69, 72-74, 76, 77.* ***H.G. Peter*** *a-58-74, 76, 77, 87.* ***Paul Reinman*** *a-49.* ***Rico*** *a-31. Captain Tootsie by* ***Beck****-31, 32. Painted-c #16 on. Hydroman c-1-11. Music Master c-12, 13, 15. Rainbow Boy c-14.*

HERO INITIATIVE: MIKE WIERINGO BOOK (Also see Hero Comics)
Marvel Comics: Aug, 2008 ($4.99)

	GD 2.0	VG 4.0	FN 6.0	VF 8.0	VF/NM 9.0	NM- 9.2
1-The "What If" Fantastic Four story with Wieringo-a (7 pgs.) finished by other artists after his passing; art by Davis, Immonen, Ramos, Kitson and others; written tributes						5.00

HERO ZERO (Also see Comics' Greatest World & Godzilla Versus Hero Zero)
Dark Horse Comics: Sept, 1994 ($2.50)

	GD 2.0	VG 4.0	FN 6.0	VF 8.0	VF/NM 9.0	NM- 9.2
0						3.00

HEX (Replaces Jonah Hex)
DC Comics: Sept, 1985 - No. 18, Feb, 1987 (Story cont'd from Jonah Hex # 92)

	GD 2.0	VG 4.0	FN 6.0	VF 8.0	VF/NM 9.0	NM- 9.2
1-Hex in post-atomic war world; origin	2	4	6	8	10	12
2-10,14-18: 6-Origin Stiletta	1	2	3	4	5	7
11-13: All contain future Batman storyline. 13-Intro The Dogs of War (origin #15)	1	3	4	6	8	10

NOTE: ***Giffen*** *a(p)-15-18; c(p)-15,17,18.* ***Texeira*** *a-1, 2p, 3p, 5-7p, 9p, 11-14p; c(p)-1, 2, 4-7, 12.*

HEXBREAKER (See First Comics Graphic Novel #15)

HEY THERE, IT'S YOGI BEAR (See Movie Comics)

HI-ADVENTURE HEROES (TV)
Gold Key: May, 1969 - No. 2, Aug, 1969 (Hanna-Barbera)

	GD 2.0	VG 4.0	FN 6.0	VF 8.0	VF/NM 9.0	NM- 9.2
1-Three Musketeers, Gulliver, Arabian Knights	5	10	15	32	51	70
2-Three Musketeers, Micro-Venture, Arabian Knights	4	8	12	28	44	60

HI AND LOIS
Dell Publishing Co.: No. 683, Mar, 1956 - No. 955, Nov, 1958

	GD 2.0	VG 4.0	FN 6.0	VF 8.0	VF/NM 9.0	NM- 9.2
Four Color 683 (#1)	5	10	15	30	48	65
Four Color 774(3/57),955	4	8	12	24	37	50

HI AND LOIS
Charlton Comics: Nov, 1969 - No. 11, July, 1971

	GD 2.0	VG 4.0	FN 6.0	VF 8.0	VF/NM 9.0	NM- 9.2
1	3	6	9	14	20	25
2-11	2	4	6	9	12	15

HICKORY (See All Humor Comics)
Quality Comics Group: Oct, 1949 - No. 6, Aug, 1950

	GD 2.0	VG 4.0	FN 6.0	VF 8.0	VF/NM 9.0	NM- 9.2
1-Sahl-c/a in all; Feldstein?-a	20	40	60	114	182	250
2	12	24	36	69	97	125
3-6	10	20	30	58	79	100

HIDDEN CREW, THE (See The United States Air Force Presents:...)

HIDE-OUT (See Zane Grey, Four Color No. 346)

HIDING PLACE, THE
Spire Christian Comics (Fleming H. Revell Co.): 1973 (39¢/49¢)

	GD 2.0	VG 4.0	FN 6.0	VF 8.0	VF/NM 9.0	NM- 9.2
nn	2	4	6	10	14	18

HIGH ADVENTURE
Red Top(Decker) Comics (Farrell): Oct, 1957

	GD 2.0	VG 4.0	FN 6.0	VF 8.0	VF/NM 9.0	NM- 9.2
1-Krigstein-r from Explorer Joe (re-issue on-c)	5	10	15	23	28	32

HIGH ADVENTURE (TV)
Dell Publishing Co.: No. 949, Nov, 1958 - No. 1001, Aug-Oct, 1959 (Lowell Thomas)

	GD 2.0	VG 4.0	FN 6.0	VF 8.0	VF/NM 9.0	NM- 9.2
Four Color 949 (#1)-Photo-c	6	12	18	37	59	80
Four Color 1001-Lowell Thomas'...(#2)	5	10	15	34	55	75

HIGH CHAPPARAL (TV)
Gold Key: Aug, 1968 (Photo-c)

	GD 2.0	VG 4.0	FN 6.0	VF 8.0	VF/NM 9.0	NM- 9.2
1 (10226-808)-Tufts-a	6	12	18	37	59	80

HIGHLANDER
Dynamite Entertainment: No. 0, 2006 - No. 12, 2007 (25¢/$2.99)

	GD 2.0	VG 4.0	FN 6.0	VF 8.0	VF/NM 9.0	NM- 9.2
0-(25¢-c) Takes place after the first movie; photo-c and Dell'Otto painted-c						3.00
1-12: 1-($2.99) Three covers; Moder-a/Jerwa & Oeming-s. 2-Three covers						3.00
... Origins: The Kurgan 1,2 (2009 - No. 2, 2009, $4.99) Three covers; Rafael-a						5.00
...: Way of the Sword (2007 - No. 4, 2008, $3.50) Two interlocking covers for each						3.50

HIGH ROADS
DC Comics (Cliffhanger): June, 2002 - No. 6, Nov, 2002 ($2.95, limited series)

	GD 2.0	VG 4.0	FN 6.0	VF 8.0	VF/NM 9.0	NM- 9.2
1-6-Leinil Yu-c/a; Lobdell-s						3.00
TPB (2003, $14.95) r/#1-6; sketch pages						15.00

HIGH SCHOOL CONFIDENTIAL DIARY (Confidential Diary #12 on)
Charlton Comics: June, 1960 - No. 11, Mar, 1962

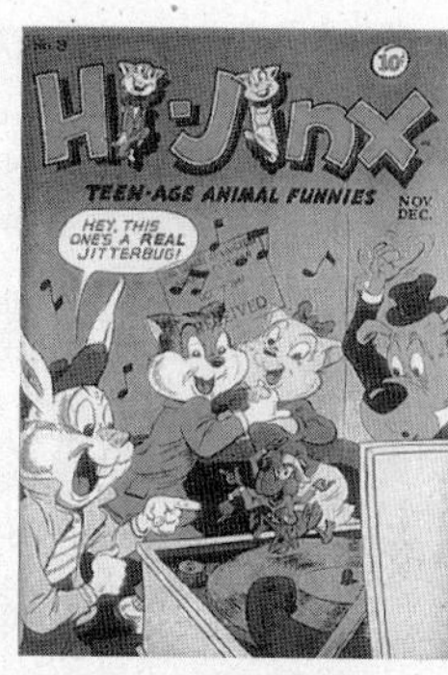

Hi-Jinx #3 © ACG

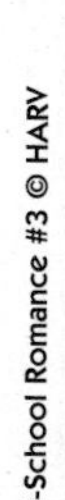
Hi-School Romance #3 © HARV

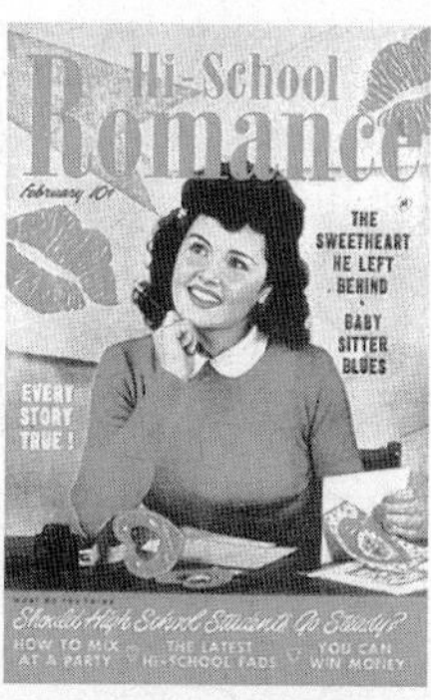

Hit Comics #52 © QUA

	GD 2.0	VG 4.0	FN 6.0	VF 8.0	VF/NM 9.0	NM- 9.2

1 4 8 12 28 44 60
2-11 3 6 9 18 27 35

HIGHWAYMEN
DC Comics (WildStorm): Aug, 2007 - No. 5, Dec, 2007 ($2.99)
1-5-Bernardin & Freeman-s/Garbett-a 3.00
TPB (2008, $17.99) r/#1-5 18.00

HI HI PUFFY AMIYUMI (Based on Cartoon Network animated series)
DC Comics: Apr, 2006 - No. 3, June, 2006 ($2.25, limited series)
1-3-Phil Moy-a 3.00

HI-HO COMICS
Four Star Publications: nd (2/46?) - No. 3, 1946
1-Funny Animal; L. B. Cole-c 37 74 111 222 361 500
2,3: 2-L. B. Cole-c 21 42 63 122 199 275

HI-JINX (Teen-age Animal Funnies)
La Salle Publ. Co./B&I Publ. Co. (American Comics Group)/Creston: 1945; July-Aug, 1947 - No. 7, July-Aug, 1948
nn-(© 1945, 25 cents, 132 Pgs.)(La Salle) 26 52 78 154 252 350
1-Teen-age, funny animal 19 38 57 109 172 235
2,3 13 26 39 72 101 130
4-7-Milt Gross. 4-X-Mas-c 18 36 54 105 165 225

HI-LITE COMICS
E. R. Ross Publishing Co.: Fall, 1945
1-Miss Shady 20 40 60 118 192 265

HILLBILLY COMICS
Charlton Comics: Aug, 1955 - No. 4, July, 1956 (Satire)
1-By Art Gates 9 18 27 52 69 85
2-4 7 14 21 35 43 50

HILLY ROSE'S SPACE ADVENTURES
Astro Comics: May, 1995 - No. 9 ($2.95, B&W)
1 1 2 3 5 7 9
2-9 5.00
Trade Paperback (1996, $12.95)-r/#1-5 13.00

HIP FLASK UNNATURAL SELECTION
Active Images: Sept, 2002 ($2.99)
1-Casey & Starkings-s/Ladronn-a; var.-c by Madureira, Campbell, Churchill 3.00

HIP-IT-TY HOP (See March of Comics No. 15)

HIRE, THE (BMWfilms.com's...)
Dark Horse Comics: July, 2004 - No. 6 ($2.99)
1-4: 1-Matt Wagner-s/Wagner & Velasco-a. 2-Bruce Campbell-s/Plunkett-a. 3-Waid-s 3.00
TPB (4/06, $17.95) r/#1-4 18.00

HI-SCHOOL ROMANCE (...Romances No. 41 on)
Harvey Publ./True Love(Home Comics): Oct, 1949 - No. 5, June, 1950; No. 6, Dec, 1950 - No. 73, Mar, 1958; No. 74, Sept, 1958 - No. 75, Nov, 1958
1-Photo-c 15 30 45 90 140 190
2-Photo-c 10 20 30 56 76 95
3-9: 3-5-Photo-c 9 18 27 47 61 75
10-Rape story 10 20 30 56 76 95
11-20 8 16 24 40 50 60
21-31 6 12 18 31 38 45
32- "Unholy passion" story 9 18 27 50 65 80
33-36: 36-Last pre-code (2/55) 6 12 18 29 36 42
37-53,59-72,74,75 5 10 15 24 30 35
54-58,73-Kirby-c 6 12 18 31 38 45
NOTE: *Powell a-1-3, 5, 8, 12-16, 18, 21-23, 25-27, 30-34, 36, 37, 39, 45-48, 50-52, 57, 58, 60, 64, 65, 67, 69.*

HI-SCHOOL ROMANCE DATE BOOK
Harvey Publications: Nov, 1962 - No. 3, Mar, 1963 (25¢ Giants)
1-Powell, Baker-a 6 12 18 41 66 90
2,3 4 8 12 22 34 45

HIS NAME IS SAVAGE (Magazine format)
Adventure House Press: June, 1968 (35¢, 52 pgs.)
1-Gil Kane-a 5 10 15 34 55 75

HI-SPOT COMICS (Red Ryder No. 1 & No. 3 on)
Hawley Publications: No. 2, Nov, 1940
2-David Innes of Pellucidar; art by J. C. Burroughs; written by Edgar Rice Burroughs
135 270 405 864 1482 2100

HISTORY OF THE DC UNIVERSE (Also see Crisis on Infinite Earths)
DC Comics: Sept, 1986 - No. 2, Nov, 1986 ($2.95, limited series)
1,2: 1-Perez-c/a 4.00
Limited Edition hardcover 4 8 12 26 41 55
Softcover (2002, $9.95) new Alex Ross wraparound-c 10.00
Softcover (2009, $12.99) Alex Ross wraparound-c 13.00

HISTORY OF VIOLENCE, A (Inspired the 2005 movie)
DC Comics (Paradox Press) 1997 ($9.95, B&W graphic novel)
nn-Paperback ($9.95) John Wagner-s/Vince Locke-a 15.00

HITCHHIKERS GUIDE TO THE GALAXY (See Life, the Universe and Everything & Restaurant at the End of the Universe)
DC Comics: 1993 - No. 3, 1993 ($4.95, limited series)
1-3: Adaptation of Douglas Adams book 5.00
TPB (1997, $14.95) r/#1-3 15.00

HIT COMICS
Quality Comics Group: July, 1940 - No. 65, July, 1950
1-Origin/1st app. Neon, the Unknown & Hercules; intro. The Red Bee; Bob & Swab, Blaze Barton, the Strange Twins, X-5 Super Agent, Casey Jones & Jack & Jill (ends #7) begin
811 1622 2433 5920 10,460 15,000
2-The Old Witch begins, ends #14 300 600 900 1950 3375 4800
3-Casey Jones ends; transvestism story "Jack & Jill"
300 600 900 1920 3310 4700
4-Super Agent (ends #17), & Betty Bates (ends #65) begin; X-5 ends
258 516 774 1651 2826 4000
5-Classic Lou Fine cover 757 1514 2271 5526 9763 14,000
6-10: 10-Old Witch by Crandall (4 pgs.); 1st work in comics (4/41)
213 426 639 1363 2332 3300
11-Classic cover 245 490 735 1568 2684 3800
12-17: 13-Blaze Barton ends. 17-Last Neon; Crandall Hercules in all; Last Lou Fine-c
132 264 396 838 1444 2050
18-Origin & 1st app. Stormy Foster, the Great Defender (12/41); The Ghost of Flanders begins; Crandall-c 139 278 417 883 1517 2150
19,20 110 220 330 704 1202 1700
21-24: 21-Last Hercules. 24-Last Red Bee & Strange Twins
107 214 321 680 1165 1650
25-Origin & 1st app. Kid Eternity and begins by Moldoff (12/42); 1st app. The Keeper (Kid Eternity's aide) 200 400 600 1280 2190 3100
26-Blackhawk x-over in Kid Eternity 100 200 300 635 1093 1550
27-29 50 100 150 315 533 750
30,31- "Bill the Magnificent" by Kurtzman, 11 pgs. in each
45 90 135 284 480 675
32-40: 32-Plastic Man x-over. 34-Last Stormy Foster
30 60 90 177 289 400
41-50 21 42 63 126 206 285
51-60-Last Kid Eternity 20 40 60 120 195 270
61-63-Crandall-c/a; 61-Jeb Rivers begins 21 42 63 124 202 280
64,65-Crandall-a 20 40 60 120 195 270
NOTE: *Crandall a-11-17(Hercules), 23, 24(Stormy Foster); c-18-20, 23, 24.* ***Fine*** *c-1-14, 16, 17(most).* ***Ward*** *c-33. Bondage c-7, 64. Hercules c-3, 10-17. Jeb Rivers c-61-65. Kid Eternity c-25-60 (w/Keeper-28-34, 36, 39-43, 45-55). Neon the Unknown c-2, 4, 8, 9. Red Bee c-1, 5-7. Stormy Foster c-18-24.*

HITLER'S ASTROLOGER (See Marvel Graphic Novel #35)

HITMAN (Also see Bloodbath #2, Batman Chronicles #4, Demon #43-45 & Demon Annual #2)
DC Comics: May, 1996 - No. 60, Apr, 2001 ($2.25/$2.50)
1-Garth Ennis-s & John McCrea-c/a begin; Batman app.
2 4 6 8 10 12
2-Joker-c;Two Face, Mad Hatter, Batman app. 1 2 3 5 6 8
3-5: 3-Batman-c/app.; Joker app. 4-1st app. Nightfist 5.00
6-20: 8-Final Night x-over. 10-GL cameo. 11-20: 11,12-GL-c/app. 15-20-"Ace of Killers". 16-18-Catwoman app. 17-19-Demon-app. 4.00
21-59: 34-Superman-c/app. 3.00
60-($3.95) Final issue; includes pin-ups by various 4.00
#1,000,000 (11/98) Hitman goes to the 853rd Century 3.00
Annual 1 (1997, $3.95) Pulp Heroes 5.00
.../Lobo: That Stupid Bastich (7/00, $3.95) Ennis-s/Mahnke-a 4.00
TPB-(1997, $9.95) r/#1-3, Demon Ann. #2, Batman Chronicles #4 10.00
Ace of Killers TPB ('00/'11, $17.95/$17.99) r/#15-22 18.00
Local Heroes TPB ('99, $17.95) r/#9-14 & Annual #1 18.00
10,000 Bullets TPB ('98, $9.95) r/#4-8 10.00
Ten Thousand Bullets TPB ('10, $17.99) r/#4-8 & Annual #1; intro, by Kevin Smith 18.00
Who Dares Wins TPB ('01, $12.95) r/#23-28 13.00

HIT-MONKEY (See Deadpool)

Holiday Comics #1 © FAW

Hollywood Confessions #1 © STJ

Holyoke One-Shot #2 © HOKE

	GD 2.0	VG 4.0	FN 6.0	VF 8.0	VF/NM 9.0	NM- 9.2

Marvel Comics: Apr, 2010; Sept, 2010 - No. 3, Nov, 2010 ($3.99/$2.99)
1-(4/10, $3.99) Printing of story from Marvel Digital Comics; Frank Cho-c; origin revealed 4.00
1-3-Daniel Way-s/Talajic-a/Johnson-c; Bullseye app. 3.00

HI-YO SILVER (See Lone Ranger's Famous Horse... and The Lone Ranger; and March of Comics No. 215 in the Promotional Comics section)

HOBBIT, THE
Eclipse Comics: 1989 - No. 3, 1990 ($4.95, squarebound, 52 pgs.)
Book 1-3: Adapts novel; Wenzel-a 8.00
Book 1-Second printing 5.00
Graphic Novel (1990, Ballantine)-r/#1-3 25.00

HOCUS POCUS (See Funny Book #9)

HOGAN'S HEROES (TV) (Also see Wild!)
Dell Publishing Co.: June, 1966 - No. 8, Sept, 1967; No. 9, Oct, 1969
1: #1-7 photo-c 8 16 24 55 93 130
2,3-Ditko-a(p) 6 12 18 37 59 80
4-9: 9-Reprints #1 5 10 15 30 48 65

HOKUM & HEX (See Razorline)
Marvel Comics (Razorline): Sept, 1993 - No. 9, May, 1994 ($1.75/$1.95)
1-($2.50)-Foil embossed-c; by Clive Barker 3.50
2-9: 5-Hyperkind x-over 3.00

HOLIDAY COMICS
Fawcett Publications: 1942 (25¢, 196 pgs.)
1-Contains three Fawcett comics plus two page portrait of Captain Marvel; Capt. Marvel, Jungle Girl #1, & Whiz. Not rebound, remaindered comics; printed at the same time as originals (scarce in high grade) 290 580 870 1856 3178 4500

HOLIDAY COMICS (Becomes Fun Comics #9-12)
Star Publications: Jan, 1951 - No. 8, Oct, 1952
1-Funny animal contents (Frisky Fables) in all; L. B. Cole X-Mas-c
29 58 87 170 278 385
2-Classic L. B. Cole-c 31 62 93 186 303 420
3-8: 5,8-X-Mas-c; all L.B. Cole-c 19 38 57 109 172 235
Accepted Reprint 4 (nd)-L.B. Cole-c 10 20 30 58 79 100

HOLIDAY DIGEST
Harvey Comics: 1988 ($1.25, digest-size)
1 1 2 3 5 7 9

HOLIDAY PARADE (Walt Disney's...)
W. D. Publications (Disney): Winter, 1990-91(no year given) - No. 2, Winter, 1990-91 ($2.95, 68 pgs.)
1-Reprints 1947 Firestone by Barks plus new-a 5.00
2-Barks-r plus other stories 4.00

HOLI-DAY SURPRISE (Formerly Summer Fun)
Charlton Comics: V2#55, Mar, 1967 (25¢ Giant)
V2#55 4 8 12 24 37 50

HOLLYWOOD COMICS
New Age Publishers: Winter, 1944 (52 pgs.)
1-Funny animal 18 36 54 105 165 225

HOLLYWOOD CONFESSIONS
St. John Publishing Co.: Oct, 1949 - No. 2, Dec, 1949
1-Kubert-c/a (entire book) 34 68 102 204 332 460
2-Kubert-c/a (entire book) (Scarce) 36 72 108 216 351 485

HOLLYWOOD DIARY
Quality Comics Group: Dec, 1949 - No. 5, July-Aug, 1950
1-No photo-c 22 44 66 128 209 290
2-Photo-c 15 30 45 84 127 170
3-5-Photo-c. 5-June Allyson/Peter Lawford photo-c 14 28 42 78 112 145

HOLLYWOOD FILM STORIES
Feature Publications/Prize: April, 1950 - No. 4, Oct, 1950 (All photo-c; "Fumetti" type movie comic)
1-June Allyson photo-c 20 40 60 120 195 270
2-4: 2-Lizabeth Scott photo-c. 3-Barbara Stanwick photo-c. 4-Betty Hutton photo-c
15 30 45 86 133 180

HOLLYWOOD FUNNY FOLKS (Formerly Funny Folks; Becomes Nutsy Squirrel #61 on)
National Periodical Publ.: No. 27, Aug-Sept, 1950 - No. 60, July-Aug, 1954
27 14 28 42 76 108 140
28-40 10 20 30 54 72 90
41-60 9 18 27 47 61 75
NOTE: *Rube Grossman a-most issues.* ***Sheldon Mayer*** *a-27-35, 37-40, 43-46, 48-51, 53, 56, 57, 60.*

HOLLYWOOD LOVE DOCTOR (See Doctor Anthony King...)

HOLLYWOOD PICTORIAL (...Romances on cover)
St. John Publishing Co.: No. 3, Jan, 1950
3-Matt Baker-a; photo-c 29 58 87 170 278 385
(Becomes a movie magazine - Hollywood Pictorial Western with No. 4.)

HOLLYWOOD ROMANCES (Formerly Brides In Love; becomes For Lovers Only #60 on)
Charlton Comics: V2#46, 11/66; #47, 10/67; #48, 11/68;V3#49,11/69-V3#59, 6/71
V2#46-Rolling Stones-c/story 9 18 27 63 112 160
V2#47-V3#59: 56- "Born to Heart Break" begins 3 6 9 14 19 24

HOLLYWOOD SECRETS
Quality Comics Group: Nov, 1949 - No. 6, Sept, 1950
1-Ward-c/a (9 pgs.) 36 72 108 216 351 485
2-Crandall-a, Ward-c/a (9 pgs.) 25 50 75 147 241 335
3-6: All photo-c. 5-Lex Barker (Tarzan)-c 14 28 42 82 121 160
...of Romance, I.W. Reprint #9; r/#2 above w/Kinstler-c
2 4 6 11 16 20

HOLLYWOOD SUPERSTARS
Marvel Comics (Epic Comics): Nov, 1990 - No. 5, Apr, 1991 ($2.25)
1-($2.95, 52 pgs.)-Spiegle-c/a in all; Aragonés-a, inside front-c plus 2-4 pgs. 4.00
2-5 ($2.25) 3.00

HOLO-MAN (See Power Record Comics)

HOLYOKE ONE-SHOT
Holyoke Publishing Co. (Tem Publ.): 1944 - No. 10, 1945 (All reprints)
1,2: 1-Grit Grady (on cover only), Miss Victory, Alias X (origin)-All reprints from Captain Fearless. 2-Rusty Dugan (Corporal); Capt. Fearless (origin), Mr. Miracle (origin) app.
27 54 81 160 263 365
3-Miss Victory; r/Crash #4; Cat Man (origin), Solar Legion by Kirby app.; Miss Victory on cover only (1945) 39 78 117 240 395 550
4,6,8: 4-Mr. Miracle; The Blue Streak app. 6-Capt. Fearless, Alias X, Capt. Stone (splash used as-c to #10); Diamond Jim & Rusty Dugan (splash from cover of #2). 8-Blue Streak, Strong Man (story matches cover to #7)-Crash reprints
24 48 72 142 234 325
5,7: 5-U.S. Border Patrol Comics (Sgt. Dick Carter of the...), Miss Victory (story matches cover to #3), Citizen Smith, & Mr. Miracle app. 7-Secret Agent Z-2, Strong Man, Blue Streak (story matches cover to #8); Reprints from Crash #2
25 50 75 150 245 340
9-Citizen Smith, The Blue Streak, Solar Legion by Kirby & Strongman, the Perfect Human app.; reprints from Crash #4 & 5; Citizen Smith on cover only-from story in #5 (1944-before #3) 28 56 84 165 270 375
10-Captain Stone; r/Crash; Solar Legion by S&K 28 56 84 165 270 375

HOLY TERROR
Legendary Comics: Sept, 2011 ($29.95, HC graphic novel, 12-1/4" wide x 9-1/4" tall)
HC-Frank Miller-s/a/c; B&W art with spot color; The Fixer vs. Al-Qaeda in Empire City 30.00

HOMER COBB (See Adventures of...)

HOMER HOOPER
Atlas Comics: July, 1953 - No. 4, Dec, 1953
1-Teenage humor 10 20 30 58 79 100
2-4 8 16 24 40 50 60

HOMER, THE HAPPY GHOST (See Adventures of...)
Atlas(ACI/PPI/WPI)/Marvel: 3/55 - No. 22, 11/58; V2#1, 11/69 - V2#4, 5/70
V1#1-Dan DeCarlo-c/a begins, ends #22 23 46 69 136 223 310
2-1st code approved issue 14 28 42 81 118 155
3-10 13 26 39 74 105 135
11-22 11 22 33 64 90 115
V2#1 (11/69) 11 22 33 73 142 210
2-4 7 14 21 46 76 105

HOME RUN (Also see A-1 Comics)
Magazine Enterprises: No. 89, 1953 (one-shot)
A-1 89 (#3)-Powell-a; Stan Musial photo-c 15 30 45 86 133 180

HOMICIDE (Also see Dark Horse Presents)
Dark Horse Comics: Apr, 1990 ($1.95, B&W, one-shot)
1-Detective story 3.00

HONEYMOON (Formerly Gay Comics)
A Lover's Magazine(USA) (Marvel): No. 41, Jan, 1950

Hong Kong Phooey #6 © H-B

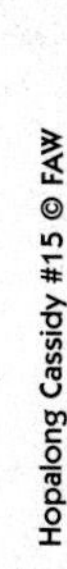

Hopalong Cassidy #15 © FAW

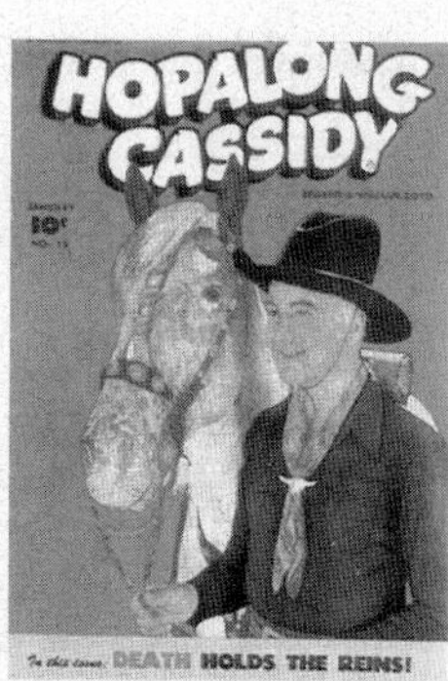

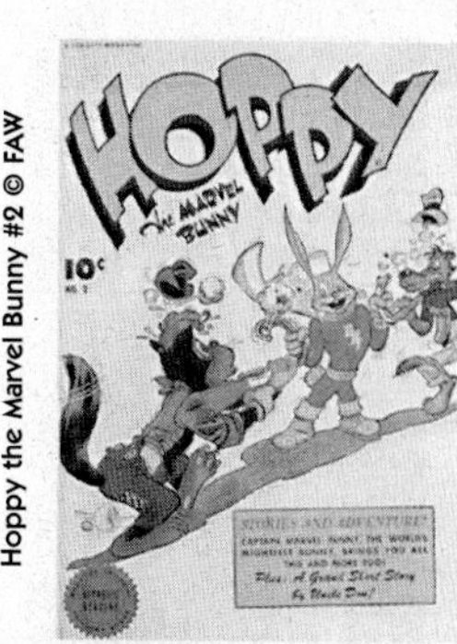

Hoppy the Marvel Bunny #2 © FAW

	GD 2.0	VG 4.0	FN 6.0	VF 8.0	VF/NM 9.0	NM- 9.2
41-Photo-c; article by Betty Grable	13	26	39	72	101	130

HONEYMOONERS, THE (TV)
Lodestone: Oct, 1986 ($1.50)

1-Photo-c 5.00

HONEYMOONERS, THE (TV)
Triad Publications: Sept, 1987 - No. 13? ($2.00)

1-13 5.00

HONEYMOON ROMANCE
Artful Publications (Canadian): Apr, 1950 - No. 2, July, 1950 (25¢, digest size)

	GD	VG	FN	VF	VF/NM	NM-
1,2-(Rare)	58	116	174	371	636	900

HONEY WEST (TV)
Gold Key: Sept, 1966 (Photo-c)

	GD	VG	FN	VF	VF/NM	NM-
1 (10186-609)	9	18	27	58	99	140

HONEY WEST (TV)
Moonstone: 2010 - Present ($5.99/$3.99)

1-($5.99) Trina Robbins-s/Cynthia Martin-a; two art covers & two photo covers 6.00
2-4-($3.99) 4.00

HONG KONG PHOOEY (TV)
Charlton Comics: June, 1975 - No. 9, Nov, 1976 (Hanna-Barbera)

	GD	VG	FN	VF	VF/NM	NM-
1	5	10	15	34	55	75
2	3	6	9	19	29	38
3-9	3	6	9	16	22	28

HONG ON THE RANGE
Image/Flypaper Press: Dec, 1997 - No. 3, Feb, 1998 ($2.50, lim. series)

1-3: Wu-s/Lafferty-a 3.00

HOOD, THE
Marvel Comics (MAX): Jul, 2002 - No. 6, Dec, 2002 ($2.99, limited series)

1-6-Vaughan-s/Hotz-c/a 3.00
Vol. 1 Blood From Stones HC (2007, $19.99, dustjacket) r/#1-6; production sketch art 20.00
Vol. 1 Blood From Stones TPB (2003, $14.99) r/#1-6 15.00

HOODED HORSEMAN, THE (Formerly Blazing West)
American Comics Group (Michel Publ.): No. 21, 1-2/52 - No. 27, 1-2/54; No. 18, 12-1/54-55 - No. 22, 8-9/55

	GD	VG	FN	VF	VF/NM	NM-
21(1-2/52)-Hooded Horseman, Injun Jones cont.	15	30	45	83	124	165
22	10	20	30	56	76	95
23,24,27(1-2/54)	9	18	27	50	65	80
25 (9-10/53)-Cowboy Sahib on cover only; Hooded Horseman i.d. revealed	9	18	27	52	69	85
26-Origin/1st app. Cowboy Sahib by L. Starr	11	22	33	62	86	110
18(12-1/54-55)(Formerly Out of the Night)	10	20	30	54	72	90
19,21,22: 19-Last precode (1-2/55)	8	16	24	44	57	70
20-Origin Johnny Injun	9	18	27	50	65	80

NOTE: ***Whitney** c/a-21('52), 20-22.*

HOODED MENACE, THE (Also see Daring Adventures)
Realistic/Avon Periodicals: 1951 (one-shot)

	GD	VG	FN	VF	VF/NM	NM-
nn-Based on a band of hooded outlaws in the Pacific Northwest, 1900-1906; reprinted in Daring Advs. #15	51	102	153	320	543	765

HOODS UP (See the Promotional Comics section)

HOOK (Movie)
Marvel Comics: Early Feb, 1992 - No. 4, Late Mar, 1992 ($1.00, limited series)

1-4: Adapts movie; Vess-c; 1-Morrow-a(p) 3.00
nn (1991, $5.95, 84 pgs.)-Contains #1-4; Vess-c 6.00
1 (1991, $2.95, magazine, 84 pgs.)-Contains #1-4; Vess-c (same cover as nn issue) 4.00

HOOT GIBSON'S WESTERN ROUNDUP (See Western Roundup under Fox Giants)

HOOT GIBSON WESTERN (Formerly My Love Story)
Fox Features Syndicate: No. 5, May, 1950 - No. 3, Sept, 1950

	GD	VG	FN	VF	VF/NM	NM-
5,6(#1,2): 5-Photo-c. 6-Photo/painted-c	21	42	63	123	197	270
3-Wood-a; painted-c	22	44	66	131	211	290

HOPALONG CASSIDY (Also see Bill Boyd Western, Master Comics, Real Western Hero, Six Gun Heroes & Western Hero; Bill Boyd starred as Hopalong Cassidy in movies, radio & TV)
Fawcett Publications: Feb, 1943; No. 2, Summer, 1946 - No. 85, Nov, 1953

	GD	VG	FN	VF	VF/NM	NM-
1 (1943, 68 pgs.)-H. Cassidy & his horse Topper begin (on sale 1/8/43)-Captain Marvel app. on-c	343	686	1029	2400	4200	6000
2-(Sum, '46)	53	106	159	334	567	800
3,4: 3-(Fall, '46, 52 pgs. begin)	26	52	78	154	252	350
5- "Mad Barber" story mentioned in **SOTI**, pgs. 308,309; photo-c	24	48	72	142	234	325
6-10: 8-Photo-c	18	36	54	105	165	225
11-19: 11,13-19-Photo-c	15	30	45	85	130	175
20-29 (52 pgs.)-Painted/photo-c	14	28	42	76	108	140
30,31,33,34,37-39,41 (52 pgs.)-Painted-c	11	22	33	64	90	115
32,40 (36pgs.)-Painted-c	10	20	30	58	79	100
35,42,43,45-47,49-51,53,54,56 (52 pgs.)-Photo-c	11	22	33	60	83	105
36,44,48 (36 pgs.)-Photo-c	10	20	30	56	76	95
52,55,57-70 (36 pgs.)-Photo-c	9	18	27	52	69	85
71-84-Photo-c	8	16	24	44	57	70
85-Last Fawcett issue; photo-c	10	20	30	54	72	90

NOTE: *Line-drawn c-1-4, 6, 7, 9, 10, 12.*

... & The 5 Men of Evil (AC Comics, 1991, $12.95) r/newspaper strips and Fawcett story "Signature of Death" 13.00

HOPALONG CASSIDY
National Periodical Publications: No. 86, Feb, 1954 - No. 135, May-June, 1959 (All-36 pgs.)

	GD	VG	FN	VF	VF/NM	NM-
86-Gene Colan-a begins, ends #117; photo covers continue	36	72	108	216	351	485
87	20	40	60	118	189	260
88-91: 91-1 pg. Superboy-sty (7/54)	15	30	45	83	124	165
92-99 (98 has #93 on-c; last precode issue, 2/55). 95-Reversed photo-c to #52. 98-Reversed photo-c to #61. 99-Reversed photo-c to #60	14	28	42	76	108	140
100-Same cover as #50	15	30	45	83	124	165
101-108: 105-Same photo-c as #54. 107-Same photo-c as #51. 108-Last photo-c	7	14	21	44	72	100
109-130: 118-Gil Kane-a begins. 123-Kubert-a (2 pgs.). 124-Grey tone-c	6	12	18	41	66	90
131-135	6	12	18	42	69	95

HOPELESS SAVAGES (Also see Too Much Hopeless Savages)
Oni Press: Aug, 2001 - No. 4, Nov, 2001 ($2.95, B&W, limited series)

1-4-Van Meter-s/Norrie-a/Clugston-Major-a/Watson-c 3.00
Free Comic Book Day giveaway (5/02) r/#1 with "Free Comic Book Day" banner on-c 3.00
TPB (2002, $13.95, 8" x 5.75") r/#1-4; plus color stories; Watson-c 14.00

HOPELESS SAVAGES: GROUND ZERO
Oni Press: June, 2002 - No. 4, Oct, 2002 ($2.95, B&W, limited series)

1-4-Van Meter-s/O'Malley-a/Dodson-c. 1-Watson-a 3.00
TPB (2003, $11.95, 8" x 5.75") r/#1-4; Dodson-c 12.00

HOPE SHIP
Dell Publishing Co.: June-Aug, 1963

	GD	VG	FN	VF	VF/NM	NM-
1	3	6	9	16	22	28

HOPPY THE MARVEL BUNNY (See Fawcett's Funny Animals)
Fawcett Publications: Dec, 1945 - No. 15, Sept, 1947

	GD	VG	FN	VF	VF/NM	NM-
1	28	56	84	165	270	375
2	14	28	42	82	121	160
3-15: 7-Xmas-c	12	24	36	67	94	120

HORACE & DOTTY DRIPPLE (Dotty Dripple No. 1-24)
Harvey Publications: No. 25, Aug, 1952 - No. 43, Oct, 1955

	GD	VG	FN	VF	VF/NM	NM-
25-43	4	9	13	18	22	26

HORIZONTAL LIEUTENANT, THE (See Movie Classics)

HOROBI
Viz Premiere Comics: 1990 - No. 8, 1990 ($3.75, B&W, mature readers, 84 pgs.) V2#1, 1990 - No. 7, 1991 ($4.25, B&W, 68 pgs.)

1-8: Japanese manga, Part Two, #1-7 5.00

HORRIFIC (Terrific No. 14 on)
Artful/Comic Media/Harwell/Mystery: Sept, 1952 - No. 13, Sept, 1954

	GD	VG	FN	VF	VF/NM	NM-
1	69	138	207	442	759	1075
2	43	86	129	271	461	650
3-Bullet in head-c	87	174	261	553	952	1350
4,5,7,9,10: 4-Shrunken head-c. 7-Guillotine-c	40	80	120	246	411	575
6-Jack The Ripper story	41	82	123	256	428	600
8-Origin & 1st app. The Teller (E.C. parody)	43	86	129	271	461	650
11-13: 11-Swipe/Witches Tales #6,27; Devil-c	34	68	102	206	336	465

NOTE: ***Don Heck** a-8; c-3-13. **Hollingsworth** a-4. **Morisi** a-8. **Palais** a-5, 7-12.*

HORRORCIDE
IDW Publishing: Sept, 2004 ($6.99)

1-Steve Niles short stories; art by Templesmith, Medors and Chee 7.00

Horse Feathers Comics #1 © LEV

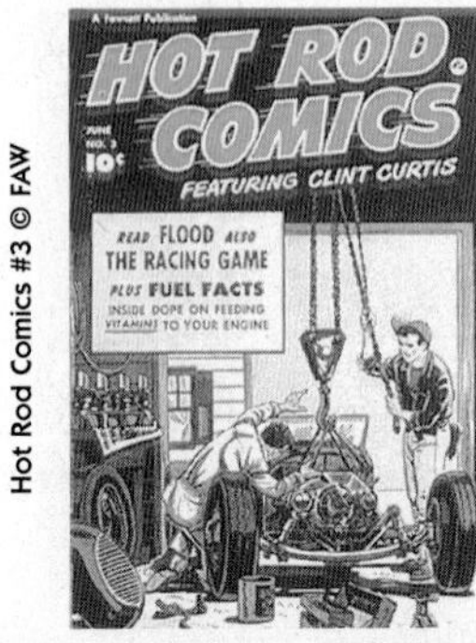

Hot Rod Comics #3 © FAW

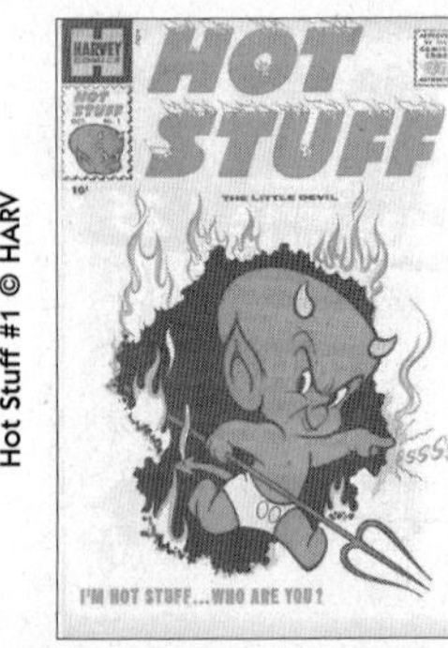

Hot Stuff #1 © HARV

HORROR FROM THE TOMB (Mysterious Stories No. 2 on)
Premier Magazine Co.: Sept, 1954

	GD 2.0	VG 4.0	FN 6.0	VF 8.0	VF/NM 9.0	NM- 9.2
1-Woodbridge/Torres, Check-a; The Keeper of the Graveyard is host	45	90	135	284	480	675

HORRORIST, THE (Also see Hellblazer)
DC Comics (Vertigo): Dec, 1995 - No. 2, Jan, 1996 ($5.95, lim. series, mature)

	GD 2.0	VG 4.0	FN 6.0	VF 8.0	VF/NM 9.0	NM- 9.2
1,2: Jamie Delano scripts, David Lloyd-c/a; John Constantine (Hellblazer) app.						6.00

HORROR OF COLLIER COUNTY
Dark Horse Comics: Oct, 1999 - No. 5, Feb, 2000 ($2.95, B&W, limited series)

	GD 2.0	VG 4.0	FN 6.0	VF 8.0	VF/NM 9.0	NM- 9.2
1-5-Rich Tommaso-s/a						3.00

HORRORS, THE (Formerly Startling Terror Tales #10)
Star Publications: No. 11, Jan, 1953 - No. 15, Apr, 1954

	GD 2.0	VG 4.0	FN 6.0	VF 8.0	VF/NM 9.0	NM- 9.2
11-Horrors of War; Disbrow-a(2)	30	60	90	177	289	400
12-Horrors of War; color illo in **POP**	28	56	84	165	270	375
13-Horrors of Mystery; crime stories	26	52	78	154	252	350
14,15-Horrors of the Underworld; crime stories	28	56	84	165	270	375

NOTE: *All have* ***L. B. Cole*** *covers; a-12.* ***Hollingsworth*** *a-13.* ***Palais*** *a-13r.*

HORROR TALES (Magazine)
Eerie Publications: V1#7, 6/69 - V6#6, 12/74; V7#1, 2/75; V7#2, 5/76 - V8#5, 1977; V9#1-3, 8/78; V10#1(2/79) (V1-V6: 52 pgs.; V7, V8#2: 112 pgs.; V8#4 on: 68 pgs.) (No V5#3, V8#1,3)

	GD 2.0	VG 4.0	FN 6.0	VF 8.0	VF/NM 9.0	NM- 9.2
V1#7	7	14	21	44	72	100
V1#8,9	5	10	15	30	48	65
V2#1-6('70), V3#1-6('71), V4#1-3,5-7('72)	4	8	12	26	41	55
V4#4-LSD story reprint/Weird V3#5	5	10	15	35	55	75
V5#1,2,4,5(6/73),5(10/73),6(12/73),V6#1-6('74),V7#1,2,4('76),V7#3('76)-Giant issue, V8#2,4,5('77)	4	8	12	26	41	55
V9#1-3(11/78, $1.50), V10#1(2/79)	4	8	12	28	44	60

NOTE: *Bondage-c-V6#1, 3, V7#2.*

HORSE FEATHERS COMICS
Lev Gleason Publ.: Nov, 1945 - No. 4, July(Summer on-c), 1948 (52 pgs.) (#2,3 are oversized)

	GD 2.0	VG 4.0	FN 6.0	VF 8.0	VF/NM 9.0	NM- 9.2
1-Wolverton's Scoop Scuttle, 2 pgs.	19	38	57	109	172	235
2	11	22	33	60	83	105
3,4: 3-(5/48)	9	18	27	47	61	75

HORSEMAN
Crusade Comics/Kevlar Studios: Mar, 1996 - No. 3, Nov, 1997 ($2.95)

	GD 2.0	VG 4.0	FN 6.0	VF 8.0	VF/NM 9.0	NM- 9.2
0-1st Kevlar Studios issue, 1-(3/96)-Crusade issue; Shi-c/app., 1-(11/96)-3-(11/97)-Kevlar Studios						3.00

HORSEMASTERS, THE (Disney)(TV, Movie)
Dell Publishing Co.: No. 1260, Dec-Feb, 1961/62

	GD 2.0	VG 4.0	FN 6.0	VF 8.0	VF/NM 9.0	NM- 9.2
Four Color 1260-Annette Funicello photo-c	11	22	33	76	151	225

HORSE SOLDIERS, THE
Dell Publishing Co.: No. 1048, Nov-Jan, 1959/60 (John Wayne movie)

	GD 2.0	VG 4.0	FN 6.0	VF 8.0	VF/NM 9.0	NM- 9.2
Four Color 1048-Painted-c, Sekowsky-a	12	24	36	79	160	240

HORSE WITHOUT A HEAD, THE (See Movie Comics)

HOT DOG
Magazine Enterprises: June-July, 1954 - No. 4, Dec-Jan, 1954-55

	GD 2.0	VG 4.0	FN 6.0	VF 8.0	VF/NM 9.0	NM- 9.2
1(A-1 #107)	9	18	27	47	61	75
2,3(A-1 #115),4(A-1 #136)	6	12	18	31	38	45

HOT DOG (See Jughead's Pal, Hotdog)

HOTEL DEPAREE - SUNDANCE (TV)
Dell Publishing Co.: No. 1126, Aug-Oct, 1960 (one-shot)

	GD 2.0	VG 4.0	FN 6.0	VF 8.0	VF/NM 9.0	NM- 9.2
Four Color 1126-Earl Holliman photo-c	6	12	18	42	69	95

HOT ROD AND SPEEDWAY COMICS
Hillman Periodicals: Feb-Mar, 1952 - No. 5, Apr-May, 1953

	GD 2.0	VG 4.0	FN 6.0	VF 8.0	VF/NM 9.0	NM- 9.2
1	27	54	81	158	259	360
2-Krigstein-a	18	36	54	105	165	225
3-5	13	26	39	72	101	130

HOT ROD COMICS (...Featuring Clint Curtis) (See XMas Comics)
Fawcett Publications: Nov, 1951 (no month given) - V2#7, Feb, 1953

	GD 2.0	VG 4.0	FN 6.0	VF 8.0	VF/NM 9.0	NM- 9.2
nn (V1#1)-Powell-c/a in all	29	58	87	170	278	385
2 (4/52)	15	30	45	90	140	190
3-6, V2#7	13	26	39	72	101	130

HOT ROD KING (Also see Speed Smith the Hot Rod King)
Ziff-Davis Publ. Co.: Fall, 1952

	GD 2.0	VG 4.0	FN 6.0	VF 8.0	VF/NM 9.0	NM- 9.2
1-Giacoia-a; Saunders painted-c	25	50	75	150	245	340

HOT ROD RACERS (Grand Prix No. 16 on)
Charlton Comics: Dec, 1964 - No. 15, July, 1967

	GD 2.0	VG 4.0	FN 6.0	VF 8.0	VF/NM 9.0	NM- 9.2
1	8	16	24	53	89	125
2-5	5	10	15	32	51	70
6-15	4	8	12	24	37	50

HOT RODS AND RACING CARS
Charlton Comics (Motor Mag. No. 1): Nov, 1951 - No. 120, June, 1973

	GD 2.0	VG 4.0	FN 6.0	VF 8.0	VF/NM 9.0	NM- 9.2
1-Speed Davis begins; Indianapolis 500 story	28	56	84	165	270	375
2	15	30	45	86	133	180
3-10	12	24	36	67	94	120
11-20	10	20	30	54	72	90
21-33,36-40	8	16	24	44	57	70
34, 35 (? & 6/58, 68 pgs.)	11	22	33	60	83	105
41-60	7	14	21	37	46	55
61-80	3	6	9	20	30	40
81-100	3	6	9	16	23	30
101-120	3	6	9	14	19	24

HOT SHOT CHARLIE
Hillman Periodicals: 1947 (Lee Elias)

	GD 2.0	VG 4.0	FN 6.0	VF 8.0	VF/NM 9.0	NM- 9.2
1	12	24	36	69	97	125

HOT SHOTS: AVENGERS
Marvel Comics: Oct, 1995 ($2.95, one-shot)

	GD 2.0	VG 4.0	FN 6.0	VF 8.0	VF/NM 9.0	NM- 9.2
nn-pin-ups						3.00

HOTSPUR
Eclipse Comics: Jun, 1987 - No. 3, Sep, 1987 ($1.75, lim. series, Baxter paper)

	GD 2.0	VG 4.0	FN 6.0	VF 8.0	VF/NM 9.0	NM- 9.2
1-3						3.00

HOT STUFF (See Stumbo Tinytown)
Harvey Comics: V2#1, Sept, 1991 - No. 12, June, 1994 ($1.00)

	GD 2.0	VG 4.0	FN 6.0	VF 8.0	VF/NM 9.0	NM- 9.2
V2#1-Stumbo back-up story						5.00
2-12 ($1.50)						4.00
...Big Book 1 (11/92), 2 (6/93) (Both $1.95, 52 pgs.)						5.00

HOT STUFF CREEPY CAVES
Harvey Publications: Nov, 1974 - No. 7, Nov, 1975

	GD 2.0	VG 4.0	FN 6.0	VF 8.0	VF/NM 9.0	NM- 9.2
1	4	8	12	22	34	45
2-7	3	6	9	15	21	26

HOT STUFF DIGEST
Harvey Comics: July, 1992 - No. 5, Nov, 1993 ($1.75, digest-size)

	GD 2.0	VG 4.0	FN 6.0	VF 8.0	VF/NM 9.0	NM- 9.2
V2#1-Hot Stuff, Stumbo, Richie Rich stories						6.00
2-5						4.00

HOT STUFF GIANT SIZE
Harvey Comics: Oct, 1992 - No. 3, Oct, 1993 ($2.25, 68 pgs.)

	GD 2.0	VG 4.0	FN 6.0	VF 8.0	VF/NM 9.0	NM- 9.2
V2#1-Hot Stuff & Stumbo stories						5.00
2,3						4.00

HOT STUFF SIZZLERS
Harvey Publications: July, 1960 - No. 59, Mar, 1974; V2#1, Aug, 1992

	GD 2.0	VG 4.0	FN 6.0	VF 8.0	VF/NM 9.0	NM- 9.2
1- 84 pgs. begin, ends #5; Hot Stuff, Stumbo begin	13	26	39	90	195	300
2-5	8	16	24	56	96	135
6-10: 6-68 pgs. begin, ends #45	6	12	18	41	66	90
11-20	4	8	12	28	44	60
21-45	3	6	9	20	30	40
46-52: 52 pgs. begin	3	6	9	16	23	30
53-59	2	4	6	10	14	18
V2#1-(8/92, $1.25)-Stumbo back-up						5.00

HOT STUFF, THE LITTLE DEVIL (Also see Devil Kids & Harvey Hits)
Harvey Publications (Illustrated Humor): 10/57 - No. 141, 7/77; No. 142, 2/78 - No. 164, 8/82; No. 165, 10/86 - No. 171, 11/87; No. 172, 11/88; No. 173, Sept, 1990 - No. 177, 1/91

	GD 2.0	VG 4.0	FN 6.0	VF 8.0	VF/NM 9.0	NM- 9.2
1	59	118	177	478	1039	1600
2-Stumbo-like giant 1st app. (12/57)	24	48	72	168	359	550
3-Stumbo the Giant debut (2/58)	19	38	57	133	287	440
4,5	17	34	51	119	260	400
6-10	11	22	33	73	142	210
11-20	9	18	27	58	99	140
21-40	6	12	18	39	62	85
41-60	4	8	12	26	41	55
61-80	3	6	9	20	30	40
81-105	3	6	9	16	22	28
106-112: All 52 pg. Giants	3	6	9	18	27	35

Hot Wheels #1 © DC

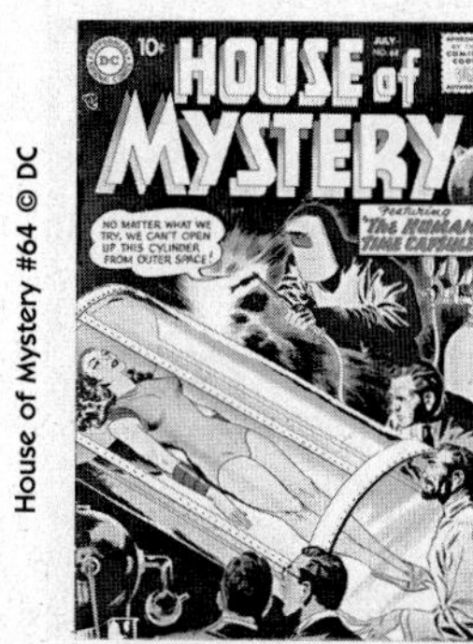

House of Mystery #64 © DC

House of Mystery #313 © DC

	GD 2.0	VG 4.0	FN 6.0	VF 8.0	VF/NM 9.0	NM- 9.2
113-125	2	4	6	9	12	15
126-141	1	2	3	5	7	9
142-177: 172-177-($1.00)						6.00
Harvey Comics Classics Vol. 3 TPB (Dark Horse Books, 3/08, $19.95) Reprints Hot Stuff's earliest appearances in this title and Devil Kids, mostly B&W with some color stories; history, early concept drawings; foreword by Mark Arnold						20.00

HOT WHEELS (TV)
National Periodical Publications: Mar-Apr, 1970 - No. 6, Jan-Feb, 1971

	GD 2.0	VG 4.0	FN 6.0	VF 8.0	VF/NM 9.0	NM- 9.2
1	10	20	30	65	118	170
2,4,5	6	12	18	39	62	85
3-Neal Adams-c	7	14	21	48	79	110
6-Neal Adams-c/a	8	16	24	56	96	135

NOTE: *Toth a-1p, 2-5; c-1p, 5.*

HOURMAN (Justice Society member, see Adventure Comics #48)

HOURMAN (See JLA and DC One Million)
DC Comics: Apr, 1999 - No. 25, Apr, 2001 ($2.50)

	GD 2.0	VG 4.0	FN 6.0	VF 8.0	VF/NM 9.0	NM- 9.2
1-25: 1-JLA app.; McDaniel-c. 2-Tomorrow Woman-c/app. 6,7-Amazo app. 11-13-Justice Legion A app. 16-Silver Age flashback. 18,19-JSA-c/app. 22-Harris-c/a. 24-Hourman Vs. Rex Tyler						3.00

HOUSE OF M (Also see miniseries with Fantastic Four, Iron Man and Spider-Man)
Marvel Comics: Aug, 2005 - No. 8, Dec, 2005 ($2.99, limited series)

	GD 2.0	VG 4.0	FN 6.0	VF 8.0	VF/NM 9.0	NM- 9.2
1-Bendis-s/Coipel-a/Ribic-c; Scarlet Witch changes reality; Quesada variant-c						3.00
2-8-Variant covers for each. 3-Hawkeye returns						3.00
... MGC #1 (6/11, $1.00) r/#1 with "Marvel's Greatest Comics" logo on cover						3.00
Secrets Of The House Of M (2005, $3.99, one-shot) profile pages and background info						4.00
... Sketchbook (6/05) B&W preview sketches by Coipel, Davis, Hairsine, Quesada						3.00
TPB (2006, $24.99) r/#1-8 and The Pulse: House of M Special Edition newspaper						25.00
...: Fantastic Four/ Iron Man TPB (2006, $13.99) r/ both House of M mini-series						14.00
...: World of M Featuring Wolverine TPB (2006, $13.99) r/2005 x-over issues Wolverine #33-35, Black Panther #7, Captain America #10 and The Pulse #10						14.00
HC (2008, $29.99, oversized with d.j.) r/#1-8, The Pulse: House of M Special Edition newspaper and Secrets Of The House Of M one-shot; script pages; cover gallery						30.00

HOUSE OF M: AVENGERS
Marvel Comics: Jan, 2008 - No. 5, Apr, 2008 ($2.99, limited series)

	GD 2.0	VG 4.0	FN 6.0	VF 8.0	VF/NM 9.0	NM- 9.2
1-5-Gage-s/Perkins-a; Luke Cage, Iron Fist, Hawkeye, Tigra, Misty Knight, Shang-Chi						3.00

HOUSE OF M: MASTERS OF EVIL
Marvel Comics: Oct, 2009 - No. 4, Jan, 2010 ($3.99, limited series)

	GD 2.0	VG 4.0	FN 6.0	VF 8.0	VF/NM 9.0	NM- 9.2
1-4-Gage-s/Garcia-a/Perkins-c; The Hood app.						4.00

HOUSE OF MYSTERY
DC Comics: Dec/Jan. 1951

nn - Ashcan comic, not distributed to newsstands, only for in-house use. Cover art is Danger Trail #3 with interior being Star Spangled Comics #109. A VG+ copy sold for $2,357.50 in 2002.

HOUSE OF MYSTERY (See Brave and the Bold #93, Elvira's House of Mystery, Limited Collectors' Edition & Super DC Giant)

HOUSE OF MYSTERY, THE
National Periodical Publications/DC Comics: Dec-Jan, 1951-52 - No. 321, Oct, 1983 (No. 194-203: 52 pgs.)

	GD 2.0	VG 4.0	FN 6.0	VF 8.0	VF/NM 9.0	NM- 9.2
1-DC's first horror comic	252	504	756	1613	2757	3900
2	95	190	285	603	1039	1475
3	65	130	195	416	708	1000
4,5	53	106	159	334	567	800
6-10	47	94	141	296	498	700
11-15	40	80	120	246	411	575
16(7/53)-25	34	68	102	199	325	450
26-35(2/55)-Last pre-code issue; 30-Woodish-a	26	52	78	154	252	350
36-50: 50-Text story of Orson Welles' War of the Worlds broadcast	13	26	39	88	189	290
51-60: 55-1st S.A. issue	12	24	36	79	160	240
61,63,65,66,69,70,72,76,85-Kirby-a	12	24	36	84	177	270
62,64,67,68,71,73-75,77-83,86-99	11	22	33	73	142	210
84-Prototype of Negative Man (Doom Patrol)	12	24	36	84	177	270
100 (7/60)	11	22	33	77	154	230
101-116: 109-Toth, Kubert-a. 116-Last 10¢ issue	10	20	30	68	127	185
117-130: 117-Swipes-c to HOS #20. 120-Toth-a	9	18	27	63	112	160
131-142	9	18	27	58	99	140
143-J'onn J'onzz, Manhunter begins (6/64), ends #173; story continues from Detective #326; intro. Idol-Head of Diabolu	17	34	51	119	260	400
144	9	18	27	58	99	140
145-155,157-159: 149-Toth-a. 155-The Human Hurricane app. (12/65), Red Tornado prototype. 158-Origin Diabolu Idol-Head	6	12	18	41	66	90
156-Robby Reed begins (origin/1st app.), ends #173	8	16	24	51	86	120
160-(7/66)-Robby Reed becomes Plastic Man in this issue only; 1st S.A. app. Plastic Man; intro Marco Xavier (Martian Manhunter) & Vulture Crime Organization; ends #173	9	18	27	63	112	160
161-173: 169-Origin/1st app. Gem Girl	5	10	15	30	48	65
174-Mystery format begins.	12	24	36	79	160	240
175-1st app. Cain (House of Mystery host); Adams-c	10	20	30	68	127	185
176,177-Neal Adams-c	9	18	27	61	106	150
178-Neal Adams-c/a (2/69)	10	20	30	65	118	170
179-Neal Adams/Orlando, Wrightson-a (1st pro work, 3 pgs.); Adams-c	11	22	33	73	142	210
180,181,183: Wrightson-a (3,10, & 3 pgs.); Adams-c. 180-Last 12¢ issue; Kane/Wood-a(2). 183-Wood-a	9	18	27	61	106	150
182,184-Adams-c. 182-Toth-a. 184-Kane/Wood, Toth-a	7	14	21	44	72	100
185-Williamson/Kaluta-a; Howard-a (3 pgs.); Adams-c	7	14	21	48	79	110
186-N. Adams-c/a; Wrightson-a (10 pgs.)	10	20	30	64	115	165
187,190: Adams-c. 187-Toth-a. 190-Toth-a(r)	6	12	18	42	69	95
188-Wrightson-a (8 & 3pgs.); Adams-c	8	16	24	53	89	125
189,192,197: Adams-c on all. 189-Wood-a(i). 192-Last 15¢-c	6	12	18	42	69	95
191-Wrightson-a (8 & 3pgs.); Adams-c	8	16	24	53	89	125
193-Wrightson-c	6	12	18	42	69	95
194-Wrightson-c; 52 pgs begin, end #203; Toth,Kirby-a	8	16	24	55	93	130
195: Wrightson-c. Swamp creature story by Wrightson similar to Swamp Thing (10 pgs.)(10/71)	10	20	30	66	121	175
196,198	6	12	18	37	59	80
199-Adams-c; Wood-a(8pgs.); Kirby-a	7	14	21	46	76	105
200-(25¢, 52 pgs.)-One third-r (3/72)	7	14	21	44	72	100
201-203-(25¢, 52 pgs.)-One third-r	5	10	15	32	51	70
204-Wrightson-c/a, 9 pgs.	6	12	18	37	59	80
205,206,208,210,212,215,216,218	3	6	9	21	32	42
207-Wrightson-c/a; Starlin, Redondo-a	6	12	18	37	59	80
209,211,213,214,217,219-Wrightson-c	5	10	15	30	48	65
220,222,223	3	6	9	19	29	38
221-Wrightson/Kaluta-a(8 pgs.); Wrightson-c	5	10	15	35	55	75
224-229: 224-Wrightson-r from Spectre #9; Dillin/Adams-r from House of Secrets #82; begin 100 pg. issues; Phantom Stranger-r. 225,227-(100 pgs.): 225-Spectre app. 226-Wrightson/Redondo-a Phantom Stranger-r. 228-N. Adams inks; Wrightson-r. 229-Wrightson-a(r); Toth-r; last 100 pg. issue	6	12	18	41	66	90
230,232-235,237-250	3	6	9	14	19	24
231-Classic Wrightson-c	5	10	15	35	55	75
236-Wrightson-c; Ditko-a(p); N. Adams-i	4	8	12	26	41	55
251-254-(84 pgs.)-Adams-c. 251-Wood-a	4	8	12	28	44	60
255,256-(84 pgs.)-Wrightson-c	4	8	12	28	44	60
257-259-(84 pgs.)	3	6	9	19	29	38
260-289: 282-(68 pgs.)-Has extra story "The Computers That Saved Metropolis" Radio Shack giveaway by Jim Starlin	2	4	6	8	10	12
290-1st "I, Vampire"	3	6	9	17	25	32
291-299: 291,293,295-299- "I, Vampire"	2	4	6	10	14	18
300,319-"I, Vampire"	2	4	6	11	16	20
301-318,320: 301-318-"I, Vampire"	2	4	6	10	14	18
321-Death of "I, Vampire"	3	6	9	14	20	25
Welcome to the House of Mystery (7/98, $5.95) reprints stories with new framing story by Gaiman and Aragonés						6.00

NOTE: ***Neal Adams** a-236i; c-175-192, 197, 199, 251-254. **Alcala** a-209, 217, 219, 224, 227. **M. Anderson** a-212; c/a-37. **Aparo** a-209. **Aragones** a-185, 186, 194, 196, 200, 202, 229, 251. **Baily** a-279p. **Cameron** a-76, 79. **Colan** a-202r. **Craig** a-263, 275, 295, 300. **Dillin/Adams** r-224. **Ditko** a-236p, 247, 254, 258, 276; c-277. **Drucker** a-37. **Evans** c-218. **Fradon** a-251. **Giffen** a-284. **Giunta** a-199, 227r. **Golden** a-257, 259. **Heath** a-194r; c-203. **Howard** a-182, 185, 187, 196, 229r, 247i, 254, 279i. **Kaluta** a-195, 200, 250r; c-200-202, 210, 212, 233, 260, 261, 263, 265, 267, 268, 273, 276, 284, 287, 288, 293-295, 300, 302, 304, 305, 309-319, 321. **Bob Kane** a-84. **Gil Kane** a-196p, 253p, 300p. **Kirby** a-194r, 199r; c-65, 76, 78, 79, 85. **Kubert** c-282, 283, 285, 286, 289-292, 297-299, 301, 303, 306-308. **Maneely** a-68, 227r. **Mayer** a-317p. **Meskin** a-52-144 (most), 195r, 224r, 229r; c-63, 66, 124, 127. **Mooney** a-24, 159, 160. **Moreira** a-3, 4, 20-50, 58, 59, 62, 68, 77, 79, 90, 108, 113, 123, 201r, 228; c-4-28, 44, 47, 50, 54, 59, 62, 64, 68, 70, 73. **Morrow** a-192, 196, 255, 320i. **Mortimer** a-204(3 pgs.). **Nasser** a-276. **Newton** a-259, 272. **Nino** a-204, 212, 213, 220, 224, 225, 245, 250, 252-256, 283. **Orlando** a-175(2 pgs.), 178, 240i; c-240, 258p, 262, 264p, 270p, 271, 272, 274, 275, 278, 296i. **Redondo** a-194, 195, 197, 202, 203, 207, 211, 214, 217, 219, 226, 227, 229, 235, 241, 287(layout), 302p, 303i, 308; c-229. **Reese** a-195, 200, 205i. **Rogers** a-254, 274, 277. **Roussos** a-65, 84, 224i. **Sekowsky** a-282p. **Sparling** a-203. **Starlin** a-207(2 pgs.), 282p; c-281. **Leonard Starr** a-9. **Staton** a-300p. **Sutton** a-189, 271, 290, 291, 293, 295, 297-299, 302, 303, 306-309, 310-313i, 314. **Tuska** a-293p, 294p, 316p. **Wrightson** c-193-195, 204, 207, 209, 211, 213, 214, 217, 219, 221, 231, 236, 255, 256; r-224.*

HOUSE OF MYSTERY
DC Comics (Vertigo): Jul, 2008 - No. 42, Dec, 2011 ($2.99)

	GD 2.0	VG 4.0	FN 6.0	VF 8.0	VF/NM 9.0	NM- 9.2
1-12,14-42: 1-Cain & Abel app.; Rossi-a/Weber-c. 9-Wrightson-a (6 pgs.). 16-Corben-a						3.00
1-Variant-c by Bernie Wrightson						5.00

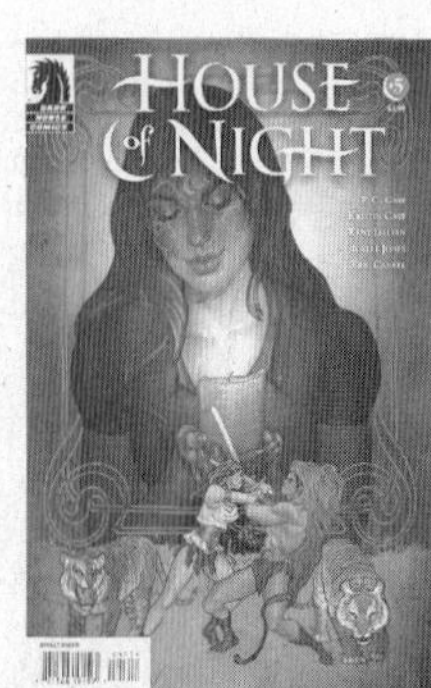

House of Night #5 © PC Cast

House of Secrets #106 © DC

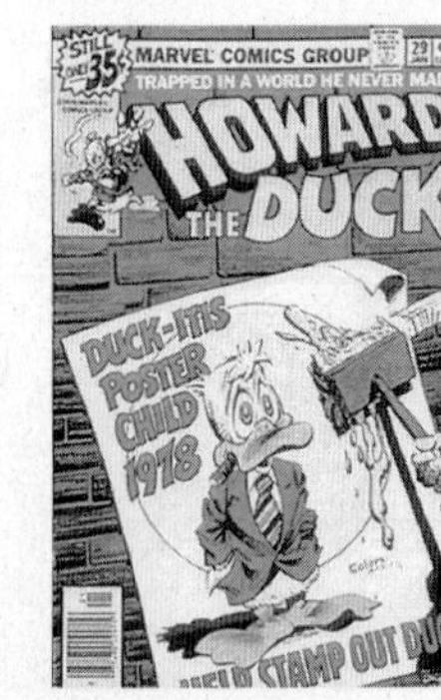

Howard the Duck #29 © MAR

	GD 2.0	VG 4.0	FN 6.0	VF 8.0	VF/NM 9.0	NM- 9.2
13-Art by Neal Adams, Ralph Reese, Eric Powell, Sergio Aragonés						3.00
13-Variant-c by Neal Adams						5.00
... Halloween Annual #1 (12/09, $4.99) short stories by various incl. Hadley, Allred, Nowlan						5.00
... Halloween Annual #2 (12/10, $4.99) short stories by various incl. Carey, Allred, Gross						5.00
...: Love Stories for Dead People TPB (2009, $14.99) r/#6-10						15.00
...: Room and Boredom TPB (2008, $9.99) r/#1-5						10.00
...: Safe as Houses TPB (2011, $14.99) r/#26-30						15.00
...: The Beauty of Decay TPB (2010, $17.99) r/#16-20 & Halloween Annual #1						18.00
...: The Space Between TPB (2010, $14.99) r/#11-15; sketch pages						15.00
...: Under New Management TPB (2011, $14.99) r/#20-25						15.00

HOUSE OF NIGHT (Based on the series of novels by P.C. Cast and Kristin Cast)
Dark Horse Comics: Nov, 2011 - No. 5, Mar, 2012 ($1.00/$2.99, limited series)

	GD	VG	FN	VF	VF/NM	NM-
1-($1.00) Cast, Cast & Dalian-s/Joëlle Jones & Kerschl-a; Frison-c						3.00
1-($1.00) Variant-c by Steve Morris						4.00
2-5-($2.99) Jones-a; two covers by Jones & Ryan Hill on each						3.00

HOUSE OF SECRETS (Combined with The Unexpected after #154)
National Periodical Publications/DC Comics: 11-12/56 - No. 80, 9-10/66; No. 81, 8-9/69 - No. 140, 2-3/76; No. 141, 8-9/76 - No. 154, 10-11/78

	GD	VG	FN	VF	VF/NM	NM-
1-Drucker-a; Moreira-c	111	222	333	900	1950	3000
2-Moreira-a	39	78	117	296	641	985
3-Kirby-c/a	33	66	99	239	520	800
4-Kirby-a	25	50	75	171	366	560
5-7	17	34	51	119	260	400
8-Kirby-a	19	38	57	133	287	440
9-11: 11-Lou Cameron-a (unsigned)	15	30	45	104	227	350
12-Kirby-c/a; Lou Cameron-a	16	32	48	111	243	375
13-15: 14-Flying saucer-c	12	24	36	83	172	260
16-20	12	24	36	78	157	235
21,22,24-30	11	22	33	73	142	210
23-1st app. Mark Merlin & begin series (8/59)	11	22	33	75	148	220
31-50: 48-Toth-a. 50-Last 10¢ issue	10	20	30	67	124	180
51-60: 58-Origin Mark Merlin	9	18	27	60	103	145
61-First Eclipso (7-8/63) and begin series	14	28	42	93	202	310
62	8	16	24	54	90	125
63-65-Toth-a on Eclipso (see Brave and the Bold #64)	6	12	18	42	69	95
66-1st Eclipso-c (also #67,70,78,79); Toth-a	8	16	24	53	89	125
67,73: 67-Toth-a on Eclipso. 73-Mark Merlin becomes Prince Ra-Man (1st app.)	6	12	18	42	69	95
68-72,74-80: 76-Prince Ra-Man vs. Eclipso. 80-Eclipso, Prince Ra-Man end	6	12	18	39	62	85
81-Mystery format begins; 1st app. Abel (House Of Secrets host); (cameo in DC Special #4)	12	24	36	81	166	250
82-84: 82-Neal Adams-c(i)	8	16	24	51	86	120
85,90: 85-N. Adams-a(i). 90-Buckler (early work)/N. Adams-a(i)	8	16	24	53	89	125
86,88,89,91	7	14	21	46	76	105
87-Wrightson & Kaluta-a	8	16	24	55	93	130
92-1st app. Swamp Thing-c/story (8 pgs.)(6-7/71) by Berni Wrightson(p) w/JeffJones/Kaluta/Weiss ink assists; classic-c.	46	92	138	352	764	1175
93,94,96-(52 pgs.)-Wrightson-c. 94-Wrightson-a(i); 96-Wood-a	8	16	24	51	86	120
95,97,98-(52 pgs.)	6	12	18	39	62	85
99-Wrightson splash pg.	6	12	18	37	59	80
100-Classic Wrightson-c	8	16	24	55	93	130
101,102,104,105,108-111,113-120	3	6	9	18	27	35
103,106,107-Wrightson-c	5	10	15	32	51	70
112-Grey tone-c	3	6	9	21	32	42
121-133	2	4	6	11	16	20
134-Wrightson-a	3	6	9	18	27	35
135,136,139-Wrightson-a/c	3	6	9	21	32	42
137,138,141-153	2	4	6	8	10	12
140-1st solo origin of the Patchworkman (see Swamp Thing #3)	3	6	9	16	23	30
154 (10-11/78, 44 pgs.) Last issue	2	4	6	9	13	16

NOTE: ***Neal Adams*** *c-81, 82, 84-88, 90, 91.* ***Alcala*** *a-104-107.* ***Anderson*** *a-91. Aparo a-93, 97, 105.* ***B. Bailey*** *a-107.* ***Cameron*** *a-13, 15.* ***Colan*** *a-63.* ***Ditko*** *a-139p, 148.* ***Elias*** *a-58.* ***Evans*** *a-118.* ***Finlay*** *a-7r(Real Fact?).* ***Glanzman*** *a-91.* ***Golden*** *a-151.* ***Heath*** *a-31.* ***Heck*** *a-85.* ***Kaluta*** *a-87, 98, 99; c-98, 99, 101, 102, 105, 149, 151, 154.* ***Bob Kane*** *a-18, 21.* ***G. Kane*** *a-85p.* ***Kirby*** *c-3, 11, 12.* ***Kubert*** *a-39.* ***Meskin*** *a-2-68 (most), 94r; c-55-60.* ***Moreira*** *a-7, 8, 51, 54, 102-104, 106, 108, 113, 116, 118, 121, 123, 127; c-1, 2, 4-10, 13-20.* ***Morrow*** *a-86, 89, 90; c-89, 146-148.* ***Nino*** *a-101, 103, 106, 109, 115, 117, 126, 128, 131, 147, 153.* ***Redondo*** *a-95, 99, 102, 104p, 113, 116, 134, 136, 139, 140.* ***Reese*** *a-85.* ***Severin*** *a-91.* ***Starlin*** *c-150.* ***Sutton*** *a-154.* ***Toth*** *a-63-67, 83, 93r, 94r, 96r-98r, 123.* ***Tuska*** *a-90, 104.* ***Wrightson*** *a-134; c-92-94, 96, 100, 103, 106, 107, 135, 136, 139.*

HOUSE OF SECRETS
DC Comics (Vertigo): Oct, 1996 - No. 25, Dec, 1998 ($2.50) (Creator-owned series)

	GD	VG	FN	VF	VF/NM	NM-
1-Steven Seagle-s/Kristiansen-c/a.						3.50
2-25: 5,7-Kristiansen-c/a. 6-Fegrado-a						3.00
TPB-(1997, $14.95) r/1-5						15.00

HOUSE OF SECRETS: FACADE
DC Comics (Vertigo): 2001 - No. 2, 2001 ($5.95, limited series)

	GD	VG	FN	VF	VF/NM	NM-
1,2-Steven Seagle-s/Teddy Kristiansen-c/a.						6.00

HOUSE OF TERROR (3-D)
St. John Publishing Co.: Oct, 1953 (25¢, came w/glasses)

	GD	VG	FN	VF	VF/NM	NM-
1-Kubert, Baker-a	27	54	81	158	259	360

HOUSE OF YANG, THE (See Yang)
Charlton Comics: July, 1975 - No. 6, June, 1976; 1978

	GD	VG	FN	VF	VF/NM	NM-
1-Sanho Kim-a in all	2	4	6	13	18	22
2-6	2	4	6	8	10	12
Modern Comics #1,2(1978)						6.00

HOUSE ON THE BORDERLAND
DC Comics (Vertigo): 2000 ($29.95, hardcover, one-shot)

	GD	VG	FN	VF	VF/NM	NM-
HC-Adaptation of William Hope Hodgson book; Corben-a						30.00
SC (2003, $19.95)						20.00

HOUSE II: THE SECOND STORY
Marvel Comics: Oct, 1987 (One-shot)

	GD	VG	FN	VF	VF/NM	NM-
1-Adapts movie						3.00

HOWARD CHAYKIN'S AMERICAN FLAGG (See American Flagg!)
First Comics: V2#1, May, 1988 - V2#12, Apr, 1989 ($1.75/$1.95, Baxter paper)

	GD	VG	FN	VF	VF/NM	NM-
V2#1-9,11,12-Chaykin-c(p) in all						3.00
10-Elvis Presley photo-c						4.00

HOWARD THE DUCK (See Bizarre Adventures #34, Crazy Magazine, Fear, Man-Thing, Marvel Treasury Edition & Sensational She-Hulk #14-17)
Marvel Comics Group: Jan, 1976 - No. 31, May, 1979; No. 32, Jan, 1986; No. 33, Sept, 1986

	GD	VG	FN	VF	VF/NM	NM-
1-Brunner-c/a; Spider-Man x-over (low distr.)	4	8	12	24	37	50
2-Brunner-c/a	2	4	6	11	16	20
3,4-(Regular 25¢ edition). 3-Buscema-a(p), (7/76)	2	4	6	8	11	14
3,4-(30¢-c, limited distribution)	3	6	9	16	22	28
5	2	4	6	8	11	14
6-11: 8-Howard The Duck for president. 9-1st Sgt. Preston Dudley of RCMP. 10-Spider-Man-c/sty	1	2	3	5	7	9
12-1st brief app. Kiss (3/77)	4	8	12	24	37	50
13-(30¢-c) 1st full app. Kiss (6/77); Daimon Hellstrom app. plus cameo of Howard as Son of Satan	4	8	12	28	44	60
13-(35¢-c, limited distribution)	9	18	27	63	112	160
14-32: 14-17-(Regular 30¢-c). 14-Howard as Son of Satan-c/story; Son of Satan app. 16-Album issue; 3 pgs. comics. 22,23-Man-Thing-c/stories; Star Wars parody. 30,32-P. Smith-a						6.00
14-17-(35¢-c, limited distribution)	3	6	9	14	20	25
33-Last issue; low print run	1	2	3	5	6	8
Annual 1(1977, 52 pgs.)-Mayerik-a	2	3	4	6	8	10
... Omnibus HC (2008, $99.99, dustjacket) r/#1-33 & Annual #1, Adventure Into Fear #19, Man-Thing #1, Giant-Size Man-Thing #4&5, Marvel Treasury Ed. #12, Marvel Team-Up #96 and FOOM #15; Gerber foreword; creator interviews; bonus art; 2 covers						100.00

NOTE: ***Austin*** *c-29i.* ***Bolland*** *c-33.* ***Brunner*** *a-1p, 2p; c-1, 2.* ***Buckler*** *c-3p.* ***Buscema*** *a-3p.* ***Colan*** *a(p)-4-15, 17-20, 24-27, 30, 31; c(p)-4-31, Annual 1p.* ***Leialoha*** *a-1-13i; c(i)-3-5, 8-11.* ***Mayerik*** *a-22, 23, 33.* ***Paul Smith*** *a-30p, 32. Man-Thing app. in #22, 23.*

HOWARD THE DUCK (Magazine)
Marvel Comics Group: Oct, 1979 - No. 9, Mar, 1981 (B&W, 68 pgs.)

	GD	VG	FN	VF	VF/NM	NM-
1-Art by Colan, Janson, Golden. Kidney Lady app.	2	4	6	8	10	12
2,3,5-9 (nudity in most): 2-Mayerick-c. 3-Xmas issue; Jack Davis-c; Duck World flashback. 5-Dracula app. 6-1st Street People back-up story. 7-Has pin-up by Byrne; Man-Thing-c/s (46 pgs.). 8-Batman parody w/Marshall Rogers-a; Dave Sim-a (1 pg.). 9-Marie Severin-a; John Pound painted-c						6.00
4-Beatles, John Lennon, Elvis, Kiss & Devo cameos; Hitler app.	2	4	6	9	12	15

NOTE: ***Buscema*** *a-4p.* ***Colan*** *a-1-5p, 7-9p.* ***Jack Davis*** *c-3.* ***Golden*** *a(p)-1, 5, 6(51pgs.).* ***Rogers*** *a-7, 8.* ***Simonson*** *a-7.*

HOWARD THE DUCK (Volume 2)
Marvel Comics: Mar, 2002 - No. 6, Aug, 2002 ($2.99)

	GD	VG	FN	VF	VF/NM	NM-
1-Gerber-s/Winslade-a/Fabry-c						4.00
2-6: 2,4-6-Gerber-s/Winslade-a/Fabry-c. 3-Fabry-a/c						3.00
TPB (9/02, $14.99) r/#1-6						15.00

Howdy Doody #7 © CNP

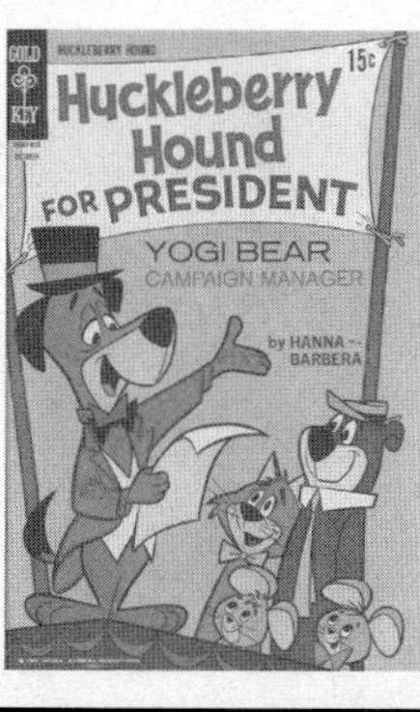

Huckleberry Hound #35 © H-B

Hulk (2008) #2 © MAR

	GD 2.0	VG 4.0	FN 6.0	VF 8.0	VF/NM 9.0	NM- 9.2

HOWARD THE DUCK (Volume 3)
Marvel Comics: Dec, 2007 - No. 4, Feb, 2008 ($2.99, limited series)

1-4-Templeton-s/Bobillo-a/c; She-Hulk app. 3.00
...: Media Duckling TPB (2008, $11.99) r/#1-4; Howard the Duck #1 (1/76) and pages from Civil War: Choosing Sides 12.00

HOWARD THE DUCK HOLIDAY SPECIAL
Marvel Comics: Feb, 1997 ($2.50, one-shot)

1-Wraparound-c; Hama-s 4.00

HOWARD THE DUCK: THE MOVIE
Marvel Comics Group: Dec, 1986 - No. 3, Feb, 1987 (Limited series)

1-3: Movie adaptation; r/Marvel Super Special 3.00

HOW BOYS AND GIRLS CAN HELP WIN THE WAR
The Parents' Magazine Institute: 1942 (10¢, one-shot)

1-All proceeds used to buy war bonds	28	56	84	165	270	375

HOWDY DOODY (TV)(See Jackpot of Fun-- & Poll Parrot)(Some have stories by John Stanley)
Dell Publishing Co.: 1/50 - No. 38, 7-9/56; No. 761, 1/57; No. 811, 7/57

1-(Scarce)-Photo-c; 1st TV comic	74	148	222	600	1300	2000
2-Photo-c	35	70	105	250	545	840
3-5: All photo-c	20	40	60	140	300	460
6-Used in **SOTI**, pg. 309; classic-c; painted covers begin	22	44	66	154	327	500
7-10	13	26	39	87	186	285
11-20: 13-X-Mas-c	11	22	33	77	154	230
21-38, Four Color 761,811	10	20	30	68	127	185

HOW IT BEGAN
United Features Syndicate: No. 15, 1939 (one-shot)

Single Series 15	34	68	102	199	325	450

HOW SANTA GOT HIS RED SUIT (See March of Comics No. 2)

HOW THE WEST WAS WON (See Movie Comics)

HOW TO DRAW FOR THE COMICS
Street and Smith: No date (1942?) (10¢, 64 pgs., B&W & color, no ads)

nn-Art by Robert Winsor McCay (recreating his father's art), George Marcoux (Supersnipe artist), Vernon Greene (The Shadow artist), Jack Binder (with biog.), Thorton Fisher, Jon Small, & Jack Farr; has biographies of each artist	31	62	93	182	296	410

H. P. LOVECRAFT'S CTHULHU
Millennium Publications: Dec, 1991 - No. 3, May, 1992 ($2.50, limited series)

1-3: 1-Contains trading cards on thin stock 3.00

H. R. PUFNSTUF (TV) (See March of Comics #360)
Gold Key: Oct, 1970 - No. 8, July, 1972

1-Photo-c	11	22	33	71	136	200
2-8-Photo-c on all. 6-8-Both Gold Key and Whitman editions exist	8	16	24	53	89	125

HUBERT AT CAMP MOONBEAM
Dell Publishing Co.: No. 251, Oct, 1949 (one shot)

Four Color 251	8	16	24	51	86	120

HUCK & YOGI JAMBOREE (TV)
Dell Publishing Co.: Mar, 1961 ($1.00, 6-1/4x9", 116 pgs., cardboard-c, high quality paper) (B&W original material)

nn (scarce)	9	18	27	61	106	150

HUCK & YOGI WINTER SPORTS (TV)
Dell Publishing Co.: No. 1310, Mar, 1962 (Hanna-Barbara) (one-shot)

Four Color 1310	8	16	24	55	93	130

HUCK FINN (See The New Adventures of... & Power Record Comics)

HUCKLEBERRY FINN (Movie)
Dell Publishing Co.: No. 1114, July, 1960

Four Color 1114-Photo-c	5	10	15	34	55	75

HUCKLEBERRY HOUND (See Dell Giant #31,44, Golden Picture Story Book, Kite Fun Book, March of Comics #199, 214, 235, Spotlight #1 & Whitman Comic Books)

HUCKLEBERRY HOUND (TV)
Dell/Gold Key No. 18 (10/62) on: No. 990, 5-7/59 - No. 43, 10/70 (Hanna-Barbera)

Four Color 990(#1)-1st app. Huckleberry Hound, Yogi Bear, & Pixie & Dixie & Mr. Jinks	11	22	33	77	154	230
Four Color 1050,1054 (12/59)	8	16	24	56	96	135
3(1-2/60) - 7 (9-10/60), Four Color 1141 (10/60)	8	16	24	51	86	120
8-10	6	12	18	42	69	95
11,13-17 (6-8/62)	5	10	15	32	51	70
12-1st Hokey Wolf & Ding-a-Ling	6	12	18	37	59	80
18,19 (84pgs.; 18-20 titled ...Chuckleberry Tales)	8	16	24	51	86	120
20-Titled Chuckleberry Tales	5	10	15	30	48	65
21-30: 28-30-Reprints	4	8	12	24	37	50
31-43: 31,32,35,37-43-Reprints	3	6	9	20	30	40

HUCKLEBERRY HOUND (TV)
Charlton Comics: Nov, 1970 - No. 8, Jan, 1972 (Hanna-Barbera)

1	5	10	15	32	51	70
2-8	3	6	9	18	27	35

HUEY, DEWEY, & LOUIE (See Donald Duck, 1938 for 1st app. Also see Mickey Mouse Magazine V4#2, V5#7 & Walt Disney's Junior Woodchucks Limited Series)

HUEY, DEWEY, & LOUIE BACK TO SCHOOL (See Dell Giant #22, 35, 49 & Dell Giants)

HUEY, DEWEY, AND LOUIE JUNIOR WOODCHUCKS (Disney)
Gold Key No. 1-61/Whitman No. 62 on: Aug, 1966 - No. 81, July, 1984
(See Walt Disney's Comics & Stories #125)

1	6	12	18	41	66	90
2,3(12/68)	4	8	12	22	34	45
4,5(4/70)-r/two WDC&S D.Duck stories by Barks	3	6	9	20	30	40
6-17	3	6	9	18	27	35
18,27-30	3	6	9	15	21	26
19-23,25-New storyboarded scripts by Barks, 13-25 pgs. per issue	3	6	9	19	29	38
24,26: 26-r/Barks Donald Duck WDC&S stories	3	6	9	16	23	30
31-57,60,61: 35,41-r/Barks J.W. scripts	2	4	6	8	11	14
58,59: 58-r/Barks Donald Duck WDC&S stories	2	4	6	9	13	16
62-64 (Whitman)	2	4	6	9	13	16
65-(9/80), 66 (Pre-pack? scarce)	4	8	12	22	34	45
67 (1/81),68	2	4	6	9	13	16
67-40¢ cover variant	4	8	12	17	21	24
69-74: 72(2/82), 73(2-3/82), 74(3/82)	2	4	6	8	11	14
75-81 (all #90183; pre-pack; nd, nd code; scarce): 75(4/83), 76(5/83), 77(7/83), 78(8/83), 79(4/84), 80(5/84), 81(7/84)	3	6	9	14	20	25

HUGGA BUNCH (TV)
Marvel Comics (Star Comics): Oct, 1986 - No. 6, Aug, 1987

1-6 5.00

HULK (Magazine)(Formerly The Rampaging Hulk)(Also see The Incredible Hulk)
Marvel Comics: No. 10, Aug., 1978 - No. 27, June, 1981 ($1.50)

10-18: 10-Bill Bixby interview. 11-Moon Knight begins. 12-15,17,18-Moon Knight stories. 12-Lou Ferrigno interview.	2	4	6	10	14	18
19-27: 20-Moon Knight story. 23-Last full color issue; Banner is attacked. 24-Part color, Lou Ferrigno interview. 25-Part color. 26,27-are B&W	2	4	6	9	12	15

NOTE: #10-20 have fragile spines which split easily. ***Alcala*** *a(i)-15, 17-20, 22, 24-27.* ***Buscema*** *a-23; c-26.* ***Chaykin*** *a-21-25.* ***Colan*** *a(p)-11, 19, 24-27.* ***Jusko*** *painted c-12.* ***Nebres*** *a-16.* ***Severin*** *a-19i. Moon Knight by* ***Sienkiewicz*** *in 13-15, 17, 18, 20.* ***Simonson*** *a-27; c-23. Dominic Fortune appears in #21-24.*

HULK (Becomes Incredible Hulk Vol. 2 with issue #12) (Also see Marvel Age Hulk)
Marvel Comics: Apr, 1999 - No. 11, Feb, 2000 ($2.99/$1.99)

1-($2.99) Byrne-s/Garney-a 5.00
1-Variant-c 9.00
1-DFE Remarked-c 50.00
1-Gold foil variant 10.00
2-7-($1.99): 2-Two covers. 5-Art by Jurgens, Buscema & Texeira. 7-Avengers app. 4.00
8-Hulk battles Wolverine 7.00
9-11: 11-She-Hulk app. 3.00
1999 Annual ($3.50) Chapter One story; Byrne-s/Weeks-a 4.00
Hulk Vs. The Thing (12/99, $3.99, TPB) reprints their notable battles 4.00

HULK (Also see Fall of the Hulks and King-Size Hulk)
Marvel Comics: Mar, 2008 - Present ($2.99/$3.99)

1-Red Hulk app.; Abomination killed; Loeb-s/McGuinness-a/c 5.00
1-Variant-c by Acuña 10.00
1-Variant-c with Incredible Hulk #1 cover swipe by McGuinness 20.00
1,2-2nd printings with wraparound McGuinness variant-c 3.00
2-22: 2-Iron Man app.; Rick Jones becomes the new Abomination. 4,6-Red Hulk vs. green Hulk; two covers (each Hulk); Thor app. 7-9-Art Adams & Cho-a (2 covers) 10-Defenders re-form. 14,15-X-Force, Elektra & Deadpool app. 15-Red She-Hulk app. 19-21-Fall of the Hulks x-over. 19-FF app. 22-World War Hulks 4.00
2-9: 2-Variant-c by Djurdjevic. 3-Var-c by Finch. 5-Var-c by Coipel. 6,7-Var-c by Turner

Hulk: Nightmerica #1 © MAR

Human Target (2010) #1 © DC

Human Torch #3 (#2) © MAR

GD VG FN VF VF/NM NM-
2.0 4.0 6.0 8.0 9.0 9.2

8-Var-c by Sal Buscema. 9-Two covers w/Hulks as Santa 6.00
23-($4.99) Origin of the Red Hulk; art by Sale, Romita, Deodato, Trimpe, Yu, others 5.00
24-31-($3.99): 24-World war Hulks. 25,26-Iron Man app. 26-Thor app. 4.00
30.1, 32-49 ($2.99): 34-Planet Red Hulk begins. 37-38-Fear Itself tie-in 3.00
... Family: Green Genes 1 (2/09, $4.99) new She-Hulk, Scorpion, Skaar & Mr. Fixit stories 5.00
... Let the Battle Begin 1 (5/10, $3.99) Snider-s/Kurth-a; Del Mundo-c; McGuinness-a 4.00
... MGC #1 (6/10, $1.00) r/#1 with "Marvel's Greatest Comics" logo on cover 3.00
... Monster-Size Special (12/08, $3.99) monster-themed stories by Niles, David & others 4.00
...: Raging Thunder 1 (8/08, $3.99) Hulk vs. Thundra; Breitweiser-a; r/FF #133; Land-c 4.00
Hulk-Sized Mini-Hulks ('11, $2.99) Red, Green & Blue Hulks all-ages humor; Giarrusso-a 3.00
... Vs. Fin Fang Foom (2/08, $3.99) new re-telling of first meeting; r/Strange Tales #89 4.00
... Vs. Hercules (6/08, $3.99) Djurdjevic-c; new story w/art by various; r/Tales To Ast. #79 4.00
...: Winter Guard (2/10, $3.99) Darkstar, Crimson Dynamo app. Steve Ellis-a/c 4.00
Hulk 100 Project (2008, $10.00, SC, charity book for the HERO Initiative) collection of 100 variant covers by Adams, Romita Sr. & Jr., Cho, McGuinness and more 10.00

HULK AND POWER PACK (All ages series)
Marvel Comics: May, 2007 - No. 4, Aug, 2007 ($2.99, limited series)

1-4-Sumerak-s. 1,2,4-Williams-a. 1-Absorbing Man app. 3-Kuhn-a; Abomination app. 3.00
...: Pack Smash! (2007, $6.99, digest) r/#1-4 7.00

HULK & THING: HARD KNOCKS
Marvel Comics: Nov, 2004 - No. 4, Feb, 2005 ($3.50, limited series)

1-4-Bruce Jones-s/Jae Lee-a/c 3.50
TPB (2005, $13.99) r/#1-4 and Giant-Size Super-Stars #1 14.00

HULK: BROKEN WORLDS
Marvel Comics: May, 2009 -No. 2, July, 2009 ($3.99, limited series)

1,2-Short stories of alternate world Hulks by various, incl. Trimpe, David, Warren 4.00

HULK CHRONICLES: WWH
Marvel Comics: Oct, 2008 - No. 6, Mar, 2009 ($4.99, limited series)

1-6-Reprints stories from World War Hulk x-over. 1-R/Inc. Hulk #106 & WWH Prologue 5.00

HULK: DESTRUCTION
Marvel Comics: Sept, 2005 - No. 4, Dec, 2005 ($2.99, limited series)

1-4-Origin of the Abomination; Peter David-s/Jim Muniz-a 3.00

HULKED-OUT HEROES
Marvel Comics: Jun, 2010 - No. 2, Jun, 2010 ($3.99, limited series)

1,2-World War Hulks tie-in; Deadpool app.; Ramos-a 4.00

HULK: FUTURE IMPERFECT
Marvel Comics: Jan, 1993 - No. 2, Dec, 1992 (In error) ($5.95, 52 pgs., squarebound, limited series)

1,2: Embossed-c; Peter David story & George Perez-c/a. 1-1st app. Maestro.
1 2 3 5 6 8

HULK: GRAY
Marvel Comics: Dec, 2003 - No. 6, Apr, 2004 ($3.50, limited series)

1-6-Hulk's origin & early days; Loeb-s/Sale-a/c 3.50
HC (2004, $21.99, with dust jacket) oversized r/#1-6 22.00
SC (2005, $19.99) r/#1-6 20.00

HULK: NIGHTMERICA
Marvel Comics: Aug, 2003 - No. 6, May, 2004 ($2.99, limited series)

1-6-Brian Ashmore painted-a/c 3.00

HULK/ PITT
Marvel Comics: 1997 ($5.99, one-shot)

1-David-s/Keown-c/a 6.00

HULK SMASH
Marvel Comics: Mar, 2001 - No. 2, Apr, 2001 ($2.99, limited series)

1,2-Ennis-s/McCrea & Janson-a/Nowlan painted-c 3.00

HULK: THE MOVIE
Marvel Comics

...Adaptation (8/03, $3.50) Bruce Jones-s/Bagley-a/Keown-c 3.50
TPB (2003, $12.99) r/Adaptation, Ultimates #5, Inc. Hulk #34, Ult. Marvel Team-Up #2&3 13.00

HULK 2099
Marvel Comics: Dec, 1994 - No. 10, Sept, 1995 ($1.50/$1.95)

1-($2.50)-Green foil-c 3.50
2-10: 2-A. Kubert-c 3.00

HULK/WOLVERINE: 6 HOURS
Marvel Comics: Mar, 2003 - No. 4, May, 2003 ($2.99, limited series)

1-4-Bruce Jones-s/Scott Kolins-a; Bisley-c 3.00
Hulk Legends Vol. 1: Hulk/Wolverine: 6 Hours (2003, $13.99, TPB) r/#1-4 & 1st Wolverine app. from Incredible Hulk #181 14.00

HUMAN DEFENSE CORPS
DC Comics: Jul, 2003 - No. 6, Dec, 2003 ($2.50, limited series)

1-6-Ty Templeton-s/Sauve, Jr & Vlasco-a. 1-Lois Lane app. 3.00

HUMAN FLY
I.W. Enterprises/Super: 1963 - 1964 (Reprints)

I.W. Reprint #1-Reprints Blue Beetle #44('46) 2 4 6 13 18 22
Super Reprint #10-R/Blue Beetle #46('47) 2 4 6 13 18 22

HUMAN FLY, THE
Marvel Comics Group: Sept, 1977 - No. 19, Mar, 1979

1,2,9,19: 1,2-(Regular 30¢-c). 1-Origin; Spider-Man x-over. 2-Ghost Rider app. 9-Daredevil x-over; Byrne-c(p). 19-Last issue 2 3 4 6 8 10
1,2-(35¢-c, limited distribution) 3 6 9 20 30 40
3-8,10-18 5.00
NOTE: ***Austin** c-4i, 9i. **Elias** a-1, 3p, 4p, 7p, 10-12p, 15p, 18p, 19p. **Layton** c-19.*

HUMANKIND
Image Comics (Top Cow): Sept, 2004 - No. 5, Mar, 2005 ($2.99, limited series)

1-5-Tony Daniel-a. 1-Three covers by Daniel, Silvestri, and Land 3.00

HUMAN RACE, THE
DC Comics: May, 2005 - No. 7, Nov, 2005 ($2.99, limited series)

1-7-Raab-s/Justiniano-a/c 3.00

HUMAN TARGET
DC Comics (Vertigo): Apr, 1999 - No. 4, July, 1999 ($2.95, limited series)

1-4-Milligan-s/Bradstreet-c/Biuković-a 3.00
1-Special Edition (6/10, $1.00) r/#1 with "What's Next?" logo on cover 3.00
TPB (2000, $12.95) new Bradstreet-c 13.00
...: Chance Meetings TPB (2010, $14.99) r/#1-4 and Human Target: Final Cut GN 15.00

HUMAN TARGET
DC Comics (Vertigo): Oct, 2003 - No. 21, June, 2005 ($2.95)

1-21: 1-5-Milligan-s/Pulido-a/c. 6-Chiang-a 3.00
...: Living in Amerika TPB (2004, $14.95) r/#6-10; Chiang sketch pages 15.00
...: Second Chances TPB (2011, $19.99) r/#1-10; Chiang sketch pages 20.00
...: Strike Zones TPB (2004, $9.95) r/#1-5 10.00

HUMAN TARGET (Based on the Fox TV series)
DC Comics: Apr, 2010 - No. 6, Sept, 2010 ($2.99, limited series)

1-6-Wein-s/Redondo-a; back-up stories by various. 1-Bermejo-c. 5-Sook-c 3.00
TPB (2010, $17.99) r/#1-6 18.00

HUMAN TARGET: FINAL CUT
DC Comics (Vertigo): 2002 ($29.95/$19.95, graphic novel)

Hardcover (2002, $29.95) Milligan-s/Pulido-a/c 30.00
Softcover (2003, $19.95) 20.00

HUMAN TARGET SPECIAL (TV)
DC Comics: Nov, 1991 ($2.00, 52 pgs., one-shot)

1 4.00

HUMAN TORCH, THE (Red Raven #1)(See All-Select, All Winners, Marvel Mystery, Men's Adventures, Mystic Comics (2nd series), Sub-Mariner, USA & Young Men)
Timely/Marvel Comics (TP 2,3/TCI 4-9/SePI 10/SnPC 11-25/CnPC 26-35/Atlas Comics (CPC 36-38)): No. 2, Fall, 1940 - No. 15, Spring, 1944; No. 16, Fall, 1944 - No. 35, Mar, 1949 (Becomes Love Tales #36 on); No. 36, April, 1954 - No. 38, Aug, 1954

2(#1)-Intro & Origin Toro; The Falcon, The Fiery Mask, Mantor the Magician, & Microman only app.; Human Torch by Burgos, Sub-Mariner by Everett begin (origin of each in text)
3000 6000 9000 21,000 43,500 66,000
3(#2)-40 pg. H.T. story; H.T. & S.M. battle over who is best artist in text-Everett or Burgos
584 1168 1752 4263 7532 10,800
4(#3)-Origin The Patriot in text; last Everett Sub-Mariner; Sid Greene-a
454 908 1362 3314 5857 8400
5(#4)-The Patriot app; Angel x-over in Sub-Mariner (Summer, 1941); 1st Nazi war-c this title; back-c ad for Young Allies #1 with diff. cover-a 400 800 1200 2800 4900 7000
5-Human Torch battles Sub-Mariner (Fall, '41); 60 pg. story
632 1264 1896 4614 8157 11,700
6 303 606 909 2121 3711 5300
7-1st Japanese war-c 326 652 978 2282 3991 5700
8-Human Torch battles Sub-Mariner; 52 pg. story; Wolverton-a, 1 pg.
423 846 1269 3067 5384 7700
9 320 640 960 2032 3816 5600
10-Human Torch battles Sub-Mariner, 45 pg. story; Wolverton-a, 1 pg.

Humdinger V2 #2 © Premium

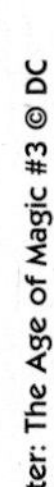
Hunter: The Age of Magic #3 © DC

Huntress (2011 series) #1 © DC

	GD 2.0	VG 4.0	FN 6.0	VF 8.0	VF/NM 9.0	NM- 9.2
	354	708	1062	2478	4339	6200
11,13-15: 14-1st Atlas Globe logo (Winter, 1943-44; see All Winners #11 also)	277	554	831	1759	3030	4300
12-Classic-c	423	846	1269	3067	5384	7700
16-20: 20-Last War issue	187	374	561	1197	2049	2900
21,22,24-30: 27-2nd app. (1st-c) Asbestos Lady (see Capt. America Comics #63 for 1st app.)	152	304	456	965	1658	2350
23 (Sum/46)-Becomes Junior Miss 24? Classic Schomburg Robot-c	187	374	561	1197	2049	2900
31,32: 31-Namora x-over in Sub-Mariner (also #30); last Toro. 32-Sungirl, Namora app.; Sungirl-c	135	270	405	864	1482	2100
33-Capt. America x-over	139	278	417	883	1517	2150
34-Sungirl solo	126	252	378	806	1378	1950
35-Captain America & Sungirl app. (1949)	129	258	387	826	1413	2000
36-38(1954)-Sub-Mariner in all	108	216	324	686	1181	1675

NOTE: ***Ayers** Human Torch in 36(3). **Brodsky** c-25, 31-33?, 37, 38, **Burgos** c-36. **Everett** a-1-3, 27, 28, 30, 37, 38. **Powell** a-36(Sub-Mariner). **Schomburg** c-1-3, 5-8, 10-23. **Sekowsky** c-28, 34?, 35? **Shores** c-24, 26, 27, 29, 30. **Mickey Spillane** text 4-6. Bondage c-2, 12, 19.*

HUMAN TORCH, THE (Also see Avengers West Coast, Fantastic Four, The Invaders, Saga of the Original... & Strange Tales #101)
Marvel Comics Group: Sept, 1974 - No. 8, Nov, 1975

	GD	VG	FN	VF	VF/NM	NM-
1: 1-8-r/stories from Strange Tales #101-108	3	6	9	16	23	30
2-8: 1st H.T. title since G.A. 7-vs. Sub-Mariner	2	4	6	11	16	20

NOTE: *Golden Age & Silver Age Human Torch-r #1-8. **Ayers** r-6, 7. **Kirby/Ayers** r-1-5, 8.*

HUMAN TORCH (From the Fantastic Four)
Marvel Comics: June, 2003 - No. 12, Jun, 2004 ($2.50/$2.99)

1-7-Skottie Young-c/a; Karl Kesel-s 3.00
8-12-($2.99) 8,10-Dodd-a. 9-Young-a. 11-Porter-a. 12-Medina-a 3.00
... Vol. 1: Burn TPB (2005, $7.99, digest size) r/#1-6 8.00

HUMAN TORCH COMICS 70TH ANNIVERSARY SPECIAL
Marvel Comics: July, 2009 ($3.99, one-shot)

1-Covers by Granov and Martin; new story and r/1st app Toro from Human Torch #2 5.00

HUMBUG (Satire by Harvey Kurtzman)
Humbug Publications: Aug, 1957 - No. 9, May, 1958; No. 10, June, 1958; No. 11, Oct, 1958

	GD	VG	FN	VF	VF/NM	NM-
1-Wood-a (intro pgs. only)	27	54	81	158	259	360
2	15	30	45	85	130	175
3-9: 8-Elvis in Jailbreak Rock	14	28	42	76	108	140
10,11-Magazine format. 10-Photo-c	15	30	45	90	140	190
Bound Volume(#1-9)(extremely rare)	65	130	195	416	708	1000

NOTE: ***Davis** a-1-11. **Elder** a-2-4, 6-9, 11. **Heath** a-2, 4-8, 10. **Jaffee** a-2, 4-9. **Kurtzman** a-11.*

HUMDINGER (Becomes White Rider and Super Horse #3 on?)
Novelty Press/Premium Group: May-June, 1946 - V2#2, July-Aug, 1947

	GD	VG	FN	VF	VF/NM	NM-
1-Jerkwater Line, Mickey Starlight by Don Rico, Dink begin	36	72	108	211	343	475
2	16	32	48	94	147	200
3-6, V2#1,2	12	24	36	69	97	125

HUMONGOUS MAN
Alternative Press (Ikon Press): Sept, 1997 -No. 3 ($2.25, B&W)

1-3-Stepp & Harrison-c/s/a. 3.00

HUMOR (See All Humor Comics)

HUMPHREY COMICS (Joe Palooka Presents...; also see Joe Palooka)
Harvey Publications: Oct, 1948 - No. 22, Apr, 1952

	GD	VG	FN	VF	VF/NM	NM-
1-Joe Palooka's pal (r); (52 pgs.)-Powell-a	14	28	42	80	115	150
2,3: Powell-a	9	18	27	47	61	75
4-Boy Heroes app.; Powell-a	9	18	27	50	65	80
5-8,10: 5,6-Powell-a. 7-Little Dot app.	8	16	24	40	50	60
9-Origin Humphrey	9	18	27	47	61	75
11-22	7	14	21	37	46	55

HUNCHBACK OF NOTRE DAME, THE
Dell Publishing Co.: No. 854, Oct, 1957 (one shot)

	GD	VG	FN	VF	VF/NM	NM-
Four Color 854-Movie, photo-c	11	22	33	76	151	225

HUNGER, THE
Speakeasy Comics: May, 2005 ($2.99)

1-Andy Bradshaw-s/a; Eric Powell-c 3.00

HUNGER DOGS, THE (See DC Graphic Novel #4)

HUNK
Charlton Comics: Aug, 1961 - No. 11, 1963

	GD	VG	FN	VF	VF/NM	NM-
1	4	8	12	24	37	50
2-11	3	6	9	14	20	25

HUNTED (Formerly My Love Memoirs)
Fox Features Syndicate: No. 13, July, 1950; No. 2, Sept, 1950

	GD	VG	FN	VF	VF/NM	NM-
13(#1)-Used in **SOTI**, pg. 42 & illo. "Treating police contemptuously" (lower left); Hollingsworth bondage-c	37	74	111	222	361	500
2	18	36	54	105	165	225

HUNTER-KILLER
Image Comics (Top Cow): Nov, 2004 - No. 12, Mar, 2007 ($2.99)

0-(11/04, 25¢) Prelude with Silvestri sketch page and Waid afterword 3.00
1-12: 1-(3/05, $2.99) Waid-s/Silvestri-a; four covers. 2-Linsner variant-c 3.00
... Collected Edition Vol. 1 (9/05, $4.99) r/#0-3 5.00
...Dossier 1 (9/05, $2.99) character profiles with art by various; Migliari-c 3.00
... Volume 1 TPB (1/08, $24.99) r/#0-12; Dossier and Script Book; variant covers 25.00

HUNTER: THE AGE OF MAGIC (See Books of Magic)
DC Comics (Vertigo): Sept, 2001 - No. 25, Sept, 2003 ($2.50/$2.75)

1-25: Horrocks-s/Case-a. 1-8-Bolton-c. 14-Begin $2.75-c. 19-Bachalo-c 3.00

HUNTRESS, THE (See All-Star Comics #69, Batman Family, DC Super Stars #17, Detective #652, Infinity, Inc. #1 & Wonder Woman #271)
DC Comics: Apr, 1989 - No. 19, Oct, 1990 ($1.00, mature)

1-16: Staton-c/a(p) in all 3.00
17-19-Batman-c/stories 3.00
...: Darknight Daughter TPB (2006, $19.99) r/origin & early apps. in DC Super Stars #17, Batman Family #18-20 & Wonder Woman #271-287,289,290,294,295; Bolland-c 20.00

HUNTRESS, THE
DC Comics: June, 1994 - No. 4, Sept, 1994 ($1.50, limited series)

1-4-Netzer-c/a: 2-Batman app. 3.00

HUNTRESS (Leads into 2012 World's Finest series)
DC Comics: Dec, 2011 - No. 6, May, 2012 ($2.99, limited series)

1-6-Levitz-s/To-a/March-c 3.00

HUNTRESS: YEAR ONE
DC Comics: Early July, 2008 - No. 6, Late Sept, 2008 ($2.99, limited series)

1-6-Origin re-told; Cliff Richards-a/Ivory Madison-s 3.00
TPB (2009, $17.99) r/#1-6; intro. by Paul Levitz 18.00

HURRICANE COMICS
Cambridge House: 1945 (52 pgs.)

	GD	VG	FN	VF	VF/NM	NM-
1-(Humor, funny animal)	23	46	69	136	223	310

HUSK
Marvel Comics (Soleil): May, 2010 - No. 2, Jun, 2010 ($5.99, limited series)

1,2-English version of French comic; L'Homme-s/Boudoiron-a 6.00

HYBRIDS
Continuity Comics: Jan, 1994 ($2.50, one-shot)

1-Neal Adams-c(p) & part-a(i); embossed-c. 3.50

HYBRIDS DEATHWATCH 2000
Continuity Comics: Apr, 1993 - No. 3, Aug, 1993 ($2.50)

0-(Giveaway)-Foil-c; Neal Adams-c(i) & plots (also #1,2) 3.50
1-3: 1-Polybagged w/card; die-cut-c. 2-Thermal-c. 3-Polybagged w/card; indestructible-c; Adams plot 4.00

HYBRIDS ORIGIN
Continuity Comics: 1993 - No. 5, Jan, 1994 ($2.50)

1-5: 2,3-Neal Adams-c. 4,5-Valeria the She-Bat app. Adams-c(i) 3.00

HYDE
IDW Publ.: Oct, 2004 ($7.49, one-shot)

1-Steve Niles-s/Nick Stakal 7.50

HYDE-25
Harris Publications: Apr, 1995 ($2.95, one-shot)

0-Coupon for poster; r/Vampirella's 1st app. 3.00

HYDROMAN (See Heroic Comics)

HYPERKIND (See Razorline)
Marvel Comics: Sept, 1993 - No. 9, May, 1994 ($1.75/$1.95)

1-($2.50)-Foil embossed-c; by Clive Barker 3.50
2-9 3.00

HYPERKIND UNLEASED
Marvel Comics: Aug, 1994 ($2.95, 52 pgs., one-shot)

I Am an Avenger #5 © MAR

Ibis, The Invincible #1 © FAW

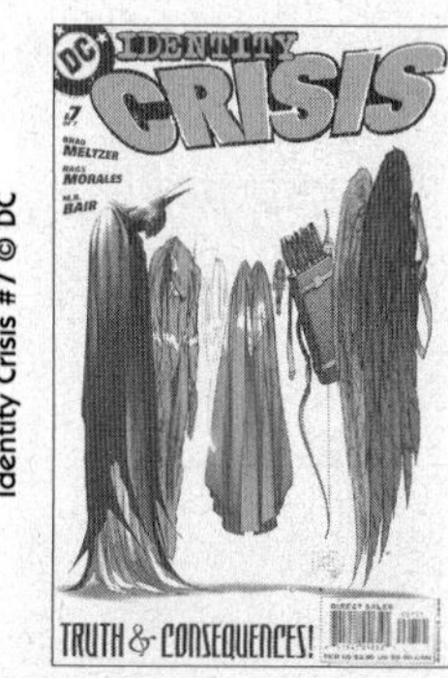

Identity Crisis #7 © DC

	GD 2.0	VG 4.0	FN 6.0	VF 8.0	VF/NM 9.0	NM- 9.2
1						4.00

HYPER MYSTERY COMICS
Hyper Publications: May, 1940 - No. 2, June, 1940 (68 pgs.)

	GD 2.0	VG 4.0	FN 6.0	VF 8.0	VF/NM 9.0	NM- 9.2
1-Hyper, the Phenomenal begins; Calkins-a	213	426	639	1363	2332	3300
2	107	214	321	680	1165	1650

HYPERSONIC
Dark Horse Comics: Nov, 1997 - No. 4, Feb, 1998 ($2.95, limited series)

1-4: Abnett & White/Erskine-a 3.00

I AIM AT THE STARS (Movie)
Dell Publishing Co.: No. 1148, Nov-Jan/1960-61 (one-shot)

	GD 2.0	VG 4.0	FN 6.0	VF 8.0	VF/NM 9.0	NM- 9.2
Four Color 1148-The Werner Von Braun Sty-photo-c	7	14	21	46	76	105

I AM AN AVENGER (See Avengers, Young Avengers and Pet Avengers)
Marvel Comics: Nov, 2010 - No. 5, Mar, 2011 ($3.99, limited series)

1-5-Short stories by various. 1-Yu-c. 2-Land-c. 2-4-Mayhew-a. 3-Noto-c. 4-Acuña-c 4.00

I AM CAPTAIN AMERICA
Marvel Comics: Jan, 2012 ($3.99, one-shot)

1-Collection of Captain America-themed 70th Anniversary covers with artist profiles 4.00

I AM COYOTE (See Eclipse Graphic Album Series & Eclipse Magazine #2)

I AM LEGEND
Eclipse Books: 1991 - No. 4, 1991 ($5.95, B&W, squarebound, 68 pgs.)

	GD 2.0	VG 4.0	FN 6.0	VF 8.0	VF/NM 9.0	NM- 9.2
1-4: Based on 1954 novel by Richard Matheson	1	2	3	5	6	8

I AM LEGION (English version of French graphic novel Je Suis Légion)
Devils Due Publishing: Jan, 2009 - No. 6, July, 2009 ($3.50)

1-6-John Cassaday-a/Fabien Nury-s; two covers 3.50

IBIS, THE INVINCIBLE (See Fawcett Miniatures, Mighty Midget & Whiz)
Fawcett Publications: 1942 (Fall?); #2, Mar.,1943; #3, Wint, 1945 - #5, Fall, 1946; #6, Spring, 1948

	GD 2.0	VG 4.0	FN 6.0	VF 8.0	VF/NM 9.0	NM- 9.2
1-Origin Ibis; Raboy-c; on sale 1/2/43	245	490	735	1568	2684	3800
2-Bondage-c (on sale 2/5/43)	107	214	321	680	1165	1650
3-Wolverton-a #3-6 (4 pgs. each)	74	148	222	470	810	1150
4-6: 5-Bondage-c	51	102	153	320	543	765

NOTE: ***Mac Raboy** c(p)-3-5. **Schaffenberger** c-6.*

I-BOTS (See Isaac Asimov's I-BOTS)

ICE AGE ON THE WORLD OF MAGIC: THE GATHERING (See Magic The Gathering)

ICE KING OF OZ, THE (See First Comics Graphic Novel #13)

ICEMAN (Also see The Champions & X-Men #94)
Marvel Comics Group: Dec, 1984 - No. 4, June, 1985 (Limited series)

1,2,4: Zeck covers on all 4.00
3-The Defenders, Champions (Ghost Rider) & the original X-Men x-over 5.00

ICEMAN (X-Men)
Marvel Comics: Dec, 2001 - No. 4, Mar, 2002 ($2.50, limited series)

1-4-Abnett & Lanning-s/Kerschl-a 3.00

ICEMAN AND ANGEL (X-Men)
Marvel Comics: May, 2011 ($2.99, one-shot)

1-Brian Clevinger-s/Juan Doe-a; Goom & Googam app. 3.00

ICON
DC Comics (Milestone): May, 1993 - No. 42, Feb, 1997($1.50/$1.75/$2.50)

1-($2.95)-Collector's Edition polybagged w/poster & trading card (direct sale only) 4.00
1-24,30-42: 9-Simonson-c. 15,16-Worlds Collide Pt. 4 & 11. 15-Superboy app. 16-Superman-c/story. 40-Vs. Blood Syndicate 3.00
25-($2.95, 52 pgs.) 4.00
... A Hero's Welcome SC (2009, $19.99) r/#1-8; intro. by Reginald Hudlin 20.00
...: Mothership Connection SC (2010, $24.99) r/#13,19-22,24-27,30 25.00

IDAHO
Dell Publishing Co.: June-Aug, 1963 - No. 8, July-Sept, 1965

	GD 2.0	VG 4.0	FN 6.0	VF 8.0	VF/NM 9.0	NM- 9.2
1	3	6	9	17	25	32
2-8: 5-7-Painted-c	2	4	6	9	13	16

IDEAL (... a Classical Comic) (2nd Series) (Love Romances No. 6 on)
Timely Comics: July, 1948 - No. 5, March, 1949 (Feature length stories)

	GD 2.0	VG 4.0	FN 6.0	VF 8.0	VF/NM 9.0	NM- 9.2
1-Antony & Cleopatra	37	74	111	222	361	500
2-The Corpses of Dr. Sacotti	31	62	93	186	303	420
3-Joan of Arc; used in **SOTI**, pg. 310 'Boer War'	29	58	87	172	281	390
4-Richard the Lion-hearted; titled "...the World's Greatest Comics"; The Witness story	40	80	120	246	411	575
5-Ideal Love & Romance; change to love; photo-c	20	40	60	117	189	260

IDEAL COMICS (1st Series) (Willie Comics No. 5 on)
Timely Comics (MgPC): Fall, 1944 - No. 4, Spring, 1946

	GD 2.0	VG 4.0	FN 6.0	VF 8.0	VF/NM 9.0	NM- 9.2
1-Funny animal; Super Rabbit in all	29	58	87	170	278	385
2	15	30	45	90	140	190
3,4	15	30	45	86	133	180

IDEAL LOVE & ROMANCE (See Ideal, A Classical Comic)

IDEAL ROMANCE (Formerly Tender Romance)
Key Publ.: No. 3, April, 1954 - No. 8, Feb, 1955 (Diary Confessions No. 9 on)

	GD 2.0	VG 4.0	FN 6.0	VF 8.0	VF/NM 9.0	NM- 9.2
3-Bernard Baily-c	10	20	30	54	72	90
4-8: 4-6-B. Baily-c	8	16	24	40	50	60

IDEALS (Secret Stories)
Ideals Publ., USA: 1981 (68 pgs, graphic novels, 7x10", stiff-c)

	GD 2.0	VG 4.0	FN 6.0	VF 8.0	VF/NM 9.0	NM- 9.2
Captain America - Star Spangled Super Hero	3	6	9	18	27	35
Fantastic Four - Cosmic Quartet	3	6	9	18	27	35
Incredible Hulk - Gamma Powered Goliath	3	6	9	18	27	35
Spider-Man - World Famous Wall Crawler	4	8	12	22	34	45

IDENTITY CRISIS
DC Comics: Aug, 2004 - No. 7, Feb, 2005 ($3.95, limited series)

1-Meltzer-s/Morales-a/Turner-c in all; Sue Dibny murdered 5.00
1-(Second printing) black-c with white sketch lines 5.00
1-(3rd & 4th) 3rd-Bloody broken photo glass image-c by Morales. 4th-Turner red-c 4.00
1-Diamond Retailer Summit Edition with sketch-c 30.00
1-Special Edition (6/09, $1.00) r/#1 with "After Watchmen" cover frame 3.00
2-7: 2-4-Deathstroke app. 5-Firestorm, Jack Drake, Capt. Boomerang killed 4.00
2-(Second printing) new Morales sketch-c 4.00
Final printings for all issues with red background variant covers 4.00
HC (2005, $24.99, dust jacket) r/series; Director's Cut extras; cover gallery; Whedon intro.; 2 covers: Direct Market-c by Turner, Bookstore-c with Morales-a 25.00
SC (2006, $14.99) r/series; Director's Cut extras; cover gallery; Whedon intro 15.00

IDENTITY DISC
Marvel Comics: Aug, 2004 - No. 5, Dec, 2004 ($2.99, limited series)

1-5-Sabretooth, Bullseye, Sandman, Vulture, Deadpool, Juggernaut app.; Higgins-a 4.00
TPB (2004, $13.99) r/#1-5 14.00

IDES OF BLOOD
DC Comics (WildStorm): Oct, 2010 - No. 6, Mar, 2011 ($3.99/$2.99, limited series)

1-6-Stuart Paul-s/Christian Duce-a/Michael Geiger-c; Roman Empire vampires 4.00

I DIE AT MIDNIGHT (Vertigo V2K)
DC Comics (Vertigo): 2000 ($6.95, prestige format, one-shot)

1-Kyle Baker-s/a 7.00

IDOL
Marvel Comics (Epic Comics): 1992 - No. 3, 1992 ($2.95, mini-series, 52 pgs.)

Book 1-3 4.00

I DREAM OF JEANNIE (TV)
Dell Publishing Co.: Apr, 1965 - No. 2, Dec, 1966 (Photo-c)

	GD 2.0	VG 4.0	FN 6.0	VF 8.0	VF/NM 9.0	NM- 9.2
1-Barbara Eden photo-c, each	12	24	36	83	172	260
2	10	20	30	70	133	195

I FEEL SICK
Slave Labor Graphics: Aug, 1999 - No. 2, May, 2000 ($3.95, limited series)

1,2-Jhonen Vasquez-s/a 4.00

I HATE GALLANT GIRL
Image Comics (Shadowline): Nov, 2008 - No. 3, Jan, 2009 ($3.50, limited series)

1-3-Kat Cahill-s/Seth Damoose-a 3.50

I (heart) MARVEL
Marvel Comics: Apr, 2006; May, 2006 ($2.99, one-shots)

...: Marvel AI 1 (4/06) Cebulski-s; manga art by various; Vision, Daredevil, Elektra app. 3.00
...: Masked Intentions 1 (5/06) Squirrel Girl, Speedball, Firestar, Justice app.; Nicieza-s 3.00
...: My Mutant Heart 1 (4/06) Wolverine, Cannonball, Doop app. 3.00
...: Outlaw Love 1 (4/06) Bullseye, The Answer, Ruby Thursday app.; Nicieza-s 3.00
...: Web of Romance 1 (4/06) Spider-Man, Mary Jane, The Avengers app. 3.00

ILLUMINATOR
Marvel Comics/Nelson Publ.: 1993 - No. 4, 1993 ($4.99/$2.95, 52 pgs.)

1,2-($4.99) Religious themed 5.00
3,4 4.00

ILLUSTRATED GAGS

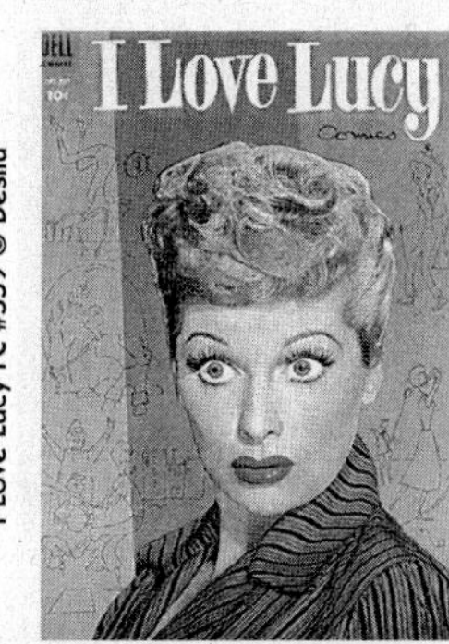

I Love Lucy FC #559 © Desilu

I, Luciphur #2 © Drew Hayes

Image Two-In-One #1 © Larsen & Eliopolis

	GD 2.0	VG 4.0	FN 6.0	VF 8.0	VF/NM 9.0	NM- 9.2

United Features Syndicate: No. 16, 1940

Single Series 16	17	34	51	98	154	210

ILLUSTRATED LIBRARY OF..., AN (See Classics Illustrated Giants)

ILLUSTRATED STORIES OF THE OPERAS
Baily (Bernard) Publ. Co.: 1943 (16 pgs.; B&W) (25 cents) (cover-B&W & red)

nn-(Rare)(4 diff. issues)-Faust (part-r in Cisco Kid #1), nn-Aida, nn-Carmen; Baily-a, nn-Rigoleito	58	116	174	371	636	900

ILLUSTRATED STORY OF ROBIN HOOD & HIS MERRY MEN, THE (See Classics Giveaways, 12/44)

ILLUSTRATED TARZAN BOOK, THE (See Tarzan Book)

I LOVED (Formerly Rulah; Colossal Features Magazine No. 33 on)
Fox Features Syndicate: No. 28, July, 1949 - No. 32, Mar, 1950

28	14	28	42	80	115	150
29-32	10	20	30	58	79	100

I LOVE LUCY
Eternity Comics : 6/90 - No. 6, 1990;V2#1, 11/90 - No. 6, 1991 ($2.95, B&W, mini-series)

1-6: Reprints 1950s comic strip; photo-c 4.00
Book II #1-6: Reprints comic strip; photo-c 4.00

...In Full Color 1 (1991, $5.95, 52 pgs.)-Reprints I Love Lucy Comics #4,5,8,16; photo-c with embossed logo (2 versions exist, one with pgs. 18 & 19 reversed, the other corrected)	1	2	3	5	6	8

...In 3-D 1 (1991, $3.95, w/glasses)-Reprints I Love Lucy Comics; photo-c; bagged 6.00

I LOVE LUCY COMICS (TV) (Also see The Lucy Show)
Dell Publishing Co.: No. 535, Feb, 1954 - No. 35, Apr-June, 1962 (Lucille Ball photo-c on all)

Four Color 535(#1)	39	78	117	293	634	975
Four Color 559(#2, 5/54)	25	50	75	175	375	575
3 (8-10/54) - 5	14	28	42	97	211	325
6-10	12	24	36	83	172	260
11-20	10	20	30	68	127	185
21-35	9	18	27	61	106	150

I LOVE NEW YORK
Linsner.com: 2002 ($2.95, B&W, one-shot)

1-Linsner-s/a; benefit book for the Sept. 11 charities 3.00

I LOVE YOU
Fawcett Publications: June, 1950 (one-shot)

1-Photo-c	15	30	45	83	124	165

I LOVE YOU (Formerly In Love)
Charlton Comics: No. 7, 9/55 - No. 121, 12/76; No. 122, 3/79 - No. 130, 5/80

7-Kirby-c; Powell-a	9	18	27	61	106	150
8-10	5	10	15	32	51	70
11-16,18-20	4	8	12	28	44	60
17-(68 pg. Giant)	7	14	21	48	79	110
21-50: 26-No Torres-a	3	6	9	21	32	42
51-59	3	6	9	16	23	30
60-(1/66)-Elvis Presley line drawn c/story	14	28	42	97	211	325
61-85	2	4	6	11	16	20
86-90,92-98,100-110	2	4	6	8	10	12
91-(5/71) Ditko-a (5 pgs.)	2	4	6	13	18	22
99-David Cassidy pin-up	2	4	6	10	14	18
111-113,115-130	1	3	4	6	8	10
114-Psychedelic cover	3	6	9	18	27	35

I, LUSIPHUR (Becomes Poison Elves, 1st series #8 on)
Mulehide Graphics: 1991 - No. 7, 1992 (B&W, magazine size)

1-Drew Hayes-c/a/scripts	4	8	12	26	41	55
2,4,5	3	6	9	14	20	25
3-Low print run	4	8	12	28	44	60
6,7	2	4	6	8	11	14

Poison Elves: Requiem For An Elf (Sirius Ent., 6/96, $14.95, trade paperback) -Reprints I, Lusiphur #1,2 as text, and 3-6 15.00

I'M A COP
Magazine Enterprises: 1954 - No. 3, 1954

1(A-1 #111)-Powell-c/a in all	15	30	45	88	137	185
2(A-1 #126), 3(A-1 #128)	10	20	30	56	76	95

IMAGE COMICS HARDCOVER
Image Comics: 2005 ($24.99, hardcover with dust jacket)

Vol. 1-New Spawn by McFarlane-s/a; Savage Dragon origin by Larsen; CyberForce by Silvestri; ShadowHawk by Valentino; intro by Marder; Image timeline 25.00

IMAGE COMICS SUMMER SPECIAL
Image Comics: July, 2004 (Free Comic Book Day giveaway)

1-New short stories of Spawn, Invincible, Savage Dragon and Witchblade 3.00

IMAGE FIRST
Image Comics: 2005 ($6.99, TPB)

Vol. 1 (2005) r/Strange Girl #1, Sea of Red #1, The Walking Dead #1 and Girls #1 7.00

IMAGE GRAPHIC NOVEL
Image Int.: 1984 ($6.95)(Advertised as Pacific Comics Graphic Novel #1)

1-The Seven Samuroid; Brunner-c/a 7.00

IMAGE HOLIDAY SPECIAL 2005
Image Comics: 2005 ($9.99, TPB)

nn-Holiday-themed short stories by various incl. Larsen, Kurtz, Kirkman, Valentino 10.00

IMAGE INTRODUCES...
Image Comics: Oct, 2001 - June, 2002 ($2.95, anthology)

Believer #1-Schamberger-s/Thurman & Molder-a; Legend of Isis preview 3.00
Cryptopia #1-Raab-s/Quinn-a 3.00
Dog Soldiers #1-Hunter-s/Pachoumis-a 3.00
Legend of Isis #1-Valdez-a 3.00
Primate #1-Two covers; Beau Smith & Bernhardt-s/Byrd-a 3.00

IMAGES OF A DISTANT SOIL
Image Comics: Feb, 1997 ($2.95, B&W, one-shot)

1-Sketches by various 3.00

IMAGES OF SHADOWHAWK (Also see Shadowhawk)
Image Comics: Sept, 1993 - No. 3, 1994 ($1.95, limited series)

1-3: Keith Giffen-c/a; Trencher app. 3.00

IMAGE TWO-IN-ONE
Image Comics: Mar, 2001 ($2.95, 48 pgs., B&W, one-shot)

1-Two stories; 24 pages produced in 24 hrs. by Larsen and Eliopoulos 4.00

IMAGE UNITED
Image Comics: No. 0, Mar, 2010; Nov, 2009 - No. 6 ($3.99, limited series)

0-(3/10, $2.99) Fortress and Savage Dragon app. 3.00
1-3-($3.99) Image character crossover; Kirkman-s; art by Larsen, Liefeld, McFarlane, Portacio, Silvestri and Valentino; Spawn, Witchblade, Savage Dragon, Youngblood, Cyberforce and Shadowhawk app. Multiple covers on each 4.00
1-Jim Lee variant-c 8.00

IMAGE ZERO
Image Comics: 1993 (Received through mail w/coupons from Image books)

0-Savage Dragon, StormWatch, Shadowhawk, Strykeforce; 1st app. Troll; 1st app. McFarlane's Freak, Blotch, Sweat and Bludd 5.00

IMAGINARIES, THE
Image Comics: Mar, 2005 - No. 4, June, 2005 ($2.95, limited series)

1-4-Mike S. Miller & Ben Avery-s; Miller & Titus-a 3.00

I'M DICKENS - HE'S FENSTER (TV)
Dell Publishing Co.: May-July, 1963 - No. 2, Aug-Oct, 1963 (Photo-c)

1	6	12	18	37	59	80
2	5	10	15	32	51	70

I MET A HANDSOME COWBOY
Dell Publishing Co.: No. 324, Mar, 1951

Four Color 324	8	16	24	55	93	130

IMMORTAL DOCTOR FATE, THE
DC Comics: Jan, 1985 - No. 3, Mar, 1985 ($1.25, limited series)

1-3: 1-Simonson-c/a. 2-Giffen-c/a(p) 4.00

IMMORTAL IRON FIST, THE (Also see Iron Fist)
Marvel Comics: Jan, 2007 - No. 27, Aug, 2009 ($2.99/$3.99)

1-Brubaker & Fraction-s/Aja-c/a; origin retold; intro. Orson Randall 5.00
1-Variant-c by Dell'Otto 8.00
1-Director's Cut ($3.99) r/#1 and 8-page story from Civil War: Choosing Sides; script excerpt; character designs; sketch and inks art; cover variant and concepts 4.00
2-13,15-26: 6,17-20-Flashback-a by Heath. 21-Green-a 3.00
14,27: 14-($3.99) Heroes For Hire app. 27-Last issue; 2 covers; Foreman & Lapham-a 4.00
Annual 1 (11/07, $3.99) Brubaker & Fraction-s/Chaykin, Brereton & J. Djurdjevic-a 4.00
... Orson Randall and the Death Queen of California (11/08, $3.99) art by Camuncoli 4.00
... Orson Randall and the Green Mist of Death (4/08, $3.99) art by Heath and various 4.00
...: The Origin of Danny Rand (2008, $3.99) r/Marvel Premiere #15-16 recolored 4.00
... Vol. 1: The Last Iron Fist Story HC (2007, $19.99, dustjacket) r/#1-6, story from Civil War:

Impact #1 © WMG

Impulse #9 © DC

Incredible Hulk #105 © MAR

GD VG FN VF VF/NM NM-
2.0 4.0 6.0 8.0 9.0 9.2

Choosing Sides; sketch pages 20.00
... Vol. 1: The Last Iron Fist Story SC (2007, $14.99) same content as HC 15.00
... Vol. 2: The Seven Capital Cities HC (2008, $24.99, dustjacket) r/#8-14 & Annual #1 25.00

IMMORTALIS (See Mortigan Goth: Immortalis)

IMMORTAL II
Image Comics: Apr, 1997 - No. 5, Feb, 1998 ($2.50, B&W&Grey, limited series)
1-5: 1-B&W w/ color pull-out poster 3.00

IMMORTAL WEAPONS (Also see Immortal Iron Fist)
Marvel Comics: Sept, 2009 - No. 5, Jan, 2010 ($3.99, limited series)
1-5: Back-up Iron Fist stories in all. 1-Origin of Fat Cobra. 2-Brereton-a 4.00

IMPACT
E. C. Comics: Mar-Apr, 1955 - No. 5, Nov-Dec, 1955
1-Not code approved 19 38 57 152 239 325
1-Variant printed by Charlton. Title logo is white instead of yellow and print quality is inferior. Distributed to newsstands before being destroyed & reprinted (scarce) 23 46 69 184 292 400
2 11 22 33 88 144 200
3-5: 4-Crandall-a 10 20 30 80 128 175
NOTE: ***Crandall*** *a-1-4.* ***Davis*** *a-2-4; c-1-5.* ***Evans*** *a-1, 4, 5.* ***Ingels*** *a-in all.* ***Kamen*** *a-3.* ***Krigstein*** *a-1, 5.* ***Orlando*** *a-2, 5.*

IMPACT
Gemstone Publishing: Apr, 1999 - No. 5, Aug, 1999 ($2.50)
1-5-Reprints E.C. series 3.00

IMPACT CHRISTMAS SPECIAL
DC Comics (Impact Comics): 1991 ($2.50, 68 pgs.)
1-Gift of the Magi by Infantino/Rogers; The Black Hood, The Fly, The Jaguar, & The Shield stories 4.00

IMPERIAL GUARD
Marvel Comics: Jan, 1997 - No. 3, Mar, 1997 ($1.95, limited series)
1-3: Augustyn-s in all; 1-Wraparound-c 3.00

IMPOSSIBLE MAN SUMMER VACATION SPECTACULAR, THE
Marvel Comics: Aug, 1990; No. 2, Sept, 1991 ($2.00, 68 pgs.) (See Fantastic Four#11)
1-Spider Man, Quasar, Dr. Strange, She-Hulk, Punisher & Dr. Doom stories; Barry Crain, Guice-a; Art Adams-c(i) 4.00
2-Ka Zar & Thor app.; Cable Wolverine-c app. 4.00

IMPULSE (See Flash #92, 2nd Series for 1st app.) (Also see Young Justice)
DC Comics: Apr, 1995 - No. 89, Oct, 2002 ($1.50/$1.75/$1.95/$2.25/$2.50)
1-Mark Waid scripts & Humberto Ramos-c/a(p) begin; brief retelling of origin 6.00
2-12: 9-XS from Legion (Impulse's cousin) comes to the 20th Century, returns to the 30th Century in #12. 10-Dead Heat Pt. 3 (cont'd in Flash #110). 11-Dead Heat Pt. 4 (cont'd in Flash #111); Johnny Quick dies. 4.00
13-25: 14-Trickster app. 17-Zatanna-c/app. 21-Legion-c/app. 22-Jesse Quick-c/app. 24-Origin; Flash app. 25-Last Ramos-a. 3.00
26-55: 26-Rousseau-a begins. 28-1st new Arrowette (see World's Finest #113). 30-Genesis x-over. 47-Superman-c/app. 50-Batman & Joker-c/app. Van Sciver-a begins 3.00
56-62: 56-Young Justice app. 3.00
63-89: 63-Begin $2.50-c. 66-JLA,JSA-c/app. 68,69-Adam Strange, GL app. 77-Our Worlds at War x-over; Young Justice-c/app. 85-World Without Young Justice x-over pt. 2. 3.00
#1,000,000 (11/98) John Fox app. 3.00
Annual 1 (1996, $2.95)-Legends of the Dead Earth; Parobeck-a 4.00
Annual 2 (1997, $3.95)-Pulp Heroes stories; Orbik painted-c 4.00
.../Atom Double-Shot 1(2/98, $1.95) Jurgens-s/Mhan-a 3.00
...: Bart Saves the Universe (4/99, $5.95) JSA app. 6.00
...Plus(9/97, $2.95) w/Gross Out (Scare Tactics)-c/app. 3.00
...Reckless Youth (1997, $14.95, TPB) r/Flash #92-94, Impulse #1-6 15.00

INCAL, THE
Marvel Comics (Epic): Nov, 1988 - No. 3, Jan, 1989 ($10.95/$12.95, mature)
1-3: Moebius-c/a in all; sexual content 16.00

INCOGNEGRO
DC Comics (Vertigo): 2008 ($19.99, B&W, hardcover graphic novel with dustjacket)
HC-Mat Johnson-s/Warren Pleece-a 20.00

INCOGNITO
Marvel Comics (Icon): Dec, 2008 - No. 6, Aug, 2009 ($3.50/$3.99, limited series)
1-5-Brubaker-s/Phillips-a/c; pulp noir-style 3.50
6-($3.99) Bonus history of the Zeppelin pulps 4.00
...: Bad Influences (10/10 - No. 5, 4/11, $3.50) 1-5 Brubaker-s/Phillips-a/c 3.50

INCOMPLETE DEATH'S HEAD (Also see Death's Head)
Marvel Comics UK: Jan, 1993 - No. 12, Dec, 1993 ($1.75, limited series)
1-($2.95, 56 pgs.)-Die-cut cover 4.00
2-11: 2-Re-intro original Death's Head. 3-Original Death's Head vs. Dragon's Claws 3.00
12-($2.50, 52 pgs.)-She Hulk app. 4.00

INCORRUPTIBLE (Also see Irredeemable)
BOOM! Studios: Dec, 2000 - Present ($3.99)
1-27: 1-Waid-s/Diaz-a; 3 covers 4.00
1-Artist Edition (12/11, $3.99) r/#1 in B&W with bonus sketch and design art 4.00

INCREDIBLE HERCULES (Continued from Incredible Hulk #112, Jan, 2008)
Marvel Comics: No. 113, Feb, 2008 - No. 141, Apr, 2010 ($2.99/$3.99)
113-125: 113-Ares and Wonder Man app.; Art Adams-c. 116-Romita Jr-c; Eternals app. 3.00
113-Variant-c by Pham 5.00
126-($3.99) Hercules origin retold; back-up story w/Miyazawa-a 4.00
127-137: 128-Dark Avengers app. 132-Replacement Thor. 136-Thor app. 3.00
138-141-($3.99) Assault on New Olympus; Avengers app. 4.00

INCREDIBLE HULK, THE (See Aurora, The Avengers #1, The Defenders #1, Giant-Size..., Hulk, Marvel Collectors Item Classics, Marvel Comics Presents #26, Marvel Fanfare, Marvel Treasury Edition, Power Record Comics, Rampaging Hulk, She-Hulk, 2099 Unlimited & World War Hulk)

INCREDIBLE HULK, THE
Marvel Comics: May, 1962 - No. 6, Mar, 1963; No. 102, Apr, 1968 - No. 474, Mar, 1999
1-Origin & 1st app. (skin is grey colored); Kirby pencils begin, end #5 1800 3600 5400 26,000 58,000 90,000
2-1st green skinned Hulk; Kirby/Ditko-a 293 586 879 2550 5525 8500
3-Origin retold; 1st app. Ringmaster (9/62) 196 392 588 1646 3573 5500
4,5: 4-Brief origin retold 161 322 483 1352 2926 4500
6-(3/63) Intro. Teen Brigade; all Ditko-a 171 342 513 1436 3118 4800
102-(4/68) (Formerly Tales to Astonish)-Origin retold; story continued from Tales to Astonish #101 21 42 63 148 317 485
103 10 20 30 69 130 190
104-Rhino app. 10 20 30 69 130 190
105-108: 105-1st Missing Link. 107-Mandarin app.(9/68). 108-Mandarin & Nick Fury app. (10/68) 8 16 24 53 89 125
109,110: 109-Ka-Zar app. 7 14 21 46 76 105
111-117: 117-Last 12¢ issue 6 12 18 37 59 80
118-Hulk vs. Sub-Mariner 7 14 21 46 76 105
119,120,123-125 4 8 12 28 44 60
121-1st app. The Glob 5 10 15 30 48 65
122-Hulk battles Thing (12/69) 9 18 27 60 103 145
126-1st Barbara Norriss (Valkyrie) 5 10 15 30 48 65
127-139: 131-Hulk vs. Iron Man; 1st Jim Wilson, Hulk's new sidekick. 136-1st Xeron, The Star-Slayer 3 6 9 20 30 40
140-Written by Harlan Ellison; 1st Jarella, Hulk's love 4 8 12 22 34 45
140-2nd printing (1994) 2 4 6 8 10 12
141-1st app. Doc Samson (7/71) 10 20 30 64 115 165
142-144: 144-Last 15¢ issue 3 6 9 19 29 38
145-(52 pgs.)-Origin retold 5 10 15 30 48 65
146-160: 149-1st app. The Inheritor. 155-1st app. Shaper. 158-Warlock cameo(12/72) 3 6 9 17 25 32
161-The Mimic dies; Beast app. 5 10 15 30 48 65
162-1st app. The Wendigo (4/73); Beast app. 7 14 21 49 82 115
163-171,173-176: 163-1st app. The Gremlin. 164-1st Capt. Omen & Colonel John D. Armbruster. 166-1st Zzzax. 168-1st The Harpy; nudity panels of Betty Ross. 169-1st app. Bi-Beast.176-Warlock cameo (2 panels only); same date as Strange Tales #178 (6/74) 3 6 9 14 20 26
172-X-Men cameo; origin Juggernaut retold 4 8 12 28 44 60
177-1st actual death of Warlock (last panel only) 3 6 9 16 22 28
178-Rebirth of Warlock 3 6 9 16 22 28
179 3 6 9 14 19 24
180-(10/74)-1st brief app. Wolverine (last pg.) 16 32 48 107 234 360
181-(11/74)-1st full Wolverine story; Trimpe-a 64 128 192 518 1122 1725
182-Wolverine cameo; see Giant-Size X-Men #1 for next app.; 1st Crackajack Jackson 11 22 33 73 142 210
183-199: 185-Death of Col. Armbruster. 195,196-Abomination app. 197,198-Man-Thing-c/s 2 4 6 10 14 18
198,199, 201,202-(30¢-c variants, lim. distribution) 3 6 9 18 27 35
200-(25¢-c) Silver Surfer app.; anniversary issue 3 6 9 20 30 40
200-(30¢-c variant, limited distribution)(6/76) 6 12 18 39 62 85
201-220: 201-Conan swipe-c/sty. 212-1st app. The Constrictor 1 2 3 5 7 9
212-216-(35¢-c variant, limited distribution) 4 8 12 24 37 50
221-249: 227-Original Avengers app. 232-Capt. America x-over from C.A. #230. 233-Marvel Man app. 234-(4/79)-1st app. Quasar (formerly called Marvel Man. 243-Cage app.

Incredible Hulk #461 © MAR

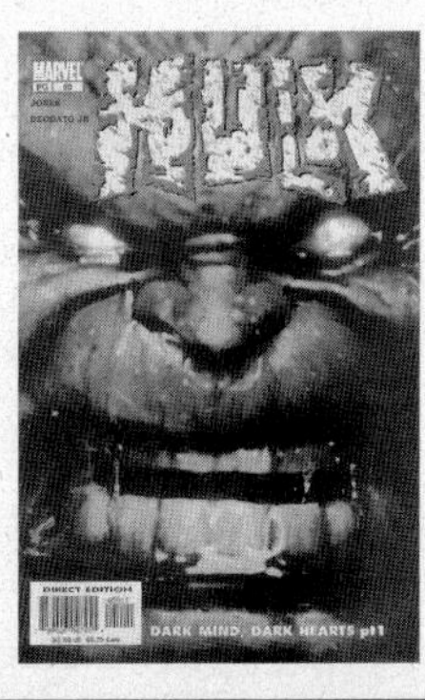

Incredible Hulk V2 #50 © MAR

Incredible Hulks #612 © MAR

	GD 2.0	VG 4.0	FN 6.0	VF 8.0	VF/NM 9.0	NM- 9.2
	1	2	3	4	5	7
250-Giant size; Silver Surfer app.	2	4	6	9	12	15
251-277,280-299: 271-Rocket Raccoon app. 272-Sasquatch & Wendigo app.; Wolverine & Alpha Flight cameo in flashback. 282-284-She-Hulk app. 293-F.F. app.						5.00
278,279-Most Marvel characters app. (Wolverine in both). 279-X-Men & Alpha Flight cameos						6.00
300-(11/84, 52 pgs.)-Spider-Man app in new black costume on-c & 2 pg. cameo	1	2	3	5	6	8
301-313: 312-Origin Hulk retold						4.00
314-Byrne-c/a begins, ends #319						6.00
315-319: 319-Bruce Banner & Betty Talbot wed						5.00
320-323,325,327-329						4.00
324-1st app. Grey Hulk since #1 (c-swipe of #1)	2	4	6	8	10	12
326-Grey vs. Green Hulk						6.00
330,331: 330-1st McFarlane ish (4/87); Thunderbolt Ross dies. 331-Grey Hulk series begins	3	6	9	17	25	32
332-334,336-339: 336,337-X-Factor app.	2	4	6	9	12	15
335-No McFarlane-a						6.00
340-Hulk battles Wolverine by McFarlane	4	8	12	26	41	55
341-346: 345-($1.50, 52 pgs.). 346-Last McFarlane issue	1	3	4	6	8	10
347-349,351-358,360-366: 347-1st app. Marlo						3.00
350-Hulk/Thing battle						6.00
359-Wolverine app. (illusion only)						3.00
367,372,377: 367-1st Dale Keown-a on Hulk (3/90). 372-Green Hulk app.;Keown-c/a. 377-1st all new Hulk; fluorescent-c; Keown-c/a	1	2	3	5	6	8
368-371,373-376: 368-Sam Kieth-c/a, 1st app. Pantheon. 369,370-Dale Keown-c/a. 370,371-Original Defenders app. 371,373-376: Keown-c/a. 376-Green vs. Grey Hulk						5.00
377-Fluorescent green logo 2nd printing						3.00
378,380,389: No Keown-a. 380-Doc Samson app.						3.00
379,381-388,390-392-Keown-a. 385-Infinity Gauntlet x-over. 389-Last $1.00-c. 392-X-Factor app.						4.00
393-($2.50, 72 pgs.)-30th anniversary issue; green foil stamped-c; swipes-c to #1; has pin-ups of classic battles; Keown-c/a						6.00
393,400-2nd printings: 400-2nd print-Diff. color foil-c.						4.00
394-399: 394-No Keown-c/a; intro Trauma. 395,396-Punisher-c/stories; Keown-c/a. 397-Begin "Ghost of the Past" 4-part sty; Keown c/a. 398-Last Keown-c/a						3.00
400-($2.50, 68 pgs.)-Holo-grafx foil-c & r/TTA #63						5.00
401-416: 402-Return of Doc Samson						3.00
417-424: 417-Begin $1.50-c; Rick Jones' bachelor party; Hulk returns from "Future Imperfect"; bound-in trading card sheet. 418-(Regular edition)-Rick Jones marries Marlo; includes cameo apps of various Marvel characters as well as DC's Death & Peter David. 420-Death of Jim Wilson						3.00
418-($2.50)-Collector's Edition w/gatefold die-cut-c						4.00
425 ($2.25, 52 pgs.)						4.00
425 ($3.50, 52 pgs.)-Holographic-c						5.00
426-434, 436-442: 426-Begin $1.95-c. 427, 428-Man-Thing app. 431,432-Abomination app. 434-Funeral for Nick Fury. 436-Ghosts of the Future begins, ends #440. 439-Hulk becomes Maestro, Avengers app. 440-Thor-c/app. 441,442-She-Hulk-c/app.						3.00
435 ($2.50)-Rhino-app; excerpt from "What Savage Beast"						4.00
443,446-448: 443-Begin $1.50-c; re-app. of Hulk. 446-w/card insert. 447-Begin Deodato-c/a(p)						3.00
444,445: 444-Cable-c/app.; "Onslaught". 445-"Onslaught"						4.00
447-Variant cover						4.00
449-1st app. Thunderbolts						6.00
450-($2.95)-Thunderbolts app.; 2 stories; Heroes Reborn-c/app.						5.00
451-470: 455-X-Men-c/app. 460-Bruce Banner returns. 464-Silver Surfer-c/app. 466,467: Betty dies. 467-Last Peter David-s/Kubert-a. 468-Casey-s/Pulido-a begin						3.00
471-473						4.00
474-($2.99) Last issue; Abomination app.						5.00
#(-1) Flashback (7/97) Kubert-a						3.00
Special 1 (10/68, 25¢, 68 pg.)-New 51 pg. story, Hulk battles The Inhumans (early app.); Steranko-c.	11	22	33	73	142	210
Special 2 (10/69, 25¢, 68 pg.)-Origin retold	6	12	18	42	69	95
Special 3,4: 3-(1/71, 25¢, 68 pg.). 4-(1/72, 52pgs.)	4	8	12	22	34	45
Annual 5 (1976)	2	4	6	10	14	18
Annual 6-8 ('77-79): 7-Byrne/Layton-c/a; Iceman & Angel app. in book-length story. 8-Book-length Sasquatch-c/sty	2	4	6	8	10	12
Annual 9,10: 9('80). 10 ('81)						6.00
Annual 11('82)-Doc Samson back-up by Miller(p)(5 pgs.); Spider-Man & Avengers app. Buckler-a(p)						6.00
Annual 12-17: 12 ('83). 13('84). 14('85). 15('86). 16('90, $2.00, 68 pgs.)-She-Hulk app. 17(1991, $2.00)-Origin retold						4.00
Annual 18-20 ('92-'94 68 pgs.)-18-Return of the Defenders, Pt. I; no Keown-c/a						

	GD 2.0	VG 4.0	FN 6.0	VF 8.0	VF/NM 9.0	NM- 9.2
19-Bagged w/card						4.00
...'97 ($2.99) Pollina-c						4.00
...And Wolverine 1 (10/86, $2.50)-r/1st app. (#180-181)	1	3	4	6	8	10
...: Beauty and the Behemoth ('98, $19.95, TPB) r/Bruce & Betty stories						20.00
...Ground Zero ('95, $12.95) r/#340-346						13.00
...Hercules Unleashed (10/96, $2.50) David-s/Deodato-c/a						4.00
... Omnibus Vol. 1 HC (2008, $99.99, dustjacket) r/#1-6 & 102, Tales To Astonish #59-101 bonus art, cover reprints; afterword by Peter David; 2 covers (Kirby & Ross swipe)						100.00
.../Sub-Mariner '98 Annual ($2.99)						3.00
...Versus Quasimodo 1 (3/83, one-shot)-Based on Saturday morning cartoon						4.00
...Vs. Superman 1 (7/99, $5.95, one-shot)-painted-c by Rude						6.00
...Versus Venom 1 (4/94, $2.50, one-shot)-Embossed-c; red foil logo						4.00
... Visionaries: Peter David Vol. 1 (2005, $19.99) r/#331-339 written by Peter David						20.00
... Visionaries: Peter David Vol. 2 (2005, $19.99) r/#340-348						20.00
... Visionaries: Peter David Vol. 3 (2006, $19.99) r/#349-354, Web of Spider-Man #44, and Fantastic Four #320						20.00
... Visionaries: Peter David Vol. 4 (2007, $19.99) r/#355-363 and Marvel Comics Presents #26,45						20.00
... Visionaries: Peter David Vol. 5 (2008, $19.99) r/#364-372 and Annual #16						20.00
Wizard #1 Ace Edition - Reprints #1 with new Andy Kubert-c						14.00
Wizard #181 Ace Edition - Reprints #181 with new Chen-c						14.00

(Also see titles listed under **Hulk**)

NOTE: **Adkins** *a-111-116i.* **Austin** *a(i)-350, 351, 353, 354; c-302i, 350i.* **Ayers** *a-3-5i.* **Buckler** *a-Annual 5; c-252.* **John Buscema** *c-202p.* **Byrne** *a-314-319p; c-314-316, 318, 319, 359, Annual 14i.* **Colan** *c-363.* **Ditko** *a-2i, 6, 249, Annual 2r(5), 3r, 9p; c-2i, 6, 235, 249.* **Everett** *c-133i.* **Golden** *c-248, 251.* **Kane** *c(p)-193, 194, 196, 198.* **Dale Keown** *a(p)-367, 369-377, 379, 381-388, 390-393, 395-398; c-369-377p, 381, 382p, 384, 385, 386, 387p, 388, 390p, 391-393, 395p, 396, 397p, 398.* **Kirby** *a-1-5p, Special 2, 3p, Annual 5p; c-1-5, Annual 5.* **McFarlane** *a-330-334p, 336-339p, 340-343, 344-346p; c-330p, 340p, 341-343, 344p, 345, 346p.* **Mignola** *c-302, 305, 313.* **Miller** *c-258p, 261, 264, 268.* **Mooney** *a-230p, 287i, 288i.* **Powell** *a-Special 3r(2).* **Romita** *a-Annual 17p.* **Severin** *a(i)-108-110, 131-133, 141-151, 153-155; c(i)-109, 110, 132, 142, 144-155.* **Simonson** *c-283, 364-367.* **Starlin** *a-222p; c-217.* **Staton** *a(i)-187-189, 191-209.* **Tuska** *a-102i, 105i, 106i, 218p.* **Williamson** *a-310i; c-310i, 311i.* **Wrightson** *c-197.*

INCREDIBLE HULK (Vol. 2) (Formerly Hulk #1-11; becomes Incredible Hercules with #113) (Re-titled Incredible Hulks #612-on)(Also see World War Hulk)
Marvel Comics: No. 12, Mar, 2000 - No. 112, Jan, 2008 ($1.99-$3.50)
No. 600, Sept, 2009 - No. 625, Oct, 2011 ($3.99/$4.99)

	GD 2.0	VG 4.0	FN 6.0	VF 8.0	VF/NM 9.0	NM- 9.2
12-Jenkins-s/Garney & McKone-a						4.00
13,14-($1.99) Garney & Buscema-a						3.00
15-24,26-32: 15-Begin $2.25-c. 21-Maximum Security x-over. 24-($1.99-c)						3.00
25-($2.99) Hulk vs. The Abomination; Romita Jr.-a						4.00
33-($3.50, 100 pgs.) new Bogdanove-a/Priest-s; reprints						4.00
34-Bruce Jones-s begin; Romita Jr.-a						5.00
35-49,51-54: 35-39-Jones-s/Romita Jr.-a. 40-43-Weeks-a. 44-49-Immonen-a						3.00
50-($3.50) Deodato-a begins; Abomination app. thru #54						4.00
55-74,77-91: 55(25¢-c) Absorbing Man returns; Fernandez-a. 60-65,70-72-Deodato-a. 66-69-Braithwaite-a. 71-74-Iron Man app. 77-($2.99-c) Peter David-s begin/Weeks-a. 80-Wolverine-c. 82-Jae Lee-c/a. 83-86-House of M x-over. 87-Scorpion app.						3.00
75,76-($3.50) The Leader app. 75-Robertson-a/Frank-c. 76-Braithwaite-a						4.00
92-Planet Hulk begins; Ladronn-c						5.00
92-2nd printing with variant-c by Bryan Hitch						4.00
93-99,101-105 Planet Hulk; Ladronn-c						3.00
100-($3.99) Planet Hulk continues; back-up w/Frank-a; r/#152,153; Ladronn-c						5.00
100-($3.99) Green Hulk variant-c by Michael Turner						10.00
100-($3.99) Gray Hulk variant-c by Michael Turner						30.00
106-World War Hulk begins; Gary Frank-a/c						6.00
106-2nd printing with new cover of Hercules and Angel						3.00
107-112: 107-Hercules vs. Hulk. 108-Rick Jones app. 112-Art Adams-c						3.00
600-(9/09, $4.99) Covers by Ross, Sale and wraparound-c by McGuinness; back-up with Stan Lee-s; r/Hulk: Gray #1; cover gallery						5.00
601-611-($3.99): 601-605-Olivetti-a. 603-Wolverine app. 606-608-Fall of the Hulks						4.00
(Title becomes Incredible Hulks with #612, Nov, 2010)						
612-621: 612-617-Dark Son. 618-620-Chaos War. 621-Hercules app.						4.00
622-634-($2.99) 623-625-Ka-Zar app.; Eaglesham-a. 626-629-Grummett-a						3.00
635-($3.99) Fin Fang Foom & Dr. Strange app.; Greg Pak interview						4.00
Annual 2000 ($3.50) Texeira-a/Jenkins-s; Avengers app.						4.00
Annual 2001 ($2.99) Thor-c/app.; Larsen-s/Williams III-c						4.00
Annual 1 (8/11, $3.99) Identity Wars; Spider-Man and Deadpool app.; Barrionuevo-a						4.00
... & The Human Torch: From the Marvel Vault 1 (8/11, $2.99) unpublished story w/Ditko-a						3.00
... : Boiling Point (Volume 2, 2002, $8.99, TPB) r/#40-43; Andrews-c						9.00
Dogs of War (6/01, $19.95, TPB) r/#12-20						20.00
House of M (2006, $13.99) r/House of M tie-in issues Incredible Hulk #83-87						14.00
Hulk: Planet Hulk HC (2007, $39.99, dustjacket) oversized r/#92-105, Planet Hulk: Gladiator Guidebook, stories from Amazing Fantasy (2004) #15 and Giant-Size Hulk #1						40.00
Hulk: Planet Hulk SC (2008, $34.99) same content as HC						35.00
Planet Hulk: Gladiator Guidebook (2006, $3.99) bios of combatants and planet history						4.00

Incredible Hulk (2011 series) #1 © MAR

The Incredibles #15 © DIS & Pixar

Indian Chief #23 © DELL

GD 2.0 | VG 4.0 | FN 6.0 | VF 8.0 | VF/NM 9.0 | NM- 9.2

...: Prelude to Planet Hulk (2006, $13.99, TPB) r/#88-91 & Official Handbook: Hulk 2004 14.00
...: Return of the Monster (7/02, $12.99, TPB) r/#34-39 13.00
...: The End (8/02, $5.95) David-s/Keown-a; Hulk in the far future 6.00
...: The End HC (2008, $19.99, dustjacket) r/The End and Hulk: Future Imperfect #1-2 20.00
...Volume 1 HC (2002, $29.99, oversized) r/#34-43 & Startling Stories: Banner #1-4 30.00
...Volume 2 HC (2003, $29.99, oversized) r/#44-54; sketch pages and cover gallery 30.00
Volume 3: Transfer of Power (2003, $12.99, TPB) r/#44-49 13.00
Volume 4: Abominable (2003, $11.99, TPB) r/#50-54; Abomination app.; Deodato-a 12.00
Volume 5: Hide in Plain Sight (2003, $11.99, TPB) r/#55-59; Fernandez-a 12.00
Volume 6: Split Decisions (2004, $12.99, TPB) r/#60-65; Deodato-a 13.00
Volume 7: Dead Like Me (2004, $12.99, TPB) r/#66-69 & Hulk Smash #1&2 13.00
Volume 8: Big Things (2004, $17.99, TPB) r/#70-76; Iron Man app. 18.00
Volume 9: Tempest Fugit (2005, $14.99, TPB) r/#77-82 15.00

INCREDIBLE HULK
Marvel Comics: Dec, 2011 - Present ($3.99)
1-Aaron-s/Silvestri-a; bonus interview with Aaron; cover by Silvestri 4.00
1-Variant covers by Neal Adams, Whilce Portacio & Ladronn 8.00
2-6: 2-Silvestri, Portacio & Tan-a 4.00

INCREDIBLE HULKS: ENIGMA FORCE
Marvel Comics: Nov, 2010 - No. 3, Jan, 2011 ($3.99, limited series)
1-3-Reed-s/Munera-a/Pagulayan-c; Bug app. 4.00

INCREDIBLE MR. LIMPET, THE (See Movie Classics)

INCREDIBLES, THE
Image Comics: Nov, 2004 - No. 4, Feb, 2005 ($2.99, limited series)
1-4-Adaptation of 2004 Pixar movie; Ricardo Curtis-a 3.00
TPB (2005, $12.95) r/#1-4; cover gallery 13.00

INCREDIBLES, THE (Pixar characters)
BOOM! Studios: No. 0, Jul, 2009 - Present ($2.99)
0-15: 0-3-City of Incredibles; Waid & Walker-s. 0,1-Wagner-c. 8-15-Walker-s 3.00
...: Family Matters 1-4 (3/09 - No. 4, 6/09) Waid-s/Takara-a. 1-Five covers 3.00

INCREDIBLE SCIENCE FICTION (Formerly Weird Science-Fantasy)
E. C. Comics: No. 30, July-Aug, 1955 - No. 33, Jan-Feb, 1956

	GD	VG	FN	VF	VF/NM	NM-
30-Davis-c begin, end #32	39	78	117	312	499	685
31-Williamson/Krenkel-a, Wood-a(2)	40	80	120	320	510	700
32-Williamson/Krenkel-a	40	80	120	320	510	700
33-Classic Wood-c; "Judgment Day" story-r/Weird Fantasy #18; final issue & last E.C. comic book	41	82	123	328	524	720

NOTE: ***Davis** a-30, 32, 33; c-30-32. **Krigstein** a-in all. **Orlando** a-30, 32, 33. **Wood** a-30, 31, 33; c-33.*

INCREDIBLE SCIENCE FICTION (Formerly Weird Science-Fantasy)
Russ Cochran/Gemstone Publ.: No. 8, Aug, 1994 - No. 11, May, 1995 ($2.00)
8-11: Reprints #30-33 of E.C. series 3.00

INDEPENDENCE DAY (Movie)
Marvel Comics: No. 0, June, 1996 - No. 2, Aug, 1996 ($1.95, limited series)
0-Special Edition; photo-c 5.00
0-2 3.00

INDIANA JONES (Title series), **Dark Horse Comics**
--ADVENTURES, 6/08 ($6.95, digest-sized) Vol. 1 - new all-ages adventures; Beavers-a 7.00
--AND THE ARMS OF GOLD, 2/94 - 5/94 ($2.50) 1-4 3.00
--AND THE FATE OF ATLANTIS, 3/91 - 9/91 ($2.50) 1-4-Dorman painted-c on all; contain trading cards (#1 has a 2nd printing, 10/91) 3.00
--AND THE GOLDEN FLEECE, 6/94 - 7/94 ($2.50) 1,2 3.00
--AND THE IRON PHOENIX, 12/94 - 3/95 ($2.50) 1-4 3.00

INDIANA JONES AND THE KINGDOM OF THE CRYSTAL SKULL
Dark Horse Comics: May, 2008 - No. 2, May, 2008 ($5.99, limited series, movie adaptation)
1,2-Luke Ross-a/John Jackson Miller-adapted-s; two covers by Struzan & Fleming 6.00
TPB (5/08, $12.95) r/#1,2; Struzan-c 13.00

INDIANA JONES AND THE LAST CRUSADE
Marvel Comics: 1989 - No. 4, 1989 ($1.00, limited series, movie adaptation)
1-4: Williamson-i assist 3.00
1-(1989, $2.95, B&W mag., 80 pgs.) 4.00

--AND THE SHRINE OF THE SEA DEVIL: Dark Horse, 9/94 ($2.50, one shot)
1-Gary Gianni-a 3.00
--AND THE SARGASSO PIRATES: Dark Horse, 12/95 - 3/96 ($2.50) 1-4: 1,2-Ross-c 3.00
--AND THE SPEAR OF DESTINY: Dark Horse, 4/95 - 8/95 ($2.50) 1-4 3.00
--AND THE TOMB OF THE GODS, 6/08 - No. 4, 3/09 ($2.99) 1-4: 1-Tony Harris-c 3.00

GD 2.0 | VG 4.0 | FN 6.0 | VF 8.0 | VF/NM 9.0 | NM- 9.2

--THUNDER IN THE ORIENT: Dark Horse, 9/93 - '94 ($2.50)
1-6: Dan Barry story & art in all; 1-Dorman painted-c 3.00

INDIANA JONES AND THE TEMPLE OF DOOM
Marvel Comics Group: Sept, 1984 - No. 3, Nov, 1984 (Movie adaptation)
1-3-r/Marvel Super Special; Guice-a 3.00

INDIANA JONES OMNIBUS
Dark Horse Books: Feb, 2008; June 2008; Feb, 2009 ($24.95, digest-size)
Volume One - Reprints Indiana Jones and the Fate of Atlantis, Indiana Jones: Thunder in the Orient; and Indiana Jones and the Arms of Gold mini-series 25.00
Volume Two - Reprints I.J. and the Golden Fleece, I.J. and the Shrine of the Sea Devil, I.J. and the Iron Phoenix, I.J. and the Spear of Destiny, I.J. and the Sargasso Pirates 25.00
The Further Adventures Volume One - (2/09) r/Raiders of the Lost Ark #1-3 & The Further Adventures of Indiana Jones #1-12 25.00

INDIAN BRAVES (Baffling Mysteries No. 5 on)
Ace Magazines: March, 1951 - No. 4, Sept, 1951

	GD	VG	FN	VF	VF/NM	NM-
1-Green Arrowhead begins, apps. in all	15	30	45	84	127	170
2	9	18	27	52	69	85
3,4	8	16	24	44	57	70
I.W. Reprint #1 (nd)-r/Indian Braves #4	2	4	6	9	13	16

INDIAN CHIEF (White Eagle...) (Formerly The Chief, Four Color 290)
Dell Publ. Co.: No. 3, July-Sept, 1951 - No. 33, Jan-Mar, 1959 (All painted-c)

	GD	VG	FN	VF	VF/NM	NM-
3	5	10	15	34	55	75
4-11: 6-White Eagle app.	4	8	12	28	44	60
12-1st White Eagle(10-12/53)-Not same as earlier character	5	10	15	34	55	75
13-29	4	8	12	23	36	48
30-33-Buscema-a	4	8	12	24	37	50

INDIAN CHIEF (See March of Comics No. 94, 110, 127, 140, 159, 170, 187)

INDIAN FIGHTER, THE (Movie)
Dell Publishing Co.: No. 687, May, 1956 (one-shot)

	GD	VG	FN	VF	VF/NM	NM-
Four Color 687-Kirk Douglas photo-c	7	14	21	49	82	115

INDIAN FIGHTER
Youthful Magazines: May, 1950 - No. 11, Jan, 1952

	GD	VG	FN	VF	VF/NM	NM-
1	15	30	49	85	130	175
2-Wildey-a/c(bondage)	11	22	33	60	83	105
3-11: 3,4-Wildey-a	9	18	27	47	61	75

NOTE: ***Hollingsworth** a-5. **Walter Johnson** c-1, 3, 4, 6. **Palais** a-10. **Stallman** a-5-8. **Wildey** a-2-4; c-2, 5.*

INDIAN LEGENDS OF THE NIAGARA (See American Graphics)

INDIANS
Fiction House Magazines (Wings Publ. Co.): Spring, 1950 - No. 17, Spr, 1953 (1-8: 52 pgs.)

	GD	VG	FN	VF	VF/NM	NM-
1-Manzar The White Indian, Long Bow & Orphan of the Storm begin	30	60	90	177	289	400
2-Starlight begins	15	30	45	90	140	190
3-5: 5-17-Most-c by Whitman	14	28	42	81	118	155
6-10	13	26	39	72	101	130
11-17	11	22	33	64	90	115

INDIANS OF THE WILD WEST
I. W. Enterprises: Circa 1958? (no date) (Reprints)

	GD	VG	FN	VF	VF/NM	NM-
9-Kinstler-c; Whitman-a; r/Indians #?	2	4	6	10	14	18

INDIANS ON THE WARPATH
St. John Publishing Co.: No date (Late 40s, early 50s) (132 pgs.)

	GD	VG	FN	VF	VF/NM	NM-
nn-Matt Baker-c; contains St. John comics rebound. Many combinations possible	39	78	117	234	385	535

INDIAN TRIBES (See Famous Indian Tribes)

INDIAN WARRIORS (Formerly White Rider and Super Horse; becomes Western Crime Cases #9)
Star Publications: No. 7, June, 1951 - No. 8, Sept, 1951

	GD	VG	FN	VF	VF/NM	NM-
7-White Rider & Superhorse continue; "Last of the Mohicans" serial begins; L.B. Cole-c	18	36	54	105	165	225
8-L.B. Cole-c	17	34	51	98	154	210
3-D 1(12/53, 25¢)-Came w/glasses; L.B. Cole-c	34	68	102	199	325	450
Accepted Reprint(nn)(inside cover shows White Rider & Superhorse #11)-r/cover to #7; origin White Rider &...; L.B. Cole-c	8	16	24	40	50	60
Accepted Reprint #8 (nd); L.B. Cole-c (r-cover to #8)	8	16	24	40	50	60

INDOORS-OUTDOORS (See Wisco)

INDOOR SPORTS
National Specials Co.: nd (6x9", 64 pgs., B&W-r, hard-c)

Infamous #1 © Sony

Inferior Five #6 © DC

Inhumans V6 #1 © MAR

GD 2.0 | VG 4.0 | FN 6.0 | VF 8.0 | VF/NM 9.0 | NM- 9.2

nn-By Tad 5 10 15 24 30 35

INDUSTRIAL GOTHIC
DC Comics (Vertigo): Dec, 1995 - No. 5, Apr, 1996 ($2.50, limited series)
1-5: Ted McKeever-c/a/scripts 3.00

INFAMOUS (Based on the Sony videogame)
DC Comics: Early May, 2011 - No. 6, Late July, 2011 ($2.99, limited series)
1-6: 1-William Harms-s/Eric Nguyen-a/Doug Mahnke-c. 3-6-Benes-c 3.00

INFERIOR FIVE, THE (Inferior 5 #11, 12) (See Showcase #62, 63, 65)
National Periodical Publications (#1-10: 12¢): 3-4/67 - No. 10, 9-10/68; No. 11, 8-9/72 - No. 12, 10-11/72
1-(3-4/67)-Sekowsky-a(p); 4th app. 6 12 18 37 59 80
2-5: 2-Plastic Man, F.F. app. 4-Thor app. 3 6 9 20 30 40
6-9: 6-Stars DC staff 3 6 9 16 23 30
10-Superman x-over; F.F., Spider-Man & Sub-Mariner app. 3 6 9 19 29 38
11,12: Orlando-c/a; both r/Showcase #62,63 2 4 6 11 16 20

INFERNO
Caliber Comics: 1995 - No. 5 ($2.95, B&W)
1-5 3.00

INFERNO (See Legion of Super-Heroes)
DC Comics: Oct, 1997 - No. 4, Feb, 1998 ($2.50, limited series)
1-Immonen-s/c/a in all 4.00
2-4 3.00

INFERNO: HELLBOUND
Image Comics (Top Cow): Jan, 2002 - No. 3 ($2.50/$2.99)
1,2: 1-Seven covers; Silvestri-a/Silvestri and Wohl-s 3.00
3-($2.99) Tan-a 3.00
#0 (7/02, $3.00) Tan-a 3.00
Wizard #0- Previews series; bagged with Wizard Top Cow Special mag 3.00

INFESTATION (Zombie crossover with G.I. Joe, Star Trek, Transformers and Ghostbusters)
IDW Publishing: Jan, 2011 - No. 2, Apr, 2011 ($3.99, limited series)
1,2-Abnett & Lanning-s/Messina-a; two covers by Messina & Snyder III 4.00
...: Outbreak 1-4 (6/11 - No. 4, 9/11, $3.99) Messina-a; Covert Vampiric Operations app. 4.00

INFINITE, THE
Image Comics (SkyBound): Aug, 2011 - No. 4, Nov, 2011 ($2.99)
1-4: 1-Robert Kirkman-s/Rob Liefeld-a; at least 11 covers. 2-Six covers 3.00

INFINITE CRISIS
DC Comics: Dec, 2005 - No. 7, Jun, 2006 ($3.99, limited series)
1-Johns-s/Jimenez-a; two covers by Jim Lee and George Pérez 5.00
1-RRP Edition with Jim Lee sketch-c 275.00
2-7: 4-New Spectre; Earth-2 returns. 5-Earth-2 Lois dies; new Blue Beetle debut. 6-Superboy killed, new Earth formed. 7-Earth-2 Superman dies 4.00
HC (2006, $24.99, dustjacket) r/#1-7; DiDio intro.; sketch cover gallery; interview/commentary with Johns, Jimenez and editors; sketch art 25.00
... Companion TPB (2006, $14.99) r/Day of Vengeance: Infinite Crisis Special #1, Rann-Thanagar War: ICS #1, The Omac Project: ICS #1, Villains United: ICS #1 15.00
... Secret Files 2006 (4/06, $5.99) tie-in story with Earth-2 Lois and Superman, Earth-Prime Superboy and Alexander Luthor; art by various; profile pages 6.00

INFINITE CRISIS AFTERMATH (See Crisis Aftermath:...)

INFINITE VACATION
Image Comics (Shadowline): Jan, 2011 - No. 5 ($3.50)
1-3-Nick Spencer-s/Christian Ward-a/c 3.50

INFINITY ABYSS (Also see Marvel Universe: The End)
Marvel Comics: Aug, 2002 - No. 6, Oct, 2002 ($2.99, limited series)
1-5-Starlin-s/a; Thanos, Captain Marvel, Spider-Man, Dr. Strange app. 3.00
6-($3.50) 3.50
Thanos Vol. 2: Infinity Abyss TPB (2003, $17.99) r/ #1-6 25.00

INFINITY CRUSADE
Marvel Comics: June, 1993 - No. 6, Nov, 1993 ($3.50/$2.50, limited series, 52 pgs.)
1-6: By Jim Starlin & Ron Lim. 1-($3.50). 2-6-($2.99) 4.00

INFINITY GAUNTLET (The... #2 on; see Infinity Crusade, The Infinity War & Warlock & the Infinity Watch)
Marvel Comics: July, 1991 - No. 6, Dec, 1991 ($2.50, limited series)
1-6: Thanos-c/stories in all; Starlin scripts in all; 5,6-Ron Lim-c/a 4.00
TPB (4/99, $24.95) r/#1-6 25.00

NOTE: *Lim a-3p(part), 5p, 6p; c-5i, 6i. Perez a-1-3p, 4p(part); c-1(painted), 2-4, 5i, 6i.*

INFINITY, INC. (See All-Star Squadron #25)
DC Comics: Mar, 1984 - No. 53, Aug, 1988 ($1.25, Baxter paper, 36 pgs.)
1-Brainwave, Jr., Fury, The Huntress, Jade, Northwind, Nuklon, Obsidian, Power Girl, Silver Scarab & Star Spangled Kid begin 4.00
2-13,38-49,51-53: 2-Dr. Midnite, G.A. Flash, W. Woman, Dr. Fate, Hourman, Green Lantern, Wildcat app. 5-Nudity panels. 46,47-Millennium tie-ins 3.00
14-Todd McFarlane-a (5/85, 2nd full story) 1 2 3 6 8 9
15-37-McFarlane-a (20,23,24: 5 pgs. only; 33: 2 pgs.); 18-24-Crisis x-over. 21-Intro new Hourman & Dr. Midnight. 26-New Wildcat app. 31-Star Spangled Kid becomes Skyman. 32-Green Fury becomes Green Flame. 33-Origin Obsidian. 35-1st modern app. G.A. Fury 4.00
50 ($2.50, 52 pgs.) 4.00
Annual 1,2: 1(12/85)-Crisis x-over. 2('88, $2.00), Special 1 ('87, $1.50) 4.00
...: The Generations Saga Volume One HC (2011, $39.99) r/#1-4, All-Star Squadron #25,26 & All-Star Squadron Annual #2 40.00

NOTE: *Kubert r-4. McFarlane a-14-37p, Annual 1p; c(p)-14-19, 22, 25, 26, 31-33, 37, Annual 1. Newton a-12p, 13p(last work 4/85). Tuska a-11p. JSA app. 3-10.*

INFINITY, INC. (See 52)
DC Comics: Nov, 2007 - No. 12, Oct, 2008 ($2.99)
1-12: 1-Milligan-s; Steel app. 3.00
...: Luthor's Monsters TPB (2008, $14.99) r/#1-5 15.00
...: The Bogeyman TPB (2008, $14.99) r/#6-10 15.00

INFINITY WAR, THE (Also see Infinity Gauntlet & Warlock and the Infinity...)
Marvel Comics: June, 1992 - No. 6, Nov, 1992 ($2.50, mini-series)
1-Starlin scripts, Lim-c/a(p), Thanos app. in all 4.00
2-6: All have wraparound gatefold covers 4.00
TPB (2006, $29.99) r/#1-6, Marvel Comics Presents #108-111, Warlock and the Infinity Watch #7-10; cover gallery and synopses of Infinity War crossovers 30.00

INFORMER, THE
Feature Television Productions: April, 1954 - No. 5, Dec, 1954
1-Sekowsky-a begins 12 24 36 69 97 125
2 9 18 27 47 61 75
3-5 8 16 24 42 54 65

IN HIS STEPS
Spire Christian Comics (Fleming H. Revell Co.): 1973, 1977 (39/49¢)
nn 2 4 6 10 14 18

INHUMANOIDS, THE (TV)
Marvel Comics (Star Comics): Jan, 1987 - No. 4, July 1987
1-4: Based on Hasbro toys 3.00

INHUMANS, THE (See Amazing Adventures, Fantastic Four #54 & Special #5, Incredible Hulk Special #1, Marvel Graphic Novel & Thor #146)
Marvel Comics Group: Oct, 1975 - No. 12, Aug, 1977
1: #1-4,6 are 25¢ issues 3 6 9 16 23 30
2-4-Peréz-a 2 4 6 9 12 15
5-12: 9-Reprints Amazing Adventures #1,2('70). 12-Hulk app. 2 4 6 8 10 12
4-(30¢-c variant, limited distribution)(4/76) Peréz-a 3 6 9 17 25 32
6-(30¢-c variant, limited distribution)(8/76) 3 6 9 17 25 32
11,12-(35¢-c variants, limited distribution) 4 8 12 24 37 50
Special 1(4/90, $1.50, 52 pgs.)-F.F. cameo 4.00
...: The Great Refuge (5/95, $2.95) 4.00

NOTE: *Buckler c-2-4p, 5. Gil Kane a-5-7p; c-1p, 7p, 8p. Kirby a-9r. Mooney a-11i. Perez a-1-4p, 8p.*

INHUMANS (Marvel Knights)
Marvel Comics: Nov, 1998 - No. 12, Oct, 1999 ($2.99, limited series)
1-Jae Lee-c/a; Paul Jenkins-s 10.00
1-($6.95) DF Edition; Jae Lee variant-c 7.00
2-Two covers by Lee and Darrow 4.00
3-12 3.00
TPB (10/00, $24.95) r/#1-12 25.00

INHUMANS (Volume 3)
Marvel Comics: Jun, 2000 - No. 4, Oct, 2000 ($2.99, limited series)
1-4-Ladronn-c/Pacheco & Marin-s. 1-3-Ladronn-a. 4-Lucas-a 3.00

INHUMANS (Volume 6)
Marvel Comics: Jun, 2003 - No. 12, Jun, 2004 ($2.50/$2.99)
1-12: 1-6-McKeever-s/Clark-a/JH Williams III-c. 7-Begin $2.99-c. 7,8-Teranishi-a 3.00
Vol. 1: Culture Shock (2005, $7.99, digest) r/#1-6; story pitch and sketch pages 8.00

INHUMANS 2099

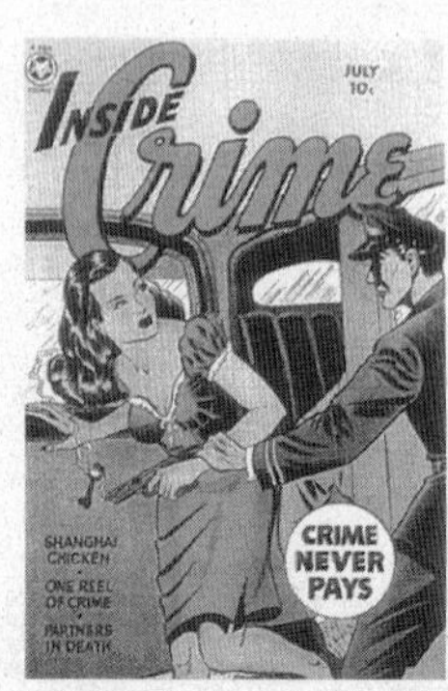

Inside Crime #3 © FOX

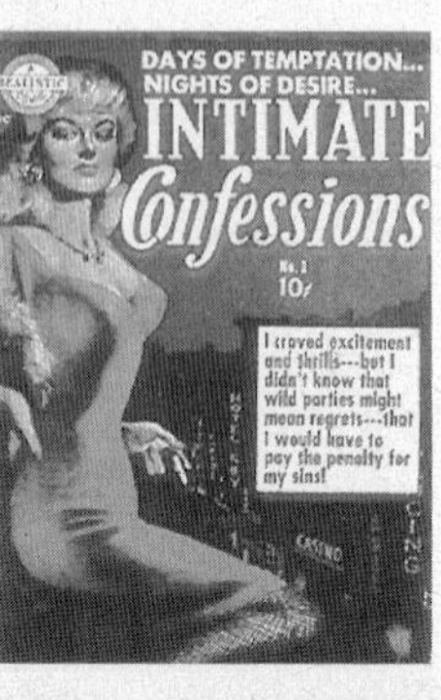

Intimate Confessions #1 © REAL

Invaders #10 © MAR

	GD 2.0	VG 4.0	FN 6.0	VF 8.0	VF/NM 9.0	NM- 9.2

Marvel Comics: Nov, 2004 ($2.99, one-shot)

1-Kirkman-s/Rathburn-a/Pat Lee-c						3.00

INKY & DINKY (See Felix's Nephews...)

IN LOVE (...Magazine on-c; I Love You No. 7 on)
Mainline/Charlton No. 5 (5/55)-on: Aug-Sept, 1954 - No. 6, July, 1955 ('Adult Reading' on-c)

1-Simon & Kirby-a; book-length novel in all issues	41	82	123	256	428	600
2,3-S&K-a. 3-Last pre-code (12-1/54-55)	25	50	75	150	245	340
4-S&K-a.(Rare)	28	56	84	165	270	375
5-S&K-c only	15	30	45	85	130	175
6-No S&K-a	10	20	30	58	79	100

INNOVATION SPECTACULAR
Innovation Publishing: 1991 - No. 2, 1991 ($2.95, squarebound, 100 pgs.)

1,2: Contains rebound comics w/o covers						4.00

INNOVATION SUMMER FUN SPECIAL
Innovation Publishing: 1991 ($3.50, B&W/color, squarebound)

1-Contains rebound comics (Power Factory)						4.00

IN SEARCH OF THE CASTAWAYS (See Movie Comics)

INSIDE CRIME (Formerly My Intimate Affair)
Fox Features Syndicate (Hero Books): No. 3, July, 1950 - No. 2, Sept, 1950

3-Wood-a (10 pgs.); L. B. Cole-c	30	60	90	177	289	400
2-Used in **SOTI**, pg. 182,183; r/Spook #24	23	46	69	136	223	310
nn(no publ. listed, nd)	11	22	33	62	86	110

INSPECTOR, THE (TV) (Also see The Pink Panther)
Gold Key: July, 1974 - No. 19, Feb, 1978

1	3	6	9	19	29	38
2-5	2	4	6	13	18	22
6-9	2	4	6	10	14	18
10-19: 11-Reprints	2	4	6	8	10	12

INSPECTOR GILL OF THE FISH POLICE (See Fish Police)

INSPECTOR WADE
David McKay Publications: No. 13, May, 1938

Feature Books 13	29	58	87	170	278	385

INSTANT PIANO
Dark Horse Comics: Aug, 1994 - No. 4, Feb, 1995 ($3.95, B&W, bimonthly, mature)

1-4						4.00

INTERFACE
Marvel Comics (Epic Comics): Dec, 1989 - No. 8, Dec, 1990 ($1.95, mature, coated paper)

1-8: Cont. from 1st ESPers series; painted-c/a						3.00
Espers: Interface TPB ('98, $16.95) r/#1-6						17.00

INTERNATIONAL COMICS (...Crime Patrol No. 6)
E. C. Comics: Spring, 1947 - No. 5, Nov-Dec, 1947

1-Schaffenberger-a begins, ends #4	64	128	192	406	696	985
2	43	86	129	271	461	650
3-5	40	80	120	243	402	560

INTERNATIONAL CRIME PATROL (Formerly International Comics #1-5; becomes Crime Patrol No. 7 on)
E. C. Comics: No. 6, Spring, 1948

6-Moon Girl app.	64	128	192	406	696	985

IN THE DAYS OF THE MOB (Magazine)
Hampshire Dist. Ltd. (National): Fall, 1971 (B&W)

1-Kirby-a; John Dillinger wanted poster inside (1/2 value if poster is missing)	8	16	24	51	86	120

IN THE PRESENCE OF MINE ENEMIES
Spire Christian Comics/Fleming H. Revell Co.: 1973 (35/49¢)

nn	2	4	6	9	13	16

IN THE SHADOW OF EDGAR ALLAN POE
DC Comics (Vertigo): 2002 (Graphic novel)

Hardcover (2002, $24.95) Fuqua-s/Phillips and Parke photo-a						25.00
Softcover (2003, $17.95)						18.00

INTIMATE
Charlton Comics: Dec, 1957 - No. 3, May, 1958

1	6	12	18	28	34	40
2,3	4	8	12	18	22	25

INTIMATE CONFESSIONS (See Fox Giants)

INTIMATE CONFESSIONS
Country Press Inc.: 1942

nn-Ashcan comic, not distributed to newsstands, only for in house use. A VF copy sold for $1,000 in 2007, and a VF+ copy sold for $1,525 in 2007.

INTIMATE CONFESSIONS
Realistic Comics: July-Aug, 1951 - No. 7, Aug, 1952; No. 8, Mar, 1953 (All painted-c)

1-Kinstler-a; c/Avon paperback #222	116	232	348	742	1271	1800
2	29	58	87	170	278	385
3-c/Avon paperback #250; Kinstler-c/a	32	64	96	192	314	435
4-8: 4-c/Avon paperback #304; Kinstler-c. 6-c/Avon paperback #120. 8-c/Avon paperback #375; Kinstler-a	28	56	84	165	270	375

INTIMATE CONFESSIONS
I. W. Enterprises/Super Comics: 1964

I.W. Reprint #9,10, Super Reprint #10,12,18	2	4	6	11	16	20

INTIMATE LOVE
Standard Comics: No. 5, 1950 - No. 28, Aug, 1954

5-8: 6-8-Severin/Elder-a	11	22	33	60	83	105
9	8	16	24	44	57	70
10-Jane Russell, Robert Mitchum photo-c	14	28	42	82	121	160
11-18,20,23,25,27,28	8	16	24	42	54	65
19,21,22,24,26-Toth-a	9	18	27	50	65	80

NOTE: ***Celardo** a-8, 10. **Colletta** a-23. **Moreira** a-13(2). Photo-c-6, 7, 10, 12, 14, 15, 18-20, 24, 26, 27.*

INTIMATES, THE
DC Comics (WildStorm): Jan, 2005 - No. 12, Dec, 2005 ($2.95/$2.99)

1-12: 1-Joe Casey-s/Jim Lee-c/Lee and Giuseppe Camuncoli-a						3.00

INTIMATE SECRETS OF ROMANCE
Star Publications: Sept, 1953 - No. 2, Apr, 1954

1,2-L. B. Cole-c	19	38	57	109	172	235

INTRIGUE
Quality Comics Group: Jan, 1955

1-Horror; Jack Cole reprint/Web of Evil	34	68	102	199	325	450

INTRIGUE
Image Comics: Aug, 1999 - No. 3, Feb, 2000 ($2.50/$2.95)

1,2: 1-Two covers (Andrews, Wieringo); Shum-s/Andrews-a						3.00
3-($2.95)						3.00

INTRUDER
TSR, Inc.: 1990 - No. 10, 1991 ($2.95, 44 pgs.)

1-10						4.00

INVADERS, THE (TV)
Gold Key: Oct, 1967 - No. 4, Oct, 1968 (All have photo-c)

1-Spiegle-a in all	9	18	27	58	99	140
2-4: 2-Pin-up on back-c	6	12	18	41	66	90

INVADERS, THE (Also see The Avengers #71 & Giant-Size Invaders)
Marvel Comics Group: August, 1975 - No. 40, May, 1979; No. 41, Sept, 1979

1-Captain America & Bucky, Human Torch & Toro, & Sub-Mariner begin; cont'd. from Giant Size Invaders #1; #1-7 are 25¢ issues	6	12	18	42	69	95
2-5: 2-1st app. Brain-Drain. 3-Battle issue; Cap vs. Namor vs. Torch; intro U-Man	3	6	9	18	27	35
6-10: 6,7-(Regular 25¢ edition). 6-(7/76) Liberty Legion app. 7-Intro Baron Blood & intro/1st app. Union Jack; Human Torch origin retold. 8-Union Jack-c/story. 9-Origin Baron Blood. 10-G.A. Capt. America-r/C.A #22	2	4	6	11	16	20
6,7-(30¢-c variants, limited distribution)	4	8	12	24	37	50
11-19: 11-Origin Spitfire; intro The Blue Bullet. 14-1st app. The Crusaders. 16-Re-intro The Destroyer. 17-Intro Warrior Woman. 18-Re-intro The Destroyer w/new origin. 19-Hitler-c/story	2	4	6	8	11	14
17-19,21-(35¢-c variants, limited distribution)	4	8	12	28	44	60
20-(Regular 30¢-c) Reprints origin/1st app. Sub-Mariner from Motion Picture Funnies Weekly with color added & brief write-up about MPFW; 1st app. new Union Jack II	2	4	6	10	14	18
20-(35¢-c variant, limited distribution)	5	10	15	32	51	70
21-(Regular 30¢ edition)-r/Marvel Mystery #10 (battle issue)	2	4	6	9	13	16
22-30,34-40: 22-New origin Toro. 24-r/Marvel Mystery #17 (team-up issue; all-r). 25-All new-a begins. 28-Intro new Human Top & Golden Girl. 29-Intro Teutonic Knight. 34-Mighty Destroyer joins. 35-The Whizzer app.	1	2	3	5	7	9
31-33: 31-Frankenstein-c/sty. 32,33-Thor app.	2	4	6	8	11	14

Invincible #60 © Kirkman & Walker

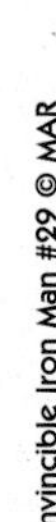
Invincible Iron Man #29 © MAR

The Invisibles #16 © Grant Morrison

	GD	VG	FN	VF	VF/NM	NM-
	2.0	4.0	6.0	8.0	9.0	9.2

41-Double size last issue 3 6 9 14 19 24
Annual 1 (9/77)-Schomburg, Rico stories (new); Schomburg-c/a (1st for Marvel in 30 years); Avengers app.; re-intro The Shark & The Hyena 5 10 15 35 55 75
... Classic Vol. 1 TPB (2007, $24.99) r/#1-9, Giant-Size Invaders #1 and Marvel Premiere #29,30; cover pencils and cover inks 25.00
NOTE: **Buckler** *a-5.* **Everett** *r-20('39), 21(1940), 24, Annual 1.* **Gil Kane** *c(p)-13, 17, 18, 20-27.* **Kirby** *c(p)-3-12, 14-16, 32, 33.* **Mooney** *a-5i, 16, 22.* **Robbins** *a-1-4, 6-9, 10(3 pg.), 11-15, 17-21, 23, 25-28; c-28.*

INVADERS (See Namor, the Sub-Mariner #12)
Marvel Comics Group: May, 1993 - No. 4, Aug, 1993 ($1.75, limited series)
1-4 3.00

INVADERS (2004 title - see New Invaders)

INVADERS FROM HOME
DC Comics (Piranha Press): 1990 - No. 6, 1990 ($2.50, mature)
1-6 3.00

INVADERS NOW! (See Avengers/Invaders and The Torch series)
Marvel Comics: Nov, 2010 - No. 5, Mar, 2011 ($3.99, limited series)
1-5-Alex Ross-c; Steve Rogers, Bucky, Human Torch & Toro, Sub-Mariner app. 4.00

INVASION
DC Comics: Holiday, 1988-'89 - No. 3, Jan, 1989 ($2.95, lim. series, 84 pgs.)
1-3:1-McFarlane/Russell-a. 2-McFarlane/Russell & Giffen/Gordon-a 4.00
Invasion! TPB (2008, $24.99) r/#1-3 25.00

INVINCIBLE (Also see The Pact #4)
Image Comics: Jan, 2003 - Present ($2.95/$2.99)
1-Kirkman-s/Walker-a 40.00
2-8-Kirkman-s/Walker-a. 4-Preview of The Moth 12.00
9-14: 11-Origin of Omni-Man. 14-Cho-c 6.00
15-24,26-41,43-49: 33-Tie-in w/Marvel Team-Up #14 4.00
25-($4.95) Science Dog app.; back-up stories w/origins of Science Dog and teammates 6.00
42-($1.99) Includes re-cap of the entire series 3.00
50-(6/08, $4.99) Two covers; back-up origin of Cecil Stedman; Science Dog app. 6.00
51-59,61-74,76-89: 51-Jim Lee-c; new costumes. 57-Continues in Astounding Wolf-Man #11. 71-74-Viltrumite War. 89-Intro. Zandale 3.00
60-($3.99) Invincible War; Witchblade, Savage Dragon, Spawn, Youngblood app. 4.00
75-($5.99) Viltrumite War; Science Dog back-up; 2 covers 6.00
#0-(4/05, 50¢) Origin of Invincible; Ottley-a 3.00
Image Firsts: Invincible #1 (4/10, $1.00) r/#1 with "Image Firsts" cover logo 3.00
Official Handbook of the Invincible Universe 1,2 (11/06, 1/07, $4.99) profile pages 5.00
Official Handbook of the Invincible Universe Vol. 1 (2007, $12.99) r/#1-2; sketch pages 13.00
... Presents Atom Eve 1,2 (12/07, 3/08, $2.99) origin of Atom Eve; Bellegarde-a 3.00
... Presents Atom Eve & Rex Splode 1-3 (10/09 - 2/10, $2.99) origin of Rex 3.00
... Returns (4/10, $3.99) Leads into Viltrumite War in #71; 4 covers 4.00
... Universe Primer 1 (5/08, $5.99) r/Invincible #1, Brit #1, Astounding Wolf-Man #1 6.00
The Complete Invincible Library Vol. 1 Slipcase HC (2006, $125.00) oversized r/#1-24, #0 and story from Image Comics Summer Special (FCBD 2004); sketch pages; script for #1 125.00
..., Ultimate Collection Vol. 1 HC (2005, $34.95) oversized r/#1-13; sketch pages 35.00
..., Ultimate Collection Vol. 2 HC (2006, $34.99) oversized r/#14-24, #0 and story from Image Comics Summer Special (FCBD 2004); sketch pages and script for #23; intro by Damon Lindelof; afterword by Robert Kirkman 35.00
..., Ultimate Collection Vol. 3 HC (2007, $34.95) oversized r/#25-35 & The Pact #4; sketch pages and script for #28; afterword by Robert Kirkman 35.00
..., Ultimate Collection Vol. 4 HC (2008, $34.99) oversized r/#36-47; sketch & script pgs. 35.00
Vol. 1: Family Matters TPB (8/03, $12.95) r/#1-4; intro. by Busiek; sketch pages 13.00
Vol. 2: Eight in Enough TPB (3/04, $12.95) r/#5-8; intro. by Larsen; sketch pages 13.00
Vol. 3: Perfect Strangers TPB (2004, $12.95) r/#9-12; intro. by Brevoort; sketch pages 13.00
Vol. 4: Head of the Class TPB (1/05, $14.95) r/#14-19; intro. by Waid; sketch pages 15.00
Vol. 5: The Facts of Life TPB (2005, $14.99) r/#0,20-24; intro. by Wieringo; sketch pages 15.00
Vol. 6: A Different World TPB (2006, $14.99) r/#25-30; intro. by Brubaker; sketch pages 15.00
Vol. 7: Three's Company TPB (2006, $14.99) r/#31-35 & The Pact #4; sketch pages 15.00
Vol. 8: My Favorite Martian TPB (2007, $14.99) r/#36-41; sketch pages 15.00
Vol. 9: Out of This World TPB (2008, $14.99) r/#42-47; sketch pages 15.00

INVINCIBLE FOUR OF KUNG FU & NINJA
Leung Publications: April, 1988 - No. 6, 1989 ($2.00)
1-($2.75) 4.00
2-6: 2-Begin $2.00-c 3.00

INVINCIBLE IRON MAN
Marvel Comics: July, 2008 - No. 33, Feb, 2011; No. 500, Mar, 2011 - Present ($2.99/$3.99)
1-Fraction-s/Larroca-a; covers by Larroca & Quesada 4.00
1-Downey movie photo wraparound 5.00
1-Secret Movie Variant white-c with movie cast 30.00
2-18: 2-War Machine and Thor app. 7-Spider-Man app. 8-10-Dark Reign. 11-War Machine app.; Pepper gets her armor suit. 12-Namor app. 3.00
19,20-($3.99) 20-Stark Disassembled starts; back-up synopsis of recent storylines 4.00
21-24-Covers by Larocca and Zircher: 21-Thor & Capt. America app. 22-Dr. Strange app. 3.00
25-($3.99) Fraction-s/Larroca-a; new armor 4.00
26-31-($2.99) 29-New Rescue armor 3.00
32,33-($3.99)-War Machine app.; back-up w/McKelvie-a 4.00
(After #33, numbering reverts to original Vol. 1 as #500)
500-(3/11, $4.99) Two covers by Larroca; Mandarin & Spider-Man app.; cover gallery 5.00
500-Variant-c by Romita Jr. 10.00
500.1 (4/11, $2.99) Histroy re-told; Fraction-s/Larroca-a/c 3.00
501-513-($3.99) 501-503-Doctor Octopus app. 503-Back-up w/Chaykin-a. 504-509-Fear Itself tie-in; Grey Gargoyle app. 4.00
Annual 1 (8/10, $4.99) Larroca-c; history of the Mandarin; Di Giandomenico-a 5.00
...MGC #1 (4/10, free) r/#1 with "Marvel's Greatest Comics" cover logo 3.00

INVISIBLE BOY (See Approved Comics)

INVISIBLE MAN, THE (See Superior Stories #1 & Supernatural Thrillers #2)

INVISIBLE PEOPLE
Kitchen Sink Press: 1992 (B&W, lim. series)
Book One: Sanctum; Book Two: "The Power": Will Eisner-s/a in all 3.00
Book Three: "Mortal Combat" 4.00
Hardcover ($34.95) 35.00
TPB (DC Comics, 9/00, $12.95) reprints series 13.00

INVISIBLES, THE (1st Series)
DC Comics (Vertigo): Sept, 1994 - No. 25, Oct, 1996 ($1.95/$2.50, mature)
1-($2.95, 52 pgs.)-Intro King Mob, Ragged Robin, Boy, Lord Fanny & Dane (Jack Frost); Grant Morrison scripts in all 6.00
2-8: 4-Includes bound-in trading cards. 5-1st app. Orlando; brown paper-c 4.00
9-25: 10-Intro Jim Crow. 13-15-Origin Lord Fanny. 19-Origin King Mob; polybagged. 20-Origin Boy. 21-Mister Six revealed. 25-Intro Division X 3.00
Apocalipstick (2001, $19.95, TPB)-r/#9-16; Bolland-c 20.00
Entropy in the U.K. (2001, $19.95, TPB)-r/#17-25; Bolland-c 20.00
Say You Want A Revolution (1996, $17.50, TPB)-r/#1-8 18.00
NOTE: **Buckingham** *a-25p.* **Rian Hughes** *c-1, 5.* **Phil Jimenez** *a-17p-19p.* **Paul Johnson** *a-16, 21.* **Sean Phillips** *c-2-4, 6-25.* **Weston** *a-10p.* **Yeowell** *a-1p-4p, 22p-24p.*

INVISIBLES, THE (2nd Series)
DC Comics (Vertigo): V2#1, Feb, 1997 - No. 22, Feb, 1999 ($2.50, mature)
1-Intro Jolly Roger; Grant Morrison scripts, Phil Jimenez-a, & Brian Bolland-c begins 4.00
2-22: 9,14-Weston-a 3.00
Bloody Hell in America TPB ('98, $12.95) r/#1-4 13.00
Counting to None TPB ('99, $19.95) r/#5-13 20.00
Kissing Mr. Quimper TPB ('00, $19.95) r/#14-22 20.00

INVISIBLES, THE (3rd Series) (Issue #'s go in reverse from #12 to #1)
DC Comics (Vertigo): V3#12, Apr, 1999 - No. 1, June, 2000 ($2.95, mature)
1-12-Bolland-c; Morrison-s on all. 1-Quitely-a. 2-4-Art by various. 5-8-Phillips-a. 9-12-Phillip Bond-a. 3.00
The Invisible Kingdom TPB ('02, $19.95) r/#12-1; new Bolland-c 20.00

INVISIBLE SCARLET O'NEIL (Also see Famous Funnies #81 & Harvey Comics Hits #59)
Famous Funnies (Harvey): Dec, 1950 - No. 3, Apr, 1951 (2-3 pgs. of Powell-a in each issue.)
1 15 30 45 86 133 180
2,3 12 24 36 67 94 120

ION (Green Lantern Kyle Rayner) (See Countdown)
DC Comics: Jun, 2006 - No. 12, May, 2007 ($2.99)
1-12: 1-Marz-s/Tocchini-a. 3-Mogo app. 9,10-Tangent Green Lantern app. 12-Monitor app. 3.00
...: The Torchbearer TPB (2007, $14.99) r/#1-6 15.00

I, PAPARAZZI
DC Comics (Vertigo): 2001 ($29.95, HC, digitally manipulated photographic art)
nn-Pat McGreal-s/Steven Parke-digital-a/Stephen John Phillips-photos 30.00

IRON AGE
Marvel Comics: Aug, 2011 - No. 3, Oct, 2011 ($4.99, limited series)
1-3-Iron Man time travels. 1-Avengers. 2-Fantastic Four. 3-Dazzler & X-Men 5.00
...: Alpha (8/11, $2.99) First part of the series; Dark Phoenix app.; Issacs-a 3.00
...: Omega (10/11, $2.99) Conclusion of the series; Olivetti-c/Issacs-a 3.00

IRON AND THE MAIDEN
Aspen MLT: Sept, 2007 - No. 4, Dec, 2007 ($3.99)
1-4: 1-Two covers by Manapul and Madureira/Matsuda; Jason Rubin-s 4.00
...: Brutes, Bims and the City (2/08, $2.99) character backgrounds/development art 3.00

IRON CORPORAL, THE (See Army War Heroes #22)

Iron Fist (2004 series) #1 © MAR

Iron Man #100 © MAR

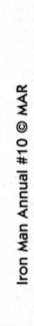

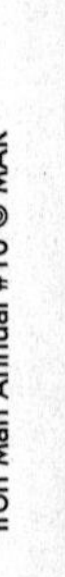
Iron Man Annual #10 © MAR

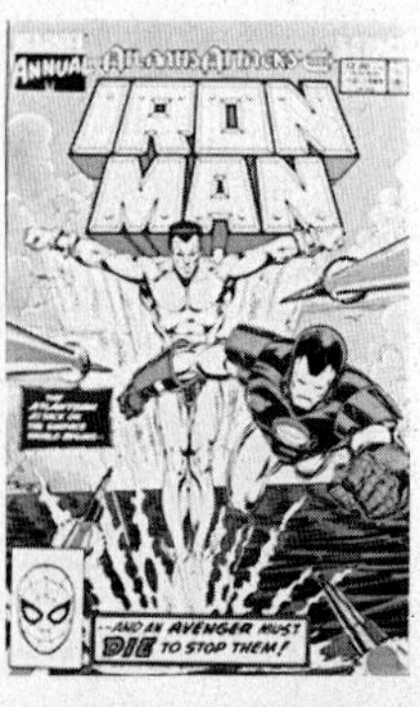

GD VG FN VF VF/NM NM-
2.0 4.0 6.0 8.0 9.0 9.2

Charlton Comics: No. 23, Oct, 1985 - No. 25, Feb, 1986
23-25: Glanzman-a(r); low print 6.00

IRON FIST (See Immortal Iron Fist, Deadly Hands of Kung Fu, Marvel Premiere & Power Man)
Marvel Comics: Nov, 1975 - No. 15, Sept, 1977
1-Iron Fist battles Iron Man (#1-6: 25¢) 7 14 21 48 79 110
2 4 8 12 24 37 50
3-10: 4-6-(Regular 25¢ edition)(4-6/76). 8-Origin retold
3 6 9 19 29 38
4-6-(30¢-c variant, limited distribution) 6 12 18 37 59 80
11,13: 13-(30¢-c) 3 6 9 16 23 30
12-Capt. America app. 3 6 9 20 30 40
13-(35¢-c variant, limited distribution) 7 14 21 48 79 110
14-1st app. Sabretooth (8/77)(see Power Man) 14 28 42 97 211 325
14-(35¢-c variant, limited distribution) 63 126 189 510 1105 1700
15-(Regular 30¢ ed.) X-Men app., Byrne-a 7 14 21 48 79 110
15-(35¢-c variant, limited distribution) 16 32 48 111 243 375
NOTE: ***Adkins** a-8p, 10i, 13i; c-8i. **Byrne** a-1-15p; c-8p, 15p. **G. Kane** c-4-6p. **McWilliams** a-1i.*

IRON FIST
Marvel Comics: Sept, 1996 - No. 2, Oct, 1996 ($1.50, limited series)
1,2 3.00

IRON FIST
Marvel Comics: Jul, 1998 - No. 3, Sept, 1998 ($2.50, limited series)
1-3: Jurgens-s/Guice-a 3.00

IRON FIST (Also see Immortal Iron Fist)
Marvel Comics: May, 2004 - No. 6, Oct, 2004 ($2.99)
1-6: 1-4,6-Kevin Lau-c/a. 5-Mays-c/a 3.00

IRON FIST: WOLVERINE
Marvel Comics: Nov, 2000 - No. 4, Feb, 2001 ($2.99, limited series)
1-4-Igle-c/a; Kingpin app. 2-Iron Man app. 3,4-Capt. America app. 3.00

IRON GHOST
Image Comics: Apr, 2005 - No. 6, Mar, 2006 ($2.95/$2.99, limited series)
1-6-Chuck Dixon-s/Sergio Cariello-a; flip cover on each 3.00

IRONHAND OF ALMURIC (Robert E. Howard's...)
Dark Horse Comics: Aug, 1991 - No. 4, 1991 ($2.00, B&W, mini-series)
1-4: 1-Conrad painted-c 3.00

IRON HORSE (TV)
Dell Publishing Co.: March, 1967 - No. 2, June, 1967
1-Dale Robertson photo covers on both 3 6 9 18 27 35
2 3 6 9 15 21 26

IRONJAW (Also see The Barbarians)
Atlas/Seaboard Publ.: Jan, 1975 - No. 4, July, 1975
1,2-Neal Adams-c. 1-1st app. Iron Jaw; Sekowsky-a(p); Fleisher-s
2 4 6 11 16 20
3,4-Marcos. 4-Origin 2 4 6 8 11 14

IRON LANTERN
Marvel Comics (Amalgam): June, 1997 ($1.95, one-shot)
1-Kurt Busiek-s/Paul Smith & Al Williamson-a 3.00

IRON MAN (Also see The Avengers #1, Giant-Size..., Marvel Collectors Item Classics, Marvel Double Feature, Marvel Fanfare, Tales of Suspense #39 & Uncanny Tales #52)
Marvel Comics: May, 1968 - No. 332, Sept, 1996
1-Origin; Colan-c/a(p); story continued from Iron Man & Sub-Mariner #1
37 74 111 278 602 925
2 13 26 39 90 195 300
3 10 20 30 68 127 185
4,5 9 18 27 61 106 150
6-10: 9-Iron Man battles green Hulk-like android 7 14 21 48 79 110
11-15: 15-Last 12¢ issue 6 12 18 41 66 90
16-20 5 10 15 32 51 70
21-24,26-30: 22-Death of Janice Cord. 27-Intro Firebrand
4 8 12 24 37 50
25-Iron Man battles Sub-Mariner 4 8 12 28 44 60
31-42: 33-1st app. Spymaster. 35-Nick Fury & Daredevil x-over. 42-Last 15¢ issue
3 6 9 19 29 38
43-Intro The Guardsman; 25¢ giant (52 pgs.) 5 10 15 30 48 65
44-46,48-50: 43-Giant-Man back-up by Ayers. 44-Ant-Man by Tuska. 46-The Guardsman dies. 50-Princess Python app. 3 6 9 17 25 32
47-Origin retold; Barry Smith-a(p) 4 8 12 24 37 50
51-53: 53-Starlin part pencils 3 6 9 16 22 28
54-Iron Man battles Sub-Mariner; 1st app. Moondragon (1/73) as Madame MacEvil; Everett part-c 5 10 15 35 55 75
55-1st app. Thanos, Drax the Destroyer, Mentor, Starfox & Kronos (2/73); Starlin-c/a
15 30 45 102 221 340
56-Starlin-a 5 10 15 35 55 75
57-65,67-70: 59-Firebrand returns. 65-Origin Dr. Spectrum. 67-Last 20¢ issue. 68-Sunfire & Unicorn app.; origin retold; Starlin-c 2 4 6 13 18 22
66-Iron Man vs. Thor. 3 6 9 20 30 40
71-84: 72-Cameo portraits of N. Adams. 73-Rename Stark Industries to Stark International; Brunner. 76-r/#9. 2 4 6 9 13 16
85-89-(Regular 25¢ editions): 86-1st app. Blizzard. 87-Origin Blizzard. 88-Thanos app. 89-Daredevil app.; last 25¢-c 2 4 6 9 13 16
85-89-(30¢-c variants, limited distribution)(4-8/76) 4 8 12 22 34 45
90-99: 96-1st app. new Guardsman 2 4 6 8 11 14
99,101-103-(35¢-c variants, limited dist.) 4 8 12 28 44 60
100-(7/77)-Starlin-c 3 6 9 21 32 42
100-(35¢-c variant, limited dist.) 9 18 27 60 100 140
101-117: 101-Intro DreadKnight. 109-1st app. new Crimson Dynamo; 1st app. Vanguard. 110-Origin Jack of Hearts retold; death of Count Nefaria. 114-Avengers app.
2 4 6 8 10 12
118-Byrne-a(p); 1st app. Jim Rhodes 3 6 9 16 23 30
119-127: 120,121-Sub-Mariner x-over. 122-Origin. 123-128-Tony Stark treated for alcohol problem. 125-Ant-Man app. 2 4 6 11 16 20
128-(11/79) Classic Tony Stark alcoholism cover 4 8 12 22 34 45
129,130,134-149 1 2 3 5 6 8
131-133: 131,132-Hulk x-over. 133-Hulk/Ant Man-c 1 3 4 6 8 10
150-Double size 2 4 6 8 10 12
151-168: 152-New armor. 161-Moon Knight app. 167-Tony Stark alcohol problem resurfaces
6.00
169-New Iron Man (Jim Rhodes replaces Tony Stark) 1 3 4 6 8 10
170,171 6.00
172-199: 172-Captain America x-over. 186-Intro Vibro. 190-Scarlet Witch app. 191-198-Tony Stark returns as original Iron Man. 192-Both Iron Men battle 5.00
200-(11/85, $1.25, 52 pgs.)-Tony Stark returns as new Iron Man (red & white armor) thru #230 1 2 3 5 6 8
201-213,215-224: 213-Intro new Dominic Fortune 4.00
214,225,228,231,234,247: 214-Spider-Woman app. in new black costume (1/87). 225-Double size ($1.25). 228-vs. Capt. America. 231-Intro new Iron Man. 234-Spider-Man x-over. 247-Hulk x-over 5.00
226,227,229,230,232,233,235-243,245,246,248,249: 233-Ant-Man app. 243-Tony Stark loses use of legs 3.00
244-($1.50, 52 pgs.)-New Armor makes him walk 4.00
250-($1.50, 52 pgs.)-Dr. Doom-c/story 4.00
251-274,276-281,283,285-287,289,291-299: 258-277-Byrne scripts. 271-Fin Fang Foom app. 276-Black Widow-c/story; last $1.00-c. 281-1st brief app. War Machine. 283-2nd full app. War Machine 3.00
275-($1.50, 52 pgs.) 4.00
282-1st full app. War Machine (7/92) 5.00
284-Death of Iron Man (Tony Stark) 5.00
288-($2.50, 52pg.)-Silver foil stamped-c; Iron Man's 350th app. in comics 4.00
290-($2.95, 52pg.)-Gold foil stamped-c; 30th ann. 4.00
300-($3.95, 68 pgs.)-Collector's Edition w/embossed foil-c; anniversary issue; War Machine-c/story 5.00
300-($2.50, 68 pgs.)-Newsstand Edition 4.00
301-303: 302-Venom-c/story (cameo #301) 3.00
304-316,318-324,326-331: 304-Begin $1.50-c; bound-in trading card sheet; Thunderstrike-c/story. 310-Orange logo. 312-w/bound-in Power Ranger Card. 319-Prologue to "The Crossing." 326-New Tony Stark; Pratt-c. 330-War Machine & Stockpile app; return of Morgan Stark 3.00
310,325: 310 ($2.95)-Polybagged w/ 16 pg. Marvel Action Hour preview & acetate print; white logo. 325-($2.95)-Wraparound-c 4.00
317-($2.50)-Flip book 4.00
332-Onslaught x-over 5.00
Special 1 (8/70)-Sub-Mariner x-over; Everett-c 5 10 15 35 55 75
Special 2 (11/71, 52 pgs.)-r/TOS #81,82,91 (all-r) 3 6 9 20 30 40
Annual 3 (1976)-Man-Thing app. 3 6 9 14 20 25
King Size 4 (8/77)-The Champions (w/Ghost Rider) app.; Newton-a(i)
2 4 6 11 16 20
Annual 5 ('82) New-a 1 2 3 5 6 8
Annual 6-8: ('83-'85) 6-New Iron Man (J. Rhodes) app. 8-X-Factor app. 5.00
Annual 9-15: ('86-'94) 10-Atlantis Attacks x-over; P. Smith-a; Layton/Guice-a; Sub-Mariner app. 11-(1990)-Origin of Mrs. Arbogast by Ditko (p&i). 12-1 pg. origin recap; Ant-Man back-up-s. 13-Darkhawk & Avengers West Coast app.; Colan/Williamson-a. 14-Bagged w/card 4.00

Iron Man V3 #55 © MAR

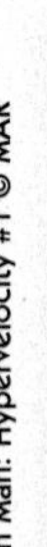
Iron Man: Hypervelocity #1 © MAR

Iron Man Noir #3 © MAR

GD 2.0 | VG 4.0 | FN 6.0 | VF 8.0 | VF/NM 9.0 | NM- 9.2

...: Armor Wars TPB (2007, $24.99) r/#225-232; Michelinie intro. 25.00
Manual 1 (1993, $1.75)-Operations handbook 3.00
Graphic Novel: Crash (1988, $12.95, Adults, 72 pgs.)-Computer generated art & color; violence & nudity 13.00
...Collector's Preview 1(11/94, $1.95)-wraparound-c; text & illos-no comics 3.00
...: Demon in a Bottle HC (2008, $24.99) r/#120-128; two covers 25.00
...: Demon in a Bottle TPB (2006, $24.99) r/#120-128 25.00
...: Many Armors of Iron Man (2008, $24.99) r/#47, 142-144, 152-153, 200, 218 25.00
...Vs. Dr. Doom (12/94, $12.95)-r/#149-150, 249,250. Julie Bell-c 13.00
...Vs. Dr. Doom: Doomquest HC (2008, $19.99, dustjacket)-r/#149-150, 249,250; new Michelinie intro.; bonus art 20.00
...: War Machine TPB (2008, $29.99) r/#280-291 30.00
The Invincible Iron Man Omnibus Vol. 1 HC (2008, $99.99, dustjacket) r/Iron Man stories from Tales of Suspense #39-83 & Tales To Astonish #82; 1992 intro. by Stan Lee; 1975 essay by Lee; 2008 essay by Layton; gallery of original art and covers; creator bios 100.00

NOTE: **Austin** *c-105i, 109-111i, 151i.* **Byrne** *a-118p; c-109p, 197, 253.* **Colan** *a-1p, 253, Special 1p(3); c-1p.* **Craig** *a-1i, 2-4, 5-13i, 14, 15-19i, 24p, 25p, 26-28i; c-2-4.* **Ditko** *a-160p.* **Everett** *c-29.* **Guice** *a-233-241p.* **G. Kane** *c(p)-52-54, 63, 67, 72-75, 77-79, 88, 98.* **Kirby** *a-Special 1p; c-13, 80p, 90, 92-95.* **Mooney** *a-40i, 43i, 47i.* **Perez** *c-103p.* **Simonson** *c-Annual 8.* **B. Smith** *a-232p, 243i; c-232.* **P. Smith** *a-159p, 245p, Annual 10p; c-159.* **Starlin** *a-53p(part), 55p, 56p; c-55p, 160, 163.* **Tuska** *a-5-13p, 15-23p, 24i, 32p, 38-46p, 48-54p, 57-61p, 63-69p, 70-72p, 78p, 86-92p, 95-106p, Annual 4p.* **Wood** *a-Special 1i.*

IRON MAN (The Invincible...) (Volume Two)
Marvel Comics: Nov, 1996 - No. 13, Nov, 1997 ($2.95/$1.95/$1.99)
(Produced by WildStorm Productions)

V2#1-3-Heroes Reborn begins; Scott Lobdell scripts & Whilce Portacio-c/a begin; new origin Iron Man & Hulk. 2-Hulk app. 3-Fantastic Four app. 4.00
1-Variant-c 5.00
4-11: 4-Two covers. 6-Fantastic Four app.; Industrial Revolution; Hulk app. 7-Return of Rebel. 11-($1.99) Dr. Doom-c/app. 3.00
12-($2.99) "Heroes Reunited"-pt. 3; Hulk-c/app. 4.00
13-($1.99) "World War 3"-pt. 3, x-over w/Image 3.00
Heroes Reborn: Iron Man (2006, $29.99, TPB) r/#1-12; Heroes Reborn #1/2; pin-ups 30.00

IRON MAN (The Invincible...) (Volume Three)
Marvel Comics: Feb, 1998 - No. 89, Dec, 2004 ($2.99/$1.99/$2.25)

V3#1-($2.99)-Follows Heroes Return; Busiek scripts & Chen-c/a begin; Deathsquad app. 6.00
1-Alternate Ed. 1 2 3 5 7 9
2-12: 2-Two covers. 6-Black Widow-c/app. 7-Warbird-c/app. 8-Black Widow app. 9-Mandarin returns 4.00
13-($2.99) battles the Controller 5.00
14-24: 14-Fantastic Four-c/app. 3.00
25-($2.99) Iron Man and Warbird battle Ultimo; Avengers app. 4.00
26-30-Quesada-s. 28-Whiplash killed. 29-Begin $2.25-c. 3.00
31-45,47-49,51-54: 35-Maximum Security x-over; FF-c/app. 41-Grant-a begins. 44-New armor debut. 48-Ultron-c/app. 3.00
46-($3.50, 100 pgs.) Sentient armor returns; r/V1#78,140,141 4.00
50-($3.50) Grell-s begin; Black Widow app. 4.00
55-($3.50) 400th issue; Asamiya-c; back-up story Stark reveals ID; Grell-a 4.00
56-66: 56-Reis-a. 57,58-Ryan-a. 59-61-Grell-c/a. 62,63-Ryan-a. 64-Davis-a; Thor-c/app. 3.00
67-89: 67-Begin $2.99-c; Gene Ha-c. 75-83-Granov-c. 84-Avengers Disassembled prologue 85-89-Avengers Disassembled. 85-88-Harris-a. 86-89-Pat Lee-c. 87-Rumiko killed 3.00
.../Captain America '98 Annual ($3.50) vs. Modok 4.00
1999, 2000 Annual ($3.50) 4.00
2001 Annual ($2.99) Claremont-s/Ryan-a 4.00
Avengers Disassembled: Iron Man TPB (2004, $14.99) r/#84-89 15.00
Mask in the Iron Man (5/01, $14.95, TPB) r/#26-30, #1/2 15.00

IRON MAN (The Invincible...)
Marvel Comics: Jan, 2005 - No. 35, Jan, 2009 ($3.50/$2.99)

1-($3.50-c) Warren Ellis-s/Adi Granov-c/a 4.00
2-14-($2.99) 5-Flashback to origin; Stark gets new abilities. 7-Knauf-s/Zircher-a 13,14-Civil War 3.00
15-24,26,27,29-35: 15-Stark becomes Director of S.H.I.E.L.D. 19,20-World War Hulk. 33-Secret Invasion; War Machine app. 34,35-War Machine title logo 3.00
25,28-($3.99) 25-Includes movie preview & armor showcase. 28-Red & white armor 4.00
All-New Iron Manual (2/08, $4.99) Handbook-style guide to characters & armor suits 5.00
... By Design 1 (11/10, $3.99) Gallery of 2010 variant covers with artist commentary 4.00
.../Captain America: Casualities of War (2/07, $3.99) two covers; flashbacks 4.00
...: Director of S.H.I.E.L.D. Annual 1 (1/08, $3.99) Madame Hydra app.; Cheung-c 4.00
Free Comic Book Day 2010 (Iron Man: Supernova) #1 (5/10, 9-1/2" x 6-1/4") Nova app. 3.00
Free Comic Book Day 2010 (Iron Man/Thor) #1 (5/10, 9-1/2" x 6-1/4") Romita Jr.-a/c 3.00
...Golden Avenger 1 (11/08, $2.99) Santacruz-a; movie photo-c 3.00
.../Hulk/Fury 1 (2/09, $3.99) crossover of movie-version characters 4.00
Indomitable Iron Man (4/10, $3.99) B&W stories; Chaykin-s/a; Rosado-a; Parrillo-c 4.00
Iron Manual Mark 3 (6/10, $3.99) Handbook-format profiles of characters 4.00

...: Iron Protocols (12/09, $3.99) Olivetti-c/Nelson-a 4.00
...: Kiss and Kill (8/10, $3.99) Black Widow and Wolverine app. 4.00
...: Requiem (2009, $4.99) r/TOS #39, Iron Man #144 (1981); armor profiles 5.00
...: The End (1/09, $4.99) future Tony Stark retires; Michelinie-s/Chang & Layton-a 5.00
...: Titanium! 1 (12/10, $4.99) short stories by various; Yardin-c 5.00
Civil War: Iron Man TPB (2007, $11.99) r/#13,14, .../Captain America: Casualities of War, and Civil War: The Confession 12.00
HC (2006, $19.99, dust jacket) r/#1-6 and Granov covers from Iron Man V3 #75-83 20.00
...: Director of S.H.I.E.L.D. TPB (2007, $14.99) r/#15-18; Strange Tales #135 (1965) and Iron Man #129; profile pages for Iron Man and S.H.I.E.L.D.; creator interviews 15.00
...: Extremis SC (2007, $14.99) r/#1-6 and Granov covers from Iron Man V3 #75-83 15.00
...: Execute Program SC (2007, $14.99) r/#7-12; cover layouts and sketches 15.00

IRON MAN AND POWER PACK
Marvel Comics: Jan, 2008 - No. 4, Apr, 2008 ($2.99, limited series)

1-4-Gurihiru-c/Sumerak-s; Puppet Master app.; Mini Marvels back-ups in each 3.00
...: Armored and Dangerous TPB (2008, $7.99, digest size) r/series 8.00

IRON MAN & SUB-MARINER
Marvel Comics Group: Apr, 1968 (12¢, one-shot) (Pre-dates Iron Man #1 & Sub-Mariner #1)

1-Iron Man story by Colan/Craig continued from Tales of Suspense #99 & continued in Iron Man #1; Sub-Mariner story by Colan continued from Tales to Astonish #101 & continued in Sub-Mariner #1; Colan/Everett-c 14 28 42 97 211 325

IRON MAN AND THE ARMOR WARS
Marvel Comics: Oct, 2009 - No. 4, Jan, 2010 ($2.99, limited series)

1-4-Rousseau-a; Crimson Dynamo & Omega Red app. 3.00

IRON MAN: ARMORED ADVENTURES
Marvel Comics: Sept, 2009 ($3.99, one-shot)

1-Based on the 2009 cartoon; Brizuela-a; Nick Fury & Living Laser app. 4.00

IRON MAN: BAD BLOOD
Marvel Comics: Sept, 2000 - No. 4, Dec, 2000 ($2.99, limited series)

1-4-Micheline-s/Layton-a 3.00

IRON MAN: ENTER THE MANDARIN
Marvel Comics: Nov, 2007 - No. 6, Apr, 2008 ($2.99, limited series)

1-6-Casey-s/Canete-a; retells first meeting 3.00
TPB (2008, $14.99) r/#1-6 15.00

IRON MAN: EXTREMIS DIRECTOR'S CUT
Marvel Comics: Jun, 2010 - No. 6, Sept, 2010 ($3.99, limited series)

1-6-Reprints Iron Man #1-6 (2005 series) with script pages and design art 4.00

IRON MAN: HOUSE OF M (Also see House of M and related x-overs)
(Reprinted in House of M: Fantastic Four/ Iron Man TPB)
Marvel Comics: Sept, 2005 - No. 3, Nov, 2005 ($2.99, limited series)

1-3-Pat Lee-a/c; Greg Pak-s 3.00

IRON MAN: HYPERVELOCITY
Marvel Comics: Mar, 2007 - No. 6, Aug, 2007 ($2.99, limited series)

1-6-Adam Warren-s/Brian Denham-a/c 3.00
TPB (2007, $14.99) r/#1-6; layout pages and armor design sketches 15.00

IRON MAN: I AM IRON MAN
Marvel Comics: Mar, 2010 - No. 2, Apr, 2010 ($3.99, limited series)

1,2-Adaptation of the first movie; Peter David-s/Sean Chen-a/Adi Granov-c 4.00

IRON MAN: INEVITABLE
Marvel Comics: Feb, 2006 - No. 6, July, 2006 ($2.99, limited series)

1-6-Joe Casey-s/Frazer Irving; Spymaster and the Living Laser app. 3.00
TPB (2006, $14.99) r/#1-6; cover sketches 15.00

IRON MAN: LEGACY
Marvel Comics: Jun, 2010 - No. 11, Apr, 2011 ($3.99/$2.99)

1-Van Lente-s/Kurth-a; Dr. Doom app.; back-up r/debut in Tales of Suspense #39 4.00
2-11-($2.99) 4-Titanium Man & Crimson Dynamo app. 6-The Pride app. 3.00

IRON MAN: LEGACY OF DOOM
Marvel Comics: Jun, 2008 - No. 4, Sept, 2008 ($2.99, limited series)

1-4-Michelinie-s/Lim & Layton-a; Dr. Doom app. 3.00

IRON MAN NOIR
Marvel Comics: Jun, 2010 - No. 4, Sept, 2010 ($3.99, limited series)

1-4-Pulp-style set in 1939; Snyder-s/Garcia-a 4.00

IRON MAN: RAPTURE
Marvel Comics: Jan, 2011 - No. 4, Feb, 2011 ($3.99, limited series)

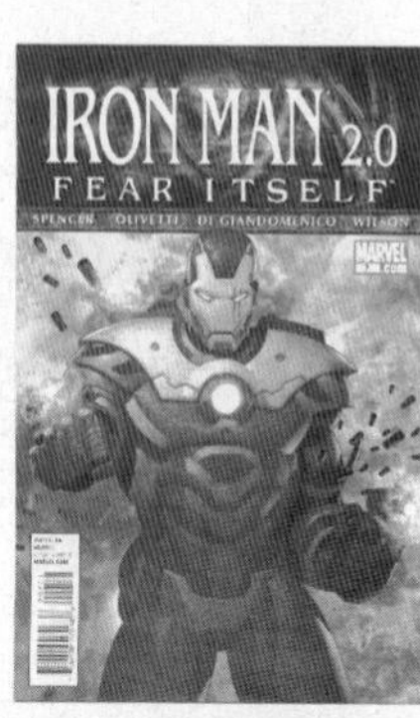

Iron Man 2.0 #7 © MAR

Irredeemable #14 © BOOM

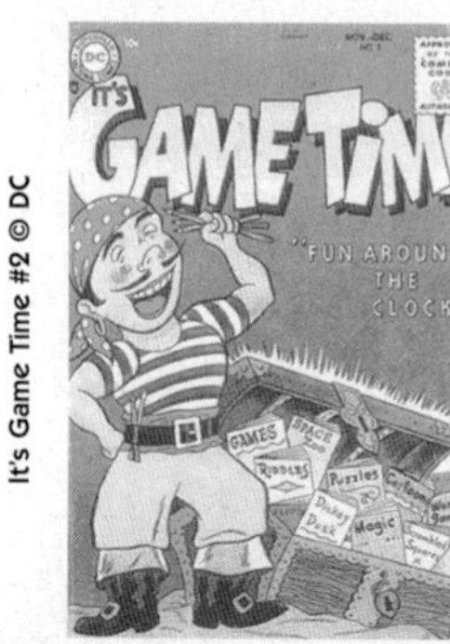

It's Game Time #2 © DC

	GD 2.0	VG 4.0	FN 6.0	VF 8.0	VF/NM 9.0	NM- 9.2
1-4-Irvine-s/Medina-a/Bradstreet-c. 3,4-War Machine app.						4.00

IRON MAN: THE IRON AGE
Marvel Comics: Aug, 1998 - No. 2, Sept, 1998 ($5.99, limited series)

1,2-Busiek-s; flashback story from gold armor days						6.00

IRON MAN: THE LEGEND
Marvel Comics: Sept, 1996 ($3.95, one-shot)

1-Tribute issue						4.50

IRON MAN/ THOR
Marvel Comics: Jan, 2011 - No. 4, Apr, 2011 ($3.99, limited series)

1-4-Eaton-a; Crimson Dynamo & Diablo app.						4.00

IRON MAN 2: ... (Follows the first movie)
Marvel Comics: Jun, 2010 - Nov, 2010 ($3.99, limited series)

Agents of S.H.I.E.L.D. 1 (11/10, $3.99) Nick Fury, Agent Coulson & Black Widow app.						4.00
Public Identity (6/10 - No. 3, 7/10, $3.99) 1-3-Kitson & Lim-a/Granov-c						4.00
Spotlight (4/10, $3.99) Interviews with Granov, Guggenheim, Fraction, Ellis, Michelinie						4.00

IRON MAN 2.0
Marvel Comics: Apr, 2011 - No. 12, Feb, 2012 ($3.99/$2.99)

1-($3.99) Spencer-s/Kitson-c; back-up history of War Machine						4.00
1-Variant-c by Djurdjevic						6.00
2-7,(7.1),8-12-($2.99) 2,3-Kitson, Kano & Di Giandomenico-a. 5-7-Fear Itself tie-in						3.00
...: Modern Warfare 1 (10/11, $4.99) r/#1-3 with variant covers						5.00

IRON MAN 2020 (Also see Machine Man limited series)
Marvel Comics: June, 1994 ($5.95, one-shot)

nn						6.00

IRON MAN: VIVA LAS VEGAS
Marvel Comics: Jul, 2008 - No. 2 ($3.99, unfinished limited series)

1,2-Jon Favreau-s/Adi Granov-a/c						4.00

IRON MAN VS WHIPLASH
Marvel Comics: Jan, 2010 - No. 4, Apr, 2010 ($3.99, limited series)

1-4-Briones-a/Peterson-c; origin of new Whiplash						4.00

IRON MAN/X-O MANOWAR: HEAVY METAL (See X-O Manowar/Iron Man: In Heavy Metal)
Marvel Comics: Sept, 1996 ($2.50, one-shot) (1st Marvel/Valiant x-over)

1-Pt. II of Iron Man/X-O Manowar x-over; Fabian Nicieza scripts; 1st app. Rand Banion						4.00

IRON MARSHALL
Jademan Comics: July, 1990 - No. 32, Feb, 1993 ($1.75, plastic coated-c)

1,32: Kung Fu stories. 1-Poster centerfold						4.00
2-31-Kung Fu stories in all						3.00

IRON VIC (See Comics Revue No. 3 & Giant Comics Editions)
United Features Syndicate/St. John Publ. Co.: 1940

Single Series 22	34	68	102	199	325	450

IRONWOLF
DC Comics: 1986 ($2.00, one shot)

1-r/Weird Worlds #8-10; Chaykin story & art						4.00

IRONWOLF: FIRES OF THE REVOLUTION (See Weird Worlds #8-10)
DC Comics: 1992 ($29.95, hardcover)

nn-Chaykin/Moore story, Mignola-a w/Russell inks.						30.00

IRREDEEMABLE (Also see Incorruptible)
BOOM! Studios: Apr, 2009 - Present ($3.99)

1-35: 1-Waid-s/Krause-a; 3 covers; Grant Morrison afterword. 2-32-Three covers						4.00
1-Artist Edition (12/11, $3.99) r/#1 in B&W with bonus sketch and design art						4.00
... Special 1 (4/10, $3.99) Art by Azaceta, Rios & Chaykin; three covers						4.00

IRREDEEMABLE ANT-MAN, THE
Marvel Comics: Dec, 2006 - No. 12, Nov, 2007 ($2.99)

1-12-Kirkman-s/Hester-a/c; intro. Eric O'Grady as the new Ant-Man. 7-Ms. Marvel app. 10-World War Hulk x-over						3.00
... Vol. 1: Lowlife (2007, $9.99, digest) r/#1-6						10.00
... Vol. 2: Small-Minded (2007, $9.99, digest) r/#7-12						10.00

ISAAC ASIMOV'S I-BOTS
Tekno Comix: Dec, 1995 - No. 7, May, 1996 ($1.95)

1-7: 1-6-Perez-c/a. 2-Chaykin variant-c exists. 3-Polybagged. 7-Lady Justice-c/app.						3.00

ISAAC ASIMOV'S I-BOTS
BIG Entertainment: V2#1, June, 1996 - No. 9, Feb, 1997 ($2.25)

	GD 2.0	VG 4.0	FN 6.0	VF 8.0	VF/NM 9.0	NM- 9.2
V2#1-9: 1-Lady Justice-c/app. 6-Gil Kane-c						3.00

ISIS (TV) (Also see Shazam)
National Per.l Publ./DC Comics: Oct-Nov, 1976 - No. 8, Dec-Jan, 1977-78

1-Wood inks	2	4	6	10	14	18
2-8: 5-Isis new look. 7-Origin	2	3	4	6	8	10

ISLAND AT THE TOP OF THE WORLD (See Walt Disney Showcase #27)

ISLAND OF DR. MOREAU, THE (Movie)
Marvel Comics Group: Oct, 1977 (52 pgs.)

1-Gil Kane-c	1	2	3	5	6	8

I SPY (TV)
Gold Key: Aug, 1966 - No. 6, Sept, 1968 (All have photo-c)

1-Bill Cosby, Robert Culp photo covers	11	22	33	73	142	210
2-6: 3,4-McWilliams-a. 5-Last 12¢-c	7	14	21	44	72	100

IT! (See Astonishing Tales No. 21-24 & Supernatural Thrillers No. 1)

ITCHY & SCRATCHY COMICS (The Simpsons TV show)
Bongo Comics: 1993 - No. 3, 1993 ($1.95)

1-3: 1-Bound-in jumbo poster. 3-w/decoder screen trading card						4.00
Holiday Special ('94, $1.95)						4.00

IT GIRL (Also see Atomics, and Madman Comics)
Oni Press: May, 2002 ($2.95, one-shot)

1-Allred-s/Clugston-Major-c/a; Atomics and Madman app.						3.00

IT REALLY HAPPENED
William H. Wise No. 1,2/Standard (Visual Editions): 1944 - No. 11, Oct, 1947

1-Kit Carson & Ben Franklin stories	24	48	72	140	230	320
2,3-Nazi WWII-c	14	28	42	82	121	160
4,6,9,11: 4-D-Day story. 6-Ernie Pyle WWII-c; Joan of Arc story. 9-Captain Kidd & Frank Buck stories	13	26	39	72	101	130
5-Lou Gehrig & Lewis Carroll stories	18	36	54	103	162	220
7-Teddy Roosevelt story	14	28	42	81	118	155
8-Story of Roy Rogers	17	34	51	98	154	210
10-Honus Wagner & Mark Twain stories	15	30	45	86	133	180

NOTE: ***Guardineer** a-7(2), 8(2), 10, 11. **Schomburg** c-1-7, 9-11.*

IT RHYMES WITH LUST (Also see Bold Stories & Candid Tales)
St. John Publishing Co.: 1950 (Digest size, 128 pgs., 25¢)

nn (Rare)-Matt Baker & Ray Osrin-a	142	284	426	909	1555	2200

IT'S A BIRD...
DC Comics: 2004 ($24.95, hardcover with dust jacket)

HC-Semi-autobiographical story of Steven Seagle writing Superman; Kristiansen-a						25.00
SC-($17.95)						18.00

IT'S ABOUT TIME (TV)
Gold Key: Jan, 1967

1 (10195-701)-Photo-c	4	8	12	28	44	60

IT'S A DUCK'S LIFE
Marvel Comics/Atlas(MMC): Feb, 1950 - No. 11, Feb, 1952

1-Buck Duck, Super Rabbit begin	15	30	45	90	140	190
2	10	20	30	56	76	95
3-11	9	18	27	52	69	85

IT'S GAMETIME
National Periodical Publications: Sept-Oct, 1955 - No. 4, Mar-Apr, 1956

1-(Scarce)-Infinity-c; Davy Crockett app. in puzzle	87	174	261	553	952	1350
2,3 (Scarce): 2-Dodo & The Frog	63	126	189	403	689	975
4 (Rare)	66	132	198	419	722	1025

IT'S LOVE, LOVE, LOVE
St. John Publishing Co.: Nov, 1957 - No. 2, Jan, 1958 (10¢)

1,2	7	14	21	35	43	50

IT! THE TERROR FROM BEYOND SPACE
IDW Publishing: Jul, 2010 - No. 3, Sept, 2010 ($3.99, limited series)

1-3-Naraghi-s/Dos Santos-a/Mannion-c						4.00

I, VAMPIRE (DC New 52)
DC Comics: Nov, 2011 - Present ($2.99)

1-7: 1-Fialkov-s/Sorrentino-a/Frison-c. 4-Constantine app. 5-7-Batman app. 7-Crossover with Justice League Dark #7,8						3.00

IVANHOE (See Fawcett Movie Comics No. 20)

IVANHOE

I, Zombie #3 © Monkeybrain & Mike Allred

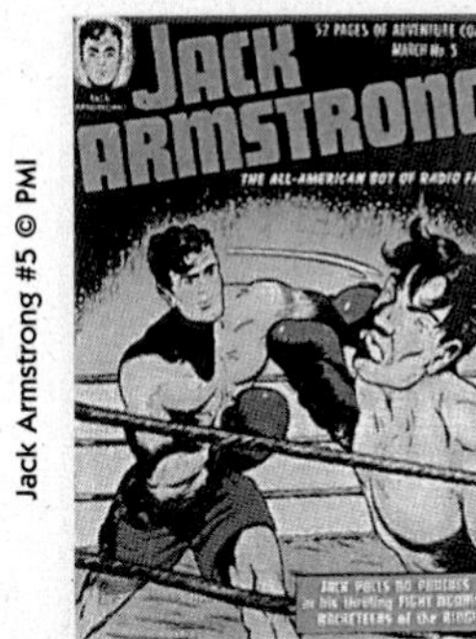

Jack Armstrong #5 © PMI

Jackie Robinson #2 © FAW

	GD 2.0	VG 4.0	FN 6.0	VF 8.0	VF/NM 9.0	NM- 9.2

Dell Publishing Co.: July-Sept, 1963

	GD	VG	FN	VF	VF/NM	NM-
1 (12-372-309)	3	6	9	21	32	42

IWO JIMA (See Spectacular Features Magazine)

I, ZOMBIE (Also see House of Mystery Halloween Annual #1)
DC Comics (Vertigo): July, 2010 - Present ($1.00/$2.99)

1-($1.00) Allred-a/Roberson-s; 2 covers by Allred & Cooke 3.00
2-24-($2.99) Allred-c/a in most. 12-Gilbert Hernandez-a. 18-Jay Stephens-a. 25-Rugg-a 3.00
...: Dead to the World TPB (2011, $14.99) r/#1-5 & House of Mystery Hall. Ann. #1 15.00

JACE PEARSON OF THE TEXAS RANGERS (Radio/TV)(4-Color #396 is titled Tales of the Texas Rangers; ...'s Tales of ... #11-on)(See Western Roundup under Dell Giants)
Dell Publishing Co.: No. 396, 5/52 - No. 1021, 8-10/59 (No #10) (All-Photo-c)

	GD	VG	FN	VF	VF/NM	NM-
Four Color 396 (#1)	10	20	30	68	127	185
2(5-7/53) - 9(2-4/55)	7	14	21	46	76	105
Four Color 648(#10, 9/55)	6	12	18	41	66	90
11(11-2/55-56) - 14,17-20(6-8/58)	6	12	18	37	59	80
15,16-Toth-a	6	12	18	39	62	85
Four Color 961,1021: 961-Spiegle-a	6	12	18	37	59	80

NOTE: *Joel McCrea photo c-1-9, F.C. 648 (starred on radio show only); Willard Parker photo c-11-on (starred on TV series).*

JACK ARMSTRONG (Radio)(See True Comics)
Parents' Institute: Nov, 1947 - No. 9, Sept, 1948; No. 10, Mar, 1949 - No. 13, Sept, 1949

nn (6/47) Ashcan edition; full color slick cover (a FN/VF sold for $485 in 2011)

	GD	VG	FN	VF	VF/NM	NM-
1-(Scarce) (odd size) Cast intro. inside front-c; Vic Hardy's Crime Lab begins	43	86	129	271	461	650
2	20	40	60	114	182	250
3-5	15	30	45	83	124	165
6-13	13	26	39	72	101	130

JACK CROSS
DC Comics: Oct, 2005 - No. 4, Jan, 2006 ($2.50)

1-4-Warren Ellis-s/Gary Erskine-a 3.00
DC Comics Presents: Jack Cross #1 (12/10, $7.99, squarebound) r/#1-4 8.00

JACK HUNTER
Blackthorne Publishing: July, 1987 - No. 3 ($1.25)

1-3 3.00

JACKIE CHAN'S SPARTAN X
Topps Comics: May, 1997 - No. 3 ($2.95, limited series)

1-3-Michael Golden-s/a; variant photo-c 3.00

JACKIE CHAN'S SPARTAN X: HELL BENT HERO FOR HIRE
Image Comics (Little Eva Ink): Mar, 1998 - No. 3 ($2.95, B&W)

1-3-Michael Golden-s/a: 1-variant photo-c 3.00

JACKIE GLEASON (TV) (Also see The Honeymooners)
St. John Publishing Co.: Sept, 1955 - No. 4, Dec, 1955?

	GD	VG	FN	VF	VF/NM	NM-
1(1955)(TV)-Photo-c	62	124	186	394	680	965
2-4	42	84	126	265	445	625

JACKIE GLEASON AND THE HONEYMOONERS (TV)
National Periodical Publications: June-July, 1956 - No. 12, Apr-May, 1958

	GD	VG	FN	VF	VF/NM	NM-
1-1st app. Ralph Kramden	90	180	270	576	988	1400
2	53	106	159	334	567	800
3-11: 8-Statue of Liberty-c	42	84	126	265	445	625
12 (Scarce)	60	120	180	380	653	925

JACKIE JOKERS (Became Richie Rich &...)
Harvey Publications: March, 1973 - No. 4, Sept, 1973 (#5 was advertised, but not published)

	GD	VG	FN	VF	VF/NM	NM-
1-1st app.	3	6	9	16	22	28
2-4: 2-President Nixon app.	2	4	6	8	11	14

JACKIE ROBINSON (Famous Plays of...) (Also see Negro Heroes #2 & Picture News #4)
Fawcett Publications: May, 1950 - No. 6, 1952 (Baseball hero) (All photo-c)

	GD	VG	FN	VF	VF/NM	NM-
nn	97	194	291	621	1061	1500
2	55	110	165	352	601	850
3-6	47	94	141	296	498	700

JACK IN THE BOX (Formerly Yellowjacket Comics #1-10; becomes Cowboy Western Comics #17 on)
Frank Comunale/Charlton Comics No. 11 on: Feb, 1946; No. 11, Oct, 1946 - No. 16, Nov-Dec, 1947

	GD	VG	FN	VF	VF/NM	NM-
1-Stitches, Marty Mouse & Nutsy McKrow	20	40	60	114	182	250
11-Yellowjacket (early Charlton comic)	22	44	66	132	216	300
12,14,15	14	28	42	80	115	150
13-Wolverton-a	21	42	63	126	206	285
16-12 pg. adapt. of Silas Marner; Kiefer-a	15	30	45	83	124	165

JACK KIRBY OMNIBUS, THE
DC Comics: 2011 ($49.99, hardcover with dustjacket)

Vol. 1 ('11) Recolored reprints of Kirby's DC work from 1946, 1957-1959; Evanier intro 50.00

JACK KIRBY'S FOURTH WORLD (See Mister Miracle & New Gods, 3rd Series)
DC Comics: Mar, 1997 - No. 20, Oct, 1998 ($1.95/$2.25)

1-20: 1-Byrne-a/scripts & Simonson-c begin; story cont'd from New Gods, 3rd Series #15; retells "The Pact" (New Gods, 1st Series #7); 1st brief DC app. Thor. 2-Thor vs. Big Barda; "Apokolips Then" back-up begins; Kirby-c/swipe (Thor #126) 8-Genesis x-over. 10-Simonson-s/a 13-Simonson back-up story. 20-Superman-c/app. 3.00

JACK KIRBY'S FOURTH WORLD OMNIBUS
DC Comics: 2007 - Vol. 4, 2008 ($49.99, hardcovers with dustjackets)

Vol. 1 ('07) Recolored reprints in chronological order of Superman's Pal, Jimmy Olsen #133-139, Forever People #1-3, New Gods #1-3, and Mister Miracle #1-3; Morrison intro, bonus art 50.00
Vol. 2 ('07) r/Jimmy Olsen #141-145, F.P. #4-6, N.G. #4-6 & M.M. #4-6; bonus art 50.00
Vol. 3 ('07) r/Jimmy Olsen #146-148, F.P. #7-10, N.G. #7-10 & M.M. #7-9; bonus art 50.00
Vol. 4 ('08) r/F.P. #11, M.M. #10-18, N.G. #11 & reprint series #6, & DC Graphic Novel #6 (The Hunger Dogs); Levitz intro.; Evanier afterword; character profile pages 50.00

JACK KIRBY'S GALACTIC BOUNTY HUNTERS
Marvel Comics (Icon): July, 2006 - No. 6, Nov, 2007 ($3.99)

1-6-Based on a Kirby concept; Mike Thibodeaux-a; Lisa Kirby, Thibodeaux and others-s 4.00
HC (2007, $24.99) r/series; pin-ups and supplemental art and interviews 25.00

JACK KIRBY'S SECRET CITY SAGA
Topps Comics (Kirbyverse): No. 0, Apr, 1993; No. 1, May, 1993 - No. 4, Aug, 1993 ($2.95, limited series)

0-(No cover price, 20 pgs.)-Simonson-c/a 3.00
0-Red embossed-c (limited ed.) 5.00
1-4-Bagged w/3 trading cards; Ditko-c/a: 1-Ditko/Art Adams-c. 2-Ditko/Byrne-c; has coupon for Pres. Clinton holo-foil trading card. 3-Dorman poster; has coupon for Gore holo-foil trading card. 4-Ditko/Perez-c 3.00

NOTE: *Issues #1-4 contain coupons redeemable for Kirbychrome version of #1*

JACK KIRBY'S SILVER STAR (Also see Silver Star)
Topps Comics (Kirbyverse): Oct, 1993 ($2.95)(Intended as a 4-issue limited series)

1-Silver ink-c; Austin-c/a(i); polybagged w/3 cards 3.00

JACK KIRBY'S TEENAGENTS (See Satan's Six)
Topps Comics (Kirbyverse): Aug, 1993 - No. 4, Nov, 1993 ($2.95, limited series)

1-4: Bagged with/3 trading cards; Busiek-s/Austin-c(i): 3-Liberty Project app. 3.00

JACK OF FABLES (See Fables)
DC Comics (Vertigo): Sept, 2006 - No. 50, Apr, 2011 ($2.99)

1-49: 1-Willingham & Sturges-s/Akins-a. 33-35-Crossover with Fables and The Literals 3.00
50-($4.99) Akins & Braun-a; Bolland-c 5.00
1-Special Edition (8/10, $1.00) r/#1 with "What's Next?" logo on cover 3.00
...: Americana TPB (2008, $14.99) r/#17-21 15.00
...: Jack of Hearts TPB (2007, $14.99) r/#6-11 15.00
...: The Bad Prince TPB (2008, $14.99) r/#12-16 15.00
...: The Big Book of War TPB (2009, $14.99) r/#28-32 15.00
...: The End TPB (2011, $17.99) r/#46-50 18.00
...: The Fulminate Blade TPB (2011, $14.99) r/#41-45 15.00
...: The (Nearly) Great Escape TPB (2007, $14.99) r/#1-5; Akins sketch pages 15.00
...: The New Adventures of Jack and Jack TPB (2010, $14.99) r/#36-40 15.00
...: Turning Pages TPB (2009, $14.99) r/#22-27 15.00

JACK OF HEARTS (Also see The Deadly Hands of Kung Fu #22 & Marvel Premiere #44)
Marvel Comics Group: Jan, 1984 - No. 4, Apr, 1984 (60¢, limited series)

1-4 3.00

JACKPOT COMICS (Jolly Jingles #10 on)
MLJ Magazines: Spring, 1941 - No. 9, Spring, 1943

	GD	VG	FN	VF	VF/NM	NM-
1-The Black Hood, Mr. Justice, Steel Sterling & Sgt. Boyle begin; Biro-c	326	652	978	2282	3991	5700
2-S. Cooper-c	148	296	444	947	1624	2300
3-Hubbell-c	110	220	330	704	1202	1700
4-Archie begins (Win/41; on sale 12/41)-(also see Pep Comics #22); 1st app. Mrs. Grundy, the principal; Novick-c	486	972	1458	3550	6275	9000
5-Hitler, Tojo, Mussolini-c by Montana; 1st definitive Mr. Weatherbee; 1st brief app. Reggie in 1 panel	206	412	618	1318	2259	3200
6-9: 6,7-Bondage-c by Novick. 8,9-Sahle-c	116	232	348	742	1271	1800

JACK Q FROST (See Unearthly Spectaculars)

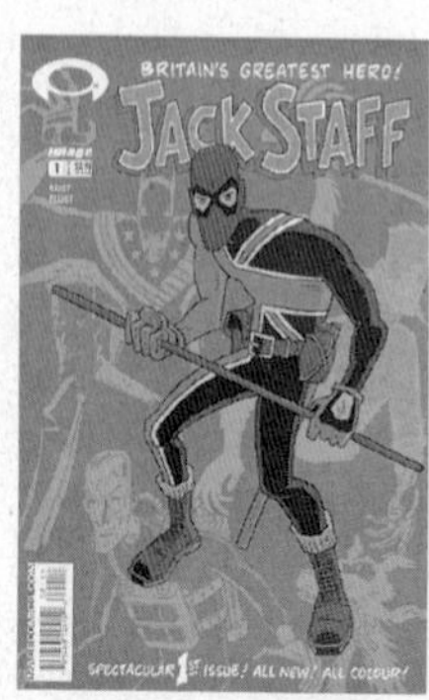

Jack Staff V2 #1 © Paul Grist

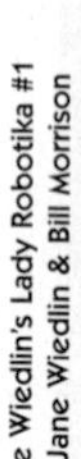
Jane Wiedlin's Lady Robotika #1 © Jane Wiedlin & Bill Morrison

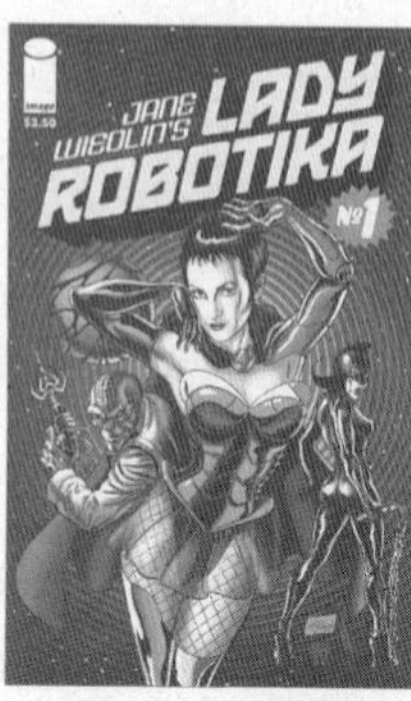

Jay & Silent Bob #3 © View Askew

GD VG FN VF VF/NM NM-
2.0 4.0 6.0 8.0 9.0 9.2

JACK STAFF (Vol. 2; previously published in Britain)
Image Comics: Feb, 2003 - No. 20, May, 2009 ($2.95/$3.50)
1-5-Paul Grist-s/a 3.50
6-20-($3.50) 6-Flashback to the WW2 Freedom Fighters 3.50
... Special 1 (1/08, $3.50) Molachi the Immortal app. 3.50
The Weird World of Jack Staff King Size Special 1 (7/07, $5.99, B&W) r/story serialized in Comics International magazine; afterword by Grist 6.00
Vol. 1: Everything Used to Be Black and White TPB (12/03, $19.95) r/British issues 20.00
Vol. 2: Soldiers TPB (2005, $15.95) r/#1-5; cover gallery 16.00
Vol. 3: Echoes of Tomorrow TPB (2006, $16.99) r/#6-12; cover gallery 17.00

JACK THE GIANT KILLER (See Movie Classics)

JACK THE GIANT KILLER (New Adventures of...)
Bimfort & Co.: Aug-Sept, 1953
V1#1-H. C. Kiefer-c/a 25 50 75 150 245 340

JACKY'S DIARY
Dell Publishing Co.: No. 1091, Apr-June, 1960 (one-shot)
Four Color 1091 5 10 15 30 48 65

JADEMAN COLLECTION
Jademan Comics: Dec, 1989 - No. 3, 1990 ($2.50, plastic coated-c, 68 pgs.)
1-3: 1-Wraparound-c w/fold-out poster 4.00

JADEMAN KUNG FU SPECIAL
Jademan Comics: 1988 ($1.50, 64 pgs.)
1 4.00

JADE WARRIORS (Mike Deodato's...)
Image Comics (Glass House Graphics): Nov, 1999 - No. 3, 2000 ($2.50)
1-3-Deodato-a 3.00
1-Variant-c 3.00

JAGUAR, THE (Also see The Adventures of...)
Impact Comics (DC): Aug, 1991 - No. 14, Oct, 1992 ($1.00)
1-14: 4-The Black Hood x-over. 7-Sienkiewicz-c. 9-Contains Crusaders trading card 3.00
Annual 1 (1992, $2.50, 68 pgs.)-With trading card 4.00

JAGUAR GOD
Verotik: Mar, 1995 - No. 7, June, 1997 ($2.95, mature)
0 (2/96, $3.50)-Embossed Frazetta-c; Bisley-a; w/pin-ups. 5.00
1-Frazetta-c. 5.00
2-7: 2-Frazetta-c. 3-Bisley-c. 4-Emond-c. 7-($2.95)-Frazetta-c 4.00

JAKE THRASH
Aircel Publishing: 1988 - No. 3, 1988 ($2.00)
1-3 3.00

JAM, THE (...Urban Adventure)
Slave Labor Nos. 1-5/Dark Horse Comics Nos. 6-8/Caliber Comics No. 9 on: Nov, 1989 - No. 14, 1997 ($1.95/$2.50/$2.95, B&W)
1-14: Bernie Mireault-c/a/scripts. 6-1st Dark Horse issue. 9-1st Caliber issue 3.00

JAMBOREE COMICS
Round Publishing Co.: Feb, 1946(no month given) - No. 3, Apr, 1946
1-Funny animal 21 42 63 122 199 275
2,3 15 30 45 85 130 175

JAMES BOND 007: A SILENT ARMAGEDDON
Dark Horse Comics/Acme Press: Mar, 1993 - Apr 1993 (limited series)
1,2 3.50

JAMES BOND 007: GOLDENEYE (Movie)
Topps Comics: Jan, 1996 ($2.95, unfinished limited series of 3)
1-Movie adaptation; Stelfreeze-c 3.00

JAMES BOND 007: SERPENT'S TOOTH
Dark Horse Comics/Acme Press: July 1992 - Aug 1992 ($4.95, limited series)
1-3-Paul Gulacy-c/a 5.00

JAMES BOND 007: SHATTERED HELIX
Dark Horse Comics: Jun 1994 - July 1994 ($2.50, limited series)
1,2 3.00

JAMES BOND 007: THE QUASIMODO GAMBIT
Dark Horse Comics: Jan 1995 - May 1995 ($3.95, limited series)
1-3 4.50

GD VG FN VF VF/NM NM-
2.0 4.0 6.0 8.0 9.0 9.2

JAMES BOND FOR YOUR EYES ONLY
Marvel Comics Group: Oct, 1981 - No. 2, Nov, 1981
1,2-Movie adapt.; r/Marvel Super Special #19 4.00

JAMES BOND JR. (TV)
Marvel Comics: Jan, 1992 - No. 12, Dec, 1992 (#1: $1.00, #2-on: $1.25)
1-12: Based on animated TV show 3.00

JAMES BOND: LICENCE TO KILL (See Licence To Kill)

JAMES BOND: PERMISSION TO DIE
Eclipse Comics/ACME Press: 1989 - No. 3, 1991 ($3.95, lim. series, squarebound, 52 pgs.)
1-3: Mike Grell-c/a/scripts in all. 3-($4.95) 5.00

JAM, THE: SUPER COOL COLOR INJECTED TURBO ADVENTURE #1 FROM HELL!
Comico: May, 1988 ($2.50, 44 pgs., one-shot)
1 4.00

JANE ARDEN (See Feature Funnies & Pageant of Comics)
St. John (United Features Syndicate): Mar, 1948 - No. 2, June, 1948
1-Newspaper reprints 15 30 45 88 137 185
2 12 24 36 67 94 120

JANE WIEDLIN'S LADY ROBOTIKA
Image Comics: Jul, 2010 - No. 2, Aug, 2010 ($3.50, unfinished limited series)
1,2-Wiedlin & Bill Morrison-s. 1-Morrison & Rodriguez-a. 2-Moy-a 3.50

JANN OF THE JUNGLE (Jungle Tales No. 1-7)
Atlas Comics (CSI): No. 8, Nov, 1955 - No. 17, June, 1957
8(#1) 37 74 111 222 361 500
9,11-15 21 42 63 122 199 275
10-Williamson/Colletta-c 21 42 63 124 202 280
16,17-Williamson/Mayo-a(3), 5 pgs. each 22 44 66 128 209 290
NOTE: *Everett c-15-17. Heck a-8, 15, 17. Maneely c-11. Shores a-8.*

JASON & THE ARGOBOTS
Oni Press: Aug, 2002 - No. 4, Dec, 2002 ($2.95, B&W, limited series)
1-4-Torres-s/Norton-c/a 3.00
Vol. 1 Birthquake TPB (6/03, $11.95, digest size) r/#1-4, Sunday comic strips 12.00
Vol. 2 Machina Ex Deus TPB (9/03, $11.95, digest size) new story 12.00

JASON & THE ARGONAUTS (See Movie Classics)

JASON GOES TO HELL: THE FINAL FRIDAY (Movie)
Topps Comics: July, 1993 - No. 3, Sept, 1993 ($2.95, limited series)
1-3: Adaptation of film. 1-Glow-in-the-dark-c 3.00

JASON'S QUEST (See Showcase #88-90)

JASON VS. LEATHERFACE
Topps Comics: Oct, 1995 - No. 3, Jan, 1996 ($2.95, limited series)
1-3: Collins scripts; Bisley-c 5.00

JAWS 2 (See Marvel Comics Super Special, A)

JAY & SILENT BOB (See Clerks, Oni Double Feature, and Tales From the Clerks)
Oni Press: July, 1998 - No. 4, Oct, 1999 ($2.95, B&W, limited series)
1-Kevin Smith-s/Fegredo-a; photo-c & Quesada/Palmiotti-c 8.00
1-San Diego Comic Con variant covers (2 different covers, came packaged with action figures) 10.00
1-2nd & 3rd printings, 2-4: 2-Allred-c. 3-Flip-c by Jaime Hernandez 3.00
Chasing Dogma TPB (1999, $11.95) r/#1-4; Alanis Morissette intro. 12.00
Chasing Dogma TPB (2001, $12.95) r/#1-4 in color; Morissette intro. 13.00
Chasing Dogma HC (1999, $69.95, S&N) r/#1-4 in color; Morissette intro. 70.00

JCP FEATURES
J.C. Productions (Archie): Feb, 1982-c; Dec, 1981-indicia ($2.00, one-shot, B&W magazine)
1-T.H.U.N.D.E.R. Agents; Black Hood by Morrow & Neal Adams; Texeira-a; 2 pgs. S&K-a from Fly #1 2 4 6 8 10 12

JEANIE COMICS (Formerly All Surprise; Cowgirl Romances #28)
Marvel Comics/Atlas(CPC): No. 13, April, 1947 - No. 27, Oct, 1949
13-Mitzi, Willie begin 22 44 66 132 216 300
14,15 15 30 45 90 140 190
16-Used in Love and Death by Legman; Kurtzman's "Hey Look" 19 38 57 109 172 235
17-19,21,22-Kurtzman's "Hey Look" (1-3 pgs. each) 14 28 42 82 121 160
20,23-27 14 28 42 78 112 145

JEEP COMICS (Also see G.I. Comics and Overseas Comics)
R. B. Leffingwell & Co.: Winter, 1944, No. 2, Spring, 1945 - No. 3, Mar-Apr, 1948

Jennifer Blood #2 © Spitfire & DE

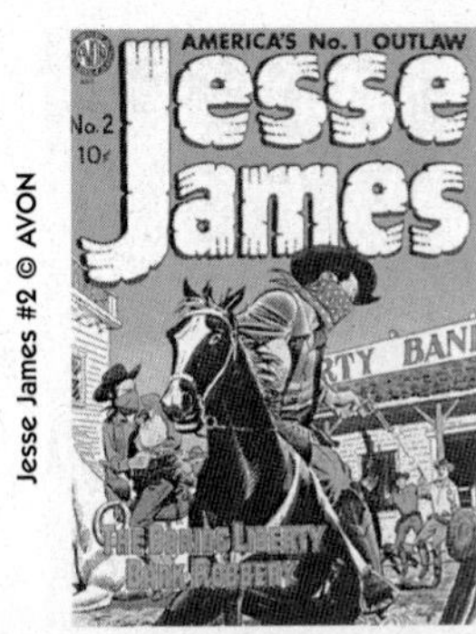

Jesse James #2 © AVON

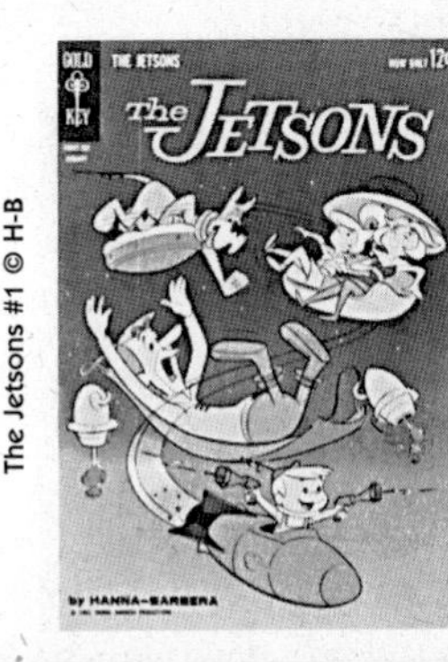

The Jetsons #1 © H-B

GD 2.0 | VG 4.0 | FN 6.0 | VF 8.0 | VF/NM 9.0 | NM- 9.2

1-Capt. Power, Criss Cross & Jeep & Peep (costumed) begin
65 130 195 416 708 1000
2- Jeep & Peep-c 41 82 123 256 428 600
3-L. B. Cole dinosaur-c 52 104 156 322 549 775

JEFF JORDAN, U.S. AGENT
D. S. Publishing Co.: Dec, 1947 - Jan, 1948
1 15 30 45 88 137 185

JEMM, SON OF SATURN
DC Comics: Sept, 1984 - No. 12, Aug, 1985 (Maxi-series, mando paper)
1-12: 3-Origin 3.00
NOTE: *Colan a-1-12p; c-1-5, 7-12p.*

JENNIFER BLOOD
Dynamite Entertainment: 2011 - Present ($3.99)
1-11: 1-3-Garth Ennis-s/Adriano Batista-a; four covers on each. 4-The Ninjettes app. 4.00

JENNIFER'S BODY (Based on the 2009 movie)
BOOM! Studios: Aug, 2009 ($24.99, hardcover graphic novel)
HC-Short stories of Jennifer and her victims; Spears-s/art by various; pin-up art 25.00

JENNY FINN
Oni Press: June, 1999 - No. 2, Sept, 1999 ($2.95, B&W, unfinished lim. series)
1,2-Mignola & Nixey-s/Nixey-a/Mignola-c 3.00
...: Doom (Atomeka, 2005, $6.99, TPB) r/#1 & 2 with new supplemental material 7.00

JENNY SPARKS: THE SECRET HISTORY OF THE AUTHORITY
DC Comics (WildStorm): Aug, 2000 - No. 5, Mar, 2001 ($2.50, limited series)
1-Millar-s/McCrea & Hodgkins-a/Hitch & Neary-c 3.50
1-Variant-c by McCrea 1 3 4 6 8 10
2-5: 2-Apollo & Midnighter. 3-Jack Hawksmoor. 4-Shen. 5-Engineer 3.00
TPB (2001, $14.95) r/#1-5; Ellis intro. 15.00

JERICHO (Based on the TV series)
Devil's Due Publishing/IDW Publishing: Oct, 2009 - Present ($3.99)
... Redux (IDW, 2/11, $7.99) r/Season 3: Civil War #1-3 8.00
... Season 3: Civil War 1-4: 1-Story by the show's writing staff 4.00

JERRY DRUMMER (Formerly Soldier & Marine V2#9)
Charlton Comics: V2#10, Apr, 1957 - V3#12, Oct, 1957
V2#10, V3#11,12: 11-Whitman-c/a 6 12 18 29 36 42

JERRY IGER'S... (All titles, Blackthorne/First)(Value: cover or less)

JERRY LEWIS (See The Adventures of...)

JERSEY GODS
Image Comics: Feb, 2009 - No. 12, May, 2010 ($3.50)
1-11: 1-Brunswick-s/McDaid-a; two covers by McDaid and Allred 3.50
12-($4.99) Wraparound cover swipe of Superman #252 by Allred 5.00

JESSE JAMES (The True Story Of..., also seeThe Legend of...)
Dell Publishing Co.: No. 757, Dec, 1956 (one shot)
Four Color 757-Movie, photo-c 8 16 24 56 96 135

JESSE JAMES (See Badmen of the West & Blazing Sixguns)
Avon Periodicals: 8/50 - No. 9, 11/52; No. 15, 10/53 - No. 29, 8-9/56
1-Kubert Alabam-r/Cowpuncher #1 17 34 51 98 154 210
2-Kubert-a(3) 14 28 42 80 115 150
3-Kubert Alabam-r/Cowpuncher #2 14 28 42 76 108 140
4,9-No Kubert 8 16 24 44 57 70
5,6-Kubert Jesse James-a(3); 5-Wood-a(1pg.) 14 28 42 76 108 140
7-Kubert Jesse James-a(2) 12 24 36 67 94 120
8-Kinstler-a(3) 9 18 27 50 65 80
15-Kinstler-r/#3 8 16 24 40 50 60
16-Kinstler-r/#3 & story-r/Butch Cassidy #1 8 16 24 42 54 65
17-19,21: 17-Jesse James-r/#4; Kinstler-c idea from Kubert splash in #6. 18-Kubert Jesse James-r/#5. 19-Kubert Jesse James-r/#6. 21-Two Jesse James-r/#4, Kinstler-r/#4
7 14 21 37 46 55
20-Williamson/Frazetta-a; r/Chief Vic. Apache Massacre; Kubert Jesse James-r/#6; Kit West story by Larsen 14 28 42 80 115 150
22-29: 22,23-No Kubert. 24-New McCarty strip by Kinstler; Kinstler-r. 25-New McCarty Jesse James strip by Kinstler; Jesse James-r/#7,9. 26,27-New McCarty Jesse James strip plus a Kinstler/McCann Jesse James-r. 28-Reprints most of Red Mountain, Featuring Quantrells Raiders 7 14 21 37 46 55
Annual nn (1952; 25¢, 100 pgs.)- "...Brings Six-Gun Justice to the West"- 3 earlier issues rebound; Kubert, Kinstler-a(3) 29 58 87 170 278 385
NOTE: *Mostly reprints #10 on.* ***Fawcette*** *c-1, 2.* ***Kida*** *a-5.* ***Kinstler*** *a-3, 4, 7-9, 15r, 16r(2), 21-27; c-3, 4, 9, 17-27. Painted c-5-8. 22 has 2 stories r/Sheriff Bob Dixon's Chuck Wagon #1 with name changed to Sheriff Bob Trent.*

JESSE JAMES
Realistic Publications: July, 1953
nn-Reprints Avon's #1; same-c, colors different 9 18 27 52 69 85

JEST (Formerly Snap; becomes Kayo #12)
Harry 'A' Chesler: No. 10, 1944; No. 11, 1944
10-Johnny Rebel & Yankee Boy app. in text 18 36 54 103 162 220
11-Little Nemo in Adventure Land 18 36 54 103 162 220

JESTER
Harry 'A' Chesler: No. 10, 1945
10 15 30 45 90 140 190

JESUS
Spire Christian Comics (Fleming H. Revell Co.): 1979 (49¢)
nn 2 4 6 10 14 18

JET (See Jet Powers)

JET (Crimson from Wildcore & Backlash)
DC Comics (WildStorm): Nov, 2000 - No. 4, Feb, 2001 ($2.50, limited series)
1-4-Nguyen-a/Abnett & Lanning-s 3.00

JET ACES
Fiction House Magazines: 1952 - No. 4, 1953
1- Sky Advs. of American War Aces (on sale 6/20/52)
17 34 51 98 154 210
2-4 11 22 33 62 86 110

JETCAT CLUBHOUSE (Also see Land of Nod, The)
Oni Press: Apr, 2001 - No. 3, Aug, 2001 ($3.25)
1-3-Jay Stephens-s/a. 1-Wraparound-c 3.25
TPB (8/02, $10.95, 8 3/4" x 5 3/4") r/#1-3 & stories from Nickelodeon mag. & other 11.00

JET DREAM (...and Her Stunt-Girl Counterspies)(See The Man from Uncle #7)
Gold Key: June, 1968 (12¢)
1-Painted-c 4 8 12 22 34 45

JET FIGHTERS (Korean War)
Standard Magazines: No. 5, Nov, 1952 - No. 7, Mar, 1953
5,7-Toth-a. 5-Toth-c 13 26 39 74 105 135
6-Celardo-a 9 18 27 47 61 75

JET POWER
I.W. Enterprises: 1963
I.W. Reprint 1,2-r/Jet Powers #1,2 3 6 9 17 25 32

JET POWERS (American Air Forces No. 5 on)
Magazine Enterprises: 1950 - No. 4, 1951
1(A-1 #30)-Powell-c/a begins 38 76 114 226 368 510
2(A-1 #32) Classic Powell dinosaur-c/a 38 76 114 226 368 510
3(A-1 #35)-Williamson/Evans-a 40 80 120 244 407 570
4(A-1 #38)-Williamson/Wood-a; "The Rain of Sleep" drug story
40 80 120 244 407 570

JET PUP (See 3-D Features)

JETSONS, THE (TV) (See March of Comics #276, 330, 348 & Spotlight #3)
Gold Key: Jan, 1963 - No. 36, Oct, 1970 (Hanna-Barbera)
1-1st comic book app. 20 40 60 137 294 450
2 11 22 33 73 142 210
3-10 9 18 27 58 99 140
11-22 7 14 21 46 76 105
23-36-Reprints 4 8 12 28 44 60

JETSONS, THE (TV) (Also see Golden Comics Digest)
Charlton Comics: Nov, 1970 - No. 20, Dec, 1973 (Hanna-Barbera)
1 8 16 24 55 93 130
2 5 10 15 30 48 65
3-10: Flintstones x-over 3 6 9 21 32 42
11-20 3 6 9 17 25 32
nn (1973, digest, 60¢, 100 pgs.) B&W one page gags 4 8 12 24 37 50

JETSONS, THE (TV)
Harvey Comics: V2#1, Sept, 1992 - No. 5, Nov, 1993 ($1.25/$1.50) (Hanna-Barbera)
V2#1-5 5.00
...Big Book V2#1,2,3 ($1.95, 52 pgs.): 1-(11/92). 2-(4/93). 3-(7/93) 5.00
...Giant Size 1,2,3 ($2.25, 68 pgs): 1-(10/92). 2-(4/93). 3-(10/93) 5.00

JETSONS, THE (TV)

Jetta of the 21st Century #6 © STD

Jim Dandy #1 © LEV

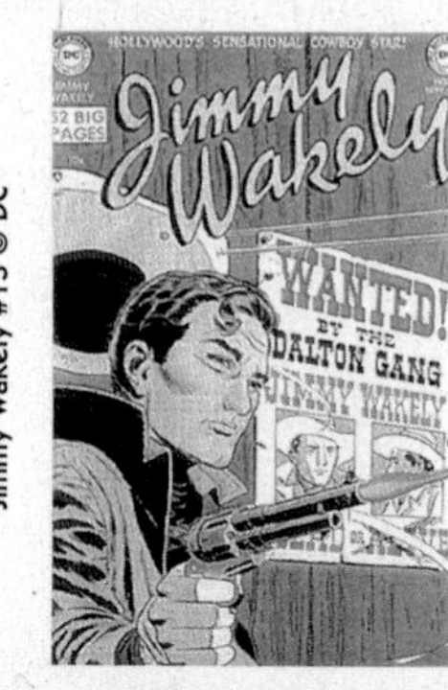

Jimmy Wakely #13 © DC

	GD 2.0	VG 4.0	FN 6.0	VF 8.0	VF/NM 9.0	NM- 9.2

Archie Comics: Sept, 1995 - No. 8, Apr, 1996 ($1.50)

1-8						3.00

JETTA OF THE 21ST CENTURY
Standard Comics: No. 5, Dec, 1952 - No. 7, Apr, 1953 (Teen-age Archie type)

5-Dan DeCarlo-a	23	46	69	136	223	310
6,7: 6-Robot-c	15	30	45	84	127	170
TPB (Airwave Publ., 2006, $9.99) B&W reprint of series; Bill Morrison intro./back-c						10.00

JEW GANGSTER
DC Comics: 2005 ($14.99, SC graphic novel)

SC-Joe Kubert-s/a						15.00

JEZEBEL JADE (Hanna-Barbara)
Comico: Oct, 1988 - No. 3, Dec, 1988 ($2.00, mini-series)

1-3: Johnny Quest spin-off						3.00

JEZEBELLE (See Wildstorm 2000 Annuals)
DC Comics (WildStorm): Mar, 2001 - No. 6, Aug, 2001 ($2.50, limited series)

1-6-Ben Raab-s/Steve Ellis-a						3.00

JIGGS & MAGGIE
Dell Publishing Co.: No. 18, 1941 (one shot)

Four Color 18 (#1)-(1936-38-r)	48	96	144	302	514	725

JIGGS & MAGGIE
Standard Comics/Harvey Publications No. 22 on: No. 11, 1949 (June) - No. 21, 2/53; No. 22, 4/53 - No. 27, 2-3/54

11	16	32	48	94	147	200
12-15,17-21	11	22	33	62	86	110
16-Wood text illos.	11	22	33	64	90	115
22-24-Little Dot app.	11	22	33	62	86	110
25,27	10	20	30	54	72	90
26-Four pgs. partially in 3-D	14	28	42	80	115	150

NOTE: *Sunday page reprints by McManus loosely blended into story continuity. Based on Bringing Up Father strip. Advertised on covers as "All New."*

JIGSAW (Big Hero Adventures)
Harvey Publ. (Funday Funnies): Sept, 1966 - No. 2, Dec, 1966 (36 pgs.)

1-Origin & 1st app.; Crandall-a (5 pgs.)	4	8	12	22	34	45
2-Man From S.R.A.M.	3	6	9	16	22	28

JIGSAW OF DOOM (See Complete Mystery No. 2)

JIM BOWIE (Formerly Danger?; Black Jack No. 20 on)
Charlton Comics: No. 16, Mar, 1956 - No. 19, Apr, 1957

16	8	16	24	42	54	65
17-19: 18-Giordano-c	6	12	18	29	36	42

JIM BOWIE (TV, see Western Tales)
Dell Publishing Co.: No. 893, Mar, 1958 - No. 993, May-July, 1959

Four Color 893 (#1)	6	12	18	39	62	85
Four Color 993-Photo-c	5	10	15	35	55	75

JIM BUTCHER'S THE DRESDEN FILES: FOOL MOON (Based on the Dresden Files novels)
Dynamite Entertainment: 2011 - Present ($3.99, limited series)

1-4: 1-Jim Butcher & Mark Powers-s/Chase Conley-a/Brett Booth-c						4.00

JIM BUTCHER'S THE DRESDEN FILES: STORM FRONT (Based on the Dresden Files novels)
Dabel Bros. Productions: Oct, 2008 (Nov. on-c) - No. 4, Apr, 2009 ($3.99, limited series)

1-4-Jim Butcher & Mark Powers-s/Ardian Syaf-a; covers by Syaf & Tsai						4.00
Vol. 2: 1,2 (7/09 - No. 4)						4.00

JIM BUTCHER'S THE DRESDEN FILES: WELCOME TO THE JUNGLE
Dabel Bros. Productions: Mar, 2008 (Apr. on-c) - No. 4, Jul, 2008 ($3.99, limited series)

1-Jim Butcher-s/Ardian Syaf-a; Ardian Syaf-c						5.00
1-Variant-c by Chris McGrath						8.00
1-New York Comic-Con 2008 variant-c						15.00
1-Second printing						4.00
2-4-Two covers on each						4.00
HC (2008, $19.95, dustjacket) r/#1-4; Butcher intro.; concept art pages						20.00

JIM DANDY
Dandy Magazine (Lev Gleason): May, 1956 - No. 3, Sept, 1956 (Charles Biro)

1-Jim Dandy adventures w/Cup, an alien & his flying saucer (both invisible) from the planet Zikalug begins; ends #3. Biro-c. 1,2-Bammy Boozle app.	9	18	27	52	69	85
2,3: 2-Two pg. actual flying saucer reports	7	14	21	35	43	50

JIM HARDY (See Giant Comics Eds., Sparkler & Treasury of Comics #2 & 5)
United Features Syndicate/Spotlight Publ.: 1939; 1942; 1947 - No. 2, 1947

Single Series 6 ('39)	41	82	123	256	428	600
Single Series 27('42)	36	72	108	211	343	475
1('47)-Spotlight Publ.	15	30	45	85	130	175
2	10	20	30	54	72	90

JIM HARDY
Spotlight/United Features Synd.: 1944 (25¢, 132 pgs.) (Tip Top, Sparkler-r)

nn-Origin Mirror Man; Triple Terror app.	40	80	120	231	378	525

JIMINY CRICKET (Disney,, see Mickey Mouse Mag. V5#3 & Walt Disney Showcase #37)
Dell Publishing Co.: No. 701, May, 1956 - No. 989, May-July, 1959

Four Color 701	8	16	24	55	93	130
Four Color 795, 897, 989	6	12	18	42	69	95

JIM LEE SKETCHBOOK
DC Comics (WildStorm): 2002 (no price, 16 pgs.)

nn-Various DC and WildStorm character sketches by Lee						3.00

JIMMY CORRIGAN (See Acme Novelty Library)

JIMMY DURANTE (Also see A-1 Comics)
Magazine Enterprises: No. 18, 1949 - No. 20, 1949

A-1 18,20-Photo-c (scarce)	48	96	144	302	514	725

JIMMY OLSEN (See Superman's Pal...)

JIMMY OLSEN
DC Comics: May, 2011 ($5.99, one-shot)

1-Reprints back-up feature from Action Comics #893-896 plus new material; Conner-c						6.00

JIMMY OLSEN: ADVENTURES BY JACK KIRBY
DC Comics: 2003, 2004 ($19.95, TPB)

nn-(2003) Reprints Jack Kirby's early issues of Superman's Pal Jimmy Olsen #133-139,141; Mark Evanier intro.; cover by Kirby and Steve Rude						20.00
Vol. 2 (2004) Reprints #142-148; Evanier intro.; cover gallery and sketch pages						20.00

JIMMY WAKELY (Cowboy movie star)
National Per. Publ.: Sept-Oct, 1949 - No. 18, July-Aug, 1952 (1-13: 52pgs.)

1-Photo-c, 52 pgs. begin; Alex Toth-a; Kit Colby Girl Sheriff begins	41	82	123	256	428	600
2-Toth-a	18	36	54	105	165	225
3,4,6,7-Frazetta-a in all, 3 pgs. each; Toth-a in all. 7-Last photo-c. 4-Kurtzman "Pot-Shot Pete", 1 pg; Toth-a	21	42	63	122	199	275
5,8-15-Toth-a; 12,14-Kubert-a (3 & 2 pgs.)	16	32	48	94	147	200
16-18	15	30	45	83	124	165

NOTE: ***Gil Kane** c-10-18p.*

JIM RAY'S AVIATION SKETCH BOOK
Vital Publishers: Mar-Apr, 1946 - No. 2, May-June, 1946 (15¢)

1-Picture stories of planes and pilots	39	78	117	231	378	525
2-Story of General "Nap" Arnold	25	50	75	147	241	335

JIM SOLAR (See Wisco/Klarer in the Promotional Comics section)

JINGLE BELLE (Paul Dini's...)
Oni Press/Top Cow: Nov, 1999 - No. 2, Dec, 1999 ($2.95, B&W, limited series)

1,2-Paul Dini-s. 2-Alex Ross flip-c						3.00
Jingle Belle: Dash Away All (12/03, $11.95, digest-size) Dini-s/Garibaldi-a						12.00
Jingle Belle: Gift-Wrapped (Top Cow, 12/11, $3.99) Dini-s/Gladden-a						4.00
Jingle Belle: Santa Claus vs. Frankenstein (Top Cow, 12/08, $2.99) Dini-s/Gladden-a						3.00
Jingle Belle's Cool Yule (11/02, $13.95,TPB) r/All-Star Holiday Hullabaloo, The Mighty Elves, and Jubilee; internet strips and a color section w/DeStefano-a						14.00
Paul Dini's Jingle Belle Jubilee (11/01, $2.95) Dini-s; art by Rolston, DeCarlo, Morrison and Bone; pin-ups by Thompson and Aragonés						3.00
Paul Dini's Jingle Belle's All-Star Holiday Hullabaloo (11/00, $4.95) stories by various including Dini, Aragonés, Jeff Smith, Bill Morrison; Frank Cho-c						5.00
Paul Dini's Jingle Belle: The Fight Before Christmas (12/05, $2.99) Dini-s/Bone & others-a						3.00
Paul Dini's Jingle Belle: The Mighty Elves (7/01, $2.95) Dini-s/Bone-a						3.00
Paul Dini's Jingle Belle Winter Wingding (11/02, $2.95) Dini-s/Clugston-Major-c						3.00
The Bakers Meet Jingle Belle (12/06, $2.99) Dini-s/Kyle Baker-a						3.00
TPB (10/00, $8.95) r/#1&2, and app. from Oni Double Feature #13						9.00

JINGLE BELLE (Paul Dini's...)
Dark Horse Comics: Nov, 2004 - No. 4, Apr, 2005 ($2.99, limited series)

1-4-Paul Dini-s/Jose Garibaldi-a						3.00
TPB (9/05, $12.95) r/#1-4						13.00

JINGLE BELLS (See March of Comics No. 65)

JINGLE DINGLE CHRISTMAS STOCKING COMICS (See Foodini #2)

Jinx #5 © Brian Michael Bendis

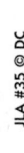

JLA #35 © DC

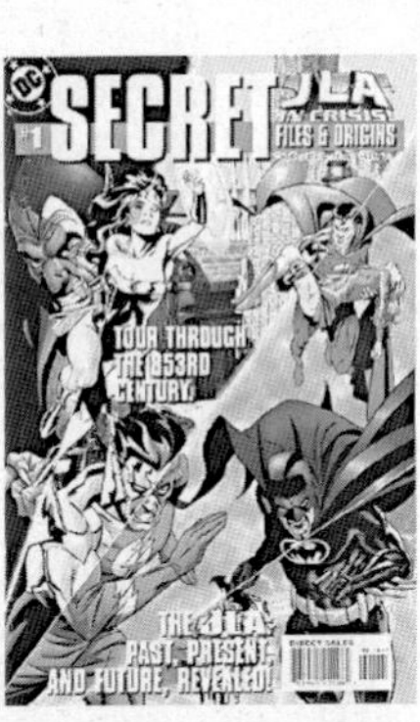

JLA in Crisis Secret Files #1 © DC

	GD 2.0	VG 4.0	FN 6.0	VF 8.0	VF/NM 9.0	NM- 9.2

Stanhall Publications: V2#1, 1951 (no date listed) (25¢, 100 pgs.; giant-size) (Publ. annually)

	GD	VG	FN	VF	VF/NM	NM-
V2#1-Foodini & Pinhead, Silly Pilly plus games & puzzles	20	40	60	118	192	265

JINGLE JANGLE COMICS (Also see Puzzle Fun Comics)
Eastern Color Printing Co.: Feb, 1942 - No. 42, Dec, 1949

	GD	VG	FN	VF	VF/NM	NM-
1-Pie-Face Prince of Old Pretzleburg, Jingle Jangle Tales by George Carlson, Hortense, & Benny Bear begin	44	88	132	277	469	660
2-4: 2,3-No Pie-Face Prince. 4-Pie-Face Prince-c	20	40	60	120	195	270
5 (10/42)	19	38	57	111	176	240
6-10: 8-No Pie-Face Prince	15	30	45	85	130	175
11-15	12	24	36	69	97	125
16-30: 17,18-No Pie-Face Prince. 24,30-XMas-c	10	20	30	56	76	95
31-42: 36,42-Xmas-c	9	18	27	52	69	85

*NOTE: **George Carlson** a-(2) in all except No. 2, 3, 8; c-1-6. **Carlson** 1 pg. puzzles in 9, 10, 12-15, 18, 20. **Carlson** illustrated a series of Uncle Wiggily books in 1930's.*

JING PALS
Victory Publishing Corp.: Feb, 1946 - No. 4, Aug?, 1946 (Funny animal)

	GD	VG	FN	VF	VF/NM	NM-
1-Wishing Willie, Puggy Panda & Johnny Rabbit begin	15	30	45	86	133	180
2-4	10	20	30	54	72	90

JINKS, PIXIE, AND DIXIE (See Kite Fun Book & Whitman Comic Books)

JINX
Caliber Press: 1996 - No. 7, 1996 ($2.95, B&W, 32 pgs.)

1-7: Brian Michael Bendis-c/a/scripts. 2-Photo-c 3.00

JINX (Volume 2)
Image Comics: 1997 - No. 5, 1998 ($2.95, B&W, bi-monthly)

1-4: Brian Michael Bendis-c/a/scripts. 3.00
5-($3.95) Brereton-c 4.00
...Buried Treasures ('98, $3.95) short stories, ...Confessions ('98, $3.95) short stories, ...Pop Culture Hoo-Hah ('98, $3.95) humor shorts 4.00
TPB (1997, $10.95) r/Vol 1,#1-4 11.00
...: The Definitive Collection ('01, $24.95) remastered #1-5, sketch pages, art gallery, script excerpts, Mack intro. 25.00

JINX: TORSO
Image Comics: 1998 - No. 6, 1999 ($3.95/$4.95, B&W)

1-6-Based on Eliot Ness' pursuit of America's first serial killer; Brian Michael Bendis & Marc Andreyko-s/Bendis-a. 3-6-($4.95) 5.00
Softcover (2000, $24.95) r/#1-6; intro. by Greg Rucka; photo essay of the actual murders and police documents 25.00
Hardcover (2000, $49.95) signed & numbered 50.00

JLA (See Justice League of America and Justice Leagues)
DC Comics: Jan, 1997 - No. 125, Apr, 2006 ($1.95/$1.99/$2.25/$2.50)

	GD	VG	FN	VF	VF/NM	NM-
1-Morrison-s/Porter & Dell-a. The Hyperclan app.	2	4	6	9	12	15
2	1	3	4	6	8	10
3,4	1	2	3	5	7	9

5-Membership drive; Tomorrow Woman app. 6.00
6-9: 8-Green Arrow joins. 6.00
10-21: 10-Rock of Ages begins. 11-Joker and Luthor-c/app. 15-($2.95) Rock of Ages concludes. 16-New members join; Prometheus app. 17,20-Jorgensen-a. 18-21-Waid-s. 20,21-Adam Strange c/app. 5.00
22-40: 22-Begin $1.99-c; Sandman (Daniel) app. 27-Amazo app. 28-31-JSA app. 35-Hal Jordan/Spectre app. 36-40-World War 3 3.00
41-($2.99) Conclusion of World War 3; last Morrison-s 4.00
42-46: 43-Waid-s; Ra's al Ghul app. 44-Begin $2.25-c. 46-Batman leaves 3.00
47-49: 47-Hitch & Neary-a begins; JLA battles Queen of Fables 3.00
50-($3.75) JLA vs. Dr. Destiny; art by Hitch & various 4.00
51-74: 52-55-Hitch-a. 59-Joker: Last Laugh. 61-68-Kelly-s/Mahnke-a. 69-73-Hunt for Aquaman; bi-monthly with alternating art by Mahnke and Guichet 3.00
75-(1/03, $3.95) leads into Aquaman (4th series) #1 4.00
76-93: 76-Firestorm app. 77-Banks-a. 79-Kanjar Ro app. 91-93-O'Neil-s/Huat-a 3.00
94-99-Byrne & Ordway-a/Claremont-s; Doom Patrol app. 3.00
100-($3.50) Intro. Vera Black; leads into Justice League Elite #1 4.00
101-114: 101-106-Austen-s/Garney-a/c. 107-114-Crime Syndicate app.; Busiek-s 3.00
115-125: 115-Begin $2.50-c; Johns & Heinberg-s;Secret Society of Super-Villains app. 3.00
#1,000,000 (11/98) 853rd Century x-over 3.00
Annual 1 (1997, $3.95) Pulp Heroes; Augustyn-s/Olivetti & Ha-a 4.00
Annual 2 (1998, $2.95) Ghosts; Wrightson-c 4.00
Annual 3 (1999, $2.95) JLApe; Art Adams-c 4.00
Annual 4 (2000, $3.50) Planet DC x-over; Steve Scott-c/a 4.00
... American Dreams (1998, $7.95, TPB) r/#5-9 8.00
...: Crisis of Conscience TPB (2006, $12.99) r/#115-119 13.00
.../ Cyberforce (DC/Top Cow, 2005, $5.99) Kelly-s/Mahnke-a/Silvestri-c 6.00
Divided We Fall (2001, $17.95, TPB) r/#47-54 18.00
...80-Page Giant 1 (7/98, $4.95) stories & art by various 6.00
...80-Page Giant 2 (11/99, $4.95) Green Arrow & Hawkman app. Hitch-c 6.00
...80-Page Giant 3 (10/00, $5.95) Pariah & Harbinger; intro. Moon Maiden 6.00
...Foreign Bodies (1999, $5.95, one-shot) Kobra app.; Semeiks-a 6.00
...Gallery (1997, $2.95) pin-ups by various; Quitely-c 3.00
...God & Monsters (2001, $6.95, one-shot) Benefiel-a/c 7.00
Golden Perfect (2003, $12.95, TPB) r/#61-65 13.00
.../ Haven: Anathema (2002, $6.95) Concludes the Haven: The Broken City series 7.00
.../ Haven: Arrival (2001, $6.95) Leads into the Haven: The Broken City series 7.00
...In Crisis Secret Files 1 (11/98, $4.95) recap of JLA in DC x-overs 5.00
...: Island of Dr. Moreau, The (2002, $6.95, one-shot) Elseworlds; Pugh-c/a; Thomas-s 7.00
.../ JSA Secret Files & Origins (1/03, $4.95) prelude to JLA/JSA: Virtue & Vice; short stories and pin-ups by various; Pacheco-c 5.00
.../ JSA: Virtue and Vice HC (2002, $24.95) Teams battle Despero & Johnny Sorrow; Goyer & Johns-s/Pacheco-a/c 25.00
.../ JSA: Virtue and Vice SC (2003, $17.95) 18.00
Justice For All (1999, $14.95, TPB) r/#24-33 15.00
New World Order (1997, $5.95, TPB) r/#1-4 6.00
...: Obsidian Age Book One, The (2003, $12.95) r/#66-71 13.00
...: Obsidian Age Book Two, The (2003, $12.95) r/#72-76 13.00
One Million (2004, $19.95, TPB) r/#DC One Million #1-4 and other #1,000,000 x-overs 20.00
...: Our Worlds at War (9/01, $2.95) Jae Lee-c; Aquaman presumed dead 3.00
...: Pain of the Gods (2005, $12.99) r/#101-106 13.00
...Primeval (1999, $5.95, one-shot) Abnett & Lanning-s/Olivetti-a 6.00
...: Riddle of the Beast HC (2001, $24.95) Grant-s/painted-a by various; Sweet-c 25.00
...: Riddle of the Beast SC (2003, $14.95) Grant-s/painted-a by various; Kaluta-c 15.00
Rock of Ages (1998, $9.95, TPB) r/#10-15 10.00
Rules of Engagement (2004, $12.95, TPB) r/#77-82 13.00
...: Seven Caskets (2000, $5.95, one-shot) Brereton-s/painted-c/a 6.00
...: Shogun of Steel (2002, $6.95, one-shot) Elseworlds; Justiniano-c/a 7.00
...Showcase 80-Page Giant (2/00, $4.95) Hitch-c 5.00
Strength in Numbers (1998, $12.95, TPB) r/#16-23, Secret Files #2 and Prometheus #1 13.00
...Superpower (1999, $5.95, one-shot) Arcudi-s/Eaton-a; Mark Antaeus joins 6.00
Syndicaté Rules (2005, $17.99, TPB) r/#107-114, Secret Files #4 18.00
Terror Incognita (2002, $12.95, TPB) r/#55-60 13.00
...: The Deluxe Edition Vol. 1 HC (2008, $29.99, dustjacket) oversized r/#1-9 and JLA Secret Files #1 30.00
...: The Deluxe Edition Vol. 2 HC (2009, $29.99, dustjacket) oversized r/#10-17, JLA/Wildcats, and Prometheus #1 30.00
...: The Deluxe Edition Vol. 3 HC (2010, $29.99, dustjacket) oversized r/#22-26, 28-31 & #1,000,000 30.00
...: The Deluxe Edition Vol. 4 HC (2010, $34.99, dustjacket) oversized r/#34, 36-41, JLA Classified #1-3 and JLA: Earth 2 GN 35.00
The Tenth Circle (2004, $12.95, TPB) r/#94-99 13.00
...: The Greatest Stories Ever Told TPB (2006, $19.99) r/Justice League of America #19,71,122, 166-168,200, Justice League #1, JLA Secret Files #1 and JLA #61; Alex Ross-c 20.00
Tower of Babel (2001, $12.95, TPB) r/#42-46, Secret Files #3, 80-Page Giant #1 13.00
Trial By Fire (2004, $12.95, TPB) r/#84-89 13.00
...Vs. Predator (DC/Dark Horse, 2000, $5.95, one-shot) Nolan-c/a 6.00
...: Welcome to the Working Week (2003, $6.95, one-shot) Patton Oswalt-s 7.00
...: World War III (2000, $12.95, TPB) r/#34-41 13.00
...: World Without a Justice League (2006, $12.99, TPB) r/#120-125 13.00
...: Zatanna's Search (2003, $12.95, TPB) rep. Zatanna's early app. & origin; Bolland-c 13.00

JLA: ACT OF GOD
DC Comics: 2000 - No. 3, 2001 ($4.95, limited series)

1-3-Elseworlds; metahumans lose their powers; Moench-s/Dave Ross-a 5.00

JLA: AGE OF WONDER
DC Comics: 2003 - No. 2, 2003 ($5.95, limited series)

1,2-Elseworlds; Superman and the League of Science during the Industrial Revolution 6.00

JLA: A LEAGUE OF ONE
DC Comics: 2000 (Graphic novel)

Hardcover ($24.95) Christopher Moeller-s/painted-a 25.00
Softcover (2002, $14.95) 15.00

JLA/AVENGERS (See Avengers/JLA for #2 & #4)
Marvel Comics: Sept, 2003; No. 3, Dec, 2003 ($5.95, limited series)

1-Busiek-s/Pérez-a; wraparound-c; Krona, Starro, Grandmaster, Terminus app. 6.00
3-Busiek-s/Pérez-a; wraparound-c; Phantom Stranger app. 6.00
SC (2008, $19.99) r/4-issue series; cover gallery; intros by Stan Lee & Julius Schwartz 20.00

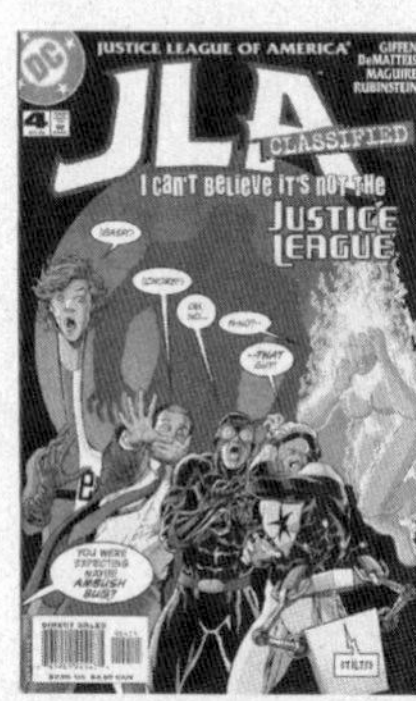

JLA Classified #4 © DC

JLA: Scary Monsters #1 © DC

JLA: World Without Grown-Ups #1 © DC

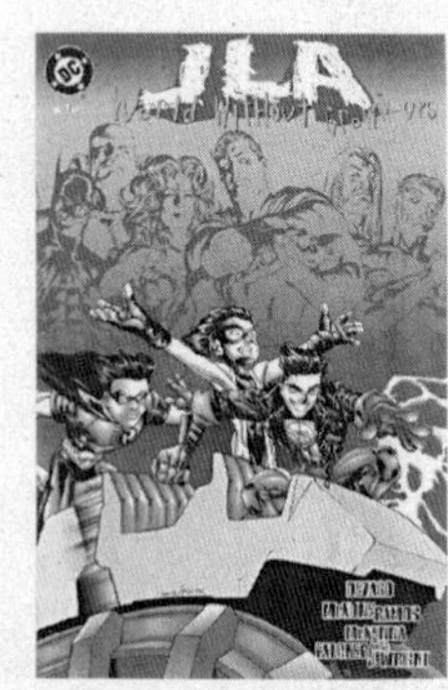

GD 2.0 | VG 4.0 | FN 6.0 | VF 8.0 | VF/NM 9.0 | NM- 9.2

JLA: BLACK BAPTISM
DC Comics: May, 2001 - No. 4, Aug, 2001 ($2.50, limited series)
1-4-Saiz-a(p)/Bradstreet-c; Zatanna app. 3.00

JLA: CLASSIFIED
DC Comics: Jan, 2005 - No. 54, May, 2008 ($2.95/$2.99)
1-3-Morrison-s/McGuinness-a/c; Ultramarines app. 3.00
4-9-"I Can't Believe It's Not The Justice League," Giffen & DeMatteis-s/Maguire-a 3.00
10-31,33-54: 10-15-New Maps of Hell; Ellis-s/Guice-a. 16-21-Garcia-Lopez-a. 22-25-Detroit League & Royal Flush Gang app.; Englehart-s. 26-28-Chaykin-s. 37-41-Kid Amazo. 50-54-Byrne-a/Middleston-c 3.00
32-($3.99) Dr. Destiny app.; Jurgens-a 4.00
I Can't Believe It's Not The Justice League TPB (2005, $12.99) r/#4-9 13.00
...: Kid Amazo TPB (2007, $12.99) r/#37-41 13.00
...: New Maps of Hell TPB (2006, $12.99) r/#10-15 13.00
...: That Was Now, This Is Then TPB (2008, $14.99) r/#50-54 15.00
...: The Hypothetical Woman TPB (2008, $12.99) r/#16-21 13.00
...: Ultramarine Corps TPB (2007, $14.99) r/#1-3, JLA/WildC.A.T.s #1 and JLA Secret Files 2004 #1 15.00

JLA CLASSIFIED: COLD STEEL
DC Comics: 2005 - No. 2, 2006 ($5.99, limited series, prestige format)
1,2-Chris Moeller-s/a; giant robot Justice League 6.00

JLA: CREATED EQUAL
DC Comics: 2000 - No. 2, 2000 ($5.95, limited series, prestige format)
1,2-Nicieza-s/Maguire-a; Elseworlds-Superman as the last man on Earth 6.00

JLA: DESTINY
DC Comics: 2002 - No. 4, 2002 ($5.95, prestige format, limited series)
1-4-Elseworlds; Arcudi-s/Mandrake-a 6.00

JLA: EARTH 2
DC Comics: 2000 (Graphic novel)
Hardcover ($24.95) Morrison-s/Quitely-a; Crime Syndicate app. 25.00
Softcover ($14.95) 15.00

JLA: GATEKEEPER
DC Comics: 2001 - No. 3, 2001 ($4.95, prestige format, limited series)
1-3-Truman-s/a 5.00

JLA: HEAVEN'S LADDER
DC Comics: 2000 ($9.95, Treasury-size one-shot)
nn-Bryan Hitch & Paul Neary-c/a; Mark Waid-s 10.00

JLA/HITMAN (Justice League/Hitman in indicia)
DC Comics: Nov, 2007 - No. 2, Dec, 2007 ($3.99, limited series)
1,2-Ennis-s/McCrea-a; Bloodlines creatures return 4.00

JLA: INCARNATIONS
DC Comics: Jul, 2001 - No. 7, Feb, 2002 ($3.50, limited series)
1-7-Ostrander-s/Semeiks-a; different eras of the Justice League 3.50

JLA: LIBERTY AND JUSTICE
DC Comics: Nov, 2003 ($9.95, Treasury-size one-shot)
nn-Alex Ross-c/a; Paul Dini-s; story of the classic Justice League 10.00

JLA PARADISE LOST
DC Comics: Jan, 1998 - No. 3, Mar, 1998 ($1.95, limited series)
1-3-Millar-s/Olivetti-a 3.00

JLA: SCARY MONSTERS
DC Comics: May, 2003 - No. 6, Oct, 2003 ($2.50, limited series)
1-6-Claremont-s/Art Adams-c 3.00

JLA SECRET FILES
DC Comics: Sept, 1997 - 2004 ($4.95)
1-Standard Ed. w/origin-s & pin-ups 5.00
1-Collector's Ed. w/origin-s & pin-ups; cardstock-c 6.00
2,3: 2-(8/98) origin-s of JLA #16's newer members. 3-(12/00) 5.00
... 2004 (11/04) Justice League Elite app.; Mahnke & Byrne-a; Crime Syndicate app. 5.00

JLA: SECRET ORIGINS
DC Comics: Nov, 2002 ($7.95, Treasury-size one-shot)
nn-Alex Ross 2-page origins of Justice League members; text by Paul Dini 8.00

JLA: SECRET SOCIETY OF SUPER-HEROES
DC Comics: 2000 - No. 2, 2000 ($5.95, limited series, prestige format)
1,2-Elseworlds JLA; Chaykin and Tischman-s/McKone-a 6.00

JLA /SPECTRE: SOUL WAR
DC Comics: 2003 - No. 2, 2003 ($5.95, limited series, prestige format)
1,2-DeMatteis-s/Banks & Neary-a 6.00

JLA: THE NAIL (Elseworlds) (Also see Justice League of America: Another Nail)
DC Comics: Aug, 1998 - No. 3, Oct, 1998 ($4.95, prestige format)
1-3-JLA in a world without Superman; Alan Davis-s/a(p) 5.00
TPB ('98, $12.95) r/series w/new Davis-c 13.00

JLA / TITANS
DC Comics: Dec, 1998 - No. 3, Feb, 1999 ($2.95, limited series)
1-3-Grayson-s; P. Jimenez-c/a 3.00
...:The Technis Imperative ('99, $12.95, TPB) r/#1-3; Titans Secret Files 13.00

JLA: TOMORROW WOMAN (Girlfrenzy)
DC Comics: June, 1998 ($1.95, one-shot)
1-Peyer-s; story takes place during JLA #5 3.00

JLA / WILDC.A.T.S
DC Comics: 1997 ($5.95, one-shot, prestige format)
1-Morrison-s/Semeiks & Conrad-a 6.00

JLA /WITCHBLADE
DC Comics/Top Cow: 2000 ($5.95, prestige format, one-shot)
1-Pararillo-c/a 6.00

JLA / WORLD WITHOUT GROWN-UPS (See Young Justice)
DC Comics: Aug, 1998 - No. 2, Sept, 1998 ($4.95, prestige format)
1,2-JLA, Robin, Impulse & Superboy app.; Ramos & McKone-a 6.00
TPB ('98, $9.95) r/series & Young Justice: The Secret #1 10.00

JLA: YEAR ONE
DC Comics: Jan, 1998 - No. 12, Dec, 1998 ($2.95/$1.95, limited series)
1-($2.95)-Waid & Augustyn-s/Kitson-a 5.00
1-Platinum Edition 10.00
2-8-($1.95): 5-Doom Patrol-c/app. 7-Superman app. 4.00
9-12 3.00
TPB ('99,'09; $19.95/$19.99) r/#1-12; Busiek intro. 20.00

JLA-Z
DC Comics: Nov, 2003 - No. 3, Jan, 2004 ($2.50, limited series)
1-3-Pin-ups and info on current and former JLA members and villains; art by various 3.00

JLX
DC Comics (Amalgam): Apr, 1996 ($1.95, one-shot)
1-Mark Waid scripts 3.00

JLX UNLEASHED
DC Comics (Amalgam): June, 1997 ($1.95, one-shot)
1-Priest-s/ Oscar Jimenez & Rodriquez/a 3.00

JOAN OF ARC (Also see A-1 Comics & Ideal a Classical Comic)
Magazine Enterprises: No. 21, 1949 (one shot)

	GD	VG	FN	VF	VF/NM	NM-
A-1 21-Movie adaptation; Ingrid Bergman photo-covers & interior photos; Whitney-a	29	58	87	170	278	385

JOE COLLEGE
Hillman Periodicals: Fall, 1949 - No. 2, Wint, 1950 (Teen-age humor, 52 pgs.)

	GD	VG	FN	VF	VF/NM	NM-
1-Powell-a; Briefer-a	13	26	39	72	101	130
2-Powell-a	10	20	30	54	72	90

JOE JINKS
United Features Syndicate: No. 12, 1939

	GD	VG	FN	VF	VF/NM	NM-
Single Series 12	31	62	93	182	296	410

JOE LOUIS (See Fight Comics #2, Picture News #6 & True Comics #5)
Fawcett Publications: Sept, 1950 - No. 2, Nov, 1950 (Photo-c) (Boxing champ) (See Dick Cole #10)

	GD	VG	FN	VF	VF/NM	NM-
1-Photo-c; life story	55	110	165	352	601	850
2-Photo-c	39	78	117	240	395	550

JOE PALOOKA (1st Series)(Also see Big Shot Comics, Columbia Comics & Feature Funnies)
Columbia Comic Corp. (Publication Enterprises): 1942 - No. 4, 1944

	GD	VG	FN	VF	VF/NM	NM-
1-1st to portray American president; gov't permission required	103	206	309	659	1130	1600
2 (1943)-Hitler-c	71	142	213	454	777	1100
3-Nazi Sub-c	41	82	123	256	428	600
4	34	68	102	206	336	465

JOE PALOOKA (2nd Series) (Battle Adv. #68-74; ...Advs. #75, 77-81, 83-85, 87; Champ of

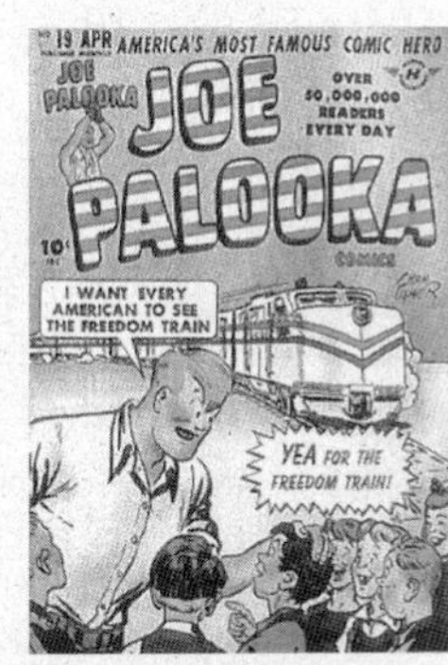

Joe Palooka #19 © HARV

John Byrne's Next Men (2010 series) #6 © John Byrne

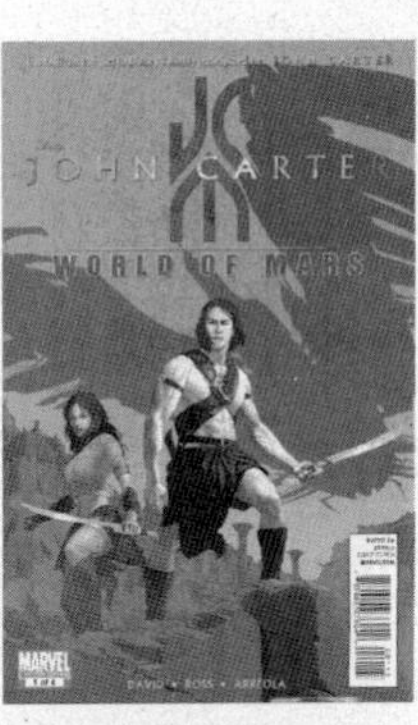

John Carter: The World of Mars #1 © DIS

GD VG FN VF VF/NM NM-
2.0 4.0 6.0 8.0 9.0 9.2

the Comics #76, 82, 86, 89-93) (See All-New)
Harvey Publications: Nov, 1945 - No. 118, Mar, 1961

1-By Ham Fisher 49 98 147 309 522 735
2 24 48 72 142 234 325
3,4,6,7-1st Flyin' Fool, ends #25 16 32 48 94 147 200
5-Boy Explorers by S&K (7-8/46) 21 42 63 122 199 275
8-10 14 28 42 80 115 150
11-14,16,18-20: 14-Black Cat text-s(2). 18-Powell-a.; Little Max app. 19-Freedom Train-c
11 22 33 64 90 115
15-Origin & 1st app. Humphrey (12/47); Super-heroine Atoma app. by Powell
15 30 45 90 140 190
17-Humphrey vs. Palooka-c/s; 1st app. Little Max 15 30 45 90 140 190
21-26,29,30: 22-Powell-a. 30-Nude female painting 10 20 30 56 76 95
27-Little Max app.; Howie Morenz-s 10 20 30 58 79 100
28-Babe Ruth 4 pg. sty. 10 20 30 58 79 100
31,39,51: 31-Dizzy Dean 4 pg. sty. 39-(12/49) Humphrey & Little Max begin; Sonny Baugh football-s; Sherlock Max-s. 51-Babe Ruth 2 pg. sty; Jake Lamotta 1/2 pg. sty
9 18 27 50 65 80
32-38,40-50,52-61: 35-Little Max-c/story(4 pgs.); Joe Louis 1 pg. sty. 36-Humphrey story. 41-Bing Crosby photo on-c. 44-Palooka marries Ann Howe. 50-(11/51)-Becomes Harvey Comics Hits #51 8 16 24 44 57 70
62-S&K Boy Explorers-r 9 18 27 50 65 80
63-65,73-80,100: 79-Story of 1st meeting with Ann 8 16 24 40 50 60
66,67-'Commie' torture story "Drug-Diet Horror" 11 22 33 64 90 115
68,70-72: 68,70-Joe vs. "Gooks"-c. 71-Bloody bayonets-c. 72-Tank-c
11 22 33 62 86 110
69-1st "Battle Adventures" issue; torture & bondage 11 22 33 64 90 115
81-99,101-115: 104,107-Humphrey & Little Max-s 7 14 21 37 46 55
116-S&K Boy Explorers-r (Giant, '60) 9 18 27 47 61 75
117-(84 pg. Giant) r/Commie issues #66,67; Powell-a 9 18 27 52 69 85
118-(84 pg. Giant) Jack Dempsey 2 pg. sty, Powell-a 9 18 27 47 61 75
...**Visits the Lost City** nn (1945)(One Shot)(50¢)-164 page continuous story strip reprint. Has biography & photo of Ham Fisher; possibly the single longest comic book story published in that era (159 pgs.?) (scarce) 200 400 600 1280 2190 3100

NOTE: *Nostrand/Powell a-73. Powell a-7, 8, 10, 12, 14, 17, 19, 26-45, 47-53, 70, 73 at least. Black Cat text stories #8, 12, 13, 19.*

JOE PSYCHO & MOO FROG
Goblin Studios: 1996 - No. 5, 1997 ($2.50, B&W)

1-5: 4-Two covers 3.00
...Full Color Extravagarbonzo ($2.95, color) 3.00

JOE THE BARBARIAN
DC Comics (Vertigo): Mar, 2010 - No. 8, May, 2011 ($1.00/$2.99/$3.99)

1-($1.00) Grant Morrison-s/Sean Murphy-a 3.00
2-7-($2.99) 3.00
8-($3.99) 4.00

JOE YANK (Korean War)
Standard Comics (Visual Editions): No. 5, Mar, 1952 - No. 16, 1954

5-Toth, Celardo, Tuska-a 10 20 30 56 76 95
6-Toth, Severin/Elder-a 10 20 30 54 72 90
7-Pinhead Perkins by Dan DeCarlo (in all?) 8 16 24 42 54 65
8-Toth-c 9 18 27 47 61 75
9-16: 9-Andru-c. 12-Andru-a 8 16 24 40 50 60

JOHN BOLTON'S HALLS OF HORROR
Eclipse Comics: June, 1985 - No. 2, June, 1985 ($1.75, limited series)

1,2-British-r; Bolton-c/a 3.00

JOHN BOLTON'S STRANGE WINK
Dark Horse Comics: Mar, 1998 - No. 3, May, 1998 ($2.95, B&W, limited series)

1-3-Anthology; Bolton-s/c/a 3.00

JOHN BYRNE'S NEXT MEN (See Dark Horse Presents #54)
Dark Horse Comics (Legend imprint #19 on): Jan, 1992 - No. 30, Dec, 1994 ($2.50, mature)

1-Silver foil embossed-c; Byrne-c/a/scripts in all 4.00
1-4: 1-2nd printing with gold ink logo 3.00
0-(2/92)-r/chapters 1-4 from DHP w/new Byrne-c 3.00
5-20,22-30: 7-10-MA #1-4 mini-series on flip side. 16-Origin of Mark IV. 17-Miller-c. 19-22-Faith storyline. 23-26-Power storyline. 27-30-Lies storyline Pt. 1-4 3.00
21-(12/93) 2nd Hellboy; cover and Hellboy pages by Mike Mignola; Byrne other pages (see San Diego Comic Con Comics #2 for 1st app.) 4 8 12 24 37 50
...Parallel, Book 2 ($16.95)-TPB; r/#7-12 17.00
...Fame, Book 3($16.95)-TPB r/#13-18 17.00
...Faith, Book 4($14.95)-TPB r/#19-22 15.00

GD VG FN VF VF/NM NM-
2.0 4.0 6.0 8.0 9.0 9.2

NOTE: *Issues 1 through 6 contain certificates redeemable for an exclusive Next Men trading card set by Byrne. Prices are for complete books. Cody painted c-23-26. Mignola a-21(part); c-21.*

JOHN BYRNE'S NEXT MEN
IDW Publishing: Dec, 2010 - Present ($3.99)

1-9-John Byrne-s/a/c in all. 1-Origin retold. 6,7-Abraham Lincoln app. 4.00

JOHN BYRNE'S 2112
Dark Horse Comics (Legend): Oct, 1994 ($9.95, TPB)

1-Byrne-c/a/s 10.00

JOHN CARTER OF MARS (See The Funnies & Tarzan #207)
Dell Publishing Co.: No. 375, Mar-May, 1952 - No. 488, Aug-Oct, 1953
(Edgar Rice Burroughs)

Four Color 375 (#1)-Origin; Jesse Marsh-a 26 52 78 182 391 600
Four Color 437, 488-Painted-c 14 28 42 97 211 325

JOHN CARTER OF MARS
Gold Key: Apr, 1964 - No. 3, Oct, 1964

1(10104-404)-r/4-Color #375; Jesse Marsh-a 7 14 21 44 72 100
2(407), 3(410)-r/4-Color #437 & 488; Marsh-a 5 10 15 30 48 65

JOHN CARTER OF MARS
House of Greystroke: 1970 (10-1/2x16-1/2", 72 pgs., B&W, paper-c)

1941-42 Sunday strip-r; John Coleman Burroughs-a 4 8 12 24 37 50

JOHN CARTER OF MARS: A PRINCESS OF MARS
Marvel Comics: Nov, 2011 - No. 5, Mar, 2012 ($2.99, limited series)

1-5: 1-Langridge-s/Andrade-a; covers by Young and Andrade. 2-4-Young-c 3.00

JOHN CARTER: THE WORLD OF MARS
Marvel Comics: Dec, 2011 - No. 4, Mar, 2012 ($3.99, limited series)

1-4-Movie prequel; Peter David-s/Luke Ross-a. 1-Ribic-c. 4-Olivetti-c 4.00

JOHN CARTER, WARLORD OF MARS (Also see Tarzan #207-209 and Weird Worlds)
Marvel Comics: June, 1977 - No. 28, Oct, 1979

1,18: 1-Origin. 18-Frank Miller-a(p)(1st publ. Marvel work)
2 4 6 11 16 20
1-(35¢-c variant, limited dist.) 4 8 12 24 37 50
2-5-(35¢-c variants, limited dist.) 3 6 9 20 30 40
2-17,19-28: 11-Origin Dejah Thoris 8.00
Annuals 1-3: 1(1977). 2(1978). 3(1979)-All 52 pgs. with new book-length stories 8.00
Edgar Rice Burroughs' John Carter of Mars: Weird Worlds TPB (Dark Horse Books, Jan. 2011, $14.99) r/stories from Tarzan #207-209 and Weird Worlds #1-7; Marv Wolfman intro. 15.00

NOTE: *Austin c-24i. Gil Kane a-1-10p; c-1p, 2p, 3, 4-9p, 10, 15p, Annual 1p. Layton a-17i. Miller c-25, 26p. Nebres a-2-4i, 8-16i; c(i)-6-9, 11-22, 25, Annual 1. Perez c-24p. Simonson a-15p. Sutton a-7i.*

JOHN CONSTANTINE - HELLBLAZER SPECIAL: PAPA MIDNITE
DC Comics (Vertigo): April, 2005 - No. 5, Aug, 2005 ($2.95/$2.99, limited series)

1-5-Origin of Papa Midnite; Akins-a/Johnson-s 3.00

JOHN F. KENNEDY, CHAMPION OF FREEDOM
Worden & Childs: 1964 (no month) (25¢)

nn-Photo-c 8 16 24 53 89 125

JOHN F. KENNEDY LIFE STORY
Dell Publishing Co.: Aug-Oct, 1964; Nov, 1965; June, 1966 (12¢)

12-378-410-Photo-c 7 14 21 48 79 110
12-378-511 (reprint, 11/65) 4 8 12 22 34 45
12-378-606 (reprint, 6/66) 3 6 9 20 30 40

JOHN FORCE (See Magic Agent)

JOHN HIX SCRAP BOOK, THE
Eastern Color Printing Co. (McNaught Synd.): Late 1930's (no date)
(10¢, 68 pgs., regular size)

1-Strange As It Seems (resembles Single Series books)
39 78 117 231 378 525
2-Strange As It Seems 25 50 75 147 241 335

JOHN JAKES' MULLKON EMPIRE
Tekno Comix: Sept, 1995 - No. 6, Feb, 1996 ($1.95)

1-6 3.00

JOHN LAW DETECTIVE (See Smash Comics #3)
Eclipse Comics: April, 1983 ($1.50, Baxter paper)

1-Three Eisner stories originally drawn in 1948 for the never published John Law #1; original cover pencilled in 1948 & inked in 1982 by Eisner 3.00

JOHN McCAIN (See Presidential Material: John McCain)

JOHNNY APPLESEED (See Story Hour Series)

Johnny Hazard #8 © STD

John Wayne Adventure Comics #28 © TOBY

Jo-Jo Comics #17 © FOX

GD 2.0 | VG 4.0 | FN 6.0 | VF 8.0 | VF/NM 9.0 | NM- 9.2

JOHNNY CASH (See Hello, I'm...)

JOHNNY DANGER (See Movie Comics, 1946)
Toby Press: 1950 (Based on movie serial)
1-Photo-c; Sparling-a 20 40 60 114 182 250

JOHNNY DANGER PRIVATE DETECTIVE
Toby Press: Aug, 1954 (Reprinted in Danger #11 by Super)
1-Photo-c; Opium den story 17 34 51 98 154 210

JOHNNY DYNAMITE (Formerly Dynamite #1-9; Foreign Intrigues #14 on)
Charlton Comics: No. 10, June, 1955 - No. 12, Oct, 1955
10-12 12 24 36 69 97 125

JOHNNY DYNAMITE
Dark Horse Comics: Sept, 1994 - Dec, 1994 ($2.95, B&W & red, limited series)
1-4: Max Allan Collins scripts in all; Terry Beatty-a 3.00
...: Underworld GN (AiT/Planet Lar, 3/03, $12.95, B&W) r/#1-4 in B&W without red 13.00

JOHNNY HAZARD
Best Books (Standard Comics) (King Features): No. 5, Aug, 1948 - No. 8, May, 1949; No. 35, date?
5-Strip reprints by Frank Robbins (c/a) 18 36 54 105 165 225
6,8-Strip reprints by Frank Robbins 15 30 45 88 137 185
7,35: 7-New art, not Robbins 12 24 36 67 94 120

JOHNNY JASON (...Teen Reporter)
Dell Publishing Co.: Feb-Apr, 1962 - No. 2, June-Aug, 1962
Four Color 1302, 2(01380-208) 4 8 12 24 37 50

JOHNNY LAW, SKY RANGER
Good Comics (Lev Gleason): Apr, 1955 - No. 3, Aug, 1955; No. 4, Nov, 1955
1-Edmond Good-c/a 10 20 30 56 76 95
2-4 7 14 21 35 43 50

JOHNNY MACK BROWN (Western star; see Western Roundup under Dell Giants)
Dell Publishing Co.: No. 269, Mar, 1950 - No. 963, Feb, 1959 (All Photo-c)
Four Color 269(#1)(3/50, 52pgs.)-Johnny Mack Brown & his horse Rebel begin; photo front/back-c begin; Marsh-a in #1-9 19 38 57 128 277 425
2(10-12/50, 52pgs.) 11 22 33 71 136 200
3(1-3/51, 52pgs.) 9 18 27 61 106 150
4-10 (9-11/52)(36pgs.), Four Color 455,493,541,584,618,645,685,722,776,834,963 7 14 21 46 76 105
Four Color 922-Manning-a 7 14 21 48 79 110

JOHNNY NEMO
Eclipse Comics: Sept, 1985 - No. 3, Feb, 1986 (Mini-series)
1-3 3.00

JOHNNY PERIL (See Comic Cavalcade #15, Danger Trail #5, Sensation Comics #107 & Sensation Mystery)

JOHNNY RINGO (TV)
Dell Publishing Co.: No. 1142, Nov-Jan, 1960/61 (one shot)
Four Color 1142-Photo-c 7 14 21 46 76 105

JOHNNY STARBOARD (See Wisco)

JOHNNY THE HOMICIDAL MANIAC (Also see Squee)
Slave Labor Graphics: Aug, 1995 - No. 7, Jan, 1997 ($2.95, B&W, lim. series)
1-Jhonen Vasquez-c/s/a 1 3 4 6 8 10
1-Signed & numbered edition 2 4 6 9 12 15
2,3: 2-(11/95). 3-(2/96) 6.00
4-7: 4-(5-96). 5-(8/96) 4.00
Hardcover-($29.95) r/#1-7 30.00
TPB-($19.95) 20.00

JOHNNY THUNDER
National Periodical Publications: Feb-Mar, 1973 - No. 3, July-Aug, 1973
1-Johnny Thunder & Nighthawk-r. in all 2 4 6 13 18 22
2,3: 2-Trigger Twins app. 2 4 6 8 11 14
NOTE: *All contain 1950s DC reprints from All-American Western.* ***Drucker*** *r-2, 3.* ***G. Kane*** *r-2, 3.* ***Moreira*** *r-1.* ***Toth*** *r-1, 3; c-1r, 3r. Also see All-American, All-Star Western, Flash Comics, Western Comics, World's Best & World's Finest.*

JOHN PAUL JONES
Dell Publishing Co.: No. 1007, July-Sept, 1959 (one-shot)
Four Color 1007-Movie, Robert Stack photo-c 5 10 15 35 55 75

JOHN ROMITA JR. 30TH ANNIVERSARY SPECIAL
Marvel Comics: 2006 ($3.99, one-shot)
nn-r/1st story in Amazing Spider-Man Annual #11; timeline, sketch pages, interviews 4.00

JOHN STEED & EMMA PEEL (See The Avengers, Gold Key series)

JOHN STEELE SECRET AGENT (Also see Freedom Agent)
Gold Key: Dec, 1964
1-Freedom Agent 6 12 18 37 59 80

JOHN WAYNE ADVENTURE COMICS (Movie star; See Big Tex, Oxydol-Dreft, Tim McCoy, & With The Marines...#1)
Toby Press: Winter, 1949-50 - No. 31, May, 1955 (Photo-c: 1-12,17,25-on)
1 (36pgs.)-Photo-c begin (1st time in comics on-c) 161 322 483 1030 1765 2500
2-4: 2-(4/50, 36pgs.)-Williamson/Frazetta-a(2) 6 & 2 pgs. (one story-r/Billy the Kid #1); photo back-c. 3-(36pgs.)-Williamson/Frazetta-a(2), 16 pgs. total; photo back-c. 4-(52pgs.)-Williamson/Frazetta-a(2), 16 pgs. total 69 138 207 442 759 1075
5 (52pgs.)-Kurtzman-a-(Alfred "L" Newman in Potshot Pete) 51 102 153 321 541 760
6 (52pgs.)-Williamson/Frazetta-a (10 pgs.); Kurtzman-a "Pot-Shot Pete", (5 pgs.); & "Genius Jones", (1 pg.) 60 120 180 381 653 925
7 (52pgs.)-Williamson/Frazetta-a (10 pgs.) 52 104 156 328 557 785
8 (36pgs.)-Williamson/Frazetta-a(2) (12 & 9 pgs.) 64 128 192 406 696 985
9-11: Photo western-c 39 78 117 230 375 520
12,14-Photo war-c. 12-Kurtzman-a(2 pg.) "Genius" 39 78 117 230 375 520
13,15: 13,15-Line-drawn-c begin, end #24 32 64 96 192 314 435
16-Williamson/Frazetta-r/Billy the Kid #1 36 72 108 211 343 475
17-Photo-c 36 72 108 211 343 475
18-Williamson/Frazetta-a (r/#4 & 8, 19 pgs.) 39 78 117 234 385 535
19-24: 23-Evans-a? 28 56 84 168 274 380
25-Photo-c resume; end #31; Williamson/Frazetta-r/Billy the Kid #3 39 78 117 234 385 535
26-28,30-Photo-c 32 64 96 192 314 435
29,31-Williamson/Frazetta-a in each (r/#4, 2) 37 74 111 222 361 500
NOTE: *Williamsonish art in later issues by* ***Gerald McCann.***

JO-JO COMICS (...Congo King #7-29; My Desire #30 on)(Also see Fantastic Fears and Jungle Jo)
Fox Feature Syndicate: 1945 - No. 29, July, 1949 (Two No.7's; no #13)
nn(1945)-Funny animal, humor 21 42 63 122 199 275
2(Sum,'46)-6(4-5/47): Funny animal. 2-Ten pg. Electro story (Fall/46) 15 30 45 83 124 165
7(7/47)-Jo-Jo, Congo King begins (1st app.); Bronze Man & Purple Tigress app. 97 194 291 621 1061 1500
7(#8) (9/47) 69 138 207 442 759 1075
8(#9) Classic Kamen mountain of skulls-c; Tanee begins 61 122 183 390 670 950
9,10(#10,11) 58 116 174 371 636 900
11,12(#12,13),14,16: 11,16-Kamen bondage-c 52 104 156 328 552 775
15,17: 15-Cited by Dr. Wertham in 5/47 Saturday Review of Literature. 17-Kamen bondage-c 53 106 159 334 567 800
18-20 52 104 156 328 552 775
21-29: 21-Hollingsworth-a(4 pgs.; 23-1 pg.) 41 82 123 256 428 600
NOTE: *Many bondage-c/a by* ***Baker/Kamen/Feldstein/Good.*** *No. 7's have Princesses Gwenna, Geesa, Yolda, & Safra before settling down on Tanee.*

JOKEBOOK COMICS DIGEST ANNUAL (...Magazine No. 5 on)
Archie Publications: Oct, 1977 - No. 13, Oct, 1983 (Digest Size)
1(10/77)-Reprints; Neal Adams-a 2 4 6 13 18 22
2(4/78)-5 2 4 6 9 12 15
6-13 1 3 4 6 8 10

JOKER
DC Comics: 2008 ($19.99, hardcover graphic novel with dustjacket)
HC-Joker is released from Arkham; Azzarello-s/Bermejo-a 20.00

JOKER, THE (See Batman #1, Batman: The Killing Joke, Brave & the Bold, Detective, Greatest Joker Stories & Justice League Annual #2)
National Periodical Publications: May, 1975 - No. 9, Sept-Oct, 1976
1-Two-Face app. 6 12 18 41 66 90
2,3: 3-The Creeper app. 4 8 12 22 34 45
4-9: 4-Green Arrow-c/sty. 6-Sherlock Holmes-c/sty. 7-Lex Luthor-c/story. 8-Scarecrow-c/story. 9-Catwoman-c/story 3 6 9 18 27 35
...: The Greatest Stories Ever Told TPB (2008, $19.99) r/Batman #1 and other apps. 20.00

JOKER, THE (See Tangent Comics/ The Joker)

JOKER COMICS (Adventures Into Terror No. 43 on)
Timely/Marvel Comics No. 36 on (TCI/CDS): Apr, 1942 - No. 42, Aug, 1950
1-(Rare)-Powerhouse Pepper (1st app.) begins by Wolverton; Stuporman app. from Daring Comics 300 600 900 1980 3440 4900
2-Wolverton-a; 1st app. Tessie the Typist & begin series

Joker: Last Laugh #1 © DC

Jonah Hex (2006 series) #53 © DC

Jonny Double #1 © DC

	GD 2.0	VG 4.0	FN 6.0	VF 8.0	VF/NM 9.0	NM- 9.2
	103	206	309	659	1130	1600
3-5-Wolverton-a	57	114	171	362	619	875
6-10-Wolverton-a. 6-Tessie-c begin	43	86	129	271	461	650
11-20-Wolverton-a	40	80	120	246	411	575
21,22,24-27,29,30-Wolverton cont'd. & Kurtzman's "Hey Look" in #23-27	36	72	108	214	347	480
23-1st "Hey Look" by Kurtzman; Wolverton-a	38	76	114	226	368	510
28,32,34,37-41: 28-Millie the Model begins. 32-Hedy begins. 41-Nellie the Nurse app.	16	32	48	94	147	200
31-Last Powerhouse Pepper; not in #28	30	60	90	177	289	400
33,35,36-Kurtzman's "Hey Look"	17	34	51	98	154	210
42-Only app. 'Patty Pinup,' clone of Millie the Model	17	34	51	98	154	210

JOKER: DEVIL'S ADVOCATE
DC Comics: 1996 ($24.95/$12.95, one-shot)

nn-(Hardcover)-Dixon scripts/Nolan & Hanna-a 25.00
nn-(Softcover) 13.00

JOKER: LAST LAUGH (See Batman: The Joker's Last Laugh for TPB)
DC Comics: Dec, 2001 - No. 6, Jan, 2002 ($2.95, weekly limited series)

1-6: 1,6-Bolland-c 3.00
...Secret Files (12/01, $5.95) Short stories by various; Simonson-c 6.00

JOKER / MASK
Dark Horse Comics: May, 2000 - No. 4, Aug, 2000 ($2.95, limited series)

1-4-Batman, Harley Quinn, Poison Ivy app. 3.00

JOKER'S ASYLUM
DC Comics: Sept, 2008 ($2.99, weekly limited series of one-shots)

...: Joker - Andy Kubert-c, Sanchez-a; ...: Penguin - Pearson-c/a; ...: Poison Ivy - Guillem March-c/a; ...: Scarecrow - Juan Doe-c/a; ...: Two-Face - Andy Clarke-c/a 3.00
Batman: The Joker's Asylum TPB (2008, $14.99) r/one-shots 15.00

JOKER'S ASYLUM II
DC Comics: Aug, 2010 ($2.99, weekly limited series of one-shots)

...: Clayface - Kelley Jones-c/a; ...: Harley Quinn - Quinones-a; ...: Killer Croc - Mattina-c; Mad Hatter - Giffen & Sienkiewicz-a, Sienkiewicz-c; ...: Riddler - Van Sciver-c 3.00
Batman: The Joker's Asylum Volume 2 TPB (2011, $14.99) r/one-shots 15.00

JOLLY CHRISTMAS, A (See March of Comics No. 269)

JOLLY COMICS: Four Star Publishing Co.: 1947 (Advertised, not published)

JOLLY JINGLES (Formerly Jackpot Comics)
MLJ Magazines: No. 10, Sum, 1943 - No. 16, Wint, 1944/45

10-Super Duck begins (origin & 1st app.); Woody The Woodpecker begins (not same as Lantz character)	42	84	126	265	445	625
11 (Fall, '43)-2nd Super Duck(see Hangman #8)	22	44	66	132	216	300
12-Hitler-c	43	86	129	271	461	650
13-16: 13-Sahle-c. 15,16-Vigoda-c	15	30	45	88	137	185

JONAH HEX (See All-Star Western, Hex and Weird Western Tales)
National Periodical Pub./DC Comics: Mar-Apr, 1977 - No. 92, Aug, 1985

1	11	22	33	76	151	225
2	7	14	21	44	72	100
3,4,9: 9-Wrightson-c.	6	12	18	37	59	80
5,6,10: 5-Rep 1st app. from All-Star Western #10	5	10	15	32	51	70
7,8-Explains Hex's face disfigurement (origin)	6	12	18	41	66	90
11-20: 12-Starlin-c	3	6	9	20	30	40
21-32: 31,32-Origin retold	2	4	6	13	18	22
33-50	2	4	6	8	11	14
51-80	1	2	3	5	7	9
81-91: 89-Mark Texeira-a. 91-Cover swipe from Superman #243 (hugging a mystery woman)	2	4	6	8	10	12
92-Story cont'd in Hex #1	3	6	9	20	30	40

*NOTE: **Ayers** a(p)-35-37, 40, 41, 44-53, 56, 58-82. **Buckler** a-11; c-11, 13-16. **Kubert** c-43-46. **Morrow** a-90-92; c-10. **Spiegle(Tothish)** a-34, 38, 40, 49, 52. **Texeira** a-89p. Batlash back-ups in 49, 52. El Diablo back-ups in 48, 56-60, 73-75. Scalphunter back-ups in 40, 41, 45-47.*

JONAH HEX (Also see All Star Western [2011 DC New 52 title])
DC Comics: Jan, 2006 - No. 70, Oct, 2011 ($2.99)

1-Justin Gray & Jimmy Palmiotti-s/Luke Ross-a/Quitely-c 5.00
1-Special Edition (7/10, $1.00) r/#1 with "What's Next?" logo on cover 3.00
2-49,51-70: 3-Bat Lash app. 10,16,17,19,20,22-Noto-a. 11-El Diablo app.; Beck-a. 13-15-Origin retold. 21,23,27,30,32,37,38,42,52,54,57,59,61,63,67-Bernet-a. 33-Darwyn Cooke-a/c. 34-Sparacio-a. 51-Giordano-c. 53-Tucci-c/a. 62-Risso-a 3.00
50-($3.99) Darwyn Cooke-a/c 4.00
...: Bullets Don't Lie TPB (2009, $14.99) r/#31-36 15.00
...: Counting Corpses TPB (2010, $14.99) r/#43,50-54 15.00
...: Face Full of Violence TPB (2006, $12.99) r/#1-6 13.00
...: Guns of Vengeance TPB (2007, $12.99) r/#7-12 13.00
...: Lead Poisoning TPB (2009, $14.99) r/#37-42 15.00
...: Luck Runs Out TPB (2008, $12.99) r/#25-30 13.00
...: No Way Back HC (2010, $19.99) new GN; Gray & Palmiotti-s/DeZuniga-a 20.00
...: No Way Back SC (2011, $14.99) new GN; Gray & Palmiotti-s/DeZuniga-a 15.00
...: Only the Good Die Young TPB (2008, $12.99) r/#19-24 13.00
...: Origins TPB (2007, $12.99) r/#13-18 13.00
...: Tall Tales TPB (2011, $14.99) r/#55-60 15.00
...: The Six Gun War TPB (2010, $14.99) r/#44-49 15.00
...: Welcome to Paradise TPB (2010, $17.99) r/debut in All-Star Western #10 plus early apps. in Weird Western Tales and Jonah Hex #2,4 (1977 series) 18.00

JONAH HEX AND OTHER WESTERN TALES (Blue Ribbon Digest)
DC Comics: Sept-Oct, 1979 - No. 3, Jan-Feb, 1980 (100 pgs.)

1-3: 1-Origin Scalphunter-r, Ayers/Evans, Neal Adams-a.; painted-c. 2-Weird Western Tales-r; Neal Adams, Toth, Aragones-a. 3-Outlaw-r, Scalphunter-r; Gil Kane, Wildey-a	2	4	6	11	16	20

JONAH HEX: RIDERS OF THE WORM AND SUCH
DC Comics (Vertigo): Mar, 1995 - No. 5, July, 1995 ($2.95, limited series)

1-5-Lansdale story, Truman -a 4.00

JONAH HEX: SHADOWS WEST
DC Comics (Vertigo): Feb, 1999 - No. 3, Apr, 1999 ($2.95, limited series)

1-3-Lansdale-s/Truman -a 4.00

JONAH HEX SPECTACULAR (See DC Special Series No. 16)

JONAH HEX: TWO-GUN MOJO
DC Comics (Vertigo): Aug, 1993 - No. 5, Dec, 1993 ($2.95, limited series)

1-Lansdale scripts in all; Truman/Glanzman-a in all w/Truman-c 6.00
1-Platinum edition with no price on cover 20.00
2-5 4.00
TPB-(1994, $12.95) r/#1-5 13.00

JONESY (Formerly Crack Western)
Comic Favorite/Quality Comics Group: No. 85, Aug, 1953; No. 2, Oct, 1953 - No. 8, Oct, 1954

85(#1)-Teen-age humor	9	18	27	47	61	75
2	6	12	18	28	34	40
3-8	5	10	15	24	30	35

JON JUAN (Also see Great Lover Romances)
Toby Press: Spring, 1950

1-All Schomburg-a (signed Al Reid on-c); written by Siegel; used in **SOTI**, pg. 38 (Scarce)	65	130	195	416	708	1000

JONNI THUNDER (...A.K.A. Thunderbolt)
DC Comics: Feb, 1985 - No. 4, Aug, 1985 (75¢, limited series)

1-4: 1-Origin & 1st app. 3.00

JONNY DOUBLE
DC Comics (Vertigo): Sept, 1998 - No. 4, Dec, 1998 ($2.95, limited series)

1-4-Azzarello-s 3.00
TPB (2002, $12.95) r/#1-4; Chiarello-c 13.00

JONNY QUEST (TV)
Gold Key: Dec, 1964 (Hanna-Barbera)

1 (10139-412)	29	58	87	206	446	685

JONNY QUEST (TV)
Comico: June 1986 - No. 31, Dec, 1988 ($1.50/$1.75)(Hanna-Barbera)

1 5.00
2,3,5: 3,5-Dave Stevens-c 4.00
4,6-31: 30-Adapts TV episode 3.00
Special 1(9/88, $1.75), 2(10/88, $1.75) 4.00

*NOTE: **M. Anderson** a-9. **Mooney** a-Special 1. **Pini** a-2. **Quagmire** a-31p. **Rude** a-1; c-2i. **Sienkiewicz** c-11. **Spiegle** a-7, 12, 21; c-21 **Staton** a-2i, 11p. **Steacy** c-8. **Stevens** a-4i; c-3,5. **Wildey** a-1, c-1, 7, 12. **Williamson** a-4i; c-4i.*

JONNY QUEST CLASSICS (TV)
Comico: May, 1987 - No. 3, July, 1987 ($2.00) (Hanna-Barbera)

1-3: Wildey-c/a; 3-Based on TV episode 3.00

JON SABLE, FREELANCE (Also see Mike Grell's Sable & Sable)
First Comics: 6/83 - No. 56, 2/88 (#1-17, $1; #18-33, $1.25, #34-on, $1.75)

1-Mike Grell-c/a/scripts 4.00
2-56: 3-5-Origin, parts 1-3. 6-Origin, part 4. 11-1st app. of Maggie the Cat. 14-Mando paper begins. 16-Maggie the Cat. app. 25-30-Shatter app. 34-Deluxe format begins ($1.75) 3.00

Journey Into Fear #3 © SUPR

Journey Into Mystery #95 © MAR

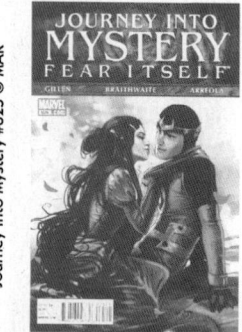

Journey Into Mystery #625 © MAR

GD VG FN VF VF/NM NM-
2.0 4.0 6.0 8.0 9.0 9.2

The Complete Jon Sable, Freelance: Vol. 1 (IDW, 2005, $19.99) r/#1-6 20.00
The Complete Jon Sable, Freelance: Vol. 2 (IDW, 2005, $19.99) r/#7-11 20.00
The Complete Jon Sable, Freelance: Vol. 3 (IDW, 2005, $19.99) r/#12-16 20.00
The Complete Jon Sable, Freelance: Vol. 4 (IDW, 2005, $19.99) r/#17-21 20.00
*NOTE: **Aragones** a-33; c-33(part). **Grell** a-1-43;c-1-52, 53p, 54-56.*

JON SABLE, FREELANCE
IDW Publ.: (Limited series)

...: Ashes of Eden 1-5 (2009 - No. 5, 2/10, $3.99) Mike Grell-c/a/scripts 4.00
...: Bloodtrail 1-6 (4/05 - No. 6, 11/05, $3.99) Mike Grell-c/a/scripts 4.00
...: Bloodtrail TPB (4/06, $19.99) r/#1-6; cover gallery 20.00

JOSEPH & HIS BRETHREN (See The Living Bible)

JOSIE (She's... #1-16) (...& the Pussycats #45 on) (See Archie's Pals 'n' Gals #23 for 1st app.) (Also see Archie Giant Series Magazine #528, 540, 551, 562, 571, 584, 597, 610, 622)
Archie Publ./Radio Comics: Feb, 1963; No. 2, Aug, 1963 - No. 106, Oct, 1982

	GD 2.0	VG 4.0	FN 6.0	VF 8.0	VF/NM 9.0	NM- 9.2
1	14	28	42	93	202	310
2	9	18	27	62	109	155
3-5	7	14	21	46	76	105
6-10: 6-(5/64) Book length Haunted Mansion-c/s. 7-(8/64) 1st app. Alexandra Cabot?	5	10	15	32	51	70
11-20	4	8	12	24	37	50
21, 23-30	3	6	9	19	29	38
22 (9/66)-Mighty Man & Mighty (Josie Girl) app.	4	8	12	26	41	55
31-44	3	6	9	16	23	30
45 (12/69)-Josie and the Pussycats begins (Hanna Barbera TV cartoon); 1st app. of the Pussycats	11	22	33	73	142	210
46-2nd app./1st cover Pussycats	8	16	24	56	96	135
47-3rd app. of the Pussycats	6	12	18	39	62	85
48,49-Pussycats band-c/s	6	12	18	42	69	95
50-J&P-c; go to Hollywood, meet Hanna & Barbera	7	14	21	48	79	110
51-54	3	6	9	19	29	38
55-74 (2/74)(52 pg. issues)	3	6	9	19	29	38
75-90(8/76)	2	4	6	13	18	22
91-99	2	4	6	10	14	18
100 (10/79)	2	4	6	13	18	22
101-106	2	4	6	11	16	20

JOSIE & THE PUSSYCATS (TV)
Archie Comics: 1993 - No. 2, 1994 ($2.00, 52 pgs.)(Published annually)

1,2-Bound-in pull-out poster in each. 2-(Spr/94) 5.00

JOURNAL OF CRIME (See Fox Giants)

JOURNEY
Aardvark-Vanaheim #1-14/Fantagraphics Books #15-on: 1983 - No. 14, Sept, 1984; No. 15, Apr, 1985 - No. 27, July, 1986 (B&W)

1 3.50
2-27: 20-Sam Kieth-a 3.00

JOURNEY INTO FEAR
Superior-Dynamic Publications: May, 1951 - No. 21, Sept, 1954

	GD 2.0	VG 4.0	FN 6.0	VF 8.0	VF/NM 9.0	NM- 9.2
1-Baker-r(2)	69	138	207	442	759	1075
2	47	94	141	296	498	700
3,4	40	80	120	246	411	575
5-10,15: 15-Used in **SOTI**, pg. 389	33	66	99	194	317	440
11-14,16-21	30	60	90	177	289	400

*NOTE: Kamenish 'headlight'-a most issues. **Robinson** a-10.*

JOURNEY INTO MYSTERY (1st Series) (Thor Nos. 126-502)
Atlas(CPS No. 1-48/AMI No. 49-68/Marvel No. 69 (6/61) on): 6/52 - No. 48, 8/57; No. 49, 11/58 - No. 125, 2/66; 503, 11/96 - No. 521, June, 1998

	GD 2.0	VG 4.0	FN 6.0	VF 8.0	VF/NM 9.0	NM- 9.2
1-Weird/horror stories begin	354	708	1062	2478	4339	6200
2	116	232	348	742	1271	1800
3,4	87	174	261	553	952	1350
5-11	61	122	183	390	670	950
12-20,22: 15-Atomic explosion panel. 22-Davis*esque*-a; last pre-code issue (2/55)	50	100	150	315	533	750
21-Kubert-a; Tothish-a by Andru	51	102	153	318	539	760
23-32,35-38,40: 24-Torres?-a. 38-Ditko-a	39	78	117	236	388	540
33-Williamson-a; Ditko-a (his 1st for Atlas?)	40	80	120	246	411	575
34,39: 34-Krigstein-a. 39-1st S.A. issue; Wood-a	39	78	117	240	395	550
41-Crandall-a; Frazetta*esque*-a by Morrow	21	42	63	146	311	475
42,46,48: 42,48-Torres-a. 46-Torres & Krigstein-a	21	42	63	142	304	465
43,44-Williamson/Mayo-a in both. 43-Invisible Woman prototype	21	42	63	146	311	475
45,47	20	40	60	137	294	450
49-Matt Fox, Check-a	21	42	63	142	304	465
50,52-54: Ditko/Kirby-a. 50-Davis-a. 54-Williamson-a	24	48	72	168	359	550
51-Kirby/Wood-a	25	50	75	171	366	560
55-61,63-65,67-69,71,72,74,75: 74-Contents change to Fantasy. 75-Last 10¢ issue	24	48	72	168	359	550
62-Prototype ish. (The Hulk); 1st app. Xemnu (Titan) called "The Hulk"	32	64	96	232	504	775
66-Prototype ish. (The Hulk)-Return of Xemnu "The Hulk"	29	58	87	210	455	700
70-Prototype ish. (The Sandman)(7/61); similar to Spidey villain	27	54	81	196	423	650
73-Story titled "The Spider" where a spider is exposed to radiation & gets powers of a human and shoots webbing; a reverse prototype of Spider-Man's origin	38	76	114	285	618	950
76,77,80-82: 80-Anti-communist propaganda story	21	42	63	146	311	475
76-(10¢ cover price blacked out, 12¢ printed on)	37	74	111	278	602	925
78-The Sorceror (Dr. Strange prototype) app. (3/62)	27	54	81	196	423	650
79-Prototype issue. (Mr. Hyde)	25	50	75	175	375	575
83-Origin & 1st app. The Mighty Thor by Kirby (8/62) and begin series; Thor-c also begin	1050	2100	3150	12,000	26,000	40,000
83-Reprint from the Golden Record Comic Set	17	34	51	119	260	400
With the record (1966)	26	52	78	182	391	600
84-2nd app. Thor	207	414	621	1739	3770	5800
85-1st app. Loki & Heimdall; 1st brief app. Odin (1 panel); 1st app. Asgard	150	300	450	1260	2730	4200
86-1st full app. Odin	85	170	255	689	1495	2300
87-89: 89-Origin Thor retold	67	134	201	545	1173	1800
90-No Kirby-a	54	108	162	437	944	1450
91,92,94,96-Sinnott-a	42	84	126	315	683	1050
93,97-Kirby-a; Tales of Asgard series begins #97 (origin which concludes in #99); origin/1st app. Lava Man	46	92	138	352	764	1175
95-Sinnott-a; Thor vs. Thor	46	92	138	359	780	1200
98,99-Kirby/Heck-a. 98-Origin/1st app. The Human Cobra. 99-1st app. Surtur & Mr. Hyde	34	68	102	247	536	825
100-Kirby/Heck-a; Thor battles Mr. Hyde	34	68	102	247	536	825
101,108: 101-(2/64)-2nd Avengers x-over (w/o Capt. America); see Tales Of Suspense #49 for 1st x-over. 108-(9/64)-Early Dr. Strange & Avengers x-over; ten extra pgs. Kirby-a	24	48	72	168	359	550
102,104-107,110: 102-Intro Sif. 105-109-Ten extra pgs. Kirby-a in each. 107-1st app. Grey Gargoyle. 110,111-Two part battle vs. The Human Cobra & Mr. Hyde	22	44	66	154	327	500
103-1st app. Enchantress	27	54	81	196	423	650
109-Magneto-c & app. (1st x-over, 10/64)	44	88	132	330	715	1100
111,113: 113-Origin Loki	17	34	51	119	260	400
112-Thor Vs. Hulk (1/65); Origin Loki	54	108	162	437	944	1450
114-Origin/1st app. Absorbing Man	24	48	72	168	359	550
115-Detailed origin of Loki	21	42	63	146	311	475
116,117,120-123,125	14	28	42	97	211	325
118-1st app. Destroyer	21	42	63	146	311	475
119-Intro Hogun, Fandral, Volstagg; 2nd Destroyer	16	32	48	111	243	375
124-Hercules-c/story	15	30	45	102	221	340

503-521: 503-(11/96, $1.50)-The Lost Gods begin; Tom DeFalco scripts & Deodato Studios-c/a. 505-Spider-Man-c/app. 509-Loki-c/app. 514-516-Shang-Chi 3.00
#(-1) Flashback (7/97) Tales of Asgard Donald Blake app. 3.00

	GD 2.0	VG 4.0	FN 6.0	VF 8.0	VF/NM 9.0	NM- 9.2
Annual 1(1965, 25¢, 72 pgs.)-New Thor vs. Hercules(1st app.)-c/story (see Incredible Hulk #3); Kirby-c/a; r/#85,93,95,97	23	46	69	161	343	525

*NOTE: **Ayers** a-14, 39, 64i, 71i, 74i, 80i. **Bailey** a-43. **Briefer** a-5, 12. **Cameron** a-35. **Check** a-17. **Colan** a-23, 81; c-14. **Ditko** a-33, 38, 50-96; c-58, 67, 71, 88i. **Kirby/Ditko** a-50-83. **Everett** a-20, 48; c-4-7, 9, 36, 37, 39-42, 44, 45, 47. **Forte** a-19, 35, 40, 53. **Heath** a-4-6, 11, 14; c-1, 8, 11, 15, 51. **Heck** a-53, 73. **Kirby** a(p)-51, 52, 56, 57-60, 62-64, 66, 67, 69-89, 93, 97, 98, 100(w/**Heck**), 101-125; c-50-57, 59-66, 68-70, 72-82, 88(w/**Ditko**), 83 & 84(w/**Sinnott**), 85-96(w/**Ayers**), 97-125p. **Leiber/Fox** a-93, 98-102. **Maneely** c-20-22. **Morisi** a-42. **Morrow** a-41, 42. **Orlando** a-30, 45, 57. **Mac Pakula** (Tothish) a-9, 35, 41. **Powell** a-20, 27, 34. **Reinman** a-39, 87, 92, 96i. **Robinson** a-9. **Roussos** a-39. **Robert Sale** a-14. **Severin** a-27; c-30. **Sinnott** a-41; c-50. **Tuska** a-11. **Wildey** a-16.*

JOURNEY INTO MYSTERY (Series and numbering continue from Thor #621)
Marvel Comics: No. 622, Jun, 2011 - Present ($3.99/$2.99)

622-Reincarnated young Loki; Thor app.; Braithwaite-a; Hans-c 4.00
622-Variant covers by Art Adams and Lee Weeks 6.00
623-626, 626.1, 627-630-($2.99) Fear Itself tie-in. 628,629-Portacio-a 3.00
631-634: 631-Portacio-a; Aftermath. 632-Hellstrom app. 3.00

JOURNEY INTO MYSTERY (2nd Series)
Marvel Comics: Oct, 1972 - No. 19, Oct, 1975

	GD 2.0	VG 4.0	FN 6.0	VF 8.0	VF/NM 9.0	NM- 9.2
1-Robert Howard adaptation; Starlin/Ploog-a	4	8	12	24	37	50
2-5: 2,3,5-Bloch adapt. 4-H. P. Lovecraft adapt.	3	6	9	16	23	30

Journey Into Unknown Worlds #13 © MAR

JSA #7 © DC

JSA Classified #1 © DC

	GD 2.0	VG 4.0	FN 6.0	VF 8.0	VF/NM 9.0	NM- 9.2
6-19: Reprints	3	6	9	14	20	25

NOTE: ***N. Adams*** *a-2i.* ***Ditko*** *r-7, 10, 12, 14, 15, 19; c-10.* ***Everett*** *r-9, 14.* ***G. Kane*** *a-1p, 2p; c-1-3p.* ***Kirby*** *r-7, 13, 15, 18, 19; c-7.* ***Mort Lawrence*** *r-2.* ***Maneely*** *r-3.* ***Orlando*** *r-16.* ***Reese*** *a-1, 2i.* ***Starlin*** *a-1p, 3p.* ***Torres*** *r-16.* ***Wildey*** *r-9, 14.*

JOURNEY INTO UNKNOWN WORLDS (Formerly Teen)
Atlas Comics (WFP): No. 36, Sept, 1950 - No. 38, Feb, 1951;
No. 4, Apr, 1951 - No. 59, Aug, 1957

	GD	VG	FN	VF	VF/NM	NM-
36(#1)-Science fiction/weird; "End Of The Earth" c/story	271	542	813	1734	2967	4200
37(#2)-Science fiction; "When Worlds Collide" c/story; Everett-c/a; Hitler story	110	220	330	704	1202	1700
38(#3)-Science fiction	92	184	276	584	1005	1425
4-6,8,10-Science fiction/weird	56	112	168	356	611	865
7-Wolverton-a "Planet of Terror", 6 pgs; electric chair c-inset/story	94	188	282	597	1024	1450
9-Giant eyeball story	74	148	222	470	810	1150
11,12-Krigstein-a	42	84	126	265	445	625
13,16,17,20	39	78	117	231	378	525
14-Wolverton-a "One of Our Graveyards Is Missing", 4 pgs; Tuska-a	69	138	207	442	759	1075
15-Wolverton-a "They Crawl by Night", 5 pgs.; 2 pg. Maneely s/f story	69	138	207	442	759	1075
18,19-Matt Fox-a	42	84	126	265	445	625
21-33: 21-Decapitation-c. 24-Sci/fic story. 26-Atom bomb panel. 27-Sid Check-a. 33-Last pre-code (2/55)	29	58	87	170	278	385
34-Kubert, Torres-a	22	44	66	132	216	300
35-Torres-a	20	40	60	120	195	270
36-45,48,50,53,55,59: 43-Krigstein-a. 44-Davis-a. 45,55,59-Williamson-a in all; with Mayo #55,59. 55-Crandall-a. 48,53-Crandall-a (4 pgs. #48). 48-Check-a. 50-Davis, Crandall-a	20	40	60	117	189	260
46,47,49,52,54,56-58: 54-Torres-a	19	38	57	109	172	235
51-Ditko, Wood-a	21	42	63	126	206	285

NOTE: ***Ayers*** *a-24, 43,* ***Berg*** *a-38(#3), 43.* ***Lou Cameron*** *a-33.* ***Colan*** *a-37(#2), 6, 17, 19, 20, 23, 39.* ***Ditko*** *a-45, 51.* ***Drucker*** *a-35, 58.* ***Everett*** *a-37(#2), 11, 14, 41, 55, 56; c-37(#2), 11, 13, 14, 17, 22, 47, 48, 50, 53-55, 59.* ***Forte*** *a-49.* ***Fox*** *a-21i.* ***Heath*** *a-36(#1), 4, 6-8, 17, 20, 22, 36i; c-18.* ***Keller*** *a-15.* ***Mort Lawrence*** *a-38, 39.* ***Maneely*** *a-7, 8, 15, 16, 22, 49, 58; c-19, 25, 52.* ***Morrow*** *a-48.* ***Orlando*** *a-44, 57.* ***Pakula*** *a-36.* ***Powell*** *a-42, 53, 54.* ***Reinman*** *a-8.* ***Rico*** *a-21.* ***Robert Sale*** *a-24, 49.* ***Sekowsky*** *a-4, 5, 9.* ***Severin*** *a-38, 51; c-38, 48i, 56.* ***Sinnott*** *a-9, 21, 24.* ***Tuska*** *a-38(#3), 14.* ***Wildey*** *a-25, 43, 44.*

JOURNEYMAN
Image Comics: Aug, 1999 - No. 3, Oct, 1999 ($2.95, B&W, limited series)

1-3-Brandon McKinney-s/a 3.00

JOURNEY TO THE CENTER OF THE EARTH (Movie)
Dell Publishing Co.: No. 1060, Nov-Jan, 1959/60 (one-shot)

	GD	VG	FN	VF	VF/NM	NM-
Four Color 1060-Pat Boone & James Mason photo-c	10	20	30	71	128	185

JSA (Justice Society of America) (Also see All Star Comics)
DC Comics: Aug, 1999 - No. 87, Sept, 2006 ($2.50/$2.99)

	GD	VG	FN	VF	VF/NM	NM-
1-Robinson and Goyer-s; funeral of Wesley Dodds	2	4	6	8	10	12
25-($3.75) Hawkman rejoins the JSA	1	2	3	5	7	9

2-5: 4-Return of Dr. Fate 6.00
6-24: 6-Black Adam-c/app. 11,12-Kobra. 16-20-JSA vs. Johnny Sorrow. 19,20-Spectre app. 22-Hawkgirl origin. 23-Hawkman returns 4.00
26-36, 38-49: 27-Capt. Marvel app. 29-Joker: Last Laugh. 31,32-Snejbjerg-a. 33-Ultra-Humanite. 34-Intro. new Crimson Avenger and Hourman. 42-G.A. Mr. Terrific and the Freedom Fighters app. 46-Eclipso returns 3.00
37-($3.50) Johnny Thunder merges with the Thunderbolt; origin new Crimson Avenger 4.00
50-($3.95) Wraparound-c by Pacheco; Sentinel becomes Green Lantern again 4.00
51-74,76-82: 51-Kobra killed. 54-JLA app. 55-Ma Hunkle (Red Tornado) app. 56-58-Black Reign x-over with Hawkman #23-25. 64-Sand returns. 67-Identity Crisis tie-in; Gibbons-a. 68,69,72-81-Ross-c. 73,74-Day of Vengeance tie-in. 76-OMAC tie-in. 82-Infinite Crisis x-over; Levitz-s/Perez-a 3.00
75-($2.99) Day of Vengeance tie-in; Alex Ross Spectre-c 4.00
83-87: One Year Later; Pérez-c. 83-85,87-Morales-a; Gentleman Ghost app. 85-Begin $2.99-c; Earth-2 Batman, Atom, Sandman, Mr. Terrific app. 86,87-Ordway-a. 3.00
Annual 1 (10/00, $3.50) Planet DC; intro. Nemesis 4.00
...: Black Reign TPB (2005, $12.99) r/#56-58, Hawkman #23-25; Watson cover gallery 13.00
...: Black Vengeance TPB (2006, $19.99) r/#66-75 20.00
...: Darkness Falls TPB (2002, $19.95) r/#6-15 20.00
...: Fair Play TPB (2003, $14.95) r/#26-31 & Secret Files #2 15.00
...: Ghost Stories TPB (2006, $14.99) r/#82-87 15.00
...: Justice Be Done TPB (2000, $14.95) r/Secret Files & #1-5 15.00
...: Lost TPB (2005, $19.99) r/#59-67 20.00
...: Mixed Signals TPB (2006, $14.99) r/#76-81 15.00
...: Our Worlds at War 1 (9/01, $2.95) Jae Lee-c; Saltares-a 3.00
... Presents Green Lantern TPB (2008, $14.99) r/JSA Classified #25,32,33 and Green Lantern: Brightest Day, Blackest Night 15.00
...: Princes of Darkness TPB (2005, $19.95) r/#46-55 20.00
...: Savage Times TPB (2004, $14.95) r/#39-45 15.00
... Secret Files 1 (8/99, $4.95) Origin stories and pin-ups; death of Wesley Dodds (G.A. Sandman); intro new Hawkgirl 5.00
... Secret Files 2 (9/01, $4.95) Short stories and profile pages 5.00
...: Stealing Thunder TPB (2003, $14.95) r/#32-38; JSA vs. The Ultra-Humanite 15.00
...: The Golden Age TPB (2005, $19.99) r/"The Golden Age" Elseworlds mini-series 20.00
...: The Return of Hawkman TPB (2002, $19.95) r/#16-26 & Secret Files #1 20.00

JSA: ALL STARS
DC Comics: July, 2003 - No. 8, Feb, 2004 ($2.50/$3.50, limited series, back-up stories in Golden Age style)

1-6,8-Goyer & Johns-s/Cassaday-c. 1-Velluto-a; intro. Legacy. 2-Hawkman by Loeb/Sale 3-Dr. Fate by Cooke. 4-Starman by Robinson/Harris. 5-Hourman by Chaykin. 6-Dr. Mid-nite by Azzarello/Risso 3.00
7-($3.50) Mr. Terrific back-up story by Chabon; Lark-a 4.00
TPB (2004, $14.95) r/#1-8 15.00

JSA: ALL STARS
DC Comics: Feb, 2010 - No. 18, Jul, 2011 ($3.99/$2.99)

1-13-Younger JSA members form team. 1-Covers by Williams and Sook 4.00
14-18-($2.99) 3.00
...: Constellations TPB (2010, $14.99) r/#1-6 and sketch art 15.00
...: Glory Days TPB (2011, $17.99) r/#7-13 18.00

JSA: CLASSIFIED (Issues #1-4 reprinted in Power Girl TPB)
DC Comics: Sept, 2005 - No. 39, Aug, 2008 ($2.50/$2.99)

1-(1st printing) Conner-c/a; origin of Power Girl 3.00
1-(1st printing) Adam Hughes variant-c 5.00
1-(2nd & 3rd printings) 2nd-Hughes B&W sketch-c. 3rd-Close-up of Conner-c 3.00
2-11: 2-LSH app. 4-Leads into Infinite Crisis #2. 5-7-Injustice Society app. 10-13-Vandal Savage origin retold; Gulacy-a/c 3.00
12-39: 12-Begin $2.99-c. 17,18-Bane app. 19,20-Morales-a. 21,22-Simonson-s/a 3.00
...: Honor Among Thieves TPB (2007, $14.99) r/#5-9 15.00

JSA STRANGE ADVENTURES
DC Comics: Oct, 2004 - No. 6, Mar, 2005 ($3.50, limited series)

1-6-Johnny Thunder as pulp writer; Kitson-a/Watson-c/ Kevin Anderson-s 3.50
TPB (2010, $14.99) r/#1-6 15.00

JSA: THE LIBERTY FILE (Elseworlds)
DC Comics: Feb, 2000 - No. 2, Mar, 2000 ($6.95, limited series)

1,2-Batman, Dr. Mid-Nite and Hourman vs. WW2 Joker; Tony Harris-c/a 7.00
JSA: The Liberty Files TPB (2004, $19.95) r/The Liberty File and The Unholy Three series 20.00

JSA: THE UNHOLY THREE (Elseworlds)(Sequel to JSA: The Liberty File)
DC Comics: 2003 - No. 2, 2003 ($6.95, limited series)

1,2-Batman, Superman and Hourman; Tony Harris-c/a 7.00

JSA VS. KOBRA
DC Comics: Aug, 2009 - No. 6, Jan, 2010 ($2.99, limited series)

1-6-Kramer-a/Ha-c; Jason Burr app. 3.00
TPB (2010, $14.99) r/#1-6; cover gallery 15.00

J2 (Also see A-Next and Juggernaut)
Marvel Comics: Oct, 1998 - No. 12, Sept, 1999 ($1.99)

1-12:1-Juggernaut's son; Lim-a. 2-Two covers; X-People app. 3-J2 battles the Hulk 3.00
Spider-Girl Presents Juggernaut Jr. Vol.1: Secrets & Lies (2006, $7.99, digest) r/#1-6 8.00

JUBILEE (X-Men)
Marvel Comics: Nov, 2004 - No. 6, Apr, 2005 ($2.99)

1-6: 1-Jubilee in a Los Angeles high school; Kirkman-s; Casey Jones-c 3.00

JUDENHASS
Aardvark-Vanaheim Press: 2008 ($4.00, B&W, squarebound)

nn-Dave Sim-writer/artist; The Shoah and Jewish persecution through history 4.00

JUDE, THE FORGOTTEN SAINT
Catechetical Guild Education Soc.: 1954 (16 pgs.; 8x11"; full color; paper-c)

	GD	VG	FN	VF	VF/NM	NM-
nn	6	12	18	28	34	40

J.U.D.G.E.: THE SECRET RAGE
Image Comics: Mar, 2000 - No. 3, May, 2000 ($2.95)

1-3-Greg Horn-s/c/a 3.00

JUDGE COLT
Gold Key: Oct, 1969 - No. 4, Sept, 1970

Judomaster #92 © CC

Juggernaut (1999) #1 © MAR

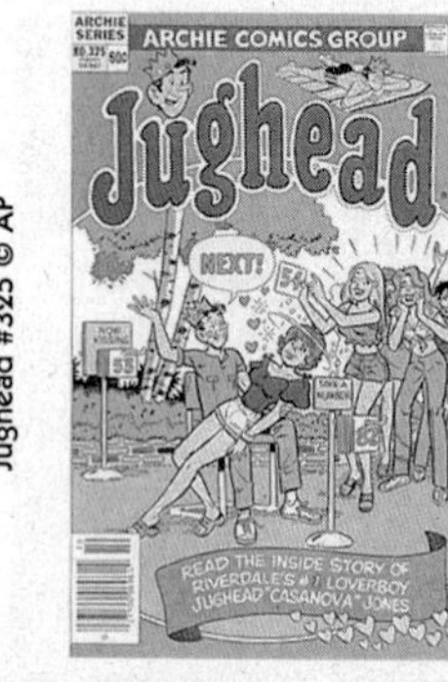

Jughead #325 © AP

	GD 2.0	VG 4.0	FN 6.0	VF 8.0	VF/NM 9.0	NM- 9.2
1	3	6	9	16	23	30
2-4	2	4	6	9	13	16

JUDGE DREDD (...Classics #62 on; also see Batman - Judge Dredd, The Law of Dredd & 2000 A.D. Monthly)
Eagle Comics/IPC Magazines Ltd./Quality Comics #34-35, V2#1-37/ Fleetway #38 on: Nov, 1983 - No. 35, 1986; V2#1, Oct, 1986 - No. 77, 1993

	GD	VG	FN	VF	VF/NM	NM-
1-Bolland-c/a						6.00
2-35						3.00
V2#1-77: 1-('86)-New look begins. 20-Begin $1.50-c. 21/22, 23/24-Two issue numbers in one. 28-1st app. Megaman (super-hero). 39-Begin $1.75-c. 51-Begin $1.95-c. 53-Bolland-a. 57-Reprints 1st published Judge Dredd story						3.00
Special 1						4.00

NOTE: ***Bolland** a-1-6, 8, 10; c-1-10, 15.* ***Guice** c-V2#23/24, 26, 27.*

JUDGE DREDD (3rd Series)
DC Comics: Aug, 1994 - No. 18, Jan, 1996 ($1.95)

	GD	VG	FN	VF	VF/NM	NM-
1-18: 12-Begin $2.25-c						3.00
nn ($5.95)-Movie adaptation, Sienkiewicz-c						6.00

JUDGE DREDD'S CRIME FILE
Eagle Comics: Aug, 1989 - No. 6, Feb, 1986 ($1.25, limited series)

	GD	VG	FN	VF	VF/NM	NM-
1-6: 1-Byrne-a						3.00

JUDGE DREDD: LEGENDS OF THE LAW
DC Comics: Dec, 1994 - No. 13, Dec, 1995 ($1.95)

	GD	VG	FN	VF	VF/NM	NM-
1-13: 1-5-Dorman-c						3.00

JUDGE DREDD: THE EARLY CASES
Eagle Comics: Feb, 1986 - No. 6, Jul, 1986 ($1.25, Mega-series, Mando paper)

	GD	VG	FN	VF	VF/NM	NM-
1-6: 2000 A.D.-r						3.00

JUDGE DREDD: THE JUDGE CHILD QUEST (Judge Child in indicia)
Eagle Comics: Aug, 1984 - No. 5, Oct, 1984 ($1.25, Lim. series, Baxter paper)

	GD	VG	FN	VF	VF/NM	NM-
1-5: 2000A.D.-r; Bolland-c/a						3.00

JUDGE DREDD: THE MEGAZINE
Fleetway/Quality: 1991 - Present ($4.95, stiff-c, squarebound, 52 pgs.)

	GD	VG	FN	VF	VF/NM	NM-
1-3						5.00

JUDGE DREDD VS. ALIENS: INCUBUS
Dark Horse Comics: March, 2003 - No. 4, June, 2003 ($2.99, limited series)

	GD	VG	FN	VF	VF/NM	NM-
1-4-Flint-a/Wagner & Diggle-s						3.00

JUDGE PARKER
Argo: Feb, 1956 - No. 2, 1956

	GD	VG	FN	VF	VF/NM	NM-
1-Newspaper strip reprints	7	14	21	35	43	50
2	5	10	15	24	30	35

JUDGMENT DAY
Awesome Entertainment: June, 1997 - No. 3, Oct, 1997 ($2.50, limited series)

	GD	VG	FN	VF	VF/NM	NM-
1-3: 1 Alpha-Moore-s/Liefeld-c/a(p) flashback art by various in all. 2 Omega. 3 Final Judgment. All have a variant cover by Dave Gibbons						3.00
...Aftermath-($3.50) Moore-s/Kane-a; Youngblood, Glory, New Men, Maximage, Allies and Spacehunter short stories. Also has a variant cover by Dave Gibbons						4.00
TPB (Checker Books, 2003, $16.95) r/series						17.00

JUDO JOE
Jay-Jay Corp.: Aug, 1953 - No. 3, Dec, 1953 (Judo lessons in each issue)

	GD	VG	FN	VF	VF/NM	NM-
1-Drug ring story	11	22	33	62	86	110
2,3: 3-Hypo needle story	8	16	24	42	54	65

JUDOMASTER (Gun Master #84-89) (Also see Crisis on Infinite Earths, Sarge Steel #6, Special War Series, & Thunderbolt)
Charlton Comics: No. 89, May-June, 1966 - No. 98, Dec, 1967 (Two No. 89's)

	GD	VG	FN	VF	VF/NM	NM-
89-3rd app. Judomaster	4	8	12	26	41	55
90-Origin of Thunderbolt	4	8	12	24	37	50
91-Sarge Steel begins	4	8	12	22	34	45
92-98: 93-Intro. Tiger	3	6	9	21	32	42
93,94,96,98 (Modern Comics reprint, 1977)						6.00

NOTE: ***Morisi** Thunderbolt #90. #91 has 1 pg. biography on writer/artist Frank McLaughlin.*

JUDY CANOVA (Formerly My Experience) (Stage, screen, radio)
Fox Features Syndicate: No. 23, May, 1950 - No. 3, Sept, 1950

	GD	VG	FN	VF	VF/NM	NM-
23(#1)-Wood-c,a(p)?	24	48	72	144	237	330
24-Wood-a(p)	24	48	72	140	230	320
3-Wood-c; Wood/Orlando-a	26	52	78	154	252	350

JUDY GARLAND (See Famous Stars)

JUDY JOINS THE WAVES
Toby Press: 1951 (For U.S. Navy)

	GD	VG	FN	VF	VF/NM	NM-
nn	7	14	21	35	43	50

JUGGERNAUT (See X-Men)
Marvel Comics: Apr, 1997, Nov, 1999 ($2.99, one-shots)

	GD	VG	FN	VF	VF/NM	NM-
1-(4/97) Kelly-s/ Rouleau-a						3.00
1-(11/99) Casey-s; Eighth Day x-over; Thor, Iron Man, Spidey app.						3.00

JUGHEAD (Formerly Archie's Pal...)
Archie Publications: No. 127, Dec, 1965 - No. 352, June, 1987

	GD	VG	FN	VF	VF/NM	NM-
127-130: 129-LBJ on cover	3	6	9	18	27	35
131,133,135-160(9/68)	3	6	9	16	22	28
132,134: 132-Shield-c; The Fly & Black Hood app.; Shield cameo. 134-Shield-c	4	8	12	28	44	60
161-180	2	4	6	13	18	22
181-199	2	4	6	9	13	16
200(1/'72)	2	4	6	11	16	20
201-240(5/75)	2	4	6	8	10	12
241-270(11/77)	1	2	3	5	7	9
271-299	1	2	3	4	5	7
300(5/80)-Anniversary issue; infinity-c	1	2	3	5	6	8
301-320(1/82)						5.00
321-324,326-352						4.00
325-(10/82) Cheryl Blossom app. (not on cover); same month as intro. (cover & story) in Archie's Girls, Betty & Veronica #320; Jason Blossom app.; DeCarlo-a	3	6	9	20	30	40

JUGHEAD (2nd Series)(Becomes Archie's Pal Jughead Comics #46 on)
Archie Enterprises: Aug, 1987 - No. 45, May, 1993 (.75/$1.00/$1.25)

	GD	VG	FN	VF	VF/NM	NM-
1	1	2	3	4	5	7
2-10						4.00
11-45: 4-X-Mas issue. 17-Colan-c/a						3.00

JUGHEAD & FRIENDS DIGEST MAGAZINE
Archie Publ.: June, 2005 - No. 38, Aug, 2010 ($2.39/$2.49/$2.69, digest-size)

	GD	VG	FN	VF	VF/NM	NM-
1-38: 1-That Wilkin Boy app.						3.00

JUGHEAD AS CAPTAIN HERO (See Archie as Pureheart the Powerful, Archie Giant Series Magazine #142 & Life With Archie)
Archie Publications: Oct, 1966 - No. 7, Nov, 1967

	GD	VG	FN	VF	VF/NM	NM-
1-Super hero parody	7	14	21	48	79	110
2	5	10	15	30	48	65
3-7	4	8	12	26	41	55

JUGHEAD COMICS. NIGHT AT GEPPI'S ENTERTAINMENT MUSEUM
Archie Comic Publ. Inc: 2008

	GD	VG	FN	VF	VF/NM	NM-
Free Comic Book Day giveaway - New story; Archie gang visits GEM; Steve Geppi app.						3.00

JUGHEAD JONES COMICS DIGEST, THE (...Magazine No. 10-64; Jughead Jones Digest Magazine #65)
Archie Publ.: June, 1977 - No. 100, May, 1996 ($1.35/$1.50/$1.75, digest-size, 128 pgs.)

	GD	VG	FN	VF	VF/NM	NM-
1-Neal Adams-a; Capt. Hero-r	3	6	9	21	32	42
2(9/77)-Neal Adams-a	3	6	9	16	22	28
3-6,8-10	2	4	6	11	16	20
7-Origin Jaguar-r; N. Adams-a.	2	4	6	13	18	22
11-20: 13-r/1957 Jughead's Folly	2	4	6	8	10	12
21-50	1	2	3	4	5	7
51-70						5.00
71-100						3.00

JUGHEAD'S BABY TALES
Archie Comics: Spring, 1994 - No. 2, Wint. 1994 ($2.00, 52 pgs.)

	GD	VG	FN	VF	VF/NM	NM-
1,2: 1-Bound-in pull-out poster						4.00

JUGHEAD'S DINER
Archie Comics: Apr, 1990 - No. 7, Apr, 1991 ($1.00)

	GD	VG	FN	VF	VF/NM	NM-
1						4.00
2-7						3.00

JUGHEAD'S DOUBLE DIGEST (...Magazine #5)
Archie Comics: Oct, 1989 - Present ($2.25 - $3.99)

	GD	VG	FN	VF	VF/NM	NM-
1	2	4	6	8	10	12
2-10: 2,5-Capt. Hero stories	1	2	3	5	6	8
11-25						5.00
26-181: 58-Begin $2.99-c. 66-Begin $3.19-c. 91-Begin $3.59-c. 138-Reprints entire Jughead #1 (1949). 139-142-"New Look" Jughead; Staton-a. 148-Begin $3.99-c						4.00

Jughead's Jokes #5 © AP

Jumbo Comics #25 © FH

Jungle Action #16 © MAR

	GD 2.0	VG 4.0	FN 6.0	VF 8.0	VF/NM 9.0	NM- 9.2
Archie New Look Series Book 2, Jughead "The Matchmakers" TPB (2009, $10.95) r/new look series in #139-142; new cover by Staton & Milgrom						11.00

JUGHEAD'S EAT-OUT COMIC BOOK MAGAZINE (See Archie Giant Series Magazine No. 170)

JUGHEAD'S FANTASY
Archie Publications: Aug, 1960 - No. 3, Dec, 1960

	GD 2.0	VG 4.0	FN 6.0	VF 8.0	VF/NM 9.0	NM- 9.2
1	15	30	45	102	221	340
2	11	22	33	71	136	200
3	9	18	27	63	112	160

JUGHEAD'S FOLLY
Archie Publications (Close-Up): 1957 (36 pgs.)(one-shot)

	GD 2.0	VG 4.0	FN 6.0	VF 8.0	VF/NM 9.0	NM- 9.2
1-Jughead a la Elvis (Rare) (1st reference to Elvis in comics?)	54	108	162	343	574	825

JUGHEAD'S JOKES
Archie Publications: Aug, 1967 - No. 78, Sept, 1982
(No. 1-8, 38 on: reg. size; No. 9-23: 68 pgs.; No. 24-37: 52 pgs.)

	GD 2.0	VG 4.0	FN 6.0	VF 8.0	VF/NM 9.0	NM- 9.2
1	6	12	18	42	69	95
2	4	8	12	24	37	50
3-8	3	6	9	17	25	32
9,10 (68 pgs.)	3	6	9	19	29	38
11-23(4/71) (68 pgs.)	3	6	9	16	23	30
24-37(1/74) (52 pgs.)	2	4	6	11	16	20
38-50(9/76)	1	3	4	6	8	10
51-78						6.00

JUGHEAD'S PAL HOT DOG (See Laugh #14 for 1st app.)
Archie Comics: Jan, 1990 - No. 5, Oct, 1990 ($1.00)

	GD 2.0	VG 4.0	FN 6.0	VF 8.0	VF/NM 9.0	NM- 9.2
1						4.00
2-5						3.00

JUGHEAD'S SOUL FOOD
Spire Christian Comics (Fleming H. Revell Co.): 1979 (49¢/59¢)

	GD 2.0	VG 4.0	FN 6.0	VF 8.0	VF/NM 9.0	NM- 9.2
nn-Low print run	3	6	9	14	19	24

JUGHEAD'S TIME POLICE
Archie Comics: July, 1990 - No. 6, May, 1991 ($1.00, bi-monthly)

	GD 2.0	VG 4.0	FN 6.0	VF 8.0	VF/NM 9.0	NM- 9.2
1						4.00
2-6: Colan a-3-6p; c-3-6						3.00

JUGHEAD WITH ARCHIE DIGEST (...Plus Betty & Veronica & Reggie Too No. 1,2; ...Magazine #33-?, 101-on; ...Comics Digest Mag.)
Archie Pub.: Mar, 1974 - No. 200, May, 2005 ($1.00-$2.39)

	GD 2.0	VG 4.0	FN 6.0	VF 8.0	VF/NM 9.0	NM- 9.2
1	5	10	15	34	55	75
2	4	8	12	22	34	45
3-10	3	6	9	18	27	35
11-13,15-17,19,20: Capt. Hero-r in #14-16; Capt. Pureheart #17,19	2	4	6	10	14	18
14,18,21,22-Pureheart the Powerful in #18,21,22	2	4	6	11	16	20
23-30: 29-The Shield-r. 30-The Fly-r	1	3	4	6	8	10
31-50,100	1	2	3	5	6	8
51-99	1	2	3	4	5	7
101-121						4.00
122-200: 156-Begin $2.19-c. 180-Begin $2.39-c						3.00

JUKE BOX COMICS
Famous Funnies: Mar, 1948 - No. 6, Jan, 1949

	GD 2.0	VG 4.0	FN 6.0	VF 8.0	VF/NM 9.0	NM- 9.2
1-Toth-c/a; Hollingsworth-a	37	74	111	222	361	500
2-Transvestism story	22	44	66	132	216	300
3-6: 3-Peggy Lee story. 4-Jimmy Durante line drawn-c. 6-Features Desi Arnaz plus Arnaz line drawn-c	18	36	54	105	165	225

JUMBO COMICS (Created by S.M. Iger)
Fiction House Magazines (Real Adv. Publ. Co.): Sept, 1938 - No. 167, Mar, 1953 (No. 1-3: 68 pgs.; No. 4-8: 52 pgs.)(No. 1-8 oversized-10-1/2x14-1/2"; black & white)

	GD 2.0	VG 4.0	FN 6.0	VF 8.0	VF/NM 9.0	NM- 9.2
1-(Rare)-Sheena Queen of the Jungle(1st app.) by Meskin, Hawks of the Seas (The Hawk #10 on; see Feature Funnies #3) by Eisner, The Hunchback by Dick Briefer (ends #8), Wilton of the West (ends #24), Inspector Dayton (ends #67) & ZX-5 (ends #140) begin; 1st comic art by Jack Kirby (Count of Monte Cristo & Wilton of the West); Mickey Mouse appears (1 panel) with brief biography of Walt Disney; 1st app. Peter Pupp by Bob Kane. Note: Sheena was created by Iger for publication in England as a newspaper strip. The early issues of Jumbo contain Sheena strip-r; multiple panel-c 1,2,7	2200	4400	6600	22,000	-	-
2-(Rare)-Origin Sheena. Diary of Dr. Hayward by Kirby (also #3) plus 2 other stories; contains strip from Universal Film featuring Edgar Bergen & Charlie McCarthy plus-c (preview of film)	720	1440	2160	7200	-	-
3-Last Kirby issue	520	1040	1560	5200	-	-
4-(Scarce)-Origin The Hawk by Eisner; Wilton of the West by Fine (ends #14)(1st comic work); Count of Monte Cristo by Fine (ends #15); The Diary of Dr. Hayward by Fine (cont'd #8,9)	480	960	1440	4800	-	-
5-Christmas-c	420	840	1260	4200	-	-
6-8-Last B&W issue. #8 was a 1939 N. Y. World's Fair Special Edition; Frank Buck's Jungleland story	380	760	1140	3800	-	-
9-Stuart Taylor begins by Fine (ends #140); Fine-c; 1st color issue (8-9/39)-1st Sheena (jungle) cover; 8-1/4x10-1/4" (oversized in width only)	450	900	1350	4500	-	-
10-Regular size 68 pg. issues begin; Sheena dons new costume w/origin costume; Stuart Taylor sci/fi-c; classic Lou Fine-c.	300	600	900	2010	3505	5000
11-13: 12-The Hawk-c by Eisner. 13-Eisner-c	158	316	474	1003	1727	2450
14-Intro. Lightning (super-hero) on-c only	161	322	483	1030	1765	2500
15-1st Lightning story and begins, ends #41	116	232	348	742	1271	1800
16-Lightning-c	129	258	387	826	1413	2000
17,18,20: 17-Lightning part-c	97	194	291	621	1061	1500
19	116	232	348	742	1276	1800
21-30: 22-1st Tom, Dick & Harry; origin The Hawk retold. 25-Midnight the Black Stallion begins, ends #65	68	136	204	435	743	1050
31-40: 31-(9/41)-1st app. Mars God of War in Stuart Taylor story (see Planet Comics #15. 35-Shows V2#11 (correct number does not appear)	54	108	162	346	591	835
41-50: 42-Ghost Gallery begins, ends #167	42	84	126	265	445	625
51-60: 52-Last Tom, Dick & Harry	39	78	117	231	378	525
61-70: 68-Sky Girl begins, ends #130; not in #79	31	62	93	186	303	420
71-93,95-99: 89-ZX5 becomes a private eye.	25	50	75	150	245	340
94-Used in Love and Death by Legman	27	54	81	160	263	365
100	27	54	81	160	263	365
101-121	22	44	66	128	209	290
121-140,150-158: 155-Used in **POP**, pg. 98	20	40	60	117	189	260
141-149-Two Sheena stories. 141-Long Bow, Indian Boy begins, ends #160	20	40	60	120	195	270
159-163: Space Scouts serial in all. 160-Last jungle-c (6/52). 161-Ghost Gallery covers begin, end #167. 163-Suicide Smith app.	19	38	57	109	172	235
164-The Star Pirate begins, ends #165	19	38	57	109	172	235
165-167: 165,167-Space Rangers app.	19	38	57	109	172	235

NOTE: *Bondage covers, negligee panels, torture, etc. are common in this series. Hawks of the Seas, Inspector Dayton, Spies in Action, Sports Shorts, & Uncle Otto by Eisner, #1-7. Hawk by* **Eisner***-#10-15.* **Eisner** *c-1-8, 12-14. 1pg. Patsy pin-ups in 92-97, 99-101. Sheena by* **Meskin***-#1, 4; by* **Powell***-#2, 3, 5-28;* **Powell** *c-14, 16, 17, 19.* **Powell/Eisner** *c-15. Sky Girl by* **Matt Baker***-#69-78, 80-130. ZX-5 & Ghost Gallery by* **Kamen***-#90-130.* **Bailey** *a-3-8.* **Briefer** *a-1-8, 10.* **Fine** *a-14; c-9-11.* **Kamen** *a-101, 105, 123, 132; c-105, 121-145.* **Bob Kane** *a-1-8.* **Whitman** *c-146-167(most). Jungle c-9, 13, 15, 17 on.*

JUMPER: JUMPSCARS
Oni Press: Jan, 2008 ($14.95, graphic novel)

	GD 2.0	VG 4.0	FN 6.0	VF 8.0	VF/NM 9.0	NM- 9.2
SC-Prelude to 2008 movie Jumper; Brian Hurtt-a/c						15.00

JUNGLE ACTION
Atlas Comics (IPC): Oct, 1954 - No. 6, Aug, 1955

	GD 2.0	VG 4.0	FN 6.0	VF 8.0	VF/NM 9.0	NM- 9.2
1-Leopard Girl begins by Al Hartley (#1,3); Jungle Boy by Forte; Maneely-a in all	39	78	117	231	378	525
2-(3-D effect cover)	39	78	117	231	378	525
3-6: 3-Last precode (2/55)	24	48	72	142	234	325

NOTE: **Maneely** *c-1, 2, 5, 6.* **Romita** *a-3, 6.* **Shores** *a-3, 6; c-3, 4?.*

JUNGLE ACTION (...& Black Panther #18-21?)
Marvel Comics Group: Oct, 1972 - No. 24, Nov, 1976

	GD 2.0	VG 4.0	FN 6.0	VF 8.0	VF/NM 9.0	NM- 9.2
1-Lorna, Jann-r (All reprints in 1-4)	3	6	9	14	20	25
2-4	2	4	6	9	12	15
5-Black Panther begins (r/Avengers #62)	3	6	9	20	30	40
6-New solo Black Panther stories begin	3	6	9	18	27	35
7,9,10: 9-Contains pull-out centerfold ad by Mark Jewelers	2	4	6	11	16	20
8-Origin Black Panther	3	6	9	14	20	26
11-20,23,24: 19-23-KKK x-over. 23-r/#22. 24-1st Wind Eagle; story contd in Marvel Premiere #51-#53	2	4	6	8	11	14
21,22-(Regular 25¢ edition)(5,7/76)	2	4	6	8	11	14
21,22-(30¢-c variant, limited distribution)	3	6	9	18	27	35

NOTE: **Buckler** *a-6-9p, 22; c-8p, 12p.* **Buscema** *a-5p; c-22.* **Byrne** *c-23.* **Gil Kane** *a-8p; c-2, 4, 10p, 11p, 13-17, 19, 24.* **Kirby** *c-18.* **Maneely** *r-1.* **Russell** *a-13i.* **Starlin** *c-3p.*

JUNGLE ADVENTURES
Super Comics: 1963 - 1964 (Reprints)

10,12,15,17,18: 10-r/Terrors of the Jungle #4 & #10(Rulah). 12-r/Zoot #14(Rulah).15-r/Kaanga from Jungle #152 & Tiger Girl. 17-All Jo-Jo-r. 18-Reprints/White Princess of the Jungle #1; no Kinstler-a; origin of both White Princess & Cap'n Courage

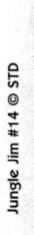

Jungle Comics #5 © FH

Jungle Jim #14 © STD

Jungle Tales #3 © MAR

GD 2.0 VG 4.0 FN 6.0 VF 8.0 VF/NM 9.0 NM- 9.2

3 6 9 19 29 38

JUNGLE ADVENTURES
Skywald Comics: Mar, 1971 - No. 3, June, 1971 (25¢, 52 pgs.) (Pre-code reprints & new-s)
1-Zangar origin; reprints of Jo-Jo, Blue Gorilla(origin)/White Princess #3, Kinstler-r/White Princess #2 3 6 9 20 30 40
2,3: 2-Zangar, Sheena-r/Sheena #17 & Jumbo #162, Jo-Jo, origin Slave Girl-r. 3-Zangar, Jo-Jo, White Princess, Rulah-r 3 6 9 16 22 28

JUNGLE BOOK (See King Louie and Mowgli, Movie Comics, Mowgli..., Walt Disney Showcase #45 & Walt Disney's The Jungle Book)

JUNGLE CAT (Disney)
Dell Publishing Co.: No. 1136, Sept-Nov, 1960 (one shot)
Four Color 1136-Movie, photo-c 6 12 18 42 69 95

JUNGLE COMICS
Fiction House Magazines: 1/40 - No. 157, 3/53; No. 158, Spr, 1953 - No. 163, Summer, 1954
1-Origin The White Panther, Kaanga, Lord of the Jungle, Tabu, Wizard of the Jungle; Wambi, the Jungle Boy, Camilla & Capt. Terry Thunder begin (all 1st app.). Lou Fine-c 476 952 1428 3475 6138 8800
2-Fantomah, Mystery Woman of the Jungle begins, ends #51; The Red Panther begins, ends #26 174 348 522 1114 1907 2700
3,4 139 278 417 883 1517 2150
5-Classic Eisner-c 158 316 474 1003 1727 2450
6-10: 7,8-Powell-c 81 162 243 518 884 1250
11-20: 13-Tuska-c 55 110 165 352 601 850
21-30: 25-Shows V2#1 (correct number does not appear). #27-New origin Fantomah, Daughter of the Pharoahs; Camilla dons new costume 48 96 144 302 514 725
31-40 39 78 117 236 388 540
41,43-50 34 68 102 206 336 465
42-Kaanga by Crandall, 12 pgs. 36 72 108 216 351 485
51-60 31 62 93 182 296 410
61-70: 67-Cover swipes Crandall splash pg. in #42 27 54 81 158 259 360
71-80: 79-New origin Tabu 24 48 72 140 230 320
81-97,99 22 44 66 132 216 300
98-Used in **SOTI**, pg. 185 & illo "In ordinary comic books, there are pictures within pictures for children who know how to look;" used by N.Y. Legis. Comm. 34 68 102 206 336 465
100 27 54 81 158 259 360
101-110: 104-In Camilla story, villain is Dr. Wertham 22 44 66 128 209 290
111-120: 118-Clyde Beatty app. 21 42 63 122 199 275
121-130 20 40 60 117 189 260
131-163: 135-Desert Panther begins in Terry Thunder (origin), not in #137; ends (dies) #138. 139-Last 52 pg. issue. 141-Last Tabu. 143,145-Used in **POP**, pg. 99. 151-Last Camilla & Terry Thunder. 152-Tiger Girl begins. 158-Last Wambi; Sheena app. 19 38 57 109 172 235
I.W. Reprint #1,9: 1-r/? 9-r/#151 3 6 9 17 25 32
NOTE: *Bondage covers, negligee panels, torture, etc. are common to this series. Camilla by* **Fran Hopper***-#70-92; by* **Baker***-#69, 100-113, 115, 116; by* **Lubbers***-#97-99 by* **Tuska***-#63, 65. Kaanga by* **John Celardo***-#80-113; by* **Larsen***-#71, 75-79; by* **Moreira***-#58, 60, 61, 63-70, 72-74; by* **Tuska***-#37, 62; by* **Whitman***-#114-163. Tabu by* **Larsen***-#59-75, 82-92; by* **Whitman***-#93-115. Terry Thunder by* **Hopper***-#71, 72; by* **Celardo***-#78, 79; by* **Lubbers***-#80-85. Tiger Girl-r by* **Baker***-#152, 153, 155-157, 159. Wambi by* **Baker***-#62-67, 74.* **Astarita** *c-45, 46.* **Celardo** *a-78; c-98-113.* **Crandall** *c-67 from splash pg.* **Eisner** *c-2, 5, 6.* **Fine** *c-1.* **Larsen** *a-65, 66, 71, 72, 74, 75, 79, 83, 84, 87-90.* **Moreira** *c-43, 44.* **Morisi** *a-51.* **Powell** *c-7, 8.* **Sultan** *c-3, 4.* **Tuska** *c-13.* **Whitman** *c-132-163(most).* **Zolnerowich** *c-11, 12, 18-41.*

JUNGLE COMICS
Blackthorne Publishing: May, 1988 - No. 4 ($2.00, B&W/color)
1-Dave Stevens-c; B. Jones scripts in all. 5.00
2-4: 2-B&W-a begins 3.00

JUNGLE GIRL (See Lorna, the...)

JUNGLE GIRL (Nyoka, Jungle Girl No. 2 on)
Fawcett Publications: Fall, 1942 (one-shot)(No month listed)
1-Bondage-c; photo of Kay Aldridge who played Nyoka in movie serial app. on-c. Adaptation of the classic Republic movie serial Perils of Nyoka. 1st comic to devote entire contents to a movie serial adaptation 126 252 378 806 1378 1950

JUNGLE GIRL
Dynamite Entertainment: No. 0, 2007 - 2009 (25¢/$2.99/$3.50)
0-(25¢-c) Eight page preview; preview of Superpowers w/Alex Ross-a 3.00
1-5-Frank Cho-plot/cover; Batista-a/variant-c 3.00
... Season 2 ($3.50) 1-5-Two covers by Cho & Batista 3.50

JUNGLE GIRLS
AC Comics: 1989 - No. 16, 1993 (B&W)
1-16: 1-4,10,13-16-New story & "good girl" reprints. 5-9,11,12-All g.g. reprints (Baker, Powell, Lubbers, others) 3.00

JUNGLE JIM (Also see Ace Comics)
Standard Comics (Best Books): No. 11, Jan, 1949 - No. 20, Apr, 1951
11 11 22 33 62 86 110
12-20 8 16 24 42 54 65

JUNGLE JIM
Dell Publishing Co.: No. 490, 8/53 - No. 1020, 8-10/59 (Painted-c)
Four Color 490(#1) 7 14 21 48 79 110
Four Color 565(#2, 6/54) 5 10 15 30 48 65
3(10-12/54)-5 4 8 12 28 44 60
6-19(1-3/59), Four Color 1020(#20) 4 8 12 26 41 55

JUNGLE JIM
King Features Syndicate: No. 5, Dec, 1967
5-Reprints Dell #5; Wood-c 2 4 6 10 14 18

JUNGLE JIM (Continued from Dell series)
Charlton Comics: No. 22, Feb, 1969 - No. 28, Feb, 1970 (#21 was an overseas edition only)
22-Dan Flagg begins; Ditko/Wood-a 3 6 9 21 32 42
23-26: 23-Last Dan Flagg; Howard-c. 24-Jungle People begin 3 6 9 15 21 26
27,28: 27-Ditko/Howard-a. 28-Ditko-a 3 6 9 17 25 32
NOTE: *Ditko cover of #22 reprints story panels*

JUNGLE JO
Fox Feature Syndicate (Hero Books): Mar, 1950 - No. 3, Sept, 1950
nn-Jo-Jo blanked out in titles of interior stories, leaving Congo King; came out after Jo-Jo #29 (intended as Jo-Jo #30?) 53 106 159 334 567 800
1-Tangi begins; part Wood-a 54 108 162 343 574 825
2,3 41 82 123 256 428 600

JUNGLE LIL (Dorothy Lamour #2 on; also see Feature Stories Magazine)
Fox Feature Syndicate (Hero Books): April, 1950
1 43 86 129 271 461 650

JUNGLE TALES (Jann of the Jungle No. 8 on)
Atlas Comics (CSI): Sept, 1954 - No. 7, Sept, 1955
1-Jann of the Jungle 39 78 117 240 395 550
2-7: 3-Last precode (1/55) 27 54 81 160 263 365
NOTE: **Heath** *c-5.* **Heck** *a-6, 7.* **Maneely** *a-2; c-1, 3.* **Shores** *a-5-7; c-4, 6.* **Tuska** *a-2.*

JUNGLE TALES OF TARZAN
Charlton Comics: Dec, 1964 - No. 4, July, 1965
1 6 12 18 37 59 80
2-4 4 8 12 24 37 50
NOTE: **Giordano** *c-3p.* **Glanzman** *a-1-3.* **Montes/Bache** *a-4.*

JUNGLE TERROR (See Harvey Comics Hits No. 54)

JUNGLE THRILLS (Formerly Sports Thrills; Terrors of the Jungle #17 on)
Star Publications: No. 16, Feb, 1952; Dec, 1953; No. 7, 1954
16-Phantom Lady & Rulah story-reprint/All Top No. 15; used in **POP**, pg. 98,99; L. B. Cole-c 51 102 153 320 543 765
3-D 1(12/53, 25¢)-Came w/glasses; Jungle Lil & Jungle Jo appear; L. B. Cole-c 51 102 153 320 543 765
7-Titled 'Picture Scope Jungle Adventures;' (1954, 36 pgs, 15¢)-3-D effect c/stories; story & coloring book; Disbrow-a/script; L.B. Cole-c 51 102 153 320 543 765

JUNGLE TWINS, THE (Tono & Kono)
Gold Key/Whitman No. 18: Apr, 1972 - No. 17, Nov, 1975; No. 18, May, 1982
1 3 6 9 16 22 28
2-5 2 4 6 8 11 14
6-18: 18(Whitman, 5/82)-Reprints 1 2 3 5 7 9
NOTE: *UFO c/story No. 13. Painted-c No. 1-17.* **Spiegle** *c-18.*

JUNGLE WAR STORIES (Guerrilla War No. 12 on)
Dell Publishing Co.: July-Sept, 1962 - No. 11, Apr-June, 1965 (Painted-c)
01-384-209 (#1) 4 8 12 22 34 45
2-11 3 6 9 16 23 30

JUNIE PROM (Also see Dexter Comics)
Dearfield Publishing Co.: Winter, 1947-48 - No. 7, Aug, 1949
1-Teen-age 15 30 45 84 127 170
2 9 18 27 52 69 85
3-7 8 16 24 44 57 70

JUNIOR

Junior Comics #10 © FOX

Jurassic Park #1 © Universal

Justice, Inc. #2 © DC

	GD 2.0	VG 4.0	FN 6.0	VF 8.0	VF/NM 9.0	NM- 9.2

Fantagraphics Books: June, 2000 - No. 5, Jan, 2001 ($2.95, B&W)

1-5-Peter Bagge-s/a 3.00

JUNIOR CARROT PATROL (Jr. Carrot Patrol #2)
Dark Horse Comics: May, 1989; No. 2, Nov, 1990 ($2.00, B&W)

1,2-Flaming Carrot spin-off. 1-Bob Burden-c(i) 3.00

JUNIOR COMICS (Formerly Li'l Pan; becomes Western Outlaws with #17)
Fox Feature Syndicate: No. 9, Sept, 1947 - No. 16, July, 1948

	GD	VG	FN	VF	VF/NM	NM-
9-Feldstein-c/a; headlights-c	142	284	426	909	1555	2200
10-16-Feldstein-c/a; headlights-c on all	129	258	387	826	1413	2000

JUNIOR FUNNIES (Formerly Tiny Tot Funnies No. 9)
Harvey Publ. (King Features Synd.): No. 10, Aug, 1951 - No. 13, Feb, 1952

	GD	VG	FN	VF	VF/NM	NM-
10-Partial reprints in all; Blondie, Dagwood, Daisy, Henry, Popeye, Felix, Katzenjammer Kids	6	12	18	28	34	40
11-13	5	10	15	24	30	35

JUNIOR HOPP COMICS
Stanmor Publ.: Feb, 1952 - No. 3, July, 1952

	GD	VG	FN	VF	VF/NM	NM-
1-Teenage humor	10	20	30	58	79	100
2,3: 3-Dave Berg-a	7	14	21	35	43	50

JUNIOR MEDICS OF AMERICA, THE
E. R. Squire & Sons: No. 1359, 1957 (15¢)

	GD	VG	FN	VF	VF/NM	NM-
1359	4	8	12	17	21	24

JUNIOR MISS
Timely/Marvel (CnPC): Wint, 1944; No. 24, Apr, 1947 - No. 39, Aug, 1950

	GD	VG	FN	VF	VF/NM	NM-
1-Frank Sinatra & June Allyson life story	32	64	96	192	314	435
24-Formerly The Human Torch #23?	16	32	48	94	147	200
25-38: 29,31,34-Cindy-c/stories (others?)	11	22	33	60	83	105
39-Kurtzman-a	12	24	36	69	97	125

NOTE: *Painted-c 35-37. 35, 37-all romance. 36, 38-mostly teen humor.* ***Louise Alston*** *c-36.*

JUNIOR PARTNERS (Formerly Oral Roberts' True Stories)
Oral Roberts Evangelistic Assn.: No. 120, Aug, 1959 - V3#12, Dec, 1961

	GD	VG	FN	VF	VF/NM	NM-
120(#1)	4	8	12	24	37	50
2(9/59)	3	6	9	17	25	32
3-12(7/60)	2	4	6	13	18	22
V2#1(8/60)-5(12/60)	2	4	6	9	13	16
V3#1(1/61)-12	2	4	6	8	10	12

JUNIOR TREASURY (See Dell Junior...)

JUNIOR WOODCHUCKS GUIDE (Walt Disney's...)
Danbury Press: 1973 (8-3/4"x5-3/4", 214 pgs., hardcover)

	GD	VG	FN	VF	VF/NM	NM-
nn-Illustrated text based on the long-standing J.W. Guide used by Donald Duck's nephews Huey, Dewey & Louie by Carl Barks. The guidebook was a popular plot device to enable the nephews to solve problems facing their uncle or Scrooge McDuck (scarce)	5	10	15	35	55	75

JUNIOR WOODCHUCKS LIMITED SERIES (Walt Disney's...)
W. D. Publications (Disney): July, 1991 - No. 4, Oct, 1991 ($1.50, limited series; new & reprint-a)

1-4: 1-The Beagle Boys app.; Barks-r 3.00

JUNIOR WOODCHUCKS (See Huey, Dewey & Louie...)

JURASSIC PARK
Topps Comics: June, 1993 - No. 4, Aug, 1993; No. 5, Oct, 1994 - No. 10, Feb, 1995

	GD	VG	FN	VF	VF/NM	NM-
1-($2.50)-Newsstand Edition; Kane/Perez-a in all; 1-4: movie adaptation						3.00
1-($2.95)-Collector's Ed.; polybagged w/3 cards						4.00
1-Amberchrome Edition w/no price or ads	1	2	3	4	5	7
2-4-($2.50)-Newsstand Edition						3.00
2,3-($2.95)-Collector's Ed.; polybagged w/3 cards						4.00
4-10: 4-($2.95)-Collector's Ed.; polybagged w/1 of 4 different action hologram trading card; Gil Kane/Perez-a. 5-becomes Advs. of						3.00
Annual 1 ($3.95, 5/95)						4.00
Trade paperback (1993, $9.95)-r/#1-4; bagged w/#0						10.00

JURASSIC PARK
IDW Publishing: Jun, 2010 - No. 5, Oct, 2010 ($3.99, limited series)

1-5: Takes place 13 years after the first movie; Schreck-s. 1-Covers by Yeates & Miller 4.00

JURASSIC PARK: DANGEROUS GAMES
IDW Publishing: Sept, 2011 - No. 5, Jan, 2012 ($3.99, limited series)

1-5-Erik Bear-s/Jorge Jimenez-a, 1-Covers by Darrow & Zornow 4.00

JURASSIC PARK: RAPTOR
Topps Comics: Nov, 1993 - No. 2, Dec, 1993 ($2.95, limited series)

1,2: 1-Bagged w/3 trading cards & Zorro #0; Golden c-1,2 3.00

JURASSIC PARK: RAPTORS ATTACK
Topps Comics: Mar, 1994 - No. 4, June, 1994 ($2.50, limited series)

1-4-Michael Golden-c/frontispiece 3.00

JURASSIC PARK: RAPTORS HIJACK
Topps Comics: July, 1994 - No. 4, Oct, 1994 ($2.50, limited series)

1-4: Michael Golden-c/front piece 3.00

JURASSIC PARK: THE DEVILS IN THE DESERT
IDW Publishing: Jan, 2011 - No. 4, Apr, 2011 ($3.99, limited series)

1-4-John Byrne-s/a/c 4.00

JUST A PILGRIM
Black Bull Entertainment: May, 2001 - No. 5, Sept, 2001 ($2.99)

Limited Preview Edition (12/00, $7.00) Ennis & Ezquerra interviews 7.00
1-Ennis-s/Ezquerra-a; two covers by Texeira & JG Jones 3.00
2-5: 2-Fabry-c. 3-Nowlan-c. 4-Sienkiewicz-c 3.00
TPB (11/01, $12.99) r/#1-5; Waid intro. 13.00

JUST A PILGRIM: GARDEN OF EDEN
Black Bull Entertainment: May, 2002 - No. 4, Aug, 2002 ($2.99, limited series)

Limited Preview Ed. (1/02, $7.00) Ennis & Ezquerra interviews; Jones-c 7.00
1-4-Ennis-s/Ezquerra-a 3.00
TPB (11/02, $12.99) r/#1-4; Gareb Shamus intro. 13.00

JUSTICE
Marvel Comics Group (New Universe): Nov, 1986 - No. 32, June, 1989

1-32: 26-32-$1.50-c (low print run) 3.00

JUSTICE
DC Comics: Oct, 2005 - No. 12, Aug, 2007 ($2.99/$3.50/$3.99, bi-monthly maxi-series)

1-Classic Justice League vs. The Legion of Doom; Alex Ross & Doug Braithwaite-a; Jim Krueger-s; two covers by Ross; Ross sketch pages 5.00
1-2nd & 3rd printings 4.00
2-($3.50) 4.00
2 (2nd printing), 3-11-($3.50) 3.50
12-($3.99) Two covers (Heroes & Villains) 4.00
Absolute Justice HC (2009, $99.99, slipcased book with dustjacket) oversized r/#1-12; afterwords by creators; Ross sketch and design art; photo gallery of action figures 100.00
HC (2011, $39.99, dustjacket) r/#1-12 40.00
... Volume One HC (2006, $19.99, dustjacket) r/#1-4; Krueger intro.; sketch pages 20.00
... Volume One SC (2008, $14.99) r/#1-4; Krueger intro.; sketch pages 15.00
... Volume Two HC (2007, $19.99, dustjacket) r/#5-8; Krueger intro.; sketch pages 20.00
... Volume Two SC (2008, $14.99) r/#5-8; Krueger intro.; sketch pages 15.00
... Volume Three HC (2007, $19.99, dustjacket) r/#9-12; Ross intro.; sketch pages 20.00
... Volume Three SC (2007, $14.99) r/#9-12; Ross intro.; sketch pages 15.00

JUSTICE COMICS (Formerly Wacky Duck; Tales of Justice #53 on)
Marvel/Atlas Comics (NPP 7-9,4-19/CnPC 20-23/MjMC 24-38/Male 39-52:
No. 7, Fall/47 - No. 9, 6/48; No. 4, 8/48 - No. 52, 3/55

	GD	VG	FN	VF	VF/NM	NM-
7(#1, 1947)	30	60	90	177	289	400
8(#2)-Kurtzman-a "Giggles 'n' Grins" (3)	20	40	60	117	189	260
9(#3, 6/48)	18	36	54	105	165	225
4	16	32	48	94	147	200
5(9/48)-9: 8-Anti-Wertham editorial	15	30	45	83	124	165
10-15-Photo-c	13	26	39	72	101	130
16-30	11	22	33	62	86	110
31-40,42-52: 35-Gene Colan-a. 48-Last precode; Pakula & Tuska-a.	10	20	30	58	79	100
41-Electrocution-c	17	34	51	98	154	210

NOTE: ***Hartley*** *a-48.* ***Heath*** *a-24.* ***Maneely*** *c-44, 52.* ***Pakula*** *a-43, 45, 47, 48.* ***Louis Ravielli*** *a-39, 47.* ***Robinson*** *a-22, 25, 41.* ***Sale*** *c-45.* ***Shores*** *c-7(#1), 8(#2)?* ***Tuska*** *a-41, 48.* ***Wildey*** *a-52.*

JUSTICE: FOUR BALANCE
Marvel Comics: Sept, 1994 - No. 4, Dec, 1994 ($1.75, limited series)

1-4: 1-Thing & Firestar app. 3.00

JUSTICE, INC. (The Avenger) (Pulp)
National Periodical Publications: May-June, 1975 - No. 4, Nov-Dec, 1975

	GD	VG	FN	VF	VF/NM	NM-
1-McWilliams-a, Kubert-c; origin	2	4	6	11	16	20
2-4: 2-4-Kirby-a(p), c-2,3p. 4-Kubert-c	2	4	6	11	16	20

NOTE: *Adapted from Kenneth Robeson novel, creator of Doc Savage.*

JUSTICE, INC. (Pulp)
DC Comics: 1989 - No. 2, 1989 ($3.95, 52 pgs., squarebound, mature)

Justice League (2011 series) #2 © DC

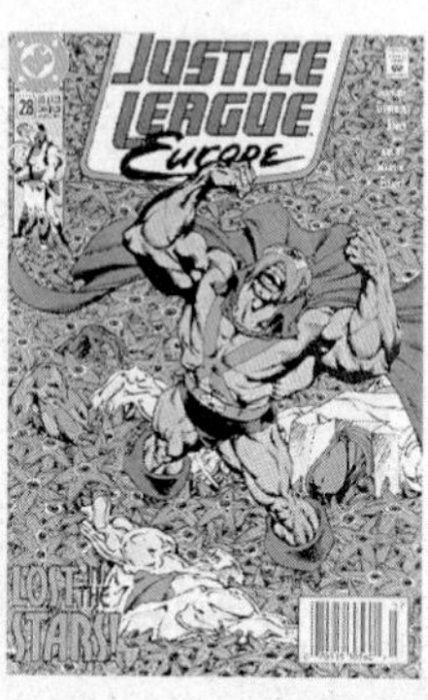

Justice League Europe #28 © DC

Justice League of America #4 © DC

GD VG FN VF VF/NM NM-
2.0 4.0 6.0 8.0 9.0 9.2

GD VG FN VF VF/NM NM-
2.0 4.0 6.0 8.0 9.0 9.2

1,2: Re-intro The Avenger; Andrew Helfer scripts & Kyle Baker-c/a 4.00

JUSTICE LEAGUE (...International #7-25; ...America #26 on)
DC Comics: May, 1987 - No. 113, Aug, 1996 (Also see Legends #6)

1-Batman, Green Lantern (Guy Gardner), Blue Beetle, Mr. Miracle, Capt. Marvel & Martian Manhunter begin 1 2 3 5 6 8
2,3: 3-Regular-c (white background) 5.00
3-Limited-c (yellow background, Superman logo) 4 8 12 24 37 50
4-6,8-10: 4-Booster Gold joins. 5-Origin Gray Man; Batman vs. Guy Gardner; Creeper app. 9,10-Millennium x-over 4.00
7-($1.25, 52 pgs.)-Capt. Marvel & Dr. Fate resign; Capt. Atom & Rocket Red join 5.00
11-17,22,23,25-49,51-68,71-82: 16-Bruce Wayne-c/story. 31,32-J. L. Europe x-over. 58-Lobo app. 61-New team begins; swipes-c to J.L. of A. #1('60). 70-Newsstand version w/o outer-c. 71-Direct sales version w/black outer-c. 71-Newsstand version w/o outer-c. 80-Intro new Booster Gold. 82,83-Guy Gardner-c/stories 3.00
18-21,24,50: 18-21-Lobo app. 24-($1.50)-1st app. Justice League Europe. 50-($1.75, 52 pgs.) 4.00
69-Doomsday tie-in; takes place between Superman: The Man of Steel #18 & Superman #74 5.00
69,70-2nd printings 3.00
70-Funeral for a Friend part 1; red 3/4 outer-c 4.00
83-99,101-113: 92-(9/94)-Zero Hour x-over; Triumph app. 113-Green Lantern, Flash & Hawkman app. 3.00
100 ($3.95)-Foil-c; 52 pgs. 5.00
100 ($2.95)-Newstand 4.00
#0-(10/94) Zero Hour (publ between #92 & #93); new team begins (Hawkman, Flash, Wonder Woman, Metamorpho, Nuklon, Crimson Fox, Obsidian & Fire) 3.00
Annual 1-8,10 ('87-'94, '96, 68 pgs.): 2-Joker-c/story; Batman cameo. 5-Armageddon 2001 x-over; Silver ink 2nd print. 7-Bloodlines x-over. 8-Elseworlds story. 10-Legends of the Dead Earth 4.00
Annual 9 (1995, $3.50)-Year One story 4.00
Special 1,2 ('90,'91, 52 pgs.): 1-Giffen plots. 2-Staton-a(p) 4.00
Spectacular 1 (1992, $1.50, 52 pgs.)-Intro new JLI & JLE teams; ties into JLI #61 & JLE #37; two interlocking covers by Jurgens 4.00
A New Beginning Trade Paperback (1989, $12.95)-r/#1-7 13.00
... International Vol. 1 HC (2008, $24.99) r/#1-7; new intro. by Giffen 25.00
... International Vol. 1 SC (2009, $17.99) r/#1-7; new intro. by Giffen 18.00
... International Vol. 2 HC (2008, $24.99) r/#8-13, Annual #1 and Suicide Squad #13 25.00
... International Vol. 2 SC (2009, $17.99) r/#8-13, Annual #1 and Suicide Squad #13 18.00
... International Vol. 3 SC (2009, $19.99) r/#14-22 20.00
... International Vol. 4 SC (2010, $17.99) r/#23-30 18.00
... International Vol. 5 SC (2011, $19.99) r/#Annual #2,3 & Justice League Europe #1-6 20.00
... International Vol. 6 SC (2011, $24.99) r/#31-35 & Justice League Europe #7-11 25.00
NOTE: ***Anderson*** *c-61i.* ***Austin*** *a-1i, 60i; c-1i.* ***Giffen*** *a-13; c-21p.* ***Guice*** *a-62i.* ***Maguire*** *a-1-12, 16-19, 22, 23.* ***Russell*** *a-Annual 1i; c-54i.* ***Willingham*** *a-30p, Annual 2.*

JUSTICE LEAGUE (DC New 52)
DC Comics: Oct, 2011 - Present ($3.99)

1-Johns-s/Jim Lee-a/c; Batman, Green Lantern & Superman app.; orange background-c 4.00
1-Combo-Pack edition ($4.99) polybagged with digital download code; blue background-c 5.00
1-Variant-c by Finch 15.00
1-Second printing 20.00
2-7: 3-Wonder Woman & Aquaman arrive. 4-Darkseid arrives. 6-Pandora back-up app. 7-Gene Ha-a; back-up Shazam origin begins; Frank-a 4.00
2-7-Combo-Pack edition ($4.99) polybagged with digital download code 5.00

JUSTICE LEAGUE ADVENTURES (Based on Cartoon Network series)
DC Comics: Jan, 2002 - No. 34, Oct, 2004 ($1.99/$2.25)

1-Timm & Ross-c 4.00
2-32: 3-Nicieza-s. 5-Starro app. 10-Begin $2.25-c. 14-Includes 16 pg. insert for VERB with Haberlin CG-art. 15,29-Amancio-a. 16-McCloud-s. 20-Psycho Pirate app. 25,26-Adam Strange-c/app. 28-Legion of Super-Heroes app. 30-Kamandi app. 3.00
Free Comic Book Day giveaway - (5/02) r/#1 with "Free Comic Book Day" banner on-c 4.00
TPB (2003, $9.95) r/#1,3,6,10-13; Timm/Ross-c from #1 10.00
...Vol. 1: The Magnificent Seven (2004, $6.95) digest-size reprints #3,6,10-12 7.00
...Vol. 2: Friends and Foes (2004, $6.95) digest-size reprints #13,14,16,19,20 7.00

JUSTICE LEAGUE: A MIDSUMMER'S NIGHTMARE
DC Comics: Sept, 1996 - No. 3, Nov, 1996 ($2.95, limited series, 38 pgs.)

1-3: Re-establishes Superman, Batman, Green Lantern, The Martian Manhunter, Flash, Aquaman & Wonder Woman as the Justice League; Mark Waid & Fabian Nicieza co-scripts; Jeff Johnson & Darick Robertson-a(p); Kevin Maguire-c 5.00
TPB-(1997, $8.95) r/1-3 9.00

JUSTICE LEAGUE: CRY FOR JUSTICE
DC Comics: Sept, 2009 - No. 7, Apr, 2010 ($3.99, limited series)

1-7-James Robinson-s/Mauro Cascioli-a/c. 1-Two covers; Congorilla origin 4.00
HC (2010, $24.99, d.j.) r/#1-7, Face of Evil: Prometheus 25.00
SC (2011, $19.99) r/#1-7, Face of Evil: Prometheus 20.00

JUSTICE LEAGUE DARK (DC New 52)
DC Comics: Nov, 2011 - Present ($2.99)

1-7: 1-Milligan-s; Deadman, Madame Xanadu, Zatanna, Shade, John Constantine app. 7-Crossover with I,Vampire #6,7; Batgirl app. 3.00

JUSTICE LEAGUE ELITE (See JLA #100 and JLA Secret Files 2004)
DC Comics: Sept, 2004 - No. 12, Aug, 2005 ($2.50)

1-12-Flash, Green Arrow, Vera Black and others; Kelly-s/Mahnke-a. 5,6-JSA app. 3.00
JL Elite TPB (2005, $19.99) r/#1-4, Action #775, JLA #100, JLA Secret Files 2004 20.00
... Vol. 2 TPB (2007, $19.99) r/#5-12 20.00

JUSTICE LEAGUE EUROPE (Justice League International #51 on)
DC Comics: Apr, 1989 - No. 68, Sept., 1994 (75¢/ $1.00/$1.25/$1.50)

1-Giffen plots in all, breakdowns in #1-8,13-30; Justice League #1-c/swipe 4.00
2-10: 7-9-Batman app. 7,8-JLA x-over. 8,9-Superman app. 3.00
11-49: 12-Metal Men app. 20-22-Rogers-c/a(p). 33,34-Lobo vs. Despero. 37-New team begins; swipes-c to JLA #9; see JLA Spectacular 3.00
50-($2.50, 68 pgs.)-Battles Sonar 4.00
51-68: 68-Zero Hour x-over; Triumph joins Justice League Task Force (See JLTF #17) 3.00
Annual 1-5 ('90-'94, 68 pgs.)-1-Return of the Global Guardians; Giffen plots/breakdowns. 2-Armageddon 2001; Giffen-a(p); Rogers-a(p); Golden-a(i). 5-Elseworlds story 4.00
NOTE: ***Phil Jimenez*** *a-68p.* ***Rogers*** *c/a-20-22.* ***Sears*** *a-1-12, 14-19, 23-29; c-1-10, 12, 14-19, 23-29.*

JUSTICE LEAGUE: GENERATION LOST (Brightest Day)
DC Comics: Early July, 2010 - No. 24, Early Jun, 2011 ($2.99, bi-weekly limited series)

1-23: 1-Maxwell Lord's return; Winick & Giffen-s. 1-5,7-Harris-c. 13-Magog killed 3.00
24-($4.99) Wonder Woman vs. Omac Prime; Lopresti-a/Nguyen-c 5.00
... Volume One HC (2010, $39.99, dustjacket) r/#1-12; cover gallery 40.00

JUSTICE LEAGUE INTERNATIONAL (See Justice League Europe)

JUSTICE LEAGUE INTERNATIONAL (DC New 52)
DC Comics: Nov, 2011 - Present ($2.99)

1-8: 1-Jurgens-s/Lopresti-a/c; Batman, Booster Gold, Guy Gardner, Vixen, Fire, Ice. 8-Batwing joins; OMAC app. 3.00

JUSTICE LEAGUE OF AMERICA (See Brave & the Bold #28-30, Mystery In Space #75 & Official... Index) (See Crisis on Multiple Earths TPBs for reprints of JLA/JSA crossovers)
National Periodical Publ./DC Comics: Oct-Nov, 1960 - No. 261, Apr, 1987 (#91-99,139-157: 52 pgs.)

1-(10-11/60)-Origin & 1st app. Despero; Aquaman, Batman, Flash, Green Lantern, J'onn J'onzz, Superman & Wonder Woman continue from Brave and the Bold 400 800 1200 4400 10,200 16,000
2 107 214 321 867 1884 2900
3-Origin/1st app. Kanjar Ro (see Mystery in Space #75)(scarce in high grade due to black-c) 93 186 279 753 1627 2500
4-Green Arrow joins JLA 62 124 186 502 1089 1675
5-Origin & 1st app. Dr. Destiny 51 102 153 413 894 1375
6-8,10: 6-Origin & 1st app. Prof. Amos Fortune. 7-(10-11/61)-Last 10¢ issue. 10-(3/62)-Origin & 1st app. Felix Faust; 1st app. Lord of Time 41 82 123 308 667 1025
9-(2/62)-Origin JLA (1st origin) 47 94 141 381 828 1275
11-15: 12-(6/62)-Origin & 1st app. Dr. Light. 13-(8/62)-Speedy app. 14-(9/62)-Atom joins JLA. 27 54 81 191 413 635
16-20: 17-Adam Strange flashback 23 46 69 163 349 535
21-(8/63)-"Crisis on Earth-One"; re-intro. of JSA in this title (see Flash #129) (1st S.A. app. Hourman & Dr. Fate) 38 76 114 285 618 950
22- "Crisis on Earth-Two"; JSA x-over (story continued from #21) 31 62 93 225 488 750
23-28: 24-Adam Strange app. 27-Robin app. 16 32 48 111 243 375
29-JSA x-over; 1st S.A. app. Starman; "Crisis on Earth-Three" 20 40 60 140 300 460
30-JSA x-over 19 38 57 132 284 435
31-Hawkman joins JLA, Hawkgirl cameo (11/64) 14 28 42 93 202 310
32,34: 32-Intro & Origin Brain Storm. 34-Joker-c/sty 11 22 33 76 151 225
33,35,36,40,41: 40-3rd S.A. Penguin app. 41-Intro & origin The Key 11 22 33 73 142 210
37-39: 37,38-JSA x-over. 37-1st S.A. app. Mr. Terrific; Batman cameo. 38-"Crisis on Earth-A". 39-Giant G-16; r/B&B #28,30 & JLA #5 12 24 36 84 177 270
42-45: 42-Metamorpho app. 43-Intro. Royal Flush Gang 9 18 27 63 112 160
46-JSA x-over; 1st S.A. app. Sandman; 3rd S.A. app. of G.A. Spectre (8/66) 12 24 36 81 166 250
47-JSA x-over; 4th S.A. app of G.A. Spectre. 10 20 30 67 124 180

Justice League of America #107 © DC

Justice League of America #228 © DC

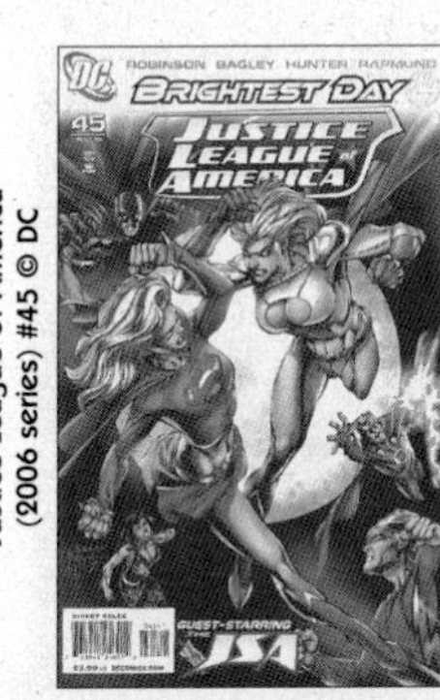

Justice League of America (2006 series) #45 © DC

GD VG FN VF VF/NM NM-
2.0 4.0 6.0 8.0 9.0 9.2

48-Giant G-29; r/JLA #2,3 & B&B #29 10 20 30 65 118 170
49-54,57,59,60 8 16 24 53 89 125
55-Intro. Earth 2 Robin (1st G.A. Robin in S.A.) 10 20 30 64 115 165
56-JLA vs. JSA (1st G.A. Wonder Woman in S.A.) 9 18 27 60 103 145
58-Giant G-41; r/JLA #6,8,1 9 18 27 60 103 145
61-63,66,68-72: 69-Wonder Woman quits. 71-Manhunter leaves. 72-Last 12¢ issue
6 12 18 41 66 90
64,65-JSA story. 64-(8/68)-Origin/1st app. S.A. Red Tornado
6 12 18 42 69 95
67-Giant G-53; r/JLA #4,14,31 8 16 24 53 89 125
73-1st S.A. app. of G.A. Superman 7 14 21 46 76 105
74-Black Canary joins; Larry Lance dies; 1st meeting of G.A. & S.A. Superman;
Neal Adams-c 7 14 21 49 82 115
75-2nd app. Green Arrow in new costume (see Brave & the Bold #85)
7 14 21 46 76 105
76-Giant G-65 7 14 21 44 72 100
77-80: 78-Re-intro Vigilante (1st S.A. app?) 4 8 12 28 44 60
81-84,86-90: 82-1st S.A. app. of G.A. Batman (cameo). 83-Apparent death of The Spectre.
90-Last 15¢ issue 4 8 12 26 41 55
85,93-(Giant G-77,G-89; 68 pgs.) 5 10 15 35 55 75
91,92: 91-1st meeting of the G.A. & S.A. Robin; begin 25¢, 52 pgs. issues, ends #99.
92-S.A. Robin tries on costume that is similar to that of G.A. Robin in All Star Comics #58
5 10 15 30 48 65
94-Reprints 1st Sandman story (Adv. #40) & origin/1st app. Starman (Adventure #61);
Deadman x-over; N. Adams-a (4 pgs.) 9 18 27 60 103 145
95,96: 95-Origin Dr. Fate & Dr. Midnight -r/ More Fun #67, All-American #25).
96-Origin Hourman (Adv. #48); Wildcat-r 5 10 15 32 51 70
97-99: 97-Origin JLA retold; Sargon, Starman-r. 98-G.A. Sargon, Starman-r.
99-G.A. Sandman, Atom-r; last 52 pg. issue 4 8 12 28 44 60
100-(8/72)-1st meeting of G.A. & S.A. W. Woman 5 10 15 32 51 70
101,102: JSA x-overs. 102-Red Tornado destroyed 4 8 12 26 41 55
103-106,109: 103-Rutland Vermont Halloween x-over; Phantom Stranger joins.
105-Elongated Man joins. 106-New Red Tornado joins. 109-Hawkman resigns
3 6 9 18 27 35
107,108-JSA x-over; 1st revival app. of G.A. Uncle Sam, Black Condor, The Ray, Dollman,
Phantom Lady & The Human Bomb 3 6 9 20 30 40
110,112-116: All 100 pgs. 112-Amazo app; Crimson Avenger, Vigilante-r; origin Starman-r/
Adv. #81. 115-Martian Manhunter app. 5 10 15 32 51 70
111-JLA vs. Injustice Gang; intro. Libra (re-appears in 2008's Final Crisis); Shining Knight,
Green Arrow-r 5 10 15 35 55 75
117-122,125-134: 117-Hawkman rejoins. 120,121-Adam Strange app. 125,126-Two-Face-app.
128-Wonder Woman rejoins. 129-Destruction of Red Tornado
3 6 9 16 22 28
123-(10/75),124: JLA/JSA x-over. DC editor Julie Schwartz & JLA writers Cary Bates & Elliot
S! Maggin appear in story as themselves. 1st named app. Earth-Prime (3rd app. after
Flash; 1st Series #179 & 228) 3 6 9 17 25 32
135-136: 135-137-G.A. Bulletman, Bulletgirl, Spy Smasher, Mr. Scarlet, Pinky & Ibis x-over, 1st
appearances since G.A. 3 6 9 17 25 32
137-Superman battles G.A. Capt. Marvel 3 6 9 19 29 38
138-Adam Strange app. w/c by Neal Adams; 1st app. Green Lantern of the 73rd Century
3 6 9 16 23 30
139-157: 139-157-(52 pgs.): 139-Adam Strange app. 144-Origin retold; origin J'onn J'onzz.
145-Red Tornado resurrected. 147,148-Legion of Super-Heroes x-over
2 4 6 10 14 18
158-160-(44 pgs.) 2 4 6 8 11 14
158,160-162,169,171,172,173,176-179,181-(Whitman variants; low print run,
none show issue # on cover) 2 4 6 10 14 18
161-165,169-182: 161-Zatanna joins & new costume. 171,172-JSA x-over. 171-Mr. Terrific
murdered. 178-Cover similar to #1; J'onn J'onzz app. 179-Firestorm joins.
181-Green Arrow leaves JLA 1 2 3 5 6 8
166-168- "Identity Crisis (2004)" precursor; JSA app. vs. Secret Society of Super-Villains
3 6 9 16 23 30
166-168-Whitman variants (no issue # on covers) 4 8 12 24 37 50
183-185-JSA/New Gods/Darkseid/Mr. Miracle x-over 2 4 6 8 10 12
186-194,198,199: 192,193-Real origin Red Tornado. 193-1st app. All-Star Squadron
as free 16 pg. insert 6.00
195-197-JSA app. vs. Secret Society of Super-Villains 1 2 3 5 6 8
200 ($1.50, Anniversary issue, 76 pgs.)-JLA origin retold; Green Arrow rejoins; Bolland, Aparo,
Giordano, Gil Kane, Infantino, Kubert-a; Pérez-c/a 1 3 4 6 8 10
201-206,209-243,246-259: 203-Intro/origin new Royal Flush Gang. 219,220-True origin Black
Canary. 228-Re-intro Martian Manhunter. 228-230-War of the Worlds storyline;
JLA Satellite destroyed by Martians. 233-Story cont'd from Annual #2. 243-Aquaman
leaves. 250-Batman rejoins. 253-Origin Despero. 258-Death of Vibe. 258-261-Legends
x-over 5.00

GD VG FN VF VF/NM NM-
2.0 4.0 6.0 8.0 9.0 9.2

207,208-JSA, JLA, & All-Star Squadron team-up 1 2 3 4 5 7
244,245-Crisis x-over 6.00
260-Death of Steel 1 2 3 4 5 7
261-Last issue 1 3 4 6 8 10
Annual 1-3 ('83-'85), 2-Intro new J.L.A. (Aquaman, Martian Manhunter, Steel, Gypsy, Vixen,
Vibe, Elongated Man & Zatanna). 3-Crisis x-over 5.00
... Hereby Elects (2006, $14.99, TPB) reprints issues where new members joined;
JLofA #4,75,105,106,146,161,173 &174; roster of various incarnations; Ordway-c 15.00

NOTE: ***Neal Adams*** *c-63, 66, 67, 70, 74, 79, 81, 82, 86-89, 91, 92, 94, 96-98, 138, 139.* ***M. Anderson*** *c-1-4, 6, 7, 10, 12-14.* ***Aparo*** *a-200.* ***Austin*** *a-200i.* ***Baily*** *a-96r.* ***Bolland*** *a-200.* ***Buckler*** *c-158, 163, 164.* ***Burnley*** *r-94, 98, 99.* ***Greene*** *a-46-61i, 64-73i, 110i(r).* ***Grell*** *c-117, 122.* ***Kaluta*** *c-154p.* ***Gil Kane*** *a-200.* ***Krigstein*** *a-96(r/Sensation #84).* ***Kubert*** *a-200; c-72, 73.* ***Nino*** *a-228i, 230i.* ***Orlando*** *c-151i.* ***Perez*** *a-184-186p, 192-197p, 200p; c-184p, 186, 192-195, 196p, 197p, 199, 200, 201p, 202, 203-205p, 207-209, 212-215, 217, 219, 220.* ***Reinman*** *r-97.* ***Roussos*** *a-62i.* ***Sekowsky*** *a-37, 38, 44-63p, 110-112p(r); c-46-48p, 51p.* ***Sekowsky/Anderson*** *c-5, 8, 9, 11, 15.* ***B. Smith*** *c-185i.* ***Starlin*** *c-178-180, 183, 185p.* ***Staton*** *a-244p; c-157p, 244p.* ***Toth*** *r-110.* ***Tuska*** *a-153, 228p, 241-243p. JSA x-overs-21, 22, 29, 30, 37, 38, 46, 47, 55, 56, 64, 65, 73, 74, 82, 83, 91, 92, 100, 101, 102, 107, 108, 110, 113, 115, 123, 124, 135-137, 147, 148, 159, 160, 171, 172, 183-185, 195-197, 207-209, 219, 220, 231, 232, 244.*

JUSTICE LEAGUE OF AMERICA
DC Comics: No. 0, Sept, 2006 - No. 60, Oct, 2011 ($2.99/$3.99)

0-Meltzer-s; history of the JLA; art by various incl. Lee, Giordano, Benes; Turner-c 5.00
0-Variant-c by Campbell 12.00
1-($3.99) Two interlocking covers by Benes; Benes-a 5.00
1-Variant-c by Turner 8.00
1-RRP Edition; sideways composite of both Benes covers 80.00
1-Second printing; Benes cover image between black bars 4.00
2-5-($2.99) Turner-c 4.00
2-5: Variant-c: 2-Jimenez. 3-Sprouse. 4-JG Jones. 5-Art Adams 5.00
6,7-($3.50) 6-JLA vs. Amazo; covers by Turner and Hughes. 7-Roster picked, new HQs;
two Benes covers and Turner cover. 4.00
8-11,13-24,26-38-($2.99) 8-11-JLA/JSA team-up; covers by Turner & Jimenez. 10-Wally West
returns. 13-Two covers. 13-15-Injustice Gang. 16-Tangent Flash. 20-Queen Bee app.
21-Libra app.; leads into Final Crisis #1. 35,36-Royal Flush Gang app. 38-Bagley-a begins
3.00
12-($3.50) Two Ross covers; origin retold with Wight-a; Benes-a 4.00
25-($3.99) McDuffie-s/art by various; Benes-c 4.00
39-49,51,52-($3.99) 39,40-Blackest Night. 41-New team; 2 covers. 44-48-Justice Society app.
44-Jade returns. 4.00
50-($4.99) Crime Syndicate app.; Bagley-a; wraparound-c by Van Sciver 5.00
50-Variant-c by Bagley, swipe of Quitely's JLA: Earth 2 cover 8.00
50-Variant-c by Jim Lee; swipe of Brave and the Bold #28 Starro cover 12.00
53-60-($2.99) 54-Booth-a; Eclipso returns. 55-Doomsday app. 3.00
... 80 Page Giant (11/09, $5.99) Anacleto-c; short stories by various; Ra's al Ghul app. 6.00
... 80 Page Giant 2011 (6/11, $5.99) Lau-c; chapters by various; JLA goes to Hell 6.00
Free Comic Book Day giveaway - (2007) r/#0 with "Free Comic Book Day" banner on-c 3.00
Justice League Wedding Special 1 (11/07, $3.99) McKone-a; Injustice League forms 4.00
...: Dark Things HC (2011, $24.99, dustjacket) r/#44-48 & J.S.A. #41,42 25.00
...: The Injustice Gang HC (2008, $19.99, dustjacket) r/#13-16; Wedding Special 20.00
...: The Lightning Saga HC (2008, $24.99, dustjacket) r/#0,8-12 & Justice Society of
America #5,6; intro. by Patton Oswalt 25.00
...: The Lightning Saga SC (2008, $17.99) r/#0,8-12 & J.S.A. #5,6; intro. by Oswalt 18.00
...: Sanctuary SC (2009, $14.99) r/#17-21 15.00
...: Second Coming HC (2009, $19.99, dustjacket) r/#22-26 20.00
...: Second Coming SC (2010, $17.99) r/#22-26 18.00
...: Team History HC (2010, $19.99, dustjacket) r/#38-43 20.00
...: The Tornado's Path HC (2007, $24.99, dustjacket) r/#1-7; variant cover gallery; Lindelof
intro.; commentary by Meltzer & Benes 25.00
...: The Tornado's Path SC (2008, $17.99) r/#1-7; variant cover gallery; Lindelof
intro.; commentary by Meltzer & Benes 18.00
...: When Worlds Collide HC (2009, $24.99, dustjacket) r/#27,28,30-34 25.00
...: When Worlds Collide SC (2010, $14.99) r/#27,28,30-34 15.00

JUSTICE LEAGUE OF AMERICA : ANOTHER NAIL (Elseworlds) (Also see JLA: The Nail)
DC Comics: 2004 - No. 3, 2004 ($5.95, prestige format)

1-3-Sequel to JLA: The Nail; Alan Davis-s/a(p) 6.00
TPB (2004, $12.95) r/series 13.00

JUSTICE LEAGUE OF AMERICA SUPER SPECTACULAR
DC Comics: 1999 ($5.95, mimics format of DC 100 Page Super Spectaculars)

1-Reprints Silver Age JLA and Golden Age JSA 6.00

JUSTICE LEAGUE OF AMERICA/ THE 99
DC Comics: Dec, 2010 - No. 6, May, 2011 ($3.99/$2/99, limited series)

1-3-($3.99) Derenick-a/Massaferra-c; JLA meets Teshkeel Comics characters 4.00
4-6-($2.99) Starro app. 3.00

JUSTICE LEAGUE QUARTERLY (...International Quarterly #6 on)

Justice League Task Force #26 © DC

Justice Society of America (2007 series) #3 © DC

Justice Traps the Guilty #1 © PRIZE

	GD 2.0	VG 4.0	FN 6.0	VF 8.0	VF/NM 9.0	NM- 9.2

DC Comics: Winter, 1990-91 - No. 17, Winter, 1994 ($2.95/$3.50, 84 pgs.)

1-12,14-17: 1-Intro The Conglomerate (Booster Gold, Praxis, Gypsy, Vapor, Echo, Maxi-Man, & Reverb); Justice League #1-c/swipe. 1,2-Keith Giffen plots/breakdowns. 3-Giffen plot; 72 pg. story. 4-Rogers/Russell-a in back-up. 5,6-Mark Waid scripts. 8,17-Global Guardians app. 4.00
13-Linsner-c 6.00
NOTE: ***Phil Jimenez** a-17p. **Sprouse** a-1p.*

JUSTICE LEAGUE: RISE AND FALL
DC Comics: 2010, 2011

Justice League: The Rise and Fall Special #1 (5/10, $3.99) Hunt for Green Arrow 4.00
HC-(2011, $24.99) Reprints Justice League of America #43, Justice League: The Rise and Fall Special #1, Green Arrow #31,32 and Justice League: The Rise of Arsenal #1-4 25.00

JUSTICE LEAGUES...
DC Comics: Mar, 2001 ($2.50, limited series)

JL?, Justice League of Amazons, Justice League of Atlantis, Justice League of Arkham, Justice League of Aliens, JLA: JLA split by the Advance Man; Perez-c in all; s&a by various 3.00

JUSTICE LEAGUE TASK FORCE
DC Comics: June, 1993 - No. 37, Aug, 1996 ($1.25/$1.50/$1.75)

1-16,0,17-37: Aquaman, Nightwing, Flash, J'onn J'onzz, & Gypsy form team. 5,6-Knight-quest tie-ins (new Batman cameo #5, 1 pg.). 15-Triumph cameo. 16-(9/94)-Zero Hour x-over; Triumph app. 0-(10/94). 17-(11/94)-Triumph becomes part of Justice League Task Force (See JLE #68). 26-Impulse app. 35-Warlord app. 37-Triumph quits team 3.00

JUSTICE LEAGUE: THE NEW FRONTIER SPECIAL (Also see DC: The New Frontier)
DC Comics: May, 2008 ($4.99, one-shot)

1-Short stories by Darwyn Cooke, J.Bone and Dave Bullock; bonus storyboards from the movie 5.00

JUSTICE LEAGUE: THE RISE OF ARSENAL (Follows Justice League: Cry For Justice)
DC Comics: May, 2010 - No. 4, Aug, 2010 ($3.99, limited series)

1-4-Horn-c/Borges-a/Krul-s. 2,3-Cheshire app. 4.00

JUSTICE LEAGUE UNLIMITED (Based on Cartoon Network animated series)
DC Comics: Nov, 2004 - No. 46, Aug, 2008 ($2.25)

1-46: 1-Zatanna app. 2,23,42-Royal Flush Gang app. 4-Adam Strange app. 10-Creeper app. 17-Freedom Fighters app. 18-Space Cabby app. 27-Black Lightning app. 34-Zod app. 3.00
Free Comic Book Day giveaway (5/06) r/#1 with "Free Comic Book Day" banner on-c 3.00
Jam Packed Action (2005, $7.99, digest) adaptations of two TV episodes 8.00
... Vol. 1: United They Stand (2005, $6.99, digest) r/#1-5 7.00
... Vol. 2: World's Greatest Heroes (2006, $6.99, digest) r/#6-10 7.00
... Vol. 3: Champions of Justice (2006, $6.99, digest) r/#11-15 7.00
...: Heroes (2009, $12.99, full-size) r/#23-29 13.00
...: The Ties That Bind (2008, $12.99, full-size) r/#16-22 13.00

JUSTICE MACHINE, THE
Noble Comics: June, 1981 - No. 5, Nov, 1983 ($2.00, nos. 1-3 are mag. size)

	GD 2.0	VG 4.0	FN 6.0	VF 8.0	VF/NM 9.0	NM- 9.2
1-Byrne-c(p)	3	6	9	15	21	26
2-Austin-c(i)	2	4	6	9	12	15
3	1	3	4	6	8	10

4,5, Annual 1: Ann. 1-(1/84, 68 pgs.)(published by Texas Comics); 1st app. The Elementals; Golden-c(p); new Thunder Agents story (43 pgs.) 6.00

JUSTICE MACHINE (Also see The New Justice Machine)
Comico/Innovation Publishing: Jan, 1987 - No. 29, May 1989 ($1.50/$1.75)

1-29 3.00
Annual 1(6/89, $2.50, 36 pgs.)-Last Comico ish. 3.00
Summer Spectacular 1 ('89, $2.75)-Innovation Publ.; Byrne/Gustovich-c 3.00

JUSTICE MACHINE, THE
Innovation Publishing: 1990 - No. 4, 1990 ($1.95/$2.25, deluxe format, mature)

1-4: Gustovich-c/a in all 3.00

JUSTICE MACHINE FEATURING THE ELEMENTALS
Comico: May, 1986 - No. 4, Aug, 1986 ($1.50, limited series)

1-4 3.00

JUSTICE RIDERS
DC Comics: 1997 ($5.95, one-shot, prestige format)

1-Elseworlds; Dixon-s/Williams & Gray-a 6.00

JUSTICE SOCIETY
DC Comics: 2006; 2007 ($14.99, TPB)

Vol. 1 - Rep. from 1976 revival in All Star Comics #58-67 & DC Special #29; Bolland-c 15.00
Vol. 2 - R/All Star Comics #68-74 & Adventure Comics #461-466; new Bolland-c 15.00

JUSTICE SOCIETY OF AMERICA (See Adventure #461 & All-Star #3)
DC Comics: April, 1991 - No. 8, Nov, 1991 ($1.00, limited series)

1-8: 1-Flash. 2-Black Canary. 3-Green Lantern. 4-Hawkman. 5-Flash/Hawkman. 6-Green Lantern/Black Canary. 7-JSA 3.00

JUSTICE SOCIETY OF AMERICA (Also see Last Days of the... Special)
DC Comics: Aug, 1992 - No. 10, May, 1993 ($1.25)

1-10 3.00

JUSTICE SOCIETY OF AMERICA (Follows JSA series)
DC Comics: Feb, 2007 - No. 54, Oct, 2011 ($3.99/$2.99)

1-($3.99) New team selected; intro. Maxine Hunkle; Alex Ross-c 4.00
1-Variant-c by Eaglesham 6.00
2-49,51-54: 1-Covers by Ross & Eaglesham. 3,4-Vandal Savage app. 5,6-JLA/JSA team-up. 9-22-Kingdom Come Superman app.18-Magog app. 22-Superman returns to Kingdom Come Earth; Ross partial art. 23-25-Ordway-a. 26-Triptych cover by Ross. 33-Team splits. 34,35-Mordru app. 41,42-Justice League x-over. 52-54-Challengers of the Unknown app. 54-Darwyn Cooke-c 3.00
50-($4.99) Degaton app.; art by Derenick, Chaykin, Williams II, and Pérez; Massafera-c 5.00
JSA Annual 1 (9/08, $3.99) Power Girl on Earth-2; Ross-c/Ordway-a 5.00
JSA Annual 2 (4/10, $4.99) All Star team app.; Magog quits; Williams-a 5.00
... 80 Page Giant (1/10, $5.99) short stories by various incl. Ordway, S. Hampton 6.00
... 80 Page Giant 2010 (12/10, $5.99) short stories by various 6.00
... 80 Page Giant 2011 (8/11, $5.99) short stories by various incl. Chaykin, Hampton 6.00
... Special (11/10, $4.99) Scott Kolins-s/a; spotlight on Magog 5.00
...: Axis of Evil SC (2010, $14.99) r/#34-40 15.00
...: Black Adam and Isis HC (2009, $19.99, d.j.) r/#23-28 20.00
...: Black Adam and Isis SC (2010, $14.99) r/#23-28 15.00
... Kingdom Come Special: Magog (1/09, $3.99) Pasarin-a; origin re-told; 2 covers 4.00
... Kingdom Come Special: Superman (1/09, $3.99) Lois' death re-told; Alex Ross-s/a/c; thumbnails, photo references, sketch art 4.00
... Kingdom Come Special: Superman (1/09, $3.99) Eaglesham variant cover 8.00
... Kingdom Come Special: The Kingdom (1/09, $3.99) Pasarin-a; 2 covers 4.00
...: The Bad Seed SC (2010, $14.99) r/#29-33 15.00
...: The Next Age SC (2008, $14.99) r/#1-4; Ross and Eaglesham sketch pages 15.00
...: Thy Kingdom Come Part One HC (2008, $19.99, d.j.) r/#7-12; Ross sketch pages 20.00
...: Thy Kingdom Come Part One SC (2009, $14.99) r/#7-12; Ross sketch pages 15.00
...: Thy Kingdom Come Part Two HC (2008, $24.99, d.j.) r/#13-18 & Annual #1; Ross sketch pages 25.00
...: Thy Kingdom Come Part Two SC (2009, $19.99) r/#13-18 & Ann. #1; Ross sketch-a 20.00
...: Thy Kingdom Come Part Three HC (2009, $24.99, d.j.) r/#19-22 & K.C. Specials - Superman, Magog and The Kingdom; Ross sketch pages 25.00
...: Thy Kingdom Come Part Three SC (2010, $19.99) same contents as HC 20.00

JUSTICE SOCIETY OF AMERICA 100-PAGE SUPER SPECTACULAR
DC Comics: 2000 ($6.95, mimics format of DC 100 Page Super Spectaculars)

1-"1975 Issue" reprints Flash team-up and Golden Age JSA 7.00

JUSTICE SOCIETY RETURNS, THE (See All Star Comics (1999) for related titles)
DC Comics: 2003 ($19.95, TPB)

TPB-Reprints 1999 JSA x-over from All-Star Comics #1,2 and related one-shots 20.00

JUSTICE TRAPS THE GUILTY (Fargo Kid V11#3 on)
Prize/Headline Publications: Oct-Nov, 1947 - V11#2(#92), Apr-May, 1958 (True FBI Cases)

	GD 2.0	VG 4.0	FN 6.0	VF 8.0	VF/NM 9.0	NM- 9.2
V2#1-S&K-c/a; electrocution-c	61	122	183	390	670	950
2-S&K-c/a	36	72	108	216	351	485
3-5-S&K-c/a	34	68	102	199	325	450
6-S&K-c/a; Feldstein-a	36	72	108	211	343	475
7,9-S&K-c/a. 7-9-V2#1-3 in indicia; #7-9 on-c	30	60	90	177	289	400
8-Krigstein-a; S&K-c; electric chair-c	27	54	81	160	263	365
10-Krigstein-a; S&K-c/a	30	60	90	177	289	400
11,18,19-S&K-c	17	34	51	98	154	210
12,14-17,20-No S&K. 14-Severin/Elder-a (8pg.)	11	22	33	62	86	110
13-Used in **SOTI**, pg. 110-111	13	26	39	74	105	135
21,30-S&K-c/a	18	36	54	103	162	220
22,23-S&K-c	14	28	42	78	112	145
24-26,27,29,31-50: 32-Meskin story	11	22	33	60	83	105
28-Kirby-c	13	26	39	74	105	135
51-55,57,59-70	10	20	30	54	72	90
56-Ben Oda, Joe Simon, Joe Genola, Mort Meskin & Jack Kirby app. in police line-up on classic-c	14	28	42	82	121	160
58-Illo. in **SOTI**, "Treating police contemptuously" (top left); text on heroin	26	52	78	154	252	350
71-92: 76-Orlando-a	8	16	24	44	57	70

Just Married #28 © CC

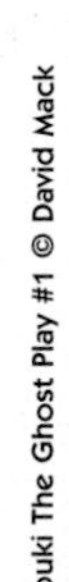

Kabuki The Ghost Play #1 © David Mack

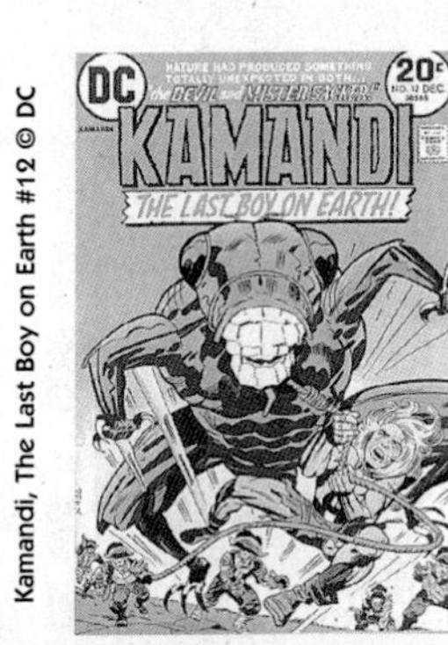

Kamandi, The Last Boy on Earth #12 © DC

NOTE: ***Bailey** a-12, 13. **Elder** a-8. **Kirby** a-19p. **Meskin** a-22, 27, 63, 64; c-45, 46. **Robinson/Meskin** a-5, 19. **Severin** a-8, 11p. Photo c-12, 15-17.*

JUST IMAGINE STAN LEE WITH... (Stan Lee re-invents DC icons)
DC Comics: 2001 - 2002 ($5.95, prestige format, one-shots)
(Adam Hughes back-c on all)(Michael Uslan back-up stories in all, diff. artists)

	GD 2.0	VG 4.0	FN 6.0	VF 8.0	VF/NM 9.0	NM- 9.2
Scott McDaniel Creating **Aquaman**- Back-up w/Fradon-a						6.00
Joe Kubert Creating **Batman**- Back-up w/Kaluta-a						6.00
Chris Bachalo Creating **Catwoman**- Back-up w/Cooke & Allred-a						6.00
John Cassaday Creating **Crisis**- no back-up story						6.00
Kevin Maguire Creating **The Flash**- Back-up w/Aragonés-a						6.00
Dave Gibbons Creating **Green Lantern**- Back-up w/Giordano-a						6.00
Jerry Ordway Creating **JLA**						6.00
John Byrne Creating **Robin**- Back-up w/John Severin-a						6.00
Walter Simonson Creating **Sandman**- Back-up w/Corben-a						6.00
Gary Frank Creating **Shazam!**- Back-up w/Kano-a						6.00
John Buscema Creating **Superman**- Back-up w/Kyle Baker-a						6.00
Jim Lee Creating **Wonder Woman**- Back-up w/Gene Colan-a						6.00
Secret Files and Origins #1 (3/02, $4.95) Crisis prologue; Jurgens-a						5.00
TPB -Just Imagine Stan Lee Creating the DC Universe: Book One (2002, $19.95) r/Batman, Wonder Woman, Superman, Green Lantern						20.00
TPB -Just Imagine Stan Lee Creating the DC Universe: Book Two (2003, $19.95) r/Flash, JLA, Secret Files and Origins, Robin, Shazam; sketch pages						20.00
TPB -Just Imagine Stan Lee Creating the DC Universe: Book Three (2004, $19.95) r/Aquaman, Catwoman, Sandman, Crisis; profile pages						20.00

JUST MARRIED
Charlton Comics: January, 1958 - No. 114, Dec, 1976

	GD 2.0	VG 4.0	FN 6.0	VF 8.0	VF/NM 9.0	NM- 9.2
1	6	12	18	41	66	90
2	4	8	12	22	34	45
3-10	3	6	9	18	27	35
11-30	3	6	9	14	20	26
31-50	2	4	6	11	16	20
51-70	2	4	6	9	13	16
71-78,80-89	2	4	6	8	11	14
79-Ditko-a (7 pages)	2	4	6	10	14	18
90-Susan Dey and David Cassidy full page poster	2	4	6	11	16	20
91-114	2	4	6	8	10	12

KA'A'NGA COMICS (...Jungle King)(See Jungle Comics)
Fiction House Magazines (Glen-Kel Publ. Co.): Spring, 1949 - No. 20, Summer, 1954

	GD 2.0	VG 4.0	FN 6.0	VF 8.0	VF/NM 9.0	NM- 9.2
1-Ka'a'nga, Lord of the Jungle begins	52	104	156	327	556	785
2 (Winter, '49-'50)	31	62	93	182	296	410
3,4	23	46	69	136	223	310
5-Camilla app.	21	42	63	126	206	285
6-10: 7-Tuska-a. 9-Tabu, Wizard of the Jungle app. 10-Used in **POP**, pg. 99	15	30	45	90	140	190
11-15: 15-Camilla-r by Baker/Jungle #106	14	28	42	80	115	150
16-Sheena app.	14	28	42	82	121	160
17-20	13	26	39	74	105	135
I.W. Reprint #1,8: 1-r/#18; Kinstler-c. 8-r/#10	3	6	9	14	20	25

NOTE: ***Celardo** c-1. **Whitman** c-8-20(most).*

KABOOM
Awesome Entertainment: Sept, 1997 - No. 3, Nov, 1997 ($2.50)

	GD 2.0	VG 4.0	FN 6.0	VF 8.0	VF/NM 9.0	NM- 9.2
1-3: 1-Matsuda-a/Loeb-s; 4 covers exist (Matsuda, Sale, Pollina and McGuinness), 1-Dynamic Forces Edition, 2-Regular, 2-Alicia Watcher variant-c, 2-Gold logo variant-c, 3-Two covers by Liefeld & Matsuda, 3-Dynamic Forces Ed., Prelude Ed.						3.00
Prelude Gold Edition						4.00

KABOOM (2nd series)
Awesome Entertainment: July, 1999 - No. 3, Dec, 1999 ($2.50)

	GD 2.0	VG 4.0	FN 6.0	VF 8.0	VF/NM 9.0	NM- 9.2
1-3: 1-Grant-a(p); at least 4 variant covers						3.00

KABUKI
Caliber: Nov, 1994 ($3.50, B&W, one-shot)

	GD 2.0	VG 4.0	FN 6.0	VF 8.0	VF/NM 9.0	NM- 9.2
nn-(Fear The Reaper) 1st app.; David Mack-c/a/s	1	2	3	5	6	8
Color Special (1/96, $2.95)-Mack-c/a/scripts; pin-ups by Tucci, Harris & Quesada						4.00
Gallery (8/95, $2.95)- pinups from Mack, Bradstreet, Paul Pope & others						3.00

KABUKI
Image Comics: Oct, 1997 - No. 9, Mar, 2000 ($2.95, color)

	GD 2.0	VG 4.0	FN 6.0	VF 8.0	VF/NM 9.0	NM- 9.2
1-David Mack-c/s/a						5.00
1-($10.00)-Dynamic Forces Edition	1	3	4	6	8	10
2-5						4.00
6-9						3.00
#1/2 (9/01, $2.95) r/Wizard 1/2; Eklipse Mag. article; bio						3.00
...Classics (2/99, $3.95) Reprints Fear the Reaper						4.00
...Classics 2 (3/99, $3.95) Reprints Dance of Dance						4.00
...Classics 3-5 (3-6/99, $4.95) Reprints Circle of Blood-Acts 1-3						5.00
...Classics 6-12 (7/99-3/00, $3.25) Various reprints						3.25
...Images (6/98, $4.95) r/#1 with new pin-ups						5.00
...Images 2 (1/99, $4.95) r/#1 with new pin-ups						5.00
...Metamorphosis TPB (10/00, $24.95) r/#1-9; Sienkiewicz intro.; 2nd printing exists						25.00
...Reflections 1-4 (7/98-5/02; $4.95) new story plus art techniques						5.00
... The Ghost Play (11/02, $2.95) new story plus interview						3.00

KABUKI
Marvel Comics (Icon): July, 2004 - Present ($2.99, color)

	GD 2.0	VG 4.0	FN 6.0	VF 8.0	VF/NM 9.0	NM- 9.2
1-9: 1-David Mack-c/s/a in all; variant-c by Alex Maleev. 4-Variant-c by Adam Hughes. 6-Variant-c by Mignola. 8-Variant-c by Kent Williams. 9-Allred var-c						3.00
...: The Alchemy HC (2008, $29.99, dust jacket) oversized r/#1-9; bonus art & content						30.00
... Reflections 5-15 (7/05-10/09, $5.99) paintings & sketches of recent work; photos						6.00

KABUKI AGENTS (SCARAB)
Image Comics: Aug, 1999 - No. 8, Aug, 2001 ($2.95, B&W)

	GD 2.0	VG 4.0	FN 6.0	VF 8.0	VF/NM 9.0	NM- 9.2
1-8-David Mack-s/Rick Mays-a						3.00
Lost in Translation HC (3/02, $29.95) r/#1-8; intro. by Paul Pope						30.00
Lost in Translation SC (3/02, $19.95) r/#1-8; intro. by Paul Pope						20.00

KABUKI: CIRCLE OF BLOOD
Caliber Press: Jan, 1995 - No. 6, Nov, 1995 ($2.95, B&W)

	GD 2.0	VG 4.0	FN 6.0	VF 8.0	VF/NM 9.0	NM- 9.2
1-David Mack story/a in all						5.00
2-6: 3-#1 on inside indicia.						3.00
6-Variant-c						3.00
TPB ($16.95) r/#1-6, intro. by Steranko						17.00
TPB (1997, $17.95) Image Edition-r/#1-6, intro. by Steranko						18.00
TPB ($24.95) Deluxe Edition						25.00

KABUKI: DANCE OF DEATH
London Night Studios: Jan, 1995 ($3.00, B&W, one-shot)

	GD 2.0	VG 4.0	FN 6.0	VF 8.0	VF/NM 9.0	NM- 9.2
1-David Mack-c/a/scripts	1	2	3	5	6	8

KABUKI: DREAMS
Image Comics: Jan, 1998 ($4.95, TPB)

	GD 2.0	VG 4.0	FN 6.0	VF 8.0	VF/NM 9.0	NM- 9.2
nn-Reprints Color Special & Dreams of the Dead						5.00

KABUKI: DREAMS OF THE DEAD
Caliber: July, 1996 ($2.95, one-shot)

	GD 2.0	VG 4.0	FN 6.0	VF 8.0	VF/NM 9.0	NM- 9.2
nn-David Mack-c/a/scripts						3.00

KABUKI FAN EDITION
Gemstone Publ./Caliber: Feb, 1997 (mail-in offer, one-shot)

	GD 2.0	VG 4.0	FN 6.0	VF 8.0	VF/NM 9.0	NM- 9.2
nn-David Mack-c/a/scripts						4.00

KABUKI: MASKS OF THE NOH
Caliber: May, 1996 - No. 4, Feb, 1997 ($2.95, limited series)

	GD 2.0	VG 4.0	FN 6.0	VF 8.0	VF/NM 9.0	NM- 9.2
1-4: 1-Three-c (1A-Quesada, 1B-Buzz, &1C-Mack). 3-Terry Moore pin-up						3.00
TPB-(4/98, $10.95) r/#1-4; intro by Terry Moore						11.00

KABUKI: SKIN DEEP
Caliber Comics: Oct, 1996 - No. 3, May, 1997 ($2.95)

	GD 2.0	VG 4.0	FN 6.0	VF 8.0	VF/NM 9.0	NM- 9.2
1-3:David Mack-c/a/scripts. 2-Two-c (1-Mack, 1-Ross)						3.00
TPB-(5/98, $9.95) r/#1-3; intro by Alex Ross						10.00

KAMANDI: AT EARTH'S END
DC Comics: June, 1993 - No. 6, Nov, 1993 ($1.75, limited series)

	GD 2.0	VG 4.0	FN 6.0	VF 8.0	VF/NM 9.0	NM- 9.2
1-6: Elseworlds storyline						3.00

KAMANDI, THE LAST BOY ON EARTH (Also see Alarming Tales #1, Brave and the Bold #120 & 157, Cancelled Comic Cavalcade & Wednesday Comics)
National Periodical Publ./DC Comics: Oct-Nov, 1972 - No. 59, Sept-Oct, 1978

	GD 2.0	VG 4.0	FN 6.0	VF 8.0	VF/NM 9.0	NM- 9.2
1-Origin & 1st app. Kamandi	8	16	24	51	86	120
2,3	5	10	15	30	48	65
4,5: 4-Intro. Prince Tuftan of the Tigers	4	8	12	26	41	55
6-10	3	6	9	19	29	38
11-20	3	6	9	16	22	28
21-28,30,31,33-40: 24-Last 20¢ issue. 31-Intro Pyra.	2	4	6	13	18	22
29,32: 29-Superman x-over. 32-(68 pgs.)-r/origin from #1 plus one new story; 4 pg. biog. of Jack Kirby with B&W photos	3	6	9	14	20	26
41-57	2	4	6	10	14	18
58-(44 pgs.)-Karate Kid x-over from LSH	3	6	9	14	19	24
59-(44 pgs.)-Cont'd in B&B #157; The Return of Omac back-up by Starlin-c/a(p)	3	6	9	16	23	30

NOTE: ***Ayers** a(p)-48-59 (most). **Giffen** a-44p, 45p. **Kirby** a-1-40p; c-1-33. **Kubert** c-34-41. **Nasser** a-45p, 46p.*

Karate Kid #6 © DC

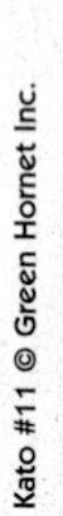
Kato #11 © Green Hornet Inc.

Katy Keene #37 © AP

Starlin a-59p; c-57, 59p.

KAMUI (Legend Of...#2 on)
Eclipse Comics/Viz Comics: May 12, 1987 - No. 37, Nov. 15, 1988 ($1.50, B&W, bi-weekly)

	GD 2.0	VG 4.0	FN 6.0	VF 8.0	VF/NM 9.0	NM- 9.2
1-37: 1-3 have 2nd printings						3.00

KANE & LYNCH (Based on the video games)
DC Comics (WildStorm): Oct, 2010 - No. 6, Apr, 2011 ($3.99/$2.99, limited series)

	GD 2.0	VG 4.0	FN 6.0	VF 8.0	VF/NM 9.0	NM- 9.2
1-4-($3.99) Templesmith-c/Edginton-s/Mitten-a						4.00
5,6-($2.99)						3.00
TPB (2011, $17.99) r/#1-6; cover gallery						18.00

KAOS MOON (Also see Negative Burn #34)
Caliber Comics: 1996 - No. 4, 1997 ($2.95, B&W)

	GD 2.0	VG 4.0	FN 6.0	VF 8.0	VF/NM 9.0	NM- 9.2
1-4-David Boller-s/a						3.00
3,4-Limited Alternate-c						4.00
3,4-Gold Alternate-c, Full Circle TPB ($5.95) r/#1,2						6.00

KARATE KID (See Action, Adventure, Legion of Super-Heroes, & Superboy)
National Periodical Publications/DC Comics: Mar-Apr, 1976 - No. 15, July-Aug, 1978 (Legion of Super-Heroes spin-off)

	GD 2.0	VG 4.0	FN 6.0	VF 8.0	VF/NM 9.0	NM- 9.2
1,15: 1-Meets Iris Jacobs; Estrada/Staton-a. 15-Continued into Kamandi #58	2	4	6	11	16	20
2-14: 2-Major Disaster app. 14-Robin x-over	2	3	4	6	8	10

NOTE: ***Grell** c-1-4, 5p, 6p, 7, 8. **Staton** a-1-9i. Legion x-over-No. 1, 2, 4, 6, 10, 12, 13. Princess Projectra x-over-#8, 9.*

KATHY
Standard Comics: Sept, 1949 - No. 17, Sept, 1955

	GD 2.0	VG 4.0	FN 6.0	VF 8.0	VF/NM 9.0	NM- 9.2
1-Teen-age	15	30	45	86	133	180
2-Schomburg-c	12	24	36	67	94	120
3-5	9	18	27	50	65	80
6-17: 17-Code approved	8	16	24	44	57	70

KATHY (The Teenage Tornado)
Atlas Comics/Marvel (ZPC): Oct, 1959 - No. 27, Feb, 1964 (most issues contain paper dolls and pin-up pages)

	GD 2.0	VG 4.0	FN 6.0	VF 8.0	VF/NM 9.0	NM- 9.2
1-The Teen-age Tornado; Goldberg-c/a in all	9	18	27	61	106	150
2	6	12	18	37	59	80
3-15	5	10	15	30	48	65
16-23,25,27	4	8	12	22	34	45
24-(8/63) Frank Sinatra, Cary Grant, Ed Sullivan & Liz Taylor-c	4	8	12	28	44	60
26-(12/63) Kathy becomes a model; Millie app.	4	8	12	24	37	50

KAT KARSON
I. W. Enterprises: No date (Reprint)

	GD 2.0	VG 4.0	FN 6.0	VF 8.0	VF/NM 9.0	NM- 9.2
1-Funny animals	2	4	6	10	12	15

KATO (Also see The Green Hornet)
Dynamite Entertainment: 2010 - No. 14, 2011 ($3.99)

	GD 2.0	VG 4.0	FN 6.0	VF 8.0	VF/NM 9.0	NM- 9.2
1-14: 1-Kato and daughter origin; Garza-a/Parks-s. 2-10 Bernard-a						4.00
Annual 1 (2011, $4.99) Parks-s/Salazar-a						5.00

KATO OF THE GREEN HORNET (Also see The Green Hornet)
Now Comics: Nov, 1991 - No. 4, Feb, 1992 ($2.50, mini-series)

	GD 2.0	VG 4.0	FN 6.0	VF 8.0	VF/NM 9.0	NM- 9.2
1-4: Brent Anderson-c/a						3.00

KATO OF THE GREEN HORNET II (Also see The Green Hornet)
Now Comics: Nov, 1992 - No. 2, Dec, 1993 ($2.50, mini-series)

	GD 2.0	VG 4.0	FN 6.0	VF 8.0	VF/NM 9.0	NM- 9.2
1,2-Baron-s/Mayerik & Sherman-a						3.00

KATO ORIGINS (Also see The Green Hornet: Year One)
Dynamite Entertainment: 2010 - No. 11, 2011 ($3.99)

	GD 2.0	VG 4.0	FN 6.0	VF 8.0	VF/NM 9.0	NM- 9.2
1-11-Kato in 1942; Jai Nitz-s/Colton Worley-a; covers by Worley & Francavilla						4.00

KATY KEENE (Also see Kasco Komics, Laugh, Pep, Suzie, & Wilbur)
Archie Publ./Close-Up/Radio Comics: 1949 - No. 4, 1951; No. 5, 3/52 - No. 62, Oct, 1961 (50-53-Adventures of...on-c) (Cut and missing pages are common)

	GD 2.0	VG 4.0	FN 6.0	VF 8.0	VF/NM 9.0	NM- 9.2
1-Bill Woggon-c/a begins; swipes-c to Mopsy #1	174	348	522	1114	1907	2700
2-(1950)	61	122	183	390	670	950
3-5: 3-(1951). 4-(1951)	50	100	150	315	533	750
6-10	37	74	111	222	361	500
11,13-21: 21-Last pre-code issue (3/55)	31	62	93	182	296	410
12-(Scarce)	37	74	111	222	361	500
22-40	21	42	63	126	206	285
41-60: 54-Wedding Album plus wedding pin-up	18	36	54	103	162	220
61,62: 62-Robot-c	20	40	60	114	182	250
Annual 1('54, 25¢)-All new stories; last pre-code	55	110	165	352	601	850
Annual 2-6('55-59, 25¢)-All new stories	32	64	96	188	307	425
3-D 1(1953, 25¢, large size)-Came w/glasses	39	78	117	231	378	525
Charm 1(9/58)-Woggon-c/a; new stories, and cut-outs	29	58	87	170	278	385
Glamour 1(1957)-Puzzles, games, cut-outs	29	58	87	170	278	385
Spectacular 1('56)	30	60	90	177	289	400

NOTE: *Debby's Diary in #45, 47-49, 52, 57.*

KATY KEENE COMICS DIGEST MAGAZINE
Close-Up, Inc. (Archie Ent.): 1987 - No. 10, July, 1990 ($1.25/$1.35/$1.50, digest size)

	GD 2.0	VG 4.0	FN 6.0	VF 8.0	VF/NM 9.0	NM- 9.2
1	2	4	6	10	14	18
2-10	1	3	4	6	8	10

NOTE: *Many used copies are cut-up inside.*

KATY KEENE FASHION BOOK MAGAZINE
Radio Comics/Archie Publications: 1955 - No. 13, Sum, '56 - N. 23, Wint, '58-59 (nn 3-10)

	GD 2.0	VG 4.0	FN 6.0	VF 8.0	VF/NM 9.0	NM- 9.2
1-Bill Woggon-c/a	54	108	162	343	574	825
2	31	62	93	182	296	410
11-18: 18-Photo Bill Woggon	22	44	66	132	216	300
19-23	19	38	57	111	176	240

KATY KEENE HOLIDAY FUN (See Archie Giant Series Magazine No. 7, 12)

KATY KEENE MODEL BEHAVIOR
Archie Comic Publications: 2008 ($10.95, TPB)

	GD 2.0	VG 4.0	FN 6.0	VF 8.0	VF/NM 9.0	NM- 9.2
Vol. 1 - New story and reprinted apps./pin-ups from Archie & Friends #101-112						11.00

KATY KEENE PINUP PARADE
Radio Comics/Archie Publications: 1955 - No. 15, Summer, 1961 (25¢) (Cut-out & missing pages are common)

	GD 2.0	VG 4.0	FN 6.0	VF 8.0	VF/NM 9.0	NM- 9.2
1-Cut-outs in all?; last pre-code issue	54	108	162	343	574	825
2-(1956)	31	62	93	182	296	410
3-5: 3-(1957)	26	52	78	154	252	350
6-10,12-14: 8-Mad parody. 10-Bill Woggon photo	22	44	66	128	209	290
11-Story of how comics get CCA approved, narrated by Katy	27	54	81	158	259	360
15(Rare)-Photo artist & family	41	82	123	251	418	585

KATY KEENE SPECIAL (Katy Keene #7 on; see Laugh Comics Digest)
Archie Ent.: Sept, 1983 - No. 33, 1990 (Later issues published quarterly)

	GD 2.0	VG 4.0	FN 6.0	VF 8.0	VF/NM 9.0	NM- 9.2
1-10: 1-Woggon-r; new Woggon-c. 3-Woggon-r						5.00
11-25: 12-Spider-Man parody						6.00
26-32-(Low print run)	1	2	3	5	7	9
33	2	4	6	8	10	12

KATZENJAMMER KIDS, THE (See Captain & the Kids & Giant Comic Album)
David McKay Publ./Standard No. 12-21(Spring/'50 - 53)/Harvey No. 22, 4/53 on: 1945-1946; Summer, 1947 - No. 27, Feb-Mar, 1954

	GD 2.0	VG 4.0	FN 6.0	VF 8.0	VF/NM 9.0	NM- 9.2
Feature Books 30	20	40	60	114	182	250
Feature Books 32,35('45),41,44('46)	18	36	54	103	162	220
Feature Book 37-Has photos & biography of Harold Knerr	19	38	57	109	172	235
1(1947)-All new stories begin	19	38	57	109	172	235
2	11	22	33	64	90	115
3-11	9	18	27	52	69	85
12-14(Standard)	8	16	24	42	54	65
15-21(Standard)	8	16	24	40	50	60
22-25,27(Harvey): 22-24-Henry app.	7	14	21	35	43	50
26-Half in 3-D	16	32	48	94	147	200

KAYO (Formerly Bullseye & Jest; becomes Carnival Comics)
Harry 'A' Chesler: No. 12, Mar, 1945

	GD 2.0	VG 4.0	FN 6.0	VF 8.0	VF/NM 9.0	NM- 9.2
12-Green Knight, Capt. Glory, Little Nemo (not by McCay)	20	40	60	114	182	250

KA-ZAR (Also see Marvel Comics #1, Savage Tales #6 & X-Men #10)
Marvel Comics Group: Aug, 1970 - No. 3, Mar, 1971 (Giant-Size, 68 pgs.)

	GD 2.0	VG 4.0	FN 6.0	VF 8.0	VF/NM 9.0	NM- 9.2
1-Reprints earlier Ka-Zar stories; Avengers x-over in Hercules; Daredevil, X-Men app.; hidden profanity-c	4	8	12	28	44	60
2,3-Daredevil-r. 2-r/Daredevil #13 w/Kirby layouts; Ka-Zar origin, Angel-r from X-Men by Tuska. 3-Romita & Heck-a (no Kirby)	3	6	9	18	27	35

NOTE: ***Buscema** r-2. **Colan** a-1p(r). **Kirby** c/a-1, 2. #1-Reprints X-Men #10 & Daredevil #24*

KA-ZAR
Marvel Comics Group: Jan, 1974 - No. 20, Feb, 1977 (Regular Size)

	GD 2.0	VG 4.0	FN 6.0	VF 8.0	VF/NM 9.0	NM- 9.2
1	3	6	9	14	19	24
2-10	2	4	6	8	10	12

Ka-Zar (2011 series) #1 © MAR

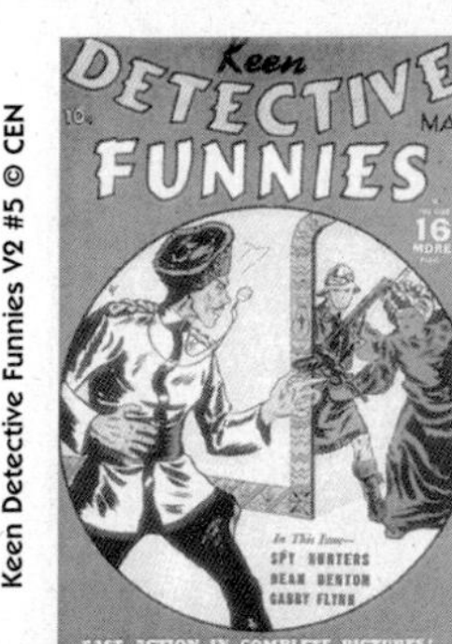

Keen Detective Funnies V2 #5 © CEN

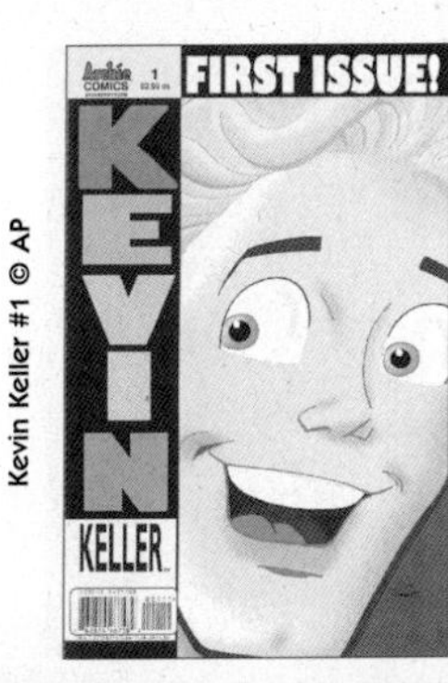

Kevin Keller #1 © AP

GD 2.0 | VG 4.0 | FN 6.0 | VF 8.0 | VF/NM 9.0 | NM- 9.2

11-14,16,18-20: 16-Only a 30 ¢ edition exists 1 2 3 5 6 8
15,17-(Regular 25¢ edition)(8/76) 1 2 3 5 6 8
15,17-(30¢-c variants, limited distribution) 3 6 9 16 22 28
NOTE: ***Alcala** a-6i, 8i. **Brunner** c-4. **J. Buscema** a-6-10p; c-1, 5, 7. **Heath** a-12. **G. Kane** c(p)-3, 5, 8-11, 15, 20. **Kirby** c-12p. **Reinman** a-1p.*

KA-ZAR (Volume 2)
Marvel Comics: May, 1997 - No. 20, Dec, 1998 ($1.95/$1.99)

1-Waid-s/Andy Kubert-c/a. thru #4 4.00
1-2nd printing; new cover 3.00
2,4: 2-Two-c 3.00
3-Alpha Flight #1 preview 4.00
5-13,15-20: 8-Includes Spider-Man Cybercomic CD-ROM. 9-11-Thanos app. 15-Priest-s/Martinez & Rodriguez-a begin; Punisher app. 3.00
14-($2.99) Last Waid/Kubert issue; flip book with 2nd story previewing new creative team of Priest-s/Martinez & Rodriguez-a 4.00
'97 Annual ($2.99)-Wraparound-c 4.00

KA-ZAR
Marvel Comics: Aug, 2011 - No. 5, Dec, 2011 ($2.99, limited series)

1-5-Jenkins-s/Alixe-a/c 3.00

KA-ZAR OF THE SAVAGE LAND
Marvel Comics: Feb, 1997 ($2.50, one-shot)

1-Wraparound-c 4.00

KA-ZAR: SIBLING RIVALRY
Marvel Comics: July, 1997 ($1.95, one-shot)

(# -1) Flashback story w/Alpha Flight #1 preview 3.00

KA-ZAR THE SAVAGE (See Marvel Fanfare)
Marvel Comics Group: Apr, 1981 - No. 34, Oct, 1984 (Regular size)(Mando paper #10 on)

1 5.00
2-20,24,27,28,30-34: 11-Origin Zabu. 12-One of two versions with panel missing on pg. 10. 20-Kraven the Hunter-c/story (also apps. in #21) 3.00
12-Version with panel on pg. 10 (1600 printed) 1 2 3 5 6 8
21-23, 25,26-Spider-Man app. 26-Photo-c. 4.00
29-Double size; Ka-Zar & Shanna wed 4.00
NOTE: ***B. Anderson** a-1-15p, 18, 19; c-1-17, 18p, 20(back). **G. Kane** a(back-up)-11, 12, 14.*

KEEN DETECTIVE FUNNIES (Formerly Detective Picture Stories?)
Centaur Publications: No. 8, July, 1938 - No. 24, Sept, 1940

V1#8-The Clock continues-r/Funny Picture Stories #1; Roy Crane-a (1st?)
271 542 813 1734 2967 4200
9-Tex Martin by Eisner; The Gang Buster app. 110 220 330 704 1202 1700
10,11: 11-Dean Denton story (begins?) 100 200 300 635 1093 1550
V2#1,2-The Eye Sees by Frank Thomas begins; ends #23(Not in V2#3&5). 2-Jack Cole-a
90 180 270 576 988 1400
3-6: 3-TNT Todd begins. 4-Gabby Flynn begins. 5,6-Dean Denton story
84 168 252 538 919 1300
7-The Masked Marvel by Ben Thompson begins (7/39, 1st app.)(scarce)
265 530 795 1694 2897 4100
8-Nudist ranch panel w/four girls 97 194 291 621 1061 1500
9-11 87 174 261 553 952 1350
12(12/39)-Origin The Eye Sees by Frank Thomas; death of Masked Marvel's sidekick ZL
107 214 321 680 1165 1650
V3#1,2 77 154 231 493 847 1200
18-Bondage/torture-c 87 174 261 553 952 1350
19,21,22 77 154 231 493 847 1200
20-Classic Eye Sees-c by Thomas 119 238 357 762 1306 1850
23-Air Man begins (intro); Air Man-c 103 206 309 659 1130 1600
24-(scarce) Air Man-c 110 220 330 704 1202 1700
NOTE: ***Burgos** a-V2#2. **Jack Cole** a-V2#2. **Eisner** a-10, V2#6r. **Ken Ernst** a-V2#4-7, 9, 10, 19, 21; c-V2#4. **Everett** a-V2#6, 7, 9, 11, 12, 20. **Guardineer** a-V2#5, 66. **Gustavson** a-V2#4-6. **Simon** c-V3#1. **Thompson** c-V2#7, 9, 10, 22.*

KEEN KOMICS
Centaur Publications: V2#1, May, 1939 - V2#3, Nov, 1939

V2#1(Large size)-Dan Hastings (s/f), The Big Top, Bob Phantom the Magician, The Mad Goddess app. 113 226 339 718 1234 1750
V2#2(Reg. size)-The Forbidden Idol of Machu Picchu; Cut Carson by Burgos begins
68 136 204 435 743 1050
V2#3-Saddle Sniffl by Jack Cole, Circus Pays, Kings Revenge app.
68 136 204 435 743 1050
NOTE: ***Binder** a-V2#2. **Burgos** a-V2#2, 3. **Ken Ernst** a-V2#3. **Gustavson** a-V2#2. **Jack Cole** a-V2#3.*

KEEN TEENS (Girls magazine)
Life's Romances Publ./Leader/Magazine Ent.: 1945 - No. 6, Aug-Sept, 1947

nn (#1)-14 pgs. Claire Voyant (cont'd. in other nn issue) movie photos, Dotty Dripple, Gertie O'Grady & Sissy; Van Johnson, Sinatra photo-c
40 80 120 246 411 575
nn (#2, 1946)-16 pgs. Claire Voyant & 16 pgs. movie photos
29 58 87 172 281 390
3-6: 4-Glenn Ford photo-c. 5-Perry Como-c 15 30 45 86 133 180

KELLYS, THE (Formerly Rusty Comics; Spy Cases No. 26 on)
Marvel Comics (HPC): No. 23, Jan, 1950 - No. 25, June, 1950 (52 pgs.)

23-Teenage 14 28 42 80 115 150
24,25: 24-Margie app. 10 20 30 54 72 90

KEN MAYNARD WESTERN (Movie star)(See Wow Comics, 1936)
Fawcett Publ.: Sept, 1950 - No. 8, Feb, 1952 (All 36 pgs; photo front/back-c)

1-Ken Maynard & his horse Tarzan begin 37 74 111 222 361 500
2 20 40 60 120 195 270
3-8: 6-Atomic bomb explosion panel 15 30 45 88 137 185

KEN SHANNON (Becomes Gabby #11 on) (Also see Police Comics #103)
Quality Comics Group: Oct, 1951 - No. 10, Apr, 1953 (A private eye)

1-Crandall-a 40 80 120 246 411 575
2-Crandall c/a(2) 31 62 93 182 296 410
3-Horror-c; Crandall-a 34 68 102 199 325 450
4,5-Crandall-a 22 44 66 132 216 300
6-Crandall-c/a; "The Weird Vampire Mob"-c/s 32 64 96 192 314 435
7-"The Ugliest Man Alive"-c; Crandall-a 26 52 78 154 252 350
8,9: 8-Opium den drug use story 19 38 57 111 176 240
10-Crandall-c 20 40 60 114 182 250
NOTE: ***Crandall/Cuidera** c-1-10. **Jack Cole** a-1-9. #1-15 published after title change to Gabby.*

KEN STUART
Publication Enterprises: Jan, 1949 (Sea Adventures)

1-Frank Borth-c/a 10 20 30 54 72 90

KENT BLAKE OF THE SECRET SERVICE (Spy)
Marvel/Atlas Comics (20CC): May, 1951 - No. 14, July, 1953

1-Injury to eye, bondage, torture; Brodsky-c 22 44 66 132 216 300
2-Drug use w/hypo scenes; Brodsky-c 15 30 45 90 140 190
3-14: 8-R.Q. Sale-a (2 pgs.) 11 22 33 60 83 105
NOTE: ***Heath** c-5, 7, 8. **Infantino** c-12. **Maneely** c-3. **Sinnott** a-2(3). **Tuska** a-8(3pg.).*

KENTS, THE
DC Comics: Aug, 1997 - No. 12, July, 1998 ($2.50, limited series)

1-12-Ostrander-s/art by Truman and Bair (#1-8), Mandrake (#9-12) 3.00
TPB ($19.95) r/#1-12 20.00

KERRY DRAKE (Also see A-1 Comics)
Argo: Jan, 1956 - No. 2, March, 1956

1,2-Newspaper-r 8 16 24 44 57 70

KERRY DRAKE DETECTIVE CASES (...Racket Buster No. 32,33)
(Also see Chamber of Clues & Green Hornet Comics #42-47)
Life's Romances/Com/Magazine Ent. No.1-5/Harvey No.6 on: 1944 - No. 5, 1944; No. 6, Jan, 1948 - No. 33, Aug, 1952

nn(1944)(A-1 Comics)(slightly over-size) 30 60 90 177 289 400
2 18 36 54 107 169 230
3-5(1944) 15 30 45 90 140 190
6,8(1948): Lady Crime by Powell. 8-Bondage-c 12 24 36 67 94 120
7-Kubert-a; biog of Andriola (artist) 13 26 39 74 105 135
9,10-Two-part marijuana story; Kerry smokes marijuana in #10
15 30 45 88 137 185
11-15 10 20 30 58 79 100
16-33 9 18 27 50 65 80
NOTE: ***Andiola** c-6-9. **Berg** a-5. **Powell** a-10-23, 28, 29.*

KEVIN KELLER (Also see Veronica #202 for 1st app. & #207-210 for first mini-series)
Archie Comics Publications: Apr, 2012 - Present ($2.99)

1-3-Two covers on each 3.00

KEWPIES
Will Eisner Publications: Spring, 1949

1-Feiffer-a; Kewpie Doll ad on back cover; used in **SOTI**, pg. 35
49 98 147 309 522 735

KEY COMICS
Consolidated Magazines: Jan, 1944 - No. 5, Aug, 1946

1-The Key, Will-O-The-Wisp begin 43 86 129 271 461 650
2 (3/44) 24 48 72 142 234 325

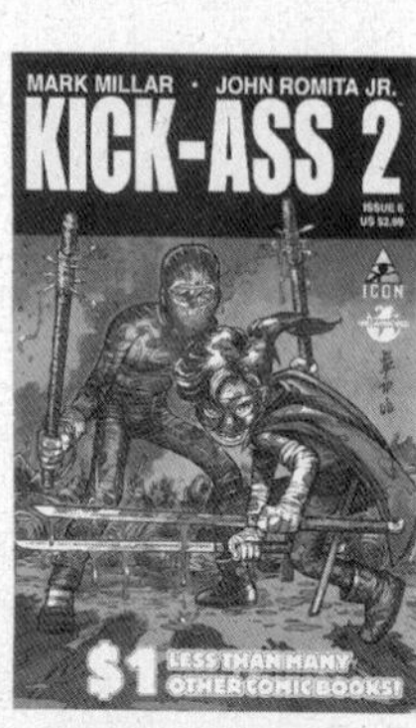

Kick-Ass 2 #6 © Millarworld & JR, Jr.

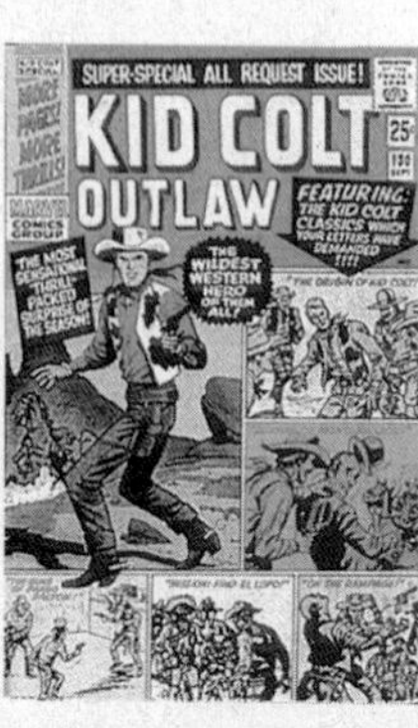

Kid Colt Outlaw #130 © MAR

Kid Eternity (1993 series) #7 © DC

GD VG FN VF VF/NM NM-
2.0 4.0 6.0 8.0 9.0 9.2

3,4: 4-(5/46)-Origin John Quincy The Atom (begins); Walter Johnson c-3-5
21 42 63 124 202 280
5-4pg. Faust Opera adaptation; Kiefer-a; back-c advertises "Masterpieces Illustrated" by Lloyd Jacquet after he left Classic Comics (no copies of Masterpieces Illustrated known)
27 54 81 158 259 360

KEY OF Z
BOOM! Studios: Oct, 2011 - No. 4, Jan, 2012 ($3.99, limited series)
1-4: 1-Claudio Sanchez & Chondra Echert-s/Aaron Kuder-a; covers by Fox & Moore 4.00

KEY RING COMICS
Dell Publishing Co.: 1941 (16 pgs.; two colors) (sold 5 for 10¢)
1-Sky Hawk, 1-Viking Carter, 1-Features Sleepy Samson, 1-Origin Greg Gilday; r/War Comics #2 9 18 27 52 69 85
1-Radior (Super hero) 11 22 33 62 86 110
NOTE: *Each book has two holes in spine to put in binder.*

KICK-ASS
Marvel Comics (Icon): April, 2008 - No. 8, Mar, 2010 ($2.99)
1-Mark Millar-s/John Romita Jr.-a/c 15.00
1-Red variant cover by McNiven 20.00
1-2nd printing 4.00
1-Director's Cut (8/08, $3.99) r/#1 with script and sketch pages; Millar afterword 4.00
2 8.00
3-8: 5-Intro. Red Mist 4.00
NOTE: *Multiple printings exist for most issues.*

KICK-ASS 2
Marvel Comics (Icon): Dec, 2010 - Present ($2.99)
1-6-Mark Millar-s/John Romita Jr.-a/c. 1-Five printings 3.00
1,2-Variant covers. 1-Edwards. 2-Yu. 5-Photo & Hitch. 6-Photo 5.00

KID CARROTS
St. John Publishing Co.: September, 1953
1-Funny animal 8 16 24 44 57 70

KID COLT ONE-SHOT
Marvel Comics: Sept, 2009 ($3.99)
1-DeFalco-s/Burchett-a/Luke Ross-c 4.00

KID COLT OUTLAW (Kid Colt #1-4; ...Outlaw #5-on)(Also see All Western Winners, Best Western, Black Rider, Giant-Size..., Two-Gun Kid, Two-Gun Western, Western Winners, Wild Western, Wisco)
Marvel Comics(LCC) 1-16; Atlas(LMC) 17-102; Marvel 103-on: 8/48 - No. 139, 3/68; No. 140, 11/69 - No. 229, 4/79
1-Kid Colt & his horse Steel begin. 129 258 387 826 1413 2000
2 57 114 171 362 619 875
3-5: 4-Anti-Wertham editorial; Tex Taylor app. 5-Blaze Carson app.
48 96 144 302 514 725
6-8: 6-Tex Taylor app; 7-Nimo the Lion begins, ends #10
32 64 96 192 314 435
9,10 (52 pgs.) 32 64 96 192 314 435
11-Origin (10/50) 38 76 114 228 369 510
12-20 22 44 66 128 209 290
21-32 18 36 54 107 169 230
33-45: Black Rider in all 15 30 45 85 130 175
46,47,49,50 14 28 42 78 112 145
48-Kubert-a 14 28 42 80 115 150
51-53,55,56 11 22 33 64 90 115
54-Williamson/Maneely-c 12 24 36 69 97 125
57-60,66: 4-pg. Williamson-a in all 8 16 24 55 93 130
61-63,67-78,80-86: 70-Severin-c. 69,73-Maneely-c. 86-Kirby-a(r).
7 14 21 44 72 100
64,65-Crandall-a 7 14 21 46 76 105
79,87: 79-Origin retold. 87-Davis-a(r) 7 14 21 46 76 105
88,89-Williamson-a in both (4 pgs.). 89-Redrawn Matt Slade #2
7 14 21 48 79 110
90-99,101-106,108,109: 91-Kirby/Ayers-c. 95-Kirby/Ayers-c/story. 102-Last 10¢ issue
6 12 18 41 66 90
100 7 14 21 44 72 100
107-Only Kirby sci-fi cover of title; Kirby-a. 8 16 24 53 89 125
110-(5/63)-1st app. Iron Mask (Iron Man type villain) 7 14 21 48 79 110
111-120: 114-(1/64)-2nd app. Iron Mask 6 12 18 37 59 80
121-129,133-139: 121-Rawhide Kid x-over. 125-Two-Gun Kid x-over. 139-Last 12¢ issue
5 10 15 30 48 65
130-132 (68 pgs.)-one new story each. 130-Origin 6 12 18 39 62 85
140-155: 140-Reprints begin (later issues mostly-r). 155-Last 15¢ issue

GD VG FN VF VF/NM NM-
2.0 4.0 6.0 8.0 9.0 9.2

3 6 9 16 23 30
156-Giant; reprints (52 pgs.) 3 6 9 21 32 42
157-180,200: 170-Origin retold. 3 6 9 14 20 25
181-199 2 4 6 11 16 20
201-229: 201-New material w/Rawhide Kid app; Kane-c. 229-Rawhide Kid-r
2 4 6 10 14 18
205-209-(30¢-c variants, limited dist.) 6 12 18 39 62 85
218-220-(35¢-c variants, limited dist.) 9 18 27 61 106 150
...Album (no date; 1950's; Atlas Comics)-132 pgs.; cardboard cover, B&W stories; (Rare) 103 206 309 659 1130 1600
NOTE: ***Ayers** a-many. **Colan** a-52, 53, 84, 112, 114; c(p)-223, 228, 229. **Crandall** a-140r, 167r. **Everett** a-90, 137i, 225i(r). **Heath** a-8(2); c-34, 35, 39, 44, 46, 48, 49, 57, 64. **Heck** a-135, 139. **Jack Keller** a-25(2), 26-68(3-4), 73, 78, 84, 85, 88, 92, 94p, 98, 99, 101, 106-108, 110-112, 114, 115, 117-127, 129, 130, 132, 140-150r. **Kirby** a-86r, 93, 96, 107, 119, 176(part); c-87, 92-95, 97, 99-112, 114-117, 121-123, 197r; w/**Ditko** c-89. **Maneely** a-12, 68, 81; c-17, 19, 40-43, 47, 52, 53, 62, 65, 68, 73, 78, 81, 142r, 150r. **Morrow** a-173r, 216r. **Rico** a-13, 18. **Severin** c-55, 58, 59, 84, 143, 148, 149i. **Shores** a-39, 41-43, 143r; c-1-10(most), 24. **Sutton** a-136, 137p, 225p(r). **Wildey** a-47, 54, 82, 144r. **Williamson** r-147, 170, 172, 216. **Woodbridge** a-64, 81. Black Rider in #33-45, 74, 86. Iron Mask in #110, 114, 121, 127. Sam Hawk in #80, 84, 101, 111, 121, 146, 174, 181, 188.*

KID COWBOY (Also see Approved Comics #4 & Boy Cowboy)
Ziff-Davis Publ./St. John (Approved Comics) #11,14: 1950 - No. 11, Wint, '52-'53; No. 13, April 1953; No. 14, June, 1954 (No #12) (Painted covers #1-10,13,14)
1-Lucy Belle & Red Feather begin 16 32 48 94 147 200
2-Maneely-c 11 22 33 62 86 110
3-11,13,14: (#3, spr. '51). 5-Berg-a. 14-Code approved
10 20 30 56 76 95

KID DEATH & FLUFFY HALLOWEEN SPECIAL
Event Comics: Oct, 1997 ($2.95, B&W, one-shot)
1-Variant-c by Cebollero & Quesada/Palmiotti 3.00

KID DEATH & FLUFFY SPRING BREAK SPECIAL
Event Comics: July, 1996 ($2.50, B&W, one-shot)
1-Quesada & Palmiotti-c/scripts 3.00

KIDDIE KAPERS
Kiddie Kapers Co., 1945/Decker Publ. (Red Top-Farrell): 1945?(nd); Oct, 1957; 1963 - 1964
1(nd, 1945-46?, 36 pgs.)-Infinity-c; funny animal 10 20 30 54 72 90
1(10/57)(Decker)-Little Bit-r from Kiddie Karnival 5 10 15 22 26 30
Super Reprint #7, 10('63), 12, 14('63), 15,17('64), 18('64): 10, 14-r/Animal Adventures #1. 15-Animal Advs. #? 17-Cowboys 'N' Injuns #? 2 4 6 8 11 14

KIDDIE KARNIVAL
Ziff-Davis Publ. Co. (Approved Comics): 1952 (25¢, 100 pgs.) (One Shot)
nn-Rebound Little Bit #1,2; painted-c 36 72 108 211 343 475

KID ETERNITY (Becomes Buccaneers) (See Hit Comics)
Quality Comics Group: Spring, 1946 - No. 18, Nov, 1949
1 90 180 270 576 988 1400
2 39 78 117 240 395 550
3-Mac Raboy-a 40 80 120 246 411 575
4-10 25 50 75 147 241 335
11-18 19 38 57 112 179 245

KID ETERNITY
DC Comics: 1991 - No. 3, Nov, 1991 ($4.95, limited series)
1-3: Grant Morrison scripts/Duncan Fegredo-a/c 6.00
TPB (2006, $14.99) r/#1-3 15.00

KID ETERNITY
DC Comics (Vertigo): May, 1993 - No. 16, Sept, 1994 ($1.95, mature)
1-16: 1-Gold ink-c. 6-Photo-c. All Sean Phillips-c/a except #15 (Phillips-c/i only) 3.00

KID FROM DODGE CITY, THE
Atlas Comics (MMC): July, 1957 - No. 2, Sept, 1957
1-Don Heck-c 10 20 30 56 76 95
2-Everett-c 7 14 21 37 46 55

KID FROM TEXAS, THE (A Texas Ranger)
Atlas Comics (CSI): June, 1957 - No. 2, Aug, 1957
1-Powell-a; Severin-c 10 20 30 56 76 95
2 7 14 21 37 46 55

KID KOKO
I. W. Enterprises: 1958
Reprint #1,2-(r/M.E.'s Koko & Kola #4, 1947) 2 4 6 8 11 14

KID KOMICS (Kid Movie Komics No. 11)
Timely Comics (USA 1,2/FCI 3-10): Feb, 1943 - No. 10, Spring, 1946

Kid Komics #8 © MAR

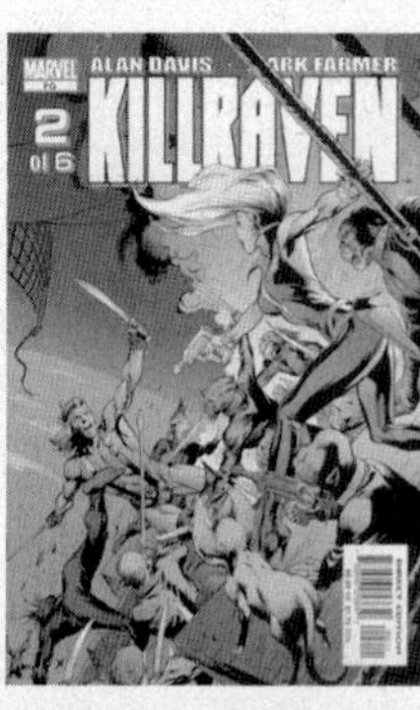

Killraven (2002 series) #2 © MAR

Kin #6 © Gary Frank

GD VG FN VF VF/NM NM-
2.0 4.0 6.0 8.0 9.0 9.2

1-Origin Captain Wonder & sidekick Tim Mullrooney, & Subbie; intro the Sea-Going Lad, Pinto Pete, & Trixie Trouble; Knuckles & Whitewash Jones (from Young Allies) app.; Wolverton-a (7 pgs.) 459 918 1377 3350 5925 8500
2-The Young Allies, Red Hawk, & Tommy Tyme begin; last Captain Wonder & Subbie; Schomburg Japanese WWII bondage-c 239 478 717 1530 2615 3700
3-The Vision, Daredevils & Red Hawk app. 161 322 483 1030 1765 2500
4-The Destroyer begins; Sub-Mariner app.; Red Hawk & Tommy Tyme end; classic Schomburg WWII human meat grinder-c 181 362 543 1158 1979 2800
5,6: 5-Tommy Tyme begins, ends #10 107 214 321 680 1165 1650
7-10: 7,10-The Whizzer app. Destroyer not in #7,8. 10-Last Destroyer, Young Allies & Whizzer 90 180 270 576 988 1400

NOTE: ***Brodsky** c-5. **Schomburg** c-2-4, 6-10. **Shores** c-1. Captain Wonder c-1, 2. The Young Allies c-3-10.*

KID MONTANA (Formerly Davy Crockett Frontier Fighter; The Gunfighters No. 51 on)
Charlton Comics: V2#9, Nov, 1957 - No. 50, Mar, 1965

V2#9 (#1) 4 8 12 28 44 60
10 3 6 9 20 30 40
11,12,14-20 3 6 9 16 22 28
13-Williamson-a 3 6 9 20 30 40
21-35: 25,31-Giordano-c. 32-Origin Kid Montana. 34-Geronimo-c/s. 35-Snow Monster-c/s 2 4 6 11 16 20
36-50: 36-Dinosaur-c/s. 37,48-Giordano-c 2 4 6 9 12 15

NOTE: *Title change to Montana Kid on cover only #44 & 45; remained Kid Montana on inside. **Chasal** a-29,30. **Giordano** c-25,31,37,48. **Giordano/Alascia** c-12. **Mastroserio** a-9,11,13,14,22; c-11,14. **Masulli/Mastroserio** c-13. **Montes/Bache** c-42. **Morisi** c-16,32-34,36?,40,41,44,46; a-13,15;16,31-50. **Nicholas/Alascia** a-44,48.*

KID MOVIE KOMICS (Formerly Kid Komics; Rusty Comics #12 on)
Timely Comics: No. 11, Summer, 1946

11-Silly Seal & Ziggy Pig; 2 pgs. Kurtzman "Hey Look" plus 6 pg. "Pigtales" story 27 54 81 158 259 360

KIDNAPPED (See Marvel Illustrated: Kidnapped)

KIDNAPPED (Robert Louis Stevenson's...also see Movie Comics)(Disney)
Dell Publishing Co.: No. 1101, May, 1960

Four Color 1101-Movie, photo-c 6 12 18 42 69 95

KIDNAP RACKET (See Harvey Comics Hits No. 57)

KID SLADE GUNFIGHTER (Formerly Matt Slade...)
Atlas Comics (SPI): No. 5, Jan, 1957 - No. 8, July, 1957

5-Maneely, Roth, Severin-a in all; Maneely-c 13 26 39 72 101 130
6,8-Severin-c 8 16 24 44 57 70
7-Williamson/Mayo-a, 4 pgs.; Maneely-c 10 20 30 56 76 95

KID SUPREME (See Supreme)
Image Comics (Extreme Studios): Mar, 1996 - No. 3, July, 1996 ($2.50)

1-3: Fraga-a/scripts. 3-Glory-c/app. 3.00

KID TERRIFIC
Image Comics: Nov, 1998 ($2.95, B&W)

1-Snyder & Diliberto-s/a 3.00

KID ZOO COMICS
Street & Smith Publications: July, 1948 (52 pgs.)

1-Funny Animal 32 64 96 188 307 425

KILL ALL PARENTS
Image Comics: June, 2008 ($3.99, one-shot)

1-Marcelo Di Chiara-a/Mark Andrew Smith-s 4.00

KILLAPALOOZA
DC Comics (WildStorm): July, 2009 - No. 6, Dec, 2009 ($2.99, limited series)

1-6: 1-Beechen-s/Hairsine-a/c 3.00
TPB (2010, $19.99) r/#1-6 20.00

KILLER (...Tales By Timothy Truman)
Eclipse Comics: March, 1985 ($1.75, one-shot, Baxter paper)

1-Timothy Truman-c/a 3.00

KILLER INSTINCT (Video game)
Acclaim Comics: June, 1996 - No. 6 ($2.50, limited series)

1-6: 1-Bart Sears-a(p). 4-Special #1. 5-Special #2. 6-Special #3 3.00

KILLERS, THE
Magazine Enterprises: 1947 - No. 2, 1948 (No month)

1-Mr. Zin, the Hatchet Killer; mentioned in **SOTI**, pgs. 179,180; used by N.Y. Legis. Comm.; L. B. Cole-c 135 270 405 864 1482 2100
2-(Scarce)-Hashish smoking story; "Dying, Dying, Dead" drug story; Whitney, Ingels-a; Whitney hanging-c 110 220 330 704 1202 1700

GD VG FN VF VF/NM NM-
2.0 4.0 6.0 8.0 9.0 9.2

KILLING GIRL
Image Comics: Aug, 2007 - No. 5, Dec, 2007 ($2.99, limited series)

1-5: 1-Frank Espinosa-a/Glen Brunswick-s; covers by Espinosa and Frank Cho 3.00

KILLING JOKE, THE (See Batman: The Killing Joke under Batman one-shots)

KILLPOWER: THE EARLY YEARS
Marvel Comics UK: Sept, 1993 - No. 4, Dec, 1993 ($1.75, mini-series)

1-($2.95)-Foil embossed-c 4.00
2-4: 2-Genetix app. 3-Punisher app. 3.00

KILLRAVEN (See Amazing Adventures #18 (5/73))
Marvel Comics: Feb, 2001 ($2.99, one-shot)

1-Linsner-s/a/c 3.00

KILLRAVEN
Marvel Comics: Dec, 2002 - No. 6, May, 2003 ($2.99, limited series)

1-6-Alan Davis-s/a(p)/Mark Farmer-i 3.00
HC (2007, $19.99) r/#1-6; cover gallery, pencil art; foreward by Alan Davis 20.00

KILLRAZOR
Image Comics (Top Cow Productions): Aug, 1995 ($2.50, one-shot)

1 3.00

KILL YOUR BOYFRIEND
DC Comics (Vertigo): June, 1995 ($4.95, one-shot)

1-Grant Morrison story 6.00
1 ($5.95, 1998) 2nd printing 6.00

KILROY (Volume 2)
Caliber Press: 1998 ($2.95, B&W)

1-Pruett-s 3.00

KILROY IS HERE
Caliber Press: 1995 ($2.95, B&W)

1-10 3.00

KILROYS, THE
B&I Publ. Co. No. 1-19/American Comics Group: June-July, 1947 - No. 54, June-July, 1955

1 22 44 66 132 216 300
2 14 28 42 80 115 150
3-5: 5-Gross-a 13 26 39 72 101 130
6-10: 8-Milt Gross's Moronica 10 20 30 56 76 95
11-20: 14-Gross-a 9 18 27 50 65 80
21-30 8 16 24 44 57 70
31-47,50-54 8 16 24 42 54 65
48,49-(3-D effect-c/stories) 18 36 54 103 162 220

KILROY: THE SHORT STORIES
Caliber Press: 1995 ($2.95, B&W)

1 3.00

KIN
Image Comics (Top Cow): Mar, 2000 - No. 6, Sept, 2000 ($2.95)

1-5-Gary Frank-s/c/a 3.00
1-($6.95) DF Alternate footprint cover 7.00
6-($3.95) 4.00
... Descent of Man TPB (2002, $19.95) r/ #1-6 20.00

KINDRED, THE
Image Comics (WildStorm Productions): Mar, 1994 - No. 4, July, 1995 ($1.95, lim. series)

1-($2.50)-Grifter & Backlash app. in all; bound-in trading card 3.00
2-4 3.00
2,3: 2-Variant-c. 3-Alternate-c by Portacio, see Deathblow #5 4.00
Trade paperback (2/95, $9.95) 10.00

NOTE: ***Booth** c/a-1-4. The first four issues contain coupons redeemable for a Jim Lee Grifter/Backlash print.*

KINDRED II, THE
DC Comics (WildStorm): Mar, 2002 - No. 4, June, 2002 ($2.50, limited series)

1-4-Booth-s/Booth & Regla-a 3.00

KINETIC
DC Comics (Focus): May, 2004 - No. 8, Dec, 2004 ($2.50)

1-8-Puckett-s/Pleece-a/c 3.00
TPB (2005, $9.99) r/#1-8; cover gallery and sketch pages 10.00

KING (Magazine)
Skywald Publ.: Mar, 1971 - No. 2, July, 1971

1-Violence; semi-nudity; Boris Vallejo-a (2 pgs.) 5 10 15 35 55 75
2-Photo-c 4 8 12 22 34 45

King Comics #39 © KING

The Kingdom #1 © DC

King of the Royal Mounted #8 © DELL

	GD 2.0	VG 4.0	FN 6.0	VF 8.0	VF/NM 9.0	NM- 9.2

KING ARTHUR AND THE KNIGHTS OF JUSTICE
Marvel Comics UK: Dec, 1993 - No. 3, Feb, 1994 ($1.25, limited series)

1-3: TV adaptation						3.00

KING CLASSICS
King Features : 1977 (36 pgs., cardboard-c) (Printed in Spain for U.S. distr.)

1-Connecticut Yankee, 2-Last of the Mohicans, 3-Moby Dick, 4-Robin Hood, 5-Swiss Family Robinson, 6-Robinson Crusoe, 7-Treasure Island, 8-20,000 Leagues, 9-Christmas Carol, 10-Huck Finn, 11-Around the World in 80 Days, 12-Davy Crockett, 13-Don Quixote, 14-Gold Bug, 15-Ivanhoe, 16-Three Musketeers, 17-Baron Munchausen, 18-Alice in Wonderland, 19-Black Arrow, 20-Five Weeks in a Balloon, 21-Great Expectations, 22-Gulliver's Travels, 23-Prince & Pauper, 24-Lawrence of Arabia (Originals, 1977-78)

each....	2	4	6	10	14	18
Reprints (1979; HRN-24)	2	4	6	8	10	12

NOTE: *The first eight issues were not numbered. Issues No. 25-32 were advertised but not published. The 1977 originals have HRN 32a; the 1978 originals have HRN 32b.*

KING COLT (See Luke Short's Western Stories)

KING COMICS (Strip reprints)
David McKay Publications/Standard #156-on: 4/36 - No. 155, 11-12/49; No. 156, Spr/50 - No. 159, 2/52 (Winter on-c)

1-1st app. Flash Gordon by Alex Raymond; Brick Bradford (1st app.), Popeye, Henry (1st app.) & Mandrake the Magician (1st app.) begin; Popeye-c begin

	1250	2500	3750	10,000	-	-
2	360	720	1080	1980	2790	3600
3	245	490	735	1348	1899	2450
4	190	380	570	1045	1473	1900
5	140	280	420	770	1085	1400
6-10: 9-X-Mas-c	95	190	285	523	737	950
11-20	75	150	225	413	582	750
21-30: 21-X-Mas-c	55	110	165	303	427	550
31-40: 33-Last Segar Popeye	45	90	135	248	349	450
41-50: 46-Text illos by Marge Buell contain characters similar to Lulu, Alvin & Tubby. 50-The Lone Ranger begins	31	62	93	182	296	410
51-60: 52-Barney Baxter begins?	22	44	66	130	213	295
61-The Phantom begins	23	46	69	136	223	310
62-80: 76-Flag-c. 79-Blondie begins	17	34	51	98	154	210
81-99	14	28	42	81	118	155
100	16	32	48	92	144	195
101-114: 114-Last Raymond issue (1 pg.); Flash Gordon by Austin Briggs begins, ends #155	14	28	42	76	108	140
115-145: 117-Phantom origin retold	10	20	30	56	76	95
146,147-Prince Valiant in both	9	18	27	50	65	80
148-155: 155-Flash Gordon ends (11-12/49)	9	18	27	50	65	80
156-159: 156-New logo begins (Standard)	9	18	27	47	61	75

NOTE: *Marge Buell text illos in No. 24-46 at least.*

KING CONAN (Conan The King No. 20 on)
Marvel Comics Group: Mar, 1980 - No. 19, Nov, 1983 (52 pgs.)

1	1	2	3	5	6	8
2-19: 4-Death of Thoth Amon. 7-1st Paul Smith-a, 1 pg. pin-up (9/81)						5.00

NOTE: ***J. Buscema** a-1-9p, 17p; c(p)-1-5, 7-9, 14, 17. **Kaluta** c-19. **Nebres** a-17i, 18, 19i. **Severin** c-18. **Simonson** c-6.*

KING CONAN: THE PHOENIX ON THE SWORD
Dark Horse Comics: Jan, 2012 - No. 4 ($3.50, limited series)

1,2-Truman-s/Giorello-a/Robinson-c. 1-Variant-c by Parel						3.50

KING CONAN: THE SCARLET CITADEL
Dark Horse Comics: Feb, 2011 - No. 4, May, 2011 ($3.50, limited series)

1-4-Truman-s/Giorello-a/Robertson-c. 1-Variant-c by Parel						3.50

KING DAVID
DC Comics (Vertigo): 2002 ($19.95, 8 1/2" x 11")

nn-Story of King David; Kyle Baker-s/a						20.00

KINGDOM, THE
DC Comics: Feb, 1999 - No. 2, Feb, 1999 ($2.95/$1.99, limited series)

1,2-Waid-s; sequel to Kingdom Come; introduces Hypertime						4.00
...: Kid Flash 1 (2/99, $1.99) Waid-s/Pararillo-a, ...: Nightstar 1 (2/99, $1.99) Waid-s/Haley-a, ...: Offspring 1 (2/99, $1.99) Waid-s/Quitely-a, ...: Planet Krypton 1 (2/99, $1.99) Waid-s/Kitson-a, ...: Son of the Bat 1 (2/99, $1.99) Waid-s/Apthorp-a						3.00

KINGDOM COME (Also see Justice Society of America #9-22)
DC Comics: 1996 - No. 4, 1996 ($4.95, painted limited series)

1-Mark Waid scripts & Alex Ross-painted c/a in all; tells the last days of the DC Universe; 1st app. Magog	1	2	3	5	6	8
2-Superman forms new Justice League	1	2	3	4	5	7
3-Return of Captain Marvel						6.00
4-Final battle of Superman and Captain Marvel	1	2	3	4	5	7
Deluxe Slipcase Edition-($89.95) w/Revelations companion book, 12 new story pages, foil stamped covers, signed and numbered						120.00
Hardcover Edition-($29.95)-Includes 12 new story pages and artwork from Revelations, new cover artwork with gold foil inlay						35.00
Hardcover 2nd printing						30.00
Softcover Ed.-($14.95)-Includes 12 new story pgs. & artwork from Revelations, new c-artwork						15.00
Softcover Ed.-(2008, $17.99)-New wraparound gatefold cover by Ross						18.00

KING KONG (See Movie Comics)

KING KONG: THE 8TH WONDER OF THE WORLD (Adaptation of 2005 movie)
Dark Horse Comics: Dec, 2005 ($3.99, planned limited series completed in TPB)

1-Photo-c; Dustin Weaver-a/Christian Gossett-s						4.00
TPB (11/06, $12.95) r/#1 and unpublished parts 2&3; photo-c; Dorman paintings						13.00

KING LEONARDO & HIS SHORT SUBJECTS (TV)
Dell Publishing Co./Gold Key: Nov-Jan, 1961-62 - No. 4, Sept, 1963

Four Color 1242,1278	11	22	33	74	145	215
01390-207(5-7/62)(Dell)	9	18	27	60	103	145
1 (10/62)	10	20	30	67	124	180
2-4	8	16	24	55	93	130

KING LOUIE & MOWGLI (See Jungle Book under Movie Comics)
Gold Key: May, 1968 (Disney)

1 (#10223-805)-Characters from Jungle Book	3	6	9	20	30	40

KING OF DIAMONDS (TV)
Dell Publishing Co.: July-Sept, 1962

01-391-209-Photo-c	4	8	12	26	41	55

KING OF KINGS (Movie)
Dell Publishing Co.: No. 1236, Oct-Nov, 1961

Four Color 1236-Photo-c	7	14	21	49	82	115

KING OF THE BAD MEN OF DEADWOOD
Avon Periodicals: 1950 (See Wild Bill Hickok #16)

nn-Kinstler-c; Kamen/Feldstein-r/Cowpuncher #2	15	30	45	94	147	200

KING OF THE ROYAL MOUNTED (See Famous Feature Stories, King Comics, Red Ryder #3 & Super Book #2, 6)

KING OF THE ROYAL MOUNTED (Zane Grey's...)
David McKay/Dell Publishing Co.: No. 1, May, 1937; No. 9, 1940; No. 207, Dec, 1948 - No. 935, Sept-Nov, 1958

Feature Books 1 (5/37)(McKay)	94	188	282	597	1024	1450
Large Feature Comic 9 (1940)	48	96	144	302	514	725
Four Color 207(#1, 12/48)	12	24	36	81	166	250
Four Color 265,283	8	16	24	56	96	135
Four Color 310,340	6	12	18	42	69	95
Four Color 363,384, 8(6-8/52)-10	6	12	18	39	62	85
11-20	5	10	15	35	55	75
21-28(3-5/58), Four Color 935(9-11/58)	4	8	12	28	44	60

NOTE: *4-Color No. 207, 265, 283, 310, 340, 363, 384 are all newspaper reprints with **Jim Gary** art. No. 8 on are all Dell originals. Painted c-No. 9-on.*

KINGPIN
Marvel Comics: Nov, 1997 ($5.99, squarebound, one-shot)

nn-Spider-Man & Daredevil vs. Kingpin; Stan Lee-s/ John Romita Sr.-a						6.00

KINGPIN
Marvel Comics: Aug, 2003 - No. 7, Jan, 2004 ($2.50/$2.99, limited series)

1-6-Bruce Jones-s/Sean Phillips & Klaus Janson-a						3.00
7-($2.99)						3.00

KING RICHARD & THE CRUSADERS
Dell Publishing Co.: No. 588, Oct, 1954

Four Color 588-Movie, Matt Baker-a, photo-c	9	18	27	61	106	150

KING-SIZE CABLE SPECTACULAR (Takes place between Cable (2008 series) #6 & #7)
Marvel Comics: Nov, 2008 ($4.99, one-shot)

1-Lashley-a; Deadpool #1 preview; cover gallery of variants from 2008 series						5.00

KING-SIZE HULK (Takes place between Hulk (2008 series) #3 & #4)
Marvel Comics: July, 2008 ($4.99, one-shot)

1-Art Adams, Frank Cho, & Herb Trimpe-a; double-c by Cho & Adams; Red Hulk, She-Hulk & Wendigo app.; origin Abomination; r/Incr. Hulk #180,181 & Avengers #83						5.00

KING-SIZE SPIDER-MAN SUMMER SPECIAL
Marvel Comics: Oct, 2008 ($4.99, one-shot)

Kirby: Genesis #1 © Roz Kirby Family

Kitty Pryde, Agent of S.H.I.E.L.D. #3 © MAR

Knights of Pendragon #17 © MAR

GD VG FN VF VF/NM NM-
2.0 4.0 6.0 8.0 9.0 9.2

GD VG FN VF VF/NM NM-
2.0 4.0 6.0 8.0 9.0 9.2

1-Short stories by various; Falcon app.; Burchett, Giarrusso & Coover-a 5.00

KINGS OF THE NIGHT
Dark Horse Comics: 1990 - No. 2, 1990 ($2.25, limited series)
1,2-Robert E. Howard adaptation; Bolton-c 3.00

KING SOLOMON'S MINES (Movie)
Avon Periodicals: 1951
nn (#1 on 1st page) 40 80 120 242 401 560

KIPLING, RUDYARD (See Mowgli, The Jungle Book)

KIRBY: GENESIS
Dynamite Entertainment: No. 0, 2011 - Present ($1.00/$3.99)
0-($1.00) Busiek-s; art by Alex Ross & Jack Herbert; series preview, sketch-a 13.00
1-5-($3.99) Ross & Herbert-a. 1-Seven covers. 2-5-Covers by Ross & Sook 4.00

KIRBY: GENESIS - CAPTAIN VICTORY
Dynamite Entertainment: 2011 - Present ($3.99)
1-4: 1-Origin retold; four covers; Sterling Gates-s/Wagner Reis-a 4.00

KIRBY: GENESIS - DRAGONSBANE
Dynamite Entertainment: 2012 - Present ($3.99)
1,2-Rodi & Ross-s/Casas-a; covers by Ross and Herbert 4.00

KIRBY: GENESIS - SILVER STAR
Dynamite Entertainment: 2011 - Present ($3.99)
1-3-Jai Nitz-s/Johnny Desjardins-a. 1-Four covers 4.00

KISS (See Crazy Magazine, Howard the Duck #12, 13, Marvel Comics Super Special #1, 5, Rock Fantasy Comics #10 & Rock N' Roll Comics #9)

KISS
Dark Horse Comics: June, 2002 - No. 13, Sept, 2003 ($2.99, limited series)
1-Photo-c and J. Scott Campbell-c; Casey-s 5.00
2-13: 2-Photo-c and J. Scott Campbell-c. 3-Photo-c and Leinil Yu-c 4.00
...: Men and Monsters TPB (9/03, $12.95) r/#7-10 13.00
...: Rediscovery TPB (2003, $9.95) r/#1-3 10.00
...: Return of the Phantom TPB (2003, $9.95) r/#4-6 10.00
...: Unholy War TPB (2004, $9.95) r/#11-13 10.00

KISS 4K
Platinum Studios Comics: May, 2007 - No. 6, Apr, 2008 ($3.99/$2.99)
1-Sprague-s/Crossley & Campos-a/Migliari-c 4.00
1-B&W sketch-c 6.00
1-Destroyer Edition ($50.00, 30"x18", edition of 5000) 50.00
2-6-($2.99) 3.00
KISSMAS (12/07, $4.99) Christmas-themed issue; re-cap of issues #1-4 5.00

KISS: THE PSYCHO CIRCUS
Image Comics: Aug, 1997 - No. 31, June, 2000 ($1.95/$2.25/$2.50)
1-Holguin-s/Medina-a(p) 1 3 4 6 8 10
1-2nd & 3rd printings 3.00
2 6.00
3,4: 4-Photo-c 5.00
5-8: 5-Begin $2.25-c 4.00
9-29 4.00
30,31: 30-Begin $2.50-c 4.00
Book 1 TPB ('98, $12.95) r/#1-6 13.00
Book 2 Destroyer TPB (8/99, $9.95) r/#10-13 10.00
Book 3 Whispered Scream TPB ('00, $9.95) r/#7-9,18 10.00
...Magazine 1 ($6.95) r/#1-3 plus interviews 7.00
...Magazine 2-5 ($4.95) 2-r/#4,5 plus interviews. 3-r/#6,7. 4-r/#8,9 5.00
Wizard Edition ('98, supplement) Bios, tour preview and interviews 3.00

KISSING CHAOS
Oni Press: Sept, 2001 - No. 8, Mar, 2002 ($2.25, B&W, 6" x 9", limited series)
1-8-Arthur Dela Cruz-s/a 3.00
...: Nine Lives (12/03, $2.99, regular comic-sized) 3.00
...: 1000 Words (7/03, $2.99, regular comic-sized) 3.00
TPB (9/02, $17.95) r/#1-8 18.00

KISSING CHAOS: NONSTOP BEAUTY
Oni Press: Oct, 2002 - No. 4, March, 2003 ($2.95, B&W, 6" x 9", limited series)
1-4-Arthur Dela Cruz-s/a 3.00
TPB (9/03, $11.95) r/#1-4 12.00

KISS KISS BANG BANG
CrossGen Comics: Feb, 2004 - No. 5, Jun, 2004 ($2.95)
1-5-Bedard-s/Perkins-a 3.00

KISSYFUR (TV)
DC Comics: 1989 (Sept.) ($2.00, 52 pgs., one-shot)
1-Based on Saturday morning cartoon 4.00

KIT CARSON (Formerly All True Detective Cases No. 4; Fighting Davy Crockett No. 9; see Blazing Sixguns & Frontier Fighters)
Avon Periodicals: 1950; No. 2, 8/51 - No. 3, 12/51; No. 5, 11-12/54 - No. 8, 9/55 (No #4)
nn(#1) (1950)- "...Indian Scout" ; r-Cowboys 'N' Injuns #? 14 28 42 76 108 140
2(8/51) 10 20 30 56 76 95
3(12/51)- "...Fights the Comanche Raiders" 9 18 27 50 65 80
5-6,8(11-12/54-9/55): 5-Formerly All True Detective Cases (last pre-code); titled "...and the Trail of Doom" 9 18 27 47 61 75
7-McCann-a? 9 18 27 47 61 75
I.W. Reprint #10('63)-r/Kit Carson #1; Severin-c 2 4 6 11 16 20
NOTE: *Kinstler c-1-3, 5-8.*

KIT CARSON & THE BLACKFEET WARRIORS
Realistic: 1953
nn-Reprint; Kinstler-c 9 18 27 52 69 85

KIT KARTER
Dell Publishing Co.: May-July, 1962
1 3 6 9 19 29 38

KITTY
St. John Publishing Co.: Oct, 1948
1-Teenage; Lily Renee-c/a 9 18 27 50 65 80

KITTY PRYDE, AGENT OF S.H.I.E.L.D. (Also see Excalibur and Mekanix)
Marvel Comics: Dec, 1997 - No. 3, Feb, 1998 ($2.50, limited series)
1-3-Hama-s 3.00

KITTY PRYDE AND WOLVERINE (Also see Uncanny X-Men & X-Men)
Marvel Comics Group: Nov, 1984 - No. 6, Apr, 1985 (Limited series)
1-6: Characters from X-Men 5.00
X-Men: Kitty Pryde and Wolverine HC (2008, $19.99) r/series 20.00

KLARER GIVEAWAYS (See Wisco in the Promotional Comics section)

KLAWS OF THE PANTHER (Also see Black Panther)
Marvel Comics: Dec, 2010 - No. 4, Feb, 2011 ($3.99, limited series)
1-4-Maberry-s/Gugliotta-a/Del Mundo-c. 1-Ka-Zar & Shanna app. 3-Spider-Man app. 4.00

KNIGHT AND SQUIRE (Also see Batman #667-669)
DC Comics: Dec, 2010 - No. 6, May, 2011 ($2.99, limited series)
1-6-Cornell-s/Broxton-a. 1-Two covers by Paquette & Tucci. 5,6-Joker app. 3.00
TPB (2011, $14.99) r/#1-6; sketch and design art 15.00

KNIGHTHAWK
Acclaim Comics (Windjammer): Sept, 1995 - No. 6, Nov, 1995 ($2.50, lim. series)
1-6: 6-origin 3.00

KNIGHTMARE
Antarctic Press: July, 1994 - May, 1995 ($2.75, B&W, mature readers)
1-6 3.00

KNIGHTMARE
Image Comics (Extreme Studios): Feb, 1995 - No. 5, June, 1995 ($2.50)
0 ($3.50) 4.00
1-5: 4-Quesada & Palmiotti variant-c, 5-Flip book w/Warcry 3.00

KNIGHTS 4 (See Marvel Knights 4)

KNIGHTS OF PENDRAGON, THE (Also see Pendragon)
Marvel Comics Ltd.: July, 1990 - No. 18, Dec, 1991 ($1.95)
1-18: 1-Capt. Britain app. 2,8-Free poster inside. 9,10-Bolton-c. 11,18-Iron Man app. 3.00

KNIGHTS OF THE ROUND TABLE
Dell Publishing Co.: No. 540, Mar, 1954
Four Color 540-Movie, photo-c 7 14 21 46 76 105

KNIGHTS OF THE ROUND TABLE
Pines Comics: No. 10, April, 1957
10 5 10 15 24 30 35

KNIGHTS OF THE ROUND TABLE
Dell Publishing Co.: Nov-Jan, 1963-64
1 (12-397-401)-Painted-c 3 6 9 21 32 42

KNIGHTSTRIKE (Also see Operation: Knightstrike)

Kobra #1 © DC

Koko and Kola #3 © ME

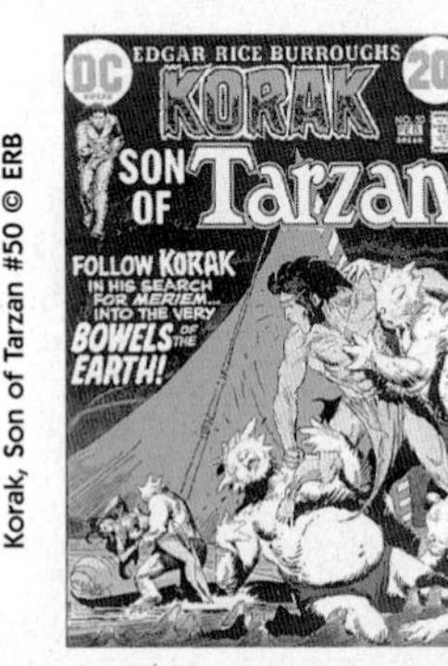

Korak, Son of Tarzan #50 © ERB

GD 2.0 | VG 4.0 | FN 6.0 | VF 8.0 | VF/NM 9.0 | NM- 9.2

Image Comics (Extreme Studios): Jan, 1996 ($2.50)
1-Rob Liefeld & Eric Stephenson story; Extreme Destroyer Part 6. 3.00

KNIGHT WATCHMAN (See Big Bang Comics & Dr. Weird)
Image Comics: June, 1998 - No. 4, Oct, 1998 ($2.95/$3.50, B&W, lim. series)
1-3-Ben Torres-c/a in all 3.00
4-($3.50) 3.50

KNIGHT WATCHMAN: GRAVEYARD SHIFT
Caliber Press: 1994 ($2.95, B&W)
1,2-Ben Torres-a 3.00

KNOCK KNOCK (...Who's There?)
Dell Publ./Gerona Publications: No. 801, 1936 (52 pgs.) (8x9", B&W)
801-Joke book; Bob Dunn-a 11 22 33 62 86 110

KNOCKOUT ADVENTURES
Fiction House Magazines: Winter, 1953-54
1-Reprints Fight Comics #53 w/Rip Carson-c/s 14 28 42 76 108 140

KNUCKLES (Spin-off of Sonic the Hedgehog)
Archie Publications: Apr, 1997 - No. 32, Feb, 2000 ($1.50/$1.75/$1.79)
1-32 4.00

KNUCKLES' CHAOTIX
Archie Publications: Jan, 1996 ($2.00, annual)
1 5.00

KOBALT
DC Comics (Milestone): June, 1994 - No. 16, Sept, 1995 ($1.75/$2.50)
1-16: 1-Byrne-c. 4-Intro Page. 16-Kent Williams-c 3.00

KOBRA (Unpublished #8 appears in DC Special Series No. 1)
National Periodical Publications: Feb-Mar, 1976 - No. 7, Mar-Apr, 1977
1-1st app.; Kirby-a redrawn by Marcos; only 25¢-c 2 4 6 8 11 14
2-7: (All 30¢ issues) 3-Giffen-a 1 2 3 5 6 8
...: Resurrection TPB (2010, $19.99) r/#1, DC Special Series No. 1 and later apps. in Checkmate #23-25, Faces of Evil: Kobra #1 and various Who's Who issues 20.00
NOTE: *Austin a-3i. Buckler a-5p; c-5p. Kubert c-4. Nasser a-6p, 7; c-7.*

KOKEY KOALA (...and the Magic Button)
Toby Press: May, 1952
1-Funny animal 12 24 36 69 97 125

KOKO AND KOLA (Also see A-1 Comics #16 & Tick Tock Tales)
Com/Magazine Enterprises: Fall, 1946 - No. 5, May, 1947; No. 6, 1950
1-Funny animal 13 26 39 74 105 135
2-X-Mas-c 9 18 27 52 69 85
3-6: 6(A-1 28) 9 18 27 47 61 75

KO KOMICS
Gerona Publications: Oct, 1945 (scarce)
1-The Duke of Darkness & The Menace (hero) 74 148 222 470 810 1150

KOLCHAK: THE NIGHT STALKER (TV)
Moonstone: 2002 - Present ($6.50/$6.95)
1-($6.50) Jeff Rice-s/Gordon Purcell-a 6.50
... Black & White & Read All Over (2005, $4.95) short stories by various; 2 covers 5.00
... Devil in the Details (2003, $6.95) Trevor Von Eeden-a 7.00
... Eve of Terror (2005, $5.95) Gentile-s/Figueroa-a/Beck-c 6.00
... Fever Pitch (2002, $6.95) Christopher Jones-a 7.00
... Get of Belial (2002, $6.95) Art Nichols-a 7.00
... Lambs to the Slaughter (2003, $6.95) Trevor Von Eeden-a 7.00
... Pain Most Human (2004, $6.95) Greg Scott-a 7.00
... Tales: The Frankenstein Agenda 1 (2007 - No. 3, $3.50) Michelinie-s 3.50
... Tales of the Night Stalker 1-7 (2003-Present, $3.50) two covers by Moore & Ulanski 3.50
TPB (2004, $17.95) r/#1, Get of Belial & Fever Pitch 18.00
Vol. 2: Terror Within TPB (2006, $16.95) r/Pain Most Human, Pain Without Tears & Devil in the Details 17.00

KOMIC KARTOONS
Timely Comics (EPC): Fall, 1945 - No. 2, Winter, 1945
1,2-Andy Wolf, Bertie Mouse 23 46 69 138 227 310

KOMIK PAGES (Formerly Snap; becomes Bullseye #11)
Harry 'A' Chesler, Jr. (Our Army, Inc.): Apr, 1945 (All reprints)
10(#1 on inside)-Land O' Nod by Rick Yager (2 pgs.), Animal Crackers, Foxy GrandPa, Tom, Dick & Mary, Cheerio Minstrels, Red Starr plus other 1-2 pg. strips; Cole-a
23 46 69 136 223 310

KONA (...Monarch of Monster Isle)
Dell Publishing Co.: Feb-Apr, 1962 - No. 21, Jan-Mar, 1967 (Painted-c)
Four Color 1256 (#1) 9 18 27 63 112 160
2-10: 4-Anak begins. 6-Gil Kane-c 6 12 18 37 59 80
11-21 5 10 15 30 48 65
NOTE: *Glanzman a-all issues.*

KONGA (Fantastic Giants No. 24) (See Return of...)
Charlton Comics: 1960; No. 2, Aug, 1961 - No. 23, Nov, 1965
1(1960)-Based on movie; Giordano-c 22 44 66 154 327 500
2-5: 2-Giordano-c; no Ditko-a 11 22 33 73 142 210
6-9-Ditko-c/a 10 20 30 65 118 170
10-15 9 18 27 61 106 150
16-23 6 12 18 41 66 90
NOTE: *Ditko a-1, 3-15; c-4, 6-9, 11. Glanzman a-12. Montes & Bache a-16-23.*

KONGA'S REVENGE (Formerly Return of...)
Charlton Comics: No. 2, Summer, 1963 - No. 3, Fall, 1964; Dec, 1968
2,3: 2-Ditko-c/a 8 16 24 51 86 120
1(12/68)-Reprints Konga's Revenge #3 3 6 9 17 25 32

KONG THE UNTAMED
National Periodical Publications: June-July, 1975 - V2#5, Feb-Mar, 1976
1-1st app. Kong; Wrightson-c; Alcala-a 2 4 6 11 16 20
2-Wrightson-c; Alcala-a 2 4 6 9 13 16
3-5: 3-Alcala-a 1 2 3 5 6 8

KOOKABURRA K
Marvel Comics (Soleil): 2009 - No. 3, 2010 ($5.99, limited series)
1-3-Humbertos Ramos-a/c 6.00

KOOKIE
Dell Publishing Co.: Feb-Apr, 1962 - No. 2, May-July, 1962 (15 cents)
1-Written by John Stanley; Bill Williams-a 8 16 24 53 89 125
2 7 14 21 48 79 110

KOOSH KINS
Archie Comics: Oct, 1991 - No. 3, Feb, 1992 ($1.00, bi-monthly, limited series)
1-3 3.00
NOTE: *No. 4 was planned, but cancelled.*

KORAK, SON OF TARZAN (Edgar Rice Burroughs)(See Tarzan #139)
Gold Key: Jan, 1964 - No. 45, Jan, 1972 (Painted-c No. 1-?)
1-Russ Manning-a 9 18 27 63 112 160
2-5-Russ Manning-a 6 12 18 37 59 80
6-11-Russ Manning-a 5 10 15 32 51 70
12-23: 12,13-Warren Tufts-a. 14-Jon of the Kalahari ends. 15-Mabu, Jungle Boy begins. 21-Manning-a. 23-Last 12¢ issue 4 8 12 28 44 60
24-30 4 8 12 22 34 45
31-45 3 6 9 18 27 35

KORAK, SON OF TARZAN (Tarzan Family #60 on; see Tarzan #230)
National Periodical Publications: V9#46, May-June, 1972 - V12#56, Feb-Mar, 1974; No. 57, May-June, 1975 - No. 59, Sept-Oct, 1975 (Edgar Rice Burroughs)
46-(52 pgs.)-Carson of Venus begins (origin), ends #56; Pellucidar feature; Weiss-a 3 6 9 16 22 28
47-59: 49-Origin Korak retold 2 4 6 8 11 14
NOTE: *All have covers by Joe Kubert. Manning strip reprints-No. 57-59. Murphy Anderson a-52. Michael Kaluta a-46-56. Frank Thorne a-46-51.*

KORE
Image Comics: Apr, 2003 - No. 5, Sept, 2003 ($2.95)
1-5: 1-Two covers by Capullo and Seeley; Seeley-a (p) 3.00

KORG: 70,000 B. C. (TV)
Charlton Publications: May, 1975 - No. 9, Nov, 1976 (Hanna-Barbera)
1,2: 1-Boyette-c/a. 2-Painted-c; Byrne text illos 2 4 6 11 16 20
3-9 2 4 6 8 11 14

KORNER KID COMICS: Four Star Publications: 1947 (Advertised, not pub.)

KOSMIC KAT ACTIVITY BOOK (See Deity)
Image Comics: Aug, 1999 ($2.95, one-shot)
1-Stories and games by various 3.00

KRAZY KAT
Holt: 1946 (Hardcover)
Reprints daily & Sunday strips by Herriman 56 112 168 353 597 840

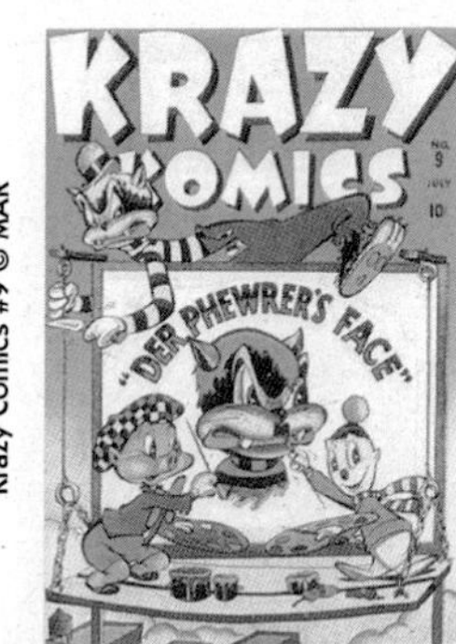

Krazy Comics #9 © MAR

Kull (2009) #1 © Kull Prods.

Kung Fu Panda 2 #1 © DW

	GD	VG	FN	VF	VF/NM	NM-
	2.0	4.0	6.0	8.0	9.0	9.2

dust jacket only 42 84 126 265 445 625

KRAZY KAT (See Ace Comics & March of Comics No. 72, 87)

KRAZY KAT COMICS (...& Ignatz the Mouse early issues)
Dell Publ. Co./Gold Key: May-June, 1951 - F.C. #696, Apr, 1956; Jan, 1964 (None by Herriman)

1(1951) 9 18 27 60 103 145
2-5 (#5, 8-10/52) 5 10 15 35 55 75
Four Color 454,504 5 10 15 32 51 70
Four Color 548,619,696 (4/56) 5 10 15 30 48 65
1(10098-401)(1/64-Gold Key)(TV) 4 8 12 26 41 55

KRAZY KOMICS (1st Series) (Cindy Comics No. 27 on) (Also see Ziggy Pig)
Timely Comics (USA No. 1-21/JPC No. 22-26): July, 1942 - No. 26, Spr, 1947

1-Toughy Tomcat, Ziggy Pig (by Jaffee) & Silly Seal begin
90 180 270 576 988 1400
2 39 78 117 231 378 525
3-8,10 26 52 78 154 252 350
9-Hitler parody-c 28 56 84 165 270 375
11,13,14 19 38 57 111 176 240
12-Timely's entire art staff drew themselves into a Creeper story
30 60 90 177 289 400
15-(8-9/44)-Has "Super Soldier" by Pfc. Stan Lee 20 40 60 114 182 250
16-24,26: 16-(10-11/44). 26-Super Rabbit-c/story 15 30 45 90 140 190
25-Wacky Duck-c/story & begin; Kurtzman-a (6pgs.) 19 38 57 109 172 235

KRAZY KOMICS (2nd Series)
Timely/Marvel Comics: Aug, 1948 - No. 2, Nov, 1948

1-Wolverton (10 pgs.) & Kurtzman (8 pgs.)-a; Eustice Hayseed begins (Li'l Abner swipe)
45 90 135 284 480 675
2-Wolverton-a (10 pgs.); Powerhouse Pepper cameo
32 64 96 192 314 435

KRAZY KROW (Also see Dopey Duck, Film Funnies, Funny Frolics & Movie Tunes)
Marvel Comics (ZPC): Summer, 1945 - No. 3, Wint, 1945/46

1 23 46 69 136 223 310
2,3 15 30 45 86 133 180
I.W. Reprint #1('57), 2('58), 7 2 4 6 11 16 20

KRAZYLIFE (Becomes Nutty Life #2)
Fox Feature Syndicate: 1945 (no month)

1-Funny animal 22 44 66 132 216 300

KREE/SKRULL WAR STARRING THE AVENGERS, THE
Marvel Comics: Sept, 1983 - No. 2, Oct, 1983 ($2.50, 68 pgs., Baxter paper)

1,2 4.00
NOTE: ***Neal Adams** p-1r, 2. **Buscema** a-1r, 2r. **Simonson** a-1p; c-1p.*

KROFFT SUPERSHOW (TV)
Gold Key: Apr, 1978 - No. 6, Jan, 1979

1-Photo-c 3 6 9 18 27 35
2-6: 6-Photo-c 3 6 9 14 19 24

KRULL
Marvel Comics Group: Nov, 1983 - No. 2, Dec, 1983

1,2-Adaptation of film; r/Marvel Super Special. 1-Photo-c from movie 3.00

KRUSTY COMICS (TV)(See Simpsons Comics)
Bongo Comics: 1995 - No. 3, 1995 ($2.25, limited series)

1-3 3.00

KRYPTON CHRONICLES
DC Comics: Sept, 1981 - No. 3, Nov, 1981

1-3: 1-Buckler-c(p) 4.00

KRYPTO THE SUPERDOG (TV)
DC Comics: Nov, 2006 - No. 6, Apr, 2007 ($2.25)

1-6-Based on Cartoon Network series. 1-Origin retold 3.00

KULL
Dark Horse Comics: Nov, 2008 - No. 6, May, 2009 ($2.99)

1-6: 1-Nelson-s/Conrad-a; two covers by Andy Brase and Joe Kubert 3.00

KULL AND THE BARBARIANS
Marvel Comics: May, 1975 - No. 3, Sept, 1975 ($1.00, B&W, magazine)

1-(84 pgs.) Andru/Wood-r/Kull #1; 2 pgs. Neal Adams; Gil Kane(p), Marie & John Severin-a(r); Krenkel text illo. 3 6 9 17 25 32
2,3: 2-(84 pgs.) Red Sonja by Chaykin begins; Solomon Kane by Weiss/Adams; Gil Kane-a; Solomon Kane pin-up by Wrightson. 3-(76 pgs.) Origin Red Sonja by Chaykin; Adams-a; Solomon Kane app. 3 6 9 14 19 24

KULL: THE CAT AND THE SKULL
Dark Horse Comics: Oct, 2011 - No. 4, Jan, 2012 ($3.50, limited series)

1-4-Lapham-s/Guzman-a/Chen-c. 1-Variant-c by Hans 3.50

KULL THE CONQUEROR (...the Destroyer #11 on; see Conan #1, Creatures on the Loose #10, Marvel Preview, Monsters on the Prowl)
Marvel Comics Group: June, 1971 - No. 2, Sept, 1971; No. 3, July, 1972 - No. 15, Aug, 1974; No. 16, Aug, 1976 - No. 29, Oct, 1978

1-Andru/Wood-a; 2nd app. & origin Kull; 15¢ issue 6 12 18 41 66 90
2-5: 2-3rd Kull app. Last 15¢ iss. 3-13: 20¢ issues. 3-Thulsa Doom-c/app.
3 6 9 18 27 35
6-10: 7-Thulsa Doom-c/app 2 4 6 10 14 18
11-15: 11-15-Ploog-a. 14,15: 25¢ issues 2 4 6 8 11 14
16-(Regular 25¢ edition)(8/76) 2 3 4 6 8 10
16-(30¢-c variant, limited distribution) 3 6 9 16 23 30
17-29: 21-23-(Reg. 30¢ editions) 2 3 4 6 8 10
21-23-(35¢-c variants, limited distribution) 5 10 15 30 48 65
NOTE: *No. 1, 2, 7-9, 11 are based on Robert E. Howard stories. **Alcala** a-17p, 18-20i; c-24. **Ditko** a-12r, 15r. **Gil Kane** c-15p, 21. **Nebres** a-22i-27i; c-25i, 27i. **Ploog** c-11, 12p, 13. **Severin** a-2-9i; c-2-10i, 19. **Starlin** c-14.*

KULL THE CONQUEROR
Marvel Comics Group: Dec, 1982 - No. 2, Mar, 1983 (52 pgs., Baxter paper)

1,2: 1-Buscema-a(p) 4.00

KULL THE CONQUEROR (No. 9,10 titled "Kull")
Marvel Comics Group: 5/83 - No. 10, 6/85 (52 pgs., Baxter paper)

V3#1-10: Buscema-a in #1-3,5-10 4.00
NOTE: *Bolton a-4. Golden painted c-3-8. Guice a-4p. Sienkiwicz a-4; c-2.*

KULL: THE HATE WITCH
Dark Horse Comics: Nov, 2010 - No. 4, Feb, 2011 ($3.50)

1-4-Lapham-s/Guzman-a/Fleming-c 3.50

KUNG FU (See Deadly Hands of..., & Master of...)

KUNG FU FIGHTER (See Richard Dragon...)

KUNG FU PANDA 2
Ape Entertainment: 2011 - No. 4, 2011 ($3.95, limited series)

1-4-Short stories by various 4.00

KURT BUSIEK'S ASTRO CITY (Limited series) (Also see Astro City: Local Heroes)
Image Comics (Juke Box Productions): Aug, 1995 - No. 6, Jan, 1996 ($2.25)

1-Kurt Busiek scripts, Brent Anderson-a & Alex Ross front & back-c begins; 1st app. Samaritan & Honor Guard (Cleopatra, MHP, Beautie, The Black Rapier, Quarrel & N-Forcer) 2 4 6 8 10 12
2-6: 2-1st app. The Silver Agent, The Old Soldier, & the "original" Honor Guard (Max O'Millions, Starwoman, the "original" Cleopatra, the "original" N-Forcer, the Bouncing Beatnik, Leopardman & Kitkat). 3-1st app. Jack-in-the-Box & The Deacon. 4-1st app. Winged Victory (cameo), The Hanged Man & The First Family. 5-1st app. Crackerjack, The Astro City Irregulars, Nightingale & Sunbird. 6-Origin Samaritan; 1st full app. Winged Victory 1 3 4 6 8 10
Life In The Big City-(8/96, $19.95, trade paperback)-r/Image Comics limited series w/sketchbook & cover gallery; Ross-c 20.00
Life In The Big City-(8/96, $49.95, hardcover, 1000 print run)-r/Image Comics limited series w/sketchbook & cover gallery; Ross-c 50.00

KURT BUSIEK'S ASTRO CITY (1st Homage Comics series)
Image Comics (Homage Comics): V2#1, Sept, 1996 - No. 15, Dec, 1998;
DC Comics (Homage Comics): No. 16, Mar, 1999 - No. 22, Aug, 2000 ($2.50)

1/2-(10/96)-The Hanged Man story; 1st app. The All-American & Slugger, The Lamplighter, The Time-Keeper & Eterneon 1 3 4 6 8 10
1/2-(1/98) 2nd printing w/new cover 3.00
1- Kurt Busiek scripts, Alex Ross-c, Brent Anderson-p & Will Blyberg-i begin; intro The Gentleman, Thunderhead & Helia. 1 2 3 5 6 8
1-(12/97, $4.95) "3-D Edition" w/glasses 5.00
2-Origin The First Family; Astra story 1 2 3 4 5 7
3-5: 4-1st app. The Crossbreed, Ironhorse, Glue Gun & The Confessor (cameo) 6.00
6-10 5.00
11-22: 14-20-Steeljack story arc. 16-(3/99) First DC issue 3.00
TPB-($19.95) Ross-c, r/#4-9, #1/2 w/sketchbook 20.00
Family Album TPB ($19.95) r/#1-3,10-13 20.00
The Tarnished Angel HC ($29.95) r/#14-20; new Ross dust jacket; sketch pages by Anderson & Ross; cover gallery with reference photos 30.00
The Tarnished Angel SC ($19.95) r/#14-20; new Ross-c 20.00

Lab Rats #3 © John Byrne

Lady Death (2010 series) #5 © Avatar

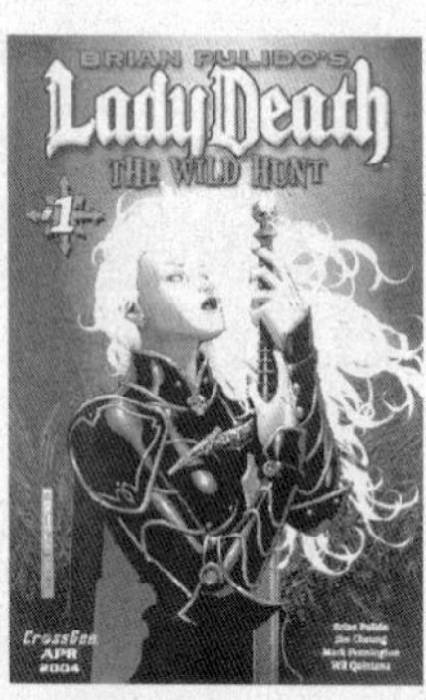

Lady Death: The Wild Hunt #1 © CRO

	GD 2.0	VG 4.0	FN 6.0	VF 8.0	VF/NM 9.0	NM- 9.2

LABMAN
Image Comics: Nov, 1996 ($3.50, one-shot)

1-Allred-c 4.00

LAB RATS
DC Comics: June, 2002 - No. 8, Jan, 2003 ($2.50)

1-8-John Byrne-s/a. 5,6-Superman app. 3.00

LABYRINTH
Marvel Comics Group: Nov, 1986 - No. 3, Jan, 1987 (Limited series)

1-3: David Bowie movie adaptation; r/Marvel Super Special #40 5.00

LA COSA NOSTROID (See Scud: The Disposible Assassin)
Fireman Press: Mar, 1996 - No. 9, 1998 ($2.95, B&W)

1-9-Dan Harmon-s/Rob Schrab-c/a 3.00

LAD: A DOG (Movie)
Dell Publishing Co.: 1961 - No. 2, July-Sept, 1962

	GD	VG	FN	VF	VF/NM	NM-
Four Color 1303	4	8	12	28	44	60
2	4	8	12	24	37	50

LADY AND THE TRAMP (Disney, See Dell Giants & Movie Comics)
Dell Publishing Co.: No. 629, May, 1955 - No. 634, June, 1955

	GD	VG	FN	VF	VF/NM	NM-
Four Color 629 (#1)-..with Jock	7	14	21	46	76	105
Four Color 634-...Album	5	10	15	32	51	70

LADY COP (See 1st Issue Special)

LADY DEADPOOL
Marvel Comics: Sept, 2010 ($3.99, one-shot)

1-Land-c/Lashley-a 4.00

LADY DEATH (See Evil Ernie)
Chaos! Comics: Jan, 1994 - No. 3, Mar, 1994 ($2.75, limited series)

	GD	VG	FN	VF	VF/NM	NM-
1/2-S. Hughes-c/a in all, 1/2 Velvet	1	2	3	4	5	7
1/2 Gold	1	3	4	6	8	10
1/2 Signed Limited Edition	2	4	6	8	10	12
1-($3.50)-Chromium-c	2	4	6	10	14	18
1-Commemorative	2	4	6	9	13	16
1-(9/96, $2.95) "Encore Presentation"; r/#1						3.00
2	1	2	3	5	6	8
3						5.00
... And Jade (4/02, $2.99) Augustyn-s/Reis-a						3.00
...And The Women of Chaos! Gallery #1 (11/96, $2.25) pin-ups by various						3.00
.../Bad Kitty (9/01, $2.99) Mota-c/a						3.00
.../Bedlam (6/02, $2.99) Augustyn-s/Reis-c						3.00
...By Steven Hughes (6/00, $2.95) Tribute issue to Steven Hughes						3.00
...By Steven Hughes Deluxe Edition(6/00, $15.95)						16.00
.../Chastity (1/02, $2.99) Mota-c/a; Augustyn-s						3.00
...Death Becomes Her #0 (11/97, $2.95) Hughes-c/a						3.00
...FAN Edition: All Hallow's Eve #1 (1/97, mail-in)						5.00
...In Lingerie #1 (8/95, $2.95) pin-ups, wraparound-c						3.00
...In Lingerie #1-Leather Edition (10,000)						12.00
...In Lingerie #1-Micro Premium Edition; Lady Demon-c (2,000)						35.00
...: Love Bites (3/01, $2.99) Kaminski-s/Luke Ross-a						3.00
.../Medieval Witchblade (8/01, $3.50) covers by Molenaar and Silvestri						3.50
.../Medieval Witchblade Preview Ed. (8/01, $1.99) Molenaar-c						3.00
...: Mischief Night (11/01, $2.99) Ostrander-s/Reis-a						3.00
...: Re-Imagined (7/02, $2.99) Gossett-c						3.00
...: River of Fear (4/01, $2.99) Bennett-a(p)/Cleavenger-c						3.00
...Swimsuit Special #1-($2.50)-Wraparound-c						3.00
...Swimsuit Special #1-Red velvet-c						14.00
...Swimsuit 2001 #1-(2/01, $2.99)-Reis-c; art by various						3.00
...: The Reckoning (7/94, $6.95)-r/#1-3						7.00
...: The Reckoning (8/95, $12.95)- new printing including Lady Death 1/2 & Swimsuit Special #1						13.00
.../Vampirella (3/99, $3.50) Hughes-c/a						3.50
.../Vampirella 2 (3/00, $3.50) Deodato-c/a						3.50
... Vs. Purgatori (12/99, $3.50) Deodato-a						3.50
... Vs. Vampirella Preview (2/00, $1.00) Deodato-a/c						3.00

LADY DEATH (Ongoing series)
Chaos! Comics: Feb, 1998 - No. 16, May, 1999 ($2.95)

1-16: 1-4: Pulido-s/Hughes-c/a. 5-8,13-16-Deodato-a. 9-11-Hughes-a 3.00
...Retribution (8/98, $2.95) Jadsen-a 3.00
...Retribution Premium Ed. 6.00

LADY DEATH
Boundless Comics: No. 0, Nov, 2010 - Present ($3.99)

0-15-Pulido & Wolfer-s/Mueller-a on most; multiple covers on all 4.00
... Origins Annual 1 (8/11, $4.99) Martin-a/Pulido-s 5.00
... Premiere (7/10, free) previews series; five covers 3.00

LADY DEATH: ALIVE
Chaos! Comics: May, 2001 - No. 4, Aug, 2001 ($2.99, limited series)

1-4-Ivan Reis-a; Lady Death becomes mortal 3.00

LADY DEATH: A MEDIEVAL TALE (Brian Pulido's...)
CG Entertainment: Mar, 2003 - No. 12, Apr, 2004 ($2.95)

1-12: 1-Brian Pulido-s/Ivan Reis-a; Lady Death in the CrossGen Universe 3.00
Vol.1 TPB (2003, $9.95) digest-sized reprint of #1-6 10.00

LADY DEATH: DARK ALLIANCE
Chaos! Comics: July, 2002 - No. 5, ($2.99, limited series)

1-3-Reis-a/Ostrander-s 3.00

LADY DEATH: DARK MILLENNIUM
Chaos! Comics: Feb, 2000 - No. 3, Apr, 2000 ($2.95, limited series)

Preview (6/00, $5.00) 5.00
1-3-Ivan Reis-a 3.00

LADY DEATH: GODDESS RETURNS
Chaos! Comics: Jun, 2002 - No. 2, Aug, 2002 ($2.99, limited series)

1,2-Mota-a/Ostrander-s 3.00

LADY DEATH: HEARTBREAKER
Chaos! Comics: Mar, 2002 - No. 4, ($2.99, limited series)

1-Molenaar-a/Ostrander-s 3.00

LADY DEATH: JUDGEMENT WAR
Chaos! Comics: Nov, 1999 - No. 3, Jan, 2000 ($2.95, limited series)

Prelude (10/99) two covers 3.00
1-3-Ivan Reis-a 3.00

LADY DEATH: LAST RITES
Chaos! Comics: Oct, 2001 - No. 4, Feb, 2001 ($2.99, limited series)

1-4-Ivan Reis-a/Ostrander-s 3.00

LADY DEATH: THE CRUCIBLE
Chaos! Comics: Nov, 1996 - No. 6, Oct, 1997 ($3.50/$2.95, limited series)

1/2 4.00
1/2 Cloth Edition 8.00
1-Wraparound silver foil embossed-c 4.00
2-6-($2.95) 3.00

LADY DEATH: THE GAUNTLET
Chaos! Comics: Apr, 2002 - No. 2, May, 2002 ($2.99, limited series)

1,2: 1-J. Scott Campbell-c/redesign of Lady Death's outfit; Mota-a 3.00

LADY DEATH: THE ODYSSEY
Chaos! Comics: Apr, 1996 - No. 4, Aug, 1996 ($3.50/$2.95)

	GD	VG	FN	VF	VF/NM	NM-
1-($1.50)-Sneak Peek Preview						3.00
1-($1.50)-Sneak Peek Preview Micro Premium Edition (2500 print run)	2	4	6	8	10	12
1-($3.50)-Embossed, wraparound goil foil-c						5.00
1-Black Onyx Edition (200 print run)	6	12	18	37	59	80
1-($19.95)-Premium Edition (10,000 print run)						20.00
2-4-($2.95)						3.00

LADY DEATH: THE RAPTURE
Chaos! Comics: Jun, 1999 - No. 4, Sept, 1999 ($2.95, limited series)

1-4-Ivan Reis-c/a; Pulido-s 3.00

LADY DEATH: THE WILD HUNT (Brian Pulido's...)
CG Entertainment: Apr, 2004 - No. 2, May, 2005 ($2.95)

1-2: 1-Brian Pulido-s/Jim Cheung-a 3.00

LADY DEATH: TRIBULATION
Chaos! Comics: Dec, 2000 - No. 4, Mar, 2001 ($2.95, limited series)

1-4-Ivan Reis-a; Kaminski-s 3.00

LADY DEATH II: BETWEEN HEAVEN & HELL
Chaos! Comics: Mar, 1995 - No. 4, July, 1995 ($3.50, limited series)

	GD	VG	FN	VF	VF/NM	NM-
1-Chromium wraparound-c; Evil Ernie cameo						5.00
1-Commemorative (4,000), 1-Black Velvet-c	2	4	6	10	14	18
1-Gold	1	3	4	6	8	10
1-"Refractor" edition (5,000)	2	4	6	11	16	20

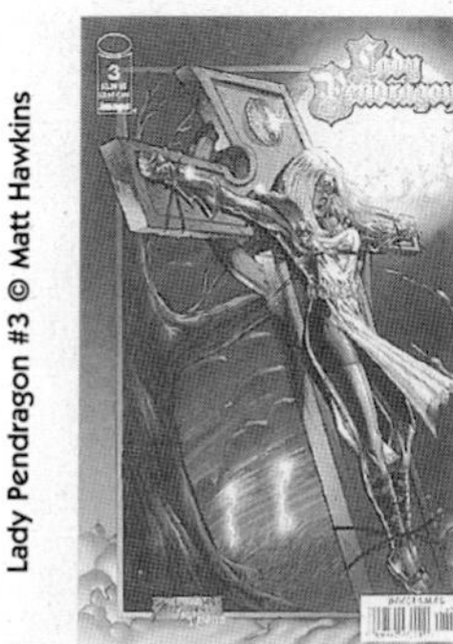

Lady Pendragon #3 © Matt Hawkins

Laff-A-Lympics #13 © H-B

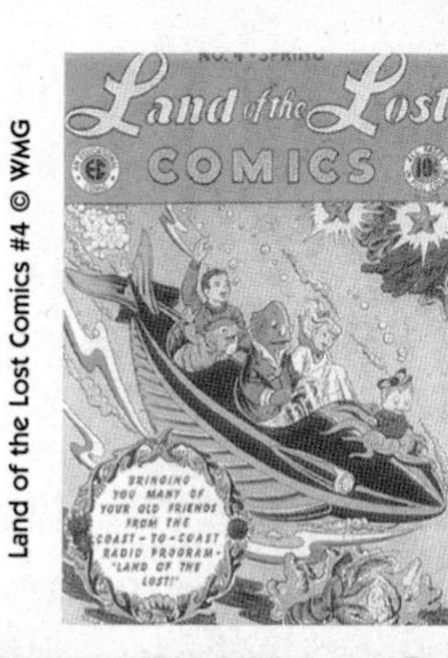

Land of the Lost Comics #4 © WMG

	GD 2.0	VG 4.0	FN 6.0	VF 8.0	VF/NM 9.0	NM- 9.2
2-4						3.50
4-Lady Demon variant-c	1	2	3	5	7	9
Trade paperback-($12.95)-r/#1-4						13.00

LADY DEMON
Chaos! Comics: Mar, 2000 - No. 3, May, 2000 ($2.95, limited series)

	GD 2.0	VG 4.0	FN 6.0	VF 8.0	VF/NM 9.0	NM- 9.2
1-3-Kaminski-s/Brewer-a						3.00

LADY FOR A NIGHT (See Cinema Comics Herald)

LADY JUSTICE (See Neil Gaiman's...)

LADY LUCK (Formerly Smash #1-85) (Also see Spirit Sections #1)
Quality Comics Group: No. 86, Dec, 1949 - No. 90, Aug, 1950

	GD 2.0	VG 4.0	FN 6.0	VF 8.0	VF/NM 9.0	NM- 9.2
86(#1)	95	190	285	603	1039	1475
87-90	65	130	195	416	708	1000

LADY MECHANIKA
Aspen MLT: No. 0, Oct, 2010 - Present ($2.50/$2.99)

	GD 2.0	VG 4.0	FN 6.0	VF 8.0	VF/NM 9.0	NM- 9.2
0-Joe Benitez-s/a; two covers; Benitez interview and sketch pages						3.00
1-(1/11, $2.99) Multiple covers						10.00
2,3-Multiple covers on each						5.00

LADY PENDRAGON
Maximum Press: Mar, 1996 ($2.50)

	GD 2.0	VG 4.0	FN 6.0	VF 8.0	VF/NM 9.0	NM- 9.2
1-Matt Hawkins script						3.00

LADY PENDRAGON
Image Comics: Nov, 1998 - No. 3, Jan, 1999 ($2.50, mini-series)

	GD 2.0	VG 4.0	FN 6.0	VF 8.0	VF/NM 9.0	NM- 9.2
Preview (6/98) Flip book w/ Deity preview						3.00
1-3: 1-Matt Hawkins-s/Stinsman-a						3.00
1-($6.95) DF Ed. with variant-c by Jusko						7.00
2-($4.95)Variant edition						5.00
0-(3/99) Origin; flip book						3.00

LADY PENDRAGON (Volume 3)
Image Comics: Apr, 1999 - No. 9, Mar, 2000 ($2.50, mini-series)

	GD 2.0	VG 4.0	FN 6.0	VF 8.0	VF/NM 9.0	NM- 9.2
1,2,4-6,8-10: 1-Matt Hawkins-s/Stinsman-a. 2-Peterson-c						3.00
3-Flip book w/Alley Cat preview (1st app.)						4.00
7-($3.95) Flip book; Stinsman-a/Cleavenger painted-a						4.00
Gallery Edition (10/99, $2.95) pin-ups						3.00
...Merlin (1/00, $2.95) Stinsman-a						3.00
.../ More Than Mortal (5/99, $2.50) Scott-s/Norton-a; 2 covers by Norton & Finch						3.00
.../ More Than Mortal Preview (2/99) Diamond Dateline supplement						3.00
Pilot Season: Lady Pendragon (5/08, $3.99) Hawkins-s/Eru-a; wraparound-c by Struzan						4.00

LADY RAWHIDE
Topps Comics: July, 1995 - No. 5, Mar, 1996 ($2.95, bi-monthly, limited series)

	GD 2.0	VG 4.0	FN 6.0	VF 8.0	VF/NM 9.0	NM- 9.2
1-5: Don McGregor scripts & Mayhew-a. in all. 2-Stelfreeze-c. 3-Hughes-c. 4-Golden-c. 5-Julie Bell-c.						3.00
It Can't Happen Here TPB (8/99, $16.95) r/#1-5						17.00
Mini Comic 1 (7/95) Maroto-a; Zorro app.						3.00
Special Edition 1 (6/95, $3.95)-Reprints						4.00

LADY RAWHIDE (Volume 2)
Topps Comics: Oct, 1996 -No. 5, June, 1997 ($2.95, limited series)

	GD 2.0	VG 4.0	FN 6.0	VF 8.0	VF/NM 9.0	NM- 9.2
1-5: 1-Julie Bell-c.						3.00

LADY RAWHIDE OTHER PEOPLE'S BLOOD (ZORRO'S ...)
Image Comics: Mar, 1999 - No. 5, July, 1999 ($2.95, B&W)

	GD 2.0	VG 4.0	FN 6.0	VF 8.0	VF/NM 9.0	NM- 9.2
1-5-Reprints Lady Rawhide series in B&W						3.00

LADY SUPREME (See Asylum)(Also see Supreme & Kid Supreme)
Image Comics (Extreme): May, 1996 - No. 2, June, 1996 ($2.50, limited series)

	GD 2.0	VG 4.0	FN 6.0	VF 8.0	VF/NM 9.0	NM- 9.2
1,2-Terry Moore -s: 1-Terry Moore-c. 2-Flip book w/Newmen preview						3.00

LAFF-A-LYMPICS (TV)(See The Funtastic World of Hanna-Barbera)
Marvel Comics: Mar, 1978 - No. 13, Mar, 1979 (Newsstand sales only)

	GD 2.0	VG 4.0	FN 6.0	VF 8.0	VF/NM 9.0	NM- 9.2
1-Yogi Bear, Scooby Doo, Pixie & Dixie, etc.	3	6	9	18	27	35
2-8	3	6	9	14	19	24
9-13: 11-Jetsons x-over; 1 pg. illustrated bio of Mighty Mightor, Herculoids, Shazzan, Galaxy Trio & Space Ghost	3	6	9	16	23	30

LAFFY-DAFFY COMICS
Rural Home Publ. Co.: Feb, 1945 - No. 2, Mar, 1945

	GD 2.0	VG 4.0	FN 6.0	VF 8.0	VF/NM 9.0	NM- 9.2
1-Funny animal	11	22	33	60	83	105
2-Funny animal	10	20	30	56	76	95

LANA (Little Lana No. 8 on)
Marvel Comics (MjMC): Aug, 1948 - No. 7, Aug, 1949 (Also see Annie Oakley)

	GD 2.0	VG 4.0	FN 6.0	VF 8.0	VF/NM 9.0	NM- 9.2
1-Rusty, Millie begin	32	64	96	188	307	425
2-Kurtzman's "Hey Look" (1); last Rusty	16	32	48	94	147	200
3-7: 3-Nellie begins	13	26	39	74	105	135

LANCELOT & GUINEVERE (See Movie Classics)

LANCELOT LINK, SECRET CHIMP (TV)
Gold Key: Apr, 1971 - No. 8, Feb, 1973

	GD 2.0	VG 4.0	FN 6.0	VF 8.0	VF/NM 9.0	NM- 9.2
1-Photo-c	6	12	18	41	66	90
2-8: 2-Photo-c	4	8	12	24	37	50

LANCELOT STRONG (See The Shield)

LANCE O'CASEY (See Mighty Midget & Whiz Comics)
Fawcett Publications: Spring, 1946 - No. 3, Fall, 1946; No. 4, Summer, 1948

	GD 2.0	VG 4.0	FN 6.0	VF 8.0	VF/NM 9.0	NM- 9.2
1-Captain Marvel app. on-c	26	52	78	154	252	350
2	16	32	48	94	147	200
3,4	14	28	42	80	115	150

NOTE: *The cover for the 1st issue was done in 1942 but was not published until 1946. The cover shows 68 pages but actually has only 36 pages.*

LANCER (TV)(Western)
Gold Key: Feb, 1969 - No. 3, Sept, 1969 (All photo-c)

	GD 2.0	VG 4.0	FN 6.0	VF 8.0	VF/NM 9.0	NM- 9.2
1	4	8	12	24	37	50
2,3	3	6	9	18	27	35

LAND OF NOD, THE
Dark Horse Comics: July, 1997 - No. 3, Feb, 1998 ($2.95, B&W)

	GD 2.0	VG 4.0	FN 6.0	VF 8.0	VF/NM 9.0	NM- 9.2
1-3-Jetcat; Jay Stephens-s/a						3.00

LAND OF OZ
Arrow Comics: 1998 - No. 9 ($2.95, B&W)

	GD 2.0	VG 4.0	FN 6.0	VF 8.0	VF/NM 9.0	NM- 9.2
1-9-Bishop-s/Bryan-s/a						3.00

LAND OF THE DEAD (George A. Romaro's...)
IDW Publishing: Aug, 2005 - No. 5 ($3.99, limited series)

	GD 2.0	VG 4.0	FN 6.0	VF 8.0	VF/NM 9.0	NM- 9.2
1-4-Adaptation of 2005 movie; Ryall-s/Rodriguez-a						4.00
TPB (3/06, $19.99) r/#1-5; cover gallery						20.00

LAND OF THE GIANTS (TV)
Gold Key: Nov, 1968 - No. 5, Sept, 1969 (All have photo-c)

	GD 2.0	VG 4.0	FN 6.0	VF 8.0	VF/NM 9.0	NM- 9.2
1	6	12	18	42	69	95
2-5	4	8	12	26	41	55

LAND OF THE LOST COMICS (Radio)
E. C. Comics: July-Aug, 1946 - No. 9, Spring, 1948

	GD 2.0	VG 4.0	FN 6.0	VF 8.0	VF/NM 9.0	NM- 9.2
1	39	78	117	240	395	550
2	24	48	72	144	237	330
3-9	21	42	63	124	202	280

LAND UNKNOWN, THE (Movie)
Dell Publishing Co.: No. 845, Sept, 1957

	GD 2.0	VG 4.0	FN 6.0	VF 8.0	VF/NM 9.0	NM- 9.2
Four Color 845-Alex Toth-a	11	22	33	71	136	200

LA PACIFICA
DC Comics (Paradox Press): 1994/1995 ($4.95, B&W, limited series, digest size, mature)

	GD 2.0	VG 4.0	FN 6.0	VF 8.0	VF/NM 9.0	NM- 9.2
1-3						5.00

LARAMIE (TV)
Dell Publishing Co.: Aug, 1960 - July, 1962 (All photo-c)

	GD 2.0	VG 4.0	FN 6.0	VF 8.0	VF/NM 9.0	NM- 9.2
Four Color 1125-Gil Kane/Heath-a	8	16	24	56	96	135
Four Color 1223,1284, 01-418-207 (7/62)	6	12	18	42	69	95

LAREDO (TV)
Gold Key: June, 1966

	GD 2.0	VG 4.0	FN 6.0	VF 8.0	VF/NM 9.0	NM- 9.2
1 (10179-606)-Photo-c	4	8	12	22	34	45

LARGE FEATURE COMIC (Formerly called Black & White in previous guides)
Dell Publishing Co.: 1939 - No. 13, 1943

Note: See individual alphabetical listings for prices

1 (Series I)-Dick Tracy Meets the Blank
3-Heigh-Yo Silver! The Lone Ranger (text & ill.)(76 pgs.); also exists as a Whitman #710; based on radio
6-Terry & the Pirates & The Dragon Lady; reprints dailies from 1936
8-Dick Tracy the Racket Buster
9-King of the Royal Mounted (Zane Grey's...)
10-(Scarce)-Gang Busters (No.
2-Terry and the Pirates (#1)
4-Dick Tracy Gets His Man
5-Tarzan of the Apes (#1) by Harold Foster (origin); reprints 1st Tarzan dailies from 1929
7-(Scarce, 52 pgs.)-Hi-Yo Silver the Lone Ranger to the Rescue; also exists as a Whitman #715, based on radio program
11-Dick Tracy Foils the Mad Doc

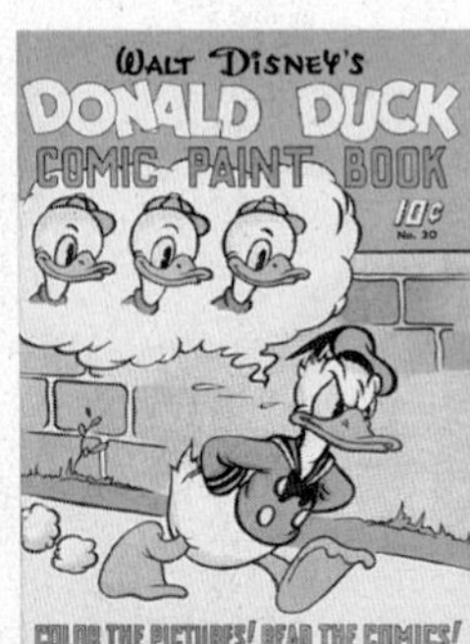

Large Feature Comic #20 © DIS

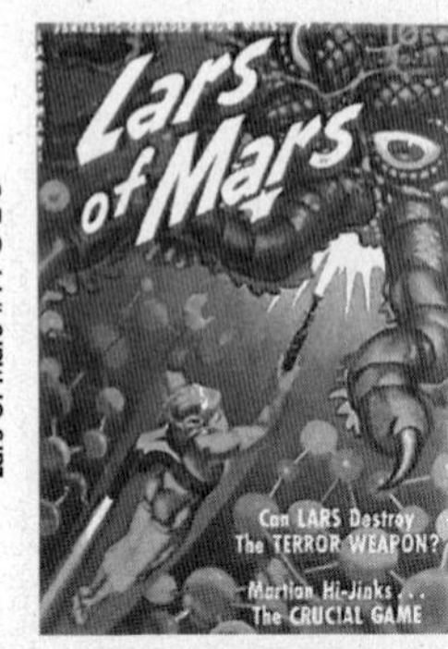

Lars of Mars #11 © Z-D

Lassie #37 © MGM

GD VG FN VF VF/NM NM-
2.0 4.0 6.0 8.0 9.0 9.2

GD VG FN VF VF/NM NM-
2.0 4.0 6.0 8.0 9.0 9.2

appears on inside front cover); first slick cover (based on radio program)
13-Dick Tracy and Scottie of Scotland Yard
15-Dick Tracy and the Kidnapped Princes
17-Gang Busters (1941)
18-Phantasmo (see The Funnies #45)
20-Donald Duck Comic Paint Book (rarer than #16) (Disney)
21,22: 21-Private Buck. 22-Nuts & Jolts
24-Popeye in "Thimble Theatre" by Segar
26-Smitty
28-Grin and Bear It
30-Tillie the Toiler
2-Winnie Winkle (#1)
3-Dick Tracy
4-Tiny Tim (#1)
6-Terry and the Pirates; Caniff-a
8-Bugs Bunny (#1)('42)
9-Bringing Up Father
10-Popeye (Thimble Theatre)
11-Barney Google and Snuffy Smith
13-(nn)-1001 Hours Of Fun; puzzles & games; by A. W. Nugent. This book was bound as #13 with Large Feature Comics in publisher's files

Hump
12-Smilin' Jack; no number on-c
14-Smilin' Jack Helps G-Men Solve a Case!
16-Donald Duck; 1st app. Daisy Duck on back cover (6/41-Disney)
19-Dumbo Comic Paint Book (Disney); partial-r from 4-Color #17
23-The Nebbs
25-Smilin' Jack-1st issue to show title on-c
27-Terry and the Pirates; Caniff-c/a
29-Moon Mullins
1 (Series II)-Peter Rabbit by Harrison Cady; arrival date-3/27/42
5-Toots and Casper
7-Pluto Saves the Ship (#1) (Disney)-Written by Carl Barks, Jack Hannah, & Nick George (Barks' 1st comic book work)
12-Private Buck

NOTE: *The Black & White Feature Books are oversized 8-1/2x11-3/8" comics with color covers and black and white interiors. The first nine issues all have rough, heavy stock covers and, except for #7, all have 76 pages, including covers. #7 and #10-on all have 52 pages. Beginning with #10 the covers are slick and thin and, because of their size, are difficult to handle without damaging. For this reason, they are seldom found in fine to mint condition. The paper stock, unlike Wow #1 and Capt. Marvel #1, is itself not unstable ...just thin. Issues #2,6, and 27 were reprinted in the early 1980s, identical except for the copyright notice on the first page.*

LARRY DOBY, BASEBALL HERO
Fawcett Publications: 1950 (Cleveland Indians)

nn-Bill Ward-a; photo-c 77 154 231 493 847 1200

LARRY HARMON'S LAUREL AND HARDY (...Comics)
National Periodical Publ.: July-Aug, 1972 (Digest advertised, not published)

1-Low print run 9 18 27 63 112 160

LARS OF MARS
Ziff-Davis Publishing Co.: No. 10, Apr-May, 1951 - No. 11, July-Aug, 1951 (Painted-c) (Created by Jerry Siegel, editor)

10-Origin; Anderson-a(3) in each; classic robot-c 92 184 276 584 1005 1425
11-Gene Colan-a; classic-c 69 138 207 442 759 1075

LARS OF MARS 3-D
Eclipse Comics: Apr, 1987 ($2.50)

1-r/Lars of Mars #10,11 in 3-D plus new story 4.00
2-D limited edition (B&W, 100 copies) 10.00

LASER ERASER & PRESSBUTTON (See Axel Pressbutton & Miracle Man 9)
Eclipse Comics: Nov, 1985 - No. 6, 1987 (95¢/$2.50, limited series)

1-6: 5,6-(95¢) 3.00
...In 3-D 1 (8/86, $2.50) 4.00
2-D 1 (B&W, limited to 100 copies signed & numbered) 10.00

LASH LARUE WESTERN (Movie star; King of the bullwhip)(See Fawcett Movie Comic, Motion Picture Comics & Six-Gun Heroes)
Fawcett Publications: Sum, 1949 - No. 46, Jan, 1954 (36 pgs., 1-6,9,13,16-on)

1-Lash & his horse Black Diamond begin; photo front/back-c begin
58 116 174 371 636 900
2(11/49) 28 56 84 165 270 375
3-5 21 42 63 126 206 285
6,9: 6-Last photo back-c; intro. Frontier Phantom (Lash's twin brother)
19 38 57 109 172 235
7,8,10 (52pgs.) 20 40 60 114 182 250
11,12,14,15 (52pgs.) 15 30 45 84 127 170
13,16-20 (36pgs.) 14 28 42 80 115 150
21-30: 21-The Frontier Phantom app. 12 24 36 69 97 125
31-45 11 22 33 60 83 105
46-Last Fawcett issue & photo-c 11 22 33 64 90 115

LASH LARUE WESTERN (Continues from Fawcett series)
Charlton Comics: No. 47, Mar-Apr, 1954 - No. 84, June, 1961

47-Photo-c 14 28 42 80 115 150
48 11 22 33 60 83 105
49-60, 67,68-(68 pgs.). 68-Check-a 9 18 27 52 69 85
61-66,69,70: 52-r/#8; 53-r/#22 9 18 27 47 61 75
71-83 8 16 24 40 50 60
84-Last issue 9 18 27 47 61 75

LASH LARUE WESTERN
AC Comics: 1990 ($3.50, 44 pgs) (24 pgs. of color, 16 pgs. of B&W)

1-Photo covers; r/Lash #6; r/old movie posters 4.00
Annual 1 (1990, $2.95, B&W, 44 pgs.)-Photo covers 4.00

LASSIE (TV)(M-G-M's... #1-36; see Kite Fun Book)
Dell Publ. Co./Gold Key No. 59 (10/62) on: June, 1950 - No. 70, July, 1969

1 (52 pgs.)-Photo-c; inside lists One Shot #282 in error
17 34 51 114 250 385
2-Painted-c begin 9 18 27 58 99 140
3-10 6 12 18 41 66 90
11-19: 12-Rocky Langford (Lassie's master) marries Gerry Lawrence. 15-1st app. Timbu
5 10 15 30 48 65
20-22-Matt Baker-a 5 10 15 35 55 75
23-38: 33-Robinson-a. 4 8 12 28 44 60
39-1st app. Timmy as Lassie picks up her TV family; photo-c
6 12 18 39 62 85
40-50-Photo-c on all 4 8 12 28 44 60
51-58-Photo-c on all 4 8 12 26 41 55
59 (10/62)-1st Gold Key 4 8 12 28 44 60
60-70: 63-Last Timmy (10/63). 64-r/#19. 65-Forest Ranger Corey Stuart begins, ends #69. 70-Forest Rangers Bob Ericson & Scott Turner app. (Lassie's new masters)
4 8 12 24 37 50
11193(1978, $1.95, 224 pgs., Golden Press)-Baker-r (92 pgs.)
4 8 12 26 41 55

NOTE: *Also see March of Comics #210, 217, 230, 254, 266, 278, 296, 308, 324,334, 346, 358, 370, 381, 394, 411, 432.*

LAST AMERICAN, THE
Marvel Comics (Epic): Dec, 1990 - No. 4, March, 1991 ($2.25, mini-series)

1-4: Alan Grant scripts 3.00

LAST AVENGERS STORY, THE (Last Avengers #1)
Marvel Comics: Nov, 1995 - No. 2, Dec, 1995 ($5.95, painted, limited series) (Alterniverse)

1,2: Peter David story; acetate-c in all. 1-New team (Hank Pym, Wasp, Human Torch, Cannonball, She-Hulk, Hotshot, Bombshell, Tommy Maximoff, Hawkeye & Mockingbird) forms to battle Ultron 59, Kang the Conqueror, The Grim Reaper & Oddball 6.00

LAST BATTLE, THE
Image Comics: Dec, 2011 ($7.99, square-bound, one-shot)

1-Facari-s/Brereton-painted art/c; Roman gladiator story; bonus Brereton sketch pages 8.00

LAST CHRISTMAS, THE
Image Comics: May, 2006 - No. 5, Oct, 2006 ($2.99, limited series)

1-5-Gerry Duggan & Brian Posehn-s/Rick Remender & Hilary Barta-a 3.00
TPB (2006, $14.99) r/#1-5; Patton Oswalt intro.; sketch pages and art 15.00

LAST DAY IN VIETNAM
Dark Horse Books: July, 2000 ($10.95, graphic novel)

nn-Will Eisner-s/a/c 11.00

LAST DAYS OF ANIMAL MAN, THE
DC Comics: July, 2009 - No. 6, Dec, 2009 ($2.99, limited series)

1-6: 1-Conway-s/Batista-a/Bolland-c. 3,4-Starfire app. 5,6-Future Justice League app. 3.00
TPB (2010, $17.99) r/#1-6 18.00

LAST DAYS OF THE JUSTICE SOCIETY SPECIAL
DC Comics: 1986 ($2.50, one-shot, 68 pgs.)

1-62 pg. JSA story plus unpubbed G.A. pg. 2 4 6 8 10 12

LAST DEFENDERS, THE
Marvel Comics: May, 2008 - No. 6, Oct, 2008 ($2.99, limited series)

1-6-Nighthawk, She-Hulk, Colossus, and Blazing Skull; Muniz-a. 2-Deodato-c 3.00

LAST FANTASTIC FOUR STORY, THE
Marvel Comics: Oct, 2007 ($4.99, one-shot)

1-Stan Lee-s/John Romita, Jr.-a/c; Galactus app. 5.00

LAST GENERATION, THE
Black Tie Studios: 1986 - No. 5, 1989 ($1.95, B&W, high quality paper)

1-5 3.00
Book 1 (1989, $6.95)-By Caliber Press 7.00

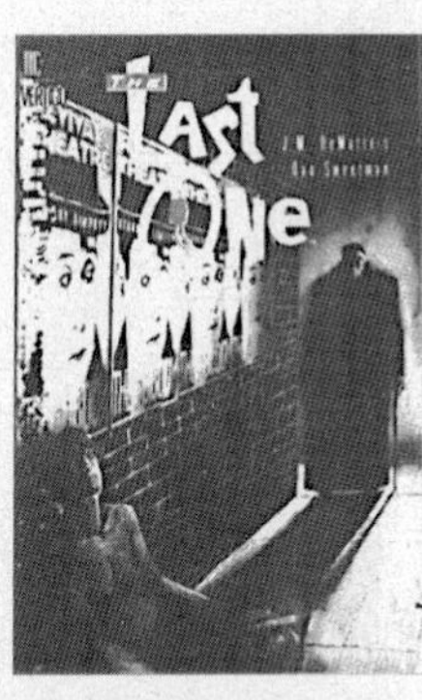
The Last One #2 © DeMatteis & Sweetman

The Last Phantom #6 © KING

Laugh Comics #21 © AP

	GD 2.0	VG 4.0	FN 6.0	VF 8.0	VF/NM 9.0	NM- 9.2

LAST HERO STANDING (Characters from Spider-Girl's M2 universe)
Marvel Comics: Aug, 2005 - No. 5, Aug, 2005 ($2.99, weekly limited series)

1-5: 1-DeFalco-s/Olliffe-a. 4-Thor app. 5-Capt. America dies 3.00
TPB (2005, $13.99) r/#1-5 14.00

LAST HUNT, THE
Dell Publishing Co.: No. 678, Feb, 1956

Four Color 678-Movie, photo-c 7 14 21 44 72 100

LAST KISS
ACME Press (Eclipse): 1988 ($3.95, B&W, squarebound, 52 pgs.)

1-One story adapts E.A. Poe's The Black Cat 4.00

LAST OF THE COMANCHES (Movie) (See Wild Bill Hickok #28)
Avon Periodicals: 1953

nn-Kinstler-c/a, 21pgs.; Ravielli-a 15 30 45 88 137 185

LAST OF THE ERIES, THE (See American Graphics)

LAST OF THE FAST GUNS, THE
Dell Publishing Co.: No. 925, Aug, 1958

Four Color 925-Movie, photo-c 6 12 18 432 69 95

LAST OF THE MOHICANS (See King Classics & White Rider and...)

LAST OF THE VIKING HEROES, THE (Also see Silver Star #1)
Genesis West Comics: Mar, 1987 - No. 12 ($1.50/$1.95)

1-4,5A,5B,6-12: 4-Intro The Phantom Force, 1-Signed edition ($1.50), 5A-Kirby/Stevens-c. 5B,6 ($1.95). 7-Art Adams-c. 8-Kirby back-c. 4.00
Summer Special 1-3: 1-(1988)-Frazetta-c & illos. 2 (1990, $2.50)-A TMNT app. 3 (1991, $2.50)-Teenage Mutant Ninja Turtles 4.00
Summer Special 1-Signed edition (sold for $1.95) 4.00
NOTE: ***Art Adams** c-7. **Byrne** c-3. **Kirby** c-1p, 5p. **Perez** c-2i. **Stevens** c-5Ai.*

LAST ONE, THE
DC Comics (Vertigo): July, 1993 - No. 6, Dec, 1993 ($2.50, lim. series, mature)

1-6 3.00

LAST PHANTOM, THE (Lee Falk's Phantom)
Dynamite Entertainment: 2010 - No. 12, 2012 ($3.99)

1-12-Beatty-s/Ferigato-a; 1-Two covers by Alex Ross; Neves & Prado var. covers 4.00
Annual 1 (2011, $4.99) Beatty-s/Desjardins-a; two covers by Desjardins & Ross 5.00

LAST PLANET STANDING
Marvel Comics: July, 2006 - No. 5, Sept, 2006 ($2.99, limited series)

1-5-Galactus threatens Spider-Girl & Fantastic Five's M2 Earth; Avengers app.; Olliffe-a 3.00
TPB (2006, $13.99) r/series 14.00

LAST SHOT
Image Comics: Aug, 2001 - No. 4, Mar, 2002 ($2.95, limited series)

1-4: 1-Wraparound-c; by Studio XD 3.00
...: First Draw (5/01, $2.95) Introductory one-shot 3.00

LAST STARFIGHTER, THE
Marvel Comics Group: Oct, 1984 - No. 3, Dec, 1984 (75¢, movie adaptation)

1-3: r/Marvel Super Special; Guice-c 3.00

LAST TEMPTATION, THE
Marvel Comics: 1994 - No. 3, 1994 ($4.95, limited series)

1-3-Alice Cooper story; Neil Gaiman scripts; McKean-c; Zulli-a: 1-Two covers 5.00
HC (Dark Horse Comics, 2005, $14.95) r/#1-3; Gaiman intro. 15.00

LAST TRAIN FROM GUN HILL
Dell Publishing Co.: No. 1012, July, 1959

Four Color 1012-Movie, photo-c 8 16 24 55 93 130

LAST TRAIN TO DEADSVILLE: A CAL McDONALD MYSTERY (See Criminal Macabre)
Dark Horse Comics: May, 2004 - No. 4, Sept, 2004 ($2.99, limited series)

1-4-Steve Niles-s/Kelley Jones-a/c 3.00
TPB (2005, $14.95) r/series 15.00

LATEST ADVENTURES OF FOXY GRANDPA (See Foxy Grandpa)

LATEST COMICS (Super Duper No. 3?)
Spotlight Publ./Palace Promotions (Jubilee): Mar, 1945 - No. 2, 1945?

1-Super Duper 16 32 48 94 147 200
2-Bee-29 (nd); Jubilee in indicia blacked out 14 28 42 76 108 140

LAUGH
Archie Enterprises: June, 1987 - No. 29, Aug, 1991 (75¢/$1.00)

V2#1 5.00
2-10,14,24: 5-X-Mas issue. 14-1st app. Hot Dog. 24-Re-intro Super Duck 4.00
11-13,15-23,25-29: 19-X-Mas issue 3.00

LAUGH COMICS (Teenage) (Formerly Black Hood #9-19) (Laugh #226 on)
Archie Publications (Close-Up): No. 20, Fall, 1946 - No. 400, Apr, 1987

	GD	VG	FN	VF	VF/NM	NM-
20-Archie begins; Katy Keene & Taffy begin by Woggon; Suzie & Wilbur also begin; Archie covers begin	103	206	309	659	1130	1600
21-23,25	42	84	126	267	451	635
24- "Pipsy" by Kirby (6 pgs.)	43	86	129	271	461	650
26-30	30	60	90	177	289	400
31-40	21	42	63	122	199	275
41-60: 41,54-Debbi by Woggon	15	30	45	86	133	180
61-80: 67-Debbi by Woggon	12	24	36	67	94	120
81-99	7	14	21	44	72	100
100	7	14	21	48	79	110
101-105,110,112,114-126: 125-Debbi app.	5	10	15	32	51	70
106-109,111,113-Neal Adams-a (1 pg.) in each	5	10	15	35	55	75
127-144: Super-hero app. in all (see note)	6	12	18	41	66	90
145-(4/63) Josie by DeCarlo begins	6	12	18	41	66	90
146-149-early Josie app. by DeCarlo	5	10	15	30	48	65
150,162,163,165,167,169,170-No Josie	3	6	9	20	30	40
151-161,164,168-Josie app. by DeCarlo	4	8	12	26	41	55
166-Beatles-c (1/65)	6	12	18	42	69	95
171-180, 200 (12/67)	3	6	9	17	25	32
181-199	3	6	9	14	20	26
201-240(3/71)	2	4	6	11	16	20
241-280(7/74)	2	4	6	9	13	16
281-299	2	4	6	8	10	12
300(3/76)	2	4	6	8	11	14
301-340 (7/79)	1	2	3	5	7	9
341-370 (1/82)	1	2	3	4	5	7
371-379,385-399						5.00
380-Cheryl Blossom app.	1	2	3	5	6	8
381-384,400: 381-384-Katy Keene app.; by Woggon-381,382						6.00

NOTE: *The Fly app. in 128, 129, 132, 134, 138, 139. Flygirl app. in 136, 137, 143. Flyman app. in 137. The Jaguar app. in 127, 130, 131, 133, 135, 140-142, 144. Josie app. in 145-149, 151-161, 164, 168. Katy Keene app. in 20-125, 129, 130, 133. Horror/Sci-Fi covers on 128-135, 137, 139. Many issues contain paper dolls. **Al Fagaly** c-20-29. **Montana** c-33, 36, 37, 42. **Bill Vigoda** c-30, 50.*

LAUGH COMICS DIGEST (...Magazine #23-89; Laugh Digest Mag. #90 on)
Archie Publ. (Close-Up No. 1, 3 on): 8/74; No. 2, 9/75; No. 3, 3/76 - No. 200, Apr, 2005 (Digest-size) (Josie and Sabrina app. in most issues)

	GD	VG	FN	VF	VF/NM	NM-
1-Neal Adams-a	5	10	15	35	55	75
2,7,8,19-Neal Adams-a	3	6	9	20	30	40
3-6,9,10	3	6	9	16	22	28
11-18,20	2	4	6	11	16	20
21-40	2	4	6	9	13	16
41-60	1	3	4	6	8	10
61-80	1	2	3	5	6	8
81-99						5.00
100						6.00
101-138						4.00
139-200: 139-Begin $1.95-c. 148-Begin $1.99-c. 156-Begin $2.19-c. 180-Begin $2.39-c						3.00

NOTE: *Katy Keene in 23, 25, 27, 32-38, 40, 45-48, 50. The Fly-r in 19, 20. The Jaguar-r in 25, 27. Mr. Justice-r in 21. The Web-r in 23.*

LAUGH COMIX (Laugh Comics inside)(Formerly Top Notch Laugh; Suzie Comics No. 49 on)
MLJ Magazines: No. 46, Summer, 1944 - No. 48, Winter, 1944-45

46-Wilbur & Suzie in all; Harry Sahle-c 25 50 75 150 245 340
47,48: 47-Sahle-c. 48-Bill Vigoda-c 18 36 54 105 165 225

LAUGH-IN MAGAZINE (TV)(Magazine)
Laufer Publ. Co.: Oct, 1968 - No. 12, Oct, 1969 (50¢) (Satire)

V1#1 5 10 15 32 51 70
2-12 4 8 12 22 34 45

LAUREL & HARDY (See Larry Harmon's... & March of Comics No. 302, 314)

LAUREL AND HARDY (...Comics)
St. John Publ. Co.: 3/49 - No. 3, 9/49; No. 26, 11/55 - No. 28, 3/56 (No #4-25)

1 74 148 222 470 810 1150
2 40 80 120 242 401 560
3 31 62 93 182 296 410
26-28 (Reprints) 15 30 45 92 144 195

LAUREL AND HARDY (TV)
Dell Publishing Co.: Oct, 1962 - No. 4, Sept-Nov, 1963

12-423-210 (8-10/62) 6 12 18 42 69 95

The L.A.W. #1 © DC

Leading Comics #4 © DC

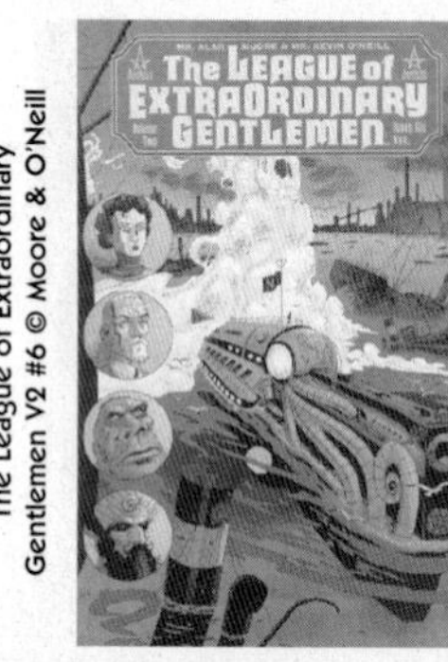

The League of Extraordinary Gentlemen V2 #6 © Moore & O'Neill

	GD 2.0	VG 4.0	FN 6.0	VF 8.0	VF/NM 9.0	NM- 9.2
2-4 (Dell)	4	8	12	28	44	60

LAUREL AND HARDY (Larry Harmon's...)
Gold Key: Jan, 1967 - No. 2, Oct, 1967

	GD	VG	FN	VF	VF/NM	NM-
1-Photo back-c	4	8	12	28	44	60
2	4	8	12	22	34	45

LAUREL AND HARDY DIGEST: DC Comics. 1972 (Advertised, not published)

L.A.W., THE (LIVING ASSAULT WEAPONS)
DC Comics: Sept, 1999 - No. 6, Feb, 2000 ($2.50, limited series)

1-6-Blue Beetle, Question, Judomaster, Capt. Atom app.; Giordano-a. 5-JLA app. 3.00

LAW AGAINST CRIME (Law-Crime on cover)
Essenkay Publishing Co.: April, 1948 - No. 3, Aug, 1948 (Real Stories from Police Files)

	GD	VG	FN	VF	VF/NM	NM-
1-(#1-3 are half funny animal, half crime stories)-L. B. Cole-c/a in all; electrocution-c	77	154	231	493	847	1200
2-L. B. Cole-c/a	56	112	168	356	611	865
3-Used in **SOTI**, pg. 180,181 & illo "The wish to hurt or kill couples in lovers' lanes;" reprinted in All-Famous Crime #9	71	142	213	454	777	1100

LAW AND ORDER
Maximum Press: Sept, 1995 - No. 2, 1995 ($2.50, unfinished limited series)

1,2 3.00

LAWBREAKERS (...Suspense Stories No. 10 on)
Law and Order Magazines (Charlton): Mar, 1951 - No. 9, Oct-Nov, 1952

	GD	VG	FN	VF	VF/NM	NM-
1	41	82	123	256	428	600
2	24	48	72	142	234	325
3,5,6,8,9	20	40	60	118	192	265
4- "White Death" junkie story	28	56	84	165	270	375
7- "The Deadly Dopesters" drug story	28	56	84	165	270	375

LAWBREAKERS ALWAYS LOSE!
Marvel Comics (CBS): Spring, 1948 - No. 10, Oct, 1949

	GD	VG	FN	VF	VF/NM	NM-
1-2pg. Kurtzman-a, "Giggles 'n' Grins"	39	78	117	230	375	520
2	20	40	60	117	189	260
3-5: 4-Vampire story	16	32	48	94	147	200
6(2/49)-Has editorial defense against charges of Dr. Wertham	18	36	54	105	165	225
7-Used in **SOTI**, illo "Comic-book philosophy"	32	64	96	192	314	435
8-10: 9,10-Photo-c	15	30	45	85	130	175

NOTE: ***Brodsky** c-4, 5. **Shores** c-1-3, 6-8.*

LAWBREAKERS SUSPENSE STORIES (Formerly Lawbreakers; Strange Suspense Stories No. 16 on)
Capitol Stories/Charlton Comics: No. 10, Jan, 1953 - No. 15, Nov, 1953

	GD	VG	FN	VF	VF/NM	NM-
10	43	86	129	271	461	650
11 (3/53)-Severed tongues-c/story & woman negligee scene	181	362	543	1158	1979	2800
12-14: 13-Giordano-c begin, end #15	30	60	90	177	289	400
15-Acid-in-face-c/story; hands dissolved in acid story	63	126	189	403	689	975

LAW-CRIME (See Law Against Crime)

LAWDOG
Marvel Comics (Epic Comics): May, 1993 - No. 10, Feb, 1993

1-10 3.00

LAWDOG/GRIMROD: TERROR AT THE CROSSROADS
Marvel Comics (Epic Comics): Sept, 1993 ($3.50)

1 3.50

LAWMAN (TV)
Dell Publishing Co.: No. 970, Feb, 1959 - No. 11, Apr-June, 1962 (All photo-c)

	GD	VG	FN	VF	VF/NM	NM-
Four Color 970(#1)	11	22	33	76	151	225
Four Color 1035('60), 3(2-4/60)-Toth-a	8	16	24	53	89	125
4-11	6	12	18	42	69	95

LAW OF DREDD, THE (Also see Judge Dredd)
Quality Comics/Fleetway #8 on: 1989 - No. 33, 1992 ($1.50/$1.75)

1-33: Bolland a-1-6,8,10-12,14(2 pg),15,19 3.00

LAWRENCE (See Movie Classics)

LAZARUS CHURCHYARD
Tundra Publishing: June, 1992 - No. 3, 1992 ($3.95/$4.50, 44 pgs., coated stock)

1-3 5.00
The Final Cut (Image, 1/01, $14.95, TPB) Reprints Ellis/D'Israeli strips 15.00

LAZARUS FIVE
DC Comics: July, 2000 - No. 5, Nov, 2000 ($2.50, limited series)

1-5-Harris-c/Abell-a(p) 3.00

LEADING COMICS
DC Comics: Jan. 1942

nn - Ashcan comic, not distributed to newsstands, only for in-house use. Cover art is Detective Comics #57 with interior being Star Spangled Comics #2 (no known sales)

LEADING COMICS (...Screen Comics No. 42 on)
National Periodical Publications: Winter, 1941-42 - No. 41, Feb-Mar, 1950

	GD	VG	FN	VF	VF/NM	NM-
1-Origin The Seven Soldiers of Victory; Crimson Avenger, Green Arrow & Speedy, Shining Knight, The Vigilante, Star Spangled Kid & Stripesy begin; The Dummy (Vigilante villain) 1st app.	343	686	1029	2400	4200	6000
2-Meskin-a; Fred Ray-c	116	232	348	742	1271	1800
3	90	180	270	576	988	1400
4,5	65	130	195	416	708	1000
6-10	50	100	150	315	533	750
11,12,14(Spring, 1945)	39	78	117	240	395	550
13-Classic robot-c	87	174	261	553	952	1350
15-(Sum,'45)-Contents change to funny animal	26	52	78	154	252	350
16-22,24-30: 16-Nero Fox-c begin, end #22	14	28	42	80	115	150
23-1st app. Peter Porkchops by Otto Feuer & begins	26	52	78	154	252	350
31,32,34-41: 34-41-Leading Screen... on-c only	12	24	36	67	94	120
33-(Scarce)	20	40	60	114	182	250

NOTE: ***Otto Feuer**-a most #15-on; **Rube Grossman**-a most #15-on;c-15-41. **Post** a-23-37, 39, 41.*

LEADING MAN
Image Comics: June, 2006 - No. 5, Feb, 2007 ($3.50, limited series)

1-5-B. Clay Moore-s/Jeremy Haun-a 3.50
TPB (2/07, $14.95) r/#1-5; sketch gallery 15.00

LEADING SCREEN COMICS (Formerly Leading Comics)
National Periodical Publ.: No. 42, Apr-May, 1950 - No. 77, Aug-Sept, 1955

	GD	VG	FN	VF	VF/NM	NM-
42-Peter Porkchops-c/stories continue	12	24	36	67	94	120
43-77	11	22	33	60	83	105

NOTE: ***Grossman** a-most. **Mayer** a-45-48, 50, 54-57, 60, 62-74, 75(3), 76, 77.*

LEAGUE OF CHAMPIONS, THE (Also see The Champions)
Hero Graphics: Dec, 1990 - No. 12, 1992 ($2.95, 52 pgs.)

1-12: 1-Flare app. 2-Origin Malice 4.00

LEAGUE OF EXTRAORDINARY GENTLEMEN, THE
America's Best Comics: Mar, 1999 - No. 6, Sept, 2000 ($2.95, limited series)

	GD	VG	FN	VF	VF/NM	NM-
1-Alan Moore-s/Kevin O'Neill-a	2	4	6	8	10	12
1-DF Edition ($10.00) O'Neill-c	2	4	6	9	12	15
2,3						6.00
4-6: 5-Revised printing with "Amaze 'Whirling Spray' Syringe" parody ad						4.00
5-Initial printing recalled because of "Marvel Co. Syringe" parody ad	12	24	36	84	177	270
... Compendium 1,2: 1-r/#1,2. 2-r/#3,4						6.00
Hardcover (2000, $24.95) r/#1-6 plus cover gallery						25.00

LEAGUE OF EXTRAORDINARY GENTLEMEN, THE (Volume 2)
America's Best Comics: Sept, 2002 - No. 6, Nov, 2003 ($3.50, limited series)

1-6-Alan Moore-s/Kevin O'Neill-a 4.00
... Bumper Compendium 1,2: 1-r/#1,2. 2-r/#3,4 6.00
... Black Dossier (HC, 2007, $29.99) new graphic novel; 3-D section with glasses; extras 30.00

LEAGUE OF EXTRAORDINARY GENTLEMEN CENTURY: 1910
Top Shelf Productions/Knockabout Comics: 2009 ($7.95, squarebound one-shot)

1-Alan Moore-s/Kevin O'Neill-a 8.00

LEAGUE OF JUSTICE
DC Comics (Elseworlds): 1996 - No. 2, 1996 ($5.95, 48 pgs., squarebound)

1,2: Magic-based alternate DC Universe story; Giordano-i 6.00

LEATHERFACE
Arpad Publishing: May (April on-c), 1991 - No. 4, May, 1992 ($2.75, painted-c)

	GD	VG	FN	VF	VF/NM	NM-
1-4-Based on Texas Chainsaw movie; Dorman-c	1	2	3	5	7	9

LEATHERNECK THE MARINE (See Mighty Midget Comics)

LEAVE IT TO BEAVER (TV)
Dell Publishing Co.: No. 912, June, 1958; May-July, 1962 (All photo-c)

	GD	VG	FN	VF	VF/NM	NM-
Four Color 912	13	26	39	90	195	300
Four Color 999,1103,1191,1285, 01-428-207	12	24	36	81	166	250

LEAVE IT TO BINKY (Binky No. 72 on) (Super DC Giant) (No. 1-22: 52 pgs.)

Leave It to Chance FCBD 2003 © Robinson & Smith

Legends of Daniel Boone #4 © DC

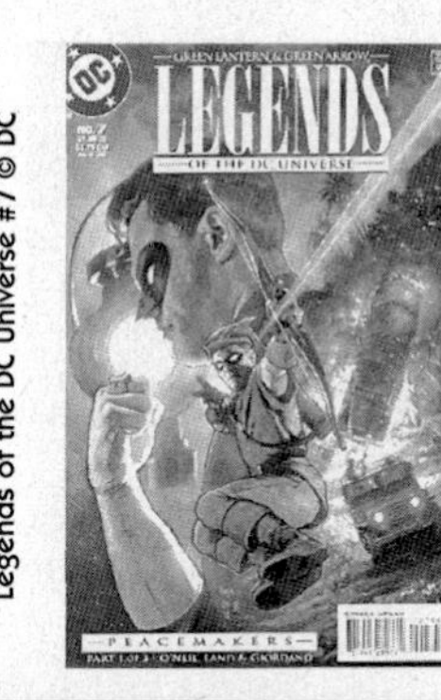

Legends of the DC Universe #7 © DC

	GD 2.0	VG 4.0	FN 6.0	VF 8.0	VF/NM 9.0	NM- 9.2

National Periodical Publications: 2-3/48 - #60, 10/58; #61, 6-7/68 - #71, 2-3/70 (Teen-age humor)

	GD	VG	FN	VF	VF/NM	NM-
1-Lucy wears Superman costume	37	74	111	222	361	500
2	20	40	60	117	189	260
3,4	14	28	42	82	121	160
5-Superman cameo	19	38	57	109	172	235
6-10	13	26	39	72	101	130
11-14,16-22: Last 52 pg. issue	11	22	33	62	86	110
15-Scribbly story by Mayer	13	26	39	72	101	130
23-28,30-45: 45-Last pre-code (2/55)	10	20	30	54	72	90
29-Used in **POP**, pg. 78	10	20	30	56	76	95
46-60: 60-(10/58)	6	12	18	39	62	85
61 (6-7/68) 1950's reprints with art changes	6	12	18	39	62	85
62-69: 67-Last 12¢ issue	4	8	12	28	44	60
70-7pg. app. Bus Driver who looks like Ralph from Honeymooners	5	10	15	32	51	70
71-Last issue	5	10	15	30	48	65

NOTE: ***Aragones**-a-61, 62, 67. **Drucker** a-28. **Mayer** a-1, 2, 15. Created by **Mayer**.*

LEAVE IT TO CHANCE
Image Comics (Homage Comics): Sept, 1996 - No. 11, Sept, 1998; No. 13, July, 2002
DC Comics (Homage Comics): No. 12, Jun, 1999 ($2.50/$2.95/$4.95)

1-3: 1-Intro Chance Falconer & St. George; James Robinson scripts & Paul Smith-c/a 5.00
4-12: 12-(6/99) 3.00
13-(7/02, $4.95) includes sketch pages and pin-ups 5.00
Free Comic Book Day Edition (2003) - James Robinson-s/Paul Smith-a 3.00
Shaman's Rain TPB (1997, $9.95) r/#1-4 10.00
Shaman's Rain HC (2002, $14.95, over-sized 8 1/4" x 12") r/#1-4 15.00
Trick or Threat TPB (1997, $12.95) r/#5-8 13.00
Trick or Threat HC (2002, $14.95, over-sized 8 1/4" x 12") r/#5-8 15.00
Vol. 3: Monster Madness and Other Stories HC (2003, $14.95, 8 1/4" x 12") r/#9-11 15.00

LEE HUNTER, INDIAN FIGHTER
Dell Publishing Co.: No. 779, Mar, 1957; No. 904, May, 1958

	GD	VG	FN	VF	VF/NM	NM-
Four Color 779 (#1)	5	10	15	35	55	75
Four Color 904	4	8	12	26	41	55

LEFT-HANDED GUN, THE (Movie)
Dell Publishing Co.: No. 913, July, 1958

	GD	VG	FN	VF	VF/NM	NM-
Four Color 913-Paul Newman photo-c	9	18	27	61	106	150

LEGACY
Majestic Entertainment: Oct, 1993 - No. 2, Nov, 1993; No. 0, 1994 ($2.25)

1-2,0: 1-Glow-in-the-dark-c. 0-Platinum 3.00

LEGACY
Image Comics: May, 2003 - No. 4, Feb, 2004 ($2.95)

1-4: 1-Francisco-a/Treffiletti-s 3.00

LEGACY OF KAIN (Based on the Eidos video game)
Top Cow Productions: Oct, 1999; Jan, 2004 ($2.99)

...Defiance 1 (1/04, $2.99) Cha-c; Kirkham-a 3.00
...Soul Reaver 1 (10/99, Diamond Dateline supplement) Benitez-c 3.00

LEGEND
DC Comics (WildStorm): Apr, 2005 - No. 4, July, 2005 ($5.95/$5.99, limited series)

1-4-Howard Chaykin-s/Russ Heath-a; inspired by Philip Wylie's novel "Gladiator" 6.00

LEGENDARY TALESPINNERS
Dynamite Entertainment: 2010 - No. 3, 2010 ($3.99)

1-3-Kuhoric-s/Bond-a; two covers 4.00

LEGEND OF CUSTER, THE (TV)
Dell Publishing Co.: Jan, 1968

	GD	VG	FN	VF	VF/NM	NM-
1-Wayne Maunder photo-c	3	6	9	18	27	35

LEGEND OF ISIS
Alias Entertainment: May, 2005 - No. 5 ($2.99)

1-5: 1-Three covers; Ottney-s/Fontana-a 3.00
...: Beginnings TPB (5/05, $9.99) Ottney-s 10.00

LEGEND OF JESSE JAMES, THE (TV)
Gold Key: Feb, 1966

	GD	VG	FN	VF	VF/NM	NM-
10172-602-Photo-c	3	6	9	18	27	35

LEGEND OF KAMUI, THE (See Kamui)

LEGEND OF LOBO, THE (See Movie Comics)

LEGEND OF MOTHER SARAH (Manga)
Dark Horse Comics: Apr, 1995 - No. 8, Nov, 1995 ($2.50, limited series)

1-8: Katsuhiro Otomo scripts 4.00

LEGEND OF MOTHER SARAH: CITY OF THE ANGELS (Manga)
Dark Horse Comics: Oct, 1996 - No. 9 ($3.95, B&W, limited series)

1(10/96), 2(12/97),3-9: Otomo scripts 4.00

LEGEND OF MOTHER SARAH: CITY OF THE CHILDREN (Manga)
Dark Horse Comics: Jan, 1996 - No. 7, July, 1996 ($3.95, B&W, limited series)

1-7: Otomo scripts 4.00

LEGEND OF SUPREME
Image Comics (Extreme): Dec, 1994 - No. 3, Feb, 1995 ($2.50, limited series)

1-3 3.00

LEGEND OF THE ELFLORD
DavDez Arts: July, 1998 - No. 2, Sept, 1998 ($2.95)

1,2-Barry Blair & Colin Chin-s/a 3.00

LEGEND OF THE HAWKMAN
DC Comics: 2000 - No. 3, 2000 ($4.95, limited series)

1-3-Raab-s/Lark-c/a 5.00

LEGEND OF THE SHIELD, THE
DC Comics (Impact Comics): July, 1991 - No. 16, Oct, 1992 ($1.00)

1-16: 6,7-The Fly x-over. 12-Contains trading card 4.00
Annual 1 (1992, $2.50, 68 pgs.)-Snyder-a; w/trading card 4.00

LEGEND OF WONDER WOMAN, THE
DC Comics: May, 1986 - No. 4, Aug, 1986 (75¢, limited series)

1-4 4.00

LEGEND OF YOUNG DICK TURPIN, THE (Disney)(TV)
Gold Key: May, 1966

	GD	VG	FN	VF	VF/NM	NM-
1 (10176-605)-Photo/painted-c	3	6	9	18	27	35

LEGEND OF ZELDA, THE (Link: The Legend... in indicia)
Valiant Comics: 1990 - No. 4, 1990 ($1.95, coated stiff-c) V2#1, 1990 - No. 5, 1990 ($1.50)

	GD	VG	FN	VF	VF/NM	NM-
1-4: 4-Layton-c(i)	1	2	3	5	6	8
V2#1-5						6.00

LEGENDS
DC Comics: Nov, 1986 - No. 6, Apr, 1987 (75¢, limited series)

	GD	VG	FN	VF	VF/NM	NM-
1-5: 1-Byrne-c/a(p) in all; 1st app. new Capt. Marvel. 3-1st app. new Suicide Squad; death of Blockbuster						5.00
6-1st app. new Justice League	1	2	3	4	5	7

LEGENDS OF DANIEL BOONE, THE (...Frontier Scout)
National Periodical Publications: Oct-Nov, 1955 - No. 8, Dec-Jan, 1956-57

	GD	VG	FN	VF	VF/NM	NM-
1 (Scarce)-Nick Cardy c-1-8	54	108	162	346	591	835
2 (Scarce)	40	80	120	246	411	575
3-8 (Scarce)	34	68	102	199	325	450

LEGENDS OF NASCAR, THE
Vortex Comics: Nov, 1990 - No. 14, 1992? (#1 3rd printing (1/91) says 2nd printing inside)

1-Bill Elliott biog.; Trimpe-a ($1.50) 5.00
1-2nd printing (11/90, $2.00) 3.00
1-3rd print; contains Maxx racecards ($3.00) 3.00
2-14: 2-Richard Petty. 3-Ken Schrader (7/91). 4-Bobby Allison; Spiegle-a(p); Adkins part-i. 5-Sterling Marlin. 6-Bill Elliott. 7-Junior Johnson; Spiegle-c/a. 8-Benny Parsons; Heck-a 3.00
1-13-Hologram cover versions. 2-Hologram shows Bill Elliott's car by mistake (all are numbered & limited) 5.00
2-Hologram corrected version 5.00
Christmas Special ($5.95) 6.00

LEGENDS OF THE DARK CLAW
DC Comics (Amalgam): Apr, 1996 ($1.95)

1-Jim Balent-c/a 3.00

LEGENDS OF THE DARK KNIGHT (See Batman: ...)

LEGENDS OF THE DC UNIVERSE
DC Comics: Feb, 1998 - No. 41, June, 2001 ($1.95/$1.99/$2.50)

1-13,15-21: 1-3-Superman; Robinson-s/Semeiks-a/Orbik-painted-c. 4,5-Wonder Woman; Deodato-a/Rude painted-c. 8-GL/GA, O'Neil-s. 10,11-Batgirl; Dodson-a. 12,13-Justice League. 15-17-Flash. 18-Kid Flash; Guice-a. 19-Impulse; prelude to JLApe Annuals. 20,21-Abin Sur 4.00
14-($3.95) Jimmy Olsen; Kirby-esque-c by Rude 5.00
22-27,30: 22,23-Superman; Rude-c/Ladronn-a. 26,27-Aquaman/Joker 3.00

L.E.G.I.O.N. '89 #7 © DC

Legion Lost (2011 series) #1 © DC

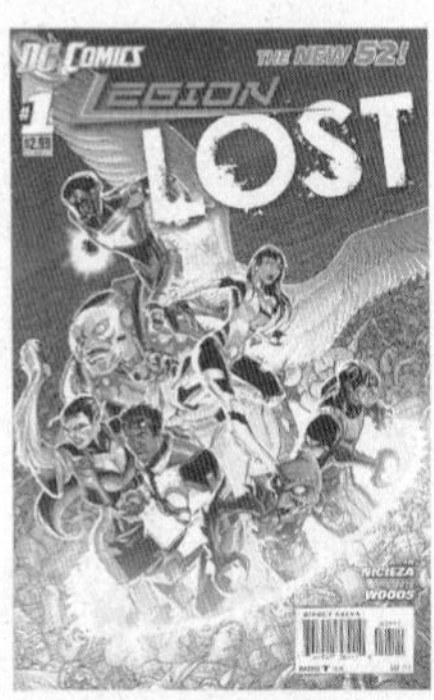

Legion of Super-Heroes (2nd series) #301 © DC

	GD	VG	FN	VF	VF/NM	NM-
	2.0	4.0	6.0	8.0	9.0	9.2

28,29: Green Lantern & the Atom; Gil Kane-a; covers by Kane and Ross 3.00
31,32: 32-Begin $2.50-c; Wonder Woman; Texeira-c 3.00
33-36-Hal Jordan as The Spectre; DeMatteis-s/Zulli-a; Hale painted-c 3.00
37-41: 37,38-Kyle Rayner. 39-Superman. 40,41-Atom; Harris-c 3.00
... Crisis on Infinite Earths 1 (2/99, $4.95) Untold story during and after Crisis on Infinite Earths #4; Wolfman-s/Ryan-a/Orbik-c 5.00
... 80 Page Giant 1 (9/98, $4.95) Stories and art by various incl. Ditko, Perez, Gibbons, Mumy; Joe Kubert-c 5.00
... 80 Page Giant 2 (1/00, $4.95) Stories and art by various incl. Challengers by Art Adams; Sean Phillips-c 5.00
... 3-D Gallery (12/98, $2.95) Pin-ups w/glasses 3.00

LEGENDS OF THE LEGION (See Legion of Super-Heroes)
DC Comics: Feb, 1998 - No. 4, May, 1998 ($2.25, limited series)
1-4:1-Origin-s of Ultra Boy. 2-Spark. 3-Umbra. 4-Star Boy 3.00

LEGENDS OF THE STARGRAZERS (See Vanguard Illustrated #2)
Innovation Publishing: Aug, 1989 - No. 6, 1990 ($1.95, limited series, mature)
1-6: 1-Redondo part inks 3.00

LEGENDS OF THE WORLD'S FINEST (See World's Finest)
DC Comics: 1994 - No. 3, 1994 ($4.95, squarebound, limited series)
1-3: Simonson scripts; Brereton-c/a; embossed foil logos 6.00
TPB-(1995, $14.95) r/#1-3 15.00

L.E.G.I.O.N. (The # to right of title represents year of print)(Also see Lobo & R.E.B.E.L.S.)
DC Comics: Feb, 1989 - No. 70, Sept, 1994 ($1.50/$1.75)
1-Giffen plots/breakdowns in #1-12,28 5.00
2-22,24-47: 3-Lobo app. #3 on. 4-1st Lobo-c this title. 5-Lobo joins L.E.G.I.O.N. 13-Lar Gand app. 16-Lar Gand joins L.E.G.I.O.N., leaves #19. 31-Capt. Marvel app. 35-L.E.G.I.O.N. '92 begins 3.00
23,70-($2.50, 52 pgs.)-L.E.G.I.O.N. '91 begins. 70-Zero Hour 4.00
48,49,51-69: 48-Begin $1.75-c. 63-L.E.G.I.O.N. '94 begins; Superman x-over 3.00
50-($3.50, 68 pgs.) 4.00
Annual 1-5 ('90-94, 68 pgs.): 1-Lobo, Superman app. 2-Alan Grant scripts. 5-Elseworlds story; Lobo app. 4.00
NOTE: *Alan Grant scripts in #1-39, 51, Annual 1, 2.*

LEGION, THE (Continued from Legion Lost & Legion Worlds)
DC Comics: Dec, 2001 - No. 38, Oct, 2004 ($2.50)
1-Abnett & Lanning-s; Coipel & Lanning-c/a 4.00
2-24: 3-8-Ra's al Ghul app. 5-Snejbjerg-a. 9-DeStefano-a. 12-Legion vs. JLA. 16-Fatal Five app.; Walker-a 17,18-Ra's al Ghul app. 20-23-Universo app. 3.00
25-($3.95) Art by Harris, Cockrum, Rivoche; teenage Clark Kent app.; Harris-c 4.00
26-38-Superboy in classic costume. 26-30-Darkseid app. 31-Giffen-a. 35-38-Jurgens-a 3.00
...Secret Files 3003 (1/04, $4.95) Kirk-a, Harris-c/a; Superboy app. 5.00
...Foundations TPB (2004, $19.95) r/#25-30 & Secret Files 3003; Harris-c 20.00

LEGION LOST (Continued from Legion of Super-Heroes [4th series] #125)
DC Comics: May, 2000 - No. 12, Apr, 2001 ($2.50, limited series)
1-Abnett & Lanning-s. Coipel & Lanning-c/a 1 2 3 4 5 7
2-12-Abnett & Lanning-s. Coipel & Lanning-c/a in most. 4,9-Alixe-a 3.00
HC (2011, $39.99, dustjacket) r/#1-12 40.00

LEGION LOST (DC New 52)
DC Comics: Nov, 2011 - Present ($2.99)
1-8: 1-Nicieza-s/Woods/a/c; group of Legionnaires trapped in the 21st century. 7,8-DeFalco-s. 8-Prelude to The Culling; Ravagers app. 3.00

LEGIONNAIRES (See Legion of Super-Heroes #40, 41 & Showcase 95 #6)
DC Comics: Apr, 1992 - No. 81, Mar, 2000 ($1.25/$1.50/$2.25)
0-(10/94)-Zero Hour restart of Legion; released between #18 & #19 3.00
1-49,51-77: 1-(4/92)-Chris Sprouse-c/a; polybagged w/SkyBox trading card. 11-Kid Quantum joins. 18-(9/94)-Zero Hour. 19(11/94). 37-Valor (Lar Gand) becomes M'onel (5/96). 43-Legion tryouts; reintro Princess Projectra, Shadow Lass & others. 47-Forms one cover image with LSH #91. 60-Karate Kid & Kid Quantum join. 61-Silver Age & 70's Legion app. 76-Return of Wildfire. 79,80-Coipel-c/a; Legion vs. the Blight 3.00
50-($3.95) Pullout poster by Davis/Farmer 4.00
#1,000,000 (11/98) Sean Phillips-a 3.00
Annual 1,3 ('94,'96 $2.95)-1-Elseworlds-s. 3-Legends of the Dead Earth-s 4.00
Annual 2 (1995, $3.95)-Year One-s 4.50

LEGIONNAIRES THREE
DC Comics: Jan, 1986 - No. 4, May, 1986 (75¢, limited series)
1-4 3.00

LEGION OF MONSTERS (Also see Marvel Premiere #28 & Marvel Preview #8)
Marvel Comics Group: Sept, 1975 ($1.00, B&W, magazine, 76 pgs.)
1-Origin & 1st app. Legion of Monsters; Neal Adams-c; Morrow-a; origin & only app. The Manphibian; Frankenstein by Mayerik; Bram Stoker's Dracula adaptation; Reese-a; painted-c (#2 was advertised with Morbius & Satana, but was never published) 6 12 18 39 62 85

LEGION OF MONSTERS (One-shots)
Marvel Comics: Apr, 2007 - Sept, 2007 ($2.99)
... Man-Thing (5/07) Huston-s/Janson-a/Land-c; Simon Garth: Zombie by Ted McKeever 3.00
... Morbius (9/07) Cahill-s/Gaydos-a/Land-c; Dracula w/Finch-a/Cebulski-s 3.00
... Satana (8/07) Furth-s/Andrasofszky-a/Land-c; Living Mummy by Hickman 3.00
... Werewolf By Night (4/07) Carey-s/Land-a/c; Monster of Frankenstein by Skottie Young 3.00
HC (2007, $24.99, dustjacket) oversized r/series and classic stories; sketch pages 25.00

LEGION OF MONSTERS
Marvel Comics: Dec, 2011 - No. 4, Mar, 2012 ($3.99, limited series)
1-4-Hopeless-s/Doe-a/c; Morbius, Manphibian, Elsa Bloodstone app. 4.00

LEGION OF NIGHT, THE
Marvel Comics: Oct, 1991 - No. 2, Oct, 1991 ($4.95, 52 pgs.)
1,2-Whilce Portacio-c/a(p) 5.00

LEGION OF SUBSTITUTE HEROES SPECIAL (See Adventure Comics #306)
DC Comics: July, 1985 ($1.25, one-shot, 52 pgs.)
1-Giffen-c/a(p) 4.00

LEGION OF SUPER-HEROES (See Action Comics, Adventure, All New Collectors Edition, Legionnaires, Legends of the Legion, Limited Collectors Edition, Secrets of the..., Superboy & Superman)
National Periodical Publications: Feb, 1973 - No. 4, July-Aug, 1973
1-Legion & Tommy Tomorrow reprints begin 3 6 9 18 27 35
2-4: 2-Forte-r. 3-r/Adv. #340. Action #240. 4-r/Adv. #341, Action #233; Mooney-r 2 4 6 11 16 20

LEGION OF SUPER-HEROES, THE (Formerly Superboy and...; Tales of The Legion #314 on)
DC Comics: No. 259, Jan, 1980 - No. 313, July, 1984
259(#1)-Superboy leaves Legion 2 4 6 8 11 14
260-270,285-289: 265-Contains 28 pg. insert "Superman & the TRS-80 computer"; origin Tyroc; Tyroc leaves Legion 6.00
261,263,264,266-(Whitman variants; low print run; no cover #'s) 2 4 6 8 11 14
271-284: 272-Blok joins; origin; 20 pg. insert-Dial 'H' For Hero. 277-Intro. Reflecto. 280-Superboy re-joins Legion. 282-Origin Reflecto. 283-Origin Wildfire 6.00
290-294-Great Darkness saga. 294-Double size (52 pgs.) 1 2 3 5 7 9
295-299,301-313: 297-Origin retold. 298-Free 16 pg. Amethyst preview. 306-Brief origin Star Boy (Swan art). 311-Colan-a 4.00
300-(68 pgs., Mando paper)-Anniversary issue; has c/a by almost everyone at DC 5.00
Annual 1-3(82-84, 52 pgs.)-1-Giffen-c/a; 1st app./origin new Invisible Kid who joins Legion. 2-Karate Kid & Princess Projectra wed & resign 4.00
...The Great Darkness Saga (1989, $17.95, 196 pgs.)-r/LSH #287,290-294 & Annual #3; Giffen-c/a 2 4 6 10 14 18
...The Great Darkness Saga The Deluxe Edition HC (2010, $39.99, dj)-r/LSH #284-296 & Annual #1; new intro. by Levitz, script for #290, Giffen design sketches 40.00
NOTE: ***Aparo** c-282, 283, 300(part). **Austin** c-268i. **Buckler** c-273p, 274p, 276p. **Colan** a-311p. **Ditko** a(p)-267, 268, 272, 274, 276, 281. **Giffen** a-285-313p, Annual 1p; c-287p, 288p, 289, 290p, 291p, 292, 293, 294-299p, 300, 301-313p, Annual 1p, 2p. **Perez** c-268p, 277-280, 281p. **Starlin** a-265. **Staton** a-259p, 260p, 280. **Tuska** a-308p.*

LEGION OF SUPER-HEROES (3rd Series) (Reprinted in Tales of the Legion)
DC Comics: Aug, 1984 - No. 63, Aug, 1989 ($1.25/$1.75, deluxe format)
1-Silver ink logo 5.00
2-36,39-44,46-49,51-62: 4-Death of Karate Kid. 5-Death of Nemesis Kid. 12-Cosmic Boy, Lightning Lad, & Saturn Girl resign. 14-Intro new members: Tellus, Sensor Girl, Quislet. 15-17-Crisis tie-ins. 18-Crisis x-over. 25-Sensor Girl i.d. revealed as Princess Projectra. 35-Saturn Girl rejoins. 42,43-Millennium tie-ins. 44-Origin Quislet 3.00
37,38-Death of Superboy 2 4 6 8 11 14
45,50: 45 ($2.95, 68 pgs.)-Anniversary ish. 50-Double size ($2.50-c) 4.00
63-Final issue 4.00
Annual 1-4 (10/85-'88, 52 pgs.)-1-Crisis tie-in 4.00
...: An Eye For An Eye TPB (2007, $17.99)-r/#1-6; intro by Paul Levitz; cover gallery 18.00
...: The More Things Change TPB (2008, $17.99)-r/#7-13; cover gallery 18.00
NOTE: ***Byrne** c-36p. **Giffen** a(p)-1, 2, 50-55, 57-63, Annual 1p, 2; c-1-5p, 54p, Annual 1. **Orlando** a-6p. **Steacy** c-45-50, Annual 3.*

LEGION OF SUPER-HEROES (4th Series)
DC Comics: Nov, 1989 - No. 125, Mar, 2000 ($1.75/$1.95/$2.25)
0-(10/94)-Zero Hour restart of Legion; released between #61 & #62 3.00
1-Giffen-c/a(p)/scripts begin (4 pg.-a only #18) 6.00

Legion of Super-Heroes (4th series) #100 © DC

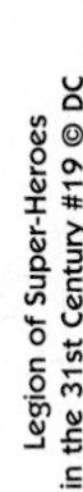
Legion of Super-Heroes in the 31st Century #19 © DC

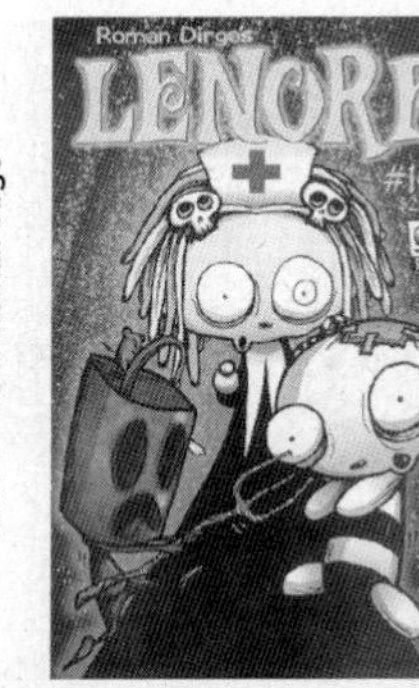
Lenore #10 © Roman Dirge

GD 2.0 | VG 4.0 | FN 6.0 | VF 8.0 | VF/NM 9.0 | NM- 9.2

2-20,26-49,51-53,55-58: 4-Mon-El (Lar Gand) destroys Time Trapper, changes reality. 5-Alt. reality story where Mordru rules all; Ferro Lad app. 6-1st app. of Laurel Gand (Lar Gand's cousin). 8-Origin. 13-Free poster by Giffen showing new costumes. 15-(2/91)-1st reference of Lar Gand as Valor. 26-New map of headquarters. 34-Six pg. preview of Timber Wolf mini-series. 40-Minor Legionnaires app. 41-(3/93)-SW6 Legion renamed Legionnaires w/new costumes and some new code-names 4.00
21-25: 21-24-Lobo & Darkseid storyline. 24-Cameo SW6 younger Legion duplicates. 25-SW6 Legion full intro. 4.50
50-($3.50, 68 pgs.) 5.00
54-($2.95)-Die-cut & foil stamped-c 5.00
59-99: 61-(9/94)-Zero Hour. 62-(11/94). 75-XS travels back to the 20th Century (cont'd in Impulse #9). 77-Origin of Brainiac 5. 81-Reintro Sun Boy. 85-Half of the Legion sent to the 20th century, Superman-c/app. 86-Final Night. 87-Deadman-c/app. 88-Impulse-c/app. Adventure Comics #247 cover swipe. 91-Forms one cover image with Legionnaires #47. 96-Wedding of Ultra Boy and Apparition. 99-Robin, Impulse, Superboy app. 3.00
100-($5.95, 96 pgs.)-Legionnaires return to the 30th Century; gatefold-c; 5 stories-art by Simonson, Davis and others 1 2 3 4 5 7
101-121: 101-Armstrong-a(p) begins. 105-Legion past & present vs. Time Trapper. 109-Moder-a. 110-Thunder joins. 114,115-Bizarro Legion. 120,121-Fatal Five. 3.00
122-124: 122,123-Coipel-c/a. 124-Coipel-c 3.50
125-Leads into "Legion Lost" maxi-series; Coipel-c 5.00
#1,000,000 (11/98) Giffen-a 3.00
Annual 1-5 (1990-1994, $3.50, 68 pgs.): 4-Bloodlines. 5-Elseworlds story 4.00
Annual 6 (1995,$3.95)-Year One story 4.00
Annual 7 (1996, $3.50, 48 pgs.)-Legends of the Dead Earth story; intro 75th Century Legion of Super-Heroes; Wildfire app. 4.00
Legion: Secret Files 1 (1/98, $4.95) Retold origin & pin-ups 5.00
Legion: Secret Files 2 (6/99, $4.95) Story and profile pages 5.00
The Beginning of Tomorrow TPB ('99, $17.95) r/post-Zero Hour reboot 18.00
NOTE: ***Giffen** a-1-24; breakdowns-26-32, 34-36; c-1-7, 8(part), 9-24. **Brandon Peterson** a(p)-15(1st for DC), 16, 18, Annual 2(54 pgs.); c-Annual 2p. **Swan/Anderson** c-8(part).*

LEGION OF SUPER-HEROES (5th Series) (Title becomes Supergirl and the Legion of Super-Heroes #16-36) (Intro. in Teen Titans/Legion Special)
DC Comics: Feb, 2005 - No. 15, Apr, 2006; No. 37, Feb, 2008 - No. 50, Mar, 2009 ($2.95/$2.99)

1-15: 1-Waid-s/Kitson-a/c. 4-Kirk & Gibbons-a. 9-Jeanty-a. 15-Dawnstar, Tyroc, Blok-c 3.00
37-50: 37-Shooter-s/Manapul-a begin; two interlocking covers. 50-Wraparound cover 3.00
44-Variant-c by Neal Adams 5.00
... Death of a Dream TPB ('06, $14.99) r/#7-13 15.00
... Enemy Manifest HC ('09, $24.99, dustjacket) r/#45-50 25.00
... Enemy Manifest SC ('10, $14.99) r/#45-50 15.00
... Enemy Rising HC ('08, $19.99, dustjacket) r/#37-44 20.00
... Enemy Rising SC ('09, $14.99) r/#37-44 15.00
...: 1050 Years of the Future TPB ('08, $19.99) r/greatest tales of their 50 year history 20.00
... Teenage Revolution TPB ('05, $14.99) r/#1-6 & Teen Titans/Legion Spec.; sketch pages 15.00

LEGION OF SUPER-HEROES (6th Series)
DC Comics: Jul, 2010 - No. 16, Oct, 2011 ($3.99/$2.99)

1-9: 1-Earth-Man app.; Titan destroyed; Levitz-s/Cinar-a/c. 6-Jimenez back-up-a 4.00
1-6-Variant covers by Jim Lee 8.00
10-16-($2.99) 12-16-Legion of Super-Villains app. 3.00
Annual 1 (2/11, $4.99) New Emerald Empress; Levitz-s/Giffen-a 5.00
...: The Choice HC (2011, $24.99, dustjacket) r/#1-6; variant-c gallery and Cinar art 25.00

LEGION OF SUPER-HEROES (DC New 52)(Also see Legion Lost)
DC Comics: Nov, 2011 - Present ($2.99)

1-7: 1-4-Levitz-s/Portela-a. 5-Simonson-c/a 3.00

LEGION OF SUPER-HEROES IN THE 31ST CENTURY (Based on the animated series)
DC Comics: June, 2007 - No. 20, Jan, 2009 ($2.25)

1-20: 1-Chynna Clugston-a; Fatal Five app. 6-Green Lantern Corps app. 15-Impulse app. 3.00
1-(6/07) Free Comic Book Day giveaway 3.00
...: Tomorrow's Heroes (2008, $14.99) r/#1-7; cover gallery 15.00

LEGION OF SUPER-VILLAINS
DC Comics: May, 2011 ($4.99, one-shot)

1-Levitz-s/Portela-a; Saturn Queen, Lightning Lord, Sun-Killer, Micro Lad app. 5.00

LEGION: PROPHETS (Prelude to 2010 movie)
IDW Publishing: Nov, 2009 - No. 4, Dec, 2009 ($3.99, limited series)

1-4: Stewart & Waltz-s. 1-Muriel-a. 2-Holder-a. 3-Paronzini-a. 4-Gaydos-a 4.00

LEGION: SCIENCE POLICE (See Legion of Super-Heroes)
DC Comics: Aug, 1998 - No. 4, Nov, 1998 ($2.25, limited series)

1-4-Ryan-a 3.00

LEGION: SECRET ORIGIN (Legion of Super-Heroes)
DC Comics: Dec, 2011 - No. 6, May, 2012 ($2.99, limited series)

1-6-Levitz-s/Batista-a; formation of the Legion retold 3.00

LEGION WORLDS (Follows Legion Lost series)
DC Comics: Jun, 2001 - No. 6, Nov, 2001 ($3.95, limited series)

1-6-Abnett & Lanning-s; art by various. 5-Dillon-a. 6-Timber Wolf app. 4.00

LEMONADE KID, THE (See Bobby Benson's B-Bar-B Riders)
AC Comics: 1990 ($2.50, 28 pgs.)

1-Powell-c(r); Red Hawk-r by Powell; Lemonade Kid-r/Bobby Benson by Powell (2 stories) 3.00

LENNON SISTERS LIFE STORY, THE
Dell Publishing Co.: No. 951, Nov, 1958 - No. 1014, Aug, 1959

Four Color 951 (#1)-Toth-a, 32pgs, photo-c 12 24 36 79 160 240
Four Color 1014-Toth-a, photo-c 11 22 33 76 151 225

LENORE
Slave Labor Graphics: Feb, 1998 - Present ($2.95/$3.95, B&W, color #13-on)

1-12: 1-Roman Dirge-s/a, 1,2-2nd printing 3.00
13-($3.95, color) 4.00
Vol. 2 (8/09 - Present) 1-4: 1-1st and 2nd printings; Lenore's origin 4.00
...: Noogies TPB ($11.95) r/#1-4 12.00
...: Wedgies TPB (2000, $13.95) r/#5-8 14.00
...: Cooties TPB (3/06, $13.95) r/#9-12; pin-ups by various 14.00

LEONARD NIMOY'S PRIMORTALS
Tekno Comix: Mar, 1995 - No. 15, May, 1996 ($1.95)

1-15: Concept by Leonard Nimoy & Isaac Asimov 1-3-w/bound-in game piece & trading card. 4-w/Teknophage Steel Edition coupon. 13,14-Art Adams-c. 15-Simonson-c 3.00

LEONARD NIMOY'S PRIMORTALS
BIG Entertainment: V2#0, June, 1996 - No. 8, Feb, 1997 ($2.25)

V2#0-8: 0-Includes Pt. 9 of "The Big Bang" x-over. 0,1-Simonson-c. 3-Kelley Jones-c 3.00

LEONARD NIMOY'S PRIMORTALS ORIGINS
Tekno Comix: Nov, 1995 - No. 2, Dec, 1995 ($2.95, limited series)

1,2: Nimoy scripts; Art Adams-c; polybagged 3.00

LEONARDO (Also see Teenage Mutant Ninja Turtles)
Mirage Studios: Dec, 1986 ($1.50, B&W, one-shot)

1 1 2 3 5 6 8

LEO THE LION
I. W. Enterprises: No date(1960s) (10¢)

1-Reprint 2 4 6 9 13 16

LEROY (Teen-age)
Standard Comics: Nov, 1949 - No. 6, Nov, 1950

1 15 30 45 85 130 175
2-Frazetta text illo. 11 22 33 60 83 105
3-6: 3-Lubbers-a 10 20 30 54 72 90

LETHAL (Also see Brigade)
Image Comics (Extreme Studios): Feb, 1996 ($2.50, unfinished limited series)

1-Marat Mychaels-c/a. 3.00

LETHAL FOES OF SPIDER-MAN (Sequel to Deadly Foes of Spider-Man)
Marvel Comics: Sept, 1993 - No. 4, Dec, 1993 ($1.75, limited series)

1-4 3.00

LETHARGIC LAD
Crusade Ent.: June, 1996 - No. 3, Sept, 1996 ($2.95, B&W, limited series)

1,2 3.00
3-Alex Ross-c/swipe (Kingdom Come) 4.00
...Jumbo Sized Annual #1 (Summer 2002, $3.99) prints comic stories from internet 4.00

LETHARGIC LAD ADVENTURES
Crusade Ent./Destination Ent.#3 on: Oct, 1997 - No. 12, Sept./Oct. 1999 ($2.95, B&W)

1-12-Hyland-s/a. 9-Alex Ross sketch page & back-c 3.00

LET ME IN: CROSSROADS (Based on the 2010 movie Let Me In)
Dark Horse Comics: Dec, 2010 - No. 4, Mar, 2011 ($3.99, limited series)

1-4-Prelude to the film; Andreyko-s/Reynolds-a/Phillips-c 4.00
1-4 Variant photo-c 8.00

LET'S PRETEND (CBS radio)
D. S. Publishing Co.: May-June, 1950 - No. 3, Sept-Oct, 1950

1 18 36 54 105 165 225

Liberty Comics #12 © Green Publ.

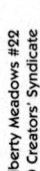

Liberty Meadows #22 © Creators' Syndicate

The Life of Captain Marvel #3 © MAR

	GD 2.0	VG 4.0	FN 6.0	VF 8.0	VF/NM 9.0	NM- 9.2
2,3	14	28	42	82	121	160

LET'S READ THE NEWSPAPER
Charlton Press: 1974

	GD 2.0	VG 4.0	FN 6.0	VF 8.0	VF/NM 9.0	NM- 9.2
nn-Features Quincy by Ted Sheares	1	3	4	6	8	10

LET'S TAKE A TRIP (TV) (CBS Television Presents)
Pines Comics: Spring, 1958

	GD 2.0	VG 4.0	FN 6.0	VF 8.0	VF/NM 9.0	NM- 9.2
1-Marv Levy-c/a	5	10	15	23	28	32

LETTERS TO SANTA (See March of Comics No. 228)

LEX LUTHOR: MAN OF STEEL
DC Comics: May, 2005 - No. 5, Sept, 2005 ($2.99, limited series)

	GD 2.0	VG 4.0	FN 6.0	VF 8.0	VF/NM 9.0	NM- 9.2
1-5: 1-Azzarello-s/Bermejo-a/c in all. 3-Batman-c/app.						3.00
TPB (2005, $12.99) r/series						13.00
Luthor HC (2010, $19.99, d.j.) r/#1-5 with 10 new story pages; cover gallery & sketch-a						20.00

LEX LUTHOR: THE UNAUTHORIZED BIOGRAPHY
DC Comics: 1989 ($3.95, 52 pgs., one-shot, squarebound)

	GD 2.0	VG 4.0	FN 6.0	VF 8.0	VF/NM 9.0	NM- 9.2
1-Painted-c; Clark Kent app.						4.00

LIBERTY COMICS (Miss Liberty No. 1)
Green Publishing Co.: No. 5, May, '46 - No. 15, July, 1946 (MLJ & other-r)

	GD 2.0	VG 4.0	FN 6.0	VF 8.0	VF/NM 9.0	NM- 9.2
5 (5/46)-The Prankster app; Starr-a	22	44	66	132	216	300
10-Hangman & Boy Buddies app.; reprints 3 Hangman stories, incl. Hangman #8	22	44	66	132	216	300
11 (V2#2, 1/46)-Wilbur in women's clothes	18	36	54	105	165	225
12 (V2#4)-Black Hood & Suzie app.; classic Skull-c	61	122	183	390	670	950
14,15-Patty of Airliner; Starr-a in both	20	40	60	114	182	250

LIBERTY COMICS (The CBLDF Presents...)
Image Comics: July, 2008; Oct, 2009 ($3.99/$4.99, Comic Book Legal Defense Fund benefit)

	GD 2.0	VG 4.0	FN 6.0	VF 8.0	VF/NM 9.0	NM- 9.2
1-Two covers by Campbell & Mignola; art by Cooke, Aragones, A. Adams & others						4.00
1-(12/08) Second printing with Thor-c by Simonson						4.00
2-(10/09, $4.99) two covers by Romita Jr. & Sale; art by Allred, Templesmith, Jim Lee						5.00
Liberty Annual 2011 (10/11, $4.99) Covers by Wagner & Cassaday						5.00

LIBERTY COMICS
Heroic Publishing: Sept, 2007 ($4.50)

	GD 2.0	VG 4.0	FN 6.0	VF 8.0	VF/NM 9.0	NM- 9.2
1-Mark Sparacio-c						4.50

LIBERTY GIRL
Heroic Publishing: Aug, 2006 - No. 3, May, 2007 ($3.25/$2.99)

	GD 2.0	VG 4.0	FN 6.0	VF 8.0	VF/NM 9.0	NM- 9.2
1-3-Mark Sparacio-c/a						3.25

LIBERTY GUARDS
Chicago Mail Order: No date (1946?)

	GD 2.0	VG 4.0	FN 6.0	VF 8.0	VF/NM 9.0	NM- 9.2
nn-Reprints Man of War #1 with cover of Liberty Scouts #1; Gustavson-c	36	72	108	211	343	475

LIBERTY MEADOWS
Insight Studios Group/Image Comics #27 on: 1999 - Present ($2.95, B&W)

	GD 2.0	VG 4.0	FN 6.0	VF 8.0	VF/NM 9.0	NM- 9.2
1-Frank Cho-s/a; reprints newspaper strips	3	6	9	14	20	25
1-2nd & 3rd printings	1	2	3	4	5	7
2,3	2	4	6	8	11	14
4-10	1	2	3	4	5	7
11-25,27-37: 20-Adam Hughes-c. 22-Evil Brandy vs. Brandy. 27-1st Image issue, printed sideways						3.00
..., Cover Girl HC (Image, 2006, $24.99, with dustjacket) r/color covers of #1-19,21-37 along with B&W inked versions, sketches and pin-up art						25.00
...: Eden Book 1 SC (Image, 2002, $14.95) r/#1-9; sketch gallery						15.00
...: Eden Book 1 SC 2nd printing (Image, 2004, $19.95) r/#1-9; sketch gallery						20.00
...: Eden Book 1 HC (Image, 2003, $24.95, with dustjacket) r/#1-9; sketch gallery						25.00
...: Creature Comforts Book 2 HC (Image, 2004, $24.95, with d.j.) r/#10-18; sketch gallery						25.00
...: Creature Comforts Book 2 SC (Image, 12/04, $14.95) r/#10-18; sketch gallery						15.00
...Book 3: Summer of Love HC (Image, 12/04, $24.95) r/#19-27; sketch gallery						25.00
...Book 3: Summer of Love SC (Image, 7/05, $14.95) r/#19-27; sketch gallery						15.00
...Book 4: Cold, Cold Heart HC (Image, 9/05, $24.95) r/#28-36; sketch gallery						25.00
...Book 4: Cold, Cold Heart SC (Image, 2006, $14.99) r/#28-36; sketch gallery						15.00
Image Firsts: Liberty Meadows #1 (9/10, $1.00) r/#1						3.00
... Sourcebook (5/04, $4.95) character info and unpublished strips						5.00
... Wedding Album (#26) (2002, $2.95)						3.00

LIBERTY PROJECT, THE
Eclipse Comics: June, 1987 - No. 8, May, 1988 ($1.75, color, Baxter paper)

	GD 2.0	VG 4.0	FN 6.0	VF 8.0	VF/NM 9.0	NM- 9.2
1-8: 6-Valkyrie app.						3.00

LIBERTY SCOUTS (See Liberty Guards & Man of War)
Centaur Publications: No. 2, June, 1941 - No. 3, Aug, 1941

	GD 2.0	VG 4.0	FN 6.0	VF 8.0	VF/NM 9.0	NM- 9.2
2(#1)-Origin The Fire-Man, Man of War; Vapo-Man & Liberty Scouts begin; intro Liberty Scouts; Gustavson-c/a in both	135	270	405	864	1482	2100
3(#2)-Origin & 1st app. The Sentinel	94	188	282	597	1024	1450

LICENCE TO KILL (James Bond 007) (Movie)
Eclipse Comics: 1989 ($7.95, slick paper, 52 pgs.)

	GD 2.0	VG 4.0	FN 6.0	VF 8.0	VF/NM 9.0	NM- 9.2
nn-Movie adaptation; Timothy Dalton photo-c	1	2	3	5	6	8
Limited Hardcover ($24.95)						25.00

LIDSVILLE (TV)
Gold Key: Oct, 1972 - No. 5, Oct, 1973

	GD 2.0	VG 4.0	FN 6.0	VF 8.0	VF/NM 9.0	NM- 9.2
1-Photo-c	5	10	15	35	55	75
2-5	4	8	12	22	34	45

LIEUTENANT, THE (TV)
Dell Publishing Co.: April-June, 1964

	GD 2.0	VG 4.0	FN 6.0	VF 8.0	VF/NM 9.0	NM- 9.2
1-Photo-c	3	6	9	18	27	35

LIEUTENANT BLUEBERRY (Also see Blueberry)
Marvel Comics (Epic Comics): 1991 - No. 3, 1991 (Graphic novel)

	GD 2.0	VG 4.0	FN 6.0	VF 8.0	VF/NM 9.0	NM- 9.2
1,2 ($8.95)-Moebius-a in all	2	4	6	11	16	20
3 ($14.95)	3	6	9	16	22	28

LT. ROBIN CRUSOE, U.S.N. (See Movie Comics & Walt Disney Showcase #26)

LIFE EATERS, THE
DC Comics (WildStorm): 2003 ($29.95, hardcover with dust jacket)

	GD 2.0	VG 4.0	FN 6.0	VF 8.0	VF/NM 9.0	NM- 9.2
HC-David Brin-s; Scott Hampton-painted-a/c; Norse Gods team with the Nazis						30.00
SC-(2004, $19.95)						20.00

LIFE OF CAPTAIN MARVEL, THE
Marvel Comics Group: Aug, 1985 - No. 5, Dec, 1985 ($2.00, Baxter paper)

	GD 2.0	VG 4.0	FN 6.0	VF 8.0	VF/NM 9.0	NM- 9.2
1-5: 1-All reprint Starlin issues of Iron Man #55, Capt. Marvel #25-34 plus Marvel Feature #12 (all with Thanos). 4-New Thanos back-c by Starlin						4.00

LIFE OF CHRIST, THE
Catechetical Guild Educational Society: No. 301, 1949 (35¢, 100 pgs.)

	GD 2.0	VG 4.0	FN 6.0	VF 8.0	VF/NM 9.0	NM- 9.2
301-Reprints from Topix(1949)-V5#11,12	9	18	27	50	65	80

LIFE OF CHRIST: THE CHRISTMAS STORY, THE
Marvel Comics/Nelson: Feb, 1993 ($2.99, slick stock)

	GD 2.0	VG 4.0	FN 6.0	VF 8.0	VF/NM 9.0	NM- 9.2
nn						5.00

LIFE OF CHRIST: THE EASTER STORY, THE
Marvel Comics/Nelson: 1993 ($2.99, slick stock)

	GD 2.0	VG 4.0	FN 6.0	VF 8.0	VF/NM 9.0	NM- 9.2
nn						5.00

LIFE OF CHRIST VISUALIZED
Standard Publishers: 1942 - No. 3, 1943

	GD 2.0	VG 4.0	FN 6.0	VF 8.0	VF/NM 9.0	NM- 9.2
1-3: All came in cardboard case, each...	9	18	27	50	65	80
Case only.....	10	20	30	54	72	90

LIFE OF CHRIST VISUALIZED
The Standard Publ. Co.: 1946? (48 pgs. in color)

	GD 2.0	VG 4.0	FN 6.0	VF 8.0	VF/NM 9.0	NM- 9.2
nn	7	14	21	37	46	55

LIFE OF ESTHER VISUALIZED
The Standard Publ. Co.: No. 2062, 1947 (48 pgs. in color)

	GD 2.0	VG 4.0	FN 6.0	VF 8.0	VF/NM 9.0	NM- 9.2
2062	7	14	21	37	46	55

LIFE OF JOSEPH VISUALIZED
The Standard Publ. Co.: No. 1054, 1946 (48 pgs. in color)

	GD 2.0	VG 4.0	FN 6.0	VF 8.0	VF/NM 9.0	NM- 9.2
1054	7	14	21	37	46	55

LIFE OF PAUL (See The Living Bible)

LIFE OF POPE JOHN PAUL II, THE
Marvel Comics Group: Jan, 1983 ($1.50/$1.75)

	GD 2.0	VG 4.0	FN 6.0	VF 8.0	VF/NM 9.0	NM- 9.2
1	1	3	4	6	8	10

LIFE OF RILEY, THE (TV)
Dell Publishing Co.: No. 917, July, 1958

	GD 2.0	VG 4.0	FN 6.0	VF 8.0	VF/NM 9.0	NM- 9.2
Four Color 917-Photo-c	10	20	30	66	121	175

LIFE ON ANOTHER PLANET
Kitchen Sink Press: 1978 (B&W, graphic novel, magazine size)

	GD 2.0	VG 4.0	FN 6.0	VF 8.0	VF/NM 9.0	NM- 9.2
nn-Will Eisner-s/a						13.00
Reprint (DC Comics, 5/00, $12.95)						13.00

LIFE'S LIKE THAT

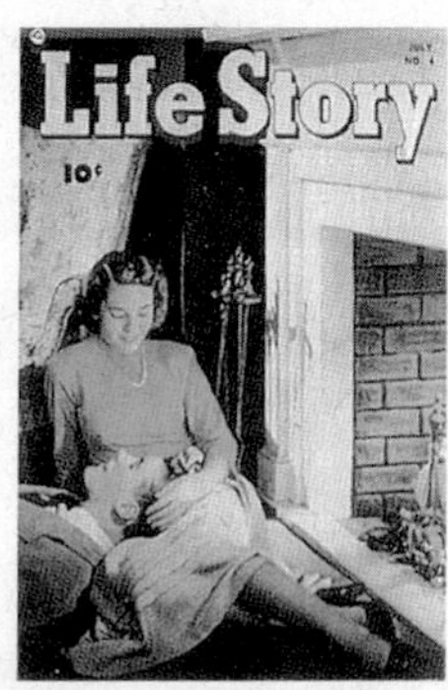

Life Story #4 © FAW

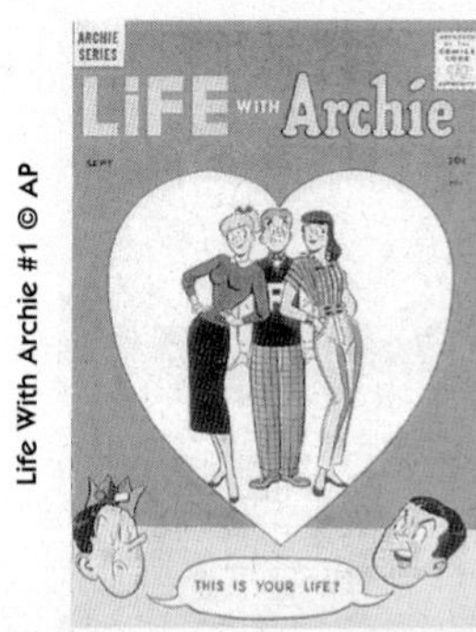

Life With Archie #1 © AP

Limited Collectors' Edition C-22 © ERB

	GD 2.0	VG 4.0	FN 6.0	VF 8.0	VF/NM 9.0	NM- 9.2

Croyden Publ. Co.: 1945 (25¢, B&W, 68 pgs.)
nn-Newspaper Sunday strip-r by Neher 7 14 21 35 43 50

LIFE STORIES OF AMERICAN PRESIDENTS (See Dell Giants)

LIFE STORY
Fawcett Publications: Apr, 1949 - V8#46, Jan, 1953; V8#47, Apr, 1953 (All have photo-c?)
V1#1 15 30 45 84 127 170
2 9 18 27 52 69 85
3-6, V2#7-12 8 16 24 44 57 70
V3#13-Wood-a 15 30 45 84 127 170
V3#14-18, V4#19-24, V5#25-30, V6#31-35 8 16 24 40 50 60
V6#36- "I sold drugs" on-c 12 24 36 69 97 125
V7#37,40-42, V8#44,45 7 14 21 37 46 55
V7#38, V8#43-Evans-a 8 16 24 40 50 60
V7#39-Drug Smuggling & Junkie story 10 20 30 58 79 100
V8#46,47 (Scarce) 9 18 27 50 65 80
NOTE: *Powell a-13, 23, 24, 26, 28, 30, 32, 39. Marcus Swayze a-1-3, 10-12, 15, 16, 20, 21, 23-25, 31, 35, 37, 40, 44, 46.*

LIFE, THE UNIVERSE AND EVERYTHING (See Hitchhikers Guide to the Galaxy & Restaurant at the End of the Universe)
DC Comics: 1996 - No. 3, 1996 ($6.95, squarebound, limited series)
1-3: Adaptation of novel by Douglas Adams. 1 2 3 4 5 7

LIFE WITH ARCHIE
Archie Publications: Sept, 1958 - No. 286, Sept, 1991
1 25 50 75 175 375 575
2-(9/59) 13 26 39 85 180 275
3-5: 3-(7/60) 10 20 30 65 118 170
6-8,10 8 16 24 55 93 130
9,11-Horror/SciFi-c 9 18 27 63 112 160
12-20 6 12 18 42 69 95
21(7/63)-30 5 10 15 35 55 75
31-34,36-38,40,41 4 8 12 28 44 60
35,39-Horror/Sci-Fi-c 6 12 18 39 62 85
42-Pureheart begins (1st app.-c/s, 10/65) 8 16 24 55 93 130
43,44 6 12 18 37 59 80
45(1/66) 1st Man From R.I.V.E.R.D.A.L.E. 7 14 21 46 76 105
46-Origin Pureheart 6 12 18 39 62 85
47-49 4 8 12 28 44 60
50-United Three begin: Pureheart (Archie), Superteen (Betty), Captain Hero (Jughead) 6 12 18 41 66 90
51-59: 59-Pureheart ends 4 8 12 28 44 60
60-Archie band begins, ends #66 6 12 18 37 59 80
61-66: 61-Man From R.I.V.E.R.D.A.L.E.-c/s 4 8 12 24 37 50
67-80 3 6 9 17 25 32
81-99 3 6 9 16 22 28
100 (8/70), 113-Sabrina & Salem app. 3 6 9 19 29 38
101-112, 114-130(2/73), 139(11/73)-Archie Band c/s 2 4 6 11 16 20
131,134-138,140-146,148-161,164-170(6/76) 2 4 6 9 12 15
132,133,147,163-all horror-c/s 3 6 9 14 20 26
162-UFO c/s 3 6 9 14 19 24
171,173-175,177-184,186,189,191-194,196 2 3 4 6 8 10
172,185,197 : 172-(9/77)-Bi-Cent. spec. ish, 185-2nd 24th cent.-c/s, 197-Time machine/SF-c/s 2 4 6 8 10 12
176(12/76)-1st app. Capt. Archie of Starship Rivda, in 24th century c/s; 1st app. Stella the Robot 3 6 9 14 19 24
187,188,195,198,199-all horror-c/s 2 4 6 9 13 16
190-1st Dr. Doom-c/s 2 4 6 9 13 16
200 (12/78) Maltese Pigeon-s 2 4 6 8 11 14
201-203,205-237,239,240(1/84): 208-Reintro Veronica 1 2 3 5 6 8
204-Flying saucer-c/s 2 3 4 6 8 10
238-(9/83)-25th anniversary issue; Ol' Betsy (jalopy) replaced 1 2 3 5 7 9
241-278,280-285: 250-Comic book convention-s 5.00
279,286: 279-Intro Mustang Sally ($1.00, 7/90) 6.00
NOTE: *Gene Colan a-272-279, 285, 286. Horror/Sci-Fi-c 9, 11, 35, 39, 162.*

LIFE WITH ARCHIE (The Married Life) (Magazine)
Archie Publications: Sept, 2010 - Present ($3.99, magazine-size)
1-15,17-20: Continuation of Married Life stories from Archie #600-605; articles/interviews 4.00
16-Kevin Keller gay wedding 12.00

LIFE WITH MILLIE (Formerly A Date With Millie) (Modeling With Millie #21 on)
Atlas/Marvel Comics Group: No. 8, Dec, 1960 - No. 20, Dec, 1962
8-Teenage 9 18 27 61 106 150
9-11 7 14 21 44 72 100
12-20 6 12 18 41 66 90

LIFE WITH SNARKY PARKER (TV)
Fox Feature Syndicate: Aug, 1950
1-Early TV comic; photo-c from TV puppet show 27 54 81 160 263 365

LIGHT AND DARKNESS WAR, THE
Marvel Comics (Epic Comics): Oct, 1988 - No. 6, Dec, 1989 ($1.95, lim. series)
1-6 3.00

LIGHT BRIGADE, THE
DC Comics: 2004 - No. 4, 2004 ($5.95, limited series)
1-4-Archangels in World War II; Tomasi-s/Snejbjerg-a 6.00
TPB (2005, 2009, $19.99) r/series; cover galery 20.00

LIGHT FANTASTIC, THE (Terry Pratchett's)
Innovation Publishing: June, 1992 - No. 4, Sept, 1992 ($2.50, mini-series)
1-4: Adapts 2nd novel in Discworld series 3.00

LIGHT IN THE FOREST (Disney)
Dell Publishing Co.: No. 891, Mar, 1958
Four Color 891-Movie, Fess Parker photo-c 7 14 21 49 82 115

LIGHTNING COMICS (Formerly Sure-Fire No. 1-3)
Ace Magazines: No. 4, Dec, 1940 - No. 13(V3#1), June, 1942
4-Characters continue from Sure-Fire 103 206 309 659 1130 1600
5,6: 6-Dr. Nemesis begins 71 142 213 454 777 1100
V2#1-6: 2- "Flash Lightning" becomes "Lash..." 56 112 168 356 611 865
V3#1-Intro. Lightning Girl & The Sword 56 112 168 356 611 865
NOTE: *Anderson a-V2#6. Mooney c-V1#5, 6, V2#1-6, V3#1. Bondage c-V2#6. Lightning-c on all.*

LIGHTNING COMICS PRESENTS
Lightning Comics: May, 1994 ($3.50)
1-Red foil-c distr. by Diamond Distr., 1-Black/yellow/blue-c distrib. by Capital Distr., 1-Red/yellow-c distributed by H. World, 1-Platinum 3.50

LI'L ... (These titles are listed under Little ...)

LILI
Image Comics: No. 0, 1999 ($4.95, B&W)
0-Bendis & Yanover-s 5.00

LILLITH (See Warrior Nun...)
Antarctic Press: Sept, 1996 - No. 3, Feb, 1997 ($2.95, limited series)
1-3: 1-Variant-c 3.00

LIMITED COLLECTORS' EDITION (See Famous First Edition, Marvel Treasury #28, Rudolph The Red-Nosed Reindeer, & Superman Vs. The Amazing Spider-Man; becomes All-New Collectors' Edition)
National Periodical Publications/DC Comics:
(#21-34,51-59: 84 pgs.; #35-41: 68 pgs.; #42-50: 60 pgs.)
C-21, Summer, 1973 - No. C-59, 1978 ($1.00) (10x13-1/2")
(Rudolph...C-20 (implied), 12/72)-See Rudolph The Red-Nosed Reindeer
C-21: Shazam (TV); r/Captain Marvel Jr. #11 by Raboy; C.C. Beck-c, biog. & photo 3 6 9 20 30 40
C-22: Tarzan; complete origin reprinted from #207-210; all Kubert-c/a; Joe Kubert biography & photo inside 3 6 9 17 25 32
C-23: House of Mystery; Wrightson, N. Adams/Orlando, G. Kane/Wood, Toth, Aragones, Sparling reprints 4 8 12 24 37 50
C-24: Rudolph The Red-Nosed Reindeer 7 14 21 45 73 100
C-25: Batman; Neal Adams-c/a(r); G.A. Joker-r; Batman/Enemy Ace-r; Novick-a(r); has photos from TV show 4 8 12 26 41 55
C-26: See Famous First Edition C-26 (same contents)
C-27,C-29,C-31: C-27: Shazam (TV); G.A. Capt. Marvel & Mary Marvel-r; Beck-r. C-29: Tarzan; reprints "Return of Tarzan" from #219-223 by Kubert; Kubert-c. C-31: Superman; origin-r; Giordano-a; photos of George Reeves from 1950s TV show on inside b/c; Burnley, Boring-r 3 6 9 16 23 30
C-32: Ghosts (new-a) 4 8 12 22 34 45
C-33: Rudolph The Red-Nosed Reindeer(new-a) 6 12 18 41 66 90
C-34: Christmas with the Super-Heroes; unpublished Angel & Ape story by Oksner & Wood; Batman & Teen Titans-r 3 6 9 16 23 30
C-35: Shazam (TV); photo cover features TV's Captain Marvel, Jackson Bostwick; Beck-r; TV photos inside b/c 3 6 9 16 22 28
C-36: The Bible; all new adaptation beginning with Genesis by Kubert, Redondo & Mayer; Kubert-c 3 6 9 16 22 28
C-37: Batman; r-1946 Sundays; inside b/c photos of Batman TV show villains (all villain issue; r/G.A. Joker, Catwoman, Penguin, Two-Face, & Scarecrow stories plus 1946 Sundays-r)

Linda #4 © AJAX

Li'l Abner #73 © TOBY

Little Archie #38 © AP

	GD 2.0	VG 4.0	FN 6.0	VF 8.0	VF/NM 9.0	NM- 9.2
	3	6	9	18	27	35
C-38: Superman; 1 pg. N. Adams; part photo-c; photos from TV show on inside back-c	3	6	9	16	22	28
C-39: Secret Origins of Super-Villains; N. Adams-i(r); collection reprints 1950's Joker origin, Luthor origin from Adv. Comics #271, Captain Cold origin from Showcase #8 among others; G.A. Batman-r; Beck-r	3	6	9	16	22	28
C-40: Dick Tracy by Gould featuring Flattop; newspaper-r from 12/21/43 - 5/17/44; biog. of Chester Gould	3	6	9	16	22	28
C-41: Super Friends (TV); JLA-r(1965); Toth-c/a	3	6	9	16	23	30
C-42: Rudolph	4	8	12	28	44	60
C-43-C-47: C-43: Christmas with the Super-Heroes; Wrightson, S&K, Neal Adams-a. C-44: Batman; N. Adams-p(r) & G.A.-r; painted-c. C-45: More Secret Origins of Super-Villains; Flash-r/#105; G.A. Wonder Woman & Batman/Catwoman-r. C-46: Justice League of America(1963-r); 3 pgs. Toth-a C-47: Superman Salutes the Bicentennial (Tomahawk interior); 2 pgs. new-a	3	6	9	14	20	26
C-48,C-49: C-48: Superman Vs. The Flash (Superman/Flash race); swipes-c to Superman #199; r/Superman #199 & Flash #175; 6 pgs. Neal Adams-a. C-49: Superboy & the Legion of Super-Heroes	3	6	9	16	23	30
C-50: Rudolph The Red-Nosed Reindeer; contains poster (1/2 price if poster is missing)	4	8	12	28	44	60
C-51: Batman; Neal Adams-c/a	3	6	9	17	25	32
C-52,C-57: C-52: The Best of DC; Neal Adams-c/a; Toth, Kubert-a. C-57: Welcome Back, Kotter-r(TV)(5/78) includes unpublished #11	3	6	9	16	22	28
C-53 thru C-56, C-58, C-60 thru C-62 (See All-New Collectors' Edition)						
C-59: Batman's Strangest Cases; N. Adams-r; Wrightson-r/Swamp Thing #7; N. Adams/Wrightson-c	3	6	9	16	22	28

NOTE: *All-r with exception of some special features and covers.* ***Aparo*** *a-52r; c-37.* ***Grell*** *c-49.* ***Infantino*** *a-25, 39, 44, 45, 52.* ***Bob Kane*** *r-25.* ***Robinson*** *r-25, 44.* ***Sprang*** *r-44. Issues #21-31, 35-39, 45, 48 have back cover cut-outs.*

LINDA (Everybody Loves...) (Phantom Lady No. 5 on)
Ajax-Farrell Publ. Co.: Apr-May, 1954 - No. 4, Oct-Nov, 1954

	GD 2.0	VG 4.0	FN 6.0	VF 8.0	VF/NM 9.0	NM- 9.2
1-Kamenish-a	15	30	45	85	130	175
2-Lingerie panel	13	26	39	72	101	130
3,4	10	20	30	56	76	95

LINDA CARTER, STUDENT NURSE
Atlas Comics (AMI): Sept, 1961 - No. 9, Jan, 1963

	GD 2.0	VG 4.0	FN 6.0	VF 8.0	VF/NM 9.0	NM- 9.2
1-Al Hartley-c	7	14	21	44	72	100
2-9	5	10	15	30	48	65

LINDA LARK
Dell Publishing Co.: Oct-Dec, 1961 - No. 8, Aug-Oct, 1963

	GD 2.0	VG 4.0	FN 6.0	VF 8.0	VF/NM 9.0	NM- 9.2
1	3	6	9	19	29	38
2-8	3	6	9	14	19	24

LINUS, THE LIONHEARTED (TV)
Gold Key: Sept, 1965

	GD 2.0	VG 4.0	FN 6.0	VF 8.0	VF/NM 9.0	NM- 9.2
1 (10155-509)	7	14	21	44	72	100

LION, THE (See Movie Comics)

LIONHEART
Awesome Comics: Sept, 1999 - No. 2, Dec, 1999 ($2.99/$2.50)

	GD 2.0	VG 4.0	FN 6.0	VF 8.0	VF/NM 9.0	NM- 9.2
1-Ian Churchill-story/a, Jeph Loeb-s; Coven app.						3.50
2-Flip book w/Coven #4						3.00

LION OF SPARTA (See Movie Classics)

LIPPY THE LION AND HARDY HAR HAR (TV)
Gold Key: Mar, 1963 (12¢) (See Hanna-Barbera Band Wagon #1)

	GD 2.0	VG 4.0	FN 6.0	VF 8.0	VF/NM 9.0	NM- 9.2
1 (10049-303)	8	16	24	53	89	125

LISA COMICS (TV)(See Simpsons Comics)
Bongo Comics: 1995 ($2.25)

	GD 2.0	VG 4.0	FN 6.0	VF 8.0	VF/NM 9.0	NM- 9.2
1-Lisa in Wonderland						3.00

LITERALS, THE (See Fables and Jack of Fables)
DC Comics (Vertigo): June, 2009 - No. 3, Aug, 2009 ($2.99)

	GD 2.0	VG 4.0	FN 6.0	VF 8.0	VF/NM 9.0	NM- 9.2
1-3-Crossover with Fables #83-85 and Jack of Fables #33-35; Buckingham-c/a						3.00

LI'L ABNER (See Comics on Parade, Sparkle, Sparkler Comics, Tip Top Comics & Tip Topper)
United Features Syndicate: 1939 - 1940

	GD 2.0	VG 4.0	FN 6.0	VF 8.0	VF/NM 9.0	NM- 9.2
Single Series 4 ('39)	81	162	243	518	884	1250
Single Series 18 ('40) (#18 on inside, #2 on-c)	61	122	183	390	670	950

LI'L ABNER (Al Capp's; continued from Comics on Parade #58)
Harvey Publ. No. 61-69 (2/49)/Toby Press No. 70 on: No. 61, Dec, 1947 - No. 97, Jan, 1955
(See Oxydol-Dreft in Promotional Comics section)

	GD 2.0	VG 4.0	FN 6.0	VF 8.0	VF/NM 9.0	NM- 9.2
61(#1)-Wolverton & Powell-a	23	46	69	136	223	310
62-65: 63-The Wolf Girl app. 65-Powell-a	15	30	45	85	130	175
66,67,69,70	14	28	42	82	121	160
68-Full length Fearless Fosdick-c/story	15	30	45	88	137	185
71-74,76,80	13	26	39	74	105	135
75,77-79,86,91-All with Kurtzman art; 86-Sadie Hawkins Day. 91-r/#77	15	30	45	83	124	165
81-85,87-90,92-94,96,97: 83-Evil-Eye Fleegle & Double Whammy app. 88-Cousin Weakeyes goes hunting. 94-Six lessons from Adam Lazonga. 96-Football issue	12	24	36	69	97	125
95-Full length Fearless Fosdick story	14	28	42	76	108	140

LI'L ABNER
Toby Press: 1951

	GD 2.0	VG 4.0	FN 6.0	VF 8.0	VF/NM 9.0	NM- 9.2
1	18	36	54	103	162	220

LI'L ABNER'S DOGPATCH (See Al Capp's...)

LITTLE AL OF THE F.B.I.
Ziff-Davis Publications: No. 10, 1950 (no month) - No. 11, Apr-May, 1951 (Saunders painted-c)

	GD 2.0	VG 4.0	FN 6.0	VF 8.0	VF/NM 9.0	NM- 9.2
10(1950)	17	34	51	98	154	210
11(1951)	14	28	42	80	115	150

LITTLE AL OF THE SECRET SERVICE
Ziff-Davis Publications: No. 10, 7-8/51; No, 2, 9-10/51; No. 3, Winter, 1951 (Saunders painted-c)

	GD 2.0	VG 4.0	FN 6.0	VF 8.0	VF/NM 9.0	NM- 9.2
10(#1)	16	32	48	92	144	195
2,3	14	28	42	76	108	140

LITTLE AMBROSE
Archie Publications: September, 1958

	GD 2.0	VG 4.0	FN 6.0	VF 8.0	VF/NM 9.0	NM- 9.2
1-Bob Bolling-c	15	30	45	85	130	175

LITTLE ANGEL
Standard (Visual Editions)/Pines: No. 5, Sept, 1954; No. 6, Sept, 1955 - No. 16, Sept, 1959

	GD 2.0	VG 4.0	FN 6.0	VF 8.0	VF/NM 9.0	NM- 9.2
5-Last pre-code issue	8	16	24	40	50	60
6-16	5	10	15	24	30	35

LITTLE ANNIE ROONEY (Also see Henry)
David McKay Publ.: 1935 (25¢, B&W dailies, 48 pgs.)(10"x10", cardboard-c)

	GD 2.0	VG 4.0	FN 6.0	VF 8.0	VF/NM 9.0	NM- 9.2
Book 1-Daily strip-r by Darrell McClure	38	76	114	226	368	510

LITTLE ANNIE ROONEY (See King Comics & Treasury of Comics)
David McKay/St. John/Standard: 1938; Aug, 1948 - No. 3, Oct, 1948

	GD 2.0	VG 4.0	FN 6.0	VF 8.0	VF/NM 9.0	NM- 9.2
Feature Books 11 (McKay, 1938)	39	78	117	231	378	525
1 (St. John)	15	30	45	88	137	185
2,3	10	20	30	54	72	90

LITTLE ARCHIE (The Adventures of... #13-on) (See Archie Giant Series Mag. #527, 534, 538, 545, 549, 556, 560, 566, 570, 583, 594, 596, 607, 609, 619)
Archie Publications: 1956 - No. 180, Feb, 1983 (Giants No. 3-84)

	GD 2.0	VG 4.0	FN 6.0	VF 8.0	VF/NM 9.0	NM- 9.2
1-(Scarce)	59	118	177	478	1039	1600
2 (1957)	24	48	72	168	359	550
3-5: 3-(1958)-Bob Bolling-c & giant issues begin	14	28	42	93	202	310
6-10	11	22	33	73	142	210
11-17,19,21 (84 pgs.)	9	18	27	58	99	140
18,20,22 (84 pgs.)-Horror/Sci-Fi-c	10	20	30	67	124	180
23-39 (68 pgs.)	7	14	21	44	72	100
40 (Fall/66)-Intro. Little Pureheart-c/s (68 pgs.)	7	14	21	48	79	110
41,44-Little Pureheart (68 pgs.)	6	12	18	42	69	95
42-Intro The Little Archies Band, ends #66 (68 pgs.)	7	14	21	46	76	105
43-1st Boy From R.I.V.E.R.D.A.L.E. (68 pgs.)	7	14	21	44	72	100
45-58 (68 pgs.)	5	10	15	35	55	75
59 (68 pgs.)-Little Sabrina begins	8	16	24	55	93	130
60-66 (68 pgs.)	4	8	12	28	44	60
67(9/71)-84: 84-Last 52pg. Giant-Size (2/74)	3	6	9	18	27	35
85-99	2	4	6	10	14	18
100	2	4	6	13	18	22
101-112,114-116,118-129	2	4	6	8	10	12
113,117,130: 113-Halloween Special issue(12/76). 117-Donny Osmond-c cameo 130-UFO cover (5/78)	2	4	6	9	13	16
131-150(1/80), 180(Last issue, 2/83)	1	2	3	5	7	9
151-179						5.00
...In Animal Land 1 (1957)	12	24	36	83	172	260
...In Animal Land 17 (Winter, 1957-58)-19 (Summer,1958)-Formerly Li'l Jinx	8	16	24	55	93	130
Archie Classics - The Adventures of Little Archie Vol. 1 TPB (2004, $10.95) reprints						11.00
Vol. 2 TPB (2008, $9.95) reprints plus new 22 pg. story with Bolling-s/a						10.00

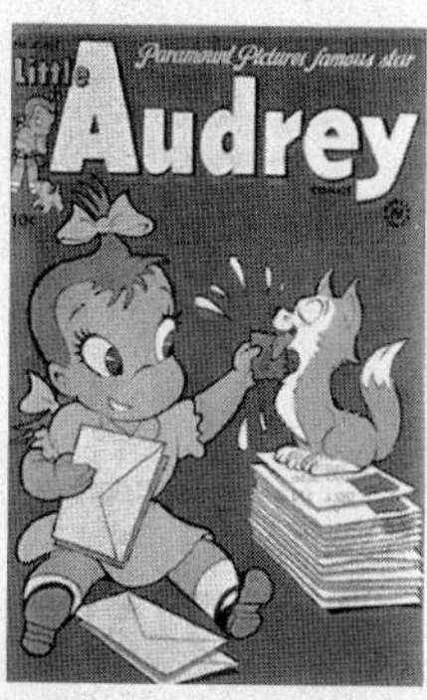

Little Audrey #27 © HARV

Li'l Depressed Boy #4 © S. Steven Struble

Little Dot #4 © HARV

NOTE: *Little Archie Band app. 42-66. Little Sabrina in 59-78,80-180*

LITTLE ARCHIE CHRISTMAS SPECIAL (See Archie Giant Series #581)

LITTLE ARCHIE COMICS DIGEST ANNUAL (...Magazine #5 on)
Archie Publications: 10/77 - No. 48, 5/91 (Digest-size, 128 pgs., later issues $1.35-$1.50)

	GD 2.0	VG 4.0	FN 6.0	VF 8.0	VF/NM 9.0	NM- 9.2
1(10/77)-Reprints	3	6	9	20	30	40
2(4/78,3(11/78)-Neal Adams-a. 3-The Fly-r by S&K	3	6	9	14	20	26
4(4/79) - 10	2	4	6	10	14	18
11-20	2	4	6	8	10	12
21-30: 28-Christmas-c	1	2	3	5	6	8
31-48: 40,46-Christmas-c						5.00

NOTE: *Little Archie, Little Jinx, Little Jughead & Little Sabrina in most issues.*

LITTLE ARCHIE DIGEST MAGAZINE
Archie Comics: July, 1991 - No. 21, Mar, 1998 ($1.50/$1.79/$1.89, digest size, bi-annual)

	GD 2.0	VG 4.0	FN 6.0	VF 8.0	VF/NM 9.0	NM- 9.2
V2#1						6.00
2-10						4.00
11-21						3.00

LITTLE ARCHIE MYSTERY
Archie Publications: Aug, 1963 - No. 2, Oct, 1963 (12¢ issues)

	GD 2.0	VG 4.0	FN 6.0	VF 8.0	VF/NM 9.0	NM- 9.2
1	11	22	33	71	136	200
2	7	14	21	44	72	100

LITTLE ASPIRIN (See Little Lenny & Wisco)
Marvel Comics (CnPC): July, 1949 - No. 3, Dec, 1949 (52 pgs.)

	GD 2.0	VG 4.0	FN 6.0	VF 8.0	VF/NM 9.0	NM- 9.2
1-Oscar app.; Kurtzman-a (4 pgs.)	17	34	51	98	154	210
2-Kurtzman-a (4 pgs.)	11	22	33	60	83	105
3-No Kurtzman-a	9	18	27	47	61	75

LITTLE AUDREY (Also see Playful...)
St. John Publ.: Apr, 1948 - No. 24, May, 1952

	GD 2.0	VG 4.0	FN 6.0	VF 8.0	VF/NM 9.0	NM- 9.2
1-1st app. Little Audrey	58	116	174	371	636	900
2	28	56	84	165	270	375
3-5	19	38	57	111	176	240
6-10	14	28	42	82	121	160
11-20: 16-X-Mas-c	11	22	33	62	86	110
21-24	10	20	30	54	72	90

LITTLE AUDREY (See Harvey Hits #11, 19)
Harvey Publications: No. 25, Aug, 1952 - No. 53, April, 1957

	GD 2.0	VG 4.0	FN 6.0	VF 8.0	VF/NM 9.0	NM- 9.2
25-(Paramount Pictures Famous Star... on-c); 1st Harvey Casper and Baby Huey (1 month earlier than Harvey Comic Hits #60(9/52))	13	26	39	90	195	300
26-30: 26-28-Casper app.	8	16	24	56	96	135
31-40: 32-35-Casper app.	7	14	21	46	76	105
41-53	5	10	15	34	55	75
...Clubhouse 1 (9/61, 68 pg. Giant)-New stories & reprints	9	18	27	58	99	140

LITTLE AUDREY
Harvey Comics: Aug, 1992 - No. 8, July, 1994 ($1.25/$1.50)

	GD 2.0	VG 4.0	FN 6.0	VF 8.0	VF/NM 9.0	NM- 9.2
V2#1						3.50
2-8						3.00

LITTLE AUDREY (...Yearbook)
St. John Publishing Co.: 1950 (50¢, 260 pgs.)

	GD 2.0	VG 4.0	FN 6.0	VF 8.0	VF/NM 9.0	NM- 9.2
Contains 8 complete 1949 comics rebound; Casper, Alice in Wonderland, Little Audrey, Abbott & Costello, Pinocchio, Moon Mullins, Three Stooges (from Jubilee), Little Annie Rooney app. (Rare)	129	258	387	826	1413	2000

(Also see All Good & Treasury of Comics)
NOTE: *This book contains remaindered St. John comics; many variations possible.*

LITTLE AUDREY & MELVIN (Audrey & Melvin No. 62)
Harvey Publications: May, 1962 - No. 61, Dec, 1973

	GD 2.0	VG 4.0	FN 6.0	VF 8.0	VF/NM 9.0	NM- 9.2
1	10	20	30	65	118	170
2-5	6	12	18	39	62	85
6-10	5	10	15	30	48	65
11-20	3	6	9	19	29	38
21-40: 22-Richie Rich app.	3	6	9	14	20	26
41-50,55-61	2	4	6	11	16	20
51-54: All 52 pg. Giants	3	6	9	14	20	26

LITTLE AUDREY TV FUNTIME
Harvey Publ.: Sept, 1962 - No. 33, Oct, 1971 (#1-31: 68 pgs.; #32,33: 52 pgs.)

	GD 2.0	VG 4.0	FN 6.0	VF 8.0	VF/NM 9.0	NM- 9.2
1-Richie Rich app.	10	20	30	65	118	170
2,3: Richie Rich app.	6	12	18	39	62	85
4,5: 5-25¢ & 35¢ issues exist	5	10	15	32	51	70
6-10	3	6	9	21	32	42
11-20	3	6	9	16	23	28
21-33	3	6	9	14	19	24

LITTLE BAD WOLF (Disney; see Walt Disney's C&S #52, Walt Disney Showcase #21 & Wheaties)
Dell Publishing Co.: No. 403, June, 1952 - No. 564, June, 1954

	GD 2.0	VG 4.0	FN 6.0	VF 8.0	VF/NM 9.0	NM- 9.2
Four Color 403 (#1)	7	14	21	46	76	105
Four Color 473 (6/53), 564	5	10	15	32	51	70

LITTLE BEAVER
Dell Publishing Co.: No. 211, Jan, 1949 - No. 870, Jan, 1958 (All painted-c)

	GD 2.0	VG 4.0	FN 6.0	VF 8.0	VF/NM 9.0	NM- 9.2
Four Color 211('49)-All Harman-a	8	16	24	55	93	130
Four Color 267,294,332(5/51)	5	10	15	35	55	75
3(10-12/51)-8(1-3/53)	5	10	15	32	51	70
Four Color 483(8-10/53),529	5	10	15	30	48	65
Four Color 612,660,695,744,817,870	5	10	15	30	48	65

LITTLE BIT
Jubilee/St. John Publishing Co.: Mar, 1949 - No. 2, June, 1949

	GD 2.0	VG 4.0	FN 6.0	VF 8.0	VF/NM 9.0	NM- 9.2
1-Kid humor	10	20	30	58	79	100
2	8	16	24	42	54	65

LI'L DEPRESSED BOY
Image Comics: Feb, 2011 - Present ($2.99)

	GD 2.0	VG 4.0	FN 6.0	VF 8.0	VF/NM 9.0	NM- 9.2
1-9-S. Steven Struble-s/Sina Grace-a. 5-Guillory-c. 6-Adlard-c. 7-Rolston-c						3.00
Vol. 0 (12/11, $9.99) reprints earlier stories from webcomics & anthologies; various-a						10.00

LITTLE DOT (See Humphrey, Li'l Max, Sad Sack, and Tastee-Freez Comics)
Harvey Publications: Sept, 1953 - No. 164, Apr, 1976

	GD 2.0	VG 4.0	FN 6.0	VF 8.0	VF/NM 9.0	NM- 9.2
1-Intro./1st app. Richie Rich & Little Lotta	343	686	1029	2400	4200	6000
2-1st app. Freckles & Pee Wee (Richie Rich's poor friends)	110	220	330	704	1202	1700
3	68	136	204	435	743	1050
4	61	122	183	390	670	950
5-Origin dots on Little Dot's dress	68	136	204	435	743	1050
6-Richie Rich, Little Lotta, & Little Dot all on cover; 1st Richie Rich cover featured	68	136	204	435	743	1050
7-10: 9-Last pre-code issue (1/55)	40	80	120	246	411	575
11-20	28	56	84	165	270	375
21-30	18	36	54	105	165	225
31-40	14	28	42	80	115	150
41-50	11	22	33	62	86	110
51-60	9	18	27	52	69	85
61-80	4	8	12	28	44	60
81-100	3	6	9	20	30	40
101-141	3	6	9	16	23	30
142-145: All 52 pg. Giants	3	6	9	18	27	35
146-164	2	4	6	11	16	20

NOTE: *Richie Rich & Little Lotta in all.*

LITTLE DOT
Harvey Comics: Sept, 1992 - No. 7, June, 1994 ($1.25/$1.50)

	GD 2.0	VG 4.0	FN 6.0	VF 8.0	VF/NM 9.0	NM- 9.2
V2#1-Little Dot, Little Lotta, Richie Rich in all						3.50
2-7 ($1.50)						3.00

LITTLE DOT DOTLAND (Dot Dotland No. 62, 63)
Harvey Publications: July, 1962 - No. 61, Dec, 1973

	GD 2.0	VG 4.0	FN 6.0	VF 8.0	VF/NM 9.0	NM- 9.2
1-Richie Rich begins	12	24	36	79	160	240
2,3	8	16	24	51	86	120
4,5	6	12	18	41	66	90
6-10	5	10	15	32	51	70
11-20	4	8	12	24	37	50
21-30	3	6	9	18	27	35
31-50	3	6	9	16	23	30
51-54: All 52 pg. Giants	3	6	9	18	27	35
55-61	2	4	6	11	16	20

LITTLE DOT'S UNCLES & AUNTS (See Harvey Hits No. 4, 13, 24)
Harvey Enterprises: Oct, 1961; No. 2, Aug, 1962 - No. 52, Apr, 1974

	GD 2.0	VG 4.0	FN 6.0	VF 8.0	VF/NM 9.0	NM- 9.2
1-Richie Rich begins; 68 pgs. begin	13	26	39	86	183	280
2,3	9	18	27	58	99	140
4,5	6	12	18	41	66	90
6-10	5	10	15	34	55	75
11-20	4	8	12	24	37	50
21-37: Last 68 pg. issue	3	6	9	19	29	38
38-52: All 52 pg. Giants	3	6	9	16	23	30

LITTLE DRACULA

Little Eva #3 © STJ

Li'l Genius #55 © CC

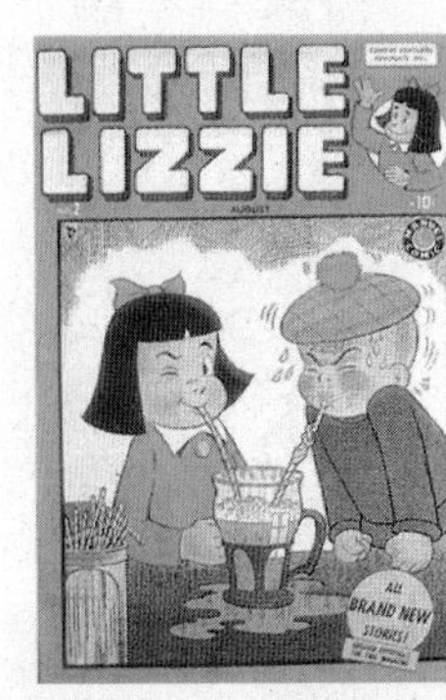

Little Lizzie #2 © MAR

Harvey Comics: Jan, 1992 - No. 3, May, 1992 ($1.25, quarterly, mini-series)

	GD 2.0	VG 4.0	FN 6.0	VF 8.0	VF/NM 9.0	NM- 9.2
1-3						3.00

LITTLE ENDLESS STORYBOOK, THE (See The Sandman titles and Delirium's Party)
DC Comics: 2001 ($5.95, Prestige format, one-shot)

	GD 2.0	VG 4.0	FN 6.0	VF 8.0	VF/NM 9.0	NM- 9.2
nn-Jill Thompson-s/painted-a/c; puppy Barnabas searches for Delirium						20.00
HC (2011, $14.99) r/story plus original character sketches and merchandise design						15.00

LITTLE EVA
St. John Publishing Co.: May, 1952 - No. 31, Nov, 1956

	GD 2.0	VG 4.0	FN 6.0	VF 8.0	VF/NM 9.0	NM- 9.2
1	16	32	48	94	147	200
2	10	20	30	58	79	100
3-5	9	18	27	47	61	75
6-10	8	16	24	42	54	65
11-31	7	14	21	37	46	55
3-D 1,2(10/53, 11/53, 25¢)-Both came w/glasses. 1-Infinity-c	18	36	54	107	169	230
I.W. Reprint #1-3,6-8: 1-r/Little Eva #28. 2-r/Little Eva #29. 3-r/Little Eva #24	2	4	6	8	11	14
Super Reprint #10,12('63),14,16,18('64): 18-r/Little Eva #25.	2	4	6	8	11	14

LI'L GENIUS (Formerly Super Brat; Summer Fun No. 54) (See Blue Bird & Giant Comics #3)
Charlton Comics: No. 6, 1954 - No. 52, 1/65; No. 53, 10/65; No. 54, 10/85 - No. 55, 1/86

	GD 2.0	VG 4.0	FN 6.0	VF 8.0	VF/NM 9.0	NM- 9.2
6 (#1)	11	22	33	62	86	110
7-10	7	14	21	37	46	55
11-1st app. Li'l Tomboy (10/56); same month as 1st issue of Li'l Tomboy (V14#92)	4	8	12	22	34	45
12-15,19,20	6	12	18	29	36	42
16,17-(68 pgs.)	8	16	24	40	50	60
18-(100 pgs., 10/58)	11	22	33	60	83	105
21-35: 34-Atomic bomb explosion	3	6	9	16	22	28
36-53	2	4	6	10	14	18
54,55 (Low print)						5.00

LI'L GHOST
St. John Publ. Co./Fago No. 1 on: 2/58; No. 2,1/59 - No. 3, Mar, 1959

	GD 2.0	VG 4.0	FN 6.0	VF 8.0	VF/NM 9.0	NM- 9.2
1(St. John)	9	18	27	50	65	80
2,3	6	12	18	28	34	40

LITTLE GIANT COMICS
Centaur Publications: 7/38 - No. 3, 10/38; No. 4, 2/39 (132 pgs.) (6-3/4x4-1/2")

	GD 2.0	VG 4.0	FN 6.0	VF 8.0	VF/NM 9.0	NM- 9.2
1-B&W with color-c; stories, puzzles, magic	135	270	405	864	1482	2100
2,3-B&W with color-c	90	180	270	576	988	1400
4 (6-5/8x9-3/8")(68 pgs., B&W inside)	90	180	270	576	988	1400

NOTE: *Filchock c-2, 4. Gustavson a-1. Pinajian a-4. Bob Wood a-1.*

LITTLE GIANT DETECTIVE FUNNIES
Centaur Publ.: Oct, 1938; No. 4, Jan, 1939 (6-3/4x4-1/2", 132 pgs., B&W)

	GD 2.0	VG 4.0	FN 6.0	VF 8.0	VF/NM 9.0	NM- 9.2
1-B&W with color-c	135	270	405	864	1482	2100
4(1/39, B&W; color-c; 68 pgs., 6-1/2x9-1/2")-Eisner-r	90	180	270	576	988	1400

LITTLE GIANT MOVIE FUNNIES
Centaur Publ.: Aug, 1938 - No. 2, Oct, 1938 (6-3/4x4-1/2", 132 pgs., B&W)

	GD 2.0	VG 4.0	FN 6.0	VF 8.0	VF/NM 9.0	NM- 9.2
1-Ed Wheelan's "Minute Movies" reprints	135	270	405	864	1482	2100
2-Ed Wheelan's "Minute Movies" reprints	90	180	270	576	988	1400

LITTLE GROUCHO (...the Red-Headed Tornado; ...Grouchy No. 2)
Reston Publ. Co.: No. 16; Feb-Mar, 1955 - No. 2, June-July, 1955 (See Tippy Terry)

	GD 2.0	VG 4.0	FN 6.0	VF 8.0	VF/NM 9.0	NM- 9.2
16, 1 (2-3/55)	8	16	24	42	54	65
2(6-7/55)	6	12	18	27	33	38

LITTLE HIAWATHA (Disney; see Walt Disney's C&S #143)
Dell Publishing Co.: No. 439, Dec, 1952 - No. 988, May-July, 1959

	GD 2.0	VG 4.0	FN 6.0	VF 8.0	VF/NM 9.0	NM- 9.2
Four Color 439 (#1)	6	12	18	39	62	85
Four Color 787 (4/57), 901 (5/58), 988	5	10	15	30	48	65

LITTLE IKE
St. John Publishing Co.: April, 1953 - No. 4, Oct, 1953

	GD 2.0	VG 4.0	FN 6.0	VF 8.0	VF/NM 9.0	NM- 9.2
1-Kid humor	10	20	30	54	72	90
2	6	12	18	31	38	45
3,4	5	10	15	24	30	35

LITTLE IODINE (See Giant Comic Album)
Dell Publ. Co.: No. 224, 4/49 - No. 257, 1949; 3-5/50 - No. 56, 4-6/62 (1-4-52pgs.)

	GD 2.0	VG 4.0	FN 6.0	VF 8.0	VF/NM 9.0	NM- 9.2
Four Color 224-By Jimmy Hatlo	11	22	33	76	151	225
Four Color 257	8	16	24	56	96	135
1(3-5/50)	10	20	30	65	118	170
2-5	6	12	18	39	62	85
6-10	5	10	15	30	48	65
11-20	4	8	12	24	37	50
21-30: 27-Xmas-c	4	8	12	22	34	45
31-40	3	6	9	20	30	40
41-56	3	6	9	18	27	35

LITTLE JACK FROST
Avon Periodicals: 1951

	GD 2.0	VG 4.0	FN 6.0	VF 8.0	VF/NM 9.0	NM- 9.2
1	12	24	36	67	94	120

LI'L JINX (Little Archie in Animal Land #17) (Also see Pep Comics #62)
Archie Publications: No. 1(#11), Nov, 1956 - No. 16, Sept, 1957

	GD 2.0	VG 4.0	FN 6.0	VF 8.0	VF/NM 9.0	NM- 9.2
1(#11)-By Joe Edwards; "First Issue" on cover	14	28	42	80	115	150
12(1/57)-16	10	20	30	54	72	90

LI'L JINX (See Archie Giant Series Magazine No. 223)

LI'L JINX CHRISTMAS BAG (See Archie Giant Series Mag. No. 195, 206, 219)

LI'L JINX GIANT LAUGH-OUT (See Archie Giant Series Mag. No. 176, 185)
Archie Publications: No. 33, Sept, 1971 - No. 43, Nov, 1973 (52 pgs.)

	GD 2.0	VG 4.0	FN 6.0	VF 8.0	VF/NM 9.0	NM- 9.2
33-43 (52 pgs.)	2	4	6	13	18	22

LITTLE JOE (See Popular Comics & Super Comics)
Dell Publishing Co.: No. 1, 1942

	GD 2.0	VG 4.0	FN 6.0	VF 8.0	VF/NM 9.0	NM- 9.2
Four Color 1	52	104	156	421	911	1400

LITTLE JOE
St. John Publishing Co.: Apr, 1953

	GD 2.0	VG 4.0	FN 6.0	VF 8.0	VF/NM 9.0	NM- 9.2
1	6	12	18	31	38	45

LI'L KIDS (Also see Li'l Pals)
Marvel Comics Group: 8/70 - No. 2, 10/70; No. 3, 11/71 - No. 12, 6/73

	GD 2.0	VG 4.0	FN 6.0	VF 8.0	VF/NM 9.0	NM- 9.2
1	8	16	24	53	89	125
2-9	4	8	12	28	44	60
10-12-Calvin app.	5	10	15	30	48	65

LITTLE KING
Dell Publishing Co.: No. 494, Aug, 1953 - No. 677, Feb, 1956

	GD 2.0	VG 4.0	FN 6.0	VF 8.0	VF/NM 9.0	NM- 9.2
Four Color 494 (#1)	9	18	27	58	99	140
Four Color 597, 677	5	10	15	35	55	75

LITTLE LANA (Formerly Lana)
Marvel Comics (MjMC): No. 8, Nov, 1949; No. 9, Mar, 1950

	GD 2.0	VG 4.0	FN 6.0	VF 8.0	VF/NM 9.0	NM- 9.2
8,9	13	26	39	74	105	135

LITTLE LENNY
Marvel Comics (CDS): June, 1949 - No. 3, Nov, 1949

	GD 2.0	VG 4.0	FN 6.0	VF 8.0	VF/NM 9.0	NM- 9.2
1-Little Aspirin app.	13	26	39	74	105	135
2,3	9	18	27	47	61	75

LITTLE LIZZIE
Marvel Comics (PrPl)/Atlas (OMC): 6/49 - No. 5, 4/50; 9/53 - No. 3, Jan, 1954

	GD 2.0	VG 4.0	FN 6.0	VF 8.0	VF/NM 9.0	NM- 9.2
1-Kid humor	14	28	42	82	121	160
2-5	9	18	27	50	65	80
1 (9/53, 2nd series by Atlas)-Howie Post-c	10	20	30	56	76	95
2,3	8	16	24	42	54	65

LITTLE LOTTA (See Harvey Hits No. 10)
Harvey Publications: 11/55 - No. 110, 11/73; No. 111, 9/74 - No. 120, 5/76
V2#1, Oct, 1992 - No. 4, July, 1993 ($1.25)

	GD 2.0	VG 4.0	FN 6.0	VF 8.0	VF/NM 9.0	NM- 9.2
1-Richie Rich (r) & Little Dot begin	36	72	108	270	585	900
2,3	15	30	45	104	227	350
4,5	11	22	33	73	142	210
6-10	8	16	24	53	89	125
11-20	6	12	18	41	66	90
21-40	4	8	12	24	37	50
41-60	3	6	9	19	29	38
61-80: 62-1st app. Nurse Jenny	3	6	9	16	22	28
81-99	2	4	6	11	16	20
100-103: All 52 pg. Giants	3	6	9	14	19	24
104-120	2	4	6	8	10	12
V2#1-4 (1992-93)						4.00

NOTE: *No. 121 was advertised, but never released.*

LITTLE LOTTA FOODLAND
Harvey Publications: 9/63 - No. 14, 10/67; No. 15, 10/68 - No. 29, Oct, 1972

	GD 2.0	VG 4.0	FN 6.0	VF 8.0	VF/NM 9.0	NM- 9.2
1-Little Lotta, Little Dot, Richie Rich, 68 pgs. begin	12	24	36	79	160	240

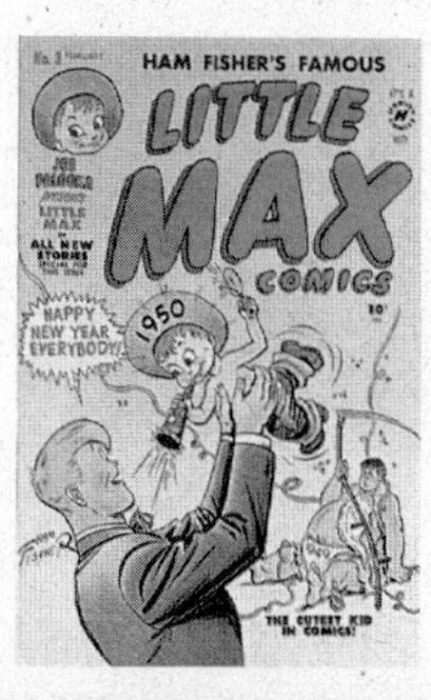

Little Max Comics #3 © HARV

Little Miss Muffet #12 © STD

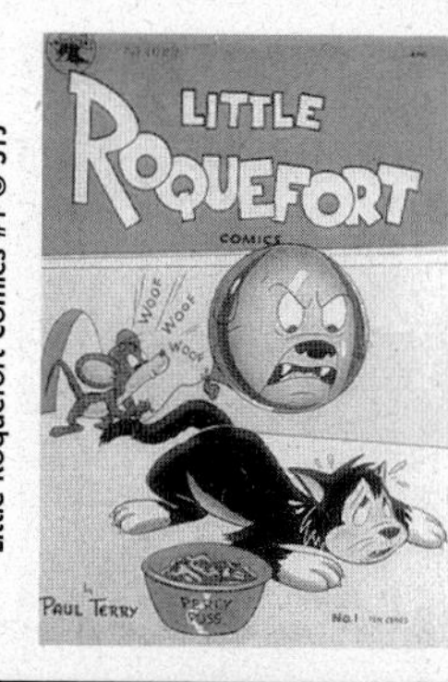

Little Roquefort Comics #1 © STJ

	GD 2.0	VG 4.0	FN 6.0	VF 8.0	VF/NM 9.0	NM- 9.2
2,3	9	18	27	58	99	140
4,5	7	14	21	44	72	100
6-10	5	10	15	32	51	70
11-20	3	6	9	20	30	40
21-26: 26-Last 68 pg. issue	3	6	9	16	23	30
27,28: Both 52 pgs.	3	6	9	14	19	24
29-(36 pgs.)	2	4	6	9	13	16

LITTLE LULU (Formerly Marge's Little Lulu)
Gold Key 207-257/Whitman 258 on: No. 207, Sept, 1972 - No. 268, Mar, 1984

	GD	VG	FN	VF	VF/NM	NM-
207,209,220-Stanley-r. 207-1st app. Henrietta	2	4	6	11	16	20
208,210-219: 208-1st app. Snobbly, Wilbur's butler	2	4	6	9	12	15
221-240,242-249, 250(r/#166), 251-254(r/#206)	1	3	4	6	8	10
241,263-Stanley-r	2	4	6	8	10	12
255-257(Gold Key): 256-r/#212	1	2	3	5	7	9
258,259,262(50¢-c),264(2/82),265(3/82) (Whitman)	2	4	6	9	13	16
260-(9/80)(Whitman pre-pack only - low distribution)	13	26	39	85	180	275
261-(11/80)(Whitman pre-pack only)	4	8	12	28	44	60
262-(1/81) Variant 40¢-c price error (reg. ed. 50¢-c)	3	6	9	14	19	24
266-268 (All #90028 on-c; no date, no date code; 3-pack): 266(7/83). 267(8/83). 268(3/84)-Stanley-r	3	6	9	16	23	30

LITTLE MARY MIXUP (See Comics On Parade)
United Features Syndicate: No. 10, 1939, - No. 26, 1940

	GD	VG	FN	VF	VF/NM	NM-
Single Series 10, 26	34	68	102	199	325	450

LITTLE MAX COMICS (Joe Palooka's Pal; see Joe Palooka)
Harvey Publications: Oct, 1949 - No. 73, Nov, 1961

	GD	VG	FN	VF	VF/NM	NM-
1-Infinity-c; Little Dot begins; Joe Palooka on-c	22	44	66	128	209	290
2-Little Dot app.; Joe Palooka on-c	14	28	42	78	112	145
3-Little Dot app.; Joe Palooka on-c	10	20	30	58	79	100
4-10: 5-Little Dot app., 1pg.	9	18	27	47	61	75
11-20	8	16	24	40	50	60
21-40: 23-Little Dot app. 38-r/#20	6	12	18	31	38	45
41-62,66	3	6	9	18	27	35
63-65,67-73-Include new five pg. Richie Rich stories. 70-73-Little Lotta app.	3	6	9	19	29	38

LI'L MENACE
Fago Magazine Co.: Dec, 1958 - No. 3, May, 1959

	GD	VG	FN	VF	VF/NM	NM-
1-Peter Rabbit app.	8	16	24	44	57	70
2-Peter Rabbit (Vincent Fago's)	7	14	21	35	43	50
3	6	12	18	28	34	40

LITTLE MERMAID, THE (Walt Disney's...; also see Disney's...)
W. D. Publications (Disney): 1990 (no date given)($5.95, no ads, 52 pgs.)

	GD	VG	FN	VF	VF/NM	NM-
nn-Adapts animated movie	1	2	3	4	5	7
nn-Comic version ($2.50)						4.00

LITTLE MERMAID, THE
Disney Comics: 1992 - No. 4, 1992 ($1.50, mini-series)

	GD	VG	FN	VF	VF/NM	NM-
1-4: Based on movie						4.00
1-4: 2nd printings sold at Wal-Mart w/different-c						4.00

LITTLE MISS MUFFET
Best Books (Standard Comics)/King Features Synd.: No. 11, Dec, 1948 - No. 13, March, 1949

	GD	VG	FN	VF	VF/NM	NM-
11-Strip reprints; Fanny Cory-c/a	9	18	27	50	65	80
12,13-Strip reprints; Fanny Cory-c/a	7	14	21	35	43	50

LITTLE MISS SUNBEAM COMICS
Magazine Enterprises/Quality Bakers of America: June-July, 1950 - No. 4, Dec-Jan, 1950-51

	GD	VG	FN	VF	VF/NM	NM-
1	15	30	45	94	147	200
2-4	10	20	30	56	76	95
...Advs. In Space ('55)	7	14	21	35	43	50

LITTLE MONSTERS, THE (See March of Comics #423, Three Stooges #17)
Gold Key: Nov, 1964 - No. 44, Feb, 1978

	GD	VG	FN	VF	VF/NM	NM-
1	6	12	18	37	59	80
2	3	6	9	20	30	40
3-10	3	6	9	17	25	32
11-20	3	6	9	15	21	26
21-30: 19-21-Reprints	2	4	6	11	16	20
31-44: 34-39,43-Reprints	2	4	6	8	11	14

LITTLE MONSTERS (Movie)
Now Comics: 1989 - No. 6, June, 1990 ($1.75)

	GD	VG	FN	VF	VF/NM	NM-
1-6: Photo-c from movie						3.00

LITTLE NEMO (See Cocomalt, Future Comics, Help, Jest, Kayo, Punch, Red Seal, & Superworld; most by Winsor McCay Jr., son of famous artist) (Other McCay books: see Little Sammy Sneeze & Dreams of the Rarebit Fiend)

LITTLE NEMO (...in Slumberland)
McCay Features/Nostalgia Press('69): 1945 (11x7-1/4", 28 pgs., B&W)

	GD	VG	FN	VF	VF/NM	NM-
1905 & 1911 reprints by Winsor McCay	10	20	30	56	76	95
1969-70 (Exact reprint)	2	4	6	9	12	15

LITTLE ORPHAN ANNIE (See Annie, Famous Feature Stories, Marvel Super Special, Merry Christmas..., Popular Comics, Super Book #7, 11, 23 & Super Comics)

LITTLE ORPHAN ANNIE
David McKay Publ./Dell Publishing Co.: No. 7, 1937 - No. 3, Sept-Nov, 1948; No. 206, Dec, 1948

	GD	VG	FN	VF	VF/NM	NM-
Feature Books(McKay) 7-(1937) (Rare)	100	200	300	635	1093	1550
Four Color 12(1941)	58	116	174	371	636	900
Four Color 18(1943)-Flag-c	31	62	93	225	488	750
Four Color 52(1944)	23	46	69	163	349	535
Four Color 76(1945)	19	38	57	130	280	430
Four Color 107(1946)	16	32	48	110	240	370
Four Color 152(1947)	11	22	33	77	154	230
1(3-5/48)-r/strips from 5/7/44 to 7/30/44	11	22	33	76	151	225
2-r/strips from 7/21/40 to 9/9/40	9	18	27	58	99	140
3-r/strips from 9/10/40 to 11/9/40	9	18	27	58	99	140
Four Color 206(12/48)	8	16	24	53	89	125

LI'L PALS (Also see Li'l Kids)
Marvel Comics Group: Sept, 1972 - No. 5, May, 1973

	GD	VG	FN	VF	VF/NM	NM-
1	7	14	21	46	76	105
2-5	4	8	12	28	44	60

LI'L PAN (Formerly Rocket Kelly; becomes Junior Comics with #9)
Fox Features Syndicate: No. 6, Dec-Jan, 1946-47 - No. 8, Apr-May, 1947
(Also see Wotalife Comics)

	GD	VG	FN	VF	VF/NM	NM-
6	11	22	33	62	86	110
7,8: 7-Atomic bomb story; robot-c	9	18	27	50	65	80

LITTLE PEOPLE (Also see Darby O'Gill & the...)
Dell Publishing Co.: No. 485, Aug-Oct, 1953 - No. 1062, Dec, 1959 (Walt Scott's)

	GD	VG	FN	VF	VF/NM	NM-
Four Color 485 (#1)	8	16	24	51	86	120
Four Color 573(7/54), 633(6/55)	5	10	15	32	51	70
Four Color 692(3/56),753(11/56),809(7/57),868(12/57),908(5/58), 959(12/58), 1062	5	10	15	32	51	70

LITTLE RASCALS
Dell Publishing Co.: No. 674, Jan, 1956 - No. 1297, Mar-May, 1962

	GD	VG	FN	VF	VF/NM	NM-
Four Color 674 (#1)	9	18	27	58	99	140
Four Color 778(3/57),825(8/57)	6	12	18	39	62	85
Four Color 883(3/58),936(9/58),974(3/59),1030(9/59),1079(2-4/60),1137(9-11/60)	6	12	18	37	59	80
Four Color 1174(3-5/61),1224(10-12/61),1297	5	10	15	30	48	65

LI'L RASCAL TWINS (Formerly Nature Boy)
Charlton Comics: No. 6, 1957 - No. 18, Jan, 1960

	GD	VG	FN	VF	VF/NM	NM-
6-Li'l Genius & Tomboy in all	6	12	18	29	36	42
7-18: 7-Timmy the Timid Ghost app.	4	8	12	18	22	25

LITTLE RED HOT: (CHANE OF FOOLS)
Image Comics: Feb, 1999 - No. 3, Apr, 1999 ($2.95/$3.50, B&W, limited series)

	GD	VG	FN	VF	VF/NM	NM-
1-3-Dawn Brown-s/a. 2,3-($3.50-c)						3.50
The Foolish Collection TPB ($12.95) r/#1-3						13.00

LITTLE RED HOT: BOUND
Image Comics: July, 2001 - No. 3, Nov, 2001 ($2.95, color, limited series)

	GD	VG	FN	VF	VF/NM	NM-
1-3-Dawn Brown-s/a.						3.00

LITTLE ROQUEFORT COMICS (See Paul Terry's Comics #105)
St. John Publishing Co.(all pre-code)/Pines No. 10: June, 1952 - No. 9, Oct, 1953; No. 10, Summer, 1958

	GD	VG	FN	VF	VF/NM	NM-
1-By Paul Terry; Funny Animal	10	20	30	54	72	90
2	6	12	18	31	38	45
3-10: 10-CBS Television Presents on-c	5	10	15	24	30	35

LITTLE SAD SACK (See Harvey Hits No. 73, 76, 79, 81, 83)
Harvey Publications: Oct, 1964 - No. 19, Nov, 1967

	GD	VG	FN	VF	VF/NM	NM-
1-Richie Rich app. on cover only	5	10	15	32	51	70
2-10	3	6	9	18	27	35
11-19	3	6	9	16	22	28

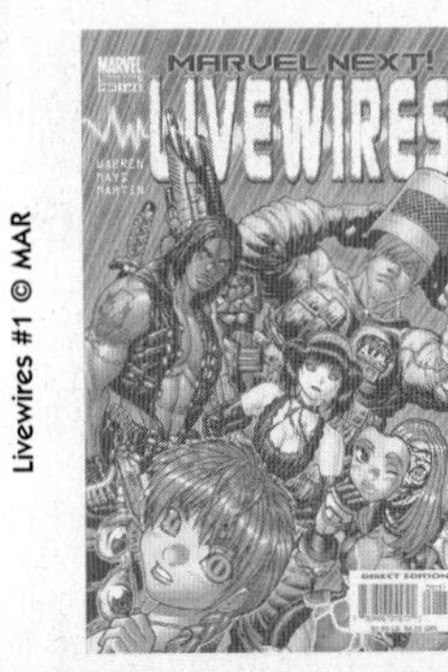

Livewires #1 © MAR

Lobo #4 © DC

Locke & Key: Clockworks #5 © Joe Hill & IDW

	GD 2.0	VG 4.0	FN 6.0	VF 8.0	VF/NM 9.0	NM- 9.2

LITTLE SCOUTS
Dell Publishing Co.: No. 321, Mar, 1951 - No. 587, Oct, 1954

	GD	VG	FN	VF	VF/NM	NM-
Four Color 321 (#1, 3/51)	5	10	15	30	48	65
2(10-12/51) - 6(10-12/52)	4	8	12	24	37	50
Four Color 462,506,550,587	4	8	12	24	37	50

LITTLE SHOP OF HORRORS SPECIAL (Movie)
DC Comics: Feb, 1987 ($2.00, 68 pgs.)

1-Colan-c/a 4.00

LITTLE SPUNKY
I. W. Enterprises: No date (1963?) (10¢)

	GD	VG	FN	VF	VF/NM	NM-
1-r/Frisky Fables #1	2	4	6	8	11	14

LITTLE STAR
Oni Press: Feb, 2005 - No. 6, Dec, 2005 ($2.99, B&W, limited series)

1-6-Andi Watson-s/a 3.00
TPB (4/06, $19.95) r/#1-6 20.00

LITTLE STOOGES, THE (The Three Stooges' Sons)
Gold Key: Sept, 1972 - No. 7, Mar, 1974

	GD	VG	FN	VF	VF/NM	NM-
1-Norman Maurer cover/stories in all	3	6	9	19	29	38
2-7	2	4	6	13	18	22

LITTLEST OUTLAW (Disney)
Dell Publishing Co.: No. 609, Jan, 1955

	GD	VG	FN	VF	VF/NM	NM-
Four Color 609-Movie, photo-c	6	12	18	42	69	95

LITTLEST SNOWMAN, THE
Dell Publishing Co.: No. 755, 12/56; No. 864, 12/57; 12-2/1963-64

	GD	VG	FN	VF	VF/NM	NM-
Four Color 755,864, 1(1964)	5	10	15	32	51	70

LI'L TOMBOY (Formerly Fawcett's Funny Animals; see Giant Comics #3)
Charlton Comics: V14#92, Oct, 1956; No. 93, Mar, 1957 - No. 107, Feb, 1960

	GD	VG	FN	VF	VF/NM	NM-
V14#92-Ties as 1st app. with Li'l Genius #11	6	12	18	27	33	38
93-107: 97-Atomic Bunny app.	5	10	14	20	24	28

LI'L WILLIE COMICS (Formerly & becomes Willie Comics #22 on)
Marvel Comics (MgPC): No. 20, July, 1949 - No. 21, Sept, 1949

	GD	VG	FN	VF	VF/NM	NM-
20,21: 20-Little Aspirin app.	14	28	42	76	108	140

LITTLE WOMEN (See Power Record Comics)

LIVE IT UP
Spire Christian Comics (Fleming H. Revell Co.): 1973, 1974 (39-49 cents)

	GD	VG	FN	VF	VF/NM	NM-
nn-1973 Edition	2	4	6	11	16	20
nn-1974 Edition	2	4	6	8	11	14

LIVEWIRES
Marvel Comics: Apr, 2005 - No. 6, Sept, 2005 ($2.99, limited series)

1-6-Adam Warren-s/c; Rick Mays-a 3.00
...: Clockwork Thugs, Yo (2005, $7.99, digest) r/#1-6 8.00

LIVING BIBLE, THE
Living Bible Corp.: Fall, 1945 - No. 3, Spring, 1946

	GD	VG	FN	VF	VF/NM	NM-
1-The Life of Paul; all have L. B. Cole-c	39	78	117	231	378	525
2-Joseph & His Brethren; Jonah & the Whale	27	54	81	158	259	360
3-Chaplains At War (classic-c)	40	80	120	246	411	575

LIVING WITH THE DEAD
Dark Horse Comics: Oct, 2007 - No. 3, Nov, 2007 ($2.99, limited series)

1-3-Zombies; Mike Richardson-s/Ben Stenbeck-a/Richard Corben-c 3.00

LOADED BIBLE
Image Comics: Apr, 2006; May, 2007; Feb, 2008 ($4.99)

...: Jesus vs. Vampires (4/06) Tim Seeley-s/Nate Bellegarde-a 5.00
...2: Blood of Christ (5/07) Seeley-s/Mike Norton-a. ...3: Communion (2/08) 5.00

LOBO
Dell Publishing Co.: Dec, 1965; No. 2, Oct, 1966

	GD	VG	FN	VF	VF/NM	NM-
1-1st black character to have his own title	5	10	15	32	51	70
2	4	8	12	22	34	45

LOBO (Also see Action #650, Adventures of Superman, Demon (2nd series), Justice League, L.E.G.I.O.N., Mister Miracle, Omega Men #3 & Superman #41)
DC Comics: Nov, 1990 - No. 4, Feb, 1991 ($1.50, color, limited series)

1-(99¢)-Giffen plots/Breakdowns in all 5.00
1-2nd printing 3.00
2-4: 2-Legion '89 spin-off. 1-4 have Bisley painted covers & art 3.00
...: Blazing Chain of Love 1 (9/92, $1.50)-Denys Cowan-c/a; Alan Grant scripts, ...Convention Special 1 (1993, $1.75), ...: Portrait of a Victim 1 (1993, $1.75) 3.00
... Paramilitary Christmas Special 1 (1991, $2.39, 52 pgs.) Bisley-c/a 4.00
...: Portrait of a Bastich TPB (2008, $19.99) r/#1-4 & Lobo's Back #1-4 20.00

LOBO (Also see Showcase '95 #9)
DC Comics: Dec, 1993 - No. 64, Jul, 1999 ($1.75/$1.95/$2.25/$2.50, mature)

1 ($2.95)-Foil enhanced-c; Alan Grant scripts begin 4.00
2-9,0,10-64: 2-7-Alan Grant scripts. 9-(9/94). 0-(10/94)-Origin retold. 50-Lobo vs. the DCU. 58-Giffen-a 3.00
#1,000,000 (11/98) 853rd Century x-over 3.00
Annual 1 (1993, $3.50, 68 pgs.)-Bloodlines x-over 4.00
Annual 2 (1994, $3.50)-21 artists (20 listed on-c); Alan Grant script; Elseworlds story 4.00
Annual 3 (1995, $3.95)-Year One story 4.00
.../Authority: Holiday Hell TPB (2006, $17.99) r/Lobo Paramilitary Christmas Special; Authority/Lobo: Jingle Hell and Spring Break Massacre; WildStorm Winter Special 18.00
...Big Babe Spring Break Special (Spr, '95, $1.95)-Balent-a 3.00
...Bounty Hunting for Fun and Profit ('95)-Bisley-c 5.00
... Chained (5/97, $2.50)-Alan Grant story 3.00
.../Deadman: The Brave And The Bald (2/95, $3.50) 4.00
.../Demon: Helloween (12/96, $2.25)-Giarrano-a 3.00
...Fragtastic Voyage 1 ('97, $5.95)-Mejia painted-c/a 6.00
...Gallery (9/95, $3.50)-pin-ups. 3.50
...In the Chair 1 (8/94, $1.95, 36 pgs.), ...I Quit-(12/95, $2.25) 3.00
.../Judge Dredd ('95, $4.95). 5.00
...Lobocop 1 (2/94, $1.95)-Alan Grant scripts; painted-c 3.00

LOBO: (Title Series), DC Comics

--A CONTRACT ON GAWD, 4/94 - 7/94 (mature) 1-4: Alan Grant scripts. 3-Groo cameo 3.00

--DEATH AND TAXES, 10/96 - No. 4, 1/97, 1-4-Giffen/Grant scripts 3.00

--GOES TO HOLLYWOOD, 8/96 ($2.25), 1-Grant scripts 3.00

--HIGHWAY TO HELL, 1/10 - No. 2, 2/10 ($6.99), 1,2-Scott Ian-s/Sam Kieth-a/c 7.00
TPB (2010, $19.99) r/#1,2; intro. by Scott Ian; Kieth B&W art pages 20.00

--INFANTICIDE, 10/92 - 1/93 ($1.50, mature), 1-4-Giffen-c/a; Grant scripts 3.00

--/ MASK, 2/97 - No. 2, 3/97 ($5.95), 1,2 6.00

--'S BACK, 5/92 - No. 4, 11/92 ($1.50, mature), 1-4: 1-Has 3 outer covers. Bisley painted-c 1,2; a-1-3. 3-Sam Kieth-c; all have Giffen plots/breakdown & Grant scripts 3.00
Trade paperback (1993, $9.95)-r/1-4 10.00

--THE DUCK, 6/97 ($1.95), 1-A. Grant-s/V. Semeiks & R. Kryssing-a 3.00

--UNAMERICAN GLADIATORS, 6/93 - No. 4, 9/93 ($1.75, mature), 1-4-Mignola-c; Grant/Wagner scripts 3.00

--UNBOUND, 8/03 - No. 6, 5/04 ($2.95), 1-6-Giffen-s/Horley-c/a. 4-6-Ambush Bug app. 3.00

LOBSTER JOHNSON: THE BURNING HAND (See B.P.R.D. and Hellboy titles)
Dark Horse Comics: Jan, 2012 - No. 5, ($3.50, limited series)

1-3-Mignola & Arcudi-s; Zonjic-a. 1-Two covers by Dave Johnson & Mignola 3.50

LOBSTER JOHNSON: THE IRON PROMETHEUS (See B.P.R.D. and Hellboy titles)
Dark Horse Comics: Sept, 2007 - No. 5, Jan, 2008 ($2.99, limited series)

1-5-Mignola-s/c; Armstrong-a 3.00

LOCKE & KEY
IDW Publ.: Feb, 2008 - No. 6, July, 2008 ($3.99, limited series)

1-Joe Hill-s/Gabriel Rodriguez-a 20.00
1-Second printing 5.00
2 10.00
3-6 5.00
...: Free Comic Book day Edition (5/11) r/story from Crown of Shadows 3.00
...: Welcome to Lovecraft Legacy Edition #1 (8/10, $1.00) r/#1; synopsis of later issues 3.00
...: Welcome to Lovecraft Special Edition #1 SC (9/09, $5.99) Hill-s/Rodriguez-a; script; back-up story with final art from Seth Fisher 6.00

LOCKE & KEY: CLOCKWORKS
IDW Publ.: Jun, 2011 - Present ($3.99, limited series)

1-5: 1-Hill-s/Rodriguez-a; set in 1776 4.00

LOCKE & KEY: CROWN OF SHADOWS
IDW Publ.: Nov, 2009 - No. 6, Apr, 2010 ($3.99, limited series)

1-6-Joe Hill-s/Gabriel Rodriguez-a 4.00

LOCKE & KEY: HEAD GAMES
IDW Publ.: Jan, 2009 - No. 6, Jun, 2009 ($3.99, limited series)

1-6-Joe Hill-s/Gabriel Rodriguez-a. 3-EC style-c 4.00

LOCKE & KEY: KEYS TO THE KINGDOM
IDW Publ.: Sept, 2010 - Present ($3.99, limited series)

Logan: Path of the Warlord #1 © MAR

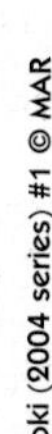
Loki (2004 series) #1 © MAR

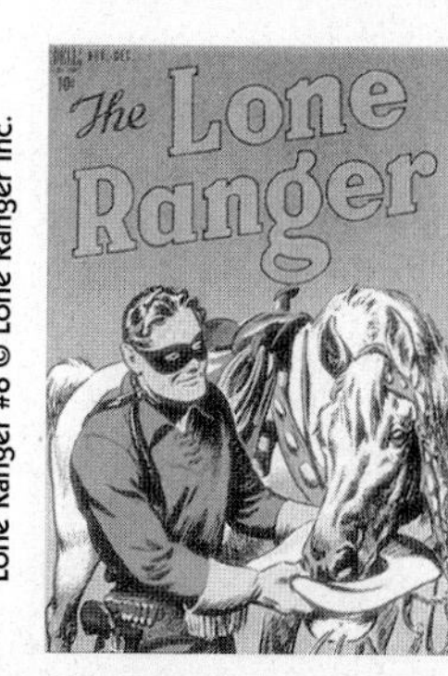

Lone Ranger #6 © Lone Ranger Inc.

GD 2.0 | VG 4.0 | FN 6.0 | VF 8.0 | VF/NM 9.0 | NM- 9.2

1-5-Joe Hill-s/Gabriel Rodriguez-a 4.00

LOCKJAW AND THE PET AVENGERS (Also see Tails of the Pet Avengers)
Marvel Comics: July, 2009 - No. 4, Oct, 2009 ($2.99, limited series)
1-4-Lockheed, Frog Thor, Zabu, Lockjaw and Redwing team up; 2 covers on each 3.00

LOCKJAW AND THE PET AVENGERS UNLEASHED
Marvel Comics: May, 2010 - No. 4, Aug, 2010 ($2.99, limited series)
1-4-Eliopoulos-s/Guara-a; 2 covers on each 3.00

LOCO (Magazine) (Satire)
Satire Publications: Aug, 1958 - V1#3, Jan, 1959
V1#1-Chic Stone-a 9 18 27 47 61 75
V1#2,3-Severin-a, 2 pgs. Davis; 3-Heath-a 7 14 21 35 43 50

LOGAN (Wolverine)
Marvel Comics: May, 2008 - No. 3, Jul, 2008 ($3.99, limited series)
1-3-Vaughan-s/Risso-a/c; regular & B&W editions for each 4.00

LOGAN: PATH OF THE WARLORD
Marvel Comics: Feb, 1996 ($5.95, one-shot)
1-John Paul Leon-a 6.00

LOGAN: SHADOW SOCIETY
Marvel Comics: 1996 ($5.95, one-shot)
1 6.00

LOGAN'S RUN
Marvel Comics Group: Jan, 1977 - No. 7, July, 1977
1: 1-5-Based on novel & movie 2 4 6 8 10 12
2-5,7: 6,7-New stories adapted from novel 1 2 3 5 6 8
6-1st Thanos (also see Iron Man #55) solo story (back-up) by Zeck (6/77)
4 8 12 24 37 50
6-(35¢-c variant, limited distribution) 8 16 24 53 89 125
7-(35¢-c variant, limited distribution) 3 6 9 20 30 40
NOTE: ***Austin*** *a-6i.* ***Gulacy*** *c-6.* ***Kane*** *c-7p.* ***Perez*** *a-1-5p; c-1-5p.* ***Sutton*** *a-6p, 7p.*

LOIS & CLARK, THE NEW ADVENTURES OF SUPERMAN
DC Comics: 1994 ($9.95, one-shot)
1-r/Man of Steel #2, Superman Ann. 1, Superman #9 & 11, Action #600 & 655, Adventures of Superman #445, 462 & 466 1 3 4 6 8 10

LOIS LANE (Also see Daring New Adventures of Supergirl, Showcase #9,10 & Superman's Girlfriend...)
DC Comics: Aug, 1986 - No. 2, Sept, 1986 ($1.50, 52 pgs.)
1,2-Morrow-c/a in each 4.00

LOKI (Thor)
Marvel Comics: Sept, 2004 - No. 4, Nov, 2004 ($3.50)
1-4-Rodi-s/Ribic-a/c 3.50
HC (2005, $17.99, with dustjacket) oversized r/#1-4; original proposal and sketch pages 18.00
SC (2007, $12.99) r/#1-4; original proposal and sketch pages 13.00

LOKI (Thor)
Marvel Comics: Dec, 2010 - No. 4, May, 2011 ($3.99, limited series)
1-4-Aguirre-Sacasa-s/Fiumara-a. 2-Balder dies 4.00

LOLLY AND PEPPER
Dell Publishing Co.: No. 832, Sept, 1957 - July, 1962
Four Color 832(#1) 5 10 15 30 48 65
Four Color 940,978,1086,1206 4 8 12 22 34 45
01-459-207 (7/62) 3 6 9 18 27 35

LOMAX (See Police Action)

LONDON'S DARK
Escape/Titan: 1989 ($8.95, B&W, graphic novel)
nn-James Robinson script; Paul Johnson-c/a 1 2 3 5 7 9

LONE
Dark Horse Comics: Sept, 2003 - No. 6, Mar, 2004 ($2.99)
1-6-Stuart Moore-s/Jerome Opeña-a/Templesmith-c 3.00

LONE EAGLE (The Flame No. 5 on)
Ajax/Farrell Publications: Apr-May, 1954 - No. 4, Oct-Nov, 1954
1 13 26 39 74 105 135
2-4: 3-Bondage-c 9 18 27 50 65 80

LONE GUNMEN, THE (From the X-Files)
Dark Horse Comics: June, 2001 ($2.99, one-shot)
1-Paul Lee-a; photo-c 3.00

LONELY HEART (Formerly Dear Lonely Hearts; Dear Heart #15 on)
Ajax/Farrell Publ. (Excellent Publ.): No. 9, Mar, 1955 - No. 14, Feb, 1956
9-Kamen*esque*-a; (Last precode) 11 22 33 60 83 105
10-14 8 16 24 42 54 65

LONE RANGER, THE (See Ace Comics, Aurora, Dell Giants, Future Comics, Golden Comics Digest #48, King Comics, Magic Comics & March of Comics #165, 174, 193, 208, 225, 238, 310, 322, 338, 350)

LONE RANGER, THE
Dell Publishing Co.: No. 3, 1939 - No. 167, Feb, 1947
Large Feature Comic 3(1939)-Heigh-Yo Silver; text with illus. by Robert Weisman; also exists as a Whitman #710 194 388 582 1242 2121 3000
Large Feature Comic 7(1939)-Illustr. by Henry Vallely; Hi-Yo Silver the Lone Ranger to the Rescue; also exists as a Whitman #715 181 362 543 1158 1979 2800
Feature Book 21(1940), 24(1941) 92 184 276 584 1005 1425
Four Color 82(1945) 35 70 105 254 552 850
Four Color 98(1945),118(1946) 26 52 78 182 391 600
Four Color 125(1946),136(1947) 17 34 51 119 260 400
Four Color 151,167(1947) 15 30 45 102 221 340

LONE RANGER, THE (Movie, radio & TV; Clayton Moore starred as Lone Ranger in the movies; No. 1-37: strip reprints)(See Dell Giants)
Dell Publishing Co.: Jan-Feb, 1948 - No. 145, May-July, 1962
1 (36 pgs.)-The Lone Ranger, his horse Silver, companion Tonto & his horse Scout begin
56 112 168 454 977 1500
2 (52 pgs. begin, end #41) 26 52 78 182 391 600
3-5 20 40 60 137 294 450
6,7,9,10 16 32 48 107 234 360
8-Origin retold; Indian back-c begin, end #35 18 36 54 126 273 420
11-20: 11- "Young Hawk" Indian boy serial begins, ends #145
12 24 36 81 166 250
21,22,24-31: 51-Reprint. 31-1st Mask logo 10 20 30 69 130 190
23-Origin retold 12 24 36 81 166 250
32-37: 32-Painted-c begin. 36-Animal photo back-c begin, end #49. 37-Last newspaper-r issue; new outfit; red shirt becomes blue; most known copies show the blue shirt on-c & inside 9 18 27 63 112 160
37-Variant issue; Long Ranger wears a red shirt on-c and inside. A few copies of the red shirt outfit were printed before catching the mistake and changing the color to blue (rare)
15 30 45 104 227 350
38-41 (All 52 pgs.) 38-Paul S. Newman-s (wrote most of the stories #38-on)
9 18 27 61 106 150
42-50 (36 pgs.) 8 16 24 53 89 125
51-74 (52 pgs.): 56-One pg. origin story of Lone Ranger & Tonto. 71-Blank inside-c
7 14 21 49 82 115
75,77-99: 79-X-mas-c 7 14 21 46 76 105
76-Classic flag-c 7 14 21 49 82 115
100 8 16 24 53 89 125
101-111: Last painted-c 6 12 18 42 69 95
112-Clayton Moore photo-c begin, end #145 15 30 45 104 227 350
113-117: 117-10¢ &15¢-c exist 10 20 30 67 124 180
118-Origin Lone Ranger, Tonto, & Silver retold; Special anniversary issue
20 40 60 137 294 450
119-140: 139-Fran Striker-s 9 18 27 63 112 160
141-145 10 20 30 65 118 170
NOTE: ***Hank Hartman*** *painted c(signed)-65, 66, 70, 75, 82; unsigned-64?, 67-69?, 71, 72, 73?, 74?, 76-78, 80, 81, 83-91, 92?, 93-111.* ***Ernest Nordli*** *painted c(signed)-42, 50, 52, 53, 56, 59, 60; unsigned-39-41, 44-49, 51, 54, 55, 57, 58, 61-63?*

LONE RANGER, THE
Gold Key (Reprints in #13-20): 9/64 - No. 16, 12/69; No. 17, 11/72; No. 18, 9/74 - No. 28, 3/77
1-Retells origin 6 12 18 41 66 90
2 4 8 12 22 34 45
3-10: Small Bear-r in #6-12. 10-Last 12¢ issue 3 6 9 20 30 40
11-17 3 6 9 16 22 28
18-28 2 4 6 11 16 20
Golden West 1(30029-610, 10/66)-Giant; r/most Golden West #3 including Clayton Moore photo front/back-c 7 14 21 44 72 100

LONE RANGER
Dynamite Entertainment: 2006 - No. 25, 2011 ($2.99/$3.50/$3.99)
1-Retells origin; Carriello-a/Matthews-s; badge cover by Cassaday 4.00
1-Variant mask cover by Cassaday 5.00
1-Baltimore Comic-Con 2006 variant cover with masked face and horse silhouette 12.00
1-Directors' Cut ($4.99) r/#1 with comments at page bottoms, script and sketches 5.00
2-23: 2-Origin continues; Tonto app. 3.50

Lone Ranger V2 #1 © Classic Media

Lone Rider #8 © Farrell

Looney Tunes #75 © WB

GD VG FN VF VF/NM NM-
2.0 4.0 6.0 8.0 9.0 9.2

GD VG FN VF VF/NM NM-
2.0 4.0 6.0 8.0 9.0 9.2

24-($3.99) 4.00
25-($4.99) Carriello-a 5.00
... and Tonto 1-4 (200-2010, $4.99) Cassaday-c 5.00
... Volume 1: Now and Forever TPB (2007, $19.99) r/#1-6; sketch pages 20.00

LONE RANGER, THE (Volume 2)
Dynamite Entertainment: 2012 - Present ($3.99)
1-3: 1-Parks-s/Polls-a; two covers by Ross & Francavilla 4.00

LONE RANGER AND TONTO, THE
Topps Comics: Aug, 1994 - No. 4, Nov, 1994 ($2.50, limited series)
1-4: 3-Origin of Lone Ranger; Tonto leaves; Lansdale story, Truman-c/a in all. 3.00
1-4: Silver logo. 1-Signed by Lansdale and Truman 6.00
Trade paperback (1/95, $9.95) 10.00

LONE RANGER AND ZORRO: THE DEATH OF ZORRO, THE
Dynamite Entertainment: 2011 - No. 5, 2011 ($3.99, limited series)
1-5: 1-Four covers by Alex Ross and others; Parks-s/Polls-a 4.00

LONE RANGER'S COMPANION TONTO, THE (TV)
Dell Publishing Co.: No. 312, Jan, 1951 - No. 33, Nov-Jan/58-59 (All painted-c)
Four Color 312(#1, 1/51) 10 20 30 69 130 190
2(8-10/51),3: (#2 titled "Tonto") 6 12 18 42 69 95
4-10 6 12 18 37 59 80
11-20 5 10 15 32 51 70
21-33 4 8 12 28 44 60
NOTE: ***Ernest Nordli*** *painted c(signed)-2, 7; unsigned-3-6, 8-11, 12?, 13, 14, 18?, 22-24? See Aurora Comic Booklets.*

LONE RANGER'S FAMOUS HORSE HI-YO SILVER, THE (TV)
Dell Publishing Co.: No. 369, Jan, 1952 - No. 36, Oct-Dec, 1960 (All painted-c, most by Sam Savitt) (Lone Ranger appears in most issues)
Four Color 369(#1)-Silver's origin as told by The Lone Ranger
10 20 30 67 124 180
Four Color 392(#2, 4/52) 6 12 18 41 66 90
3(7-9/52)-10(4-6/52) 5 10 15 35 55 75
11-36 4 8 12 28 44 60

LONE RIDER (Also see The Rider)
Superior Comics(Farrell Publ.): Apr, 1951 - No. 26, Jul, 1955 (#3-on: 36 pgs.)
1 (52 pgs.)-The Lone Rider & his horse Lightnin' begin; Kamenish-a begins
32 64 96 188 307 425
2 (52 pgs.)-The Golden Arrow begins (origin) 20 40 60 120 195 220
3-6: 6-Last Golden Arrow 17 34 51 98 154 210
7-Golden Arrow becomes Swift Arrow; origin of his shield
20 40 60 120 195 220
8-Origin Swift Arrow 18 36 54 107 169 230
9,10 12 24 36 69 97 125
11-14 10 20 30 54 72 90
15-Golden Arrow origin-r from #2, changing name to Swift Arrow
10 20 30 58 79 100
16-20,22-26: 23-Apache Kid app. 9 18 27 50 65 80
21-3-D effect-c 16 32 48 94 147 200

LONERS, THE
Marvel Comics: June, 2007 - No. 6, Jan, 2008 ($2.99, limited series)
1-6-Cebulski-s/Moline-a/Pearson-c; Lightspeed, Spider-Woman, Ricochet app. 3.00
...: The Secret Lives of Super Heroes TPB (2008, $14.99) r/#1-6; sketch pages 15.00

LONE WOLF AND CUB
First Comics: May, 1987 - No. 45, Apr, 1991 ($1.95-$3.25, B&W, deluxe size)
1-Frank Miller-c & intro.; reprints manga series by Koike & Kojima
1 2 3 6 8 10
1-2nd print, 3rd print, 2-2nd print 4.00
2-12: 6-72 pgs. origin issue 5.50
13-38,40: 40-Ploog-c 4.00
39-($5.95, 120 pgs.)-Ploog-c 6.50
41-44: 41-($3.95, 84 pgs.)-Ploog-c. 42-Ploog-c 6.00
45-Last issue; low print 2 4 6 8 10 12
Deluxe Edition ($19.95, B&W) 20.00
NOTE: ***Sienkiewicz*** *c-13-24.* ***Matt Wagner*** *c-25-30.*

LONE WOLF AND CUB (Trade paperbacks)
Dark Horse Comics: Aug, 2000 - No. 28 ($9.95, B&W, 4" x 6", approx. 300 pgs.)
1-Collects First Comics reprint series; Frank Miller-c 18.00
1-(2nd printing) 12.00
1-(3rd-5th printings) 10.00
2,3-(1st printings) 12.00
2,3-(2nd printings) 10.00
4-28 10.00

LONE WOLF 2100 (Also see Reveal)
Dark Horse Comics: May, 2002 - No. 11, Dec, 2003 ($2.99, color)
1-New homage to Lone Wolf and Cub; Kennedy-s/Velasco-a 4.00
2-11 3.00
...: The Red File (1/03, $2.99) character and story background files 3.00
... Vol. 1 - Shadows on Saplings TPB (2003, $12.95, 6" x 9") r/#1-4 13.00
... Vol. 2 - The Language of Chaos TPB (2003, $12.95, 6" x 9") r/#5-8, Dirty Tricks short story from Reveal 13.00

LONG BOW (...Indian Boy)(See Indians & Jumbo Comics #141)
Fiction House Mag. (Real Adventures Publ.): 1951 - No. 9, Wint, 1952/53
1-Most covers by Maurice Whitman 18 36 54 103 162 220
2 11 22 33 62 86 110
3-9 10 20 30 56 76 95

LONG HOT SUMMER, THE
DC Comics (Milestone): Jul, 1995 - No. 3, Sept, 1995 ($2.95/$2.50, lim. series)
1-3: 1-($2.95-c). 2,3-($2.50-c) 3.00

LONG JOHN SILVER & THE PIRATES (Formerly Terry & the Pirates)
Charlton Comics: No. 30, Aug, 1956 - No. 32, March, 1957 (TV)
30-32: Whitman-c 10 20 30 54 72 90

LONGSHOT (Also see X-Men, 2nd Series #10)
Marvel Comics: Sept, 1985 - No. 6, Feb, 1986 (60¢, limited series)
1-6: 1-Art Adams/Whilce Portacio-c/a in all. 4-Spider-Man app. 6-Double size
1 2 3 4 5 7
Trade Paperback (1989, $16.95)-r/#1-6 17.00

LONGSHOT
Marvel Comics: Feb, 1998 ($3.99, one-shot)
1-DeMatteis-s/Zulli-a 4.00

LOOKING GLASS WARS: HATTER M
Image Comics (Desperado): Dec, 2005 - No. 4, Nov, 2006 ($3.99)
1-4-Templesmith-a/c 4.00

LOONEY TUNES (2nd Series) (TV)
Gold Key/Whitman: April, 1975 - No. 47, June, 1984
1-Reprints 4 8 12 22 34 45
2-10: 2,4-reprints 2 4 6 13 18 22
11-20: 16-reprints 2 4 6 9 12 15
21-30 2 3 4 6 8 10
31,32,36-42(2/82) 1 2 3 5 6 8
33-(8/80)-35 (Whitman pre-pack only, scarce) 3 6 9 17 25 32
43(4/82),44(6/83) (low distribution) 2 4 6 9 13 16
45-47 (All #90296 on-c; nd, nd code, pre-pack) 45(8/83), 46(3/84), 47(6/84)
3 6 9 14 20 26

LOONEY TUNES (3rd Series) (TV)
DC Comics: Apr, 1994 - Present ($1.50/$1.75/$1.95/$1.99/$2.25/$2.50/$2.99)
1-10,120: 1-Marvin Martian-c/sty; Bugs Bunny, Roadrunner, Daffy begin. 120-($2.95-C) 4.00
11-119,121-187: 23-34-($1.75-c). 35-43-($1.95-c). 44-Begin $1.99-c. 93-Begin $2.25-c. 100-Art by various incl. Kyle Baker, Marie Severin, Darwyn Cooke, Jill Thompson 3.00
188-206: 188-Begin $2.99-c; Scooby-Doo spoof. 193-Christmas-c 3.00
...Back In Action Movie Adaptation (12/03, $3.95) photo-c 4.00

LOONEY TUNES AND MERRIE MELODIES COMICS ("Looney Tunes" #166(8/55) on)
(Also see Porky's Duck Hunt)
Dell Publishing Co.: 1941 - No. 246, July-Sept, 1962
1-Porky Pig, Bugs Bunny, Daffy Duck, Elmer Fudd, Mary Jane & Sniffles, Pat Patsy and Pete begin (1st comic book app. of each). Bugs Bunny story by Win Smith (early Mickey Mouse artist) 1150 2300 3450 8700 15,850 23,000
2 (11/41) 154 308 462 1294 2797 4300
3-Kandi the Cave Kid begins by Walt Kelly; also in #4-6,8,11,15
107 214 321 867 1884 2900
4-Kelly-a 107 214 321 867 1884 2900
5-Bugs Bunny The Super-Duper Rabbit story (1st funny animal super hero, 3/42; also see Coo Coo); Kelly-a 80 160 240 648 1399 2150
6,8-Kelly-a 63 126 189 510 1105 1700
7,9,10: 9-Painted-c. 10-Flag-c 46 92 138 373 812 1250
11,15-Kelly-a; 15-X-Mas-c 47 94 141 381 828 1275
12-14,16-19 36 72 108 270 585 900
20-25: Pat, Patsy & Pete by Walt Kelly in all. 20-War Bonds-c
31 62 93 225 488 750

Looney Tunes & Merrie Melodies #21 © WB

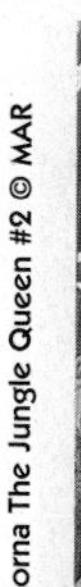

Lorna The Jungle Queen #2 © MAR

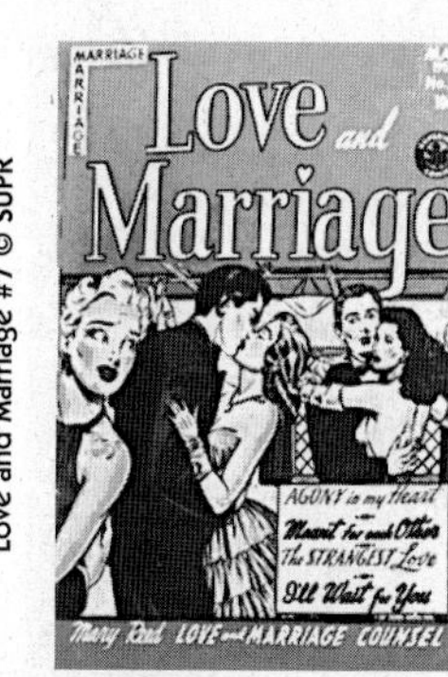
Love and Marriage #7 © SUPR

	GD 2.0	VG 4.0	FN 6.0	VF 8.0	VF/NM 9.0	NM- 9.2
26-30	23	46	69	166	353	540
31-40: 33-War Bonds-c. 39-X-Mas-c	19	38	57	132	284	435
41-50: 45-War Bonds-c	14	28	42	97	211	325
51-60	12	24	36	81	166	250
61-80	9	18	27	63	112	160
81-99: 87-X-Mas-c	8	16	24	56	96	135
100	9	18	27	60	103	145
101-120	7	14	21	46	76	105
121-150	6	12	18	41	67	90
151-200: 159-X-Mas-c	6	12	18	37	59	80
201-240	5	10	15	35	55	75
241-246	6	12	18	37	59	80

LOONY SPORTS (Magazine)
3-Strikes Publishing Co.: Spring, 1975 (68 pgs.)

	GD	VG	FN	VF	VF/NM	NM-
1-Sports satire	2	4	6	8	11	14

LOOSE CANNON (Also see Action Comics Annual #5 & Showcase '94 #5)
DC Comics: June, 1995 - No. 4, Sept, 1995 ($1.75, limited series)

1-4: Adam Pollina-a. 1-Superman app. 3.00

LOOY DOT DOPE
United Features Syndicate: No. 13, 1939

	GD	VG	FN	VF	VF/NM	NM-
Single Series 13	30	60	90	177	289	400

LORD JIM (See Movie Comics)

LORD OF THE JUNGLE
Dynamite Entertainment: 2012 - Present ($1.00/$3.99)

1-($1.00) Retelling of Tarzan's origin; Nelson-s/Castro-a; four covers 3.00
2-($3.99) Three covers 4.00

LORD PUMPKIN
Malibu Comics (Ultraverse): Oct, 1994 ($2.50, one-shot)

0-Two covers 3.00

LORD PUMPKIN/NECROMANTRA
Malibu Comics (Ultraverse): Apr, 1995 - No. 4, July, 1995 ($2.95, limited series, flip book)

1-4 3.00

LORDS OF AVALON: KNIGHT OF DARKNESS
Marvel Comics: Jan, 2008 - No. 6, July, 2009 ($3.99, limited series)

1-6-($3.99)-Kenyon & Furth-s; Ohtsuka-a/c 4.00

LORDS OF AVALON: SWORD OF DARKNESS
Marvel Comics: Apr, 2008 - No. 6, Sept, 2006 ($3.99/$2.99, limited series)

1-($3.99)-Adaptation of Sherrilyn Kenyon's Arthurian fantasy; Ohtsuka-a/c 4.00
2-6-($2.99) 3.00
HC (2008, $19.99) r/#1-6; two covers 20.00

LORNA, RELIC WRANGLER
Image Comics: Mar, 2011 ($3.99, one-shot)

1-Micah Harris-s; J. Bone-c 4.00

LORNA THE JUNGLE GIRL (...Jungle Queen #1-5)
Atlas Comics (NPI 1/OMC 2-11/NPI 12-26): July, 1953 - No. 26, Aug, 1957

	GD	VG	FN	VF	VF/NM	NM-
1-Origin & 1st app.	40	80	120	246	411	575
2-Intro. & 1st app. Greg Knight	21	42	63	122	199	275
3-5	18	36	54	107	169	230
6-11: 11-Last pre-code (1/55)	15	30	45	88	137	185
12-17,19-26: 14-Colletta & Maneely-c	14	28	42	81	118	155
18-Williamson/Colletta-c	15	30	45	83	124	165

NOTE: ***Brodsky** c-1-3, 5, 9. **Everett** c-21, 23-26. **Heath** c-6, 7. **Maneely** c-12, 15. **Romita** a-18, 20, 22, 24, 26. **Shores** a-14-16, 18, 24, 26; c-11, 13, 16. **Tuska** a-6.*

LOSERS (Inspired the 2010 movie)
DC Comics (Vertigo): Aug, 2003 - No. 32, Mar, 2006 ($2.95/$2.99)

1-Andy Diggle-s/Jock-a 4.00
1-Special Edition (6/10, $1.00) r/#1 with "What's Next?" logo on cover 3.00
2-32: 15-Bagged with Sky Captain CD. 20-Oliver-a. 27-Wilson-a 3.00
...: Ante Up TPB (2004, $9.95) r/#1-6 10.00
...: Book Two TPB (2010, $24.99) r/#13-32; Ian Rankin intro.; preliminary art pages 25.00
...: Close Quarters TPB (2005, $14.99) r/#20-25 15.00
...: Double Down TPB (2004, $12.95) r/#7-12 13.00
...: Endgame TPB (2006, $14.99) r/#26-32 15.00
...: Trifecta TPB (2005, $14.99) r/#13-19 15.00
...: Volumes One and Two TPB (2010, $19.99) r/#1-12; new intro. by Diggle 20.00

LOSERS SPECIAL (See Our Fighting Forces #123)(Also see G.I. Combat & Our Fighting Forces)
DC Comics: Sept, 1985 ($1.25, one-shot)

1-Capt. Storm, Gunner & Sarge; Crisis on Infinite Earths x-over 6.00

LOST, THE
Chaos! Comics: Dec, 1997 - No. 3 ($2.95, B&W, unfinished limited series)

1-3-Andreyko-script: 1-Russell back-c 3.00

LOST BOYS: REIGN OF FROGS (Based on the 1987 vampire movie)
DC Comics (WildStorm): Jul, 2008 - No. 4, Oct, 2008 ($3.50, limited series)

1-4-Rodionoff-s/Gomez-a; Edgar Frog app. 3.50
TPB (2009, $12.99) r/#1-4 13.00

LOST CONTINENT
Eclipse Int'l: Sept, 1990 - No. 6, 1991 ($3.50, B&W, squarebound, 60 pgs.)

1-6: Japanese story translated to English 4.00

LOST IN SPACE (Movie)
Dark Horse Comics: Apr, 1998 - No. 3, July, 1998 ($2.95, limited series)

1-3-Continuation of 1998 movie; Erskine-c 3.00

LOST IN SPACE (TV)(Also see Space Family Robinson)
Innovation Publishing: Aug, 1991 - No. 12, Jan, 1993 ($2.50, limited series)

1-12: Bill Mumy (Will Robinson) scripts in #1-9. 9-Perez-c 3.00
1,2-Special Ed.; r/#1,2 plus new art & new-c 3.00
Annual 1,2 (1991, 1992, $2.95, 52 pgs.) 4.00
...: Project Robinson (11/93, $2.50) 1st & only part of intended series 3.00

LOST IN SPACE: VOYAGE TO THE BOTTOM OF THE SOUL
Innovation Publishing: No. 13, Aug, 1993 - No. 18, 1994 ($2.50, limited series)

13(V1#1, $2.95)-Embossed silver logo edition; Bill Mumy scripts begin; painted-c 3.00
13(V1#1, $4.95)-Embossed gold logo edition bagged w/poster 5.00
14-18: Painted-c 3.00
NOTE: *Originally intended to be a 12 issue limited series.*

LOST ONES, THE
Image Comics: Mar, 2000 ($2.95)

1-Ken Penders-s/a 3.00

LOST PLANET
Eclipse Comics: 5/87 - No. 5, 2/88; No. 6, 3/89 (Mini-series, Baxter paper)

1-6-Bo Hampton-c/a in all 3.00

LOST WAGON TRAIN, THE (See Zane Grey Four Color 583)

LOST WORLD, THE
Dell Publishing Co.: No. 1145, Nov-Jan, 1960-61

	GD	VG	FN	VF	VF/NM	NM-
Four Color 1145-Movie, Gil Kane-a, photo-c; 1pg. Conan Doyle biography by Torres	9	18	27	62	109	155

LOST WORLD, THE (See Jurassic Park)
Topps Comics: May, 1997 - No. 4, Aug, 1997 ($2.95, limited series)

1-4-Movie adaption 3.00

LOST WORLDS (Weird Tales of the Past and Future)
Standard Comics: No. 5, Oct, 1952 - No. 6, Dec, 1952

	GD	VG	FN	VF	VF/NM	NM-
5- "Alice in Terrorland" by Alex Toth; J. Katz-a	45	90	135	284	480	675
6-Toth-a	37	74	111	222	361	500

LOTS 'O' FUN COMICS
Robert Allen Co.: 1940's? (5¢, heavy stock, blue covers)

nn-Contents can vary; Felix, Planet Comics known; contents would determine value. Similar to Up-To-Date Comics. Remainders - re-packaged.

LOU GEHRIG (See The Pride of the Yankees)

LOVE ADVENTURES (Actual Confessions #13)
Marvel (IPS)/Atlas Comics (MPI): Oct, 1949; No. 2, Jan, 1950; No. 3, Feb, 1951 - No. 12, Aug, 1952

	GD	VG	FN	VF	VF/NM	NM-
1-Photo-c	19	38	57	111	176	240
2-Powell-a; Tyrone Power, Gene Tierney photo-c	15	30	45	88	137	185
3-8,10-12: 8-Robinson-a	11	22	33	60	83	105
9-Everett-a	11	22	33	62	86	110

LOVE AND MARRIAGE
Superior Comics Ltd. (Canada): Mar, 1952 - No. 16, Sept, 1954

	GD	VG	FN	VF	VF/NM	NM-
1	15	30	45	88	137	185
2	10	20	30	54	72	90
3-10	9	18	27	50	65	80
11-16	8	16	24	44	57	70

I.W. Reprint #1,2,8,11,14: 8-r/Love and Marriage #3. 11-r/Love and Marriage #11

Love and Rockets V2 #3 © Fantagraphics

Love Classics #2 © MAR

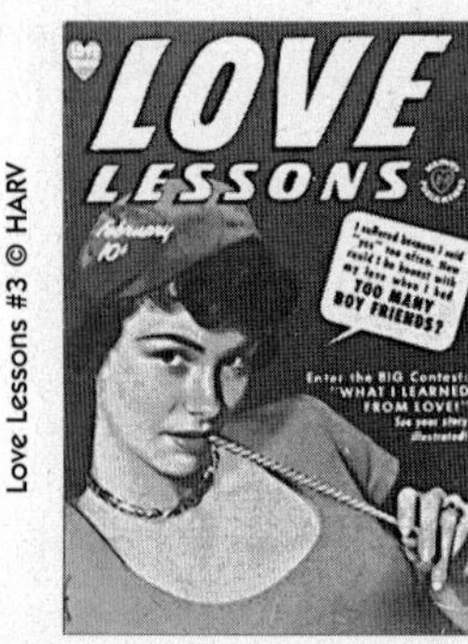
Love Lessons #3 © HARV

	GD 2.0	VG 4.0	FN 6.0	VF 8.0	VF/NM 9.0	NM- 9.2
	2	4	6	9	13	16
Super Reprint #10('63),15,17('64):15-Love and Marriage #?	2	4	6	9	13	16

NOTE: *All issues have* ***Kamenish*** *art.*

LOVE AND ROCKETS
Fantagraphics Books: July, 1982 - No. 50, May, 1996 ($2.95/$2.50/$4.95, B&W, mature)

	GD 2.0	VG 4.0	FN 6.0	VF 8.0	VF/NM 9.0	NM- 9.2
1-B&W-c (6/82, $2.95; small size, publ. by Hernandez Bros.)(800 printed)	6	12	18	42	69	95
1 (Fall, '82; color-c)	4	8	12	24	37	50
1-2nd & 3rd printing, 2-11,29-31: 2nd printings						4.00
2	2	4	6	13	18	22
3-10	1	3	4	6	8	10
11-49: 30 ($2.95, 52 pgs.)						5.00
50-($4.95)						6.00

LOVE AND ROCKETS (Volume 2)
Fantagraphics Books: Spring, 2001 - Present ($3.95-$7.99, B&W, mature)

	GD 2.0	VG 4.0	FN 6.0	VF 8.0	VF/NM 9.0	NM- 9.2
1-9-Gilbert, Jaime and Mario Hernandez-s/a						5.00
10-($5.95)						6.00
11-19-($4.50)						4.50
20-($7.99)						8.00

LOVE AND ROMANCE
Charlton Comics: Sept, 1971 - No. 24, Sept, 1975

	GD 2.0	VG 4.0	FN 6.0	VF 8.0	VF/NM 9.0	NM- 9.2
1	3	6	9	18	27	35
2-5,7-10	2	4	6	10	14	18
6-David Cassidy pin-up; grey-tone cover	3	6	9	14	19	24
11,13-24	2	4	6	8	10	12
12-Susan Dey poster	2	4	6	10	14	18

LOVE AT FIRST SIGHT
Ace Magazines (RAR Publ. Co./Periodical House): Oct, 1949 - No. 43, Nov, 1956 (Photo-c: 18-42)

	GD 2.0	VG 4.0	FN 6.0	VF 8.0	VF/NM 9.0	NM- 9.2
1-Painted-c	18	36	54	103	162	220
2-Painted-c	11	22	33	62	86	110
3-10: 4,7-Painted-c	10	20	30	56	76	95
11-20	9	18	27	52	69	85
21-33: 33-Last pre-code	9	18	27	50	65	80
34-43	9	18	27	47	61	75

LOVE BUG, THE (See Movie Comics)

LOVEBUNNY AND MR. HELL
Devil's Due Publ./Image Comics: 2002 - 2004 ($2.95, B&W, one-shots)

	GD 2.0	VG 4.0	FN 6.0	VF 8.0	VF/NM 9.0	NM- 9.2
1-Tim Seeley-s						3.00
...: A Day in the Lovelife (Image, 2003) Blaylock-a						3.00
...: Savage Love (Image, 2003) Seeley-s/a; Savage Dragon app.; Seeley & Larsen-c						3.00
TPB (4/04, $9.95, digest-sized) reprints						10.00

LOVE CLASSICS
A Lover's Magazine/Marvel: Nov, 1949 - No. 2, Feb, 1950 (Photo-c, 52 pgs.)

	GD 2.0	VG 4.0	FN 6.0	VF 8.0	VF/NM 9.0	NM- 9.2
1,2: 2-Virginia Mayo photo-c; 30 pg. story "I Turned Into a Small-Town Flirt"	17	34	51	98	154	210

LOVE CONFESSIONS
Quality Comics: Oct, 1949 - No. 54, Dec, 1956 (Photo-c: 3,4,6,7,9,11-18,21,24,25)

	GD 2.0	VG 4.0	FN 6.0	VF 8.0	VF/NM 9.0	NM- 9.2
1-Ward-c/a, 9 pgs; Gustavson-a	33	66	99	194	317	440
2-Gustavson-a; Ward-c	17	34	51	98	154	210
3	12	24	36	67	94	120
4-Crandall-a	13	26	39	74	105	135
5-Ward-a, 7 pgs.	14	28	42	81	118	155
6,7,9,11-13,15,16,18: 7-Van Johnson photo-c. 8-Robert Mitchum & Jane Russell photo-c	10	20	30	56	76	95
8,10-Ward-a (2 stories in #10)	14	28	42	81	118	155
14,17,19,22-Ward-a; 17-Faith Domerque photo-c	14	28	42	78	112	145
20-Ward-a(2)	14	28	42	81	118	155
21,23-28,30-38,40-42: Last precode, 4/55	9	18	27	50	65	80
29-Ward-a	13	26	39	74	105	135
39,53-Matt Baker-a	11	22	33	64	90	115
43,44,46,47,50-52,54: 47-Ward-c?	9	18	27	47	61	75
45,48-Ward-a	10	20	30	56	76	95
49-Baker-c/a	14	28	42	76	108	140

LOVECRAFT
DC Comics: 2003 (graphic novel)

	GD 2.0	VG 4.0	FN 6.0	VF 8.0	VF/NM 9.0	NM- 9.2
Hardcover ($24.95) Rodionoff & Giffen-s/Breccia-a; intro. by John Carpenter						25.00
Softcover ($17.95)						18.00

LOVE DIARY
Our Publishing Co./Toytown/Patches: July, 1949 - No. 48, Oct, 1955 (Photo-c: 1-24,27-29) (52 pgs. #1-11?)

	GD 2.0	VG 4.0	FN 6.0	VF 8.0	VF/NM 9.0	NM- 9.2
1-Krigstein-a	22	44	66	128	209	290
2,3-Krigstein & Mort Leav-a in each	15	30	45	84	127	170
4-8	11	22	33	62	86	110
9,10-Everett-a	12	24	36	67	94	120
11-15,17-20	10	20	30	56	76	95
16- Mort Leav-a, 3 pg. Baker-sty. Leav-a	11	22	33	60	83	105
21-30,32-48: 45-Leav-a. 47-Last precode(12/54)	9	18	27	52	69	85
31-John Buscema headlights-c	12	24	36	67	94	120

LOVE DIARY (Diary Loves #2 on; title change due to previously published title)
Quality Comics Group: Sept, 1949

	GD 2.0	VG 4.0	FN 6.0	VF 8.0	VF/NM 9.0	NM- 9.2
1-Ward-c/a, 9 pgs.	32	64	96	192	314	435

LOVE DIARY
Charlton Comics: July, 1958 - No. 102, Dec, 1976

	GD 2.0	VG 4.0	FN 6.0	VF 8.0	VF/NM 9.0	NM- 9.2
1	11	22	33	62	86	110
2	8	16	24	40	50	60
3-5,7-10: 10-Photo-c	7	14	21	35	43	50
6-Torres-a	7	14	21	37	46	55
11-20: 20-Photo-c	3	6	9	18	27	35
21-40	3	6	9	16	22	28
41-60	2	4	6	13	18	22
61-78,80,100-102	2	4	6	9	13	16
79-David Cassidy pin-up	2	4	6	13	18	22
81,83,84,86-99	2	4	6	8	10	12
82,85: 82-Partridge Family poster. 85-Danny poster	2	4	6	10	14	18

LOVE DOCTOR (See Dr. Anthony King...)

LOVE DRAMAS (True Secrets No. 3 on?)
Marvel Comics (IPS): Oct, 1949 - No. 2, Jan, 1950

	GD 2.0	VG 4.0	FN 6.0	VF 8.0	VF/NM 9.0	NM- 9.2
1-Jack Kamen-a; photo-c	20	40	60	114	182	250
2-Photo-c	14	28	42	82	121	160

LOVE EXPERIENCES (Challenge of the Unknown No. 6)
Ace Periodicals (A.A. Wyn/Periodical House): Oct, 1949 - No. 5, June, 1950; No. 6, Apr, 1951 - No. 38, June, 1956

	GD 2.0	VG 4.0	FN 6.0	VF 8.0	VF/NM 9.0	NM- 9.2
1-Painted-c	17	34	51	98	154	210
2	11	22	33	60	83	105
3-5: 5-Painted-c	10	20	30	56	76	95
6-10	9	18	27	52	69	85
11-30: 30-Last pre-code (2/55)	9	18	27	47	61	75
31-38: 38-Indicia date-6/56; c-date-8/56	8	16	24	44	57	70

NOTE: ***Anne Brewster*** *a-15. Photo c-4, 15-35, 38.*

LOVE FIGHTS (Also see Free Comic Book Day Edition in the Promotional Comics section)
Oni Press: June, 2003 - No. 12, Aug, 2004 ($2.99, B&W)

	GD 2.0	VG 4.0	FN 6.0	VF 8.0	VF/NM 9.0	NM- 9.2
1-12-Andi Watson-s/a						3.00
Vol. 1 TPB (4/04, $14.95, digest-size) r/#1-6						15.00

LOVE JOURNAL
Our Publishing Co.: No. 10, Oct, 1951 - No. 25, July, 1954

	GD 2.0	VG 4.0	FN 6.0	VF 8.0	VF/NM 9.0	NM- 9.2
10	15	30	45	85	130	175
11-15,17-25: 19-Mort Leav-a	11	22	33	60	83	105
16-Buscema headlight-c	13	26	39	74	105	135

LOVELAND
Mutual Mag./Eye Publ. (Marvel): Nov, 1949 - No. 2, Feb, 1950 (52 pgs.)

	GD 2.0	VG 4.0	FN 6.0	VF 8.0	VF/NM 9.0	NM- 9.2
1,2-Photo-c	14	28	42	80	115	150

LOVELESS
DC Comics: Dec, 2005 - No. 24, Jun, 2008 ($2.99)

	GD 2.0	VG 4.0	FN 6.0	VF 8.0	VF/NM 9.0	NM- 9.2
1-24: 1-Azzarello-s/Frusin-a. 6-8,15,22,23,24-Zezelj-a. 11,12,16-21-Dell'Edera-a						3.00
...: A Kin of Homecoming TPB (2006, $9.99) r/#1-5						10.00
...: Blackwater Falls TPB (2008, $19.99) r/#13-24						20.00
...: Thicker Than Blackwater TPB (2007, $14.99) r/#6-12						15.00

LOVE LESSONS
Harvey Comics/Key Publ. No. 5: Oct, 1949 - No. 5, June, 1950

	GD 2.0	VG 4.0	FN 6.0	VF 8.0	VF/NM 9.0	NM- 9.2
1-Metallic silver-c printed over the cancelled covers of Love Letters #1; indicia title is "Love Letters"	15	30	45	85	130	175
2-Powell-a; photo-c	9	18	27	52	69	85
3-5: 3,4-Photo-c	8	16	24	42	54	65

LOVE LETTERS (10/49, Harvey; advertised but never published; covers were printed before cancellation and were used as the cover to Love Lessons #1)

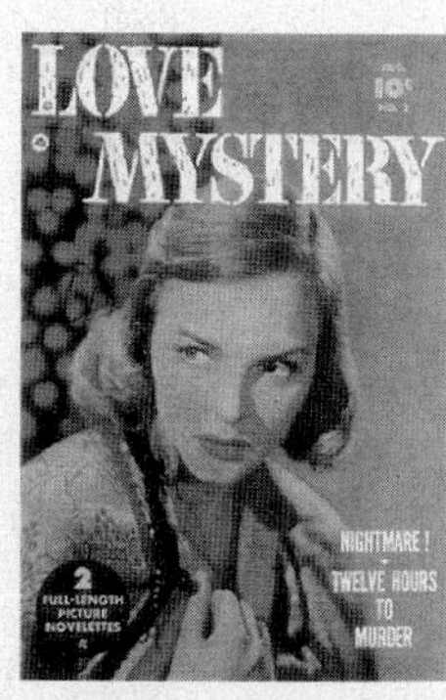

Love Mystery #2 © FAW

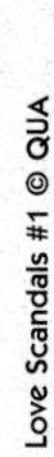
Love Scandals #1 © QUA

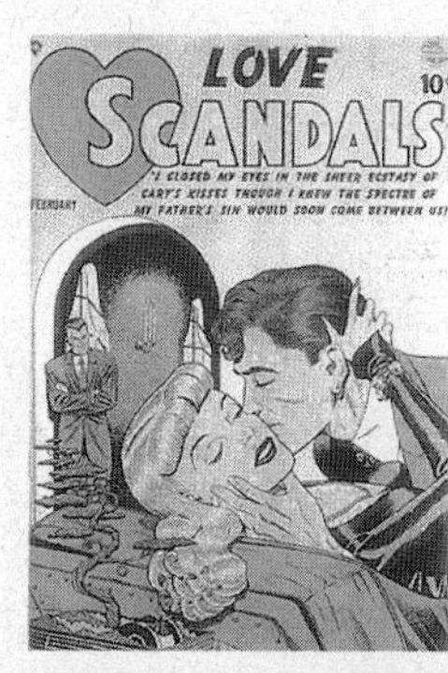

Love Secrets #2 © QUA

LOVE LETTERS (Love Secrets No. 32 on)
Quality Comics: 11/49 - #6, 9/50; #7, 3/51 - #31, 6/53; #32, 2/54 - #51, 12/56

	GD 2.0	VG 4.0	FN 6.0	VF 8.0	VF/NM 9.0	NM- 9.2
1-Ward-c, Gustavson-a	26	52	78	154	252	350
2-Ward-c, Gustavson-a	21	42	63	122	199	275
3-Gustavson-a	15	30	45	86	133	180
4-Ward-a, 9 pgs.; photo-c	20	40	60	114	182	250
5-8,10	11	22	33	64	90	110
9-One pg. Ward "Be Popular with the Opposite Sex"; Robert Mitchum photo-c	12	24	36	69	97	125
11-Ward-r/Broadway Romances #2 & retitled	12	24	36	69	97	125
12-15,18-20	10	20	30	56	76	95
16,17-Ward-a; 16-Anthony Quinn photo-c. 17-Jane Russell photo-c	15	30	45	84	127	170
21-29	10	20	30	54	72	90
30,31(6/53)-Ward-a	11	22	33	62	86	110
32(2/54)-39: 37-Ward-a. 38-Crandall-a. 39-Last precode (4/55)	9	18	27	50	65	80
40-48	9	18	27	47	61	75
49-51: 49,50-Baker-a. 51-Baker-c	13	26	39	72	101	130

NOTE: *Photo-c on most 3-28.*

LOVE LIFE
P. L. Publishing Co.: Nov, 1951

	GD 2.0	VG 4.0	FN 6.0	VF 8.0	VF/NM 9.0	NM- 9.2
1	11	22	33	62	86	110

LOVELORN (Confessions of the Lovelorn #52 on)
American Comics Group (Michel Publ./Regis Publ.): Aug-Sept, 1949 - No. 51, July, 1954 (No. 1-26: 52 pgs.)

	GD 2.0	VG 4.0	FN 6.0	VF 8.0	VF/NM 9.0	NM- 9.2
1	18	36	54	103	162	220
2	11	22	33	62	86	110
3-10	10	20	30	54	72	90
11-20,22-48: 18-Drucker-a(2 pgs.). 46-Lazarus-a	9	18	27	47	61	75
21-Prostitution story	11	22	33	62	86	110
49-51-Has 3-D effect-c/stories	17	34	51	98	154	210

LOVE MEMORIES
Fawcett Publications: 1949 (no month) - No. 4, July, 1950 (All photo-c)

	GD 2.0	VG 4.0	FN 6.0	VF 8.0	VF/NM 9.0	NM- 9.2
1	15	30	45	88	137	185
2-4: 2-(Win/49-50)	10	20	30	56	76	95

LOVE ME TENDERLOIN: A CAL McDONALD MYSTERY
Dark Horse Comics: Jan, 2004 ($2.99, one-shot)

	GD 2.0	VG 4.0	FN 6.0	VF 8.0	VF/NM 9.0	NM- 9.2
1-Niles-s/Templesmith-a/c						3.00

LOVE MYSTERY
Fawcett Publications: June, 1950 - No. 3, Oct, 1950 (All photo-c)

	GD 2.0	VG 4.0	FN 6.0	VF 8.0	VF/NM 9.0	NM- 9.2
1-George Evans-a	21	42	63	124	202	280
2,3-Evans-a. 3-Powell-a	16	32	48	92	144	195

LOVE PROBLEMS (See Fox Giants)

LOVE PROBLEMS AND ADVICE ILLUSTRATED (see True Love...)

LOVE ROMANCES (Formerly Ideal #5)
Timely/Marvel/Atlas(TCI No. 7-71/Male No. 72-106): No. 6, May, 1949 - No. 106, July, 1963

	GD 2.0	VG 4.0	FN 6.0	VF 8.0	VF/NM 9.0	NM- 9.2
6-Photo-c	20	40	60	114	182	250
7-Photo-c; Kamen-a	13	26	39	74	105	135
8-Kubert-a; photo-c	13	26	39	74	105	135
9-20: 9-12-Photo-c	12	24	36	67	94	120
21,24-Krigstein-a	12	24	36	69	97	125
22,23,25-35,37,39,40	11	22	33	62	86	110
36,38-Krigstein-a	11	22	33	64	90	115
41-44,46,47: Last precode (2/55)	11	22	33	60	83	105
45,57-Matt Baker-a	13	26	39	72	101	130
48,50-52,54-56,58-74	6	12	18	41	66	90
49,53-Toth-a, 6 & ? pgs.	7	14	21	44	72	100
75,77,82-Matt Baker-a	8	16	24	51	86	120
76,78-81,86,88-90,92-95: 80-Heath-c. 95-Last 10¢-c?	6	12	18	39	62	85
83,84,87,91-Kirby-c. 83-Severin-a	7	14	21	48	79	110
85,96,97,99-106-Kirby-c/a. 97-10¢ cover price blacked out, 12¢ printed on cover	8	16	24	55	93	130
98-Kirby-c/a	8	16	24	55	93	130

NOTE: ***Anne Brewster** a-67, 72. **Colletta** a-37, 40, 42, 44, 67(2); c-42, 44, 49, 54, 80. **Everett** c-70. **Hartley** c-20, 21, 30, 31. **Heath** a-87. **Kirby** c-80, 85, 88. **Robinson** a-29.*

LOVERS (Formerly Blonde Phantom)
Marvel Comics No. 23,24/Atlas No. 25 on (ANC): No. 23, May, 1949 - No. 86, Aug?, 1957

	GD 2.0	VG 4.0	FN 6.0	VF 8.0	VF/NM 9.0	NM- 9.2
23-Photo-c begin, end #29	20	40	60	114	182	250
24-Toth-*ish* plus Robinson-a	12	24	36	69	97	125
25,30-Kubert-a; 7, 10 pgs.	13	26	39	72	101	130
26-29,31-36,39,40: 35-Maneely-c	11	22	33	62	86	110
37,38-Krigstein-a	12	24	36	69	97	125
41-Everett-a(2)	12	24	36	69	97	125
42,44-65: 65-Last pre-code (1/55)	10	20	30	54	72	90
43-Frazetta 1 pg. ad	10	20	30	56	76	95
66,68-80,82-86	9	18	27	52	69	85
67-Toth-a	10	20	30	56	76	95
81-Baker-a	10	20	30	58	79	100

NOTE: ***Anne Brewster** a-86. **Colletta** a-54, 59, 62, 64, 65, 69, 85; c-61, 64, 65, 75. **Hartley** c-37, 53, 54. **Heath** a-61. **Maneely** a-57. **Powell** a-27, 30. **Robinson** a-42, 54, 56.*

LOVERS' LANE
Lev Gleason Publications: Oct, 1949 - No. 41, June, 1954 (No. 1-18: 52 pgs.)

	GD 2.0	VG 4.0	FN 6.0	VF 8.0	VF/NM 9.0	NM- 9.2
1-Biro-c	15	30	45	90	140	190
2-Biro-c	10	20	30	58	79	100
3-20: 3,4-Painted-c. 20-Frazetta 1 pg. ad	10	20	30	54	72	90
21-38,40,41	9	18	27	47	61	75
39-Story narrated by Frank Sinatra	10	20	30	58	79	100

NOTE: ***Briefer** a-6, 13, 21. **Esposito** a-5. **Fuje** a-4, 16; c-many. **Guardineer** a-1, 3. **Kinstler** c-41. **Sparling** a-3. **Tuska** a-6. Painted c-3-18. Photo c-19-22, 26-28.*

LOVE SCANDALS
Quality Comics: Feb, 1950 - No. 5, Oct, 1950 (Photo-c #2-5) (All 52 pgs.)

	GD 2.0	VG 4.0	FN 6.0	VF 8.0	VF/NM 9.0	NM- 9.2
1-Ward-c/a, 9 pgs.	27	54	81	160	263	365
2,3: 2-Gustavson-a	14	28	42	80	115	150
4-Ward-a, 18 pgs; Gil Fox-a	21	42	63	124	202	280
5-C. Cuidera-a; tomboy story "I Hated Being a Woman"	15	30	45	88	137	185

LOVE SECRETS
Marvel Comics(IPC): Oct, 1949 - No. 2, Jan, 1950 (52 pgs., photo-c)

	GD 2.0	VG 4.0	FN 6.0	VF 8.0	VF/NM 9.0	NM- 9.2
1	18	36	54	103	162	220
2	12	24	36	69	97	125

LOVE SECRETS (Formerly Love Letters #31)
Quality Comics Group: No. 32, Aug, 1953 - No. 56, Dec, 1956

	GD 2.0	VG 4.0	FN 6.0	VF 8.0	VF/NM 9.0	NM- 9.2
32	14	28	42	76	108	140
33,35-39	10	20	30	54	72	90
34-Ward-a	14	28	42	76	108	140
40-Matt Baker-c	13	26	39	74	105	135
41-43: 43-Last precode (3/55)	10	20	30	54	72	90
44,47-50,53,54	9	18	27	47	61	75
45-Ward-a	11	22	33	62	86	110
46-Ward-a; Baker-a	12	24	36	69	97	125
51,52-Ward(r). 52-r/Love Confessions #17	10	20	30	54	72	90
55,56: 55-Baker-a. 56-Baker-c	11	22	33	64	90	115

LOVE STORIES (See Top Love Stories)

LOVE STORIES (Formerly Heart Throbs)
National Periodical Publ.: No. 147, Nov, 1972 - No. 152, Oct-Nov, 1973

	GD 2.0	VG 4.0	FN 6.0	VF 8.0	VF/NM 9.0	NM- 9.2
147-152	3	6	9	14	20	26

LOVE STORIES OF MARY WORTH (See Harvey Comics Hits #55 & Mary Worth)
Harvey Publications: Sept, 1949 - No. 5, May, 1950

	GD 2.0	VG 4.0	FN 6.0	VF 8.0	VF/NM 9.0	NM- 9.2
1-1940's newspaper reprints-#1-4	9	18	27	47	61	75
2-5: 3-Kamen/Baker-a?	6	12	18	31	38	45

LOVE TALES (Formerly The Human Torch #35)
Marvel/Atlas Comics (ZPC No. 36-50/MMC No. 67-75): No. 36, 5/49 - No. 58, 8/52; No. 59, date? - No. 75, Sept, 1957

	GD 2.0	VG 4.0	FN 6.0	VF 8.0	VF/NM 9.0	NM- 9.2
36-Photo-c	18	36	54	107	169	230
37	11	22	33	64	90	115
38-44,46-50: 39-41-Photo-c	11	22	33	60	83	105
45,51,52,69: 45-Powell-a. 51,69-Everett-a. 52-Krigstein-a	11	22	33	62	86	110
53-60: 60-Last pre-code (2/55)	9	18	27	52	69	85
61-68,70-75: 75-Brewster, Cameron, Colletta-a	9	18	27	50	65	80

LOVE THRILLS (See Fox Giants)

LOVE TRAILS (Western romance)
A Lover's Magazine (CDS)(Marvel): Dec, 1949 - No. 2, Mar, 1950 (52 pgs.)

	GD 2.0	VG 4.0	FN 6.0	VF 8.0	VF/NM 9.0	NM- 9.2
1,2: 1-Photo-c	15	30	45	86	133	180

LOWELL THOMAS' HIGH ADVENTURE (See High Adventure)

Lucifer #20 © DC

Lucky Star #3 © Nationwide

Lyndon B. Johnson © DELL

GD VG FN VF VF/NM NM-
2.0 4.0 6.0 8.0 9.0 9.2

LT. (See Lieutenant)

LUCIFER (See The Sandman #4)
DC Comics (Vertigo): Jun, 2000 - No. 75, Aug, 2006 ($2.50/$2.75)

1-Carey-s/Weston-a/Fegredo-c 8.00
2,3-Carey-s/Weston-a/Fegredo-c 5.00
4-10: 4-Pleece-a. 5-Gross-a 4.00
11-49,51-73: 16-Moeller-c begin. 25,26-Death app. 45-Naifeh-a. 53-Kaluta-c begin. 62-Doran-a. 63-Begin $2.75-c 3.00
50-($3.50) P. Craig Russell-a; Mazikeen app. 4.00
74-($2.99) Kaluta-c 3.00
75-($3.99) Last issue; Lucifer's origins retold; Morpheus app.; Gross-a/Moeller-c 4.00
Preview-16 pg. flip book w/Swamp Thing Preview 3.00
...: A Dalliance With the Damned TPB ('02, $14.95) r/#14-20 15.00
...: Children and Monsters TPB ('01, $17.95) r/#5-13 18.00
...: Crux TPB (2006, $14.99) r/#55-61 15.00
...: Devil in the Gateway TPB ('01, $14.95) r/#1-4 & Sandman Presents:..#1-3 15.00
...: Evensong TPB (2007, $14.99) r/#70-75 & Lucifer: Nirvana one-shot 15.00
...: Exodus TPB (2005, $14.95) r/#42-44,46-49 15.00
...: Inferno TPB (2003, $14.95) r/#29-35 15.00
...: Mansions of the Silence TPB (2004, $14.95) r/#36-41 15.00
...: Morningstar TPB (2006, $14.99) r/#62-69 15.00
...: Nirvana (2002, $5.95) Carey-s/Muth-painted-c/a; Daniel app. 6.00
...: The Divine Comedy TPB (2003, $17.95) r/#21-28 18.00
...: The Wolf Beneath the Tree TPB (2005, $14.99) r/#45,50-54 15.00

LUCIFER'S HAMMER (Larry Niven & Jerry Pournelle's...)
Innovation Publishing: Nov, 1993 - No. 6, 1994 ($2.50, painted, limited series)

1-6: Adaptatin of novel, painted-c & art 3.00

LUCKY COMICS
Consolidated Magazines: Jan, 1944; No. 2, Sum, 1945 - No. 5, Sum, 1946

1-Lucky Starr & Bobbie begin 23 46 69 136 223 310
2-5: 5-Devil-c by Walter Johnson 14 28 42 81 118 155

LUCKY DUCK
Standard Comics (Literary Ent.): No. 5, Jan, 1953 - No. 8, Sept, 1953

5-Funny animal; Irving Spector-a 11 22 33 60 83 105
6-8-Irving Spector-a 10 20 30 54 72 90
NOTE: *Harvey Kurtzman tried to hire Spector for Mad #1.*

LUCKY "7" COMICS
Howard Publishers Ltd.: 1944 (No date listed)

1-Pioneer, Sir Gallagher, Dick Royce, Congo Raider, Punch Powers; bondage-c 40 80 120 246 411 575

LUCKY STAR (Western)
Nation Wide Publ. Co.: 1950 - No. 7, 1951; No. 8, 1953 - No. 14, 1955 (5x7-1/4"; full color, 5¢)

nn (#1)-(5¢, 52 pgs.)-Davis-a 19 38 57 111 176 240
2,3-(5¢, 52 pgs.)-Davis-a 13 26 39 74 105 135
4-7-(5¢, 52 pgs.)-Davis-a 12 24 36 69 97 125
8-14-(36 pgs.)(Exist?) 12 24 36 69 97 125
Given away with Lucky Star Western Wear by the Juvenile Mfg. Co. 7 14 21 35 43 50

LUCY SHOW, THE (TV) (Also see I Love Lucy)
Gold Key: June, 1963 - No. 5, June, 1964 (Photo-c: 1,2)

1 11 22 33 76 151 225
2 7 14 21 48 79 110
3-5: Photo back c-1,2,4,5 6 12 18 42 69 95

LUCY, THE REAL GONE GAL (Meet Miss Pepper #5 on)
St. John Publishing Co.: June, 1953 - No. 4, Dec, 1953

1-Negligee panels 16 32 48 94 147 200
2 10 20 30 58 79 100
3,4: 3-Drucker-a 10 20 30 54 72 90

LUDWIG BEMELMAN'S MADELEINE & GENEVIEVE
Dell Publishing Co.: No. 796, May, 1957

Four Color 796 4 8 12 24 37 50

LUDWIG VON DRAKE (TV)(Disney)(See Walt Disney's C&S #256)
Dell Publishing Co.: Nov-Dec, 1961 - No. 4, June-Aug, 1962

1 7 14 21 44 72 100
2-4 5 10 15 32 51 70

LUFTWAFFE: 1946 (Volume 1)
Antarctic Press: July, 1996 - No. 4, Jan, 1997 ($2.95, B&W, limited series)

1-4-Ben Dunn & Ted Nomura-s/a, ...Special Ed. 3.00

LUFTWAFFE: 1946 (Volume 2)
Antarctic Press: Mar, 1997 - No. 18 ($2.95/$2.99, B&W, limited series)

1-18: 8-Reviews Tigers of Terra series 3.00
Annual 1 (4/98, $2.95)-Reprints early Nomura pages 4.00
...Color Special (4/98) 3.00
...Technical Manual 1,2 (2/98, 4/99) 4.00

LUGER
Eclipse Comics: Oct, 1986 - No. 3, Feb, 1987 ($1.75, miniseries, Baxter paper)

1-3: Bruce Jones scripts; Yeates-c/a 3.00

LUKE CAGE (See Cage & Hero for Hire)

LUKE CAGE NOIR
Marvel Comics: Oct, 2009 - No. 4, Jan, 2010 ($3.99, limited series)

1-4-Glass & Benson-a/Martinbrough-a; covers by Bradstreet and Calero 4.00

LUKE SHORT'S WESTERN STORIES
Dell Publishing Co.: No. 580, Aug, 1954 - No. 927, Aug, 1958

Four Color 580(8/54), 651(9/55)-Kinstler-a 4 8 12 28 44 60
Four Color 739,771,807,848,875,927 4 8 12 26 41 55

LUNATIC FRINGE, THE
Innovation Publishing: July, 1989 - No. 2, 1989 ($1.75, deluxe format)

1,2 3.00

LUNATICKLE (Magazine) (Satire)
Whitstone Publ.: Feb, 1956 - No. 2, Apr, 1956

1,2-Kubert-a (scarce) 9 18 27 47 61 75

LUNATIK
Marvel Comics: Dec, 1995 - No. 3, Feb, 1996 ($1.95, limited series)

1-3 3.00

LURKERS, THE
IDW Publ.: Oct, 2004 - No. 4, Jan, 2005 ($3.99)

1-4-Niles-s/Casanova-a 4.00

LUST FOR LIFE
Slave Labor Graphics: Feb, 1997 - No. 4, Jan, 1998 ($2.95, B&W)

1-4: 1-Jeff Levin-s/a 3.00

LUTHOR (See Lex Luthor: Man of Steel)

LYCANTHROPE LEO
Viz Communications: 1994 - No. 7($2.95, B&W, limited series, 44 pgs.)

1-7 4.00

LYNCH (See Gen 13)
Image Comics (WildStorm Productions): May, 1997 ($2.50, one-shot)

1-Helmut-c/app. 3.00

LYNCH MOB
Chaos! Comics: June, 1994 - No. 4, Sept, 1994 ($2.50, limited series)

1-4 5.00
1-Special edition full foil-c 1 2 3 5 6 8

LYNDON B. JOHNSON
Dell Publishing Co.: Mar, 1965

12-445-503-Photo-c 3 6 9 20 30 40

M
Eclipse Books: 1990 - No. 4, 1991 ($4.95, painted, 52 pgs.)

1-Adapts movie; contains flexi-disc ($5.95) 6.00
2-4 5.00

MACE GRIFFIN BOUNTY HUNTER (Based on video game)
Image Comics (Top Cow): May, 2003 ($2.99, one-shot)

1-Nocon-a 3.00

MACHETE (Based on the Robert Rodriguez movie)
IDW Publishing: No. 0, Sept, 2010 ($3.99)

0-Origin story; Rodriguez & Kaufman-s/Sayger-a; 3 covers 4.00

MACHINE, THE
Dark Horse Comics: Nov, 1994 - No. 4, Feb, 1995 ($2.50, limited series)

1-4 3.00

MACHINE MAN (Also see 2001, A Space Odyssey)
Marvel Comics Group: Apr, 1978 - No. 9, Dec, 1978; No. 10, Aug, 1979 - No. 19, Feb, 1981

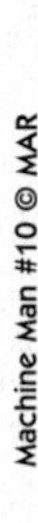
Machine Man #10 © MAR

Mad #8 © E.C. Publ.

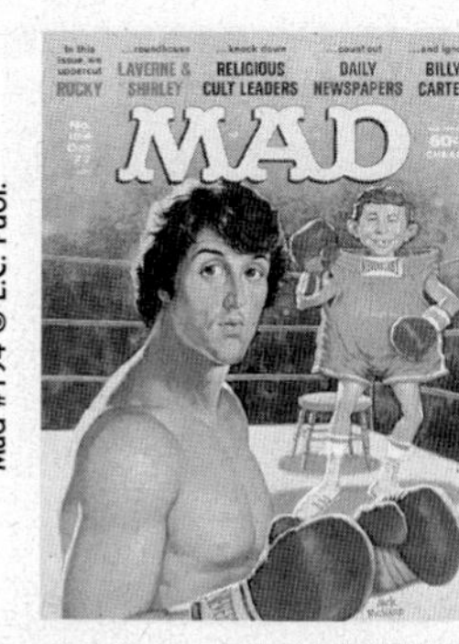

Mad #194 © E.C. Publ.

GD VG FN VF VF/NM NM-
2.0 4.0 6.0 8.0 9.0 9.2

1-Jack Kirby-c/a/scripts begin; end #9 3 6 9 16 23 30
2-9-Kirby-c/a/s. 9-(12/78) 2 4 6 9 12 15
10-17: 10-(8/79) Marv Wolfman scripts & Ditko-a begins
1 3 4 6 8 10
18-Wendigo, Alpha Flight-ties into X-Men #140 3 6 9 16 23 30
19-Intro/1st app. Jack O'Lantern (Macendale), later becomes 2nd Hobgoblin
3 6 9 14 20 25

NOTE: ***Austin*** *c-7i, 19i.* ***Buckler*** *c-17p, 18p.* ***Byrne*** *c-14p.* ***Ditko*** *a-10-19; c-10-13, 14i, 15, 16.* ***Kirby*** *a-1-9p; c-1-5, 7-9p.* ***Layton*** *c-7i.* ***Miller*** *c-19p.* ***Simonson*** *c-6.*

MACHINE MAN (Also see X-51)
Marvel Comics Group: Oct, 1984 - No. 4, Jan, 1985 (limited series)

1-4-Barry Smith-c/a(i) & colors in all 5.00
TPB (1988, $6.95) r/ #1-4; Barry Smith-c 7.00
.../Bastion '98 Annual ($2.99) wraparound-c 4.00

MACHINE MAN 2020
Marvel Comics: Aug, 1994 - Nov, 1994 ($2.00, 52 pgs., limited series)

1-4: Reprints Machine Man limited series; Barry Windsor-Smith-c/i(r) 4.00

MACHINE TEEN
Marvel Comics: July, 2005 - No. 5, Nov, 2005 ($2.99, limited series)

1-5-Sumerak-s/Hawthorne-a. 1-James Jean-c 3.00
...: History (2005, $7.99, digest) r/#1-5 8.00

MACK BOLAN: THE EXECUTIONER (Don Pendleton's...)
Innovation Publishing: July, 1993 ($2.50)

1-3-($2.50) 3.00
1-($3.95)-Indestructible Cover Edition 4.00
1-($2.95)-Collector's Gold Edition; foil stamped 3.00
1-($3.50)-Double Cover Edition; red foil outer-c 3.50

MACKENZIE'S RAIDERS (Movie, TV)
Dell Publishing Co.: No. 1093, Apr-June, 1960

Four Color 1093-Richard Carlson photo-c from TV show
6 12 18 42 69 95

MACROSS (Becomes Robotech: The Macross Saga #2 on)
Comico: Dec, 1984 ($1.50)(Low print run)

1-Early manga app. 3 6 9 14 20 25

MACROSS II
Viz Select Comics: 1992 - No. 10, 1993 ($2.75, B&W, limited series)

1-10: Based on video series 4.00

MAD (Tales Calculated to Drive You...)
E. C. Comics (Educational Comics): Oct-Nov, 1952 - Present (No. 24-on are magazine format) (Kurtzman editor No. 1-28, Feldstein No. 29 - No. ?)

1-Wood, Davis, Elder start as regulars 417 834 1251 3336 5318 7300
2-Dick Tracy cameo 110 220 330 880 1403 1925
3,4: 3-Stan Lee mentioned. 4-Reefer mention story "Flob Was a Slob" by Davis; Superman parody 77 154 231 616 983 1350
5-Low distr.; W.M. Gaines biog. 157 314 471 1256 2003 2750
6-11: 6-Popeye cameo. 7,8- "Hey Look" reprints by Kurtzman. 11-Wolverton-a; Davis story was-r/Crime Suspenstories #12 w/new Kurtzman dialogue
60 120 180 480 765 1050
12-15: 15,18-Pot Shot Pete-r by Kurtzman 48 96 144 384 612 840
16-23(5/55): 18-Alice in Wonderland by Jack Davis. 21-1st app. Alfred E. Neuman on-c in fake ad. 22-All by Elder plus photo-montages by Kurtzman. 23-Special cancel announcement 40 80 120 320 510 700
24(7/55)-1st magazine issue (25¢); Kurtzman logo & border on-c; 1st "What? Me Worry?" on-c; 2nd printing exists 94 188 282 752 1201 1650
25-Jaffee starts as regular writer 44 88 132 352 564 775
26,27: 27-Jaffee starts as story artist; new logo 39 78 117 312 499 685
28-Last issue edited by Kurtzman; (three cover variations exist with different wording on contents banner on lower right of cover; value of each the same)
36 72 108 216 351 485
29-Kamen-a; Don Martin starts as regular; Feldstein editing begins
36 72 108 216 351 485
30-1st A. E. Neuman cover by Mingo; last Elder-a; Bob Clarke starts as regular; Disneyland & Elvis Presley spoof 50 100 150 315 533 750
31-Freas starts as regular; last Davis-a until #99 32 64 96 192 314 435
435
32,33: 32-Orlando, Drucker, Woodbridge start as regulars; Wood back-c. 33-Orlando back-c
27 54 81 162 266 370
34-Berg starts as regular 22 44 66 132 216 300
35-Mingo wraparound-c; Crandall-a 22 44 66 132 216 300

GD VG FN VF VF/NM NM-
2.0 4.0 6.0 8.0 9.0 9.2

36-40 (7/58): 39-Beall-c 18 36 54 105 165 225
41-50: 42-Danny Kaye-s. 44-Xmas-c. 47-49-Sid Caesar-s. 48-Uncle Sam-c. 50 (10/59)-Peter Gunn-s 15 30 45 90 140 190
51-59: 52-Xmas-c; 77 Sunset Strip. 53-Rifleman-s. 54-Jaffee-a begins. 55-Sid Caesar-s. 59-Strips of Superman, Flash Gordon, Donald Duck & others. 59-Halloween/Headless Horseman-c 14 28 42 80 115 150
60 (1/61)-JFK/Nixon flip-c; 1st Spy vs. Spy by Prohias, who starts as regular
15 30 45 86 133 180
61-70: 64-Rickard starts as regular. 65-JFK-s. 66-JFK-c. 68-Xmas-c by Martin. 70-Route 66-s
7 14 21 48 79 110
71-75,77-80 (7/63): 72-10th Anniv. special; 1/3 pg. strips of Superman, Tarzan & others. 73-Bonanza-s. 74-Dr. Kildare-s 5 10 15 35 55 75
76-Aragonés starts as regular 6 12 18 39 62 85
81-85: 81-Superman strip. 82-Castro-c. 85-Lincoln-c 5 10 15 30 48 65
86-1st Fold-in; commonly creased back covers makes these and later issues scarcer in NM
6 12 18 37 59 80
87,88 5 10 15 35 55 75
89,90: 89-One strip by Walt Kelly; Frankenstein-c; Fugitive-s. 90-Ringo back-c by Frazetta; Beatles app. 6 12 18 37 59 80
91,94,96,100: 94-King Kong-c. 96-Man From U.N.C.L.E. 100-(1/66)-Anniversary issue
5 10 15 30 48 65
92,93,95,97-99: 99-Davis-a resumes 4 8 12 28 44 60
101,104,106,108,114,115,119,121: 101-Infinity-c; Voyage to the Bottom of the Sea-s. 104-Lost in Space-s. 106-Tarzan back-c by Frazetta; 2 pg. Batman by Aragonés. 108-Hogan's Heroes by Davis. 114-Rat Patrol-s. 115-Star Trek. 119-Invaders (TV). 121-Beatles-c; Ringo pin-up; flip-c of Sik-Teen; Flying Nun-s 3 6 9 21 32 42
102,103,107,109-113,116-118,120(7/68): 118-Beatles cameo
3 6 9 19 29 38
105-Batman-c/s, TV show parody (9/66) 4 8 12 24 37 50
122,124,126,128,129,131-134,136,137,139,140: 122-Ronald Reagan photo inside; Drucker & Mingo-c. 126-Family Affair-s. 128-Last Orlando. 131-Reagan photo back-c. 132-Xmas-c. 133-John Wayne/True Grit. 136-Room 222 3 6 9 16 22 28
123-Four different covers 3 6 9 16 23 30
125,127,130,135,138: 125-2001 Space Odyssey; Hitler back-c. 127-Mod Squad-c/s. 130-Land of the Giants-s; Torres begins as reg. 135-Easy Rider-c by Davis. 138-Snoopy-c; MASH-s
3 6 9 17 25 32
141-149,151-156,158-165,167-170: 141-Hawaii Five-0. 147-All in the Family-s. 153-Dirty Harry-s. 155-Godfather-c/s. 156-Columbo-s. 159-Clockwork Orange-c/s. 161-Tarzan-s. 164-Kung Fu (TV)-s. 165-James Bond-s; Dean Martin-c. 169-Drucker-c; McCloud-s. 170-Exorcist-s 3 6 9 14 19 24
150-(4/72) Partridge Family-s 3 6 9 15 21 26
157-(3/73) Planet of the Apes-c/s 3 6 9 16 23 30
166-(4/74) Classic finger-c 3 6 9 16 23 30
171-185,187,189-192,194,195,198,199: 172-Six Million Dollar Man-s; Hitler back-c. 178-Godfather II-c/s. 180-Jaws-c/s (1/76). 182-Bob Jones starts as regular.185-Starsky & Hutch-s. 187-Fonz/Happy Days-c/s; Harry North starts as regular. 189-Travolta/Kotter-c/s. 190-John Wayne-c/s. 192-King Kong-c/s. 194-Rocky-c/s; Laverne & Shirley-s. 199-James Bond-s 2 4 6 10 14 18
186,188,197,200: 186-Star Trek-c/s. 188-Six Million Dollar Man/ Bionic Woman. 197-Spock-s; Star Wars-s. 200-Close Encounters 2 4 6 13 18 22
193,196: 193-Farrah/Charlie's Angels-c/s. 196-Star Wars-c/s
3 6 9 14 19 24
201,203,205,220: 201-Sat. Night Fever-c/s. 203-Star Wars. 205-Travolta/Grease. 220-Yoda-c, Empire Strikes Back-s 2 4 6 9 13 16
202,204,206,207,209,211-219,221-227,229,230: 204-Hulk TV show. 206-Tarzan. 208-Superman movie. 209-Mork & Mindy. 212-Spider-Man-s; Alien (movie)-s. 213-James Bond, Dracula, Rocky II-s 216-Star Trek. 219-Martin-c. 221-Shining-s. 223-Dallas-c/s. 225-Popeye. 226-Superman II. 229-James Bond. 230-Star Wars
1 3 4 6 8 10
208,228: 208-Superman movie-c/s; Battlestar Galactica-s. 228-Raiders of the Lost Ark-c/s
2 4 6 9 12 15
210-Lord of the Rings 2 4 6 9 13 16
231-235,237-241,243-249,251-260: 233-Pac-Man-c. 234-MASH-c/s. 235-Flip-c with Rocky III & Conan; Boris-a. 239-Mickey Mouse-c. 241-Knight Rider-s. 243-Superman III. 245- Last Rickard-a. 247-Seven Dwarfs-c. 253-Supergirl movie-s; Prince/Purple Rain-s. 254-Rock stars-s. 255-Reagan-c; Cosby-s. 256-Last issue edited by Feldstein; Dynasty, Bev. Hills Cop. 259-Rambo. 260-Back to the Future-c/s; Honeymooners-s
1 2 3 5 6 8
236,242,250: 236-E.T.-c/s;Star Trek II-s. 242-Star Wars/A-Team-c/s. 250-Temple of Doom-c/s; Tarzan-s 1 2 3 5 7 9
261-267,269-276,278-288,290-297: 261-Miami Vice. 262-Rocky IV-c/s, Leave It To Beaver-s. 263-Young Sherlock Holmes-s. 264-Hulk Hogan-c; Rambo-s. 267-Top Gun. 271-Star Trek IV-c/s. 272-ALF-c; Get Smart-s. 273-Pee Wee Herman-c/s. 274-Last Martin-a. 281-California Raisins-c. 282-Star Trek:TNG-s; ALF-s. 283-Rambo III-c/s. 284-Roger

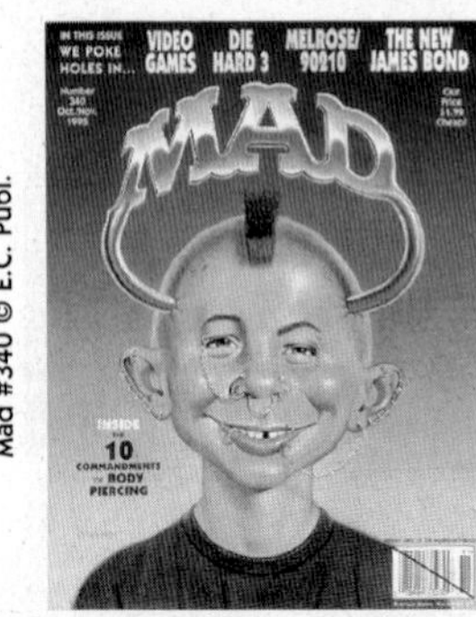

Mad #340 © E.C. Publ.

Madame Xanadu #29 © DC

Madman Adventures #1 © Mike Allred

GD VG FN VF VF/NM NM-
2.0 4.0 6.0 8.0 9.0 9.2

Rabbit-c/s. 285-Hulk Hogan-c. 287-3 pgs. Eisner-a. 291-TMNT-c; Indiana Jones-s. 292-Super Mario Bros.-c; Married with Children-s. 295-Back to the Future II. 297-Mike Tyson-c 1 2 3 4 5 7
268,277,289,298-300: 268-Aliens-c/s. 277-Michael Jackson-c/s; Robocop-s. 289-Batman movie parody. 298-Gremlins II-c/s; Robocop II. Batman-s. 299-Simpsons-c/story; Total Recall-s. 300(1/91) Casablanca-s, Dick Tracy-s, Wizard of Oz-s, Gone With The Wind-s 1 2 3 5 6 8
300-303 (1/91-6/91)-Special Hussein Asylum Editions; only distributed to the troops in the Middle East (see Mad Super Spec.) 2 4 6 13 18 22
301-310,312,313,315-320,322,324,326-334,337-349: 303-Home Alone-c/s. 305-Simpsons-s. 306-TMNT II movie. 308-Terminator II. 315-Tribute to William Gaines. 316-Photo-c. 319-Dracula-c/s. 320-Disney's Aladdin-s. 322-Batman Animated series. 327-Seinfeld-s; X-Men-s. 331-Flintstones-c/s. 332-O.J. Simpson-c/s; Simpsons app. in Lion King. 334-Frankenstein-c/s. 338-Judge Dredd-c by Frazetta. 341-Pocahontas-s. 345-Beatles app. (1 pg.) 347-Broken Arrow & Mission Impossible 5.00
311,314,321,323,325,335,336,350,354,358: 311-Addams Family-c/story, Home Improvement-s. 314-Batman Returns-c/story. 321-Star Trek DS9-c/s. 323-Jurassic Park-c/s. 325,336-Beavis & Butthead-c/s. 335-X-Files-s; Pulp Fiction-s; Interview with the Vampire-s. 336-Lois & Clark-s. 350-Polybagged w/CD Rom. 354-Star Wars; Beavis & Butthead-s. 358-X-Files 6.00
351-353,355-357,359-500 5.00
501-503-($5.99) 6.00
Mad About Super Heroes (2002, $9.95) r/super hero app.; Alex Ross-c 10.00

NOTE: **Aragones** *c-210, 293.* **Beall** *c-39.* **Davis** *c-2, 27, 135, 139, 173, 178, 212, 213, 219, 246, 260, 296, 308.* **Drucker** *a-35-62; c-122, 169, 176, 225, 234, 264, 266, 274, 280, 285, 297, 299, 303, 314, 315, 321.* **Elder** *c-5, 259, 261, 268.* **Elder/Kurtzman** *a-258-274.* **Jules Feiffer** *a(r)-42.* **Freas** *c-40-59, 62-67, 69-70, 72, 74.* **Heath** *a-14, 27.* **Jaffee** *c-199, 217, 224, 258.* **Kamen** *a-29.* **Krigstein** *a-12, 17, 24, 26.* **Kurtzman** *c-1, 3, 4, 6-10, 13, 16, 18.* **Martin** *a-29-62; c-68, 165, 229.* **Mingo** *c-30-37, 61, 71, 75-80, 82-114, 117-124, 126, 129, 131, 133, 134, 136, 140, 143-148, 150-162, 164, 166-168, 171, 172, 174, 175, 177, 179, 181, 183, 185, 198, 206, 209, 211, 214, 218, 221, 222, 300.* **John Severin** *a-1-6, 9, 10.* **Wolverton** *c-11; a-11, 17, 29, 31, 36, 40, 82, 137.* **Wood** *a-1-21, 23-62; c-26, 28, 29.* **Woodbridge** *a-35-62. Issues 1-23 are 36 pgs.; 24-28 are 58 pgs.; 29 on are 52 pgs.*

MAD (See Mad Follies, ...Special, More Trash from..., and The Worst from...)

MAD ABOUT MILLIE (Also see Millie the Model)
Marvel Comics Group: April, 1969 - No. 16, Nov, 1970

1-Giant issue 10 20 30 65 118 170
2,3 (Giants) 7 14 21 44 72 100
4-10 5 10 15 32 51 70
11-16: 16-r 5 10 15 30 48 65
Annual 1(11/71, 52 pgs.) 5 10 15 32 51 70

MADAME MIRAGE
Image Comics (Top Cow): June, 2007 - No. 6, May, 2008 ($2.99)

1-6: 1-Paul Dini-s/Kenneth Rocafort-a; two covers by Horn and Rocafort 3.00
... First Look (5/07, 99¢) preview of series; Dini interview; cover gallery 3.00
Volume 1 TPB (7/08, $14.99) r/#1-6; cover gallery; cover and design sketches 15.00

MADAME XANADU
DC Comics: July, 1981 ($1.00, no ads, 36 pgs.)

1-Marshall Rogers-a (25 pgs.); Kaluta-c/a (2pgs.); pin-up 1 2 3 5 6 8

MADAME XANADU (Also see Doorway to Nightmare)
DC Comics (Vertigo): Aug, 2008 - No. 29, Jan, 2011 ($2.99)

1-Matt Wagner-s/Amy Reeder Hadley-a/c; Phantom Stranger app. 4.00
1,2-Variant covers. 1-Wagner. 2-Kaluta 5.00
2-29: 2-10-Amy Reeder Hadley-a/c; Phantom Stranger app. 6-Death (from The Sandman) app.; covers by Hadley & Quitely. 9-Zatara app. 10-Jim Corrigan becomes The Spectre. 11-15-Kaluta-a. 14,15-Sandman (Wesley Dodds) app. 16-18-Hadley-a; Det. Jones app. 3.00
...: Broken House of Cards TPB (2011, $17.99) r/#16-23 and story from House of Mystery Halloween Annual #1 18.00
...: Disenchanted TPB (2009, $12.99) r/#1-10; James Robinson intro.; Hadley sketch-a 13.00
...: Exodus TPB (2010, $12.99) r/#11-15; Chris Roberson intro. 13.00
...: Extra-Sensory TPB (2011, $17.99) r/#24-29 18.00

MADBALLS
Star Comics/Marvel Comics #9 on: Sept, 1986 - No. 3, Nov, 1986; No. 4, June, 1987 - No. 10, June, 1988

1-10: Based on toys. 9-Post-a 4.00

MAD DISCO
E.C. Comics: 1980 (one-shot, 36 pgs.)

1-Includes 30 minute flexi-disc of Mad disco music 2 4 6 11 16 20

MAD-DOG
Marvel Comics: May, 1993 - No. 6, Oct, 1993 ($1.25)

1-6-Flip book w/2nd story "created" by Bob Newhart's character from his TV show "Bob" set at a comic book company; actual s/a-Ty Templeton 3.00

GD VG FN VF VF/NM NM-
2.0 4.0 6.0 8.0 9.0 9.2

MAD DOGS
Eclipse Comics: Feb, 1992 - No. 3, July, 1992 ($2.50, B&W, limited series)

1-3 3.00

MAD 84 (Mad Extra)
E.C. Comics: 1984 (84 pgs.)

1 1 3 4 6 8 10

MAD FOLLIES (Special)
E. C. Comics: 1963 - No. 7, 1969

nn(1963)-Paperback book covers 20 40 60 135 290 445
2(1964)-Calendar 15 30 45 102 221 340
3(1965)-Mischief Stickers 12 24 36 81 166 250
4(1966)-Mobile; Frazetta-r/back-c Mad #90 10 20 30 64 115 165
5,6: 5(1967)-Stencils. 6(1968)-Mischief Stickers 8 16 24 51 86 120
7(1969)-Nasty Cards 8 16 24 51 86 120
(If bonus is missing, issue is half price)

NOTE: ***Clarke*** *c-4.* ***Frazetta*** *r-4, 6 (1 pg. ea.).* ***Mingo*** *c-1-3.* ***Orlando*** *a-5.*

MAD HATTER, THE (Costumed Hero)
O. W. Comics Corp.: Jan-Feb, 1946; No. 2, Sept-Oct, 1946

1-Freddy the Firefly begins; Giunta-c/a 77 154 231 493 847 1200
2-Has ad for E.C.'s Animal Fables #1 40 80 120 246 411 575

MADHOUSE
Ajax/Farrell Publ. (Excellent Publ./4-Star): 3-4/54 - No. 4, 9-10/54; 6/57 - No. 4, Dec?, 1957

1(1954) 32 64 96 192 314 435
2,3 18 36 54 107 169 230
4-Surrealistic-c 24 48 72 142 234 325
1(1957, 2nd series) 15 30 45 83 124 165
2-4 (#4 exist?) 10 20 30 56 76 95

MAD HOUSE (Formerly Madhouse Glads; ...Comics #104? on)
Red Circle Productions/Archie Publications: No. 95, 9/74 - No. 97, 1/75; No. 98, 8/75 - No. 130, 10/82

95,96-Horror stories through #97; Morrow-c 2 4 6 11 16 20
97-Intro. Henry Hobson; Morrow-a/c, Thorne-a 2 4 6 10 14 18
98,99,101-120-Satire/humor stories. 110-Sabrina app.,1pg. 1 3 4 6 8 10
100 2 4 6 8 10 12
121-129 2 4 6 8 10 12
130 2 4 6 9 13 16
Annual 8(1970-71)-Formerly Madhouse Ma-ad Annual; Sabrina app. (6 pgs.) 4 8 12 26 41 55
Annual 9-12(1974-75): 11-Wood-a(r) 3 6 9 14 20 25
...Comics Digest 1('75-76) 2 4 6 10 14 18
2-8(8/82)(...Mag. #5 on)-Sabrina in many 2 4 6 8 11 14

NOTE: ***B. Jones*** *a-96.* ***McWilliams*** *a-97.* ***Wildey*** *a-95, 96. See Archie Comics Digest #1, 13.*

MADHOUSE GLADS (Formerly ...Ma-ad; Madhouse #95 on)
Archie Publ.: No. 73, May, 1970 - No. 94, Aug, 1974 (No. 78-92: 52 pgs.)

73-77,93,94: 74-1 pg. Sabrina 2 4 6 9 13 16
78-92 (52 pgs.) 2 4 6 11 16 20

MADHOUSE MA-AD (...Jokes #67-70; ...Freak-Out #71-74)
(Formerly Archie's Madhouse) (Becomes Madhouse Glads #73 on)
Archie Publications: No. 67, April, 1969 - No. 72, Jan, 1970

67-71: 70-1 pg. Sabrina 3 6 9 16 22 28
72-6 pgs. Sabrina 4 8 12 26 41 55
...Annual 7(1969-70)-Formerly Archie's Madhouse Annual; becomes Madhouse Annual; 6 pgs. Sabrina 4 8 12 28 44 60

MADMAN (See Creatures of the Id #1)
Tundra Publishing: Mar, 1992 - No. 3, 1992 ($3.95, duotone, high quality, lim. series, 52 pgs.)

1-Mike Allred-c/a in all 2 4 6 8 10 12
1-2nd printing 4.00
2,3 6.00

MADMAN ADVENTURES
Tundra Publishing: 1992 - No. 3, 1993 ($2.95, limited series)

1-Mike Allred-c/a in all 1 2 3 5 7 9
2,3 5.00
TPB (Oni Press, 2002, $14.95) r/#1-3 & first app. of Frank Einstein from Creatures of the Id in color; gallery pages 15.00

MADMAN ATOMIC COMICS (Also see The Atomics)
Image Comics: Apr, 2007 - Present ($2.99/$3.50)

1-12-Mike Allred-s/c/a. 1-Origin re-told; pin-ups by Rivoche and Powell. 3-Sale back-c 3.50

Mad Super Special #108 © E.C. Publ.

Magdalena V3 #6 © TCOW

Mage - The Hero Defined #5 © Matt Wagner

GD 2.0 | VG 4.0 | FN 6.0 | VF 8.0 | VF/NM 9.0 | NM- 9.2

13-17-($3.50) Wraparound-c. 14-Back up w/Darwyn Cooke-a 3.50
All-New Giant-Size Super Ginchy Special (4/11, $5.99) Allred-s/a; back-ups/pin-ups 6.00
... Vol. 1 (2008, $19.99) r/#1-7; bonus art; Jamie Rich intro. 20.00

MADMAN COMICS (Also see The Atomics)
Dark Horse Comics (Legend No. 2 on): Apr, 1994 - No. 20, Dec, 2000 ($2.95/$2.99)

1-Allred-c/a; F. Miller back-c. 1 2 3 5 6 8
2-3: 3-Alex Toth back-c. 5.00
4-11: 4-Dave Stevens back-c. 6,7-Miller/Darrow's Big Guy app. 6-Bruce Timm back-c. 7-Darrow back-c. 8-Origin?; Bagge back-c. 10-Allred/Ross-c; Ross back-c. 11-Frazetta back-c 4.00
12-16: 12-(4/99) 3.50
17-20: 17-The G-Men From Hell #1 on cover; Brereton back-c. 18-(#2). 19,20-($2.99-c). 20-Clowes back-c 3.50
... Boogaloo TPB (6/99, $8.95) r/Nexus Meets Madman & Madman/The Jam 9.00
... Gargantua! (2007, $125.00, HC with dustjacket) r/Madman#1-3, Madman Adventures #1-3, Madman Comics #1-20 and Madman King-Size Super Groovy Special; pin-ups 125.00
Image Firsts: Madman #1 (10/10, $1.00) r/#1 3.00
Ltd. Ed. Slipcover (1997, $99.95, signed and numbered) w/Vol.1 & Vol. 2. Vol.1- reprints #1-5; Vol. 2- reprints #6-10 100.00
The Complete Madman Comics: Vol. 2 (11/96, $17.95, TPB) r/#6-10 plus new material 18.00
Madman King-Size Super Groovy Special (Oni Press, 7/03, $6.95) new short stories by Allred, Derington, Krall and Weissman 7.00
Madman Picture Exhibition No. 1-4 (4-7/02, $3.95) pin-ups by various 4.00
Madman Picture Exhibition Limited Edition (10/02, $29.95) Hardcover collects MPE #1-4 30.00
... Volume 2 SC (2007, $17.99) r/#1-11; Erik Larsen intro. 18.00
... Volume 3 SC (2007, $17.99) r/#12-20 and story from King-Size Groovy; Allred intro. 18.00
Yearbook '95 (1996, $17.95, TPB)-r/#1-5, intro by Teller 18.00

MADMAN / THE JAM
Dark Horse Comics: Jul, 1998 - No. 2, Aug, 1998 ($2.95, mini-series)

1,2-Allred & Mireault-s/a 4.00

MAD MONSTER PARTY (See Movie Classics)

MADNESS IN MURDERWORLD
Marvel Comics: 1989 (Came with computer game from Paragon Software)

V1#1-Starring The X-Men 3.00

MADRAVEN HALLOWEEN SPECIAL
Hamilton Comics: Oct, 1995 ($2.95, one-shot)

nn-Morrow-a 3.00

MADROX (from X-Factor)
Marvel Comics (Marvel Knights): Nov, 2004 - No. 5, Mar, 2005 ($2.99)

1-5-Peter David-s/Pablo Raimondi-a; Strong Guy app. 3.00
...: Multiple Choice TPB (2005, $13.99) r/#1-5 14.00
X-Factor: Madrox - Multiple Choice HC (2008, $19.99) r/#1-5 20.00

MAD SPECIAL (...Super Special)
E. C. Publications, Inc.: Fall, 1970 - No. 141, Nov, 1999 (84 - 116 pgs.)
(If bonus is missing, issue is one half price)

Fall 1970(#1)-Bonus-Voodoo Doll; contains 17 pgs. new material 10 20 30 65 118 170
Spring 1971(#2)-Wall Nuts; 17 pgs. new material 6 12 18 37 59 80
3-Protest Stickers 6 12 18 37 59 80
4-8: 4-Mini Posters. 5-Mad Flag. 6-Mad Mischief Stickers. 7-Presidential candidate posters, Wild Shocking Message posters. 8-TV Guise 5 10 15 32 51 70
9(1972)-Contains Nostalgic Mad #1 (28 pgs.) 4 8 12 26 41 55
10-13: 10-Nonsense Stickers (Don Martin). 13-Sickie Stickers; 3 pgs. Wolverton-r/Mad #137. 11-Contains 33-1/3 RPM record. 12-Contains Nostalgic Mad #2 (36 pgs.); Davis, Wolverton-a 3 6 9 20 30 40
14,16-21,24: 4-Vital Message posters & Art Depreciation paintings. 16-Mad-hesive Stickers. 17-Don Martin posters. 20-Martin Stickers. 18-Contains Nostalgic Mad #4 (36 pgs.). 21,24-Contains Nostalgic Mad #5 (28 pgs.) & #6 (28 pgs.) 3 6 9 16 23 30
15-Contains Nostalgic Mad #3 (28 pgs.) 3 6 9 17 25 32
22,23,25,27-29,30: 22-Diplomas. 23-Martin Stickers. 25-Martin Posters. 27-Mad Shock-Sticks. 28-Contains Nostalgic Mad #7 (36 pgs.). 29-Mad Collectable-Connectables Posters. 30-The Movies 2 4 6 9 13 16
26-Has 33-1/3 RPM record 2 4 6 13 18 22
31,33-35,37-50 2 4 6 8 11 14
32-Contains Nostalgic Mad #8. 36-Has 96 pgs. of comic book & comic strip spoofs: titles "The Comics" on-c 2 4 6 9 13 16
51-70 1 3 4 6 8 10
71-88,90-100: 71-Batman parodies-r by Wood, Drucker. 72-Wolverton-c r-from 1st panel in Mad #11; Wolverton-s r/new dialogue. 83-All Star Trek spoof issue 1 2 3 5 6 8
76-(Fall, 1991)-Special Hussein Asylum Edition; distributed only to the troops in the Middle East (see Mad #300-303) 2 4 6 13 18 22
89-($3.95)-Polybaged w/1st of 3 Spy vs. Spy hologram trading cards (direct sale only issue) (other cards came w/card set) 1 3 4 6 8 10
101-141: 117-Sci-Fi parodies-r. 4.00
NOTE: *#28-30 have no number on cover.* ***Freas*** *c-76.* ***Mingo*** *c-9, 11, 15, 19, 23.*

MAGDALENA, THE (See The Darkness #15-18)
Image Comics (Top Cow): Apr, 2000 - No. 3, Jan, 2001 ($2.50)

Preview Special ('00, $4.95) Flip book w/Blood Legacy preview 5.00
1-Benitez-c/a; variant covers by Silvestri & Turner 3.00
2,3: 2-Two covers 3.00
.../Angelus #1/2 (11/01, $2.95) Benitez-c/Ching-a 3.00
...Blood Divine (2002, $9.95) r/#1-3 & #1/2; cover gallery 10.00
.../Vampirella (7/03, $2.99) Wohl-s/Benitez-a; two covers 3.00

MAGDALENA, THE (Volume 2)
Image Comics (Top Cow): Aug, 2003 - No. 4, Dec, 2003 ($2.99)

Preview (6/03) B&W preview; Wizard World East logo on cover 3.00
1-4-Holguin-s/Basaldua-a 3.00
1-Variant-c by Jim Silke benefitting ACTOR charity 5.00
TPB Volume 1 (12/06, $19.99) r/both series, Darkness #15-18 & Magdalena/Angelus 20.00
.../Daredevil (5/08, $3.99) Phil Hester-s/a; Hester & Sejic-c 4.00
.../Vampirella (12/04, $2.99) Kirkman-s/Manapul-a; two covers by Manapul and Bachalo 3.00
... Vs. Dracula Monster War 2005 (6/05, $2.99) four covers; Joyce Chin-a 3.00

MAGDALENA, THE (Volume 3)
Image Comics (Top Cow): Apr, 2010 - Present ($3.99)

1-11: 1-Marz-s/Blake-a/Sook-c. 7,8-Keu Cha-a 4.00

MAGE (The Hero Discovered...; also see Grendel #16)
Comico: Feb, 1984 (no month) - No. 15, Dec, 1986 ($1.50, Mando paper)

1-Comico's 1st color comic 2 4 6 8 11 14
2-5: 3-Intro Edsel 6.00
6-Grendel begins (1st in color) 3 6 9 14 20 25
7-1st new Grendel story 2 4 6 8 10 12
8-14: 13-Grendel dies. 14-Grendel story ends 6.00
15-($2.95) Double size w/pullout poster 1 2 3 5 6 8
Image Firsts: Mage - The Hero Discovered #1 (10/10, $1.00) r/#1 w/"Image Firsts" logo 3.00
TPB Volume 1-4 (Image, $5.95) 1- r/#1,2. 2- r/#3,4. 3- r/#5,6. 4- r/#7,8 7.00
TPB Volume 5-7 (Image, $6.95) 5- r/#9,10. 6- r/#11,12. 7- r/#13,14 7.00
TPB Volume 8 (Image, 9/99, $7.50) r/#15 7.50
..., Vol. 1 TPB (Image, 2004, $29.99) r/#1-15; cover gallery, promo artwork, bonus art 30.00

MAGE (The Hero Defined) (Volume 2)
Image Comics: July, 1997 - No. 15, Oct, 1999 ($2.50)

0-(7/97, $5.00) American Ent. Ed. 5.00
1-14:Matt Wagner-c/s/a in all. 13-Three covers 3.00
1-"3-D Edition" (2/98, $4.95) w/glasses 5.00
15-($5.95) Acetate cover 6.00
Volume 1,2 TPB ('98,'99, $9.95) 1- r/#1-4. 2-r/#5-8 10.00
Volume 3 TPB ('00, $12.95) r/#9-12 13.00
Volume 4 TPB ('01, $14.95) r/#13-15 15.00
Hardcover Vol. 2 (2005, $49.95) r/#1-15; cover gallery, character design & sketch pages 50.00

MAGE KNIGHT: STOLEN DESTINY (Based on the fantasy game Mage Knight)
Idea + Design Works: Oct, 2002 - No. 5, Feb, 2003 ($3.50, limited series)

1-5: 1-J. Scott Campbell-c; Cabrera-a/Dezago-s, 2-Dave Johnson-c 3.50

MAGGIE AND HOPEY COLOR SPECIAL (See Love and Rockets)
Fantagraphics Books: May, 1997 ($3.50, one-shot)

1 3.50

MAGGIE THE CAT (Also see Jon Sable, Freelance #11 & Shaman's Tears #12)
Image Comics (Creative Fire Studio): Jan, 1996 - No. 2, Feb, 1996 ($2.50, unfinished limited series)

1,2: Mike Grell-c/a/scripts 3.00

MAGICA DE SPELL (See Walt Disney Showcase #30)

MAGIC AGENT (See Forbidden Worlds & Unknown Worlds)
American Comics Group: Jan-Feb, 1962 - No. 3, May-June, 1962

1-Origin & 1st app. John Force 4 8 12 26 41 55
2,3 3 6 9 19 29 38

MAGICAL POKÉMON JOURNEY
Viz Comics: 2000 - Present ($4.95, B&W, magazine-size)

Magic Comics #15 © KING

Magneto: Not a Hero #1 © MAR

Magnus Robot Fighter #17 © GK

GD 2.0 | VG 4.0 | FN 6.0 | VF 8.0 | VF/NM 9.0 | NM- 9.2

1-4 5.00
Part 2: 1-3; Part 3: 1-4: 1-Includes color poster; Part 4: 1-4; Part 5: 1-4; Part 6: 1-4 5.00

MAGIC COMICS
David McKay Publications: Aug, 1939 - No. 123, Nov-Dec, 1949

1-Mandrake the Magician, Henry, Popeye , Blondie, Barney Baxter, Secret Agent X-9 (not by Raymond), Bunky by Billy DeBeck & Thornton Burgess text stories illustrated by Harrison Cady begin; Henry covers begin 352 704 1056 2024 3212 4400
2 124 248 372 713 1132 1550
3 92 184 276 529 840 1150
4 74 148 222 426 676 925
5 61 122 183 351 556 760
6-10: 8-11,21-Mandrake/Henry-c 48 96 144 276 438 600
11-16,18,20: 12-Mandrake-c begin. 40 80 120 230 365 500
17-The Lone Ranger begins 46 92 138 265 426 575
19-Classic robot-c (scarce) 100 200 300 575 913 1250
21-30: 25-Only Blondie-c. 26-Dagwood-c begin 28 56 84 165 270 375
31-40: 36-Flag-c 20 40 60 114 182 250
41-50 15 30 45 88 137 185
51-60 14 28 42 80 115 150
61-70 11 22 33 64 90 115
71-99, 107,108-Flash Gordon app; not by Raymond 10 20 30 54 72 90
100 10 20 30 58 79 100
101-106,109-123: 123-Last Dagwood-c 9 18 27 50 65 80

MAGIC FLUTE, THE (See Night Music #9-11)

MAGICIAN: APPRENTICE
Dabel Brothers/Marvel Comics (Dabel Brothers) #3 on: Mar, 2007 - No. 12, Dec, 2007 ($2.95/$2.99)

1-12-Adaptation of the Raymond E. Feist Riftwar Saga series 3.00
1,2-($5.95) 1-Wraparound variant-c by Maitz. 2-Wraparound variant-c by Booth 6.00
Collected Edition (10/06, $3.99) r/#1&2 4.00
Vol. 1 HC (2007, $19.99, dustjacket) r/#1-6; foreword by Feist 20.00
Vol. 1 SC (2007, $15.99) r/#1-6; foreword by Feist 16.00
Vol. 2 HC (2008, $19.99, dustjacket) r/#7-12 20.00

MAGIC PICKLE
Oni Press: Sept, 2001 - No. 4, Dec, 2001 ($2.95, limited series)

1-4-Scott Morse-s/a; Mahfood-a (2 pgs.) 3.00

MAGIC SWORD, THE (See Movie Classics)

MAGIC THE GATHERING (Title Series), **Acclaim Comics (Armada)**

...ANTIQUITIES WAR,11/95 - 2/96 ($2.50), 1-4-Paul Smith-a(p) 3.00
...ARABIAN NIGHTS, 12/95 - 1/96 ($2.50), 1,2 3.00
...COLLECTION ,'95 ($4.95), 1,2-polybagged 5.00
...CONVOCATIONS, '95 ($2.50), 1-nn-pin-ups 3.00
...ELDER DRAGONS ,'95 ($2.50), 1,2-Doug Wheatley-a 3.00
...FALLEN ANGEL ,'95 ($5.95), nn 6.00
...FALLEN EMPIRES ,9/95 - 10/95 ($2.75), 1,2 3.00
...Collection ($4.95)-polybagged 5.00
...HOMELANDS ,'95 ($5.95), nn-polybagged w/card; Hildebrandts-c 6.00
... ICE AGE (On The World of...) ,7/5 -11/95 ($2.50), 1-4: 1,2-bound-in Magic Card. 3,4-bound-in insert 3.00
...LEGEND OF JEDIT OJANEN, '96 ($2.50), 1,2 3.00
...NIGHTMARE, '95 ($2.50, one shot), 1 3.00
...THE SHADOW MAGE, 7/95 - 10/95 ($2.50), 1-4-bagged w/Magic The Gathering card 3.00
...Collection 1,2 (1995, $4.95)-Trade paperback; polybagged 5.00
...SHANDALAR ,'96 ($2.50), 1,2 3.00
...WAYFARER ,11/95 - 2/96 ($2.50), 1-5 3.00

MAGIC: THE GATHERING
IDW Publishing: Dec, 2011 - Present ($3.99)

1-Forbeck-s/Cóccolo-a 4.00

MAGIC: THE GATHERING: GERRARD'S QUEST
Dark Horse Comics: Mar, 1998 - No. 4, June, 1998 ($2.95, limited series)

1-4: Grell-s/Mhan-a 3.00

MAGIK (Illyana and Storm Limited Series)
Marvel Comics Group: Dec, 1983 - No. 4, Mar, 1984 (60¢, limited series)

1-4: 1-Characters from X-Men; Inferno begins; X-Men cameo (Buscema pencils in #1,2; c-1p. 2-4: 2-Nightcrawler app. & X-Men cameo 4.00

MAGIK (See Black Sun mini-series)
Marvel Comics: Dec, 2000 - No. 4, Mar, 2001 ($2.99, limited series)

1-4-Liam Sharp-a/Abnett & Lanning-s; Nightcrawler app. 3.00

MAGILLA GORILLA (TV) (See Kite Fun Book)
Gold Key: May, 1964 - No. 10, Dec, 1968 (Hanna-Barbera)

1-1st comic app. 9 18 27 63 112 160
2-4: 3-Vs. Yogi Bear for President. 4-1st Punkin Puss & Mushmouse, Ricochet Rabbit & Droop-a-Long 6 12 18 37 59 80
5-10: 10-Reprints 5 10 15 30 48 65

MAGILLA GORILLA (TV)(See Spotlight #4)
Charlton Comics: Nov, 1970 - No. 5, July, 1971 (Hanna-Barbera)

1 5 10 15 35 55 75
2-5 4 8 12 22 34 45

MAGNETIC MEN FEATURING MAGNETO
Marvel Comics (Amalgam): June, 1997 ($1.95, one-shot)

1-Tom Peyer-s/Barry Kitson & Dan Panosian-a 3.00

MAGNETO (See X-Men #1)
Marvel Comics: nd (Sept, 1993) (Giveaway) (one-shot)

0-Embossed foil-c by Sienkiewicz; r/Classic X-Men #19 & 12 by Bolton 5.00

MAGNETO
Marvel Comics: Nov, 1996 - No. 4, Feb, 1997 ($1.95, limited series)

1-4: Peter Milligan scripts & Kelley Jones-a(p) 3.00

MAGNETO
Marvel Comics: Mar, 2011 ($2.99, one-shot)

1-Howard Chaykin-s/a; Roger Cruz-c 3.00

MAGNETO AND THE MAGNETIC MEN
Marvel Comics (Amalgam): Apr, 1996 ($1.95, one-shot)

1-Jeff Matsuda-a(p) 3.00

MAGNETO ASCENDANT
Marvel Comics: May, 1999 ($3.99, squarebound one-shot)

1-Reprints early Magneto appearances 4.00

MAGNETO: DARK SEDUCTION
Marvel Comics: Jun, 2000 - No. 4, Sept, 2000 ($2.99, limited series)

1-4: Nicieza-s/Cruz-a. 3,4-Avengers-c/app. 3.00

MAGNETO: NOT A HERO (X-Men Regenesis)
Marvel Comics: Jan, 2012 - No. 4, Apr, 2012 ($2.99, limited series)

1-4-Skottie Young-s/Clay Mann-a; Joseph returns 3.00

MAGNETO REX
Marvel Comics: Apr, 1999 - No. 3, July, 1999 ($2.50, limited series)

1-3-Rogue, Quicksilver app.; Peterson-a(p) 3.00

MAGNUS, ROBOT FIGHTER (...4000 A.D.)(See Doctor Solar)
Gold Key: Feb, 1963 - No. 46, Jan, 1977 (All painted covers except #5,30,31)

1-Origin & 1st app. Magnus; Aliens (1st app.) series begins 22 44 66 154 327 500
2,3 11 22 33 71 136 200
4-10: 10-Simonson fan club illo (5/65, 1st-a?) 7 14 21 49 82 115
11-20 5 10 15 35 55 75
21,24-28: 28-Aliens ends 4 8 12 24 37 50
22,23: 22-Origin-r/#1; last 12¢ issue 4 8 12 26 41 55
29-46-Mostly reprints 2 4 6 13 18 22
...: One For One (Dark Horse Comics, 9/10, $1.00) r/#1 3.00
Russ Manning's Magnus Robot Fighter - Vol. 1 HC (Dark Horse, 2004, $49.95) r/#1-7 70.00
Russ Manning's Magnus Robot Fighter - Vol. 2 HC (DH, 6/05, $49.95) r/#8-14; forward by Steve Rude 50.00
Russ Manning's Magnus Robot Fighter - Vol. 3 HC (Dark Horse, 10/06, $49.95) r/#15-21 50.00
NOTE: *Manning a-1-22, 28-43(r). Spiegle a-23, 44r.*

MAGNUS ROBOT FIGHTER (Also see Vintage Magnus)
Valiant/Acclaim Comics: May, 1991 - No. 64, Feb, 1996 ($1.75/$1.95/$2.25/$2.50)

1-Nichols/Layton-c/a; 1-8 have trading cards 1 3 4 6 8 10
2-8: 4-Rai cameo. 5-Origin & 1st full app. Rai (10/91); 5-8 are in flip book format and back-c & half of book are Rai #1-4 mini-series. 6-1st Solar x-over. 7-Magnus vs. Rai-c/story; 1st X-O Armor 6.00
0-Origin issue; Layton-a; ordered through mail w/coupons from 1st 8 issues plus 50¢; B. Smith trading card 2 4 6 11 16 20
0-Sold thru comic shops without trading card 2 4 6 8 10 12

Magog #7 © DC

Major Victory Comics #3 © CHES

Man Comics #16 © MAR

GD VG FN VF VF/NM NM-
2.0 4.0 6.0 8.0 9.0 9.2

9-11 4.00
12-(3.25, 44 pgs.)-Turok-c/story (1st app. in Valiant universe, 5/92); has 8 pg. Magnus story insert 2 4 6 11 16 20
13-24,26-48: 14-1st app. Isak. 15,16-Unity x-overs. 15-Miller-c. 16-Birth of Magnus. 21-New direction & new logo. 21-Gold ink variant. 24-Story cont'd in Rai & the Future Force #9. 33-Timewalker app.36-Bound-in trading cards. 37-Rai & Starwatchers app. 44-Bound-in sneak peek card. 3.00
25-($2.95)-Embossed silver foil-c; new costume 4.00
49-63 3.00
64-($2.50): 64-Magnus dies? 4.00
...Invasion (1994, $9.95)-r/Rai #1-4 & Magnus #5-8 10.00
Magnus Steel Nation (1994, $9.95) r/#1-4 10.00
Yearbook (1994, $3.95, 52 pgs.) 4.00
NOTE: ***Ditko/Reese*** *a-18.* ***Layton*** *a(i)-5; c-6-9i, 25; back(i)-5-8.* ***Reese*** *a(i)-22, 25, 28; c(i)-22, 24, 28.* ***Simonson*** *c-16. Prices for issues 1-8 are for trading cards and coupons intact.*

MAGNUS ROBOT FIGHTER
Acclaim Comics (Valiant Heroes): V2#1, May, 1997 - No. 18, Jun, 1998 ($2.50)
1-18: 1-Reintro Magnus; Donavon Wylie (X-O Manowar) cameo; Tom Peyer scripts & Mike McKone-c/a begin; painted variant-c exists 3.00

MAGNUS ROBOT FIGHTER
Dark Horse Comics: Aug, 2010 - No. 4, May, 2011 ($3.50)
1-4: 1-Shooter-s/Reinhold-a; covers by Swanland & Reinhold; back-up r/#1 (1963) 3.50

MAGNUS ROBOT FIGHTER/NEXUS
Valiant/Dark Horse Comics: Dec, 1993 - No. 2, Apr, 1994 ($2.95, lim. series)
1,2: Steve Rude painted-c & pencils in all 3.00

MAGOG (See Justice Society of America 2007 series)(Continues in Justice Society Special #1)
DC Comics: Nov, 2009 - No.12, Ot. 2010 ($2.99)
1-12: 1-Giffen-s/Porter-a/Fabry-c; variant-c by Porter. 7-Zatanna app. 3.00
...: Lethal Force TPB (2010, $14.99) r/#1-5 15.00

MAID OF THE MIST (See American Graphics)

MAI, THE PSYCHIC GIRL
Eclipse Comics: May, 1987 - No. 28, July, 1989 ($1.50, B&W, bi-weekly, 44pgs.)
1-28, 1,2-2nd print 4.00

MAJESTIC (Mr. Majestic from WildCATS)
DC Comics: Oct, 2004 - No. 4, Jan, 2005 ($2.95, limited series)
1-4-Kerschl-a/Abnett & Lanning-s. 1-Superman app.; Superman #1 cover swipe 3.00
...: Strange New Visitor TPB (2005, $14.99) r/#1-4 & Action #811, Advs. of Superman #624 & Superman #201 15.00

MAJESTIC (Mr. Majestic from WildCATS)
DC Comics (WildStorm): Mar, 2005 - No. 17, July, 2006 ($2.95/$2.99)
1-17: 1-Googe-a/Abnett & Lanning-s; Superman app. 9-Jeanty-a; Zealot app. 3.00
...: Meanwhile, Back on Earth... TPB (2006, $14.99) r/#8-12 15.00
...: The Final Cut TPB (2007, $14.99) r/#13-17 & story fro WildStorm Winter Special 15.00
...: While You Were Out TPB (2006, $12.99) r/#1-7 13.00

MAJOR BUMMER
DC Comics: Aug, 1997 - No. 15, Oct, 1998 ($2.50)
1-15: 1-Origin and 1st app. Major Bummer 3.00

MAJOR HOOPLE COMICS (See Crackajack Funnies)
Nedor Publications: nd (Jan, 1943)
1-Mary Worth, Phantom Soldier app. by Moldoff 38 76 114 219 352 485

MAJOR VICTORY COMICS (Also see Dynamic Comics)
H. Clay Glover/Service Publ./Harry 'A' Chesler: 1944 - No. 3, Summer, 1945
1-Origin Major Victory (patriotic hero) by C. Sultan (reprint from Dynamic #1); 1st app. Spider Woman 66 132 198 419 722 1025
2-Dynamic Boy app. 40 80 120 246 411 575
3-Rocket Boy app. 39 78 117 231 378 525

MALIBU ASHCAN: RAFFERTY (See Firearm #12)
Malibu Comics (Ultraverse): Nov, 1994 (99¢, B&W w/color-c; one-shot)
1-Previews "The Rafferty Saga" storyline in Firearm; Chaykin-c 3.00

MALTESE FALCON
David McKay Publications: No. 48, 1946
Feature Books 48-by Dashiell Hammett 87 174 261 553 952 1350

MALU IN THE LAND OF ADVENTURE
I. W. Enterprises: 1964 (See White Princess of Jungle #2)
1-r/Avon's Slave Girl Comics #1; Severin-c 5 10 15 30 48 65

MAMMOTH COMICS
Whitman Publishing Co.(K. K. Publ.): 1938 (84 pgs.) (B&W, 8-1/2x11-1/2")
1-Alley Oop, Terry & the Pirates, Dick Tracy, Little Orphan Annie, Wash Tubbs, Moon Mullins, Smilin' Jack, Tailspin Tommy, Don Winslow, Dan Dunn, Smokey Stover & other reprints (scarce) 206 412 618 1318 2259 3200

MAN AGAINST TIME
Image Comics (Motown Machineworks): May, 1996 - No. 4, Aug, 1996 ($2.25, lim. series)
1-4: 1-Simonson-c. 2,3-Leon-c. 4-Barreto & Leon-c 3.00

MAN-BAT (See Batman Family, Brave & the Bold, & Detective #400)
National Periodical Publ./DC Comics: Dec-Jan, 1975-76 - No. 2, Feb-Mar, 1976; Dec, 1984
1-Ditko-a(p); Aparo-c; Batman app.; 1st app. She-Bat? 3 6 9 16 23 30
2-Aparo-c 2 4 6 10 14 18
1 (12/84)-N. Adams-r(3)/Det.(Vs. Batman on-c) 5.00

MAN-BAT
DC Comics: Feb, 1996 - No. 3, Apr, 1996 ($2.25, limited series)
1-3: Dixon scripts in all. 2-Killer Croc-c/app. 3.00

MAN-BAT
DC Comics: Jun, 2006 - No. 5, Oct, 2006 ($2.99, limited series)
1-5: Bruce Jones-s/Mike Huddleston-a/c. 1-Hush app. 3.00

MAN CALLED A-X, THE
Malibu Comics (Bravura): Nov, 1994 - No. 4, Jun, 1995 ($2.95, limited series)
0-4: Marv Wolfman scripts & Shawn McManus-c/a. 0-(2/95). 1-"1A" on cover 3.00

MAN CALLED A-X, THE
DC Comics: Oct, 1997 - No. 8, May, 1998 ($2.50)
1-8: Marv Wolfman scripts & Shawn McManus-c/a. 3.00

MAN CALLED KEV, A (See The Authority)
DC Comics (WildStorm): Sept, 2006 - No. 5, Feb, 2007 ($2.99, limited series)
1-5-Ennis-s/Ezquerra-a/Fabry-c 3.00
TPB (2007, $14.99) r/#1-5; cover gallery 15.00

MAN COMICS
Marvel/Atlas Comics (NPI): Dec, 1949 - No. 28, Sept, 1953 (#1-6: 52 pgs.)
1-Tuska-a 24 48 72 144 237 330
2-Tuska-a 15 30 45 84 127 170
3-6 13 26 39 72 101 130
7,8 12 24 36 67 94 120
9-13,15: 9-Format changes to war 10 20 30 56 76 95
14-Henkel (3 pgs.); Pakula-a 10 20 30 58 79 100
16-21,23-28: 28-Crime issue (Bob Brant) 9 18 27 52 69 85
22-Krigstein-a, 5 pgs. 11 22 33 60 83 105
NOTE: ***Berg*** *a-14, 15, 19.* ***Colan*** *a-9, 21, 23.* ***Everett*** *a-8, 22; c-22, 25.* ***Heath*** *a-11, 13, 16, 17, 21. Kubertish a-by* ***Bob Brown****-3.* ***Maneely*** *a-11-13; c-10, 11, 16.* ***Reinman*** *a-11.* ***Robinson*** *a-7, 10, 14.* ***Robert Sale*** *a-9, 11.* ***Sinnott*** *a-22, 23.* ***Tuska*** *a-14, 23.*

MANDRAKE THE MAGICIAN (See Defenders Of The Earth, 123, 46, 52, 55, Giant Comic Album, King Comics, Magic Comics, The Phantom #21, Tiny Tot Funnies & Wow Comics, '36)

MANDRAKE THE MAGICIAN (See Harvey Comics Hits #53)
David McKay Publ./Dell/King Comics (All 12¢): 1938 - 1948; Sept, 1966 - No. 10, Nov, 1967
Feature Books 18,19,23 (1938) 77 154 231 493 847 1200
Feature Books 46 48 96 144 302 514 725
Feature Books 52,55 40 80 120 246 411 575
Four Color 752 (11/56) 10 20 30 66 121 175
1-Begin S.O.S. Phantom, ends #3 6 12 18 37 59 80
2-7,9: 4-Girl Phantom app. 5-Flying Saucer-c/story. 5,6-Brick Bradford app. 7-Origin Lothar. 9-Brick Bradford app. 4 8 12 22 34 45
8-Jeff Jones-a (4 pgs.) 4 8 12 24 37 50
10-Rip Kirby app.; Raymond-a (14 pgs.) 4 8 12 28 44 60

MANDRAKE THE MAGICIAN
Marvel Comics: Apr, 1995 - No. 2, May, 1995 ($2.95, unfinished limited series)
1,2: Mike Barr scripts 3.00

MAN-EATING COW (See Tick #7,8)
New England Comics: July, 1992 - No. 10, 1994? ($2.75, B&W, limited series)
1-10 3.00
Man-Eating Cow Bonanza (6/96, $4.95, 128 pgs.)-r/#1-4. 5.00

MAN FROM ATLANTIS (TV)
Marvel Comics: Feb, 1978 - No. 7, Aug, 1978
1-(84 pgs.)-Sutton-a(p), Buscema-c; origin & cast photos 2 4 6 8 12 12

Manga Darkchylde #1 © Darkchylde Ent.

Manhunter #18 © DC

Man O' Mars #1 © FH

GD 2.0 | VG 4.0 | FN 6.0 | VF 8.0 | VF/NM 9.0 | NM- 9.2

2-7 6.00

MAN FROM PLANET X, THE
Planet X Productions: 1987 (no price; probably unlicensed)

1-Reprints Fawcett Movie Comic 3.00

MAN FROM U.N.C.L.E., THE (TV) (Also see The Girl From Uncle)
Gold Key: Feb, 1965 - No. 22, Apr, 1969 (All photo-c)

1 12 24 36 79 160 240
2-Photo back c-2-8 7 14 21 49 82 115
3-10: 7-Jet Dream begins (1st app., also see Jet Dream) (all new stories)
6 12 18 37 59 80
11-22: 19-Last 12¢ issue. 21,22-Reprint #10 & 7 5 10 15 32 51 70

MAN FROM U.N.C.L.E., THE (TV)
Entertainment Publishing: 1987 - No. 11 ($1.50/$1.75, B&W)

1-7 ($1.50), 8-11 ($1.75) 4.00

MAN FROM WELLS FARGO (TV)
Dell Publishing Co.: No. 1287, Feb-Apr, 1962 - May-July, 1962 (Photo-c)

Four Color 1287, #01-495-207 6 12 18 37 59 80

MANGA DARKCHYLDE (Also see Darkchylde titles)
Dark Horse Comics: Feb, 2005 - No. 5 ($2.99, limited series)

1,2-Randy Queen-s/a; manga-style pre-teen Ariel Chylde 3.00

MANGA SHI (See Tomoe)
Crusade Entertainment: Aug, 1996 ($2.95)

1-Printed backwards (manga-style) 3.00

MANGA SHI 2000
Crusade Entertainment: Feb, 1997 - No. 3, June, 1997 ($2.95, mini-series)

1-3: 1-Two covers 3.00

MANGA ZEN (Also see Zen Intergalactic Ninja)
Zen Comics (Fusion Studios): 1996 - No. 3, 1996 ($2.50, B&W)

1-3 3.00

MANGAZINE
Antarctic Press: Aug, 1985 - No. 4, Sept, 1986 (B&W)

1-Soft paper-c 2 4 6 11 16 20
2-4 2 4 6 8 11 14

MANGLE TANGLE TALES
Innovation Publishing: 1990 ($2.95, deluxe format)

1-Intro by Harlan Ellison 3.00

MANHUNT! (Becomes Red Fox #15 on)
Magazine Enterprises: 10/47 - No. 11, 8/48; #13,14, 1953 (no #12)

1-Red Fox by L. B. Cole, Undercover Girl by Whitney, Space Ace begin (1st app.); negligee panels 54 108 162 343 574 825
2-Electrocution-c 42 84 126 265 445 625
3-6: 6-Bondage-c 34 68 102 206 336 465
7-10: 7-Space Ace ends. 8-Trail Colt begins (intro/1st app., 5/48) by Guardineer; Trail Colt-c. 10-G. Ingels-a 30 60 90 177 289 400
11(8/48)-Frazetta-a, 7 pgs.; The Duke, Scotland Yard begin
41 82 123 256 428 600
13(A-1 #63)-Frazetta, r-/Trail Colt #1, 7 pgs. 39 78 117 234 385 535
14(A-1 #77)-Bondage/hypo-c; last L. B. Cole Red Fox; Ingels-a
40 80 120 246 411 575

NOTE: ***Guardineer** a-1-5; c-8. **Whitney** a-2-14; c-1-6, 10. Red Fox by **L. B. Cole**-#1-14. #15 was advertised but came out as Red Fox #15.*

MANHUNTER (See Adventure #58, 73, Brave & the Bold, Detective Comics, 1st Issue Special, House of Mystery #143 and Justice League of America)
DC Comics: 1984 ($2.50, 76 pgs; high quality paper)

1-Simonson-c/a(r)/Detective; Batman app. 4.00

MANHUNTER
DC Comics: July, 1988 - No. 24, Apr, 1990 ($1.00)

1-24: 8,9-Flash app. 9-Invasion. 17-Batman-c/sty 3.00

MANHUNTER
DC Comics: No. 0, Nov, 1994 - No. 12, Nov, 1995 ($1.95/$2.25)

0-12 3.00

MANHUNTER (Also see Batman: Streets of Gotham)
DC Comics: Oct, 2004 - No. 38, Mar, 2009 ($2.50/$2.99)

1-21: 1-Intro. Kate Spencer; Saiz-a/Jae Lee-c/Andreyko-s. 2,3 Shadow Thief app. 13,14-Omac x-over. 20-One Year Later 3.00
22-30: 22-Begin $2.99-c. 23-Sandra Knight app. 27-Chaykin-c. 28-Batman app. 3.00
31-38: 31-(8/08) Gaydos-a. 33,34-Suicide Squad app. 3.00
...: Forgotten (2009, $17.99) r/#31-38 18.00
...: Origins (2007, $17.99) r/#15-23 18.00
...: Street Justice (2005, $12.99) r/#1-5; Andreyko intro. 13.00
...: Trial By Fire (2007, $17.99) r/#6-14 18.00
...: Unleashed (2008, $17.99) r/#24-30 18.00

MANHUNTER: ...
DC Comics: 1979, 1999

The Complete Saga TPB (1979) Reprints stories from Detective Comics #437-443 by Goodwin and Simonson 40.00
The Special Edition TPB (1999, $9.95) r/stories from Detective Comics #437-443 10.00

MANIFEST ETERNITY
DC Comics: Aug, 2006 - No. 6, Jan, 2007 ($2.99)

1-6-Lobdell-s/Nguyen-a/c 3.00

MAN IN BLACK (See Thrill-O-Rama) (Also see All New Comics, Front Page, Green Hornet #31, Strange Story & Tally-Ho Comics)
Harvey Publications: Sept, 1957 - No. 4, Mar, 1958

1-Bob Powell-c/a 18 36 54 105 165 225
2-4: Powell-c/a 14 28 42 80 115 150

MAN IN BLACK
Lorne-Harvey Publications (Recollections): 1990 - No. 2, July, 1991 (B&W)

1,2 4.00

MAN IN FLIGHT (Disney, TV)
Dell Publishing Co.: No. 836, Sept, 1957

Four Color 836 7 14 21 46 76 105

MAN IN SPACE (Disney, TV, see Dell Giant #27)
Dell Publishing Co.: No. 716, Aug, 1956 - No. 954, Nov, 1958

Four Color 716-A science feat. from Tomorrowland 8 16 24 55 93 130
Four Color 954-Satellites 7 14 21 46 76 105

MANKIND (WWF Wrestling)
Chaos Comics: Sept, 1999 ($2.95, one-shot)

1-Regular and photo-c 3.00
1-Premium Edition ($10.00) Dwayne Turner & Danny Miki-c 10.00

MANN AND SUPERMAN
DC Comics: 2000 ($5.95, prestige format, one-shot)

nn-Michael T. Gilbert-s/a 6.00

MAN OF STEEL, THE (Also see Superman: The Man of Steel)
DC Comics: 1986 (June release) - No. 6, 1986 (75¢, limited series)

1-6: 1-Silver logo; Byrne-c/a/scripts in all; origin, 1-Alternate-c for newsstand sales,1-Distr. to toy stores by So Much Fun, 2-6: 2-Intro. Lois Lane, Jimmy Olsen. 3-Intro/origin Magpie; Batman-c/story. 4-Intro. new Lex Luthor 4.00
1-6-Silver Editions (1993, $1.95)-r/1-6 3.00
...The Complete Saga nn (SC)-Contains #1-6, given away in contest; limited edition
4 8 12 28 44 60

NOTE: *Issues 1-6 were released between Action #583 (9/86) & Action #584 (1/87) plus Superman #423 (9/86) & Advs. of Superman #424 (1/87).*

MAN OF THE ATOM (See Solar, Man of the Atom Vol. 2)

MAN OF WAR (See Liberty Guards & Liberty Scouts)
Centaur Publications: Nov, 1941 - No. 2, Jan, 1942

1-The Fire-Man, Man of War, The Sentinel, Liberty Guards, & Vapo-Man begin; Gustavson-c/a; Flag-c 177 354 531 1124 1937 2750
2-Intro The Ferret; Gustavson-c/a 126 252 378 806 1378 1950

MAN OF WAR
Eclipse Comics: Aug, 1987 - No. 3, Feb, 1988 ($1.75, Baxter paper)

1-3: Bruce Jones scripts 3.00

MAN OF WAR (See The Protectors)
Malibu Comics: 1993 - No, 8, Feb, 1994 ($1.95/$2.50/$2.25)

1-5 ($1.95)-Newsstand Editions w/different-c 3.00
1-8: 1-5-Collector's Edi. w/poster. 6-8 ($2.25): 6-Polybagged w/Skycap. 8-Vs. Rocket Rangers 4.00

MAN O' MARS
Fiction House Magazines: 1953; 1964

1-Space Rangers; Whitman-c 47 94 141 296 498 700
I.W. Reprint #1-r/Man O'Mars #1 & Star Pirate; Murphy Anderson-a
6 12 18 39 62 85

Man-Thing (2004 series) #1 © MAR

Many Loves of Dobie Gillis #1 © DC

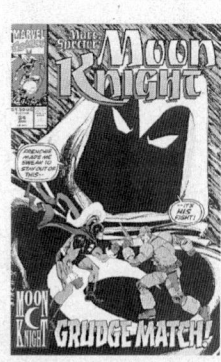

Marc Spector: Moon Knight #34 © MAR

MANTECH ROBOT WARRIORS
Archie Enterprises, Inc.: Sept, 1984 - No. 4, Apr, 1985 (75¢)

	GD 2.0	VG 4.0	FN 6.0	VF 8.0	VF/NM 9.0	NM- 9.2
1-4: Ayers-c/a(p). 1-Buckler-c(i)						3.00

MAN-THING (See Fear, Giant-Size..., Marvel Comics Presents, Marvel Fanfare, Monsters Unleashed, Power Record Comics & Savage Tales)
Marvel Comics Group: Jan, 1974 - No. 22, Oct, 1975; V2#1, Nov, 1979 - V2#11, July, 1981

	GD 2.0	VG 4.0	FN 6.0	VF 8.0	VF/NM 9.0	NM- 9.2
1-Howard the Duck(2nd app.) cont'd/Fear #19	6	12	18	41	66	90
2	3	6	9	18	27	35
3-1st app. original Foolkiller	3	6	9	16	22	28
4-Origin Foolkiller; last app. 1st Foolkiller	3	6	9	14	20	26
5-11-Ploog-a. 11-Foolkiller cameo (flashback)	3	6	9	14	20	26
12-22: 19-1st app. Scavenger. 20-Spidey cameo. 21-Origin Scavenger, Man-Thing. 22-Howard the Duck cameo	2	4	6	9	13	16
V2#1(1979)	2	4	6	8	10	12
V2#2-11: 4-Dr. Strange-c/app. 11-Mayerik-a						6.00

NOTE: ***Alcala** a-14. **Brunner** c-1. J. **Buscema** a-12p, 13p, 16p. **Gil Kane** c-4p, 10p, 12-20p, 21. **Mooney** a-17, 18, 19p, 20-22, V2#1-3p. **Ploog** Man-Thing-5p, 6p, 7, 8, 9-11p; c-5, 6, 8, 9, 11. **Sutton** a-13i. No. 19 says #10 in indicia.*

MAN-THING (Volume Three, continues in Strange Tales #1 (9/98))
Marvel Comics: Dec, 1997 - No. 8, July, 1998 ($2.99)

	GD 2.0	VG 4.0	FN 6.0	VF 8.0	VF/NM 9.0	NM- 9.2
1-8-DeMatteis-s/Sharp-a. 2-Two covers. 6-Howard the Duck-c/app.						3.00

MAN-THING (Prequel to 2005 movie)
Marvel Comics: Sept, 2004 - No. 3, Nov, 2004 ($2.99, limited series)

	GD 2.0	VG 4.0	FN 6.0	VF 8.0	VF/NM 9.0	NM- 9.2
1-3-Hans Rodionoff-s/Kyle Hotz-a						3.00
...: Whatever Knows Fear... (2005, $12.99, TPB) r/#1-3, Savage Tales #1, Adv. Into Fear #16						13.00

MANTRA
Malibu Comics (Ultraverse): July, 1993 - No. 24, Aug, 1995 ($1.95/$2.50)

	GD 2.0	VG 4.0	FN 6.0	VF 8.0	VF/NM 9.0	NM- 9.2
1-Polybagged w/trading card & coupon						4.00
1-Newsstand edition w/o trading card or coupon						3.00
1-Full cover holographic edition	1	3	4	6	8	10
1-Ultra-limited silver foil-c						5.00
2,3,5-9,11-24: 2-($2.50-Newsstand edition bagged w/card. 3-Intro Warstrike & Kismet. 6-Break-Thru x-over. 7-Prime app.; origin Prototype by Jurgens/Austin (2 pgs.). 11-New costume. 17-Intro NecroMantra & Pinnacle; prelude to Godwheel						3.00
4-($2.50, 48 pgs.)-Rune flip-c/story by B. Smith (3 pgs.)						4.00
10-($3.50, 68 pgs.)-Flip-c w/Ultraverse Premiere #2						4.00
Giant Size 1 (7/94, $2.50, 44 pgs.)						4.00
...Spear of Destiny 1,2 (4/95, $2.50, 36pgs.)						3.00

MANTRA (2nd Series) (Also See Black September)
Malibu Comics (Ultraverse): Infinity, Sept, 1995 - No. 7, Apr, 1996 ($1.50)

	GD 2.0	VG 4.0	FN 6.0	VF 8.0	VF/NM 9.0	NM- 9.2
Infinity (9/95, $1.50)-Black September x-over, Intro new Mantra						3.00
1-7: 1-(10/95). 5-Return of Eden (original Mantra). 6,7-Rush app.						3.00

MAN WITH NO NAME, THE (Based on the Clint Eastwood gunslinger character)
Dynamite Entertainment: 2008 - No. 11, 2009 ($3.50)

	GD 2.0	VG 4.0	FN 6.0	VF 8.0	VF/NM 9.0	NM- 9.2
1-11: 1-Gage-s/Dias-a/Isanove-c. 7-Bernard-a						3.50

MAN WITH THE SCREAMING BRAIN (Based on screenplay by Bruce Campbell & David Goodman)
Dark Horse Comics: Apr, 2005 - No. 4, July, 2005 ($2.99, limited series)

	GD 2.0	VG 4.0	FN 6.0	VF 8.0	VF/NM 9.0	NM- 9.2
1-4-Campbell & Goodman-s; Remender-a/c. 1-Variant-c by Noto. 3-Powell var-c. 4-Mignola var-c						3.00
TPB (11/05, $13.95) r/#1-4; David Goodman intro.; cover gallery						14.00

MAN WITH THE X-RAY EYES, THE (See X,... under Movie Comics)

MANY GHOSTS OF DR. GRAVES, THE (Doctor Graves #73 on)
Charlton Comics: 5/67 - No. 60, 12/76; No. 61, 9/77 - No. 62, 10/77; No. 63, 2/78 - No. 65, 4/78; No. 66, 6/81 - No. 72, 5/82

	GD 2.0	VG 4.0	FN 6.0	VF 8.0	VF/NM 9.0	NM- 9.2
1-Ditko-a; Palais-a; early issues 12¢-c	7	14	21	46	76	105
2-6,8,10	3	6	9	20	30	40
7,9-Ditko-a	4	8	12	24	37	50
11-13,16-18-Ditko-c/a	3	6	9	20	30	40
14,19,23,25	2	4	6	10	14	18
15,20,21-Ditko-a	3	6	9	14	20	25
22,24,26,27,29-35,38,40-Ditko-c/a	3	6	9	16	22	28
28-Ditko-c	3	6	9	14	20	25
36,46,56,57,59,61,66,67,69,71	2	4	6	8	10	12
37,41,43,51,60-Ditko-a	2	4	6	9	13	16
39,58-Ditko-c. 39-Sutton-a. 58-Ditko-a	2	4	6	9	13	16
42,44,53-Sutton-c; Ditko-a. 42-Sutton-a	2	4	6	9	13	16
45-(5/74) 2nd Newton comic work (8 pgs.); new logo; Sutton-c	2	4	6	11	16	20
47-Newton, Sutton, Ditko-a	2	4	6	10	14	18
48-Ditko, Sutton-a	2	4	6	9	13	16
49-Newton-c/a; Sutton-a.	2	4	6	8	11	14
50-Sutton-a	2	4	6	8	10	12
52-Newton-c; Ditko-a	2	4	6	9	13	16
54-Early Byrne-c; Ditko-a	2	4	6	10	14	18
55-Ditko-c; Sutton-a	2	4	6	9	13	16
62-65,68-Ditko-c/a. 65-Sutton-a	2	4	6	11	16	20
70,72-Ditko-a	2	4	6	10	14	18
Modern Comics Reprint 12,25 (1978)						6.00

NOTE: ***Aparo** a-4, 5, 7, 8, 66r, 69r; c-8, 14, 19, 66r, 67r. **Byrne** c-54. **Ditko** a-1, 7, 9, 11-13, 15-18, 20-22, 24, 26, 27, 29, 30-35, 37, 38, 40-44, 47, 48, 51-54, 58, 60r-65r, 70, 72; c-11-13, 16-18, 22, 24, 26-35, 38, 40, 55, 58, 62-65. **Howard** a-38, 39, 45i, 65; c-48. **Kim** a-36, 46, 52. **Larson** a-58. **Morisi** a-13, 14, 23, 26. **Newton** a-45, 47p, 49p; c-49, 52. **Staton** a-36, 37, 41, 43. **Sutton** a-39, 42, 47-50, 55, 65; c-42, 44, 45; painted c-53. **Zeck** a-56, 59.*

MANY LOVES OF DOBIE GILLIS (TV)
National Periodical Publications: May-June, 1960 - No. 26, Oct, 1964

	GD 2.0	VG 4.0	FN 6.0	VF 8.0	VF/NM 9.0	NM- 9.2
1-Most covers by Bob Oskner	20	40	60	140	300	460
2-5	11	22	33	77	154	230
6-10: 10-Last 10¢-c	9	18	27	60	103	145
11-26: 20-Drucker-a. 24-(3-4/64). 25-(9/64)	8	16	24	53	89	125

MANY WORLDS OF TESLA STRONG, THE (Also see Tom Strong)
America's Best Comics: July, 2003 ($5.95, one-shot)

	GD 2.0	VG 4.0	FN 6.0	VF 8.0	VF/NM 9.0	NM- 9.2
1-Two covers by Timm & Art Adams; art by various incl. Campbell, Cho, Noto, Hughes						6.00

MARAUDER'S MOON (See Luke Short, Four Color #848)

MARCH OF COMICS (See Promotional Comics section)

MARCH OF CRIME (Formerly My Love Affair #1-6) (See Fox Giants)
Fox Features Synd.: No. 7, July, 1950 - No. 2, Sept, 1950; No. 3, Sept, 1951

	GD 2.0	VG 4.0	FN 6.0	VF 8.0	VF/NM 9.0	NM- 9.2
7(#1)(7/50)-True crime stories; Wood-a	41	82	123	256	428	600
2(9/50)-Wood-a (exceptional)	40	80	120	246	411	575
3(9/51)	21	42	63	122	199	275

MARCO POLO
Charlton Comics Group: 1962 (Movie classic)

	GD 2.0	VG 4.0	FN 6.0	VF 8.0	VF/NM 9.0	NM- 9.2
nn (Scarce)-Glanzman-c/a (25 pgs.)	10	20	30	66	121	175

MARC SILVESTRI SKETCHBOOK
Image Comics (Top Cow): Jan, 2004 ($2.99, one-shot)

	GD 2.0	VG 4.0	FN 6.0	VF 8.0	VF/NM 9.0	NM- 9.2
1-Character sketches, concept artwork, storyboards of Witchblade, Darkness & others						3.00

MARC SPECTOR: MOON KNIGHT (Also see Moon Knight)
Marvel Comics: June, 1989 - No. 60, Mar, 1994 ($1.50/$1.75, direct sales)

	GD 2.0	VG 4.0	FN 6.0	VF 8.0	VF/NM 9.0	NM- 9.2
1-24,26-49,51-54,58,59: 4-Intro new Midnight. 8,9-Punisher app. 15-Silver Sable app. 19-21-Spider-Man & Punisher app. 32,33-Hobgoblin II (Macendale) & Spider-Man (in black costume) app. 35-38-Punisher story. 42-44-Infinity War x-over. 46-Demogoblin app. 51,53-Gambit app. 55-New look. 57-Spider-Man-c/story. 60-Moon Knight dies						3.00
25,50: 25-(52 pgs.)-Ghost Rider app. 50-(56 pgs.)-Special die-cut-c						4.00
55-57,60-Platt a						4.00
...: Divided We Fall ($4.95, 52 pgs.)						5.00
Special 1 (1992, $2.50)						4.00

NOTE: *Cowan c(p) 20-23. Guice c-20. Heath c/a-4. Platt -a 55-57,60; c-55-60.*

MARGARET O'BRIEN (See The Adventures of...)

MARGE'S LITTLE LULU (Continues as Little Lulu from #207 on)
Dell Publishing Co./Gold Key #165-206: No. 74, 6/45 - No. 164, 7-9/62; No. 165, 10/62 - No. 206, 8/72

Marjorie Henderson Buell, born in Philadelphia, Pa., in 1904, created Little Lulu, a cartoon character that appeared weekly in the Saturday Evening Post from Feb. 23, 1935 through Dec. 30, 1944. She was not responsible for any of the comic books. **John Stanley** did pencils only on all Little Lulu comics through at least #135 (1959). He did pencils and inks on Four Color #74 & 97. **Irving Tripp** began inking stories from #1 on, and remained the comic's illustrator throughout its entire run. **Stanley** did storyboards (layouts), pencils, and scripts in all cases and inking only on covers. His word balloons were written in cursive. **Tripp** and occasionally other artists at Western Publ. in Poughkeepsie, N.Y. blew up the pencilled pages, inked the blowups, and lettered them. **Arnold Drake** did storyboards, pencils and scripts starting with #197 (1970) on, amidst reprinted issues. **Buell** sold her rights exclusively to Western Publ. in Dec., 1971. The earlier issues had to be approved by **Buell** prior to publication.

	GD 2.0	VG 4.0	FN 6.0	VF 8.0	VF/NM 9.0	NM- 9.2
Four Color 74('45)-Intro Lulu, Tubby & Alvin	143	286	429	1200	2600	4000
Four Color 97(2/46)	56	112	168	454	977	1500
(Above two books are all John Stanley - cover, pencils, and inks.)						
Four Color 110('46)-1st Alvin Story Telling Time; 1st app. Willy; variant cover exists	37	74	111	278	602	925
Four Color 115-1st app. Boys' Clubhouse	36	72	108	270	585	900
Four Color 120, 131: 120-1st app. Eddie	31	62	93	225	488	750
Four Color 139('47),146,158	30	60	90	218	472	725
Four Color 165 (10/47)-Smokes doll hair & has wild hallucinations. 1st Tubby detective story	30	60	90	218	472	725
1(1-2/48)-Lulu's Diary feature begins	67	134	201	545	1173	1800

Marge's Little Lulu #44 © M. Buell

Marineman #4 © Ian Churchill

The Mark #3 © DH

GD VG FN VF VF/NM NM-
2.0 4.0 6.0 8.0 9.0 9.2

2-1st app. Gloria; 1st app. Miss Feeny 30 60 90 218 472 725
3-5 27 54 81 196 423 650
6-10: 7-1st app. Annie; Xmas-c 22 44 66 154 327 500
11-20: 18-X-Mas-c. 19-1st app. Wilbur. 20-1st app. Mr. McNabbem
17 34 51 114 250 385
21-30: 26-r/F.C. 110. 30-Xmas-c 15 30 45 100 218 335
31-38,40: 35-1st Mumday story 12 24 36 84 175 265
39-Intro. Witch Hazel in "That Awful Witch Hazel" 12 24 36 84 177 270
41-60: 42-Xmas-c. 45-2nd Witch Hazel app. 49-Gives Stanley & others credit
11 22 33 75 148 220
61-80: 63-1st app. Chubby (Tubby's cousin). 68-1st app. Prof. Cleff.
78-Xmas-c. 80-Intro. Little Itch (2/55) 10 20 30 64 115 165
81-99: 90-Xmas-c 8 16 24 53 89 125
100 8 16 24 56 96 135
101-130: 123-1st app. Fifi 6 12 18 42 69 95
131-164: 135-Last Stanley-p 6 12 18 37 59 80
165-Giant; ...in Paris ('62) 10 20 30 68 127 185
166-Giant; ...Christmas Diary (1962 - '63) 10 20 30 68 127 185
167-169 5 10 15 30 48 65
170,172,175,176,178-196,198-200-Stanley-r. 182-1st app. Little Scarecrow Boy
3 6 9 18 27 35
171,173,174,177,197 3 6 9 16 23 30
201,203,206-Last issue to carry Marge's name 3 6 9 14 20 26
202,204,205-Stanley-r 3 6 9 16 23 30
...& Tubby in Japan (12¢)(5-7/62) 01476-207 8 16 24 51 86 120
...Summer Camp 1(8/67-G.K.-Giant) '57-58-r 6 12 18 41 66 90
...Trick 'N' Treat 1(12¢)(12/62-Gold Key) 7 14 21 46 76 105

NOTE: *See Dell Giant Comics #23, 29, 36, 42, 50, & Dell Giants for annuals. All Giants not by Stanley from L.L. on Vacation (7/54) on. Irving Tripp a-#1-on. Christmas c-7, 18, 30, 42, 78, 90, 126, 166, 250. Summer Camp issues #173, 177, 181, 189, 197, 201, 206.*

MARGE'S LITTLE LULU (See Golden Comics Digest #19, 23, 27, 29, 33, 36, 40, 43, 46, & March of Comics #251, 267, 275, 293, 307, 323, 335, 349, 355, 369, 385, 406, 417, 427, 439, 456, 468, 475, 488)

MARGE'S TUBBY (Little Lulu)(See Dell Giants)
Dell Publishing Co./Gold Key: No. 381, Aug, 1952 - No. 49, Dec-Feb, 1961-62

Four Color 381(#1)-Stanley script; Irving Tripp-a 17 34 51 119 260 400
Four Color 430,444-Stanley-a 11 22 33 75 148 220
Four Color 461 (4/53)-1st Tubby & Men From Mars story; Stanley-a
10 20 30 69 130 190
5 (7-9/53)-Stanley-a 9 18 27 60 103 145
6-10 8 16 24 51 86 120
11-20 6 12 18 39 62 85
21-30 5 10 15 32 51 70
31-49 4 8 12 28 44 60
...& the Little Men From Mars No. 30020-410(10/64-G.K.)-25¢, 68 pgs.
8 16 24 51 86 120

NOTE: ***John Stanley** did all storyboards & scripts through at least #35 (1959). **Lloyd White** did all art except F.C. 381, 430, 444, 461 & #5.*

MARGIE (See My Little...)

MARGIE (TV)
Dell Publ. Co.: No. 1307, Mar-May, 1962 - No. 2, July-Sept, 1962 (Photo-c)

Four Color 1307(#1) 6 12 18 37 59 80
2 5 10 15 30 48 65

MARGIE COMICS (Formerly Comedy Comics; Reno Browne #50 on)
(Also see Cindy Comics & Teen Comics)
Marvel Comics (ACI): No. 35, Winter, 1946-47 - No. 49, Dec, 1949

35 20 40 60 114 182 250
36-38,42,45,47-49 12 24 36 69 97 125
39,41,43(2),44,46-Kurtzman's "Hey Look" 14 28 42 76 108 140
40-Three "Hey Looks", three "Giggles 'n' Grins" by Kurtzman
14 28 42 82 121 160

MARINEMAN (Ian Churchill's...)
Image Comics: Dec, 2010 - No. 6, Jun, 2011 ($3.99/$4.99)

1-5-Ian Churchill-s/a/c 4.00
6-($4.99) Origin revealed 5.00

MARINES (See Tell It to the...)

MARINES ATTACK
Charlton Comics: Aug, 1964 - No. 9, Feb-Mar, 1966

1-Glanzman-a begins 4 8 12 22 34 45
2-9: 8-1st Vietnam war-c/story 3 6 9 14 19 24

MARINES AT WAR (Formerly Tales of the Marines #4)
Atlas Comics (OPI): No. 5, Apr, 1957 - No. 7, Aug, 1957

5-7 10 20 30 56 76 95

NOTE: ***Colan** a-5. **Drucker** a-5. **Everett** a-5. **Maneely** a-5. **Orlando** a-7. **Severin** c-5.*

MARINES IN ACTION
Atlas News Co.: June, 1955 - No. 14, Sept, 1957

1-Rock Murdock, Boot Camp Brady begin 14 28 42 78 112 145
2-14 10 20 30 56 76 95

NOTE: ***Berg** a-2, 8, 9, 11, 14. **Heath** c-2, 9. **Maneely** c-1, 3. **Severin** a-4; c-7-11, 14.*

MARINES IN BATTLE
Atlas Comics (ACI No. 1-12/WPI No. 13-25): Aug, 1954 - No. 25, Sept, 1958

1-Heath-c; Iron Mike McGraw by Heath; history of U.S. Marine Corps. begins
22 44 66 132 216 300
2-Heath-c 14 28 42 81 118 155
3-6,8-10: 4-Last precode (2/55); Romita-a 11 22 33 62 86 110
7-Kubert/Moskowitz-a (6 pgs.) 11 22 33 64 90 115
11-16,18-21,24 10 20 30 58 79 100
17-Williamson-a (3 pgs.) 12 24 36 67 94 120
22,25-Torres-a 10 20 30 58 79 100
23-Crandall-a; Mark Murdock app. 11 22 33 60 83 105

NOTE: ***Berg** a-22. **G. Colan** a-22, 23. **Drucker** a-6. **Everett** a-4, 15; c-21. **Heath** c-1, 2, 4. **Maneely** c-23, 24. **Orlando** a-14. **Pakula** a-6, 23. **Powell** a-16. **Severin** a-22; c-12. **Sinnott** a-23. **Tuska** a-15.*

MARINE WAR HEROES (Charlton Premiere #19 on)
Charlton Comics: Jan, 1964 - No. 18, Mar, 1967

1-Montes/Bache-c/a 4 8 12 23 36 48
2-18: 11-Vietnam sty w/VC tunnels & moles.14,18-Montes/Bache-a. 17-Tojo's plan to bomb
Pearl Harbor & 1st Atomic bomb blast on Japan 3 6 9 14 20 26

MARK, THE (Also see Mayhem)
Dark Horse Comics: Dec, 1993 - No. 4, Mar, 1994 ($2.50, limited series)

1-4 3.00

MARK HAZZARD: MERC
Marvel Comics Group: Nov, 1986 - No. 12, Oct, 1987 (75¢)

1-12: Morrow-a 3.00
Annual 1 (11/87, $1.25) 4.00

MARK OF CHARON (See Negation)
CG Entertainment: Apr, 2003 - No. 5, Aug, 2003 ($2.95, limited series)

1-5-Bedard-s/Bennett-a 3.00

MARK OF ZORRO (See Zorro, Four Color #228)

MARK 1 COMICS (Also see Shaloman)
Mark 1 Comics: Apr, 1988 - No. 3, Mar, 1989 ($1.50)

1-3: Early Shaloman app. 2-Origin 3.00

MARKSMAN, THE (Also see Champions)
Hero Comics: Jan, 1988 - No. 5, 1988 ($1.95)

1-5: 1-Rose begins. 1-3-Origin The Marksman 3.00
Annual 1 ('88, $2.75, 52 pgs.)-Champions app. 4.00

MARK TRAIL
Standard Magazines (Hall Syndicate)/Fawcett Publ. No. 5: Oct, 1955; No. 5, Summer, 1959

1(1955)-Sunday strip-r 7 14 21 37 46 55
5(1959) 5 10 15 22 26 30
...Adventure Book of Nature 1 (Summer, 1958, 25¢, Pines)-100 pg. Giant; Special Camp Issue;
contains 78 Sunday strip-r 9 18 27 52 69 85

MARMADUKE MONK
I. W. Enterprises/Super Comics: No date; 1963 (10¢)

I.W. Reprint 1 (nd) 2 4 6 8 11 14
Super Reprint 14 (1963)-r/Monkeyshines Comics #? 2 4 6 8 10 12

MARMADUKE MOUSE
Quality Comics Group (Arnold Publ.): Spring, 1946 - No. 65, Dec, 1956 (Early issues: 52 pgs.)

1-Funny animal 17 34 51 98 154 210
2 11 22 33 60 83 105
3-10 9 18 27 47 61 75
11-30 7 14 21 35 43 50
31-65: Later issues are 36 pgs. 6 12 18 28 34 40
Super Reprint #14(1963) 2 4 6 9 12 15

MARQUIS, THE
Oni Press

...: A Sin of One ($2.99, 5/03) Guy Davis-s/a; Michael Gaydos-c 3.00
...: Intermezzo TPB ($11.95, 12/03) r/A Sin of One and Hell's Courtesan #1,2 12.00

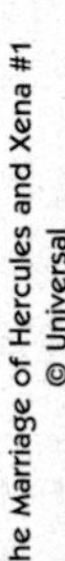
The Marriage of Hercules and Xena #1 © Universal

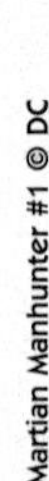
Martian Manhunter #1 © DC

Marvel Adventures #15 © MAR

GD 2.0 | VG 4.0 | FN 6.0 | VF 8.0 | VF/NM 9.0 | NM- 9.2

MARQUIS, THE: DANSE MACABRE
Oni Press: May, 2000 - No. 5, Feb, 2001 ($2.95, B&W, limited series)
1-5-Guy Davis-s/a. 1-Wagner-c. 2-Mignola-c. 3-Vess-c. 5-K. Jones-c 3.00
TPB (8/2001, $18.95) r/1-5 & Les Preludes; Seagle intro. 19.00

MARQUIS, THE: DEVIL'S REIGN: HELL'S COURTESAN
Oni Press: Feb, 2002 - No. 2, Apr, 2002 ($2.95, B&W, limited series)
1,2-Guy Davis-s/a 3.00

MARRIAGE OF HERCULES AND XENA, THE
Topps Comics: July, 1998 ($2.95, one-shot)
1-Photo-c; Lopresti-a; Alex Ross pin-up, 1-Alex Ross painted-c 3.00
1-Gold foil logo-c 5.00

MARRIED ... WITH CHILDREN (TV)(Based on Fox TV show)
Now Comics: June, 1990 - No. 7, Feb, 1991(12/90 inside) ($1.75)
V2#1, Sept, 1991 - No. 7, Apr, 1992 ($1.95)
1-7: 2-Photo-c, 1,2-2nd printing, V2#1-7: 1,4,6-Photo-c 3.00
...Buck's Tale (6/94, $1.95) 3.00
...1994 Annual nn (2/94, $2.50, 52 pgs.)-Flip book format 4.00
Special 1 (7/92, $1.95)-Kelly Bundy photo-c/poster 3.00

MARRIED ... WITH CHILDREN: KELLY BUNDY
Now Comics: Aug, 1992 - No. 3, Oct, 1992 ($1.95, limited series)
1-3: Kelly Bundy photo-c & poster in each 3.00

MARRIED ... WITH CHILDREN: QUANTUM QUARTET
Now Comics: Oct, 1993 - No. 4, 1994, ($1.95, limited series)
1-4: Fantastic Four parody 3.00

MARRIED ... WITH CHILDREN: 2099
Now Comics: June, 1993 - No. 3, Aug, 1993 ($1.95, limited series)
1-3 3.00

MARS
First Comics: Jan, 1984 - No. 12, Jan, 1985 ($1.00, Mando paper)
1-12: Marc Hempel & Mark Wheatley story & art. 2-The Black Flame begins. 10-Dynamo Joe begins 3.00
TPB (IDW Publ., 8/05, $39.99) r/#1-12, creator commentary; bonus art; new Hempel-c 40.00

MARS & BEYOND (Disney, TV)
Dell Publishing Co.: No. 866, Dec, 1957
Four Color 866-A Science feat. from Tomorrowland 8 16 24 55 93 130

MARS ATTACKS
Topps Comics: May, 1994 - No. 5, Sept, 1994 ($2.95, limited series)
1-5-Giffen story; flip books 1 3 4 6 8 10
Special Edition 2 4 6 8 10 12
Trade paperback (12/94, $12.95)-r/limited series plus new 8 pg. story 13.00

MARS ATTACKS
Topps Comics: V2#1, 8/95 - V2#3, 10/95; V2#4, 1/96 - No. 7, 5/96($2.95, bi-monthly #6 on)
V2#1-7: 1-Counterstrike storyline begins. 4-(1/96). 5-(1/96). 5,7-Brereton-c. 6-(3/96)-Simonson-c. 7-Story leads into Baseball Special #1 4.00
Baseball Special 1 (6/96, $2.95)-Bisley-c. 4.00

MARS ATTACKS HIGH SCHOOL
Topps Comics: May, 1997 - No. 2, Sept, 1997 ($2.95, B&W, limited series)
1,2-Stelfreeze-c 4.00

MARS ATTACKS IMAGE
Topps Comics: Dec, 1996 - No. 4, Mar, 1997 ($2.50, limited series)
1-4-Giffen-s/Smith/Sienkiewicz-a 4.00

MARS ATTACKS THE SAVAGE DRAGON
Topps Comics: Dec, 1996 - No. 4, Mar, 1997 ($2.95, limited series)
1-4: 1-w/bound-in card 4.00

MARSHAL BLUEBERRY (See Blueberry)
Marvel Comics (Epic Comics): 1991 ($14.95, graphic novel)
1-Moebius-a 3 6 9 14 19 24

MARSHAL LAW (Also see Crime And Punishment: Marshall Law...)
Marvel Comics (Epic Comics): Oct, 1987 - No. 6, May, 1989 ($1.95, mature)
1-6 3.00

M.A.R.S. PATROL TOTAL WAR (Formerly Total War #1,2)
Gold Key: No. 3, Sept, 1966 - No. 10, Aug, 1969 (All-Painted-c except #7)
3-Wood-a; aliens invade USA 6 12 18 41 66 90
4-10 4 8 12 24 37 50
Wally Wood's M.A.R.S. Patrol Total War TPB (Dark Horse, 9/04, $12.95) r/#3 & Total War #1&2; foreward by Batton Lash; afterword by Dan Adkins 13.00

MARTHA WASHINGTON (Also see Dark Horse Presents Fifth Anniversary Special, Dark Horse Presents #100-4, Give Me Liberty, Happy Birthday Martha Washington & San Diego Comicon Comics #2)

MARTHA WASHINGTON... (one-shots)
Dark Horse Comics (Legend): ($2.95/$3.50, one-shots)
... Dies (7/07, $3.50) Miller-s/Gibbons-a; r/Miller's original outline for Give Me Liberty 3.50
... Stranded in Space (11/95, $2.95) Miller-s/Gibbons-a; Big Guy app. 4.00

MARTHA WASHINGTON GOES TO WAR
Dark Horse Comics (Legend): May, 1994 - No. 5, Sep, 1994 ($2.95, lim. series)
1-5-Miller scripts; Gibbons-c/a 4.00
TPB ($17.95) r/#1-5 18.00

MARTHA WASHINGTON SAVES THE WORLD
Dark Horse Comics: Dec, 1997 - No. 3, Feb, 1998 ($2.95/$3.95, lim. series)
1,2-Miller scripts; Gibbons-c/a in all 4.00
3-($3.95) 4.00

MARTHA WAYNE (See The Story of...)

MARTIAN MANHUNTER (See Detective Comics & Showcase '95 #9)
DC Comics: May, 1988 - No. 4, Aug,. 1988 ($1.25, limited series)
1-4: 1,4-Batman app. 2-Batman cameo 3.00
Special 1-(1996, $3.50) 4.00

MARTIAN MANHUNTER (See JLA)
DC Comics: No. 0, Oct, 1998 - No. 36, Nov, 2001 ($1.99)
0-(10/98) Origin retold; Ostrander-s/Mandrake-c/a 3.00
1-36: 1-(12/98). 6-9-JLA app. 18,19-JSA app. 24-Mahnke-a 3.00
#1,000,000 (11/98) 853rd Century x-over 3.00
Annual 1,2 (1998,1999; $2.95) 1-Ghosts; Wrightson-c. 2-JLApe 4.00

MARTIAN MANHUNTER (See DCU Brave New World)
DC Comics: Oct, 2006 - No. 8, May, 2007 ($2.99, limited series)
1-8-Lieberman-s/Barrionuevo-a/c 3.00
...: The Others Among Us TPB (2007, $19.99) r/#1-8 & story from DCU Brave New World 20.00

MARTIAN MANHUNTER: AMERICAN SECRETS
DC Comics: 1992 - Book Three, 1992 ($4.95, limited series, prestige format)
1-3: Barreto-a 5.00

MARTIN KANE (William Gargan as... Private Eye)(Stage/Screen/Radio/TV)
Fox Features Syndicate (Hero Books): No. 4, June, 1950 - No. 2, Aug, 1950 (Formerly My Secret Affair)
4(#1)-True crime stories; Wood-c/a(2); used in **SOTI**, pg. 160; photo back-c 32 64 96 192 314 435
2-Wood/Orlando story, 5 pgs; Wood-a(2) 24 48 72 140 230 320

MARTIN MYSTERY
Dark Horse (Bonelli Comics): Mar, 1999 - No. 6, Aug, 1999 ($4.95, B&W, digest size)
1-6-Reprints Italian series in English; Gibbons-c on #1-3 5.00

MARTY MOUSE
I. W. Enterprises: No date (1958?) (10¢)
1-Reprint 2 4 6 9 12 15

MARVEL ACTION HOUR FEATURING IRON MAN (TV cartoon)
Marvel Comics: Nov, 1994 - No. 8, June, 1995 ($1.50/$2.95)
1-8: Based on cartoon series 3.00
1 ($2.95)-Polybagged w/16 pg Marvel Action Hour Preview & acetate print 4.00

MARVEL ACTION HOUR FEATURING THE FANTASTIC FOUR (TV cartoon)
Marvel Comics: Nov, 1994 - No. 8, June, 1995 ($1.50/$2.95)
1-8: Based on cartoon series 3.00
1-($2.95)-Polybagged w/ 16 pg. Marvel Action Hour Preview & acetate print 4.00

MARVEL ACTION UNIVERSE (TV cartoon)
Marvel Comics: Jan, 1989 ($1.00, one-shot)
1-r/Spider-Man And His Amazing Friends 4.00

MARVEL ADVENTURES
Marvel Comics: Apr, 1997 - No. 18, Sept, 1998 ($1.50)
1-18-"Animated style": 1,4,7-Hulk-c/app. 2,11-Spider-Man. 3,8,15-X-Men. 5-Spider-Man & X-Men. 6-Spider-Man & Human Torch. 9,12-Fantastic Four. 10,16-Silver Surfer. 13-Spider-Man & Silver Surfer. 14-Hulk & Dr. Strange. 18-Capt. America 3.00

MARVEL ADVENTURES...

Marvel Adventures Spider-Man (2nd series) #7 © MAR

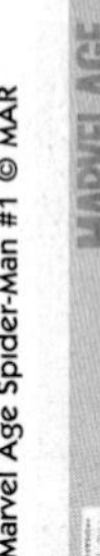

Marvel Age Spider-Man #1 © MAR

Marvel Boy #1 © MAR

GD 2.0 | VG 4.0 | FN 6.0 | VF 8.0 | VF/NM 9.0 | NM- 9.2

GD 2.0 | VG 4.0 | FN 6.0 | VF 8.0 | VF/NM 9.0 | NM- 9.2

Marvel Comics: 2007, 2008 (Free Comic Book Day giveaways)

... Free Comic Book Day 2007 (6/07) 1-Iron Man, Hulk and Franklin Richards app. 3.00
... Free Comic Book Day 2008 - Iron Man, Hulk, Ant-Man and Spider-Man app. 3.00

MARVEL ADVENTURES FANTASTIC FOUR (All ages title)
Marvel Comics: No. 0, July, 2005 - No. 48, July, 2009 ($1.99/$2.50/$2.99)

0-($1.99) Movie version characters; Dr. Doom app.; Eaton-a 3.00
1-10-($2.50) 1-Skrulls app.; Pagulayan-a. 7-Namor app. 3.00
11-48-($2.99) 12,42-Dr. Doom app. 24-Namor app. 26,28-Silver Surfer app. 3.00
... Vol. 1: Family of Heroes (2005, $6.99, digest) r/#1-4 7.00
... Vol. 2: Fantastic Voyages (2006, $6.99, digest) r/#5-8 7.00
... Vol. 3: World's Greatest (2006, $6.99, digest) r/#9-12 7.00
... Vol. 4: Cosmic Threats (2006, $6.99, digest) r/#13-16 7.00
... Vol. 5: All 4 One, 4 For All (2007, $6.99, digest) r/#17-20 7.00
... Vol. 6: Monsters & Mysteries (2007, $6.99, digest) r/#21-24 7.00
... Vol. 7: The Silver Surfer (2007, $6.99, digest) r/#25-28 7.00
... Vol. 8: Monsters, Moles, Cowboys & Coupons (2008, $7.99, digest) r/#29-32 8.00

MARVEL ADVENTURES FLIP MAGAZINE (All ages title)
Marvel Comics: Aug, 2005 - Present ($3.99/$4.99)

1-11: 1-10-Rep. Marvel Advs. Fantastic Four and Marvel Advs. Spider-Man in flip format 4.00
12-14-($4.99) Reprints Marvel Advs. Spider-Man & X-Men/Power Pack in flip format 5.00
15-26-Rep. Marvel Advs. Fantastic Four and Marvel Advs. Spider-Man in flip format 5.00

MARVEL ADVENTURES HULK (All ages title)
Marvel Comics: Sept, 2007 - No. 16, Dec, 2008 ($2.99)

1-16: 1-New version of Hulk's origin; Pagulayan-c. 2-Jamie Madrox app. 13-Mummies 3.00
... Vol. 1: Misunderstood Monster (2007, $6.99, digest) r/#1-4 7.00

MARVEL ADVENTURES IRON MAN (All ages title)
Marvel Comics: July, 2007 - No. 13, Jul, 2008 ($2.99)

1-13: 1-4-Michael Golden-c. 1-New version of Iron Man's origin. 2-Intro. the Mandarin 3.00
... Vol. 1: Heart of Steel (2007, $6.99, digest) r/#1-4 7.00
... Vol. 2: Iron Armory (2008, $7.99, digest) r/#5-8 8.00

MARVEL ADVENTURES SPIDER-MAN (All ages title)
Marvel Comics: May, 2005 - No. 61, May, 2010 ($2.50/$2.99)

1-13-Lee & Ditko stories retold with new art. 13-Conner-c 3.00
14-48: 14-Begin $2.99-c. 14-16-Conner-c. 22,23-Black costume. 35-Venom app. 3.00
50-($3.99) Sinister Six app.; back-up w/Sonny Liew-a 4.00
51-61: 53-Emma Frost becomes a regular; intro. Chat; Skottie Young-c begin 3.00
... Vol. 1 HC (2006, $19.99, with dustjacket) r/#1-8; plot for #7; sketch pages from #6,8 20.00
... Vol. 1: The Sinister Six (2005, $6.99, digest) r/#1-4 7.00
... Vol. 2: Power Struggle (2005, $6.99, digest) r/#5-8 7.00
... Vol. 3: Doom With a View (2006, $6.99, digest) r/#9-12 7.00
... Vol. 4: Concrete Jungle (2006, $6.99, digest) r/#13-16 7.00
... Vol. 5: Monsters on the Prowl (2007, $6.99, digest) r/#17-20 7.00
... Vol. 6: The Black Costume (2007, $6.99, digest) r/#21-24 7.00
... Vol. 7: Secret Identity (2007, $6.99, digest) r/#25-28 7.00
... Vol. 8: Forces of Nature (2008, $7.99, digest) r/#29-32 8.00
... Vol. 9: Fiercest Foes (2008, $7.99, digest) r/#33-36 8.00

MARVEL ADVENTURES SPIDER-MAN (All ages title)
Marvel Comics: June, 2010 - No. 24, May, 2012 ($3.99/$2.99)

1-($3.99) Tobin-s; Franklin Richards back-up 4.00
2-23-($2.99): 3,7-Wolverine app. 3,4-Bullseye app. 6-Doctor Octopus app. 3.00

MARVEL ADVENTURES STARRING DAREDEVIL (...Adventure #3 on)
Marvel Comics Group: Dec, 1975 - No. 6, Oct, 1976

	GD	VG	FN	VF	VF/NM	NM-
1	2	4	6	9	13	16
2-6-r/Daredevil #22-27 by Colan. 3-5-(25¢-c)	1	3	4	6	8	10
3-5-(30¢-c variants, limited distribution)(4,6,8/76)	3	6	9	14	20	25

MARVEL ADVENTURES SUPER HEROES (All ages title)
Marvel Comics: Sept, 2008 - No. 21, May, 2010 ($2.99)

1-21: 1-4: Spider-Man, Hulk and Iron Man team-ups. 1-Hercules app. 5-Dr. Strange app. 6-Ant-Man origin re-told. 7-Thor. 8,12-Capt. America. 17-Avengers begin 3.00

MARVEL ADVENTURES SUPER HEROES (All ages title)
Marvel Comics: June, 2010 - No. 24, May, 2012 ($3.99/$2.99)

1-($3.99) Iron Man and Avengers vs. Magneto 4.00
2-24-($2.99) 4-Deadpool app. 5-Rhino app. 11,12,22-Hulk app. 13,14,19-Thor 3.00

MARVEL ADVENTURES THE AVENGERS (All ages title)
Marvel Comics: July, 2006 - No. 39, Oct, 2009 ($2.99)

1-39-Spider-Man, Wolverine, Hulk, Iron Man, Capt. America, Storm, Giant-Girl app. 3.00
... Vol. 1: Heroes Assembled (2006, $6.99, digest) r/#1-4 7.00
... Vol. 2: Mischief (2007, $6.99, digest) r/#5-8 7.00
... Vol. 3: Bizarre Adventures (2007, $6.99, digest) r/#9-12 7.00
... Vol. 4: The Dream Team (2007, $6.99, digest) r/#13-15 & Giant-Size #1 7.00
... Vol. 5: Some Assembling Required (2008, $7.99, digest) r/#16-19 8.00

MARVEL ADVENTURES TWO-IN-ONE
Marvel Comics: Oct, 2007 - No. 18 ($4.99, bi-weekly)

1-18: 1-9-Reprints Marvel Adventures Spider-Man and Fantastic Four stories. 10-Hulk 5.00

MARVEL AGE FANTASTIC FOUR (All ages title)
Marvel Comics: Jun, 2004 - No. 12, Mar, 2005 ($2.25)

1-12-Lee & Kirby stories retold with new art by various. 11-Impossible Man app. 3.00
...Tales (4/05, $2.25) retells first meeting with the Black Panther; O'Hare & Lim-a 3.00
Vol. 1: All For One TPB (2004, $5.99, digest size) r/#1-4 6.00
Vol. 2: Doom TPB (2004, $5.99, digest size) r/#5-8 6.00
Vol. 3: The Return of Doctor Doom TPB (2005, $5.99, digest size) r/#9-12 6.00

MARVEL AGE HULK (All ages title)
Marvel Comics: Nov, 2004 - No. 4, Feb, 2005 ($1.75)

1-3-Lee & Kirby stories retold with new art by various 3.00
Vol. 1: Incredible TPB (2005, $5.99, digest size) r/#1-4 6.00
Vol. 2: Defenders (2008, $7.99, digest) r/#5-8 8.00

MARVEL AGE SPIDER-MAN (All ages title)
Marvel Comics: May, 2004 - No. 20, Mar, 2005 ($2.25)

1-20-Lee & Ditko stories retold with new art. 4-Doctor Doom app. 5-Lizard app. 3.00
1-(Free Comic Book Day giveaway, 8/04) Spider-Man vs. The Vulture; Brooks-a 3.00
Vol. 1 TPB (2004, $5.99, digest) 1-r/#1-4 6.00
Vol. 2: Everyday Hero TPB (2004, $5.99, digest) r/#5-8 6.00
Vol. 3: Swingtime TPB (2004, $5.99, digest) r/#9-12 6.00
Spidey Strikes Back TPB (2005, 5.99, digest) r/#17-20 6.00

MARVEL AGE SPIDER-MAN TEAM-UP (Marvel Adventures on cover)
Marvel Comics: June, 2005 (Free Comic Book Day giveaway)

1-Spider-Man meets the Fantastic Four 3.00

MARVEL AGE TEAM-UP (All ages Spider-Man team-ups) (Also see Free Comic Book Day edition in the Promotional Comics section)
Marvel Comics: Nov, 2004 - No. 5, Apr, 2005 ($1.75)

1-5-Stories retold with new art by various. 1-Fantastic Four app. 3-Kitty Pryde app. 3.00
... Vol. 1: A Little Help From My Friends (2005, $7.99, digest) r/#1-5 8.00

MARVEL AND DC PRESENT FEATURING THE UNCANNY X-MEN AND THE NEW TEEN TITANS
Marvel Comics/DC Comics: 1982 ($2.00, 68 pgs., one-shot, Baxter paper)

	GD	VG	FN	VF	VF/NM	NM-
1-3rd app. Deathstroke the Terminator; Darkseid app.; Simonson/Austin-c/a	2	4	6	11	16	20

MARVEL APES
Marvel Comics: Nov, 2008 - No. 4, Dec, 2008 ($3.99, limited series)

1-4: 1-Kesel-s/Bachs-a; back-up history story with Peyer-s/Kitson-a; two covers 4.00
1-($10.00) Hero Initiative edition with Daredevil gorilla cover by Mike Wieringo 10.00
#0-(2008, $3.99) r/Amazing Spider-Man #110,111; gallery of Marvel Apes variant covers 4.00
...: Amazing Spider-Monkey Special 1 (6/09, $3.99) Sandmonk and the Apevengers app. 4.00
...: Grunt Line 1 (7/09, $3.99) Kesel-s; Charles Darwin app. 4.00
...: Speedball Special 1 (5/09, $3.99) Bachs & Hardin-a 4.00

MARVEL ASSISTANT-SIZED SPECTACULAR
Marvel Comics: Jun, 2009 - No. 2, Jun, 2009 ($3.99, limited series)

1,2-Short stories by various incl. Isanove, Giarrusso, Nauck, Wyatt Cenak, Warren 4.00

MARVEL ATLAS (Styled after the Official Marvel Handbooks)
Marvel Comics: 2007 - No. 2, 2008 ($3.99, limited series)

1,2-Profiles and maps of countries in the Marvel Universe 4.00

MARVEL BOY (Astonishing #3 on; see Marvel Super Action #4)
Marvel Comics (MPC): Dec, 1950 - No. 2, Feb, 1951

	GD	VG	FN	VF	VF/NM	NM-
1-Origin Marvel Boy by Russ Heath	118	236	354	749	1287	1825
2-Everett-a; Washington DC under attack	81	162	243	518	884	1250

MARVEL BOY (Marvel Knights)
Marvel Comics: Aug, 2000 - No. 6, Mar, 2001 ($2.99, limited series)

1-Intro. Marvel Boy; Morrison-s/J.G. Jones-c/a 3.50
1-DF Variant-c 5.00
2-6 3.00
TPB (6/01, $15.95) 16.00

MARVEL BOY: THE URANIAN (Agents of Atlas)
Marvel Comics: Mar, 2010 - No. 3, May, 2010 ($3.99, limited series)

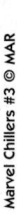

Marvel Chillers #3 © MAR

Marvel Comics Presents #134 © MAR

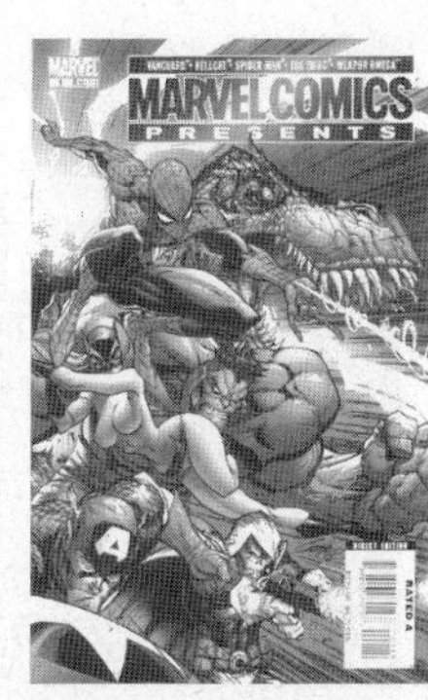

Marvel Comics Presents (2007 series) #1 © MAR

GD 2.0 | VG 4.0 | FN 6.0 | VF 8.0 | VF/NM 9.0 | NM- 9.2

1-3-Origin re-told; back-up reprints from 1950s; Heath & Everett-a 4.00

MARVEL CHILLERS (Also see Giant-Size Chillers)
Marvel Comics Group: Oct, 1975 - No. 7, Oct, 1976 (All 25¢ issues)

1-Intro. Modred the Mystic, ends #2; Kane-c(p) 3 6 9 14 19 24
2,4,5,7: 4-Kraven app. 5,6-Red Wolf app. 7-Kirby-c; Tuska-p 2 4 6 8 11 14
3-Tigra, the Were-Woman begins (origin), ends #7 (see Giant-Size Creatures #1). Chaykin/Wrightson-c. 3 6 9 18 27 35
4-6-(30¢-c variants, limited distribution)(4-8/76) 3 6 9 20 30 40
6-Byrne-a(p); Buckler-c(p) 2 4 6 11 16 20
NOTE: *Bolle a-1. Buckler c-2. Kirby c-7.*

MARVEL CLASSICS COMICS SERIES FEATURING...
(Also see Pendulum Illustrated Classics)
Marvel Comics Group: 1976 - No. 36, Dec, 1978 (52 pgs., no ads)

1-Dr. Jekyll and Mr. Hyde 2 4 6 10 14 18
2-10,28: 28-1st Golden-c/a; Pit and the Pendulum 2 4 6 8 10 12
11-27,29-36 1 2 3 5 7 9
NOTE: ***Adkins** c-1i, 4i, 12i. **Alcala** a-34i; c-34. **Bolle** a-35. **Buscema** c-17p, 19p, 26p. **Golden** c/a-28. **Gil Kane** c-1-16p, 21p, 22p, 24p, 32p. **Nebres** a-5; c-24i. **Nino** a-2, 8, 12. **Redondo** a-1, 9. No. 1-12 were reprinted from Pendulum Illustrated Classics.*

MARVEL COLLECTIBLE CLASSICS: AVENGERS
Marvel Comics: 1998 ($10.00, reprints with chromium wraparound-c)

1-Reprints Avengers Vol.3, #1; Perez-c 10.00

MARVEL COLLECTIBLE CLASSICS: SPIDER-MAN
Marvel Comics: 1998 ($10.00, reprints with chromium wraparound-c)

1-Reprints Amazing Spider-Man #300; McFarlane-c 10.00
2-Reprints Spider-Man #1; McFarlane-c 10.00

MARVEL COLLECTIBLE CLASSICS: X-MEN
Marvel Comics: 1998 ($10.00, reprints with chromium wraparound-c)

1-6: 1-Reprints (Uncanny) X-Men #1 & 2; Adam Kubert-c. 2-Reprints Uncanny X-Men #141 & 142; Byrne-c. 3-Reprints (Uncanny) X-Men #137; Larroca-c. 4-Reprints X-Men #25; Andy Kubert-c. 5-Reprints Giant Size X-Men #1; Gary Frank-c. 6-Reprints X-Men V2#1; Ramos-c 10.00

MARVEL COLLECTOR'S EDITION
Marvel Comics: 1992 (Ordered thru mail with Charleston Chew candy wrapper)

1-Flip-book format; Spider-Man, Silver Surfer, Wolverine (by Sam Kieth), & Ghost Rider stories; Wolverine back-c by Kieth 5.00

MARVEL COLLECTORS' ITEM CLASSICS (Marvel's Greatest #23 on)
Marvel Comics Group(ATF): Feb, 1965 - No. 22, Aug, 1969 (25¢, 68 pgs.)

1-Fantastic Four, Spider-Man, Thor, Hulk, Iron Man-r begin 11 22 33 73 142 210
2 (4/66) 7 14 21 46 76 105
3,4 6 12 18 39 62 85
5-10 5 10 15 35 55 75
11-22: 22-r/The Man in the Ant Hill/TTA #27 4 8 12 28 44 60
NOTE: *All reprints; **Ditko, Kirby** art in all.*

MARVEL COMICS (Marvel Mystery Comics #2 on)
Timely Comics (Funnies, Inc.): Oct, Nov, 1939

NOTE: The first issue was originally dated October 1939. Most copies have a black circle stamped over the date (on cover and inside) with "November" printed over it. However, some copies do not have the November overprint and could have a higher value. Most No. 1's have printing defects, i.e., tilted pages which caused trimming into the panels usually on right side and bottom. Covers exist with and without gloss finish.

1-Origin Sub-Mariner by Bill Everett(1st newsstand app.); 1st 8 pgs. were produced for Motion Picture Funnies Weekly #1 which was probably not distributed outside of advance copies; intro Human Torch by Carl Burgos, Kazar the Great (1st Tarzan clone), & Jungle Terror(only app.); intro. The Angel by Gustavson, The Masked Raider & his horse Lightning (ends #12); cover by sci/fi pulp illustrator Frank R. Paul 21,500 43,000 64,500 137,500 237,500 475,000

MARVEL COMICS
Marvel Comics: 1990 ($17.95, hardcover)

1-Reprint of entire Marvel Comics #1 3 6 9 16 23 30

MARVEL COMICS 70th ANNIVERARY SPECIAL
Marvel Comics: Oct, 2009 ($4.99, one-shot)

1-Re-colored reprint of entire Marvel Comics #1; cover swipe by Jelena Djurdjevic 5.00

MARVEL COMICS PRESENTS
Marvel Comics (Midnight Sons imprint #143 on): Early Sept, 1988 - No. 175, Feb, 1995 ($1.25/$1.50/$1.75, bi-weekly)

1-Wolverine by Buscema in #1-10 1 2 3 5 6 8
2-5 5.00
6-10: 6-Sub-Mariner app. 10-Colossus begins 4.00
11-47,51-71: 17-Cyclops begins. 19-1st app. Damage Control. 24-Havok begins. 25-Origin/1st app. Nth Man. 26-Hulk begins by Rogers. 29-Quasar app. 31-Excalibur begins by Austin (i). 32-McFarlane-a(p). 33-Capt. America; Jim Lee-a. 37-Devil-Slayer app. 38-Wolverine begins by Buscema; Hulk app. 39-Spider-Man app. 46-Liefeld Wolverine-c. 51-53-Wolverine by Rob Liefeld. 54-61-Wolverine/Hulk story: 54-Werewolf by Night begins; The Shroud by Ditko. 58-Iron Man by Ditko. 59-Punisher. 62-Deathlok & Wolverine stories 63-Wolverine. 64-71-Wolverine/Ghost Rider 8-part story. 70-Liefeld Ghost Rider/ Wolverine-c 3.00
48-50-Wolverine & Spider-Man team-up by Erik Larsen-c/a. 48-Wasp app. 49,50-Savage Dragon prototype app. by Larsen. 50-Silver Surfer. 50-53-Comet Man; Mumy scripts 5.00
72-Begin 13-part Weapon-X story (Wolverine origin) by B. Windsor-Smith (prologue) 5.00
73-Weapon-X part 1; Black Knight, Sub-Mariner 4.00
74-84: 74-Weapon-X part 2; Black Knight, Sub-Mariner. 76-Death's Head story. 77-Mr. Fantastic story. 78-Iron Man by Steacy. 80,81-Capt. America by Ditko/Austin. 81-Daredevil by Rogers/Williamson. 82-Power Man. 83-Human Torch by Ditko(a&scripts); $1.00-c direct, $1.25 newsstand. 84-Last Weapon-X (24 pg. conclusion) 3.00
85-Begin 8-part Wolverine story by Sam Kieth (c/a); 1st Kieth-a on Wolverine; begin 8-part Beast story by Jae Lee(p) with Liefeld part pencils #85,86; 1st Jae Lee-a (assisted w/Liefeld, 1991) 4.00
86-90: 86-89-Wolverine, Beast stories continue. 90-Begin 8-part Ghost Rider & Cable story, ends #97; begin flip book format w/two-c 3.00
91-175: 93-Begin 6-part Wolverine story, ends #98. 98-Begin 2-part Ghost Rider story. 99-Spider-Man story. 100-Full-length Ghost Rider/Wolverine story by Sam Kieth w/Tim Vigil assists; anniversary issue, non flip-book. 101-Begin 6-part Ghost Rider/Dr. Strange story & begin 8-part Wolverine/Nightcrawler story by Colan/Williamson; Punisher story. 107-Begin 6-part Ghost Rider/Werewolf by Night story. 109-Begin 8 part Wolverine/Typhoid Mary story. 111-Iron Fist. 113-Begin 6-part Giant-Man & begin 6-part Ghost Rider/Iron Fist stories. 117-Preview of Ravage 2099 (1st app.); begin 6 part Wolverine/Venom story w/Kieth-a. 118-Preview of Doom 2099 (1st app.). 119-Begin Ghost Rider/Cloak & Dagger by Colan. 120,136,138-Spider-Man. 123-Begin 8-part Ghost Rider/Typhoid Mary story; begin 4-part She Hulk story; begin 8-part Wolverine/Lynx story. 125-Begin 6-part Iron Fist story. 130-Begin 6-part Ghost Rider/ Cage story. 136-Daredevil. 137-Begin 6-part Wolverine story & 6-part Ghost Rider story. 147-Begin 2-part Vengeance-c/story w/new Ghost Rider. 149-Vengeance-c/story w/new Ghost Rider. 150-Silver ink-c; begin 2-part Bloody Mary story w/Typhoid Mary,Wolverine, Daredevil, new Ghost Rider; intro Steel Raven. 152-Begin 4-part Wolverine, 4-part War Machine, 4-part Vengeance, 3-part Moon Knight stories; same date as War Machine #1. 143-146: Siege of Darkness parts 3,6,11,14; all have spot-varnished-c. 143-Ghost Rider/Scarlet Witch; intro new Werewolf. 144-Begin 2-part Morbius story. 145-Begin 2-part Nightstalkers story. 153-155-Bound-in Spider-Man trading card sheet 3.00
...Colossus: God's Country (1994, $6.95) r/#10-17 1 2 3 4 5 7
....: Wolverine Vol. 1 TPB (2005, $12.99) r/Wolverine stories from #1-10 13.00
....: Wolverine Vol. 2 TPB (2006, $12.99) r/from #39-50 and Marvel Age Annual #4 13.00
....: Wolverine Vol. 3 TPB (2006, $12.99) r/from #51-61 13.00
....: Wolverine Vol. 4 TPB (2006, $12.99) r/from #62-71 13.00
NOTE: ***Austin** a-31-37i; c(i)-48, 50, 99, 122. **Buscema** a-1-10, 38-47; c-6. **Byrne** a-79; c-71. **Colan** a(p)-36, 37. **Colan/Williamson** a-101-108. **Ditko** a-7p, 10, 56p, 58, 80, 81, 83. **Guice** a-62. **Sam Kieth** a-85-92, 117-122; c-85-98, 99p, 100-108, 117, 118, 120-122; back c-109-113, 117. **Jae Lee** c-129(back). **Liefeld** a-51, 52, 53p(2), 85p; c-46, 70. **McFarlane** c-32. **Mooney** a-73. **Rogers** a-26, 38, 46i, 81p. **Russell** a-10-14,16,17i; c-4,19, 30,31i. **Saltares** a-8p(early), 38-45p. **Simonson** c-1. **B. Smith** a-72-84; c-72-84. **P. Smith** c-34. **Sparling** a-33. **Starlin** a-89i. **Staton** a-74. **Steacy** a-78. **Sutton** a-101-105. **Williamson** c-62i. Two Gun Kid by **Gil Kane** in #116, 122.*

MARVEL COMICS PRESENTS
Marvel Comics: Nov, 2007 - No. 12, Oct, 2008 ($3.99)

1-12-Short stories by various. 1-Wraparound-c by Campbell 4.00

MARVEL COMICS SUPER SPECIAL, A (Marvel Super Special #5 on)
Marvel Comics: Sept, 1977 - No. 41(?), Nov, 1986 (nn 7) ($1.50, magazine)

1-Kiss, 40 pgs. comics plus photos & features; John Buscema-a(p); also see Howard the Duck #12; ink contains real KISS blood; Dr. Doom, Spider-Man, Avengers, Fantastic Four, Mephisto app. 11 22 33 76 151 225
2-Conan (1978) 3 6 9 14 19 24
3-Close Encounters of the Third Kind (1978); Simonson-a 2 4 6 9 13 16
4-The Beatles Story (1978)-Perez/Janson-a; has photos & articles 5 10 15 32 51 70
5-Kiss (1978)-Includes poster 11 22 33 76 151 225
6-Jaws II (1978) 2 4 6 9 13 16
7-Sgt. Pepper; Beatles movie adaptation; withdrawn from U.S. distribution (French ed. exists)
8-Battlestar Galactica; tabloid size ($1.50, 1978); adapts TV show 2 4 6 13 18 20
8-Modern-r of tabloid size 2 4 6 10 14 18
8-Battlestar Galactica; publ. in regular magazine format; low distribution ($1.50, 8-1/2x11") 3 6 9 14 19 24

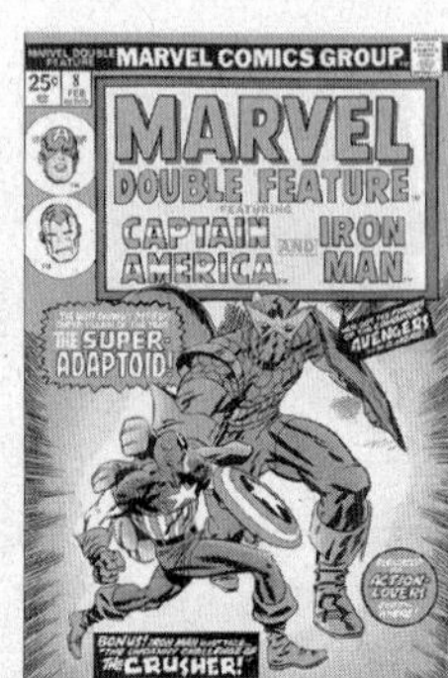

Marvel Double Feature #8 © MAR

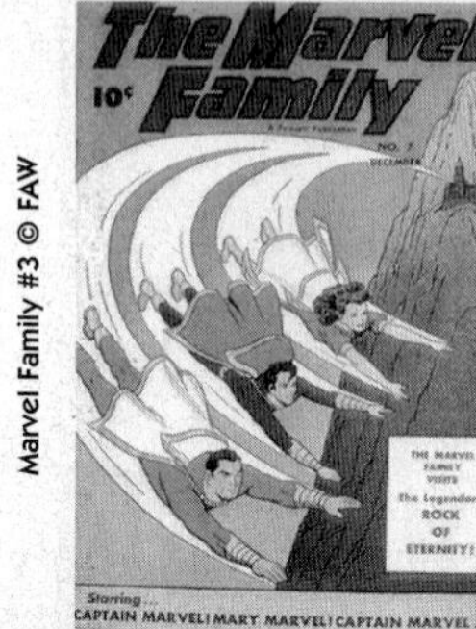

Marvel Family #3 © FAW

Marvel Fanfare #57 © MAR

GD VG FN VF VF/NM NM-
2.0 4.0 6.0 8.0 9.0 9.2

9-Conan 2 4 6 11 16 20
10-Star-Lord 2 4 6 9 13 16
11-13-Weirdworld begins #11; 25 copy special press run of each with gold seal and signed by artists (Proof quality), Spring-June, 1979 8 16 24 53 89 125
11-15: 11-13-Weirdworld (regular issues): 11-Fold-out centerfold. 14-Miller-c(p); adapts movie "Meteor." 15-Star Trek with photos & pin-ups ($1.50-c) 1 3 4 6 8 10
15-With $2.00 price; the price was changed at tail end of a 200,000 press run 2 4 6 8 10 12
16-Empire Strikes Back adaption; Williamson-a 2 4 6 9 12 15
17-20 (Movie adaptations): 17-Xanadu. 18-Raiders of the Lost Ark. 19-For Your Eyes Only (James Bond). 20-Dragonslayer 6.00
21-26,28-30 (Movie adaptations): 21-Conan. 22-Blade Runner; Williamson-a; Steranko-c. 23-Annie. 24-The Dark Crystal. 25-Rock and Rule-w/photos; artwork is from movie. 26-Octopussy (James Bond). 28-Krull; photo-c. 29-Tarzan of the Apes (Greystoke movie). 30-Indiana Jones and the Temple of Doom 1 2 3 4 5 7
27,31-41: 27-Return of the Jedi. 31-The Last Star Fighter. 32-The Muppets Take Manhattan. 33-Buckaroo Banzai. 34-Sheena. 35-Conan The Destroyer. 36-Dune. 37-2010. 38-Red Sonja. 39-Santa Claus:The Movie. 40-Labyrinth. 41-Howard The Duck 1 2 3 5 7 9

NOTE: ***J. Buscema** a-1, 2, 9, 11-13, 18p, 21, 35, 40; c-11(part), 12. **Chaykin** a-9, 19p; c-18, 19. **Colan** a(p)-6, 10, 14. **Morrow** a-34; c-1i, 34. **Nebres** a-11. **Spiegle** a-29. **Stevens** a-27. **Williamson** a-27. #22-28 contain photos from movies.*

MARVEL COMICS: 2001
Marvel Comics: 2001 (no cover price, one-shot)

1-Previews new titles for Fall 2001; Wolverine-c 3.00

MARVEL DABEL BROTHERS SAMPLER
Marvel Comics: Dec, 2006 (no cover price, one-shot)

1-Profiles and sample pages of Anita Blake, Magician: Apprentice, Red Prophet, Ptolus 3.00

MARVEL DIVAS
Marvel Comics: Sept, 2009 - No. 4, Dec, 2009 ($3.99, limited series)

1-4-Black Cat, Firestar, Hellcat and Photon app. 1-Campbell-c 4.00

MARVEL DOUBLE FEATURE
Marvel Comics Group: Dec, 1973 - No. 21, Mar, 1977

1-Capt. America, Iron Man-r/T.O.S. begin 2 4 6 11 16 20
2-10: 3-Last 20¢ issue 2 4 6 8 10 12
11-17,20,21:17-Story-r/Iron Man & Sub-Mariner #1; last 25¢ issue 1 2 3 5 6 8
15-17-(30¢-c variants, limited distribution)(4,6,8/76) 2 4 6 9 13 16
18,19-Colan/Craig-r from Iron Man #1 in both 2 3 4 6 8 10

NOTE: ***Colan** r-1-19p. **Craig** r-17-19i. **G. Kane** r-15p; c-15p. **Kirby** r-1-16p, 20, 21; c-17-20.*

MARVEL DOUBLE SHOT
Marvel Comics: Jan, 2003 - No. 4, April, 2003 ($2.99, limited series)

1-4: 1-Hulk by Haynes; Thor w/Asamiya-a; Jusko-c. 2-Dr. Doom by Rivera; Simpsons-style Avengers by Bill Morrison 3.00

MARVEL FAMILY (Also see Captain Marvel Adventures No. 18)
Fawcett Publications: Dec, 1945 - No. 89, Jan, 1954

1-Origin Captain Marvel, Captain Marvel Jr., Mary Marvel, & Uncle Marvel retold; origin/1st app. Black Adam 181 362 543 1158 1979 2800
2-The 3 Lt. Marvels & Uncle Marvel app. 77 154 231 493 847 1200
3 54 108 162 343 574 825
4,5 44 88 132 277 469 660
6-10: 7-Shazam app. 39 78 117 230 375 520
11-20 30 60 90 177 289 400
21-30 26 52 78 154 252 350
31-40 22 44 66 128 209 290
41-46,48-50 19 38 57 111 176 240
47-Flying Saucer-c/story (5/50) 24 48 72 144 237 330
51-76 18 36 54 103 162 220
77-Communist Threat-c 28 56 84 165 270 375
78,81-Used in **POP**, pg. 92,93. 20 40 60 117 189 260
79,80,82-88: 79-Horror satire-c 20 40 60 114 182 250
89-Last issue; last Fawcett Captain Marvel app. (low distribution) 24 48 72 142 234 325

MARVEL FANFARE (1st Series)
Marvel Comics Group: Mar, 1982 - No. 60, Jan, 1992 ($1.25/$2.25, slick paper, direct sales)

1-Spider-Man/Angel team-up; 1st Paul Smith-a (1st full story; see King Conan #7); Daredevil app. (many copies were printed missing the centerfold) 1 3 4 6 8 10
2-Spider-Man, Ka-Zar, The Angel. F.F. origin retold 1 2 3 5 6 8

GD VG FN VF VF/NM NM-
2.0 4.0 6.0 8.0 9.0 9.2

3,4-X-Men & Ka-Zar. 4-Deathlok, Spidey app. 6.00
5-14: 5-Dr. Strange, Capt. America. 6-Spider-Man, Scarlet Witch. 7-Incredible Hulk; D.D. back-up(also 15). 8-Dr. Strange; Wolf Boy begins. 9-Man-Thing. 10-13-Black Widow. 14-The Vision 4.00
15,24,33: 15-The Thing by Barry Smith, c/a. 24-Weirdworld; Wolverine back-up. 33-X-Men, Wolverine app.; Punisher pin-up 5.00
16-23,25-32,34-44,46-50: 16,17-Skywolf. 16-Sub-Mariner back-up. 17-Hulk back-up. 18-Capt. America by Miller. 19-Cloak and Dagger. 20-Thing/Dr. Strange. 21-Thing/Dr. Strange /Hulk. 22,23-Iron Man vs. Dr. Octopus. 25,26-Weirdworld. 27-Daredevil/Spider-Man. 28-Alpha Flight. 29-Hulk. 30-Moon Knight. 31,32-Captain America. 34-37-Warriors Three. 38-Moon Knight/Dazzler. 39-Moon Knight/Hawkeye. 40-Angel/Rogue & Storm. 41-Dr. Strange. 42-Spider-Man. 43-Sub-Mariner/Human Torch. 44-Iron Man vs. Dr. Doom by Ken Steacy. 46-Fantastic Four. 47-Hulk. 48-She-Hulk/Vision. 49-Dr. Strange/Nick Fury. 50-X-Factor 3.00
45-All pin-up issue by Steacy, Art Adams & others 5.00
51-($2.95, 52 pgs.)-Silver Surfer; Fantastic Four & Capt. Marvel app.; 51,52-Colan/Williamson back-up (Dr. Strange) 4.00
52,53,56-60: 52,53-Black Knight; 53-Iron Man back up. 56-59-Shanna the She-Devil. 58-Vision & Scarlet Witch back-up. 60-Black Panther/Rogue/Daredevil stories 3.00
54,55-Wolverine back-ups. 54-Black Knight. 55-Power Pack 4.00
... Vol. 1 TPB (2008, $24.99) r/#1-7 25.00

NOTE: ***Art Adams** c-13. **Austin** a-1i, 4i, 33i, 38i; c-8i, 33i. **Buscema** a-51p. **Byrne** a-1p, 29, 48; c-29. **Chiodo** painted c-56-59. **Colan** a-51p. **Cowan/Simonson** c/a-60. **Golden** a-1, 2, 4p, 47; c-1, 2, 47. **Infantino** c/a(p)-8. **Gil Kane** a-8-11p. **Miller** a-18; c-1(Back-c), 18. **Perez** a-10, 11p, 12, 13p; c-10-13p. **Rogers** a-5p; c-5p. **Russell** a-5i, 6, 8-11i, 43i; c-5i, 6. **Paul Smith** a-1p, 4p, 32, 60; c-4p. Staton c/a-50(p). **Williamson** a-30i, 51i.*

MARVEL FANFARE (2nd Series)
Marvel Comics: Sept, 1996 - No. 6, Feb, 1997 (99¢)

1-6: 1-Capt. America & The Falcon-c/story; Deathlok app. 2-Wolverine & Hulk-c/app. 3-Ghost Rider & Spider-Man-c/app. 5-Longshot-c/app. 6-Sabretooth, Power Man, & Iron Fist-c/app 3.00

MARVEL FEATURE (See Marvel Two-In-One)
Marvel Comics Group: Dec, 1971 - No. 12, Nov, 1973 (1,2: 25¢, 52 pg. giants) (#1-3: quarterly)

1-Origin/1st app. The Defenders (Sub-Mariner, Hulk & Dr. Strange); see Sub-Mariner #34,35 for prequel; Dr. Strange solo story (predates Dr.Strange #1) plus 1950s Sub-Mariner-r; Neal Adams-c 16 32 48 107 234 360
2-2nd app. Defenders; 1950s Sub-Mariner-r. Rutland, Vermont Halloween x-over 10 20 30 64 115 165
3-Defenders ends 7 14 21 46 76 105
4-Re-intro Antman (1st app. since 1960s), begin series; brief origin; Spider-Man app. 5 10 15 35 55 75
5-7,9,10: 6-Wasp app. & begins team-ups. 9-Iron Man app. 10-Last Antman 3 6 9 21 32 42
8-Origin Antman & Wasp-r/TTA #44; Kirby-a 4 8 12 23 36 48
11-Thing vs. Hulk; 1st Thing solo book (9/73); origin Fantastic Four retold 8 16 24 56 96 135
12-Thing/Iron Man; early Thanos app.; occurs after Capt. Marvel #33; Starlin-a(p) 6 12 18 37 59 80

NOTE: ***Bolle** a-9i. **Everett** a-1i, 3i. **Hartley** r-10. **Kane** c-3p, 7p. **Russell** a-7-10p. **Starlin** a-8, 11, 12; c-8.*

MARVEL FEATURE (Also see Red Sonja)
Marvel Comics: Nov, 1975 - No. 7, Nov, 1976 (Story cont'd in Conan #68)

1,7: 1-Red Sonja begins (pre-dates Red Sonja #1); adapts Howard short story; Adams-r/Savage Sword of Conan #1. 7-Battles Conan 2 4 6 10 14 18
2-6: Thorne-c/a in #2-7. 4,5-(Regular 25¢ edition)(5,7/76) 1 3 4 6 8 10
4,5-(30¢-c variants, limited distribution) 3 6 9 16 23 30

MARVEL FRONTIER COMICS UNLIMITED
Marvel Frontier Comics: Jan, 1994 ($2.95, 68 pgs.)

1-Dances with Demons, Immortalis, Children of the Voyager, Evil Eye, The Fallen stories 4.00

MARVEL FUMETTI BOOK
Marvel Comics Group: Apr, 1984 ($1.00, one-shot)

1-All photos; Stan Lee photo-c; Art Adams touch-ups 5.00

MARVEL FUN & GAMES
Marvel Comics Group: 1979/80 (color comic for kids)

1,11: 1-Games, puzzles, etc. 11-X-Men-c 2 3 4 6 8 10
2-10,12,13: (beware marked pages) 1 2 3 4 5 7

MARVEL GIRL
Marvel Comics: Apr, 2011 ($2.99, one-shot)

1-Early X-Men days of Jean Grey; Fialkov-s/Plati-a/Cruz-c 3.00

MARVEL GRAPHIC NOVEL

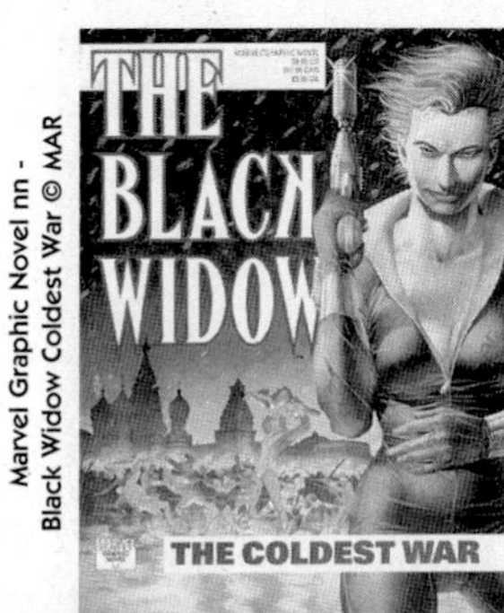

Marvel Graphic Novel nn - Black Widow Coldest War © MAR

Marvel - Heroes and Legends 1997 © MAR

Marvel Illustrated: Treasure Island #4 © MAR

GD 2.0 | VG 4.0 | FN 6.0 | VF 8.0 | VF/NM 9.0 | NM- 9.2

Marvel Comics Group (Epic Comics): 1982 - No. 38, 1990? ($5.95/$6.95)

1-Death of Captain Marvel (2nd Marvel graphic novel); Capt. Marvel battles Thanos by Jim Starlin (c/a/scripts) 3 6 9 14 19 24
1 (2nd & 3rd printings) 1 2 3 5 6 8
2-Elric: The Dreaming City 2 4 6 8 10 12
3-Dreadstar; Starlin-c/a, 52 pgs. 2 4 6 8 11 14
4-Origin/1st app. The New Mutants (1982) 2 4 6 8 11 14
4,5-2nd printings 1 2 3 4 5 7
5-X-Men; book-length story (1982) 3 6 9 14 20 25
6-15,20,23,25,30,31: 6-The Star Slammers. 7-Killraven. 8-Super Boxers; Byrne scripts. 9-The Futurians. 10-Heartburst. 11-Void Indigo. 12-Dazzler. 13-Starstruck. 14-The Swords Of The Swashbucklers. 15-The Raven Banner (a Tale of Asgard). 20-Greenberg the Vampire. 23-Dr. Strange. 25-Alien Legion. 30-A Sailor's Story. 31-Wolfpack 1 2 3 5 7 9
16,17,21,29: 16-The Aladdin Effect (Storm, Tigra, Wasp, She-Hulk). 17-Revenge Of The Living Monolith (Spider-Man, Avengers, FF app.). 21-Marada the She-Wolf. 29-The Big Chance (Thing vs. Hulk) 1 2 3 5 7 9
18,19,26-28: 18-She Hulk. 19-Witch Queen of Acheron (Conan). 26-Dracula. 27-Avengers (Emperor Doom). 28-Conan the Reaver 2 4 6 9 11 13
22-Amaz. Spider-Man in Hooky by Wrightson 2 4 6 9 12 15
24-Love and War (Daredevil); Miller scripts 2 4 6 8 11 14
32-Death of Groo 2 4 6 9 12 15
32-2nd printing ($5.95) 1 2 3 5 6 8
33,34,36,37: 33-Thor. 34-Predator & Prey (Cloak & Dagger). 36-Willow (movie adapt.). 37-Hercules 1 3 4 6 8 10
35-Hitler's Astrologer (The Shadow, $12.95, HC) 2 4 6 9 13 16
35-Soft-c reprint (1990, $10.95) 2 4 6 8 10 12
38-Silver Surfer (Judgement Day)($14.95, HC) 2 4 6 10 14 18
38-Soft-c reprint (1990, $10.95) 2 4 6 8 11 14
nn-Abslom Daak: Dalak Killer (1990, $8.95) Dr. Who 1 3 4 6 8 10
nn-Arena by Bruce Jones (1989, $5.95) Dinosaurs 1 2 3 5 6 8
nn- A-Team Storybook Comics Illustrated (1983) r/ A-Team mini-series #1-3 1 3 4 6 8 10
nn-Ax (1988, $5.95) Ernie Colan-s/a 1 3 4 6 8 10
nn-Black Widow Coldest War (4/90, $9.95) 2 4 6 8 10 12
nn-Chronicles of Genghis Grimtoad (1990, $8.95)-Alan Grant-s 1 3 4 6 8 10
nn-Conan the Barbarian in the Horn of Azoth (1990, $8.95) 2 4 6 8 11 16
nn-Conan of Isles ($8.95) 2 4 6 8 11 16
nn-Conan Ravagers of Time (1992, $9.95) Kull & Red Sonja app. 2 4 6 8 11 16
nn-Conan -The Skull of Set 2 4 6 8 11 16
nn-Doctor Strange and Doctor Doom Triumph and Torment (1989, $17.95, HC) 2 4 6 13 18 22
nn-Dreamwalker (1989, $6.95)-Morrow-a 1 2 3 5 7 9
nn-Excalibur Weird War III (1990, $9.95) 2 4 6 8 10 12
nn-G.I. Joe - The Trojan Gambit (1983, 68 pgs.) 2 4 6 8 10 12
nn-Harvey Kurtzman Strange Adventures (Epic, $19.95, HC) Aragonés, Crumb 3 6 9 14 20 25
nn-Hearts and Minds (1990, $8.95) Heath-a 1 3 4 6 8 10
nn-Inhumans (1988, $7.95)-Williamson-i 1 2 3 5 7 9
nn-Jhereg (Epic, 1990, $8.95) 1 3 4 6 8 10
nn-Kazar-Guns of the Savage Land (7/90, $8.95) 1 3 4 6 8 10
nn-Kull-The Vale of Shadow ('89, $6.95) 2 4 6 8 10 12
nn-Last of the Dragons (1988, $6.95) Austin-a(i) 1 2 3 4 5 7
nn-Nightraven: House of Cards (1991, $14.95) 2 4 6 9 12 15
nn-Nightraven: The Collected Stories (1990, $9.95) Bolton-r/British Hulk mag.; David Lloyd-c/a 2 4 6 8 10 12
nn-Original Adventures of Cholly and Flytrap (Epic, 1991, $9.95) Suydam-s/c/a 2 4 6 9 12 15
nn-Rick Mason Agent (1989, $9.95) 1 3 4 6 8 10
nn-Roger Rabbit In The Resurrection Of Doom (1989, $8.95) 1 3 4 6 8 10
nn-A Sailor's Story Book II: Winds, Dreams and Dragons ('86, $6.95, softcover) Glansman-s/c/a 1 3 4 6 8 10
nn-Squadron Supreme: Death of a Universe (1989, $9.95) Gruenwald-s; Ryan & Williamson-a 3 6 9 14 20 25
nn-Who Framed Roger Rabbit (1989, $6.95) 1 3 4 6 8 10

NOTE: ***Aragones** a-27, 32. **Buscema** a-38. **Byrne** c/a-18. **Heath** a-35i. **Kaluta** a-13, 35p; c-13. **Miller** a-24p. **Simonson** a-6; c-6. **Starlin** c/a-1,3. **Williamson** a-34. **Wrightson** c-29i.*

MARVEL HEARTBREAKERS
Marvel Comics: Apr, 2010 ($3.99, one-shot)

1-Romance short stories; Spider-Man, MJ & Gwen app.; Casagrande-a; Beast app. 4.00

MARVEL - HEROES & LEGENDS
Marvel Comics: Oct, 1996; 1997 ($2.95)

nn-Wraparound-c, ...1997 ($2.99) -Original Avengers story 3.00

MARVEL HEROES FLIP MAGAZINE
Marvel Comics: Aug, 2005 - No. 26, Sept, 2007 ($3.99/$4.99)

1-11-Reprints New Avengers and Captain America (2005 series) in flip format thru #13 4.00
12-26: 14-19-Reprints New Avengers and Young Avengers in flip format. 20-Ghost Rider 5.00

MARVEL HOLIDAY SPECIAL
Marvel Comics: No. 1, 1991 ($2.25, 84 pgs.) - Present

1-X-Men, Fantastic Four, Punisher, Thor, Capt. America, Ghost Rider, Capt. Ultra, Spidey stories; Art Adams-c/a 4.00
nn (1/93)-Wolverine, Thanos (by Starlin/Lim/Austin) 4.00
nn (1994)-Capt. America, X-Men, Silver Surfer 4.00
... 1996-Spider-Man by Waid & Olliffe; X-Men, Silver Surfer 4.00
... 2004-Spider-Man by DeFalco & Miyazawa; X-Men, Fantastic Four 4.00
... 2004 TPB ($15.99) r/M.H.S. 2004 & past Christmas-themed stories 16.00
1 (1/06, $3.99) new Christmas-themed stories by various; Immonen-c 4.00
... 2006 (2/07, $3.99) Fin Fang Foom, Hydra, AIM app.; gallery of past covers; Irving-c 4.00
... 2007 (2/08, $3.99) Spider-Man & Wolverine stories; Hembeck-a 4.00
... 2011 (2/12, $3.99) Seeley-c; Spider-Man, Wolverine, Nick Fury, The Thing app. 4.00
Marvel Holiday (2006, $7.99, digest) reprints from M.H.S. 2004, 2006 & TPB 8.00
Marvel Holiday Spectacular Magazine (2009, $9.99, magazine) reprints from M.H.S. '93, '94, & Amazing Spider-Man #166; and new material w/Doe, Semeiks & Nauck-a 10.00

NOTE: ***Art Adams** c-'93. **Golden** a-'93. **Perez** c-'94.*

MARVEL ILLUSTRATED...
Marvel Comics: 2007 ($2.99)

...Jungle Book - reprints from Marvel Fanfare #8-11; Gil Kane-s/a(p); P. Craig Russell-i 3.00

MARVEL ILLUSTRATED: KIDNAPPED (Title changes to Kidnapped with #5)
Marvel Comics: Jan, 2009 - No. 5, May, 2009 ($3.99, limited series)

1-5-Adaptation of the Stevenson novel; Roy Thomas-s/Mario Gully-a/Parel-c 4.00

MARVEL ILLUSTRATED: LAST OF THE MOHICANS
Marvel Comics: July, 2007 - No. 6, Dec, 2007 ($2.99, limited series)

1-6-Adaptation of the Cooper novel; Roy Thomas-s/Steve Kurth-a. 1-Jo Chen-c 3.00
HC (2008, $19.99) r/#1-6 20.00

MARVEL ILLUSTRATED: MOBY DICK
Marvel Comics: Apr, 2008 - No. 6, Sept, 2008 ($2.99, limited series)

1-6-Adaptation of the Melville novel; Roy Thomas-s/Alixe-a/Watson-c 3.00

MARVEL ILLUSTRATED: PICTURE OF DORIAN GRAY
Marvel Comics: Jan, 2008 - No. 6, July, 2008 ($2.99, limited series)

1-6-Adaptation of the Wilde novel; Roy Thomas-s/Fiumara-a. 1-Parel-c 3.00

MARVEL ILLUSTRATED: SWIMSUIT ISSUE (Also see Marvel Swimsuit Special)
Marvel Comics: 1991 ($3.95, magazine, 52 pgs.)

V1#1-Parody of Sports Illustrated swimsuit issue; Mary Jane Parker centerfold pin-up by Jusko; 2nd print exists 1 3 4 6 8 10

MARVEL ILLUSTRATED: THE ILIAD
Marvel Comics: Feb, 2008 - No. 8, Sept, 2008 ($2.99, limited series)

1-8-Adaptation of Homer's Epic Poem; Roy Thomas-s/Sepulveda-a/Rivera-c 3.00

MARVEL ILLUSTRATED: THE MAN IN THE IRON MASK
Marvel Comics: Sept, 2007 - No. 6, Feb, 2008 ($2.99, limited series)

1-6-Adaptation of the Dumas novel; Roy Thomas-s/Hugo Petrus-a. 1-Djurdjevic-c 3.00
HC (2008, $19.99) r/#1-6 20.00

MARVEL ILLUSTRATED: THE ODYSSEY (Title changes to The Odyssey with #7)
Marvel Comics: Nov, 2008 - No. 8, June, 2009 ($3.99, limited series)

1-8-Adaptation of Homer's Epic Poem; Roy Thomas-s/Greg Tocchini-a/c 4.00

MARVEL ILLUSTRATED: THE THREE MUSKETEERS
Marvel Comics: Aug, 2008 - No. 6, Jan, 2009 ($3.99, limited series)

1-6-Adaptation of the Dumas novel; Roy Thomas-s/Hugo Petrus-a/Parel-c 4.00

MARVEL ILLUSTRATED: TREASURE ISLAND
Marvel Comics: Aug, 2007 - No. 6, Jan, 2008 ($2.99, limited series)

1-6-Adaptation of the Stevenson novel; Roy Thomas-s/Mario Gully-a/Greg Hildebrandt-c 3.00
HC (2008, $19.99) r/#1-6 20.00

MARVEL KNIGHTS (See Black Panther, Daredevil, Inhumans, & Punisher)
Marvel Comics: 1998 (Previews for upcoming series)

Sketchbook-Wizard suppl.; Quesada & Palmiotti-c 3.00
Tourbook-($2.99) Interviews and art previews 3.00

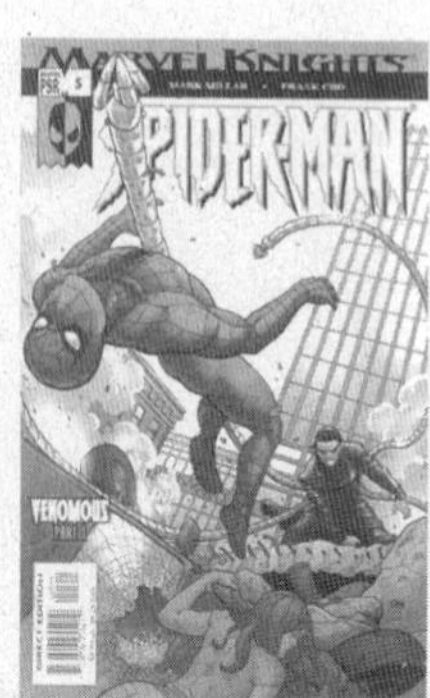

Marvel Knights Spider-Man #5 © MAR

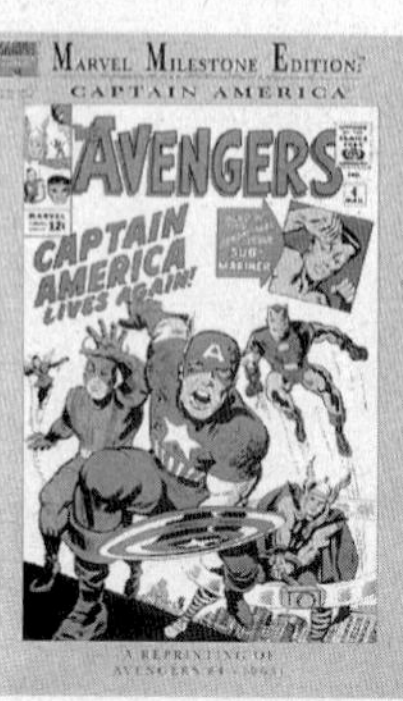

Marvel Milestone Editon: Avengers #4 © MAR

Marvel Monsters: Devil Dinosaur © MAR

	GD 2.0	VG 4.0	FN 6.0	VF 8.0	VF/NM 9.0	NM- 9.2

MARVEL KNIGHTS
Marvel Comics: July, 2000 - No. 15, Sept, 2001 ($2.99)

1-Daredevil, Punisher, Black Widow, Shang-Chi, Dagger app. 4.00
2-15: 2-Two covers by Barreto & Quesada 3.00
.../Marvel Boy Genesis Edition (6/00) Sketchbook preview 3.00
...: Millennial Visions (2/02, $3.99) Pin-ups by various; Harris-c 4.00

MARVEL KNIGHTS (Volume 2)
Marvel Comics: May, 2002 - No. 6, Oct, 2002 ($2.99)

1-6-Daredevil, Punisher, Black Widow app.; Ponticelli-a 3.00

MARVEL KNIGHTS: DOUBLE SHOT
Marvel Comics: June, 2002 - No. 4, Sept, 2002 ($2.99, limited series)

1-4: 1-Punisher by Ennis & Quesada; Daredevil by Haynes; Fabry-c 3.00

MARVEL KNIGHTS 4 (Fantastic Four) (Issues #1&2 are titled **Knights 4**) (#28-30 titled **Four**)
Marvel Comics: Apr, 2004 - No. 30, July, 2006 ($2.99)

1-30: 1-7-McNiven-c/a; Aguirre-Sacasa-a. 8,9-Namor app. 13-Cho-c. 14-Land-c. 21-Flashback meeting with Black Panther. 30-Namor app. 3.00
...Vol. 1: The Wolf at the Door (2004, $16.99, TPB) r/#1-7 17.00
...Vol. 2: The Stuff of Nightmares (2005, $13.99, TPB) r/#8-12 14.00
...Vol. 3: Divine Time (2005, $14.99, TPB) r/#13-18 15.00
...Vol. 4: Impossible Things Happen Every Day (2006, $14.99, TPB) r/#19-24 15.00
Fantastic Four: The Resurrection of Nicholas Scratch TPB (2006, $14.99) r/#25-30 15.00

MARVEL KNIGHTS MAGAZINE
Marvel Comics: May, 2001 - No. 6, Oct, 2001 ($3.99, magazine size)

1-6-Reprints of recent Daredevil, Punisher, Black Widow, Inhumans 4.00

MARVEL KNIGHTS SPIDER-MAN (Title continues in Sensational Spider-Man #23)
Marvel Comics: Jun, 2004 - No. 22, Mar, 2006 ($2.99)

1-Wraparound-c by Dodson; Millar-s/Dodson-a; Green Goblin app. 4.00
2-12: 2-Avengers app. 2,3-Vulture & Electro app. 5,8-Cho-c/a. 6-8-Venom app. 3.00
13-18-Reginald Hudlin-s/Billy Tan-a. 13,14,18-New Avengers app. 15-Punisher app. 3.00
19-22-The Other x-over pts. 2,5,8,11; Pat Lee-a 3.00
19-22-var-c: 19-Black costume. 20-Scarlet Spider. 21-Spider-Armor. 22-Peter Parker 5.00
... Vol. 1 HC (2005, $29.99, over-sized with d.j.) r/#1-12; Stan Lee intro.; Dodson & Cho sketch pages 30.00
... Vol. 1: Down Among the Dead Men (2004, $9.99, TPB) r/#1-4 10.00
... Vol. 2: Venomous (2005, $9.99, TPB) r/#5-8 10.00
... Vol. 3: The Last Stand (2005, $9.99, TPB) r/#9-12 10.00
... Vol. 4: Wild Blue Yonder (2005, $14.99, TPB) r/#13-18 15.00

MARVEL KNIGHTS 2099
Marvel Comics: 2005 ($13.99, TPB)

nn-Reprints one shots: Daredevil 2099, Punisher 2099, Black Panther 2099, Inhumans 2099 and Mutant 2099; Pat Lee-c 14.00

MARVEL LEGACY: ...
Marvel Comics: 2006, 2007 ($4.99, one-shots)

... The 1960s Handbook - Profiles of 1960s iconic and minor characters; info thru 1969 5.00
... The 1970s Handbook - Profiles of 1970s iconic and minor characters; info thru 1979 5.00
... The 1980s Handbook - Profiles of 1980s iconic and minor characters; info thru 1989 5.00
... The 1990s Handbook - Profiles of 1990s iconic and minor characters; Lim-c 5.00
...: The 1960s-1990s Handbook TPB (207, $19.99) r/one-shots 20.00

MARVELMAN CLASSIC
Marvel Comics: 2010 ($34.99, B&W)

HC-(2010, $34.99) Reprints of 1950s British Marvelman stories; character history 35.00
... Primer (8/10, $3.99) Character history; Mick Anglo interview; Quesada-c 4.00

MARVELMAN FAMILY'S FINEST
Marvel Comics: 2010 - No. 6 ($3.99, B&W, limited series)

1-6-Reprints of 1950s Marvelman, Young Marvelman and Marvelman Family stories 4.00

MARVEL MANGAVERSE:... (one-shots)
Marvel Comics: March, 2002 ($2.25, manga-inspired one-shots)

Avengers Assemble! - Udon Studio-s/a 3.00
Eternity Twilight ($3.50) - Ben Dunn-s/a/wrap-around-c 4.00
Fantastic Four - Adam Warren-s/Keron Grant-a 3.00
Ghost Riders - Chuck Austen-s/a 3.00
Punisher - Peter David-s/Lea Hernandez-a 3.00
Spider-Man - Kaare Andrews-s/a 3.00
X-Men - C.B. Cebulski-s/Jeff Matsuda-a 3.00

MARVEL MANGAVERSE (Manga series)
Marvel Comics: June, 2002 - No. 6, Nov., 2002 ($2.25)

1-6: 1-Ben Dunn-s/a; intro. manga Captain Marvel 3.00

	GD 2.0	VG 4.0	FN 6.0	VF 8.0	VF/NM 9.0	NM- 9.2

Vol. 1 TPB (2002, $24.95) r/one-shots 25.00
Vol. 2 TPB (2002, $12.99) r/#1-6 13.00
Vol. 3: Spider-Man-Legend of the Spider-Clan (2003, $11.99, TPB) r/series 12.00

MARVEL MASTERPIECES COLLECTION, THE
Marvel Comics: May, 1993 - No. 4, Aug, 1993 ($2.95, coated paper, lim. series)

1-4-Reprints Marvel Masterpieces trading cards w/ new Jusko paintings in each; Jusko painted-c/a 3.00

MARVEL MASTERPIECES 2 COLLECTION, THE
Marvel Comics: July, 1994 - No. 3, Sept, 1994 ($2.95, limited series)

1-3: 1-Kaluta-c; r/trading cards; new Steranko centerfold 3.00

MARVEL MILESTONE EDITION
Marvel Comics: 1991 - 1999 ($2.95, coated stock)(r/originals with original ads w/silver ink-c)

...: X-Men #1-Reprints X-Men #1 (1991) 3.00
...: Giant Size X-Men #1-(1991, $3.95, 68 pgs.) 4.00
...: Fantastic Four #1 (11/91), ...: Incredible Hulk #1 (3/92, says 3/91 by error), ...: Amazing Fantasy #15 (3/92), ...: Fantastic Four #5 (11/92), ...: Amazing Spider-Man #129 (11/92), ...: Iron Man #55 (11/92), ...: Iron Fist #14 (11/92), ...: Amazing Spider-Man #1 (1/93), ...: Amazing Spider-Man #1 (1/93) variation- no price on-c, ...: Tales of Suspense #39 (3/93), ...: Avengers #1 (9/93), ...: X-Men #9 (10/93), ...: Avengers #16 (10/93), ...:Amazing Spider-Man #149 (11/94, $2.95), ...:X-Men #28 (11/94, $2.95) 3.00
...:Captain America #1 (3/95, $3.95) 4.00
...:Amazing Spider-Man #3 (3/95, $2.95), ...:Avengers #4 (3/95, $2.95), ...:Strange Tales-r/Dr. Strange stories from #110, 111, 114, & 115 3.00
....:Hulk #181 (8/99, $2.99) 3.00

MARVEL MILESTONES
Marvel Comics: 2005 - Present ($3.99, coated stock)(r/originals w/silver ink-c)

...: Beast & Kitty Pryde-r/from Amazing Adventures #11 & Uncanny X-Men #153 4.00
...: Black Panther, Storm & Ka-Zar-r/from Black Panther #26, Marvel Team-Up #100 and Marvel Mystery Comics #7 4.00
...: Blade, Man-Thing & Satana-r/from Tomb of Dracula #10, Adv. Into Fear #16 and Vampire Tales #2 4.00
...: Captain Britain, Psylocke & Sub-Mariner-r/from Spect. Spidey #114, Uncanny X-Men #213 and Human Torch #2 4.00
...: Doom, Sub-Mariner & Red Skull -r/from FF Ann. #2, Sub-Mariner Comics #1, Captain America Comics #1 4.00
...: Dragon Lord, Speedball and The Man in the Sky -r/from Marvel Spotlight #5, Speedball #1 and Amazing Adult Fantasy #14; Ditko-a on all 4.00
...: Dr. Strange, Silver Surfer, Sub-Mariner, & Hulk -r/from Marvel Premiere #3, FF Ann. #5, Marvel Comics #1, Incredible Hulk #3 4.00
...: Ghost Rider, Black Widow & Iceman -r/from Marvel Spotlight #5, Daredevil #81, X-Men #47 4.00
...: Iron Man, Ant-Man & Captain America -r/from TOS #39,40, TTA #27, Capt. America #1 4.00
...: Legion of Monsters, Spider-Man and Brother Voodoo -r/Marvel Premiere #28 & others 4.00
...: Millie the Model & Patsy Walker-r/from Millie the Model #100, Defenders #65 4.00
...: Onslaught -r/Onslaught: Marvel; wraparound-c 4.00
...: Rawhide Kid & Two-Gun Kid-r/Two-Gun Kid #60 and Rawhide Kid #17 4.00
...: Special: Bloodstone, X-51 & Captain Marvel II ($4.99) -r/from Marvel Presents #1, Machine Man #1, Amazing Spider-Man Ann. #19, and Bloodstone #1 5.00
...: Star Brand & Quasar -r/from Star Brand #1 & Quasar #1 4.00
...: Ultimate Spider-Man, Ult. X-Men, Microman & Mantor -r/from Ultimate Spider-Man #1/2, Ultimate X-Men #1/2 and Human Torch #2 4.00
...: Venom & Hercules -r/Marvel S-H Secret Wars #8, Journey Into Mystery Ann. #1 4.00
...: Wolverine, X-Men & Tuk: Caveboy -r/from Marvel Comics Presents #1, Uncanny X-Men #201, Capt. America Comics #1,2 4.00
...: (Jim Lee and Chris Claremont) X-Men and the Starjammers Pt. 1 -r/Unc. X-Men #275 4.00
...: X-Men and the Starjammers Pt. 2 -r/Unc. X-Men #276,277 4.00

MARVEL MINI-BOOKS (See Promotional Comics section)

MARVEL MONSTERS:... (one-shots)
Marvel Comics: Dec, 2005 ($3.99)

...Devil Dinosaur 1 - Hulk app.; Eric Powell-c/a; Sniegoski-s; r/Journey Into Mystery #62 5.00
...Fin Fang Four 1 - FF app.; Powell-c; Langridge-s/Gray-a; r/Strange Tales #89 5.00
...From the Files of Ulysses Bloodstone 1 - Guide to classic Marvel monsters; Powell-c 5.00
...Monsters on the Prowl 1 - Niles-s/Fegredo-a/Powell-c; Thing, Hulk, Giant-Man & Beast app. 5.00
...Where Monsters Dwell 1 - Giffen-s/a; David-s/Pander-a; Parker-s/Braun-s; Powell-c 5.00
HC (2006, $20.99, dust jacket) r/one-shots 21.00

MARVEL MOVIE PREMIERE (Magazine)
Marvel Comics Group: Sept, 1975 (B&W, one-shot)

1-Burroughs' "The Land That Time Forgot" adapt. 2 4 6 9 13 16

MARVEL MOVIE SHOWCASE FEATURING STAR WARS
Marvel Comics Group: Nov, 1982 - No. 2, Dec, 1982 ($1.25, 68 pgs.)

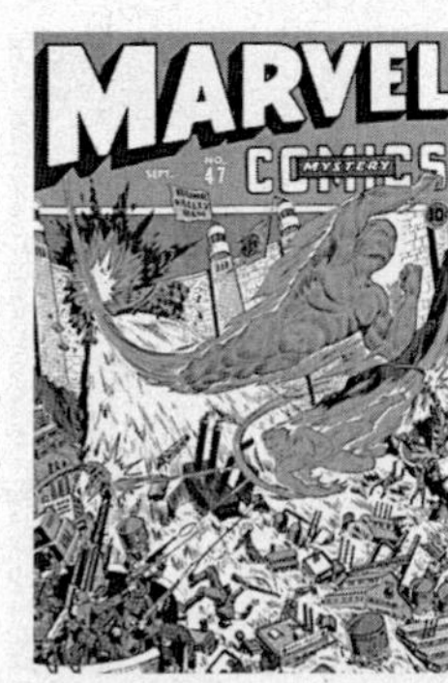
Marvel Mystery Comics #47 © MAR

Marvel No-Prize Book #1 © MAR

Marvelous Land of Oz #6 © MAR

GD VG FN VF VF/NM NM-
2.0 4.0 6.0 8.0 9.0 9.2

1,2-Star Wars movie adaptation; reprints Star Wars #1-6 by Chaykin;
1-Reprints-c to Star Wars #1. 2-Stevens-r 4.00

MARVEL MOVIE SPOTLIGHT FEATURING RAIDERS OF THE LOST ARK
Marvel Comics Group: Nov, 1982 ($1.25, 68 pgs.)
1-Edited-r/Raiders of the Lost Ark #1-3; Buscema-c/a(p); movie adapt. 4.00

MARVEL MUST HAVES (Reprints of recent sold-out issues)
Marvel Comics: Dec, 2001 - Present ($2.99/$3.99/$4.99)
1,2,4-6: 1-r/Wolverine: Origin #1, Startling Stories: Banner #1, Tangled Web #4 and Cable #97. 2-Amazing Spider-Man #36 and others. 4-Truth #1, Capt. America V4 #1, and The Ultimates #1. 5-r/Ultimate War #1, Ult. X-Men #26, Ult Spider-Man #33. 6-Ult. Spider-Man #33-36 4.00
3-r/Call of Duty: The Brotherhood #1 & Daredevil #32,33 3.00
Amazing Spider-Man #30-32; Incredible Hulk #34-36; The Ultimates #1-3; Ultimate Spider-Man #1-3; Ultimate X-Men #1-3; (New) X-Men #114-116 each.... 4.00
NYX #1-3; NYX #4-5 with sketch & cover gallery; Ultimates 2 #1-3 each... 5.00
Spider-Man and the Black Cat #1-3; preview of #4 5.00

MARVEL MYSTERY COMICS (Formerly Marvel Comics) (Becomes Marvel Tales No. 93 on)
Timely /Marvel Comics (TP #2-17/TCI #18-54/MCI #55-92): No. 2, Dec, 1939 - No. 92, June, 1949 (Some material from #8-10 reprinted in 2004's Marvel 65th Anniversary Special #1)
2-(Rare)-American Ace begins, ends #3; Human Torch (blue costume) by Burgos, Sub-Mariner by Everett continue; 2 pg. origin recap of Human Torch; Angel-c
3250 6500 9750 24,400 47,200 70,000
3-New logo from Marvel pulp begins; 1st app. of television in comics? in Human Torch story (1/40); Angel-c 2000 4000 6000 14,500 27,250 40,000
4-Intro. Electro, the Marvel of the Age (ends #19), The Ferret, Mystery Detective (ends #9); 1st Sub-Mariner-c by Schomburg; 2nd German swastika on-c of a comic (2/40); one month after Top-Notch Comics #2 1900 3800 5700 14,000 26,000 38,000
5 Classic Schomburg Torch-c, his 1st ever (Scarce)
2800 5600 8400 21,000 40,000 60,000
6-Angel-c; Gustavson Angel story 970 1940 2910 7180 12,590 18,000
7-Sub-Mariner attacks N.Y. city & Torch joins police force setting up battle in #8-10. Classic Schomburg Torch-c, his 2nd ever 1,000 2,000 3,000 7500 13,500 19,500
8-1st Human Torch & Sub-Mariner battle(6/40) 1350 2700 4050 10,000 19,000 28,000
9-(Scarce)-Human Torch & Sub-Mariner battle (cover/story); classic-c by Everett
4500 9000 13,500 34,000 59,000 85,000
10-Human Torch & Sub-Mariner battle, conclusion, 1 pg.; Terry Vance, the Schoolboy Sleuth begins, ends #57 1250 2500 3750 9500 17,750 26,000
11-Schomburg Torch-c, his 3rd ever 432 864 1296 3154 5577 8000
12-Classic Angel-c by Kirby 476 952 1428 3475 6138 8800
13-Intro. of The Vision by S&K (11/40); Sub-Mariner dons new costume, ends #15; Schomburg's 4th Human Torch-c 649 1298 1947 4738 8369 12,000
14-16: 14-Shows-c to Human Torch #1 on-c (12/40). 15-S&K Vision, Gustavson Angel story
349 698 1047 2443 4272 6100
17-Human Torch/Sub-Mariner team-up by Burgos/Everett; Human Torch pin-up on back-c; shows-c to Human Torch #2 on-c 377 754 1131 2639 4620 6600
18 326 652 978 2282 3991 5700
19,20: 19-Origin Toro in text; shows-c to Sub-Mariner #1 on-c. 20-Origin The Angel in text
331 662 993 2317 4059 5800
21-The Patriot begins, (intro. in Human Torch #4 (#3)); not in #46-48; Sub-Mariner pin-up on back-c (7/41) 331 662 993 2317 4059 5800
22-25: 23-Last Gustavson Angel; origin The Vision in text. 24-Injury-to-eye story
314 628 942 2198 3849 5500
26-29: 27-Ka-Zar ends; last S&K Vision who battles Satan. 28-Jimmy Jupiter in the Land of Nowhere begins, ends #48; Sub-Mariner vs. The Flying Dutchman
300 600 900 2070 3635 5200
30-"Remember Pearl Harbor" Japanese war-c 314 628 942 2198 3849 5500
31,32-"Remember Pearl Harbor" Japanese war-c. 31-Sub-Mariner by Everett ends, resumes #84. 32-1st app. The Boboes 297 594 891 2070 3635 5200
33,35,36,38,39 300 600 900 1950 3375 4800
34-Everett, Burgos, Martin Goodman, Funnies, Inc. office appear in story & battles Hitler; last Burgos Human Torch 300 600 900 2070 3635 5200
37-Classic Hitler-c 320 640 960 2240 3920 5600
40-Classic Zeppelin-c 371 742 1113 2600 4550 6500
41-43,47 277 554 831 1759 3030 4300
44-Classic Super Plane-c 371 742 1113 2600 4550 6500
45-Red Skull, Nazi hooded Vigilante war-c 300 600 900 2010 3505 5000
46-Classic Hitler-c 371 742 1113 2600 4550 6500
48-Last Vision; flag-c 284 568 852 1818 3109 4400
49-Origin Miss America 290 580 870 1856 3178 4500
50-Mary becomes Miss Patriot (origin) 277 554 831 1759 3030 4300
51-60: 54-Bondage-c 232 464 696 1485 2543 3600
61,62,64-Last German war-c 213 426 639 1363 2332 3300

GD VG FN VF VF/NM NM-
2.0 4.0 6.0 8.0 9.0 9.2

63-Classic Hitler War-c; The Villainess Cat-Woman only app.
277 554 831 1759 3030 4300
65,66-Last Japanese War-c 213 426 639 1363 2332 3300
67-78: 74-Last Patriot. 75-Young Allies begin. 76-Ten Chapter Miss America serial begins, ends #85 135 2070 405 864 1482 2100
79-New cover format; Super Villains begin on cover; last Angel
148 296 444 947 1624 2300
80-1st app. Capt. America in Marvel Comics 165 330 495 1048 1799 2550
81-Captain America app. 135 270 405 864 1482 2100
82-Origin & 1st app. Namora (5/47); 1st Sub-Mariner/Namora team-up; Captain America app.
300 600 900 1920 3310 4700
83,85: 83-Last Young Allies. 85-Last Miss America; Blonde Phantom app.
126 252 378 806 1378 1950
84-Blonde Phantom begins (on-c of #84,88,89); Sub-Mariner by Everett begins; Captain America app.; Everett-c 165 330 495 1048 1799 2550
86-Blonde Phantom i.d. revealed; Captain America app.; last Bucky app.
132 264 396 838 1444 2050
87-1st Capt. America/Golden Girl team-up; last Toro app. (8/48)
142 284 426 909 1555 2200
88-Golden Girl, Namora, & Sun Girl (1st in Marvel Comics) x-over; Captain America, Blonde Phantom app. 134 268 402 851 1463 2075
89-1st Human Torch/Sun Girl team-up; 1st Captain America solo; Blonde Phantom app.
132 264 396 838 1444 2050
90,91: 90-Blonde Phantom un-masked; Captain America app. 91-Capt. America app.; Blonde Phantom & Sub-Mariner end; early Venus app. (4/49) (scarce)
187 374 561 1197 2049 2900
92-Feature story on the birth of the Human Torch and the death of Professor Horton (his creator); 1st app. The Witness in Marvel Comics; Captain America app. (scarce)
360 720 1080 2520 4410 6300
132 Pg. issue, B&W, 25¢ (1943-44)-printed in N. Y.; square binding, blank inside covers); has Marvel No. 33-c in color; contains Capt. America #18 & Marvel Mystery Comics #33; same contents as Captain America Annual (Less than 5 copies known to exist)
7000 14,000 21,000 42,000 - -
132 Pg. issue (with variant contents), B&W, 25¢ (1942-'43)- square binding, blank inside covers; has same Marvel No. 33-c in color but contains Capt. America #22 & Marvel Mystery Comics #41 instead (possibly scarcer than other version)
(a VG+ copy sold in 2007 for $28,680 and a VG copy sold in 2009 for $19,120)
NOTE: ***Brodsky** c-49, 72, 86, 88-92. **Crandall** a-26i. **Everett** c-9, 27, 84. **Gabrielle** c-30-32. **Schomburg** c-3-11, 13-29, 33-36, 39-48, 50-59, 63-69, 74, 76, 132 pg. issue. **Shores** c-37, 38, 75p, 77, 78p, 79p, 80, 81p, 82-84, 85p, 87p. **Sekowsky** c-73. Bondage covers-3, 4, 7, 12, 28, 29, 49, 50, 52, 56, 57, 58, 59, 65. Angel c-2, 3, 8, 12. Remember Pearl Harbor issues-#30-32.*

MARVEL MYSTERY COMICS
Marvel Comics: Dec, 1999 ($3.95, reprints)
1-Reprints original 1940s stories; Schomburg-c from #74 5.00

MARVEL MYSTERY COMICS 70th ANNIVERARY SPECIAL
Marvel Comics: Jul, 2009 ($3.99, one-shot)
1-Rivera-c; new Sub-Mariner/Human Torch team-up set in 1941; reps. from #4 & 5 5.00

MARVEL MYSTERY HANDBOOK: 70th ANNIVERARY SPECIAL
Marvel Comics: 2009 ($4.99, one-shot)
1-Official Handbook-style profile pages of characters from Marvel's first year 5.00

MARVEL NEMESIS: THE IMPERFECTS (EA Games characters)
Marvel Comics: July, 2005 - No. 6, Dec, 2005 ($2.99, limited series)
1-6-Jae Lee-c/Greg Pak-s/Renato Arlem-a; Spider-Man, Thing, Wolverine, Elektra app 3.00
Digest (2005, $7.99) r/#1-6 8.00

MARVEL 1985
Marvel Comics: July, 2008 - No. 6, Dec, 2008 ($3.99, limited series)
1-6: 1-Marvel villains come to the real world; Millar-s/Edwards-a; three covers 4.00
HC (2009, $24.99) r/#1-6; intro. by Lindelof; Edwards production art 25.00

MARVEL NO-PRIZE BOOK, THE (The Official... on-c)
Marvel Comics Group: Jan, 1983 (one-shot, direct sales only)
1-Golden-c; Kirby-a 4.00

MARVELOUS ADVENTURES OF GUS BEEZER
Marvel Comics: May, 2003; Feb, 2004 ($2.99, one-shots)
...: Gus Beezer & Spider-Man 1 - (5/03) Gurihiru-a 3.00
...: Hulk 1 - (5/03) Simone-s/Lethcoe-a; She-Hulk app. 3.00
...: Spider-Man 1 - (5/03) Simone-s/Lethcoe-a; The Lizard & Dr. Doom app. 3.00
...: X-Men 1 - (5/03) Simone-s/Lethcoe-a 3.00

MARVELOUS LAND OF OZ (Sequel to Wonderful Wizard of Oz)
Marvel Comics: Jan, 2010 - No. 8, Sept, 2010 ($3.99, limited series)
1-8-Eric Shanower-a/Skottie Young-a/c. 1-Two covers by Young 4.00

Marvel Premiere #48 © MAR

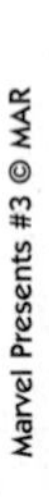

Marvel Presents #3 © MAR

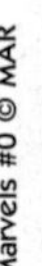

Marvels #0 © MAR

GD 2.0 | VG 4.0 | FN 6.0 | VF 8.0 | VF/NM 9.0 | NM- 9.2

1-Variant Pumpkinhead/Saw-Horse cover by McGuinness 6.00

MARVEL PETS HANDBOOK (Also see "Lockjaw and the Pet Avengers")
Marvel Comics: 2009 ($3.99, one-shot)

1-Official Handbook-style profile pages of animal characters 4.00

MARVEL PREMIERE
Marvel Comics Group: April, 1972 - No. 61, Aug, 1981 (A tryout book for new characters)

1-Origin Warlock (pre-#1) by Gil Kane/Adkins; origin Counter-Earth; Hulk & Thor cameo (#1-14 are 20¢-c) 8 16 24 51 86 120
2-Warlock ends; Kirby Yellow Claw-r 4 8 12 26 41 55
3-Dr. Strange series begins (pre #1, 7/72), B. Smith-c/a(p) 8 16 24 55 93 130
4-Smith/Brunner-a 4 8 12 24 37 50
5-9: 8-Starlin-c/a(p) 3 6 9 17 25 32
10-Death of the Ancient One 3 6 9 19 29 38
11-14: 11-Dr. Strange origin-r by Ditko. 14-Last Dr. Strange (3/74), gets own title 3 months later 2 4 6 13 18 22
15-Origin/1st app. Iron Fist (5/74), ends #25 10 20 30 64 115 165
16,25: 16-2nd app. Iron Fist; origin cont'd from #15; Hama's 1st Marvel-a. 25-1st Byrne Iron Fist (moves to own title next) 5 10 15 30 48 65
17-24: Iron Fist in all 3 6 9 21 32 42
26-Hercules. 2 4 6 8 10 12
27-Satana 2 4 6 9 12 15
28-Legion of Monsters (Ghost Rider, Man-Thing, Morbius, Werewolf) 3 6 9 19 29 38
29-46,49: 29,30-The Liberty Legion. 29-1st modern app. Patriot. 31-1st app. Woodgod; last 25¢ issue. 32-1st app. Monark Starstalker. 33,34-1st color app. Solomon Kane (Robert E. Howard adaptation "Red Shadows".) 35-Origin/1st app. 3-D Man. 36,37-3-D Man. 38-1st Weirdworld. 39,40-Torpedo. 41-1st Seeker 3000! 42-Tigra. 43-Paladin. 44-Jack of Hearts (1st solo book, 10/78). 45,46-Man-Wolf. 49-The Falcon (1st solo book, 8/79) 1 2 3 5 6 8
29-31-(30¢-c variants, limited distribution)(4,6,8/76) 3 6 9 14 19 24
36-38-(35¢-c variants, limited distribution)(6,8,10/77) 3 6 9 20 30 40
47,48-Byrne-a: 47-Origin/1st app. new Ant-Man. 48-Ant-Man 2 4 6 13 18 22
50-1st app. Alice Cooper; co-plotted by Alice 2 4 6 9 13 16
51-56,58-61: 51-53-Black Panther. 54-1st Caleb Hammer. 55-Wonder Man. 56-1st color app. Dominic Fortune. 58-60-Dr. Who. 61-Star Lord 6.00
57-Dr. Who (2nd U.S. app.-see Movie Classics) 1 3 4 6 8 10

NOTE: ***N. Adams*** *(Crusty Bunkers) part inks-10, 12, 13.* ***Austin*** *a-50i, 56i; c-46i, 50i, 56i, 58.* ***Brunner*** *a-4i, 6p, 9-14p; c-9-14.* ***Byrne*** *a-47p, 48p.* ***Chaykin*** *a-32-34; c-32, 33, 56.* ***Giffen*** *a-31p, 44p; c-44.* ***Gil Kane*** *a(p)-1, 2, 15; c(p)-1, 2, 15, 16, 22-24, 27, 36, 37.* ***Kirby*** *c-26, 29-31, 35.* ***Layton*** *a-47i, 48i; c-47.* ***McWilliams*** *a-25i.* ***Miller*** *c-49p, 53p, 58p.* ***Nebres*** *a-44i; c-38i.* ***Nino*** *a-38i.* ***Perez*** *c/a-38p, 45p, 46p.* ***Ploog*** *a-38; c-5-7.* ***Russell*** *a-7p.* ***Simonson*** *a-60(2pgs.); c-57.* ***Starlin*** *a-8p; c-8.* ***Sutton*** *a-41, 43, 50p, 61; c-50p, 61. #57-60 publ'd w/two different prices on-c.*

MARVEL PRESENTS
Marvel Comics: October, 1975 - No. 12, Aug, 1977 (#1-6 are 25¢ issues)

1-Origin & 1st app. Bloodstone 2 4 6 9 13 16
2-Origin Bloodstone continued; Kirby-c 2 3 4 6 8 10
3-Guardians of the Galaxy (1st solo book, 2/76) begins, ends #12 2 4 6 11 16 20
4-7,9-12: 9,10-Origin Starhawk 2 3 4 6 8 10
4-6-(30¢-c variants, limited distribution)(4-8/76) 3 6 9 18 27 35
8-r/story from Silver Surfer #2 plus 4 pgs. new-a 2 3 4 6 8 10
11,12-(35¢-c variants, limited distribution)(6,8/77) 4 8 12 26 41 55

NOTE: ***Austin*** *a-6i.* ***Buscema*** *r-8p.* ***Chaykin*** *a-5p.* ***Kane*** *c-1p.* ***Starlin*** *layouts-10.*

MARVEL PREVIEW (Magazine) (Bizarre Adventures #25 on)
Marvel Comics: Feb (no month), 1975 - No. 24, Winter, 1980 (B&W) ($1.00)

1-Man-Gods From Beyond the Stars; Crusty Bunkers (Neal Adams)-a(i) & cover; Nino-a 3 6 9 16 23 30
2-1st origin The Punisher (see Amaz. Spider-Man #129 & Classic Punisher); 1st app. Dominic Fortune; Morrow-c 11 22 33 73 142 210
3,8,10: 3-Blade the Vampire Slayer. 8-Legion of Monsters; Morbius app. 10-Thor the Mighty; Starlin frontispiece 3 6 9 18 27 35
4,5: 4-Star-Lord & Sword in the Star (origins & 1st app.). 5,6-Sherlock Holmes. 3 6 9 14 19 24
6,9: 6-Sherlock Holmes; N. Adams frontispiece. 9-Man-God; origin Star Hawk, ends #20 2 4 6 11 16 20
7-Satana, Sword in the Star app. 2 4 6 13 18 22
11,12,16,19,21,23: 11-Star-Lord; Byrne-a; Starlin frontispiece. 12-Haunt of Horror. 16-Masters of Terror. 19-Kull. 21-Moon Knight (Spr/80)-Predates Moon Knight #1; The Shroud by Ditko. 23-Bizarre Advs.; Miller-a. 2 4 6 8 10 12
13-15,17,18,20,22,24: 14,15-Star-Lord. 14-Starlin painted-c. 17-Blackmark by G. Kane (see SSOC #1-3). 18-Star-Lord; Sienkiewicz-a; Veitch & Bissette-a. 20-Bizarre Advs. 22-King Arthur. 24-Debut Paradox 1 2 3 5 6 8

NOTE: ***N. Adams*** *(C. Bunkers) r-20i.* ***Buscema*** *a-22, 23.* ***Byrne*** *a-11.* ***Chaykin*** *a-20r; c-20 (new).* ***Colan*** *a-8, 16p(3), 18p, 23p; c-16p.* ***Elias*** *a-18.* ***Giffen*** *a-7.* ***Infantino*** *a-14p.* ***Kaluta*** *a-12; c-15.* ***Miller*** *a-23.* ***Morrow*** *a-8i; c-2-4.* ***Perez*** *a-20p.* ***Ploog*** *a-8.* ***Starlin*** *c-13, 14. Nudity in some issues.*

MARVEL RIOT
Marvel Comics: Dec, 1995 ($1.95, one-shot)

1-"Age of Apocalypse" spoof; Lobdell script 3.00

MARVEL ROMANCE
Marvel Comics: 2006 ($19.99, TPB)

nn-Reprints romance stories from 1960-1972; art by Kirby, Buscema, Colan, Romita 20.00

MARVEL ROMANCE REDUX (Humor stories using art reprinted from Marvel romance comics)
Marvel Comics: Apr, 2006 - Aug, 2006 ($2.99, one-shots)

...: But I Thought He Loved Me Too (4/06) art by Kirby, Colan, Buscema & Romita; Giffen-c 3.00
...: Guys & Dolls (5/06) art by Starlin, Heck, Colan & Buscema; Conner-c 3.00
...: I Should Have Been a Blonde (7/06) art by Brodsky Colletta & Colan; Cho-c 3.00
...: Love is a Four Letter Word (8/06) art by Kirby, Buscema, Colan & Heck; Land-c 3.00
...: Restraining Orders are For Other Girls (6/06) art by Giordano, Kirby; Baker-c 3.00
...: Another Kind of Love TPB (2007, $13.99) r/one-shots 14.00

MARVELS (Also see Marvels: Eye of the Camera)
Marvel Comics: Jan, 1994 - No. 4, Apr, 1994 ($5.95, painted lim. series)
No. 1 (2nd Printing), Apr, 1996 - No. 4 (2nd Printing), July, 1996 ($2.95)

1-4: Kurt Busiek scripts & Alex Ross painted-c/a in all; double-c w/acetate overlay 1 2 3 5 6 8
Marvel Classic Collectors Pack ($11.90)-Issues #1 & 2 boxed (1st printings). 2 4 6 9 13 16
0-(8/94, $2.95)-no acetate overlay. 4.00
1-4-(2nd printing): r/original limited series w/o acetate overlay 3.00
Hardcover (1994, $59.95)-r/#0-4; w/intros by Stan Lee, John Romita, Sr., Kurt Busiek & Scott McCloud. 60.00
...: 10th Anniversary Edition (2004, $49.99, hardcover w/dustjacket) r/#0-4; scripts and commentaries; Ross sketch pages, cover gallery, behind the scenes art 50.00
Trade paperback ($19.95) 20.00

MARVEL SAGA, THE
Marvel Comics Group: Dec, 1985 - No. 25, Dec, 1987

1-25 3.00

NOTE: ***Williamson*** *a(i)-9, 10; c(i)-7, 10-12, 14, 16.*

MARVELS COMICS: ... (Marvel-type comics read in the Marvel Universe)
Marvel Comics: Jul, 2000 ($2.25, one-shots)

...Captain America #1 -Frenz & Sinnott-a; ...Daredevil #1 -Isabella-s/Newell-a; ...Fantastic Four #1 -Kesel-s/Paul Smith-a; Spider-Man #1 -Oliff-a; ...Thor #1 -Templeton-s/Aucoin-a 3.00
...X-Men #1 -Millar-s/ Sean Phillips & Duncan Fegredo-a 3.00
The History of Marvels Comics (no cover price)-Faux history; previews titles 3.00

MARVEL SELECT FLIP MAGAZINE
Marvel Comics: Aug, 2005 - No. 24 ($3.99/$4.99)

1-11-Reprints Astonishing X-Men and New X-Men: Academy X in flip format 4.00
12-24-($4.99) Reprints recent X-Men mini-series in flip format 5.00

MARVEL SELECTS:
Marvel Comics: Jan, 2000 - No. 6, June, 2000 ($2.75/$2.99, reprints)

...Fantastic Four 1-6: Reprints F.F. #107-112; new Davis-c 3.00
...Spider-Man 1,2,4-6: Reprints AS-M #100,101,103,104,93; Wieringo-c 3.00
...Spider-Man 3 ($2.99): Reprints AS-M #102; new Wieringo-c 3.00

MARVELS: EYE OF THE CAMERA (Sequel to Marvels)
Marvel Comics: Feb, 2009 - No. 6, Apr, 2010 ($3.99, limited series)

1-6-Kurt Busiek-s/Jay Anacleto-a; continuing story of photographer Phil Sheldon 4.00
1-6-B&W edition 4.00

MARVEL'S GREATEST COMICS (Marvel Collectors' Item Classics #1-22)
Marvel Comics Group: No. 23, Oct, 1969 - No. 96, Jan, 1981

23-34 (Giants). Begin Fantastic Four-r/#30s?-116 3 6 9 18 27 35
35-37-Silver Surfer-r/Fantastic Four #48-50 2 4 6 9 12 15
38-50: 42-Silver Surfer-r/F.F.(others?) 1 2 3 5 7 9
51-70: 63,64-(25¢ editions) 6.00
63,64-(30¢-c variants, limited distribution)(5,7/76) 3 6 9 14 19 24
71-96: 71-73-(30¢ editions) 5.00
71-73-(35¢-c variants, limited distribution)(7,9-10/77) 3 6 9 20 30 40
...: Fantastic Four #52 (2006, $2.99) reprints entire comic with ads and letter column 3.00

NOTE: *Dr. Strange, Fantastic Four, Iron Man, Watcher-#23, 24. Capt. America, Dr. Strange, Iron Man, Fantastic Four-#25-28. Fantastic Four-#38-96.* ***Buscema*** *r-85-92; c-87-92r.* ***Ditko*** *r-23-28.* ***Kirby*** *r-23-82; c-75, 77p, 80p. #81 reprints Fantastic Four #100.*

Marvel: 1602 #1 © MAR

Marvel Spotlight #19 © MAR

Marvel's The Avengers Prelude #1 © MAR

GD 2.0 | VG 4.0 | FN 6.0 | VF 8.0 | VF/NM 9.0 | NM- 9.2

MARVEL'S GREATEST SUPERHERO BATTLES (See Fireside Book Series)

MARVEL: SHADOWS AND LIGHT
Marvel Comics: Feb, 1997 ($2.95, B&W, one-shot)
1-Tony Daniel-c 3.00

MARVEL 1602
Marvel Comics: Nov, 2003 - No. 8, June, 2004 ($3.50/$3.99, limited series)
1-7-Neil Gaiman-s; Andy Kubert & Richard Isanove-a 3.50
8-($3.99) 4.00
... MGC #1 (7/10, $1.00) r/#1 with "Marvel's Greatest Comics" logo on cover 3.00
HC (2004, $24.99) r/series; script pages for #1, sketch pages and Gaiman afterword 25.00
SC (2005, $19.99) 20.00

MARVEL 1602: FANTASTICK FOUR
Marvel Comics: Nov, 2006 - No. 5, Mar, 2007s ($3.50, limited series)
1-5-Peter David-s/Pascal Alixe-a/Leinil Yu-c 3.50
TPB (2007, $14.99) r/#1-5; sketch page 15.00

MARVEL 1602: NEW WORLD
Marvel Comics: Oct, 2005 - No. 5, Jan, 2006 ($3.50, limited series)
1-5-Greg Pak-s/Greg Tocchini-a; "Hulk" and "Iron Man" app. 3.50
TPB (2006, $14.99) r/#1-5 15.00

MARVEL 65TH ANNIVERSARY SPECIAL
Marvel Comics: 2004 ($4.99, one-shot)
1-Reprints Sub-Mariner & Human Torch battle from Marvel Mystery Comics #8-10 5.00

MARVELS OF SCIENCE
Charlton Comics: March, 1946 - No. 4, June, 1946
1-A-Bomb story 23 46 69 136 223 310
2-4 14 28 42 80 115 150

MARVEL SPECIAL EDITION FEATURING... (Also see Special Collectors' Ed.)
Marvel Comics Group: 1975 - 1978 (84 pgs.) (Oversized)
1-The Spectacular Spider-Man ($1.50); r/Amazing Spider-Man #6,35, Annual 1; Ditko-a(r) 3 6 9 20 30 40
1,2-Star Wars ('77,'78; r/Star Wars #1-3 & #4-6; regular edition and Whitman variant exist 2 4 6 11 16 20
3-Star Wars ('78, $2.50, 116 pgs.); r/S. Wars #1-6; regular edition and Whitman variant exist 3 6 9 14 20 26
3-Close Encounters of the Third Kind (1978, $1.50, 56 pgs.)-Movie adaptation; Simonson-a(p) 2 4 6 10 14 18
V2#2(Spring, 1980, $2.00, oversized)- "Star Wars: The Empire Strikes Back"; r/Marvel Comics Super Special #16 3 6 9 16 23 30
NOTE: ***Chaykin*** *c/a(r)-1(1977), 2, 3.* ***Stevens*** *a(r)-2i, 3i.* ***Williamson*** *a(r)-V2#2.*

MARVEL SPECTACULAR
Marvel Comics Group: Aug, 1973 - No. 19, Nov, 1975
1-Thor-r from mid-sixties begin by Kirby 2 4 6 9 13 16
2-19 1 3 4 6 8 10

MARVELS: PORTRAITS
Marvel Comics: Mar, 1995 - No. 4, June, 1995 ($2.95, limited series)
1-4:Different artists renditions of Marvel characters 3.00

MARVEL SPOTLIGHT (...& Son of Satan #19, 20, 23, 24)
Marvel Comics Group: Nov, 1971 - No. 33, Apr, 1977; V2#1, July, 1979 - V2#11, Mar, 1981
(A try-out book for new characters)
1-Origin Red Wolf (western hero)(1st solo book, pre-#1); Wood inks, Neal Adams-c; only 15¢ issue 6 12 18 39 62 85
2-(25¢, 52 pgs.)-Venus-r by Everett; origin/1st app. Werewolf By Night (begins) by Ploog; N. Adams-c 19 38 57 132 284 435
3,4: 4-Werewolf By Night ends (6/72); gets own title 9/72 7 14 21 46 76 105
5-Origin/1st app. Ghost Rider (8/72) & begins 26 52 78 182 391 600
6-8: 6-Origin G.R. retold. 8-Last Ploog issue 9 18 27 58 99 140
9-11-Last Ghost Rider (gets own title next mo.) 6 12 18 42 69 95
12-Origin & 2nd full app. The Son of Satan (10/73); story cont'd from Ghost Rider #2 & into #3; series begins, ends #24 4 8 12 28 44 60
13-24: 13-Partial origin Son of Satan. 14-Last 20¢ issue. 22-Ghost Rider-c & cameo (5 panels). 24-Last Son of Satan (10/75); gets own title 12/75 2 4 6 9 12 15
25,27,30,31: 27-(Regular 25¢-c), Sub-Mariner app. 30-The Warriors Three. 31-Nick Fury 6.00
26-Scarecrow 1 3 4 6 8 10
27-(30¢-c variant, limited distribution) 3 6 9 14 20 25
28-(Regular 25¢-c) 1st solo Moon Knight app. 4 8 12 24 37 50
28-(30¢-c variant, limited distribution) 8 16 24 56 96 135
29-(Regular 25¢-c) (8/76) Moon Knight app.; last 25¢ issue 3 6 9 16 23 30
29-(30¢-c variant, limited distribution) 7 14 21 44 72 100
32-1st app./partial origin Spider-Woman (2/77); Nick Fury app. 3 6 9 16 23 30
33-Deathlok; 1st app. Devil-Slayer 2 3 4 6 8 10
V2#1-7,9-11: 1-4-Capt. Marvel. 5-Dragon Lord. 6,7-StarLord; origin #6. 9-11-Capt. Universe (see Micronauts #8) 5.00
1-Variant copy missing issue #1 on cover 2 4 6 9 12 15
8-Capt. Marvel; Miller-c/a(p) 1 3 4 6 8 10
NOTE: ***Austin*** *c-V2#2i, 8.* ***J. Buscema*** *c/a-30p.* ***Chaykin*** *a-31; c-26, 31.* ***Colan*** *a-18p, 19p.* ***Ditko*** *a-V2#4, 5, 9-11; c-V2#4, 9-11.* ***Kane*** *c-21p, 32p.* ***Kirby*** *c-29p.* ***McWilliams*** *a-20i.* ***Miller*** *a-V2#8p; c(p)-V2#2, 5, 7, 8.* ***Mooney*** *a-8i, 10i, 14p, 15, 16p, 17p, 24p, 27, 32i.* ***Nasser*** *a-33p.* ***Ploog*** *a-2-5, 6-8p; c-3-9.* ***Romita*** *c-13.* ***Sutton*** *a-9-11p, V2#6, 7. #29-25¢ & 30¢ issues exist.*

MARVEL SPOTLIGHT (Most issues spotlight one Marvel artist and one Marvel writer)
Marvel Comics: 2005 - Present ($2.99/$3.99)
...Brian Bendis/Mark Bagley; Daniel Way/Olivier Coipel; David Finch/Roberto Aguirre-Sacasa; Ed Brubaker/Billy Tan; John Cassaday/Sean McKeever; Joss Whedon/Michael Lark; Laurell K. Hamilton/George R.R. Martin; Neil Gaiman/Salvador Larroca; Robert Kirkman/Greg Land; Stan Lee/Jack Kirby; Warren Ellis/Jim Cheung each... 3.00
...Steve McNiven/Mark Millar - Civil War 10.00
...: Captain America (2009) interviews with Brubaker & Hitch; Reborn preview 3.00
...: Captain America Remembered (2007) character features; creator interviews 3.00
...: Civil War Aftermath (2007) Top 10 Moments, casualty list, previews of upcoming series 3.00
...: Dark Reign (2009) features on the Avengers, Fury and others; creator interview 4.00
...: Dark Tower (2007) previews the Stephen King adaptation; creator interviews 5.00
...: Deadpool (2009) character features; interviews with Kelly, Way, Medina & Benson 3.00
...: Fantastic Four and Silver Surfer (2007) character features; creator interviews 3.00
...: Ghost Rider (2007) character and movie features; creator interviews 3.00
...: Halo (2007) a World of Halo feature; Bendis & Maleev interviews 3.00
...: Heroes Reborn/Onslaught Reborn (2006) 3.00
...: Hulk Movie (2008) character and movie features; comic & movie creator interviews 3.00
...: Iron Man Movie (2008) character and movie features; Terrence Howard interview 3.00
...: Iron Man 2 (4/10) movie preview; Granov, Fraction interviews; Whiplash profile 4.00
...: Marvel Knights 10th Anniversary (2008) Quesada interview; series synopsies 3.00
...: Marvel Zombies/Mystic Arcana (2008) character features; creator interviews 3.00
...: Marvel Zombies Return (2009) character features; creator interviews 3.00
...: New Mutants (2009) character features; Claremont & McLeod interviews 3.00
...: Punisher Movie (2008) character and movie features; creator interviews 3.00
...: Secret Invasion (2008) features on the Skrulls; Bendis, Reed & Yu interviews 3.00
...: Secret Invasion Aftermath (2008) Skrull profiles; Bendis, Reed & Diggle interviews 4.00
...: Spider-Man (2007) character features; creator interviews; Ditko art showcase 3.00
...: Spider-Man - Brand New Day (2008) storyline features; Romitas interviews 3.00
...: Spider-Man-One More Day/Brand New Day (2008) storyline features; interviews 3.00
...: Summer Events (2009, $3.99) 2009 title previews; creator interviews 4.00
...: Thor (2007) character features; Straczynski interview; Romita Jr. art showcase 3.00
...: Ultimates 3 (2008) character features; Loeb & Madureira interviews 3.00
...: Ultimatum (2008) previews the limited series; Loeb & Bendis interviews 3.00
...: Uncanny X-Men 500 Issues Celebration (2008) creator interviews; timeline 3.00
...: War of Kings (2009) character features; Abnett, Lanning, Pelletier interviews 3.00
...: Wolverine (2009, $3.99) preview of 2009 Wolverine stories; creator interviews 4.00
...: World War Hulk (2007) character features; creator interviews; early art showcase 3.00
...: X-Men: Messiah Complex (2008) X-Men crossover features; creator interviews 3.00

MARVELS PROJECT, THE
Marvel Comics: Oct, 2009 - No. 8, July, 2010 ($3.99, limited series)
1-8-Emergence of Marvel heroes in 1939-40; Brubaker-s/Epting-a; Epting & McNiven-c 4.00
1-8-Variant covers by Parel 5.00

MARVEL'S THE AVENGERS PRELUDE
Marvel Comics: May, 2012 - No. 4 ($2.99, limited series)
1-Prelude to 2012 movie; Luke Ross & Daniel HDR-a 3.00

MARVEL SUPER ACTION (Magazine)
Marvel Comics Group: Jan, 1976 (B&W, 76 pgs.)
1-2nd app. Dominic Fortune (see Marvel Preview); early Punisher app.; Weird World & The Huntress; Evans, Ploog-a 9 18 27 61 106 150

MARVEL SUPER ACTION
Marvel Comics Group: May, 1977 - No. 37, Nov, 1981
1-Reprints Capt. America #100 by Kirby 2 4 6 11 16 20
2-13: 2,3,5-13 reprint Capt. America #101,102,103-111. 4-Marvel Boy-r(origin)/M. Boy #1. 11-Origin-r. 12,13-Classic Steranko-c/a(r). 2 4 6 8 10 12
2,3-(35¢-c variants, limited distribution)(6,8/77) 4 8 12 24 37 50
14-20: r/Avengers #55,56, Annual 2, others 1 2 3 5 6 8
21-37: 30-r/Hulk #6 from U.K. 6.00

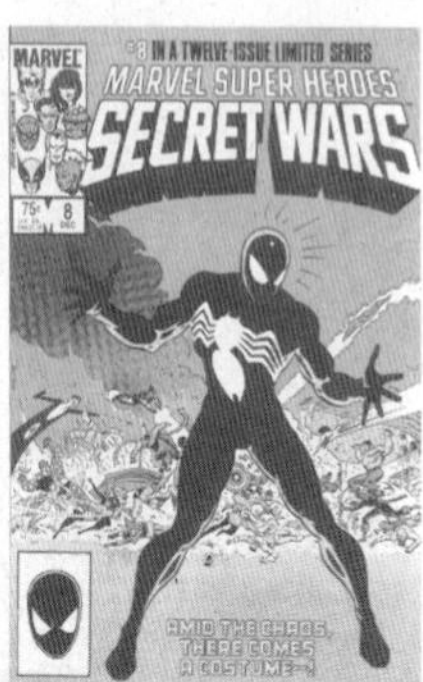

Marvel Super-Heroes Secret Wars #8 © MAR

Marvel Super Hero Squad #12 © MAR

Marvel Tales #96 © MAR

GD VG FN VF VF/NM NM-
2.0 4.0 6.0 8.0 9.0 9.2

NOTE: ***Buscema*** *a(r)-14p, 15p; c-18-20, 22, 35r-37.* ***Everett*** *a-4.* ***Heath*** *a-4r.* ***Kirby*** *r-1-3, 5-11.* ***B. Smith*** *a-27r, 28r.* ***Steranko*** *a(r)-12p, 13p; c-12r, 13r.*

MARVEL SUPER HERO CONTEST OF CHAMPIONS
Marvel Comics Group: June, 1982 - No. 3, Aug, 1982 (Limited series)
1-3: Features nearly all Marvel characters currently appearing in their comics; 1st Marvel limited series 1 2 3 5 6 8

MARVEL SUPER HEROES
Marvel Comics Group: October, 1966 (25¢, 68 pgs.) (1st Marvel one-shot)
1-r/origin Daredevil from D.D. #1; r/Avengers #2; G.A. Sub-Mariner-r/Marvel Mystery #8 (Human Torch app.). Kirby-a 11 22 33 76 151 225

MARVEL SUPER-HEROES (Formerly Fantasy Masterpieces #1-11)
(Also see Giant-Size Super Heroes) (#12-20: 25¢, 68 pgs.)
Marvel Comics: No. 12, 12/67 - No. 31, 11/71; No. 32, 9/72 - No. 105, 1/82
12-Origin & 1st app. Capt. Marvel of the Kree; G.A. Human Torch, Destroyer, Capt. America, Black Knight, Sub-Mariner-r (#12-20 all contain new stories and reprints) 12 24 36 83 172 260
13-2nd app. Capt. Marvel; G.A. Black Knight, Torch, Vision, Capt. America, Sub-Mariner-r 8 16 24 55 93 130
14-Amazing Spider-Man (5/68, new-a by Andru/Everett); G.A. Sub-Mariner, Torch, Mercury (1st Kirby-a at Marvel), Black Knight, Capt. America reprints 10 20 30 68 127 185
15-17: 15-Black Bolt cameo in Medusa (new-a); Black Knight, Sub-Mariner, Black Marvel, Capt. America-r. 16-Origin & 1st app. S. A. Phantom Eagle; G.A. Torch, Capt. America, Black Knight, Patriot, Sub-Mariner-r. 17-Origin Black Knight (new-a); G.A. Torch, Sub-Mariner-r; reprint from All-Winners Squad #21 (cover & story) 5 10 15 32 51 70
18-Origin/1st app. Guardians of the Galaxy (1/69); G.A. Sub-Mariner, All-Winners Squad-r 7 14 21 49 82 115
19-Ka-Zar (new-a); G.A. Torch, Marvel Boy, Black Knight, Sub-Mariner reprints; Smith-c(p); Tuska-a(r) 4 8 12 26 41 55
20-Doctor Doom (5/69); r/Young Men #24 w/-c 5 10 15 30 48 65
21-31: All-r issues. 21-X-Men, Daredevil, Iron Man-r begin, end #31. 31-Last Giant issue 3 6 9 16 23 30
32-50: 32-Hulk/Sub-Mariner-r begin from TTA. 1 2 3 5 7 9
51-70,100: 56-r/origin Hulk/Inc. Hulk #102; Hulk-r begin 6.00
57,58-(30¢-c variants, limited distribution)(5,7/76) 3 6 9 14 19 24
65,66-(35¢-c variants, limited distribution)(7,9/77) 3 6 9 19 29 38
71-99,101-105 5.00
NOTE: ***Austin*** *a-104.* ***Colan*** *a(p)-12, 13, 15, 18; c-12, 13, 15, 18.* ***Everett*** *a-14i(new); r-14, 15i, 18, 19, 33; c-85(r). New* ***Kirby*** *c-22, 27, 54.* ***Maneely*** *r-14, 15, 19.* ***Severin*** *r-83-85i, 100-102; c-100-102r.* ***Starlin*** *c-47.* ***Tuska*** *a-19p. Black Knight-r by* ***Maneely*** *in 12-16, 19. Sub-Mariner-r by* ***Everett*** *in 12-20.*

MARVEL SUPER-HEROES
Marvel Comics: May, 1990 - V2#15, Oct, 1993 ($2.95/$2.50, quart., 68-84 pgs.)
1-Moon Knight, Hercules, Black Panther, Magik, Brother Voodoo, Speedball (by Ditko) & Hellcat; Hembeck-a 5.00
2,4,5,V2#3,6-15: 2-Summer Special(7/90); Rogue, Speedball (by Ditko), Iron Man, Falcon, Tigra & Daredevil. 4-Spider-Man/Nick Fury, Daredevil,Speedball, Wonder Man, Spitfire & Black Knight; Byrne-c. 5-Thor, Dr. Strange, Thing & She-Hulk; Speedball by Ditko(p). V2#3-Retells origin Capt. America w/new facts; Blue Shield, Capt. Marvel,Speedball, Wasp; Hulk by Ditko/Rogers V2#6-9: 6-8-$2.25-c. 6,7-X-Men, Cloak & Dagger, The Shroud (by Ditko) & Marvel Boy in each. 8-X-Men, Namor & Iron Man (by Ditko); Larsen-c. 9-West Coast Avengers, Iron Man app.; Kieth-c(p). V2#10-Ms. Marvel/Sabretooth-c/story (intended for Ms. Marvel #24; shows-c to #24); Namor, Vision, Scarlet Witch stories. V2#11,12 :11-Original Ghost Rider-c/story; Giant-Man, Ms. Marvel stories. 12-Dr. Strange, Falcon, Iron Man. V2#13-15 ($2.75, 84 pgs.): 13-All Iron Man 30th anniversary. 15-Iron Man/Thor/Volstagg/Dr. Druid 4.00

MARVEL SUPER-HEROES MEGAZINE
Marvel Comics: Oct, 1994 - No. 6, Mar, 1995 ($2.95, 100 pgs.)
1-6: 1-r/FF #232, DD #159, Iron Man #115, Incred. Hulk #314 4.00

MARVEL SUPER-HEROES SECRET WARS (See Secret Wars II)
Marvel Comics Group: May, 1984 - No. 12, Apr, 1985 (limited series)
1 1 2 3 5 6 8
1-3-(2nd printings, sold in multi-packs) 3.00
2-6,9-11: 6-The Wasp dies 6.00
7,12: 7-Intro. new Spider-Woman. 12-($1.00, 52 pgs.) 1 2 3 4 5 7
8-Spider-Man's new black costume explained as alien costume (1st app. Venom as alien costume) 3 6 9 20 30 40
Secret Wars Omnibus HC (2008, $99.99, dustjacket) r/#1-12, Thor #383, She-Hulk (2004) #10 and What If? (1989) #4 & #114; photo gallery of related toys; pencil-a from #1 100.00
NOTE: ***Zeck*** *a-1-12; c-1,3,8-12. Additional artists (John Romita Sr., Art Adams and others) had uncredditted art in #12.*

MARVEL SUPER HERO SQUAD (All ages)
Marvel Comics: Mar, 2009; Nov, 2009 - No. 4, Feb, 2010 ($3.99/$2.99)
1-4-Based on the animated series; back-up humor strips and pin-ups 3.00
...Hero Up! (3/09, $3.99) Collects humor strips from MarvelKids.com; 2 covers 4.00

MARVEL SUPER HERO SQUAD (All ages)
Marvel Comics: Mar, 2010 - No. 12, Feb, 2011 ($2.99)
1-12-Based on the animated series. 1-Wraparound-c 3.00
Super Hero Squad Spectacular 1 (4/11, $3.99) The Beyonder app. 4.00

MARVEL SUPER SPECIAL, A (See Marvel Comics Super...)

MARVEL SWIMSUIT SPECIAL (Also see Marvel Illustrated...)
Marvel Comics: 1992 - No. 4, 1995 ($3.95/$4.50, magazine, 52 pgs.)
1-4-Silvestri-c; pin-ups by diff. artists. 2-Jusko-c. 3-Hughes-c 1 3 4 6 8 10

MARVEL TAILS STARRING PETER PORKER THE SPECTACULAR SPIDER-HAM
(Also see Peter Porker...)
Marvel Comics Group: Nov, 1983 (one-shot)
1-Peter Porker, the Spectacular Spider-Ham, Captain Americat, Goose Rider, Hulk Bunny app. 4.00

MARVEL TALES (Formerly Marvel Mystery Comics #1-92)
Marvel/Atlas Comics (MCI): No. 93, Aug, 1949 - No. 159, Aug, 1957
93-Horror/weird stories begin 161 322 483 1030 1765 2500
94-Everett-a 98 196 294 622 1074 1525
95-New logo 73 146 219 467 796 1125
96,99,101,103,105 61 122 183 390 670 950
97-Sun Girl, 2 pgs; Kirbyish-a; one story used in N.Y. State Legislative document 82 164 246 528 902 1275
98,100: 98-Krigstein-a 62 124 186 394 680 965
102-Wolverton-a "The End of the World", (6 pgs.) 87 174 261 553 952 1350
104-Wolverton-a "Gateway to Horror", (6 pgs.) 87 174 261 553 952 1350
106,107-Krigstein-a. 106-Decapitation story 50 100 150 315 533 750
108-120: 116-(7/53) Werewolf By Night story. 118-Hypo-c/panels in End of World story. 120-Jack Katz-a 37 74 111 222 361 500
121,123-131: 128-Flying Saucer-c. 131-Last precode (2/55) 30 60 90 177 289 400
122-Kubert-a 31 62 93 182 296 410
132,133,135-141,143,145 22 44 66 132 216 300
134-Krigstein, Kubert-a; flying saucer-c 24 48 72 144 237 330
142-Krigstein-a 23 46 69 136 223 310
144-Williamson/Krenkel-a, 3 pgs. 23 46 69 136 223 310
146,148-151,154-156,158: 150-1st S.A. issue. 156-Torres-a 19 38 57 109 172 235
147,152: 147-Ditko-a. 152-Wood, Morrow-a 20 40 60 120 195 270
153-Everett End of World c/story 22 44 66 132 216 300
157,159-Krigstein-a 20 40 60 114 182 250
NOTE: ***Andru*** *a-103.* ***Briefer*** *a-118.* ***Check*** *a-147.* ***Colan*** *a-102, 105, 107, 118, 120, 121, 127, 131.* ***Drucker*** *a-127, 135, 141, 146, 150.* ***Everett*** *a-98, 104, 106(2), 108(2), 131, 148, 151, 153, 155; c-107, 109, 111, 112, 114, 117, 127, 143, 147-151, 153, 155, 156.* ***Forte*** *a-119, 125, 130, 158.* ***Heath*** *a-110, 113, 118, 119; c-104-106, 110, 130.* ***Gil Kane*** *a-117.* ***Lawrence*** *a-130.* ***Maneely*** *a-111, 126, 129; c-108, 116, 120, 129, 152.* ***Mooney*** *a-114.* ***Morisi*** *a-153.* ***Morrow*** *a-150, 152, 156.* ***Orlando*** *a-149, 151, 157.* ***Pakula*** *a-119, 121, 133, 135, 144, 150, 152, 156.* ***Powell*** *a-136, 137, 150, 154.* ***Ravielli*** *a-117, 123.* ***Rico*** *a-97, 99.* ***Romita*** *a-108.* ***Sekowsky*** *a-96-98.* ***Shores*** *a-110; c-96.* ***Sinnott*** *a-105, 116, 144.* ***Tuska*** *a-114.* ***Whitney*** *a-107.* ***Wildey*** *a-126, 138.*

MARVEL TALES (...Annual #1,2; ...Starring Spider-Man #123 on)
Marvel Comics Group (NPP earlier issues): 1964 - No. 291, Nov, 1994 (No. 1-32: 72 pgs.)
(#1-3 have Canadian variants; back & inside-c are blank, same value)
1-Reprints origins of Spider-Man/Amazing Fantasy #15, Hulk/Inc. Hulk#1, Ant-Man/T.T.A. #35, Giant Man/T.T.A. #49, Iron Man/T.O.S. #39,48, Thor/J.I.M. #83 & r/Sgt. Fury #1 28 56 84 198 429 660
2 ('65)-r/X-Men #1(origin), Avengers #1(origin), origin Dr. Strange-r/Strange Tales #115 & origin Hulk(Hulk #3) 11 22 33 71 136 200
3 (7/66)-Spider-Man, Strange Tales (H. Torch), Journey into Mystery (Thor), Tales to Astonish (Ant-Man)-r begin (r/Strange Tales #101) 7 14 21 44 72 100
4,5 5 10 15 32 51 70
6-8,10: 10-Reprints 1st Kraven/Amaz. S-M #15 4 8 12 22 34 45
9-r/Amazing Spider-Man #14 w/cover 4 8 12 24 37 50
11-33: 11-Spider-Man battles Daredevil-r/Amaz. Spider-Man #16. 13-Origin Marvel Boy-r from M. Boy #1. 22-Green Goblin-c/story-r/Amaz. Spider-Man #27. 30-New Angel story (x-over w/Ka-Zar #2,3). 32-Last 72 pg. iss. 33-(52 pgs.) Kraven-r 3 6 9 16 23 30
34-50: 34-Begin regular size issues 2 3 4 6 8 10
51-65 1 2 3 5 6 8
66-70-(Regular 25¢ editions)(4-8/76) 1 2 3 5 6 8

Marvel Tales #290 © MAR

Marvel Team-Up #76 © MAR

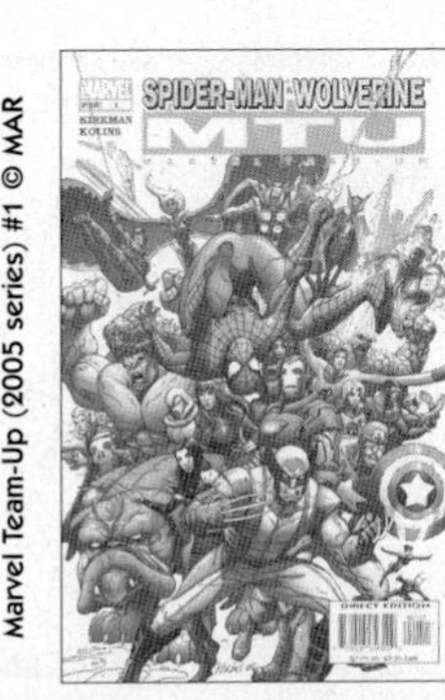

Marvel Team-Up (2005 series) #1 © MAR

GD VG FN VF VF/NM NM-
2.0 4.0 6.0 8.0 9.0 9.2

66-70-(30¢-c variants, limited distribution) 3 6 9 20 30 40

71-105: 75-Origin Spider-Man-r. 77-79-Drug issues-r/Amaz. Spider-Man #96-98. 98-Death of Gwen Stacy-r/Amaz. Spider-Man #121 (Green Goblin). 99-Death Green Goblin-r/Amaz. Spider-Man #122. 100-(52 pgs.)-New Hawkeye/Two Gun Kid story. 101-105-All Spider-Man-r 6.00

80-84-(35¢-c variants, limited distribution)(6-10/77) 3 6 9 18 27 35

106-r/1st Punisher-Amazing Spider-Man #129 1 2 3 5 7 9

107-136: 107-133-All Spider-Man-r. 111,112-r/Spider-Man #134,135 (Punisher). 113,114-r/Spider-Man #136,137(Green Goblin). 126-128-r/clone story from Amazing Spider-Man #149-151. 134-136-Dr. Strange-r begin; SpM stories continue. 134-Dr. Strange-r/Strange Tales #110 5.00

137-Origin-r Dr. Strange; shows original unprinted-c & origin Spider-Man/Amazing Fantasy #15 1 2 3 5 7 9

137-Nabisco giveaway 1 2 3 5 7 9

138-Reprints all Amazing Spider-Man #1; begin reprints of Spider-Man with covers similar to originals 1 2 3 5 6 8

139-144: r/Amazing Spider-Man #2-7 6.00

145-149,151-190,193-199: Spider-Man-r continue w/#8 on. 149-Contains skin "Tattooz" decals. 153-r/1st Kraven/Spider-Man #15. 155-r/2nd Green Goblin/Spider-Man #17. 161,164,165-Gr. Goblin-c/stories-r/Spider-Man #23,26,27. 178,179-Green Goblin-c/story-r/ Spider-Man #39,40. 187,189-Kraven-r. 193-Byrne-r/Marvel Team-Up begin w/scripts 4.00

150,191,192,200: 150-($1.00, 52pgs.)-r/Spider-Man Annual #1(Kraven app.). 191-($1.50, 68 pgs.)-r/Spider-Man #96-98. 192-($1.25, 52 pgs.)-r/Spider-Man #121,122. 200-Double size ($1.25)-Miller-c & r/Annual #14 5.00

201-249,251,252,254-257: 208-Last Byrne-r. 210,211-r/Spidey #134,135. 212,213-r/Giant-Size Spidey #4. 213-r/1st solo Silver Surfer story/F.F. Annual #5. 214,215-r/Spidey #161,162. 222-Reprints origin Punisher/Spect. Spider-Man #83; last Punisher reprint. 209-Reprints 1st app. The Punisher/Amazing Spider-Man #129; Punisher reprints begin, end #222. 223-McFarlane-c begins, end #239. 233-Spider-Man/X-Men team-ups begin; r/X-Men #35. 234-r/Marvel Team-Up #4. 235,236-r/M. Team-Up Annual #1. 237,238-r/M. Team-Up #150. 239,240-r/M. Team-Up #38,90(Beast). 242-r/M.Team-Up #89. 243-r/M. Team-Up #117 (Wolverine). 251-r/Spider-Man #100 (Green Goblin-c/story). 252-r/1st app. Morbius/Amaz. Spider-Man #101. 254-r/M. Team-Up #15(Ghost Rider); new painted-c. 255,256-Spider-Man & Ghost Rider-r/Marvel Team-Up #58,91. 257-Hobgoblin-r begin (r/ASM #238) 3.00

250.253: 250-($1.50, 52 pgs.)-r/1st Karma/M. Team-Up #100. 253-($1.50, 52 pgs.) -r/Amaz. S-M #102 4.00

258-291: 258-261-r/A. Spider-Man #239,249-251(Hobgoblin). 262,263-r/Marv. Team-Up #53,54. 262-New X-Men vs. Sunstroke story. 263-New Woodgod origin story. 264,265-r/Amazing Spider-Man Annual 5. 266-273-Reprints alien costume stories/A. S-M 252-259. 277-r/1st Silver Sable/A. S-M 265. 283-r/A. S-M 275 (Hobgoblin). 284-r/A. S-M 276 (Hobgoblin) 3.00

285-variant w/Wonder-Con logo on c-no price-giveaway 3.00

286-($2.95)-p/bagged w/16 page insert & animation print 4.00

NOTE: *All contain reprints; some have new art. #89-97-r/Amazing Spider-Man #110-118; #98-136-r/#121-159; #137-150-r/Amazing Fantasy #15, #1-12 & Annual 1; #151-167-r/#13-28 & Annual 2; #168-186-r/#29-46.* **Austin** *a-100i; c-272i, 273i.* **Byrne** *a(r)-193-198p, 201-208p.* **Ditko** *a-1-30, 83, 100, 137-155.* **G. Kane** *a-71, 81, 98-101p, 249r; c-125-127p, 130p, 137-155.* **Sam Kieth** *c-255, 262, 263.* **Ron Lim** *c-266p-281p, 283p-285p.* **McFarlane** *c-223-239.* **Mooney** *a-63, 95-97i, 103(i).* **Nasser** *a-100p.* **Nebres** *a-242i.* **Perez** *c-259-261.* **Rogers** *c-240, 241, 243-252.*

MARVEL TALES FLIP MAGAZINE
Marvel Comics: Sept, 2005 - No. 25, Sept, 2007 ($3.99/$4.99)

1-6-Reprints Amazing Spider-Man #30-up and Amazing Fantasy (2004) in flip format 4.00

7-10-Reprints Amazing Spider-Man #36-up and Runaways Vol. 2 in flip format 4.00

11-25-($4.99) Reprints Amazing Spider-Man #36-up and Runaways Vol. 2 in flip format 5.00

MARVEL TAROT, THE
Marvel Comics: 2007 ($3.99, one-shot)

1-Marvel characters featured in Tarot deck images; Djurdjevic-c 4.00

MARVEL TEAM-UP (See Marvel Treasury Edition #18 & Official Marvel Index To...)
(Replaced by Web of Spider-Man)
Marvel Comics Group: March, 1972 - No. 150, Feb, 1985
NOTE: *Spider-Man team-ups in all but Nos. 18, 23, 26, 29, 32, 35, 97, 104, 105, 137.*

1-Human Torch 12 24 36 83 172 260

2-Human Torch 6 12 18 41 66 90

3-Spider-Man/Human Torch vs. Morbius (part 1); 3rd app. of Morbius (7/72) 7 14 21 48 79 110

4-Spider-Man/X-Men vs. Morbius (part 2 of story); 4th app. of Morbius 7 14 21 48 79 110

5-10: 5-Vision. 6-Thing. 7-Thor. 8-The Cat (4/73, came out between The Cat #3 & 4). 9-Iron Man. 10-H-T 3 6 9 21 32 42

11,13,14,16-20: 11-Inhumans. 13-Capt. America. 14-Sub-Mariner. 16-Capt. Marvel. 17-Mr. Fantastic. 18-H-T/Hulk. 19-Ka-Zar. 20-Black Panther; last 20¢ issue 2 4 6 13 18 22

12-Werewolf (By Night) (8/73) 3 6 9 20 30 40

15-1st Spider-Man/Ghost Rider team-up (11/73) 3 6 9 21 32 42

21-30: 21-Dr. Strange. 22-Hawkeye. 23-H-T/Iceman (X-Men cameo). 24-Brother Voodoo. 25-Daredevil. 26-H-T/Thor. 27-Hulk. 28-Hercules. 29-H-T/Iron Man. 30-Falcon 2 4 6 8 10 12

31-45,47-50: 31-Iron Fist. 32-H-T/Son of Satan. 33-Nighthawk. 34-Valkyrie. 35-H-T/Dr. Strange. 36-Frankenstein. 37-Man-Wolf. 38-Beast. 39-H-T. 40-Sons of the Tiger/H-T. 41-Scarlet Witch. 42-The Vision. 43-Dr. Doom; retells origin. 44-Moondragon. 45-Killraven. 47-Thing. 48-Iron Man; last 25¢ issue. 49-Dr. Strange; Iron Man app. 50-Iron Man; Dr. Strange app. 1 2 3 5 6 8

44-48-(30¢-c variants, limited distribution)(4-8/76) 4 8 12 24 37 50

46-Spider-Man/Deathlok team-up 1 2 3 5 7 9

51,52,56,57: 51-Iron Man; Dr. Strange app. 52-Capt. America. 56-Daredevil. 57-Black Widow 1 2 3 4 5 7

53-Hulk; Woodgod & X-Men app., 1st Byrne-a on X-Men (1/77) 3 6 9 20 30 40

54,55,58-60: 54,59,60: 54-Hulk; Woodgod app. 59-Yellowjacket/The Wasp. 60-The Wasp (Byrne-a in all). 55-Warlock-c/story; Byrne-a. 58-Ghost Rider 2 3 4 6 8 10

58-62-(35¢-c variants, limited distribution)(6-10/77) 5 10 15 35 55 75

61-70: All Byrne-a; 61-H-T. 62-Ms. Marvel; last 30¢ issue. 63-Iron Fist. 64-Daughters of the Dragon. 65-Capt. Britain (1st U.S. app.). 66-Capt. Britain; 1st app. Arcade. 67-Tigra; Kraven the Hunter app. 68-Man-Thing. 69-Havok (from X-Men). 70-Thor 1 2 3 5 7 9

71-74,76-78,80: 71-Falcon. 72-Iron Man. 73-Daredevil. 74-Not Ready for Prime Time Players (Belushi). 76-Dr. Strange. 77-Ms. Marvel. 78-Wonder Man. 80-Dr. Strange/Clea; last 35¢ issue 6.00

75,79,81: Byrne-a(p). 75-Power Man; Cage app. 79-Mary Jane Watson as Red Sonja; Clark Kent cameo (1 panel, 3/79). 81-Death of Satana 1 2 3 5 6 8

82-99: 82-Black Widow. 83-Nick Fury. 84-Shang-Chi. 86-Guardians of the Galaxy. 89-Nightcrawler (from X-Men). 91-Ghost Rider. 92-Hawkeye. 93-Werewolf by Night. 94-Spider-Man vs. The Shroud. 95-Mockingbird (intro.); Nick Fury app. 96-Howard the Duck; last 40¢ issue. 97-Spider-Woman/ Hulk. 98-Black Widow. 99-Machine Man. 85-Shang-Chi/ Black Widow/Nick Fury. 87-Black Panther. 88-Invisible Girl. 90-Beast 5.00

100-(Double-size)-Spider-Man & Fantastic Four story with origin/1st app. Karma, one of the New Mutants; X-Men & Professor X cameo; Miller-c/a(p); Storm & Black Panther story; brief origins; Byrne-a(p) 1 3 4 6 8 10

101-116: 101-Nighthawk(Ditko-a). 102-Doc Samson. 103-Ant-Man. 104-Hulk/Ka-Zar. 105-Hulk/Powerman/Iron Fist. 106-Capt. America. 107-She-Hulk. 108-Paladin; Dazzler cameo. 109-Dazzler; Paladin app. 110-Iron Man. 111-Devil-Slayer. 112-King Kull; last 50¢ issue. 113-Quasar. 114-Falcon. 115-Thor. 116-Valkyrie 4.00

117-Wolverine-c/story 2 4 6 8 10 12

118-140,142-149: 118-Professor X; Wolverine app. (4 pgs.); X-Men cameo. 119-Gargoyle. 120-Dominic Fortune. 121-Human Torch. 122-Man-Thing. 123-Daredevil. 124-The Beast. 125-Tigra. 126-Hulk & Powerman/Son of Satan. 127-The Watcher. 128-Capt. America; Spider-Man/Capt. America photo-c. 129-The Vision. 130-Scarlet Witch. 131-Frogman. 132-Mr. Fantastic. 133-Fantastic Four. 134-Jack of Hearts. 135-Kitty Pryde; X-Men cameo. 136-Wonder Man. 137-Aunt May/Franklin Richards. 138-Sandman. 139-Nick Fury. 140-Black Widow. 142-Capt. Marvel. 143-Starfox. 144-Moon Knight. 145-Iron Man. 146-Nomad. 147-Human Torch; Spider-Man back to old costume. 148-Thor. 149-Cannonball 4.00

141-Daredevil; SpM/Black Widow app. (Spidey in new black costume; ties w/ Amazing Spider-Man #252 for 1st black costume) 2 4 6 10 14 18

150-X-Men ($1.00, double-size); B. Smith-c 6.00

Annual 1 (1976)-Spider-Man/X-Men (early app.) 4 8 12 22 34 45

Annual 2 (1979)-Spider-Man/Hulk 1 3 4 6 8 10

Annuals 3,4: 3 (1980)-Hulk/Power Man/Machine Man/Iron Fist; Miller-c(p). 4 (1981)-Spider-Man /Daredevil/Moon Knight/Power Man/Iron Fist; brief origins of each; Miller-c; Miller scripts on Daredevil 1 2 3 4 5 7

Annuals 5-7: 5 (1982)-SpM/The Thing/Scarlet Witch/Dr. Strange/Quasar. 6 (1983)-Spider-Man/ New Mutants (early app.), Cloak & Dagger. 7(1984)-Alpha Flight; Byrne-c(i) 6.00

NOTE: **Art Adams** *c-141p.* **Austin** *a-79i; c-76i, 79i, 96i, 101i, 112i, 130i.* **Bolle** *a-9i.* **Byrne** *a(p)-53-55, 59-70, 75, 79, 100; c-68p, 70p, 72p, 75, 76p, 79p, 129i, 133i.* **Colan** *a-87p.* **Ditko** *a-101.* **Kane** *a(p)-4-6, 13, 14, 16-19, 23; c(p)-4, 13, 14, 17-19, 23, 25, 26, 32-35, 37, 41, 44, 45, 47, 53, 54.* **Miller** *a-100p; c-95p, 99p, 100p, 102p, 106.* **Mooney** *a-2i, 7i, 8, 10p, 11p, 16i, 24-31p, 72, 93i, Annual 5i.* **Nasser** *a-89p; c-101p.* **Simonson** *c-99i, 148.* **Paul Smith** *c-131, 132.* **Starlin** *c-27.* **Sutton** *a-93p. "H-T" means Human Torch; "SpM" means Spider-Man; "S-M" means Sub-Mariner.*

MARVEL TEAM-UP (2nd Series)
Marvel Comics: Sept, 1997 - No. 11, July, 1998 ($1.99)

1-11: 1-Spider-Man team-ups begin, Generation x-app. 2-Hercules-c/app.; two covers. 3-Sandman. 4-Man-Thing. 7-Blade. 8-Namor team-ups begin, Dr. Strange app. 9-Capt. America. 10-Thing. 11-Iron Man 3.00

MARVEL TEAM-UP
Marvel Comics: Jan, 2005 - No. 25, Dec, 2006 ($2.25/$2.99)

1-7,9: 1,2-Spider-Man & Wolverine; Kirkman-s/Kolins-a. 5,6-X-23 app. 3.00

Marvel Treasury Edition #10 © MAR

Marvel Triple Action #40 © MAR

Marvel Universe vs. Wolverine #1 © MAR

8,10-25 ($2.99-c) 10-Spider-Man & Daredevil. 12-Origin of Titannus. 14-Invincible app. 3.00
... Vol. 1: The Golden Child TPB (2005, $12.99) r/#1-6 13.00
... Vol. 2: Master of the Ring TPB (2005, $17.99) r/#7-13 18.00
... Vol. 3: League of Losers TPB (2006, $13.99) r/#14-18 14.00
... Vol. 4: Freedom Ring TPB (2007, $17.99) r/#19-25 18.00

MARVEL: THE LOST GENERATION
Marvel Comics: No. 12, Mar, 2000 - No. 1, Feb, 2001 ($2.99, issue #s go in reverse)

1-12-Stern-s/Byrne-s/a; untold story of The First Line. 5-Thor app. 3.00

MARVEL/ TOP COW CROSSOVERS
Image Comics (Top Cow): Nov, 2005 ($24.99, TPB)

Vol. 1-Reprints crossovers with Wolverine, Witchblade, Hulk, Darkness; Devil's Reign 25.00

MARVEL TREASURY EDITION
Marvel Comics Group/Whitman #17,18: 1974; #2, Dec, 1974 - #28, 1981 ($1.50/$2.50, 100 pgs., oversized, new-a &-r)(Also see Amazing Spider-Man, The, Marvel Spec. Ed. Feat.--, Savage Fists of Kung Fu, Superman Vs., & 2001, A Space Odyssey)

1-Spectacular Spider-Man; story-r/Marvel Super-Heroes #14; Romita-c/a(r); G. Kane, Ditko-r; Green Goblin/Hulk-r 6 12 18 37 59 80
1-1,000 numbered copies signed by Stan Lee & John Romita on front-c & sold thru mail for $5.00; these were the1st 1,000 copies off the press 11 22 33 71 136 200
2-10: 2-Fantastic Four-r/F.F. 6,11,48-50(Silver Surfer). 3-The Mighty Thor-r/Thor #125-130. 4-Conan the Barbarian; Barry Smith-c/a(r)/Conan #11. 5-The Hulk (origin-r/Hulk #3). 6-Dr. Strange. 7-Mighty Avengers. 8-Giant Superhero Holiday Grab-Bag; Spider-Man, Hulk, Nick Fury. 9-Giant; Super-hero Team-up. 10-Thor; r/Thor #154-157 3 6 9 18 27 35
11-20: 11-Fantastic Four. 12-Howard the Duck (r/#H. the Duck #1 & G.S. Man-Thing #4,5) plus new Defenders story. 13-Giant Super-Hero Holiday Grab-Bag. 14-The Sensational Spider-Man; r/1st Morbius from Amazing S-M #101,102 plus #100 & r/Not Brand Echh #6. 15-Conan; B. Smith, Neal Adams-i; r/Conan #24. 16-The Defenders (origin) & Valkyrie; r/Defenders #1,4,13,14. 17-Incredible Hulk; Blob, Havok, Rhino and The Leader app. 18-The Astonishing Spider-Man; r/Spider-Man's 1st team-ups with Iron Fist, The X-Men, Ghost Rider & Werewolf by Night; inside back-c has photos from 1978 Spider-Man TV show. 19-Conan the Barbarian. 20-Hulk 3 6 9 14 20 25
21-24,27: 21-Fantastic Four. 22-Spider-Man. 23-Conan. 24-Rampaging Hulk. 27-Spider-Man 3 6 9 14 20 25
25-Spider-Man vs. The Hulk new story 3 6 9 16 23 30
26-The Hulk; 6 pg. new Wolverine/Hercules-s 3 6 9 16 22 28
28-Spider-Man/Superman; (origin of each) 5 10 15 32 51 70

NOTE: *Reprints-2, 3, 5, 7-9, 13, 14, 16, 17.* ***Neal Adams*** *a(i)-6, 15.* ***Brunner*** *a-6, 12; c-6.* ***Buscema*** *a-15, 19, 28; c-28.* ***Colan*** *a-6r; c-12p.* ***Ditko*** *a-1, 6.* ***Gil Kane*** *c-16p.* ***Kirby*** *a-1-3, 5, 7, 9-11; c-7.* ***Perez*** *a-26.* ***Romita*** *c-1, 5.* ***B. Smith*** *a-4, 15, 19; c-4, 19.*

MARVEL TREASURY OF OZ FEATURING THE MARVELOUS LAND OF OZ
Marvel Comics Group: 1975 ($1.50, oversized) (See MGM's Marvelous...)

1-Roy Thomas-s/Alfredo Alcala-a; Romita-c & bk-c 3 6 9 16 23 30

MARVEL TREASURY SPECIAL (Also see 2001: A Space Odyssey)
Marvel Comics Group: 1974; 1976 ($1.50, oversized, 84 pgs.)

Vol. 1-Spider-Man, Torch, Sub-Mariner, Avengers "Giant Superhero Holiday Grab-Bag"; Wood, Colan/Everett, plus 2 Kirby-r; reprints Hulk vs. Thing from Fantastic Four #25,26 3 6 9 17 25 32
Vol. 1-... Featuring Captain America's Bicentennial Battles (6/76)-Kirby-a; B. Smith inks, 11 pgs. 3 6 9 18 27 35

MARVEL TRIPLE ACTION (See Giant-Size...)
Marvel Comics Group: Feb, 1972 - No. 24, Mar, 1975; No. 25, Aug, 1975 - No. 47, Apr, 1979

1-(25¢ giant, 52 pgs.)-Dr. Doom, Silver Surfer, The Thing begin, end #4 ('66 reprints from Fantastic Four) 4 8 12 24 37 50
2-5 2 4 6 10 14 18
6-10 1 3 4 6 8 10
11-47: 45-r/X-Men #45. 46-r/Avengers #53(X-Men) 1 2 3 5 6 8
29,30-(30¢-c variants, limited distribution)(5,7/76) 3 6 9 16 23 30
36,37-(35¢-c variants, limited distribution)(7,9/77) 4 8 12 22 34 45

NOTE: *#5-44, 46, 47 reprint Avengers #11 thru ?. #40-r/Avengers #48(1st Black Knight).* ***Buscema*** *a(r)-35p, 36p, 38p, 39p, 41, 42, 43p, 44p, 46p, 47p.* ***Ditko*** *a-2r; c-47.* ***Kirby*** *a(r)-1-4p; c-1-4, 9-19, 22, 24, 29.* ***Starlin*** *c-7.* ***Tuska*** *a(r)-40p, 43i, 46i, 47i. #2 through #17 are 20¢-c.*

MARVEL TRIPLE ACTION
Marvel Comics: May, 2009 - No. 2, Jun, 2009 ($5.99, limited series)

1,2-Reprints stories from Wolverine First Class, Marvel Adventures Avengers & Marvel Super Heroes 6.00

MARVEL TV: GALACTUS - THE REAL STORY
Marvel Comics: Apr, 2009 ($3.99, one-shot)

1-The "hoax" of Galactus, Tieri-s/Santacruz-a; r/Fantastic Four #50 4.00

GD VG FN VF VF/NM NM-
2.0 4.0 6.0 8.0 9.0 9.2

MARVEL TWO-IN-ONE (...Featuring ... #82 on; also see The Thing)
Marvel Comics Group: January, 1974 - No. 100, June, 1983

1-Thing team-ups begin; Man-Thing 7 14 21 48 79 110
2,3: 2-Sub-Mariner; last 20¢ issue. 3-Daredevil 3 6 9 21 32 42
4-6: 4-Capt. America. 5-Guardians of the Galaxy (9/74, 2nd app.?). 6-Dr. Strange (11/74) 3 6 9 16 22 28
7,9,10 2 4 6 10 14 18
8-Early Ghost Rider app. (3/75) 3 6 9 16 22 28
11-14,19,20: 13-Power Man. 14-Son of Satan (early app.) 1 3 4 6 8 10
15-18-(Regular 25¢ editions)(5-7/76) 17-Spider-Man 1 3 4 6 8 10
15-18-(30¢-c variants, limited distribution) 4 8 12 22 34 45
21-29: 27-Deathlok. 29-Master of Kung Fu; Spider-Woman cameo 1 2 3 5 6 8
28,29,31-(35¢-c variants, limited distribution) 4 8 12 26 41 55
30-2nd full app. Spider-Woman (see Marvel Spotlight #32 for 1st app.) 2 4 6 8 10 12
30-(35¢-c variant, limited distribution)(8/77) 5 10 15 35 55 75
31-33-Spider-Woman app. 1 3 4 6 8 10
34-40: 39-Vision 1 2 3 4 5 7
41,42,44,45,47-49: 42-Capt. America. 45-Capt. Marvel 6.00
43,50,53,55-Byrne-a(p). 53-Quasar(7/79, 2nd app.) 1 2 3 5 7 9
46-Thing battles Hulk-c/story 2 4 6 8 10 12
51-The Beast, Nick Fury, Ms. Marvel; Miller-p 1 2 3 5 7 9
52-Moon Knight app. 6.00
54-Death of Deathlok; Byrne-a 2 4 6 8 11 14
56-60,64-74,76-79,81,82: 60-Intro. Impossible Woman. 68-Angel. 69-Guardians of the Galaxy. 71-1st app. Maelstrom. 76-Iceman 4.00
61-63: 61-Starhawk (from Guardians); "The Coming of Her" storyline begins, ends #63; cover similar to F.F. #67 (Him-c). 62-Moondragon; Thanos & Warlock cameo in flashback; Starhawk app. 63-Warlock revived shortly; Starhawk & Moondragon app. 5.00
75-Avengers (52 pgs.) 5.00
80,90,100: 80-Ghost Rider. 90-Spider-Man. 100-Double size, Byrne-s 5.00
83-89,91-99: 83-Sasquatch. 84-Alpha Flight app. 93-Jocasta dies. 96-X-Men-c & cameo 4.00
Annual 1 (1976, 52 pgs.)-Thing/Liberty Legion; Kirby-c 2 4 6 10 14 18
Annual 2 (1977, 52 pgs.)-Thing/Spider-Man; 2nd death of Thanos; end of Thanos saga; Warlock app.; Starlin-c/a 6 12 18 37 59 80
Annual 3,4 (1978-79, 52 pgs.): 3-Nova. 4-Black Bolt 1 2 3 4 5 7
Annual 5-7 (1980-82, 52 pgs.): 5-Hulk. 6-1st app. American Eagle. 7-The Thing/Champion; Sasquatch, Colossus app.; X-Men cameo (1 pg.) 5.00

NOTE: ***Austin*** *c(i)-42, 54, 56, 58, 61, 63, 66.* ***John Buscema*** *a-30p, 45; c-30p.* ***Byrne*** *(p)-43, 50, 53-55; c-43, 53p, 56p, 98i, 99i.* ***Gil Kane*** *a-1p, 2p; c(p)-1-3, 9, 11, 14, 28.* ***Kirby*** *c-10, 12, 19p, 20, 25, 27.* ***Mooney*** *a-18i, 38i, 90i.* ***Nasser*** *a-70p.* ***Perez*** *a(p)-56-58, 60, 64, 65; c(p)-32, 33, 42, 50-52, 54, 55, 57, 58, 61-66, 70.* ***Roussos*** *a-Annual 1i.* ***Simonson*** *c-43i, 97p, Annual 6i.* ***Starlin*** *c-6, Annual 1.* ***Tuska*** *a-6p.*

MARVEL TWO-IN-ONE
Marvel Comics: Sept, 2007 - Present ($4.99, 64 pgs.)

1-8,13-16-Reprints Marvel Adventures Avengers and X-Men: First Class stories 5.00
9-12,17-Reprints Marvel Adventures Iron Man and Avengers stories 5.00

MARVEL UNIVERSE (See Official Handbook Of The...)

MARVEL UNIVERSE (Title on variant covers for newsstand editions of some 2001 Marvel titles. See indicia for actual titles and issue numbers)

MARVEL UNIVERSE
Marvel Comics: June, 1998 - No. 7, Dec, 1998 ($2.99/$1.99)

1-($2.99)-Invaders stories from WW2; Stern-s 4.00
2-7-($1.99): 2-Two covers. 4-7-Monster Hunters; Manley-a/Stern-s 3.00

MARVEL UNIVERSE: MILLENNIAL VISIONS
Marvel Comics: Feb, 2002 ($3.99, one-shot)

1-Pin-ups by various; wraparound-c by JH Williams & Gray 4.00

MARVEL UNIVERSE: THE END (Also see Infinity Abyss)
Marvel Comics: May, 2003 - No. 6, Aug, 2003 ($3.50/$2.99, limited series)

1-($3.50)-Thanos, X-Men, FF, Avengers, Spider-Man, Daredevil app.; Starlin-s/a(p) 3.50
2-6-($2.99) Akhenaten, Eternity, Living Tribunal app. 3.00
Thanos Vol. 3: Marvel Universe - The End (2003, $16.99) r/#1-6 17.00

MARVEL UNIVERSE VS. THE PUNISHER
Marvel Comics: Oct, 2010 - No. 4, Nov, 2010 ($3.99, limited series)

1-4-Punisher vs. Marvel Zombies; Maberry-s/Parlov-a/c 4.00

MARVEL UNIVERSE VS. WOLVERINE
Marvel Comics: Aug, 2011 - No. 4, Nov, 2011 ($3.99, limited series)

1-4-Wolverine vs. Marvel Zombies; Maberry-s/Laurence Campbell-a/c 4.00

MARVEL UNLIMITED (Title on variant covers for newsstand editions of some 2001 Daredevil issues.

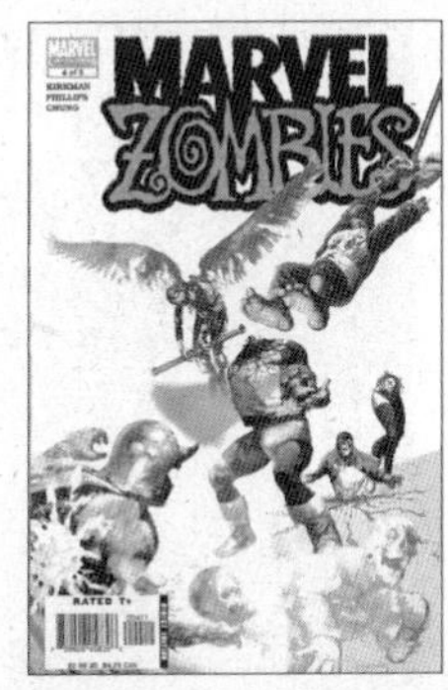

Marvel Zombies #4 © MAR

Mary Jane: Homecoming #1 © MAR

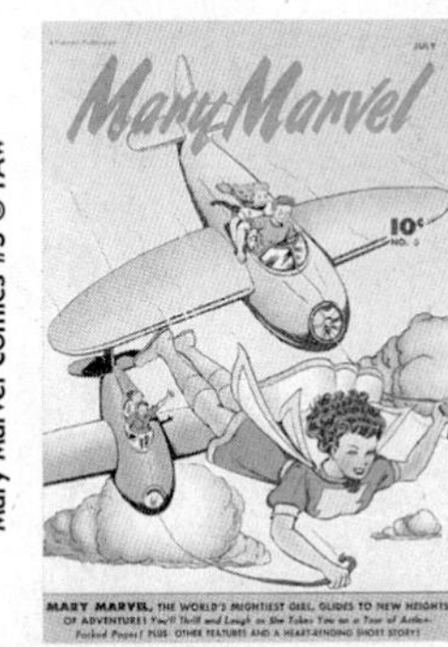

Mary Marvel Comics #3 © FAW

See indicia for actual titles and issue numbers)

MARVEL VALENTINE SPECIAL
Marvel Comics: Mar, 1997 ($2.99, one-shot)

1-Valentine stories w/Spider-Man, Daredevil, Cyclops, Phoenix 3.00

MARVEL VERSUS DC (See DC Versus Marvel) (Also see Amazon, Assassins, Bruce Wayne: Agent of S.H.I.E.L.D., Bullets & Bracelets, Doctor Strangefate, JLX, Legend of the Dark Claw, Magneto & The Magnetic Men, Speed Demon, Spider-Boy, Super Soldier, & X-Patrol)
Marvel Comics: No. 2, 1996 - No. 3, 1996 ($3.95, limited series)

2,3: 2-Peter David script. 3-Ron Marz script; Dan Jurgens-a(p). 1st app. of Super Soldier, Spider-Boy, Dr. Doomsday, Doctor Strangefate, The Dark Claw, Nightcreeper, Amazon, Wraith & others. Storyline continues in Amalgam books. 4.00

MARVEL VISIONARIES
Marvel Comics: 2002 - Present (various prices, HC and TPB)

...: Chris Claremont (2005, $29.99) r/X-Men #137, Uncanny X-Men #153,205,268 & Ann. #12, Iron Fist #14, Wolverine #3, New Mutants #21 and other highlights 30.00
...: Gil Kane (8/02, $24.95) r/Amazing Spider-Man #99, Marvel Premiere #1,#15, TOA #76 & others; plus sketch pages and a cover gallery 25.00
...: Jack Kirby HC (2004, $29.99) r/career highlights- Red Raven Comics #1 (1st work), Captain America Comics #1, Avengers #4, Fantastic Four #48-50 and more 30.00
...: Jack Kirby Vol. 2 HC (2006, $34.99) r/career highlights- Captain America, Two-Gun Kid, Fantastic Four, Thor, Fin Fang Foom, Devil Dinosaur, romance and more 35.00
...: Jim Steranko (9/02, $14.95) r/Captain America #110,111,113; X-Men #50,51 and stories from Tower of Shadows #1 and Our Love Story #5; plus a cover gallery 15.00
...: John Buscema (2007, $34.99) r/career highlights-Avengers, Silver Surfer, Thor, FF, Hulk, Wolverine and others; Roy Thomas intro.; sketch pages and pin-up art 35.00
...: John Romita Jr. (2005, $29.99) r/various stories 1977-2002; debut in AS-M Ann. #11; Iron Man #128, AS-M V2 #36, issues of Hulk, Daredevil: The Man Without Fear, Punisher; sketch pages; intro. by John Romita Sr. 30.00
...: John Romita Sr. (2005, $29.99) r/various stories 1951-1997 including Young Men #24&26, Daredevil #16, ASM #39,42,50; sketch pages; intro. by John Romita Jr. 30.00
...: Roy Thomas (2006, $34.99) r/career highlights; intro. by Stan Lee 35.00
...: Steve Ditko (2005, $29.99) r/various stories 1961-1992; intro. by Blake Bell 30.00
...: Stan Lee HC (2005, $29.99) r/career highlights- Captain America Comics #3 (1st work), and various Spider-Man, FF, Thor, Daredevil stories; 1940-1995; Roy Thomas intro. 30.00

MARVEL WEDDINGS
Marvel Comics: 2005 ($19.99, TPB)

TPB-Reprints weddings of Peter & Mary Jane, Reed & Sue, Scott & Jean, and others 20.00

MARVEL WESTERNS: ...
Marvel Comics: 2006 ($3.99, one-shots)

... Kid Colt and the Arizona Girl 1 (9/06) 2 short stories & 3 Kirby/Ayers reps.; Powell-c 4.00
... Outlaw Files-Profiles and essays about Marvel western characters 4.00
... Strange Westerns Starring The Black Rider 1 (10/06) Englehart-s/Rogers-a & 2 Kirby Rawhide Kid reprints; Rogers-c 4.00
... The Two-Gun Kid 1 (8/06) 2 short stories & a Kirby/Ayers reprint; Powell-c 4.00
... Western Legends 1 (9/06) 2 short stories & r/Rawhide Kid origin by Kirby; Powell-c 4.00
HC (2006, $20.99, dustjacket) r/one-shots 21.00

MARVEL X-MEN COLLECTION, THE
Marvel Comics: Jan, 1994 - No. 3, Mar, 1994 ($2.95, limited series)

1-3-r/X-Men trading cards by Jim Lee 3.00

MARVEL - YEAR IN REVIEW (Magazine)
Marvel Comics: 1989 - No. 3, 1991 (52 pgs.)

1-3: 1-Spider-Man-c by McFarlane. 2-Capt. America-c. 3-X-Men/Wolverine-c 5.00

MARVEL: YOUR UNIVERSE
Marvel Comics: 2008; May, 2009 - No. 3, July, 2009 ($5.99)

1-3-Reprints of 5 recent comics (Ms. Marvel, Nova, Immortal Iron Fist & others) 6.00
...Saga (2008, no cover price) - Re-caps of crossovers (Secret War thru Secret Invasion) 3.00

MARVEL ZOMBIES (See Ultimate Fantastic Four #21-23, 30-32)
Marvel Comics: Feb, 2006 - No. 5, June, 2006 ($2.99, limited series)

1-Zombies vs. Magneto; Kirkman-s/Phillips-a/Suydam-c swipe of A.F. #15 25.00
1-(2nd-4th printings) Variant Suydam-c swipes of Spider-Man #1, Amazing Spider-Man #50 and Incredible Hulk #1 5.00
2-Avengers #4 cover swipe by Suydam 10.00
3-5: 3-Inc. Hulk #340 c-swipe. 4-X-Men #1 c-swipe. 5-AS-M Ann. #21 c-swipe 6.00
3-5-(2nd printings) 3-Daredevil #179 c-swipe. 4-AS-M #39 c-swipe. 5-Silver Surfer #1 3.00
...: Dead Days (7/07, $3.99) Early days of the plaque; Kirkman-s/Phillips-a/Suydam-c 5.00
...: Dead Days HC (2008, $29.99, oversized) r/Dead Days one-shot, Ultimate Fantastic Four #21-23, 30-32, and Black Panther #28-30 30.00
...: Evil Evolution (1/10, $4.99) Apes vs. Zombies; Marcos Martin-c 5.00
... MGC #1 (7/10, $1.00) r/#1 with "Marvel's Greatest Comics" logo on cover 3.00
...: The Book of Angels, Demons and Various Monstrosities (2007, $3.99) profile pages 5.00
...: The Covers HC (2007, $19.99, d.j.) Suydam's covers with originals and commentary 20.00
HC (2006, $19.99) r/#1-5; Kirkman foreword; cover gallery with variants 20.00

MARVEL ZOMBIES 2
Marvel Comics: Dec, 2007 - No. 5, Apr, 2008 ($2.99, limited series)

1-5-Kirkman-s/Phillips-a/Suydam zombie-fied cover swipes 5.00
HC (2008, $19.99) r/#1-5; cover swipe gallery 20.00

MARVEL ZOMBIES 3
Marvel Comics: Dec, 2008 - No. 4, Mar, 2009 ($3.99, limited series)

1-4-Van Lente-s/Walker-a/Land-c; Machine Man, Jocasta and Morbius app. 5.00

MARVEL ZOMBIES 4
Marvel Comics: Jun, 2009 - No. 4, Sept, 2009 ($3.99, limited series)

1-4-Van Lente-s/Walker-a/Land-c; Zombie Deadpool head app. 4.00

MARVEL ZOMBIES 5
Marvel Comics: Jun, 2010 - No. 5, Sept, 2010 ($3.99, limited series)

1-5-Van Lente-s; Machine Man and Howard the Duck app. 3-Kaluta-a 4.00

MARVEL ZOMBIES / ARMY OF DARKNESS
Marvel Comics/Dynamite Entertainment: May, 2007 - No. 5, Aug, 2007($2.99, limited series)

1-Zombies vs. Ash during the start of the plaque; Layman-s/Neves-a/Suydam-c 7.00
1-Second printing with Suydam zombie-fied Captain America Comics #1 cover swipe 3.00
2-5-Suydam zombie-fied cover swipes on all 5.00
HC (2007, $19.99) r/#1-5; cover gallery with variants and non-zombied original covers 20.00

MARVEL ZOMBIES CHRISTMAS CAROL ("Zombies Christmas Carol" on cover)
Marvel Comics: Aug, 2011 - No. 5, Oct, 2011 ($3.99, limited series)

1-5-Adaptation of the Dickens classic with zombies; Kaluta-c/Baldeon-a 4.00

MARVEL ZOMBIES RETURN
Marvel Comics: Nov, 2009 - No. 5, Nov, 2009 ($3.99, weekly limited series)

1-5-Suydam-c. 1-Zombie Spider-Man eats the Earth-Z Sinister Six; Dragotta-a. 4.00

MARVEL ZOMBIES SUPREME
Marvel Comics: May, 2011 - No. 5, Aug, 2011 ($3.99, limited series)

1-5-Zombies in Squadron Supreme dimension; Blanco-a/Komarck-c; Jack of Hearts app. 4.00

MARVILLE
Marvel Comics: Nov, 2002 - No. 7, Jul, 2003 ($2.25, limited series)

1-6-Satire on DC/AOL-Time-Warner; Jemas-a/Bright-a/Horn-c 3.00
1-($3.95) Variant foil cover by Udon Studios; bonus sketch pages and Jemas afterword 4.00
7-($2.99) Intro. to Epic Comics line with submission guidelines 3.00

MARVIN MOUSE
Atlas Comics (BPC): September, 1957

	GD 2.0	VG 4.0	FN 6.0	VF 8.0	VF/NM 9.0	NM- 9.2
1-Everett-c/a; Maneely-a	14	28	42	81	118	155

MARY JANE (Spider-Man) (Also see Spider-Man Loves Mary Jane)
Marvel Comics: Aug, 2004 - No. 4, Nov, 2004 ($2.25, limited series)

1-4-Marvel Age series with teen-age MJ Watson; Miyazawa-c/a; McKeever-s 3.00
... Vol. 1: Circle of Friends (2004, $5.99, digest-size) r/#1-4 6.00

MARY JANE & SNIFFLES (See Looney Tunes)
Dell Publishing Co.: No. 402, June, 1952 - No. 474, June, 1953

	GD 2.0	VG 4.0	FN 6.0	VF 8.0	VF/NM 9.0	NM- 9.2
Four Color 402 (#1)	7	14	21	49	82	115
Four Color 474	7	14	21	46	76	105

MARY JANE: HOMECOMING (Spider-Man)
Marvel Comics: May, 2005 - No. 4, Aug, 2005 ($2.99, limited series)

1-4-Teen-age MJ Watson in high school; Miyazawa-c/a; McKeever-s 3.00
... Vol. 2 (2005, $6.99, digest-size) r/#1-4 7.00

MARY MARVEL COMICS (Monte Hale #29 on) (Also see Captain Marvel #18, Marvel Family, Shazam, & Wow Comics)
Fawcett Publications: Dec, 1945 - No. 28, Sept, 1948

	GD 2.0	VG 4.0	FN 6.0	VF 8.0	VF/NM 9.0	NM- 9.2
1-Captain Marvel introduces Mary on-c; intro/origin Georgia Sivana	161	322	483	1030	1765	2500
2	65	130	195	416	708	1000
3,4: 3-New logo	47	94	141	296	498	700
5-8: 8-Bulletgirl x-over in Mary Marvel; X-Mas-c	40	80	120	244	402	560
9,10	37	74	111	218	354	490
11-20	25	50	75	147	241	335
21-28: 28-Western-c	21	42	63	124	202	280

MARY POPPINS (See Movie Comics & Walt Disney Showcase No. 17)

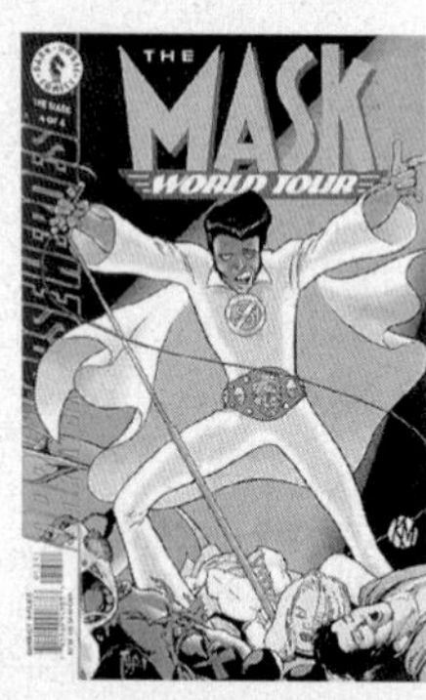
The Mask World Tour #4 © DH

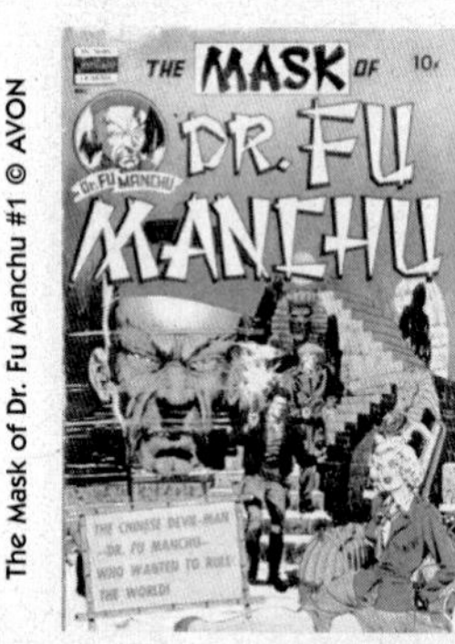

The Mask of Dr. Fu Manchu #1 © AVON

Masks: Too Hot for TV! #1 © WSP

GD VG FN VF VF/NM NM-
2.0 4.0 6.0 8.0 9.0 9.2

MARY SHELLEY'S FRANKENSTEIN
Topps Comics: Oct, 1994 - Jan, 1995 ($2.95, limited series)
1-4-polybagged w/3 trading cards 4.00
1-4 ($2.50)-Newstand ed. 3.00

MARY WORTH (See Harvey Comics Hits #55 & Love Stories of...)
Argo: March, 1956 (Also see Romantic Picture Novelettes)
1 8 16 24 42 54 65

MASK (TV)
DC Comics: Dec, 1985 - No. 4, Mar, 1986; Feb, 1987 - No. 9, Oct, 1987
1-4; 1-9 (2nd series)-Sat. morning TV show. 4.00

MASK, THE (Also see Mayhem)
Dark Horse Comics: Aug, 1991 - No. 4, Oct, 1991; No. 0, Dec, 1991 ($2.50, 36 pgs., limited series)
1-4: 1-1st app. Lt. Kellaway as The Mask (see Dark Horse Presents #10 for 1st app.) 5.00
0-(12/91, B&W, 56 pgs.)-r/Mayhem #1-4 4.00
...Omnibus Vol. 1 (8/08, $24.95) r/#1-4, Mask Returns and Mask Strikes Back series 25.00
...Omnibus Vol. 2 (4/09, $24.95) r/#1-4, The Hunt For Green October, World Tour, Southern Discomfort, Toys in the Attic series and short stories from DHP 25.00
...: HUNT FOR GREEN OCTOBER July, 1995 - Oct, 1995 ($2.50, lim. series)
1-4-Evan Dorkin scripts 3.00
.../ MARSHALL LAW Feb, 1998 - No. 2, Mar, 1998 ($2.95, lim. series)
1,2-Mills-s/O'Neill-a 3.00
...: OFFICIAL MOVIE ADAPTATION July, 1994 - Aug, 1994 ($2.50, lim. series)
1,2 3.00
... RETURNS Oct, 1992 - No. 4, Mar, 1993 ($2.50, limited series)
1-4 4.00
... SOUTHERN DISCOMFORT Mar, 1996 - No. 4, July, 1996 ($2.50, lim. series)
1-4 3.00
... STRIKES BACK Feb, 1995 - No. 5, Jun, 1995 ($2.50, limited series)
1-5 3.00
... SUMMER VACATION July, 1995 ($10.95, one shot, hard-c)
1-nn-Rick Geary-c/a 11.00
... TOYS IN THE ATTIC Aug, 1998 - No. 4, Nov, 1998 ($2.95, limited series)
1-4-Fingerman-s 3.00
... VIRTUAL SURREALITY July, 1997 ($2.95, one shot)
nn-Mignola, Aragonés, and others-s/a 3.00
... WORLD TOUR Dec, 1995 - No. 4, Mar, 1996 ($2.50, limited series)
1-4: 3-X & Ghost-c/app. 3.00

MASK COMICS
Rural Home Publ.: Feb-Mar, 1945 - No. 2, Apr-May, 1945; No. 2, Fall, 1945
1-Classic L. B. Cole Satan-c/a; Palais-a 300 600 900 2070 3635 5200
2-(Scarce)-Classic L. B. Cole Satan-c; Black Rider, The Boy Magician, & The Collector app. 213 426 639 1363 2332 3300
2-(Fall, 1945)-No publ.-same as regular #2; L. B. Cole-c 168 336 504 1075 1838 2600

MASKED BANDIT, THE
Avon Periodicals: 1952
nn-Kinstler-a 16 32 48 94 147 200

MASKED MAN, THE
Eclipse Comics: 12/84 - #10, 4/86; #11, 10/87; #12, 4/88 ($1.75/$2.00, color/B&W #9 on, Baxter paper)
1-12: 1-Origin retold. 3-Origin Aphid-Man; begin $2.00-c 3.00

MASKED MARVEL (See Keen Detective Funnies)
Centaur Publications: Sept, 1940 - No. 3, Dec, 1940
1-The Masked Marvel begins 168 336 504 1075 1838 2600
2,3: 2-Gustavson, Tarpe Mills-a 110 220 330 704 1202 1700

MASKED RAIDER, THE (Billy The Kid #9 on; Frontier Scout, Daniel Boone #10-13) (Also see Blue Bird)
Charlton Comics: June, 1955 - No. 8, July, 1957; No. 14, Aug, 1958 - No. 30, June, 1961
1-Masked Raider & Talon the Golden Eagle begin; painted-c 13 26 39 72 101 130
2 8 16 24 42 54 65
3-8,15: 8-Billy The Kid app. 15-Williamson-a, 7 pgs. 6 12 18 31 38 45
14,16-30: 22-Rocky Lane app. 5 10 15 24 30 35

MASKED RANGER
Premier Magazines: Apr, 1954 - No. 9, Aug, 1955
1-The Masked Ranger, his horse Streak, & The Crimson Avenger (origin) begin, end #9; Woodbridge/Frazetta-a 40 80 120 246 411 575
2,3 15 30 45 88 137 185
4-8-All Woodbridge-a. 5-Jesse James by Woodbridge. 6-Billy The Kid by Woodbridge. 7-Wild Bill Hickok by Woodbridge. 8-Jim Bowie's Life Story 15 30 45 90 140 190
9-Torres-a; Wyatt Earp by Woodbridge; Says Death of Masked Ranger on-c 17 34 51 98 154 210
NOTE: ***Check** a-1. **Woodbridge** c/a-1, 4-9.*

MASK OF DR. FU MANCHU, THE (See Dr. Fu Manchu)
Avon Periodicals: 1951
1-Sax Rohmer adapt.; Wood-c/a (26 pgs.); Hollingsworth-a 100 200 300 635 1093 1550

MASK OF ZORRO, THE
Image Comics: Aug, 1998 - No. 4, Dec, 1998 ($2.95, limited series)
1-4-Movie adapt. Photo variant-c 3.00

MASKS: TOO HOT FOR TV!
DC Comics (WildStorm): Feb, 2004 ($4.95)
1-Short stories by various incl. Thompson, Brubaker, Mahnke, Conner; Fabry-c 5.00

MASQUE OF THE RED DEATH (See Movie Classics)

MASQUERADE (See Project Superpowers)
Dynamite Entertainment: 2009 - No. 4, 2009 ($3.50, limited series)
1-4-Alex Ross & Phil Hester-s/Carlos Paul-a; covers by Ross & others 3.50

MASS EFFECT: EVOLUTION (2nd series based on the EA video game)
Dark Horse Comics: Jan, 2011 - No. 4, Apr, 2011 ($3.50, limited series)
1-4-Walters & Jackson Miller-s/Carnevale-c 3.50

MASS EFFECT: INVASION (3rd series based on the EA video game)
Dark Horse Comics: Oct, 2011 - No. 4, Jan, 2012 ($3.50, limited series)
1-4-Walters & Jackson Miller-s/Carnevale-c 3.50

MASS EFFECT: REDEMPTION (Based on the EA video game)
Dark Horse Comics: Jan, 2010 - No. 4, Apr, 2010 ($3.50, limited series)
1-4-Walters & Jackson Miller-s/Francia-a 3.50

MASTER COMICS (Combined with Slam Bang Comics #7 on)
Fawcett Publications: Mar, 1940 - No. 133, Apr, 1953 (No. 1-6: oversized issues) (#1-3: 15¢, 52 pgs.; #4-6: 10¢, 36 pgs.; #7-Begin 68 pg. issues)
1-Origin & 1st app. Master Man; The Devil's Dagger, El Carim, Master of Magic, Rick O'Say, Morton Murch, White Rajah, Shipwreck Roberts, Frontier Marshal, Streak Sloan, Mr. Clue begin (all features end #6) 811 1622 2433 5920 10,460 15,000
2 252 504 756 1613 2757 3900
3-6: 6-Last Master Man 181 362 543 1158 1979 2800
NOTE: *#1-6 rarely found in near mint or very fine condition due to large-size format.*
7-(10/40)-Bulletman, Zoro, the Mystery Man (ends #22), Lee Granger, Jungle King, & Buck Jones begin; only app. The War Bird & Mark Swift & the Time Retarder; Zoro, Lee Granger, Jungle King & Mark Swift all continue from Slam Bang; Bulletman moves from Nickel 300 600 900 1935 3343 4750
8-The Red Gaucho (ends #13), Captain Venture (ends #22) & The Planet Princess begin 160 320 480 1016 1746 2475
9,10: 10-Lee Granger ends 127 254 381 807 1391 1975
11-Origin & 1st app. Minute-Man (2/41) 274 548 822 1740 2995 4250
12 129 258 387 826 1413 2000
13-Origin & 1st app. Bulletgirl; Hitler-c 216 432 648 1372 2361 3350
14-16: 14-Companions Three begins, ends #31 115 230 345 730 1253 1775
17-20: 17-Raboy-a on Bulletman begins. 20-Captain Marvel cameo app. in Bulletman 105 210 315 667 1146 1625
21-(12/41; Scarce)-Captain Marvel & Bulletman team up against Capt. Nazi; origin & 1st app. Capt. Marvel Jr's most famous nemesis Captain Nazi who will cause creation of Capt. Marvel Jr. in Whiz #25. Part I of trilogy origin of Capt. Marvel Jr.; 1st Mac Raboy-c for Fawcett; Capt. Nazi-c 622 1244 1866 4541 8021 11,500
22-(1/42)-Captain Marvel Jr. moves over from Whiz #25 & teams up with Bulletman against Captain Nazi; part III of trilogy origin of Capt. Marvel Jr. & his 1st cover and adventure 568 1136 1704 4146 7323 10,500
23-Capt. Marvel Jr. c/stories begin (1st solo story); fights Capt. Nazi by himself. 300 600 900 1950 3375 4800
24,25 111 222 333 705 1215 1725
26-28,30-Captain Marvel Jr. vs. Capt. Nazi. 28-Liberty Bell-c. 30-Flag-c 103 206 309 659 1130 1600
29-Hitler & Hirohito-c 161 322 483 1030 1765 2500
31-33,35: 32-Last El Carim & Buck Jones; intro Balbo, the Boy Magician in El Carim story;

Master Comics #41 © FAW

Master of Kung Fu #125 © MAR

Masters of the Universe V2 #1 © Mattel

GD VG FN VF VF/NM NM-
2.0 4.0 6.0 8.0 9.0 9.2

classic Eagle-c by Raboy. 33-Balbo, the Boy Magician (ends #47), Hopalong Cassidy (ends #49) begins 84 168 252 538 919 1300
34-Capt. Marvel Jr. vs. Capt. Nazi-c/story; 1st mention of Capt. Nippon 90 180 270 576 988 1400
36-39 68 136 204 435 743 1050
40-Classic flag-c 90 180 270 576 988 1400
41-(8/43)-Bulletman, Capt. Marvel Jr. & Bulletgirl x-over in Minute-Man; only app. Crime Crusaders Club (Capt. Marvel Jr., Minute-Man, Bulletman & Bulletgirl) 71 142 213 454 777 1100
42-47,49: 47-Hitler becomes Corpl. Hitler Jr. 49-Last Minute-Man 42 84 126 267 451 635
48-Intro. Bulletboy; Capt. Marvel cameo in Minute-Man 49 98 147 309 522 735
50-Intro Radar & Nyoka the Jungle Girl & begin series (5/44); Radar also intro in Captain Marvel #35 (same date); Capt. Marvel x-over in Radar; origin Radar; Capt. Marvel & Capt. Marvel, Jr. introduce Radar on-c 43 86 129 271 461 650
51-58 27 54 81 158 259 360
59-62: Nyoka serial "Terrible Tiara" in all; 61-Capt. Marvel Jr. 1st meets Uncle Marvel 29 58 87 170 278 385
63-80 21 42 63 122 199 275
81,83-87,89-91,95-99: 88-Hopalong Cassidy begins (ends #94). 95-Tom Mix begins (cover only in #123, ends #133) 19 38 57 111 176 240
82,88,92-94-Krigstein-a 20 40 60 114 182 250
100 20 40 60 114 182 250
101-106-Last Bulletman (not in #104) 18 36 54 107 169 230
107-120: 118-Mary Marvel 18 36 54 103 162 220
121-131-(lower print run): 123-Tom Mix-c only 19 38 57 111 176 240
132-B&W and color illos in **POP**; last Nyoka 19 38 57 112 179 245
133-Bill Battle app. 24 48 72 140 230 320

NOTE: ***Mac Raboy** a-15-39, 40(part), 42, 58. c-21-49, 51, 52, 54, 56, 58, 68(part), 69(part). Bulletman c-7-11, 13(half), 15, 18(part), 19, 20, 21(w/Capt. Marvel & Capt. Nazi), 22(w/Capt. Marvel, Jr.). Capt. Marvel, Jr. c-23-133. Master Man c-1-6. Minute Man c-12, 13(half), 14, 16, 17, 18(part).*

MASTER DARQUE
Acclaim Comics (Valiant): Feb, 1998 ($3.95)

1-Manco-a/Christina Z.-s 4.00

MASTER DETECTIVE
Super Comics: 1964 (Reprints)

17-r/Criminals on the Loose V4 #2; r/Young King Cole #?; McWilliams-r 2 4 6 8 11 14

MASTER OF KUNG FU (Formerly Special Marvel Edition; see Deadly Hands of Kung Fu & Giant-Size...)
Marvel Comics Group: No. 17, April, 1974 - No. 125, June, 1983

17-Starlin-a; intro Black Jack Tarr; 3rd Shang-Chi (ties w/Deadly Hands #1) 4 8 12 26 41 55
18,20 3 6 9 16 22 28
19-Man-Thing-c/story 3 6 9 18 27 35
21-23,25-30 2 4 6 10 14 18
24-Starlin, Simonson-a 2 4 6 11 16 20
31-50: 33-1st Leiko Wu. 43-Last 25¢ issue 1 3 4 6 8 10
39-43-(30¢-c variants, limited distribution)(5-7/76) 3 6 9 17 25 32
51-75 6.00
53-57-(35¢-c variants, limited distribution)(6-10/77) 3 6 9 20 30 40
76-99 5.00
100,118,125-Double size 6.00
101-117,119-124 4.00
Annual 1(4/76)-Iron Fist app. 3 6 9 18 27 35

NOTE: ***Austin** c-63i, 74i. **Buscema** c-44p. **Gulacy** a(p)-18-20, 22, 25, 29-31, 33-35, 38, 39, 40(p&i), 42-50, 53r(#20); c-51, 55, 64, 67. **Gil Kane** c(p)-20, 38, 39, 42, 45, 59, 63. **Nebres** c-73i. **Starlin** a-17p, 24; c-54. **Sutton** a-42i. #53 reprints #20.*

MASTER OF KUNG-FU, SHANG-CHI:... (2002 series, see Shang Chi:...)

MASTER OF KUNG-FU: BLEEDING BLACK
Marvel Comics: Feb, 1991 ($2.95, 84 pgs., one-shot)

1-The Return of Shang-Chi 4.00

MASTER OF THE WORLD
Dell Publishing Co.: No. 1157, July, 1961

Four Color 1157-Movie based on Jules Verne's "Master of the World" and "Robur the Conqueror" novels; with Vincent Price & Charles Bronson 7 14 21 44 72 100

MASTERS OF TERROR (Magazine)
Marvel Comics Group: July, 1975 - No. 2, Sept, 1975 (B&W) (All reprints)

1-Brunner, Barry Smith-a; Morrow/Steranko-c; Starlin-a(p); Gil Kane-a 3 6 9 18 27 35
2-Reese, Kane, Mayerik-a; Adkins/Steranko-c 2 4 6 13 18 22

MASTERS OF THE UNIVERSE (See DC Comics Presents #47 for 1st app.)
DC Comics: Dec, 1982 - No. 3, Feb, 1983 (Mini-series)

1 6.00
2,3: 2-Origin He-Man & Ceril 4.00

NOTE: ***Alcala** a-1i,, 2i. **Tuska** a-1-3p; c-1-3p. #2 has 75 & 95 cent cover price.*

MASTERS OF THE UNIVERSE (Comic Album)
Western Publishing Co.: 1984 (8-1/2x11", $2.95, 64 pgs.)

11362-Based on Mattel toy & cartoon 2 4 6 11 16 20

MASTERS OF THE UNIVERSE
Star Comics/Marvel #7 on: May 1986 - No. 13, May, 1988 (75¢/$1.00)

1 1 2 3 5 6 8
2-11: 8-Begin $1.00-c 6.00
12-Death of He-Man (1st Marvel app.) 2 4 6 8 11 14
13-Return of He-Man & death of Skeletor 2 4 6 8 11 14
The Motion Picture (11/87, $2.00)-Tuska-p 1 2 3 4 5 7

MASTERS OF THE UNIVERSE
Image Comics: Nov, 2002 - No. 4, March, 2003 ($2.95, limited series)

1-($2.95) Two covers by Santalucia and Campbell; Santalucia-a 3.00
1-($5.95) Variant-c by Norem w/gold foil logo 6.00
2-4($2.95) 2-Two covers by Santalucia and Manapul. 3,4-Two covers 3.00
TPB (CrossGen, 2003, $9.95, 8-1/4" x 5-1/2") digest-sized reprints #1-4 10.00

MASTERS OF THE UNIVERSE (Volume 2)
Image Comics: March, 2003 - No. 6, Aug, 2003 ($2.95)

1-6-($2.95) 1-Santalucia-c. 2-Two covers by Santalucia & JJ Kirby 3.00
1-($5.95) Wraparound variant-c by Struzan w/silver foil logo 6.00
3,4-($5.95) Wraparound variant holofoil-c. 3-By Edwards 4-By Boris Vallejo & Julie Bell 6.00
Volume 2 Dark Reflections TPB (2004, $18.95) r/#1-6 19.00

MASTERS OF THE UNIVERSE (Volume 3)
MVCreations: Apr, 2004 - No. 8, Dec, 2004 ($2.95)

1-8: 1-Santalucia-c 3.00

MASTERS OF THE UNIVERSE...
CrossGen Comics

...Rise of the Snake-Men (Nov, 2003 - No. 3, $2.95) Meyers-a 3.00
...The Power of Fear (12/03, $2.95, one-shot) Santalucia-a 3.00

MASTERS OF THE UNIVERSE, ICONS OF EVIL
Image Comics/CrossGen Comics: 2003 ($4.95, one-shots)

...Beastman -(Image) Origin of Beast Man; Tony Moore-a 5.00
...Mer-Man -(CrossGen) 5.00
...Trapjaw -(CrossGen) 5.00
...Tri-Klops -(CrossGen) Walker-c 5.00
TPB (3/04, $18.95, MVCreations) r/one-shots; sketch pages 19.00

MASTERWORKS SERIES OF GREAT COMIC BOOK ARTISTS, THE
Sea Gate Dist./DC Comics: May, 1983 - No. 3, Dec, 1983 (Baxter paper)

1-3: 1,2-Shining Knight by Frazetta r-/Adventure. 2-Tomahawk by Frazetta-r. 3-Wrightson-c/a(r) 6.00

MATADOR
DC Comics (WildStorm): July, 2005 - No. 6, May, 2006 ($2.99, limited series)

1-6-Devin Grayson-s/Brian Stelfreeze-a/c 3.00

MATRIX COMICS, THE (Movie)
Burlyman Entertainment: 2003; 2004 ($21.95, trade paperback)

nn-Short stories by various incl. Wachowskis, Darrow, Gaiman, Sienkiewicz, Bagge 22.00
...Volume One Preview (7/03, no cover price) bios of creators; Chadwick-s/a 3.00
Volume 2-(2004) Short stories by various incl. Wachowskis, Sale, McKeever, Dorman 22.00

MATT SLADE GUNFIGHTER (Kid Slade Gunfighter #5 on; See Western Gunfighters)
Atlas Comics (SPI): May, 1956 - No. 4, Nov, 1956

1-Intro Matt & horse Eagle; Williamson/Torres-a 18 36 54 107 169 230
2-Williamson-a 13 26 39 74 105 135
3,4 10 20 30 56 76 95

NOTE: ***Maneely** a-1, 3, 4; c-1, 2, 4. **Roth** a-2-4. **Severin** a-1, 3, 4. **Maneely** c/a-1. Issue #s stamped on cover after printing.*

MAUS: A SURVIVOR'S TALE (First graphic novel to win a Pulitzer Prize)
Pantheon Books: 1986, 1991 (B&W)

Vol. 1-(...: My Father Bleeds History)(1986) Art Spiegelman-s/a; recounts stories of Spiegelman's father in 1930s-40s Nazi-occupied Poland; collects first six stories serialized in Raw Magazine from 1980-1985 20.00

Maverick #7 © MAR

The Maze Agency #1 © Mike Barr

McHale's Navy #2 © DELL

	GD	VG	FN	VF	VF/NM	NM-
	2.0	4.0	6.0	8.0	9.0	9.2

Vol. 2-(...: And Here My Troubles Began)(1991) 20.00
Complete Maus Survivor's Tale -HC Vols. 1& 2 w/slipcase 35.00
Hardcover Vol. 1 (1991) 24.00
Hardcover Vol. 2 (1991) 24.00
TPB (1992, $14.00) Vols. 1& 2 14.00

MAVERICK (TV)
Dell Publishing Co.: No. 892, 4/58 - No. 19, 4-6/62 (All have photo-c)

Four Color 892 (#1)-James Garner photo-c begin 19 38 57 128 277 425
Four Color 930,945,962,980,1005 (6-8/59): 945-James Garner/Jack Kelly photo-c begin 10 20 30 69 130 190
7 (10-12/59) - 14: 11-Variant edition has "Time For Change" comic strip on back-c. 14-Last Garner/Kelly-c 9 18 27 61 106 150
15-18: Jack Kelly/Roger Moore photo-c 8 16 24 51 86 120
19-Jack Kelly photo-c (last issue) 8 16 24 53 89 125

MAVERICK (See X-Men)
Marvel Comics: Jan, 1997 ($2.95, one-shot)

1-Hama-s 4.00

MAVERICK (See X-Men)
Marvel Comics: Sept, 1997 - No. 12, Aug, 1998 ($2.99/$1.99)

1,12: 1-($2.99)-Wraparound-c. 12-($2.99) Battles Omega Red 4.00
2-11: 2-Two covers. 4-Wolverine app. 6,7-Sabretooth app. 3.00

MAVERICK MARSHAL
Charlton Comics: Nov, 1958 - No. 7, May, 1960

1 6 12 18 33 41 48
2-7 5 10 15 23 28 32

MAVERICKS
Daggar Comics Group: Jan, 1994 - No. 5, 1994 (#1-$2.75, #2-5-$2.50)

1-5: 1-Bronze. 1-Gold. 1-Silver 3.00

MAX BRAND (See Silvertip)

MAX HAMM FAIRY TALE DETECTIVE
Nite Owl Comix: 2002 - 2004 ($4.95, B&W, 6 1/2" x 8")

1-(2002) Frank Cammuso-s/a 5.00
Vol. 2 #1-3 (2003-2004) Frank Cammuso-s/a 5.00

MAXIMAGE
Image Comics (Extreme Studios): Dec, 1995 - No. 7, June 1996 ($2.50)

1-7: 1-Liefeld-c. 2-Extreme Destroyer Pt. 2; polybagged w/card. 4-Angela & Glory-c/app. 3.00

MAXIMO
Dreamwave Prods.: Jan, 2004 ($3.95, one-shot)

1-Based on the Capcom video game 4.00

MAXIMUM SECURITY (Crossover)
Marvel Comics: Oct, 2000 - No. 3, Jan, 2001 ($2.99)

1-3-Busiek-s/Ordway-a; Ronan the Accuser, Avengers app. 3.00
...Dangerous Planet 1: Busiek-s/Ordway-a; Ego, the Living Planet 3.00
Thor vs. Ego (11/00, $2.99) Reprints Thor #133,160,161; Kirby-a 3.00

MAXX (Also see Darker Image, Primer #5, & Friends of Maxx)
Image Comics (I Before E): Mar, 1993 - No. 35, Feb, 1998 ($1.95)

1/2 1 3 4 6 8 10
1/2 (Gold) 20.00
1-Sam Kieth-c/a/scripts 4.00
1-Glow-in-the-dark variant 2 4 6 8 10 12
1-"3-D Edition" (1/98, $4.95) plus new back-up story 5.00
2-12: 6-Savage Dragon cameo(1 pg.). 7,8-Pitt-c & story 3.00
13-16 3.00
17-35: 21-Alan Moore-s 3.00
Volume 1 TPB (DC/WildStorm, 2003, $17.95) r/#1-6 18.00
Volume 2 TPB (DC/WildStorm, 2004, $17.95) r/#7-13 18.00
Volume 3 TPB (DC/WildStorm, 2004, $17.95) r/#14-20 18.00
Volume 4 TPB (DC/WildStorm, 2005, $17.95) r/#21-27 18.00
Volume 5 TPB (DC/WildStorm, 2005, $19.99) r/#28-35 20.00
Volume 6 TPB (DC/WildStorm, 2006, $19.99) r/Friends of Maxx #1-3 & The Maxx 3-D 20.00

MAYA (See Movie Classics)
Gold Key: Mar, 1968

1 (10218-803)(TV) 3 6 9 17 25 32

MAYHEM
Dark Horse Comics: May, 1989 - No. 4, Sept, 1989 ($2.50, B&W, 52 pgs.)

1- Four part Stanley Ipkiss/Mask story begins; Mask-c 1 3 4 6 8 10
2-4: 2-Mask 1/2 back-c. 4-Mask-c 1 2 3 5 7 9

	GD	VG	FN	VF	VF/NM	NM-
	2.0	4.0	6.0	8.0	9.0	9.2

MAYHEM (Tyrese Gibson's...)
Image Comics: Aug, 2009 - No. 3, Oct, 2009 ($2.99, limited series)

1-3-Tyrese Gibson co-writer; Tone Rodriguez-a/c 3.00

MAZE AGENCY, THE
Comico/Innovation Publ. #8 on: Dec, 1988 - No. 20, 1991 ($1.95-$2.50, color)

1-20: 9-Ellery Queen app. 7 ($2.50)-Last Comico issue 3.00
Annual 1 (1990, $2.75)-Ploog-c; Spirit tribute ish 4.00
Special 1 (1989, $2.75)-Staton-p (Innovation) 4.00
TPB (IDW Publ., 11/05, $24.99) r/#1-5 25.00

MAZE AGENCY, THE (Vol. 2)
Caliber Comics: July, 1997 - No. 3, 1998 ($2.95, B&W)

1-3: 1-Barr-s/Gonzales-a(p). 3-Hughes-c 3.00

MAZE AGENCY, THE
Caliber Comics: Nov, 2005 - No. 3, Jan, 2006 ($3.99, limited series)

1-3-Barr-s/Padilla-a(p)/c 4.00

MAZIE (...& Her Friends) (See Flat-Top, Mortie, Stevie & Tastee-Freez)
Mazie Comics(Magazine Publ.)/Harvey Publ. No. 13-on: 1953 - #12, 1954; #13, 12/54 - #22, 9/56; #23, 9/57 - #28, 8/58

1-(Teen-age)-Stevie's girlfriend 10 20 30 58 79 100
2 7 14 21 35 43 50
3-10 6 12 18 31 38 45
11-28 5 10 15 24 30 35

MAZIE
Nation Wide Publishers: 1950 - No. 7, 1951 (5¢) (5x7-1/4"-miniature)(52 pgs.)

1-Teen-age 18 36 54 105 165 225
2-7 12 24 36 69 97 125

MAZINGER (See First Comics Graphic Novel #17)

'MAZING MAN
DC Comics: Jan, 1986 - No. 12, Dec, 1986

1-11: 7,8-Hembeck-a 3.00
12-Dark Knight part-c by Miller 3.50
Special 1 ('87), 2 (4/88), 3 ('90)-All $2.00, 52pgs. 3.00

McCANDLESS & COMPANY
Mandalay Books: 2001 ($7.95)

...: Dead Razor - J.C. Vaughn-s/Busch & Sheehan-a; 3 covers 8.00
Crime Scenes: A McCandless & Company Reader TPB (Spring 2006, $17.95) Vaughn-s 18.00

McHALE'S NAVY (TV) (See Movie Classics)
Dell Publ. Co.: May-July, 1963 - No. 3, Nov-Jan, 1963-64 (All have photo-c)

1 7 14 21 44 72 100
2,3 5 10 15 32 51 70

McKEEVER & THE COLONEL (TV)
Dell Publishing Co.: Feb-Apr, 1963 - No. 3, Aug-Oct, 1963

1-Photo-c 6 12 18 39 62 85
2,3 5 10 15 30 48 65

McLINTOCK (See Movie Comics)

MD
E. C. Comics: Apr-May, 1955 - No. 5, Dec-Jan, 1955-56

1-Not approved by code; Craig-c 16 32 48 128 204 280
2-5 10 20 30 80 130 180

NOTE: ***Crandall, Evans, Ingels, Orlando*** *art in all issues;* ***Craig*** *c-1-5.*

MD
Russ Cochran/Gemstone Publishing: Sept, 1999 - No. 5, Jan, 2000 ($2.50)

1-5-Reprints original EC series 3.00
Annual 1 (1999, $13.50) r/#1-5 14.00

MEASLES
Fantagraphics Books: Christmas 1998 - No. 8 ($2.95, B&W, quarterly)

1-8-Anthology: 1-Venus-s by Hernandez 3.00

MECHA (Also see Mayhem)
Dark Horse Comics: June, 1987 - No. 6, 1988 ($1.50/$1.95, color/B&W)

1-6: 1,2 ($1.95, color), 3,4-($1.75, B&W), 5,6-($1.50, B&W) 3.00

MECHANIC, THE
Image Comics: 1998 ($5.95, one-shot, squarebound)

Meet Miss Bliss #1 © MAR

Megalith #8 © Continuity

Megaman #1 © Capcom

GD VG FN VF VF/NM NM-
2.0 4.0 6.0 8.0 9.0 9.2

1-Chiodo-painted art; Peterson-s 6.00
1-($10.00) DF Alternate Cover Ed. 10.00

MECHA SPECIAL
Dark Horse Comics: May, 1995 ($2.95, one-shot)
1 3.00

MECH DESTROYER
Image Comics: Apr, 2001 - No. 4, Sept, 2001 ($2.95, limited series)
1-4-Jae Kim-c/a; Robert Chong-s 3.00

MEDAL FOR BOWZER, A (See Promotional Comics section)

MEDAL OF HONOR COMICS
A. S. Curtis: Spring, 1946
1-War stories 14 28 42 78 112 145

MEDAL OF HONOR SPECIAL
Dark Horse Comics: 1994 ($2.50, one-shot)
1-Kubert-c/a (first story) 3.00

MEDIA STARR
Innovation Publ.: July, 1989 - No. 3, Sept, 1989 ($1.95, mini-series, 28 pgs.)
1-3: Deluxe format 3.00

MEDIEVAL SPAWN/WITCHBLADE
Image Comics (Top Cow Productions): May, 1996 - No. 3, June, 1996 ($2.95, limited series)
1-3-Garth Ennis scripts in all 6.00
1-Platinum foil-c (500 copies from Pittsburgh Con) 35.00
1-Gold 10.00
1-ETM Exclusive Edition; gold foil logo 7.00
TPB ($9.95) r/#1-3 10.00

MEET ANGEL (Formerly Angel & the Ape)
National Periodical Publications: No. 7, Nov-Dec, 1969
7-Wood-a(i) 3 6 9 20 30 40

MEET CORLISS ARCHER (Radio/Movie)(My Life #4 on)
Fox Features Syndicate: Mar, 1948 - No. 3, July, 1948
1-(Teen-age)-Feldstein-c/a; headlight-c 113 226 339 718 1234 1750
2 57 114 171 362 619 875
3-Part Feldstein-c only 53 106 159 334 567 800
NOTE: *No. 1-3 used in Seduction of the Innocent, pg. 39.*

MEET HERCULES (See Three Stooges)

MEET MERTON
Toby Press: Dec, 1953 - No. 4, June, 1954
1-(Teen-age)-Dave Berg-c/a 10 20 30 58 79 100
2-Dave Berg-c/a 7 14 21 35 43 50
3,4-Dave Berg-c/a 6 12 18 31 38 45
I.W. Reprint #9, Super Reprint #11('63), 18 2 4 6 8 11 14

MEET MISS BLISS (Becomes Stories Of Romance #5 on)
Atlas Comics (LMC): May, 1955 - No. 4, Nov, 1955
1-Al Hartley-c/a 14 28 42 81 118 155
2-4 10 20 30 56 76 95

MEET MISS PEPPER (Formerly Lucy, The Real Gone Gal)
St. John Publishing Co.: No. 5, April, 1954 - No. 6, June, 1954
5-Kubert/Maurer-a 21 42 63 126 206 285
6-Kubert/Maurer-a; Kubert-c 19 38 57 109 172 235

MEGACITY909
Devil's Due Publ.: Sept, 2004 - No. 8, Aug, 2005 ($2.95)
1-8-Kano Kang & Zack Suh-a 3.00

MEGA DRAGON & TIGER
Image Comics: Mar, 1999 - No. 5 ($2.95)
1-5-Tony Wong-s/a 3.00

MEGAHURTZ
Image Comics: Aug, 1997 - No. 3, Oct, 1997 ($2.95, B&W)
1-3-St. Pierre-s 3.00

MEGALITH (Megalith Deathwatch 2000 #1,2 of second series)
Continuity: 1989 - No. 9, Mar, 1992; No, 0, Apr, 1993 - No. 7, Jan, 1994
1-9-($2.00-c) 1-Neal Adams & Mark Texiera-c/Texiera & Nebres-a 3.00
2nd series: 0-(4/93)-Foil-c; no c-price, giveaway; Adams plot 3.00
1-7: 1-3-Bagged w/card: 1-Gatefold-c by Nebres; Adams plot. 2-Fold-out-c; Adams plot. 3-Indestructible-c. 4-7-Embossed-c: 4-Adams/Nebres-c; Adams part-i. 5-Sienkiewicz-i. 6-Adams part-i. 7-Adams-c(p); Adams plot 3.00

MEGAMAN
Dreamwave Productions: Sept, 2003 - No. 4, Dec, 2003 ($2.95)
1-4-Brian Augustyn-s/Mic Fong-a 3.00
1-($5.95) Chromium wraparound variant-c 6.00

MEGA MAN (Based on the Capcom video game character)
Archie Comics Publications: Jul, 2011 - Present ($2.99)
1-14: 1-Spaziante-a 3.00

MEGAMIND: BAD. BLUE. BRILLIANT (DreamWorks'...) (Based on the 2010 movie)
Ape Entertainment: 2010 - No. 4, 2011 ($3.95, limited series)
1-4: 1-High school flashback 4.00
nn-($6.95, 9x6") Prequel to the movie; Joe Kelly-s 7.00

MEGA MORPHS
Marvel Comics: Oct, 2005 - No. 4, Dec, 2005 ($2.99, limited series)
1-4-Giant robots based on action figures; McKeever-s; Kang-a 3.00
Digest (2006, $7.99) r/#1-4 plus mini-comics 8.00

MEGATON (A super hero)
Megaton Publ.: Nov, 1983; No. 2, Oct, 1985 - No. 8, Aug, 1987 (B&W)
1-($2.00, 68 pgs.)-Erik Larsen's 1st pro work; Vanguard by Larsen begins (1st app.), ends #4; 1st app. Megaton, Berzerker, & Ethrian; Guice-c/a(p); Gustovich-a(p) in #1,2 2 4 6 10 14 18
2-($2.00, 68 pgs.)-1st brief app. The Dragon (1 pg.) by Larsen (later The Savage Dragon in Image Comics); Guice-c/a(p) 2 4 6 9 12 15
3-(44 pgs.)-1st full app. Savage Dragon-c/story by Larsen; 1st comic book work by Angel Medina (pin-up) 2 4 6 13 18 22
4-(52 pgs.)-2nd full app. Savage Dragon by Larsen; 4,5-Wildman by Grass Green 2 4 6 8 10 12
5-1st Liefeld published-a (inside f/c, 6/86) 1 2 3 5 7 9
6,7: 6-Larsen-c 1 2 3 4 5 7
8-1st Liefeld story-a (7 pg. super hero story) plus 1 pg. Youngblood ad 1 3 4 6 8 10
...Explosion (6/87, 16 pg. color giveaway)-1st app. Youngblood by Rob Liefeld (2 pg. spread); shows Megaton heroes 3 6 9 14 20 25
...Holiday Special 1 (1994, $2.95, color, 40 pgs., publ. by Entity Comics)-Gold foil logo; bagged w/Kelley Jones card; Vanguard, Megaton plus shows unpublished-c to 1987 Youngblood #1 by Liefeld/Ordway 5.00
NOTE: *Copies of Megaton Explosion were also released in early 1992 all signed by Rob Liefeld and were made available to retailers.*

MEGATON MAN (See Don Simpson's Bizarre Heroes)
Kitchen Sink Enterprises: Nov, 1984 - No. 10, 1986
1-10, 1-2nd printing (1989) 3.00
...Meets The Uncategorizable X-Thems 1 (4/89, $2.00) 3.00

MEGATON MAN: BOMB SHELL
Image Comics: Jul, 1999 - No. 2 ($2.95, B&W, mini-series)
1-Reprints stories from Megaton Man internet site 3.00

MEGATON MAN: HARD COPY
Image Comics: Feb, 1999 - No. 2, Apr, 1999 ($2.95, B&W, mini-series)
1,2-Reprints stories from Megaton Man internet site 3.00

MEGATON MAN VS. FORBIDDEN FRANKENSTEIN
Fiasco Comics: Apr, 1996 ($2.95, B&W, one-shot)
1-Intro The Tomb Team (Forbidden Frankenstein, Drekula, Bride of the Monster, & Moon Wolf). 3.00

MEK (See Reload/Mek flipbook for TPB reprint)
DC Comics (Homage): Jan, 2003 - No. 3, Mar, 2003 ($2.95, limited series)
1-3-Warren Ellis-s/Steve Rolston-a 3.00

MEKANIX (See X-Men titles) (See X-Treme X-Men Vol. 4 for TPB)
Marvel Comics: Dec, 2002 - No. 6, May, 2003 ($2.99, limited series)
1-6-Kitty Pryde in college; Claremont-s/Bobillo & Sosa-a 3.00

MEL ALLEN SPORTS COMICS (The Voice of the Yankees)
Standard Comics: No. 5, Nov, 1949; No. 6, June, 1950
5(#1 on inside)-Tuska-a 23 46 69 136 223 310
6(#2)-Lou Gehrig story 16 32 48 94 147 200

MELTDOWN
Image Comics: Dec, 2006 - No. 2, Jan, 2007 ($5.95, squarebound, limited series)
1,2-Schwartz-s/Wang-a. 1-Bachalo-c. 2-Horn-c 6.00

MELVIN MONSTER

Menace #7 © ATLAS

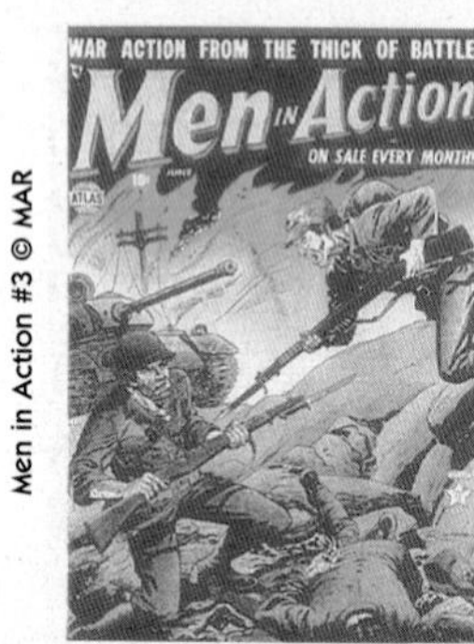

Men in Action #3 © MAR

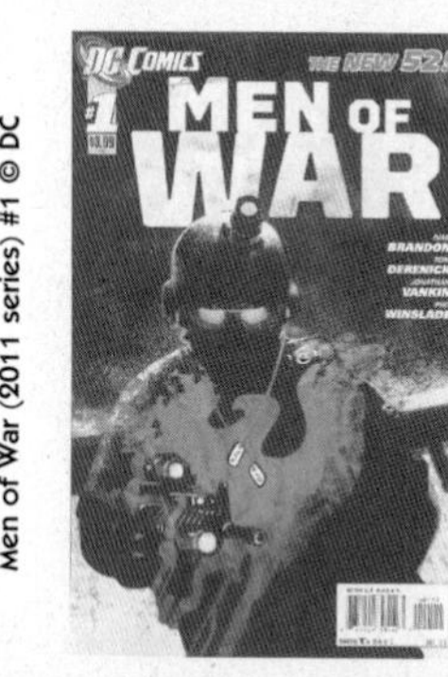

Men of War (2011 series) #1 © DC

GD 2.0 | VG 4.0 | FN 6.0 | VF 8.0 | VF/NM 9.0 | NM- 9.2

Dell Publishing Co.: Apr-June, 1965 - No. 10, Oct, 1969
1-By John Stanley 7 14 21 46 76 105
2-10-All by Stanley. #10-r/#1 5 10 15 32 51 70

MELVIN THE MONSTER (See Peter, the Little Pest & Dexter The Demon #7)
Atlas Comics (HPC): July, 1956 - No. 6, July, 1957
1-Maneely-c/a 14 28 42 82 121 160
2-6: 4-Maneely-c/a 10 20 30 56 76 95

MENACE
Atlas Comics (HPC): Mar, 1953 - No. 11, May, 1954
1-Horror & sci/fi stories begin; Everett-c/a 84 168 252 538 919 1300
2-Post-atom bomb disaster by Everett; anti-Communist propaganda/torture scenes; Sinnott sci/fi story "Rocket to the Moon" 54 108 162 343 574 825
3,4,6-Everett-a. 4-Sci/fi story "Escape to the Moon". 6-Romita sci/fi story "Science Fiction" 45 90 135 284 480 675
5-Origin & 1st app. The Zombie by Everett (reprinted in Tales of the Zombie #1)(7/53); 5-Sci/fi story "Rocket Ship" 68 136 204 435 743 1050
7,8,10,11: 7-Frankenstein story. 8-End of world story; Heath 3-D art(3 pgs.). 10-H-Bomb panels 39 78 117 231 378 525
9-Everett-a r-in Vampire Tales #1 40 80 120 246 411 575
NOTE: ***Brodsky*** *c-7, 8, 11.* ***Colan*** *a-6; c-9.* ***Everett*** *a-1-6, 9; c-1-6.* ***Heath*** *a-1-8; c-10.* ***Katz*** *a-11.* ***Maneely*** *a-3, 5, 7-9.* ***Powell*** *a-11.* ***Romita*** *a-3, 6, 8, 11.* ***Shelly*** *a-10.* ***Shores*** *a-7.* ***Sinnott*** *a-2, 7.* ***Tuska*** *a-1, 2, 5.*

MENACE
Awesome-Hyperwerks: Nov, 1998 ($2.50)
1-Jada Pinkett Smith-s/Fraga-a 3.00

MEN AGAINST CRIME (Formerly Mr. Risk; Hand of Fate #8 on)
Ace Magazines: No. 3, Feb, 1951 - No. 7, Oct, 1951
3-Mr. Risk app. 11 22 33 60 83 105
4-7: 4-Colan-a; entire book-r as Trapped! #4. 5-Meskin-a 8 16 24 44 57 70

MEN, GUNS, & CATTLE (See Classics Illustrated Special Issue)

MEN IN ACTION (Battle Brady #10 on)
Atlas Comics (IPS): April, 1952 - No. 9, Dec, 1952 (War stories)
1-Berg, Reinman-a 18 36 54 107 169 230
2,3: 3-Heath-c/a 11 22 33 64 90 115
4-6,8,9 10 20 30 58 79 100
7-Krigstein-a; Heath-c 11 22 33 64 90 115
NOTE: ***Brodsky*** *a-3; c-1, 4-6.* ***Maneely*** *c-5.* ***Pakula*** *a-1, 6.* ***Robinson*** *c-8.* ***Shores*** *c-9.* ***Sinnott*** *a-6.*

MEN IN ACTION
Ajax/Farrell Publications: April, 1957 - No. 6, 1958
1 10 20 30 56 76 95
2 7 14 21 35 43 50
3-6 6 12 18 31 38 45

MEN IN BLACK, THE (1st series)
Aircel Comics (Malibu): Jan, 1990 - No. 3 Mar, 1990 ($2.25, B&W, lim. series)
1-Cunningham-s/a in all 5 10 15 32 51 70
2,3 3 6 9 18 27 35
Graphic Novel (Jan, 1991) r/#1-3 3 6 9 16 23 30

MEN IN BLACK (2nd series)
Aircel Comics (Malibu): May, 1991 - No. 3, Jul, 1991 ($2.50, B&W, lim. series)
1-Cunningham-s/a in all 3 6 9 18 27 35
2,3 2 4 6 10 14 18

MEN IN BLACK: FAR CRY
Marvel Comics: Aug, 1997 ($3.99, color, one-shot)
1-Cunningham-s 4.00

MEN IN BLACK: RETRIBUTION
Marvel Comics: Dec, 1997 ($3.99, color, one-shot)
1-Cunningham-s; continuation of the movie 4.00

MEN IN BLACK: THE MOVIE
Marvel Comics: Oct, 1997 ($3.99, one-shot, movie adaptation)
1-Cunningham-s 4.00

MEN INTO SPACE
Dell Publishing Co.: No. 1083, Feb-Apr, 1960
Four Color 1083-Anderson-a, photo-c 5 10 15 35 55 75

MEN OF BATTLE (Also see New Men of Battle)
Catechetical Guild: V1#5, March, 1943 (Hardcover)
V1#5-Topix reprints 6 12 18 28 34 40

MEN OF WAR
DC Comics, Inc.: August, 1977 - No. 26, March, 1980 (#9,10: 44 pgs.)
1-Enemy Ace, Gravedigger (origin #1,2) begin 3 6 9 16 23 30
2-4,8-10,12-14,19,20: All Enemy Ace stories. 4-1st Dateline Frontline. 9-Unknown Soldier app. 2 4 6 10 14 18
5-7,11,15-18,21-25: 17-1st app. Rosa 2 4 6 8 11 14
26-Sgt. Rock & Easy Co.-c/s 3 6 9 14 19 24
NOTE: ***Chaykin*** *a-9, 10, 12-14, 19, 20.* ***Evans*** *c-25.* ***Kubert*** *c-2-23, 24p, 26.*

MEN OF WAR (DC New 52)
DC Comics: Nov, 2011 - No. 8, Jun, 2012 ($3.99)
1-8: 1-Sgt. Rock's grandson in modern times; Derenick-a; Navy Seals back-up; Winslade-a 6-Back-up w/Corben-a. 8-Frankenstein & G.I. Robot app. 4.00

MEN'S ADVENTURES (Formerly True Adventures)
Marvel/Atlas Comics (CCC): No. 4, Aug, 1950 - No. 28, July, 1954
4(#1)(52 pgs.) 34 68 102 206 336 465
5-Flying Saucer story 22 44 66 132 216 300
6-8: 7-Buried alive story. 8-Sci/fic story 20 40 60 115 185 265
9-20: All war format 14 28 42 82 121 160
21,22,24,26: All horror format 25 50 75 150 245 340
23-Crandall-a; Fox-a(i); horror format 26 52 78 154 252 350
25-Shrunken head-c 39 78 117 231 378 525
27,28-Human Torch & Toro-c/stories; Captain America & Sub-Mariner stories in each (also see Young Men #24-28) 126 252 378 806 1378 1950
NOTE: ***Ayers*** *a-20, 27(H. Torch).* ***Berg*** *a-15, 16.* ***Brodsky*** *c-4-9, 11, 12, 16-18, 24.* ***Burgos*** *c-27, 28 (Human Torch).* ***Colan*** *a-13, 14, 19.* ***Everett*** *a-10, 14, 22, 25, 28; c-14, 21-23.* ***Hartley*** *a-12.* ***Heath*** *a-8, 11, 24; c-13, 20, 26.* ***Lawrence*** *a-23; 27(Captain America).* ***Maneely*** *a-24; c-10, 15.* ***Mac Pakula*** *a-15, 25.* ***Post*** *a-23.* ***Powell*** *a-27(Sub-Mariner).* ***Reinman*** *a-11, 12, 16.* ***Robinson*** *c-19.* ***Romita*** *a-22.* ***Sale*** *a-12.* ***Shores*** *c-25.* ***Sinnott*** *a-13, 21.* ***Tuska*** *a-24. Adventure-#4-8; War-#9-20; Weird/Horror-#21-26.*

MENZ INSANA
DC Comics (Vertigo): 1997 ($7.95, one-shot)
nn-Fowler-s/Bolton painted art 1 2 3 5 6 8

MEPHISTO VS... (See Silver Surfer #3)
Marvel Comics Group: Apr, 1987 - No. 4, July, 1987 ($1.50, mini-series)
1-4: 1-Fantastic Four; Austin-i. 2-X-Factor. 3-X-Men. 4-Avengers 3.00

MERC (See Mark Hazzard: Merc)

MERCENARIES (Based on the Pandemic video game)
Dynamite Entertainment: 2007 - No. 3, 2008 ($3.99, limited series)
1-3-Michael Turner-c; Brian Reed-s/Edgar Salazar-a 4.00

MERCHANTS OF DEATH
Acme Press (Eclipse): Jul, 1988 - No. 4, Nov, 1988 ($3.50, B&W/16 pgs. color, 44 pg. mag.)
1-4: 4-Toth-c 4.00

MERCY THOMPSON: HOMECOMING (Patricia Briggs'...)
Dabel Brothers Prods.: Oct, 2008 (Nov. on-c) - No. 4 ($3.99, limited series)
1-Characters from the Patricia Briggs werewolf novels; Francis Tsai-a 4.00

MERIDIAN
CrossGeneration Comics: Jul, 2000 - No. 44, Apr, 2004 ($2.95)
1-44: Barbara Kesel-s 3.00
Flying Solo Vol. 1 TPB (2001, $19.95) r/#1-7; cover by Steve Rude 20.00
Going to Ground Vol. 2 TPB (2002, $19.95) r/#8-14 20.00
Taking the Skies Vol. 3 TPB (2002, $15.95) r/#15-20 16.00
Vol. 4: Coming Home (12/02, $15.95) r/#21-26 16.00
Vol. 5: Minister of Cadador (7/03, $15.95) r/#27-32 16.00
Vol. 6: Changing Course (1/04, $15.95) r/#33-38 16.00
Traveler Vol. 1-4 ($9.95): Digest-size reprints of TPBs 10.00

MERLIN JONES AS THE MONKEY'S UNCLE (See Movie Comics and The Misadventures of... under Movie Comics)

MERRILL'S MARAUDERS (See Movie Classics)

MERRY CHRISTMAS (See A Christmas Adventure, Donald Duck..., Dell Giant #39, & March of Comics #153 in the Promotional Comics section)

MERRY COMICS
Carlton Publishing Co.: Dec, 1945 (10¢)
nn-Boogeyman app. 20 40 60 114 182 250

MERRY COMICS: Four Star Publications: 1947 (Advertised, not published)

MERRY-GO-ROUND COMICS
LaSalle Publ. Co./Croyden Publ./Rotary Litho.: 1944 (25¢, 132 pgs.); 1946; 9-10/47 - No. 2, 1948

Metallix #1 © Michelinie & Layton

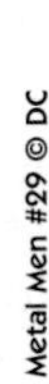

Metal Men #29 © DC

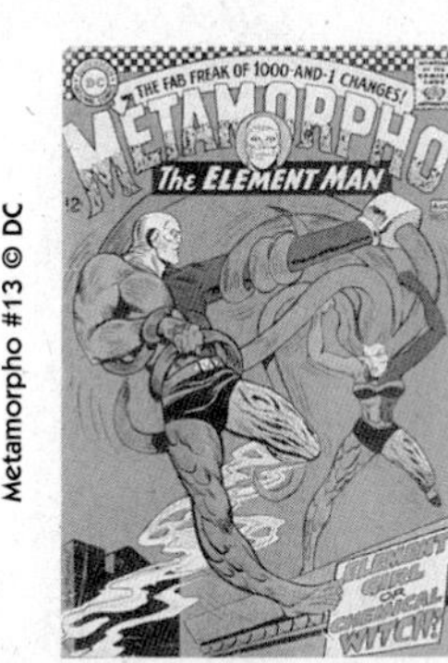
Metamorpho #13 © DC

	GD 2.0	VG 4.0	FN 6.0	VF 8.0	VF/NM 9.0	NM- 9.2
nn(1944)(LaSalle)-Funny animal; 29 new features	18	36	54	105	165	225
21 (Publisher?)	9	18	27	47	61	75
1(1946)(Croyden)-Al Fago-c; funny animal	11	22	33	60	83	105
V1#1,2(1947-48; 52 pgs.)(Rotary Litho. Co. Ltd., Canada); Ken Hultgren-a	9	18	27	47	61	75

MERRY MAILMAN (See Fawcett's Funny Animals #87-89)

MERRY MOUSE (Also see Funny Tunes & Space Comics)
Avon Periodicals: June, 1953 - No. 4, Jan-Feb, 1954

	GD 2.0	VG 4.0	FN 6.0	VF 8.0	VF/NM 9.0	NM- 9.2
1-1st app.; funny animal; Frank Carin-c/a	10	20	30	54	72	90
2-4	7	14	21	35	43	50

MERV PUMPKINHEAD, AGENT OF D.R.E.A.M. (See The Sandman)
DC Comics (Vertigo): 2000 ($5.95, one-shot)

1-Buckingham-a(p); Nowlan painted-c 6.00

META-4
First Comics: Feb, 1991 - No. 4, 1991 ($2.25)

1-($3.95, 52pgs.) 4.00
2-4 3.00

METAL GEAR SOLID (Based on the video game)
IDW Publ.: Sept, 2004 - No. 12, Aug, 2005 ($3.99)

1-12: 1-Two covers; Ashley Wood-a/Kris Oprisko-s 4.00
1-Retailer edition with foil cover 15.00

METAL GEAR SOLID: SONS OF LIBERTY
IDW Publ.: Sept, 2005 - No. 12, Sept, 2007 ($3.99)

#0 (9/05) profile pages on characters; Ashley Wood-a 4.00
1-12: 1-Two covers; Ashley Wood-a/Alex Garner-s 4.00

METALLIX
Future Comics: Dec, 2002 - No. 6, June, 2003 ($3.50)

0-6-Ron Lim-a. 0-(6/03) Origin. 1-Layton-c 3.50
1-Collector's Edition with variant cover by Lim 3.50
1-Free Comic Book Day Edition (4/03) Layton-c 3.00

METAL MEN (See Brave & the Bold, DC Comics Presents, and Showcase #37-40)
National Periodical Publications/DC Comics: 4-5/63 - No. 41, 12-1/69-70; No. 42, 2-3/73 - No. 44, 7-8/73; No. 45, 4-5/76 - No. 56, 2-3/78

	GD 2.0	VG 4.0	FN 6.0	VF 8.0	VF/NM 9.0	NM- 9.2
1-(4-5/63)-5th app. Metal Men	52	104	156	421	911	1400
2	21	42	63	142	304	465
3-5	13	26	39	90	195	300
6-10	10	20	30	66	121	175
11-20: 12-Beatles cameo (2-3/65)	8	16	24	53	89	125
21-Batman, Robin & Flash x-over	6	12	18	42	69	95
22-26,28-30	6	12	18	39	62	85
27-Origin Metal Men retold	7	14	21	49	82	115
31-41(1968-70): 38-Last 12¢ issue. 41-Last 15¢	5	10	15	34	55	75
42-44(1973)-Reprints	2	4	6	10	14	18
45('76)-49-Simonson-a in all: 48,49-Re-intro Eclipso	2	4	6	10	14	18
50-56: 50-Part-r. 54,55-Green Lantern x-over	2	4	6	9	12	15

NOTE: ***Andru/Esposito** c-1-30. **Aparo** c-53-56. **Giordano** c-45, 46. **Kane/Esposito** a-30, 31; c-31. **Simonson** a-45-49; c-47-52. **Staton** a-50-56.*

METAL MEN (Also see Tangent Comics/ Metal Men)
DC Comics: Oct, 1993 - No. 4, Jan, 1994 ($1.25, mini-series)

1-($2.50)-Multi-colored foil-c 4.00
2-4: 2-Origin 3.00

METAL MEN (Also see 52)
DC Comics: Oct, 2007 - No. 8, Jul, 2008 ($2.99, limited series)

1-8-Duncan Rouleau-s/a; origin re-told. 3-Chemo returns 3.00
HC (2008, $24.99, dustjacket) r/#1-8; cover gallery and sketch pages 25.00
SC (2009, $14.99) r/#1-8; cover gallery and sketch pages 15.00

METAMORPHO (See Action Comics #413, Brave & the Bold #57,58, 1st Issue Special, & World's Finest #217)
National Periodical Publications: July-Aug, 1965 - No. 17, Mar-Apr, 1968 (All 12¢ issues)

	GD 2.0	VG 4.0	FN 6.0	VF 8.0	VF/NM 9.0	NM- 9.2
1-(7-8/65)-3rd app. Metamorpho	12	24	36	83	172	260
2,3	8	16	24	51	86	120
4-6,10:10-Origin & 1st app. Element Girl (1-2/67)	6	12	18	42	69	95
7-9	6	12	18	37	59	80
11-17: 17-Sparling-c/a	5	10	15	32	51	70

NOTE: ***Ramona Fradon** a-B&B 57, 58, 1-4. **Orlando** a-5, 6; c-5-9, 11. **Trapani** a(p)-7-16; i-16.*

METAMORPHO
DC Comics: Aug, 1993 - No. 4, Nov, 1993 ($1.50, mini-series)

1-4 3.00

METAMORPHO: YEAR ONE
DC Comics: Early Dec, 2007 - No. 6, Late Feb, 2008 ($2.99, limited series)

1-6-Origin re-told; Jurgens-s/Jurgens & Delperdang-a/Nowlan-c. 6-Justice League app. 3.00
TPB ('08, $14.99) r/#1-6 15.00

METAPHYSIQUE
Malibu Comics (Bravura): Apr, 1995 - No. 6, Oct, 1995 ($2.95, limited series)

1-6: Norm Breyfogle-c/a/scripts 3.00

METEOR COMICS
L. L. Baird (Croyden): Nov, 1945

	GD 2.0	VG 4.0	FN 6.0	VF 8.0	VF/NM 9.0	NM- 9.2
1-Captain Wizard, Impossible Man, Race Wilkins app.; origin Baldy Bean, Capt. Wizard's sidekick; bare-breasted mermaids story	40	80	120	246	411	575

METEOR MAN
Marvel Comics: Aug, 1993 - No. 6, Jan, 1994 ($1.25, limited series)

1-6: 1-Regular unbagged. 4-Night Thrasher-c/story. 6-Terry Austin-c(i) 3.00
1-Polybagged w/button & rap newspaper 4.00
...: The Movie (4/93 [7/93 on cover], $2.25) movie adaptation 3.00

METROPOL (See Ted McKeever's...)

METROPOL A.D. (See Ted McKeever's...)

METROPOLIS S.C.U. (Also see Showcase '96 #1)
DC Comics: Nov, 1995 - No. 4, Feb, 1996 ($1.50, limited series)

1-4:1-Superman-c & app. 3.00

MEZZ: GALACTIC TOUR 2494 (Also See Nexus)
Dark Horse Comics: May, 1994 ($2.50, one-shot)

1 3.00

MGM'S MARVELOUS WIZARD OF OZ (See Marvel Treasury of Oz)
Marvel Comics Group/National Periodical Publications: 1975 ($1.50, 84 pgs.; oversize)

	GD 2.0	VG 4.0	FN 6.0	VF 8.0	VF/NM 9.0	NM- 9.2
1-Adaptation of MGM's movie; J. Buscema-a	3	6	9	16	23	30

M.G.M'S MOUSE MUSKETEERS (Formerly M.G.M.'s The Two Mouseketeers)
Dell Publishing Co.: No. 670, Jan, 1956 - No. 1290, Mar-May, 1962

	GD 2.0	VG 4.0	FN 6.0	VF 8.0	VF/NM 9.0	NM- 9.2
Four Color 670 (#4)	5	10	15	35	55	75
Four Color 711,728,764	4	8	12	26	41	55
8 (4-6/57) - 21 (3-5/60)	4	8	12	24	37	50
Four Color 1135,1175,1290	4	8	12	24	37	50

M.G.M.'S SPIKE AND TYKE (also see Tom & Jerry #79)
Dell Publishing Co.: No. 499, Sept, 1953 - No. 1266, Dec-Feb, 1961-62

	GD 2.0	VG 4.0	FN 6.0	VF 8.0	VF/NM 9.0	NM- 9.2
Four Color 499 (#1)	7	14	21	44	72	100
Four Color 577,638	5	10	15	30	48	65
4(12-2/55-56)-10	4	8	12	26	41	55
11-24(12-2/60-61)	4	8	12	22	34	45
Four Color 1266	4	8	12	24	37	50

M.G.M.'S THE TWO MOUSKETEERS
Dell Publishing Co.: No. 475, June, 1953 - No. 642, July, 1955

	GD 2.0	VG 4.0	FN 6.0	VF 8.0	VF/NM 9.0	NM- 9.2
Four Color 475 (#1)	8	16	24	51	86	120
Four Color 603 (11/54), 642	6	12	18	37	59	80

MICE TEMPLAR, THE
Image Comics: Sept, 2007 - No. 6, Oct, 2008 ($3.99/$2.99)

1-($3.99)-Bryan Glass-s/Michael Avon Oeming-a/c 4.00
2-6-($2.99) 3.00

MICE TEMPLAR, THE , VOLUME 2: DESTINY
Image Comics: July, 2009 - No. 9, May, 2010 ($3.99/$2.99/$4.99)

1,2-($3.99) 1-Bryan Glass-s/Oeming & Santos-a; 2 covers. 2-Santos-a 4.00
3-8-($2.99)-Santos-a; 2 covers by Oeming & Santos 3.00
9-($4.99) 5.00

MICE TEMPLAR, THE , VOLUME 3: A MIDWINTER NIGHT'S DREAM
Image Comics: Dec, 2010 - No. 8, Mar, 2012 ($3.99/$2.99)

1,8-($3.99) 1-Bryan Glass-s/Oeming & Santos-a; 2 covers 4.00
2-7-($2.99)-Santos-a; 2 covers by Oeming & Santos 3.00

MICHAELANGELO CHRISTMAS SPECIAL (See Teenage Mutant Ninja Turtles Christmas Special)

MICHAELANGELO, TEENAGE MUTANT NINJA TURTLE
Mirage Studios: 1986 (One shot) ($1.50, B&W)

	GD 2.0	VG 4.0	FN 6.0	VF 8.0	VF/NM 9.0	NM- 9.2
1-Christmas-c/story	1	3	4	6	8	10
1-2nd printing ('89, $1.75)-Reprint plus new-a						4.00

MICHAEL CHABON PRESENTS THE AMAZING ADVENTURES OF THE ESCAPIST

Michael Chabon Presents The Escapist #3 © Michael Chabon

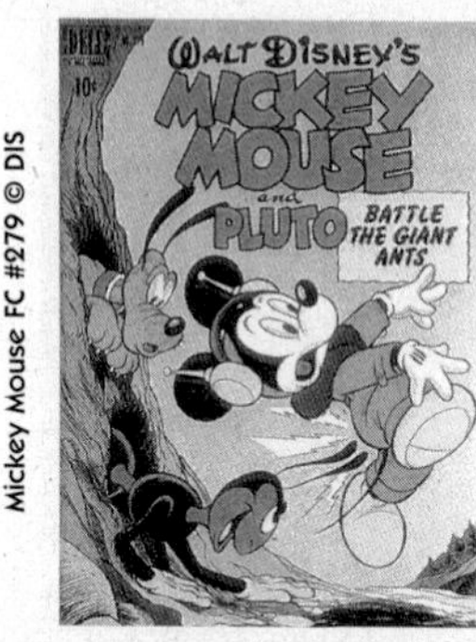

Mickey Mouse FC #279 © DIS

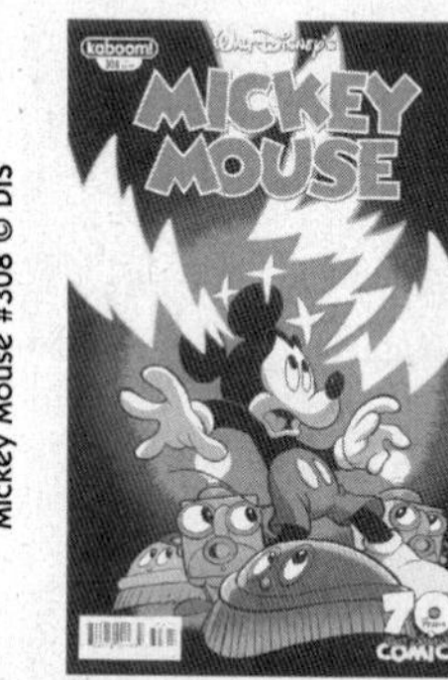

Mickey Mouse #308 © DIS

Dark Horse Comics: Feb, 2004 - Present ($8.95, squarebound)

	GD 2.0	VG 4.0	FN 6.0	VF 8.0	VF/NM 9.0	NM- 9.2
1-5,7,8-Short stories by Chabon and various incl. Chaykin, Starlin, Brereton, Baker						9.00
6-Includes 6 pg. Spirit & Escapist story (Will Eisner's last work); Spirit on cover						9.00
... Vol. 1 (5/04, $17.95, digest-size) r/#1&2; wraparound-c by Chris Ware						18.00
... Vol. 2 (11/04, $17.95, digest-size) r/#3&4; wraparound-c by Matt Kindt						18.00
... Vol. 3 (4/06, $14.95, digest-size) r/#5&6; Tim Sale-c						15.00

MICHAEL MOORCOCK'S ELRIC: THE MAKING OF A SORCEROR
DC Comics: 2004 - No. 4, 2006 ($5.95, prestige format, limited series)

	GD 2.0	VG 4.0	FN 6.0	VF 8.0	VF/NM 9.0	NM- 9.2
1-4-Moorcock-s/Simonson-a						6.00
TPB (2007, $19.99) r/#1-4						20.00

MICHAEL MOORCOCK'S MULTIVERSE
DC Comics (Helix): Nov, 1997 - No. 12, Oct, 1998 ($2.50, limited series)

	GD 2.0	VG 4.0	FN 6.0	VF 8.0	VF/NM 9.0	NM- 9.2
1-12: Simonson, Reeve & Ridgway-a						3.00
TPB (1999, $19.95) r/#1-12						20.00

MICHAEL TURNER, A TRIBUTE TO...
Aspen MLT: 2008 ($8.99, squarebound)

	GD 2.0	VG 4.0	FN 6.0	VF 8.0	VF/NM 9.0	NM- 9.2
nn-Pin-ups and tributes from Turner's colleagues and friends; Turner & Ross-c						9.00

MICHAEL TURNER PRESENTS: ASPEN (See Aspen)

MICKEY AND DONALD (See Walt Disney's...)

MICKEY AND DONALD IN VACATIONLAND (See Dell Giant No. 47)

MICKEY & THE BEANSTALK (See Story Hour Series)

MICKEY & THE SLEUTH (See Walt Disney Showcase #38, 39, 42)

MICKEY FINN (Also see Big Shot Comics #74 & Feature Funnies)
Eastern Color 1-4/McNaught Synd. #5 on (Columbia)/Headline V3#2:
Nov?, 1942 - V3#2, May, 1952

	GD 2.0	VG 4.0	FN 6.0	VF 8.0	VF/NM 9.0	NM- 9.2
1	30	60	90	177	289	400
2	15	30	45	90	140	190
3-Charlie Chan story	12	24	36	69	97	125
4	10	20	30	56	76	95
5-10	9	18	27	47	61	75
11-15(1949): 12-Sparky Watts app.	8	16	24	40	50	60
V3#1,2(1952)	6	12	18	31	38	45

MICKEY MALONE
Hale Nass Corp.: 1936 (Color, punchout-c) (B&W-a on back)

	GD 2.0	VG 4.0	FN 6.0	VF 8.0	VF/NM 9.0	NM- 9.2
nn - 1pg. of comics	200	400	800	-	-	-

MICKEY MANTLE (See Baseball's Greatest Heroes #1)

MICKEY MOUSE (See Adventures of Mickey Mouse, The Best of Walt Disney Comics, Cheerios giveaways, Donald and ..., Dynabrite Comics, 40 Big Pages..., Gladstone Comic Album, Merry Christmas From..., Walt Disney's Mickey and Donald, Walt Disney's Comics & Stories, Walt Disney's..., & Wheaties)

MICKEY MOUSE (...Secret Agent #107-109; Walt Disney's... #148-205?)
(See Dell Giants for annuals) (#204 exists from both G.K. & Whitman)
Dell Publ. Co./Gold Key #85-204/Whitman #204-218/Gladstone #219 on:
#16, 1941 - #84, 7-9/62; #85, 11/62 - #218, 6/84; #219, 10/86 - #256, 4/90

	GD 2.0	VG 4.0	FN 6.0	VF 8.0	VF/NM 9.0	NM- 9.2
Four Color 16(1941)-1st Mickey Mouse comic book; "...vs. the Phantom Blot" by Gottfredson	1250	2500	3750	16,500	-	-
Four Color 27(1943)- "7 Colored Terror"	73	146	219	591	1283	1975
Four Color 79(1945)-By Carl Barks (1 story)	89	178	267	721	1561	2400
Four Color 116(1946)	24	48	72	168	359	550
Four Color 141,157(1947)	21	42	63	142	304	465
Four Color 170,181,194('48)	17	34	51	119	260	400
Four Color 214('49),231,248,261	13	26	39	90	195	300
Four Color 268-Reprints/WDC&S #22-24 by Gottfredson ("Surprise Visitor")	13	26	39	85	180	275
Four Color 279,286,296	11	22	33	73	142	210
Four Color 304,313(#1),325(#2),334	10	20	30	68	127	185
Four Color 343,352,362,371,387	9	18	27	61	106	150
Four Color 401,411,427(10-11/52)	8	16	24	51	86	120
Four Color 819-Mickey Mouse in Magicland	6	12	18	39	62	85
Four Color 1057,1151,1246(1959-61)-Album; #1057 has 10¢ & 12¢ editions; back covers are different	5	10	15	35	55	75
28(12-1/52-53)-32,34	7	14	21	46	76	105
33-(Exists with 2 dates, 10-11/53 & 12-1/54)	7	14	21	46	76	105
35-50	6	12	18	41	66	90
51-73,75-80	5	10	15	35	55	75
74-Story swipe "The Rare Stamp Search" from 4-Color #422- "The Gilded Man"	6	12	18	37	59	80
81-105: 93,95-titled "Mickey Mouse Club Album". 100-105: Reprint 4-Color #427,194,279, 170,343,214 in that order	4	8	12	26	41	55
106-120	3	6	9	20	30	40
121-130	3	6	9	16	23	30
131-146	3	6	9	14	20	25
147,148: 147-Reprints "The Phantom Fires" from WDC&S #200-202.148-Reprints "The Mystery of Lonely Valley" from WDC&S #208-210	3	6	9	14	20	25
149-158	2	4	6	10	14	18
159-Reprints "The Sunken City" from WDC&S #205-207	2	4	6	10	14	18
160-178: 162-165,167-170-r	2	4	6	10	14	18
179-(52 pgs.)	2	4	6	11	16	20
180-203: 200-r/Four Color #371	2	4	6	8	10	12
204-(Whitman or G.K.), 205,206	2	4	6	9	13	16
207(8/80), 209(pre-pack?)	5	10	15	30	48	65
208-(8-12/80)-Only distr. in Whitman 3-pack	10	20	30	66	121	175
210(2/81),211-214	2	4	6	9	13	16
215-218: 215(2/82), 216(4/82), 217(3/84), 218(misdated 8/82; actual date 7/84)	2	4	6	10	14	18
219-1st Gladstone issue; The Seven Ghosts serial-r begins by Gottfredson	2	4	6	11	16	20
220,221	2	3	4	6	8	10
222-225: 222-Editor-in Grief strip-r						5.00
226-230						5.00
231-243,246-254: 240-r/March of Comics #27. 245-r/F.C. #279. 250-r/F.C. #248						4.00
244 (1/89, $2.95, 100 pgs.)-Squarebound 60th anniversary issue; gives history of Mickey						5.00
245, 256: 245-r/F.C. #279. 256-$1.95, 68 pgs.						5.00
255 ($1.95, 68 pgs.)						5.00

NOTE: *Reprints #195-197, 198(2/3), 199(1/3), 200-208, 211(1/2), 212, 213, 215(1/3), 216-on.* ***Gottfredson*** *Mickey Mouse serials in #219-239, 241-244, 246-249, 251-253, 255.*

	GD 2.0	VG 4.0	FN 6.0	VF 8.0	VF/NM 9.0	NM- 9.2
Album 01-518-210(Dell), 1(10082-309)(9/63-Gold Key)	4	8	12	22	34	45
...Club 1(1/64-Gold Key)(TV)	4	8	12	23	36	48
Mini Comic 1(1976)(3-1/4x6-1/2")-Reprints 158	1	2	3	5	6	8
Surprise Party 1(30037-901, G.K.)(1/69)-40th Anniversary (see Walt Disney Showcase #47)	3	6	9	21	32	42
Surprise Party 1(1979)-r/1969 issue	1	2	3	5	6	8

MICKEY MOUSE (Continued from Mickey Mouse and Friends)
BOOM! Studios: No. 304, Jan, 2011 - No. 309, Jun, 2011 ($3.99)

	GD 2.0	VG 4.0	FN 6.0	VF 8.0	VF/NM 9.0	NM- 9.2
304-309: 304-Peg-Leg Pete app. 309-Continues in Walt Disney's C&S #720						4.00

MICKEY MOUSE ADVENTURES
Disney Comics: June, 1990 - No. 18, Nov, 1991 ($1.50)

	GD 2.0	VG 4.0	FN 6.0	VF 8.0	VF/NM 9.0	NM- 9.2
1,8,9: 1-Bradbury, Murry-r/M.M. #45,73 plus new-a. 8-Byrne-c. 9-Fantasia 50th ann. issue w/new adapt. of movie						4.00
2-7,10-18: 2-Begin all new stories. 10-r/F.C. #214						3.00

MICKEY MOUSE AND FRIENDS (Continued from Walt Disney's Mickey Mouse and Friends)
(Title continues as Mickey Mouse #304-on)
BOOM! Studios: No. 296, Sept, 2009 - No. 303, Dec, 2010 ($2.99/$3.99)

	GD 2.0	VG 4.0	FN 6.0	VF 8.0	VF/NM 9.0	NM- 9.2
296-299,301-303: 296-299-Wizards of Mickey stories. 301-Conclusion to story in #300						3.00
300-($3.99, 9/10) Petrucha-s/Pelaez-a; back-up Tanglefoot story w/Gottfredson-a						4.00
300 Deluxe Edition ($6.99) Variant cover by Daan Jippes						7.00

MICKEY MOUSE CLUB FUN BOOK
Golden Press: 1977 (1.95, 228 pgs.)(square bound)

	GD 2.0	VG 4.0	FN 6.0	VF 8.0	VF/NM 9.0	NM- 9.2
11190-1950s-r; 20,000 Leagues, M. Mouse Silly Symphonys, The Reluctant Dragon, etc.	4	8	12	28	44	60

MICKEY MOUSE CLUB MAGAZINE (See Walt Disney...)

MICKEY MOUSE COMICS DIGEST
Gladstone: 1986 - No. 5, 1987 (96 pgs.)

	GD 2.0	VG 4.0	FN 6.0	VF 8.0	VF/NM 9.0	NM- 9.2
1 ($1.25-c)	1	2	3	5	6	8
2-5: 3-5 ($1.50-c)						5.00

MICKEY MOUSE IN COLOR
Another Rainbow/Pantheon: 1988 (Deluxe, 13"x17", hard-c, $250.00)
(Trade, 9-7/8"x11-1/2", hard-c, $39.95)

	GD 2.0	VG 4.0	FN 6.0	VF 8.0	VF/NM 9.0	NM- 9.2
Deluxe limited edition of 3,000 copies signed by Floyd Gottfredson and Carl Barks, designated as the "Official Mickey Mouse 60th Anniversary" book. Mickey Sunday and daily reprints, plus Barks "Riddle of the Red Hat" from Four Color #79. Comes with 45 r.p.m. record interview with Gottfredson and Barks. 240 pgs.	13	26	39	85	180	275
Deluxe, limited to 100 copies, as above, but with a unique colored pencil original drawing of Mickey Mouse by Carl Barks.						800.00
Pantheon trade edition, edited down & without Barks, 192 pgs.	3	6	9	20	30	40

MICKEY MOUSE MAGAZINE (Becomes Walt Disney's Comics & Stories)(Also see 40 Big

Mickey Mouse Magazine #1 © DIS

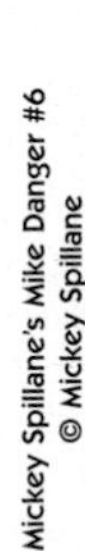
Mickey Spillane's Mike Danger #6 © Mickey Spillane

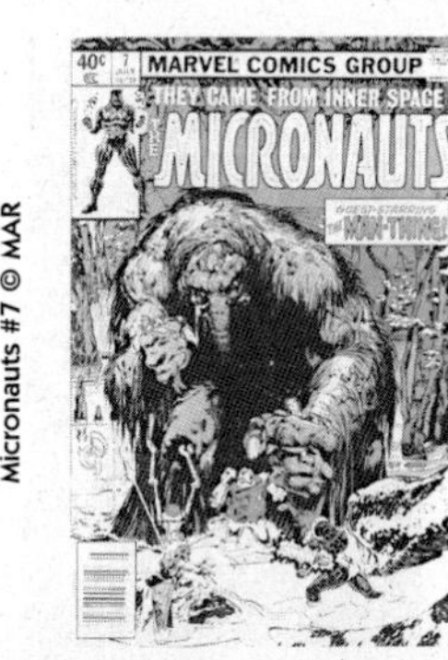

Micronauts #7 © MAR

GD 2.0 | VG 4.0 | FN 6.0 | VF 8.0 | VF/NM 9.0 | NM- 9.2

Pages of Mickey Mouse)
K. K. Publ./Western Publishing Co.: Summer, 1935 (June-Aug, indicia) - V5#12, Sept, 1940; V1#1-5, V3#11,12, V4#1-3 are 44 pgs; V2#3-100 pgs; V5#12-68 pgs; rest are 36 pgs.(No V3#1, V4#6)

V1#1 (Large size, 13-1/4x10-1/4"; 25¢)-Contains puzzles, games, cels, stories & comics of Disney characters. Promotional magazine for Disney cartoon movies and paraphernalia 1425 2850 4275 9200 19,000 -

Note: *Some copies were autographed by the editors & given away with all early one year subscriptions.*

2 (Size change, 11-1/2x8-1/2"; 10/35; 10¢)-High quality paper begins; Messmer-a 282 564 846 2400 - -
3,4: 3-Messmer-a 153 306 459 1300 - -
5-1st Donald Duck solo-c; 2nd cover app. ever; last 44 pg. & high quality paper issue 271 542 813 2300 - -
6-9: 6-36 pg. issues begin; Donald becomes editor. 8-2nd Donald solo-c. 9-1st Mickey/Minnie-c 141 282 423 1200 - -
10-12, V2#1,2: 11-1st Pluto/Mickey-c; Donald fires himself and appoints Mickey as editor 135 270 405 1150 - -
V2#3-Special 100 pg. Christmas issue (25¢); Messmer-a; Donald becomes editor of Wise Quacks 447 894 1341 3800 - -
4-Mickey Mouse Comics & Roy Ranger (adventure strip) begin; both end V2#9; Messmer-a 115 230 345 975 - -
5-9: 5-Ted True (adventure strip, ends V2#9) & Silly Symphony Comics (ends V3#3) begin. 6-1st solo Minnie-c. 6-9-Mickey Mouse Movies cut-out in each 54 108 162 343 584 825
10-1st full color issue; Mickey Mouse (by Gottfredson; ends V3#12) & Silly Symphony (ends V3#3) full color Sunday-r, Peter The Farm Detective (ends V5#8) & Ole Of The North (ends V3#3) begins 81 162 243 518 884 1250
11-13: 12-Hiawatha-c & feature story 53 106 159 334 567 800
V3#2-Big Bad Wolf Halloween-c 60 120 180 381 653 925
3 (12/37)-1st app. Snow White & The Seven Dwarfs (before release of movie) (possibly 1st in print); Mickey X-Mas-c 107 214 321 680 1165 1650
4 (1/38)-Snow White & The Seven Dwarfs serial begins (on stands before release of movie); Ducky Symphony (ends V3#11) begins 89 178 267 565 970 1375
5-1st Snow White & Seven Dwarfs-c (St. Valentine's Day) 107 214 321 680 1165 1650
6-Snow White serial ends; Lonesome Ghosts app. (2 pp.) 60 120 180 381 658 935
7-Seven Dwarfs Easter-c 56 112 168 355 615 875
8-10: 9-Dopey-c. 10-1st solo Goofy-c 48 96 144 302 514 725
11,12 (44 pgs; 8 more pgs. color added). 11-Mickey the Sheriff serial (ends V4#3) & Donald Duck strip-r (ends V3#12) begin. Color feature on Snow White's Forest Friends 52 104 156 328 552 775
V4#1 (10/38; 44 pgs.)-Brave Little Tailor-c/feature story, nominated for Academy Award; Bobby & Chip by Otto Messmer (ends V4#2) & The Practical Pig (ends V4#2) begin 52 104 156 328 552 775
2 (44 pgs.)-1st Huey, Dewey & Louie-c 53 106 159 334 567 800
3 (12/38, 44 pgs.)-Ferdinand The Bull-c/feature story, Academy Award winner; Mickey Mouse & The Whalers serial begins, ends V4#12 52 104 156 328 552 775
4-Spotty, Mother Pluto strip-r begin, end V4#8 48 96 144 302 514 725
5-St. Valentine's day-c. 1st Pluto solo-c 54 108 162 343 584 825
7 (3/39)-The Ugly Duckling-c/feature story, Academy Award winner 52 104 156 328 552 775
7 (4/39)-Goofy & Wilbur The Grasshopper classic-c/feature story from 1st Goofy solo cartoon movie; Timid Elmer begins, ends V5#5 52 104 156 328 552 775
8-Big Bad Wolf-c from Practical Pig movie poster; Practical Pig feature story 52 104 156 328 552 775
9-Donald Duck & Mickey Mouse Sunday-r begin; The Pointer feature story, nominated for Academy Award 52 104 156 328 552 775
10-Classic July 4th drum & fife-c; last Donald Sunday-r 62 124 186 394 680 965
11-1st slick-c; last over-sized issue 48 96 144 302 514 725
12 (9/39; format change, 10-1/4x8-1/4")-1st full color, cover to cover issue; Donald's Penguin-c/feature story 55 110 165 352 601 850
V5#1-Black Pete-c; Officer Duck-c/feature story; Autograph Hound feature story; Robinson Crusoe serial begins 54 108 162 346 591 835
2-Goofy-c; 1st brief app. Pinocchio 71 142 213 454 777 1100
3 (12/39)-Pinocchio Christmas-c (Before movie release). 1st app. Jiminy Cricket; Pinocchio serial begins 84 168 252 538 919 1300
4,5: 5-Jiminy Cricket-c; Pinocchio serial ends; Donald's Dog Laundry feature story 56 112 168 348 594 840

GD 2.0 | VG 4.0 | FN 6.0 | VF 8.0 | VF/NM 9.0 | NM- 9.2

6,7: 6-Tugboat Mickey feature story; Rip Van Winkle feature begins, ends V5#8. 7-2nd Huey, Dewey & Louie-c 54 108 162 336 573 810
8-Last magazine size issue; 2nd solo Pluto-c; Figaro & Cleo feature story 56 112 168 348 594 840
9-11: 9 (6/40; change to comic book size)-Jiminy Cricket feature story; Donald-c & Sunday-r begin. 10-Special Independence Day issue. 11-Hawaiian Holiday & Mickey's Trailer feature stories; last 36 pg. issue 60 120 180 381 653 925
12 (Format change)-The transition issue (68 pgs.) becoming a comic book. With only a title change to follow, becomes Walt Disney's Comics & Stories #1 with the next issue 465 930 1395 3395 5998 8600

NOTE: ***Otto Messmer**-a is in many issues of the first two-three years. The following story titles and issues have gags created by **Carl Barks**: V4#3(12/38)-'Donald's Better Self' & 'Donald's Golf Game;' V4#4(1/39)-'Donald's Lucky Day;' V4#7(3/39)-'Hockey Champ;' V4#7(4/39)-'Donald's Cousin Gus;' V4#9(6/39)-'Sea Scouts;' V4#12(9/39)-'Donald's Penguin;' V5#9 (6/40)-'Donald's Vacation;' V5#10(7/40)-'Bone Trouble;' V5#12(9/40)-'Window Cleaners.'*

MICKEY MOUSE MAGAZINE (Russian Version)
May 16, 1991 (1st Russian printing of a modern comic book)
1-Bagged w/gold label commemoration in English 10.00

MICKEY MOUSE MARCH OF COMICS (See March of Comics #8,27,45,60,74)

MICKEY MOUSE'S SUMMER VACATION (See Story Hour Series)

MICKEY MOUSE SUMMER FUN (See Dell Giants)

MICKEY SPILLANE'S MIKE DANGER
Tekno Comix: Sept, 1995 - No. 11, May, 1996 ($1.95)
1-11: 1-Frank Miller-c. 7-polybagged; Simonson-c. 8,9-Simonson-c 3.00

MICKEY SPILLANE'S MIKE DANGER
Big Entertainment: V2#1, June, 1996 - No. 10, Apr, 1997 ($2.25)
V2#1-10: Max Allan Collins scripts 3.00

MICKEY'S TWICE UPON A CHRISTMAS (Disney)
Gemstone Publishing: 2004 ($3.95, square-bound, one-shot)
nn-Christmas short stories with Mickey, Minnie, Donald, Uncle Scrooge, Goofy and others 4.00

MICROBOTS, THE
Gold Key: Dec, 1971 (one-shot)
1 (10271-112) 3 6 9 16 22 28

MICRONAUTS (Toys)
Marvel Comics Group: Jan, 1979 - No. 59, Aug, 1984 (Mando paper #53 on)
1-Intro/1st app. Baron Karza 1 2 3 5 7 9
2-10,35,37,57: 7-Man-Thing app. 8-1st app. Capt. Universe (8/79). 9-1st app. Cilicia. 35-Double size; origin Microverse; intro Death Squad; Dr. Strange app. 37-Nightcrawler app.; X-Men cameo (2 pgs.). 57-(52 pgs.) 5.00
11-34,36,38-56,58,59: 13-1st app. Jasmine. 15-Death of Microtron. 15-17-Fantastic Four app. 17-Death of Jasmine. 20-Ant-Man app. 21-Microverse series begins. 25-Origin Baron Karza. 25-29-Nick Fury app. 27-Death of Biotron. 34-Dr. Strange app. 38-First direct sale. 40-Fantastic Four app. 48-Early Guice-a begins. 59-Golden painted-c 4.00
nn-Blank UPC; diamond on top 3.00
Annual 1,2 (12/79,10/80)-Ditko-c/a 5.00

NOTE: *#38-on distributed only through comic shops. **N. Adams** c-7i. **Chaykin** a-13-18p. **Ditko** a-39p. **Giffen** a-36p, 37p(part). **Golden** a-1-12p; c-2-7p, 8-23, 24p, 38, 39, 59. **Guice** a-48-58p; c-49-58. **Gil Kane** a-38, 40-45p; c-40-45. **Layton** c-33-37. **Miller** c-31.*

MICRONAUTS (Micronauts: The New Voyages on cover)
Marvel Comics Group: Oct, 1984 - No. 20, May, 1986
V2#1-20 3.00

NOTE: ***Kelley Jones** a-1; c-1, 6. **Guice** a-4p; c-2p.*

MICRONAUTS
Image Comics: 2002 - No. 11, Sept, 2003 ($2.95)
2002 Convention Special (no cover price, B&W) previews series 3.00
1-11: 1-3-Hanson-a; Dave Johnson-c. 4-Su-a; 2 covers by Linsner & Hanson 3.00
...Vol. 1: Revolution (2003, $12.95, digest size) r/#1-5 13.00

MICRONAUTS (Volume 2)
Devil's Due Publishing: Mar, 2004 - No. 3, May, 2004 ($2.95)
1-3-Jolley-s/Broderick-a 3.00

MICRONAUTS: KARZA
Image Comics: Feb, 2003 - No. 4, May, 2003 ($2.95)
1-4-Krueger-s/Kurth-a 3.00

MICRONAUTS SPECIAL EDITION
Marvel Comics Group: Dec, 1983 - No. 5, Apr, 1984 ($2.00, limited series, Baxter paper)
1-5: r-/original series 1-12; Guice-c(p)-all 4.00

MIDGET COMICS (Fighting Indian Stories)

Midnight Tales #5 © CC

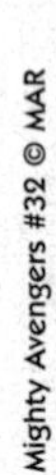

Mighty Avengers #32 © MAR

The Mighty Crusaders #10 © AP

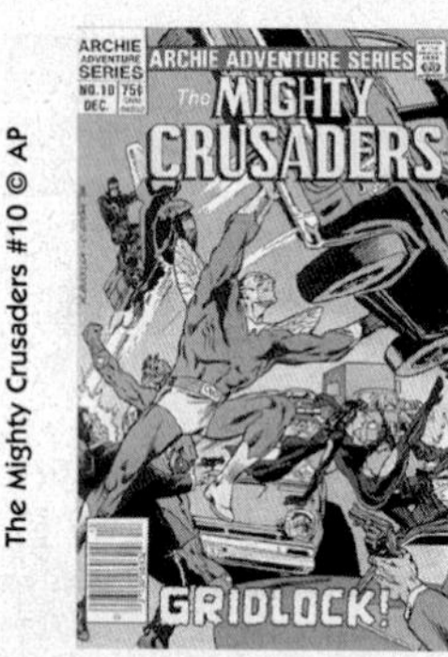

	GD 2.0	VG 4.0	FN 6.0	VF 8.0	VF/NM 9.0	NM- 9.2

St. John Publishng Co.: Feb, 1950 - No. 2, Apr, 1950 (5-3/8x7-3/8", 68 pgs.)

1-Fighting Indian Stories; Matt Baker-c	21	42	63	126	206	285
2-Tex West, Cowboy Marshal (also in #1)	12	24	36	69	97	125

MIDNIGHT (See Smash Comics #18)

MIDNIGHT
Ajax/Farrell Publ. (Four Star Comic Corp.): Apr, 1957 - No. 6, June, 1958

1-Reprints from Voodoo & Strange Fantasy with some changes	15	30	45	90	140	190
2-6	11	22	33	60	83	105

MIDNIGHTER (See The Authority)
DC Comics (WildStorm): Jan, 2007 - No. 20, Aug, 2008 ($2.99)

1-20: 1-Ennis-s/Sprouse-a/c. 6-Fabry-a. 7-Vaughan-s. 8-Gage-s. 9-Stelfreeze-a 3.00
1-4-Variant covers. 1-Michael Golden. 2-Art Adams 3-Jason Pearson. 4-Glenn Fabry 4.00
...: Anthem TPB (2008, $14.99) r/#7,10-15 15.00
...: Armageddon (12/07, $2.99) Gage-s/Coleby-a/McKone-c 3.00
...: Assassin8 TPB (2009, $14.99) r/#16-20 15.00
...: Killing Machine TPB (2008, $14.99) r/#1-6 15.00

MIDNIGHT MASS
DC Comics (Vertigo): Jun, 2002 - No. 8, Jan, 2003 ($2.50)

1-8-Rozum-s/Saiz & Palmiotti-a 3.00

MIDNIGHT MASS: HERE THERE BE MONSTERS
DC Comics (Vertigo): March, 2004 - No. 6, Aug, 2004 ($2.95, limited series)

1-6-Rozum-s/Paul Lee-a 3.00

MIDNIGHT MEN
Marvel Comics (Epic Comics/Heavy Hitters): June, 1993 - No. 4, Sept, 1993 ($2.50/$1.95, limited series)

1-($2.50)-Embossed-c; Chaykin-c/a & scripts in all 4.00
2-4 3.00

MIDNIGHT MYSTERY
American Comics Group: Jan-Feb, 1961 - No. 7, Oct, 1961

1-Sci/Fi story	8	16	24	56	96	135
2-7: 7-Gustavson-a	5	10	15	30	48	65

NOTE: *Reinman a-1, 3.* ***Whitney*** *a-1, 4-6; c-1-3, 5, 7.*

MIDNIGHT NATION
Image Comics (Top Cow): Oct, 2000 - No. 12, July, 2002 ($2.50/$2.95)

1-Straczynski-s/Frank-a; 2 covers 3.50
2-11: 9-Twin Towers cover 3.00
12-($2.95)Last issue 3.00
Wizard #1/2 (2001) Michael Zulli-a; two covers by Frank 3.00
Vol. 1 ('03, $29.99, TPB) r/#1-12 & Wizard #1/2; cover gallery; afterword by Straczynski 30.00

MIDNIGHT SONS UNLIMITED
Marvel Comics (Midnight Sons imprint #4 on): Apr, 1993 - No. 9, May, 1995 ($3.95, 68 pgs.)

1-9: Blaze, Darkhold (by Quesada #1), Ghost Rider, Morbius & Nightstalkers in all. 1-Painted-c. 3-Spider-Man app. 4-Siege of Darkness part 17; new Dr. Strange & new Ghost Rider app.; spot varnish-c 4.00
NOTE: ***Sears*** *a-2.*

MIDNIGHT TALES
Charlton Press: Dec, 1972 - No. 18, May, 1976

V1#1	3	6	9	16	23	30
2-10	2	4	6	10	14	18
11-18: 11-14-Newton-a(p)	2	4	6	8	11	14
12,17(Modern Comics reprint, 1977)						6.00

NOTE: ***Adkins*** *a-12i, 13i.* ***Ditko*** *a-12.* ***Howard*** *(Wood imitator) a-1-15, 17, 18; c-1-18.* ***Don Newton*** *a-11-14p.* ***Staton*** *a-1, 3-11, 13.* ***Sutton*** *a-3-10.*

MIGHTY, THE
DC Comics: Apr, 2009 - No. 12, Mar, 2010 ($2.99)

1-12: Tomasi & Champagne-s/Dave Johnson-c. 1-4-Snejbjerg-a. 5-12-Samnee-a 3.00
...: Volume 1 TPB (2009, $17.99) r/#1-6 18.00
...: Volume 2 TPB (2010, $17.99) r/#7-12 18.00

MIGHTY ATOM, THE (...& the Pixies #6) (Formerly The Pixies #1-5)
Magazine Enterprises: No. 6, 1949; Nov, 1957 - No. 6, Aug-Sept, 1958

6(1949-M.E.)-no month (1st Series)	7	14	21	35	43	50
1-6(2nd Series)-Pixies-r	4	8	12	18	22	25
I.W. Reprint #1(nd)	2	4	6	8	11	14

MIGHTY AVENGERS
Marvel Comics: May, 2007 - No. 36, Jun, 2010 ($3.99/$2.99)

	GD 2.0	VG 4.0	FN 6.0	VF 8.0	VF/NM 9.0	NM- 9.2

1-($3.99) Iron Man, Ms. Marvel select new team; Bendis-s/Cho-a/c; Mole Man app. 5.00
2-6-($2.99) Ultron returns 3.00
7-15: 7-Bagley-a begins; Venom on-c. 9-11-Dr. Doom app. 3.00
12-20-Secret Invasion: 12,13-Maleev-a. 15-Romita Jr.-a. 16-Elektra. 20-Wasp funeral 3.00
21-($3.99) Dark Reign; Scarlet Witch returns; new team assembled; Pham-a 4.00
22-36: 25,26-Fantastic Four app. 35,36-Siege; Ultron returns 3.00
...: Most Wanted Files (2007, $3.99) profiles of members, accomplices & adversaries 4.00
... Vol. 1: The Ultron Initiative HC (2008, $19.99) r/#1-6; variant covers and sketch art 20.00
... Vol. 2: Venom Bomb HC (2008, $19.99) r/#7-11; B&W cover art 20.00

MIGHTY BEAR (Formerly Fun Comics; becomes Unsane #15)
Star Publ. No. 13,14/Ajax-Farrell (Four Star): No. 13, Jan, 1954 - No. 14, Mar, 1954; 9/57 - No. 3, 2/58

13,14-L. B. Cole-c	18	36	54	103	162	220
1-3('57-58)Four Star; becomes Mighty Ghost #4	7	14	21	35	43	50

MIGHTY COMICS (...Presents) (Formerly Flyman)
Radio Comics (Archie): No. 40, Nov, 1966 - No. 50, Oct, 1967 (All 12¢ issues)

40-Web	5	10	15	32	51	70
41-50: 41-Shield, Black Hood. 42-Black Hood. 43-Shield, Web & Black Hood. 44-Black Hood, Steel Sterling & The Shield. 45-Shield & Hangman; origin Web retold. 46-Steel Sterling, Web & Black Hood. 47-Black Hood & Mr. Justice. 48-Shield & Hangman; Wizard x-over in Shield. 49-Steel Sterling & Fox; Black Hood x-over in Steel Sterling. 50-Black Hood & Web; Inferno x-over in Web	5	10	15	30	48	65

NOTE: ***Paul Reinman*** *a-40-50.*

MIGHTY CRUSADERS, THE (Also see Adventures of the Fly, The Crusaders & Fly Man)
Mighty Comics Group (Radio Comics): Nov, 1965 - No. 7, Oct, 1966 (All 12¢)

1-Origin The Shield	8	16	24	57	86	120
2-Origin Comet	5	10	15	30	48	65
3,5-7: 3-Origin Fly-Man. 5-Intro. Ultra-Men (Fox, Web, Capt. Flag) & Terrific Three (Jaguar, Mr. Justice, Steel Sterling). 7-Steel Sterling feature; origin Fly-Girl	4	8	12	28	44	60
4-1st S.A. app. Fireball, Inferno & Fox; Firefly, Web, Bob Phantom, Blackjack, Hangman, Zambini, Kardak, Steel Sterling, Mr. Justice, Wizard, Capt. Flag, Jaguar x-over	5	10	15	30	48	65
Volume 1: Origin of a Super Team TPB (2003, $12.95) r/#1 & Fly Man #31-33						13.00

NOTE: ***Reinman*** *a-6.*

MIGHTY CRUSADERS, THE (All New Advs. of...#2)
Red Circle Prod./Archie Ent. No. 6 on: Mar, 1983 - No. 13, Sept, 1985 ($1.00, 36 pgs, Mando paper)

1-Origin Black Hood, The Fly, Fly Girl, The Shield, The Wizard, The Jaguar, Pvt. Strong & The Web.	1	2	3	4	5	7
2-10: 2-Mister Midnight begins. 4-Darkling replaces Shield. 5-Origin Jaguar, Shield begins. 7-Untold origin Jaguar. 10-Veitch-a						5.00
11-13-Lower print run						6.00

NOTE: ***Buckler*** *a-1-3, 4i, 5p, 7p, 8i, 9i; c-1-10p.*

MIGHTY CRUSADERS, THE (Also see The Shield, The Web and The Red Circle)
DC Comics: Sept, 2010 - No. 6, Feb, 2011 ($3.99, limited series)

1-6-The Shield, The Web, Fly-Girl, Inferno, War Eagle & The Comet team-up 4.00
... Special 1 (7/10, $4.99) Prequel to series; Pina-a/Lau-c 5.00

MIGHTY GHOST (Formerly Mighty Bear #1-3)
Ajax/Farrell Publ.: No. 4, June, 1958

4	7	14	21	35	43	50

MIGHTY HERCULES, THE (TV)
Gold Key: July, 1963 - No. 2, Nov, 1963

1 (10072-307)	12	24	36	82	169	255
2 (10072-311)	12	24	36	79	160	240

MIGHTY HEROES, THE (TV) (Funny)
Dell Publishing Co.: Mar, 1967 - No. 4, July, 1967

1-Also has a 1957 Heckle & Jeckle-r	11	22	33	71	136	200
2-4: 4-Has two 1958 Mighty Mouse-r	8	16	24	51	86	120

MIGHTY HEROES
Spotlight Comics: 1987 (B&W, one-shot)

1-Heckle & Jeckle backup 5.00

MIGHTY HEROES
Marvel Comics: Jan, 1998 ($2.99, one-shot)

1-Origin of the Mighty Heroes 3.00

MIGHTY LOVE
DC Comics: 2003 ($24.99/$17.95, graphic novel)

Mighty Marvel Western #17 © MAR

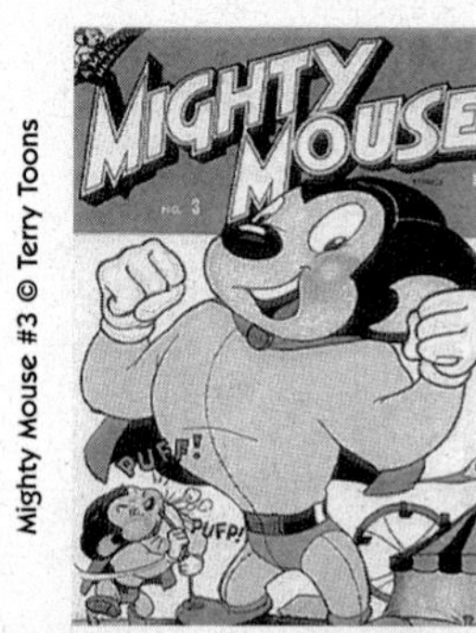

Mighty Mouse #3 © Terry Toons

Mighty Samson #31 © GK

	GD 2.0	VG 4.0	FN 6.0	VF 8.0	VF/NM 9.0	NM- 9.2

HC-($24.95) Howard Chaykin-s/a; intro. Skylark and the Iron Angel 25.00
SC-($17.95) 18.00

MIGHTY MAN (From Savage Dragon titles)
Image Comics: Dec, 2004 ($7.95, one-shot)

1-Reprints seriaizedl back-up from Savage Dragon #109-118 8.00

MIGHTY MARVEL TEAM-UP THRILLERS
Marvel Comics: 1983 ($5.95, trade paperback)

1-Reprints team-up stories 3 6 9 19 29 38

MIGHTY MARVEL WESTERN, THE
Marvel Comics Group (LMC earlier issues): Oct, 1968 - No. 46, Sept, 1976 (#1-14: 68 pgs.; #15,16: 52 pgs.)

1-Begin Kid Colt, Rawhide Kid, Two-Gun Kid-r 6 12 18 41 66 90
2-5: (2-14 are 68 pgs.) 4 8 12 28 44 60
6-16: (15,16 are 52 pgs.) 4 8 12 22 34 45
17-20 2 4 6 13 18 22
21-30,32,37: 24-Kid Colt-r end. 25-Matt Slade-r begin. 32-Origin-r/Rawhide Kid #23; Williamson-r/Kid Slade #7. 37-Williamson, Kirby-r/Two-Gun Kid 51
2 4 6 9 13 16
31,33-36,38-46: 31-Baker-r. 2 4 6 8 11 14
45-(30¢-c variant, limited distribution)(6/76) 4 8 12 28 44 60

NOTE: *Jack Davis a(r)-21-24.* ***Keller*** *r-1-13, 22.* ***Kirby*** *a(r)-1-3, 6, 9, 12-14, 16, 25-29, 32-38, 40, 41, 43-46; c-29.* ***Maneely*** *a(r)-22.* ***Severin*** *c-3i, 9. No Matt Slade-#43.*

MIGHTY MIDGET COMICS, THE (Miniature)
Samuel E. Lowe & Co.: No date; circa 1942-1943 (Sold 2 for 5¢, B&W and red, 36 pgs, approx. 5x4")

Bulletman #11(1943)-r/cover/Bulletman #3 16 32 48 94 147 200
Captain Marvel Adventures #11 16 32 48 94 147 200
Captain Marvel #11 (Same as above except for full color ad on back cover; this issue was glued to cover of Captain Marvel #20 and is not found in fine-mint condition)
340 680 1020 - - -
Captain Marvel Jr. #11 (Same-c as Master #27 16 32 48 94 147 200
Captain Marvel Jr. #11 (Same as above except for full color ad on back-c; this issue was glued to cover of Captain Marvel #21 and is not found in fine-mint condition)
340 680 1020 - - -
Golden Arrow #11 15 30 45 86 133 180
Golden Arrow #11 (Same as above except for full color ad on back-c; this issue was glued to cover of Captain Marvel #21 and is not found in fine-mint condition)
280 560 840 - - -
Ibis the Invincible #11(1942)-Origin; reprints cover to Ibis #1 (Predates Fawcett's Ibis the Invincible #1). 16 32 48 94 147 200
Spy Smasher #11(1942) 16 32 48 94 147 200

NOTE: *The above books came in a box called "box full of books" and was distributed with other Samuel Lowe puzzles, paper dolls, coloring books, etc. They are not titled Mighty Midget Comics. All have a war bond seal on back cover which is otherwise blank. These books came in a "Mighty Midget" flat cardboard counter display rack.*

Balbo, the Boy Magician #12 (1943)-1st book devoted entirely to character.
10 20 30 54 72 90
Bulletman #12 12 24 36 69 97 125
Commando Yank #12 (1943)-Only comic devoted entirely to character.
10 20 30 56 76 95
Dr. Voltz the Human Generator (1943)-Only comic devoted entirely to character.
10 20 30 54 72 90
Lance O'Casey #12 (1943)-1st comic devoted entirely to character (Predates Fawcett's Lance O'Casey #1). 10 20 30 54 72 90
Leatherneck the Marine (1943)-Only comic devoted entirely to character.
10 20 30 54 72 90
Minute Man #12 12 24 36 67 94 120
Mister "Q" (1943)-Only comic devoted entirely to character.
10 20 30 54 72 90
Mr. Scarlet and Pinky #12 (1943)-Only comic devoted entirely to character.
10 20 30 58 79 100
Pat Wilton and His Flying Fortress (1943)-1st comic devoted entirely to character. 10 20 30 54 72 90
The Phantom Eagle #12 (1943)-Only comic devoted entirely to character.
10 20 30 54 72 90
State Trooper Stops Crime (1943)-Only comic devoted entirely to character.
10 20 30 54 72 90
Tornado Tom (1943)-Origin, r/from Cyclone #1-3; only comic devoted entirely to character.
10 20 30 54 72 90

MIGHTY MORPHIN' POWER RANGERS: THE MOVIE (Also see Saban's Mighty Morphin' Power Rangers)
Marvel Comics: Sept, 1995 ($3.95, one-shot)

nn-Adaptation of movie 5.00

MIGHTY MOUSE (See Adventures of..., Dell Giant #43, Giant Comics Edition, March of Comics #205, 237, 247, 257, 447, 459, 471, 483, Oxydol-Dreft, Paul Terry's, & Terry-Toons Comics)

MIGHTY MOUSE (1st Series)
Timely/Marvel Comics (20th Century Fox): Fall, 1946 - No. 4, Summer, 1947

1 181 362 543 1158 1979 2800
2 69 138 207 442 759 1075
3,4 43 86 129 271 461 650

MIGHTY MOUSE (2nd Series) (Paul Terry's... #62-71)
St. John Publishing Co./Pines No. 68 (3/56) on (TV issues #72 on): Aug, 1947 - No. 67, 11/55; No. 68, 3/56 - No. 83, 6/59

5(#1) 39 78 117 240 395 550
6-10: 10-Over-sized issue 20 40 60 117 189 260
11-19 14 28 42 80 115 150
20 (11/50) - 25-(52 pg. editions) 11 22 33 62 86 110
20-25-(36 pg. editions) 10 20 30 54 72 90
26-37: 35-Flying saucer-c 9 18 27 50 65 80
38-45-(100 pgs.) 18 36 54 107 169 230
46-83: 62-64,67-Painted-c. 82-Infinity-c 9 18 27 47 61 75
Album nn (nd, 1952/53?, St. John)(100 pgs.)(Rebound issues w/new cover)
22 44 66 128 209 290
Album 1(10/52, 25¢, 100 pgs., St. John)-Gandy Goose app.
28 56 84 165 270 375
Album 2,3(11/52 & 12/52, St. John) (100 pgs.) 22 44 66 128 209 290
Fun Club Magazine 1(Fall, 1957-Pines, 25¢, 100 pgs.) (CBS TV)-Tom Terrific, Heckle & Jeckle, Dinky Duck, Gandy Goose 15 30 45 90 140 190
Fun Club Magazine 2-6(Winter, 1958-Pines) 11 22 33 62 86 110
3-D 1-(1st printing-9/53, 25¢)(St. John)-Came w/glasses; stiff covers; says World's First! on-c; 1st 3-D comic 28 56 84 165 270 375
3-D 1-(2nd printing-10/53, 25¢)-Came w/glasses; slick, glossy covers, slightly smaller
20 40 60 114 182 250
3-D 2,3(11/53, 12/53, 25¢)-(St. John)-With glasses 20 40 60 114 182 250

MIGHTY MOUSE (TV)(3rd Series)(Formerly Adventures of Mighty Mouse)
Gold Key/Dell Publ. Co. No. 166-on: No. 161, Oct, 1964 - No. 172, Oct, 1968

161(10/64)-165(9/65)-(Becomes Adventures of... No. 166 on)
5 10 15 30 48 65
166(3/66), 167(6/66)-172 3 6 9 21 32 42

MIGHTY MOUSE (TV)
Spotlight Comics: 1987 - No. 2, 1987 ($1.50, color)

1,2-New stories 4.00
...And Friends Holiday Special (11/87, $1.75) 4.00

MIGHTY MOUSE (TV)
Marvel Comics: Oct, 1990 - No. 10, July, 1991 ($1.00)(Based on Sat. cartoon)

1-10: 1-Dark Knight-c parody. 2-10: 3-Intro Bat-Bat; Byrne-c. 4,5-Crisis-c/story parodies w/Perez-c. 6-Spider-Man-c parody. 7-Origin Bat-Bat 3.00

MIGHTY MOUSE ADVENTURE MAGAZINE
Spotlight Comics: 1987 ($2.00, B&W, 52 pgs., magazine size, one-shot)

1-Deputy Dawg, Heckle & Jeckle backup stories 5.00

MIGHTY MOUSE ADVENTURES (Adventures of... #2 on)
St. John Publishing Co.: November, 1951

1 36 72 108 211 343 475

MIGHTY MOUSE ADVENTURE STORIES (Paul Terry's... on-c only)
St. John Publishing Co.: 1953 (50¢, 384 pgs.)

nn-Rebound issues 48 96 144 302 514 725

MIGHTY MUTANIMALS (See Teenage Mutant Ninja Turtles Adventures #19)
May, 1991 - No. 3, July, 1991 ($1.00, limited series)
Archie Comics: Apr, 1992 - No. 8, June, 1993 ($1.25)

1-3: 1-Story cont'd from TMNT Advs. #19. 6.00
1-4 (1992) 6.00
5-8: 7-1st app. Merdude 1 2 3 5 7 9

MIGHTY SAMSON (Also see Gold Key Champion)
Gold Key/Whitman #32: July, 1964 - No. 20, Nov, 1969; No. 21, Aug, 1972; No. 22, Dec, 1973 - No. 31, Mar, 1976; No. 32, Aug, 1982 (Painted-c #1-31)

1-Origin/1st app.; Thorne-a begins 8 16 24 53 89 125
2-5 5 10 15 30 48 65
6-10: 7-Tom Morrow begins, ends #20 3 6 9 20 30 40
11-20 3 6 9 16 23 30
21-31: 21,22-r 2 4 6 11 16 20
32(Whitman, 8/82)-r 2 4 6 8 10 12

The Mighty Thor #2 © MAR

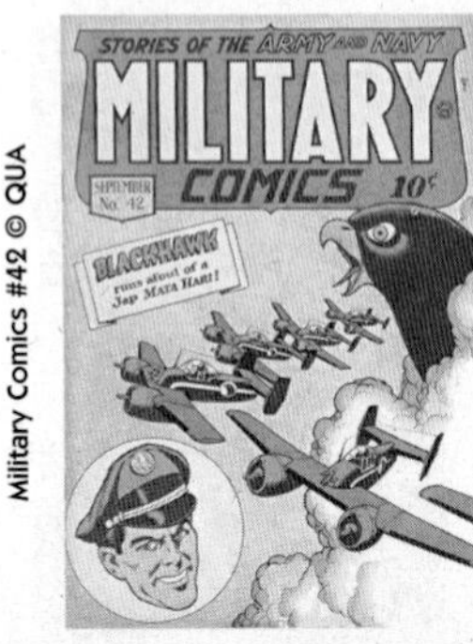

Military Comics #42 © QUA

Millie the Model #129 © MAR

MIGHTY SAMSON
Dark Horse Comics: Dec, 2010 - No. 4, Oct, 2011 ($3.50)

	GD 2.0	VG 4.0	FN 6.0	VF 8.0	VF/NM 9.0	NM- 9.2
1-4: 1-Origin retold; Shooter & Vaughn-s/Olliffe-a/Swanland-c; r/1st app. from 1964						3.50
1-Variant-c by Olliffe						4.00

MIGHTY THOR, THE
Marvel Comics: Jun, 2011 - Present ($3.99)

	GD 2.0	VG 4.0	FN 6.0	VF 8.0	VF/NM 9.0	NM- 9.2
1-Fraction-s/Coipel-a; Silver Surfer app.; bonus concept art from the movie						4.00
1-Variant-c by Charest						6.00
1-Variant-c by Simonson						10.00
2-11: 3-6-Galactus app. 7-Fear Itself tie-in; Odin's 1st battle vs. the Serpent. 8-Tanarus						4.00

MIKE BARNETT, MAN AGAINST CRIME (TV)
Fawcett Publications: Dec, 1951 - No. 6, Oct, 1952

	GD 2.0	VG 4.0	FN 6.0	VF 8.0	VF/NM 9.0	NM- 9.2
1	19	38	57	111	176	240
2	13	26	39	74	105	135
3,4,6	11	22	33	60	83	105
5- "Market for Morphine" cover/story	14	28	42	82	121	160

MIKE DANGER (See Mickey Spillane's...)

MIKE DEODATO'S...
Caliber Comics: 1996, ($2.95, B&W)

	GD 2.0	VG 4.0	FN 6.0	VF 8.0	VF/NM 9.0	NM- 9.2
...FALLOUT 3000 #1, **...JONAS** (mag. size) #1,**...PRIME CUTS** (mag. size) #1, **...PROTHEUS** #1,2, **...RAMTHAR** #1,**...RAZOR NIGHTS** #1						3.00

MIKE GRELL'S SABLE (Also see Jon Sable & Sable)
First Comics: Mar, 1990 - No. 10, Dec, 1990 ($1.75)

	GD 2.0	VG 4.0	FN 6.0	VF 8.0	VF/NM 9.0	NM- 9.2
1-10: r/Jon Sable Freelance #1-10 by Grell						3.00

MIKE MIST MINUTE MIST-ERIES (See Ms. Tree/Mike Mist in 3-D)
Eclipse Comics: April, 1981 ($1.25, B&W, one-shot)

	GD 2.0	VG 4.0	FN 6.0	VF 8.0	VF/NM 9.0	NM- 9.2
1						3.00

MIKE SHAYNE PRIVATE EYE
Dell Publishing Co.: Nov-Jan, 1962 - No. 3, Sept-Nov, 1962

	GD 2.0	VG 4.0	FN 6.0	VF 8.0	VF/NM 9.0	NM- 9.2
1	4	8	12	24	37	50
2,3	3	6	9	17	25	32

MILESTONE FOREVER
DC Comics: Apr, 2010 - No. 2, May, 2010 ($5.99, squarebound, limited series)

	GD 2.0	VG 4.0	FN 6.0	VF 8.0	VF/NM 9.0	NM- 9.2
1,2-McDuffie-s/Leon & Bright-a; Icon, Blood Syndicate, Hardware and Static app.						6.00

MILITARY COMICS (Becomes Modern Comics #44 on)
Quality Comics Group: Aug, 1941 - No. 43, Oct, 1945

	GD 2.0	VG 4.0	FN 6.0	VF 8.0	VF/NM 9.0	NM- 9.2
1-Origin/1st app. Blackhawk by C. Cuidera (Eisner scripts); Miss America, The Death Patrol by Jack Cole (also #2-7,27-30), & The Blue Tracer by Guardineer; X of the Underground, The Yankee Eagle, Q-Boat & Shot & Shell, Archie Atkins, Loops & Banks by Bud Ernest (Bob Powell)(ends #13) begin	432	864	1296	3154	5577	8000
2-Secret War News begins (by McWilliams #2-16); Cole-a; new uniform with yellow circle & hawk's head for Blackhawk	135	270	405	864	1482	2100
3-Origin/1st app. Chop Chop (9/41)	116	232	348	742	1271	1800
4	103	206	309	659	1130	1600
5-The Sniper begins; Miss America in costume #4-7	90	180	270	576	988	1400
6-9: 8-X of the Underground begins (ends #13). 9-The Phantom Clipper begins (ends #16)	71	142	213	454	777	1100
10-Classic Eisner-c	90	180	270	576	988	1400
11-Flag-c	68	136	204	435	743	1050
12-Blackhawk by Crandall begins, ends #22	71	142	213	454	777	1100
13-15: 14-Private Dogtag begins (ends #83)	58	116	174	371	636	900
16-20: 16-Blue Tracer ends. 17-P.T. Boat begins	53	106	159	334	567	800
21-31: 22-Last Crandall Blackhawk. 23-Shrunken head-c. 27-Death Patrol revived	47	94	141	296	498	700
32-43	41	82	123	256	428	600

NOTE: *Berg a-6.* ***Al Bryant*** *c-31-34, 38, 40-43.* ***J. Cole*** *a-1-3, 27-32.* ***Crandall*** *a-12-22; c-13-20.* ***Cuidera*** *c-2-9.* ***Eisner*** *c-1, 2(part), 9, 10.* ***Kotsky*** *c-21-29, 35, 37, 39.* ***McWilliams*** *a-2-16.* ***Powell*** *a-1-13.* ***Ward*** *Blackhawk-30, 31(15 pgs. each); c-30.*

MILK AND CHEESE (Also see Cerebus Bi-Weekly #20)
Slave Labor: 1991 - Present ($2.50, B&W)

	GD 2.0	VG 4.0	FN 6.0	VF 8.0	VF/NM 9.0	NM- 9.2
1-Evan Dorkin story & art in all	4	8	12	24	37	50
1-2nd-6th printings						4.00
2-"Other #1"	3	6	9	16	23	30
2-reprint						3.00
3-"Third #1"	2	4	6	11	16	20
4-"Fourth #1", 5-"First Second Issue"	1	3	4	6	8	10
6,7: 6-"#666"						5.00

NOTE: *Multiple printings of all issues exist and are worth cover price unless listed here.*

MILKMAN MURDERS, THE
Dark Horse Comics: Jun, 2004 - No. 4, Aug, 2004 ($2.99, limited series)

	GD 2.0	VG 4.0	FN 6.0	VF 8.0	VF/NM 9.0	NM- 9.2
1-4-Casey-s/Parkhouse-a						3.00

MILLENNIUM
DC Comics: Jan, 1988 - No. 8, Feb, 1988 (Weekly limited series)

	GD 2.0	VG 4.0	FN 6.0	VF 8.0	VF/NM 9.0	NM- 9.2
1-Englehart-s/Staton c/a(p)						4.00
2-8						3.00
TPB (2008, $19.99) r/#1-8						20.00

MILLENNIUM EDITION:... (Reprints of classic DC issues)
DC Comics: Feb, 2000 - Feb, 2001 (gold foil cover stamps)

	GD 2.0	VG 4.0	FN 6.0	VF 8.0	VF/NM 9.0	NM- 9.2
Action Comics #1, Adventure Comics #61, All Star Comics #3, All Star Comics #8, Batman #1, Detective Comics #1, Detective Comics #27, Detective Comics #38, Flash Comics #1, Military Comics #1, More Fun Comics #73, Police Comics #1, Sensation Comics #1, Superman #1, Whiz Comics #2, Wonder Woman #1 -($3.95-c)						4.00
Action Comics #252, Adventure Comics #247, Brave and the Bold #28, Brave and the Bold #85, Crisis on Infinte Earths #1, Detective #225, Detective #327, Detective #359, Detective #395, Flash #123, Gen13 #1, Green Lantern #76, House of Mystery #1, House of Secrets #92, JLA #1, Justice League #1, Mad #1, Man of Steel #1, Mysterious Suspense #1, New Gods, #1, New Teen Titans #1, Our Army at War #81, Plop! #1, Saga of the Swamp Thing #21, Shadow #1, Showcase #4, Showcase #9, Showcase #22, Superman #233, Superman (2nd) #75, Superman's Pal Jimmy Olsen #1, Watchmen #1, WildC.A.T.s #1, Wonder Woman (2nd) #1, World's Finest #71 -($2.50-c)						3.00
All-Star Western #10, Hellblazer #1, More Fun Comics #101, Preacher #1, Sandman #1, Spirit #1, Superboy #1, Superman #76, Young Romance #1-($2.95-c)						3.00
Batman: The Dark Knight Returns #1, Kingdom Come #1 -($5.95-c)						6.00
All Star Comics #3, Batman #1, Justice League #1: Chromium cover						10.00
Crisis on Infinite Earths #1 Chromium cover						20.00

MILLENNIUM FEVER
DC Comics (Vertigo): Oct, 1995 - No.4, Jan, 1996 ($2.50, limited series)

	GD 2.0	VG 4.0	FN 6.0	VF 8.0	VF/NM 9.0	NM- 9.2
1-4: Duncan Fegredo-c/a						3.00

MILLENNIUM INDEX
Independent Comics Group: Mar, 1988 - No. 2, Mar, 1988 ($2.00)

	GD 2.0	VG 4.0	FN 6.0	VF 8.0	VF/NM 9.0	NM- 9.2
1,2						3.00

MILLENNIUM 2.5 A.D.
ACG Comics: No. 1, 2000 ($2.95)

	GD 2.0	VG 4.0	FN 6.0	VF 8.0	VF/NM 9.0	NM- 9.2
1-Reprints 1934 Buck Rogers daily strips #1-48						3.00

MILLIE, THE LOVABLE MONSTER
Dell Publishing Co.: Sept-Nov, 1962 - No. 6, Jan, 1973

	GD 2.0	VG 4.0	FN 6.0	VF 8.0	VF/NM 9.0	NM- 9.2
12-523-211-Bill Woggon c/a in all	5	10	15	35	55	75
2(8-10/63)	5	10	15	30	48	65
3(8-10/64)	4	8	12	26	41	55
4(7/72), 5(10/72), 6(1/73)	3	6	9	14	19	24

NOTE: ***Woggon*** *a-3-6; c-3-6. 4 reprints 1; 5 reprints 2; 6 reprints 3.*

MILLIE THE MODEL (See Comedy Comics, A Date With..., Joker Comics #28, Life With..., Mad About..., Marvel Mini-Books, Misty & Modeling With...)
Marvel/Atlas/Marvel Comics(CnPC #1)(SPI/Male/VPI):1945 - No. 207, Dec, 1973

	GD 2.0	VG 4.0	FN 6.0	VF 8.0	VF/NM 9.0	NM- 9.2
1-Origin	110	220	330	704	1202	1700
2 (10/46)-Millie becomes The Blonde Phantom to sell Blonde Phantom perfume; a pre-Blonde Phantom app. (see All-Select #11, Fall, 1946)	48	96	144	302	514	725
3-8,10: 4-7-Willie app. 7-Willie smokes extra strong tobacco. 8,10-Kurtzman's "Hey Look". 8-Willie & Rusty app.	39	78	117	231	378	525
9-Powerhouse Pepper by Wolverton, 4 pgs.	39	78	117	240	395	550
11-Kurtzman-a, "Giggles 'n' Grins"	23	46	69	136	223	310
12,15,17,19,20: 12-Rusty & Hedy Devine app.	20	40	60	115	185	255
13,14,16,18: 13,14,16-Kurtzman's "Hey Look". 13-Hedy Devine app. 18-Dan DeCarlo-a begins	20	40	60	118	192	265
21-30	15	30	45	85	130	175
31-40	9	18	27	61	106	150
41-60	8	16	24	51	86	120
61-99	7	14	21	44	72	100
100	7	14	21	48	79	110
101-106,108-130	6	12	18	39	62	85
107-Jack Kirby app. in story	6	12	18	42	69	95
131-134,136,138-153: 141-Groovy Gears-c/s	5	10	15	30	48	65
135-(2/66) 1st app. Groovy Gears	6	12	18	37	59	80
137-2nd app. Groovy Gears	5	10	15	32	51	70
154-New Millie begins (10/67)	7	14	21	44	72	100

Ministry of Space #1 © Ellis & Weston

Miracleman #19 © ECL

Miss America Magazine #3 © MAR

	GD 2.0	VG 4.0	FN 6.0	VF 8.0	VF/NM 9.0	NM- 9.2

155-190 5 10 15 30 48 65
191,193-199,201-206 4 8 12 26 41 55
192-(52 pgs.) 5 10 15 30 48 65
200,207(Last issue) 5 10 15 30 48 65
(Beware: cut-up pages are common in all Annuals)
Annual 1(1962)-Early Marvel annual (2nd?) 17 34 51 119 260 400
Annual 2(1963) 12 24 36 81 166 250
Annual 3-5 (1964-1966) 9 18 27 61 106 150
Annual 6-10(1967-11/71) 7 14 21 48 79 110
Queen-Size 11(9/74), 12(1975) 6 12 18 42 69 95
NOTE: *Dan DeCarlo a-18-93.*

MILLION DOLLAR DIGEST (Richie Rich... #23 on; also see Richie Rich...)
Harvey Publications: 11/86 - No. 7, 11/87; No. 8, 4/88 - No. 34, Nov, 1994 ($1.25/$1.75, digest size)
1 1 2 3 5 6 8
2-8: 8-(68 pgs.) 6.00
9-20: 9-Begin $1.75-c. 14-May not exist 1 2 3 4 5 7
21-34 1 3 4 6 8 10

MILT GROSS FUNNIES (Also see Picture News #1)
Milt Gross, Inc. (ACG?): Aug, 1947 - No. 2, Sept, 1947
1 22 44 66 132 216 300
2 15 30 45 90 140 190

MILTON THE MONSTER & FEARLESS FLY (TV)
Gold Key: May, 1966
1 (10175-605) 9 18 27 61 106 150

MINDFIELD
Aspen MLT: No. 0, May, 2010 - No. 6, Sept, 2011 ($2.50/$2.99)
0-($2.50) Krul-s/Konat-a; 3 covers 3.00
1-6-($2.99) Multiples covers on each 3.00

MINIMUM WAGE
Fantagraphics Books: V1#1, July, 1995 ($9.95, B&W, graphic novel, mature)
V2#1, 1995 - 1997 ($2.95, B&W, mature)
V1#1-Bob Fingerman story & art 1 3 4 6 8 10
V2#1-9($2.95): Bob Fingerman story & art. 2-Kevin Nowlan back-c. 4-w/pin-ups. 5-Mignola back-c 3.00
Book Two TPB ('97, $12.95) r/V2#1-5 13.00

MINISTRY OF SPACE
Image Comics: Apr, 2001 - No. 3, Apr, 2004 ($2.95, limited series)
1-3-Warren Ellis-s/Chris Weston-a 3.00
...Vol. 1 Omnibus (3/04, $4.95) r/1&2 5.00
TPB (12/04, $12.95) r/series; sketch & design pages; intro by Mark Millar 13.00

MINOR MIRACLES
DC Comics: 2000 ($12.95, B&W, squarebound)
nn-Will Eisner-s/a 13.00

MINUTE MAN (See Master Comics & Mighty Midget Comics)
Fawcett Publications: Summer, 1941 - No. 3, Spring, 1942 (68 pgs.)
1 213 426 639 1363 2332 3300
2,3: 2-Japanese WWII-c 123 246 369 787 1344 1900

MINX, THE
DC Comics (Vertigo): Oct, 1998 - No. 8, May, 1999 ($2.50, limited series)
1-8-Milligan-s/Phillips-c/a 3.00

MIRACLE COMICS
Hillman Periodicals: Feb, 1940 - No. 4, Mar, 1941
1-Sky Wizard Master of Space, Dash Dixon, Man of Might, Pinkie Parker, Dusty Doyle, The Kid Cop, K-7, Secret Agent, The Scorpion, & Blandu, Jungle Queen begin; Masked Angel only app. (all 1st app.) 200 400 600 1280 2190 3100
2 100 200 300 635 1093 1550
3,4: 3-Devil-c; Bill Colt, the Ghost Rider begins. 4-The Veiled Prophet & Bullet Bob (by Burnley) app. 84 168 252 538 919 1300

MIRACLEMAN
Eclipse Comics: Aug, 1985 - No. 15, Nov, 1988; No. 16, Dec, 1989 - No. 24, Aug, 1993
1-r/British Marvelman series; Alan Moore scripts in #1-16 2 3 4 6 8 10
1-Gold variant (edition of 400, signed by Alan Moore, came with signed & #'d certificate of authenticity) 56 112 168 454 977 1500
1-Blue variant (edition of 600, came with signed certificate of authenticity) 33 66 99 239 520 800
2-10: 8-Airboy preview. 6,9,10-Origin Miracleman. 9-Shows graphic scenes of childbirth. 10-Snyder-c 1 2 3 5 6 8
11-14(5/87-4/88) Totleben-a 2 4 6 11 16 20
15-($1.75-c, scarce) end of Kid Miracleman 6 12 18 41 66 90
16-Last Alan Moore-s; 1st $1.95-c (low print) 3 6 9 16 23 30
17-22: 17-"The Golden Age" begins, ends #22. Dave McKean-c begins, end #22; Neil Gaiman scripts in #17-24 2 4 6 10 14 18
23-"The Silver Age" begins; Barry W. Smith-c 2 4 6 11 16 20
24-Last issue; Smith-c 3 6 9 14 20 25
3-D #1 (12/85) 1 2 3 5 7 9
3-D #1 Blue variant (edition of 99) 3 6 9 16 23 30
3-D #1 Gold variant (edition of 199) 2 4 6 11 16 20
NOTE: *Miracleman 3-D #1 (12/85) (2D edition) Interior is the same as the 3-D version except in non 3-D format. Indicia are the same for both versions of the book with only the non 3-D art distinguishing this book from the standard 3-D version. Standard 3-D edition has house ad mentioning the non 3-D edition. Two known copies exist, one in the Michigan State University Special Collection Department. (No known sales)*
Book One: A Dream of Flying (1988, $9.95, TPB) r/#1-5; Leach-c 22.00
Book One: A Dream of Flying-Hardcover (1988, $29.95) r/#1-5 70.00
Book Two: The Red King Syndrome (1990, $12.95, TPB) r/#6-10; Bolton-c 30.00
Book Two: The Red King Syndrome-Hardcover (1990, $30.95) r/#6-10 85.00
Book Three: Olympus (1990, $12.95, TPB) r/#11-16 130.00
Book Three: Olympus-Hardcover (1990, $30.95) r/#11-16 250.00
Book Four: The Golden Age (1992, $15.95, TPB) r/#17-22 30.00
Book Four: The Golden Age Hardcover (1992, $33.95) r/#17-22 50.00
Book Four: The Golden Age (1993, $12.99, TPB) new McKean-c 15.00
NOTE: *Eclipse archive copies exist for #4,5,8,17,23. Each has a small Miracleman image foil-stamped on the cover.* ***Chaykin*** *c-3.* ***Gulacy*** *c-7.* ***McKean*** *c-17-22.* ***B. Smith*** *c-23, 24.* ***Starlin*** *c-4.* ***Totleben*** *a-11-13; c-9, 11-13.* ***Truman*** *c-6.*

MIRACLEMAN: APOCRYPHA
Eclipse Comics: Nov, 1991 - No. 3, Feb, 1992 ($2.50, limited series)
1-3: 1-Stories by Neil Gaiman, Mark Buckingham, Alex Ross & others. 3-Stories by James Robinson, Kelley Jones, Matt Wagner, Neil Gaiman, Mark Buckingham & others 1 2 3 4 5 7
TPB (12/92, $15.95) r/#1-3; Buckingham-c 20.00

MIRACLEMAN FAMILY
Eclipse Comics: May, 1988 - No. 2, Sept, 1988 ($1.95, lim. series, Baxter paper)
1,2: 2-Gulacy-c 5.00

MIRACLE OF THE WHITE STALLIONS, THE (See Movie Comics)

MIRROR'S EDGE (Based on the EA video game)
DC Comics (WildStorm): Dec, 2008 - No. 6, Jun, 2009 ($3.99, limited series)
1-6: 1-Origin of Faith; Rhianna Pratchett-s/Matthew Dow Smith-a 4.00
TPB (2009, $19.99) r/#1-6 20.00

MISADVENTURES OF ADAM WEST, THE
Bluewater Comics: Jul, 2011 - Present ($3.99)
1-4: 1-Two covers; co-created by Adam West 4.00
Second series 1,2 (1/12 - Present) 4.00

MISADVENTURES OF MERLIN JONES, THE (See Movie Comics & Merlin Jones as the Monkey's Uncle under Movie Comics)

MISPLACED
Image Comics: May, 2003 - No. 4, Dec, 2004 ($2.95)
1-4: 1-Three covers by Blaylock, Green and Clugston-Major; Blaylock-s/a 3.00
... @17 (12/04, $4.95) Nara from "Dead @17 " app.; Blaylock-s/a 5.00

MISS AMERICA COMICS (Miss America Magazine #2 on; also see Blonde Phantom & Marvel Mystery Comics)
Marvel Comics (20CC): 1944 (one-shot)
1-2 pgs. pin-ups 206 412 618 1318 2259 3200

MISS AMERICA COMICS 70th ANNIVERARY SPECIAL
Marvel Comics: Aug, 2009 ($3.99, one-shot)
1-Eaglesham-c; new Miss America & Whizzer story; reps. from All Winners #9-11 5.00

MISS AMERICA MAGAZINE (Formerly Miss America; Miss America #51 on)
Miss America Publ. Corp./Marvel/Atlas (MAP): V1#2, Nov, 1944 - No. 93, Nov, 1958
V1#2-Photo-c of teenage girl in Miss America costume; Miss America, Patsy Walker (intro.) comic stories plus movie reviews & stories; intro. Buzz Baxter & Hedy Wolfe; 1 pg. origin Miss America 155 310 465 992 1696 2400
3-5-Miss America & Patsy Walker stories 68 136 204 435 743 1050
6-Patsy Walker only 39 78 117 240 395 550
V2#1(4/45)-6(9/45)-Patsy Walker continues 15 30 45 88 137 185
V3#1(10/45)-6(4/46) 14 28 42 80 115 150
V4#1(5/46),2,5(9/46) 13 26 39 74 105 135
V4#3(7/46)-Liz Taylor photo-c 34 68 102 199 325 450

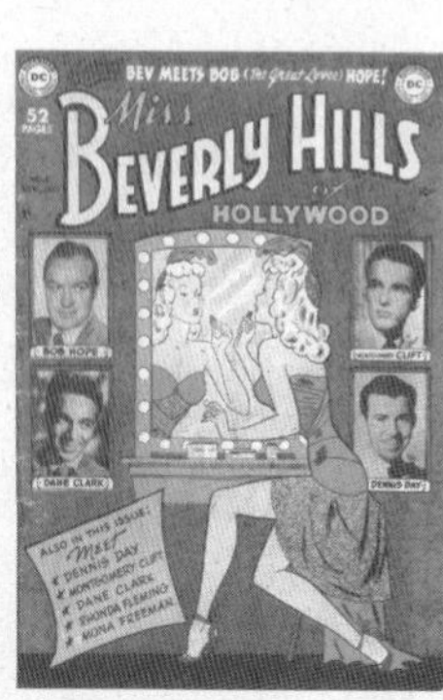

Miss Beverly Hills of Hollywood #5 © DC

Mister E #3 © DC

Mister Miracle #24 © DC

	GD 2.0	VG 4.0	FN 6.0	VF 8.0	VF/NM 9.0	NM- 9.2
V4#4 (8/46; 68 pgs.), V4#6 (10/46; 92 pgs.)	12	24	36	69	97	125
V5#1(11/46)-6(4/47), V6#1(5/47)-3(7/47)	12	24	36	67	94	120
V7#1(8/47)-23(#56, 6/49)	11	22	33	64	90	115
V7#24(#57, 7/49)-Kamen-a (becomes Best Western #58 on?)	12	24	36	67	94	120
V7#25(8/49), 27-44(3/52), VII,nn(5/52)	11	22	33	62	86	110
V7#26(9/49)-All comics	12	24	36	69	97	125
V1,nn(7/52)-V1,nn(1/53)(#46-49), V7#50(Spring '53), V1#51-V7?#54(7/53), 55-93	11	22	33	60	83	105

NOTE: *Photo-c #1, 4, V2#1, 4, 5, V3#5, V4#3, 4, 6, V7#15, 16, 24, 26, 34, 37, 38. Painted c-3.* **Powell** *a-V7#31.*

MISS BEVERLY HILLS OF HOLLYWOOD (See Adventures of Bob Hope)
National Periodical Publ.: Mar-Apr, 1949 - No. 9, July-Aug, 1950 (52 pgs.)

	GD	VG	FN	VF	VF/NM	NM-
1 (Meets Alan Ladd)	58	116	174	371	636	900
2-William Holden photo on-c	42	84	126	265	450	635
3-5: 2-9-Part photo-c. 5-Bob Hope photo on-c	39	78	117	232	381	530
6,7,9: 6-Lucille Ball photo on-c	35	70	105	208	339	470
8-Reagan photo on-c	39	78	117	240	395	550

NOTE: *Beverly meets Alan Ladd in #1, Eve Arden #2, Betty Hutton #4, Bob Hope #5.*

MISS CAIRO JONES
Croyden Publishers: 1945

	GD	VG	FN	VF	VF/NM	NM-
1-Bob Oksner daily newspaper-r (1st strip story); lingerie panels	20	40	60	114	182	250

MISS FURY COMICS (Newspaper strip reprints)
Timely Comics (NPI 1/CmPI 2/MPC 3-8): Winter, 1942-43 - No. 8, Winter, 1946 (Published twice a year)

	GD	VG	FN	VF	VF/NM	NM-
1-Origin Miss Fury by Tarpe' Mills (68 pgs.) in costume w/paper dolls with cut-out costumes	417	834	1251	2919	5110	7300
2-(60 pgs.)-In costume w/paper dolls; hooded Nazi-c	213	426	639	1363	2332	3300
3-(60 pgs.)-In costume w/paper dolls; Hitler-c	174	348	522	1114	1907	2700
4-(52 pgs.)-Classic Nazi WWII-c with giant swastika, Tojo & Hitler photo on wall; in costume, 2 pgs. w/paper dolls	148	296	444	947	1624	2300
5-(52 pgs.)-In costume w/paper dolls; Japanese WWII-c	113	226	339	718	1234	1750
6-(52 pgs.)-Not in costume in inside stories, w/paper dolls	102	204	306	648	1112	1575
7,8-(36 pgs.)-In costume 1 pg. each; no paper dolls	82	164	246	528	902	1275

NOTE: **Schomburg** *c-1, 5, 6.*

MISS FURY
Adventure Comics: 1991 - No. 4, 1991 ($2.50, limited series)

	GD	VG	FN	VF	VF/NM	NM-
1-4: 1-Origin; granddaughter of original Miss Fury						3.00
1-Limited ed. ($4.95)						5.00

MISSION IMPOSSIBLE (TV) (Also see Wild!)
Dell Publ. Co.: May, 1967 - No. 4, Oct, 1968; No. 5, Oct, 1969 (All have photo-c)

	GD	VG	FN	VF	VF/NM	NM-
1	8	16	24	56	96	135
2-5: 5-Reprints #1	6	12	18	41	66	90

MISSION IMPOSSIBLE (Movie) (1st Paramount Comics book)
Marvel Comics (Paramount Comics): May, 1996 ($2.95, one-shot)

	GD	VG	FN	VF	VF/NM	NM-
1-Liefeld-c & back-up story						3.00

MISS LIBERTY (Becomes Liberty Comics)
Burten Publishing Co.: 1945 (MLJ reprints)

	GD	VG	FN	VF	VF/NM	NM-
1-The Shield & Dusty, The Wizard, & Roy, the Super Boy app.; r/Shield-Wizard #13	30	60	90	177	289	400

MISS MELODY LANE OF BROADWAY (See The Adventures of Bob Hope)
National Periodical Publ.: Feb-Mar, 1950 - No. 3, June-July, 1950 (52 pgs.)

	GD	VG	FN	VF	VF/NM	NM-
1-Movie stars photos app. on all-c.	60	120	180	381	653	925
2,3: 3-Ed Sullivan photo on-c.	39	78	117	231	378	525

MISS PEACH
Dell Publishing Co.: Oct-Dec, 1963; 1969

	GD	VG	FN	VF	VF/NM	NM-
1-Jack Mendelsohn-a/script	8	16	24	51	86	120
...Tells You How to Grow (1969; 25¢)-Mel Lazarus-a; also given away (36 pgs.)	5	10	15	32	51	70

MISS PEPPER (See Meet Miss Pepper)

MISS SUNBEAM (See Little Miss...)

MISS VICTORY (See Captain Fearless #1,2, Holyoke One-Shot #3, Veri Best Sure Fire & Veri Best Sure Shot Comics)

MISTER AMERICA
Endeavor Comics: Apr, 1994 - No. 2, May, 1994 ($2.95, limited series)

	GD	VG	FN	VF	VF/NM	NM-
1,2						3.00

MR. & MRS. BEANS
United Features Syndicate: No. 11, 1939

	GD	VG	FN	VF	VF/NM	NM-
Single Series 11	34	68	102	199	325	450

MR. & MRS. J. EVIL SCIENTIST (TV)(See The Flintstones & Hanna-Barbera Band Wagon #3)
Gold Key: Nov, 1963 - No. 4, Sept, 1966 (Hanna-Barbera, all 12¢)

	GD	VG	FN	VF	VF/NM	NM-
1	6	12	18	41	66	90
2-4	4	8	12	24	37	50

MR. ANTHONY'S LOVE CLINIC (Based on radio show)
Hillman Periodicals: Nov, 1949 - No. 5, Apr-May, 1950 (52 pgs.)

	GD	VG	FN	VF	VF/NM	NM-
1-Photo-c on all	16	32	48	94	147	200
2	11	22	33	62	86	110
3-5	10	20	30	58	79	100

MISTER BLANK
Amaze Ink: No. 0, Jan, 1996 - No. 14, May, 2000 ($1.75/$2.95, B&W)

	GD	VG	FN	VF	VF/NM	NM-
0-($1.75, 16 pgs.) Origin of Mr. Blank						3.00
1-14-($2.95) Chris Hicks-s/a						3.00

MR. DISTRICT ATTORNEY (Radio/TV)
National Per. Publ.: Jan-Feb, 1948 - No. 67, Jan-Feb, 1959 (1-23: 52 pgs.)

	GD	VG	FN	VF	VF/NM	NM-
1-Howard Purcell c-5-23 (most)	87	174	261	553	952	1350
2	41	82	123	256	428	600
3-5	29	58	87	170	278	385
6-10: 8-Rise & fall of Lucky Lynn	22	44	66	132	216	300
11-20	17	34	51	98	154	210
21-43: 43-Last pre-code (1-2/55)	14	28	42	76	108	140
44-67: 55-UFO story	11	22	33	62	86	110

MR. DISTRICT ATTORNEY (SeeThe Funnies #35)
Dell Publishing Co.: No. 13, 1942

	GD	VG	FN	VF	VF/NM	NM-
Four Color 13-See The Funnies #35 for 1st app.	25	50	75	171	366	560

MISTER E (Also see Books of Magic limited series)
DC Comics: Jun, 1991- No. 4, Sept, 1991($1.75, limited series)

	GD	VG	FN	VF	VF/NM	NM-
1-4-Snyder III-c/a; follow-up to Books of Magic limited series						3.00

MISTER ED, THE TALKING HORSE (TV)
Dell Publishing Co./Gold Key: Mar-May, 1962 - No. 6, Feb, 1964 (All photo-c; photo back-c: 1-6)

	GD	VG	FN	VF	VF/NM	NM-
Four Color 1295	11	22	33	76	151	225
1(11/62) (Gold Key)-Photo-c	9	18	27	58	99	140
2-6: Photo-c	6	12	18	37	59	80

(See March of Comics #244, 260, 282, 290)

MR. GUM (From The Atomics)
Oni Press: April, 2003 ($2.99, one-shot)

	GD	VG	FN	VF	VF/NM	NM-
1-Mike Allred-s/J. Bone-a; Madman & The Atomics app.						3.00

MR. HERO, THE NEWMATIC MAN (See Neil Gaiman's...)

MR. MAGOO (TV) (The Nearsighted..., ...& Gerald McBoing Boing 1954 issues; formerly Gerald McBoing-Boing And ...)
Dell Publishing Co.: No. 6, Nov-Jan, 1953-54; 5/54 - 3-5/62; 9-11/63 - 3-5/65

	GD	VG	FN	VF	VF/NM	NM-
6	10	20	30	65	118	170
Four Color 561(5/54),602(11/54)	10	20	30	65	118	170
Four Color 1235(#1, 12-2/62),1305(#2, 3-5/62)	8	16	24	55	93	130
3(9-11/63) - 5	7	14	21	49	82	115
Four Color 1235(12-536-505)(3-5/65)-2nd Printing	6	12	18	41	66	90

MR. MAJESTIC (See WildC.A.T.S.)
DC Comics (WildStorm): Sept, 1999 - No. 9, May, 2000 ($2.50)

	GD	VG	FN	VF	VF/NM	NM-
1-9: 1-McGuinness-a/Casey & Holguin-s. 2-Two covers						3.00
TPB (2002, $14.95) r/#1-6 & Wildstorm Spotlight #1						15.00

MISTER MIRACLE (1st series) (See Cancelled Comic Cavalcade)
National Periodical Publications/DC Comics: 3-4/71 - V4#18, 2-3/74; V5#19, 9/77 - V6#25, 8-9/78; 1987 (Fourth World)

	GD	VG	FN	VF	VF/NM	NM-
1-1st app. Mr. Miracle (#1-3 are 15¢)	8	16	24	55	93	130
2,3: 2-Intro. Granny Goodness. 3-Last 15¢ issue	5	10	15	30	48	65
4-8: 4-Intro. Barda; Boy Commandos-r begin; all 52 pgs.	5	10	15	30	48	65
9-18: 9-Origin Mr. Miracle; Darkseid cameo. 15-Intro/1st app. Shilo Norman. 18-Barda & Scott Free wed; New Gods app. & Darkseid cameo; Last Kirby issue.	3	6	9	16	23	30
19-25 (1977-78)	2	4	6	8	10	12

Mister Mystery #8 © Media Publ.

Mister Terrific #1 © DC

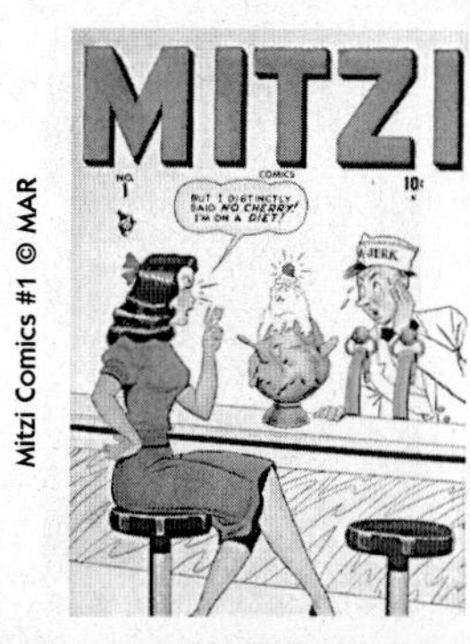

Mitzi Comics #1 © MAR

	GD 2.0	VG 4.0	FN 6.0	VF 8.0	VF/NM 9.0	NM- 9.2

Special 1(1987, $1.25, 52 pgs.) 4.00
Jack Kirby's Fourth World TPB ('01, $12.95) B&W&Grey-toned reprint of #11-18; Mark Evanier intro. 13.00
Jack Kirby's Mister Miracle TPB ('98, $12.95) B&W&Grey-toned reprint of #1-10; David Copperfield intro. 13.00
*NOTE: **Austin** a-19i. **Ditko** a-6r. **Golden** a-23-25p; c-25p. **Heath** a-24i, 25i; c-25i. **Kirby** a(p)/c-1-18. **Nasser** a-19i. **Rogers** a-19-22p; c-19, 20p, 21p, 22-24. 4-8 contain **Simon & Kirby** Boy Commandos reprints from Detective 82,76, Boy Commandos 1, 3 & Detective 64 in that order.*

MISTER MIRACLE (2nd Series) (See Justice League)
DC Comics: Jan, 1989 - No. 28, June, 1991 ($1.00/$1.25)
1-28: 13,14-Lobo app. 22-1st new Mr. Miracle w/new costume 3.00

MISTER MIRACLE (3rd Series)
DC Comics: Apr, 1996 - No. 7, Oct, 1996 ($1.95)
1-7: 2-Vs. JLA. 6-Simonson-c 3.00

MR. MIRACLE (See Capt. Fearless #1 & Holyoke One-Shot #4)

MR. MONSTER (1st Series)(Doc Stearn... #7 on; See Airboy-Mr. Monster Special, Dark Horse Presents, Super Duper Comics & Vanguard Illustrated #7)
Eclipse Comics: Jan, 1985 - No. 10, June, 1987 ($1.75, Baxter paper)
1-3: 1-1st story-r from Vanguard Ill. #7(1st app.). 2-Dave Stevens-c. 3-Alan Moore scripts; Wolverton-r/Weird Mysteries #5. 5.00
4-10: 6-Ditko-r/Fantastic Fears #5 plus new Giffen-a. 10- "6-D" issue 4.00

MR. MONSTER
Dark Horse Comics: Feb, 1988 - No. 8, July, 1991 ($1.75, B&W)
1-7 3.00
8-($4.95, 60 pgs.)-Origins conclusion 5.00

MR. MONSTER ATTACKS! (Doc Stearn...)
Tundra Publ.: Aug, 1992 - No. 3, Oct, 1992 ($3.95, limited series, 32 pgs.)
1-3: Michael T. Gilbert-a/scripts; Gilbert/Dorman painted-c 4.00

MR. MONSTER PRESENTS (CRACK-A-BOOM!)
Caliber Comics: 1997 - No. 3, 1997 ($2.95, B&W&Red, limited series)
1-3: Michael T. Gilbert-a/scripts: 1-Wraparound-c 3.00

MR. MONSTER'S GAL FRIDAY...KELLY!
Image Comics: Jan, 2000 - No. 3, May, 2004 ($3.50, B&W)
1-3-Michael T. Gilbert-c; story & art by various. 3-Alan Moore-s 3.50

MR. MONSTER'S SUPER-DUPER SPECIAL
Eclipse Comics: May, 1986 - No. 8, July, 1987
1-(5/86)...3-D High Octane Horror #1 5.00
1-(5/86)...2-D version, 100 copies 2 4 6 9 13 16
2-(8/86)...High Octane Horror #1, 3-(9/86)...True Crime #1, 4-(11/86)...True Crime #2, 5-(1/87)...Hi-Voltage Super Science #1, 6-(3/87)...High Shock Schlock #1, 7-(5/87)...High Shock Schlock #2, 8-(7/87)...Weird Tales Of The Future #1 4.00
*NOTE: **Jack Cole** r-3, 4. **Evans** a-2r. **Kubert** a-1r. **Powell** a-5r. **Wolverton** a-2r, 7r, 8r.*

MR. MONSTER VS. GORZILLA
Image Comics: July, 1998 ($2.95, one-shot)
1-Michael T. Gilbert-a 3.00

MR. MONSTER: WORLDS WAR TWO
Atomeka Press: 2004 ($6.99, one-shot)
nn-Michael T. Gilbert-s/George Freeman-a; two covers by Horley & Dorman 7.00

MR. MUSCLES (Formerly Blue Beetle #18-21)
Charlton Comics: No. 22, Mar, 1956; No. 23, Aug, 1956
22,23 9 18 27 50 65 80

MR. MXYZPTLK (VILLAINS)
DC Comics: Feb, 1998 ($1.95, one-shot)
1-Grant-s/Morgan-a/Pearson-c 3.00

MISTER MYSTERY (Tales of Horror and Suspense)
Mr. Publ. (Media Publ.) No. 1-3/SPM Publ./Stanmore (Aragon): Sept, 1951 - No. 19, Oct, 1954
1-Kurtzman*esque* horror story 103 206 309 659 1130 1600
2,3-Kurtzman*esque* story. 3-Anti-Wertham edit. 65 130 195 416 708 1000
4-Bondage-c 65 130 195 416 708 1000
5,8,10 58 116 174 371 636 900
6-Classic torture-c 97 194 291 621 1061 1500
7- "The Brain Bats of Venus" by Wolverton; partially re-used in Weird Tales of the Future #7 135 270 405 864 1482 2100
9-Nostrand-a 58 116 174 371 636 900
11-Wolverton "Robot Woman" story/Weird Mysteries #2, cut up, rewritten & partially redrawn 89 178 267 565 970 1375
12-Classic injury to eye-c 181 362 543 1158 1979 2800
13-17,19: 15- "Living Dead" junkie story. 16-Bondage-c. 17-Severed heads-c. 19-Reprints 47 94 141 296 498 700
18- "Robot Woman" by Wolverton reprinted from Weird Mysteries #2; decapitation, bondage-c 77 154 231 493 847 1200
*NOTE: **Andru** a-1, 2p, 3p. **Andru/Esposito** c-1-3. **Baily** c-10-18(most). **Mortellaro** c-5-7. Bondage c-7, 16. Some issues have graphic dismemberment scenes.*

MR. PUNCH
DC Comics (Vertigo): 1994 ($24.95, one-shot)
nn (Hard-c)-Gaiman scripts; McKean-c/a 40.00
nn (Soft-c) 15.00

MISTER Q (See Mighty Midget Comics & Our Flag Comics #5)

MR. RISK (Formerly All Romances; Men Against Crime #3 on)(Also see Our Flag Comics & Super-Mystery Comics)
Ace Magazines: No. 7, Oct, 1950; No. 2, Dec, 1950
7,2 12 24 36 67 94 120

MR. SCARLET & PINKY (See Mighty Midget Comics)

MR. T
APComics: May, 2005 ($3.50)
1-Chris Bunting-s/Neil Edwards-a 3.50

MR. T AND THE T-FORCE
Now Comics: June, 1993 - No. 10, May, 1994 ($1.95, color)
1-10-Newsstand editions: 1-7-polybagged with photo trading card in each. 1,2-Neal Adams-c/a(p). 3-Dave Dorman painted-c 3.00
1-10-Direct Sale editions polybagged w/line drawn trading cards. 1-Contains gold foil trading card by Neal Adams 3.00

MISTER TERRIFIC (DC New 52)(Leads into Earth 2 series)
DC Comics: Nov, 2011 - No. 8, Jun, 2012 ($2.99)
1-8: 1-Wallace-s/Gugliotta-a/JG Jones-c; origin re-told. 2-Intro. Brainstorm 3.00

MISTER UNIVERSE (Professional wrestler)
Mr. Publications Media Publ. (Stanmor, Aragon): July, 1951; No. 2, Oct, 1951 - No. 5, April, 1952
1 22 44 66 132 216 300
2- "Jungle That Time Forgot", (24 pg. story); Andru/Esposito-c 14 28 42 82 121 160
3-Marijuana story 14 28 42 82 121 160
4,5- "Goes to War" cover/stories 11 22 33 64 90 115

MISTER X (See Vortex)
Mr. Publications/Vortex Comics/Caliber V3#1 on: 6/84 - No. 14, 8/88 ($1.50/$2.25, direct sales, coated paper);V2#1, Apr, 1989 - V2#12, Mar, 1990 ($2.00/$2.50, B&W, newsprint) V3#1, 1996 - Present ($2.95, B&W)
1-14: 11-Dave McKean story & art (6 pgs.) 4.00
V2 #1-12: 1-11 (Second Coming, B&W): 1-Four diff.-c. 10-Photo-c 3.00
V3 #1-4 3.00
Return of... ($11.95, graphic novel)-r/V1#1-4 12.00
Return of... ($34.95, hardcover limited edition)-r/1-4 35.00
Special (no date, 1990?) 3.00

MISTER X: CONDEMNED
Dark Horse Comics: Dec, 2008 - No. 4, Mar, 2009 ($3.50, limited series)
1-4-Dean Motter-s/a 3.50

MISTY
Marvel Comics (Star Comics): Dec, 1985 - No. 6, May, 1986 (Limited series)
1-6: Millie The Model's niece 4.00

MITZI COMICS (Becomes Mitzi's Boy Friend #2-7)(See All Teen)
Timely Comics: Spring, 1948 (one-shot)
1-Kurtzman's "Hey Look" plus 3 pgs. "Giggles 'n' Grins" 32 64 96 188 307 425

MITZI'S BOY FRIEND (Formerly Mitzi Comics; becomes Mitzi's Romances)
Marvel Comics (TCI): No. 2, June, 1948 - No. 7, April, 1949
2 16 32 48 94 147 200
3-7 14 28 42 80 115 150

MITZI'S ROMANCES (Formerly Mitzi's Boy Friend)
Timely/Marvel Comics (TCI): No. 8, June, 1949 - No. 10, Dec, 1949
8-Becomes True Life Tales #8 (10/49) on? 14 28 42 82 121 160
9,10: 10-Painted-c 13 26 39 72 101 130

MNEMOVORE

Modeling With Millie #48 © MAR

Mod Wheels #12 © GK

The Monkees #4 © Raybert Prods.

	GD 2.0	VG 4.0	FN 6.0	VF 8.0	VF/NM 9.0	NM- 9.2
DC Comics (Vertigo): Jun, 2005 - No. 6, Nov, 2005 ($2.99, limited series)						
1-6-Rodionoff & Fawkes-s/Huddleston-a/c						3.00
MOBY DICK (See Feature Presentations #6, and King Classics)						
Dell Publishing Co.: No. 717, Aug, 1956						
Four Color 717-Movie, Gregory Peck photo-c	8	16	24	55	93	130
MOBY DUCK (See Donald Duck #112 & Walt Disney Showcase #2,11)						
Gold Key (Disney): Oct, 1967 - No. 11, Oct, 1970; No. 12, Jan, 1974 - No. 30, Feb, 1978						
1	3	6	9	21	32	42
2-5	2	4	6	11	16	20
6-11	2	4	6	9	13	16
12-30: 21,30-r	1	3	4	6	8	10
MODEL FUN (With Bobby Benson)						
Harle Publications: No. 2, Fall, 1954 - No. 5, July, 1955						
2-Bobby Benson	7	14	21	35	43	50
3-5-Bobby Benson	5	10	15	23	28	32
MODELING WITH MILLIE (Formerly Life With Millie)						
Atlas/Marvel Comics (Male Publ.): No. 21, Feb, 1963 - No. 54, June, 1967						
21	9	18	27	63	112	160
22-30	6	12	18	39	62	85
31-53	5	10	15	32	51	70
54-Last issue; Gears-c & 6 pg. story; Beatles swipe imitators; FF #63 comic appears in story; "Millie the Marvel" 6 pg. story as super-hero	6	12	18	37	59	80
MODELS, INC.						
Marvel Comics: Oct, 2009 - No. 4, Jan, 2010 ($3.99, limited series)						
1-4-Millie the Model, Patsy Walker, Mary Jane Watson app.; Land-c. 1-Tim Gunn app.						4.00
MODERN COMICS (Formerly Military Comics #1-43)						
Quality Comics Group: No. 44, Nov, 1945 - No. 102, Oct, 1950						
44-Blackhawk continues	52	104	156	328	557	785
45-52: 49-1st app. Fear, Lady Adventuress	38	76	114	228	369	510
53-Torchy by Ward begins (9/46)	42	84	126	265	445	625
54-60: 55-J. Cole-a	32	64	96	192	314	435
61-Classic-c	39	78	117	231	378	525
62-64,66-77,79,80: 73-J. Cole-a	31	62	93	182	296	410
65-Classic Grim Reaper Skull-c	50	100	150	315	533	750
78-1st app. Madame Butterfly	34	68	102	199	325	450
81-99,101: 82,83-One pg. J. Cole-a. 83-Last 52 pg. issue 99-Blackhawks on the moon-c/story	29	58	87	170	278	385
100	31	62	93	186	303	420
102-(Scarce)-J. Cole-a; Spirit by Eisner app.	38	76	114	229	375	520

NOTE: ***Al Bryant** c-44-51, 54, 55, 66, 69. **Jack Cole** a-55, 73. **Crandall** Blackhawk-#46, 47, 50, 51, 54, 56, 58-60, 64, 67-70, 73, 74, 76-78, 80-83; c-60-65, 67, 68, 70-95. **Crandall/Cuidera** c-56-59, 96-102. **Gustavson** a-47, 49. **Ward** Blackhawk-#52, 53, 55 (15 pgs. each). Torchy in #53-102; by **Ward** only in #53-89(9/49); by **Gil Fox** #92, 93, 102.*

	GD 2.0	VG 4.0	FN 6.0	VF 8.0	VF/NM 9.0	NM- 9.2
MODERN LOVE						
E. C. Comics: June-July, 1949 - No. 8, Aug-Sept, 1950						
1-Feldstein, Ingels-a	87	174	261	553	952	1350
2-Craig/Feldstein-c/s	54	108	162	343	574	825
3	48	96	144	302	514	725
4-6 (Scarce): 4-Bra/panties panels	60	120	180	381	653	925
7,8	48	96	144	302	514	725

NOTE: ***Craig** a-3. **Feldstein** a-in most issues; c-1, 2i, 3-8. **Harrison** a-4. **Iger** a-6-8. **Ingels** a-1, 2, 4-7. **Palais** a-5. **Wood** a-7. **Wood/Harrison** a-5-7. (Canadian reprints known; see Table of Contents.)*

	GD 2.0	VG 4.0	FN 6.0	VF 8.0	VF/NM 9.0	NM- 9.2
MODERN WARFARE 2: GHOST (Based on the videogame)						
DC Comics (WildStorm): Jan, 2010 - No. 6, Sept, 2010 ($3.99, limited series)						
1-6: 1-Two covers; Lapham-s/West-a						4.00
TPB (2010, $17.99) r/#1-6; cover sketches and sketch art						18.00
MOD LOVE						
Western Publishing Co.: 1967 (50¢, 36 pgs.)						
1-(Low print)	6	12	18	39	66	90
MODNIKS, THE						
Gold Key: Aug, 1967 - No. 2, Aug, 1970						
10206-708(#1)	4	8	12	22	34	45
2	3	6	9	16	22	28
M.O.D.O.K.: REIGN DELAY						
Marvel Comics: Nov, 2009 ($3.99, one-shot)						
1-M.O.D.O.K. cartoony humor stories from Marvel Digital Comics; Ryan Dunlavey-s/a						4.00
MOD SQUAD (TV)						
Dell Publishing Co.: Jan, 1969 - No. 3, Oct, 1969 - No. 8, April, 1971						
1-Photo-c	7	14	21	44	72	100
2-4: 2-4-Photo-c	4	8	12	28	44	60
5-8: 8-Photo-c; Reprints #2	4	8	12	24	37	50
MOD WHEELS						
Gold Key: Mar, 1971 - No. 19, Jan, 1976						
1	4	8	12	26	41	55
2-9	3	6	9	16	23	30
10-19: 11,15-Extra 16 pgs. ads	3	6	9	14	19	24
MOE & SHMOE COMICS						
O. S. Publ. Co.: Spring, 1948 - No. 2, Summer, 1948						
1	9	18	27	47	61	75
2	6	12	18	31	38	45
MOEBIUS (Graphic novel)						
Marvel Comics (Epic Comics): Oct, 1987 - No. 6, 1988; No. 7, 1990; No. 8, 1991 ($9.95, 8x11", mature)						
1,2,4-6,8: (#2, 2nd printing, $9.95)	3	6	9	16	22	28
3,7,0: 3-(1st & 2nd printings, $12.95). 0 (1990, $12.95)	3	6	9	17	25	32
Moebius I-Signed & #'d hard-c ($45.95, Graphitti Designs, 1,500 copies printed)-r/#1-3	5	10	15	32	51	70
MOEBIUS COMICS						
Caliber: May, 1996 - No. 6 ($2.95, B&W)						
1-6: Moebius-c/a. 1-William Stout-a						4.00
MOEBIUS: THE MAN FROM CIGURI						
Dark Horse Comics: 1996 ($7.95, digest-size)						
nn-Moebius-c/a	1	2	3	5	7	9
MOLLY MANTON'S ROMANCES (Romantic Affairs #3)						
Marvel Comics (SePI): Sept, 1949 - No. 2, Dec, 1949 (52 pgs.)						
1-Photo-c (becomes Blaze the Wonder Collie #2 (10/49) on? & Molly Manton's Romances #2	19	38	57	111	176	240
2-Titled "Romances of..."; photo-c	14	28	42	80	115	150
MOLLY O'DAY (Super Sleuth)						
Avon Periodicals: February, 1945 (1st Avon comic)						
1-Molly O'Day, The Enchanted Dagger by Tuska (r/Yankee #1), Capt'n Courage, Corporal Grant app.	60	120	180	381	653	925
MOMENT OF SILENCE						
Marvel Comics: Feb, 2002 ($3.50, one-shot)						
1-Tributes to the heroes and victims of Sept. 11; s/a by various						3.50
MONARCHY, THE (Also see The Authority and StormWatch)						
DC Comics (WildStorm): Apr, 2001 - No. 12, May, 2002 ($2.50)						
1-12: 1-McCrea & Leach-a/Young-s						3.00
Bullets Over Babylon TPB (2001, $12.95) r/#1-4, Authority #21						13.00
MONKEES, THE (TV)(Also see Circus Boy, Groovy, Not Brand Echh #3, Teen-Age Talk, Teen Beam & Teen Beat)						
Dell Publishing Co.: March, 1967 - No. 17, Oct, 1969						
1-Photo-c	10	20	30	66	121	175
2-17: All photo-c. 17-Reprints #1	6	12	18	42	69	95
MONKEY AND THE BEAR, THE						
Atlas Comics (ZPC): Sept, 1953 - No. 3, Jan, 1954						
1-Howie Post-c/a in all; funny animal	10	20	30	54	72	90
2,3	8	16	24	40	50	60
MONKEYMAN AND O'BRIEN (Also see Dark Horse Presents #80, 100-5, Gen13/..., Hellboy: Seed of Destruction, & San Diego Comic Con #2)						
Dark Horse Comics (Legend): Jul, 1996 - No. 3, Sept, 1996 ($2.95, lim. series)						
1-3: New stories; Art Adams-c/a/scripts						4.00
nn-(2/96, $2.95)-r/back-up stories from Hellboy: Seed of Destruction; Adams-c/a/scripts						4.00
MONKEYSHINES COMICS						
Ace Periodicals/Publishers Specialists/Current Books/Unity Publ.: Summer, 1944 - No. 27, July, 1949						
1-Funny animal	15	30	45	84	127	170
2-(Aut/44)	10	20	30	54	72	90
3-10: 3-(Win/44)	9	18	27	50	65	80
11-18,20-27: 23,24-Fago-c/a	8	16	24	40	50	60
19-Frazetta-a	9	18	27	50	65	80

Monster Crime Comics #1 © HILL

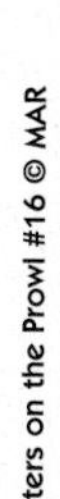

Monsters on the Prowl #16 © MAR

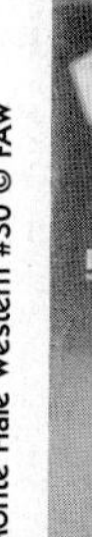

Monte Hale Western #30 © FAW

GD VG FN VF VF/NM NM-
2.0 4.0 6.0 8.0 9.0 9.2

MONKEY'S UNCLE, THE (See Merlin Jones As... under Movie Comics)

MONOLITH, THE
DC Comics: Apr, 2004 - No. 12, Mar, 2005 ($3.50/$2.95)

1-($3.50) Palmiotti & Gray-s/Winslade-a 3.50
2-12-($2.95): 6-8-Batman app.; Coker-a 3.00

MONROES, THE (TV)
Dell Publishing Co.: Apr, 1967

1-Photo-c 3 6 9 18 27 35

MONSTER
Fiction House Magazines: 1953 - No. 2, 1953

1-Dr. Drew by Grandenetti; reprint from Rangers Comics #48; Whitman-c
53 106 159 334 567 800
2-Whitman-c 40 80 120 242 401 560

MONSTER CRIME COMICS (Also see Crime Must Stop)
Hillman Periodicals: Oct, 1952 (15¢, 52 pgs.)

1 (Scarce) 181 362 543 1158 1979 2800

MONSTER HOUSE (Companion to the 2006 movie)
IDW Publishing: June, 2006 ($7.99, one-shot)

nn-Two stories about Bones and Skull by Joshua Dysart and Simeon Wilkins 8.00

MONSTER HOWLS (Magazine)
Humor-Vision: December, 1966 (Satire) (35¢, 68 pgs.)

1-John Severin 6 12 18 39 62 85

MONSTER HUNTERS
Charlton Comics: Aug, 1975 - No. 9, Jan, 1977; No. 10, Oct, 1977 - No. 18, Feb, 1979

1-Howard-a; Newton-c; 1st Countess Von Bludd and Colonel Whiteshroud
3 6 9 18 27 35
2-Sutton-c/a; Ditko-a 3 6 9 14 19 24
3,4,5,7: 4-Sutton-c/a 2 4 6 9 12 15
6,8,10: 6,8,10-Ditko-a 2 4 6 10 14 18
9,11,12 1 3 4 6 8 10
13,15,18-Ditko-c/a. 18-Sutton-a 2 4 6 10 14 18
14-Special all-Ditko issue 3 6 9 17 25 32
16,17-Sutton-a 2 3 4 6 8 10
1,2 (Modern Comics reprints, 1977) 6.00

NOTE: ***Ditko** a-2, 6, 8, 10, 13-15r, 18r; c-13-15, 18. **Howard** a-1, 3, 17; r-13. **Morisi** a-1. **Staton** a-1, 13. **Sutton** a-2, 4; c-2, 4; r-16-18. **Zeck** a-4-9. Reprints in #12-18.*

MONSTER MADNESS (Magazine)
Marvel Comics: 1972 - No. 3, 1973 (60¢, B&W)

1-3: Stories by "Sinister" Stan Lee. 1-Frankenstein photo-c. 2-Son of Frankenstein photo-c. 3-Bride of Frankenstein photo-c 4 8 12 26 41 55

MONSTER MAN
Image Comics (Action Planet): Sept, 1997 ($2.95, B&W)

1-Mike Manley-c/s/a 3.00

MONSTER MASTERWORKS
Marvel Comics: 1989 ($12.95, TPB)

nn-Reprints 1960's monster stories; art by Kirby, Ditko, Ayers, Everett 20.00

MONSTER MATINEE
Chaos! Comics: Oct, 1997 - No. 3, Oct, 1997 ($2.50, limited series)

1-3: pin-ups 3.00

MONSTER MENACE
Marvel Comics: Dec, 1993 - No. 4, Mar, 1994 ($1.25, limited series)

1-4: Pre-code Atlas horror reprints. 6.00

NOTE: ***Ditko**-r & **Kirby**-r in all.*

MONSTER OF FRANKENSTEIN (See Frankenstein and Essential Monster of Frankenstein)

MONSTER PILE-UP
Image Comics: Aug, 2008 ($1.99)

1-New short stories of Astounding Wolf-Man, Firebreather, Perhapanauts, Proof 3.00

MONSTERS ATTACK (Magazine)
Globe Communications Corpse: Sept, 1989 - No. 5, Dec, 1990 (B&W)

1-5-Ditko, Morrow, J. Severin-a. 5-Toth, Morrow-a 1 2 3 4 5 7

MONSTERS, INC. (Based on the Disney/Pixar movie)
BOOM! Studios: Jun, 2009 - No. 4, Nov, 2009 ($2.99, limited series)

...: Laugh Factory 1-4: 1,3-Three covers. 2,4-Two covers 3.00

MONSTERS ON THE PROWL (Chamber of Darkness #1-8)
Marvel Comics Group (No. 13,14: 52 pgs.): No. 9, 2/71 - No. 27, 11/73; No. 28, 6/74 - No. 30, 10/74

9-Barry Smith inks 4 8 12 28 44 60
10-12,15: 12-Last 15¢ issue 3 6 9 17 25 32
13,14-(52 pgs.) 3 6 9 20 30 40
16-(4/72)-King Kull 4th app.; Severin-c 3 6 9 20 30 40
17-30 3 6 9 14 20 26

NOTE: ***Ditko** r-9, 14, 16. **Kirby** r-10-17, 21, 23, 25, 27, 28, 30; c-9, 25. **Kirby/Ditko** r-14, 17-20, 22, 24, 26, 29. **Marie/John Severin** a-16(Kull). 9-13, 15 contain one new story. Woodish art by **Reese**-11. King Kull created by Robert E. Howard.*

MONSTERS TO LAUGH WITH (Magazine) (Becomes Monsters Unlimited #4)
Marvel Comics Group: 1964 - No. 3, 1965 (B&W)

1-Humor by Stan Lee 8 16 24 51 86 120
2,3 5 10 15 32 51 70

MONSTERS UNLEASHED (Magazine)
Marvel Comics Group: July, 1973 - No. 11, Apr, 1975; Summer, 1975 (B&W)

1-Soloman Kane sty; Werewolf app. 5 10 15 30 48 65
2-4: 2-The Frankenstein Monster begins, ends #10. 3-Neal Adams-c/a; The Man-Thing begins (origin-r); Son of Satan preview. 4-Werewolf app. 4 8 12 24 37 50
5-7: Werewolf in all. 5-Man-Thing. 7-Williamson-a(r) 3 6 9 18 27 35
8-11: 8-Man-Thing; N. Adams-r. 9-Man-Thing; Wendigo app. 10-Origin Tigra
3 6 9 19 29 38
Annual 1 (Summer,1975, 92 pgs.)-Kane-a 3 6 9 18 27 35

NOTE: ***Boris** c-2, 6. **Brunner** a-2; c-11. **J. Buscema** a-2p, 4p, 5p. **Colan** a-1, 4r. **Davis** a-3r. **Everett** a-2r. **G. Kane** a-3. **Krigstein** r-4. **Morrow** a-3; c-1. **Perez** a-8. **Ploog** a-6. **Reese** a-1, 2. **Tuska** a-3p. **Wildey** a-1r.*

MONSTERS UNLIMITED (Magazine) (Formerly Monsters To Laugh With)
Marvel Comics Group: No. 4, 1965 - No. 7, 1966 (B&W)

4-7: 4,7-Frankenstein photo-c 5 10 15 32 51 70

MONSTER WORLD
DC Comics (WildStorm): Jul, 2001 - No. 4, Oct, 2001 ($2.50, limited series)

1-4-Lobdell-s/Meglia-c/a 3.00

MONTANA KID, THE (See Kid Montana)

MONTE HALE WESTERN (Movie star; Formerly Mary Marvel #1-28; also see Fawcett Movie Comic, Motion Picture Comics, Picture News #8, Real Western Hero, Six-Gun Heroes, Western Hero & XMas Comics)
Fawcett Publ./Charlton No. 83 on: No. 29, Oct, 1948 - No. 88, Jan, 1956

29-(#1, 52 pgs.)-Photo-c begin, end #82; Monte Hale & his horse Pardner begin
26 52 78 154 252 350
30-(52 pgs.)-Big Bow and Little Arrow begin, end #34; Captain Tootsie by Beck
14 28 42 80 115 150
31-36,38-40-(52 pgs.): 34-Gabby Hayes begins, ends #80. 39-Captain Tootsie by Beck
12 24 36 67 94 120
37,41,45,49-(36 pgs.) 10 20 30 54 72 90
42-44,46-48,50-(52 pgs.): 47-Big Bow & Little Arrow app.
10 20 30 58 79 100
51,52,54-56,58,59-(52 pgs.) 9 18 27 52 69 85
53,57-(36 pgs.): 53-Slim Pickens app. 8 16 24 44 57 70
60-81: 36 pgs. #60-on. 80-Gabby Hayes ends 8 16 24 42 54 65
82-Last Fawcett issue (6/53) 9 18 27 52 69 85
83-1st Charlton issue (2/55); B&W photo back-c begin. Gabby Hayes returns, ends #86
10 20 30 58 79 100
84 (4/55) 8 16 24 44 57 70
85-86 8 16 24 42 54 65
87,88: 87-Wolverton-r, 1/2 pg. 88-Last issue 8 16 24 44 57 70

NOTE: ***Gil Kane** a-33?, 34? Rocky Lane -1 pg. (Carnation ad)-38, 40, 41, 43, 44, 46, 55.*

MONTY HALL OF THE U.S. MARINES (See With the Marines...)
Toby Press: Aug, 1951 - No. 11, Apr, 1953

1 12 24 36 69 97 125
2 8 16 24 42 54 65
3-5 8 16 24 40 50 60
6-11 7 14 21 37 46 55

NOTE: *Full page pin-ups (Pin-Up Pete) by **Jack Sparling** in #1-9.*

MOON, A GIRL...ROMANCE, A (Becomes Weird Fantasy #13 on; formerly Moon Girl #1-8)
E. C. Comics: No. 9, Sept-Oct, 1949 - No. 12, Mar-Apr, 1950

9-Moon Girl cameo 83 166 249 527 906 1285
10,11 68 136 204 432 746 1060
12-(Scarce) 83 166 249 527 906 1285

NOTE: ***Feldstein, Ingels** art in all. **Feldstein** c-9-12. **Wood/Harrison** a-10-12. Canadian reprints known; see Table of Contents.*

MOON GIRL AND THE PRINCE (#1) (Moon Girl #2-6; Moon Girl Fights Crime #7, 8; becomes

Moon Knight #17 © MAR

Moonshadow #7 © DeMatteis & Muth

Mopsy #2 © STJ

GD VG FN VF VF/NM NM-
2.0 4.0 6.0 8.0 9.0 9.2

GD VG FN VF VF/NM NM-
2.0 4.0 6.0 8.0 9.0 9.2

A Moon, A Girl, Romance #9 on)(Also see Animal Fables #7, Int. Crime Patrol #6, Happy Houlihans & Tales From The Crypt #22)
E. C. Comics: Fall, 1947 - No. 8, Summer, 1949

1-Origin Moon Girl (see Happy Houlihans #1). Intro Santana, Queen of the Underworld
110 220 330 704 1202 1700
2-Moon Girl battles Futureman 64 128 192 406 696 985
3,4: 3-Santana, Queen of the Underworld returns. 4-Moon Girl vs. a vampire
55 110 165 352 601 850
5-E.C.'s 1st horror story, "Zombie Terror" 123 246 369 787 1344 1900
6-8 (Scarce): 7-Origin Star (Moongirl's sidekick) 64 128 192 406 696 985
NOTE: *Craig a-2, 5; c-1, 2.* ***Moldoff*** *a-1-8; c-3-8 (Shelly).* ***Wheelan's*** *Fat and Slat app. in #3, 4, 6. #2 & #3 are 52 pgs., #4 on, 36 pgs. Canadian reprints known; (see Table of Contents.)*

MOON KNIGHT (Also see The Hulk, Marc Spector..., Marvel Preview #21, Marvel Spotlight & Werewolf by Night #32)
Marvel Comics Group: Nov, 1980 - No. 38, Jul, 1984 (Mando paper #33 on)

1-Origin resumed in #4 6.00
2-15,25,35: 4-Intro Midnight Man. 25-Double size. 35-($1.00, 52 pgs.)-X-Men app.; F.F. cameo 4.00
16-24,26-28,30-34,36-38: 16-The Thing app. 3.00
29,30-Werewolf By Night app. 4.00
NOTE: ***Austin*** *c-27i, 31i.* ***Cowan*** *a-16; c-16, 17.* ***Kaluta*** *c-36-38; back c-35.* ***Miller*** *c-9, 12p, 13p, 15p, 27p.* ***Ploog*** *back c-35.* ***Sienkiewicz*** *a-1-15, 17-20, 22-26, 28-30, 33i, 36(4), 37; c-1-5, 7, 8, 10, 11, 14-16, 18-26, 28-30, 31p, 33, 34.*

MOON KNIGHT
Marvel Comics Group: June, 1985 - V2#6, Dec, 1985

V2#1-Double size; new costume 4.00
V2#2-6: 6-Sienkiewicz painted-c 3.00

MOON KNIGHT
Marvel Comics: Jan, 1998 - No. 4, Apr, 1998 ($2.50, limited series)

1-4-Moench-s/Edwards-c/a 3.00

MOON KNIGHT (Volume 3)
Marvel Comics: Jan, 1999 - No. 4, Feb, 1999 ($2.99, limited series)

1-4-Moench-s/Texeira-a(p) 3.00

MOON KNIGHT (Fourth series) (Leads into Vengeance of the Moon Knight)
Marvel Comics: June, 2006 - No. 30, Jul, 2009 ($2.99)

1-Finch-a/c; Huston-s 4.00
1-B&W sketch variant-c 6.00
2-19,21-26: 7-Spider-Man app. 9,10-Punisher app. 13-Suydam-c begin. 23-25-Bullseye 3.00
20-($3.99) Deodato-a; back-up r/1st app. in Werewolf By Night #32,33 4.00
Annual 1 (1/08, $3.99) Swierczynski-s/Palo-a 4.00
... Saga (2009, free) synopsis of origin and major storylines 3.00
...: Silent Knight 1 (1/09, $3.99) Milligan-s/Laurence Campbell-a/Crain-c 4.00
... Vol. 1: The Bottom HC (2006, $19.99) r/#1-6; Huston afterword; 2 covers 20.00
... Vol. 1: The Bottom SC (2007, $14.99) r/#1-6; Huston afterword 15.00
... Vol. 2: Midnight Sun HC (2008, $19.99) r/#7-13 & Annual #1 20.00
... Vol. 2: Midnight Sun SC (2008, $14.99) r/#7-13 & Annual #1 15.00

MOON KNIGHT (Fifth series)
Marvel Comics: Jul, 2011 - Present ($3.99, limited series)

1-Bendis-s/Maleev-a/c; Wolverine, Spider-Man and Capt. America "app." 4.00
2-10: 2-Echo returns. 3-Bullseye-c 4.00

MOON KNIGHT: DIVIDED WE FALL
Marvel Comics: 1992 ($4.95, 52 pgs.)

nn-Denys Cowan-c/a(p) 5.00

MOON KNIGHT SPECIAL
Marvel Comics: Oct, 1992 ($2.50, 52 pgs.)

1-Shang Chi, Master of Kung Fu-c/story 4.00

MOON KNIGHT SPECIAL EDITION
Marvel Comics Group: Nov, 1983 - No. 3, Jan, 1984 ($2.00, limited series, Baxter paper)

1-3: Reprints from Hulk mag. by Sienkiewicz 4.00

MOON MULLINS (See Popular Comics, Super Book #3 & Super Comics)
Dell Publishing Co.: 1941 - 1945

Four Color 14(1941) 45 90 135 284 480 675
Large Feature Comic 29(1941) 36 72 108 211 343 475
Four Color 31(1943) 15 30 45 102 221 340
Four Color 81(1945) 10 20 30 68 127 185

MOON MULLINS
Michel Publ. (American Comics Group)#1-6/St. John #7,8: Dec-Jan, 1947-48 - No. 8, Mar-May, 1949 (52 pgs)

1-Alternating Sunday & daily strip-r 22 44 66 128 209 290
2 14 28 42 78 112 145
3-8: 7,8-St. John Publ. 8-...Featuring Kayo on-c 13 26 39 74 105 135
NOTE: ***Milt Gross*** *a-2-6, 8.* ***Frank Willard*** *r-all.*

MOON PILOT
Dell Publishing Co.: No. 1313, Mar-May, 1962

Four Color 1313-Movie, photo-c 7 14 21 46 76 105

MOONSHADOW (Also see Farewell, Moonshadow)
Marvel Comics (Epic Comics): 5/85 - #12, 2/87 ($1.50/$1.75, mature)
(1st fully painted comic book)

1-Origin; J. M. DeMatteis scripts & Jon J. Muth painted-c/a. 6.00
2-12: 11-Origin 4.00
Trade paperback (1987?)-r/#1-12 14.00
Signed & #ed HC ($39.95, 1,200 copies)-r/#1-12 4 8 12 28 44 60

MOONSHADOW
DC Comics (Vertigo): Oct, 1994 - No. 12, Aug, 1995 ($2.25/$2.95)

1-11: Reprints Epic series. 3.00
12 ($2.95)-w/expanded ending 4.00
The Complete Moonshadow TPB ('98, $39.95) r/#1-12 and Farewell Moonshadow; new Muth painted-c 40.00

MOON-SPINNERS, THE (See Movie Comics)

MOONSTONE MONSTERS
Moonstone: 2003 - 2005 ($2.95, B&W)

...: Demons ($2.95) - Short stories by various; Frenz-c 3.00
...: Ghosts ($2.95) - Short stories by various; Frenz-c 3.00
...: Sea Creatures ($2.95) - Short stories by various; Frenz-c 3.00
...: Witches ($2.95) - Short stories by various; Frenz-c 3.00
...: Zombies ($2.95) - Short stories by various; Frenz-c 3.00
Volume 1 (2004, $16.95, TPB) r/short stories from series; Wolak-c 17.00

MOONSTONE NOIR
Moonstone: 2003 - Present ($2.95/$4.95/$5.50, B&W)

...: Bulldog Drummond (2004, $4.95) - Messner-Loebs-s/Barkley-a 5.00
...: Johnny Dollar ($4.95) - Gallaher-s/Theriault-a 5.00
...: Mr. Keen, Tracer of Lost Persons 1,2 ($2.95, limited series) - Ferguson-a 3.00
...: Mysterious Traveler (2003, $5.50) - Trevor Von Eeden-a/Joe Gentile-s 5.50
...: Mysterious Traveler Returns (2004, $4.95) - Trevor Von Eeden-a/Joe Gentile-s 5.00
...: The Lone Wolf ($4.95) - Jolley-s/Croall-a 5.00

MOPSY (See Pageant of Comics & TV Teens)
St. John Publ. Co.: Feb, 1948 - No. 19, Sept, 1953

1-Part-r; reprints "Some Punkins" by Neher 18 36 54 103 162 220
2 11 22 33 62 86 110
3-10(1953): 8-Lingerie panels 10 20 30 56 76 95
11-19: 19-Lingerie-c 9 18 27 52 69 85
NOTE: *#1-7, 13, 18, 19 have paper dolls.*

MORBIUS REVISITED
Marvel Comic: Aug, 1993 - No. 5, Dec, 1993 ($1.95, mini-series)

1-5-Reprints Fear #27-31 3.00

MORBIUS: THE LIVING VAMPIRE (Also see Amazing Spider-Man #101,102, Fear #20, Marvel Team-Up #3, 4, Midnight Sons Unl. & Vampire Tales)
Marvel Comics (Midnight Sons imprint #16 on): Sep, 1992 - No. 32, Apr, 1995 ($1.75/$1.95)

1-($2.75, 52 pgs.)-Polybagged w/poster; Ghost Rider & Johnny Blaze x-over (part 3 of Rise of the Midnight Sons) 4.00
2-11,13-24,26-32: 3,4-Vs. Spider-Man-c/s.15-Ghost Rider app. 16-Spot varnish-c. 16,17-Siege of Darkness, parts 5 &13. 18-Deathlok app. 21-Bound-in Spider-Man trading card sheet; Spider-Man app. 3.00
12-($2.25)-Outer-c is a Darkhold envelope made of black parchment w/gold ink; Midnight Massacre x-over 3.00
25-($2.50, 52 pgs.)-Gold foil logo 4.00

MORE FUN COMICS (Formerly New Fun Comics #1-6)
National Periodical Publs: No. 7, Jan, 1936 - No. 127, Nov-Dec, 1947 (No. 7,9-11: paper-c)

7(1/36)-Oversized, paper-c; 1 pg. Kelly-a 850 1700 2550 6800 - -
8(2/36)-Oversized (10x12"), paper-c; 1 pg. Kelly-a; Sullivan-c
850 1700 2550 6800 - -
9(3-4/36)(Very rare, 1st standard-sized comic book with original material)-Last multiple panel-c 1025 2050 3075 8200 - -
10,11(7/36): 10-Last Henri Duval by Siegel & Shuster. 11-1st "Calling All Cars" by Siegel & Shuster; new classic logo begins 594 1188 1782 4750 - -

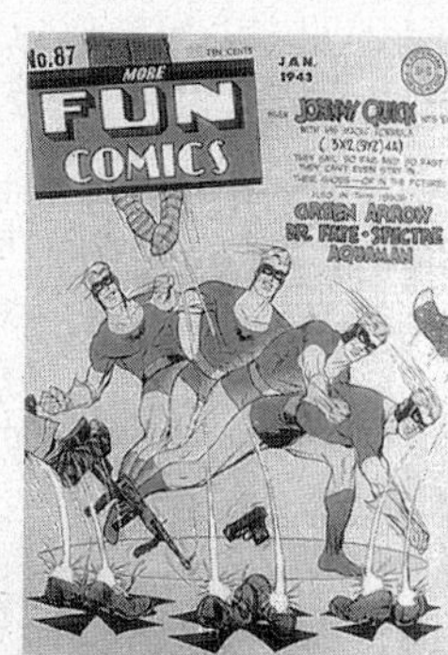

More Fun Comics #87 © DC

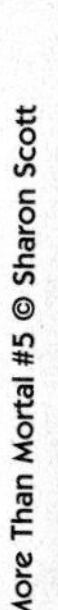

More Than Mortal #5 © Sharon Scott

Morning Glories #7 © Spencer & Eisma

	GD 2.0	VG 4.0	FN 6.0	VF 8.0	VF/NM 9.0	NM- 9.2
12(8/36)-Slick-c begin	463	926	1389	3700	-	-
V2#1(9/36, #13) 1 pg. Fred Astaire photo/bio	425	850	1275	3400	-	-
2(10/36, #14)-Dr. Occult in costume (1st in color)(Superman proto-type; 1st DC appearance) continues from The Comics Magazine, ends #17	1938	3876	5814	15,500	-	-
V2#3(11/36, #15), 17(V2#5)	788	1576	2364	6300	-	-
16(V2#4)-Cover numbering begins; ties with New Comics #11 as 1st DC Christmas-c; last Superman tryout issue	813	1626	2439	6500	-	-
18-20(V2#8, 5/37)	338	676	1014	2700	-	-
21(V2#9)-24(V2#12, 9/37)	276	552	828	1518	2309	3100
25(V3#1, 10/37)-27(V3#3, 12/37): 27-Xmas-c	276	552	828	1518	2309	3100
28-30: 30-1st non-funny cover	250	500	750	1375	2088	2800
31-Has ad for Action Comics #1	265	530	795	1458	2204	2950
32-35: 32-Last Dr. Occult	250	500	750	1375	2088	2800
36-40: 36-(10/38)-The Masked Ranger & sidekick Pedro begins; Ginger Snap by Bob Kane (2 pgs.; 1st-a?). 39-Xmas-c	250	500	750	1375	2088	2800
41-50: 41-Last Masked Ranger	212	424	636	1166	1833	2500
51-The Spectre app. (in costume) in one panel ad at end of Buccaneer story	741	1482	2223	4076	6038	8000
52-(2/40)-Origin/1st app. The Spectre (in costume splash panel only), part 1 by Bernard Baily (parts 1 & 2 written by Jerry Siegel; Spectre's costume changes color from purple & blue to green & grey; last Wing Brady; Spectre-c	8000	16,000	24,000	60,000	105,000	150,000
53-Origin The Spectre (in costume at end of story), part 2; Capt. Desmo begins; Spectre-c	3250	6500	9750	22,750	49,875	77,000
54-The Spectre in costume; last King Carter; classic-Spectre-c	1800	3600	5400	13,500	24,750	36,000
55-(Scarce, 5/40)-Dr. Fate begins (1st app.); last Bulldog Martin; Spectre-c	1700	3400	5100	12,750	23,375	34,000
56-1st Dr. Fate-c (classic), origin continues. Congo Bill begins (6/40), 1st app.;	865	1730	2595	6315	11,158	16,000
57-60-All Spectre-c	443	886	1329	3234	5717	8200
61,65: 61-Classic Dr. Fate-c. 65-Classic Spectre-c	423	846	1269	3000	5250	7500
62-64,66: 63-Last Lt. Bob Neal. 64-Lance Larkin begins; all Spectre-c	331	662	993	2317	4059	5800
67-(5/41)-Origin (1st) Dr. Fate; last Congo Bill & Biff Bronson (Congo Bill continues in Action Comics #37, 6/41)-Spectre-c	622	1244	1866	4541	8021	11,500
68-70: 68-Clip Carson begins. 70-Last Lance Larkin; all Dr. Fate-c	290	580	870	1856	3178	4500
71-Origin & 1st app. Johnny Quick by Mort Weisinger (9/41); classic sci/fi Dr. Fate-c	432	864	1296	3154	5577	8000
72-Dr. Fate's new helmet; last Sgt. Carey, Sgt. O'Malley & Captain Desmo; German submarine-c (Nazi war-c)	284	568	852	1818	3109	4400
73-Origin & 1st app. Aquaman (11/41) by Paul Norris; intro. Green Arrow & Speedy; Dr. Fate-c	1600	3200	4800	12,000	21,500	31,000
74-2nd Aquaman; 1st Percival Popp, Supercop; Dr. Fate-c	300	600	900	2010	3505	5000
75,76: 75-New origin Spectre; Nazi spy ring cover w/Hitler's photo. 76-Last Dr. Fate-c; Johnny Quick (by Meskin #76-97) begins, ends #107; last Clip Carson	258	516	774	1651	2826	4000
77-80: 77-Green Arrow-c begin	155	310	465	992	1696	2400
81-83,85,88,90: 81-Last large logo. 82-1st small logo.	103	206	309	659	1130	1600
84-Green Arrow Japanese war-c	110	220	330	704	1202	1700
86,87-Johnny Quick-c. 87-Last Radio Squad	103	206	309	659	1130	1600
89-Origin Green Arrow & Speedy Team-up	110	220	330	704	1202	1700
91-97,99: 91-1st bi-monthly issue. 93-Dover & Clover begin (1st app., 9-10/43). 97-Kubert-a	77	154	231	493	847	1200
98-Last Dr. Fate (scarce)	97	194	291	621	1061	1500
100 (11-12/44)-Johnny Quick-c	90	180	270	576	988	1400
101-Origin & 1st app. Superboy (1-2/45)(not by Siegel & Shuster); last Spectre issue; Green Arrow-c	757	1514	2271	5526	9763	14,000
102-2nd Superboy app; 1st Dover & Clover-c	145	290	435	921	1586	2250
103-3rd Superboy app; last Green Arrow-c	103	206	309	659	1130	1600
104-1st Superboy-c w/Dover & Clover	90	180	270	576	988	1400
105,106-Superboy-c	82	164	246	528	902	1275
107-Last Johnny Quick & Superboy	82	164	246	528	902	1275
108-120: 108-Genius Jones begins; 1st c-app. (3-4/46; cont'd from Adventure Comics #102)	26	52	78	154	252	350
121-124,126: 121-123,126-Post funny animal (Jimminy & the Magic Book)-c	24	48	72	142	234	325
125-Superman c-app.w/Jimminy	82	164	246	528	902	1275
127-(Scarce)-Post-c/a	39	78	117	231	378	525

NOTE: *All issues are scarce to rare. Cover features: The Spectre-#52-55, 57-60, 62-67. Dr. Fate-#56, 61, 68-76. The Green Arrow & Speedy-#77-85, 88-97, 99, 101 (w/Dover & Clover-#98, 103). Johnny Quick-#86, 87, 100. Dover & Clover-#102, (104, 106 w/Superboy), 107, 108(w/Genius Jones), 110, 112, 114, 117, 119. Genius Jones-#109, 111, 113, 115, 116, 118, 120.* **Baily** *a-45, 52-on; c-52-55, 57-60, 62-67.* **Al Capp** *a-45(signed Koppy).* **Ellsworth** *c-7.* **Creig Flessel** *c-30, 31, 35-48(most).* **Guardineer** *c-47, 49, 50.* **Kiefer** *a-20.* **Meskin** *c-86, 87, 100?* **Moldoff** *c-51.* **George Papp** *c-77-85.* **Post** *c-121-127.* **Vincent Sullivan** *c-8-28, 32-34.*

MORE FUND COMICS (Benefit book for the Comic Book Legal Defense Fund)
(Also see Even More Fund Comics)
Sky Dog Press: Sept, 2003 ($10.00, B&W, trade paperback)

	GD 2.0	VG 4.0	FN 6.0	VF 8.0	VF/NM 9.0	NM- 9.2
nn-Anthology of short stories and pin-ups by various; Hulk-c by Pérez						10.00

MORE SEYMOUR (See Seymour My Son)
Archie Publications: Oct, 1963

	GD 2.0	VG 4.0	FN 6.0	VF 8.0	VF/NM 9.0	NM- 9.2
1-DeCarlo-a?	3	6	9	20	30	40

MORE THAN MORTAL (Also see Lady Pendragon/...)
Liar Comics: June, 1997 - No. 4, Apr, 1998 ($2.95, limited series)
Image Comics: No. 5, Dec, 1999 - No. 6, Mar, 2000 ($2.95)

	GD 2.0	VG 4.0	FN 6.0	VF 8.0	VF/NM 9.0	NM- 9.2
1-Blue forest background-c, 1-Variant-c						4.00
1-White-c						6.00
1-2nd printing; purple sky cover						3.00
2-4: 3-Silvestri-c, 4-Two-c, one by Randy Queen						3.00
5,6: 5-1st Image Comics issue						3.00

MORE THAN MORTAL: OTHERWORLDS
Image Comics: July, 1999 - No. 4, Dec, 1999 ($2.95, limited series)

	GD 2.0	VG 4.0	FN 6.0	VF 8.0	VF/NM 9.0	NM- 9.2
1-4-Firchow-a. 1-Two covers						3.00

MORE THAN MORTAL SAGAS
Liar Comics: Jun, 1998 - No. 3, Dec, 1998 ($2.95, limited series)

	GD 2.0	VG 4.0	FN 6.0	VF 8.0	VF/NM 9.0	NM- 9.2
1,2-Painted art by Romano. 2-Two-c, one by Firchow						3.00
1-Variant-c by Linsner						5.00

MORE THAN MORTAL TRUTHS AND LEGENDS
Liar Comics: Aug, 1998 - No. 6, Apr, 1999 ($2.95)

	GD 2.0	VG 4.0	FN 6.0	VF 8.0	VF/NM 9.0	NM- 9.2
1-6-Firchow-a(p)						3.00
1-Variant-c by Dan Norton						4.50

MORE TRASH FROM MAD (Annual)
E. C. Comics: 1958 - No. 12, 1969
(Note: Bonus missing = half price)

	GD 2.0	VG 4.0	FN 6.0	VF 8.0	VF/NM 9.0	NM- 9.2
nn(1958)-8 pgs. color Mad reprint from #20	17	34	51	114	250	385
2(1959)-Market Product Labels	12	24	36	81	166	250
3(1960)-Text book covers	11	22	33	76	151	225
4(1961)-Sing Along with Mad booklet	11	22	33	76	151	225
5(1962)-Window Stickers; r/from Mad #39	9	18	27	61	106	150
6(1963)-TV Guise booklet	9	18	27	61	106	150
7(1964)-Alfred E. Neuman commemorative stamps	8	16	24	51	86	120
8(1965)-Life size poster-Alfred E. Neuman	6	12	18	41	66	90
9-12: 9,10(1966-67)-Mischief Sticker. 11(1968)-Campaign poster & bumper sticker. 12(1969)-Pocket medals	6	12	18	41	66	90

NOTE: **Kelly Freas** *c-1, 2, 4.* **Mingo** *c-3, 5-9, 12.*

MORGAN THE PIRATE (Movie)
Dell Publishing Co.: No. 1227, Sept-Nov, 1961

	GD 2.0	VG 4.0	FN 6.0	VF 8.0	VF/NM 9.0	NM- 9.2
Four Color 1227-Photo-c	7	14	21	49	82	115

MORLOCKS
Marvel Comics: June, 2002 - No. 4, Sept, 2002 ($2.50, limited series)

	GD 2.0	VG 4.0	FN 6.0	VF 8.0	VF/NM 9.0	NM- 9.2
1-4-Johns-s/Martinbrough-c/a						3.00

MORLOCK 2001
Atlas/Seaboard Publ.: Feb, 1975 - No. 3, July, 1975

	GD 2.0	VG 4.0	FN 6.0	VF 8.0	VF/NM 9.0	NM- 9.2
1,2: 1-(Super-hero)-Origin & 1st app.; Milgrom-c	2	4	6	9	13	16
3-Ditko/Wrightson-a; origin The Midnight Man & The Mystery Men	3	6	9	14	19	24

MORNING GLORIES
Image Comics: Aug, 2010 - Present ($3.99/$3.50/$2.99)

	GD 2.0	VG 4.0	FN 6.0	VF 8.0	VF/NM 9.0	NM- 9.2
1-($3.99) Nick Spencer-s/Joe Eisma-a/Rodin Esquejo-c; group cover						8.00
1-Second-Fourth printings						4.00
2-($3.50) Regular cover and white background 2nd printing						5.00
3-6-Regular covers and white background 2nd printings						4.00
7-16-($2.99)						3.00
...Vol. 1 TPB (2/11, $9.99) r/#1-6						10.00

MORNINGSTAR SPECIAL
Comico: Apr, 1990 ($2.50)

	GD 2.0	VG 4.0	FN 6.0	VF 8.0	VF/NM 9.0	NM- 9.2
1-From the Elementals; Willingham-c/a/scripts						3.00

MORTAL KOMBAT
Malibu Comics: July, 1994 - No. 6, Dec, 1994 ($2.95)

Mostly Wanted #4 © DC

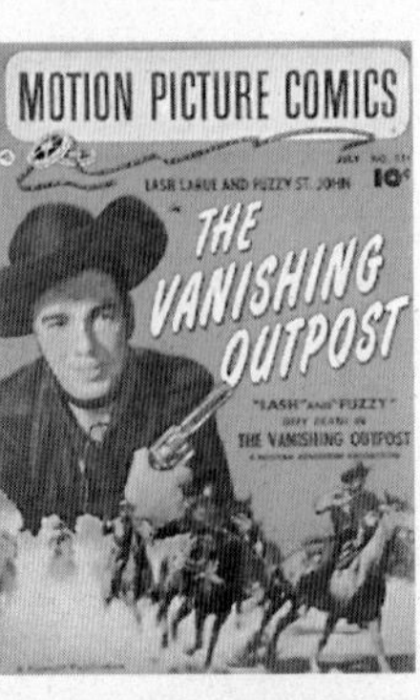

Motion Picture Comics #111 © FAW

Movie Classics - El Dorado © DELL

GD VG FN VF VF/NM NM-
2.0 4.0 6.0 8.0 9.0 9.2

1-6: 1-Two diff. covers exist 3.00
1-Limited edition gold foil embossed-c 4.00
0 (12/94), Special Edition 1 (11/94) 3.00
Tournament Edition I12/94, $3.95), II('95)($3.95) 4.00
...: **BARAKA** ,June, 1995 ($2.95, one-shot) #1; ...**BATTLEWAVE** ,2/95 - No. 6, 7/95 , #1-6; ...**GORO, PRINCE OF PAIN** ,9/94 - No. 3, 11/94, #1-3; ...**KITANA AND MILEENA** ,8/95 , ...**KUNG LAO** ,7/95 , #1; ... **RAYDON & KANO** ,3/95 - No. 3, 5/95, #1-3: ...(all $2.95-c) 3.00
...: **U.S. SPECIAL FORCES** ,1/95 - No. 2, ($3.50), #1,2 3.50

MORTIE (Mazie's Friend; also see Flat-Top)
Magazine Publishers: Dec, 1952 - No. 4, June, 1953?

1 9 18 27 50 65 80
2-4 6 12 18 28 34 40

MORTIGAN GOTH: IMMORTALIS (See Marvel Frontier Comics Unlimited)
Marvel Comics: Sept, 1993 - No. 4, Mar, 1994 ($1.95, mini-series)

1-($2.95)-Foil-c 3.50
2-4 3.00

MORT THE DEAD TEENAGER
Marvel Comics: Nov, 1993 - No. 4, Mar, 1994 ($1.75, mini-series)

1-4 3.00

MORTY MEEKLE
Dell Publishing Co.: No. 793, May, 1957

Four Color 793 4 8 12 24 37 50

MOSES & THE TEN COMMANDMENTS (See Dell Giants)

MOSTLY WANTED
DC Comics (WildStorm): Jul, 2000 - No. 4, Nov, 2000 ($2.50, limited series)

1-4-Lobdell-s/Flores-a 3.00

MOTEL HELL (Based on the 1980 movie)
IDW Publishing: Oct, 2010 - No. 3, Dec, 2010 ($3.99, limited series)

1-3-Matt Nixon-s/Chris Moreno-a. 1,2-Bradstreet-c. 3-Moreno-c 4.00

MOTH, THE
Dark Horse Comics: Apr, 2004 - No. 4, Aug, 2004 ($2.99)

1-4-Steve Rude-c/a; Gary Martin-s 3.00
... Special (3/04, $4.95) 5.00
TPB (5/05, $12.95) r/#1-4 and Special; gallery of extras 13.00

MOTH, THE
Rude Dude Productions: May 2008 (Free Comic Book Day giveaway)

... Special Edition - Steve Rude-s/a; sketch pages 3.00

MOTHER GOOSE AND NURSERY RHYME COMICS (See Christmas With Mother Goose)
Dell Publishing Co.: No. 41, 1944 - No. 862, Nov, 1957

Four Color 41-Walt Kelly-c/a 20 40 60 137 294 450
Four Color 59, 68-Kelly c/a 16 32 48 109 237 365
Four Color 862-The Truth About..., Movie (Disney) 7 14 21 48 79 110

MOTHER TERESA OF CALCUTTA
Marvel Comics Group: 1984

1-(52 pgs.) No ads 1 2 3 5 6 8

MOTION PICTURE COMICS (See Fawcett Movie Comics)
Fawcett Publications: No. 101, 1950 - No. 114, Jan, 1953 (All-photo-c)

101- "Vanishing Westerner"; Monte Hale (1950) 15 30 45 90 140 190
102- "Code of the Silver Sage"; Rocky Lane (1/51) 15 30 45 83 124 165
103- "Covered Wagon Raid"; Rocky Lane (3/51) 15 30 45 83 124 165
104- "Vigilante Hideout"; Rocky Lane (5/51)-Book length Powell-a 15 30 45 83 124 165
105- "Red Badge of Courage"; Audie Murphy; Bob Powell-a (7/51) 18 36 54 105 165 225
106- "The Texas Rangers"; George Montgomery (9/51) 15 30 45 83 124 165
107- "Frisco Tornado"; Rocky Lane (11/51) 14 28 42 80 115 150
108- "Mask of the Avenger"; John Derek 12 24 36 69 97 125
109- "Rough Rider of Durango"; Rocky Lane 14 28 42 80 115 150
110- "When Worlds Collide"; George Evans-a (5/52); Williamson & Evans drew themselves in story; (also see Famous Funnies No. 72-88) 77 154 231 493 847 1200
111- "The Vanishing Outpost"; Lash LaRue 15 30 45 90 140 190
112- "Brave Warrior"; Jon Hall & Jay Silverheels 12 24 36 67 94 120
113- "Walk East on Beacon"; George Murphy; Schaffenberger-a 10 20 30 54 72 90
114- "Cripple Creek"; George Montgomery (1/53) 10 20 30 58 79 100

MOTION PICTURE FUNNIES WEEKLY (See Promotional Comics section)

MOTORHEAD (See Comic's Greatest World)
Dark Horse Comics: Aug, 1995 - No. 6, Jan, 1996 ($2.50)

1-6: Bisley-c on all. 1-Predator app. 3.00
Special 1 (3/94, $3.95, 52pgs.)-Jae Lee-c; Barb Wire, The Machine & Wolf Gang app. 4.00

MOTORMOUTH (... & Killpower #7? on)
Marvel Comics UK: June, 1992 - No. 12, May, 1993 ($1.75)

1-13: 1,2-Nick Fury app. 3-Punisher-c/story. 5,6-Nick Fury & Punisher app. 6-Cable cameo. 7-9-Cable app. 3.00

MOUNTAIN MEN (See Ben Bowie)

MOUSE MUSKETEERS (See M.G.M.'s...)

MOUSE ON THE MOON, THE (See Movie Classics)

MOVIE CARTOONS
DC Comics: Dec, 1944 (cover only ashcan)

nn-Ashcan comic, not distributed to newsstands, only for in house use. Covers were produced, but not the rest of the book. A copy sold in 2006 for $500.

MOVIE CLASSICS
Dell Publishing Co.: Apr, 1956; May-Jul, 1962 - Dec, 1969

(Before 1963, most movie adaptations were part of the 4-Color series)
(Disney movie adaptations after 1970 are in Walt Disney Showcase)

Around the World Under the Sea 12-030-612 (12/66) 3 6 9 20 30 40
Bambi 3(4/56)-Disney; r/4-Color #186 4 8 12 24 37 50
Battle of the Bulge 12-056-606 (6/66) 3 6 9 21 32 42
Beach Blanket Bingo 12-058-509 7 14 21 46 76 105
Bon Voyage 01-068-212 (12/62)-Disney; photo-c 4 8 12 22 34 45
Castilian, The 12-110-401 3 6 9 20 30 40
Cat, The 12-109-612 (12/66) 3 6 9 19 29 38
Cheyenne Autumn 12-112-506 (4-6/65) 5 10 15 35 55 75
Circus World, Samuel Bronston's 12-115-411; John Wayne app.; John Wayne photo-c 9 18 27 63 112 160
Countdown 12-150-710 (10/67)-James Caan photo-c 3 6 9 21 32 42
Creature, The 1 (12-142-302) (12-2/62-63) 9 18 27 60 103 145
Creature, The 12-142-410 (10/64) 5 10 15 32 51 70
David Ladd's Life Story 12-173-212 (10-12/62)-Photo-c 7 14 21 46 76 105
Die, Monster, Die 12-175-603 (3/66)-Photo-c 6 12 18 37 59 80
Dirty Dozen 12-180-710 (10/67) 4 8 12 28 44 60
Dr. Who & the Daleks 12-190-612 (12/66)-Peter Cushing photo-c; 1st U.S. app. of Dr. Who 10 20 30 70 133 195
Dracula 12-231-212 (10-12/62) 8 16 24 55 93 130
El Dorado 12-240-710 (10/67)-John Wayne; photo-c 11 22 33 71 136 200
Ensign Pulver 12-257-410 (8-10/64) 3 6 9 19 29 38
Frankenstein 12-283-305 (3-5/63)(see Frankenstein 8-10/64 for 2nd printing) 8 16 24 56 96 135
Great Race, The 12-299-603 (3/66)-Natallie Wood, Tony Curtis photo-c 4 8 12 28 44 60
Hallelujah Trail, The 12-307-602 (2/66) (Shows 1/66 inside); Burt Lancaster, Lee Remick photo-c 5 10 15 32 51 70
Hatari 12-340-301 (1/63)-John Wayne 8 16 24 51 86 120
Horizontal Lieutenant, The 01-348-210 (10/62) 3 6 9 19 29 38
Incredible Mr. Limpet, The 12-370-408; Don Knotts photo-c 5 10 15 32 51 70
Jack the Giant Killer 12-374-301 (1/63) 8 16 24 51 86 120
Jason & the Argonauts 12-376-310 (8-10/63)-Photo-c 9 18 27 60 103 145
Lancelot & Guinevere 12-416-310 (10/63) 5 10 15 32 51 70
Lawrence 12-426-308 (8/63)-Story of Lawrence of Arabia; movie ad on back-c; not exactly like movie 5 10 15 32 51 70
Lion of Sparta 12-439-301 (1/63) 4 8 12 22 34 45
Mad Monster Party 12-460-801 (9/67)-Based on Kurtzman's screenplay 9 18 27 58 99 140
Magic Sword, The 01-496-209 (9/62) 5 10 15 35 55 75
Masque of the Red Death 12-490-410 (8-10/64)-Vincent Price photo-c 6 12 18 41 66 90
Maya 12-495-612 (12/66)-Clint Walker & Jay North part photo-c 4 8 12 24 37 50
McHale's Navy 12-500-412 (10-12/64) 4 8 12 28 44 60
Merrill's Marauders 12-510-301 (1/63)-Photo-c 3 6 9 19 29 38
Mouse on the Moon, The 12-530-312 (10/12/63)-Photo-c

Movie Classics - Tomb of Ligeia © DELL

Movie Comics #2 © DC

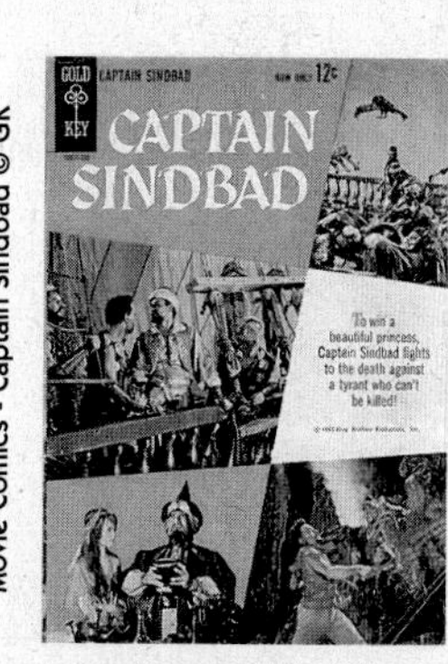

Movie Comics - Captain Sindbad © GK

GD VG FN VF VF/NM NM-
2.0 4.0 6.0 8.0 9.0 9.2

4 8 12 22 34 45
Mummy, The 12-537-211 (9-11/62) 2 versions with different back-c
9 18 27 58 99 140
Music Man, The 12-538-301 (1/63) 3 6 9 20 30 40
Naked Prey, The 12-545-612 (12/66)-Photo-c 5 10 15 35 55 75
Night of the Grizzly, The 12-558-612 (12/66)-Photo-c 4 8 12 22 34 45
None But the Brave 12-565-506 (4-6/65) 5 10 15 35 55 75
Operation Bikini 12-597-310 (10/63)-Photo-c 3 6 9 20 30 40
Operation Crossbow 12-590-512 (10-12/65) 3 6 9 20 30 40
Prince & the Pauper, The 01-654-207 (5-7/62)-Disney
4 8 12 22 34 45
Raven, The 12-680-309 (9/63)-Vincent Price photo-c 6 12 18 41 66 90
Ring of Bright Water 01-701-910 (10/69) (inside shows #12-701-909)
4 8 12 22 34 45
Runaway, The 12-707-412 (10-12/64) 3 6 9 19 29 38
Santa Claus Conquers the Martians #? (1964)-Photo-c
10 20 30 64 115 165
Santa Claus Conquers the Martians 12-725-603 (3/66, 12¢)-Reprints 1964 issue;
photo-c 7 14 21 46 76 105
Another version given away with a Golden Record, SLP 170, nn, no price
(3/66)-Complete with record 11 22 33 76 151 225
Six Black Horses 12-750-301 (1/63)-Photo-c 3 6 9 20 30 40
Ski Party 12-743-511 (9-11/65)-Frankie Avalon photo-c; photo inside-c; Adkins-a
5 10 15 30 48 65
Smoky 12-746-702 (2/67) 3 6 9 19 29 38
Sons of Katie Elder 12-748-511 (9-11/65); John Wayne app.; photo-c
11 22 33 71 136 200
Tales of Terror 12-793-302 (2/63)-Evans-a 5 10 15 35 55 75
Three Stooges Meet Hercules 01-828-208 (8/62)-Photo-c
9 18 27 58 99 140
Tomb of Ligeia 12-830-506 (4-6/65) 5 10 15 35 55 75
Treasure Island 01-845-211 (7-9/62)-Disney; r/4-Color #624
3 6 9 20 30 40
Twice Told Tales (Nathaniel Hawthorne) 12-840-401 (11-1/63-64);
Vincent Price photo-c 6 12 18 37 59 80
Two on a Guillotine 12-850-506 (4-6/65) 4 8 12 22 34 45
Valley of Gwangi 01-880-912 (12/69) 9 18 27 58 99 140
War Gods of the Deep 12-900-509 (7-9/65) 3 6 9 20 30 40
War Wagon, The 12-533-709 (9/67); John Wayne app.
8 16 24 53 89 125
Who's Minding the Mint? 12-924-708 (8/67) 3 6 9 19 29 38
Wolfman, The 12-922-308 (6-8/63) 8 16 24 56 96 135
Wolfman, The 1(12-922-410)(8-10/64)-2nd printing; r/#12-922-308
4 8 12 23 36 48
Zulu 12-950-410 (8-10/64)-Photo-c 7 14 21 48 79 110

MOVIE COMICS (See Cinema Comics Herald & Fawcett Movie Comics)

MOVIE COMICS
National Periodical Publications/Picture Comics: April, 1939 - No. 6, Sept-Oct, 1939 (Most all photo-c)

1- "Gunga Din", "Son of Frankenstein", "The Great Man Votes", "Fisherman's Wharf", & "Scouts to the Rescue" part 1; Wheelan "Minute Movies" begin
366 732 1098 2562 4481 6400
2- "Stagecoach", "The Saint Strikes Back", "King of the Turf","Scouts to the Rescue" part 2, "Arizona Legion", Andy Devine photo-c 252 504 756 1613 2757 3900
3- "East Side of Heaven", "Mystery in the White Room", "Four Feathers", "Mexican Rose" with Gene Autry, "Spirit of Culver", "Many Secrets", "The Mikado" (1st Gene Autry photo cover) 177 354 531 1124 1937 2750
4- "Captain Fury", Gene Autry in "Blue Montana Skies", "Streets of N.Y." with Jackie Cooper, "Oregon Trail" part 1 with Johnny Mack Brown, "Big Town Czar" with Barton MacLane, & "Star Reporter" with Warren Hull 148 296 444 947 1624 2300
5- "The Man in the Iron Mask", "Five Came Back", "Wolf Call", "The Girl & the Gambler", "The House of Fear", "The Family Next Door", "Oregon Trail" part 2
161 322 483 1030 1765 2500
6- "The Phantom Creeps", "Chumps at Oxford", & "The Oregon Trail" part 3; 2nd Robot-c
206 412 618 1318 2259 3200

NOTE: *Above books contain many original movie stills with dialogue from movie scripts. All issues are scarce.*

MOVIE COMICS
Fiction House Magazines: Dec, 1946 - No. 4, 1947

1-Big Town (by Lubbers), Johnny Danger begin; Celardo-a; Mitzi of the Movies by Fran Hopper 41 82 123 256 428 600
2-(2/47)- "White Tie & Tails" with William Bendix; Mitzi of the Movies begins; Matt Baker-a 31 62 93 186 303 420
3-(6/47)-Andy Hardy starring Mickey Rooney 31 62 93 186 303 420

GD VG FN VF VF/NM NM-
2.0 4.0 6.0 8.0 9.0 9.2

4-Mitzi In Hollywood by Matt Baker; Merton of the Movies with Red Skelton; Yvonne DeCarlo & George Brent in "Slave Girl" 39 78 117 231 378 525

MOVIE COMICS
Gold Key/Whitman: Oct, 1962 - 1984

Alice in Wonderland 10144-503 (3/65)-Disney; partial reprint of 4-Color #331
4 8 12 22 34 45
Alice In Wonderland #1 (Whitman pre-pack, 3/84) 2 4 6 10 14 18
Aristocats, The 1 (30045-103)(3/71)-Disney; with pull-out poster (25¢)
(No poster = half price) 7 14 21 46 76 105
Bambi 1 (10087-309)(9/63)-Disney; r/4-C #186 4 8 12 24 37 50
Bambi 2 (10087-607)(7/66)-Disney; r/4-C #186 3 6 9 20 30 40
Beneath the Planet of the Apes 30044-012 (12/70)-with pull-out poster; photo-c
(No poster = half price) 9 18 27 61 106 150
Big Red 10026-211 (11/62)-Disney; photo-c 3 6 9 20 30 40
Big Red 10026-503 (3/65)-Disney; reprints 10026-211; photo-c
3 6 9 16 23 30
Blackbeard's Ghost 10222-806 (6/68)-Disney 3 6 9 19 29 38
Bullwhip Griffin 10181-706 (6/67)-Disney; Spiegle-a; photo-c
4 8 12 22 34 45
Captain Sindbad 10077-309 (9/63)-Manning-a; photo-c
6 12 18 41 66 90
Chitty Chitty Bang Bang 1 (30038-902)(2/69)-with pull-out poster; Disney; photo-c
(No poster = half price) 6 12 18 42 69 95
Cinderella 10152-508 (8/65)-Disney; r/4-C #786 4 8 12 26 41 55
Darby O'Gill & the Little People 10251-001(1/70)-Disney; reprints 4-Color #1024 (Toth-a);
photo-c 5 10 15 30 48 65
Dumbo 1 (10090-310)(10/63)-Disney; r/4-C #668 3 6 9 21 32 42
Emil & the Detectives 10120-502 (11/64)-Disney; photo-c & back-c photo pin-up
3 6 9 20 30 40
Escapade in Florence 1 (10043-301)(1/63)-Disney; starring Annette Funicello
8 16 24 51 86 120
Fall of the Roman Empire 10118-407 (7/64); Sophia Loren photo-c
4 8 12 24 37 50
Fantastic Voyage 10178-702 (2/67)-Wood/Adkins-a; photo-c
6 12 18 37 59 80
55 Days at Peking 10081-309 (9/63)-Photo-c 3 6 9 20 30 40
Fighting Prince of Donegal, The 10193-701 (1/67)-Disney
3 6 9 19 29 38
First Men in the Moon 10132-503 (3/65)-Fred Fredericks-a; photo-c
4 8 12 24 37 50
Gay Purr-ee 30017-301(1/63, 84 pgs.) 5 10 15 32 51 70
Gnome Mobile, The 10207-710 (10/67)-Disney; Walter Brennan photo-c & back-c photo pin-up
4 8 12 22 34 45
Goodbye, Mr. Chips 10246-006 (6/70)-Peter O'Toole photo-c
3 6 9 20 30 40
Happiest Millionaire, The 10221-804 (4/68)-Disney 4 8 12 22 34 45
Hey There, It's Yogi Bear 10122-409 (9/64)-Hanna-Barbera
6 12 18 42 69 95
Horse Without a Head, The 10109-401 (1/64)-Disney 3 6 9 19 29 38
How the West Was Won 10074-307 (7/63)-Based on the L'Amour novel; Tufts-a
4 8 12 28 44 60
In Search of the Castaways 10048-303 (3/63)-Disney; Hayley Mills photo-c
6 12 18 42 69 95
Jungle Book, The 1 (6022-801)(1/68-Whitman)-Disney; large size (10x13-1/2"); 59¢
6 12 18 42 69 95
Jungle Book, The 1 (30033-803)(3/68, 68 pgs.)-Disney; same contents as Whitman #1
4 8 12 24 37 50
Jungle Book, The 1 (6/78, $1.00 tabloid) 3 6 9 16 23 30
Jungle Book (7/84)-r/Giant; Whitman pre-pack 2 4 6 10 14 18
Kidnapped 10080-306 (6/63)-Disney; reprints 4-Color #1101; photo-c
3 6 9 20 30 40
King Kong 30036-809(9/68-68 pgs.)-painted-c 4 8 12 26 41 55
King Kong nn-Whitman Treasury($1.00, 68 pgs.,1968), same cover as Gold Key issue
5 10 15 35 55 75
King Kong 11299(#1-786, 10x13-1/4", 68 pgs., $1.00, 1978)
3 6 9 18 27 35
Lady and the Tramp 10042-301 (1/63)-Disney; r/4-Color #629
3 6 9 21 32 42
Lady and the Tramp 1 (1967-Giant; 25¢)-Disney; reprints part of Dell #1
5 10 15 35 55 75
Lady and the Tramp 2 (10042-203)(3/72)-Disney; r/4-Color #629
3 6 9 16 23 30
Legend of Lobo, The 1 (10059-303)(3/63)-Disney; photo-c
3 6 9 16 23 30

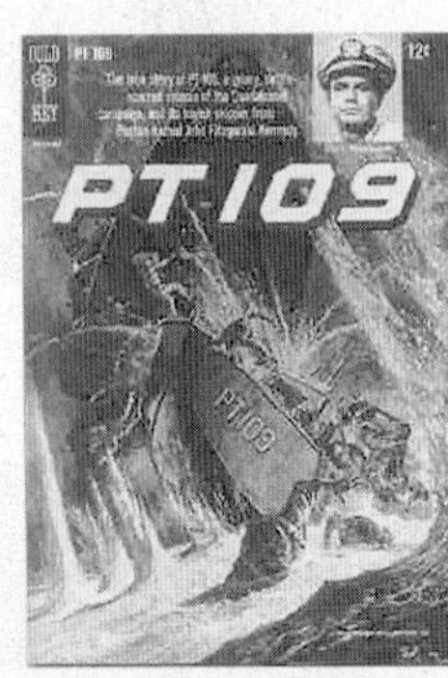

Movie Comics - P.T. 109 © GK

Movie Love #2 © FF

M. Rex #1 © Kelly & Rouleau

GD VG FN VF VF/NM NM-
2.0 4.0 6.0 8.0 9.0 9.2

GD VG FN VF VF/NM NM-
2.0 4.0 6.0 8.0 9.0 9.2

Lt. Robin Crusoe, U.S.N. 10191-610 (10/66)-Disney; Dick Van Dyke photo-c & back-c photo
pin-up 3 6 9 18 27 35
Lion, The 10035-301 (1/63)-Photo-c 3 6 9 17 25 32
Lord Jim 10156-509 (9/65)-Photo-c 3 6 9 17 25 32
Love Bug, The 10237-906 (6/69)-Disney; Buddy Hackett photo-c
4 8 12 22 34 45
Mary Poppins 10136-501 (1/65)-Disney; photo-c 5 10 15 30 48 65
Mary Poppins 30023-501 (1/65-68 pgs.)-Disney; photo-c
7 14 21 46 76 105
McLintock 10110-403 (3/64); John Wayne app.; John Wayne & Maureen O'Hara photo-c
11 22 33 73 142 210
Merlin Jones as the Monkey's Uncle 10115-510 (10/65)-Disney; Annette Funicello
front/back photo-c 6 12 18 39 62 85
Miracle of the White Stallions, The 10065-306 (6/63)-Disney
3 6 9 19 29 38
Misadventures of Merlin Jones, The 10115-405 (5/64)-Disney; Annette Funicello
photo front/back-c 6 12 18 39 62 85
Moon-Spinners, The 10124-410 (10/64)-Disney; Hayley Mills photo-c
6 12 18 42 69 95
Mutiny on the Bounty 1 (10040-302)(2/63)-Marlon Brando photo-c
4 8 12 22 34 45
Nikki, Wild Dog of the North 10141-412 (12/64)-Disney; reprints 4-Color #1226
3 6 9 16 23 30
Old Yeller 10168-601 (1/66)-Disney; reprints 4-Color #869; photo-c
3 6 9 16 23 30
One Hundred & One Dalmations 1 (10247-002) (2/70)-Disney; reprints Four Color #1183
3 6 9 18 27 35
Peter Pan 1 (10086-309)(9/63)-Disney; reprints Four Color #442
3 6 9 21 32 42
Peter Pan 2 (10086-909)(9/69)-Disney; reprints Four Color #442
3 6 9 16 23 30
Peter Pan 1 (3/84)-r/4-Color #442; Whitman pre-pack 2 4 6 11 16 20
P.T. 109 10123-409 (9/64)-John F. Kennedy 5 10 15 30 48 65
Rio Conchos 10143-503(3/65) 4 8 12 22 34 45
Robin Hood 10163-506 (6/65)-Disney; reprints Four Color #413
3 6 9 17 25 32
Shaggy Dog & the Absent-Minded Professor 30032-708 (8/67-Giant, 68 pgs.) Disney;
reprints 4-Color #985,1199 5 10 15 32 51 70
Sleeping Beauty 1 (30042-009)(9/70)-Disney; reprints Four Color #973; with pull-out poster
(No poster = half price) 6 12 18 42 69 95
Snow White & the Seven Dwarfs 1 (10091-310)(10/63)-Disney; reprints Four Color #382
3 6 9 20 30 40
Snow White & the Seven Dwarfs 10091-709 (9/67)-Disney; reprints Four Color #382
3 6 9 16 23 30
Snow White & the Seven Dwarfs 90091-204 (2/84)-Reprints Four Color #382;
Whitman pre-pack 2 4 6 11 16 20
Son of Flubber 1 (10057-304)(4/63)-Disney; sequel to "The Absent-Minded Professor"
4 8 12 22 34 45
Summer Magic 10076-309 (9/63)-Disney; Hayley Mills photo-c; Manning-a
6 12 18 42 69 95
Swiss Family Robinson 10236-904 (4/69)-Disney; reprints Four Color #1156; photo-c
3 6 9 18 27 35
Sword in the Stone, The 30019-402 (2/64-Giant, 68 pgs.)-Disney (see March of Comics #258
& Wart and the Wizard 6 12 18 42 69 95
That Darn Cat 10171-602 (2/66)-Disney; Hayley Mills photo-c
6 12 18 42 69 95
Those Magnificent Men in Their Flying Machines 10162-510 (10/65); photo-c
3 6 9 20 30 40
Three Stooges in Orbit 30016-211 (11/62-Giant, 32 pgs.)-All photos from movie; stiff-photo-c
9 18 27 63 112 160
Tiger Walks, A 10117-406 (6/64)-Disney; Torres?, Tufts-a; photo-c
4 8 12 24 37 50
Toby Tyler 10142-502 (2/65)-Disney; reprints Four Color #1092; photo-c
3 6 9 18 27 35
Treasure Island 1 (10200-703)(3/67)-Disney; reprints Four Color #624; photo-c
3 6 9 16 23 30
20,000 Leagues Under the Sea 1 (10095-312)(12/63)-Disney; reprints Four Color #614
3 6 9 18 27 35
Wonderful Adventures of Pinocchio, The 1 (10089-310)(10/63)-Disney; reprints Four Color #545
(see Wonderful Advs. of...) 3 6 9 21 32 42
Wonderful Adventures of Pinocchio, The 10089-109 (9/71)-Disney; reprints Four Color #545
3 6 9 16 23 30
Wonderful World of the Brothers Grimm 1 (10008-210)(10/62)
4 8 12 28 44 60

X, the Man with the X-Ray Eyes 10083-309 (9/63)-Ray Milland photo on-c
7 14 21 49 80 110
Yellow Submarine 35000-902 (2/69-Giant, 68 pgs.)-With pull-out poster;
The Beatles cartoon movie; Paul S. Newman-s 20 40 60 137 294 450
Without poster 9 18 27 63 112 160

MOVIE FABLES
DC Comics: Dec, 1944 (cover only ashcan)

nn-Ashcan comic, not distributed to newsstands, only for in house use. Covers were produced, but not the rest of the book. A copy sold in 2006 for $500.

MOVIE GEMS
DC Comics: Dec, 1944 (cover only ashcan)

nn-Ashcan comic, not distributed to newsstands, only for in house use. Covers were produced, but not the rest of the book. A copy sold in 2006 for $500.

MOVIE LOVE (Also see Personal Love)
Famous Funnies: Feb, 1950 - No. 22, Aug, 1953 (All photo-c)

1-Dick Powell, Evelyn Keyes, & Mickey Rooney photo-c
20 40 60 114 182 250
2-Myrna Loy photo-c 12 24 36 69 97 125
3-7,9: 6-Ricardo Montalban photo-c. 9-Gene Tierney, John Lund, Glenn Ford,
& Rhonda Fleming photo-c. 11 22 33 64 90 115
8-Williamson/Frazetta-a, 6 pgs. 47 94 141 298 504 710
10-Frazetta-a, 6 pgs. 48 96 144 302 514 725
11,14-16: 14-Janet Leigh photo-c 11 22 33 62 86 110
12-Dean Martin & Jerry Lewis photo-c (12/51, pre-dates Advs. of Dean Martin &
Jerry Lewis comic) 21 42 63 122 199 275
13-Ronald Reagan photo-c with 1 pg. biog. 28 56 84 165 270 375
17-Leslie Caron & Ralph Meeker photo-c; 1 pg. Frazetta ad
11 22 33 64 90 115
18-22: 19-John Derek photo-c. 20-Donald O'Connor & Debbie Reynolds photo-c.
21-Paul Henreid & Patricia Medina photo-c. 22-John Payne & Coleen Gray photo-c
11 22 33 60 83 105

NOTE: *Each issue has a full-length movie adaptation with photo covers.*

MOVIE MONSTERS (Magazine)
Atlas/Seaboard: Dec, 1974 - No. 4, Aug, 1975 (B&W; Film, photo & article magazine)

1-(84 pages) Planet of the Apes, King Kong, Sindbad & Harryhausen, Christopher Lee
Dracula, Star Trek, Werewolf, Creature from the Black Lagoon, Hammer's Mummy,
Gorgo, & Exorcist 4 8 12 22 34 45
2-(2/1975) 2001: Planet of the Apes-c; 2001: A Space Odyssey; Doc Savage; Frankenstein;
Rodan; One Million Years BC; (lower print run) 4 8 12 22 34 45
3-(4/1975) Phantom of the Opera-c; Wolfman, Godzilla, Boris Karloff, Batman, Forbidden
Planet, Jack the Giant Killer 4 8 12 22 34 45
4-(8/1975) Thing, Flash Gordon, Lon Chaney Jr., Lost Worlds, Loch Ness Monster, Day the
Earth Stood Still, Star Trek 4 8 12 22 34 45

MOVIE THRILLERS (Movie)
Magazine Enterprises: 1949

1-Adaptation of "Rope of Sand" w/Burt Lancaster; Burt Lancaster photo-c
28 56 84 165 270 375

MOVIE TOWN ANIMAL ANTICS (Formerly Animal Antics; becomes Raccoon Kids #52 on)
National Periodical Publ.: No. 24, Jan-Feb, 1950 - No. 51, July-Aug, 1954

24-Raccoon Kids continue 12 24 36 67 94 120
25-51 10 20 30 54 72 90

NOTE: ***Sheldon Mayer** a-28-33, 35, 37-41, 43, 44, 47, 49-51.*

MOVIE TUNES COMICS (Formerly Animated...; Frankie No. 4 on)
Marvel Comics (MgPC): No. 3, Fall, 1946

3-Super Rabbit, Krazy Krow, Silly Seal & Ziggy Pig 15 30 45 88 137 185

MOWGLI JUNGLE BOOK (Rudyard Kipling's...)
Dell Publ. Co.: No. 487, Aug-Oct, 1953 - No. 620, Apr, 1955

Four Color 487 (#1) 6 12 18 37 59 80
Four Color 582 (8/54), 620 5 10 15 30 48 65

MR. (See Mister)

M. REX
Image Comics: July, 1999 - No. 2, Dec, 1999 ($2.95)

Preview ($5.00) B&W pages and sketchbook; Rouleau-a 5.00
1,2-($2.95) 1-Joe Kelly-s/Rouleau-a/Anacleto-c. 2-Rouleau-c 3.00

MS. MARVEL (Also see The Avengers #183)
Marvel Comics Group: Jan, 1977 - No. 23, Apr, 1979

1-1st app. Ms. Marvel; Scorpion app. in #1,2 2 4 6 11 16 20
2-10: 2-Origin. 5-Vision app. 6-10-(Reg. 30¢-c). 10-Last 30¢ issue

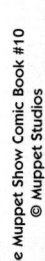

Ms. Marvel #49 © MAR

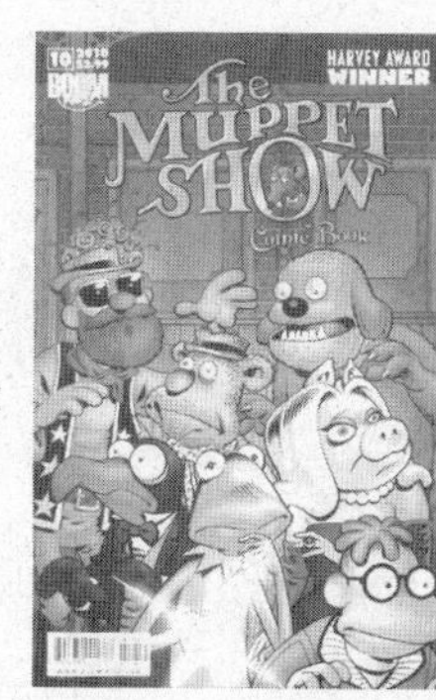

The Muppet Show Comic Book #10 © Muppet Studios

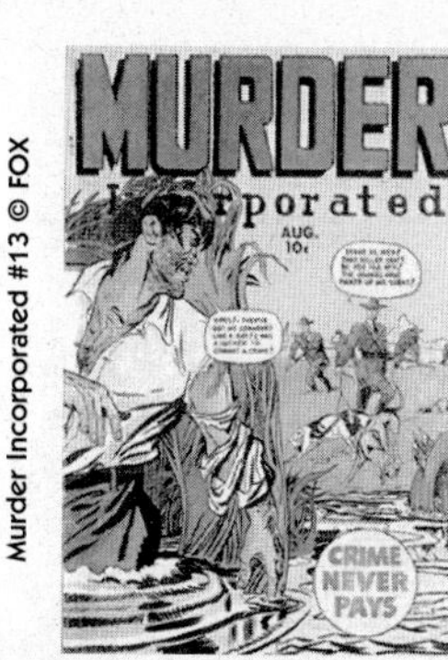

Murder Incorporated #13 © FOX

	GD 2.0	VG 4.0	FN 6.0	VF 8.0	VF/NM 9.0	NM- 9.2
	1	2	3	5	7	9
6-10-(35¢-c variants, limited dist.)(6/77)	4	8	12	22	34	45
11-15,19-23: 19-Capt. Marvel app. 20-New costume. 23-Vance Astro (leader of the Guardians) app.						6.00
16,17-1st brief app. Mystique	3	6	9	16	22	28
18-1st full app. Mystique; Avengers x-over	5	10	15	30	48	65

NOTE: ***Austin*** *c-14i, 16i, 17i, 22i.* ***Buscema*** *a-1-3p; c(p)-2, 4, 6, 7, 15.* ***Infantino*** *a-14p, 19p.* ***Gil Kane*** *c-8.* ***Mooney*** *a-4-8p, 13p, 15-18p.* ***Starlin*** *c-12.*

MS. MARVEL (Also see New Avengers)
Marvel Comics: May, 2006 - Present ($2.99)

1-24: 1-Cho-c/Reed-s/De La Torre-a; Stilt-Man app. 4,5-Dr. Strange app. 6,7-Araña app. 3.00
1-Variant cover by Michael Turner 5.00
25-($3.99) Two covers by Horn and Dodson; Secret Invasion 4.00
26-49: 26-31-Secret Invasion. 34-Spider-Man app. 35-Dark Reign. 37-Carol explodes. 39,40,46,48,49-Takeda-a. 41-Carol returns. 47-Spider-Man app. 3.00
50-($3.99) Mystique and Captain Marvel app.; Takeda & Oliver-a 4.00
... Annual 1 (11/08, $3.99) Spider-Man app.; Horn-c 4.00
... Special (3/07, $2.99) Reed-s/Camuncoli-a/c 3.00
... Storyteller (1/09, $2.99) Reed-s/Camuncoli-a/c 3.00
... Vol. 1: Best of the Best HC (2006, $19.99) r/#1-5 & Giant-Size Ms. Marvel #1 20.00
... Vol. 1: Best of the Best SC (2007, $14.99) r/#1-5 & Giant-Size Ms. Marvel #1 15.00
... Vol. 2: Civil War HC (2007, $19.99) r/#6-10 & Ms. Marvel Special #1 20.00
... Vol. 2: Civil War SC (2007, $14.99) r/#6-10 & Ms. Marvel Special #1 15.00
... Vol. 3: Operation Lightning Storm HC (2007, $19.99) r/#11-17 20.00
... Vol. 4: Monster Smash HC (2008, $19.99) r/#18-24 20.00

MS. MYSTIC
Pacific Comics: Oct, 1982 - No. 2, Feb, 1984 ($1.00/$1.50)

1,2: Neal Adams-c/a/script. 1-Origin; intro Erth, Ayre, Fyre & Watr 4.00

MS. MYSTIC
Continuity Comics: 1988 - No. 9, May, 1992 ($2.00)

1-9: 1,2-Reprint Pacific Comics issues 3.00

MS. MYSTIC
Continunity Comics: V2#1, Oct, 1993 - V2#4, Jan, 1994 ($2.50)

V2#1-4: 1-Adams-c(i)/part-i. 2-4-Embossed-c. 2-Nebres part-i. 3-Adams-c(i)/plot. 4-Adams-c(p)/plot 3.00

MS. MYSTIC DEATHWATCH 2000 (Ms. Mystic #3)
Continuity: May, 1993 - No. 3, Aug, 1993 ($2.50)

1-3-Bagged w/card; Adams plots 3.00

MS. TREE QUARTERLY / SPECIAL
DC Comics: Summer, 1990 -No. 10, 1992 ($3.95/$3.50, 84 pgs, mature)

1-10: 1-Midnight story; Batman text story, Grell-a. 2,3-Midnight stories; The Butcher text stories 4.00

NOTE: ***Cowan*** *c-2.* ***Grell*** *c-1, 6.* ***Infantino*** *a-8.*

MS. TREE'S THRILLING DETECTIVE ADVS (Ms. Tree #4 on; also see The Best of Ms. Tree) (Baxter paper #4-9)
Eclipse Comics/Aardvark-Vanaheim 10-18/Renegade Press 19 on: 2/83 - #9, 7/84; #10, 8/84 - #18, 5/85; #19, 6/85 - #50, 6/89

1 4.00
2-49: 2-Schythe begins. 9-Last Eclipse & last color issue. 10,11-two-tone 3.00
50-Contains flexi-disc ($3.95, 52 pgs.) 4.00
Summer Special 1 (8/86) 3.00
1950s 3-D Crime (7/87, no glasses)-Johnny Dynamite in 3-D 3.00
Mike Mist in 3-D (8/85)-With glasses 3.00

NOTE; ***Miller*** *pin-up 1-4. Johnny Dynamite-r begin #36 by* ***Morisi.***

MS. VICTORY SPECIAL(Also see Capt. Paragon & Femforce)
Americomics: Jan, 1985 (nd)

1 3.00

MUCHA LUCHA (Based on Kids WB animated TV show)
DC Comics: Jun, 2003 - No. 3, Aug, 2003 ($2.25, limited series)

1-3-Rikochet, Buena Girl and The Flea app. 3.00

MUDMAN
Image Comics: Nov, 2011 - Present ($3.50)

1,2-Paul Grist-s/a 3.50

MUGGSY MOUSE (Also see Tick Tock Tales)
Magazine Enterprises: 1951 - No. 3, 1951; No. 4, 1954 - No. 5, 1954; 1963

	GD 2.0	VG 4.0	FN 6.0	VF 8.0	VF/NM 9.0	NM- 9.2
1(A-1 #33)	10	20	30	54	72	90
2(A-1 #36)-Racist-c	14	28	42	80	115	150
3(A-1 #39), 4(A-1 #95), 5(A-1 #99)	8	16	24	40	50	60
Super Reprint #14(1963), I.W. Reprint #1,2 (nd)	2	4	6	8	11	14

MUGGY-DOO, BOY CAT
Stanhall Publ.: July, 1953 - No. 4, Jan, 1954

	GD 2.0	VG 4.0	FN 6.0	VF 8.0	VF/NM 9.0	NM- 9.2
1-Funny animal; Irving Spector-a	9	18	27	47	61	75
2-4	6	12	18	27	33	38
Super Reprint #12('63), 16('64)	2	4	6	8	11	14

MULLKON EMPIRE (See John Jake's...)

MUMMY, THE (See Universal Presents... under Dell Giants & Movie Classics)

MUMMY, THE: THE RISE AND FALL OF XANGO'S AX (Based on the Brendan Fraser movies)
IDW Publishing: Apr, 2008 - No. 4, July, 2008 ($3.99, limited series)

1-4-Prequel to '08 movie The Mummy: Tomb of the Dragon Emperor; Stephen Mooney-a 4.00

MUNDEN'S BAR ANNUAL
First Comics: Apr, 1988; 1989 ($2.95/$5.95)

1-($2.95)-r/from Grimjack; Fish Police story; Ordway-c 3.00
2-($5.95)-Teenage Mutant Ninja Turtles app. 6.00

MUNSTERS, THE (TV)
Gold Key: Jan, 1965 - No. 16, Jan, 1968 (All photo-c)

	GD 2.0	VG 4.0	FN 6.0	VF 8.0	VF/NM 9.0	NM- 9.2
1 (10134-501)	15	30	45	102	221	340
2	9	18	27	63	112	160
3-5	8	16	24	53	89	125
6-16	7	14	21	46	76	105

MUNSTERS, THE (TV)
TV Comics!: Aug, 1997 - No. 4 ($2.95, B&W)

1-4-All have photo-c 3.00
1,4-($7.95)-Variant-c 8.00
2-Variant-c w/Beverly Owens as Marilyn 3.00
Special Comic Con Ed. (7/97, $9.95) 10.00

MUPPET... (TV)
BOOM! Studios

... King Arthur 1-4 (12/09 - No. 4, 3/10, $2.99) Benjamin & Storck-s/Alvarez-a; 2 covers 3.00
... Peter Pan 1-4 (8/09 - No. 4, 11/09, $2.99) Randolph-s/Mebberson-a; multiple covers 3.00
... Robin Hood 1-4 (4/09 - No. 4, 7/09, $2.99) Beedle-s/Villavert Jr.-a; multiple covers 3.00
... Sherlock Holmes 1-4 (8/10 - No. 4, 11/10, $2.99) Storck-s/Mebberson-a/c 3.00
... Snow White 1-4 (4/10 - No. 4, 7/10, $2.99) Snider & Storck-s/Paroline-a; 2 covers 3.00

MUPPET BABIES, THE (TV)(See Star Comics Magazine)
Marvel Comics (Star Comics)/Marvel #18 on: Aug, 1985 - No. 26, July, 1989 (Children's book)

1-26 4.00

MUPPET SHOW, THE (TV)
BOOM! Studios: Mar, 2009 - No. 4, Jun, 2009 ($2.99, limited series)

1-4-Roger Landridge-s/a; multiple covers 3.00
...: The Treasure of Peg Leg Wilson (7/09 - No. 4, 10/09) 1-4-Landridge-s/a; multiple-c 3.00

MUPPET SHOW COMIC BOOK, THE (TV)
BOOM! Studios: No. 0, Nov, 2009 - Present ($2.99)

0-11: 0-3-Roger Landridge-s/a; multiple covers. 0-Paroline-a; Pigs in Space 3.00

MUPPETS TAKE MANHATTAN, THE
Marvel Comics (Star Comics): Nov, 1984 - No. 3, Jan, 1985

1-3-Movie adapt. r-/Marvel Super Special 4.00

MURCIELAGA, SHE-BAT
Heroic Publishing: Jan, 1993 - No. 2, 1993 (B&W)

1-($1.50, 28 pgs.) 3.00
2-($2.95, 36 pgs.)-Coated-c 3.00

MURDER CAN BE FUN
Slave Labor Graphics: Feb, 1996 - No. 12 ($2.95, B&W)

1-12: 1-Dorkin-c. 2-Vasquez-c. 3.00

MURDER INCORPORATED (My Private Life #16 on)
Fox Feature Syndicate: 1/48 - No. 15, 12/49; (2 No.9's); 6/50 - No. 3, 8/51

	GD 2.0	VG 4.0	FN 6.0	VF 8.0	VF/NM 9.0	NM- 9.2
1 (1st Series); 1,2 have 'For Adults Only' on-c	54	108	162	343	574	825
2-Electrocution story	41	82	123	249	417	585
3-7,9(4/49),10(5/49),11-15	26	52	78	154	252	350
8-Used in **SOTI**, pg. 160	29	58	87	170	278	385
9(3/49)-Possible use in **SOTI**, pg. 145; r/Blue Beetle #56('48)	26	52	78	154	252	350

5(#1, 6/50)(2nd Series)-Formerly My Desire #4; bondage-c.

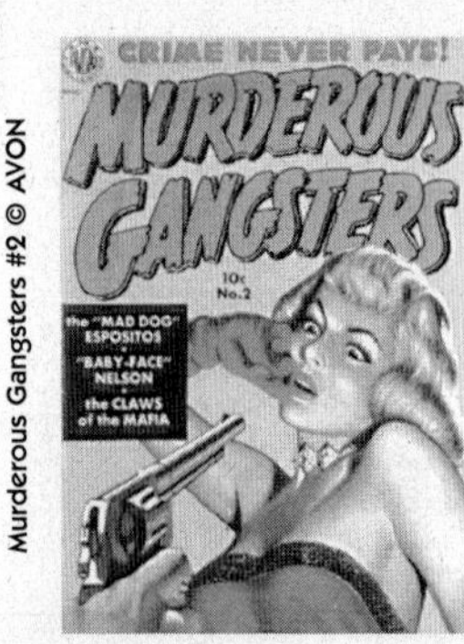

Murderous Gangsters #2 © AVON

Mutant X #8 © MAR

Mutt & Jeff #17 © DC

	GD 2.0	VG 4.0	FN 6.0	VF 8.0	VF/NM 9.0	NM- 9.2
	21	42	63	122	199	275
2(8/50)-Morisi-a	19	38	57	111	176	240
3(8/51)-Used in **POP**, pg. 81; Rico-a; lingerie-c/panels	21	42	63	126	206	285

MURDERLAND
Image Comics: Aug, 2010 - No. 3, Nov, 2010 ($2.99)

	GD	VG	FN	VF	VF/NM	NM-
1-3-Stephen Scott-s/David Haun-a						3.00

MURDER ME DEAD
El Capitán Books: July, 2000 - No. 9, Oct, 2001 ($2.95/$4.95, B&W)

	GD	VG	FN	VF	VF/NM	NM-
1-8-David Lapham-s/a						3.00
9-($4.95)						5.00

MURDEROUS GANGSTERS
Avon Per./Realistic No. 3 on: Jul, 1951; No. 2, Dec, 1951 - No. 4, Jun, 1952

	GD	VG	FN	VF	VF/NM	NM-
1-Pretty Boy Floyd, Leggs Diamond; 1 pg. Wood-a	45	90	135	284	480	675
2-Baby-Face Nelson; 1 pg. Wood-a; painted-c	29	58	87	170	278	385
3-Painted-c	24	48	72	140	230	320
4- "Murder by Needle" drug story; Mort Lawrence-a; Kinstler-c	30	60	90	177	289	400

MURDER MYSTERIES (Neil Gaiman's...)
Dark Horse Comics: 2002 ($13.95, HC, one-shot)

	GD	VG	FN	VF	VF/NM	NM-
HC-Adapts Gaiman story; P. Craig Russell-script/art						14.00

MURDER TALES (Magazine)
World Famous Publications: V1#10, Nov, 1970 - V1#11, Jan, 1971 (52 pgs.)

	GD	VG	FN	VF	VF/NM	NM-
V1#10-One pg. Frazetta ad	4	8	12	28	44	60
11-Guardineer-r; bondage-c	4	8	12	24	37	50

MUSHMOUSE AND PUNKIN PUSS (TV)
Gold Key: September, 1965 (Hanna-Barbera)

	GD	VG	FN	VF	VF/NM	NM-
1 (10153-509)	8	16	24	56	96	135

MUSIC BOX (Jennifer Love Hewitt's...)
IDW Publishing: Nov, 2009 - No. 5, Apr, 2010 ($3.99, lim. series)

	GD	VG	FN	VF	VF/NM	NM-
1-5-Anthology; Scott Lobdell-s/art by various. 1-Gaydos-a. 3-Archer-a						4.00

MUSIC MAN, THE (See Movie Classics)

MUTANT CHRONICLES (Video game)
Acclaim Comics (Armada): May, 1996 - No. 4, Aug, 1996 ($2.95, lim. series)

	GD	VG	FN	VF	VF/NM	NM-
1-4: Simon Bisley-c on all, Sourcebook (#5)						3.00

MUTANT EARTH (Stan Winston's...)
Image Comics: April, 2002 - No. 4, Jan, 2003 ($2.95)

	GD	VG	FN	VF	VF/NM	NM-
1-4-Flip book w/Realm of the Claw						3.00
Trakk...His Adventures in Mutant Earth TPB (2003, $16.95) r/#1-4; Winston interview						17.00

MUTANT MISADVENTURES OF CLOAK AND DAGGER, THE
(Becomes Cloak and Dagger #14 on)
Marvel Comics: Oct, 1988 - No. 19, Aug, 1991 ($1.25/$1.50)

	GD	VG	FN	VF	VF/NM	NM-
1-8,10-15: 1-X-Factor app. 10-Painted-c. 12-Dr. Doom app. 14-Begin new direction						3.00
9,16-19: 9-(52 pgs.) The Avengers x-over; painted-c. 16-18-Spider-Man x-over. 18-Infinity Gauntlet x-over; Thanos cameo; Ghost Rider app. 19-(52 pgs.) Origin Cloak & Dagger						4.00

NOTE: *Austin a-12i; c(i)-4, 12, 13; scripts-all.* ***Russell*** *a-2i.* ***Williamson*** *a-14i-16i; c-15i.*

MUTANTS & MISFITS
Silverline Comics (Solson): 1987 - No. 3, 1987 ($1.95)

	GD	VG	FN	VF	VF/NM	NM-
1-3						3.00

MUTANTS VS. ULTRAS
Malibu Comics (Ultraverse): Nov, 1995 ($6.95, one-shot)

	GD	VG	FN	VF	VF/NM	NM-
1-r/Exiles vs. X-Men, Night Man vs. Wolverine, Prime vs. Hulk						7.00

MUTANT, TEXAS: TALES OF SHERIFF IDA RED (Also see Jingle Belle)
Oni Press: May, 2002 - No. 4, Nov, 2002 ($2.95, B&W, limited series)

	GD	VG	FN	VF	VF/NM	NM-
1-4-Paul Dini-s/J. Bone-c/a						3.00
TPB (2003, $11.95) r/#1-4; intro. by Joe Lansdale						12.00

MUTANT 2099
Marvel Comics (Marvel Knights): Nov, 2004 ($2.99, one-shot)

	GD	VG	FN	VF	VF/NM	NM-
1-Kirkman-s/Pat Lee-c						3.00

MUTANT X (See X-Factor)
Marvel Comics: Nov, 1998 - No. 32, June, 2001 ($2.99/$1.99/$2.25)

	GD	VG	FN	VF	VF/NM	NM-
1-($2.99) Alex Summers with alternate world's X-Men						4.00
2-11,13-19-($1.99): 2-Two covers. 5-Man-Spider-c/app.						3.00
12,25-($2.99): 12-Pin-up gallery by Kaluta, Romita, Byrne						4.00
20-24,26-32: 20-Begin $2.25-c. 28-31-Logan-c/app. 32-Last issue						3.00
Annual '99, '00 (5/99,'00, $3.50) '00-Doran-a(p)						4.00
Annual 2001 ($2.99) Story occurs between #31 & #32; Dracula app.						4.00

MUTANT X (Based on TV show)
Marvel Comics: May, 2002; June, 2002 ($3.50)

	GD	VG	FN	VF	VF/NM	NM-
...: Dangerous Decisions (6/02) -Kuder-s/Immonen-a						3.50
...: Origin (5/02) -Tischman & Chaykin-s/Ferguson-a						3.50

MUTATIS
Marvel Comics (Epic Comics): 1992 - No. 3, 1992 ($2.25, mini-series)

	GD	VG	FN	VF	VF/NM	NM-
1-3: Painted-c						3.00

MUTIES
Marvel Comics: Apr, 2002 - No. 6, Sept, 2002 ($2.50)

	GD	VG	FN	VF	VF/NM	NM-
1-6: 1-Bollars-s/Ferguson-a. 2-Spaziante-a. 3-Haspiel-a. 4-Kanuiga-a						3.00

MUTINY (Stormy Tales of the Seven Seas)
Aragon Magazines: Oct, 1954 - No. 3, Feb, 1955

	GD	VG	FN	VF	VF/NM	NM-
1	16	32	48	94	147	200
2,3: 2-Capt. Mutiny. 3-Bondage-c	14	28	42	76	108	140

MUTINY ON THE BOUNTY (See Classics Illustrated #100 & Movie Comics)

MUTOPIA X (Also see House of M and related titles)
Marvel Comics: Sept, 2005 - No. 5, Jan, 2006 ($2.99, limited series)

	GD	VG	FN	VF	VF/NM	NM-
1-5-Medina-a/Hine-s						3.00
House of M: Mutopia X (2006, $13.99, TPB) r/series						14.00

MUTT AND JEFF (See All-American, All-Flash #18, Cicero's Cat, Comic Cavalcade, Famous Feature Stories, The Funnies, Popular & Xmas Comics)
All American/National 1-103(6/58)/Dell 104(10/58)-115 (10-12/59)/ Harvey 116(2/60)-148: Summer, 1939 (nd) - No. 148, Nov, 1965

	GD	VG	FN	VF	VF/NM	NM-
1(nn)-Lost Wheels	148	296	444	947	1624	2300
2(nn)-Charging Bull (Summer, 1940, nd; on sale 6/20/40)	70	140	210	445	765	1085
3(nn)-Bucking Broncos (Summer, 1941, nd)	51	102	153	318	539	760
4(Winter, '41), 5(Summer, '42)	47	94	141	296	498	700
6-10: 6-Includes Minute Man Answers the Call	28	56	84	165	270	375
11-20: 20-X-Mas-c	20	40	60	117	189	260
21-30	15	30	45	88	137	185
31-50: 32-X-Mas-c	14	28	42	78	112	145
51-75-Last Fisher issue. 53-Last 52 pgs.	11	22	33	62	86	110
76-99,101-103: 76-Last pre-code issue(1/55)	6	12	18	39	62	85
100	6	12	18	41	66	90
104-115,132-148	5	10	15	30	48	65
116-131-Richie Rich app.	5	10	15	32	51	70
...Jokes 1-3(8/60-61, Harvey)-84 pgs.; Richie Rich in all; Little Dot in #2,3; Lotta in #2	5	10	15	30	48	65
...New Jokes 1-4(10/63-11/65, Harvey)-68 pgs.; Richie Rich in #1-3; Stumbo in #1	4	8	12	24	37	50

NOTE: *Most all issues by* ***Al Smith****. Issues from 1963 on have* ***Fisher*** *reprints. Clarification: early issues signed by Fisher are mostly drawn by Smith.*

MY BROTHERS' KEEPER
Spire Christian Comics (Fleming H. Revell Co.): 1973 (35/49¢, 36 pgs.)

	GD	VG	FN	VF	VF/NM	NM-
nn	2	4	6	10	14	18

MY CONFESSIONS (My Confession #7&8; formerly Western True Crime; A Spectacular Feature Magazine #11)
Fox Feature Syndicate: No. 7, Aug, 1949 - No. 10, Jan-Feb, 1950

	GD	VG	FN	VF	VF/NM	NM-
7-Wood-a (10 pgs.)	25	50	75	150	245	340
8,9: 8-Harrison/Wood-a (19 pgs.). 9-Wood-a	23	46	69	136	223	310
10	14	28	42	80	115	150

MY DATE COMICS (Teen-age)
Hillman Periodicals: July, 1947 - V1#4, Jan, 1948 (2nd Romance comic; see Young Romance)

	GD	VG	FN	VF	VF/NM	NM-
1-S&K-c/a	39	78	117	240	395	550
2-4-S&K-c/a; Dan Barry-a	27	54	81	160	263	365

MY DESIRE (Formerly Jo-Jo Comics; becomes Murder, Inc. #5 on)
Fox Feature Syndicate: No. 30, Aug, 1949 - No. 4, April, 1950

	GD	VG	FN	VF	VF/NM	NM-
30(#1)	19	38	57	109	172	235
31 (#2, 10/49),3(2/50),4	14	28	42	82	121	160
31 (Canadian edition)	9	18	27	50	65	80
32(12/49)-Wood-a	22	44	66	132	216	300

MY DIARY (Becomes My Friend Irma #3 on?)
Marvel Comics (A Lovers Mag.): Dec, 1949 - No. 2, Mar, 1950

My Experience #19 © FOX

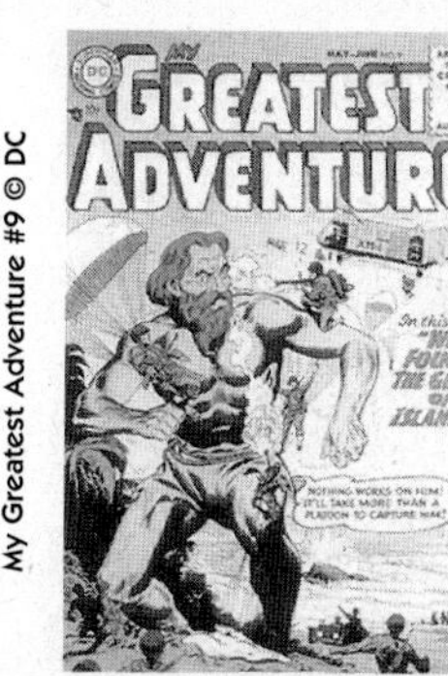

My Greatest Adventure #9 © DC

My Love Affair #1 © FOX

	GD 2.0	VG 4.0	FN 6.0	VF 8.0	VF/NM 9.0	NM- 9.2
1,2-Photo-c	15	30	45	90	140	190

MY EXPERIENCE (Formerly All Top; becomes Judy Canova #23 on)
Fox Feature Syndicate: No. 19, Sept, 1949 - No. 22, Mar, 1950

	GD 2.0	VG 4.0	FN 6.0	VF 8.0	VF/NM 9.0	NM- 9.2
19,21: 19-Wood-a. 21-Wood-a(2)	26	52	78	154	252	350
20	14	28	42	82	121	160
22-Wood-a (9 pgs.)	22	44	66	132	216	300

MY FAITH IN FRANKIE
DC Comics (Vertigo): March, 2004 - No. 4, June, 2004 ($2.95, limited series)

	GD 2.0	VG 4.0	FN 6.0	VF 8.0	VF/NM 9.0	NM- 9.2
1-4-Mike Carey-s/Sonny Liew & Marc Hempel-a						3.00
TPB (2004, $6.95, digest-size) r/series in B&W; Dead Boy Detectives preview						7.00

MY FAVORITE MARTIAN (TV)
Gold Key: 1/64; No.2, 7/64 - No. 9, 10/66 (No. 1,3-9 have photo-c)

	GD 2.0	VG 4.0	FN 6.0	VF 8.0	VF/NM 9.0	NM- 9.2
1-Russ Manning-a	11	22	33	76	151	225
2	7	14	21	48	79	110
3-9	6	12	18	41	66	90

MY FRIEND IRMA (Radio/TV) (Formerly My Diary? and/or Western Life Romances?)
Marvel/Atlas Comics (BFP): No. 3, June, 1950 - No. 47, Dec, 1954; No. 48, Feb, 1955

	GD 2.0	VG 4.0	FN 6.0	VF 8.0	VF/NM 9.0	NM- 9.2
3-Dan DeCarlo-a in all; 52 pgs. begin, end ?	20	40	60	117	189	260
4-Kurtzman-a (10 pgs.)	19	38	57	111	176	240
5- "Egghead Doodle" by Kurtzman (4 pgs.)	15	30	45	86	133	180
6,8-10: 9-Paper dolls, 1 pg; Millie app. (5 pgs.)	14	28	42	76	108	140
7-One pg. Kurtzman-a	14	28	42	78	112	145
11-23: 23-One pg. Frazetta-a	10	20	30	58	79	100
24-48: 41,48-Stan Lee & Dan DeCarlo app.	9	18	27	52	69	85

MY GIRL PEARL
Atlas Comics: 4/55 - #4, 10/55; #5, 7/57 - #6, 9/57; #7, 8/60 - #11, ?/61

	GD 2.0	VG 4.0	FN 6.0	VF 8.0	VF/NM 9.0	NM- 9.2
1-Dan DeCarlo-c/a in #1-6	16	32	48	94	147	200
2	10	20	30	58	79	100
3-6	9	18	27	50	65	80
7-11	5	10	15	32	51	70

MY GREATEST ADVENTURE (Doom Patrol #86 on)
National Periodical Publications: Jan-Feb, 1955 - No. 85, Feb, 1964

	GD 2.0	VG 4.0	FN 6.0	VF 8.0	VF/NM 9.0	NM- 9.2
1-Before CCA	122	244	366	988	2144	3300
2	45	90	135	338	732	1125
3-5	32	64	96	232	504	775
6-10: 6-Science fiction format begins	27	54	81	184	397	610
11-14: 12-1st S.A. issue	20	40	60	137	294	450
15-17: Kirby-a in all	21	42	63	148	317	485
18-Kirby-c/a	24	48	72	168	359	550
19,23-25	16	32	48	111	243	375
20,21,28-Kirby-a	20	40	60	137	294	450
22-Space Ranger prototype (7-8/58)(see Showcase #15 for Space Ranger debut)	17	34	51	119	260	400
26,27,29,30	13	26	39	87	186	285
31-40	11	22	33	76	151	225
41,42,44-57,59	10	20	30	67	124	180
43-Kirby-a	10	20	30	70	133	195
58,60,61-Toth-a; Last 10¢ issue	10	20	30	68	127	185
62-76,78,79: 79-Promotes "Legion of the Strange" for next issue; renamed Doom Patrol for #80	8	16	24	56	96	135
77-Toth-a; Robotman prototype	9	18	27	58	99	140
80-(6/63)-Intro/origin Doom Patrol and begin series; origin & 1st app. Negative Man, Elasti-Girl & S.A. Robotman	46	92	138	373	812	1250
81,85-Toth-a	17	34	51	119	260	400
82-84	16	32	48	111	243	375

NOTE: ***Anderson** a-42. **Cameron** a-24. **Colan** a-77. **Meskin** a-25, 26, 32, 39, 45, 50, 56, 57, 61, 64, 70, 73, 74, 76, 79; c-76. **Moreira** a-11, 12, 15, 17, 20, 23, 25, 27, 37, 40-43, 46, 48, 55-57, 59, 60, 62-65, 67, 69, 70; c-1-4, 7-10. **Roussos** c/a-71-73. **Wildey** a-32.*

MY GREATEST ADVENTURE (Also see 2011 Weird Worlds series)
DC Comics: Dec, 2011 - No. 6, May, 2012 ($3.99, limited series)

	GD 2.0	VG 4.0	FN 6.0	VF 8.0	VF/NM 9.0	NM- 9.2
1-6-Short stories of Tanga, Robotman, and Garbage Man; Lopresti-s/a, Maguire-s/a						4.00

MY GREAT LOVE (Becomes Will Rogers Western #5)
Fox Feature Syndicate: Oct, 1949 - No. 4, Apr, 1950

	GD 2.0	VG 4.0	FN 6.0	VF 8.0	VF/NM 9.0	NM- 9.2
1	17	34	51	98	154	210
2-4	11	22	33	60	83	105

MY INTIMATE AFFAIR (Inside Crime #3)
Fox Feature Syndicate: Mar, 1950 - No. 2, May, 1950

	GD 2.0	VG 4.0	FN 6.0	VF 8.0	VF/NM 9.0	NM- 9.2
1	17	34	51	98	154	210
2	11	22	33	60	83	105

MY LIFE (Formerly Meet Corliss Archer)
Fox Feature Syndicate: No. 4, Sept, 1948 - No. 15, July, 1950

	GD 2.0	VG 4.0	FN 6.0	VF 8.0	VF/NM 9.0	NM- 9.2
4-Used in **SOTI**, pg. 39; Kamen/Feldstein-a	42	84	126	265	445	625
5-Kamen-a	26	52	78	154	252	350
6-Kamen/Feldstein-a	29	58	87	170	278	385
7-Wood-a; wash cover	22	44	66	132	216	300
8,9,11-15	14	28	42	80	115	150
10-Wood-a	20	40	60	118	192	265

MY LITTLE MARGIE (TV)
Charlton Comics: July, 1954 - No. 54, Nov, 1964

	GD 2.0	VG 4.0	FN 6.0	VF 8.0	VF/NM 9.0	NM- 9.2
1-Photo front/back-c	37	74	111	218	354	490
2-Photo front/back-c	18	36	54	107	169	230
3-7,10	12	24	36	69	97	125
8,9-Infinity-c	13	26	39	72	101	130
11-14: Part-photo-c (#13, 8/56). 14-UFO cover	10	20	30	58	79	100
15-19	10	20	30	54	72	90
20-(25¢, 100 pg. issue)	15	30	45	86	133	180
21-40: 40-Last 10¢ issue	5	10	15	32	51	70
41-53	4	8	12	28	44	60
54-(11/64) Beatles on cover; lead story spoofs the Beatle haircut craze of the 1960's; Beatles app. (scarce)	14	28	42	97	211	325

NOTE: *Doll cut-outs in 32, 33, 40, 45, 50.*

MY LITTLE MARGIE'S BOY FRIENDS (TV) (Freddy V2#12 on)
Charlton Comics: Aug, 1955 - No. 11, Apr?, 1958

	GD 2.0	VG 4.0	FN 6.0	VF 8.0	VF/NM 9.0	NM- 9.2
1-Has several Archie swipes	15	30	45	84	127	170
2	9	18	27	52	69	85
3-11	8	16	24	44	57	70

MY LITTLE MARGIE'S FASHIONS (TV)
Charlton Comics: Feb, 1959 - No. 5, Nov, 1959

	GD 2.0	VG 4.0	FN 6.0	VF 8.0	VF/NM 9.0	NM- 9.2
1	14	28	42	76	108	140
2-5	8	16	24	44	57	70

MY LOVE (Becomes Two Gun Western #5 (11/50) on?)
Marvel Comics (CLDS): July, 1949 - No. 4, Apr, 1950 (All photo-c)

	GD 2.0	VG 4.0	FN 6.0	VF 8.0	VF/NM 9.0	NM- 9.2
1	18	36	54	103	162	220
2,3	12	24	36	69	97	125
4-Bettie Page photo-c (see Cupid #2)	42	84	126	265	445	625

MY LOVE
Marvel Comics Group: Sept, 1969 - No. 39, Mar, 1976

	GD 2.0	VG 4.0	FN 6.0	VF 8.0	VF/NM 9.0	NM- 9.2
1	8	16	24	55	93	130
2-9: 4-6-Colan-a	5	10	15	30	48	65
10-Williamson-r/My Own Romance #71; Kirby-a	5	10	15	32	51	70
11-13,15-19	4	8	12	26	41	55
14-(52 pgs.)-Woodstock-c/sty; Morrow-c/a; Kirby/Colletta-r	6	12	18	41	66	90
20-Starlin-a	4	8	12	28	44	60
21,22,24-27,29-38: 38-Reprints	4	8	12	22	34	45
23-Steranko-r/Our Love Story #5	4	8	12	26	41	55
28-Kirby-a	4	8	12	24	37	50
39-Last issue; reprints	4	8	12	24	37	50
Special 1 (12/71)(52 pgs.)	6	12	18	37	59	80

NOTE: ***John Buscema** a-1-7, 10, 18-21, 22r(2), 24r, 25r, 29r, 34r, 36r, 37r, Spec. (r)(4); c-13, 15, 25, 27, Spec. **Colan** a-4, 5, 6, 8, 9, 16, 17, 20, 21, 22, 24r, 27r, 30r, 35r, 39r. **Colan/Everett** a-13, 15, 16, 27(r/#13). **Kirby** a-(r)-10, 14, 26, 28. **Romita** a-1-3, 19, 20, 25, 34, 38; c-1-3, 15.*

MY LOVE AFFAIR (March of Crime #7 on)
Fox Feature Syndicate: July, 1949 - No. 6, May, 1950

	GD 2.0	VG 4.0	FN 6.0	VF 8.0	VF/NM 9.0	NM- 9.2
1	17	34	51	98	154	210
2	11	22	33	60	83	105
3-6-Wood-a. 5-(3/50)-Becomes Love Stories #6	20	40	60	115	185	255

MY LOVE LIFE (Formerly Zegra)
Fox Feature Synd.: No. 6, June, 1949 - No. 13, Aug, 1950; No. 13, Sept, 1951

	GD 2.0	VG 4.0	FN 6.0	VF 8.0	VF/NM 9.0	NM- 9.2
6-Kamenish-a	17	34	51	98	154	210
7-13	11	22	33	60	83	105
13 (9/51)(Formerly My Story #12)	10	20	30	56	76	95

MY LOVE MEMOIRS (Formerly Women Outlaws; Hunted #13 on)
Fox Feature Syndicate: No. 9, Nov, 1949 - No. 12, May, 1950

	GD 2.0	VG 4.0	FN 6.0	VF 8.0	VF/NM 9.0	NM- 9.2
9,11,12-Wood-a	20	40	60	115	185	255
10	11	22	33	60	83	105

MY LOVE SECRET (Formerly Phantom Lady; Animal Crackers #31)
Fox Feature Syndicate/M. S. Distr.: No. 24, June, 1949 - No. 30, June, 1950; No. 53, 1954

My Love Story #4 © FOX

My Name is Holocaust #3 © Milestone

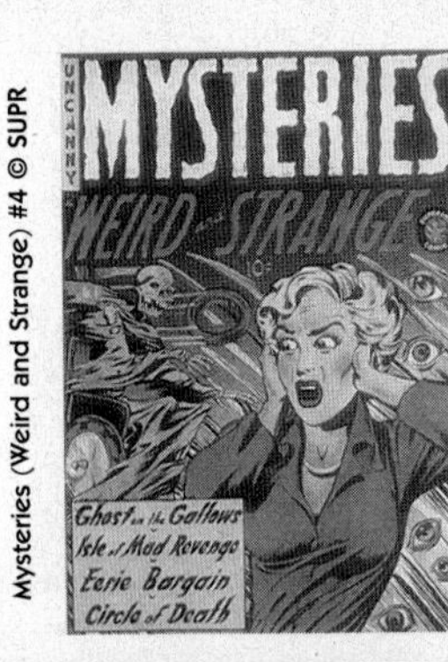

Mysteries (Weird and Strange) #4 © SUPR

	GD 2.0	VG 4.0	FN 6.0	VF 8.0	VF/NM 9.0	NM- 9.2
24-Kamen/Feldstein-a	20	40	60	118	192	265
25-Possible caricature of Wood on-c?	14	28	42	78	112	145
26,28-Wood-a	20	40	60	115	185	255
27,29,30: 30-Photo-c	12	24	36	69	97	125
53-(Reprint, M.S. Distr.) 1954? nd given; formerly Western Thrillers; becomes Crimes by Women #54; photo-c	8	16	24	40	50	60

MY LOVE STORY (Hoot Gibson Western #5 on)
Fox Feature Syndicate: Sept, 1949 - No. 4, Mar, 1950

	GD 2.0	VG 4.0	FN 6.0	VF 8.0	VF/NM 9.0	NM- 9.2
1	17	34	51	98	154	210
2	11	22	33	60	83	105
3,4-Wood-a	20	40	60	115	185	255

MY LOVE STORY
Atlas Comics (GPS): April, 1956 - No. 9, Aug, 1957

	GD 2.0	VG 4.0	FN 6.0	VF 8.0	VF/NM 9.0	NM- 9.2
1	14	28	42	80	115	150
2	9	18	27	47	61	75
3,7: Matt Baker-a. 7-Toth-a	11	22	33	62	86	110
4-6,8,9	8	16	24	44	57	70

NOTE: ***Brewster** a-3. **Colletta** a-1(2), 3, 4(2), 5; c-3.*

MY NAME IS BRUCE
Dark Horse Comics: Sept, 2008 ($3.50, one-shot)

	GD 2.0	VG 4.0	FN 6.0	VF 8.0	VF/NM 9.0	NM- 9.2
nn-Adaptation of the Bruce Campbell movie; Cliff Richards-a/Bart Sears-c						3.50

MY NAME IS HOLOCAUST
DC Comics: May, 1995 - No. 5, Sept, 1995 ($2.50, limited series)

	GD 2.0	VG 4.0	FN 6.0	VF 8.0	VF/NM 9.0	NM- 9.2
1-5						3.00

MY ONLY LOVE
Charlton Comics: July, 1975 - No. 9, Nov, 1976

	GD 2.0	VG 4.0	FN 6.0	VF 8.0	VF/NM 9.0	NM- 9.2
1	3	6	9	14	19	24
2,4-9	2	4	6	9	13	16
3-Toth-a	2	4	6	11	16	20

MY OWN ROMANCE (Formerly My Romance; Teen-Age Romance #77 on)
Marvel/Atlas (MjPC/RCM No. 4-59/ZPC No. 60-76): No. 4, Mar, 1949 - No. 76, July, 1960

	GD 2.0	VG 4.0	FN 6.0	VF 8.0	VF/NM 9.0	NM- 9.2
4-Photo-c	17	34	51	98	154	210
5-10: 5,6,8-10-Photo-c	11	22	33	64	90	115
11-20: 14-Powell-a	10	20	30	58	79	100
21-42,55: 42-Last precode (2/55). 55-Toth-a	10	20	30	54	72	90
43-54,56-60	5	10	15	35	55	75
61-70,72,73,75,76	5	10	15	30	48	65
71-Williamson-a	6	12	18	37	59	80
74-Kirby-a	6	12	18	37	59	80

NOTE: ***Brewster** a-59. **Colletta** a-45(2), 48, 50, 55, 57(2), 59; c-58i, 59, 61. **Everett** a-25; c-58p. **Kirby** c-71, 75, 76. **Morisi** a-18. **Orlando** a-61. **Romita** a-36. **Tuska** a-10.*

MY PAL DIZZY (See Comic Books, Series I)

MY PAST (...Confessions) (Formerly Western Thrillers)
Fox Feature Syndicate: No. 7, Aug, 1949 - No. 11, Apr, 1950 (Crimes Inc. #12)

	GD 2.0	VG 4.0	FN 6.0	VF 8.0	VF/NM 9.0	NM- 9.2
7	17	34	51	98	154	210
8-10	11	22	33	60	83	105
11-Wood-a	20	40	60	115	185	255

MY PERSONAL PROBLEM
Ajax/Farrell/Steinway Comic: 11/55; No. 2, 2/56; No. 3, 9/56 - No. 4, 11/56; 10/57 - No. 3, 5/58

	GD 2.0	VG 4.0	FN 6.0	VF 8.0	VF/NM 9.0	NM- 9.2
1	9	18	27	52	69	85
2-4	7	14	21	35	43	50
1-3('57-'58)-Steinway	6	12	18	28	34	40

MY PRIVATE LIFE (Formerly Murder, Inc.; becomes Pedro #18)
Fox Feature Syndicate: No. 16, Feb, 1950 - No. 17, April, 1950

	GD 2.0	VG 4.0	FN 6.0	VF 8.0	VF/NM 9.0	NM- 9.2
16,17	14	28	42	81	118	155

MYRA NORTH (See The Comics, Crackajack Funnies & Red Ryder)
Dell Publishing Co.: No. 3, Jan, 1940

	GD 2.0	VG 4.0	FN 6.0	VF 8.0	VF/NM 9.0	NM- 9.2
Four Color 3	97	194	291	621	1061	1500

MY REAL LOVE
Standard Comics: No. 5, June, 1952 (Photo-c)

	GD 2.0	VG 4.0	FN 6.0	VF 8.0	VF/NM 9.0	NM- 9.2
5-Toth-a, 3 pgs.; Tuska, Cardy, Vern Greene-a	14	28	42	78	112	145

MY ROMANCE (Becomes My Own Romance #4 on)
Marvel Comics (RCM): Sept, 1948 - No. 3, Jan, 1949

	GD 2.0	VG 4.0	FN 6.0	VF 8.0	VF/NM 9.0	NM- 9.2
1	20	40	60	117	189	260
2,3: 2-Anti-Wertham editorial (11/48)	14	28	42	78	112	145

MY ROMANTIC ADVENTURES (Formerly Romantic Adventures)
American Comics Group: No. 68, 8/56 - No. 115, 12/60; No. 116, 7/61 - No. 138, 3/64

	GD 2.0	VG 4.0	FN 6.0	VF 8.0	VF/NM 9.0	NM- 9.2
68	8	16	24	42	54	65
69-85	7	14	21	35	43	50
86-Three pg. Williamson-a (2/58)	8	16	24	44	57	70
87-100	3	6	9	20	30	40
101-138	3	6	9	16	23	30

NOTE: ***Whitney** art in most issues.*

MY SECRET (Becomes Our Secret #4 on)
Superior Comics, Ltd.: Aug, 1949 - No. 3, Oct, 1949

	GD 2.0	VG 4.0	FN 6.0	VF 8.0	VF/NM 9.0	NM- 9.2
1	18	36	54	105	165	225
2,3	14	28	42	80	115	150

MY SECRET AFFAIR (Becomes Martin Kane #4)
Hero Book (Fox Feature Syndicate): Dec, 1949 - No. 3, April, 1950

	GD 2.0	VG 4.0	FN 6.0	VF 8.0	VF/NM 9.0	NM- 9.2
1-Harrison/Wood-a (10 pgs.)	24	48	72	144	237	330
2,3-Wood-a	20	40	60	115	185	255

MY SECRET CONFESSION
Sterling Comics: September, 1955

	GD 2.0	VG 4.0	FN 6.0	VF 8.0	VF/NM 9.0	NM- 9.2
1-Sekowsky-a	9	18	27	52	69	85

MY SECRET LIFE (Formerly Western Outlaws; Romeo Tubbs #26 on)
Fox Feature Syndicate: No. 22, July, 1949 - No. 27, July, 1950; No. 27, 9/51

	GD 2.0	VG 4.0	FN 6.0	VF 8.0	VF/NM 9.0	NM- 9.2
22	14	28	42	80	115	150
23,26-Wood-a, 6 pgs.	20	40	60	115	185	255
24,25,27	12	24	36	69	97	125
27 (9/51)	10	20	30	56	76	95

NOTE: *The title was changed to Romeo Tubbs after #25 even though #26 & 27 did come out.*

MY SECRET LIFE (Formerly Young Lovers; Sue & Sally Smith #48)
Charlton Comics: No. 19, Aug, 1957 - No. 47, Sept, 1962

	GD 2.0	VG 4.0	FN 6.0	VF 8.0	VF/NM 9.0	NM- 9.2
19	4	8	12	26	41	55
20-35	3	6	9	16	23	30
36-47: 44-Last 10¢ issue. 47-1st app. Sue & Sally Smith	3	6	9	14	20	26

MY SECRET MARRIAGE
Superior Comics, Ltd.: May, 1953 - No. 24, July, 1956 (Canadian)

	GD 2.0	VG 4.0	FN 6.0	VF 8.0	VF/NM 9.0	NM- 9.2
1	15	30	45	84	127	170
2	9	18	27	52	69	85
3-24	8	16	24	44	57	70
I.W. Reprint #9	2	4	6	8	11	14

NOTE: *Many issues contain **Kamen-ish** art.*

MY SECRET ROMANCE (Becomes A Star Presentation #3)
Hero Book (Fox Feature Syndicate): Jan, 1950 - No. 2, March, 1950

	GD 2.0	VG 4.0	FN 6.0	VF 8.0	VF/NM 9.0	NM- 9.2
1	16	32	48	94	147	200
2-Wood-a	20	40	60	115	185	255

MY SECRETS (Magazine) (Also see Gothic Romances)
Atlas/Seaboard: Feb, 1975 (B&W, 68 pgs.)

	GD 2.0	VG 4.0	FN 6.0	VF 8.0	VF/NM 9.0	NM- 9.2
Vol. 1 #1	8	16	24	53	89	125

MY SECRET STORY (Formerly Captain Kidd #25; Sabu #30 on)
Fox Feature Syndicate: No. 26, Oct, 1949 - No. 29, April, 1950

	GD 2.0	VG 4.0	FN 6.0	VF 8.0	VF/NM 9.0	NM- 9.2
26	15	30	45	88	137	185
27-29	11	22	33	60	83	105

MYSPACE DARK HORSE PRESENTS
Dark Horse Books: Sept, 2008 - Feb, 2011 ($19.95/$19.99, TPB)

	GD 2.0	VG 4.0	FN 6.0	VF 8.0	VF/NM 9.0	NM- 9.2
Vol. 1 - Short stories previously appearing on Dark Horse's MySpace.com webpage; s/a by various incl. Whedon, Bá, Bagge, Mignola, Moon, Nord, Trimpe, Warren, Way						20.00
Vol. 2 - Collects stories from online #7-12; s/a by Way, Niles, Dorkin, Hotz & others						20.00
Vol. 3 - Collects stories from online #13-19; s/a by Mignola, Cloonan & others						20.00
Vol. 4 - Collects stories from online #20-24; s/a by Whedon, Chen & others						20.00
Vol. 5 - Collects stories from online #25-30; s/a by Thompson, Aragonés & others						20.00
Vol. 6 - Collects stories from online #31-36; s/a by Sakai, Dorkin & others						20.00

MYSTERIES (...Weird & Strange)
Superior/Dynamic Publ. (Randall Publ. Ltd.): May, 1953 - No. 11, Jan, 1955

	GD 2.0	VG 4.0	FN 6.0	VF 8.0	VF/NM 9.0	NM- 9.2
1-All horror stories	43	86	129	268	454	640
2-A-Bomb blast story	27	54	81	160	263	365
3-11: 10-Kamenish-c/a reprinted from Strange Mysteries #2; cover is from a panel in Strange Mysteries #2	24	48	72	142	234	325

MYSTERIES IN SPACE (See Fireside Book Series)

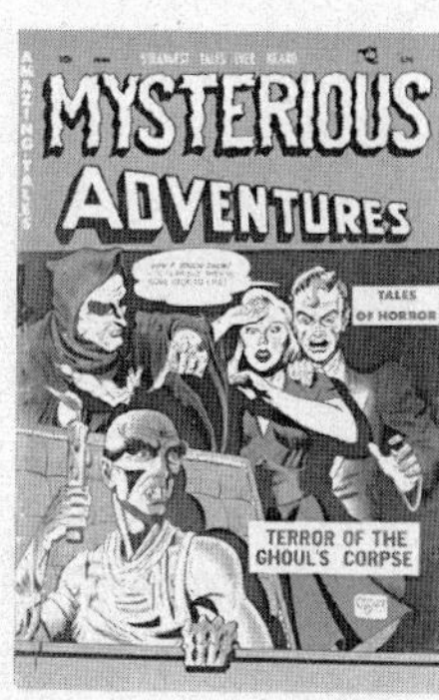

Mysterious Adventures #2 © Story

Mystery Comics #7 © WHW

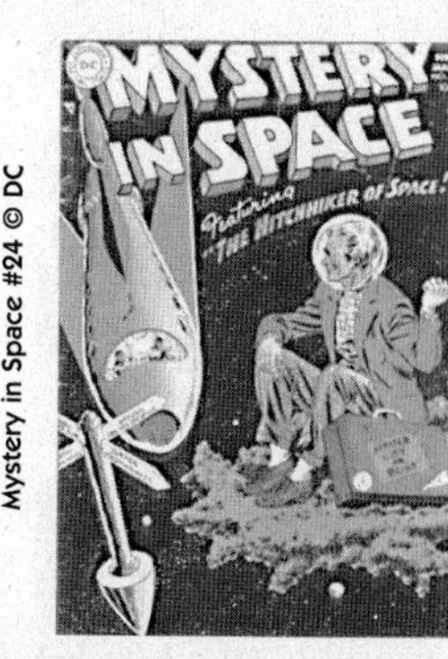

Mystery in Space #24 © DC

GD VG FN VF VF/NM NM-
2.0 4.0 6.0 8.0 9.0 9.2

MYSTERIES OF SCOTLAND YARD (Also see A-1 Comics)
Magazine Enterprises: No. 121, 1954 (one shot)
A-1 121-Reprinted from Manhunt (5 stories) 15 30 45 85 130 175

MYSTERIES OF UNEXPLORED WORLDS (See Blue Bird)(Becomes Son of Vulcan V2#49 on)
Charlton Comics: Aug, 1956; No. 2, Jan, 1957 - No. 48, Sept, 1965
1 37 74 111 222 361 500
2-No Ditko 16 32 48 94 147 200
3,4,8,9 Ditko-a. 3-Diko c/a (4). 4-Ditko c/a (2). 30 60 90 177 289 400
5,6,10,11: 5,6-Ditko-c/a (all). 10-Ditko-c/a(4). 11-Ditko-c/a(3); signed J. Kotdi
31 62 93 186 303 420
7-(2/58, 68 pgs.) 4 stories w/Ditko-a 34 68 102 204 332 460
12-Ditko sty (3); Baker story "The Charm Bracelet" 30 60 90 177 289 400
13-18,20 10 20 30 56 76 95
19,21-24,26-Ditko-a 23 46 69 136 223 310
25,27-30: 28-Communist A-bomb story w/Khrushchev
5 10 15 35 55 75
31-45: Atomic bomb panel 4 8 12 26 41 55
46(5/65)-Son of Vulcan begins (origin/1st app.) 4 8 12 28 44 60
47,48 4 8 12 23 34 45
NOTE: ***Ditko** c-3-6, 10, 11, 19, 21-24. Covers to #19, 21-24 reprint story panels.*

MYSTERIOUS ADVENTURES
Story Comics: Mar, 1951 - No. 24, Mar, 1955; No. 25, Aug, 1955
1-All horror stories 79 158 237 502 864 1225
2-(6/51) 43 86 129 271 461 650
3,4,6,10 41 82 123 256 428 600
5-Seered heads/bondage-c 43 86 129 271 461 650
7-Dagger in eye panel; dismemberment stories 48 96 144 302 514 725
8-Eyeball story 54 108 162 343 574 825
9-Extreme violence (8/52) 45 90 135 284 480 675
11-(12/52)-Used in **SOTI**, pg. 84 45 90 135 284 480 675
12,14: 14-E.C. Old Witch swipe 41 82 123 256 428 600
13-Classic skull-c 55 110 165 352 601 850
15-21: 18-Used in Senate Investigative report, pgs. 5,6; E.C. swipe/TFTC #35; The Coffin-Keeper & Corpse (hosts). 20-Electric chair-c; used by Wertham in the Senate hearings. 21-Bondage/beheading-c; extreme violence
48 96 144 302 514 725
22- "Cinderella" parody 42 84 126 265 445 625
23-Disbrow-a (6 pgs.); E.C. swipe "The Mystery Keeper's Tale" (host) and "Mother Ghoul's Nursery Tale" 42 84 126 265 445 625
24,25 32 64 96 188 307 425
NOTE: *Tothish art by **Ross Andru**-#22, 23. **Bache** a-8. **Cameron** a-5-7. **Harrison** a-12. **Hollingsworth** a-3-8, 12. **Schaffenberger** a-24, 25. **Wildey** a-15, 17.*

MYSTERIOUS ISLAND
Dell Publishing Co.: No. 1213, July-Sept, 1961
Four Color 1213-Movie, photo-c 8 16 24 55 93 130

MYSTERIOUS ISLE
Dell Publishing Co.: Nov-Jan, 1963/64 (Jules Verne)
1 4 8 12 22 34 45

MYSTERIOUS RIDER, THE (See Zane Grey, 4-Color 301)

MYSTERIOUS STORIES (Formerly Horror From the Tomb #1)
Premier Magazines: No. 2, Dec-Jan, 1954-1955 - No. 7, Dec, 1955
2-Woodbridge-c; last pre-code issue 50 100 150 315 533 750
3-Woodbridge-c/a 36 72 108 211 343 475
4-7: 5-Cinderella parody. 6-Woodbridge-c 32 64 96 192 314 435
NOTE: ***Hollingsworth** a-2, 4.*

MYSTERIOUS STRANGER
DC Comics: Aug/Sept. 1952
nn-Ashcan comic, not distributed to newsstands, only for in-house use. Cover art is All Star Western #60 with interior being Sensation Comics #100. A FN/VF copy sold for $2,357.50 in 2002.

MYSTERIOUS SUSPENSE (Also see Blue Beetle #1 (1967))
Charlton Comics: Oct, 1968 (12¢)
1-Return of the Question by Ditko (c/a) 7 14 21 46 76 105

MYSTERIOUS TRAVELER (See Tales of the...)

MYSTERIOUS TRAVELER COMICS (Radio)
Trans-World Publications: Nov, 1948
1-Powell-c/a(2); Poe adaptation, "Tell Tale Heart" 63 126 189 403 689 975

MYSTERIUS
DC Comics (WildStorm): Mar, 2009 - No. 6, Aug, 2009 ($2.99, limited series)
1-6-Jeff Parker-a/Tom Fowler-a 3.00
TPB (2010, $17.99) r/#1-6 18.00

MYSTERY COMICS
William H. Wise & Co.: 1944 - No. 4, 1944 (No months given)
1-The Magnet, The Silver Knight, Brad Spencer, Wonderman, Dick Devins, King of Futuria, & Zudo the Jungle Boy begin (all 1st app.); Schomburg-c on all
129 258 387 826 1413 2000
2-Bondage-c 71 142 213 454 777 1100
3,4: 3-Lance Lewis, Space Detective begins (1st app.); Robot-c. 4-(V2#1 inside); KKK-c
65 130 195 416 708 1000

MYSTERY COMICS DIGEST
Gold Key/Whitman?: Mar, 1972 - No. 26, Oct, 1975
1-Ripley's Believe It or Not; reprint of Ripley's #1 origin Ra-Ka-Tep the Mummy; Wood-a
4 8 12 26 41 55
2-9: 2-Boris Karloff Tales of Mystery; Wood-a; 1st app. Werewolf Count Wulfstein. 3-Twilight Zone (TV); Crandall, Toth & George Evans-a; 1st app. Tragg & Simbar the Lion Lord; (2) Crandall/Frazetta-r/Twilight Zone #1 4-Ripley's Believe It or Not; 1st app. Baron Tibor, the Vampire. 5-Boris Karloff Tales of Mystery; 1st app. Dr. Spektor. 6-Twilight Zone (TV); 1st app. U.S. Marshal Reid & Sir Duane; Evans-r. 7-Ripley's Believe It or Not; origin The Lurker in the Swamp; 1st app. Duroc. 8-Boris Karloff Tales of Mystery; McWilliams-r; Orlando-r. 9-Twilight Zone (TV); Williamson, Crandall, McWilliams-a; 2nd Tragg app.;Torres, Evans, Heck/Tuska-r 3 6 9 20 30 40
10-26: 10,13-Ripley's Believe It or Not: 13-Orlando-r. 11,14-Boris Karloff Tales of Mystery. 14-1st app. Xorkon. 12,15-Twilight Zone (TV). 16,19,22,25-Ripley's Believe It or Not. 17-Boris Karloff Tales of Mystery; Williamson-r; Orlando-r. 18,21,24-Twilight Zone (TV). 20,23,26-Boris Karloff Tales of Mystery 3 6 9 16 23 30
NOTE: *Dr. Spektor app.-#5, 10-12, 21. Durak app.-#15. Duroc app.-#14 (later called Durak). King George 1st app.-#8.*

MYSTERY IN SPACE (Also see Fireside Book Series and Pulp Fiction Library: ...)
National Periodical Pub.: 4-5/51 - No. 110, 9/66; No. 111, 9/80 - No. 117, 3/81 (#1-3: 52 pgs.)
1-Frazetta-a, 8 pgs.; Knights of the Galaxy begins, ends #8
232 464 696 1950 4225 6500
2 83 166 249 672 1461 2250
3 64 128 192 518 1122 1725
4,5 52 104 156 421 911 1400
6-10: 7-Toth-a 40 80 120 300 650 1000
11-15 33 66 99 235 510 785
16-18,20-25: Interplanetary Insurance feature by Infantino in all. 21-1st app. Space Cabbie. 24-Last pre-code issue 29 58 87 205 445 685
19-Virgil Finlay-a 31 62 93 220 478 735
26-40: 26-Space Cabbie feature begins. 34-1st S.A. issue. 40-Grey-tone-c
23 46 69 164 350 535
41-52: 47-Space Cabbie feature ends 17 34 51 114 250 385
53-Adam Strange begins (8/59, 10pg. sty); robot-c 154 308 462 1294 2797 4300
54 44 88 132 330 715 1100
55-Grey tone-c 40 80 120 300 650 1000
56-60: 59-Kane/Anderson-a 23 46 69 161 343 525
61-71: 61-1st app. Adam Strange foe Ulthoon. 62-1st app. A.S. foe Mortan. 63-Origin Vandor. 66-Star Rovers begin (1st app.). 68-1st app. Dust Devils (6/61). 69-1st Mailbag. 70-2nd app. Dust Devils. 71-Last 10¢ issue 18 36 54 126 273 420
72-74,76-80 13 26 39 86 183 280
75-JLA x-over in Adam Strange (5/62)(sequel to J.L.A. #3, 2nd app. of Kanjar Ro)
22 44 66 154 327 500
81-86 11 22 33 71 136 200
87-(11/63)-Adam Strange/Hawkman double feat begins; 3rd Hawkman tryout series
15 30 45 102 221 340
88-Adam Strange & Hawkman stories 13 26 39 90 195 300
89-Adam Strange & Hawkman stories 13 26 39 88 189 290
90-Book-length Adam Strange & Hawkman story; 1st team-up (3/64); Hawkman moves to own title next month; classic-c 15 30 45 102 221 340
91-102: 91-End Infantino art on Adam Strange; double-length Adam Strange story. 92-Space Ranger begins (6/64), ends #103. 92-94,96,98-Space Ranger-c. 94,98-Adam Strange/Space Ranger team-up. 102-Adam Strange ends (no Space Ranger)
7 14 21 49 82 115
103-Origin Ultra, the Multi-Alien; last Space Ranger 6 12 18 41 66 90
104-110: 110-(9/66)-Last 12¢ issue 5 10 15 32 51 70
V17#111(9/80)-117: 117-Newton-a(3 pgs.) 2 4 6 8 11 14
NOTE: ***Anderson** a-2, 4, 8-10, 12-17, 19, 45-48, 51, 57, 59i, 61-64, 70, 76, 87-91; c-9, 10, 15-25, 87, 89, 105-108, 110. **Aparo** a-111. **Austin** a-112i. **Bolland** a-115. **Craig** a-114, 116. **Ditko** a-111, 114-116. **Drucker** a-13, 14. **Elias** a-98, 102, 103. **Golden** a-113p. **Sid Greene** a-78, 91. **Infantino** a-1-8, 11, 14-25, 27-46, 48, 49, 51, 53-91, 103, 117; c-60-86, 88, 90, 91, 105, 107. **Gil Kane** a-14p, 15p, 18p, 19p, 26p, 29-59p(most), 100-102; c-52, 101. **Kubert** a-113; c-111-115. **Moreira** c-27, 28. **Rogers** a-111. **Sekowsky** a-52. **Simon & Kirby** a-4(2 pgs.). **Spiegle** a-111, 114. **Starlin** c-116. **Sutton** a-112. **Tuska** a-115p, 117p.*

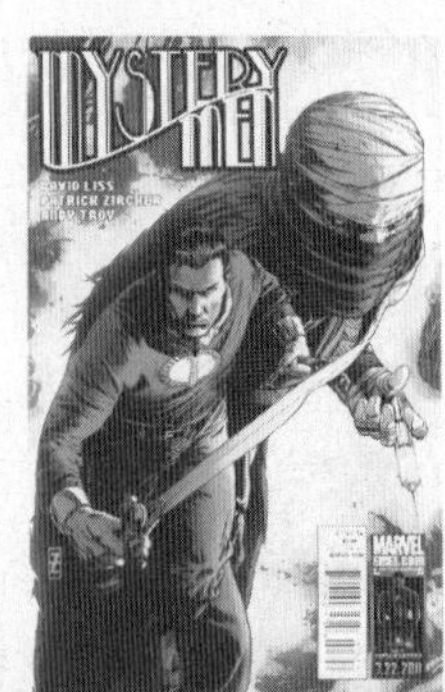

Mystery Men #3 © MAR

Mystery Tales #40 © MAR

Mystic (2011 series) #1 © DIS

GD VG FN VF VF/NM NM-
2.0 4.0 6.0 8.0 9.0 9.2

MYSTERY IN SPACE
DC Comics: Nov, 2006 - No. 8, Jul, 2007 ($3.99, limited series)

1-8: 1-Captain Comet's rebirth; Starlin-s/Shane Davis-a; The Weird by Starlin 4.00
1-Variant cover by Neal Adams 10.00
Volume One TPB (2007, $17.99) r/#1-5 18.00
Volume Two TPB (2007, $17.99) r/#6-8 and The Weird from #1-4 18.00

MYSTERY MEN
Marvel Comics: Aug, 2011 - No. 5, Nov, 2011 ($2.99, limited series)

1-5-Zircher-a/c; Liss-s; Pulp-era characters in 1932 3.00

MYSTERY MEN COMICS
Fox Features Syndicate: Aug, 1939 - No. 31, Feb, 1942

1-Intro. & 1st app. The Blue Beetle, The Green Mask, Rex Dexter of Mars by Briefer, Zanzibar by Tuska, Lt. Drake, D-13-Secret Agent by Powell, Chen Chang, Wing Turner, & Captain Denny Scott 1000 2000 3000 7500 13,500 19,500
2-Robot & sci/fi-c (2nd Robot-c w/Movie #6) 354 708 1062 2478 4339 6200
3 (10/39)-Classic Lou Fine-c 470 940 1410 3431 6066 8700
4,5: 4-Capt. Savage begins (11/39) 297 594 891 1901 3251 4600
6-Tuska-c 245 490 735 1568 2684 3800
7-1st Blue Beetle-c app. 300 600 900 1950 3375 4800
8-Lou Fine bondage-c 284 568 852 1818 3109 4400
9-The Moth begins; Lou Fine-c 142 284 426 909 1555 2200
10-12: All Joe Simon-c. 10-Wing Turner by Kirby; Simon bondage-c. 11-Intro. Domino
123 246 369 787 1344 1900
13-Intro. Lynx & sidekick Blackie (8/40) 71 142 213 454 777 1100
14-18 66 132 198 419 722 1025
19-Intro. & 1st app. Miss X (ends #21) 71 142 213 454 777 1100
20-31: 26-The Wraith begins 63 126 189 403 689 975

NOTE: ***Briefer** a-1-15, 20, 24; c-9. **Cuidera** a-22. **Lou Fine** c-1-5,8,9. **Powell** a-1-15, 24. **Simon** c-10-12. **Tuska** a-1-16, 22, 24, 27; c-6. Bondage-c 1, 3, 7, 8, 10, 25, 27-29, 31. Blue Beetle c-7, 8, 10-31. D-13 Secret Agent c-6. Green Mask c-1, 3-5. Rex Dexter of Mars c-2, 9.*

MYSTERY MEN MOVIE ADAPTION
Dark Horse Comics: July, 1999 - No. 2, Aug, 1999 ($2.95, mini-series)

1,2-Fingerman-s; photo-c 3.00

MYSTERY PLAY, THE
DC Comics (Vertigo): 1994 ($19.95, one-shot)

nn-Hardcover-Morrison-s/Muth-painted art 25.00
Softcover ($9.95)-New Muth cover 10.00

MYSTERY SOCIETY
IDW Publishing: May, 2010 - No. 5, Oct, 2010 ($3.99, limited series)

1-5-Niles-s/Staples-a 4.00

MYSTERY TALES
Atlas Comics (20CC): Mar, 1952 - No. 54, Aug, 1957

1-Horror/weird stories in all 103 206 309 659 1130 1600
2-Krigstein-a 53 106 159 334 567 800
3-10: 6-A-Bomb panel. 10-Story similar to "The Assassin" from Shock SuspenStories
47 94 141 296 498 700
11,13-21: 14-Maneely s/f story. 20-Electric chair issue. 21-Matt Fox-a; decapitation story 32 64 96 192 314 435
12,22: 12-Matt Fox-a. 22-Forte/Matt Fox-c; a(i) 36 72 108 216 351 485
23-26 (2/55)-Last precode issue 26 52 78 154 252 350
27,29-35,37,38,41-43,48,49: 43-Morisi story contains Frazetta art swipes from Untamed Love
21 42 63 122 199 275
28,36,39,40,45: 28-Jack Katz-a. 36,39-Krigstein-a. 40,45-Ditko-a (#45 is 3 pgs. only)
21 42 63 126 206 285
44,51-Williamson/Krenkel-a 22 44 66 132 216 300
46-Williamson/Krenkel-a; Crandall text illos 22 44 66 132 216 300
47-Crandall, Ditko, Powell-a 22 44 66 132 216 300
50,52,53: 50-Torres, Morrow-a 21 42 63 122 199 275
54-Crandall, Check-a 21 42 63 126 206 285

NOTE: ***Ayers** a-18, 49, 52. **Berg** a-17, 51. **Colan** a-1, 3, 18, 35, 43. **Colletta** a-18. **Drucker** a-41. **Everett** a-2, 29, 33, 35, 41; c-8-11, 14, 38, 39, 41, 43, 44, 46, 48-51, 53. **Fass** a-16. **Forte** a-21, 22, 45, 46. **Matt Fox** a-12?, 21, 22; c-22. **Heath** a-3; c-3, 15, 17, 26. **Heck** a-25. **Kinstler** a-15. **Mort Lawrence** a-26, 32, 34. **Maneely** a-1, 9, 14, 22; c-12, 23, 24, 27. **Mooney** a-3, 40. **Morisi** a-43, 49, 52. **Morrow** a-50. **Orlando** a-51. **Pakula** a-16. **Powell** a-21, 29, 37, 38, 47. **Reinman** a-1, 14, 17. **Robinson** a-7p, 42. **Romita** a-37. **Roussos** a-4, 44. **R.Q. Sale** a-45, 46, 49. **Severin** c-52. **Shores** a-17, 45. **Tuska** a-10, 12, 14. **Whitney** a-2. **Wildey** a-37.*

MYSTERY TALES
Super Comics: 1964

Super Reprint #16,17('64): 16-r/Tales of Horror #2. 17-r/Eerie #14(Avon), 18-Kubert-r/Strange Terrors #4 3 6 9 14 20 25

MYSTERY TRAIL
DC Comics: Feb/Mar 1950

nn - Ashcan comic, not distributed to newsstands, only for in-house use. Cover art is Danger Trail #3 with interior being Star Spangled Comics #109. A FN/VF copy sold for $2,357.50 in 2002.

MYSTIC (3rd Series)
Marvel/Atlas Comics (CLDS 1/CSI 2-21/OMC 22-35/CSI 35-61): March, 1951 - No. 61, Aug, 1957

1-Atom bomb panels; horror/weird stories in all 103 206 309 659 1130 1600
2 53 106 159 334 567 800
3-Eyes torn out 48 96 144 302 514 725
4- "The Devil Birds" by Wolverton (6 pgs.) 82 164 246 528 902 1275
5,7-10 39 78 117 236 388 540
6- "The Eye of Doom" by Wolverton (7 pgs.) 82 164 246 528 902 1275
11-20: 16-Bondage/torture c/story 32 64 96 188 307 425
21-25,27-36-Last precode (3/55). 25-E.C. swipe 25 50 75 150 245 340
26-Atomic War story; severed head story/cover 32 64 96 188 307 425
37-51,53-56,61 21 42 63 124 202 280
52-Wood-a; Crandall-a? 22 44 66 132 216 300
57-Story "Trapped in the Ant-Hill" (1957) is very similar to "The Man in the Ant Hill" in TTA #27
26 52 78 154 252 350
58,59-Krigstein-a 21 42 63 126 206 285
60-Williamson/Mayo-a (4 pgs.) 22 44 66 128 209 290

NOTE: ***Andru** a-23, 25. **Ayers** a-35, 53; c-8. **Berg** a-49. **Cameron** a-49, 51. **Check** a-31, 60. **Colan** a-3, 7, 12, 21, 37, 60. **Colletta** a-29. **Drucker** a-46, 52, 56. **Everett** a-8, 9, 17, 40, 44, 57; c-13, 18, 21, 42, 47, 49, 51-55, 57-59, 61. **Forte** a-35, 52, 58. **Fox** a-24i. **Al Hartley** a-35. **Heath** a-10; c-10, 20, 22, 23, 25, 30. **Infantino** a-12. **Kane** a-8, 24p. **Jack Katz** a-31, 33. **Mort Law.rence** a-19, 37. **Maneely** a-22, 24, 58; c-7, 15, 28, 29, 31. **Moldoff** a-29. **Morisi** a-48, 49, 52. **Morrow** a-51. **Orlando** a-57, 61. **Pakula** a-52, 57, 59. **Powell** a-52, 54-56. **Robinson** a-5. **Romita** a-11, 15. **R.Q. Sale** a-35, 53, 58. **Sekowsky** a-1, 2, 4, 5. **Severin** c-56, 60. **Tuska** a-15. **Whitney** a-33. **Wildey** a-28, 30. **Ed Win** a-17, 20. Canadian reprints known-title 'Startling.'*

MYSTIC (Also see CrossGen Chronicles)
CrossGeneration Comics: Jul, 2000 - No. 43, Jan, 2004 ($2.95)

1-43: 1-Marz-s/Peterson & Dell-a. 15-Cameos by DC & Marvel characters 3.00
...: Rite of Passage Vol. 1 TPB (5/01, $19.95) r/#1-7; Linsner-c 20.00
...: The Demon Queen Vol. 2 TPB (2002, $19.95) r/#8-14 20.00
...: Siege of Scales Vol. 3 TPB (2002, $15.95) r/#15-20 16.00
...: Out All Night Vol.4 TPB (2003, $15.95) r/#21-26 16.00
Vol. 5: Master Class (2003, $15.95) r/#27-32 16.00

MYSTIC (CrossGen characters)
Marvel Comics: Oct, 2011 - No. 4, Jan, 2012 ($2.99, limited series)

1-4-G. Willow Wilson-s/David López-a/Amanda Conner-c 3.00

MYSTICAL TALES
Atlas Comics (CCC 1/EPI 2-8): June, 1956 - No. 8, Aug, 1957

1-Everett-c/a 50 100 150 315 533 750
2-4: 2-Berg-a. 3,4-Crandall-a. 27 54 81 158 259 360
5-Williamson-a (4 pgs.) 29 58 87 170 278 385
6-Torres, Krigstein-a 26 52 78 154 252 350
7-Bolle, Forte, Torres, Orlando-a 25 50 75 150 245 340
8-Krigstein, Check-a 26 52 78 154 252 350

NOTE: ***Everett** a-1; c-1-4, 6, 7. **Orlando** a-1, 2, 7. **Pakula** a-3. **Powell** a-1, 4.*

MYSTIC ARCANA
Marvel Comics: Aug, 2007 - Jan, 2008 ($2.99)

1-Magik on-c; art by Scott and Nguyen; Ian McNee and Dani Moonstar app. 3.00
(#2)...: Black Knight 1 (9/07, $2.99) Djurdjevic-c/Grummett & Hanna-a; origin retold 3.00
3-("Scarlet Witch" on cover)(10/07, $2.99) Djurdjevic-c/Santacruz-a; childhood 3.00
(#4)...: Sister Grimm 1 (1/08, $2.99) Nico Minoru from Runaways; Djurdjevic-c/Noto-a 3.00
...: The Book of Marvel Magic ('07, $3.99) Official Handbook profiles of the magic-related 4.00
HC (2007, $24.99, d.j.) r/series and ...: The Book of Marvel Magic 25.00

MYSTIC COMICS (1st Series)
Timely Comics (TPI 1-5/TCI 8-10): March, 1940 - No. 10, Aug, 1942

1-Origin The Blue Blaze, The Dynamic Man, & Flexo the Rubber Robot; Zephyr Jones, 3X's & Deep Sea Demon app.; The Magician begins (all 1st app.);
c-from Spider pulp V18#1, 6/39 1400 2800 4200 10,700 19,850 29,000
2-The Invisible Man & Master Mind Excello begin; Space Rangers, Zara of the Jungle, Taxi Taylor app. (scarce) 541 1082 1623 3950 6975 10,000
3-Origin Hercules, who last appears in #4 383 766 1149 2681 4691 6700
4-Origin The Thin Man & The Black Widow; Merzak the Mystic app.; last Flexo, Dynamic Man, Invisible Man & Blue Blaze (some issues have date sticker on cover; others have July w/August overprint in silver color); Roosevelt assassination-c
432 864 1296 3154 5577 8000
5-(3/41)-Origin The Black Marvel, The Blazing Skull, The Sub-Earth Man, Super Slave & The Terror; The Moon Man & Black Widow app.; 5-German war-c begin, end #10

Mystic Comics #9 © MAR

Mystique #2 © MAR

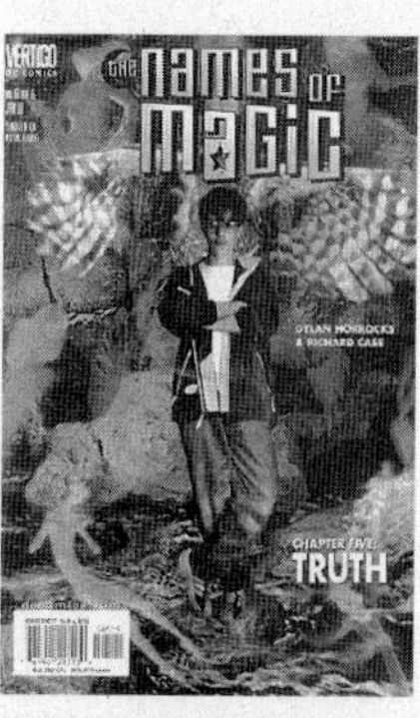

The Names of Magic #5 © DC

GD VG FN VF VF/NM NM-
2.0 4.0 6.0 8.0 9.0 9.2

377 754 1131 2639 4620 6600
6-(10/41)-Origin The Challenger & The Destroyer (1st app.?; also see All-Winners #2, Fall, 1941) 443 886 1329 3234 5717 8200
7-The Witness begins (12/41, origin & 1st app.); origin Davey & the Demon; last Black Widow; Hitler opens his trunk of terror-c by Simon & Kirby (classic-c) 503 1006 1509 3672 6486 9300
8,10: 10-Father Time, World of Wonder, & Red Skeleton app.; last Challenger & Terror 300 600 900 2070 3635 5200
9-Gary Gaunt app.; last Black Marvel, Mystic & Blazing Skull; Hitler-c 366 732 1098 2562 4481 6400
NOTE: *Gabrielle c-8-10. **Kirby/Schomburg** c-6. **Rico** a-9(2). **Schomburg** a-1-4; c-1-5. **Sekowsky** a-9. **Sekowsky/Klein** a-8(Challenger). Bondage c-1, 2, 9.*

MYSTIC COMICS (2nd Series)
Timely Comics (ANC): Oct, 1944 - No. 3, Win, 1944-45; No. 4, Mar, 1945
1-The Angel, The Destroyer, The Human Torch, Terry Vance the Schoolboy Sleuth, & Tommy Tyme begin 277 554 831 1759 3030 4300
2-(Fall/44)-Last Human Torch & Terry Vance; bondage/hypo-c 148 296 444 947 1624 2300
3-Last Angel (two stories) & Tommy Tyme 127 254 381 807 1391 1975
4-The Young Allies-c & app.; Schomburg-c 116 232 348 742 1271 1800

MYSTIC COMICS 70th ANNIVERARY SPECIAL
Marvel Comics: Oct, 2009 ($3.99, one-shot)
1-New story of The Vision; r/G.A. Vision app. from Marvel Myst. Comics #13 & 16 5.00

MYSTIC HANDS OF DR. STRANGE
Marvel Comics: May, 2010 ($3.99, B&W, one-shot)
1-Short stories; art by Irving, Brunner, McKeever & Marcos Martin; Parrillo-c 4.00

MYSTIQUE (See X-Men titles)
Marvel Comics: June, 2003 - No. 24, Apr, 2005 ($2.99)
1-24: 1-6-Linsner-c/Vaughan-s/Lucas-a. 7-Ryan-a begins. 8-Horn-c. 9-24-Mayhew-c 23-Wolverine & Rogue app. 3.00
... Vol. 1: Drop Dead Gorgeous TPB (2004, $14.99) r/#1-6 15.00
... Vol. 2: Tinker, Tailor, Mutant, Spy TPB (2004, $17.99) r/#7-13 18.00
... Vol. 3: Unnatural TPB (2004, $13.99) r/#14-18 14.00

MYSTIQUE & SABRETOOTH (Sabretooth and Mystique on-c)
Marvel Comics: Dec, 1996 - No. 4, Mar, 1997 ($1.95, limited series)
1-4: Characters from X-Men 3.00

MY STORY (...True Romances in Pictures #5,6; becomes My Love Life #13) (Formerly Zago)
Hero Books (Fox Features Syndicate): No. 5, May, 1949 - No. 12, Aug, 1950
5-Kamen/Feldstein-a 22 44 66 128 209 290
6-8,11,12: 12-Photo-c 13 26 39 74 105 135
9,10-Wood-a 20 40 60 115 185 255

MYTHOS
Marvel Comics: Mar, 2006 - Dec, 2007 ($3.99)
1-Retelling of X-Men #1 with painted-a by Paolo Rivera; Paul Jenkins-s 4.00
...: Captain America 1 (8/08) Retelling of origin; painted-a by Rivera; Jenkins-s 4.00
...: Fantastic Four 1 (12/07) Retelling of Fantastic Four #1; painted-a by Rivera; Jenkins-s 4.00
...: Ghost Rider 1 (3/07) Retelling of Marvel Spotlight #5; painted-a by Rivera; Jenkins-s 4.00
...: Hulk 1 (10/06) Retelling of Incredible Hulk #1; painted-a by Rivera; Jenkins-s 4.00
...: Spider-Man 1 (8/07) Retelling of Amazing Fantasy #15; painted-a by Rivera; Jenkins-s 4.00

MYTHOS: THE FINAL TOUR
DC Comics/Vertigo: Dec, 1996 - No. 3, Feb, 1997 ($5.95, limited series)
1-3: 1-Ney Rieber-s/Amaro-a. 2-Snejbjerg-a; Constantine-app. 3-Kristiansen-a; Black Orchid-app. 6.00

MYTHSTALKERS
Image Comics: Mar, 2003 - No. 8, Mar, 2004 ($2.95)
1-8-Jiro-a 3.00

MY TRUE LOVE (Formerly Western Killers #64; Frank Buck #70 on)
Fox Features Syndicate: No. 65, July, 1949 - No. 69, March, 1950
65 17 34 51 98 154 210
66,68,69: 69-Morisi-a 12 24 36 69 97 125
67-Wood-a 20 40 60 115 185 255

NAIL, THE
Dark Horse Comics: June, 2004 - No. 4, Oct, 2004 ($2.99, limited series)
1-4-Rob Zombie & Steve Niles-s/Nat Jones-a/Simon Bisley-c 3.00
TPB (2005, $12.95) r/series 13.00

NAKED BRAIN (Marc Hempel's...)
Insight Studios Group: 2002 - No. 3, 2002 ($2.95, B&W, limited series)
1-3-Marc Hempel cartoons and sketches; Tug & Buster app. 3.00

NAKED PREY, THE (See Movie Classics)

'NAM, THE (See Savage Tales #1, 2nd series & Punisher Invades...)
Marvel Comics Group: Dec, 1986 - No. 84, Sept, 1993
1-Golden a(p)/c begins, ends #13 6.00
1 (2nd printing) 3.00
2-7,9-19,21-66,70-74: 7-Golden-a (2 pgs.). 32-Death R. Kennedy. 52,53-Frank Castle (The Punisher) app. 52,53-Gold 2nd printings. 58-Silver logo. 65-Heath-c/a. 70-Lomax scripts begin 3.00
8-1st app. Fudd Verzyl, Tunnel Rat 5.00
20-2nd app. Fudd Verzyl, Tunnel Rat 4.00
67-69-Punisher 3 part story 4.00
75-($2.25, 52 pgs.) 6.00
76-84 3.00
Trade Paperback 1,2: 1-r/#1-4. 2-r/#5-8 5.00
TPB ('99, $14.95) r/#1-4; recolored 15.00

'NAM MAGAZINE, THE
Marvel Comics: Aug, 1988 - No. 10, May, 1989 ($2.00, B&W, 52pgs.)
1-10: Each issue reprints 2 issues of the comic 4.00

NAMELESS, THE
Image Comics: May, 1997 - No. 5, Sept, 1997 ($2.95, B&W)
1-5: Pruett/Hester-s/a 3.00
...: The Director's Cut TPB (2006, $15.99) r/#1-5; original proposal by Pruett 16.00

NAMES OF MAGIC, THE (Also see Books of Magic)
DC Comics (Vertigo): Feb, 2001 - No. 5, June, 2001 ($2.50, limited series)
1-5: Bolton painted-c on all; Case-a; leads into Hunter: The Age of Magic 3.00
TPB (2002, $14.95) r/#1-5 15.00

NAME OF THE GAME, THE
DC Comics: 2001 ($29.95, graphic novel)
Hardcover ($29.95) Will Eisner-s/a 30.00

NAMOR (Volume 2)
Marvel Comics: June, 2003 - No. 12, May, 2004 (25¢/$2.25/$2.99)
1-(25¢-c)Young Namor in the 1920s; Larroca-c/a 3.00
2-6-($2.25) Larroca-a 3.00
7-12-($2.99): 7-Olliffe-a begins 3.00

NAMORA (See Marvel Mystery Comics #82 & Sub-Mariner Comics)
Marvel Comics (PrPl): Fall, 1948 - No. 3, Dec, 1948
1-Sub-Mariner x-over in Namora; Namora by Everett(2), Sub-Mariner by Rico (10 pgs.) 284 568 852 1818 3109 4400
2-The Blonde Phantom & Sub-Mariner story; Everett-a 161 322 483 1030 1765 2500
3-(Scarce)-Sub-Mariner app.; Everett-a 174 348 522 1114 1907 2700

NAMORA (See Agents of Atlas)
Marvel Comics: Aug, 2010 ($3.99, one-shot)
1-Parker-s/Pichelli-a 4.00

NAMOR: THE FIRST MUTANT (Curse of the Mutants x-over with X-Men titles)
Marvel Comics: Oct, 2010 - No. 11, Aug, 2011 ($3.99/$2.99)
1-($3.99) Olivetti-a/Stuart Moore-s/Jae Lee-c; back-up retelling of origin and history 4.00
2-11-($2.99) 2-Emma Frost app. 5-Mayhew-c. 6-10-Noto-c 3.00
... Annual 1 (7/11, $3.99) Part 3 of "Escape From the Negative Zone" x-over; Fiumara-a 4.00

NAMOR, THE SUB-MARINER (See Prince Namor & Sub-Mariner)
Marvel Comics: Apr, 1990 - No. 62, May, 1995 ($1.00/$1.25/$1.50)
1-Byrne-c/a/scripts in 1-25 (scripts only #26-32) 5.00
2-5: 5-Iron Man app. 4.00
6-11,13-23,25,27-49,51-62: 16-Re-intro Iron Fist (8-cameo only). 18-Punisher cameo (1 panel); 21-23,25-Wolverine cameos. 22,23-Iron Fist app. 28-Iron Fist-c/story. 31-Dr. Doom-c/story. 33,34-Iron Fist cameo. 35-New Tiger Shark-c/story. 37-Aqua holografx foil-c. 48-The Thing app. 3.00
12,24: 12-(52pgs.)-Re-intro. The Invaders. 24-Namor vs. Wolverine 4.00
26-Namor w/new costume; 1st Jae Lee-c/a this title (5/92) & begins 4.00
50-($1.75, 52 pgs.)-Newsstand ed.; w/bound-in S-M trading card sheet (both versions) 4.00
50-($2.95, 52 pgs.)-Collector edition w/foil-c 4.00
Annual 1-4 ('91-94, 68 pgs.): 1-3 pg. origin recap. 2-Return/Defenders. 3-Bagged w/card. 4-Painted-c 4.00
NOTE: ***Jae Lee** a-26-30p, 31-37, 38p, 39, 40; c-26-40.*

NANCY AND SLUGGO (See Comics On Parade & Sparkle Comics)
United Features Syndicate: No. 16, 1949 - No. 23, 1954

Nancy and Sluggo #187 © DELL

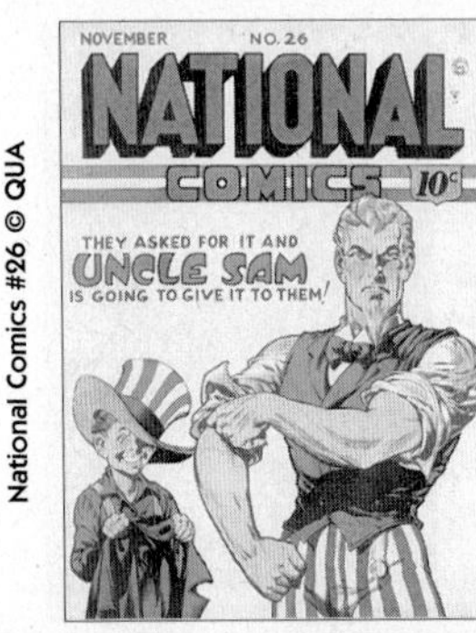

National Comics #26 © QUA

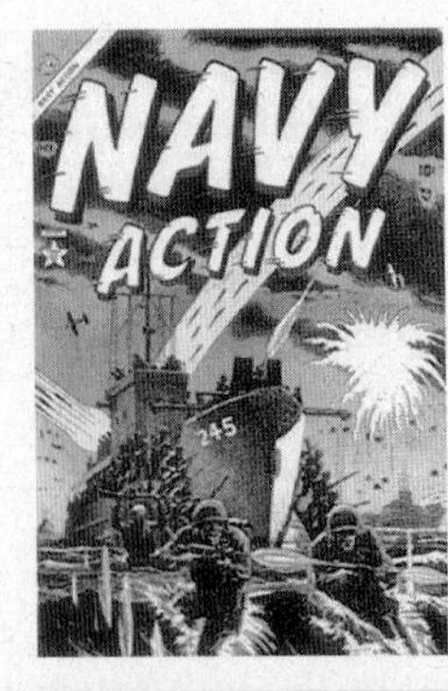

Navy Action #2 © MAR

	GD 2.0	VG 4.0	FN 6.0	VF 8.0	VF/NM 9.0	NM- 9.2
16(#1)	10	20	30	58	79	100
17-23	8	16	24	40	50	60

NANCY & SLUGGO (Nancy #146-173; formerly Sparkler Comics)
St. John/Dell #146-187/Gold Key #188 on: No. 121, Apr, 1955-No. 192, Oct, 1963

	GD 2.0	VG 4.0	FN 6.0	VF 8.0	VF/NM 9.0	NM- 9.2
121(4/55)(St. John)	10	20	30	54	72	90
122-145(7/57)(St. John)	8	16	24	44	57	70
146(9/57)-Peanuts begins, ends #192 (Dell)	9	18	27	63	112	160
147-161 (Dell) Peanuts in all	8	16	24	51	86	120
162-165,177-180-John Stanley-a	8	16	24	51	86	120
166-176-Oona & Her Haunted House series; Stanley-a	8	16	24	56	96	135
181-187(3-5/62)(Dell)	6	12	18	41	66	90
188(10/62)-192 (Gold Key)	6	12	18	41	66	90
Four Color 1034(9-11/59)-Summer Camp	5	10	15	32	51	70

(See Dell Giant #34, 45 & Dell Giants)

NANNY AND THE PROFESSOR (TV)
Dell Publishing Co.: Aug, 1970 - No. 2, Oct, 1970 (Photo-c)

	GD 2.0	VG 4.0	FN 6.0	VF 8.0	VF/NM 9.0	NM- 9.2
1-(01-546-008)	5	10	15	32	51	70
2	4	8	12	26	41	55

NAPOLEON
Dell Publishing Co.: No. 526, Dec, 1953

	GD 2.0	VG 4.0	FN 6.0	VF 8.0	VF/NM 9.0	NM- 9.2
Four Color 526	4	8	12	24	37	50

NAPOLEON & SAMANTHA (See Walt Disney Showcase No. 10)

NAPOLEON & UNCLE ELBY (See Clifford McBride's...)
Eastern Color Printing Co.: July, 1942 (68 pgs.) (One Shot)

	GD 2.0	VG 4.0	FN 6.0	VF 8.0	VF/NM 9.0	NM- 9.2
1	43	86	129	268	454	640
1945-American Book-Strafford Press (128 pgs.) (8x10-1/2"; B&W reprints; hardcover)	15	30	45	83	124	165

NARRATIVE ILLUSTRATION, THE STORY OF THE COMICS (Also see Good Triumphs Over Evil!)
M.C. Gaines: Summer, 1942 (32 pgs., 7-1/4"x10", B&W w/color inserts)

nn-16 pgs. text with illustrations of ancient art, strips and comic covers; 4 pg. WWII War Bond promo, "The Minute Man Answers the Call" color comic drawn by Shelly and a special 8-page color comic insert of "The Story of Saul" (from Picture Stories from the Bible #10 or soon to appear in PS #10) or "Noah and His Ark" or "The Story of Ruth". Insert has special title page indicating it was part of a Sunday newspaper supplement insert series that had already run in a New England "Sunday Herald." Another version exists with insert from Picture Stories from the Bible #7.
(very rare) Estimated value... 1500.00

NOTE: ***Print, A Quarterly Journal of the Graphic Arts*** *Vol. 3 No. 2 (88 pg., square bound) features the 1st printing of Narrative Illustration, The Story of The Comics. A VG+ copy sold for $750 in 2005.*

NASCAR HEROES
Starbridge Media: 2007 - No. 3 ($3.95)

	GD 2.0	VG 4.0	FN 6.0	VF 8.0	VF/NM 9.0	NM- 9.2
1-3: 1-Origin of fictional racer Jimmy Dash. 3-Origin of the Daytona 500; DeStefano-s						4.00
nn-(2008, Free Comic Book Day giveaway) The Mystery of Driver Z						3.00

NASH (WCW Wrestling)
Image Comics: July, 1999 - No. 2, July, 1999 ($2.95)

	GD 2.0	VG 4.0	FN 6.0	VF 8.0	VF/NM 9.0	NM- 9.2
1,2-Regular and photo-c						3.00
1-($6.95) Photo-split-cover Edition						7.00

NATHANIEL DUSK
DC Comics: Feb, 1984 - No. 4, May, 1984 ($1.25, mini-series, direct sales, Baxter paper)

	GD 2.0	VG 4.0	FN 6.0	VF 8.0	VF/NM 9.0	NM- 9.2
1-4: 1-Intro/origin; Gene Colan-c/a in all						3.00

NATHANIEL DUSK II
DC Comics: Oct, 1985 - No. 4, Jan, 1986 ($2.00, mini-series, Baxter paper)

	GD 2.0	VG 4.0	FN 6.0	VF 8.0	VF/NM 9.0	NM- 9.2
1-4: Gene Colan-c/a in all						3.00

NATIONAL COMICS
Quality Comics Group: July, 1940 - No. 75, Nov, 1949

	GD 2.0	VG 4.0	FN 6.0	VF 8.0	VF/NM 9.0	NM- 9.2
1-Uncle Sam begins (1st app.); origin sidekick Buddy by Eisner; origin Wonder Boy & Kid Dixon; Merlin the Magician (ends #45); Cyclone, Kid Patrol, Sally O'Neil Policewoman, Pen Miller (by Klaus Nordling; ends #22), Prop Powers (ends #26), & Paul Bunyan (ends #22) begin	568	1136	1704	4146	7323	10,500
2	245	490	735	1568	2684	3800
3-Last Eisner Uncle Sam	177	354	531	1124	1937	2750
4-Last Cyclone	135	270	405	864	1482	2100
5-(11/40)-Quicksilver begins (1st app.; 3rd w/lightning speed?; re-intro'd by DC in 1993 as Max Mercury in Flash #76, 2nd series); origin Uncle Sam; bondage-c	155	310	465	992	1696	2400
6,8-11: 8-Jack & Jill begins (ends #22). 9-Flag-c	129	258	387	826	1413	2000
7-Classic Lou Fine-c	271	542	813	1734	2967	4200
12	89	178	267	565	970	1375
13-16-Lou Fine-a	90	180	270	576	988	1400
17,19-22: 21-Classic Nazi swastika cover. 22-Last Pen Miller (moves to Crack #23)	69	138	207	442	759	1075
18-(12/41)-Shows Asians attacking Pearl Harbor; on stands one month before actual event	139	278	417	883	1517	2150
23-The Unknown & Destroyer 171 begin	71	142	213	454	777	1100
24-Japanese War-c	71	142	213	454	777	1100
25-30: 25-Nazi drug usage/hypodermic needle in story. 26-Wonder Boy ends. 27- G-2 the Unknown begins (ends #46). 29-Origin The Unknown	52	104	156	328	552	775
31-33: 33-Chic Carter begins (ends #47)	47	94	141	296	498	700
34-37,40: 35-Last Kid Patrol	41	82	123	249	417	585
38-Hitler, Tojo, Mussolini-c	66	132	198	419	722	1025
39-Hitler-c	68	136	204	435	743	1050
41,43-50: 48-Origin The Whistler	28	56	84	165	270	375
42-The Barker begins (1st app?, 5/44); The Barker covers begin	41	82	123	256	428	600
51-Sally O'Neil by Ward, 8 pgs. (12/45)	30	60	90	117	289	400
52-60	20	40	60	118	192	265
61-67: 67-Format change; Quicksilver app.	15	30	45	90	140	190
68-75: The Barker ends	15	30	45	83	124	165

NOTE: ***Cole*** *Quicksilver-13; Barker-43; c-43, 46, 47, 49-51.* ***Crandall*** *Uncle Sam-11-13 (with* ***Fine****), 25, 26; c-24-26, 30-33, 43.* ***Crandall*** *Paul Bunyan-10-13.* ***Fine*** *Uncle Sam-13 (w/****Crandall****), 17, 18; c-1-14, 16, 18, 21.* ***Gill Fox*** *c-69-74.* ***Guardineer*** *Quicksilver-27, 35.* ***Gustavson*** *Quicksilver-14-26.* ***McWilliams*** *a-23-28, 55, 57. Uncle Sam c-1-41. Barker c-42-75.*

NATIONAL COMICS (Also see All Star Comics 1999 crossover titles)
DC Comics: May, 1999 ($1.99, one-shot)

	GD 2.0	VG 4.0	FN 6.0	VF 8.0	VF/NM 9.0	NM- 9.2
1-Golden Age Flash and Mr. Terrific; Waid-s/Lopresti-a						3.00

NATIONAL CRUMB, THE (Magazine-Size)
Mayfair Publications: August, 1975 (52 pgs., B&W) (Satire)

	GD 2.0	VG 4.0	FN 6.0	VF 8.0	VF/NM 9.0	NM- 9.2
1-Grandenetti-c/a, Ayers-a	2	4	6	11	16	20

NATIONAL VELVET (TV)
Dell Publishing Co./Gold Key: May-July, 1961 - No. 2, Mar, 1963 (All photo-c)

	GD 2.0	VG 4.0	FN 6.0	VF 8.0	VF/NM 9.0	NM- 9.2
Four Color 1195 (#1)	7	14	21	48	79	110
Four Color 1312, 01-556-207, 12-556-210 (Dell)	4	8	12	28	44	60
1,2: 1(12/62) (Gold Key). 2(3/63)	4	8	12	28	44	60

NATION OF SNITCHES
Piranha Press (DC): 1990 ($4.95, color, 52 pgs.)

	GD 2.0	VG 4.0	FN 6.0	VF 8.0	VF/NM 9.0	NM- 9.2
nn						5.00

NATION X (X-Men on the Utopia island)
Marvel Comics: Feb, 2010 - No. 4, May, 2010 ($3.99, limited series)

	GD 2.0	VG 4.0	FN 6.0	VF 8.0	VF/NM 9.0	NM- 9.2
1-4-Short stories by various. 1,4-Allred-a. 2-Choi, Cloonan-a. 4-Doop app.						4.00
...: X-Factor (3/10, $3.99) David-s/DeLandro-a						4.00

NATURE BOY (Formerly Danny Blaze; Li'l Rascal Twins #6 on)
Charlton Comics: No. 3, March, 1956 - No. 5, Feb, 1957

	GD 2.0	VG 4.0	FN 6.0	VF 8.0	VF/NM 9.0	NM- 9.2
3-1st app./origin; Blue Beetle story (last Golden Age app.); Buscema-c/a	22	44	66	130	213	295
4,5	15	30	45	92	144	195

NOTE: ***John Buscema*** *a-3, 4p, 5; c-3.* ***Powell*** *a-4.*

NATURE OF THINGS (Disney, TV/Movie)
Dell Publishing Co.: No. 727, Sept, 1956 - No. 842, Sept, 1957

	GD 2.0	VG 4.0	FN 6.0	VF 8.0	VF/NM 9.0	NM- 9.2
Four Color 727 (#1), 842-Jesse Marsh-a	5	10	15	35	55	75

NAUSICAA OF THE VALLEY OF WIND
Viz Comics: 1988 - No. 7, 1989; 1989 - No. 4, 1990 ($2.50, B&W, 68pgs.)

	GD 2.0	VG 4.0	FN 6.0	VF 8.0	VF/NM 9.0	NM- 9.2
Book 1-7: 1-Contains Moebius poster						4.00
Part II, Book 1-4 ($2.95)						4.00

NAVY ACTION (Sailor Sweeney #12-14)
Atlas Comics (CDS): Aug, 1954 - No. 11, Apr, 1956; No. 15, 1/57 - No. 18, 8/57

	GD 2.0	VG 4.0	FN 6.0	VF 8.0	VF/NM 9.0	NM- 9.2
1-Powell-a	20	40	60	117	189	260
2-Lawrence-a; RQ Sale-a	13	26	39	72	101	130
3-11: 4-Last precode (2/55)	10	20	30	58	79	100
15-18	10	20	30	56	76	95

NOTE: ***Berg*** *a-7, 9.* ***Colan*** *a-8.* ***Drucker*** *a-7, 17.* ***Everett*** *a-3, 7, 16; c-16, 17.* ***Heath*** *c-1, 2, 5, 6.* ***Maneely*** *a-5, 7, 8, 18; c-9, 11.* ***Pakula*** *a-2, 3, 9.* ***Reinman*** *a-17.*

NAVY COMBAT
Atlas Comics (MPI): June, 1955 - No. 20, Oct, 1958

	GD 2.0	VG 4.0	FN 6.0	VF 8.0	VF/NM 9.0	NM- 9.2
1-Torpedo Taylor begins by Don Heck; Heath-c	20	40	60	117	189	260

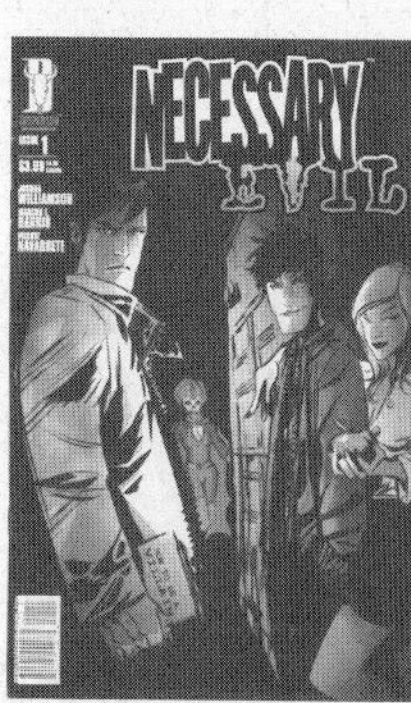

Necessary Evil #1 © Williamson & Harris

Negative Burn #47 © Caliber

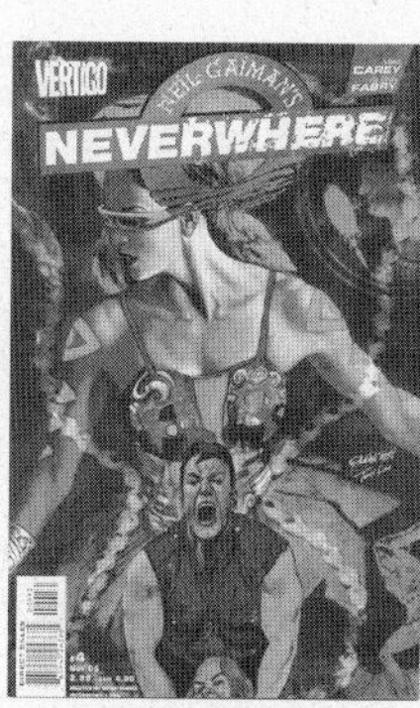

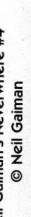

Neil Gaiman's Neverwhere #4 © Neil Gaiman

	GD 2.0	VG 4.0	FN 6.0	VF 8.0	VF/NM 9.0	NM- 9.2
2	13	26	39	72	101	130
3-10	10	20	30	58	79	100
11,13-16,18-20: 14-Torres-a	10	20	30	56	76	95
12-Crandall-a	11	22	33	62	86	110
17-Williamson-a, 4 pgs.; Torres-a	11	22	33	60	83	105

NOTE: *Ayers a-15. Berg a-10, 11. Colan a-11. Drucker a-7. Everett a-3, 20; c-8 & 9 w/Tuska, 10, 13-16. Forte a-15, 18. Heck a-11(2), 15, 19. Maneely c-1, 6, 11, 17. Morisi a-8. Pakula a-7, 18. Powell a-20. Reinman a-18.*

NAVY HEROES
Almanac Publishing Co.: 1945

	GD	VG	FN	VF	VF/NM	NM-
1-Heavy in propaganda	14	28	42	82	121	160

NAVY PATROL
Key Publications: May, 1955 - No. 4, Nov, 1955

	GD	VG	FN	VF	VF/NM	NM-
1	9	18	27	47	61	75
2-4	6	12	18	31	38	45

NAVY TALES
Atlas Comics (CDS): Jan, 1957 - No. 4, July, 1957

	GD	VG	FN	VF	VF/NM	NM-
1-Everett-c; Berg, Powell-a	18	36	54	103	162	220
2-Williamson/Mayo-a(5 pgs); Crandall-a	14	28	42	81	118	155
3,4-Reinman-a; Severin-c. 4-Crandall-a	13	26	39	72	101	130

NOTE: *Colan a-4. Maneely c-2. Reinman a-2-4. Sinnott a-4.*

NAVY TASK FORCE
Stanmor Publications/Aragon Mag. No. 4-8: Feb, 1954 - No. 8, April, 1956

	GD	VG	FN	VF	VF/NM	NM-
1	9	18	27	52	69	85
2	7	14	21	35	43	50
3-8: #8-r/Navy Patrol #1	6	12	18	31	38	45

NAVY WAR HEROES
Charlton Comics: Jan, 1964 - No. 7, Mar-Apr, 1965

	GD	VG	FN	VF	VF/NM	NM-
1	3	6	9	20	30	40
2-7	3	6	9	14	19	24

NAZA (Stone Age Warrior)
Dell Publishing Co.: Nov-Jan, 1963-64 - No. 9, March, 1966

	GD	VG	FN	VF	VF/NM	NM-
12-555-401 (#1)-Painted-c	5	10	15	35	55	75
2-9: 2-4-Painted-c	4	8	12	24	37	50

NEBBS, THE (Also see Crackajack Funnies)
Dell Publishing Co./Croydon Publishing Co.: 1941; 1945

	GD	VG	FN	VF	VF/NM	NM-
Large Feature Comic 23(1941)	21	42	63	124	202	280
1(1945, 36 pgs.)-Reprints	13	26	39	74	105	135

NECESSARY EVIL
Desperado Publishing: Oct, 2007 - No. 9, Nov, 2008 ($3.99)

1-9: 1-Joshua Williamson-s/Marcus Harris-a/Dustin Nguyen-c — 4.00

NECROMANCER
Image Comics (Top Cow): Sept, 2005 - No. 6, July 2006 ($2.99)

1-6: 1-Manapul-a/Ortega-s; three covers by Manapul, Horn & Bachalo — 3.00
... Pilot Season Vol. 1 #1 (11/07, $2.99) Ortega-s/Meyers-a/Manapul-c — 3.00

NECROMANCER: THE GRAPHIC NOVEL
Marvel Comics (Epic Comics): 1989 ($8.95)

nn — 9.00

NECROWAR
Dreamwave Productions: July, 2003 - No. 3, Sept, 2003 ($2.95)

1-3-Furman-s/Granov-digital art — 3.00

NEGATION
CrossGeneration Comics: Dec, 2001 - No. 27, Mar, 2004 ($2.95)

Prequel (12/01) — 3.00
1-27: 1-(1/02) Pelletier-a/Bedard & Waid-s — 3.00
... Lawbringer (11/02, $2.95) Nebres-a — 3.00
Vol. 1: Bohica! (10/02, $19.95, TPB) r/ Prequel & #1-6 — 20.00
Vol. 2: Baptism of Fire (5/03, $15.95, TPB) r/#7-12 — 16.00
Vol. 3: Hounded (12/03, $15.95, TPB) r/#13-18 — 16.00

NEGATION WAR
CrossGeneration Comics: Apr, 2004 - No. 6 ($2.95)

1-4-Bedard-s/Pelletier-a — 3.00

NEGATIVE BURN
Caliber: 1993 - No. 50, 1997 ($2.95, B&W, anthology)

1,2,4-12,14-47: Anthology by various including Bolland, Burden, Doran, Gaiman, Moebius, Moore, & Pope — 4.00

	GD	VG	FN	VF	VF/NM	NM-
3,13: 3-Bone story. 13-Strangers in Paradise story	2	4	6	8	10	12

48,49-($4.95) — 5.00
50-($6.95, 96 pgs.)-Gaiman, Robinson, Bolland — 7.00
...Summer Special 2005 (Image, 2005, $9.99) new short stories by various — 10.00
...: The Best From 1993-1998 (Image, 1/05, $19.95) r/short stories by various — 20.00
...Winter Special 2005 (Image, 2005, $9.95) new short stories by various — 10.00

NEGATIVE BURN
Image Comics (Desperado): May, 2006 - Present ($5.99, B&W, anthology)

1-21: 1-Art by Bolland, Powell, Luna, Smith, Hester. 2-Milk & Cheese by Dorkin — 6.00

NEGRO (See All-Negro)

NEGRO HEROES (Calling All Girls, Real Heroes, & True Comics reprints)
Parents' Magazine Institute: Spring, 1947 - No. 2, Summer, 1948

	GD	VG	FN	VF	VF/NM	NM-
1	135	270	405	864	1482	2100
2-Jackie Robinson-c/story	135	270	405	864	1482	2100

NEGRO ROMANCE (Negro Romances #4)
Fawcett Publications: June, 1950 - No. 3, Oct, 1950 (All photo-c)

	GD	VG	FN	VF	VF/NM	NM-
1-Evans-a (scarce)	161	300	483	1030	1765	2500
2,3 (scarce)	129	258	387	826	1413	2000

NEGRO ROMANCES (Formerly Negro Romance; Romantic Secrets #5 on)
Charlton Comics: No. 4, May, 1955

	GD	VG	FN	VF	VF/NM	NM-
4-Reprints Fawcett #2 (scarce)	90	180	270	576	988	1400

NEIL GAIMAN AND CHARLES VESS' STARDUST
DC Comics (Vertigo): 1997 - No. 4, 1998 ($5.95/$6.95, square-bound, lim. series)

1-4: Gaiman text with Vess paintings in all — 7.00
Hardcover (1998, $29.95) r/series with new sketches — 35.00
Softcover (1999, $19.95) oversized; new Vess-c — 20.00

NEIL GAIMAN'S LADY JUSTICE
Tekno Comix: Sept, 1995 - No. 11, May, 1996 ($1.95/$2.25)

1-11: 1-Sienkiewicz-c; pin-ups. 1-5-Brereton-c. 7-Polybagged. 11-The Big Bang Pt. 7 — 3.00

NEIL GAIMAN'S LADY JUSTICE
BIG Entertainment: V2#1, June, 1996 - No. 9, Feb, 1997 ($2.25)

V2#1-9: Dan Brereton-c on all. 6-8-Dan Brereton script — 3.00

NEIL GAIMAN'S MIDNIGHT DAYS
DC Comics (Vertigo): 1999 ($17.95, trade paperback)

nn-Reprints Gaiman's short stories; new Swamp Thing w/ Bissette-a — 18.00

NEIL GAIMAN'S MR. HERO-THE NEWMATIC MAN
Tekno Comix: Mar, 1995 - No. 17, May, 1996 ($1.95/$2.25)

1-17: 1-Intro Mr. Hero & Teknophage; bound-in game piece and trading card. 4-w/Steel edition Neil Gaiman's Teknophage #1 coupon. 13-Polybagged — 3.00

NEIL GAIMAN'S MR. HERO-THE NEWMATIC MAN
BIG Entertainment: V2#1, June, 1996 ($2.25)

V2#1-Teknophage destroys Mr. Hero; includes The Big Bang Pt. 10 — 3.00

NEIL GAIMAN'S NEVERWHERE
DC Comics (Vertigo): Aug, 2005 - No. 9, Sept, 2006 ($2.99, limited series)

1-9-Adaptation of Gaiman novel; Carey-s/Fabry-a/c — 3.00
TPB (2007, $19.99) r/series; intro. by Carey — 20.00

NEIL GAIMAN'S PHAGE-SHADOWDEATH
BIG Entertainment: June, 1996 - No. 6, Nov, 1996 ($2.25, limited series)

1-6: Bryan Talbot-c & scripts in all. 1-1st app. Orlando Holmes — 3.00

NEIL GAIMAN'S TEKNOPHAGE
Tekno Comix: Aug, 1995 - No. 10, Mar, 1996 ($1.95/$2.25)

1-6-Rick Veitch scripts & Bryan Talbot-c/a. — 3.00
1-Steel Edition — 4.00
7-10: Paul Jenkins scripts in all. 8-polybagged — 3.00

NEIL GAIMAN'S WHEEL OF WORLDS
Tekno Comix: Apr, 1995 - No. 1, May, 1996 ($2.95/$3.25)

0-1st app. Lady Justice; 48 pgs.; bound-in poster — 4.00
0-Regular edition — 3.00
1 ($3.25, 5/96)-Bruce Jones scripts; Lady Justice & Teknophage app.; CGI photo-c — 4.00

NEIL THE HORSE (See Charlton Bullseye #2)
Aardvark-Vanaheim #1-10/Renegade Press #11 on: 2/83 - No. 10, 12/84; No. 11, 4/85 - #15, 1985 (B&W)

1($1.40) — 4.00
1-2nd print — 3.00

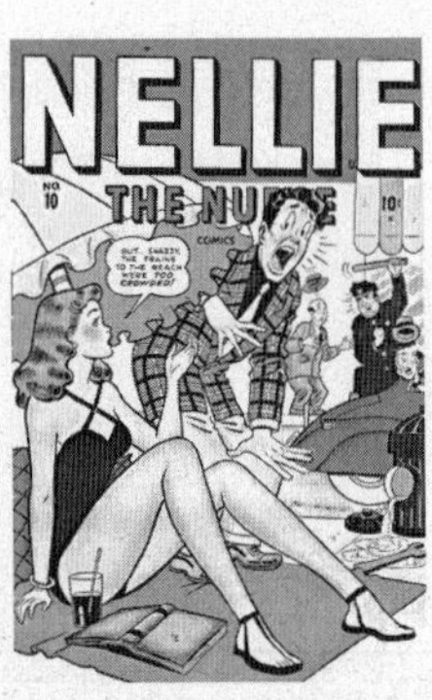

Nellie the Nurse #10 © MAR

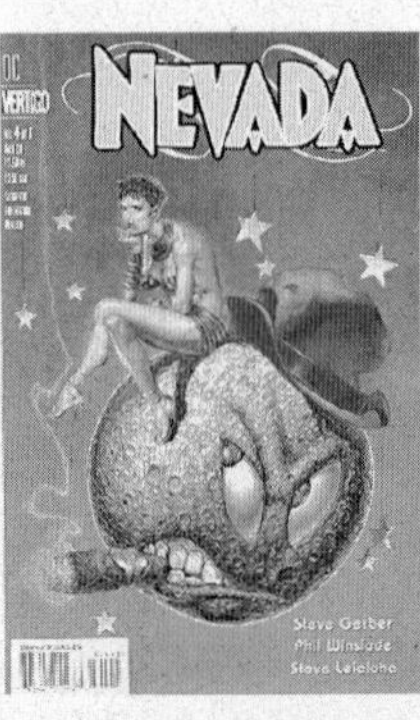

Nevada #4 © Gerber & DC

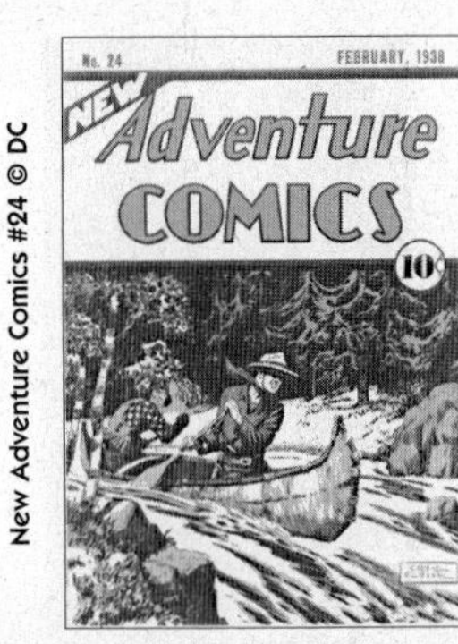

New Adventure Comics #24 © DC

	GD 2.0	VG 4.0	FN 6.0	VF 8.0	VF/NM 9.0	NM- 9.2

2-12: 11-w/paperdolls 3.00
13-15: Double size ($3.00). 13-w/paperdolls. 15 is a flip book(2-c) 4.00

NEIL YOUNG'S GREENDALE
DC Comics (Vertigo): 2010 ($19.99, hardcover graphic novel)

HC-Story based on the Neil Young album; Dysart-s/Chiang-a; intro. by Neil Young 20.00

NELLIE THE NURSE (Also see Gay Comics & Joker Comics)
Marvel/Atlas Comics (SPI/LMC): 1945 - No. 36, Oct, 1952; 1957

1-(1945) 47 94 141 296 498 700
2-(Spring/46) 24 48 72 140 230 320
3,4: 3-New logo (9/46) 19 38 57 112 179 245
5-Kurtzman's "Hey Look" (3); Georgie app. 20 40 60 117 189 260
6-8,10: 7,8-Georgie app. 10-Millie app. 18 36 54 105 165 225
9-Wolverton-a (1 pg.); Mille the Model app. 18 36 54 107 169 230
11,14-16,18-Kurtzman's "Hey Look" 19 38 57 109 172 235
12- "Giggles 'n' Grins" by Kurtzman 18 36 54 105 165 225
13,17,19,20: 17-Annie Oakley app. 15 30 45 83 124 165
21-30: 28-Mr. Nexdoor-r (3 pgs.) by Kurtzman/Rusty #22
13 26 39 74 105 135
31-36: 36-Post-c 11 22 33 64 90 115
1('57)-Leading Mag. (Atlas)-Everett-a, 20 pgs 12 24 36 69 97 125

NELLIE THE NURSE
Dell Publishing Co.: No. 1304, Mar-May, 1962

Four Color 1304-Stanley-a 7 14 21 46 76 105

NEMESIS (Millar & McNiven's...)
Marvel Comics (Icon): May, 2010 - No. 4, Feb, 2011 ($2.99)

1-4-Millar-s/McNiven-a 3.00
1,2-Variant covers: 1-Yu. 2-Cassaday 8.00

NEMESIS ARCHIVES (Listed with Adventures Into the Unknown)

NEMESIS: THE IMPOSTERS
DC Comics: May, 2010 - No. 4, Aug, 2010 ($2.99, limited series)

1-4-Richards-a/Luvisi-c. 1-Joker app. 2-4-Batman app. 3.00

NEMESIS THE WARLOCK (Also see Spellbinders)
Eagle Comics: Sept, 1984 - No. 7, Mar, 1985 (limited series, Baxter paper)

1-7: 2000 A.D. reprints 3.00

NEMESIS THE WARLOCK
Quality Comics/Fleetway Quality #2 on: 1989 - No. 19, 1991 ($1.95, B&W)

1-19 3.00

NEUTRO
Dell Publishing Co.: Jan, 1967

1-Jack Sparling-c/a (super hero); UFO-s 4 8 12 26 41 55

NEVADA (See Zane Grey's Four Color 412, 996 & Zane Grey's Stories of the West #1)

NEVADA (Also see Vertigo Winter's Edge #1)
DC Comics (Vertigo): May, 1998 - No. 6, Oct, 1998 ($2.50, limited series)

1-6-Gerber-s/Winslade-c/a 3.00
TPB-(1999, $14.95) r/#1-6 & Vertigo Winter's Edge preview 15.00

NEVER AGAIN (War stories; becomes Soldier & Marine V2#9)
Charlton Comics: Aug, 1955; No. 8, July, 1956 (No #2-7)

1 10 20 30 54 72 90
8-(Formerly Foxhole?) 6 12 18 31 38 45

NEVERMEN, THE (See Dark Horse Presents #148-150)
Dark Horse Comics: May, 2000 - No. 4, Aug, 2000 ($2.95, limited series)

1-4-Phil Amara-s/Guy Davis-a 3.00

NEVERMEN, THE: STREETS OF BLOOD
Dark Horse Comics: Jan, 2003 - No. 3, Apr, 2003 ($2.99, limited series)

1-3-Phil Amara-s/Guy Davis-a 3.00
TPB (7/03, $9.95) r/#1-3; Paul Jenkins intro.; Davis sketch pages 10.00

NEVERMORE (DEAN KOONTZ'S:...)
Dabel Brothers Prods.: Mar, 2009 - No. 5 ($3.99, limited series)

1-Keith Champagne-s/Andy Smith-a 4.00

NEW ADVENTURE COMICS (Formerly New Comics; becomes Adventure Comics #32 on; V1#12 indicia says NEW COMICS #12)
National Periodical Publications: V1#12, Jan, 1937 - No. 31, Oct, 1938

V1#12-Federal Men by Siegel & Shuster continues; Jor-L mentioned;
Whitney Ellsworth-c begin, end #14 550 1100 1650 4400 - -

	GD 2.0	VG 4.0	FN 6.0	VF 8.0	VF/NM 9.0	NM- 9.2

V2#1(2/37, #13)-(Rare) 525 1050 1575 4200 - -
V2#2 (#14) 475 950 1425 3800 - -
15(V2#3)-20(V2#8): 15-1st Adventure logo; Creig Flessel-c begin, end #31.
16-1st non-funny cover. 17-Nadir, Master of Magic begins, ends #30
367 734 1100 2020 3210 4400
21(V2#9),22(V2#10, 2/37): 22-X-Mas-c 333 666 1000 1830 2915 4000
23-25,28-31 292 584 876 1600 2550 3500
26(5/38) (scarce) has house ad for Action Comics #1 showing B&W image of cover
(early published image of Superman)(prices vary widely on this book)
(A CGC 5.0 sold in 2006 for $5377.50)
27(6/38) has house ad for Action Comics #1 showing B&W image of cover (scarce)
(early published image of Superman) 600 1200 1800 3600 4800 6000

NEW ADVENTURES OF ABRAHAM LINCOLN, THE
Image Comics (Homage): 1998 ($19.95, one-shot)

1-Scott McCloud-s/computer art 20.00

NEW ADVENTURES OF CHARLIE CHAN, THE (TV)
National Periodical Publications: May-June, 1958 - No. 6, Mar-Apr, 1959

1 (Scarce)-John Broome-s/Sid Greene-a in all 77 154 231 493 847 1200
2 (Scarce) 48 96 144 302 514 725
3-6 (Scarce)-Greene/Giella-a 41 82 123 256 428 600

NEW ADVENTURES OF HUCK FINN, THE (TV)
Gold Key: December, 1968 (Hanna-Barbera)

1- "The Curse of Thut"; part photo-c 4 8 12 22 34 45

NEW ADVENTURES OF PINOCCHIO (TV)
Dell Publishing Co.: Oct-Dec, 1962 - No. 3, Sept-Nov, 1963

12-562-212(#1) 8 16 24 55 93 130
2,3 7 14 21 44 72 100

NEW ADVENTURES OF ROBIN HOOD (See Robin Hood)

NEW ADVENTURES OF SHERLOCK HOLMES (Also see Sherlock Holmes)
Dell Publishing Co.: No. 1169, Mar-May, 1961 - No. 1245, Nov-Jan, 1961/62

Four Color 1169(#1) 12 24 36 83 172 260
Four Color 1245 11 22 33 77 154 230

NEW ADVENTURES OF SPEED RACER
Now Comics: Dec, 1993 - No. 7, 1994? ($1.95)

1-7 3.00
0-(Premiere)-3-D cover 3.00

NEW ADVENTURES OF SUPERBOY, THE (Also see Superboy)
DC Comics: Jan, 1980 - No. 54, June, 1984

1 5.00
2-6,8-10 4.00
11-49,51-54: 11-Superboy gets new power. 14-Lex Luthor app. 15-Superboy gets new parents. 28-Dial "H" For Hero begins, ends #49. 45-47-1st app. Sunburst. 48-Begin 75¢-c. 3.00
1,2,5,6,8 (Whitman variants; low print run; no issue # shown on cover)
2 4 6 8 10 12
7,50: 7-Has extra story "The Computers That Saved Metropolis" by Starlin (Radio Shack giveaway w/indicia). 50-Legion app. 5.00

NOTE: *Buckler a-9p; c-36p. Giffen a-50; c-50. 40i. Gil Kane c-32p, 33p, 35, 39, 41-49. Miller c-51. Starlin a-7. Krypto back-ups in 17, 22. Superbaby in 11, 14, 19, 24.*

NEW ADVENTURES OF THE PHANTOM BLOT, THE (See The Phantom Blot)

NEW AMERICA
Eclipse Comics: Nov, 1987 - No. 4, Feb, 1988 ($1.75, Baxter paper)

1-4: Scout limited series 3.00

NEW ARCHIES, THE (TV)
Archie Comic Publications: Oct, 1987 - No. 22, May, 1990 (75¢)

1 5.00
2-10: 3-Xmas issue 4.00
11-22: 17-22 (95¢-$1.00): 21-Xmas issue 3.00

NEW ARCHIES DIGEST (TV)(...Comics Digest Magazine #4?-10; ...Digest Magazine #11 on)
Archie Comics: May, 1988 - No. 14, July, 1991 ($1.35/$1.50, quarterly)

1 6.00
2-14: 6-Begin $1.50-c 3.50

NEW AVENGERS, THE (Also see Promotional section for military giveaway)
Marvel Comics: Jan, 2005 - No. 64, Jun, 2010 ($2.25/$2.50/$2.99/$3.99)

1-Bendis-s/Finch-a; Spider-Man app.; re-intro The Sentry; 4 covers by McNiven, Quesada & Finch; variants from #1-6 combine for one team image 5.00
1-Director's Cut ($3.99) includes alternate covers, script, villain gallery 4.00

New Avengers #3 © MAR

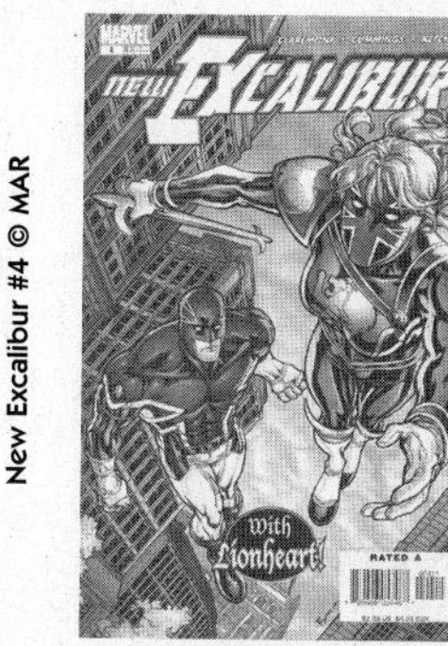

New Excalibur #4 © MAR

New Fun Comics #1 © DC

GD VG FN VF VF/NM NM-
2.0 4.0 6.0 8.0 9.0 9.2

1-MGC (6/10 $1.00) r/#1 with "Marvel's Greatest Comics" cover logo 3.00
2-20: 2-6-Finch-a. 5-Wolverine app. 7-10-Origin of the Sentry; McNiven-a. 11-Debut of Ronin. 14,15-Cho-c/a. 17-20-Deodato-a 3.00
21-48: 21-26-Civil War. 21-Chaykin-a/c. 26-Maleev-a. 27-31-Yu-a; Echo & "Elektra" app. 33-37-The Hood app. 38-Gaydos-a. 39-Mack-a. 40-47-Secret Invasion 3.00
49-($3.99) Dark Reign 4.00
50-($4.99) Dark Reign; Tan, Hitch, McNiven, Yu, Horn & others-a; Tan wraparound-c 5.00
50-($4.99) Adam Kubert variant-c 6.00
51-64-($3.99) Dark Reign. 51,52-Tan & Bachalo-a. 54-Brother Voodoo becomes Sorceror Supreme. 56-Wrecking Crew app. 61-64-Siege; Steve Rogers app. 4.00
51-54-Variant covers by Bachalo 7.00
56,57-Variant covers. 56-70th Anniversary frame. 57-Super Hero Squad 6.00
Annual 1 (6/06, $3.99) Wedding of Luke Cage and Jessica Jones; Bendis-s/Coipel-a 4.00
Annual 2 (2/08, $3.99) Avengers vs. The Hood's gang; Bendis-s/Pagulayan-a 4.00
Annual 3 (2/10, $4.99) Mayhew-c/a; Dark Avengers app.; Siege preview 5.00
... Finale (6/10, $4.99) Follows Siege #4; Bendis-s/Hitch-a/c; Count Nefaria app. 5.00
...: Illuminati (5/06, $3.99) Bendis-s/Maleev-a; leads into Planet Hulk; Civil War preview 4.00
... Most Wanted Files (2006, $3.99) profile pages of Avenger villains 4.00
... Vol. 1: Breakout HC (2005, $19.99) r/#1-6; gallery of variant covers 20.00
... Vol. 1: Breakout SC (2006, $14.99) r/#1-6; gallery of variant covers 15.00
... Vol. 2: Sentry HC (2006, $19.99) r/#7-10 & ... Most Wanted Files 20.00
... Vol. 2: Sentry SC (2006, $14.99) r/#7-10 & ... Most Wanted Files 15.00
... Vol. 3: Secrets and Lies HC (2006, $19.99) r/#11-15 & Giant-Size Spider-Woman #1 20.00
... Vol. 3: Secrets and Lies SC (2006, $14.99) r/#11-15 & Giant-Size Spider-Woman #1 15.00
... Vol. 4: The Collective HC (2006, $19.99) r/#16-20 20.00
... Vol. 4: The Collective SC (2007, $14.99) r/#16-20 15.00
... Vol. 5: Civil War HC (2007, $19.99) r/#21-25 20.00
... Vol. 5: Civil War SC (2007, $14.99) r/#21-25 15.00
... Vol. 6: Revolution HC (2007, $19.99) r/#26-31 20.00
... Vol. 6: Revolution SC (2007, $14.99) r/#26-31 15.00
... Volume 1 HC (2007, $29.99) oversized r/#1-10, ... Most Wanted Files, and ... Guest Starring the Fantastic Four (militiary giveaway); new intro. by Bendis; script & sketch pages 30.00
... Volume 2 HC (2008, $29.99) oversized r/#11-20, ... Annual #1, and story from Giant-Size Spider-Woman; variant covers & sketch pages 30.00

NEW AVENGERS (The Heroic Age)
Marvel Comics: Aug, 2010 - Present ($3.99)

1-Bendis-s/Immonen-a/c; Luke Cage forms new team; back-up text Avengers history 4.00
1-Variant-c by Djurdjevic 6.00
2-16: Hellstrom & Doctor Voodoo app.; back-up text Avengers history. 6-Doctor Voodoo killed. 9-13-Nick Fury flashback w/Chaykin-a. 14-16-Fear Itself. 16-Daredevil joins 4.00
16.1 (11/11, $2.99) Neal Adams-a/c; Bendis-s; Norman Osborn app. 3.00
17-22-($3.99) 17-Norman Osborn attacks; Iron Man app.; Deodato-a 4.00
Annual 1 (11/11, $4.99) Dell'Otto-a; Wonder Man app.; continues in Avengers Annual #1 5.00

NEW AVENGERS: ILLUMINATI (Also see Civil War and Secret Invasion)
Marvel Comics: Feb, 2007 - No. 5, Jan, 2008 ($2.99, limited series)

1-5-Bendis & Reed-s/Cheung-a. 3-Origin of The Beyonder. 5-Secret Invasion 3.00
HC (2008, $19.99, dustjacket) r/#1-5; cover sketch art 20.00
SC (2008, $14.99) r/#1-5; cover sketch art 15.00

NEW AVENGERS: LUKE CAGE
Marvel Comics: Jun, 2010 - No. 3, Aug, 2010 ($3.99, limited series)

1-3-Arcudi-s/Canete-a; Spider-Man & Ronin app. 4.00

NEW AVENGERS: THE REUNION
Marvel Comics: May, 2009 - No. 4, Aug, 2009 ($3.99, limited series)

1-4-Mockingbird and Ronin (Hawkeye); McCann-s/López-a/Jo Chen-c 4.00

NEW AVENGERS/TRANSFORMERS
Marvel Comics: Sept, 2007 - No. 4, Dec, 2007 ($2.99, limited series)

1-4-Kirkham-a; Capt. America app. 1-Cheung-c. 2-Pearson-c 3.00
TPB (2008, $10.99) r/#1-4 11.00

NEW BOOK OF COMICS (Also see Big Book Of Fun)
National Periodical Publ.: 1937; No. 2, Spring, 1938 (100 pgs. each) (Reprints)

1(Rare)-1st regular size comic annual; 2nd DC annual; contains r/New Comics #1-4 & More Fun #9; r/Federal Men (8 pgs.), Henri Duval (1 pg.), & Dr. Occult in costume (1 pg.) by Siegel & Shuster; Moldoff, Sheldon Mayer (15 pgs.)-a
1850 3700 5550 12,000 21,000 30,000
2-Contains-r/More Fun #15 & 16; r/Dr. Occult in costume (a Superman prototype), & Calling All Cars (4 pgs.) by Siegel & Shuster 950 1900 2850 6175 11,088 16,000

NEW COMICS (New Adventure #12 on)
National Periodical Publ.: 12/35 - No. 11, 12/36 (No. 1-6: paper cover) (No. 1-5: 84 pgs.)

V1#1-Billy the Kid, Sagebrush 'n' Cactus, Jibby Jones, Needles, The Vikings, Sir Loin of Beef, Now-When I Was a Boy, & other 1-2 pg. strips; 2 pgs. Kelly art(1st)-(Gulliver's Travels); Sheldon Mayer-a(1st)(2 2pg. strips); Vincent Sullivan-c(1st)
2333 4666 7000 14,000 - -
2-1st app. Federal Men by Siegel & Shuster & begins (also see The Comics Magazine #2); Mayer, Kelly-a (Rare)(1/36) 1250 2500 3750 7500 - -
3-6: 3,4-Sheldon Mayer-a which continues in The Comics Magazine #1. 3-Vincent Sullivan-c. 4-Dickens' "A Tale of Two Cities" adaptation begins. 5-Junior Federal Men Club; Kiefer-a. 6- "She" adaptation begins 800 1600 2400 4800 - -
7-10 550 1100 1650 3300 - -
11-Ties with More Fun #16 as DC's 1st Christmas-c 600 1200 1800 3600 - -
NOTE: *#1-6 rarely occur in mint condition.* ***Whitney Ellsworth** c-4-11.*

NEW DEADWARDIANS, THE
DC Comics (Vertigo): May, 2012 - No. 8 ($2.99, limited series)

1-Abnett-s/Culbard-a 3.00

NEW DEFENDERS (See Defenders)

NEW DNAGENTS, THE (Formerly DNAgents)
Eclipse Comics: V2#1, Oct, 1985 - V2#17, Mar, 1987 (Whole #s 25-40; Mando paper)

V2#1-17: 1-Origin recap. 7-Begin 95 cent-c. 9,10-Airboy preview 3.00
3-D 1 (1/86, $2.25) 3.00
2-D 1 (1/86)-Limited ed. (100 copies) 10.00

NEW DYNAMIX
DC Comics (WildStorm): May, 2008 - No. 5, Sept, 2008 ($2.99, limited series)

1-5-Warner-s/J.J. Kirby-a/c. 1-Variant-c by Jim Lee. 1-Convention Ed. with Lee-c 3.00

NEW ETERNALS: APOCALYPSE NOW (Also see Eternals, The)
Marvel Comics: Feb, 2000 ($3.99, one-shot)

1-Bennett & Hanna-a; Ladronn-c 4.00

NEW EXCALIBUR
Marvel Comics: Jan, 2006 - No. 24, Dec, 2007 ($2.99)

1-24: 1-Claremont-s/Ryan-a; Dazzler app. 3-Juggernaut app. 4-Lionheart app. 3.00
... Vol. 1: Defenders of the Realm TPB (2006, $17.99) r/#1-7 18.00
... Vol. 2: Last Days of Camelot TPB (2007, $19.99) r/#8-15 20.00
... Vol. 3: Battle for Eternity TPB (2007, $24.99) r/#16-24; sketch pages 25.00

NEW EXILES (Continued from Exiles #100 and Exiles - Days of Then and Now)
Marvel Comics: Mar, 2008 - No. 18, Apr, 2009 ($2.99)

1-18: 1-Claremont-s/Grummett-a; 2 covers by Land & Golden; new team 3.00
1-2nd printing with Grummett-c 3.00
Annual 1 (2/09, $3.99) Claremont-s/Grummett-a 4.00

NEWFORCE (Also see Newmen)
Image Comics (Extreme Studios): Jan, 1996-No. 4, Apr, 1996 ($2.50, lim. series)

1-4: 1-"Extreme Destroyer" Pt. 8; polybagged w/gaming card. 4-Newforce disbands 3.00

NEW FUN COMICS (More Fun #7 on; see Big Book of Fun Comics)
National Periodical Publications: Feb, 1935 - No. 6, Oct, 1935 (10x15", No. 1-4,: slick-c) (No. 1-5: 36 pgs; 40 pgs. No. 6)

V1#1 (1st DC comic); 1st app. Oswald The Rabbit; Jack Woods (cowboy) begins
7571 15,142 22,713 53,000 - -
2(3/35)-(Very Rare) 3283 6572 9858 23,000 - -
3-5(8/35): 3-Don Drake on the Planet Soro-c/story (sci/fi, 4/35); early (maybe 1st) DC letter column. 5-Soft-c 2000 4000 6000 14,000 - -
6(10/35)-1st Dr. Occult by Siegel & Shuster (Leger & Reuths); last "New Fun" title. "New Comics" #1 begins in Dec. which is reason for title change to More Fun; Henri Duval (ends #10) by Siegel & Shuster begins; paper-c
3571 7142 10,713 25,000 - -

NEW FUNNIES (The Funnies #1-64; Walter Lantz...#109 on; New TV... #259, 260, 272, 273; TV Funnies #261-271)
Dell Publishing Co.: No. 65, July, 1942 - No. 288, Mar-Apr, 1962

65(#1)-Andy Panda in a world of real people, Raggedy Ann & Andy, Oswald the Rabbit (with Woody Woodpecker x-overs), Li'l Eight Ball & Peter Rabbit begin; Bugs Bunny and Elmer app. 70 140 210 567 1234 1900
66-70: 66-Felix the Cat begins. 67-Billy & Bonny Bee by Frank Thomas begins. 69-Kelly-a (2 pgs.); The Brownies begin (not by Kelly) 31 62 93 220 478 735
71-75: 72-Kelly illos. 75-Brownies by Kelly? 21 42 63 146 311 475
76-Andy Panda (Carl Barks & Pabian-a); Woody Woodpecker x-over in Oswald ends
69 138 207 559 1205 1850
77,78: 77-Kelly-c. 78-Andy Panda in a world with real people ends
20 40 60 137 294 450
79-81 13 26 39 88 189 290
82-Brownies by Kelly begins 14 28 42 93 202 310
83-85-Brownies by Kelly in ea. 83-X-mas-c; Homer Pigeon begins. 85-Woody Woodpecker, 1 pg. strip begins 13 26 39 91 198 305

New Gods #10 © DC

New Kids on the Block Chillin' #1 © NKOTB

New Mutants #13 © MAR

	GD 2.0	VG 4.0	FN 6.0	VF 8.0	VF/NM 9.0	NM- 9.2
86-90: 87-Woody Woodpecker stories begin	11	22	33	75	148	220
91-99	10	20	30	64	115	165
100 (6/45)	10	20	30	66	121	175
101-120: 119-X-Mas-c	8	16	24	53	89	125
121-150: 131,143-X-Mas-c	7	14	21	46	76	105
151-200: 155-X-Mas-c. 167-X-Mas-c. 182-Origin & 1st app. Knothead & Splinter. 191-X-Mas-c	6	12	18	41	66	90
201-240	6	12	18	37	59	80
241-288: 270,271-Walter Lantz c-app. 281-1st story swipes/WDC&S #100	5	10	15	32	51	70

NOTE: *Early issues written by* ***John Stanley.***

NEW GODS, THE (1st Series)(New Gods #12 on)(See Adventure #459, DC Graphic Novel #4, 1st Issue Special #13 & Super-Team Family)
National Periodical Publications/DC Comics: 2-3/71 - V2#11, 10-11/72; V3#12, 7/77 - V3#19, 7-8/78 (Fourth World)

	GD	VG	FN	VF	VF/NM	NM-
1-Intro/1st app. Orion; 4th app. Darkseid (cameo; 3 weeks after Forever People #1) (#1-3 are 15¢ issues)	9	18	27	63	112	160
2-Darkseid-c/story (2nd full app., 4-5/71)	5	10	15	35	55	75
3-1st app. Black Racer; last 15¢ issue	4	8	12	24	37	50
4-9: (25¢, 52 pg. giants): 4-Darkseid cameo; origin Manhunter-r. 5,7,8-Young Gods feature. 7-Darkseid app. (2-3/72); origin Orion; 1st origin of all New Gods as a group. 9-1st app. Forager	4	8	12	24	37	50
10,11: 11-Last Kirby issue.	3	6	9	20	30	40
12-19: Darkseid storyline w/minor apps. 12-New costume Orion (see 1st Issue Special #13 for 1st new costume). 19-Story continued in Adventure Comics #459,460	2	4	6	8	10	12

Jack Kirby's New Gods TPB ('98, $11.95, B&W&Grey) r/#1-11 plus cover gallery of original series and "84 reprints 12.00

NOTE: *#4-9(25¢, 52 pgs.) contain Manhunter-r by* ***Simon*** *&* ***Kirby*** *from Adventure #73, 74, 75, 76, 77, 78 with covers in that order.* ***Adkins*** *i-12-14, 17-19.* ***Buckler*** *a(p)-15.* ***Kirby*** *c/a-1-11p.* ***Newton*** *a(p)-12-14, 16-19.* ***Starlin*** *c-17.* ***Staton*** *c-19p.*

NEW GODS (Also see DC Graphic Novel #4)
DC Comics: June, 1984 - No. 6, Nov, 1984 ($2.00, Baxter paper)

1-5: New Kirby-c; r/New Gods #1-10. 4.00
6-Reprints New Gods #11 w/48 pgs of new Kirby story & art; leads into DC Graphic Novel #4 — 2 4 6 8 10 12

NEW GODS (2nd Series)
DC Comics: Feb, 1989 - No. 28, Aug, 1991 ($1.50)

1-28 3.00

NEW GODS (3rd Series) (Becomes Jack Kirby's Fourth World) (Also see Showcase '94 #1 & Showcase '95 #7)
DC Comics: Oct, 1995 - No. 15, Feb, 1997 ($1.95)

1-11,13-15: 9-Giffen-a(p). 10,11-Superman app. 13-Takion, Mr. Miracle & Big Barda app. 13-15-Byrne-a(p)/scripts & Simonson-c. 15-Apokolips merged w/ New Genesis; story cont'd in Jack Kirby's Fourth World 3.00
12-(11/96, 99¢)-Byrne-a(p)/scripts & Simonson-c begin; Takion cameo; indicia reads October 1996 3.00
...Secret Files 1 (9/98, $4.95) Origin-s 5.00

NEW GUARDIANS, THE
DC Comics: Sept, 1988 - No. 12, Sept, 1989 ($1.25)

1-($2.00, 52 pgs)-Staton-c/a in #1-9 4.00
2-12 3.00

NEW HEROIC (See Heroic)

NEW INVADERS (Titled Invaders for #0 & #1) (See Avengers V3#83,84)
Marvel Comics: No. 0, Aug, 2004 - No. 9, June, 2005 ($2.99)

0-9-Roster of U.S. Agent, Sub-Mariner, Blazing Skull and others. 0-Avengers app. 3.00

NEW JUSTICE MACHINE, THE (Also see The Justice Machine)
Innovation Publishing: 1989 - No. 3, 1989 ($1.95, limited series)

1-3 3.00

NEW KIDS ON THE BLOCK, THE (Also see Richie Rich and...)
Harvey Comics: Dec, 1990 - No. 8, Dec, 1991 ($1.25)

1-8 4.00
...**Back Stage Pass** 1(12/90) - 7(11/91) **Chillin'** 1(12/90) - 7(12/91): 1-Photo-c ...**Comic Tour** '90/91 1 (12/90) - 7(12/91) **Digest** 1(1/91) - 5(1/92) **Hanging Tough** 1 (2/91) **Magic Summer Tour** 1 (Fall/90) **Magic Summer Tour** nn (Fall/90, sold at concerts) **Step By Step** 1 (Fall/90, one-shot) **Valentine Girl** 1 (Fall/90, one-shot)-Photo-c 4.00

NEW LINE CINEMA'S TALES OF HORROR (Anthology)
DC Comics (WildStorm): Nov, 2007 ($2.99, one-shot)

1-Freddy Krueger and Leatherface app.; Darick Robertson-c 3.00

NEW LOVE (See Love & Rockets)
Fantagraphics Books: Aug, 1996 - No. 6, Dec, 1997 ($2.95, B&W, lim. series)

1-6: Gilbert Hernandez-s/a 3.00

NEWMAN
Image Comics (Extreme Studios): Jan, 1996 - No. 4, Apr, 1996 ($2.50, lim. series)

1-4: 1-Extreme Destroyer Pt. 3; polybagged w/card. 4-Shadowhunt tie-in; Eddie Collins becomes new Shadowhawk 3.00

NEW MANGVERSE (Also see Marvel Mangaverse)
Marvel Comics: Mar, 2006 - No. 5, July, 2006 ($2.99, lim. series)

1-5: Cebulski-s/Ohtsuka-a; The Hand and Elektra app. 3.00
...: The Rings of Fate (2006, $7.99, digest) r/#1-5 8.00

NEWMEN (becomes The Adventures Of The...#22)
Image Comics (Extreme Studios): Apr, 1994 - No. 20, Nov, 1995; No. 21, Nov, 1996 ($1.95/$2.50)

1-21: 1-5: Matsuda-c/a. 10-Polybagged w/trading card. 11-Polybagged. 20-Has a variant-c; Babewatch! x-over. 21-(11/96)-Series relaunch; Chris Sprouse-a begins; pin-up. 16-Has a variant-c by Quesada & Palmiotti 3.00
TPB-(1996, $12.95) r/#1-4 w/pin-ups 13.00

NEW MEN OF BATTLE, THE
Catechetical Guild: 1949 (nn) (Carboard-c)

	GD	VG	FN	VF	VF/NM	NM-
nn(V8#1-3,5,6)-192 pgs.; contains 6 issues of Topix rebound	9	18	27	50	65	80
nn(V8#7-V8#11)-160 pgs.; contains 5 iss. of Topix	9	18	27	50	65	80

NEW MUTANTS, THE (See Marvel Graphic Novel #4 for 1st app.)(Also see X-Force & Uncanny X-Men #167)
Marvel Comics Group: Mar, 1983 - No. 100, Apr, 1991

1 6.00
2-10: 3,4-Ties into X-Men #167. 10-1st app. Magma 4.00
11-17,19,20: 13-Kitty Pryde app. 16-1st app. Warpath (w/out costume); see X-Men #193 3.00
18,21: 18-Intro. new Warlock. 21-Double size; origin new Warlock; newsstand version has cover price written in by Sienkiewicz 4.00
22-24,27-30: 23-25-Cloak & Dagger app. 3.00
25,26: 25-1st brief app. Legion. 26-1st full Legion app. 5.00
31-49,51-58: 35-Magneto intro'd as new headmaster. 43-Portacio-i. 58-Contains pull-out mutant registration form 3.00
50,73: 50-Double size. 73-(52 pgs.). 4.00
59-61: Fall of The Mutants series. 60-(52 pgs.) 4.00
62-72,74-85: 68-Intro Spyder. 63-X-Men & Wolverine clones app. 76-X-Factor & X-Terminator app. 85-Liefeld-c begin 3.00

	GD	VG	FN	VF	VF/NM	NM-
86-Rob Liefeld-a begins; McFarlane-c(i) swiped from Ditko splash pg.; 1st brief app. Cable (last page teaser)	1	2	3	5	6	8
87-1st full app. Cable (3/90)	3	6	9	18	27	35

87-2nd printing; gold metallic ink-c ($1.00) 3.00
88-2nd app. Cable — 1 3 4 6 8 10
92-No Liefeld-a; Liefeld-c 4.00
89,90,91,93-97,99,100: 89-3rd app. Cable. 90-New costumes. 90,91-Sabretooth app. 93,94-Cable vs. Wolverine. 95-97-X-Tinction Agenda x-over. 95-Death of new Warlock. 97-Wolverine & Cable-c, but no app. 99-1st app. of Feral (of X-Force); Byrne-c/swipe (X-Men, 1st Series #138). 100-(52 pgs.)-1st brief app. X-Force 5.00
95,100-Gold 2nd printing. 100-Silver ink 3rd printing 4.00
98-1st app. Deadpool, Gideon & Domino (2/91); 2nd Shatterstar (cameo); Liefeld-c/a — 4 8 12 24 37 50
Annual 1 (1984) 5.00
Annual 2 (1986, $1.25)-1st Psylocke — 2 4 6 8 10 12
Annual 3,4,6,7 ('87, '88,'90,'91, 68 pgs.): 4-Evolutionary War x-over. 6-1st new costumes by Liefeld (3 pgs.); 1st brief app. Shatterstar (of X-Force). 7-Liefeld pin-up only; X-Terminators back-up story; 2nd app. X-Force (cont'd in New Warriors Annual #1) 4.00
Annual 5 (1989, $2.00, 68 pgs.)-Atlantis Attacks; 1st Liefeld-a on New Mutants 5.00
... Classic Vol. 1 TPB (2006, $24.99) r/#1-7, Marvel Graphic Novel #4, Uncanny X-Men #167 25.00
... Classic Vol. 2 TPB (2007, $24.99) r/#8-17 25.00
... Classic Vol. 3 TPB (2008, $24.99) r/#18-25 & Annual #1 25.00
Special 1-Special Edition ('85, 68 pgs.)-Ties in w/X-Men Alpha Flight limited series; cont'd in X-Men Annual #9; Art Adams/Austin-a 5.00
Summer Special 1(Sum/90, $2.95, 84 pgs.) 4.00

NOTE: ***Art Adams*** *c-38, 39.* ***Austin*** *c-57i.* ***Byrne*** *c/a-75p.* ***Liefeld*** *a-86-91p, 93-96p, 98-100, Annual 5p, 6(3 pgs.); c-85-91p, 92, 93p, 94, 95, 96p, 97-100, Annual 5, 6p.* ***McFarlane*** *c-85-89i, 93i.* ***Portacio*** *a(i)-43.* ***Russell*** *a-48i.* ***Sienkiewicz*** *a-18-31, 35-38i; c-17-31, 35i, 37i, Annual 1.* ***Simonson*** *c-11p.* ***B. Smith*** *c-36, 40-48.* ***Williamson*** *a(i)-69, 71-73, 78-80, 82, 83; c(i)-69, 72, 73, 78i.*

NEW MUTANTS (Continues as New X-Men (Academy X))
Marvel Comics: July, 2003 - No. 13, June, 2004 ($2.50/$2.99)

New Mutants (2009 series) #14 © MAR

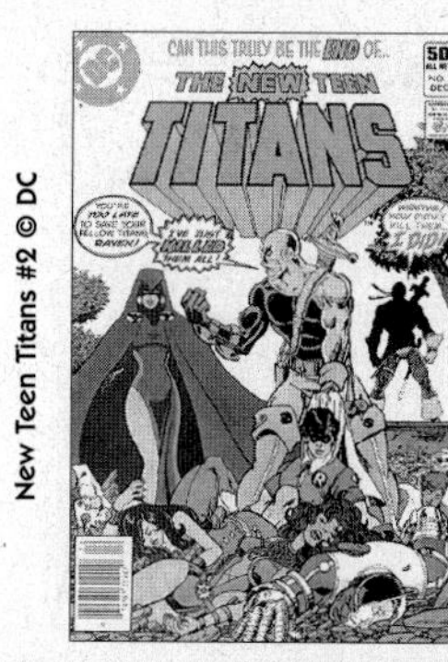

New Teen Titans #2 © DC

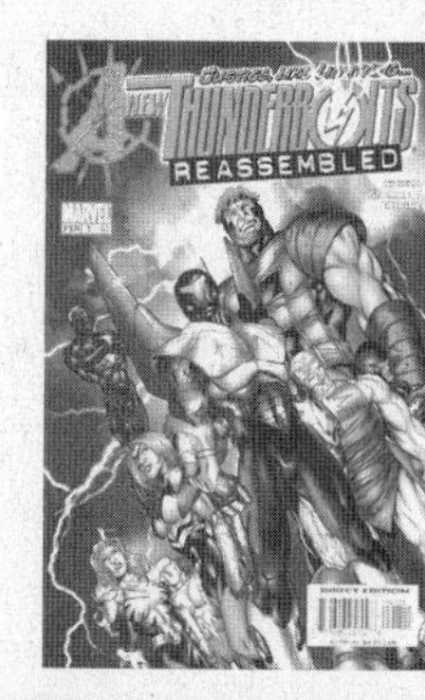

New Thunderbolts #1 © MAR

GD 2.0 | VG 4.0 | FN 6.0 | VF 8.0 | VF/NM 9.0 | NM- 9.2

1-7: 1-6-Josh Middleton-c. 7-Bachalo-c 3.00
8-13 ($2.99) 8-11-Bachalo-c 3.00
... Vol. 1: Back To School TPB (2005, $16.99) r/#1-6; new Middleton-c 17.00

NEW MUTANTS
Marvel Comics: July, 2009 - Present ($3.99/$2.99)

1-($3.99) Neves-a; Legion app.; covers by Ross, Adam Kubert, McLeod, Benjamin 4.00
2-24-($2.99) 2-10-Adam Kubert-c. 11-Siege; Dodson-c. 12-14-Second Coming 3.00
25-($3.99) Fernandez-a; wraparound-c by Djurdjevic; Nate Grey returns 4.00
26-38: 29-32-Fear Itself tie-in. 33-Regenesis. 34-Blink returns 3.00
... Saga (2009, giveaway) New Mutants character profiles and story synopsies; Neves-c 3.00

NEW MUTANTS FOREVER
Marvel Comics: Oct, 2010 - No. 5, Feb, 2011 ($3.99, limited series)

1-5-Claremont-s/Rio & McLeod-a; Red Skull app. 1-Back-up history of New Mutants 4.00

NEW MUTANTS, THE: TRUTH OR DEATH
Marvel Comics: Nov, 1997 - No. 3, Jan, 1998 ($2.50, limited series)

1-3-Raab-s/Chang-a(p) 3.00

NEW ORDER, THE
CFD Publishing: Nov, 1994 ($2.95)

1 3.00

NEW PEOPLE, THE (TV)
Dell Publishing Co.: Jan, 1970 - No. 2, May, 1970

	GD	VG	FN	VF	VF/NM	NM-
1	3	6	9	17	25	32
2-Photo-c	3	6	9	15	21	26

NEW ROMANCES
Standard Comics: No. 5, May, 1951 - No. 21, May, 1954

	GD	VG	FN	VF	VF/NM	NM-
5-Photo-c	15	30	45	90	140	190
6-9: 6-Barbara Bel Geddes, Richard Basehart "Fourteen Hours" photo-c. 7-Ray Milland & Joan Fontaine photo-c. 9-Photo-c from '50s movie	11	22	33	62	86	110
10,14,16,17-Toth-a	12	24	36	67	94	120
11-Toth-a; Liz Taylor, Montgomery Clift photo-c	32	64	96	188	307	425
12,13,15,18-21	10	20	30	56	76	95

NOTE: *Celardo a-9. **Moreira** a-6. **Tuska** a-7, 20. Photo c-5-16.*

NEWSBOY LEGION BY JOE SIMON AND JACK KIRBY, THE
DC Comics: 2010 ($49.99, hardcover with dustjacket)

Vol. 1 - Reprints apps. in Star Spangled Comics #7-32; new intro. by Joe Simon 50.00

NEW SHADOWHAWK, THE (Also see Shadowhawk & Shadowhunt)
Image Comics (Shadowline Ink): June, 1995 - No. 7, Mar, 1996 ($2.50)

1-7: Kurt Busiek scripts in all 3.00

NEW STATESMEN, THE
Fleetway Publications (Quality Comics): 1989 - No. 5, 1990 ($3.95, limited series, mature readers, 52pgs.)

1-5: Futuristic; squarebound; 3-Photo-c 4.00

NEWSTRALIA
Innovation Publ.: July, 1989 - No. 5, 1989 ($1.75, color)(#2 on, $2.25, B&W)

1-5: 1,2: Timothy Truman-c/a; Gustovich-i 3.00

NEW TALENT SHOWCASE (Talent Showcase #16 on)
DC Comics: Jan, 1984 - No. 19, Oct, 1985 (Direct sales only)

1-19: Features new strips & artists. 18-Williamson-c(i) 3.00

NEW TEEN TITANS, THE (See DC Comics Presents #26, Marvel and DC Present & Teen Titans; Tales of the Teen Titans #41 on)
DC Comics: Nov, 1980 - No. 40, Mar, 1984

	GD	VG	FN	VF	VF/NM	NM-
1-Robin, Kid Flash, Wonder Girl, The Changeling (1st app.), Starfire, The Raven, Cyborg begin; partial origin	3	6	9	16	23	30
2-1st app. Deathstroke the Terminator	4	8	12	22	34	45
3-10: 3-Origin Starfire; Intro The Fearsome Five. 4-Origin continues; J.L.A. app. 6-Origin Raven. 7-Cyborg origin. 8-Origin Kid Flash retold. 9-Minor app. Deathstroke on last pg. 10-2nd app. Deathstroke the Terminator (see Marvel & DC Present for 3rd app.); origin Changeling retold	1	3	4	6	8	10
11-20: 13-Return of Madame Rouge & Capt. Zahl; Robotman revived. 14-Return of Mento; origin Doom Patrol. 15-Death of Madame Rouge & Capt. Zahl; intro. new Brotherhood of Evil. 16-1st app. Captain Carrot (free 16 pg. preview). 18-Return of Starfire. 19-Hawkman teams-up	1	2	3	4	5	7

21-40: 21-Intro Night Force in free 16 pg. insert; intro Brother Blood. 23-1st app. Vigilante (not in costume), & Blackfire. 24-Omega Men app. 25-Omega Men cameo; free 16 pg. preview Masters of the Universe. 26-1st app. Terra. 27-Free 16 pg. preview Atari Force. 29-The New Brotherhood of Evil & Speedy app. 30-Terra joins the Titans. 34-4th app. Deathstroke the Terminator. 37-Batman & The Outsiders x-over. 38-Origin Wonder Girl. 39-Last Dick Grayson as Robin; Kid Flash quits 5.00
Annual 1(11/82)-Omega Men app. 6.00
Annual V2#2(9/83)-1st app. Vigilante in costume; 1st app. Lyla 6.00
Annual 3 (See Tales of the Teen Titans Annual #3)
...: Games GN (2011, $24.99, HC) Wolfman-s/Pérez-a/c; original GN started in 1988, finished in 2011; '80s NTT roster; afterword by Pérez; Wolfman's original plot 25.00
...: Terra Incognito TPB (2006, $19.99) r/#26,28-34 & Annual #2 20.00
...: The Judas Contract TPB (2003, $19.95) r/#39,40 plus Tales of the Teen Titans #41-44 & Annual #3 20.00
...: Who is Donna Troy? TPB (2005, $19.99) r/#38,Tales of the Teen Titans #50, New Titans #50-55 and Teen Titans/Outsiders Secret Files 2003 20.00

NOTE: ***Pérez** a-1-4p, 6-34p, 37-40p, Annual 1p, 2p; c-1-12, 13-17p, 18-21, 22p, 23p, 24-37, 38, 39(painted), 40, Annual 1, 2.*

NEW TEEN TITANS, THE (Becomes The New Titans #50 on)
DC Comics: Aug, 1984 - No. 49, Nov, 1988 ($1.25/$1.75; deluxe format)

	GD	VG	FN	VF	VF/NM	NM-
1-New storyline; Pérez-c/a begins	1	3	4	6	8	10

2,3: 2-Re-intro Lilith 6.00
4-10: 5-Death of Trigon. 7-9-Origin Lilith. 8-Intro Kole. 10-Kole joins 5.00
11-49: 13,14-Crisis x-over. 20-Robin (Jason Todd) joins; original Teen Titans return. 38-Infinity, Inc. x-over. 47-Origin of all Titans; Titans (East & West) pin-up by Pérez 4.00
Annual 1-4 (9/85-'88): 1-Intro. Vanguard. 2-Byrne c/a(p); origin Brother Blood; intro new Dr. Light. 3-Intro. Danny Chase. 4-Pérez-c 4.00
...: The Terror of Trigon TPB (2003, $17.95) r/#1-5; new cover by Phil Jimenez 18.00

NOTE: ***Buckler** c-10. **Kelley Jones** a-47, Annual 4. **Erik Larsen** a-33. **Orlando** c-33p. **Perez** a-1-5; c-1-7, 19-23, 43. **Steacy** c-47.*

NEW TERRYTOONS (TV)
Dell Publishing Co./Gold Key: 6-8/60 - No. 8, 3-5/62; 10/62 - No. 54, 1/79

	GD	VG	FN	VF	VF/NM	NM-
1(1960-Dell)-Deputy Dawg, Dinky Duck & Hashimoto-San begin (1st app. of each)	10	20	30	69	130	190
2-8(1962)	7	14	21	46	76	105
1(30010-210)(10/62-Gold Key, 84 pgs.)-Heckle & Jeckle begins	10	20	30	64	115	165
2(30010-301)-84 pgs.	8	16	24	58	97	135
3-5	4	8	12	28	44	60
6-10	4	8	12	22	34	45
11-20	3	6	9	16	22	28
21-30	2	4	6	9	13	16
31-43	1	3	4	6	8	10
44-54: Mighty Mouse-c/s in all	2	4	6	8	11	14

NOTE: *Reprints: #4-12, 38, 40, 47. (See March of Comics #379, 393, 412, 435)*

NEW TESTAMENT STORIES VISUALIZED
Standard Publishing Co.: 1946 - 1947

	GD	VG	FN	VF	VF/NM	NM-
"New Testament Heroes–Acts of Apostles Visualized, Book I" "New Testament Heroes–Acts of Apostles Visualized, Book II" "Parables Jesus Told" Set....	17	34	51	98	154	210

NOTE: *All three are contained in a cardboard case, illustrated on front and info about the set.*

NEW THUNDERBOLTS (Continues in Thunderbolts #100)
Marvel Comics: Jan, 2005 - No. 18, Apr, 2006 ($2.99)

1-18: 1-Grummett-a/Nicieza-s. 1-Captain Marvel app. 2-Namor app. 4-Wolverine app. 3.00
... Vol. 1: One Step Forward (2005, $14.99) r/#1-6 15.00
... Vol. 2: Modern Marvels (2005, $14.99) r/#7-12 15.00
... Vol. 3: Right of Power (2006, $17.99) r/#13-18 & Thunderbolts #100 18.00

NEW TITANS, THE (Formerly The New Teen Titans)
DC Comics: No. 50, Dec, 1988 - No. 130, Feb, 1996 ($1.75/$2.25)

50-Perez-c/a begins; new origin Wonder Girl 6.00
51-59: 50-55-Painted-c. 55-Nightwing (Dick Grayson) forces Danny Chase to resign; Batman app. in flashback, Wonder Girl becomes Troia 4.00
60,61: 60-A Lonely Place of Dying Part 2 continues from Batman #440; new Robin tie-in; Timothy Drake app. 61-A Lonely Place of Dying Part 4 4.00
62-70,72-99,101-124,126-130: 62-65: Deathstroke the Terminator app. 65-Tim Drake (Robin) app. 70-1st Deathstroke solo cover/sty. 72-79-Deathstroke in all: 74-Intro. Pantha. 79-Terra brought back to life; 1 panel cameo Team Titans (1st app.). Deathstroke in #80-84,86. 80-2nd full app. Team Titans. 83,84-Deathstroke kills his son, Jericho. 85-Team Titans app. 86-Deathstroke vs. Nightwing-c/story; last Deathstroke app. 87-New costume Nightwing. 90-92-Parts 2,5,8 Total Chaos (Team Titans). 115-(11/94) 3.00
71-(44 pgs.)-10th anniversary issue; Deathstroke cameo 4.00
100-($3.50, 52 pgs.)-Holo-grafx foil-c 4.00
125 (3.50)-wraparound-c 4.00
#0-(10/94) Zero Hour, released between #114 & 115 3.00
Annual 5-10 ('89-'94, 68 pgs.. 7-Armaggedon 2001 x-over; 1st full app. Teen (Team) Titans

New Warriors V2 #9 © MAR

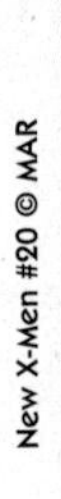

New X-Men #20 © MAR

Next Nexus #3 © FC

GD 2.0 | VG 4.0 | FN 6.0 | VF 8.0 | VF/NM 9.0 | NM- 9.2

(new group). 8-Deathstroke app.; Eclipso app. (minor). 10-Elseworlds story 4.00
Annual 11 (1995, $3.95)-Year One story 4.00
NOTE: *Perez a-50-55p, 57,60p, 58,59,61(layouts); c-50-61, 62-67i, Annual 5i; co-plots-66.*

NEW TV FUNNIES (See New Funnies)

NEW TWO-FISTED TALES, THE
Dark Horse Comics/Byron Preiss: 1993 ($4.95, limited series, 52 pgs.)
1-Kurtzman-r & new-a 5.00
NOTE: *Eisner c-1i. Kurtzman c-1p, 2.*

NEWUNIVERSAL
Marvel Comics: Feb, 2007 - No. 6, July, 2007 ($2.99)
1-6-Warren Ellis-s/Salvador Larroca-a. 1,2-Variant covers by Ribic 3.00
...: 1959 (9/08, $3.99) Aftermath of the White Event of 1953; Tony Stark app. 4.00
...: Conqueror (10/08, $3.99) The White Event of 2689 B.C.; Eric Nguyen-a 4.00
... : Everything Went White HC (2007, $19.99) r/#1-6; sketch pages 20.00
... : Everything Went White SC (2008, $14.99) r/#1-6; sketch pages 15.00

NEWUNIVERSAL: SHOCKFRONT
Marvel Comics: Jul, 2008 - Present ($2.99)
1,2-Warren Ellis-s/Steve Kurth-a 3.00

NEW WARRIORS, THE (See Thor #411,412)
Marvel Comics: July, 1990 - No. 75, 1996 ($1.00/$1.25/$1.50)
1-Williamson-i; Bagley-c/a(p) in 1-13, Annual 1 6.00
1-Gold 2nd printing (7/91) 3.00
2-5: 1,3-Guice-c(i). 2-Williamson-c/a(i). 4.00
6-24,26-49,51-75: 7-Punisher cameo (last pg.). 8,9-Punisher app. 14-Darkhawk & Namor x-over. 17-Fantastic Four & Silver Surfer x-over. 19-Gideon (of X-Force) app. 28-Intro Turbo & Cardinal. 31-Cannonball & Warpath app. 42-Nova vs. Firelord. 46-Photo-c. 47-Bound-in S-M trading card sheet. 52-12 pg. ad insert. 62-Scarlet Spider-c/app. 70-Spider-Man-c/app. 72-Avengers-c/app. 3.00
25-($2.50, 52 pgs.)-Die-cut cover 4.00
40,60: 40-($2.25)-Gold foil collector's edition 4.00
50-($2.95, 52 pgs.)-Glow in the dark-c 4.00
Annual 1-4('91-'94,68 pgs.)-1-Origins all members; 3rd app. X-Force (cont'd from New Mutants Ann. #7 & cont'd in X-Men Ann. #15); x-over before X-Force #1. 3-Bagged w/card 4.00

NEW WARRIORS, THE
Marvel Comics: Oct, 1999 - No. 10, July, 2000 ($2.99/$2.50)
0-Wizard supplement; short story and preview sketchbook 3.00
1-($2.99) 4.00
2-10: 2-Two covers. 5-Generation X app. 9-Iron Man-c 3.00

NEW WARRIORS (See Civil War #1)
Marvel Comics: Aug, 2005 - No. 6, Feb, 2006 ($2.99, limited series)
1-6-Scottie Young-a 3.00
...: Reality Check TPB (2006, $14.99) r/#1-6 15.00

NEW WARRIORS (The Initiative)
Marvel Comics: Aug, 2007 - No. 20, Mar, 2009 ($2.99)
1-19: 1-Medina-a; new team is formed. 2-Jubilee app. 14-16-Secret Invasion 3.00
20-($3.99) 4.00
...: Defiant TPB (2008, $14.99) r/#1-6 15.00

NEW WAVE, THE
Eclipse Comics: 6/10/86 - No. 13, 3/87 (#1-8: bi-weekly, 20pgs; #9-13: monthly)
1-13:1-Origin, concludes #5. 6-Origin Megabyte. 8,9-The Heap returns. 13-Snyder-c 3.00
...Versus the Volunteers 3-D #1,2(4/87): 1-Snyder-c 3.00

NEW WEST, THE
Black Bull Comics: Mar, 2005 - No. 2, Jun, 2005 ($4.99, limited series)
1,2-Phil Noto-a/c; Jimmy Palmiotti-s 5.00

NEW WORLD (See Comic Books, series I)

NEW WORLDS
Caliber: 1996 - No. 6 ($2.95/$3.95, 80 pgs., B&W, anthology)
1-6: 1-Mister X & other stories 4.00

NEW X-MEN (See X-Men *2nd series* #114-156)

NEW X-MEN (Academy X) (Continued from New Mutants)
Marvel Comics: July, 2004 - Present ($2.99)
1-46: 1,2-Green-c/a. 16-19-House of M. 20,21-Decimation. 40-Endangered Species back-ups begin. 44-46-Messiah Complex x-over; Ramos-a 3.00
Yearbook 1 (12/05, $3.99) new story and profile pages 4.00
...: Childhood's End Vol. 1 TPB (2006, $10.99) r/#20-23 11.00
...: Childhood's End Vol. 2 TPB (2006, $10.99) r/#24-27 11.00
...: Childhood's End Vol. 3 TPB (2006, $10.99) r/#28-32 11.00
...: Childhood's End Vol. 4 TPB (2007, $10.99) r/#33-36 11.00
...: Childhood's End Vol. 5 TPB (2007, $17.99) r/#37-43 18.00
House of M: New X-Men TPB (2006, $13.99) r/#16-19 and selections from Secrets Of The House of M one-shot 14.00
... Vol. 1: Choosing Sides TPB (2004, $14.99) r/#1-6 15.00
... Vol. 2: Haunted TPB (2005, $14.99) r/#7-12 15.00
... Vol. 3: X-Posed TPB (2006, $14.99) r/#12-15 & Yearbook Special 15.00

NEW X-MEN: HELLIONS
Marvel Comics: July, 2005 - No. 4, Oct, 2005 ($2.99, limited series)
1-4-Henry-a/Weir & DeFilippis-s 3.00
TPB (2006, $9.99) r/#1-4 10.00

NEW YORK FIVE, THE
DC Comics (Vertigo): Mar, 2011 - No. 4, Jun, 2011 ($2.99, B&W, limited series)
1-4-Brian Wood-s/Ryan Kelly-a 3.00

NEW YORK GIANTS (See Thrilling True Story of the Baseball Giants)

NEW YORK STATE JOINT LEGISLATIVE COMMITTEE TO STUDY THE PUBLICATION OF COMICS, THE
N.Y. State Legislative Document: 1951, 1955
This document was referenced by Wertham for **Seduction of the Innocent.** Contains numerous repros from comics showing violence, sadism, torture, and sex. 1955 version (196p, No. 37, 2/23/55) - Sold for $180 in 1986.

NEW YORK, THE BIG CITY
Kitchen Sink Press: 1986 ($10.95, B&W); **DC Comics:** July, 2000 ($12.95, B&W)
nn-Will Eisner-s/a 13.00

NEW YORK WORLD'S FAIR (Also see Big Book of Fun & New Book of Fun)
National Periodical Publ.: 1939, 1940 (100 pgs.; cardboard covers)
(DC's 4th & 5th annuals)
1939-Scoop Scanlon, Superman (blond haired Superman on-c), Sandman, Zatara, Slam Bradley, Ginger Snap by Bob Kane begin; 1st published app. The Sandman (see Adventure #40 for his 1st drawn story); Vincent Sullivan-c; cover background by Guardineer
1700 3400 5100 12,750 29,000 –
1940-Batman, Hourman, Johnny Thunderbolt, Red, White & Blue & Hanko (by Creig Flessel) app.; Superman, Batman & Robin-c (1st time they all appear together); early Robin app.; 1st Burnley-c/a (per Burnley) 922 1844 2766 6915 15,500 –
NOTE: *The 1939 edition was published 4/29/39 and released 4/30/39, the day the fair opened, at 25¢, and was first sold only at the fair. Since all other comics were 10¢, it didn't sell. Remaining copies were advertised beginning in the August issues of most DC comics for 25¢, but soon the price was dropped to 15¢. Everyone that sent a quarter through the mail for it received a free Superman #1 or a #2 to make up the dime difference. 15¢ stickers were placed over the 25¢ price. Four variations on the 15¢ stickers are known. The 1940 edition was published 5/11/40 and was priced at 15¢. It was a precursor to World's Best #1.*

NEW YORK: YEAR ZERO
Eclipse Comics: July, 1988 - No. 4, Oct, 1988 ($2.00, B&W, limited series)
1-4 3.00

NEXT, THE
DC Comics: Sept, 2006 - No. 6, Feb, 2007 ($2.99, limited series)
1-6-Tad Williams-s/Dietrich Smith-a; Superman app. 3.00

NEXT MEN (See John Byrne's...)

NEXT NEXUS, THE
First Comics: Jan, 1989 - No. 4, April, 1989 ($1.95, limited series, Baxter paper)
1-4: Mike Baron scripts & Steve Rude-c/a. 3.00
TPB (10/89, $9.95) r/series 10.00

NEXTWAVE: AGENTS OF H.A.T.E
Marvel Comics: Mar, 2006 - No. 12, Mar, 2007 ($2.99)
1-12-Warren Ellis-s/Stuart Immonen-a. 2-Fin Fang Foom app. 12-Devil Dinosaur app. 3.00
Vol. 1 - This Is What They Want HC (2006, $19.99) r/#1-6; Ellis original pitch 20.00
Vol. 1 - This Is What They Want SC (2007, $14.99) r/#1-6; Ellis original pitch 15.00
Vol. 2 - I Kick Your Face HC (2007, $19.99) r/#7-12 20.00
Vol. 2 - I Kick Your Face SC (2008, $14.99) r/#7-12 15.00

NEXUS (See First Comics Graphic Novel #4, 19 & The Next Nexus)
Capital Comics/First Comics No. 7 on: June, 1981 - No. 6, Mar, 1984; No. 7, Apr, 1985 - No. 80?, May, 1991 (Direct sales only, 36 pgs.; V2#1('83)-printed on Baxter paper)
1-B&W version; mag. size; w/double size poster 3 6 9 14 20 26
1-B&W 1981 limited edition; 500 copies printed and signed; same as above except this version has a 2-pg. poster & a pencil sketch on paperboard by Steve Rude
4 8 12 24 37 50
2-B&W, magazine size 2 4 6 11 16 20
3-B&W, magazine size; Brunner back-c; contains 33-1/3 rpm record ($2.95 price)
2 4 6 9 13 16

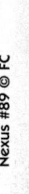

Nexus #89 © FC

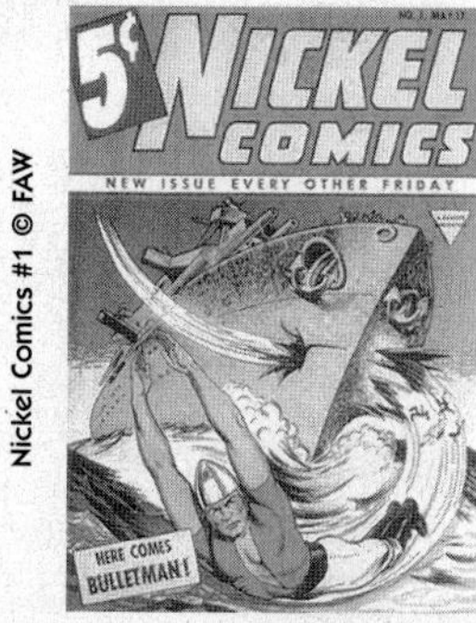

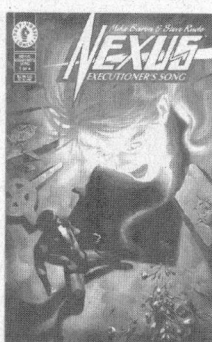

Nickel Comics #1 © FAW

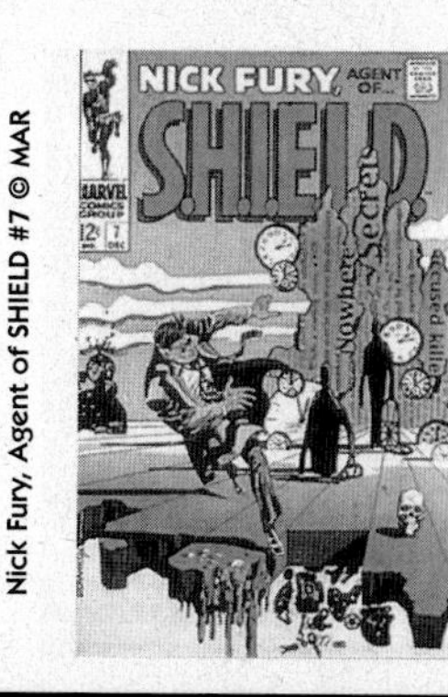

Nick Fury, Agent of SHIELD #7 © MAR

	GD 2.0	VG 4.0	FN 6.0	VF 8.0	VF/NM 9.0	NM- 9.2

V2#1-Color version 4.00
2-49,51-80: 2-Nexus' origin begins. 67-Snyder-c/a 3.00
50-($3.50, 52 pgs.) 4.00
Hardcover Volume One (Dark Horse Books, 11/05, $49.95) r/#1-3 & V2 #1-4; creator bios 50.00
HC Volume Two (Dark Horse Books, 3/06, $49.95) r/V2 #5-11; creator bios 50.00
HC Volume Three (Dark Horse Books, 5/06, $49.95) r/V2 #12-18; Marz forward 50.00
HC Volume Four (Dark Horse Books, 8/06, $49.95) r/V2 #19-25; Powell forward 50.00
HC Volume Five (Dark Horse Books, 2/07, $49.95) r/V2 #26-32; Brubaker forward 50.00
HC Volume Six (Dark Horse Books, 2/07, $49.95) r/V2 #33-39; Evanier forward 50.00
HC Volume Seven (Dark Horse Books, 2/08, $49.95) r/V2 #40-46; Brunning forward 50.00
HC Volume Eight (Dark Horse Books, 1/09, $49.95) r/V2 #47-52 and The Next Nexus #1; interview with original publishers John Davis and Milton Griepp 50.00
HC Volume Nine (Dark Horse Books, 8/09, $49.95) r/V2 #53-57 & The Next Nexus #2-4 50.00

NOTE: ***Bissette** c-V2#29. **Giffen** c/a-V2#23. **Gulacy** c-1 (B&W), 2(B&W). **Mignola** c/a-V2#28. **Rude** c-3(B&W), V2#1-22, 24-27, 33-36, 39-42, 45-48, 50, 58-60, 75; a-1-3, V2#1-7, 8-16p, 18-22p, 24-27p, 33-36p, 39-42p, 45-48p, 50, 58, 59p, 60. **Paul Smith** a-V2#37, 38, 43, 44, 51-55p; c-V2#37, 38, 43, 44, 51-55.*

NEXUS
Rude Dude Productions: No. 99, July, 2007 - No. 102, Jun, 2009 ($2.99)

99-Mike Baron scripts & Steve Rude-c/a 3.00
100-($4.99) Part 2 of Space Opera; back-up feature: History of Nexus 5.00
101/102-(6/09, $4.95) Combined issue 5.00
..., Free Comic Book Day 2007 - Excerpts from previous issues and preview of #99 3.00
... Greatest Hits (8/07, $1.99) same content as Free Comic Book Day 2007 3.00
...: The Origin (11/07, $3.99) reprints the 7/96 one-shot 4.00

NEXUS: ALIEN JUSTICE
Dark Horse Comics: Dec, 1992 - No. 3, Feb, 1993 ($3.95, limited series)

1-3: Mike Baron scripts & Steve Rude-c/a 4.00

NEXUS: EXECUTIONER'S SONG
Dark Horse Comics: June, 1996 - No. 4, Sept, 1996 ($2.95, limited series)

1-4: Mike Baron scripts & Steve Rude-c/a 3.00

NEXUS FILES
First Comics: 1989 ($4.50, color/16pgs. B&W, one-shot, squarebound, 52 pgs.)

1-New Rude-a; info on Nexus 4.50

NEXUS: GOD CON
Dark Horse Comics: Apr, 1997 - No. 2, May, 1997 ($2.95, limited series)

1,2-Baron-s/Rude-c/a 3.00

NEXUS LEGENDS
First Comics: May, 1989 - No. 23, Mar, 1991 ($1.50, Baxter paper)\

1-23: R/1-3(Capital) & early First Comics issues w/new Rude covers #1-6,9,10 3.00

NEXUS MEETS MADMAN (...Special)
Dark Horse Comics: May, 1996 ($2.95, one-shot)

nn-Mike Baron & Mike Allred scripts, Steve Rude-c/a. 3.00

NEXUS: NIGHTMARE IN BLUE
Dark Horse Comics: July, 1997 - No. 4, Oct, 1997 ($2.95, limited series)

1-4: 1,2,4-Adam Hughes-c 3.00

NEXUS: THE LIBERATOR
Dark Horse Comics: Aug, 1992 - No. 4, Nov, 1992 ($2.95, limited series)

1-4 3.00

NEXUS: THE ORIGIN
Dark Horse Comics: July, 1996 ($3.95, one-shot)

nn-Mike Baron- scripts, Steve Rude-c/a. 4.00

NEXUS: THE WAGES OF SIN
Dark Horse Comics: Mar, 1995 - No. 4, June, 1995 ($2.95, limited series)

1-4 3.00

NFL SUPERPRO
Marvel Comics: Oct, 1991 - No. 12, Sept, 1992 ($1.00)

1-12: 1-Spider-Man-c/app. 3.00
Special Edition (9/91, $2.00) Jusko painted-c 4.00
Super Bowl Edition (3/91, squarebound) Jusko painted-c 4.00

NICKEL COMICS
Dell Publishing Co.: 1938 (Pocket size - 7-1/2x5-1/2")(68 pgs.)

1- "Bobby & Chip" by Otto Messmer, Felix the Cat artist. Contains some English reprints
81 162 243 518 884 1250

NICKEL COMICS
Fawcett Publications: Feb 1940

nn - Ashcan comic, not distributed to newsstands, only for in-house use. A CGC certified 9.6 copy sold for $7,200 in 2003. In 2008, a CGC certified 8.5 sold for $2,390 and an uncertified Near Mint copy sold for $3,100.

NICKEL COMICS
Fawcett Publications: May, 1940 - No. 8, Aug, 1940 (36 pgs.; Bi-Weekly; 5¢)

	GD	VG	FN	VF	VF/NM	NM-
1-Origin/1st app. Bulletman	371	742	1113	2600	4550	6500
2	118	236	354	749	1287	1825
3	86	172	258	546	936	1325
4-The Red Gaucho begins	68	136	204	435	743	1050
5-7	67	134	201	426	731	1035
8-World's Fair-c; Bulletman moved to Master Comics #7 in October (scarce)	89	178	267	565	970	1375

NOTE: ***Beck** c-5-8. **Jack Binder** c-1-4. Bondage c-5. Bulletman c-1-8.*

NICK FURY, AGENT OF SHIELD (See Fury, Marvel Spotlight #31 & Shield)
Marvel Comics Group: 6/68 - No. 15, 11/69; No. 16, 11/70 - No. 18, 3/71

	GD	VG	FN	VF	VF/NM	NM-
1	13	26	39	87	186	285
2-4: 4-Origin retold	8	16	24	56	96	135
5-Classic-c	9	18	27	60	103	145
6,7: 7-Salvador Dali painting swipe	8	16	24	53	89	125
8-11,13: 9-Hate Monger begins, ends #11. 10-Smith layouts/pencil. 11-Smith-c. 13-1st app. Super-Patriot; last 12¢ issue	5	10	15	30	48	65
12-Smith-c/a	5	10	15	32	51	70
14-Begin 15¢ issues	4	8	12	26	41	55
15-1st app. & death of Bullseye-c/story(11/69); Nick Fury shot & killed; last 15¢ issue	8	16	24	55	93	130
16-18-(25¢, 52 pgs.)-r/Str. Tales #135-143	3	6	9	21	32	42

TPB (May 2000, $19.95) r/ Strange Tales #150-168 20.00
...: Who is Scorpio? TPB (11/00, $12.95) r/#1-3,5; Steranko-c 13.00

NOTE: ***Adkins** a-3i. **Craig** a-10i. **Sid Greene** a-12i. **Kirby** a-16-18r. **Springer** a-4, 6, 7, 8p, 9, 10p, 11; c-8, 9. **Steranko** a(p)-1-3, 5; c-1-7.*

NICK FURY AGENT OF SHIELD (Also see Strange Tales #135)
Marvel Comics: Dec, 1983 - No. 2, Jan, 1984 (2.00, 52 pgs., Baxter paper)

1,2-r/Nick Fury #1-4; new Steranko-c 4.00

NICK FURY, AGENT OF S.H.I.E.L.D.
Marvel Comics: Sept, 1989 - No. 47, May, 1993 ($1.50/$1.75)

V2#1-26,30-47: 10-Capt. America app. 13-Return of The Yellow Claw. 15-Fantastic Four app. 30,31-Deathlok app. 36-Cage app. 37-Woodgod c/story. 38-41-Flashes back to pre-Shield days after WWII. 44-Capt. America-c/s. 45-Viper-c/s. 46-Gideon x-over 3.00
27-29-Wolverine-c/stories 4.00

NOTE: ***Alan Grant** scripts-11. **Guice** a(p)-20-23, 25, 26; c-20-28.*

NICK FURY'S HOWLING COMMANDOS
Marvel Comics: Dec, 2005 - No. 6, May, 2006 ($2.99)

1-6: 1-Giffen-s/Francisco-a 3.00
1-Director's Cut ($3.99) r/#1 with original script and sketch design pages 4.00

NICK FURY VS. S.H.I.E.L.D.
Marvel Comics: June, 1988 - No. 6, Nov, 1988 ($3.50, 52 pgs, deluxe format)

1,2: 1-Steranko-c. 2-(Low print run) Sienkiewicz-c 5.00
3-6 4.00

NICK HALIDAY (Thrill of the Sea)
Argo: May, 1956

1-Daily & Sunday strip-r by Petree 8 16 24 44 57 70

NIGHT AND THE ENEMY (Graphic Novel)
Comico: 1988 (8-1/2x11") ($11.95, color, 80 pgs.)

1-Harlan Ellison scripts/Ken Steacy-c/a; r/Epic Illustrated & new-a (1st & 2nd printings) 12.00
1-Limited edition ($39.95) 40.00

NIGHT BEFORE CHRISTMAS, THE (See March of Comics No. 152 in the Promotional Comics section)

NIGHT BEFORE CHRISTMASK, THE
Dark Horse Comics: Nov, 1994 ($9.95, one-shot)

nn-Hardcover book; The Mask; Rick Geary-c/a 10.00

NIGHTBREED (See Clive Barker's Nightbreed)

NIGHT CLUB
Image Comics: Apr, 2005 - No. 4, Dec, 2006 ($2.95/$2.99, limited series)

1-4: 1-Mike Baron-s/Mike Norton-a 3.00

NIGHTCRAWLER (X-Men)
Marvel Comics Group: Nov, 1985 - No. 4, Feb, 1986 (Mini-series from X-Men)

1-4: 1-Cockrum-c/a 4.00

NIGHTCRAWLER (Volume 2)

Night Force (2012 series) #1 © DC

Nightmare #3 © Skywald

Nightmares #2 © ECL

GD 2.0 | VG 4.0 | FN 6.0 | VF 8.0 | VF/NM 9.0 | NM- 9.2

Marvel Comics: Feb, 2002 - No. 4, May, 2002 ($2.50, limited series)

1-4-Matt Smith-a 3.00

NIGHTCRAWLER
Marvel Comics: Nov, 2004 - No. 12, Jan, 2006 ($2.99)

1-12: 1-6-Robertson-a/Land-c. 2-Magik app. 8-Wolverine app. 10-Man-Thing app. 3.00
...: The Devil Inside TPB (2005, $14.99) r/#1-6 15.00
...: The Winding Way TPB (2006, $14.99) r/#7-12 15.00

NIGHTFALL: THE BLACK CHRONICLES
DC Comics (Homage): Dec, 1999 - No. 3, Feb, 2000 ($2.95, limited series)

1-3-Coker-a/Gilmore-s 3.00

NIGHT FORCE, THE (See New Teen Titans #21)
DC Comics: Aug, 1982 - No. 14, Sept, 1983 (60¢)

1 4.00
2-14: 13-Origin Baron Winter. 14-Nudity panels 3.00
NOTE: ***Colan*** *c/a-1-14p.* ***Giordano*** *c-1i, 2i, 4i, 5i, 7i, 12i.*

NIGHT FORCE
DC Comics: Dec, 1996 - No. 12, Nov, 1997 ($2.25)

1-12: 1-3-Wolfman-s/Anderson-a(p). 8-"Convergence" part 2 3.00

NIGHT FORCE
DC Comics: May, 2012 - No. 7 ($2.99, limited series)

1,2-Wolfman-s/Mandrake-a/Manco-c 3.00

NIGHT GLIDER
Topps Comics (Kirbyverse): April, 1993 ($2.95, one-shot)

1-Kirby c-1, Heck-a; polybagged w/Kirbychrome trading card 3.00

NIGHTHAWK
Marvel Comics: Sept, 1998 - No. 3, Nov, 1998 ($2.99, mini-series)

1-3-Krueger-s; Daredevil app. 3.00

NIGHTINGALE, THE
Henry H. Stansbury Once-Upon-A-Time Press, Inc.: 1948 (10¢, 7-1/4x10-1/4", 14 pgs., 1/2 B&W)

(Very Rare)-Low distribution; distributed to Westchester County & Bronx, N.Y. only; used in **Seduction of the Innocent**, pg. 312,313 as the 1st and only "good" comic book ever published. Ill. by Dong Kingman; 1,500 words of text, printed on high quality paper & no word balloons. Copyright registered 10/22/48, distributed week of 12/5/48. (By Hans Christian Andersen)
Estimated value........ 250.00

NIGHT MAN, THE (See Sludge #1)
Malibu Comics (Ultraverse): Oct, 1993 - No. 23, Aug, 1995 ($1.95/$2.50)

1-($2.50, 48 pgs.)-Rune flip-c/story by B. Smith (3 pgs.) 3.00
1-Ultra-Limited silver foil-c 6.00
2-15, 17: 3-Break-Thru x-over; Freex app. 4-Origin Firearm (2 pgs.) by Chaykin. 6-TNTNT app. 8-1st app. Teknight 3.00
16 ($3.50)-flip book (Ultraverse Premiere #11) 4.00
...:The Pilgrim Conundrum Saga (1/95, $3.95, 68 pgs.)-Strangers app. 4.00
18-23: 22-Loki-c/app. 3.00
Infinity ($1.50) 3.00
...Vs. Wolverine #0-Kelley Jones-c; mail in offer 1 3 4 6 8 10
NOTE: ***Zeck*** *a-16.*

NIGHT MAN, THE
Malibu Comics (Ultraverse): Sept, 1995 - No.4, Dec, 1995 ($1.50, lim. series)

1-4: Post Black September storyline 3.00

NIGHT MAN, THE /GAMBIT
Malibu Comics (Ultraverse): Mar, 1996 - No. 3, May, 1996 ($1.95, lim. series)

0-Limited Premium Edition 4.00
1-3: David Quinn scripts in all. 3-Rhiannon discovered to be The Night Man's mother 3.00

NIGHTMARE
Ziff-Davis (Approved Comics)/St. John No. 3: Summer, 1952 - No. 3, Winter, 1952, 53 (Painted-c)

1-1 pg. Kinstler-a; Tuska-a(2) 58 116 174 371 636 900
2-Kinstler-a-Poe's "Pit & the Pendulum" 41 82 123 256 428 600
3-Kinstler-a 39 78 117 231 378 525

NIGHTMARE (Weird Horrors #1-9) (Amazing Ghost Stories #14 on)
St. John Publishing Co.: No. 10, Dec, 1953 - No. 13, Aug, 1954

10-Reprints Ziff-Davis Weird Thrillers #2 w/new Kubert-c plus 2 pgs. Kinstler-a; Anderson, Colan & Toth-a 55 110 165 352 601 850
11-Krigstein-a; painted-c; Poe adapt., "Hop Frog" 41 82 123 256 428 600
12-Kubert bondage-c; adaptation of Poe's "The Black Cat"; Cannibalism story 40 80 120 246 411 575
13-Reprints Z-D Weird Thrillers #3 with new cover; Powell-a(2), Tuska-a; Baker-c 32 64 96 188 307 425

NIGHTMARE (Magazine) (Also see Psycho)
Skywald Publishing Corp.: Dec, 1970 - No. 23, Feb, 1975 (B&W, 68 pgs.)

1-Everett-a; Heck-a; Shores-a 10 20 30 65 118 170
2-5,8,9: 2,4-Decapitation story. 5-Nazi-s; Boris Karloff 4 pg. photo/text-s. 8-Features E.C. movie "Tales From the Crypt"; reprints some E.C. comics panels. 9-Wrightson-a; bondage-c; 1st Lovecraft Saggoth Chronicles/Cthulhu 6 12 18 39 62 85
6-Kaluta-a; Jeff Jones-c, photo & interview; 1st Living Gargoyle; Love Witch-s w/nudity; Boris Karloff-s 6 12 18 41 66 90
7 5 10 15 32 51 70
10-Wrightson-a (1 pg.); Princess of Earth-c/s; Edward & Mina Sartyros, the Human Gargoyles series continues from Psycho #8 6 12 18 41 66 90
11-19: 12-Excessive gore, severed heads. 13-Lovecraft-s. 15-Dracula-c/s. 17-Vampires issue; Autobiography of a Vampire series begins 4 8 12 26 41 55
20-John Byrne's 1st artwork (2 pgs.)(8/74); severed head-c; Hitler app. 8 16 24 55 93 130
21-23: 21-(1974 Summer Special)-Kaluta-a. 22-Tomb of Horror issue. 23-(1975 Winter Special) 5 10 15 30 48 65
Annual 1(1972)-Squarebound; B. Jones-a 5 10 15 30 48 65
Winter Special 1(1973)-All new material 4 8 12 26 41 55
Yearbook nn(1974)-B. Jones, Reese, Wildey-a 4 8 12 26 41 55
NOTE: ***Adkins*** *a-5.* ***Boris*** *c-2, 3, 5 (#4 is not by Boris).* ***Buckler*** *a-3, 15.* ***Byrne*** *a-20p.* ***Everett*** *a-1, 2, 4, 5, 12.* ***Jeff Jones*** *a-6, 21r(Psycho #6); c-6.* ***Katz*** *a-3, 5, 21.* ***Reese*** *a-4, 5.* ***Wildey*** *a-4, 5, 6, 21, '74 Yearbook.* ***Wrightson*** *a-9, 10.*

NIGHTMARE (Alex Nino's)
Innovation Publishing: 1989 ($1.95)

1-Alex Nino-a 3.00

NIGHTMARE
Marvel Comics: Dec, 1994 - No. 4, Mar, 1995 ($1.95, limited series)

1-4 3.00

NIGHTMARE & CASPER (See Harvey Hits #71) (Casper & Nightmare #6 on) (See Casper The Friendly Ghost #19)
Harvey Publications: Aug, 1963 - No. 5, Aug, 1964 (25¢)

1-All reprints? 8 16 24 53 89 125
2-5: All reprints? 5 10 15 32 51 70

NIGHTMARE ON ELM STREET, A (Also see Freddy Krueger's...)
DC Comics (WildStorm): Dec, 2006 - Present ($2.99)

1-8: 1-Two covers by Harris & Bradstreet; Dixon-s/West-a 3.00

NIGHTMARES (See Do You Believe in Nightmares)

NIGHTMARES
Eclipse Comics: May, 1985 - No. 2, May, 1985 ($1.75, Baxter paper)

1,2 3.00

NIGHTMARE THEATER
Chaos! Comics: Nov, 1997 - No. 4, Nov, 1997 ($2.50, mini-series)

1-4-Horror stories by various; Wrightson-a 3.00

NIGHTMARK: BLOOD & HONOR
Alpha Productions: 1994 - No. 3, 1994 ($2.50, B&W, mini-series)

1,2 3.00

NIGHTMARK MYSTERY SPECIAL
Alpha Productions: Jan, 1994 ($2.50, B&W)

1 3.00

NIGHTMASK
Marvel Comics Group: Nov, 1986 - No. 12, Oct, 1987

1-12 3.00

NIGHT MASTER
Silverwolf: Feb, 1987 ($1.50, B&W)

1-Tim Vigil-c/a 3.00

NIGHTMASTER (See Shadowpact)
DC Comics: Jan, 2011 ($2.99, one-shot)

1-Wrightson-c/Beechen-s/Dwyer-a; Shadowpact app. 3.00

NIGHT MUSIC (See Eclipse Graphic Album Series, The Magic Flute)
Eclipse Comics: Dec, 1984 - No. 11, 1990 ($1.75/$3.95/$4.95, Baxter paper)

1-7: 3-Russell's Jungle Book adapt. 4,5-Pelleas And Melisande (double titled) 6-Salomé (double titled). 7-Red Dog #1 3.00

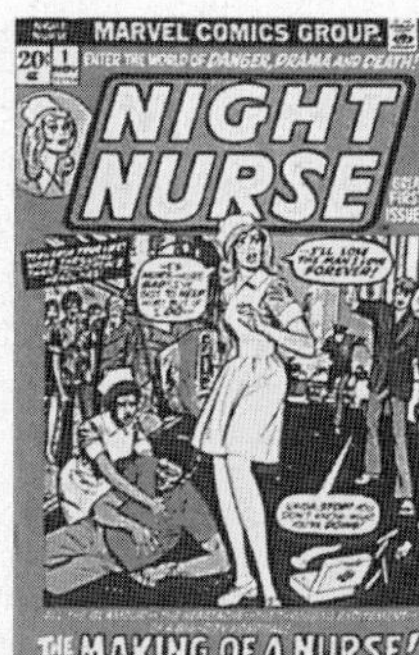

Night Nurse #1 © MAR

Nightstalkers #12 © MAR

Nightwing #6 © DC

	GD	VG	FN	VF	VF/NM	NM-
	2.0	4.0	6.0	8.0	9.0	9.2

8-($3.95) Ariane and Bluebeard 4.00
9-11-($4.95) The Magic Flute; Russell adapt. 5.00

NIGHT NURSE
Marvel Comics Group: Nov, 1972 - No. 4, May, 1973

1	12	24	36	79	160	240
2-4	9	18	27	63	112	160

NIGHT OF MYSTERY
Avon Periodicals: 1953 (no month) (one-shot)

nn-1 pg. Kinstler-a, Hollingsworth-c	48	96	144	302	514	725

NIGHT OF THE GRIZZLY, THE (See Movie Classics)

NIGHTRAVEN (See Marvel Graphic Novel)

NIGHT RIDER (Western)
Marvel Comics Group: Oct, 1974 - No. 6, Aug, 1975

1: 1-6 reprint Ghost Rider #1-6 (#1-origin)	2	4	6	10	14	18
2-6	2	4	6	8	10	12

NIGHT'S CHILDREN: THE VAMPIRE
Millenium: July, 1995 - No. 2, Aug, 1995 ($2.95, B&W)

1,2: Wendy Snow-Lang story & art 3.00

NIGHTSIDE
Marvel Comics: Dec, 2001 - No. 4, Mar, 2002 ($2.99)

1-4: 1-Weinberg-s/Derenick-a; intro Sydney Taine 3.00

NIGHTS INTO DREAMS (Based on video game)
Archie Comics: Feb, 1998 -No. 6, Oct, 1998 ($1.75, limited series)

1-6 3.00

NIGHTSTALKERS (Also see Midnight Sons Unlimited)
Marvel Comics (Midnight Sons #14 on): Nov, 1992 - No. 18, Apr, 1994 ($1.75)

1-($2.75, 52 pgs.)-Polybagged w/poster; part 5 of Rise of the Midnight Sons storyline; Garney/Palmer-c/a begins; Hannibal King, Blade & Frank Drake begin (see Tomb of Dracula for & Dr. Strange) 4.00
2-9,11-18: 5-Punisher app. 7-Ghost Rider app. 8,9-Morbius app. 14-Spot varnish-c. 14,15-Siege of Darkness Pts 1 & 9 3.00
10-($2.25)-Outer-c is a Darkhold envelope made of black parchment w/gold ink; Midnight Massacre part 1 3.00

NIGHT TERRORS,THE
Chanting Monks Studios: 2000 ($2.75, B&W)

1-Bernie Wrightson-c; short stories, one by Wrightson-s/a 3.00

NIGHT THRASHER (Also see The New Warriors)
Marvel Comics: Aug, 1993 - No. 21, Apr, 1995 ($1.75/$1.95)

1-($2.95, 52 pgs.)-Red holo-grafx foil-c; origin 4.00
2-21: 2-Intro Tantrum. 3-Gideon (of X-Force) app. 10-Bound-in trading card sheet; Iron Man app. 15-Hulk app. 3.00

NIGHT THRASHER: FOUR CONTROL
Marvel Comics: Oct, 1992 - No. 4, Jan, 1993 ($2.00, limited series)

1-4: 2-Intro Tantrum. 3-Gideon (of X-Force) app. 3.00

NIGHT TRIBES
DC Comics (WildStorm): July, 1999 ($4.95, one-shot)

1-Golden & Sniegoski-s/Chin-a 5.00

NIGHTVEIL (Also see Femforce)
Americomics/AC Comics: Nov, 1984 - No. 7, 1987 ($1.75)

1-7 3.00
...'s Cauldron Of Horror 1 (1989, B&W)-Kubert, Powell, Wood-r plus new Nightveil story 3.00
...'s Cauldron Of Horror 2 (1990, $2.95, B&W)-Pre-code horror-r by Kubert & Powell 3.00
...'s Cauldron Of Horror 3 (1991) 3.00
Special 1 ('88, $1.95)-Kaluta-c 3.00
One Shot ('96, $5.95)-Flip book w/ Colt 6.00

NIGHTWATCH
Marvel Comics: Apr, 1994 - No. 12, Mar, 1995 ($1.50)

1-($2.95)-Collectors edition; foil-c; Ron Lim-c/a begins; Spider-Man app. 4.00
1-12-Regular edition. 2-Bound-in S-M trading card sheet; 5,6-Venom-c & app. 7,11-Cardiac app. 3.00

NIGHTWING (Also see New Teen Titans, New Titans, Showcase '93 #11,12, Tales of the New Teen Titans & Teen Titans Spotlight)
DC Comics: Sept, 1995 - No. 4, Dec, 1995 ($2.25, limited series)

1-Dennis O'Neil story/Greg Land-a in all 5.00
2-4 4.00
...: Alfred's Return (7/95, $3.50) Giordano-a 4.00
...Ties That Bind (1997, $12.95, TPB) r/mini-series & Alfred's Return 13.00

NIGHTWING
DC Comics: Oct, 1996 - No. 153, Apr, 2009 ($1.95/$1.99/$2.25/$2.50/$2.99)

1-Chuck Dixon scripts & Scott McDaniel-c/a	2	4	6	9	11	12

2,3 6.00
4-10: 6-Robin-c/app. 5.00
11-20: 13-15-Batman app. 19,20-Cataclysm pts. 2,11 4.00
21-49,51-64: 23-Green Arrow app. 26-29-Huntress-c/app. 30-Superman-c/app. 35-39-No Man's Land. 41-Land/Geraci-a begins. 46-Begin $2.25-c. 47-Texiera-c. 52-Catwoman-c/app. 54-Shrike app. 3.00
50-($3.50) Nightwing battles Torque 4.00
65-74,76-99: 65,66-Bruce Wayne: Murderer x-over pt. 3,9. 68,69: B.W.: Fugitive pt. 6,9. 70-Last Dixon-s. 71-Devin Grayson-s begin. 81-Batgirl vs. Deathstroke. 93-Blockbuster killed. 94-Copperhead app. 96-Bagged w/CD. 96-98-War Games 3.00
75-(1/03, $2.95) Intro. Tarantula 4.00
100-(2/05, $2.95) Tarantula app. 4.00
101-117: 101-Year One begins. 103-Jason Todd & Deadman app. 107-110-Hester-a. 109-Begin $2.50-c. 109,110-Villains United tie-ins. 112-Deathstroke app. 3.00
118-149,151-153: 118-One Year Later; Jason Todd as 2nd Nightwing. 120-Begin $2.99-c. 138,139-Resurrection of Ra's al Ghul x-over. 138-2nd printing. 147-Two-Face app. 3.00
150-($3.99) Batman R.I.P. x-over; Nightwing vs. Two-Face; Tan-c 4.00
#1,000,000 (11/98) teams with future Batman 3.00
Annual 1(1997, $3.95) Pulp Heroes 4.00
Annual 2 (6/07, $3.99) Dick Grayson and Barbara Gordon's shared history 4.00
...Eighty Page Giant 1 (12/00, $5.95) Intro. of Hella; Dixon-s/Haley-c 6.00
...: Big Guns (2004, $14.95, TPB) r/#47-50; Secret Files 1, Eighty Page Giant 1 15.00
...: Brothers in Blood (2007, $14.99, TPB) r/#118-124 15.00
...: A Darker Shade of Justice (2001, $19.95, TPB) r/#30-39, Secret Files #1 20.00
...: Freefall (2008, $17.99, TPB) r/#140-146 18.00
...: A Knight in Blüdhaven (1998, $14.95, TPB) r/#1-8 15.00
...: Love and Bullets (2000, $17.95, TPB) r/#1/2, 19,21,22,24-29 18.00
...: Love and War (2007, $14.99, TPB) r/#125-132 15.00
...: On the Razor's Edge (2005, $14.99, TPB) r/#52,54-60 15.00
...: Our Worlds at War (9/01, $2.95) Jae Lee-c 3.00
...: Renegade TPB (2006, $17.95) r/#112-117 18.00
...: Rough Justice (1999, $17.95, TPB) r/#9-18 18.00
Secret Files 1 (10/99, $4.95) Origin-s and pin-ups 5.00
...: The Great Leap (2009, $19.99) r/#147-153 20.00
...: The Hunt for Oracle (2003, $14.95, TPB) r/#41-46 & Birds of Prey #20,21 15.00
...: The Lost Year (2008, $14.99) r/#133-137 & Annual #2 15.00
...: The Target (2001, $5.95) McDaniel-c/a 6.00
Wizard 1/2 (Mail offer) 5.00
...: Year One (2005, $14.99) r/#101-106 15.00

NIGHTWING (DC New 52)
DC Comics: Nov, 2011 - Present ($2.99)

1-7: 1-Dick Grayson in black/red costume; Higgins-s/Barrows-a/c. 4-Batgirl app. 3.00

NIGHTWING (See Tangent Comics/ Nightwing)

NIGHTWING AND HUNTRESS
DC Comics: May, 1998 - No. 4, Aug, 1998 ($1.95, limited series)

1-4-Grayson-s/Land & Sienkiewicz-a 3.00
TPB (2003, $9.95) r/#1/4; cover gallery 10.00

NIGHTWINGS (See DC Science Fiction Graphic Novel)

NIKKI, WILD DOG OF THE NORTH (Disney, see Movie Comics)
Dell Publishing Co.: No. 1226, Sept, 1961

Four Color 1226-Movie, photo-c	5	10	15	35	55	75

9-11 - ARTISTS RESPOND
Dark Horse Comics: 2002 ($9.95, TPB, proceeds donated to charities)

Volume 1-Short stories about the September 11 tragedies by various Dark Horse, Chaos! and Image writers and artists; Eric Drooker-c 10.00

9-11: EMERGENCY RELIEF
Alternative Comics: 2002 ($14.95, TPB, proceeds donated to the Red Cross)

nn-Short stories by various inc. Pekar, Eisner, Hester, Oeming, Noto; Cho-c 15.00

9-11 - THE WORLD'S FINEST COMIC BOOK WRITERS AND ARTISTS TELL STORIES TO REMEMBER
DC Comics: 2002 ($9.95, TPB, proceeds donated to charities)

Volume 2-Short stories about the September 11 tragedies by various DC, MAD, and WildStorm writers and artists ; Alex Ross-c 10.00

Ninjak #2 © VAL

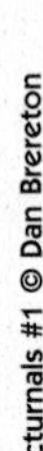

Nocturnals #1 © Dan Brereton

No Honor #2 © TCOW

GD 2.0 | VG 4.0 | FN 6.0 | VF 8.0 | VF/NM 9.0 | NM- 9.2

NINE RINGS OF WU-TANG
Image Comics: July, 1999 - No. 5, July, 2000 ($2.95)

Preview (7/99, $5.00, B&W) 5.00
1-5: 1-(11/99, $2.95) Clayton Henry-a 3.00
Tower Records Variant-c 5.00
Wizard #0 Prelude 3.00
TPB (1/01, $19.95) r/#1-5, Preview & Prelude; sketchbook & cover gallery 20.00

1963
Image Comics (Shadowline Ink): Apr, 1993 - No. 6, Oct, 1993 ($1.95, lim. series)

1-6: Alan Moore scripts; Veitch, Bissette & Gibbons-a(p) 3.00
1-Gold 4.00
*NOTE: **Bissette** a-2-4; **Gibbons** a-1i, 2i, 6i; c-2.*

1984 (Magazine) (1994 #11 on)
Warren Publishing Co.: June, 1978 - No. 10, Jan, 1980 ($1.50, B&W with color inserts, mature content with nudity; 84 pgs. except #4 has 92 pgs.)

1-Nino-a in all; Mutant World begins by Corben 3 6 9 14 19 24
2-10: 4-Rex Havoc begins. 7-1st Ghita of Alizarr by Thorne. 9-1st Starfire 2 4 6 9 13 16
NOTE: ***Alcala** a-1-3,5,7i. **Corben** a-1-8; c-1,2. **Nebres** a-1-8,10. **Thorne** a-7,8,10. **Wood** a-1,2,5i.*

1994 (Formerly 1984) (Magazine)
Warren Publishing Co.: No. 11, Feb, 1980 - No. 29, Feb, 1983 (B&W with color; mature; #11-(84 pgs.); #12-16,18-21,24-(76 pgs.); #17,22,23,25-29-(68 pgs.)

11,17,18,20,22,23,29: 11,17-8 pgs. color insert. 18-Giger-c. 20-1st Diana Jacklighter Manhuntress by Maroto. 22-1st Sigmund Pavlov by Nino; 1st Ariel Hart by Hsu. 23-All Nino issue 2 4 6 8 11 14
12-16,19,21,24-28: 21-1st app. Angel by Nebres. 27-The Warhawks return 1 3 4 6 8 10
NOTE: ***Corben** c-26. **Maroto** a-20, 21, 24-28. **Nebres** a-11-13, 15, 16, 18, 21, 22, 25, 28. **Nino** a-11-19, 20(2), 21, 25, 26, 28; c-21. **Redondo** c-20. **Thorne** a-11-14, 17-21, 24-26, 28, 29.*

NINJA BOY
DC Comics (WildStorm): Oct, 2001 - No. 6, Mar, 2002 ($3.50/$2.95)

1-($3.50) Ale Garza-a/c 3.50
2-6-($2.95) 3.00
...: Faded Dreams TPB (2003, $14.95) r/#1-6; sketch pages 15.00

NINJA HIGH SCHOOL (1st series)
Antarctic Press: 1986 - No. 3, Aug, 1987 (B&W)

1-Ben Dunn-s/c/a; early Manga series 2 4 6 9 12 15
2,3 1 3 4 6 8 10

NINJAK (See Bloodshot #6, 7 & Deathmate)
Valiant/Acclaim Comics (Valiant) No. 16 on: Feb, 1994 - No. 26, Nov. 1995 ($2.25/$2.50)

1 ($3.50)-Chromium-c; Quesada-c/a(p) in #1-3 4.00
1-Gold 5.00
2-13: 3-Batman, Spawn & Random (from X-Factor) app. as costumes at party (cameo). 4-w/bound-in trading card. 5,6-X-O app. 3.00
0,00,14-26: 14-(4/95)-Begin $2.50-c. 0-(6/95, $2.50). 00-(6/95, $2.50) 3.00
Yearbook 1 (1994, $3.95) 4.00

NINJAK
Acclaim Comics (Valiant Heroes): V2#1, Mar, 1997 -No. 12, Feb, 1998 ($2.50)

V2#1-12: 1-Intro new Ninjak; 1st app. Brutakon; Kurt Busiek scripts begin; painted variant-c exists. 2-1st app. Karnivor & Zeer. 3-1st app. Gigantik, Shurikai, & Nixie. 4-Origin; 1st app. Yasuiti Motomiya; intro The Dark Dozen; Colin King cameo. 9-Copycat-c 3.00

NINJA SCROLL
DC Comics (WildStorm): Nov, 2006 - No. 12, Oct, 2007 ($2.99)

1-12: 1-J. Torres-s/Michael Chang Ting Yu-a/c. 11-Puckett-s/Meyers-a 3.00
1-3-Variant covers by Jim Lee 5.00
TPB (2007, $19.99) r/#1-3,5-7 20.00

NINJETTES (See Jennifer Blood #4)
Dynamite Entertainment: 2012 - Present ($3.99)

1,2-Origin of the team; Ewing-s/Casallos-a 4.00

NINTENDO COMICS SYSTEM (Also see Adv. of Super Mario Brothers)
Valiant Comics: Feb, 1990 - No. 9, Oct, 1991 ($4.95, card stock-c, 68pgs.)

1-9: 1-Featuring Game Boy, Super Mario, Clappwall. 3-Layton-c. 5-8-Super Mario Bros. 9-Dr. Mario 1st app. 5.00

NOAH'S ARK
Spire Christian Comics/Fleming H. Revell Co.: 1973 (35/49¢)

nn-By Al Hartley 2 4 6 10 14 18

NOBLE CAUSES
Image Comics: July, 2001; Jan, 2002 - No. 4, May, 2002 ($2.95)

...First Impressions (7/01) Intro. the Noble family; Faerber-s 3.00
1-4: 1-(1/02) Back-up-s with Conner-a. 2-Igle back-up-a. 2-4-Two covers 3.00
...: Extended Family (5/03, $6.95) short stories by various 7.00
...: Extended Family 2 (6/04, $7.95) short stories by various 8.00
Vol. 1: In Sickness and in Health (2003, $12.95) r/#1-4 & ...First Impresssions 13.00

NOBLE CAUSES (Volume 3)
Image Comics: July, 2004 - No. 40, Mar, 2009 ($3.50)

1-24,26-40-Faerber-s. 1-Two covers. 2-Venture app. 5-Invincible app. 3.50
25-($4.99) Art by various; Randolph-c 5.00
Vol. 4: Blood and Water (2005, $14.95) r/#1-6 15.00
Vol. 5: Betrayals (2006, $14.99) r/#7-12 & The Pact V2 #2 15.00
Vol. 6: Hidden Agendas (2006, $15.99) r/#13-18 and Image Holiday Spec. 2005 story 16.00
Vol. 7: Powerless (2007, $15.99) r/#19-25; Wieringo sketch page 16.00

NOBLE CAUSES: DISTANT RELATIVES
Image Comics: Jul, 2003 - No. 4, Oct, 2003 ($2.95, B&W, limited series)

1-4-Faerber-s/Richardson & Ponce-a 3.00
Vol. 3: Distant Relatives (1/05, $12.95) r/#1-4; intro. by Joe Casey 13.00

NOBLE CAUSES: FAMILY SECRETS
Image Comics: Oct, 2002 - No. 4, Jan, 2003 ($2.95, limited series)

1-4-Faerber-s/Oeming-c. 1-Variant cover by Walker. 2,3-Valentino var-c. 4-Hester var-c 3.00
Vol. 2: Family Secrets (2004, $12.95) r/#1-4; sketch pages 13.00

NOBODY (Amado, Cho & Adlard's...)
Oni Press: Nov, 1998 - No. 4, Feb, 1999 ($2.95, B&W, mini-series)

1-4 3.00

NOCTURNALS, THE
Malibu Comics (Bravura): Jan, 1995 - No. 6, Aug, 1995 ($2.95, limited series)

1-6: Dan Brereton painted-c/a & scripts 3.00
1-Glow-in-the-Dark premium edition 5.00

NOCTURNALS, THE
Dark Horse Comics/Image Comics/Oni Press: one-shots and trade paperbacks

Black Planet TPB (Oni Press, 1998, $19.95) r/#1-6 (Malibu Comics series) 20.00
Black Planet and Other Stories HC (Olympian Publ.; 7/07, $39.95) r/Black Planet & Witching Hour contents; cover & sketch gallery with Brereton interviews 40.00
Carnival of Beasts (Image, 7/08, $6.99) short stories; Brereton-s/Brereton & others-a 7.00
Troll Bridge (Oni Press, 2000, $4.95, B&W & orange) Brereton-s/painted-c; art by Brereton, Chin, Art Adams, Sakai, Timm, Warren, Thompson, Purcell, Stephens and others 5.00
Unhallowed Eve TPB (Oni Press, 10/02, $9.95) r/Witching Hour & Troll Bridge one-shots 10.00
Witching Hour (Dark Horse, 5/98, $4.95) Brereton-s/a; reprints DHP stories + 8 new pgs. 5.00

NOCTURNALS: THE DARK FOREVER
Oni Press: Jul, 2001 -No. 3, Feb, 2002 ($2.95, limited series)

1-3-Brereton-s/painted-a/c 3.00
TPB (5/02, $9.95) r/#1-3; afterword & pin-ups by Alex Ross 10.00

NOCTURNE
Marvel Comics: June, 1995 - No. 4, Sept. 1995 ($1.50, limited series)

1-4 3.00

NO ESCAPE (Movie)
Marvel Comics: June, 1994 - No. 3, Aug, 1994 ($1.50)

1-3: Based on movie 3.00

NO HONOR
Image Comics (Top Cow): Feb, 2001 - No. 4, July, 2001 ($2.50)

Preview (12/00, B&W) Silvestri-c 3.00
1-4-Avery-s/Crain-a 3.00
TPB (8/03, $12.99) r/#1-4; intro. by Straczynski 13.00

NOMAD (See Captain America #180)
Marvel Comics: Nov, 1990 - No. 4, Feb, 1991 ($1.50, limited series)

1-4: 1,4-Captain America app. 3.00

NOMAD
Marvel Comics: V2#1, May, 1992 - No. 25, May, 1994 ($1.75)

V2#1-25: 1-Has gatefold-c w/map/wanted poster. 4-Deadpool x-over. 5-Punisher vs. Nomad-c/story. 6-Punisher & Daredevil-c/story cont'd in Punisher War Journal #48. 7-Gambit-c/story. 10-Red Wolf app. 21-Man-Thing-c/story. 25-Bound-in trading card sheet 3.00

NOMAD: GIRL WITHOUT A WORLD (Rikki Barnes from Captain America V2 Heroes Reborn)
Marvel Comics: Nov, 2009 - No. 4, Feb, 2010 ($3.99, limited series)

1-4-McKeever-s. 2-Falcon app. 4-Young Avengers app. 4.00

Northanger Abbey #1 © MAR

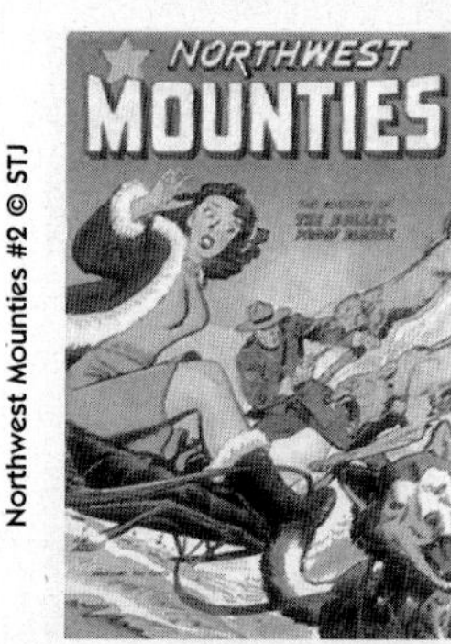

Northwest Mounties #2 © STJ

Nova #10 © MAR

GD 2.0 | VG 4.0 | FN 6.0 | VF 8.0 | VF/NM 9.0 | NM- 9.2

NOMAN (See Thunder Agents)
Tower Comics: Nov, 1966 - No. 2, March, 1967 (25¢, 68 pgs.)

1-Wood/Williamson-c; Lightning begins; Dynamo cameo; Kane-a(p) & Whitney-a 9 18 27 61 106 150
2-Wood-c only; Dynamo x-over; Whitney-a 6 12 18 39 62 85

NONE BUT THE BRAVE (See Movie Classics)

NOODNIK COMICS (See Pinky the Egghead)
Comic Media/Mystery/Biltmore: Dec, 1953; No. 2, Feb, 1954 - No. 5, Aug, 1954

3-D(1953, 25¢; Comic Media)(#1)-Came w/glasses 29 58 87 170 278 385
2-5 9 18 27 52 69 85

NORMALMAN (See Cerebus the Aardvark #55, 56)
Aardvark-Vanaheim/Renegade Press #6 on: Jan, 1984 - No. 12, Dec, 1985 ($1.70/$2.00)

1-12: 1-Jim Valentino-c/a in all. 6-12 ($2.00, B&W): 10-Cerebus cameo; Sim-a (2 pgs.) 3.00
...- Megaton Man Special 1 (Image Comics, 8/94, $2.50) 3.00
...3-D 1 (Annual, 1986, $2.25) 3.00
...Twentieth Anniversary Special (7/04, $2.95) 3.00

NORTHANGER ABBEY (Adaptation of the Jane Austen novel)
Marvel Comics: Jan, 2012 - No. 5, May, 2012 ($3.99, mini-series)

1-5-Nancy Butler-s/Janet K. Lee-a/Julian Tedesco-c 4.00

NORTH AVENUE IRREGULARS (See Walt Disney Showcase #49)

NORTH 40
DC Comics (WildStorm): Sept, 2009 - No. 6, Feb, 2010 ($2.99)

1-6-Aaron Williams-s/Fiona Staples-a 3.00
TPB (2010, $17.99) r/#1-6 18.00

NORTHLANDERS
DC Comics (Vertigo): Feb, 2008 - No. 50, Jun, 2012 ($2.99)

1-50: 1-Vikings in 980 A.D.; Wood-s/Gianfelice-a; covers by Carnivale. 35-Cloonan-a 3.00
1-3-Variant covers. 1-Adam Kubert. 2-Andy Kubert. 3-Dave Gibbons 5.00
...: Blood in the Snow TPB (2010, $14.99) r/#9,10,17-20 15.00
...: Metal and Other Stories TPB (2011, $17.99) r/#29-36 18.00
...: Sven the Returned TPB (2008, $9.99) r/#1-8; cover gallery 10.00
...: The Cross + The Hammer TPB (2009, $14.99) r/#11-16 15.00
...: The Plague Widow TPB (2010, $16.99) r/#21-28 17.00

NORTHSTAR
Marvel Comics: Apr, 1994 - No. 4, July, 1994 ($1.75, mini-series)

1-4: Character from Alpha Flight 3.00

NORTH TO ALASKA
Dell Publishing Co.: No. 1155, Dec, 1960

Four Color 1155-Movie, John Wayne photo-c 14 28 42 95 205 315

NORTHWEST MOUNTIES (Also see Approved Comics #12)
Jubilee Publications/St. John: Oct, 1948 - No. 4, July, 1949

1-Rose of the Yukon by Matt Baker; Walter Johnson-a; Lubbers-c 47 94 141 296 498 700
2-Baker-a; Lubbers-c. Ventrilo app. 39 78 117 231 378 525
3-Bondage-c, Baker-a; Sky Chief, K-9 app. 39 78 117 240 395 550
4-Baker-c/a(2 pgs.); Blue Monk & The Desperado app. 41 82 123 256 428 600

NO SLEEP 'TIL DAWN
Dell Publishing Co.: No. 831, Aug, 1957

Four Color 831-Movie, Karl Malden photo-c 6 12 18 42 69 95

NOSTALGIA ILLUSTRATED
Marvel Comics: Nov, 1974 - V2#8, Aug, 1975 (B&W, 76 pgs.)

V1#1 4 8 12 22 34 45
V1#2, V2#1-8 3 6 9 16 22 28

NOT BRAND ECHH (Brand Echh #1-4; See Crazy, 1973)
Marvel Comics Group (LMC): Aug, 1967 - No. 13, May, 1969
(1st Marvel parody book)

1: 1-8 are 12¢ issues 7 14 21 49 82 115
2-8: 3-Origin Thor, Hulk & Capt. America; Monkees, Alfred E. Neuman cameo. 4-X-Men app. 5-Origin/intro. Forbush Man. 7-Origin Fantastical-4 & Stuporman. 8-Beatles cameo; X-Men satire; last 12¢-c 4 8 12 26 41 55
9-13 (25¢, 68 pgs., all Giants) 9-Beatles cameo. 10-All-r; The Old Witch, Crypt Keeper & Vault Keeper cameos. 12,13-Beatles cameo 5 10 15 32 51 70

NOTE: ***Colan** a(p)-4, 5, 8, 9, 13. **Everett** a-1i. **Kirby** a(p)-1, 3, 5-7, 10r; c-1p. **J. Severin** a-1; c-3, 6-8, 11. **M. Severin** a-1-13; c-2, 9, 10, 12, 13. **Sutton** a-3, 4, 5i, 6i, 8, 9, 10r, 11-13; c-5. Archie satire in #9. Avengers satire in #8, 12.*

NOTHING CAN STOP THE JUGGERNAUT
Marvel Comics: 1989 ($3.95)

1-r/Amazing Spider-Man #229 & 230 4.00

NO TIME FOR SERGEANTS (TV)
Dell Publ. Co.: No. 914, July, 1958; Feb-Apr, 1965 - No. 3, Aug-Oct, 1965

Four Color 914 (Movie)-Toth-a; Andy Griffith photo-c 9 18 27 63 112 160
1(2-4/65) (TV): Photo-c 6 12 18 39 62 85
2,3 (TV): Photo-c 5 10 15 30 48 65

NOVA (The Man Called... No. 22-25)(See New Warriors)
Marvel Comics Group: Sept, 1976 - No. 25, May, 1979

1-Origin/1st app. Nova 3 6 9 14 20 25
2,3 2 4 6 8 10 12
4,12: 4-Thor x-over. 12-Spider-Man x-over 2 4 6 9 12 15
5-11 1 2 3 5 7 9
10,11-(35¢-c variants, limited distribution)(6,7/77) 4 8 12 28 44 60
12-(35¢-c variant, limited distribution)(8/77) 5 10 15 35 55 75
13,14-(Regular 30¢ editions)(9/77) 13-Intro Crime-Buster 1 2 3 5 6 8
13,14-(35¢-c variants, limited distribution) 4 8 12 26 41 55
15-24: 18-Yellow Claw app. 19-Wally West (Kid Flash) cameo 1 2 3 5 6 8
25-Last issue 2 3 4 6 8 10

NOTE: ***Austin** c-21i, 23i. **John Buscema** a(p)-1-3, 8, 21; c-1p, 2, 15. **Infantino** a(p)-15-20, 22-25; c-17-20, 21p, 23p, 24p. **Kirby** c-4p, 5, 7. **Nebres** c-25i. **Simonson** a-23i.*

NOVA
Marvel Comics: Jan, 1994 - June, 1995 ($1.75/$1.95) (Started as 4-part mini-series)

1-($2.95, 52 pgs.)-Collector's Edition w/gold foil-c; new Nova costume 5.00
1-($2.25, 52 pgs.)-Newsstand Edition w/o foil-c 4.00
2-18: 3-Spider-Man-c/story. 5-Stan Lee app. 5-Bound-in card sheet. 13-Firestar & Night Thrasher app.14-Darkhawk 3.00

NOVA
Marvel Comics: May, 1999 - No. 7, Nov, 1999 ($2.99/$1.99)

1-($2.99) Larsen-s/Bennett-a; wraparound-c by Larsen 4.00
2-7-($1.99): 2-Two covers; Capt. America app. 5-Spider-Man. 7-Venom 3.00

NOVA (See Secret Avengers and The Thanos Imperative)
Marvel Comics: June, 2007 - No. 36, Jun, 2010 ($2.99)

1-36: 1-Sean Chen-a/Granov-c. 2,3-Iron Man app. 3-Thunderbolts app. 14,15-Silver Surfer & Galactus app. 16-18-Secret Invasion. 21-Fantastic Four app. 23-28-War of Kings 3.00
... Annual 1 (4/08, $3.99) Origin retold; Annihilation: Conquest tie-in 4.00
...: Origin of Richard Rider (2009, $4.99) origin retold from Nova #1 & 4 ('76) 5.00
... Vol. 1: Annihilation - Conquest TPB (2007, $17.99) r/#1-7; cover sketches 18.00

NOW AGE ILLUSTRATED (See Pendulum Illustrated Classics)

NOW AGE BOOKS ILLUSTRATED (See Pendulum Illustrated Classics)

NOWHERE MAN
Dynamite Entertainment: 2011 - Present ($3.99)

1,2-Marc Guggenheim-s/Jeevan J. Kang-a 4.00

NTH MAN THE ULTIMATE NINJA (See Marvel Comics Presents #25)
Marvel Comics: Aug, 1989 - No. 16, Sept, 1990 ($1.00)

1-16-Ninja mercenary. 8-Dale Keown's 1st Marvel work (1/90, pencils) 3.00

NUCLEUS (Also see Cerebus)
Heiro-Graphic Publications: May, 1979 ($1.50, B&W, adult fanzine)

1-Contains "Demonhorn" by Dave Sim; early app. of Cerebus The Aardvark (4 pg. story) 6 12 18 37 59 80

NUKLA
Dell Publishing Co.: Oct-Dec, 1965 - No. 4, Sept, 1966

1-Origin & 1st app. Nukla (super hero) 5 10 15 30 48 65
2,3 3 6 9 20 30 40
4-Ditko-a, c(p) 4 8 12 24 37 50

NUMBER OF THE BEAST
DC Comics (WildStorm): June, 2008 - No. 8, Sept, 2008 ($2.99, limited series)

1-8-Beatty-s/Sprouse-a/c. 1-Variant-c by Mahnke. 6-The Authority app. 3.00
TPB (2008, $19.99) r/#1-8; character dossiers 20.00

NURSE BETSY CRANE (Formerly Teen Secret Diary) (Also see Registered Nurse for reprints)
Charlton Comics: V2#12, Aug, 1961 - V2#27, Mar, 1964 (See Soap Opera Romances)

V2#12-27 3 6 9 16 23 30

NURSE HELEN GRANT (See The Romances of...)

Nuts! #3 © PG

NYX #3 © MAR

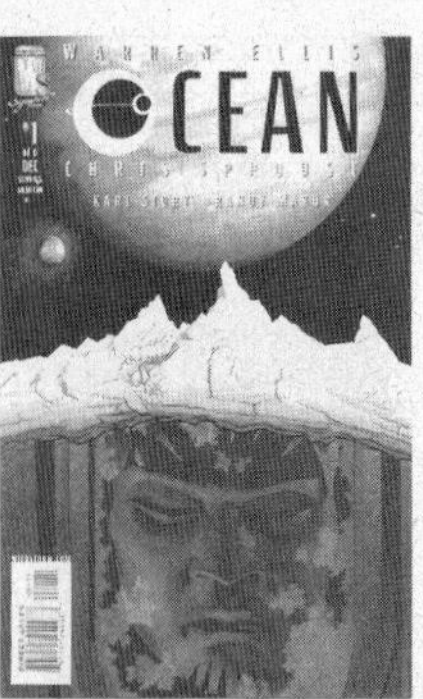

Ocean #1 © Ellis & Sprouse

	GD 2.0	VG 4.0	FN 6.0	VF 8.0	VF/NM 9.0	NM- 9.2

NURSE LINDA LARK (See Linda Lark)

NURSERY RHYMES
Ziff-Davis Publ. Co. (Approved Comics): No. 10, July-Aug, 1951 - No. 2, Winter, 1951 (Painted-c)

10 (#1), 2: 10-Howie Post-a 16 32 48 94 147 200

NURSES, THE (TV)
Gold Key: April, 1963 - No. 3, Oct, 1963 (Photo-c: #1,2)

1 4 8 12 24 37 50
2,3 3 6 9 18 27 35

NUTS! (Satire)
Premiere Comics Group: March, 1954 - No. 5, Nov, 1954

1-Hollingsworth-a 31 62 93 186 303 420
2,4,5: 5-Capt. Marvel parody 20 40 60 120 195 270
3-Drug "reefers" mentioned 21 42 63 122 199 275

NUTS (Magazine) (Satire)
Health Knowledge: Feb, 1958 - No. 2, April, 1958

1 10 20 30 54 72 90
2 7 14 21 37 46 55

NUTS & JOLTS
Dell Publishing Co.: No. 22, 1941

Large Feature Comic 22 18 36 54 105 165 225

NUTSY SQUIRREL (Formerly Hollywood Funny Folks)(See Comic Cavalcade)
National Periodical Publications: #61, 9-10/54 - #69, 1-2/56; #70, 8-9/56 - #71, 10-11/56; #72, 11/57

61-Mayer-a; Grossman-a in all 14 28 42 76 108 140
62-72: Mayer a-62,65,67-72 10 20 30 54 72 90

NUTTY COMICS
Fawcett Publications: Winter, 1946

1-Capt. Kidd story; 1 pg. Wolverton-a 14 28 42 80 115 150

NUTTY COMICS
Home Comics (Harvey Publications): 1945; No. 4, May-June, 1946 - No. 8, June-July, 1947 (No #2,3)

nn-Helpful Hank, Bozo Bear & others (funny animal) 9 18 27 50 65 80
4 7 14 21 37 46 55
5-Rags Rabbit begins(1st app.); infinity-c 8 16 24 40 50 60
6-8 6 12 18 31 38 45

NUTTY LIFE (Formerly Krazy Life #1; becomes Wotalife Comics #3 on)
Fox Features Syndicate: No. 2, Summer, 1946

2 17 34 51 98 154 210

NYOKA, THE JUNGLE GIRL (Formerly Jungle Girl; see The Further Adventures of..., Master Comics #50 & XMas Comics)
Fawcett Publications: No. 2, Winter, 1945 - No. 77, June, 1953 (Movie serial)

2 60 120 180 381 653 925
3 34 68 102 199 325 450
4,5 28 56 84 165 270 375
6-11,13,14,16-18-Krigstein-a: 17-Sam Spade ad by Lou Fine
20 40 60 114 182 250
12,15,19,20 18 36 54 105 165 225
21-30: 25-Clayton Moore photo-c? 14 28 42 76 108 140
31-40 11 22 33 62 86 110
41-50 10 20 30 56 76 95
51-60 9 18 27 50 65 80
61-77 8 16 24 44 57 70

NOTE: *Photo-c from movies 25, 30-70, 72, 75-77. Bondage c-4, 5, 7, 8, 14, 24.*

NYOKA, THE JUNGLE GIRL (Formerly Zoo Funnies; Space Adventures #23 on)
Charlton Comics: No. 14, Nov, 1955 - No. 22, Nov, 1957

14 11 22 33 62 86 110
15-22 9 18 27 52 69 85

NYX (Also see X-23 title)
Marvel Comics: Nov, 2003 - No. 7, Oct, 2005 ($2.99)

1,2: 1-Quesada-s/Middleton-a/c; intro. Kiden Nixon 3.00
3-1st app. X-23 1 3 4 6 8 10
4-6: 5,6-Teranishi-a 3.00
7-($3.99) Teranishi-a 4.00
NYX X-23 (2005, $34.99, oversized with d.j.) r/X-23 #1-6 & NYX #1-7; intro by Craig Kyle; sketch pages, development art and unused covers 35.00
...: Wannabe TPB (2006, $19.99) r/#1-7; development art and unused covers 20.00

NYX: NO WAY HOME
Marvel Comics: Oct, 2008 - No. 6, Apr, 2009 ($3.99)

1-6: 1-Andrasofszky-a/Liu-s/Urusov-c; sketch pages, character and cover design art 4.00

OAKLAND PRESS FUNNYBOOK, THE
The Oakland Press: 9/17/78 - 4/13/80 (16 pgs.) (Weekly)
Full color in comic book form; changes to tabloid size 4/20/80-on

Contains Tarzan by Manning, Marmaduke, Bugs Bunny, etc. (low distribution); 9/23/79 - 4/13/80 contain Buck Rogers by Gray Morrow & Jim Lawrence 3.00

OAKY DOAKS (See Famous Funnies #190)
Eastern Color Printing Co.: July, 1942 (One Shot)

1 34 68 102 199 325 450

OBERGEIST: RAGNAROK HIGHWAY
Image Comics (Top Cow/Minotaur): May, 2001 - No. 6, Nov, 2001 ($2.95, limited series)

Preview ('01, B&W, 16 pgs.) Harris painted-c 3.00
1-6-Harris-c/a/Jolley-s. 1-Three covers 3.00
... :The Directors' Cut (2002, $19.95, TPB) r/#1-6; Bruce Campbell intro. 20.00
... :The Empty Locket (3/02, $2.95, B&W) Harris & Snyder-a 3.00

OBIE
Store Comics: 1953 (6¢)

1 6 12 18 28 34 40

OBJECTIVE FIVE
Image Comics: July, 2000 - No. 6, Jan, 2001($2.95)

1-6-Lizalde-a 3.00

OBLIVION
Comico: Aug, 1995 - No. 3, May, 1996 ($2.50)

1-3: 1-Art Adams-c. 2-(1/96)-Bagged w/gaming card. 3-(5/96)-Darrow-c 3.00

OBNOXIO THE CLOWN (Character from Crazy Magazine)
Marvel Comics Group: April, 1983 (one-shot)

1-Vs. the X-Men 4.00

OCCULT CRIMES TASKFORCE
Image Comics: July, 2006 - No. 4, May, 2007 ($2.99, limited series)

1-4-Rosario Dawson & David Atchison-s/Tony Shasteen-a 3.00
... Vol. 1 TPB (2007, $14.99) r/#1-4; sketch and cover development art 15.00

OCCULTIST, THE
Dark Horse Comics: Dec, 2010 ($3.50, one-shot)

1-Richardson & Seeley-sDrujiniu-a/Morris-c 3.50

OCCULTIST, THE
Dark Horse Comics: Nov, 2011 - No. 3, Jan, 2012 ($3.50, limited series)

1-3-Seeley-s/Drujiniu-a/Morris-c. 1-Variant-c by Frison 3.50

OCCULT FILES OF DR. SPEKTOR, THE
Gold Key/Whitman No. 25: Apr, 1973 - No. 24, Feb, 1977; No. 25, May, 1982 (Painted-c #1-24)

1-1st app. Lakota; Baron Tibor begins 5 10 15 35 55 75
2-5: 3-Mummy-c/s. 5-Jekyll & Hyde-c/s 3 6 9 18 27 35
6-10: 6,9-Frankenstein. 8,9-Dracula c/s. 9.-Jekyll & Hyde c/s. 9,10-Mummy-c/s
3 6 9 14 20 25
11-13,15-17,19-22,24: 11-1st app. Spektor as Werewolf. 11-13-Werewolf-c/s. 12,16-Frankenstein c/s. 17-Zombie/Voodoo-c. 19-Sea monster-c/s. 20-Mummy-s. 21-Swamp monster-c/s. 24-Dragon-c/s 2 4 6 10 14 18
14-Dr. Solar app. 3 6 9 16 23 30
18,23-Dr. Solar cameo 2 4 6 11 16 20
22-Return of the Owl c/s 2 4 6 11 16 20
25(Whitman, 5/82)-r/#1 with line drawn-c 2 4 6 8 11 14

NOTE: *Also see Dan Curtis, Golden Comics Digest 33, Gold Key Spotlight, Mystery Comics Digest 5, & Spine Tingling Tales.*

OCEAN
DC Comics (WildStorm): Dec, 2005 - No. 6, Sept, 2005 ($2.95/$2.99/$3.99, limited series)

1-5-Warren Ellis-s/Chris Sprouse-a 3.00
6-($3.99) Conclusion 4.00

ODELL'S ADVENTURES IN 3-D (See Adventures in 3-D)

ODYSSEY, THE (See Marvel Illustrated: The Odyssey)

OFFCASTES
Marvel Comics (Epic Comics/Heavy Hitters): July, 1993 - No. 3, Sept, 1993 ($1.95, limited series)

1-3: Mike Vosburg-c/a/scripts in all 3.00

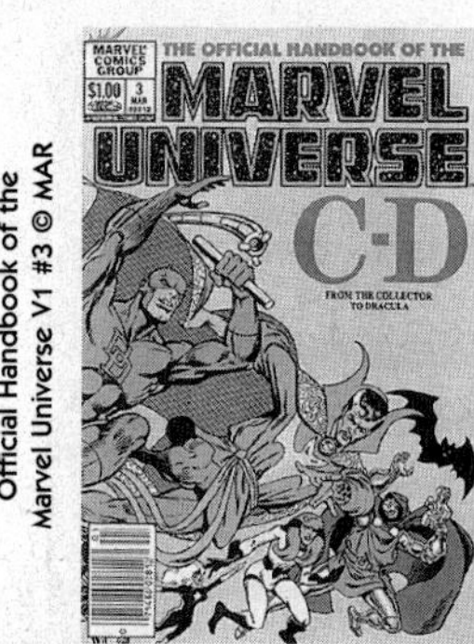
Official Handbook of the Marvel Universe V1 #3 © MAR

Official True Crime Cases #25 © MAR

Oh My Goddess Pt. #2 © Kosuke Fujishima

GD 2.0 | VG 4.0 | FN 6.0 | VF 8.0 | VF/NM 9.0 | NM- 9.2

OFFICIAL CRISIS ON INFINITE EARTHS INDEX, THE
Independent Comics Group (Eclipse): Mar, 1986 ($1.75)

1 5.00

OFFICIAL CRISIS ON INFINITE EARTHS CROSSOVER INDEX, THE
Independent Comics Group (Eclipse): July, 1986 ($1.75)

1-Perez-c. 5.00

OFFICIAL DOOM PATROL INDEX, THE
Independent Comics Group (Eclipse): Feb, 1986 - No. 2, Mar, 1986 ($1.50, limited series)

1,2: Byrne-c. 4.00

OFFICIAL HANDBOOK OF THE CONAN UNIVERSE (See Handbook of...)

OFFICIAL HANDBOOK OF THE MARVEL UNIVERSE, THE
Marvel Comics Group: Jan, 1983 - No. 15, May, 1984 (Limited series)

1-Lists Marvel heroes & villains (letter A) 5.00
2-15: 2 (B-C, 3-(C-D). 4-(D-G). 5-(H-J), 6-(K-L). 7-(M). 8-(N-P); Punisher-c. 9-(Q-S), 10-(S). 11-(S-U). 12-(V-Z); Wolverine-c. 13,14-Book of the Dead. 15-Weaponry catalogue 4.00

NOTE: **Bolland** *a-8.* **Byrne** *c/a(p)-1-14; c-15p.* **Grell** *a-6, 9.* **Kirby** *a-1, 3.* **Layton** *a-2, 5, 7.* **Mignola** *a-3, 4, 5, 6, 8, 12.* **Miller** *a-4-6, 8, 10.* **Nebres** *a-3, 4, 8.* **Redondo** *a-3, 4, 8, 13, 14.* **Simonson** *a-1, 4, 6-13.* **Paul Smith** *a-1-12.* **Starlin** *a-5, 7, 8, 10, 13, 14.* **Steranko** *a-8p.* **Zeck***-2-14.*

OFFICIAL HANDBOOK OF THE MARVEL UNIVERSE, THE
Marvel Comics Group: Dec, 1985 - No. 20, Feb, 1988 ($1.50, maxi-series)

V2#1-Byrne-c 5.00
2-20: 2,3-Byrne-c 4.00
Trade paperback Vol. 1-10 ($6.95) 1 3 4 6 8 10

NOTE: **Art Adams** *a-7, 8, 11, 12, 14.* **Bolland** *a-8, 10, 13.* **Buckler** *a-1, 3, 5, 10.* **Buscema** *a-1, 5, 8, 9, 10, 13, 14.* **Byrne** *a-1-14; c-1-11.* **Ditko** *a-1, 2, 4, 6, 7, 11, 13. a-7, 11.* **Mignola** *a-2, 4, 9, 11, 13.* **Miller** *a-2, 4, 12.* **Simonson** *a-1, 2, 4-13, 15.* **Paul Smith** *a-1-5, 7-12, 14.* **Starlin** *a-6, 8, 9, 12, 16.* **Zeck** *a-1-4, 6, 7, 9-14, 16.*

OFFICIAL HANDBOOK OF THE MARVEL UNIVERSE, THE
Marvel Comics: July, 1989 - No. 8, Mid-Dec, 1990 ($1.50, lim. series, 52 pgs.)

V3#1-8: 1-McFarlane-a (2 pgs.) 4.00

OFFICIAL HANDBOOK OF THE MARVEL UNIVERSE, THE (Also see Spider-Man)
Marvel Comics: 2004 - Present ($3.99, one-shots)

...: Alternate Universes 2005 - Profile pages of 1602, MC2, 2099, Earth X, Mangaverse, Days of Future Past, Squadron Supreme, Spider-Ham's Larval Earth and others 4.00
...: Avengers 2004 - Profile pages; art by various; lists of character origins and 1st apps. 4.00
...: Avengers 2005 - Profile pages and info for New Avengers, Young Avengers & others 4.00
...: Book of the Dead 2004 - Profile pages of deceased Marvel characters; art by various; 4.00
...: Daredevil 2004 - Profile pages; art by various; lists of character origins and 1st apps. 4.00
...: Fantastic Four 2005 - Profile pages of members, friends & enemies 4.00
...: Golden Age 2005 - Profile pages; art by various; lists of character origins and 1st apps. 4.00
...: Horror 2005 - Profile pages; art by various; lists of character origins and 1st apps. 4.00
...: Hulk 2004 - Profile pages; art by various; lists of character origins and 1st apps. 4.00
...: Marvel Knights 2005 - Profile pages of characters from Marvel Knights line 4.00
...: Spider-Man 2004 - Profile pages; art by various; lists of character origins and 1st apps. 4.00
...: Spider-Man 2005 - Profile pages of Spidey's friends and foes, emphasizing the recent 4.00
...: Wolverine 2004 - Profile pages; art by various; lists of character origins and 1st apps. 4.00
...: Teams 2005 - Profile pages of Avengers, X-Men and other teams 4.00
...: Women of Marvel 2005 - Profile pages; art by various; Greg Land-c 4.00
...: X-Men 2004 - Profile pages; art by various; lists of character origins and 1st apps. 4.00
...: X-Men 2005 - Profile pages; art by various; lists of character origins and 1st apps. 4.00
...: X-Men - The Age of Apocalypse 2005 - Profile pages of characters plus Exiles 4.00

OFFICIAL HANDBOOK OF THE MARVEL UNIVERSE A-Z UPDATE
Marvel Comics: Apr, 2010 - No. 5, 2010 ($3.99, limited series)

1-5-Profile pages; Andrasofszky-c 4.00

OFFICIAL HANDBOOK OF THE ULTIMATE MARVEL UNIVERSE, THE
Marvel Comics: 2005 ($3.99, one-shots)

... 2005: The Fantastic Four and Spider-Man - Profile pages; art by various 4.00
... The Ultimates and X-Men 2005 - Profile pages; art by various; Bagley-c 4.00

OFFICIAL HAWKMAN INDEX, THE
Independent Comics Group: Nov, 1986 - No. 2, Dec, 1986 ($2.00)

1,2 4.00

OFFICIAL INDEX TO THE MARVEL UNIVERSE (Also see "Avengers, Thor...")
Marvel Comics: 2009 - No. 14, April, 2010 ($3.99)

1-14-Each issue has chronological synopsies, creator credits, character lists for 40-50 issues of apps. for Iron Man, Spider-Man and the X-Men starting with 1st apps. in issue #1 4.00

OFFICIAL JUSTICE LEAGUE OF AMERICA INDEX, THE
Independent Comics Group (Eclipse): April, 1986 - No. 8, Mar, 1987 ($2.00, Baxter paper)

1-8: 1,2-Perez-c. 6.00

GD 2.0 | VG 4.0 | FN 6.0 | VF 8.0 | VF/NM 9.0 | NM- 9.2

OFFICIAL LEGION OF SUPER-HEROES INDEX, THE
Independent Comics Group (Eclipse): Dec, 1986 - No. 5, 1987 ($2.00, limited series) (No Official in Title #2 on)

1-5: 4-Mooney-c 6.00

OFFICIAL MARVEL INDEX TO MARVEL TEAM-UP
Marvel Comics Group: Jan, 1986 - No. 6, 1987 ($1.25, limited series)

1-6 4.00

OFFICIAL MARVEL INDEX TO THE AMAZING SPIDER-MAN
Marvel Comics Group: Apr, 1985 - No. 9, Dec, 1985 ($1.25, limited series)

1 ($1.00)-Byrne-c. 5.00
2-9: 5,6,8,9-Punisher-c. 4.00

OFFICIAL MARVEL INDEX TO THE AVENGERS, THE
Marvel Comics: Jun, 1987 - No. 7, Aug, 1988 ($2.95, limited series)

1-7 5.00

OFFICIAL MARVEL INDEX TO THE AVENGERS, THE
Marvel Comics: V2#1, Oct, 1994 - V2#6, 1995 ($1.95, limited series)

V2#1-#6 4.00

OFFICIAL MARVEL INDEX TO THE FANTASTIC FOUR
Marvel Comics Group: Dec, 1985 - No. 12, Jan, 1987 ($1.25, limited series)

1-12: 1-Byrne-c. 1,2-Kirby back-c (unpub. art) 4.00

OFFICIAL MARVEL INDEX TO THE X-MEN, THE
Marvel Comics: May, 1987 - No. 7, July, 1988 ($2.95, limited series)

1-7 5.00

OFFICIAL MARVEL INDEX TO THE X-MEN, THE
Marvel Comics: V2#1, Apr, 1994 - V2#5, 1994 ($1.95, limited series)

V2#1-5: 1-Covers X-Men #1-51. 2-Covers #52-122,Special #1,2,Giant-Size #1,2. 3-Byrne-c; covers #123-177, Annuals 3-7, Spec. Ed. #1. 4-Covers Uncanny X-Men #178-234, Annuals 8-12. 5-Covers #235-287, Annuals 13-15 4.00

OFFICIAL SOUPY SALES COMIC (See Soupy Sales)

OFFICIAL TEEN TITANS INDEX, THE
Indep. Comics Group (Eclipse): Aug, 1985 - No. 5, 1986 ($1.50, lim. series)

1-5 4.00

OFFICIAL TRUE CRIME CASES (Formerly Sub-Mariner #23; All-True Crime Cases #26 on)
Marvel Comics (OCI): No. 24, Fall, 1947 - No. 25, Winter, 1947-48

24(#1)-Burgos-a; Syd Shores-c 23 46 69 136 223 310
25-Syd Shores-c; Kurtzman's "Hey Look" 18 36 54 107 169 230

OF SUCH IS THE KINGDOM
George A. Pflaum: 1955 (15¢, 36 pgs.)

nn-Reprints from 1951 Treasure Chest 4 7 10 14 17 20

O.G. WHIZ (See Gold Key Spotlight #10)
Gold Key: 2/71 - No. 6, 5/72; No. 7, 5/78 - No. 11, 1/79 (No. 7: 52 pgs.)

1-John Stanley script 5 10 15 35 55 75
2-John Stanley script 4 8 12 24 37 50
3-6(1972) 3 6 9 18 27 35
7-11(1978-79)-Part-r: 9-Tubby issue 2 4 6 9 12 15

OH, BROTHER! (Teen Comedy)
Stanhall Publ.: Jan, 1953 - No. 5, Oct, 1953

1-By Bill Williams 9 18 27 52 69 85
2-5 7 14 21 35 43 50

OH MY GODDESS! (Manga)
Dark Horse Comics: Aug, 1994 - Present ($2.50-$3.99, B&W)

1-6-Kosuke Fujishima-s/a in all 3.00
... PART II 2/95 - No. 9, 9/95 ($2.50, B&W, lim.series) #1-9 3.00
... PART III 11/95 - No. 11, 9/96 ($2.95, B&W, lim. series) #1-11 3.00
... PART IV 12/96 - No. 8, 7/97 ($2.95, B&W, lim. series) #1-8 3.00
... PART V 9/97 - Np. 12, 8/98 ($2.95, B&W, lim. series)
1,2,5,8: 5-Ninja Master pt. 1 3.00
3,4,6,7,10-12-($3.95, 48 pgs.) 10-Fallen Angel. 11-Play The Game 4.00
9-($3.50) "It's Lonely At The Top" 3.50
... PART VI 10/98 - No. 5, 3/99 ($3.50/$2.95, B&W, lim. series)
1-($3.50) 3.50
2-6-($2.95)-6-Super Urd one-shot 3.00
... PART VII 5/99 - No. 8, 12/99 ($2.95, B&W, lim. series) #1-3 3.00
4-8-($3.50) 3.50
... PART VIII 1/00 - No. 6, 6/00 ($3.50, B&W, lim. series) #1-3,5,7 3.50

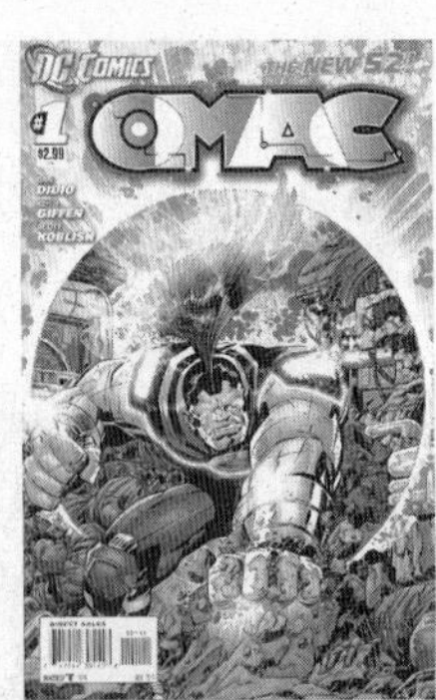

O.M.A.C. #1 © DC

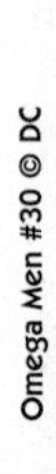
Omega Men #30 © DC

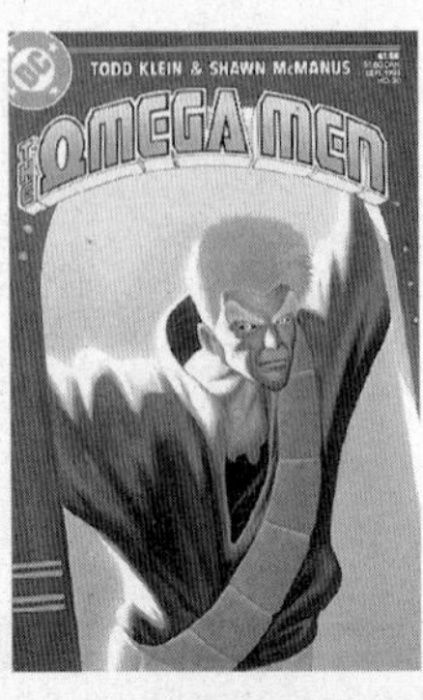

The Omen #1 © Chaos!

GD 2.0 | VG 4.0 | FN 6.0 | VF 8.0 | VF/NM 9.0 | NM- 9.2

4-($2.95) "Hail To The Chief" begins 3.00
... **PART IX** 7/00 - No. 7, 1/01 ($3.50/$2.99) #1-4: 3-Queen Sayoko 3.50
5-7-($2.99) 3.00
... **PART X** 2/01 - No. 5, 6/01 ($3.50) #1-5 3.50
... **PART XI** 10/01 - No. 10, 3/02 ($3.50) #1,2,7,8 3.50
3-6,9-($2.99) Mystery Child 3.00
10-($3.99) 4.00
(Series adapts new numbering) 88-90-($3.50) Learning to Love 3.50
91-94,96-103,105,107-110: 91-94 ($2.99) Traveler. 96-98-The Phantom Racer 3.00
95,104,106-($3.50) 95-Traveler pt. 5 3.50
111,112-($3.99) 4.00

OH SUSANNA (TV)
Dell Publishing Co.: No. 1105, June-Aug, 1960 (Gale Storm)
Four Color 1105-Toth-a, photo-c 10 20 30 70 133 195

OKAY COMICS
United Features Syndicate: July, 1940
1-Captain & the Kids & Hawkshaw the Detective reprints 45 90 135 279 465 650

O.K. COMICS
Hit Publications: May, 1940 (ashcan)
nn-Ashcan comic, not distributed to newsstands, only for in house use. A CGC certified 8.0 copy sold in 2003 for $1,000.

O.K. COMICS
United Features Syndicate/Hit Publications: July, 1940 - No. 2, Oct, 1940
1-Little Giant (w/super powers), Phantom Knight, Sunset Smith, & The Teller Twins begin 76 152 228 486 831 1175
2 (Rare)-Origin Mister Mist by Chas. Quinlan 77 154 231 493 847 1200

OKLAHOMA KID
Ajax/Farrell Publ.: June, 1957 - No. 4, 1958
1 11 22 33 60 83 105
2-4 7 14 21 37 46 55

OKLAHOMAN, THE
Dell Publishing Co.: No. 820, July, 1957
Four Color 820-Movie, photo-c 8 16 24 56 96 135

OKTANE
Dark Horse Comics: Aug, 1995 - Nov, 1995 ($2.50, color, limited series)
1-4-Gene Ha-a 3.00

OKTOBERFEST COMICS
Now & Then Publ.: Fall 1976 (75¢, Canadian, B&W, one-shot)
1-Dave Sim-s/a; Gene Day-a; 1st app. Uncle Hans & Natter P. Bombast; The Beavers sty; 1st Cap'n Riverrat, Sim-s/Day-a 3 6 9 16 23 30

OLD GLORY COMICS
DC Comics: 1941
nn - Ashcan comic, not distributed to newsstands, only for in-house use. Cover art is Flash Comics #12 with interior being Action Comics #37 (no known sales)

OLD IRONSIDES (Disney)
Dell Publishing Co.: No. 874, Jan, 1958
Four Color 874-Movie w/Johnny Tremain 6 12 18 42 69 95

OLD YELLER (Disney, see Movie Comics, and Walt Disney Showcase #25)
Dell Publishing Co.: No. 869, Jan, 1958
Four Color 869-Movie, photo-c 5 10 15 35 55 75

OMAC (One Man Army; ...Corps. #4 on; also see Kamandi #59 & Warlord)
(See Cancelled Comic Cavalcade)
National Periodical Publications: Sept-Oct, 1974 - No. 8, Nov-Dec, 1975
1-Origin 6 12 18 37 59 80
2-8: 8-2 pg. Neal Adams ad 3 6 9 18 27 35
Jack Kirby's Omac: One Man Army Corps HC (2008, $24.99, d.j.) r/#1-8; Evanier intro. 25.00
NOTE: *Kirby a-1-8p; c-1-7p. Kubert c-8.*

OMAC (See DCU Brave New World)
DC Comics: Sept, 2006 - No. 8, Apr, 2007 ($2.99, limited series)
1-8: 1-Bruce Jones-s/Renato Guedes-a. 1-3-Firestorm & Cyborg app. 8-Superman app. 3.00

O.M.A.C. (DC New 52)
DC Comics: Nov, 2011 - No. 8, Jun, 2012 ($2.99)
1-8: 1-DiDio-s/Giffen-a/c; Dubbilex and Brother Eye app. 2-Max Lord & Sarge Steel app. 5-Crossover with Frankenstein, Agent of SHADE #5. 6-Kolins-a 3.00

OMAC: ONE MAN ARMY CORPS
DC Comics: 1991 - No. 4, 1991 ($3.95, B&W, mini-series, mature, 52 pgs.)
Book One - Four: John Byrne-c/a & scripts 4.00

OMAC PROJECT, THE
DC Comics: June, 2005 - No. 6, Nov, 2005 ($2.50, limited series)
1-6-Prelude to Infinite Crisis x-over; Rucka-s/Saiz-a 3.00
...: Infinite Crisis Special 1 (5/06, $4.99) Rucka-s/Saiz-a; follows destruction of satellite 5.00
TPB (2005, $14.99) r/#1-6, Countdown to Infinite Crisis, Wonder Woman #219 15.00

O'MALLEY AND THE ALLEY CATS
Gold Key: April, 1971 - No. 9, Jan, 1974 (Disney)
1 3 6 9 16 23 30
2-9 2 4 6 9 13 16

OMEGA ELITE
Blackthorne Publishing: 1987 ($1.25)
1-Starlin-c 3.00

OMEGA FLIGHT
Marvel Comics: Jun, 2007 - No. 5, Oct, 2007 ($2.99, limited series)
1-Oeming-s/Kolins-a; Wrecking Crew app. 4.00
1-Second printing with Sasquatch variant-c 3.00
2-5: 5-Beta Ray Bill app. 3.00
...: Alpha to Omega TPB ('07, $13.99) r/#1-5, USAgent story/Civil War: Choosing Sides 14.00

OMEGA MEN, THE (See Green Lantern #141)
DC Comics: Dec, 1982 - No. 38, May, 1986 ($1.00/$1.25/$1.50; Baxter paper)
1,20: 20-2nd full Lobo story 4.00
2,4-9,11-19,21-25,28-30,32,33,36,38: 2-Origin Broot. 5,9-2nd & 3rd app. Lobo (cameo, 2 pgs. each). 7-Origin The Citadel. 19-Lobo cameo. 30-Intro new Primus 3.00
3-1st app. Lobo (5 pgs.)(6/83); Lobo-c 1 2 3 4 5 7
10-1st full Lobo story 5.00
26,27,31,34,35: 26,27-Alan Moore scripts. 31-Crisis x-over. 34,35-Teen Titans x-over 4.00
37-1st solo Lobo story (8 pg. back-up by Giffen) 4.00
Annual 1(11/84, 52 pgs.), 2(11/85) 4.00
NOTE: *Giffen c/a-1-6p. Morrow a-24r. Nino c/a-16, 21; a-Annual 1i.*

OMEGA MEN, THE
DC Comics: Dec, 2006 - No. 6, May, 2007 ($2.99, limited series)
1-6: 1-Superman, Wonder Girl, Green Lantern app.; Flint-a/Gabrych-s 3.00

OMEGA THE UNKNOWN
Marvel Comics Group: March, 1976 - No. 10, Oct, 1977
1-1st app. Omega 2 4 6 11 16 20
2,3-(Regular 25¢ editions). 2-Hulk-c/story. 3-Electro-c/story. 2 3 4 6 8 10
2,3-(30¢-c variants, limited distribution) 3 6 9 18 27 35
4-10: 8-1st brief app. 2nd Foolkiller (Greg Salinger), 1 panel only. 9,10-(Reg. 30¢ editions). 9-1st full app. 2nd Foolkiller 1 2 3 5 6 8
9,10-(35¢-c variants, limited distribution) 4 8 12 22 34 45
... Classic TPB (2005, $29.99) r/#1-10 30.00
NOTE: *Kane c(p)-3, 5, 8, 9. Mooney a-1-3, 4p, 5, 6p, 7, 8i, 9, 10.*

OMEGA: THE UNKNOWN
Marvel Comics: Dec, 2007 - No. 10, Sept, 2008 ($2.99, limited series)
1-10-Jonathan Lethem-s/Farel Dalrymple-a 3.00

OMEN
Northstar Publishing: 1989 - No. 3, 1989 ($2.00, B&W, mature)
1-Tim Vigil-c/a in all 1 2 3 5 7 9
1, (2nd printing) 3.00
2,3 6.00

OMEN, THE
Chaos! Comics: May, 1998 - No. 5, Sept, 1998 ($2.95, limited series)
1-5: 1-Six covers, ...: Vexed (10/98, $2.95) Chaos! characters appear 3.00

OMNI MEN
Blackthorne Publishing: 1987 - No. 3, 1987 ($1.25)
1-3 3.00
Graphic Novel (1989, $3.50) 4.00

ONE, THE
Marvel Comics (Epic Comics): July, 1985 - No. 6, Feb, 1986 (Limited series, mature)
1-6: Post nuclear holocaust super-hero. 2-Intro The Other 3.00

ONE-ARM SWORDSMAN, THE
Victory Prod./Lueng's Publ. #4 on: 1987 - No. 12, 1990 ($2.75/$1.80, 52 pgs.)

100 Bullets #28 © Azzarello & Risso & DC

One Plus One #3 © Shaffer & Krall

Oni Double Feature #6 © Oni Press

GD 2.0 | VG 4.0 | FN 6.0 | VF 8.0 | VF/NM 9.0 | NM- 9.2

1-3 ($2.75) 4.00
4-12: 4-6-$1.80-c. 7-12-$2.00-c 4.00

ONE HUNDRED AND ONE DALMATIANS (Disney, see Cartoon Tales, Movie Comics, and Walt Disney Showcase #9, 51)
Dell Publishing Co.: No. 1183, Mar, 1961
Four Color 1183-Movie 10 20 30 65 118 170

101 DALMATIONS (Movie)
Disney Comics: 1991 (52 pgs., graphic novel)
nn-($4.95, direct sales)-r/movie adaptation & more 5.00
1-($2.95, newsstand edition) 3.00

101 WAYS TO END THE CLONE SAGA (See Spider-Man)
Marvel Comics: Jan, 1997 ($2.50, one-shot)
1 3.00

100 BULLETS
DC Comics (Vertigo): Aug, 1999 - No. 100, Jun, 2009 ($2.50/$2.75/$2.99)
1-Azzarello-s/Risso-a/Dave Johnson-c 4.00
2-5 3.00
6-49,51-61: 26-Series summary; art by various. 45-Preview of Losers 3.00
50-($3.50) History of the Trust 4.00
62-71: 62-Begin $2.75-c. 64-Preview of Loveless 3.00
72-99: 72-Begin $2.99-c 3.00
100-($4.99) Final issue 5.00
...#1/Crime Line Sampler Flip-Book (9/09, $1.00) r/#1 with previews of upcoming GNs 3.00
...: A Foregone Tomorrow TPB (2002, $17.95) r/#20-30 18.00
...: Decayed TPB (2006, $14.99) r/#68-75; Darwyn Cooke intro. 15.00
...: First Shot, Last Call TPB (2000, $9.95) r/#1-5, Vertigo Winter's Edge #3 10.00
...: Hang Up on the Hang Low TPB (2001, $9.95) r/#15-19; Jim Lee intro. 10.00
...: Once Upon a Crime TPB (2007, $12.99) r/#76-83 13.00
...: Samurai TPB (2003, $12.95) r/#43-49 13.00
...: Six Feet Under the Gun TPB (2003, $12.95) r/#37-42 13.00
...: Split Second Chance TPB (2001, $14.95) r/#6-14 15.00
...: Strychnine Lives TPB (2006, $14.99) r/#59-67; Manuel Ramos intro. 15.00
...: The Counterfifth Detective TPB (2003, $12.95) r/#31-36 13.00
...: The Hard Way TPB (2005, $14.99) r/#50-58 15.00
...: Wilt TPB (2009, $19.99) r/#89-100; Azzarello intro. 20.00

100 GREATEST MARVELS OF ALL TIME
Marvel Comics: Dec, 2001 ($7.50/$3.50, limited series)
1-5-Reprints top #6-#25 stories voted by poll for Marvel's 40th ann. 7.50
6-($3.50) (#5 on-c) Reprints X-Men (2nd series) #1 4.00
7-($3.50) (#4 on-c) Reprints Giant-Size X-Men #1 4.00
8-($3.50) (#3 on-c) Reprints (Uncanny) X-Men #137 (Death of Jean Grey) 4.00
9-($3.50) (#2 on-c) Reprints Fantastic Four #1 4.00
10-($3.50) (#1 on-c) Reprints Amazing Fantasy #15 (1st app. Spider-Man) 4.00

100 PAGES OF COMICS
Dell Publishing Co.: 1937 (Stiff covers, square binding)
101(Found on back cover)-Alley Oop, Wash Tubbs, Capt. Easy, Og Son of Fire, Apple Mary, Tom Mix, Dan Dunn, Tailspin Tommy, Doctor Doom 148 296 444 947 1624 2300

100 PAGE SUPER SPECTACULAR (See DC 100 Page Super Spectacular)

100%
DC Comics (Vertigo): Aug, 2002 - No. 5, July, 2003 ($5.95, B&W, limited series)
1-5-Paul Pope-s/a 6.00
HC (2009, $39.99, dustjacket) r/#1-5; sketch pages and background info 40.00
TPB (2005, $24.99) r/#1-5; sketch pages and background info 25.00
TPB (2009, $29.99) r/#1-5; sketch pages and background info 30.00

100% TRUE?
DC Comics (Paradox Press): Summer 1996 - No. 2 ($4.95, B&W)
1,2-Reprints stories from various Paradox Press books. 5.00

$1,000,000 DUCK (See Walt Disney Showcase #5)

ONE MILLION YEARS AGO (Tor #2 on)
St. John Publishing Co.: Sept, 1953
1-Origin & 1st app. Tor; Kubert-c/a; Kubert photo inside front cover 19 38 57 109 172 235

ONE MONTH TO LIVE ("Heroic Age: ..." in indicia)
Marvel Comics: Nov, 2010 - No. 5, Nov, 2010 ($2.99, weekly limited series)
1-5-Remender-s; Spider-Man and the Fantastic Four app. 3.00

ONE PLUS ONE
Oni Press: Sept, 2002 - No. 5, March, 2003 ($2.95, B&W, limited series)
1-5-Shaffer-s/Krall-a 3.00
TPB (9/03, $14.95, digest-size) r/#1-5 & story from Oni Press Color Special 2002 15.00

ONE SHOT (See Four Color...)

1001 HOURS OF FUN
Dell Publishing Co.: No. 13, 1943
Large Feature Comic 13 (nn)-Puzzles & games; by A.W. Nugent. This book was bound as #13 w/Large Feature Comics in publisher's files 29 58 87 170 278 385

ONE TRICK RIP OFF, THE (See Dark Horse Presents)

ONI (Adaption of video game)
Dark Horse Comics: Feb, 2001 - No. 3, Apr, 2001 ($2.99, limited series)
1-3-Sunny Lee-a(p) 3.00

ONI DOUBLE FEATURE (See Clerks: The Comic Book and Jay & Silent Bob)
Oni Press: Jan, 1998 - No. 13, Sept, 1999 ($2.95, B&W)
1-Jay & Silent Bob; Kevin Smith-s/Matt Wagner-a 1 3 4 6 8 10
1-2nd printing 3.00
2-11,13: 2,3-Paul Pope-s/a. 3,4-Nixey-s/a. 4,5-Sienkewicz-s/a. 6,7-Gaiman-s. 9-Bagge-c. 13-All Paul Dini-s; Jingle Belle 3.00
12-Jay & Silent Bob as Bluntman & Chronic; Smith-s/Allred-a 5.00

ONI PRESS COLOR SPECIAL
Oni Press: Jun, 2001; Jul, 2002 ($5.95, annual)
...2001-Oeming "Who Killed Madman?" cover; stories & art by various 6.00
...2002-Allred wraparound-c; stories & art by various 6.00

ONSLAUGHT: EPILOGUE
Marvel Comics: Feb, 1997 ($2.95, one-shot)
1-Hama-s/Green-a; Xavier-c; Bastion-app. 3.00

ONSLAUGHT: MARVEL
Marvel Comics: Oct, 1996 ($3.95, one-shot)
1-Conclusion to Onslaught x-over; wraparound-c 1 2 3 4 5 7

ONSLAUGHT REBORN
Marvel Comics: Jan, 2007 - No. 5, Feb, 2008 ($2.99, limited series)
1-5-Loeb-s/Liefeld-a; female Bucky app. 2-Variant-c by Joe Madureira. 3-McGuiness var-c. 4-Campbell var-c. 5-Bianchi var-c; female Bucky goes to regular Marvel Universe 3.00
1-Variant-c by Michael Turner 4.00
HC (2008, $19.99) r/#1-5; sketch pages; foreword by Liefeld 20.00

ONSLAUGHT UNLEASHED
Marvel Comics: Apr, 2011 - No. 4, Jul, 2011 ($3.99, limited series)
1-4-McKeever-s/Andrade-a/Ramos-c; Secret Avengers & Young Allies app. 4.00

ONSLAUGHT: X-MEN
Marvel Comics: Aug, 1996 ($3.95, one-shot)
1-Waid & Lobdell script; Fantastic Four & Avengers app.; Xavier as Onslaught 5.00
1-Variant-c 2 4 6 8 10 12

ON STAGE
Dell Publishing Co.: No. 1336, Apr-June, 1962
Four Color 1336-Not by Leonard Starr 5 10 15 30 48 65

ON THE DOUBLE (Movie)
Dell Publishing Co.: No. 1232, Sept-Nov, 1961
Four Color 1232 5 10 15 30 48 65

ON THE ROAD TO PERDITION (Movie)
DC Comics (Paradox Press): 2003 - Book 3, 2004 ($7.95, 8"x5 1/2", B&W, limited series)
...: Oasis, Book 1-Max Allan Collins-s/José Luis García-López-a/David Beck-c 8.00
...: Sanctuary, Book 2-Max Allan Collins-s/Steve Lieber-a/José Luis García-López-c 8.00
...: Detour, Book 3-Max Allan Collins-s/José Luis García-López-a/Steve Lieber-c/a(i) 8.00
Road to Perdition 2: On the Road (2004, $14.95) r/series; Collins intro. 15.00

ON THE ROAD WITH ANDRAE CROUCH
Spire Christian Comics (Fleming H. Revell): 1973, 1974 (39¢)
nn-1973 Edition 2 4 6 11 16 20
nn-1974 Edition 2 4 6 8 11 14

ON THE SCENE PRESENTS:...
Warren Publishing Co.: Oct, 1966 - No. 2, 1967 (B&W magazine, two #1 issues)
#1 "Super Heroes" (68 pgs.) Batman 1966 movie photo-c/s; has articles/photos/comic art from serials on Superman, Flash Gordon, Capt. America, Capt. Marvel and The Phantom 5 10 15 30 48 65
#1 "Freak Out, USA" (Fall/1966, 60 pgs.) (lower print run) articles on musicians like Zappa,

Operation Peril #11 © ACG

Orchid #1 © Tom Morello

Original Ghost Rider #12 © MAR

GD VG FN VF VF/NM NM-
2.0 4.0 6.0 8.0 9.0 9.2

Jefferson Airplane, Supremes 5 10 15 32 51 70
#2 "Freak Out, USA" (2/67, 52 pgs.) Beatles, Country Joe, Doors/Jim Morrison, Bee Gees
5 10 15 32 51 70

ON THE SPOT (Pretty Boy Floyd...)
Fawcett Publications: Fall, 1948
nn-Pretty Boy Floyd photo on-c; bondage-c 34 68 102 199 325 450

ONYX OVERLORD
Marvel Comics (Epic): Oct, 1992 - No. 4, Jan, 1993 ($2.75, mini-series)
1-4: Moebius scripts 3.00

OPEN SPACE
Marvel Comics: Mid-Dec, 1989 - No. 4, Aug, 1990 ($4.95, bi-monthly, 68 pgs.)
1-4: 1-Bill Wray-a; Freas-c 5.00
0-(1999) Wizard supplement; unpubl. early Alex Ross-a; new Ross-c 3.00

OPERATION BIKINI (See Movie Classics)

OPERATION: BROKEN WINGS, 1936
BOOM! Studios: Nov, 2011 - No. 3, Jan, 2012 ($3.99, limited series)
1-3-Hanna-s/Hairsine-a; English translation of French comic 4.00

OPERATION BUCHAREST (See The Crusaders)

OPERATION CROSSBOW (See Movie Classics)

OPERATION: KNIGHTSTRIKE (See Knightstrike)
Image Comics (Extreme Studios): May, 1995 - No.3, July, 1995 ($2.50)
1-3 3.00

OPERATION PERIL
American Comics Group (Michel Publ.): Oct-Nov, 1950 - No. 16, Apr-May, 1953 (#1-5: 52 pgs.)
1-Time Travelers, Danny Danger (by Leonard Starr) & Typhoon Tyler
(by Ogden Whitney) begin 40 80 120 242 401 560
2-War-c 23 46 69 136 223 310
3-War-c; horror story 21 42 63 126 206 285
4,5-Sci/fi-c/story 23 46 69 136 223 310
6-10: 6,8,9,10-Sci/fi-c. 6-Tank vs. T-Rex-c. 7-Sabretooth-c
21 42 63 122 199 275
11,12-War-c; last Time Travelers 14 28 42 80 115 150
13-16: All war format 10 20 30 56 76 95
NOTE: ***Starr** a-2, 5. **Whitney** a-1, 2, 5-10, 12; c-1, 3, 5, 8, 9.*

OPERATION: STORMBREAKER
Acclaim Comics (Valiant Heroes): Aug, 1997 ($3.95, one-shot)
1-Waid/Augustyn-s, Braithwaite-a 4.00

OPTIC NERVE
Drawn and Quarterly: Apr, 1995 - Present ($2.95-$3.95, bi-annual)
1-7: Adrian Tomine-c/a/scripts in all 3.00
8-11: 8-($3.50). 9-11-($3.95) 4.00
12-($5.95) Half front-c; Amber Sweet story 6.00
32 Stories-($9.95, trade paperback)-r/Optic Nerve mini-comics 10.00
32 Stories-($29.95, hardcover)-r/Optic Nerve mini-comics; signed & numbered 30.00

ORACLE: THE CURE
DC Comics: May, 2009 - No. 3, Jul, 2009 ($2.99, limited series)
1-3-Guillem March-c; Calculator app. 3.00
TPB (2010, $17.99) r/#1-3 and Birds of Prey #126,127 18.00

ORAL ROBERTS' TRUE STORIES (Junior Partners #120 on)
TelePix Publ. (Oral Roberts' Evangelistic Assoc./Healing Waters): 1956 (no month) - No. 119, 7/59 (15¢)(No. 102: 25¢)
V1#1(1956)-(Not code approved)- "The Miracle Touch"
19 38 57 109 172 235
102-(Only issue approved by code, 10/56) "Now I See"
13 26 39 74 105 135
103-119: 115-(114 on inside) 10 20 30 54 72 90
NOTE: *Also see Happiness & Healing For You.*

ORANGE BIRD, THE
Walt Disney Educational Media Co.: No date (1980) (36 pgs.; in color; slick cover)
nn-Included with educational kit on foods, ...in Nutrition Adventures nn (1980)
...and the Nutrition Know-How Revue nn (1983) 3.00

ORB (Magazine)
Orb Publishing: 1974 - No. 6, Mar/Apr 1976 (B&W/color)
1-1st app. Northern Light & Kadaver, both series begin
5 10 15 32 51 70
2,3 (72 pgs.) 3 6 9 16 23 30
4-6 (60 pgs.): 4,5-origin Northern Light 2 4 6 10 14 18
NOTE: ***Allison** a-1-3. **Gene Day** a-1-6. **P. Hsu** a-4-6. **Steacy** s/a-3,4.*

GD VG FN VF VF/NM NM-
2.0 4.0 6.0 8.0 9.0 9.2

ORBIT
Eclipse Books: 1990 - No. 3, 1990 ($4.95, 52 pgs., squarebound)
1-3: Reprints from Isaac Asimov's Science Fiction Magazine; 1-Dave Stevens-c, Bolton-a.
3-Bolton-c/a, Yeates-a 5.00

ORBITER
DC Comics (Vertigo): 2003 ($24.95, hardcover with dust jacket)
HC-Warren Ellis-s/Colleen Doran-a 25.00
SC-(2004, $17.95) Warren Ellis-s/Colleen Doran-a 18.00

ORCHID
Dark Horse Comics: Oct, 2011 - Present ($1.00/$3.50)
1-Tom Morello-s/Scott Hepburn-a; covers by Carnevale & Fairey 3.00
2-5-($3.50) Carnevale-c 3.50

ORDER, THE (cont'd from Defenders V2#12)
Marvel Comics: Apr, 2002 - No. 6, Sept, 2002 ($2.25, limited series)
1-6: 1-Haley-a/Duffy & Busiek-s. 3-Avengers-c/app. 4-Jurgens-a 3.00

ORDER, THE (The Initiative following Civil War)
Marvel Comics: Sept, 2007 - No. 10, Jun, 2008 ($2.99)
1-10-California's Initiative team; Fraction-s/Kitson-a/c 3.00
... Vol. 1: The Next Right Thing TPB (2008, $14.99) r/#1-7 15.00

ORIENTAL HEROES
Jademan Comics: Aug, 1988 - No. 55, Feb, 1993 ($1.50/$1.95, 68 pgs.)
1,55 5.00
2-54 4.00

ORIGINAL ADVENTURES OF CHOLLY & FLYTRAP, THE
Image Comics: Feb, 2006 - No. 2, June, 2006 ($5.99, limited series)
1,2-Arthur Suydam-s/a; interview with Suydam and art pages 6.00

ORIGINAL ASTRO BOY, THE
Now Comics: Sept, 1987 - No. 20, Jun, 1989 ($1.50/$1.75)
1-20-All have Ken Steacy painted-c/a 3.00

ORIGINAL BLACK CAT, THE
Recollections: Oct. 6, 1988 - No. 9, 1992 ($2.00, limited series)
1-9: Elias-r; 1-Bondage-c. 2-Murphy Anderson-c 4.00

ORIGINAL DICK TRACY, THE
Gladstone Publishing: Sept, 1990 - No. 5, 1991 ($1.95, bi-monthly, 68pgs.)
1-5: 1-Vs. Pruneface. 2-& the Evil influence; begin $2.00-c 4.00
NOTE: *#1 reprints strips 7/16/43 - 9/30/43. #2 reprints strips 12/1/46 - 2/2/47. #3 reprints 8/31/46 - 11/14/46. #4 reprints 9/17/45 - 12/23/45. #5 reprints 6/10/46 - 8/28/46.*

ORIGINAL DOCTOR SOLAR, MAN OF THE ATOM, THE
Valiant: Apr, 1995 ($2.95, one-shot)
1-Reprints Doctor Solar, Man of the Atom #1,5; Bob Fugitani-r; Paul Smith-c;
afterword by Seaborn Adamson 4.00

ORIGINAL E-MAN AND MICHAEL MAUSER, THE
First Comics: Oct, 1985 - No. 7, April, 1986 ($1.75/$2.00, Baxter paper)
1-6: 1-Has r-/Charlton's E-Man, Vengeance Squad. 2-Shows #4 in indicia by mistake 3.00
7-($2.00, 44 pgs.)-Staton-a 4.00

ORIGINAL GHOST RIDER, THE
Marvel Comics: July, 1992 - No. 20, Feb, 1994 ($1.75)
1-20: 1-7-r/Marvel Spotlight #5-11 by Ploog w/new-c. 3-New Phantom Rider (former Night Rider) back-ups begin by Ayers. 4-Quesada-c(p). 8-Ploog-c. 8,9-r/Ghost Rider #1,2. 10-r/Marvel Spotlight #12. 11-18,20-r/Ghost Rider #3-12. 19-r/Marvel Two-in-One #8 3.00

ORIGINAL GHOST RIDER RIDES AGAIN, THE
Marvel Comics: July, 1991 - No. 7, Jan, 1992, ($1.50, limited series, 52 pgs.)
1-7: 1-r/Ghost Rider #68(origin),69 w/covers. 2-7: R/ G.R. #70-81 w/covers 4.00

ORIGINAL MAGNUS ROBOT FIGHTER, THE
Valiant: Apr, 1995 ($2.95, one-shot)
1-Reprints Magnus, Robot Fighter 4000 #2; Russ Manning-r; Rick Leonardi-c;
afterword by Seaborn Adamson 4.00

ORIGINAL NEXUS GRAPHIC NOVEL (See First Comics Graphic Novel #19)

ORIGINALS, THE
DC Comics (Vertigo): 2004 ($24.95/$17.99, B&W graphic novel)
HC (2004, $24.95) Dave Gibbons-s/a 25.00

Orion #25 © DC

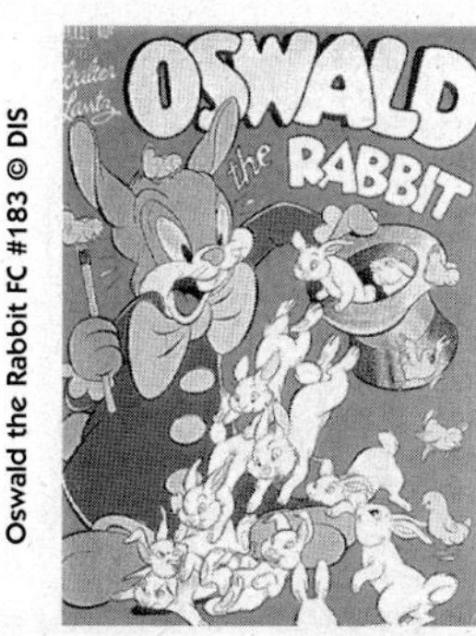

Oswald the Rabbit FC #183 © DIS

Our Army at War #138 © DC

GD 2.0 | VG 4.0 | FN 6.0 | VF 8.0 | VF/NM 9.0 | NM- 9.2

SC (2005, $17.99) 18.00

ORIGINAL SHIELD, THE
Archie Enterprises, Inc.: Apr, 1984 - No. 4, Oct, 1984
1-4: 1,2-Origin Shield; Ayers p-1-4, Nebres c-1,2 4.00

ORIGINAL SWAMP THING SAGA, THE (See DC Special Series #2, 14, 17, 20)

ORIGINAL TUROK, SON OF STONE, THE
Valiant: Apr, 1995 - No. 2, May, 1995 ($2.95, limited series)
1,2: 1-Reprints Turok, Son of Stone #24,25,42; Alberto Gioletti-r; Rags Morales-c; afterword by Seaborn Adamson. 2-Reprints Turok, Son of Stone #24,33; Gioletti-r; McKone-c 4.00

ORIGIN OF GALACTUS (See Fantastic Four #48-50)
Marvel Comics: Feb, 1996 ($2.50, one-shot)
1-Lee & Kirby reprints w/pin-ups 4.00

ORIGIN OF THE DEFIANT UNIVERSE, THE
Defiant Comics: Feb, 1994 ($1.50, 20 pgs., one-shot)
1-David Lapham, Adam Pollina & Alan Weiss-a; Weiss-c 5.00
NOTE: *The comic was originally published as Defiant Genesis and was distributed at the 1994 Philadelphia ComicCon.*

ORIGINS OF MARVEL COMICS (Also see Fireside Book Series)
Marvel Comics: July, 2010 ($3.99, one-shot)
1-Single page origins of prominent Marvel characters; text and art by various 4.00
...: X-Men (11/10, $3.99) single page origins of X-Men and other mutants; s/a-various 4.00

ORION (Manga)
Dark Horse Comics: Sept, 1992 - No. 6, July, 1993 ($2.95/$3.95, B&W, bimonthly, lim. series)
1-6:1,2,6-Squarebound): 1-Masamune Shirow-c/a/s in all 4.00

ORION (See New Gods)
DC Comics: June, 2000 - No. 25, June, 2002 ($2.50)
1-14-Simonson-s/a. 3-Back-up story w/Miller-a. 4-Gibbons-a back-up. 7-Chaykin back-up. 8-Loeb/Liefeld back-up. 10-A. Adams back-up-a 12-Jim Lee back-up-a. 13-JLA-c/app.; Byrne-a 3.00
15-($3.95) Black Racer app.; back-up story w/J.P. Leon-a 4.00
16-24-Simonson-s/a: 19-Joker: Last Laugh x-over 3.00
25-($3.95) Last issue; Mister Miracle-c/app. 4.00
The Gates of Apocalypse (2001, $12.95, TPB) r/#1-5 & various short-s 13.00

ORORO: BEFORE THE STORM (Storm from X-Men)
Marvel Comics: Aug, 2005 - No. 4, Nov, 2005 ($2.99, limited series)
1-4-Barberi-a/Sumerak-s; young Storm in Egypt 3.00
... Digest (2006, $6.99) r/#1-4 7.00

OSBORN (Green Goblin)
Marvel Comics: Jan, 2011 - No. 5, Jun, 2011 ($3.99, limited series)
1-5-Deconnick-s/Rios-a/Oliver-c 4.00

OSBORN JOURNALS (See Spider-Man titles)
Marvel Comics: Feb, 1997 ($2.95, one-shot)
1-Hotz-c/a 3.00

OSCAR COMICS (Formerly Funny Tunes; Awful...#11 & 12) (Also see Cindy Comics)
Marvel Comics: No. 24, Spring, 1947 - No. 10, Apr, 1949; No. 13, Oct, 1949
24(#1, Spring, 1947) 19 38 57 111 176 240
25(#2, Sum, 1947)-Wolverton-a plus Kurtzman's "Hey Look" 20 40 60 117 189 260
26(#3)-Same as regular #3 except #26 was printed over in black ink with #3 appearing on-c below the over print 14 28 42 78 112 145
3-9,13: 8-Margie app. 14 28 42 78 112 145
10-Kurtzman's "Hey Look" 15 30 45 83 124 165

OSWALD THE RABBIT (Also see New Fun Comics #1)
Dell Publishing Co.: No. 21, 1943 - No. 1268, 12-2/61-62 (Walter Lantz)
Four Color 21(1943) 39 78 117 293 634 975
Four Color 39(1943) 26 52 78 182 391 600
Four Color 67(1944) 15 30 45 102 221 340
Four Color 102(1946)-Kelly-a, 1 pg. 13 26 39 85 180 275
Four Color 143,183 9 18 27 61 106 150
Four Color 225,273 7 14 21 44 72 100
Four Color 315,388 6 12 18 39 62 85
Four Color 458,507,549,593 5 10 15 32 51 70
Four Color 623,697,792,894,979,1268 4 8 12 28 44 60

OSWALD THE RABBIT (See The Funnies, March of Comics #7, 38, 53, 67, 81, 95, 111, 126, 141, 156, 171, 186, New Funnies & Super Book #8, 20)

OTHER SIDE, THE
DC Comics (Vertigo): Dec, 2006 - No. 5, Apr, 2007 ($2.99, limited series)
1-5-Soldiers from both sides of the Vietnam War; Aaron-s/Stewart-a/c 3.00
TPB (2007, $12.99) r/#1-5; sketch pages, Stewart's travelogue to Saigon 13.00

OTHERWORLD
DC Comics (Vertigo): May, 2005 - No. 7, Nov, 2005 ($2.99)
1-7-Phil Jimenez-s/a(p) 3.00
...: Book One TPB (2006, $19.99) r/#1-7; cover gallery 20.00

OUR ARMY AT WAR (Becomes Sgt. Rock #302 on; also see Army At War)
National Periodical Publications: Aug, 1952 - No. 301, Feb, 1977
1 189 378 567 1588 3444 5300
2 82 164 246 664 1432 2200
3,4: 4-Krigstein-a 61 122 183 494 1072 1650
5-7 47 94 141 381 828 1275
8-11,14-Krigstein-a 46 92 138 359 780 1200
12,15-20 41 82 123 308 667 1025
13-Krigstein-c/a; flag-c 46 92 138 373 812 1250
21-31: Last precode (2/55) 29 58 87 210 448 685
32-40 25 50 75 175 375 575
41-60: 51-1st S.A. issue. 60-Grey tone-c 22 44 66 154 327 500
61-70: 61-(8/57) Pre-Sgt. Rock Easy Co.-c/s. 67-Minor Sgt. Rock prototype 20 40 60 137 294 450
71-80 17 34 51 119 260 400
81-(4/59) "The Rock of Easy" - Sgt. Rock prototype. Part of lead-up trio to 1st definitive Sgt. Rock. Story features a character named "Sgt. Rocky" as a "4th grade rate" sergeant (three stripes/chevrons) who is referred to as "The Rock of Easy". Editor also promises more stories of "...Rock-like Sergeant". Andru & Esposito-a/Haney-s 275 550 825 2310 5005 7700
82-(5/59) "Hold up Easy"- 1st app. of a Sgt. Rock. Part of lead-up trio to 1st definitive Sgt. Rock. Character named Sgt. Rock appears in a supporting "motivator" role as a "4th grade rate" sergeant (three stripes/chevrons) in six panels in six page story; Haney-s/Drucker-a 89 178 267 721 1561 2400
83-(6/59) "The Rock and Wall" - 1st true appearance of Sgt. Rock. Sgt. Rock finally introduced as a Master Sergeant (three chevrons and three rockers) and is main character of story. 1st specific narration that defines the "Rock of Easy" as Sgt. Rock. 1st actual "Sgt. Rock" collaboration between creators Robert Kanigher and Joe Kubert 328 656 984 2850 6175 9500
84-(7/59) "Laughter on Snakehead Hill" - 2nd appearance of Sgt. Rock. Story advances true Sgt. Rock continuity in 13-page title story featuring Sgt. Rock and Easy Co.; Kanigher-s/Novick-a/Kubert-c 50 100 150 405 878 1350
85-Origin & 1st app. Ice Cream Soldier 53 106 159 429 927 1425
86,87-Early Sgt. Rock; Kubert-a 44 88 132 330 715 1100
88-1st Sgt. Rock-c; Kubert-c/a 56 112 168 454 977 1500
89-"No Shot From Easy!" story; Heath-c 38 76 114 285 618 950
90-Kubert-c/a; How Rock got his stripes 52 104 156 421 911 1400
91-All-Sgt. Rock issue; Grandenetti-c/Kubert-a 100 200 300 810 1755 2700
92,94,96-99: 97-Regular Kubert-c begin 27 54 81 196 423 650
93-1st Zack Nolan 29 58 87 210 455 700
95,100: 95-1st app. Bulldozer 30 60 90 218 472 725
101,105,108,113,114: 101-1st app. Buster. 105-1st app. Junior. 113-1st app. Wildman & Jackie Johnson 21 42 63 148 317 485
102-104,106,107,109,110,114,116-120: 104-Nurse Jane-c/s. 109-Pre Easy Co. Sgt. Rock-s. 118-Sunny injured 19 38 57 132 284 435
111-1st app. Wee Willie & Sunny 27 54 81 189 407 625
112-Classic Easy Co. roster-c 35 70 105 254 552 850
115-Rock revealed as orphan; 1st x-over Mlle. Marie. 1st Sgt. Rock's battle family 26 52 78 182 391 600
121-125 14 28 42 97 211 325
126-1st app. Canary; grey tone-c 20 40 60 137 294 450
127-2nd all-Sgt. Rock issue; 1st app. Little Sure Shot 23 46 69 161 343 525
128-Training & origin Sgt. Rock; 1st Sgt. Krupp 36 72 108 270 585 900
129-139: 138-1st Sparrow. 141-1st Shaker 13 26 39 90 195 300
140-3rd all-Sgt. Rock issue 16 32 48 109 237 365
141-150: 147,148-Rock becomes a General 12 24 36 81 166 250
151-Intro. Enemy Ace by Kubert (2/65), black-c 44 88 132 330 715 1100
152-4th all-Sgt. Rock issue 14 28 42 97 211 325
153-2nd app. Enemy Ace (4/65) 21 42 63 146 311 475
154,156,157,159-161,165-167: 157-2 pg. centerfold spread pin-up as part of story. 159-1st Nurse Wendy Winston-c/s. 165-2nd Iron Major 11 22 33 71 136 200
155-3rd app. Enemy Ace (6/65)(see Showcase) 14 28 42 97 211 325
158-Origin & 1st app. Iron Major(9/65), formerly Iron Captain 12 24 36 78 157 235
162,163-Viking Prince x-over in Sgt. Rock 11 22 33 76 151 225
164-Giant G-19 15 30 45 104 227 350

Our Army at War (2011) TPB © DC

Our Fighting Forces #1 © DC

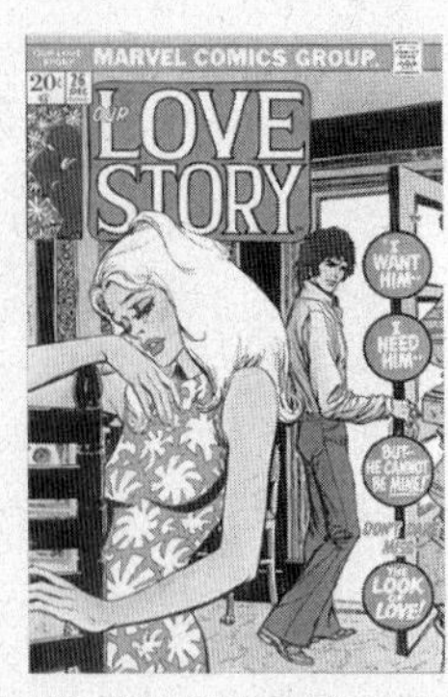

Our Love Story #26 © MAR

	GD 2.0	VG 4.0	FN 6.0	VF 8.0	VF/NM 9.0	NM- 9.2
168-1st Unknown Soldier app.; referenced in Star-Spangled War Stories #157; (Sgt. Rock x-over) (6/66)	15	30	45	104	227	350
169,170	9	18	27	63	112	160
171-176,178-181: 171-1st Mad Emperor	9	18	27	58	99	140
177-(80 pg. Giant G-32)	11	22	33	71	136	200
182,183,186-Neal Adams-a. 186-Origin retold	10	20	30	64	115	165
184-Wee Willie dies	10	20	30	68	127	185
185,187,188,193-195,197-199	7	14	21	48	79	110
189,191,192,196: 189-Intro. The Teen-age Underground Fighters of Unit 3. 196-Hitler cameo	7	14	21	49	82	115
190-(80 pg. Giant G-44)	9	18	27	61	106	150
200-12 pg. Rock story told in verse; Evans-a	8	16	24	51	86	120
201,202,204-207: 201-Krigstein-r/#14. 204,205-All reprints; no Sgt. Rock. 207-Last 12¢ cover	6	12	18	39	62	85
203-(80 pg. Giant G-56)-All-r, Sgt. Rock story	8	16	24	55	93	130
208-215	4	8	12	28	44	60
216,229-(80 pg. Giants G-68, G-80): 216-Has G-58 on-c by mistake	7	14	21	46	76	105
217-219: 218-1st U.S.S. Stevens	4	8	12	26	41	55
220-Classic dinosaur/Sgt. Rock-c/s	5	10	15	30	48	65
221-228,230-234: 231-Intro/death Rock's brother. 234-Last 15¢ issue	4	8	12	22	34	45
235-239,241: 52 pg. Giants	4	8	12	28	44	60
240-Neal Adams-a; 52 pg. Giant	5	10	15	35	55	75
242-Also listed as DC 100 Page Super Spectacular #9	10	20	30	65	118	170
243-246: (All 52 pgs.) 244-No Adams-a	4	8	12	26	41	55
247-250,254-268,270: 247-Joan of Arc	3	6	9	16	22	28
251-253-Return of Iron Major	3	6	9	17	25	32
269,275-(100 pgs.)	5	10	15	35	55	75
271,272,274,276-279	3	6	9	14	19	24
273-Crucifixion-c	3	6	9	17	25	32
280-(68 pgs.)-200th app. Sgt. Rock; reprints Our Army at War #81,83	4	8	12	25	36	48
281-299,301: 295-Bicentennial cover	2	4	6	13	18	22
300-Sgt. Rock-s by Kubert (2/77)	3	6	9	16	22	28

NOTE **Alcala** *a-251.* **Drucker** *a-27, 67, 68, 79, 82, 83, 96, 164, 177, 203, 212, 243r, 244, 269r, 275r, 280r.* **Evans** *a-165-175, 200, 266, 269, 270, 274, 276, 278, 280.* **Glanzman** *a-218, 220, 222, 223, 225, 227, 230-232, 238-241, 244, 247, 248, 256-259, 261, 265-267, 271, 282, 283, 298.* **Grandenetti** *c-91,120.* **Grell** *a-287.* **Heath** *a-50, 164, & most 176-281.* **Kubert** *a-38, 59, 67, 68 & most issues from 83-165, 171, 233, 236, 267, 275, 300; c-84, 280.* **Maurer** *a-233, 237, 239, 240, 45, 280, 284, 288, 290, 291, 295.* **Severin** *a-236, 252, 265, 267, 269r, 272.* **Toth** *a-235, 241, 254.* **Wildey** *a-283-285, 287p.* **Wood** *a-249.*

OUR ARMY AT WAR
DC Comics: Nov, 2010 ($3.99, one-shot)

	GD 2.0	VG 4.0	FN 6.0	VF 8.0	VF/NM 9.0	NM- 9.2
1-Joe Kubert-c; Mike Marts-s/Victor Ibáñez-a						4.00
TPB (2011, $14.99) r/#1 and other 2010 war one-shots Weird War Tales #1, Our Fighting Forces #1, G.I. Combat #1 and Star-Spangled War Stories #1						15.00

OUR FIGHTING FORCES
National Per. Publ./DC Comics: Oct-Nov, 1954 - No. 181, Sept-Oct, 1978

	GD 2.0	VG 4.0	FN 6.0	VF 8.0	VF/NM 9.0	NM- 9.2
1-Grandenetti-c/a	126	252	378	1021	2211	3400
2	46	92	138	373	812	1250
3-Kubert-c; last precode issue (3/55)	40	80	120	300	650	1000
4,5	34	68	102	247	536	825
6-9: 7-1st S.A. issue	28	56	84	203	439	675
10-Wood-a	29	58	87	205	445	685
11-19	25	50	75	172	369	565
20-Grey tone-c (4/57)	32	64	96	230	498	765
21-30	20	40	60	137	294	450
31-40	17	34	51	119	260	400
41-Unknown Soldier tryout	21	42	63	146	311	475
42-44	16	32	48	111	243	375
45-1st app. of Gunner & Sarge, app. thru #94	50	100	150	405	878	1350
46	24	48	72	168	359	550
47	19	38	57	128	277	425
48,50	15	30	45	104	227	350
49-1st Pooch	23	46	69	161	343	525
51-Grey tone-c	22	44	66	154	327	500
52-64: 64-Last 10¢ issue	13	26	39	85	180	275
65-70	11	22	33	71	136	200
71-Classic grey tone-c; Pooch fires machine gun	14	28	42	97	211	325
72-80	9	18	27	63	112	160
81-90	8	16	24	51	86	120
91-98: 95-Devil-Dog begins, ends #98.	6	12	18	42	69	95
99-Capt. Hunter begins, ends #106	7	14	21	44	72	100
100	7	14	21	44	72	100
101-105,107-120: 116-Mlle. Marie app. 120-Last 12¢ issue	5	10	15	32	51	70
106-Hunters Hellcats begin	5	10	15	35	55	75
121,122: 121-Intro. Heller	4	8	12	28	44	60
123-The Losers (Capt. Storm, Gunner & Sarge, Johnny Cloud) begin	9	18	27	61	106	150
124-132: 132-Last 15¢ issue	4	8	12	24	37	50
133-137 (Giants). 134-Toth-a	4	8	12	28	44	60
138-145,147-150	3	6	9	16	23	30
146-Classic "Burma Sky" story; Toth-a/Goodwin-s	3	6	9	18	27	35
151-162-Kirby a(p)	3	6	9	19	29	38
163-180	3	6	9	14	19	24
181-Last issue	3	6	9	16	23	30
... (War One-Shot) 1 (11/10, $3.99) The Losers app.; B. Clay Moore-s/Chad Hardin-a						4.00

NOTE: **N. Adams** *c-147.* **Drucker** *a-28, 37, 39, 42-44, 49, 53, 133r.* **Evans** *a-149, 164-174, 177-181.* **Glanzman** *a-125-128, 132, 134, 138-141, 143, 144.* **Heath** *a-2, 16, 18, 28, 41, 44, 49, 114, 135-138r; c-51.* **Kirby** *a-151-162p; c-152-159.* **Kubert** *c/a in many issues.* **Maurer** *a-135.* **Redondo** *a-166.* **Severin** *a-123-130, 131i, 132-150.*

OUR FIGHTING MEN IN ACTION (See Men In Action)

OUR FLAG COMICS
Ace Magazines: Aug, 1941 - No. 5, April, 1942

	GD 2.0	VG 4.0	FN 6.0	VF 8.0	VF/NM 9.0	NM- 9.2
1-Captain Victory, The Unknown Soldier (intro.) & The Three Cheers begin	258	516	774	1651	2826	4000
2-Origin The Flag (patriotic hero); 1st app?	110	220	330	704	1202	1700
3-5: 5-Intro & 1st app. Mr. Risk	84	168	252	538	919	1300

NOTE: **Anderson** *a-1, 4.* **Mooney** *a-1, 2; c-2.*

OUR GANG COMICS (With Tom & Jerry #39-59; becomes Tom & Jerry #60 on; based on film characters)
Dell Publishing Co.: Sept-Oct, 1942 - No. 59, June, 1949

	GD 2.0	VG 4.0	FN 6.0	VF 8.0	VF/NM 9.0	NM- 9.2
1-Our Gang & Barney Bear by Kelly, Tom & Jerry, Pete Smith, Flip & Dip, The Milky Way begin (all 1st app.)	63	126	189	510	1105	1700
2-Benny Burro begins (#2 by Kelly)	32	64	96	232	504	775
3-5	22	44	66	157	334	510
6-Bumbazine & Albert only app. by Kelly	30	60	90	203	457	710
7-No Kelly story	16	32	48	111	243	375
8-Benny Burro begins by Barks	38	76	114	285	618	950
9-Barks-a(2): Benny Burro & Happy Hound; no Kelly story	35	70	105	254	547	840
10-Benny Burro by Barks	26	52	78	182	391	600
11-1st Barney Bear & Benny Burro by Barks (5-6/44); Happy Hound by Barks	35	70	105	254	547	840
12-20	16	32	48	109	237	365
21-30: 30-X-Mas-c	12	24	36	82	169	255
31-36-Last Barks issue	10	20	30	70	133	195
37-40	8	16	24	51	86	120
41-50	7	14	21	44	72	100
51-57	6	12	18	41	66	90
58,59-No Kelly art or Our Gang stories	6	12	18	37	59	80
Our Gang Volume 1 (Fantagraphics Books, 2006, $12.95, TPB) r/Our Gang stories written and by Walt Kelly from #1-8; Leonard Maltin intro.; Jeff Smith-c						13.00
Our Gang Volume 2 (Fantagraphics Books, 2007, $12.95, TPB) r/Our Gang stories written and by Walt Kelly from #9-15; Steve Thompson intro.; Jeff Smith-c						13.00
Our Gang Volume 3 (Fantagraphics Books, 2008, $14.99, TPB) r/Our Gang stories written and by Walt Kelly from #16-23; Steve Thompson intro.; Jeff Smith-c						15.00

NOTE: **Barks** *art in part only.* **Barks** *did not write Barney Bear stories #30-34. (See March of Comics #3, 26). Early issues have photo back-c.*

OUR LADY OF FATIMA
Catechetical Guild Educational Society: 3/11/55 (15¢) (36 pgs.)

	GD 2.0	VG 4.0	FN 6.0	VF 8.0	VF/NM 9.0	NM- 9.2
395	6	12	18	28	34	40

OUR LOVE (True Secrets #3 on? or Romantic Affairs #3 on?)
Marvel Comics (SPC): Sept, 1949 - No. 2, Jan, 1950

	GD 2.0	VG 4.0	FN 6.0	VF 8.0	VF/NM 9.0	NM- 9.2
1-Photo-c	18	36	54	103	162	220
2-Photo-c	12	24	36	69	97	125

OUR LOVE STORY
Marvel Comics Group: Oct, 1969 - No. 38, Feb, 1976

	GD 2.0	VG 4.0	FN 6.0	VF 8.0	VF/NM 9.0	NM- 9.2
1	8	16	24	56	96	135
2-4,6-8,10,11	5	10	15	30	48	65
5-Steranko-a	11	22	33	73	142	210
9,12-Kirby-a	5	10	15	32	51	70
13-(10/71, 52 pgs.)	6	12	18	37	59	80
14-New story by Gary Fredrich & Tarpe' Mills	5	10	15	32	51	70
15-20,27:27-Colan/Everett-a(r?); Kirby/Colletta-r	4	8	12	22	34	45

Out for Blood #3 © Part & Grant

Outlaw Nation #3 © Delano & Sudzuka

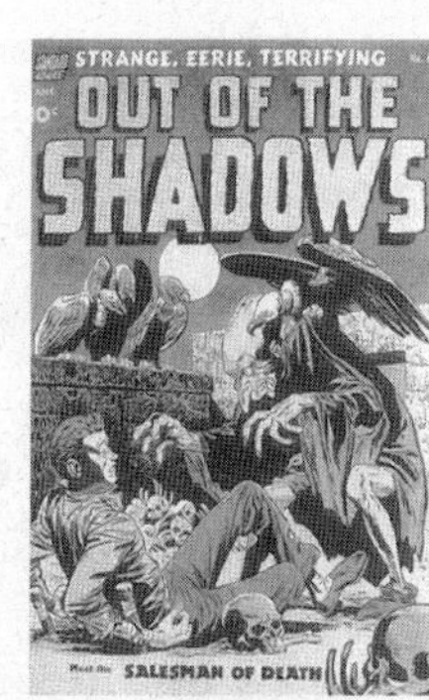
Out of the Shadows #6 © STD

	GD 2.0	VG 4.0	FN 6.0	VF 8.0	VF/NM 9.0	NM- 9.2
21-26,28-37	3	6	9	20	30	40
38-Last issue	4	8	12	24	37	50

NOTE: ***J. Buscema*** *a-1-3, 5-7, 9, 13r, 16r, 19r(2), 21r, 22r(2), 23r, 34r, 35r; c-11, 13, 16, 22, 23, 24, 27, 35.* ***Colan*** *a-3-6, 21r(#6), 22r, 23r(#3), 24r(#4), 27; c-19.* ***Katz*** *a-17.* ***Maneely*** *a-13r.* ***Romita*** *a-13r; c-1, 2, 4-6.* ***Weiss*** *a-16, 17, 29r(#17).*

OUR MEN AT WAR
DC Comics: Aug/Sept 1952

nn - Ashcan comic, not distributed to newsstands, only for in-house use. Cover art is All Star Western #60 with interior being Detective Comics #181 (no known sales)

OUR MISS BROOKS
Dell Publishing Co.: No. 751, Nov, 1956

	GD	VG	FN	VF	VF/NM	NM-
Four Color 751-Photo-c	7	14	21	49	82	115

OUR SECRET (Exciting Love Stories)(Formerly My Secret)
Superior Comics Ltd.: No. 4, Nov, 1949 - No. 8, Jun, 1950

	GD	VG	FN	VF	VF/NM	NM-
4-Kamen-a; spanking scene	20	40	60	114	182	250
5,6,8	13	26	39	72	101	130
7-Contains 9 pg. story intended for unpublished Ellery Queen #5; lingerie panels	14	28	42	76	108	140

OUTBREED 999
Blackout Comics: May, 1994 - No. 6, 1994 ($2.95)

1-6: 4-1st app. of Extreme Violet in 7 pg. backup story 3.00

OUTCAST, THE
Valiant: Dec, 1995 ($2.50, one-shot)

1-Breyfogle-a. 3.00

OUTCASTS
DC Comics: Oct, 1987 - No. 12, Sept, 1988 ($1.75, limited series)

1-12: John Wagner & Alan Grant scripts in all 3.00

OUTER LIMITS, THE (TV)
Dell Publishing Co.: Jan-Mar, 1964 - No. 18, Oct, 1969 (Most painted-c)

	GD	VG	FN	VF	VF/NM	NM-
1	11	22	33	76	151	225
2-5	7	14	21	48	79	110
6-10	6	12	18	41	66	90
11-18: 17-Reprints #1. 18-r/#2	5	10	15	35	55	75

OUTER SPACE (Formerly This Magazine Is Haunted, 2nd Series)
Charlton Comics: No. 17, May, 1958 - No. 25, Dec, 1959; Nov, 1968

	GD	VG	FN	VF	VF/NM	NM-
17-Williamson/Wood-a	14	28	42	80	115	150
18-20-Ditko-a	23	46	69	136	223	310
21-Ditko-c	20	40	60	114	182	250
22-25	14	28	42	80	115	150
V2#1(11/68)-Ditko-a, Boyette-c	5	10	15	32	51	70

OUT FOR BLOOD
Dark Horse: Sept, 1999 - No. 4, Dec, 1999 ($2.95, B&W, limited series)

1-4-Kelley Jones-c; Erskine-a 3.00

OUTLANDERS (Manga)
Dark Horse Comics: Dec, 1988 - No. 33, Sept,1991 ($2.00-$2.50, B&W, 44 pgs.)

1-33: Japanese Sci-fi manga 4.00

OUTLAW (See Return of the...)

OUTLAW FIGHTERS
Atlas Comics (IPC): Aug, 1954 - No. 5, Apr, 1955

	GD	VG	FN	VF	VF/NM	NM-
1-Tuska-a	14	28	42	76	108	140
2-5: 5-Heath-c/a, 7 pgs.	9	18	27	50	65	80

NOTE: ***Hartley*** *a-3.* ***Heath*** *c/a-5.* ***Maneely*** *c-2.* ***Pakula*** *a-2.* ***Reinman*** *a-2.* ***Tuska*** *a-1-3.*

OUTLAW KID, THE (1st Series; see Wild Western)
Atlas Comics (CCC No. 1-11/EPI No. 12-29): Sept, 1954 - No. 19, Sept, 1957

	GD	VG	FN	VF	VF/NM	NM-
1-Origin; The Outlaw Kid & his horse Thunder begin; Black Rider app.	27	54	81	158	259	360
2-Black Rider app.	14	28	42	80	115	150
3-7,9: 3-Wildey-a(3)	12	24	36	69	97	125
8-Williamson/Woodbridge-a, 4 pgs.	13	26	39	74	105	135
10-Williamson-a	13	26	39	74	105	135
11-17,19: 13-Baker text illo. 15-Williamson text illo (unsigned)	9	18	27	52	69	85
18-Williamson/Mayo-a	10	20	30	56	76	95

NOTE: ***Berg*** *a-4, 7, 13.* ***Maneely*** *c-1-3, 5-8, 11-13, 15, 16, 18.* ***Pakula*** *a-3.* ***Severin*** *c-10, 17, 19.* ***Shores*** *a-1.* ***Wildey*** *a-1(3), 2-8, 10, 11, 12(4), 13(4), 15-19(4 each); c-4.*

OUTLAW KID, THE (2nd Series)
Marvel Comics Group: Aug, 1970 - No. 30, Oct, 1975

	GD	VG	FN	VF	VF/NM	NM-
1-Reprints; 1-Orlando-r, Wildey-r(3)	3	6	9	20	30	40
2,3,9: 2-Reprints. 3,9-Williamson-a(r)	2	4	6	13	18	22
4-7: 7-Last 15¢ issue	2	4	6	11	16	20
8-Double size (52 pgs.); Crandall-r	3	6	9	17	25	32
10-Origin	3	6	9	20	30	40
11-20: new-a in #10-16	2	4	6	13	18	22
21-30: 27-Origin-r/#10	2	4	6	9	13	16

NOTE: ***Ayers*** *a-10, 27r.* ***Berg*** *a-7, 25r.* ***Everett*** *a-2(2 pgs.).* ***Gil Kane*** *c-10, 11, 15, 27r, 28.* ***Roussos*** *a-10i, 27i(r).* ***Severin*** *c-1, 9, 20, 25.* ***Wildey*** *r-1-4, 6-9, 19-22, 25, 26.* ***Williamson*** *a-28r.* ***Woodbridge/Williamson*** *a-9r.*

OUTLAW NATION
DC Comics (Vertigo): Nov, 2000 - No. 19, May, 2002 ($2.50)

1-19-Fabry painted-c/Delano-s/Sudzuka-a 3.00
TPB (Image Comics, 11/06, $15.99) B&W reprint of #1-19; Delano intro. 16.00

OUTLAWS
D. S. Publishing Co.: Feb-Mar, 1948 - No. 9, June-July, 1949

	GD	VG	FN	VF	VF/NM	NM-
1-Violent & suggestive stories	34	68	102	204	332	460
2-Ingels-a; Baker-a	34	68	102	204	332	460
3,5,6: 3-Not Frazetta. 5-Sky Sheriff by Good app. 6-McWilliams-a	17	34	51	98	154	210
4-Orlando-a	18	36	54	103	162	220
7,8-Ingels-a in each	24	48	72	142	234	325
9-(Scarce)-Frazetta-a (7 pgs.)	48	96	144	302	514	725

NOTE: *Another #3 was printed in Canada with* ***Frazetta*** *art "Prairie Jinx," 7 pgs.*

OUTLAWS, THE (Formerly Western Crime Cases)
Star Publishing Co.: No. 10, May, 1952 - No. 13, Sep, 1953; No. 14, Apr, 1954

	GD	VG	FN	VF	VF/NM	NM-
10-L. B. Cole-c	21	42	63	122	199	275
11-14-L. B. Cole-c. 14-Reprints Western Thrillers #4 (Fox) w/new L.B. Cole-c; Kamen, Feldstein-r	16	32	48	92	144	195

OUTLAWS
DC Comics: Sept, 1991 - No. 8, Apr, 1992 ($1.95, limited series)

1-8: Post-apocalyptic Robin Hood. 3.00

OUTLAWS OF THE WEST (Formerly Cody of the Pony Express #10)
Charlton Comics: No. 11, 7/57 - No. 81, 5/70; No. 82, 7/79 - No. 88, 4/80

	GD	VG	FN	VF	VF/NM	NM-
11	8	16	24	44	57	70
12,13,15-17,19,20	6	12	18	27	33	38
14-(68 pgs., 2/58)	9	18	27	50	65	80
18-Ditko-a	10	20	30	56	76	95
21-30	3	6	9	16	23	30
31-50: 34-Gunmaster app.	2	4	6	13	18	22
51-63,65,67-70: 54-Kid Montana app.	2	4	6	10	14	18
64,66: 64-Captain Doom begins (1st app.). 68-Kid Montana series begins	2	4	6	13	18	22
71-79: 73-Origin & 1st app. The Sharp Shooter, last app. #74. 75-Last Capt. Doom	2	4	6	9	12	15
80,81-Ditko-a	2	4	6	13	18	22
82-88						6.00
64,79(Modern Comics-r, 1977, '78)						6.00

OUTLAWS OF THE WILD WEST
Avon Periodicals: 1952 (25¢, 132 pgs.) (4 rebound comics)

	GD	VG	FN	VF	VF/NM	NM-
1-Wood back-c; Kubert-a (3 Jesse James-r)	34	68	102	206	336	465

OUTLAW TRAIL (See Zane Grey 4-Color 511)

OUT OF SANTA'S BAG (See March of Comics #10 in the Promotional Comics section)

OUT OF THE NIGHT (The Hooded Horseman #18 on)
Amer. Comics Group (Creston/Scope): Feb-Mar, 1952 - No. 17, Oct-Nov, 1954

	GD	VG	FN	VF	VF/NM	NM-
1-Williamson/LeDoux-a (9 pgs.); ACG's 1st editor's page	67	134	201	426	731	1035
2-Williamson-a (5 pgs.)	47	94	141	296	498	700
3,5-10: 9-Sci/Fic story	30	60	90	117	289	400
4-Williamson-a (7 pgs.)	40	80	120	246	411	575
11-17: 13-Nostrand-a? 17-E.C. Wood swipe	22	44	66	132	216	300

NOTE: ***Landau*** *a-14, 16, 17.* ***Shelly*** *a-12.*

OUT OF THE SHADOWS
Standard Comics/Visual Editions: No. 5, July, 1952 - No. 14, Aug, 1954

	GD	VG	FN	VF	VF/NM	NM-
5-Toth-p; Moreira, Tuska-a; Roussos-c	57	114	171	362	619	875
6-Toth/Celardo-a; Katz-a(2)	41	82	123	249	417	585
7,9: 7-Jack Katz-c/a(2). 9-Crandall-a(2)	36	72	108	211	343	475
8-Katz shrunken head-c	56	112	168	356	613	870
10-Spider-c; Sekowsky-a	37	74	111	222	361	500
11-Toth-a, 2 pgs.; Katz-a; Andru-c	36	72	108	211	343	475

Outsiders (2003 series) #1 © DC

Ozark Ike #12 © KING

Ozma of Oz #4 © MAR

	GD 2.0	VG 4.0	FN 6.0	VF 8.0	VF/NM 9.0	NM- 9.2
12-Toth/Peppe-a(2); Katz-a	41	82	123	249	417	585
13-Cannabalism story; Sekowsky-a; Roussos-c	39	78	117	240	395	550
14-Toth-a	36	72	108	211	343	475

OUT OF THE VORTEX (Comics' Greatest World:... #1-4)
Dark Horse Comics: Oct., 1993 - No. 12, Oct, 1994 ($2.00, limited series)

	GD 2.0	VG 4.0	FN 6.0	VF 8.0	VF/NM 9.0	NM- 9.2
1-11: 1-Foil logo. 4-Dorman-c(p). 6-Hero Zero x-over						3.00
12 ($2.50)						3.00

NOTE: *Art Adams c-7. Golden c-8. Mignola c-2. Simonson c-3. Zeck c-10.*

OUT OF THIS WORLD
Charlton Comics: Aug, 1956 - No. 16, Dec, 1959

	GD 2.0	VG 4.0	FN 6.0	VF 8.0	VF/NM 9.0	NM- 9.2
1	27	54	81	160	263	365
2	15	30	45	86	133	180
3-6-Ditko-c/a (3) each	32	64	96	192	314	435
7-(2/58, 15¢, 68 pgs.)-Ditko-c/a(4)	34	68	102	204	332	460
8-(5/58, 15¢, 68 pgs.)-Ditko-a(2)	31	62	93	182	296	410
9,10,12,16-Ditko-a	24	48	72	140	230	320
11-Ditko c/a (3)	27	54	81	160	263	365
13,15	13	26	39	74	105	135
14-Matt Baker-a, 7 pg. story	14	28	42	78	112	145

NOTE: *Ditko c-3-12, 16. Reinman a-10.*

OUT OF THIS WORLD
Avon Periodicals: June, 1950; Aug, 1950

	GD 2.0	VG 4.0	FN 6.0	VF 8.0	VF/NM 9.0	NM- 9.2
1-Kubert-a(2) (one reprinted/Eerie #1, 1947) plus Crom the Barbarian by Gardner Fox & John Giunta (origin); Fawcette-c	81	162	243	518	884	1250
1-(8/50) Reprint; no month on cover	48	96	144	302	514	725

OUT OF THIS WORLD ADVENTURES
Avon Periodicals: July, 1950 - No. 2, Apr, 1951 (25¢ sci-fi pulp magazine with 32-page color comic insert)

	GD 2.0	VG 4.0	FN 6.0	VF 8.0	VF/NM 9.0	NM- 9.2
1-Kubert-a(2); Crom the Barbarian by Fox & Giunta; text stories by Cummings, Van Vogt, del Rey, Chandler	74	148	222	470	810	1150
2-Kubert-a plus The Spider God of Akka by Gardner Fox & John Giunta pulp magazine w/comic insert; Wood-a (21 pgs.); mentioned in **SOTI,** page 120	52	104	156	322	549	775

OUT OUR WAY WITH WORRY WART
Dell Publishing Co.: No. 680, Feb, 1956

	GD 2.0	VG 4.0	FN 6.0	VF 8.0	VF/NM 9.0	NM- 9.2
Four Color 680	4	8	12	24	37	50

OUTPOSTS
Blackthorne Publishing: June, 1987 - No. 4, 1987 ($1.25)

	GD 2.0	VG 4.0	FN 6.0	VF 8.0	VF/NM 9.0	NM- 9.2
1-4: 1-Kaluta-c(p)						3.00

OUTSIDERS, THE
DC Comics: Nov, 1985 - No. 28, Feb, 1988

	GD 2.0	VG 4.0	FN 6.0	VF 8.0	VF/NM 9.0	NM- 9.2
1						4.00
2-17						3.00
18-28: 18-26-Batman returns. 21-Intro. Strike Force Kobra; 1st app. Clayface IV 22-E.C. parody; Orlando-a. 21- 25-Atomic Knight app. 27,28-Millennium tie-ins						3.00
Annual 1 (12/86, $2.50), Special 1 (7/87, $1.50)						4.00

NOTE: *Aparo a-1-7, 9-14, 17-22, 25, 26; c-1-7, 9-14, 17, 19-26. Byrne a-11. Bolland a-6, 18; c-16. Ditko a-13p. Erik Larsen a-24, 27 28; c-27, 28. Morrow a-12.*

OUTSIDERS
DC Comics: Nov, 1993 - No. 24, Nov, 1995 ($1.75/$1.95/$2.25)

	GD 2.0	VG 4.0	FN 6.0	VF 8.0	VF/NM 9.0	NM- 9.2
1-11,0,12-24: 1-Alpha; Travis Charest-c. 1-Omega; Travis Charest-c. 5-Atomic Knight app. 8-New Batman-c/story. 11-(9/94)-Zero Hour. 0-(10/94).12-(11/94). 21-Darkseid cameo. 22-New Gods app.						3.00

OUTSIDERS (See Titans/Young Justice: Graduation Day)(Leads into Batman and the Outsiders)
DC Comics: Aug, 2003 - No. 50, Nov, 2007 ($2.50/$2.99)

	GD 2.0	VG 4.0	FN 6.0	VF 8.0	VF/NM 9.0	NM- 9.2
1-Nightwing, Arsenal, Metamorpho app.; Winick-s/Raney-a						5.00
2-Joker and Grodd app.						3.50
3-33: 3-Joker-c. 5,6-ChrisCross-a. 8-Huntress app. 9,10-Capt. Marvel Jr. app. 24,25-X-over with Teen Titans. 26,27-Batman & old Outsiders						3.00
34-50: 34-One Year Later. 36-Begin $2.99-c. 37-Superman app. 44-Red Hood app.						3.00
Annual 1 (6/07, $3.99) McDaniel-a; Black Lightning app.						4.00
.../Checkmate: Checkout TPB (2008, $14.99) r/#47-49 & Checkmate #13-15						15.00
... Double Feature (10/03, $4.95) r/#1,2						5.00
...: Crisis Intervention TPB (2006, $12.99) r/#29-33						13.00
...: Looking For Trouble TPB (2004, $12.95) r/#1-7 & Teen Titans/Outsiders Secret Files & Origins 2003; intro. by Winick						13.00
...: Pay As You Go TPB (2007, $14.99) r/#42-46 & Annual #1						15.00
...: Sum of All Evil TPB (2004, $14.95) r/#8-15						15.00
...: The Good Fight TPB (2006, $14.99) r/#34-41						15.00
...: Wanted TPB (2005, $14.99) r/#16-23						15.00

OUTSIDERS, THE (See Batman and the Outsiders for #1-14 and #40)
DC Comics: No. 15, Apr, 2009 - No. 39, Jun, 2011 ($2.99)

	GD 2.0	VG 4.0	FN 6.0	VF 8.0	VF/NM 9.0	NM- 9.2
15-23,26-39: 15-Alfred assembles a new team; Garbett-a. 17-19-Deathstroke app.						3.00
24,25-($3.99) Blackest Night; Terra rises as a Black Lantern						4.00
...: The Deep TPB (2009, $14.99) r/#15-20 & Batman and the Outsiders Special #1						15.00
...: The Great Divide TPB (2011, $17.99) r/#32-40; cover gallery						18.00
...: The Hunt TPB (2010, $14.99) r/#21-25						15.00
...: The Road to Hell TPB (2010, $14.99) r/#26-31						15.00

OUTSIDERS: FIVE OF A KIND (Bridges Outsiders #49 & 50)
DC Comics: Oct, 2007 ($2.99, weekly limited series)

	GD 2.0	VG 4.0	FN 6.0	VF 8.0	VF/NM 9.0	NM- 9.2
...Katana/Shazam! (part 2 of 5) - Barr-s/Sharpe-a						3.00
...Metamorpho/Aquaman (part 4 of 5) - Wilson-s/Middleton-a						3.00
...Nightwing/Captain Boomerang (part 1 of 5) - DeFilippis & Weir-s/Willams-a						3.00
...Thunder/Martian Manhunter (part 3 of 5) - Bedard-s/Turnbull-a; Grayven app.						3.00
...Wonder Woman/Grace (part 5 of 5) - Andreyko-s/Richards-a						3.00
TPB (2008, $14.99) r/series & Outsiders #50						15.00

OUT THERE
DC Comics(Cliffhanger): July, 2001 - No. 18, Aug, 2003 ($2.50/$2.95)

	GD 2.0	VG 4.0	FN 6.0	VF 8.0	VF/NM 9.0	NM- 9.2
1-Humberto Ramos-c/a; Brian Augustyn-s						3.00
1-Variant-c by Carlos Meglia						4.00
2-8: 3-Variant-c by Bruce Timm						3.00
9-18: 9-Begin $2.95-c						3.00
...: The Evil Within TPB (2002, $12.95) r/#1-6; Ramos sketch pages						13.00

OVERKILL: WITCHBLADE/ ALIENS/ DARKNESS/ PREDATOR
Image Comics/Dark Horse Comics: Dec, 2000 - No. 2, 2001 ($5.95)

	GD 2.0	VG 4.0	FN 6.0	VF 8.0	VF/NM 9.0	NM- 9.2
1,2-Jenkins-s/Lansing, Ching & Benitez-a						6.00

OVER THE EDGE
Marvel Comics: Nov, 1995 - No. 10, Aug, 1996 (99¢)

	GD 2.0	VG 4.0	FN 6.0	VF 8.0	VF/NM 9.0	NM- 9.2
1-10: 1,6,10-Daredevil-c/story. 2,7-Dr. Strange-c/story. 3-Hulk-c/story. 4,9-Ghost Rider-c/story. 5-Punisher-c/story. 8-Elektra-c/story						3.00

OWL, THE (See Crackajack Funnies #25, Popular Comics #72 and Occult Files of Dr. Spektor #22)
Gold Key: April, 1967; No. 2, April, 1968

	GD 2.0	VG 4.0	FN 6.0	VF 8.0	VF/NM 9.0	NM- 9.2
1-Written by Jerry Siegel; '40s super hero	6	12	18	39	62	85
2	5	10	15	30	48	65

OZ (See First Comics Graphic Novel, Marvel Treaury Of Oz & MGM's Marvelous...)

OZ
Caliber Press: 1994 - 1997 ($2.95, B&W)

	GD 2.0	VG 4.0	FN 6.0	VF 8.0	VF/NM 9.0	NM- 9.2
0-20: 0-Released between #10 & #11						3.00
1 ($5.95)-Limited Edition; double-c						6.00
...Specials: Freedom Fighters. Lion. Scarecrow. Tin Man						3.00

OZARK IKE
Dell Publishing Co./Standard Comics B11 on: Feb, 1948; Nov, 1948 - No. 24, Dec, 1951; No. 25, Sept, 1952

	GD 2.0	VG 4.0	FN 6.0	VF 8.0	VF/NM 9.0	NM- 9.2
Four Color 180(1948-Dell)	10	20	30	64	115	165
B11, B12, 13-15	10	20	30	56	76	95
16-25	9	18	27	50	65	80

OZ: DAEMONSTORM
Caliber Press: 1997 ($3.95, B&W, one-shot)

	GD 2.0	VG 4.0	FN 6.0	VF 8.0	VF/NM 9.0	NM- 9.2
1						4.00

OZMA OF OZ (Dorothy Gale from Wonderful Wizard of Oz)
Marvel Comics: Jan, 2011 - No. 8, Sept, 2011 ($3.99, limited series)

	GD 2.0	VG 4.0	FN 6.0	VF 8.0	VF/NM 9.0	NM- 9.2
1-6-Eric Shanower-s/Skottie Young-a/c						4.00
Oz Primer (5/11, $3.99) creator interviews and character profiles						4.00

OZ: ROMANCE IN RAGS
Caliber Press: 1996 ($2.95, B&W, limited series)

	GD 2.0	VG 4.0	FN 6.0	VF 8.0	VF/NM 9.0	NM- 9.2
1-3, ..Special						3.00

OZ SQUAD
Brave New Worlds/Patchwork Press: 1992 - No. 4, 1994 ($2.50/$2.75, B&W)

	GD 2.0	VG 4.0	FN 6.0	VF 8.0	VF/NM 9.0	NM- 9.2
1-4-Patchwork Press						3.00

OZ SQUAD
Patchwork Press: Dec, 1995 - No. 10, 1996 ($3.95/$2.95, B&W)

	GD 2.0	VG 4.0	FN 6.0	VF 8.0	VF/NM 9.0	NM- 9.2
1-($3.95)						4.00
2-10						3.00

The Pact #3 © Image

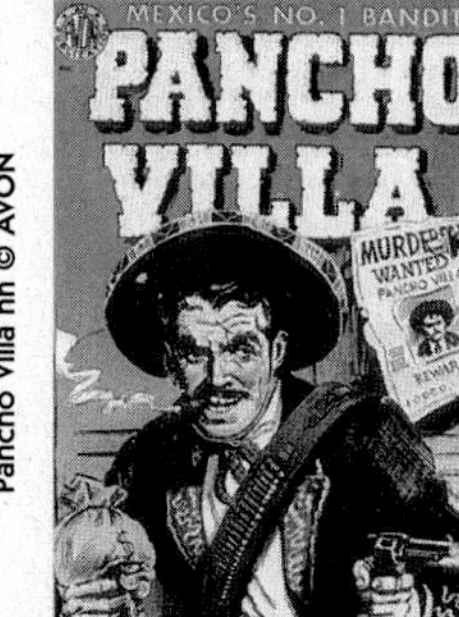

Pancho Villa nn © AVON

Panic #3 © WMG

OZ: STRAW AND SORCERY
Caliber Press: 1997 ($2.95, B&W, limited series)

	GD 2.0	VG 4.0	FN 6.0	VF 8.0	VF/NM 9.0	NM- 9.2
1-3						3.00

OZ-WONDERLAND WARS, THE
DC Comics: Jan, 1986 - No. 3, March, 1986 (Mini-series)(Giants)

	GD 2.0	VG 4.0	FN 6.0	VF 8.0	VF/NM 9.0	NM- 9.2
1-3-Capt. Carrot app.; funny animals						4.00

OZZIE & BABS (TV Teens #14 on)
Fawcett Publications: Dec, 1947 - No. 13, Fall, 1949

	GD 2.0	VG 4.0	FN 6.0	VF 8.0	VF/NM 9.0	NM- 9.2
1-Teen-age	10	20	30	54	72	90
2	6	12	18	31	38	45
3-13	6	12	18	27	33	38

OZZIE AND HARRIET (The Adventures of... on cover) (Radio)
National Periodical Publications: Oct-Nov, 1949 - No. 5, June-July, 1950

	GD 2.0	VG 4.0	FN 6.0	VF 8.0	VF/NM 9.0	NM- 9.2
1-Photo-c	94	188	282	597	1024	1450
2	47	94	141	296	498	700
3-5	39	78	117	240	395	550

OZZY OSBOURNE (Todd McFarlane Presents)
Image Comics (Todd McFarlane Prod.): June, 1999 ($4.95, magazine-sized)

	GD 2.0	VG 4.0	FN 6.0	VF 8.0	VF/NM 9.0	NM- 9.2
1-Bio, interview and comic story; Ormston painted-a; Ashley Wood-c						5.00

PACIFIC COMICS GRAPHIC NOVEL (See Image Graphic Novel)

PACIFIC PRESENTS (Also see Starslayer #2, 3)
Pacific Comics: Oct, 1982 - No. 2, Apr, 1983; No. 3, Mar, 1984 - No. 4, Jun, 1984

	GD 2.0	VG 4.0	FN 6.0	VF 8.0	VF/NM 9.0	NM- 9.2
1-Chapter 3 of The Rocketeer; Stevens-c/a; Bettie Page model	2	4	6	9	12	15
2-Chapter 4 of The Rocketeer (4th app.); nudity; Stevens-c/a	2	4	6	9	12	15
3,4: 3-1st app. Vanity						3.00

NOTE: ***Conrad** a-3, 4; c-3. **Ditko** a-1-3; c-1(1/2). **Dave Stevens** a-1, 2; c-1(1/2), 2.*

PACT, THE
Image Comics: Feb, 1994 - No. 3, June, 1994 ($1.95, limited series)

	GD 2.0	VG 4.0	FN 6.0	VF 8.0	VF/NM 9.0	NM- 9.2
1-3: Valentino co-scripts & layouts						3.00

PACT, THE
Image Comics: Apr, 2005 - No. 4, Jan, 2006 ($2.99/$2.95)

	GD 2.0	VG 4.0	FN 6.0	VF 8.0	VF/NM 9.0	NM- 9.2
1-4: Invincible, Shadowhawk, Firebreather & Zephyr team-up. 1-Valentino-s/a						3.00

PAGEANT OF COMICS (See Jane Arden & Mopsy)
Archer St. John: Sept, 1947 - No. 2, Oct, 1947

	GD 2.0	VG 4.0	FN 6.0	VF 8.0	VF/NM 9.0	NM- 9.2
1,2: 1-Mopsy strip-r. 2-Jane Arden strip-r	10	20	30	56	76	95

PAINKILLER JANE
Event Comics: June, 1997 - No. 5, Nov, 1997 ($3.95/$2.95)

	GD 2.0	VG 4.0	FN 6.0	VF 8.0	VF/NM 9.0	NM- 9.2
1-Augustyn/Waid-s/Leonardi/Palmiotti-a, variant-c						4.00
2-5: Two covers (Quesada, Leonardi)						3.00
0-(1/99, $3.95) Retells origin; two covers						4.00
Essential Painkiller Jane TPB (2007, $19.99) r/#0-5; cover gallery and pin-ups						20.00

PAINKILLER JANE
Dynamite Entertainment: 2006 - No. 3, 2006 ($2.99)

	GD 2.0	VG 4.0	FN 6.0	VF 8.0	VF/NM 9.0	NM- 9.2
1-3-Quesada & Palmiotti-s/Moder-a. 1-Four covers by Q&P, Moder, Tan and Conner						3.00
Volume #1 TPB (2007, $9.99) r/#1-3; cover gallery and Palmiotti interview						10.00

PAINKILLER JANE
Dynamite Entertainment: No. 0, 2007 - Present ($3.50)

	GD 2.0	VG 4.0	FN 6.0	VF 8.0	VF/NM 9.0	NM- 9.2
0-(25¢) Quesada & Palmiotti-s/Moder-a						3.00
1-5-($3.50) 1-Continued from #0; 5 covers. 4,5-Crossover with Terminator 2 #6,7						3.50
Volume #2 TPB (2007, $11.99) r/#0-3; cover gallery						12.00

PAINKILLER JANE / DARKCHYLDE
Event Comics: Oct, 1998 ($2.95, one-shot)

	GD 2.0	VG 4.0	FN 6.0	VF 8.0	VF/NM 9.0	NM- 9.2
Preview-($6.95) DF Edition, 1-($6.95) DF Edition						7.00
1-Three covers; J.G. Jones-a						3.00

PAINKILLER JANE / HELLBOY
Event Comics: Aug, 1998 ($2.95, one-shot)

	GD 2.0	VG 4.0	FN 6.0	VF 8.0	VF/NM 9.0	NM- 9.2
1-Leonardi & Palmiotti-a						3.00

PAINKILLER JANE VS. THE DARKNESS
Event Comics: Apr, 1997 ($2.95, one-shot)

	GD 2.0	VG 4.0	FN 6.0	VF 8.0	VF/NM 9.0	NM- 9.2
1-Ennis-s; four variant-c (Conner, Hildebrandts, Quesada, Silvestri)						3.50

PAKKINS' LAND
Caliber Comics (Tapestry): Oct, 1996 - No. 6, July, 1997 ($2.95, B&W)

	GD 2.0	VG 4.0	FN 6.0	VF 8.0	VF/NM 9.0	NM- 9.2
1-Gary and Rhoda Shipman-s/a						6.00
2,3						4.00
1-3-2nd printing						3.00
4-6						3.00
0-(6/97, $1.95)						3.00

PAKKINS' LAND
Alias Enterprises: Apr, 2005 - No. 2 ($2.99)

	GD 2.0	VG 4.0	FN 6.0	VF 8.0	VF/NM 9.0	NM- 9.2
1,2-Gary Shipman-s/a						3.00

PAKKINS' LAND: FORGOTTEN DREAMS
Caliber Comics/Image Comics #4: Apr, 1998 - No. 4, Mar, 2000 ($2.95, B&W)

	GD 2.0	VG 4.0	FN 6.0	VF 8.0	VF/NM 9.0	NM- 9.2
1-4-Gary and Rhoda Shipman-s/a						3.00

PAKKINS' LAND: QUEST FOR KINGS
Caliber Comics: Aug, 1997 - No. 6, Mar, 1998 ($2.95, B&W)

	GD 2.0	VG 4.0	FN 6.0	VF 8.0	VF/NM 9.0	NM- 9.2
1-6: 1-Gary and Rhoda Shipman-s/a; Jeff Smith var-c						3.00

PANCHO VILLA
Avon Periodicals: 1950

	GD 2.0	VG 4.0	FN 6.0	VF 8.0	VF/NM 9.0	NM- 9.2
nn-Kinstler-c	23	46	69	136	223	310

PANHANDLE PETE AND JENNIFER (TV) (See Gene Autry #20)
J. Charles Laue Publishing Co.: July, 1951 - No. 3, Nov, 1951

	GD 2.0	VG 4.0	FN 6.0	VF 8.0	VF/NM 9.0	NM- 9.2
1	10	20	30	54	72	90
2,3: 2-Interior photo-cvrs	7	14	21	37	46	55

PANIC (Companion to Mad)
E. C. Comics (Tiny Tot Comics): Feb-Mar, 1954 - No. 12, Dec-Jan, 1955-56

	GD 2.0	VG 4.0	FN 6.0	VF 8.0	VF/NM 9.0	NM- 9.2
1-Used in Senate Investigation hearings; Elder draws entire E. C. staff; Santa Claus & Mickey Spillane parody	36	72	108	288	457	625
2	17	34	51	136	218	300
3,4: 3-Senate Subcommittee parody; Davis draws Gaines, Feldstein & Kelly, 1 pg.; Old King Cole smokes marijuana. 4-Infinity-c; John Wayne parody	14	28	42	112	176	240
5-11: 8-Last pre-code issue (5/55). 9-Superman, Smilin' Jack & Dick Tracy app. on-c; has photo of Walter Winchell on-c. 11-Wheedies cereal box-c	13	26	39	104	162	220
12 (Low distribution; thousands were destroyed)	16	32	48	128	204	280

NOTE: ***Davis** a-1-12; c-12. **Elder** a-1-12. **Feldstein** c-1-3, 5. **Kamen** a-1. **Orlando** a-1-9. **Wolverton** c-4, panel-3. **Wood** a-2-9, 11, 12.*

PANIC (Magazine) (Satire)
Panic Publ.: July, 1958 - No. 6, July, 1959; V2#10, Dec, 1965 - V2#12, 1966

	GD 2.0	VG 4.0	FN 6.0	VF 8.0	VF/NM 9.0	NM- 9.2
1	14	28	42	76	108	140
2-6	9	18	27	50	65	80
V2#10-12: Reprints earlier issues	3	6	9	18	27	35

NOTE: ***Davis** a-3(2 pgs.), 4, 5, 10; c-10. **Elder** a-5. **Powell** a-V2#10, 11. **Torres** a-1-5. **Tuska** a-V2#11.*

PANIC
Gemstone Publishing: March, 1997 - No. 12, Dec, 1999 ($2.50, quarterly)

	GD 2.0	VG 4.0	FN 6.0	VF 8.0	VF/NM 9.0	NM- 9.2
1-12: E.C. reprints						3.00

PANTHA (See Vampirella-The New Monthly #16,17)

PANTHA: HAUNTED PASSION (Also see Vampirella Monthly #0)
Harris Comics: May, 1997 ($2.95, B&W, one-shot)

	GD 2.0	VG 4.0	FN 6.0	VF 8.0	VF/NM 9.0	NM- 9.2
1-r/Vampirella #30,31						3.00

PANTHEON
IDW Publishing: Apr, 2010 - No. 5, Aug, 2010 ($3.99)

	GD 2.0	VG 4.0	FN 6.0	VF 8.0	VF/NM 9.0	NM- 9.2
1-5-Andreyko-s/Molnar-a; co-created by Michael Chiklis						4.00

PAPA MIDNITE (See John Constantine - Hellblazer Special:...)

PARADE (See Hanna-Barbera...)

PARADE COMICS (See Frisky Animals on Parade)

PARADE OF PLEASURE
Derric Verschoyle Ltd., London, England: 1954 (192 pgs.) (Hardback book)

	GD 2.0	VG 4.0	FN 6.0	VF 8.0	VF/NM 9.0	NM- 9.2
By Geoffrey Wagner. Contains section devoted to the censorship of American comic books with illustrations in color and black and white. (Also see **Seduction of the Innocent**). Distributed in USA by Library Publishers, N. Y.	117	234	351	503	602	700
with dust jacket....	217	434	651	933	1117	1300

PARADISE TOO!
Abstract Studios: 2000 - No. 14, 2003 ($2.95, B&W)

	GD 2.0	VG 4.0	FN 6.0	VF 8.0	VF/NM 9.0	NM- 9.2
1-14-Terry Moore's unpublished newspaper strips and sketches						3.00
...: Checking For Weirdos TPB (4/03, $14.95) r/#8-12						15.00
...: Drunk Ducks! TPB (7/02, $15.95) r/#1-7						16.00

Parliament of Justice #1 © Oeming & Vokes

Pat Boone #2 © DC

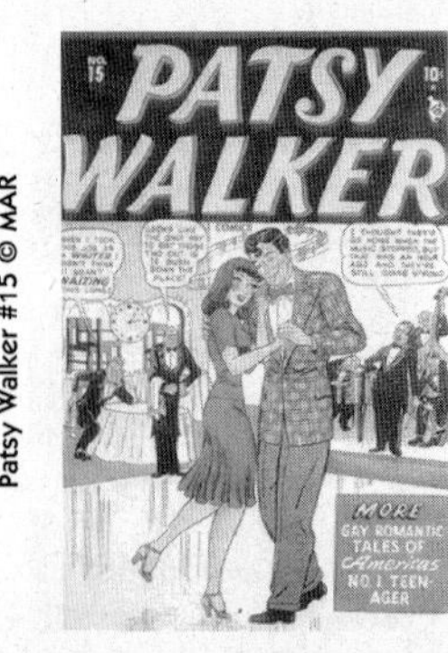

Patsy Walker #15 © MAR

GD 2.0 | VG 4.0 | FN 6.0 | VF 8.0 | VF/NM 9.0 | NM- 9.2

GD 2.0 | VG 4.0 | FN 6.0 | VF 8.0 | VF/NM 9.0 | NM- 9.2

PARADISE X (Also see Earth X and Universe X)
Marvel Comics: Apr, 2002 - No. 12, Aug, 2003 ($4.50/$2.99)

0-Ross-c; Braithwaite-a 4.50
1-12-($2.99) Ross-c; Braithwaite-a. 7-Punisher on-c. 10-Kingpin on-c 3.00
...:A (10/03, $2.99) Braithwaite-a; Ross-c 3.00
...:Devils (11/02, $4.50) Sadowski-a; Ross-c 4.50
...:Ragnarok 1,2 (3/02, 4/03; $2.99) Yeates-a; Ross-c 3.00
...:X (11/03, $2.99) Braithwaite-a; Ross-c; conclusion of story 3.00
...:Xen (7/02, $4.50) Yeowell & Sienkiewicz-a; Ross-c 4.50
Earth X Vol. 4: Paradise X Book 1 (2003, $29.99, TPB) r/#0,1-5, ...: Xen; Heralds #1-3 30.00
Vol. 5: Paradise X Book 2 (2004, $29.99, TPB) r/#6-12, Ragnarok #1&2; Devils, A & X 30.00

PARADISE X: HERALDS (Also see Earth X and Universe X)
Marvel Comics: Dec, 2001 - No. 3, Feb, 2002 ($3.50)

1-3-Prelude to Paradise X series; Ross-c; Pugh-a 3.50
Special Edition (Wizard preview) Ross-c 3.00

PARADOX
Dark Visions Publ: June, 1994 - No. 2, Aug, 1994 ($2.95, B&W, mature)

1,2: 1-Linsner-c. 2-Boris-c. 3.00

PARALLAX: EMERALD NIGHT (See Final Night)
DC Comics: Nov, 1996 ($2.95, one-shot, 48 pgs.)

1-Final Night tie-in; Green Lantern (Kyle Rayner) app. 4.00

PARAMOUNT ANIMATED COMICS (See Harvey Comics Hits #60, 62)
Harvey Publications: No. 3, Feb, 1953 - No. 22, July, 1956

3-Baby Huey, Herman & Katnip, Buzzy the Crow begin
24 48 72 142 234 325
4-6 14 28 42 76 108 140
7-Baby Huey becomes permanent cover feature; cover title becomes Baby Huey with #9
22 44 66 132 216 300
8-10: 9-Infinity-c 12 24 36 69 97 125
11-22 10 20 30 54 72 90

PARENT TRAP, THE (Disney)
Dell Publishing Co.: No. 1210, Oct-Dec, 1961

Four Color 1210-Movie, Hayley Mills photo-c 9 18 27 58 99 140

PARLIAMENT OF JUSTICE
Image Comics: Mar, 2003 ($5.95, B&W, one-shot, square-bound)

1-Michael Avon Oeming-c/s; Neil Vokes-a 6.00

PARODY
Armour Publishing: Mar, 1977 - No. 3, Aug, 1977 (B&W humor magazine)

1 3 6 9 14 19 24
2,3: 2-King Kong, Happy Days. 3-Charlie's Angels, Rocky
2 4 6 10 14 18

PAROLE BREAKERS
Avon Periodicals/Realistic #2 on: Dec, 1951 - No. 3, July, 1952

1(#2 on inside)-r-c/Avon paperback #283 (painted-c)
44 88 132 277 469 660
2-Kubert-a; r-c/Avon paperback #114 (photo-c) 31 62 93 182 296 410
3-Kinstler-c 27 54 81 160 263 365

PARTRIDGE FAMILY, THE (TV)(Also see David Cassidy)
Charlton Comics: Mar, 1971 - No. 21, Dec, 1973

1-(2 versions: B&W photo-c & tinted color photo-c) 7 14 21 48 79 110
2-4,6-10 4 8 12 26 41 55
5-Partridge Family Summer Special (52 pgs.); The Shadow, Lone Ranger, Charlie McCarthy, Flash Gordon, Hopalong Cassidy, Gene Autry & others app.
8 16 24 53 89 125
11-21 4 8 12 22 34 45

PARTS OF A HOLE
Caliber Press: 1991 ($2.50, B&W)

1-Short stories & cartoons by Brian Michael Bendis 3.00

PARTS UNKNOWN
Eclipse Comics/FX: July, 1992 - No. 4, Oct, 1992 ($2.50, B&W, mature)

1-4: All contain FX gaming cards 3.00

PARTS UNKNOWN
Image Comics: May, 2000 - Sept, 2000 ($2.95, B&W)

...: Killing Attractions 1 (5/00) Beau Smith-s/Brad Gorby-a 3.00
...: Hostile Takeover 1-4 (6-9/00) 3.00

PASSION, THE
Catechetical Guild: No. 394, 1955

394 6 12 18 31 38 45

PASSOVER (See Avengelyne)
Maximum Press: Dec, 1996 ($2.99, one-shot)

1 3.00

PAT BOONE (TV)(Also see Superman's Girlfriend Lois Lane #9)
National Per. Publ.: Sept-Oct, 1959 - No. 5, May-Jun, 1960 (All have photo-c)

1 42 84 126 265 445 625
2-5: 3-Fabian, Connie Francis & Paul Anka photos on-c. 4-Previews "Journey To The Center Of The Earth". 4-Johnny Mathis & Bobby Darin photos on-c. 5-Dick Clark & Frankie Avalon photos on-c 34 68 102 199 325 450

PATCHES
Rural Home/Patches Publ. (Orbit): Mar-Apr, 1945 - No. 11, Nov, 1947

1-L. B. Cole-c 39 78 117 240 395 550
2 15 30 45 88 137 185
3,4,6,8-11: 6-Henry Aldrich story. 8-Smiley Burnette-c/s (6/47); pre-dates Smiley Burnette #1. 9-Mr. District Attorney story (radio). Leav/Keigstein-a (16 pgs.). 9-11-Leav-c. 10-Jack Carson (radio) c/story; Leav-c. 11-Red Skelton story 15 30 45 85 130 175
5-Danny Kaye-c/story; L.B. Cole-c. 20 40 60 115 185 255
7-Hopalong Cassidy-c/story 18 36 54 103 162 220

PATH, THE (Also see Negation War)
CrossGeneration Comics: Apr, 2002 - No. 23, Apr, 2004 ($2.95)

1-23: 1-Ron Marz-s/Bart Sears-a. 13-Matthew Smith-a begins 3.00
Vol. 1: Crisis of Faith (2002, $15.95, TPB) r/#1-6 16.00
Vol. 2: Blood on Snow (5/03, $15.95, TPB) r/#7-12 16.00
Vol. 3: Death and Dishonor ('03, $15.95, TPB) r/#13-18 16.00

PATHWAYS TO FANTASY
Pacific Comics: July, 1984

1-Barry Smith-c/a; Jeff Jones-a (4 pgs.) 4.00

PATIENT ZERO
Image Comics: Mar, 2004 - No. 4, Jun, 2004 ($2.95, limited series)

1-4-Brent White-a/John McLean-Foreman-s 3.00

PATORUZU (See Adventures of...)

PATRIOTS, THE
DC Comics (WildStorm): Jan, 2000 - No. 10, Oct, 2000 ($2.50)

1-10-Choi and Peterson-s/Ryan-a 3.00

PATSY & HEDY (Teenage)(Also see Hedy Wolfe)
Atlas Comics/Marvel (GPI/Male): Feb, 1952 - No. 110, Feb, 1967

1-Patsy Walker & Hedy Wolfe; Al Jaffee-c 28 56 84 165 270 375
2 15 30 45 86 133 180
3-10: 3,7,8,9-Al Jaffee-c 14 28 42 78 112 145
11-20: 17,19,20-Al Jaffee-c 12 24 36 67 94 120
21-40 10 20 30 56 76 95
41-50 6 12 18 39 62 85
51-60 6 12 18 37 59 80
61-80,100: 88-Lingerie panel 5 10 15 32 51 70
81-87,89-99,101-110 5 10 15 30 48 65
Annual 1(1963)-Early Marvel annual 10 20 30 64 115 165

PATSY & HER PALS (Teenage)
Atlas Comics (PPI): May, 1953 - No. 29, Aug, 1957

1-Patsy Walker 20 40 60 120 195 270
2 13 26 39 74 105 135
3-10 12 24 36 67 94 120
11-29: 24-Everett-c 10 20 30 56 76 95

PATSY WALKER (See All Teen, A Date With Patsy, Girls' Life, Miss America Magazine, Patsy & Hedy, Patsy & Her Pals & Teen Comics)
Marvel/Atlas Comics (BPC): 1945 (no month) - No. 124, Dec, 1965

1-Teenage 60 120 180 381 653 925
2 34 68 102 199 325 450
3,4,6-10 27 54 81 160 263 365
5-Injury-to-eye-c 32 64 96 188 307 425
11,12,15,16,18 17 34 51 98 154 210
13,14,17,19-22-Kurtzman's "Hey Look" 18 36 54 103 162 220
23,24 15 30 45 84 127 170
25-Rusty by Kurtzman; painted-c 18 36 54 103 162 220
26-29,31: 26-31: 52 pgs. 14 28 42 76 108 140
30(52 pgs.)-Egghead Doodle by Kurtzman (1 pg.) 14 28 42 80 115 150

Pat the Brat #29 © AP

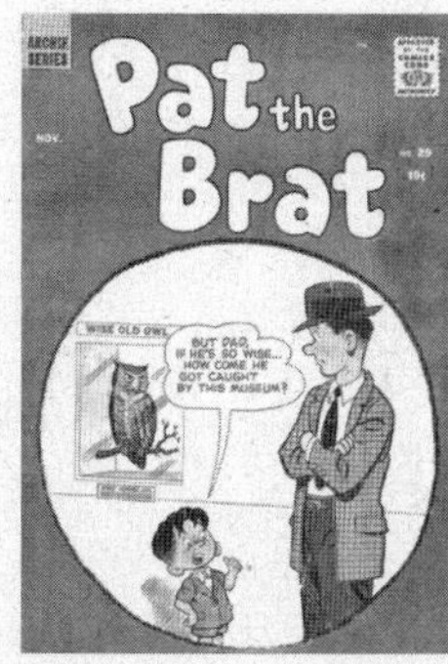

Peanuts (2011 series) #1 © Peanuts WW

Pebbles and Bamm-Bamm Giant Size #1 © H-B

	GD 2.0	VG 4.0	FN 6.0	VF 8.0	VF/NM 9.0	NM- 9.2
32-57: Last precode (3/55)	11	22	33	62	86	110
58-80,100	6	12	18	41	66	90
81-99: 92,98-Millie x-over. 99-Linda Carter x-over	6	12	18	37	59	80
101-124	5	10	15	32	51	70
Fashion Parade 1(1966, 68 pgs.) (Beware cut-out & marked pages)	9	18	27	58	99	140

NOTE: *Painted c-25-28. Anti-Wertham editorial in #21. Georgie app. in #8, 11, 17. Millie app. in #10, 92, 98. Mitzi app. in #11. Rusty app. in #12, 25. Willie app. in #12.* ***Al Jaffee*** *c-44, 47, 49, 51, 57, 58.*

PATSY WALKER: HELLCAT
Marvel Comics: Sept, 2008 - No. 5, Feb, 2009 ($2.99, limited series)

1-5-Lafuente-a/Kathryn Immonen-s/Stuart Immonen-c; Hellcat joins The Initiative 3.00

PAT THE BRAT (Adventures of Pipsqueak #34 on)
Archie Publications (Radio): June, 1953; Summer, 1955 - No. 4, 5/56; No. 15, 7/56 - No. 33, 7/59

	GD	VG	FN	VF	VF/NM	NM-
nn(6/53)	14	28	42	76	108	140
1(Summer, 1955)	10	20	30	54	72	90
2-4-(5/56) (#5-14 not published). 3-Early Bolling-a	7	14	21	37	46	55
15-(7/56)-33: 18-Early Bolling-a	4	8	12	22	34	45

PAT THE BRAT COMICS DIGEST MAGAZINE
Archie Publications: October, 1980

1-Li'l Jinx & Super Duck app. 2 4 6 9 13 16

PATTY CAKE
Permanent Press: Mar, 1995 - No. 9, Jul, 1996 ($2.95, B&W)

1-9: Scott Roberts-s/a 3.00

PATTY CAKE
Caliber Press (Tapestry): Oct, 1996 - No. 3, Apr, 1997 ($2.95, B&W)

1-3: Scott Roberts-s/a, ...Christmas (12/96) 3.00

PATTY CAKE & FRIENDS
Slave Labor Graphics: Nov, 1997 - Nov, 2000 ($2.95, B&W)

Here There Be Monsters (10/97), 1-14: Scott Roberts-s/a 3.00
Volume 2 #1 (11/00, $4.95) 5.00

PATTY POWERS (Formerly Della Vision #3)
Atlas Comics: No. 4, Oct, 1955 - No. 7, Oct, 1956

	GD	VG	FN	VF	VF/NM	NM-
4	11	22	33	64	90	115
5-7	8	16	24	42	54	65

PAT WILTON (See Mighty Midget Comics)

PAUL
Spire Christian Comics (Fleming H. Revell Co.): 1978 (49¢)

nn 2 4 6 10 14 18

PAULINE PERIL (See The Close Shaves of...)

PAUL REVERE'S RIDE (TV, Disney, see Walt Disney Showcase #34)
Dell Publishing Co.: No. 822, July, 1957

Four Color 822-w/Johnny Tremain, Toth-a 8 16 24 56 96 135

PAUL TERRY (See Heckle and Jeckle)

PAUL TERRY'S ADVENTURES OF MIGHTY MOUSE (See Adventures of...)

PAUL TERRY'S COMICS (Formerly Terry-Toons Comics; becomes Adventures of Mighty Mouse No. 126 on)
St. John Publishing Co.: No. 85, Mar, 1951 - No. 125, May, 1955

	GD	VG	FN	VF	VF/NM	NM-
85,86-Same as Terry-Toons #85, & 86 with only a title change; published at same time?; Mighty Mouse, Heckle & Jeckle & Gandy Goose continue from Terry-Toons	12	24	36	67	94	120
87-99	9	18	27	50	65	80
100	10	20	30	54	72	90
101-104,107-125: 121,122,125-Painted-c	9	18	27	47	61	75
105,106-Giant Comics Edition (25¢, 100 pgs.) (9/53 & ?). 105-Little Roquefort-c/story	18	36	54	105	165	225

PAUL TERRY'S MIGHTY MOUSE (See Mighty Mouse)

PAUL TERRY'S MIGHTY MOUSE ADVENTURE STORIES (See Mighty Mouse Adventure Stories)

PAUL THE SAMURAI (See The Tick #4)
New England Comics: July, 1992 - No. 6, July, 1993 ($2.75, B&W)

1-6 3.00

PAWNEE BILL
Story Comics (Youthful Magazines?): Feb, 1951 - No. 3, July, 1951

	GD	VG	FN	VF	VF/NM	NM-
1-Bat Masterson, Wyatt Earp app.	13	26	39	72	101	130
2,3: 3-Origin Golden Warrior; Cameron-a	8	16	24	42	54	65

PAY-OFF (This Is the..., ...Crime, ...Detective Stories)
D. S. Publishing Co.: July-Aug, 1948 - No. 5, Mar-Apr, 1949 (52 pgs.)

	GD 2.0	VG 4.0	FN 6.0	VF 8.0	VF/NM 9.0	NM- 9.2
1-True Crime Cases #1,2	27	54	81	158	259	360
2	15	30	45	94	147	200
3-5-Thrilling Detective Stories	14	28	42	82	121	160

PEACEMAKER, THE (Also see Fightin' Five)
Charlton Comics: V3#1, Mar, 1967 - No. 5, Nov, 1967 (All 12¢ cover price)

	GD	VG	FN	VF	VF/NM	NM-
1-Fightin' Five begins	5	10	15	35	55	75
2,3,5	3	6	9	21	32	42
4-Origin The Peacemaker	4	8	12	26	41	55
1,2(Modern Comics reprint, 1978)						6.00

PEACEMAKER (Also see Crisis On Infinite Earths & Showcase '93 #7,9,10)
DC Comics: Jan, 1988 - No. 4, Apr, 1988 ($1.25, limited series)

1-4 3.00

PEANUTS (Charlie Brown) (See Fritzi Ritz, Nancy & Sluggo, Sparkle & Sparkler, Tip Top, Tip Topper & United Comics)
United Features Syndicate/Dell Publishing Co./Gold Key: 1953-54; No. 878, 2/58 - No. 13, 5-7/62; 5/63 - No. 4, 2/64

	GD	VG	FN	VF	VF/NM	NM-
1(U.F.S.)(1953-54)-Reprints United Features' Strange As It Seems, Willie, Ferdnand	43	86	129	271	461	650
Four Color 878(#1) (Dell) Schulz-s/a, with assistance from Dale Hale and Jim Sasseville thru #4	21	42	63	148	317	485
Four Color 969,1015('59)	13	26	39	87	186	285
4(2-4/60) Schulz-s/a; one story by Anthony Pocrnich, Schulz's assistant cartoonist	12	24	36	80	163	245
5-13-Schulz-c only; s/a by Pocrnich	11	22	33	71	136	200
1(Gold Key, 5/63)	11	22	33	75	148	220
2-4	8	16	24	56	96	135

PEANUTS (Charlie Brown)
BOOM! Entertainment: No. 0, Nov, 2011 - Present ($1.00/$3.99)

0-(11/11, $1.00) New short stories and Sunday page reprints 1.00
1,2: 1-(1/12, $3.99) New short stories and Sunday page reprints; Snoopy sled cover 4.00
1,2-Variant-c with first appearance image. 1-Charlie Brown. 2-Lucy 6.00
Happiness is a Warm Blanket, Charlie Brown HC (Boom Entertainment, 3/2011, $19.99) adaptation of new animated special 20.00

PEBBLES & BAMM BAMM (TV) (See Cave Kids #7, 12)
Charlton Comics: Jan, 1972 - No. 36, Dec, 1976 (Hanna-Barbera)

	GD	VG	FN	VF	VF/NM	NM-
1-From the Flintstones; "Teen Age..." on cover	5	10	15	30	48	65
2-10	3	6	9	17	25	32
11-20	2	4	6	13	18	22
21-36	2	4	6	9	13	16
nn (1973, digest, 100 pgs.) B&W one page gags	3	6	9	18	27	35

PEBBLES & BAMM BAMM (TV)
Harvey Comics: Nov, 1993 - No. 3, Mar, 1994 ($1.50) (Hanna-Barbera)

V2#1-3 3.00
...Giant Size 1 (10/93, $2.25, 68 pgs.)("Summer Special" on-c) 4.00

PEBBLES FLINTSTONE (TV) (See The Flintstones #11)
Gold Key: Sept, 1963 (Hanna-Barbera)

1 (10088-309)-Early Pebbles app. 9 18 27 58 99 140

PEDRO (Formerly My Private Life #17; also see Romeo Tubbs)
Fox Features Syndicate: No. 18, June, 1950 - No. 2, Aug, 1950?

	GD	VG	FN	VF	VF/NM	NM-
18(#1)-Wood-c/a(p)	22	44	66	132	216	300
2-Wood-a?	15	30	45	88	137	185

PEE-WEE PIXIES (See The Pixies)

PELLEAS AND MELISANDE (See Night Music #4, 5)

PENALTY (See Crime Must Pay the...)

PENANCE: RELENTLESS (See Civil War, Thunderbolts and related titles)
Marvel Comics: Nov, 2007 - No. 5 ($2.99)

1-5-Speedball/Penance; Jenkins-s/Gulacy-a. 3-Wolverine app. 3.00
TPB (2008, $13.99) r/#1-5 14.00

PENDRAGON (Knights of... #5 on; also see Knights of...)
Marvel Comics UK, Ltd.: July, 1992 - No. 15, Sept, 1993 ($1.75)

1-15: 1-4-Iron Man app. 6-8-Spider-Man app. 3.00

PENDULUM ILLUSTRATED BIOGRAPHIES
Pendulum Press: 1979 (B&W)

19-355x-George Washington/Thomas Jefferson, 19-3495-Charles Lindbergh/Amelia Earhart, 19-3509-Harry

Penguins of Madagascar #1 © DW

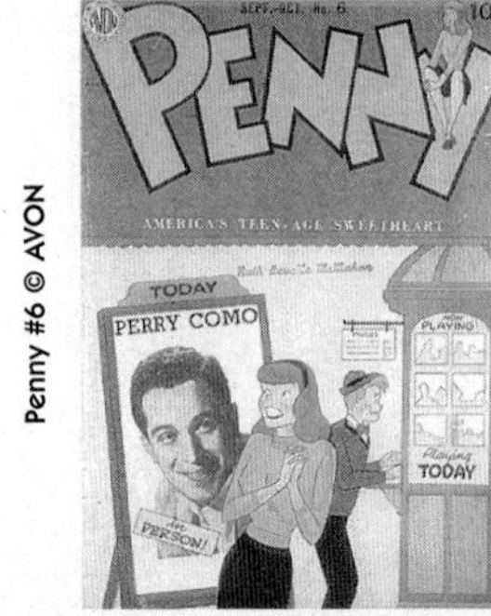

Penny #6 © AVON

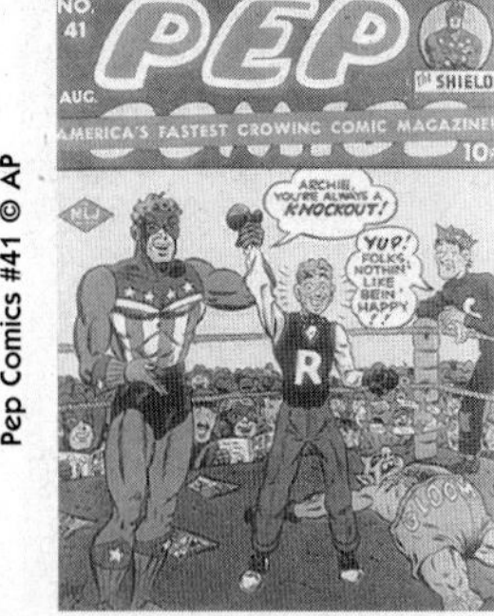

Pep Comics #41 © AP

GD 2.0 | VG 4.0 | FN 6.0 | VF 8.0 | VF/NM 9.0 | NM- 9.2

Houdini/Walt Disney, 19-3517-Davy Crockett/Daniel Boone-Redondo-a, 19-3525-Elvis Presley/Beatles, 19-3533-Benjamin Franklin/Martin Luther King Jr, 19-3541-Abraham Lincoln/Franklin D. Roosevelt, 19-3568-Marie Curie/Albert Einstein-Redondo-a, 19-3576-Thomas Edison/Alexander Graham Bell-Redondo-a, 19-3584-Vince Lombardi/Pele, 19-3592-Babe Ruth/Jackie Robinson, 19-3606-Jim Thorpe/Althea Gibson

Softback 5.00
Hardback 1 2 3 4 5 7

PENDULUM ILLUSTRATED CLASSICS (Now Age Illustrated)
Pendulum Press: 1973 - 1978 (75¢, 62pp, B&W, 5-3/8x8")
(Also see Marvel Classics)

64-100x(1973)-Dracula-Redondo art, 64-131x-The Invisible Man-Nino art, 64-0968-Dr. Jekyll and Mr. Hyde-Redondo art, 64-1005-Black Beauty, 64-1010-Call of the Wild, 64-1020-Frankenstein, 64-1025-Hucklebury Finn, 64-1030-Moby Dick-Nino-a, 64-1040-Red Badge of Courage, 64-1045-The Time Machine-Nino-a, 64-1050-Tom Sawyer, 64-1055-Twenty Thousand Leagues Under the Sea, 64-1069-Treasure Island, 64-1328(1974)-Kidnapped, 64-1336-Three Musketeers-Nino art, 64-1344-A Tale of Two Cities, 64-1352-Journey to the Center of the Earth, 64-1360-The War of the Worlds-Nino-a, 64-1379-The Greatest Advs. of Sherlock Holmes-Redondo art, 64-1387-Mysterious Island, 64-1395-Hunchback of Notre Dame, 64-1409-Helen Keller-story of my life, 64-1417-Scarlet Letter, 64-1425-Gulliver's Travels, 64-2618(1977)-Around the World in Eighty Days, 64-2626-Captains Courageous, 64-2634-Connecticut Yankee, 64-2642-The Hound of the Baskervilles, 64-2650-The House of Seven Gables, 64-2669-Jane Eyre, 64-2677-The Last of the Mohicans, 64-2685-The Best of O'Henry, 64-2693-The Best of Poe-Redondo-a, 64-2707-Two Years Before the Mast, 64-2715-White Fang, 64-2723-Wuthering Heights, 64-3126(1978)-Ben Hur-Redondo art, 64-3134-A Christmas Carol, 64-3142-The Food of the Gods, 64-3150-Ivanhoe, 64-3169-The Man in the Iron Mask, 64-3177-The Prince and the Pauper, 64-3185-The Prisoner of Zenda, 64-3193-The Return of the Native, 64-3207-Robinson Crusoe, 64-3215-The Scarlet Pimpernel, 64-3223-The Sea Wolf, 64-3231-The Swiss Family Robinson, 64-3851-Billy Budd, 64-386x-Crime and Punishment, 64-3878-Don Quixote, 64-3886-Great Expectations, 64-3894-Heidi, 64-3908-The Iliad, 64-3916-Lord Jim, 64-3924-The Mutiny on Board H.M.S. Bounty, 64-3932-The Odyssey, 64-3940-Oliver Twist, 64-3959-Pride and Prejudice, 64-3967-The Turn of the Screw

Softback 6.00
Hardback 1 2 3 5 6 8

NOTE: *All of the above books can be ordered from the publisher; some were reprinted as Marvel Classic Comics #1-12. In 1972 there was another brief series of 12 titles which contained Classics Ill. artwork. They were entitled* ***Now Age Books*** *Illustrated, but can be easily distinguished from later series by the small Classics Illustrated logo at the top of the front cover. The format is the same as the later series. The 48 pg. C.I. art was stretched out to make 62 pgs. After Twin Circle Publ. terminated the Classics Ill. series in 1971, they made a one year contract with Pendulum Press to print these twelve titles of C.I. art. Pendulum was unhappy with the contract, and at the end of 1972 began their own art series, utilizing the talents of the Filipino artist group. One detail which makes this rather confusing is that when they redid the art in 1973, they gave it the same identifying no. as the 1972 series. All 12 of the 1972 C.I. editions have new covers, taken from internal art panels. In spite of their recent age, all of the 1972 C.I. series are very rare. Mint copies would fetch at least $50. Here is a list of the 1972 series, with C.I. title no. counterpart:*

64-1005 (CI#60-A2) 64-1010 (CI#91) 64-1015 (CI-Jr #503) 64-1020 (CI#26)
64-1025 (CI#19-A2) 64-1030 (CI#5-A2) 64-1035 (CI#169) 64-1040 (CI#98)
64-1045 (CI#133) 64-1050 (CI#50-A2) 64-1055 (CI#47) 64-1060 (CI-Jr#535)

PENDULUM ILLUSTRATED ORIGINALS
Pendulum Press: 1979 (In color)

94-4254-Solarman: The Beginning (See Solarman) 6.00

PENDULUM'S ILLUSTRATED STORIES
Pendulum Press: 1990 - No. 72, 1990? (No cover price ($4.95), squarebound, 68 pgs.)

1-72: Reprints Pendulum Ill. Classics series 5.00

PENGUIN: PAIN & PREJUDICE (Batman)
DC Comics: Dec, 2011 - No. 5, Apr, 2012 ($2.99, limited series)

1-5-Hurwitz-s/Kudranski-a/c; Penguin's childhood and rise to power 3.00

PENGUINS OF MADAGASCAR (Based on the DreamWorks movie and TV series)
Ape Entertainment: 2010 - No. 4 ($3.95, limited series)

1-Skipper, Kowalski, Private and Rico app. 4.00

PENNY
Avon Comics: 1947 - No. 6, Sept-Oct, 1949 (Newspaper reprints)

1-Photo & biography of creator 21 42 63 126 206 285
2-5 11 22 33 64 90 115
6-Perry Como photo on-c 12 24 36 69 97 125

PENNY CENTURY (See Love and Rockets)
Fantagraphics Books: Dec, 1997 - No. 7, Jul, 2000 ($2.95, B&W, mini-series)

1-7-Jaime Hernandez-s/a 3.00

PEP COMICS (See Archie Giant Series #576, 589, 601, 614, 624)
MLJ Magazines/Archie Publications No. 56 (3/46) on: Jan, 1940 - No. 411, Mar, 1987

1-Intro. The Shield (1st patriotic hero) by Irving Novick; origin & 1st app. The Comet by Jack Cole, The Queen of Diamonds & Kayo Ward; The Rocket, The Press Guardian (The Falcon #1 only), Sergeant Boyle, Fu Chang, & Bentley of of Scotland Yard; Robot-c; Shield-c begin
892 1784 2676 6512 11,506 16,500
2-Origin The Rocket 274 548 822 1740 2995 4250
3 206 412 618 1318 2259 3200
4-Wizard cameo; early robot-s 168 336 504 1075 1838 2600
5-Wizard cameo in Shield story 168 336 504 1075 1838 2600
6-10: 8-Last Cole Comet; no Cole-a in #6,7 132 264 396 838 1444 2050

GD 2.0 | VG 4.0 | FN 6.0 | VF 8.0 | VF/NM 9.0 | NM- 9.2

11-Dusty, Shield's sidekick begins (1st app.); last Press Guardian, Fu Chang
135 270 405 864 1482 2100
12-Origin & 1st app. Fireball (2/41); last Rocket & Queen of Diamonds; Danny in Wonderland begins 155 310 465 992 1696 2400
13-15 110 220 330 704 1202 1700
16-Origin Madam Satan; blood drainage-c 174 348 522 1114 1907 2700
17-Origin/1st app. The Hangman (7/41); death of The Comet; Comet is revealed as Hangman's brother 394 788 1182 2758 4829 6900
18,19,21: 21-Last Madam Satan 102 204 306 648 1112 1575
20-Classic Nazi swastika-c; last Fireball 161 322 483 1030 1765 2500
22-Intro. & 1st app. Archie, Betty, & Jughead(12/41); (also see Jackpot)
8000 16,000 24,000 56,000 83,000 110,000
23 400 800 1200 2800 4900 7000
24,25: 24-Coach Kleats app. (unnamed until Archie #94); bondage/torture-c. 25-1st app. Archie's jalopy; 1st skinny Mr. Weatherbee prototype 297 594 891 1901 3251 4600
26-1st app. Veronica Lodge (4/42); "Remember Pearl Harbor!" cover caption
371 742 1113 2600 4550 6500
27,29,30: 27-Bill of Rights-c. 29-Origin Shield retold; 30-Capt. Commando begins; bondage/torture-c; 1st Miss Grundy (definitive version); see Jackpot #4
213 426 639 1363 2332 3300
28-Classic swastika/Hangman-c 226 452 678 1446 2473 3500
31-33,35: 31-MLJ offices & artists are visited in Sgt. Boyle story; 1st app. Mr. Lodge. 32-Shield dons new costume. 33-Pre-Moose tryout (see Jughead #1)
181 362 543 1158 1979 2800
34-Bondage/Hypo-c 271 542 813 1734 2967 4200
36-1st Archie-c (2/43) w/Shield & Hangman 389 778 1167 2723 4762 6800
37-40 116 232 348 742 1271 1800
41-45: 41-Archie-c begin 81 162 243 518 884 1250
46,47,49,50: 47-Last Hangman issue; infinity-c 71 142 213 454 777 1100
48-Black Hood begins (5/44); ends #51,59,60; Archie fish-c
116 232 348 742 1271 1800
51-60: 52-Suzie begins; 1st Mr Weatherbee-c. 56-Last Capt. Commando. 59-Black Hood not in costume; lingerie panels; Archie dresses as his aunt; Suzie ends. 60-Katy Keene begins(3/47), ends #154 40 80 120 246 411 575
61-65-Last Shield. 62-1st app. Li'l Jinx (7/47) 36 72 108 211 343 475
66-80: 66-G-Man Club becomes Archie Club (2/48); Nevada Jones by Bill Woggon. 76-Katy Keene story. 78-1st app. Dilton 20 40 60 114 182 250
81-99 15 30 45 88 137 185
100 18 36 54 107 169 230
101-130 11 22 33 62 86 110
131(2/59)-137 6 12 18 37 59 80
138-140-Neal Adams-a (1 pg.) in each 6 12 18 41 66 90
141-149(9/61) 5 10 15 30 48 65
150-160-Super-heroes app. in each (see note). 150 (10/61?)-2nd or 3rd app. The Jaguar? 151-154,156-158-Horror/Sci/Fi-c. 157-Li'l Jinx. 159-Both 12¢ and 15¢ covers exist
6 12 18 43 69 95
161(3/63)-167,169-180: 161-3rd Josie app.; early Josie stories w/DeCarlo-a begin (see Note for others) 4 8 12 24 37 50
168,200: 168-(1/64)-Jaguar app. 200-(12/66) 4 8 12 26 41 55
181(5/65)-199: 187-Pureheart try-out story. 192-UFO-c. 198-Giantman-c(only)
3 6 9 18 27 35
201-217,219-226,228-240(4/70) 3 6 9 16 22 28
218,227-Archies Band-c only 3 6 9 17 25 32
241-270(10/72) 2 4 6 13 18 22
271-297,299 2 4 6 9 12 15
298, 300: 298-Josie and the Pussycats-c. 300(4/75) 2 4 6 13 18 22
301-340(8/78) 1 3 4 6 8 10
341-382 1 2 3 4 5 7
383(4/82),393(3/84): 383-Marvelous Maureen begins (Sci/fi). 393-Thunderbunny begins
1 2 3 5 6 8
384-392,394,395,397-399,401-410 5.00
396-Early Cheryl Blossom-c 1 2 3 5 6 8
400(5/85),411: 400-Story featuring Archie staff (DeCarlo-a)
1 2 3 4 5 7

NOTE: ***Biro*** *a-2, 4, 5.* ***Jack Cole*** *a-1-5, 8.* ***Al Fagaly*** *c-55-72.* ***Fuje*** *a-39, 45, 47; c-34.* ***Meskin*** *a-2, 4, 5, 11(2).* ***Montana*** *c-30, 32, 33, 36, 73-87(most).* ***Novick*** *c-1-28, 29(w/****Schomburg****), 31i.* ***Harry Sahle*** *c-35, 39-50.* ***Schomburg*** *c-38.* ***Bob Wood*** *a-2, 4-6, 11. The Fly app. in 151, 154, 160. Flygirl app. in 153, 155, 156, 158. Jaguar app. in 150, 152, 157, 159, 168. Josie by* ***DeCarlo*** *in 161-166, 168-171, 173, 175-177, 179, 181. Katy Keene by* ***Bill Woggon*** *in 73-126. Bondage c-7, 12, 13, 15, 18, 21, 31, 32. Cover features: Shield #1-16; Shield/Hangman #17-27, 29-41; Hangman #28. Archie #36, 41-on.*

PEP COMICS FEATURING BETTY AND VERONICA
Archie Comic Publications: May, 2011 (Giveaway)

Free Comic Book Day Edition - Little Archie flashback 3.00

PEPE

Perfect Crime #9 © Cross Pub.

Personal Love #1 © FF

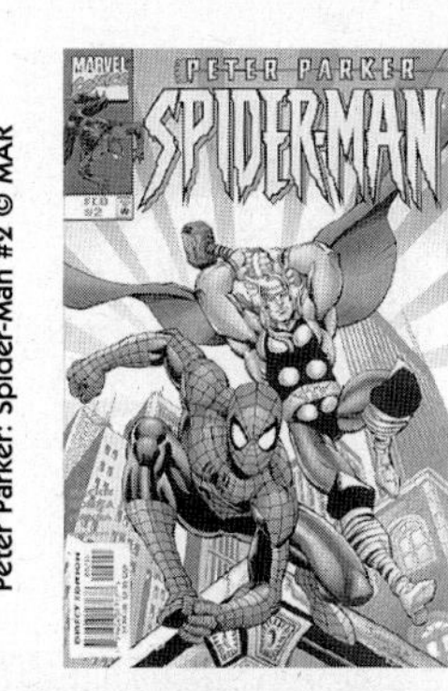

Peter Parker: Spider-Man #2 © MAR

Dell Publishing Co.: No. 1194, Apr, 1961

	GD 2.0	VG 4.0	FN 6.0	VF 8.0	VF/NM 9.0	NM- 9.2
Four Color 1194-Movie, photo-c	4	8	12	24	37	50

PERFECT CRIME, THE
Cross Publications: Oct, 1949 - No. 33, May, 1953 (#2-14, 52 pgs.)

	GD 2.0	VG 4.0	FN 6.0	VF 8.0	VF/NM 9.0	NM- 9.2
1-Powell-a(2)	39	78	117	231	378	525
2 (4/50)	20	40	60	120	195	270
3-10: 7-Steve Duncan begins, ends #30. 10-Flag-c	18	36	54	107	169	230
11-Used in **SOTI**, pg. 159	20	40	60	117	189	260
12-14	17	34	51	98	154	210
15- "The Most Terrible Menace" 2 pg. drug editorial (8/51)	19	38	57	109	172	235
16,17,19-25,27-29,31-33	14	28	42	82	121	160
18-Drug cover, heroin drug propaganda story, plus 2 pg. anti-drug editorial (11/51)	32	64	96	188	307	425
26-Drug-c with hypodermic needle; drug propaganda story (7/52)	30	60	90	177	289	400
30-Strangulation cover (11/52)	31	62	93	182	296	410

NOTE: ***Powell** a-No. 1, 2, 4. **Wildey** a-1, 5. Bondage c-11.*

PERFECT LOVE
Ziff-Davis(Approved Comics)/St. John No. 9 on: #10, 8-9/51 (cover date; 5-6/51 indicia date); #2, 10-11/51 - #10, 12/53

	GD 2.0	VG 4.0	FN 6.0	VF 8.0	VF/NM 9.0	NM- 9.2
10(#1)(8-9/51)-Painted-c	22	44	66	132	216	300
2(10-11/51)	15	30	45	88	137	185
3,5-7: 3-Painted-c. 5-Photo-c	14	28	42	80	115	150
4,8 (Fall, 1952)-Kinstler-a; last Z-D issue	14	28	42	81	118	155
9,10 (10/53, 12/53, St. John): 9-Painted-c. 10-Photo-c	14	28	42	78	112	145

PERHAPANAUTS, THE
Dark Horse Comics: Nov, 2005 - No. 4, Feb, 2006 ($2.99, limited series)

	GD 2.0	VG 4.0	FN 6.0	VF 8.0	VF/NM 9.0	NM- 9.2
1-4-Todd Dezago-s/Craig Rousseau-a/c						3.00
... Annual #1 (2/08, $3.50) Two covers by Rousseau and Allred						3.50
... Halloween Spooktacular 1 (10/09, $3.50) Hembeck, Rousseau and others-a						3.50
,,, - Molly's Story (2/10, $3.50) Copland-a						3.50
(2nd series) (4/08 - Present, $3.50) 1-6: 1-Two covers by Art Adams and Rousseau						3.50

PERHAPANAUTS: SECOND CHANCES, THE
Dark Horse Comics: Oct, 2006 - No. 4, Jan, 2007 ($2.99, limited series)

	GD 2.0	VG 4.0	FN 6.0	VF 8.0	VF/NM 9.0	NM- 9.2
1-4-Todd Dezago-s/Craig Rousseau-a/c						3.00

PERRI (Disney)
Dell Publishing Co.: No. 847, Jan, 1958

	GD 2.0	VG 4.0	FN 6.0	VF 8.0	VF/NM 9.0	NM- 9.2
Four Color 847-Movie, w/2 diff-c publ.	5	10	15	35	55	75

PERRY MASON
David McKay Publications: No. 49, 1946 - No. 50, 1946

	GD 2.0	VG 4.0	FN 6.0	VF 8.0	VF/NM 9.0	NM- 9.2
Feature Books 49, 50-Based on Gardner novels	34	68	102	199	325	450

PERRY MASON MYSTERY MAGAZINE (TV)
Dell Publishing Co.: June-Aug, 1964 - No. 2, Oct-Dec, 1964

	GD 2.0	VG 4.0	FN 6.0	VF 8.0	VF/NM 9.0	NM- 9.2
1	6	12	18	39	62	85
2-Raymond Burr photo-c	5	10	15	32	51	70

PERSONAL LOVE (Also see Movie Love)
Famous Funnies: Jan, 1950 - No. 33, June, 1955

	GD 2.0	VG 4.0	FN 6.0	VF 8.0	VF/NM 9.0	NM- 9.2
1-Photo-c	22	44	66	128	209	290
2-Kathryn Grayson & Mario Lanza photo-c	14	28	42	78	112	145
3-7,10: 7-Robert Walker & Joanne Dru photo-c. 10-Loretta Young & Joseph Cotton photo-c	13	26	39	72	101	130
8,9: 8-Esther Williams & Howard Keel photo-c. 9-Debra Paget & Louis Jourdan photo-c	13	26	39	74	105	135
11-Toth-a; Glenn Ford & Gene Tierney photo-c	14	28	42	82	121	160
12,16,17-One pg. Frazetta each. 17-Rock Hudson & Yvonne DeCarlo photo-c	13	26	39	72	101	130
13-15,18-23: 12-Jane Greer & William Lundigan photo-c. 14-Kirk Douglas photo-c. 15-Dale Robertson & Joanne Dru photo-c. 18-Gregory Peck & Susan Hayworth photo-c. 19-Anthony Quinn & Suzan Ball photo-c. 20-Robert Wagner & Kathleen Crowley photo-c. 21-Roberta Peters & Byron Palmer photo-c. 22-Dale Robertson photo-c. 23-Rhonda Fleming-c	12	24	36	67	94	120
24,27,28-Frazetta-a in each (8,8&6 pgs.). 27-Rhonda Fleming & Fernando Lamas photo-c. 28-Mitzi Gaynor photo-c	47	94	141	296	498	700
25-Frazetta-a (tribute to Bettie Page, 7 pg. story); Tyrone Power/Terry Moore photo-c from "King of the Khyber Rifles"	63	126	189	403	689	975
26,29,30,33: 26-Constance Smith & Byron Palmer photo-c. 29-Charlton Heston & Nicol Morey photo-c. 30-Johnny Ray & Mitzi Gaynor photo-c. 33-Dana Andrews & Piper Laurie photo-c	12	24	36	67	94	120
31-Marlon Brando & Jean Simmons photo-c; last pre-code (2/55)	14	28	42	82	121	160
32-Classic Frazetta-a (8 pgs.); Kirk Douglas & Bella Darvi photo-c	64	128	192	406	696	985

NOTE: *All have photo-c. Many feature movie stars.* ***Everett** a-5, 9, 10, 24.*

PERSONAL LOVE (Going Steady V3#3 on)
Prize Publ. (Headline): V1#1, Sept, 1957 - V3#2, Nov-Dec, 1959

	GD 2.0	VG 4.0	FN 6.0	VF 8.0	VF/NM 9.0	NM- 9.2
V1#1	11	22	33	62	86	110
2	8	16	24	42	54	65
3-6(7-8/58)	7	14	21	37	46	55
V2#1(9-10/58)-V2#6(7-8/59)	6	12	18	31	38	45
V3#1-Wood?/Orlando-a	7	14	21	35	43	50
2	6	12	18	29	36	42

PETER CANNON - THUNDERBOLT (See Crisis on Infinite Earths)(Also see Thunderbolt)
DC Comics: Sept, 1992 - No. 12, Aug, 1993 ($1.25)

	GD 2.0	VG 4.0	FN 6.0	VF 8.0	VF/NM 9.0	NM- 9.2
1-12						3.00

PETER COTTONTAIL
Key Publications: Jan, 1954; Feb, 1954 - No. 2, Mar, 1954 (Says 3/53 in error)

	GD 2.0	VG 4.0	FN 6.0	VF 8.0	VF/NM 9.0	NM- 9.2
1(1/54)-Not 3-D	9	18	27	52	69	85
1(2/54)-(3-D, 25¢)-Came w/glasses; written by Bruce Hamilton	21	42	63	122	199	275
2-Reprints 3-D #1 but not in 3-D	6	12	18	31	38	45

PETER GUNN (TV)
Dell Publishing Co.: No. 1087, Apr-June, 1960

	GD 2.0	VG 4.0	FN 6.0	VF 8.0	VF/NM 9.0	NM- 9.2
Four Color 1087-Photo-c	8	16	24	56	96	135

PETE ROSE: HIS INCREDIBLE BASEBALL CAREER
Masstar Creations Inc.: 1995

	GD 2.0	VG 4.0	FN 6.0	VF 8.0	VF/NM 9.0	NM- 9.2
1-John Tartaglione-a						3.00

PETER PAN (Disney) (See Hook, Movie Classics & Comics, New Adventures of... & Walt Disney Showcase #36)
Dell Publishing Co.: No. 442, Dec, 1952 - No. 926, Aug, 1958

	GD 2.0	VG 4.0	FN 6.0	VF 8.0	VF/NM 9.0	NM- 9.2
Four Color 442 (#1)-Movie	10	20	30	66	121	175
Four Color 926-Reprint of 442	4	8	12	28	44	60

PETER PAN
Disney Comics: 1991 ($5.95, graphic novel, 68 pgs.)(Celebrates video release)

	GD 2.0	VG 4.0	FN 6.0	VF 8.0	VF/NM 9.0	NM- 9.2
nn-r/Peter Pan Treasure Chest from 1953						7.00

PETER PANDA
National Periodical Publications: Aug-Sept, 1953 - No. 31, Aug-Sept, 1958

	GD 2.0	VG 4.0	FN 6.0	VF 8.0	VF/NM 9.0	NM- 9.2
1-Grossman-c/a in all	51	102	153	320	543	765
2	26	52	78	154	252	350
3,4,6-8,10	21	42	63	126	206	285
5-Classic-c (scarce)	74	148	222	470	810	1150
9-Robot-c	30	60	90	177	289	400
11-31	15	30	45	88	137	185

PETER PAN RECORDS (See Power Records)

PETER PAN TREASURE CHEST (See Dell Giants)

PETER PARKER (See The Spectacular Spider-Man)

PETER PARKER
Marvel Comics: May, 2010 - No. 5, Sept, 2010 ($3.99/$2.99)

	GD 2.0	VG 4.0	FN 6.0	VF 8.0	VF/NM 9.0	NM- 9.2
1-($3.99) Prints material from Marvel Digital Comics; Olliffe-a; back-up w/Hembeck-s/a						4.00
2-5-($2.99): 2-4-Olliffe-a. 3-Braithwaite-c. 5-Nauck-a; Thing app.						3.00

PETER PARKER: SPIDER-MAN
Marvel Comics: Jan, 1999 - No. 57, Aug, 2003 ($2.99/$1.99/$2.25)

	GD 2.0	VG 4.0	FN 6.0	VF 8.0	VF/NM 9.0	NM- 9.2
1-Mackie-s/Romita Jr.-a; wraparound-c						4.00
1-($6.95) DF Edition w/variant-c by the Romitas	1	2	3	5	6	8
2-11,13-17-($1.99): 2-Two covers; Thor app. 3-Iceman-c/app. 4-Marrow-c/app. 5-Spider-Woman app. 7,8-Blade app. 9,10-Venom app. 11-Iron Man & Thor-c/app.						3.00
12-($2.99) Sinister Six and Venom app.						4.00
18-24,26-43: 18-Begin $2.25-c. 20-Jenkins-s/Buckingham-a start. 23-Intro Typeface. 24-Maximum Security x-over. 29-Rescue of MJ. 30-Ramos-c. 42,43-Mahfood-a						3.00
25-($2.99) Two covers; Spider-Man & Green Goblin						4.00
44-47-Humberto Ramos-c/a; Green Goblin-c/app.						3.00
48,49,51-57: 48,49-Buckingham-c/a. 51,52-Herrera-a. 56,57-Kieth-a; Sandman returns						3.00
50-($3.50) Buckingham-c/a						4.00
...'99 Annual (8/99, $3.50) Man-Thing app.						4.00
...'00 Annual ($3.50) Bounty app.; Joe Bennett-a; Black Cat back-up story						4.00

Peter Porkchops #6 © DC

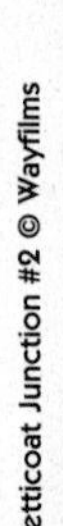
Petticoat Junction #2 © Wayfilms

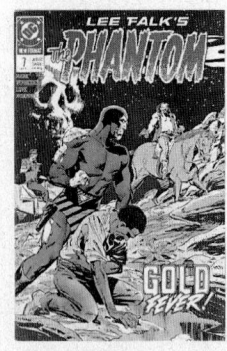

Phantom (1989 series) #7 © KING

GD 2.0 | VG 4.0 | FN 6.0 | VF 8.0 | VF/NM 9.0 | NM- 9.2

GD 2.0 | VG 4.0 | FN 6.0 | VF 8.0 | VF/NM 9.0 | NM- 9.2

...'01 Annual ($2.99) Avery-s 4.00
...: A Day in the Life TPB (5/01, $14.95) r/#20-22,26; Webspinners #10-12 15.00
...: One Small Break TPB (2002, $16.95) r/#27,28,30-34; Andrews-c 17.00
Spider-Man: Return of the Goblin TPB (2002, $8.99) r/#44-47; Ramos-c 9.00
...Vol. 4: Trials & Tribulations TPB (2003, $11.99) r/#35,37,48-50; Cho-c 12.00

PETER PAT
United Features Syndicate: No. 8, 1939

Single Series 8 36 72 108 211 343 475

PETER PAUL'S 4 IN 1 JUMBO COMIC BOOK
Capitol Stories (Charlton): No date (1953)

1-Contains 4 comics bound; Space Adventures, Space Western, Crime & Justice, Racket Squad in Action 40 80 120 242 401 560

PETER PIG
Standard Comics: No. 5, May, 1953 - No. 6, Aug, 1953

5,6 7 14 21 35 43 50

PETER PORKCHOPS (See Leading Comics #23) (Also see Capt. Carrot)
National Periodical Publications: 11-12/49 - No. 61, 9-11/59; No. 62, 10-12/60 (1-11: 52 pgs.)

1 34 68 102 199 325 450
2 15 30 45 90 140 190
3-10: 6- "Peter Rockets to Mars!" c/story 13 26 39 74 105 135
11-30 10 20 30 56 76 95
31-62 9 18 27 47 61 75

NOTE: ***Otto Feuer** a-all. **Rube Grossman**-a most issues. **Sheldon Mayer** a-30-38, 40-44, 46-52, 61.*

PETER PORKER, THE SPECTACULAR SPIDER-HAM
Star Comics (Marvel): May, 1985 - No. 17, Sept, 1987 (Also see Marvel Tails)

1-Michael Golden-c 5.00
2-17: 12-Origin/1st app. Bizarro Phil. 13-Halloween issue 4.00

NOTE: *Back-up features: 2-X-Bugs. 3-Iron Mouse. 4-Croctor Strange. 5-Thrr, Dog of Thunder.*

PETER POTAMUS (TV)
Gold Key: Jan, 1965 (Hanna-Barbera)

1-1st app. Peter Potamus & So-So, Breezly & Sneezly 9 18 27 63 112 160

PETER RABBIT (See New Funnies #65 & Space Comics)
Dell Publishing Co.: No. 1, 1942

Large Feature Comic 1 62 124 186 394 677 960

PETER RABBIT (Adventures of...; New Advs. of... #9 on)(Also see Funny Tunes & Space Comics)
Avon Periodicals: 1947 - No. 34, Aug-Sept, 1956

1(1947)-Reprints 1943-44 Sunday strips; contains a biography & drawing of Cady 36 72 108 214 347 480
2 (4/48) 24 48 72 142 234 325
3 ('48) - 6(7/49)-Last Cady issue 21 42 63 124 202 280
7-10(1950-8/51): 9-New logo 11 22 33 62 86 110
11(11/51)-34('56)-Avon's character 9 18 27 52 69 85
...Easter Parade (1952, 25¢, 132 pgs.) 20 40 60 117 189 260
...Jumbo Book (1954-Giant Size, 25¢)-Jesse James by Kinstler (6 pgs.); space ship-c 24 48 72 140 230 320

PETER RABBIT 3-D
Eternity Comics: April, 1990 ($2.95, with glasses; sealed in plastic bag)

1-By Harrison Cady (reprints) 3.00

PETER, THE LITTLE PEST (#4 titled Petey)
Marvel Comics Group: Nov, 1969 - No. 4, May, 1970

1 7 14 21 46 76 105
2-4-r-Dexter the Demon & Melvin the Monster 5 10 15 32 51 70

PETE'S DRAGON (See Walt Disney Showcase #43)

PETE THE PANIC
Stanmor Publications: November, 1955

nn-Code approved 6 12 18 28 34 40

PETEY (See Peter, the Little Pest)

PETTICOAT JUNCTION (TV, inspired Green Acres)
Dell Publ. Co.: Oct-Dec, 1964 - No. 5, Oct-Dec, 1965 (#1-3, 5 have photo-c)

1 7 14 21 46 76 105
2-5 5 10 15 32 51 70

PETUNIA (Also see Looney Tunes and Porky Pig)
Dell Publishing Co.: No. 463, Apr, 1953

Four Color 463 4 8 12 28 44 60

PHAGE (See Neil Gaiman's Teknophage & Neil Gaiman's Phage-Shadowdeath)

PHANTACEA
McPherson Publishing Co.: Sept, 1977 - No. 6, Summer, 1980 (B&W)

1-Early Dave Sim-a (32 pgs.) 5 10 15 30 48 65
2-Dave Sim-a(10 pgs.) 3 6 9 14 19 24
3-6: 3-Flip-c w/Damnation Bridge. 4-Gene Day-a 2 4 6 10 14 18

PHANTASMO (See The Funnies #45)
Dell Publishing Co.: No. 18, 1941

Large Feature Comic 18 39 78 117 231 378 525

PHANTOM, THE
David McKay Publishing Co.: 1939 - 1949

Feature Books 20 95 190 285 603 1039 1475
Feature Books 22 67 134 201 426 731 1035
Feature Books 39 51 102 153 318 539 760
Feature Books 53,56,57 41 82 123 250 418 585

PHANTOM, THE (See Ace Comics, Defenders Of The Earth, Eat Right to Work and Win, Future Comics, Harvey Comics Hits #51,56, Harvey Hits #1, 6, 12, 15, 26, 36, 44, 48, & King Comics)

PHANTOM, THE (nn (#29)-Published overseas only) (Also see Comics Reading Libraries in the Promotional Comics section)
Gold Key(#1-17)/King(#18-28)/Charlton(#30 on): Nov, 1962 - No. 17, Jul, 1966; No. 18, Sept, 1966 - No. 28, Dec, 1967; No. 30, Feb, 1969 - No. 74, Jan, 1977

1-Origin revealed on inside-c & back-c 16 32 48 111 243 375
2-King, Queen & Jack begins, ends #11 10 20 30 65 118 170
3-5 9 18 27 60 103 145
6-10 7 14 21 48 79 110
11-17: 12-Track Hunter begins 6 12 18 41 66 90
18-Flash Gordon begins; Wood-a 5 10 15 32 51 70
19-24: 20-Flash Gordon ends (both by Gil Kane). 21-Mandrake begins. 20,24-Girl Phantom app. 4 8 12 28 44 60
25-28: 25-Jeff Jones-a(4 pgs.); 1 pg. Williamson ad. 26-Brick Bradford app. 28(nn)-Brick Bradford app. 4 8 12 22 34 45
30-33: 33-Last 12¢ issue 3 6 9 17 25 32
34-40: 36,39-Ditko-a 3 6 9 16 23 30
41-66: 46-Intro. The Piranha. 51-Grey tone-c. 62-Bolle-c 3 6 9 14 19 24
67-Origin retold; Newton-c/a; Humphrey Bogart, Lauren Bacall & Peter Lorre app. 3 6 9 17 25 32
68-73-Newton-c/a 2 4 6 13 18 22
74-Classic flag-c by Newton; Newton-a; 3 6 9 16 23 30

NOTE: ***Aparo** a-31-34, 36-38; c-31-38, 60, 61. Painted c-1-17.*

PHANTOM, THE
DC Comics: May, 1988 - No. 4, Aug, 1988 ($1.25, mini-series)

1-4: Orlando-c/a in all 3.00

PHANTOM, THE
DC Comics: Mar, 1989 - No. 13, Mar, 1990 ($1.50)

1-13: 1-Brief origin 3.00

PHANTOM, THE
Wolf Publishing: 1992 - No. 8, 1993 ($2.25)

1-8 3.00

PHANTOM, THE
Moonstone: 2003 - No. 26, Dec, 2008 ($3.50/$3.99)

1-26: 1-Cassaday-c/Raab-s/Quinn-a 4.00
... Annual #1 (2007, $6.50) Blevins-c; stroy and art by various incl. Nolan 6.50
... - Captain Action 1 (2010, $3.99) covers by Thibert, Sparacio, and Gilbert 4.00

PHANTOM BLOT, THE (#1 titled New Adventures of...)
Gold Key: Oct, 1964 - No. 7, Nov, 1966 (Disney)

1 (Meets The Mysterious Mr. X) 6 12 18 41 66 90
2-1st Super Goof 5 10 15 34 55 75
3-7 4 8 12 22 34 45

PHANTOM EAGLE (See Mighty Midget, Marvel Super Heroes #16 & Wow #6)

PHANTOM FORCE
Image Comics/Genesis West #0, 3-7: 12/93 - #2, 1994; #0, 3/94; #3, 5/94 - #8, 10/94 ($2.50/$3.50, limited series)

0 (3/94, $2.50)-Kirby/Jim Lee-c; Kirby-p pgs. 1,5,24-29. 3.00
1 (12/93, $2.50)-Polybagged w/trading card; Kirby/Liefeld-c; Kirby plots/pencils w/inks by Liefeld, McFarlane, Jim Lee, Silvestri, Larsen, Williams, Ordway & Miki 3.00

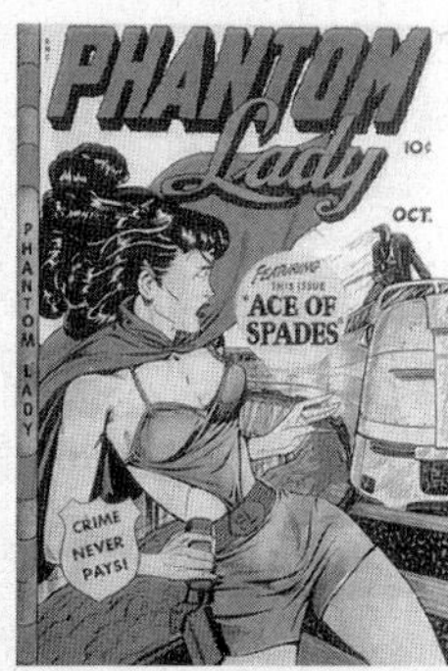

Phantom Lady #20 © FOX

Phantom Stranger #5 © DC

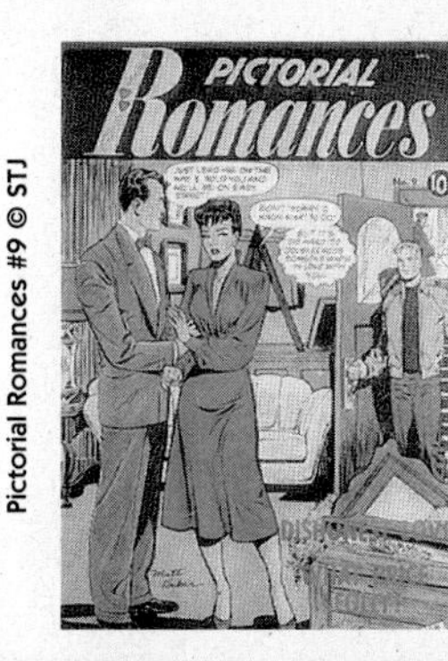

Pictorial Romances #9 © STJ

	GD 2.0	VG 4.0	FN 6.0	VF 8.0	VF/NM 9.0	NM- 9.2

2 ($3.50)-Kirby-a(p); Kirby/Larson-c 4.00
3-8: 3-(5/94, $2.50)-Kirby/McFarlane-c 4-(5/94)-Kirby-c(p). 5-(6/94) 3.00

PHANTOM GUARD
Image Comics (WildStorm Productions): Oct, 1997 - No. 6, Mar, 1998 ($2.50)

1-6: 1-Two covers 3.00
1-($3.50)-Voyager Pack w/Wildcore preview 4.00

PHANTOM JACK
Image Comics: Mar, 2004 - No. 5, July, 2004 ($2.95)

1-5-Mike San Giacomo-s/Mitchell Breitweiser-a. 4-Initial printings with errors exist 3.00
The Collected Edition (Speakeasy Comics, 2005, $17.99) r/series; Bendis intro 18.00

PHANTOM LADY (1st Series) (My Love Secret #24 on) (Also see All Top, Daring Adventures, Freedom Fighters, Jungle Thrills, & Wonder Boy)
Fox Features Syndicate: No. 13, Aug, 1947 - No. 23, Apr, 1949

	GD	VG	FN	VF	VF/NM	NM-
13(#1)-Phantom Lady by Matt Baker begins (see Police Comics #1 for 1st app.); Blue Beetle story	432	864	1296	3154	5577	8000
14-16: 14(#2)-Not Baker-c. 15-P.L. injected with experimental drug. 16-Negligee-c, panels; true crime stories begin	284	568	852	1818	3109	4400
17-Classic bondage cover; used in **SOTI**, illo "Sexual stimulation by combining 'headlights' with the sadist's dream of tying up a woman"	757	1514	2271	5526	9763	14,000
18,19	194	388	582	1242	2121	3000
20-22	165	330	495	1048	1799	2550
23-Bondage-c	194	388	582	1242	2121	3000

NOTE: ***Matt Baker** a-in all; c-13, 15-21. **Kamen** a-22, 23.*

PHANTOM LADY (2nd Series) (See Terrific Comics) (Formerly Linda)
Ajax/Farrell Publ.: V1#5, Dec-Jan, 1954/1955 - No. 4, June, 1955

	GD	VG	FN	VF	VF/NM	NM-
V1#5(#1)-By Matt Baker	126	252	378	806	1378	1950
V1#2-Last pre-code	92	184	276	584	1005	1425
3,4-Red Rocket. 3-Heroin story	73	146	219	467	796	1125

PHANTOM LADY
Verotik Publications: 1994 ($9.95)

1-Reprints G. A. stories from Phantom Lady and All Top Comics; Adam Hughes-c 10.00

PHANTOM PLANET, THE
Dell Publishing Co.: No. 1234, 1961

	GD	VG	FN	VF	VF/NM	NM-
Four Color 1234-Movie	7	14	21	46	76	105

PHANTOM STRANGER, THE (1st Series)(See Saga of Swamp Thing)
National Periodical Publications: Aug-Sept, 1952 - No. 6, June-July, 1953

	GD	VG	FN	VF	VF/NM	NM-
1(Scarce)-1st app.	213	426	639	1363	2332	3300
2 (Scarce)	116	232	348	742	1271	1800
3-6 (Scarce)	100	200	300	635	1093	1550

Ashcan (8,9/52) Not distributed to newsstands, only for in house use (no known sales)

PHANTOM STRANGER, THE (2nd Series) (See Showcase #80) (See Showcase Presents for B&W reprints)
National Periodical Publs.: May-June, 1969 - No. 41, Feb-Mar, 1976; No. 42, Mar, 2010

	GD	VG	FN	VF	VF/NM	NM-
1-2nd S.A. app. P. Stranger; only 12¢ issue	11	22	33	76	151	225
2,3	7	14	21	44	72	100
4-1st new look Phantom Stranger; N. Adams-a	7	14	21	48	79	110
5-7	5	10	15	35	55	75
8-14: 14-Last 15¢ issue	4	8	12	24	37	50
15-19: All 25¢ giants (52 pgs.)	4	8	12	26	41	55
20-Dark Circle begins, ends #24.	3	6	9	17	25	32
21,22	3	6	9	14	20	25
23-Spawn of Frankenstein begins by Kaluta	4	8	12	26	41	55
24,25,27-30-Last Spawn of Frankenstein	3	6	9	20	30	40
26- Book-length story featuring Phantom Stranger, Dr. 13 & Spawn of Frankenstein	4	8	12	22	34	45
31-The Black Orchid begins (6-7/74).	3	6	9	19	29	38
32,34-38: 34-Last 20¢ issue (#35 on are 25¢)	2	4	6	13	18	22
33,39-41: 33-Deadman-c/story. 39-41-Deadman app.	3	6	9	14	20	25

42-(3/10, $2.99) Blackest Night one-shot; Syaf-a; Spectre, Deadman and Blue Devil app. 3.00

NOTE: ***N. Adams** a-4; c-3-19. **Anderson** a-4, 5i. **Aparo** a-7-17, 19-26; c-20-24, 33-41. **B. Bailey** a-27-30. **DeZuniga** a-12-16, 18, 19, 21, 22, 31, 34. **Grell** a-33. **Kaluta** a-23-25; c-26. **Meskin** r-15, 16, 18, 19. **Redondo** a-32, 35, 36. **Sparling** a-20. **Starr** a-17r. **Toth** a-15r. Black Orchid by **Carrilo**-38-41. Dr. 13 solo in-13, 18, 19, 20, 21, 34. Frankenstein by **Kaluta**-23-25; by **Baily**-27-30. No Black Orchid-33, 34, 37.*

PHANTOM STRANGER (See Justice League of America #103)
DC Comics: Oct, 1987 - No. 4, Jan, 1988 (75¢, limited series)

1-4-Mignola/Russell-c/a & Eclipso app. in all. 3,4-Eclipso-c 4.00

PHANTOM STRANGER (See Vertigo Visions-The Phantom Stranger)

PHANTOM: THE GHOST WHO WALKS
Marvel Comics: Feb, 1995 - No. 3, Apr, 1995 ($2.95, limited series)

1-3 4.00

PHANTOM: THE GHOST WHO WALKS
Moonstone: 2003 ($16.95, TPB)

nn-Three new stories by Raab, Goulart, Collins, Blanco and others; Klauba painted-c 17.00

PHANTOM 2040 (TV cartoon)
Marvel Comics: May, 1995 - No. 4, Aug, 1995 ($1.50)

1-4-Based on animated series; Ditko-a(p) in all 3.00

PHANTOM WITCH DOCTOR (Also see Durango Kid #8 & Eerie #8)
Avon Periodicals: 1952

	GD	VG	FN	VF	VF/NM	NM-
1-Kinstler-c/a (7 pgs.)	49	98	147	309	522	735

PHANTOM ZONE, THE (See Adventure #283 & Superboy #100, 104)
DC Comics: January, 1982 - No. 4, April, 1982

1-4-Superman app. in all. 2-4: Batman, Green Lantern app. 4.00

NOTE: ***Colan** a-1-4p; c-1-4p. **Giordano** c-1-4i.*

PHAZE
Eclipse Comics: Apr, 1988 - No. 2, Oct, 1988 ($2.25)

1,2: 1-Sienkiewicz-c. 2-Gulacy painted-c 3.00

PHIL RIZZUTO (Baseball Hero)(See Sport Thrills, Accepted reprint)
Fawcett Publications: 1951 (New York Yankees)

	GD	VG	FN	VF	VF/NM	NM-
nn-Photo-c	70	140	210	445	765	1085

PHOENIX
Atlas/Seaboard Publ.: Jan, 1975 - No. 4, Oct, 1975

	GD	VG	FN	VF	VF/NM	NM-
1-Origin; Rovin-s/Amendola-a	2	4	6	9	13	16
2-4: 3-Origin & only app. The Dark Avenger. 4-New origin/costume The Protector (formerly Phoenix)	2	4	6	8	11	14

NOTE: ***Infantino** appears in #1, 2. **Austin** a-3i. **Thorne** c-3.*

PHOENIX
Ardden Entertainment (Atlas Comics): Mar, 2011 - Present ($2.99)

1-3-Krueger & Deneen-s/Zachary-a; origin re-told 3.00
... Issue Zero - NY Comicon Edtion (10/10, $2.99) Dorien-a; origin prequel to #1 3.00

PHOENIX (...The Untold Story)
Marvel Comics Group: April, 1984 ($2.00, one-shot)

	GD	VG	FN	VF	VF/NM	NM-
1-Byrne/Austin-r/X-Men #137 with original unpublished ending	2	4	6	8	10	12

PHOENIX RESURRECTION, THE
Malibu Comics (Ultraverse): 1995 - 1996 ($3.95)

Genesis #1 (12/95)-X-Men app; wraparound-c, Revelations #1 (12/95)-X-Men app; wraparound-c, Aftermath #1 (1/96)-X-Men app. 4.00
0-($1.95)-r/series 3.00
0-American Entertainment Ed. 4.00

PHOENIX WITHOUT ASHES
IDW Publishing: Aug, 2010 - No. 4, Nov, 2010 ($3.99, limited series)

1-Harlan Ellison-s/Alan Robinson-a 4.00

PICNIC PARTY (See Dell Giants)

PICTORIAL CONFESSIONS (Pictorial Romances #4 on)
St. John Publishing Co.: Sept, 1949 - No. 3, Dec, 1949

	GD	VG	FN	VF	VF/NM	NM-
1-Baker-c/a(3)	53	106	159	334	567	800
2-Baker-a; photo-c	30	60	90	177	289	400
3-Kubert, Baker-a; part Kubert-c	31	62	93	182	296	410

PICTORIAL LOVE STORIES (Formerly Tim McCoy)
Charlton Comics: No. 22, Oct, 1949 - No. 26, July, 1950 (all photo-c)

	GD	VG	FN	VF	VF/NM	NM-
22-26: All have "Me-Dan Cupid". 25-Fred Astaire-c	20	40	60	114	182	250

PICTORIAL LOVE STORIES
St. John Publishing Co.: October, 1952

	GD	VG	FN	VF	VF/NM	NM-
1-Baker-c	36	72	108	211	343	475

PICTORIAL ROMANCES (Formerly Pictorial Confessions)
St. John Publ. Co.: No. 4, Jan, 1950; No. 5, Jan, 1951 - No. 24, Mar, 1954

	GD	VG	FN	VF	VF/NM	NM-
4-Baker-a; photo-c	34	68	102	204	332	460
5,10-All Matt Baker issues. 5-Reprints all stories from #4 w/new Baker-c	32	64	96	188	307	425
6-9,12,13,15,16-Baker-c, 2-3 stories	30	60	90	177	289	400
11-Baker-c/a(3); Kubert-r/Hollywood Confessions #1	32	64	96	188	307	425

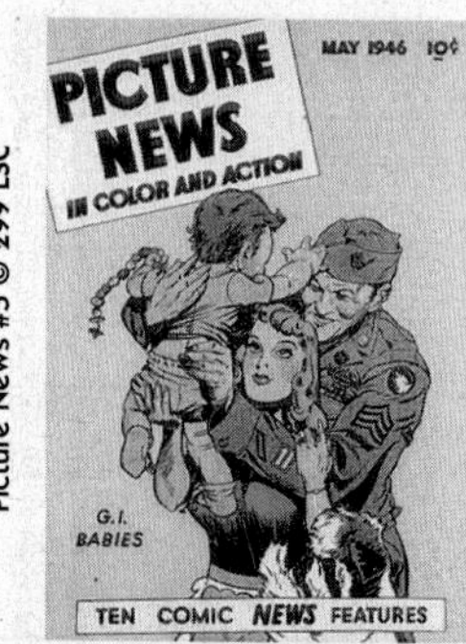

Picture News #5 © 299 LSC

Pigs #3 © Cosby & McCool

Pink Panther #44 © GK

GD VG FN VF VF/NM NM-
2.0 4.0 6.0 8.0 9.0 9.2

14,21-24: Baker-c/a each. 21,24-Each has signed story by Estrada
30 60 90 177 289 400
17-20(7/53, 25¢, 100 pgs.): Baker-c/a; each has two signed stories by Estrada
52 104 156 322 549 775
NOTE: *Matt Baker art in most issues. Estrada a-17-20(2), 21, 24.*

PICTURE CRIMES
David McKay Publ.: June, 1937

1 (a GD+ copy sold in 2012 for $478)

PICTURE NEWS
Lafayette Street Corp.: Jan, 1946 - No. 10, Jan-Feb, 1947

1-Milt Gross begins, ends No. 6; 4 pg. Kirby-a; A-Bomb-c/story
43 86 129 271 461 650
2-Atomic explosion panels; Frank Sinatra/Perry Como story
23 46 69 136 223 310
3-Atomic explosion panels; Frank Sinatra, June Allyson, Benny Goodman stories 20 40 60 120 195 270
4-Atomic explosion panels; "Caesar and Cleopatra" movie adapt. w/Claude Raines & Vivian Leigh; Jackie Robinson story 22 44 66 132 216 300
5-7: 5-Hank Greenberg story; Atomic explosion panel. 6-Joe Louis-c/story
18 36 54 103 162 220
8,10: 8-Monte Hale story (9-10/46; 1st?). 10-Dick Quick; A-Bomb story; Krigstein, Gross-a
18 36 54 107 169 230
9-A-Bomb story; "Crooked Mile" movie adaptation; Joe DiMaggio story.
20 40 60 117 189 260

PICTURE PARADE (Picture Progress #5 on)
Gilberton Company (Also see A Christmas Adventure): Sept, 1953 - V1#4, Dec, 1953 (28 pgs.)

V1#1-Andy's Atomic Adventures; A-bomb blast-c; (Teachers version distributed to schools exists) 20 40 60 114 182 250
2-Around the World with the United Nations 12 24 36 69 97 125
3-Adventures of the Lost One(The American Indian), 4-A Christmas Adventure (r-under same title in 1969) 12 24 36 69 97 125

PICTURE PROGRESS (Formerly Picture Parade)
Gilberton Corp.: V1#5, Jan, 1954 - V3#2, Oct, 1955 (28-36 pgs.)

V1#5-9,V2#1-9: 5-News in Review 1953. 6-The Birth of America. 7-The Four Seasons. 8-Paul Revere's Ride. 9-The Hawaiian Islands(5/54). V2#1-The Story of Flight(9/54). 2-Vote for Crazy River (The Meaning of Elections). 3-Louis Pasteur. 4-The Star Spangled Banner. 5-News in Review 1954. 6-Alaska: The Great Land. 7-Life in the Circus. 8-The Time of the Cave Man. 9-Summer Fun(5/55) 9 18 27 50 65 80
V3#1,2: 1-The Man Who Discovered America. 2-The Lewis & Clark Expedition
9 18 27 47 61 75

PICTURE SCOPE JUNGLE ADVENTURES (See Jungle Thrills)

PICTURE STORIES FROM AMERICAN HISTORY
National/All-American/E. C. Comics: 1945 - No. 4, Sum, 1947 (#1,2: 10¢, 56 pgs.; #3,4: 15¢, 52 pgs.)

1 30 60 90 177 289 400
2-4 24 48 72 140 230 320

PICTURE STORIES FROM SCIENCE
E.C. Comics: Spring, 1947 - No. 2, Fall, 1947

1-(15¢) 30 60 90 177 289 400
2-(10¢) 24 48 72 140 230 320

PICTURE STORIES FROM THE BIBLE (See Narrative Illustration, the Story of the Comics by M.C. Gaines)
National/All-American/E.C. Comics: 1942 - No. 4, Fall, 1943; 1944-46

1-4('42-Fall, '43)-Old Testament (DC) 24 48 72 142 234 325
Complete Old Testament Edition, (12/43-DC, 50¢, 232 pgs.);-1st printing; contains #1-4; 2nd - 8th (1/47) printings exist; later printings by E.C. some with 65¢-c
32 64 96 188 307 425
Complete Old Testament Edition (1945-publ. by Bible Pictures Ltd.)-232 pgs., hardbound, in color with dust jacket 32 64 96 188 307 425
NOTE: *Both Old and New Testaments published in England by Bible Pictures Ltd. in hardback, 1943, in color, 376 pgs. (2 vols.: O.T. 232 pgs. & N.T. 144 pgs.), and were also published by Scarf Press in 1979 (Old Test., $9.95) and in 1980 (New Test., $7.95)*

1-3(New Test.; 1944-46, DC)-52 pgs. ea. 20 40 60 114 182 250
The Complete Life of Christ Edition (1945, 25¢, 96 pgs.)-Contains #1&2 of the New Testament Edition 32 64 96 188 307 425
1,2(Old Testament-r in comic book form)(E.C., 1946; 52 pgs.)
20 40 60 114 182 250
1(DC),2(AA),3(EC)(New Testament-r in comic book form)(E.C., 1946; 52 pgs.)
20 40 60 114 182 250

GD VG FN VF VF/NM NM-
2.0 4.0 6.0 8.0 9.0 9.2

Complete New Testament Edition (1945-E.C., 40¢, 144 pgs.)-Contains #1-3
1946 printing has 50¢-c 32 64 96 188 307 425
NOTE: *Another British series entitled **The Bible Illustrated** from 1947 has recently been discovered, with the same internal artwork. This eight edition series (5-OT, 3-NT) is of particular interest to Classics Ill. collectors because it exactly copied the C.I. logo format. The British publisher was Thorpe & Porter, who in 1951 began publishing the British Classics Ill. series. All editions of The Bible Ill. have new British painted covers. While this market is still new, and not all editions have as yet been found, current market value is about the same as the first U.S. editions of Picture Stories From The Bible.*

PICTURE STORIES FROM WORLD HISTORY
E.C. Comics: Spring, 1947 - No. 2, Summer, 1947 (52, 48 pgs.)

1-(15¢) 30 60 90 177 289 400
2-(10¢) 24 48 72 140 230 320

PIGS
Image Comics: Sept, 2011 - Present ($2.99)

1-6: 1-Cosby & McCool-s/Tamura-a/Jock-c. 3-Conner-c. 5-Gibbons-c 3.00

PILGRIM, THE
IDW Publishing: 2010 - Present ($3.99, limited series)

1,2-Mike Grell-a/c; Mark Ryan-s 4.00

PILOT SEASON...
Image Comics (Top Cow): 2008 - Present ($1.00/$2.99/$3.99, one-shots)

...: Asset (9/10, $3.99) Sablik-s/Marquez-a/Frison-c 4.00
...: City of Refuge (10/11, $3.99) Foehl-s/Calero-a/c 4.00
...: Crosshair (10/10, $3.99) Katz-s/Jefferson-a/Silvestri-c 4.00
...: Declassified (10/09, $1.00) Preview of one-shots with covers, script and sketch pgs. 3.00
...: Demonic (1/10, $2.99) Kirkman-s/Benitez-a; two covers by Silvestri 3.00
...: Fleshdigger (10/11, $3.99) Denton & Keene-s; Sanchez-a; Francavilla-c 4.00
...: Forever (10/10, $3.99) Inglesby-s/Nachlik-a/Hutomo-c 4.00
...: Murdered (11/09, $2.99) Kirkman-s/Blake-a; two covers by Silvestri 3.00
...: 7 Days From Hell (10/10, $3.99) Noto-a/Hill & Levin-s/Stelfreeze-c 4.00
...: Stellar (7/10, $2.99) Kirkman-s/Chang-a/Silvestri-c 3.00
...: The Beauty (10/11, $3.99) Haun & Hurley-s/Haun-a/c 4.00
...: The Test (10/10, $3.99) Fialkov-s/Ekedal-a/Hutomo-c 4.00
...: 39 Minutes (9/10, $3.99) Harms-s/Lando-a/Albuquerque-c 4.00
...: Twilight Guardian (5/08, $3.99) Hickman-s 4.00

PINHEAD
Marvel Comics (Epic Comics): Dec, 1993 - No. 6, May, 1994 ($2.50)

1-($2.95)-Embossed foil-c by Kelley Jones; Intro Pinhead & Disciples (Snakeoil, Hangman, Fan Dancer & Dixie) 4.00
2-6 3.00

PINHEAD & FOODINI (TV)(Also see Foodini & Jingle Dingle Christmas...)
Fawcett Publications: July, 1951 - No. 4, Jan, 1952 (Early TV comic)

1-(52 pgs.)-Photo-c; based on TV puppet show 32 64 96 188 307 425
2,3-Photo-c 16 32 48 94 147 200
4 14 28 42 80 115 150

PINHEAD VS. MARSHALL LAW (Law in Hell)
Marvel Comics (Epic): Nov, 1993 - No. 2, Dec, 1993 ($2.95, lim. series)

1,2: 1-Embossed red foil-c. 2-Embossed silver foil-c 4.00

PINK DUST
Kitchen Sink Press: 1998 ($3.50, B&W, mature)

1-J. O'Barr-s/a 3.50

PINK PANTHER, THE (TV)(See The Inspector & Kite Fun Book)
Gold Key #1-70/Whitman #71-87: April, 1971 - No. 87, Mar, 1984

1-The Inspector begins 5 10 15 35 55 75
2-5 3 6 9 18 27 35
6-10 3 6 9 14 19 24
11-30: Warren Tufts-a #16-on 2 4 6 9 13 16
31-60 2 4 6 8 11 14
61-70 1 2 3 5 7 9
71-74,81-83: 81(2/82), 82(3/82), 83(4/82) 2 4 6 8 10 12
75(8/80)-77 (Whitman pre-pack) (scarce) 3 6 9 19 29 38
78(1/81)-80 (Whitman pre-pack) (not as scarce) 2 4 6 10 14 18
78 (1/81, 40¢-c) Cover price error variant 3 6 9 14 20 26
84-87(All #90266 on-c, no date or date code): 84(6/83), 85(8/83), 87(3/84)
3 6 9 14 20 26
Mini-comic No. 1(1976)(3-1/4x6-1/2") 1 3 4 6 8 10
NOTE: *Pink Panther began as a movie cartoon. (See Golden Comics Digest #38, 45 and March of Comics #376, 384, 390, 409, 418, 429, 441, 449, 461, 473, 486); #37, 72, 80-85 contain reprints.*

PINK PANTHER SUPER SPECIAL (TV)
Harvey Comics: Oct, 1993 ($2.25, 68 pgs.)

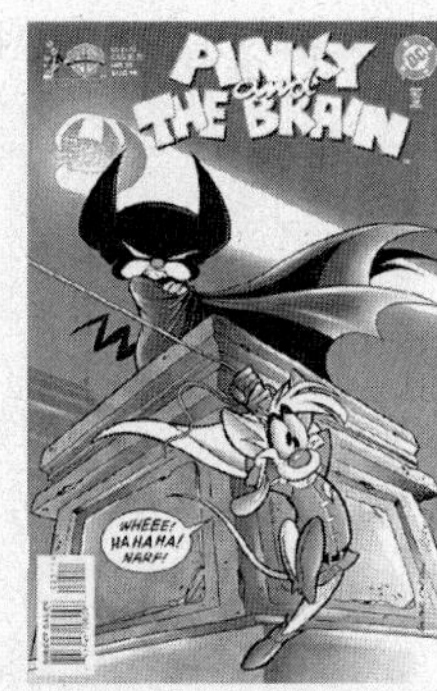

Pinky and the Brain #25 © WB

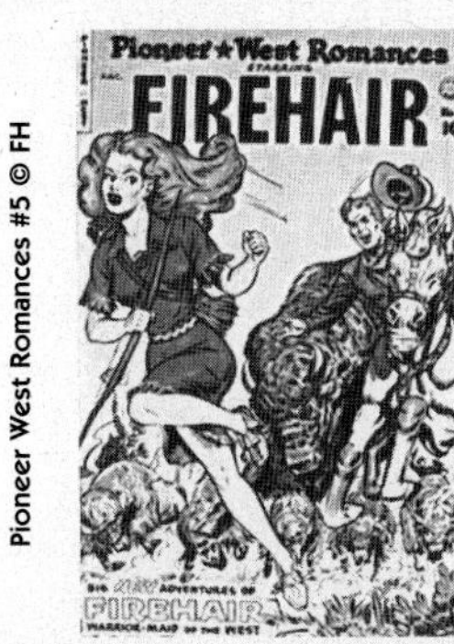

Pioneer West Romances #5 © FH

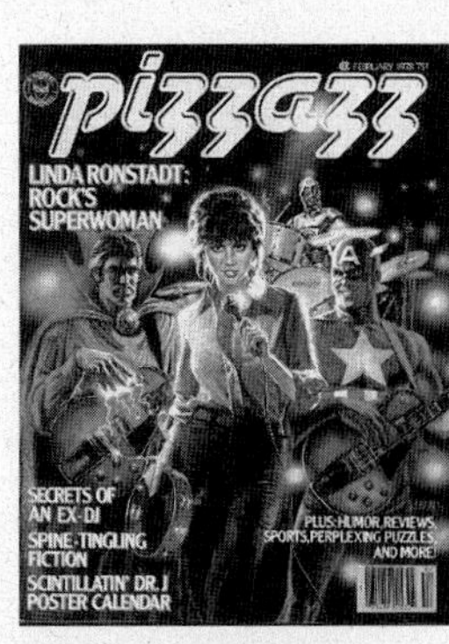

Pizzazz #5 © MAR

	GD 2.0	VG 4.0	FN 6.0	VF 8.0	VF/NM 9.0	NM- 9.2

V2#1-The Inspector & Wendy Witch stories also 4.00

PINK PANTHER, THE
Harvey Comics: Nov, 1993 - No. 9, July, 1994 ($1.50)

V2#1-9 3.00

PINKY & THE BRAIN (See Animaniacs)
DC Comics: July, 1996 - No. 27, Nov, 1998 ($1.75/$1.95/$1.99)

1-27, ...Christmas Special (1/96, $1.50) 3.00

PINKY LEE (See Adventures of...)

PINKY THE EGGHEAD
I.W./Super Comics: 1963 (Reprints from Noodnik)

I.W. Reprint #1,2(nd) 2 4 6 8 11 14
Super Reprint #14-r/Noodnik Comics #4 2 4 6 8 11 14

PINOCCHIO (See 4-Color #92, 252, 545, 1203, Mickey Mouse Mag. V5#3, Movie Comics under Wonderful Advs. of..., New Advs. of..., Thrilling Comics #2, Walt Disney Showcase, Walt Disney's..., Wonderful Advs. of..., & World's Greatest Stories #2)
Dell Publishing Co.: No. 92, 1945 - No. 1203, Mar, 1962 (Disney)

Four Color 92-The Wonderful Adventures of...; 16 pg. Donald Duck story ;
entire book by Kelly 46 92 138 345 748 1150
Four Color 252 (10/49)-Origin, not by Kelly 10 20 30 68 127 185
Four Color 545 (3/54)-The Wonderful Advs. of...; part-r of 4-Color #92; Disney-movie
7 14 21 46 76 105
Four Color 1203 (3/62) 5 10 15 35 55 75

PINOCCHIO AND THE EMPEROR OF THE NIGHT
Marvel Comics: Mar, 1988 ($1.25, 52 pgs.)

1-Adapts film 4.00

PINOCCHIO LEARNS ABOUT KITES (See Kite Fun Book)

PIN-UP PETE (Also see Great Lover Romances & Monty Hall...)
Toby Press: 1952

1-Jack Sparling pin-ups 19 38 57 111 176 240

PIONEER MARSHAL (See Fawcett Movie Comics)

PIONEER PICTURE STORIES
Street & Smith Publications: Dec, 1941 - No. 9, Dec, 1943

1-The Legless Air Ace begins 39 78 117 240 395 550
2 -True life story of Errol Flynn 20 40 60 114 182 250
3-9 15 30 45 90 140 190

PIONEER WEST ROMANCES (Firehair #1,2,7-11)
Fiction House Magazines: No. 3, Spring, 1950 - No. 6, Winter, 1950-51

3-(52 pgs.)-Firehair continues 19 38 57 109 172 235
4-6 19 38 57 109 172 235

PIPSQUEAK (See The Adventures of...)

PIRACY
E. C. Comics: Oct-Nov, 1954 - No. 7, Oct-Nov, 1955

1-Williamson/Torres-a 28 56 84 224 355 485
2-Williamson/Torres-a 18 36 54 144 227 310
3-7: 5-7-Comics Code symbol on cover 14 28 42 112 181 250

NOTE: ***Crandall** a-in all; c-2-4. **Davis** a-1, 2, 6. **Evans** a-3-7; c-7. **Ingels** a-3-7. **Krigstein** a-3-5, 7; c-5, 6. **Wood** a-1, 2; c-1.*

PIRACY
Gemstone Publishing: March, 1998 - No. 7, Sept, 1998 ($2.50)

1-7: E.C. reprints 3.00
Annual 1 ($10.95) Collects #1-4 11.00
Annual 2 ($7.95) Collects #5-7 8.00

PIRANA (See The Phantom #46 & Thrill-O-Rama #2, 3)

PIRATE CORP$, THE (See Hectic Planet)
Eternity Comics/Slave Labor Graphics: 1987 - No. 4, 1988 ($1.95)

1-4: 1,2-Color. 3,4-B&W 3.00
Special 1 ('89, B&W)-Slave Labor Publ. 3.00

PIRATE CORP$, THE (Volume 2)
Slave Labor Graphics: 1989 - No. 6, 1992 ($1.95)

1-6-Dorkin-s/a 3.00

PIRATE OF THE GULF, THE (See Superior Stories #2)

PIRATES COMICS
Hillman Periodicals: Feb-Mar, 1950 - No. 4, Aug-Sept, 1950 (All 52 pgs.)

1 24 48 72 140 230 320
2-Dave Berg-a 17 34 51 98 154 210
3,4-Berg-a 15 30 45 88 137 185

PIRATES OF CONEY ISLAND, THE
Image Comics: Oct, 2006 - No. 8 ($2.99)

1-6-Rick Spears-s/Vasilis Lolos-a; two covers. 2-Cloonan var-c 3.00

PIRATES OF DARK WATER, THE (Hanna Barbera)
Marvel Comics: Nov, 1991 - No. 9, Aug, 1992 ($1.95)

1-9: 9-Vess-c 3.00

P.I.'S: MICHAEL MAUSER AND MS. TREE, THE
First Comics: Jan, 1985 - No. 3, May, 1985 ($1.25, limited series)

1-3: Staton-c/a(p) 3.00

PITT, THE (Also see The Draft & The War)
Marvel Comics: Mar, 1988 ($3.25, 52 pgs., one-shot)

1-Ties into Starbrand, D.P.7 4.00

PITT (See Youngblood #4 & Gen 13 #3,#4)
Image Comics #1-9/Full Bleed #1/2,10-on: Jan, 1993 - No. 20 ($1.95, intended as a four part limited series)

1/2-(12/95)-1st Full Bleed issue 4.00
1-Dale Keown-c/a. 1-1st app. The Pitt 4.00
2-13: All Dale Keown-c/a. 3 (Low distribution). 10 (1/96)-Indicia reads "January 1995" 3.00
14-20: 14-Begin $2.50-c, pullout poster 3.00
TPB-(1997, $9.95) r/#1/2, 1-4 10.00
TPB 2-(1999, $11.95) r/#5-9 12.00

PITT CREW
Full Bleed Studios: Aug, 1998 - No. 5, Dec, 1999 ($2.50)

1-5: 1-Richard Pace-s/Ken Lashley-a. 2-4-Scott Lee-a 3.00

PITT IN THE BLOOD
Full Bleed Studios: Aug, 1996 ($2.50, one-shot)

nn-Richard Pace-a/script 3.00

PIXIE & DIXIE & MR. JINKS (TV)(See Jinks, Pixie, and Dixie & Whitman Comic Books)
Dell Publishing Co./Gold Key: July-Sept, 1960 - Feb, 1963 (Hanna-Barbera)

Four Color 1112 7 14 21 49 82 115
Four Color 1196,1264, 01-631-207 (Dell, 7/62) 6 12 18 37 59 80
1(2/63-Gold Key) 6 12 18 42 69 95

PIXIE PUZZLE ROCKET TO ADVENTURELAND
Avon Periodicals: Nov, 1952

1 15 30 45 83 124 165

PIXIES, THE (Advs. of...)(The Mighty Atom and ...#6 on)(See A-1 Comics #16)
Magazine Enterprises: Winter, 1946 - No. 4, Fall?, 1947; No. 5, 1948

1-Mighty Atom 9 18 27 52 69 85
2-5-Mighty Atom 6 12 18 29 36 42
I.W. Reprint #1(1958), 8-(Pee-Wee Pixies), 10-I.W. on cover, Super on inside
2 4 6 8 10 12

PIZZAZZ
Marvel Comics: Oct, 1977 - No. 16, Jan, 1979 (slick-color kids mag. w/puzzles, games, comics)

1-Star Wars photo-c/article; origin Tarzan; KISS photos/article; Iron-On bonus; 2 pg. pin-up calendars thru #8 3 6 9 20 30 40
2-Spider-Man-c; Beatles pin-up calendar 2 4 6 13 18 22
3-8: 3-Close Encounters-s; Bradbury-s. 4-Alice Cooper, Travolta; Charlie's Angels/Fonz/Hulk/Spider-Man-c. 5-Star Trek quiz. 6-Asimov-s. 7-James Bond; Spock/Darth Vader-c. 8-TV Spider-Man photo-c/article 2 4 6 11 16 20
9-14: 9-Shaun Cassidy-c. 10-Sgt. Pepper-c/s. 12-Battlestar Galactica-s; Spider-Man app. 13-TV Hulk-c/s. 14-Meatloaf-c/s 2 4 6 10 14 18
15,16: 15-Battlestar Galactica-s. 16-Movie Superman photo-c/s, Hulk.
2 4 6 11 16 20

NOTE: ***Star Wars** comics in all (1-6:Chaykin-a, 7-9: DeZuniga-a, 10-13:Simonson/Janson-a. 14-16:Cockrum-a). **Tarzan** comics, 1pg.-#1-8. 1pg. "Hey Look" by Kurtzman #12-16.*

PLANETARY (See Preview in flip book Gen13 #33)
DC Comics (WildStorm Prod.): Apr, 1999 - No. 27, Dec, 2009 ($2.50/$2.95/$2.99)

1-Ellis-s/Cassaday-a/c 1 3 4 6 8 10
1-Special Edition (6/09, $1.00) r/#1 with "After Watchmen" cover frame 3.00
2-5 6.00
6-10 5.00
11-15: 12-Fourth Man revealed 4.00
16-26: 16-Begin $2.95-c. 23-Origin of The Drummer 3.00
27-($3.99) Wraparound gatefold-c 4.00

Planet Comics #7 © FH

Planet of the Apes (2011 series) #2 © 20th Century Fox

Plastic Man #3 © DC

GD VG FN VF VF/NM NM-
2.0 4.0 6.0 8.0 9.0 9.2

...: All Over the World and Other Stories (2000, $14.95) r/#1-6 & Preview 15.00
...: All Over the World and Other Stories-Hardcover (2000, $24.95) r/#1-6 & Preview; with dustjacket 25.00
.../Batman: Night on Earth 1 (8/03, $5.95) Ellis-s/Cassaday-a 6.00
...: Crossing Worlds (2004, $14.95) r/Batman, JLA, and The Authority x-overs 15.00
.../JLA: Terra Occulta (11/02, $5.95) Elseworlds; Ellis-s/Ordway-a 6.00
...: Leaving the 20th Century -HC (2004, $24.95) r/#13-18 25.00
...: Leaving the 20th Century -SC (2004, $14.99) r/#13-18 15.00
...: Spacetime Archaeology -HC (2010, $24.99) r/#19-27 25.00
...: Spacetime Archaeology -SC (2010, $17.99) r/#19-27 18.00
.../The Authority: Ruling the World (8/00, $5.95) Ellis-s/Phil Jimenez-a 6.00
...: The Fourth Man -Hardcover (2001, $24.95) r/#7-12 25.00
...: The Planetary Reader (8/03, $5.95) r/#13-15 6.00

PLANETARY BRIGADE (Also see Hero Squared)
Boom Studios: Feb, 2006 - No. 2, Mar, 2006 ($2.99)

1-3-Giffen & DeMatteis-s/art by various; Haley-c 3.00
... Origins 1-3 (10/06-4/07, $3.99) Giffen & DeMatteis-s/Julia Bax-a 4.00

PLANET COMICS
Fiction House Magazines: 1/40 - No. 62, 9/49; No. 63, Wint, 1949-50; No. 64, Spring, 1950; No. 65, 1951(nd); No. 66-68, 1952(nd); No. 69, Wint, 1952-53; No. 70-72, 1953(nd); No. 73, Winter, 1953-54

1-Origin Auro, Lord of Jupiter by Briefer (ends #61); Flint Baker & The Red Comet begin; Eisner/Fine-c 1275 2550 3825 9500 17,250 25,000
2-Lou Fine-c (Scarce) 459 918 1377 3350 5925 8500
3-Eisner-c 320 640 960 2240 3920 5600
4-Gale Allen and the Girl Squadron begins 300 600 900 1950 3375 4800
5,6-(Scarce): 5-Eisner/Fine-c 297 594 891 1901 3251 4600
7-12: 8-Robot-c. 12-The Star Pirate begins 226 452 678 1446 2473 3500
13,14: 13-Reff Ryan begins 161 322 483 1030 1765 2500
15-(Scarce)-Mars, God of War begins (11/41); see Jumbo Comics #31 for 1st app. 314 628 942 2198 3849 5500
16-20,22 148 296 444 947 1624 2300
21-The Lost World & Hunt Bowman begin 155 310 465 992 1696 2400
23-26: 26-Space Rangers begin (9/43), end #71 135 270 405 864 1482 2100
27-30 107 214 321 680 1165 1650
31-35: 33-Origin Star Pirates Wonder Boots, reprinted in #52. 35-Mysta of the Moon begins, ends #62 94 188 282 597 1024 1450
36-45: 38-1st Mysta of the Moon-c. 41-New origin of "Auro, Lord of Jupiter". 42-Last Gale Allen. 43-Futura begins 87 174 261 553 952 1350
46-60: 48-Robot-c. 53-Used in **SOTI**, pg. 32 69 138 207 442 759 1075
61-68,70: 64,70-Robot-c. 65-70-All partial-r of earlier issues. 70-r/stories from #41 51 102 153 318 539 760
69-Used in **POP**, pgs. 101,102 52 104 156 322 549 775
71-73-No series stories. 71-Space Rangers strip 41 82 123 256 428 600
I.W. Reprint 1,8,9: 1(nd)-r/#70; cover-r from Attack on Planet Mars. 8 (r/#72), 9-r/#73 8 16 24 55 93 130

NOTE: ***Anderson** a-33-38, 40-51 (Star Pirate). **Matt Baker** a-53-59 (Mysta of the Moon). **Celardo** c-12. **Bill Discount** a-71 (Space Rangers). **Elias** c-70. **Evans** a-46-49 (Auro, Lord of Jupiter), 50-64 (Lost World). **Fine** c-2, 5. **Hopper** a-31, 35 (Gale Allen), 41, 42, 48, 49 (Mysta of the Moon). **Ingels** a-24-31 (Lost World), 56-61 (Auro, Lord of Jupiter). **Lubbers** a-44-47 (Space Rangers); c-40, 41. **Moreira** a-43, 44 (Mysta of the Moon). **Renee** a-40-49 (Lost World); c-33, 35, 39. **Tuska** a-30 (Star Pirate). **M. Whitman** a-50-52 (Mysta of the Moon), 53-58 (Star Pirate); c-71-73. **Starr** a-59. **Zolnerwich** c-10. 13-25. Bondage c-53.*

PLANET COMICS
Pacific Comics: 1984 ($5.95)

1-Reprints Planet Comics #1(1940) 1 2 3 5 6 8

PLANET COMICS
Blackthorne Publishing: Apr, 1988 - No. 3 ($2.00, color/B&W #3)

1-New stories; Dave Stevens-c 1 2 3 5 6 8
2,3: New stories 4.00

PLANET HULK (See Incredible Hulk and Giant-Size Hulk #1 (2006))

PLANET OF THE APES (Magazine) (Also see Adventures on the... & Power Record Comics)
Marvel Comics Group: Aug, 1974 - No. 29, Feb, 1977 (B&W) (Based on movies)

1-Ploog-a 4 8 12 26 41 55
2-Ploog-a 3 6 9 17 25 32
3-10 3 6 9 14 20 26
11-20 3 6 9 16 22 28
21-28 (low distribution) 3 6 9 18 27 35
29 (low distribution) 5 10 15 35 55 75

NOTE: ***Alcala** a-7-11, 17-22, 24. **Ploog** a-1-4, 6, 8, 11, 13, 14, 19. **Sutton** a-11, 12, 15, 17, 19, 20, 23, 24, 29. **Tuska** a-1-6.*

PLANET OF THE APES
Adventure Comics: Apr, 1990 - No. 24, 1992 ($2.50, B&W)

GD VG FN VF VF/NM NM-
2.0 4.0 6.0 8.0 9.0 9.2

1-New movie tie-in; comes w/outer-c (3 colors) 4.00
1-Limited serial numbered edition ($5.00) 5.00
1-2nd printing (no outer-c, $2.50) 3.00
2-24 3.00
Annual 1 ($3.50) 4.00
...Urchak's Folly 1-4 ($2.50, mini-series) 3.00

PLANET OF THE APES (The Human War)
Dark Horse Comics: Jun, 2001 - No. 3, Aug, 2001 ($2.99, limited series)

1-3-Follows the 2001 movie; Edginton-s 3.00

PLANET OF THE APES
Dark Horse Comics: Sept, 2001 - No. 6, Feb, 2002 ($2.99, ongoing series)

1-6: 1-3-Edginton-s. 1-Photo & Wagner covers. 2-Plunkett & photo-c 3.00

PLANET OF THE APES
BOOM! Studios: Apr, 2011 - Present ($3.99)

1-4,6-11-Takes place 1200 years before Taylor's arrival; Magno-a; three covers 4.00
5-($1.00) Three covers 3.00

PLANET OF VAMPIRES
Seaboard Publications (Atlas): Feb, 1975 - No. 3, July, 1975

1-Neal Adams-c(i); 1st Broderick-c/a(p); Hama-s 2 4 6 13 18 22
2,3: 2-Neal Adams-c. 3-Heath-c/a 2 4 6 9 13 16

PLANET TERRY
Marvel Comics (Star Comics)/Marvel: April, 1985 - No. 12, March, 1986 (Children's comic)

1-12 4.00
1-Variant with "Star Chase" game on last page & inside back-c 10.00

PLASM (See Warriors of Plasm)
Defiant Comics: June, 1993

0-Came bound into Diamond Previews V3#6 (6/93); price is for complete Previews with comic still attached 5.00
0-Comic only removed from Previews 3.00

PLASMER
Marvel Comics UK: Nov, 1993 - No. 4, Feb, 1994 ($1.95, limited series)

1-($2.50)-Polybagged w/4 trading cards 4.00
2-4: Capt. America & Silver Surfer app. 3.00

PLASTIC FORKS
Marvel Comis (Epic Comics): 1990 - No. 5, 1990 ($4.95, 68 pgs., limited series, mature)

Book 1-5: Squarebound 5.00

PLASTIC MAN (Also see Police Comics & Smash Comics #17)
Vital Publ. No. 1,2/Quality Comics No. 3 on: Sum, 1943 - No. 64, Nov, 1956

nn(#1)- "In The Game of Death"; Skull-c; Jack Cole-c/a begins; ends-#64? 423 846 1269 3067 5384 7700
nn(#2, 2/44)- "The Gay Nineties Nightmare" 181 362 543 1158 1979 2800
3 (Spr, '46) 118 236 354 749 1287 1825
4 (Sum, '46) 89 178 267 565 970 1375
5 (Aut, '46) 73 146 219 467 796 1125
6-10 60 120 180 381 653 925
11-15,17-20 53 106 159 334 567 800
16-Classic-c 61 122 183 390 670 950
21-30: 26-Last non-r issue? 41 82 123 256 428 600
31-40: 40-Used in POP, pg. 91 34 68 102 199 325 450
41-64: 53-Last precode issue. 54-Robot-c 26 52 78 152 249 345
Super Reprint 11,16,18: 11('63)-r/#16. 16-r/#18 & #21; Cole-a. 18('64)-Spirit-r by Eisner from Police #95 4 8 12 24 37 50

NOTE: ***Cole** r-44, 49, 56, 58, 59 at least. **Cuidera** c-32-64i.*

PLASTIC MAN (See DC Special #15 & House of Mystery #160)
National Periodical Publications/DC Comics: 11-12/66 - No. 10, 5-6/68; V4#11, 2-3/76 - No. 20, 10-11/77

1-Real 1st app. Silver Age Plastic Man (House of Mystery #160 is actually tryout); Gil Kane-c/a; 12¢ issues begin 10 20 30 67 124 180
2-5: 4-Infantino-c; Mortimer-a 5 10 15 35 55 75
6-10('68): 7-G.A. Plastic Man & Woozy Winks (1st S.A. app.) app.; origin retold. 10-Sparling-a; last 12¢ issue 4 8 12 28 44 60
V4#11('76)-20: 11-20-Fradon-p. 17-Origin retold 2 4 6 8 11 14
...80-Page Giant (2003, $6.95) reprints origin and other stories in 80-Pg. Giant format 7.00
...Special 1 (8/99, $3.95) 4.00

PLASTIC MAN
DC Comics: Nov, 1988 - No. 4, Feb, 1989 ($1.00, mini-series)

1-4: 1-Origin; Woozy Winks app. 4.00

Plop #13 © DC

Pogo Possum #3 © Oskar Lebeck

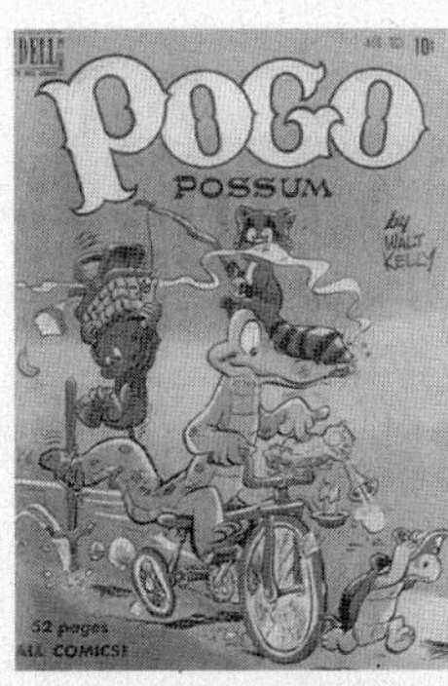

Point One #1 © MAR

	GD 2.0	VG 4.0	FN 6.0	VF 8.0	VF/NM 9.0	NM- 9.2

PLASTIC MAN
DC Comics: Feb, 2004 - No. 20, Mar, 2006 ($2.95/$2.99)

1-20-Kyle Baker-s/a in most. 1-Retells origin. 7,12-Scott Morse-s/a. 8-JLA cameo						3.00
...: On the Lam TPB (2004, $14.95) r/#1-6						15.00
...: Rubber Bandits TPB (2005, $14.99) r/#8-11,13,14						15.00

PLASTRON CAFE
Mirage Studios: Dec, 1992 - No. 4, July, 1993 ($2.25, B&W)

1-4: 1-Teenage Mutant Ninja Turtles app.; Kelly Freas-c. 2-Hildebrandt painted-c. 4-Spaced & Alien Fire stories						3.00

PLAYFUL LITTLE AUDREY (TV)(Also see Little Audrey #25)
Harvey Publications: 6/57 - No. 110, 11/73; No. 111, 8/74 - No. 121, 4/76

	GD	VG	FN	VF	VF/NM	NM-
1	23	46	69	161	343	525
2	11	22	33	77	154	230
3-5	9	18	27	61	106	150
6-10	7	14	21	46	76	105
11-20	5	10	15	35	55	75
21-40	4	8	12	26	41	55
41-60	3	6	9	20	30	40
61-84: 84-Last 12¢ issue	3	6	9	16	22	28
85-99	2	4	6	11	16	20
100-52 pg. Giant	3	6	9	16	23	30
101-103: 52 pg. Giants	3	6	9	14	20	25
104-121	1	3	4	6	8	10
...In 3-D (Spring, 1988, $2.25, Blackthorne #66)						4.00

PLOP! (Also see The Best of DC #60)
National Periodical Publications: Sept-Oct, 1973 - No. 24, Nov-Dec, 1976

	GD	VG	FN	VF	VF/NM	NM-
1-Sergio Aragonés-a begins; Wrightson-a	4	8	12	24	37	50
2-4,6-20	3	6	9	14	20	26
5-Wrightson-a	3	6	9	16	22	28
21-24 (52 pgs.). 23-No Aragonés-a	3	6	9	16	23	30

NOTE: ***Alcala** a-1-3. **Anderson** a-5. **Aragonés** a-1-22, 24. **Ditko** a-16p. **Evans** a-1. **Mayer** a-1. **Orlando** a-21, 22; c-21. **Sekowsky** a-5, 6p. **Toth** a-11. **Wolverton** r-4, 22-24(1 pg.ea.); c-1-12, 14, 17, 18. **Wood** a-14, 16i, 18-24; c-13, 15, 16, 19.*

PLUTO (See Cheerios Premiums, Four Color #537, Mickey Mouse Magazine, Walt Disney Showcase #4, 7, 13, 20, 23, 33 & Wheaties)
Dell Publ. Co.: No. 7, 1942; No. 429, 10/52 - No. 1248, 11-1/61-62 (Disney)

	GD	VG	FN	VF	VF/NM	NM-
Large Feature Comic 7(1942)-Written by Carl Barks, Jack Hannah, & Nick George (Barks' 1st comic book work)	168	336	504	1075	1838	2600
Four Color 429 (#1)	10	20	30	64	115	165
Four Color 509	6	12	18	41	66	90
Four Color 595,654,736,853	5	10	15	32	51	70
Four Color 941,1039,1143,1248	4	8	12	28	44	60

POCKET CLASSICS
Academic Inc. Publications: 1984 (B&W, 4 1/4" x 6 3/4", 68 pages)

C1(Black Beauty. C2(The Call of the Wild). C3(Dr. Jekyll and Mr. Hyde). C4(Dracula). C5(Frankenstein). C6(Huckleberry Finn). C7(Moby Dick). C8(The Red Badge of Courage). C9(The Time Machine). C10(Tom Sawyer). C11(Treasure Island). C12(20,000 Leagues Under the Sea). C13(The Great Adventures of Sherlock Holmes). C14(Gulliver's Travels). C15(The Hunchback of Notre Dame). C16(The Invisible Man). C17(Journey to the Center of the Earth). C18(Kidnapped). C19(The Mysterious Island). C20(The Scarlet Letter). C21(The Story of My Life). C22(A Tale of Two Cities). C23(The Three Musketeers). C24(The War of the Worlds). C25(Around the World in Eighty Days). C26(Captains Courageous). C27 (A Connecticut Yankee in King Arthur's Court). C28(Sherlock Holmes - The Hound of the Baskervilles). C29(The House of the Seven Gables). C30(Jane Eyre). C31(The Last of the Mohicans). C32(The Best of O. Henry). C33(The Best of Poe). C34(Two Years Before the Mast). C35(White Fang). C36(Wuthering Heights). C37(Ben Hur). C38(A Christmas Carol). C39(The Food of the Gods). C40(Ivanhoe). C41(The Man in the Iron Mask). C42(The Prince and the Pauper). C43(The Prisoner of Zenda). C44(The Return of the Native). C45(Robinson Crusoe). C46(The Scarlet Pimpernel). C47(The Sea Wolf). C48(The Swiss Family Robinson). C49(Billy Budd). C50(Crime and Punishment). C51(Don Quixote). C52(Great Expectations). C53(Heidi). C54(The Illiad). C55(Lord Jim). C56(The Mutiny on Board H.M.S. Bounty). C57(The Odyssey). C58(Oliver Twist). C59(Pride and Prejudice). C60(The Turn of the Screw) each... 8.00

Shakespeare Series:
S1(As You Like It). S2(Hamlet). S3(Julius Caesar). S4(King Lear). S5(Macbeth). S6(The Merchant of Venice). S7(A Midsummer Night's Dream). S8(Othello). S9(Romeo and Juliet). S10(The Taming of the Shrew). S11(The Tempest). S12(Twelfth Night) each... 9.00

POCKET COMICS (Also see Double Up)
Harvey Publications: Aug, 1941 - No. 4, Jan, 1942 (Pocket size; 100 pgs.)
(Tied with Spitfire Comics #1 for earliest Harvey comic)

	GD	VG	FN	VF	VF/NM	NM-
1-Origin & 1st app. The Black Cat, Cadet Blakey the Spirit of '76, The Red Blazer, The Phantom, Sphinx, & The Zebra; Phantom Ranger, British Agent #99, Spin Hawkins, Satan, Lord of Evil begin (1st app. of each); Simon-c/a in #1-3	116	232	348	742	1271	1800
2 (9/41)-Black Cat on-c #2-4	77	154	231	493	847	1200
3,4	65	130	195	416	708	1000

POE
Cheese Comics: Sept, 1996 - No. 6, Apr, 1997 ($2.00, B&W)

1-6-Jason Asala-s/a						3.00

POE
Sirius Entertainment (Dogstar Press): Oct, 1997 - No. 24 ($2.50/$2.95, B&W)

1-24-Jason Asala-s/a. 20-24 ($2.95)						3.00
... Color Special (12/98, $2.95) Linsner-c						3.00

POGO PARADE (See Dell Giants)

POGO POSSUM (Also see Animal Comics & Special Delivery)
Dell Publishing Co.: No. 105, 4/46 - No. 148, 5/47; 10-12/49 - No. 16, 4-6/54

	GD	VG	FN	VF	VF/NM	NM-
Four Color 105(1946)-Kelly-c/a	47	94	141	381	828	1275
Four Color 148-Kelly-c/a	38	76	114	285	618	950
1-(10-12/49)-Kelly-c/a in all	34	68	102	247	536	825
2	23	46	69	161	343	525
3-5	16	32	48	107	234	360
6-10: 10-Infinity-c	14	28	42	93	202	310
11-16: 11-X-Mas-c	11	22	33	76	151	225

NOTE: *#1-4, 9-13: 52 pgs.; #5-8, 14-16: 36 pgs.*

POINT BLANK (See Wildcats)
DC Comics (WildStorm): Oct, 2002 - No. 5, Feb, 2003 ($2.95, limited series)

1-5-Brubaker-s/Wilson-a/Bisley-c. 1-Variant-c by Wilson; Grifter and John Lynch app.						3.00
TPB (2003, $14.95), (2009, $14.99) r/#1-5; afterword by Brubaker						15.00

POINT ONE
Marvel Comics: Jan, 2012 ($5.99, one-shot)

1-Short story preludes to Marvel's event storylines for 2012; s/a by various						6.00

POISON ELVES (Formerly I, Lusiphur)
Mulehide Graphics: No. 8, 1993- No. 20, 1995 (B&W, magazine/comic size, mature readers)

	GD	VG	FN	VF	VF/NM	NM-
8-Drew Hayes-c/a/scripts.	2	4	6	8	10	12
9-11: 11-1st comic size issue	2	4	6	8	10	12
12,14,16	1	2	3	5	6	8
13,15-(low print)	2	4	6	8	11	14
15-2nd print						4.00
17-20	1	2	3	5	6	8
...Desert of the Third Sin-(1997, $14.95, TPB)-r/#13-18						15.00
...Patrons-($4.95, TPB)-r/#19,20						5.00
...Traumatic Dogs-(1996, $14.95,TPB)-Reprints I, Lusiphur #7, Poison Elves #8-12						15.00

POISON ELVES (See I, Lusiphur)
Sirius Entertainment: June, 1995 - No. 79, Sept, 2004 ; No. 80, Nov, 2007 ($2.50/$2.95, B&W, mature readers)

	GD	VG	FN	VF	VF/NM	NM-
1-Linsner-c; Drew Hayes-a/scripts in all.						5.00
1-2nd print						3.00
2-25: 12-Purple Marauder-c/app.						3.00
26-45, 47-49						3.00
46,50-79: 61-Fillbäch Brothers-s/a. 74-Art by Crilley (3 pgs.)						3.00
80-($3.50) Tribute issue to Drew Hayes; sketchbook and notebook art with commentary						3.50
... Baptism By Fire-(2003, $19.95, TPB)-r/#48-59						20.00
... Color Special #1 (12/98, $2.95)						5.00
... Companion (12/02, $3.50) Back-story and character bios						3.50
... : Dark Wars TPB Vol. 1 (2005, $15.95) r/#60,62-68						16.00
... FAN Edition #1 mail-in offer; Drew Hayes-c/s/a	1	2	3	5	6	8
... Rogues-(2002, $15.95, TPB)-r/#40-47						16.00
...Salvation-(2001, $19.95, TPB)-r/#26-39						20.00
...Sanctuary-(1999, $14.95, TPB)-r/#1-12						15.00

POISON ELVES: DOMINION
Sirius Entertainment: Sept, 2005 - No. 6, Sept, 2006 ($3.50, B&W, limited series)

1-6-Keith Davidsen-s/Scott Lewis-a						3.50

POISON ELVES: HYENA
Sirius Entertainment: Sept, 2004 - No. 4, Feb, 2005 ($2.95, B&W, limited series)

1-4-Keith Davidsen-s/Scott Lewis-a						3.00
Ventures TPB Vol. 1: The Hyena Collection (2006, $14.95) r/#1-4 & 2 short stories						15.00

POISON ELVES: LOST TALES
Sirius Entertainment: Jan, 2006 - No. 11 ($2.95, B&W, limited series)

Pokémon Pt. 3 #1 © Nintendo

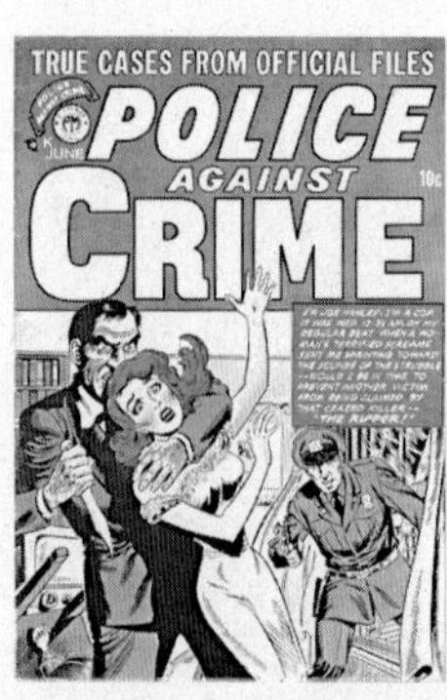

Police Against Crime #2 © PG

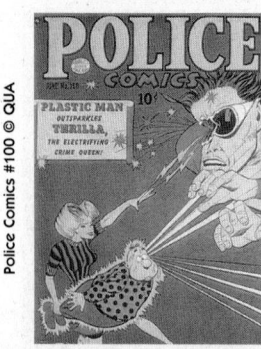

Police Comics #100 © QUA

	GD 2.0	VG 4.0	FN 6.0	VF 8.0	VF/NM 9.0	NM- 9.2

1-11-Aaron Bordner-a; Bordner & Davidsen-s 3.00

POISON ELVES: LUSIPHUR & LIRILITH
Sirius Entertainment: 2001 - No. 4, 2001 ($2.95, B&W, limited series)

1-4-Drew Hayes-s/Jason Alexander-a 3.00
TPB (2002, $11.95) r/#1-4 12.00

POISON ELVES: PARINTACHIN
Sirius Entertainment: 2001 - No. 3, 2002 ($2.95, B&W, limited series)

1-3-Drew Hayes-c/Fillbäch Brothers-s/a 3.00
TPB (2003, $8.95) r/#1-3 9.00

POISON ELVES VENTURES
Sirius Entertainment: May, 2005 - No. 4, Apr, 2006 ($3.50, B&W, limited series)

... #1: Cassanova; ...#2: Lynn; ...#3: The Purple Marauder; #4: Jace - Bordner-a 3.50

POKÉMON (TV) (Also see Magical Pokémon Journey)
Viz Comics: Nov, 1998 - 2000 ($3.25/$3.50, B&W)

...Part 1: The Electric Tale of Pikachu
1-Toshiro Ono-s/a 1 3 4 6 8 10
1-4 (2nd through current printings) 3.50
2 6.00
3,4 4.00
TPB ($12.95) 13.00
...Part 2: Pikachu Strikes Back
1 5.00
2-4 4.00
TPB 13.00
...Part 3: Electric Pikachu Boogaloo
1 5.00
2-4 ($2.95-c) 4.00
TPB 13.00
...Part 4: Surf's Up Pikachu
1,3,4 4.00
2 ($2.95-c) 4.00
TPB 13.00
NOTE: Multiple printings exist for most issues

POKÉMON ADVENTURES
Viz Comics: Sept, 1999 - No. 4 ($5.95, B&W, magazine-size)

1-4-Includes stickers bound in 6.00

POKÉMON ADVENTURES
Viz Comics: 2000 - Present ($2.95/$4.95, B&W)

Part 2 (2/00-7/00) 1-6-Includes stickers bound in 4.00
Part 3 (8/00-2/01) 1-7 4.00
Part 4 (3/00-6/01) 1-4 5.00
Part 5 (7/01-10/01) 1-4 5.00
Part 6: 1-4, Part 7 1-5 5.00

POKÉMON: THE FIRST MOVIE
Viz Comics: 1999 ($3.95)

Mewtwo Strikes Back 1-4 4.00
Pikachu's Vacation 4.00

POKÉMON: THE MOVIE 2000
Viz Comics: 2000 ($3.95)

1-Official movie adaption 4.00
Pikachu's Rescue Adventure 4.00
...:The Power of One (mini-series) 1-3 4.00

POLICE ACADEMY (TV)
Marvel Comics: Nov, 1989 - No. 6, Feb, 1990 ($1.00)

1-6: Based on TV cartoon; Post-c/a(p) in all 3.00

POLICE ACTION
Atlas News Co.: Jan, 1954 - No. 7, Nov, 1954

1-Violent-a by Robert Q. Sale 22 44 66 132 216 300
2 14 28 42 76 108 140
3-7: 7-Powell-a 12 24 36 69 97 125
NOTE: ***Ayers** a-4, 5. **Colan** a-1. **Forte** a-1, 2. **Mort Lawrence** a-5. **Maneely** a-3; c-1, 5. **Reinman** a-6, 7.*

POLICE ACTION
Atlas/Seaboard Publ.: Feb, 1975 - No. 3, June, 1975

1-3: 1-Lomax, N.Y.P.D., Luke Malone begin; McWilliams-a. 2-Origin Luke Malone, Manhunter; Ploog-a 2 4 6 9 13 16
NOTE: ***Ploog** art in all. **Sekowsky/McWilliams** a-1-3. **Thorne** c-3.*

	GD 2.0	VG 4.0	FN 6.0	VF 8.0	VF/NM 9.0	NM- 9.2

POLICE AGAINST CRIME
Premiere Magazines: April, 1954 - No. 9, Aug, 1955

1-Disbrow-a; extreme violence (man's face slashed with knife); Hollingsworth-a
34 68 102 199 325 450
2-Hollingsworth-a 18 36 54 105 165 225
3-9 15 30 45 88 137 185

POLICE BADGE #479 (Formerly Spy Thrillers #1-4)
Atlas Comics (PrPI): No. 5, Sept, 1955

5-Maneely-c/a (6 pgs.); Heck-a 11 22 33 64 90 115

POLICE CASE BOOK (See Giant Comics Editions)

POLICE CASES (See Authentic... & Record Book of...)

POLICE COMICS
Quality Comics Group (Comic Magazines): Aug, 1941 - No. 127, Oct, 1953

1-Origin/1st app. Plastic Man by Jack Cole (r-in DC Special #15), The Human Bomb by Gustavson, & No. 711; intro. The Firebrand by Reed Crandall, The Mouthpiece by Guardineer, Phantom Lady, & The Sword; Chic Carter by Eisner app.; Firebrand-c 1-4
811 1622 2433 5920 10,460 15,000
2-Plastic Man smuggles opium 314 628 942 2198 3849 5500
3 239 478 717 1530 2615 3700
4 200 400 600 1280 2190 3100
5-Plastic Man-c begin; Plastic Man forced to smoke marijuana; Plastic Man covers begin, end #102 300 600 900 1950 3375 4800
6,7 174 348 522 1114 1907 2700
8-Manhunter begins (origin/1st app.) (3/42) 200 400 600 1280 2190 3100
9,10 139 278 417 883 1517 2150
11-The Spirit strip reprints begin by Eisner (origin-strip #1); 1st comic book app. The Spirit & 1st cover app. (9/42) 300 600 900 1950 3375 4800
12-Intro. Ebony 161 322 483 1030 1765 2500
13-Intro. Woozy Winks; last Firebrand 168 336 504 1075 1838 2600
14-19: 15-Last No. 711; Destiny begins 77 154 231 493 847 1200
20-The Raven x-over in Phantom Lady; features Jack Cole himself
77 154 231 493 847 1200
21,22: 21-Raven & Spider Widow x-over in Phantom Lady (cameo in #22)
65 130 195 416 708 1000
23-30: 23-Last Phantom Lady. 24-26-Flatfoot Burns by Kurtzman in all
58 116 174 371 636 900
31-41: 37-1st app. Candy by Sahle & begins (12/44). 41-Last Spirit-r by Eisner
47 94 141 296 498 700
42,43-Spirit-r by Eisner/Fine 41 82 123 256 428 600
44-Fine Spirit-r begin, end #88,90,92 41 82 123 256 428 600
45-50: 50-(#50 on-c, #49 on inside, 1/46) 36 72 108 214 347 480
51-60: 58-Last Human Bomb 30 60 90 177 289 400
61-88,90,92: 63-(Some issues have #65 printed on cover, but #63 on inside) Kurtzman-a, 6 pgs. 90,92-Spirit by Fine 25 50 75 150 245 340
89,91,93-No Spirit stories 23 46 69 136 223 310
94-99,101,102: Spirit by Eisner in all; 101-Last Manhunter. 102-Last Spirit & Plastic Man by Jack Cole 32 64 96 192 314 435
100 39 78 117 231 378 525
103-Content change to crime; Ken Shannon & T-Man begin (1st app. of each, 12/50) 30 60 90 177 289 400
104-112,114-127: Crandall-a most issues (not in 104,105,122,125-127). 109-Atomic bomb story. 112-Crandall-a 20 40 60 114 182 250
113-Crandall-c/a(2), 9 pgs. each 21 42 63 126 206 285
NOTE: *Most Spirit stories signed by Eisner are not by him; all are reprints. **Crandall** Firebrand-1-8. Spirit by **Eisner** 1-41, 94-102; by **Eisner/Fine**-42, 43; by **Fine**-44-88, 90, 92. 103, 109. **Al Bryant** c-33, 34. **Cole** c-17-32, 35-102(most). **Crandall** c-13, 14. **Crandall/Cuidera** c-105-127. **Eisner** c-4i. **Gill Fox** c-1-3, 4p, 5-12, 15. Bondage c-103, 109, 125.*

POLICE LINE-UP
Avon Periodicals/Realistic Comics #3,4: Aug, 1951 - No. 4, July, 1952 (Painted-c #1-3)

1-Wood-a, 1 pg. plus part-c; spanking panel-r/Saint #5
40 80 120 243 404 565
2-Classic story "The Religious Murder Cult", drugs, perversion; r/Saint #5; c-r/Avon paperback #329 30 60 90 177 289 400
3,4: 3-Kubert-a(r?)/part-c; Kinstler-a (inside-c only) 20 40 60 120 195 270

POLICE TRAP (Public Defender In Action #7 on)
Mainline #1-4/Charlton #5,6: 8-9/54 - No. 4, 2-3/55; No. 5, 7/55 - No. 6, 9/55

1-S&K covers-all issues; Meskin-a; Kirby scripts 31 62 93 182 296 410
2-4 20 40 60 114 182 250
5,6-S&K-c/a 25 50 75 147 241 335

POLICE TRAP
Super Comics: No. 11, 1963; No. 16-18, 1964

Polly Pigtails #2 © PMI

Popeye #48 © KING

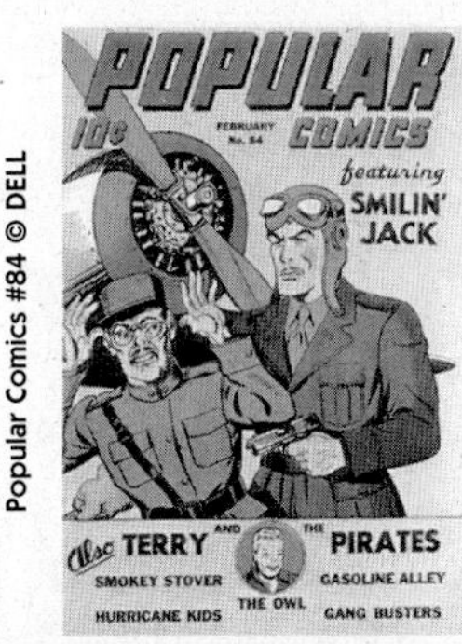

Popular Comics #84 © DELL

	GD 2.0	VG 4.0	FN 6.0	VF 8.0	VF/NM 9.0	NM- 9.2
Reprint #11,16-18: 11-r/Police Trap #3. 16-r/Justice Traps the Guilty #? 17-r/Inside Crime #3 & r/Justice Traps The Guilty #83; 18-r/Inside Crime #3	2	4	6	9	13	16

POLLY & HER PALS (See Comic Monthly #1)

POLLY & THE PIRATES
Oni Press: Sept, 2005 - No. 6, June, 2006 ($2.99, B&W, limited series)

	GD	VG	FN	VF	VF/NM	NM-
1-6-Ted Naifeh-s/a; Polly is shanghaied by the pirate ship Titania						3.00
TPB (7/06, $11.95, digest) r/#1-6						12.00

POLLYANNA (Disney)
Dell Publishing Co.: No. 1129, Aug-Oct, 1960

	GD	VG	FN	VF	VF/NM	NM-
Four Color 1129-Movie, Hayley Mills photo-c	7	14	21	49	82	115

POLLY PIGTAILS (Girls' Fun & Fashion Magazine #44 on)
Parents' Magazine Institute/Polly Pigtails: Jan, 1946 - V4#43, Oct-Nov, 1949

	GD	VG	FN	VF	VF/NM	NM-
1-Infinity-c; photo-c	17	34	51	98	154	210
2-Photo-c	11	22	33	60	83	105
3-5: 3,4-Photo-c	10	20	30	54	72	90
6-10: 7-Photo-c	9	18	27	50	65	80
11-30: 22-Photo-c	8	16	24	42	54	65
31-43	7	14	21	35	43	50

PONY EXPRESS (See Tales of the...)

PONYTAIL (Teen-age)
Dell Publishing Co./Charlton No. 13 on: 7-9/62 - No. 12, 10-12/65; No. 13, 11/69 - No. 20, 1/71

	GD	VG	FN	VF	VF/NM	NM-
12-641-209(#1)	4	8	12	24	37	50
2-12	3	6	9	18	27	35
13-20	3	6	9	14	19	24

POP COMICS
Modern Store Publ.: 1955 (36 pgs.; 5x7"; in color) (7¢)

	GD	VG	FN	VF	VF/NM	NM-
1-Funny animal	6	12	18	28	34	40

POPEYE (See Comic Album #7, 11, 15, Comics Reading Libraries *in the Promotional Comics section,* Eat Right to Work and Win, Giant Comic Album, King Comics, Kite Fun Book, Magic Comics, March of Comics #37,52, 66, 80, 96, 117, 134, 148, 157, 169, 194, 246, 264, 274, 294, 453, 465, 477 & Wow Comics, 1st series)

POPEYE
David McKay Publications: 1937 - 1939 (All by Segar)

	GD	VG	FN	VF	VF/NM	NM-
Feature Books nn (100 pgs.) (Very Rare)	703	1406	2109	5132	9066	13,000
Feature Books 2 (52 pgs.)	110	220	330	704	1202	1700
Feature Books 3 (100 pgs.)-r/nn issue with a new-c	94	188	282	597	1024	1450
Feature Books 5,10 (76 pgs.)	84	168	252	538	919	1300
Feature Books 14 (76 pgs.) (Scarce)	90	180	270	576	988	1400

POPEYE (Strip reprints through 4-Color #70)
Dell #1-65/Gold Key #66-80/King #81-92/Charlton #94-138/Gold Key #139-155/Whitman #156 on: 1941 - 1947; #1, 2-4/48 - #65, 7-9/62; #66, 10/62 - #80, 5/66; #81, 8/66 - #92, 12/67; #94, 2/69 - #138, 1/77; #139, 5/78 - #171, 6/84 (no #93,160,161)

	GD	VG	FN	VF	VF/NM	NM-
Large Feature Comic 24('41)-Half by Segar	74	148	222	470	810	1150
Four Color 25('41)-by Segar	89	178	267	565	970	1375
Large Feature Comic 10('43)	60	120	180	381	653	925
Four Color 17('43),26('43)-by Segar	40	80	120	300	650	1000
Four Color 43('44)	27	54	81	189	407	625
Four Color 70('45)-Title: ...& Wimpy	20	40	60	137	294	450
Four Color 113('46-original strips begin),127,145('47),168	12	24	36	84	175	265
1(2-4/48)(Dell)-All new stories continue	25	50	75	178	382	585
2	13	26	39	85	180	275
3-10: 5-Popeye on moon w/rocket-c	11	22	33	71	136	200
11-20	9	18	27	61	106	150
21-40,46: 46-Origin Swee' Pee	8	16	24	51	86	120
41-45,47-50	6	12	18	42	69	95
51-60	6	12	18	37	59	80
61-65 (Last Dell issue)	5	10	15	32	51	70
66(10/62),67-Both 84 pgs. (Gold Key)	7	14	21	46	76	105
68-80	4	8	12	26	41	55
81-92,94-97 (no #93): 97-Last 12¢ issue	3	6	9	21	32	42
98,99,101-107,109-138: 123-Wimpy beats Neil Armstrong to the moon. 130-1st app.Superstuff	3	6	9	14	19	24
100	3	6	9	18	27	35
108-Traces Popeye's origin from 1929	3	6	9	16	27	28
139-155: 144-50th Anniversary issue	2	4	6	8	10	12
156,157,162-167(Whitman)(no #160,161).167(3/82)	2	4	6	10	14	18
158(9/80),159(11/80)-pre-pack only	4	8	12	22	34	45
168-171:(All #90069 on-c; pre-pack) 168(6/83). 169(#168 on-c)(8/83). 170(3/84). 171(6/84)	3	6	9	16	22	28

NOTE: *Reprints-#145, 147, 149, 151, 153, 155, 157, 163-168(1/3), 170.*

POPEYE
Harvey Comics: Nov, 1993 - No. 7, Aug, 1994 ($1.50)

	GD	VG	FN	VF	VF/NM	NM-
V2#1-7						3.00
...Summer Special V2#1-(10/93, $2.25, 68 pgs.)-Sagendorf-r & others						4.00

POPEYE SPECIAL
Ocean Comics: Summer, 1987 - No. 2, Sept, 1988 ($1.75/$2.00)

	GD	VG	FN	VF	VF/NM	NM-
1,2: 1-Origin						4.00

POPPLES (TV, movie)
Star Comics (Marvel): Dec, 1986 - No. 4, Jun, 1987

	GD	VG	FN	VF	VF/NM	NM-
1-4-Based on toys						4.00

POPPO OF THE POPCORN THEATRE
Fuller Publishing Co. (Publishers Weekly): 10/29/55 - No. 13, 1956 (weekly)

	GD	VG	FN	VF	VF/NM	NM-
1	9	18	27	52	69	85
2-5	7	14	21	37	46	55
6-13	6	12	18	31	38	45

NOTE: *By **Charles Biro.** 10¢ cover, given away by supermarkets such as IGA.*

POP-POP COMICS
R. B. Leffingwell Co.: No date (Circa 1945) (52 pgs.)

	GD	VG	FN	VF	VF/NM	NM-
1-Funny animal	14	28	42	76	108	140

POPULAR COMICS
Dell Publishing Co.: Feb, 1936 - No. 145, July-Sept, 1948

	GD	VG	FN	VF	VF/NM	NM-
1-Dick Tracy (1st comic book app.), Little Orphan Annie, Terry & the Pirates, Gasoline Alley, Don Winslow (1st app.), Harold Teen, Little Joe, Skippy, Moon Mullins, Mutt & Jeff, Tailspin Tommy, Smitty, Smokey Stover, Winnie Winkle & The Gumps begin (all strip-r)	771	1542	2313	5400	-	-
2	257	514	771	1800	-	-
3	193	386	579	1350	-	-
4-6(7/36): 5-Tom Mix begins. 6-1st app. Scribbly	150	300	450	1050	-	-
7-10: 8,9-Scribbly & Reglar Fellers app.	121	242	363	850	-	-
11-20: 12-X-Mas-c	83	166	249	477	739	1000
21-27: 27-Last Terry & the Pirates, Little Orphan Annie, & Dick Tracy	63	126	189	362	556	750
28-37: 28-Gene Autry app. 31,32-Tim McCoy app. 35-Christmas-c; Tex Ritter app.	49	98	147	282	434	585
38-43: Tarzan in text only. 38-(4/39)-Gang Busters (Radio, 2nd app.) & Zane Grey's Tex Thorne begins? 43-The Masked Pilot app.; 1st non-funny-c?	47	94	141	270	415	560
44,45: 45-Hurricane Kid-c	36	72	108	207	321	435
46-Origin/1st app. Martan, the Marvel Man(12/39)	46	92	138	265	408	550
47-50	35	70	105	201	311	420
51-Origin The Voice (The Invisible Detective) strip begins (5/40)	37	74	111	213	327	440
52-Robot-c	42	84	126	242	371	500
53-59: 55-End of World story	33	66	99	190	295	400
60-Origin/1st app. Professor Supermind and Son (2/41)	34	68	102	196	303	410
61-71: 63-Smilin' Jack begins	26	52	78	150	230	310
72-The Owl & Terry & the Pirates begin (2/42); Smokey Stover reprints begin	42	84	126	242	371	500
73-75	29	58	87	167	259	350
76-78-Capt. Midnight in all (see The Funnies #57)	40	80	120	230	358	485
79-85-Last Owl	27	54	81	155	238	320
86-99: 98-Felix the Cat, Smokey Stover-r begin	18	36	54	104	157	210
100	20	40	60	115	175	235
101-130	10	20	30	58	89	120
131-145: 142-Last Terry & the Pirates	9	18	27	52	79	105

NOTE: *Martan, the Marvel Man c-47-49, 52, 57-59. Professor Supermind c-60-63, 64(1/2), 65, 66. The Voice c-53.*

POPULAR FAIRY TALES (See March of Comics #6, 18)

POPULAR ROMANCE
Better-Standard Publications: No. 5, Dec, 1949 - No. 29, July, 1954

	GD	VG	FN	VF	VF/NM	NM-
5	15	30	45	83	124	165
6-9: 7-Palais-a; lingerie panels	11	22	33	62	86	110
10-Wood-a (2 pgs.)	13	26	39	74	105	135
11,12,14-16,18-21,28,29	10	20	30	54	72	90
13,17-Severin/Elder-a (3&8 pgs.)	10	20	30	58	79	100
22-27-Toth-a	11	22	33	64	90	115

NOTE: *All have photo-c. **Tuska** art in most issues.*

Popular Teen-agers #9 © STAR

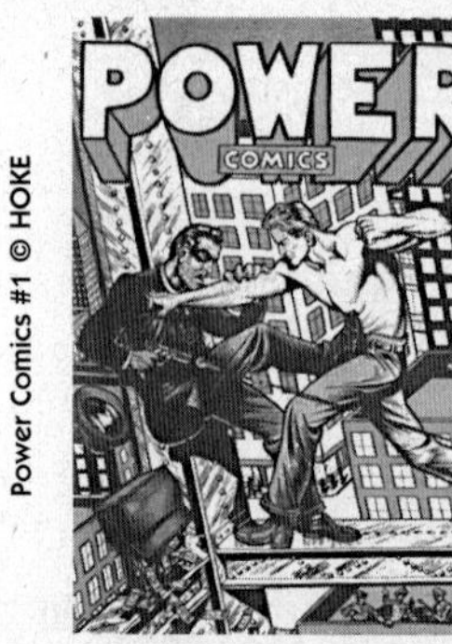

Power Comics #1 © HOKE

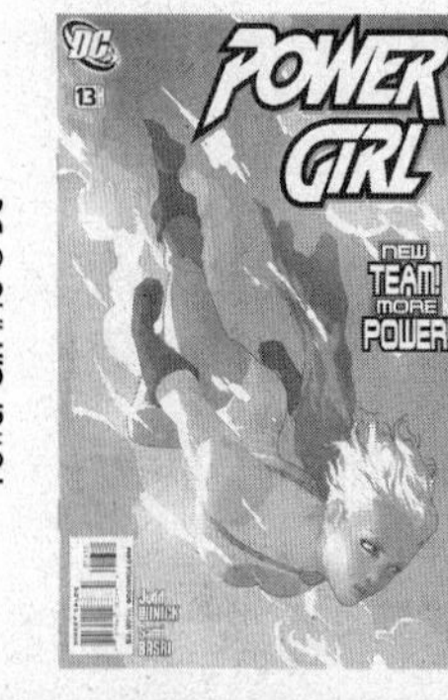

Power Girl #13 © DC

	GD 2.0	VG 4.0	FN 6.0	VF 8.0	VF/NM 9.0	NM- 9.2

POPULAR TEEN-AGERS (Secrets of Love) (School Day Romances #1-4)
Star Publications: No. 5, Sept, 1950 - No. 23, Nov, 1954

	GD	VG	FN	VF	VF/NM	NM-
5-Toni Gay, Midge Martin & Eve Adams continue from School Day Romances; Ginger Bunn (formerly Ginger Snapp & becomes Honey Bunn #6 on) begins; all features end #8	27	54	81	158	259	360
6-8 (7/51)-Honey Bunn begins; all have L. B. Cole-c; 6-Negligee panels	22	44	66	128	209	290
9-(...Romances; 1st romance issue, 10/51)	18	36	54	105	165	225
10-(...Secrets of Love thru #23)	17	34	51	98	154	210
11,16,18,19,22,23	15	30	45	83	124	165
12,13,17,20,21-Disbrow-a	15	30	45	88	137	185
14-Harrison/Wood-a	21	42	63	122	199	275
15-Wood?, Disbrow-a	16	32	48	94	147	200
Accepted Reprint 5,6 (nd); L.B. Cole-c	9	18	27	47	61	75

NOTE: *All have **L. B. Cole** covers.*

PORKY PIG (See Bugs Bunny &..., Kite Fun Book, Looney Tunes, March of Comics #42, 57, 71, 89, 99, 113, 130, 143, 164, 175, 192, 209, 218, 367, and Super Book #6, 18, 30)

PORKY PIG (...& Bugs Bunny #40-69)
Dell Publishing Co./Gold Key No. 1-93/Whitman No. 94 on: No. 16, 1942 - No. 81, Mar-Apr, 1962; Jan, 1965 - No. 109, June, 1984

	GD	VG	FN	VF	VF/NM	NM-
Four Color 16(#1, 1942)	80	160	240	648	1399	2150
Four Color 48(1944)-Carl Barks-a	83	166	249	672	1461	2250
Four Color 78(1945)	24	48	72	168	359	550
Four Color 112(7/46)	14	28	42	97	211	325
Four Color 156,182,191('49)	11	22	33	76	151	225
Four Color 226,241('49),260,271,277,284,295	10	20	30	66	121	175
Four Color 303,311,322,330: 322-Sci/fi-c/story	8	16	24	53	89	125
Four Color 342,351,360,370,385,399,410,426	6	12	18	42	69	95
25 (11-12/52)-30	6	12	18	37	59	80
31-40	5	10	15	32	51	70
41-60	4	8	12	26	41	55
61-81(3-4/62)	4	8	12	22	34	45
1(1/65-Gold Key)(2nd Series)	5	10	15	35	55	75
2,4,5-r/4-Color 226,284 & 271 in that order	3	6	9	20	30	40
3,6-10: 3-r/Four Color #342	3	6	9	17	25	32
11-30	3	6	9	14	19	24
31-54	2	4	6	10	14	18
55-70	2	4	6	8	11	14
71-93(Gold Key)	2	3	4	6	8	10
94-96	2	4	6	8	10	12
97(9/80),98-pre-pack only (99 known not to exist)	3	6	9	21	32	42
100	2	4	6	10	14	18
101-105: 104(2/82). 105(4/82)	2	4	6	8	11	14
106-109 (All #90140 on-c, no date or date code): 106(7/83), 107(8/83), 108(2/84), 109(6/84) low print run	3	6	9	14	20	26

NOTE: *Reprints-#1-8, 9-35(2/3); 36-46(1/4-1/2), 58, 67, 69-74, 76, 78, 102-109(1/3-1/2).*

PORKY PIG'S DUCK HUNT
Saalfield Publishing Co.: 1938 (12pgs.)(large size)(heavy linen-like paper)

	GD	VG	FN	VF	VF/NM	NM-
2178-1st app. Porky Pig & Daffy Duck by Leon Schlesinger. Illustrated text story book written in verse. 1st book ever devoted to these characters. (see Looney Tunes #1 for their 1st comic book app.)	73	146	219	467	796	1125

PORTENT, THE
Image Comics: Feb, 2006 - No. 4, Aug, 2006 ($2.99)

1-4-Peter Bergting-s/a 3.00
Vol. 1: Duende TPB (2006, 12.99) r/#1-4; pin-up art; intro. by Kaluta 13.00

PORTIA PRINZ OF THE GLAMAZONS
Eclipse Comics: Dec, 1986 - No. 6, Oct, 1987 ($2.00, B&W, Baxter paper)

1-6 3.00

POSSESSED, THE
DC Comics (Cliffhanger): Sept, 2003 - No. 6, March, 2004 ($2.95, limited series)

1-6-Johns & Grimminger-s/Sharp-a 3.00
TPB (2004, $14.95) r/#1-6; promo art and sketch pages 15.00

POST GAZETTE (See Meet the New... in the Promotional Comics section)

POWDER RIVER RUSTLERS (See Fawcett Movie Comics)

POWER & GLORY (See American Flagg! & Howard Chaykin's American Flagg!
Malibu Comics (Bravura): Feb, 1994 - No. 4, May, 1994 ($2.50, limited series, mature)

1A, 1B-By Howard Chaykin; w/Bravura stamp 3.00
1-Newsstand ed. (polybagged w/children's warning on bag), Gold ed., Silver-foil ed., Blue-foil ed.(print run of 10,000), Serigraph ed. (print run of 3,000)($2.95)-Howard Chaykin-c/a begin 4.00
2-4-Contains Bravura stamp 3.00
Holiday Special (Win '94, $2.95) 3.00

POWER COMICS
Holyoke Publ. Co./Narrative Publ.: 1944 - No. 4, 1945

	GD	VG	FN	VF	VF/NM	NM-
1-L. B. Cole-c	142	284	426	909	1555	2200
2-Hitler, Hirohito-c (scarce)	155	310	465	992	1696	2400
3-Classic L.B. Cole-c; Dr. Mephisto begins?	177	354	531	1124	1937	2750
4-L.B. Cole-c; Miss Espionage app. #3,4; Leav-a	142	284	426	909	1555	2200

POWER COMICS
Power Comics Co.: 1977 - No. 5, Dec, 1977 (B&W)

	GD	VG	FN	VF	VF/NM	NM-
1- "A Boy And His Aardvark" by Dave Sim; first Dave Sim aardvark (not Cerebus)	3	6	9	16	23	30
1-Reprint (3/77, black-c)	1	2	3	5	6	8
2-Cobalt Blue by Gustovich	1	3	4	6	8	10
3-5: 3-Nightwitch. 4-Northern Light. 5-Bluebird	1	3	4	6	8	10

POWER COMICS
Eclipse Comics (Acme Press): Mar, 1988 - No. 4, Sept, 1988 ($2.00, B&W, mini-series)

1-4: Bolland, Gibbons-r in all 3.00

POWER COMPANY, THE
DC Comics: Apr, 2002 - No. 18, Sep, 2003 ($2.50/$2.75)

1-6-Busiek-s/Grummett-a. 6-Green Arrow & Black Canary-c/app. 3.00
7-18: 7:Begin $2.75-c. 8,9-Green Arrow app. 11-Firestorm joins. 15-Batman app. 3.00
...Bork (3/02) Busiek-s/Dwyer-a; Batman & Flash (Barry Allen) app. 3.00
...Josiah Power (3/02) Busiek-s/Giffen-a; Superman app. 3.00
...Manhunter (3/02) Busiek-s/Jurgens-a; Nightwing app. 3.00
...Sapphire (3/02) Busiek-s/Bagley-a; JLA & Kobra app. 3.00
...Skyrocket (3/02) Busiek-s/Staton-a; Green Lantern (Hal Jordan) app. 3.00
...Striker Z (3/02) Busiek-s/Bachs-a; Superboy app. 3.00
...Witchfire (3/02) Busiek-s/Haley-a; Wonder Woman app. 3.00

POWER FACTOR
Wonder Color Comics #1/Pied Piper #2: May, 1987 - No. 2, 1987 ($1.95)

1,2: Super team. 2-Infantino-c 3.00

POWER FACTOR
Innovation Publishing: Oct, 1990 - No. 3, 1991 ($1.95/$2.25)

1-3: 1-R-/1st story + new-a, 2-r/2nd story + new-a. 3-Infantino-a 3.00

POWER GIRL (See All-Star #58, Infinity, Inc., JSA Classified, Showcase #97-99)
DC Comics: June, 1988 - No. 4, Sept, 1988 ($1.00, color, limited series)

1-4 4.00
TPB (2006, $14.99) r/Showcase #97-99; Secret Origins #11; JSA Classified #1-4 and pages from JSA #32,39; cover gallery 15.00

POWER GIRL
DC Comics: Jul, 2009 - No. 27, Oct, 2011 ($2.99)

1-12: 1,2-Amanda Conner-a; covers by Conner and Hughes; Ultra-Humanite app. 3-6-Covers by Conner and March 3.00
13-27: 13-23-Winick-s/Basri-a. 20,21-Crossover with Justice League: Generation Lost #18-22 23-Zatanna app. 24,25-Batman app.; Prasetya-a. 27-Cyclone app. 3.00
...: Aliens and Apes SC (2010, $17.99) r/#7-12 18.00
...: A New Beginning SC (2010, $17.99) r/#1-6; gallery of variant covers 18.00
...: Bomb Squad SC (2011, $14.99) r/#13-18 15.00

POWERHOUSE PEPPER COMICS (See Gay Comics, Joker Comics & Tessie the Typist)
Marvel Comics (20CC): No. 1, 1943; No. 2, May, 1948 - No. 5, Nov, 1948

	GD	VG	FN	VF	VF/NM	NM-
1-(60 pgs.)-Wolverton-a in all; c-2,3	216	432	648	1372	2361	3350
2	92	184	276	584	1005	1425
3,4	86	172	258	546	936	1325
5-(Scarce)	97	194	291	621	1061	1500

POWERLESS
Marvel Comics: Aug, 2004 - No. 6, Jan, 2005 ($2.99, limited series)

1-6-Peter Parker, Matt Murdock and Logan without powers; Gaydos-a 3.00
TPB (2005, $14.99) r/series; sketch page by Gaydos 15.00

POWER LINE
Marvel Comics (Epic Comics): May, 1988 - No. 8, Sept, 1989 ($1.25/$1.50)

1-8: 2-Williamson-i. 3-Dr. Zero app. 4-7-Morrow-a. 8-Williamson-i 3.00

POWER LORDS
DC Comics: Dec, 1983 - No. 3, Feb, 1984 (Limited series, Mando paper)

1-3: Based on Revell toys 4.00

Power Man and Iron Fist #59 © MAR

Powerpuff Girls #24 © Cartoon Network

Powers #7 © Bendis & Oeming

GD 2.0 VG 4.0 FN 6.0 VF 8.0 VF/NM 9.0 NM- 9.2

POWER MAN (Formerly Hero for Hire; ...& Iron Fist #50 on; see Cage & Giant-Size...)
Marvel Comics Group: No. 17, Feb, 1974 - No. 125, Sept, 1986

17-Luke Cage continues; Iron Man app. 3 6 9 18 27 35
18-20: 18-Last 20¢ issue 2 4 6 11 16 20
21-30 2 4 6 8 10 12
30-(30¢-c variant, limited distribution)(4/76) 3 6 9 17 25 32
31-46: 31-Part Neal Adams-i. 34-Last 25¢ issue. 36-r/Hero For Hire #12. 41-1st app. Thunderbolt. 45-Starlin-c. 1 3 4 6 8 10
31-34-(30¢-c variants, limited distribution)(5-8/76) 3 6 9 19 29 38
44-46-(35¢-c variants, limited distribution)(6-8/77) 4 8 12 24 37 50
47-Barry Smith-a 2 4 6 8 10 12
47-(35¢-c variant, limited distribution)(10/77) 4 8 12 28 44 60
48-50-Byrne-a(p); 48-Power Man/Iron Fist 1st meet. 50-Iron Fist joins Cage 2 4 6 10 14 18
51-56,58-65,67-77: 58-Intro El Aguila. 75-Double size. 77-Daredevil app. 6.00
57-New X-Men app. (6/79) 4 8 12 26 41 55
66-2nd app. Sabretooth (see Iron Fist #14) 6 12 18 39 62 85
78,84: 78-3rd app. Sabretooth (cameo under cloak). 84-4th app. Sabretooth 4 8 12 24 37 50
79-83,85-99,101-124: 87-Moon Knight app. 109-The Reaper app. 4.00
100,125-Double size: 100-Origin K'un L'un. 125-Death of Iron Fist 6.00
Annual 1(1976)-Punisher cameo in flashback 2 4 6 13 18 22

NOTE: ***Austin** c-102i. **Byrne** a-48-50; c-102, 104, 106, 107, 112-116. **Kane** c(p)-24, 25, 28, 48. **Miller** a-68, 76(2 pgs.); c-66-68, 70-74, 80i. **Mooney** a-38i, 53i, 55i. **Nebres** a-76p. **Nino** a-42i, 43i. **Perez** a-27. **B. Smith** a-47i. **Tuska** a(p)-17, 20, 24, 26, 28, 29, 36, 47. Painted c-75, 100.*

POWER MAN AND IRON FIST
Marvel Comics: Apr, 2011 - No. 5, Jul, 2011 ($2.99, limited series)

1-5-Van Lente-s/Alves-a; Victor Alvarez as Power Man 3.00

POWER OF PRIME
Malibu Comics (Ultraverse): July, 1995 - No. 4, Nov, 1995 ($2.50, lim. series)

1-4 3.00

POWER OF SHAZAM!, THE (See SHAZAM!)
DC Comics: 1994 (Painted graphic novel) (Prequel to new series)

Hardcover-($19.95)-New origin of Shazam!; Ordway painted-c/a & script 3 6 9 14 20 25
Softcover-($7.50), Softcover-($9.95)-New-c. 2 4 6 8 10 12

POWER OF SHAZAM!, THE
DC Comics: Mar, 1995 - No. 47, Mar, 1999; No. 48, Mar, 2010 ($1.50/$1.75/$1.95/$2.50)

1-Jerry Ordway scripts begin 4.00
2-20: 4-Begin $1.75-c. 6:Re-intro of Capt. Nazi. 8-Re-intro of Spy Smasher, Bulletman & Minuteman; Swan-a (7 pgs.). 11-Re-intro of Ibis, Swan-a(2 pgs.). 14-Gil Kane-a(p). 20-Superman-c/app.; "Final Night" 3.00
21-47: 21-Plastic Man-c/app. 22-Batman-c/app. 35,36-X-over w/Starman #39,40. 38-41-Mr. Mind. 43-Bulletman app. 45-JLA-c/app. 3.00
48-(3/10, $2.99) Blackest Night one-shot; Osiris rises as a Black Lantern; Kramer-a 3.00
#1,000,000 (11/98) 853rd Century x-over; Ordway-c/s/a 3.00
Annual 1 (1996, $2.95)-Legends of the Dead Earth story; Jerry Ordway-c; Mike Manley-a 4.00

POWER OF STRONGMAN, THE (Also see Strongman)
AC Comics: 1989 ($2.95)

1-Powell G.A.-r 3.00

POWER OF THE ATOM (See Secret Origins #29)
DC Comics: Aug, 1988 - No. 18, Nov, 1989 ($1.00)

1-18: 6-Chronos returns; Byrne-p. 9-JLI app. 3.00

POWER PACHYDERMS
Marvel Comics: Sept, 1989 ($1.25, one-shot)

1-Elephant super-heroes; parody of X-Men, Elektra, & 3 Stooges 3.00

POWER PACK
Marvel Comics Group: Aug, 1984 - No. 62, Feb, 1991

1-($1.00, 52 pgs.)-Origin & 1st app. Power Pack 4.00
2-18,20-26,28,30-45,47-62 3.00
19-(52 pgs.)-Cloak & Dagger, Wolverine app. 4.00
27-Mutant massacre; Wolverine & Sabretooth app. 5.00
29,46: 29-Spider-Man & Hobgoblin app. 46-Punisher app. 3.50
Graphic Novel: Power Pack & Cloak & Dagger: Shelter From the Storm ('89, SC, $7.95) Velluto/Farmer-a 10.00
...Holiday Special 1 (2/92, $2.25, 68 pgs.) 4.00

NOTE: ***Austin** scripts-53. **Mignola** c-20. **Morrow** a-51. **Spiegle** a-55i. **Williamson** a(i)-43, 50, 52.*

POWER PACK (Volume 2)
Marvel Comics: Aug, 2000 - No. 4, Nov, 2000 ($2.99, limited series)

1-4-Doran & Austin-c/a 3.00

POWER PACK
Marvel Comics: June, 2005 - No. 4, Aug, 2005 ($2.99, limited series)

1-4-Sumerak-s/Gurihiru-a; back-up Franklin Richards story. 3-Fantastic Four app. 3.00
... Digest (2006, $6.99) r/#1-4 7.00

POWER PACK: DAY ONE
Marvel Comics: May, 2008 - No. 4, Aug, 2008($2.99, limited series)

1-4-Van Lente-s/Gurihiru-a; origin retold; Coover-a back-ups. 1-Fantastic Four cameo 3.00

POWERPUFF GIRLS, THE (Also see Cartoon Network Starring... #1)
DC Comics: May, 2000 - No. 70, Mar, 2006 ($1.99/$2.25)

1 5.00
2-55,57-70: 25-Pin-ups by Allred, Byrne, Baker, Mignola, Hernandez, Warren 3.00
56-($2.95) Bonus pages; Mojo Jojo-c 4.00
...Double Whammy (12/00, $3.95) r/#1,2 & a Dexter's Lab story 4.00
...Movie: The Comic (9/02, $2.95) Movie adaptation; Phil Moy & Chris Cook-a 3.00

POWER RANGERS ZEO (TV)(Saban's...)(Also see Saban's Mighty Morphin Power Rangers)
Image Comics (Extreme Studios): Aug, 1996 ($2.50)

1-Based on TV show 4.00

POWER RECORD COMICS (Named Peter Pan Record Comics for #34-47)
Marvel Comics/Power Records: 1974 - 1978 ($1.49, 7x10" comics, 20 pgs. with 45 R.P.M. record) (Clipped corners - reduce value 20%) (Comic alone - 50%; record alone - 50%)

PR10-Spider-Man-r/from #124,125; Man-Wolf app. PR18-Planet of the Apes-r. PR19-Escape From the Planet of the Apes-r. PR20-Beneath the Planet of the Apes-r. PR21-Battle for the Planet of the Apes-r. PR24-Spider-Man II-New-a begins. PR27-Batman "Stacked Cards"; N. Adams-a(p). PR30-Batman; N. Adams-r/Det.(7 pgs.).
With record; each... 6 12 18 37 59 80
PR11-Hulk-r. PR12-Captain America-r/#168. PR13-Fantastic Four-r/#126. PR14-Frankenstein -Ploog-r/#1. PR15-Tomb of Dracula-Colan-r/#2. PR16-Man-Thing-Ploog-r/#5. PR17-Werewolf By Night-Ploog-r/Marvel Spotlight #2. PR28-Superman "Alien Creatures". PR29-Space: 1999 "Breakaway". PR31-Conan-N. Adams-a; reprinted in Conan #116. PR32-Space: 1999 "Return to the Beginning". PR33-Superman-G.A. origin, Buckler-a(p). PR34-Superman. PR35-Wonder Woman-Buckler-a(p)
With record; each... 5 10 15 32 51 70
PR11-(1981 Peter Pan records re-issue) new Abomination & Rhino-c
With record 5 10 15 35 55 75
PR25-Star Trek "Passage to Moauv". PR26-Star Trek "Crier in Emptiness." PR36-Holo-Man. PR37-Robin Hood. PR39-Huckleberry Finn. PR40-Davy Crockett. PR41-Robinson Crusoe. PR42-20,000 Leagues Under the Sea. PR45-Star Trek "Dinosaur Planet". PR46-Star Trek "The Robot Masters". PR47-Little Women
With record; each... 4 8 12 28 44 60

NOTE: *Peter Pan re-issues exist for #25-34 and are valued the same.*

POWERS
Image Comics: 2000 - No. 37, Feb, 2004 ($2.95)

1-Bendis-s/Oeming-a; murder of Retro Girl 1 3 4 6 8 10
2-6: 6-End of Retro Girl arc. 5.00
7-14: 7-Warren Ellis app. 12-14-Death of Olympia 3.50
15-37: 31-36-Origin of the Powers 3.00
Annual 1 (2001, $3.95) 4.00
...: Anarchy TPB (11/03, $14.95) r/#21-24; interviews, sketchbook, cover gallery 15.00
...Coloring/Activity Book (2001, $1.50, B&W, 8 x 10.5") Oeming-a 3.00
...: Forever TPB (2005, $19.95) r/#31-37; script for #31, sketchbook, cover gallery 20.00
...: Little Deaths TPB (2002, $19.95) r/#7,12-14, Ann. #1, Coloring/Activity Book; sketch pages, cover gallery 20.00
...: Roleplay TPB (2001, $13.95) r/#8-11; sketchbook, cover gallery 14.00
... Scriptbook (2001, $19.95) scripts for #1-11; Oeming sketches 20.00
...: Supergroup TPB (2003, $19.95) r/#15-20; sketchbook, cover gallery 20.00
...: The Definitive Collection Vol. 1 HC (2006, $29.99, dust jacket) r/#1-11 & Coloring/Activity Book, script for #1, sketch pages and covers, interviews, letter column highlights 30.00
...: The Definitive Collection Vol. 2 HC (2009, $29.99, dust jacket) r/#12-24 & Annual #1; cover gallery; 1st Bendis/Oeming Jinx story; interviews, letter column highlights 30.00
..: Who Killed Retro Girl TPB (2000, $21.95) r/#1-6; sketchbook, cover gallery, and promotional strips from Comic Shop News 22.00

POWERS
Marvel Comics (Icon): Jul, 2004 - No. 30, Sept, 2008 ($2.95/$3.95)

1-11,13-24-Bendis-s/Oeming-a. 14-Cover price error 3.00
12-($3.95, 64 pages) 2 covers; Bendis & Oeming interview 4.00
25-30-($3.95, 40 pages) 25-Two covers; Bendis interview 4.00
Annual 2008 (5/08, $4.95) Bendis-s/Oeming-a; interview with Brubaker, Simone, others 5.00
...: Legends TPB (2005, $17.95) r/#1-6; sketchbook, cover gallery 18.00

Preacher #34 © Ennis & Dillon

Predator: Big Game #2 © 20th Century Fox

Predator: Strange Roux nn © 20th Century Fox

GD VG FN VF VF/NM NM-
2.0 4.0 6.0 8.0 9.0 9.2

...: Psychotic TPB (1/06, $19.95) r/#7-12; Bendis & Oeming interview, cover gallery 20.00
...: Cosmic TPB (10/07, $19.95) r/#13-18; script and sketch pages 20.00
...: Secret Identity TPB (12/07, $19.95) r/#19-24; script pages 20.00

POWERS (Volume 3)
Marvel Comics (Icon): Nov, 2009 - Present ($3.95)

1-9-Bendis-s/Oeming-a 4.00

POWERS THAT BE (Becomes Star Seed No.7 on)
Broadway Comics: Nov, 1995 - No. 6, June, 1996 ($2.50)

1-6: 1-Intro of Fatale & Star Seed. 6-Begin $2.95-c. 3.00
Preview Editions 1-3 (9/95 - 11/95, B&W) 3.00

POW MAGAZINE (Bob Sproul's) (Satire Magazine)
Humor-Vision: Aug, 1966 - No. 3, Feb, 1967 (30¢)

1,2: 2-Jones-a 5 10 15 30 48 65
3-Wrightson-a 6 12 18 39 62 85

PREACHER
DC Comics (Vertigo): Apr, 1995 - No. 66, Oct, 2000 ($2.50, mature)

nn-Preview 2 4 6 11 16 20
1 ($2.95)-Ennis scripts, Dillon-a & Fabry-c in all; 1st app. Jesse, Tulip, & Cassidy
2 4 6 8 11 14
1-Special Edition (6/09, $1.00) r/#1 with "After Watchmen" cover frame 3.00
2,3: 2-1st app. Saint of Killers. 1 2 3 5 7 9
4,5 1 2 3 4 5 7
6-10 5.00
11-20: 12-Polybagged w/videogame w/Ennis text. 13-Hunters storyline begins; ends #17. 19-Saint of Killers app.; begin "Crusaders", ends #24 4.00
21-25: 21-24-Saint of Killers app. 25-Origin of Cassidy. 3.00
26-49,52-64: 52-Tulip origin 3.00
50-($3.75) Pin-ups by Jim Lee, Bradstreet, Quesada and Palmiotti 4.00
51-Includes preview of 100 Bullets; Tulip origin 4.00
65,66-($3.75) 65-Almost everyone dies. 66-Final issue 5.00
Alamo (2001, $17.95, TPB) r/#59-66; Fabry-c 18.00
All Hell's a-Coming (2000, $17.95, TPB)-r/#51-58, ...:Tall in the Saddle 18.00
... Book One HC (2009, $39.99, d.j.) r/#1-12; new Ennis intro.; pin-ups from #50,66 40.00
... Book Two HC (2010, $39.99, d.j.) r/#13-26; new Stuart Moore intro. 40.00
... Book Three HC (2010, $39.99, d.j.) r/#27-33, ...Special: Saint of Killers #1-4 & ...Special: Cassidy: Blood & Whiskey #1; new Ennis intro. 40.00
... Book Four HC (2011, $39.99, d.j.) r/#34-40, ...Special: One Man's War, ...Special: The Story of You-Know-Who, & ...Special: The Good Old Boys; new Dillon intro. 40.00
...: Dead or Alive HC (2000, $29.95) Gallery of Glenn Fabry's cover paintings for every Preacher issue; commentary by Fabry & Ennis 30.00
...: Dead or Alive SC (2003, $19.95) 20.00
Dixie Fried (1998, $14.95, TPB)-r/#27-33, Special: Cassidy 15.00
Gone To Texas (1996, $14.95, TPB)-r/#1-7; Fabry-c 15.00
Proud Americans (1997, $14.95, TPB)-r/#18-26; Fabry-c 15.00
Salvation (1999, $14.95, TPB)-r/#41-50; Fabry-c 15.00
Until the End of the World (1996, $14.95, TPB)-r/#8-17; Fabry-c 15.00
War in the Sun (1999, $14.95, TPB)-r/#34-40 15.00

PREACHER SPECIAL: CASSIDY: BLOOD & WHISKEY
DC Comics (Vertigo): 1998 ($5.95, one-shot)

1-Ennis-scripts/Fabry-c/Dillon-a 6.00

PREACHER SPECIAL: ONE MAN'S WAR
DC Comics (Vertigo): Mar, 1998 ($4.95, one-shot)

1-Ennis-scripts/Fabry-c /Snejbjerg-a 5.00

PREACHER SPECIAL: SAINT OF KILLERS
DC Comics (Vertigo): Aug, 1996 - No. 4, Nov, 1996 ($2.50, lim. series, mature)

1-4: Ennis-scripts/Fabry-c. 1,2-Pugh-a. 3,4-Ezquerra-a 3.00
1-Signed & numbered 20.00

PREACHER SPECIAL: THE GOOD OLD BOYS
DC Comics (Vertigo): Aug, 1997 ($4.95, one-shot, mature)

1-Ennis-scripts/Fabry-c /Esquerra-a 5.00

PREACHER SPECIAL: THE STORY OF YOU-KNOW-WHO
DC Comics (Vertigo): Dec, 1996 ($4.95, one-shot, mature)

1-Ennis-scripts/Fabry-c/Case-a 5.00

PREACHER: TALL IN THE SADDLE
DC Comics (Vertigo): 2000 ($5.95, one-shot)

1-Ennis-scripts/Fabry-c/Dillon-a; early romance of Tulip and Jesse 6.00

PREDATOR (Also see Aliens Vs. ..., Batman vs. ..., Dark Horse Comics, & Dark Horse Presents)
Dark Horse Comics: June, 1989 - No. 4, Mar, 1990 ($2.25, limited series)

1-Based on movie; 1st app. Predator 1 2 3 4 5 7
1-2nd printing 3.00
2 5.00
3,4 4.00
Trade paperback (1990, $12.95)-r/#1-4 13.00
... Omnibus Volume 1 (8/07, $24.95, 6" x 9") r/#1-4, ... Cold War, ... Dark River, ...Bloody Sands of Time mini-series and stories from Dark Horse Comics #1,2,4-7,10-12 25.00
... Omnibus Volume 2 (2/08, $24.95, 6" x 9") r/ ... Big Game, ... Race War, ...Invaders From The, Fourth Dimension mini-series and stories from Dark Horse Comics #16-18,20,21; Dark Horse Presents #46 and A Decade of Dark Horse 25.00
... Omnibus Volume 3 (6/08, $24.95, 6" x 9") r/ ... Bad Blood, ... Kindred, ...Hell and Hot Water, ... Strange Roux mini-series and stories from Dark Horse Comics #12-14 and Dark Horse Presents #119 & 124 25.00

PREDATOR
Dark Horse Comics: June, 2009 - No. 4, Jan, 2010 ($3.50, limited series)

1-4-Arcudi-s/Saltares-a/Swanland-c; variant-c by Warner 3.50

PREDATOR: (title series) **Dark Horse Comics**

--BAD BLOOD, 12/93 - No. 4, 1994 ($2.50) 1-4 3.00
--BIG GAME, 3/91 - No. 4, 6/91 ($2.50) 1-4: 1-3-Contain 2 Dark Horse trading cards 3.00
--BLOODY SANDS OF TIME, 2/92 - No. 2, 2/92 ($2.50) 1,2-Dan Barry-c/a(p)/scripts 3.00
--CAPTIVE, 4/98 ($2.95, one-shot) 1 3.00
--COLD WAR, 9/91 - No. 4, 12/91 ($2.50) 1-4: All have painted-c 3.00
--DARK RIVER, 7/96 - No.4, 10/96 ($2.95)1-4: Miran Kim-c 3.00
--HELL & HOT WATER, 4/97 - No. 3, 6/97 ($2.95) 1-3 3.00
--HELL COME A WALKIN', 2/98 - No. 2, 3/98 ($2.95) 1,2-In the Civil War 3.00
--HOMEWORLD, 3/99 - No. 4, 6/99 ($2.95) 1-4 3.00
--INVADERS FROM THE FOURTH DIMENSION, 7/94 ($3.95, one-shot, 52 pgs.) 1 4.00
--JUNGLE TALES. 3/95 ($2.95t) 1-r/Dark Horse Comics 3.00
--KINDRED, 12/96 - No. 4, 3/97 ($2.50) 1-4 3.00
--NEMESIS, 12/97 - No. 2, 1/98 ($2.95) 1,2-Predator in Victorian England; Taggart-c 3.00
--PRIMAL, 7/97 - No. 2, 8/97 ($2.95) 1,2 3.00
--RACE WAR (See Dark Horse Presents #67), 2/93 - No. 4,10/93 ($2.50, color) 1-4,0: 1-4-Dorman painted-c #1-4, 0(4/93) 3.00
--STRANGE ROUX, 11/96 ($2.95, one-shot) 1 3.00
--XENOGENESIS (Also see Aliens Xenogenesis), 8/99 - No. 4, 11/99 ($2.95) 1,2-Edginton-s 3.00

PREDATORS (Based on the 2010 movie)
Dark Horse Comics: Jun, 2010 - No. 4, Jun, 2010 ($2.99, weekly limited series)

1-4-Prequel to the 2010 movie; stories by Andreyko and Lapham; Paul Lee-c 3.00
... Film Adaptation (7/10, $6.99) Tobin-s/Drujiniu-s/photo-c 7.00
...: Preserve the Game (7/10, $3.50) Sequel to the movie; Lapham-s/Jefferson-a 3.50

PREDATOR 2
Dark Horse Comics: Feb, 1991 - No. 2, June, 1991 ($2.50, limited series)

1,2: 1-Adapts movie; both w/trading cards & photo-c 3.00

PREDATOR VS. JUDGE DREDD
Dark Horse Comics: Oct, 1997 - No. 3 ($2.50, limited series)

1-3-Wagner-s/Alcatena-a/Bolland-c 3.00

PREDATOR VS. MAGNUS ROBOT FIGHTER
Dark Horse/Valiant: Oct, 1992 - No. 2, 1993 ($2.95, limited series)
(1st Dark Horse/Valiant x-over)

1,2: (Reg.)-Barry Smith-c; Lee Weeks-a. 2-w/trading cards 3.00
1 (Platinum edition, 11/92)-Barry Smith-c 10.00

PREHISTORIC WORLD (See Classics Illustrated Special Issue)

PRELUDE TO DEADPOOL CORPS (Leads into Deadpool Corps #1)
Marvel Comics: May, 2010 - No. 5, May, 2010 ($3.99/$2.99, weekly limited series)

1-($3.99) Deadpool & Lady Deadpool vs. alternate dimension Capt. America; Liefeld-a 4.00
2-5-($2.99) Alternate reality Deadpools team-up; Dave Johnson interlocking covers 3.00

PRELUDE TO INFINITE CRISIS
DC Comics: 2005 ($5.99, squarebound)

nn-Reprints stories and panels with commentary leading into Infinite Crisis series 6.00

PREMIERE (See Charlton Premiere)

Pride & Joy #2 © Ennis & Higgins

Prime #8 © MAL

Prince Valiant (1994 series) #4 © KING

GD 2.0 | VG 4.0 | FN 6.0 | VF 8.0 | VF/NM 9.0 | NM- 9.2

PRESIDENTIAL MATERIAL
IDW Publishing: Oct, 2008 ($3.99/$7.99)

...: Barack Obama - Biography of the candidate; Mariotte-s/Morgan-a/Campbell-c 4.00
...: John McCain - Biography of the candidate; Helfer-s/Thompson-a/Campbell-c 4.00
Flipbook ($7.99) Both issues in flipbook format 8.00

PRESTO KID, THE (See Red Mask)

PRETTY BOY FLOYD (See On the Spot)

PREZ (See Cancelled Comic Cavalcade, Sandman #54 & Supergirl #10)
National Periodical Publications: Aug-Sept, 1973 - No. 4, Feb-Mar, 1974

1-Origin; Joe Simon scripts 3 6 9 18 27 35
2-4 2 4 6 13 18 22

PRICE, THE (See Eclipse Graphic Album Series)

PRIDE & JOY
DC Comics (Vertigo): July, 1997 - No. 4, Oct, 1997 ($2.50, limited series)

1-4-Ennis-s 3.00
TPB (2004, $14.95) r/#1-4 15.00

PRIDE & PREJUDICE
Marvel Comics: June, 2009 - No. 5, Oct, 2009 ($3.99, limited series)

1-5-Adaptation of the Jane Austen novel; Nancy Butler-s/Hugo Petrus-a 4.00

PRIDE AND THE PASSION, THE
Dell Publishing Co.: No. 824, Aug, 1957

Four Color 824-Movie, Frank Sinatra & Cary Grant photo-c
9 18 27 61 106 150

PRIDE OF BAGHDAD
DC Comics (Vertigo): 2006 ($19.99, hardcover with dustjacket)

HC-A pride of lions escaping from the Baghdad zoo in 2003; Vaughan-s/Henrichon-a 20.00
SC-(2007, $12.99) 13.00

PRIDE OF THE YANKEES, THE (See Real Heroes & Sport Comics)
Magazine Enterprises: 1949 (The Life of Lou Gehrig)

nn-Photo-c; Ogden Whitney-a 83 166 249 527 906 1285

PRIEST (Also see Asylum)
Maximum Press: Aug, 1996 - No. 2, Oct, 1996 ($2.99)

1,2 3.00

PRIMAL FORCE
DC Comics: No. 0, Oct, 1994 - No. 14, Dec, 1995 ($1.95/$2.25)

0-14: 0- Teams Red Tornado, Golem, Jack O'Lantern, Meridian & Silver Dragon. 9-begin $2.25-c 3.00

PRIMAL MAN (See The Crusaders)

PRIMAL RAGE
Sirius Entertainment: 1996 ($2.95)

1-Dark One-c; based of video game 3.00

PRIME (See Break-Thru, Flood Relief & Ultraforce)
Malibu Comics (Ultraverse): June, 1993 - No. 26, Aug, 1995 ($1.95/$2.50)

1-1st app. Prime; has coupon for Ultraverse Premiere #0 3.00
1-With coupon missing 2.00
1-Full cover holographic edition; 1st of kind w/Hardcase #1 & Strangers #1 6.00
1-Ultra 5,000 edition w/silver ink-c 4.00
2-4,6-11,14-26: 2-Polybagged w/card & coupon for U. Premiere #0. 3,4-Prototype app. 4-Direct sale w/o card.4-($2.50)-Newsstand ed. polybagged w/card. 6-Bill & Chelsea Clinton app.115-Intro Papa Verite; Pérez-c/a. 16-Intro Turbo Charge 3.00
5-($2.50, 48 pgs.)-Rune flip-c/story part B by Barry Smith; see Sludge #1 for 1st app. Rune; 3-pg. Night Man preview 4.00
12-($3.50, 68 pgs.)-Flip book w/Ultraverse Premiere #3; silver foil logo 4.00
13-($2.95, 52 pgs.)-Variant covers 4.00
...: Gross and Disgusting 1 (10/94, $3.95)-Boris-c; "Annual" on cover, published monthly in indicia 4.00
...Month "Ashcan" (8/94, 75¢)-Boris-c 3.00
... Time: A Prime Collection (1994, $9.95)-r/1-4 10.00
...Vs. The Incredible Hulk (1995)-mail away limited edition 10.00
...Vs. The Incredible Hulk Premium edition 10.00
...Vs. The Incredible Hulk Super Premium edition 15.00
NOTE: *Perez a-15; c-15, 16.*

PRIME (Also see Black September)
Malibu Comics (Ultraverse): Infinity, Sept, 1995 - V2#15, Dec, 1996 ($1.50)

Infinity, V2#1-8: Post Black September storyline. 6-8-Solitaire app. 9-Breyfogle-c/a. 10-12-Ramos-c. 15-Lord Pumpkin app. 3.00
Infinity Signed Edition (2,000 printed) 5.00

PRIME/CAPTAIN AMERICA
Malibu Comics: Mar, 1996 ($3.95, one-shot)

1-Norm Breyfogle-a 4.00

PRIME8: CREATION
Two Morrows Publishing: July, 2001 ($3.95, B&W)

1-Neal Adams-c 4.00

PRIMER (Comico...)
Comico: Oct (no month), 1982 - No. 6, Feb, 1984 (B&W)

1 (52 pgs.) 2 4 6 11 16 20
2-1st app. Grendel & Argent by Wagner 9 18 27 63 112 160
3,4 2 4 6 9 12 15
5-1st Sam Kieth art in comics ('83) & 1st The Maxx 4 8 12 24 37 50
6-Intro & 1st app. Evangeline 2 4 6 13 18 22

PRIMORTALS (Leonard Nimoy's...)

PRIMUS (TV)
Charlton Comics: Feb, 1972 - No. 7, Oct, 1972

1-Staton-a in all 2 4 6 11 16 20
2-7: 6-Drug propaganda story 2 4 6 8 11 14

PRINCE NAMOR, THE SUB-MARINER (Also see Namor ...)
Marvel Comics Group: Sept, 1984 - No. 4, Dec, 1984 (Limited-series)

1-4 4.00

PRINCE OF PERSIA: BEFORE THE SANDSTORM (Based on the 2010 movie)
Dynamite Entertainment: 2010 - No. 4, 2010 ($3.99, limited series)

1-4-Art by Fowler and various. 1-Chang-a. 2-Lopez-a. 3-Edwards-a 5.00

PRINCESS SALLY (Video game)
Archie Publications: Apr, 1995 - No. 3, June, 1995 ($1.50, limited series)

1-3: Spin-off from Sonic the Hedgehog 4.00

PRINCE VALIANT (See Ace Comics, Comics Reading Libraries *in the Promotional Comics section*, & King Comics #146, 147)
David McKay Publ./Dell: No. 26, 1941; No. 67, June, 1954 - No. 900, May, 1958

Feature Books 26 ('41)-Harold Foster-c/a; newspaper strips reprinted, pgs. 1-28,30-63; color & 68 pgs; Foster cover is only original comic book artwork by him
110 220 330 704 1202 1700
Four Color 567 (6/54)(#1)-By Bob Fuje-Movie, photo-c
10 20 30 68 127 185
Four Color 650 (9/55), 699 (4/56), 719 (8/56),-Fuje-a 7 14 21 49 82 115
Four Color 788 (4/57), 849 (1/58), 900-Fuje-a 7 14 21 46 76 105

PRINCE VALIANT
Marvel Comics: Dec, 1994 - No. 4, Mar, 1995 ($3.95, limited series)

1-4; Kaluta-c in all. 4.00

PRINCE VANDAL
Triumphant Comics: Nov, 1993 - Apr?, 1994 ($2.50)

1-6: 1,2-Triumphant Unleashed x-over 3.00

PRIORITY: WHITE HEAT
AC Comics: 1986 - No. 2, 1986 ($1.75, mini-series)

1,2-Bill Black-a 3.00

PRISCILLA'S POP
Dell Publishing Co.: No. 569, June, 1954 - No. 799, May, 1957

Four Color 569 (#1), 630 (5/55), 704 (5/56),799 4 8 12 26 41 55

PRISON BARS (See Behind...)

PRISON BREAK!
Avon Per./Realistic No. 3 on: Sept, 1951 - No. 5, Sept, 1952 (Painted c-3)

1-Wood-c & 1 pg.; has-r/Saint #7 retitled Michael Strong Private Eye
41 82 123 256 428 600
2-Wood-c; Kubert-a; Kinstler inside front-c 30 60 90 177 289 400
3-Orlando, Check-a; c-/Avon paperback #179 24 48 72 140 230 320
4,5: 4-Kinstler-c & inside f/c; Lawrence, Lazarus-a. 5-Kinstler-c; Infantino-a
21 42 63 122 199 275

PRISONER, THE (TV)
DC Comics: 1988 - No. 4, 1989 ($3.50, squarebound, mini-series)

1-4 (Books a-d) 4.00

PRISON RIOT

Prize Comics #23 © QUA

Professor Xavier and the X-Men #10 © MAR

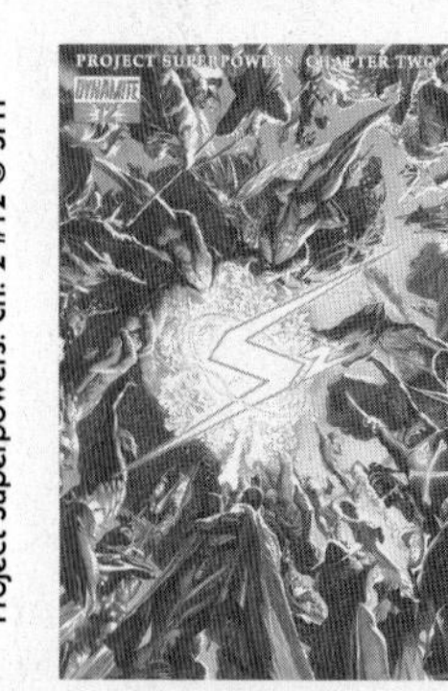

Project Superpowers: Ch. 2 #12 © SPH

	GD 2.0	VG 4.0	FN 6.0	VF 8.0	VF/NM 9.0	NM- 9.2

Avon Periodicals: 1952

1-Marijuana Murders-1 pg. text; Kinstler-c; 2 Kubert illos on text pages
29 58 87 170 278 385

PRISON TO PRAISE
Logos International: 1974 (35¢) (Religious, Christian)

nn-True Story of Merlin R. Carothers 2 4 6 11 16 20

PRIVATE BUCK
Dell Publishing Co./Rand McNally: No. 21, 1941 - No. 12, 1942 (4-1/2" x 5-1/2", 1942)

Large Feature Comic 21 (#1)(1941)(Series I), 22 (1941)(Series I), 12 (1942)(Series II)
17 34 51 98 154 210
382-Rand McNally, one panel per page; small size 10 20 30 58 79 100

PRIVATE EYE (Cover title: Rocky Jorden...#6-8)
Atlas Comics (MCI): Jan, 1951 - No. 8, March, 1952

1-Cover title: Crime Cases... #1-5 21 42 63 124 202 280
2,3-Tuska c/a(3) 14 28 42 76 108 140
4-8 11 22 33 60 83 105

NOTE: *Henkel a-6(3), 7; c-7. Sinnott a-6.*

PRIVATE EYE (See Mike Shayne...)

PRIVATE SECRETARY
Dell Publishing Co.: Dec-Feb, 1962-63 - No. 2, Mar-May, 1963

1 3 6 9 21 32 42
2 3 6 9 17 25 32

PRIVATE STRONG (See The Double Life of...)

PRIZE COMICS (...Western #69 on) (Also see Treasure Comics)
Prize Publications: March, 1940 - No. 68, Feb-Mar, 1948

1-Origin Power Nelson, The Futureman & Jupiter, Master Magician; Ted O'Neil, Secret Agent M-11, Jaxon of the Jungle, Bucky Brady & Storm Curtis begin (1st app. of each)
277 554 831 1759 3030 4300
2-The Black Owl begins (1st app.) 129 258 387 826 1413 2000
3 119 238 357 762 1306 1850
4-Classic robot-c 142 284 426 909 1555 2200
5,6: Dr. Dekkar, Master of Monsters app. in each 110 220 330 704 1202 1700
7-(Scarce)-1st app. The Green Lama (12/40); Black Owl by S&K; origin/1st app. Dr. Frost & Frankenstein; Capt. Gallant, The Great Voodini & Twist Turner begin;
245 490 735 1568 2684 3800
8,9-Black Owl & Ted O'Neil by S&K 110 220 330 704 1202 1700
10-12,14,15: 11-Origin Bulldog Denny. 14-War-c 77 154 231 493 847 1200
13-Yank & Doodle begin (8/41, origin/1st app.) 90 180 270 576 988 1400
16-19: 16-Spike Mason begins 71 142 213 454 777 1100
20-(Rare) Frankenstein, Black Owl, Green Lama, Yank and Doodle WWII parade-c
90 180 270 576 988 1400
21,25,27,28,31-All WWII covers 60 120 180 381 653 925
22-24,26: 22-Statue of Liberty Japanese attack war-c. 23-Uncle Sam patriotic war-c. 24-Lincoln statue patriotic-c. 26-Liberty Bell-c 71 142 213 454 777 1100
29,30 46 92 138 290 488 685
32 41 82 123 249 417 585
33-Classic bondage/torture-c 65 130 195 416 708 1000
34-Origin Airmale, Yank & Doodle; The Black Owl joins army, Yank & Doodle's father assumes Black Owl's role 39 78 117 240 395 550
35-36,38-39: 35-Flying Fist & Bingo begin 30 60 90 177 289 400
37-Intro. Stampy, Airmale's sidekick; Hitler-c 55 110 165 352 601 850
40-Nazi WWII-c 36 72 108 216 351 485
41-45,47-50: 45-Yank & Doodle learn Black Owl's I.D. (their father). 48-Prince Ra begins
24 48 72 142 234 325
46-Classic Zombie Horror-c/story 43 86 129 271 461 650
51-62,64,67,68: 53-Transvestism story. 55-No Frankenstein. 57-X-Mas-c. 64-Black Owl retires 18 36 54 105 165 225
63-Simon & Kirby c/a 21 42 63 122 199 275
65,66-Frankenstein-c by Briefer 20 40 60 114 182 250

NOTE: ***Briefer** a 7-on; c-65, 66. **J. Binder** a-16; c-21-29. **Guardineer** a-62. **Kiefer** c-62. **Palais** c-68. **Simon & Kirby** c-63, 75, 83.*

PRIZE COMICS WESTERN (Formerly Prize Comics #1-68)
Prize Publications (Feature): No. 69(V7#2), Apr-May, 1948 - No. 119, Nov-Dec, 1956 (No. 69-84: 52 pgs.)

69(V7#2) 14 28 42 80 115 150
70-75: 74-Kurtzman-a (8 pgs.) 12 24 36 67 94 120
76-Randolph Scott photo-c; "Canadian Pacific" movie adaptation
13 26 39 72 101 130
77-Photo-c; Severin/Elder, Mart Bailey-a; "Streets of Laredo" movie adaptation
12 24 36 67 94 120
78-Photo-c; S&K-a, 10 pgs.; Severin, Mart Bailey-a; "Bullet Code", & "Roughshod" movie adaptations 15 30 45 90 140 190
79-Photo-c; Kurtzman-a, 8 pgs.; Severin/Elder, Severin, Mart Bailey-a; "Stage To Chino" movie adaptation w/George O'Brien 15 30 45 90 140 190
80-82-Photo-c; 80,81-Severin/Elder-a(2). 82-1st app. The Preacher by Mart Bailey; Severin/Elder-a(3) 13 26 39 72 101 130
83,84 10 20 30 58 79 100
85-1st app. American Eagle by John Severin & begins (V9#6, 1-2/51)
19 38 57 111 176 240
86,101-105, 109-Severin/Williamson-a 11 22 33 64 90 115
87-99,110,111-Severin/Elder-a(2-3) each 12 24 36 69 97 125
100 13 26 39 74 105 135
106-108,112 9 18 27 47 61 75
113-Williamson/Severin-a(2)/Frazetta? 12 24 36 69 97 125
114-119: Drifter series in all; by Mort Meskin #114-118
8 16 24 42 54 65

NOTE: ***Fass** a-81. **Severin & Elder** c-84-99. **Severin** a-72, 75, 77-79, 83-86, 96, 97, 100-105; c-92,100-109(most), 110-119. **Simon & Kirby** c-75, 83.*

PRIZE MYSTERY
Key Publications: May, 1955 - No. 3, Sept, 1955

1 11 22 33 60 83 105
2,3 8 16 24 44 57 70

PRO, THE
Image Comics: July, 2002 ($5.95, squarebound, one-shot)

1-Ennis-s/Conner & Palmiotti-a; prostitute gets super-powers 8.00
1-Second printing with different cover 6.00
Hardcover Edition (10/04, $14.95) oversized reprint plus new 8 pg. story; sketch pages 15.00

PROFESSIONAL FOOTBALL (See Charlton Sport Library)

PROFESSOR COFFIN
Charlton Comics: No. 19, Oct, 1985 - No. 21, Feb, 1986

19-21: Wayne Howard-a(r); low print run 1 2 3 5 6 8

PROFESSOR OM
Innovation Publishing: May, 1990 - No. 2, 1990 ($2.50, limited series)

1,2-East Meets West spin-off 3.00

PROFESSOR XAVIER AND THE X-MEN (Also see X-Men, 1st series)
Marvel Comics: Nov, 1995 - No. 18 (99¢)

1-18: Stories featuring the Original X-Men. 2-vs. The Blob. 5-Vs. the Original Brotherhood of Evil Mutants. 10-Vs. The Avengers 3.00

PROGRAMME, THE
DC Comics (WildStorm): Sept, 2007 - No. 12, Aug, 2008 ($2.99, limited series)

1-12: 1-Milligan-s/C.P. Smith-a; covers by Smith & Van Sciver 3.00
Book One TPB (2008, $17.99) r/#1-6; cover sketches 18.00
Book Two TPB (2008, $17.99) r/#7-12; cover sketches 18.00

PROJECT A-KO (Manga)
Malibu Comics: Mar, 1994 - No. 4, June, 1994 ($2.95)

1-4-Based on anime film 3.00

PROJECT A-KO 2 (Manga)
CPM Comics: May, 1995 - No. 3, Aug, 1995 ($2.95, limited series)

1-3 3.00

PROJECT A-KO VERSUS THE UNIVERSE (Manga)
CPM Comics: Oct, 1995 - No. 5, June, 1996 ($2.95, limited series, bi-monthly)

1-5 3.00

PROJECT SUPERPOWERS
Dynamite Entertainment: 2008 - No. 7, 2008 ($1.00/$3.50/$2.99)

0-($1.00) Two connecting covers by Alex Ross; re-intro of Golden Age heroes 3.00
0-($1.00) Variant cover by Michael Turner 5.00
1-($3.50) Covers by Ross and Turner; Jim Krueger-s/Carlos Paul-a 3.50
2-7-($2.99) 3.00
... Chapter One HC (2008, $29.99, dustjacket) r/#0-7; Ross sketch pages; layout art 30.00

PROJECT SUPERPOWERS: CHAPTER TWO
Dynamite Entertainment: 2009 - No. 12, 2010 ($1.00/$2.99)

... Chapter Two Prelude (2008, $1.00) Ross sketch pages and mini-series previews 3.00
0-($1.00) Three connecting covers by Alex Ross; The Inheritors assemble 3.00
1-12-($2.99) 1-Krueger & Ross-s/Salazar-a; Ross sketch pages; 2 Ross covers 3.00
... X-Mas Carol (2010, $5.99) Berkenkotter-a/Ross-c 6.00

PROJECT SUPERPOWERS: MEET THE BAD GUYS
Dynamite Entertainment: 2009 - No. 4, 2009 ($2.99)

Promethea #32 © ABC

Prototype #9 © MAL

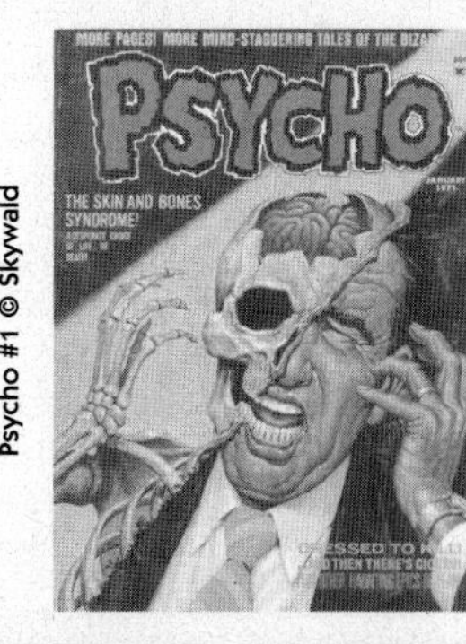

Psycho #1 © Skywald

	GD 2.0	VG 4.0	FN 6.0	VF 8.0	VF/NM 9.0	NM- 9.2

1-4: Ross & Casey-s. 1-Bloodlust. 2-The Revolutionary. 3-Dagon. 4-Supremacy 3.00

PROMETHEA
America's Best Comics: Aug, 1999 - No. 32, Apr, 2005 ($3.50/$2.95)

1-Alan Moore-s/Williams III & Gray-a; Alex Ross painted-c 3.50
1-Variant-c by Williams III & Gray 3.50
2-31-($2.95): 7-Villarrubia photo-a. 10-"Sex, Stars & Serpents". 26-28-Tom Strong app. 27-Cover swipe of Superman vs. Spider-Man treasury ed. 3.00
32-($3.95) Final issue; pages can be cut & assembled into a 2-sided poster 6.00
32-Limited edition of 1000; variant issue printed as 2-sided poster, signed by Moore and Williams; each came with a 48 page book of Promethea covers 120.00
Book 1 Hardcover ($24.95, dust jacket) r/#1-6 25.00
Book 1 TPB ($14.95) r/#1-6 15.00
Book 2 Hardcover ($24.95, dust jacket) r/#7-12 25.00
Book 2 TPB ($14.95) r/#7-12 15.00
Book 3 Hardcover ($24.95, dust jacket) r/#13-18 25.00
Book 3 TPB ($14.95) r/#13-18 15.00
Book 4 Hardcover ($24.95, dust jacket) r/#19-25 25.00
Book 4 TPB ($14.99) r/#19-25 15.00
Book 5 Hardcover ($24.95, d.j.) r/#26-32; includes 2-sided poster image from #32 25.00
Book 5 TPB ($14.99) r/#26-32; includes 2-sided poster image from #32 15.00

PROMETHEUS (VILLAINS) (Leads into JLA #16,17)
DC Comics: Feb, 1998 ($1.95, one-shot)

1-Origin & 1st app.; Morrison-s/Pearson-c 3.00

PROPELLERMAN
Dark Horse Comics: Jan, 1993 - No. 8, Mar, 1994 ($2.95, limited series)

1-8: 2,4,8-Contain 2 trading cards 3.00

PROPHET (See Youngblood #2)
Image Comics (Extreme Studios): Oct, 1993 - No. 10, 1995 ($1.95)

1-($2.50)-Liefeld/Panosian-c/a; 1st app. Mary McCormick; Liefeld scripts in 1-4; #1-3 contain coupons for Prophet #0 3.00
1-Gold foil embossed-c edition rationed to dealers 4.00
2-10: 2-Liefeld-c(p). 3-1st app. Judas. 4-1st app. Omen; Black and White Pt. 3 by Thibert. 4-Alternate-c by Stephen Platt. 5,6-Platt-c/a. 7-(9/94, $2.50)-Platt-c/a. 8-Bloodstrike app. 10-Polybagged w/trading card; Platt-c. 3.00
0-(7/94, $2.50)-San Diego Comic Con ed. (2200 copies) 3.00

PROPHET
Image Comics (Extreme Studios): V2#1, Aug, 1995 - No. 8 ($3.50)

V2#1-8: Dixon scripts in all. 1-4-Platt-a. 1-Boris-c; F. Miller variant-c. 4-Newmen app. 5,6-Wraparound-c 3.50
Annual 1 (9/95, $2.50)-Bagged w/Youngblood gaming card; Quesada-c 3.00
Babewatch Special 1 (12/95, $2.50)-Babewatch tie-in 3.00
1995 San Diego Edition-B&W preview of V2#1. 3.00
TPB-(1996, $12.95) r/#1-7 13.00

PROPHET (Volume 3)
Awesome Comics: Mar, 2000 ($2.99)

1-Flip-c by Jim Lee and Liefeld 3.00

PROPHET
Image Comics: No. 21, Jan, 2012 - Present ($2.99)

21-24: 21-Two covers; Graham-s 3.00

PROPHET/CABLE
Image Comics (Extreme): Jan, 1997 - No. 2, Mar, 1997 ($3.50, limited series)

1,2-Liefeld-c/a: 2-#1 listed on cover 3.50

PROPHET/CHAPEL: SUPER SOLDIERS
Image Comics (Extreme): May, 1996 - No. 2, June, 1996 ($2.50, limited series)

1,2: 1-Two covers exist 3.00
1-San Diego Edition; B&W-c 3.00

PROPOSITION PLAYER
DC Comics (Vertigo): Dec, 1999 - No. 6, May, 2000 ($2.50, limited series)

1-6-Willingham-s/Guinan-a/Bolton-c 3.00
TPB (2003, $14.95) r/#1-6; intro. by James McManus 15.00

PROTECTORS (Also see The Ferret)
Malibu Comics: Sept, 1992 - No. 20, May, 1994 ($1.95-$2.95)

1-20 ($2.50, direct sale)-With poster & diff-c: 1-Origin; has 3/4 outer-c. 3-Polybagged w/Skycap 3.50
1-12 ($1.95, newsstand)-Without poster 3.00

PROTOTYPE (Also see Flood Relief & Ultraforce)
Malibu Comics (Ultraverse): Aug, 1993 - No. 18, Feb, 1995 ($1.95/$2.50)

1-Holo-c 6.00
1-Ultra Limited silver foil-c 4.00
1,2,4-12,14-18: 4-Intro Wrath. 5-Break-Thru & Strangers x-over. 6-Arena cameo. 7,8-Arena-c/story. 12-(7/94). 14 (10/94) 3.00
3-($2.50, 48 pgs.)-Rune flip-c/story by B. Smith (3 pgs.) 4.00
13 (8/94, $3.50)-Flip book (Ultraverse Premiere #6) 4.00
#0-(8/94, $2.50, 44 pgs.) 4.00
Giant Size 1 (10/94, $2.50, 44 pgs.) 4.00

PROTOTYPE (Based on the Activision video game)
DC Comics (WildStorm): Jun, 2009 - No. 6, Nov, 2009 ($3.99, limited series)

1-6-Darick Robertson-c/a 4.00
TPB (2010, $19.99) r/#1-6 20.00

PRUDENCE & CAUTION (Also see Dogs of War & Warriors of Plasm)
Defiant: May, 1994 - No. 2, June, 1994 ($3.50/$2.50)(Spanish versions exist)

1-($3.50, 52 pgs.)-Chris Claremont scripts in all 4.00
2-($2.50) 3.00

PRYDE AND WISDOM (Also see Excalibur)
Marvel Comics: Sept, 1996 - No. 3, Nov, 1996 ($1.95, limited series)

1-3: Warren Ellis scripts; Terry Dodson & Karl Story-c/a 3.00

PSI-FORCE
Marvel Comics Group: Nov, 1986 - No. 32, June, 1989 (75¢/$1.50)

1-25: 11-13-Williamson-i 3.00
26-32 3.00
Annual 1 (10/87) 4.00
... Classic Vol. 1 TPB (2008, $24.99) r/#1-9 25.00

PSI-JUDGE ANDERSON
Fleetway Publications (Quality): 1989 - No. 15, 1990 ($1.95, B&W)

1-15 3.00

PSI-LORDS
Valiant: Sept, 1994 - No. 10, June, 1995 ($2.25)

1-($3.50)-Chromium wraparound-c 4.00
1-Gold 5.00
2-10: 3-Chaos Effect Epsilon Pt. 2 3.00

PSYBA-RATS (Also see Showcase '94 #3,4)
DC Comics: Apr, 1995-No. 3, June, 1995 ($2.50, limited series)

1-3 3.00

PSYCHO (Magazine) (Also see Nightmare)
Skywald Publ. Corp.: Jan, 1971 - No. 24, Mar, 1975 (68 pgs.; B&W)

	GD 2.0	VG 4.0	FN 6.0	VF 8.0	VF/NM 9.0	NM- 9.2
1-All reprints	9	18	27	58	99	140
2-Origin & 1st app. The Heap, series begins	6	12	18	41	66	90
3-Frankenstein series by Adkins begins	6	12	18	39	62	85
4,7,9,10: 4-7-Squarebound. 4-1st Out of Chaos/Satan-c/s	5	10	15	35	55	75
8-(Squarebound)1st app. Edward & Mina Sartyros, the Human Gargoyles	6	12	18	39	62	85
11-18: 13-Cannabalism; 3 pgs of Christopher Lee as Dracula photos. 18-Injury to eye-c.	4	8	12	26	41	55
19-Origin Dracula.	4	8	12	28	44	60
20-Severed Head-c	5	10	15	35	55	75
21-24: 22-1974 Fall Special; Reese, Wildey-a(r). 24-1975 Winter Special; Dave Sim scripts (1st pro work)	5	10	15	30	48	65
Annual 1 (1972)(68 pgs.) Dracula & the Heap app.	5	10	15	30	48	65
Yearbook (1974-nn)-Everett, Reese-a	4	8	12	26	41	55

NOTE: ***Boris** c-3, 5. **Buckler** a-2, 4, 5. **Gene Day** a-21, 23, 24. **Everett** a-3-6. **B. Jones** a-4. **Jeff Jones** a-6, 7, 9; c-12. **Kaluta** a-13. **Katz/Buckler** a-3. **Kim** a-24. **Morrow** a-1. **Reese** a-5. **Dave Sim** s-24. **Sutton** a-3. **Wildey** a-5.*

PSYCHO, THE
DC Comics: 1991 - No. 3, 1991 ($4.95, squarebound, limited series)

1-3-Hudnall-s/Brereton painted-a/c 5.00
TPB (Image Comics, 2006, $17.99) r/series; Brereton sketch pages; Hudnall afterword 18.00

PSYCHOANALYSIS
E. C. Comics: Mar-Apr, 1955 - No. 4, Sept-Oct, 1955

	GD 2.0	VG 4.0	FN 6.0	VF 8.0	VF/NM 9.0	NM- 9.2
1-All Kamen-c/a; not approved by code	21	42	63	168	272	375
2-4-Kamen-c/a in all	14	28	42	112	181	250

PSYCHOANALYSIS
Gemstone Publishing: Oct, 1999 - No. 4, Jan, 2000 ($2.50)

1-4-Reprints E.C. series 3.00

The Pulse #4 © MAR

Punch Comics #12 © CHES

Punisher #50 © MAR

	GD 2.0	VG 4.0	FN 6.0	VF 8.0	VF/NM 9.0	NM- 9.2

Annual 1 (2000, $10.95) r/#1-4 11.00

PSYCHOBLAST
First Comics: Nov, 1987 - No. 9, July, 1988 ($1.75)

1-9 3.00

PSYCHONAUTS
Marvel Comics (Epic Comics): Oct, 1993 - No. 4, Jan, 1994 ($4.95, lim. series)

1-4: American/Japanese co-produced comic 5.00

PSYLOCKE
Marvel Comics: Jan, 2010 - No. 4, Apr, 2010 ($3.99, limited series)

1-4-Finch-c/Yost-s/Tolibao-a. 3,4-Wolverine app. 4.00

PSYLOCKE & ARCHANGEL CRIMSON DAWN
Marvel Comics: Aug, 1997 - No. 4, Nov, 1997 ($2.50, limited series)

1-4-Raab-s/Larroca-a(p) 3.00

PTOLUS: CITY BY THE SPIRE
Dabel Brothers Productions/Marvel Comics (Dabel Brothers) #2 on: June, 2006 - No. 6, Mar, 2007 ($2.99)

1-(1st printing, Dabel) Adaptation of the Monte Cook novel; Cook-s 3.00
1-(2nd printing, Marvel), 2-6 3.00
Monte Cooke's Ptolus: City By the Spire TPB (2007, $14.99) r/#1-6 15.00

P.T. 109 (See Movie Comics)

PUBLIC DEFENDER IN ACTION (Formerly Police Trap)
Charlton Comics: No. 7, Mar, 1956 - No. 12, Oct, 1957

	GD 2.0	VG 4.0	FN 6.0	VF 8.0	VF/NM 9.0	NM- 9.2
7	10	20	30	58	79	100
8-12	8	16	24	40	50	60

PUBLIC ENEMIES
D. S. Publishing Co.: 1948 - No. 9, June-July, 1949

	GD 2.0	VG 4.0	FN 6.0	VF 8.0	VF/NM 9.0	NM- 9.2
1-True Crime Stories	28	56	84	165	270	375
2-Used in **SOTI**, pg. 95	23	46	69	136	223	310
3-5: 5-Arrival date of 10/1/48	15	30	45	90	140	190
6,8,9	15	30	45	86	133	180
7-McWilliams-a; injury to eye panel	15	30	45	90	140	190

PUBO
Dark Horse Comics: Dec, 2002 - No. 3, Mar, 2003 ($3.50, B&W, limited series)

1-3-Leland Purvis-s/a 3.50

PUDGY PIG
Charlton Comics: Sept, 1958 - No. 2, Nov, 1958

	GD 2.0	VG 4.0	FN 6.0	VF 8.0	VF/NM 9.0	NM- 9.2
1,2	3	6	9	17	25	32

PUFFED
Image Comics: Jul, 2003 - No. 3, Sept, 2003 ($2.95, B&W)

1-3-Layman-s/Crosland-a. 1-Two covers by Crosland & Quitely 3.00

PULP FANTASTIC (Vertigo V2K)
DC Comics (Vertigo): Feb, 2000 - No. 3, Apr, 2000 ($2.50, limited series)

1-3-Chaykin & Tischman-s/Burchett-a 3.00

PULP FICTION LIBRARY: MYSTERY IN SPACE
DC Comics: 1999 ($19.95, TPB)

nn-Reprints classic sci-fi stories from Mystery in Space, Strange Adventures, Real Fact Comics and My Greatest Adventure 20.00

PULSE, THE (Also see Alias and Deadline)
Marvel Comics: Apr, 2004 - No. 14, May, 2006 ($2.99)

1-14: 1-5-Bendis-s/Bagley-a; Jessica Jones, Ben Urich, Kat Farrell app. 3-5-Green Goblin app. 6,7-Brent Anderson-a 9-Wolverine app. 10-House of M. 11-14-Gaydos-a 3.00
...: House of M Special (9/05, 50¢) tabloid newspaper format; Mayhew- "photos" 3.00
Vol. 1: Thin Air (2004, $13.99) r/#1-5, gallery of cover layouts and sketches 14.00
Vol. 2: Secret War (2005, $11.99) r/#6-9 12.00
Vol. 3: Fear (2006, $14.99) r/#11-14 and New Avengers Annual #1 15.00

PUMA BLUES
Aardvark One International/Mirage Studios #21 on: 1986 - No. 26, 1990 ($1.70-$1.75, B&W)

1-19, 21-26: 1-1st & 2nd printings. 25,26-$1.75-c 3.00
20 ($2.25)-By Alan Moore, Miller, Grell, others 5.00
Trade Paperback (12/88, $14.95) 15.00

PUMPKINHEAD: THE RITES OF EXORCISM (Movie)
Dark Horse Comics: 1993 - No. 2, 1993 ($2.50, limited series)

1,2: Based on movie; painted-c by McManus 3.00

PUNCH & JUDY COMICS
Hillman Per.: 1944; No. 2, Fall, 1944 - V3#2, 12/47; V3#3, 6/51 - V3#9, 12/51

	GD 2.0	VG 4.0	FN 6.0	VF 8.0	VF/NM 9.0	NM- 9.2
V1#1-(60 pgs.)	23	46	69	136	223	310
2	14	28	42	80	115	150
3-12(7/46)	11	22	33	64	90	115
V2#1(8/49),3-9	9	18	27	50	65	80
V2#2,10-12, V3#1-Kirby-a(2) each	21	42	63	122	199	275
V3#2-Kirby-a	19	38	57	112	179	245
3-9	9	18	27	47	61	75

PUNCH COMICS
Harry 'A' Chesler: 12/41; #2, 2/42; #9, 7/44 - #19, 10/46; #20, 7/47 - #23, 1/48

	GD 2.0	VG 4.0	FN 6.0	VF 8.0	VF/NM 9.0	NM- 9.2
1-Mr. E, The Sky Chief, Hale the Magician, Kitty Kelly begin	155	310	465	992	1696	2400
2-Captain Glory app.	95	190	285	603	1039	1475
9-Rocketman & Rocket Girl & The Master Key begin; classic-c	107	214	321	680	1165	1650
10-Sky Chief app.; J. Cole-a; Master Key-r/Scoop #3	64	128	192	406	696	985
11-Origin Master Key-r/Scoop #1; Sky Chief, Little Nemo app.; Jack Cole-a; Fine-*ish* art by Sultan	60	120	180	381	653	925
12-Rocket Boy & Capt. Glory app; classic Skull-c	300	600	900	1950	3375	4800
13-Cover has list of 4 Chesler artists' names on tombstone	71	142	213	454	777	1100
14,15,19,21: 21-Hypo needle story	56	112	168	356	611	865
16,17-Gag-c	39	78	117	240	395	550
18-Bondage-c; hypodermic panels	68	136	204	435	743	1050
20-Unique cover with bare-breasted women. Rocket Girl-c	123	246	369	787	1344	1900
22,23-Little Nemo-not by McCay. 22-Intro Baxter (teenage)(68 pgs.)	24	48	72	140	230	320

PUNCHY AND THE BLACK CROW
Charlton Comics: No. 10, Oct, 1985 - No. 12, Feb, 1986

10-12: Al Fago funny animal-r; low print run 6.00

PUNISHER (See Amazing Spider-Man #129, Blood and Glory, Born, Captain America #241, Classic Punisher, Daredevil #182-184, 257, Daredevil and the..., Ghost Rider V2#5, 6, Marc Spector #8 & 9, Marvel Preview #2, Marvel Super Action, Marvel Tales, Power Pack #46, Spectacular Spider-Man #81-83, 140, 141, 143 & new Strange Tales #13 & 14)

PUNISHER (The...)
Marvel Comics Group: Jan, 1986 - No. 5, May, 1986 (Limited series)

	GD 2.0	VG 4.0	FN 6.0	VF 8.0	VF/NM 9.0	NM- 9.2
1-Double size	3	6	9	14	20	25
2-5	2	4	6	8	11	14

Trade Paperback (1988)-r/#1-5 11.00
Circle of Blood TPB (8/01, $15.95) Zeck-c 16.00
Circle of Blood HC (2008, $19.99) two covers 20.00
NOTE: *Zeck a-1-4; c-1-5.*

PUNISHER (The...) (Volume 2)
Marvel Comics: July, 1987 - No. 104, July, 1995

	GD 2.0	VG 4.0	FN 6.0	VF 8.0	VF/NM 9.0	NM- 9.2
1	1	3	4	6	8	10
2-9: 8-Portacio/Williams-c/a begins, ends #18. 9-Scarcer, low dist.						6.00
10-Daredevil app; ties in w/Daredevil #257	1	3	4	6	8	10
11-25,50: 13-18-Kingpin app. 19-Stroman-c/a. 20-Portacio-c(p). 24-1st app. Shadowmasters. 25,50:($1.50,52 pgs.). 25-Shadowmasters app.						4.00
26-49,51-74,76-85,87-89: 57-Photo-c; came w/outer-c (newsstand ed. w/o outer-c). 59-Punisher is severely cut & has skin grafts (has black skin). 60-62-Luke Cage app. 62-Punisher back to white skin. 68-Tarantula-c/story. 85-Prequel to Suicide Run Pt. 0. 87,88-Suicide Run Pt. 6 & 9						3.00
75-($2.75, 52 pgs.)-Embossed silver foil-c						4.00
86-($2.95, 52 pgs.)-Embossed & foil stamped-c; Suicide Run part 3						4.00
90-99: 90-bound-in cards. 99-Cringe app.						3.00
100,104: 100-($2.95, 68 pgs.). 104-Last issue						4.00
100-($3.95, 68 pgs.)-Foil cover						5.00
101-103: 102-Bullseye						3.50
"Ashcan" edition (75¢)-Joe Kubert-c						3.00
Annual 1-7 ('88-'94, 68 pgs.) 1-Evolutionary War x-over. 2-Atlantis Attacks x-over; Jim Lee-a(p) (back-up story, 6 pgs.); Moon Knight app. 4-Golden-c(p). 6-Bagged w/card.						4.00
...: A Man Named Frank (1994, $6.95, TPB)						7.00
...and Wolverine in African Saga nn (1989, $5.95, 52 pgs.)-Reprints Punisher War Journal #6 & 7; Jim Lee-c/a(r)						6.00
... Assassin Guild ('88, $6.95, graphic novel)						10.00
Back to School Special 1-3 (11/92-10/94, $2.95, 68 pgs.)						4.00
.../Batman: Deadly Knights (10/94, $4.95)						5.00
.../Black Widow: Spinning Doomsday's Web (1992, $9.95, graphic novel)						12.00
...Bloodlines nn (1991, $5.95, 68 pgs.)						6.00

Punisher V3 #6 © MAR

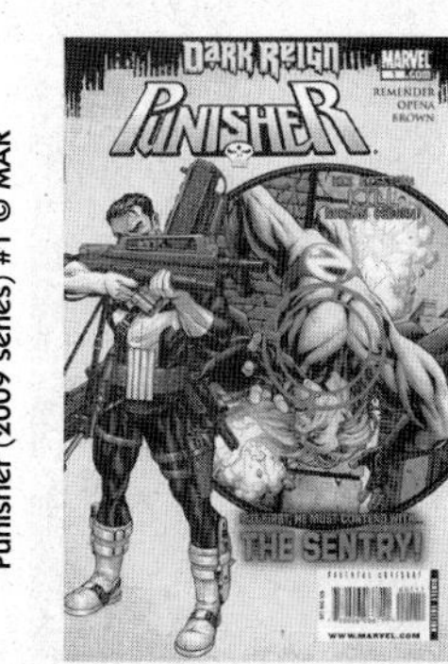

Punisher (2009 series) #1 © MAR

PunisherMax #6 © MAR

	GD	VG	FN	VF	VF/NM	NM-
	2.0	4.0	6.0	8.0	9.0	9.2

...: Die Hard in the Big Easy nn ('92, $4.95, 52 pgs.) 5.00
...: Empty Quarter nn ('94, $6.95) 7.00
...G-Force nn (1992, $4.95, 52 pgs.)-Painted-c 5.00
...Holiday Special 1-3 (1/93-1/95,, 52 pgs.,68pgs.)-1-Foil-c 4.00
...Intruder Graphic Novel (1989, $14.95, hardcover) 20.00
...Intruder Graphic Novel (1991, $9.95, softcover) 12.00
...Invades the 'Nam: Final Invasion nn (2/94, $6.95)-J. Kubert-c & chapter break art; reprints The 'Nam #84 & unpublished #85,86 7.00
...Kingdom Gone Graphic Novel (1990, $16.95, hardcover) 20.00
...Meets Archie (8/94, $3.95, 52 pgs.)-Die cut-c; no ads; same contents as Archie Meets The Punisher 5.00
...Movie Special 1 (6/90, $5.95, squarebound, 68 pgs.) painted-c; Brent Anderson-a; contents intended for a 3 issue series which was advertised but not published 6.00
...: No Escape nn (1990, $4.95, 52 pgs.)-New-a 5.00
...Return to Big Nothing Graphic Novel (Epic, 1989, $16.95, hardcover) 25.00
...Return to Big Nothing Graphic Novel (Marvel, 1989, $12.95, softcover) 15.00
...The Prize nn (1990, $4.95, 68 pgs.)-New-a 5.00
Summer Special 1-4(8/91-7/94, 52 pgs.):1-No ads. 2-Bisley-c; Austin-a(i). 3-No ads 4.00

NOTE: ***Austin*** *c(i)-47, 48.* ***Cowan*** *c-39.* ***Golden*** *c-50, 85, 86, 100.* ***Heath*** *a-26, 27, 89, 90, 91; c-26, 27.* ***Quesada*** *c-56p, 62p.* ***Sienkiewicz*** *c-Back to School 1.* ***Stroman*** *a-76p(9 pgs.).* ***Williamson*** *a(i)-25, 60-62i, 64-70, 74, Annual 5; c(i)-62, 65-68.*

PUNISHER (Also see Double Edge)
Marvel Comics: Nov, 1995 - No. 18, Apr, 1997 ($2.95/$1.95/$1.50)

1 ($2.95)-Ostrander scripts begin; foil-c. 4.00
2-18: 7-Vs. S.H.I.E.L.D. 11-"Onslaught." 12-17-X-Cutioner-c/app. 17-Daredevil, Spider-Man-c/app. 3.00

PUNISHER (Marvel Knights)
Marvel Comics: Nov, 1998 - No. 4, Feb, 1999 ($2.99, limited series)

1-4: 1-Wrightson-a; Wrightson & Jusko-c 3.00
1-($6.95) DF Edition; Jae Lee variant-c 7.00

PUNISHER (Marvel Knights) (Volume 3)
Marvel Comics: Apr, 2000 - No. 12, Mar, 2001 ($2.99, limited series)

1-Ennis-s/Dillon & Palmiotti-a/Bradstreet-c 5.00
1-Bradstreet white variant-c 10.00
1-($6.95) DF Edition; Jurgens & Ordway variant-c 7.00
2-Two covers by Bradstreet & Dillon 3.00
3-($3.99) Bagged with Marvel Knights Genesis Edition; Daredevil app. 4.00
4-12: 9-11-The Russian app. 3.00
HC (6/02, $34.95) r/#1-12, Punisher Kills the Marvel Universe, and Marvel Knights Double Shot #1 35.00
... By Garth Ennis Omnibus (2008, $99.99) oversized r/#1-12, #1-7 & #13-37 of 2001 series, Punisher Kills the Marvel Universe, and Marvel Knights Double Shot #1; extras 100.00
.../Painkiller Jane (1/01, $3.50) Jusko-c; Ennis-s/Jusko and Dave Ross-a(p) 3.50
...: Welcome Back Frank TPB (4/01, $19.95) r/#1-12 20.00

PUNISHER (Marvel Knights) (Volume 4)
Marvel Comics: Aug, 2001 - No. 37, Feb, 2004 ($2.99)

1-Ennis-s/Dillon & Palmiotti-a/Bradstreet-c; The Russian app. 4.00
2-Two covers (Dillon & Bradstreet) Spider-Man-c/app. 3.00
3-37: 3-7-Ennis-s/Dillon-a. 9-12-Peyer-s/Gutierrez-a. 13,14-Ennis-s/Dilllon-a. 16,17-Wolverine app.; Robertson-a. 18-23,32-Dillon-a. 24-27-Mandrake-a. 27-Elektra app. 33-37-Spider-Man, Daredevil, & Wolverine app. 36,37-Hulk app. 3.00
...Army of One TPB (2/02, $15.95) r/#1-7; Bradstreet-c 16.00
Vol. 2 HC (2003, $29.95) r/#1-7,13-18; intro. by Mike Millar 30.00
Vol. 3 HC (2004, $29.95) r/#19-27; script pages for #19 30.00
Vol. 3: Business as Usual TPB (2003, $14.99) r/#13-18; Bradstreet-c 15.00
Vol. 4: Full Auto TPB (2003, $17.99) r/#20-26; Bradstreet-c 18.00
Vol. 5: Streets of Laredo TPB (2003, $17.99) r/#19,27-32 18.00
Vol. 6: Confederacy of Dunces TPB (2004, $13.99) r/#33-37 14.00

PUNISHER (Marvel MAX)(Title becomes "Punisher: Frank Castle MAX" with #66)
Marvel Comics: Mar, 2004 - No. 75, Dec, 2009 ($2.99/$3.99)

1-49,51-60: 1-Ennis-s/LaRosa-a/Bradstreet-c; flashback to his family's murder; Micro app. 6-Micro killed. 7-12,19-25-Fernandez-a. 13-18-Braithwaite-a. 31-36-Barracuda. 43-49-Medina-a. 51-54-Barracuda app. 60-Last Ennis-s/Bradstreet-c 3.00
50-($3.99) Barracuda returns; Chaykin-a 4.00
61-65-Gregg Hurwitz-s/Dave Johnson-c/Laurence Campbell-a 3.00
66-73-($3.99) 66-70-Six Hours to Kill; Swierczynski-s. 71-73-Parlov-a 4.00
74,75-($4.99) 74-Parlov-a. 75-Short stories; art by Lashley, Coker, Parlov & others 5.00
Annual (11/07, $3.99) Mike Benson-s/Laurence Campbell-a 4.00
...: Bloody Valentine (4/06, $3.99) Palmiotti & Gray-s/Gulacy & Palmiotti-a; Gulacy-c 4.00
...: Force of Nature (4/08, $4.99) Swierczynski-s/Lacombe-a/Deodato-c 5.00
...: MAX MGC #1 (5/10, $1.00) reprints #1 with "Marvel's Greatest Comics" cover logo 3.00
...: MAX: Naked Kill (8/09, $3.99) Campbell-a/Bradstreet-c 4.00
...: MAX Special: Little Black Book (8/08, $3.99) Gischler-s/Palo-a/Johnson-c 4.00
...: MAX X-Mas Special (2/09, $3.99) Aaron-s/Boschi-a/Bachalo-c 4.00
...: Red X-Mas (2/05, $3.99) Palmiotti & Gray-s/Texeira & Palmiotti-a; Texeira-c 4.00
...: Silent Night (2/06, $3.99) Diggle-s/Hotz-a/Deodato-c 4.00
...: The Cell (7/05, $4.99) Ennis-s/LaRosa-a/Bradstreet-c 5.00
...: The Tyger (2/06, $4.99) Ennis-s/Severin-a/Bradstreet-c; Castle's childhood 5.00
...: Very Special Holidays TPB ('06, $12.99) r/Red X-Mas, Bloody Valentine and Silent Night 13.00
...: X-Mas Special (1/07, $3.99) Stuart Moore-s/CP Smith-a 4.00
... MAX: From First to Last HC (2006, $19.99) r/The Tyger, The Cell and The End 1-shots 20.00
... MAX Vol. 1 (2005, $29.99) oversized r/#1-12; gallery of Fernandez art from #7 shown from layout to colored pages 30.00
... MAX Vol. 2 (2006, $29.99) oversized r/#13-24; gallery of Fernandez pencil art 30.00
... MAX Vol. 3 (2007, $29.99) oversized r/#25-36; gallery of Fernandez & Parlov art 30.00
... MAX Vol. 4 (2008, $29.99) oversized r/#37-49; gallery of Fernandez & Medina art 30.00
Vol. 1: In the Beginning TPB (2004, $14.99) r/#1-6 15.00
Vol. 2: Kitchen Irish TPB (2004, $14.99) r/#7-12 15.00
Vol. 3: Mother Russia TPB (2005, $14.99) r/#13-18 15.00
Vol. 4: Up is Down and Black is White TPB (2005, $14.99) r/#19-24 15.00
Vol. 5: The Slavers TPB (2006, $15.99) r/#25-30; Fernandez pencil pages 16.00
Vol. 6: Barracuda TPB (2006, $15.99) r/#31-36; Parlov sketch page 16.00
Vol. 7: Man of Stone TPB (2007, $15.99) r/#37-42 16.00
Vol. 8: Widowmaker TPB (2007, $17.99) r/#43-49 18.00
Vol. 9: Long Cold Dark TPB (2008, $15.99) r/#50-54 16.00

PUNISHER (Frank Castle in the Marvel Universe after Secret Invasion)
(Title changes to Franken-Castle for #17-21)
Marvel Comics: Mar, 2009 - No. 21, Nov, 2010 ($3.99/$2.99)

1-($3.99) Dark Reign; Sentry app.; Remender-s/Opena-a; character history; 2 covers 4.00
2-5,710($2.99) 2-7-The Hood app. 4-Microchip returns. 5-Daredevil #183 cover swipe 3.00
6-($3.99) Huat-a/McKone-c; profile pages of resurrected villains 4.00
11-Follows Dark Reign: The List - Punisher; Franken-Castle begins; Tony Moore-a 4.00
12-16-Franken-Castle continues; Legion of Monsters app. 14-Brereton & Moore-a 3.00
Franken-Castle 17-20: 19, 20-Wolverine & Daken app. 3.00
Franken-Castle 21-($3.99) Brereton-a/c; Legion of Monsters app.; Frank gets body back 4.00
Annual 1 (11/09, $3.99) Pearson-a/c; Spider-Man app. 4.00
...: Franken-Castle - The Birth of the Monster 1 (7/10, $4.99) r/#11 & Dark Reign: The List 5.00

PUNISHER (Frank Castle in the Marvel Universe)
Marvel Comics: Oct, 2011 - Present ($3.99/$2.99)

1-($3.99) Rucka-s/Checchetto-a/Hitch-c 4.00
1-Variant-c by Sal Buscema 6.00
1-Variant-c by Neal Adams 10.00
2-9-($2.99): 2,3-Vulture app. 3.00
..., Moon Knight & Daredevil: The Big Shots (10/11, $3.99) Previews new series for Punisher, Moon Knight & Daredevil; creator interviews and production art 4.00

PUNISHER AND WOLVERINE: DAMAGING EVIDENCE (See Wolverine and...)

PUNISHER ARMORY, THE
Marvel Comics: 7/90 ($1.50); No. 2, 6/91; No. 3, 4/92 - 10/94($1.75/$2.00)

1-10: 1-r/weapons pgs. from War Journal. 1,2-Jim Lee-c. 3-10- All new material. 3-Jusko painted-c 3.00

PUNISHER: IN THE BLOOD (Marvel Universe Frank Castle)
Marvel Comics: Jan, 2011 - No. 5, May, 2011 ($3.99, limited series)

1-5-Remender-s/Boschi-a; Jigsaw & Microchip app. 4.00

PUNISHER KILLS THE MARVEL UNIVERSE
Marvel Comics: Nov, 1995 ($5.95, one-shot)

1-Garth Ennis script/Doug Braithwaite-a 7.00
1-2nd printing (3/00) Steve Dillon-c 6.00
1-3rd printing (2008, $4.99) original 1995 cover 5.00

PUNISHER MAGAZINE, THE
Marvel Comics: Oct, 1989 - No. 16, Nov, 1990 ($2.25, B&W, Magazine, 52 pgs.)

1-16: 1-r/Punisher #1('86). 2,3-r/Punisher 2-5. 4-16: 4-7-r/Punisher V2#1-8. 4-Chiodo-c. 8-r/Punisher #10 & Daredevil #257; Portacio & Lee-r. 14-r/Punisher War Journal #1,2 w/new Lee-c. 16-r/Punisher W. J. #3,8 4.00

NOTE: ***Chiodo*** *painted c-4, 7, 16.* ***Jusko*** *painted c-6, 8.* ***Jim Lee*** *r-8, 14-16; c-14.* ***Portacio/Williams*** *r-7-12.*

PUNISHERMAX
Marvel Comics (MAX): Jan, 2010 - No. 22, Apr, 2012 ($3.99)

1-22-Aaron-s/Dillon-a/Johnson-c. 1-5-Rise of the Kingpin. 6-11-Bullseye. 17-20-Elektra app. 21-Castle dies. 22-Afterword by Aaron 4.00
...: Butterfly (5/10, $4.99) Valerie D'Orazio-s/Laurence Campbell-a/c 5.00
...: Get Castle (3/10, $4.99) Rob Williams-s/Laurence Campbell-a/Bradstreet-c 5.00

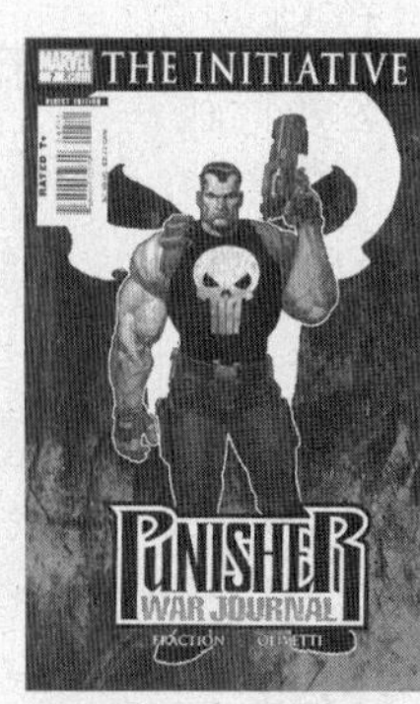

Punisher War Journal (2007 series) #7 © MAR

Punisher War Zone #10 © MAR

Purgatori #5 © Chaos!

	GD 2.0	VG 4.0	FN 6.0	VF 8.0	VF/NM 9.0	NM- 9.2

...: Happy Ending (10/10, $3.99) Milligan-s/Ryp-a/c 4.00
...: Hot Rods of Death (11/10, $4.99) Huston-s/Martinbrough-a/Bradstreet-c 5.00
...: Tiny Ugly World (12/10, $4.99) Lapham-s/Talajic-a/Bradstreet-c 5.00

PUNISHER NOIR
Marvel Comics: Oct, 2009 - No. 4, Jan, 2010 ($3.99, limited series)

1-4-Pulp-style set in 1935; Tieri-s/Azaceta-a 4.00

PUNISHER: OFFICIAL MOVIE ADAPTATION
Marvel Comics: May, 2004 - No. 3, May, 2004 ($2.99, limited series)

1-3-Photo-c of Thomas Jane; Milligan-s/Olliffe-a 3.00

PUNISHER: ORIGIN OF MICRO CHIP, THE
Marvel Comics: July, 1993 - No. 2, Aug, 1993 ($1.75, limited series)

1,2 3.00

PUNISHER: P.O.V.
Marvel Comics: 1991 - No. 4, 1991 ($4.95, painted, limited series, 52 pgs.)

1-4: Starlin scripts & Wrightson painted-c/a in all. 2-Nick Fury app. 5.00

PUNISHER PRESENTS: BARRACUDA MAX
Marvel Comics (MAX): Apr, 2007 - No. 5, Aug, 2007 ($3.99, limited series)

1-5-Ennis-s/Parlov-a/c 4.00
SC (2007, $17.99) r/series; sketch pages 18.00

PUNISHER: THE END
Marvel Comics: June, 2004 ($4.50, one-shot)

1-Ennis-s/Corben-a/c 4.50

PUNISHER: THE GHOSTS OF INNOCENTS
Marvel Comics: Jan, 1993 - No. 2, Jan, 1993 ($5.95, 52 pgs.)

1,2-Starlin scripts 6.00

PUNISHER: THE MOVIE
Marvel Comics: 2004 ($12.99,TPB)

nn-Reprints Amazing Spider-Man #129; Official Movie Adaptation and Punisher V3 #1 13.00

PUNISHER 2099 (See Punisher War Journal #50)
Marvel Comics: Feb, 1993 - No. 34, Nov, 1995 ($1.25/$1.50/$1.95)

1-24,26-34: 1-Foil stamped-c. 1-Second printing. 13-Spider-Man 2099 x-over; Ron Lim-c(p). 16-bound-in card sheet 3.00
25 ($2.95, 52 pgs.)-Deluxe edition; embossed foil-cover 4.00
25 ($2.25, 52 pgs.) 4.00
(Marvel Knights) #1 (11/04, $2.99) Kirkman-s/Mhan-a/Pat Lee-c 3.00

PUNISHER VS. BULLSEYE
Marvel Comics: Jan, 2006 - No. 5, May, 2006 ($2.99, limited series)

1-5-Daniel Way-s/Steve Dillon-a 3.00
TPB (2006, $13.99) r/#1-5; cover sketch pages 14.00

PUNISHER VS. DAREDEVIL
Marvel Comics: Jun, 2000 ($3.50, one-shot)

1-Reprints Daredevil #183,#184 & #257 4.00

PUNISHER WAR JOURNAL, THE
Marvel Comics: Nov, 1988 - No. 80, July, 1995 ($1.50/$1.75/$1.95)

1-Origin The Punisher; Matt Murdock cameo; Jim Lee inks begin 5.00
2-7: 2,3-Daredevil x-over; Jim Lee-c(i). 4-Jim Lee c/a begins. 6-Two part Wolverine story begins. 7-Wolverine-c, story ends 4.00
8-49,51-60,62,63,65: 13-16,20-22: No Jim Lee-a. 13-Lee-c only. 13-15-Heath-i. 14,15-Spider-Man x-over. 19-Last Jim Lee-c/a.29,30-Ghost Rider app. 31-Andy & Joe Kubert art. 36-Photo-c. 47,48-Nomad/Daredevil-c/stories; see Nomad. 57,58-Daredevil & Ghost Rider-c/stories. 62,63-Suicide Run Pt. 4 & 7 3.00
50,61,64($2.95, 52 pgs.): 50-Preview of Punisher 2099 (1st app.); embossed-c. 61-Embossed foil cover; Suicide Run Pt. 1. 64-Die-cut-c; Suicide Run Pt. 10 4.00
64-($2.25, 52 pgs.)-Regular cover edition 4.00
66-74,76-80: 66-Bound-in card sheet 3.00
75 ($2.50, 52 pgs.) 4.00
NOTE: ***Golden** c-25-30, 40, 61, 62.* ***Jusko** painted c-31, 32.* ***Jim Lee** a-1i-3i, 4p-13p, 17p-19p; c-2i, 3i, 4p-15p, 17p, 18p, 19p. Painted c-40.*

PUNISHER WAR JOURNAL (Frank Castle back in the regular Marvel Universe)
Marvel Comics: Jan, 2007 - No. 26, Feb, 2009 ($2.99)

1-Civil War tie-in; Spider-Man app; Fraction-s/Olivetti-a 5.00
1-B&W edition (11/06) 5.00
2-5: 2,3-Civil War tie-in. 4-Deodato-a 4.00
6-11,13-24,26: 6-10-Punisher dons Captain America-*esque* outfit. 7-Two covers. 11-Winter Soldier app. 16-23-Chaykin-a. 18-23-Jigsaw app. 24-Secret Invasion 3.00
12,25-($3.99) 12-World War Hulk x-over; Fraction-s/Olivetti-a. 25-Secret Invasion 4.00
... Annual 1 (1/09, $3.99) Spurrier-s/Dell'edera-a 4.00
... Vol. 1: Civil War HC (2007, $19.99) r/#1-4 and #1 B&W edition; Olivetti sketch pages 20.00
... Vol. 1: Civil War SC (2007, $14.99) r/#1-4 and #1 B&W edition; Olivetti sketch pages 15.00
... Vol. 2: Goin' Out West HC (2007, $24.99) r/#5-11; Olivetti sketch page 25.00
... Vol. 2: Goin' Out West SC (2008, $17.99) r/#5-11; Olivetti sketch page 18.00
... Vol. 3: Hunter Hunted HC (2008, $19.99) r/#12-17 20.00

PUNISHER: WAR ZONE, THE
Marvel Comics: Mar, 1992 - No. 41, July, 1995 ($1.75/$1.95)

1-($2.25, 40 pgs.)-Die cut-c; Romita, Jr.-c/a begins 4.00
2-22,24,26,27-41: 8-Last Romita, Jr.-c/a. 19-Wolverine app. 24-Suicide Run Pt. 5. 27-Bound-in card sheet. 31-36-Joe Kubert-a 3.00
23-($2.95, 52 pgs.)-Embossed foil-c; Suicide Run part 2; Buscema-a(part) 4.00
25-($2.25, 52 pgs.)-Suicide Run part 8; painted-c 4.00
Annual 1,2 ('93, 94, $2.95, 68 pgs.)-1-Bagged w/card; John Buscema-a 4.00
...: River Of Blood TPB (2006, $15.99) r/#31-36; Joe Kubert-a 16.00
NOTE: ***Golden** c-23.* ***Romita, Jr.** c/a-1-8.*

PUNISHER: WAR ZONE
Marvel Comics: Feb, 2009 - No. 6, Mar, 2009 ($3.99, weekly limited series)

1-6-Ennis-s/Dillon-a/c; return of Ma Gnucci 4.00
1-Variant cover by John Romita, Jr. 6.00

PUNISHER: YEAR ONE
Marvel Comics: Dec, 1994 - No. 4, Apr, 1995 ($2.50, limited series)

1-4 3.00

PUNX
Acclaim (Valiant): Nov, 1995 - No. 3, Jan, 1996 ($2.50, unfinished lim. series)

1-3: Giffen story & art in all. 2-Satirizes Scott McCloud's Understanding Comics 3.00
(Manga) Special 1 (3/96, $2.50)-Giffen scripts 3.00

PUPPET COMICS
George W. Dougherty Co.: Spring, 1946 - No. 2, Summer, 1946

	GD 2.0	VG 4.0	FN 6.0	VF 8.0	VF/NM 9.0	NM- 9.2
1-Funny animal in both	15	30	45	83	124	165
2	11	22	33	62	86	110

PUPPETOONS (See George Pal's...)

PUREHEART (See Archie as...)

PURGATORI
Chaos! Comics: Prelude #-1, 5/96 ($1.50, 16 pgs.); 1996 - No. 3 Dec, 1996 ($3.50/$2.95, limited series)

Prelude #-1-Pulido story; Balent-c/a; contains sketches & interviews 3.00
0-(2/01, $2.99) Prelude to "Love Bites"; Rio-c/a 3.00
1/2 (12/00, $2.95) Al Rio-c/a 3.00
1-($3.50)-Wraparound cover; red foil embossed-c; Jim Balent-a 5.00
1-($19.95)-Premium Edition (1000 print run) 20.00
2-($3.00)-Wraparound-c 3.00
2-Variant-c 5.00
...: Heartbreaker 1 (3/02, $2.99) Jolley-s 3.00
...: Love Bites 1 (3/01, $2.99) Turnbull-a/Kaminski-s 3.00
...: Mischief Night 1 (11/01, $2.99) 3.00
...: Re-Imagined 1 (7/02, $2.99) Jolley-s/Neves-a 3.00
...The Dracula Gambit-($2.95) 3.00
...The Dracula Gambit Sketchbook-($2.95) 3.00
...The Vampire's Myth 1-($19.95) Premium Ed. (10,000) 20.00
...Vs. Chastity (7/00, $2.95) Two versions (Alpha and Omega) with different endings; Rio-a 3.00
...Vs. Lady Death (1/01, $2.95) Kaminski-s 3.00
...Vs. Vampirella (4/00, $2.95) Zanier-a; Chastity app. 3.00

PURGATORI
Chaos! Comics: Oct, 1998 - No. 7, Apr, 1999 ($2.95)

1-7-Quinn-s/Rio-c/a. 2-Lady Death-c 3.00

PURGATORI: DARKEST HOUR
Chaos! Comics: Sept, 2001 - No. 2, Oct, 2001 ($2.99, limited series)

1,2 3.00

PURGATORI: EMPIRE
Chaos! Comics: May, 2000 - No. 3, July, 2000 ($2.95, limited series)

1-3-Cleavenger-c 3.00

PURGATORI: GODDESS RISING
Chaos! Comics: July, 1999 - No. 4, Oct, 1999 ($2.95, limited series)

1-4-Deodato-c/a 3.00

PURGATORI: GOD HUNTER
Chaos! Comics: Apr, 2002 - No. 2, May, 2002 ($2.99, limited series)

Purple Claw #2 © TOBY

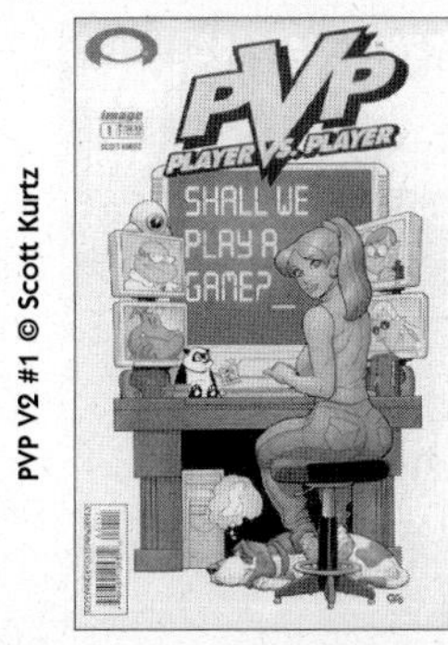

PVP V2 #1 © Scott Kurtz

Queen Sonja #14 © RSLLC

GD 2.0 | VG 4.0 | FN 6.0 | VF 8.0 | VF/NM 9.0 | NM- 9.2

GD 2.0 | VG 4.0 | FN 6.0 | VF 8.0 | VF/NM 9.0 | NM- 9.2

1,2-Molenaar-a/Jolley-s 3.00

PURGATORI: GOD KILLER
Chaos! Comics: Jun, 2002 - No. 2, July, 2002 ($2.99, limited series)

1,2-Molenaar-a/Jolley-s 3.00

PURGATORI: THE HUNTED
Chaos! Comics: Jun, 2001 - No. 2, Aug, 2001 ($2.99, limited series)

1,2 3.00

PURPLE CLAW, THE (Also see Tales of Horror)
Minoan Publishing Co./Toby Press: Jan, 1953 - No. 3, May, 1953

1-Origin; horror/weird stories in all 34 68 102 199 325 450
2,3: 1-3 r-in Tales of Horror #9-11 24 48 72 142 234 325
I.W. Reprint #8-Reprints #1 3 6 9 16 23 30

PUSH (Based on the 2009 movie)
DC Comics (WildStorm): Early Jan, 2009 - No. 6, Apr, 2009 ($3.50, limited series)

1-6-Movie prequel; Bruno Redondo-a. 1-Jock-c 3.50
TPB (2009, $19.99) r/#1-6 20.00

PUSSYCAT (Magazine)
Marvel Comics Group: Oct, 1968 (B&W reprints from Men's magazines)

1-(Scarce)-Ward, Everett, Wood-a; Everett-c 17 34 51 114 250 385

PUZZLE FUN COMICS (Also see Jingle Jangle)
George W. Dougherty Co.: Spring, 1946 - No. 2, Summer, 1946 (52 pgs.)

1-Gustavson-a 24 48 72 142 234 325
2 15 30 45 90 140 190
NOTE: *#1 & 2('46) each contain a* ***George Carlson*** *cover plus a 6 pg. story "Alec in Fumbleland"; also many puzzles in each.*

PvP (Player vs. Player)
Image Comics: Mar, 2003 - No. 45, Mar, 2010 ($2.95/$2.99/$3.50, B&W, reads sideways)

1-34,36-Scott Kurtz-s/a in all. 1,16-Frank Cho-c. 11-Savage Dragon-c/app. 14-Invincible app. 19-Jonathan Luna-c. 25-Cho-a (2 pgs.) 3.00
35,37-45 ($3.50): 45-Brandy from Liberty Meadows app. 3.50
#0 (7/05, 50¢) Secret Origin of Skull 3.00
...: At Large TPB (7/04, $11.95) r/#1-6 12.00
... Vol. 2: Reloaded TPB (12/04, $11.95) r/#7-12 12.00
... Vol. 3: Rides Again TPB (2005, $11.99) r/#13-18 12.00
... Vol. 4: PVP Goes Bananas TPB (2007, $12.99) r/#19-24 13.00
... Vol. 5: PVP Treks On TPB (2008, $14.99) r/#25-31 15.00
...: The Dork Ages TPB (2/04, $11.95) r/#1-6 from Dork Storm Press 12.00

QUACK!
Star Reach Productions: July, 1976 - No. 6, 1977? ($1.25, B&W)

1-Brunner-c/a on Duckaneer (Howard the Duck clone); Dave Stevens, Gilbert, Shaw-a 2 4 6 10 14 18
1-2nd printing (10/76) 5.00
2-6: 2-Newton the Rabbit Wonder by Aragonés/Leialoha; Gilbert, Shaw-a; Leialoha-c. 3-The Beavers by Dave Sim begin, end #5; Gilbert, Shaw-a; Sim/Leialoha-c. 6-Brunner-a (Duckeneer); Gilbert-a 2 4 6 8 10 12

QUADRANT
Quadrant Publications: 1983 - No. 8, 1986 (B&W, nudity, adults)

1-Peter Hsu-c/a in all 2 4 6 10 14 18
2-8 2 3 4 6 8 10

QUANTUM & WOODY
Acclaim Comics: June, 1997 - No. 17, No. 32 (9/99), No. 18 - No. 21, Feb, 2000 ($2.50)

1-17: 1-1st app.; two covers. 6-Copycat-c. 9-Troublemakers app. 3.00
32-(9/99); 18-(10/99),19-21 3.00
The Director's Cut TPB ('97, $7.95) r/#1-4 plus extra pages 8.00

QUANTUM LEAP (TV) (See A Nightmare on Elm Street)
Innovation Publishing: Sept, 1991 - No. 12, Jun, 1993 ($2.50, painted-c)

1-12: Based on TV show; all have painted-c. 8-Has photo gallery 4.00
Special Edition 1 (10/92)-r/#1 w/8 extra pgs. of photos & articles 4.00
Time and Space Special 1 (#13) ($2.95)-Foil logo 4.00

QUANTUM TUNNELER, THE
Revolution Studio: Oct, 2001 (no cover price, one-shot)

1-Prequel to "The One" movie; Clayton Henry-a 3.00

QUASAR (See Avengers #302, Captain America #217, Incredible Hulk #234, Marvel Team-Up #113 & Marvel Two-in-One #53)
Marvel Comics: Oct, 1989 - No. 60, Jul, 1994 ($1.00/$1.25, Direct sales #17 on)

1-Origin; formerly Marvel Boy/Marvel Man 4.00
2-15,17-24,26-49,51-60: 3-Human Torch app. 6-Venom cameo (2 pgs.). 7-Cosmic Spidey. 11-Excalibur x-over. 14-McFarlane-c. 17-Flash parody (Buried Alien). 20-Fantastic Four app. 23-Ghost Rider x-over. 26-Infinity Gauntlet x-over; Thanos-c/story. 27-Infinity Gauntlet x-over. 30-Thanos cameo in flashback; last $1.00-c. 31-Begin $1.25-c; D.P. 7 guest stars. 38-40-Infinity War x-overs. 38-Battles Warlock. 39-Thanos-c & cameo. 40-Thanos app. 42-Punisher-c/story. 53-Warlock & Moondragon app. 58-w/bound-in card sheet 3.00
16,25,50: 16-($1.50, 52 pgs.). 25-($1.50, 52 pgs.)-New costume Quasar. 50-($2.95, 52 pgs.)-Holo-grafx foil-c; Silver Surfer, Man-Thing, Ren & Stimpy app. 4.00
Special #1-3 ($1.25, newsstand)-Same as #32-34 3.00

QUEEN & COUNTRY (See Whiteout)
Oni Press: Mar, 2001 - No. 32, Aug, 2007 ($2.95/$2.99, B&W)

1-Rucka-s in all. Rolston-a/Sale-c 1 2 3 4 5 7
2-5: 2-4-Rolston-a/Sale-c. 5-Snyder-c/Hurtt-a 4.00
6-24,26-32: 6,7-Snyder-c/Hurtt-a. 13-15-Alexander-a. 16-20-McNeil-a. 21-24-Hawthorne-a 26-28-Norton-a 3.00
25-($5.99) Rolston-a 6.00
Free Comic Book Day giveaway (5/02) r/#1 with "Free Comic Book Day" banner on-c 3.00
Operation: Blackwall (10/03, $8.95, TPB) r/#13-15; John Rogers intro. 9.00
Operation: Broken Ground (2002, $11.95, TPB) r/#1-4; Ellis intro. 12.00
Operation: Crystal Ball (1/03, $14.95, TPB) r/#8-12; Judd Winick intro. 15.00
Operation: Dandelion HC (8/04, $25.00) r/#21-24; Jamie S. Rich intro. 25.00
Operation: Dandelion (8/04, $11.95, TPB) r/#21-24; Jamie S. Rich intro. 12.00
Operation: Morningstar (9/02, $8.95, TPB) r/#5-7; Stuart Moore intro. 9.00
Operation: Storm Front (3/04, $14.95, TPB) r/#16-20; Geoff Johns intro. 15.00

QUEEN & COUNTRY: DECLASSIFIED
Oni Press: Nov, 2002 - No. 3, Jan, 2003 ($2.95, B&W, limited series)

1-3-Rucka-s/Hurtt-a/Morse-c 3.00
TPB (7/03, $8.95) r/#1-3; intro. by Micah Wright 9.00

QUEEN & COUNTRY: DECLASSIFIED (Volume 2)
Oni Press: Jan, 2005 - No. 3, Feb, 2006 ($2.95/$2.99, B&W, limited series)

1-3-Rucka-s/Burchett-a/c 3.00
TPB (3/06, $8.95) r/#1-3 9.00

QUEEN & COUNTRY: DECLASSIFIED (Volume 3)
Oni Press: Jun, 2005 - No. 3, Aug, 2005 ($2.95, B&W, limited series)

1-3- "Sons & Daughters;" Johnston-s/Mitten-a/c 3.00
TPB (3/06, $8.95) r/#1-3 9.00

QUEEN OF THE WEST, DALE EVANS (TV)(See Dale Evans Comics, Roy Rogers & Western Roundup under Dell Giants)
Dell Publ. Co.: No. 479, 7/53 - No. 22, 1-3/59 (All photo-c; photo back c-4-8,15)

Four Color 479(#1, '53) 16 32 48 109 237 365
Four Color 528(#2, '54) 10 20 30 66 121 175
3,4: 3(4-6/54)-Toth-a. 4-Toth, Manning-a 8 16 24 53 89 125
5-10-Manning-a. 5-Marsh-a 7 14 21 46 76 105
11,19,21-No Manning 21-Tufts-a 5 10 15 35 55 75
12-18,20,22-Manning-a 6 12 18 39 62 85

QUEEN SONJA (See Red Sonja)
Dynamite Entertainment: 2009 - Present ($2.99/$3.99)

1-10: 1-Rubi-a/Ortega-s; 3 covers; back-up r/Marvel Feature #1 3.00
11-27-($3.99) 16-Thulsa Doom returns 4.00

QUENTIN DURWARD
Dell Publishing Co.: No. 672, Jan, 1956

Four Color 672-Movie, photo-c 7 14 21 44 72 100

QUESTAR ILLUSTRATED SCIENCE FICTION CLASSICS
Golden Press: 1977 (224 pgs.) ($1.95)

11197-Stories by Asimov, Sturgeon, Silverberg & Niven; Starstream-r 3 6 9 20 30 40

QUEST FOR CAMELOT
DC Comics: July, 1998 ($4.95)

1-Movie adaption 5.00

QUEST FOR DREAMS LOST (Also see Word Warriors)
Literacy Volunteers of Chicago: July 4, 1987 ($2.00, B&W, 52 pgs.)(Proceeds donated to help fight illiteracy)

1-Teenage Mutant Ninja Turtles by Eastman/Laird, Trollords, Silent Invasion, The Realm, Wordsmith, Reacto Man, Eb'nn, Aniverse 4.00

QUESTION, THE (See Americomics, Blue Beetle (1967), Charlton Bullseye & Mysterious Suspense)

QUESTION, THE (Also see Showcase '95 #3)
DC Comics: Feb, 1987 - No. 36, Mar, 1990; No. 37, Mar, 2010 ($1.50)

The Question (2005 series) #1 © DC

Quicksilver #13 © MAR

Rachel Rising #1 © Terry Moore

GD 2.0 | VG 4.0 | FN 6.0 | VF 8.0 | VF/NM 9.0 | NM- 9.2

1-36: Denny O'Neil scripts in all 3.00
37-(3/10, $2.99) Blackest Night one-shot; Victor Sage rises; Shiva app.; Cowan-a 3.00
Annual 1 (1988, $2.50) 4.00
Annual 2 (1989, $3.50) 4.00
...: Epitaph For a Hero TPB (2008, $19.99) r/#13-18 20.00
...: Peacemaker TPB (2010, $19.99) r/#31-36 20.00
...: Pipeline TPB (2011, $14.99) r/stories from Detective Comics #854-865; sketch-a 15.00
...: Poisoned Ground TPB (2008, $19.99) r/#7-12 20.00
...: Riddles TPB (2009, $19.99) r/#25-30 20.00
...: Welcome to Oz TPB (2009, $19.99) r/#19-24 20.00
...: Zen and Violence TPB (2007, $19.99) r/#1-6 20.00

QUESTION, THE (Also see Crime Bible and 52)
DC Comics: Jan, 2005 - No. 6, Jun, 2005 ($2.95, limited series)
1-6-Rick Veitch-s/Tommy Lee Edwards-a. 4,6-Superman app. 3.00

QUESTION QUARTERLY, THE
DC Comics: Summer, 1990 - No. 5, Spring, 1992 ($2.50/$2.95, 52pgs.)
1-5 4.00
NOTE: ***Cowan** a-1, 2, 4, 5; c-1-3, 5. **Mignola** a-5i. **Quesada** a-3-5.*

QUESTION RETURNS, THE
DC Comics: Feb, 1997 ($3.50, one-shot)
1-Brereton-c 4.00

QUESTPROBE
Marvel Comics: 8/84; No. 2, 1/85; No. 3, 11/85 (lim. series)
1-3: 1-The Hulk app. by Romita. 2-Spider-Man; Mooney-a(i). 3-Human Torch & Thing 3.00

QUICK DRAW McGRAW (TV) (Hanna-Barbera)(See Whitman Comic Books)
Dell Publishing Co./Gold Key No. 12 on: No. 1040, 12-2/59-60 - No. 11, 7-9/62; No. 12, 11/62; No. 13, 2/63; No. 14, 4/63; No. 15, 6/69 (1st show aired 9/29/59)
Four Color 1040(#1) 1st app. Quick Draw & Baba Looey, Augie Doggie & Doggie Daddy and Snooper & Blabber 12 24 36 79 160 240
2(4-6/60)-4,6: 2-Augie Doggie & Snooper & Blabber stories (8 pgs. each); pre-dates both of their #1 issues. 4-Augie Doggie & Snooper & Blabber stories. 6 12 18 41 66 90
5-1st Snagglepuss app.; last 10¢ issue 7 14 21 44 72 100
7-11 5 10 15 32 51 70
12,13-Title change to ...Fun-Type Roundup (84pgs.) 7 14 21 44 72 100
14,15: 15-Reprints 4 8 12 28 44 60

QUICK DRAW McGRAW (TV)(See Spotlight #2)
Charlton Comics: Nov, 1970 - No. 8, Jan, 1972 (Hanna-Barbera)
1 5 10 15 32 51 70
2-8 3 6 9 19 29 38

QUICKSILVER (See Avengers)
Marvel Comics: Nov, 1997 - No. 13, Nov, 1998 ($2.99/$1.99)
1-($2.99)-Peyer-s/Casey Jones-a; wraparound-c 4.00
2-11: 2-Two covers-variant by Golden. 4-6-Inhumans app. 3.00
12-($2.99) Siege of Wundagore pt. 4 4.00
13-Magneto-c/app.; last issue 3.00

QUICK-TRIGGER WESTERN (...Action #12; Cowboy Action #5-11)
Atlas Comics (ACI #12/WPI #13-19): No. 12, May, 1956 - No. 19, Sept, 1957
12-Baker-a 15 30 45 90 140 190
13-Williamson-a, 5 pgs. 15 30 45 84 127 170
14-Everett, Crandall, Torres-a; Heath-c 14 28 42 81 118 155
15,16: 15-Torres, Crandall-a. 16-Orlando, Kirby-a 12 24 36 69 97 125
17,18: 18-Baker-a 12 24 36 67 94 120
19 10 20 30 54 72 90
NOTE: ***Ayers** a-17. **Colan** a-16. **Maneely** a-15, 17; c-15, 18. **Morrow** a-18. **Powell** a-14. **Severin** a-19; c-12, 13, 16, 17, 19. **Shores** a-16. **Tuska** a-17.*

QUINCY (See Comics Reading Libraries in the Promotional Comics section)

QUITTER, THE
DC Comics (Vertigo): 2005 ($19.99, B&W graphic novel)
HC ($19.99) Autobiography of Harvey Pekar; Pekar-s/Daen Haspiel-a 20.00
SC (2006, $12.99) 13.00

RACCOON KIDS, THE (Formerly Movietown Animal Antics)
National Periodical Publications (Arleigh No. 63,64): No. 52, Sept-Oct, 1954 - No. 62, Oct-Nov, 1956; No. 63, Sept, 1957; No. 64, Nov, 1957
52-Doodles Duck by Mayer 15 30 45 83 124 165
53-64: 53-62-Doodles Duck by Mayer 11 22 33 62 86 110
NOTE: ***Otto Feuer**-a most issues. **Rube Grossman**-a most issues.*

RACE FOR THE MOON
Harvey Publications: Mar, 1958 - No. 3, Nov, 1958
1-Powell-a(5); 1/2-pg. S&K-a; cover redrawn from Galaxy Science Fiction pulp (5/53) 18 36 54 103 162 220
2-Kirby/Williamson-c(r)/a(3); Kirby-p 7 more stys 26 52 78 154 252 350
3-Kirby/Williamson-c/a(4); Kirby-p 6 more stys 28 56 84 165 270 375

RACER-X
Now Comics: 8/88 - No. 11, 8/89; V2#1, 9/89 - V2#10, 1990 ($1.75)
0-Deluxe ($3.50) 4.00
1 (9/88) - 11, V2#1-10 3.00

RACER X (See Speed Racer)
DC Comics (WildStorm): Oct, 2000 - No. 3, Dec, 2000 ($2.95, limited series)
1-3: 1-Tommy Yune-s/Jo Chen-a; 2 covers by Yune. 2,3-Kabala app. 3.50

RACHEL RISING
Abstract Studio: 2011 - Present ($3.99, B&W)
1-Terry Moore-s/a/c; back cover by Fabio Moon 5.00
1-(2nd printing), 2-6 4.00

RACING PETTYS
STP Corp.: 1980 ($2.50, 68 pgs., 10 1/8" x 13 1/4")
1-Bob Kane-a. Kane bio on inside back-c. 10.00

RACK & PAIN
Dark Horse Comics: Mar, 1994 - No. 4, June, 1994 ($2.50, limited series)
1-4: Brian Pulido scripts in all. 1-Greg Capullo-c 3.00

RACK & PAIN: KILLERS
Chaos! Comics: Sept, 1996 - No. 4, Jan, 1997 ($2.95, limited series)
1-4: Reprints Dark Horse series; Jae Lee-c 3.00

RACKET SQUAD IN ACTION
Capitol Stories/Charlton Comics: May-June, 1952 - No. 29, Mar, 1958
1 30 60 90 177 289 400
2-4,6: 3,4,6-Dr. Neff, Ghost Breaker app. 15 30 45 88 137 185
5-Dr. Neff, Ghost Breaker app; headlights-c 22 44 66 132 216 300
7-10: 10-Explosion-c 14 28 42 82 121 160
11-Ditko-c/a 32 64 96 188 307 425
12-Ditko explosion-c (classic); Shuster-a(2) 53 106 159 334 567 800
13-Shuster-c(p)/a. 13 26 39 74 105 135
14-Marijuana story "Shakedown"; Giordano-c 15 30 45 90 140 190
15-28: 15,20,22,23-Giordano-c 11 22 33 64 90 115
29-(15¢, 68 pgs.) 14 28 42 81 118 155

RADIANT LOVE (Formerly Daring Love #1)
Gilmor Magazines: No. 2, Dec, 1953 - No. 6, Aug, 1954
2 14 28 42 80 115 150
3-6 10 20 30 54 72 90

RADICAL DREAMER
Blackball Comics: No. 0, May, 1994 - No. 4, Nov, 1994 ($1.99, bi-monthly)
(1st poster format comic)
0-4: 0-2-($1.99, poster format): 0-1st app. Max Wrighter. 3,4-($2.50-c) 3.00

RADICAL DREAMER
Mark's Giant Economy Size Comics: V2#1, June, 1995 - V2#6, Feb, 1996 ($2.95, B&W, limited series)
V2#1-6 3.00
Prime (5/96, $2.95) 3.00
Dreams Cannot Die!-(1996, $20.00, softcover)-Collects V1#0-4 & V2#1-6; intro by Kurt Busiek; afterward by Mark Waid 20.00
Dreams Cannot Die!-(1996, $60.00, hardcover)-Signed & limited edition; collects V1#0-4 & V2#1-6; intro by Kurt Busiek; afterward by Mark Waid 60.00

RADIOACTIVE MAN (Simpsons TV show)
Bongo Comics: 1993 - No. 6, 1994 ($1.95/$2.25, limited series)
1-($2.95)-Glow-in-the-dark-c; bound-in jumbo poster; origin Radioactive Man; (cover dated Nov. 1952) 5.00
2-6: 2-Says #88 on-c & inside & dated May 1962; cover parody of Atlas Kirby monster-c; Superior Squad app.; origin Fallout Boy. 3-($1.95)-Cover "dated" Aug 1972 #216. 4-($2.25)-Cover "dated" Oct 1980 #412; w/trading card. 5-Cover "dated" Jan 1986 #679; w/trading card. 6-(Jan 1995 #1000) 4.00
Colossal #1-($4.95) 7.00
#4 (2001, $2.50) Faux 1953 issue; Murphy Anderson-i (6 pgs.) 3.00
#100 (2000, $2.50) Comic Book Guy-c/app.; faux 1963 issue inside 3.00
#136 (2001, $2.50) Dan DeCarlo-c/a 3.00
#222 (2001, $2.50) Batton Lash-s; Radioactive Man in 1972-style 3.00

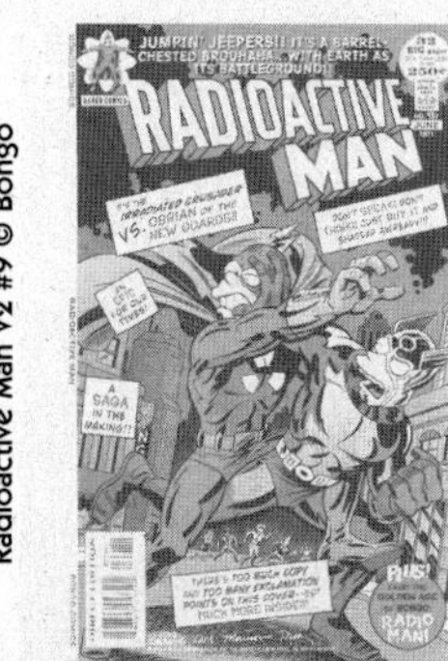

Radioactive Man V2 #9 © Bongo

Rai #26 © VAL

Rampaging Hulk (1998 series) #1 © MAR

GD VG FN VF VF/NM NM-
2.0 4.0 6.0 8.0 9.0 9.2

#575 (2002, $2.50) Chaykin-c; Radioactive Man in 1984-style 3.00
1963-106 (2002, $2.50) Radioactive Man in 1960s Gold Key-style; Groening-c 3.00
#7 Bongo Super Heroes Starring... (2003, $2.50) Marvel Silver Age-style Superior Squad 3.00
#8 Official Movie Adaptation (2004, $2.99) starring Rainier Wolfcastle and Milhouse 3.00
#9 (#197 on-c) (2004, $2.50) Kirby-esque New Gods spoof; Golden Age Radio Man app. 3.00

RADIO FUNNIES
DC Comics: Mar. 1939; undated variant

nn-(3/39) Ashcan comic, not distributed to newsstands, only for in-house use. Cover art is Adventure Comics #39 with interior being Detective Comics #19 (no known sales)
nn - Ashcan comic. No date. Cover art is Detective #26 with interior from Detective #17; one copy, graded at GD/VG, sold at auction for $4481.25 in Nov, 2009. Another copy graded at GD/VG sold at auction for $3346 in Feb, 2010.

RAGAMUFFINS
Eclipse Comics: Jan, 1985 ($1.75, one shot)

1-Eclipse Magazine-r, w/color; Colan-a 3.00

RAGE (Based on the id video game)
Dark Horse Comics: Jun, 2011 - No. 3, Aug, 2011 ($3.50, limited series)

1-3-Nelson-s/Mutti-a/Fabry-c. 1-Variant-c by Martiniere 3.50

RAGGEDY ANN AND ANDY (See Dell Giants, March of Comics #23 & New Funnies)
Dell Publishing Co.: No. 5, 1942 - No. 533, 2/54; 10-12/64 - No. 4, 3/66

Four Color 5(1942) 43 86 129 323 704 1085
Four Color 23(1943) 31 62 93 225 488 750
Four Color 45(1943) 26 52 78 182 391 600
Four Color 72(1945) 21 42 63 148 317 485
1(6/46)-Billy & Bonnie Bee by Frank Thomas 29 58 87 210 455 700
2,3: 3-Egbert Elephant by Dan Noonan begins 15 30 45 102 221 340
4-Kelly-a, 16 pgs. 16 32 48 107 234 360
5,6,8-10 12 24 36 84 175 265
7-Little Black Sambo, Black Mumbo & Black Jumbo only app; Christmas-c
14 28 42 96 208 320
11-20 11 22 33 71 136 200
21-Alice In Wonderland cover/story 12 24 36 84 175 265
22-27,29-39(8/49), Four Color 262 (1/50): 34-"...In Candyland"
10 20 30 64 115 165
28-Kelly-c 10 20 30 66 121 175
Four Color 306,354,380,452,533 7 14 21 49 82 115
1(10-12/64-Dell) 4 8 12 24 37 50
2,3(10-12/65), 4(3/66) 3 6 9 16 23 30
NOTE: *Kelly art ("Animal Mother Goose")-#1-34, 36, 37; c-28. Peterkin Pottle by **John Stanley** in 32-38.*

RAGGEDY ANN AND ANDY
Gold Key: Dec, 1971 - No. 6, Sept, 1973

1 3 6 9 19 29 38
2-6 3 6 9 15 21 26

RAGGEDY ANN & THE CAMEL WITH THE WRINKLED KNEES (See Dell Jr. Treasury #8)

RAGMAN (See Batman Family #20, The Brave & The Bold #196 & Cancelled Comic Cavalcade)
National Per. Publ./DC Comics No. 5: Aug-Sept, 1976 - No. 5, Jun-Jul, 1977

1-Origin & 1st app. 2 4 6 11 16 20
2-5: 2-Origin ends; Kubert-c. 4-Drug use story 2 4 6 8 10 12
NOTE: ***Kubert** a-4, 5; c-1-5. **Redondo** studios a-1-4.*

RAGMAN (2nd Series)
DC Comics: Oct, 1991 - No. 8, May, 1992 ($1.50, limited series)

1-8: 1-Giffen plots/breakdowns. 3-Origin. 8-Batman-c/story 3.00

RAGMAN: CRY OF THE DEAD
DC Comics: Aug, 1993 - No. 6, Jan, 1994 ($1.75, limited series)

1-6: Joe Kubert-c 3.00

RAGMAN: SUIT OF SOULS
DC Comics: Dec, 2010 ($3.99, one-shot)

1-Gage-s/Segovia-a/Saiz-c; origin retold 4.00

RAGS RABBIT (Formerly Babe Ruth Sports #10 or Little Max #10?; also see Harvey Hits #2, Harvey Wiseguys & Tastee Freez)
Harvey Publications: No. 11, June, 1951 - No. 18, March, 1954 (Written & drawn for little folks)

11-(See Nutty Comics #5 for 1st app.) 6 12 18 31 38 45
12-18 5 10 15 24 30 35

RAI (Rai and the Future Force #9-23) (See Magnus #5-8)
Valiant: Mar, 1992 - No. 0, Oct, 1992; No. 9, May, 1993 - No. 33, Jun, 1995 ($1.95/$2.25)

1-Valiant's 1st original character 2 4 6 9 13 16
2-4,0: 4-Low print run. 0-(11/92)-Origin/1st app. new Rai (Rising Spirit) & 1st full app. & partial origin Bloodshot; also see Eternal Warrior #4; tells future of all characters
2 4 6 8 10 12
5-10: 6,7-Unity x-overs. 7-Death of Rai. 9-($2.50)-Gatefold-c; story cont'd from Magnus #24; Magnus, Eternal Warrior & X-O app. 5.00
11-33: 15-Manowar Armor app. 17-19-Magnus x-over. 21-1st app. The Starwatchers (cameo); trading card. 22-Death of Rai. 26-Chaos Effect Epsilon Pt. 3 3.00
NOTE: ***Layton** c-2i, 9i. **Miller** c-6. **Simonson** c-7.*

RAIDERS OF THE LOST ARK (Movie)
Marvel Comics Group: Sept, 1981 - No. 3, Nov, 1981 (Movie adaptation)

1-r/Marvel Comics Super Special #18 6.00
2,3 4.00
NOTE: ***Buscema** a(p)-1-3; c(p)-1. **Simonson** a-3i; scripts-1-3.*

RAINBOW BRITE AND THE STAR STEALER
DC Comics: 1985

nn-Movie adaptation 2 4 6 8 10 12

RAISE THE DEAD
Dynamite Entertainment: 2007 - No. 4, Aug, 2007 ($3.50)

1-4-Arthur Suydam-c/Leah Moore & John Reppion-s/Petrus-a; Phillips var-c on all 3.50
... Vol. 1 HC (2007, $19.99) r/#1-4; script, interview & sketch pages; cover gallery 20.00

RAISE THE DEAD 2
Dynamite Entertainment: 2010 - No. 4, 2011 ($3.99)

1-4-Leah Moore & John Reppion-s/Vilanova-a 4.00

RALPH KINER, HOME RUN KING
Fawcett Publications: 1950 (Pittsburgh Pirates)

nn-Photo-c; life story 60 120 180 381 653 925

RALPH SNART ADVENTURES
Now Comics: June, 1986 - V2#9, 1987; V3#1 - #26, Feb, 1991; V4#1, 1992 - #4, 1992

1-3, V2#1-7,V3#1-23,25,26:1-($1.00, B&W)-1(B&W),V2#1(11/86), B&W), 8,9-color. V3#1(9/88)-Color begins 3.00
V3#24-($2.50)-3-D issue, V4#1-3-Direct sale versions w/cards 3.00
V4#1-3-Newsstand versions w/random cards 3.00
Book 1 1 2 3 5 6 8
3-D Special (11/92, $3.50)-Complete 12-card set w/3-D glasses 4.00

RAMAR OF THE JUNGLE (TV)
Toby Press No. 1/Charlton No. 2 on: 1954 (no month); No. 2, Sept, 1955 - No. 5, Sept, 1956

1-Jon Hall photo-c; last pre-code issue 21 42 63 124 202 280
2-5: 2-Jon Hall photo-c 15 30 45 86 133 180

RAMAYAN 3392 A.D.
Virgin Comics: Sept, 2006 - No. 8, Aug, 2008 ($2.99)

1-8: 1-Alex Ross-c; re-imagining of the Indian myth of Ramayana; poster of cover inside 3.00
... Reloaded (8/07 - No. 7, 7/08, $2.99) 1-7: 1-Two covers by Kang and Oeming 3.00
... Reloaded Guidebook (4/08, $2.99) Profiles of characters and weapons 3.00

RAMM
Megaton Comics: May, 1987 - No. 2, Sept, 1987 ($1.50, B&W)

1,2-Both have 1 pg. Youngblood ad by Liefeld 3.00

RAMPAGING HULK (The Hulk #10 on; also see Marvel Treasury Edition)
Marvel Comics Group: Jan, 1977 - No. 9, June, 1978 ($1.00, B&W magazine)

1-Bloodstone story w/Buscema & Nebres-a. Origin re-cap w/Simonson-a; Gargoyle, UFO story; Ken Barr-c 3 6 9 19 29 38
2-Old X-Men app; origin old w/Simonson-a & new X-Men in text w/Cockrum illos; Bloodstone story w/Brown & Nebres-a 3 6 9 16 22 28
3-9: 3-Iron Man app.; Norem-c. 4-Gallery of villains w/Giffen-a. 5,6-Hulk vs. Sub-Mariner. 7-Man-Thing story. 8-Original Avengers app. 9-Thor vs. Hulk battle; Shanna the She-Devil story w/DeZuniga-a 2 4 6 13 18 22
NOTE: ***Alcala** a-1-3i, 5i, 8i. **Buscema** a-1. **Giffen** a-4. **Nino** a-4i. **Simonson** a-1-3p. **Starlin** a-4(w/**Nino**), 7; c-4, 5, 7.*

RAMPAGING HULK
Marvel Comics: Aug, 1998 - No. 6, Jan, 1999 ($2.99/$1.99)

1-($2.99) Flashback stories of Savage Hulk; Leonardi-a 4.00
2-6-($1.99): 2-Two covers 3.00

RAMPAGING WOLVERINE
Marvel Comics: June, 2009 ($3.99, B&W, one-shot)

1-Short stories by Fialkov, Luque, Ted McKeever, Yost, Santolouco, Firth, Nelson 4.00

RANDOLPH SCOTT (Movie star)(See Crack Western #67, Prize Comics Western #76, Western Hearts #8, Western Love #1 & Western Winners #7)

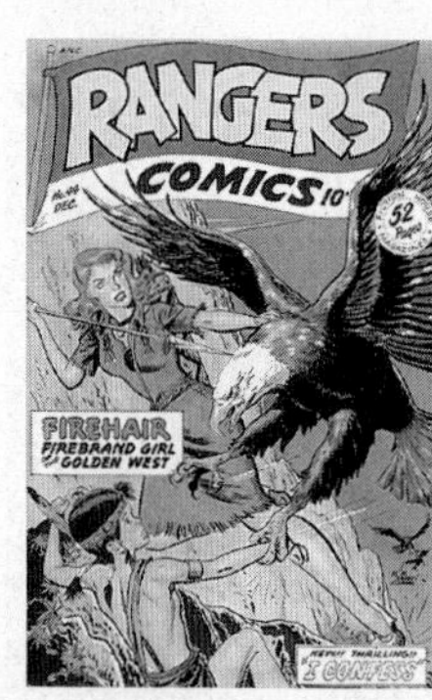

Rangers Comics #44 © FH

Rasl #11 © Jeff Smith

Rawhide Kid #2 © MAR

GD 2.0 | VG 4.0 | FN 6.0 | VF 8.0 | VF/NM 9.0 | NM- 9.2

RANGE BUSTERS
Fox Features Syndicate: Sept, 1950 (One shot)
1 (Exist?) 19 38 57 112 179 245

RANGE BUSTERS (Formerly Cowboy Love?; Wyatt Earp, Frontier Marshall #11 on)
Charlton Comics: No. 8, May, 1955 - No. 10, Sept, 1955
8 8 16 24 42 54 65
9,10 6 12 18 28 34 40

RANGELAND LOVE
Atlas Comics (CDS): Dec, 1949 - No. 2, Mar, 1950 (52 pgs.)
1-Robert Taylor & Arlene Dahl photo-c 17 34 51 98 154 210
2-Photo-c 14 28 42 80 115 150

RANGER, THE (See Zane Grey, Four Color #255)

RANGE RIDER, THE (TV)(See Flying A's...)

RANGE ROMANCES
Comic Magazines (Quality Comics): Dec, 1949 - No. 5, Aug, 1950 (#5: 52 pg)
1-Gustavson-c/a 26 52 78 152 244 335
2-Crandall-c/a 26 52 78 152 244 335
3-Crandall, Gustavson-a; photo-c 22 44 66 127 204 280
4-Crandall-a; photo-c 19 38 57 112 176 240
5-Gustavson-a; Crandall-a(p); photo-c 19 38 57 112 176 240

RANGERS COMICS (...of Freedom #1-7)
Fiction House Magazines: 10/41 - No. 67, 10/52; No. 68, Fall, 1952; No. 69, Winter, 1952-53 (Flying stories)
1-Intro. Ranger Girl & The Rangers of Freedom; ends #7, cover app. only #5
331 662 993 2317 4059 5800
2 97 194 291 621 1061 1500
3 71 142 213 454 777 1100
4,5 64 128 192 406 696 985
6-10-All Japanese war covers. 8-U.S. Rangers begin
53 106 159 334 567 800
11,12-Commando Rangers app. 50 100 150 315 533 750
13-Commando Ranger begins-not same as Commando Rangers; Nazi war-c
48 96 144 302 514 725
14-20: 15,17,19-Japanese war-c. 18-Nazi war-c 42 84 126 265 445 625
21-Intro/origin Firehair (begins, 2/45) 43 86 129 271 461 650
22-30: 22-25,27-Japanese war-c. 23-Kazanda begins, ends #28. 28-Tiger Man begins (origin/1st app., 4/46), ends #46. 30-Crusoe Island begins, ends #40
34 68 102 204 332 460
31-40: 33-Hypodermic panels 30 60 90 177 289 400
41-46: 41-Last Werewolf Hunter 24 48 72 142 234 325
47-56- "Eisnerish" Dr. Drew by Grandenetti. 48-Last Glory Forbes. 53-Last 52 pg. issue. 55-Last Sky Rangers 22 44 66 132 216 300
57-60-Straight run of Dr. Drew by Grandenetti 18 36 54 103 162 220
61-69: 64-Suicide Smith begins. 63-Used in **POP**, pgs. 85, 99. 67-Space Rangers begin, end #69 15 30 45 88 137 185

NOTE: *Bondage, discipline covers, lingerie panels are common. Crusoe Island by* ***Larsen****-#30-36. Firehair by* ***Lubbers****-#30-49. Glory Forbes by* ***Baker****-#36-45, 47; by* ***Whitman****-#34, 35. I Confess in #41-53. Jan of the Jungle in #42-58. King of the Congo in #49-53. Tiger Man by* ***Celardo****-#30-39.* ***M. Anderson*** *a-30?* ***Baker*** *a-36-38, 42, 44.* ***John Celardo*** *a-34, 36-39.* ***Lee Elias*** *a-21-28.* ***Evans*** *a-19, 38-46, 48-52.* ***Hopper*** *a-25, 26.* ***Ingels*** *a-13-16.* ***Larsen*** *a-34.* ***Bob Lubbers*** *a-30-38, 40-44; c-40-45.* ***Moreira*** *a-41-47.* ***Tuska*** *a-16, 17, 19, 22.* ***M. Whitman*** *c-61-66.* ***Zolnerwich*** *c-1-17.*

RANGO (TV)
Dell Publishing Co.: Aug, 1967
1-Photo-c of comedian Tim Conway 4 8 12 24 37 50

RANN-THANAGAR HOLY WAR (Also see Hawkman Special #1)
DC Comics: July, 2008 - No. 8, Feb, 2009 ($3.50, limited series)
1-8-Adam Strange & Hawkman app.; Starlin-s/Lim-a. 1-Two covers by Starlin & Lim 3.50
Volume One TPB (2009, $19.99) r/#1-4 & Hawkman Special #1 20.00
Volume Two TPB (2009, $19.99) r/#5-8 & Adam Strange Special #1 20.00

RANN-THANAGAR WAR (See Adam Strange 2004 mini-series)(Prelude to Infinite Crisis)
DC Comics: July, 2005 - No. 6, Dec, 2005 ($2.50, limited series)
1-6-Adam Strange, Hawkman and Green Lantern (Kyle Rayner) app.; Gibbons-s/Reis-a 3.00
...: Infinite Crisis Special (4/06, $4.99) Kyle Rayner becomes Ion again; Jade dies 5.00
TPB (2005, $12.99) r/#1-6; cover gallery; new Bolland-c 13.00

RAPHAEL (See Teenage Mutant Ninja Turtles)
Mirage Studios: 1985 ($1.50, 7-1/2x11", B&W w/2 color cover, one-shot)
1-1st Turtles one-shot spin-off; contains 1st drawing of the Turtles as a group from 1983
2 4 6 8 10 12
1-2nd printing (11/87); new-c & 8 pgs. art 5.00

RAPHAEL BAD MOON RISING (See Teenage Mutant Ninja Turtles)
Mirage Publishing: July, 2007 - No. 4, Oct, 2007 ($3.25, B&W, limited series)
1-4-Continued from Tales of the TMNT #7; Lawson-a 3.25

RAPTURE
Dark Horse Comics: May, 2009 - No. 6, Jan, 2010 ($2.99, limited series)
1-6-Taki Soma & Michael Avon Oeming-s/a/c. 1-Maleev var-c. 2-Mack var-c 3.00

RASCALS IN PARADISE
Dark Horse Comics: Aug, 1994 - No. 3, Dec, 1994 ($3.95, magazine size)
1-3-Jim Silke-a/story 4.00
Trade paperback-($16.95)-r/#1-3 17.00

RASL
Cartoon Books: Mar, 2008 - Present ($3.50, B&W)
1-13-Jeff Smith-s/a/c 3.50

RATCHET & CLANK (Based on the Sony videogame)
DC Comics (WildStorm thru #4): Nov, 2010 - No. 6, Apr, 2011 ($3.99/$2.99, limited series)
1-4-Fixman-s/Archer-a 4.00
5,6-($2.99) 3.00
TPB (2011, $17.99) r/#1-6 18.00

RATFINK (See Frantic, Zany, & Ed "Big Daddy" Roth's Ratfink Comix)
Canrom, Inc.: Oct, 1964
1-Woodbridge-a 8 16 24 53 89 125

RAT PATROL, THE (TV) (Also see Wild!)
Dell Publishing Co.: Mar, 1967 - No. 5, Nov, 1967; No. 6, Oct, 1969
1-Christopher George photo-c 7 14 21 46 76 105
2-6: 3-6-Photo-c 4 8 12 28 44 60

RAVAGE 2099 (See Marvel Comics Presents #117)
Marvel Comics: Dec, 1992 - No. 33, Aug, 1995($1.25/$1.50)
1-($1.75)-Gold foil stamped-c; Stan Lee scripts 4.00
1-($1.75)-2nd printing 3.00
2-24,26-33: 5-Last Ryan-c. 6-Last Ryan-a. 14-Punisher 2099 x-over. 15-Ron Lim-c(p). 18-Bound-in card sheet 3.00
25 ($2.25, 52 pgs.) 4.00
25 ($2.95, 52 pgs.)-Silver foil embossed-c 4.50

RAVEN (See DC Special: Raven and Teen Titans titles)

RAVEN, THE (See Movie Classics)

RAVEN CHRONICLES
Caliber (New Worlds): 1995 - No. 16 ($2.95, B&W)
1-16: 10-Flip book w/Wordsmith #6. 15-Flip book w/High Caliber #4 3.00

RAVENS AND RAINBOWS
Pacific Comics: Dec, 1983 (Baxter paper)(Reprints fanzine work in color)
1-Jeff Jones-c/a(r); nudity scenes 3.00

RAWHIDE (TV)
Dell Publishing Co./Gold Key: Sept-Nov, 1959 - June-Aug, 1962; July, 1963 - No. 2, Jan, 1964
Four Color 1028 (#1) 20 40 60 137 294 450
Four Color 1097,1160,1202,1261,1269 12 24 36 84 177 270
01-684-208 (8/62, Dell) 11 22 33 76 151 225
1(10071-307) (7/63, Gold Key) 11 22 33 76 151 225
2-(12¢) 11 22 33 71 136 200

NOTE: *All have Clint Eastwood photo-c.* ***Tufts*** *a-1028.*

RAWHIDE KID
Atlas/Marvel Comics (CnPC No. 1-16/AMI No. 17-30): Mar, 1955 - No. 16, Sept, 1957; No. 17, Aug, 1960 - No. 151, May, 1979
1-Rawhide Kid, his horse Apache & sidekick Randy begin; Wyatt Earp app.; #1 was not code approved; Maneely splash pg. 103 206 309 659 1130 1600
2 41 82 123 256 428 600
3-5 32 64 96 192 314 435
6-10: 7-Williamson-a (4 pgs.) 25 50 75 150 245 340
11-16: 16-Torres-a 20 40 60 118 192 265
17-Origin by Jack Kirby; Kirby-a begins 45 90 135 284 480 675
18-21,24-30 12 24 36 78 157 235
22-Monster-c/story by Kirby/Ayers 13 26 39 90 195 300
23-Origin retold by Jack Kirby 16 32 48 109 237 365
31-35,40: 31,32-Kirby-a. 33-35-Davis-a. 34-Kirby-a. 35-Intro & death of The Raven. 40-Two-Gun Kid x-over. 11 22 33 71 136 200
36,37,39,41,42-No Kirby. 42-1st Larry Lieber issue 10 20 30 64 115 165
38-Red Raven-c/story; Kirby-c (2/64); Colan-a 11 22 33 76 151 225

Rawhide Kid (2003 series) #1 © MAR

The Ray (2012 series) #1 © DC

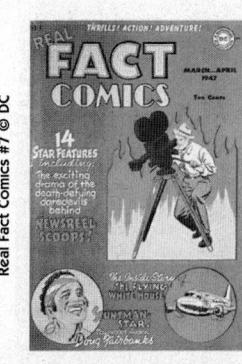

Real Fact Comics #7 © DC

GD VG FN VF VF/NM NM-
2.0 4.0 6.0 8.0 9.0 9.2

43-Kirby-a (beware: pin-up often missing) 11 22 33 76 151 225
44,46: 46-Toth-a. 46-Doc Holliday-c/s 9 18 27 62 109 155
45-Origin retold, 17 pgs. 11 22 33 71 136 200
47-49,51-60 7 14 21 44 72 100
50-Kid Colt x-over; vs. Rawhide Kid 7 14 21 48 79 110
61-70: 64-Kid Colt story. 66-Two-Gun Kid story. 67-Kid Colt story. 70-Last 12¢ issue
5 10 15 35 55 75
71-78,80-83,85 3 6 9 20 30 40
79,84,86,95: 79-Williamson-a(r). 84,86: Kirby-a. 86-Origin-r; Williamson-r/Ringo Kid #13 (4 pgs.) 3 6 9 21 32 42
87-91: 90-Kid Colt app. 91-Last 15¢ issue 3 6 9 18 27 35
92,93 (52 pg.Giants). 92-Kirby-a 4 8 12 24 37 50
94,96-99 3 6 9 16 23 30
100 (6/72)-Origin retold & expanded 3 6 9 21 32 42
101-120: 115-Last new story 2 4 6 13 18 22
121-151 2 4 6 9 13 16
133,134-(30¢-c variants, limited distribution)(5,7/76) 4 8 12 28 44 60
140,141-(35¢-c variants, limited distribution)(7,9/77) 6 12 18 41 66 90
Special 1(9/71, 25¢, 68 pgs.)-All Kirby/Ayers-r 5 10 15 32 51 70

NOTE: ***Ayers*** *a-13, 14, 16, 29, 37-39, 61.* ***Colan*** *a-5, 35, 37, 38; c-145p, 148p, 149p.* ***Davis*** *a-125r.* ***Everett*** *a-54i, 65, 66, 88, 96i, 148i(r).* ***Gulacy*** *c-147.* ***Heath*** *c-4.* ***G. Kane*** *c-101, 144.* ***Keller*** *a-5, 39, 41, 144r.* ***Kirby*** *a-17-32, 34, 42, 43, 84, 86, 92, 109r, 112r, 116r, 117r, 137r, Spec. 1; c-17-35, 37, 38, 40, 41, 43-47, 137r.* ***Maneely*** *c-1, 2, 5, 6, 14.* ***Morisi*** *a-13.* ***Morrow/Williamson*** *r-111.* ***Roussos*** *r-146i, 147i, 149-151i.* ***Severin*** *a-16; c-8, 13.* ***Sutton*** *a-61, 93.* ***Torres*** *a-99r.* ***Tuska*** *a-14.* ***Wildey*** *r-146-151(Outlaw Kid).* ***Williamson*** *r-79, 86, 95.*

RAWHIDE KID
Marvel Comics Group: Aug, 1985 - No. 4, Nov, 1985 (Mini-series)

1-4 5.00

RAWHIDE KID
Marvel Comics (MAX): Apr, 2003 - No. 5, June, 2003 ($2.99, limited series)

1-John Severin-a/Ron Zimmerman-s; Dave Johnson-c 3.00
2-5: 3-Dodson-c. 4-Darwyn Cooke-c. 5-J. Scott Campbell-c 3.00
Vol. 1: Slap Leather TPB (2003, $12.99) r/#1-5 13.00

RAWHIDE KID (The Sensational Seven)
Marvel Comics: Aug, 2010 - No. 4, Nov, 2010 ($3.99, limited series)

1-4-Chaykin-a/Zimmerman-s. 1-Cassaday-c. 2-Dave Johnson-c. 4-Suydam-c 4.00

RAY, THE (See Freedom Fighters & Smash Comics #14)
DC Comics: Feb, 1992 - No. 6, July, 1992 ($1.00, mini-series)

1-Sienkiewicz-c; Joe Quesada-a(p) in 1-5 5.00
2-6: 3-6-Quesada-c(p). 6-Quesada layouts only 3.00
...In a Blaze of Power (1994, $12.95)-r/#1-6 w/new Quesada-c 13.00

RAY, THE
DC Comics: May, 1994 - No. 28, Oct, 1996 ($1.75/$1.95/$2.25)

1-Quesada-c(p); Superboy app. 3.00
1-($2.95)-Collectors Edition w/diff. Quesada-c; embossed foil-c 4.00
2-5,0,6-24,26-28: 2-Quesada-c(p); Superboy app. 5-(9/94). 0-(10/94) 3.00
25-($3.50)-Future Flash (Bart Allen)-c/app; double size 4.00
Annual 1 ($3.95, 68 pgs.)-Superman app. 4.00

RAY, THE
DC Comics: Feb, 2012 - No. 4, May, 2012 ($2.99, limited series)

1-4: 1-Igle-a/Palmiotti & Gray-s; origin of the new Ray; intro. Lucien Gates 3.00

RAY BRADBURY COMICS
Topps Comics: Feb, 1993 - V4#1, June, 1994 ($2.95)

1-5-Polybagged w/3 trading cards each. 1-All dinosaur issue; Corben-a; Williamson/Torres/Krenkel-r/Weird Science-Fantasy #25. 3-All dinosaur issue; Steacy painted-c; Stout-a 3.00
Special Edition 1 (1994, $2.95)-The Illustrated Man 3.00
...Special: Tales of Horror #1 ($2.50), ...Trilogy of Terror V3#1 (5/94, $2.50), ...Martian Chronicles V4#1 (6/94, $2.50)-Steranko-c 3.00

NOTE: ***Kelley Jones*** *a-Trilogy of Terror V3#1.* ***Kaluta*** *a-Martian Chronicles V4#1.* ***Kurtzman/Matt Wagner*** *c-2.* ***McKean*** *c-4.* ***Mignola*** *a-4.* ***Wood*** *a-Trilogy of Terror V3#1r.*

RAZORLINE
Marvel Comics: Sept, 1993 (75¢, one-shot)

1-Clive Barker super-heroes: Ectokid, Hokum & Hex, Hyperkind & Saint Sinner 3.00

RAZOR'S EDGE, THE
DC Comics (WildStorm): Dec, 2004 - No. 5, Apr, 2005 ($2.95)

1-5-Warblade; Bisley-c/a; Ridley-s 3.00

REAL ADVENTURE COMICS (Action Adventure #2 on)
Gillmor Magazines: Apr, 1955

1 9 18 27 47 61 75

GD VG FN VF VF/NM NM-
2.0 4.0 6.0 8.0 9.0 9.2

REAL ADVENTURES OF JONNY QUEST, THE
Dark Horse Comics: Sept, 1996 - No. 12, Sept, 1997 ($2.95)

1-12 3.00

REAL CLUE CRIME STORIES (Formerly Clue Comics)
Hillman Periodicals: V2#4, June, 1947 - V8#3, May, 1953

V2#4(#1)-S&K c/a(3); Dan Barry-a 49 98 147 309 522 735
5-7-S&K c/a(3-4). 7-Iron Lady app. 39 78 117 240 395 550
8-12 14 28 42 81 118 155
V3#1-8,10-12, V4#1-3,5-8,11,12 13 26 39 72 101 130
V3#9-Used in **SOTI**, pg. 102 15 30 45 83 124 165
V4#4-S&K-a 15 30 45 84 127 170
V4#9,10-Krigstein-a 13 26 39 74 105 135
V5#1-5,7,8,10,12 10 20 30 56 76 95
6,9,11(1/54)-Krigstein-a 11 22 33 60 83 105
V6#1-5,8,9,11 9 18 27 52 69 85
6,7,10,12-Krigstein-a. 10-Bondage-c 11 22 33 60 83 105
V7#1-3,5-11, V8#1-3: V7#6-1 pg. Frazetta ad "Prayer" - 1st app.?
10 20 30 56 76 95
4,12-Krigstein-a 11 22 33 60 83 105

NOTE: ***Barry*** *a-9, 10; c-V2#8.* ***Briefer*** *a-V6#6.* ***Fuje*** *a- V2#7(2), 8, 11.* ***Infantino*** *a-V2#8; c-V2#11.* ***Lawrence*** *a-V3#8, V5#7.* ***Powell*** *a-V4#11, 12. V5#4, 5, 7 are 68 pgs.*

REAL EXPERIENCES (Formerly Tiny Tessie)
Atlas Comics (20CC): No. 25, Jan, 1950

25-Virginia Mayo photo-c from movie "Red Light" 12 24 36 67 94 120

REAL FACT COMICS
National Periodical Publications: Mar-Apr, 1946 - No. 21, July-Aug, 1949

1-S&K-c/a; Harry Houdini story; Just Imagine begins (not by Finlay); Fred Ray-a
47 94 141 296 498 700
2-S&K-a; Rin-Tin-Tin & P. T. Barnum stories 28 56 84 165 270 375
3-H.G. Wells, Lon Chaney stories; early DC letter column (New Fun Comics #3 from 1935 may be the 1st) 26 52 78 154 252 350
4-Virgil Finlay-a on 'Just Imagine' begins, ends #12 (2 pgs. each); Jimmy Stewart & Jack London stories; Joe DiMaggio 1 pg. biography 29 58 87 172 281 390
5-Batman/Robin-c taken from cover of Batman #9; 5 pg. story about creation of Batman & Robin; Tom Mix story 155 310 465 992 1696 2400
6-Origin & 1st app. Tommy Tomorrow by Weisinger and Sherman (1-2/47); Flag-c; 1st writing by Harlan Ellison (letter column, non-professional); "First Man to Reach Mars" epic-c/story
84 168 252 538 919 1300
7-(No. 6 on inside)-Roussos-a; D. Fairbanks sty. 15 30 45 94 147 200
8-2nd app. Tommy Tomorrow by Finlay (5-6/47) 48 96 144 302 514 725
9-S&K-a; Glenn Miller, Indianapolis 500 stories 21 42 63 122 199 275
10-Vigilante by Meskin (based on movie serial); 4 pg. Finlay s/f story
20 40 60 118 192 265
11,12: 11-Annie Oakley, G-Men stories; Kinstler-a 14 28 42 82 121 160
13-Dale Evans and Tommy Tomorrow-c/stories 37 74 111 222 361 500
14,17,18: 14-Will Rogers story 14 28 42 80 115 150
15-Nuclear explosion part-c ("Last War on Earth" story); Clyde Beatty story
15 30 45 94 147 200
16-Tommy Tomorrow app.; 1st Planeteers? 36 72 108 211 343 475
19-Sir Arthur Conan Doyle story 15 30 45 83 124 165
20-Kubert-a, 4 pgs; Daniel Boone story 15 30 45 88 137 185
21-Kubert-a, 2 pgs; Kit Carson story 14 28 42 80 115 150
Ashcan (2/46) nn-Not distributed to newsstands, only for in house use. Covers were produced, but not the rest of the book. A copy sold in 2008 for $500.

NOTE: ***Barry*** *c-16.* ***Virgil Finlay*** *c-6, 8.* ***Meskin*** *c-10.* ***Roussos*** *a-1-4, 6.*

REAL FUNNIES
Nedor Publishing Co.: Jan, 1943 - No. 3, June, 1943

1-Funny animal, humor; Black Terrier app. (clone of The Black Terror)
32 64 96 188 307 425
2,3 15 30 45 94 147 200

REAL GHOSTBUSTERS, THE (Also see Slimer)
Now Comics: Aug, 1988 - No. 32, 1991 ($1.75/$1.95)

1-32: 1-Based on Ghostbusters movie. #29-32 exist? 3.00

REAL HEROES COMICS
Parents' Magazine Institute: Sept, 1941 - No. 16, Oct, 1946

1-Roosevelt-c/story 32 64 96 188 307 425
2-J. Edgar Hoover-c/story 15 30 45 83 124 165
3-5,7-10: 4-Churchill, Roosevelt stories 14 28 42 76 108 140
6-Lou Gehrig-c/story 19 38 57 112 179 245
11-16: 13-Kiefer-a 10 20 30 54 72 90

Real Life Comics #26 © Pict. Mag.

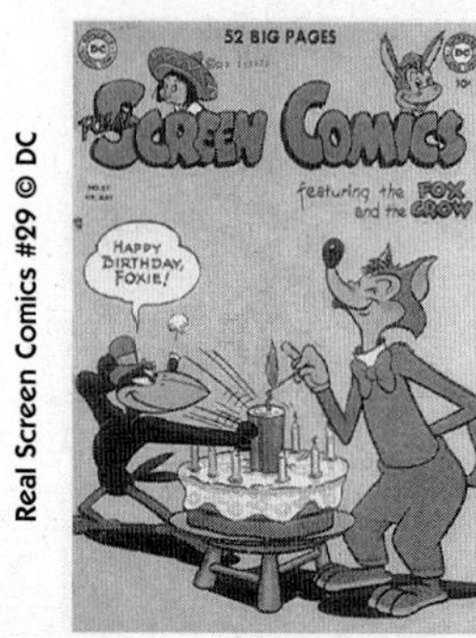

Real Screen Comics #29 © DC

Real West Romances #2 © PRIZE

REALISTIC ROMANCES
Realistic Comics/Avon Periodicals: July-Aug, 1951 - No. 17, Aug-Sept, 1954 (No #9-14)

	GD 2.0	VG 4.0	FN 6.0	VF 8.0	VF/NM 9.0	NM- 9.2
1-Kinstler-a; c-/Avon paperback #211	32	64	96	188	307	425
2	16	32	48	94	147	200
3,4	15	30	45	90	140	190
5,8-Kinstler-a	16	32	48	92	144	195
6-c-/Diversey Prize Novels #6; Kinstler-a	16	32	48	94	147	200
7-Evans-a?; c-/Avon paperback #360	16	32	48	94	147	200
15,17: 17-Kinstler-c	15	30	45	86	133	180
16-Kinstler marijuana story-r/Romantic Love #6	16	32	48	92	144	195
I.W. Reprint #1,8,9: #1-r/Realistic Romances #4; Astarita-a. 9-r/Women To Love #1	2	4	6	11	16	20

NOTE: ***Astarita** a-2-4, 7, 8, 17. Photo c-1, 2. Painted c-3, 4.*

REAL LIFE COMICS
Nedor/Better/Standard Publ./Pictorial Magazine No. 13: Sept, 1941 - No. 59, Sept, 1952

	GD 2.0	VG 4.0	FN 6.0	VF 8.0	VF/NM 9.0	NM- 9.2
1-Uncle Sam-c/story; Daniel Boone story	63	126	189	403	689	975
2	32	64	96	188	307	425
3-Hitler cover	206	412	618	1318	2259	3200
4,5: 4-Story of American flag "Old Glory"	20	40	60	118	192	265
6-10: 6-Wild Bill Hickok story	20	40	60	115	185	255
11-14,16-20: 17-Albert Einstein story	18	36	54	107	169	230
15-Japanese WWII-c by Schomburg	20	40	60	114	182	250
21-23,25,26,28-30: 29-A-Bomb story	16	32	48	94	147	200
24-Story of Baseball (Babe Ruth)	22	44	66	132	216	300
27-Schomburg A-Bomb-c; story of A-Bomb	21	42	63	126	206	285
31-33,35,36,42-44,48,49: 49-Baseball issue	15	30	45	85	130	175
34,37-41,45-47: 34-Jimmy Stewart story. 37-Story of motion pictures; Bing Crosby story. 38-Jane Froman story. 39- "1,000,000 A.D." story. 40-Bob Feller. 41-Jimmie Foxx story ("Jimmy" on-c); "Home Run" Baker story. 45-Story of Olympic games; Burl Ives & Kit Carson story. 46-Douglas Fairbanks Jr. & Sr. story. 47-George Gershwin story	15	30	45	90	140	190
50-Frazetta-a (5 pgs.)	30	60	90	177	289	400
51-Jules Verne "Journey to the Moon" by Evans; Severin/Elder-a	21	42	63	124	202	280
52-Frazetta-a (4 pgs.); Severin/Elder-a(2); Evans-a	33	66	99	194	317	440
53-57-Severin/Elder-a. 54-Bat Masterson-c/story	17	34	51	98	154	210
58-Severin/Elder-a(2)	17	34	51	100	158	215
59-1 pg. Frazetta; Severin/Elder-a	17	34	51	100	158	215

NOTE: ***Guardineer** a-40(2), 44. **Meskin** a-52. **Roussos** a-50. **Schomburg** c-1, 2, 4, 5, 7, 11, 13-21, 23, 24, 26, 28, 30-32, 34-40, 42, 44-47, 55. **Tuska** a-53. Photo-c 5, 6.*

REAL LIFE SECRETS (Real Secrets #2 on)
Ace Periodicals: Sept, 1949 (one-shot)

	GD 2.0	VG 4.0	FN 6.0	VF 8.0	VF/NM 9.0	NM- 9.2
1-Painted-c	15	30	45	83	124	165

REAL LIFE STORY OF FESS PARKER (Magazine)
Dell Publishing Co.: 1955

	GD 2.0	VG 4.0	FN 6.0	VF 8.0	VF/NM 9.0	NM- 9.2
1	9	18	27	60	103	145

REAL LIFE TALES OF SUSPENSE (See Suspense)

REAL LOVE (Formerly Hap Hazard)
Ace Periodicals (A. A. Wyn): No. 25, April, 1949 - No. 76, Nov, 1956

	GD 2.0	VG 4.0	FN 6.0	VF 8.0	VF/NM 9.0	NM- 9.2
25	15	30	45	83	124	165
26	11	22	33	62	86	110
27-L. B. Cole-a	12	24	36	69	97	125
28-35	10	20	30	56	76	95
36-66: 66-Last pre-code (2/55)	9	18	27	52	69	85
67-76	8	16	24	44	57	70

NOTE: *Photo c-50-76. Painted c-46.*

REALM, THE
Arrow Comics/WeeBee Comics #13/Caliber Press #14 on: Feb, 1986 - No. 21, 1991 (B&W)

	GD 2.0	VG 4.0	FN 6.0	VF 8.0	VF/NM 9.0	NM- 9.2
1-3,5-21						3.00
4-1st app. Deadworld (9/86)						4.00
Book 1 ($4.95, B&W)						5.00

REAL McCOYS, THE (TV)
Dell Publ. Co.: No. 1071, 1-3/60 - 5-7/1962 (All have Walter Brennan photo-c)

	GD 2.0	VG 4.0	FN 6.0	VF 8.0	VF/NM 9.0	NM- 9.2
Four Color 1071,1134-Toth-a in both	9	18	27	58	99	140
Four Color 1193,1265	8	16	24	55	93	130
01-689-207 (5-7/62)	7	14	21	49	82	115

REALM OF KINGS (Also see Guardians of the Galaxy and Nova)
Marvel Comics: Jan, 2010 ($3.99, one-shot)

	GD 2.0	VG 4.0	FN 6.0	VF 8.0	VF/NM 9.0	NM- 9.2
1-Abnett & Lanning-s/Manco & Asrar-a; Guardians of the Galaxy app.						4.00

REALM OF KINGS: IMPERIAL GUARD
Marvel Comics: Jan, 2010 - No. 5, May, 2010 ($3.99, limited series)

	GD 2.0	VG 4.0	FN 6.0	VF 8.0	VF/NM 9.0	NM- 9.2
1-5-Abnett & Lanning-s/Walker-a; Starjammers app.						4.00

REALM OF KINGS: INHUMANS
Marvel Comics: Jan, 2010 - No. 5, May, 2010 ($3.99, limited series)

	GD 2.0	VG 4.0	FN 6.0	VF 8.0	VF/NM 9.0	NM- 9.2
1-5-Abnett & Lanning-s/Raimondi-a; Mighty Avengers app.						4.00

REALM OF KINGS: SON OF HULK
Marvel Comics: Apr, 2010 - No. 4, July, 2010 ($3.99, limited series)

	GD 2.0	VG 4.0	FN 6.0	VF 8.0	VF/NM 9.0	NM- 9.2
1-4-Reed-s/Munera-a; leads into Incredible Hulk #609						4.00

REALM OF THE CLAW (Also see Mutant Earth as part of a flipbook)
Image Comics: Oct, 2003 - No. 2 ($2.95)

	GD 2.0	VG 4.0	FN 6.0	VF 8.0	VF/NM 9.0	NM- 9.2
0-(7/03, $5.95) Convention Special; cover has gold-foil title logo						6.00
1,2-Two covers by Yardin						3.00
Vol. 1 TPB (2006, $16.99) r/series; concept art & sketch pages						17.00

REAL SCREEN COMICS (#1 titled Real Screen Funnies; TV Screen Cartoons #129-138)
National Periodical Publications: Spring, 1945 - No. 128, May-June, 1959 (#1-40: 52 pgs.)

	GD 2.0	VG 4.0	FN 6.0	VF 8.0	VF/NM 9.0	NM- 9.2
1-The Fox & the Crow, Flippity & Flop, Tito & His Burrito begin	102	204	306	648	1112	1575
2	47	94	141	296	498	700
3-5	32	64	96	188	307	425
6-10 (2-3/47)	21	42	63	122	199	275
11-20 (10-11/48): 13-The Crow x-over in Flippity & Flop	16	32	48	94	147	200
21-30 (6-7/50)	14	28	42	76	108	140
31-50	11	22	33	60	83	105
51-99	10	20	30	54	72	90
100	10	20	30	56	76	95
101-128	8	16	24	44	57	70

REAL SCREEN FUNNIES
DC Comics: Spring 1945

1-Ashcan comic, not distributed to newsstands, only for in-house use. Cover art is Real Screen Funnies #1 with interior being Detective Comics #92. Only ashcan cover to be produced using the regular production first issue art and only using the color yellow. A copy sold in 2008 for $3,000.

REAL SECRETS (Formerly Real Life Secrets)
Ace Periodicals: No. 2, Nov, 1950 - No. 5, May, 1950

	GD 2.0	VG 4.0	FN 6.0	VF 8.0	VF/NM 9.0	NM- 9.2
2-Painted-c	11	22	33	62	86	110
3-5: 3-Photo-c	9	18	27	50	65	80

REAL SPORTS COMICS (All Sports Comics #2 on)
Hillman Periodicals: Oct-Nov, 1948 (52 pgs.)

	GD 2.0	VG 4.0	FN 6.0	VF 8.0	VF/NM 9.0	NM- 9.2
1-Powell-a (12 pgs.)	39	78	117	240	395	550

REAL WAR STORIES
Eclipse Comics: July, 1987; No. 2, Jan, 1991 ($2.00, 52 pgs.)

	GD 2.0	VG 4.0	FN 6.0	VF 8.0	VF/NM 9.0	NM- 9.2
1-Bolland-a(p), Bissette-a, Totleben-a(i); Alan Moore scripts (2nd printing exists, 2/88)						5.00
2-($4.95)						5.00

REAL WESTERN HERO (Formerly Wow #1-69; Western Hero #76 on)
Fawcett Publications: No. 70, Sept, 1948 - No. 75, Feb, 1949 (All 52 pgs.)

	GD 2.0	VG 4.0	FN 6.0	VF 8.0	VF/NM 9.0	NM- 9.2
70(#1)-Tom Mix, Monte Hale, Hopalong Cassidy, Young Falcon begin	22	44	66	132	216	300
71-75: 71-Gabby Hayes begins. 71,72-Captain Tootsie by Beck. 75-Big Bow and Little Arrow app.	15	30	45	85	130	175

NOTE: *Painted/photo c-70-73; painted c-74, 75.*

REAL WEST ROMANCES
Crestwood Publishing Co./Prize Publ.: 4-5/49 - V1#6, 3/50; V2#1, Apr-May, 1950 (All 52 pgs. & photo-c)

	GD 2.0	VG 4.0	FN 6.0	VF 8.0	VF/NM 9.0	NM- 9.2
V1#1-S&K-a(p)	26	52	78	154	252	350
2-Gail Davis and Rocky Shahan photo-c	14	28	42	80	115	150
3-Kirby-a(p) only	14	28	42	82	121	160
4-S&K-a; Whip Wilson, Reno Browne photo-c	19	38	57	111	176	240
5-Audie Murphy, Gale Storm photo-c; S&K-a	17	34	51	98	154	210
6-Produced by S&K, no S&K-a; Robert Preston & Cathy Downs photo-c	13	26	39	74	105	135
V2#1-Kirby-a(p)	13	26	39	74	105	135

NOTE: ***Meskin** a-V1#5, 6. **Severin/Elder** a-V1#3-6, V2#1. **Meskin** a-V1#6. **Leonard Starr** a-1-3. Photo-c V1#1-6, V2#1.*

REALWORLDS :...
DC Comics: 2000 ($5.95, one-shots, prestige format)

R.E.B.E.L.S. '95 #6 © DC

Red Dragon Comics (2nd series) #5 © CN

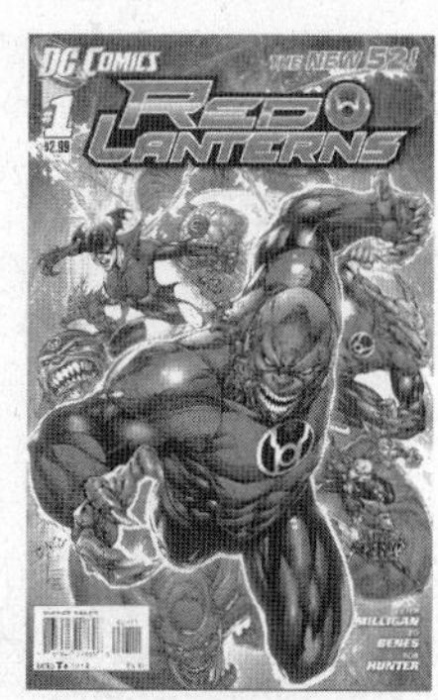

Red Lanterns #1 © DC

GD VG FN VF VF/NM NM-
2.0 4.0 6.0 8.0 9.0 9.2

Batman - Marshall Rogers-a/Golden & Sniegoski-s; Justice League of America -Dematteis-s/ Barr-painted art; Superman - Vance-s/García-López & Rubenstein-a; Wonder Woman - Hanson & Neuwirth-s/Sam-a 6.00

RE-ANIMATOR IN FULL COLOR
Adventure Comics: Oct, 1991 - No. 3, 1992 ($2.95, mini-series)
1-3: Adapts horror movie. 1-Dorman painted-c 3.00

REAP THE WILD WIND (See Cinema Comics Herald)

REBEL, THE (TV)
Dell Publishing Co.: No. 1076, Feb-Apr, 1960 - No. 1262, Dec-Feb, 1961-62
Four Color 1076 (#1)-Sekowsky-a, photo-c 9 18 27 63 112 160
Four Color 1138 (9-11/60), 1207 (9-11/61), 1262-Photo-c
8 16 24 55 93 130

R.E.B.E.L.S.
DC Comics: Apr, 2009 - No. 28, Jul, 2011 ($2.99)
1-9,12-28: 1-Bedard-s/Clarke-a; Vril Dox returns; Supergirl app.; 2 covers. 15-Starfire app. 19-28-Lobo app. 3.00
10,11-($3.99) Blackest Night x-over; Vril Dox joins the Sinestro Corps 4.00
Annual 1 (12/09, $4.99) Origin on Starro the Conqueror; Despero app. 5.00
...: Sons of Brainiac TPB (2011, $14.99) r/#15-20 15.00
...: Strange Companions TPB (2010, $14.99) r/#7-9 & Annual #1 15.00
...: The Coming of Starro TPB (2010, $17.99) r/#1-6 18.00
...: The Son and the Stars TPB (2010, $17.99) r/#10-14 18.00

R.E.B.E.L.S. '94 (Becomes R.E.B.E.L.S. '95 & R.E.B.E.L.S. '96)
DC Comics: No. 0, Oct, 1994 - No. 17, Mar, 1996 ($1.95/$2.25)
0-17: 8-$2.25-c begins. 15-R.E.B.E.L.S '96 begins. 3.00

RECORD BOOK OF FAMOUS POLICE CASES
St. John Publishing Co.: 1949 (25¢, 132 pgs.)
nn-Kubert-a(3); r/Son of Sinbad; Baker-c 42 84 126 265 445 625

RED (Inspired the 2010 Bruce Willis movie)
DC Comics (Homage): Sept, 2003 - No. 3, Feb, 2004 ($2.95, limited series)
1-3-Warren Ellis-s/Cully Hamner-a/c 5.00
Red/Tokyo Storm Warning TPB (2004, $14.95) Flip book r/both series 15.00
Red: Eyes Only (2/11, $4.99) comic prequel; Hamner-s/a/c 5.00
Red: Frank (11/10, $3.99) movie prequel; Noveck-s/Masters-a/Hamner & photo-c 4.00
Red: Joe (11/10, $3.99) movie prequel; Wagner-s/Redondo-a/Hamner & photo-c 4.00
Red: Marvin (11/10, $3.99) movie prequel; Hoeber-s/Olmos-a/Hamner & photo-c 4.00
Red: Victoria (11/10, $3.99) movie prequel; Hoeber-s/Hahn-a/Hamner & photo-c 4.00
...: Better R.E.D. Than Dead TPB (2011, $14.99) r/movie prequel issues; sketch-a 15.00

RED ARROW
P. L. Publishing Co.: May-June, 1951 - No. 3, Oct, 1951
1 11 22 33 60 83 105
2,3 9 18 27 47 61 75

RED BAND COMICS
Enwil Associates: Nov, 1944, No. 2, Jan, 1945 - No. 4, May, 1945
1-Bogeyman-c/intro. (The Spirit swipe) 41 82 123 249 417 585
2-Origin Bogeyman & Santanas; c-reprint/#1 29 58 87 170 278 385
3,4-Captain Wizard app. in both (1st app.); each has identical contents/cover
27 54 81 158 259 360

REDBLADE
Dark Horse Comics: Apr, 1993 - No. 3, July, 1993 ($2.50, mini-series)
1-3: 1-Double gatefold-c 3.00

RED CIRCLE, THE (Re-introduction of characters from MLJ/Archie publications)
DC Comics: Oct, 2009 ($2.99, series of one-shots)
...Inferno 1 - Hangman app.; Straczynski-s/Greg Scott-a 5.00
...The Hangman 1 - Origin retold; Straczynski-s/Derenick & Sienkiewicz-a 5.00
...The Shield 1 - Origin retold; Straczynski-s/McDaniel-a 5.00
...The Web 1 - Straczynski-s/Robinson-a 5.00

RED CIRCLE COMICS (Also see Blazing Comics & Blue Circle Comics)
Rural Home Publications (Enwil): Jan, 1945 - No. 4, April, 1945
1-The Prankster & Red Riot begin 50 100 150 315 533 750
2-Starr-a; The Judge (costumed hero) app. 32 64 96 188 307 425
3,4-Starr-c/a. 3-The Prankster not in costume 26 52 78 154 252 350
4-(Dated 4/45)-Leftover covers to #4 were later restapled over early 1950s coverless comics; variations in the coverless comics used are endless; Woman Outlaws, Dorothy Lamour, Crime Does Not Pay, Sabu, Diary Loves, Love Confessions & Young Love V3#3 known
19 38 57 109 172 235

GD VG FN VF VF/NM NM-
2.0 4.0 6.0 8.0 9.0 9.2

RED CIRCLE SORCERY (Chilling Adventures in Sorcery #1-5)
Red Circle Prod. (Archie): No. 6, Apr, 1974 - No. 11, Feb, 1975 (All 25¢ iss.)
6,8,9,11: 6-Early Chaykin-a. 7-Pino-a. 8-Only app. The Cobra
2 4 6 9 13 16
7-Bruce Jones-a with Wrightson, Kaluta, Jeff Jones 3 6 9 14 19 24
10-Wood-a(i) 2 4 6 10 14 18
NOTE: ***Chaykin*** *a-6, 10.* ***McWilliams*** *a-10(2 & 3 pgs.).* ***Mooney*** *a-11p.* ***Morrow*** *a-6-8, 9(text illos), 10, 11i; c-6-11.* ***Thorne*** *a-8, 10.* ***Toth*** *a-8, 9.*

RED DOG (See Night Music #7)

RED DRAGON
Comico: June, 1996 ($2.95)
1-Bisley-c 3.00

RED DRAGON COMICS (1st Series) (Formerly Trail Blazers; see Super Magician V5#7, 8)
Street & Smith Publications: No. 5, Jan, 1943 - No. 9, Jan, 1944
5-Origin Red Rover, the Crimson Crimebuster; Rex King, Man of Adventure, Captain Jack Commando, & The Minute Man begin; text origin Red Dragon; Binder-c
77 154 231 493 847 1200
6-Origin The Black Crusader & Red Dragon (3/43); 1st story app. Red Dragon & 1st cover (classic-c) 181 362 543 1158 1979 2800
7-Classic WWII-c 219 438 657 1402 2401 3400
8-The Red Knight app. 61 122 183 390 670 950
9-Origin Chuck Magnon, Immortal Man 61 122 183 390 670 950

RED DRAGON COMICS (2nd Series)(See Super Magician V2#8)
Street & Smith Publications: Nov, 1947 - No. 6, Jan, 1949; No. 7, July, 1949
1-Red Dragon begins; Elliman, Nigel app.; Edd Cartier-c/a
90 180 270 576 988 1400
2-Cartier-c 53 106 159 334 567 800
3-1st app. Dr. Neff Ghost Breaker by Powell; Elliman, Nigel app.
43 86 129 271 461 650
4-Cartier c/a 58 116 174 371 636 900
5-7 34 68 102 199 325 450
NOTE: ***Maneely*** *a-5, 7.* ***Powell*** *a-2-7; c-3, 5, 7.*

RED EAGLE
David McKay Publications: No. 16, Aug, 1938
Feature Books 16 28 56 84 165 270 375

REDEYE (See Comics Reading Libraries in the Promotional Comics section)

RED FOX (Formerly Manhunt! #1-14; also see Extra Comics)
Magazine Enterprises: No. 15, 1954
15(A-1 #108)-Undercover Girl story; L.B. Cole-c/a (Red Fox); r-from Manhunt; Powell-a
19 38 57 109 172 235

RED GOOSE COMIC SELECTIONS (See Comic Selections)

RED HAWK (See A-1 Comics, Bobby Benson's ..#14-16 & Straight Arrow #2)
Magazine Enterprises: No. 90, 1953
11-(A-1 Comics #90)-Powell-c/a 13 26 39 72 101 130

RED HERRING
DC Comics (WildStorm): Oct, 2009 - No. 6, Mar, 2010 ($2.99, limited series)
1-6-Tischman-s/Bond-a 3.00

RED HOOD AND THE OUTLAWS
DC Comics: Nov, 2011 - Present ($2.99)
1-7: 1-Jason Todd, Starfire, Roy Harper app.; Lobdell-s/Rocafort-a/c 3.00

RED HOOD: THE LOST DAYS
DC Comics: Aug, 2010 - No. 6, Jan, 2011 ($2.99, limited series)
1-6-The Return of Jason Todd; Winick-s/Raimondi-a/Tucci-c. 6-Joker & Hush app. 3.00
TPB (2011, $14.99) r/#1-6 15.00

RED LANTERNS (DC New 52)
DC Comics: Nov, 2011 - Present ($2.99)
1-8: 1-Milligan-s/Benes-a/c; Atrocitus, Dex-Starr & Bleez app. 6-8-Guy Gardner app. 3.00

RED MASK (Formerly Tim Holt; see Best Comics, Blazing Six-Guns)
Magazine Enterprises No. 42-53/Sussex No. 54 (M.E. on-c): No. 42, June-July, 1954 - No. 53, May, 1956; No. 54, Sept, 1957
42-Ghost Rider by Ayers continues, ends #50; Black Phantom continues; 3-D effect c/stories begin 21 42 63 122 199 275
43- 3-D effect-c/stories 19 38 57 109 172 235
44-52: 3-D effect stories only. 47-Last pre-code issue. 50-Last Ghost Rider. 51-The Presto Kid begins by Ayers (1st app.); Presto Kid-c begins; last 3-D effect story.
52-Origin The Presto Kid 17 34 51 98 154 210

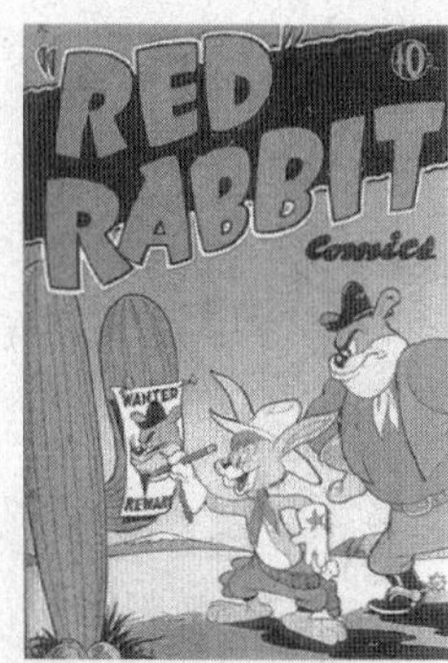

Red Rabbit Comics #1 © Dearfield

Red Robin #22 © DC

Red Sonja #8 © MAR

	GD 2.0	VG 4.0	FN 6.0	VF 8.0	VF/NM 9.0	NM- 9.2
53,54-Last Black Phantom; last Presto Kid-c	15	30	45	83	124	165
I.W. Reprint #1 (r-/#52). 2 (nd, r/#51 w/diff.-c). 3, 8 (nd; Kinstler-c); 8-r/Red Mask #52	3	6	9	16	22	28

NOTE: *Ayers art on Ghost Rider & Presto Kid.* ***Bolle*** *art in all (Red Mask); c-43, 44, 49.* ***Guardineer*** *a-52. Black Phantom in #42-44, 47-50, 53, 54.*

REDMASK OF THE RIO GRANDE
AC Comics: 1990 ($2.50, 28pgs.)(Has photos of movie posters)

1-Bolle-c/a(r); photo inside-c 3.00

RED MENACE
DC Comics (WildStorm): Jan, 2007 - No. 6, Jun, 2007 ($2.99, limited series)

1-6-Ordway-a/c; Bilson, DeMeo & Brody-s 3.00
TPB (2007, $17.99) r/series, sketch pages & variant covers 18.00

RED MOUNTAIN FEATURING QUANTRELL'S RAIDERS (Movie)(Also see Jesse James #28)
Avon Periodicals: 1952

nn-Alan Ladd; Kinstler-c	28	56	84	165	270	375

RED PROPHET: THE TALES OF ALVIN MAKER
Dabel Brothers Prods./Marvel Comics (Dabel Brothers): Mar, 2006 - No. 12, Mar, 2008 ($2.99)

1-12-Adaptation of Orson Scott Card novel. 1-Miguel Montenegro-a 3.00
... Vol. 1 HC (2007, $19.99, dustjacket) r/#1-6 20.00
... Vol. 1 SC (2007, $15.99) r/#1-6 16.00
... Vol. 2 HC (2008, $19.99, dustjacket) r/#7-12 20.00

"RED" RABBIT COMICS
Dearfield Comic/J. Charles Laue Publ. Co.: Jan, 1947 - No. 22, Aug-Sep, 1951

1	14	28	42	76	108	140
2	8	16	24	44	57	70
3-10	7	14	21	37	46	55
11-17,19-22	7	14	21	35	43	50
18-Flying Saucer-c (1/51)	8	16	24	44	57	70

RED RAVEN COMICS (Human Torch #2 on)(Also see X-Men #44 & Sub-Mariner #26, 2nd series)
Timely Comics: August, 1940

1-Origin & 1st app. Red Raven; Comet Pierce & Mercury by Kirby, The Human Top & The Eternal Brain; intro. Magar, the Mystic & only app.; Kirby-c (his 1st signed work)	1400	2800	4200	10,500	19,250	28,000

RED ROBIN (Batman: Reborn)
DC Comics: Aug, 2009 - No. 26, Oct, 2011 ($2.99)

1-26-Tim (Drake) Wayne in the Kingdom Come costume; Bachs-a. 1-Two covers 3.00
...: Collision SC (2010, $19.99) r/#6-12 and Batgirl (2009 series) #8 20.00
...: The Grail SC (2010, $17.99) r/#1-5 18.00
...: The Hit List SC (2011, $17.99) r/#13-17 18.00

RED ROCKET 7
Dark Horse Comics: Aug, 1997 - No. 7, June, 1998 ($3.95, square format, limited series)

1-7-Mike Allred-c/s/a 4.00

RED RYDER COMICS (Hi Spot #2)(Movies, radio)(See Crackajack Funnies & Super Book of Comics)
Hawley Publ. No. 1/Dell Publishing Co.(K.K.) No. 3 on: 9/40; No. 3, 8/41 - No. 5, 12/41; No. 6, 4/42 - No. 151, 4-6/57

1-Red Ryder, his horse Thunder, Little Beaver & his horse Papoose strip reprints begin by Fred Harman; 1st meeting of Red & Little Beaver; Harman line-drawn-c #1-85	245	490	735	1568	2684	3800
3-(Scarce)-Alley Oop, Capt. Easy, Dan Dunn, Freckles & His Friends, King of the Royal Mtd., Myra North strip-r begin	52	104	156	421	911	1400
4-6: 6-1st Dell issue (4/42)	26	52	78	182	391	600
7-10	22	44	66	154	327	500
11-20	15	30	45	104	227	350
21-32-Last Alley Oop, Dan Dunn, Capt. Easy, Freckles	11	22	33	76	151	225
33-40 (52 pgs.): 40-Photo back-c begin, end #57	10	20	30	65	118	170
41 (52 pgs.)-Rocky Lane photo back-c	10	20	30	67	124	180
42-46 (52 pgs.): 46-Last Red Ryder strip-r	8	16	24	56	96	135
47-53 (52 pgs.): 47-New stories on Red Ryder begin. 49,52-Harmon photo back-c	7	14	21	48	79	110
54-92: 54-73 (36 pgs.). 59-Harmon photo back-c. 73-Last King of the Royal Mtd; strip-r by Jim Gary. 74-85 (52 pgs.)-Harman line-drawn-c. 86-92 (52 pgs.)-Harman painted-c	6	12	18	42	69	95
93-99,101-106: 94-96 (36 pgs.)-Harman painted-c. 97,98,(36 pgs.)-Harman line-drawn-c. 99,101-106 (36 pgs.)-Jim Bannon Photo-c	6	12	18	37	59	80
100 (36 pgs.)-Bannon photo-c	6	12	18	39	62	85
107-118 (52 pgs.)-Harman line-drawn-c	5	10	15	35	55	75
119-129 (52 pgs.): 119-Painted-c begin, not by Harman, end #151	5	10	15	32	51	70
130-151 (36 pgs.): 145-Title change to Red Ryder Ranch Magazine; 149-Title change to Red Ryder Ranch Comics	5	10	15	30	48	65
Four Color 916 (7/58)	5	10	15	30	48	65

NOTE: ***Fred Harman*** *a-1-99; c-1-98, 107-118. Don Red Barry, Allan Rocky Lane, Wild Bill Elliott & Jim Bannon starred as Red Ryder in the movies. Robert Blake starred as Little Beaver.*

RED RYDER PAINT BOOK
Whitman Publishing Co.: 1941 (8-1/2x11-1/2", 148 pgs.)

nn-Reprints 1940 daily strips	76	152	228	479	810	1140

RED SEAL COMICS (Formerly Carnival Comics, and/or Spotlight Comics?)
Harry 'A' Chesler/Superior Publ. No. 19 on: No. 14, 10/45 - No. 18, 10/46; No. 19, 6/47 - No. 22, 12/47

14-The Black Dwarf begins (continued from Spotlight?); Little Nemo app; bondage/hypo-c; Tuska-a	82	164	246	528	902	1275
15-Torture story; funny-c	41	82	123	256	428	600
16-Used in **SOTI**, pg. 181, illo "Outside the forbidden pages of de Sade, you find draining a girl's blood only in children's comics;" drug club story r-later in Crime Reporter #1; Veiled Avenger & Barry Kuda app; Tuska-a; funny-c	63	126	189	403	689	975
17,18,20: Lady Satan, Yankee Girl & Sky Chief app; 17-Tuska-a	52	104	156	322	549	775
19-No Black Dwarf (on-c only); Zor, El Tigre app.	46	92	138	290	488	685
21-Lady Satan & Black Dwarf app.	33	66	99	194	317	440
22-Zor, Rocketman app. (68 pgs.)	33	66	99	194	317	440

REDSKIN (Thrilling Indian Stories)(Famous Western Badmen #13 on)
Youthful Magazines: Sept, 1950 - No. 12, Oct, 1952

1-Walter Johnson-a (7 pgs.)	17	34	51	98	154	210
2	11	22	33	62	86	110
3-12: 3-Daniel Boone story. 6-Geronimo story	10	20	30	54	72	90

NOTE: ***Walter Johnson*** *c-3, 4.* ***Palais*** *a-11.* ***Wildey*** *a-5, 11. Bondage c-6, 12.*

RED SKULL
Marvel Comics: Sept, 2011 - No. 5, Jan, 2012 ($2.99, limited series)

1-5-Pak-s/Colak-a/Aja-c; Red Skull's childhood and origin 3.00

RED SONJA (Also see Conan #23, Kull & The Barbarians, Marvel Feature & Savage Sword Of Conan #1)
Marvel Comics Group: 1/77 - No. 15, 5/79; V1#1, 2/83 - V2#2, 3/83; V3#1, 8/83 - V3#4, 2/84; V3#5, 1/85 - V3#13, 5/86

1-Created by Robert E. Howard	3	6	9	14	20	25
2-10: 5-Last 30¢ issue	2	4	6	8	10	12
4,5-(35¢-c variants, limited distribution)(7,9/77)	3	6	9	20	30	40
11-15, V1#1,V2#2: 14-Last 35¢ issue	1	3	4	6	8	10

V3#1-13: #1-4 ($1.00, 52 pgs.) 4.00

NOTE: ***Brunner*** *c-12-14.* ***J. Buscema*** *a(p)-12, 13, 15; c-V#1.* ***Nebres*** *a-V3#3i(part).* ***N. Redondo*** *a-8i, V3#2i, 3i.* ***Simonson*** *a-V3#1.* ***Thorne*** *c/a-1-11.*

RED SONJA (Continues in Queen Sonja) (Also see Classic Red Sonja)
Dynamite Entertainment: No. 0, Apr, 2005 - Present (25¢/$2.99/$3.99)

0-(4/05, 25¢) Greg Land-c/Mel Rubi-a/Oeming & Carey-s 3.00
1-(6/05, $2.99) Five covers by Ross, Linsner, Cassaday, Turner, Rivera; Rubi-a 3.00
2-46-Multiple covers on all. 29-Sonja dies. 34-Sonja reborn 3.00
5-RRP Edition with Red Foil logo and Isanove-a 10.00
50-('10, $4.99) new stories and reprints; Marcos, Chin, Desjardins-a; 4 covers 5.00
51-64-($3.99): 51-56-Geovani-a; multiple covers on each 4.00
Annual #1 (2007, $3.50) Oeming-s/Sadowski-a; Red Sonja Comics Chronology 4.00
Annual #2 (2009, $3.99) Gage-s/Marcos-a; wraparound Prado-c & Marcos-c 4.00
Annual #3 (2010, $5.99) Brereton-s/c/a; Batista-a 6.00
... Blue (2011, $4.99) Brett-s/Geovani-a; covers by Geovani & Rubi 5.00
... Break the Skin (2011, $4.99) Winslade-c/Van Meter-s/Salazar-a 5.00
... Cover Showcase Vol. 1 (2007, $5.99) gallery of variant covers; Cho sketches 6.00
... Deluge (2011, $4.99) Brereton-s/c; Bolson-a/var-c; reprint from Conan #48 ('74) 5.00
Giant Size Red Sonja #1 (2007, $4.99) Chaykin-c; new story and reprints and pin-ups 5.00
Giant Size Red Sonja #2 (2008, $4.99) Segovia-c; new story and reprints and pin-ups 5.00
... Goes East ($4.99) three covers; Joe Ng-a 5.00
...: Monster Isle ($4.99) two covers; Pablo Marcos-a/Roy Thomas-s 5.00
... One More Day ($4.99) two covers; Liam Sharp-a 5.00
... Raven ('12, $4.99) Antonio-a/Martin-c; bonus pin-up gallery 5.00
...: Revenge of the Gods 1-5 (2011 - No. 5, 2011, $3.99) Sampare-a/Lieberman-s 4.00
... Vacant Shell ($4.99) two covers; Remender-s/Renaud-a 5.00
...: Wrath of the Gods 1-5 (2010 - No. 5, 2010, $3.99) Geovani-a 4.00
The Adventures of Red Sonja TPB (2005, $19.99) r/Marvel Feature #1-7 20.00
The Adventures of Red Sonja Vol. 2 TPB (2007, $19.99) r/#1-7 of '77 Marvel series 20.00

Red Sonja / Claw: The Devil's Hands #1 © WSP & RSLLC

The Red Star #9 © Christian Gossett

Reg'lar Fellers #6 © STD

	GD 2.0	VG 4.0	FN 6.0	VF 8.0	VF/NM 9.0	NM- 9.2

... Vol. 1 TPB (2006, $19.99) r/#0-6; gallery of covers and variants; creators interview 20.00
... Vol. 2 Arrowsmith TPB (2007, $19.99) r/#7-12; gallery of covers and variants 20.00
... Vol. 3 The Rise of Gath TPB (2007, $19.99) r/#13-18; gallery of covers and variants 20.00
... Vol. 4 Animals & More TPB (2007, $24.99) r/#19-24; gallery of covers and variants 25.00

RED SONJA/CLAW: THE DEVIL'S HANDS (See Claw the Unconquered)
DC Comics (WildStorm)/Dynamite Ent.: May, 2006 - No. 4, Aug, 2006 ($2.99, limited series)

1-4-Covers by Jim Lee & Dell'Otto.; Andy Smith-a 1-Alex Ross var-c. 2-Dell'Otto var-c. 3-Bermejo var-c. 4-Andy Smith var-c 3.00
TPB (2007, $12.99) r/#1-4; cover gallery 13.00

RED SONJA: SCAVENGER HUNT
Marvel Comics: Dec, 1995 ($2.95, one-shot)

1 3.00

RED SONJA: THE MOVIE
Marvel Comics Group: Nov, 1985 - No. 2, Dec, 1985 (Limited series)

1,2-Movie adapt-r/Marvel Super Spec. #38 3.00

RED SONJA VS. THULSA DOOM
Dynamite Entertainment: 2005 - No. 4, 2006 ($3.50)

1-4-Conrad-a; Conrad & Dell'Otto covers 3.50
..., Volume 1 TPB (2006, $14.99) r/series; cover gallery 15.00

RED STAR, THE
Image Comics/Archangel Studios: June, 2000 - No. 9, June, 2002 ($2.95)

1-Christian Gossett-s/a(p) 4.00
2-9: 9-Beck-c 3.00
#(7.5) Reprints Wizard #1/2 story with new pages 3.00
Annual 1 (Archangel Studios, 11/02, $3.50) "Run Makita Run" 4.00
TPB (4/01, $24.95, 9x12") oversized r/#1-4; intro. by Bendis 25.00
Nokgorka TPB (8/02, $24.95, 9x12") oversized r/#6-9; w/sketch pages 25.00
Wizard 1/2 (mail order) 10.00

RED STAR, THE (Volume 2)
CrossGen #1,2/Archangel Studios #3 on: Feb, 2003 - No. 5, July, 2004 ($2.95/$2.99)

1-5-Christian Gossett-s/a(p) 3.00
Prison of Souls TPB (8/04, $24.95, 9x12") oversized r/#1-5; w/sketch pages 25.00

RED STAR, THE: SWORD OF LIES
Archangel Studios: Aug, 2006 ($4.50)

1-Christian Gossett-s/a(p); origin of the Red Star team 4.50

RED TORNADO (See All-American #20 & Justice League of America #64)
DC Comics: July, 1985 - No. 4, Oct, 1985 (Limited series)

1-4: Kurt Busiek scripts in all. 1-3-Superman & Batman cameos 4.00

RED TORNADO
DC Comics: Nov, 2009 - No. 6, Apr, 2010 ($2.99, limited series)

1-6: 1-3-Benes-c. 5,6-Vixen app. 3.00
...: Family Reunion TPB (2010, $17.99) r/#1-6 18.00

RED WARRIOR
Marvel/Atlas Comics (TCI): Jan, 1951 - No. 6, Dec, 1951

	GD	VG	FN	VF	VF/NM	NM-
1-Red Warrior & his horse White Wing; Tuska-a	16	32	48	92	144	195
2-Tuska-c	10	20	30	56	76	95
3-6: 4-Origin White Wing. 6-Maneely-c	9	18	27	47	61	75

RED, WHITE & BLUE COMICS
DC Comics: 1941

nn - Ashcan comic, not distributed to newsstands, only for in-house use. Cover art is All-American Comics #20 with interior being Flash Comics #17 (no known sales)

RED WING
Image Comics: Jul, 2011 - No. 4, Oct, 2011 ($3.50, limited series)

1-4-Hickman-s/Pitarra-a 3.50

RED WOLF (See Avengers #80 & Marvel Spotlight #1)
Marvel Comics Group: May, 1972 - No. 9, Sept, 1973

	GD	VG	FN	VF	VF/NM	NM-
1-(Western hero); Gil Kane/Severin-c; Shores-a	3	6	9	18	27	35
2-9: 2-Kane-c; Shores-a. 6-Tuska-r in back-up. 7-Red Wolf as super hero begins. 9-Origin sidekick, Lobo (wolf)	2	4	6	13	18	22

REESE'S PIECES
Eclipse Comics: Oct, 1985 - No.2, Oct, 1985 ($1.75, Baxter paper)

1,2-B&W-r in color 3.00

REFORM SCHOOL GIRL!
Realistic Comics: 1951

	GD	VG	FN	VF	VF/NM	NM-
nn-Used in **SOTI**, pg. 358, & cover ill. with caption "Comic books are supposed to be like fairy tales"; classic photo-c	497	994	1491	3628	6414	9200

(Prices vary widely on this book)

NOTE: *The cover and title originated from a digest-sized book published by Diversey Publishing Co. of Chicago in 1948. The original book "House of Fury", Doubleday, came out in 1941. The girl's real name which appears on the cover of the digest and comic is Marty Collins, Canadian model and ice skating star who posed for this special color photograph for the Diversey novel.*

REGENTS ILLUSTRATED CLASSICS
Prentice Hall Regents, Englewood Cliffs, NJ 07632: 1981 (Plus more recent reprintings) (48 pgs., B&W-a with 14 pgs. of teaching helps)

NOTE: *This series contains Classics Ill. art, and was produced from the same illegal source as* **Cassette Books.** *But when Twin Circle sued to stop the sale of the Cassette Books, they decided to permit this series to continue. This series was produced as a teaching aid. The 20 title series is divided into four levels based upon number of basic words used therein. There is also a teacher's manual for each level. All of the titles are still available from the publisher for about $5 each retail. The number to call for mail order purchases is (201)767-5937. Almost all of the issues have new covers taken from some interior art panel. Here is a list of the series by Regents ident. no. and the Classics Ill. counterpart.*

16770(CI#24-A2)18333(CI#3-A2)21668(CI#13-A2)32224(CI#21)33051(CI#26)35788(CI#84)37153(CI#16)44460(CI#19-A2)44808(CI#18-A2)52395(CI#4-A2)58627(CI#5-A2)60067(CI#30)68405(CI#23A1)70302(CI#29)78192(CI#7-A2)78193(CI#10-A2)79679(CI#85)92046(CI#1-A2)93062(CI#64)93512(CI#25)

RE: GEX
Awesome-Hyperwerks: Jul, 1998 - No. 0, Dec, 1998; ($2.50)

Preview (7/98) Wizard Con Edition 3.00
0-(12/98) Loeb-s/Liefeld-a/Pat Lee-c, 1-(9/98) Loeb-s/Liefeld-a/c 3.00

REGGIE (Formerly Archie's Rival...; Reggie & Me #19 on)
Archie Publications: No. 15, Sept, 1963 - No. 18, Nov, 1965

	GD	VG	FN	VF	VF/NM	NM-
15(9/63), 16(10/64), 17(8/65), 18(11/65)	5	10	15	32	51	70

NOTE: *Cover title No. 15 & 16 is Archie's Rival Reggie.*

REGGIE AND ME (Formerly Reggie)
Archie Publ.: No. 19, Aug, 1966 - No. 126, Sept, 1980 (No. 50-68: 52 pgs.)

	GD	VG	FN	VF	VF/NM	NM-
19-Evilheart app.	4	8	12	24	37	50
20-23-Evilheart app.; with Pureheart #22	3	6	9	20	30	40
24-40(3/70)	3	6	9	14	20	26
41-49(7/71)	2	4	6	11	16	20
50(9/71)-68 (1/74, 52 pgs.)	3	6	9	14	19	24
69-99	2	4	6	8	10	12
100(10/77)	2	4	6	9	12	15
101-126	1	2	3	5	7	9

REGGIE'S JOKES (See Reggie's Wise Guy Jokes)

REGGIE'S REVENGE!
Archie Comic Publications, Inc.: Spring, 1994 - No. 3 ($2.00, 52 pgs.) (Published semi-annually)

1-Bound-in pull-out poster 5.00
2,3 4.00

REGGIE'S WISE GUY JOKES
Archie Publications: Aug, 1968 - No. 55, 1980 (#5-28 are Giants)

	GD	VG	FN	VF	VF/NM	NM-
1	4	8	12	28	44	60
2-4	3	6	9	14	20	26
5-16 (1/71)(68 pg. Giants)	3	6	9	17	25	32
17-28 (52 pg. Giants)	2	4	6	13	18	22
29-40(1/77)	1	3	4	6	8	10
41-55	1	2	3	5	6	8

REGISTERED NURSE
Charlton Comics: Summer, 1963

	GD	VG	FN	VF	VF/NM	NM-
1-r/Nurse Betsy Crane & Cynthia Doyle	3	6	9	17	25	32

REG'LAR FELLERS
Visual Editions (Standard): No. 5, Nov, 1947 - No. 6, Mar, 1948

	GD	VG	FN	VF	VF/NM	NM-
5,6	9	18	27	47	61	75

REG'LAR FELLERS HEROIC (See Heroic Comics)

REID FLEMING, WORLD'S TOUGHEST MILKMAN
Eclipse Comics/ Deep Sea Comics: 1980; 8/86; V2#1, 12/86 - V2#3, 12/88; V2#4, 11/89; V2#5, 11/90 (B&W)

1-(1980, self-published) David Boswell-s/a 5.00
1-2nd, 4th & 5th printings ($2.50); (3rd print, large size, 8/86, $2.50) 3.00
V2#1 (10/86, regular size, $2.00), 1-2nd print, 3rd print ($2.00, 2/89) 3.00
2-8 , V2#2-2nd & 3rd printings, V2#4-2nd printing, V2#5 ($2.00) 3.00

REIGN IN HELL
DC Comics: Sept, 2008 - No. 8, Apr, 2009 ($3.50, limited series)

1-8-Neron, Shadowpact app.; Giffen-s; Dr. Occult back-up w/Segovia-a. 1-Two covers 3.50

The Ren & Stimpy Show #23 © Nickelodeon

The Resistance #1 © WSP

Resurrection Man (2011 series) #1 © DC

GD VG FN VF VF/NM NM-
2.0 4.0 6.0 8.0 9.0 9.2

GD VG FN VF VF/NM NM-
2.0 4.0 6.0 8.0 9.0 9.2

TPB (2009, $19.99) r/#1-8 20.00

REIGN OF THE ZODIAC
DC Comics: Oct, 2003 - No. 8, May, 2004 ($2.75)

1-8: 1-6,8-Giffen-s/Doran-a/Harris-c. 7-Byrd-a 3.00

RELATIVE HEROES
DC Comics: Mar, 2000 - No. 6, Aug, 2000 ($2.50, limited series)

1-6-Grayson-s/Guichet & Sowd-a. 6-Superman-c/app. 3.00

RELOAD
DC Comics (Homage): May, 2003 - No. 3, Sept, 2003 ($2.95, limited series)

1-3-Warren Ellis-s/Paul Gulacy & Jimmy Palmiotti-a 3.00
.../Mek TPB (2004, $14.95, flip book) r/Reload #1-3 & Mek #1-3 15.00

RELUCTANT DRAGON, THE (Walt Disney's...)
Dell Publishing Co.: No. 13, 1940

Four Color 13-Contains 2 pgs. of photos from film; 2 pg. foreword to Fantasia by Leopold Stokowski; Donald Duck, Goofy, Baby Weems & Mickey Mouse (as the Sorcerer's Apprentice) app. 219 438 657 1402 2401 3400

REMAINS
IDW Publishing: May, 2004 - No. 5, Sept, 2004 ($3.99)

1-5-Steve Niles-s/Kieron Dwyer-a 4.00

REMARKABLE WORLDS OF PROFESSOR PHINEAS B. FUDDLE, THE
DC Comics (Paradox Press): 2000 - No. 4, 2000 ($5.95, limited series)

1-4-Boaz Yakin-s/Erez Yakin-a 6.00
TPB (2001, $19.95) r/series 20.00

REMEMBER PEARL HARBOR
Street & Smith Publications: 1942 (68 pgs.) (Illustrated story of the battle)

nn-Uncle Sam-c; Jack Binder-a 52 104 156 322 549 775

REN & STIMPY SHOW, THE (TV) (Nicklodeon cartoon characters)
Marvel Comics: Dec, 1992 - No. 44, July, 1996 ($1.75/$1.95)

1-($2.25)-Polybagged w/scratch & sniff Ren or Stimpy air fowler (equal numbers of each were made) 1 2 3 5 6 8
1-2nd & 3rd printing; different dialogue on-c 3.00
2-6: 4-Muddy Mudskipper back-up. 5-Bill Wray painted-c. 6-Spider-Man vs. Powdered Toast Man 4.00
7-17: 12-1st solo back-up story w/Tank & Brenner 3.00
18-44: 18-Powered Toast Man app. 3.00
25 ($2.95) Deluxe edition w/die cut cover 4.00
...Don't Try This at Home (3/94, $12.95, TPB)-r/#9-12 13.00
...Eenteractive Special ('95, $2.95) 4.00
...Holiday Special 1994 (2/95, $2.95, 52 pgs.) 4.00
...Mini Comic (1995) 5.00
...Pick of the Litter nn (1993, $12.95, TPB)-r/#1-4 13.00
...Radio Daze (11/95, $1.95) 3.00
...Running Joke nn (1993, $12.95, TPB)-r/#1-4 plus new-a 13.00
...Seeck Little Monkeys (1/95, $12.95)-r/#17-20 13.00
...Special 2 (7/94, $2.95, 52 pgs.), ...Special 3 (10/94, $2.95, 52 pgs.)-Choose adventure, ...Special: Around the World in a Daze ($2.95), ...Special: Four Swerks (1/95, $2.95, 52 pgs.)-FF #1 cover swipe; cover reads "Four Swerks w/5 pg. coloring book.", ...Special: Powdered Toast Man 1 (4/94, $2.95, 52 pgs.), ...Special: Powdered Toast Man's Cereal Serial (4/95, $2.95), ...Special: Sports (10/95, $2.95) 4.00
...Tastes Like Chicken nn (11/93,$12.95,TPB)-r/#5-8 13.00
...Your Pals (1994, $12.95, TPB)-r/#13-16 13.00

RENFIELD
Caliber Press:1994 - No. 3, 1995 ($2.95, B&W, limited series)

1-3 3.00

RENO BROWNE, HOLLYWOOD'S GREATEST COWGIRL (Formerly Margie Comics; Apache Kid #53 on; also see Western Hearts, Western Life Romances & Western Love)
Marvel Comics (MPC): No. 50, April, 1950 - No. 52, Sept, 1950 (52 pgs.)

50-Reno Browne photo-c on all 29 58 87 170 278 385
51,52 24 48 72 142 234 325

REPLACEMENT GOD
Amaze Ink: June, 1995 - No. 8 ($2.95, B&W)

1-8-Zander Cannon-s/a 3.00

REPLACEMENT GOD
Image Comics: May, 1997 - No. 5 ($2.95, B&W)

1-5: 1-Flip book w/"Knute's Escapes", r/original series. 2-Flip book w/"Harris Thermidor". 3-5: 3-Flip book w/"Myth and Legend" 3.00

REPTILICUS (Becomes Reptisaurus #3 on)
Charlton Comics: Aug, 1961 - No. 2, Oct, 1961

1 (Movie) 20 40 60 137 294 450
2 11 22 33 73 142 210

REPTISAURUS (Reptilicus #1,2)
Charlton Comics: V2#3, Jan, 1962 - No. 8, Dec, 1962; Summer, 1963

V2#3-8: 3-Flying saucer-c/s. 8-Montes/Bache-c/a 6 12 18 41 66 90
Special Edition 1 (Summer, 1963) 6 12 18 39 62 85

REQUIEM FOR DRACULA
Marvel Comics: Feb, 1993 ($2.00, 52 pgs.)

nn-r/Tomb of Dracula #69,70 by Gene Colan 4.00

RESCUE (Pepper Potts in Iron Man armor)
Marvel Comics: July, 2010 ($3.99, one-shot)

1-DeConnick-s/Mutti-a/Foreman-c 4.00

RESCUERS, THE (See Walt Disney Showcase #40)

RESIDENT EVIL (Based on video game)
Image Comics (WildStorm): Mar, 1998 - No. 5 ($4.95, quarterly magazine)

1 7.00
2-5 5.00
...Code: Veronica 1-4 (2002, $14.95) English reprint of Japanese comics 15.00
...Collection One ('99, $14.95, TPB) r/#1-4 15.00

RESIDENT EVIL (Volume 2)
DC Comics (WildStorm): May, 2009 - No. 6, Feb, 2011 ($3.99)

1-6: 1,2-Liam Sharpe-a. 1-Two covers 4.00
...: Volume 2 TPB (2011, $19.99) r/#1-6 20.00

RESIDENT EVIL: FIRE AND ICE
DC Comics (WildStorm): Dec, 2000 - No. 4, May, 2001 ($2.50, limited series)

1-4-Bermejo-c 3.00
TPB (2009, $24.99) r/#1-4 plus short stories from Resident Evil magazine 25.00

RESISTANCE (Based on the video game)
DC Comics (WildStorm): Early Mar, 2009 - No. 6, Jul, 2009 ($3.99, limited series)

1-6-Ramón Pérez-a/C.P. Smith-c 4.00
TPB (2010, $19.99) r/#1-6 20.00

RESISTANCE, THE
DC Comics (WildStorm): Nov, 2002 - No. 8, June, 2003 ($2.95)

1-8-Palmiotti & Gray-s/Santacruz-a 3.00

REST (Milo Ventimiglia Presents...)
Devil's Due Publ.: No. 0, Aug, 2008 - Present (99¢/$3.50)

0-(99¢) Prelude to series; Powers-s/McManus-a 3.00
1,2-($3.50) 1-Two covers (Tim Sale art & Milo Ventimiglia photo) 3.50

RESTAURANT AT THE END OF THE UNIVERSE, THE (See Hitchhiker's Guide to the Galaxy & Life, the Universe & Everything)
DC Comics: 1994 - No. 3, 1994 ($6.95, limited series)

1-3 7.00

RESTLESS GUN (TV)
Dell Publishing Co.: No. 934, Sept, 1958 - No. 1146, Nov-Jan, 1960-61

Four Color 934 (#1)-Photo-c 10 20 30 67 124 180
Four Color 986 (5/59), 1045 (11-1/60), 1089 (3/60), 1146-Wildey-a; all photo-c 8 16 24 51 86 120

RESURRECTION MAN
DC Comics: May, 1997 - No. 27, Aug, 1999 ($2.50)

1-Lenticular disc on cover 5.00
2-5: 2-JLA app. 4.00
6-10: 6-Genesis-x-over. 7-Batman app. 10-Hitman-c/app. 3.00
11-27: 16,17-Supergirl x-over. 18-Deadman & Phantom Stranger-c/app. 21-JLA-c/app. 3.00
#1,000,000 (11/98) 853rd Century x-over 3.00

RESURRECTION MAN (DC New 52)
DC Comics: Nov, 2011 - Present ($2.99)

1-8: 1-Abnett & Lanning-s/Dagnino-a/Reis-c; Body Doubles app. 5-Blanco-a 3.00

RETIEF (Keith Laumer's)
Adventure Comics (Malibu): Dec, 1989 - Vol. 2, No.6, ($2.25, B&W)

1-6,Vol. 2, #1-6,Vol. 3 (...of The CDT) #1-6 3.00
...and The Warlords #1-6, ...: Diplomatic Immunity #1 (4/91), ...: Giant Killer #1 (9/91), ...: Crime & Punishment #1 (11/91) 3.00

Return of the Outlaw #6 © TOBY

Rex Mundi #0 © Nelson & Johnson

Richard Dragon, Kung-Fu Fighter #5 © DC

GD 2.0 | VG 4.0 | FN 6.0 | VF 8.0 | VF/NM 9.0 | NM- 9.2

RETURN FROM WITCH MOUNTAIN (See Walt Disney Showcase #44)

RETURN OF ALISON DARE: LITTLE MISS ADVENTURES, THE (Also see Alison Dare: Little Miss Adventures)
Oni Press: Apr, 2001 - No. 3, Sept, 2001 ($2.95, B&W, limited series)
1-3-J. Torres-s/J.Bone-c/a 3.00

RETURN OF GORGO, THE (Formerly Gorgo's Revenge)
Charlton Comics: No. 2, Aug, 1963; No. 3, Fall, 1964 (12¢)
2,3-Ditko-c/a; based on M.G.M. movie 8 16 24 56 96 135

RETURN OF KONGA, THE (Konga's Revenge #2 on)
Charlton Comics: 1962
nn 8 16 24 56 96 135

RETURN OF MEGATON MAN
Kitchen Sink Press: July, 1988 - No. 3, 1988 ($2.00, limited series)
1-3: Simpson-c/a 3.00

RETURN OF THE GREMLINS (The Roald Dahl characters)
Dark Horse Comics: Mar, 2008 - No. 3, May, 2008 ($2.99, limited series)
1-3-Richardson-s/Yeagle-a. 1-Back-up reprint of intro. from 1943. 2-Back-up reprints of three Gremlin Gus 2-pagers from 1943. 3-Back-up reprints 3.00

RETURN OF THE OUTLAW
Toby Press (Minoan): Feb, 1953 - No. 11, 1955
1-Billy the Kid 10 20 30 54 72 90
2 7 14 21 35 43 50
3-11 6 12 18 31 38 45

RETURN TO JURASSIC PARK
Topps Comics: Apr, 1995 - No. 9, Feb, 1996 ($2.50/$2.95)
1-9: 3-Begin $2.95-c. 9-Artist's Jam issue 3.00

RETURN TO THE AMALGAM AGE OF COMICS: THE MARVEL COMICS COLLECTION
Marvel Comics: 1997 ($12.95, TPB)
nn-Reprints Amalgam one-shots: Challengers of the Fantastic #1, The Exciting X-Patrol #1, Iron Lantern #1, The Magnetic Men Featuring Magneto #1, Spider-Boy Team-Up #1 & Thorion of the New Asgods #1 13.00

REVEAL
Dark Horse Comics: Nov, 2002 ($6.95, squarebound)
1-Short stories of Dark Horse characters by various; Lone Wolf 2100, Buffy, Spyboy app. 7.00

REVEALING LOVE STORIES (See Fox Giants)

REVEALING ROMANCES
Ace Magazines: Sept, 1949 - No. 6, Aug, 1950
1 15 30 45 86 133 180
2 10 20 30 54 72 90
3-6 9 18 27 50 65 80

REVELATIONS
Dark Horse Comics: Aug, 2005 - No. 6, Jan, 2006 ($2.99, limited series)
1-6-Paul Jenkins-s/Humberto Ramos-a/c 3.00

REVENGE OF THE PROWLER (Also see The Prowler)
Eclipse Comics: Feb, 1988 - No. 4, June, 1988 ($1.75/$1.95)
1,3,4: 1-$1.75. 3,4-$1.95-c; Snyder III-a(p) 3.00
2 ($2.50)-Contains flexi-disc 4.00

REVOLUTION ON THE PLANET OF THE APES
Mr. Comics: Dec, 2005 - No. 6, Aug, 2006 ($3.95)
1-6: 1,2-Salgood Sam-a 4.00

REX ALLEN COMICS (Movie star)(Also see Four Color #877 & Western Roundup under Dell Giants)
Dell Publ. Co.: No. 316, Feb, 1951 - No. 31, Dec-Feb, 1958-59 (All-photo-c)
Four Color 316(#1)(52 pgs.)-Rex Allen & his horse Koko begin; Marsh-a 12 24 36 84 175 265
2 (9-11/51, 36 pgs.) 9 18 27 61 106 150
3-10 7 14 21 44 72 100
11-20 6 12 18 39 62 85
21-23,25-31 5 10 15 35 55 75
24-Toth-a 6 12 18 39 62 85
NOTE: *Manning a-20, 27-30. Photo back-c F.C. #316, 2-12, 20, 21.*

REX DEXTER OF MARS (See Mystery Men Comics)
Fox Features Syndicate: Fall, 1940 (68 pgs.)
1-Rex Dexter, Patty O'Day, & Zanzibar (Tuska-a) app.; Briefer-c/a 206 412 618 1318 2259 3200

REX HART (Formerly Blaze Carson; Whip Wilson #9 on)
Timely/Marvel Comics (USA): No. 6, Aug, 1949 - No. 8, Feb, 1950 (All photo-c)
6-Rex Hart & his horse Warrior begin; Black Rider app; Captain Tootsie by Beck 26 52 78 152 249 345
7,8: 18 pg. Thriller in each. 8-Blaze the Wonder Collie app. in text 18 36 54 103 162 220

REX MORGAN, M.D. (Also see Harvey Comics Library)
Argo Publ.: Dec, 1955 - No. 3, Apr?, 1956
1-r/Rex Morgan daily newspaper strips & daily panel-r of "These Women" by D'Alessio & "Timeout" by Jeff Keate 14 28 42 76 108 140
2,3 10 20 30 54 72 90

REX MUNDI (Latin for "King of the World")
Image Comics: No. 0, Aug, 2002 - No. 18, Apr, 2006 ($2.95/$2.99)
0-18-Arvid Nelson-s. 0-13-Eric Johnson-a. 14,15-Jim DiBartolo-a. 18-Ramos-c 3.00
Vol. 1: The Guardian of the Temple TPB (1/04, $14.95) r/#0-5 15.00
Book 1: The Guardian of the Temple TPB (Dark Horse, 11/06, $16.95) r/#0-5 & Brother Matthew web comic; Dysart intro. 17.00
Vol. 2: The River Underground TPB (4/05, $14.95) r/#6-11 15.00
Book 2: The River Underground (Dark Horse, 2006, $16.95) r/#6-11 17.00
Vol. 3: The Lost Kings TPB (Dark Horse, 9/06, $16.95) r/#12-17 17.00
Book Four: Crowd and Sword TPB (Dark Horse, 12/07, $16.95) r/#18 plus V2 #1-5 and story from Dark Horse Book of Monsters 17.00

REX MUNDI (Volume 2)
Dark Horse Comics: July, 2006 - No. 19, Aug, 2009 ($2.99)
1-19-Arvid Nelson-s. 1-JH Williams-c. 16-Chen-c. 18-Linsner-c 3.00
Book Five: The Valley at the End of the World TPB (11/08, $17.95) r/#6-12 18.00

REX THE WONDER DOG (See The Adventures of...)

RHUBARB, THE MILLIONAIRE CAT
Dell Publishing Co.: No. 423, Sept-Oct, 1952 - No. 563, June, 1954
Four Color 423 (#1) 6 12 18 39 62 85
Four Color 466(5/53),563 5 10 15 35 55 75

RIB
Dilemma Productions: Oct, 1995 - April, 1996 ($1.95, B&W)
Ashcan, 1 3.00

RIB
Bookmark Productions: 1996 ($2.95, B&W)
1-Sakai-c; Andrew Ford-s/a 3.00

RIB
Caliber Comics: May, 1997 - No. 5, 1998 ($2.95, B&W)
1-5: 1-"Beginnings" pts. 1 & 2 3.00

RIBIT! (Red Sonja imitation)
Comico: Jan, 1989 - No. 4, April?, 1989 ($1.95, limited series)
1-4: Frank Thorne-c/a/scripts 3.00

RIBTICKLER (Also see Fox Giants)
Fox Feature Synd./Green Publ. (1957)/Norlen (1959): 1945, No. 2, 1946, No. 3, Jul-Aug, 1946 - No. 9, Jul-Aug, 1947; 1957; 1959
1-Funny animal 15 30 45 90 140 190
2-(1946) 10 20 30 54 72 90
3-9: 3,5,7-Cosmo Cat app. 9 18 27 47 61 75
3,7,8 (Green Publ.-1957), 3,7,8 (Norlen Mag.-1959) 3 6 9 16 23 30

RICHARD DRAGON
DC Comics: July, 2004 - No. 12, Jun, 2005 ($2.50)
1-12: 1-Dixon-s/McDaniel-a/c; Ben Turner app. 2,3-Nightwing app. 4-6,11,12-Lady Shiva 3.00

RICHARD DRAGON, KUNG-FU FIGHTER (See The Batman Chronicles #5, Brave & the Bold, & The Question)
National Periodical Publ./DC Comics: Apr-May, 1975 - No. 18, Nov-Dec, 1977
1-Intro Richard Dragon, Ben Stanley & O-Sensei; 1st app. Barney Ling; adaptation of Jim Dennis novel "Dragon's Fists" begins, ends #4 3 6 9 14 20 26
2,3: 2-Intro Carolyn Woosan; Starlin/Weiss-c/a; bondage-c. 3-Kirby-a(p); Giordano bondage-c 2 4 6 9 12 15
4-8-Wood inks. 4-Carolyn Woosan dies. 5-1st app. Lady Shiva 2 4 6 8 10 12
9-13,15-18: 9-Ben Stanley becomes Ben Turner; intro Preying Mantis. 16-1st app. Prof Ojo. 18-1st app. Ben Turner as The Bronze Tiger 1 3 4 6 8 10
14-"Spirit of Bruce Lee" 3 6 9 14 20 26

Richie Rich #18 © HARV

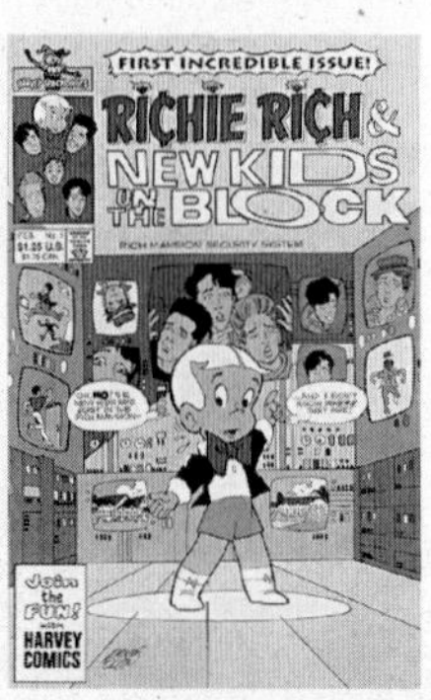

Richie Rich and the New Kids on the Block #1 © HARV

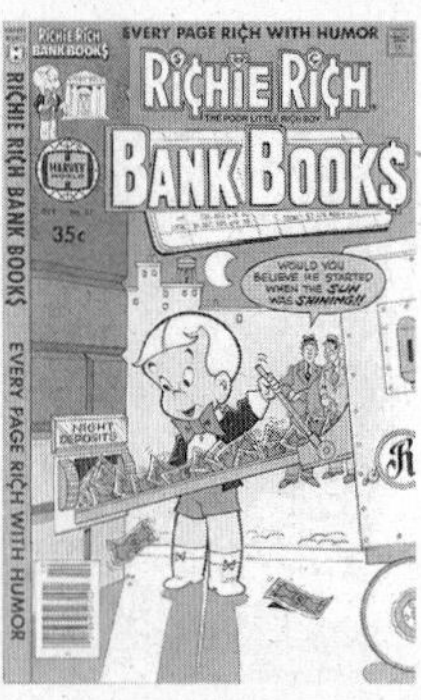

Richie Rich Bank Books #37 © HARV

NOTE: **Buckler** *a-14. c-15, 18.* **Chua** *c-13.* **Estrada** *a-9, 13-18.* **Estrada/Abel** *a-10-12.* **Estrada/Wood** *a-4-8.* **Giordano** *c-1, 3-11.* **Weiss** *a-2(partial) c-2i.*

RICHARD THE LION-HEARTED (See Ideal a Classical Comic)

RICHIE RICH (See Harvey Collectors Comics, Harvey Hits, Little Dot, Little Lotta, Little Sad Sack, Million Dollar Digest, Mutt & Jeff, Super Richie & 3-D Dolly; also Tastee-Freez Comics in the Promotional Comics section)

RICHIE RICH (...the Poor Little Rich Boy) (See Harvey Hits #3, 9)
Harvey Publ.: Nov, 1960 - #218, Oct, 1982; #219, Oct, 1986 - #254, Jan, 1991

	GD 2.0	VG 4.0	FN 6.0	VF 8.0	VF/NM 9.0	NM- 9.2
1-(See Little Dot #1 for 1st app.)	250	500	750	2100	4550	7000
2	72	144	216	583	1267	1950
3-5	46	92	138	345	748	1150
6-10: 8-Christmas-c	27	54	81	189	407	625
11-20	17	34	51	114	250	385
21-30	12	24	36	81	166	250
31-40	10	20	30	68	127	185
41-50: 42(2/66)-X-mas-c	8	16	24	56	96	135
51-55,57-60: 59-Buck, prototype of Dollar the Dog	6	12	18	41	66	90
56-1st app. Super Richie	7	14	21	48	79	110
61-64,66-80: 71-Nixon & Robert Kennedy caricatures; outer space-c	5	10	15	30	48	65
65-Buck the Dog (Dollar prototype) on cover	6	12	18	42	69	95
81-99	4	8	12	22	34	45
100(12/70)-1st app. Irona the robot maid	4	8	12	26	41	55
101-111,117-120	3	6	9	14	20	26
112-116: All 52 pg. Giants	3	6	9	17	25	32
121-140: 137-1st app. Mr. Cheepers and Professor Keenbean	2	4	6	9	13	16
141-160: 145-Infinity-c. 155-3rd app. The Money Monster	2	4	6	8	10	12
161-180	1	3	4	6	8	10
181-199	1	2	3	5	6	8
200	1	3	4	6	8	10
201-218: 210-Stone-Age Riches app	1	2	3	4	5	7
219-254: 237-Last original material						6.00
Harvey Comics Classics Vol. 2 TPB (Dark Horse Books, 10/07, $19.95) Reprints Richie Rich's early appearances in this title, Little Dot and Richie Rich Success Stories, mostly B&W with some color stories; history and interview with Ernie Colón						20.00

RICHIE RICH
Harvey Comics: Mar, 1991 - No. 28, Nov, 1994 ($1.00, bi-monthly)

	GD 2.0	VG 4.0	FN 6.0	VF 8.0	VF/NM 9.0	NM- 9.2
1-28: Reprints best of Richie Rich						3.00
Giant Size 1-4 (10/91-10/93, $2.25, 68 pgs.)						4.00

RICHIE RICH ADVENTURE DIGEST MAGAZINE
Harvey Comics: 1992 - No. 7, Sept, 1994 ($1.25, quarterly, digest-size)

	GD 2.0	VG 4.0	FN 6.0	VF 8.0	VF/NM 9.0	NM- 9.2
1-7						4.00

RICHIE RICH AND...
Harvey Comics: Oct, 1987 - No. 11, May, 1990 ($1.00)

	GD 2.0	VG 4.0	FN 6.0	VF 8.0	VF/NM 9.0	NM- 9.2
1-Professor Keenbean						4.00
2-11: 2-Casper. 3-Dollar the Dog. 4-Cadbury. 5 Mayda Munny. 6-Irona. 7-Little Dot. 8-Professor Keenbean. 9-Little Audrey. 10-Mayda Munny. 11-Cadbury						3.00

RICHIE RICH AND BILLY BELLHOPS
Harvey Publications: Oct, 1977 (52 pgs., one-shot)

	GD 2.0	VG 4.0	FN 6.0	VF 8.0	VF/NM 9.0	NM- 9.2
1	2	4	6	11	16	20

RICHIE RICH AND CADBURY
Harvey Publ.: 10/77; #2, 9/78 - #23, 7/82; #24, 7/90 - #29, 1/91 (1-10: 52pgs.)

	GD 2.0	VG 4.0	FN 6.0	VF 8.0	VF/NM 9.0	NM- 9.2
1-(52 pg. Giant)	2	4	6	11	16	20
2-10-(52 pg. Giant)	2	4	6	8	10	12
11-23						6.00
24-29: 24-Begin $1.00-c						4.00

RICHIE RICH AND CASPER
Harvey Publications: Aug, 1974 - No. 45, Sept, 1982

	GD 2.0	VG 4.0	FN 6.0	VF 8.0	VF/NM 9.0	NM- 9.2
1	3	6	9	20	30	40
2-5	2	4	6	13	18	22
6-10: 10-Xmas-c	2	4	6	9	13	16
11-20	1	3	4	6	8	10
21-45: 22-Xmas-c						6.00

RICHIE RICH AND DOLLAR THE DOG (See Richie Rich #65)
Harvey Publications: Sept, 1977 - No. 24, Aug, 1982 (#1-10: 52 pgs.)

	GD 2.0	VG 4.0	FN 6.0	VF 8.0	VF/NM 9.0	NM- 9.2
1-(52 pg. Giant)	2	4	6	11	16	20
2-10-(52 pg. Giant)	2	4	6	8	10	12
11-24						6.00

RICHIE RICH AND DOT
Harvey Publications: Oct, 1974 (one-shot)

	GD 2.0	VG 4.0	FN 6.0	VF 8.0	VF/NM 9.0	NM- 9.2
1	3	6	9	16	22	28

RICHIE RICH AND GLORIA
Harvey Publications: Sept, 1977 - No. 25, Sept, 1982 (#1-11: 52 pgs.)

	GD 2.0	VG 4.0	FN 6.0	VF 8.0	VF/NM 9.0	NM- 9.2
1-(52 pg. Giant)	2	4	6	11	16	20
2-11-(52 pg. Giant)	2	4	6	8	10	12
12-25						6.00

RICHIE RICH AND HIS GIRLFRIENDS
Harvey Publications: April, 1979 - No. 16, Dec, 1982

	GD 2.0	VG 4.0	FN 6.0	VF 8.0	VF/NM 9.0	NM- 9.2
1-(52 pg. Giant)	2	4	6	9	13	16
2-(52 pg. Giant)	1	3	4	6	8	10
3-10	1	2	3	5	6	8
11-16						6.00

RICHIE RICH AND HIS MEAN COUSIN REGGIE
Harvey Publications: April, 1979 - No. 3, 1980 (50¢) (#1,2: 52 pgs.)

	GD 2.0	VG 4.0	FN 6.0	VF 8.0	VF/NM 9.0	NM- 9.2
1	2	4	6	9	13	16
2-3:	1	3	4	6	8	10

NOTE: *No. 4 was advertised, but never released.*

RICHIE RICH AND JACKIE JOKERS (Also see Jackie Jokers)
Harvey Publications: Nov, 1973 - No. 48, Dec, 1982

	GD 2.0	VG 4.0	FN 6.0	VF 8.0	VF/NM 9.0	NM- 9.2
1: 52 pg. Giant; contains material from unpublished Jackie Jokers #5	4	8	12	24	37	50
2,3-(52 pg. Giants). 2-R.R. & Jackie 1st meet	3	6	9	16	22	28
4,5	2	4	6	13	18	22
6-10	2	4	6	9	13	16
11-20,26: 11-1st app. Kool Katz. 26-Star Wars parody	1	3	4	6	8	10
21-25,27-40	1	2	3	4	5	7
41-48						6.00

RICHIE RICH AND PROFESSOR KEENBEAN
Harvey Comics: Sept, 1990 - No. 2, Nov, 1990 ($1.00)

	GD 2.0	VG 4.0	FN 6.0	VF 8.0	VF/NM 9.0	NM- 9.2
1,2						3.00

RICHIE RICH AND THE NEW KIDS ON THE BLOCK
Harvey Publications: Feb, 1991 - No. 3, June, 1991 ($1.25, bi-monthly)

	GD 2.0	VG 4.0	FN 6.0	VF 8.0	VF/NM 9.0	NM- 9.2
1-3: 1,2-New Richie Rich stories						4.00

RICHIE RICH AND TIMMY TIME
Harvey Publications: Sept, 1977 (50¢, 52 pgs, one-shot)

	GD 2.0	VG 4.0	FN 6.0	VF 8.0	VF/NM 9.0	NM- 9.2
1	2	4	6	11	16	20

RICHIE RICH BANK BOOK
Harvey Publications: Oct, 1972 - No. 59, Sept, 1982

	GD 2.0	VG 4.0	FN 6.0	VF 8.0	VF/NM 9.0	NM- 9.2
1	5	10	15	30	48	65
2-5: 2-2nd app. The Money Monster	3	6	9	16	23	30
6-10	2	4	6	11	16	20
11-20: 18-Super Richie app.	2	4	6	8	10	12
21-30	1	2	3	5	7	9
31-40	1	2	3	4	5	7
41-59						6.00

RICHIE RICH BEST OF THE YEARS
Harvey Publications: Oct, 1977 - No. 6, June, 1980 (128 pgs., digest-size)

	GD 2.0	VG 4.0	FN 6.0	VF 8.0	VF/NM 9.0	NM- 9.2
1(10/77)-Reprints	2	4	6	9	12	15
2-6(11/79-6/80, 95¢). #2(10/78)-Rep.. #3(6/79, 75¢)	1	2	3	5	7	9

RICHIE RICH BIG BOOK
Harvey Publications: Nov, 1992 - No. 2, May, 1993 ($1.50, 52 pgs.)

	GD 2.0	VG 4.0	FN 6.0	VF 8.0	VF/NM 9.0	NM- 9.2
1,2						4.00

RICHIE RICH BIG BUCKS
Harvey Publications: Apr, 1991 - No. 8, July, 1992 ($1.00, bi-monthly)

	GD 2.0	VG 4.0	FN 6.0	VF 8.0	VF/NM 9.0	NM- 9.2
1-8						3.00

RICHIE RICH BILLIONS
Harvey Publications: Oct, 1974 - No. 48, Oct, 1982 (#1-33: 52 pgs.)

	GD 2.0	VG 4.0	FN 6.0	VF 8.0	VF/NM 9.0	NM- 9.2
1	4	8	12	22	34	45
2-5: 2-Christmas issue	3	6	9	14	20	25
6-10	2	4	6	10	14	18
11-20	2	4	6	8	10	12
21-33	1	2	3	5	6	8
34-48: 35-Onion app.						6.00

RICHIE RICH CASH

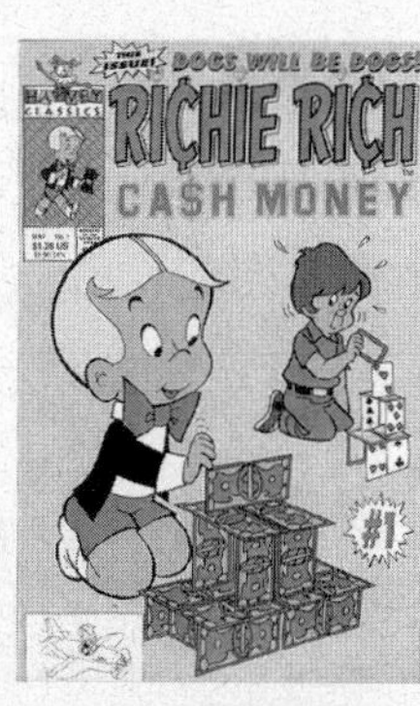

Richie Rich Cash Money #1 © HARV

Richie Rich Dollars & Cents #69 © HARV

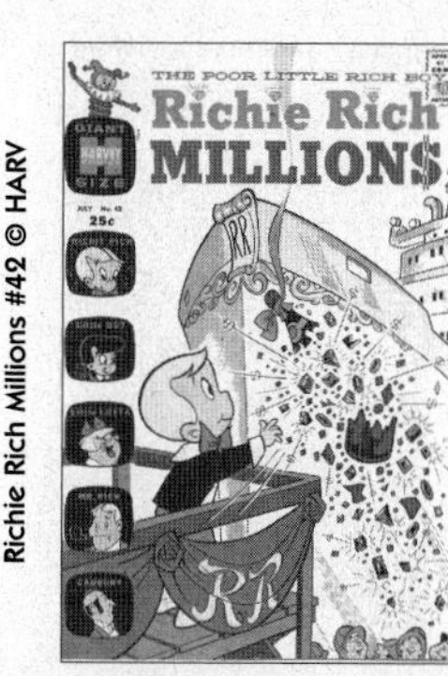

Richie Rich Millions #42 © HARV

Harvey Publications: Sept, 1974 - No. 47, Aug, 1982

	GD 2.0	VG 4.0	FN 6.0	VF 8.0	VF/NM 9.0	NM- 9.2
1-1st app. Dr. N-R-Gee	3	6	9	20	30	40
2-5	2	4	6	13	18	22
6-10	2	4	6	9	13	16
11-20	1	3	4	6	8	10
21-30	1	2	3	4	5	7
31-47: 33-Dr. Blemish app.						6.00

RICHIE RICH CASH MONEY
Harvey Comics: May, 1992 - No. 2, Aug, 1992 ($1.25)

	GD 2.0	VG 4.0	FN 6.0	VF 8.0	VF/NM 9.0	NM- 9.2
1,2						3.00

RICHIE RICH, CASPER AND WENDY - NATIONAL LEAGUE
Harvey Comics: June, 1976 (50¢)

	GD 2.0	VG 4.0	FN 6.0	VF 8.0	VF/NM 9.0	NM- 9.2
1-Newsstand version of the baseball giveaway	2	4	6	13	18	22

RICHIE RICH COLLECTORS COMICS (See Harvey Collectors Comics)

RICHIE RICH DIAMONDS
Harvey Publications: Aug, 1972 - No. 59, Aug, 1982 (#1, 23-45: 52 pgs.)

	GD 2.0	VG 4.0	FN 6.0	VF 8.0	VF/NM 9.0	NM- 9.2
1-(52 pg. Giant)	5	10	15	32	51	70
2-5	3	6	9	16	23	30
6-10	2	4	6	11	16	20
11-22	2	4	6	8	10	12
23-30-(52 pg. Giants)	2	4	6	8	11	14
31-45: 39-r/Origin Little Dot	1	2	3	5	7	9
46-50	1	2	3	4	5	7
51-59						6.00

RICHIE RICH DIGEST MAGAZINE
Harvey Publications: Oct, 1986 - No. 42, Oct, 1994 ($1.25/$1.75, digest-size)

	GD 2.0	VG 4.0	FN 6.0	VF 8.0	VF/NM 9.0	NM- 9.2
1	1	2	3	5	6	8
2-10						5.00
11-20						4.00
21-42						4.00

RICHIE RICH DIGEST STORIES (...Magazine #?-on)
Harvey Publications: Oct, 1977 - No., 17, Oct, 1982 (75¢/95¢, digest-size)

	GD 2.0	VG 4.0	FN 6.0	VF 8.0	VF/NM 9.0	NM- 9.2
1-Reprints	2	4	6	9	12	15
2-10: Reprints	1	2	3	5	7	9
11-17: Reprints						6.00

RICHIE RICH DIGEST WINNERS
Harvey Publications: Dec, 1977 - No. 16, Sept, 1982 (75¢/95¢, 132 pgs., digest-size)

	GD 2.0	VG 4.0	FN 6.0	VF 8.0	VF/NM 9.0	NM- 9.2
1	2	4	6	9	12	15
2-5	1	2	3	5	7	9
6-16						6.00

RICHIE RICH DOLLARS & CENTS
Harvey Publications: Aug, 1963 - No. 109, Aug, 1982 (#1-43: 68 pgs.; 44-60, 71-94: 52 pgs.)

	GD 2.0	VG 4.0	FN 6.0	VF 8.0	VF/NM 9.0	NM- 9.2
1: (#1-64 are all reprint issues)	16	32	48	109	237	365
2	10	20	30	67	124	180
3-5: 5-r/1st app. of R.R. from Little Dot #1	9	18	27	61	106	150
6-10	7	14	21	46	76	105
11-20	5	10	15	30	48	65
21-30: 25-r/1st app. Nurse Jenny (Little Lotta #62)	4	8	12	22	34	45
31-43: 43-Last 68 pg. issue	3	6	9	18	27	35
44-60: All 52 pgs.	3	6	9	14	19	25
61-71	1	3	4	6	8	10
72-94: All 52 pgs.	2	4	6	8	10	12
95-99,101-109						6.00
100-Anniversary issue	1	2	3	5	7	9

RICHIE RICH FORTUNES
Harvey Publications: Sept, 1971 - No. 63, July, 1982 (#1-15: 52 pgs.)

	GD 2.0	VG 4.0	FN 6.0	VF 8.0	VF/NM 9.0	NM- 9.2
1	6	12	18	39	62	85
2-5	3	6	9	20	30	40
6-10	2	4	6	13	18	22
11-15: 11-r/1st app. The Onion	2	4	6	9	12	15
16-30	1	2	3	5	7	9
31-40	1	2	3	4	5	7
41-63: 62-Onion app.						6.00

RICHIE RICH GEMS
Harvey Publications: Sept, 1974 - No. 43, Sept, 1982

	GD 2.0	VG 4.0	FN 6.0	VF 8.0	VF/NM 9.0	NM- 9.2
1	3	6	9	20	30	40
2-5	2	4	6	13	18	22
6-10	2	4	6	9	13	16
11-20	1	3	4	6	8	10
21-30	1	2	3	4	5	7
31-43: 36-Dr. Blemish, Onion app. 38-1st app. Stone-Age Riches						6.00
44 (Ape Entertainment, 2011, $3.99) new story w/Colon-a & reprints						4.00
... Valentines Special (Ape Entertainment, 2012, $3.99) new story w/Colon-a & reprints						4.00
... Winter Special (Ape Entertainment, 2011, $3.99) new story w/Colon-a & reprints						4.00

RICHIE RICH GOLD AND SILVER
Harvey Publications: Sept, 1975 - No. 42, Oct, 1982 (#1-27: 52 pgs.)

	GD 2.0	VG 4.0	FN 6.0	VF 8.0	VF/NM 9.0	NM- 9.2
1	3	6	9	18	27	35
2-5	2	4	6	11	16	20
6-10	2	4	6	8	11	14
11-27	1	2	3	5	7	9
28-42: 34-Stone-Age Riches app.						6.00

RICHIE RICH GOLD NUGGETS DIGEST
Harvey Publications: Dec., 1990 - No. 4, June, 1991 ($1.75, digest-size)

	GD 2.0	VG 4.0	FN 6.0	VF 8.0	VF/NM 9.0	NM- 9.2
1-4						3.00

RICHIE RICH HOLIDAY DIGEST MAGAZINE (...Digest #4)
Harvey Publications: Jan, 1980 - #3, Jan, 1982; #4, 3/88; #5, 2/89 (annual)

	GD 2.0	VG 4.0	FN 6.0	VF 8.0	VF/NM 9.0	NM- 9.2
1-X-Mas-c	1	3	4	6	8	10
2-5: 2,3: All X-Mas-c. 4-(3/88, $1.25), 5-(2/89, $1.75)	1	2	3	4	5	7

RICHIE RICH INVENTIONS
Harvey Publications: Oct, 1977 - No. 26, Oct, 1982 (#1-11: 52 pgs.)

	GD 2.0	VG 4.0	FN 6.0	VF 8.0	VF/NM 9.0	NM- 9.2
1	2	4	6	11	16	20
2-5	2	4	6	8	10	12
6-11	1	2	3	5	6	8
12-26						6.00

RICHIE RICH JACKPOTS
Harvey Publications: Oct, 1972 - No. 58, Aug, 1982 (#41-43: 52 pgs.)

	GD 2.0	VG 4.0	FN 6.0	VF 8.0	VF/NM 9.0	NM- 9.2
1-Debut of Cousin Jackpots	5	10	15	30	48	65
2-5	3	6	9	16	23	30
6-10	2	4	6	11	16	20
11-15,17-20	2	4	6	8	10	12
16-Super Richie app.	2	4	6	9	12	15
21-30	1	2	3	5	7	9
31-40,44-50: 37-Caricatures of Frank Sinatra, Dean Martin, Sammy Davis, Jr. 45-Dr. Blemish app.	1	2	3	4	5	7
41-43 (52 pgs.)	1	3	4	6	8	10
51-58						6.00

RICHIE RICH MILLION DOLLAR DIGEST (...Magazine #?-on)(See Million Dollar Digest)
Harvey Publications: Oct, 1980 - No. 10, Oct, 1982 ($1.50)

	GD 2.0	VG 4.0	FN 6.0	VF 8.0	VF/NM 9.0	NM- 9.2
1	1	3	4	6	8	10
2-10						6.00

RICHIE RICH MILLIONS
Harvey Publ.: 9/61; #2, 9/62 - #113, 10/82 (#1-48: 68 pgs.; 49-64, 85-97: 52 pgs.)

	GD 2.0	VG 4.0	FN 6.0	VF 8.0	VF/NM 9.0	NM- 9.2
1: (#1-3 are all reprint issues)	19	38	57	128	277	425
2	11	22	33	71	136	200
3-5: All other giants are new & reprints. 5-1st 15 pg. Richie Rich story	9	18	27	63	112	160
6-10	8	16	24	56	96	135
11-20	6	12	18	41	66	90
21-30	4	8	12	28	44	60
31-48: 31-1st app. The Onion. 48-Last 68 pg. Giant	3	6	9	20	30	40
49-64: 52 pg. Giants	3	6	9	14	20	25
65-67,69-73,75-84	2	4	6	8	10	12
68-1st Super Richie-c (11/74)	2	4	6	13	18	22
74-1st app. Mr. Woody; Super Richie app.	2	4	6	8	11	14
85-97: 52 pg. Giants	2	4	6	8	11	14
98,99	1	2	3	4	5	7
100	1	2	3	5	7	9
101-113						6.00

RICHIE RICH MONEY WORLD
Harvey Publications: Sept, 1972 - No. 59, Sept, 1982

	GD 2.0	VG 4.0	FN 6.0	VF 8.0	VF/NM 9.0	NM- 9.2
1-(52 pg. Giant)-1st app. Mayda Munny	6	12	18	37	59	80
2-Super Richie app.	3	6	9	18	27	35
3-5	3	6	9	16	23	30
6-10: 9,10-Richie Rich mistakenly named Little Lotta on covers	2	4	6	11	16	20
11-20: 16,20-Dr. N-R-Gee	2	4	6	8	10	12
21-30	1	2	3	5	7	9

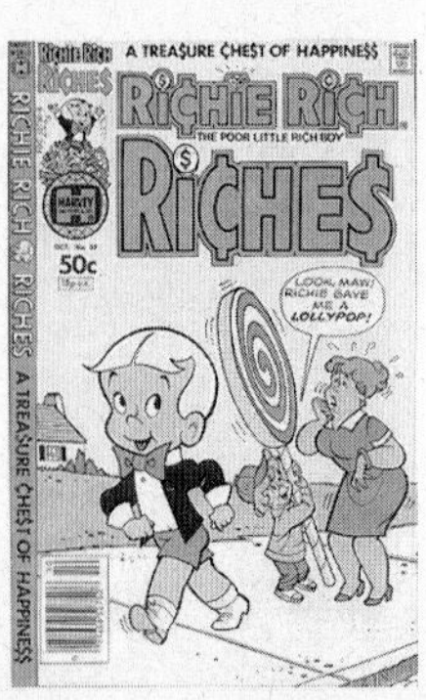

Richie Rich Riches #55 © HARV

Richie Rich: Rich Rescue #3 © Classic Media

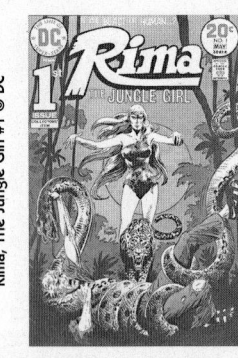

Rima, The Jungle Girl #1 © DC

	GD 2.0	VG 4.0	FN 6.0	VF 8.0	VF/NM 9.0	NM- 9.2
31-50	1	2	3	4	5	7
51-59						6.00
Digest 1 (2/91, $1.75)						5.00
2-8 (12/93, $1.75)						3.00

RICHIE RICH PROFITS
Harvey Publications: Oct, 1974 - No. 47, Sept, 1982

	GD 2.0	VG 4.0	FN 6.0	VF 8.0	VF/NM 9.0	NM- 9.2
1	3	6	9	20	30	40
2-5	2	4	6	13	18	22
6-10: 10-Origin of Dr. N-R-Gee	2	4	6	9	13	16
11-20: 15-Christmas-c	1	3	4	6	8	10
21-30	1	2	3	4	5	7
31-47						6.00

RICHIE RICH RELICS
Harvey Comics: Jan, 1988 - No.4, Feb, 1989 (75¢/$1.00, reprints)

	GD 2.0	VG 4.0	FN 6.0	VF 8.0	VF/NM 9.0	NM- 9.2
1-4						3.00

RICHIE RICH RICHES
Harvey Publications: July, 1972 - No. 59, Aug, 1982 (#1, 2, 41-45: 52 pgs.)

	GD 2.0	VG 4.0	FN 6.0	VF 8.0	VF/NM 9.0	NM- 9.2
1-(52 pg. Giant)-1st app. The Money Monster	6	12	18	37	59	80
2-(52 pg. Giant)	3	6	9	20	30	40
3-5	3	6	9	16	23	30
6-10: 7-1st app. Aunt Novo	2	4	6	11	16	20
11-20: 17-Super Richie app. (3/75)	2	4	6	8	10	12
21-40	1	2	3	5	6	8
41-45: 52 pg. Giants	1	3	4	6	8	10
46-59: 56-Dr. Blemish app.						6.00

RICHIE RICH: RICH RESCUE
Ape Entertainment: 2011 - No. 4, 2011 ($3.95, limited series)

	GD 2.0	VG 4.0	FN 6.0	VF 8.0	VF/NM 9.0	NM- 9.2
1-4-New short stories by various incl. Ernie Colon; Jack Lawrence-c						4.00
FCBD Edition (2011, giveaway) Flip book with Kung Fu Panda						3.00

RICHIE RICH SUCCESS STORIES
Harvey Publications: Nov, 1964 - No. 105, Sept, 1982 (#1-38: 68 pgs., 39-55, 67-90: 52 pgs.)

	GD 2.0	VG 4.0	FN 6.0	VF 8.0	VF/NM 9.0	NM- 9.2
1	15	30	45	102	221	340
2	10	20	30	64	115	165
3-5	9	18	27	58	99	140
6-10	6	12	18	41	66	90
11-20	5	10	15	35	55	75
21-30: 27-1st Penny Van Dough (8/69)	4	8	12	24	37	50
31-38: 38-Last 68 pg. Giant	3	6	9	20	30	40
39-55-(52 pgs.): 44-Super Richie app.	3	6	9	14	20	25
56-66	2	4	6	8	10	12
67-90: 52 pgs.	2	4	6	8	11	14
91-99,101-105: 91-Onion app. 101-Dr. Blemish app.						6.00
100	1	2	3	5	7	9

RICHIE RICH SUMMER BONANZA
Harvey Comics: Oct, 1991 ($1.95, one-shot, 68 pgs.)

	GD 2.0	VG 4.0	FN 6.0	VF 8.0	VF/NM 9.0	NM- 9.2
1-Richie Rich, Little Dot, Little Lotta						4.00

RICHIE RICH TREASURE CHEST DIGEST (...Magazine #3)
Harvey Publications: Apr, 1982 - No. 3, Aug, 1982 (95¢, Digest Mag.)
(#4 advertised but not publ.)

	GD 2.0	VG 4.0	FN 6.0	VF 8.0	VF/NM 9.0	NM- 9.2
1	1	2	3	5	7	9
2,3	1	2	3	4	5	7

RICHIE RICH VACATION DIGEST
Harvey Comics: Oct, 1991; Oct, 1992; Oct, 1993 ($1.75, digest-size)

	GD 2.0	VG 4.0	FN 6.0	VF 8.0	VF/NM 9.0	NM- 9.2
1-(10/91), 1-(10/92), 1-(10/93)						4.00

RICHIE RICH VACATIONS DIGEST
Harvey Publ.: 11/77; No. 2, 10/78 - No. 7, 10/81; No. 8, 8/82; No. 9, 10/82 (Digest, 132 pgs.)

	GD 2.0	VG 4.0	FN 6.0	VF 8.0	VF/NM 9.0	NM- 9.2
1-Reprints	2	4	6	9	12	15
2-6	1	2	3	5	7	9
7-9						6.00

RICHIE RICH VAULT OF MYSTERY
Harvey Publications: Nov, 1974 - No. 47, Sept, 1982

	GD 2.0	VG 4.0	FN 6.0	VF 8.0	VF/NM 9.0	NM- 9.2
1	3	6	9	20	30	40
2-5: 5-The Condor app.	2	4	6	13	18	22
6-10	2	4	6	9	13	16
11-20	1	3	4	6	8	10
21-30	1	2	3	4	5	7
31-47						6.00

RICHIE RICH ZILLIONZ
Harvey Publ.: Oct, 1976 - No. 33, Sept, 1982 (#1-4: 68 pgs.; #5-18: 52 pgs.)

	GD 2.0	VG 4.0	FN 6.0	VF 8.0	VF/NM 9.0	NM- 9.2
1	3	6	9	18	27	35
2-4: 4-Last 68 pg. Giant	2	4	6	11	16	20
5-10	2	4	6	8	10	12
11-18: 18-Last 52 pg. Giant	1	2	3	5	6	8
19-33						6.00

RICKY
Standard Comics (Visual Editions): No. 5, Sept, 1953

	GD 2.0	VG 4.0	FN 6.0	VF 8.0	VF/NM 9.0	NM- 9.2
5-Teenage humor	6	12	18	29	36	42

RICKY NELSON (TV)(See Sweethearts V2#42)
Dell Publishing Co.: No. 956, Dec, 1958 - No. 1192, June, 1961 (All photo-c)

	GD 2.0	VG 4.0	FN 6.0	VF 8.0	VF/NM 9.0	NM- 9.2
Four Color 956,998	15	30	45	102	221	340
Four Color 1115,1192: 1192-Manning-a	12	24	36	84	175	265

RIDE, THE (Also see Gun Candy flip-book)
Image Comics: June, 2004 - No. 2, July, 2004 ($2.95, B&W, anthology)

	GD 2.0	VG 4.0	FN 6.0	VF 8.0	VF/NM 9.0	NM- 9.2
1,2: Hughes-c/Wagner-s. 1-Hamner & Stelfreeze-a. 2-Jeanty & Pearson-a						3.00
... Die Valkyrie 1-3 (6/07 - No. 3, 2/08, $2.99) Stelfreeze-a/Wagner-s/Pearson-c						3.00
... Foreign Parts 1 (1/05, $2.95) Dixon-s/Haynes-a; Marz-s/Brunner-a; Pearson-c						3.00
... Halloween Special: The Key to Survival (10/07, $3.50) Tomm Coker-s/a						3.50
... Savannah 1 (4/07, $4.99) s/a by students of Savannah College of Art						5.00
... 2 For the Road 1 (10/04, $2.95) Dixon-s/Hamner & Gregory-a/Johnson-c						3.00
Vol. 1 TPB (2005, $9.99) r/#1,2, Foreign Parts, 2 For the Road; Chaykin intro.						10.00
Vol. 2 TPB (2005, $15.99) r/Gun Candy #1,2 & Die Valkyrie #1-3; sketch pages						16.00

RIDER, THE (Frontier Trail #6; also see Blazing Sixguns I.W. Reprint #10, 11)
Ajax/Farrell Publ. (Four Star Comic Corp.): Mar, 1957 - No. 5, 1958

	GD 2.0	VG 4.0	FN 6.0	VF 8.0	VF/NM 9.0	NM- 9.2
1-Swift Arrow, Lone Rider begin	13	26	39	72	101	130
2-5	8	16	24	42	54	65

RIDERS OF THE PURPLE SAGE (See Zane Grey & Four Color #372)

RIFLEMAN, THE (TV)
Dell Publ. Co./Gold Key No. 13 on: No. 1009, 7-9/59 - No. 12, 7-9/62; No. 13, 11/62 - No. 20, 10/64

	GD 2.0	VG 4.0	FN 6.0	VF 8.0	VF/NM 9.0	NM- 9.2
Four Color 1009 (#1)	19	38	57	128	277	425
2 (1-3/60)	11	22	33	71	136	200
3-Toth-a (4 pgs.); variant edition has back-c with "Something Special" comic strip	11	22	33	71	136	200
4-10: 6-Toth-a (4 pgs.)	10	20	30	66	121	175
11-20	8	16	24	53	89	125

NOTE: ***Warren Tufts** a-2-9. All have Chuck Connors & Johnny Crawford photo-c. Photo back c-13-15.*

RIFTWAR
Marvel Comics: July, 2009 - No. 5, Dec, 2009 ($3.99, limited series)

	GD 2.0	VG 4.0	FN 6.0	VF 8.0	VF/NM 9.0	NM- 9.2
1-5-Adaptation of Raymond E. Feist novel; Glass-s/Stegman-a						4.00

RIMA, THE JUNGLE GIRL
National Periodical Publications: Apr-May, 1974 - No. 7, Apr-May, 1975

	GD 2.0	VG 4.0	FN 6.0	VF 8.0	VF/NM 9.0	NM- 9.2
1-Origin, part 1 (#1-5: 20¢; 6,7: 25¢)	2	4	6	13	18	22
2-7: 2-4-Origin, parts 2-4. 7-Origin & only app. Space Marshal	2	3	4	6	8	10

NOTE: ***Kubert** c-1-7. **Nino** a-1-7. **Redondo** a-1-7.*

RING OF BRIGHT WATER (See Movie Classics)

RING OF THE NIBELUNG, THE
DC Comics: 1989 - No. 4, 1990 ($4.95, squarebound, 52 pgs., mature readers)

	GD 2.0	VG 4.0	FN 6.0	VF 8.0	VF/NM 9.0	NM- 9.2
1-4: Adapts Wagner cycle of operas, Gil Kane-c/a						5.00

RING OF THE NIBELUNG, THE
Dark Horse Comics: Feb, 2000 - Sept, 2001 ($2.95/$2.99/$5.99, limited series)

	GD 2.0	VG 4.0	FN 6.0	VF 8.0	VF/NM 9.0	NM- 9.2
Vol. 1 (The Rhinegold) 1-4: Adapts Wagner; P. Craig Russell-s/a						3.00
Vol. 2,3: Vol. 2 (The Valkyrie) 1-3: 1-(8/00). Vol. 3 (Siegfried) 1-3: 1-(12/00)						3.00
Vol. 4 (The Twilight of the Gods) 1-3: 1-(6/01)						3.00
4-(9/01, $5.99, 64 pgs.) Conclusion with sketch pages						6.00

RINGO KID, THE (2nd Series)
Marvel Comics Group: Jan, 1970 - No. 23, Nov, 1973; No. 24, Nov, 1975 - No. 30, Nov, 1976

	GD 2.0	VG 4.0	FN 6.0	VF 8.0	VF/NM 9.0	NM- 9.2
1-Williamson-a r-from #10, 1956.	3	6	9	18	27	35
2-11: 2-Severin-c. 11-Last 15¢ issue	2	4	6	11	16	20
12 (52 pg. Giant)	3	6	9	16	22	28
13-20: 13-Wildey-r. 20-Williamson-r/#1	2	4	6	9	13	16
21-30	2	4	6	8	10	12
27,28-(30¢-c variant, limited distribution)(5,7/76)	3	6	9	20	30	40

RINGO KID WESTERN, THE (1st Series) (See Wild Western & Western Trails)

The Rinse #1 © BOOM & Phillips

Riot #3 © MAR

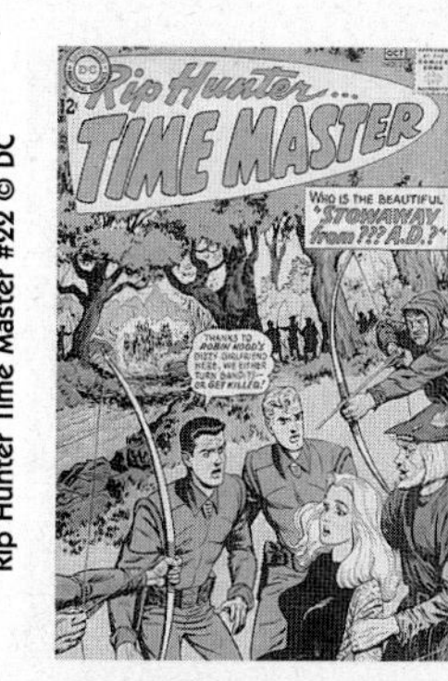

Rip Hunter Time Master #22 © DC

	GD 2.0	VG 4.0	FN 6.0	VF 8.0	VF/NM 9.0	NM- 9.2

Atlas Comics (HPC)/Marvel Comics: Aug, 1954 - No. 21, Sept, 1957

	GD	VG	FN	VF	VF/NM	NM-
1-Origin; The Ringo Kid begins	30	60	90	177	289	400
2-Black Rider app.; origin/1st app. Ringo's Horse Arab	15	30	45	90	140	190
3-5	12	24	36	69	97	125
6-8-Severin-a(3) each	13	26	39	74	105	135
9,11,12,14-21: 12-Orlando-a (4 pgs.)	10	20	30	56	76	95
10,13-Williamson-a (4 pgs.)	11	22	33	60	83	105

NOTE: *Berg a-8. Maneely a-1-5, 15, 16(text illos only), 17(4), 18, 20, 21; c-1-6, 8, 13, 15-18, 20. J. Severin c-10, 11. Sinnott a-1. Wildey a-16-18.*

RINSE, THE
Boom! Studios: Sept, 2011 - No. 4, Dec, 2011 ($1.00/$3.99)

	GD	VG	FN	VF	VF/NM	NM-
1-($1.00)-Phillips-s/Laming-a						3.00
2-4-($3.99)						4.00

RIN TIN TIN (See March of Comics #163,180,195)

RIN TIN TIN (TV) (...& Rusty #21 on; see Western Roundup under Dell Giants)
Dell Publishing Co./Gold Key: Nov, 1952 - No. 38, May-July, 1961; Nov, 1963 (All Photo-c)

	GD	VG	FN	VF	VF/NM	NM-
Four Color 434 (#1)	13	26	39	85	180	275
Four Color 476,523	8	16	24	55	93	130
4(3-5/54)-10	7	14	21	44	72	100
11-17,19,20	6	12	18	42	69	95
18-(4-5/57) 1st app. of Rusty and the Cavalry of Fort Apache; photo-c	8	16	24	53	89	125
21-38: 36-Toth-a (4 pgs.)	5	10	15	35	55	75
... & Rusty 1 (11/63-Gold Key)	6	12	18	37	59	80

RIO (Also see Eclipse Monthly)
Comico: June, 1987 ($8.95, 64 pgs.)

	GD	VG	FN	VF	VF/NM	NM-
1-Wildey-c/a						9.00

RIO AT BAY
Dark Horse Comics: July, 1992 - No. 2, Aug, 1992 ($2.95, limited series)

	GD	VG	FN	VF	VF/NM	NM-
1,2-Wildey-c/a						3.00

RIO BRAVO (Movie) (See 4-Color #1018)
Dell Publishing Co.: June, 1959

	GD	VG	FN	VF	VF/NM	NM-
Four Color 1018-Toth-a; John Wayne, Dean Martin, & Ricky Nelson photo-c.	20	40	60	137	294	450

RIO CONCHOS (See Movie Comics)

RIOT (Satire)
Atlas Comics (ACI No. 1-5/WPI No. 6): Apr, 1954 - No. 3, Aug, 1954; No. 4, Feb, 1956 - No. 6, June, 1956

	GD	VG	FN	VF	VF/NM	NM-
1-Russ Heath-a	34	68	102	206	336	465
2-Li'l Abner satire by Post	24	48	72	142	234	325
3-Last precode (8/54)	21	42	63	126	206	285
4-Infinity-c; Marilyn Monroe "7 Year Itch" movie satire; Mad Rip-off ads	27	54	81	162	266	370
5-Marilyn Monroe, John Wayne parody; part photo-c	28	56	84	165	270	375
6-Lorna of the Jungle satire by Everett; Dennis the Menace satire-c/story; part photo-c	21	42	63	126	206	285

NOTE: *Berg a-3. Burgos c-1, 2. Colan a-1. Everett a-4, 6. Heath a-1. Maneely a-1, 2, 4-6; c-3, 4, 6. Post a-1-4. Reinman a-2. Severin a-4-6.*

RIOT GEAR
Triumphant Comics: Sept, 1993 - No. 11, July, 1994 ($2.50, serially numbered)

	GD	VG	FN	VF	VF/NM	NM-
1-11: 1-2nd app. Riot Gear. 2-1st app. Rabin. 3,4-Triumphant Unleashed x-over. 3-1st app. Surzar. 4-Death of Captain Tich						3.00
Violent Past 1,2: 1-(2/94, $2.50)						3.00

R.I.P.
TSR, Inc.:1990 - No. 8, 1991 ($2.95, 44 pgs.)

	GD	VG	FN	VF	VF/NM	NM-
1-8-Based on TSR game						4.00

RIPCLAW (See Cyberforce)
Image Comics (Top Cow Prod.): Apr, 1995 - No. 3, June, 1995 (Limited series)

	GD	VG	FN	VF	VF/NM	NM-
1/2-Gold, 1/2-San Diego ed., 1/2-Chicago ed.	1	3	4	6	8	10
1-3: Brandon Peterson-a(p)						3.00
Special 1 (10/95, $2.50)						3.00

RIPCLAW
Image Comics (Top Cow Prod.): V2#1, Dec, 1995 - No. 6, June, 1996 ($2.50)

	GD	VG	FN	VF	VF/NM	NM-
V2#1-6: 5-Medieval Spawn/Witchblade Preview						3.00
...: Pilot Season 1 (2007, $2.99) Jason Aaron-s/Jorge Lucas-a/Tony Moore-c						3.00

RIPCORD (TV)
Dell Publishing Co.: Mar-May, 1962

	GD	VG	FN	VF	VF/NM	NM-
Four Color 1294	7	14	21	46	76	105

R.I.P.D.
Dark Horse Comics: Oct, 1999 - No. 4, Jan, 2000 ($2.95, limited series)

	GD	VG	FN	VF	VF/NM	NM-
1-4						3.00
TPB (2003, $12.95) r/#1-4						13.00

RIP HUNTER TIME MASTER (See Showcase #20, 21, 25, 26 & Time Masters)
National Periodical Publications: Mar-Apr, 1961 - No. 29, Nov-Dec, 1965

	GD	VG	FN	VF	VF/NM	NM-
1-(3-4/61)	50	100	150	405	878	1350
2	25	50	75	171	366	560
3-5: 5-Last 10¢ issue	15	30	45	102	221	340
6,7-Toth-a in each	11	22	33	73	142	210
8-15	9	18	27	61	106	150
16-19	7	14	21	48	79	110
20-Hitler-c/s	8	16	24	53	89	125
21-29: 29-Gil Kane-c	6	12	18	42	69	95

RIP IN TIME (Also see Teenage Mutant Ninja Turtles #5-7)
Fantagor Press: Aug, 1986 - No.5, 1987 ($1.50, B&W)

	GD	VG	FN	VF	VF/NM	NM-
1-5: Corben-c/a in all						3.00

RIP KIRBY (Also see Harvey Comics Hits #57, & Street Comix)
David McKay Publications: 1948

	GD	VG	FN	VF	VF/NM	NM-
Feature Books 51,54: Raymond-c; 51-Origin	36	72	108	211	343	475

RIPLEY'S BELIEVE IT OR NOT! (See Ace Comics, All-American Comics, Mystery Comics Digest #1, 4, 7, 10, 13, 16, 19, 22, 25)

RIPLEY'S BELIEVE IT OR NOT!
Harvey Publications: Sept, 1953 - No. 4, March, 1954

	GD	VG	FN	VF	VF/NM	NM-
1-Powell-a	14	28	42	76	108	140
2-4	10	20	30	54	72	90

RIPLEY'S BELIEVE IT OR NOT! (Continuation of Ripleys'...True Ghost Stories & Ripley's...True War Stories)
Gold Key: No. 4, April, 1967 - No. 94, Feb, 1980

	GD	VG	FN	VF	VF/NM	NM-
4-Shrunken head photo-c; McWilliams-a	4	8	12	24	37	50
5-Subtitled "True War Stories"; Evans-a; 1st Jeff Jones-a in comics? (2 pgs.)	4	8	12	24	37	50
6-10: 6-McWilliams-a. 10-Evans-a(2)	3	6	9	20	30	40
11-20: 15-Evans-a	3	6	9	16	23	30
21-30	2	4	6	13	18	22
31-38,40-60	2	4	6	9	13	16
39-Crandall-a	2	4	6	10	14	18
61-73	1	3	4	6	8	10
74,77-83-(52 pgs.)	2	4	6	9	13	16
75,76,84-94	1	2	3	5	6	8
Story Digest Mag. 1(6/70)-4-3/4x6-1/2", 148pp.	5	10	15	35	55	75

NOTE: *Evanish art by Luiz Dominguez #22-25, 27, 30, 31, 40. Jeff Jones a-5(2 pgs.). McWilliams a-65, 66, 70, 89. Orlando a-8. Sparling c-68. Reprints-74, 77-84, 87 (part); 91, 93 (all). Williamson, Wood a-80r/#1.*

RIPLEY'S BELIEVE IT OR NOT!
Dark Horse Comics: May, 2002 - No. 3, Oct, 2002 ($2.99, B&W, unfinished limited series)

	GD	VG	FN	VF	VF/NM	NM-
1-3-Nord-c/a. 1-Stories of Amelia Earhart & D.B. Cooper						3.00

RIPLEY'S BELIEVE IT OR NOT! TRUE GHOST STORIES (Along with Ripley's...True War Stories, the three issues together precede the 1967 series that starts its numbering with #4) (Also see Dan Curtis)
Gold Key: June, 1965 - No. 2, Oct, 1966

	GD	VG	FN	VF	VF/NM	NM-
1-Williamson, Wood & Evans-a; photo-c	8	16	24	51	86	120
2-Orlando, McWilliams-a; photo-c	4	8	12	28	44	60
Mini-Comic 1(1976-3-1/4x6-1/2")	2	4	6	8	11	14
11186(1977)-Golden Press; ($1.95, 224 pgs.)-All-r	4	8	12	24	37	50
11401(3/79)-Golden Press; ($1.00, 96 pgs.)-All-r	3	6	9	15	21	26

RIPLEY'S BELIEVE IT OR NOT! TRUE WAR STORIES (Along with Ripley's...True Ghost Stories, the three issues together precede the 1967 series that starts its numbering with #4)
Gold Key: Nov, 1965 (Aug, 1965 in indicia)

	GD	VG	FN	VF	VF/NM	NM-
1-No Williamson-a	4	8	12	28	44	60

RIPLEY'S BELIEVE IT OR NOT! TRUE WEIRD
Ripley Enterprises: June, 1966 - No. 2, Aug, 1966 (B&W Magazine)

	GD	VG	FN	VF	VF/NM	NM-
1,2-Comic stories & text	3	6	9	18	27	35

RISE OF APOCALYPSE
Marvel Comics: Oct, 1996 - No. 4, Jan, 1997 ($1.95, limited series)

Rising Stars #1 © JMS

Roarin' Rick's Rare Bit Fiends #1 © Rick Veitch

Robin #172 © DC

	GD	VG	FN	VF	VF/NM	NM-
	2.0	4.0	6.0	8.0	9.0	9.2

1-4: Adam Pollina-c/a 3.00

RISING STARS
Image Comics (Top Cow): Mar, 1999 - No. 24, Mar, 2005 ($2.50/$2.99)

	GD	VG	FN	VF	VF/NM	NM-
Preview-(3/99, $5.00) Straczynski-s						6.00
0-(6/00, $2.50) Gary Frank-a/c						3.00
1/2-(8/01, $2.95) Anderson-c; art & sketch pages by Zanier						3.00
1-Four covers; Keu Cha-c/a	1	2	3	5	7	9
1-($10.00) Gold Editions-four covers						10.00
1-($50.00) Holofoil-c						50.00
2-7: 5-7-Zanier & Lashley-a(p)	1	2	3	5	7	9
8-23: 8-13-Zanier & Lashley-a(p). 14-Immonen-a. 15-Flip book B&W preview of Universe. 15-23-Brent Anderson-a						3.00
24-($3.99) Series finale; Anderson-a/c						4.00
Born In Fire TPB (11/00, $19.95) r/#1-8; foreword by Neil Gaiman						20.00
Power TPB (2002, $19.95) r/#9-16						20.00
Prelude-(10/00, $2.95) Cha-a/Lashley-c						3.00
...: Visitations (2002, $8.99) r/#0, 1/2, Preview; new Anderson-c; cover gallery						9.00
Vol. 3: Fire and Ash TPB (2005, $19.99) r/#17-24; design pages & cover gallery						20.00
Vol. 4 TPB (2006, $19.99) r/Rising Stars Bright #1-3 and Voices of the Dead #1-6						20.00
Vol. 5 TPB (2007, $16.99) r/Rising Stars: Untouchable #1-5 and ...: Visitations						17.00
Wizard #0-(3/99) Wizard supplement; Straczynski-s						3.00
Wizard #1/2						10.00

RISING STARS BRIGHT
Image Comics (Top Cow): Mar, 2003 - No. 3, May, 2003 ($2.99, limited series)

1-3-Avery-s/Jurgens & Gorder-a/Beck-c 3.00

RISING STARS: UNTOUCHABLE
Image Comics (Top Cow): Mar, 2006 - No. 5, July, 2006 ($2.99, limited series)

1-5-Avery-s/Anderson-a 3.00

RISING STARS: VOICES OF THE DEAD
Image Comics (Top Cow): June, 2005 - No. 6, Dec, 2005 ($2.99, limited series)

1-6-Avery-s/Staz Johnson-a 3.00

RIVERDALE HIGH (Archie's... #7,8)
Archie Comics: Aug, 1990 - No. 8, Oct, 1991 ($1.00, bi-monthly)

1 4.00
2-8 3.00

RIVER FEUD (See Zane Grey & Four Color #484)

RIVETS
Dell Publishing Co.: No. 518, Nov, 1953

	GD	VG	FN	VF	VF/NM	NM-
Four Color 518	4	8	12	24	37	50

RIVETS (A dog)
Argo Publ.: Jan, 1956 - No. 3, May, 1956

	GD	VG	FN	VF	VF/NM	NM-
1-Reprints Sunday & daily newspaper strips	6	12	18	31	38	45
2,3	5	10	15	22	26	30

ROACHMILL
Blackthorne Publ.: Dec, 1986 - No. 6, Oct, 1987 ($1.75, B&W)

1-6 3.00

ROACHMILL
Dark Horse Comics: May, 1988 - No. 10, Dec, 1990 ($1.75, B&W)

1-10: 10-Contains trading cards 3.00

ROAD RUNNER (See Beep Beep, the...)

ROAD TO PERDITION (Inspired the 2002 Tom Hanks/Paul Newman movie)
(Also see On the Road to Perdition)
DC Comics/Paradox Press: 1998, 2002 ($13.95, B&W paperback graphic novel)

nn-(1st printing) Max Allan Collins-s/Richard Piers Rayner-a 30.00
2nd & 3rd printings (2002, $13.95) 14.00
Movie photo cover edition (2002) 14.00

ROADTRIP
Oni Press: Aug, 2000 ($2.95, B&W, one-shot)

1-Reprints Judd Winick's back-up stories from Oni Double Feature #9,10 3.00

ROADWAYS
Cult Press: May, 1994 ($2.75, B&W, limited series)

1 3.00

ROARIN' RICK'S RARE BIT FIENDS
King Hell Press: July, 1994 - No. 21, Aug, 1996 ($2.95, B&W, mature)

1-21: Rick Veitch-c/a/scripts in all. 20-(5/96). 21-(8/96)-Reads Subtleman #1 on cover 3.00

	GD	VG	FN	VF	VF/NM	NM-
	2.0	4.0	6.0	8.0	9.0	9.2

Rabid Eye: The Dream Art of Rick Veitch ($14.95, B&W, TPB)-r/#1-8 & the appendix from #12 15.00
Pocket Universe (6/96, $14.95, B&W, TPB)-Reprints 15.00

ROBERT E. HOWARD'S CONAN THE BARBARIAN
Marvel Comics: 1983 ($2.50, 68 pgs., Baxter paper)

1-r/Savage Tales #2,3 by Smith, c-r/Conan #21 by Smith. 4.00

ROBERT LOUIS STEVENSON'S KIDNAPPED (See Kidnapped)

ROBIN (See Aurora, Birds of Prey, Detective Comics #38, New Teen Titans, Robin II, Robin III, Robin 3000, Star Spangled Comics #65, Teen Titans & Young Justice)

ROBIN (See Batman #457)
DC Comics: Jan, 1991 - No. 5, May, 1991 ($1.00, limited series)

1-Free poster by N. Adams; Bolland-c on all 5.00
1-2nd & 3rd printings (without poster) 3.00
2-5 4.00
2-2nd printing 3.00
Annual 1,2 (1992-93, $2.50, 68 pgs.): 1-Grant/Wagner scripts; Sam Kieth-c. 2-Intro Razorsharp; Jim Balent-c(p) 4.00

ROBIN (See Detective #668) (Also see Red Robin)
DC Comics: Nov, 1993 - No. 183, Apr, 2009 ($1.50/$1.95/$1.99/$2.25/$2.50/$2.99)

1-($2.95)-Collector's edition w/foil embossed-c; 1st app. Robin's car, The Redbird; Azrael as Batman app. 5.00
1-Newsstand ed. 3.00
0,2-49,51-66-Regular editions: 3-5-The Spoiler app. 6-The Huntress-c/story cont'd from Showcase '94 #5. 7-Knightquest: The Conclusion w/new Batman (Azrael) vs. Bruce Wayne. 8-KnightsEnd Pt. 5. 9-KnightsEnd Aftermath; Batman-c & app. 10-(9/94)-Zero Hour. 0-(10/94). 11-(11/94). 25-Green Arrow-c/app. 26-Batman app. 27-Contagion Pt. 3; Catwoman-c/app; Penguin & Azrael app. 28-Contagion Pt. 11. 29-Penguin app. 31-Wildcat-c/app. 32-Legacy Pt. 3. 33-Legacy Pt. 7. 35-Final Night. 46-Genesis. 52,53-Cataclysm pt. 7, conclusion. 55-Green Arrow app. 62-64-Flash-c/app. 3.50
14 ($2.50)-Embossed-c; Troika Pt. 4 4.00
50-($2.95)-Lady Shiva & King Snake app. 4.00
67-74,76-78: 67-72-No Man's Land 3.00
75-($2.95) 4.00
79-97: 79-Begin $2.25-c; Green Arrow app. 86-Pander Bros.-a 3.00
98,99-Bruce Wayne: Murderer x-over pt. 6, 11 3.00
100-($3.50) Last Dixon-s 4.00
101-147: 101-Young Justice x-over. 106-Kevin Lau-c. 121,122-Willingham-s/Mays-a. 125-Tim Drake quits. 126-Spoiler becomes the new Robin. 129-131-War Games. 132-Robin moves to Bludhaven, Batgirl app. 138-Begin $2.50-c. 139-McDaniel-a begins. 146-147-Teen Titans app. 3.00
148-174: 148-One Year Later; new costume. 150-Begin $2.99-c. 152,153-Boomerang app. 168,169-Resurrection of Ra's al Ghul x-over. 174 Spoiler unmasked 3.00
175-183: 175,176-Batman R.I.P. x-over. 180-Robin vs. Red Robin 3.00
#1,000,000 (11/98) 853rd Century x-over 3.00
Annual 3-5: 3-(1994, $2.95)-Elseworlds story. 4-(1995, $2.95)-Year One story. 5-(1996, $2.95)-Legends of the Dead Earth story 4.00
Annual 6 (1997, $3.95)-Pulp Heroes story. 4.00
Annual 7 (12/07, $3.99)-Pearson-c/a; prelude to Resurrection of Ra's al Ghul x-over 4.00
.../Argent 1 (2/98, $1.95) Argent (Teen Titans) app. 3.00
.../Batgirl: Fresh Blood TPB (2005, $12.99) r/#132,133 & Batgirl #58,59 13.00
...: Days of Fire and Madness (2006, $12.99, TPB) r/#140-145 13.00
...Eighty-Page Giant 1 (9/00, $5.95) Chuck Dixon-s/Diego Barreto-a 6.00
...: Flying Solo (2000, $12.95, TPB) r/#1-6, Showcase '94 #5,6 13.00
...Plus 1 (12/96, $2.95) Impulse-c/app.; Waid-s 4.00
...Plus 2 (12/97, $2.95) Fang (Scare Tactics) app. 4.00
...: Search For a Hero (2009, $19.99, TPB) r/#175-183; cover gallery 20.00
.../Spoiler Special 1 (8/08, $3.99) Follows Spoiler's return in Robin #174; Dixon-s 4.00
...: Teenage Wasteland (2007, $17.99, TPB) r/#154-162 18.00
...: The Big Leagues (2008, $12.99, TPB) r/#163-167 13.00
...: Unmasked (2004, $12.95, TPB) r/#121-125; Pearson-c 13.00
...: Violent Tendencies (2008, $17.99, TPB) r/#170-174 & Robin/Spoiler Special 1 18.00
...: Wanted (2007, $12.99, TPB) r/#148-153 13.00

ROBIN: A HERO REBORN
DC Comics: 1991 ($4.95, squarebound, trade paperback)

nn-r/Batman #455-457 & Robin #1-5; Bolland-c 5.00

ROBIN HOOD (See The Advs. of..., Brave and the Bold, Four Color #413, 669, King Classics, Movie Comics & Power Record Comics)

ROBIN HOOD (...& His Merry Men, The Illustrated Story of...) (See Classic Comics #7 & Classics Giveaways, 12/44)

ROBIN HOOD (Disney)

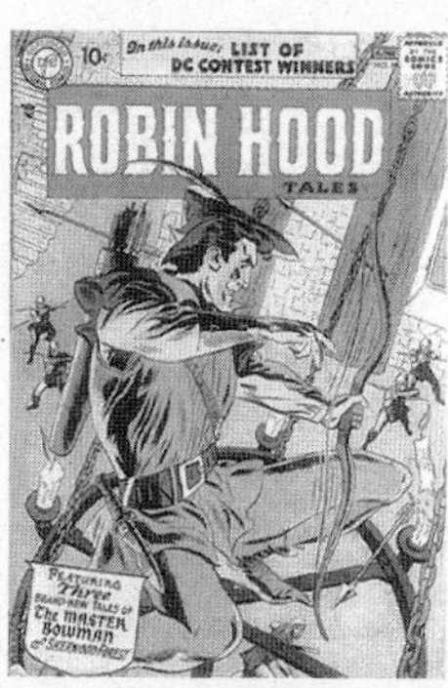

Robin Hood Tales #9 © DC

Robin II #2 © DC

Robocop #14 © Orion Pict.

GD 2.0 | VG 4.0 | FN 6.0 | VF 8.0 | VF/NM 9.0 | NM- 9.2

Dell Publishing Co.: No. 413, Aug, 1952; No. 669, Dec, 1955
Four Color 413-(1st Disney movie Four Color book)(8/52)-Photo-c 9 18 27 63 112 160
Four Color 669 (12/55)-Reprints #413 plus photo-c 6 12 18 37 59 80

ROBIN HOOD (Adventures of... #7, 8)
Magazine Enterprises (Sussex Pub. Co.): No. 52, Nov, 1955 - No. 6, Jun, 1957
52 (#1)-Origin Robin Hood & Sir Gallant of the Round Table 15 30 45 85 130 175
53 (#2), 3-6: 6-Richard Greene photo-c (TV) 12 24 36 67 94 120
I.W. Reprint #1,2,9: 1-r/#3. 2-r/#4. 9-r/#52 (1963) 2 4 6 9 13 16
Super Reprint #10,15: 10-r/#53. 15-r/#5 2 4 6 9 13 16
NOTE: *Bolle a-in all; c-52. Powell a-6.*

ROBIN HOOD (Not Disney)
Dell Publishing Co.: May-July, 1963 (one-shot)
1 3 6 9 16 23 30

ROBIN HOOD (Disney) (Also see Best of Walt Disney)
Western Publishing Co.: 1973 ($1.50, 8-1/2x11", 52 pgs., cardboard-c)
96151- "Robin Hood", based on movie, 96152- "The Mystery of Sherwood Forest", 96153- "In King Richard's Service", 96154- "The Wizard's Ring" each.... 3 6 9 16 22 28

ROBIN HOOD
Eclipse Comics: July, 1991 - No. 3, Dec, 1991 ($2.50, limited series)
1-3: Timothy Truman layouts 3.00

ROBIN HOOD AND HIS MERRY MEN (Formerly Danger & Adventure)
Charlton Comics: No. 28, Apr, 1956 - No. 38, Aug, 1958
28 10 20 30 54 72 90
29-37 8 16 24 42 54 65
38-Ditko-a (5 pgs.); Rocke-c 14 28 42 76 108 140

ROBIN HOOD TALES (Published by National Periodical #7 on)
Quality Comics Group (Comic Magazines): Feb, 1956 - No. 6, Nov-Dec, 1956
1-All have Baker/Cuidera-c 32 64 96 188 307 425
2-6-Matt Baker-a 30 60 90 177 289 400

ROBIN HOOD TALES (Cont'd from Quality series)(See Brave & the Bold #5)
National Periodical Publ.: No. 7, Jan-Feb, 1957 - No. 14, Mar-Apr, 1958
7-All have Andru/Esposito-c 36 72 108 211 343 475
8-14 30 60 90 177 289 400

ROBINSON CRUSOE (See King Classics & Power Record Comics)
Dell Publishing Co.: Nov-Jan, 1963-64
1 3 6 9 15 21 26

ROBIN II (The Joker's Wild)
DC Comics: Oct, 1991 - No. 4, Dec, 1991 ($1.50, mini-series)
1-(Direct sales, $1.50)-With 4 diff.-c; same hologram on each 4.00
1-(Newsstand, $1.00)-No hologram; 1 version 3.00
1-Collector's set ($10.00)-Contains all 5 versions bagged with hologram trading card inside 15.00
2-(Direct sales, $1.50)-With 3 different-c 3.50
2-4-(Newsstand, $1.00)-1 version of each 3.00
2-Collector's set ($8.00)-Contains all 4 versions bagged with hologram trading card inside 10.00
3-(Direct sale, $1.50)-With 2 different-c 3.50
3-Collector's set ($6.00)-Contains all 3 versions bagged with hologram trading card inside 8.00
4-(Direct sales, $1.50)-Only one version 3.50
4-Collector's set ($4.00)-Contains both versions bagged with Bat-Signal hologram trading card 6.00
Multi-pack (All four issues w/hologram sticker) 12.00
Deluxe Complete Set ($30.00)-Contains all 14 versions of #1-4 plus a new hologram trading card; numbered & limited to 25,000; comes with slipcase & 2 acid free backing boards 40.00

ROBIN III: CRY OF THE HUNTRESS
DC Comics: Dec, 1992 - No. 6, Mar, 1993 (Limited series)
1-6 ($2.50, collector's ed.)-Polybagged w/movement enhanced-c plus mini-poster of newsstand-c by Zeck 4.00
1-6 ($1.25, newsstand ed.): All have Zeck-c 3.00

ROBIN 3000
DC Comics (Elseworlds): 1992 - No. 2, 1992 ($4.95, mini-series, 52 pgs.)
1,2-Foil logo; Russell-c/a 5.00

ROBIN: YEAR ONE
DC Comics: 2000 - No. 4, 2001 ($4.95, square-bound, limited series)
1-4: Earliest days of Robin's career; Javier Pulido-c/a. 2,4-Two-Face app. 5.00
TPB (2002, 2008, $14.95/$14.99, 2 printings) r/#1-4 15.00

ROBOCOP
Marvel Comics: Oct, 1987 ($2.00, B&W, magazine, one-shot)
1-Movie adaptation 5.00

ROBOCOP (Also see Dark Horse Comics)
Marvel Comics: Mar, 1990 - No. 23, Jan, 1992 ($1.50)
1-Based on movie 4.00
2-23 3.00
nn (7/90, $4.95, 52 pgs.)-r/B&W magazine in color; adapts 1st movie 5.00

ROBOCOP
Dynamite Entertainment: 2010 - No. 6, 2010 ($3.50, limited series)
1-6-Follows the events of the first film; Neves-a 3.50

ROBOCOP (FRANK MILLER'S...)
Avatar Press: July, 2003 - No. 9, Jan, 2006 ($3.50/$3.99, limited series)
1-9-Frank Miller-s/Juan Ryp-a. 1-Three covers by Miller, Ryp, and Barrows. 2-Two covers 4.00
Free Comic Book Day Edition (4/03) Previews Robocop & Stargate SG•1; Busch-c 3.00

ROBOCOP: MORTAL COILS
Dark Horse Comics: Sept, 1993 - No. 4, Dec, 1993 ($2.50, limited series)
1-4: 1,2-Cago painted-c 3.00

ROBOCOP: PRIME SUSPECT
Dark Horse Comics: Oct, 1992 - No. 4, Jan, 1993 ($2.50, limited series)
1-4: 1,3-Nelson painted-c. 2,4-Bolton painted-c 3.00

ROBOCOP: ROAD TRIP
Dynamite Entertainment: 2012 - Present ($3.99, limited series)
1-3-De Zarate-a 4.00

ROBOCOP: ROULETTE
Dark Horse Comics: Dec, 1993 - No. 4, 1994 ($2.50, limited series)
1-4: 1,3-Nelson painted-c. 2,4-Bolton painted-c 3.00

ROBOCOP 2
Marvel Comics: Aug, 1990 ($2.25, B&W, magazine, 68 pgs.)
1-Adapts movie sequel 4.00

ROBOCOP 2
Marvel Comics: Aug, 1990; Late Aug, 1990 - #3, Late Sept, 1990 ($1.00, limited series)
nn-(8/90, $4.95, 68 pgs., color)-Same contents as B&W magazine 5.00
1: #1-3 reprint no number issue 3.00
2,3: 2-Guice-c(i) 3.00

ROBOCOP 3
Dark Horse Comics: July, 1993 - No. 3, Nov, 1993 ($2.50, limited series)
1-3: Nelson painted-c; Nguyen-a(p) 3.00

ROBOCOP VERSUS THE TERMINATOR
Dark Horse Comics: Sept, 1992 - No. 4, 1992 (Dec.) ($2.50, limited series)
1-4: Miller scripts & Simonson-c/a in all 3.00
1-Platinum Edition 6.00
NOTE: *All contain a different Robocop cardboard cut-out stand-up.*

ROBO DOJO
DC Comics (WildStorm): Apr, 2002 - No. 6, Sept, 2002 ($2.95, limited series)
1-6-Wolfman-s 3.00

ROBO-HUNTER (Also see Sam Slade...)
Eagle Comics: Apr, 1984 - No. 5, 1984 ($1.00)
1-5-2000 A.D. 3.00

R.O.B.O.T. BATTALION 2050
Eclipse Comics: Mar, 1988 ($2.00, B&W, one-shot)
1 3.00

ROBOT COMICS
Renegade Press: No. 0, June, 1987 ($2.00, B&W, one-shot)
0-Bob Burden story & art 3.00

ROBOTECH
Antarctic Press: Mar, 1997 - No. 11, Nov, 1998 ($2.95)
1-11, Annual 1 (4/98, $2.95) 4.00
...Class Reunion (12/98, $3.95, B&W) 4.00

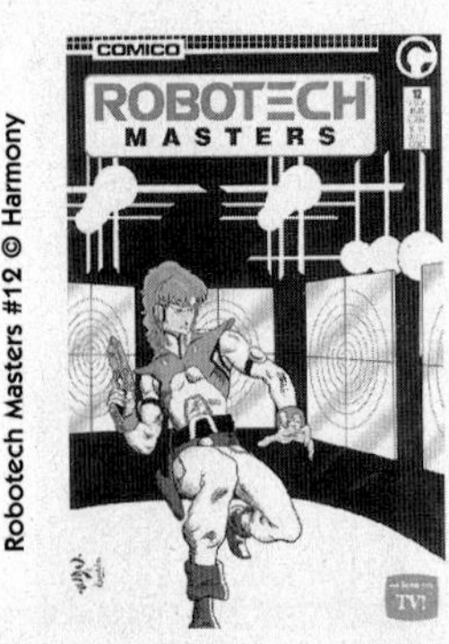

Robotech Masters #12 © Harmony

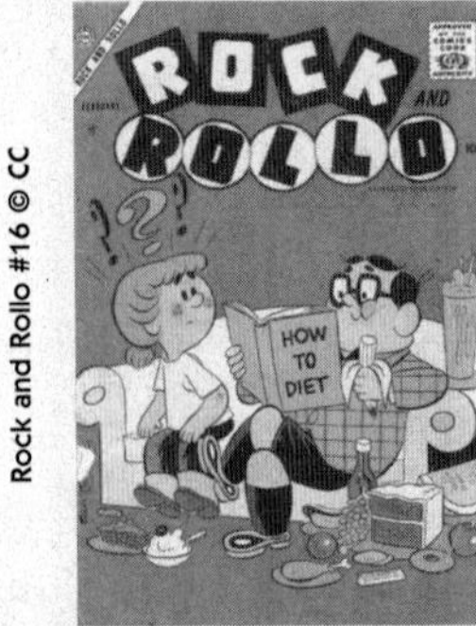

Rock and Rollo #16 © CC

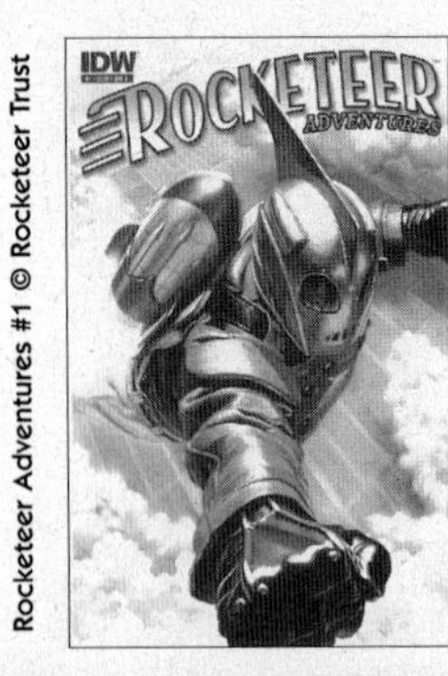

Rocketeer Adventures #1 © Rocketeer Trust

	GD 2.0	VG 4.0	FN 6.0	VF 8.0	VF/NM 9.0	NM- 9.2

...Escape (5/98, $2.95, B&W), ...Final Fire (12/98, $2.95, B&W) 4.00

ROBOTECH
DC Comics (WildStorm): No. 0, Feb, 2003 - No. 6, Jul, 2003 ($2.50/$2.95, limited series)

0-Tommy Yune-s; art by Jim Lee, Garza, Bermejo and others; pin-up pages by various 3.00
1-6 ($2.95)-Long Vo-a 3.00
...: From the Stars (2003, $9.95, digest-size) r/#0-6 & Sourcebook 10.00
... Sourcebook (3/03, $2.95) pin-ups and info on characters and mecha; art by various 3.00

ROBOTECH: COVERT-OPS
Antarctic Press: Aug, 1998 - No. 2, Sept, 1998 ($2.95, B&W, limited series)

1,2-Gregory Lane-s/a 4.00

ROBOTECH DEFENDERS
DC Comics: Mar, 1985 - No. 2, Apr, 1985 (Mini-series)

1,2 4.00

ROBOTECH IN 3-D (TV)
Comico: Aug, 1987 ($2.50)

1-Steacy painted-c 4.00

ROBOTECH: INVASION
DC Comics (WildStorm): Feb, 2004 - No. 5, July, 2004 ($2.95, limited series)

1-5-Faerber & Yune-s/Miyazawa & Dogan-a 3.00

ROBOTECH: LOVE AND WAR
DC Comics (WildStorm): Aug, 2003 - No. 6, Jan, 2004 ($2.95, limited series)

1-6-Long Vo & Charles Park-a/Faerber & Yune-s. 2-Variant-c by Warren 3.00

ROBOTECH MASTERS (TV)
Comico: July, 1985 - No. 23, Apr, 1988 ($1.50)

1 6.00
2-23 4.00

ROBOTECH: PRELUDE TO THE SHADOW CHRONICLES
DC Comics (WildStorm): Dec, 2005 - No. 5, Mar, 2006 ($3.50, limited series)

1-5-Yune-s/Dogan & Udon Studios-a 3.50
TPB (2010, $17.99) r/#1-5; production art 18.00

ROBOTECH: SENTINELS - RUBICON
Antarctic Press: July, 1998 ($2.95, B&W)

1 4.00

ROBOTECH SPECIAL
Comico: May, 1988 ($2.50, one-shot, 44 pgs.)

1-Steacy wraparound-c; partial photo-c 5.00

ROBOTECH THE GRAPHIC NOVEL
Comico: Aug, 1986 ($5.95, 8-1/2x11", 52 pgs.)

1-Origin SDF-1; intro T.R. Edwards, Steacy-c/a; 2nd printing also exists (12/86) 7.00

ROBOTECH: THE MACROSS SAGA (TV)(Formerly Macross)
Comico: No. 2, Feb, 1985 - No. 36, Feb, 1989 ($1.50)

2 1 2 3 5 6 8
3-10 5.00
11-36: 12,17-Ken Steacy painted-c. 26-Begin $1.75-c. 35,36-($1.95) 4.00
Volume 1-4 TPB (WildStorm, 2003, $14.95, 5-3/4" x 8-1/4")1-Reprints #2-6 & Macross #1. 2- r/#7-12. 3-r/#13-18. 4-r/#19-24 15.00

ROBOTECH: THE NEW GENERATION
Comico: July, 1985 - No. 25, July, 1988

1 6.00
2-25 4.00

ROBOTECH: VERMILION
Antarctic Press: Mar, 1997 - No. 4, ($2.95, B&W, limited series)

1-4 4.00

ROBOTECH: WINGS OF GIBRALTAR
Antarctic Press: Aug, 1998 - No. 2, Sept, 1998 ($2.95, B&W, limited series)

1,2-Lee Duhig-s/a 4.00

ROBOTIX
Marvel Comics: Feb, 1986 (75¢, one-shot)

1-Based on toy 4.00

ROBOTMEN OF THE LOST PLANET (Also see Space Thrillers)
Avon Periodicals: 1952 (Also see Strange Worlds #19)

1-McCann-a (3 pgs.); Fawcette-a 129 258 387 826 1413 2000

ROB ROY
Dell Publishing Co.: 1954 (Disney-Movie)

Four Color 544-Manning-a, photo-c 7 14 21 49 82 115

ROCK, THE (WWF Wrestling)
Chaos! Comics: June, 2001 ($2.99, one-shot)

1-Photo-c; Grant-s/Neves-a 4.00

ROCK & ROLL HIGH SCHOOL
Roger Corman's Cosmic Comics: Oct, 1995 ($2.50)

1-Bob Fingerman scripts 3.00

ROCK AND ROLLO (Formerly TV Teens)
Charlton Comics: V2#14, Oct, 1957 - No. 19, Sept, 1958

V2#14-19 6 12 18 31 38 45

ROCK COMICS
Landgraphic Publ.: Jul/Aug, 1979 ($1.25, tabloid size, 28 pgs.)

1-N. Adams-c; Thor(not Marvel's) story by Adams 3 6 9 14 20 25

ROCKET COMICS
Hillman Periodicals: Mar, 1940 - No. 3, May, 1940

1-Rocket Riley, Red Roberts the Electro Man (origin), The Phantom Ranger, The Steel Shark, The Defender, Buzzard Barnes and his Sky Devils, Lefty Larson, & The Defender, the Man with a Thousand Faces begin (1st app. of each); all have Rocket Riley-c 271 542 813 1734 2967 4200
2,3 135 270 405 864 1482 2100

ROCKET COMICS: IGNITE
Dark Horse Comics: Apr, 2003 (Free Comic Book Day giveaway)

1-Previews Dark Horse series Syn, Lone, and Go Boy 7 3.00

ROCKETEER, THE (See Eclipse Graphic Album Series, Pacific Presents & Starslayer)

ROCKETEER ADVENTURE MAGAZINE, THE
Comico/Dark Horse Comics No. 3: July, 1988 ($2.00); No. 2, July, 1989 ($2.75); No. 3, Jan, 1995 ($2.95)

1-(7/88, $2.00)-Dave Stevens-c/a in all; Kaluta back-up-a; 1st app. Jonas (character based on The Shadow) 2 4 6 8 10 12
2-(7/89, $2.75)-Stevens/Dorman painted-c 1 2 3 5 6 8
3-(1/95, $2.95)-Includes pinups by Stevens, Gulacy, Plunkett, & Mignola 5.00
Volume 2-(9/96, $9.95, magazine size TPB)-Reprints #1-3 10.00

ROCKETEER ADVENTURES
IDW Publishing: May, 2011 - No. 4, Aug, 2011 ($3.99, limited series)

1-4-Anthology of new stories by various; covers by Alex Ross and Dave Stevens 4.00

ROCKETEER JETPACK TREASURY EDITION
IDW Publishing: Nov, 2011 ($9.99, oversized 13" x 9-3/4" format)

1-Recolored r/Starslayer #1-3, Pacific Presents #1,2 & Rocketeer Special Edition 10.00

ROCKETEER SPECIAL EDITION, THE
Eclipse Comics: Nov, 1984 ($1.50, Baxter paper)(Chapter 5 of Rocketeer serial)

1-Stevens-c/a; Kaluta back-c; pin-ups inside 2 4 6 9 12 15
NOTE: *Originally intended to be published in Pacific Presents.*

ROCKETEER, THE: THE COMPLETE ADVENTURES
IDW Publishing: Oct, 2009 ($29.99/$75.00, hardcover)

HC-Reprints of Dave Stevens' Rocketeer stories in Starslayer #1-3, Pacific Presents #1,2, Rocketeer Special Edition and Rocketeer Adventure Magazine #1-3; all re-colored 30.00
... Deluxe Edition ($75.00, 8"x12" slipcased HC) larger size reprints of HC content plus 100 bonus pages of sketch art, layouts, design work; intro. by Thomas Jane 110.00
... Deluxe Edition 2nd printing ($75.00, oversized slipcased HC) 75.00

ROCKETEER, THE: THE OFFICIAL MOVIE ADAPTATION
W. D. Publications (Disney): 1991

nn-($5.95, 68 pgs.)-Squarebound deluxe edition 6.00
nn-($2.95, 68 pgs.)-Stapled regular edition 4.00
3-D Comic Book (1991, $7.98, 52 pgs.) 8.00

ROCKET KELLY (See The Bouncer, Green Mask #10); becomes Li'l Pan #6)
Fox Feature Syndicate: 1944; Fall, 1945 - No. 5, Oct-Nov, 1946

nn (1944), 1 (Fall, 1945) 37 74 111 222 361 500
2-The Puppeteer app. (costumed hero) 25 50 75 150 245 340
3-5: 5-(#5 on cover, #4 inside) 22 44 66 132 216 300

ROCKETMAN (Strange Fantasy #2 on) (See Hello Pal & Scoop Comics)
Ajax/Farrell Publications: June, 1952 (Strange Stories of the Future)

1-Rocketman & Cosmo 41 82 123 249 417 585

ROCKET RACCOON (Also see Incredible Hulk #271)

Rock Fantasy Comics #9 © RFC

Rocky Lane Western #20 © FAW

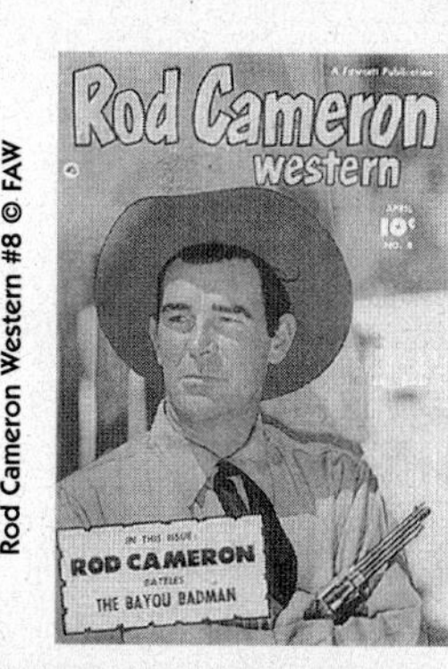

Rod Cameron Western #8 © FAW

GD 2.0 | VG 4.0 | FN 6.0 | VF 8.0 | VF/NM 9.0 | NM- 9.2

Marvel Comics: May, 1985 - No. 4, Aug, 1985 (color, limited series)
1-4: Mignola-a 4.00

ROCKET SHIP X
Fox Features Syndicate: September, 1951; 1952
1 64 128 192 406 696 985
1952 (nn, nd, no publ.)-Edited 1951-c (exist?) 39 78 117 231 378 525

ROCKET TO ADVENTURE LAND (See Pixie Puzzle...)

ROCKET TO THE MOON
Avon Periodicals: 1951
nn-Orlando-c/a; adapts Otis Adelbert Kline's "Maza of the Moon"
129 258 387 826 1413 2000

ROCK FANTASY COMICS
Rock Fantasy Comics: Dec, 1989 - No. 16?, 1991 ($2.25/$3.00, B&W)(No cover price)
1-Pink Floyd part 1 5.00
1-2nd printing ($3.00-c) 3.00
2,3: 2-Rolling Stones #1. 3-Led Zeppelin #1 4.00
2,3: 2nd printings ($3.00-c, 1/90 & 2/90) 3.00
4-Stevie Nicks Not published
5-Monstrosities of Rock #1; photo back-c 4.00
5-2nd printing ($3.00, 3/90 indicia, 2/90-c) 3.00
6-9,11-15,17,18: 6-Guns n' Roses #1 (1st & 2nd printings, 3/90)-Begin $3.00-c. 7-Sex Pistols #1. 8-Alice Cooper; not published. 9-Van Halen #1; photo back-c. 11-Jimi Hendrix #1; wraparound-c 3.00
10-Kiss #1; photo back-c 2 4 6 8 10 12
16-($5.00, 68 pgs.)-The Great Gig in the Sky(Floyd) 5.00

ROCK HAPPENING (See Bunny and Harvey Pop Comics:...)

ROCK N' ROLL COMICS
DC Comics: Dec./Jan 1956 (ashcan)
nn-Ashcan comic, not distributed to newsstands, only for in house use (no known sales)

ROCK N' ROLL COMICS
Revolutionary Comics: Jun, 1989 - No. 65 ($1.50/$1.95/$2.50, B&W/col. #15 on)
1-Guns N' Roses 1 2 3 5 6 8
1-2nd thru 7th printings. 7th printing (full color w/new-c/a) 3.00
2-Metallica 1 3 4 6 8 10
2-2nd thru 6th printings (6th in color) 3.00
3-Bon Jovi (no reprints) 1 2 3 5 6 8
4-8,10-65: 4-Motley Crue(2nd printing only, 1st destroyed). 5-Def Leppard (2 printings). 6-Rolling Stones(4 printings). 7-The Who (3 printings). 8-Skid Row; not published. 10-Warrant/Whitesnake(2 printings; 1st has 2 diff.-c). 11-Aerosmith (2 printings?). 12-New Kids on the Block(2 printings). 12-3rd printing; rewritten & titled NKOTB Hate Book. 13-Led Zeppelin. 14-Sex Pistols. 15-Poison; 1st color issue. 16-Van Halen. 17-Madonna. 18-Alice Cooper. 19-Public Enemy/2 Live Crew. 20-Queensryche/Tesla. 21-Prince? 22-AC/DC; begin $2.50-c. 23-Living Colour. 26-Michael Jackson. 29-Ozzy. 45,46-Grateful Dead. 49-Rush. 50,51-Bob Dylan. 56-David Bowie 5.00
9-Kiss 2 4 6 8 10 12
9-2nd & 3rd printings 3.00
NOTE: *Most issues were reprinted except #3. Later reprints are in color. #8 was not released.*

ROCKO'S MODERN LIFE (TV)
Marvel Comics: June, 1994 - No. 7, Dec, 1994 ($1.95) (Nickelodeon cartoon)
1-7 3.00

ROCKY AND HIS FIENDISH FRIENDS (TV)(Bullwinkle)
Gold Key: Oct, 1962 - No. 5, Sept, 1963 (Jay Ward)
1 (25¢, 80 pgs.) 13 26 39 88 189 290
2,3 (25¢, 80 pgs.) 10 20 30 69 130 190
4,5 (Regular size, 12¢) 8 16 24 53 89 125

ROCKY AND HIS FRIENDS (See Kite Fun Book & March of Comics #216 in the Promotional Comics section)

ROCKY AND HIS FRIENDS (TV)
Dell Publishing Co.: No. 1128, 8-10/60 - No.1311,1962 (Jay Ward)
Four Color 1128 (#1) (8-10/60) 26 52 78 182 391 600
Four Color 1152 (12-2/61), 1166, 1208, 1275, 1311('62)
16 32 48 109 237 365

ROCKY HORROR PICTURE SHOW THE COMIC BOOK, THE
Caliber Press: Jul, 1990 - No. 3, Jan, 1991 ($2.95, mini-series, 52 pgs.)
1-3: 1-Adapts cult film plus photos, etc., 1-2nd printing 4.00
...Collection ($4.95) 5.00

ROCKY JONES SPACE RANGER (See Space Adventures #15-18)

ROCKY JORDEN PRIVATE EYE (See Private Eye)

ROCKY LANE WESTERN (Allan Rocky Lane starred in Republic movies & TV for a short time as Allan Lane, Red Ryder & Rocky Lane) (See Black Jack Fawcett Movie Comics, Motion Picture Comics & Six-Gun Heroes)
Fawcett Publications/Charlton No. 56 on: May, 1949 - No. 87, Nov, 1959
1 (36 pgs.)-Rocky, his stallion Black Jack, & Slim Pickens begin; photo-c begin, end #57; photo back-c 55 110 165 352 601 850
2 (36 pgs.)-Last photo back-c 22 44 66 132 216 300
3-5 (52 pgs.): 4-Captain Tootsie by Beck 17 34 51 98 154 210
6,10 (36 pgs.): 10-Complete western novelette "Badman's Reward"
14 28 42 76 108 140
7-9 (52 pgs.) 14 28 42 82 121 160
11-13,15-17,19,20 (52 pgs.): 15-Black Jack's Hitching Post begins, ends #25. 20-Last Slim Pickens 12 24 36 67 94 120
14,18 (36 pgs.) 10 20 30 58 79 100
21,23,24 (52 pgs.): 21-Dee Dickens begins, ends #55,57,65-68
10 20 30 58 79 100
22,25-28,30 (36 pgs. begin) 10 20 30 54 72 90
29-Classic complete novel "The Land of Missing Men" with hidden land of ancient temple ruins (r-in #65) 14 28 42 76 108 140
31-40 9 18 27 52 69 85
41-54 9 18 27 47 61 75
55-Last Fawcett issue (1/54) 9 18 27 52 69 85
56-1st Charlton issue (2/54)-Photo-c 14 28 42 82 121 160
57,60-Photo-c 10 20 30 54 72 90
58,59,61-64,66-78,80-86: 59-61-Young Falcon app. 64-Slim Pickens app. 66-68: Reprints #30,31,32 8 16 24 44 57 70
65-r/#29, "The Land of Missing Men" 9 18 27 50 65 80
79-Giant Edition (68 pgs.) 10 20 30 58 79 100
87-Last issue 9 18 27 52 69 85
NOTE: *Complete novels in #10, 14, 18, 22, 25, 30-32, 36, 38, 39, 49. Captain Tootsie in #4, 12, 20. Big Bow and Little Arrow in #11, 28, 63. Black Jack's Hitching Post in #15-25, 64, 73.*

ROCKY LANE WESTERN
AC Comics: 1989 ($2.50, B&W, one-shot?)
1-Photo-c; Giordano reprints 4.00
Annual 1 (1991, $2.95, B&W, 44 pgs.)-photo front/back & inside-c; reprints 4.00

ROD CAMERON WESTERN (Movie star)
Fawcett Publications: Feb, 1950 - No. 20, Apr, 1953
1-Rod Cameron, his horse War Paint, & Sam The Sheriff begin; photo front/back-c begin
30 60 90 177 289 400
2 15 30 45 86 133 180
3-Novel length story "The Mystery of the Seven Cities of Cibola"
14 28 42 82 121 160
4-10: 9-Last photo back-c 12 24 36 69 97 125
11-19 10 20 30 58 79 100
20-Last issue & photo-c 11 22 33 62 86 110
NOTE: *Novel length stories in No. 1-8, 12-14.*

RODEO RYAN (See A-1 Comics #8)

ROGAN GOSH
DC Comics (Vertigo): 1994 ($6.95, one-shot)
nn-Peter Milligan scripts 7.00

ROGER DODGER (Also in Exciting Comics #57 on)
Standard Comics: No. 5, Aug, 1952
5-Teen-age 6 12 18 31 38 45

ROGER RABBIT (Also see Marvel Graphic Novel)
Disney Comics: June, 1990 - No. 18, Nov, 1991 ($1.50)
1-18-All new stories 3.00
In 3-D 1 (1992, $2.50)-Sold at Wal-Mart?; w/glasses 4.00

ROGER RABBIT'S TOONTOWN
Disney Comics: Aug, 1991 - No. 5, Dec, 1991 ($1.50)
1-5 3.00

ROGER ZELAZNY'S AMBER: THE GUNS OF AVALON
DC Comics: 1996 - No. 3, 1996 ($6.95, limited series)
1-3: Based on novel 7.00

ROG 2000
Pacific Comics: June, 1982 ($2.95, 44 pgs., B&W, one-shot, magazine)
nn-Byrne-c/a (r) 2 4 6 8 10 12
2nd printing (7/82) 1 2 3 4 5 7

Rogue (2004 series) #1 © MAR

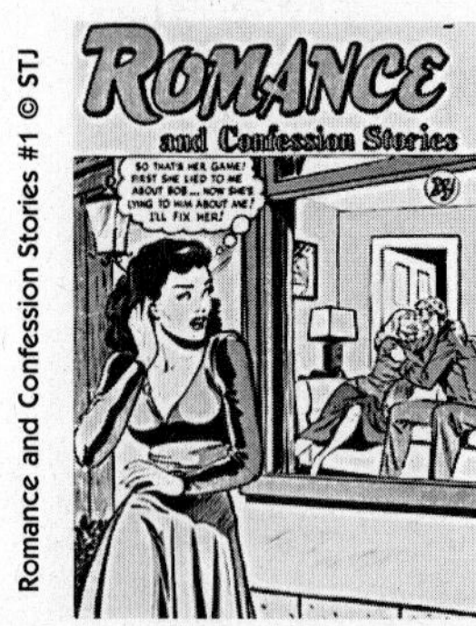

Romance and Confession Stories #1 © STJ

Romantic Adventures #3 © ACG

GD VG FN VF VF/NM NM-
2.0 4.0 6.0 8.0 9.0 9.2

ROG 2000
Fantagraphics Books: 1987 - No. 2, 1987 ($2.00, limited series)
1,2-Byrne-r 3.00

ROGUE (From X-Men)
Marvel Comics: Jan, 1995 - No. 4, Apr, 1995 ($2.95, limited series)
1-4: 1-Gold foil logo 4.00
TPB-($12.95) r/#1-4 13.00

ROGUE (Volume 2)
Marvel Comics: Sept, 2001 - No. 4, Dec, 2001 ($2.50, limited series)
1-4-Julie Bell painted-c/Lopresti-a; Rogue's early days with X-Men 3.00

ROGUE (From X-Men)
Marvel Comics: Sept, 2004 - No. 12, Aug, 2005 ($2.99)
1-12: 1-Richards-a. 4-Gambit app. 11-Sunfire dies, Rogue absorbs his powers 3.00
...: Going Rogue TPB (2005, $14.99) r/#1-6 15.00
...: Forget-Me-Not TPB (2006, $14.99) r/#7-12 15.00

ROGUE ANGEL: TELLER OF TALL TALES (Based on the Alex Archer novels)
IDW Publishing: Feb, 2008 - No. 5, Jun, 2008 ($3.99)
1-5-Annja Creed adventures; Barbara-Kesel-s/Renae De Liz-a 4.00

ROGUES GALLERY
DC Comics: 1996 ($3.50, one-shot)
1-Pinups of DC villains by various artists 4.00

ROGUES, THE (VILLAINS) (See The Flash)
DC Comics: Feb, 1998 ($1.95, one-shot)
1-Augustyn-s/Pearson-c 3.00

ROKKIN
DC Comics (WildStorm): Sept, 2006 - No. 6, Feb, 2007 ($2.99, limited series)
1-6-Hartnell-s/Bradshaw-a 3.00

ROLLING STONES: VOODOO LOUNGE
Marvel Comics: 1995 ($6.95, Prestige format, one-shot)
nn-Dave McKean-script/design/art 7.00

ROLY POLY COMIC BOOK
Green Publishing Co.: 1945 - No. 15, 1946 (MLJ reprints)
1-(No number on cover or indicia, "1945 issue" on cover) Red Rube & Steel Sterling begin; Sahle-c 32 64 96 192 314 435
6-The Blue Circle & The Steel Fist app. 20 40 60 118 192 265
10-Origin Red Rube retold; Steel Sterling story (Zip #41) 28 56 84 165 270 375
11,12: The Black Hood app. in both 20 40 60 117 189 260
14-Classic decapitation-c; the Black Hood app. 77 154 231 493 847 1200
15-The Blue Circle & The Steel Fist app.; cover exact swipe from Fox Blue Beetle #1 33 66 99 194 317 440

ROM (Based on the Parker Brothers toy)
Marvel Comics Group: Dec, 1979 - No. 75, Feb, 1986
1-Origin/1st app. 3 6 9 14 20 25
2-16,19-23,28-30: 5-Dr. Strange. 13-Saga of the Space Knights begins. 19-X-Men cameo. 23-Powerman & Iron Fist app. 1 2 3 5 6 8
17,18-X-Men app. 2 4 6 9 12 15
24-27: 24-F.F. cameo; Skrulls, Nova & The New Champions app. 25-Double size. 26,27-Galactus app. 1 2 3 5 7 9
31-49,51-60: 31,32-Brotherhood of Evil Mutants app. 32-X-Men cameo. 34,35-Sub-Mariner app. 41,42-Dr. Strange app. 56,57-Alpha Flight app. 58,59-Ant-Man app. 6.00
50-Skrulls app. (52 pgs.) Pin-ups by Konkle, Austin 1 2 3 4 5 7
61-74: 65-West Coast Avengers & Beta Ray Bill app. 65,66-X-Men app. 6.00
75-Last issue 2 4 6 9 12 15
Annual 1-4: (1982-85, 52 pgs.) 6.00
NOTE: ***Austin*** *c-3i, 18i, 61i.* ***Byrne*** *a-74i; c-56, 57, 74.* ***Ditko*** *a-59-75p, Annual 4.* ***Golden*** *c-7-12, 19.* ***Guice*** *a-61i; c-55, 58, 60p, 70p.* ***Layton*** *a-59i, 72i; c-15, 59i, 69.* ***Miller*** *c-2p?, 3p, 17p, 18p.* ***Russell*** *a(i)-64, 65, 67, 69, 71, 75; c-64, 65i, 66, 71i, 75.* ***Severin*** *c-41p.* ***Sienkiewicz*** *a-53i; c-46, 47, 52-54, 68, 71p, Annual 2.* ***Simonson*** *c-18.* ***P. Smith*** *c-59p.* ***Starlin*** *c-67.* ***Zeck*** *c-50.*

ROMANCE (See True Stories of...)

ROMANCE AND CONFESSION STORIES (See Giant Comics Edition)
St. John Publishing Co.: No date (1949) (25¢, 100 pgs.)
1-Baker-c/a; remaindered St. John love comics 52 104 156 328 557 785

ROMANCE DIARY
Marvel Comics (CDS)(CLDS): Dec, 1949 - No. 2, Mar, 1950
1,2 16 32 48 94 147 200

GD VG FN VF VF/NM NM-
2.0 4.0 6.0 8.0 9.0 9.2

ROMANCE OF FLYING, THE
David McKay Publications: 1942
Feature Books 33 (nn)-WW II photos 15 30 45 86 133 180

ROMANCES OF MOLLY MANTON (See Molly Manton)

ROMANCES OF NURSE HELEN GRANT, THE
Atlas Comics (VPI): Aug, 1957
1 9 18 27 52 69 85

ROMANCES OF THE WEST (Becomes Romantic Affairs #3?)
Marvel Comics (SPC): Nov, 1949 - No. 2, Mar, 1950 (52 pgs.)
1-Movie photo-c of Yvonne DeCarlo & Howard Duff (Calamity Jane & Sam Bass) 23 46 69 136 223 310
2-Photo-c 15 30 45 85 130 175

ROMANCE STORIES OF TRUE LOVE (Formerly True Love Problems & Advice Illustrated)
Harvey Publications: No. 45, 5/57 - No. 50, 3/58; No. 51, 9/58 - No. 52, 11/58
45-51: 45,46,48-50-Powell-a 6 12 18 31 38 45
52-Matt Baker-a 9 18 27 47 61 75

ROMANCE TALES (Formerly Western Winners #6?)
Marvel Comics (CDS): No. 7, Oct, 1949 - No. 9, April, 1950 (7-9: photo-c)
7 15 30 45 85 130 175
8,9: 8-Everett-a 11 22 33 60 83 105

ROMANCE TRAIL
National Periodical Publications: July-Aug, 1949 - No. 6, May-June, 1950
(All photo-c & 52 pgs.)
1-Kinstler, Toth-a; Jimmy Wakely photo-c 55 110 165 352 601 850
2-Kinstler-a; Jim Bannon photo-c 31 62 93 182 296 410
3-Tex Williams photo-c; Kinstler, Toth-a 32 64 96 192 314 435
4-Jim Bannon as Red Ryder photo-c; Toth-a 24 48 72 140 230 320
5,6: Photo-c on both. 5-Kinstler-a 22 44 66 128 209 290

ROMAN HOLIDAYS, THE (TV)
Gold Key: Feb, 1973 - No. 4, Nov, 1973 (Hanna-Barbera)
1 4 8 12 28 44 60
2-4 3 6 9 18 27 35

ROMANTIC ADVENTURES (My... #49-67, covers only)
American Comics Group (B&I Publ. Co.): Mar-Apr, 1949 - No. 67, July, 1956 (Becomes My... #68 on)
1 20 40 60 114 182 250
2 12 24 36 69 97 125
3-10 10 20 30 56 76 95
11-20 (4/52) 9 18 27 50 65 80
21-45,51,52: 52-Last Pre-code (2/55) 8 16 24 44 57 70
46-49-3-D effect-c/stories (TrueVision) 14 28 42 78 112 145
50-Classic cover/story "Love of A Lunatic" 13 26 39 74 105 135
53-67 8 16 24 40 50 60
NOTE: *#1-23, 52 pgs.* ***Shelly*** *a-40.* *Whitney c/art in many issues.*

ROMANTIC AFFAIRS (Formerly Molly Manton's Romances #2 and/or Romances of the West #2 and/or Our Love #2?)
Marvel Comics (SPC): No. 3, Mar, 1950
3-Photo-c from Molly Manton's Romances #2 11 22 33 60 83 105

ROMANTIC CONFESSIONS
Hillman Periodicals: Oct, 1949 - V3#1, Apr-May, 1953
V1#1-McWilliams-a 18 36 54 107 169 230
2-Briefer-a; negligee panels 11 22 33 64 90 115
3-12 10 20 30 56 76 95
V2#1,2,4-8,10-12: 2-McWilliams-a 9 18 27 52 69 85
3-Krigstein-a 10 20 30 58 79 100
9-One pg. Frazetta ad 9 18 27 52 69 85
V3#1 9 18 27 50 65 80

ROMANTIC HEARTS
Story Comics/Master/Merit Pubs.: Mar, 1951 - No. 10, Oct, 1952; July, 1953 - No. 12, July, 1955
1(3/51) (1st Series) 15 30 45 86 133 180
2 10 20 30 54 72 90
3-10: Cameron-a 9 18 27 50 65 80
1(7/53) (2nd Series)-Some say #11 on-c 11 22 33 60 83 105
2 9 18 27 47 61 75
3-12 8 16 24 42 54 65

ROMANTIC LOVE

Romantic Secrets #34 © FAW

Ronald McDonald #4 © McDonald's

Rose and Thorn #2 © DC

	GD 2.0	VG 4.0	FN 6.0	VF 8.0	VF/NM 9.0	NM- 9.2

Avon Periodicals/Realistic (No #14-19): 9-10/49 - #3, 1-2/50; #4, 2-3/51 - #13, 10/52; #20, 3-4/54 - #23, 9-10/54

	GD	VG	FN	VF	VF/NM	NM-
1-c-/Avon paperback #252	34	68	102	199	325	450
2-5: 3-c-/paperback Novel Library #12. 4-c-/paperback Diversey Prize Novel #5. 5-c-/paperback Novel Library #34	20	40	60	118	192	265
6- "Thrill Crazy" marijuana story; c-/Avon paperback #207; Kinstler-a	29	58	87	170	278	385
7,8: 8-Astarita-a(2)	20	40	60	114	182	250
9-12: 9-c-/paperback Novel Library #41; Kinstler-a. 10-c-/Avon paperback #212. 11-c-/paperback Novel Library #17; Kinstler-a. 12-c-/paperback Novel Library #13	21	42	63	122	199	275
13,21-23: 22,23-Kinstler-c	20	40	60	114	182	250
20-Kinstler-c/a	20	40	60	118	192	265
nn(1-3/53)(Realistic-r)	14	28	42	80	115	150

NOTE: *Astarita a-7, 10, 11, 21. Painted c-1-3, 5, 7-11, 13. Photo c-4, 6.*

ROMANTIC LOVE
Quality Comics Group: 1963-1964

	GD	VG	FN	VF	VF/NM	NM-
I.W. Reprint #2,3,8,11: 2-r/Romantic Love #2	2	4	6	11	16	20

ROMANTIC MARRIAGE (Cinderella Love #25 on)
Ziff-Davis/St. John No. 18 on (#1-8: 52 pgs.): #1-3 (1950, no months); #4, 5-6/51 - #17, 9/52; #18, 9/53 - #24, 9/54

	GD	VG	FN	VF	VF/NM	NM-
1-Photo-c; Cary Grant/Betsy Drake photo back-c.	22	44	66	128	209	290
2-Painted-c; Anderson-a (also #15)	15	30	45	85	130	175
3-9: 3,4,8,9-Painted-c; 5-7-Photo-c	14	28	42	81	118	155
10-Unusual format; front-c is a painted-c; back-c is a photo-c complete with logo, price, etc.	21	42	63	126	206	285
11-17 13-Photo-c. 15-Signed story by Anderson. 17-(9/52)-Last Z-D issue	14	28	42	76	108	140
18-22,24: 20-Photo-c	14	28	42	76	108	140
23-Baker-c; all stories are reprinted from #15	15	30	45	85	130	175

ROMANTIC PICTURE NOVELETTES
Magazine Enterprises: 1946

	GD	VG	FN	VF	VF/NM	NM-
1-Mary Worth-r; Creig Flessel-c	16	32	48	94	147	200

ROMANTIC SECRETS (Becomes Time For Love)
Fawcett/Charlton Comics No. 5 (10/55) on: Sept, 1949 - No. 39, 4/53; No. 5, 10/55 - No. 52, 11/64 (#1-39: photo-c)

	GD	VG	FN	VF	VF/NM	NM-
1-(52 pg. issues begin, end #?)	18	36	54	103	162	220
2,3	11	22	33	62	86	110
4,9-Evans-a	12	24	36	67	94	120
5-8,10(9/50)	9	18	27	52	69	85
11-23	9	18	27	47	61	75
24-Evans-a	9	18	27	52	69	85
25-39('53)	8	16	24	44	57	70
5 (Charlton, 2nd Series)(10/55, formerly Negro Romances #4)	10	20	30	58	79	100
6-10	8	16	24	44	57	70
11-20	4	8	12	23	36	48
21-35	3	6	9	20	30	40
36-52('64)	3	6	9	16	23	30

NOTE: ***Bailey** a-20. **Powell** a(1st series)-5, 7, 10, 12, 16, 17, 20, 26, 29, 33, 34, 36, 37. **Sekowsky** a-26. **Swayze** a(1st series)-16, 18, 19, 23, 26-28, 31, 32, 39.*

ROMANTIC STORY (Cowboy Love #28 on)
Fawcett/Charlton Comics No. 23 on: 11/49 - #22, Sum, 1953; #23, 5/54 - #27, 12/54; #28, 8/55 - #130, 11/73

	GD	VG	FN	VF	VF/NM	NM-
1-Photo-c begin, end #24; 52 pgs. begins	18	36	54	103	162	220
2	11	22	33	62	86	110
3-5	10	20	30	54	72	90
6-14	9	18	27	50	65	80
15-Evans-a	10	20	30	54	72	90
16-22(Sum, '53; last Fawcett issue). 21-Toth-a?	8	16	24	42	54	65
23-39: 26,29-Wood swipes	7	14	21	37	46	55
40-(100 pgs.)	11	22	33	64	90	115
41-50	3	6	9	21	32	42
51-80: 57-Hypo needle story	3	6	9	16	23	30
81-99	2	4	6	10	14	18
100	2	4	6	13	28	22
101-130: 120-Bobby Sherman pin-up	2	4	6	9	12	15

NOTE: ***Jim Aparo** a-94. **Powell** a-7, 8, 16, 20, 30. **Marcus Swayze** a-2, 12, 20, 32.*

ROMANTIC THRILLS (See Fox Giants)

ROMANTIC WESTERN
Fawcett Publications: Winter, 1949 - No. 3, June, 1950 (All Photo-c)

	GD	VG	FN	VF	VF/NM	NM-
1	22	44	66	128	209	290
2-(Spr/50)-Williamson, McWilliams-a	20	40	60	114	182	250
3	15	30	45	85	130	175

ROMEO TUBBS (...That Lovable Teenager; formerly My Secret Life)
Fox Feature Syndicate/Green Publ. Co. No. 27: No. 26, 5/50 - No. 28, 7/50; No. 1, 1950; No. 27, 12/52

	GD	VG	FN	VF	VF/NM	NM-
26-Teen-age	11	22	33	64	90	115
28 (7/50)	10	20	30	58	79	100
27 (12/52)-Contains Pedro on inside; Wood-a (exist?)	15	30	45	84	127	170

RONALD McDONALD (TV)
Charlton Press: Sept, 1970 - No. 4, March, 1971

	GD	VG	FN	VF	VF/NM	NM-
1-Bill Yates-a in all	8	16	24	55	93	130
2-4: 2 & 3 both dated Jan, 1971	5	10	15	32	51	70
V2#1-4-Special reprint for McDonald systems; new cover art on each; "Not for resale" on cover	6	12	18	39	62	85

RONIN
DC Comics: July, 1983 - No. 6, Aug, 1984 ($2.50, limited series, 52 pgs.)

	GD	VG	FN	VF	VF/NM	NM-
1-5-Frank Miller-c/a/scripts in all	2	3	4	6	8	10
6-Scarcer; has fold-out poster.	2	4	6	8	10	12
Trade paperback (1987, $12.95)-Reprints #1-6						13.00

RONNA
Knight Press: Apr, 1997 ($2.95, B&W, one-shot)

	GD	VG	FN	VF	VF/NM	NM-
1-Beau Smith-s						3.00

ROOK (See Eerie Magazine & Warren Presents: The Rook)
Warren Publications: Oct, 1979 - No. 14, April, 1982 (B&W magazine)

	GD	VG	FN	VF	VF/NM	NM-
1-Nino-a/Corben-c; with 8 pg. color insert	3	6	9	16	23	30
2-4,6,7: 2-Voltar by Alcala begins. 3,4-Toth-a	2	4	6	9	13	16
5,8-14: 11-Zorro-s. 12-14-Eagle by Severin	2	4	6	9	13	16

ROOK
Harris Comics: No. 0, Jun, 1995 - No. 4, 1995 ($2.95)

	GD	VG	FN	VF	VF/NM	NM-
0-4: 0-short stories (3) w/preview. 4-Brereton-c.						3.00

ROOKIE COP (Formerly Crime and Justice?)
Charlton Comics: No. 27, Nov, 1955 - No. 33, Aug, 1957

	GD	VG	FN	VF	VF/NM	NM-
27	9	18	27	47	61	75
28-33	6	12	18	31	38	45

ROOM 222 (TV)
Dell Publishing Co.: Jan, 1970; No. 2, May, 1970 - No. 4, Jan, 1971

	GD	VG	FN	VF	VF/NM	NM-
1	5	10	15	35	55	75
2-4: 2,4-Photo-c. 3-Marijuana story. 4 r/#1	4	8	12	22	34	45

ROOTIE KAZOOTIE (TV)(See 3-D-ell)
Dell Publishing Co.: No. 415, Aug, 1952 - No. 6, Oct-Dec, 1954

	GD	VG	FN	VF	VF/NM	NM-
Four Color 415 (#1)	9	18	27	63	112	160
Four Color 459,502(#2,3), 4(4-6/54)-6	7	14	21	46	76	105

ROOTS OF THE SWAMP THING
DC Comics: July, 1986 - No.5, Nov, 1986 ($2.00, Baxter paper, 52 pgs.)

	GD	VG	FN	VF	VF/NM	NM-
1-5: r/Swamp Thing #1-10 by Wrightson & House of Mystery-r. 1-new Wrightson-c (2-5 reprinted covers).						4.00

ROSE (See Bone)
Cartoon Books: Nov, 2000 - No. 3, Feb, 2002 ($5.95, lim. series, square-bound)

	GD	VG	FN	VF	VF/NM	NM-
1-3-Prequel to Bone; Jeff Smith-s/Charles Vess painted-a/c						6.00
HC (2001, $29.95) r/#1-3; new Vess cover painting						30.00
SC (2002, $19.95) r/#1-3; new Vess cover painting						20.00
1-($6.00)-Blood & Glory Edition						6.00

ROSE AND THORN
DC Comics: Feb, 2004 - No. 6, July, 2004 ($2.95, limited series)

	GD	VG	FN	VF	VF/NM	NM-
1-6-Simone-s/Melo-a/Hughes-c						3.00

ROSWELL: LITTLE GREEN MAN (See Simpsons Comics #19-22)
Bongo Comics: 1996 - No. 6 ($2.95, quarterly)

	GD	VG	FN	VF	VF/NM	NM-
1-6						4.00
...Walks Among Us ('97, $12.95, TPB) r/ #1-3 & Simpsons flip books						13.00

ROUND TABLE OF AMERICA: PERSONALITY CRISIS (See Big Bang Comics)
Image Comics: Aug, 2005 ($3.50, one-shot)

	GD	VG	FN	VF	VF/NM	NM-
1-Carlos Rodriguez-a/Pedro Angosto-s						3.50

ROUNDUP (...Western Crime Stories)

Roy Rogers Comics #4 © Roy Rogers

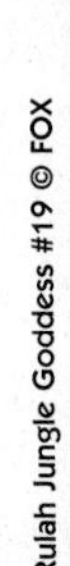
Rulah Jungle Goddess #19 © FOX

Runaways (2005 series) #1 © DC

D. S. Publishing Co.: July-Aug, 1948 - No. 5, Mar-Apr, 1949 (All 52 pgs.)

	GD 2.0	VG 4.0	FN 6.0	VF 8.0	VF/NM 9.0	NM- 9.2
1-Kiefer-a	18	36	54	107	169	230
2-5: 2-Marijuana drug mention story	14	28	42	82	121	160

ROUTE 666
CrossGeneration Comics: July, 2002 - No. 22, Jun, 2004 ($2.95)

	GD 2.0	VG 4.0	FN 6.0	VF 8.0	VF/NM 9.0	NM- 9.2
1-22-Bedard-s/Moline-a in most. 5-Richards-a. 15-McCrea-a						3.00
...: Highway to Horror (4/03, $15.95, TPB) r/#1-6						16.00
Vol. 2: Three-Ring Circus (2003, $15.95) r/#7-12						16.00

ROYAL ROY
Marvel Comics (Star Comics): May, 1985 - No.6, Mar, 1986 (Children's book)

	GD 2.0	VG 4.0	FN 6.0	VF 8.0	VF/NM 9.0	NM- 9.2
1-6						4.00

ROY CAMPANELLA, BASEBALL HERO
Fawcett Publications: 1950 (Brooklyn Dodgers)

	GD 2.0	VG 4.0	FN 6.0	VF 8.0	VF/NM 9.0	NM- 9.2
nn-Photo-c; life story	60	120	180	381	658	935

ROY ROGERS (See March of Comics #17, 35, 47, 62, 68, 73, 77, 86, 91, 100, 105, 116, 121, 131, 136, 146, 151, 161, 167, 176, 191, 206, 221, 236, 250)

ROY ROGERS AND TRIGGER
Gold Key: Apr, 1967

	GD 2.0	VG 4.0	FN 6.0	VF 8.0	VF/NM 9.0	NM- 9.2
1-Photo-c; reprints	4	8	12	28	44	60

ROY ROGERS ANNUAL
Wilson Publ. Co., Toronto/Dell: 1947 ("Giant Edition" on-c)(132 pgs., 50¢)

nn-Less than 5 known copies. Front and back cover art are from Roy Rogers #2. Stories reprinted from Roy Rogers #2, Four Color #137 and Four Color #153. (A copy in VG/FN was sold in 1986 for $400, in 1996 for $1200 & in 2000 for $1500; a FN+ sold for $1,650; a GD sold for $448 in 2008 and a FN sold for $717 in 2009.)

ROY ROGERS COMICS (See Western Roundup under Dell Giants)
Dell Publishing Co.: No. 38, 4/44 - No. 177, 12/47 (#38-166: 52 pgs.)

	GD 2.0	VG 4.0	FN 6.0	VF 8.0	VF/NM 9.0	NM- 9.2
Four Color 38 (1944)-49 pg. story; photo front/back-c on all 4-Color issues (1st western comic with photo-c)	146	292	438	1226	2663	4100
Four Color 63 (1945)-Color photos on all four-c	36	72	108	261	568	875
Four Color 86,95 (1945)	26	52	78	182	391	600
Four Color 109 (1946)	20	40	60	137	294	450
Four Color 117,124,137,144	16	32	48	107	234	360
Four Color 153,160,166: 166-48 pg. story	14	28	42	97	211	325
Four Color 177 (36 pgs.)-32 pg. story	14	28	42	93	202	310
HC (Dark Horse Books, 8/08, $49.95) r/Four Color #38,63,86,95,109; Roy Rogers Jr intro.						50.00

ROY ROGERS COMICS (...& Trigger #92(8/55)-on)(Roy starred in Republic movies, radio & TV) (Singing cowboy) (Also see Dale Evans, It Really Happened #8, Queen of the West Dale Evans, & Roy Rogers' Trigger)
Dell Publishing Co.: Jan, 1948 - No. 145, Sept-Oct, 1961 (#1-19: 36 pgs.)

	GD 2.0	VG 4.0	FN 6.0	VF 8.0	VF/NM 9.0	NM- 9.2
1-Roy, his horse Trigger, & Chuck Wagon Charley's Tales begin; photo-c begin, end #145	57	114	171	462	1006	1550
2	21	42	63	142	304	465
3-5	14	28	42	97	211	325
6-10	12	24	36	84	175	265
11-19: 19-Chuck Wagon Charley's Tales ends	11	22	33	75	148	220
20 (52 pgs.)-Trigger feature begins, ends #46	11	22	33	76	151	225
21-30 (52 pgs.)	10	20	30	67	124	180
31-46 (52 pgs.): 37-X-Mas-c	9	18	27	58	99	140
47-56 (36 pgs.): 47-Chuck Wagon Charley's Tales returns, ends #133. 49-X-mas-c. 55-Last photo back-c	7	14	21	46	76	105
57 (52 pgs.)-Heroin drug propaganda story	7	14	21	48	76	110
58-70 (52 pgs.): 58-Heroin drug use/dealing story. 61-X-Mas-c	7	14	21	46	76	105
71-80 (52 pgs.): 73-X-Mas-c	6	12	18	41	66	90
81-91 (36 pgs. #81-on): 85-X-Mas-c	6	12	18	39	62	85
92-99,101-110,112-118: 92-Title changed to Roy Rogers and Trigger (8/55)	6	12	18	37	59	80
100-Trigger feature returns, ends #131	6	12	18	42	69	95
111,119-124-Toth-a	7	14	21	44	72	100
125-131: 125-Toth-a (1 pg.)	5	10	15	35	55	75
132-144-Manning-a. 132-1st Dale Evans-sty by Russ Manning. 138,144-Dale Evans featured	6	12	18	39	62	85
145-Last issue	7	14	21	46	76	105

NOTE: ***Buscema** a-74-108(2 stories each). **Manning** a-123, 124, 132-144. **Marsh** a-110. Photo back-c No. 1-9, 11-35, 38-55.*

ROY ROGERS' TRIGGER
Dell Publishing Co.: No. 329, May, 1951 - No. 17, June-Aug, 1955

	GD 2.0	VG 4.0	FN 6.0	VF 8.0	VF/NM 9.0	NM- 9.2
Four Color 329 (#1)-Painted-c	12	24	36	84	175	265
2 (9-11/51)-Photo-c	10	20	30	70	133	195
3-5: 3-Painted-c begin, end #17, most by S. Savitt	6	12	18	42	69	95
6-17: Title merges with Roy Rogers after #17	5	10	15	35	55	75

ROY ROGERS WESTERN CLASSICS
AC Comics: 1989 -No. 4 ($2.95/$3.95, 44pgs.) (24 pgs. color, 16 pgs. B&W)

	GD 2.0	VG 4.0	FN 6.0	VF 8.0	VF/NM 9.0	NM- 9.2
1-4: 1-Dale Evans-r by Manning, Trigger-r by Buscema; photo covers & interior photos by Roy & Dale. 2-Buscema-r (3); photo-c & B&W photos inside. 3-Dale Evans-r by Manning; Trigger-r by Buscema plus other Buscema-r; photo-c						4.00

RUDOLPH, THE RED-NOSED REINDEER
National Per. Publ.: 1950 - No. 13, Winter, 1962-63 (Issues are not numbered)

	GD 2.0	VG 4.0	FN 6.0	VF 8.0	VF/NM 9.0	NM- 9.2
1950 issue (#1); Grossman-c/a in all	22	44	66	132	216	300
1951-53 issues (3 total)	14	28	42	80	115	150
1954/55, 55/56, 56/57	12	24	36	72	101	130
1957/58, 58/59, 59/60, 60/61, 61/62	7	14	21	49	82	115
1962/63 (rare)(84 pgs.)(shows "Annual" in indicia)	11	22	33	73	142	210

NOTE: *13 total issues published. Has games & puzzles also.*

RUDOLPH, THE RED-NOSED REINDEER (Also see Limited Collectors' Edition C-20, C-24, C-33, C-42, C-50; and All-New Collectors' Edition C-53 & C-60)
National Per. Publ.: Christmas 1972 (Treasury-size)

	GD 2.0	VG 4.0	FN 6.0	VF 8.0	VF/NM 9.0	NM- 9.2
nn-Precursor to Limited Collectors' Edition title (scarce) (implied to be Lim. Coll .Ed. C-20)	18	36	54	123	267	410

RUFF AND REDDY (TV)
Dell Publ. Co.: No. 937, 9/58 - No. 12, 1-3/62 (Hanna-Barbera)(#9 on: 15¢)

	GD 2.0	VG 4.0	FN 6.0	VF 8.0	VF/NM 9.0	NM- 9.2
Four Color 937(#1)(1st Hanna-Barbera comic book)	11	22	33	74	145	215
Four Color 981,1038	8	16	24	51	86	120
4(1-3/60)-12: 8-Last 10¢ issue	7	14	21	44	72	100

RUGGED ACTION (Strange Stories of Suspense #5 on)
Atlas Comics (CSI): Dec, 1954 - No. 4, June, 1955

	GD 2.0	VG 4.0	FN 6.0	VF 8.0	VF/NM 9.0	NM- 9.2
1-Brodsky-c	14	28	42	80	115	150
2-4: 2-Last precode (2/55)	10	20	30	58	79	100

NOTE: ***Ayers** a-2, 3. **Maneely** c-2, 3. **Severin** a-2.*

RUINS
Marvel Comics (Alterniverse): July, 1995 - No. 2, Sept, 1995 ($5.00, painted, limited series)

	GD 2.0	VG 4.0	FN 6.0	VF 8.0	VF/NM 9.0	NM- 9.2
1,2: Phil Sheldon from Marvels; Warren Ellis scripts; acetate-c						5.00
Reprint (2009, $4.99) r/#1,2; cover gallery						5.00

RULAH JUNGLE GODDESS (Formerly Zoot; I Loved #28 on) (Also see All Top Comics & Terrors of the Jungle)
Fox Features Syndicate: No. 17, Aug, 1948 - No. 27, June, 1949

	GD 2.0	VG 4.0	FN 6.0	VF 8.0	VF/NM 9.0	NM- 9.2
17	129	258	387	826	1413	2000
18-Classic girl-fight interior splash	81	162	243	518	884	1250
19,20	73	146	219	467	796	1125
21-Used in **SOTI**, pg. 388,389	76	152	228	486	831	1175
22-Used in **SOTI**, pg. 22,23	76	152	228	486	831	1175
23-27	55	110	165	352	601	850

NOTE: ***Kamen** c-17-19, 21, 22.*

RUNAWAY, THE (See Movie Classics)

RUNAWAYS
Marvel Comics: July, 2003 - No. 18, Nov, 2004 ($2.95/$2.25/$2.99)

	GD 2.0	VG 4.0	FN 6.0	VF 8.0	VF/NM 9.0	NM- 9.2
1-($2.95) Vaughan-s/Alphona-a/Jo Chen-c						4.00
2-9-($2.50)						3.00
10-18-($2.99) 11,12-Miyazawa-a; Cloak and Dagger app. 16-The mole revealed						3.00
Hardcover (2005, $34.99) oversized r/#1-18; proposal & sketch pages; Vaughan intro.						35.00
Marvel Age Runaways Vol. 1: Pride and Joy (2004, $7.99, digest size) r/#1-6						8.00
...Vol. 2: Teenage Wasteland (2004, $7.99, digest size) r/#7-12						8.00
...Vol. 3: The Good Die Young (2004, $7.99, digest size) r/#13-18						8.00

RUNAWAYS (Also see X-Men/Runaways 2006 FCBD Edition in the Promotional Section)
Marvel Comics: Apr, 2005 - No. 30, Aug, 2008 ($2.99)

	GD 2.0	VG 4.0	FN 6.0	VF 8.0	VF/NM 9.0	NM- 9.2
1-24: 1-6-Vaughan-s/Alphona-a/Jo Chen-c. 7,8-Miyazawa-a/Bachalo-c. 11-Spider-Man app. 12-New Avengers app. 18-Gert killed						3.00
25-30-Joss Whedon-s/Michael Ryan-a. 25-Punisher app.						3.00
...: Dead End Kids HC (2008, $19.99) r/#25-30						20.00
... Saga (2007, $3.99) re-caps the 2 series thru #24; 4 new pages w/Ramos-a; Ramos-c						4.00
Hardcover (2006, $24.99) oversized r/#1-12 & X-Men/Runaways; script & sketch pages						25.00
Hardcover Vol. 3 (2007, $24.99) oversized r/#13-24; sketch pages						25.00
...Vol. 4: True Believers (2006, $7.99, digest size) r/#1-6						8.00
...Vol. 5: Escape To New York (2006, $7.99, digest size) r/#7-12						8.00
...Vol. 6: Parental Guidance (2006, $7.99, digest size) r/#13-18						8.00

RUNAWAYS (3rd series)

Ruse #4 © CRO

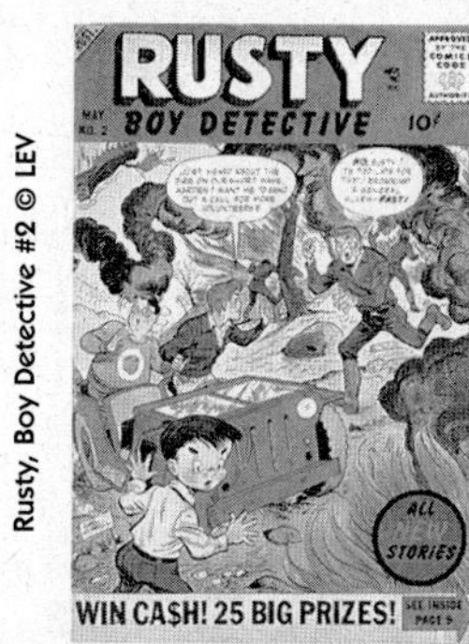

Rusty, Boy Detective #2 © LEV

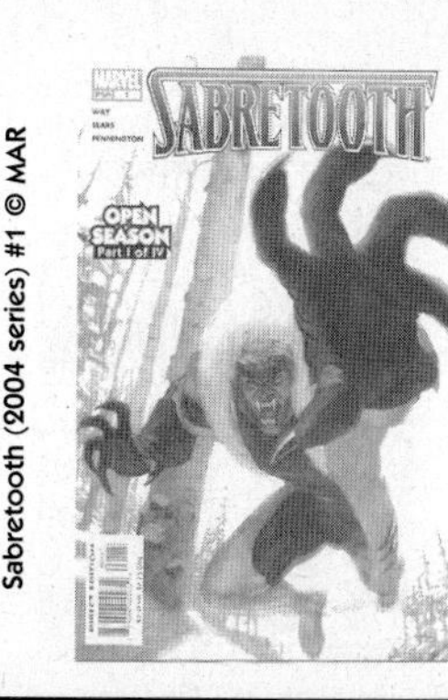

Sabretooth (2004 series) #1 © MAR

GD VG FN VF VF/NM NM-
2.0 4.0 6.0 8.0 9.0 9.2

Marvel Comics: Oct, 2008 - No. 14, Nov, 2009 ($2.99/$3.99)
1-9,11-14: 1-6-Terry Moore-s/Humberto Ramos-a/c. 7-9-Miyazawa-a 3.00
10-($3.99) Wolverine & the X-Men app.; Yost & Asmus-s; Pichelli & Rios-a; Lafuente-c 4.00

RUN BABY RUN
Logos International: 1974 (39¢, Christian religious)
nn-By Tony Tallarico from Nicky Cruz's book 2 4 6 11 16 20

RUN, BUDDY, RUN (TV)
Gold Key: June, 1967 (Photo-c)
1 (10204-706) 3 6 9 18 27 35

RUNE (See Curse of Rune, Sludge & all other Ultraverse titles for previews)
Malibu Comics (Ultraverse): 1994 - No. 9, Apr, 1995 ($1.95)
0-Obtained by sending coupons from 11 comics; came w/Solution #0, poster, temporary tattoo, card 1 2 3 5 6 8
1,2,4-9: 1-Barry Windsor-Smith-c/a/stories begin, ends #6. 5-1st app. of Gemini. 6-Prime & Mantra app. 3.00
1-(1/94)-"Ashcan" edition flip book w/Wrath #1 3.00
1-Ultra 5000 Limited silver foil edition 4.00
3-(3/94, $3.50, 68 pgs.)-Flip book w/Ultraverse Premiere #1 4.00
Giant Size 1 ($2.50, 44 pgs.)-B.Smith story & art. 4.00

RUNE (2nd Series)(Formerly Curse of Rune)(See Ultraverse Unlimited #1)
Malibu Comics (Ultraverse): Infinity, Sept, 1995 - V2#7, Apr, 1996 ($1.50)
Infinity, V2#1-7: Infinity-Black September tie-in; black-c & painted-c exist. 1,3-7-Marvel's Adam Warlock app; regular & painted-c exist. 2-Flip book w/ "Phoenix Resurrection" Pt. 6 3.00
...Vs. Venom 1 (12/95, $3.95) 4.00

RUNE: HEARTS OF DARKNESS
Malibu Comics (Ultraverse): Sept, 1996 - No. 3, Nov, 1996 ($1.50, lim. series)
1-3: Moench scripts & Kyle Hotz-c/a; flip books w/6 pg. Rune story by the Pander Bros. 3.00

RUNE/SILVER SURFER
Marvel Comics/Malibu Comics (Ultraverse): Apr, 1995 ($5.95/$2.95, one-shot)
1 ($5.95, direct market)-BWS-c 6.00
1 ($2.95, newstand)-BWS-c 3.00
1-Collector's limited edition 6.00

RUSE (Also see Archard's Agents)
CrossGeneration Comics: Nov, 2001 - No. 26, Jan, 2004 ($2.95)
1-Waid-s/Guice & Perkins-a 5.00
2-26: 6-Jeff Johnson-a. 11,15-Paul Ryan-a. 12-Last Waid-s 3.00
Enter the Detective Vol. 1 TPB (2002, $15.95) r/#1-6; Guice-c 16.00
...: The Silent Partner Vol. 2 (3/03, $15.95, TPB) r/#7-12 16.00
...: Criminal Intent Vol. 3 ('03, $15.95, TPB) r/#13-18 16.00
Traveler 1,2 ($9.95): Digest-size editions of the TPBs 10.00

RUSE
Marvel Comics: May, 2011 - No. 4 ($2.99, limited series)
1-4-Waid-s/Guice-c. 1,3,4-Pierfederici-a 3.00

RUSH CITY
DC Comics: Sept, 2006 - No. 6, May, 2007 ($2.99, limited series)
1-6: 1-Dixon-s/Green-a/Jock-c. 2,3-Black Canary app. 3.00

RUSTLERS, THE (See Zane Grey Four Color 532)

RUSTY, BOY DETECTIVE
Good Comics/Lev Gleason: Mar-April, 1955 - No. 5, Nov, 1955
1-Bob Wood, Carl Hubbell-a begins 9 18 27 47 61 75
2-5 6 12 18 31 38 45

RUSTY COMICS (Formerly Kid Movie Comics; Rusty and Her Family #21, 22; The Kelleys #23 on; see Millie The Model)
Marvel Comics (HPC): No. 12, Apr, 1947 - No. 22, Sept, 1949
12-Mitzi app. 23 46 69 136 223 310
13 14 28 42 82 121 160
14-Wolverton's Powerhouse Pepper (4 pgs.) plus Kurtzman's "Hey Look" 22 44 66 132 216 300
15-17-Kurtzman's "Hey Look" 16 32 48 94 147 200
18,19 14 28 42 78 112 145
20-Kurtzman-a (5 pgs.) 17 34 51 98 154 210
21,22-Kurtzman-a (17 & 22 pgs.) 21 42 63 126 206 285

RUSTY DUGAN (See Holyoke One-Shot #2)

RUSTY RILEY
Dell Publishing Co.: No. 418, Aug, 1952 - No. 554, April, 1954 (Frank Godwin strip reprints)
Four Color 418 (...a Boy, a Horse, and a Dog #1) 5 10 15 32 51 70
Four Color 451(2/53), 486 ('53), 554 4 8 12 26 41 50

RUULE
Beckett Comics: Dec, 2003 - No. 5, Apr, 2004 ($2.99)
1-5-David Mack-c/Mike Hawthorne-a 3.00

RUULE: KISS & TELL
Beckett Comics: Jun, 2004 - No. 8 ($1.99)
1-8: 1-Amano-s/c; Rousseau-a. 4-Maleev-c 3.00
TPB (2005, $19.99) r/#1-8 20.00

RYDER OF THE STORM
Radical Comics: Oct, 2010 - No. 3, Apr, 2011 ($4.99, limited series)
1-3-David Hine-s/Wayne Nichols-a 5.00

SAARI ("The Jungle Goddess")
P. L. Publishing Co.: November, 1951
1 47 94 141 296 498 700

SABAN POWERHOUSE (TV)
Acclaim Books: 1997 ($4.50, digest size)
1,2-Power Rangers, BeetleBorgs, and others 4.50

SABAN PRESENTS POWER RANGERS TURBO VS. BEETLEBORGS METALLIX (TV)
Acclaim Books: 1997 ($4.50, digest size, one-shot)
nn 4.50

SABAN'S MIGHTY MORPHIN POWER RANGERS
Hamilton Comics: Dec, 1994 - No. 6, May, 1995 ($1.95, limited series)
1-6: 1-w/bound-in Power Ranger Barcode Card 4.00

SABAN'S MIGHTY MORPHIN POWER RANGERS (TV)
Marvel Comics: 1995 - No. 8, 1996 ($1.75)
1-8 4.00

SABLE (Formerly Jon Sable, Freelance; also see Mike Grell's...)
First Comics: Mar, 1988 - No. 27, May, 1990 ($1.75/$1.95)
1-27: 10-Begin $1.95-c 3.00

SABLE & FORTUNE (Also see Silver Sable and the Wild Pack)
Marvel Comics: Mar, 2006 - No. 4, June, 2006 ($2.99, limited series)
1-4-John Burns-a/Brendan Cahill-s 3.00

SABRE (See Eclipse Graphic Album Series)
Eclipse Comics: Aug, 1982 - No. 14, Aug, 1985 (Baxter paper #4 on)
1-14: 1-Sabre & Morrigan Tales begin. 4-6-Incredible Seven origin 3.00

SABRETOOTH (See Iron Fist, Power Man, X-Factor #10 & X-Men)
Marvel Comics: Aug, 1993 - No. 4, Nov, 1993 ($2.95, lim. series, coated paper)
1-4: 1-Die-cut-c. 3-Wolverine app. 4.00
...Special 1 "In the Red Zone" (1995, $4.95) Chromium wraparound-c 6.00
V2 #1 (1/98, $5.95, one-shot) Wildchild app. 6.00
Trade paperback (12/94, $12.95) r/#1-4 13.00

SABRETOOTH
Marvel Comics: Dec, 2004 - No. 4, Feb, 2005 ($2.99, limited series)
1-4-Sears-a. 3,4-Wendigo app. 3.00
...: Open Season TPB (2005, $9.99) r/#1-4 10.00

SABRETOOTH AND MYSTIQUE (See Mystique and Sabretooth)

SABRETOOTH CLASSIC
Marvel Comics: May, 1994 - No. 15, July, 1995 ($1.50)
1-15: 1-3-r/Power Man & Iron Fist #66,78,84. 4-r/Spec. S-M #116. 9-Uncanny X-Men #212, 10-r/Uncanny X-Men #213. 11-r/ Daredevil #238. 12-r/Classic X-Men #10 3.00

SABRETOOTH: MARY SHELLEY OVERDRIVE
Marvel Comics: Aug, 2002 - No. 4, Nov, 2002 ($2.99, limited series)
1-4-Jolley-s; Harris-c 3.00

SABRINA (Volume 2) (Based on animated series)
Archie Publications: Jan, 2000 - No. 104, Sept, 2009 ($1.79/$1.99/$2.19/$2.25/$2.50)
1-Teen-age Witch magically reverted to 12 years old 5.00
2-10: 4-Begin $1.99-c 4.00
11-104: 38-Sabrina aged back to 16 years old. 39-Begin $2.19-c. 58-Manga-style begins; Tania Del Rio-a. 67-Josie and the Pussycats app. 101-Young Salem; begin $2.50-c 3.00

SABRINA'S CHRISTMAS MAGIC (See Archie Giant Series Magazine #196, 207, 220, 231, 243, 455, 467, 479, 491, 503, 515)

SABRINA'S HALLOWEEN SPOOOKTACULAR

Sabrina V2 #58 © AP

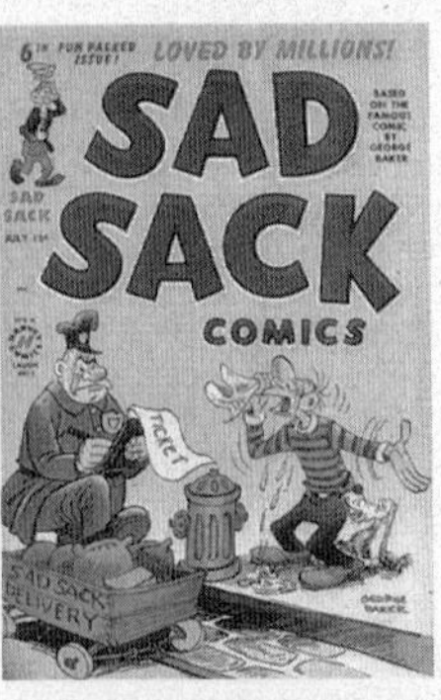

Sad Sack Comics #6 © HARV

Sad Sack Laugh Special #1 © HARV

	GD 2.0	VG 4.0	FN 6.0	VF 8.0	VF/NM 9.0	NM- 9.2

Archie Publications: 1993 - 1995 ($2.00, 52 pgs.)

1-Neon orange ink-c; bound-in poster	1	2	3	5	6	8
2,3-Titled "Sabrina's Holiday Spectacular"						5.00

SABRINA, THE TEEN-AGE WITCH (TV)(See Archie Giant Series, Archie's Madhouse 22, Archie's TV..., Chilling Advs. In Sorcery, Little Archie #59)
Archie Publications: April, 1971 - No. 77, Jan, 1983 (52 pg.Giants No. 1-17)

1-52 pgs. begin, end #17	13	26	39	88	189	290
2-Archie's group x-over	9	18	27	60	103	145
3-5: 3,4-Archie's Group x-over	6	12	18	41	66	90
6-10	5	10	15	35	55	75
11-17(2/74)	4	8	12	26	41	55
18-30	3	6	9	19	29	38
31-40(8/77)	3	6	9	14	20	26
41-60(6/80)	2	4	6	10	14	18
61-70	2	4	6	8	11	14
71-76-low print run	2	4	6	11	16	20
77-Last issue; low print run	3	6	9	14	20	26

SABRINA, THE TEEN-AGE WITCH
Archie Publications: 1996 ($1.50, 32 pgs., one-shot)

1-Updated origin						6.00

SABRINA, THE TEEN-AGE WITCH (Continues in Sabrina, Vol. 2)
Archie Publications: May, 1997 - No. 32, Dec, 1999 ($1.50/$1.75/$1.79)

1-Photo-c with Melissa Joan Hart	1	3	4	6	8	10
2-10: 9-Begin $1.75-c						6.00
11-20						5.00
21-32: 24-Begin $1.79-c. 28-Sonic the Hedgehog-c/app.						4.00

SABU, "ELEPHANT BOY" (Movie; formerly My Secret Story)
Fox Features Syndicate: No. 30, June, 1950 - No. 2, Aug, 1950

30(#1)-Wood-a; photo-c from movie	26	52	78	154	252	350
2-Photo-c from movie; Kamen-a	19	38	57	111	176	240

SACHS & VIOLENS
Marvel Comics (Epic Comics): Nov, 1993 - No. 4, July, 1994 ($2.25, limited series, mature)

1-($2.75)-Embossed-c w/bound-in trading card						3.00
1-($3.50)-Platinum edition (1 for each 10 ordered)						4.00
2-4: Perez-c/a; bound-in trading card: 2-(5/94)						3.00
TPB (DC, 2006, $14.99) r/series; intro. by Peter David; creator bios.						15.00

SACRAMENTS, THE
Catechetical Guild Educational Society: Oct, 1955 (35¢)

30304	6	12	18	31	38	45

SACRED AND THE PROFANE, THE (See Eclipse Graphic Album Series #9 & Epic Illustrated #20)

SADDLE JUSTICE (Happy Houlihans #1,2) (Saddle Romances #9 on)
E. C. Comics: No. 3, Spring, 1948 - No. 8, Sept-Oct, 1949

3-The 1st E.C. by Bill Gaines to break away from M. C. Gaines' old Educational Comics format. Craig, Feldstein, H. C. Kiefer, & Stan Asch-a; mentioned in Love and Death	54	108	162	343	574	825
4-1st Graham Ingels-a for E.C.	47	94	141	296	498	700
5-8-Ingels-a in all	42	84	126	265	445	625

NOTE: ***Craig** and **Feldstein** art in most issues. Canadian reprints known; see Table of Contents. **Craig** c-3, 4. **Ingels** c-5-8. #4 contains a biography of **Craig**.*

SADDLE ROMANCES (Saddle Justice #3-8; Weird Science #12 on)
E. C. Comics: No. 9, Nov-Dec, 1949 - No. 11, Mar-Apr, 1950

9,11: 9-Ingels-c/a. 11-Ingels-a; Feldstein-c	47	94	141	296	498	700
10-Wally Wood's 1st work at E. C.; Ingels-a; Feldstein-c	48	96	144	302	514	725

NOTE: *Canadian reprints known; see Table of Contents. **Wood/Harrison** a-10, 11.*

SADHU
Virgin Comics: July, 2006 - No. 8, June, 2007 ($2.99)

1-8: 1,2-Gotham Chopra-s/Jeevan Kang-a						3.00
...: The Silent Ones (8/07 - No. 5, 2/08, $2.99) 1-5						3.00
...: Wheel of Destiny (4/08 - No. 5, $2.99) 1,2						3.00

SADIE SACK (See Harvey Hits #93)

SAD SACK AND THE SARGE
Harvey Publications: Sept, 1957 - No. 155, June, 1982

1	12	24	36	81	166	250
2	8	16	24	52	86	120
3-10	6	12	18	41	66	90
11-20	5	10	15	32	51	70
21-30	3	6	9	20	30	40
31-50	3	6	9	14	20	25
51-70	2	4	6	9	13	16
71-90,97-99	1	3	4	6	8	10
91-96: All 52 pg. Giants	2	4	6	9	13	16
100	2	4	6	8	10	12
101-120	1	2	3	4	5	7
121-155						5.00

NOTE: ***George Baker** covers on numerous issues.*

SAD SACK COMICS (See Harvey Collector's Comics #16, Little Sad Sack, Tastee Freez Comics #4 & True Comics #55)
Harvey Publications/Lorne-Harvey Publications (Recollections) #288 On: Sept, 1949 - No. 287, Oct, 1982; No. 288, 1992 - No. 291, 1993

1-Infinity-c; Little Dot begins (1st app.); civilian issues begin, end #21; based on comic strip	104	208	312	842	1821	2800
2-Flying Fool by Powell	29	58	87	210	455	700
3	17	34	51	119	260	400
4-10	12	24	36	83	172	260
11-21	9	18	27	61	106	150
22-("Back In The Army Again" on covers #22-36); "The Specialist" story about Sad Sack's return to Army	10	20	30	66	121	175
23-30	6	12	18	39	62	85
31-50	5	10	15	30	48	65
51-80,100: 62-"The Specialist" reprinted	4	8	12	22	34	45
81-99	3	6	9	16	23	30
101-140	3	6	9	14	19	24
141-170,200	2	4	6	11	16	20
171-199	2	4	6	9	13	16
201-207: 207-Last 12¢ issue	2	4	6	8	11	14
208-222	1	3	4	6	8	10
223-228 (25¢ Giants, 52 pgs.)	2	4	6	8	11	14
229-250	1	3	4	6	8	10
251-285						6.00
286,287-Limited distribution	1	2	3	5	7	9
288,289 ($2.75, 1992): 289-50th anniversary issue						6.00
290,291 ($1.00, 1993, B&W)						3.00
3-D 1 (1/54, 25¢)-Came with 2 pairs of glasses; titled "Harvey 3-D Hits"	14	28	42	95	205	315
...At Home for the Holidays 1 (1993, no-c price)-Publ. by Lorne-Harvey' X-Mas issue						4.00

NOTE: *The Sad Sack Comics comic book was a spin-off from a Sunday Newspaper strip launched through John Wheeler's Bell Syndicate. The previous Sunday page and the first 21 comics depicted the Sad Sack in civvies. Unpopularity caused the Sunday page to be discontinued in the early '50s. Meanwhile Sad Sack returned to the Army, by popular demand, in issue No. 22, remaining there ever since. Incidentally, relatively few of the first 21 issues were ever collected and remain scarce due to this. **George Baker** covers on numerous issues.*

SAD SACK FUN AROUND THE WORLD
Harvey Publications: 1974 (no month)

1-About Great Britain	2	4	6	11	16	20

SAD SACK GOES HOME
Harvey Publications: 1951 (16 pgs. in color, no cover price)

nn-By George Baker	5	10	15	35	55	75

SAD SACK LAUGH SPECIAL
Harvey Publications: Winter, 1958-59 - No. 93, Feb, 1977 (#1-9: 84 pgs.; #10-60: 68 pgs.; #61-76: 52 pgs.)

1-Giant 25¢ issues begin	10	20	30	67	124	180
2	6	12	18	41	66	90
3-10	5	10	15	32	51	70
11-30	4	8	12	26	41	55
31-60: 31-Hi-Fi Tweeter app. 60-Last 68 pg. Giant	3	6	9	16	23	30
61-76-(All 52 pg. issues)	2	4	6	10	14	18
77-93	1	2	3	5	6	8

SAD SACK NAVY, GOBS 'N' GALS
Harvey Publications: Aug, 1972 - No. 8, Oct, 1973

1: 52 pg. Giant	3	6	9	16	23	30
2-8	2	4	6	9	12	15

SAD SACK'S ARMY LIFE (See Harvey Hits #8, 17, 22, 28, 32, 39, 43, 47, 51, 55, 58, 61, 64, 67, 70)

SAD SACK'S ARMY LIFE (...Parade #1-57, ...Today #58 on)
Harvey Publications: Oct, 1963 - No. 60, Nov, 1975; No. 61, May, 1976

1-(68 pg. issues begin)	8	16	24	51	86	120
2-10	4	8	12	28	44	60
11-20	3	6	9	20	30	40
21-34: Last 68 pg. issue	3	6	9	16	23	30

Saga #1 © Vaughan & Staples

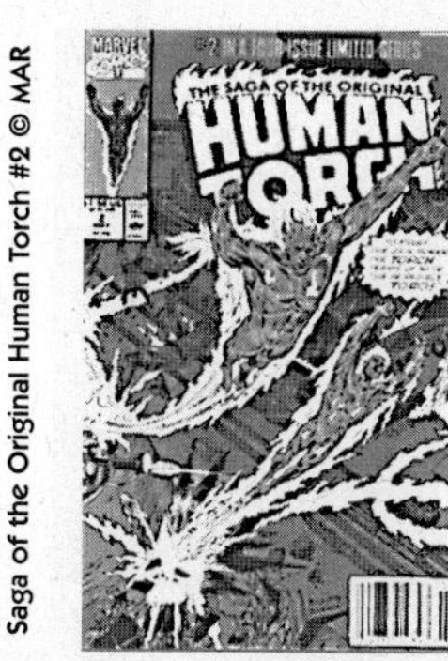

Saga of the Original Human Torch #2 © MAR

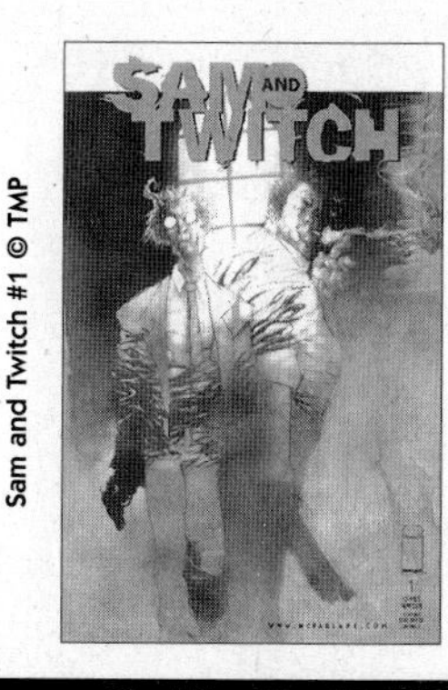

Sam and Twitch #1 © TMP

	GD 2.0	VG 4.0	FN 6.0	VF 8.0	VF/NM 9.0	NM- 9.2
35-51: All 52 pgs.	2	4	6	10	14	18
52-61	1	3	4	6	8	10

SAD SACK'S FUNNY FRIENDS (See Harvey Hits #75)
Harvey Publications: Dec, 1955 - No. 75, Oct, 1969

	GD 2.0	VG 4.0	FN 6.0	VF 8.0	VF/NM 9.0	NM- 9.2
1	10	20	30	67	124	180
2-10	6	12	18	41	66	90
11-20	4	8	12	24	37	50
21-30	3	6	9	18	27	35
31-50	3	6	9	14	20	25
51-75	2	4	6	9	13	16

SAD SACK'S MUTTSY (See Harvey Hits #74, 77, 80, 82, 84, 87, 89, 92, 96, 99, 102, 105, 108, 111, 113, 115, 117, 119, 121)

SAD SACK USA (...Vacation #8)
Harvey Publications: Nov, 1972 - No. 7, Nov, 1973; No. 8, Oct, 1974

	GD 2.0	VG 4.0	FN 6.0	VF 8.0	VF/NM 9.0	NM- 9.2
1	3	6	9	14	20	25
2-8	2	4	6	8	10	12

SAD SACK WITH SARGE & SADIE
Harvey Publications: Sept, 1972 - No. 8, Nov, 1973

	GD 2.0	VG 4.0	FN 6.0	VF 8.0	VF/NM 9.0	NM- 9.2
1-(52 pg. Giant)	3	6	9	14	20	25
2-8	2	4	6	8	10	12

SAD SAD SACK WORLD
Harvey Publ.: Oct, 1964 - No. 46, Dec, 1973 (#1-31: 68 pgs.; #32-38: 52 pgs.)

	GD 2.0	VG 4.0	FN 6.0	VF 8.0	VF/NM 9.0	NM- 9.2
1	7	14	21	48	79	110
2-10	4	8	12	26	41	55
11-20	3	6	9	20	30	40
21-31: 31-Last 68 pg. issue	3	6	9	16	23	30
32-39-(All 52 pgs)	2	4	6	10	14	18
40-46	1	3	4	6	8	10

SAFEST PLACE IN THE WORLD, THE
Dark Horse Comics: 1993 ($2.50, one-shot)

1-Steve Ditko-c/a/scripts 3.00

SAFETY-BELT MAN
Sirius Entertainment: June, 1994 - No. 6, 1995 ($2.50, B&W)

1-6: 1-Horan-s/Dark One-a/Sprouse-c. 2,3-Warren-c. 4-Linsner back-up story. 5,6-Crilley-a 3.00

SAFETY-BELT MAN ALL HELL
Sirius Entertainment: June, 1996 - No. 6, Mar, 1997 ($2.95, color)

1-6-Horan-s/Fillbach Bros.-a 3.00

SAGA
Image Comics: Mar, 2012 - Present ($2.99)

1-Brian K. Vaughan-s/Fiona Staples-a/c 5.00

SAGA OF BIG RED, THE
Omaha World-Herald: Sept, 1976 ($1.25) (In color)

nn-by Win Mumma; story of the Nebraska Cornhuskers (sports) 6.00

SAGA OF CRYSTAR, CRYSTAL WARRIOR, THE
Marvel Comics: May, 1983 - No. 11, Feb, 1985 (Remco toy tie-in)

1,6: 1-(Baxter paper). 6-Nightcrawler app; Golden-c 4.00
2-5,7-11: 3-Dr. Strange app. 3-11-Golden-c (painted-4,5). 11-Alpha Flight app. 3.00

SAGA OF RA'S AL GHUL, THE
DC Comics: Jan, 1988 - No. 4, Apr, 1988 ($2.50, limited series)

1-4-r/N. Adams Batman 6.00

SAGA OF SABAN'S MIGHTY MORPHIN POWER RANGERS (Also see Saban's Mighty Morphin Power Rangers)
Hamilton Comics: 1995 - No. 4, 1995 ($1.95, limited series)

1-4 4.00

SAGA OF SEVEN SUNS, THE : VEILED ALLIANCES
DC Comics (WildStorm): 2004 ($24.95, hardcover graphic novel with dustjacket)

HC-Kevin J. Anderson-s/Robert Teranishi-a 25.00
SC-(2004, $17.95) 18.00

SAGA OF THE ORIGINAL HUMAN TORCH
Marvel Comics: Apr, 1990 - No. 4, July, 1990 ($1.50, limited series)

1-4: 1-Origin; Buckler-c/a(p). 3-Hitler-c 3.00

SAGA OF THE SUB-MARINER, THE
Marvel Comics: Nov, 1988 - No. 12, Oct, 1989 ($1.25/$1.50 #5 on, maxi-series)

1-12: 9-Original X-Men app. 3.00

SAGA OF THE SWAMP THING, THE (See Swamp Thing)

SAILOR MOON (Manga)
Mixx Entertainment Inc.: 1998 - Present ($2.95)

	GD 2.0	VG 4.0	FN 6.0	VF 8.0	VF/NM 9.0	NM- 9.2
1	3	6	9	14	20	25
1-(San Diego edition)	3	6	9	16	23	30
2-5	2	4	6	9	12	15
6-10	1	3	4	6	8	10
11-25	1	2	3	4	5	7
26-35						5.00
... Rini's Moon Stick 1						15.00

SAILOR ON THE SEA OF FATE (See First Comics Graphic Novel #11)

SAILOR SWEENEY (Navy Action #1-11, 15 on)
Atlas Comics (CDS): No. 12, July, 1956 - No. 14, Nov, 1956

	GD 2.0	VG 4.0	FN 6.0	VF 8.0	VF/NM 9.0	NM- 9.2
12-14: 12-Shores-a. 13,14-Severin-c	10	20	30	54	72	90

SAINT, THE (Also see Movie Comics(DC) #2 & Silver Streak #18)
Avon Periodicals: Aug, 1947 - No. 12, Mar, 1952

	GD 2.0	VG 4.0	FN 6.0	VF 8.0	VF/NM 9.0	NM- 9.2
1-Kamen bondage-c/a	90	180	270	576	988	1400
2	42	84	126	265	445	625
3-5: 4-Lingerie panels	39	78	117	231	378	525
6-Miss Fury app. by Tarpe Mills (14 pgs.)	52	104	156	328	557	785
7-c-/Avon paperback #118	31	62	93	182	296	410
8,9(12/50): Saint strip-r in #8-12; 9-Kinstler-c	27	54	81	160	263	365
10-Wood-a, 1 pg; c-/Avon paperback #289	27	54	81	160	263	365
11	21	42	63	122	199	275
12-c-/Avon paperback #123	22	44	66	132	216	300

NOTE: *Lucky Dale, Girl Detective in #1,2,4,6.* **Hollingsworth** *a-4, 6. Painted-c 7, 8, 10-12.*

SAINT ANGEL
Image Comics: Mar, 2000 - No. 4, Mar, 2001 ($2.95/$3.95)

0-Altstaetter & Napton-s/Altstaetter-a 3.00
1-4-($3.95) Flip book w/Deity. 1-(6/00). 2-(10/00) 4.00

ST. GEORGE
Marvel Comics (Epic Comics): June, 1988 - No.8, Oct, 1989 ($1.25,/$1.50)

1-8: Sienkiewicz-c. 3-begin $1.50-c 3.00

SAINT GERMAINE
Caliber Comics: 1997 - No. 8, 1998 ($2.95)

1-8: 1,5-Alternate covers 3.00

ST. SWITHIN'S DAY
Trident Comics: Apr, 1990 ($2.50, one-shot)

1-Grant Morrison scripts 3.00

ST. SWITHIN'S DAY
Oni Press: Mar, 1998 ($2.95, B&W, one-shot)

1-Grant Morrison-s/Paul Grist-a 3.00

SALOMÉ (See Night Music #6)

SALVATION RUN
DC Comics: Jan, 2008 - No. 7, Jul, 2008 ($2.99/$3.50, limited series)

1-6-DC villains banished to an alien planet; Willingham-s/Chen-a/c. 1-Var-c by Corroney 3.00
7-($3.50) Luthor cover by Chen 3.50
7-($3.50) Variant Joker cover by Neal Adams 5.00

SAM AND MAX, FREELANCE POLICE SPECIAL
Fishwrap Prod./Comico: 1987 ($1.75, B&W); Jan, 1989 ($2.75, 44 pgs.)

1 ($1.75, B&W, Fishwrap) 4.00
2 ($2.75, color, Comico) 4.00

SAM AND TWITCH (See Spawn and Case Files:...)
Image Comics (Todd McFarlane Prod.): Aug, 1999 - No. 26, Feb, 2004 ($2.50)

1-26: 1-19-Bendis-s. 1-14-Medina-a. 15-19-Maleev-a. 20-24-McFarlane-s/Maleev-a 3.00
Book One: Udaku (2000, $21.95, TPB) B&W reprint of #1-8 22.00
...: The Brian Michael Bendis Collection Vol. 1 (2/06, $24.95) r/#1-9 in color; sketch pages 25.00
...: The Brian Michael Bendis Collection Vol. 2 (6/07, $24.95) r/#10-19; cover gallery 25.00

SAM AND TWITCH: THE WRITER
Image Comics (Todd McFarlane Prod.): May, 2010 - No. 4, Jun, 2010 ($2.99)

1-4-Blengino-s/Erbetta-a/c 3.00

SAM HILL PRIVATE EYE
Close-Up (Archie): 1950 - No. 7, 1951

	GD 2.0	VG 4.0	FN 6.0	VF 8.0	VF/NM 9.0	NM- 9.2
1	17	34	51	98	154	210

Samson #3 © FOX

Samurai #3 © Aircel

Sandman #17 © DC

GD VG FN VF VF/NM NM-
2.0 4.0 6.0 8.0 9.0 9.2

2 11 22 33 60 83 105
3-7 10 20 30 54 72 90

SAMSON (1st Series) (Captain Aero #7 on; see Big 3 Comics)
Fox Features Syndicate: Fall, 1940 - No. 6, Sept, 1941 (See Fantastic Comics)

1-Samson begins, ends #6; Powell-a, signed 'Rensie;' Wing Turner by Tuska app; Fine-c? 194 388 582 1242 2121 3000
2-Dr. Fung by Powell; Fine-c? 80 160 240 508 874 1240
3-Navy Jones app.; Joe Simon-c 60 120 180 381 653 925
4-Yarko the Great, Master Magician begins 53 106 159 334 567 800
5,6: 6-Origin The Topper 43 86 129 271 461 650

SAMSON (2nd Series) (Formerly Fantastic Comics #10, 11)
Ajax/Farrell Publications (Four Star): No. 12, April, 1955 - No. 14, Aug, 1955

12-Wonder Boy 30 60 90 177 289 400
13,14: 13-Wonder Boy, Rocket Man 26 52 78 154 252 350

SAMSON (See Mighty Samson)

SAMSON & DELILAH (See A Spectacular Feature Magazine)

SAMUEL BRONSTON'S CIRCUS WORLD (See Circus World under Movie Classics)

SAMURAI (Also see Eclipse Graphic Album Series #14)
Aircel Publications: 1985 - No. 23, 1987 ($1.70, B&W)

1, 14-16-Dale Keown-a 4.00
1-(reprinted),2-12,17-23: 2 (reprinted issue exists) 3.00
13-Dale Keown's 1st published artwork (1987) 6.00

SAMURAI
Warp Graphics: May, 1997 ($2.95, B&W)

1 3.00

SAMURAI CAT
Marvel Comics (Epic Comics): June, 1991 - No. 3, Sept, 1991 ($2.25, limited series)

1-3: 3-Darth Vader-c/story parody 3.00

SAMURAI: HEAVEN & EARTH
Dark Horse Comics: Dec, 2004 - No. 5, Dec, 2005 ($2.99)

1-5-Luke Ross-a/Ron Marz-s 3.00
TPB (4/06, $14.95) r/#1-5; sketch pages and cover and pin-up gallery 15.00

SAMURAI: HEAVEN & EARTH (Volume 2)
Dark Horse Comics: Nov, 2006 - No. 5, June, 2007 ($2.99)

1-5-Luke Ross-a/Ron Marz-s 3.00
TPB (10/07, $14.95) r/#1-5; sketch pages and cover and pin-up gallery 15.00

SAMURAI JACK SPECIAL (TV)
DC Comics: Sept, 2002 ($3.95, one-shot)

1-Adaptation of pilot episode with origin story; Tartakovsky-s 4.00

SAMURAI: LEGEND
Marvel Comics (Soleil): 2008 - No. 4, 2009 ($5.99)

1-4-Genet-a/DiGiorgio-s; English version of French comic; preview of other titles 6.00

SAMUREE
Continuity Comics: May, 1987 - No. 9, Jan, 1991

1-9 3.00

SAMUREE
Continuity Comics: V2#1, May, 1993 - V2#4, Jan,1994 ($2.50)

V2#1-4-Embossed-c: 2,4-Adams plot, Nebres-i. 3-Nino-c(i) 3.00

SAMUREE
Acclaim Comics (Windjammer): Oct, 1995 - No. 2, Nov,1995 ($2.50, lim. series)

1,2 3.00

SAN DIEGO COMIC CON COMICS
Dark Horse Comics: 1992 - No.4, 1995 (B&W, promo comic for the San Diego Comic Con)

1-(1992)-Includes various characters published from Dark Horse including Concrete, The Mask, RoboCop and others; 1st app. of Sprint from John Byrne's Next Men; art by Quesada, Byrne, Rude, Burden, Moebius & others; pin-ups by Rude, Dorkin, Allred & others; Chadwick-c 1 3 4 6 8 10
2-(1993)-Intro of Legend imprint; 1st app. of John Byrne's Danger Unlimited, Mike Mignola's Hellboy (also see John Byrne's Next Men #21), Art Adams' Monkeyman & O'Brien; contains stories featuring Concrete, Sin City, Martha Washington & others; Grendel, Madman, & Big Guy pin-ups; Don Martin-c 2 4 6 11 16 20
3-(1994)-Contains stories featuring Barb Wire, The Mask, The Dirty Pair, & Grendel by Matt Wagner; contains pin-ups of Ghost, Predator & Rascals In Paradise; The Mask-c 1 2 3 5 6 8
4-(1995)-Contains Sin City story by Miller (3pg.), Star Wars, The Mask, Tarzan, Foot Soldiers; Sin City & Star Wars flip-c 1 2 3 5 6 8

SANDMAN, THE (1st Series) (Also see Adventure Comics #40, New York World's Fair & World's Finest #3)
National Periodical Publ.: Winter, 1974; No. 2, Apr-May, 1975 - No. 6, Dec-Jan, 1975-76

1-1st app. Bronze Age Sandman by Simon & Kirby (last S&K collaboration) 7 14 21 48 79 110
2-6: 6-Kirby/Wood-c/a 4 8 12 22 34 45
The Sandman By Joe Simon & Jack Kirby HC (2009, $39.99, d.j.) r/Sandman app. from World's Finest #6,7, Adventure Comics #72-102 and Sandman #1; Morrow intro. 40.00

NOTE: ***Kirby** a-1p, 4-6p; c-1-5, 6p.*

SANDMAN (2nd Series) (See Books of Magic, Vertigo Jam & Vertigo Preview)
DC Comics (Vertigo imprint #47 on): Jan, 1989 - No. 75, Mar, 1996 ($1.50-$2.50, mature)

1 ($2.00, 52 pgs.)-1st app. Modern Age Sandman (Morpheus); Neil Gaiman scripts begin; Sam Kieth-a(p) in #1-5; Wesley Dodds (G.A. Sandman) cameo. 4 8 12 24 37 50
2-Cain & Abel app. (from HOM & HOS) 3 6 9 14 19 24
3-5: 3-John Constantine app. 2 4 6 10 14 18
6,7 2 4 6 8 11 14
8-Death-c/story (1st app.)-Regular ed. has Jeanette Kahn publishorial & American Cancer Society ad w/no indicia on inside front-c 3 6 9 16 23 30
8-Limited ed. (600+ copies?); has Karen Berger editorial and next issue teaser on inside covers (has indicia) 6 12 18 39 62 85
9-14: 10-Has explaination about #8 mixup; has bound-in Shocker movie poster. 14-(52 pgs.)-Bound-in Nightbreed fold-out 2 4 6 8 10 12
15-20: 16-Photo-c. 17,18-Kelley Jones-a. 19-Vess-a 1 2 3 5 6 8
18-Error version w/1st 3 panels on pg. 1 in blue ink 3 6 9 20 30 40
19-Error version w/pages 18 & 20 facing each other 3 6 9 18 27 35
21,23-27: Seasons of Mist storyline. 22-World Without End preview. 24-Kelley Jones/Russell-a 6.00
22-1st Daniel (Later becomes new Sandman) 2 4 6 8 10 12
28-30 5.00
31-49,51-74: 36-(52 pgs.). 41,44-48-Metallic ink on-c. 48-Cerebus appears as a doll. 54-Re-intro Prez; Death app.; Belushi, Nixon & Wildcat cameos. 57-Metallic ink on c. 65-w/bound-in trading card. 69-Death of Sandman. 70-73-Zulli-a. 74-Jon J. Muth-a. 4.00
50-($2.95, 52 pgs.)-Black-c w/metallic ink by McKean; Russell-a; McFarlane pin-up 5.00
50-($2.95)-Signed & limited (5,000) Treasury Edition with sketch of Neil Gaiman 1 2 3 5 6 8
50-Platinum 20.00
75-($3.95)-Vess-a. 5.00
Special 1 (1991, $3.50, 68 pgs.)-Glow-in-the-dark-c 5.00
Absolute Sandman Special Edition #1 (2006, 50¢) sampling from HC; recolored r/#1 3.00
Absolute Sandman Volume One (2006, $99.00, slipcased hardcover) recolored r/#1-20; Gaiman's original proposal; script and pencils from #19; character sketch gallery 100.00
Absolute Sandman Volume Two (2007, $99.00, slipcased hardcover) recolored r/#21-39; r/A Gallery of Dreams one-shot; bonus stories, scripts and pencil art 100.00
Absolute Sandman Volume Three (2008, $99.00, slipcased hardcover) recolored r/#40-56; & Special #1; bonus galleries, scripts and pencil art; Jill Thompson intro. 100.00
Absolute Sandman Volume Four (2008, $99.00, slipcased hardcover) recolored r/#57-75; scripts & sketch pages for #57 & 75; gallery of Dreaming memorabilia; Berger intro. 100.00
...: A Gallery of Dreams ($2.95)-Intro by N. Gaiman 3.00
...: Preludes & Nocturnes ($29.95, HC)-r/#1-8. 30.00
...: The Doll's House (1990, $29.95, HC)-r/#8-16. 30.00
...: Dream Country ($29.95, HC)-r/#17-20. 30.00
...: Season of Mists ($29.95, Leatherbound HC)-r/#21-28. 50.00
...: A Game of You ($29.95, HC)-r/32-37, ...: Fables and Reflections ($29.95, HC)-r/Vertigo Preview #1, Sandman Special #1, #29-31, #38-40 & #50. ...: Brief Lives ($29.95, HC)-r/#41-49. ...: World's End ($29.95, HC)-r/#51-56 30.00
...: The Kindly Ones (1996, $34.95, HC)-r/#57-69 & Vertigo Jam #1 35.00
...: The Wake ($29.95, HC)-r/#70-75. 30.00

NOTE: *A new set of hardcover printings with new covers was introduced in 1998-99. Multiple printings exist of softcover collections. Recolored (from the Absolute HC) softcover editions were released in 2010. **Bachalo** a-12; **Kelley Jones** a-17, 18, 22, 23, 26, 27. **Vess** a-19, 75.*

SANDMAN: ENDLESS NIGHTS
DC Comics (Vertigo): 2003 ($24.95, hardcover, with dust jacket)

HC-Neil Gaiman stories of Morpheus and the Endless illustrated by Fabry, Manara, Prado, Quitely, Russell, Sienkiewicz, and Storey; McKean-c 25.00
...Special (11/03, $2.95) Previews hardcover; Dream story w/Prado-a; McKean-c 3.00
SC (2004, $17.95) 18.00

SANDMAN MIDNIGHT THEATRE
DC Comics (Vertigo): Sept, 1995 ($6.95, squarebound, one-shot)

nn-Modern Age Sandman (Morpheus) meets G.A. Sandman; Gaiman & Wagner story;

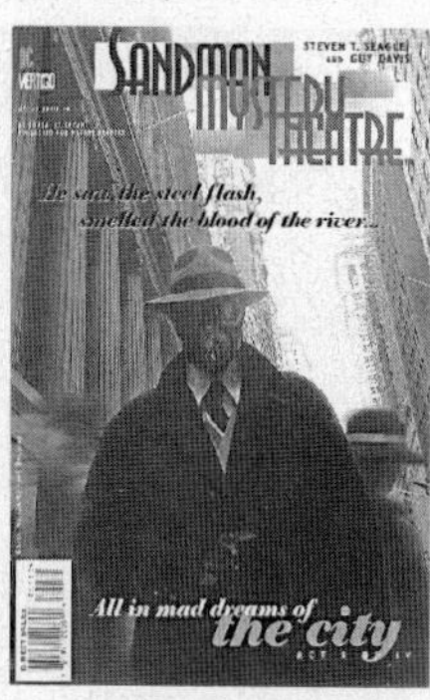

Sandman Mystery Theater #61 © DC

Sandman Presents: The Dead Boy Detectives #2 © DC

Sarge Snorkel #10 © CC

	GD 2.0	VG 4.0	FN 6.0	VF 8.0	VF/NM 9.0	NM- 9.2
McKean-c; Kristiansen-a						7.00

SANDMAN MYSTERY THEATRE (Also see Sandman (2nd Series) #1)
DC Comics (Vertigo): Apr, 1993 - No. 70, Feb, 1999 ($1.95/$2.25/$2.50)

	NM- 9.2
1-G.A. Sandman advs. begin; Matt Wagner scripts begin	5.00
2-49: 5-Neon ink logo. 29-32-Hourman app. 38-Ted Knight (G.A. Starman) app. 42-Jim Corrigan (Spectre) app. 45-48-Blackhawk app.	3.00
50-($3.50, 48 pgs.) w/bonus story of S.A. Sandman, Torres-a	4.00
51-70	3.00
Annual 1 (10/94, $3.95, 68 pgs.)-Alex Ross, Bolton & others-a	5.00
...: Dr. Death and the Night of the Butcher (2007, $19.99) r/#21-28	20.00
...: The Blackhawk and The Return of the Scarlet Ghost (2010, $19.99) r/#45-52	20.00
...: The Face and the Brute (2004, $19.95) r/#5-12	20.00
...: The Hourman and The Python (2008, $19.99) r/#29-36	20.00
...: The Mist and The Phantom of the Fair (2009, $19.99) r/#37-44	20.00
...: The Scorpion (2006, $12.99) r/#17-20	13.00
...: The Tarantula (1995, $14.95) r/#1-4	15.00
...: The Vamp (2005, $12.99) r/#13-16	13.00

SANDMAN MYSTERY THEATRE (2nd Series)
DC Comics (Vertigo): Feb, 2007 - No. 5, Jun, 2007 ($2.99, limited series)

1-5-Wesley Dodds and Dian in 1997; Rieber-s/Nguyen-a 3.00

SANDMAN PRESENTS...
DC Comics (Vertigo)

Taller Tales TPB (2003, $19.95) r/S.P: The Thessaliad #1-4; Merv Pumpkinhead, Agent...; The Dreaming #55; S.P. Everything You Always...; new McKean-c; intro by Willingham 20.00

SANDMAN PRESENTS: BAST
DC Comics (Vertigo): Mar, 2003 - No. 3, May, 2003 ($2.95, limited series)

1-3-Kiernan-s/Bennett-a/McKean-c 3.00

SANDMAN PRESENTS: DEADBOY DETECTIVES (See Sandman #21-28)
DC Comics (Vertigo): Aug, 2001 - No. 4, Nov, 2001 ($2.50, limited series)

1-4:Talbot-a/McKean-c/Brubaker-s 3.00
TPB (2008, $12.99) r/#1-4 13.00

SANDMAN PRESENTS: EVERYTHING YOU ALWAYS WANTED TO KNOW ABOUT DREAMS...BUT WERE AFRAID TO ASK
DC Comics (Vertigo): Jul, 2001 ($3.95, one-shot)

1-Short stories by Willingham; art by various; McKean-c 4.00

SANDMAN PRESENTS: LOVE STREET
DC Comics (Vertigo): Jul, 1999 - No. 3, Sept, 1999 ($2.95, limited series)

1-3: Teenage Hellblazer in 1968 London; Zulli-a 3.00

SANDMAN PRESENTS: LUCIFER
DC Comics (Vertigo): Mar, 1999 - No. 3, May, 1999 ($2.95, limited series)

1-3: Scott Hampton painted-c/a 3.00

SANDMAN PRESENTS: PETREFAX
DC Comics (Vertigo): Mar, 2000 - No. 4, Jun, 2000 ($2.95, limited series)

1-4-Carey-s/Leialoha-a 3.00

SANDMAN PRESENTS: THE CORINTHIAN
DC Comics (Vertigo): Dec, 2001 - No. 3, Feb, 2002 ($2.95, limited series)

1-3-Macan-s/Zezelj-a/McKean-c 3.00

SANDMAN PRESENTS, THE: THE FURIES
DC Comics (Vertigo): 2002 ($24.95, one-shot)

Hardcover-Mike Carey-s/John Bolton-painted art; Lyta Hall's reunion with Daniel 30.00
Softcover-(2003, $17.95) 18.00

SANDMAN PRESENTS, THE: THESSALY: WITCH FOR HIRE
DC Comics (Vertigo): Apr, 2004 - No. 4, July, 2004 ($2.95, limited series)

1-4-Willingham-s/McManus-a/McPherson-c 3.00
TPB-(2005, $12.99) r/#1-4 13.00

SANDMAN PRESENTS, THE: THE THESSALIAD
DC Comics (Vertigo): Mar, 2002 - No. 4, Jun, 2002 ($2.95, limited series)

1-4-Willingham-s/McManus-a/McKean-c 3.00

SANDMAN, THE: THE DREAM HUNTERS
DC Comics (Vertigo): Oct, 1999 ($29.95/$19.95, one-shot graphic novel)

Hardcover-Neil Gaiman-s/Yoshitaka Amano-painted art 30.00
Softcover-(2000, $19.95) new Amano-c 20.00

SANDMAN, THE: THE DREAM HUNTERS
DC Comics (Vertigo): Jan, 2009 - No. 4, Apr, 2009 ($2.99, limited series)

1-4-Adaptation of the Gaiman/Amano GN by P. Craig Russell-s/a; 2 covers on each 3.00
HC (2009, $24.99) afterwords by Gaiman, Russell, Berger; cover gallery & sketch art 25.00
SC (2010, $19.99) afterwords by Gaiman, Russell, Berger; cover gallery & sketch art 20.00

SANDS OF THE SOUTH PACIFIC
Toby Press: Jan, 1953

	GD 2.0	VG 4.0	FN 6.0	VF 8.0	VF/NM 9.0	NM- 9.2
1	20	40	60	117	189	260

SANTA AND HIS REINDEER (See March of Comics #166)

SANTA AND THE ANGEL (See Dell Junior Treasury #7)
Dell Publishing Co.: Dec, 1949 (Combined w/Santa at the Zoo) (Gollub-a condensed from FC#128)

	GD 2.0	VG 4.0	FN 6.0	VF 8.0	VF/NM 9.0	NM- 9.2
Four Color 259	5	10	15	35	55	75

SANTA AT THE ZOO (See Santa And The Angel)

SANTA CLAUS AROUND THE WORLD (See March of Comics #241 in Promotional Comics section)

SANTA CLAUS CONQUERS THE MARTIANS (See Movie Classics)

SANTA CLAUS FUNNIES (Also see Dell Giants)
Dell Publishing Co.: Dec?, 1942 - No. 1274, Dec, 1961

	GD 2.0	VG 4.0	FN 6.0	VF 8.0	VF/NM 9.0	NM- 9.2
nn(#1)(1942)-Kelly-a	32	64	96	232	504	775
2(12/43)-Kelly-a	21	42	63	148	317	485
Four Color 61(1944)-Kelly-a	21	42	63	146	311	475
Four Color 91(1945)-Kelly-a	15	30	45	104	227	350
Four Color 128('46),175('47)-Kelly-a	13	26	39	85	180	275
Four Color 205,254-Kelly-a	12	24	36	79	160	240
Four Color 302,361,525,607,666,756,867	7	14	21	44	72	100
Four Color 958,1063,1154,1274	6	12	18	41	66	90

NOTE: *Most issues contain only one Kelly story.*

SANTA CLAUS PARADE
Ziff-Davis (Approved Comics)/St. John Publishing Co.: 1951; No. 2, Dec, 1952; No. 3, Jan, 1955 (25¢)

	GD 2.0	VG 4.0	FN 6.0	VF 8.0	VF/NM 9.0	NM- 9.2
nn(1951-Ziff-Davis)-116 pgs. (Xmas Special 1,2)	31	62	93	182	296	410
2(12/52-Ziff-Davis)-100 pgs.; Dave Berg-a	23	46	69	136	223	310
V1#3(1/55-St. John)-100 pgs.; reprints-c/#1	19	38	57	111	176	240

SANTA CLAUS' WORKSHOP (See March of Comics #50,168 in Promotional Comics section)

SANTA IS COMING (See March of Comics #197 in Promotional Comics section)

SANTA IS HERE (See March of Comics #49 in Promotional Comics section)

SANTA'S BUSY CORNER (See March of Comics #31 in Promotional Comics section)

SANTA'S CANDY KITCHEN (See March of Comics #14 in Promotional Comics section)

SANTA'S CHRISTMAS BOOK (See March of Comics #123 in Promotional Comics section)

SANTA'S CHRISTMAS COMICS
Standard Comics (Best Books): Dec, 1952 (100 pgs.)

	GD 2.0	VG 4.0	FN 6.0	VF 8.0	VF/NM 9.0	NM- 9.2
nn-Supermouse, Dizzy Duck, Happy Rabbit, etc.	19	38	57	111	176	240

SANTA'S CHRISTMAS LIST (See March of Comics #255 in Promotional Comics section)

SANTA'S HELPERS (See March of Comics #64, 106, 198 in Promotional Comics section)

SANTA'S LITTLE HELPERS (See March of Comics #270 in Promotional Comics section)

SANTA'S SHOW (See March of Comics #311 in Promotional Comics section)

SANTA'S SLEIGH (See March of Comics #298 in Promotional Comics section)

SANTA'S SURPRISE (See March of Comics #13 in Promotional Comics section)

SANTA'S TINKER TOTS
Charlton Comics: 1958

	GD 2.0	VG 4.0	FN 6.0	VF 8.0	VF/NM 9.0	NM- 9.2
1-Based on "The Tinker Tots Keep Christmas"	4	8	12	26	41	55

SANTA'S TOYLAND (See March of Comics #242 in Promotional Comics section)

SANTA'S TOYS (See March of Comics #12 in Promotional Comics section)

SANTA'S VISIT (See March of Comics #283 in Promotional Comics section)

SANTA THE BARBARIAN
Maximum Press: Dec, 1996 ($2.99, one-shot)

1-Fraga/Mhan-s/a 3.00

SANTIAGO (Movie)
Dell Publishing Co.: Sept, 1956 (Alan Ladd photo-c)

	GD 2.0	VG 4.0	FN 6.0	VF 8.0	VF/NM 9.0	NM- 9.2
Four Color 723-Kinstler-a	9	18	27	61	106	150

SARGE SNORKEL (Beetle Bailey)
Charlton Comics: Oct, 1973 - No. 17, Dec, 1976

	GD 2.0	VG 4.0	FN 6.0	VF 8.0	VF/NM 9.0	NM- 9.2
1	2	4	6	11	16	20
2-10	2	4	6	8	10	12

Satan's Six #1 © Jack Kirby

Savage Dragon #48 © Erik Larsen

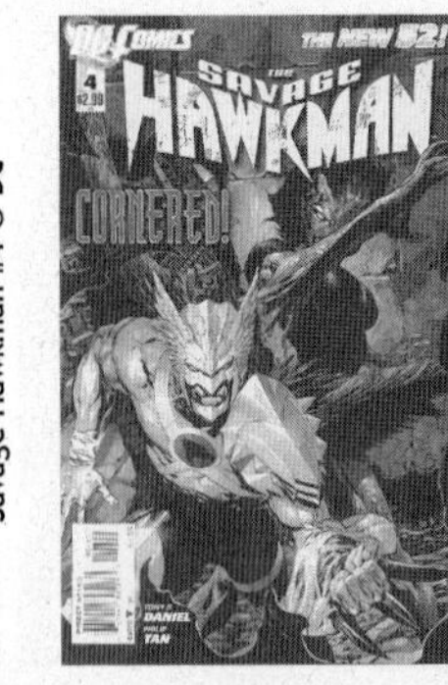

Savage Hawkman #4 © DC

	GD 2.0	VG 4.0	FN 6.0	VF 8.0	VF/NM 9.0	NM- 9.2

11-17 1 2 3 5 7 9

SARGE STEEL (Becomes Secret Agent #9 on; also see Judomaster)
Charlton Comics: Dec, 1964 - No. 8, Mar-Apr, 1966 (All 12¢ issues)

1-Origin & 1st app. 4 8 12 24 37 50
2-5,7,8 3 6 9 16 23 30
6-2nd app. Judomaster 3 6 9 20 30 40

SATAN'S SIX
Topps Comics (Kirbyverse): Apr, 1993 - No. 4, July, 1993 ($2.95, lim. series)

1-4: 1-Polybagged w/Kirbychrome trading card; Kirby/McFarlane-c plus 8 pgs. Kirby-a(p); has coupon for Kirbychrome ed. of Secret City Saga #0. 2-4-Polybagged w/3 cards. 4-Teenagents preview 4.00
NOTE: *Ditko a-1. Miller a-1.*

SATAN'S SIX: HELLSPAWN
Topps Comics (Kirbyverse): June, 1994 - No. 3, July, 1994 ($2.50, limited series)

1-3: 1-(6/94)-Indicia incorrectly shows "Vol 1 #2". 2-(6/94) 3.00

SAUCER COUNTRY
DC Comics (Vertigo): May, 2012 - Present ($2.99)

1,2-Cornell-s/Kelly-a 3.00

SAURIANS: UNNATURAL SELECTION (See Sigil)
CrossGeneration Comics: Feb, 2002 - No. 2, Mar, 2002 ($2.95, limited series)

1,2-Waid-s/DiVito-a 3.00

SAVAGE
Image Comics (Shadowline): Oct, 2008 - No. 4, Jan, 2009 ($3.50, limited series)

1-4-Mayhew-c/a; Niles and Frank-s 3.50

SAVAGE AXE OF ARES
Marvel Comics: June, 2010 ($3.99, B&W, one-shot)

1-B&W short stories by Hurwitz, Palo, McKeever, Swierczynski, Manco and others 4.00

SAVAGE COMBAT TALES
Atlas/Seaboard Publ.: Feb, 1975 - No. 3, July, 1975

1,3: 1-Sgt. Stryker's Death Squad begins (origin); Goodwin-s 2 4 6 8 11 14
2-Toth-a; only app. War Hawk; Goodwin-s 2 4 6 9 13 16
NOTE: *Buckler c-3. McWilliams a-1-3; c-1. Sparling a-1, 3.*

SAVAGE DRAGON, THE (See Megaton #3 & 4)
Image Comics (Highbrow Entertainment): July, 1992 - No. 3, Dec, 1992 ($1.95, lim. series)

1-Erik Larsen-c/a/scripts & bound-in poster in all; 4 cover color variations w/4 different posters; 1st Highbrow Entertainment title 5.00
2-Intro SuperPatriot-c/story (10/92) 4.00
3-Contains coupon for Image Comics #0 4.00
3-With coupon missing 2.00
...Vs. Savage Megaton Man 1 (3/93, $1.95)-Larsen & Simpson-c/a. 4.00
TPB-('93, $9.95) r/#1-3 10.00

SAVAGE DRAGON, THE
Image Comics (Highbrow Entertainment): June, 1993 - Present ($1.95/$2.50/$2.99/$3.50)

1-Erik Larsen-c/a/scripts 5.00
2-($2.95, 52 pgs.)-Teenage Mutant Ninja Turtles-c/story; flip book features Vanguard #0 (See Megaton for 1st app.); 1st app. Supreme 4.00
3-30: 3-7: Erik Larsen-c/a/scripts. 3-Mighty Man back-up story w/Austin-a(i). 4-Flip book w/Ricochet. 5-Mighty Man flip-c & back-up plus poster. 6-Jae Lee poster. 7-Vanguard poster. 8-Deadly Duo poster by Larsen. 13A (10/94)-Jim Lee-c/a; 1st app. Max Cash (Condition Red). 13B (6/95)-Larsen story. 15-Dragon poster by Larsen. 22-TMNT-c/a; Bisley pin-up. 27-"Wondercon Exclusive" new-c. 28-Maxx-c/app. 29-Wildstar-c/app. 30-Spawn app. 3.50
25 ($3.95)-variant-c exists. 4.00
31-49,51-71: 31-God vs. The Devil; alternate version exists w/o expletives (has "God Is Good" inside Image logo) 33-Birth of Dragon/Rapture's baby. 34,35-Hellboy-c/app. 51-Origin of She-Dragon. 70-Ann Stevens killed 3.50
50-($5.95, 100 pgs.) Kaboom and Mighty Man app.; Matsuda back-c; pin-ups by McFarlane, Simonson, Capullo and others 6.00
72-74: 72-Begin $2.95-c 3.50
75-($5.95) 6.00
76-99,101-106,108-114,116-124,126-127,129-131,133-136,138: 76-New direction starts. 83,84-Madman-c/app. 84-Atomics app. 97-Dragon returns home; Mighty Man app. 134-Bomb Queen app. 3.50
100-($8.95) Larsen-s/a; inked by various incl. Sienkiewicz, Timm, Austin, Simonson, Royer; plus pin-ups by Timm, Silvestri, Miller, Cho, Art Adams, Pacheco 9.00
107-($3.95) Firebreather, Invincible, Major Damage-c/app.; flip book w/Major Damage 4.00
115-($7.95, 100 pgs.) Wraparound-c; Freak Force app.; Larsen & Englert-a 8.00
125-($4.99, 64 pgs.) new story, The Fly, & various Mr. Glum reprints 5.00
128-Wesley and the villains from Wanted app.; J.G. Jones-c 4.00
132-($6.99, 80 pgs.) new story with Larsen-a; back-up story with Fosco-a 7.00
137-(8/08) Madman and Amazing Joy Buzzards-c/app. 4.00
137-(8/08) Variant cover with Barack Obama endorsed by Savage Dragon; yellow bkgrd 10.00
137-(8/08) 2nd printing of variant cover with Barack Obama and red background 3.50
137-3rd & 4th printings: 3rd-Blue background. 4th-Purple background 3.50
139-149,151-174,176-178: 139-Start $3.50-c; Invincible app. 140,141-Witchblade, Spawn app. 145-Obama-c/app. 148-Also a FCBD edition.155-160-Dragon War. 160-163-Flip book 3.50
150-($5.99, 100 pgs.) back up r/Daredevil's origin from Daredevil #18 (1943) 6.00
175-($3.99, 48 pgs.) Darklord app.; Vanguard back-c and back-up story 4.00
#0-(7/06, $1.95) reprints origin story from 2005 Image Comics Hardcover 3.50
...Archives Vol. 1 (12/06, $19.99) B&W rep. 1st mini-series #1-3 & #1-21 20.00
...Archives Vol. 2 (2007, $19.99) B&W rep. #22-50; roster pages of Dragon's fellow cops 20.00
...Companion (7/02, $2.95) guide to issues #1-100, character backgrounds 3.50
...Endgame (2/04, $15.95, TPB) r/#47-52 16.00
The Fallen (11/97, $12.95, TPB) r/#7-11, ...Possessed (9/98, $12.95, TPB) r/#12-16, ...Revenge (1998, $12.95, TPB) r/#17-21 13.00
...Gang War (4/00, $16.95, TPB) r/#22-26 17.00
.../Hellboy (10/02, $5.95) r/#34 & #35; Mignola-c 6.00
Image Firsts: Savage Dragon #1 (4/10, $1.00) reprints #1 3.00
...Team-Ups (10/98, $19.95, TPB) r/team-ups 20.00
...: Terminated HC (2/03, $28.95) r/#34-40 & #1/2 29.00
...: This Savage World HC (2002, $24.95) r/#76-81; intro. by Larsen 25.00
...: This Savage World SC (2003, $15.95) r/#76-81; intro. by Larsen 16.00
...: Worlds at War SC (2004, $16.95) r/#41-46; intro. by Larsen; sketch pages 17.00

SAVAGE DRAGON ARCHIVES (Also see Dragon Archives, The)

SAVAGE DRAGONBERT: FULL FRONTAL NERDITY
Image Comics: Oct, 2002 ($5.95, B&W, one-shot)

1-Reprints of the Savage Dragon/Dilbert spoof strips 6.00

SAVAGE DRAGON/DESTROYER DUCK, THE
Image Comics/ Highbrow Entertainment: Nov, 1996 ($3.95, one-shot)

1 4.00

SAVAGE DRAGON: GOD WAR
Image Comics: July, 2004 - No. 4, Oct, 2005 ($2.95, limited series)

1-4-Kirkman-s/Englert-a 3.50

SAVAGE DRAGON/MARSHALL LAW
Image Comics: July, 1997 - No. 2, Aug, 1997 ($2.95, B&W, limited series)

1,2-Pat Mills-s, Kevin O'Neill-a 3.50

SAVAGE DRAGON: SEX & VIOLENCE
Image Comics: Aug, 1997 - No. 2, Sept, 1997 ($2.50, limited series)

1,2-T&M Bierbaum-s, Mays, Lupka, Adam Hughes-a 3.50

SAVAGE DRAGON/TEENAGE MUTANT NINJA TURTLES CROSSOVER
Mirage Studios: Sept, 1993 ($2.75, one-shot)

1-Erik Larsen-c(i) only 4.00

SAVAGE DRAGON: THE RED HORIZON
Image Comics/ Highbrow Entertainment: Feb, 1997 - No. 3 ($2.50, lim. series)

1-3 3.50

SAVAGE FISTS OF KUNG FU
Marvel Comics Group: 1975 (Marvel Treasury)

1-Iron Fist, Shang Chi, Sons of Tiger; Adams, Starlin-a 3 6 9 18 27 35

SAVAGE HAWKMAN, THE (DC New 52)
DC Comics: Nov, 2011 - Present ($2.99)

1-7: 1-Tony Daniel-s/Philip Tan-a/c; Carter Hall bonds with the Nth metal 3.00

SAVAGE HULK, THE (Also see Incredible Hulk)
Marvel Comics: Jan, 1996 ($6.95, one-shot)

1-Bisley-c; David, Lobdell, Wagner, Loeb, Gibbons, Messner-Loebs scripts; McKone, Kieth, Ramos & Sale-a. 7.00

SAVAGE RAIDS OF GERONIMO (See Geronimo #4)

SAVAGE RANGE (See Luke Short, Four Color 807)

SAVAGE RED SONJA: QUEEN OF THE FROZEN WASTES
Dynamite Entertainment: 2006 - No. 4, 2006 ($3.50, limited series)

1-4: 1-Three covers by Cho, Texeira & Homs; Cho & Murray-s/Homs-a 3.50
TPB (2007, $14.99) r/series; cover gallery and sketch pages 15.00

SAVAGE RETURN OF DRACULA

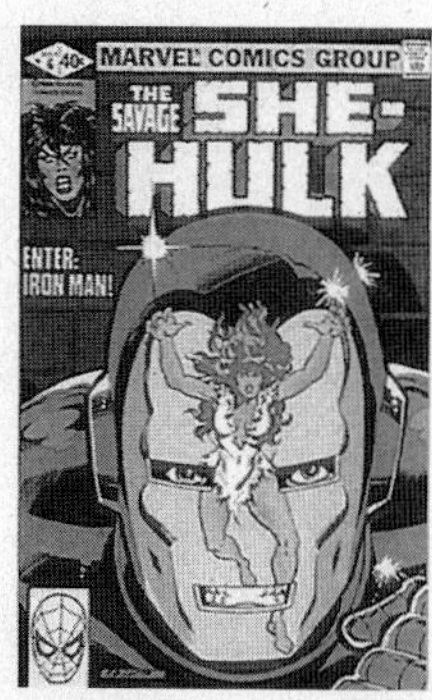

Savage She-Hulk #6 © MAR

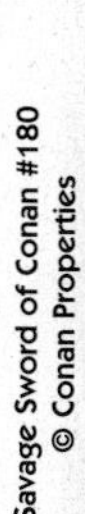
Savage Sword of Conan #180 © Conan Properties

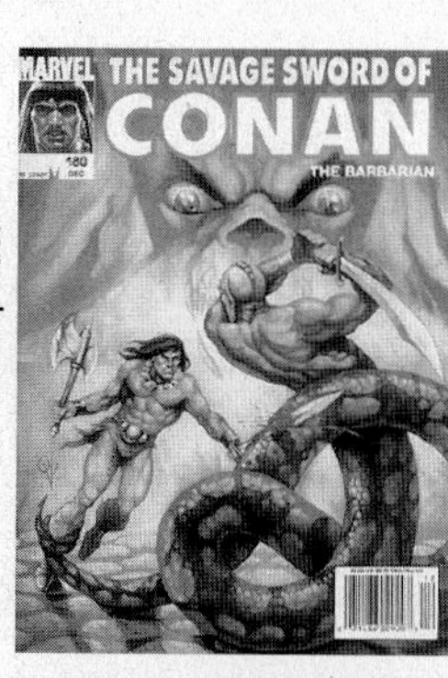

Scalped #56 © Aaron & Milosevic

GD VG FN VF VF/NM NM-
2.0 4.0 6.0 8.0 9.0 9.2

Marvel Comics: 1992 ($2.00, 52 pgs.)
1-r/Tomb of Dracula #1,2 by Gene Colan 4.00

SAVAGE SHE-HULK, THE (See The Avengers, Marvel Graphic Novel #18 & The Sensational She-Hulk)
Marvel Comics Group: Feb, 1980 - No. 25, Feb, 1982
1-Origin & 1st app. She-Hulk 2 4 6 9 12 15
2-5,25: 25-(52 pgs.) 6.00
6-24: 6-She-Hulk vs. Iron Man. 8-Vs. Man-Thing 5.00
NOTE: ***Austin*** *a-25i; c-23i-25i.* ***J. Buscema*** *a-1p; c-1, 2p.* ***Golden*** *c-8-11.*

SAVAGE SHE-HULK (Titled All New Savage She Hulk for #3,4)
Marvel Comics: Jun, 2009 - No. 4, Sept, 2009 ($3.99, limited series)
1-4-Lyra, daughter of the Hulk; She-Hulk & Dark Avengers app. 2-Campbell-c 4.00

SAVAGE SWORD (ROBERT E. HOWARD'S...)
Dark Horse Comics: Dec, 2010 - Present ($7.99, squarebound)
1-3-Short stories by various incl. Roy Thomas, Barry-Windsor-Smith; Conan app. 8.00

SAVAGE SWORD OF CONAN (The...: #41 on; ...The Barbarian #175 on)
Marvel Comics Group: Aug, 1974 - No. 235, July, 1995 ($1.00/$1.25/$2.25, B&W magazine, mature)
1-Smith-r; J. Buscema/N. Adams/Krenkel-a; origin Blackmark by Gil Kane (part 1, ends #3); Blackmark's 1st app. in magazine form-r/from paperback) & Red Sonja (3rd app.) 10 20 30 69 130 190
2-Neal Adams-c; Chaykin/N. Adams-a 6 12 18 39 62 85
3-Severin/B. Smith-a; N. Adams-a 4 8 12 28 44 60
4-Neal Adams/Kane-a(r) 4 8 12 22 34 45
5-10: 5-Jeff Jones frontispiece (r) 3 6 9 18 27 35
11-20 2 4 6 13 18 22
21-30 2 4 6 10 14 18
31-50: 34-3 pg. preview of Conan newspaper strip. 35-Cover similar to Savage Tales #1. 45-Red Sonja returns; begin $1.25-c 2 4 6 8 11 14
51-99: 63-Toth frontispiece. 65-Kane-a w/Chaykin/Miller/Simonson/Sherman finishes. 70-Article on movie. 83-Red Sonja-r by Neal Adams from #1 1 2 3 5 7 9
100 1 3 4 6 8 10
101-176: 163-Begin $2.25-c. 169-King Kull story. 171-Soloman Kane by Williamson (i). 172-Red Sonja story 6.00
177-199: 179,187,192-Red Sonja app. 190-193-4 part King Kull story. 196-King Kull story 5.00
200-220: 200-New Buscema-a; Robert E. Howard app. with Conan in story. 202-King Kull story. 204-60th anniversary (1932-92). 211-Rafael Kayanan's 1st Conan-a. 214-Sequel to Red Nails by Howard 6.00
221-230 1 2 3 5 7 9
231-234 2 4 6 9 12 15
235-Last issue 3 6 9 16 22 28
Special 1(1975, B&W)-B. Smith-r/Conan #10,13 3 6 9 17 25 32
Volume 1 TPB (Dark Horse Books, 12/07, $17.95, B&W) r/#1-10 and selected stories from Savage Tales #1-5 with covers 18.00
Volume 2 TPB (Dark Horse Books, 3/08, $17.95, B&W) r/#11-24 18.00
Volume 3 TPB (Dark Horse Books, 5/08, $19.95, B&W) r/#25-36 and selected pin-ups 20.00
Volume 4 TPB (Dark Horse Books, 9/08, $19.95, B&W) r/#37-48 and selected pin-ups 20.00
Volume 5 TPB (Dark Horse Books, 2/09, $19.95, B&W) r/#49-60 and selected pin-ups 20.00
NOTE: ***N. Adams*** *a-14p, 60, 83p(r).* ***Alcala*** *a-2 ,4, 7, 12, 15-20, 23, 24, 28, 59, 67, 69, 75, 76i, 80i, 82i, 83i, 89, 180i, 184i, 187i, 189i, 216p.* ***Austin*** *a-78i.* ***Boris*** *painted c-1, 4, 5, 7, 9, 10, 12, 15.* ***Brunner*** *a-30; c-8, 30.* ***Buscema*** *a-1-5, 7, 10-12, 15-24, 26-28, 31, 32, 36-43, 45, 47-58p, 60-67p, 70, 71-74p, 76-81p, 87-96p, 98, 99-101p, 190-204p; painted c-40.* ***Chaykin*** *c-31.* ***Chiodo*** *painted c-71, 76, 79, 81, 84, 85, 178.* ***Conrad*** *c-215, 217.* ***Corben*** *a-4, 16, 29.* ***Finlay*** *a-16.* ***Golden*** *a-98, 101; c-98, 101, 105, 106, 117, 124, 150.* ***Kaluta*** *a-11, 18; c-3, 91, 93.* ***Gil Kane*** *a-2, 3, 8, 13r, 29, 47, 64, 65, 67, 85p, 86p.* ***Rafael Kayanan*** *a-211-213, 215, 217.* ***Krenkel*** *a-9, 11, 14, 16, 24.* ***Morrow*** *a-7.* ***Nebres*** *a-93i, 101i, 107, 114.* ***Newton*** *a-6.* ***Nino*** *c/a-6.* ***Redondo*** *painted c-48-50, 52, 56, 57, 85i, 90, 96i.* ***Marie & John Severin*** *a-Special 1.* ***Simonson*** *a-7, 8, 12, 15-17.* ***Barry Smith*** *a-7, 16, 24, 82r, Special 1r.* ***Starlin*** *c-26.* ***Toth*** *a-64.* ***Williamson*** *a(i)-162, 171, 186. No. 8 , 10 & 16 contain a Robert E. Howard Conan adaptation.*

SAVAGE TALES (...Featuring Conan #4 on)(Magazine)
Marvel Comics Group: May, 1971; No. 2, 10/73; No. 3, 2/74 - No. 12, Summer, 1975 (B&W)
1-Origin/1st app. The Man-Thing by Morrow; Conan the Barbarian by Barry Smith (1st Conan x-over outside his own title); Femizons by Romita-r/in #3; Ka-Zar story by Buscema 15 30 45 104 227 350
2-B. Smith, Brunner, Morrow, Williamson-a; Wrightson King Kull reprint/ Creatures on the Loose #10 6 12 18 41 66 90
3-B. Smith, Brunner, Steranko, Williamson-a 5 10 15 32 51 70
4,5-N. Adams-c; last Conan (Smith-r/#4) plus Kane/N. Adams-a. 5-Brak the Barbarian begins, ends #8 4 8 12 28 44 60
6-Ka-Zar begins; Williamson-r; N. Adams-c 3 6 9 20 30 40
7-N. Adams-i 3 6 9 16 22 28
8,9,11: 8-Shanna, the She-Devil app. thru #10; Williamson-r 3 6 9 14 20 26
10-Neal Adams-a(i), Williamson-r 3 6 9 16 22 28
...Featuring Ka-Zar Annual 1 (Summer, '75, B&W)(#12 on inside)-Ka-Zar origin by Gil Kane; B. Smith-r/Astonishing Tales 3 6 9 17 25 32
NOTE: ***Boris*** *c-7, 10.* ***Buscema*** *a-5r, 6p, 8p; c-2.* ***Colan*** *a-1p.* ***Fabian*** *c-8.* ***Golden*** *a-1, 4; c-1.* ***Heath*** *a-10p, 11p.* ***Kaluta*** *c-9.* ***Maneely*** *r-2, 4(The Crusader in both).* ***Morrow*** *a-1, 2, Annual 1.* ***Reese*** *a-2.* ***Severin*** *a-1-7.* ***Starlin*** *a-5. Robert E. Howard adaptations-1-4.*

SAVAGE TALES
Marvel Comics Group: Nov, 1985 - No. 8, Dec, 1986 ($1.50, B&W, magazine, mature)
1-1st app. The Nam; Golden, Morrow-a 6.00
2-8: 2,7-Morrow-a. 4-2nd Nam story; Golden-a 4.00

SAVAGE TALES
Dynamite Entertainment: 2007 - Present ($4.99)
1-10: 1-Anthology; Red Sonja app.; three covers 5.00

SAVANT GARDE (Also see WildC.A.T.S...)
Image Comics/WildStorm Productions: Mar, 1997 - No. 7, Sept, 1997 ($2.50)
1-7 3.00

SAVED BY THE BELL (TV)
Harvey Comics: Mar, 1992 - No. 5, May, 1993 ($1.25, limited series)
1-5, Holiday Special (3/92), Special 1 (9/92, $1.50)-photo-c, Summer Break 1 (10/92) 3.00

SAW: REBIRTH (Based on 2004 movie Saw)
IDW Publ.: Oct, 2005 ($3.99, one-shot)
1-Guedes-a 4.00

SCALPED
DC Comics (Vertigo): Mar, 2007 - Present ($2.99, limited series)
1-57: 1-Aaron-s/Guera-a/Jock-c. 12-Leon-a. 50-Bonus pin-ups by various 3.00
1-Special Edition (7/10, $1.00) r/#1 with "What's Next?" cover frame 3.00
...: Casino Blood TPB (2008, $14.99) r/#6-11; intro. by Garth Ennis 15.00
...: Dead Mothers TPB (2008, $17.99) r/#12-18 18.00
...: High Lonesome TPB (2009, $14.99) r/#25-29; intro. by Jason Starr 15.00
...: Indian Country TPB (2007, $9.99) r/#1-5; intro. by Brian K. Vaughan 10.00
...: Rez Blues (2011, $17.99) r/#35-42 18.00
...: The Gnawing (2010, $14.99) r/#30-34; intro. by Matt Fraction 15.00
...: The Gravel in Your Guts (2009, $14.99) r/#19-24; intro. by Ed Brubaker 15.00

SCAMP (Walt Disney)(See Walt Disney's Comics & Stories #204)
Dell Publ. Co./Gold Key: No. 703, 5/56 - No. 1204, 8-10/61; 11/67 - No. 45, 1/79
Four Color 703(#1) 8 16 24 56 96 135
Four Color 777,806('57),833 6 12 18 42 69 95
5(3-5/58)-10(6-8/59) 5 10 15 35 55 75
11-16(12-2/60-61), Four Color 1204(1961) 4 8 12 28 44 60
1(12/67-Gold Key)-Reprints begin 4 8 12 26 41 55
2(3/69)-10 2 4 6 13 18 22
11-20 2 4 6 8 11 14
21-45 1 2 3 4 5 7
NOTE: *New stories-#20(in part), 22-25, 27, 29-31, 34, 36-40, 42-45. New covers-#11, 12, 14, 15, 17-25, 27, 29-31, 34, 36-38.*

SCARAB
DC Comics (Vertigo): Nov, 1993 - No. 8, June, 1994 ($1.95, limited series)
1-8-Glenn Fabry painted-c: 1-Silver ink-c. 2-Phantom Stranger app. 3.00

SCARECROW OF ROMNEY MARSH, THE (See W. Disney Showcase #53)
Gold Key: April, 1964 - No. 3, Oct, 1965 (Disney TV Show)
10112-404 (#1) 6 12 18 37 59 80
2,3 4 8 12 24 37 50

SCARECROW (VILLAINS) (See Batman)
DC Comics: Feb, 1998 ($1.95, one-shot)
1-Fegredo-a/Milligan-s/Pearson-c 3.00

SCARE TACTICS
DC Comics: Dec, 1996 - No. 12, Mar, 1998 ($2.25)
1-12: 1-1st app. 3.00

SCAR FACE (See The Crusaders)

SCARFACE: SCARRED FOR LIFE (Based on the 1983 movie)
IDW Publishing: Dec, 2006 - No. 5, Apr, 2007 ($3.99, limited series)
1-5-Tony Montana survives his shooting; Layman-s/Crosland-a 4.00
Scarface: Devil in Disguise (7/07 - No. 4, 10/07, $3.99) Alberto Dose-a 4.00

SCARLET
Marvel Comics (ICON): July, 2010 - Present ($3.95)

Scarlet Spider (2012 series) #1 © MAR

Science Comics #3 © FOX

Scion #25 © CRO

	GD 2.0	VG 4.0	FN 6.0	VF 8.0	VF/NM 9.0	NM- 9.2
1-5-Bendis-s/Maleev-a. 1-Second printing exists						4.00
1,2-Variant covers. 1-Deodato & Lafuente. 2-Oeming & Mack. 3,4-Oeming. 5-Bendis						6.00

SCARLET O'NEIL (See Harvey Comics Hits #59 & Invisible...)

SCARLET SPIDER
Marvel Comics: Nov, 1995 - No. 2, Jan, 1996 ($1.95, limited series)

	GD	VG	FN	VF	VF/NM	NM-
1,2: Replaces Spider-Man title						3.00

SCARLET SPIDER
Marvel Comics: Mar, 2012 - Present ($3.99/$2.99)

	GD	VG	FN	VF	VF/NM	NM-
1-Kaine following "Spider Island"; Yost-s/Stegman-a; 2 covers by Stegman						4.00
2,3-($2.99)						

SCARLET SPIDER UNLIMITED
Marvel Comics: Nov, 1995 ($3.95, one-shot)

	GD	VG	FN	VF	VF/NM	NM-
1-Replaces Spider-Man Unlimited title						4.00

SCARLET WITCH (See Avengers #16, Vision &... & X-Men #4)
Marvel Comics: Jan, 1994 - No. 4, Apr, 1994 ($1.75, limited series)

	GD	VG	FN	VF	VF/NM	NM-
1-4						3.00

SCARY GODMOTHER (Hardcover story books)
Sirius: 1997 - Present ($19.95, HC with dust jackets, one-shots)

	GD	VG	FN	VF	VF/NM	NM-
Volume 1 (9/97) Jill Thompson-s/a; first app. of Scary Godmother						20.00
Vol. 2 - The Revenge of Jimmy (9/98, $19.95)						20.00
Vol. 3 - The Mystery Date (10/99, $19.95)						20.00
Vol. 4 - The Boo Flu (9/02, $19.95)						20.00

SCARY GODMOTHER
Sirius: 2001 - No. 6, 2002 ($2.95, B&W, limited series)

	GD	VG	FN	VF	VF/NM	NM-
1-6-Jill Thompson-s/a						3.00
...: Activity Book (12/00, $2.95, B&W) Jill Thompson-s/a						3.00
...: Bloody Valentine Special (2/98, $3.95, B&W) Jill Thompson-s/a; pin-ups by Ross, Mignola, Russell						4.00
...: Ghoul's Out For Summer (2002,$14.95, B&W) r/#1-6						15.00
...: Holiday Spooktakular (11/98, $2.95, B&W) Jill Thompson-s/a; pin-ups by Brereton, LaBan, Dorkin, Fingerman						3.00

SCARY GODMOTHER: WILD ABOUT HARRY
Sirius: 2000 - No. 3 ($2.95, B&W, limited series)

	GD	VG	FN	VF	VF/NM	NM-
1-3-Jill Thompson-s/a						3.00
TPB (2001, $9.95) r/series						10.00

SCARY TALES
Charlton Comics: 8/75 - #9, 1/77; #10, 9/77 - #20, 6/79; #21, 8/80 - #46, 10/84

	GD	VG	FN	VF	VF/NM	NM-
1-Origin/1st app. Countess Von Bludd, not in #2	3	6	9	19	29	38
2,4,6,9,10: 4,9-Sutton-c/a. 4-Man-Thing copy	2	4	6	9	13	16
3-Sutton painted-c; Ditko-a	2	4	6	11	16	20
5,11-Ditko-c/a.	3	6	9	14	19	24
7,8-Ditko-a	2	4	6	10	14	18
12,15,16,19,21,39-Ditko-a	2	4	6	9	13	16
13,17,20	2	4	6	8	10	12
14,18,30,32-Ditko-c/a	2	4	6	11	16	20
22-29,33-37,39,40: 37,38,40-New-a. 39-All Ditko reprints and cover	1	3	4	6	8	10
31,38: 31-Newton-c/a. 38-Mr. Jigsaw app.	1	3	4	6	8	10
41-45-New-a. 41-Ditko-a(3). 42-45-(Low print)	2	4	6	8	10	12
46-Reprints (Low print)	2	4	6	10	14	18
1(Modern Comics reprint, 1977)						6.00

NOTE: ***Adkins** a-31i; c-31i. **Ditko** a-3, 5, 7, 8(2), 11, 12, 14-16r, 18(3)r, 19r, 21r, 30r, 32, 39r, 41(3); c-5, 11, 14, 18, 30, 32. **Newton** a-31p; c-31p. **Powell** a-18r. **Staton** a-1(2 pgs.), 4, 20r; c-1, 20. **Sutton** a-4, 9; c-4, 9. **Zeck** a-9.*

SCATTERBRAIN
Dark Horse Comics: Jun, 1998 - No. 4, Sept, 1998 ($2.95, limited series)

	GD	VG	FN	VF	VF/NM	NM-
1-4-Humor anthology by Aragonés, Dorkin, Stevens and others						3.00

SCAVENGERS
Quality Comics: Feb, 1988 - No. 14, 1989 ($1.25/$1.50)

	GD	VG	FN	VF	VF/NM	NM-
1-14: 9-13-Guice-c						3.00

SCAVENGERS
Triumphant Comics: 1993(nd, July) - No. 11, May, 1994 ($2.50, serially numbered)

	GD	VG	FN	VF	VF/NM	NM-
1-9,0,10,11: 5,6-Triumphant Unleashed x-over. 9-(3/94). 0-Retail ed. (3/94, $2.50, 36 pgs.). 0-Giveaway edition (3/94, 20 pgs.). 0-Coupon redemption edition. 10-(4/94)						3.00

SCENE OF THE CRIME (Also see Vertigo: Winter's Edge #2)
DC Comics (Vertigo): May, 1999 - No. 4, Aug, 1999 ($2.50, limited series)

	GD	VG	FN	VF	VF/NM	NM-
1-4-Brubaker-s/Lark-a						3.00
...: A Little Piece of Goodnight TPB ('00, $12.95) r/#1-4; Winter's Edge #2						13.00

SCHOOL DAY ROMANCES (...of Teen-Agers #4; Popular Teen-Agers #5 on)
Star Publications: Nov-Dec, 1949 - No. 4, May-June, 1950 (Teenage)

	GD	VG	FN	VF	VF/NM	NM-
1-Toni Gayle (later Toni Gay), Ginger Snapp, Midge Martin & Eve Adams begin	27	54	81	158	259	360
2,3: 3-Jane Powell photo on-c & true life story	20	40	60	115	185	255
4-Ronald Reagan photo on-c; L.B. Cole-c	30	60	90	177	289	400

NOTE: *All have **L. B. Cole** covers.*

SCHWINN BICYCLE BOOK (...Bike Thrills, 1959)
Schwinn Bicycle Co.: 1949; 1952; 1959 (10¢)

	GD	VG	FN	VF	VF/NM	NM-
1949	6	12	18	28	34	40
1952-Believe It or Not facts; comic format; 36 pgs.	5	10	14	20	24	28
1959	3	6	8	11	13	15

SCIENCE COMICS (1st Series)
Fox Features Syndicate: Feb, 1940 - No. 8, Sept, 1940

	GD	VG	FN	VF	VF/NM	NM-
1-Origin Dynamo (1st app., called Electro in #1), The Eagle (1st app.), & Navy Jones; Marga, The Panther Woman (1st app.), Cosmic Carson & Perisphere Payne, Dr. Doom begin; bondage/hypo-c; Electro-c	486	972	1458	3550	6275	9000
2-Classic Lou Fine Dynamo-c	258	516	774	1651	2826	4000
3-Classic Lou Fine Dynamo-c	206	412	618	1318	2259	3200
4-Kirby-a; Cosmic Carson-c by Joe Simon	181	362	543	1158	1979	2800
5-8: 5,8-Eagle-c. 6,7-Dynamo-c	107	214	321	680	1165	1650

NOTE: *Cosmic Carson by **Tuska**-#1-3; by **Kirby**-#4. **Lou Fine** c-1-3 only.*

SCIENCE COMICS (2nd Series)
Humor Publications (Ace Magazines?): Jan, 1946 - No. 5, 1946

	GD	VG	FN	VF	VF/NM	NM-
1-Palais-c/a in #1-3; A-Bomb-c	20	40	60	114	182	250
2	12	24	36	67	94	120
3-Feldstein-a (6 pgs.)	16	32	48	94	147	200
4,5: 4-Palais-c	10	20	30	54	72	90

SCIENCE COMICS
Ziff-Davis Publ. Co.: May, 1947 (8 pgs. in color)

	GD	VG	FN	VF	VF/NM	NM-
nn-Could be ordered by mail for 10¢; like the nn Amazing Adventures (1950) & Boy Cowboy (1950); used to test the market	41	82	123	256	428	600

SCIENCE COMICS (True Science Illustrated)
Export Publication Ent., Toronto, Canada: Mar, 1951 (Distr. in U.S. by Kable News Co.)

	GD	VG	FN	VF	VF/NM	NM-
1-Science Adventure stories plus some true science features; man on moon story	14	28	42	76	108	140

SCIENCE DOG SPECIAL (Also see Invincible)
Image Comics: Aug, 2010; No. 2, May, 2011 ($3.50)

	GD	VG	FN	VF	VF/NM	NM-
1,2: 1-Kirkman-s/Walker-a/c; leads into Invincible #75						3.50

SCIENCE FICTION SPACE ADVENTURES (See Space Adventures)

SCION (Also see CrossGen Chronicles)
CrossGeneration Comics: July, 2000 - No. 43, Apr, 2004 ($2.95)

	GD	VG	FN	VF	VF/NM	NM-
1-43: 1-Marz-s/Cheung-a						3.00
...: Conflict of Conscience Vol. 1 TPB (5/01, $19.95) r/#1-7; Adam Hughes-c						20.00
...: Blood For Blood Vol. 2 TPB (2002, $19.95) r/#8-14 & CrossGen Chronicles #2						20.00
...: Divided Loyalties Vol. 3 TPB (2002, $15.95) r/#15-21						16.00
...: Sanctuary Vol. 4 TPB (2003, $15.95) r/#22-27						16.00
Vol. 5: The Far Kingdom (2003, $15.95) r/#28-33						16.00
Vol. 6: The Royal Wedding (2004, $15.95) r/#34-39						16.00
Traveler Vol. 1-3 ($9.95) Digest-sized reprints of TPBs						10.00

SCI-SPY
DC Comics (Vertigo): Apr, 2002 - No. 6, Sept, 2002 ($2.50, limited series)

	GD	VG	FN	VF	VF/NM	NM-
1-6-Moench-s/Gulacy-c/a						3.00

SCI-TECH
DC Comics (WildStorm): Sept, 1999 - No. 4, Dec, 1999 ($2.50, limited series)

	GD	VG	FN	VF	VF/NM	NM-
1-4-Benes-a/Choi & Peterson-s						3.00

SCOOBY DOO (TV)(...Where are you? #1-16,26; ...Mystery Comics #17-25, 27 on)
(See March Of Comics #356, 368, 382, 391 in the Promotional Comics section)
Gold Key: Mar, 1970 - No. 30, Feb, 1975 (Hanna-Barbera)

	GD	VG	FN	VF	VF/NM	NM-
1	13	26	39	90	195	300
2-5	8	16	24	56	96	135
6-10	7	14	21	48	79	110
11-20: 11-Tufts-a	6	12	18	39	62	85
21-30	5	10	15	30	48	65

SCOOBY DOO (TV)

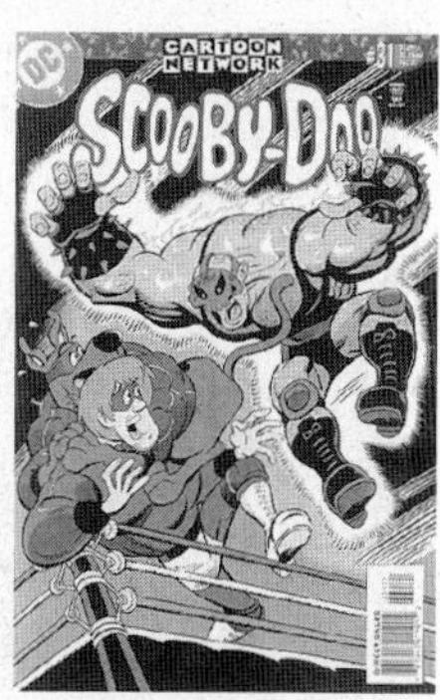

Scooby-Doo (1997 series) #31 © H-B

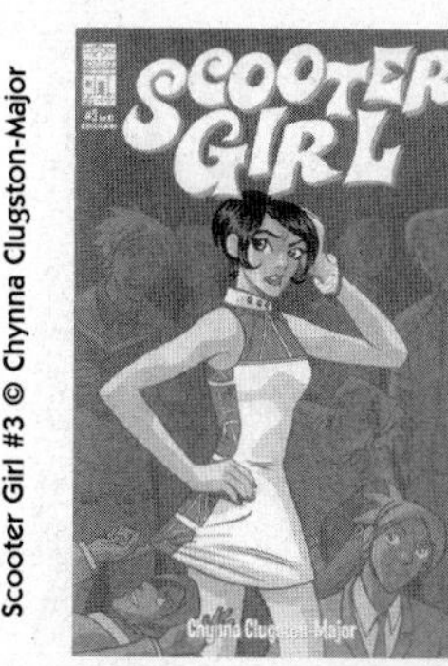

Scooter Girl #3 © Chynna Clugston-Major

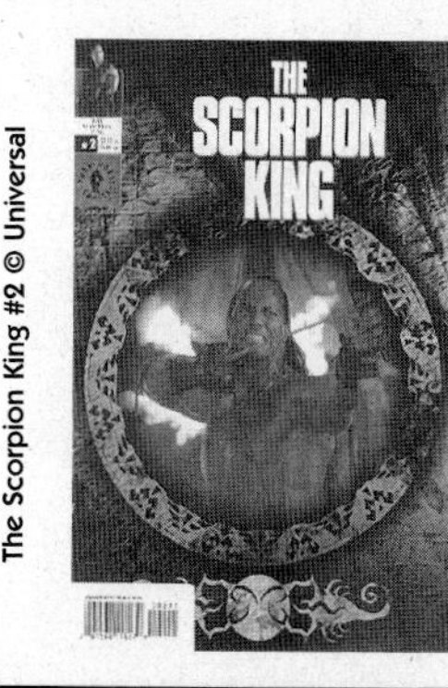

The Scorpion King #2 © Universal

Charlton Comics: Apr, 1975 - No. 11, Dec, 1976 (Hanna-Barbera)

	GD 2.0	VG 4.0	FN 6.0	VF 8.0	VF/NM 9.0	NM- 9.2
1	7	14	21	44	72	100
2-5	4	8	12	28	44	60
6-11	4	8	12	24	37	50
nn-(1976, digest, 68 pgs., B&W)	4	8	12	26	41	55

SCOOBY-DOO (TV)(Newsstand sales only) (See Dynamutt & Laff-A-Lympics)
Marvel Comics Group: Oct, 1977 - No. 9, Feb, 1979 (Hanna-Barbera)

	GD 2.0	VG 4.0	FN 6.0	VF 8.0	VF/NM 9.0	NM- 9.2
1,6-9: 1-Dyno-Mutt begins	3	6	9	20	30	40
1-(35¢-c variant, limited distribution)(10/77)	8	16	24	56	96	135
2-5	3	6	9	17	25	32

SCOOBY-DOO (TV)
Harvey Comics: Sept, 1992 - No. 3, May, 1993 ($1.25)

	GD 2.0	VG 4.0	FN 6.0	VF 8.0	VF/NM 9.0	NM- 9.2
V2#1,2	1	2	3	4	5	7
Big Book 1,2 (11/92, 4/93, $1.95, 52 pgs.)	1	2	3	5	7	9
Giant Size 1,2 (10/92, 3/93, $2.25, 68 pgs.)	1	2	3	5	7	9

SCOOBY DOO (TV)
Archie Comics: Oct, 1995 -No. 21, June, 1997 ($1.50)

	GD 2.0	VG 4.0	FN 6.0	VF 8.0	VF/NM 9.0	NM- 9.2
1	1	2	3	5	6	8
2-21: 12-Cover by Scooby Doo creative designer Iwao Takamoto						5.00

SCOOBY DOO (TV)
DC Comics: Aug, 1997 - No. 159, Oct, 2010 ($1.75/$1.95/$1.99/$2.25/$2.50/$2.99)

	GD 2.0	VG 4.0	FN 6.0	VF 8.0	VF/NM 9.0	NM- 9.2
1						6.00
2-10: 5-Begin-$1.95-c						4.00
11-45: 14-Begin $1.99-c						3.00
46-89,91-157: 63-Begin $2.25-c. 75-With 2 Garbage Pail Kids stickers. 100-Wray-c						3.00
90,158,159: 90-($2.95) Bonus stories. 158,159-($2.99-c)						4.00
...Spooky Spectacular 1 (10/99, $3.95) Comic Convention story						4.00
...Spooky Spectacular 2000 (10/00, $3.95)						4.00
...Spooky Summer Special 2001 (8/01, $3.95) Staton-a						4.00
...Super Scarefest (8/02, $3.95) r/#20,25,30-32						4.00
Vol. 1: You Meddling Kids (2003, $6.95, digest-size) r/#1-5						7.00
Vol. 2: Ruh-Roh! (2003, $6.95, digest-size) r/#6-10						7.00
Vol. 3: All Wrapped Up! (2005, $6.95, digest-size) r/#11-15						7.00
Vol. 4: The Big Squeeze! (2005, $6.95, digest-size) r/#16-20						7.00
Vol. 5: Surf's Up! (2006, $6.99, digest-size) r/#21-25						7.00
Vol. 5: Space Fright! (2006, $6.99, digest-size) r/#26-30						7.00

SCOOBY DOO: WHERE ARE YOU? (TV)
DC Comics: Nov, 2010 - Present ($2.99)

	GD 2.0	VG 4.0	FN 6.0	VF 8.0	VF/NM 9.0	NM- 9.2
1-20						3.00

SCOOP COMICS (Becomes Yankee Comics #4-7, a digest sized cartoon book; then after #8 it becomes Snap #9)
Harry 'A' Chesler (Holyoke): November, 1941 - No. 3, Mar, 1943; No. 8, 1944

	GD 2.0	VG 4.0	FN 6.0	VF 8.0	VF/NM 9.0	NM- 9.2
1-Intro. Rocketman & Rocketgirl & begins; origin The Master Key & begins; Dan Hastings begins; Charles Sultan-c/a	155	310	465	992	1696	2400
2-Rocket Boy begins; injury to eye story (reprinted in Spotlight #3); classic-c	181	362	543	1158	1979	2800
3-Injury to eye story-r from #2; Rocket Boy	74	128	222	470	810	1150
8-Formerly Yankee Comics; becomes Snap	48	96	114	302	514	725

SCOOTER (See Swing With...)

SCOOTER COMICS
Rucker Publ. Ltd. (Canadian): Apr, 1946

	GD 2.0	VG 4.0	FN 6.0	VF 8.0	VF/NM 9.0	NM- 9.2
1-Teen-age/funny animal	11	22	33	62	86	110

SCOOTER GIRL
Oni Press: May, 2003 - No. 6, Feb, 2004 ($2.99, B&W, limited series)

	GD 2.0	VG 4.0	FN 6.0	VF 8.0	VF/NM 9.0	NM- 9.2
1-6-Chynna Clugston-Major-s/a						3.00
TPB (5/04, $14.95, digest size) r/series; sketch pages						15.00

SCORPION
Atlas/Seaboard Publ.: Feb, 1975 - No. 3, July, 1975

	GD 2.0	VG 4.0	FN 6.0	VF 8.0	VF/NM 9.0	NM- 9.2
1-Intro.; bondage-c by Chaykin	2	4	6	13	18	22
2-Chaykin-a w/Wrightson, Kaluta, Simonson assists(p)	2	4	6	13	18	22
3-Jim Craig-c/a	2	4	6	10	14	18

NOTE: ***Chaykin** a-1, 2; c-1. **Colon** c-2. **Craig** c/a-3.*

SCORPION KING, THE (Movie)
Dark Horse Comics: March, 2002 - No. 2, Apr, 2002 ($2.99, limited series)

	GD 2.0	VG 4.0	FN 6.0	VF 8.0	VF/NM 9.0	NM- 9.2
1,2-Photo-c of the Rock; Richards-a						3.00

SCORPIO ROSE
Eclipse Comics: Jan, 1983 - No. 2, Oct, 1983 ($1.25, Baxter paper)

	GD 2.0	VG 4.0	FN 6.0	VF 8.0	VF/NM 9.0	NM- 9.2
1,2: Dr. Orient back-up story begins. 2-origin.						4.00

SCOTLAND YARD (Inspector Farnsworth of)(Texas Rangers in Action #5 on?)
Charlton Comics Group: June, 1955 - No. 4, Mar, 1956

	GD 2.0	VG 4.0	FN 6.0	VF 8.0	VF/NM 9.0	NM- 9.2
1-Tothish-a	14	28	42	80	115	150
2-4: 2-Tothish-a	10	20	30	54	72	90

SCOTT PILGRIM, ... (Inspired the 2010 movie)
Oni Press: Jul, 2004 - Vol. 6, Jul, 2010 ($11.99, B&W, 7-1/2" x 5", multiple printings exist)

	GD 2.0	VG 4.0	FN 6.0	VF 8.0	VF/NM 9.0	NM- 9.2
Scott Pilgrim's Precious Little Life (Vol. 1) Bryan Lee O'Malley-s/a in all						12.00
Scott Pilgrim Vs. The World (Vol. 2), S.P. & The Infinite Sadness (Vol. 3), S.P. Gets it Together (Vol. 4), S.P. Vs. The Universe (Vol. 5), Scott Pilgrim's Finest Hour (Vol. 6) each						12.00
Free Scott Pilgrim #1 (Free Comic Book Day Edition, 2006)						15.00
Full-Colour Odds & Ends 2008						8.00

SCOURGE, THE
Aspen MLT: No. 0, Aug, 2010 - No. 6, Dec, 2011 ($2.50/$2.99)

	GD 2.0	VG 4.0	FN 6.0	VF 8.0	VF/NM 9.0	NM- 9.2
0-($2.50) Lobdell-s/Battle-a; multiple covers						3.00
1-6-($2.99) Lobdell-s/Battle-a; multiple covers						3.00

SCOURGE OF THE GODS
Marvel Comics (Soleil): 2009 - No. 3, 2009 ($5.99, limited series)

	GD 2.0	VG 4.0	FN 6.0	VF 8.0	VF/NM 9.0	NM- 9.2
1-3-Mangin-s/Gajic-a; English version of French comic						6.00
...: The Fall 1-3 (2009 - No. 3, 2009)						6.00

SCOUT (See Eclipse Graphic Album #16, New America & Swords of Texas) (Becomes Scout: War Shaman)
Eclipse Comics: Dec, 1985 - No. 24, Oct, 1987($1.75/$1.25, Baxter paper)

	GD 2.0	VG 4.0	FN 6.0	VF 8.0	VF/NM 9.0	NM- 9.2
1-15,17,18,20-24: 19-Airboy preview. 10-Bissette-a. 11-Monday, the Eliminator begins. 15-Swords of Texas						3.00
16,19: 16-Scout 3-D Special ($2.50), 16-Scout 2-D Limited Edition, 19-contains flexidisk ($2.50)						4.00
...Handbook 1 (8/87, $1.75, B&W)						3.00
Mount Fire (1989, $14.95, TPB) r/#8-14						15.00

SCOUT: WAR SHAMAN (Formerly Scout)
Eclipse Comics: Mar, 1988 - No. 16, Dec, 1989 ($1.95)

	GD 2.0	VG 4.0	FN 6.0	VF 8.0	VF/NM 9.0	NM- 9.2
1-16						3.00

SCRATCH
DC Comics: Aug, 2004 - No. 5, Dec, 2004 ($2.50, limited series)

	GD 2.0	VG 4.0	FN 6.0	VF 8.0	VF/NM 9.0	NM- 9.2
1-5-Sam Kieth-s/a/c; Batman app.						3.00

SCREAM (...Comics) (Andy Comics #20 on)
Humor Publications/Current Books(Ace Magazines): Autumn, 1944 - No. 19, Apr, 1948

	GD 2.0	VG 4.0	FN 6.0	VF 8.0	VF/NM 9.0	NM- 9.2
1-Teenage humor	16	32	48	92	144	195
2	10	20	30	56	76	95
3-16: 11-Racist humor (Indians). 16-Intro. Lily-Belle	9	18	27	47	61	75
17,19	8	16	24	42	54	65
18-Hypo needle story	9	18	27	47	61	75

SCREAM (Magazine)
Skywald Publ. Corp.: Aug, 1973 - No. 11, Feb, 1975 (68 pgs., B&W) (Painted-c on all)

	GD 2.0	VG 4.0	FN 6.0	VF 8.0	VF/NM 9.0	NM- 9.2
1-Nosferatu-c/1st app. (series thru #11); Morrow-a. Cthulhu/Necronomicon-s	8	16	24	51	86	120
2,3: 2-(10/73) Lady Satan 1st app. & series begins; Edgar Allan Poe adaptations begin (thru #11); Phantom of the Opera-s. 3-(12/73) Origin Lady Satan	5	10	15	35	55	75
4-1st Cannibal Werewolf and 1st Lunatic Mummy	5	10	15	30	48	65
5,7,8: 5,7-Frankenstein app. 8-Buckler-a; Werewolf-s; Slither-Slime Man-s	5	10	15	30	48	65
6, 9,10: 6-(6/74) Saga of The Victims/ I Am Horror, classic GGA Hewetson series begins (thru #11); Frankenstein 2073-s. 9-Severed head-c; Marcos-a. 9,10-Werewolf-s. 10-Dracula-c/s	5	10	15	32	51	70
11- (1975 Winter Special) "Mr. Poe and the Raven" story	5	10	15	35	55	75

NOTE: ***Buckler** a-8. **Hewetson** s-1-11. **Marcos** a-9. **Miralles** c-2. **Morrow** a-1. **Poe** s-2-11. **Segrelles** a-7; c-1.*

SCREEN CARTOONS
DC Comics: Dec, 1944 (cover only ashcan)

nn-Ashcan comic, not distributed to newsstands, only for in house use. Covers were produced, but not the rest of the book. A copy sold in 2006 for $400 and in 2008 for $500.

SCREEN COMICS
DC Comics: Dec, 1944 (cover only ashcan)

nn-Ashcan comic, not distributed to newsstands, only for in house use. Covers were produced, but not the rest of the book. A copy sold in 2006 for $400 and in 2008 for $500.

SCREEN FABLES

Scribbly #9 © DC

Sea Devils #10 © DC

Second Life of Doctor Mirage #1 © VAL

	GD 2.0	VG 4.0	FN 6.0	VF 8.0	VF/NM 9.0	NM- 9.2

DC Comics: Dec, 1944 (cover only ashcan)

nn-Ashcan comic, not distributed to newsstands, only for in house use. Covers were produced, but not the rest of the book. A copy sold in 2006 for $400 and in 2008 for $500.

SCREEN FUNNIES
DC Comics: Dec, 1944 (cover only ashcan)

nn-Ashcan comic, not distributed to newsstands, only for in house use. Covers were produced, but not the rest of the book. A copy sold in 2006 for $400 and in 2008 for $500.

SCREEN GEMS
DC Comics: Dec, 1944 (cover only ashcan)

nn-Ashcan comic, not distributed to newsstands, only for in house use. Covers were produced, but not the rest of the book. A copy sold in 2010 for $891 and a VF copy sold for $775.

SCREWBALL SQUIRREL
Dark Horse Comics: July, 1995 - No. 3, Sept, 1995 ($2.50, limited series)

1-3: Characters created by Tex Avery 3.00

SCRIBBLY (See All-American Comics, Buzzy, The Funnies, Leave It To Binky & Popular Comics)
National Periodical Publ.: 8-9/48 - No. 13, 8-9/50; No. 14, 10-11/51 - No. 15, 12-1/51-52

	GD	VG	FN	VF	VF/NM	NM-
1-Sheldon Mayer-c/a in all; 52 pgs. begin	87	174	261	553	952	1350
2	55	110	165	352	601	850
3-5	45	90	135	284	480	675
6-10	36	72	108	216	351	485
11-15: 13-Last 52 pgs.	31	62	93	184	300	415

SCUD: TALES FROM THE VENDING MACHINE
Fireman Press: 1998 - No. 5 ($2.50, B&W)

1-5: 1-Kaniuga-a. 2-Ruben Martinez-a 3.00

SCUD: THE DISPOSABLE ASSASSIN
Fireman Press: Feb, 1994 - No. 20, 1997 ($2.95, B&W)
Image Comics: No. 21, Feb, 2008 - No. 24, May, 2008 ($3.50, B&W)

1 6.00
1-2nd printing in color 3.00
2,3 4.00
4-20 3.00
21-24: 21-(2/08, $3.50) Ashley Wood-c. 22-Mahfood-c 3.50
Heavy 3PO ($12.95, TPB) r/#1-4 13.00
Programmed For Damage ($14.95, TPB) r/#5-9 15.00
Solid Gold Bomb ($17.95, TPB) r/#10-15 18.00

SEA DEVILS (See Limited Collectors' Edition #39,45, & Showcase #27-29)
National Periodical Publications: Sept-Oct, 1961 - No. 35, May-June, 1967

	GD	VG	FN	VF	VF/NM	NM-
1-(9-10/61)	55	110	165	446	961	1475
2-Last 10¢ issue; grey-tone-c	28	56	84	199	430	660
3-Begin 12¢ issues thru #35; grey-tone-c	18	36	54	123	267	410
4,5-Grey-tone-c	16	32	48	107	234	360
6-10	11	22	33	76	151	225
11,12,14-20: 12-Grey-tone-c	9	18	27	61	106	150
13-Kubert, Colan-a; Joe Kubert app. in story	9	18	27	62	109	155
21-35: 22-Intro. International Sea Devils; origin & 1st app. Capt. X & Man Fish. 33,35-Grey-tone-c	7	14	21	46	76	105

NOTE: *Heath a-Showcase 27-29, 1-10; c-Showcase 27-29, 1-10, 14-16.* ***Moldoff*** *a-16i.*

SEA DEVILS (See Tangent Comics/ Sea Devils)

SEADRAGON (Also see the Epsilion Wave)
Elite Comics: May, 1986 - No. 8, 1987 ($1.75)

1-8: 1-1st & 2nd printings exist 3.00

SEAGUY
DC Comics (Vertigo): July, 2004 - No. 3, Sept, 2004 ($2.95, limited series)

1-3-Grant Morrison-s/Cameron Stewart-a/c 3.00
TPB (2005, $9.95) r/#1-3 10.00

SEAGUY: THE SLAVES OF MICKEY EYE
DC Comics (Vertigo): Jun, 2009 - No. 3, Aug, 2009 ($3.99, limited series)

1-3-Grant Morrison-s/Cameron Stewart-a/c 4.00

SEA HOUND, THE (Captain Silver's Log Of The...)
Avon Periodicals: 1945 (no month) - No. 2, Sept-Oct, 1945

	GD	VG	FN	VF	VF/NM	NM-
nn (#1)-29 pg. novel length sty-"The Esmeralda's Treasure"	18	36	54	105	165	225
2	13	26	39	74	105	135

SEA HOUND, THE (Radio)
Capt. Silver Syndicate: No. 3, July, 1949 - No. 4, Sept, 1949

	GD	VG	FN	VF	VF/NM	NM-
3,4	10	20	30	54	72	90

SEA HUNT (TV)
Dell Publishing Co.: No. 928, 8/58 - No. 1041, 10-12/59; No. 4, 1-3/60 - No. 13, 4-6/62 (All have Lloyd Bridges photo-c)

	GD	VG	FN	VF	VF/NM	NM-
Four Color 928(#1)	11	22	33	71	136	200
Four Color 994(#2), 4-13: Manning-a #4-6,8-11,13	8	16	24	53	89	125
Four Color 1041(#3)-Toth-a	8	16	24	53	89	125

SEA OF RED
Image Comics: Mar, 2005 - No. 13, Nov, 2006 ($2.95/$2.99/$3.50)

1-12-Vampirates at sea; Remender & Dwyer-s/Dwyer & Sam-a 3.00
13-($3.50) 3.50
Vol. 1: No Grave But The Sea (9/05, $8.95) r/#1-4 9.00
Vol. 2: No Quarter (2006, $11.99) r/#5-8 12.00
Vol. 3: The Deadlights (2006, $14.99) r/#9-13 15.00

SEAQUEST (TV)
Nemesis Comics: Mar, 1994 ($2.25)

1-Has 2 diff-c stocks (slick & cardboard); Alcala-i 3.00

SEARCH FOR LOVE
American Comics Group: Feb-Mar, 1950 - No. 2, Apr-May, 1950 (52 pgs.)

	GD	VG	FN	VF	VF/NM	NM-
1	12	24	36	69	97	125
2	9	18	27	47	61	75

SEARCHERS, THE (Movie)
Dell Publishing Co.: No. 709, 1956

	GD	VG	FN	VF	VF/NM	NM-
Four Color 709-John Wayne photo-c	20	40	60	137	294	450

SEARCHERS, THE
Caliber Comics: 1996 - No. 4, 1996 ($2.95, B&W)

1-4 3.00

SEARCHERS, THE : APOSTLE OF MERCY
Caliber Comics: 1997 - No. 2, 1997 ($2.95/$3.95, B&W)

1-($2.95) 3.00
2-($3.95) 4.00

SEARS (See Merry Christmas From...)

SEASON'S GREETINGS
Hallmark (King Features): 1935 (6-1/4x5-1/4", 24 pgs. in color)

nn-Cover features Mickey Mouse, Popeye, Jiggs & Skippy. "The Night Before Christmas" told one panel per page, each panel by a famous artist featuring their character. Art by Alex Raymond, Gottfredson, Swinnerton, Segar, Chic Young, Milt Gross, Sullivan (Messmer), Herriman, McManus, Percy Crosby & others (22 artists in all)
Estimated value... 950.00

SEBASTIAN O
DC Comics (Vertigo): May, 1993 - No. 3, July, 1993 ($1.95, limited series)

1-3-Grant Morrison scripts; Steve Yeowell-a 3.00
TPB (2004, $9.95) r/#1-3; intro. chronology by Morrison 10.00

SECOND LIFE OF DOCTOR MIRAGE, THE (See Shadowman #16)
Valiant: Nov, 1993 - No. 18, May, 1995 ($2.50)

1-18: 1-With bound-in poster. 5-Shadowman x-over. 7-Bound-in trading card 3.00
1-Gold ink logo edition; no price on-c 4.00

SECRET AGENT (Formerly Sarge Steel)
Charlton Comics: V2#9, Oct, 1966; V2#10, Oct, 1967

	GD	VG	FN	VF	VF/NM	NM-
V2#9-Sarge Steel part-r begins	3	6	9	17	25	32
10-Tiffany Sinn, CIA app. (from Career Girl Romances #39); Aparo-a	3	6	9	14	19	24

SECRET AGENT (TV) (See Four Color #1231)
Gold Key: Nov, 1966; No. 2, Jan, 1968

	GD	VG	FN	VF	VF/NM	NM-
1-Photo-c	8	16	24	56	96	135
2-Photo-c	6	12	18	41	66	90

SECRET AGENT X-9 (See Flash Gordon #4 by King)
David McKay Publ.: 1934 (Book 1: 84 pgs.; Book 2: 124 pgs.) (8x7-1/2")

	GD	VG	FN	VF	VF/NM	NM-
Book 1-Contains reprints of the first 13 weeks of the strip by Alex Raymond; complete except for 2 dailies	43	86	129	271	461	650
Book 2-Contains reprints immediately following contents of Book 1, for 20 weeks by Alex Raymond; complete except for two dailies. Note: Raymond mis-dated the last five strips from 6/34, and while the dating sequence is confusing, the continuity is correct	39	78	117	234	385	535

SECRET AGENT X-9 (See Magic Comics)
Dell Publishing Co.: Dec, 1937 (Not by Raymond)

Secret Avengers #13 © MAR

Secret Hearts #26 © DC

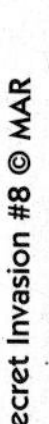
Secret Invasion #8 © MAR

	GD 2.0	VG 4.0	FN 6.0	VF 8.0	VF/NM 9.0	NM- 9.2
Feature Books 8	47	94	141	296	498	700

SECRET AGENT Z-2 (See Holyoke One-Shot No. 7)

SECRET AVENGERS (The Heroic Age)
Marvel Comics: Jul, 2010 - Present ($3.99)

	NM- 9.2
1-Bendis-s/Deodato-a/Djurdjevic-c; Steve Rogers assembles covert squad	4.00
1-Variant-c by Yardin	6.00
2-12: 2-Two covers. 2-4-Deodato-a. 5-Nick Fury app.; Aja-a	4.00
12.1 ($2.99) Spencer-s/Eaton-a/Deodato-c	3.00
13-21: 13-15-Fear Itself tie-in; Granov-c. 15-Aftermath of Bucky's demise. 16-21-Ellis-s	4.00
21.2-($2.99) Remender-s/Zircher-a; intro. new Masters of Evil	3.00
22,23-Remenber-s/Hardman-a/Art Adams-c. 23-Venom joins	4.00

SECRET CITY SAGA (See Jack Kirby's Secret City Saga)

SECRET DEFENDERS (Also see The Defenders & Fantastic Four #374)
Marvel Comics: Mar, 1993 - No. 25, Mar, 1995 ($1.75/$1.95)

	NM- 9.2
1-($2.50)-Red foil stamped-c; Dr. Strange, Nomad, Wolverine, Spider Woman & Darkhawk begin	4.00
2-11,13-24: 9-New team w/Silver Surfer, Thunderstrike, Dr. Strange & War Machine. 13-Thanos replaces Dr. Strange as leader; leads into Cosmic Powers limited series; 14-Dr. Druid. 15-Bound in card sheet. 18-Giant Man & Iron Fist app.	3.00
12,25: 12-($2.50)-Prismatic foil-c. 25 ($2.50, 52 pgs.)	4.00

SECRET DIARY OF EERIE ADVENTURES
Avon Periodicals: 1953 (25¢ giant, 100 pgs., one-shot)

	GD 2.0	VG 4.0	FN 6.0	VF 8.0	VF/NM 9.0	NM- 9.2
nn-(Rare)-Kubert-a; Hollingsworth-c; Sid Check back-c	226	452	678	1446	2473	3500

SECRET FILES & ORIGINS GUIDE TO THE DC UNIVERSE
DC Comics: Mar, 2000; Feb, 2002 ($6.95/$4.95)

	NM- 9.2
2000 (3/00, $6.95)-Overview of DC characters; profile pages by various	7.00
2001-2002 (2/02, $4.95) Olivetti-c	5.00

SECRET FILES PRESIDENT LUTHOR
DC Comics: Mar, 2001 ($4.95, one-shot)

	NM- 9.2
1-Short stories & profile pages by various; Harris-c	5.00

SECRET HEARTS
National Periodical Publications (Beverly)(Arleigh No. 50-113):
9-10/49 - No. 6, 7-8/50; No. 7, 12-1/51-52 - No. 153, 7/71

	GD 2.0	VG 4.0	FN 6.0	VF 8.0	VF/NM 9.0	NM- 9.2
1-Kinstler-a; photo-c begin, end #6	57	114	171	362	619	875
2-Toth-a (1 pg.); Kinstler-a	31	62	93	182	296	410
3,6 (1950)	27	54	81	158	259	360
4,5-Toth-a	27	54	81	160	263	365
7(12-1/51-52) (Rare)	41	82	123	249	417	585
8-10 (1952)	20	40	60	117	189	260
11-20	15	30	45	90	140	190
21-26: 26-Last precode (2-3/55)	14	28	42	81	118	155
27-40	7	14	21	48	79	110
41-50	6	12	18	37	59	80
51-60	5	10	15	32	51	70
61-75,100: 75-Last 10¢ issue	5	10	15	30	48	65
76-99,101-109	4	8	12	23	36	48
110- "Reach for Happiness" serial begins, ends #138	4	8	12	26	41	55
111-119,121-126	3	6	9	18	27	35
120,134-Neal Adams-c	4	8	12	26	41	55
127 (4/68)-Beatles cameo	4	8	12	26	41	55
128-133,135-142: 141,142- "20 Miles to Heartbreak", Chapter 2 & 3 (see Young Love for Chapters 1 & 4); Toth, Colletta-a	3	6	9	17	25	32
143-148,150-152: 144-Morrow-a	3	6	9	14	20	26
149,153: 149-Toth-a. 153-Kirby-i	3	6	9	16	22	28

SECRET HISTORY OF THE AUTHORITY: HAWKSMOOR
DC Comics (WildStorm): May, 2008 - No. 6, Oct, 2008 ($2.99, limited series)

	NM- 9.2
1-6-Costa-s/Staples-a/Hamner-c	3.00
TPB (2009, $19.99) r/#1-6	20.00

SECRET INVASION (Also see Mighty Avengers, New Avengers, and Skrulls!)
Marvel Comics: June, 2008 - No. 8, Jan, 2009 ($3.99, limited series)

	NM- 9.2
1-Skrull invasion; Bendis-s/Yu-a/Dell'Otto-c	4.00
1-Variant cover with blank area for sketches	4.00
1-McNiven variant-c	12.00
1-Yu variant-c	30.00
1-2nd printing with old Avengers variant-c by Yu	4.00
1 Director's Cut (2008, $4.99) r/#1 with script; concept and promo art; cover gallery	5.00
2-8-Dell'Otto-c. 8-Wasp killed	4.00
2-4-McNiven variant-c. 2-Avengers. 3-Nick Fury. 4-Tony Stark, Spider-Woman, Black Widow	6.00
2-8-Yu variant-c. 2-Hawkeye & Mockingbird. 3-Spider-Woman. 4-Nick Fury	10.00
5-Rubi variant-c	5.00
6-Cho Spider-Woman variant-c	8.00
...:Aftermath: Beta Ray Bill - The Green of Eden (6/09, $3.99) Brereton-a	4.00
...: Chronicles 1,2 (4/09,6/09, $5.99) reprints from New Avengers & Illuminati issues	6.00
... Dark Reign (2/09, $3.99) villain meeting after #8; previews new series; Maleev-a/c	4.00
... Dark Reign (2/09, $3.99) Variant Green Goblin cover by Bryan Hitch	8.00
... Requiem (2009, $3.99) Hank Pym becomes The Wasp; r/TTA #44 & Avengers #215	4.00
... Saga (2008, giveaway) history of the Skrulls told through reprint panels and text	3.00
...: The Infiltration TPB (2008, $19.99) r/FF #2; New Avengers #31,32,38,39; New Avengers: Illuminati #1,5; Mighty Avengers #7; and Avengers: The Initiative Annual #1	20.00
...: War of Kings (2/09, $3.99) Black Bolt and the Inhumans; Pelletier & Dazo-a	4.00
...: Who Do You Trust? (8/08, $3.99) short tie-in stories by various; Jimenez-c	4.00

SECRET INVASION: AMAZING SPIDER-MAN
Marvel Comics: Oct, 2008 - No. 3, Dec, 2008 ($2.99, limited series)

	NM- 9.2
1-3-Jackpot battles a Super-Skrull; Santucci-a. 2-Menace app.	3.00

SECRET INVASION: FANTASTIC FOUR
Marvel Comics: July, 2008 - No. 3, Sept, 2008 ($2.99, limited series)

	NM- 9.2
1-3-Skrulls and Lyja invade; Kitson-a/Davis-c	3.00
1-Variant Skrull cover by McKone	5.00

SECRET INVASION: FRONT LINE
Marvel Comics: Sept, 2008 - No. 5, Jan, 2009 ($2.99, limited series)

	NM- 9.2
1-5-Ben Urich covering the Skrull invasion; Reed-s/Castiello-a	3.00

SECRET INVASION: INHUMANS
Marvel Comics: Oct, 2008 - No. 4, Jan, 2009 ($2.99, limited series)

	NM- 9.2
1-4-Raney-a/Sejic-c/Pokasky-s; search for Black Bolt	3.00

SECRET INVASION: RUNAWAYS/YOUNG AVENGERS (Follows Runaways #30)
Marvel Comics: Aug, 2008 - No. 3, Nov, 2008 ($2.99, limited series)

	NM- 9.2
1-3-Miyazawa-a/Ryan-c	3.00

SECRET INVASION: THOR
Marvel Comics: Oct, 2008 - No. 3, Dec, 2008 ($2.99, limited series)

	NM- 9.2
1-3-Fraction-s/Braithwaite-a; Skrulls invade Asgard; Beta Ray Bill app.	3.00
1-2nd printing with Beta Ray Bill cover	3.00

SECRET INVASION: X-MEN
Marvel Comics: Oct, 2008 - No. 4, Jan, 2009 ($2.99, limited series)

	NM- 9.2
1-4-Carey-s/Nord-a/Dodson-c; Skrulls invade San Francisco	3.00
1-2nd printing with variant Nord-c	3.00

SECRET ISLAND OF OZ, THE (See First Comics Graphic Novel)

SECRET LOVE (See Fox Giants & Sinister House of...)

SECRET LOVE
Ajax-Farrell/Four Star Comic Corp. No. 2 on: 12/55 - No. 3, 8/56; 4/57 - No. 5, 2/58; No. 6, 6/58

	GD 2.0	VG 4.0	FN 6.0	VF 8.0	VF/NM 9.0	NM- 9.2
1(12/55-Ajax, 1st series)	10	20	30	58	79	100
2,3	8	16	24	40	50	60
1(4/57-Ajax, 2nd series)	9	18	27	47	61	75
2-6: 5-Bakerish-a	7	14	21	35	43	50

SECRET LOVES
Comic Magazines/Quality Comics Group: Nov, 1949 - No. 6, Sept, 1950

	GD 2.0	VG 4.0	FN 6.0	VF 8.0	VF/NM 9.0	NM- 9.2
1-Ward-c	26	52	78	154	252	350
2-Ward-c	21	42	63	126	206	285
3-Crandall-a	15	30	45	84	127	170
4,6	13	26	39	72	101	130
5-Suggestive art "Boom Town Babe"; photo-c	15	30	45	85	130	175

SECRET LOVE STORIES (See Fox Giants)

SECRET MISSIONS (Admiral Zacharia's...)
St. John Publishing Co.: February, 1950

	GD 2.0	VG 4.0	FN 6.0	VF 8.0	VF/NM 9.0	NM- 9.2
1-Joe Kubert-c; stories of U.S. foreign agents	20	40	60	114	182	250

SECRET MYSTERIES (Formerly Crime Mysteries & Crime Smashers)
Ribage/Merit Publications No. 17 on: No. 16, Nov, 1954 - No. 19, July, 1955

	GD 2.0	VG 4.0	FN 6.0	VF 8.0	VF/NM 9.0	NM- 9.2
16-Horror, Palais-a; Myron Fass-c	32	64	96	188	307	425
17-19-Horror. 17-Fass-c; mis-dated 3/54?	22	44	66	132	216	300

SECRET ORIGINS (1st Series) (See 80 Page Giant #8)
National Periodical Publications: Aug-Oct, 1961 (Annual) (Reprints)

Secret Origins (2nd series) #5 © DC

Secret Six #34 © DC

Secrets of Haunted House #18 © DC

GD 2.0 VG 4.0 FN 6.0 VF 8.0 VF/NM 9.0 NM- 9.2

1-Origin Adam Strange (Showcase #17), Green Lantern (Green Lantern #1), Challengers (partial-r/Showcase #6, 6 pgs. Kirby-a), J'onn J'onzz (Det. #225), The Flash (Showcase #4), Green Arrow (1 pg. text), Superman-Batman team (World's Finest #94), Wonder Woman (Wonder Woman #105) 44 88 132 352 714 1075
Replica Edition (1998, $4.95) r/entire book and house ads 5.00
Even More Secret Origins (2003, $6.95) reprints origins of Hawkman, Eclipso, Kid Flash, Blackhawks, Green Lantern's oath, and Jimmy Olsen-Robin team in 80 pg. Giant style 7.00

SECRET ORIGINS (2nd Series)
National Periodical Publications: Feb-Mar, 1973 - No. 6, Jan-Feb, 1974; No. 7, Oct-Nov, 1974 (All 20¢ issues) (All origin reprints)

1-Superman(r/1 pg. origin/Action #1, 1st time since G.A.), Batman(Detective #33), Ghost(Flash #88), The Flash(Showcase #4) 5 10 15 32 51 70
2-7: 2-Green Lantern & The Atom(Showcase #22 & 34), Supergirl(Action #252). 3-Wonder Woman (W.W. #1), Wildcat (Sensation #1). 4-Vigilante (Action #42) by Meskin, Kid Eternity(Hit #25). 5-The Spectre by Baily (More Fun #52,53). 6-Blackhawk(Military #1) & Legion of Super-Heroes(Superboy #147). 7-Robin (Detective #38), Aquaman (More Fun #73) 3 6 9 19 29 38
NOTE: *Infantino a-1. Kane a-2. Kubert a-1.*

SECRET ORIGINS (3rd Series)
DC Comics: 4/86 - No. 50, 8/90 (All origins)(52 pgs. #6 on)(#27 on: $1.50)

1-Origin Superman 1 2 3 5 6 8
2-6: 2-Blue Beetle. 3-Shazam. 4-Firestorm. 5-Crimson Avenger. 6-Halo/G.A. Batman 4.00
7-9,11,12,14-20,22-26: 7-Green Lantern (Guy Gardner)/G.A. Sandman. 8-Shadow Lass/Doll Man. 9-G.A. Flash/Skyman.11-G.A. Hawkman/Power Girl. 12-Challengers of Unknown/ G.A. Fury (2nd modern app.). 14-Suicide Squad; Legends spin-off. 15-Spectre/Deadman. 16-G.A. Hourman/Warlord. 17-Adam Strange story by Carmine Infantino; Dr. Occult. 18-G.A. Gr. Lantern/The Creeper. 19-Uncle Sam/The Guardian. 20-Batgirl/G.A. Dr. Mid-Nite. 22-Manhunters. 23-Floronic Man/Guardians of the Universe. 24-Blue Devil/Dr. Fate. 25-LSH/Atom. 26-Black Lightning/Miss America 4.00
10-Phantom Stranger w/Alan Moore scripts; Legends spin-off 4.00
13-Origin Nightwing; Johnny Thunder app. 4.00
21-Jonah Hex/Black Condor 4.00
27-30,36-38,40-49: 27-Zatara/Zatanna. 28-Midnight/Nightshade. 29-Power of the Atom/Mr. America; new 3 pg. Red Tornado story by Mayer (last app. of Scribbly, 8/88). 30-Plastic Man/Elongated Man. 36-Poison Ivy by Neil Gaiman & Mark Buckingham/Green Lantern. 37-Legion Of Substitute Heroes/Doctor Light. 38-Green Arrow/Speedy; Grell scripts. 40-All Ape issue. 41-Rogues Gallery of Flash. 42-Phantom Girl/GrimGhost. 43-Original Hawk & Dove/Cave Carson/Chris KL-99. 44-Batman app.; story based on Det. #40. 45-Blackhawk/ El Diablo. 46-JLA/LSH/New Titans. 47-LSH. 48-Ambush Bug/Stanley & His Monster/Rex the Wonder Dog/Trigger Twins. 49-Newsboy Legion/Silent Knight/Bouncing Boy 3.00
31-35,39: 31-JSA. 32-JLA. 33-35-JLI. 39-Animal Man-c/story continued in Animal Man #10; Grant Morrison scripts; Batman app. 3.00
50-($3.95, 100 pgs.)-Batman & Robin in text, Flash of Two Worlds, Johnny Thunder, Dolphin, Black Canary & Space Museum 5.00
Annual 1 (8/87)-Capt. Comet/Doom Patrol 4.00
Annual 2 ('88, $2.00)-Origin Flash II & Flash III 4.00
Annual 3 ('89, $2.95, 84 pgs.)-Teen Titans; 1st app. new Flamebird who replaces original Bat-Girl 4.00
Special 1 (10/89, $2.00)-Batman villains: Penguin, Riddler, & Two-Face; Bolland-c; Sam Kieth-a; Neil Gaiman scripts(2) 5.00
NOTE: ***Art Adams** a-33i(part). **M. Anderson** 8, 19, 21, 25i; c-19(part). **Aparo** c/a-10. **Bissette** c-23. **Bolland** c-7. **Byrne** c/a-Annual 1. **Colan** c/a-5p. **Forte** a-37. **Giffen** a-18p, 44p, 48. **Infantino** a-17, 50p. **Kaluta** c-39. **Gil Kane** a-2, 28; c-2p. **Kirby** c-19(part). **Erik Larsen** a-13. **Mayer** a-29. **Morrow** a-21. **Orlando** a-10. **Perez** a-50i, Annual 3i; c- Annual 3. **Rogers** a-6p. **Russell** a-27i. **Simonson** c-22. **Staton** a-36, 50p. **Steacy** a-35. **Tuska** a-4p, 9p.*

SECRET ORIGINS 80 PAGE GIANT (Young Justice)
DC Comics: Dec, 1998 ($4.95, one-shot)

1-Origin-s of Young Justice members; Ramos-a (Impulse) 5.00

SECRET ORIGINS FEATURING THE JLA
DC Comics: 1999 ($14.95, TPB)

1-Reprints recent origin-s of JLA members; Cassaday-c 15.00

SECRET ORIGINS OF SUPER-HEROES (See DC Special Series #10, 19)

SECRET ORIGINS OF SUPER-VILLAINS 80 PAGE GIANT
DC Comics: Dec, 1999 ($4.95, one-shot)

1-Origin-s of Sinestro, Amazo and others; Gibbons-c 5.00

SECRET ORIGINS OF THE WORLD'S GREATEST SUPER-HEROES
DC Comics: 1989 ($4.95, 148 pgs.)

nn-Reprints Superman, JLA origins; new Batman origin-s; Bolland-c 1 2 3 4 5 7

SECRET ROMANCE
Charlton Comics: Oct, 1968 - No. 41, Nov, 1976; No. 42, Mar, 1979 - No. 48, Feb, 1980

1-Begin 12¢ issues, ends #? 3 6 9 18 27 35
2-10: 9-Reese-a 2 4 6 11 16 20
11-16,18,19,21-30 2 4 6 9 13 16
17,20: 17-Susan Dey poster. 20-David Cassidy pin-up 2 4 6 11 16 20
31-48 2 4 6 8 10 12
NOTE: *Beyond the Stars app.-No. 9, 11, 12, 14.*

SECRET ROMANCES (Exciting Love Stories)
Superior Publications Ltd.: Apr, 1951 - No. 27, July, 1955

1 16 32 48 94 147 200
2 12 24 36 67 94 120
3-10 10 20 30 54 72 90
11-13,15-18,20-27 9 18 27 47 61 75
14,19-Lingerie panels 9 18 27 50 65 80

SECRET SERVICE (See Kent Blake of the...)

SECRET SIX (See Action Comics Weekly)
National Periodical Publications: Apr-May, 1968 - No. 7, Apr-May, 1969 (12¢)

1-Origin/1st app. 6 12 18 41 66 90
2-7 4 8 12 22 34 45

SECRET SIX (See Tangent Comics/ Secret Six)

SECRET SIX (See Villains United)
DC Comics: Jul, 2006 - No. 6, Jan, 2007 ($2.99, limited series)

1-6-Gail Simone-s/Brad Walker-a. 4-Doom Patrol app. 3.00
...: Six Degrees of Devastation TPB (2007, $14.99) r/#1-6 15.00

SECRET SIX
DC Comics: Nov, 2008 - No. 36, Oct, 2011 ($2.99)

1-36: 1-Gail Simone-s/Nicola Scott-a. 2-Batman app. 8-Rodriguez-a. 11-13-Wonder Woman & Artemis app. 16-Black Alice app. 17,18-Blackest Night 3.00
...: Cats in the Cradle TPB (2011, $14.99) r/#19-24 15.00
...: Danse Macabre TPB (2010, $14.99) r/#15-18 & Suicide Squad #67 (Blackest Night) 15.00
...: Depths TPB (2010, $14.99) r/#8-14 15.00
...: The Reptile Brain TPB (2011, $14.99) r/#25-29 15.00
...: Unhinged TPB (2009, $14.99) r/#1-7; intro. by Paul Cornell 15.00

SECRET SKULL
IDW Publ.: Aug, 2004 - No. 4, Nov, 2004 ($3.99)

1-4-Steve Niles-s/Chuck BB-a 4.00

SECRET SOCIETY OF SUPER-VILLAINS
National Per. Publ./DC Comics: May-June, 1976 - No. 15, June-July, 1978

1-Origin; JLA cameo & Capt. Cold app. 3 6 9 14 19 24
2-5,15: 2-Re-intro/origin Capt. Comet; Green Lantern x-over. 5-Green Lantern, Hawkman x-over; Darkseid app. 15-G.A. Atom, Dr. Midnite, & JSA app. 2 4 6 8 11 14
6-14: 9,10-Creeper x-over. 11-Capt. Comet; Orlando-i 2 3 4 6 8 10

SECRET SOCIETY OF SUPER-VILLAINS SPECIAL (See DC Special Series #6)

SECRETS OF HAUNTED HOUSE
National Periodical Publications/DC Comics: 4-5/75 - #5, 12-1/75-76; #6, 6-7/77 - #14, 10-11/78; #15, 8/79 - #46, 3/82

1 6 12 18 39 62 85
2-4 3 6 9 20 30 40
5-Wrightson-c 4 8 12 24 37 50
6-14 2 4 6 11 16 20
15-30 2 4 6 8 11 14
31,44: 31-(12/80) Mr. E series begins (1st app.), ends #41. 44-Wrightson-c 2 4 6 9 13 16
32-(1/81) Origin of Mr. E 2 4 6 8 11 14
33-43,45,46: 34,35-Frankenstein Monster app. 1 3 4 6 8 10
NOTE: ***Aparo** c-7. **Aragones** a-1. **B. Bailey** a-8. **Bissette** a-46. **Buckler** c-32-40p. **Ditko** a-9, 12, 41, 45. **Golden** a-10. **Howard** a-13i. **Kaluta** c-8, 10, 11, 14, 16, 29. **Kubert** c-41, 42. **Sheldon Mayer** a-43p. **McWilliams** a-35. **Nasser** a-24. **Newton** a-30p. **Nino** a-1, 13, 19. **Orlando** c-13, 30, 43, 45i. **N. Redondo** a-4, 5, 29. **Rogers** c-26. **Spiegle** a-31-41. **Wrightson** c-5, 44.*

SECRETS OF HAUNTED HOUSE SPECIAL (See DC Special Series #12)

SECRETS OF LIFE (Movie)
Dell Publishing Co.: 1956 (Disney)

Four Color 749-Photo-c 5 10 15 32 51 70

SECRETS OF LOVE (See Popular Teen-Agers...)

SECRETS OF LOVE AND MARRIAGE
Charlton Comics: V2#1, Aug, 1956 - V2#25, June, 1961

V2#1-Matt Baker-c? 5 10 15 30 48 65

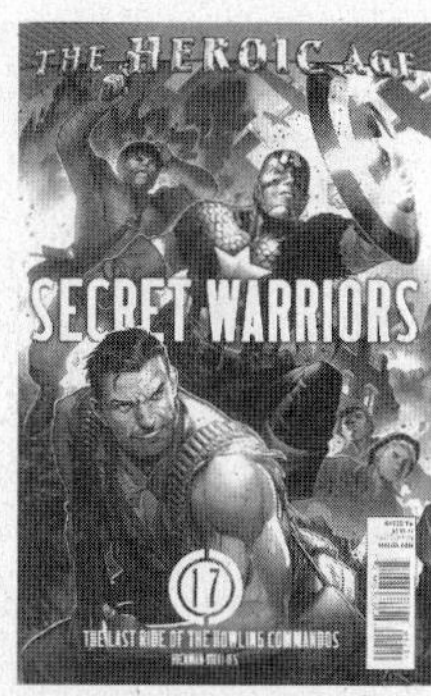

Secret Warriors #17 © MAR

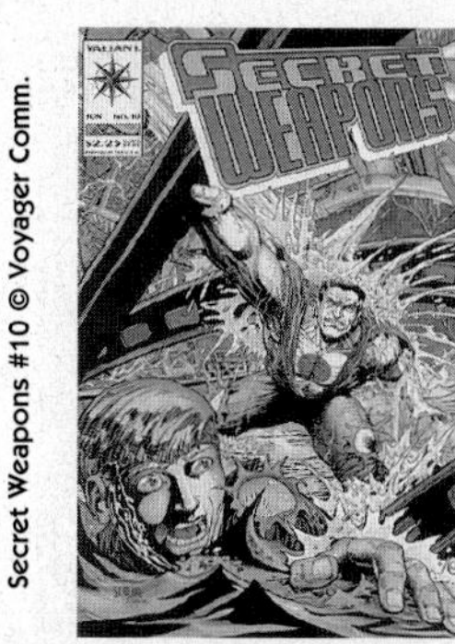

Secret Weapons #10 © Voyager Comm.

Sensational She-Hulk #20 © MAR

	GD 2.0	VG 4.0	FN 6.0	VF 8.0	VF/NM 9.0	NM- 9.2
V2#2-6	3	6	9	20	30	40
V2#7-9-(All 68 pgs.)	5	10	15	32	51	70
10-25	3	6	9	17	25	32

SECRETS OF MAGIC (See Wisco)

SECRETS OF SINISTER HOUSE (Sinister House of Secret Love #1-4)
National Periodical Publ.: No. 5, June-July, 1972 - No. 18, June-July, 1974

	GD	VG	FN	VF	VF/NM	NM-
5-(52 pgs.).	6	12	18	41	66	90
6-9: 7-Redondo-a	4	8	12	24	37	50
10-Neal Adams-a(i)	4	8	12	26	41	55
11-18: 15-Redondo-a. 17-Barry-a; early Chaykin 1 pg. strip	3	6	9	16	23	30

NOTE: ***Alcala** a-6, 13, 14. **Glanzman** a-7. **Kaluta** c-6, 7. **Nino** a-8, 11-13. Ambrose Bierce adapt.-#14.*

SECRETS OF THE LEGION OF SUPER-HEROES
DC Comics: Jan, 1981 - No. 3, Mar, 1981 (Limited series)

1-3: 1-Origin of the Legion. 2-Retells origins of Brainiac 5, Shrinking Violet, Sun-Boy, Bouncing Boy, Ultra-Boy, Matter-Eater Lad, Mon-El, Karate Kid & Dream Girl 5.00

SECRETS OF TRUE LOVE
St. John Publishing Co.: Feb, 1958

	GD	VG	FN	VF	VF/NM	NM-
1	8	16	24	42	54	65

SECRETS OF YOUNG BRIDES
Charlton Comics: No. 5, Sept, 1957 - No. 44, Oct, 1964; July, 1975 - No. 9, Nov, 1976

	GD	VG	FN	VF	VF/NM	NM-
5	5	10	15	32	51	70
6-10: 8-Negligee panel	4	8	12	22	34	45
11-20	3	6	9	20	30	40
21-30: Last 10¢ issue?	3	6	9	18	27	35
31-44(10/64)	3	6	9	14	19	24
1-(2nd series) (7/75)	3	6	9	14	20	26
2-9	2	4	6	8	11	14

SECRET SQUIRREL (TV)(See Kite Fun Book)
Gold Key: Oct, 1966 (12¢) (Hanna-Barbera)

	GD	VG	FN	VF	VF/NM	NM-
1-1st Secret Squirrel and Morocco Mole, Squiddly Diddly, Winsome Witch	10	20	30	68	127	185

SECRET STORY ROMANCES (Becomes True Tales of Love)
Atlas Comics (TCI): Nov, 1953 - No. 21, Mar, 1956

	GD	VG	FN	VF	VF/NM	NM-
1-Everett-a; Jay Scott Pike-c	17	34	51	98	154	210
2	11	22	33	60	83	105
3-11: 11-Last pre-code (2/55)	10	20	30	54	72	90
12-21	9	18	27	47	61	75

NOTE: ***Colletta** a-10, 14, 15, 17, 21; c-10, 14, 17.*

SECRET VOICE, THE (See Great American Comics Presents...)

SECRET WAR
Marvel Comics: Apr, 2004 - No. 5, Dec, 2005 ($3.99, limited series)

1-Bendis-s/Dell'Otto painted-a/c; 5.00
1-2nd printing with gold logo on white cover and full-color Spider-Man 4.00
1-3rd printing with white cover and B&W sketched Spider-Man 4.00
2-5: 2-Wolverine-c. 3-Capt. America-c. 4-Black Widow-c. 5-Daredevil-c 4.00
2-2nd printing with white cover and B&W sketched Wolverine 4.00
... : From the Files of Nick Fury (2005, $3.99) Fury's journal entries; profiles of characters 4.00
HC (2005, $29.99, dust jacket) r/#1-5 & ...From the Files of Nick Fury; additional art 30.00
SC (2006, $24.99) r/#1-5 & ...From the Files of Nick Fury; additional art 25.00

SECRET WARRIORS (Also see 2009 Dark Reign titles)
Marvel Comics: Apr, 2009 - No. 28, Sept, 2011 ($3.99/$2.99)

1-Bendis & Hickman-s/Caselli-a/Cheung-c; Nick Fury app.; Hydra dossier; sketch pages 4.00
2-24,26-28-($2.99) 8-Dark Avengers app. 17-19-Howling Commandos return 3.00
25-($3.99) Baron Strucker app.; Vitti-a 4.00

SECRET WARS II (Also see Marvel Super Heroes...)
Marvel Comics Group: July, 1985 - No. 9, Mar, 1986 (Maxi-series)

1,9: 9-(52 pgs.) X-Men app., Spider-Man app. 6.00
2-8: 2,8-X-Men app. 5-1st app. Boom Boom. 5,8-Spider-Man app. 4.00

SECRET WEAPONS
Valiant: Sept, 1993 - No. 21, May, 1995 ($2.25)

1-10,12-21: 3-Reese-a(i). 5-Ninjak app. 9-Bound-in trading card. 12-Bloodshot app. 3.00
11-(Sept. on envelope, Aug on-c, $2.50)-Enclosed in manilla envelope; Bloodshot app; intro new team. 3.00

SECTAURS
Marvel Comics: June, 1985 - No. 8, Sept, 1986 (75¢) (Based on Coleco Toys)

1-8, 1-Giveaway; same-c with "Coleco 1985 Toy Fair Collectors' Edition" 4.00

SECTION ZERO
Image Comics (Gorilla): June, 2000 - No. 3, Sept, 2000 ($2.50)

1-3-Kesel-s/Grummett-a 3.00

SEDUCTION OF THE INNOCENT (Also see New York State Joint Legislative Committee to Study...)
Rinehart & Co., Inc., N. Y.: 1953, 1954 (400 pgs.) (Hardback, $4.00)(Written by Fredric Wertham, M.D.)(Also printed in Canada by Clarke, Irwin & Co. Ltd.)

	GD	VG	FN	VF	VF/NM	NM-
(1st Version)-with bibliographical note intact (pages 399 & 400)(several copies got out before the comic publishers forced the removal of this page)	167	334	501	718	859	1000
Dust jacket only	37	74	111	222	361	500
(1st Version)-without bibliographical note	83	166	249	357	429	500
Dust jacket only	20	40	60	114	182	250
(2nd Version)-Published in England by Rinehart, 1954, 399 pgs. has bibliographical page; "Second print" listed on inside flap of the dust jacket; publication page has no "R" colophon; unlike 1st version	15	30	45	85	130	175
1972 r-/of 2nd version; 400 pgs. w/bibliography page; Kennikat Press	5	10	15	30	48	65

NOTE: *Material from this book appeared in the November, 1953 (Vol.70, pp50-53,214) issue of the **Ladies' Home Journal** under the title "What Parents Don't Know About Comic Books". With the release of this book, Dr. Wertham reveals seven years of research attempting to link juvenile delinquency to comic books. Many illustrations showing excessive violence, sex, sadism, and torture are shown. This book was used at the Kefauver Senate hearings which led to the Comics Code Authority. Because of the influence this book had on the comic industry and the collector's interest in it, we feel this listing is justified. Modern printings exist in limited editions. Also see **Parade of Pleasure.***

SEDUCTION OF THE INNOCENT! (Also see Halloween Horror)
Eclipse Comics: Nov, 1985 - 3-D#2, Apr, 1986 ($1.75)

1-6: Double listed under cover title from #7 on 4.00
3-D 1 (10/85, $2.25, 36 pgs.)-contains unpublished Advs. Into Darkness #15 (pre-code); Dave Stevens-c 5.00

	GD	VG	FN	VF	VF/NM	NM-
2-D 1 (100 copy limited signed & #ed edition)(B&W)	1	3	4	6	8	10

3-D 2 (4/86)-Baker, Toth, Wrightson-c 5.00

	GD	VG	FN	VF	VF/NM	NM-
2-D 2 (100 copy limited signed & #ed edition)(B&W)	1	3	4	6	8	10

NOTE: ***Anderson** r-2, 3. **Crandall** c/a(r)-1. **Meskin** c/a(r)-3, 3-D 1. **Moreira** r-2. **Toth** a-1-6r; c-4r. **Tuska** r-6.*

SEEKER
Sky Comics: Apr, 1994 ($2.50, one-shot)

1 3.00

SEEKERS INTO THE MYSTERY
DC Comics (Vertigo): Jan, 1996 - No. 15, Apr, 1997 ($2.50)

1-14: J.M. DeMatteis scripts in all. 1-4-Glenn Barr-a. 5,10-Muth-c/a. 6-9-Zulli-c/a. 11-14-Bolton-c; Jill Thompson-a 3.00
15-($2.95)-Muth-c/a 3.00

SEEKER 3000 (See Marvel Premiere #41)
Marvel Comics: Jun, 1998 - No. 4, Sept, 1998 ($2.99/$2.50, limited series)

1-($2.99)-Set 25 years after 1st app.; wraparound-c 4.00
2-4-($2.50) 3.00
...Premiere 1 (6/98, $1.50) Reprints 1st app. from Marvel Premiere #41; wraparound-c 3.00

SELECT DETECTIVE (Exciting New Mystery Cases)
D. S. Publishing Co.: Aug-Sept, 1948 - No. 3, Dec-Jan, 1948-49

	GD	VG	FN	VF	VF/NM	NM-
1-Matt Baker-a	30	60	90	177	289	400
2-Baker, McWilliams-a	20	40	60	117	189	260
3	15	30	45	90	140	190

SEMPER FI (Tales of the Marine Corp)
Marvel Comics: Dec, 1988- No.9, Aug, 1989 (75¢)

1-9: Severin-c/a 3.00

SENSATIONAL POLICE CASES (Becomes Captain Steve Savage, 2nd Series)
Avon Periodicals: 1952; No. 2, 1954 - No. 4, July-Aug, 1954

	GD	VG	FN	VF	VF/NM	NM-
nn-(1952, 25¢, 100 pgs.)-Kubert-a?; Check, Larsen, Lawrence & McCann-a; Kinstler-c	42	84	126	265	445	625
2-4: 2-Kirbyish-a (3-4/54). 4-Reprint/Saint #5	15	30	45	90	140	190
I.W. Reprint #5-(1963?, nd)-Reprints Prison Break #5(1952-Realistic); Infantino-a	3	6	9	16	23	30

SENSATIONAL SHE-HULK, THE (She-Hulk #21-23) (See Savage She-Hulk)
Marvel Comics: V2#1, 5/89 - No. 60, Feb, 1994 ($1.50/$1.75, deluxe format)

V2#1-Byrne-c/a(p)/scripts begin, end #8 4.00
2,3,5-8: 3-Spider-Man app. 3.00
4,14-17,21-23: 4-Reintro G.A. Blonde Phantom. 14-17-Howard the Duck app. 21-23-Return of the Blonde Phantom. 22-All Winners Squad app. 3.00
9-13,18-20,24-49,51-60: 25-Thor app. 26-Excalibur app.; Guice-c. 29-Wolverine app. (3 pgs.). 30-Hobgoblin-c & cameo. 31-Byrne-c/a/scripts begin again. 35-Last $1.50-c.

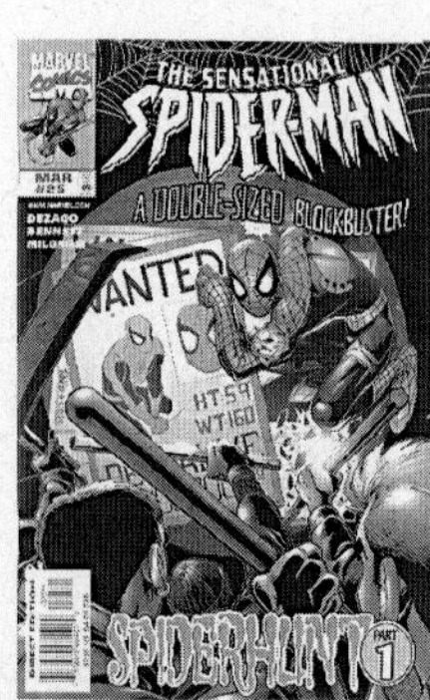

Sensational Spider-Man #25 © MAR

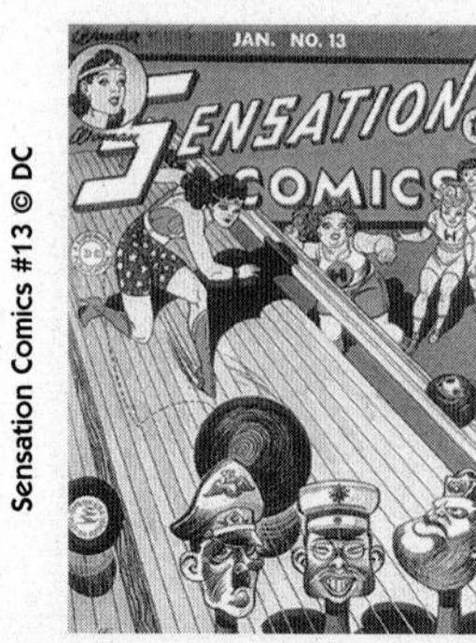

Sensation Comics #13 © DC

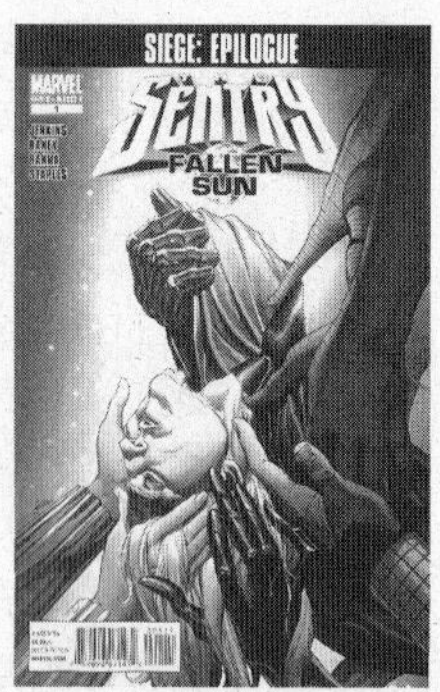

Sentry: Fallen Sun #1 © MAR

GD VG FN VF VF/NM NM-
2.0 4.0 6.0 8.0 9.0 9.2

37-Wolverine/Punisher/Spidey-c, but no app. 39-Thing app. 56-War Zone app.; Hulk cameo. 57-Vs. Hulk-c/story. 58-Electro-c/story. 59-Jack O'Lantern app. 3.00
50-($2.95, 52 pgs.)-Embossed green foil-c; Byrne app.; last Byrne-c/a; Austin, Chaykin, Simonson-a; Miller-a(2 pgs.) 4.00
NOTE: *Dale Keown a(p)-13, 15-22.*

SENSATIONAL SHE-HULK IN CEREMONY, THE
Marvel Comics: 1989 - No. 2, 1989 ($3.95, squarebound, 52 pgs.)
nn-Part 1, nn-Part 2 4.00

SENSATIONAL SPIDER-MAN
Marvel Comics: Apr, 1989 ($5.95, squarebound, 80 pgs.)
1-r/Amazing Spider-Man Annual #14,15 by Miller & Annual #8 by Kirby & Ditko 6.00

SENSATIONAL SPIDER-MAN, THE
Marvel Comics: Jan, 1996 - No. 33, Nov, 1998 ($1.95/$1.99)
0 ($4.95)-Lenticular-c; Jurgens-a/scripts 5.00
1 5.00
1-($2.95) variant-c; polybagged w/cassette 1 2 3 5 6 8
2-5: 2-Kaine & Rhino app. 3-Giant-Man app. 4.00
6-18: 9-Onslaught tie-in; revealed that Peter & Mary Jane's unborn baby is a girl. 11-Revelations. 13-15-Ka-Zar app. 14,15-Hulk app. 3.00
19-24: Living Pharoah app. 22,23-Dr. Strange app. 3.00
25-($2.99) Spiderhunt pt. 1; Normie Osborne kidnapped 4.00
25-Variant-c 1 2 3 5 6 8
26-33: 26-Nauck-a. 27-Double-c with "The Sensational Hornet #1"; Vulture app. 28-Hornet vs. Vulture. 29,30-Black Cat-c/app. 33-Last issue; Gathering of Five concludes 3.00
#(-1) Flashback(7/97) Dezago-s/Wieringo-a 3.00
'96 Annual ($2.95) 4.00

SENSATIONAL SPIDER-MAN, THE (Previously Marvel Knights Spider-Man #1-22)
Marvel Comics: No. 23, Apr, 2006 - No. 41, Dec, 2007 ($2.99)
23-40: 23-25-Aguirre-Sacasa-s/Medina-a. 23-Wraparound-c. 24,34,37-Black Cat app. 26-New costume. 28-Unmasked; Dr. Octopus app.; Crain-a. 35-Black costume resumes 3.00
41-($3.99) One More Day pt. 3; Straczynski-s/Quesada-a/c 4.00
... Annual 1 (2007, $3.99) Flashbacks of Peter & MJ's relationship; Larroca-a/Fraction-s 4.00
... Feral HC (2006, $19.99, dustjacket) r/#23-27; sketch pages 20.00
Civil War: Peter Parker, Spider-Man TPB (2007, $17.99) r/#28-34; Crain cover concepts 18.00

SENSATION COMICS (Sensation Mystery #110 on)
National Per. Publ./All-American: Jan, 1942 - No. 109, May-June, 1952
1-Origin Mr. Terrific(1st app.), Wildcat(1st app.), The Gay Ghost, & Little Boy Blue; Wonder Woman (cont'd from All Star #8), The Black Pirate begin; intro. Justice & Fair Play Club 2950 5900 8850 22,000 42,000 62,000
1-Reprint, Oversize 13-1/2x10". WARNING: This comic is an exact duplicate reprint of the original except for its size. DC published it in 1974 with a second cover titling it as a Famous First Edition. There have been many reported cases of the outer cover being removed and the interior sold as the original edition. The reprint with the new outer cover removed is practically worthless. See Famous First Edition for value.

	GD 2.0	VG 4.0	FN 6.0	VF 8.0	VF/NM 9.0	NM- 9.2
2-Etta Candy begins	476	952	1428	3475	6138	8800
3-W. Woman gets secretary's job	300	600	900	1950	3375	4800
4-1st app. Stretch Skinner in Wildcat	213	426	639	1363	2332	3300
5-Intro. Justin, Black Pirate's son	171	342	513	1086	1868	2650
6-Origin/1st app. Wonder Woman's magic lasso	174	348	522	1114	1907	2700
7-10	123	246	369	787	1344	1900
11,12,14-20	103	206	309	659	1130	1600
13-Hitler, Tojo, Mussolini-c (as bowling pins)	174	348	522	1114	1907	2700
21-30	82	164	246	528	902	1275
31-33	63	126	189	403	689	975
34-Sargon, the Sorcerer begins (10/44), ends #36; begins again #52	66	132	198	419	722	1025
35-40: 38-X-Mas-c	60	120	180	381	653	925
41-50: 43-The Whip app.	57	114	171	362	619	875
51-60: 51-Last Black Pirate. 56,57-Sargon by Kubert	55	110	165	352	601	850
61-67,69-80: 63-Last Mr. Terrific. 66-Wildcat by Kubert	50	100	150	315	533	750
68-Origin & 1st app. Huntress (8/47)	55	110	165	352	601	850
81-Used in **SOTI**, pg. 33,34; Krigstein-a	54	108	162	343	574	825
82-93: 83-Last Sargon. 86-The Atom app. 90-Last Wildcat. 91-Streak begins by Alex Toth. 92-Toth-a (2 pgs.)	50	100	150	315	533	750
94-1st all girl issue	81	162	243	518	884	1250
95-99,101-106: 95-Unmasking of Wonder Woman-c/story. 99-1st app. Astra, Girl of the Future, ends #106. 103-Robot-c. 105-Last 52 pgs. 106-Wonder Woman ends	68	136	204	435	743	1050
100-(11-12/50)	77	154	231	493	847	1200
107-(Scarce, 1-2/52)-1st mystery issue; Johnny Peril by Toth(p), 8 pgs. & begins; continues from Danger Trail #5 (3-4/51)(see Comic Cavalcade #15 for 1st app.)	77	154	231	493	847	1200
108-(Scarce)-Johnny Peril by Toth(p)	66	132	198	419	722	1025
109-(Scarce)-Johnny Peril by Toth(p)	77	154	231	493	847	1200

NOTE: ***Krigstein** a-(Wildcat)-81, 83, 84. **Moldoff** Black Pirate-1-25; Black Pirate not in 34-36, 43-48. **Oskner** c(i)-89-91, 94-106. Wonder Woman by **H. G. Peter**, all issues except #8, 17-19, 21; c-4-7, 9-18, 20-88, 92, 93. **Toth** a-91, 98; c-107. Wonder Woman c-1-106.*

GD VG FN VF VF/NM NM-
2.0 4.0 6.0 8.0 9.0 9.2

SENSATION COMICS (Also see All Star Comics 1999 crossover titles)
DC Comics: May, 1999 ($1.99, one-shot)
1-Golden Age Wonder Woman and Hawkgirl; Robinson-s 3.00

SENSATION MYSTERY (Formerly Sensation Comics #1-109)
National Periodical Publ.: No. 110, July-Aug, 1952 - No. 116, July-Aug, 1953
110-Johnny Peril continues 51 102 153 318 539 760
111-116-Johnny Peril in all. 116-M. Anderson-a 51 102 153 318 539 760
NOTE: ***M. Anderson** c-110. **Colan** a-114p. **Giunta** a-112. **G. Kane** c(p)-108, 109, 111-115.*

SENSE & SENSABILITY
Marvel Comics: July, 2010 - No. 5, Nov, 2010 ($3.99, limited series)
1-5-Adaptation of the Jane Austen novel; Nancy Butler-s/Sonny Liew-a/c 4.00

SENSUOUS STREAKER
Marvel Publ.: 1974 (B&W magazine, 68pgs.)
1 4 8 12 26 41 55

SENTENCES: THE LIFE OF M.F. GRIMM
DC Comics (Vertigo): 2007 ($19.99, B&W graphic novel)
HC-Autobiography of Percy Carey (M.F. Grimm); Ronald Wimberly-a 20.00
SC (2008, $14.99) 15.00

SENTINEL
Marvel Comics: June, 2003 - No. 12, April, 2004 ($2.99/$2.50)
1-Sean McKeever-s/Udon Studios-a 3.00
2-12 3.00
Marvel Age Sentinel Vol. 1: Salvage (2004, $7.99, digest size) r/#1-6 8.00
Vol. 2: No Hero (2004, $7.99, digest size) r/#7-12; sketch pages 8.00

SENTINEL (2nd series)
Marvel Comics: Jan, 2006 - No. 5, May, 2006 ($2.99, limited series)
1-5-Sean McKeever-s/Joe Vriens-a 3.00
Vol. 3: Past Imperfect (2006, $7.99, digest size) r/#1-5 8.00

SENTINELS OF JUSTICE, THE (See Americomics & Captain Paragon &...)

SENTINEL SQUAD O*N*E
Marvel Comics: Mar, 2006 - No. 5, July, 2006 ($2.99, limited series)
1-5-Lopresti-a/Layman-s 3.00
Decimation: Sentinel Squad O*N*E (2006, $13.99, TPB) r/series; sketch pg. by Caliafore 14.00

SENTRY (Also see New Avengers and Siege)
Marvel Comics: Sept, 2000 - No. 5, Jan, 2001 ($2.99, limited series)
1-5-Paul Jenkins-s/Jae Lee-a. 3-Spider-Man-c/app. 4-X-Men, FF app. 3.00
.../Fantastic Four (2/01, $2.99) Continues story from #5; Winslade-a 3.00
.../Hulk (2/01, $2.99) Sienkiewicz-c/a 3.00
.../Spider-Man (2/01, $2.99) back story of the Sentry; Leonardi-a 3.00
.../The Void (2/01, $2.99) Conclusion of story; Jae Lee-a 3.00
.../X-Men (2/01, $2.99) Sentry and Archangel; Texeira-a 3.00
TPB (10/01, $24.95) r/#1-5 & all one-shots; Stan Lee interview 25.00
TPB (2nd edition, 2005, $24.99) 25.00

SENTRY (Follows return in New Avengers #10)
Marvel Comics: Nov, 2005 - No. 8, Jun, 2006 ($2.99, limited series)
1-8-Paul Jenkins-s/John Romita Jr.-a. 1-New Avengers app. 3-Hulk app. 3.00
1-(Rough Cut) (12/05, $3.99) Romita sketch art and Jenkins script; cover sketches 4.00
...: Fallen Sun (7/10, $3.99) Siege epilogue; Jenkins-s/Raney-a/Yu-c 4.00
...: Reborn TPB (2006, $21.99) r/#1-8 22.00

SENTRY SPECIAL
Innovation Publishing: 1991 ($2.75, one-shot)(Hero Alliance spin-off)
1-Lost in Space preview (3 pgs.) 3.00

SERAPHIM
Innovation Publishing: May, 1990 ($2.50, mature readers)
1 3.00

SERENITY (Based on 2005 movie Serenity and 2003 TV series Firefly)
Dark Horse Comics: July, 2005 - No. 3, Sept, 2005 ($2.99, limited series)
1-3: Whedon & Matthews-s/Conrad-a. Three covers for each issue by various 4.00
...: Float Out (6/10, $3.50) Story of Wash; Patton Oswalt-s; covers by Jo Chen & Stockton 3.50

Sgt Bilko's Pvt. Doberman #11 © DC

Sgt. Fury #7 © MAR

Sgt. Rock #347 © DC

	GD 2.0	VG 4.0	FN 6.0	VF 8.0	VF/NM 9.0	NM- 9.2
...: One For One (9/10, $1.00) reprints #1, Cassaday-c with red cover frame						3.00
...: Those Left Behind HC (11/07, $19.95, dustjacket) r/series; intro. by Nathan Fillion; pre-production art for the movie; Hughes-c						20.00
...: Those Left Behind TPB (1/06, $9.95) r/series; intro. by Nathan Fillion; Hughes-c						10.00

SERENITY BETTER DAYS (Firefly)
Dark Horse Comics: Mar, 2008 - No. 3, May, 2008 ($2.99, limited series)

	GD 2.0	VG 4.0	FN 6.0	VF 8.0	VF/NM 9.0	NM- 9.2
1-3: Whedon & Matthews-s/Conrad-a; Adam Hughes-c						3.00

SERGEANT BARNEY BARKER (Becomes G. I. Tales #4 on)
Atlas Comics (MCI): Aug, 1956 - No. 3, Dec, 1956

	GD 2.0	VG 4.0	FN 6.0	VF 8.0	VF/NM 9.0	NM- 9.2
1-Severin-c/a(4)	18	36	54	105	165	225
2,3: 2-Severin-c/a(4). 3-Severin-c/a(5)	14	28	42	76	108	140

SERGEANT BILKO (Phil Silvers Starring as...) (TV)
National Periodical Publications: May-June, 1957 - No. 18, Mar-Apr, 1960

	GD 2.0	VG 4.0	FN 6.0	VF 8.0	VF/NM 9.0	NM- 9.2
1-All have Bob Oskner-c	58	116	174	371	636	900
2	31	62	93	186	303	420
3-5	26	52	78	154	252	350
6-18: 11,12,15,17-Photo-c	21	42	63	124	202	280

SGT. BILKO'S PVT. DOBERMAN (TV)
National Periodical Publications: June-July, 1958 - No. 11, Feb-Mar, 1960

	GD 2.0	VG 4.0	FN 6.0	VF 8.0	VF/NM 9.0	NM- 9.2
1-Bob Oskner c-1-4,7,11	22	44	66	154	327	500
2	12	24	36	83	172	260
3-5: 5-Photo-c	10	20	30	67	124	180
6-11: 6,9-Photo-c	8	16	24	52	86	120

SGT. DICK CARTER OF THE U.S. BORDER PATROL (See Holyoke One-Shot)

SGT. FURY (& His Howling Commandos)(See Fury & Special Marvel Edition)
Marvel Comics Group (BPC earlier issues): May, 1963 - No. 167, Dec, 1981

	GD 2.0	VG 4.0	FN 6.0	VF 8.0	VF/NM 9.0	NM- 9.2
1-1st app. Sgt. Nick Fury (becomes agent of Shield in Strange Tales #135); Kirby/Ayers-c/a; 1st Dum-Dum Dugan & the Howlers	268	536	804	2250	4875	7500
2-Kirby-a	52	104	156	421	911	1400
3-5: 3-Reed Richards x-over. 4-Death of Junior Juniper. 5-1st Baron Strucker app.; Kirby-a	27	54	81	196	423	650
6-10: 8-Baron Zemo, 1st Percival Pinkerton app. 9-Hitler-c & app. 10-1st app. Capt. Savage (the Skipper)(9/64)	14	28	42	97	211	325
11,12,14-20: 14-1st Blitz Squad. 18-Death of Pamela Hawley	10	20	30	66	121	175
13-Captain America & Bucky app.(12/64); 2nd solo Capt. America x-over outside The Avengers; Kirby-a	38	76	114	285	618	950
13-2nd printing (1994)	2	4	6	8	10	12
21-24,26,28-30	7	14	21	46	76	105
25,27: 25-Red Skull app. 27-1st app. Eric Koenig; origin Fury's eye patch	7	14	21	48	79	110
31-33,35-50: 35-Eric Koenig joins Howlers. 43-Bob Hope, Glen Miller app. 44-Flashback on Howlers' 1st mission	4	8	12	28	44	60
34-Origin Howling Commandos	5	10	15	30	48	65
51-60	4	8	12	24	37	50
61-67: 64-Capt. Savage & Raiders x-over; peace symbol-c. 67-Last 12¢ issue; flag-c	3	6	9	20	30	40
68-80: 76-Fury's Father app. in WWI story	3	6	9	17	25	32
81-91: 91-Last 15¢ issue	3	6	9	14	20	26
92-(52 pgs.)	3	6	9	17	25	32
93-99: 98-Deadly Dozen x-over	3	6	9	14	19	24
100-Capt. America, Fantastic 4 cameos; Stan Lee, Martin Goodman & others app.	3	6	9	17	25	32
101-120: 101-Origin retold	2	4	6	10	14	18
121-130: 121-123-r/#19-21	2	4	6	8	11	14
131-167: 167-Reprints (from 1963)	2	4	6	8	10	12
133,134-(30¢-c variants, limited dist.)(5,7/76)	3	6	9	16	22	28
141,142-(35¢-c variants, limited dist.)(7,9/77)	4	8	12	22	34	45
Annual 1(1965, 25¢, 72 pgs.)-r/#4,5 & new-a	13	26	39	90	195	300
Special 2(1966)	7	14	21	46	76	105
Special 3(1967) All new material	5	10	15	32	51	70
Special 4(1968)	4	8	12	22	34	45
Special 5-7(1969-11/71)	3	6	9	18	27	35

NOTE: ***Ayers*** *a-8, Annual 1.* ***Ditko*** *a-15i.* ***Gil Kane*** *c-37, 96.* ***Kirby*** *a-1-7, 13p, 167p(r). Special 5; c-1-8, 10-20, 25, 167p.* ***Severin*** *a-44-46, 48, 162, 164; inks-49-79, Special 4, 6; c-4i, 5, 6, 44, 46, 110, 149i, 155i, 162-166.* ***Sutton*** *a-57p. Reprints in #80, 82, 85, 87, 89, 91, 93, 95, 99, 101, 103, 105, 107, 109, 111, 121-123, 145-155, 167.*

SGT. FURY AND HIS HOWLING COMMANDOS
Marvel Comics: July, 2009 ($3.99, one-shot)

	GD 2.0	VG 4.0	FN 6.0	VF 8.0	VF/NM 9.0	NM- 9.2
1-John Paul Leon-a/c; WWII tale set in 1942; Baron Strucker app.						4.00

SGT. FURY AND HIS HOWLING DEFENDERS (See The Defenders #147)

SERGEANT PRESTON OF THE YUKON (TV)
Dell Publishing Co.: No. 344, Aug, 1951 - No. 29, Nov-Jan, 1958-59

	GD 2.0	VG 4.0	FN 6.0	VF 8.0	VF/NM 9.0	NM- 9.2
Four Color 344(#1)-Sergeant Preston & his dog Yukon King begin; painted-c begin, end #18	11	22	33	73	142	210
Four Color 373,397,419('52)	8	16	24	51	86	120
5(11-1/52-53)-10(2-4/54): 6-Bondage-c.	6	12	18	41	66	90
11,12,14-17	6	12	18	37	59	80
13-Origin Sgt. Preston	6	12	18	41	66	90
18-Origin Yukon King; last painted-c	6	12	18	41	66	90
19-29: All photo-c	7	14	21	48	79	110

SGT. ROCK (Formerly Our Army at War; see Brave & the Bold #52 & Showcase #45)
National Periodical Publications/DC Comics: No. 302, Mar, 1977 - No. 422, July, 1988

	GD 2.0	VG 4.0	FN 6.0	VF 8.0	VF/NM 9.0	NM- 9.2
302	5	10	15	30	48	65
303-310	3	6	9	16	23	30
311-320: 318-Reprints	2	4	6	10	16	20
321-350	2	4	6	8	11	14
329-Whitman variant	3	6	9	14	19	24
351-399,401-421: 412-Mlle Marie & Haunted Tank	1	2	3	5	7	9
400-(6/85) Anniversary issue	2	4	6	8	11	14
422-1st Joe, Adam, Andy Kubert-a team; last issue	2	4	6	10	14	18
Annual 2-4: 2(1982)-Formerly Sgt. Rock's Prize Battle Tales #1. 3(1983). 4(1984)	2	4	6	8	10	12

NOTE: ***Estrada*** *a-322, 327, 331, 336, 337, 341, 342i.* ***Glanzman*** *a-384, 421.* ***Kubert*** *a-302, 303, 305r, 306, 328, 351, 356, 368, 373, 422; c-317, 318r, 319-323, 325-333-on, Annual 2, 3.* ***Severin*** *a-347.* ***Spiegle*** *a-382, Annual 2, 3.* ***Thorne*** *a-384.* ***Toth*** *a-385r.* ***Wildey*** *a-307, 311, 313, 314.*

SGT. ROCK: BETWEEN HELL AND A HARD PLACE
DC Comics (Vertigo): 2003 ($24.95, hardcover one-shot)

	GD 2.0	VG 4.0	FN 6.0	VF 8.0	VF/NM 9.0	NM- 9.2
HC-Joe Kubert-a/c; Brian Azzarello-s						25.00
SC (2004, $17.95)						18.00

SGT. ROCK'S COMBAT TALES
DC Comics: 2005 ($9.99, digest)

	GD 2.0	VG 4.0	FN 6.0	VF 8.0	VF/NM 9.0	NM- 9.2
Vol. 1-Reprints early app. in Our Army at War, G.I. Combat, Star Spangled War Stories						10.00

SGT. ROCK SPECIAL (Sgt. Rock #14 on; see DC Special Series #3)
DC Comics: Oct, 1988 - No. 21, Feb, 1992; No. 1, 1992; No. 2, 1994
($2.00, quarterly/monthly, 52 pgs)

	GD 2.0	VG 4.0	FN 6.0	VF 8.0	VF/NM 9.0	NM- 9.2
1-Reprint begin	2	4	6	8	11	14
2-21: All-r; 5-r/early Sgt. Rock/Our Army at War #81. 7-Tomahawk-r by Thorne. 9-Enemy Ace-r by Kubert. 10-All Rock issue. 11-r/1st Haunted Tank story. 12-All Kubert issue; begins monthly. 13-Dinosaur story by Heath(r). 14-Enemy Ace-r (22 pgs.) by Adams/Kubert. 15-Enemy Ace (22 pgs.) by Kubert. 16-Iron Major-c/story. 16,17-Enemy Ace-r. 19-r/Batman/Sgt. Rock team-up/B&B #108 by Aparo	1	2	3	5	6	8
1 (1992, $2.95, 68 pgs.)-Simonson-c; unpubbed Kubert-a; Glanzman, Russell, Pratt, & Wagner-a						6.00
2 (1994, $2.95) Brereton painted-c						4.00

NOTE: ***Neal Adams*** *r-1, 8, 14p.* ***Chaykin*** *a-2; r-3, 9(2pgs.); c-3.* ***Drucker*** *r-6.* ***Glanzman*** *r-20.* ***Golden*** *a-1.* ***Heath*** *a-2; r-5, 9-13, 16, 19, 21.* ***Krigstein*** *r-4, 8.* ***Kubert*** *r-1-17, 20, 21; c-1p, 2, 8, 14-21.* ***Miller*** *r-6p.* ***Severin*** *r-3, 6, 10.* ***Simonson*** *r-2, 4; c-4.* ***Thorne*** *r-7.* ***Toth*** *r-2, 8, 11.* ***Wood*** *r-4.*

SGT. ROCK SPECTACULAR (See DC Special Series #13)

SGT. ROCK'S PRIZE BATTLE TALES (Becomes Sgt. Rock Annual #2 on; see DC Special Series #18 & 80 Page Giant #7)
National Periodical Publications: Winter, 1964 (Giant - 80 pgs., one-shot)

	GD 2.0	VG 4.0	FN 6.0	VF 8.0	VF/NM 9.0	NM- 9.2
1-Kubert, Heath-r; new Kubert-c	33	66	99	239	520	800
... Replica Edition (2000, $5.95) Reprints entire issue						6.00

SGT. ROCK: THE LOST BATTALION
DC Comics: Jan, 2009 - No. 6, Jun, 2009 ($2.99, limited series)

	GD 2.0	VG 4.0	FN 6.0	VF 8.0	VF/NM 9.0	NM- 9.2
1-6-Billy Tucci-s/a. 1-Tucci & Sparacio-c						3.00
HC (2009, $24.99, d.j.) r/#1-6; production art; cover art gallery						25.00
SC (2010, $17.99) r/#1-6; production art; cover art gallery						18.00

SGT. ROCK: THE PROPHECY
DC Comics: Mar, 2006 - No. 6, Aug, 2006 ($2.99, limited series)

	GD 2.0	VG 4.0	FN 6.0	VF 8.0	VF/NM 9.0	NM- 9.2
1-6-Joe Kubert-s/a/c. 1-Variant covers by Andy and Adam Kubert						3.00
TPB (2007, $17.99) r/#1-6						18.00

SGT. STRYKER'S DEATH SQUAD (See Savage Combat Tales)

SERGIO ARAGONÉS' ACTIONS SPEAK
Dark Horse Comics: Jan, 2001 - No. 6, Jun, 2001 ($2.99, B&W, limited series)

	GD 2.0	VG 4.0	FN 6.0	VF 8.0	VF/NM 9.0	NM- 9.2
1-6-Aragonés-c/a; wordless one-page cartoons						3.00

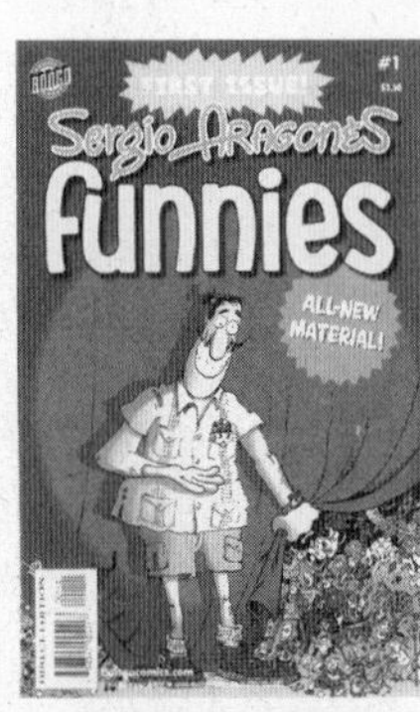

Sergio Aragonés Funnies #1 © Sergio Aragonés

Seven Seas Comics #6 © UPF

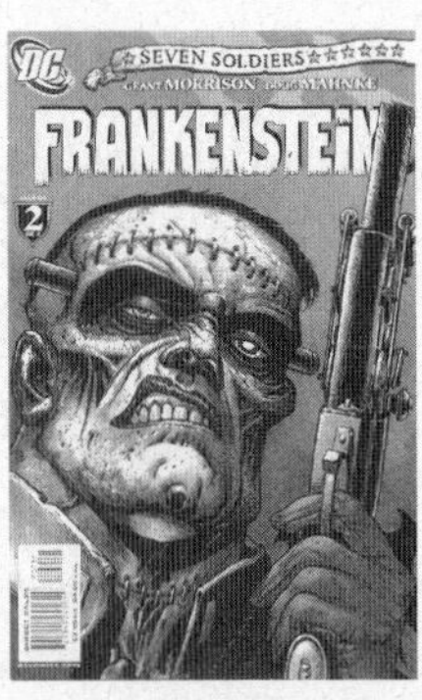

Seven Soldiers: Frankenstein #2 © DC

	GD 2.0	VG 4.0	FN 6.0	VF 8.0	VF/NM 9.0	NM- 9.2

SERGIO ARAGONÉS' BLAIR WHICH?
Dark Horse Comics: Dec, 1999 ($2.95, B&W, one-shot)
nn-Aragonés-c/a; Evanier-s. Parody of "Blair Witch Project" movie 3.00

SERGIO ARAGONÉS' BOOGEYMAN
Dark Horse Comics: June, 1998 - No. 4, Sept, 1998 ($2.95, B&W, lim. series)
1-4-Aragonés-c/a 3.00

SERGIO ARAGONÉS DESTROYS DC
DC Comics: June, 1996 ($3.50, one-shot)
1-DC Superhero parody book; Aragonés-c/a; Evanier scripts 3.50

SERGIO ARAGONÉS' DIA DE LOS MUERTOS
Dark Horse Comics: Oct, 1998 ($2.95, one-shot)
1-Aragonés-c/a; Evanier scripts 3.00

SERGIO ARAGONÉS FUNNIES
Bongo Comics: 2011 - Present ($3.50)
1-7-Color and B&W humor strips by Aragonés 3.50

SERGIO ARAGONÉS' GROO & RUFFERTO
Dark Horse Comics: Dec, 1998 - No. 4, Mar, 1999 ($2.95, lim. series)
1-3-Aragonés-c/a 3.00

SERGIO ARAGONÉS' GROO: DEATH AND TAXES
Dark Horse Comics: Dec, 2001 - No. 4, Apr, 2002 ($2.99, lim. series)
1-4-Aragonés-c/a; Evanier-s 3.00

SERGIO ARAGONÉS' GROO: HELL ON EARTH
Dark Horse Comics: Nov, 2007 - No. 4, Apr, 2008 ($2.99, lim. series)
1-4-Aragonés-c/a; Evanier-s 3.00

SERGIO ARAGONÉS' GROO: MIGHTIER THAN THE SWORD
Dark Horse Comics: Jan, 2000 - No. 4, Apr, 2000 ($2.95, lim. series)
1-4-Aragonés-c/a; Evanier-s 3.00

SERGIO ARAGONÉS' GROO: THE HOGS OF HORDER
Dark Horse Comics: Oct, 2009 - No. 4, Mar, 2010 ($3.99, lim. series)
1-4-Aragonés-c/a; Evanier-s 4.00

SERGIO ARAGONÉS' GROO THE WANDERER (See Groo...)

SERGIO ARAGONÉS' GROO: 25TH ANNIVERSARY SPECIAL
Dark Horse Comics: Aug, 2007 ($5.99, one-shot)
nn-Aragonés-c/a; Evanier scripts; wraparound cover 6.00

SERGIO ARAGONÉS' LOUDER THAN WORDS
Dark Horse Comics: July, 1997 - No. 6, Dec, 1997 ($2.95, B&W, limited series)
1-6-Aragonés-c/a 3.00

SERGIO ARAGONÉS MASSACRES MARVEL
Marvel Comics: June, 1996 ($3.50, one-shot)
1-Marvel Superhero parody book; Aragonés-c/a; Evanier scripts 3.50

SERGIO ARAGONÉS STOMPS STAR WARS
Marvel Comics: Jan, 2000 ($2.95, one-shot)
1-Star Wars parody; Aragonés-c/a; Evanier scripts 3.00

SEVEN
Intrinsic Comics: July, 2007 ($3.00)
1-Jim Shooter-s/Paul Creddick-a 3.00

SEVEN BLOCK
Marvel Comics (Epic Comics): 1990 ($4.50, one-shot, 52 pgs.)
1-Dixon-s/Zaffino-a 6.00
nn-(IDW Publ., 2004, $5.99) reprints #1 6.00

SEVEN BROTHERS (John Woo's...)
Virgin Comics: Oct, 2006 - No. 5, Feb, 2007 ($2.99)
1-5-Garth Ennis-s/Jeevan Kang-a. 1-Two covers by Amano & Horn. 2-Kang var-c 3.00
TPB (6/07, $14.99) r/#1-5; cover gallery, deleted scenes and concept art 15.00
Volume 2 (9/07 - No. 5, 2/08) 1-Edison George-a. 4,5-David Mack-c 3.00

SEVEN DEAD MEN (See Complete Mystery #1)

SEVEN DWARFS (Also see Snow White)
Dell Publishing Co.: No. 227, 1949 (Disney-Movie)
Four Color 227 9 18 27 63 112 160

SEVEN MILES A SECOND
DC Comics (Vertigo Verité): 1996 ($7.95, one-shot)
nn-Wojnarowicz-s/Romberg-a 8.00

SEVEN SAMUROID, THE (See Image Graphic Novel)

SEVEN SEAS COMICS
Universal Phoenix Features/Leader No. 6: Apr, 1946 - No. 6, 1947(no month)
1-South Sea Girl by Matt Baker, Capt. Cutlass begin; Tugboat Tessie by Baker app.
90 180 270 576 988 1400
2-Swashbuckler-c 68 136 204 432 746 1060
3,5,6: 3-Six pg. Feldstein-a 69 138 207 442 759 1075
4-Classic Baker-c 90 180 270 576 988 1400
NOTE: *Baker a-1-6; c-3-6.*

SEVEN SOLDIERS OF VICTORY (Book-ends for seven related mini-series)
DC Comics: No. 0, Apr, 2005; No. 1; Dec, 2006 ($2.95/$3.99)
0-Grant Morrison-s/J.H. Williams-a 3.00
1-($3.99) Series conclusion; Grant Morrison-s/J.H. Williams-a 4.00
... Volume One (2006, $14.99) r/#0, Shining Knight #1,2; Zatanna #1,2; Guardian #1,2; and Klarion the Witch Boy #1; intro. by Morrison; character design sketches 15.00
... Volume Two (2006, $14.99) r/Shining Knight #3,4; Zatanna #3; Guardian #3,4; and Klarion the Witch Boy #2,3 15.00
... Volume Three ('06, $14.99) r/Zatanna #4; Mister Miracle #1,2; Bulleteer #1,2; Frankenstein #1 and Klarion the Witch Boy #4; 15.00
... Volume Four ('07, $14.99) r/Mister Miracle #3,4; Bulleteer #3,4; Frankenstein #2-4 and Seven Soldiers of Victory #1; script pages 15.00

SEVEN SOLDIERS: BULLETEER
DC Comics: Jan, 2006 - No. 4, May, 2006 ($2.99, limited series)
1-4-Grant Morrison-s/Yanick Paquette-a/c 3.00

SEVEN SOLDIERS: FRANKENSTEIN
DC Comics: Jan, 2006 - No. 4, May, 2006 ($2.99, limited series)
1-4-Grant Morrison-s/Doug Mahnke-a/c 3.00

SEVEN SOLDIERS: GUARDIAN
DC Comics: May, 2005 - No. 4, Nov, 2005 ($2.99, limited series)
1-4-Grant Morrison-s/Cameron Stewart-a; Newsboy Army app. 3.00

SEVEN SOLDIERS: KLARION THE WITCH BOY
DC Comics: June, 2005 - No. 4, Dec, 2005 ($2.99, limited series)
1-4-Grant Morrison-s/Frazer Irving-a 3.00

SEVEN SOLDIERS: MISTER MIRACLE
DC Comics: Nov, 2005 - No. 4, May, 2006 ($2.99, limited series)
1-4: 1-Grant Morrison-s/Pasqual Ferry-a/c. 3,4-Freddie Williams II-a/c 3.00

SEVEN SOLDIERS: SHINING KNIGHT
DC Comics: May, 2005 - No. 4, Oct, 2005 ($2.99, limited series)
1-4-Grant Morrison-s/Simone Bianchi-a 3.00

SEVEN SOLDIERS: ZATANNA
DC Comics: June, 2005 - No. 4, Dec, 2005 ($2.99, limited series)
1-4-Grant Morrison-s/Ryan Sook-a 3.00

1776 (See Charlton Classic Library)

7TH VOYAGE OF SINBAD, THE (Movie)
Dell Publishing Co.: Sept, 1958 (photo-c)
Four Color 944-Buscema-a 11 22 33 76 151 225

77 SUNSET STRIP (TV)
Dell Publ. Co./Gold Key: No. 1066, Jan-Mar, 1960 - No. 2, Feb, 1963 (All photo-c)
Four Color 1066-Toth-a 10 20 30 67 124 180
Four Color 1106,1159-Toth-a 8 16 24 56 96 135
Four Color 1211,1263,1291, 01-742-209(7-9/62)-Manning-a in all
8 16 24 53 89 125
1,2: Manning-a. 1(11/62-G.K.) 8 16 24 53 89 125

77TH BENGAL LANCERS, THE (TV)
Dell Publishing Co.: May, 1957
Four Color 791-Photo-c 7 14 21 46 76 105

SEVERED
Image Comics: Aug, 2011 - No. 7, Feb, 2012 ($2.99)
1-7-Scott Snyder & Scott Tuft-s/Attila Futaki-a/c 3.00

SEYMOUR, MY SON (See More Seymour)
Archie Publications (Radio Comics): Sept, 1963
1-DeCarlo-c/a 4 8 12 22 34 45

The Shade (2012 series) #7 © DC

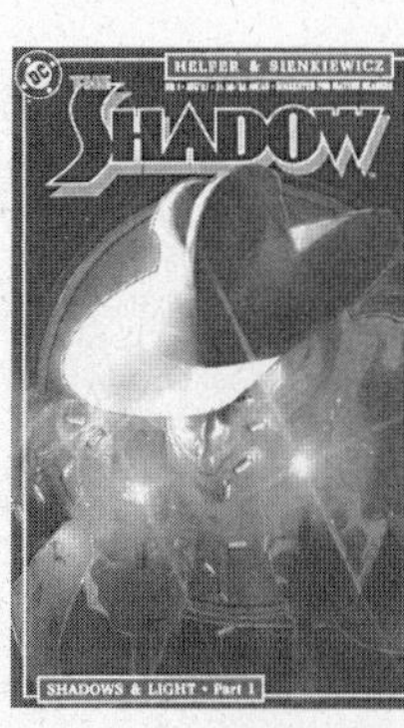

The Shadow (1987 series) #1 © CN

Shadow Comics #2 © CN

GD VG FN VF VF/NM NM-
2.0 4.0 6.0 8.0 9.0 9.2

SHADE, THE (See Starman)
DC Comics: Apr, 1997 - No. 4, July, 1997 ($2.25, limited series)
1-4-Robinson-s/Harris-c: 1-Gene Ha-a. 2-Williams/Gray-a 3-Blevins-a. 4-Zulli-a 3.00

SHADE, THE (From Starman)
DC Comics: Dec, 2011 - No. 12 ($2.99, limited series)
1-7: 1-Robinson-s/Hamner-a/Harris-c; Deathstroke app. 4-Cooke-a 3.00
1-7-Variant covers. 1-3-Hamner. 4-Darwyn Cooke. 5-7-Pulido 4.00

SHADE, THE CHANGING MAN (See Cancelled Comic Cavalcade)
National Per. Publ./DC Comics: June-July, 1977 - No. 8, Aug-Sept, 1978
1-1st app. Shade; Ditko-c/a in all 2 4 6 11 16 20
2-8 2 3 4 6 8 10

SHADE, THE CHANGING MAN (2nd series) (Also see Suicide Squad #16)
DC Comics (Vertigo imprint #33 on): July, 1990 - No. 70, Apr, 1996 ($1.50-$2.25, mature)
1-($2.50, 52 pgs.)-Peter Milligan scripts in all 4.00
2-41,45-49,51-59: 6-Preview of World Without End. 17-Begin $1.75-c. 33-Metallic ink on-c. 41-Begin $1.95-c 3.00
42-44-John Constantine app. 3.50
50-($2.95, 52 pgs.) 4.00
60-70: 60-begin $2.25-c 3.00
...: Edge of Vision TPB (2009, $19.99) r/#7-13 20.00
...: Scream Time TPB (2010, $19.99) r/#14-19 20.00
...: The American Scream TPB (2003, 2009, $17.95/$17.99) r/#1-6 18.00
NOTE: ***Bachalo*** *a-1-9, 11-13, 15-21, 23-26, 33-39, 42-45, 47, 49, 50; c-30, 33-41.*

SHADO: SONG OF THE DRAGON (See Green Arrow #63-66)
DC Comics: 1992 - No. 4, 1992 ($4.95, limited series, 52 pgs.)
Book One - Four: Grell scripts; Morrow-a(i) 5.00

SHADOW, THE (See Batman #253, 259 & Marvel Graphic Novel #35)

SHADOW, THE (Pulp, radio)
Archie Comics (Radio Comics): Aug, 1964 - No. 8, Sept, 1965 (All 12¢)
1-Jerrry Siegel scripts in all; Shadow-c. 9 18 27 61 106 150
2-8: 2-App. in super-hero costume on-c only; Reinman-a(backup). 3-Superhero begins; Reinman-a (book-length novel). 3,4,6,7-The Fly 1 pg. strips. 4-8-Reinman-a. 5-8-Siegel scripts. 7-Shield app. 6 12 18 37 59 80

SHADOW, THE
National Periodical Publications: Oct-Nov, 1973 - No. 12, Aug-Sept, 1975
1-Kaluta-a begins 6 12 18 42 69 95
2 4 8 12 22 34 45
3-Kaluta/Wrightson-a 4 8 12 24 37 50
4,6-Kaluta-a ends. 4-Chaykin, Wrightson part-i 3 6 9 19 29 38
5,7-12: 11-The Avenger (pulp character) x-over 2 4 6 13 18 22
NOTE: ***Craig*** *a-10.* ***Cruz*** *a-10-12.* ***Kaluta*** *a-1, 2, 3p, 4, 6; c-1-4, 6, 10-12.* ***Kubert*** *c-9.* ***Robbins*** *a-5, 7-9; c-5, 7, 8.*

SHADOW, THE
DC Comics: May, 1986 - No. 4, Aug, 1986 (limited series)
1-4: Howard Chaykin art in all 4.00
Blood & Judgement ($12.95)-r/1-4 13.00

SHADOW, THE
DC Comics: Aug, 1987 - No. 19, Jan, 1989 ($1.50)
1-19: Andrew Helfer scripts in all. 4.00
Annual 1,2 (12/87, '88,)-2-The Shadow dies; origin retold (story inspired by the movie "Citizen Kane"). 5.00
NOTE: ***Kyle Baker*** *a-7i, 8-19, Annual 2.* ***Chaykin*** *c-Annual 1.* ***Helfer*** *scripts in all.* ***Orlando*** *a-Annual 1.* ***Rogers*** *c/a-7.* ***Sienkiewicz*** *c/a-1-6.*

SHADOW, THE (Movie)
Dark Horse Comics: June, 1994 - No. 2, July, 1994 ($2.50, limited series)
1,2-Adaptation from Universal Pictures film 4.00
NOTE: ***Kaluta*** *c/a-1, 2.*

SHADOW AND DOC SAVAGE, THE
Dark Horse Comics: July, 1995 - No. 2, Aug, 1995 ($2.95, limited series)
1,2 4.00

SHADOW AND THE MYSTERIOUS 3, THE
Dark Horse Comics: Sept, 1994 ($2.95, one-shot)
1-Kaluta co-scripts. 4.00
NOTE: ***Stevens*** *c-1.*

SHADOW CABINET (See Heroes)
DC Comics (Milestone): No. 0, Jan, 1994 - No. 17, Oct, 1995 ($1.75/$2.50)
0-(1/94, $2.50, 52 pgs.)-Silver ink-c; Simonson-c 4.00
1-17: 1-(6/94) Byrne-c 3.00

GD VG FN VF VF/NM NM-
2.0 4.0 6.0 8.0 9.0 9.2

SHADOW COMICS (Pulp, radio)
Street & Smith Publications: Mar, 1940 - V9#5, Aug-Sept, 1949
NOTE: *The Shadow first appeared on radio in 1929 and was featured in pulps beginning in April, 1931, written by Walter Gibson. The early covers of this series were reprinted from the pulp covers.*
V1#1-Shadow, Doc Savage, Bill Barnes, Nick Carter (radio), Frank Merriwell, Iron Munro, the Astonishing Man begin 486 972 1458 3550 6275 9000
2-The Avenger begins, ends #6; Capt. Fury only app. 216 432 648 1372 2361 3350
3(nn-5/40)-Norgil the Magician app.; cover is exact swipe of Shadow pulp from 1/33 155 310 465 992 1696 2400
4,5: 4-The Three Musketeers begins, ends #8. 5-Doc Savage ends 115 230 345 730 1253 1775
6,8,9: 9-Norgil the Magician app. 97 194 291 621 1061 1500
7-Origin/1st app. The Hooded Wasp & Wasplet (11/40); series ends V3#8; Hooded Wasp/Wasplet app. on-c thru #9 102 204 306 648 1112 1575
10-Origin The Iron Ghost, ends #11; The Dead End Kids begins, ends #14 95 190 285 603 1039 1475
11-Origin Hooded Wasp & Wasplet retold 95 190 285 603 1039 1475
12-Dead End Kids app. 89 178 267 565 970 1375
V2#1(11/41, Vol.II#2 in indicia) Dead End Kids -s 87 174 261 553 952 1350
2-(Rare, Vol.II#3 in indicia) Giant ant-c 165 330 495 1048 1799 2550
3-Origin & 1st app. Supersnipe (3/42); series begins; Little Nemo story (Vol.II#4 in indicia) 139 278 417 883 1517 2150
4,5: 4,8-Little Nemo story 76 152 228 486 831 1175
6-9: 6-Blackstone the Magician story 73 146 219 467 796 1125
10,12: 10-Supersnipe app. Skull-c 71 142 213 454 777 1100
11-Classic Devil Kyoti World War 2 sunburst-c 87 174 261 553 952 1350
V3#1,2,5,7-12: 10-Doc Savage begins, not in V5#5, V6#10-12, V8#4 69 138 207 442 759 1075
3-1st Monstrodamus-c/sty 84 168 252 538 919 1300
4-2nd Monstrodamus; classic-c of giant salamander getting shot in the head 90 180 270 576 988 1400
6-Classic underwater-c 97 194 291 621 1061 1500
V4#1-12: 2-Severed head-c 50 100 150 315 533 750
V5#1-12 43 86 129 271 461 650
V6#1-11: 9-Intro. Shadow, Jr. (12/46) 40 80 120 246 411 575
12-Powell-c/a; atom bomb panels 43 86 129 271 461 650
V7#1,2,5,7-9,12: 2,5-Shadow, Jr. app.; Powell-a 40 80 120 246 411 575
3,6,11-Powell-c/a 45 90 135 284 480 675
4-Powell-c/a; Atom bomb panels 47 94 141 296 498 700
10(1/48)-Flying Saucer-c/story (2nd of this theme; see The Spirit 9/28/47); Powell-c/a 60 120 180 381 653 925
V8#1-12-Powell-a. 3-Powell Spider-c/a 45 90 135 284 480 675
V9#1,5-Powell-a 43 86 129 271 461 650
2-4-Powell-c/a 45 90 135 284 480 675
NOTE: ***Binder*** *c-V3#1.* ***Powell*** *art in most issues beginning V6#12. Painted c-1-6.*

SHADOWDRAGON
DC Comics: 1995 ($3.50, annual)
Annual 1-Year One story 4.00

SHADOW EMPIRES: FAITH CONQUERS
Dark Horse Comics: Aug, 1994 - No. 4, Nov, 1994 ($2.95, limited series)
1-4 3.00

SHADOWHAWK (See Images of Shadowhawk, New Shadowhawk, Shadowhawk II, Shadowhawk III & Youngblood #2)
Image Comics (Shadowline Ink): Aug, 1992 - No. 4, Mar, 1993; No. 12, Aug, 1994 - No. 18, May, 1995 ($1.95/$2.50)
1-($2.50)-Embossed silver foil stamped-c; Valentino/Liefeld-c; Valentino-c/a/ scripts in all; has coupon for Image #0; 1st Shadowline Ink title 5.00
1-With coupon missing 2.00
1-($1.95)-Newsstand version w/o foil stamp 3.00
2-13,0,1418: 2-Shadowhawk poster w/McFarlane-i; brief Spawn app.; wraparound-c w/silver ink highlights. 3-($2.50)-Glow-in-the-dark-c. 4-Savage Dragon-c/story; Valentino/Larsen-c. 5-11-(See Shadowhawk II and III). 12-Cont'd from Shadowhawk III; pull-out poster by Texeira.13-w/ShadowBone poster; WildC.A.T.s app. 0 (10/94)-Liefeld c/a/story; ShadowBart poster. 14-(10/94, $2.50)-The Others app. 16-Supreme app. 17-Spawn app.; story cont'd from Badrock & Co. #6. 18-Shadowhawk dies; Savage Dragon & Brigade app. 3.00
Special 1(12/94, $3.50, 52 pgs.)-Silver Age Shadowhawk flip book 4.00
Gallery (4/94, $1.95) 3.00
Out of the Shadows ($19.95)-r/Youngblood #2, Shadowhawk #1-4, Image Zero #0, Operation: Urban Storm (Never published) 20.00
.../Vampirella (2/95, $4.95)-Pt.2 of x-over (See Vampirella/Shadowhawk for Pt. 1) 5.00
NOTE: *Shadowhawk was originally a four issue limited series. The story continued in Shadowhawk II, Shadowhawk III & then became Shadowhawk again with issue #12.*

Shadowhawk V3 #1 © Jim Valentino

Shadowland: Elektra #1 © MAR

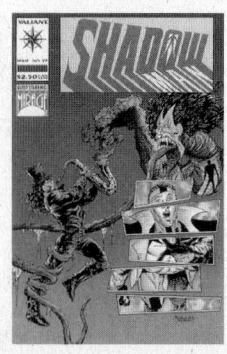

Shadowman #23 © Voyager Comm.

GD VG FN VF VF/NM NM-
2.0 4.0 6.0 8.0 9.0 9.2

GD VG FN VF VF/NM NM-
2.0 4.0 6.0 8.0 9.0 9.2

SHADOWHAWK II (Follows Shadowhawk #4)
Image Comics (Shadowline Ink): V2#1, May, 1993 - V2#3, Aug, 1993 ($3.50/$1.95/$2.95, limited series)

V2#1 ($3.50)-Cont'd from Shadowhawk #4; die-cut mirricard-c 4.00
2 ($1.95)-Foil embossed logo; reveals identity; gold-c variant exists 3.00
3 ($2.95)-Pop-up-c w/Pact ashcan insert 4.00

SHADOWHAWK III (Follows Shadowhawk II #3)
Image Comics (Shadowline Ink): V3#1, Nov, 1993 - V3#4, Mar, 1994 ($1.95, limited series);

V3#1-4: 1-Cont'd from Shadowhawk II; intro Valentine; gold foil & red foil stamped-c variations. 2-(52 pgs.)-Shadowhawk contracts HIV virus; U.S. Male by M. Anderson (p) in free 16 pg.insert. 4-Continues in Shadowhawk #12 3.00

SHADOWHAWK (Volume 2) (Also see New Man #4)
Image Comics: May, 2005 - No. 15, Sept, 2006 ($2.99/$3.50)

1-4-Eddie Collins as Shadowhawk; Rodríguez-a; Valentino-co-plotter 3.50
5-15-($3.50) 5-Cover swipe of Superman Vs. Spider-Man treasury edition 3.50
...One Shot #1 (7/06, $1.99) r/Return of Shadowhawk 3.00
Return of Shadowhawk (12/04, $2.99) Valentino-s/a/c; Eddie Collins origin retold 3.00

SHADOWHAWK (Volume 3)
Image Comics: May, 2010 - No. 5, Dec, 2010 ($3.50)

1-5-Rodríguez-a. 1-Back-up with Valentino-a/Niles-s 3.50

SHADOWHAWKS OF LEGEND
Image Comics (Shadowline Ink): Nov, 1995 ($4.95, one-shot)

nn-Stories of past Shadowhawks by Kurt Busiek, Beau Smith & Alan Moore 5.00

SHADOW, THE: HELL'S HEAT WAVE (Movie, pulp, radio)
Dark Horse Comics: Apr, 1995 - No. 3, June, 1995 ($2.95, limited series)

1-3: Kaluta story 4.00

SHADOW HUNTER (Jenna Jameson's...)
Virgin Comics: No. 0, Dec, 2007 - No. 3 ($2.99)

0-Preview issue; creator interviews; gallery of covers for upcoming issues; Greg Horn-c 3.00
1-3: 1-Two covers by Horn & Land; Jameson & Christina Z-s/Singh-a. 2-Three covers 3.00

SHADOWHUNT SPECIAL
Image Comics (Extreme Studios): Apr, 1996 ($2.50)

1-Retells origin of past Shadowhawks; Valentino script; Chapel app. 3.00

SHADOW, THE: IN THE COILS OF THE LEVIATHAN (Movie, pulp, radio)
Dark Horse Comics: Oct, 1993 - No. 4, Apr, 1994 ($2.95, limited series)

1-4-Kaluta-c & co-scripter 4.00
Trade paperback (10/94, $13.95)-r/1-4 14.00

SHADOWLAND (Also see Daredevil #508-512 & Black Panther: The Man Without Fear #513)
Marvel Comics: Sept, 2010 - No. 5, Jan, 2011 ($3.99, limited series)

1-5: 1-Diggle-s/Tan-a; Bullseye killed; Cassaday-c. 2-Ghost Rider app. 4.00
1-Variant-c by Tan 6.00
...: After the Fall 1 (2/11, $3.99) Finch-c; Black Panther app. 4.00
...: Bullseye 1 (10/10, $3.99) Chen-a; Bullseye's funeral 4.00
...: Elektra 1 (11/10, $3.99) Wells-s/Rios-a/Takeda-c 4.00
...: Ghost Rider 1 (11/10, $3.99) Williams-s/Crain-a/c 4.00
...: Spider-Man 1 (12/10, $3.99) Shang-Chi & Mr. Negative app.; Siqueira-a 4.00

SHADOWLAND: BLOOD IN THE STREETS (Leads into Heroes For Hire)
Marvel Comics: Oct, 2010 - No. 4, Jan, 2011 ($3.99, limited series)

1-4-Johnston-s/Alves-a; Misty Knight, Silver Sable, Paladin, Shroud app. 4.00

SHADOWLAND: DAUGHTERS OF THE SHADOW
Marvel Comics: Oct, 2010 - No. 3, Dec, 2010 ($3.99, limited series)

1-3-Henderson-s/Rodriguez-a; Colleen Wing app. 3-Preview of Black Panther #513 4.00

SHADOWLAND: MOON KNIGHT
Marvel Comics: Oct, 2010 - No. 3, Dec, 2010 ($3.99, limited series)

1-3-Hurwitz-s/Dazo-a 4.00

SHADOWLAND: POWER MAN
Marvel Comics: Oct, 2010 - No. 4, Jan, 2011 ($3.99, limited series)

1-4-Van Lente-s/Asrar-a. 1-New Power Man debut; Iron Fist app. 4.00

SHADOWLINE SAGA: CRITICAL MASS, A
Marvel Comics (Epic): Jan, 1990 - No. 7, July, 1990 ($4.95, lim. series, 68 pgs)

1-6: Dr. Zero, Powerline, St. George 5.00
7 ($5.95, 84 pgs.)-Morrow-a, Williamson-c(i) 6.00

SHADOWMAN (See X-O Manowar #4)
Valiant/Acclaim Comics (Valiant): May, 1992 - No. 43, Dec, 1995 ($2.50)

1-Partial origin 5.00
2-5: 3-1st app. Sousa the Soul Eater 4.00
6-43: 8-1st app. Master Darque. 16-1st app. Dr. Mirage (8/93). 15-Minor Turok app. 17,18-Archer & Armstrong x-over. 19-Aerosmith-c/story. 23-Dr. Mirage x-over. 24-(4/94). 25-Bound-in trading card. 29-Chaos Effect. 43-Shadowman jumps to his death 3.00
0-($2.50, 4/94)-Regular edition 3.00
0-($3.50)-Wraparound chromium-c edition 4.00
0-Gold 15.00
Yearbook 1 (12/94, $3.95) 4.00

SHADOWMAN (Volume 2)
Acclaim Comics (Valiant Heroes): Mar, 1997 - No. 20 ($2.50, mature)

1-20: 1-1st app. Zero; Garth Ennis scripts begin, end #4. 2-Zero becomes new Shadowman. 4-Origin; Jack Boniface (original Shadowman) rises from the grave. 5-Jamie Delano scripts begin. 9-Copycat-c 3.00
1-Variant painted cover 3.00
#0 Gold 5.00

SHADOWMAN (Volume 3)
Acclaim Comics: July, 1999 - No. 5, Nov, 1999 ($3.95/$2.50)

1-($3.95)-Abnett & Lanning-s/Broome & Benjamin-a 4.00
2-5-($2.50): 3,4-Flip book with Unity 2000 3.00

SHADOWMASTERS
Marvel Comics: Oct, 1989 - No.4, Jan, 1990 ($3.95, squarebound, 52 pgs.)

1-4: Heath-a(i). 1-Jim Lee-c; story cont'd from Punisher 4.00

SHADOW OF THE BATMAN
DC Comics: Dec, 1985 - No. 5, Apr, 1986 ($1.75, limited series)

1-Detective-r (all have wraparound-c) 1 2 3 5 6 8
2,3,5: 3-Penguin-c & cameo. 5-Clayface app. 6.00
4-Joker-c/story 1 2 3 4 5 7

NOTE: ***Austin*** *a(new)-2i, 3i; r-2-4i.* ***Rogers*** *a(new)-1, 2p, 3p, 4, 5; r-1-5p; c-1-5.* ***Simonson*** *a-1r.*

SHADOW OF THE TORTURER, THE
Innovation: July, 1991 - No. 3, 1992 ($2.50, limited series)

1-3: Based on Pocket Books novel 3.00

SHADOW ON THE TRAIL (See Zane Grey & Four Color #604)

SHADOWPACT (See Day of Vengeance)
DC Comics: Jul, 2006 - No. 25, Jul, 2008 ($2.99)

1-25: 1-Bill Willingham-s; Detective Chimp, Ragman, Blue Devil, Nightshade, Enchantress and Nightmaster app. 1-Superman app. 13-Zauriel app.; S. Hampton-a 3.00
...: Cursed TPB (2007, $14.99) r/#4,9-13 15.00
...: Darkness and Light TPB (2008, $14.99) r/#14-19 15.00
...: The Burning Age TPB (2008, $17.99) r/#20-25 18.00
...: The Pentacle Plot TPB (2007, $14.99) r/#1-3,5-8 15.00

SHADOW PLAY (Tales of the Supernatural)
Whitman Publications: June, 1982

1-Painted-c 1 2 3 5 6 8

SHADOWPLAY
IDW Publ.: Sept, 2005 - No. 4, Dec, 2005 ($3.99)

1-4-Benson-s/Templesmith-a; Christina Z-s/Wood-a; 2 covers by Templesmith & Wood 4.00
TPB (3/06, $17.99) r/series; flip book format 18.00

SHADOW REAVERS
Black Bull Ent.: Oct, 2001 - No. 5, Mar, 2002 ($2.99)

1-5-Nelson-a; two covers for each issue 3.00
Limited Preview Edition (5/01, no cover price) 3.00

SHADOW RIDERS
Marvel Comics UK, Ltd.: June, 1993 - No. 4, Sept, 1993 ($1.75, limited series)

1-($2.50)-Embossed-c; Cable-c/story 4.00
2-4-Cable app. 2-Ghost Rider app. 3.00

SHADOWS
Image Comics: Feb, 2003 - No. 4, Nov, 2003 ($2.95)

1-4-Jade Dodge-s/Matt Camp-a/c 3.00

SHADOWS & LIGHT
Marvel Comics: Feb, 1998 - No. 3, July, 1998 ($2.99, B&W, quarterly)

1-3: 1-B&W anthology of Marvel characters; Black Widow art by Gene Ha, Hulk by Wrightson, Iron Man by Ditko & Daredevil by Stelfreeze; Stelfreeze painted-c. 2-Weeks, Sharp, Starlin, Thompson-a. 3-Buscema, Grindberg, Giffen, Layton-a 3.00

SHADOW'S FALL
DC Comics (Vertigo): Nov, 1994 - No. 6, Apr, 1995 ($2.95, limited series)

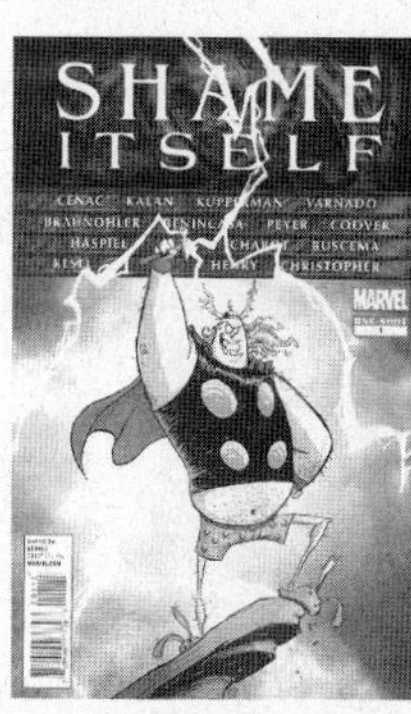

Shame Itself #1 © MAR

Shanna, The She-Devil #5 © MAR

Shazam! #15 © DC

	GD 2.0	VG 4.0	FN 6.0	VF 8.0	VF/NM 9.0	NM- 9.2
1-6: Van Fleet-c/a in all.						3.00

SHADOWS FROM BEYOND (Formerly Unusual Tales)
Charlton Comics: V2#50, October, 1966

V2#50-Ditko-c	4	8	12	23	36	48

SHADOW STATE
Broadway Comics: Dec, 1995 - No. 5, Apr, 1996 ($2.50)

1-5: 1,2-Fatale back-up story; Cockrum-a(p) 3.00
Preview Edition 1,2 (10-11/95, $2.50, B&W) 3.00

SHADOW STRIKES!, THE (Pulp, radio)
DC Comics: Sept, 1989 - No.31, May, 1992 ($1.75)

1-4,7-31: 31-Mignola-c 4.00
5,6-Doc Savage x-over 5.00
Annual 1 (1989, $3.50, 68 pgs.)-Spiegle a; Kaluta-c 5.00

SHADOW WAR OF HAWKMAN
DC Comics: May, 1985 - No. 4, Aug, 1985 (limited series)

1-4 3.00

SHAGGY DOG & THE ABSENT-MINDED PROFESSOR (See Four Color #1199, Movie Comics & Walt Disney Showcase #46)(Disney-Movie)
Dell Publ. Co.: No. 985, May, 1959

Four Color 985	7	14	21	49	82	115

SHALOMAN (Jewish-themed stories and history)
Al Wiesner/ Mark 1 Comics: 1988 - Present (B&W)

V1#1-Al Wiesner-s/a in all 5.00
2-9 3.00
V2 #1(The New Adventures)-4,6-10, V3 (The Legend of...) #1-12 3.00
V2 #5 (Color)-Shows Vol 2, No. 4 in indicia 3.00
V4 (The Saga of ...) #1(2004), 2-8: 8-Chanukah & The Holocaust 3.00
...: The Sequel (2010) "11-9" , ...: The Sequel 2 (2011) Genesis #2 Jews in Space 3.00
...: The Sequel 3 (2012) Purim and the X-Suit 3.00
The Saga of Shaloman (20th Anniversary Edition) TPB (10/08, $15.99) r/V4 #1-8 16.00

SHAMAN'S TEARS (Also see Maggie the Cat)
Image Comics (Creative Fire Studio): 5/93 - No. 2, 8/93; No. 3, 11/94 - No. 0, 1/96 ($2.50/$1.95)

0-2: 0-(DEC-c, 1/96)-Last Issue. 1-(5/93)-Embossed red foil-c; Grell-c/a & scripts in all. 2-Cover unfolds into poster (8/93-c, 7/93 inside) 3.00
3-12: 3-Begin $1.95-c. 5-Re-intro Jon Sable. 12-Re-intro Maggie the Cat (1 pg.) 3.00

SHAME ITSELF
Marvel Comics: Jan, 2012 ($3.99, one-shot)

1-Spoof of "Fear Itself" x-over event; short stories by various incl. Cenac & Kupperman 4.00

SHANG-CHI: MASTER OF KUNG-FU ("Master of Kung Fu" on cover for #1&2)
Marvel Comics: Nov, 2002 - No. 6, Apr, 2003 ($2.99, limited series)

1-6-Moench-s/Gulacy-c/a 3.00
...One-Shot 1 (11/09, $3.99, B&W) Deadpool app. 4.00
... Vol. 1: The Hellfire Apocalypse TPB (2003, $14.99) r/#1-6 15.00

SHANGRI-LA
Image Comics: Jan, 2004 ($7.95, B&W, square-bound graphic novel)

1-Marc Bryant-s/Shepherd Hendrix-a 8.00

SHANNA, THE SHE-DEVIL (See Savage Tales #8)
Marvel Comics Group: Dec, 1972 - No. 5, Aug, 1973 (All are 20¢ issues)

1-1st app. Shanna; Steranko-c; Tuska-a(p)	4	8	12	26	41	55
2-Steranko-c; heroin drug story	4	8	12	22	34	45
3-5	3	6	9	14	20	25

SHANNA, THE SHE-DEVIL
Marvel Comics: Apr, 2005 - No. 7, Oct, 2005 ($3.50, limited series)

1-7-Reintro of Shanna; Frank Cho-s/a/c in all 3.50
HC (2005, $24.99, dust jacket) r/#1-7 25.00
SC (2006, $16.99) r/#1-7 17.00

SHANNA, THE SHE-DEVIL: SURVIVAL OF THE FITTEST
Marvel Comics: Oct, 2007 - No. 4, Jan, 2008 ($2.99, limited series)

1-4-Khari Evans-a/c; Gray & Palmiotti-s 3.00
SC (2008, $10.99) r/#1-4 11.00

SHAOLIN COWBOY
Burlyman Entertainment: Dec, 2004 - No. 7 ($3.50)

1-7-Geof Darrow-s/a. 3-Moebius-c 3.50

SHARK FIGHTERS, THE (Movie)
Dell Publishing Co.: Jan, 1957

Four Color 762-Buscema-a; photo-c	7	14	21	49	82	115

SHARK-MAN
Thrill House/Image Comics: Jul, 2006; Jul, 2007; Jan, 2008 - No. 3, Jun, 2008 ($3.99/$3.50)

1,2: 1-(Thrill House, 7/06, $3.99)-Steve Pugh-s/a. 2-(Image Comics, 7/07) 4.00
1-3: 1-(Image, 1/08, $3.50) reprints Thrill House #1 3.50

SHARKY
Image Comics: Feb, 1998 - No. 4, 1998 ($2.50, bi-monthly)

1-4: 1-Mask app.; Elliot-s/a. Horley painted-c. 3-Three covers by Horley, Bisley, & Horley/Elliot. 4-Two covers (swipe of Avengers #4 and wraparound) 3.00
1-($2.95) "$1,000,000" variant 3.00
2-($2.50) Savage Dragon variant-c 3.00

SHARP COMICS (Slightly large size)
H. C. Blackerby: Winter, 1945-46 - V1#2, Spring, 1946 (52 pgs.)

V1#1-Origin Dick Royce Planetarian	41	82	123	249	417	585
2-Origin The Pioneer; Michael Morgan, Dick Royce, Sir Gallagher, Planetarian, Steve Hagen, Weeny and Pop app.	36	72	108	216	351	485

SHARPY FOX (See Comic Capers & Funny Frolics)
I. W. Enterprises/Super Comics: 1958; 1963

1,2-I.W. Reprint (1958): 2-r/Kiddie Kapers #1	2	4	6	8	10	12
14-Super Reprint (1963)	2	4	6	8	10	12

SHATTER (See Jon Sable #25-30)
First Comics: June, 1985; Dec, 1985 - No. 14, Apr, 1988. ($1.75, Baxter paper/deluxe paper)

1 (6/85)-1st computer generated-a in a comic book (1st printing) 4.00
1-(2nd print.); 1(12/85)-14: computer generated-a & lettering in all 3.00
Special 1 (1988) 3.00

SHATTERED IMAGE
Image Comics (WildStorm Productions): Aug, 1996 - No. 4, Dec, 1996 ($2.50, lim. series)

1-4: 1st Image company-wide x-over; Kurt Busiek scripts in all. 1-Tony Daniel-c/a(p). 2-Alex Ross-c/swipe (Kingdom Come) by Ryan Benjamin & Travis Charest 3.00

SHAUN OF THE DEAD (Movie)
IDW Publishing: June, 2005 - No. 4, Sept, 2005 ($3.99, limited series)

1-4-Adaptation of 2004 movie; Zach Howard-a 4.00
TPB (12/05, $17.99) r/series; sketch pages and cover gallery 18.00

SHAZAM (See Billy Batson and the Magic of Shazam!, Giant Comics to Color, Limited Collectors' Edition, Power Of Shazam! and Trials of Shazam!)

SHAZAM! (TV)(See World's Finest #253 for story from unpublished #36)
National Periodical Publ./DC Comics: Feb, 1973 - No. 35, May-June, 1978

1-1st revival of original Captain Marvel since G.A. (origin retold), by C.C. Beck; Mary Marvel & Captain Marvel Jr. app.; Superman-c	6	12	18	42	69	95
2-5: 2-Infinity photo-c.; re-intro Mr. Mind & Tawny. 3-Capt. Marvel-r. (10/46). 4-Origin retold; Capt. Marvel-r. (1949). 5-Capt. Marvel Jr. origin retold; Capt. Marvel-r. (1948, 7 pgs.)	3	6	9	18	27	35
6,7,9-11: 6-photo-c; Capt. Marvel-r (1950, 6 pgs.). 9-Mr. Mind app. 10-Last C.C. Beck issue. 11-Schaffenberger-a begins.	3	6	9	14	20	26
8 (100 pgs.) 8-r/Capt. Marvel Jr. by Raboy; origin/C.M. #80; origin Mary Marvel/C.M.A. #18; origin Mr. Tawny/C.M.A. #79	6	12	18	41	66	90
12-17-(All 100 pgs.). 15-vs. Lex Luthor & Mr. Mind	5	10	15	32	51	70
18-24,26-30: 21-24-All reprints. 26-Sivana app. (10/76). 27-Kid Eternity teams up w/Capt. Marvel. 28-1st S.A. app. of Black Adam. 30-1st DC app. 3 Lt. Marvels	2	4	6	11	16	20
25-1st app. Isis	3	6	9	14	19	24
31-35: 31-1st DC app. Minuteman. 34-Origin Capt. Nazi & Capt. Marvel Jr. retold	3	6	9	14	19	24

...: The Greatest Stories Ever Told TPB (2008, $24.99) reprints; Alex Ross-c 25.00

NOTE: *Reprints in #1-8, 10, 12-17, 21-24.* ***Beck*** *a-1-10, 12-17r, 21-24r; c-1, 3-9.* ***Nasser*** *c-35p.* ***Newton*** *a-35p.* ***Raboy*** *a-5r, 8r, 17r.* ***Schaffenberger*** *a-11, 14-20, 25, 26, 27p, 28, 29-31p, 33i, 35i; c-20, 22, 23, 25, 26i, 27i, 28-33.*

SHAZAM!
DC Comics: March, 2011 ($2.99, one-shot)

1-Richards-a/Chiang-c; Blaze app.; story continues in Titans #32 3.00

SHAZAM! AND THE SHAZAM FAMILY! ANNUAL
DC Comics: 2002 ($5.95, squarebound, one-shot)

1-Reprints Golden Age stories including 1st Mary Marvel and 1st Black Adam 6.00

SHAZAM!: POWER OF HOPE
DC Comics: Nov, 2000 ($9.95, treasury size, one-shot)

nn-Painted art by Alex Ross; story by Alex Ross and Paul Dini 10.00

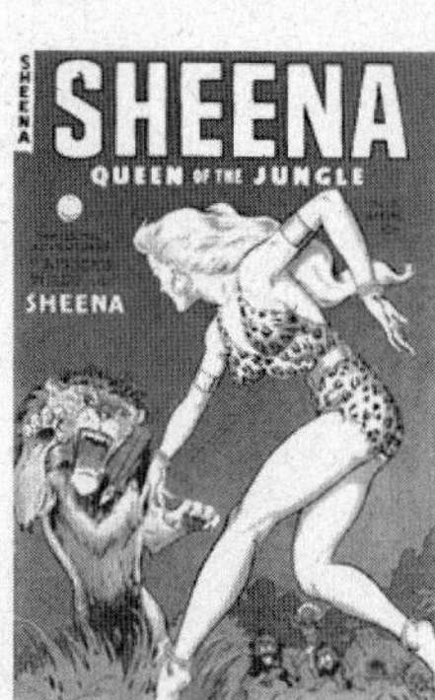

Sheena, Queen of the Jungle #15 © FH

She-Hulk (2005 series) #3 (#100) © MAR

Sherry the Showgirl #1 © MAR

GD VG FN VF VF/NM NM-
2.0 4.0 6.0 8.0 9.0 9.2

SHAZAM!: THE MONSTER SOCIETY OF EVIL
DC Comics: 2007 - No. 4, 2007 ($5.99, square-bound, limited series)
1-4: Jeff Smith-s/a/c in all. 1-Retelling of origin. 2-Mary Marvel & Dr. Sivana app. 6.00
HC (2007, $29.99, over-sized with dust jacket that unfolds to a poster) r/#1-4; Alex Ross intro.; Smith afterword; sketch pages, script pages and production notes 30.00
SC (2009, $19.99) r/#1-4; Alex Ross intro. 20.00

SHAZAM: THE NEW BEGINNING
DC Comics: Apr, 1987 - No. 4, July, 1987 (Legends spin-off) (Limited series)
1-4: 1-New origin & 1st modern app. Captain Marvel; Marvel Family cameo. 2-4-Sivana & Black Adam app. 4.00

SHEA THEATRE COMICS
Shea Theatre: No date (1940's) (32 pgs.)
nn-Contains Rocket Comics; MLJ cover in one color 11 22 33 62 86 110

SHE-BAT (See Murcielaga, She-Bat & Valeria the She-Bat)

SHE-DRAGON (See Savage Dragon #117)
Image Comics: July, 2006 ($5.99, one-shot)
nn- She-Dragon in Dimension-X; origin retold; Franchesco-a/Larsen-s; sketch pages 6.00

SHEENA (Movie)
Marvel Comics: Dec, 1984 - No. 2, Feb, 1985 (limited series)
1,2-r/Marvel Comics Super Special #34; Tanya Roberts movie 4.00

SHEENA, QUEEN OF THE JUNGLE (See Jerry Iger's Classic..., Jumbo Comics, & 3-D Sheena)
Fiction House Magazines: Spr, 1942; No. 2, Wint, 1942-43; No. 3, Spr, 1943; No. 4, Fall, 1948; No. 5, Sum, 1949; No. 6, Spr, 1950; No. 7-10, 1950(nd); No. 11, Spr, 1951 - No. 18, Wint, 1952-53 (#1-3: 68 pgs.; #4-7: 52 pgs.)
1-Sheena begins 284 568 852 1818 3109 4400
2 (Winter, 1942-43) 129 258 387 826 1413 2000
3 (Spring, 1943) 97 194 291 621 1061 1500
4,5 (Fall, 1948, Sum, 1949): 4-New logo; cover swipe from Jumbo #20 54 108 162 343 574 825
6,7 (Spring, 1950, 1950) 45 90 135 284 480 675
8-10(1950 - Win/50, 36 pgs.) 41 82 123 256 428 600
11-17: 15-Cover swipe from Jumbo #43 37 74 111 222 361 500
18-Used in **POP**, pg. 98 39 78 117 240 395 550
I.W. Reprint #9-r/#18; c-r/White Princess #3 4 8 12 28 44 60
NOTE: ***Baker** c-5-10? **Whitman** c-11-18(most).*

SHEENA, QUEEN OF THE JUNGLE
Devil's Due Publishing: Mar, 2007; Jun, 2007 - No. 5, Jan, 2008 (99¢/$3.50)
1-5: 1-Rodi-s/Merhoff-a; 5 covers 3.50
... 99¢ Special (3/07) Revival of the character; Rodi-s/Cummings-a; sketch pages; history 3.00
...: Dark Rising (10/08 - No. 3, 12/08) 1-3 3.50
... Trail of the Mapinguari (4/08, $5.50) Two covers 5.50

SHEENA 3-D SPECIAL (Also see Blackthorne 3-D Series #1)
Eclipse Comics: Jan, 1985 ($2.00)
1-Dave Stevens-c 1 2 3 5 6 8

SHE-HULK (Also see The Savage She-Hulk & The Sensational She-Hulk)
Marvel Comics: May, 2004 - No. 12, Apr, 2005 ($2.99)
1-4-Bobillo-a/Slott-s/Granov-c. 1-Avengers app. 4-Spider-Man-c/app. 3.00
5-12: Mayhew-c. 9-12-Pelletier-a. 10-Origin of Titania 3.00
Vol. 1: Single Green Female TPB (2004, $14.99) r/#1-6 15.00
Vol. 2: Superhuman Law TPB (2005, $14.99) r/#7-12 15.00

SHE-HULK (2nd series)
Marvel Comics: Dec, 2005 - No. 38, Apr, 2009 ($2.99)
1,2,4-7,9-24: 1-Bobillo-a/Slott-s/Horn-c. 1-New Avengers app. 2-Hawkeye-c/app. 9-Jen marries John Jameson. 12-Thanos app. 16-Wolverine app. 3.00
3-($3.99) 100th She-Hulk issue; new story w/art by various incl. Bobillo, Conner, Mayhew & Powell; r/Savage She-Hulk #1 and r/Sensational She-Hulk #1 4.00
8-Civil War 15.00
8-2nd printing with variant Bobillo-c 3.00
25-($3.99) Intro. the Behemoth; Juggernaut cameo; Handbook bio pages of She-Hulk 4.00
26-37: 27-Iron Man app. 30-Hercules app. 31-X-Factor app. 32,33-Secret Invasion 3.00
38-($3.99) Thundra, Valkyrie and Invisible Woman app. 4.00
...: Cosmic Collision 1 (2/09, $3.99) Lady Liberators app.; David-s/Asrar-a/Sejic-c 4.00
... Sensational 1 (5/10, $4.99) 30th Anniversary celebration; Stan Lee app.; Frank-c 5.00
Vol. 3: Time Trials (2006, $14.99) r/#1-5; Bobillo sketch page 15.00
Vol. 4: Laws of Attraction (2007, $19.99) r/#6-12; Paul Smith sketch page 20.00
Vol. 5: Planet Without a Hulk (2007, $19.99) r/#14-21; Slott's original series pitch 20.00
...: Jaded HC (2008, $19.99) r/#22-27; cover gallery 20.00

SHE-HULKS
Marvel Comics: Jan, 2011 - No. 4, Apr, 2011 ($3.99/$2.99, limited series)
1-($3.99) She-Hulk & Lyra team-up; Stegman-a/McGuinness-c; character profile pages 4.00
2-4-($2.99) McGuinness-c 3.00

SHERIFF BOB DIXON'S CHUCK WAGON (TV) (See Wild Bill Hickok #22)
Avon Periodicals: Nov, 1950
1-Kinstler-c/a(3) 14 28 42 80 115 150

SHERIFF OF TOMBSTONE
Charlton Comics: Nov, 1958 - No. 17, Sept, 1961
V1#1-Giordano-c; Severin-a 6 12 18 41 66 90
2 4 8 12 22 34 45
3-10 3 6 9 17 25 32
11-17 3 6 9 14 20 25

SHERLOCK HOLMES (See Marvel Preview, New Adventures of..., & Spectacular Stories)

SHERLOCK HOLMES (All New Baffling Adventures of...)(Young Eagle #3 on?)
Charlton Comics: Oct, 1955 - No. 2, Mar, 1956
1-Dr. Neff, Ghost Breaker app. 40 80 120 243 402 560
2 35 70 105 208 339 470

SHERLOCK HOLMES (Also see The Joker)
National Periodical Publications: Sept-Oct, 1975
1-Cruz-a; Simonson-c 3 6 9 16 23 30

SHERLOCK HOLMES
Dynamite Entertainment: 2009 - No. 5, 2009 ($3.50, limited series)
1-5-Cassaday-c/Moore & Reppion-s/Aaron Campbell-a 3.50

SHERLOCK HOLMES: YEAR ONE
Dynamite Entertainment: 2011 - No. 6, 2011 ($3.99, limited series)
1-6-Beatty-s; multiple covers on each 4.00

SHERRY THE SHOWGIRL (Showgirls #4)
Atlas Comics: July, 1956 - No. 3, Dec, 1956; No. 5, Apr, 1957 - No. 7, Aug, 1957
1-Dan DeCarlo-c/a in all 20 40 60 117 189 260
2 14 28 42 80 115 150
3,5-7 13 26 39 72 101 130

SHE'S JOSIE (See Josie)

SHEVA'S WAR
DC Comics (Helix): Oct, 1998 - No. 5, Feb, 1999 ($2.95, mini-series)
1-5-Christopher Moeller-s/painted-a/c 3.00

SHI (one-shots and TPBs)
Crusade Comics
...: Akai (2001, $2.99)-Intro. Victoria Cross; Tucci-a/c; J.C. Vaughn-s 3.00
...: Akai Victoria Cross Ed. ($5.95, edition of 2000) variant Tucci-c 6.00
...: C.G.I. (2001, $4.99) preview of unpublished series 5.00
.../ Cyblade: The Battle for the Independents (9/95, $2.95) Tucci-c; Hellboy, Bone app. 3.00
.../ Cyblade: The Battle for the Independents (9/95, $2.95) Silvestri variant-c 3.00
.../ Daredevil: Honor Thy Mother (1/97, $2.95) Flip book 3.00
...: Judgment Night (200, $3.99) Wolverine app.; Battlebook card and pages; Tucci-a 4.00
...: Kaidan (10/96, $2.95) Two covers; Tucci-c; Jae Lee wraparound-c 3.00
...: Masquerade (3/98, $3.50) Painted art by Lago, Texeira, and others 3.50
...: Nightstalkers (9/97, $3.50) Painted art by Val Mayerik 3.50
...: Rekishi (1/97, $2.95) Character bios and story summaries of Shi: The Way of the Warrior told in Detective Joe Labianca's point of view; Christopher Golden script; Tucci-c; J.G. Jones-a; flip book w/Shi: East Wind Rain preview 3.00
...: The Art of War Tourbook (1998, $4.95) Blank cover for sketches; early Tucci-a inside 5.00
.../ Vampirella (10/97, $2.95) Ellis-s/Lau-a 3.00
... Vs. Tomoe (8/96, $3.95) Tucci-a/scripts; wraparound foil-c 4.00
... Vs. Tomoe (6/96, $5.00. B&W)-Preview Ed.; sold at San Diego Comic Con 5.00
The Definitive Shi Vol. 1 (2006-2007, $24.99, TPB) B&W r/Way of the Warrior, Tomoe, Rekishi, and Senryaku series; cover gallery with sketches; Tucci & Sparacio-c 25.00

SHI: BLACK, WHITE AND RED
Crusade Comics: Mar, 1998 - No. 2, May, 1998 ($2.95, B&W&Red, mini-series)
1,2-J.G. Jones-painted art 3.00
...- Year of the Dragon Collected Edition (2000, $5.95) r/#1&2 6.00

SHIDIMA
Image Comics: Jan, 2001 - No. 7, Nov, 2002 ($2.95, limited series)
1-7-Prequel to Warlands 3.00
#0-(10/01, $2.25) Short story and sketch pages 3.00

SHI: EAST WIND RAIN

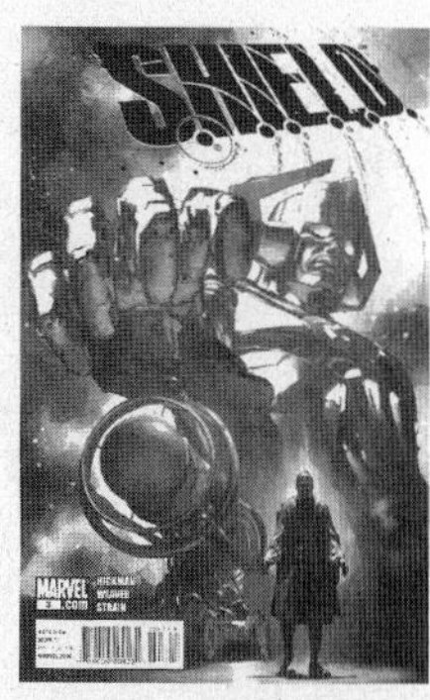
S.H.I.E.L.D. #3 © MAR

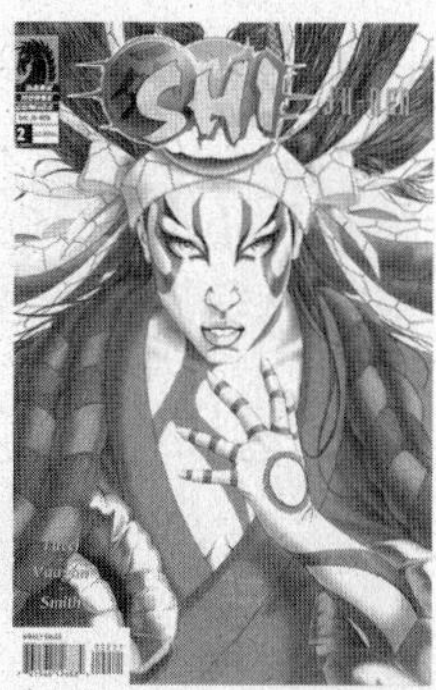
Shi: Ju-Nen #2 © Billy Tucci

Shinku #1 © Marz & Moder

	GD 2.0	VG 4.0	FN 6.0	VF 8.0	VF/NM 9.0	NM- 9.2

Crusade Comics: Nov, 1997 - No. 2, Feb, 1998 ($3.50, limited series)

1,2-Shi at WW2 Pearl Harbor 3.50

S.H.I.E.L.D. (Nick Fury & His Agents of...) (Also see Nick Fury)
Marvel Comics Group: Feb, 1973 - No. 5, Oct, 1973 (All 20¢ issues)

1-All contain reprint stories from Strange Tales #146-155; new Steranko-c 3 6 9 16 22 28
2-New Steranko flag-c 2 4 6 11 16 20
3-5: 3-Kirby/Steranko-c(r). 4-Steranko-c(r) 2 4 6 8 11 14
NOTE: *Buscema a-3p(r). Kirby layouts 1-5; c-3 (w/Steranko). Steranko a-3r, 4r(2).*

S.H.I.E.L.D.
Marvel Comics: Jun, 2010 - No. 6, Apr, 2011; Aug, 2011 - Present ($3.99/$2.99)

1-($3.99) Leonardo DaVinci app.; Weaver-a/Hickman-s/Parel-c; 4 printings 4.00
1-Variant-c by Weaver 6.00
1-Director's Cut (9/10, $4.99) r/#1 with character sketch-a and bios; design-a 5.00
2-6-($2.99) 2-Three printings. 3-Galactus app. 3.00
Infinity (6/11, $4.99) DaVinci, Nostradamus, Newton & Tesla app.; Parel-c 5.00
1 (2nd series) (8/11, $3.99) Weaver-a/Hickman-s/Parel-c; profile pgs of main characters 4.00
2-4-($2.99) 3.00

SHIELD, THE (Becomes Shield-Steel Sterling #3; #1 titled Lancelot Strong; also see Advs. of the Fly, Double Life of Private Strong, Fly Man, Mighty Comics, The Mighty Crusaders, The Original... & Pep Comics #1)
Archie Enterprises, Inc.: June, 1983 - No. 2, Aug, 1983

1,2: Steel Sterling app. 2-Kanigher-s 5.00
America's 1st Patriotic Comic Book Hero, The Shield (2002, $12.95, TPB) r/Pep Comics #1-5, Shield-Wizard Comics #1; foreward by Robert M. Overstreet 13.00

SHIELD, THE (Archie Ent. character) (Continued from The Red Circle)
DC Comics: Nov, 2009 - No. 10, Aug, 2010 ($3.99)

1-10: 1-Magog app.; Inferno back-up feature thru #6; Green Arrow app. 2,3-Grodd app. 7-10-The Fox back-up feature; Oeming-a 4.00
...: Kicking Down the Door TPB ('10, $19.99) r/#1-6, Red Circle: The Web & RC: The Shield 20.00

SHIELD, THE: SPOTLIGHT (TV)
IDW Publishing: Jan, 2004 - No. 5, May, 2004 ($3.99)

1-5-Jeff Marriote-s/Jean Diaz-a/Tommy Lee Edwards-c 4.00
TPB (7/04, $19.99) r/#1-5; Michael Chiklis photo-c 20.00

SHIELD-STEEL STERLING (Formerly The Shield)
Archie Enterprises, Inc.: No. 3, Dec, 1983 (Becomes Steel Sterling No. 4)

3-Nino-a; Steel Sterling by Kanigher & Barreto 3.00

SHIELD WIZARD COMICS (Also see Pep Comics & Top-Notch Comics)
MLJ Magazines: Summer, 1940 - No. 13, Spring, 1944

1-(V1#5 on inside)-Origin The Shield by Irving Novick & The Wizard by Ed Ashe, Jr; Flag-c 514 1028 1542 3750 6625 9500
2-(Winter/40)-Origin The Shield retold; Wizard's sidekick, Roy the Super Boy begins (see Top-Notch #8 for 1st app.) 271 542 813 1734 2967 4200
3,4 174 348 522 1114 1907 2700
5-Dusty, the Boy Detective begins; Nazi bondage-c 155 310 465 992 1696 2400
6,7: 6-Roy the Super Boy app. 7-Shield dons new costume (Summer, 1942); S & K-c? 148 296 444 947 1624 2300
8-Nazi bondage-c; Hitler photo on-c 168 336 504 1075 1838 2600
9-Japanese WWII bondage-c 116 232 348 742 1271 1800
10-Nazi swastica-c 123 246 369 787 1344 1900
11,12 103 206 309 659 1130 1600
13-Japanese WWII bondage/torture-c (scarce) 129 258 387 826 1413 2000
NOTE: *Bob Montana c-13. Novick c-1,3-6,8-11. Harry Sahle c-12.*

SHI: FAN EDITIONS
Crusade Comics: 1997

1-3-Two covers polybagged in FAN #19-21 3.00
1-3-Gold editions 4.00

SHI: HEAVEN AND EARTH
Crusade Comics: June, 1997 - No. 4, Apr, 1998 ($2.95)

1-4 3.00
4-($4.95) Pencil-c variant 5.00
Rising Sun Edition-signed by Tucci in FanClub Starter Pack 4.00
"Tora No Shi" variant-c 3.00

SHI: JU-NEN
Dark Horse Comics: July, 2004 - No. 4, May, 2005 ($2.99, mini-series)

1-4-Tucci-a/Tucci & Vaughn-s; origin retold 3.00
TPB (2/06, $12.95) r/#1-4; Tucci and Sparacio-c 13.00

SHINING KNIGHT (See Adventure Comics #66)

SHINKU
Image Comics: Jun, 2011 - Present ($2.99)

1-4-Marz-s/Moder-a 3.00

SHINOBI (Based on Sega video game)
Dark Horse Comics: Aug, 2002 ($2.99, one-shot)

1-Medina-a/c 3.00

SHIP AHOY
Spotlight Publishers: Nov, 1944 (52 pgs.)

1-L. B. Cole-c 19 38 57 111 176 240

SHIP OF FOOLS
Image Comics: Aug, 1997 - No. 3 ($2.95, B&W)

0-3-Glass-s/Oeming-a 3.00

SHI: POISONED PARADISE
Avatar Press: July, 2002 - No. 2, Aug, 2002 ($3.50, limited series)

1,2-Vaughn and Tucci-s/Waller-a; 1-Four covers 3.50

SHIPWRECKED! (Disney-Movie)
Disney Comics: 1990 ($5.95, graphic novel, 68 pgs.)

nn-adaptation; Spiegle-a 6.00

SHI: SEMPO
Avatar Press: Aug, 2003 - No. 2, ($3.50, B&W, limited series)

1,2-Vaughn and Tucci-s/Alves-a; 1-Four covers 3.50

SHI: SENRYAKU
Crusade Comics: Aug, 1995 - No. 3, Nov, 1995 ($2.95, limited series)

1-3: 1-Tucci-c; Quesada, Darrow, Sim, Lee, Smith-a. 2-Tucci-c; Silvestri, Balent, Perez, Mack-a. 3-Jusko-c; Hughes, Ramos, Bell, Moore-a 3.00
1-variant-c (no logo) 4.00
Hardcover ($24.95)-r/#1-3; Frazetta-c. 25.00
Trade Paperback ($13.95)-r/#1-3; Frazetta-c. 14.00

SHI: THE ILLUSTRATED WARRIOR
Crusade Comics: 2002 - No. 7, 2003 ($2.99, B&W)

1-7-Story text with Tucci full page art 3.00

SHI: THE SERIES
Crusade Comics: Aug, 1997 - No. 13 ($2.95, color #1-10, B&W #11)

1-10 3.00
11-13: 11-B&W. 12-Color; Lau-a 3.00
#0 Convention Edition 5.00

SHI: THE WAY OF THE WARRIOR
Crusade Comics: Mar, 1994 - No. 12, Apr, 1997 ($2.50/$2.95)

1/2 4.00
1 2 4 6 8 10 12
1-Commemorative ed., B&W, new-c; given out at 1994 San Diego Comic Con 2 4 6 10 14 18
1-Fan appreciation edition -r/#1 3.00
1-Fan appreciation edition (variant) 6.00
1- 10th Anniversary Edition (2004, $2.99) 3.00
2 5.00
2-Commemorative edition (3,000) 2 4 6 9 13 16
2-Fan appreciation edition -r/#2 3.00
3 4.00
4-7: 4-Silvestri poster. 7-Tomoe app. 3.00
5,6: 5-Silvestri variant-c. 6-Tomoe #1 variant-c 3.50
5-Gold edition 12.00
6,8-12: 6-Fan appreciation edition 3.00
8-Combo Gold edition 6.00
8-Signed Edition-(5000) 4.00
Trade paperback (1995, $12.95)-r/#1-4 13.00
Trade paperback (1995, $14.95)-r/#1-4 revised; Julie Bell-c 15.00

SHI: YEAR OF THE DRAGON
Crusade Comics: 2000 - No. 3, 2000 ($2.99, limited series)

1-3: 1-Two covers; Tucci-a/c; flashback to teen-aged Ana 3.00

SHMOO (See Al Capp's... & Washable Jones &...)

SHOCK (Magazine)
Stanley Publ.: May, 1969 - V3#4, Sept, 1971 (B&W reprints from horror comics, including some pre-code) (No V2#1,3)

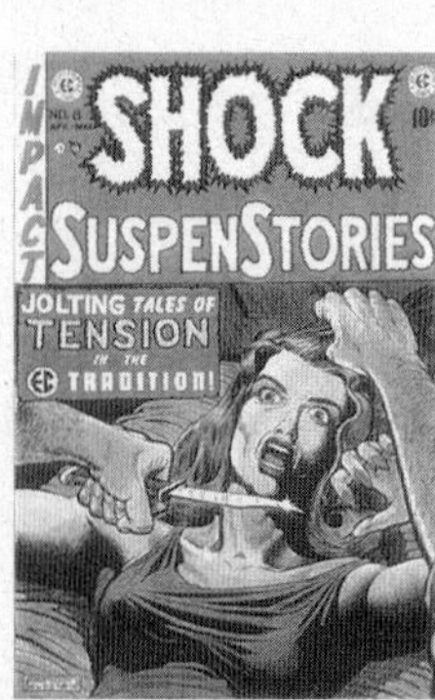

Shock SuspenStories #8 © WMG

Showcase #17 © DC

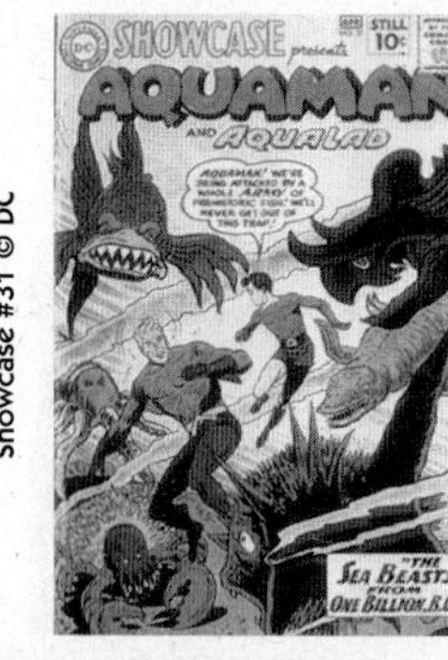

Showcase #31 © DC

GD 2.0 | VG 4.0 | FN 6.0 | VF 8.0 | VF/NM 9.0 | NM- 9.2

V1#1-Cover-r/Weird Tales of the Future #7 by Bernard Baily; r/Weird Chills #1
8 16 24 51 86 120
2-Wolverton-r/Weird Mysteries 5; r-Weird Mysteries #7 used in **SOTI**; cover reprints cover to Weird Chills #1 6 12 18 39 62 85
3,5,6 4 8 12 28 44 60
4-Harrison/Williamson-r/Forbid. Worlds #6 5 10 15 30 48 65
V2#2(5/70), V1#8(7/70), V2#4(9/70)-6(1/71), V3#1-4: V2#4-Cover swipe from Weird Mysteries #6 4 8 12 26 41 55
NOTE: ***Disbrow*** *r-V2#4; Bondage c-V1#4, V2#6, V3#1.*

SHOCK DETECTIVE CASES (Formerly Crime Fighting Detective)
(Becomes Spook Detective Cases No. 22)
Star Publications: No. 20, Sept, 1952 - No. 21, Nov, 1952
20,21-L.B. Cole-c; based on true crime cases 23 46 69 136 223 310
NOTE: ***Palais*** *a-20. No. 21-Fox-r.*

SHOCK ILLUSTRATED (...Adult Crime Stories; Magazine format)
E. C. Comics: Sept-Oct, 1955 - No. 3, Spring, 1956 (Adult Entertainment on-c #1,2)(All 25¢)
1-All by Kamen; drugs, prostitution, wife swapping 19 38 57 111 176 240
2-Williamson-a redrawn from Crime SuspenStories #13 plus Ingels, Crandall, Evans & part Torres-i; painted-c 20 40 60 114 182 250
3-Only 100 known copies bound & given away at E.C. office; Crandall, Evans-a; painted-c; shows May, 1956 on-c 123 246 369 787 1344 1900

SHOCKING MYSTERY CASES (Formerly Thrilling Crime Cases)
Star Publications: No. 50, Sept, 1952 - No. 60, Oct, 1954 (All crime reprints?)
50-Disbrow "Frankenstein" story 43 86 129 271 461 650
51-Disbrow-a 28 56 84 165 270 375
52-60: 56-Drug use story 26 52 78 154 252 350
NOTE: ***L. B. Cole*** *covers on all; a-60(2 pgs.).* ***Hollingsworth*** *a-52.* ***Morisi*** *a-55.*

SHOCKING TALES DIGEST MAGAZINE
Harvey Publications: Oct, 1981 (95¢)
1-1957-58-r; Powell, Kirby, Nostrand-a 2 4 6 9 13 16

SHOCK ROCKETS
Image Comics (Gorilla): Apr, 2000 - No. 6, Oct, 2000 ($2.50)
1-6-Busiek-s/Immonen & Grawbadger-a. 6-Flip book w/Superstar preview 3.00
...: We Have Ignition TPB (Dark Horse, 8/04, $14.95, 6" x 9") r/#1-6 15.00

SHOCK SUSPENSTORIES (Also see EC Archives • Shock SuspenStories)
E. C. Comics: Feb-Mar, 1952 - No. 18, Dec-Jan, 1954-55
1-Classic Feldstein electrocution-c 91 182 273 728 1164 1600
2 49 98 147 392 621 850
3,4: 4-Used in **SOTI**, pg. 387,388 37 74 111 296 473 650
5-Hanging-c 44 88 132 352 564 775
6-Classic hooded vigilante bondage-c 63 126 189 504 802 1100
7-Classic face melting-c 56 112 168 448 717 985
8-Williamson-a 36 72 108 288 457 625
9-11: 9-Injury to eye panel. 10-Junkie story 30 60 90 240 383 525
12- "The Monkey" classic junkie cover/story; anti-drug propaganda issue
40 80 120 320 510 700
13-Frazetta's only solo story for E.C., 7 pgs. 43 86 129 344 547 750
14-Used in Senate Investigation hearings 26 52 78 208 329 450
15-Used in 1954 Reader's Digest article, "For the Kiddies to Read"
23 46 69 184 292 400
16-18: 16- "Red Dupe" editorial; rape story 21 42 63 168 272 375
NOTE: ***Ray Bradbury*** *adaptations-1, 7, 9.* ***Craig*** *a-11; c-11.* ***Crandall*** *a-9-13, 15-18.* ***Davis*** *a-1-5.* ***Evans*** *a-7, 8, 14-18; c-16-18.* ***Feldstein*** *c-1, 7-9, 12.* ***Ingels*** *a-1, 2, 6.* ***Kamen*** *a-in all; c-10, 13, 15.* ***Krigstein*** *a-14, 18.* ***Orlando*** *a-1, 3-7, 9, 10, 12, 16, 17.* ***Wood*** *a-2-15; c-2-6, 14.*

SHOCK SUSPENSTORIES (Also see EC Archives • Shock SuspenStories)
Russ Cochran/Gemstone Publishing: Sept, 1992 - No. 18, Dec, 1996 ($1.50/$2.00/$2.50, quarterly)
1-18: 1-3: Reprints with original-c. 17-r/HOF #17 3.00

SHOGUN WARRIORS
Marvel Comics Group: Feb, 1979 - No. 20, Sept, 1980 (Based on Mattel toys of the classic Japanese animation characters) (1-3: 35¢; 4-19: 40¢; 20: 50¢)
1-Raydeen, Combatra, & Dangard Ace begin; Trimpe-a
2 4 6 9 12 15
2-20: 2-Lord Maurkon & Elementals of Evil app.; Rok-Korr app. 6-Shogun vs. Shogun. 7,8-Cerberus. 9-Starchild. 11-Austin-c. 12-Simonson-c. 14-16-Doctor Demonicus. 17-Juggernaut. 19,20-FF x-over 2 3 4 6 8 10

SHOOK UP (Magazine) (Satire)
Dodsworth Publ. Co.: Nov, 1958
V1#1 4 8 12 28 44 60

SHORT RIBS
Dell Publishing Co.: No. 1333, Apr - June, 1962
Four Color 1333 5 10 15 35 55 75

SHORTSTOP SQUAD (Baseball)
Ultimate Sports Ent. Inc.: 1999 ($3.95, one-shot)
1-Ripken Jr., Larkin, Jeter, Rodriguez app.; Edwards-c/a 4.00

SHORT STORY COMICS (See Hello Pal,...)

SHORTY SHINER (The Five-Foot Fighter in the Ten Gallon Hat)
Dandy Magazine (Charles Biro): June, 1956 - No. 3, Oct, 1956
1 7 14 21 37 46 55
2,3 5 10 15 24 30 35

SHOTGUN SLADE (TV)
Dell Publishing Co.: No. 1111, July-Sept, 1960
Four Color 1111-Photo-c 6 12 18 41 66 90

SHOWCASE (See Cancelled Comic Cavalcade & New Talent...)
National Per. Publ./DC Comics: 3-4/56 - No. 93, 9/70; No. 94, 8-9/77 - No. 104, 9/78
1-Fire Fighters; w/Fireman Farrell 275 550 825 2310 5005 7700
2-Kings of the Wild; Kubert-a (animal stories) 89 178 267 721 1561 2400
3-The Frogmen by Russ Heath; Heath greytone-c (early DC example, 7-8/56)
93 186 279 753 1627 2500
4-Origin/1st app. The Flash (1st DC Silver Age hero, Sept-Oct, 1956); Kanigher-s; Infantino & Kubert-c/a; 1st app. Iris West and The Turtle; r/in Secret Origins #1 ('61 & '73); Flash shown reading G.A. Flash Comics #13; back-up story w/Broome-s/Infantino & Kubert-a
1750 3500 5250 18,500 39,250 60,000
5-Manhunters; Meskin-a 87 174 261 705 1528 2350
6-Origin/1st app. Challengers of the Unknown by Kirby, partly r/in Secret Origins #1 & Challengers #64,65 (1st S.A. hero team & 1st original concept S.A. series)(1-2/57)
293 586 879 2550 5525 8500
7-Challengers of the Unknown by Kirby (2nd app.) reprinted in Challengers of the Unknown #75 146 292 438 1226 2663 4100
8-The Flash (5-6/57, 2nd app.); origin & 1st app. Captain Cold
840 1680 2520 7600 13,050 18,500
9-Lois Lane (Pre-#1, 7-8/57) (1st Showcase character to win own series)
Superman app. on-c 660 1320 1980 5280 9640 14,000
10-Lois Lane; Jor-El cameo; Superman app. on-c 229 458 687 1924 4162 6400
11-Challengers of the Unknown by Kirby (3rd) 139 278 417 1126 2438 3750
12-Challengers of the Unknown by Kirby (4th) 139 278 417 1126 2438 3750
13-The Flash (3rd app.); origin Mr. Element 303 606 909 2636 5718 8800
14-The Flash (4th app.); origin Dr. Alchemy, former Mr. Element (rare in NM)
324 648 972 2819 6110 9400
15-Space Ranger (7-8/58, 1st app., also see My Greatest Adventure #22)
154 308 462 1294 2797 4300
16-Space Ranger (9-10/58, 2nd app.) 76 152 228 616 1333 2050
17-(11-12/58)-Adventures on Other Worlds; origin/1st app. Adam Strange by Gardner Fox & Mike Sekowsky 204 408 612 1714 3707 5700
18-Adventures on Other Worlds (2nd A. Strange) 93 186 279 753 1627 2500
19-Adam Strange; 1st Adam Strange logo 104 208 312 842 1821 2800
20-Rip Hunter; origin & 1st app. (5-6/59); Moreira-a 85 170 255 689 1495 2300
21-Rip Hunter (7-8/59, 2nd app.); Sekowsky-c/a 46 92 138 345 748 1150
22-Origin & 1st app. Silver Age Green Lantern by Gil Kane and John Broome (9-10/59); reprinted in Secret Origins #2 700 1400 2800 8000 16,000 24,000
23-Green Lantern (11-12/59, 2nd app.); nuclear explosion-c
179 358 537 1500 3250 5000
24-Green Lantern (1-2/60, 3rd app.) 161 322 483 1352 2926 4500
25,26-Rip Hunter by Kubert. 25-Grey tone-c 38 76 114 285 618 950
27-Sea Devils (7-8/60, 1st app.); Heath-c/a; Grey tone-c
78 156 234 632 1366 2100
28-Sea Devils (9-10/60, 2nd app.); Heath-c/a; Grey tone-c
39 78 117 293 634 975
29-Sea Devils; Heath-c/a; grey tone c-27-29 42 84 126 315 683 1050
30-Origin Silver Age Aquaman (1-2/61) (see Adventure #260 for 1st S.A. origin)
74 148 222 600 1300 2000
31,32-Aquaman 39 78 117 293 634 975
33-Aquaman 39 78 117 293 634 975
34-Origin & 1st app. Silver Age Atom by Gil Kane & Murphy Anderson (9-10/61); reprinted in Secret Origins #2 111 222 333 900 1950 3000
35-The Atom by Gil Kane (2nd); last 10¢ issue 52 104 156 421 911 1400
36-The Atom by Gil Kane (1-2/62, 3rd app.) 42 84 126 315 683 1050
37-Metal Men (3-4/62, 1st app.) 57 114 171 462 994 1525
38-Metal Men (5-6/62, 2nd app.) 32 64 96 228 494 760
39-Metal Men (7-8/62, 3rd app.) 25 50 75 171 366 560

Showcase #97 © DC

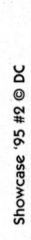

Showcase '95 #2 © DC

Showcase Presents: The Doom Patrol Vol. 2 © DC

	GD 2.0	VG 4.0	FN 6.0	VF 8.0	VF/NM 9.0	NM- 9.2
40-Metal Men (9-10/62, 4th app.)	22	44	66	154	327	500
41,42-Tommy Tomorrow (parts 1 & 2). 42-Origin	14	28	42	93	202	310
43-Dr. No (James Bond); Nodel-a; originally published as British Classics Illustrated #158A & as #6 in a European Detective series, all with diff. painted-c. This Showcase #43 version is actually censored, deleting all racial skin color and dialogue thought to be racially demeaning (1st DC S.A. movie adaptation)(based on Ian Fleming novel & movie)	46	92	138	345	748	1150
44-Tommy Tomorrow	11	22	33	73	142	210
45-Sgt. Rock (7-8/63); pre-dates B&B #52; origin retold; Heath-c	34	68	102	247	536	825
46,47-Tommy Tomorrow	10	20	30	68	127	185
48,49-Cave Carson (3rd tryout series; see B&B)	9	18	27	61	106	150
50,51-I Spy (Danger Trail-r by Infantino), King Farady story (#50 has new 4 pg. story)	8	16	24	55	93	130
52-Cave Carson	8	16	24	56	96	135
53,54-G.I. Joe (11-12/64, 1-2/65); Heath-a	11	22	33	73	142	210
55-Dr. Fate & Hourman (3-4/65); origin of each in text; 1st solo app. G.A. Green Lantern in Silver Age (pre-dates Gr. Lantern #40); 1st S.A. app. Solomon Grundy	22	44	66	154	327	500
56-Dr. Fate & Hourman	13	26	39	87	186	285
57-Enemy Ace by Kubert (7-8/65, 4th app. after Our Army at War #155)	20	40	60	137	294	450
58-Enemy Ace by Kubert (5th app.)	16	32	48	109	237	365
59-Teen Titans (11-12/65, 3rd app.)	15	30	45	102	221	340
60-1st S. A. app. The Spectre; Anderson-a (1-2/66); origin in text	25	50	75	175	375	575
61-The Spectre by Anderson (2nd app.)	13	26	39	85	180	275
62-Origin & 1st app. Inferior Five (5-6/66)	9	18	27	63	112	160
63,65-Inferior Five. 63-Hulk parody. 65-X-Men parody (11-12/66)	6	12	18	42	69	95
64-The Spectre by Anderson (5th app.)	12	24	36	84	175	265
66,67-B'wana Beast	6	12	18	41	66	90
68-Maniaks (1st app., spoof of The Monkees)	6	12	18	41	66	90
69,71-Maniaks. 71-Woody Allen-c/app.	6	12	18	39	62	85
70-Binky (9-10/67)-Tryout issue; 1950's Leave It To Binky reprints with art changes	6	12	18	42	69	95
72-Top Gun (Johnny Thunder-r)-Toth-a	5	10	15	35	55	75
73-Origin/1st app. Creeper; Ditko-c/a (3-4/68)	11	22	33	76	151	225
74-Intro/1st app. Anthro; Post-c/a (5/68)	8	16	24	56	96	135
75-Origin/1st app. Hawk & the Dove; Ditko-c/a	11	22	33	71	136	200
76-1st app. Bat Lash (8/68)	8	16	24	56	96	135
77-1st app. Angel & The Ape (9/68)	7	14	21	48	79	110
78-1st app. Jonny Double (11/68)	5	10	15	32	51	70
79-1st app. Dolphin (12/68); Aqualad origin-r	6	12	18	42	69	95
80-1st S.A. app. Phantom Stranger (1/69); Neal Adams-c	10	20	30	68	127	185
81-Windy & Willy; r/Many Loves of Dobie Gillis #26 with art changes	6	12	18	39	62	85
82-1st app. Nightmaster (5/69) by Grandenetti & Giordano; Kubert-c	7	14	21	48	79	110
83,84-Nightmaster by Wrightson w/Jones/Kaluta ink assist in each; Kubert-c. 83-Last 12¢ issue 84-Origin retold; begin 15¢	7	14	21	48	79	110
85-87-Firehair; Kubert-a	3	6	9	16	23	30
88-90-Jason's Quest: 90-Manhunter 2070 app.	3	6	9	14	20	25
91-93-Manhunter 2070: 92-Origin. 93-(9/70) Last 15¢ issue	3	6	9	14	20	25
94-Intro/origin new Doom Patrol & Robotman(8-9/77)	2	4	6	11	16	20
95,96-The Doom Patrol. 95-Origin Celsius	2	3	4	6	8	10
97-99-Power Girl; origin-97,98; JSA cameos	2	4	6	8	10	12
100-(52 pgs.)-Most Showcase characters featured	2	4	6	11	16	20
101-103-Hawkman; Adam Strange x-over	2	3	4	6	8	10
104-(52 pgs.)-O.S.S. Spies at War	2	3	4	6	8	10

NOTE: ***Anderson*** *a-22-24i, 34-36i, 55, 56, 60, 61, 64, 101-103i; c-50i, 51i, 55, 56, 60, 61, 64.* ***Aparo*** *c-94-96.* ***Boring*** *c-10.* ***Estrada*** *a-104.* ***Fraden*** *c(p)-30, 31, 33.* ***Heath*** *c-3, 27-29.* ***Infantino*** *c/a(p)-4, 8, 13, 14; c-50p, 51p.* ***Gil Kane*** *a-22-24p, 34-36p; c-17-19, 22-24p(w/****Giella****), 31.* ***Kane/Anderson*** *c-34-36.* ***Kirby*** *c-11, 12.* ***Kirby/Stein*** *c-6, 7.* ***Kubert*** *a-2, 4i, 25, 26, 45, 53, 54, 72; c-25, 26, 53, 54, 57, 58, 82-87, 101-104; c-2, 4i.* ***Moreira*** *c-5.* ***Orlando*** *a-62p, 63p, 97i; c-62, 63, 97i.* ***Sekowsky*** *a-65p.* ***Sparling*** *a-78.* ***Staton*** *a-94, 95-99p, 100; c-97-100p.*

SHOWCASE '93

DC Comics: Jan, 1993 - No. 12, Dec, 1993 ($1.95, limited series, 52 pgs.)

1-12: 1-Begin 4 part Catwoman story & 6 part Blue Devil story; begin Cyborg story; Art Adams/Austin-c. 3-Flash by Charest (p). 6-Azrael in Bat-costume (2 pgs.). 7,8-Knightfall parts 13 & 14. 6-10-Deathstroke app. (6,10-cameo). 9,10-Austin-i. 10-Azrael as Batman in new costume app.; Gulacy-c. 11-Perez-c. 12-Creeper app.; Alan Grant scripts 4.00

NOTE: ***Chaykin*** *c-9.* ***Fabry*** *c-8.* ***Giffen*** *a-12.* ***Golden*** *c-3.* ***Zeck*** *c-6.*

GD 2.0 VG 4.0 FN 6.0 VF 8.0 VF/NM 9.0 NM- 9.2

SHOWCASE '94

DC Comics: Jan, 1994 - No. 12, Dec, 1994 ($1.95, limited series, 52 pgs.)

1-12: 1,2-Joker & Gunfire stories. 1-New Gods. 4-Riddler story. 5-Huntress-c/story w/app. new Batman. 6-Huntress-c/story w/app. Robin; Atom story. 7-Penguin story by Peter David, P. Craig Russell, & Michael T. Gilbert; Penguin-c by Jae Lee. 8,9-Scarface origin story by Alan Grant, John Wagner,& Teddy Kristiansen; Prelude to Zero Hour. 10-Zero Hour tie-in story. 11-Man-Bat. 4.00

NOTE: ***Alan Grant*** *scripts-3, 4.* ***Kelley Jones*** *c-12.* ***Mignola*** *c-3.* ***Nebres*** *a(i)-2.* ***Quesada*** *c-10.* ***Russell*** *a-7p.* ***Simonson*** *c-5.*

SHOWCASE '95

DC Comics: Jan, 1995 - No. 12, Dec, 1995 ($2.50/$2.95, limited series)

1-4-Supergirl story. 3-Eradicator-c.; The Question story. 4-Thorn c/story 4.00

5-12: 5-Thorn-c/story; begin $2.95-c. 8-Spectre story. 12-The Shade story by James Robinson & Wade Von Grawbadger; Maitresse story by Claremont & Alan Davis 4.00

SHOWCASE '96

DC Comics: Jan, 1996 - No. 12, Dec, 1996 ($2.95, limited series)

1-12: 1-Steve Geppi cameo. 3-Black Canary & Lois Lane-c/story; Deadman story by Jamie Delano & Wade Von Grawbadger, Gary Frank-c. 4-Firebrand & Guardian-c/story; The Shade & Dr. Fate "Times Past" story by James Robinson & Matt Smith begins, ends #5. 6-Superboy-c/app.; Atom app.; Capt. Marvel (Mary Marvel)-c/app. 8-Supergirl by David & Dodson. 11-Scare Tactics app. 11,12-Legion of Super-Heroes vs. Brainiac. 12-Jesse Quick app. 4.00

SHOWCASE PRESENTS... (B&W archive reprints of DC Silver Age stories)

DC Comics: 2005 - Present ($9.99/$16.99/$17.99/$19.99, B&W, over 500 pgs., squarebound)

Adam Strange Vol. 1 (2007, $16.99) r/Showcase #17-19 & Mystery in Space #53-84 17.00
Ambush Bug (2009, $16.99) r/first app. in DC Comics Presents #52 other early app. 17.00
Aquaman Vol. 1 (2007, $16.99) r/Aquaman #1-6 & other early app. 17.00
Aquaman Vol. 2 (2008, $16.99) r/Aquaman #7-23 & other early app. 17.00
Aquaman Vol. 3 (2009, $16.99) r/Aquaman #24-39 & other early app. 17.00
The Atom Vol. 1 (2007, $16.99) r/Showcase #34-36 & The Atom #1-17 17.00
The Atom Vol. 2 (2008, $16.99) r/The Atom #18-38 17.00
Batgirl Vol. 1 (2007, $16.99) r/early apps. from Detective #359 (1967) thru 1975 17.00
Bat Lash Vol. 1 (2009, $9.99) r/#1-7, Showcase #76, DC Special Series #16, and Jonah Hex #49,51,52 10.00
Batman Vol. 1 (2006, $16.99) r/"new look" from Detective #327-342, Batman #164-174 17.00
Batman Vol. 2 (2007, $16.99) r/"new look" from Detective #343-358, Batman #175-188 17.00
Batman Vol. 3 (2008, $16.99) r/"new look" from Detective #359-375, Batman #189, 190-192,194-197,199-202 17.00
Batman and the Outsiders Vol. 1 (2007, $16.99) r/#1-19, Annual #1; Brave and the Bold #200; and New Teen Titans #37 17.00
Blackhawk Vol. 1 (2008, $16.99) r/#108-127 17.00
Booster Gold Vol. 1 (2008, $16.99) r/#1-25 & Action Comics #594 17.00
The Brave and the Bold Batman Team-ups Vol. 1 (2007, $16.99) r/#59,64,67-71,74-87 17.00
The Brave and the Bold Batman Team-ups Vol. 2 (2007, $16.99) r/#88-108 17.00
The Brave and the Bold Batman Team-ups Vol. 3 (2008, $16.99) r/#109-134 17.00
Challengers of the Unknown Vol. 1 (2006, $16.99) r/#1-17 & Showcase #6,7,11,12 17.00
Challengers of the Unknown Vol. 2 (2008, $16.99) r/#18-37 17.00
DC Comics Presents: The Superman Team-ups Vol. 1 (2009, $17.99) r/#1-26 18.00
Dial H For Hero ('10, $9.99) r/early apps. in House of Mystery #156-173 10.00
Doc Savage ('11, $19.99) r/Doc Savage #1-8 (1975-77 Marvel B&W magazine) 20.00
The Doom Patrol Vol. 1 (2009, $16.99) r/#86-101 and My Greatest Adventure #80-85 17.00
The Doom Patrol Vol. 2 (2010, $19.99) r/#102-121 20.00
The Elongated Man Vol. 1 ('06, $16.99) r/early apps. in Flash & Detective ('60-'68) 17.00
Eclipso Vol. 1 (2009, $9.99) r/stories from House of Secrets #61-80 10.00
Enemy Ace Vol. 1 (2008, $16.99) r/Our Army at War #151 & other early app. 17.00
The Flash Vol. 1 (2007, $16.99) r/Flash Comics #104 (last G.A. issue), Showcase #4,8,13,14 & The Flash #105-119 17.00
The Flash Vol. 2 (2008, $16.99) r/The Flash #120-140 17.00
The Flash Vol. 3 (2009, $16.99) r/The Flash #141-161 17.00
The Flash, The Trial of ... (2011, $19.99) r/The Flash #323-327,329-336,340-350 20.00
The Great Disaster Featuring The Atomic Knights and Hercules Vol. 1 (2007, $16.99) 17.00
Green Arrow Vol. 1 (2006, $16.99) r/Adventure #250-269, Brave and the Bold #50,71,85; Justice League of America #4; World's Finest #95-134,136,138,140 17.00
Green Lantern Vol. 1 (2005, $9.99) r/Showcase #22-24 & Green Lantern #1-17 10.00
Green Lantern Vol. 1 (2010, $19.99) r/Showcase #22-24 & Green Lantern #1-17 20.00
Green Lantern Vol. 2 (2007, $16.99) r/Green Lantern #18-38 17.00
Green Lantern Vol. 3 (2008, $16.99) r/Green Lantern #39-59 17.00
Green Lantern Vol. 4 (2009, $16.99) r/Green Lantern #60-75 17.00
Green Lantern Vol. 5 (2011, $19.99) r/Green Lantern #76-87,89 and back up stories from Flash #217-246 20.00
Haunted Tank Vol. 1 ('06, $16.99) r/G.I. Combat #87-119, Brave & The Bold #52 and Our Army at War #155; Russ Heath-c 17.00

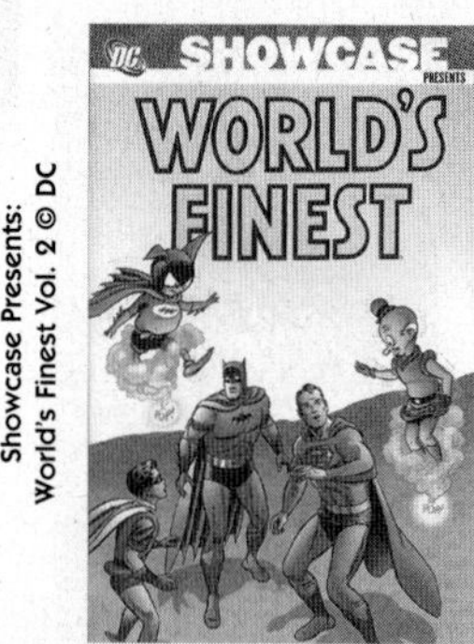

Showcase Presents: World's Finest Vol. 2 © DC

Shrek #2 © Dreamworks

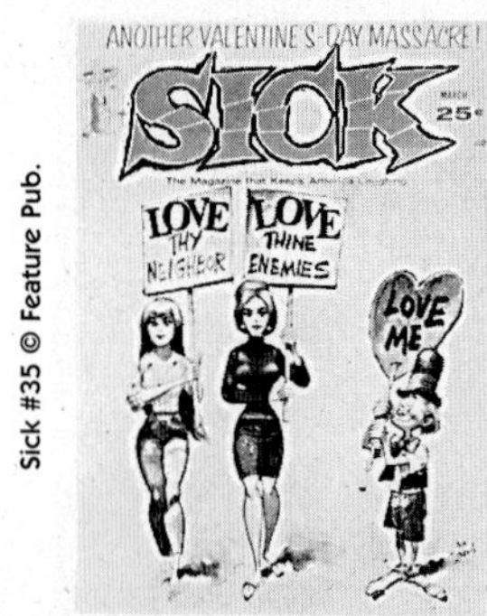

Sick #35 © Feature Pub.

	GD 2.0	VG 4.0	FN 6.0	VF 8.0	VF/NM 9.0	NM- 9.2

Haunted Tank Vol. 2 ('08, $16.99) r/G.I. Combat #120-156 17.00
Hawkman Vol. 1 ('07, $16.99) r/Brave & The Bold #34-36,42-44, Mystery in Space #87-90, Hawkman #1-11, and The Atom #7 17.00
Hawkman Vol. 2 ('08, $16.99) r/Brave & The Bold #70, Hawkman #12-27, The Atom #31, & The Atom and Hawkman #39-45 17.00
The House of Mystery Vol. 1 ('06, $16.99) r/House of Mystery #174-194 ('68-'71) 17.00
The House of Mystery Vol. 2 ('07, $16.99) r/House of Mystery #195-211 ('71-'73) 17.00
The House of Mystery Vol. 3 ('09, $16.99) r/House of Mystery #212-226 ('73-'74) 17.00
The House of Secrets Vol. 1 ('08, $16.99) r/House of Secrets #81-98 ('69-'72) 17.00
The House of Secrets Vol. 2 ('09, $17.99) r/House of Secrets #99-119 ('72-'74) 18.00
Jonah Hex Vol. 1 (2005, $16.99) r/All Star Western #10-12, Weird Western Tales #13,14, 16-33; plus the complete adventures of Outlaw from All Star Western #2-8 17.00
Justice League of America Vol. 1 ('05, $16.99) r/Brave & the Bold #28-30, J.L. of A. #1-16 and Mystery in Space #75 17.00
Justice League of America Vol. 2 ('07, $16.99) r/Justice League of America #17-36 17.00
Justice League of America Vol. 3 ('07, $16.99) r/Justice League of America #37-60 17.00
Justice League of America Vol. 4 ('09, $16.99) r/Justice League of America #61-83 17.00
Justice League of America Vol. 5 ('11, $19.99) r/Justice League of America #84-106 20.00
Legion of Super-Heroes Vol. 1 ('07, $16.99) r/Adventure #247 & early app. thru 1964 17.00
Legion of Super-Heroes Vol. 2 ('08, $16.99) r/app. in Adventure & Superboy 1964-66 17.00
Legion of Super-Heroes Vol. 3 ('09, $16.99) r/Adventure #349-368 & S.P. Jimmy Olsen #106 17.00
Legion of Super-Heroes Vol. 4 ('10, $19.99) r/app. in Adv., Action & Superboy 1968-72 20.00
Martian Manhunter Vol. 1 (2007, $16.99) r/Detective #225-304 & Batman #78 (prototype) 17.00
Martian Manhunter Vol. 2 ('09, $16.99) r/Detective #305-326 & House of Myst. #143-173 17.00
Metal Men Vol. 1 (2007, $16.99) r/#1-16; Brave & Bold #55, Showcase #37-40 17.00
Metamorpho Vol. 1 ('05, $16.99) r/Brave&Bold #57,58,66,68; Metamorpho #1-17;JLA #42 17.00
Our Army at War Vol. 1 ('10, $19.99) r/#1-20 20.00
Phantom Stranger Vol. 1 (2006, $16.99) r/#1-21 (2nd series) & Showcase #80 17.00
Phantom Stranger Vol. 2 (2008, $16.99) r/#22-41 and various 1970-1978 appearances 17.00
Robin The Boy Wonder Vol. 1 (2007, $16.99) r/back-ups from Batman, Detective, WF 17.00
Secrets of Sinister House ('10, $17.99) r/#5-18 and Sinister House of Secret Love #1-4 18.00
Sgt. Rock Vol. 1 ('07, $16.99) r/G.I. Combat #68, Our Army at War #81-117 17.00
Sgt. Rock Vol. 2 ('08, $16.99) r/Our Army at War #118-148 17.00
Sgt. Rock Vol. 3 ('10, $19.99) r/Our Army at War #149-163,165-172,174-176,178-180 20.00
Shazam! Vol. 1 ('06, $16.99) r/#1-33 17.00
Strange Adventures Vol. 1 ('08, $16.99) r/#54-73 17.00
Supergirl Vol. 1 ('07, $16.99) r/prototype from Superman #123 (8/58); 1st app. Action #252 (5/59) and early appearances thru Nov. 1961 17.00
Supergirl Vol. 2 ('08, $16.99) r/appearances in Action Comics #283-321 (1961-1965) 17.00
Superman Vol. 1 ('05, $9.99) r/Action #241-257 & Superman #122-134 (1958-59) 10.00
Superman Vol. 1 ('10, $19.99) r/Action #241-257 & Superman #122-134 (1958-59) 20.00
Superman Vol. 2 ('06, $16.99) r/Action #258-275 & Superman #134-145 (1959-61) 17.00
Superman Vol. 3 ('07, $16.99) r/Action #279-292 & Superman #146-156 & Annual #3,4 17.00
Superman Vol. 4 ('08, $16.99) r/Action #293-309 & Superman #157-166 (1962-64) 17.00
Superman Family Vol. 1 ('06, $16.99) Superman's Pal, Jimmy Olsen #1-22; Showcase #9 and Superman #22 17.00
Superman Family Vol. 2 ('08, $16.99) Superman's Pal, Jimmy Olsen #23-34; Showcase #10 and Superman's Girl Friend, Lois Lane #1-7 17.00
Superman Family Vol. 3 ('09, $16.99) Superman's Pal, Jimmy Olsen #35-44 and Superman's Girl Friend, Lois Lane #8-16 17.00
Teen Titans Vol. 1 ('06, $16.99) r/#1-18; Brave & the Bold #54,60; Showcase #59 17.00
Teen Titans Vol. 2 ('07, $16.99) r/#19-37, World's Finest #205 and Brave & Bold #83,94 17.00
The Unknown Soldier Vol. 1 ('06, $16.99) r/Star Spangled War Stories #158-188 17.00
The War That Time Forgot Vol. 1 ('07, $16.99) r/S.S.W.S. #90,92,94-125,127,128 17.00
Warlord Vol. 1 ('09, $16.99) r/#1-28 and debut in 1st Issue Special #1 17.00
The Witching Hour Vol. 1 ('11, $19.99) r/#1-19 20.00
Wonder Woman Vol. 1 ('07, $16.99) r/#98-117 17.00
Wonder Woman Vol. 2 ('08, $16.99) r/#118-137 17.00
World's Finest Vol. 1 ('07, $16.99) r/#71-111 & Superman #76 17.00
World's Finest Vol. 2 ('08, $16.99) r/#112-145 17.00
World's Finest Vol. 3 ('10, $17.99) r/#146-160,162-169,171-173 ('64-'68) 18.00

SHOWGIRLS (Formerly Sherry the Showgirl #3)
Atlas Comics (MPC No. 2): No. 4, 2/57; June, 1957 - No. 2, Aug, 1957

4-(2/57) Dan DeCarlo-c/a begins 13 26 39 72 101 130
1-(6/57) Millie, Sherry, Chili, Pearl & Hazel begin 14 28 42 82 121 160
2 12 24 36 67 94 120

SHREK (Movie)
Dark Horse Comics: Sept, 2003 - No. 3, Dec, 2003 ($2.99, limited series)

1-3-Takes place after 1st movie; Evanier-s/Bachs-a; CGI cover 4.00

SHREK (Movie)
Ape Entertainment: 2010 - No. 4, 2011 ($3.95, limited series)

1-3-Short stories by various 4.00

	GD 2.0	VG 4.0	FN 6.0	VF 8.0	VF/NM 9.0	NM- 9.2

SHROUD, THE (See Super-Villain Team-Up #5)
Marvel Comics: Mar, 1994 - No. 4, June, 1994 ($1.75, mini-series)

1-4: 1,2,4-Spider-Man & Scorpion app. 3.00

SHROUD OF MYSTERY
Whitman Publications: June, 1982

1 1 2 3 4 5 7

SHRUGGED
Aspen MLT, Inc.: No. 0, June, 2006 - No. 8, Feb, 2009 ($2.50/$2.99)

0-($2.50) Turner & Mastromauro-s/Gunnell-a; intro. story and character profiles 3.00
1-8-($2.99) 1-Six covers. 2-Three covers 3.00
... : Beginnings (5/06, $1.99) Prequel intro. to Ange and Dev; Gunnell-a; development art 3.00

SHUT UP AND DIE
Image Comics/Halloween: 1998 - No. 3, 1998 ($2.95,B&W, bi-monthly)

1-3: Hudnall-s 3.00

SICK (Sick Special #131) (Magazine) (Satire)
Feature Publ./Headline Publ./Crestwood Publ. Co./Hewfred Publ./ Pyramid Comm./Charlton Publ. No. 109 (4/76) on: Aug, 1960 - No. 134, Fall, 1980

V1#1-Jack Paar photo on-c; Torres-a; Untouchables-s; Ben Hur movie photo-s 14 28 42 95 205 315
2-Torres-a; Elvis app.; Lenny Bruce app. 10 20 30 67 124 180
3-5-Torres-a in all. 3-Khruschev-c; Hitler-s. 4-Newhart-s; Castro-s; John Wayne. 5-JFK/Castro-c; Elvis pin-up; Hitler. 9 18 27 61 106 150
6-Photo-s of Ricky Nelson & Marilyn Monroe; JFK 9 18 27 63 112 160
V2#1,2,4-8 (#7,8,10-14): 1-(#7) Hitler-s; Brando photo-s. 2-(#8) Dick Clark-s. 4-(#10) Untouchables-c; Candid Camera-s. 5-(#11) Nixon-c; Lone Ranger-s; JFK-s. 6-(#12) Beatnik-c/s. 8-(#14) Liz Taylor pin-up, JFK-s; Dobie Gillis-s; Sinatra & Dean Martin photo-s 8 16 24 56 96 135
3-(#9) Marilyn Monroe/JFK-c; Kingston Trio-s 9 18 27 61 106 150
V3#1-7(#15-21): 1-(#15) JFK app.; Liz Tayor/Richard Burton-s. 2-(#16) Ben Casey/ Frankenstein-c/s; Hitler photo-s. 5-(#19) Nixon back-c/s; Sinatra photo-s. 6-(#20) 1st Huckleberry Fink-c 5 10 15 35 55 75
8-(#22) Cassius Clay vs. Liston-s; 1st Civil War Blackouts-/Pvt. Bo Reargard w/ Jack Davis-a 6 12 18 39 62 85
V4#1-5 (#23-27): Civil War Blackouts-/Pvt. Bo Reargard w/ Jack Davis-a in all. 1-(#23) Smokey Bear-c; Tarzan-s. 2-(#24) Goldwater & Paar-s; Castro-s. 3-(#25) Frankenstein-c; Cleopatra/Liz Taylor-s; Steve Reeves photo-s. 4-(#26) James Bond-s; Hitler-s. 5-(#27) Taylor/Burton pin-up; Sinatra, Martin, Andress, Ekberg photo-s 4 8 12 28 44 60
28,31,36,39: 31-Pink Panther movie photo-s; Burke's Law-s. 39-Westerns; Elizabeth Montgomery photo-s; Beat mag-s 4 8 12 24 37 50
29,34,37,38: 29-Beatles-c by Jack Davis. 34-Two pg. Beatles-s & photo pin-up. 37-Playboy parody issue. 38-Addams Family-s 4 8 12 28 44 60
30,32,35,40: 30-Beatles photo pin-up; James Bond photo-s. 32-Ian Fleming-s; LBJ-s; Tarzan-s. 35-Beatles cameo; Three Stooges parody. 40-Tarzan-s; Crosby/Hope-s; Beatles parody 5 10 15 30 48 65
33-Ringo Starr photo-c & spoof on "A Hard Day's Night"; inside-c has Beatles photos 6 12 18 41 66 90
41,50,51,53,54,60: 41-Sports Illustrated parody-c/s. 50-Mod issue; flip-c w/1967 calendar w/Bob Taylor-a. 51-Get Smart-s. 53-Beatles cameo; nudity panels. 54-Monkees-c. 60-TV Daniel Boone-s 3 6 9 20 30 40
42-Fighting American-c revised from Simon/Kirby-c; "Good girl" art by Sparling; profile on Bob Powell; superhero parodies 6 12 18 37 59 80
43-49,52,55-59: 43-Sneaker set begins by Sparling. 45-Has #44 on-c & #45 on inside; TV Westerns-s; Beatles cameo. 46-Hell's Angels-s; NY Mets-s. 47-UFO/Space-c. 49-Men's Adventure mag. parody issue; nudity. 52-LBJ-s. 55-Underground culture special. 56-Alfred E. Neuman-c; inventors issue. 58-Hippie issue-c/s. 59-Hippie-s 3 6 9 17 25 32
61-64,66-69,71,73,75-80: 63-Tiny Tim-c & poster; Monkees-s. 64-Flip-c. 66-Flip-c; Mod Squad-s. 69-Beatles cameo; Peter Sellers photo-s. 71-Flip-c; Clint Eastwood-s. 76-Nixon-s; Marcus Welby-s. 78-Ma Barker-s; Courtship of Eddie's Father-s; Abbie Hoffman-s 3 6 9 16 22 28
65,70,74: 65-Cassius Clay/Brando/J. Wayne-c; Johnny Carson-s. 70-(9/69) John & Yoko-c, 1/2 pg. story. 74-Clay, Agnew, Namath & others as superheroes-c/s; Easy Rider-s; Ghost and Mrs. Muir-s 3 6 9 17 25 32
72-(84 pgs.) Xmas issue w/2 pg. slick color poster; Tarzan-s; 2 pg. Superman & superheroes-s 4 8 12 22 34 45
81-85,87-95,98,99: 81-(2/71) Woody Allen photo-s. 85 Monster Mag. parody-s; Nixon-s w/Ringo & John cameo. 88-Klute photo-s; Nixon paper dolls page. 92-Lily Tomlin; Archie Bunker pin-up. 93-Woody Allen 2 4 6 13 18 22
86,96,97,100: 86-John & Yoko, Tiny Tim-c; Love Story movie photo-s. 96-Kung Fu-c;

Siege: Embedded #1 © MAR

Sigil #4 © DIS

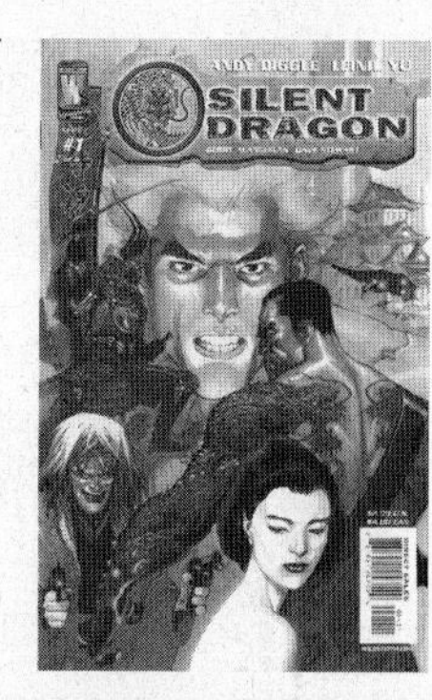

Silent Dragon #1 © Yu & Diggle

GD VG FN VF VF/NM NM-
2.0 4.0 6.0 8.0 9.0 9.2

Mummy-s, Dracula & Frankenstein app. 97-Superman-s; 1974 Calendar; Charlie Brown & Snoopy pin-up. 100-Serpico-s; Cosell-s; Jacques Cousteau-s
3 6 9 14 19 24

101-103,105-114,116,119,120: 101-Three Musketeers-s; Dick Tracy-s. 102-Young Frankenstein-s. 103-Kojak-s; Evel Knievel-s. 105-Towering Inferno-s; Peanuts/Snoopy-s. 106-Cher-c/s. 10 7-Jaws-c/s. 108-Pink Panther-c/s; Archie-s. 109-Adam & Eve-s(nudity). 110-Welcome Back Kotter-s. 111-Sonny & Cher-s. 112-King Kong-c/s. 120-Star Trek-s
2 4 6 9 13 16

104,115,117,118: 104-Muhammad Ali-c/s. 115-Charlie's Angels-s. 117-Bionic Woman & Six Million $ Man-c/s; Cher D'Flower begins by Sparling (nudity). 118-Star Wars-s; Popeye-s
2 4 6 11 16 20

121-125,128-130: 122-Darth Vader-s. 123-Jaws II-s. 128-Superman-c/movie parody. 130-Alien movie-s 2 4 6 10 14 18

126,127: 126-(68 pgs.) Battlestar Galactica-c/s; Star Wars-s; Wonder Woman-s. 127-Mork & Mindy-s; Lord of the Rings-s 2 4 6 13 18 22

131-(1980 Special) Star Wars/Star Trek/Flash Gordon wraparound-c/s; Superman parody; Battlestar Galactica-s 3 6 9 14 19 24

132,133: 132-1980 Election-c/s; Apocalypse Now-s. 133-Star Trek-s; Chips-s; Superheroes page 2 4 6 13 18 22

134 (scarce)(68 pg. Giant)-Star Wars-c; Alien-s; WKRP-s; Mork & Mindy-s; Taxi-s; MASH-s
4 8 12 21 30 40

Annual 1- Birthday Annual (1966)-3 pg. Huckleberry Fink fold out
4 8 12 23 34 50

Annual 2- 7th Annual Yearbook (1967)-Davis-c, 2 pg. glossy poster insert
4 8 12 23 34 50

Annual 3 (1968) "Big Sick Laff-in" on-c (84 pgs.)-w/psychedelic posters; Frankenstein poster
3 6 9 18 27 35

Annual 1969 "Great Big Fat Annual Sick", 1969 "9th Year Annual Sick", 1970, 1971
3 6 9 17 25 32

Annual 12,13-(1972,1973, 84 pgs.) 13-Monster-c 3 6 9 17 25 32
Annual 14,15-(1974,1975, 84 pgs.) 14-Hitler photo-s 3 6 9 17 25 32
Annual 2-4 (1980) 2 4 6 9 13 16
Special 1 (1980) Buck Rogers-c/s; MASH-s 3 6 9 14 19 24
Special 2 (1980) Wraparound Star Wars:Empire Strikes Back-c; Charlie's Angels/Farrah-s; Rocky-s; plus reprints 3 6 9 14 19 24
Yearbook 15(1975, 84 pgs.) Paul Revere-c 3 6 9 16 23 30

NOTE: ***Davis*** *a-42, 87; c-22, 23, 25, 29, 31, 32.* ***Powell*** *a-7, 31, 57.* ***Simon*** *a-1-3, 10, 41, 42, 87, 99; c-1, 47, 57, 59, 69, 91, 95-97, 99, 100, 102, 107, 112.* ***Torres*** *a-1-3, 29, 31, 47, 49.* ***Tuska*** *a-14, 41-43. Civil War Blackouts-23, 24. #42 has biography of Bob Powell.*

SIDEKICK (Paul Jenkins'...)
Image Comics (Desperado): June, 2006 - No. 5, May, 2007 ($3.50, limited series)
1-5-Paul Jenkins-s/Chris Moreno-a 3.50
... Super Summer Sidekick Spectacular 1 (7/07, $2.99) 3.50
... Super Summer Sidekick Spectacular 2 (9/07, $3.50) 3.50

SIDEKICKS
Fanboy Ent., Inc.: Jun, 2000 - No. 3, Apr, 2001 ($2.75, B&W, lim. series)
1-3-J.Torres-s/Takesi Miyazawa-a. 3-Variant-c by Wieringo 3.00
...: Super Fun Summer Special (Oni Press, 7/03, $2.99) art by various incl. Wieringo 3.00
...: The Substitute (Oni Press, 7/02, $2.95) 3.00
...: The Transfer Student TPB (Oni Press, 6/02, $8.95, 9" x 6") r/#1-3 9.00
...: The Transfer Student TPB 2nd Ed. (10/03, $11.95, 9" x 6") r/#1-3; The Substitute 12.00

SIDESHOW
Avon Periodicals: 1949 (one-shot)
1-(Rare)-Similar to Bachelor's Diary 58 116 174 371 636 900

SIEGE
Marvel Comics: Mar, 2010 - No. 4, Jun, 2010 ($3.99, limited series)
1-4-Asgard is invaded; Bendis-s/Coipel-a. 4-End of The Sentry 4.00
1-4-Variant covers by Dell'Otto 8.00
...: Captain America (6/10, $2.99) Gage-s/Dallocchio-a/Djurdjevic-c; both Caps app. 4.00
...: Loki (6/10, $2.99) Gillen-s/McKelvie-a/Djurdjevic-c; Hela & Mephisto app. 4.00
...: Secret Warriors (6/10, $2.99) Hickman-s/Vitti-a/Djurdjevic-c; Phobos attacks 4.00
...: Spider-Man (6/10, $2.99) Reed-s/Santucci-a/Djurdjevic-c; Venom & Ms. Marvel app. 4.00
...: Storming Asgard - Heroes & Villains (3/10, $3.99) Dossiers on participants; Land-c 4.00
...: The Cabal (2/10, $3.99) series prelude; Bendis-s/Lark-a; covers by Finch & Davis 4.00
...: Young Avengers (6/10, $2.99) McKeever-s/Asrar-a/Djurdjevic-c; Wrecking Crew app. 4.00

SIEGE: EMBEDDED
Marvel Comics: Mar, 2010 - No. 4, Jul, 2010 ($3.99, limited series)
1-4-Reed-s/Samnee-a/Granov-c; Ben Urich & Volstagg cover the invasion 4.00

SIEGEL AND SHUSTER: DATELINE 1930s
Eclipse Comics: Nov, 1984 - No. 2, Sept, 1985 ($1.50/$1.75, Baxter paper #1)
1,2: 1-Unpublished samples of strips from the '30s; includes 'Interplanetary Police'; Shuster-c. 2 ($1.75, B&W)-unpublished strips; Shuster-c 3.00

GD VG FN VF VF/NM NM-
2.0 4.0 6.0 8.0 9.0 9.2

SIF (See Thor titles)
Marvel Comics: Jun, 2010 ($3.99, one shot)
1-Deconnick-s/Stegman-a/Foreman-c; Beta Ray Bill app. 4.00

SIGIL (Also see CrossGen Chronicles)
CrossGeneration Comics: Jul, 2000 - No. 43, Jan, 2004 ($2.95)
1-43: 1-Barbara Kesel-s/Ben & Ray Lai-a. 12-Waid-s begin. 21-Chuck Dixon-s begin 3.00
...: Mark of Power TPB (5/01, $19.95) r/#1-7; Moeller painted-c 20.00
...: The Marked Man Vol. 2 TPB (2002, $19.95) r/#8-14 20.00
...: The Lizard God Vol. 3 TPB (2002, $15.95) r/#15-20 16.00
Vol. 4: Hostage Planet (4/03, $15.95) r/#21-26 16.00
Vol. 5: Death Match (2003, $15.95) r/#27-32 16.00

SIGIL
Marvel Comics: May, 2011 - No. 4, Aug, 2011 ($2.99)
1-4-Carey-s/Kirk-a 3.00
1-Variant-c by McGuinness 5.00

SIGMA
Image Comics (WildStorm): March, 1996 - No. 3, June, 1996 ($2.50, limited series)
1-3: 1-"Fire From Heaven" prelude #2; Coker-a. 2-"Fire From Heaven" pt. 6. 3-"Fire From Heaven" pt. 14. 3.00

SILENT DRAGON
DC Comics (WildStorm): Sept, 2005 - No. 6, Feb, 2006 ($2.99, limited series)
1-6-Tokyo 2066 A.D.; Leinil Yu-a/c; Andy Diggle-s 3.00
TPB (2006, $19.99) r/series; sketch page 20.00

SILENT HILL: DEAD/ALIVE
IDW Publishing: Dec, 2005 - No. 5, Apr, 2006 ($3.99, limited series)
1-5-Stakal-a/Ciencin-s. 1-Four covers. 2-5-Two covers 4.00

SILENT HILL: DYING INSIDE
IDW Publishing: Feb, 2004 - No. 5, June, 2004 ($3.99, limited series)
1-5-Based on the Konami computer game. 1-Templesmith-a; Ashley Wood-c 4.00
...: Paint It Black (2/05, $7.49) Ciencin-s/Thomas-a 7.50
...: The Grinning Man 5/05, $7.49) Ciencin-s/Stakal-a 7.50
TPB (8/04, $19.99) r/#1-5; Ashley Wood-c 20.00

SILENT HILL: PAST LIFE
IDW Publishing: Oct, 2010 - No. 4, Jan, 2011 ($3.99, limited series)
1-4-Waltz-s; two covers on each 4.00

SILENT HILL: SINNER'S REWARD
IDW Publishing: Feb, 2008 - No. 4, Apr, 2008 ($3.99, limited series)
1-4-Waltz-s/Stamb-a 4.00

SILENT INVASION, THE
Rengade Press: Apr, 1986 - No.12, Mar, 1988 ($1.70/$2.00, B&W)
1-12-UFO sightings of the '50's 3.00
Book 1- reprints ($7.95) 8.00

SILENT MOBIUS
Viz Select Comics: 1991 - No. 5, 1992 ($4.95, color, squarebound, 44 pgs.)
1-5: Japanese stories translated to English 5.00

SILENT SCREAMERS (Based on the Aztech Toys figures)
Image Comics: Oct, 2000 ($4.95)
Nosferatu Issue - Alex Ross front & back-c 5.00

SILENT WAR
Marvel Comics: Mar, 2007 - No. 6, Aug, 2007 ($2.99, limited series)
1-6-Inhumans, Black Bolt and Fantastic Four app.; Hine-s/Irving-a/Watson-c 3.00
TPB (2007, $14.99) r/series 15.00

SILKE
Dark Horse Comics: Jan, 2001 - No. 4, Sept, 2001 ($2.95)
1-4-Tony Daniel-s/a 3.00

SILKEN GHOST
CrossGen Comics: June, 2003 - No. 5, Oct, 2003 ($2.95, limited series)
1-5-Dixon-s/Rosado-a 3.00
Traveler Vol. 1 (2003, $9.95) digest-sized reprint #1-5 10.00

SILLY PILLY (See Frank Luther's...)

SILLY SYMPHONIES (See Dell Giants)

SILLY TUNES

Silver Sable and the Wild Pack #28 © MAR

Silver Streak Comics #5 © LEV

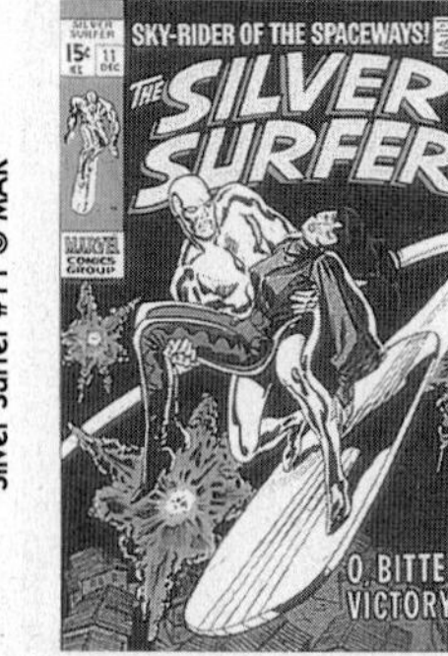

Silver Surfer #11 © MAR

GD 2.0 | VG 4.0 | FN 6.0 | VF 8.0 | VF/NM 9.0 | NM- 9.2

Timely Comics: Fall, 1945 - No. 7, June, 1947

1-Silly Seal, Ziggy Pig begin 24 48 72 140 230 320
2-(2/46) 14 28 42 82 121 160
3-7: 6-New logo 13 26 39 72 101 130

SILVER (See Lone Ranger's Famous Horse...)

SILVER AGE
DC Comics: July, 2000 ($3.95, limited series)

1-Waid-s/Dodson-a; "Silver Age" style x-over; JLA & villains switch bodies 4.00
...: Challengers of the Unknown ($2.50) Joe Kubert-c; vs. Chronos 3.00
...: Dial H For Hero ($2.50) Jim Mooney-c; vs. Martian Manhunter 3.00
...: Doom Patrol ($2.50) Ramona Fradon-c/Peyer-s 3.00
...: Flash ($2.50) Carmine Infantino-c; Kid Flash and Elongated Man app. 3.00
...: Green Lantern ($2.50) Gil Kane-c/Busiek-s/Anderson-a; vs. Sinestro 3.00
...: Justice League of America ($2.50) Ty Templeton-c 3.00
...: Showcase ($2.50) Dick Giordano-c/a; Batgirl, Adam Strange app. 3.00
... Secret Files ($4.95) Intro. Agamemno; short stories & profile pages 5.00
...: Teen Titans ($2.50) Nick Cardy-c; vs. Penguin, Mr. Element, Black Manta 3.00
...: The Brave and the Bold ($2.50) Jim Aparo-c; Batman & Metal Men 3.00
... 80-Page Giant ($5.95) Conclusion of x-over; "lost" Silver Age stories 6.00

SILVERBACK
Comico: 1989 - No. 3, 1990 ($2.50, color, limited series, mature readers)

1-3: Character from Grendel: Matt Wagner-a 3.00

SILVERBLADE
DC Comics: Sept, 1987 - No. 12, Sept, 1988

1-12: Colan-c/a in all 3.00

SILVERHAWKS
Star Comics/Marvel Comics #6: Aug, 1987 - No. 6, June, 1988 ($1.00)

1-6 3.00

SILVERHEELS
Pacific Comics: Dec, 1983 - No. 3, May, 1984 ($1.50)

1-3 3.00

SILVER KID WESTERN
Key/Stanmor Publications: Oct, 1954 - No. 5, July, 1955

1 10 20 30 54 72 90
2 6 12 18 31 38 45
3-5 6 12 18 28 34 40
I.W. Reprint #1,2-Severin-c: 1-r/#? 2-r/#1 2 4 6 8 11 14

SILVER SABLE AND THE WILD PACK (See Amazing Spider-Man #265 and Sable & Fortune)
Marvel Comics: June, 1992 - No. 35, Apr, 1995 ($1.25/$1.50

1-($2.00)-Embossed & foil stamped-c; Spider-Man app. 4.00
2-24,26-35: 4,5-Dr. Doom-c/story. 6,7-Deathlok-c/story. 9-Origin Silver Sable. 10-Punisher-c/s. 15-Capt. America-c/s. 16,17-Intruders app. 18,19-Venom-c/s. 19-Siege of Darkness x-over. 23-Daredevil (in new costume) & Deadpool app. 24-Bound-in card sheet. Li'l Sylvie backup story 3.00
25-($2.00, 52 pgs.)-Li'l Sylvie backup story 4.00

SILVER STAR (Also see Jack Kirby's...)
Pacific Comics: Feb, 1983 - No. 6, Jan, 1984 ($1.00)

1-6: 1-1st app. Last of the Viking Heroes. 1-5-Kirby-c/a. 2-Ditko-a 5.00
...: Graphite Edition TPB (TwoMorrows Publ., 3/06, $19.95) r/series in B&W including Kirby's original pencils; sketch pages; original screenplay 20.00
Jack Kirby's Silver Star, Volume 1 HC (Image Comics, 2007, $34.99) r/series in color; sketch pages; original screenplay 35.00

SILVER STREAK COMICS (Crime Does Not Pay #22 on)
Your Guide Publs. No. 1-7/New Friday Publs. No. 8-17/Comic House Publ./ Newsbook Publ.: Dec, 1939 - No. 21, May, 1942; No. 23, 1946; No # 22 (Silver logo-#1-5)

1-(Scarce)-Intro the Claw by Cole (r-in Daredevil #21), Red Reeves Boy Magician (ends #2), Captain Fearless (ends #2), The Wasp (ends #2), Mister Midnight (ends #2) begin; Spirit Man only app. Calling The Duke begins (ends #2). Barry Lane only app. Silver Metallic-c begin, end #5; Claw-c 1,2,6-8 1000 2000 3000 7500 13,500 19,500
2-The Claw ends (by Cole); makes pact w/Hitler; Simon-c/a (The Claw); ad for Marvel Mystery Comics #2 (12/39). Lance Hale begins (receives super powers). Solar Patrol app. 400 800 1200 2800 4900 7000
3-1st app. & origin Silver Streak (2nd with Lightning speed); Dickie Dean the Boy Inventor, Lance Hale, Ace Powers (ends #6), Bill Wayne The Texas Terror (ends #6) & The Planet Patrol (ends #6) begin. Detective Snoop, Sergeant Drake only app. 343 686 1029 2400 4200 6000
4-Sky Wolf begins (ends #6); Silver Streak by Jack Cole (new costume); 1st app. Jackie, Lance Hale's sidekick. Lance Hale gains immortality 168 336 504 1075 1838 2600
5-Cole c/a(2); back-c ad for Claw app. in #6 194 388 582 1242 2121 3000
6-(Scarce, 9/40)-Origin & 1st app. Daredevil (blue & yellow costume) by Jack Binder; The Claw returns as the Green Claw; classic Cole Claw-c 1400 2800 4200 10,500 19,250 28,000
7-Claw vs. Daredevil serial begins c/sty, ends #11. Daredevil new costume-blue & red by Jack Cole & 3 other Cole stories (38 pgs.). Origin Whiz, S. S.'s Falcon 2nd app. Daredevil & 1st Daredevil-c (by Cole). Cloud Curtis, Presto Martin begins. Dynamo Hill & Zongar The Miracleman only app. 784 1568 2352 5723 10,112 14,500
8-Claw vs. Daredevil by Cole c/sty; last Cole Silver streak. Dan Dearborn begins (ends) #12. Secret Agent X-101 begins, ends #9 400 800 1200 2800 4900 7000
9-Claw vs. Daredevil by Cole. Silver Streak-c by Bob Wood 226 452 678 1446 2473 3500
10-Origin & 1st app. Captain Battle (5/41) by Binder; Claw vs. Daredevil by Cole; Silver Streak/robot-c by Bob Wood 177 354 531 1124 1937 2750
11-Intro. Mercury by Bob Wood, Silver Streak's sidekick; conclusion Claw vs. Daredevil by Rico; in 'Presto Martin,' 2nd pg., newspaper says 'Roussos does it again' 129 258 387 826 1413 2000
12-Daredevil-c by Rico; Lance Hale finds lost valley w/cave men, battles dinosaurs, sabre-toothed cats; his last app. 103 206 309 659 1130 1600
13-15: 13-Origin Thun-Dohr. Bingham Boys app. 90 180 270 576 988 1400
16-Hitler-c 113 226 339 718 1234 1750
17-Last Daredevil issue. 89 178 267 565 970 1375
18-The Saint begins (2/42, 1st app.) by Leslie Charteris (see Movie Comics #2 by DC); The Saint-c 81 162 243 518 884 1250
19-21 (1942): 19,20-Ned of the Navy app.; Wolverton's Scoop Scuttle in 20,21. 20-Last Captain Battle, Dickie Dean & Cloud Curtis; Red Reed, Alonzo Appleseed only app. 21-Hitler app. in strip on cover 53 106 159 334 567 800
23(1946(An Atomic Comic)-Reprints; bondage-c 57 114 171 362 619 875
nn(11/46)(Newsbook Publ.)-R-/S.S. story from #4-7 plus 2 Captain Fearless stories, all in color; bondage/torture-c (scarce) 71 142 213 454 777 1100

NOTE: ***Jack Binder** a-8-12, 15; c-3, 4, 13-15, 17. **Dick Briefer** a-9-20. **Jack Cole** a-(Claw)-#2, 3, 6-10. (Daredevil)-#6-10, (Dickie Dean)-#3-10, (Pirate Prince)-#7, (Silver Streak)-#4-8, nn; c-5 (Silver Streak), 6 (Claw), 7, 8 (Daredevil). **Bill Everett** Red Reed begins #20. **Fred Guardineer** a-#8-12. **Don Rico** a-11-17 (Daredevil), 15, 19 (Silver Streak); c-11, 12, 16. **Joe Simon** a-2 (Solar Patrol), 3 (Silver Streak); c-2. **Basil Wolverton** a-20. **Bob Wood** a-8-15 (Presto Martin), 9 (Silver Streak); c-9, 10. Captain Battle c-11, 13-15, 17. Claw c-#1, 2, 6-8. Daredevil c-7, 8, 12. Dickie Dean c-19. Ned of the Navy c-20 (war). The Saint c-18. Silver Streak c-5, 10, 16, 23.*

SILVER STREAK COMICS (Homage with Golden Age size and Golden Age art styles)
Image Comics: No. 24, Dec, 2009 ($3.99, one-shot)

24-New Daredevil, Claw, Silver Streak & Captain Battle stories; Larsen, Grist, Gilbert-a 4.00

SILVER SURFER (See Fantastic Four, Fantasy Masterpieces V2#1, Fireside Book Series, Marvel Graphic Novel, Marvel Presents #8, Marvel's Greatest Comics & Tales To Astonish #92)

SILVER SURFER, THE (Also see Essential Silver Surfer)
Marvel Comics Group: Aug, 1968 - No. 18, Sept, 1970; June, 1982

1-More detailed origin by John Buscema (p); The Watcher back-up stories begin (origin), end #7; (No. 1-7: 25¢, 68 pgs.) 48 96 144 389 845 1300
2-1st app. Badoon 20 40 60 137 294 450
3-1st app. Mephisto 18 36 54 123 267 410
4-Lower distribution; Thor & Loki app. 42 84 126 315 683 1050
5-7-Last giant size. 5-The Stranger app.; Fantastic Four app. 6-Brunner inks. 7-(8/69)-Early cameo Frankenstein's monster (see X-Men #40) 13 26 39 87 186 285
8-10: 8-18-(15¢ issues) 11 22 33 73 142 210
11-13,15-18: 15-Silver Surfer vs. Human Torch; Fantastic Four app. 17-Nick Fury app. 18-Vs. The Inhumans; Kirby-c/a 10 20 30 69 130 190
14-Spider-Man x-over 14 28 42 97 211 325
... Omnibus Vol. 1 Hardcover (2007, $74.99, dustjacket) r/#1-18 re-colored with original letter pages, Fantastic Four Annual #5 & Not Brand Echh #13; Lee and Buscema bios 75.00
V2#1 (6/82, 52 pgs.)-Byrne-c/a 2 4 6 8 10 12

NOTE: ***Adkins** a-8-15i. **Brunner** a-6i. **J. Buscema** a-1-17p. **Colan** a-1-3p. **Reinman** a-1-4i. #1-14 were reprinted in Fantasy Masterpieces V2#1-14.*

SILVER SURFER (Volume 3) (See Marvel Graphic Novel #38)
Marvel Comics Group: V3#1, July, 1987 - No. 146, Nov, 1998

1-Double size ($1.25) 1 3 4 6 8 10
2-17: 15-Ron Lim-c/a begins (9/88) 5.00
18-33,39-43: 25,31 ($1.50, 52 pgs.). 25-Skrulls app. 32,39-No Ron Lim-c/a. 39-Alan Grant scripts 4.00
34-Thanos returns (cameo); Starlin scripts begin 5.00
35-38: 35-1st full Thanos app. in Silver Surfer (3/90); reintro Drax the Destroyer on last pg. (cameo). 36-Recaps history of Thanos; Capt. Marvel & Warlock app. in recap. 37-1st full app. Drax the Destroyer; Drax-c. 38-Silver Surfer battles Thanos 6.00
44,45,49-Thanos stories (c-44,45) 5.00
46-48: 46-Return of Adam Warlock (2/91); re-intro Gamora & Pip the Troll. 47-Warlock battles Drax. 48-Last Starlin scripts (also #50) 5.00

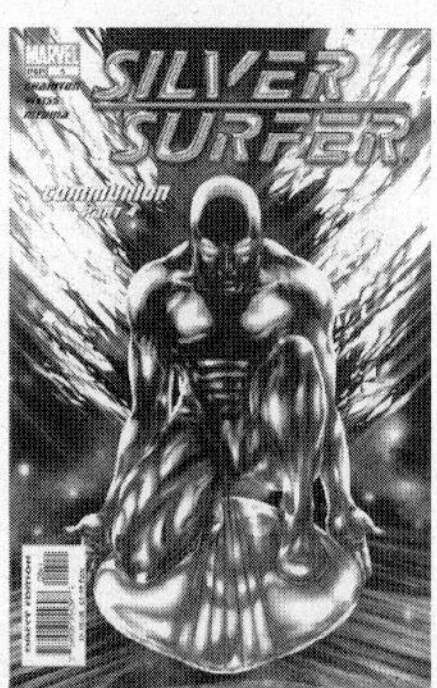
Silver Surfer V4 #4 © MAR

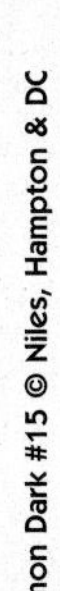
Simon Dark #15 © Niles, Hampton & DC

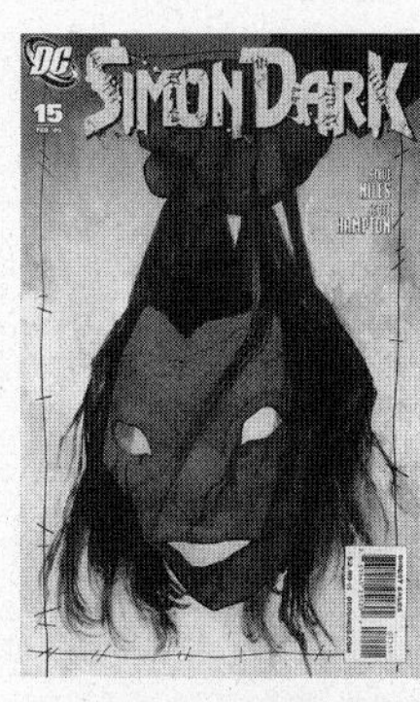

Simpsons Comics #169 © Bongo

GD VG FN VF VF/NM NM-
2.0 4.0 6.0 8.0 9.0 9.2

50-($1.50, 52 pgs.)-Embossed & silver foil-c; Silver Surfer has brief battle w/Thanos; story cont'd in Infinity Gauntlet #1 1 2 3 5 6 8
50-2nd & 3rd printings 4.00
51-59: 51-53: Infinity Gauntlet x-over . 54-57: Infinity Gauntlet x-overs. 54-Rhino app. 55,56-Thanos-c & app. 57-Thanos-c & cameo. 58,59-Infinity Gauntlet x-overs; 58-Lim-c only. 59-Thanos battles Silver Surfer-c/story; Thanos joins 4.00
60-74,76-81-,83-99,101-124,126-139: 63-Capt. Marvel app. 67-69-Infinity War x-overs. 76-78-Jack of Hearts-c/s. 83-85-Infinity Crusade x-over; 83,84-Thanos cameo. 85-Storm, Wonder Man x-over. 86-Thor-c/s. 87-Dr. Strange & Warlock app. 88-Thanos-c/s. 95-FF app. 96-Hulk & FF app. 97-Terrax & Nova app. 101-Bound in card sheet. 106-Doc Doom app. 121-Quasar & Beta Ray Bill app. 123-w/card insert; begin Garney-a. 126-Dr. Strange-c/app. 128-Spider-Man & Daredevil-c/app. 138-Thing-c 3.00
75,82: 75-($2.50, 52 pgs.)-Embossed foil-c; Lim-c/a. 82-(52 pgs.) 4.00
100 ($2.25, 52 pgs.)-Wraparound-c 4.00
100 ($3.95, 52 pgs.)-Enhanced-c 5.00
125 ($2.95)-Wraparound-c; Vs. Hulk-c/app. 4.00
140-146: 140-142,144,145-Muth-c/a. 143,146-Cowan-a. 146-Last issue 3.00
#(-1) Flashback (7/97) 3.00
Annual 1 (1988, $1.75)-Evolutionary War app.; 1st Ron Lim-a on Silver Surfer (20 pg. back-up story & pin-ups) 5.00
Annual 2-7 ('89-'94, 68 pgs.): 2-Atlantis Attacks. 4-3 pg. origin story; Silver Surfer battles Guardians of the Galaxy. 5-Return of the Defenders, part 3; Lim-c/a (3 pgs. of pin-ups only). 6-Polybagged w/trading card; 1st app. Legacy; card is by Lim/Austin 4.00
Annual '97 ($2.99), .../Thor Annual '98 ($2.99) 4.00
Ashcan (1995, 75¢) reprints part of V1#3; Lim-c 3.00
...Dangerous Artifacts-(1996, $3.95)-Ron Marz scripts; Galactus-c/app. 4.00
Graphic Novel (1988, HC, $14.95) Judgment Day; Lee-s/Buscema-a 15.00
The Enslavers Graphic Novel (1990, $16.95) 17.00
Homecoming Graphic Novel (1991, $12.95, softcover) Starlin-s 15.00
Inner Demons TPB (4/98, $3.50)r/#123,125,126 4.00
...: Rebirth of Thanos TPB (2006, $24.99) r/#34-38, Thanos Quest #1,2; Logan's Run #6 25.00
...: The First Coming of Galactus nn (11/92, $5.95, 68 pgs.)-Reprints Fantastic Four #48-50 with new Lim-c 6.00
Wizard 1/2 2 4 6 9 12 15

NOTE: ***Austin*** *c(i)-7, 8, 71, 73, 74, 76, 79.* ***Cowan*** *a-143,146.* ***Cully Hamner*** *a-83p.* ***Ron Lim*** *a(p)-15-31, 33-38, 40-55, (56, 57-part-p), 60-65, 73-82, Annual 2, 4; c(p)-15-31, 32-38, 40-84, 86-92, Annual 2, 4-6.* ***Muth*** *c/a-140-142,144,145.* ***M. Rogers*** *a-1-10, 12, 19, 21; c-1-9, 11, 12, 21.*

SILVER SURFER (Volume 4)
Marvel Comics: Sept, 2003 - No. 14, Dec, 2004 ($2.25/$2.99)

1-6: 1-Milx-a; Jusko-c. 2-Jae Lee-c 3.00
7-14-($2.99) 3.00
...Vol. 1: Communion (2004, $14.99) r/#1-6 15.00

SILVER SURFER (Volume 5)
Marvel Comics: Apr, 2011 - No. 5, Aug, 2011 ($2.99, limited series)

1-5-Pagulayan-c. 1-Segovia-a. 4,5-Fantastic Four app. 3.00

SILVER SURFER, THE
Marvel Comics (Epic): Dec, 1988 - No. 2, Jan, 1989 ($1.00, lim. series)

1,2: By Stan Lee scripts & Moebius-c/a 5.00
HC (1988, $19.95, dust jacket) r/#1,2; "Making Of" text section and sketch pages 30.00
...: Parable ('98, $5.99) r/#1&2 6.00

SILVER SURFER: IN THY NAME
Marvel Comics: Jan, 2008 - No. 4, Apr, 2008 ($2.99, limited series)

1-4-Spurrier-s/Huat-a. 1-Turner-c. 2-Dell'Otto-c. 3-Paul Pope-c. 4-Galactus app. 3.00

SILVER SURFER: LOFTIER THAN MORTALS
Marvel Comics: Oct, 1999 - No. 2, Oct, 1999 ($2.50, limited series)

1,2-Remix of Fantastic Four #57-60; Velluto-a 3.00

SILVER SURFER: REQUIEM
Marvel Comics: July, 2007 - No. 4, Oct, 2007 ($3.99, limited series)

1-4-Straczynski-s/Ribic-a. 1-Origin retold; Fantastic Four app. 4.00
HC (2007, $19.99) r/#1-4, Ribic cover sketches 20.00

SILVER SURFER/SUPERMAN
Marvel Comics: 1996 ($5.95,one-shot)

1-Perez-s/Lim-c/a(p) 6.00

SILVER SURFER VS. DRACULA
Marvel Comics: Feb, 1994 ($1.75, one-shot)

1-r/Tomb of Dracula #50; Everett Vampire-r/Venus #19; Howard the Duck back-up by Brunner; Lim-c(p) 4.00

SILVER SURFER/WARLOCK: RESURRECTION
Marvel Comics: Mar, 1993 - No. 4, June, 1993 ($2.50, limited series)

1-4: Starlin-c/a & scripts 3.00

SILVER SURFER/WEAPON ZERO
Marvel Comics: Apr, 1997 ($2.95, one-shot)

1-"Devil's Reign" pt. 8 3.00

SILVERTIP (Max Brand)
Dell Publishing Co.: No. 491, Aug, 1953 - No. 898, May, 1958

Four Color 491 (#1); all painted-c 8 16 24 51 86 120
Four Color 572,608,637,667,731,789,898-Kinstler-a 5 10 15 30 48 65
Four Color 835 5 10 15 30 48 65

SIMON DARK
DC Comics: Dec, 2007 - No. 18, May, 2009 ($2.99)

1-Intro. Simon Dark; Steve Niles-s/Scott Hampton-a/c 4.00
1-Second printing with full face variant cover 3.00
2-18 3.00
...: Ashes TPB (2009, $17.99) r/#7-12 18.00
...: The Game of Life TPB (2009, $17.99) r/#13-18 18.00
...: What Simon Does TPB (2008, $14.99) r/#1-6 15.00

SIMPSONS COMICS (See Bartman, Futurama, Itchy & Scratchy & Radioactive Man)
Bongo Comics Group: 1993 - Present ($1.95/$2.50/$2.99)

1-($2.25)-FF#1-c swipe; pull-out poster; flip book 1 3 4 6 8 10
2-5: 2-Patty & Selma flip-c/sty. 3-Krusty, Agent of K.L.O.W.N. flip-c/story. 4-Infinity-c; flip-c of Busman #1; w/trading card. 5-Wraparound-c w/trading card 6.00
6-40: All Flip books. 6-w/Chief Wiggum's "Crime Comics". 7-w/"McBain Comics". 8-w/"Edna, Queen of the Congo". 9-w/"Barney Gumble". 10-w/"Apu". 11-w/"Homer". 12-w/"White Knuckled War Stories". 13-w/"Jimbo Jones' Wedgie Comics". 14-w/"Grampa". 15-w/"Itchy & Scratchy". 16-w/"Bongo Grab Bag". 17-w/"Headlight Comics". 18-w/"Milhouse". 19,20-w/"Roswell." 21,22-w/"Roswell". 23-w/"Hellfire Comics". 24-w/"Lil' Homey". 36-39-Flip book w/Radioactive Man 5.00
41-49,51-99: 43-Flip book w/Poochie. 52-Dini-s. 77-Dixon-s. 85-Begin $2.99-c 4.00
50-($5.95) Wraparound-c; 80 pgs.; square-bound 1 2 3 5 6 8
100-($6.99) 100 pgs.; square-bound; clip issue of past highlights 1 2 3 5 6 8
101-182,185-188: 102-Barks Ducks homage. 117-Hank Scorpio app. 122-Archie spoof. 132-Movie poster enclosed. 132-133-Two-parter. 144-Flying Hellfish flashback. 150-w/Poster. 163-Aragonés-s/a 3.00
183-Archie Comics #1 cover swipe; Archie homage with Stan Goldberg-a 3.00
... A Go-Go (1999, $11.95)-r/#32-35; ...Big Bonanza (1998, $11.95)-r/#28-31, ...Extravaganza (1994, $10.00)-r/#1-4; infinity-c, ...On Parade (1998, $11.95)-r/#24-27, ...Simpsorama (1996, $10.95)-r/#11-14 12.00
Simpsons Classics 1-30 (2004-Present, $3.99, magazine-size, quarterly) reprints 4.00
Simpsons Comics Barn Burner ('04, $14.95) r/#57-61,63 15.00
Simpsons Comics Beach Blanket Bongo ('07, $14.95) r/#71-75,77 15.00
Simpsons Comics Belly Buster ('04, $14.95) r/#49,51,53-56 15.00
Simpsons Comics Hit the Road! ('08, $15.95) r/#85,86,88,89,90 16.00
Simpsons Comics Jam-Packed Jamboree ('06, $14.95) r/#64-69 15.00
Simpsons Comics Madness ('03, $14.95) r/#43-48 15.00
Simpsons Comics Royale ('01, $14.95) r/various Bongo issues 15.00
Simpsons Comics Treasure Trove 1-4 ('08-'09, $3.99, 6" x 8") r/various Bongo issues 4.00
Simpsons Summer Shindig ('07-'11, $4.99) 1-5-Anthology. 1-Batman/Ripken insert 5.00
Simpsons Winter Wing Ding ('06-'11, $4.99) 1-6-Holiday anthology. 1-Dini-s 5.00

SIMPSONS COMICS AND STORIES
Welsh Publishing Group: 1993 ($2.95, one-shot)

1-(Direct Sale)-Polybagged w/Bartman poster 1 2 3 5 6 8
1-(Newsstand Edition)-Without poster 5.00

SIMPSONS COMICS PRESENTS BART SIMPSON
Bongo Comics Group: 2000 - Present ($2.50/$2.99)

1-68: 7-9-Dan DeCarlo-layouts. 13-Begin $2.99-c. 17,37-Bartman app. 50-Aragonés-s/a 3.00
The Big Book of Bart Simpson TPB (2002, $12.95) r/#1-4 13.00
The Big Bad Book of Bart Simpson TPB (2003, $12.95) r/#5-8 13.00
The Big Bratty Book of Bart Simpson TPB (2004, $12.95) r/#9-12 13.00
The Big Beefy Book of Bart Simpson TPB (2005, $13.95) r/#13-16 14.00
The Big Bouncy Book of Bart Simpson TPB (2006, $13.95) r/#17-20 14.00
The Big Beastly Book of Bart Simpson TPB (2007, $14.95) r/#21-24 15.00
The Big Brilliant Book of Bart Simpson TPB (2008, $14.95) r/#25-28 15.00

SIMPSONS FUTURAMA CROSSOVER CRISIS II (TV) (Also see Futurama/Simpsons Infinitely Secret Crossover Crisis)
Bongo Comics: 2005 - No. 2, 2005 ($3.00, limited series)

1,2-The Professor brings the Simpsons' Springfield crew to the 31st century 3.00

SIMPSONS ILLUSTRATED (TV)

Simpsons Super Spectacuar #3 © Bongo

Sin City: Hell and Back #1 © Frank Miller

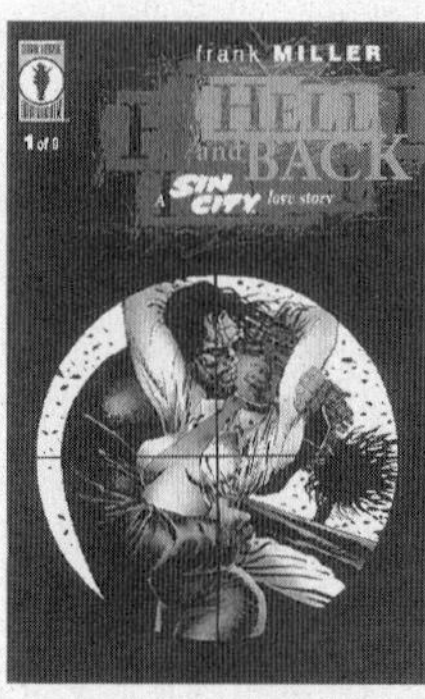

Single Series #17 © UFS

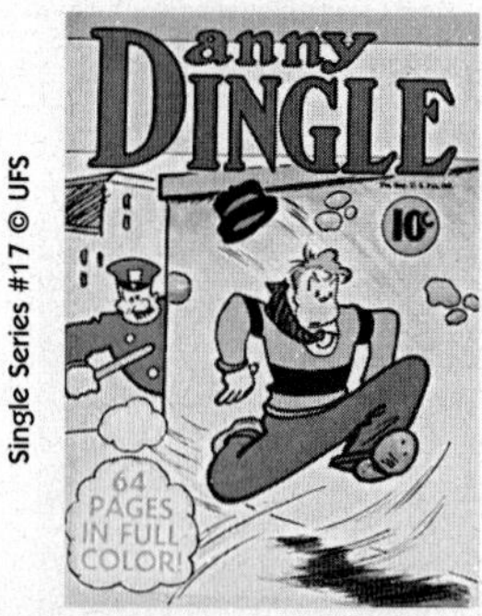

GD VG FN VF VF/NM NM-
2.0 4.0 6.0 8.0 9.0 9.2

Bongo Comics: 2012 - Present ($3.99, quarterly)

1-Reprints 4.00

SIMPSONS ONE-SHOT WONDERS (TV)
Bongo Comics: 2012 - Present ($2.99)

...: Ralph Wiggums Comics 1 - Short stories by Aragonés and others 3.00

SIMPSONS SUPER SPECTACULAR (TV)
Bongo Comics: 2006 - Present ($2.99)

1-14: 2-Bartman, Stretch Dude and The Cupcake Kid team up; back-up story Brereton-a. 5-Fradon-a on Metamorpho spoof. 8-Spirit spoof. 9,10,14-Radioactive Man app. 3.00

SINBAD, JR (TV Cartoon)
Dell Publishing Co.: Sept-Nov, 1965 - No. 3, May, 1966

	GD	VG	FN	VF	VF/NM	NM-
1	4	8	12	24	37	50
2,3	3	6	9	18	27	35

SIN CITY (See Dark Horse Presents, A Decade of Dark Horse, & San Diego Comic Con Comics #2,4)
Dark Horse Comics (Legend)

TPB ($15.00) Reprints early DHP stories 15.00
Booze, Broads & Bullets TPB ($15.00) 15.00
Frank Miller's Sin City: One For One (8/10, $1.00) reprints debut story from DHP #51 3.00

SIN CITY (FRANK MILLER'S...) (Reissued TPBs to coincide with the April 2005 movie)
Dark Horse Books: Feb, 2005 ($17.00/$19.00, 6" x 9" format with new Miller covers)

Volume 1: The Hard Goodbye ($17.00) reprints stories from Dark Horse Presents #51-62 and DHP Fifth Anniv. Special; covers and publicity pieces 17.00
Volume 2: A Dame to Kill For ($17.00) r/Sin City: A Dame to Kill For #1-6 17.00
Volume 3: The Big Fat Kill ($17.00) r/Sin City: The Big Fat Kill #1-5; pin-up gallery 17.00
Volume 4: That Yellow Bastard ($19.00) r/Sin City: That Yellow Bastard #1-6; pin-up gallery by Mike Allred, Kyle Baker, Jeff Smith and Bruce Timm; cover gallery 19.00
Volume 5: Family Values ($12.00) r/Sin City: Family Values GN 12.00
Volume 6: Booze, Broads & Bullets ($15.00) r/Sin City: The Babe Wore Red and Other Stories; Silent Night; story from A Decade of Dark Horse; Lost Lonely & Lethal; Sex & Violence; and Just Another Saturday Night 15.00
Volume 7: Hell and Back ($28.00) r/Sin City: Hell and Back #1-9; pin-up gallery 28.00

SIN CITY: A DAME TO KILL FOR
Dark Horse Comics (Legend): Nov, 1993 - No. 6, May, 1994 ($2.95, B&W, limited series)

1-6: Frank Miller-c/a & story in all. 1-1st app. Dwight. 6.00
Limited Edition Hardcover 85.00
Hardcover 25.00
TPB ($15.00) 15.00

SIN CITY: FAMILY VALUES
Dark Horse Comics (Legend): Oct, 1997 ($10.00, B&W, squarebound, one-shot)

nn-Miller-c/a & story 10.00
Limited Edition Hardcover 75.00

SIN CITY: HELL AND BACK
Dark Horse (Maverick): Jul, 1999 - No. 9 ($2.95/$4.95, B&W, limited series)

1-8-Miller-c/a & story. 7-Color 4.00
9-($4.95) 6.00

SIN CITY: JUST ANOTHER SATURDAY NIGHT
Dark Horse Comics (Legend): Aug, 1997 (Wizard 1/2 offer, B&W, one-shot)

	GD	VG	FN	VF	VF/NM	NM-
1/2-Miller-c/a & story	1	2	3	5	6	8

nn (10/98, $2.50) r/#1/2 3.00

SIN CITY: LOST, LONELY & LETHAL
Dark Horse Comics (Legend): Dec, 1996 ($2.95, B&W and blue, one-shot)

nn-Miller-c/s/a; w/pin-ups 5.00

SIN CITY: SEX AND VIOLENCE
Dark Horse Comics (Legend): Mar, 1997 ($2.95, B&W and blue, one-shot)

nn-Miller-c/a & story 5.00

SIN CITY: SILENT NIGHT
Dark Horse Comics (Legend): Dec, 1995 ($2.95, B&W, one-shot)

1-Miller-c/a & story; Marv app. 5.00

SIN CITY: THAT YELLOW BASTARD (Second Ed. TPB listed under Sin City (Frank Miller's...)
Dark Horse Comics (Legend): Feb, 1996 - No. 6, July, 1996 ($2.95/$3.50, B&W and yellow, limited series)

1-5: Miller-c/a & story in all. 1-1st app. Hartigan. 5.00
6-($3.50) Error & corrected 5.00
Limited Edition Hardcover 25.00
TPB ($15.00) 15.00

SIN CITY: THE BABE WORE RED AND OTHER STORIES
Dark Horse Comics (Legend): Nov, 1994 ($2.95, B&W and red, one-shot)

1-r/serial run in Previews as well as other stories; Miller-c/a & scripts; Dwight app. 4.00

SIN CITY: THE BIG FAT KILL (Second Edition TPB listed under Sin City (Frank Miller's...)
Dark Horse Comics (Legend): Nov, 1994 - No. 5, Mar, 1995 ($2.95, B&W, limited series)

1-5-Miller story & art in all; Dwight app. 5.00
Hardcover 25.00
TPB ($15.00) 15.00

SIN CITY: THE FRANK MILLER LIBRARY
Dark Horse Books: Set 1, Nov, 2005; Set 2, Mar, 2006 ($150, slipcased hardcover, 8" x 12")

Set 1 - Individual hardcovers for Volume 1: The Hard Goodbye, Volume 2: A Dame to Kill For, Volume 3: The Big Fat Kill, Volume 4: That Yellow Bastard; new red foil stamped covers; slipcase box is black with red foil graphics 150.00
Set 2 - Individual hardcovers for Volume 5: Family Values, Volume 6: Booze, Broads & Bullets, Volume 7: Hell and Back, new red foil stamped covers; The Art of Sin City red hardcover; slipcase box is black with red foil graphics 150.00

SINDBAD (See Capt. Sindbad under Movie Comics, and Fantastic Voyages of Sindbad)

SINGING GUNS (See Fawcett Movie Comics)

SINGLE SERIES (Comics on Parade #30 on)(Also see John Hix...)
United Features Syndicate: 1938 - No. 28, 1942 (All 68 pgs.)

Note: See Individual Alphabetical Listings for prices

1-Captain and the Kids (#1)
2-Broncho Bill (1939) (#1)
3-Ella Cinders (1939)
4-Li'l Abner (1939) (#1)
5-Fritzi Ritz (#1)
6-Jim Hardy by Dick Moores (#1)
7-Frankie Doodle
8-Peter Pat (On sale 7/14/39)
9-Strange As It Seems
10-Little Mary Mixup
11-Mr. and Mrs. Beans
12-Joe Jinks
13-Looy Dot Dope
14-Billy Make Believe
15-How It Began (1939)
16-Illustrated Gags (1940)-Has ad for Captain and the Kids #1 reprint listed below
17-Danny Dingle
18-Li'l Abner (#2 on-c)
19-Broncho Bill (#2 on-c)
20-Tarzan by Hal Foster
21-Ella Cinders (#2 on-c; on sale 3/19/40)
22-Iron Vic
23-Tailspin Tommy by Hal Forrest (#1)
24-Alice in Wonderland (#1)
25-Abbie and Slats
26-Little Mary Mixup (#2 on-c, 1940)
27-Jim Hardy by Dick Moores (1942)
28-Ella Cinders & Abbie and Slats (1942)
1-Captain and the Kids (1939 reprint)-2nd Edition
1-Fritzi Ritz (1939 reprint)-2nd ed.

NOTE: *Some issues given away at the 1939-40 New York World's Fair (#6).*

SINGULARITY 7
IDW Publ.: July, 2004 - No. 4, Oct, 2004 ($3.99, limited series)

1-4-Templesmith-s/a 4.00

SINISTER HOUSE OF SECRET LOVE, THE (Becomes Secrets of Sinister House No. 5 on)
National Periodical Publ.: Oct-Nov, 1971 - No. 4, Apr-May, 1972

	GD	VG	FN	VF	VF/NM	NM-
1 (All 52 pgs.) -Grey-tone-c	13	26	39	90	195	300
2,4: 2-Jeff Jones-c	8	16	24	53	89	125
3-Toth-a; Grey-tone-c	8	16	24	56	96	135

SINS OF YOUTH... (Also see Young Justice: Sins of Youth)
DC Comics: May 2000 ($4.95/$2.50, limited crossover series)

Secret Files 1 ($4.95) Short stories and profile pages; Nauck-c 5.00
...Aquaboy/Lagoon Man; Batboy and Robin; JLA Jr.; Kid Flash/Impulse; Starwoman and the JSA, Superman, Jr./Superboy, Sr.; The Secret/ Deadboy, Wonder Girls ($2.50-c) Old and young heroes switch ages 3.00

SIR CHARLES BARKLEY AND THE REFEREE MURDERS
Hamilton Comics: 1993 ($9.95, 8-1/2" x 11", 52 pgs.)

	GD	VG	FN	VF	VF/NM	NM-
nn-Photo-c; Sports fantasy comic book fiction (uses real names of NBA superstars). Script by Alan Dean Foster, art by Joe Staton. Comes with bound-in sheet of 35 gummed "Moods of Charles Barkley" stamps. Photo/story on Barkley	2	4	6	8	10	12

Special Edition of 100 copies for charity signed on an affixed book plate by Barkley, Foster & Staton 150.00

	GD	VG	FN	VF	VF/NM	NM-
Ashcan edition given away to dealers, distributors & promoters (low distribution). Four pages in color, balance of story in b&w	2	4	6	8	10	12

SIR EDWARD GREY, WITCHFINDER: IN THE SERVICE OF ANGELS (From Hellboy)
Dark Horse Comics: July, 2009 - No. 5, Nov, 2009 ($2.99, limited series)

1-5-Mignola-s/c; Stenbeck-a 3.00

SIREN (Also see Eliminator & Ultraforce)
Malibu Comics (Ultraverse): Sept, 1995 - No. 3, Dec, 1995 ($1.50)

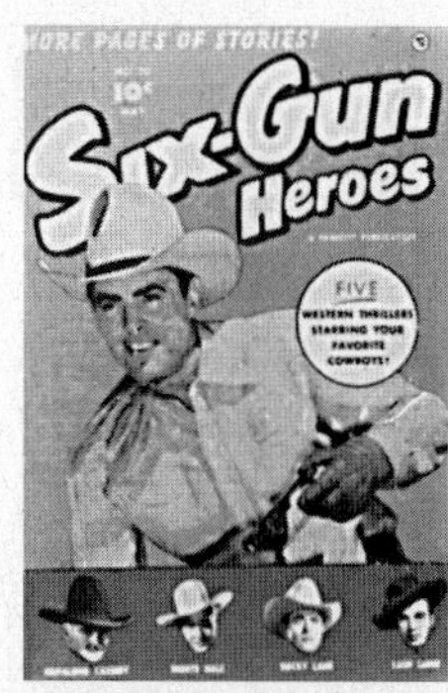

Six-Gun Heroes #20 © FAW

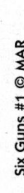

Six Guns #1 © MAR

Skeleton Hand #2 © ACG

	GD 2.0	VG 4.0	FN 6.0	VF 8.0	VF/NM 9.0	NM- 9.2
Infinity, 1-3: Infinity-Black-c & painted-c exists. 1-Regular-c & painted-c; War Machine app.						
2-Flip book w/Phoenix Resurrection Pt. 3						3.00
Special 1-(2/96, $1.95, 28 pgs.)-Origin Siren; Marvel Comic's Juggernaut-c/app.						3.00

SIREN: SHAPES
Image Comics: May, 1998 - No. 3, Nov, 1998 ($2.95, B&W, limited series)

	GD	VG	FN	VF	VF/NM	NM-
1-3-J. Torres -s						3.00

SIR LANCELOT (TV)
Dell Publishing Co.: No. 606, Dec, 1954 - No. 775, Mar, 1957

	GD	VG	FN	VF	VF/NM	NM-
Four Color 606 (not TV)	7	14	21	48	79	110
Four Color 775(...and Brian)-Buscema-a; photo-c	9	18	27	63	112	160

SIR WALTER RALEIGH (Movie)
Dell Publishing Co.: May, 1955 (Based on movie "The Virgin Queen")

	GD	VG	FN	VF	VF/NM	NM-
Four Color 644-Photo-c	7	14	21	44	72	100

SISTERHOOD OF STEEL (See Eclipse Graphic Adventure Novel #13)
Marvel Comics (Epic Comics): Dec, 1984 -No. 8, Feb, 1986 ($1.50, Baxter paper, mature)

	GD	VG	FN	VF	VF/NM	NM-
1-8						3.00

SIX
Image Comics: Aug, 2004 ($5.95, B&W)

	GD	VG	FN	VF	VF/NM	NM-
1-Oeming-s/c; Beavers-a						6.00

6 BLACK HORSES (See Movie Classics)

SIX FROM SIRIUS
Marvel Comics (Epic Comics): July, 1984 - No. 4, Oct, 1984 ($1.50, limited series, mature)

	GD	VG	FN	VF	VF/NM	NM-
1-4: Moench scripts; Gulacy-c/a in all						3.00

SIX FROM SIRIUS II
Marvel Comics (Epic Comics): Feb, 1986 - No. 4, May, 1986 ($1.50, limited series, mature)

	GD	VG	FN	VF	VF/NM	NM-
1-4: Moench scripts; Gulacy-c/a in all						3.00

SIX-GUN HEROES
Fawcett Publications: March, 1950 - No. 23, Nov, 1953 (Photo-c #1-23)

	GD	VG	FN	VF	VF/NM	NM-
1-Rocky Lane, Hopalong Cassidy, Smiley Burnette begin (same date as Smiley Burnette #1)	31	62	93	186	303	420
2	16	32	48	94	147	200
3-5: 5-Lash LaRue begins	14	28	42	76	108	140
6-15	11	22	33	62	86	110
16-22: 17-Last Smiley Burnette. 18-Monte Hale begins	10	20	30	54	72	90
23-Last Fawcett issue	10	20	30	58	79	100

NOTE: *Hopalong Cassidy photo c-1-3. Monte Hale photo c-18. Rocky Lane photo c-4, 5, 7, 9, 11, 13, 15, 17, 20, 21, 23. Lash LaRue photo c-6, 8, 10, 12, 14, 16, 19, 22.*

SIX-GUN HEROES (Cont'd from Fawcett; Gunmasters #84 on) (See Blue Bird)
Charlton Comics: No. 24, Jan, 1954 - No. 83, Mar-Apr, 1965 (All Vol. 4)

	GD	VG	FN	VF	VF/NM	NM-
24-Lash LaRue, Hopalong Cassidy, Rocky Lane & Tex Ritter begin; photo-c	14	28	42	80	115	150
25	10	20	30	54	72	90
26-30: 26-Rod Cameron story. 28-Tom Mix begins?	9	18	27	47	61	75
31-40: 38-40-Jingles & Wild Bill Hickok (TV)	8	16	24	42	54	65
41-46,48,50: 41-43-Wild Bill Hickok (TV)	8	16	24	40	50	60
47-Williamson-a, 2 pgs; Torres-a	8	16	24	42	54	65
49-Williamson-a (5 pgs.)	9	18	27	50	65	80
51-56,58-60: 58-Gunmaster app.	3	6	9	20	30	40
57-Origin & 1st app. Gunmaster	4	8	12	26	41	55
61,63-70	3	6	9	16	23	30
62-Origin Gunmaster	3	6	9	20	30	40
71-75,77,78,80-83	2	4	6	13	18	22
76,79: 76-Gunmaster begins. 79-1st app. & origin of Bullet, the Gun-Boy	3	6	9	14	19	24

SIXGUN RANCH (See Luke Short & Four Color #580)

SIX GUNS
Marvel Comics: Jan, 2012 - No. 5, Apr, 2012 ($2.99, limited series)

	GD	VG	FN	VF	VF/NM	NM-
1-5-Diggle-s/Gianfelice-a; Tarantula and Tex Dawson app.						3.00

SIX-GUN WESTERN
Atlas Comics (CDS): Jan, 1957 - No. 4, July, 1957

	GD	VG	FN	VF	VF/NM	NM-
1-Crandall-a; two Williamson text illos	18	36	54	105	165	225
2,3-Williamson-a in both	14	28	42	80	115	150
4-Woodbridge-a	10	20	30	58	79	100

NOTE: ***Ayers** a-2, 3. **Maneely** a-1; c-2, 3. **Orlando** a-2. **Pakula** a-2. **Powell** a-3. **Romita** a-1, 4. **Severin** c-1, 4. **Shores** a-2.*

SIX MILLION DOLLAR MAN, THE (TV) (Also see The Bionic Man)
Charlton Comics: 6/76 - No. 4, 12/76; No. 5, 10/77; No. 6, 2/78 - No. 9, 6/78

	GD	VG	FN	VF	VF/NM	NM-
1-Staton-c/a; Lee Majors photo on-c	3	6	9	18	27	35
2-Neal Adams-c; Staton-a	3	6	9	14	20	25
3-9	2	4	6	13	18	22

SIX MILLION DOLLAR MAN, THE (TV)(Magazine)
Charlton Comics: July, 1976 - No. 7, Nov, 1977 (B&W)

	GD	VG	FN	VF	VF/NM	NM-
1-Neal Adams-c/a	4	8	12	22	34	45
2-Neal Adams-c	3	6	9	16	23	30
3-N. Adams part inks; Chaykin-a	3	6	9	14	19	24
4-7	2	4	6	11	16	20

SIX STRING SAMURAI
Awesome-Hyperwerks: Sept, 1998 ($2.95)

	GD	VG	FN	VF	VF/NM	NM-
1-Stinsman & Fraga-a						3.00

67 SECONDS
Marvel Comics (Epic Comics): 1992 ($15.95, 54 pgs., graphic novel)

	GD	VG	FN	VF	VF/NM	NM-
nn-James Robinson scripts; Steve Yeowell-c/a	2	4	6	11	14	18

SKAAR: KING OF THE SAVAGE LAND
Marvel Comics: Jun, 2011 - No. 5 ($2.99, limited series)

	GD	VG	FN	VF	VF/NM	NM-
1-5-Shanna & Ka-Zar app.; Ching-a. 1-Komarck-c. 2-McGuinness-c						3.00

SKAAR: SON OF HULK (Title continues in Son of Hulk #13)(Also see World War Hulk x-over)
Marvel Comics: Aug, 2008 - No. 12, Aug, 2009 ($2.99)

	GD	VG	FN	VF	VF/NM	NM-
1-Garney-a/Pak-s; 2 covers by Pagulayan and Julie Bell; origin						4.00
1-Second printing - 2 covers by Garney and Hulk movie image						3.00
1-Third printing - Garney sketch variant-c						3.00
2-12: 2-6-Back-up story with Guice-a. 7-12-Silver Surfer app.						3.00
Planet Skaar Prologue 1 (7/09, $3.99) Panosian-a; Fantastic Four & She-Hulk app.						4.00
... Presents - Savage World of Sakaar (11/08, $3.99) Pak-s/art by various; Garney-c						4.00

SKATEMAN
Pacific Comics: Nov, 1983 (Baxter paper, one-shot)

	GD	VG	FN	VF	VF/NM	NM-
1-Adams-c/a						4.00

SKELETON HAND (...In Secrets of the Supernatural)
American Comics Gr. (B&M Dist. Co.): Sept-Oct, 1952 - No. 6, Jul-Aug, 1953

	GD	VG	FN	VF	VF/NM	NM-
1	47	94	141	296	498	700
2	34	68	102	206	336	465
3-6	27	54	81	160	263	365

SKELETON KEY
Amaze Ink: July, 1995 - No. 30, Jan, 1998 ($1.25/$1.50/$1.75, B&W)

	GD	VG	FN	VF	VF/NM	NM-
1-30						3.00
Special #1 (2/98, $4.95) Unpublished short stories						5.00
Sugar Kat Special (10/98, $2.95) Halloween stories						3.00
Beyond The Threshold TPB (6/96. $11.95)-r/#1-6						12.00
Cats and Dogs TPB ($12.95)-r/#25-30						13.00
The Celestial Calendar TPB ($19.95)-r/#7-18						20.00
Telling Tales TPB ($12.95)-r/#19-24						13.00

SKELETON KEY (Volume 2)
Amaze Ink: 1999 - No. 4, 1999 ($2.95, B&W)

	GD	VG	FN	VF	VF/NM	NM-
1-4-Andrew Watson-s/a						3.00

SKELETON WARRIORS
Marvel Comics: Apr, 1995 - No. 4, July, 1995 ($1.50)

	GD	VG	FN	VF	VF/NM	NM-
1-4: Based on animated series.						3.00

SKIN GRAFT: THE ADVENTURES OF A TATTOOED MAN
DC Comics (Vertigo): July, 1993 - No. 4, Oct, 1993 ($2.50, lim. series, mature)

	GD	VG	FN	VF	VF/NM	NM-
1-4						3.00

SKINWALKER
Oni Press: May, 2002 - No. 4, Sept, 2002 ($2.95, limited series)

	GD	VG	FN	VF	VF/NM	NM-
1-4-Hurtt & Dela Cruz-a; Talon-c						3.00
1-(5/05) Free Comic Book Day Edition						3.00

SKI PARTY (See Movie Classics)

SKREEMER
DC Comics: May, 1989 - No. 6, Oct, 1989 ($2.00, limited series, mature)

	GD	VG	FN	VF	VF/NM	NM-
1-6: Contains graphic violence; Milligan-s						3.00
TPB (2002, $19.95) r/#1-6						20.00

SKRULL KILL KREW
Marvel Comics: Sept, 1995 - No. 5, Dec, 1995 ($2.95, limited series)

Skullkickers #9 © Jim Zubkavich

Skyman #1 © CCG

Sleepwalkers #2 © MAR

GD 2.0 | VG 4.0 | FN 6.0 | VF 8.0 | VF/NM 9.0 | NM- 9.2

1-5: Grant Morrison & Mark Millar scripts; Steve Yeowell-a. 2,3-Cap America app. 3.00
TPB (2006, $16.99) r/#1-5 17.00

SKRULL KILL KREW
Marvel Comics: Jun, 2009 - No. 5, Dec, 2009 ($3.99, limited series)
1-5-Felber-s/Robinson-a 4.00

SKRULLS! (Tie-in to Secret Invasion crossover)
Marvel Comics: 2008 ($4.99, one-shot)
1-Skrull history, profiles of Skrulls, their allies & foes; checklist of appearances; Horn-c 5.00

SKRULLS VS. POWER PACK (Tie-in to Secret Invasion crossover)
Marvel Comics: Sept, 2008 - No. 4 ($2.99, limited series)
1-4-Van Lente-s/Hamscher-a; Franklin Richards app. 3.00

SKUL, THE
Virtual Comics (Byron Preiss Multimedia): Oct, 1996 - No. 3, Dec, 1996 ($2.50, lim. series)
1-3: Ron Lim & Jimmy Palmiotti-a 3.00

SKULL & BONES
DC Comics: 1992 - No. 3, 1992 ($4.95, limited series, 52 pgs.)
Book 1-3: 1-1st app. 5.00

SKULLKICKERS
Image Comics: Sept, 2010 - Present ($2.99)
1-Jim Zubkavich-s/Edwin Huang-a; two covers 4.00
1-(2nd & 3rd printings), 2-12 3.00

SKULL, THE SLAYER
Marvel Comics Group: Aug, 1975 - No. 8, Nov, 1976 (20¢/25¢)
1-Origin & 1st app.; Gil Kane-c 2 4 6 11 16 20
2-8: 2-Gil Kane-c. 5,6-(Regular 25¢-c). 8-Kirby-c 2 4 6 8 10 12
5,6-(30¢-c variants, limited distribution)(5,7/76) 3 6 9 18 27 35

SKY BLAZERS (CBS Radio)
Hawley Publications: Sept, 1940 - No. 2, Nov, 1940
1-Sky Pirates, Ace Archer, Flying Aces begin 60 120 180 381 658 935
2 39 78 117 231 378 525

SKY DOLL
Marvel Comics (Soleil): 2008 - No. 3, 2008 ($5.99, mature)
1-3-Barbucci & Canepa-s/a; English version of French comic; preview of other titles 6.00
...: Doll's Factory 1,2 (2009 - No. 2, 2009, $5.99) Barbucci & Canepa-s/a 6.00
...: Lacrima Christi 1,2 (9/10 - No. 2, 10/10, $5.99) Barbucci & Canepa and others-s/a 6.00
...: Space Ship 1,2 (7/10 - No. 2, 8/10, $5.99) Barbucci & Canepa and others-s/a 6.00

SKYE RUNNER
DC Comics (WildStorm): June, 2006 - No. 6, Mar, 2007 ($2.99)
1-6: 1-Three covers; Warner-s/Garza-a. 2-Three covers, incl. Campbell 3.00

SKYMAN (See Big Shot Comics & Sparky Watts)
Columbia Comics Gr.: Fall?, 1941 - No. 2, Fall?, 1942; No. 3, 1948 - No. 4, 1948
1-Origin Skyman, The Face, Sparky Watts app.; Whitney-c/a; 3rd story-r from Big Shot #1; Whitney c-1-4 126 252 378 806 1378 1950
2 (1942)-Yankee Doodle 63 126 189 403 689 975
3,4 (1948) 40 80 120 246 411 575

SKYPILOT
Ziff-Davis Publ. Co.: No. 10, 1950(nd) - No. 11, Apr-May, 1951
10,11-Frank Borth-a; Saunders painted-c 15 30 45 84 127 170

SKY RANGER (See Johnny Law...)

SKYROCKET
Harry 'A' Chesler: 1944
nn-Alias the Dragon, Dr. Vampire, Skyrocket & The Desperado app.; WWII Japan zero-c 36 72 108 211 343 475

SKY SHERIFF (Breeze Lawson...) (Also see Exposed & Outlaws)
D. S. Publishing Co.: Summer, 1948
1-Edmond Good-c/a 14 28 42 76 108 140

SKY WOLF (Also see Airboy)
Eclipse Comics: Mar, 1988 - No. 3, Oct, 1988 ($1.25/$1.50/$1.95, lim. series)
1-3 3.00

SLAINE, THE BERSERKER (Slaine the King #21 on)
Quality: July, 1987 - No. 28, 1989 ($1.25/$1.50)
1-28 3.00

SLAINE, THE HORNED GOD

GD 2.0 | VG 4.0 | FN 6.0 | VF 8.0 | VF/NM 9.0 | NM- 9.2

Fleetway: 1998 - No. 3 ($6.99)
1-3-Reprints series from 2000 A.D.; Bisley-a 7.00

SLAM BANG COMICS (Western Desperado #8)
Fawcett Publications: Mar, 1940 - No. 7, Sept, 1940 (Combined with Master Comics #7)
1-Diamond Jack, Mark Swift & The Time Retarder, Lee Granger, Jungle King begin & continue in Master 226 452 678 1446 2473 3500
2 90 180 270 576 988 1400
3-Classic-c 206 412 618 1318 2259 3200
4-7: 6-Intro Zoro, the Mystery Man (also in #7) 71 142 213 454 777 1100
Ashcan (1940) Not distributed to newsstands, only for in house use. A copy sold in 2006 for $4,500.

SLAPSTICK
Marvel Comics: Nov, 1992 - No. 4, Feb, 1993 ($1.25, limited series)
1-4: Fry/Austin-c/a. 4-Ghost Rider, D.D., F.F. app. 3.00

SLAPSTICK COMICS
Comic Magazines Distributors: nd (1946?) (36 pgs.)
nn-Firetop feature; Post-a(2) 25 50 75 150 245 340

SLASH-D DOUBLECROSS
St. John Publishing Co.: 1950 (Pocket-size, 132 pgs.)
nn-Western comics 21 42 63 122 199 275

SLAUGHTERMAN
Comico: Feb, 1983 - No. 2, 1983 ($1.50, B&W)
1,2 3.00

SLAVE GIRL COMICS (See Malu... & White Princess of the Jungle #2)
Avon Periodicals/Eternity Comics (1989): Feb, 1949 - No. 2, Apr, 1949 (52 pgs.); Mar, 1989 (B&W, 44 pgs)
1-Larsen-c/a 103 206 309 659 1130 1600
2-Larsen-a 73 146 219 467 796 1125
1-(3/89, $2.25, B&W, 44 pgs.)-r/#1 4.00

SLAVE LABOR STORIES
SLG Publishing: May, 2003 (Giveaway, B&W)
1-Free Comic Book Day Edition; short stories by various; Dorkin Milk & Cheese-c 3.00

SLEDGE HAMMER (TV)
Marvel Comics: Feb, 1988 - No. 2, Mar,1988 ($1.00, limited series)
1,2 3.00

SLEEPER
DC Comics (WildStorm): Mar, 2003 - No. 12, Mar, 2004 ($2.95)
1-12-Brubaker-s/Phillips-c/a. 3-Back-up preview of The Authority: High Stakes pt. 2 3.00
...: All False Moves TPB (2004, $17.95) r/#7-12 18.00
...: Out in the Cold TPB (2004, $17.95) r/#1-6 18.00

SLEEPER: SEASON TWO
DC Comics (WildStorm): Aug, 2004 - No. 12, July, 2005 ($2.95/$2.99)
1-12-Brubaker-s/Phillips-c/a. 3.00
TPB (2009, $24.99) r/#1-12 25.00
...: A Crooked Line TPB (2005, $17.99) r/#1-6 18.00
...: The Long Way Home TPB (2005, $14.99) r/#7-12 15.00

SLEEPING BEAUTY (See Dell Giants & Movie Comics)
Dell Publishing Co.: No. 973, May, 1959 - No. 984, June, 1959 (Disney)
Four Color 973 (...and the Prince) 10 20 30 69 130 190
Four Color 984 (...Fairy Godmother's) 9 18 27 60 103 145

SLEEPWALKER
Marvel Comics: June, 1991 - No. 33, Feb, 1994 ($1.00/$1.25)
1-1st app. Sleepwalker 3.50
2-33: 4-Williamson-i. 5-Spider-Man-c/stor. 7-Infinity Gauntlet x-over. 8-Vs. Deathlok-c/story. 11-Ghost Rider-c/story. 12-Quesada-c/a(p) 14-Intro Spectra. 15-F.F.-c/story. 17-Darkhawk & Spider-Man x-over. 18-Infinity War x-over; Quesada/Williamson-c. 21,22-Hobgoblin app. 19-($2.00)-Die-cut Sleepwalker mask-c 3.00
25-($2.95, 52 pgs.)-Holo-grafx foil-c; origin 4.00
Holiday Special 1 (1/93, $2.00, 52 pgs.)-Quesada-c(p) 4.00

SLEEPWALKING
Hall of Heroes: Jan, 1996 ($2.50, B&W)
1-Kelley Jones-c 3.00

SLEEPY HOLLOW (Movie Adaption)
DC Comics (Vertigo): 2000 ($7.95, one-shot)
1-Kelley Jones-a/Seagle-s 8.00

Slingers #1 © MAR

Smallville #2 © DC

Smash Comics #36 © QUA

GD VG FN VF VF/NM NM-
2.0 4.0 6.0 8.0 9.0 9.2

GD VG FN VF VF/NM NM-
2.0 4.0 6.0 8.0 9.0 9.2

SLEEZE BROTHERS, THE
Marvel Comics (Epic Comics): Aug, 1989 - No. 6, Jan, 1990 ($1.75, mature)

1-6: 4-6 (9/89 - 11/89 indicia dates) 3.00
nn-(1991, $3.95, 52 pgs.) 4.00

SLICK CHICK COMICS
Leader Enterprises: 1947(nd) - No. 3, 1947(nd)

1-Teenage humor 14 28 42 80 115 150
2,3 10 20 30 56 76 95

SLIDERS (TV)
Acclaim Comics (Armada): June, 1996 - No. 2, July, 1996 ($2.50, lim. series)

1,2: D.G. Chichester scripts; Dick Giordano-a. 3.00

SLIDERS: DARKEST HOUR (TV)
Acclaim Comics (Armada): Oct, 1996 - No. 3, Dec, 1996 ($2.50, limited series)

1-3 3.00

SLIDERS SPECIAL
Acclaim Comics (Armada): Nov, 1996 - No 3, Mar, 1997 ($3.95, limited series)

1-3: 1-Narcotica-Jerry O'Connell-s. 2-Blood and Splendor. 3-Deadly Secrets 4.00

SLIDERS: ULTIMATUM (TV)
Acclaim Comics (Armada): Sept, 1996 - No. 2, Sept, 1996 ($2.50, lim. series)

1,2 3.00

SLIMER! (TV cartoon) (Also see the Real Ghostbusters)
Now Comics: 1989 - No. 19, Feb?, 1991 ($1.75)

1-19: Based on animated cartoon 3.00

SLIM MORGAN (See Wisco)

SLINGERS (See Spider-Man: Identity Crisis issues)
Marvel Comics: Dec, 1998 - No. 12, Nov, 1999 ($2.99/$1.99)

0-(Wizard #88 supplement) Prelude story 3.00
1-($2.99) Four editions w/different covers for each hero, 16 pages common to all, the other pages from each hero's perspective 4.00
2-12: 2-Two-c. 12-Saltares-a 3.00

SLITHISS ATTACKS! (Also see Very Weird Tales)
Oceanspray Comics Group: Dec, 2001 – No. 4, Aug, 2004 ($3.00/$4.00)

1-($3.00) Origin and 1st app. of the monster Slithiss; 1st app. Overconfident Man 15.00
2-($4.00) 2nd app. Overconfident Man; "Chris Lamo" Newport, OR murder parody 12.00
3-($3.00) Rutland Vermont Halloween x-over; 3rd app. Overconfident Man 12.00
4-($3.00) 4th app. Overconfident Man 10.00
Special Edition 1($20.00) reprints #1-2 without letter column 20.00
Special Edition 1($20.00) second printing 20.00
NOTE: *Created in prevention classes taught by Jon McClure at the Oceanspray Family Center in Newport, OR and paid for by the Housing Authority of Lincoln County, all books are b&w with color covers. Bob Overstreet and other comics' professionals wrote letters of encouragement that were published in issues #2-4. Issues #1-2 penciled and inked by various artists; #3-4 penciled by James Gilmer. All comics feature characters created by students, signed and numbered by Jon McClure. Issue #1 had a 200 issue print run, while issues #2-4 have print runs of 100 each. Special Edition #1 had a print run of 26 issues, while the second printing had a 10 issue print run. Ties in with live action movie Face Eater released in 2007 and card game FaceEater released in 2010.*

SLUDGE
Malibu Comics (Ultraverse): Oct, 1993 - No. 12, Dec, 1994 ($2.50/$1.95)

1-($2.50, 48 pgs.)-Intro/1st app. Sludge; Rune flip-c/story Pt. 1 (1st app., 3 pgs.) by Barry Smith; The Night Man app. (3 pg. preview); The Mighty Magnor 1 pg strip begins by Aragonés (cont. in other titles) 4.00
1-Ultra 5000 Limited silver foil 5.00
2-11: 3-Break-Thru x-over. 4-2 pg. Mantra origin. 8-Bloodstorm app. 3.00
12 ($3.50)-Ultraverse Premiere #8 flip book; Alex Ross poster 4.00
...:Red Xmas (12/94, $2.50, 44 pgs.) 4.00

SLUGGER (Little Wise Guys Starring...)(Also see Daredevil Comics)
Lev Gleason Publications: April, 1956

1-Biro-c 7 14 21 37 46 55

SMALL GODS
Image Comics: Jun, 2004 - No. 12, Nov, 2005 ($2.95/$2.99, B&W)

1-12-Rand-s/Ferreyna-a 3.00
... Special #1 (6/05, $2.95) flip cover 3.00
Vol. 1: Killing Grin (1/05, $9.95, TPB) r/#1-4; sketch pages, cover gallery & script page 10.00

SMALLVILLE (Based on TV series)
DC Comics: May, 2003 - No. 11 ($3.50/$3.95, bi-monthly)

1-6-Photo-c. 1-Plunkett-a; interviews with cast; season 1 episode guide begins 4.00
7-11-($3.95) 7-Chloe Chronicles begin; season 2 episode guide begins 4.00
Vol. 1 TPB (2004, $9.95) r/#1-4 & Smallville: The Comic; photo-c 10.00

SMALLVILLE: THE COMIC (Based on TV series)
DC Comics: Nov, 2002 ($3.95, 64 pages, one-shot)

1-Photo-c; art by Martinez and Leon; interviews with cast; season 2 preview 4.00

SMASH COMICS (Becomes Lady Luck #86 on)
Quality Comics Group: Aug, 1939 - No. 85, Oct, 1949

1-Origin Hugh Hazard & His Iron Man, Bozo the Robot, Espionage, Starring Black X by Eisner, & Hooded Justice (Invisible Justice #2 on); Chic Carter & Wings Wendall begin; 1st Robot on the cover of a comic book (Bozo) 331 662 993 2317 4059 5800
2-The Lone Star Rider app; Invisible Hood gains power of invisibility; bondage/torture-c 135 270 405 864 1482 2100
3-Captain Cook & Eisner's John Law begin 71 142 213 454 777 1100
4,5: 4-Flash Fulton begins 68 136 204 435 743 1050
6-12: 12-One pg. Fine-a 65 130 195 416 708 1000
13-Magno begins (8/40); last Eisner issue; The Ray app. in full page ad; The Purple Trio begins 66 132 198 419 722 1025
14-Intro. The Ray (9/40) by Lou Fine & others 300 600 900 2010 3505 5000
15-1st Ray-c, 2nd app. 142 284 426 909 1555 2200
16-The Scarlet Seal begins 126 252 378 806 1378 1950
17-Wun Cloo becomes plastic super-hero by Jack Cole (9-months before Plastic Man); Ray-c 132 264 396 838 1444 2050
18-Midnight by Jack Cole begins (origin & 1st app., 1/41) 165 330 495 1048 1799 2550
19-22: Last Ray by Fine; The Jester begins-#22. 19,21-Ray-c 89 178 267 565 970 1375
23,24: 23-Ray-c. 24-The Sword app.; last Chic Carter; Wings Wendall dons new costume #24,25 68 136 204 435 743 1050
25-Origin/1st app. Wildfire; Rookie Rankin begins; Ray-c 776 152 228 486 831 1175
26-30: 28-Midnight-c begin, end #85 64 128 192 406 696 985
31,32,34: The Ray by Rudy Palais; also #33 54 108 162 346 591 835
33-Origin The Marksman 62 124 186 394 680 965
35-37 49 98 147 309 522 735
38-The Yankee Eagle begins; last Midnight by Jack Cole; classic-c by Cole 98 196 294 622 1074 1525
39,40-Last Ray issue 50 100 150 315 533 750
41,44-50 40 80 120 246 411 575
42-Lady Luck begins by Klaus Nordling 135 270 405 864 1482 2100
43-Lady Luck-c (1st & only in Smash) 74 148 222 470 810 1150
51-60 30 60 90 177 289 400
61-70 23 46 69 136 223 310
71-85: 79-Midnight battles the Men from Mars-c/s 21 42 63 122 199 275
NOTE: ***Al Bryant** c-54, 63-68. **Cole** a-17-38, 68, 69, 72, 73, 78, 80, 83, 85; c-38, 60-62, 69-84. **Crandall** a-(Ray)-23-29, 35-38; c-36, 39, 40, 42-44, 46. **Fine** a(Ray)-14, 15, 16(w/**Tuska**), 17-22. **Fox** c-24-35. **Fuje** Ray-30. **Gil Fox** a-6-7, 9, 11-13. **Guardineer** a-(The Marksman)-39-?, 49, 52. **Gustavson** a-4-7, 9, 11-13 (The Jester)-22-46; (Magno)-13-21; (Midnight)-39(Cole inks), 49, 52, 63-65. **Kotzky** a-(Espionage)-33-38; c-45, 47-53. **Nordling** a-49, 52, 63-65. **Powell** a-11, 12, (Abdul the Arab)-13-24.Black X c-2, 6, 9, 11, 13, 16. Bozo the Robot c-1, 3, 5, 8, 10, 12, 14, 18, 20, 22, 24, 26. Midnight c-28-85. The Ray c-15, 17, 19, 21, 23, 25, 27. Wings Wendall c-4, 7.*

SMASH COMICS (Also see All Star Comics 1999 crossover titles)
DC Comics: May, 1999 ($1.99, one-shot)

1-Golden Age Doctor Mid-nite and Hourman 3.00

SMASH HIT SPORTS COMICS
Essankay Publications: V2#1, Jan, 1949

V2#1-L.B. Cole-c/a 28 56 84 165 270 375

SMAX (Also see Top Ten)
America's Best Comics: Oct, 2003 - No. 5, May, 2004 ($2.95, limited series)

1-5-Alan Moore-s/Zander Cannon-a 3.00
... Collected Edition (2004, $19.95, HC with dustjacket) r/#1-5 20.00
... Collected Edition SC (2005, $12.99) r/#1-5 13.00

SMILE COMICS (Also see Gay Comics, Tickle, & Whee)
Modern Store Publ.: 1955 (52 pgs.; 5x7-1/4") (7¢)

1 6 12 18 31 38 45

SMILEY BURNETTE WESTERN (Also see Patches #8 & Six-Gun Heroes)
Fawcett Publ.: March, 1950 - No. 4, Oct, 1950 (All photo front & back-c)

1-Red Eagle begins 25 50 75 150 245 340
2-4 16 32 48 94 147 200

SMILEY (THE PSYCHOTIC BUTTON) (See Evil Ernie)
Chaos! Comics: July, 1998 - Present ($2.95, one-shots)

1-Ivan Reis-a 3.00
... Holiday Special (1/99), ...'s Spring Break (4/99), ...Wrestling Special (5/99) 3.00

SMILIN' JACK (See Famous Feature Stories and Popular Comics) (Also see Super Book of

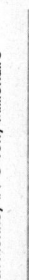

Smilin' Jack FC #58 © KING

Snarked #0 © BOOM

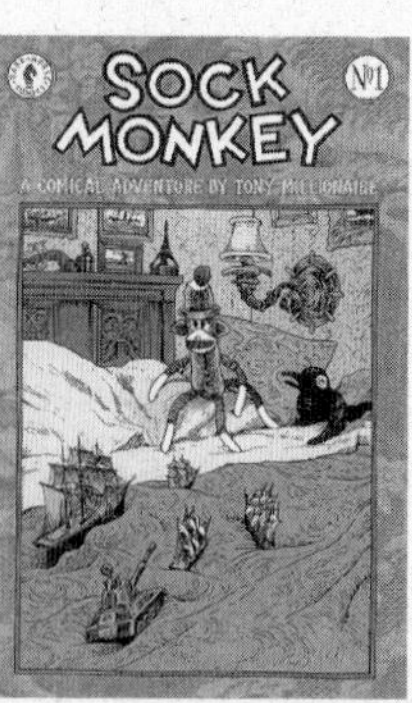

Sock Monkey #1 © Tony Millionaire

	GD 2.0	VG 4.0	FN 6.0	VF 8.0	VF/NM 9.0	NM- 9.2

Comics #1&2 and Super-Book of Comics #7&19 in the Promotional Comics section)
Dell Publishing Co.: No. 5, 1940 - No. 8, Oct-Dec, 1949

	GD	VG	FN	VF	VF/NM	NM-
Four Color 5	74	148	222	470	810	1150
Four Color 10 (1940)	62	124	186	394	680	965
Large Feature Comic 12,14,25 (1941)	60	120	180	381	653	925
Four Color 4 (1942)	35	70	105	254	552	850
Four Color 14 (1943)	27	54	81	192	414	635
Four Color 36,58 (1943-44)	20	40	60	137	294	450
Four Color 80 (1945)	13	26	39	85	180	275
Four Color 149 (1947)	10	20	30	66	121	175
1 (1-3/48)	10	20	30	67	124	180
2	6	12	18	41	66	90
3-8 (10-12/49)	5	10	15	32	51	70

SMILING SPOOK SPUNKY (See Spunky)

SMITTY (See Popular Comics, Super Book #2, 4 & Super Comics)
Dell Publishing Co.: No. 11, 1940 - No. 7, Aug-Oct, 1949; No. 909, Apr, 1958

	GD	VG	FN	VF	VF/NM	NM-
Four Color 11 (1940)	46	92	138	290	488	685
Large Feature Comic 26 (1941)	37	74	111	222	361	500
Four Color 6 (1942)	19	38	57	132	284	435
Four Color 32 (1943)	13	26	39	90	195	300
Four Color 65 (1945)	12	24	36	78	157	235
Four Color 99 (1946)	10	20	30	68	127	185
Four Color 138 (1947)	9	18	27	62	109	155
1 (2-4/48)	9	18	27	61	106	150
2-(5-7/48)	5	10	15	32	51	70
3,4: 3-(8-10/48), 4-(11-1/48-49)	4	8	12	28	44	60
5-7, Four Color 909 (4/58)	4	8	12	24	37	50

SMOKEY BEAR (TV) (See March Of Comics #234, 362, 372, 383, 407)
Gold Key: Feb, 1970 - No. 13, Mar, 1973

	GD	VG	FN	VF	VF/NM	NM-
1	3	6	9	19	29	38
2-5	2	4	6	10	14	18
6-13	2	4	6	8	10	12

SMOKEY STOVER (See Popular Comics, Super Book #5,17,29 & Super Comics)
Dell Publishing Co.: No. 7, 1942 - No. 827, Aug, 1957

	GD	VG	FN	VF	VF/NM	NM-
Four Color 7 (1942)-Reprints	25	50	75	175	375	575
Four Color 35 (1943)	14	28	42	96	208	320
Four Color 64 (1944)	12	24	36	79	160	240
Four Color 229 (1949)	6	12	18	41	66	90
Four Color 730,827	5	10	15	32	51	70

SMOKEY THE BEAR (See Forest Fire for 1st app.)
Dell Publ. Co.: No. 653, 10/55 - No. 1214, 8/61 (See March of Comics #234)

	GD	VG	FN	VF	VF/NM	NM-
Four Color 653 (#1)	10	20	30	67	124	180
Four Color 708,754,818,932	6	12	18	41	66	90
Four Color 1016,1119,1214	4	8	12	28	44	60

SMOKY (See Movie Classics)

SMURFS (TV)
Marvel Comics: 1982 (Dec) - No. 3, 1983

	GD	VG	FN	VF	VF/NM	NM-
1-3	2	4	6	11	16	20
...Treasury Edition 1 (64 pgs.)-r/#1-3	3	6	9	18	27	35

SNAFU (Magazine)
Atlas Comics (RCM): Nov, 1955 - V2#2, Mar, 1956 (B&W)

	GD	VG	FN	VF	VF/NM	NM-
V1#1-Heath/Severin-a; Everett, Maneely-a	15	30	45	86	133	180
V2#1,2-Severin-a	12	24	36	67	94	120

SNAGGLEPUSS (TV)(See Hanna-Barbera Band Wagon, Quick Draw McGraw #5 & Spotlight #4)
Gold Key: Oct, 1962 - No. 4, Sept, 1963 (Hanna-Barbera)

	GD	VG	FN	VF	VF/NM	NM-
1	8	16	24	56	96	135
2-4	6	12	18	42	69	95

SNAKE EYES (G.I. Joe)
Devil's Due Publ.: Aug, 2005 - No. 6, Jan, 2006 ($2.95)

	NM-
1-6-Santalucia-a	3.00
...: Declassified TPB (4/06, $18.95) r/series; source guide	19.00

SNAKE PLISSKEN CHRONICLES, (John Carpenter's...)
Hurricane Entertainment: June, 2003 - No. 4 ($2.99)

	NM-
Preview Issue (8/02, no cover price) B&W preview; John Carpenter interview	3.00
1-4: 1-Three covers; Rodriguez-a	3.00

SNAKES AND LADDERS
Eddie Campbell Comics: 2001 ($5.95, B&W, one-shot)

	NM-
nn-Alan Moore-s/Eddie Campbell-a	6.00

SNAKES ON A PLANE (Adaptation of the 2006 movie)
Virgin Comics: Oct, 2006 - No. 2, Nov, 2006 ($2.99, limited series)

	NM-
1,2: 1-Dixon-s/Purcell-a. JG Jones and photo-c. 2-Klebs, Jr.-a; Moore & photo-c	3.00

SNAKE WOMAN (Shekhar Kapur's...)
Virgin Comics: July, 2006 - No. 10, Apr, 2007 ($2.99)

	NM-
1-10: 1-6-Michael Gaydos-a/Zeb Wells-s. 1-Two covers by Gaydos & Singh	3.00
#0 (5/07, 99¢) origin of the Snake Goddess; background info; Gaydos-a/c	3.00
... Curse of the 68 (3/08 - No. 4, 5/08, $2.99) 1-4: 1-Ingale-a. 2-Manu-a	3.00
... Tale of the Snake Charmer 1-6 (6/07-12/07, $2.99) Vivek Shinde-a	3.00
... Vol. 1 TPB (6/07, $14.99) r/#1-5; Gaydos sketch pages; creator commentary	15.00
... Vol. 2 TPB (9/07, $14.99) r/#6-10; Cebulski intro.	15.00

SNAP (Formerly Scoop #8; becomes Jest #10,11 & Komik Pages #10)
Harry 'A' Chesler: No. 9, 1944

	GD	VG	FN	VF	VF/NM	NM-
9-Manhunter, The Voice; WWII gag-c	29	58	87	170	278	385

SNAPPY COMICS
Cima Publ. Co. (Prize Publ.): 1945

	GD	VG	FN	VF	VF/NM	NM-
1-Airmale app.; 9 pg. Sorcerer's Apprentice adapt; Kiefer-a	33	66	99	194	317	440

SNARKED
Boom Entertainment (Kaboom!): No. 0, Aug, 2011 - Present ($1.00/$3.99)

	NM-
0-($1.00) Roger Langridge-s/a; sketch gallery, bonus content and games	3.00
1-5: 1-($3.99) Covers by Langridge & Samnee	4.00

SNARKY PARKER (See Life With...)

SNIFFY THE PUP
Standard Publ. (Animated Cartoons): No. 5, Nov, 1949 - No. 18, Sept, 1953

	GD	VG	FN	VF	VF/NM	NM-
5-Two Frazetta text illos	11	22	33	62	86	110
6-10	7	14	21	37	46	55
11-18	6	12	18	31	38	45

SNOOPER AND BLABBER DETECTIVES (TV) (See Whitman Comic Books)
Gold Key: Nov, 1962 - No. 3, May, 1963 (Hanna-Barbera)

	GD	VG	FN	VF	VF/NM	NM-
1	7	14	21	48	79	110
2,3	6	12	18	37	59	80

SNOW WHITE (See Christmas With... (in Promotional Comics section), Mickey Mouse Magazine, Movie Comics & Seven Dwarfs)
Dell Publishing Co.: No. 49, July, 1944 - No. 382, Mar, 1952 (Disney-Movie)

	GD	VG	FN	VF	VF/NM	NM-
Four Color 49 (...& the Seven Dwarfs)	46	92	138	345	748	1150
Four Color 382 (1952)-origin; partial reprint of Four Color 49	9	18	27	63	112	160

SNOW WHITE
Marvel Comics: Jan, 1995 ($1.95, one-shot)

	NM-
1-r/1937 Sunday newspaper pages	3.00

SNOW WHITE AND THE SEVEN DWARFS
Whitman Publications: April, 1982 (60¢)

	GD	VG	FN	VF	VF/NM	NM-
nn-r/Four Color 49	1	2	3	5	6	8

SNOW WHITE AND THE SEVEN DWARFS GOLDEN ANNIVERSARY
Gladstone: Fall, 1987 ($2.95, magazine size, 52 pgs.)

	GD	VG	FN	VF	VF/NM	NM-
1-Contains poster	2	4	6	8	11	14

SOAP OPERA LOVE
Charlton Comics: Feb, 1983 - No. 3, June, 1983

	GD	VG	FN	VF	VF/NM	NM-
1-3-Low print run	3	6	9	18	27	35

SOAP OPERA ROMANCES
Charlton Comics: July, 1982 - No. 5, March, 1983

	GD	VG	FN	VF	VF/NM	NM-
1-5-Nurse Betsy Crane-r; low print run	3	6	9	18	27	35

SOCK MONKEY
Dark Horse Comics: Sept, 1998 - No. 2, Oct, 1998 ($2.95/$2.99, B&W)

	NM-
1,2-Tony Millionaire-s/a	4.00

Vol. 2 -(Tony Millionaire's Sock Monkey) July, 1999 - No. 2, Aug, 1999

	NM-
1,2	3.00

Vol. 3 -(Tony Millionaire's Sock Monkey) Nov, 2000 - No. 2, Dec, 2000

	NM-
1,2	3.00

Vol. 4 -(Tony Millionaire's Sock Monkey) May, 2003 - No. 2, Aug, 2003

	NM-
1,2	3.00

Sojourn #11 © CRO

Soldier Zero #7 © BOOM

Solo #1 © MAR

GD 2.0 VG 4.0 FN 6.0 VF 8.0 VF/NM 9.0 NM- 9.2

GD 2.0 VG 4.0 FN 6.0 VF 8.0 VF/NM 9.0 NM- 9.2

...The Inches Incident (Sept, 2006 - No. 4, Apr, 2007) 1-4-Tony Millionaire-s/a 3.00

SOJOURN
White Cliffs Publ. Co.: Sept, 1977 - No. 2, 1978 ($1.50, B&W & color, tabloid size)

1,2: 1-Tor by Kubert, Eagle by Severin, E. V. Race, Private Investigator by Doug Wildey, T. C. Mars by Aragonés begin plus other strips 2 4 6 8 10 12
NOTE: Most copies came folded. Unfolded copies are worth 50% more.

SOJOURN
CrossGeneration Comics: July, 2001 - No. 34, May, 2004 ($2.95)

Prequel -Ron Marz-s/Greg Land-c/a; preview pages 3.00
1-Ron Marz-s/Greg Land-c/a in most 6.00
2,3 5.00
4-24: 7-Immonen-a. 12-Brigman-a. 17-Lopresti-a. 21-Luke Ross-a 3.00
25-34: 25-$1.00-c. 34-Cariello-a 3.00
...: From the Ashes TPB (2001, $19.95) r/#1-6; Land painted-c 20.00
...: The Dragon's Tale TPB (2002, $15.95) r/#7-12; Jusko painted-c 16.00
...: The Warrior's Tale TPB (2003, $15.95) r/#13-18 16.00
Vol. 4: The Thief's Tale (2003, $15.95) r/#19-24 16.00
Vol. 5: The Sorcerer's Tale (Checker Book Publ.,2007, $17.95) r/#25-30 18.00
Vol. 6: The Berzerker's Tale (Checker Book Publ.,2007, $17.95) r/#31-34, Prequel 18.00
Traveler Vol.1,2 ($9.95) digest-sized reprints of TPBs 10.00

SOLAR (...Man of the Atom) (Also see Doctor Solar)
Valiant/Acclaim Comics (Valiant): Sept, 1991 - No. 60, Apr, 1996 ($1.75-$2.50, 44 pgs.)

1-Layton-a(i) on Solar; Barry Windsor-Smith-c/a 2 4 6 8 10 12
2-9: 2-Layton-a(i) on Solar, B. Smith-a. 3-1st app. Harada (11/91). 7-vs. X-O Armor 6.00
10-(6/92, $3.95)-1st app. Eternal Warrior (6 pgs.); black embossed-c; origin & 1st app. Geoff McHenry (Geomancer) 2 4 6 9 12 15
10-($3.95)-2nd printing 4.00
11-15: 11-1st full app. Eternal Warrior. 12,13-Unity x-overs. 14-1st app. Fred Bender (becomes Dr. Eclipse). 15-2nd Dr. Eclipse 4.00
16-60: 17-X-O Manowar app. 23-Solar splits. 29-1st Valiant Vision book. 33-Valiant Vision; bound-in trading card. 38-Chaos Effect Epsilion Pt.1. 46-52-Dan Jurgens-a(p)/scripts w/Giordano-i. 53,54-Jurgens scripts only. 60-Giffen scripts; Jeff Johnson-a(p) 3.00
0-($9.95, trade paperback)-r/Alpha and Omega origin story; polybagged w/poster 10.00
...:Second Death (1994, $9.95)-r/issues #1-4. 10.00
NOTE: *#1-10 all have free 8 pg. insert "Alpha and Omega" which is a 10 chapter Solar origin story. All 10 center-folds can pieced together to show climax of story.* ***Ditko*** *a-11p, 14p.* ***Giordano*** *a-46, 47, 48, 49, 50, 51, 52i.* ***Johnson*** *a-60p.* ***Jurgens*** *a-46, 47, 48, 49, 50 , 51, 52p.* ***Layton*** *a-1-3i; c-2i, 11i, 17i, 25i.* ***Miller*** *c-12.* ***Quesada*** *c-17p, 20-23p, 29p.* ***Simonson*** *c-13.* ***B. Smith*** *a-1-10; c-1, 3, 5, 7, 19i.* ***Thibert*** *c-22i, 23i.*

SOLAR LORD
Image Comics: Mar, 1999 - No. 7, Sept, 1999 ($2.50)

1-7-Khoo Fuk Lung-s/a 3.00

SOLARMAN (See Pendulum Ill. Originals)
Marvel Comics: Jan, 1989 - No. 2, May, 1990 ($1.00, limited series)

1,2 3.00

SOLAR, MAN OF THE ATOM (Man of the Atom on cover)
Acclaim Comics (Valiant Heroes): Vol. 2, May, 1997 ($3.95, one-shot, 46 pgs)
(1st Valiant Heroes Special Event)

Vol. 2-Reintro Solar; Ninjak cameo; Warren Ellis scripts; Darick Robertson-a 4.00

SOLAR, MAN OF THE ATOM: HELL ON EARTH
Acclaim Comics (Valiant Heroes): Jan, 1998 - No. 4 ($2.50, limited series)

1-4-Priest-s/ Zircher-a(p) 3.00

SOLAR, MAN OF THE ATOM: REVELATIONS
Acclaim Comics (Valiant Heroes): Nov, 1997 ($3.95, one-shot, 46 pgs.)

1-Krueger-s/ Zircher-a(p) 4.00

SOLDIER & MARINE COMICS (Fightin' Army #16 on)
Charlton Comics (Toby Press of Conn. V1#11): No. 11, Dec, 1954 - No. 15, Aug, 1955; V2#9, Dec, 1956

V1#11 (12/54)-Bob Powell-a 9 18 27 52 69 85
V1#12(2/55)-15: 12-Photo-c. 14-Photo-c; Colan-a 7 14 21 35 43 50
V2#9(Formerly Never Again; Jerry Drummer V2#10 on) 6 12 18 31 38 45

SOLDIER COMICS
Fawcett Publications: Jan, 1952 - No. 11, Sept, 1953

1 14 28 42 76 108 140
2 8 16 24 44 57 70
3-5 8 16 24 42 54 65
6-11: 8-Illo. in **POP** 8 16 24 40 50 60

SOLDIERS OF FORTUNE
American Comics Group (Creston Publ. Corp.): Mar-Apr, 1951 - No. 13, Feb-Mar, 1953

1-Capt. Crossbones by Shelly, Ace Carter, Lance Larson begin 23 46 69 136 223 310
2 14 28 42 81 118 155
3-10: 6-Bondage-c 12 24 36 69 97 125
11-13 (War format) 9 18 27 47 61 75
NOTE: ***Shelly*** *a-1-3, 5.* ***Whitney*** *a-6, 8-11, 13; c-1-3, 5, 6.*

SOLDIERS OF FREEDOM
Americomics: 1987 - No. 2, 1987 ($1.75)

1,2 3.00

SOLDIER X (Continued from Cable)
Marvel Comics: Sept, 2002 - No. 12, Aug, 2003 ($2.99/$2.25)

1,10,11,12-($2.99) 1-Kordey-a/Macan-s. 10-Bollers-s/Ranson-a 3.00
2-9-($2.25) 3.00

SOLDIER ZERO (From Stan Lee)
BOOM! Studios: Oct, 2010 - No. 12, Sept, 2011 ($3.99)

1-12: 1-4-Cornell-s/Pina-a 4.00

SOLITAIRE (Also See Prime V2#6-8)
Malibu Comics (Ultraverse): Nov, 1993 - No. 12, Dec, 1994 ($1.95)

1-($2.50)-Collector's edition bagged w/playing card 4.00
1-12: 1-Regular edition w/o playing card. 2,4-Break-Thru x-over. 3-2 pg. origin The Night Man. 4-Gatefold-c. 5-Two pg. origin the Strangers 3.00

SOLO
Marvel Comics: Sept, 1994 - No. 4, Dec, 1994 ($1.75, limited series)

1-4: Spider-Man app. 3.00

SOLO (Movie)
Dark Horse Comics: July, 1996 - No. 2, Aug, 1996 ($2.50, limited series)

1,2: Adaptation of film; photo-c 3.00

SOLO (Anthology showcasing individual artists)
DC Comics: Dec, 2004 - No. 12, Oct, 2006 ($4.95/$4.99)

1-11: 1-Tim Sale-a; stories by Sale and various. 2-Richard Corben-a; stories by Corben and Arcudi. 3-Paul Pope. 4-Howard Chaykin. 5-Darwyn Cooke. 6-Jordi Bernet. 7-Michael Allred; Teen Titans & Doom Patrol app. 8-Teddy Kristiansen. 9-Scott Hampton. 10-Damion Scott. 11-Sergio Aragonés. 12-Brendan McCarthy 5.00

SOLO AVENGERS (Becomes Avenger Spotlight #21 on)
Marvel Comics: Dec, 1987 - No. 20, July, 1989 (75¢/$1.00)

1-Jim Lee-a on back-up story 6.00
2-20: 11-Intro Bobcat 4.00

SOLOMON AND SHEBA (Movie)
Dell Publishing Co.: No. 1070, Jan-Mar, 1960

Four Color 1070-Sekowsky-a; photo-c 8 16 24 56 96 135

SOLOMON GRUNDY
DC Comics: May, 2009 - No. 7, Nov, 2009 ($2.99)

1-7-Scott Kolins-s/a. 2-Bizarro app. 7-Blackest Night prelude 3.00
TPB (2010, $19.99) r/#1-7 20.00

SOLOMON KANE (Based on the Robert E. Howard character. Also see Blackthorne 3-D Series #60 & Marvel Premiere)
Marvel Comics: Sept, 1985 - No. 6, July, 1986 (Limited series)

1-Double size 4.00
2-6: 3-6-Williamson-a(i) 3.00

SOLOMON KANE
Dark Horse Comics: Sept, 2008 - No. 5, Feb, 2009 ($2.99)

1-5: 1-Two covers by Cassaday and Joe Kubert; Guevara-a 3.00
...: Death's Black Riders 1-4 (1/10 - No. 4, 6/10, $3.50) Robertson-c 3.50
...: Red Shadows 1-4 (4/11 - No. 4, 7/11, $3.50) Bruce Jones-s/Rahsan Ekedal-a; two covers by Davis & Manchess on each 3.50

SOLUS
CG Entertainment, Inc.: Apr, 2003 - No. 8, Jan, 2004 ($2.95)

1-8: 1-4,6,7-George Pérez-a/c; Barbara Kesel-s. 5-Ryan-a. 8-Kirk-a 3.00
Vol. 1: Genesis (1/04, $15.95) r/#1-6 16.00

SOLUTION, THE
Malibu Comics (Ultraverse): Sept, 1993 - No. 17, Feb, 1995 ($1.95)

1,3-15: 1-Intro Meathook, Deathdance, Black Tiger, Tech. 4-Break-Thru x-over; gatefold-c. 5-2 pg. origin The Strangers. 11-Brereton-c 3.00
1-($2.50)-Newsstand ed. polybagged w/trading card 4.00

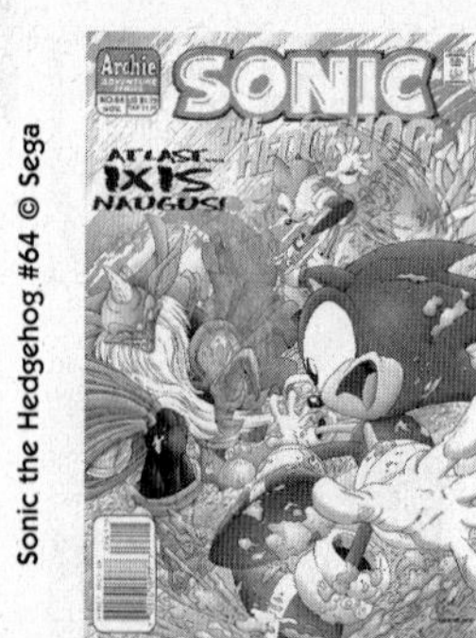

Sonic the Hedgehog #64 © Sega

Son of M #1 © MAR

Soulfire V2 #9 © Aspen MLT

GD 2.0 | VG 4.0 | FN 6.0 | VF 8.0 | VF/NM 9.0 | NM- 9.2

1-Ultra 5000 Limited silver foil 5.00
0-Obtained w/Rune #0 by sending coupons from 11 comics 4.00
2-($2.50, 48 pgs.)-Rune flip-c/story by B. Smith; The Mighty Magnor 1 pg. strip by Aragonés 4.00
16 ($3.50)-Flip-c Ultraverse Premiere #10 4.00
17 ($2.50) 3.00

SOMERSET HOLMES (See Eclipse Graphic Novel Series)
Pacific Comics/ Eclipse Comics No. 5, 6: Sept, 1983 - No. 6, Dec, 1984 ($1.50, Baxter paper)
1-6: 1-Brent Anderson-c/a. Cliff Hanger by Williamson in all 3.00

SONG OF THE SOUTH (See Brer Rabbit)

SONIC & KNUCKLES
Archie Comics: Aug, 1995 ($2.00)
1 — 1 3 4 6 8 10

SONIC DISRUPTORS
DC Comics: Dec, 1987 - No. 7, July, 1988 ($1.75, unfinished limited series)
1-7 3.00

SONIC'S FRIENDLY NEMESIS KNUCKLES
Archie Publications: July, 1996 - No. 3, Sept, 1996 ($1.50, limited series)
1-3 6.00

SONIC SUPER SPECIAL
Archie Publications: 1997 - Present ($2.00/$2.25/$2.29, 48 pgs)
1-3 5.00
4-6,8-15: 10-Sabrina-c/app. 15-Sin City spoof 4.00
7-(w/Image) Spawn, Maxx, Savage Dragon-c/app.; Valentino-a 4.00

SONIC THE HEDGEHOG (TV, video game)
Archie Comics: No. 0, Feb, 1993 - No. 3, May, 1993 ($1.25, mini-series)
0(2/93),1: Shaw-a(p) & covers on all — 4 8 12 22 34 45
2,3 — 3 6 9 16 23 30
Beginnings TPB (2003, $10.95) r/#0-3 11.00
...: The Beginning TPB (2006, $10.95) r/#0-3 11.00

SONIC THE HEDGEHOG (TV, video game)
Archie Comics: July, 1993 - Present ($1.25-$2.99)
1 — 4 8 12 24 37 50
2,3 — 3 6 9 16 23 30
4-10: 8-Neon ink-c. — 2 4 6 11 16 20
11-20 — 2 4 6 9 13 16
21-30 ($1.50): 25-Silver ink-c — 2 4 6 8 10 12
31-50 — 1 2 3 5 6 8
51-93 4.00
94-212: 117-Begin $2.19-c. 152-Begin $2.25-c. 157-Shadow app. 198-Begin $2.50 3.00
213-237: 213-Begin $2.99-c 3.00
Free Comic Book Day Edition 1 (2007)- Leads into Sonic the Hedgehog #175 3.00
Free Comic Book Day Edition 2009 - Reprints Sonic the Hedgehog #1 from July 1993 3.00
Free Comic Book Day Edition 2010 - New story 3.00
Triple Trouble Special (10/95, $2.00, 48 pgs.) — 1 3 4 6 8 10

SONIC UNIVERSE (Sonic the Hedgehog)
Archie Publications: Apr, 2009 - Present ($2.50/$2.99)
1-15 3.00
16-40: 16-Begin $2.99-c 3.00

SONIC VS. KNUCKLES "BATTLE ROYAL" SPECIAL
Archie Publications: 1997 ($2.00, one-shot)
1 — 1 2 3 5 6 8

SONIC X (Sonic the Hedgehog)
Archie Publications: Nov, 2005 - No. 40, Feb, 2009 ($2.25)
1-Sam Speed app. 4.00
2-40 3.00

SON OF AMBUSH BUG (See Ambush Bug)
DC Comics: July, 1986 - No. 6, Dec, 1986 (75¢)
1-6: Giffen-c/a in all. 5-Bissette-a. 3.00

SON OF BLACK BEAUTY (Also see Black Beauty)
Dell Publishing Co.: No. 510, Oct, 1953 - No. 566, June, 1954
Four Color 510, 566 — 4 8 12 26 41 55

SON OF FLUBBER (See Movie Comics)

SON OF HULK (Continues from Skaar: Son of Hulk #12) (See Realm of Kings)
Marvel Comics: No. 13, Sept, 2009 - No. 17, Jan, 2010 ($2.99)

GD 2.0 | VG 4.0 | FN 6.0 | VF 8.0 | VF/NM 9.0 | NM- 9.2

13-17: 13,15-17-Galactus app. 3.00

SON OF M (Also see House of M series)
Marvel Comics: Feb, 2006 - No. 6, July, 2006 ($2.99, limited series)
1-6: 1-Powerless Quicksilver; Martinez-a. 2-Quicksilver regains powers; Inhumans app. 3.00
Decimation: Son of M (2006, $13.99, TPB) r/series; Martinez sketch pages 14.00

SON OF MUTANT WORLD
Fantagor Press: 1990 - No. 5, 1990? ($2.00, bi-monthly)
1-5: 1-3: Corben-c/a. 4,5 ($1.75, B&W) 3.00

SON OF ORIGINS OF MARVEL COMICS (See Fireside Book Series)

SON OF SATAN (Also see Ghost Rider #1 & Marvel Spotlight #12)
Marvel Comics Group: Dec, 1975 - No. 8, Feb, 1977 (25¢)
1-Mooney-a; Kane-c(p), Starlin splash(p) — 3 6 9 18 27 40
2,6-8: 2-Origin The Possessor. 8-Heath-a — 2 4 6 10 14 18
3-5-(Regular 25¢ editions)(4-8/76): 5-Russell-p — 2 4 6 10 14 18
3-5-(30¢-c variants, limited distribution) — 4 8 12 20 30 40

SON OF SINBAD (Also see Abbott & Costello & Daring Adventures)
St. John Publishing Co.: Feb, 1950
1-Kubert-c/a — 50 100 150 315 533 750

SON OF SUPERMAN (Elseworlds)
DC Comics: 1999 ($14.95, prestige format, one-shot)
nn-Chaykin & Tischman-s/Williams III & Gray-a 15.00

SON OF TOMAHAWK (See Tomahawk)

SON OF VULCAN (Formerly Mysteries of Unexplored Worlds #1-48; Thunderbolt V3#51 on)
Charlton Comics: V2#49, Nov, 1965 - V2#50, Jan, 1966
V2#49,50: 50-Roy Thomas scripts (1st pro work) — 3 6 9 17 25 32

SONS OF KATIE ELDER (See Movie Classics)

SORCERY (See Chilling Adventures in... & Red Circle...)

SORORITY SECRETS
Toby Press: July, 1954
1 — 11 22 33 62 86 110

SOULFIRE (MICHAEL TURNER PRESENTS:...)
Aspen MLT, Inc.: No. 0, 2004 - No. 10, Jul, 2009 ($2.50/$2.99)
0-($2.50) Turner-a/c; Loeb-s; intro. to characters & development sketches 3.00
1-($2.99) Two covers 3.00
1-Diamond Previews Exclusive 5.00
2-9: 2,3-Two covers. 4-Four covers 3.00
10-($3.99) Benitez-a 4.00
...: The Collected Edition Vol. 1 (5/05, $6.99) r/#1,2; cover gallery 7.00
Hardcover Volume 1 (12/05, $24.99) r/#0-5 & preview from Wizard Mag.; Johns intro. 25.00

SOULFIRE (MICHAEL TURNER PRESENTS:...) (Volume 2)
Aspen MLT, Inc.: No. 0, Oct, 2009 - No. 9, Jan, 2011 ($2.50/$2.99)
0-($2.50) Marcus To-a 3.00
1-9-($2.99) 1-Five covers. 9-Covers by To and Linsner 3.00

SOULFIRE (MICHAEL TURNER'S...) (Volume 3)
Aspen MLT, Inc.: No. 0, Apr, 2011 - Present ($1.99/$2.99)
0-($1.99) Krul-s/Fabok-a; 4 covers 3.00
1-7-($2.99) 1-Four covers 3.00

SOULFIRE: CHAOS REIGN
Aspen MLT, Inc.: No. 0, June, 2006 - No. 3, Jan, 2007 ($2.50/$2.99)
0-($2.50) Three covers; Marcus To-a; J.T. Krul-s 3.00
1-3-($2.99) 1-Three covers 3.00
...: Beginnings (7/06, $1.99) Marcus To-a; J.T. Krul-s 3.00
...: Beginnings 1 (7/07, $1.99) Francisco Herrera-a; J.T. Krul-s 3.00

SOULFIRE: DYING OF THE LIGHT
Aspen MLT, Inc.: No. 0, 2004 - No. 5, Feb, 2006 ($2.50/$2.99)
0-($2.50) Three covers; Gunnell-a; Krul-s; back-story to the Soulfire universe 3.00
1-5-($2.99) 1-Five covers 3.00
... Vol. 1 TPB (2007, $14.99) r/#0-5; Gunnell sketch pages, cover gallery 15.00

SOULFIRE: NEW WORLD ORDER
Aspen MLT, Inc.: No. 0, Jul, 2007; May, 2009 - No. 5, Dec, 2009 ($2.50/$2.99)
0 (7/07, $2.50) Two covers; Herrera-a/Krul-s 3.00
1-5-($2.99) 1-Four covers 3.00

SOULFIRE: SHADOW MAGIC

Sovereign Seven #28 © Chris Claremont

Space Adventures #15 © CC

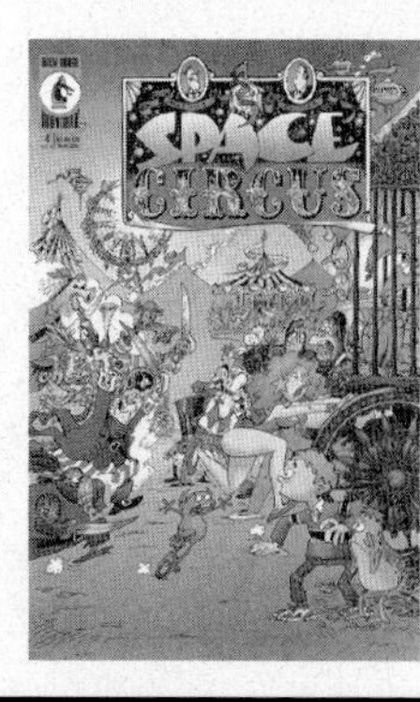

Space Circus #4 © Aragonés & Evanier

GD VG FN VF VF/NM NM-
2.0 4.0 6.0 8.0 9.0 9.2

Aspen MLT, Inc.: No. 0, Nov, 2008 - No. 5, May, 2009 ($2.50/$2.99)
0-($2.50) Two covers; Sana Takeda-a 3.00
1-5-($2.99) 1-Two covers 3.00

SOUL SAGA
Image Comics (Top Cow): Feb, 2000 - No. 5, Apr, 2001 ($2.50)
1-5: 1-Madureira-c; Platt & Batt-a 3.00

SOULSEARCHERS AND COMPANY
Claypool Comics: June, 1995 - No. 82, Jan, 2007 ($2.50, B&W)
1-10: Peter David scripts 5.00
11-25 3.00
26-82 3.00

SOULWIND
Image Comics: Mar, 1997 - No. 8 ($2.95, B&W, limited series)
1-8: 5-"The Day I Tried To Live" pt. 1 3.00
Book Five; The August Ones (Oni Press, 3/01, $8.50) 8.50
...The Kid From Planet Earth (1997, $9.95, TPB) 10.00
...The Kid From Planet Earth (Oni Press, 1/00, $8.50, TPB) 8.50
...The Day I Tried to Live (Oni Press, 4/00, $8.50, TPB) 8.50
The Complete Soulwind TPB ($29.95, 11/03, 8" x 5 1/2") r/Oni Books #1-5 30.00

SOUPY SALES COMIC BOOK (TV)(The Official...)
Archie Publications: 1965
1 9 18 27 58 99 140

SOUTHERN KNIGHTS, THE (See Crusaders #1)
Guild Publ/Fictioneer Books: No. 2, 1983 - No. 41, 1993 (B&W)
2-Magazine size 1 2 3 5 6 8
3-35, 37-41 3.00
36-($3.50-c) 4.00
Dread Halloween Special 1, Primer Special 1 (Spring, 1989, $2.25) 3.00
Graphic Novels #1-4 4.00

SOVEREIGN SEVEN (Also see Showcase '95 #12)
DC Comics: July, 1995 - No. 36, July, 1998 ($1.95) (1st creator-owned mainstream DC comic)
1-1st app. Sovereign Seven (Reflex, Indigo, Cascade, Finale, Cruiser, Network & Rampart); 1st app. Maitresse; Darkseid app.; Chris Claremont-s & Dwayne Turner-c/a begins 4.00
1-Gold 8.00
1-Platinum 40.00
2-25: 2-Wolverine cameo. 4-Neil Gaiman cameo. 5,8-Batman app. 7-Ramirez cameo (from the movie Highlander). 9-Humphrey Bogart cameo from Casablanca. 10-Impulse app; Manoli Wetherell & Neal Conan cameo from Uncanny X-Men #226. 11-Robin app. 16-Final Night. 24-Superman app. 25-Power Girl app. 3.00
26-36: 26-Begin $2.25-c. 28-Impulse-c/app. 3.00
Annual 1 (1995, $3.95)-Year One story; Big Barda & Lobo app.; Jeff Johnson-c/a 4.00
Annual 2 (1996, $2.95)-Legends of the Dead Earth; Leonardi-c/a 4.00
...Plus 1(2/97, $2.95)-Legion-c/app. 4.00
TPB-($12.95) r/#1-5, Annual #1 & Showcase '95 #12 13.00

SPACE: ABOVE AND BEYOND (TV)
Topps Comics: Jan, 1996 - No. 3, Mar, 1996 ($2.95, limited series)
1-3: Adaptation of pilot episode; Steacy-c. 3.00

SPACE: ABOVE AND BEYOND--THE GAUNTLET (TV)
Topps Comics: May, 1996 -No. 2, June, 1996 ($2.95, limited series)
1,2 3.00

SPACE ACE (Also see Manhunt!)
Magazine Enterprises: No. 5, 1952
5(A-1 #61)-Guardineer-a 57 114 171 362 619 875

SPACE ACE: DEFENDER OF THE UNIVERSE (Based on the Don Bluth video game)
CrossGen Comics: Oct, 2003 - No. 6 ($2.95, limited series)
1,2-Kirkman-s/Borges-a 3.00

SPACE ACTION
Ace Magazines (Junior Books): June, 1952 - No. 3, Oct, 1952
1-Cameron-a in all (1 story) 79 158 237 502 864 1225
2,3 54 108 162 346 591 835

SPACE ADVENTURES (War At Sea #22 on)
Capitol Stories/Charlton Comics: 7/52 - No. 21, 8/56; No. 23, 5/58 - No. 59, 11/64; V3#60, 10/67; V1#2, 7/68 - V1#8, 7/69; No. 9, 5/78 - No. 13, 3/79
1 55 110 165 352 601 850
2 29 58 87 170 278 385
3-5: 4,6-Flying saucer-c/stories 23 46 69 136 223 310
6-9: 7-Sex change story "Transformation". 8-Robot-c. 9-A-Bomb panel
21 42 63 124 202 280
10,11-Ditko-c/a. 10-Robot-c. 11-Two Ditko stories 54 108 162 343 574 825
12-Ditko-c (classic) 97 194 291 621 1061 1500
13-(Fox-r, 10-11/54); Blue Beetle-c/story 16 32 48 94 147 200
14,15,17,18: 14-Blue Beetle-c/story; Fox-r (12-1/54-55, last pre-code).
15,17,18-Rocky Jones-c/s.(TV); 15-Part photo-c 20 40 60 118 192 265
16-Krigstein-a; Rocky Jones-c/story (TV) 22 44 66 128 209 290
19 15 30 45 88 137 185
20-Reprints Fawcett's "Destination Moon" 22 44 66 132 216 300
21-(8/56) (no #22)(Becomes War At Sea) 15 30 45 88 137 185
23-(5/58; formerly Nyoka, The Jungle Girl)-Reprints Fawcett's "Destination Moon"
20 40 60 118 192 265
24,25,31,32-Ditko-a. 24-Severin-a(signed "LePoer") 20 40 60 118 192 265
26,27-Ditko-a(4) each. 26,28-Flying saucer-c 21 42 63 126 206 285
28-30 11 22 33 64 90 115
33-Origin/1st app. Capt. Atom by Ditko (3/60) 50 100 150 315 533 750
34-40,42-All Captain Atom by Ditko 21 42 63 124 202 280
41,43,45-59: 43-Alan Shephard strory, 2nd man in space. 45-Mercury Man app. 5 10
15 32 51 70
44-1st app. Mercury Man 5 10 15 35 55 75
V3#60(#1, 10/67)-Origin & 1st app. Paul Mann & The Saucers From the Future
5 10 15 32 51 70
2,5,6,8 (1968-69)-Ditko-a: 2-Aparo-c/a 3 6 9 20 30 40
3,4,7: 4-Aparo-c/a 3 6 9 16 23 30
9-13(1978-79)-Capt. Atom-r/Space Adventures by Ditko; 9-Reprints origin/1st app. Capt. Atom from #33 6.00

NOTE: ***Aparo** a-V3#60. c-V3#8. **Ditko** c-12, 31-42. **Giordano** c-3, 4, 7-9, 18p. **Krigstein** c-15. **Shuster** a-11. Issues 13 & 14 have Blue Beetle logos; #15-18 have Rocky Jones logos.*

SPACE ARK
Americomics (AC Comics)/ Apple Comics #3 on: June, 1985 - No. 5, Sept, 1987 ($1.75)
1-5: Funny animal (#1,2-color; #3-5-B&W) 3.00

SPACE BUSTERS
Ziff-Davis Publ. Co.: Spring, 1952 - No. 2, Fall, 1952
1-Krigstein-a(3); Painted-c by Norman Saunders 83 166 249 527 906 1285
2-Kinstler-a(2 pgs.); Saunders painted-c 64 128 192 406 696 985

NOTE: ***Anderson** a-2. Bondage c-2.*

SPACE CADET (See Tom Corbett,...)

SPACE CIRCUS
Dark Horse Comics: July, 2000 - No. 4, Oct, 2000 ($2.95, limited series)
1-4-Aragonés-a/Evanier-s 3.00

SPACE COMICS (Formerly Funny Tunes)
Avon Periodicals: No. 4, Mar-Apr, 1954 - No. 5, May-June, 1954
4,5-Space Mouse, Peter Rabbit, Super Pup (formerly Spotty the Pup), & Merry Mouse continue from Funny Tunes 8 16 24 40 50 60
I.W. Reprint #8 (nd)-Space Mouse-r 2 4 6 8 10 12

SPACED
Anthony Smith Publ. #1,2/Unbridled Ambition/Eclipse Comics #10 on:
1982 - No. 13, 1988 ($1.25/$1.50, B&W, quarterly)
1-($1.25-c) 4.00
2-13, Special Edition (1983, Mimeo) 3.00

SPACE DETECTIVE
Avon Periodicals: July, 1951 - No. 4, July, 1952
1-Rod Hathway, Space Detective begins, ends #4; Wood-c/a(3)-23 pgs.; "Opium Smugglers of Venus" drug story; Lucky Dale-r/Saint #4 123 246 369 787 1344 1900
2-Tales from the Shadow Squad story; Wood/Orlando-c; Wood inside layouts; "Slave Ship of Saturn" story 90 180 270 576 988 1400
3,4: 3-Kinstler-c. 4-Kinstlerish-a by McCann 45 90 135 284 480 675
I.W. Reprint #1(Reprints #2), 8(Reprints cover #1 & part Famous Funnies #191)
4 8 12 22 34 45

SPACE EXPLORER (See March of Comics #202)

SPACE FAMILY ROBINSON (TV)(...Lost in Space #15-37, ...Lost in Space On Space Station One #38 on)(See Gold Key Champion)
Gold Key: Dec, 1962 - No. 36, Oct, 1969; No. 37, 10/73 - No. 54, 11/78; No. 55, 3/81 - No. 59, 5/82 (All painted covers)
1-(Low distribution); Spiegle-a in all 21 42 63 146 311 475
2(3/63)-Family becomes lost in space 11 22 33 76 151 225
3-5 8 16 24 53 89 125
6-10: 6-Captain Venture back-up stories begin 6 12 18 42 69 95
11-20: 14-(10/65). 15-Title change (1/66) 5 10 15 30 48 65

Space Ghost #4 © H-B

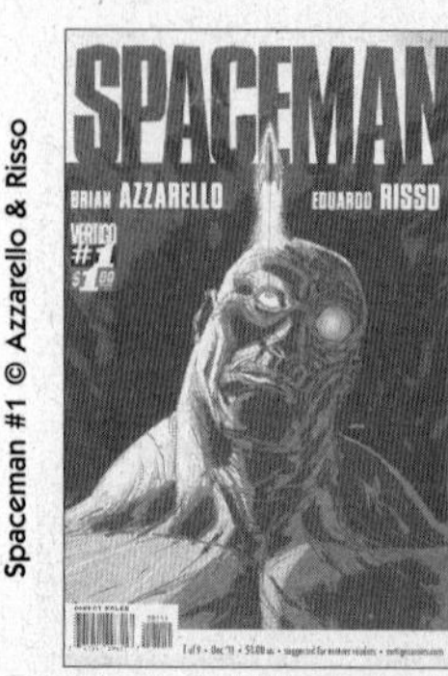

Spaceman #1 © Azzarello & Risso

Space War #16 © CC

GD VG FN VF VF/NM NM-
2.0 4.0 6.0 8.0 9.0 9.2

GD VG FN VF VF/NM NM-
2.0 4.0 6.0 8.0 9.0 9.2

21-36: 28-Last 12¢ issue. 36-Captain Venture ends 4 8 12 23 36 45
37-48: 37-Origin retold 2 4 6 10 14 18
49-59: Reprints #49,50,55-59 2 4 6 8 10 12
NOTE: *The TV show first aired on 9/15/65. Title changed after TV show debuted.*

SPACE FAMILY ROBINSON (See March of Comics #320, 328, 352, 404, 414)

SPACE GHOST (TV) (Also see Golden Comics Digest #2 & Hanna-Barbera Super TV Heroes #3-7)
Gold Key: March, 1967 (Hanna-Barbera) (TV debut was 9/10/66)
1 (10199-703)-Spiegle-a 26 52 78 182 391 600

SPACE GHOST (TV cartoon)
Comico: Mar, 1987 ($3.50, deluxe format, one-shot) (Hanna-Barbera)
1-Steve Rude-c/a 1 2 3 5 6 8

SPACE GHOST (TV cartoon)
DC Comics: Jan, 2005 - No. 6, June, 2005 ($2.95/$2.99, limited series)
1-6-Alex Ross-c/Ariel Olivetti-a/Joe Kelly-s; origin of Space Ghost 3.00
TPB (2005, $14.99) r/series; cover gallery 15.00

SPACE GIANTS, THE (TV cartoon)
FBN Publications: 1979 ($1.00, B&W, one-shots)
1-Based on Japanese TV series 2 4 6 9 12 15

SPACEHAWK
Dark Horse Comics: 1989 - No. 3, 1990 ($2.00, B&W)
1-3-Wolverton-c/a(r) plus new stories by others. 4.00

SPACE JAM
DC Comics: 1996 ($5.95, one-shot, movie adaption)
1-Wraparound photo cover of Michael Jordan 1 2 3 5 6 8

SPACE KAT-ETS (...in 3-D)
Power Publishing Co.: Dec, 1953 (25¢, came w/glasses)
1 30 60 90 177 289 400

SPACEKNIGHTS
Marvel Comics: Oct, 2000 - No. 5, Feb, 2001 ($2.99, limited series)
1-5-Starlin-s/Batista-a 3.00

SPACEMAN (Speed Carter...)
Atlas Comics (CnPC): Sept, 1953 - No. 6, July, 1954
1-Grey tone-c 74 148 222 470 810 1150
2 45 90 135 284 480 675
3-6: 4-A-Bomb explosion-c 40 80 120 246 411 575
NOTE: ***Everett** c-1, 3. **Heath** a-1. **Maneely** a-1(3), 2(4), 3(3), 4-6; c-5, 6. **Romita** a-1. **Sekowsky** c-4. **Sekowsky/Abel** a-4(3). **Tuska** a-5(3).*

SPACE MAN
Dell Publ. Co.: No. 1253, 1-3/62 - No. 8, 3-5/64; No. 9, 7/72 - No. 10, 10/72
Four Color 1253 (#1)(1-3/62)(15¢-c) 7 14 21 48 79 110
2,3: 2-(15¢-c). 3-(12¢-c) 4 8 12 28 44 60
4-8-(12¢-c) 4 8 12 22 34 45
9,10-(15¢-c): 9-Reprints #1253. 10-Reprints #2 2 4 6 9 12 15

SPACEMAN (From the Atomics)
Oni Press: July, 2002 ($2.95, one-shot)
1-Mike Allred-s/a; Lawrence Marvit additional art 3.00

SPACEMAN
DC Comics (Vertigo): Dec, 2011 - No. 9 ($1.00/$2.99, limited series)
1-($1.00) Azzarello-s/Risso-a/Johnson-c 4.00
2-5-($2.99) 3.00

SPACE MOUSE (Also see Funny Tunes & Space Comics)
Avon Periodicals: April, 1953 - No. 5, Apr-May, 1954
1 10 20 30 58 79 100
2 7 14 21 37 46 55
3-5 6 12 18 31 38 45

SPACE MOUSE (Walter Lantz...#1; see Comic Album #17)
Dell Publishing Co./Gold Key: No. 1132, Aug-Oct, 1960 - No. 5, Nov, 1963 (Walter Lantz)
Four Color 1132,1244, 1(11/62)(G.K.) 4 8 12 28 44 60
2-5 4 8 12 24 37 50

SPACE MYSTERIES
I.W. Enterprises: 1964 (Reprints)
1-r/Journey Into Unknown Worlds #4 w/new-c 3 6 9 16 22 28
8,9: 9-r/Planet Comics #73 3 6 9 16 22 28

SPACE: 1999 (TV) (Also see Power Record Comics)
Charlton Comics: Nov, 1975 - No. 7, Nov, 1976
1-Origin Moonbase Alpha; Staton-c/a 3 6 9 16 23 30
2,7: 2-Staton-a 2 4 6 13 18 22
3-6: All Byrne-a; c-3,5,6 3 6 9 16 23 30
nn (Charlton Press, digest, 100 pgs., B&W, no cover price) new stories & art 4 8 12 28 44 60

SPACE: 1999 (TV)(Magazine)
Charlton Comics: Nov, 1975 - No. 8, Nov, 1976 (B&W) (#7 shows #6 inside)
1-Origin Moonbase Alpha; Morrow-c/a 3 6 9 16 22 28
2-8: 2,3-Morrow-c/a. 4-6-Morrow-c. 5,8-Morrow-a 2 4 6 11 16 20

SPACE PATROL (TV)
Ziff-Davis Publishing Co. (Approved Comics): Summer, 1952 - No. 2, Oct-Nov, 1952 (Painted-c by Norman Saunders)
1-Krigstein-a 95 190 285 603 1039 1475
2-Krigstein-a(3) 67 134 201 426 731 1035

SPACE PIRATES (See Archie Giant Series #533)

SPACE RANGER (See Mystery in Space #92, Showcase #15 & Tales of the Unexpected)

SPACE SQUADRON (In the Days of the Rockets)(Becomes Space Worlds #6)
Marvel/Atlas Comics (ACI): June, 1951 - No. 5, Feb, 1952
1-Space team; Brodsky c-1,5 74 148 222 470 810 1150
2: Tuska c-2-4 57 114 171 362 619 875
3-5: 3-Capt. Jet Dixon by Tuska(3). 4-Weird advs. begin 50 100 150 315 533 750

SPACE THRILLERS
Avon Periodicals: 1954 (25¢ Giant)
nn-(Scarce)-Robotmen of the Lost Planet; contains 3 rebound comics of The Saint & Strange Worlds. Contents could vary 129 258 387 826 1413 2000

SPACE TRIP TO THE MOON (See Space Adventures #23)

SPACE USAGI
Mirage Studios: June, 1992 - No. 3, 1992 ($2.00, B&W, mini-series)
V2#1, Nov, 1993 - V2#3, Jan, 1994 ($2.75)
1-3: Stan Sakai-c/a/scripts, V2#1-3 3.00

SPACE USAGI
Dark Horse Comics: Jan, 1996 - No. 3, Mar, 1996 ($2.95, B&W, limited series)
1-3: Stan Sakai-c/a/scripts 3.00

SPACE WAR (Fightin' Five #28 on)
Charlton Comics: Oct, 1959 - No. 27, Mar, 1964; No. 28, Mar, 1978 - No. 34, 3/79
V1#1-Giordano-c begin, end #3 12 24 36 81 166 250
2,3 8 16 24 53 89 125
4-6,8,10-Ditko-c/a 12 24 36 81 166 250
7,9,11-15 (3/62): Last 10¢ issue 6 12 18 41 66 90
16 (6/52)-27 (3/64): 18,19-Robot-c 5 10 15 35 55 75
28 (3/78),29-31,33,34-Ditko-c/a(r): 30-Staton, Sutton/Wood-a. 31-Ditko-c/a(3); same-c as Strange Suspense Stories #2 (1968); atom blast-c 1 3 4 6 8 10
32-r/Charlton Premiere V2#2; Sutton-a 6.00

SPACE WARPED
Boom Entertainment (Kaboom!): Jun, 2011 - No. 6, Dec, 2011 ($3.99, limited series)
1-6-Star Wars spoof; Bourhis-s/Spiessert-a 4.00

SPACE WESTERN (Formerly Cowboy Western Comics; becomes Cowboy Western Comics #46 on)
Charlton Comics (Capitol Stories): No. 40, Oct, 1952 - No. 45, Aug, 1953
40-Intro Spurs Jackson & His Space Vigilantes; flying saucer story 55 110 165 352 601 850
41,43,44: 41-Flying saucer-c 41 82 123 256 428 600
42-Atom bomb explosion-c 43 86 129 271 456 640
45-"The Valley That Time Forgot", a pre-Turok story with dinosaurs & a bow-hunting Indian; Hitler app. 42 84 126 265 445 625

SPACE WORLDS (Formerly Space Squadron #1-5)
Atlas Comics (Male): No. 6, April, 1952
6-Sol Brodsky-c 47 94 141 296 498 700

SPANKY & ALFALFA & THE LITTLE RASCALS (See The Little Rascals)

SPANNER'S GALAXY
DC Comics: Dec, 1984 - No. 6, May, 1985 (limited series)

Sparkler Comics #39 © UFS

Spartacus V1 #1 © Starz

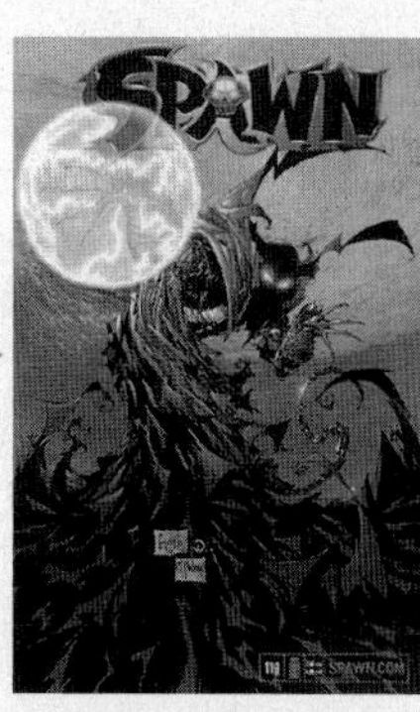

Spawn #119 © TMP

	GD 2.0	VG 4.0	FN 6.0	VF 8.0	VF/NM 9.0	NM- 9.2
1-6: Mandrake-c/a in all.						3.00

SPARKIE, RADIO PIXIE (Radio)(Becomes Big Jon & Sparkie #4)
Ziff-Davis Publ. Co.: Winter, 1951 - No. 3, July-Aug, 1952 (Painted-c)(Sparkie #2,3; #1?)

	GD 2.0	VG 4.0	FN 6.0	VF 8.0	VF/NM 9.0	NM- 9.2
1-Based on children's radio program	27	54	81	158	259	360
2,3: 3-Big Jon and Sparkie on-c only	18	36	54	105	165	225

SPARKLE COMICS
United Features Synd.: Oct-Nov, 1948 - No. 33, Dec-Jan, 1953-54

	GD 2.0	VG 4.0	FN 6.0	VF 8.0	VF/NM 9.0	NM- 9.2
1-Li'l Abner, Nancy, Captain & the Kids, Ella Cinders (#1-3: 52 pgs.)	15	30	45	83	124	165
2	9	18	27	50	65	80
3-10	8	16	24	40	50	60
11-20	7	14	21	35	43	50
21-32	6	12	18	28	34	40
33-(2-3/54) 2 pgs. early Peanuts by Schulz	10	20	30	54	72	90

SPARKLE PLENTY (See Harvey Comics Library #2 & Dick Tracy)

SPARKLER COMICS (1st series)
United Feature Comic Group: July, 1940 - No. 2, 1940

	GD 2.0	VG 4.0	FN 6.0	VF 8.0	VF/NM 9.0	NM- 9.2
1-Jim Hardy	39	78	117	231	378	525
2-Frankie Doodle	28	56	84	165	270	375

SPARKLER COMICS (2nd series)(Nancy & Sluggo #121 on)(Cover title becomes Nancy and Sluggo #101? on)
United Features Syndicate: July, 1941 - No. 120, Jan, 1955

	GD 2.0	VG 4.0	FN 6.0	VF 8.0	VF/NM 9.0	NM- 9.2
1-Origin 1st app. Sparkman; Tarzan (by Hogarth in all issues), Captain & the Kids, Ella Cinders, Danny Dingle, Dynamite Dunn, Nancy, Abbie & Slats, Broncho Bill, Frankie Doodle, begin; Spark Man c-1-9,11,12; Hap Hopper c-10,13	230	460	690	1449	2450	3450
2	76	152	228	479	807	1135
3,4	57	114	171	359	610	860
5-9: 9-Spark Man's new costume	41	82	123	256	428	600
10-Spark Man's secret ID revealed	41	82	123	256	428	600
11,12-Spark Man war-c. 12-Spark Man's new costume (color change)	37	74	111	222	361	500
13-Hap Hopper war-c	34	68	102	199	325	450
14-Tarzan-c by Hogarth	50	100	150	315	533	750
15,17: 15-Capt & Kids-c. 17-Nancy & Sluggo-c	24	48	72	142	234	325
16,18-Spark Man war-c	37	74	111	222	361	500
19-1st Race Riley and the Commandos-c/s	34	68	102	199	325	450
20-Nancy war-c	26	52	78	154	252	350
21,25,28,31,34,37,39-Tarzan-c by Hogarth	42	84	126	267	451	635
22-24,26,27,29,30: 22-Race Riley & the Commandos strips begin, ends #44	22	44	66	132	216	300
32,33,35,36,38,40	14	28	42	80	115	150
41,43,45,46,48,49	10	20	30	58	79	100
42,44,47,50-Tarzan-c (42,47,50 by Hogarth)	26	52	78	156	256	355
51,52,54-68,70: 57-Li'l Abner begins (not in #58); Fearless Fosdick app. in #58	10	20	30	56	76	95
53-Tarzan-c by Hogarth	22	44	66	132	216	300
69-Wolverton-*esque* Horror-c	16	32	48	94	147	200
71-80	9	18	27	47	61	75
81,82,84-86: 86 Last Tarzan; lingerie panels	8	16	24	40	50	60
83-Tarzan-c; Li'l Abner ends	13	26	39	74	105	135
87-96,98-99	7	14	21	37	46	55
97-Origin Casey Ruggles by Warren Tufts	8	16	24	42	54	65
100	8	16	24	42	54	65
101-107,109-112,114-119	6	12	18	31	38	45
108,113-Toth-a	7	14	21	37	46	55
120-(10-11/54) 2 pgs. early Peanuts by Schulz	10	20	30	54	72	90

SPARKLING LOVE
Avon Periodicals/Realistic (1953): June, 1950; 1953

	GD 2.0	VG 4.0	FN 6.0	VF 8.0	VF/NM 9.0	NM- 9.2
1(Avon)-Kubert-a; photo-c	27	54	81	158	259	360
nn(1953)-Reprint; Kubert-a	12	24	36	67	94	120

SPARKLING STARS
Holyoke Publishing Co.: June, 1944 - No. 33, March, 1948

	GD 2.0	VG 4.0	FN 6.0	VF 8.0	VF/NM 9.0	NM- 9.2
1-Hell's Angels, FBI, Boxie Weaver, Petey & Pop, & Ali Baba begin	20	40	60	114	182	250
2-Speed Spaulding story	12	24	36	69	97	125
3-Actual FBI case photos & war photos	10	20	30	54	72	90
4-10: 7-X-Mas-c	9	18	27	50	65	80
11-19: 13-Origin/1st app. Jungo the Man-Beast-c/s	8	16	24	44	57	70
20-Intro Fangs the Wolf Boy	9	18	27	50	65	80
21-33: 29-Bondage-c. 31-Sid Greene-a	8	16	24	42	54	65

SPARK MAN (See Sparkler Comics)
Frances M. McQueeny: 1945 (36 pgs., one-shot)

	GD 2.0	VG 4.0	FN 6.0	VF 8.0	VF/NM 9.0	NM- 9.2
1-Origin Spark Man r/Sparkler #1-3; female torture story; cover redrawn from Sparkler #1	32	64	96	188	307	425

SPARKS (William Katt Presents...)
Catastrophic Comics: June, 2008 - Present ($2.99)

	GD 2.0	VG 4.0	FN 6.0	VF 8.0	VF/NM 9.0	NM- 9.2
1,2: 1-Folino-s/Ringuet-a; origin of Sparks						3.00

SPARKY WATTS (Also see Big Shot Comics & Columbia Comics)
Columbia Comic Corp.: Nov?, 1942 - No. 10, 1949

	GD 2.0	VG 4.0	FN 6.0	VF 8.0	VF/NM 9.0	NM- 9.2
1(1942)-Skyman & The Face app; Hitler-c	82	164	246	528	902	1275
2(1943)	31	62	93	182	296	410
3(1944)	21	42	63	126	206	285
4(1944)-Origin	19	38	57	109	172	235
5(1947)-Skyman app.; Boody Rogers-c/a	15	30	45	90	140	190
6,7,9,10: 6(1947),10(1949)	11	22	33	62	86	110
8(1948)-Surrealistic-c	14	28	42	78	112	145

NOTE: ***Boody Rogers** c-1-8.*

SPARTACUS (Movie)
Dell Publishing Co.: No. 1139, Nov, 1960 (Kirk Douglas photo-c)

	GD 2.0	VG 4.0	FN 6.0	VF 8.0	VF/NM 9.0	NM- 9.2
Four Color 1139-Buscema-a	11	22	33	76	151	225

SPARTACUS (Television series)
Devil's Due Publishing: Oct, 2009 - No. 2 ($3.99)

	GD 2.0	VG 4.0	FN 6.0	VF 8.0	VF/NM 9.0	NM- 9.2
1,2: 1-DeKnight-s. 2-Palmiotti-s						4.00

SPARTAN: WARRIOR SPIRIT (Also see WildC.A.T.S: Covert Action Teams)
Image Comics (WildStorm Productions): July, 1995 - No. 4, Nov, 1995 ($2.50, lim. series)

	GD 2.0	VG 4.0	FN 6.0	VF 8.0	VF/NM 9.0	NM- 9.2
1-4: Kurt Busiek scripts; Mike McKone-c/a						3.00

SPARTA: USA
DC Comics (WildStorm): May, 2010 - No. 6, Oct, 2010 ($2.99, limited series)

	GD 2.0	VG 4.0	FN 6.0	VF 8.0	VF/NM 9.0	NM- 9.2
1-6: 1-Lapham-s/Timmons-a; covers by Timmons and Lapham						3.00

SPAWN (Also see Curse of the Spawn and Sam & Twitch)
Image Comics (Todd McFarlane Prods.): May, 1992 - Present ($1.95/$2.50/$2.99)

	GD 2.0	VG 4.0	FN 6.0	VF 8.0	VF/NM 9.0	NM- 9.2
1-1st app. Spawn; McFarlane-c/a begins; McFarlane/Steacy-c; 1st Todd McFarlane Productions title.	2	4	6	8	10	12
1-Black & white edition	2	4	6	13	18	22
2,3: 2-1st app. Violator; McFarlane/Steacy-c	1	3	4	6	8	10
4-Contains coupon for Image Comics #0	1	3	4	6	8	10
4-With coupon missing						3.00
4-Newsstand edition w/o poster or coupon						3.00
5-Cerebus cameo (1 pg.) as stuffed animal; Spawn mobile poster #1	1	2	3	5	7	8
6-8,10: 7-Spawn Mobile poster #2. 8-Alan Moore scripts; Miller poster. 10-Cerebus app.; Dave Sim scripts; 1 pg. cameo app. by Superman						5.00
9-Neil Gaiman scripts; Jim Lee poster; 1st Angela.	1	2	3	4	5	7
11-17,19,20,22-30: 11-Miller script; Darrow poster. 12-Bloodwulf poster by Liefeld. 14,15-Violator app. 16,17-Grant Morrison scripts; Capullo-c/a(p). 23,24-McFarlane-a/stories. 25-(10/94). 19-(10/94). 20-(11/94)						4.00
18-Grant Morrison script, Capullo-c/a(p); low distr.	1	2	3	5	7	9
21-low distribution	1	2	3	5	7	9
31-49: 31-1st app. The Redeemer; new costume (brief). 32-1st full app. new costume. 38-40,42,44,46,48-Tony Daniel-c/a(p). 38-1st app. Cy-Gor. 40,41-Cy-Gor & Curse app.						4.00
50-($3.95, 48 pgs.)						5.00
51-66: 52-Savage Dragon app. 56-w/ Darkchylde preview. 57-Cy-Gor-c/app. 64-Polybagged w/McFarlane Toys catalog. 65-Photo-c of movie Spawn and McFarlane						4.00
67-97: 81-Billy Kincaid returns. 97-Angela-c/app.						3.00
98,99,101-149-($2.50): 98,99-Angela app.						3.00
100-($4.95) Angela dies; 6 covers by McFarlane, Ross, Miller, Capullo, Wood, Mignola						5.00
150-($4.95) 4 covers by McFarlane, Capullo, Tan, Jim Lee						5.00
151-184: 151-($2.95) Wraparound-c by Tan. 167-Clown app. 179-Mayhew-a						3.00
185-199,201-217: 185-McFarlane & Holguin-s/Portacio-a begins. 193-Sam & Twitch app. 210-215-Michael Golden-c						3.00
200-(1/11, $3.99) 7 covers by McFarlane, Capullo, Finch, Jim Lee, Liefeld, Silvestri, Wood						4.00
Annual 1-Blood & Shadows ('99, $4.95) Ashley Wood-c/a; Jenkins-s						5.00
...: Architects of Fear (2/11, $6.99, squarebound GN) Briclot-a						7.00
...: Armegeddon Complete Collection TPB ('07, $29.95) r/#150-163						30.00
...: Armegeddon, Part 1 TPB (10/06, $14.99) r/#150-155						15.00
...: Armegeddon, Part 2 TPB (2/07, $15.95) r/#156-164						16.00
...Bible-(8/96, $1.95)-Character bios						4.00

Book 1 TPB($9.95) r/#1-5; Book 2-r/#6-9,11; Book 3 -r/#12-15, Book 4- r/#16-20;

Spawn the Undead #1 © TMP

Species #4 © MGM

Spectacular Features Magazine #3 © FOX

	GD 2.0	VG 4.0	FN 6.0	VF 8.0	VF/NM 9.0	NM- 9.2
Book 5-r/#21-25; Book 6- r/#26-30; Book 7-r/#31-34; Book 8-r/#35-38; Book 9-r/#39-42; Book 10-r/#43-47						11.00
Book 11 TPB ($10.95) r/#48-50; Book 12-r/#51-54						11.00
... Collection Vol. 1 (10/05, $19.95) r/#1-8,11,12; intro. by Frank Miller						20.00
... Collection Vol. 2 HC (7/07, $49.95) r/#13-33						50.00
... Collection Vol. 2 SC (9/06, $29.95) r/#13-33						30.00
... Collection Vol. 3 (3/07, $29.95) r/#34-54						30.00
... Collection Vol. 4 (9/07, $29.95) r/#55-75						30.00
... Collection Vol. 5 ('08, $29.95) r/#76-95						30.00
... Collection Vol. 6 (8/08, $29.95) r/#96-116; cover gallery						30.00
Image Firsts: Spawn #1 (4/10, $1.00) reprints #1						3.00
... Godslayer Vol. 1 (9/06, $6.99) Anacleto-c/a; Holguin-s; sketch pages						7.00
...: Neonoir TPB (11/08, $14.95) r/#170-175						15.00
...: New Flesh TPB ('07, $14.95) r/#166-169						15.00
...Simony (5/04, $7.95) English translation of French Spawn story; Briclot-a						8.00

NOTE: ***Capullo** a-16p-18p; c-16p-18p. **Daniel** a-38-40, 42, 44, 46. **McFarlane** a-1-15; c-1-15p. **Thibert** a-16i(part). Posters come with issues 1, 4, 7-9, 11, 12. #25 was released before #19 & 20.*

SPAWN-BATMAN (Also see Batman/Spawn: War Devil under Batman: One-Shots)
Image Comics (Todd McFarlane Productions): 1994 ($3.95, one-shot)

	GD	VG	FN	VF	VF/NM	NM-
1-Miller scripts; McFarlane-c/a						6.00

SPAWN: BLOOD FEUD
Image Comics (Todd McFarlane Prods.): June, 1995 - No. 4, Sept, 1995 ($2.25, lim. series)

	GD	VG	FN	VF	VF/NM	NM-
1-4-Alan Moore scripts, Tony Daniel-a						4.00

SPAWN FAN EDITION
Image Comics (Todd McFarlane Productions): Aug, 1996 - No. 3, Oct, 1996 (Giveaway, 12 pgs.) (Polybagged w/Overstreet's FAN)

	GD	VG	FN	VF	VF/NM	NM-
1-3: Beau Smith scripts; Brad Gorby-a(p). 1-1st app. Nordik, the Norse Hellspawn. 2-1st app. McFallon. 3-1st app. Mercy	1	2	3	5	6	8
1-3-(Gold): All retailer incentives						16.00
1-3-Variant-c	1	2	3	5	6	8
2-(Platinum)-Retailer incentive						25.00

SPAWN GODSLAYER
Image Comics (Todd McFarlane Prods.): May, 2007 - No. 8, Apr, 2008 ($2.99)

	GD	VG	FN	VF	VF/NM	NM-
1-8: 1-Holguin-s/Tan-a/Anacleto-c						3.00

SPAWN: THE DARK AGES
Image Comics (Todd McFarlane Productions): Mar, 1999 - No. 28, Oct, 2001 ($2.50)

	GD	VG	FN	VF	VF/NM	NM-
1-Fabry-c; Holguin-s/Sharp-a; variant-c by McFarlane						3.00
2-28						3.00

SPAWN THE IMPALER
Image Comics (Todd McFarlane Prods.): Oct, 1996 - No. 3, Dec, 1996 ($2.95, limited series)

	GD	VG	FN	VF	VF/NM	NM-
1-3-Mike Grell scripts, painted-a						3.00

SPAWN: THE UNDEAD
Image Comics (Todd McFarlane Prod.): Jun, 1999 - No. 9, Feb, 2000 ($1.95/$2.25)

	GD	VG	FN	VF	VF/NM	NM-
1-9-Dwayne Turner-c/a; Jenkins-s. 7-9-($2.25-c)						3.00
TPB (6/08, $24.99) r/#1-9						25.00

SPAWN/WILDC.A.T.S
Image Comics (WildStorm): Jan, 1996 - No. 4, Apr, 1996 ($2.50, lim. series)

	GD	VG	FN	VF	VF/NM	NM-
1-4: Alan Moore scripts in all.						3.00

SPEAKER FOR THE DEAD (ORSON SCOTT CARD'S...) (Ender's Game)
Marvel Comics: Mar, 2011 - No. 5, Jul, 2011 ($3.99, limited series)

	GD	VG	FN	VF	VF/NM	NM-
1-3-Johnston-s/Mhan-a/Camuncoli-c						4.00

SPECIAL AGENT (Steve Saunders...)(Also see True Comics #68)
Parents' Magazine Institute (Commended Comics No. 2): Dec, 1947 - No. 8, Sept, 1949 (Based on true FBI cases)

	GD	VG	FN	VF	VF/NM	NM-
1-J. Edgar Hoover photo on-c	12	24	36	67	94	120
2	8	16	24	40	50	60
3-8	7	14	21	35	43	50

SPECIAL COLLECTORS' EDITION (See Savage Fists of Kung-Fu)

SPECIAL COMICS (Becomes Hangman #2 on)
MLJ Magazines: Winter, 1941-42

	GD	VG	FN	VF	VF/NM	NM-
1-Origin The Boy Buddies (Shield & Wizard x-over); death of The Comet retold (see Pep #17); origin The Hangman retold; Hangman-c	343	686	1029	2400	4200	6000

SPECIAL EDITION (See Gorgo and Reptisaurus)

SPECIAL EDITION COMICS (See Promotional Section)

SPECIAL EDITION COMICS
Fawcett Publications: 1940 (August) (68 pgs., one-shot)

	GD	VG	FN	VF	VF/NM	NM-
1-1st book devoted entirely to Captain Marvel; C.C. Beck-c/a; only app. of Captain Marvel with belt buckle; Capt. Marvel appears with button-down flap; 1st story (came out before Captain Marvel #1)	811	1622	2433	5920	10,460	15,000

NOTE: *Prices vary widely on this book. Since this book is all Captain Marvel stories, it is actually a pre-Captain Marvel #1. There is speculation that this book almost became **Captain Marvel** #1. After **Special Edition** was published, there was an editor change at Fawcett. The new editor commissioned Kirby to do a nn **Captain Marvel** book early in 1941. This book was followed by a 2nd book several months later. This 2nd book was advertised as a #3 (making Special Edition the #1, & the nn issue the #2). However, the 2nd book did come out as a #2.*

SPECIAL EDITION: SPIDER-MAN VS. THE HULK (See listing under The Amazing Spider-Man)

SPECIAL EDITION X-MEN
Marvel Comics Group: Feb, 1983 ($2.00, one-shot, Baxter paper)

	GD	VG	FN	VF	VF/NM	NM-
1-r/Giant-Size X-Men #1 plus one new story	2	4	6	8	10	12

SPECIAL FORCES
Image Comics: Oct, 2007 - No. 4, Mar, 2009 ($2.99)

	GD	VG	FN	VF	VF/NM	NM-
1-4-Iraq war combat; Kyle Baker-s/a/c						3.00

SPECIAL MARVEL EDITION (Master of Kung Fu #17 on)
Marvel Comics Group: Jan, 1971 - No. 16, Feb, 1974 (#1-3: 25¢, 68 pgs.; #4: 52 pgs.; #5-16: 20¢, regular ed.)

	GD	VG	FN	VF	VF/NM	NM-
1-Thor-r by Kirby; 68 pgs.	4	8	12	24	37	50
2-4: Thor-r by Kirby; 2,3-68 pg. Giant. 4-(52 pgs.)	3	6	9	16	22	28
5-14: Sgt. Fury-r; 11-r/Sgt. Fury #13 (Capt. America)	2	4	6	9	12	15
15-Master of Kung Fu (Shang-Chi) begins (1st app., 12/73); Starlin-a; origin/1st app. Nayland Smith & Dr. Petrie	13	26	39	87	186	285
16-1st app. Midnight; Starlin-a (2nd Shang-Chi)	7	14	21	48	79	110

NOTE: ***Kirby** c-10-14.*

SPECIAL MISSIONS (See G.I. Joe...)

SPECIAL WAR SERIES (Attack V4#3 on?)
Charlton Comics: Aug, 1965 - No. 4, Nov, 1965

	GD	VG	FN	VF	VF/NM	NM-
V4#1-D-Day (also see D-Day listing)	4	8	12	24	37	50
2-Attack!	3	6	9	16	22	28
3-War & Attack (also see War & Attack)	2	4	6	13	18	22
4-Judomaster (intro/1st app.; see Sarge Steel)	8	16	24	53	89	125

SPECIES (Movie)
Dark Horse Comics: June, 1995 - No. 4, Sept, 1995 ($2.50, limited series)

	GD	VG	FN	VF	VF/NM	NM-
1-4: Adaptation of film						3.00

SPECIES: HUMAN RACE (Movie)
Dark Horse Comics: Nov, 1996 - No. 4, Feb, 1997 ($2.95, limited series)

	GD	VG	FN	VF	VF/NM	NM-
1-4						3.00

SPECTACULAR ADVENTURES (See Adventures)

SPECTACULAR FEATURE MAGAZINE, A (Formerly My Confessions) (Spectacular Features Magazine #12)
Fox Feature Syndicate: No. 11, April, 1950

	GD	VG	FN	VF	VF/NM	NM-
11 (#1)-Samson and Delilah	27	54	81	160	263	365

SPECTACULAR FEATURES MAGAZINE (Formerly A Spectacular Feature Magazine)
Fox Feature Syndicate: No. 12, June, 1950 - No. 3, Aug, 1950

	GD	VG	FN	VF	VF/NM	NM-
12 (#2)-Iwo Jima; photo flag-c	27	54	81	158	259	360
3-True Crime Cases From Police Files	22	44	66	128	209	290

SPECTACULAR SCARLET SPIDER
Marvel Comics: Nov, 1995 - No. 2, Dec, 1995 ($1.95, limited series)

	GD	VG	FN	VF	VF/NM	NM-
1,2: Replaces Spectacular Spider-Man						3.00

SPECTACULAR SPIDER-GIRL
Marvel Comics: Jul, 2010 - No. 4, Oct, 2010 ($3.99, limited series)

	GD	VG	FN	VF	VF/NM	NM-
1-4-Frenz-a; Frank Castle and the Hobgoblin app.						4.00

SPECTACULAR SPIDER-MAN, THE (See Marvel Special Edition and Marvel Treasury Edition)

SPECTACULAR SPIDER-MAN, THE (Magazine)
Marvel Comics Group: July, 1968 - No. 2, Nov, 1968 (35¢)

	GD	VG	FN	VF	VF/NM	NM-
1-(B&W)-Romita/Mooney 52 pg. story plus updated origin story with Everett-a(i)	11	22	33	75	148	220
1-Variation w/single c-price of 40¢	11	22	33	75	148	220
2-(Color)-Green Goblin-c & 58 pg. story; Romita painted-c (story reprinted in King Size Spider-Man #9); Romita/Mooney-a	10	20	30	67	124	180

SPECTACULAR SPIDER-MAN, THE (Peter Parker...#54-132, 134)
Marvel Comics Group: Dec, 1976 - No. 263, Nov, 1998

	GD	VG	FN	VF	VF/NM	NM-
1-Origin recap in text; return of Tarantula	6	12	18	41	66	90
2-Kraven the Hunter app.	3	6	9	18	27	35
3-5: 3-Intro Lightmaster. 4-Vulture app.	3	6	9	14	20	25

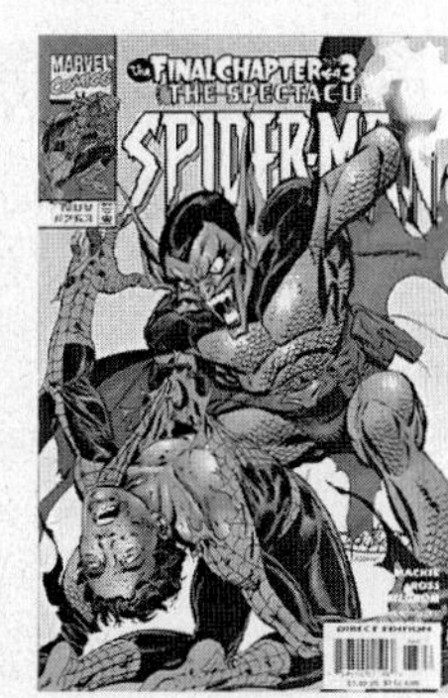

Spectacular Spider-Man #263 © MAR

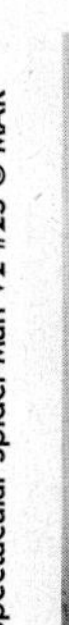
Spectacular Spider-Man V2 #23 © MAR

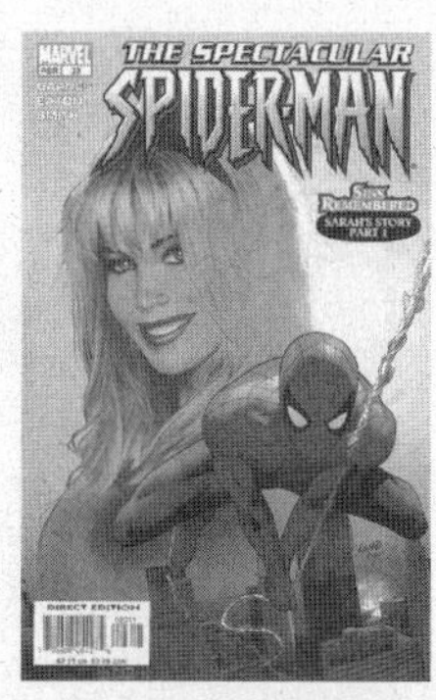

The Spectre V4 #27 © DC

GD VG FN VF VF/NM NM-
2.0 4.0 6.0 8.0 9.0 9.2

6-8-Morbius app.; 6-r/Marvel Team-Up #3 w/Morbius 3 6 9 16 22 28
7,8-(35¢-c variants, limited distribution)(6,7/77) 5 10 15 35 55 75
9-20: 9,10-White Tiger app. 11-Last 30¢-c. 17,18-Angel & Iceman app. (from Champions); Ghost Rider cameo. 18-Gil Kane-c 2 4 6 8 11 14
9-11-(35¢-c variants, limited distribution)(8-10/77) 3 6 9 20 30 40
21,24-26: 21-Scorpion app. 26-Daredevil app. 2 3 4 6 8 10
22,23-Moon Knight app. 2 4 6 8 10 12
27-Miller's 1st art on Daredevil (2/79); also see Captain America #235 6 12 18 37 59 80
28-Miller Daredevil (p) 4 8 12 26 41 55
29-55,57,59: 33-Origin Iguana. 38-Morbius app. 1 2 3 4 5 7
56-2nd app. Jack O'Lantern (Macendale) & 1st Spidey/Jack O'Lantern battle (7/81) 1 2 3 5 6 8
58-Byrne-a(p) 1 2 3 5 6 8
60-Double size; origin retold with new facts revealed 1 2 3 5 6 8
61-63,65-68,71-74: 65-Kraven the Hunter app. 6.00
64-1st app. Cloak & Dagger (3/82) 2 4 6 10 14 18
69,70-Cloak & Dagger app. 1 2 3 5 7 9
75-Double size 1 2 3 4 5 7
76-80: 78,79-Punisher cameo 6.00
81,82-Punisher, Cloak & Dagger app. 1 2 3 5 6 8
83-Origin Punisher retold (10/83) 2 4 6 8 10 12
84,86-89,91-99: 94-96-Cloak & Dagger app. 98-Intro The Spot 6.00
85-Hobgoblin (Ned Leeds) app. (12/83); gains powers of original Green Goblin (see Amazing Spider-Man #238) 2 4 6 8 10 12
90-Spider-Man's new black costume, last panel (ties w/Amazing Spider-Man #252 & Marvel Team-Up #141 for 1st app.) 2 4 6 8 11 14
100-(3/85)-Double size 1 2 3 4 5 7
101-115,117,118,120-129: 107-110-Death of Jean DeWolff. 111-Secret Wars II tie-in. 128-Black Cat new costume 5.00
116,119-Sabretooth-c/story 2 3 4 6 8 10
130-132: 130-Hobgoblin app. 131-Six part Kraven tie-in. 132-Kraven tie-in 2 3 4 6 8 10
133-140: 138-1st full app. Tombstone (origin #139). 140-Punisher cameo 5.00
141-143-Punisher app. 1 2 3 4 5 7
144-146,148-157: 151-Tombstone returns 4.00
147-1st brief app. new Hobgoblin (Macendale), 1 page; continued in Web of Spider-Man #48 2 4 6 8 11 14
158-Spider-Man gets new powers (1st Cosmic Spidey, cont'd in Web of Spider-Man #59) 1 2 3 5 6 8
159-Cosmic Spider-Man app. 1 2 3 4 5 7
160-170: 161-163-Hobgoblin app. 168-170-Avengers x-over. 169-1st app. The Outlaws 3.00
171-188,190-199: 180,181,183,184-Green Goblin app. 197-199-Original X-Men-c/story 3.00
189-($2.95, 52 pgs.)-Silver hologram on-c; battles Green Goblin; origin Spidey retold; Vess poster w/Spidey & Hobgoblin 6.00
189-(2nd printing)-Gold hologram on-c 4.00
195-(Deluxe ed.)-Polybagged w/"Dirt" magazine #2 & Beastie Boys/Smithereens music cassette 4.00
200-($2.95)-Holo-grafx foil-c; Green Goblin-c/story 4.00
201-219,221,222,224,226-228,230-247: 212-w/card sheet. 203-Maximum Carnage x-over. 204-Begin 4 part death of Tombstone story. 207,208-The Shroud-c/story. 208-Siege of Darkness x-over (#207 is a tie-in). 209-Black Cat back-up. 215,216-Scorpion app. 217-Power & Responsibility Pt. 4. 231-Return of Kaine; Spider-Man corpse discovered. 232-New Doc Octopus app. 233-Carnage-c/app. 235-Dragon Man cameo. 236-Dragon Man-c/app; Lizard app.; Peter Parker regains powers. 238,239-Lizard app. 239-w/card insert. 240-Revelations storyline begins. 241-Flashback 3.00
213-Collectors ed. polybagged w/16 pg. preview & animation cel; foil-c; 1st meeting Spidey & Typhoid Mary 4.00
213-Version polybagged w/Gamepro #7; no-c date, price 3.00
217,219 ($2.95)-Deluxe edition foil-c: flip book 4.00
220 ($2.25, 52 pgs.)-Flip book, Mary Jane reveals pregnancy 4.00
223,229: ($2.50) 229-Spidey quits 4.00
223,225: ($2.95)-223-Die Cut-c. 225-Newsstand ed. 4.00
225,229: ($3.95) 225-Direct Market Holodisk-c (Green Goblin). 229-Acetate-c, Spidey quits 5.00
240-Variant-c 4.00
248,249,251-254,256: 249-Return of Norman Osborn 256-1st app. Prodigy 3.00
250-($3.25) Double gatefold-c 4.00
255-($2.99) Spiderhunt pt. 4 4.00
257-262: 257-Double cover with "Spectacular Prodigy #1"; battles Jack O'Lantern. 258-Spidey is cleared. 259,260-Green Goblin & Hobgoblin app. 262-Byrne-s 3.00
263-Final issue; Byrne-c; Aunt May returns 5.00
#(-1) Flashback (7/97) 3.00

GD VG FN VF VF/NM NM-
2.0 4.0 6.0 8.0 9.0 9.2

1000 (6/11, $4.99) Punisher app.; Nauck & Ryan-a/Rivera-c; r/ASM #129 5.00
Annual 1 (1979)-Doc Octopus-c & 46 pg. story 2 4 6 8 11 14
Annual 2 (1980)-Origin/1st app. Rapier 1 2 3 5 6 8
Annual 3-5: ('81-'83) 3-Last Man-Wolf 5.00
Annual 6-14: 8 ('88,$ 1.75)-Evolutionary War x-over; Daydreamer returns Gwen Stacy "clone" back to real self (not Gwen Stacy). 9 ('89, $2.00, 68 pgs.)-Atlantis Attacks. 10 ('90, $2.00, 68 pgs.)-McFarlane-a. 11 ('91, $2.00, 68 pgs.)-Iron Man app. 12 ('92, $2.25, 68 pgs.)-Venom solo story cont'd from Amazing Spider-Man Annual #26. 13 ('93, $2.95, 68 pgs.)-Polybagged w/trading card; John Romita, Sr. back-up-a 4.00
Special 1 (1995, $3.95)-Flip book 4.00
NOTE: ***Austin*** *c-21i, Annual 11i.* ***Buckler*** *a-103, 107-111, 116, 117, 119, 122, Annual 1, Annual 10; c-103, 107-111, 113, 116-119, 122, Annual 1.* ***Buscema*** *a-121.* ***Byrne*** *c(p)-17, 43, 58, 101, 102.* ***Giffen*** *a-120p.* ***Hembeck*** *c/a-86p.* ***Larsen*** *c-Annual 11p.* ***Miller*** *c-46p, 48p, 50, 51p, 52p, 54p, 55, 56p, 57, 60.* ***Mooney*** *a-7i, 11i, 21p, 23p, 25p, 26p, 29-34p, 36p, 37p, 39i, 41, 42i, 49p, 50i, 51i, 53p, 54-57i, 59-66i, 68i, 71i, 73-79i, 81-83i, 85i, 87-99i, 102i, 125p, Annual 1i, 2p.* ***Nasser*** *c-37p.* ***Perez*** *c-10.* ***Simonson*** *c-54i.* ***Zeck*** *a-22, 118, 131, 132; c-131, 132.*

SPECTACULAR SPIDER-MAN (2nd series)
Marvel Comics: Sept, 2003 - No. 27, June, 2005 ($2.25/$2.99)

1-Jenkins-s/Ramos-a/c; Venom-c/app. 4.00
2-26: 2-5-Venom app. 6-9-Dr. Octopus app. 11-13-The Lizard app. 14-Rivera painted-a. 15,16-Capt. America app. 17,18-Ramos-a. 20-Spider-Man gets organic webshooters 21,22-Caldwell-a. 23-26-Sarah & Gabriel app.; Land-c 3.00
27-($2.99) Last issue; Uncle Ben app. in flashback; Buckingham-a 4.00
... Vol. 1: The Hunger TPB (2003, $11.99) r/#1-5 12.00
... Vol. 2: Countdown TPB (2004, $11.99) r/#6-10 12.00
... Vol. 3: Here There Be Monsters TPB (2004, $9.99) r/#11-14 10.00
... Vol. 4: Disassembled TPB (2004, $14.99) r/#15-20 15.00
... Vol. 5: Sins Remembered (2005, $9.99) r/#23-26 10.00
... Vol. 6: The Final Curtain (2005, $14.99) r/#21,22,27 & Peter Parker: Spider-Man #39-41 15.00

SPECTACULAR STORIES MAGAZINE (Formerly A Star Presentation)
Fox Feature Syndicate (Hero Books): No. 4, July, 1950; No. 3, Sept, 1950

4-Sherlock Holmes (true crime stories) 36 72 108 214 347 480
3-The St. Valentine's Day Massacre (true crime) 24 48 72 140 230 320

SPECTRE, THE (1st Series) (See Adventure Comics #431-440, More Fun & Showcase)
National Periodical Publ.: Nov-Dec, 1967 - No. 10, May-June, 1969 (All 12¢)

1-(11-12/67)-Anderson-c/a 13 26 39 87 186 285
2-5-Neal Adams-c/a; 3-Wildcat x-over 10 20 30 64 115 165
6-8,10: 6-8-Anderson inks. 7-Hourman app. 7 14 21 48 79 110
9-Wrightson-a 8 16 24 51 86 120

SPECTRE, THE (2nd Series) (See Saga of the Swamp Thing #58, Showcase '95 #8 & Wrath of the...)
DC Comics: Apr, 1987 - No. 31, Oct, 1989 ($1.00, new format)

1-Colan-a begins 5.00
2-32: 9-Nudity panels. 10-Batman cameo. 10,11-Millennium tie-ins 3.00
Annual 1 (1988, $2.00)-Deadman app. 4.00
NOTE: ***Art Adams*** *c-Annual 1.* ***Colan*** *a-1-6.* ***Kaluta*** *c-1-3.* ***Mignola*** *c-7-9.* ***Morrow*** *a-9-15.* ***Sears*** *c/a-22.* ***Vess*** *c-13-15.*

SPECTRE, THE (3rd Series) (Also see Brave and the Bold #72, 75, 116, 180, 199 & Showcase '95 #8)
DC Comics: Dec, 1992 - No. 62, Feb, 1998 ($1.75/$1.95/$2.25/$2.50)

1-($1.95)-Glow-in-the-dark-c; Mandrake-a begins 5.00
2,3 4.00
4-7,9-12,14-20: 10-Kaluta-c. 11-Hildebrandt painted-c. 16-Aparo/K. Jones-a. 19-Snyder III-c. 20-Sienkiewicz-c 3.00
8,13-($2.50)-Glow-in-the-dark-c 4.00
21-62: 22-(9/94)-Superman-c & app. 23-(11/94). 43-Kent Williams-c. 44-Kaluta-c. 47-Final Night x-over. 49-Begin Bolton-c. 51-Batman-c/app. 52-Gianni-c. 54-Corben-c. 60-Harris-c 3.00
#0 (10/94) Released between #22 & #23 3.00
Annual 1 (1995, $3.95)-Year One story 4.00
NOTE: ***Bisley*** *c-27.* ***Fabry*** *c-2.* ***Kelley Jones*** *c-31.* ***Vess*** *c-5.*

SPECTRE, THE (4th Series) (Hal Jordan; also see Day of Judgment #5 and Legends of the DC Universe #33-36)
DC Comics: Mar, 2001 - No. 27, May, 2003 ($2.50/$2.75)

1-DeMatteis-s/Ryan Sook-c/a 4.00
2-27: 3,4-Superman & Batman-c/app. 5-Two-Face-c/app. 20-Begin $2.75-c. 21-Sinestro returns. 24-JLA app. 3.00

SPECTRE, THE (See Crisis Aftermath: The Spectre)

SPEEDBALL (See Amazing Spider-Man Annual #12, Marvel Super-Heroes & The New Warriors)
Marvel Comics: Sept, 1988(10/88-inside) - No. 11, July, 1989 (75¢)

1-11: Ditko/Guice-a-1-4, c-1; Ditko a-1-10; c-1-11p 4.00

Speed Comics #10 © Brookwood

Speed Racer #6 © Speed Racer Ents.

Spellbound #3 © MAR

GD 2.0 | VG 4.0 | FN 6.0 | VF 8.0 | VF/NM 9.0 | NM- 9.2

SPEED BUGGY (TV)(Also see Fun-In #12, 15)
Charlton Comics: July, 1975 - No. 9, Nov, 1976 (Hanna-Barbera)

1 3 6 9 16 22 28
2-9 2 4 6 10 14 18

SPEED CARTER SPACEMAN (See Spaceman)

SPEED COMICS (New Speed)(Also see Double Up)
Brookwood Publ./Speed Publ./Harvey Publications No. 14 on:
10/39 - #11, 8/40; #12, 3/41 - #44, 1-2/47 (#14-16: pocket size, 100 pgs.)

1-Origin & 1st app. Shock Gibson; Ted Parrish, the Man with 1000 Faces begins; Powell-a; becomes Champion #2 on?; has earliest? full page panel in comics 360 720 1080 2520 4410 6300
2-Powell-a 121 242 363 768 1322 1875
3 68 136 204 435 743 1050
4,5: 4-Powell-a? 5-Dinosaur-c 55 110 165 352 601 850
6-11: 7-Mars Mason begins, ends #11 50 100 150 315 533 750
12 (3/41; shows #11 in indicia)-The Wasp begins; Major Colt app. (Capt. Colt #12) 53 106 159 334 567 800
13-Intro. Captain Freedom & Young Defenders; Girl Commandos, Pat Parker (costumed heroine), War Nurse begins; Major Colt app. 71 142 213 454 777 1100
14-16 (100 pg. pocket size, 1941): 14-2nd Harvey comic (See Pocket); Shock Gibson dons new costume; Nazi war-c. 15-Pat Parker dons costume, last in costume #23; no Girl Commandos 116 232 348 742 1271 1800
17-Black Cat begins (4/42, early app.; see Pocket #1); origin Black Cat-r/Pocket #1; not in #40,41; S&K-c 107 214 321 680 1165 1650
18-20-S&K-c. 20-Japanese war-c 90 180 270 576 988 1400
21-Hitler, Tojo-c; Kirby-c 129 258 387 826 1413 200
22-Kirby-c 87 174 261 553 952 1350
23-Origin Girl Commandos; Kirby-c 87 174 261 553 952 1350
24-Pat Parker team-up with Girl Commandos; Hitler, Tojo, & Mussolini-c 116 232 348 742 1271 1800
25,27-30 71 142 213 454 777 1100
26-Flag-c 77 154 231 493 847 1200
31-Schomburg Hitler & Tojo-c 129 258 387 826 1413 2000
32-36-Schomburg-c. 33,35,36-Japanese war-c. 34-Nazi war-c 71 142 213 454 777 1100
37,39-42,44: 37-Japanese war-c 41 82 123 256 428 600
38-Iwo-Jima Flag-c 43 86 129 271 461 650
43-Robot-c 45 90 135 284 480 675

NOTE: ***Al Avison*** *c-14-16, 30, 43.* ***Briefer*** *a-6, 7.* ***Jon Henri*** *(Kirbyesque) c-17-20.* ***Kubert*** *a-37, 38, 42-44.* ***Kirby/Caseneuve*** *c-21-23.* ***Cecelia Munson*** *a-7-11(Mars Mason).* ***Palais*** *c-37, 39-42.* ***Powell*** *a-1, 2, 4-7, 28, 31, 44.* ***Schomburg*** *c-31-36.* ***Tuska*** *a-3, 6, 7. Bondage c-18, 35. Captain Freedom c-16-24, 25(part), 26-44(w/Black Cat #27, 29, 31, 32-40). Shock Gibson c-1-15.*

SPEED DEMON (Also see Marvel Versus DC #3 & DC Versus Marvel #4)
Marvel Comics (Amalgam): Apr, 1996 ($1.95, one-shot)

1 3.00

SPEED DEMONS (Formerly Frank Merriwell at Yale #1-4?; Submarine Attack #11 on)
Charlton Comics: No. 5, Feb, 1957 - No. 10, 1958

5-10 7 14 21 35 43 50

SPEED FORCE (See The Flash 2nd Series #143-Cobalt Blue)
DC Comics: Nov, 1997 ($3.95, one-shot)

1-Flash & Kid Flash vs. Cobalt Blue; Waid-s/Aparo & Sienkiewicz-a; Flash family stories and pin-ups by various 4.00

SPEED RACER (Also see The New Adventures of...)
Now Comics: July, 1987 - No. 38, Nov, 1990 ($1.75)

1 4.00
2-38, 1-2nd printing 3.00
Special 1 (1988, $2.00) 4.00
Special 2 (1988, $3.50) 4.00

SPEED RACER (Also see Racer X)
DC Comics (WildStorm): Oct, 1999 - No. 3, Dec, 1999 ($2.50, limited series)

1-3-Tommy Yune-s/a; origin of Racer X; debut of the Mach 5 3.00
...: Born To Race (2000, $9.95, TPB) r/series & conceptual art 10.00
...: The Original Manga Vol. 1 ('00, $9.95, TPB) r/1950s B&W manga 10.00

SPEED RACER: CHRONICLES OF THE RACER
IDW Publishing: 2007 - No. 4, Apr, 2008 ($3.99)

1-4-Multiple covers for each 4.00

SPEED RACER FEATURING NINJA HIGH SCHOOL
Now Comics: Aug, 1993 - No. 2, 1993 ($2.50, mini-series)

1,2: 1-Polybagged w/card. 2-Exists? 3.00

SPEED RACER: RETURN OF THE GRX
Now Comics: Mar, 1994 - No. 2, Apr, 1994 ($1.95, limited series)

1,2 3.00

SPEED SMITH-THE HOT ROD KING (Also see Hot Rod King)
Ziff-Davis Publishing Co.: Spring, 1952

1-Saunders painted-c 23 46 69 136 223 310

SPEEDY GONZALES
Dell Publishing Co.: No. 1084, Mar, 1960

Four Color 1084 5 10 15 35 55 75

SPEEDY RABBIT (See Television Puppet Show)
Realistic/I. W. Enterprises/Super Comics: nd (1953); 1963

nn (1953)-Realistic Reprint? 2 4 6 10 14 18
I.W. Reprint #1 (2 versions w/diff. c/stories exist)-Peter Cottontail #?
Super Reprint #14(1963) 2 4 6 8 10 12

SPELLBINDERS
Quality: Dec, 1986 - No. 12, Jan, 1988 ($1.25)

1-12: Nemesis the Warlock, Amadeus Wolf 3.00

SPELLBINDERS
Marvel Comics: May, 2005 - No. 6, Oct, 2005 ($2.99, limited series)

1-6-Carey-s/Perkins-a 3.00
...: Signs and Wonders TPB (2006, $7.99, digest) r/#1-6 8.00

SPELLBOUND (See The Crusaders)

SPELLBOUND (Tales to Hold You... #1, Stories to Hold You...)
Atlas Comics (ACI 1-15/Male 16-23/BPC 24-34): Mar, 1952 - #23, June, 1954; #24, Oct, 1955 - #34, June, 1957

1-Horror/weird stories in all 81 162 243 518 884 1250
2-Edgar A. Poe app. 42 84 126 265 445 625
3-5: 3-Whitney-a; cannibalism story 39 78 117 231 378 525
6-Krigstein-a 39 78 117 231 378 525
7-10: 8-Ayers-a 32 64 96 192 314 435
11-16,18-20: 14-Ed Win-a 27 54 81 162 266 370
17-Krigstein-a 28 56 84 165 270 375
21-23: 23-Last precode (6/54) 22 44 66 132 216 300
24-28,30,31,34: 25-Orlando-a 21 42 63 122 199 275
29-Ditko-a (4 pgs.) 22 44 66 132 216 300
32,33-Torres-a 21 42 63 122 199 275

NOTE: ***Brodsky*** *a-5; c-1, 5-7, 10, 11, 13, 15, 25-27, 32.* ***Colan*** *a-17.* ***Everett*** *a-2, 5, 7, 10, 16, 28, 31; c-2, 8, 9, 14, 17-19, 28, 30.* ***Forgione/Abel*** *a-29.* ***Forte/Fox*** *a-16.* ***Al Hartley*** *a-2.* ***Heath*** *a-2, 4, 8, 9, 12, 14, 16; c-3, 4, 12, 16, 20, 21.* ***Infantino*** *a-15.* ***Keller*** *a-5.* ***Kida*** *a-2, 14.* ***Maneely*** *a-7, 14, 27; c-24, 29, 31.* ***Mooney*** *a-5, 13, 18.* ***Mac Pakula*** *a-22, 32.* ***Post*** *a-8.* ***Powell*** *a-19, 20, 32.* ***Robinson*** *a-1.* ***Romita*** *a-24, 26, 27.* ***R.Q. Sale*** *a-29.* ***Sekowsky*** *a-5.* ***Severin*** *c-29.* ***Sinnott*** *a-8, 16, 17.*

SPELLBOUND
Marvel Comics: Jan, 1988 - Apr, 1988 ($1.50, bi-weekly, Baxter paper)

1-5 3.00
6 ($2.25, 52 pgs.) 4.00

SPELLJAMMER (Also see TSR Worlds Comics Annual)
DC Comics: Sept, 1990 - No. 15, Nov, 1991 ($1.75)

1-15: Based on TSR game. 11-Heck-a. 3.00

SPENCER SPOOK (Formerly Giggle Comics)
American Comics Group: No. 100, Mar-Apr, 1955 - No. 101, May-June, 1955

100,101 7 14 21 37 46 55

SPIDER, THE
Eclipse Books: 1991 - Book 3, 1991 ($4.95, 52 pgs., limited series)

Book 1-3-Truman-c/a 5.00

SPIDER-BOY (Also see Marvel Versus DC #3)
Marvel Comics (Amalgam): Apr, 1996 ($1.95)

1-Mike Wieringo-c/a; Karl Kesel story; 1st app. of Bizarnage, Insect Queen, Challengers of the Fantastic, Sue Storm: Agent of S.H.I.E.L. D., & King Lizard 3.00

SPIDER-BOY TEAM-UP
Marvel Comics (Amalgam): June, 1997 ($1.95, one-shot)

1-Karl Kesel & Roger Stern-s/Jo Ladronn-a(p) 3.00

SPIDER-GIRL (See What If... #105)
Marvel Comics: Oct, 1998 - No. 100, Sept, 2006 ($1.99/$2.25/$2.99)

0-($2.99)-r/1st app. Peter Parker's daughter from What If #105; previews regular series, Avengers-Next and J2 1 2 3 4 5 7
1-DeFalco-s/Olliffe & Williamson-s 1 2 3 4 5 7

Spider-Girl #20 © MAR

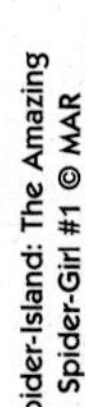
Spider-Island: The Amazing Spider-Girl #1 © MAR

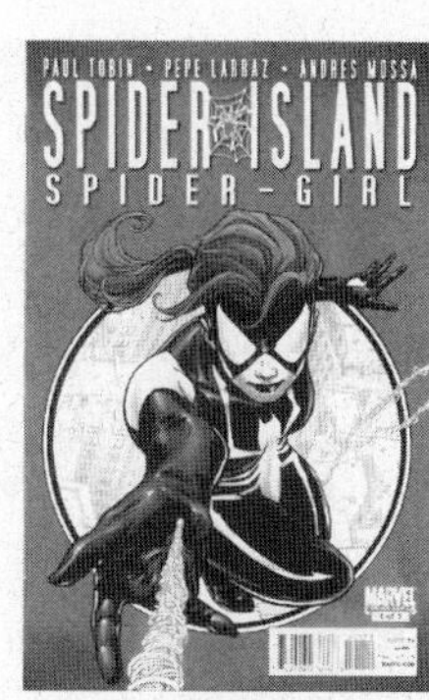

Spider-Man #93 © MAR

GD VG FN VF VF/NM NM-
2.0 4.0 6.0 8.0 9.0 9.2

2-Two covers 4.00
3-16,18-20: 3-Fantastic Five-c/app. 10,11-Spider-Girl time-travels to meet teenaged Spider-Man 3.00
17-($2.99) Peter Parker suits up 4.00
21-24,26-49,51-59: 21-Begin $2.25-c. 31-Avengers app. 3.00
25-($2.99) Spider-Girl vs. the Savage Six 4.00
50-($3.50) 4.00
59-99-($2.99) 59-Avengers app.; Ben Parker born. 75-May in Black costume. 82-84-Venom bonds with Normie Osborn. 93-Venom-c. 95-Tony Stark app. 3.00
100-($3.99) Last issue; story plus Rogues Gallery, profile pages; r/#27,53 4.00
1999 Annual ($3.99) 4.00
...: The End! (10/10, $3.99) Frenz & Buscema-a; Mayhem app. 4.00
Wizard #1/2 (1999) 3.00
... A Fresh Start (1/99,$5.99, TPB) r/#1&2 6.00
... Presents The Buzz and Darkdevil (2007, $7.99, digest) r/mini-series 8.00
TPB (10/01, $19.95) r/#0-8; new Olliffe-c 20.00
Marvel Age Spider-Girl Vol. 1: Legacy (2004, $7.99, digest size) r/#0-5 8.00
Marvel Age Spider-Girl Vol. 2: Like Father, Like Daughter (2004, $7.99, digest) r/#6-11 8.00
Spider-Girl Vol. 3: Avenging Allies (2005, $7.99, digest) r/#12-16 & 1999 Annual 8.00
Spider-Girl Vol. 4: Turning Point (2005, $7.99, digest) r/#17-21 & #1/2 8.00
Spider-Girl Vol. 5: Endgame (2006, $7.99, digest) r/#22-27 8.00
Spider-Girl Vol. 6: Too Many Spiders! (2006, $7.99, digest) r/#28-33 8.00
Spider-Girl Vol. 7: Betrayed (2006, $7.99, digest) r/#34-38 & #51 8.00
Spider-Girl Vol. 8: Duty Calls (2007, $7.99, digest) r/#39-44 8.00
Spider-Girl Vol. 9: Secret Lives (2007, $7.99, digest) r/#45-50 8.00

SPIDER-GIRL (Araña Corazon from Arana Heart of the Spider)
Marvel Comics: Jan, 2011 - No. 8, Sept, 2011 ($3.99/$2.99)

1-($3.99) Tobin-s/Henry-a/Kitson-c; back-up w/Haspiel-a; Fantastic Four app. 4.00
1-Variant-c by Del Mundo 5.00
2-8-($2.99) 2,3-Red Hulk app. 4,5-Ana Kravenoff app. 6-Hobgoblin app. 8-Powers return 3.00

SPIDER-HAM 25TH ANNIVERSARY SPECIAL
Marvel Comics: Aug, 2010 ($3.99, one-shot)

1-Jusko-c/DeFalco-s/Chabot-a; Peter Porker vs. the Swinester Six 4.00

SPIDER ISLAND... (one-shots) (See Amazing Spider-Man #666-673)
Marvel Comics

...: Deadly Foes 1 (10/11, $4.99) Hobgoblin & Jackal stories; Caselli-c 5.00
...: Emergence of Evil - Jackal & Hobgoblin 1 (10/11, $4.99) Hobgoblin & Jackal reprints 5.00
...: Heroes For Hire 1 (12/11, $2.99) Misty Knight & Paladin; Hotz-a/Yardin-c 3.00
...: I Love New York City 1 (11/11, $3.99) Short stories by various; Punisher app. 4.00
...: Spider-Woman 1 (11/11, $2.99) Van Lente-s/Camuncoli-a; Alicia Masters app. 3.00
... Spotlight 1 ('11, $3.99) Creator interviews and story previews 4.00
...: The Avengers 1 (11/11, $2.99) McKone-a/Yu-c; Frog-Man app. 3.00

SPIDER ISLAND: CLOAK & DAGGER (See Amazing Spider-Man #666-673)
Marvel Comics: Oct, 2011 - No. 3 ($2.99, limited series)

1,2-Spencer-s/Rios-a/Choi-c; Mr. Negative app. 3.00

SPIDER ISLAND: DEADLY HANDS OF KUNG FU (See Amazing Spider-Man #666-673)
Marvel Comics: Oct, 2011 - No. 3, Dec, 2011 ($2.99, limited series)

1-3-Johnston-s/Fiumara-a; Madame Web & Iron Fist app. 3.00

SPIDER ISLAND: THE AMAZING SPIDER-GIRL (Continued from Spider-Girl #8)
Marvel Comics: Oct, 2011 - No. 3, Dec, 2011 ($2.99, limited series)

1-3-Hobgoblin & Kingpin app.; Tobin-s/Larraz-a 3.00

SPIDER-MAN (See Amazing..., Friendly Neighborhood..., Giant-Size..., Marvel Age..., Marvel Knights..., Marvel Tales, Marvel Team-Up, Spectacular..., Spidey Super Stories, Ultimate Marvel Team-Up, Ultimate..., Venom, & Web Of...)

SPIDER-MAN (Peter Parker Spider-Man on cover but not indicia #75-on)
Marvel Comics: Aug, 1990 - No. 98, Nov, 1998 ($1.75/$1.95/ $1.99)

1-Silver edition, direct sale only (unbagged) 1 2 3 5 6 8
1-Silver bagged edition; direct sale, no price on comic, but $2.00 on plastic bag (125,000 print run) 2 4 6 11 16 20
1-Regular edition w/Spidey face in UPC area (unbagged); green-c 6.00
1-Regular bagged edition w/Spidey face in UPC area; green cover (125,000) 12.00
1-Newsstand bagged w/UPC code 8.00
1-Gold edition, 2nd printing (unbagged) with Spider-Man in box (400,000-450,000) 5.00
1-Gold 2nd printing w/UPC code; (less than 10,000 print run) intended for Wal-Mart; much scarcer than originally believed 8 16 24 51 86 120
1-Platinum ed. mailed to retailers only (10,000 print run); has new McFarlane-a & editorial material instead of ads; stiff-c, no cover price 8 16 24 55 93 130
2-25: 2-McFarlane-c/a/scripts continue. 6,7-Ghost Rider & Hobgoblin app. 8-Wolverine cameo; Wolverine storyline begins. 12-Wolverine storyline ends. 13-Spidey's black costume returns; Morbius app. 14-Morbius app. 15-Erik Larsen-c/a; Beast c/s. 16-X-Force-c/story w/Liefeld assists; continues in X-Force #4; reads sideways; last McFarlane issue. 17-Thanos-c/story; Leonardi/Williamson-c/a. 13,14-Spidey in black costume. 18-Ghost Rider-c/story. 18-23-Sinister Six storyline w/Erik Larsen-c/a/scripts. 19-Hulk & Hobgoblin-c & app. 20-22-Deathlok app. 22,23-Ghost Rider, Hulk, Hobgoblin app. 23-Wrap-around gatefold-c. 24-Infinity War x-over w/Demogoblin & Hobgoblin-c/story. 24-Demogoblin dons new costume & battles Hobgoblin-c/story 4.00
26-($3.50, 52 pgs.)-Silver hologram on-c w/gatefold poster by Ron Lim; origin retold 5.00
26-2nd printing; gold hologram on-c 4.00
27-45: 32-34-Punisher-c/story. 37-Maximum Carnage x-over. 39,40-Electro-c/s (cameo #38). 41-43-Iron Fist-c/stories w/Jae Lee-c/a. 42-Intro Platoon. 44-Hobgoblin app. 3.50
46-49,51-53, 55, 56,58-74,76-81: 46-Begin $1.95-c; bound-in card sheet. 51-Power & Responsibility Pt. 3. 52,53-Venom app. 60-Kaine revealed. 61-Origin Kaine. 65-Mysterio app. 66-Kaine-c/app.; Peter Parker app. 67-Carnage-c/app. 68,69-Hobgoblin-c/app. 72-Onslaught x-over; Spidey vs. Sentinels. 74-Daredevil-c/app. 77-80-Morbius-c/app. 3.00
46-($2.95)-Polybagged; silver ink-c w/16 pg. preview of cartoon series & animation style print; bound-in trading card sheet 4.00
50-($2.50)-Newsstand edition 4.00
50-($3.95)-Collectors edition w/holographic-c 5.00
51-($2.95)-Deluxe edition foil-c; flip book 4.00
54-($2.75, 52 pgs.)-Flip book 4.00
57-($2.50) 4.00
57-($2.95)-Die cut-c 5.00
65-($2.95)-Variant-c; polybagged w/cassette 4.00
75-($2.95)-Wraparound-c; Green Goblin returns; death of Ben Reilly (who was the clone) 4.00
82-97: 84-Juggernaut app. 91-Double cover with "Dusk #1"; battles the Shocker. 93-Ghost Rider app. 3.00
98-Double cover; final issue 4.00
#(-1) Flashback (7/97) 3.00
Annual '97 ($2.99), '98 ($2.99)-Devil Dinosaur-c/app. 4.00
NOTE: ***Erik Larsen** c/a-15, 18-23. **M. Rogers/Keith Williams** c/a-27, 28.*

SPIDER-MAN (one-shots, hardcovers and TPBs)
...& Arana Special: The Hunter Revealed (5/06, $3.99) Del Rio-s; art by Del Rio & various 4.00
...and Batman ('95, $5.95) DeMatteis-s; Joker, Carnage app. 6.00
...and Daredevil ('84, $2.00) 1-r/Spectacular Spider-Man #26-28 by Miller 4.00
...and The Human Torch in...Bahia de Los Muertos! 1 (5/09, $3.99) Beland-s/Juan Doe-a; Diablo app.; printed in two versions (English and Spanish language) 4.00
...: Back in Black HC (2007, $34.99, dustjacket) oversized r/Amaz. S-M #539-543, Friendly Neighborhood S-M #17-23 & Annual #1; cover pencils and sketch pages 35.00
...: Back in Black SC (2008, $24.99) same contents as HC 25.00
...: Back in Black Handbook (2007, $3.99) Official Handbook format; Lopresti-c 4.00
...: Back in Quack (11/10, $3.99) Howard the Duck, Beverly and Man-Thing app. 4.00
...: Birth of Venom TPB (2007, $29.99) r/Secret Wars #8, AS-M #252-259,298-300,315-317, AS-M Annual #25, Fantastic Four #274 and Web of Spider-Man #1 30.00
...: Brand New Day HC (2008, $24.99, dustjacket) r/Amaz. S-M #546-551, Spider-Man: Swing Shift and story from Venom Super-Special 25.00
...: Carnage nn (6/93, $6.95, TPB)-r/Amazing S-M #344,345,359-363; spot varnish-c 7.00
.../Daredevil (10/02, $2.99) Vatche Mavlian-c/a; Brett Matthews-s 3.00
...: Dead Man's Hand 1 (4/97, $2.99) 3.00
...: Death of the Stacys HC (2007, $19.99, dustjacket) r/Amazing Spider-Man #88-92 and #121,122; intro. by Gerry Conway; afterword by Romita; cover gallery incl. reprints 20.00
.../Dr. Strange: "The Way to Dusty Death" nn (1992, $6.95, 68 pgs.) 7.00
...: Election Day HC (2009, $29.99) r/#584-588; includes Barack Obama app from #583 30.00
.../Elektra '98-($2.99) vs. The Silencer 3.00
... Family (2005, $4.99, 100 pgs.) new story and reprints; Spider-Ham app. 5.00
... Fear Itself (3/09, $3.99) Spider-Man and Man-Thing; Stuart Moore-s/Joe Suitor-a 4.00
... Fear Itself Graphic Novel (2/92, $12.95) 18.00
Giant-Sized Spider-Man (12/98, $3.99) r/team-ups 4.00
...: Grim Hunt - The Kraven Saga (5/10, free) prelude to Grim Hunt arc; Kraven history 3.00
Holiday Special 1995 ($2.95) 4.00
...: Hot Shots nn (1/96, $2.95) fold out posters by various, inc. Vess and Ross 4.00
Identity Crisis (9/98, $19.95, TPB) 20.00
...: Kraven's Last Hunt HC (2006, $19.99) r/Amaz. S-M #293,294; Web of S-M #31,32 and Spect. S-M #131-132; intro. by DeMatteis; Zeck-a; cover pencils and interior pencils 20.00
...: Legacy of Evil 1 (6/96, $3.95) Kurt Busiek script & Mark Texeira-c/a 4.00
...Legends Vol. 1: Todd McFarlane ('03, $19.95, TPB)-r/Amaz. S-M #298-305 20.00
...Legends Vol. 2: Todd McFarlane ('03, $19.99, TPB)-r/Amaz. S-M #306-314, & Spec. Spider-Man Annual #10 20.00
...Legends Vol. 3: Todd McFarlane ('04, $24.99, TPB)-r/Amaz. S-M #315-323,325,328 25.00
...Legends Vol. 4: Spider-Man & Wolverine ('03, $13.95, TPB) r/Spider-Man & Wolverine #1-4 and Spider-Man/Daredevil #1 14.00
.../Marrow (2/01, $2.99) Garza-a 3.00
.../Mary Jane: ... You Just Hit the Jackpot TPB (2009, $24.99) early apps. & key stories 25.00
...: One More Day HC (2008. $24.99, dustjacket) r/Amaz. S-M #544-545, Friendly N.S-M #24, Sensational S-M #41 and Marvel Spotlight: Spider-Man-One More Day 25.00

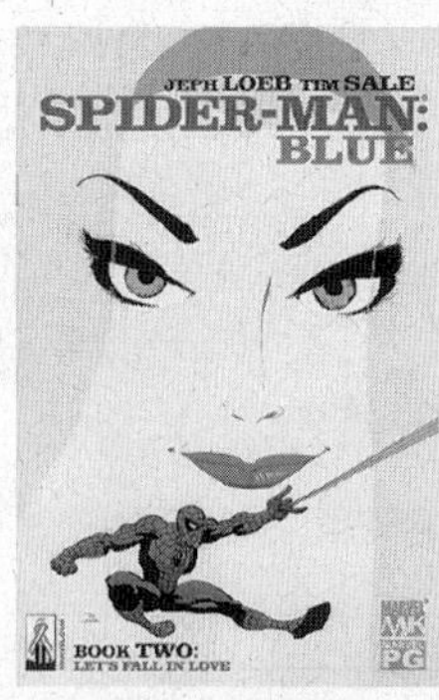

Spider-Man: Blue #2 © MAR

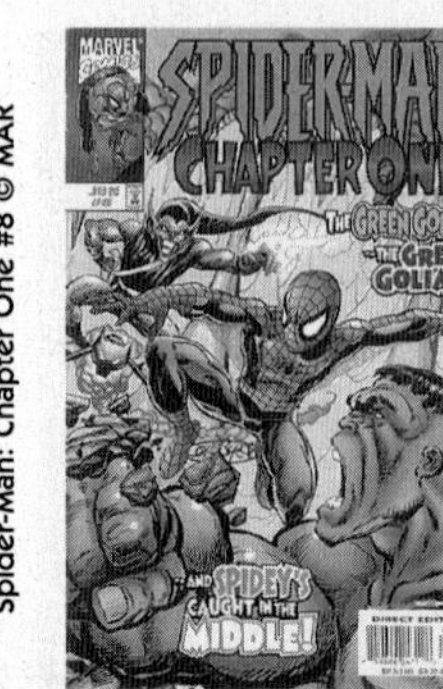

Spider-Man: Chapter One #8 © MAR

Spider-Man Classics #5 © MAR

GD 2.0 | VG 4.0 | FN 6.0 | VF 8.0 | VF/NM 9.0 | NM- 9.2

...: Origin of the Hunter (6/10, $3.99) r/Kraven apps. in ASM #15 & 34; new Mayhew-a 4.00
..., Peter Parker: Back in Black HC (2007, $34.99) oversized r/Sensational Spider-Man #35-40 & Annual #1, Spider-Man Family #1,2; Marvel Spotlight: Spider-Man and Spider-Man Back in Black Handbook; cover sketches 35.00
..., Punisher, Sabretooth: Designer Genes (1993, $8.95) 9.00
...Return of the Goblin TPB (See Peter Parker: Spider-Man)
...Revelations ('97, $14.99, TPB) r/end of Clone Saga plus 14 new pages by Romita Jr. 15.00
...: Saga of the Sandman TPB (2007, $19.99) r/1st app. Amazing S-M #4 and other app. 20.00
...: Son of the Goblin (2004, $15.99, TPB) r/AS-M#136-137,312 & Spec. S-M #189,200 16.00
... Special: Black and Blue and Read All Over 1 (11/06, $3.99) new story and r/ASM #12 4.00
Special Edition 1 (12/92-c, 11/92 inside)-The Trial of Venom; ordered thru mail with $5.00 donation or more to UNICEF; embossed metallic ink; came bagged w/bound-in poster; Daredevil app. 1 3 4 6 8 10
Super Special (7/95, $3.95)-Planet of the Symbiotes 4.00
The Best of Spider-Man Vol. 2 (2003, $29.99, HC with dust jacket) r/AS-M V2 #37-45, Peter Parker: S-M #44-47, and S-M's Tangled Web #10,11; Pearson-c 30.00
The Best of Spider-Man Vol. 3 (2004, $29.99, HC with d.j.) r/AS-M V2 #46-58, 500 30.00
The Best of Spider-Man Vol. 4 (2005, $29.99, HC with d.j.) r/#501-514; sketch pages 30.00
The Best of Spider-Man Vol. 5 (2006, $29.99, HC with d.j.) r/#515-524; sketch pages 30.00
The Complete Frank Miller Spider-Man (2002, $29.95, HC) r/Miller-s/a 30.00
The Death of Captain Stacy ($3.50) r/AS-M#88-90 4.00
The Death of Gwen Stacy ($14.95) r/AS-M#96-98,121,122 15.00
...: The Movie ($12.95) adaptation by Stan Lee-s/Alan Davis-a; plus r/Ultimate Spider-Man #8, Peter Parker #35, Tangled Web #10; photo-c 13.00
...: The Official Movie Adaptation ($5.95) Stan Lee-s/Alan Davis-a 6.00
...: The Other HC (2006, $29.99, dust jacket) r/Amazing S-M #525-528, Friendly Neighborhood S-M #1-4 and Marvel Knights S-M #19-22; gallery of variant covers 30.00
...: The Other SC (2006, $24.99) r/crossover; gallery of variant covers 25.00
...: The Other Sketchbook (2005, $2.99) sketch page preview of 2005-6 x-over 3.00
Torment TPB (5/01$15.95) r/#1-5, Spec. S-M #10 16.00
... Vs. Doctor Octopus ($17.95) reprints early battles; Sean Chen-c 18.00
... Vs. Punisher (7/00, $2.99) Michael Lopez-c/a 3.00
...Vs. Silver Sable (2006, $15.99, TPB)-r/Amazing Spider-Man #265,279-281 & Peter Parker, The Spectacular Spider-Man #128,129 16.00
...Vs. The Black Cat (2005, $14.99, TPB)-r/Amaz. S-M #194,195,204,205,226,227 15.00
...Vs. Vampires (12/10, $3.99) Blade app.; Castro-a/Grevioux-s 4.00
...Vs. Venom (1990, $8.95, TPB)-r/Amaz. S-M #300,315-317 w/new McFarlane-c 9.00
...Visionaries (10/01, $19.95, TPB)-r/Amaz. S-M #298-305; McFarlane-a 20.00
...Visionaries: John Romita (8/01, $19.95, TPB)-r/Amaz. S-M #39-42, 50,68,69,108,109; new Romita-c 20.00
...Visionaries: Kurt Busiek (2006, $19.99, TPB)-r/Untold Tales of Spider-Man #1-8 20.00
...Visionaries: Roger Stern (2007, $24.99, TPB)-r/Amazing Spider-Man #206 & Spectacular Spider-Man #43-52,54; Stern interview 25.00
Wizard 1/2 ($10.00) Leonardi-a; Green Goblin app. 10.00

SPIDER-MAN ADVENTURES
Marvel Comics: Dec, 1994 - No. 15, Mar, 1996 ($1.50)

1-15 ($1.50)-Based on animated series 3.00
1-($2.95)-Foil embossed-c 4.00

SPIDER-MAN AND HIS AMAZING FRIENDS (See Marvel Action Universe)
Marvel Comics Group: Dec, 1981 (one-shot)

1-Adapted from NBC TV cartoon show; Green Goblin-c/story; 1st Spidey, Firestar, Iceman team-up; Spiegle-p 5.00

SPIDER-MAN AND POWER PACK
Marvel Comics: Jan, 2007 - No. 4, Apr, 2007 ($2.99, limited series)

1-4-Sumerak-s/Gurihiru-a; Sandman app. 3,4-Venom app. 3.00
...: Big City Heroes (2007, $6.99, digest) r/#1-4 7.00

SPIDER-MAN AND THE FANTASTIC FOUR
Marvel Comics: Jun, 2007 - No. 4, Sept, 2007 ($2.99, limited series)

1-4-Mike Wieringo-a/c; Jeff Parker-s. 1,4-Impossible Man app. 3.00
...: Silver Rage TPB (2007, $10.99) r/#1-4; series outline and cover sketches 11.00

SPIDER-MAN AND THE SECRET WARS
Marvel Comics: Feb, 2010 - No. 4, May, 2010 ($2.99, limited series)

1-4-Tobin-s/Scherberger-a. 3-Black costume app. 3.00

SPIDER-MAN AND THE INCREDIBLE HULK (See listing under Amazing...)

SPIDER-MAN AND THE UNCANNY X-MEN
Marvel Comics: Mar, 1996 ($16.95, trade paperback)

nn-r/Uncanny X-Men #27, Uncanny X-men #35, Amazing Spider-Man #92, Marvel Team-Up Annual #1, Marvel Team-Up #150, & Spectacular Spider-Man #197-199 17.00

SPIDER-MAN & WOLVERINE (See Spider-Man Legends Vol. 4 for TPB reprint)
Marvel Comics: Aug, 2003 - No. 4, Nov, 2003 ($2.99, limited series)

1-4-Matthews-s/Mavlian-a 3.00

SPIDER-MAN AND X-FACTOR
Marvel Comics: May, 1994 - No. 3, July, 1994 ($1.95, limited series)

1-3 3.00

SPIDER-MAN /BADROCK
Maximum Press: Mar, 1997 ($2.99, mini-series)

1A, 1B(#2)-Jurgens-s 3.00

SPIDER-MAN/BLACK CAT: THE EVIL THAT MEN DO (Also see Marvel Must Haves)
Marvel Comics: Aug, 2002 - No. 6, Mar, 2006 ($2.99, limited series)

1-6-Kevin Smith-s/Terry Dodson-c/a 3.00
HC (2006, $19.99, dust jacket) r/#1-6; script to #6 with sketches 20.00

SPIDER-MAN: BLUE
Marvel Comics: July, 2002 - No. 6, Apr, 2003 ($3.50, limited series)

1-6: Jeph Loeb-s/Tim Sale-a/c; flashback to early MJ and Gwen Stacy 3.50
HC (2003, $21.99, with dust jacket) over-sized r/#1-6; intro. by John Romita 22.00
SC (2004, $14.99) r/#1-6; cover gallery 15.00

SPIDER-MAN: BRAND NEW DAY (See Amazing Spider-Man Vol. 2)

SPIDER-MAN: BREAKOUT (See New Avengers #1)
Marvel Comics: June, 2005 - No. 5, Oct, 2005 ($2.99, limited series)

1-5-Bedard-s/Garcia-a. 1-U-Foes app. 5-New Avengers app. 3.00
TPB (2006, $13.99) r/#1-5 14.00

SPIDER-MAN: CHAPTER ONE
Marvel Comics: Dec, 1998 - No. 12, Oct, 1999 ($2.50, limited series)

1-Retelling/updating of origin; John Byrne-s/c/a 3.00
1-($6.95) DF Edition w/variant-c by Jae Lee 7.00
2-11: 2-Two covers (one is swipe of ASM #1); Fantastic Four app. 9-Daredevil. 11-Giant-Man-c/app. 3.00
12-($3.50) Battles the Sandman 4.00
0-(5/99) Origins of Vulture, Lizard and Sandman 3.00

SPIDER-MAN CLASSICS
Marvel Comics: Apr, 1993 - No. 16, July, 1994 ($1.25)

1-14,16: 1-r/Amaz. Fantasy #15 & Strange Tales #115. 2-16-r/Amaz. Spider-Man #1-15. 6-Austin-c(i) 3.00
15-($2.95)-Polybagged w/16 pg. insert & animation style print; r/Amazing Spider-Man #14 (1st Green Goblin) 4.00

SPIDER-MAN COLLECTOR'S PREVIEW
Marvel Comics: Dec, 1994 ($1.50, 100 pgs., one-shot)

1-wraparound-c; no comics 4.00

SPIDER-MAN COMICS MAGAZINE
Marvel Comics Group: Jan, 1987 - No. 13, 1988 ($1.50, digest-size)

1-13-Reprints 6.00

SPIDER-MAN: DEATH AND DESTINY
Marvel Comics: Aug, 2000 - No. 3, Oct, 2000 ($2.99, limited series)

1-3-Aftermath of the death of Capt. Stacy 3.00

SPIDER-MAN/ DOCTOR OCTOPUS: OUT OF REACH
Marvel Comics: Jan, 2004 - No. 5, May, 2004 ($2.99, limited series)

1-5: 1-Keron Grant-a/Colin Mitchell-s 3.00
Marvel Age... TPB (2004, $5.99, digest size) r/#1-5 6.00

SPIDER-MAN/ DOCTOR OCTOPUS: YEAR ONE
Marvel Comics: Aug, 2004 - No. 5, Dec, 2004 ($2.99, limited series)

1-5-Kaare Andrews-a/Zeb Wells-s 3.00

SPIDER-MAN FAIRY TALES
Marvel Comics: July, 2007 - No. 4, Oct, 2007 ($2.99, limited series)

1-4: 1-Cebulski-s/Tercio-a. 2-Henrichon-a. 3-Kobayashi-a. 4-Dragotta-p/Allred-i 3.00
TPB (2007, $10.99) r/#1-4 11.00

SPIDER-MAN FAMILY (Also see Amazing Spider-Man Family)
Marvel Comics: Apr, 2007 - No. 9, Aug, 2008 ($4.99, anthology)

1-9-New tales and reprints. 1-Black costume, Sandman, Black Cat app. 4-Agents of Atlas app., Kirk-a; Puppet Master by Eliopoulos. 8-Iron Man app. 9-Hulk app. 5.00
... Featuring Spider-Clan 1 (1/07, $4.99) new Spider-Clan story; reprints w/Spider-Man 2099 and Amazing Spider-Man #252 (black costume) 5.00
... Featuring Spider-Man's Amazing Friends 1 (10/06, $4.99) new story with Iceman and Firestar; Mini Marvels w/Giarrusso-a; reprints w/Spider-Man 2099 5.00
...: Back In Black (2007, $7.99, digest) r/new content from #1-3 8.00
...: Untold Team-Ups (2008, $9.99, digest) r/new content from #4-6 10.00

Spider-Man: Funeral For an Octopus #3 © MAR

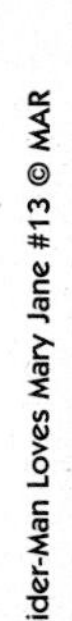
Spider-Man Loves Mary Jane #13 © MAR

Spider-Man/Red Sonja #2 © MAR & RSLLC

GD	VG	FN	VF	VF/NM	NM-
2.0	4.0	6.0	8.0	9.0	9.2

SPIDER-MAN/FANTASTIC FOUR (Spider-Man and the Fantastic Four on cover)
Marvel Comics: Sept, 2010 - No. 4, Dec, 2010 ($3.99, limited series)
1-4-Gage-s/Alberti-a; Dr. Doom app. 4.00

SPIDER-MAN: FEVER
Marvel Comics: Jun, 2010 - No. 3, Aug, 2010 ($3.99, limited series)
1-3-Brendan McCarthy-s/a; Dr. Strange app. 4.00

SPIDER-MAN: FRIENDS AND ENEMIES
Marvel Comics: Jan, 1995 - No. 4, Apr, 1995 ($1.95, limited series)
1-4-Darkhawk, Nova & Speedball app. 3.00

SPIDER-MAN: FUNERAL FOR AN OCTOPUS
Marvel Comics: Mar, 1995 - No. 3, May, 1995 ($1.50, limited series)
1-3 3.00

SPIDER-MAN/ GEN 13
Marvel Comics: Nov, 1996 ($4.95, one-shot)
nn-Peter David-s/Stuart Immonen-a 5.00

SPIDER-MAN: GET KRAVEN
Marvel Comics: Aug, 2002 - No. 6, Jan, 2003 ($2.99/$2.25, limited series)
1-($2.99) McCrea-a/Quesada-c; back-up story w/Rio-a 4.00
2-6-($2.25) 2-Sub-Mariner app. 3.00

SPIDER-MAN: HOBGOBLIN LIVES
Marvel Comics: Jan, 1997 - No. 3, Mar, 1997 ($2.50, limited series)
1-3-Wraparound-c 3.00
TPB (1/98, $14.99) r/#1-3 plus timeline 15.00

SPIDER-MAN: HOUSE OF M (Also see House of M and related x-overs)
Marvel Comics: Aug, 2005 - No. 5, Dec, 2005 ($2.99, limited series)
1-5-Waid & Peyer-s/Larroca-a; rich and famous Peter Parker in mutant-ruled world 3.00
House of M: Spider-Man TPB (2006, $13.99) r/series 14.00

SPIDER-MAN/ HUMAN TORCH
Marvel Comics: Mar, 2005 - No. 5, July, 2005 ($2.99, limited series)
1-5-Ty Templeton-a/Dan Slott-s; team-ups from early days to the present 3.00
...: I'm With Stupid (2006, $7.99, digest) r/#1-5 8.00

SPIDER-MAN: INDIA
Marvel Comics: Jan, 2005 - No. 4, Apr, 2005 ($2.99, limited series)
1-4-Pavitr Prabhakar gains spider powers; Kang-a/Seetharaman-s 3.00

SPIDER-MAN: LEGEND OF THE SPIDER-CLAN (See Marvel Mangaverse for TPB)
Marvel Comics: Dec, 2002 - No. 5, Apr, 2003 ($2.25, limited series)
1-5-Marvel Mangaverse Spider-Man; Kaare Andrews-s/Skottie Young-c/a 3.00

SPIDER-MAN: LIFELINE
Marvel Comics: Apr, 2001 - No. 3, June, 2001 ($2.99, limited series)
1-3-Nicieza-s/Rude-c/a; The Lizard app. 3.00

SPIDER-MAN LOVES MARY JANE (Also see Mary Jane limited series)
Marvel Comics: Feb, 2006 - No. 20, Sept, 2007 ($2.99)
1-20-Mary Jane & Peter in high school; McKeever-s/Miyazawa-a/c. 5-Gwen Stacy app. 16-18,20-Firestar app. 17-Felecia Hardy app. 3.00
... Vol. 1: Super Crush (2006, $7.99, digest) r/#1-5; cover concepts page 8.00
... Vol. 2: The New Girl (2006, $7.99, digest) r/#6-10; sketch pages 8.00
... Vol. 3: My Secret Life (2007, $7.99, digest) r/#11-15; sketch pages 8.00
... Vol. 4: Still Friends (2007, $7.99, digest) r/#16-20 8.00
Hardcover Vol. 1 (2007, $24.99) oversized reprints of #1-5, Mary Jane #1-4 and Mary Jane: Homecoming #1-4; series proposals, sketch pages and covers; coloring process 25.00
Hardcover Vol. 2 (2008, $39.99) oversized reprints of #6-20, sketch & layout pages 40.00

SPIDER-MAN LOVES MARY JANE SEASON 2
Marvel Comics: Oct, 2008 - No. 5, Feb, 2009 ($2.99, limited series)
1-5-Terry Moore-s/c; Craig Rousseau-a 3.00
1-Variant-c by Alphona 8.00

SPIDER-MAN: MADE MEN
Marvel Comics: Aug, 1998 ($5.99, one-shot)
1-Spider-Man & Daredevil vs. Kingpin 6.00

SPIDER-MAN MAGAZINE
Marvel Comics: 1994 - No. 3, 1994 ($1.95, magazine)
1-3: 1-Contains 4 S-M promo cards & 4 X-Men Ultra Fleer cards; Spider-Man story by Romita, Sr.; X-Men story; puzzles & games. 2-Doc Octopus & X-Men stories 4.00

SPIDER-MAN: MAXIMUM CLONAGE
Marvel Comics: 1995 ($4.95)
Alpha #1-Acetate-c, Omega #1-Chromium-c. 5.00

SPIDER-MAN MEGAZINE
Marvel Comics: Oct, 1994 - No. 6, Mar, 1995 ($2.95, 100 pgs.)
1-6: 1-r/ASM #16,224,225, Marvel Team-Up #1 4.00

SPIDER-MAN NOIR
Marvel Comics: Dec, 2008 - No. 4, May, 2009 ($3.99, limited series)
1-4-Pulp-style Spider-Man in 1933; DiGiandomenico-a; covers by Zircher & Calero 4.00
...: Eyes Without a Face 1-4 (2/10 - No. 4, 5/10) DiGiandomenico-a; Zircher & Calero-c 4.00

SPIDER-MAN: POWER OF TERROR
Marvel Comics: Jan, 1995 - No. 4, Apr, 1995 ($1.95, limited series)
1-4-Silvermane & Deathlok app. 3.00

SPIDER-MAN/PUNISHER: FAMILY PLOT
Marvel Comics: Feb, 1996 - No. 2, Mar, 1996 ($2.95, limited series)
1,2 3.00

SPIDER-MAN: QUALITY OF LIFE
Marvel Comics: Jul, 2002 - No. 4, Oct, 2002 ($2.99, limited series)
1-4-All CGI art by Scott Sava; Rucka-s; Lizard app. 3.00
TPB (2002, $12.99) r/#1-4; a "Making of..." section detailing the CGI process 13.00

SPIDER-MAN: REDEMPTION
Marvel Comics: Sept, 1996 - No. 4, Dec, 1996 ($1.50, limited series)
1-4: DeMatteis scripts; Zeck-a 3.00

SPIDER-MAN/ RED SONJA
Marvel Comics: Oct, 2007 - No. 5, Feb, 2008 ($2.99, limited series)
1-5-Rubi-a/Oeming-s/Turner-c; Venom & Kulan Gath app. 3.00
HC (2008, $19.99, dustjacket) r/#1-5 and Marvel Team-Up #79; sketch pages 20.00

SPIDER-MAN: REIGN
Marvel Comics: Feb, 2007 - No. 4, May, 2007 ($3.99, limited series)
1-Kaare Andrews-s/a; red costume on cover 4.00
1-Variant cover with black costume 10.00
2-4 4.00
HC (2007, $19.99, dustjacket) r/#1-4; sketch pages and cover variant gallery 20.00
HC 2nd printing (2007, $19.99, dustjacket) with variant black cover 20.00
SC (2008, $14.99) r/#1-4; sketch pages and cover variant gallery 15.00

SPIDER-MAN: REVENGE OF THE GREEN GOBLIN
Marvel Comics: Oct, 2000 - No. 3, Dec, 2000 ($2.99, limited series)
1-3-Frenz & Olliffe-a; continues in AS-M #25 & PP:S-M #25 3.00

SPIDER-MAN SAGA
Marvel Comics: Nov, 1991 - No. 4, Feb, 1992 ($2.95, limited series)
1-4: Gives history of Spider-Man: text & illustrations 3.00

SPIDER-MAN 1602
Marvel Comics: Dec, 2009 - No. 5, Apr, 2010 ($3.99, limited series)
1-5- Peter Parquagh from Marvel 1602; Parker-s/Rosanas-a 4.00

SPIDER-MAN: SWEET CHARITY
Marvel Comics: Aug, 2002 ($4.95, one-shot)
1-The Scorpion-c/app.; Campbell-c/Zimmerman-s/Robertson-a 5.00

SPIDER-MAN'S TANGLED WEB (Titled **"Tangled Web"** in indicia for #1-4)
Marvel Comics: Jun, 2001 - No. 22, Mar, 2003 ($2.99)
1-3: "The Thousand" on-c; Ennis-s/McCrea-a/Fabry-c 4.00
4-"Severance Package" on-c; Rucka-s/Risso-a; Kingpin-c/app. 5.00
5,6-Flowers for Rhino; Milligan-s/Fegredo-a 3.00
7-10,12,15-20,22: 7-9-Gentlemen's Agreement; Bruce Jones-s/Lee Weeks-a. 10-Andrews-s/a. 12-Fegredo-a. 15-Paul Pope-s/a. 18-Ted McKeever-s/a. 19-Mahfood-a. 20-Haspiel-a 3.00
11,13,21-($3.50) 11-Darwyn Cooke-s/a. 13-Phillips-a. 21-Christmas-s by Cooke & Bone 4.00
14-Azzarello & Scott Levy (WWE's Raven)-s about Crusher Hogan 4.00
TPB (10/01, $15.95) r/#1-6 16.00
Volume 2 TPB (4/02, $14.95) r/#7-11 15.00
Volume 3 TPB (2002, $15.99) r/#12-17; Jason Pearson-c 16.00
Volume 4 TPB (2003, $15.99) r/#18-22; Frank Cho-c 16.00

SPIDER-MAN TEAM-UP
Marvel Comics: Dec, 1995 - No. 7, June, 1996 ($2.95)
1-7: 1-w/ X-Men. 2-w/Silver Surfer. 3-w/Fantastic Four. 4-w/Avengers. 5-Gambit & Howard the Duck-c/app. 7-Thunderbolts-c/app. 4.00
... Special 1 (5/05, $2.99) Fantastic Four app.; Todd Dezago-s/Shane Davis-a 4.00

SPIDER-MAN: THE ARACHNIS PROJECT
Marvel Comics: Aug, 1994 - No. 6, Jan, 1995 ($1.75, limited series)

Spider-Man: The Manga #28 © MAR

Spider-Man 2099 Annual #1 © MAR

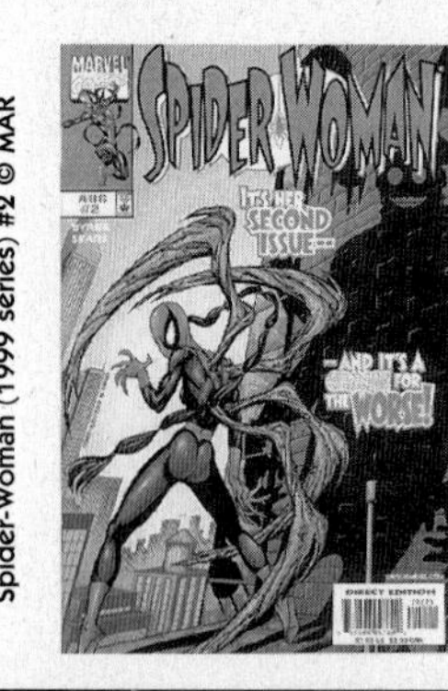

Spider-Woman (1999 series) #2 © MAR

GD 2.0 | VG 4.0 | FN 6.0 | VF 8.0 | VF/NM 9.0 | NM- 9.2

1-6-Venom, Styx, Stone & Jury app. 3.00

SPIDER-MAN: THE CLONE JOURNAL
Marvel Comics: Mar, 1995 ($2.95, one-shot)

1 4.00

SPIDER-MAN: THE CLONE SAGA
Marvel Comics: Nov, 2009 - No. 6, Apr, 2010 ($3.99, limited series)

1-6-Retelling of the saga with different ending; DeFalco & Mackie-s/Nauck-a 4.00

SPIDER-MAN: THE FINAL ADVENTURE
Marvel Comics: Nov, 1995 - No. 4, Feb, 1996 ($2.95, limited series)

1-4: 1-Nicieza scripts; foil-c 3.00

SPIDER-MAN: THE JACKAL FILES
Marvel Comics: Aug, 1995 ($1.95, one-shot)

1 3.00

SPIDER-MAN: THE LOST YEARS
Marvel Comics: Aug, 1995-No. 3, Oct, 1995; No. 0, 1996 ($2.95/$3.95,lim. series)

0-(1/96, $3.95)-Reprints. 4.00
1-3-DeMatteis scripts, Romita, Jr.-c/a 3.00
NOTE: ***Romita** c-0i. **Romita, Jr.** a-0r, 1-3p. c-0-3p. **Sharp** a-0r.*

SPIDER-MAN: THE MANGA
Marvel Comics: Dec, 1997 - No. 31, June, 1999 ($3.99/$2.99, B&W, bi-weekly)

1-($3.99)-English translation of Japanese Spider-Man 4.00
2-31-($2.99) 3.00

SPIDER-MAN: THE MUTANT AGENDA
Marvel Comics: No. 0, Feb, 1994; No. 1, Mar, 1994 - No. 3, May, 1994 ($1.75, limited series)

0-(2/94, $1.25, 52 pgs.)-Crosses over w/newspaper strip; has empty pages to paste in newspaper strips; gives origin of Spidey 4.00
1-3: Beast & Hobgoblin app. 1-X-Men app. 3.00

SPIDER-MAN: THE MYSTERIO MANIFESTO (Listed as "Spider-Man and Mysterio" in indicia)
Marvel Comics: Jan, 2001 - No. 3, Mar, 2001 ($2.99, limited series)

1-3-Daredevil-c/app.; Weeks & McLeod-a 3.00

SPIDER-MAN: THE PARKER YEARS
Marvel Comics: Nov, 1995 ($2.50, one-shot)

1 3.00

SPIDER-MAN 2: THE MOVIE
Marvel Comics: Aug, 2004 ($3.50/$12.99, one-shot)

1-($3.50) Movie adaptation; Johnson, Lim & Olliffe-a 4.00
TPB-($12.99) Movie adaptation; r/Amazing Spider-Man #50, Ultimate Spider-Man #14,15 13.00

SPIDER-MAN 2099 (See Amazing Spider-Man #365)
Marvel Comics: Nov, 1992 - No. 46, Aug, 1996 ($1.25/$1.50/$1.95)

1-(stiff-c)-Red foil stamped-c; begins origin of Miguel O'Hara (Spider-Man 2099); Leonardi/Williamson-c/a begins 4.00
1-2nd printing, 2-12,14-24,26-34,39,40: 2-Origin continued, ends #3. 4-Doom 2099 app. 19-Bound-in trading cards. 3.00
13-Extra 16 pg. insert on Midnight Sons 4.00
25-($2.25, 52 pgs.)-Newsstand edition 4.00
25-($2.95, 52 pgs.)-Deluxe edition w/embossed foil-c 4.50
35-38-Venom app. 35-Variant-c. 36-Two-c; Jae Lee-a. 37,38-Two-c 5.00
41-46: 46-The Vulture app; Mike McKone-a(p) 3.00
Annual 1 (1994, $2.95, 68 pgs.) 4.00
Special 1 (1995, $3.95) 4.00
NOTE: ***Chaykin** c-37. **Ron Lim** a(p)-18; c(p)-13, 16, 18. **Kelley Jones** c/a-9. **Leonardi/Williamson** a-1-8, 10-13, 15-17, 19, 20, 22-25; c-1-13, 15, 17-19, 20, 22-25, 35.*

SPIDER-MAN 2099 MEETS SPIDER-MAN
Marvel Comics: 1995 ($5.95, one-shot)

nn-Peter David script; Leonardi/Williamson-c/a. 6.00

SPIDER-MAN UNIVERSE
Marvel Comics: Mar, 2000 - No. 7, Oct, 2000 ($4.95/$3.99, reprints)

1-5-Reprints recent issues from the various Spider-Man titles 5.00
6,7-($3.99) 4.00

SPIDER-MAN UNLIMITED
Marvel Comics: May, 1993 - No. 22, Nov, 1998 ($3.95, #1-12 were quarterly, 68 pgs.)

1-Begin Maximum Carnage storyline, ends; Carnage-c/story 5.00
2-12: 2-Venom & Carnage-c/story; Lim-c/a(p) in #2-6. 10-Vulture app. 4.00
13-22: 13-Begin $2.99-c; Scorpion-c/app. 15-Daniel-c; Puma-c/app. 19-Lizard-c/app. 20-Hannibal King and Lilith app. 21,22-Deodato-a 3.00

SPIDER-MAN UNLIMITED (Based on the TV animated series)
Marvel Comics: Dec, 1999 - No. 5, Apr, 2000 ($2.99/$1.99)

1-($2.99) Venom and Carnage app. 4.00
2-5: 2-($1.99) Green Goblin app. 3.00

SPIDER-MAN UNLIMITED (3rd series)
Marvel Comics: Mar, 2004 - No. 15, July, 2006 ($2.99)

1-16: 1-Short stories by various incl. Miyazawa & Chen-a. 2-Mays-a. 6-Allred-c. 14-Finch-c/a; Black Cat app. 3.00

SPIDER-MAN UNMASKED
Marvel Comics: Nov, 1996 ($5.95, one-shot)

nn-Art w/text 6.00

SPIDER-MAN: VENOM AGENDA
Marvel Comics: Jan, 1998 ($2.99, one-shot)

1-Hama-s/Lyle-c/a 3.00

SPIDER-MAN VS. DRACULA
Marvel Comics: Jan, 1994 ($1.75, 52 pgs., one-shot)

1-r/Giant-Size Spider-Man #1 plus new Matt Fox-a 4.00

SPIDER-MAN VS. WOLVERINE
Marvel Comics Group: Feb, 1987; V2#1, 1990 (68 pgs.)

1-Williamson-c/a(i); intro Charlemagne; death of Ned Leeds (old Hobgoblin) 2 4 6 12 16 20
V2#1 (1990, $4.95)-Reprints #1 (2/87) 5.00

SPIDER-MAN: WEB OF DOOM
Marvel Comics: Aug, 1994 - No. 3, Oct, 1994 ($1.75, limited series)

1-3 3.00

SPIDER-MAN: WITH GREAT POWER...
Marvel Comics: Mar, 2008 - No. 5, Sept, 2008 ($3.99, limited series)

1-5-Origin and early days re-told; Lapham-s/Harris-a/c 4.00

SPIDER-MAN: WITH GREAT POWER COMES GREAT RESPONSIBILITY
Marvel Comics: Jun, 2011 - No. 7, Dec, 2011 ($3.99, limited series)

1-7: Reprints of noteworthy Spider-Man stories. 1-R/Ultimate Spider-Man #33,97, and Ultimate Comics Spider-Man #1. 4-R/ Amazing Spider-Man #1,11,20 4.00

SPIDER-MAN: YEAR IN REVIEW
Marvel Comics: Feb, 2000 ($2.99)

1-Text recaps of 1999 issues 3.00

SPIDER REIGN OF THE VAMPIRE KING, THE (Also see The Spider)
Eclipse Books: 1992 - No. 3, 1992 ($4.95, limited series, coated stock, 52 pgs.)

Book One - Three: Truman scripts & painted-c 5.00

SPIDER'S WEB, THE (See G-8 and His Battle Aces)

SPIDER-WOMAN (Also see The Avengers #240, Marvel Spotlight #32, Marvel Super Heroes Secret Wars #7, Marvel Two-In-One #29 and New Avengers)
Marvel Comics Group: April, 1978 - No. 50, June, 1983 (New logo #47 on)

1-New complete origin & mask added 2 4 6 11 16 20
2-5,7-18: 2-Excalibur app. 3,11,12-Brother Grimm app. 13,15-The Shroud-c/s. 16-Sienkiewicz-c 1 2 3 4 5 7
6,19,20,28,29,32: 6-Morgan LeFay app. 6,19,32-Werewolf by Night-c/s. 20,28,29-Spider-Man app. 32-Universal Monsters photo/Miller-c 1 2 3 5 6 8
21-27,30,31,33-36 6.00
37,38-X-Men x-over: 37-1st app. Siryn of X-Force; origin retold 2 4 6 8 10 12
39-49: 46-Kingpin app. 49-Tigra-c/story 5.00
50-(52 pgs.)-Death of Spider-Woman; photo-c 2 4 6 9 13 16
NOTE: ***Austin** a-37i. **Byrne** c-26p. **Infantino** a-1-19. **Layton** c-19. **Miller** c-32p.*

SPIDER-WOMAN
Marvel Comics: Nov, 1993 - No. 4, Feb, 1994 ($1.75, mini-series)

V2#1-4: 1,2-Origin; U.S. Agent app. 3.00

SPIDER-WOMAN
Marvel Comics: July, 1999 - No. 18, Dec, 2000 ($2.99/$1.99/$2.25)

1-($2.99) Byrne-s/Sears-a 4.00
2-18: 2-11-($1.99). 2-Two covers. 12-Begin $2.25-c. 15-Capt. America-c/app. 3.00

SPIDER-WOMAN (Printed version of the motion comic for computers)
Marvel Comics: Nov, 2009 - No. 7, May, 2010 ($3.99/$2.99)

1-($3.99) Bendis-s/Maleev-a; covers by Maleev & Alex Ross; Jessica joins S.W.O.R.D. 4.00

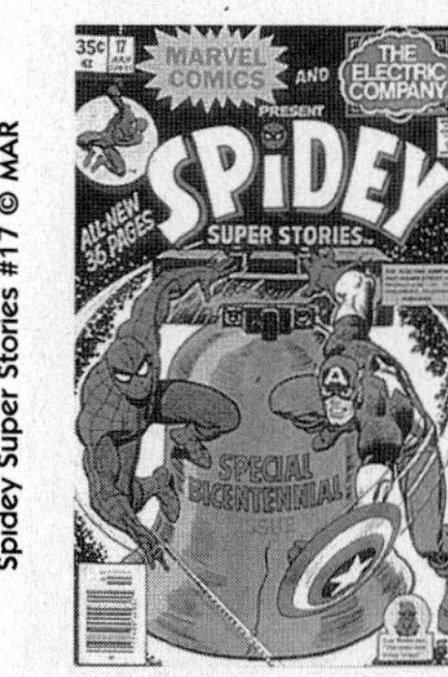

Spidey Super Stories #17 © MAR

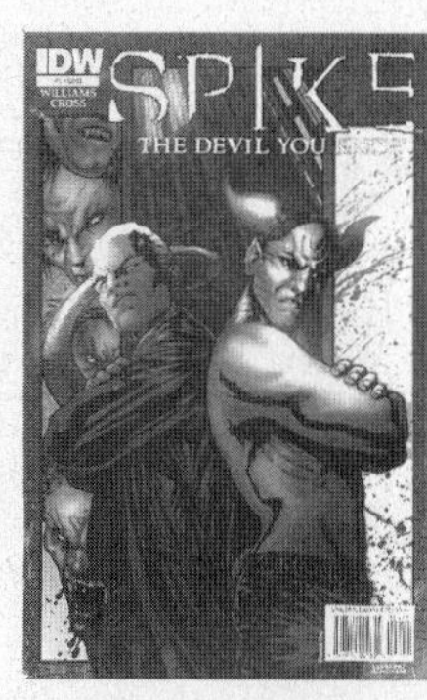

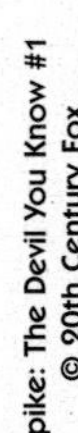
Spike: The Devil You Know #1 © 20th Century Fox

The Spirit (1966 series) #1 © Will Eisner Studios

	GD 2.0	VG 4.0	FN 6.0	VF 8.0	VF/NM 9.0	NM- 9.2

2-6-($2.99) 2-4-Madame Hydra app. 6-Thunderbolts app. 3.00
7-($3.99) New Avengers app. 4.00

SPIDER-WOMAN: ORIGIN (Also see New Avengers)
Marvel Comics: Feb, 2006 - No. 5, June, 2006 ($2.99, limited series)

1-5-Bendis & Reed-s/Jonathan & Joshua Luna-a/c 3.00
1-Variant cover by Olivier Coipel 3.00
HC (2006, $19.99) r/series 20.00
SC (2007, $13.99) r/series 14.00

SPIDEY SUPER STORIES (Spider-Man) (Also see Fireside Books)
Marvel/Children's TV Workshop: Oct, 1974 - No. 57, Mar, 1982 (35¢, no ads)

1-Origin (stories simplified for younger readers) 5 10 15 30 48 65
2-Kraven 3 6 9 18 27 35
3-10,15: 6-Iceman. 15-Storm-c/sty 3 6 9 14 20 26
11-14,16-20: 19,20-Kirby-c 3 6 9 14 19 24
21-30: 24-Kirby-c 2 4 6 13 18 22
31-53: 31-Moondragon-c/app.; Dr. Doom app. 33-Hulk. 34-Sub-Mariner. 38-F.F. 39-Thanos-c/ story. 44-Vision. 45-Silver Surfer & Dr. Doom app. 2 4 6 11 16 20
54-57: 56-Battles Jack O'Lantern-c/sty (exactly one year after 1st app. in Machine Man #19) 3 6 9 14 20 26

SPIKE AND TYKE (See M.G.M.'s...)

SPIKE... (Also see Buffy the Vampire Slayer and related titles)
IDW Publ.: Aug, 2005; Jan, 2006; Apr, 2006 ($7.49, squarebound, one-shots)

...: Lost & Found (4/06, $7.49) Scott Tipton-s/Fernando Goni-a 8.00
...: Old Times (8/05, $7.49) Peter David-s/Fernando Goni-a; Cecily/Halfrek app. 8.00
...: Old Wounds (1/06, $7.49) Tipton-s/Goni-a; flashback to Black Dahlia murder case 8.00
TPB (7/06, $19.99) r/one-shots 20.00

SPIKE (Buffy the Vampire Slayer)
IDW Publ.: Oct, 2010 - No. 8, May, 2011 ($3.99, limited series)

1-8-Lynch-s; multiple covers on each. 1,2-Urru-a. 5-7-Willow app. 4.00
... 100 Page Spectacular (6/11, $7.99) reprints of four IDW Spike stories; Frison-c 8.00

SPIKE: AFTER THE FALL (Also see Angel: After the Fall) (Follows the last Angel TV episode)
IDW Publ.: July, 2008 - No. 4, Oct, 2008 ($3.99, limited series)

1-4-Lynch-s/Urru-a; multiple covers on each 4.00

SPIKE: ASYLUM (Buffy the Vampire Slayer)
IDW Publ.: Sept, 2006 - No. 5, Jan, 2007 ($3.99, limited series)

1-5-Lynch-s/Urru-a; multiple covers on each 4.00

SPIKE: SHADOW PUPPETS (Buffy the Vampire Slayer)
IDW Publ.: June, 2007 - No. 4, Sept, 2007 ($3.99, limited series)

1-4-Lynch-s/Urru-a; multiple covers on each 4.00

SPIKE: THE DEVIL YOU KNOW (Buffy the Vampire Slayer)
IDW Publ.: Jun, 2010 - No. 4, Sept, 2010 ($3.99, limited series)

1-4-Bill Williams-s/Chris Cross-a/Urru-c 4.00

SPIKE VS. DRACULA (Buffy the Vampire Slayer)
IDW Publ.: Feb, 2006 - No. 5, Mar, 2006 ($3.99, limited series)

1-5: 1-Peter David-s/Joe Corroney-a; Dru and Bela Lugosi app. 4.00

SPIN & MARTY (TV) (Walt Disney's)(See Walt Disney Showcase #32)
Dell Publishing Co. (Mickey Mouse Club): No. 714, June, 1956 - No. 1082, Mar-May, 1960 (All photo-c)

Four Color 714 (#1) 11 22 33 76 151 225
Four Color 767,808 (#2,3) 9 18 27 61 106 150
Four Color 826 (#4)-Annette Funicello photo-c 19 38 57 128 277 425
5(3-5/58) - 9(6-8/59) 8 16 24 51 86 120
Four Color 1026,1082 8 16 24 51 86 120

SPIN ANGELS
Marvel Comics (Soleil): 2009 - No. 4, 2009 ($5.99)

1-4-English version of French comics; Jean-Luc Sala-s/Pierre-Mony Chan-a 6.00

SPINE-TINGLING TALES (Doctor Spektor Presents...)
Gold Key: May, 1975 - No. 4, Jan, 1976 (All 25¢ issues)

1-1st Tragg-r/Mystery Comics Digest #3 2 4 6 9 13 16
2-4: 2-Origin Ra-Ka-Tep-r/Mystery Comics Digest #1; Dr. Spektor #12. 3-All Durak-r issue; 4-Baron Tibor's 1st app.-r/Mystery Comics Digest #4; painted-c 1 2 3 5 7 9

SPINWORLD
Amaze Ink (Slave Labor Graphics): July, 1997 - No. 4, Jan, 1998 ($2.95/$3.95, B&W, mini-series)

1-3-Brent Anderson-a(p) 3.00
4-($3.95) 4.00

SPIRAL PATH, THE
Eclipse Comics: July, 1986 - No. 2 ($1.75, Baxter paper, limited series)

1,2 3.00

SPIRAL ZONE
DC Comics: Feb, 1988 - No. 4, May, 1988 ($1.00, mini-series)

1-4-Based on Tonka toys 3.00

SPIRIT, THE (Newspaper comics - see Promotional Comics section)

SPIRIT, THE (1st Series)(Also see Police Comics #11 and The Best of the Spirit TPB)
Quality Comics Group (Vital): 1944 - No. 22, Aug, 1950

nn(#1)- "Wanted Dead or Alive" 123 246 369 787 1344 1900
nn(#2)- "Crime Doesn't Pay" 51 102 153 320 543 765
nn(#3)- "Murder Runs Wild" 43 86 129 271 461 650
4,5: 4-Flatfoot Burns begins, ends #22. 5-Wertham app. 37 74 111 222 361 500
6-10 32 64 96 188 307 425
11-Crandall-c 30 60 90 177 289 400
12-17-Eisner-c. 19-Honeybun app. 40 80 120 246 411 575
18-21-Strip-r by Eisner; Eisner-c 53 106 159 334 567 800
22-Used by N.Y. Legis. Comm; classic Eisner-c 161 322 483 1030 1765 2500
Super Reprint #11-r/Quality Spirit #19 by Eisner 3 6 9 18 27 35
Super Reprint #12-r/Spirit #17 by Fine; Sol Brodsky-c 3 6 9 18 27 35

SPIRIT, THE (2nd Series)
Fiction House Magazines: Spring, 1952 - No. 5, 1954

1-Not Eisner 43 86 129 271 461 650
2-Eisner-c/a(2) 42 84 126 267 451 635
3-Eisner/Grandenetti-c 39 78 117 234 385 535
4-Eisner/Grandenetti-c; Eisner-a 39 78 117 240 395 550
5-Eisner-c/a(4) 41 82 123 260 435 610

SPIRIT, THE
Harvey Publications: Oct, 1966 - No. 2, Mar, 1967 (Giant Size, 25¢, 68 pgs.)

1-Eisner-r plus 9 new pgs.(origin Denny Colt, Take 3, plus 2 filler pgs.) (#3 was advertised, but never published) 9 18 27 61 106 150
2-Eisner-r plus 9 new pgs.(origin of the Octopus) 8 16 24 51 86 120

SPIRIT, THE (Underground)
Kitchen Sink Enterprises (Krupp Comics): Jan, 1973 - No. 2, Sept, 1973 (Black & White)

1-New Eisner-c & 4 pgs. new Eisner-a plus-r (titled Crime Convention) 4 8 12 24 37 50
2-New Eisner-c & 4 pgs. new Eisner-a plus-r (titled Meets P'Gell) 4 8 12 26 41 55

SPIRIT, THE (Magazine)
Warren Publ. Co./Krupp Comic Works No. 17 on: 4/74 - No. 16, 10/76; No. 17, Winter, 1977 - No. 41, 6/83 (B&W w/color) (#6-14,16 are squarebound)

1-Eisner-r begin; 8 pg. color insert 7 14 21 48 79 110
2-5: 2-Powder Pouf-s; UFO-s. 4-Silk Satin-s 4 8 12 28 44 60
6-9,11-15: 7-All Ebony issue. 8-Female Foes issue. 8,12-Sand Seref-s. 9-P'Gell & Octopus-s. 12-X-Mas issue 4 8 12 26 41 55
10-Giant Summer Special ($1.50)-Origin 4 8 12 28 44 60
16-Giant Summer Special ($1.50)-Olga Bustle-c/s 4 8 12 26 41 55
17,18(8/78): 17-Lady Luck-r 3 6 9 18 27 35
19-21-New Eisner-a. 20,21-Wood-r (#21-r/A DP on the Moon by Wood). 20-Outer Space-r 3 6 9 18 27 35
22-41: 22,23-Wood-r (#22-r/Mission the Moon by Wood). 28-r/last story (10/5/52). 30-(7/81)-Special Spirit Jam issue w/Caniff, Corben, Bolland, Byrne, Miller, Kurtzman, Rogers, Sienkiewicz-a & 40 others. 36-Begin Spirit Section-r; r/1st story (6/2/40) in color; new Eisner-c/a(18 pgs.)($2.95). 37-r/2nd story in color plus 18 pgs. new Eisner-a. 38-41: r/3rd - 6th stories in color. 41-Lady Luck Mr. Mystic in color 3 6 9 16 22 28
Special 1(1975)-All Eisner-a (mail only, 1500 printed, full color) 13 26 39 90 195 300

NOTE: *Covers pencilled/inked by* **Eisner** *only #1-9,12-16; painted by Eisner & Ken Kelly #10 & 11; painted by Eisner #17-up; one color story reprinted in #1-10.* **Austin** *a-30i.* **Byrne** *a-30p.* **Miller** *a-30p.*

SPIRIT, THE
Kitchen Sink Enterprises: Oct, 1983 - No. 87, Jan, 1992 ($2.00, Baxter paper)

1-60: 1-Origin-r/12/23/45 Spirit Section. 2-r/ 1/20/46-2/10/46. 3-r/2/17/46-3/10/46. 4-r/3/17/46-4/7/46. 11-Last color issue. 54-r/section 2/19/50 4.00
61-87: 85-87-Reprint the Outer Space Spirit stories by Wood. 86-r/A DP on the Moon by Wood from 1952 4.00

The Spirit (2010 series) #16 © Will Eisner Studios

Spongebob Comics #2 © United Plankton

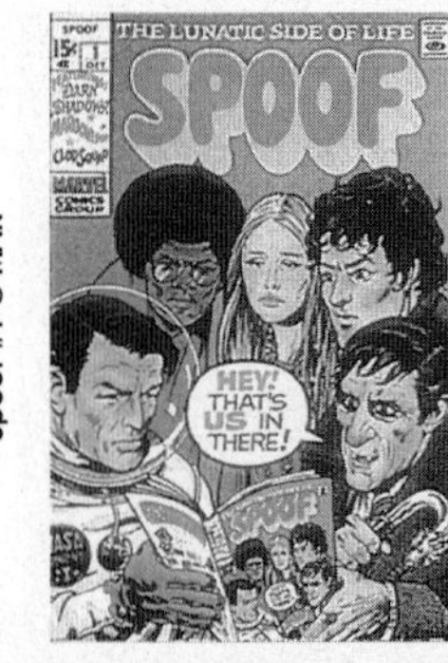

Spoof #1 © MAR

	GD	VG	FN	VF	VF/NM	NM-
	2.0	4.0	6.0	8.0	9.0	9.2

SPIRIT, THE (Also see Batman/The Spirit in Batman one-shots)
DC Comics: Feb, 2007 - No. 32, Oct, 2009 ($2.99)

1-32: 1-6,8-12-Darwyn Cooke-s/a/c. 2-P'Gell app. 3-Origin re-told. 7-Short stories by Baker, Bernet, Palmiotti, Simonson & Sprouse; Cooke-c. 13-Short stories by various 3.00
... Book One HC (2007, $24.99, die-cut dust jacket) r/#1-6 and Batman/The Spirit 25.00
... Book One SC (2007, $19.99) r/#1-6 and Batman/The Spirit 20.00
... Book Two HC (2008, $24.99, die-cut dust jacket) r/#7-13 25.00
... Book Two SC (2009, $19.99) r/#7-13 20.00
... Book Three SC (2009, $19.99) r/#14-20 20.00
... Book Four SC (2009, $19.99) r/#21-25 20.00
... Book Five SC (2009, $19.99) r/#26-32 20.00
... Femme Fatales TPB (2008, $19.99) r/1940s stories focusing on the Spirit's female adversaries like Silk Satin, P'gell, Powder Pouf and Silken Floss; Michael Uslan intro. 20.00
... Special 1 (2008, $2.99) r/stories from '47, '49, '50 newspaper strips; the Octopus app. 3.00

SPIRIT, THE (First Wave)
DC Comics: Jun, 2010 - No. 17, Oct, 2011 ($3.99/$2.99)(B&W back-up stories by various)

1-10: 1-Schultz-s/Moritat-a; covers by Ladronn and Schultz; back-up by O'Neil & Sienkiewicz. 2-Back-up by Ellison & Baker. 7-Corben-a back-up. 8-Ploog-a back-up 4.00
11-17-($2.99) 11-16-Hine-s/Moritat-a; no back-up story. 17-B&W; Bolland, Russell-a 3.00
...: Angel Smerti TPB (2011, $17.99) r/#1-7 18.00

SPIRIT JAM
Kitchen Sink Press: Aug, 1998 ($5.95, B&W, oversized, square-bound)

nn-Reprints Spirit (Magazine) #30 by Eisner & 50 others; and "Cerebus Vs. The Spirit" from Cerebus Jam #1 6.00

SPIRIT, THE: THE NEW ADVENTURES
Kitchen Sink Press: 1997 - No. 8, Nov, 1998 ($3.50, anthology)

1-Moore-s/Gibbons-c/a 4.00
2-8: 2-Gaiman-s/Eisner-c. 3-Moore-s/Bolland-c/Moebius back-c. 4-Allred-s/a; Busiek-s/Anderson-a. 5-Chadwick-s/c/a(p); Nyberg-i. 6-S.Hampton & Mandrake-a 3.50
Will Eisner's The Spirit Archives Volume 27 (Dark Horse, 2009, $49.95) r/#1-8 50.00

SPIRIT: THE ORIGIN YEARS
Kitchen Sink Press: May, 1992 - No. 10, Dec, 1993 ($2.95, B&W)

1-10: 1-r/sections 6/2/40(origin)-6/23/40 (all 1940s) 3.00

SPIRITMAN (Also see Three Comics)
No publisher listed: No date (1944) (10¢)
(Triangle Sales Co. ad on back cover)

1-Three 16pg. Spirit sections bound together, (1944, 10¢, 52 pgs.)
22 44 66 132 216 300
2-Two Spirit sections (3/26/44, 4/2/44) bound together; by Lou Fine
20 40 60 117 189 260

SPIRIT OF THE BORDER (See Zane Grey & Four Color #197)

SPIRIT OF THE TAO
Image Comics (Top Cow): Jun, 1998 - No. 15, May, 2000 ($2.50)

Preview 5.00
1-14: 1-D-Tron-s/Tan & D-Tron-a 3.00
15-($4.95) 5.00

SPIRIT WORLD (Magazine)
National Periodical Publications: Fall, 1971 (B&W)

1-New Kirby-a; Neal Adams-c; poster inside 7 14 21 46 76 105
(1/2 price without poster)

SPITFIRE (Female undercover agent)
Malverne Herald (Elliot)(J. R. Mahon): No. 132, 1944 (Aug) - No. 133, 1945

132,133: Both have Classics Gift Box ads on b/c with checklist to #20. 132-British spitfire WWII-c. 133-Female agent/Nazi WWII-c 26 52 78 154 252 350

SPITFIRE (WW2 speedster from MI:13)
Marvel Comics: Oct, 2010 ($3.99, one-shot)

1-Cornell-s/Casagrande-a; Blade app. 4.00

SPITFIRE AND THE TROUBLESHOOTERS
Marvel Comics: Oct, 1986 - No. 9, June, 1987 (Codename: Spitfire #10 on)

1-3,5-9 3.00
4-McFarlane-a 4.00

SPITFIRE COMICS (Also see Double Up) (Tied with Pocket Comics #1 for earliest Harvey)
Harvey Publications: Aug, 1941 - No. 2, Oct, 1941 (Pocket size; 100 pgs.)

1-Origin The Clown, The Fly-Man, The Spitfire & The Magician From Bagdad; British spitfire, Nazi bomber WWII-c 77 154 231 493 847 1200
2-(Rare) Fly-Man-c 71 142 213 454 777 1100

SPLITTING IMAGE
Image Comics: Mar, 1993 - No. 2, 1993 ($1.95)

1,2-Simpson-c/a; parody comic 3.00

SPONGEBOB COMICS (TV's Spongebob Squarepants)
United Plankton Pictures: 2011 - Present ($2.99)

1-7-Short stories by various. 1-Kochalka back-c. 3-Aquaman homage w/Fradon-a 3.00

SPOOF
Marvel Comics Group: Oct, 1970; No. 2, Nov, 1972 - No. 5, May, 1973

1-Infinity-c; Dark Shadows-c & parody 4 8 12 24 37 50
2-5: 2-All in the Family. 3-Beatles, Osmond's, Jackson 5, David Cassidy, Nixon & Agnew-c. 5-Rod Serling, Woody Allen, Ted Kennedy-c 3 6 9 17 25 32

SPOOK (Formerly Shock Detective Cases)
Star Publications: No. 22, Jan, 1953 - No. 30, Oct, 1954

22-Sgt. Spook-r; acid in face story; hanging-c 40 80 120 242 401 560
23,25,27: 25-Jungle Lil-r. 27-Two Sgt. Spook-r 29 58 87 172 281 390
24-Used in **SOTI**, pgs. 182,183-r/Inside Crime #2; Transvestism story
30 60 90 177 289 400
26,28-30: 26-Disbrow-a. 28,29-Rulah app. 29-Jo-Jo app. 30-Disbrow-c/a(2); only Star-c 29 58 87 172 281 390

NOTE: *L. B. Cole covers-all issues except #30; a-28(1 pg.).* ***Disbrow*** *a-26(2), 28, 29(2), 30(2); No. 30 r/Blue Bolt Weird Tales #114.*

SPOOK COMICS
Baily Publications/Star: 1946

1-Mr. Lucifer story 32 64 96 192 314 435

SPOOKY (The Tuff Little Ghost; see Casper The Friendly Ghost)
Harvey Publications: 11/55 - 139, 11/73; No. 140, 7/74 - No. 155, 3/77; No. 156, 12/77 - No. 158, 4/78; No. 159, 9/78; No. 160, 10/79; No. 161, 9/80

	GD	VG	FN	VF	VF/NM	NM-
1-Nightmare begins (see Casper #19)	44	88	132	330	715	1100
2	20	40	60	137	294	450
3-10(1956-57)	12	24	36	78	157	235
11-20(1957-58)	8	16	24	51	86	120
21-40(1958-59)	6	12	18	37	59	80
41-60	4	8	12	28	44	60
61-80,100	3	6	9	20	30	40
81-99	3	6	9	17	25	32
101-120	2	4	6	11	16	20
121-126,133-140	2	4	6	8	11	14
127-132: All 52 pg. Giants	2	4	6	11	16	20
141-161	1	2	3	5	7	9

SPOOKY
Harvey Comics: Nov, 1991 - No. 4, Sept, 1992 ($1.00/$1.25)

1 4.00
2-4: 3-Begin $1.25-c 3.00
...Digest 1-3 (10/92, 6/93, 10/93, $1.75, 100 pgs.)-Casper, Wendy, etc. 4.00

SPOOKY HAUNTED HOUSE
Harvey Publications: Oct, 1972 - No. 15, Feb, 1975

	GD	VG	FN	VF	VF/NM	NM-
1	3	6	9	18	27	35
2-5	2	4	6	10	14	18
6-10	2	4	6	8	10	12
11-15	1	2	3	5	7	9

SPOOKY MYSTERIES
Your Guide Publ. Co.: No date (1946) (10¢)

1-Mr. Spooky, Super Snooper, Pinky, Girl Detective app.
20 40 60 117 189 260

SPOOKY SPOOKTOWN
Harvey Publ.: 9/61; No. 2, 9/62 - No. 52, 12/73; No. 53, 10/74 - No. 66, 12/76

	GD	VG	FN	VF	VF/NM	NM-
1-Casper, Spooky; 68 pgs. begin	14	28	42	95	205	315
2	9	18	27	61	106	150
3-5	7	14	21	44	72	100
6-10	5	10	15	35	55	75
11-20	4	8	12	24	37	50
21-39: 39-Last 68 pg. issue	3	6	9	20	30	40
40-45: All 52 pgs.	2	4	6	11	16	20
46-66: 61-Hot Stuff/Spooky team-up story	1	2	3	5	7	9

SPORT COMICS (Becomes True Sport Picture Stories #5 on)
Street & Smith Publications: Oct, 1940 (No mo.) - No. 4, Nov, 1941

	GD	VG	FN	VF	VF/NM	NM-
1-Life story of Lou Gehrig	54	108	162	346	591	835
2	31	62	93	182	296	410

Sports Action #7 © MAR

Spotlight Comics #3 © CHES

Spy Smasher #6 © FAW

	GD 2.0	VG 4.0	FN 6.0	VF 8.0	VF/NM 9.0	NM- 9.2
3,4	26	52	78	154	252	350

SPORT LIBRARY (See Charlton Sport Library)

SPORTS ACTION (Formerly Sport Stars)
Marvel/Atlas Comics (ACI No. 2,3/SAI No. 4-14): No. 2, Feb, 1950 - No. 14, Sept, 1952

	GD 2.0	VG 4.0	FN 6.0	VF 8.0	VF/NM 9.0	NM- 9.2
2-Powell painted-c; George Gipp life story	43	86	129	269	455	640
1-(nd,no price, no publ., 52pgs, #1 on-c; has same-c as #2; blank inside-c (giveaway?)	22	44	66	132	216	300
3-Everett-a	24	48	72	142	234	325
4-11,14: Weiss-a	22	44	66	128	209	290
12,13: 12-Everett-c. 13-Krigstein-a	23	46	69	136	223	310

NOTE: *Title may have changed after No. 3, to Crime Must Lose No. 4 on, due to publisher change.* ***Sol Brodsky*** *c-4-7, 13, 14.* ***Maneely*** *c-3, 8-11.*

SPORT STARS
Parents' Magazine Institute (Sport Stars): Feb-Mar, 1946 - No. 4, Aug-Sept, 1946 (Half comic, half photo magazine)

	GD 2.0	VG 4.0	FN 6.0	VF 8.0	VF/NM 9.0	NM- 9.2
1- "How Tarzan Got That Way" story of Johnny Weissmuller	40	80	120	243	402	560
2-Baseball greats	26	52	78	154	252	350
3,4	23	46	69	136	223	310

SPORT STARS (Becomes Sports Action #2 on)
Marvel Comics (ACI): Nov, 1949 (52 pgs.)

	GD 2.0	VG 4.0	FN 6.0	VF 8.0	VF/NM 9.0	NM- 9.2
1-Knute Rockne; painted-c	45	90	135	284	480	675

SPORT THRILLS (Formerly Dick Cole; becomes Jungle Thrills #16)
Star Publications: No. 11, Nov, 1950 - No. 15, Nov, 1951

	GD 2.0	VG 4.0	FN 6.0	VF 8.0	VF/NM 9.0	NM- 9.2
11-Dick Cole begins; Ted Williams & Ty Cobb life stories	27	54	81	160	263	365
12-Joe DiMaggio, Phil Rizzuto stories & photos on-c; L.B. Cole-c/a	22	44	66	130	213	295
13-15-All L. B. Cole-c. 13-Jackie Robinson, Pee Wee Reese stories & photo on-c. 14-Johnny Weissmuler life story	22	44	66	130	213	295
Accepted Reprint #11 (#15 on-c, nd); L.B. Cole-c	10	20	30	54	72	90
Accepted Reprint #12 (nd); L.B. Cole-c; Joe DiMaggio & Phil Rizzuto life stories-r/#12	10	20	30	54	72	90

SPOTLIGHT (TV) (newsstand sales only)
Marvel Comics Group: Sept, 1978 - No. 4, Mar, 1979 (Hanna-Barbera)

	GD 2.0	VG 4.0	FN 6.0	VF 8.0	VF/NM 9.0	NM- 9.2
1-Huckleberry Hound, Yogi Bear; Shaw-a	3	6	9	20	30	40
2,4: 2-Quick Draw McGraw, Augie Doggie, Snooper & Blabber. 4-Magilla Gorilla, Snagglepuss	3	6	9	18	23	30
3-The Jetsons; Yakky Doodle	3	6	9	20	30	40

SPOTLIGHT COMICS
Country Press Inc.: Sept, 1940

nn-Ashcan, not distributed to newsstands, only for in house use. A NM copy sold in 2009 for $1015.

SPOTLIGHT COMICS (Becomes Red Seal Comics #14 on?)
Harry 'A' Chesler (Our Army, Inc.): Nov, 1944, No. 2, Jan, 1945 - No. 3, 1945

	GD 2.0	VG 4.0	FN 6.0	VF 8.0	VF/NM 9.0	NM- 9.2
1-The Black Dwarf (cont'd in Red Seal?), The Veiled Avenger, & Barry Kuda begin; Tuska-c	97	194	291	621	1061	1500
2	58	116	174	371	636	900
3-Injury to eye story (reprinted from Scoop #3)	61	122	183	390	670	950

SPOTTY THE PUP (Becomes Super Pup #4, see Television Puppet Show)
Avon Periodicals/Realistic Comics: No. 2, Oct-Nov, 1953 - No. 3, Dec-Jan, 1953-54 (Also see Funny Tunes)

	GD 2.0	VG 4.0	FN 6.0	VF 8.0	VF/NM 9.0	NM- 9.2
2,3	7	14	21	35	43	50
nn (1953, Realistic-r)	4	8	12	18	22	25

SPUNKY (...Junior Cowboy)(...Comics #2 on)
Standard Comics: April, 1949 - No. 7, Nov, 1951

	GD 2.0	VG 4.0	FN 6.0	VF 8.0	VF/NM 9.0	NM- 9.2
1-Text illos by Frazetta	11	22	33	62	86	110
2-Text illos by Frazetta	9	18	27	47	61	75
3-7	6	12	18	31	38	45

SPUNKY THE SMILING SPOOK
Ajax/Farrell (World Famous Comics/Four Star Comic Corp.): Aug, 1957 - No. 4, May, 1958

	GD 2.0	VG 4.0	FN 6.0	VF 8.0	VF/NM 9.0	NM- 9.2
1-Reprints from Frisky Fables	10	20	30	54	72	90
2-4	6	12	18	31	38	45

SPY AND COUNTERSPY (Becomes Spy Hunters #3 on)
American Comics Group: Aug-Sept, 1949 - No. 2, Oct-Nov, 1949 (52 pgs.)

	GD 2.0	VG 4.0	FN 6.0	VF 8.0	VF/NM 9.0	NM- 9.2
1-Origin, 1st app. Jonathan Kent, Counterspy	27	54	81	158	259	360
2	17	34	51	98	154	210

SPYBOY
Dark Horse Comics: Oct, 1999 - No. 17, May, 2001 ($2.50/$2.95/$2.99)

	NM- 9.2
1-17: 1-6-Peter David-s/Pop Mhan-a. 7,8-Meglia-a. 9-17-Mhan-a	3.00
13.1-13.3 (4/03-8/03, $2.99), 13.2,13.3-Mhan-a	3.00
... Special (5/02, $4.99) David-s/Mhan-a	5.00

SPYBOY: FINAL EXAM
Dark Horse Comics: May, 2004 - No. 4, Aug, 2004 ($2.99, limited series)

	NM- 9.2
1-4-Peter David-s/Pop Mhan-a/c	3.00
TPB (2005, $12.95) r/series	13.00

SPYBOY/ YOUNG JUSTICE
Dark Horse Comics: Feb, 2002 - No. 3, Apr, 2002 ($2.99, limited series)

	NM- 9.2
1-3: 1-Peter David-s/Todd Nauck-a/Pop Mhan-c. 2-Mhan-a	3.00

SPY CASES (Formerly The Kellys)
Marvel/Atlas Comics (Hercules Publ.): No. 26, Sept, 1950 - No. 19, Oct, 1953

	GD 2.0	VG 4.0	FN 6.0	VF 8.0	VF/NM 9.0	NM- 9.2
26 (#1)	24	48	72	144	237	330
27(#2),28(#3, 2/51): 27-Everett-a; bondage-c	15	30	45	83	124	165
4(4/51) - 7,9,10: 4-Heath-a	14	28	42	76	108	140
8-A-Bomb-c/story	15	30	45	83	124	165
11-19: 10-14-War format	11	22	33	62	86	110

NOTE: ***Sol Brodsky*** *c-1-5, 8, 9, 11-14, 17, 18.* ***Maneely*** *a-8; c-7, 10.* ***Tuska*** *a-7.*

SPY FIGHTERS
Marvel/Atlas Comics (CSI): March, 1951 - No. 15, July, 1953
(Cases from official records)

	GD 2.0	VG 4.0	FN 6.0	VF 8.0	VF/NM 9.0	NM- 9.2
1-Clark Mason begins; Tuska-a; Brodsky-c	25	50	75	147	241	335
2-Tuska-a	14	28	42	81	118	155
3-13: 3-5-Brodsky-c. 7-Heath-c	14	28	42	76	108	140
14,15-Pakula-a(3), Ed Win-a. 15-Brodsky-c	14	28	42	78	112	145

SPY-HUNTERS (Formerly Spy & Counterspy)
American Comics Group: No. 3, Dec-Jan, 1949-50 - No. 24, June-July, 1953 (#3-14: 52 pgs.)

	GD 2.0	VG 4.0	FN 6.0	VF 8.0	VF/NM 9.0	NM- 9.2
3-Jonathan Kent continues, ends #10	23	46	69	136	223	310
4-10: 4,8,10-Starr-a	14	28	42	80	115	150
11-15,17-22,24: 18-War-c begin. 21-War-c/stories begin	10	20	30	56	76	95
16-Williamson-a (9 pgs.)	15	30	45	88	137	185
23-Graphic torture, injury to eye panel	20	40	60	114	182	250

NOTE: ***Drucker*** *a-12.* ***Whitney*** *a-many issues; c-7, 8, 10-12, 15, 16.*

SPYMAN (Top Secret Adventures on cover)
Harvey Publications (Illustrated Humor): Sept, 1966 - No. 3, Feb, 1967 (12¢)

	GD 2.0	VG 4.0	FN 6.0	VF 8.0	VF/NM 9.0	NM- 9.2
1-Origin and 1st app. of Spyman. Steranko-a(p)-1st pro work; 1 pg. Neal Adams ad; Tuska-c/a, Crandall-a(i)	7	14	21	44	72	100
2-Simon-c; Steranko-a(p)	4	8	12	28	44	60
3-Simon-c	4	8	12	26	41	55

SPY SMASHER (See Mighty Midget, Whiz & Xmas Comics) (Also see Crime Smasher)
Fawcett Publications: Fall, 1941 - No. 11, Feb, 1943

	GD 2.0	VG 4.0	FN 6.0	VF 8.0	VF/NM 9.0	NM- 9.2
1-Spy Smasher begins; silver metallic-c	331	662	993	2317	4059	5800
2-Raboy-c	152	304	456	965	1658	2350
3,4: 3-Bondage-c. 4-Irvin Steinberg-c	102	204	306	648	1112	1575
5-7: Raboy-a; 6-Raboy-c/a. 7-Part photo-c (movie) Japanese dragon-c	87	174	261	553	952	1350
8,11: War-c	73	146	219	467	796	1125
9-Hitler, Tojo, Mussolini-c.	113	226	339	718	1234	1750
10-Hitler-c	103	206	309	659	1130	1600

SPY THRILLERS (Police Badge No. 479 #5)
Atlas Comics (PrPI): Nov, 1954 - No. 4, May, 1955

	GD 2.0	VG 4.0	FN 6.0	VF 8.0	VF/NM 9.0	NM- 9.2
1-Brodsky c-1,2	21	42	63	122	199	275
2-Last precode (1/55)	14	28	42	78	112	145
3,4	11	22	33	62	86	110

SQUADRON SUPREME (Also see Marvel Graphic Novel - ...: Death of a Universe)
Marvel Comics Group: Aug, 1985 - No. 12, Aug, 1986 (Maxi-series)

	NM- 9.2
1-Double size	4.00
2-12	3.00
TPB ($24.99) r/#1-12; Alex Ross painted-c; printing inks contain some of the cremated remains of late writer Mark Gruenwald	50.00
TPB-2nd printing ($24.99): Inks contain no ashes	25.00
...Death of a Universe TPB (2006, $24.99) r/Marvel Graphic Novel, Thor #280, Avengers #5,6; Avengers/Squadron Supreme Annual and Squadron Supreme: New World Order	25.00

SQUADRON SUPREME (Also see Supreme Power)
Marvel Comics: May, 2006 - No. 7, Nov, 2006 ($2.99)

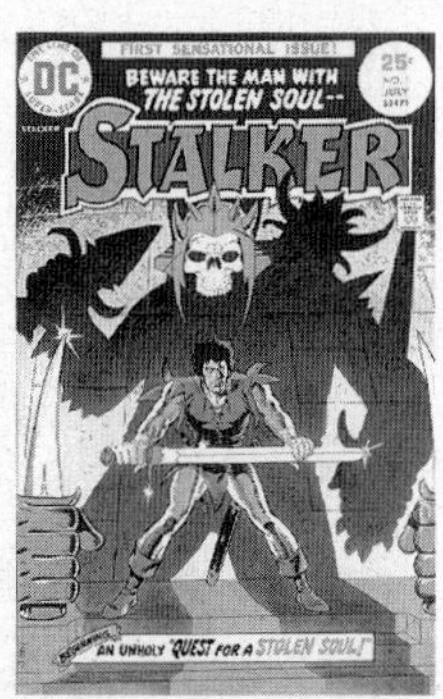

Stalker #1 © DC

The Stand: No Man's Land #1 © Stephen King

Star Comics V2 #1 © CEN

	GD	VG	FN	VF	VF/NM	NM-
	2.0	4.0	6.0	8.0	9.0	9.2

1-7-Straczynski-s/Frank-a/c 3.00
Saga of Squadron Supreme (2006, $3.99) summary of Supreme Power #1-18; plus Hyperion and Nighthawk limited series; wraparound-c; preview of Squadron Supreme #1 4.00
... Vol. 1: The Pre-War Years (2006, $20.99, dustjacket) r/#1-5 & Saga of S.S. 21.00

SQUADRON SUPREME
Marvel Comics: Sept, 2008 - No. 12, Aug, 2009 ($2.99)
1-12: 1-Set 5 years after Ultimate Power; Nick Fury app.; Chaykin-s/Turini-a/Land-c 3.00

SQUADRON SUPREME: HYPERION VS. NIGHTHAWK
Marvel Comics: Mar, 2007 - No. 4, June, 2007 ($2.99, limited series)
1-4-Hyperion and Nighthawk in Darfur; Gulacy-a/c; Guggenheim-s 3.00
TPB (2007, $10.99) r/#1-4 11.00

SQUADRON SUPREME: NEW WORLD ORDER
Marvel Comics: Sept, 1998 ($5.99, one-shot)
1-Wraparound-c; Kaminski-s 6.00

SQUALOR
First Comics: Dec, 1989 - Aug, 1990 ($2.75, limited series)
1-4: Sutton-a 3.00

SQUEE (Also see Johnny The Homicidal Maniac)
Slave Labor Graphics: Apr, 1997 - No. 4, May, 1998 ($2.95, B&W)
1-4: Jhonen Vasquez-s/a in all 3.00

SQUEEKS (Also see Boy Comics)
Lev Gleason Publications: Oct, 1953 - No. 5, June, 1954
1-Funny animal; Biro-c; Crimebuster's pet monkey "Squeeks" begins
10 20 30 54 72 90
2-Biro-c 6 12 18 31 38 45
3-5: 3-Biro-c 6 12 18 28 34 40

S.R. BISSETTE'S SPIDERBABY COMIX
SpiderBaby Grafix: Aug, 1996 - No. 2 ($3.95, B&W, magazine size)
Preview-(8/96, $3.95)-Graphic violence & nudity; Laurel & Hardy app. 4.00
1,2 4.00

S.R. BISSETTE'S TYRANT
SpiderBaby Grafix: Sept, 1994 - No. 4 ($2.95, B&W)
1-4 4.00

STALKER (Also see All Star Comics 1999 and crossover issues)
National Periodical Publications: June-July, 1975 - No. 4, Dec-Jan, 1975-76
1-Origin & 1st app; Ditko/Wood-c/a 2 4 6 10 14 18
2-4-Ditko/Wood-c/a 2 3 4 6 8 10

STALKERS
Marvel Comics (Epic Comics): Apr, 1990 - No. 12, Mar, 1991 ($1.50)
1-12: 1-Chadwick-c 3.00

STAMP COMICS (Stamps... on-c; Thrilling Adventures In...#8)
Youthful Magazines/Stamp Comics, Inc.: Oct, 1951 - No. 7, Oct, 1952
1-(15¢) ('Stamps' on indicia No. 1-3,5,7) 26 52 78 152 249 345
2 15 30 45 86 133 180
3-6: 3,4-Kiefer, Wildey-a 14 28 42 81 118 155
7-Roy Krenkel (4 pgs.) 17 34 51 98 154 210
NOTE: *Promotes stamp collecting; gives stories behind various commemorative stamps. No. 2, 10¢ printed over 15¢ c-price.* ***Kiefer*** *a-1-7.* ***Napoli*** *a-2-7.* ***Palais*** *a-2-4, 7.*

STAND, THE ... (Based on the Stephen King novel)
Marvel Comics: 2008 - Present ($3.99, limited series)
...: American Nightmares 1-5 (5/09 - No. 5, 10/09, $3.99) Aguirre-Sacasa-s/Perkins-a 4.00
...: Captain Trips 1-5 (12/08 - No. 5, 3/09, $3.99) Aguirre-Sacasa-s/Perkins-a 4.00
...: Hardcases 1-5 (8/10 - No. 5, 1/11, $3.99) Aguirre-Sacasa-s/Perkins-a 4.00
...: No Man's Land 1-5 (4/11 - No. 5, 8/11, $3.99) Aguirre-Sacasa-s/Perkins-a 4.00
...: Soul Survivors 1-5 (12/09 - No. 5, 5/10, $3.99) Aguirre-Sacasa-s/Perkins-a 4.00
...: The Night Has Come 1-6 (10/11 - No. 6, 3/12, $3.99) Aguirre-Sacasa-s/Perkins-a 4.00

STAN LEE MEETS...
Marvel Comics: Nov, 2006 - Jan, 2007 ($3.99, series of one-shots)
Doctor Doom 1 (12/06) Lee-s/Larroca-a/c; Loeb-s/McGuinness-a; r/Fantastic Four #87 4.00
Doctor Strange 1 (11/06) Lee-s/Davis-a/c; Bendis-s/Bagley-a; r/Marvel Premiere #3 4.00
Silver Surfer 1 (1/07) Lee-s/Wieringo-a/c; Jenkins-s/Buckingham-a; r/S.S. #14 4.00
Spider-Man 1 (11/06) Lee-s/Coipel-a/c; Whedon-s/Gaydos-a; Hembeck-s/a; r/AS-M #87 4.00
The Thing 1 (12/06) Lee-s/Weeks-a/c; Thomas-s/Kolins-a; r/FF #79; FF #51 cover swipe 4.00
HC (2007, $24.99, dustjacket) r/one-shots; interviews and features 25.00

STANLEY & HIS MONSTER (Formerly The Fox & the Crow)
National Periodical Publ.: No. 109, Apr-May, 1968 - No. 112, Oct-Nov, 1968

	GD	VG	FN	VF	VF/NM	NM-
	2.0	4.0	6.0	8.0	9.0	9.2

109-112 4 8 12 22 34 45

STANLEY & HIS MONSTER
DC Comics: Feb, 1993 - No. 4, May, 1993 ($1.50, limited series)
1-4 3.00

STAN SHAW'S BEAUTY & THE BEAST
Dark Horse Comics: Nov, 1993 ($4.95, one-shot)
1 5.00

STAR
Image Comics (Highbrow Entertainment): June, 1995 - No. 4, Oct, 1995 ($2.50, lim. series)
1-4 3.00

STARBLAST
Marvel Comics: Jan, 1994 - No. 4, Apr, 1994 ($1.75, limited series)
1-($2.00, 52 pgs.)-Nova, Quasar, Black Bolt; painted-c 4.00
2-4 3.00

STAR BLAZERS
Comico: Apr, 1987 - No. 4, July, 1987 ($1.75, limited series)
1-4 3.00

STAR BLAZERS
Comico: 1989 ($1.95/$2.50, limited series)
1-5- Steacy wraparound painted-c on all 3.00

STAR BLAZERS (The Magazine of Space Battleship Yamato)
Argo Press: No. 0, Aug, 1995 - No. 3, Dec, 1995 ($2.95)
0-3 3.00

STARBORN (From Stan Lee)
BOOM! Studios: Dec, 2010 - No. 12, Nov, 2011 ($3.99)
1-12: 1-9,11-Roberson-s/Randolph-a. 1-7-Three covers on each. 10-Scalera-a 4.00

STAR BRAND
Marvel Comics (New Universe): Oct, 1986 - No. 19, May, 1989 (75¢/$1.25)
1-15: 14-begin $1.25-c 3.00
16-19-Byrne story & art; low print run 5.00
Annual 1 (10/87) 4.00
... Classic Vol. 1 TPB (2006, $19.99) r/#1-7 20.00

STARCHILD
Tailspin Press: 1992 - No. 12 ($2.25/$2.50, B&W)
1,2-('92),0(4/93),3-12: 0-Illos by Chadwick, Eisner, Sim, M. Wagner. 3-(7/93). 4-(11/93). 6-(2/94) 3.00

STARCHILD: MYTHOPOLIS
Image Comics: No. 0, July, 1997 - No. 4, Apr, 1998 ($2.95, B&W, limited series)
0-4-James Owen-s/a 3.00

STAR COMICS
Ultem Publ. (Harry `A' Chesler)/Centaur Publications: Feb, 1937 - V2#7 (No. 23), Aug, 1939 (#1-6: large size)
V1#1-Dan Hastings (s/f) begins 271 542 813 1734 2967 4200
2 129 258 387 826 1413 2000
3-Classic Black Americana cover (rare) 271 542 813 1734 2967 4200
4-6 (#6, 9/37): 4,5-Little Nemo-c/stories 103 206 309 659 1130 1600
7-9: 8-Severed head centerspread; Impy & Little Nemo by Winsor McCay Jr, Popeye app. by Bob Wood; Mickey Mouse & Popeye app. as toys in Santa's bag on-c; X-Mas-c 90 180 270 576 988 1400
10 (1st Centaur; 3/38)-Impy by Winsor McCay Jr; Don Marlow by Guardineer begins
110 220 330 704 1202 1700
11-1st Jack Cole comic-a, 1 pg. (4/38) 84 168 252 538 919 1300
12-15: 12-Riders of the Golden West begins; Little Nemo app. 15-Speed Silvers by Gustavson & The Last Pirate by Burgos begins
68 136 204 435 743 1050
16 (12/38)-The Phantom Rider & his horse Thunder begins, ends V2#6
71 142 213 454 777 1100
V2#1(#17, 2/39)-Phantom Rider-c (only non-funny-c)
74 148 222 470 810 1150
2-7(#18-23): 2-Diana Deane by Tarpe Mills app. 3-Drama of Hollywood by Mills begins. 7-Jungle Queen app. 58 116 174 371 636 900
NOTE: ***Biro*** *c-6, 9, 10.* ***Burgos*** *a-15, 16, V2#1-7.* ***Ken Ernst*** *a-10, 12, 14.* ***Filchock*** *c-15, 18, 22.* ***Gill Fox*** *c-14, 19.* ***Guardineer*** *a-6, 8-14.* ***Gustavson*** *a-13-16, V2#1-7.* ***Winsor McCay*** *c-4, 5.* ***Tarpe Mills*** *a-15, V2#1-7.* ***Schwab*** *c-20, 23.* ***Bob Wood*** *a-10, 12, 13; c-7, 8.*

STAR COMICS MAGAZINE
Marvel Comics (Star Comics): Dec, 1986 - No. 13, 1988 ($1.50, digest-size)

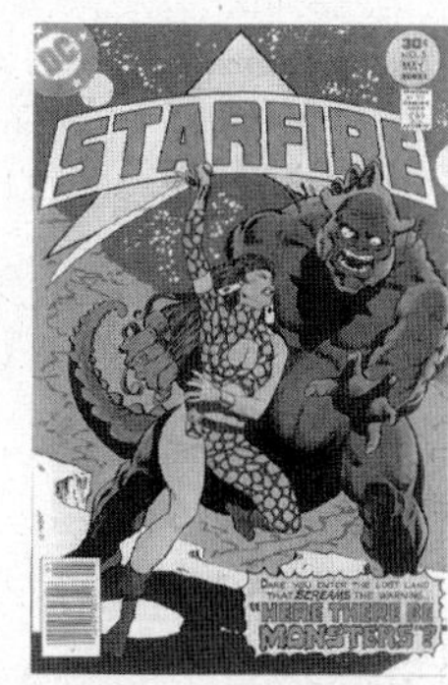

Starfire #5 © DC

Starlet O'Hara in Hollywood #1 © STD

Starman (2nd series) #57 © DC

GD 2.0 | VG 4.0 | FN 6.0 | VF 8.0 | VF/NM 9.0 | NM- 9.2

1,9-Spider-Man-c/s 2 4 6 8 11 14
2-8-Heathcliff, Ewoks, Top Dog, Madballs-r in #1-13 1 2 3 5 7 9
10-13 2 4 6 8 10 12

S.T.A.R. CORPS
DC Comics: Nov, 1993 - No. 6, Apr, 1994 ($1.50, limited series)
1-6: 1,2-Austin-c(i). 1-Superman app. 3.00

STARCRAFT (Based on the video game)
DC Comics (WildStorm): July, 2009 - No. 7, Jan, 2010 ($2.99)
1-7-Furman-s; two covers on each 3.00
HC (2010, $19.99, dustjacket) r/#1-7 20.00
SC (2011, $14.99) r/#1-7 15.00

STAR CROSSED
DC Comics (Helix): June, 1997 - No. 3, Aug, 1997 ($2.50, limited series)
1-3-Matt Howarth-s/a 3.00

STARDUST (See Neil Gaiman and Charles Vess' Stardust)

STARDUST KID, THE
Image Comics/Boom! Studios #4-on: May, 2005 - No. 4 ($3.50)
1-4-J.M. DeMatteis-s/Mike Ploog-a 3.50

STAR FEATURE COMICS
I. W. Enterprises: 1963
Reprint #9-Stunt-Man Stetson-r/Feat. Comics #141 2 4 6 10 13 16

STARFIRE (Not the Teen Titans character)
National Periodical Publ./DC Comics: Aug-Sept, 1976 - No. 8, Oct-Nov, 1977
1-Origin (CCA stamp fell off cover art; so it was approved by code)
2 4 6 8 11 14
2-8 1 2 3 5 6 8

STARGATE
Dynamite Entertainment
...: Daniel Jackson 1-4 (2010 - No. 4, 2010, $3.99) Watson-a/Murray-s 4.00
...: Vala Mal Doran 1-5 (2010 - No. 5, 2010, $3.99) Razek-a/Jerwa-s 4.00

STAR HUNTERS (See DC Super Stars #16)
National Periodical Publ./DC Comics: Oct-Nov, 1977 - No. 7, Oct-Nov, 1978
1,7: 1-Newton-a(p). 7-44 pgs. 2 4 6 8 10 12
2-6 1 2 3 4 5 7
NOTE: *Buckler a-4-7p; c-1-7p. Layton a-1-5i; c-1-6i. Nasser a-3p. Sutton a-6i.*

STARJAMMERS (See X-Men Spotlight on Starjammers)

STARJAMMERS (Also see Uncanny X-Men)
Marvel Comics: Oct, 1995 - No. 4, Jan, 1996 ($2.95, limited series)
1-4: Foil-c; Ellis scripts 4.00

STARJAMMERS
Marvel Comics: Sept, 2004 - No. 6, Jan, 2005 ($2.99, limited series)
1-6-Kevin J. Anderson-s. 1-Garza-a. 2-6-Lucas-a 3.00

STARK TERROR
Stanley Publications: Dec, 1970 - No. 5, Aug, 1971 (B&W, magazine, 52 pgs.)
(1950s Horror reprints, including pre-code)
1-Bondage, torture-c 7 14 21 48 79 110
2-4 (Gillmor/Aragon-r) 4 8 12 28 44 60
5 (ACG-r) 4 8 12 24 37 50

STARLET O'HARA IN HOLLYWOOD (Teen-age) (Also see Cookie)
Standard Comics: Dec, 1948 - No. 4, Sept, 1949
1-Owen Fitzgerald-a in all 26 52 78 154 252 350
2 15 30 45 85 130 175
3,4 14 28 42 76 108 140

STAR-LORD THE SPECIAL EDITION (Also see Marvel Comics Super Special #10, Marvel Premiere & Preview & Marvel Spotlight V2#6,7)
Marvel Comics Group: Feb, 1982 (one-shot, direct sales) (1st Baxter paper comic)
1-Byrne/Austin-a; Austin-c; 8 pgs. of new-a by Golden (p); Dr. Who story by Dave Gibbons; 1st deluxe format comic 6.00

STARLORD
Marvel Comics: Dec, 1996 - No. 3, Feb, 1997 ($2.50, limited series)
1-3-Timothy Zahn-s 3.00

STARLORD MEGAZINE
Marvel Comics: Nov, 1996 ($2.95, one-shot)
1-Reprints w/preview of new series 3.00

GD 2.0 | VG 4.0 | FN 6.0 | VF 8.0 | VF/NM 9.0 | NM- 9.2

STARMAN (1st Series) (Also see Justice League & War of the Gods)
DC Comics: Oct, 1988 - No. 45, Apr, 1992 ($1.00)
1-Origin 4.00
2-25,29-45: 4-Intro The Power Elite. 9,10,34-Batman app. 14-Superman app. 17-Power Girl app. 38-War of the Gods x-over. 42-45-Eclipso-c/stories 3.00
26-1st app. David Knight (G.A.Starman's son). 5.00
27,28: 27-Starman (David Knight) app. 28-Starman disguised as Superman; leads into Superman #50 4.00

STARMAN (2nd Series) (Also see The Golden Age, Showcase 95 #12, Showcase 96 #4,5)
DC Comics: No. 0, Oct, 1994 - No. 80, Aug, 2001; No. 81, Mar, 2010 ($1.95/$2.25/$2.50)
0,1: 0-James Robinson scripts, Tony Harris-c/a(p) & Wade Von Grawbadger-a(i) begins; Sins of the Father storyline begins, ends #3; 1st app. new Starman (Jack Knight); reintro of the G.A. Mist & G.A. Shade; 1st app. Nash; David Knight dies
1 2 3 4 5 7
2-7: 2-Reintro Charity from Forbidden Tales of Dark Mansion. 3-Reintro/2nd app. "Blue" Starman (1st app. in 1st Issue Special #12); Will Payton app. (both cameos). 5-David Knight app. 6-The Shade "Times Past" story; Kristiansen-a. 7-The Black Pirate cameo 5.00
8-17: 8-Begin $2.25-c. 10-1st app. new Mist (Nash). 11-JSA "Times Past" story; Matt Smith-a. 12-16-Sins of the Child. 17-The Black Pirate app. 4.00
18-37: 18-G.A. Starman "Times Past" story; Watkiss-a. 19-David Knight app. 20-23-G.A. Sandman app. 24-26-Demon Quest; all 3 covers make-up triptych. 33-36-Batman-c/app. 37-David Knight and deceased JSA members app. 3.00
38-49,51-56: 38-Nash vs. Justice League Europe. 39,40-Crossover w/ Power of Shazam! #35,36; Bulletman app. 42-Demon-c/app. 43-JLA-c/app. 44-Phantom Lady-c/app. 46-Gene Ha-a. 51-Jor-El app. 52,53-Adam Strange-c/app. 3.00
50-($3.95) Gold foil logo on-c; Star Boy (LSH) app. 4.00
57-79: 57-62-Painted covers by Harris and Alex Ross. 72-Death of Ted Knight 3.00
80-($3.95) Final issue; cover by Harris & Robinson 4.00
81-(3/10, $2.99) Blackest Night one-shot; The Shade vs. David Knight; Harris-c 3.00
#1,000,000 (11/98) 853rd Century x-over; Snejbjerg-a 3.00
Annual 1 (1996, $3.50)-Legends of the Dead Earth story; Prince Gavyn & G.A. Starman stories; J.H. Williams III, Bret Blevins, Craig Hamilton-c/a(p) 4.00
Annual 2 (1997, $3.95)-Pulp Heroes story; 4.00
...80 Page Giant (1/99, $4.95) Harris-c 5.00
...Secret Files 1 (4/98, $4.95)-Origin stories and profile pages 5.00
...The Mist (6/98, $1.95) Girlfrenzy; Mary Marvel app. 3.00
A Starry Knight-($17.95, TPB) r/#47-53 18.00
Grand Guignol-(2004, $19.95, TPB)-r/#61-73 20.00
Infernal Devices-($17.95, TPB) r/#29-35,37,38 18.00
Night and Day-($14.95, TPB)-r/#7-10,12-16 15.00
Sins of the Father-($12.95, TPB)-r/#0-5 13.00
Sons of the Father-($14.99, TPB)-r/#75-80 15.00
Stars My Destination-(2003, $14.95, TPB)-r/#55-60 15.00
Times Past-($17.95, TPB)-r/stories of other Starmen 18.00
The Starman Omnibus Vol. One (2008, $49.99, HC with dj) r/#0,1-16; Robinson intro. 50.00
The Starman Omnibus Vol. Two (2009, $49.99, HC with dj) r/#17-29, Annual #1, Showcase '95 #12, Showcase '96 #4,5; Harris intro.; merchandise gallery 50.00
The Starman Omnibus Vol. Three (2009, $49.99, HC with dj) r/#30-38, Annual #2, Starman Secret Files #1 and The Shade #1-4 50.00
The Starman Omnibus Vol. Four (2010, $49.99, HC with dj) r/#39-46, 80 Page Giant #1, Power of Shazam! #35,36; Starman: The Mist #1 and Batman/Hellboy/Starman #1,2 50.00
The Starman Omnibus Vol. Five (2010, $49.99, HC with dj) r/#47-60, #1,000,000; Stars and S.T.R.I.P.E. #0; All Star Comics 80 Page Giant #1; JSA: All Stars #4 50.00
The Starman Omnibus Vol. Six (2011, $49.99, HC with dj) r/#61-81, Johns intro. 50.00

STARMAN/CONGORILLA (See Justice League: Cry For Justice)
DC Comics: Mar, 2011 ($2.99, one-shot)
1-Animal Man and Rex the Wonder Dog app.; Robinson-s/Booth-a/Ha-c 3.00

STARMASTERS
Marvel Comics: Dec, 1995 - No. 3, Feb, 1996 ($1.95, limited series)
1-3-Continues in Cosmic Powers Unlimited #4 3.00

STAR PRESENTATION, A (Formerly My Secret Romance #1,2; Spectacular Stories #4 on) (Also see This Is Suspense)
Fox Features Syndicate (Hero Books): No. 3, May, 1950
3-Dr. Jekyll & Mr. Hyde by Wood & Harrison (reprinted in Startling Terror Tales #10); "The Repulsing Dwarf" by Wood; Wood-c 61 122 183 390 670 950

STAR QUEST COMIX (Warren Presents... on cover)
Warren Publications: Oct, 1978 ($1.50, B&W magazine, 84 pgs., square-bound)
1-Corben, Maroto, Neary-a; Ken Kelly-c; Star Wars 2 4 6 9 12 15

STAR RAIDERS (See DC Graphic Novel #1)

STAR RANGER (Cowboy Comics #13 on)

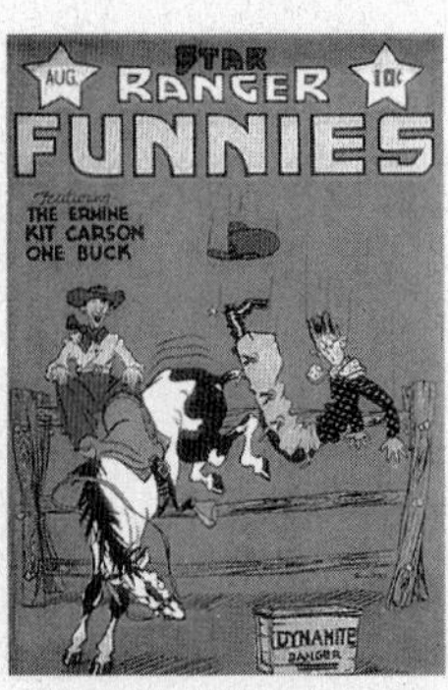

Star Ranger Funnies V2 #4 © CEN

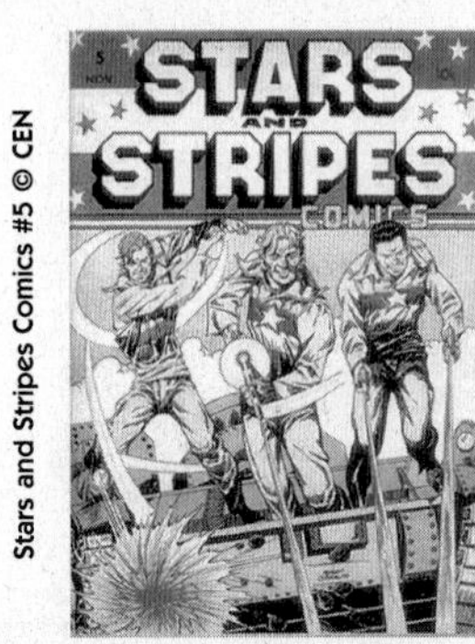

Stars and Stripes Comics #5 © CEN

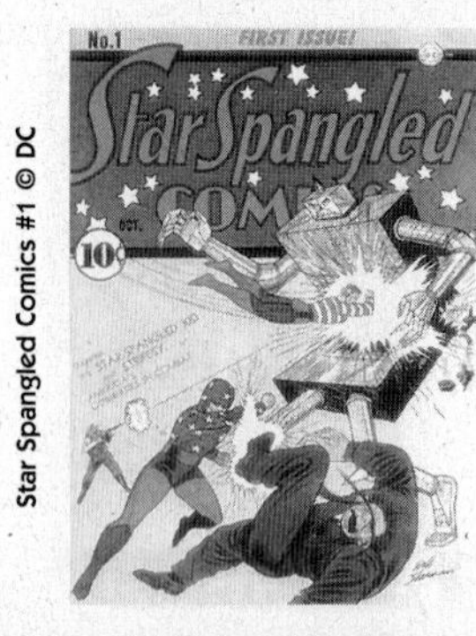

Star Spangled Comics #1 © DC

GD 2.0	VG 4.0	FN 6.0	VF 8.0	VF/NM 9.0	NM- 9.2

Chesler Publ./Centaur Publ.: Feb, 1937 - No. 12, May, 1938 (Large size: No. 1-6)

1-(1st Western comic)-Ace & Deuce, Air Plunder; Creig Flessel-a 245 490 735 1568 2684 3800
2 107 214 321 680 1165 1650
3-6 94 188 282 597 1024 1450
7-9: 8(12/37)-Christmas-c; Air Patrol, Gold coast app.; Guardineer centerfold 71 142 213 454 777 1100
V2#10 (1st Centaur; 3/38) 97 194 291 621 1061 1500
11,12 71 142 213 454 777 1100

NOTE: *J. Cole a-10, 12; c-12. Ken Ernst a-11. Gill Fox a-8(illo), 9, 10. Guardineer a-1, 3, 6, 7, 8(illos), 9, 10, 12. Gustavson a-8-10, 12. Fred Schwab c-2-11. Bob Wood a-8-10.*

STAR RANGER FUNNIES (Formerly Cowboy Comics)
Centaur Publications: V1#15, Oct, 1938 - V2#5, Oct, 1939

V1#15-Lyin Lou, Ermine, Wild West Junior, The Law of Caribou County by Eisner, Cowboy Jake, The Plugged Dummy, Spurs by Gustavson, Red Coat, Two Buckaroos & Trouble Hunters begin 97 194 291 621 1061 1500
V2#1 (1/39) 74 148 222 470 810 1150
2-5: 2-Night Hawk by Gustavson. 4-Kit Carson app. 63 126 189 403 689 975

NOTE: *Jack Cole a-V2#1, 3; c-V2#1. Filchock c-V2#2, 3. Guardineer a-V2#3. Gustavson a-V2#2. Pinajian c/a-V2#5.*

STAR REACH (Mature content)
Star Reach Publ.: Apr, 1974 - No. 18, Oct, 1979 (B&W, #12-15 w/color)

1-(75¢, 52 pgs.) Art by Starlin, Simonson. Chaykin-c/a; origin Death. Cody Starbuck-sty 3 6 9 18 27 35
1-2nd, 3th, and 4th printings ($1.00-$1.50-c) 6.00
2-11: 2-Adams, Giordano-a; 1st Stephanie Starr-c/s. 3-1st Linda Lovecraft. 4-1st Sherlock Duck. 5-1st Gideon Faust by Chaykin. 6-Elric-c. 7-BWS-c. 9-14-Sacred & Profane-c/s by Steacy. 11-Samurai 2 4 6 8 11 14
2-2nd printing 4.00
12-15 (44 pgs.): 12-Zelazny-s. Nasser-a, Brunner-c 2 4 6 9 13 16
16-18-Magazine size: 17-Poe's Raven-c/s 2 4 6 9 13 16

NOTE: *Adams c-2. Bonivert a-17. Brunner a-3,5; c-3,10,12. Chaykin a-1,4,5; c-1(1st ed),4,5; back-c-1(2nd,3rd,4th ed). Gene Day a-6,8,9,11,15. Friedrich s-2,3,8,10. Gasbarri a-7. Gilbert a-9,12. Giordano a-2. Gould a-6. Hirota/Mukaide s/a-7. Jones c-6. Konz a-17. Leialoha a-3,4,6-i, 13,15; c-13,15. Lyda a-6,12-15. Marrs a-2-5,7,10,14,15,16,18; c-18; back-c-2. Mukaide a-18. Nasser a-12. Nino a-6; Russell a-8,10; c-8. Dave Sim s-7; lettering-9. Simonson a-1. Skeates a-1,2. Starlin a-1(x2), 2(x2); back-c-1(1st ed); c-1(2nd,3rd,4th ed). Barry Smith c-7. Staton a-5,6,7. Steacy a-8-14; c-9,11,14,16. Vosburg a-2-5,7,10. Workman a-2-5,8. Nudity panels in most. Wraparound-c: 3-5,7-11,13-16,18.*

STAR REACH CLASSICS
Eclipse Comics: Mar, 1984 - No. 6, Aug, 1984 ($1.50, Baxter paper)

1-6: 1-Neal Adams-r/Star Reach #1; Sim & Starlin-a 3.00

STARR FLAGG, UNDERCOVER GIRL (See Undercover...)

STARRIORS
Marvel Comics: Aug, 1984 - Feb, 1985 (Limited series) (Based on Tomy toys)

1-4 4.00

STARR THE SLAYER
Marvel Comics (MAX): Nov, 2009 - No. 4, Feb, 2010 ($3.99, limited series)

1-4- Richard Corben-c/a; Daniel Way-s 4.00

STARS AND S.T.R.I.P.E. (Also see JSA)
DC Comics: July, 1999 - No. 14, Sept, 2000 ($2.95/$2.50)

0-($2.95) Moder and Weston-a; Starman app. 3.00
1-Johns and Robinson-s/Moder-a; origin new Star Spangled Kid 3.00
2-14: 4-Marvel Family app. 9-Seven Soldiers of Victory-c/app. 3.00
JSA Presents: Stars and S.T.R.I.P.E. Vol. 1 TPB (2007, $17.99) r/#1-8; Johns intro. 18.00
JSA Presents: Stars and S.T.R.I.P.E. Vol. 2 TPB (2008, $17.99) r/#0,9-14 18.00

STARS AND STRIPES COMICS
Centaur Publications: No. 2, May, 1941 - No. 6, Dec, 1941

2(#1)-The Shark, The Iron Skull, A-Man, The Amazing Man, Mighty Man, Minimidget begin; The Voice & Dash Dartwell, the Human Meteor, Reef Kinkaid app.; Gustavson Flag-c 232 464 696 1485 2543 3600
3-Origin Dr. Synthe; The Black Panther app. 126 252 378 806 1378 1950
4-Origin/1st app. The Stars and Stripes; injury to eye-c 107 214 321 680 1165 1650
5(#5 on cover & inside) 74 148 222 470 810 1150
5(#6)-(#5 on cover, #6 on inside) 74 148 222 470 810 1150

NOTE: *Gustavson c/a-3. Myron Strauss c-4, 5(#5), 5(#6).*

STAR SEED (Formerly Powers That Be)
Broadway Comics: No. 7, 1996 - No. 9 ($2.95)

7-9 3.00

STARSHIP TROOPERS
Dark Horse Comics: 1997 - No. 2, 1997 ($2.95, limited series)

1,2-Movie adaption 3.00

STARSHIP TROOPERS: BRUTE CREATIONS
Dark Horse Comics: 1997 ($2.95, one-shot)

1 3.00

STARSHIP TROOPERS: DOMINANT SPECIES
Dark Horse Comics: Aug, 1998 - No. 4, Nov, 1998 ($2.95, limited series)

1-4-Strnad-s/Bolton-c 3.00

STARSHIP TROOPERS: INSECT TOUCH
Dark Horse Comics: 1997 - No. 3, 1997 ($2.95, limited series)

1-3 3.00

STAR SLAMMERS (See Marvel Graphic Novel #6)
Malibu Comics (Bravura): May, 1994 - No. 4, Aug, 1994 ($2.50, unfinished limited series)

1-4: W. Simonson-a/stories; contain Bravura stamps 3.00

STAR SLAMMERS SPECIAL
Dark Horse Comics (Legend): June, 1996 ($2.95, one-shot)

nn-Simonson-c/a/scripts; concludes Bravura limited series. 3.00

STARSLAYER
Pacific Comics/First Comics No. 7 on: Feb, 1982 - No. 6, Apr, 1983; No. 7, Aug, 1983 - No. 34, Nov, 1985

1-Origin & 1st app.; 1 pg. Rocketeer brief app. which continues in #2 1 3 4 6 8 10
2-Origin/1st full app. the Rocketeer (4/82) by Dave Stevens (Chapter 1 of Rocketeer saga; see Pacific Presents #1,2) 2 4 6 10 14 18
3-Chapter 2 of Rocketeer saga by Stevens 2 4 6 8 10 12
4,6,7: 7-Grell-a ends 4.00
5-2nd app. Groo the Wanderer by Aragonés 1 2 3 5 6 8
8-34: 10-1st app. Grimjack (11/83, ends #17). 18-Starslayer meets Grimjack. 20-The Black Flame begins (9/84, 1st app.), ends #33. 27-Book length Black Flame story 3.00

NOTE: *Grell a-1-7; c-1-8. Stevens back c-2, 3. Sutton a-17p, 20-22p, 24-27p, 29-33p.*

STARSLAYER (The Director's Cut)
Acclaim Comics (Windjammer): June, 1994 - No. 8, Dec, 1995 ($2.50)

1-8: Mike Grell-c/a/scripts 3.00

STAR SPANGLED COMICS (Star Spangled War Stories #131 on)
National Periodical Publications: Oct, 1941 - No. 130, July, 1952

1-Origin/1st app. Tarantula; Captain X of the R.A.F., Star Spangled Kid (see Action #40), Armstrong of the Army begin; Robot-c 508 1016 1524 3708 6554 9400
2 168 336 504 1075 1838 2600
3-5 105 210 315 667 1146 1625
6-Last Armstrong/Army; Penniless Palmer begins 64 128 192 406 696 985
7-(4/42)-Origin/1st app. The Guardian by S&K, & Robotman (by Paul Cassidy & created by Siegel);The Newsboy Legion (1st app.), Robotman & TNT begin; last Captain X 730 1460 2190 5329 9415 13,500
8-Origin TNT & Dan the Dyna-Mite 242 484 726 1537 2644 3750
9,10 168 336 504 1075 1838 2600
11-17 123 246 369 787 1344 1900
18-Origin Star Spangled Kid 153 306 459 972 1674 2375
19-Last Tarantula 123 246 369 787 1344 1900
20-Liberty Belle begins (5/43) 142 284 426 909 1555 2200
21-29-Last S&K issue; 23-Last TNT. 25-Robotman by Jimmy Thompson begins. 29-Intro Robbie the Robotdog 103 206 309 659 1130 1600
30-40: 31-S&K-c 61 122 183 390 670 950
41-51: 41,49-Kirby-c. 51-Robot-c by Kirby 55 110 165 352 601 850
52-64: 53 by S&K. 64-Last Newsboy Legion & The Guardian 50 100 150 315 533 750
65-Robin begins with c/app. (2/47); Batman cameo in 1 panel; Robin-c begins, end #95 181 362 543 1158 1979 2800
66-Batman cameo in Robin story 86 172 258 546 936 1325
67,68,70-80: 68-Last Liberty Belle? 72-Burnley Robin-c 68 136 204 435 743 1050
69-Origin/1st app. Tomahawk by F. Ray; atom bomb story & splash (6/47); black-c (rare in high grade) 174 348 522 1114 1907 2700
81-Origin Merry, Girl of 1000 Gimmicks in Star Spangled Kid story 57 114 171 362 624 885
82,85: 82-Last Robotman? 85-Last Star Spangled Kid? 53 106 159 334 567 800

Star Spangled Comics #90 © DC

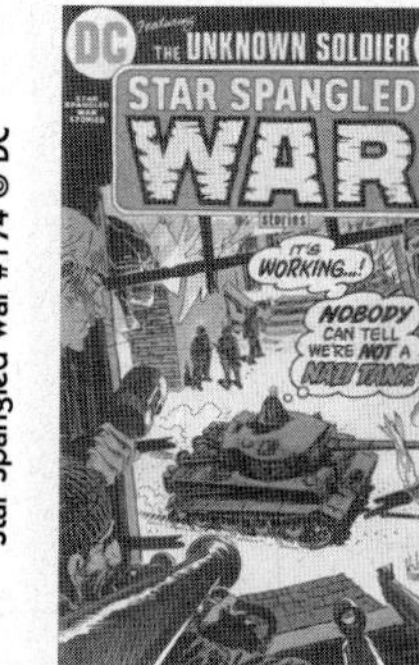

Star Spangled War #174 © DC

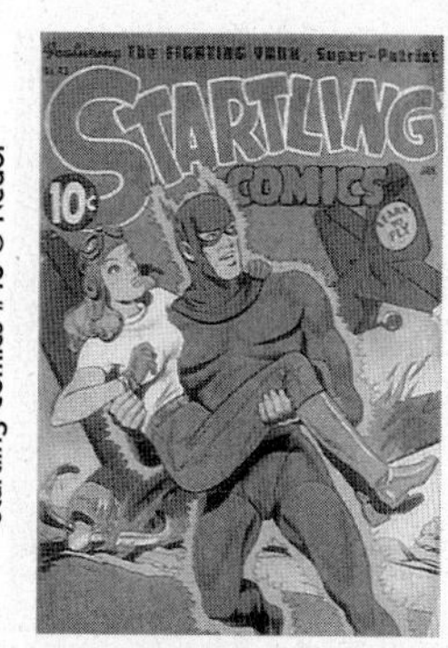

Startling Comics #43 © Nedor

	GD 2.0	VG 4.0	FN 6.0	VF 8.0	VF/NM 9.0	NM- 9.2
83-Tomahawk enters the lost valley, a land of dinosaurs; Capt. Compass begins, ends #130	54	108	162	343	574	825
84,87 (Rare): 87-Batman cameo in Robin	86	172	258	546	936	1325
86-Batman cameo in Robin story	60	120	180	381	653	925
88(1/49)-94: Batman-c/stories in all. 91-Federal Men begin, end #93. 94-Manhunters Around the World begin, end #121	63	126	189	403	689	975
95-Batman story; last Robin-c	55	110	165	352	601	850
96,98-Batman cameo in Robin stories. 96-1st Tomahawk-c (also #97-121)	40	80	120	244	405	565
97,99	36	72	108	211	343	475
100 (1/50)-Pre-Bat-Hound tryout in Robin story (pre-dates Batman #92).	41	82	123	256	428	600
101-109,118,119,121: 121-Last Tomahawk-c	32	64	96	192	314	435
110,111,120-Batman cameo in Robin stories. 120-Last 52 pg. issue	34	68	102	199	325	450
112-Batman & Robin story	36	72	108	216	351	485
113-Frazetta-a (10 pgs.)	41	82	123	256	428	600
114-Retells Robin's origin (3/51); Batman & Robin story	43	86	129	271	461	650
115,117-Batman app. in Robin stories	36	72	108	211	343	475
116-Flag-c	36	72	108	211	343	475
122-(11/51)-Ghost Breaker-c/stories begin (origin/1st app.), ends #130 (Ghost Breaker covers #122-130)	47	94	141	296	498	700
123-126,128,129	32	64	96	192	314	435
127-Batman app.	34	68	102	206	336	465
130-Batman cameo in Robin story	37	74	111	222	361	500

NOTE: *Most all issues after #29 signed by Simon & Kirby are not by them.* ***Bill Ely*** *c-122-130.* ***Mortimer*** *c-65-74(most), 76-95(most).* ***Fred Ray*** *c-96-106, 109, 110, 112, 113, 115-120.* ***S&K*** *c-7-31, 33, 34, 36, 37, 39, 40, 48, 49, 50-54, 56-58.* ***Hal Sherman*** *c-1-6.* ***Dick Sprang*** *c-75.*

STAR SPANGLED COMICS (Also see All Star Comics 1999 crossover titles)
DC Comics: May, 1999 ($1.99, one-shot)

1-Golden Age Sandman and the Star Spangled Kid — 3.00

STAR SPANGLED KID (See Action #40, Leading Comics & Star Spangled Comics)

STAR SPANGLED WAR STORIES
DC Comics: Aug/Sept 1952

nn - Ashcan comic, not distributed to newsstands, only for in-house use. Cover art is Western Comics #28 with interior being Western Comics #13 (no known sales)

STAR SPANGLED WAR STORIES (Formerly Star Spangled Comics #1-130; Becomes The Unknown Soldier #205 on) (See Showcase)
National Periodical Publications: No. 131, 8/52 - No. 133, 10/52; No. 3, 11/52 - No. 204, 2-3/77

	GD 2.0	VG 4.0	FN 6.0	VF 8.0	VF/NM 9.0	NM- 9.2
131(#1)	161	322	483	1030	1765	2500
132	94	188	282	597	1024	1450
133-Used in **POP**, pg. 94	81	162	243	518	884	1250
3-6: 4-Devil Dog Dugan app. 6-Evans-a	57	114	171	362	619	875
7-10	29	58	87	210	455	700
11-20	25	50	75	178	382	585
21-30: 30-Last precode (2/55)	21	42	63	148	317	485
31-33,35-40	17	34	51	114	250	385
34-Krigstein-a	17	34	51	119	260	400
41-44,46-50: 50-1st S.A. issue	15	30	45	104	227	350
45-1st DC grey tone war-c (5/56)	38	76	114	285	618	950
51,52,54-63,65,66, 68-83	13	26	39	90	195	300
53-"Rock Sergeant," 3rd Sgt. Rock prototype; inspired "P.I. & The Sand Fleas" in G.I. Combat #56 (1/57)	24	48	72	168	359	550
64-Pre-Sgt. Rock Easy Co. story (12/57)	17	34	51	119	260	400
67-Two Easy Co. stories without Sgt. Rock	18	36	54	123	267	410
84-Origin Mlle. Marie	24	48	72	168	359	550
85-89-Mlle. Marie in all	15	30	45	104	227	350
90-1st app. "War That Time Forgot" series; dinosaur issue-c/story (4-5/60) (also see Weird War Tales #94 & #99)	52	104	156	421	911	1400
91,93-No dinosaur stories	15	30	45	104	227	350
92-2nd dinosaur-c/s	24	48	72	168	359	550
94 (12/60)- "Ghost Ace" story; Baron Von Richter as The Enemy Ace (predates Our Army at War #151)	27	54	81	196	423	650
95-99: Dinosaur-c/s	19	38	57	128	277	425
100-Dinosaur-c/story.	21	42	63	146	311	475
101-115: All dinosaur issues	15	30	45	104	227	350
116-125,127-133,135-137: 120-1st app. Caveboy and Dino. 137-Last dinosaur story; Heath Birdman-#129,131	13	26	39	90	195	300
126-No dinosaur story	12	24	36	79	160	240
134-Dinosaur story; Neal Adams-a	15	30	45	104	227	350
138-New Enemy Ace-c/stories begin by Joe Kubert (4-5/68), end #150 (also see Our Army at War #151 and Showcase #57)	15	30	45	104	227	350
139-Origin Enemy Ace (7/68)	11	22	33	76	151	225
140-143,145: 145-Last 12¢ issue (6-7/69)	9	18	27	61	106	150
144-Neal Adams/Kubert-a	10	20	30	65	118	170
146-Enemy Ace-c/app.	7	14	21	48	79	110
147,148-New Enemy Ace stories	8	16	24	55	93	130
149,150-Last new Enemy Ace by Kubert. Viking Prince by Kubert	8	16	24	51	86	120
151-1st solo app. Unknown Soldier (6-7/70); Enemy Ace-r begin (from Our Army at War, Showcase & SSWS); end #161	17	34	51	119	260	400
152-Reprints 2nd Enemy Ace app.	7	14	21	44	72	100
153,155-Enemy Ace reprints; early Unknown Soldier stories	6	12	18	39	62	85
154-Origin Unknown Soldier	13	26	39	87	186	285
156-1st Battle Album; Unknown Soldier story; Kubert-c/a	5	10	15	35	55	75
157-Sgt. Rock x-over in Unknown Soldier story.	5	10	15	30	48	65
158-163-(52 pgs.): New Unknown Soldier stories; Kubert-c/a. 161-Last Enemy Ace-r	4	8	12	26	41	55
164-183,200: 181-183-Enemy Ace vs. Balloon Buster serial app; Frank Thorne-a. 200-Enemy Ace back-up	3	6	9	16	22	28
184-199,201-204	2	4	6	13	18	22

NOTE: ***Anderson*** *a-28.* ***Chaykin*** *a-167.* ***Drucker*** *a-59, 61, 64, 66, 67, 73-84.* ***Estrada*** *a-149.* ***John Giunta*** *a-72.* ***Glanzman*** *a-167, 171, 172, 174.* ***Heath*** *a-42,122, 132, 133; c-67, 122, 132-134.* ***Kaluta*** *a-197i; c-167.* ***G. Kane*** *a-169.* ***Kubert*** *a-6-163(most later issues), 200.* ***Maurer*** *a-160, 165.* ***Severin*** *a-65, 162.* ***S&K*** *c-7-31, 33, 34, 37, 40.* ***Simonson*** *a-170, 172, 174, 180.* ***Sutton*** *a-168.* ***Thorne*** *a-183.* ***Toth*** *a-164.* ***Wildey*** *a-161. Suicide Squad in 110, 116-118, 120, 121, 127.*

STAR SPANGLED WAR STORIES (Featuring Mademoiselle Marie)
DC Comics: Nov, 2010 ($3.99, one-shot)

1-Mademoiselle Marie in 1944 France; Tucci-s/Justiniano-a/Bolland-c — 4.00

STARSTREAM (Adventures in Science Fiction)(See Questar illustrated)
Whitman/Western Publishing Co.: 1976 (79¢, 68 pgs, cardboard-c)

	GD 2.0	VG 4.0	FN 6.0	VF 8.0	VF/NM 9.0	NM- 9.2
1-4: 1-Bolle-a. 2-4-McWilliams & Bolle-a	2	4	6	10	14	18

STARSTRUCK
Marvel Comics (Epic Comics): Feb, 1985 - No. 6, Feb, 1986 ($1.50, mature)

1-6: Kaluta-a — 4.00

STARSTRUCK
Dark Horse Comics: Aug, 1990 - No. 4, Nov?, 1990 ($2.95, B&W, 52pgs.)

1-3: Kaluta-r/Epic series plus new-c/a in all — 4.00
4 (68 pgs.)-contains 2 trading cards — 5.00
Reprint 1-13 (IDW, 8/09 - No. 13, Sept, 2010, $3.99) newly colored; Galactic Girl Guides — 4.00

STAR STUDDED
Cambridge House/Superior Publishers: 1945 (25¢, 132 pgs.); 1945 (196 pgs.)

	GD 2.0	VG 4.0	FN 6.0	VF 8.0	VF/NM 9.0	NM- 9.2
nn-Captain Combat by Giunta, Ghost Woman, Commandette, & Red Rogue app.; Infantino-a	37	74	111	222	361	500
nn-The Cadet, Edison Bell, Hoot Gibson, Jungle Lil (196 pgs.); copies vary; Blue Beetle in some	39	78	117	231	378	525

STARTLING COMICS
Better Publications (Nedor): June, 1940 - No. 53, Sept, 1948

	GD 2.0	VG 4.0	FN 6.0	VF 8.0	VF/NM 9.0	NM- 9.2
1-Origin Captain Future-Man Of Tomorrow, Mystico (By Sansone), The Wonder Man; The Masked Rider & his horse Pinto begins; Masked Rider formerly in pulps; drug use story	300	600	900	2010	3505	5000
2 -Don Davis, Espionage Ace begins	110	220	330	704	1202	1700
3	90	180	270	576	988	1400
4	63	126	189	403	689	975
5,6,9	54	108	162	343	574	825
7-8-Nazi WWII-c	58	116	174	371	636	900
10-The Fighting Yank begins (9/41, origin/1st app.); Nazi WWII-c	432	864	1296	3154	5577	8000
11-2nd app. Fighting Yank; Nazi WWII-c	142	284	426	909	1555	2200
12-Hitler, Hirohito, Mussolini-c	161	322	483	1030	1765	2500
13-15	71	142	213	454	777	1100
16-Origin The Four Comrades; not in #32,35	73	146	219	467	796	1125
17-Last Masked Rider & Mystico	54	108	162	343	574	825
18-Pyroman begins (12/42, origin)(also see America's Best Comics #3 for 1st app., 11/42)	107	214	321	680	1165	1650
19-Nazi WWII-c	58	116	174	371	636	900
20,21: 20-The Oracle begins (3/43); not in issues 26,28,33,34; Nazi WWII-c. 21-Origin The Ape, Oracle's enemy; Schomburg hypo-c	61	122	183	390	670	950

22-34: All have Schomburg WWII-c. 34-Origin The Scarab & only app.

Startling Stories: The Thing #1 © MAR

STAR TREK
A scientist escapes into Time with a doomsday bomb!

Star Trek #36 © Paramount

Star Trek (1989 series) #58 © Paramount

GD VG FN VF VF/NM NM-
2.0 4.0 6.0 8.0 9.0 9.2

60 120 180 381 653 925
35-Hypodermic syringe attacks Fighting Yank in drug story; Schomburg WWII-c
61 122 183 390 670 950
36-43: 36-Last Four Comrades. 38-Bondage/torture-c. 40-Last Capt. Future & Oracle. 41-Front Page Peggy begins; A-Bomb-c. 43-Last Pyroman
48 96 144 302 514 725
44,45: 44-Lance Lewis, Space Detective begins; Ingels-c; sci/fi-c begin. 45-Tygra begins (intro/origin, 5/47); Ingels-c/a (splash pg. & inside f/c B&W ad)
81 162 243 518 884 1250
46-Classic Ingels-c; Ingels-a 119 238 357 762 1306 1850
47,48,50-53: 50,51-Sea-Eagle app. 77 154 231 493 847 1200
49-Classic Schomburg Robot-c; last Fighting Yank 541 1082 1623 3950 6975 10,000

NOTE: ***Ingels** a-44, 45; c-44, 45, 46(wash). **Schomburg** (**Xela**) c-21-43; 47-53 (airbrush). **Tuska** c-45? Bondage c-16, 21, 37, 46-49. Captain Future c-1-9, 13, 14. Fighting Yank c-10-12, 15-17, 21, 22, 24, 26, 28, 30, 32, 34, 36, 38, 40, 42. Pyroman c-18-20, 23, 25, 27, 29, 31, 33, 35, 37, 39, 41, 43.*

STARTLING STORIES: BANNER
Marvel Comics: July, 2001 - No. 4, Oct, 2001 ($2.99, limited series)

1-4-Hulk story by Azzarello; Corben-c/a 3.00
TPB (11/01, $12.95) r/1-4 13.00

STARTLING STORIES: FANTASTIC FOUR - UNSTABLE MOLECULES (See Fantastic Four - ...)

STARTLING STORIES: THE MEGALOMANIACAL SPIDER-MAN
Marvel Comics: Jun, 2002 ($2.99, one-shot)

1-Spider-Man spoof; Peter Bagge-s/a 3.00

STARTLING STORIES: THE THING
Marvel Comics: 2003 ($3.50, one-shot)

1-Zimmerman-s/Kramer-a; Inhumans and the Hulk app. 3.50

STARTLING STORIES: THE THING - NIGHT FALLS ON YANCY STREET
Marvel Comics: Jun, 2003 - No. 4, Sept, 2003 ($3.50, limited series)

1-4-Dorkin-s/Haspiel-a. 2,3-Frightful Four app. 3.50

STARTLING TERROR TALES
Star Publications: No. 10, May, 1952 - No. 14, Feb, 1953; No. 4, Apr, 1953 - No. 11, 1954

10-(1st Series)-Wood/Harrison-a (r/A Star Presentation #3) Disbrow/Cole-c; becomes 4 different titles after #10; becomes Confessions of Love #11 on, The Horrors #11 on, Terrifying Tales #11 on, Terrors of the Jungle #11 on & continues w/Startling Terror #11
77 154 231 493 847 1200
11-(8/52)-L. B. Cole Spider-c; r-Fox's "A Feature Presentation" #5 (blue-c)
194 388 582 1242 2121 3000
11-Black-c (variant; believed to be a pressrun change) (Unique)
200 400 600 1280 2190 3100
12,14 34 68 102 199 325 450
13-Jo-Jo-r; Disbrow-a 35 70 105 208 339 470
4-9,11(1953-54) (2nd Series): 11-New logo 30 60 90 177 289 400
10-Disbrow-a 36 72 108 214 347 480

NOTE: ***L. B. Cole** covers-all issues. **Palais** a-V2#8r, V2#11r.*

STAR TREK (TV) (See Dan Curtis Giveaways, Dynabrite Comics & Power Record Comics)
Gold Key: 7/67; No. 2, 6/68; No. 3, 12/68; No. 4, 6/69 - No. 61, 3/79

1-Photo-c begin, end #9; photo back-c is on all copies, no variant exists with an ad on the back-c 52 104 156 421 911 1400
2-Regular version has an ad on back-c 22 44 66 154 327 500
2 (rare variation w/photo back-c) 33 66 99 239 520 800
3-5-All have back-c ads 14 28 42 97 211 325
3 (rare variation w/photo back-c) 24 48 72 168 359 550
6-9 11 22 33 76 151 225
10-20 6 12 18 42 69 95
21-30 6 12 18 37 59 80
31-40 4 8 12 28 44 60
41-61: 52-Drug propaganda story 4 8 12 22 34 45
...the Enterprise Logs nn (8/76)-Golden Press, ($1.95, 224 pgs.)-r/#1-8 plus 7 pgs. by McWilliams (#11185)-Photo-c 6 12 18 39 62 85
...the Enterprise Logs Vol. 2 ('76)-r/#9-17 (#11187)-Photo-c
5 10 15 35 55 75
...the Enterprise Logs Vol. 3 ('77)-r/#18-26 (#11188); McWilliams-a (4 pgs.)-Photo-c
5 10 15 35 55 75
Star Trek Vol. 4 (Winter '77)-Reprints #27,28,30-34,36,38 (#11189) plus 3 pgs. new art 5 10 15 35 55 75
... : The Key Collection (Checker Book Publ. Group, 2004, $22.95) r/#1-8 23.00
... : The Key Collection Volume 2 (Checker, 2004, $22.95) r/#9-16 23.00
... : The Key Collection Volume 3 (Checker, 2005, $22.95) r/#17-24 23.00
... : The Key Collection Volume 4 (Checker, 2005, $22.95) r/#25-33 23.00
... : The Key Collection Volume 5 (Checker, 2006, $22.95) r/#34,36,38,39,40-43 23.00

NOTE: ***McWilliams** a-38, 40-44, 46-61. #29 reprints #1; #35 reprints #4; #37 reprints #5; #45 reprints #7. The tabloids all have photo covers and blank inside covers. Painted covers #10-44, 46-59.*

STAR TREK
Marvel Comics Group: April, 1980 - No. 18, Feb, 1982

1: 1-3-r/Marvel Super Special; movie adapt. 2 4 6 10 14 18
2-16: 5-Miller-c 1 3 4 6 8 10
17-Low print run 2 4 6 8 11 14
18-Last issue; low print run 2 4 6 11 16 20

NOTE: ***Austin** c-18i. **Buscema** a-13. **Gil Kane** a-15. **Nasser** c/a-7. **Simonson** c-17.*

STAR TREK (Also see Who's Who In Star Trek)
DC Comics: Feb, 1984 - No. 56, Nov, 1988 (75¢, Mando paper)

1-Sutton-a(p) begins 1 3 4 6 8 10
2-5 6.00
6-10: 7-Origin Saavik 5.00
11-20: 19-Walter Koenig story 4.00
21-32 3.50
33-($1.25, 52 pgs.)-20th anniversary issue 4.00
34-49: 37-Painted-c 3.00
50-($1.50, 52 pgs.) 4.00
51-56 3.00
Annual 1-3: 1(1985). 2(1986). 3(1988, $1.50) 4.00
...: To Boldly Go TPB (Titan Books, 7/05, $19.95) r/#1-6; Koenig foreward; cast interviews 20.00
...: The Trial of James T. Kirk TPB (Titan Books, 6/06, $19.95) r/#7-12; cast interviews 20.00
...: The Return of the Worthy TPB (Titan Books, 12/06, $19.95) r/#13-18; cast interviews 20.00

NOTE: ***Morrow** a-28, 35, 36, 56. **Orlando** c-8i. **Perez** c-1-3. **Spiegle** a-19. **Starlin** c-24, 25. **Sutton** a-1-6p, 8-18p, 20-27p, 29p, 31-34p, 39-52p, 55p; c-4-6p, 8-22p, 46p.*

STAR TREK
DC Comics: Oct, 1989 - No. 80, Jan, 1996 ($1.50/$1.75/$1.95/$2.50)

1-Capt. Kirk and crew 6.00
2,3 4.00
4-23,25-30: 10-12-The Trial of James T. Kirk. 21-Begin $1.75-c 3.00
24-($2.95, 68 pgs.)-40 pg. epic w/pin-ups 4.00
31-49,51-60 3.00
50-($3.50, 68 pgs.)-Painted-c 4.00
61-74,76-80 3.00
75 ($3.95) 4.00
Annual 1-6('90-'95, 68 pgs.): 1-Morrow-a. 3-Painted-c 4.00
Special 1-3 ('9-'95, 68 pgs.)-1-Sutton-a. 4.00
...: The Ashes of Eden (1995, $14.95, 100 pgs.)-Shatner story 15.00
...Generations (1994, $3.95, 68 pgs.)-Movie adaptation 4.00
...Generations (1994, $5.95, 68 pgs.)-Squarebound 6.00

STAR TREK...(TV)
DC Comics (WildStorm): one-shots

All of Me (4/00, $5.95, prestige format) Lopresti-a 6.00
Enemy Unseen TPB (2001, $17.95) r/Perchance to Dream, Embrace the Wolf, The Killing Shadows; Struzan-c 18.00
Enter the Wolves (2001, $5.95) Crispin & Weinstein-s; Mota-a/c 6.00
New Frontier - Double Time (11/00, $5.95)-Captain Calhoun's USS Excalibur; Peter David-s; Stelfreeze-c 6.00
Other Realities TPB (2001, $14.95) r/All of Me, New Frontier - Double Time, and DS9-N-Vector; Van Fleet-c 15.00
Special (2001, $6.95) Stories from all 4 series by various; Van Fleet-c 7.00

STAR TREK (Further adventures of the crew from the 2009 movie)
IDW Publishing: Sept, 2011 - Present ($3.99)

1-3: 1,2-Gary Mitchell app.; Molnar-a. 1-Covers by Bradstreet & Messina 4.00

STAR TREK: ALIEN SPOTLIGHT
IDW Publishing: Sept, 2007 - Feb, 2008 ($3.99, series of one-shots)

... Andorians (11/07) Storrie-s/O'Grady-a; Counselor Troi app.; two art & one photo-c 4.00
... Borg (1/08) Harris-s/Murphy-a; Janeway & Next Gen crew app.; two art & one photo-c 4.00
... Cardassians (12/09) Padilla-a; Garak & Kira app. 4.00
... The Gorn (9/07) Messina-a; Chekov app.; two art & one photo-c 4.00
... Orions (12/07) Casagrande-a; Capt. Pike app.; two art & one photo-c 4.00
... Q (8/09) Casagrande-a; takes place after Star Trek 8 movie; two art & one photo-c 4.00
... Romulans (2/08) John Byrne-s/a; Kirk era; two art & one photo-c 4.00
... Romulans (5/09) Wagner Reis-a; David Williams-c 4.00
... Tribbles (3/09) Hawthorne-a; first encounter with Klingons; one art & one photo-c 4.00
... Vulcans (10/07) Spock's early Enterprise days with Capt. Pike; two art & one photo-c 4.00

STAR TREK: ASSIGNMENT EARTH
IDW Publishing: May, 2008 - No. 5, Sept, 2008 ($3.99, limited series)

1-5-Further adventures of Gary Seven and Roberta; John Byrne-s/a/c. 5-Nixon app. 4.00

STAR TREK: BURDEN OF KNOWLEDGE

Star Trek: Deep Space Nine #4 © Paramount

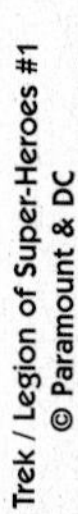

Star Trek / Legion of Super-Heroes #1 © Paramount & DC

Star Trek Movie Adaptation #6 © Paramount

GD 2.0	VG 4.0	FN 6.0	VF 8.0	VF/NM 9.0	NM- 9.2

IDW Publishing: Jun, 2010 - No. 4, Sept, 2010 ($3.99, limited series)
1-4-Original series Kirk and crew; Manfredi-a 4.00

STAR TREK: CAPTAIN'S LOG
IDW Publishing: one-shots
...: Harriman (4/10, $3.99) Captain of the Enterprise-B following Kirk's "demise"; Currie-a 4.00
...: Jellico (10/10, $3.99) Woodward-a 4.00
...: Pike (9/10, $3.99) Events that put Pike in the chair; Woodward-a 4.00
...: Sulu (1/10, $3.99) Manfredi-a 4.00

STAR TREK: COUNTDOWN (Prequel to the 2009 movie)
IDW Publishing: Jan, 2009 - No. 4, Apr, 2009 ($3.99, limited series)
1-4: 1-Ambassador Spock on Romulus; intro. Nero; Messina-a 4.00
Hundred Penny Press: Star Trek: Countdown #1 (4/11, $1.00) r/#1 w/new cover frame 3.00

STAR TREK: CREW
IDW Publishing: Mar, 2009 - No. 5, Jul, 2009 ($3.99, limited series)
1-5: John Byrne-s/a; Captain Pike era 4.00

STAR TREK: DEBT OF HONOR
DC Comics: 1992 ($24.95/$14.95, graphic novel)
Hardcover ($24.95) Claremont-s/Hughes-a(p) 25.00
Softcover ($14.95) 15.00

STAR TREK: DEEP SPACE NINE (TV)
Malibu Comics: Aug, 1993 - No. 32, Jan, 1996 ($2.50)
1-Direct Sale Edition w/line drawn-c 4.00
1-Newsstand Edition with photo-c 3.00
0-(1/95, $2.95)-Terok Nor 3.00
2-30: 2-Polybagged w/trading card. 9-4 pg. prelude to Hearts & Minds 3.00
31-($3.95) 4.00
32-($3.50) 4.00
Annual 1 (1/95, $3.95, 68 pgs.) 4.00
Special 1 (1995, $3.50) 4.00
Ultimate Annual 1 (12/95, $5.95) 6.00
...:Lightstorm (12/94, $3.50) 4.00

STAR TREK: DEEP SPACE NINE (TV)
Marvel Comics (Paramount Comics): Nov, 1996 - No. 15, Mar, 1998 ($1.95/$1.99)
1-15: 12,13-"Telepathy War" pt. 2,3 3.00

STAR TREK: DEEP SPACE NINE: FOOL'S GOLD
IDW Publishing: Dec, 2009 - No. 4, Mar, 2010 ($3.99)
1-4-Mantovani-a 4.00

STAR TREK: DEEP SPACE NINE -- N-VECTOR (TV)
DC Comics (WildStorm): Aug, 2000 - No. 4, Nov, 2000 ($2.50, limited series)
1-4-Cypress-a 3.00

STAR TREK DEEP SPACE NINE-THE CELEBRITY SERIES
Malibu Comics: May, 1995 ($2.95)
1-Blood and Honor; Mark Lenard script 3.00
1-Rules of Diplomacy; Aron Eisenberg script 3.00

STAR TREK: DEEP SPACE NINE HEARTS AND MINDS
Malibu Comics: June, 1994 - No. 4, Sept, 1994 ($2.50, limited series)
1-4 3.00
1-Holographic-c 4.00

STAR TREK: DEEP SPACE NINE, THE MAQUIS
Malibu Comics: Feb, 1995 - No. 3, Apr, 1995 ($2.50, limited series)
1-3-Newsstand-c, 1-Photo-c 3.00

STAR TREK: DEEP SPACE NINE/THE NEXT GENERATION
Malibu Comics: Oct, 1994 - No. 2, Nov, 1994 ($2.50, limited series)
1,2: Parts 2 & 4 of x-over with Star Trek: TNG/DS9 from DC Comics 3.00

STAR TREK: DEEP SPACE NINE WORF SPECIAL
Malibu Comics: Dec, 1995 ($3.95, one-shot)
1-Includes pinups 4.00

STAR TREK: DIVIDED WE FALL
DC Comics (WildStorm): July, 2001 - No. 4, Oct, 2001 ($2.95, limited series)
1-4: Ordover & Mack-s; Lenara Kahn, Verad and Odan app. 3.00

STAR TREK EARLY VOYAGES (TV)
Marvel Comics (Paramount Comics): Feb, 1997 - No. 17, Jun, 1998 ($2.95/$1.95/$1.99)
1-($2.95) 4.00
2-17 3.00

GD 2.0	VG 4.0	FN 6.0	VF 8.0	VF/NM 9.0	NM- 9.2

STAR TREK: ENTERPRISE EXPERIMENT
IDW Publishing: Apr, 2008 - No. 5, Aug, 2008 ($3.99, limited series)
1-5-Year Four story; D.C. Fontana & Derek Chester-s; Purcell-a 4.00

STAR TREK: FIRST CONTACT (Movie)
Marvel Comics (Paramount Comics): Nov, 1996 ($5.95, one-shot)
nn-Movie adaption 6.00

STAR TREK: INFESTATION (Crossover with G.I. Joe, Transformers & Ghostbusters)
IDW Publishing: Feb, 2011 - No. 2, Feb, 2011 ($3.99, limited series)
1,2-Zombies in the Kirk era; Maloney & Erskine-a; two covers on each 4.00

STAR TREK: KHAN RULING IN HELL
IDW Publishing: Oct, 2010 - No. 4, Jan, 2011 ($3.99, limited series)
1-4-Khan and the Botany Bay crew after banishment on Ceti Alpha V; Mantovani-a 4.00

STAR TREK: KLINGONS: BLOOD WILL TELL
IDW Publishing: Apr, 2007 - No. 5 ($3.99, limited series)
1-5-Star Trek TOS episodes from the Klingon viewpoint; Messina-a. 2-Tribbles 4.00
1-($4.99) Klingon Language Variant; comic with Kliingon text; English script 5.00

STAR TREK/ LEGION OF SUPER-HEROES
IDW Publishing: Oct, 2011 - No. 6 ($3.99, limited series)
1-6-Jeff Moy-a/Jimenez-c 1-Giffen var-c. 2-Lightle var-c. 3-Grell var-c. 5-Allred var-c 4.00

STAR TREK: LEONARD McCOY, FRONTIER DOCTOR
IDW Publishing: Apr, 2010 - No. 4, Jul, 2010 ($3.99, limited series)
1-4-Dr. McCoy right before Star Trek: TMP; John Byrne-s/a 4.00

STAR TREK: MIRROR IMAGES
IDW Publishing: June, 2008 - No. 5, Nov, 2008 ($3.99, limited series)
1-5-Further adventures in the Mirror Universe. 3-Mirror-Picard app. 4.00

STAR TREK: MIRROR MIRROR
Marvel Comics (Paramount Comics): Feb, 1997 ($3.95, one-shot)
1-DeFalco-s 4.00

STAR TREK: MISSION'S END
IDW Publishing: Mar, 2009 - No. 5, July, 2009 ($3.99, limited series)
1-5-Kirk, Spock, Bones crew, their last mission on the pre-movie Enterprise 4.00

STAR TREK MOVIE ADAPTATION
IDW Publishing: Feb, 2010 - No. 6, Aug, 2010 ($3.99, limited series)
1-6-Adaptation of 2009 movie; Messina-a; regular & photo-c on each 4.00

STAR TREK MOVIE SPECIAL
DC Comics: 1984 (June) - No. 2, 1987 ($1.50); No. 1, 1989 ($2.00, 52 pgs)
nn-(#1)-Adapts Star Trek III; Sutton-p (68 pgs.) 4.00
2-Adapts Star Trek IV; Sutton-a; Chaykin-c. (68 pgs.) 4.00
1 (1989)-Adapts Star Trek V; painted-c 4.00

STAR TREK: NERO
IDW Publishing: Aug, 2009 - No. 4, Nov, 2009 ($3.99, limited series)
1-4-Nero's ship after the attack on the Kelvin to the arrival of Spock 4.00

STAR TREK: NEW FRONTIER
IDW Publishing: Mar, 2008 - No. 5, July, 2008 ($3.99, limited series)
1-5-Capt. Calhoun & Adm. Shelby app.; Peter David-s 4.00

STAR TREK: OPERATION ASSIMILATION
Marvel Comics (Paramount Comics): Dec, 1996 ($2.95, one-shot)
1 4.00

STAR TREK: ROMULANS SCHISMS
IDW Publishing: Sept, 2009 - No. 3, Nov, 2009 ($3.99, limited series)
1-3-John Byrne-s/a/c 4.00

STAR TREK: ROMULANS THE HOLLOW CROWN
IDW Publishing: Sept, 2008 - No. 2, Oct, 2008 ($3.99, limited series)
1,2-John Byrne-s/a/c 4.00

STAR TREK VI: THE UNDISCOVERED COUNTRY (Movie)
DC Comics: 1992
1-($2.95, regular edition, 68 pgs.)-Adaptation of film 4.00
nn-($5.95, prestige edition)-Has photos of movie not included in regular edition; painted-c by Palmer; photo back-c 6.00

STAR TREK: SPOCK: REFLECTIONS
IDW Publishing: July, 2009 - No. 4, Oct, 2009 ($3.99, limited series)
1-4-Flashbacks of Spock's childhood and career; Messina & Manfredi-a 4.00

Star Trek: The Next Generation Annual #2 © Paramount

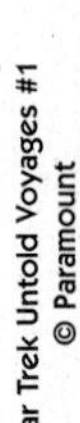

Star Trek Untold Voyages #1 © Paramount

Star Wars #65 © Lucasfilm

GD 2.0 | VG 4.0 | FN 6.0 | VF 8.0 | VF/NM 9.0 | NM- 9.2

GD 2.0 | VG 4.0 | FN 6.0 | VF 8.0 | VF/NM 9.0 | NM- 9.2

STAR TREK: STARFLEET ACADEMY
Marvel Comics (Paramount Comics): Dec, 1996 - No. 19, Jun, 1998 ($1.95/$1.99)

1-19: Begin new series. 12-"Telepathy War" pt. 1. 18-English & Klingon editions 3.00

STAR TREK: TELEPATHY WAR
Marvel Comics (Paramount Comics): Nov, 1997 ($2.99, 48 pgs., one-shot)

1-"Telepathy War" x-over pt. 6 4.00

STAR TREK - THE MODALA IMPERATIVE
DC Comics: Late July, 1991 - No. 4, Late Sept, 1991 ($1.75, limited series)

1-4 3.00
TPB ($19.95) r/series and ST:TNG - The Modala Imperative 20.00

STAR TREK: THE NEXT GENERATION (TV)
DC Comics: Feb, 1988 - No. 6, July, 1988 (limited series)

1 ($1.50, 52 pgs.)-Sienkiewicz painted-c 6.00
2-6 ($1.00) 4.00

STAR TREK: THE NEXT GENERATION (TV)
DC Comics: Oct, 1989 -No. 80, 1995 ($1.50/$1.75/$1.95)

1-Capt. Picard and crew from TV show 1 2 3 5 7 9
2,3 5.00
4-10 4.00
11-23,25-49,51-60 3.00
24,50: 24-($2.50, 52 pgs.). 50-($3.50, 68 pgs.)-Painted-c 5.00
61-74,76-80 3.00
75-($3.95, 50 pgs.) 4.00
Annual 1-6 ('90-'95, 68 pgs.) 4.00
Special 1 -3('93-'95, 68 pgs.)-1-Contains 3 stories 4.00
...-The Series Finale (1994, $3.95, 68 pgs.) 4.00

STAR TREK: THE NEXT GENERATION (TV)
DC Comics (WildStorm): one-shots

Embrace the Wolf (6/00, $5.95, prestige format) Golden & Sniegoski-s 6.00
Forgiveness (2001, $24.95, HC) David Brin-s/Scott Hampton painted-a; dust jacket-c 30.00
Forgiveness (2002, $17.95, SC) 18.00
The Gorn Crisis (1/01, $29.95, HC) Kordey painted-a/dust jacket-c 30.00
The Gorn Crisis (1/01, $17.95, SC) Kordey painted-a 18.00

STAR TREK: THE NEXT GENERATION/DEEP SPACE NINE (TV)
DC Comics: Dec, 1994 - No. 2, Jan, 1995 ($2.50, limited series)

1,2-Parts 1 & 3 of x-over with Star Trek: DS9/TNG from Malibu Comics 3.00

STAR TREK: THE NEXT GENERATION: GHOSTS
IDW Publishing: Nov, 2009 - No. 5, Mar, 2010 ($3.99)

1-5-Cannon-s/Aranda-a 4.00

STAR TREK: THE NEXT GENERATION - ILL WIND
DC Comics: Nov, 1995 - No. 4, Feb, 1996 ($2.50, limited series)

1-4: Hugh Fleming painted-c on all 3.00

STAR TREK: THE NEXT GENERATION: INTELLIGENCE GATHERING
IDW Publishing: Jan, 2008 - No. 5, May, 2008 ($3.99)

1-5-Messina-a/Scott & David Tipton-s; two covers on each 4.00

STAR TREK: THE NEXT GENERATION - PERCHANCE TO DREAM
DC Comics/WildStorm: Feb, 2000 - No. 4, May, 2000 ($2.50, limited series)

1-4-Bradstreet-c 3.00

STAR TREK: THE NEXT GENERATION - RIKER
Marvel Comics (Paramount Comics): July, 1998 ($3.50, one-shot)

1-Riker joins the Maquis 4.00

STAR TREK: THE NEXT GENERATION - SHADOWHEART
DC Comics: Dec, 1994 - No. 4, Mar, 1995 ($1.95, limited series)

1-4 3.00

STAR TREK: THE NEXT GENERATION - THE KILLING SHADOWS
DC Comics/WildStorm: Nov, 2000 - No. 4, Feb, 2001 ($2.50, limited series)

1-4-Scott Ciencin-s; Sela app. 3.00

STAR TREK: THE NEXT GENERATION: THE LAST GENERATION
IDW Publishing: Nov, 2008 - No. 5, Mar, 2009 ($3.99, limited series)

1-5-Purcell-a; alternate timeline with Klingon war; Sulu app. 4.00

STAR TREK: THE NEXT GENERATION - THE MODALA IMPERATIVE
DC Comics: Early Sept, 1991 - No. 4, Late Oct, 1991 ($1.75, limited series)

1-4 3.00

STAR TREK: THE NEXT GENERATION: THE SPACE BETWEEN
IDW Publishing: Jan, 2007 - No. 6, June, 2007 ($3.99)

1-6-Single issue stories from various seasons; photo & art covers 4.00

STAR TREK: THE WRATH OF KHAN
IDW Publishing: Jun, 2009 - No. 3, Jul, 2009 ($3.99, limited series)

1-3-Movie adaptation; Chee Yang Ong-a 4.00

STAR TREK UNLIMITED
Marvel Comics (Paramount Comics): Nov, 1996 - No. 10, July, 1998 ($2.95/$2.99)

1,2-Stories from original series and Next Generation 5.00
3-10: 3-Begin $2.99-c. 6-"Telepathy War" pt. 4. 7-Q & Trelane swap Kirk & Picard 4.00

STAR TREK UNTOLD VOYAGES
Marvel Comics (Paramount Comics): May, 1998 - No. 5, July, 1998 ($2.50)

1-5-Kirk's crew after the 1st movie 3.00

STAR TREK: VOYAGER
Marvel Comics (Paramount Comics): Nov, 1996 - No. 15, Mar, 1998 ($1.95/$1.99)

1-15: 13-"Telepathy War" pt. 5. 14-Seven of Nine joins crew 3.00

STAR TREK: VOYAGER
DC Comics/WildStorm: one-shots and trade paperbacks

- Elite Force (7/00, $5.95) The Borg app.; Abnett & Lanning-s 6.00
... Encounters With the Unknown TPB (2001, $19.95) reprints 20.00
- False Colors (1/00, $5.95) Photo-c and Jim Lee-c; Jeff Moy-a 6.00

STAR TREK: VOYAGER-- THE PLANET KILLER
DC Comics/WildStorm: Mar, 2001 - No. 3, May, 2001 ($2.95, limited series)

1-3-Voyager vs. the Planet Killer from the ST:TOS episode; Teranishi-a 3.00

STAR TREK: VOYAGER SPLASHDOWN
Marvel Comics (Paramount Comics): Apr, 1998 - No. 4, July, 1998 ($2.50, limited series)

1-4-Voyager crashes on a water planet 3.00

STAR TREK/ X-MEN
Marvel Comics (Paramount Comics): Dec, 1996 ($4.99, one-shot)

1-Kirk's crew & X-Men; art by Silvestri, Tan, Winn & Finch; Lobdell-s 5.00

STAR TREK/ X-MEN: 2ND CONTACT
Marvel Comics (Paramount Comics): May, 1998 ($4.99, 64 pgs., one-shot)

1-Next Gen. crew & X-Men battle Kang, Sentinels & Borg following First Contact movie 5.00
1-Painted wraparound variant cover 5.00

STAR TREK: YEAR FOUR (Also see Star Trek: Enterprise Experiment)
IDW Publishing: July, 2007 - No. 5, Nov, 2007 ($3.99, limited series)

1-5: 1-Original series crew; Tischman-s/Conley-a; three covers on each 4.00

STAR WARS (Movie) (See Classic..., Contemporary Motivators, Dark Horse Comics, The Droids, The Ewoks, Marvel Movie Showcase, Marvel Special Ed.)
Marvel Comics Group: July, 1977 - No. 107, Sept, 1986

1-(Regular 30¢ edition)-Price in square w/UPC code; #1-6 adapt first movie; first issue on sale before movie debuted 7 14 21 48 79 110
1-(35¢-c; limited distribution - 1500 copies?)- Price in square w/UPC code (Prices vary widely on this book. In 2005 a CGC certified 9.4 sold for $6,500, a CGC certified 9.2 sold for $3,403, and a CGC certified 6.0 sold for $610) 130 260 390 1053 2277 3500

NOTE: *The rare 35¢ edition has the cover price in a square box, and the UPC box in the lower left hand corner has the UPC code lines running through it.*

2-4-(30¢ issues). 4-Battle with Darth Vader 4 8 12 24 37 50
2-4-(35¢ with UPC code; not reprints) 15 30 45 104 227 350
5,6: 5-Begin 35¢-c on all editions. 6-Stevens-a(i). 3 6 9 16 22 28
7-20 2 4 6 9 13 16
21-70: 39-44-The Empire Strikes Back-r by Al Williamson in all. 50-Giant. 68-Reintro Boba Fett. 2 4 6 8 10 12
71-80 2 4 6 8 11 14
81-90: 81-Boba Fett app. 2 4 6 9 13 16
91,93-99: 98-Williamson-a. 2 4 6 11 16 20
92,100-106: 92,100-($1.00, 52 pgs.). 3 6 9 14 20 26
107(low dist.); Portacio-a(i) 6 12 18 39 62 85
1-9: Reprints; has "reprint" in upper lefthand corner of cover or on inside or price and number inside a diamond with no date or UPC on cover; 30¢ and 35¢ issues published 4.00
Annual 1 (12/79, 52 pgs.)-Simonson-c 2 4 6 8 11 14
Annual 2 (11/82, 52 pgs.), 3(12/83, 52 pgs.) 2 4 6 8 10 12
... A Long Time Ago...Vol. 1 TPB (Dark Horse Comics, 6/02, $29.95) r/#1-14 30.00
... A Long Time Ago...Vol. 2 TPB (Dark Horse Comics, 7/02, $29.95) r/#15-28 30.00
... A Long Time Ago...Vol. 3 TPB (Dark Horse Comics, 11/02, $29.95) r/#39-53 30.00
... A Long Time Ago...Vol. 4 TPB (Dark Horse Comics, 1/03, $29.95) r/#54-67 & Ann. 2 30.00

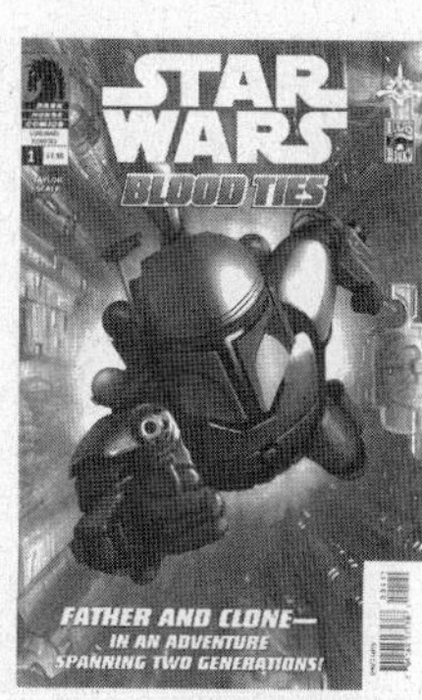

Star Wars: Blood Ties #1 © Lucasfilm

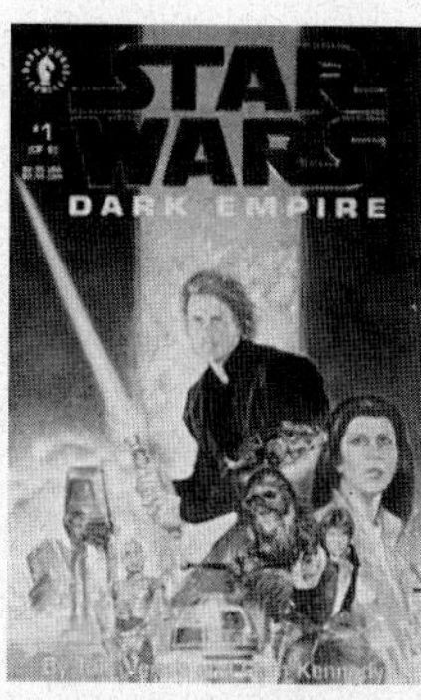

Star Wars Dark Empire #1 © Lucasfilm

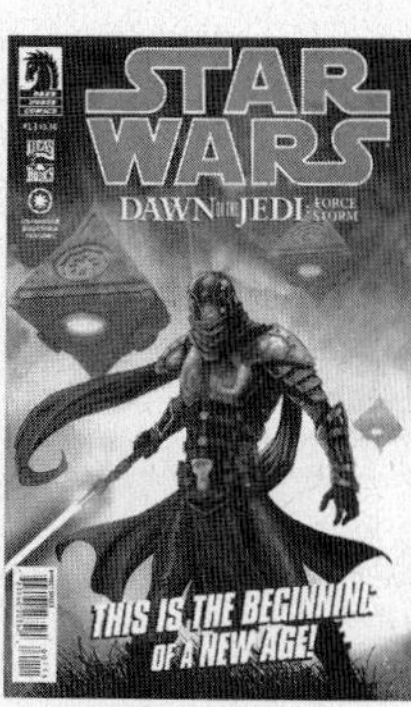

Star Wars: Dawn of the Jedi #1 © Lucasfilm

GD 2.0 | VG 4.0 | FN 6.0 | VF 8.0 | VF/NM 9.0 | NM- 9.2

... A Long Time Ago...Vol. 5 TPB (Dark Horse Comics, 3/03, $29.95) r/#68-81 & Ann. 3 — 30.00
... A Long Time Ago...Vol. 6 TPB (Dark Horse Comics, 5/03, $29.95) r/#82-93 — 30.00
... A Long Time Ago...Vol. 7 TPB (Dark Horse Comics, 6/03, $29.95) r/#96-107 — 30.00

__Austin__ a-11-15i, 21i, 38; c-12-15i, 21i. __Byrne__ c-13p. __Chaykin__ a-1-10p; c-1. __Golden__ c/a-38. __Miller__ c-47p; pin-up-43. __Nebres__ c/a-Annual 2i. __Portacio__ a-107i. __Sienkiewicz__ c-92i, 98. __Simonson__ a-16p, 49p, 51-63p, 65p, 66p; c-16, 49-51, 52p, 53-62, Annual 1. __Steacy__ painted a-105i, 106i; c-105. __Williamson__ a-39-44p, 50p, 98; c-39, 40, 41-44p. Painted c-81, 87, 92, 95, 98, 100, 105.

STAR WARS (Monthly series) (Becomes Star Wars Republic #46-on)
Dark Horse Comics: Dec, 1998 - No. 45, Aug, 2005 ($2.50/$2.95/$2.99)

1-45: 1-6-Prelude To Rebellion; Strnad-s. 4-Brereton-c. 7-12-Outlander. 13,17-18-($2.95). 13-18-Emissaries to Malastare; Truman-s. 14-16-($2.50) Schultz-c. 19-22-Twilight; Duursema-a. 23-26-Infinity's End. 42-45-Rite of Passage — 3.00
5,6 (Holochrome-c variants) — 6.00
#0 Another Universe.com Ed.($10.00) r/serialized pages from Pizzazz Magazine; new Dorman painted-c — 10.00
... A Valentine Story (2/03, $3.50) Leia & Han Solo on Hoth; Winick-s/Chadwick-a/c — 3.50
...: Rite of Passage (2004, $12.95) r/#42-45 — 13.00
...: The Stark Hyperspace War (903, $12.95) r/#36-39 — 13.00

STAR WARS
Dark Horse Comics (Free Comic Book Day giveaways)

...: Clone Wars #0 (5/09) flip book with short stories of Usagi Yojimbo, Emily the Strange — 3.00
...: Clone Wars Adventures (7/04) based on Cartoon Network series; Fillbach Bros. -a — 3.00
...: FCBD 2005 Special (5/05) Anakin & Obi-Wan during Clone Wars — 3.00
...: FCBD 2006 Special (5/06) Clone Wars story; flip book with Conan FCBD Special — 3.00
...: Tales - A Jedi's Weapon (5/02, 16 pgs.) Anakin Skywalker Episode 2 photo-c — 3.00
Free Comic Book Day and Star Wars: The Clone Wars (5/11) flip book with Avatar: The Last Airbender — 3.00

STAR WARS: AGENT OF THE EMPIRE - IRON ECLIPSE
Dark Horse Comics: Dec, 2011 - No. 5 ($3.50, limited series)

1-4: 1-Ostrander-s/Roux-a; Han Solo & Chewbacca app. — 3.50

STAR WARS: A NEW HOPE - THE SPECIAL EDITION
Dark Horse Comics: Jan, 1997 - No. 4, Apr, 1997 ($2.95, limited series)

1-4-Dorman-c — 4.00

STAR WARS: BLOOD TIES: JANGO AND BOBA FETT
Dark Horse Comics: Aug, 2010 - No. 4, Nov, 2010 ($3.50, limited series)

1-4-Scalf painted-a/c — 3.50

STAR WARS: BOBA FETT
Dark Horse Comics: Dec, 1995 - No. 3, Aug, 1997 ($3.95) (Originally intended as a one-shot)

1-Kennedy-c/a — 6.00
2,3 — 5.00
Death, Lies, & Treachery TPB (1/98, $12.95) r/#1-3 — 13.00
... - Agent of Doom (11/00, $2.99) Ostrander-s/Cam Kennedy-a — 3.00
... - Overkill (3/06, $2.99) Hughes-c/Andrews-s/Velasco-a — 3.00
Twin Engines of Destruction (1/97, $2.95) — 4.00

STAR WARS: BOBA FETT: ENEMY OF THE EMPIRE
Dark Horse Comics: Jan, 1999 - No. 4, Apr, 1999 ($2.95, limited series)

1-4-Recalls 1st meeting of Fett and Vader — 3.00

STAR WARS: CHEWBACCA
Dark Horse Comics: Jan, 2000 - No. 4, Apr, 2000 ($2.95, limited series)

1-4-Macan-s/art by various incl. Anderson, Kordey, Gibbons; Phillips-c — 3.00

STAR WARS: CLONE WARS ADVENTURES
Dark Horse Comics: 2004 - No. 10, 2007 ($6.95, digest-sized)

1-10-Short stories inspired by Clone Wars animated series — 7.00

STAR WARS: CRIMSON EMPIRE
Dark Horse Comics: Dec, 1997 - No. 6, May, 1998 ($2.95, limited series)

1-Richardson-s/Gulacy-a — 1 2 3 4 5 7
2-6 — 5.00

STAR WARS: CRIMSON EMPIRE II: COUNCIL OF BLOOD
Dark Horse Comics: Nov, 1998 - No. 6, Apr, 1999 ($2.95, limited series)

1-6-Richardson & Stradley-s/Gulacy-a — 3.00

STAR WARS: CRIMSON EMPIRE III: EMPIRE LOST
Dark Horse Comics: Oct, 2011 - No. 6 ($3.50, limited series)

1-5: 1-Richardson-s/Gulacy-a/Dorman-c — 3.50

STAR WARS: DARK EMPIRE
Dark Horse Comics: Dec, 1991 - No. 6, Oct, 1992 ($2.95, limited series)

Preview-(99¢) — 3.00
1-All have Dorman painted-c — 1 2 3 5 7 9
1-3-2nd printing — 4.00
2-Low print run — 2 4 6 8 10 12
3 — 6.00
4-6 — 4.00
Gold Embossed Set (#1-6)-With gold embossed foil logo (price is for set) — 90.00
Platinum Embossed Set (#1-6) — 120.00
Trade paperback (4/93, 16.95) — 17.00
Dark Empire 1 - TPB 3rd printing (2003, $16.95) — 17.00
Ltd. Ed. Hardcover ($99.95) Signed & numbered — 100.00

STAR WARS: DARK EMPIRE II
Dark Horse Comics: Dec, 1994 - No. 6, May, 1995 ($2.95, limited series)

1-Dave Dorman painted-c — 5.00
2-6: Dorman-c in all. — 4.00
Platinum Embossed Set (#1-6) — 35.00
Trade paperback ($17.95) — 18.00
TPB Second Edition (9/06, $19.95) r/#1-6 and Star Wars: Empire's End #1,2 — 20.00

STAR WARS: DARK FORCE RISING
Dark Horse Comics: May, 1997 - No. 6, Oct, 1997 ($2.95, limited series)

1-6 — 4.00
TPB (2/98, $17.95) r/#1-6 — 18.00

STAR WARS: DARK TIMES (Continued from Star Wars Republic #84)(Continues in Star Wars: Rebellion #15)
Dark Horse Comics: Oct, 2006 - No. 17, Jun, 2010 ($2.99)

1-17-Nineteen years before Episode IV; Doug Wheatley-a. 11-Celeste Morne awakens 13-17-Blue Harvest — 3.00
#0-(7/09, $2.99) Prologue to Blue Harvest — 3.00
... Volume 1: The Path To Nowhere (1/08, $17.95, TPB) r/#1-5 — 18.00

STAR WARS: DARK TIMES - OUT OF THE WILDERNESS
Dark Horse Comics: Aug, 2011 - No. 5 ($2.99, limited series)

1-4-Doug Wheatley-a — 3.00

STAR WARS: DARTH MAUL
Dark Horse Comics: Sept, 2000 - No. 4, Dec, 2000 ($2.95, limited series)

1-4-Photo-c and Struzan painted-c; takes place 6 months before Ep. 1 — 3.00

STAR WARS: DARTH VADER AND THE LOST COMMAND
Dark Horse Comics: Jan, 2011 - No. 5, May, 2011 ($3.50, limited series)

1-5-Blackman-s/Leonardi-a/Sanda-c. 1-Variant-c by Wheatley — 3.50

STAR WARS: DAWN OF THE JEDI
Dark Horse Comics: No. 0, Feb, 2012 - Present ($3.50)

0-Guide to the worlds, characters, sites, vehicles; Migliari-c — 3.50
1,2-Ostrander-s/Duursema-a/c — 3.50

STAR WARS: DROIDS (See Dark Horse Comics #17-19)
Dark Horse Comics: Apr, 1994 - #6, Sept, 1994; V2#1, Apr, 1995 - V2#8, Dec, 1995 ($2.50, limited series)

1-($2.95)-Embossed-c — 5.00
2-6 , Special 1 (1/95, $2.50), V2#1-8 — 4.00
Star Wars Omnibus: Droids One TPB (6/08, $24.95) r/#1-6, Special 1, V2#1-8, Star Wars: The Protocol Offensive and "Artoo's Day Out" story from Star Wars Galaxy Magazine #1 — 25.00

STAR WARS: EMPIRE
Dark Horse Comics: Sept, 2002 - No. 40, Feb, 2006 ($2.99)

1-40: 1-Benjamin-a; takes place weeks before SW: A New Hope. 7,28-Boba Fett-c. 14-Vader after the destruction of the Death Star. 15-Death of Biggs; Wheatley-a — 3.00
... Volume 1 (2003, $12.95, TPB) r/#1-4 — 13.00
... Volume 2 (2004, $17.95, TPB) r/#8-12,15 — 18.00
... Volume 3: The Imperial Perspective (2004, $17.95, TPB) r/#13,14,16-19 — 18.00
... Volume 4: The Heart of the Rebellion (2005, $17.95, TPB) r/#5,6,20-22 & Star Wars: A Valentine Story — 18.00
... Volume 5 (2006, $14.95, TPB) r/#23-27 — 18.00
... Volume 6: In the Shadows of Their Fathers (10/06, $17.95, TPB) r/#29-34 — 18.00
... Volume 7: The Wrong Side of the War (1/07, $17.95, TPB) r/#34-40 — 18.00

STAR WARS: EMPIRE'S END
Dark Horse Comics: Oct, 1995 - No. 2, Nov, 1995 ($2.95, limited series)

1,2-Dorman-c — 4.00

STAR WARS: EPISODE 1 THE PHANTOM MENACE
Dark Horse Comics: May, 1999 - No. 4 ($2.95, movie adaptation)

1-4-Regular and photo-c; Damaggio & Williamson-a — 3.00
TPB ($12.95) r/#1-4 — 13.00

Star Wars: Episode II #1 © Lucasfilm

Star Wars: Legacy #50 © Lucasfilm

Star Wars: Mara Jade #4 © Lucasfilm

	GD 2.0	VG 4.0	FN 6.0	VF 8.0	VF/NM 9.0	NM- 9.2

...Anakin Skywalker-Photo-c & Bradstreet-c, ...Obi-Wan Kenobi-Photo-c & Egeland-c,
...Queen Amidala-Photo-c & Bradstreet-c, ...Qui-Gon Jinn-Photo-c & Bradstreet-c 3.00
Gold foil covers; Wizard 1/2 10.00

STAR WARS: EPISODE II - ATTACK OF THE CLONES
Dark Horse Comics: Apr, 2002 - No. 4, May, 2002 ($3.99, movie adaptation)
1-4-Regular and photo-c; Duursema-a 4.00
TPB ($17.95) r/#1-4; Struzan-c 18.00

STAR WARS: EPISODE III - REVENGE OF THE SITH
Dark Horse Comics: May, 2005 - No. 4, May, 2005 ($2.99, movie adaptation)
1-4-Wheatley-a/Dorman-c 3.00
TPB ($12.95) r/#1-4; Dorman-c 13.00

STAR WARS: GENERAL GRIEVOUS
Dark Horse Comics: Mar, 2005 - No. 4, June, 2005 ($2.99, limited series)
1-4-Leonardi-a/Dixon-s 3.00
TPB (2005, $12.95) r/#1-4 13.00

STAR WARS HANDBOOK
Dark Horse Comics: July, 1998 - Present ($2.95, one-shots)
...X-Wing Rogue Squadron (7/98)-Guidebook to characters and spacecraft 3.00
...Crimson Empire (7/99) Dorman-c 3.00
...Dark Empire (3/00) Dorman-c 3.00

STAR WARS: HEIR TO THE EMPIRE
Dark Horse Comics: Oct, 1995 - No.6, Apr, 1996 ($2.95, limited series)
1-6: Adaptation of Zahn novel 4.00

STAR WARS: INFINITIES - A NEW HOPE
Dark Horse Comics: May, 2001 - No. 4, Oct, 2001 ($2.99, limited series)
1-4: "What If..." the Death Star wasn't destroyed in Episode 4 3.00
TPB (2002, $12.95) r/ #1-4 13.00

STAR WARS: INFINITIES - THE EMPIRE STRIKES BACK
Dark Horse Comics: July, 2002 - No. 4, Oct, 2002 ($2.99, limited series)
1-4: "What If..." Luke died on the ice planet Hoth; Bachalo-c 3.00
TPB (2/03, $12.95) r/ #1-4 13.00

STAR WARS: INFINITIES - RETURN OF THE JEDI
Dark Horse Comics: Nov, 2003 - No. 4, Mar, 2004 ($2.99, limited series)
1-4:"What If..." ; Benjamin-a 3.00

STAR WARS: INVASION
Dark Horse Comics: July, 2009 - Present ($2.99)
1-5-Jo Chen-c 3.00
#0-(10/09, $3.50) Dorman-c; Han Solo and Chewbacca app. 3.50
... - Rescues 1-6 (5/10 - No. 6, 12/10) Chen-c 3.00
... - Revelations 1-5 (7/11 - No. 5, 11/11, $3.50) Luke Skywalker app.; Scalf-c 3.50

STAR WARS: JABBA THE HUTT
Dark Horse Comics: Apr, 1995 ($2.50, one-shots)
nn, ...The Betrayal, ...The Dynasty Trap, ...The Hunger of Princess Nampi 4.00

STAR WARS: JANGO FETT - OPEN SEASONS
Dark Horse Comics: Apr, 2002 - No. 4, July, 2002 ($2.99, limited series)
1-4: 1-Bachs & Fernandez-a 3.00

STAR WARS: JEDI
Dark Horse Comics: Feb, 2003 - Jun, 2004 ($4.99, one-shots)
... - Aayla Secura (8/03) Ostrander-s/Duursema-a 5.00
... - Count Dooku (11/03) Duursema-a 5.00
... - Mace Windu (2/03) Duursema-a 5.00
... - Shaak Ti (5/03) Ostrander-s/Duursema-a 5.00
... - Yoda (6/04) Barlow-s/Hoon-a 5.00

STAR WARS: JEDI ACADEMY - LEVIATHAN
Dark Horse Comics: Oct, 1998 - No. 4, Jan, 1999 ($2.95, limited series)
1-4: 1-Lago-c. 2-4-Chadwick-c 3.00

STAR WARS: JEDI COUNCIL: ACTS OF WAR
Dark Horse Comics: Jun, 2000 - No. 4, Sept, 2000 ($2.95, limited series)
1-4-Stradley-s; set one year before Episode 1 3.00

STAR WARS: JEDI QUEST
Dark Horse Comics: Sept, 2001 - No. 4, Dec, 2001 ($2.99, limited series)
1-4-Anakin's Jedi training; Windham-s/Mhan-a 3.00

STAR WARS: JEDI - THE DARK SIDE
Dark Horse Comics: May, 2011 - No. 5, Sept, 2011 ($2.99, limited series)
1-5: 1-Qui-Gon Jinn 21 years befor Episode 1; Asrar-a 3.00

STAR WARS: JEDI VS. SITH
Dark Horse Comics: Apr, 2001 - No. 6, Sept, 2001 ($2.99, limited series)
1-6: Macan-s/Bachs-a/Robinson-c 3.00

STAR WARS: KNIGHT ERRANT
Dark Horse Comics: Oct, 2010 - No. 5, Feb, 2011 ($2.99)
1-5: 1-John Jackson Miller-s/Federico Dallocchio-a 3.00
... - Deluge 1-5 (8/11 - No. 5 12/11, $3.50) 1-Miller-s/Rodriguez-a/Quinones-c 3.50

STAR WARS: KNIGHTS OF THE OLD REPUBLIC
Dark Horse Comics: Jan, 2006 - No. 50, Feb, 2010 ($2.99)
1-50-Takes place 3,964 years before Episode IV. 1-6-Brian Ching-a/Travis Charest-c 3.00
... Handbook (11/07, $2.99) profiles of characters, ships, locales 3.00
.../Rebellion #0 (3/06, 25¢) flip book preview of both series 3.00
... - War 1-3 (1/12 - No. 5, $3.50) J.J. Miller-s/Mutti-a 3.50
... Vol. 1 Commencement TPB (11/06, $18.95) r/#0-6 19.00
... Vol. 2 Flashpoint TPB (5/07, $18.95) r/#17-12 19.00
... Vol. 3 Days of Fear, Nights of Anger TPB (1/08, $18.95) r/#13-18 19.00

STAR WARS: LEGACY
Dark Horse Comics: No. 0, June, 2006 - No. 50, Aug, 2010 ($2.99)
0-(25¢) Dossier of characters, settings, ships and weapons; Duursema-c 3.00
0 1/2-(1/08, $2.99) Updated dossier of characters, settings, ships, and history 3.00
1-50: 1-Takes place 130 years after Episode IV; Hughes-c/Duursema-a. 4-Duursema-c
7,39-Luke Skywalker on-c. 16-Obi-Wan Kenobi app. 50-Wraparound-c 3.00
...: Broken Vol. 1 TPB (4/07, $17.95) r/#1-3,5,6 18.00
...: One for One (9/10, $1.00) reprints #1 with red cover frame 3.00
... War 1-6 (12/10 - No. 6, 5/11, $3.50) 1-Ostrander-s/Duursema-a; Darth Krayt app. 3.50

STAR WARS: MARA JADE
Dark Horse Comics: Aug, 1998 - No. 6, Jan, 1999 ($2.95, limited series)
1-6-Ezquerra-a 3.00

STAR WARS: OBSESSION (Clone Wars)
Dark Horse Comics: Nov, 2004 - No. 5, Apr, 2005 ($2.99, limited series)
1-5-Blackman-s/Ching-a/c; Anakin & Obi-Wan 5 months before Episode III 3.00
...: Clone Wars Vol. 7 (2005, $17.95) r/#1-5 and 2005 Free Comic Book Day edition 18.00

STAR WARS: PURGE
Dark Horse Comics: Dec, 2005 ($2.99, one-shot)
nn-Vader vs. remaining Jedi one month after Episode III; Hughes-c/Wheatley-a 5.00
... - Seconds To Die (11/09, $3.50) Vader app.; Charest-c/Ostrander-s 3.50
... - The Hidden Blade (4/10, $3.50) Vader app.; Scalf-c/a; Blackman-s 3.50

STAR WARS: QUI-GON & OBI-WAN - LAST STAND ON ORD MANTELL
Dark Horse Comics: Dec, 2000 - No. 3, Mar, 2001 ($2.99, limited series)
1-3: 1-Three covers (photo, Tony Daniel, Bachs) Windham-s 3.00

STAR WARS: QUI-GON & OBI-WAN - THE AURORIENT EXPRESS
Dark Horse Comics: Feb, 2002 - No. 2, Mar, 2002 ($2.99, limited series)
1,2-Six years prior to Phantom Menace; Marangon-a 3.00

STAR WARS: REBELLION (Also see Star Wars: Knights of the Old Republic flip book)
Dark Horse Comics: Apr, 2006 - Present ($2.99)
1-16-Takes place 9 months after Episode IV; Luke Skywalker app. 1-Badeaux-a/c 3.00
Vol. 1 TPB (2/07, $14.95) r/#0 (flip book) & #1-5 15.00

STAR WARS: REPUBLIC (Formerly Star Wars monthly series)
Dark Horse Comics: No. 46, Sept, 2002 - No. 83, Feb, 2006 ($2.99)
46-83-Events of the Clone Wars 3.00
...: Clone Wars Vol. 1 (2003, $14.95) r/#46-50 15.00
...: Clone Wars Vol. 2 (2003, $14.95) r/#51-53 & Star Wars: Jedi - Shaak Ti 15.00
...: Clone Wars Vol. 3 (2004, $14.95) r/#55-59 15.00
...: Clone Wars Vol. 4 (2004, $16.95) r/#54, 63 & Star Wars: Jedi - Aayla Secura & Dooku 17.00
...: Clone Wars Vol. 5 (2004, $17.95) r/#60-62, 64 & Star Wars: Jedi - Yoda 18.00
...: Clone Wars Vol. 6 (2005, $17.95) r/#65-71 18.00
(Clone Wars Vol. 7 - see Star Wars: Obsession)
...: Clone Wars Vol. 8 (2006, $17.95) r/#72-78 18.00
...: Clone Wars Vol. 9 (2006, $17.95) r/#79-83 & Star Wars: Purge 18.00
...: Honor and Duty TPB (5/06, $12.95) r/#46-48,78 13.00

STAR WARS: RETURN OF THE JEDI (Movie)
Marvel Comics Group: Oct, 1983 - No. 4, Jan, 1984 (limited series)

	GD 2.0	VG 4.0	FN 6.0	VF 8.0	VF/NM 9.0	NM- 9.2
1-Williamson-p in all; r/Marvel Super Special #27	2	4	6	9	12	15
2-4-Continues r/Marvel Super Special #27	2	4	6	8	10	12

Oversized issue (1983, $2.95, 10-3/4x8-1/4", 68 pgs., cardboard-c)-r/#1-4

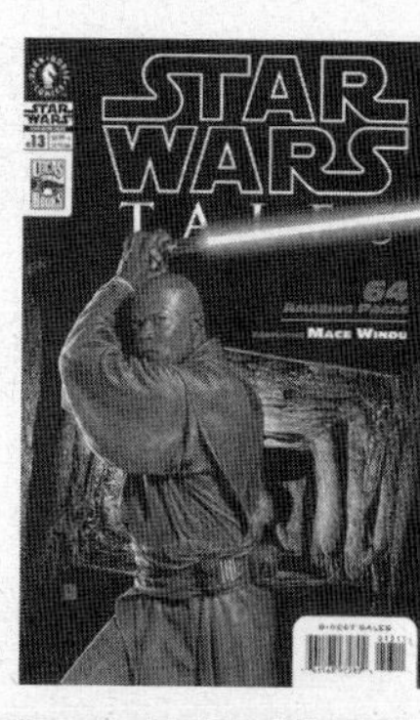

Star Wars Tales #13 © Lucasfilm

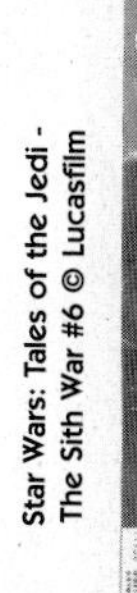
Star Wars: Tales of the Jedi - The Sith War #6 © Lucasfilm

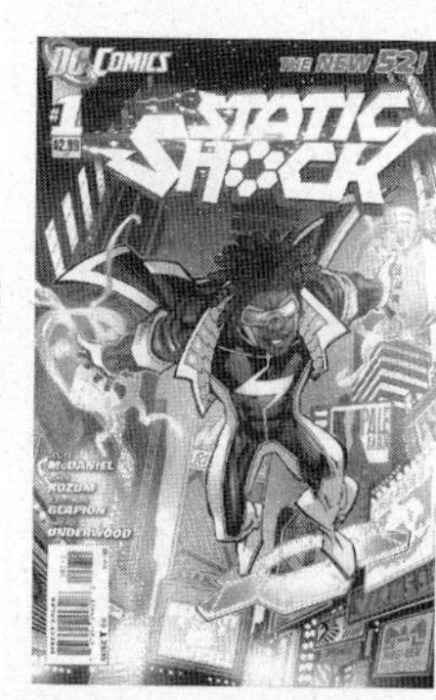

Static Shock (2011 series) #1 © Milestone

GD VG FN VF VF/NM NM-
2.0 4.0 6.0 8.0 9.0 9.2

GD VG FN VF VF/NM NM-
2.0 4.0 6.0 8.0 9.0 9.2

2 4 6 10 13 16

STAR WARS: RIVER OF CHAOS
Dark Horse Comics: June, 1995 - No. 4, Sept, 1995 ($2.95, limited series)
1-4: Louise Simonson scripts 4.00

STAR WARS: SHADOWS OF THE EMPIRE
Dark Horse Comics: May, 1996 - No. 6, Oct, 1996 ($2.95, limited series)
1-6: Story details events between The Empire Strikes Back & Return of the Jedi; Russell-a(i). 4.00

STAR WARS: SHADOWS OF THE EMPIRE - EVOLUTION
Dark Horse Comics: Feb, 1998 - No. 5, June, 1998 ($2.95, limited series)
1-5: Perry-s/Fegredo-c. 3.00

STAR WARS: SHADOW STALKER
Dark Horse Comics: Sept, 1997 ($2.95, one-shot)
nn-Windham-a. 4.00

STAR WARS: SPLINTER OF THE MIND'S EYE
Dark Horse Comics: Dec, 1995 - No. 4, June, 1996 ($2.50, limited series)
1-4: Adaption of Alan Dean Foster novel 4.00

STAR WARS: STARFIGHTER
Dark Horse Comics: Jan, 2002 - No. 3, March, 2002 ($2.99, limited series)
1-3-Williams & Gray-c 3.00

STAR WARS: TAG & BINK ARE DEAD
Dark Horse Comics: Oct, 2001 - No. 2, Nov, 2001($2.99, limited series)
1,2-Rubio-s 3.00
Star Wars: Tag & Bink Were Here TPB (11/06, $14.95) r/both SW: Tag & Bink series 15.00

STAR WARS: TAG & BINK II
Dark Horse Comics: Mar, 2006 - No. 2, Apr, 2006($2.99, limited series)
1-Tag & Bink invade Return of the Jedi; Rubio-s. 2-Tag & Bink as Jedi younglings during Ep II 3.00

STAR WARS TALES
Dark Horse Comics: Sept, 1999 - No. 24, Jun, 2005 ($4.95/$5.95/$5.99, anthology)
1-4-Short stories by various 6.00
5-24 ($5.95/$5.99-c) Art and photo-c on each 6.00
Volume 1-6 ($19.95) 1-(1/02) r/#1-4. 2-('02) r/#5-8. 3-(1/03) r/#9-12. 4-(1/04) r/#13-16 5-(1/05) r/#17-20; introduction pages from #1-20. 6-(1/06) r/#21-24 20.00

STAR WARS: TALES FROM MOS EISLEY
Dark Horse Comics: Mar, 1996 ($2.95, one-shot)
nn-Bret Blevins-a. 4.00

STAR WARS: TALES OF THE JEDI (See Dark Horse Comics #7)
Dark Horse Comics: Oct, 1993 - No. 5, Feb, 1994 ($2.50, limited series)
1-5: All have Dave Dorman painted-c. 3-r/Dark Horse Comics #7-9 w/new coloring & some panels redrawn 5.00
1-5-Gold foil embossed logo; limited # printed-7500 (set) 50.00
Star Wars Omnibus: Tales of the Jedi Volume One TPB (11/07, $24.95) r/#1-5, ... - The Golden Age of the Sith #0-5 and ... - The Fall of the Sith Empire #1-5 25.00

STAR WARS: TALES OF THE JEDI-DARK LORDS OF THE SITH
Dark Horse Comics: Oct, 1994 - No. 6, Mar, 1995 ($2.50, limited series)
1-6: 1-Polybagged w/trading card 4.00

STAR WARS: TALES OF THE JEDI-REDEMPTION
Dark Horse Comics: July, 1998 - No. 5, Nov, 1998 ($2.95, limited series)
1-5: 1-Kevin J. Anderson-s/Kordey-c 3.00

STAR WARS: TALES OF THE JEDI-THE FALL OF THE SITH EMPIRE
Dark Horse Comics: June, 1997 - No. 5, Oct, 1997 ($2.95, limited series)
1-5 4.00

STAR WARS: TALES OF THE JEDI-THE FREEDON NADD UPRISING
Dark Horse Comics: Aug, 1994 - No. 2, Nov, 1994 ($2.50, limited series)
1,2 4.00

STAR WARS: TALES OF THE JEDI-THE GOLDEN AGE OF THE SITH
Dark Horse Comics: July, 1996 - No. 5, Feb, 1997 (99¢/$2.95, limited series)
0-(99¢)-Anderson-s 3.00
1-5-Anderson-s 4.00

STAR WARS: TALES OF THE JEDI-THE SITH WAR
Dark Horse Comics: Aug, 1995 - No. 6, Jan, 1996 ($2.50, limited series)
1-6: Anderson scripts 4.00

STAR WARS: THE BOUNTY HUNTERS
Dark Horse Comics: July, 1999 - Oct, 1999 ($2.95, one-shots)
...Aurra Sing (7/99), ...Kenix Kil (10/99), ...Scoundrel's Wages (8/99) Lando Calrissian app. 3.00

STAR WARS: THE CLONE WARS (Based on the Cartoon Network series)
Dark Horse Comics: Sept, 2008 - No. 12, Jan, 2010 ($2.99)
1-12: 1-6-Gilroy-s/Hepburn-a/Filoni-c 3.00

STAR WARS: THE FORCE UNLEASHED (Based on the LucasArts video game)
Dark Horse Comics: Aug, 2008 ($15.95, one-shot graphic novel)
GN-Intro. Starkiller, Vader's apprentice; takes place 2 years before Battle of Yavin 16.00

STAR WARS: THE JABBA TAPE
Dark Horse Comics: Dec, 1998 ($2.95, one-shot)
nn-Wagner-s/Plunkett-a 3.00

STAR WARS: THE LAST COMMAND
Dark Horse Comics: Nov, 1997 - No. 6, July, 1998 ($2.95, limited series)
1-6: Based on the Timothy Zaun novel 4.00

STAR WARS: THE OLD REPUBLIC (Based on the video game)
Dark Horse Comics: July, 2010 - No. 6, Dec, 2010 ($2.99, limited series)
1-3 (Threat of Peace)-Chestny-s/Sanchez-a. 1-Two covers 3.00
4-6 (Blood of the Empire)-Freed-s/Dave Ross-a 3.00

STAR WARS: THE OLD REPUBLIC - THE LOST SUNS (Based on the video game)
Dark Horse Comics: Jun, 2011 - No. 5, Oct, 2011 ($3.50, limited series)
1-5-Freed-s/Carré-c/Freeman-a 3.50

STAR WARS: THE PROTOCOL OFFENSIVE
Dark Horse Comics: Sept, 1997 ($4.95, one-shot)
nn-Anthony Daniels & Ryder Windham-s 5.00

STAR WARS: UNDERWORLD - THE YAVIN VASSILIKA
Dark Horse Comics: Dec, 2000 - No. 5, June, 2001 ($2.99, limited series)
1-5-(Photo and Robinson covers) 3.00

STAR WARS: UNION
Dark Horse Comics: Nov, 1999 - No. 4, Feb, 2000 ($2.95, limited series)
1-4-Wedding of Luke and Mara Jade; Teranishi-a/Stackpole-s 3.00

STAR WARS: VADER'S QUEST
Dark Horse Comics: Feb, 1999 - No. 4, May, 1999 ($2.95, limited series)
1-4-Follows destruction of 1st Death Star; Gibbons-a 3.00

STAR WARS: VISIONARIES
Dark Horse Comics: Apr, 2005 ($17.95, TPB)
nn-Short stories from the concept artists for Revenge of the Sith movie 18.00

STAR WARS: X-WING ROGUE SQUADRON (Star Wars: X-Wing Rogue Squadron-The Phantom Affair #5-8 appears on cover only)
Dark Horse Comics: July, 1995 - No. 35, Nov, 1998 ($2.95)
1/2 8.00
1-24,26-35: 1-4-Baron scripts. 5-20-Stackpole scripts 4.00
25-($3.95) 5.00
The Phantom Affair TPB ($12.95) r/#5-8 13.00

STAR WARS: X-WING ROGUE SQUADRON: ROGUE LEADER
Dark Horse Comics: Sept, 2005 - No. 3, Nov, 2005 ($2.99)
1-3-Takes place one week after the Batttle of Endor 3.00

S.T.A.T.
Majestic Entertainment: Dec, 1993 ($2.25)
1 3.00

STATIC (See Charlton Action: Featuring "Static")

STATIC (See Heroes)
DC Comics (Milestone): June, 1993 - No. 45, Mar, 1997 ($1.50/$1.75/$2.50)
1-($2.95)-Collector's Edition; polybagged w/poster & trading card & backing board (direct sales only) 4.00
1-Platinum Edition with red background cover 5.00
1-13,15-24,26-45: 2-Origin. 8-Shadow War; Simonson silver ink-c. 27-Kent Williams-c 3.00
14-($2.50, 52 pgs.)-Worlds Collide Pt. 14 4.00
25 ($3.95) 4.00
...: Trial by Fire (2000, $9.95) r/#1-4; Leon-c 10.00

STATIC SHOCK (DC New 52)
DC Comics: Nov, 2011 - No. 8, Jun, 2012 ($2.99)
1-8: 1-McDaniel & Rozum-s/McDaniel-a/c. 6-Hardware & Technique app. 8-Origin retold 3.00

Steed and Mrs. Peel #1 © Studio Canal

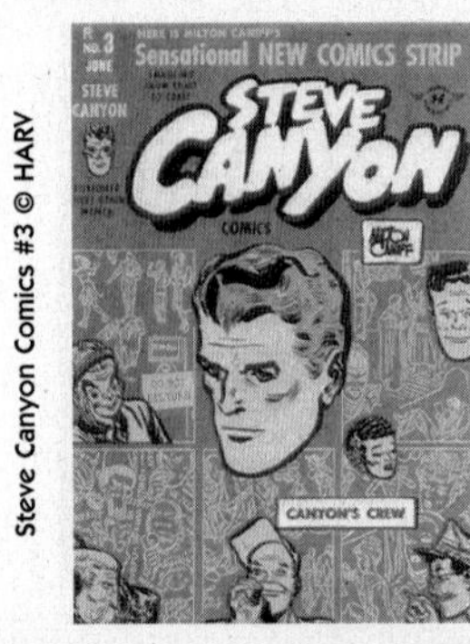

Steve Canyon Comics #3 © HARV

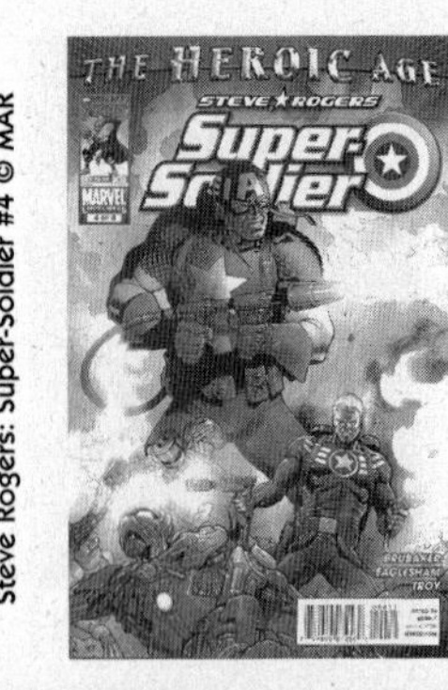

Steve Rogers: Super-Soldier #4 © MAR

	GD 2.0	VG 4.0	FN 6.0	VF 8.0	VF/NM 9.0	NM- 9.2

STATIC SHOCK!: REBIRTH OF THE COOL (TV)
DC Comics: Jan, 2001 - No. 4, Sept, 2001 ($2.50, limited series)
1-4: McDuffie-s/Leon-c/a 3.00

STATIC SHOCK SPECIAL
DC Comics: Aug, 2011 ($2.99, one-shot)
1-Cowan-a/Williams III-c; pin-ups by various; tribute to Dwayne McDuffie 3.00

STATIC-X
Chaos! Comics: Aug, 2002 ($5.99)
1-Polybagged with music CD; metal band as super-heroes; Pulido-s 6.00

STEALTH (Pilot Season: ...)
Image Comics (Top Cow): May, 2010 ($2.99)
1-Kirkman-s/Mitchell-a/Silvestri-c 3.00

STEAMPUNK
DC/WildStorm (Cliffhanger): Apr, 2000 - No. 12, Aug, 2002 ($2.50/$3.50)
Catechism (1/00) Prologue -Kelly-s/Bachalo-a 3.00
1-4,6-11: 4-Four covers by Bachalo, Madureira, Ramos, Campbell 3.00
5,12-($3.50) 4.00
...: Drama Obscura ('03, $14.95) r/#6-12 15.00
...: Manimatron ('01, $14.95) r/#1-5, Catechism, Idiosincratica 15.00

STEED AND MRS. PEEL (TV)(Also see The Avengers)
Eclipse Books/ ACME Press: 1990 - No. 3, 1991 ($4.95, limited series)
Books One - Three: Grant Morrison scripts/Ian Gibson-a 5.00
1,2: 1-(BOOM! Studios, 1/12, $3.99) r/#1 4.00

STEEL (Also see JLA)
DC Comics: Feb, 1994 - No. 52, July, 1998 ($1.50/$1.95/$2.50)
1-8,0,9-52: 1-From Reign of the Supermen storyline. 6,7-Worlds Collide Pt. 5 &12. 8-(9/94). 0-(10/94). 9-(11/94). 46-Superboy-c/app. 50-Millennium Giants x-over 3.00
1-(3/11, $2.99, one-shot) Benes-a/Garner-c; Reign of Doomsday x-over 4.00
Annual 1 (1994, $2.95)-Elseworlds story 4.00
Annual 2 (1995, $3.95)-Year One story 4.00
...Forging of a Hero TPB (1997, $19.95) reprints early app. 20.00

STEEL: THE OFFICIAL COMIC ADAPTION OF THE WARNER BROS. MOTION PICTURE
DC Comics: 1997 ($4.95, Prestige format, one-shot)
nn-Movie adaption; Bogdanove & Giordano-a 5.00

STEELGRIP STARKEY
Marvel Comics (Epic): June, 1986 - No. 6, July, 1987 ($1.50, lim. series, Baxter paper)
1-6 3.00

STEEL STERLING (Formerly Shield-Steel Sterling; see Blue Ribbon, Jackpot, Mighty Comics, Mighty Crusaders, Roly Poly & Zip Comics)
Archie Enterprises, Inc.: No. 4, Jan, 1984 - No. 7, July, 1984
4-7: 4-6-Kanigher-s; Barreto-a. 5,6-Infantino-a. 6-McWilliams-a 5.00

STEEL, THE INDESTRUCTIBLE MAN (See All-Star Squadron #8 and J.L. of A. Annual #2)
DC Comics: Mar, 1978 - No. 5, Oct-Nov, 1978
1 2 4 6 8 11 14
2-5: 5-44 pgs. 1 2 3 4 6 8

STEELTOWN ROCKERS
Marvel Comics: Apr, 1987 - No. 6, Sept, 1990 ($1.00, limited series)
1-6: Small town teens form rock band 3.00

STEPHEN COLBERT'S TEK JANSEN (From the animated shorts on The Colbert Report)
Oni Press: July, 2007 - No. 5, Jan, 2009 ($3.99, limited series)
1-Chantier-a/Layman & Peyer-s; back-up story by Massey-s/Rodriguez-a; Chantier-c 4.00
1-Variant-c by John Cassaday 6.00
1-Second printing with flip book of Cassaday & Chantier covers 4.00
2-5: 2-(6/08) Flip book with covers by Rodriguez & Wagner. 3-Flip-c by Darwyn Cooke 4.00

STEPHEN KING'S N. THE COMIC SERIES
Marvel Comics: May, 2010 - No. 4, Aug, 2010 ($3.99, limited series)
1-4-Guggenheim-s/Maleev-a/c 4.00

STEVE AUSTIN (See Stone Cold Steve Austin)

STEVE CANYON (See Harvey Comics Hits #52)
Dell Publishing Co.: No. 519, 11/53 - No. No. 1033, 9/59 (All Milton Caniff-a except #519, 939, 1033)
Four Color 519 (1, '53) 8 16 24 55 93 130
Four Color 578 (8/54), 641 (7/55), 737 (10/56), 804 (5/57), 939 (10/58), 1033 (9/59) (photo-c) 5 10 15 35 55 75

STEVE CANYON
Grosset & Dunlap: 1959 (6-3/4x9", 96 pgs., B&W, no text, hardcover)
100100-Reprints 2 stories from strip (1953, 1957) 6 12 18 31 38 45
100100 (softcover edition) 5 10 15 24 30 35

STEVE CANYON COMICS
Harvey Publ.: Feb, 1948 - No. 6, Dec, 1948 (Strip reprints, No. 4,5: 52pgs.)
1-Origin; has biography of Milton Caniff; Powell-a, 2 pgs.; Caniff-a 20 40 60 117 189 260
2-Caniff, Powell-a in #2-6 14 28 42 80 115 150
3-6: 6-Intro Madame Lynx-c/story 14 28 42 76 108 140

STEVE CANYON IN 3-D
Kitchen Sink Press: June, 1986 ($2.25, one-shot)
1-Contains unpublished story from 1954 5.00

STEVE DITKO'S STRANGE AVENGING TALES
Fantagraphics Books: Feb, 1997 ($2.95, B&W)
1-Ditko-c/s/a 3.00

STEVE DONOVAN, WESTERN MARSHAL (TV)
Dell Publishing Co.: No. 675, Feb, 1956 - No. 880, Feb, 1958 (All photo-c)
Four Color 675-Kinstler-a 8 16 24 51 86 120
Four Color 768-Kinstler-a 6 12 18 42 69 95
Four Color 880 5 10 15 30 48 65

STEVE ROGERS: SUPER-SOLDIER (Captain America - The Heroic Age)
Marvel Comics: Sept, 2010 - No. 4, Dec, 2010 ($3.99, limited series)
1-4-Brubaker-s/Eaglesham-a/Pacheco-c. 1-Back-up rep. of origin from CA #1 ('41) 4.00
Annual 1 (6/11, $3.99) Continued from Uncanny X-Men Annual #3; Roberson-a 4.00

STEVE ROPER
Famous Funnies: Apr, 1948 - No. 5, Dec, 1948
1-Contains 1944 daily newspaper-r 12 24 36 69 97 125
2 9 18 27 47 61 75
3-5 8 16 24 40 50 60

STEVE SAUNDERS SPECIAL AGENT (See Special Agent)

STEVE SAVAGE (See Captain...)

STEVE ZODIAC & THE FIRE BALL XL-5 (TV)
Gold Key: Jan, 1964
10108-401 (#1) 8 16 24 51 86 120

STEVIE (Mazie's boy friend)(Also see Flat-Top, Mazie & Mortie)
Mazie (Magazine Publ.): Nov, 1952 - No. 6, Apr, 1954
1-Teenage humor; Stevie, Mortie & Mazie begin 9 18 27 47 61 75
2-6 6 12 18 31 38 45

STEVIE MAZIE'S BOY FRIEND (See Harvey Hits #5)

STEWART THE RAT (See Eclipse Graphic Album Series)

ST. GEORGE (See listing under Saint...)

STIG'S INFERNO
Vortex/Eclipse: 1985 - No. 7, Mar, 1987 ($1.95, B&W)
1-7 ($1.95) 3.00
Graphic Album (1988, $6.95, B&W, 100 pgs.) 7.00

STING OF THE GREEN HORNET (See The Green Hornet)
Now Comics: June, 1992 - No. 4, 1992 ($2.50, limited series)
1-4: Butler-c/a 3.00
1-4 ($2.75)-Collectors Ed.; polybagged w/poster 4.00

STOKER'S DRACULA (Reprints unfinished Dracula story from 1974-75 with new ending)
Marvel Comics: 2004 - No. 4, May, 2005 ($3.99, B&W)
1-4: 1-Reprints from Dracula Lives! #5-8; Roy Thomas-s/Dick Giordano-a. 2-R/#10,11 & Legion of Monsters #1. 3,4-New story/artwork to finish story. 4-Giordano afterword 4.00
HC (2005, $24.99) r/#1-4; foreward by Thomas; Giordano afterword; bonus art & covers 25.00

STONE
Avalon Studios: Aug, 1998 - No. 4, Apr, 1999 ($2.50, limited series)
1-4-Portacio-a/Haberlin-s 3.00
1-Alternate-c 5.00
2-($14.95) DF Stonechrome Edition 15.00

STONE (Volume 2)
Avalon Studios: Aug, 1999 - No. 4, May, 2000 ($2.50)

Stories by Famous Authors #8 © FAI

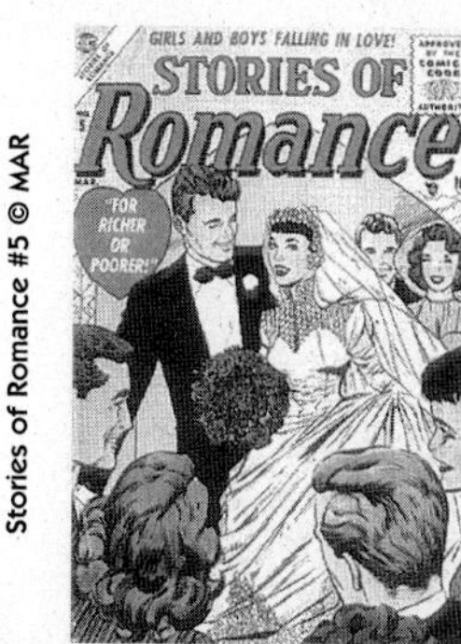

Stories of Romance #5 © MAR

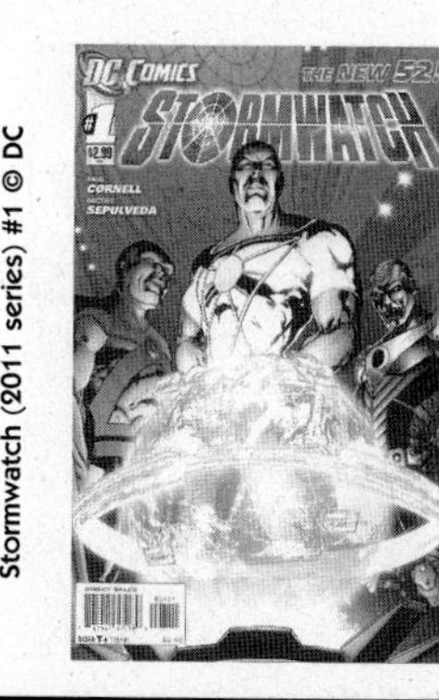

Stormwatch (2011 series) #1 © DC

GD 2.0 | VG 4.0 | FN 6.0 | VF 8.0 | VF/NM 9.0 | NM- 9.2

GD 2.0 | VG 4.0 | FN 6.0 | VF 8.0 | VF/NM 9.0 | NM- 9.2

1-4-Portacio-a/Haberlin-s 3.00
1-Chrome-c 5.00

STONE COLD STEVE AUSTIN (WWF Wrestling)
Chaos! Comics: Oct, 1999 - No. 4, Feb, 2000 ($2.95)

1-4-Reg. & photo-c; Steven Grant-s 3.00
1-Premium Ed. ($10.00) 10.00
Preview ($5.00) 5.00

STONE PROTECTORS
Harvey Pubications: May, 1994 - No. 3, Sept, 1994

nn (1993, giveaway)(limited distribution, scarce) 6.00
1-3-Ace Novelty action figures 4.00

STONEY BURKE (TV)
Dell Publishing Co.: June-Aug, 1963 - No. 2, Sept-Nov, 1963

1,2-Jack Lord photo-c on both 3 6 9 17 25 32

STONY CRAIG
Pentagon Publishing Co.: 1946 (No #)

nn-Reprints Bell Syndicate's "Sgt. Stony Craig" newspaper strips 8 16 24 40 50 60

STORIES BY FAMOUS AUTHORS ILLUSTRATED (Fast Fiction #1-5)
Seaboard Publ./Famous Authors Ill.: No. 6, Aug, 1950 - No. 13, Mar, 1951

1-Scarlet Pimpernel-Baroness Orczy 27 54 81 160 263 365
2-Capt. Blood-Raphael Sabatini 26 52 78 154 252 350
3-She, by Haggard 30 60 90 177 289 400
4-The 39 Steps-John Buchan 18 36 54 107 169 230
5-Beau Geste-P. C. Wren 18 36 54 107 169 230

NOTE: *The above five issues are exact reprints of Fast Fiction #1-5 except for the title change and new Kiefer covers on #1 and 2. Kiefer c(r)-3-5. The above 5 issues were released before Famous Authors #6.*

6-Macbeth, by Shakespeare; Kiefer art (8/50); used in **SOTI**, pg. 22,143; Kiefer-c; 36 pgs. 24 48 72 142 234 325
7-The Window; Kiefer-c/a; 52 pgs. 18 36 54 107 169 230
8-Hamlet, by Shakespeare; Kiefer-c/a; 36 pgs. 21 42 63 126 206 285
9,10: 9-Nicholas Nickleby, by Dickens; G. Schrotter-a; 52 pgs. 10-Romeo & Juliet, by Shakespeare; Kiefer-c/a; 36 pgs. 18 36 54 107 169 230
11-13: 11-Ben-Hur; Schrotter-a; 52 pgs. 12-La Svengali; Schrotter-a; 36 pgs. 13-Scaramouche; Kiefer-c/a; 36 pgs. 18 36 54 103 162 220

NOTE: *Artwork was prepared/advertised for #14, The Red Badge Of Courage. Gilberton bought out Famous Authors, Ltd. and used that story as C.I. #98. Famous Authors, Ltd. then published the Classics Junior series. The Famous Authors titles were published as part of the regular Classics Ill. Series in Brazil starting in 1952.*

STORIES FROM THE TWILIGHT ZONE
Skylark Pub: Mar, 1979, 68 pgs. (B&W comic digest, 5-1/4x7-5/8")

15405-2: Pfevfer-a, 56 pgs, new comics 3 6 9 18 27 35

STORIES OF ROMANCE (Formerly Meet Miss Bliss)
Atlas Comics (LMC): No. 5, Mar, 1956 - No. 13, Aug, 1957

5-Baker-a? 12 24 36 67 94 120
6-10,12,13 8 16 24 44 57 70
11-Baker, Romita-a; Colletta-c/a 11 22 33 62 86 110

NOTE: ***Ann Brewster** a-13. **Colletta** a-9(2), 11; c-5, 11.*

STORM
Marvel Comics: Feb, 1996 - No. 4, May, 1996 ($2.95, limited series)

1-4-Foil-c; Dodson-a(p); Ellis-s: 2-4-Callisto app. 4.00

STORM
Marvel Comics: Apr, 2006 - No. 6, Sept, 2006 ($2.99, limited series)

1-6: Ororo and T'Challa meet as teens; Eric Jerome Dickey-s 3.00
HC (2007, $19.99, dustjacket) r/#1-6 20.00
SC (2008, $14.99) r/#1-6 15.00

STORMBREAKER: THE SAGA OF BETA RAY BILL (Also see Thor)
Marvel Comics: Mar, 2005 - No. 6, Aug, 2005 ($2.99, limited series)

1-6-Oeming & Berman-s/DiVito-a; Galactus app. 6-Spider-Man app. 3.00
TPB (2006, $16.99) r/#1-6 17.00

STORMING PARADISE
DC Comics (WildStorm): Sept, 2008 - No. 6, Aug, 2009 ($2.99, limited series)

1-6-WWII invasion of Japan; Dixon-s/Guice-a/c 3.00
TPB (2009, $19.99) r/#1-6 20.00

STORM SHADOW (G.I. Joe character)
Devil's Due Publishing: May, 2007 - No. 7, Nov, 2007 ($3.50)

1-7-Larry Hama-s 3.50

STORMWATCH (Also see The Authority)
Image Comics (WildStorm Prod.): May, 1993 - No. 50, Jul, 1997 ($1.95/$2.50)

1-8,0,9-36: 1-Intro StormWatch (Battalion, Diva, Winter, Fuji, & Hellstrike); 1st app. Weatherman; Jim Lee-c & part scripts; Lee plots in all. 1-Gold edition.1-3-Includes coupon for limited edition StormWatch trading card #00 by Lee. 3-1st brief app. Backlash. 0-($2.50)-Polybagged w/card; 1st full app. Backlash. 9-(4/94, $2.50)-Intro Defile. 10-(6/94),11,12-Both (8/94). 13,14-(9/94). 15-(10/94). 21-Reads #1 on-c. 22-Direct Market; Wildstorm Rising Pt. 9, bound-in card. 23-Spartan joins team. 25-(6/94, June 1995 on-c, $2.50). 35-Fire From Heaven Pt. 5. 36-Fire From Heaven Pt. 12 3.00
10-Alternate Portacio-c, see Deathblow #5 3.00
22-($1.95)-Newsstand, Wildstorm Rising Pt. 9 3.00
37-(7/96, $3.50, 38 pgs.)-Weatherman forms new team; 1st app. Jenny Sparks, Jack Hawksmoor & Rose Tattoo; Warren Ellis scripts begin; Justice League #1-c/swipe 4.00
38-49: 44-Three covers. 3.00
50-($4.50) 4.50
Special 1 ,2(1/94, 5/95, $3.50, 52 pgs.) 4.00
Sourcebook 1 (1/94, $2.50) 3.00
Forces of Nature ('99, $14.95, TPB) r/V1 #37-42 15.00
Lightning Strikes ('00, $14.95, TPB) r/V1 #43-47 15.00

STORMWATCH (Also see The Authority)
Image Comics (WildStorm): Oct, 1997 - No. 11, Sept, 1998 ($2.50)

1-Ellis-s/Jimenez-a(p); two covers by Bennett 3.00
1-($3.50)-Voyager Pack bagged w/Gen 13 preview 4.00
2-4: 4-1st app. Midnighter and Apollo 3.00
5-11: 7,8-Freefall app. 9-Gen13 & DV8 app. 3.00
A Finer World ('99, $14.95, TPB) r/V2 #4-9 15.00
Change or Die ('99, $14.95, TPB) r/V1 #48-50 & V2 #1-3 15.00
Final Orbit ('01, $9.95, TPB) r/V2 #10,11 & WildC.A.T.S./Aliens; Hitch-c 10.00

STORMWATCH (DC New 52)
DC Comics: Nov, 2011 - Present ($2.99)

1-Cornell-s/Sepulveda-a; Martian Manhunter app.; blue bkgrd cover 4.00
1-(2nd printing, cover has red bkgrd), 2-8: 7,8-Jenkins-s 3.00

STORMWATCHER
Eclipse Comics (Acme Press): Apr, 1989 - No. 4, Dec, 1989 ($2.00, B&W)

1-4 3.00

STORMWATCH: P.H.D. (Post Human Division)
DC Comics (WildStorm): Jan, 2007 - No. 24, Jan, 2010 ($2.99)

1-24: 1-Two covers by Mahnke & Hairsine; Gage-s/Mahnke-a. 2-Var-c by Dell'Otto 3.00
...: Armageddon 1 (2/08, $2.99) Gage-s/Fernández-a/McKone-c 3.00
TPB (2007, $17.99) r/#1-4,6,7 & story from Worldstorm #1 18.00
... Book Two TPB (2008, $17.99) r/#5,8-12; sketch pages and concept art 18.00
... Book Three TPB (2009, $17.99) r/#13-19 18.00

STORMWATCH: TEAM ACHILLES
DC Comics (WildStorm): Sept, 2002 - No. 23, Aug, 2004 ($2.95)

1-8: 1-Two covers by Portacio; Portacio-a/Wright-s. 5,6-The Authority app. 3.00
9-23: 9-Back-up preview of The Authority: High Stakes pt. 1 3.00
TPB (2003, $14.95) r/Wizard Preview and #1-6; Portacio art pages 15.00
Book 2 (2004, $14.95) r/#7-11 & short story from Eye of the Storm Annual 15.00

STORMY (Disney) (Movie)
Dell Publishing Co.: No. 537, Feb, 1954

Four Color 537 (...the Thoroughbred)-on top 2/3 of each page; Pluto story on bottom 1/3 5 10 15 30 48 65

STORY OF JESUS (See Classics Illustrated Special Issue)

STORY OF MANKIND, THE (Movie)
Dell Publishing Co.: No. 851, Jan, 1958

Four Color 851-Vincent Price/Hedy Lamarr photo-c 7 14 21 46 76 105

STORY OF MARTHA WAYNE, THE
Argo Publ.: April, 1956

1-Newspaper strip-r 6 12 18 29 36 42

STORY OF RUTH, THE
Dell Publishing Co.: No. 1144, Nov-Jan, 1961 (Movie)

Four Color 1144-Photo-c 8 16 24 56 96 135

STORY OF THE COMMANDOS, THE (Combined Operations)
Long Island Independent: 1943 (15¢, B&W, 68 pgs.) (Distr. by Gilberton)

nn-All text (no comics); photos & illustrations; ad for Classic Comics on back cover (Rare) 34 68 102 199 325 450

STORY OF THE GLOOMY BUNNY, THE (See March of Comics #9)

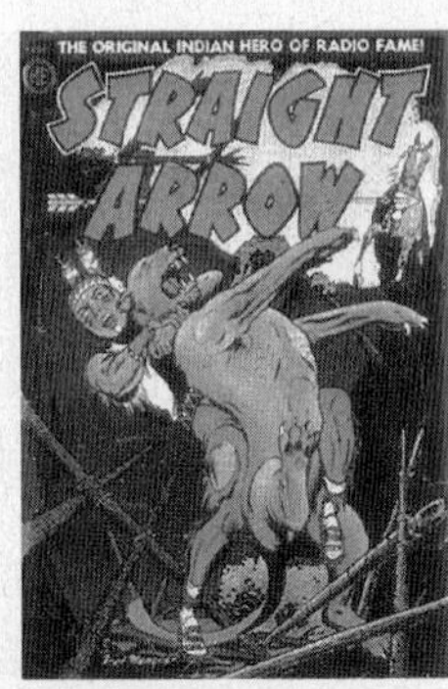
Straight Arrow #16 © ME

Strange (2004 series) #1 © MAR

Strange Adventures #24 © DC

GD VG FN VF VF/NM NM-
2.0 4.0 6.0 8.0 9.0 9.2

STRAIGHT ARROW (Radio)(See Best of the West & Great Western)
Magazine Enterprises: Feb-Mar, 1950 - No. 55, Mar, 1956 (All 36 pgs.)

1-Straight Arrow (alias Steve Adams) & his palomino Fury begin; 1st mention of Sundown Valley & the Secret Cave 46 92 138 290 488 685
2-Red Hawk begins (1st app?) by Powell (origin), ends #55 23 46 69 136 223 310
3-Frazetta-c 31 62 93 182 296 410
4,5: 4-Secret Cave-c 21 42 63 122 199 275
6-10 17 34 51 100 158 215
11-Classic story "The Valley of Time", with an ancient civilization made of gold 22 44 66 128 209 290
12-19 14 28 42 82 121 160
20-Origin Straight Arrow's Shield 16 32 48 92 144 195
21-Origin Fury 19 38 57 109 172 235
22-Frazetta-c 25 50 75 147 241 335
23,25-30: 25-Secret Cave-c. 28-Red Hawk meets The Vikings 11 22 33 62 86 110
24-Classic story "The Dragons of Doom!" with prehistoric pteradactyls 14 28 42 82 121 160
31-38: 36-Red Hawk drug story by Powell 10 20 30 54 72 90
39-Classic story "The Canyon Beast", with a dinosaur egg hatching a Tyranosaurus Rex 14 28 42 76 108 140
40-Classic story "Secret of The Spanish Specters", with Conquistadors' lost treasure 11 22 33 64 90 115
41,42,44-54: 45-Secret Cave-c 9 18 27 50 65 80
43-Intro & 1st app. Blaze, S. Arrow's Warrior dog 10 20 30 58 79 100
55-Last issue 11 22 33 62 86 110

NOTE: ***Fred Meagher** a 1-55; c-1, 2, 4-21, 23-55. **Powell** a 2-55. **Whitney** a-1. Many issues advertise the radio premiums associated with Straight Arrow.*

STRAIGHT ARROW'S FURY (Also see A-1 Comics)
Magazine Enterprises: No. 119, 1954 (one-shot)

A-1 119-Origin; Fred Meagher-c/a 15 30 45 85 130 175

STRAIN, THE (Adaptation of novels by Guillermo del Toro and Chuck Hogan)
Dark Horse Comics: Dec, 2011 - Present ($1.00/$3.50)

1-($1.00) Lapham, Hogan & del Toro-s/Huddleston-a/c; variant-c by Morris 3.50
2-4-($3.50) Lapham-s/Huddleston-a/c 3.50

STRANDED
Virgin Comics: Dec, 2007 - No. 5, June, 2008 ($2.99)

1-5-Carey-s/Kotian-a. 1-Silvestri-c. 2-5-Moeller-c 3.00

STRANGE (Tales You'll Never Forget)
Ajax-Farrell Publ. (Four Star Comic Corp.): March, 1957 - No. 6, May, 1958

1 22 44 66 132 216 300
2-Censored r/Haunted Thrills 14 28 42 80 115 150
3-6 11 22 33 62 86 110

STRANGE (Dr. Strange)
Marvel Comics (Marvel Knghts): Nov, 2004 - No. 6, July, 2005 ($3.50)

1-6-Straczynski & Barnes-s/Peterson-a; Dr. Strange's origin retold 3.50
...: Beginnings and Endings TPB (2006, $17.99) r/#1-6 18.00

STRANGE (Dr. Strange)
Marvel Comics: Jan, 2010 - No. 4, Apr, 2010 ($3.99, limited series)

1-4-Waid-s/Rios-a/Coker-c 4.00

STRANGE ADVENTURES
DC Comics: July/Aug 1950

nn - Ashcan comic, not distributed to newsstands, only for in-house use. Cover art is All Star Comics #47 with interior being Detective Comics #140. A second example has the interior of Detective Comics #146. A third example has an unidentified issue of Detective Comics as the interior. This is the only ashcan with multiple interiors. A FN+ copy sold for $1,000 in 2007.

STRANGE ADVENTURES
National Periodical Publ.: Aug-Sept, 1950 - No. 244, Oct-Nov, 1973 (No. 1-12: 52 pgs.)

1-Adaptation of "Destination Moon"; preview of movie w/photo-c from movie (also see Fawcett Movie Comic #2); adapt. of Edmond Hamilton's "Chris KL-99" in #1-3; Darwin Jones begins 161 322 483 1352 2926 4500
2 74 148 222 600 1300 2000
3,4 52 104 156 421 911 1400
5-8,10: 7-Origin Kris KL-99 46 92 138 359 780 1200
9-(6/51)-Origin/1st app. Captain Comet (c/story) 104 208 312 842 1821 2800
11-20: 12,13,17,18-Toth-a. 14-Robot-c 31 62 93 225 488 750
21-30: 28-Atomic explosion panel. 30-Robot-c 29 58 87 210 455 700
31,34-38 27 54 81 192 414 635
32,33-Krigstein-a 27 54 81 196 423 650
39-Ill. in **SOTI** "Treating police contemptuously" (top right) 31 62 93 221 478 735
40-49-Last Capt. Comet; not in 45,47,48 27 54 81 189 407 625
50-53-Last precode issue (2/55) 21 42 63 146 311 475
54-70 16 32 48 109 237 365
71-99: 80-Grey-tone-c 13 26 39 85 180 275
100 13 26 39 90 195 300
101-110: 104-Space Museum begins by Sekowsky 11 22 33 75 148 220
111-116,118,119: 114-Star Hawkins begins, ends #185; Heath-a in Wood E.C. style 11 22 33 73 142 210
117-(6/60)-Origin/1st app. Atomic Knights. 46 92 138 345 748 1150
120-2nd app. Atomic Knights 21 42 63 146 311 475
121,122,125,127,128,130,131,133,134: 134-Last 10¢ issue 10 20 30 68 127 185
123,126-3rd & 4th app. Atomic Knights 12 24 36 83 172 260
124-Intro/origin Faceless Creature 11 22 33 73 142 210
129,132,135,138,141,147-Atomic Knights app. 11 22 33 73 142 210
136,137,139,140,143,145,146,148,149,151,152,154,155,157-159: 136-Robot cover. 159-Star Rovers app.; Gil Kane/Anderson-a. 8 16 24 56 96 135
142-2nd app. Faceless Creature 9 18 27 63 112 160
144-Only Atomic Knights-c (by M. Anderson) 11 22 33 76 151 225
150,153,156,160: Atomic Knights in each. 150-Greytone-c. 153-(6/63)-3rd app. Faceless Creature; atomic explosion-c. 160-Last Atomic Knights 9 18 27 61 106 150
161-179: 161-Last Space Museum. 163-Star Rovers app. 170-Infinity-c. 177-Intro/origin Immortal Man 7 14 21 46 76 105
180-Origin/1st app. Animal Man 14 28 42 97 211 325
181-183,185-189: 187-Intro/origin The Enchantress 6 12 18 39 62 85
184-2nd app. Animal Man by Gil Kane 10 20 30 68 127 185
190-1st app. Animal Man in costume 12 24 36 79 160 240
191-194,196-200,202-204 5 10 15 35 55 75
195-1st full app. Animal Man 7 14 21 49 82 115
201-Last Animal Man; 2nd full app. 6 12 18 41 66 90
205-(10/67)-Intro/origin Deadman by Infantino & begin series, ends #216 14 28 42 97 211 325
206-Neal Adams-a begins 11 22 33 76 151 225
207-210 10 20 30 66 121 175
211-216: 211-Space Museum-r. 216-(1-2/69)-Deadman story finally concludes in Brave & the Bold #86 (10-11/69); secret message panel by Neal Adams (pg. 13); tribute to Steranko 9 18 27 61 106 150
217-r/origin & 1st app. Adam Strange from Showcase #17, begin-r; Atomic Knights-r begin 3 6 9 16 23 30
218-221,223-225: 218-Last 12¢ issue. 225-Last 15¢ issue 3 6 9 14 20 26
222-New Adam Strange story; Kane/Anderson-a 3 6 9 21 32 42
226,227,230-236-(68-52 pgs.): 226, 227-New Adam Strange text story w/illos by Anderson (8,6 pgs.) 231-Last Atomic Knights-r. 235-JLA-c/s 3 6 9 14 20 26
228,229 (68 pgs.) 3 6 9 17 25 32
237-243 2 4 6 10 14 18
244-Last issue 2 4 6 11 16 20

NOTE: ***Neal Adams** a-206-216; c-207-218, 228, 235. **Anderson** a-8-52, 94, 96, 99, 115, 117, 119-163, 217r, 218r, 222, 223-225r, 226, 229r, 242i(r); c-18, 19, 21, 23, 24, 27, 30, 32-44(most); c/r-157i, 190i, 217-224, 228-231, 233, 235-239, 241-243. **Ditko** a-188, 189. **Drucker** a-42, 43, 45. **Elias** a-212. **Finlay** a-2, 3, 6, 7, 210r, 229r. **Giunta** a-237r. **Heath** a-116. **Infantino** a-10-101, 106-151, 154, 157-163, 180, 190, 218-221r, 223-244p(r); c-50; c(r)-190p, 197, 199-211, 218-221, 223-244. **Kaluta** c-238, 240. **Gil Kane** a-8-116, 124, 125, 130, 138, 146-157, 173-186, 204r, 222r, 227-231r; c(p)-11-17, 25, 154, 157. **Kubert** a-55(2 pgs.), 226; c-219, 220, 225-227, 232, 234. **Moreira** c-26, 28, 29, 71. **Morrow** c-230. **Mortimer** c-8. **Powell** a-4. **Sekowsky** a-71p, 97-162p, 217p(r), 218p(r); c-206, 217-219r. **Simon & Kirby** a-2r (2 pgs) **Sparling** a-201. **Toth** a-8, 12, 13, 17-19. **Wood** a-154i. Atomic Knights in #117, 120, 123, 126, 129, 132, 135, 138, 141, 144, 147, 150, 153, 156, 160. Atomic Knights reprints by **Anderson** in 217-221, 223-231. Chris KL99 in 1-3, 5, 7, 9, 11, 15. Capt. Comet covers-9-14, 17-19, 24, 26, 27, 32-44.*

STRANGE ADVENTURES
DC Comics (Vertigo): Nov, 1999 - No. 4, Feb, 2000 ($2.50, limited series)

1-4: 1-Bolland-c; art by Bolland, Gibbons, Quitely 3.00

STRANGE ADVENTURES
DC Comics: May, 2009 - No. 8, Dec, 2009 ($3.99, limited series)

1-8: 1-Starlin-s in all; Adam Strange, Capt. Comet, Bizarro & Prince Gavyn app. 4.00
TPB (2010, $19.99) r/#1-8; cover gallery 20.00

STRANGE ADVENTURES
DC Comics (Vertigo): Jul, 2011 ($7.99, one-shot)

1-Short story anthology; s/a by Azzarello, Risso, Milligan and others; Paul Pope-c 8.00

STRANGE AS IT SEEMS (See Famous Funnies-A Carnival of Comics, Feature Funnies #1, The John Hix Scrap Book & Peanuts)

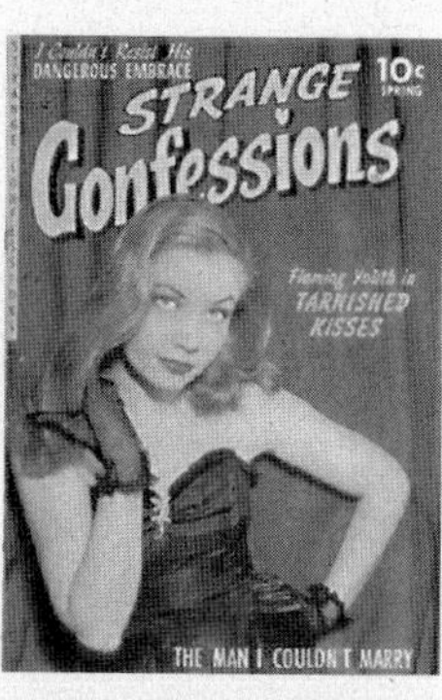

Strange Confessions #1 © Z-D

Strange Fantasy #3 © AJAX

The Strangers #2 © MAL

	GD 2.0	VG 4.0	FN 6.0	VF 8.0	VF/NM 9.0	NM- 9.2

STRANGE AS IT SEEMS
United Features Syndicate: 1939
Single Series 9, 1, 2 — 34 68 102 199 325 450

STRANGE ATTRACTORS
RetroGraphix: 1993 - No. 15, Feb, 1997 ($2.50, B&W)
1-15: 1-(5/93), 2-(8/93), 3-(11/93), 4-(2/94) — 3.00
Volume One-($14.95, trade paperback)-r/#1-7 — 15.00

STRANGE ATTRACTORS: MOON FEVER
Caliber Comics: Feb, 1997 - No. 3, June, 1997 ($2.95, B&W, mini-series)
1-3 — 3.00

STRANGE COMBAT TALES
Marvel Comics (Epic Comics): Oct, 1993 - No. 4, Jan, 1994 ($2.50, limited series)
1-4 — 3.00

STRANGE CONFESSIONS
Ziff-Davis Publ. Co.: Jan-Mar (Spring on-c), 1952 - No. 4, Fall, 1952 (All have photo-c)
1(Scarce)-Kinstler-a — 55 110 165 352 601 850
2(Scarce, 7-8/52) — 40 80 120 242 401 560
3(Scarce, 9-10/52)-#3 on-c, #2 on inside; Reformatory girl story; photo-c — 39 78 117 240 395 550
4(Scarce) — 39 78 117 231 378 525

STRANGE DAYS
Eclipse Comics: Oct, 1984 - No. 3, Apr, 1985 ($1.75, Baxter paper)
1-3: Freakwave, Johnny Nemo, & Paradax from Vanguard Illustrated; nudity, violence & strong language — 3.00

STRANGE DAYS (Movie)
Marvel Comics: Dec, 1995 ($5.95, squarebound, one-shot)
1-Adaptation of film — 6.00

STRANGE FANTASY (Eerie Tales of Suspense!)(Formerly Rocketman #1)
Ajax-Farrell: Aug, 1952 - No. 14, Oct-Nov, 1954
2(#1, 8/52)-Jungle Princess story; Kamenish-a; reprinted from Ellery Queen #1 — 50 100 150 315 533 750
2(10/52)-No Black Cat or Rulah; Bakerish, Kamenish-a; hypo/meathook-c — 45 90 135 284 480 675
3-Rulah story, called Pulah — 40 80 120 246 411 575
4-Rocket Man app. (2/53) — 39 78 117 233 384 535
5,6,8,10,12,14 — 30 60 90 177 289 400
7-Madam Satan/Slave story — 39 78 117 233 384 535
9(w/Black Cat), 9(w/Boy's Ranch; S&K-a), 9(w/War)(A rebinding of Harvey interiors; not publ. by Ajax) — 34 68 102 206 336 465
9-Regular issue; Steve Ditko's 3rd published work (tied with Captain 3D) — 48 96 144 302 514 725
11-Jungle story — 37 74 111 222 361 500
13-Bondage-c; Rulah (Kolah) story — 37 74 111 222 361 500

STRANGE GALAXY
Eerie Publications: V1#8, Feb, 1971 - No. 11, Aug, 1971 (B&W, magazine)
V1#8-Reprints-c/Fantastic V19#3 (2/70) (a pulp) — 4 8 12 22 34 45
9-11 — 3 6 9 18 27 35

STRANGE GIRL
Image Comics: June, 2005 - No. 18, Sept, 2007 ($2.95/$2.99/$3.50)
1-12: 1-Rick Remender-s/Eric Nguyen-a — 3.50
13-18-($3.50) — 3.50
... Vol. 1: Girl Afraid TPB (2005, $12.99) r/#1-4; sketch pages and pin-ups — 13.00

STRANGE JOURNEY
America's Best (Steinway Publ.) (Ajax/Farrell): Sept, 1957 - No. 4, Jun, 1958 (Farrell reprints)
1 — 20 40 60 114 182 250
2-4: 2-Flying saucer-c. 3-Titanic-c — 15 30 45 83 124 165

STRANGE LOVE (See Fox Giants)

STRANGE MYSTERIES
Superior/Dynamic Publications: Sept, 1951 - No. 21, Jan, 1955
1-Kamenish-a & horror stories begin — 71 142 213 454 777 1100
2 — 39 78 117 240 395 550
3-5 — 37 74 111 222 361 500
6-8 — 32 64 96 192 314 435
9-Bondage 3-D effect-c — 39 78 117 233 384 535
10-Used in **SOTI**, pg. 181 — 30 60 90 177 289 400
11-18 — 24 48 72 142 234 325
19-r/Journey Into Fear #1; cover is a splash from one story; Baker-r(2) — 25 50 75 150 245 340
20,21-Reprints; 20-r/#1 with new-c (The Devil) — 19 38 57 111 176 240

STRANGE MYSTERIES
I. W. Enterprises/Super Comics: 1963 - 1964
I.W. Reprint #9; Rulah-r/Spook #28; Disbrow-a — 3 6 9 20 30 40
Super Reprint #10-12,15-17(1963-64): 10,11-r/Strange #2,1. 12-r/Tales of Horror #5 (3/53) less-c. 15-r/Dark Mysteries #23. 16-r/The Dead Who Walk. 17-r/Dark Mysteries #22 — 3 6 9 20 30 40
Super Reprint #18-r/Witchcraft #1; Kubert-a — 3 6 9 20 30 40

STRANGE PLANETS
I. W. Enterprises/Super Comics: 1958; 1963-64
I.W. Reprint #1(nd)-Reprints E. C. Incredible S/F #30 plus-c/Strange Worlds #3 — 6 12 18 39 62 85
I.W. Reprint #9-Orlando/Wood-r/Strange Worlds #4; cover-r from Flying Saucers #1 — 7 14 21 48 79 110
Super Reprint #10-Wood-r (22 pg.) from Space Detective #1; cover-r/Attack on Planet Mars — 7 14 21 48 79 110
Super Reprint #11-Wood-r (25 pg.) from An Earthman on Venus — 8 16 24 53 89 125
Super Reprint #12-Orlando-r/Rocket to the Moon — 7 14 21 48 79 110
Super Reprint #15-Reprints Journey Into Unknown Worlds #8; Heath, Colan-r — 4 8 12 28 44 60
Super Reprint #16-Reprints Avon's Strange Worlds #6; Kinstler, Check-a — 5 10 15 30 48 65
Super Reprint #18-r/Great Exploits #1 (Daring Adventures #6); Space Busters, Explorer Joe, The Son of Robin Hood; Krigstein-a — 4 8 12 24 37 50

STRANGERS
Image Comics: Mar, 2003 - No. 6, Sept, 2003 ($2.95)
1-6-Randy & Jean-Marc Lofficier-s; two covers. 2-Nexus back-up story — 3.00

STRANGERS, THE
Malibu Comics (Ultraverse): June, 1993 - No. 24, May, 1995 ($1.95/$2.50)
1-4,6-12,14-20: 1-1st app. The Strangers; has coupon for Ultraverse Premiere #0; 1st app. the Night Man (not in costume). 2-Polybagged w/trading card. 7-Break-Thru x-over. 8-2 pg. origin Solution. 12-Silver foil logo; wraparound-c. 17-Rafferty app. — 3.00
1-With coupon missing — 2.00
1-Full cover holographic edition, 1st of kind w/Hardcase #1 & Prime #1 — 6.00
1-Ultra 5000 limited silver foil — 4.00
4-($2.50)-Newsstand edition bagged w/card — 4.00
5-($2.50, 52 pgs.)-Rune flip-c/story by B. Smith (3 pgs.); The Mighty Magnor 1 pg. strip by Aragones; 3-pg. Night Man preview — 4.00
13-($3.50, 68 pgs.)-Mantra app.; flip book w/Ultraverse Premiere #4 — 4.00
21-24 ($2.50) — 3.00
...:The Pilgrim Conundrum Saga (1/95, $3.95, 68pgs.) — 4.00

STRANGERS IN PARADISE
Antarctic Press: Nov, 1993 - No. 3, Feb, 1994 ($2.75, B&W, limited series)
1 — 5 10 15 35 55 75
1-2nd/3rd prints — 1 2 3 5 6 8
2 (2300 printed) — 4 8 12 22 34 45
3 — 3 6 9 16 23 30
Trade paperback (Antarctic Press, $6.95)-Red -c (5000 print run) — 10.00
Trade paperback (Abstract Studios, $6.95)-Red-c (2000 print run) — 15.00
Trade paperback (Abstract Studios, $6.95, 1st-4th printing)-Blue- — 7.00
Hardcover ('98, $29.95) includes first draft pages — 30.00
Gold Reprint Series ($2.75) 1-3-r/#1-3 — 3.00

STRANGERS IN PARADISE
Abstract Studios: Sept, 1994 - No. 14, July, 1996 ($2.75, B&W)
1 — 2 4 6 9 13 16
1,3- 2nd printings — 4.00
2,3: 2-Color dream sequence — 1 2 3 5 6 8
4-10 — 4.00
4-6-2nd printings — 3.00
11-14: 14-The Letters of Molly & Poo — 4.00
Gold Reprint Series ($2.75) 1-13-r/#1-13 — 3.00
I Dream Of You ($16.95, TPB) r/#1-9 — 17.00
It's a Good Life ($8.95, TPB) r/#10-13 — 9.00

STRANGERS IN PARADISE (Volume Three)
Homage Comics #1-8/Abstract Studios #9-on: Oct, 1996 - No. 90, May, 2007 ($2.75-$2.99, color #1-5, B&W #6-on)

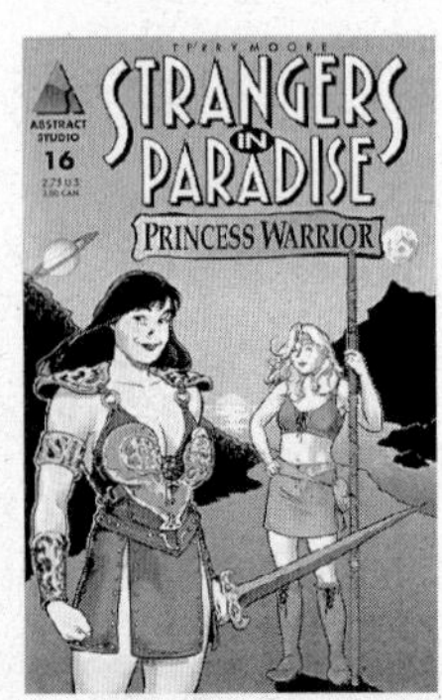

Strangers in Paradise V3 #16 © Terry Moore

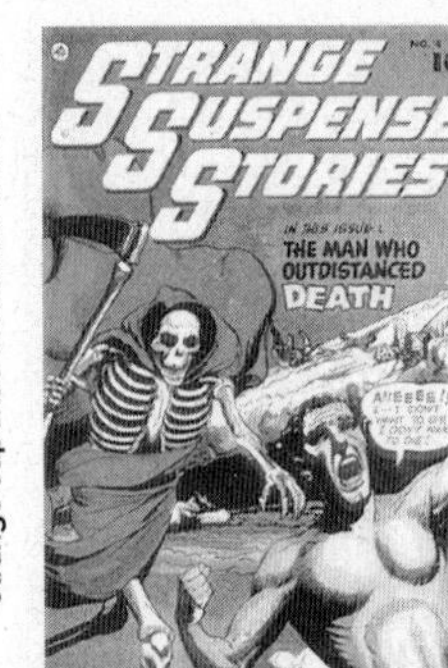

Strange Supense Stories #4 © FAW

Strange Tales #3 © MAR

	GD 2.0	VG 4.0	FN 6.0	VF 8.0	VF/NM 9.0	NM- 9.2
1-Terry Moore-c/s/a in all; dream seq. by Jim Lee-a						5.00
1-Jim Lee variant-c	1	2	3	6	7	8
2-5						4.00
6-16: 6-Return to B&W. 13-15-High school flashback. 16-Xena Warrior Princess parody; two covers						3.00
17-89: 33-Color issue. 46-Molly Lane. 49-Molly & Poo. 86-David dies						3.00
90-Last issue; 3 covers of Katchoo, Francine and David forming a triptych						3.00
...Lyrics and Poems (2/99)						3.00
...Source Book (2003, $2.95) Background on characters & story arcs, checklists						3.00
Brave New World ('02, $8.95, TPB) r/#44,45,47,48						9.00
Child of Rage ($15.95, TPB) r/#31-38						16.00
David's Story (6/04, $8.95, TPB) r/#61-63						9.00
Ever After ('07, $15.95, TPB) r/#83-90						16.00
Flower to Flame ('03, $15.95, TPB) r/#55-60						16.00
Heart in Hand ('03, $12.95, TPB) r/#50-54						13.00
High School ('98, $8.95, TPB) r/#13-16						9.00
Immortal Enemies ('98, $14.95, TPB) r/#6-12						15.00
Love & Lies (2006, $14.95, TPB)r/#77-82						15.00
Love Me Tender ($12.95, TPB) r/#1-5 in B&W w/ color Lee seq.						13.00
Molly & Poo (2005, $8.95, TPB)r/#46,49,73						9.00
My Other Life ($14.95, TPB) r/#25-30						15.00
Pocket Book 1-5 ($17.95, 5 1/2" x 8", TPB) 1-r/Vol.1 & 2. 2-r/#1-17 in B&W. 3-r/#18-24,26-32,34-38. 4-r/#41-45,47,48,50-60. 5-r/#46,49,61-76						18.00
Sanctuary ($15.95, TPB) r/#17-24						16.00
Tattoo ($14.95, TPB) r/#70-76; sketch pages and fan tattoo photos						15.00
Tomorrow Now (11/04, $14.95, TPB) r/#64-69						15.00
Tropic of Desire ($12.95, TPB) r/#39-43						13.00
The Complete... : Volume 3 Part 1 HC ($49.95) r/#1-12						50.00
The Complete... : Volume 3 Part 2 HC ($49.95) r/#13-15,17-25						50.00
The Complete... : Volume 3 Part 3 HC ('01, $49.95) r/#26-38						50.00
The Complete... : Volume 3 Part 4 HC ('02, $39.95) r/#39-46,49						40.00
The Complete... : Volume 3 Part 5 HC ('03, $49.95) r/#47,48,50-57						50.00
The Complete... : Volume 3 Part 6 HC ('04, $49.95) r/#58-69						50.00
The Complete... : Volume 3 Part 7 HC ('06, $49.95) r/#70-80						50.00

STRANGE SPORTS STORIES (See Brave & the Bold #45-49, DC Special, and DC Super Stars #10)
National Periodical Publications: Sept-Oct, 1973 - No. 6, July-Aug, 1974

	GD	VG	FN	VF	VF/NM	NM-
1-Devil-c	3	6	9	16	23	30
2-6: 2-Swan/Anderson-a	2	4	6	9	13	16

STRANGE STORIES FROM ANOTHER WORLD (Unknown World #1)
Fawcett Publications: No. 2, Aug, 1952 - No. 5, Feb, 1953

	GD	VG	FN	VF	VF/NM	NM-
2-Saunders painted-c	50	100	150	315	533	750
3-5-Saunders painted-c	39	78	117	240	395	550

STRANGE STORIES OF SUSPENSE (Rugged Action #1-4)
Atlas Comics (CSI): No. 5, Oct, 1955 - No. 16, Aug, 1957

	GD	VG	FN	VF	VF/NM	NM-
5(#1)	41	82	123	256	428	600
6,9	27	54	81	158	259	360
7-E. C. swipe cover/Vault of Horror #32	27	54	81	162	266	370
8-Morrow/Williamson-a; Pakula-a	29	58	87	170	278	385
10-Crandall, Torres, Meskin-a	27	54	81	162	266	370
11-13: 12-Torres, Pakula-a. 13-E.C. art swipes	23	46	69	136	223	310
14-16: 14-Williamson/Mayo-a. 15-Krigstein-a. 16-Fox, Powell-a	25	50	75	147	241	335

NOTE: ***Everett** a-6, 7, 13; c-8, 9, 11-14. **Forte** a-12, 16. **Heath** a-5. **Maneely** c-5. **Morisi** a-11. **Morrow** a-13. **Powell** a-8. **Sale** a-11. **Severin** c-7. **Wildey** a-14.*

STRANGE STORY (Also see Front Page)
Harvey Publications: June-July, 1946 (52 pgs.)

	GD	VG	FN	VF	VF/NM	NM-
1-The Man in Black Called Fate by Powell	34	68	102	199	325	450

STRANGE SUSPENSE STORIES (Lawbreakers Suspense Stories #10-15; This Is Suspense #23-26; Captain Atom V1#78 on)
Fawcett Publications/Charlton Comics No. 16 on: 6/52 - No. 5, 2/53; No. 16, 1/54 - No. 22, 11/54; No. 27, 10/55 - No. 77, 10/65; V3#1, 10/67 - V1#9, 9/69

	GD	VG	FN	VF	VF/NM	NM-
1-(Fawcett)-Powell, Sekowsky-a	87	174	261	553	952	1350
2-George Evans horror story	50	100	150	315	533	750
3-5 (2/53)-George Evans horror stories	41	82	123	256	428	600
16(1-2/54)-Formerly Lawbreakers S.S.	31	62	93	182	296	410
17,21: 21-Shuster-a	24	48	72	142	234	325
18-E.C. swipe/HOF 7; Ditko-c/a(2)	40	80	120	246	411	575
19-Ditko electric chair-c; Ditko-a	55	110	165	352	601	850
20-Ditko-c/a(2)	40	80	120	246	411	575
22(11/54)-Ditko-c, Shuster-a; last pre-code issue; becomes This Is Suspense	37	74	111	222	361	500
27(10/55)-(Formerly This Is Suspense #26)	15	30	45	86	133	180
28-30,38	12	24	36	69	97	125
31-33,35,37,40-Ditko-c/a(2-3 each)	21	42	63	126	206	285
34-Story of ruthless business man, Wm. B. Gaines; Ditko-c/a	47	94	141	296	498	700
36-(15¢, 68 pgs.); Ditko-a(4)	26	52	78	154	252	350
39,41,52,53-Ditko-a	19	38	57	111	176	240
42-44,46,49,54-60	6	12	18	39	62	85
45,47,48,50,51-Ditko-c/a	12	24	36	84	175	265
61-74	5	10	15	30	48	65
75(6/65)-Reprints origin/1st app. Captain Atom by Ditko from Space Advs. #33; r/Severin-a/Space Advs. #24 (75-77: 12¢ issues)	11	22	33	73	142	210
76,77-Captain Atom-r by Ditko/Space Advs.	6	12	18	42	69	95
V3#1(10/67): 12¢ issues begin	3	6	9	20	30	40
V1#2-Ditko-c/a; atom bomb-c	3	6	9	20	30	40
V1#3-9: 3-8-All 12¢ issues. 9-15¢ issue	2	4	6	13	18	22

NOTE: ***Alascia** a-19. **Aparo** a-60, V3#1, 2, 4; c-V1#4, 8, 9. **Baily** a-1-3; c-2, 5. **Evans** c-3, 4. **Giordano** c-16, 17p, 24p, 25p. **Montes/Bache** c-66. **Powell** a-4. **Shuster** a-19, 21. **Marcus Swayze** a-27.*

STRANGE TALES (...Featuring Warlock #178-181; Doctor Strange #169 on)
Atlas (CCPC #1-67/ZPC #68-79/VPI #80-85)/Marvel #86(7/61) on:
June, 1951 - No. 168, May, 1968; No. 169, Sept, 1973 - No. 188, Nov, 1976

	GD	VG	FN	VF	VF/NM	NM-
1-Horror/weird stories begin	326	652	978	2282	3991	5700
2	116	232	348	742	1271	1800
3,5: 3-Atom bomb panels	90	180	270	576	988	1400
4-Cosmic eyeball story "The Evil Eye"	94	188	282	597	1024	1450
6-9: 6-Heath-c/a. 7-Colan-a	66	132	198	419	722	1025
10-Krigstein-a	68	136	204	435	743	1050
11-14,16-20	48	96	144	302	514	725
15-Krigstein-a	49	98	147	309	522	735
21,23-27,29-34: 27-Atom bomb panels. 33-Davis-a. 34-Last pre-code issue (2/55)	41	82	123	256	428	600
22-Krigstein, Forte/Fox-a	41	82	123	259	435	610
28-Jack Katz story used in Senate Investigation report, pgs. 7 & 169	42	84	126	265	445	625
35-41,43,44: 37-Vampire story by Colan	22	44	66	154	327	500
42,45,59,61-Krigstein-a; #61 (2/58)	22	44	66	157	334	510
46-57,60: 51-(10/56) 1st S.A. issue. 53,56-Crandall-a. 60-(8/57)	21	42	63	146	311	475
58,64-Williamson-a in each, with Mayo-#58	21	42	63	148	317	485
62,63,65,66: 62-Torres-a. 66-Crandall-a	21	42	63	144	307	470
67-Prototype ish. (Quicksilver)	24	48	72	168	359	550
68,71,72,74,77,80: Ditko/Kirby-a in #67-80	23	46	69	161	343	525
69,70,73,75,76,78,79: 69-Prototype ish. (Prof. X). 70-Prototype ish. (Giant Man). 73-Prototype ish. (Ant-Man). 75-Prototype ish. (Iron Man). 76-Prototype ish. (Human Torch). 78-Prototype ish. (Ant-Man). 79-Prototype ish. (Dr. Strange) (12/60)	26	52	78	182	391	600
81-83,85-88,90,91-Ditko/Kirby-a in all: 86-Robot-c. 90-(11/61)-Atom bomb blast panel	22	44	66	154	327	500
84-Prototype ish. (Magneto)(5/61); has powers like Magneto of X-Men, but two years earlier; Ditko/Kirby-a	25	50	75	175	375	575
89-1st app. Fin Fang Foom (10/61) by Kirby	52	104	156	421	911	1400
92-Prototype ish. (Ancient One & Ant-Man); last 10¢ issue	23	46	69	161	343	525
93,95,96,98-100: Kirby-a	21	42	63	146	311	475
94-Creature similar to The Thing; Kirby-a	23	46	69	161	343	525
97-1st app. Aunt May & Uncle Ben by Ditko (6/62), before Amazing Fantasy #15; (see Tales Of Suspense #7); Kirby-a	42	84	126	315	683	1050
101-Human Torch begins by Kirby (10/62); origin recap Fantastic Four & Human Torch; Human Torch-c begin	122	244	366	988	2144	3300
102-1st app. Wizard; robot-c	41	82	123	308	667	1025
103-105: 104-1st app. Trapster. 105-2nd Wizard	35	70	105	254	552	850
106,108,109: 106-Fantastic Four guests (3/63)	27	54	81	196	423	650
107-(4/63)-Human Torch/Sub-Mariner battle; 4th S.A. Sub-Mariner app. & 1st x-over outside of Fantastic Four	42	84	126	315	683	1050
110-(7/63)-Intro Doctor Strange, Ancient One & Wong by Ditko	171	342	513	1436	3118	4800
111-2nd Dr. Strange	40	80	120	300	650	1000
112,113	20	40	60	137	294	450
114-Acrobat disguised as Captain America, 1st app. since the G.A.; intro. & 1st app. Victoria Bentley; 3rd Dr. Strange app. & begin series (11/63)	40	80	120	300	650	1000
115-Origin Dr. Strange; Human Torch vs. Sandman (Spidey villain; 2nd app. & brief origin); early Spider-Man x-over, 12/63	46	92	138	373	812	1250

Strange Tales #146 © MAR

Strange Tales: Dark Corners #1 © MAR

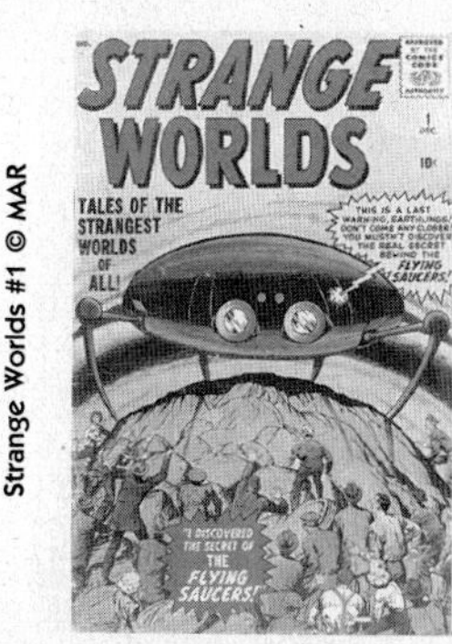

Strange Worlds #1 © MAR

GD 2.0 | VG 4.0 | FN 6.0 | VF 8.0 | VF/NM 9.0 | NM- 9.2

116-(1/64)-Human Torch battles The Thing; 1st Thing x-over 17 34 51 114 250 385
117,118,120: 120-1st Iceman x-over (from X-Men) 13 26 39 90 195 300
119-Spider-Man x-over (2 panel cameo) 15 30 45 104 227 350
121,122,124,126-134: Thing/Torch team-up in 121-134. 126-Intro Clea. 128-Quicksilver & Scarlet Witch app. (1/65). 130-The Beatles cameo. 134-Last Human Torch; The Watcher-c/story; Wood-a(i) 12 24 36 78 157 235
123-1st app. The Beetle (see Amazing Spider-Man #21 for next app.); 1st Thor x-over (8/64); Loki app. 13 26 39 85 180 275
125-Torch & Thing battle Sub-Mariner (10/64) 13 26 39 90 195 300
135-Col. (formerly Sgt.) Nick Fury becomes Nick Fury Agent of Shield (origin/1st app.) by Kirby (8/65); series begins 26 52 78 182 391 600
136-140: 138-Intro Eternity 8 16 24 56 96 135
141-147,149: 145-Begins alternating-c features w/Nick Fury (odd #'s) & Dr. Strange (even #'s). 146-Last Ditko Dr. Strange who is in consecutive stories since #113; only full Ditko Dr. Strange-c this title. 147-Dr. Strange (by Everett #147-152) continues thru #168, then Dr. Strange #169 7 14 21 44 72 100
148-Origin Ancient One 8 16 24 56 96 135
150(11/66)-John Buscema's 1st work at Marvel 7 14 21 48 79 110
151-Kirby/Steranko-c/a; 1st Marvel work by Steranko 10 20 30 65 118 170
152,153-Kirby/Steranko-a 8 16 24 51 86 120
154-158-Steranko-a/script 8 16 24 51 86 120
159-Origin Nick Fury retold; Intro Val; Captain America-c/story; Steranko-a 9 18 27 58 99 140
160-162-Steranko-a/scripts; Capt. America app. 8 16 24 51 86 120
163-166,168-Steranko-a(p). 168-Last Nick Fury (gets own book next month) & last Dr. Strange who also gets own book 7 14 21 49 82 115
167-Steranko pen/script; classic flag-c 9 18 27 58 99 140
169-1st app. Brother Voodoo(origin in #169,170) & begin series, ends #173. 3 6 9 18 27 35
170-174: 174-Origin Golem 2 4 6 13 18 22
175-177: 177-Brunner-c 2 4 6 11 16 20
178-(2/75)-Warlock by Starlin begins; origin Warlock & Him retold; 1st app. Magus; Starlin-c/a/scripts in #178-181 (all before Warlock #9) 3 6 9 21 32 42
179-181-All Warlock. 179-Intro/1st app. Pip the Troll. 180-Intro Gamora. 181-(8/75)-Warlock story continued in Warlock #9 3 6 9 17 25 32
182-188: 185,186-(Regular 25¢ editions) 1 3 4 6 8 10
185,186-(30¢-c variants, limited distribution)(5,7/76) 2 4 6 11 16 20
Annual 1(1962)-Reprints from Strange Tales #73,76,78, Tales of Suspense #7,9, Tales to Astonish #1,6,7, & Journey Into Mystery #53,55,59; (1st Marvel annual?) 52 104 156 421 911 1400
Annual 2(7/63)-Reprints from Strange Tales #67, Strange Worlds (Atlas) #1-3, World of Fantasy #16; new Human Torch vs. Spider-Man story by Kirby/Ditko (1st Spidey x-over; 4th app.); Kirby-c 82 164 246 664 1432 2200

NOTE: ***Briefer** a-17. **Burgos** a-123p. **J. Buscema** a-174p. **Colan** a-7, 11, 20, 37, 53, 169-173p, 188p. **Davis** c-71. **Ditko** a-46, 50, 67-122, 123-125p, 126-146, 175r, 182-188r; c-51, 93, 115, 121, 146. **Everett** a-4, 21, 40-42, 73, 147-152, 164i; c-8, 10, 11, 13, 15, 24, 45, 49-54, 56, 58, 60, 61, 63, 148, 150, 152, 158i. **Forte** a-27, 43, 50, 53, 54, 60. **Heath** a-2, 6; c-6, 18-20. **Kamen** a-45. **G. Kane** c-170-173, 182p. **Kirby** Human Torch-101-105, 108, 109, 114, 120; Nick Fury-135p, 141-143p; (Layouts)-135-153; other **Kirby** a-67-100p; c-68-70, 72-74, 76-92, 94, 95, 101-114, 116-123, 125-130, 132-135, 136p, 138-145, 147, 149, 151p. **Kirby/Ayers** c-101-106, 108-110. **Kirby/Ditko** a-80, 88, 121; c-75, 93, 97, 100, 139. **Lawrence** a-29. **Leiber/ Fox** a-110-113. **Maneely** a-3, 7, 37, 42; c-33, 40. **Moldoff** a-20. **Mooney** a-174i. **Morisi** a-53, 56. **Morrow** a-54. **Orlando** a-41, 44, 46, 49, 52. **Powell** a-42, 44, 49, 54, 130-134p; c-131p. **Reinman** a-11, 50, 74, 88, 91, 95, 104, 106, 112i, 124-127i. **Robinson** a-17. **Romita** c-169. **Roussos** c-201i. **R.Q. Sale** a-56; c-16. **Sekowski** a-3, 11. **Severin** a(i)-136-138; c-137. **Starlin** a-178, 179, 180p, 181p; c-178-180, 181p. **Steranko** a-151-161, 162-168p; c-151i, 153, 155, 157, 159, 161, 163, 165, 167. **Torres** a-53, 62. **Tuska** a-14, 166p. **Whitney** a-149. **Wildey** a-42, 56. **Woodbridge** a-59. Fantastic Four cameos #101-134. Jack Katz app.-26.*

STRANGE TALES
Marvel Comics Group: Apr, 1987 - No. 19, Oct, 1988

V2#1-19 3.00

STRANGE TALES
Marvel Comics: Nov, 1994 ($6.95, one-shot)

V3#1-acetate-c 7.00

STRANGE TALES (Anthology; continues stories from Man-Thing #8 and Werewolf By Night #6)
Marvel Comics: Sept, 1998 - No. 2, Oct, 1998 ($4.99)

1,2: 1-Silver Surfer app. 2-Two covers 5.00

STRANGE TALES (Humor anthology)
Marvel Comics: Nov, 2009 - No. 3, Jan, 2010 ($4.99, limited series)

1-3: 1-Paul Pope, Kochalka, Bagge and others-s/a. 2-Bagge-c/a. 3-Sakai-c/a 5.00

STRANGE TALES II (Humor anthology)
Marvel Comics: Dec, 2010 - No. 3, Feb, 2011 ($4.99, limited series)

1-3: 2-Jaime Hernandez-c. 3-Terry Moore-s/a; Pekar-s/Templeton-a 5.00

GD 2.0 | VG 4.0 | FN 6.0 | VF 8.0 | VF/NM 9.0 | NM- 9.2

STRANGE TALES: DARK CORNERS
Marvel Comics: May, 1998 ($3.99, one-shot)

1-Anthology; stories by Baron & Maleev, McGregor & Dringenberg, DeMatteis & Badger; Estes painted-c 4.00

STRANGE TALES OF THE UNUSUAL
Atlas Comics (ACI No. 1-4/WPI No. 5-11): Dec, 1955 - No. 11, Aug, 1957

1-Powell-a 46 92 138 290 488 685
2 30 60 90 177 289 400
3-Williamson-a (4 pgs.) 31 62 93 182 296 410
4,6,8,11 22 44 66 132 216 300
5-Crandall, Ditko-a 27 54 81 158 259 360
7,9: 7-Kirby, Orlando-a. 9-Krigstein-a 24 48 72 142 234 325
10-Torres, Morrow-a 22 44 66 132 216 300

NOTE: ***Baily** a-6. **Brodsky** c-2-4. **Everett** a-2, 6; c-6, 9, 11. **Heck** a-1. **Maneely** c-1. **Orlando** a-7. **Pakula** a-10. **Romita** a-1. **R.Q. Sale** a-3. **Wildey** a-3.*

STRANGE TERRORS
St. John Publishing Co.: June, 1952 - No. 7, Mar, 1953

1-Bondage-c; Zombies spelled Zoombies on-c; Fine-*esque* -a 65 130 195 416 708 1000
2 39 78 117 231 378 525
3-Kubert-a; painted-c 43 86 129 271 461 650
4-Kubert-a (reprinted in Mystery Tales #18); Ekgren painted-c; Fine-*esque* -a; Jerry Iger caricature 58 116 174 371 636 900
5-Kubert-a; painted-c 43 86 129 271 461 650
6-Giant (25¢, 100 pgs.)(1/53); bondage-c 55 110 165 352 601 850
7-Giant (25¢, 100 pgs.); Kubert-c/a 57 114 171 362 624 885

NOTE: ***Cameron** a-6, 7. **Morisi** a-6.*

STRANGE WORLD OF YOUR DREAMS
Prize Publications: Aug, 1952 - No. 4, Jan-Feb, 1953

1-Simon & Kirby-a 64 128 192 406 696 985
2,3-Simon & Kirby-c/a. 2-Meskin-a 50 100 150 315 533 750
4-S&K-c; Meskin-a 41 82 123 256 428 600

STRANGE WORLDS (#18 continued from Avon's Eerie #1-17)
Avon Periodicals: 11/50 - No. 9, 11/52; No. 18, 10-11/54 - No. 22, 9-10/55 (No #11-17)

1-Kenton of the Star Patrol by Kubert (r/Eerie #1 from 1947); Crom the Barbarian by John Giunta 148 296 444 947 1624 2300
2-Wood-a; Crom the Barbarian by Giunta; Dara of the Vikings app.; used in **SOTI**, pg. 112; injury to eye panel 129 258 387 826 1413 2000
3-Wood/Orlando-a (Kenton), Wood/Williamson/Frazetta/Krenkel/Orlando-a (7 pgs.); Malu Slave Girl Princess app.; Kinstler-c 245 490 735 1568 2684 3800
4-Wood-c/a (Kenton); Orlando-a; origin The Enchanted Daggar; Sultan-a; classic cover 148 296 444 947 1624 2300
5-Orlando/Wood-a (Kenton); Wood-c 81 162 243 518 884 1250
6-Kinstler-a(2); Orlando/Wood-c; Check-a 50 100 150 315 533 750
7-Fawcette & Becker/Alascia-a 42 84 126 265 445 625
8-Kubert, Kinstler, Hollingsworth & Lazarus-a; Lazarus Robot-c 42 84 126 265 445 625
9-Kinstler, Fawcette, Alascia-a 40 80 120 246 411 575
18-(Formerly Eerie #17)-Reprints "Attack on Planet Mars" by Kubert 32 64 96 192 314 435
19-r/Avon's "Robotmen of the Lost Planet"; last pre-code issue; Robot-c 32 64 96 192 314 435
20-War-c/story; Wood-c(r)/U.S. Paratroops #1 11 22 33 60 83 105
21,22-War-c/stories. 22-New logo 9 18 27 52 69 85
I.W. Reprint #5-Kinstler-a(r)/Avon's #9 4 8 12 24 37 50

STRANGE WORLDS
Marvel Comics (MPI No. 1,2/Male No. 3,5): Dec, 1958 - No. 5, Aug, 1959

1-Kirby & Ditko-a; flying saucer issue 94 188 282 597 1024 1450
2-Ditko-c/a 53 106 159 334 567 800
3-Kirby-a(2) 43 86 129 271 461 650
4-Williamson-a 42 84 126 265 445 625
5-Ditko-a 39 78 117 231 378 525

NOTE: ***Buscema** a-3, 4. **Ditko** a-1-5; c-2.. **Heck** a-2. **Kirby** a-1, 3. **Kirby/Brodsky** c-1, 3-5.*

STRAWBERRY SHORTCAKE
Marvel Comics (Star Comics): Jun, 1985 - No. 6, Feb, 1986 (Children's comic)

1-6: Howie Post-a 2 3 4 6 8 10

STRAWBERRY SHORTCAKE
Ape Entertainment: 2011 - No. 4, 2011 ($3.95, limited series)

1-4: 1-Scratch 'n' sniff cover 4.00

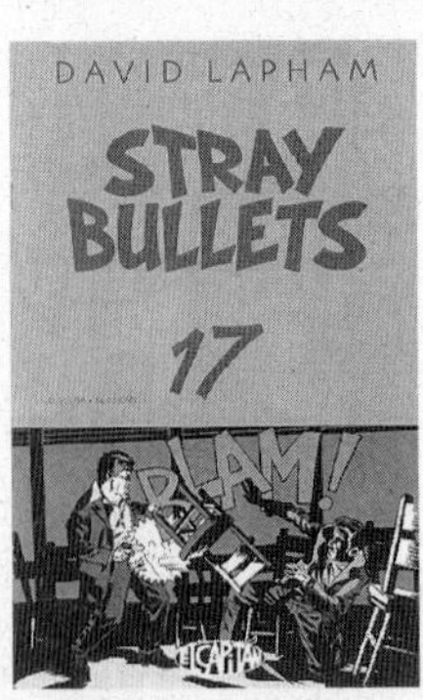

Stray Bullets #17 © David Lapham

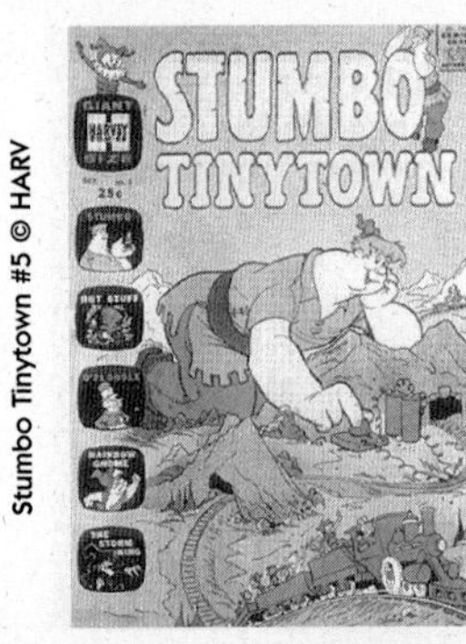

Stumbo Tinytown #5 © HARV

Stupid Comics #2 © Jim Mahfood

GD VG FN VF VF/NM NM-
2.0 4.0 6.0 8.0 9.0 9.2

STRAY
DC Comics (Homage Comics): 2001 ($5.95, prestige format, one-shot)
1-Pollina-c/a; Lobdell & Palmiotti-s 6.00

STRAY BULLETS
El Capitan Books: 1995 - No. 40, Oct, 2005 ($2.95/$3.50, B&W, mature readers)
1-David Lapham-c/a/scripts 2 4 6 8 10 12
2,3 6.00
4-8 4.00
9-21,31,32-($2.95) 3.50
22-30,33-40-($3.50) 22-Includes preview to Murder Me Dead 3.50
Free Comic Book Day giveaway (5/02) Reprints #2 with "Free Comic Book Day" banner on-c; flip book with The Matrix (printing of internet comic) 3.00
Innocence of Nihilism Volume 1 HC ($29.95, hardcover) r/#1-7 30.00
Somewhere Out West Volume 2 HC ($34.95, hardcover) r/#8-14 35.00
Other People Volume 3 HC ($34.95, hardcover) r/#15-22 35.00
Volume 1-3 TPB ($11.95, softcover) 1-r/#1-4. 2-r/#5-8. 3-r/ #9-12 12.00
Volume 4-7 TPB ($14.95) 4- r/#13-16. 5- r/#17-20. 6- r/#21-24. 7-r/#25-28 15.00
NOTE: *Multiple printings of most issues exist & are worth cover price.*

STRAY TOASTERS
Marvel Comics (Epic Comics): Jan, 1988 - No. 4, April, 1989 ($3.50, squarebound, limited series)
1-4: Sienkiewicz-c/a/scripts 4.00

STREET COMIX
Street Enterprises/King Features: 1973 (50¢, B&W, 36 pgs.)(20,000 print run)
1-Rip Kirby 2 4 6 8 11 14
2-Flash Gordon 2 4 6 10 14 18

STREETFIGHTER
Ocean Comics: Aug, 1986 - No. 4, Spr, 1987 ($1.75, limited series)
1-4: 2-Origin begins 3.00

STREET FIGHTER
Malibu Comics: Sept, 1993 - No. 3, Nov, 1993 ($2.95)
1-3: 3-Includes poster; Ferret x-over 3.00

STREET FIGHTER
Image Comics: Sept, 2003 - No. 14, Feb, 2005 ($2.95)
1-Back-up story w/Madureira-a; covers by Madureira and Tsang 3.00
2-6,8-14: 2-Two covers by Campbell and Warren; back-up story w/Warren-a 3.00
7-($4.50) Larocca-c 4.50
... Vol. 1 (3/04, $9.99, digest-size) r/main stories from #1-6 10.00

STREET FIGHTER: THE BATTLE FOR SHADALOO
DC Comics/CAP Co. Ltd.: 1995 ($3.95, one-shot)
1-Polybagged w/trading card & Tattoo 4.00

STREET FIGHTER II
Tokuma Comics (Viz): Apr, 1994 - No. 8, Nov, 1994 ($2.95, limited series)
1-8 3.00

STREET FIGHTER II
UDON Comics: No. 0, Oct, 2005 - No. 6, Nov, 2006 ($1.99/$3.95/$2.95)
0-(10/05, $1.99) prelude to series; Alvin Lee-a 3.00
1-($3.95) Two covers by Alvin Lee & Ed McGuinness 4.00
2-6-($2.95) 3.00

STREET FIGHTER LEGENDS
UDON Comics: Aug, 2006 ($3.95)
1-Spotlight on Sakura; two covers 4.00

STREETS
DC Comics: 1993 - No. 3, 1993 ($4.95, limited series, 52 pgs.)
Book 1-3-Estes painted-c 5.00

STREET SHARKS
Archie Publications: Jan, 1996 - No. 3, Mar, 1996 ($1.50, limited series)
1-3 3.00

STREET SHARKS
Archie Publications: May, 1996 - No. 6 ($1.50, published 8 times a year)
1-6 3.00

STRICTLY PRIVATE (You're in the Army Now)
Eastern Color Printing Co.: July, 1942 (#1 on sale 6/15/42)
1,2: Private Peter Plink. 2-Says 128 pgs. on-c 25 50 75 150 245 340

STRIKE!
Eclipse Comics: Aug, 1987 - No. 6, Jan, 1988 ($1.75)
1-6, ...Vs. Sgt. Strike Special 1 (5/88, $1.95) 3.00

STRIKEBACK! (The Hunt For Nikita)
Malibu Comics (Bravura): Oct, 1994 - No. 3, Jan, 1995 ($2.95, unfinished limited series)
1-3: Jonathon Peterson script, Kevin Maguire-c/a 3.00
1-Gold foil embossed-c 5.00

STRIKEBACK!
Image Comics (WildStorm Productions): Jan, 1996 - No. 5, May, 1996 ($2.50, lim. series)
1-5: Reprints original Bravura series w/additional story & art by Kevin Maguire & Jonathon Peterson; new Maguire-c in all. 4,5-New story & art 3.00

STRIKEFORCE: AMERICA
Comico: Dec, 1995 ($2.95)
V2#1-Polybagged w/gaming card; S. Clark-a(p) 3.00

STRIKEFORCE: MORITURI
Marvel Comics Group: Dec, 1986 - No. 31, July, 1989
1,13: 13-Double size 4.00
2-12,14-31: 14-Williamson-i. 25-Heath-c 3.00
... – We Who Are About To Die 1 (3/12, $0.99) r/#1 with profile pages and cover gallery 1.00

STRIKEFORCE MORITURI: ELECTRIC UNDERTOW
Marvel Comics: Dec, 1989 - No. 5, Mar, 1990 ($3.95, 52 pgs., limited series)
1-5 Squarebound 4.00

STRONG GUY REBORN (See X-Factor)
Marvel Comics: Sept, 1997 ($2.99, one-shot)
1-Dezago-s/Andy Smith, Art Thibert-a 3.00

STRONG MAN (Also see Complimentary Comics & Power of...)
Magazine Enterprises: Mar-Apr, 1955 - No. 4, Sept-Oct, 1955
1(A-1 #130)-Powell-c/a 23 46 69 136 223 310
2-4: (A-1 #132,134,139)-Powell-a. 2-Powell-c 18 36 54 105 165 225

STRONTIUM DOG
Eagle Comics: Dec, 1985 - No. 4, Mar, 1986 ($1.25, limited series)
1-4, Special 1: 4-Moore script. Special 1 (1986)-Moore script 3.00

STRYFE'S STRIKE FILE
Marvel Comics: Jan, 1993 ($1.75, one-shot, no ads)
1-Stroman, Capullo, Andy Kubert, Brandon Peterson-a; silver metallic ink-c; X-Men tie-in to X-Cutioner's Song 4.00
1-Gold metallic ink 2nd printing 3.00

STRYKEFORCE
Image Comics (Top Cow): May, 2004 - No. 5, Oct, 2004 ($2.99)
1-5-Faerber-s/Kirkham-a. 4,5-Preview of HumanKind 3.00
Vol. 1 TPB (2005, $16.99) r/#1-5 & Codename: Strykeforce #0-3; sketch pages 17.00

STUMBO THE GIANT (See Harvey Hits #49,54,57,60,63,66,69,72,78,88 & Hot Stuff #2)

STUMBO TINYTOWN
Harvey Publications: Oct, 1963 - No. 13, Nov, 1966 (All 25¢ giants)
1-Stumbo, Hot Stuff & others begin 13 26 39 88 189 290
2 9 18 27 60 103 145
3-5 7 14 21 44 72 100
6-13 6 12 18 37 59 80

STUNT DAWGS
Harvey Comics: Mar, 1993 ($1.25, one-shot)
1 3.00

STUNTMAN COMICS (Also see Thrills Of Tomorrow)
Harvey Publ.: Apr-May, 1946 - No. 2, June-July, 1946; No. 3, Oct-Nov, 1946
1-Origin Stuntman by S&K reprinted in Black Cat #9; S&K-c
116 232 348 742 1271 1800
2-S&K-c/a; The Duke of Broadway story 68 136 204 435 743 1050
3-Small size (5-1/2x8-1/2"; B&W; 32 pgs.); distributed to mail subscribers only; S&K-a; Kid Adonis by S&K reprinted in Green Hornet #37
110 220 330 704 1202 1700
(Also see All-New #15, Boy Explorers #2, Flash Gordon #5 & Thrills of Tomorrow)

STUPID COMICS (Also see 40 oz. Collected)
Oni Press/Image Comics: July, 2000; Sept, 2002 - Present ($2.95, B&W)
1-(Oni Press, 7/00) Jim Mahfood 1 page satire strips reprinted from JAVA magazine 3.00
1-3-(Image Comics, 9/02; 10/03) Jim Mahfood 1 page and 2 page satire strips 3.00

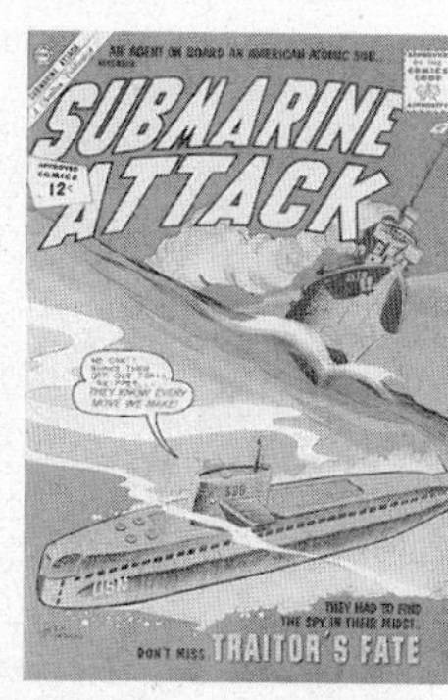

Submarine Attack #36 © CC

Sub-Mariner #6 © MAR

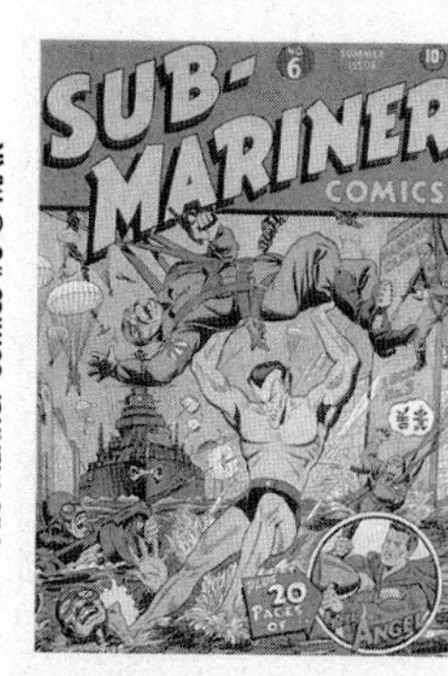

Sub-Mariner Comics #6 © MAR

GD VG FN VF VF/NM NM-
2.0 4.0 6.0 8.0 9.0 9.2

TPB (4/06, $12.99) r/#1(Oni) and #1-3(Image); Phoenix New Times strips 13.00

STUPID HEROES
Mirage Studios: Sept, 1993 - No. 3, Dec, 1994 ($2.75, unfinished limited series)
1-3-Laird-c/a & scripts; 2 trading cards bound in 3.00

STUPID, STUPID RAT TAILS (See Bone)
Cartoon Books: Dec, 1999 - No. 3, Feb, 2000 ($2.95, limited series)
1-3-Jeff Smith-a/Tom Sniegoski-s 3.00

SUBHUMAN
Dark Horse Comics: Nov, 1998 - No. 4, Feb, 1999 ($2.95, limited series)
1-4-Mark Schultz-c 3.00

SUBMARINE ATTACK (Formerly Speed Demons)
Charlton Comics: No. 11, May, 1958 - No. 54, Feb-Mar, 1966
11 4 8 12 26 41 55
12-20: 16-Atomic bomb panels 3 6 9 19 29 38
21-30 3 6 9 17 25 32
31-54: 43-Cuban missile crisis story. 47-Atomic bomb panels
3 6 9 14 20 26
NOTE: ***Glanzman** c/a-25. **Montes/Bache** a-38, 40, 41.*

SUB-MARINER (See All-Select, All-Winners, Blonde Phantom, Daring, The Defenders, Fantastic Four #4, Human Torch, The Invaders, Iron Man &..., Marvel Mystery, Marvel Spotlight #27, Men's Adventures, Motion Picture Funnies Weekly, Namora, Namor, The..., Prince Namor, The Sub-Mariner, Saga Of The..., Tales to Astonish #70 & 2nd series, USA & Young Men)

SUB-MARINER, THE (2nd Series)(Sub-Mariner #31 on)
Marvel Comics Group: May, 1968 - No. 72, Sept, 1974 (No. 43: 52 pgs.)
1-Origin Sub-Mariner; story continued from Iron Man & Sub-Mariner #1
21 42 63 146 311 475
2-Triton app. 10 20 30 68 127 185
3-5: 5-1st Tiger Shark (9/68) 8 16 24 53 89 125
6,7,9,10: 6-Tiger Shark-c & 2nd app., cont'd from #5. 7-Photo-c. (1968).
9-1st app. Serpent Crown (origin in #10 & 12) 6 12 18 37 59 80
8-Sub-Mariner vs. Thing 10 20 30 66 121 175
8-2nd printing (1994) 2 4 6 8 10 12
11-13,15: 15-Last 12¢ issue 5 10 15 30 48 65
14-Sub-Mariner vs. G.A. Human Torch; death of Toro (1st modern app. & only app. Toro, 6/69)
6 12 18 42 69 95
16-20: 19-1st Sting Ray (11/69); Stan Lee, Romita, Heck, Thomas, Everett & Kirby cameos.
20-Dr. Doom app. 4 8 12 22 34 45
21,23-33,37-39,41,42: 25-Origin Atlantis. 30-Capt. Marvel x-over. 37-Death of Lady Dorma.
38-Origin retold. 42-Last 15¢ issue. 3 6 9 17 25 32
22,40: 22-Dr. Strange x-over. 40-Spider-Man x-over 3 6 9 18 27 35
34-Prelude (w/#35) to 1st Defenders story; Hulk & Silver Surfer x-over
9 18 27 61 106 150
35-Namor/Hulk/Silver Surfer team-up to battle The Avengers-c/story (3/71);
hints at teaming up again 7 14 21 48 79 110
36-Wrightson-a(i) 3 6 9 20 30 40
43-King Size Special (52 pgs.) 3 6 9 21 32 42
44,45-Sub-Mariner vs. Human Torch 3 6 9 19 29 38
46-49,56,62,64-72: 47,48-Dr. Doom app. 49-Cosmic Cube story. 62-1st Tales of Atlantis,
ends #66. 64-Hitler cameo. 67-New costume; F.F. x-over. 69-Spider-Man x-over (6 panels)
2 4 6 9 13 16
50-1st app. Nita, Namor's niece (later Namorita in New Warriors)
2 4 6 11 16 20
51-55,57,58,60,61,63-Everett issues: 57-Venus app. (1st since 4/52); anti-Vietnam War
panels. 61-Last artwork by Everett; 1st 4 pgs. completed by Mortimer; pgs. 5-20 by Mooney
2 4 6 10 14 18
59-1st battle with Thor; Everett-a 3 6 9 21 32 42
Special 1 (1/71)-r/Tales to Astonish #70-73 3 6 9 21 32 42
Special 2 (1/72)-(52 pgs.)-r/T.T.A. #74-76; Everett-a 3 6 9 17 25 32
NOTE: ***Bolle** a-67i. **Buscema** a(p)-1-8, 20, 24. **Colan** a(p)-10, 11, 40, 43, 46-49, Special 1, 2; c(p)-10, 11, 40. **Craig** a-17i, 19-23i. **Everett** a-45r, 50-55, 57, 58, 59-61(plot), 63(plot); c-47, 48i, 55, 57, 58-59i, 61, Spec. 2. **G. Kane** c(p)-42-52, 58, 66, 70, 71. **Mooney** a-24i, 25i, 32-35i, 39i, 42i, 44i, 45i, 60i, 61i, 65p, 66p, 68i. **Severin** c/a-38i. **Starlin** c-59p. **Tuska** a-41p, 42p, 69-71p. **Wrightson** a-36i. #53, 54-r/stories Sub-Mariner Comics #41 & 39.*

SUB-MARINER (The Initiative, follows Civil War series)
Marvel Comics: Aug, 2007 - No. 6, Jan, 2008 ($2.99, limited series)
1-6: 1-Turner-c/Briones-a/Cherniss & Johnson-s; Iron Man app. 3-Yu-c; Venom app. 3.00
...: Revolution TPB (208, $14.99) r/#1-6 15.00

SUB-MARINER COMICS (1st Series) (The Sub-Mariner #1, 2, 33-42)(Official True Crime Cases #24 on; Amazing Mysteries #32 on; Best Love #33 on)
Timely/Marvel Comics (TCI 1-7/SePI 8/MPI 9-32/Atlas Comics (CCC 33-42)):
Spring, 1941 - No. 23, Sum, 1947; No. 24, Wint, 1947 - No. 31, 4/49; No. 32, 7/49; No. 33, 4/54 - No. 42, 10/55
1-The Sub-Mariner by Everett & The Angel begin
2700 5400 8100 20,000 44,000 68,000
2-Everett-a 622 1244 1866 4541 8021 11,500
3-Churchill assassination-c; 40 pg. S-M story 541 1082 1623 3950 6975 10,000
4-Everett-a, 40 pgs.; 1 pg. Wolverton-a 411 822 1233 2877 5039 7200
5-Gabrielle/Klein-c 326 652 978 2282 3991 5700
6-10: 9-Wolverton-a, 3 pgs.; flag-c 303 606 909 2121 3711 5300
11-Classic Schomburg-c 314 628 942 2198 3849 5500
12-15 245 490 735 1568 2684 3800
16-20 194 388 582 1242 2121 3000
21-Last Angel; Everett-a 135 270 405 864 1482 2100
22-Young Allies app. 135 270 405 864 1482 2100
23-The Human Torch, Namora x-over (Sum/47); 2nd app. Namora after
Marvel Mystery #82 158 316 474 1003 1727 2450
24-Namora x-over (3rd app.) 142 284 426 909 1555 2200
25-The Blonde Phantom begins (Spr/48), ends No. 31; Kurtzman-a; Namora x-over;
last quarterly issue 152 304 456 965 1658 2350
26-28: 28-Namora cover; Everett-a 139 278 417 883 1517 2150
29-31 (4/49): 29-The Human Torch app. 31-Capt. America app.
139 278 417 883 1517 2150
32 (7/49, Scarce)-Origin Sub-Mariner 271 542 813 1734 2967 4200
33 (4/54)-Origin Sub-Mariner; The Human Torch app.; Namora x-over in Sub-Mariner #33-42
116 232 348 742 1271 1800
34,35-Human Torch in each 95 190 285 603 1039 1475
36,37,39-41: 36,39-41-Namora app. 94 188 282 597 1024 1450
38-Origin Sub-Mariner's wings; Namora app.; last pre-code (2/55)
98 196 294 616 1071 1525
42-Last issue 103 206 309 659 1130 1600
NOTE: *Angel by **Gustavson**-#1, 8. **Brodsky** c-34-36, 42. **Everett** a-1-4, 22-24, 26-42; c-32, 33, 40. **Maneely** a-38; c-37, 39-41. **Rico** c-27-31. **Schomburg** c-1-4, 6, 8-18, 20. **Sekowsky** c-24. 25, 26(w/**Rico**). **Shores** c-21-23, 38. Bondage c-13, 22, 24, 25, 34.*

SUB-MARINER COMICS 70th ANNIVERARY SPECIAL
Marvel Comics: June, 2009 ($3.99, one-shot)
1-New WWII story, Breitweiser-a; Williamson-a; r/debut app. from Marvel Comics #1 5.00

SUB-MARINER: THE DEPTHS
Marvel Comics: Nov, 2008 - No. 5, May, 2009 ($3.99, limited series)
1-5-Peter Milligan-s/Esad Ribic-a/c 4.00

SUBSPECIES
Eternity Comics: May, 1991 - No. 4, Aug, 1991 ($2.50, limited series)
1-4: New stories based on horror movie 3.00

SUBTLE VIOLENTS
CFD Productions: 1991 ($2.50, B&W, mature)
1-Linsner-c & story 1 3 4 8 10 12
San Diego Limited Edition 4 8 12 24 37 50

SUE & SALLY SMITH (Formerly My Secret Life)
Charlton Comics: V2#48, Nov, 1962 - No. 54, Nov, 1963 (Flying Nurses)
V2#48-2nd app. 3 6 9 17 25 32
49-54 2 4 6 13 18 22

SUGAR & SPIKE (Also see The Best of DC & DC Silver Age Classics)
National Periodical Publications: Apr-May, 1956 - No. 98, Oct-Nov, 1971
1 (Scarce) 331 662 993 2317 4059 5800
2 126 252 378 806 1378 1950
3-5: 3-Letter column begins 77 154 231 493 847 1200
6-10 47 94 141 296 498 700
11-20 37 74 111 222 361 500
21-29: 26-Christmas-c 26 52 78 154 252 350
30-Scribbly & Scribbly, Jr. x-over 27 54 81 158 259 360
31-40 20 40 60 117 189 260
41-60 9 18 27 61 106 150
61-80: 69-1st app. Tornado-Tot-c/story. 72-Origin & 1st app. Bernie the Brain
7 14 21 49 82 115
81-84,86-95: 84-Bernie the Brain apps. as Superman in 1 panel (9/69)
6 12 18 39 62 85
85 (68 pgs.)-r/#72 6 12 18 42 69 95
96 (68 pgs.) 7 14 21 46 76 105
97,98 (52 pgs.) 6 12 18 42 69 95
No. 1 Replica Edition (2002, $2.95) reprint of #1 4.00
NOTE: *All written and drawn by **Sheldon Mayer**. Issues with Paper Doll pages cut or missing are common.*

SUGAR BOWL COMICS (Teen-age)
Famous Funnies: May, 1948 - No. 5, Jan, 1949

Suicide Squad (2011 series) #1 © DC

Sun Girl #1 © MAR

Superboy #44 © DC

	GD 2.0	VG 4.0	FN 6.0	VF 8.0	VF/NM 9.0	NM- 9.2

1-Toth-c/a 15 30 45 83 124 165
2,4,5 9 18 27 50 65 80
3-Toth-a 10 20 30 56 76 95

SUGARFOOT (TV)
Dell Publishing Co.: No. 907, May, 1958 - No. 1209, Oct-Dec, 1961

Four Color 907 (#1)-Toth-a, photo-c 11 22 33 74 145 215
Four Color 992 (5-7/59), Toth-a, photo-c 10 20 30 70 133 195
Four Color 1059 (11-1/60), 1098 (5-7/60), 1147 (11-1/61), 1209-all photo-c. 1059,1098,1147-all have variant edition, back-c comic strip 8 16 24 56 96 135

SUGARSHOCK (Also see MySpace Dark Horse Presents)
Dark Horse Comics: Oct, 2009 ($3.50, one-shot)

1-Joss Whedon-s/Fabio Moon-a/c; story from online comic; Moon sketch pgs. 3.50

SUICIDE SQUAD (See Brave & the Bold, Doom Patrol & Suicide Squad Spec., Legends #3 & note under Star Spangled War stories)
DC Comics: May, 1987 - No. 66, June, 1992; No. 67, Mar, 2010 (Direct sales only #32 on)

1-Chaykin-c 4.00
2-66: 9-Millennium x-over. 10-Batman-c/story. 13-JLI app. (Batman). 16-Re-intro Shade The Changing Man. 23-1st Oracle. 27-34,36,37-Snyder-a. 40-43-"The Phoenix Gambit" Batman storyline. 40-Free Batman/Suicide Squad poster 3.00
67-(3/10, $2.99) Blackest Night one-shot; Fiddler rises as a Black Lantern; Califiore-a 3.00
Annual 1 (1988, $1.50)-Manhunter x-over 4.00
...: Trial By Fire TPB (2011, $19.99) r/#1-8 & Secret Origins #14 20.00

SUICIDE SQUAD (2nd series)
DC Comics: Nov, 2001 - No. 12, Oct, 2002 ($2.50)

1-12-Giffen-s/Medina-a; Sgt. Rock app. 4-Heath-a. 10-J. Severin-a. 12-JSA app. 3.00

SUICIDE SQUAD (3rd series)
DC Comics: Nov, 2007 - No. 8, Jun, 2008 ($2.99, limited series)

1-8-Ostrander-s/Pina-a/Snyder III-c 3.00
...: From the Ashes TPB (2008, $19.99) r/#1-8 20.00

SUICIDE SQUAD (DC New 52)
DC Comics: Nov, 2011 - Present ($2.99)

1-8: 1-Harley Quinn, Deadshot, King Shark, El Diablo, Voltaic, Black Spider team up 3.00

SUMMER FUN (See Dell Giants)

SUMMER FUN (Formerly Li'l Genius; Holiday Surprise #55)
Charlton Comics: No. 54, Oct, 1966 (Giant)

54 4 8 12 22 34 45

SUMMER FUN (Walt Disney's...)
Disney Comics: Summer, 1991 ($2.95, annual, 68 pgs.)

1-D. Duck, M. Mouse, Brer Rabbit, Chip 'n' Dale & Pluto, Li'l Bad Wolf, Super Goof, Scamp stories 4.00

SUMMER LOVE (Formerly Brides in Love?)
Charlton Comics: V2#46, Oct, 1965; V2#47, Oct, 1966; V2#48, Nov, 1968

V2#46-Beatles-c & 8 pg. story 12 24 36 81 166 250
47-(68 pgs.) Beatles-c & 12 pg. story 10 20 30 68 127 185
48 3 6 9 16 22 28

SUMMER MAGIC (See Movie Comics)

SUNDANCE (See Hotel Deparee...)

SUNDANCE KID (Also see Blazing Six-Guns)
Skywald Publications: June, 1971 - No. 3, Sept, 1971 (52 pgs.)(Pre-code reprints & new-s)

1-Durango Kid; Two Kirby Bullseye-r 3 6 9 16 23 30
2,3: 2-Swift Arrow, Durango Kid, Bullseye by S&K; Meskin plus 1 pg. origin.
3-Durango Kid, Billy the Kid, Red Hawk-r 2 4 6 11 16 20

SUNDAY PIX (Christian religious)
David C. Cook Pub/USA Weekly Newsprint Color Comics: V1#1, Mar,1949 - V16#26, July 19, 1964 (7x10", 12 pgs., mail subscription only)

V1#1 8 16 24 42 54 65
V1#2-up 6 12 18 27 33 38
V2#1-52 (1950) 5 10 15 23 28 32
V3-V6 (1951-1953) 4 9 13 18 22 26
V7-V11#1-7,23-52 (1954-1959) 2 4 6 13 18 22
V11#8-22 (2/22-5/31/59) H.G. Wells First Men in the Moon serial 3 6 9 14 19 24
V12#1-19,21-52; V13-V15#1,2,9-52; V16#1-26(7/19/64) 2 4 6 10 14 18
V12#20 (5/15/60) 2 page interview with Peanuts' Charles Schulz 4 8 12 24 37 50
V15#3-8 (2/24/63) John Glenn, Christian astronaut 3 6 9 16 23 30

SUN DEVILS
DC Comics: July, 1984 - No. 12, June, 1985 ($1.25, maxi series)

1-12: 6-Death of Sun Devil 3.00

SUNDIATA: A LEGEND OF AFRICA
NBM Publishing Inc.: 2002 ($15.95, hardcover with dustjacket)

nn-Will Eisner-s/a; adaptation of an African folk tale 16.00

SUN FUN KOMIKS
Sun Publications: 1939 (15¢, B&W & red)

1-Satire on comics (rare) 290 580 870 1856 3178 4500
NOTE: *Hitler, Stalin and Mussolini featured gag in 1-page story written in Hebrew and English. Nazi swastika and Nazi flag app. in a different 1-page "Gussie the Gob" story. First Hitler app. in comics?*

SUNFIRE & BIG HERO SIX (See Alpha Flight)
Marvel Comics: Sept, 1998 - No. 3, Nov, 1998 ($2.50, limited series)

1-3-Lobdell-s 3.00

SUN GIRL (See The Human Torch & Marvel Mystery Comics #88)
Marvel Comics (CCC): Aug, 1948 - No. 3, Dec, 1948

1-Sun Girl begins; Miss America app. 194 388 582 1242 2121 3000
2,3: 2-The Blonde Phantom begins 129 258 387 826 1413 2000

SUNNY, AMERICA'S SWEETHEART (Formerly Cosmo Cat #1-10)
Fox Features Syndicate: No. 11, Dec, 1947 - No. 14, June, 1948

11-Feldstein-c/a 126 252 378 806 1378 1950
12-14-Feldstein-c/a; 13,14-Lingerie panels. 13-L.B. Cole-a 90 180 270 576 988 1400
I.W. Reprint #8-Feldstein-a; r/Fox issue 10 20 30 73 129 185

SUN-RUNNERS (Also see Tales of the...)
Pacific Comics/Eclipse Comics/Amazing Comics: 2/84 - No. 3, 5/84; No. 4, 11/84 - No. 7, 1986 (Baxter paper)

1-7: P. Smith-a in #2-4 3.00
Christmas Special 1 (1987, $1.95)-By Amazing 3.00

SUNSET CARSON (Also see Cowboy Western)
Charlton Comics: Feb, 1951 - No. 4, 1951 (No month) (Photo-c on each)

1-Photo/retouched-c (Scarce, all issues) 58 116 174 371 636 900
2-Kit Carson story; adapts "Kansas Raiders" w/Brian Donlevy, Audie Murphy & Margaret Chapman 41 82 123 256 428 600
3,4 34 68 102 199 325 450

SUNSET PASS (See Zane Grey & 4-Color #230)

SUPER ANIMALS PRESENTS PIDGY & THE MAGIC GLASSES
Star Publications: Dec, 1953 (25¢, came w/glasses)

1-(3-D Comics)-L. B. Cole-c 40 80 120 246 411 575

SUPER BAD JAMES DYNOMITE
5-D Comics: Dec, 2005 - No. 5, Feb, 2007 ($3.99)

1-5-Created by the Wayans brothers 4.00

SUPERBOY
DC Comics: Jan, 1942

nn-Ashcan comic, not distributed to newsstands, only for in house use. Covers were produced, but not the rest of the book. A CGC certified 9.2 copy sold in 2003 for $6,600.

SUPERBOY (See Adventure, Aurora, DC Comics Presents, DC 100 Page Super Spectacular #15, DC Super Stars, 80 Page Giant #10, More Fun Comics, The New Advs. of... & Superman Family #191, Young Justice)

SUPERBOY (1st Series)(...& the Legion of Super-Heroes with #231)
(Becomes The Legion of Super-Heroes No. 259 on)
National Periodical Publ./DC Comics: Mar-Apr, 1949 - No. 258, Dec, 1979 (#1-16: 52 pgs.)

1-Superman cover; intro in More Fun #101 (1-2/45) 892 1784 2676 6512 11,506 16,500
2-Used in **SOTI**, pg. 35-36,226 248 496 744 1575 2713 3850
3 194 388 582 1242 2121 3000
4,5: 5-1st pre-Supergirl tryout (c/story, 11-12/49) 135 270 405 864 1482 2100
6-9: 8-1st Superbaby 119 238 357 762 1306 1850
10-1st app. Lana Lang 129 258 387 826 1413 2000
11-15: 11-2nd Lana Lang app.; 1st Lana cover 87 174 261 553 952 1350
16-20: 20-2nd Jor-El cover 60 120 180 381 653 925
21-26,28-30: 21-Lana Lang app. 50 100 150 315 533 750
27-Low distribution 52 104 156 322 549 775
31-38: 38-Last pre-code issue (1/55) 42 84 126 265 445 625
39-48,50 (7/56) 39 78 117 240 395 550
49 (6/56)-1st app. Metallo (Jor-El's robot) 43 86 129 271 461 650

Superboy #223 © DC

Superboy (3rd series) #50 © DC

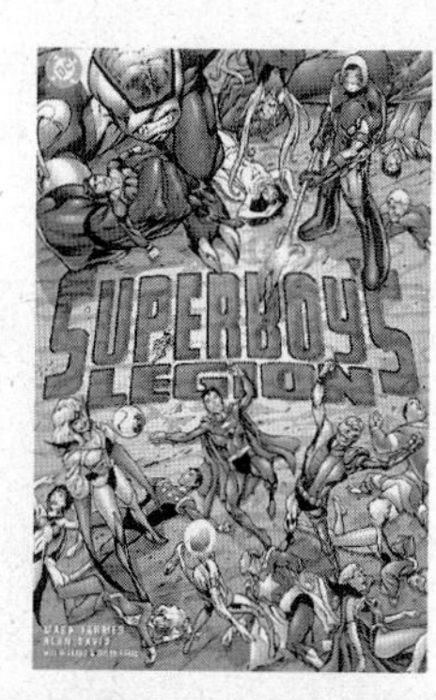

Superboy's Legion #2 © DC

	GD 2.0	VG 4.0	FN 6.0	VF 8.0	VF/NM 9.0	NM- 9.2
51-60: 52-1st S.A. issue. 56-Krypto-c	32	64	96	188	307	425
61-67	26	52	78	154	252	350
68-Origin/1st app. original Bizarro (10-11/58)	71	142	213	454	777	1100
69-77,79: 76-1st Supermonkey	22	44	66	132	216	300
78-Origin Mr. Mxyzptlk & Superboy's costume	30	60	90	177	289	400
80-1st meeting Superboy/Supergirl (4/60)	28	56	84	165	270	375
81,83-85,87,88: 83-Origin/1st app. Kryptonite Kid	13	26	39	85	180	275
82-1st Bizarro Krypto	13	26	39	87	186	285
86-(1/61)-4th Legion app; Intro Pete Ross	20	40	60	137	294	450
89-(6/61)-1st app. Mon -El; 2nd Phantom Zone	27	54	81	189	407	625
90-92: 90-Pete Ross learns Superboy's I.D. 92-Last 10¢ issue	12	24	36	79	160	240
93-10th Legion app.(12/61); Chameleon Boy app.	12	24	36	81	166	250
94-97,99: 94-1st app. Superboy Revenge Squad	11	22	33	73	142	210
98-(7/62) Legion app; origin & 1st app. Ultra Boy; Pete Ross joins Legion	13	26	39	85	180	275
100-(10/62)-Ultra Boy app; 1st app. Phantom Zone villains, Dr. Xadu & Erndine. 2 pg. map of Krypton; origin Superboy retold; r-cover of Superman #1	17	34	51	119	260	400
101-120: 104-Origin Phantom Zone. 115-Atomic bomb-c. 117-Legion app.	10	20	30	64	115	165
121-128: 124-(10/65)-1st app. Insect Queen (Lana Lang). 125-Legion cameo. 126-Origin Krypto the Super Dog retold with new facts	8	16	24	56	96	135
129-(80-pg. Giant G-22)-Reprints origin Mon-El	10	20	30	64	115	165
130-137,139,140: 131-Legion statues cameo in Dog Legionnaires story. 132-1st app. Supremo. 133-Superboy meets Robin	7	14	21	48	79	110
138 (80-pg. Giant G-35)	8	16	24	53	89	125
141-146,148-155,157: 145-Superboy's parents regain their youth. 148-Legion app. 157-Last 12¢ issue	6	12	18	41	66	90
147(6/68)-Giant G-47; 1st origin of L.S.H. (Saturn Girl, Lightning Lad, Cosmic Boy); origin Legion of Super-Pets-r/Adv. #293	7	14	21	48	79	110
147 Replica Edition (2003, $6.95) reprints entire issue; cover recreation by Ordway						7.00
156-(Giant G-59)	7	14	21	44	72	100
158-164,166-171,175: 171-1st app. Aquaboy	3	6	9	19	29	38
165,174 (Giant G-71,G-83): 165-r/1st app. Krypto the Superdog from Adventure Comics #210	6	12	18	39	62	85
172,173,176-Legion app.: 172-1st app. & origin Yango (The Super Ape). 176-Partial photo-c; last 15¢ issue	3	6	9	20	30	40
177-184,186,187 (All 52 pgs.): 182-All new origin of the classic World's Finest team (Superman & Batman) as teenagers (2/72, 22pgs). 184-Origin Dial H for Hero-r	3	6	9	21	32	42
185-Also listed as DC 100 Pg. Super Spectacular #12; Legion-c/story; Teen Titans, Kid Eternity(r/Hit #46), Star Spangled Kid-r(S.S. #55)	8	16	24	53	89	125
188-190,192,194,196: 188-Origin Karkan. 196-Last Superboy solo story	3	6	9	14	19	24
191,193,195: 191-Origin Sunboy retold; Legion app. 193-Chameleon Boy & Shrinking Violet get new costumes. 195-1st app. Erg-1/Wildfire; Phantom Girl gets new costume	3	6	9	14	20	26
197-Legion series begins; Lightning Lad's new costume	3	6	9	20	30	40
198,199: 198-Element Lad & Princess Projectra get new costumes	3	6	9	14	20	26
200-Bouncing Boy & Duo Damsel marry; J'onn J'onzz cameo	3	6	9	16	23	30
201,204,206,207,209: 201-Re-intro Erg-1 as Wildfire. 204-Supergirl resigns from Legion. 206-Ferro Lad & Invisible Kid app. 209-Karate Kid gets new costume	2	4	6	11	16	20
202,205-(100 pgs.): 202-Light Lass gets new costume; Mike Grell's 1st comic work-i (5-6/74)	5	10	15	30	48	65
203-Invisible Kid killed by Validus	3	6	9	16	22	28
208,210: 208-(68 pgs.). 208-Legion of Super-Villains app. 210-Origin Karate Kid	3	6	9	14	20	26
211-220: 212-Matter-Eater Lad resigns. 216-1st app. Tyroc, who joins the Legion in #218	2	4	6	9	13	16
221-230,246-249: 226-Intro. Dawnstar. 228-Death of Chemical King	2	4	6	8	10	12
231-245: (Giants). 240-Origin Dawnstar. 242-(52 pgs.). 243-Legion of Substitute Heroes app. 243-245-(44 pgs.).	2	4	6	9	13	16
244,245-(Whitman variants; low print run, no issue# shown on cover)	3	6	9	14	20	26
246-248-(Whitman variants; low ...)	2	4	6	11	16	20
250-258: 253-Intro Blok. 257-Return of Bouncing Boy & Duo Damsel by Ditko	2	3	4	6	8	10
251-258-(Whitman variants; low print run)	2	4	6	10	14	18
Annual 1 (Sum/64, 84 pgs.)-Origin Krypto-r	15	30	45	104	227	350
Spectacular 1 (1980, Giant)-1st comic distributed only through comic stores; mostly-r	2	4	6	8	10	12

...: The Greatest Team-Up Stories Ever Told TPB (2010, $19.99) r/team-ups with Robin, Supergirl, young versions of Aquaman, Green Arrow, Bruce Wayne; Davis-c 20.00

NOTE: ***Neal Adams*** *c-143, 145, 146, 148-155, 157-161, 163, 164, 166-168, 172, 173, 175, 176, 178.* ***M. Anderson*** *a-178,179, 245i.* ***Ditko*** *a-257p.* ***Grell*** *a-202i, 203-219, 220-224p, 235p; c-207-232, 235, 236p, 237, 239p, 240p, 243p, 246, 258.* ***Nasser*** *a(p)-222, 225, 226, 230, 231, 233, 236.* ***Simonson*** *a-237p.* ***Starlin*** *a(p)-239, 250, 251; c-238.* ***Staton*** *a-227p, 243-249p, 252-258p; c-247-251p.* ***Swan/Moldoff*** *c-109.* ***Tuska*** *a-172, 173, 176, 183, 235p.* ***Wood*** *inks-153-155, 157-161. Legion app.-172, 173, 176, 177, 183, 184, 188, 190, 191, 193, 195, 197-258.*

SUPERBOY (TV)(2nd Series)(The Adventures of...#19 on)
DC Comics: Feb, 1990 - No. 22, Dec, 1991 ($1.00/$1.25)

1-Photo-c from TV show; Mooney-a(p) 4.00
2-22: Mooney-a in 2-8,18-20; 8-Bizarro-c/story; Arthur Adams-a(i). 9-12,14-17-Swan-a 3.00
...Special 1 (1992, $1.75) Swan-a 4.00

SUPERBOY (3rd Series)
DC Comics: Feb, 1994 - No. 100, Jul, 2002 ($1.50/$1.95/$1.99/$2.25)

1-Metropolis Kid from Reign of the Supermen 4.00
2-8,0,9-24,26-76: 6,7-Worlds Collide Pts. 3 & 8. 8-(9/94)-Zero Hour x-over. 0-(10/94). 9-(11/94)-King Shark app. 21-Legion app. 28-Supergirl-c/app. 33-Final Night. 38-41-"Meltdown". 45-Legion-c/app. 47-Green Lantern-c/app. 50-Last Boy on Earth begins. 60-Crosses Hypertime. 68-Demon-c/app. 3.00
25-($2.95)-New Gods & Female Furies app.; w/pin-ups 4.00
77-99: 77-Begin $2.25-c. 79-Superboy's powers return. 80,81-Titans app. 83-New costume. 85-Batgirl app. 90,91-Our Worlds at War x-over 3.00
100-($3.50) Sienkiewicz-c; Grummett & McCrea-a; Superman cameo 4.00
#1,000,000 (11/98) 853rd Century x-over 3.00
Annual 1 (1994, $2.95, 68 pgs.)-Elseworlds story, Pt. 2 of The Super Seven (see Adventures Of Superman Annual #6) 4.00
Annual 2 (1995, $3.95)-Year One story 4.00
Annual 3 (1996, $2.95)-Legends of the Dead Earth 4.00
Annual 4 (1997, $3.95)-Pulp Heroes story 4.00
...Plus 1 (Jan, 1997, $2.95) w/Capt. Marvel Jr. 4.00
...Plus 2 (Fall, 1997, $2.95) w/Slither (Scare Tactics) 4.00
.../Risk Double-Shot 1 (Feb, 1998, $1.95) w/Risk (Teen Titans) 3.00

SUPERBOY (4th Series)
DC Comics: Jan, 2011 - No. 11, Early Oct, 2011 ($2.99)

1-11: 1-Lemire-s/Gallo-a/Albuquerque-c; Parasite & Poison Ivy app. 2,3-Noto-c 3.00
1-5: 1-Variant-c by Cassaday. 2-March-var-c. 3-Nguyen var-c. 4-Lau var-c. 5-Manapul 4.00

SUPERBOY (DC New 52)
DC Comics: Nov, 2011 - Present ($2.99)

1-8: 1-New origin; Lobdell-s/Silva-a/Canete-c; Caitlin Fairchild app. 6-Supergirl app. 8-Grunge, Beast Boy & Terra app. 3.00

SUPERBOY AND THE LEGION OF SUPER-HEROES
DC Comics: 2011 ($14.99, TPB)

SC-Reprints stories from Adventure Comics #515-520 15.00

SUPERBOY & THE RAVERS
DC Comics: Sept, 1996 - No. 19, March, 1998 ($1.95)

1-19: 4-Adam Strange app. 7-Impulse-c/app. 9-Superman-c/app. 3.00

SUPERBOY COMICS
DC Comics: Jan. 1942

nn - Ashcan comic, not distributed to newsstands, only for in-house use. Cover art is Detective Comics #57 with interior being Action Comics #38. A CGC certified 9.2 copy sold for $6,600 in 2003 and for $15,750 in 2008.

SUPERBOY/ROBIN: WORLD'S FINEST THREE
DC Comics: 1996 - No. 2, 1996 ($4.95, squarebound, limited series)

1,2: Superboy & Robin vs. Metallo & Poison Ivy; Karl Kesel & Chuck Dixon scripts; Tom Grummett-c(p)/a(p) 5.00

SUPERBOY'S LEGION (Elseworlds)
DC Comics: 2001 - No. 2, 2001 ($5.95, squarebound, limited series)

1,2-31st century Superboy forms Legion; Farmer-s/i; Davis-a(p)/c 6.00

SUPERBOY: THE BOY OF STEEL
DC Comics: 2010 ($19.99, hardcover with dustjacket)

HC-Reprints stories from Adventure Comics #0-3,5,6 & Superman Secret Files 2009 20.00
SC-(2011, $14,99) Same contents as HC 15.00

SUPER BRAT (Li'l Genius #6 on)

Super Comics #77 © DELL

Super Duck Comics #18 © AP

Super Friends #26 © DC

Toby Press: Jan, 1954 - No. 4, July, 1954

	GD 2.0	VG 4.0	FN 6.0	VF 8.0	VF/NM 9.0	NM- 9.2
1	9	18	27	47	61	75
2-4: 4-Li'l Teevy by Mel Lazarus	6	12	18	28	34	40
I.W. Reprint #1,2,3,7,8('58): 1-r/#1	2	4	6	8	10	12
I.W. (Super) Reprint #10('63)	2	4	6	8	10	12

SUPERCAR (TV)
Gold Key: Nov, 1962 - No. 4, Aug, 1963 (All painted-c)

	GD 2.0	VG 4.0	FN 6.0	VF 8.0	VF/NM 9.0	NM- 9.2
1	11	22	33	76	151	225
2,3	7	14	21	48	79	110
4-Last issue	8	16	24	53	89	125

SUPER CAT (Formerly Frisky Animals; also see Animal Crackers)
Star Publications #56-58/Ajax/Farrell Publ. (Four Star Comic Corp.): No. 56, Nov, 1953 - No. 58, May, 1954; Aug, 1957 - No. 4, May, 1958

	GD 2.0	VG 4.0	FN 6.0	VF 8.0	VF/NM 9.0	NM- 9.2
56-58-L.B. Cole-c on all	19	38	57	112	179	245
1(1957-Ajax)- "The Adventures of..." c-only	10	20	30	54	72	90
2-4	7	14	21	35	43	50

SUPER CIRCUS (TV)
Cross Publishing Co.: Jan, 1951 - No. 5, Sept, 1951 (Mary Hartline)

	GD 2.0	VG 4.0	FN 6.0	VF 8.0	VF/NM 9.0	NM- 9.2
1-(52 pgs.)-Cast photos on-c	15	30	45	85	130	175
2-Cast photos on-c	10	20	30	58	79	100
3-5	9	18	27	50	65	80

SUPER CIRCUS (TV)
Dell Publ. Co.: No. 542, Mar, 1954 - No. 694, Mar, 1956 (Mary Hartline)

	GD 2.0	VG 4.0	FN 6.0	VF 8.0	VF/NM 9.0	NM- 9.2
Four Color 542: Mary Hartline photo-c	7	14	21	46	76	105
Four Color 592,694: Mary Hartline photo-c	6	12	18	42	69	95

SUPER COMICS
Dell Publishing Co.: May, 1938 - No. 121, Feb-Mar, 1949

	GD 2.0	VG 4.0	FN 6.0	VF 8.0	VF/NM 9.0	NM- 9.2
1-Terry & The Pirates, The Gumps, Dick Tracy, Little Orphan Annie, Little Joe, Gasoline Alley, Smilin' Jack, Smokey Stover, Smitty, Tiny Tim, Moon Mullins, Harold Teen, Winnie Winkle begin	226	452	678	1446	2473	3500
2	82	164	246	528	902	1275
3	73	146	219	467	796	1125
4,5: 4-Dick Tracy-c; also #8-10,17,26(part),31	57	114	171	362	619	875
6-10	47	94	141	296	498	700
11-20: 20-Smilin' Jack-c (also #29,32)	39	78	117	240	395	550
21-29: 21-Magic Morro begins (origin & 1st app., 2/40). 22,27-Ken Ernst-c (also #25?); Magic Morro c-22,25,27,34	34	68	102	199	325	450
30- "Sea Hawk" movie adaptation-c/story with Errol Flynn	35	70	105	208	339	470
31-40: 34-Ken Ernst-c	28	56	84	165	270	375
41-50: 41-Intro Lightning Jim. 43-Terry & The Pirates ends	23	46	69	138	227	315
51-60	19	38	57	109	172	235
61-70: 62-Flag-c. 65-Brenda Starr-r begin? 67-X-Mas-c	17	34	51	98	154	210
71-80	14	28	42	80	115	150
81-99	13	26	39	74	105	135
100	14	28	42	78	112	145
101-115-Last Dick Tracy (moves to own title)	10	20	30	56	76	95
116-121: 116,118-All Smokey Stover. 117-All Gasoline Alley. 119-121-Terry & The Pirates app. in all	9	18	27	50	65	80

SUPER COPS, THE
Red Circle Productions (Archie): July, 1974 (one-shot)

	GD 2.0	VG 4.0	FN 6.0	VF 8.0	VF/NM 9.0	NM- 9.2
1-Morrow-c/a; art by Pino, Hack, Thorne	2	4	6	8	11	14

SUPER COPS
Now Comics: Sept, 1990 - No. 4, Dec?, 1990 ($1.75)

	GD 2.0	VG 4.0	FN 6.0	VF 8.0	VF/NM 9.0	NM- 9.2
1-($2.75, 52 pgs.)-Dave Dorman painted-c (both printings)						4.00
2-4						3.00

SUPER CRACKED (See Cracked)

SUPER DC GIANT (25-50¢, all 68-52 pg. Giants)
National Per. Publ.: No. 13, 9-10/70 - No. 26, 7-8/71; V3#27, Summer, 1976 (No #1-12)

	GD 2.0	VG 4.0	FN 6.0	VF 8.0	VF/NM 9.0	NM- 9.2
S-13-Binky	11	22	33	71	136	200
S-14-Top Guns of the West; Kubert-c; Trigger Twins, Johnny Thunder, Wyoming Kid-r; Moreira-r (9-10/70)	6	12	18	37	59	80
S-15-Western Comics; Kubert-c; Pow Wow Smith, Vigilante, Buffalo Bill-r; new Gil Kane-a (9-10/70)	6	12	18	37	59	80
S-16-Best of the Brave & the Bold; Batman-r & Metamorpho origin-r from Brave & the Bold; Spectre pin-up.	4	8	12	28	44	60
S-17-Love 1970 (scarce)	24	48	72	168	359	550
S-18-Three Mouseketeers; Dizzy Dog, Doodles Duck, Bo Bunny-r; Sheldon Mayer-a	10	20	30	64	115	165
S-19-Jerry Lewis; Neal Adams pin-up	10	20	30	66	121	175
S-20-House of Mystery; N. Adams-c; Kirby-r(3)	8	16	24	51	86	120
S-21-Love 1971 (scarce)	28	56	84	203	439	675
S-22-Top Guns of the West; Kubert-c	4	8	12	26	41	55
S-23-The Unexpected	5	10	15	30	48	65
S-24-Supergirl	4	8	12	26	41	55
S-25-Challengers of the Unknown; all Kirby/Wood-r	4	8	12	23	36	48
S-26-Aquaman (1971)-r/S.A. Aquaman origin story from Showcase #30	4	8	12	23	36	48
27-Strange Flying Saucers Adventures (Sum, 1976)	3	6	9	19	29	38

NOTE: ***Sid Greene** r-27p(2), **Heath** r-27. **G. Kane** a-14r(2), 15, 27r(p). **Kubert** r-16.*

SUPER DINOSAUR
Image Comics: Apr, 2011 - Present ($2.99)

	GD 2.0	VG 4.0	FN 6.0	VF 8.0	VF/NM 9.0	NM- 9.2
1-8: 1-Robert Kirkman-s/Jason Howard-a; origin story and character profiles						3.00
... Origin Special #1 FCBD Edition (5/11, giveaway) r/#1						3.00

SUPER-DOOPER COMICS
Able Mfg. Co./Harvey: 1946 - No. 7, May, 1946; No. 8, 1946 (10¢, 32 pgs., paper-c)

	GD 2.0	VG 4.0	FN 6.0	VF 8.0	VF/NM 9.0	NM- 9.2
1-The Clock, Gangbuster app. (scarce)	37	74	111	222	361	500
2	15	30	45	85	130	175
3-6	14	28	42	80	115	150
7,8-Shock Gibson. 7-Where's Theres A Will by Ed Wheelan, Steve Case Crime Rover, Penny & Ullysses Jr. 8-Sam Hill app.	15	30	45	85	130	175

SUPER DUCK COMICS (The Cockeyed Wonder) (See Jolly Jingles)
MLJ Mag. No. 1-4(9/45)/Close-Up No. 5 on (Archie): Fall, 1944 - No. 94, Dec, 1960 (Also see Laugh #24)(#1-5 are quarterly)

	GD 2.0	VG 4.0	FN 6.0	VF 8.0	VF/NM 9.0	NM- 9.2
1-Origin; Hitler & Hirohito-c	97	194	291	621	1061	1500
2-Bill Vigoda-c	30	60	90	177	289	400
3-5: 4-20-Al Fagaly-c (most)	20	40	60	117	189	260
6-10	15	30	45	83	124	165
11-20(6/48)	11	22	33	62	86	110
21,23-40 (10/51)	10	20	30	54	72	90
22-Used in **SOTI**, pg. 35,307,308	11	22	33	62	86	110
41-60 (2/55)	8	16	24	44	57	70
61-94	7	14	21	35	43	50

SUPER DUPER (Formerly Pocket Comics #1-4?)
Harvey Publications: No. 5, 1941 - No. 11, 1941

	GD 2.0	VG 4.0	FN 6.0	VF 8.0	VF/NM 9.0	NM- 9.2
5-Captain Freedom & Shock Gibson app.	32	64	96	188	307	425
8,11	20	40	60	114	182	250

SUPER DUPER COMICS (Formerly Latest Comics?)
F. E. Howard Publ.: No. 3, May-June, 1947

	GD 2.0	VG 4.0	FN 6.0	VF 8.0	VF/NM 9.0	NM- 9.2
3-1st app. Mr. Monster	22	44	66	132	216	300

SUPER FRIENDS (TV) (Also see Best of DC & Limited Collectors' Edition)
National Periodical Publications/DC Comics: Nov, 1976 - No. 47, Aug, 1981 (#14 is 44 pgs.)

	GD 2.0	VG 4.0	FN 6.0	VF 8.0	VF/NM 9.0	NM- 9.2
1-Superman, Batman, Robin, Wonder Woman, Aquaman, Atom, Wendy, Marvin & Wonder Dog begin (1st Super Friends)	5	10	15	32	51	70
2-Penguin-c/sty	3	6	9	16	23	30
3-5	3	6	9	14	20	26
6-10,14: 7-1st app. Wonder Twins & The Seraph. 8-1st app. Jack O'Lantern. 9-1st app. Icemaiden. 14-Origin Wonder Twins	2	4	6	13	18	22
11-13,15-30: 13-1st app. Dr. Mist. 25-1st app. Fire as Green Fury. 28-Bizarro app.	2	4	6	9	13	16
13-16,20-23,25,32-(Whitman variants; low print run, no issue# on cover)	2	4	6	11	16	20
31,47: 31-Black Orchid app. 47-Origin Fire & Green Fury	2	4	6	10	14	18
32-46: 36,43-Plastic Man app.	2	4	6	8	11	14
TBP (2001, $14.95) r/#1,6-9,14,21,27 & Limited Collectors' Edition C-41; Alex Ross-c						15.00
...: Truth, Justice and Peace TPB (2003, $14.95) r/#10,12,13,25,28,29,31,36,37						15.00

NOTE: ***Estrada** a-1p, 2p. **Orlando** a-1p. **Staton** a-43, 45.*

SUPER FRIENDS (All ages stories with puzzles and games)(Based on Mattel toy line)
DC Comics: May, 2008 - No. 29, Sept, 2010 ($2.25/$2.99)

	GD 2.0	VG 4.0	FN 6.0	VF 8.0	VF/NM 9.0	NM- 9.2
1-29-Superman, Batman, Wonder Woman, Aquaman, Flash & Green Lantern. 29-Begin $2.99-c; Bat-Mite & Mr. Mxyzptlk app.						3.00
...: Calling All Super Friends TPB (2009, $12.99) r/#8-14; puzzles and games						13.00
...: For Justice TPB (2009, $12.99) r/#1-7; puzzles and games						13.00
...: Head of the Class TPB (2010, $12.99) r/#15-21; puzzles and games						13.00
...: Mystery in Space TPB (2011, $12.99) r/#22-28; puzzles and games						13.00

Supergirl #1 © DC

Supergirl (2005 series) #54 © DC

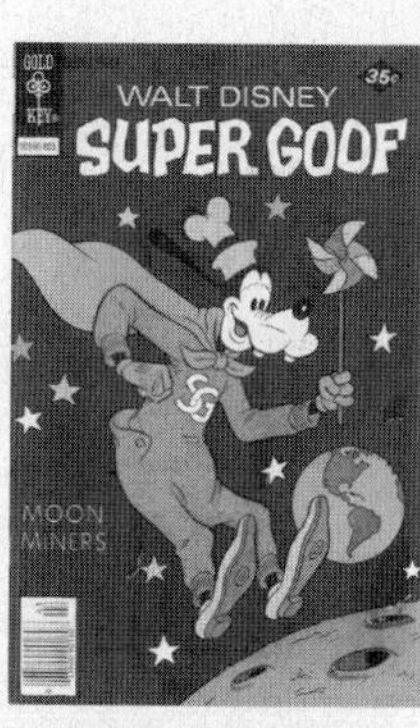

Super Goof #45 © DIS

GD VG FN VF VF/NM NM-
2.0 4.0 6.0 8.0 9.0 9.2

SUPER FUN
Gillmor Magazines: Jan, 1956 (By A.W. Nugent)

1-Comics, puzzles, cut-outs by A.W. Nugent 7 14 21 35 43 50

SUPER FUNNIES (...Western Funnies #3,4)
Superior Comics Publishers Ltd. (Canada): Dec, 1953 - No. 4, Sept, 1954

1-(3-D, 10¢)-...Presents Dopey Duck; make your own 3-D glasses cut-out inside front-c; did not come w/glasses 36 72 108 214 347 480
2-Horror & crime satire 15 30 45 83 124 165
3-Phantom Ranger-c/s; Geronimo, Billy the Kid app. 10 20 30 54 72 90
4-Phantom Ranger-c/story 10 20 30 54 72 90

SUPERGIRL
DC Comics: Feb. 1944

nn - Ashcan comic, not distributed to newsstands, only for in-house use. Cover art is Boy Commandos #1 with interior being Action Comics #80. A copy sold for $15,750 in 2008.

SUPERGIRL (See Action, Adventure #281, Brave & the Bold, Crisis on Infinite Earths #7, Daring New Advs. of..., Super DC Giant, Superman Family, & Super-Team Family)

SUPERGIRL
National Periodical Publ.: Nov, 1972 - No. 9, Dec-Jan, 1973-74; No. 10, Sept-Oct, 1974 (1st solo title)(20¢)

1-Zatanna back-up stories begin, end #5 8 16 24 51 86 120
2-4,6,7,9 4 8 12 26 41 55
5,8,10: 5-Zatanna origin-r. 8-JLA x-over; Batman cameo. 10-Prez 4 8 12 28 44 60

NOTE: *Zatanna in #1-5, 7(Guest); Prez app. in #10. #1-10 are 20¢ issues.*

SUPERGIRL (Formerly Daring New Adventures of...)
DC Comics: No. 14, Dec, 1983 - No. 23, Sept, 1984

14-23: 16-Ambush Bug app. 20-JLA & New Teen Titans app. 4.00
...Movie Special (1985)-Adapts movie; Morrow-a; photo back-c 4.00

SUPERGIRL
DC Comics: Feb, 1994 - No. 4, May, 1994 ($1.50, limited series)

1-4: Guice-a(i) 3.00

SUPERGIRL (See Showcase '96 #8)
DC Comics: Sept, 1996 - No. 80, May, 2003 ($1.95/$1.99/$2.25/$2.50)

1-Peter David scripts & Gary Frank-c/a 1 2 3 5 6 8
1-2nd printing 3.00
2,4-9: 4-Gorilla Grodd-c/app. 6-Superman-c/app. 9-Last Frank-a 4.00
3-Final Night, Gorilla Grodd app. 5.00
10-19: 14-Genesis x-over. 16-Power Girl app. 3.50
20-35: 20-Millennium Giants x-over; Superman app. 23-Steel-c/app. 24-Resurrection Man x-over. 25-Comet ID revealed; begin $1.99-c 3.00
36-46: 36,37-Young Justice x-over 3.00
47-49,51-74: 47-Begin $2.25-c. 51-Adopts costume from animated series. 54-Green Lantern app. 59-61-Our Worlds at War x-over. 62-Two-Face-c/app. 66,67-Demon-c/app. 68-74-Mary Marvel app. 70-Nauck-a. 73-Begin $2.50-c 3.00
50-($3.95) Supergirl's final battle with the Carnivore 4.00
75-80: 75-Re-intro. Kara Zor-El; cover swipe of Action Comics #252 by Haynes; Benes-a. 78-Spectre app. 80-Last issue; Romita-c 3.00
#1,000,000 (11/98) 853rd Century x-over 3.00
Annual 1 (1996, $2.95)-Legends of the Dead Earth 4.00
Annual 2 (1997, $3.95)-Pulp Heroes; LSH app.; Chiodo-c 4.00
...: Many Happy Returns TPB (2003, $14.95) r/#75-80; intro. by Peter David 15.00
...Plus (2/97, $2.95) Capt.(Mary) Marvel-c/app.; David-s/Frank-a 4.00
.../Prysm Double-Shot 1 (Feb, 1998, $1.95) w/Prysm (Teen Titans) 3.00
...: Wings (2001, $5.95) Elseworlds; DeMatteis-s/Tolagson-a 6.00
TPB-('98, $14.95) r/Showcase '96 #8 & Supergirl #1-9 15.00

SUPERGIRL (See Superman/Batman #8 & #19)
DC Comics: No. 0, Oct, 2005 - No. 67, Oct, 2011 ($2.99)

0-Reprints Superman/Batman #19 with white variant of that cover 3.00
1-Loeb-s/Churchill-a; two covers by Churchill & Turner; Power Girl app. 5.00
1-2nd printing with B&W sketch variant of Turner-c 3.00
1-3rd printing with variant-c homage to Action Comics #252 by Churchill 3.00
2-4: 2-Teen Titans app. 3-Outsiders app.; covers by Turner & Churchill 3.00
5-($3.99) Supergirl vs. Supergirl; Churchill & Turner-c 4.00
6-49: 6-9-One Year Later; Power Girl app. 11-Intro. Powerboy. 12-Terra debut; Conner-a 20-Amazons Attack x-over. 21,22-Karate Kid app. 28-31-Resurrection Man app. 35,36-New Krypton x-over; Argo City story re-told; Superwoman app. 35-Ross-c. 36-Zor-El dies 3.00
50-($4.99) Lana Lang Insect Queen app.; Superwoman returns; back-up story co-written by Helen Slater with Chiang-a; Turner-c 5.00
50-Variant cover by Middleton 6.00

GD VG FN VF VF/NM NM-
2.0 4.0 6.0 8.0 9.0 9.2

51-67: 51-52-New Krypton. 52-Brainiac 5 app. 53-57-Bizarro-Girl app. 55-63-Reeder-c 3.00
58-DC 75th Anniversary variant cover by Conner 6.00
Annual 1 (11/09, $3.99) Origin of Superwoman 4.00
Annual 2 (12/10, $4.99) Silver Age Legion of Super-Heroes app.; Reeder-c 5.00
...: Beyond Good and Evil TPB (2008, $17.99) r/#23-27 and Action Comics #850 18.00
...: Bizarrogirl TPB (2011, $19.99) r/#53-59 & Annual #2 20.00
...: Candor TPB (2007, $14.99) r/#6-9; and pages from JSA Classified #2, Superman #223, Superman/Batman #27 and JLA #122,123 15.00
...: Death & The Family TPB (2010, $17.99) r/#48-50 & Annual #1 18.00
...: Friends & Fugitives TPB (2010, $17.99) r/#43,45-47; Action Comics #881,882 18.00
...: Identity TPB (2007, $19.99) r/#10-16 and story from DCU Infinite Holiday Special 20.00
...: Power TPB (2006, $14.99) r/#1-5 and Superman/Batman #19; variant-c gallery 15.00
...: Way of the World TPB (2009, $17.99) r/#28-33 18.00
...: Who is Superwoman TPB (2009, $17.99) r/#34,37-42 18.00

SUPERGIRL (DC New 52)
DC Comics: Nov, 2011 - Present ($2.99)

1-7: 1-New origin; Green & Johnson-s/Asrar-a/c. 1-3-Superman app. 3.00

SUPERGIRL AND THE LEGION OF SUPER-HEROES (Continues from Legion of Super-Heroes #15, Apr, 2006)(Continues as Legion of Super-Heroes #37)
DC Comics: No. 16, May, 2006 - No. 36, Jan, 2008 ($2.99)

16-Supergirl appears in the 31st century 4.00
16-2nd printing 3.00
17-36: 23-Mon-El cameo. 24,25-Mon-El returns 3.00
...: Adult Education TPB (2007, $14.99) r/#20-25 & LSH #6,9,13-15 15.00
...: Dominator War TPB (2007, $14.99) r/#26-30 15.00
...: Strange Visitor From Another Century TPB (2006, $14.99) r/#16-19 & LSH #11,12,15 15.00
...: The Quest For Cosmic Boy TPB (2008, $14.99) r/#31-36 15.00

SUPERGIRL: COSMIC ADVENTURES IN THE 8TH GRADE (Cartoony all-ages title)
DC Comics: Feb, 2008 - No. 6, Jul, 2009 ($2.50, limited series)

1-6: 1-Supergirl lands on Earth; Eric Jones-a. 5,6-Comet & Streaky app. 3.00
TPB (2009, $12.99) r/#1-6; sketch art 13.00

SUPERGIRL/LEX LUTHOR SPECIAL (Supergirl and Team Luthor on-c)
DC Comics: 1993 ($2.50, 68 pgs., one-shot)

1-Pin-ups by Byrne & Thibert 4.00

SUPERGOD (Warren Ellis'...)
Avatar Press: Oct, 2009 - No. 5, Nov, 2010 ($3.99, limited series)

1-5-Warren Ellis-s/Garrie Gastony-a; multiple covers on each 4.00

SUPER GOOF (Walt Disney) (See Dynabrite & The Phantom Blot)
Gold Key No. 1-57/Whitman No. 58 on: Oct, 1965 - No. 74, July, 1984

1 4 8 12 28 44 60
2-5 3 6 9 16 23 30
6-10 3 6 9 14 19 24
11-20 2 4 6 8 11 14
21-30 1 3 4 6 8 10
31-50 1 2 3 4 5 7
51-57 6.00
58,59 (Whitman) 1 2 3 5 6 8
60(8/80), 62(11/80) 3-pack only (scarce) 4 8 12 24 37 50
61(9-10/80) 3-pack only (rare) 4 8 12 26 41 55
63-66('81) 1 2 3 5 6 8
63 (1/81, 40¢-c) Cover price error variant (scarce) 2 4 6 10 14 18
67-69: 67(2/82), 68(2-3/82), 69(3/82) 6.00
70-74 (#90180 on-c; pre-pack, nd, nd code): 70(5/83), 71(8/83), 72(5/84), 73(6/84), 74(7/84) 3 6 9 16 22 28

NOTE: *Reprints in #16, 24, 28, 29, 37, 38, 43, 45, 46, 54(1/2), 56-58, 65(1/2), 72(r-#2).*

SUPER GREEN BERET (Tod Holton...)
Lightning Comics (Milson Publ. Co.): Apr, 1967 - No. 2, Jun, 1967

1-(25¢, 68 pgs) 5 10 15 32 51 70
2-(25¢, 68 pgs) 4 8 12 22 34 45

SUPER HEROES (See Giant-Size... & Marvel...)

SUPER HEROES
Dell Publishing Co.: Jan, 1967 - No. 4, June, 1967

1-Origin & 1st app. Fab 4 4 8 12 24 37 50
2-4 3 6 9 17 25 32

SUPER-HEROES BATTLE SUPER-GORILLAS (See DC Special #16)
National Periodical Publications: Winter, 1976 (52 pgs., all reprints, one-shot)

1-Superman, Batman, Flash stories; Infantino-a(p) 2 4 6 11 16 20

SUPER HEROES VERSUS SUPER VILLAINS

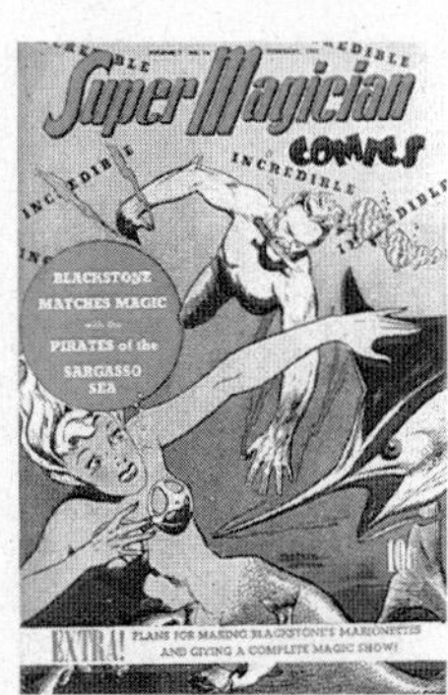

Super Magician Comics #10 © CN

Superman #2 © DC

Superman #100 © DC

GD VG FN VF VF/NM NM-
2.0 4.0 6.0 8.0 9.0 9.2

GD VG FN VF VF/NM NM-
2.0 4.0 6.0 8.0 9.0 9.2

Archie Publications (Radio Comics): July, 1966 (no month given)(68 pgs.)
1-Flyman, Black Hood, Web, Shield-r; Reinman-a 6 12 18 42 69 95

SUPER HERO SQUAD (See Marvel Super Hero Squad)

SUPERHERO WOMEN, THE - FEATURING THE FABULOUS FEMALES OF MARVEL COMICS (See Fireside Book Series)

SUPERICHIE (Formerly Super Richie)
Harvey Publications: No. 5, Oct, 1976 - No. 18, Jan, 1979 (52 pgs. giants)
5-Origin/1st app. new costumes for Rippy & Crashman 2 4 6 9 13 16
6-18 2 4 6 8 10 12

SUPERIOR
Marvel Comics (ICON): Dec, 2010 - No. 7, Mar, 2012 ($2.99/$4.99)
1-6-Mark Millar-s/Leinil Yu-a. 1-1st & 2nd printings 3.00
7-($4.99) Bonus preview of Supercrooks #1 5.00
... World Record Special 1 (12/11, $2.99, B&W) Comic created in less than 12 hours 3.00

SUPERIOR STORIES
Nesbit Publishers, Inc.: May-June, 1955 - No. 4, Nov-Dec, 1955
1-The Invisible Man by H.G. Wells 23 46 69 136 223 310
2-4: 2-The Pirate of the Gulf by J.H. Ingrahams. 3-Wreck of the Grosvenor by William Clark Russell. 4-The Texas Rangers by O'Henry 11 22 33 62 86 110
NOTE: *Morisi c/a in all. Kiwanis stories in #3 & 4. #4 has photo of Gene Autry on-c.*

SUPER MAGIC (Super Magician Comics #2 on)
Street & Smith Publications: May, 1941
V1#1-Blackstone the Magician-c/story; origin/1st app. Rex King (Black Fury); Charles Sultan-c; Blackstone-c begin 181 362 543 1158 1979 2800

SUPER MAGICIAN COMICS (Super Magic #1)
Street & Smith Publications: No. 2, Sept, 1941 - V5#8, Feb-Mar, 1947
V1#2-Blackstone the Magician continues; Rex King, Man of Adventure app. 68 136 204 435 743 1050
3-Tao-Anwar, Boy Magician begins 42 84 123 265 445 625
4-7,9-12: 4-Origin Transo. 11-Supersnipe app. 40 80 120 242 404 565
8-Abbott & Costello story (1st app?, 11/42) 40 80 120 249 417 585
V2#1-The Shadow app. 41 82 123 249 417 585
2-12: 5-Origin Tigerman. 8-Red Dragon begins 22 44 66 128 209 290
V3#1-12: 5-Origin Mr. Twilight 22 44 66 128 209 290
V4#1-12: 5-KKK-c/sty. 11-Nigel Elliman Ace of Magic begins (3/46) 18 36 54 105 165 225
V5#1-6 18 36 54 105 165 225
7,8-Red Dragon by Edd Cartier-c/a 39 78 117 236 388 540
NOTE: ***Jack Binder** c-1-14(most). Red Dragon c-V5#7, 8.*

SUPERMAN (See Action Comics, Advs. of..., All-New Coll. Ed., All-Star Comics, Best of DC, Brave & the Bold, Cosmic Odyssey, DC Comics Presents, Heroes Against Hunger, JLA, The Kents, Krypton Chronicles, Limited Coll. Ed., Man of Steel, Phantom Zone, Power Record Comics, Special Edition, Steel, Super Friends, Superman: The Man of Steel, Superman: The Man of Tomorrow, Taylor's Christmas Tabloid, Three-Dimension Advs., World Of Krypton, World Of Metropolis, World Of Smallville & World's Finest)

SUPERMAN (Becomes Adventures of...#424 on)
National Periodical Publ./DC Comics: Summer, 1939 - No. 423, Sept, 1986
(#1-5 are quarterly)
1(nn)-1st four Action stories reprinted; origin Superman by Siegel & Shuster; has a new 2 pg. origin plus 4 pgs. omitted in Action story; see The Comics Magazine #1 & More Fun #14-17 for Superman prototype app.; cover r/splash page from Action #10; 1st pin-up Superman on back-c - 1st pin-up in comics 35,000 70,000 120,000 280,000 465,000 650,000
1-Reprint, Oversize 13-1/2x10". **WARNING:** This comic is an exact duplicate reprint of the original except for its size. DC published it in 1978 with a second cover titling it as a Famous First Edition. There have been many reported cases of the outer cover being removed and the interior sold as the original edition. The reprint with the new outer cover removed is practically worthless. See Famous First Edition for value.
2-All daily strip-r; full pg. ad for N.Y. World's Fair 2250 4500 6750 17,000 31,000 45,000
3-2nd story-r from Action #5; 3rd story-r from Action #6 1250 2500 3750 9500 17,250 25,000
4-2nd mention of Daily Planet (Spr/40); also see Action #23; 2nd & 3rd app. Luthor (red-headed; also see Action #23) 757 1514 2271 5526 9763 14,000
5-4th Luthor app. (grey hair) 622 1244 1866 4540 8020 11,500
6,7: 6-1st splash pg. in a Superman comic. 7-1st Perry White? (11-12/40) 423 846 1269 3067 5384 7700
8-10: 10-5th app. Luthor (1st bald Luthor, 5-6/41) 389 778 1167 2723 4762 6800
11-13,15: 13-Jimmy Olsen & Luthor app. 300 600 900 2010 3505 5000
14-Patriotic Shield-c classic by Fred Ray 568 1136 1704 4146 7323 10,500
16,19,20: 16-1st Lois Lane-c this title (5-6/42); 2nd Lois-c after Action #29 271 542 813 1734 2967 4200
17-Hitler, Hirohito-c 432 864 1296 3154 5577 8000
18-Classic WWII-c 300 600 900 1950 3375 4800
21,22,25: 25-Clark Kent's only military service; Fred Ray's only super-hero story 174 348 522 1114 1907 2700
23-Classic periscope-c 271 542 813 1734 2967 4200
24-Classic Jack Burnley flag-c 343 686 1029 2400 4200 6000
26-Classic war-c 300 600 900 1950 3375 4800
27-29: 27,29-Lois Lane-c. 28-Lois Lane Girl Reporter series begins, ends #40,42 148 296 444 947 1624 2300
28-Overseas edition for Armed Forces; same as reg. #28 148 296 444 947 1624 2300
30-Origin & 1st app. Mr. Mxyztplk (9-10/44)(pronounced "Mix-it-plk") in comic books; name later became Mxyzptlk ("Mix-yez-pit-l-ick"); the character was inspired by a combination of the name of Al Capp's Joe Blyfstyk (the little man with the black cloud over his head) & the devilish antics of Bugs Bunny; he first app. in newspapers 3/7/44; Superman flies for the first time 284 568 852 1818 3109 4400
31-40: 33-(3-4/45)-3rd app. Mxyztplk. 35,36-Lois Lane-c. 38-Atomic bomb story (1-2/46); delayed because of gov't censorship; Superman shown reading Batman #32 on cover. 40-Mxyztplk-c 126 252 378 806 1378 1950
41-50: 42-Lois Lane-c. 45-Lois Lane as Superwoman (see Action #60 for 1st app.). 46-(5-6/47)-1st app. Superboy this title? 48-1st time Superman travels thru time 103 206 309 659 1130 1600
51,52: 51-Lois Lane-c 94 188 282 597 1024 1450
53-Third telling of Superman origin; 10th anniversary issue ('48); classic origin-c by Boring 309 618 927 2163 3782 5400
54,56-60: 57-Lois Lane as Superwoman-c. 58-Intro Tiny Trix. 59-Early use of heat vision (possibly first time) 94 188 282 597 1024 1450
55-Used in **SOTI**, pg. 33 95 190 285 603 1039 1475
61-Origin Superman retold; origin Green Kryptonite (1st Kryptonite story); Superman returns to Krypton for 1st time & sees his parents for 1st time since infancy, discovers he's not an Earth man 161 322 483 1030 1765 2500
62-70: 62-Orson Welles-c/story. 65-1st Krypton Foes: Mala, Kizo, & U-Ban. 66-2nd Superbaby story. 67-Perry Como-c/story. 68-1st Luthor-c this title (see Action Comics) 92 184 276 584 1005 1425
71-75: 74-2nd Luthor-c this title. 75-Some have #74 on-c 89 178 267 565 970 1375
76-Batman x-over; Superman & Batman learn each other's I.D. for the 1st time (5-6/52) (also see World's Finest #71) 245 490 735 1568 2684 3800
77-81: 78-Last 52 pg. issue. 81-Used in **POP**, pg. 88 79 158 237 502 864 1225
82-87,89,90: 89-1st Curt Swan-c in title 73 146 219 467 796 1125
88-Prankster, Toyman & Luthor team-up 77 154 231 493 847 1200
91-95: 95-Last precode issue (2/55) 65 130 195 416 708 1000
96-99: 96-Mr. Mxyztplk-c/story 58 116 174 371 636 900
100 (9-10/55)-Shows cover to #1 on-c 239 478 717 1530 2615 3700
101-105,107-110: 109-1st S.A. issue 52 104 156 328 589 850
106 (7/56)-Retells origin 53 106 159 334 605 875
111-120 47 94 141 296 523 750
121,122,124-127,129: 127-Origin/1st app. Titano. 129-Intro/origin Lori Lemaris, The Mermaid 41 82 123 256 453 650
123-Pre-Supergirl tryout-c/story (8/58). 63 126 189 403 952 1500
128-(4/59)-Red Kryptonite used. Bruce Wayne x-over who protects Superman's i.d. (3rd story) 42 84 126 265 470 675
130-(7/59)-2nd app, Krypto, the Superdog with Superman (see Sup.'s Pal Jimmy Olsen #29) (all other previous app. w/Superboy) 43 86 129 271 486 700
131-139: 135-2nd Lori Lemaris app. 139-Lori Lemaris app.; 34 68 102 199 342 485
140-1st Blue Kryptonite & Bizarro Supergirl; origin Bizarro Jr. #1 34 68 102 206 353 500
141-145,148: 142-2nd Batman x-over 29 58 87 170 295 420
146-(7/61)-Superman's life story; back-up hints at Earth II. Classic-c 39 78 117 235 418 600
147(8/61)-7th Legion app; 1st app. Legion of Super-Villains; 1st app. Adult Legion; swipes-c to Adv. #247 36 72 108 216 371 525
149(11/61)-8th Legion app. (cameo); "The Death of Superman" imaginary story; last 10¢ issue 34 68 102 199 350 500
150,151,153,154,157,159,160: 157-Gold Kryptonite used (see Adv. #299); Mon -El app.; Lightning Lad cameo (11/62) 13 26 39 85 180 275
152,155,156,158,162: 152(4/62)-15th Legion app. 155-(8/62)-Legion app; Lightning Man & Cosmic Man, & Adult Legion app. 156,162-Legion app. 158-1st app. Flamebird & Nightwing & Nor-Kan of Kandor (12/62) 13 26 39 87 186 285
161-1st told death of Ma and Pa Kent 13 26 39 87 186 285
161-2nd printing (1987, $1.25)-New DC logo; sold thru So Much Fun Toy Stores (cover title: Superman Classic) 4.00
163-166,168-180: 166-XMas-c. 168-All Luthor issue; JFK tribute/memorial. 169-Bizarro Invasion of Earth-c/story; last Sally Selwyn. 170-Pres. Kennedy story is finally published

Superman #233 © DC

Superman (2nd series) #29 © DC

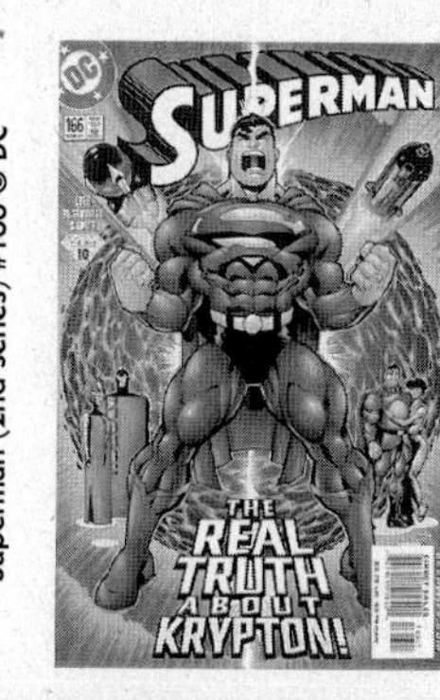

Superman (2nd series) #166 © DC

GD VG FN VF VF/NM NM-
2.0 4.0 6.0 8.0 9.0 9.2

after delay from #168 due to assassination. 172,173-Legion cameos. 174-Super-Mxyzptlk; Bizarro app. 11 22 33 75 148 220
167-New origin Brainiac, text reference of Brainiac 5 descending from adopted human son Brainiac II; intro Tharla (later Luthor's wife) 13 26 39 85 180 275
181,182,184-186,188-192,194-196,198,200: 181-1st 2465 story/series. 182-1st S.A. app. of The Toyman (1/66). 189-Origin/destruction of Krypton II.
9 18 27 63 112 160
183 (Giant G-18) 11 22 33 75 148 220
187,193,197 (Giants G-23,G-31,G-36) 10 20 30 66 121 175
199-1st Superman/Flash race (8/67): also see Flash #175 & World's Finest #198,199 (r-in Limited Coll. Ed. C-48) 27 54 81 196 423 650
201,203-206,208-211,213-216: 213-Brainiac-5 app. 216-Last 12¢ issue
6 12 18 42 69 95
202 (80-pg. Giant G-42)-All Bizarro issue 7 14 21 48 79 110
207,212,217 (Giants G-48,G-54,G-60): 207-30th anniversary Superman (6/68)
7 14 21 48 79 110
218-221,223-226,228-231 6 12 18 37 59 80
222,239(Giants, G-66,G-84) 7 14 21 44 72 100
227,232(Giants, G-72,G-78)-All Krypton issues 7 14 21 44 72 100
233-2nd app. Morgan Edge; Clark Kent switches from newspaper reporter to TV newscaster; all Kryptonite on Earth destroyed; classic Neal Adams-c; 1st Fabulous World of Krypton story; Superman pin-up by Swan 10 20 30 64 115 165
234-238 5 10 15 35 55 75
240-Kaluta-a; last 15¢ issue 4 8 12 28 44 60
241-244 (All 52 pgs.): 241-New Wonder Woman app. 243-G.A.-r/#38
5 10 15 30 48 65
245-Also listed as DC 100 Pg. Super Spectacular #7; Air Wave, Kid Eternity, Hawkman-r; Atom-r/Atom #3 10 20 30 67 124 180
246-248,250,251,253 (All 52 pgs.): 246-G.A.-r/#40. 248-World of Krypton story. 251-G.A.-r/#45. 253-Finlay-a, 2 pgs., G.A.-r/#1 5 10 15 30 48 65
249,254-Neal Adams-a. 249-(52 pgs.); 1st app. Terra-Man (Swan-a) & origin-s by Dick Dillin (p) & Neal Adams (inks) 6 12 18 41 66 90
252-Also listed as DC 100 Pg. Super Spectacular #13; Ray(r/Smash #17), Black Condor, (r/Crack #18), Hawkman(r/Flash #24); Starman-r/Adv. #67; Dr. Fate & Spectre-r/More Fun #57; N. Adams-c 11 22 33 73 142 210
255-271,273-277,279-283: 263-Photo-c. 264-1st app. Steve Lombard. 276-Intro Capt. Thunder. 279-Batman, Batgirl app. 282-Luthor battlesuit 3 6 9 14 19 24
272,278,284-All 100 pgs. G.A.-r in all. 272-r/2nd app. Mr. Mxyztplk from Action #80
5 10 15 32 51 70
285-299: 289-Partial photo-c. 292-Origin Lex Luthor retold
2 4 6 9 13 16
300-(6/76) Superman in the year 2001 3 6 9 20 30 40
301-350: 301,320-Solomon Grundy app. 323-Intro. Atomic Skull. 327-329-(44 pgs.). 327-Kobra app. 330-More facts revealed about I.D. 331,332-1st/2nd app. Master Jailer. 335-Mxyzptlk marries Ms. Bgbznz. 336-Rose & Thorn app. 338-(8/79) 40th Anniv. issue; the bottled city of Kandor enlarged. 344-Frankenstein & Dracula app.
1 3 4 6 8 10
321-323,325-327,329-332,335-345,348,350 (Whitman variants; low print run; no issue # on cover) 2 4 6 9 13 16
351-399: 353-Brief origin. 354,355,357-Superman 2020 stories (354-Debut of Superman III). 356-World of Krypton story (also #360,367,375). 366-Fan letter by Todd McFarlane. 369-Christmas-c. 372-Superman 2021 story. 376-Free 16 pg. preview Daring New Advs. of Supergirl. 377-Free 16 pg. preview Masters of the Universe
1 2 3 4 5 7
400 (10/84, $1.50, 68 pgs.)-Many top artists featured; Chaykin painted cover, Miller back-c; Steranko-s/a (10 pages) 1 3 4 6 8 10
401-422: 405-Super-Batman story. 408-Nuclear Holocaust-c/story. 411-Special Julius Schwartz tribute issue. 414,415-Crisis x-over. 422-Horror-c 6.00
409-(7/85) Variant-c with Superman/Superhombre logo (no reported sales)
423-Alan Moore scripts; Curt Swan-a/George Pérez-a(i); "Whatever Happened to the Man of Tomorrow?" story, cont'd in Action #583 2 4 6 8 10 12
Annual 1(10/60, 84 pgs.)-Reprints 1st Supergirl story/Action #252; r/Lois Lane #1; Krypto-r (1st Silver Age DC annual) 80 160 240 648 1400 2150
Annual 2(Win, 1960-61)-Super-villain issue; Brainiac, Titano, Metallo, Bizarro origin-r
35 70 105 254 552 850
Annual 3(Sum, 1961)-Strange Lives of Superman 23 46 69 164 350 535
Annual 4(Win, 1961-62)-11th Legion app; 1st Legion origins (text & pictures); advs. in time, space & on alien worlds 20 40 60 137 294 450
Annual 5(Sum, 1962)-All Krypton issue 16 32 48 111 243 375
Annual 6(Win, 1962-63)-Legion-r/Adv. #247 14 28 42 97 211 325
Annual 7(Sum, 1963)-Silver Anniversary Issue; origin-r/Superman-Batman team/Adv. #275; cover gallery of famous issues 12 24 36 80 163 245
Annual 8(Win, 1963-64)-All origins issue 11 22 33 75 148 220
Annual 9(8/64)-Was advertised but came out as 80 Page Giant #1 instead

GD VG FN VF VF/NM NM-
2.0 4.0 6.0 8.0 9.0 9.2

Annual 9(1983)-Toth/Austin-a 1 2 3 4 5 7
Annuals 10-12: 10(1984, $1.25)-M. Anderson-i. 11(1985)-Moore-s. 12(1986)-Bolland-c 6.00
Special 1-3('83-'85): 1-G. Kane-c/a; contains German-r 6.00
The Amazing World of Superman "Official Metropolis Edition" (1973, $2.00, treasury-size)-Origin retold; Wood-r(i) from Superboy #153,161; poster incl. (half price if poster missing)
4 8 12 28 44 60
11195 (2/79, $1.95, 224 pgs.)-Golden Press 4 8 12 24 37 50
NOTE: **N. Adams** *a-249i, 254p; c-204-206, 210, 212-215, 219, 231i, 233-237, 240-243, 249-252, 254, 263, 307, 308, 313, 314, 317.* **Adkins** *a-323i.* **Austin** *c-368i.* **Wayne Boring** *art-late 1940's to early 1960's.* **Buckler** *a(p)-352, 363, 364, 369; c(p)-324-327, 356, 363, 368, 369, 373, 376, 378.* **Burnley** *a-252r; c-19-25, 30, 33, 34, 35p, 38p, 39p, 45p.* **Fine** *a-252r.* **Kaluta** *a-400.* **Gil Kane** *a-272r, 367, 372, 375, Special 2; c-374p, 375p, 377, 381, 382, 384-390, 392, Annual 9, Special 2.* **Joe Kubert** *c-216.* **Morrow** *a-238.* **Mortimer** *a-250r.* **Perez** *c-364p.* **Fred Ray** *a-25; c-6, 8-18.* **Starlin** *c-355.* **Staton** *a-354i, 355i.* **Swan/Moldoff** *c-149.* **Williamson** *a(i)-408-410, 412-416; c-408i, 409i.* **Wrightson** *a-400, 416.*

SUPERMAN (2nd Series) (Title continues numbering from Adventures of Superman #649)
DC Comics: Jan, 1987 - No. 226, Apr, 2006; No. 650, May, 2006 - No. 714, Oct, 2011

0-(10/94) Zero Hour; released between #93 & #94 3.00
1-Byrne-c/a begins; intro new Metallo 6.00
2-8,10: 3-Legends x-over; Darkseid-c & app. 7-Origin/1st app. Rampage. 8-Legion app. 4.00
9-Joker-c 5.00
11-15,17-20,22-49,51,52,54-56,58-67: 11-1st new Mr. Mxyzptlk. 12-Lori Lemaris revived. 13-1st app. new Toyman. 13,14-Millennium x-over. 20-Doom Patrol app.; Supergirl cameo. 31-Mr. Mxyzptlk app. 37-Newsboy Legion app. 41-Lobo app. 44-Batman storyline, part 1. 45-Free extra 8 pgs. 54-Newsboy Legion story. 63-Aquaman x-over. 67-Last $1.00-c 3.00
16,21: 16-1st app. new Supergirl (4/88). 21-Supergirl-c/story; 1st app. Matrix who becomes new Supergirl 4.00
50-($1.50, 52 pgs.)-Clark Kent proposes to Lois 5.00
50-2nd printing 4.00
53-Clark reveals i.d. to Lois (Cont'd from Action #662) 4.00
53-2nd printing 3.00
57-($1.75, 52 pgs.) 4.00
68-72: 65,66,68-Deathstroke-c/stories. 70-Superman & Robin team-up 3.00
73-Doomsday cameo 5.00
74-Doomsday Pt. 2 (Cont'd from Justice League #69); Superman battles Doomsday 6.00
73,74-2nd printings 3.00
75-($2.50)-Collector's Ed.; Doomsday Pt. 6; Superman dies; polybagged w/poster of funeral, obituary from Daily Planet, postage stamp & armband premiums (direct sales only)
2 4 6 11 16 20
75-Direct sales copy (no upc code, 1st print) 1 3 4 6 8 10
75-Direct sales copy (no upc code, 2nd-4th prints) 4.00
75-Newsstand copy w/upc code 1 3 4 6 8 10
75-Platinum Edition; given away to retailers 4 8 12 28 44 60
76,77-Funeral For a Friend parts 4 & 8 4.00
78-($1.95)-Collector's Edition with die-cut outer-c & mini poster; Doomsday cameo 4.00
78-($1.50)-Newsstand Edition w/poster and different-c; Doomsday-c & cameo 3.00
79-81,83-89: 83-Funeral for a Friend epilogue; new Batman (Azrael) cameo. 87,88-Bizarro-c/story 3.00
82-($3.50)-Collector's Edition w/all chromium-c; real Superman revealed; Green Lantern x-over from G.L. #46; no ads 6.00
82-($2.00, 44 pgs.)-Regular Edition w/different-c 4.00
90-99: 93-(9/94)-Zero Hour. 94-(11/94). 95-Atom app. 96-Brainiac returns 3.00
100-Death of Clark Kent foil-c 4.00
100-Newsstand 3.00
101-122: 101-Begin $1.95-c; Black Adam app. 105-Green Lantern app. 110-Plastic Man-c/app. 114-Brainiac app; Dwyer-c. 115-Lois leaves Metropolis. 116-(10/96)-1st app. Teen Titans by Jurgens & Perez in 8 pg. preview. 117-Final Night. 118-Wonder Woman app. 119-Legion app. 122-New powers 3.00
123-Collector's Edition w/glow in the dark-c, new costume 6.00
123-Standard ed., new costume 4.00
124-149: 128-Cyborg-c/app. 131-Birth of Lena Luthor. 132-Superman Red/Superman Blue. 134-Millennium Giants. 136,137-Superman 2999. 139-Starlin-a. 140-Grindberg-a 3.00
150-($2.95) Standard Ed.; Brainiac 2.0 app.; Jurgens-s 3.00
150-($3.95) Collector's Ed. w/holo-foil enhanced variant-c 4.00
151-158: 151-Loeb-s begins; Daily Planet reopens 3.00
159-174: 159-$2.25-c begin. 161-Joker-c/app. 162-Aquaman-c/app. 163-Young Justice app. 165-JLA app.; Ramos; Madureira, Liefeld, A. Adams, Wieringo, Churchill-a. 166-Collector's and reg. editions. 167-Return to Krypton. 168-Batman-c/app.(cont'd in Detective #756). 171-173-Our Worlds at War. 173-Sienkiewicz-a (2 pgs.). 174-Adopts black & red "S" logo
3.00
175-($3.50) Joker: Last Laugh x-over; Doomsday-c/app. 4.00
176-189,191-199: 176,180-Churchill-a. 180-Dracula app. 181-Bizarro-c/app. 184-Return to Krypton II. 189-Van Fleet-c. 192,193,195,197-199-New Supergirl app. 3.00
190-($2.25) Regular edition 3.00
190-($3.95) Double-Feature Issue; included reprint of Superman: The 10¢ Adventure 4.00
200-($3.50) Gene Ha-c/art by various; preview art by Yu & Bermejo 4.00

Superman (2nd series) #670 © DC

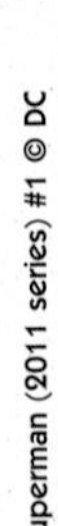
Superman (2011 series) #1 © DC

Superman Chronicles Vol. 9 © DC

	GD 2.0	VG 4.0	FN 6.0	VF 8.0	VF/NM 9.0	NM- 9.2

201-Mr Majestic-c/app.; cover swipe of Action #1 3.00
202,203-Godfall parts 3,6; Turner-c; Caldwell-a(p). 203-Jim Lee sketch pages 3.00
204-Jim Lee-c/a begins; Azzarello-s 3.00
204-Diamond Retailer Summit edition with sketch-c 8 16 24 53 89 125
205-214: 205-Two covers by Jim Lee and Michael Turner. 208-JLA app. 211-Battles Wonder Woman 3.00
215-($2.99) Conclusion to Azzarello/Lee arc 4.00
216-218,220-226: 216-Captain Marvel app. 221-Bizarro & Zoom app. 226-Earth-2 Superman story; Chaykin,Sale, Benes, Ordway-a 3.00
219-Omac/Sacrifice pt. 1; JLA app. 4.00
219-2nd printing with red background variant-c 3.00
(Title continues numbering from Adventures of Superman #649)
650-(5/06) One Year Later; Clark powerless after Infinite Crisis 4.00
651-665,667-669,671-674.676-680: 652-Begin $2.99-c. 654-658,662-664,667-Pacheco-a. 665-Origin of Jimmy Olsen. 671-673-Insect Queen. 676-680-Ross-c 3.00
666, 670,675-($3.99) 666-Simonson-a. 670-The Third Kryptonian. 675-Ross-c 4.00
681-699: 681-683-New Krypton x-over; Ross-c. 685-Mon-El freed from Phantom Zone. 694-Mon-El new costume. 698,699-Last Stand of New Krypton x-over 3.00
700-(8/10, $4.99) Cover by Gary Frank; Robinson-s; Straczynski-s begin 5.00
700-Variant-c by Risso 8.00
701-714: 701-"Grounded" begins; Straczynski-s/Cassaday-c. 704,706-Wilson-s 3.00
701-DC 75th Variant-c by Cassaday (Superman #1 swipe) 8.00
#1,000,000 (11/98) 853rd Century x-over; Gene Ha-c 3.00
Annual 1,2: 1 (1987)-No Byrne-a. 2 (1988)-Byrne-a; Newsboy Legion; Guardian returns 4.00
Annual 3-6 ('91-'94 68 pgs.): 1-Armageddon 2001 x-over; Batman app.; Austin-c(i) & part inks. 4-Eclipso app. 6-Elseworlds sty 4.00
Annual 3-2nd & 3rd printings; 3rd has silver ink 4.00
Annual 7 (1995, $3.95, 69 pgs.)-Year One story 4.00
Annual 8 (1996, $2.95)-Legends of the Dead Earth story 4.00
Annual 9 (1997, $3.95)-Pulp Heroes story 4.00
Annual 10 (1998, $2.95)-Ghosts; Wrightson-c 4.00
Annual 11 (1999, $2.95)-JLApe; Art Adams-c 4.00
Annual 12 (2000, $3.50)-Planet DC 4.00
Annual 13 (1/08, $3.99) Finale of Camelot Falls 4.00
Annual 14 (10/09, $3.99) Origin of Mon-El re-told; Pina-a/Guedes-c 4.00
...: 80 Page Giant (2/99, $4.95) Jurgens-c 5.00
...: 80 Page Giant 1 (5/10, $5.99) Lopresti-c; short stories by various 6.00
...: 80 Page Giant 2 (6/99, $4.95) Harris-c 5.00
...: 80 Page Giant 3 (11/00, $5.95) Nowlan-c; art by various 6.00
...: 80 Page Giant 2011 (4/11, $5.99) Nguyen-c; art by various; Bizarros app. 6.00
Special 1 (1992, $3.50, 68 pgs.)-Simonson-c/a 5.00

SUPERMAN (DC New 52)
DC Comics: Nov, 2011 - Present ($2.99)
1-7: 1-Pérez-s/c; Merino-a. 3-6-Nicola Scott-a. 6-Supergirl app. 3.00

SUPERMAN (Hardcovers and Trade Paperbacks)
... and the Legion of Super-Heroes HC (2008, $24.99) r/Action Comics #858-863, covers and variants; intro. by Giffen; Gary Frank design sketch pages 25.00
... and the Legion of Super-Heroes SC (2009, $14.99) same contents as HC 15.00
...: Back in Action TPB (2007, $14.99) r/Action Comics #841-843 and DC Comics Presents #4,17,24; commentary by Busiek 15.00
.../Batman: Saga of the Super Sons TPB (2007, $19.99) r/Super Sons stories from '70s World's Finest #215,216,221,222,224,228,230,231,233,242,263 & Elseworlds 80-Page Giant 20.00
...: Brainiac HC (2009, $19.99, dustjacket) r/Action Comics #866-870 & Superman: New Krypton Special #1 20.00
...: Brainiac SC (2010, $12.99) r/Action #866-870 & Superman: New Krypton Spec. #1 13.00
...: Camelot Falls HC (2007, $19.99, dustjacket) r/Superman #654-658 20.00
...: Camelot Falls SC (2008, $12.99) r/Superman #654-658 13.00
...: Camelot Falls Vol. 2 HC (2008, $19.99, dj) r/Superman #662-664,667 & Ann. #13 20.00
...: Camelot Falls Vol. 2 The Weight of the World SC (2008, $12.99) r/Superman #662-664,667 & Ann. #13 13.00
...: Chronicles Vol. 1 ('06, $14.99, TPB) r/early Superman app. in Action Comics #1-13, New York World's Fair 1939 and Superman #1 15.00
...: Chronicles Vol. 2 ('07, $14.99, TPB) r/early Superman app. in Action Comics #14-20 and Superman #2,3 15.00
...: Chronicles Vol. 3 ('07, $14.99, TPB) r/early Superman app. in Action Comics #21-25, Superman #3,4 and New York World's Fair 1940 15.00
...: Chronicles Vol. 4 ('08, $14.99, TPB) r/early Superman app. in Action Comics #26-31, Superman #6,7 15.00
...: Chronicles Vol. 5 ('08, $14.99, TPB) r/early Superman app. in Action Comics #32-36, Superman #8,9 and World's Best Comics #1 15.00
...: Chronicles Vol. 6 ('09, $14.99, TPB) r/early Superman app. in Action Comics #37-40, Superman #10,11 and World's Finest Comics #2,3 15.00
...: Chronicles Vol. 7 ('09, $14.99, TPB) r/early Superman app. in Action Comics #41-43, Superman #12,13 and World's Finest Comics #4 15.00
...: Chronicles Vol. 8 ('10, $14.99, TPB) r/early Superman app. in Action Comics #44-47, and Superman #14,15 15.00
...: Chronicles Vol. 9 ('11, $17.99, TPB) r/early Superman app. in Action Comics #48-52, and Superman #16,17 and World's Finest Comics #6 18.00
...: Codename: Patriot HC ('10, $24.99, d.j.) r/partial New Krypton storyline 25.00
...: Codename: Patriot SC ('11, $14.99) r/partial New Krypton storyline 15.00
...: Critical Condition ('03, $14.95, TPB) r/2000 Kryptonite poisoning storyline 15.00
.../ Doomsday: The Collection Edition (2006, $19.99) r/Superman/Doomsday: Hunter/Prey #1-3, Doomsday Ann. #1, Superman: The Doomsday Wars #1-3, Advs. of Superman #594 and Superman #175; intro. by Dan Jurgens 20.00
...: Daily Planet (2006, $19.99, TPB)-Reprints stories of Daily Planet staff 20.00
... Earth One HC (2010, $19.99)-Updated re-imagining of Superman's debut in Metropolis; Straczynski-s/Shane Davis-a; sketch pages b;y Davis 20.00
...: Emperor Joker TPB (2007, $14.99) reprints 2000 x-over from Superman titles 15.00
...: Endgame (2000, $14.95, TPB)-Reprints Y2K and Brainiac story line 15.00
...: Ending Battle (2009, $14.99, TPB) r/crossover of Superman titles from 2002 15.00
...: Eradication! The Origin of the Eradicator (1996, $12.95, TPB) 13.00
...: Escape From Bizarro World HC (2008, $24.99, dustjacket) r/Action #855-857; early apps. in Superman #140, DC Comics Presents #71 and Man of Steel #5; Vaughan intro. 25.00
...: Escape From Bizarro World SC (2009, $14.99) same contents as hardcover 15.00
...: Exile (1998, $14.95, TPB)-Reprints space exile following execution of Kryptonian criminals; 1st Eradicator 15.00
...: For Tomorrow Volume 1 HC (2005, $24.99, dustjacket) r/#204-209; intro by Azzarello; new cover and sketch section by Lee 25.00
...: For Tomorrow Volume 1 SC (2005, $14.99) r/#204-209; foil-stamped S emblem-c 15.00
...: For Tomorrow Volume 2 HC (2005, $24.99, dustjacket) r/#210-215; afterword and sketch section by Lee; new Lee-c with foil-stamped S emblem 25.00
...: For Tomorrow Volume 2 SC (2005, $14.99) r/#210-215; foil-stamped S emblem-c 15.00
...: Godfall HC (2004, $19.95, dustjacket) r/Action #812-813, Advs. of Superman #625-626, Superman #202-203; Caldwell sketch pages; Turner cover gallery; new Turner-c 20.00
...: Godfall SC (2004, $9.99) r/Action #812-813, Advs. of Superman #625-626, Superman #202-203; Caldwell sketch pages; Turner cover gallery; new Turner-c 10.00
...: Infinite Crisis TPB (2006, $12.99) r/Infinite Crisis #5, I.C. Secret Files and Origins 2006, Action Comics #836, Superman #226 and Advs. of Superman #649 13.00
... In the Forties ('05, $19.99, TPB) Intro. by Bob Hughes 20.00
... In the Fifties ('02, $19.95, TPB) Intro. by Mark Waid 20.00
... In the Sixties ('01, $19.95, TPB) Intro. by Mark Waid 20.00
... In the Seventies ('00, $19.95, TPB) Intro. by Christopher Reeve 20.00
... In the Eighties ('06, $19.99, TPB) Intro. by Jerry Ordway 20.00
... In the Name of Gog ('05, $17.99, TPB) r/Action Comics #820-825 18.00
... Kryptonite HC ('08, $24.99) r/Superman Confidential #1-5,11; Darwyn Cooke intro. 25.00
...: Last Son HC (2008, $19.99) r/Action Comics #844-846,851 and Annual #11; sketch pages and variant covers; Marc McClure intro. 20.00
... Mon-El HC ('10, $24.99) r/Superman #684-690, Action #874 & Annual #1, Superman: Secret Files 2009 #1 25.00
... Mon-El SC ('11, $17.99) r/Superman #684-690, Action #874 & Annual #1, Superman: Secret Files 2009 #1 18.00
... Mon-El - Man of Valor HC ('10, $24.99) r/Superman #692-697 & Annual #14, Adventure #11, Superman: Secret Files 2009 #1 25.00
... : New Krypton Vol. 1 HC ('09, $24.99, d.j.) r/Superman #681, Action #871 & one-shots 25.00
... : New Krypton Vol. 1 SC ('10, $17.99) r/Superman #681, Action #871 & one-shots 18.00
... : New Krypton Vol. 2 HC ('09, $24.99, d.j.) r/Superman #682,683, Action #872,873 & Supergirl #35,36; gallery of covers and variants 25.00
... : New Krypton Vol. 2 SC ('10, $17.99) same contents as HC 18.00
... : New Krypton Vol. 3 HC ('10, $24.99, d.j.) r/Superman: World of New Krypton #1-5 & Action Comics Annual #10; gallery of covers and variants 25.00
... : New Krypton Vol. 3 SC ('11, $17.99) same contents as HC 18.00
... : New Krypton Vol. 4 HC ('10, $24.99, d.j.) r/Superman: World of New Krypton #6-12; gallery of covers and variants; sketch and design art 25.00
... : New Krypton Vol. 4 SC ('11, $17.99) same contents as HC 18.00
... : Nightwing and Flamebird HC ('10, $24.99, d.j.) r/Action #875-879 & Annual #12 25.00
... : Nightwing and Flamebird SC ('10, $17.99) r/Action #875-879 & Annual #12 18.00
... : Nightwing and Flamebird Vol. 2 HC ('10, $24.99, d.j.) r/Action #883-889, Superman #696 & Adventure Comics #8-10 25.00
... No Limits ('00, $14.95, TPB) Reprints early 2000 stories 15.00
...: Our Worlds at War Book 1 ('02, $19.95, TPB) r/1st half of x-over 20.00
...: Our Worlds at War Book 2 ('02, $19.95, TPB) r/2nd half of x-over 20.00
...: Our Worlds at War - The Complete Collection ('06, $24.99, TPB) r/entire x-over 25.00
...: Past and Future (2008, $19.99, TPB) r/time travel stories 1947-1983 20.00
...: President Lex TPB (2003, $17.95) r/Luthor's run for the White House; Harris-c 18.00
...: Redemption TPB (2007, $12.99) r/Superman #659,666 & Action Comics #848,849 13.00
...: Return to Krypton (2004, $17.95, TPB) r/2001-2002 x-over 18.00
...: Sacrifice (2005, $14.99, TPB) prelude x-over to Infinite Crisis; r/Superman #218-220,

Superman: The Black Ring HC © DC

Superman: Infinite City HC © DC

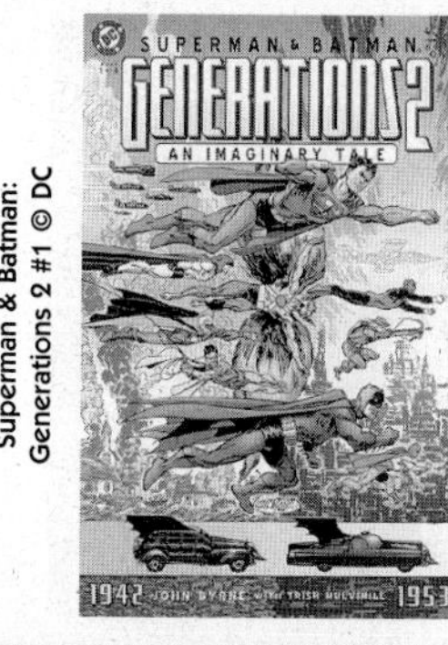

Superman & Batman: Generations 2 #1 © DC

GD VG FN VF VF/NM NM-
2.0 4.0 6.0 8.0 9.0 9.2

Advs. of Superman #642,643; Action #829, Wonder Woman #219,220 15.00
...: Shadows Linger (2008, $14.99, TPB) r/Superman #671-675 15.00
... : Strange Attractors (2006, $14.99, TPB) r/Action Comics #827,828,830-835 15.00
... : Tales From the Phantom Zone ('09, $19.99, TPB) r/Phantom Zone stories 1961-68 20.00
...: That Healing Touch TPB (2005, $14.99) r/Advs. of Superman #633-638 & Superman Secret Files 2004 15.00
...: The Adventures of Nightwing and Flamebird TPB (2009, $19.99)-reprints appearances in Superman Family #173,183-194 20.00
...: The Black Ring Volume One HC (2011, $19.99, d.j.) r/Action Comics #890-895 20.00
The Bottle City of Kandor TPB (2007, $14.99)-Reprints 1st app. in Action #242 and other stories; Nightwing and Flamebird app. 15.00
The Coming of Atlas HC (2009, $19.99, dustjacket)-r/Superman #677-680 & Atlas' debut from First Issue Special #1 (1975); intro by James Robinson 20.00
The Coming of Atlas SC (2010, $14.99) same contents as HC 15.00
The Death of Clark Kent (1997, $19.95, TPB)-Reprints Man of Steel #43 (1 page), Superman #99 (1 page),#100-102, Action #709 (1 page), #710,711, Advs. of Superman #523-525, Superman:The Man of Tomorrow #1 20.00
The Death of Superman (1993, $4.95, TPB)-Reprints Man of Steel #17-19, Superman #73-75, Advs. of Superman #496,497, Action #683,684, & Justice League #69 1 2 3 5 6 8
The Death of Superman, 2nd & 3rd printings 5.00
The Death of Superman Platinum Edition 15.00
...: The Greatest Stories Ever Told ('04, $19.95, TPB) Ross-c, Uslan intro. 20.00
...: The Greatest Stories Ever Told Vol. 2 ('06, $19.99, TPB) Ross-c, Greenberger intro. 20.00
...: The Journey ('06, $14.99, TPB) r/Action Comics #831 & Superman #217,221-225 15.00
...: The Man of Steel Vol. 2 ('03, $19.95, TPB) r/Superman #1-3, Action #584-586, Advs. of Superman #424-426 & Who's Who Update '87 20.00
...: The Man of Steel Vol. 3 ('04, $19.95, TPB) r/Superman #4-6, Action #587-589, Advs. of Superman #427-429; intro. by Ordway; new Ordway-c 20.00
...: The Man of Steel Vol. 4 ('05, $19.99, TPB) r/Superman #7,8; Action #590,591; Advs. of Superman #430,431; Legion of Super-Heroes #37,38; new Ordway-c 20.00
...: The Man of Steel Vol. 5 ('06, $19.99, TPB) r/Superman #9-11, Action #592-593, Advs. of Superman #432-435; intro. by Mike Carlin; new Ordway-c 20.00
...: The Man of Steel Vol. 6 ('08, $19.99, TPB) r/Superman #12 & Ann. #1, Action #594-595 & Ann. #1, Advs. of Superman Ann.#1; Booster Gold #23; new Ordway-c 20.00
The Third Kryptonian ('08, $14.99, TPB) r/Action #847, Superman #668-670 & Ann. #13 15.00
The Trial of Superman ('97, $14.95, TPB) reprints story arc 15.00
The World of Krypton ('08, $14.99, TPB) r/World of Krypton Vol. 2 #1-4 and various tales of Krypton and its history; Kupperberg intro. 15.00
The Wrath of Gog ('05, $14.99, TPB) reprints Action Comics #812-819 15.00
...: They Saved Luthor's Brain ('00, $14.95) r/ "death" and return of Luthor 15.00
...: 3-2-1 Action! ('08, $14.99) Jimmy Olsen super-powered stories; Steve Rude-c 15.00
...: 'Til Death Do Us Part ('01, $17.95) reprints; Mahnke-c 18.00
...: Time and Time Again (1994, $7.50, TPB)-Reprints 8.00
...: Transformed ('98, $12.95, TPB) r/post Final Night powerless Superman to Electric Superman 13.00
...: Unconventional Warfare (2005, $14.95, TPB) r/Adventures of Superman #625-632 and pages from Superman Secret Files 2004 15.00
...: Up, Up and Away! (2006, $14.99, TPB) r/Superman #650-653 and Action #837-840 15.00
... Vs. Brainiac (2008, $19.99, TPB) reprints 1st meeting in Action #242 and other duels 20.00
... Vs. Lex Luthor (2006, $19.99, TPB) reprints 1st meeting in Action #23 and 11 other classic duels 1940-2001 20.00
... Vs. The Flash (2005, $19.99, TPB) reprints their races from Superman #199, Flash #175, World's Finest #198, DC Comics Presents #1&2, Advs. of Superman #463 & DC First: Flash/Superman; new Alex Ross-c 20.00
... Vs. The Revenge Squad (1999, $12.95, TPB) 13.00
...: Whatever Happened to the Man of Tomorrow? TPB (1/97, $5.99) r/Superman #423 & Action Comics #583, intro. by Paul Kupperberg 6.00
...: Whatever Happened to the Man of Tomorrow? Deluxe Edition HC (2009, $24.99, d.j.) r/Superman #423, Action #583, DC Comics Presents #85, Superman Ann #11 25.00
...: Whatever Happened to the Man of Tomorrow? SC (2010, $14.99) r/same as HC 15.00

NOTE: ***Austin** a(i)-1-3. **Byrne** a-1-16p, 17, 19-21p, 22; c-1-17, 20-22; scripts-1-22. **Guice** c/a-64. **Kirby** c-37p. **Joe Quesada** c-Annual 4. **Russell** c/a-23i. **Simonson** c-69i. #19-21 2nd printings sold in multi-packs.*

SUPERMAN (one-shots)
Daily News Magazine Presents DC Comics' Superman nn-(1987, 8 pgs.)-Supplement to New York Daily News; Perez-c/a 5.00
...: A Nation Divided (1999, $4.95)-Elseworlds Civil War story 5.00
... & Savage Dragon: Chicago (2002, $5.95) Larsen-a; Ross-c 6.00
... & Savage Dragon: Metropolis (11/99, $4.95) Bogdanove-a 5.00
...: At Earth's End (1995, $4.95)-Elseworlds story 5.00
...Beyond #0 (10/11, $3.99) The Batman Beyond future; Frenz-a/Nguyen-c 4.00
...: Blood of My Ancestors (2003, $6.95)-Gil Kane & John Buscema-a 7.00
...: Distant Fires (1998, $5.95)-Elseworlds; Chaykin-s 6.00
...: Emperor Joker (10/00, $3.50)-Follows Action #769 4.00
...: End of the Century (2/00, $24.95, HC)-Immonen-s/a 25.00
...: End of the Century (2003, $17.95, SC)-Immonen-s/a 18.00
... For Earth (1991, $4.95, 52 pgs, printed on recycled paper)-Ordway wraparound-c 5.00
...IV Movie Special (1987, $2.00)-Movie adaptation; Heck-a 4.00
...Gallery, The 1 (1993, $2.95)-Poster-a 3.00
..., Inc. (1999, $6.95)-Elseworlds Clark as a sports hero; Garcia-Lopez-a 7.00
...: Infinite City HC (2005, $24.99, dustjacket) Mike Kennedy-s/Carlos Meglia-a 25.00
...: Infinite City SC (2006, $17.99) Mike Kennedy-s/Carlos Meglia-a 18.00
...: Kal (1995, $5.95)-Elseworlds story 6.00
...: Lex 2000 (1/01, $3.50)-Election night for the Luthor Presidency 4.00
...: Monster (1999, $5.95)-Elseworlds story; Anthony Williams-a 6.00
... Movie Special-(9/83)-Adaptation of Superman III; other versions exist with store logos on bottom 1/3 of-c 4.00
...: New Krypton Special 1-(12/08, $3.99) Funeral of Pa Kent; newly enlarged Kandor 4.00
...: Our Worlds at War Secret Files 1-(8/01, $5.95)-Stories & profile pages 6.00
... Plus 1(2/97, $2.95)-Legion of Super-Heroes-c/app. 4.00
...'s Metropolis-(1996, $5.95, prestige format)-Elseworlds; McKeever-c/a 6.00
...: Speeding Bullets-(1993, $4.95, 52 pgs.)-Elseworlds 5.00
.../Spider-Man-(1995, $3.95)-r/DC and Marvel Presents... 4.00
... 10-Cent Adventure 1 (3/02, 10¢) McDaniel-a; intro. Cir-El Supergirl 3.00
...: The Earth Stealers 1-(1988, $2.95, 52 pgs, prestige format) Byrne script; painted-c 5.00
...: The Earth Stealers 1-2nd printing 4.00
...: The Legacy of Superman #1 (3/93, $2.50, 68 pgs.)-Art Adams-c; Simonson-a 5.00
...: The Last God of Krypton ('99,$4.95) Hildebrandt Bros.-a/Simonson-s 5.00
...: The Odyssey ('99, $4.95) Clark Kent's post-Smallville journey 5.00
...: 3-D (12/98, $3.95)-with glasses 4.00
.../Thundercats (1/04, $5.95) Winick-s/Garza-a; two covers by Garza & McGuinness 6.00
.../Through the Ages (2006, $3.99) r/Action #1, Superman ('87) #7; origins and pin-ups 4.00
.../Toyman-(1996, $1.95) 3.00
...: True Brit (2004, $24.95, HC w/dust jacket) Elseworlds; Kal-El's rocket lands in England; co-written by John Cleese and Kim Howard Johnson; John Byrne-a 25.00
...: True Brit (2005, $17.99, TPB) Elseworlds; Kal-El's rocket lands in England 18.00
...: Under A Yellow Sun (1994, $5.95, 68 pgs.)-A Novel by Clark Kent; embossed-c 6.00
... Vs. Darkseid: Apokolips Now! 1 (3/03, $2.95) McKone-a; Kara (Supergirl #75) app. 4.00
...: War of the Worlds (1999, $5.95)-Battles Martians 6.00
...: Where is thy Sting? (2001, $6.95)-McCormack-Sharp-c/a 7.00
...: Y2K (2/00, $4.95)-1st Brainiac 13 app.; Guice-c/a 5.00

SUPERMAN ADVENTURES, THE (Based on animated series)
DC Comics: Oct, 1996 - No. 66, Apr, 2002 ($1.75/$1.95/$1.99)
1-Rick Burchett-c/a begins; Paul Dini script; Lex Luthor app.; silver ink, wraparound-c 4.00
2-20,22: 2-McCloud scripts begin; Metallo-c/app. 3-Brainiac-c/app. 6-Mxyzptlk-c/app. 3.00
21-($3.95) 1st animated Supergirl 5.00
23-66: 23-Begin $1.99-c; Livewire app. 25-Batgirl-c/app. 28-Manley-a. 54-Retells Superman #233 "Kryptonite Nevermore" 58-Ross-c 3.00
Annual 1 (1997, $3.95)-Zatanna and Bruce Wayne app. 4.00
Special 1 (2/98, $2.95) Superman vs. Lobo 4.00
TPB (1998, $7.95) r/#1-6 8.00
... Vol 1: Up, Up and Away (2004, $6.95, digest) r/#16,19,22-24; Amancio-a 7.00
... Vol 2: The Never-Ending Battle (2004, $6.95) r/#25-29 7.00
... Vol 3: Last Son of Krypton (2006, $6.99) r/#30-34 7.00
... Vol 4: The Man of Steel (2006, $6.99) r/#35-39 7.00

SUPERMAN ALIENS 2: GOD WAR (Also see Superman Vs. Aliens)
DC Comics/Dark Horse Comics: May, 2002 - No. 4, Nov, 2002 ($2.99, limited series)
1-4-Bogdanove & Nowlan-a; Darkseid & New Gods app. 3.00
TPB (6/03, $12.95) r/#1-4 13.00

SUPERMAN & BATMAN: GENERATIONS (Elseworlds)
DC Comics: 1999 - No. 4, 1999 ($4.95, limited series)
1-4-Superman & Batman team-up from 1939 to the future; Byrne-c/s/a 5.00
TPB (2000, $14.95) r/series 15.00

SUPERMAN & BATMAN: GENERATIONS II (Elseworlds)
DC Comics: 2001 - No. 4, 2001 ($5.95, limited series)
1-4-Superman, Batman & others team-up from 1942-future; Byrne-c/s/a 6.00
TPB (2003, $19.95) r/series 20.00

SUPERMAN & BATMAN: GENERATIONS III (Elseworlds)
DC Comics: Mar, 2003 - No. 12, Feb, 2004 ($2.95, limited series)
1-12-Superman & Batman through the centuries; Byrne-c/s/a 3.00

SUPERMAN & BATMAN VS. ALIENS AND PREDATOR
DC Comics: 2007 - No. 2, 2007 ($5.99, squarebound, limited series)
1,2-Schultz-s/Olivetti-a 6.00
TPB (2007, $12.99) r/#1,2; pencil breakdown pages 13.00

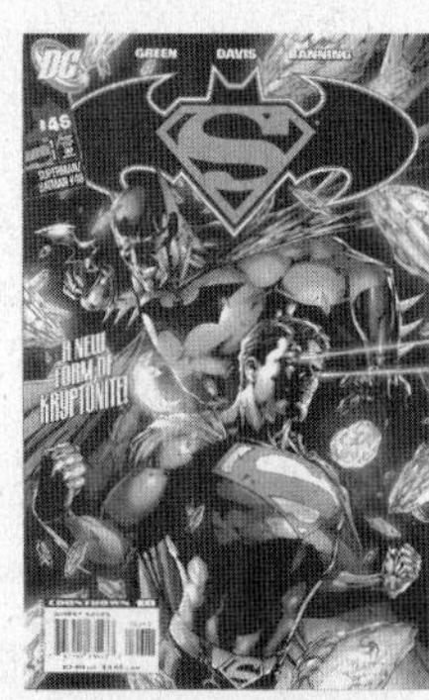
Superman / Batman #46 © DC

Superman Family #222 © DC

Superman: Last Stand on Krypton #1 © DC

	GD	VG	FN	VF	VF/NM	NM-
	2.0	4.0	6.0	8.0	9.0	9.2

SUPERMAN AND BATMAN VS. VAMPIRES AND WEREWOLVES
DC Comics: Early Dec, 2008 - No. 6, Late Feb, 2009 ($2.99, limited series)

1-6-Van Hook-s/Mandrake-a/c. 1-Wonder Woman app. 5-Demon-c/app. 3.00
TPB (2009, $14.99) r/#1-6; intro. by John Landis 15.00

SUPERMAN & BATMAN: WORLD'S FUNNEST (Elseworlds)
DC Comics: 2000 ($6.95, square-bound, one-shot)

nn-Mr. Mxyzptlk and Bat-Mite destroy each DC Universe; Dorkin-s; art by various incl. Ross, Timm, Miller, Allred, Moldoff, Gibbons, Cho, Jimenez 7.00

SUPERMAN & BUGS BUNNY
DC Comics: Jul, 2000 - No. 4, Oct, 2000 ($2.50, limited series)

1-4-JLA & Looney Tunes characters meet 3.00

SUPERMAN/BATMAN
DC Comics: Oct, 2003 - No. 87, Oct, 2011 ($2.95/$2.99)

1-Two covers (Superman or Batman in foreground) Loeb-s/McGuinness-a; Metallo app. 5.00
1-2nd printing (Batman cover) 3.00
1-3rd printing; new McGuinness cover 3.00
1-Diamond/Alliance Retailer Summit Edition-variant 7 14 21 44 72 100
1-(6/06, Free Comic Book Day giveaway) reprints #1 3.00
2-6: 2,5-Future Superman app. 6-Luthor in battlesuit 3.00
7-Pat Lee-c/a; Superboy & Robin app. 3.00
8-Michael Turner-c/a; intro. new Kara Zor-El 5.00
8-Second printing with sketch cover 3.00
8-Third printing with new Turner cover 3.00
9-13-Michael Turner-c/a; Wonder Woman app. 10,13-Variant-c by Jim Lee 3.00
14-25: 14-18-Pacheco-a; Lightning Lord, Saturn Queen & Cosmic King app. 19-Supergirl app.; leads into Supergirl #1. 21-25-Bizarro app. 25-Superman & Batman covers; 2nd printing with white bkgrd cover 3.00
26-($3.99) Sam Loeb tribute issue; 2 covers by Turner; story & art by 26 various; back-up by Loeb & Sale 5.00
27-49: 27-Flashback to Earth-2 Power Girl & Huntress; Maguire-a. 34-36-Metal Men app. 3.00
50-($3.99) Thomas Wayne meets Jor-El; Justice League app. 4.00
51-74: 51,52-Mr. Mxyzptlk app. 66,67-Blackest Night; Man-Bat and Bizarro app. 3.00
75-($4.99) Quitely-c; Legion of Super-Heroes app.; Ordway-a; 2-pg. features by various 5.00
76-87: 76-Aftermath of Batman's "death". 77-Supergirl/Damian team-up 3.00
Annual #1 (12/06, $3.99) Re-imaging of 1st meeting from World's Finest #71 4.00
Annual #2 (5/08, $3.99) Kolins-a; re-imaging of Superman as Supernova story 4.00
Annual #3 (3/09, $3.99) Composite Superman-c by Wrightson; Batista-a 4.00
Annual #4 (8/10, $4.99) Batman Beyond; Levitz-s/Guedes-a/Lau-c 8.00
Annual #5 (6/11, $4.99) Reign of Doomsday x-over, Cyborg Superman app.; Sepulveda-a 5.00
...Absolute Power HC (2005, $19.99) r/#14-18 20.00
...Absolute Power SC (2006, $12.99) r/#14-18 13.00
...Big Noise SC (2010, $14.99) r/#64,68-71 15.00
...Enemies Among Us SC (2009, $12.99) r/#28-33 13.00
...Finest Worlds SC (2010, $14.99) r/#50-56 15.00
...Night and Day HC (2010, $19.99) r/#60-63,65-67 20.00
...Public Enemies HC (2004, $19.95) r/#1-6 & Secret Files 2003; sketch art pages 20.00
...Public Enemies SC (2005, $12.99) r/#1-6 & Secret Files 2003; sketch art pages 13.00
...Public Enemies SC (2009, $14.99) r/#1-6 & Secret Files 2003; sketch art pages 15.00
...Secret Files 2003 (11/03, $4.95) Reis-a; pin-ups by various; Loeb/Sale short-s 5.00
... : Supergirl HC (2004, $19.95) r/#8-13; intro by Loeb, cover gallery, sketch pages 20.00
... : Supergirl SC (2005, $12.99) r/#8-13; intro by Loeb, cover gallery, sketch pages 13.00
... : The Search For Kryptonite HC (2008, $19.99) r/#44-49; Davis sketch pages 20.00
... : The Search For Kryptonite SC (2009, $12.99) r/#44-49; Davis sketch pages 13.00
... : Torment HC (2008, $19.99) r/#37-42; cover gallery, Nguyen sketch pages 20.00
... : Vengeance HC (2006, $19.99) r/#20-25; sketch pages 20.00
... : Vengeance SC (2008, $12.99) r/#20-25; sketch pages 13.00
... : Worship SC (2011, $17.99) r/#72-75 & Annual #4 18.00

SUPERMAN/BATMAN: ALTERNATE HISTORIES
DC Comics: 1996 ($14.95, trade paperback)

nn-Reprints Detective Comics Annual #7, Action Comics Annual #6, Steel Annual #1, Legends of the Dark Knight Annual #4 15.00

SUPERMAN: BIRTHRIGHT
DC Comics: Sept, 2003 - No. 12, Sept, 2004 ($2.95, limited series)

1-12-Waid-s/Leinil Yu-a; retelling of origin and early Superman years 3.00
HC (2004, $29.95, dustjacket) r/series; cover gallery; Waid proposal with Yu concept art 30.00
SC (2005, $19.99) r/series; cover gallery; Waid proposal with Yu concept art 20.00

SUPERMAN COMICS
DC Comics: 1939

nn - Ashcan comic, not distributed to newsstands, only for in-house use. Cover art is Action Comics #7 with interior being Action Comics #8. A CGC certified 9.0 copy sold for $37,375 in 2005 and for $90,000 in 2007.

SUPERMAN CONFIDENTIAL (See Superman Hardcovers and TPBs listings for reprint)
DC Comics: Jan, 2007 - No. 14, Jun, 2008 ($2.99)

1-14: 1-5,9-Darwyn Cooke-s/Tim Sale-a/c; origin of Kryptonite re-told. 8-10-New Gods and Darkside app. 3.00
...: Kryptonite TPB (2009, $14.99) r/#1-5,11; intro. by Darwyn Cooke; Tim Sale sketch-a 15.00

SUPERMAN: DAY OF DOOM
DC Comics: Jan, 2003 - No. 4, Feb, 2003 ($2.95, weekly limited series)

1-4-Jurgens-s/Jurgens & Sienkiewicz-a 3.00
TPB (2003, $9.95) r/#1-4 10.00

SUPERMAN/DOOMSDAY: HUNTER/PREY
DC Comics: 1994 - No. 3, 1994 ($4.95, limited series, 52 pgs.)

1-3 5.00

SUPERMAN FAMILY, THE (Formerly Superman's Pal Jimmy Olsen)
National Per. Publ./DC Comics: No. 164, Apr-May, 1974 - No. 222, Sept, 1982

	GD 2.0	VG 4.0	FN 6.0	VF 8.0	VF/NM 9.0	NM- 9.2
164-(100 pgs.) Jimmy Olsen, Supergirl, Lois Lane begin	5	10	15	30	48	65
165-169 (100 pgs.)	3	6	9	19	29	38
170-176 (68 pgs.)	3	6	9	14	19	24
177-190 (52 pgs.): 177-181-52 pgs. 182-Marshall Rogers-a; $1.00 issues begin; Krypto begins, ends #192. 183-Nightwing-Flamebird begins, ends #194. 189-Brainiac 5, Mon -El app.	2	4	6	9	13	16
191-193,195-199: 191-Superboy begins, ends #198	2	3	4	6	8	10
194,200: 194-Rogers-a. 200-Book length sty	2	4	6	8	10	12
201-210,212-222	1	2	3	5	6	8
211-Earth II Batman & Catwoman marry	2	4	6	8	11	14

NOTE: ***N. Adams** c-182-185. **Anderson** a-186i. **Buckler** c(p)-190, 191, 209, 210, 215, 217, 220. **Jones** a-191-193. **Gil Kane** c(p)-221, 222. **Mortimer** a(p)-191-193, 199, 201-222. **Orlando** a(i)-186, 187. **Rogers** a-182, 194. **Staton** a-191-194, 196p. **Tuska** a(p)-203, 207-209.*

SUPERMAN/FANTASTIC FOUR
DC Comics/Marvel Comics: 1999 ($9.95, tabloid size, one-shot)

1-Battle Galactus and the Cyborg; wraparound-c by Alex Ross and Dan Jurgens; Jurgens-s/a; Thibert-a 10.00

SUPERMAN FOR ALL SEASONS
DC Comics: 1998 - No, 4, 1998 ($4.95, limited series, prestige format)

1-Loeb-s/Sale-a/c; Superman's first year in Metropolis 6.00
2-4 5.00
Hardcover (1999, $24.95) r/#1-4 25.00

SUPERMAN FOR EARTH (See Superman one-shots)

SUPERMAN FOREVER
DC Comics: Jun, 1998 ($5.95, one-shot)

1-($5.95)-Collector's Edition with a 7-image lenticular-c by Alex Ross; Superman returns to normal; s/a by various 7.00
1-($4.95) Standard Edition with single image Ross-c 5.00

SUPERMAN/GEN13
DC Comics (WildStorm): Jun, 2000 - No. 3, Aug, 2000 ($2.50, limited series)

1-3-Hughes-s/ Bermejo-a; Campbell variant-c for each 3.00
TPB (2001, $9.95) new Bermejo-c; cover gallery 10.00

SUPERMAN: KING OF THE WORLD
DC Comics: June, 1999 ($3.95/$4.95, one-shot)

1-($3.95) Regular Ed. 4.00
1-($4.95) Collectors' Ed. with gold foil enhanced-c 5.00

SUPERMAN: LAST SON OF EARTH
DC Comics: 2000 - No. 2, 2000 ($5.95, limited series, prestige format)

1,2-Elseworlds; baby Clark rockets to Krypton; Gerber-s/Wheatley-a 6.00

SUPERMAN: LAST STAND OF NEW KRYPTON
DC Comics: May, 2010 - No. 3, Late June, 2010 ($3.99, limited series)

1-3-Robinson & Gates-s/Woods-a. 2-Pérez-c. 3-Sook-c 4.00
HC (2010, $24.99, DJ) r/#1,2, Adventure Comics #8,9, Supergirl #51 & Superman #698 25.00
Vol. 2 HC (2010, $19.99, DJ) r/#3, Adventure #10,11, Supergirl #52 & Superman #699 20.00

SUPERMAN: LAST STAND ON KRYPTON
DC Comics: 2003 ($6.95, one-shot, prestige format)

1-Sequel to Superman: Last Son of Earth; Gerber-s/Wheatley-a 7.00

SUPERMAN: LOIS LANE (Girlfrenzy)
DC Comics: Jun, 1998 ($1.95, one shot)

1-Connor & Palmiotti-a 3.00

Superman Red / Superman Blue #1 © DC

Superman's Girlfriend Lois Lane #10 © DC

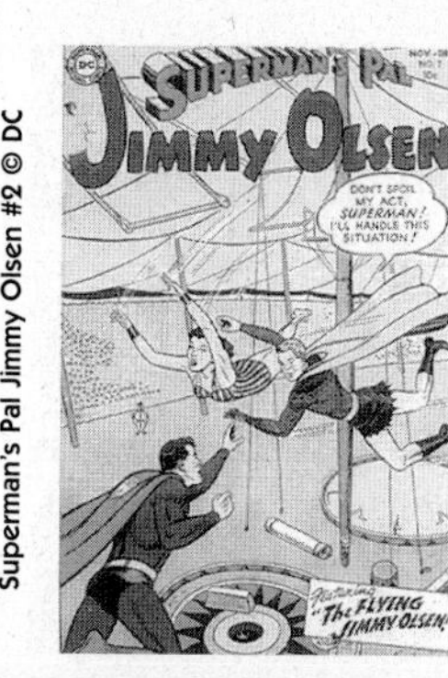

Superman's Pal Jimmy Olsen #2 © DC

GD VG FN VF VF/NM NM-
2.0 4.0 6.0 8.0 9.0 9.2

SUPERMAN/MADMAN HULLABALOO!
Dark Horse Comics: June, 1997 - No. 3, Aug, 1997 ($2.95, limited series)
1-3-Mike Allred-c/s/a 3.00
TPB (1997, $8.95) 9.00

SUPERMAN: METROPOLIS
DC Comics: Apr, 2003 - No. 12, Mar, 2004 ($2.95, limited series)
1-12-Focus on Jimmy Olsen; Austen-s. 1-6-Zezelj-a. 7-12-Kristiansen-a. 8,9-Creeper app. 3.00

SUPERMAN METROPOLIS SECRET FILES
DC Comics: Jun, 2000 ($4.95, one shot)
1-Short stories, pin-ups and profile pages; Hitch and Neary-c 5.00

SUPERMAN: PEACE ON EARTH
DC Comics: Jan, 1999 ($9.95, Treasury-sized, one-shot)
1-Alex Ross painted-c/a; Paul Dini-s 12.00

SUPERMAN: RED SON
DC Comics: 2003 - No. 3, 2003 ($5.95, limited series, prestige format)
1-Elseworlds; Superman's rocket lands in Russia; Mark Millar-s/Dave Johnson-c/a 10.00
2,3 6.00
TPB (2004, $17.95) r/#1-3; intro. by Tom DeSanto; sketch pages 18.00
... - The Deluxe Edition HC (2009, $24.99, d.j.) r/#1-3; sketch art by various 25.00

SUPERMAN RED/ SUPERMAN BLUE
DC Comics: Feb, 1998 ($4.95, one shot)
1-Polybagged w/3-D glasses and reprint of Superman 3-D (1955); Jurgens-plot/3-D cover; script and art by various 5.00
1-($3.95)-Standard Ed.; comic only, non 3-D cover 4.00

SUPERMAN RETURNS... (2006 movie)
DC Comics: Aug, 2006 ($3.99, movie tie-in stories by Singer, Dougherty and Harris)
Prequel 1 - Krypton to Earth; Olivetti-a/Hughes-c; retells Jor-El's story 6.00
Prequel 2 - Ma Kent; Kerschl-a/Hughes-c; Ma Kent during Clark childhood and absence 4.00
Prequel 3 - Lex Luthor; Leonardi-a/Hughes-c; Luthor's 5 years in prison 4.00
Prequel 4 - Lois Lane; Dias-a/Hughes-c; Lois during Superman's absence 4.00
The Movie and Other Tales of the Man of Steel (2006, $12.99, TPB) adaptation; origin from Amazing World of Superman; Action #810, Superman #185; Advs. of Superman #575 13.00
The Official Movie Adaptation (2006, $6.99) Pasko-s/Haley-a; photo-c 7.00
...: The Prequels TPB (2006, $12.99) r/the 4 prequels 13.00

SUPERMAN: SAVE THE PLANET
DC Comics: Oct, 1998 ($2.95, one-shot)
1-($2.95) Regular Ed.; Luthor buys the Daily Planet 3.00
1-($3.95) Collector's Ed. with acetate cover 4.00

SUPERMAN SCRAPBOOK (Has blank pages; contains no comics)

SUPERMAN: SECRET FILES
DC Comics: Jan, 1998; May 1999 ($4.95)
1,2: 1-Retold origin story, "lost" pages & pin-ups 5.00
... & Origins 2004 (8/04) pin-ups by Lee, Turner and others 5.00
... & Origins 2005 (1/06) short stories and pin-ups by various 5.00
... 2009 (10/09, $4.99) short stories and pin-ups about New Krypton x-over 5.00

SUPERMAN: SECRET IDENTITY
DC Comics: 2004 - No. 4, 2004 ($5.95, squarebound, limited series)
1-4-Busiek-s/Immonen-a/c 6.00

SUPERMAN: SECRET ORIGIN
DC Comics: Nov, 2009 - No. 6, Oct, 2010 ($3.99, limited series)
1-6-Geoff Johns-s/Gary Frank-a/c; origin mythos re-told. 2-Legion app. 5-Metallo app. 4.00
1-6-Variant covers by Frank 6.00
HC (2011, $29.99) r/#1-6; intro. by David Goyer; variant covers 30.00

SUPERMAN'S GIRLFRIEND LOIS LANE (See Action Comics #1, 80 Page Giant #3, 14, Lois Lane, Showcase #9, 10, Superman #28 & Superman Family)

SUPERMAN'S GIRLFRIEND LOIS LANE (See Showcase #9,10)
National Periodical Publ.: Mar-Apr, 1958 - No. 136, Jan-Feb, 1974; No. 137, Sept-Oct, 1974
1-(3-4/58) 328 656 984 2850 6175 9500
2 85 170 255 689 1495 2300
3 56 112 168 454 977 1500
4,5 44 88 132 330 715 1100
6,7 35 70 105 254 552 850
8-10: 9-Pat Boone-c/story 29 58 87 210 455 700
11-13,15-19: 12-(10/59)-Aquaman app. 17-(5/60) 2nd app. Brainiac.
18 36 54 126 273 420
14-Supergirl x-over; Batman app. on-c only 19 38 57 133 287 440
20-Supergirl-c/sty 19 38 57 130 280 430
21-28: 23-1st app. Lena Thorul, Lex Luthor's sister; 1st Lois as Elastic Lass. 27-Bizarro-c/story 14 28 42 96 208 320
29-Aquaman, Batman, Green Arrow cover app. and cameo; last 10¢ issue
15 30 45 102 221 340
30-32,34-46,48,49 10 20 30 65 116 175
33(5/62)-Mon -El app. 10 20 30 66 121 185
47-Legion app. 10 20 30 66 121 185
50(7/64)-Triplicate Girl, Phantom Girl & Shrinking Violet app.
10 20 30 66 121 185
51-55,57-67,69: 59-Jor -El app.; Batman back-up sty 8 16 24 51 86 120
56-Saturn Girl app. 8 16 24 53 89 125
68-(Giant G-26) 9 18 27 61 106 150
70-Penguin & Catwoman app. (1st S.A. Catwoman, 11/66; also see Detective #369 for 3rd app.); Batman & Robin cameo 22 44 66 154 327 500
71-Batman & Robin cameo (3 panels); Catwoman story cont'd from #70 (2nd app.); see Detective #369 for 3rd app 13 26 39 86 183 280
72,73,75,76,78 6 12 18 39 62 85
74-1st Bizarro Flash (5/67); JLA cameo 6 12 18 41 66 90
77-(Giant G-39) 7 14 21 49 82 115
79-Neal Adams-c or c(i) begin, end #95,108 6 12 18 41 66 90
80-85,87,88,90-92: 92-Last 12¢ issue 5 10 15 30 48 65
86,95 (Giants G-51,G-63)-Both have Neal Adams-c 6 12 18 42 69 95
89,93: 89-Batman x-over; all N. Adams-c. 93-Wonder Woman-c/story
5 10 15 32 51 70
94,96-99,101-103,107-110 4 8 12 24 37 50
100 4 8 12 26 41 55
104-(Giant G-75) 6 12 18 39 62 85
105-Origin/1st app. The Rose & the Thorn. 6 12 18 39 62 85
106-"I Am Curious (Black)" story; Lois changes her skin color to black
8 16 24 55 93 130
111-Justice League-c/s; Morrow-a; last 15¢ issue 4 8 12 26 41 55
112,114-123 (52 pgs.): 122-G.A. Lois Lane-r/Superman #30. 123-G.A. Batman-r/Batman #35 (w/Catwoman) 4 8 12 24 37 50
113-(Giant G-87) Kubert-a (previously unpublished G.A. story)(scarce in NM)
6 12 18 42 69 95
124-135: 130-Last Rose & the Thorn. 132-New Zatanna story
3 6 9 16 23 30
136,137: 136-Wonder Woman x-over 3 6 9 18 27 35
Annual 1(Sum, 1962)-r/L. Lane #12; Aquaman app. 19 38 57 128 277 425
Annual 2(Sum, 1963) 13 26 39 87 186 285
NOTE: ***Buckler*** *a-117-121p.* ***Curt Swan or Kurt Schaffenberger*** *a-1-81(most); c(p)-1-15.*

SUPERMAN/SHAZAM: FIRST THUNDER
DC Comics: Nov, 2005 - No. 4, Feb, 2006 ($3.50, limited series)
1-4-Retells first meeting; Winick-s/Middleton-a. Dr. Sivana app. 3.50

SUPERMAN: SILVER BANSHEE
DC Comics: Dec, 1998 - No. 2, Jan, 1999 ($2.25, mini-series)
1,2-Brereton-s/c; Chin-a 3.00

SUPERMAN'S NEMESIS: LEX LUTHOR
DC Comics: Mar, 1999 - No. 4, Jun, 1999 ($2.50, mini-series)
1-4-Semeiks-a 3.00

SUPERMAN'S PAL JIMMY OLSEN (Superman Family #164 on)
(See Action Comics #6 for 1st app. & 80 Page Giant)
National Periodical Publ.: Sept-Oct, 1954 - No. 163, Feb-Mar, 1974 (Fourth World #133-148)
1 550 1100 1650 4950 9475 14,000
2 143 286 429 1200 2600 4000
3-Last pre-code issue 85 170 255 689 1495 2300
4,5 56 112 168 454 977 1500
6-10 40 80 120 300 650 1000
11-20: 15-1st S.A. issue 28 56 84 203 439 675
21-28,30 19 38 57 128 277 425
29-(6/58) 1st app. Krypto with Superman 20 40 60 137 294 450
31-Origin & 1st app. Elastic Lad (Jimmy Olsen) 16 32 48 111 243 375
32-40: 33-One pg. biography of Jack Larson (TV Jimmy Olsen). 36-Intro Lucy Lane. 37-2nd app. Elastic Lad & 1st cover app. 13 26 39 85 180 275
41-50: 41-1st J.O. Robot. 48-Intro/origin Superman Emergency Squad
11 22 33 71 136 200
51-56: 56-Last 10¢ issue 9 18 27 61 106 150
57-62,64-70: 57-Olsen marries Supergirl. 62-Mon-El & Elastic Lad app. but not as Legionnaires. 70-Element Boy (Lad) app. 7 14 21 46 76 105
63(9/62)-Legion of Super-Villains app. 7 14 21 48 79 110
71,74,75,78,80-84,86,89,90: 86-Jimmy Olsen Robot becomes Congorilla

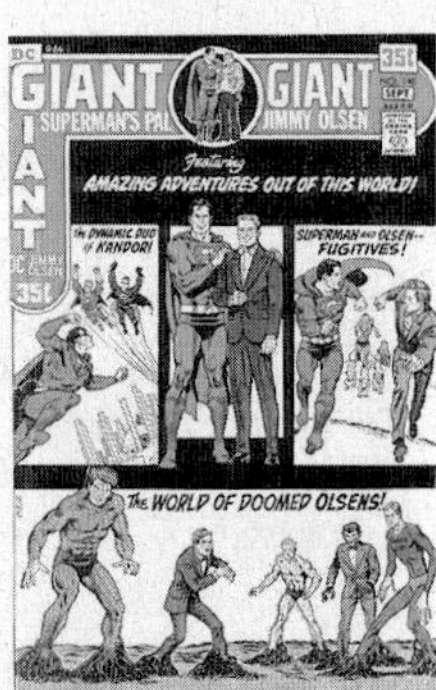

Superman's Pal Jimmy Olsen #140 © DC

Superman: The Man of Steel #81 © DC

Superman vs. Predator #1
© DC, DH & 20th Century Fox

GD VG FN VF VF/NM NM-
2.0 4.0 6.0 8.0 9.0 9.2

6 12 18 37 59 80
72,73,76,77,79,85,87,88: 72(10/63)-Legion app; Elastic Lad (Olsen) joins. 73-Ultra Boy app. 76,85-Legion app. 76-Legion app. 77-Olsen with Colossal Boy's powers & costume; origin Titano retold. 79-(9/64)-Titled The Red-headed Beatle of 1000 B.C. 85-Legion app. 87-Legion of Super-Villains app. 88-Star Boy app. 6 12 18 39 62 85
91-94,96-98 5 10 15 30 48 65
95 (Giant G-25) 7 14 21 46 76 105
99-Olsen w/powers & costumes of Lightning Lad, Sun Boy & Element Lad 5 10 15 32 51 70
100-Legion cameo 5 10 15 35 55 75
101-103,105-112,114-120: 106-Legion app. 110-Infinity-c. 117-Batman & Legion cameo. 120-Last 12¢ issue 4 8 12 24 37 50
104 (Giant G-38) 6 12 18 39 62 85
113,122,131,140 (Giants G-50,G-62,G-74,G-86) 5 10 15 35 55 75
121,123-130,132 4 8 12 22 34 45
133-(10/70)-Jack Kirby story & art begins; re-intro Newsboy Legion; 1st app. Morgan Edge 6 12 18 41 66 90
134-1st app. Darkseid (1 panel, 12/70) 7 14 21 46 76 105
135-2nd app. Darkseid (1 pg. cameo; see New Gods & Forever People); G.A. Guardian app. 5 10 15 30 48 65
136-139: 136-Origin new Guardian. 138-Partial photo-c. 139-Last 15¢ issue 4 8 12 24 37 50
141-150: (25¢,52 pgs.). 141-Photo-c; Newsboy Legion-r by S&K begin; full pg. self-portrait of Jack Kirby; Don Rickles cameo. 149,150-G.A. Plastic Man-r in both; 150-Newsboy Legion app. 4 8 12 22 34 45
151-163 3 6 9 16 23 30
... Special 1 (12/08, $4.99) New Krypton tie-in; The Guardian and Dubbilex app. 5.00
... Special 2 (10/09, $4.99) New Krypton tie-in; Mon-El app.; Chang-a 5.00
Superman: The Amazing Transformations of Jimmy Olsen TPB (2007, $14.99) reprints Olsen's transformations into Wolf-Man, Elastic Lad, Turtle Boy and others; new Bolland-c 15.00

NOTE: *Issues #141-148 contain* **Simon & Kirby** *Newsboy Legion reprints from Star Spangled #7, 8, 9, 10, 11, 12, 13, 14 in that order.* **N. Adams** *c-109-112, 115, 117, 118, 120, 121, 132, 134-136, 147, 148.* **Kirby** *a-133-139p, 141-148p; c-133, 137, 139, 142, 145p.* **Kirby/N. Adams** *c-137, 138, 141-144, 146.* **Curt Swan** *c-1-14(most)., 140.*

SUPERMAN SPECTACULAR (Also see DC Special Series #5)
DC Comics: 1982 (Magazine size, 52 pgs., square binding)
1-Saga of Superman Red/ Superman Blue; Luthor and Terra-Man app.; Gonzales & Colletta-a 1 3 4 6 8 10

SUPERMAN: STRENGTH
DC Comics: 2005 - No. 3, 2005 ($5.95, limited series)
1-3: Alex Ross-c/Scott McCloud-s/Aluir Amancio-a 6.00

SUPERMAN / SUPERGIRL: MAELSTROM
DC Comics: Early Jan, 2009 - No. 5, Mar, 2009 ($2.99, limited series)
1-5: Palmiotti & Gray-s/Noto-c/a; Darkseid app. 3.00
TPB (2009, $12.99) r/#1-5 13.00

SUPERMAN / SUPERHOMBRE
DC Comics: Apr, 1945
nn - Ashcan comic, not distributed to newsstands, only for in-house use (no known sales)

SUPERMAN / TARZAN: SONS OF THE JUNGLE
Dark Horse Comics: Oct, 2001 - No. 3, May, 2002 ($2.99, limited series)
1-3-Elseworlds; Kal-El lands in the jungle; Dixon-s/Meglia-a/Ramos-c 3.00

SUPERMAN: THE DARK SIDE
DC Comics: 1998 - No. 3, 1998 ($4.95, squarebound, mini-series)
1-3: Elseworlds; Kal-El lands on Apokolips 5.00

SUPERMAN: THE DOOMSDAY WARS
DC Comics: 1998 - No. 3, 1999 ($4.95, squarebound, mini-series)
1-3: Superman & JLA vs. Doomsday; Jurgens-s/a(p) 5.00

SUPERMAN: THE KANSAS SIGHTING
DC Comics: 2003 - No. 2, 2003 ($6.95, squarebound, mini-series)
1,2-DeMatteis-s/Tolagson-a 7.00

SUPERMAN: THE LAST FAMILY OF KRYPTON
DC Comics: Oct, 2010 - No. 3, Dec, 2010 ($4.99, limited series)
1-3-Elseworlds; the El family lands on Earth; Bates-s/Arlem-a/Massafera-c 5.00

SUPERMAN: THE MAN OF STEEL (Also see Man of Steel, The)
DC Comics: July, 1991 - No. 134, Mar, 2003 ($1.00/$1.25/$1.50/$1.95/$2.25)
0-(10/94) Zero Hour; released between #37 & #38 3.00
1-($1.75, 52 pgs.)-Painted-c 5.00
2-16: 3-War of the Gods x-over. 5-Reads sideways. 10-Last $1.00-c.

GD VG FN VF VF/NM NM-
2.0 4.0 6.0 8.0 9.0 9.2

14-Superman & Robin team-up 3.00
17-1st brief app. Doomsday 1 2 3 4 5 7
17,18: 17-2nd printing. 18-2nd & 3rd printings 3.00
18-1st full app. Doomsday 1 2 3 5 7 9
19-Doomsday battle issue (c/story) 6.00
20-22: 20,21-Funeral for a Friend. 22-($1.95)-Collector's Edition w/die-cut outer-c & bound-in poster; Steel-c/story 4.00
22-($1.50)-Newsstand Ed. w/poster & different-c 4.00
23-49,51-99: 30-Regular edition. 32-Bizarro-c/story. 35,36-Worlds Collide Pt. 1 & 10. 37-(9/94)-Zero Hour x-over. 38-(11/94). 48-Aquaman app. 54-Spectre-c/app; Lex Luthor app. 56-Mxyzptlk-c/app. 57-G.A. Flash app. 58-Supergirl app. 59-Parasite-c/app.; Steel app. 60-Reintro Bottled City of Kandor. 62-Final Night. 64-New Gods app. 67-New powers. 75-"Death" of Mxyzptlk. 78,79-Millennium Giants. 80-Golden Age style. 92-JLA app. 98-Metal Men app. 3.00
30-($2.50)-Collector's Edition; polybagged with Superman & Lobo vinyl clings that stick to wraparound-c; Lobo-c/story 4.00
50 ($2.95)-The Trial of Superman 4.00
100-($2.99) New Fortress of Solitude revealed 3.00
100-($3.99) Special edition with fold out cardboard-c 4.00
101,102-101-Batman app. 3.00
103-133: 103-Begin $2.25. 105-Batman-c/app. 111-Return to Krypton. 115-117-Our Worlds at War. 117-Maxima killed. 121-Royal Flush Gang app. 128-Return to Krypton II. 3.00
134-($2.75) Last issue; Steel app.; Bogdanove-c 3.00
#1,000,000 (11/98) 853rd Century x-over; Gene Ha-c 3.00
Annual 1-5 ('92-'96,68 pgs.): 1-Eclipso app.; Joe Quesada-c(p). 2-Intro Edge. 3 -Elseworlds; Mignola-c; Batman app. 4-Year One story. 5-Legends of the Dead Earth story 4.00
Annual 6 (1997, $3.95)-Pulp Heroes story 4.00
...Gallery (1995, $3.50) Pin-ups by various 4.00

SUPERMAN: THE MAN OF TOMORROW
DC Comics: 1995 - No. 15, Fall, 1999 ($1.95-$2.95, quarterly)
1-15: 1-Lex Luthor app. 3-Lex Luthor-c/app; Joker app. 4-Shazam! app. 5-Wedding of Lex Luthor. 10-Maxima-c/app. 13-JLA-c/app. 3.00
#1,000,000 (11/98) 853rd Century x-over; Gene Ha-c 3.00

SUPERMAN: THE SECRET YEARS
DC Comics: Feb, 1985 - No. 4, May, 1985 (limited series)
1-4-Miller-c on all 4.00

SUPERMAN: THE WEDDING ALBUM
DC Comics: Dec, 1996 ($4.95, 96 pgs, one-shot)
1-Standard Edition-Story & art by past and present Superman creators; gatefold back-c. Byrne-c 5.00
1-Collector's Edition-Embossed cardstock variant-c w/ metallic silver ink and matte and gloss varnishes 5.00
Retailer Rep. Program Edition (#'d to 250, signed by Bob Rozakis on back-c) 50.00
TPB ('97, $14.95) r/Wedding and honeymoon stories 15.00

SUPERMAN 3-D (See Three-Dimension Adventures)

SUPERMAN-TIM (See Promotional Comics section)

SUPERMAN VILLAINS SECRET FILES
DC Comics: Jun, 1998 ($4.95, one shot)
1-Origin stories, "lost" pages & pin-ups 5.00

SUPERMAN VS. ALIENS (Also see Superman Aliens 2: God War)
DC Comics/Dark Horse Comics: July, 1995 - No. 3, Sept, 1995 ($4.95, limited series)
1-3: Jurgens/Nowlan-a 5.00

SUPERMAN VS. MUHAMMAD ALI (See All-New Collectors' Edition C-56 for original 1978 printing)
DC Comics: 2010
... Deluxe Edition (2010, $19.99, HC w/dustjacket) recolored reprint in comic size; new intro. by Neal Adams; afterword by Jenette Kahn; sketch pages, key to cover celebs 20.00
... Facsimile Edition (2010, $39.99, HC no dustjacket) recolored reprint in original Treasury size; new intro. by Neal Adams; key to cover celebs 40.00

SUPERMAN VS. PREDATOR
DC Comics/Dark Horse Comics: 2000 - No. 3, 2000 ($4.95, limited series)
1-3-Micheline-s/Maleev-a 5.00
TPB (2001, $14.95) r/series 15.00

SUPERMAN VS. THE AMAZING SPIDER-MAN (Also see Marvel Treasury Edition No. 28)
National Periodical Publications/Marvel Comics Group: 1976
($2.00, Treasury sized, 100 pgs.)
1-Superman and Spider-Man battle Lex Luthor and Dr. Octopus; Andru/Giordano-a; 1st Marvel/DC x-over. 8 16 24 53 89 125
1-2nd printing; 5000 numbered copies signed by Stan Lee & Carmine Infantino on

Super-Mystery Comics V2 #4 © ACE

Supernatural V4 #1 © WB

Supernatural Thrillers #7 © MAR

	GD 2.0	VG 4.0	FN 6.0	VF 8.0	VF/NM 9.0	NM- 9.2

front cover & sold through mail 12 24 36 83 172 260
nn-(1995, $5.95)-r/#1 6.00

SUPERMAN VS. THE TERMINATOR: DEATH TO THE FUTURE
Dark Horse/DC Comics: Dec, 1999 - No. 4, Mar, 2000 ($2.95, limited series)

1-4-Grant-s/Pugh-a/c: Steel and Supergirl app. 3.00

SUPERMAN: WAR OF THE SUPERMEN
DC Comics: No. 0, Jun, 2010 - No. 4, Jul, 2010 ($2.99, limited series)

0-Free Comic Book Day issue; Barrows-c 3.00
1-4: 1-New Krypton destroyed 3.00
HC (2011, $19.99) r/#0-4 & Superman #700 20.00

SUPERMAN/WONDER WOMAN: WHOM GODS DESTROY
DC Comics: 1997 ($4.95, prestige format, limited series)

1-4-Elseworlds; Claremont-s 5.00

SUPERMAN WORKBOOK
National Periodical Publ./Juvenile Group Foundation: 1945 (B&W, reprints, 68 pgs)

nn-Cover-r/Superman #14 194 388 582 1242 2121 3000

SUPERMAN: WORLD OF NEW KRYPTON
DC Comics: May, 2009 - No. 12,Apr, 2010 ($2.99, limited series)

1-12: Robinson & Rucka-s/Woods-a; Frank-c and variant for each. 4-Green Lantern app. 3.00

SUPER MARIO BROS. (Also see Adventures of the..., Blip, Gameboy, and Nintendo Comics System)
Valiant Comics: 1990 - No. 5?, 1991 ($1.95, slick-c) V2#1, 1991 - No. 5, 1991

1-Wildman-a 1 3 4 6 8 10
2-5, V2#1-5-($1.50) 6.00
Special Edition 1 (1990, $1.95)-Wildman-a 6.00

SUPER MARKET COMICS
Fawcett Publications: No date (1950s)

nn - Ashcan comic, not distributed to newsstands, only for in-house use (no known sales)

SUPER MARKET VARIETIES
Fawcett Publications: No date (1950s)

nn - Ashcan comic, not distributed to newsstands, only for in-house use (no known sales)

SUPERMEN OF AMERICA
DC Comics: Mar, 1999 ($3.95/$4.95, one-shot)

1-($3.95) Regular Ed.; Immonen-s/art by various 4.00
1-($4.95) Collectors' Ed. with membership kit 5.00

SUPERMEN OF AMERICA (Mini-series)
DC Comics: Mar, 2000 - No. 6, Aug, 2000 ($2.50)

1-6-Nicieza-s/Braithwaite-a 3.00

SUPERMOUSE (...the Big Cheese; see Coo Coo Comics)
Standard Comics/Pines No. 35 on (Literary Ent.): Dec, 1948 - No. 34, Sept, 1955; No. 35, Apr, 1956 - No. 45, Fall, 1958

1-Frazetta text illos (3) 28 56 84 165 270 375
2-Frazetta text illos 15 30 45 84 127 170
3,5,6-Text illos by Frazetta in all 13 26 39 74 105 135
4-Two pg. text illos by Frazetta 14 28 42 78 112 145
7-10 9 18 27 47 61 75
11-20: 13-Racist humor (Indians) 7 14 21 37 46 55
21-45 6 12 18 31 38 45
1-Summer Holiday issue (Summer, 1957, 25¢, 100 pgs.)-Pines
14 28 42 80 115 150
2-Giant Summer issue (Summer, 1958, 25¢, 100 pgs.)-Pines; has games, puzzles & stories 10 20 30 58 79 100

SUPER-MYSTERY COMICS
Ace Magazines (Periodical House): July, 1940 - V8#6, July, 1949

V1#1-Magno, the Magnetic Man & Vulcan begins (1st app.); Q-13, Corp. Flint, & Sky Smith begin 320 640 960 2240 3920 5600
2 105 210 315 667 1146 1625
3-The Black Spider begins (1st app.) 84 168 252 538 919 1300
4-Origin Davy 60 120 180 381 653 925
5-Intro. The Clown & begin series (12/40) 64 128 192 406 696 985
6(2/41) 53 106 159 334 567 800
V2#1(4/41)-Origin Buckskin 52 104 156 328 552 775
2-6(2/42): 6-Vulcan begins again 49 98 147 309 522 735
V3#1(4/42),2: 1-Black Ace begins 43 86 129 271 461 650
3-Intro. The Lancer; Dr. Nemesis & The Sword begin; Kurtzman-c/a(2) (Mr. Risk & Paul Revere Jr.); Robot-c 53 106 159 334 567 800
4-Kurtzman-c/a; classic-c 94 188 282 597 1024 1450
5-Kurtzman-a(2); L.B. Cole-a; Mr. Risk app. 52 104 156 328 557 785
6(10/43)-Mr. Risk app.; Kurtzman's Paul Revere Jr.; L.B. Cole-a
52 104 156 328 557 785
V4#1(1/44)-L.B. Cole-a 46 92 138 290 488 685
2-6(4/45): 2,5,6-Mr. Risk app. 33 66 99 194 317 440
V5#1(7/45)-6 33 66 99 194 317 440
V6#1,2,4,5,6: 4-Last Magno. Mr. Risk app. in #2,4-6. 6-New logo
27 54 81 160 263 365
3-Torture c-story 37 74 111 222 361 500
V7#1-6, V8#1-4,6 25 50 75 147 241 335
V8#5-Meskin, Tuska, Sid Greene-a 25 50 75 150 245 340

NOTE: ***Sid Greene** a-V7#4. **Mooney** c-V1#5, 6, V2#1-6. **Palais** a-V5#3, 4; c-V4#6-V5#4, V6#2, V8#4. Bondage c-V2#5, 6, V3#2, 5. Magno c-V1#1-V3#6, V4#2-V5#5, V6#2. The Sword c-V4#1, 6(w/Magno).*

SUPERNATURAL (Volume 4) (Based on the CW television series)
DC Comics: Dec, 2011 - No. 6, May, 2012 ($2.99, limited series)

1-6: 1-Sam in Scotland; Brian Wood-s/Grant Bond-a 3.00

SUPERNATURAL: BEGINNING'S END (Based on the CW television series)
DC Comics (WildStorm): Mar, 2010 - No. 6, Aug, 2010 ($2.99, limited series)

1-6-Prequel to the series; Dabb & Loflin-s/Olmos-a. 1-Olmos and photo-c 3.00
TPB (2010, $14.99) r/#1-6; character sketch pages 15.00

SUPERNATURAL FREAK MACHINE: A CAL MCDONALD MYSTERY
IDW Publishing: Mar, 2005 - No. 3 ($3.99)

1-3-Steve Niles-s/Kelley Jones-a 4.00

SUPERNATURAL LAW (Formerly Wolff & Byrd, Counselors of the Macabre)
Exhibit A Press: No. 24, Oct, 1999 - Present ($2.50/$2.95/$3.50, B&W)

24-35-Batton Lash-s/a. 29-Marie Severin-c. 33-Cerebus spoof 3.00
36-40-($2.95). 37-Frank Cho pin-up and story panels 3.00
(#41) ...First Amendment Issue (2005, $3.50) anti-censorship story; CBLDF info 3.50
(#42) With a Silver Bullet (2006, $3.50) new stories and pin-ups 3.50
(#43) At the Box Office (2006, $3.50) new stories and pin-ups 3.50
(#44) Wolff & Byrd: The Movie (2007, $3.50) new stories and pin-ups 3.50
45-($3.50) Toxic Avenger and Lloyd Kaufman app. 3.50
#1 (2005, $2.95) r/Wolff & Byrd with redrawn and re-toned art; relettered 3.00

SUPERNATURAL LAW SECRETARY MAVIS
Exhibit A Press: 2001 - Present ($2.95/$3.50, B&W)

1-3: 3-DeCarlo-c 3.00
4,5-($3.50) Jaime Hernandez-c 3.50

SUPERNATURAL: ORIGINS (Based on the CW television series)
DC Comics (WildStorm): July, 2007 - No. 6, Dec, 2007 ($2.99, limited series)

1-6: 1-Bradstreet-c; Johnson-s/Smith-a; back-up w/Johns-s/Hester-a 3.00
TPB (2008, $14.99) r/#1-6; sketch pages 15.00

SUPERNATURAL: RISING SON (Based on the CW television series)
DC Comics (WildStorm): Jun, 2008 - No. 6, Nov, 2008 ($2.99, limited series)

1-6-Johnson & Dessertine-s/Olmos-a. 1-Oliver-c 3.00
1-Variant-c by Nguyen 6.00
TPB (2009, $14.99) r/#1-6 15.00

SUPERNATURALS
Marvel Comics: Dec, 1998 - No. 4, Dec, 1998 ($3.99, weekly limited series)

1-4-Pulido-s/Balent-c; bound-in Halloween masks 4.00
1-4-With bound-in Ghost Rider mask (1 in 10) 4.00

SUPERNATURAL THRILLERS
Marvel Comics Group: Dec, 1972 - No. 6, Nov, 1973; No. 7, Jun, 1974 - No. 15, Oct, 1975

1-It!; Sturgeon adap. (see Astonishing Tales #21) 4 8 12 22 34 45
2-4,6: 2-The Invisible Man; H.G. Wells adapt. 3-The Valley of the Worm; R.E. Howard adapt. 4-Dr. Jekyll & Mr. Hyde; R.L. Stevenson adapt.. 6-The Headless Horseman; last 20¢ issue
3 6 9 14 20 25
5-1st app. The Living Mummy 7 14 21 46 76 105
7-15: 7-The Living Mummy begins 3 6 9 18 27 35

NOTE: ***Brunner** c-11. **Buckler** a-5p. **Ditko** a-8r, 9r. **G. Kane** a-3p; c-3, 9p, 15p. **Mayerik** a-2p, 7, 8, 9p, 10p, 11. **McWilliams** a-14i. **Mortimer** a-4. **Steranko** c-1, 2. **Sutton** a-15. **Tuska** a-6p.*

SUPERPATRIOT (Also see Freak Force & Savage Dragon #2)
Image Comics (Highbrow Entertainment): July, 1993 - No. 4, Dec, 1993 ($1.95, lim. series)

1-4: Dave Johnson-c/a; Larsen scripts; Giffen plots 3.00

SUPERPATRIOT: AMERICA'S FIGHTING FORCE
Image Comics: July, 2002 - No. 4, Oct, 2002 ($2.95, limited series)

1-4-Cory Walker-a/c; Savage Dragon app. 3.00

Super Rabbit #13 © MAR

Supersnipe Comics V4 #6 © CN

Super-Team Family #4 © DC

	GD	VG	FN	VF	VF/NM	NM-
	2.0	4.0	6.0	8.0	9.0	9.2

GD VG FN VF VF/NM NM-
2.0 4.0 6.0 8.0 9.0 9.2

SUPERPATRIOT: LIBERTY & JUSTICE
Image Comics (Highbrow Entertainment): July, 1995 - No. 4, Oct, 1995 ($2.50, lim. series)

1-4: Dave Johnson-c/a. 1-1st app. Liberty & Justice 3.00
TPB (2002, $12.95) r/#1-4; new cover by Dave Johnson; sketch pages 13.00

SUPERPATRIOT: WAR ON TERROR
Image Comics: July, 2004 - No. 4, May, 2007 ($2.95/$2.99, limited series)

1-4-Kirkman-s/Su-a 3.00

SUPER POWERS (1st Series)
DC Comics: July, 1984 - No. 5, Nov, 1984

1-5: 1-Joker/Penguin-c/story; Batman app.; all Kirby-c. 5-Kirby c/a 5.00

SUPER POWERS (2nd Series)
DC Comics: Sept, 1985 - No. 6, Feb, 1986

1-6: Kirby-c/a; Capt. Marvel & Firestorm join; Batman cameo; Darkseid storyline in all. 4-Batman cameo. 5,6-Batman app. 5.00

SUPER POWERS (3rd Series)
DC Comics: Sept, 1986 - No. 4, Dec, 1986

1-4: 1-Cyborg joins; 1st app. Samurai from Super Friends TV show. 1-4-Batman cameos; Darkseid storyline in #1-4 4.00

SUPER PUP (Formerly Spotty The Pup) (See Space Comics)
Avon Periodicals: No. 4, Mar-Apr, 1954 - No. 5, 1954

4,5: 4-Atom bomb-c. 5-Robot-c 7 14 21 37 46 55

SUPER RABBIT (See All Surprise, Animated Movie Tunes, Comedy Comics, Comic Capers, Ideal Comics, It's A Duck's Life, Movie Tunes & Wisco)
Timely Comics (CmPl): Fall, 1944 - No. 14, Nov, 1948

1-Hitler & Hirohito-c; war effort paper recycling PSA by S&K; Ziggy Pig & Silly Seal begin
181 362 543 1158 1979 2800
2 41 82 123 256 428 600
3-5 28 56 84 165 270 375
6-Origin 30 60 90 177 289 400
7-10: 9-Infinity-c 19 38 57 111 176 240
11-Kurtzman's "Hey Look" 20 40 60 114 182 250
12-14 19 38 57 111 176 240
I.W. Reprint #1,2('58),7,10('63): 1-r/#13. 2-r/#10. 2 4 6 10 14 18

SUPER RICHIE (Superichie #5 on) (See Richie Rich Millions #68)
Harvey Publications: Sept, 1975 - No. 4, Mar, 1976 (All 52 pg. Giants)

1 3 6 9 16 23 30
2-4 2 4 6 11 16 20

SUPER SLUGGERS (Baseball)
Ultimate Sports Ent. Inc.: 1999 ($3.95, one-shot)

1-Bonds, Piazza, Caminiti, Griffey Jr. app.; Martinbrough-c/a 4.00

SUPERSNIPE COMICS (Formerly Army & Navy #1-5)
Street & Smith Publications: V1#6, Oct, 1942 - V5#1, Aug-Sept, 1949
(See Shadow Comics V2#3)

V1#6-Rex King - Man of Adventure (costumed hero, see Super Magic/Magician) by Jack Binder begins; Supersnipe by George Marcoux continues from Army & Navy #5; Bill Ward-a 71 142 213 454 777 1100
7,10-12: 10,11-Little Nemo app. 40 80 120 246 411 575
8-Hitler, Tojo, Mussolini in Hell with Devil-c 116 232 348 742 1271 1800
9-Doc Savage x-over in Supersnipe; Hitler-c 119 238 357 762 1306 1850
V2 #1: Both V2#1(2/44) & V2#2(4/44) have V2#1 on outside-c; Huck Finn by Clare Dwiggins begins, ends V3#5 (rare) 57 114 171 362 619 875
V2#2 (4/44) has V2#1 on outside-c; classic shark-c 37 74 111 222 361 500
3-12 22 44 66 132 216 300
V3#1-12: 8-Bobby Crusoe by Dwiggins begins, ends V3#12. 9-X-Mas-c
20 40 60 114 182 250
V4#1-12, V5#1: V4#10-X-Mas-c 16 32 48 94 147 200
NOTE: *George Marcoux c-V1#6-V3#4. Doc Savage app. in some issues.*

SUPER SOLDIER (See Marvel Versus DC #3)
DC Comics (Amalgam): Apr, 1996 ($1.95, one-shot)

1-Mark Waid script & Dave Gibbons-c/a. 3.00

SUPER SOLDIER: MAN OF WAR
DC Comics (Amalgam): June, 1997 ($1.95, one-shot)

1-Waid & Gibbons-s/Gibbons & Palmiotti-c/a. 3.00

SUPER SOLDIERS
Marvel Comics UK: Apr, 1993 - No. 8, Nov, 1993 ($1.75)

1-($2.50)-Embossed silver foil logo 4.00

2-8: 5-Capt. America app. 6-Origin; Nick Fury app.; neon ink-c 3.00

SUPERSPOOK (Formerly Frisky Animals on Parade)
Ajax/Farrell Publications: No. 4, June, 1958

4 8 16 24 44 57 70

SUPER SPY (See Wham Comics)
Centaur Publications: Oct, 1940 - No. 2, Nov, 1940 (Reprints)

1-Origin The Sparkler 84 168 252 538 919 1300
2-The Inner Circle, Dean Denton, Tim Blain, The Drew Ghost, The Night Hawk by Gustavson, & S.S. Swanson by Glanz app. 52 104 156 328 557 785

SUPERSTAR: AS SEEN ON TV
Image Comics (Gorilla): 2001 ($5.95)

1-Busiek-s/Immonen-a 6.00

SUPER STAR HOLIDAY SPECIAL (See DC Special Series #21)

SUPER-TEAM FAMILY
National Periodical Publ./DC Comics: Oct-Nov, 1975 - No. 15, Mar-Apr, 1978

1-Reprints by Neal Adams & Kane/Wood; 68 pgs. begin, ends #4. New Gods app.
3 6 9 16 23 30
2,3: New stories 3 6 9 14 20 25
4-7: Reprints. 4-G.A. JSA-r & Superman/Batman/Robin-r from World's Finest. 5-52 pgs. begin 2 4 6 10 14 18
8-14: 8-10-New Challengers of the Unknown stories. 9-Kirby-a. 11-14: New stories
3 6 9 14 19 24
15-New Gods app. New stories 3 6 9 14 20 26
NOTE: ***Neal Adams** r-1-3. **Brunner** c-3. **Buckler** c-8p. **Tuska** a-7r. **Wood** a-1i(r), 3.*

SUPER TV HEROES (See Hanna-Barbera...)

SUPER-VILLAIN CLASSICS
Marvel Comics Group: May, 1983

1-Galactus -The Origin; Kirby-a 6.00

SUPER-VILLAIN TEAM-UP (See Fantastic Four #6 & Giant-Size...)
Marvel Comics Group: 8/75 - No. 14, 10/77; No. 15, 11/78; No. 16, 5/79; No. 17, 6/80

1-Giant-Size Super-Villain Team-Up #2; Sub-Mariner & Dr. Doom begin, end #10
5 10 15 30 48 65
2-5: 5-1st app. The Shroud 3 6 9 14 19 24
5-(30¢-c variant, limited distribution)(4/76) 4 8 12 23 36 48
6,7-(25¢ editions) 6-(6/76)-F.F., Shroud app. 7-Origin Shroud
2 4 6 8 11 14
6,7-(30¢-c, limited distribution)(6,8/76) 3 6 9 20 30 40
8-17: 9-Avengers app. 11-15-Dr. Doom & Red Skull app.
2 4 6 8 11 14
12-14-(35¢-c variants, limited distribution)(6,8,10/77) 4 8 12 24 37 50
NOTE: ***Buckler** c-4p, 5p, 7p. **Buscema** c-1. **Byrne/Austin** c-14. **Evans** a-1p, 3p. **Everett** a-1p. **Giffen** a-8p, 13p; c-13p. **Kane** c-2p, 9p. **Mooney** a-4i. **Starlin** c-6. **Tuska** r-1p, 15p. **Wood** r-15p.*

SUPER-VILLAIN TEAM-UP/ MODOK'S 11
Marvel Comics: Sept, 2007 - No. 5, Jan, 2008 ($2.99, limited series)

1-5: 1-MODOK's origin re-told; Portela-a/Powell-c; Purple Man & Mentallo app. 3.00
... TPB (2008, $13.99) r/#1-5 14.00

SUPER WESTERN COMICS (Also see Buffalo Bill)
Youthful Magazines: Aug, 1950 (One shot)

1-Buffalo Bill begins; Wyatt Earp, Calamity Jane & Sam Slade app; Powell-c/a
15 30 45 83 124 165

SUPER WESTERN FUNNIES (See Super Funnies)

SUPERWOMAN
DC Comics: Jan 1942

nn - Ashcan comic, not distributed to newsstands, only for in-house use. Cover art is More Fun Comics #73 with interior being Action Comics #38 (no known sales)

SUPERWORLD COMICS
Hugo Gernsback (Komos Publ.): Apr, 1940 - No. 3, Aug, 1940 (68 pgs.)

1-Origin & 1st app. Hip Knox, Super Hypnotist; Mitey Powers & Buzz Allen, the Invisible Avenger, Little Nemo begin; cover by Frank R. Paul (all have sci/fi-c) (Scarce) 865 1730 2595 6315 11,158 16,000
2-Marvo 1-2 Go+, the Super Boy of the Year 2680 (1st app.); Paul-c (Scarce)
459 918 1377 3350 5925 8500
3 (Scarce) 383 766 1149 2681 4691 6700

SUPER ZOMBIES
Dynamite Entertainment: 2009 - No. 5, 2009 ($3.50)

1-5- Mel Rubi-a; Guggenheim & Gonzales-s; two covers for each by Rubi & Neves 3.50

Supreme #53 © Awesome

Supurbia #1 © BOOM & Grace Randolph

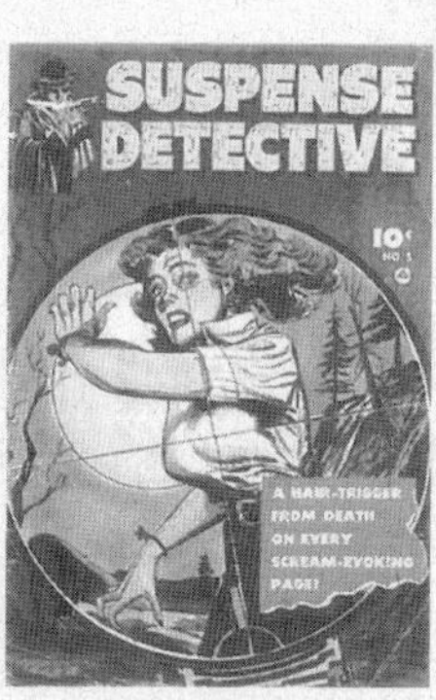

Suspense Detective #5 © FAW

GD VG FN VF VF/NM NM-
2.0 4.0 6.0 8.0 9.0 9.2

SUPREME (Becomes ...The New Adventures #43-48)(See Youngblood #3)
(Also see Bloodwulf Special, Legend of Supreme, & Trencher #3)
Image Comics (Extreme Studios)/ Awesome Entertainment #49 on:
V2#1, Nov, 1992 - V2#42, Sept, 1996; V3#49 - No. 56, Feb, 1998

V2#1-Liefeld-a(i) & scripts; embossed foil logo 4.00
1-Gold Edition 6.00
2-(3/93)-Liefeld co-plots & inks; 1st app. Grizlock 3.00
3-42: 3-Intro Bloodstrike; 1st app. Khrome. 5-1st app. Thor. 6-1st brief app. The Starguard. 7-1st full app. The Starguard. 10-Black and White Pt 1 (1st app.) by Art Thibert (2 pgs. ea. installment). 25-(5/94)-Platt-c. 11-Coupon #4 for Extreme Prejudice #0; Black and White Pt. 7 by Thibert. 12-(4/94)-Platt-c. 13,14-(6/94). 15 (7/94). 16 (7/94)-Stormwatch app. 18-Kid Supreme Sneak Preview; Pitt app.19,20-Polybagged w/trading card. 20-1st app. Woden & Loki (as a dog); Overtkill app. 21-1st app. Loki (in true form). 21-23-Poly-bagged trading card. 32-Lady Supreme cameo. 33-Origin & 1st full app. of Lady Supreme (Probe from the Starguard); Babewatch! tie-in. 37-Intro Loki; Fraga-c. 40-Retells Supreme's past advs. 41-Alan Moore scripts begin; Supreme revised; intro The Supremacy; Jerry Ordway-c (Joe Bennett variant-c exists). 42-New origin w/Rick Veitch-a; intro Radar, The Hound Supreme & The League of Infinity 3.00
28-Variant-c by Quesada & Palmiotti 3.00
(#43-48-**See Supreme: The New Adventures**)
V3#49,51: 49-Begin $2.99-c 3.00
50-($3.95)-Double sized, 2 covers, pin-up gallery 4.00
52a,52b-($3.50) 4.00
53-56: 53-Sprouse-a begins. 56-McGuinness-c 3.00
Annual 1-(1995, $2.95) 4.00
...: Supreme Sacrifice (3/06, $3.99) Flip book with Suprema; Kirkman-s/Malin-a 4.00
...: The Return TPB (Checker Book Publ., 2003, $24.95) r/#53-56 & Supreme; The Return #1-6; Ross-c; additional sketch pages by Ross 25.00
...: The Story of the Year TPB (Checker Book Publ., 2002, $26.95) r/#41-52; Ross-c 27.00
NOTE: ***Rob Liefeld** a(i)-1, 2; co-plots-2-4; scripts-1, 5, 6. **Ordway** c-41. **Platt** c-12, 25. **Thibert** c(i)-7-9.*

SUPREME
Image Comics: No. 63, APR, 2012 - Present ($2.99)
63-Moore-s; two covers by Larsen & Hamscher 3.00

SUPREME: GLORY DAYS
Image Comics (Extreme Studios): Oct, 1994 - No. 2, Dec, 1994 ($2.95/$2.50, limited series)
1,2: 2-Diehard, Roman, Superpatriot, & Glory app. 3.00

SUPREME POWER (Also see Squadron Supreme 2006 series)
Marvel Comics (MAX): Oct, 2003 - No. 18, Oct, 2005 ($2.99)
1-($2.99) Straczynski-s/Frank-a; Frank-c 3.00
1-($4.99) Special Edition with variant Quesada-c; includes r/early Squadron Supreme apps. 5.00
2-18: 4-Intro. Nighthawk. 6-The Blur debuts. 10-Princess Zarda returns. 17-Hyperion revealed as alien. 18-Continues in mini-series 3.00
... MGC #1 (7/11, $1.00) r/#1 with "Marvel's Greatest Comics" banner on cover 3.00
Vol. 1: Contact TPB (2004, $14.99) r/#1-6 15.00
Vol. 2: Powers & Principalities TPB (2004, $14.99) r/#7-12 15.00
Vol. 3: High Command TPB (2005, $14.99) r/#13-18 15.00
Vol. 1 HC (2005, $29.99, 7 1/2" x 11" with dustjacket) r/#1-12; Avengers #85 & 86, Straczynski intro., Frank cover sketches and character design pages 30.00
Vol. 2 HC (2006, $29.99, 7 1/2" x 11" with dustjacket) r/#13-18; ...: Hyperion #1-5; character design pages 30.00

SUPREME POWER
Marvel Comics (MAX): Aug, 2011 - No. 4, Nov, 2011 ($3.99, limited series)
1-4-Higgins-s/Garcia-a/Fiumara-c; Doctor Spectrum app. 4.00

SUPREME POWER: HYPERION
Marvel Comics (MAX): Nov, 2005 - No. 5, Mar, 2006 ($2.99, limited series)
1-5: 1-Straczynski-s/Jurgens-a/Dodson-c 3.00
TPB (2006, $14.99) r/#1-5 15.00

SUPREME POWER: NIGHTHAWK
Marvel Comics (MAX): Nov, 2005 - No. 6, Apr, 2006 ($2.99, limited series)
1-6-Daniel Way-s/Steve Dillon-a; origin of Whiteface 3.00
TPB (2006, $16.99) r/#1-6; cover concept art 17.00

SUPREME: THE NEW ADVENTURES (Formerly Supreme)
Maximum Press: V3#43, Oct, 1996 - V3#48, May, 1997 ($2.50)
V3#43-48: 43-Alan Moore scripts begin; Joe Bennett-a; Rick Veitch-a (8 pgs.); Dan Jurgens-a (1 pg.); intro Citadel Supreme & Suprematons; 1st Allied Supermen of America 3.00

SUPREME: THE RETURN
Awesome Entertainment: May, 1999 - No. 6, June, 2000 ($2.99)
1-6: Alan Moore-s. 1,2-Sprouse & Gordon-a/c. 2,4-Liefeld-c. 6-Kirby app. 3.00

GD VG FN VF VF/NM NM-
2.0 4.0 6.0 8.0 9.0 9.2

SUPURBIA (GRACE RANDOLPH'S...)
BOOM! Studios: Mar, 2012 - No. 4 ($3.99, limited series)
1-Grace Randolph-s; Dauterman-a/Garza-c 4.00

SURE-FIRE COMICS (Lightning Comics #4 on)
Ace Magazines: June, 1940 - No. 4, Oct, 1940 (Two No. 3's)
V1#1-Origin Flash Lightning & begins; X-The Phantom Fed, Ace McCoy, Buck Steele, Marvo the Magician, The Raven, Whiz Wilson (Time Traveler) begin (all 1st app.); Flash Lightning c-1-4 187 374 561 1197 2049 2900
2 84 168 252 538 919 1300
3(9/40), 3(#4)(10/40)-nn on-c, #3 on inside 61 122 183 390 670 950

SURF 'N' WHEELS
Charlton Comics: Nov, 1969 - No. 6, Sept, 1970
1 3 6 9 20 30 40
2-6 3 6 9 14 19 24

SURGE
Eclipse Comics: July, 1984 - No. 4, Jan, 1985 ($1.50, lim. series, Baxter paper)
1-4 Ties into DNAgents series 3.00

SURPRISE ADVENTURES (Formerly Tormented)
Sterling Comic Group: No. 3, Mar, 1955 - No. 5, July, 1955
3-5: 3,5-Sekowsky-a 9 18 27 50 65 80

SUSIE Q. SMITH
Dell Publishing Co.: No. 323, Mar, 1951 - No. 553, Apr, 1954
Four Color 323 (#1) 5 10 15 32 51 70
Four Color 377, 453 (2/53), 553 4 8 12 26 41 55

SUSPENSE (Radio/TV issues #1-11; Real Life Tales of... #1-4) (Amazing Detective Cases #3 on?)
Marvel/Atlas Comics (CnPC No. 1-10/BFP No. 11-29): Dec, 1949 - No. 29, Apr, 1953 (#1-8, 17-23: 52 pgs.)
1-Powell-a; Peter Lorre, Sidney Greenstreet photo-c from Hammett's "The Verdict" 60 120 180 381 658 935
2-Crime stories; Dennis O'Keefe & Gale Storm photo-c from Universal movie "Abandoned" 36 72 108 216 351 485
3-Change to horror 42 84 126 265 445 625
4,7-10: 7-Dracula-sty 34 68 102 199 325 450
5-Krigstein, Tuska, Everett-a 36 72 108 211 343 475
6-Tuska, Everett, Morisi-a 34 68 102 206 336 465
11-13,15-17,19,20 27 54 81 160 263 365
14-Clasic Heath Hypo-c; A-Bomb panels 39 78 117 240 395 550
18,22-Krigstein-a 28 56 84 165 270 375
21,23,24,26-29: 24-Tuska-a 24 48 72 142 234 325
25-Electric chair-c/story 34 68 102 199 325 450
NOTE: ***Ayers** a-20. **Briefer** a-5, 7, 27. **Brodsky** c-4, 6-9, 11, 16, 17, 25. **Colan** a-8(2), 9. **Everett** a-5, 6(2), 19, 23, 28; c-21-23, 26. **Fuje** a-29. **Heath** a-5, 6, 8, 10, 12, 14; c-14, 19, 24. **Maneely** a-12, 23, 24, 28, 29; c-5, 6p, 10, 13, 15, 18. **Mooney** a-24, 28. **Morisi** a-6, 12. **Palais** a-10. **Rico** a-7-9. **Robinson** a-29. **Romita** a-20(2), 25. **Sekowsky** a-11, 13, 14. **Sinnott** a-23, 25. **Tuska** a-5, 6(2), 12; c-12. **Whitney** a-15, 16, 22. **Ed Win** a-27.*

SUSPENSE COMICS
Continental Magazines: Dec, 1943 - No. 12, Sept, 1946
1-The Grey Mask begins; bondage/torture-c; L. B. Cole-a (7 pgs.) 432 864 1296 3154 5577 8000
2-Intro. The Mask; Rico, Giunta, L. B. Cole-a (7 pgs.) 274 548 822 1740 2995 4250
3-L.B. Cole-a; classic Schomburg-c (Scarce) 5200 10,400 15,600 31,200 43,100 55,000
4-6: 4-L. B. Cole-c begin 213 426 639 1363 2332 3300
7,9,10,12: 9-L.B. Cole eyeball-c 161 322 483 1030 1765 2500
8-Classic L. B. Cole spider-c 423 846 1269 3000 5250 7500
11-Classic Devil-c 320 640 960 2240 3920 5600
NOTE: ***L. B. Cole** c-4-12. **Fuje** a-8. **Larsen** a-11. **Palais** a-10, 11. Bondage c-1, 3, 4.*

SUSPENSE DETECTIVE
Fawcett Publications: June, 1952 - No. 5, Mar, 1953
1-Evans-a (11 pgs); Baily-c/a 45 90 135 284 480 675
2-Evans-a (10 pgs.) 27 54 81 160 263 365
3-5 23 46 69 136 223 310
NOTE: ***Baily** a-4, 5; c-1-3. **Sekowsky** a-2, 4, 5; c-5.*

SUSPENSE STORIES (See Strange Suspense Stories)

SUSSEX VAMPIRE, THE (Sherlock Holmes)
Caliber Comics: 1996 ($2.95, 32 pgs., B&W, one-shot)
nn-Adapts Sir Arthur Conan Doyle's story; Warren Ellis scripts 3.00

SUZIE COMICS (Formerly Laugh Comix; see Laugh Comics, Liberty Comics #10, Pep Comics & Top-Notch Comics #28)

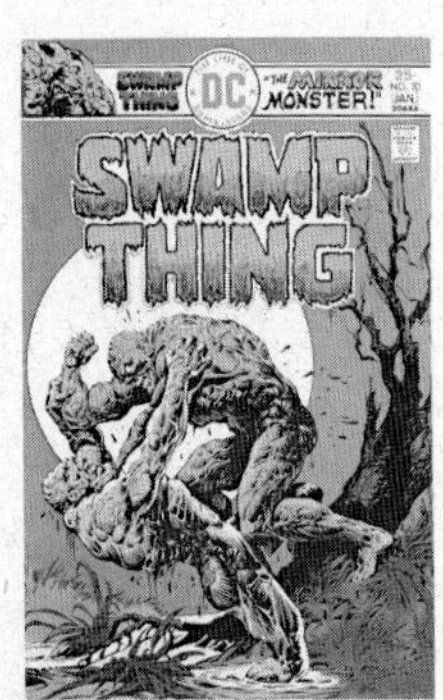

Swamp Thing #20 © DC

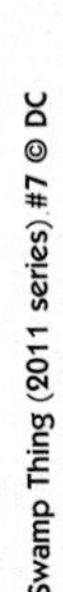

Swamp Thing (2011 series) #7 © DC

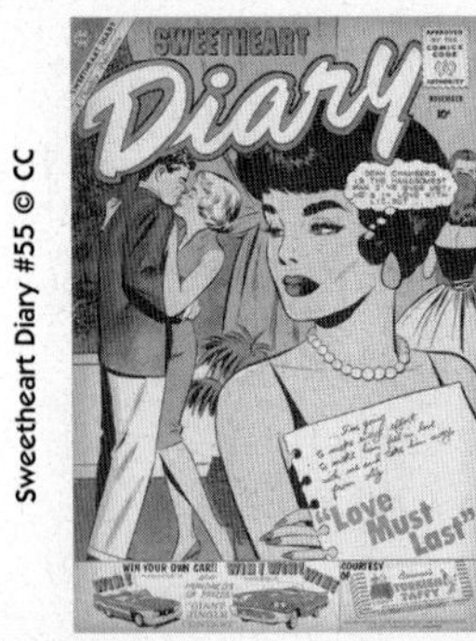

Sweetheart Diary #55 © CC

Close-Up No. 49,50/MLJ Mag./Archie No. 51 on: No. 49, Spring, 1945 - No. 100, Aug, 1954

	GD 2.0	VG 4.0	FN 6.0	VF 8.0	VF/NM 9.0	NM- 9.2
49-Ginger begins	29	58	87	170	278	385
50-55: 54-Transvestism story. 55-Woggon-a	18	36	54	105	165	225
56-Katy Keene begins by Woggon	19	38	57	109	172	235
57-65	14	28	42	80	115	150
66-80	13	26	39	74	105	135
81-87,89-99	11	22	33	62	86	110
88,100: 88-Used in **POP**, pgs. 76,77; Bill Woggon draws himself in story. 100-Last Katy Keene	13	26	39	74	105	135

NOTE: ***Al Fagaly*** *c-49-67. Katy Keene app. in 53-82, 85-100.*

SWAMP FOX, THE (TV, Disney)(See Walt Disney Presents #2)
Dell Publishing Co.: No. 1179, Dec, 1960

	GD 2.0	VG 4.0	FN 6.0	VF 8.0	VF/NM 9.0	NM- 9.2
Four Color 1179-Leslie Nielsen photo-c	8	16	24	55	93	130

SWAMP THING (See Brave & the Bold, Challengers of the Unknown #82, DC Comics Presents #8 & 85, DC Special Series #2, 14, 17, 20, House of Secrets #92, Limited Collectors' Edition C-59, & Roots of the...)

SWAMP THING
National Per. Publ./DC Comics: Oct-Nov, 1972 - No. 24, Aug-Sept, 1976

	GD 2.0	VG 4.0	FN 6.0	VF 8.0	VF/NM 9.0	NM- 9.2
1-Wrightson-c/a begins; origin	15	30	45	104	227	350
2-1st brief app. Patchwork Man (1 panel)	9	18	27	58	99	140
3-1st full app. Patchwork Man (see House of Secrets #140)	7	14	21	46	76	105
4-6,	6	12	18	39	62	85
7-Batman-c/story	6	12	18	42	69	95
8-10: 10-Last Wrightson issue	5	10	15	35	55	75
11-20: 11-19-Redondo-a. 13-Origin retold (1 pg.)	3	6	9	19	29	38
21-24: 23,24-Swamp Thing reverts back to Dr. Holland. 23-New logo	3	6	9	19	29	38
Secret of the Swamp Thing (2005, $9.99, digest) r/#1-10						10.00

NOTE: ***J. Jones*** *a-9i(assist).* ***Kaluta*** *a-9i.* ***Redondo*** *c-12-19, 21.* ***Wrightson*** *issues (#1-10) reprinted in DC Special Series #2, 14, 17, 20 & Roots of the Swamp Thing.*

SWAMP THING (Saga Of The... #1-38,42-45) (See Essential Vertigo:...)
DC Comics (Vertigo imprint #129 on): May, 1982 - No. 171, Oct, 1996 (Direct sales #65 on)

	GD 2.0	VG 4.0	FN 6.0	VF 8.0	VF/NM 9.0	NM- 9.2
1-Origin retold; Phantom Stranger series begins; ends #13; Yeates-c/a begins						6.00
2-15: 2-Photo-c from movie. 13-Last Yeates-a						4.00
16-19: Bissette-a.						5.00
20-1st Alan Moore issue	3	6	9	14	20	26
21-New origin	2	4	6	13	18	22
21 Special Editon (5/09, $1.00) reprint with "After Watchmen" cover frame						3.00
22,23,25: 25-John Constantine 1-panel cameo	2	4	6	9	12	15
24-JLA x-over; Last Yeates-c.	2	4	6	9	13	16
26-30	1	2	3	5	6	8
31-33,35,36: 33-r/1st app. from House of Secrets #92						6.00
34	1	2	3	5	7	9
37-1st app. John Constantine (Hellblazer) (6/85)	2	4	6	9	13	16
38-40: John Constantine app.	1	2	3	5	7	9
41-52,54-64: 44-Batman cameo. 44-51-John Constantine app. 46-Crisis x-over; Batman cameo. 49-Spectre app. 50-($1.25, 52 pgs.)-Deadman, Dr. Fate, Demon. 52-Arkham Asylum-c/story; Joker-c/cameo. 58-Spectre preview. 64-Last Moore issue						4.00
53-($1.25, 52 pgs.)-Arkham Asylum; Batman-c/story						5.00
65-83,85-99,101-124,126-149,151-153: 65-Direct sales only begins. 66-Batman & Arkham Asylum story. 70,76-John Constantine x-over; 76-X-over w/Hellblazer #9. 79-Superman-c/story. 85-Jonah Hex app. 102-Preview of World Without End. 116-Photo-c. 129-Metallic ink on-c. 140-Millar scripts begin, end #171						3.00
84-Sandman (Morpheus) cameo.						4.00
100,125,150: 100 ($2.50, 52 pgs.). 125-($2.95, 52 pgs.)-20th anniversary issue. 150 (52 pgs.)-Anniversary issue						4.00
154-171: 154-$2.25-c begins. 165-Curt Swan-a(p). 166,169,171-John Constantine & Phantom Stranger app. 168-Arcane returns						3.00
Annual 1,3-6('82-91): 1-Movie Adaptation; painted-c. 3-New format; Bolland-c. 4-Batman-c/story. 5-Batman cameo; re-intro Brother Power (Geek),1st app. since 1968						4.00
Annual 2 (1985)-Moore scripts; Bissette-a(p); Deadman, Spectre app.						7.00
Annual 7(1993, $3.95)-Children's Crusade						4.00
...A Murder of Crows (2001, $19.95)-r/#43-50; Moore-s						20.00
...: Earth To Earth (2002, $17.95)-r/#51-56; Batman app.						18.00
...: Infernal Triangles (2006, $19.99, TPB) r/#77-81 & Annual #3; cover gallery						20.00
...Love and Death (1990, $17.95)-r/#28-34 & Annual #2; Totleben painted-c						18.00
...: Regenesis (2004, $17.95, TPB) r/#65-70; Veitch-s						18.00
...: Reunion (2003, $19.95, TPB) r/#57-64; Moore-s						20.00
...: Roots (1998, $7.95) Jon J Muth-s/painted-a/c						8.00
Saga of the Swamp Thing ('87, '89)-r/#21-27 (1st & 2nd print)						13.00
Saga of the Swamp Thing Book One HC (2009, $24.99, d.j.) r/#20-27; Wein intro.						25.00
Saga of the Swamp Thing Book Two HC (2009, $24.99, d.j.) r/#28-34 & Annual #2						25.00
Saga of the Swamp Thing Book Three HC (2010, $24.99, d.j.) r/#35-42; Bissette intro.						25.00
Saga of the Swamp Thing Book Four HC (2010, $24.99, d.j.) r/#43-50; Gaiman foreword						25.00
Saga of the Swamp Thing Book Five HC (2011, $24.99, d.j.) r/#51-56; Bissette intro.						25.00
....: Spontaneous Generation (2005, $19.99) r/#71-76						20.00
....: The Curse (2000, $19.95, TPB) r/#35-42; Bisley-c						20.00

NOTE: ***Bissette*** *a(p)-16-19, 21-27, 29, 30, 34-36, 39-42, 44, 46, 50, 64; c-17i, 24-32p, 35-37p, 40p, 44p, 46-50p, 51-58, 61, 62, 63p.* ***Kaluta*** *c/a-74.* ***Spiegle*** *a-1-3, 6.* ***Sutton*** *a-98p.* ***Totleben*** *a(i)-10, 16-27, 29, 31, 34-40, 42, 44, 46, 48, 50, 53, 55i; c-25-32i, 33, 35-40i, 42i, 44i, 46-50i, 53, 55i, 59p, 64, 65, 68, 73, 76, 80, 82, 84, 89, 91-100, Annual 4, 5.* ***Vess*** *painted c-121, 129-139, Annual 7.* ***Williamson*** *86i.* ***Wrightson*** *a-18i(r), 33r. John Constantine appears in #37-40, 44-51, 65-67, 70-77, 80-90, 99, 114, 115, 130, 134-138.*

SWAMP THING
DC Comics (Vertigo): May, 2000 - No. 20, Dec, 2001 ($2.50)

	GD 2.0	VG 4.0	FN 6.0	VF 8.0	VF/NM 9.0	NM- 9.2
1-3-Tefé Holland's return; Vaughan-s/Petersen-a; Hale painted-c.						3.50
4-20: 7-9-Bisley-c. 10-John Constantine-c/app. 10-12-Fabry-c. 13-15-Mack-c 18-Swamp Thing app.						3.00
Preview-16 pg. flip book w/Lucifer Preview						3.00

SWAMP THING
DC Comics (Vertigo): May, 2004 - No. 29, Sept, 2006 ($2.95/$2.99)

	GD 2.0	VG 4.0	FN 6.0	VF 8.0	VF/NM 9.0	NM- 9.2
1-29: 1-Diggle-s/Breccia-a; Constantine app. 2-6-Sargon app. 7,8,20-Corben-c/a. 21-29-Eric Powell-c						3.00
...: Bad Seed (2004, $9.95) r/#1-6						10.00
...: Healing the Breach (2006, $17.99) r/#15-20						18.00
...: Love in Vain (2005, $14.99) r/#9-14						15.00

SWAMP THING (DC New 52)
DC Comics: Nov, 2011 - Present ($2.99)

	GD 2.0	VG 4.0	FN 6.0	VF 8.0	VF/NM 9.0	NM- 9.2
1-Snyder-s/Paquette-a; Superman app.						8.00
1-(2nd & 3rd printing)						3.00
2-8: 2-Abigail Arcane returns. 7-Holland transforms						3.00

SWAT MALONE (America's Home Run King)
Swat Malone Enterprises: Sept, 1955

	GD 2.0	VG 4.0	FN 6.0	VF 8.0	VF/NM 9.0	NM- 9.2
V1#1-Hy Fleishman-a	11	22	33	62	86	110

SWEATSHOP
DC Comics: Jun, 2003 - No. 6, Nov, 2003 ($2.95)

	GD 2.0	VG 4.0	FN 6.0	VF 8.0	VF/NM 9.0	NM- 9.2
1-6-Peter Bagge-s/a; Destefano-a						3.00

SWEENEY (Formerly Buz Sawyer)
Standard Comics: No. 4, June, 1949 - No. 5, Sept, 1949

	GD 2.0	VG 4.0	FN 6.0	VF 8.0	VF/NM 9.0	NM- 9.2
4,5: 5-Crane-a	9	18	27	47	61	75

SWEE'PEA (Also see Popeye #46)
Dell Publishing Co.: No. 219, Mar, 1949

	GD 2.0	VG 4.0	FN 6.0	VF 8.0	VF/NM 9.0	NM- 9.2
Four Color 219	8	16	24	56	93	130

SWEET CHILDE
Advantage Graphics Press: 1995 - No. 2, 1995 ($2.95, B&W, mature)

	GD 2.0	VG 4.0	FN 6.0	VF 8.0	VF/NM 9.0	NM- 9.2
1,2						3.00

SWEETHEART DIARY (Cynthia Doyle #66-on)
Fawcett Publications/Charlton Comics No. 32 on: Wint, 1949; #2, Spr, 1950; #3, 6/50 - #5, 10/50; #6, 1951(nd); #7, 9/51 - #14, 1/53; #32, 10/55; #33, 4/56 - #65, 8/62 (#1-14: photo-c)

	GD 2.0	VG 4.0	FN 6.0	VF 8.0	VF/NM 9.0	NM- 9.2
1	20	40	60	114	182	250
2	12	24	36	69	97	125
3,4-Wood-a	15	30	45	86	133	180
5-10: 8-Bailey-a	10	20	30	56	76	95
11-14: 13-Swayze-a. 14-Last Fawcett issue	9	18	27	47	61	75
32 (10/55; 1st Charlton issue)(Formerly Cowboy Love #31)	9	18	27	52	69	85
33-40: 34-Swayze-a	7	14	21	35	43	50
41-(68 pgs.)	8	16	24	40	50	60
42-60	3	6	9	20	30	40
61-65	3	6	9	18	27	35

SWEETHEARTS (Formerly Captain Midnight)
Fawcett Publications/Charlton No. 122 on: #68, 10/48 - #121, 5/53; #122, 3/54; V2#23, 5/54 - #137, 12/73

	GD 2.0	VG 4.0	FN 6.0	VF 8.0	VF/NM 9.0	NM- 9.2
68-Photo-c begin	18	36	54	103	162	220
69,70	11	22	33	62	86	110
71-80	9	18	27	52	69	85
81-84,86-93,95-99,105	9	18	27	47	61	75
85,94,103,110,117-George Evans-a	10	20	30	54	72	90
100	9	18	27	52	69	85
101,107-Powell-a	9	18	27	50	65	80

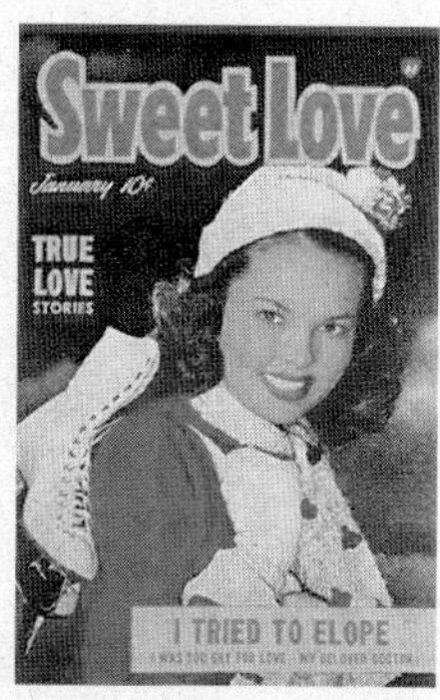

Sweet Love #3 © HARV

Swift Arrow (2nd series) #1 © AJAX

S.W.O.R.D. #1 © MAR

	GD 2.0	VG 4.0	FN 6.0	VF 8.0	VF/NM 9.0	NM- 9.2
102,104,106,108,109,112-116,118	8	16	24	44	57	70
111-1 pg. Ronald Reagan biography	10	20	30	56	76	95
119-Marilyn Monroe & Richard Widmark photo-c (1/54?); also appears in story; part Wood-a	66	132	198	419	722	1025
120-Atom Bomb story	12	24	36	67	94	120
121-Liz Taylor/Fernanado Lamas photo-c	32	64	96	192	314	435
122-(1st Charlton? 3/54)-Marijuana story	13	26	39	72	101	130
V2#23 (5/54)-28: 28-Last precode issue (2/55)	8	16	24	42	54	65
29-39,41,43,45,47-50	4	8	12	26	41	55
40-Photo-c; Tommy Sands story	4	8	12	28	44	60
42-Ricky Nelson photo-c/story	8	16	24	56	96	135
44-Pat Boone photo-c/story	4	8	12	28	44	60
46-Jimmy Rodgers photo-c/story	4	8	12	28	44	60
51-60	4	8	12	22	34	45
61-80,100	3	6	9	19	29	38
81-99	3	6	9	17	25	32
101-110	2	4	6	13	18	22
111-120,122-124,126-137	2	4	6	10	14	18
121,125-David Cassidy pin-ups	2	4	6	13	18	22

NOTE: *Photo c-68-121(Fawcett), 40, 42, 46(Charlton).* ***Swayze*** *a(Fawcett)-70-118(most).*

SWEETHEART SCANDALS (See Fox Giants)

SWEETIE PIE
Dell Publishing Co.: No. 1185, May-July, 1961 - No. 1241, Nov-Jan, 1961/62

	GD 2.0	VG 4.0	FN 6.0	VF 8.0	VF/NM 9.0	NM- 9.2
Four Color 1185 (#1)	5	10	15	30	48	65
Four Color 1241	4	8	12	24	37	50

SWEETIE PIE
Ajax-Farrell/Pines (Literary Ent.): Dec, 1955 - No. 15, Fall, 1957

	GD 2.0	VG 4.0	FN 6.0	VF 8.0	VF/NM 9.0	NM- 9.2
1-By Nadine Seltzer	10	20	30	54	72	90
2 (5/56; last Ajax?)	7	14	21	35	43	50
3-15	6	12	18	28	34	40

SWEET LOVE
Home Comics (Harvey): Sept, 1949 - No. 5, May, 1950 (All photo-c)

	GD 2.0	VG 4.0	FN 6.0	VF 8.0	VF/NM 9.0	NM- 9.2
1	10	20	30	58	79	100
2	7	14	21	37	46	55
3,4: 3-Powell-a	6	12	18	31	38	45
5-Kamen, Powell-a	9	18	27	47	61	75

SWEET ROMANCE
Charlton Comics: Oct, 1968

	GD 2.0	VG 4.0	FN 6.0	VF 8.0	VF/NM 9.0	NM- 9.2
1	3	6	9	14	20	25

SWEET SIXTEEN (...Comics and Stories for Girls)
Parents' Magazine Institute: Aug-Sept, 1946 - No. 13, Jan, 1948 (All have movie stars photos on covers)

	GD 2.0	VG 4.0	FN 6.0	VF 8.0	VF/NM 9.0	NM- 9.2
1-Van Johnson's life story; Dorothy Dare, Queen of Hollywood Stunt Artists begins (in all issues); part photo-c	23	46	69	136	223	310
2-Jane Powell, Roddy McDowall "Holiday in Mexico" photo on-c; Alan Ladd story	15	30	45	90	140	190
3,5,6,8-11: 5-Ann Francis photo on-c; Gregory Peck story. 6-Dick Haymes story. 8-Shirley Jones photo on-c. 10-Jean Simmons photo on-c; James Stewart story	13	26	39	74	105	135
4-Elizabeth Taylor photo on-c	29	58	87	170	278	385
7-Ronald Reagan's life story	23	46	69	136	223	310
12-Bob Cummings, Vic Damone story	14	28	42	78	112	145
13-Robert Mitchum's life story	14	28	42	80	115	150

SWEET XVI
Marvel Comics: May, 1991 - No. 5, Sept, 1991 ($1.00)

1-5: Barbara Slate story & art — 3.00

SWEET TOOTH
DC Comics (Vertigo): Nov, 2009 - Present ($1.00/$2.99)

1-($1.00) Jeff Lemire-s/a — 3.00
2-32-($2.99) 18-Printed sideways. 26-28-Kindt-a — 3.00
...: Animal Armies TPB (2011, $14.99) r/#12-17 — 15.00
...: In Captivity TPB (2010, $12.99) r/#6-11 — 13.00
...: Out of the Deep Woods TPB (2010, $9.99) r/#1-5 — 10.00

SWIFT ARROW (Also see Lone Rider & The Rider)
Ajax/Farrell Publications: Feb-Mar, 1954 - No. 5, Oct-Nov, 1954; Apr, 1957 - No. 3, Sept, 1957

	GD 2.0	VG 4.0	FN 6.0	VF 8.0	VF/NM 9.0	NM- 9.2
1(1954) (1st Series)	16	32	48	92	144	195
2	10	20	30	56	76	95
3-5: 5-Lone Rider story	9	18	27	50	65	80
1 (2nd Series) (Swift Arrow's Gunfighters #4)	9	18	27	50	65	80
2,3: 2-Lone Rider begins	8	16	24	40	50	60

SWIFT ARROW'S GUNFIGHTERS (Formerly Swift Arrow)
Ajax/Farrell Publ. (Four Star Comic Corp.): No. 4, Nov, 1957

	GD 2.0	VG 4.0	FN 6.0	VF 8.0	VF/NM 9.0	NM- 9.2
4	8	16	24	40	50	60

SWING WITH SCOOTER
National Periodical Publ.: June-July, 1966 - No. 35, Aug-Sept, 1971; No. 36, Oct-Nov, 1972

	GD 2.0	VG 4.0	FN 6.0	VF 8.0	VF/NM 9.0	NM- 9.2
1	9	18	27	61	106	150
2,6-10: 9-Alfred E. Newman swipe in last panel	5	10	15	35	55	75
3-5: 3-Batman cameo on-c. 4-Batman cameo inside. 5-JLA cameo	6	12	18	37	59	80
11-13,15-19: 18-Wildcat of JSA 1pg. text. 19-Last 12¢-c	3	6	9	21	32	42
14-Alfred E. Neuman cameo	4	8	12	22	34	45
20 (68 pgs.)	5	10	15	32	51	70
21-23,25-31	3	6	9	18	27	35
24-Frankenstein-c.	4	8	12	22	34	45
32-34 (68 pgs.). 32-Batman cameo. 33-Interview with David Cassidy. 34-Interview with Rick Ely (The Rebels)	5	10	15	30	48	65
35-(52 pgs.). 1 pg. app. Clark Kent and 4 full pgs. of Superman	7	14	21	49	82	115
36-Bat-signal refererence to Batman	4	8	12	22	34	45

NOTE: ***Aragonés*** *a-13 (1pg.), 18(1pg.), 30(2pgs.)* ***Orlando*** *a-1-11; c-1-11, 13. #20, 33, 34: 68 pgs.; #35: 52 pgs.*

SWISS FAMILY ROBINSON (Walt Disney's..; see King Classics & Movie Comics)
Dell Publishing Co.: No. 1156, Dec, 1960

	GD 2.0	VG 4.0	FN 6.0	VF 8.0	VF/NM 9.0	NM- 9.2
Four Color 1156-Movie-photo-c	7	14	21	48	79	110

S.W.O.R.D. (Sentient World Observation and Response Department)
Marvel Comics: Jan, 2010 - No. 5, May, 2010 ($3.99/$2.99)

1-($3.99) Cassaday-c/Gillen-s/Sanders-a; Commander Brand & Henry Gyrich app. — 4.00
2-5-($2.99): 2,3-Cassaday-c. 4,5-Del Mundo-c — 3.00

SWORD, THE
Image Comics: Oct, 2007 - No. 24, May, 2010 ($2.99/$4.99)

1-Luna Brothers-s/a — 4.00
1-(2nd printing) — 3.00
2-23: 12-Zakros killed — 3.00
24-($4.99) Final issue — 5.00
..., Vol. 1: Fire (TPB, 2008, $14.99) r/#1-6 — 15.00
..., Vol. 2: Water (TPB, 2008, $14.99) r/#7-12 — 15.00
..., Vol. 3: Earth (TPB, 2009, $14.99) r/#13-18 — 15.00
..., Vol. 4: Water (TPB, 2010, $14.99) r/#19-24 — 15.00

SWORD & THE DRAGON, THE
Dell Publishing Co.: No. 1118, June, 1960

	GD 2.0	VG 4.0	FN 6.0	VF 8.0	VF/NM 9.0	NM- 9.2
Four Color 1118-Movie, photo-c	7	14	21	49	82	115

SWORD & THE ROSE, THE (Disney)
Dell Publishing Co.: No. 505, Oct, 1953 - No. 682, Feb, 1956

	GD 2.0	VG 4.0	FN 6.0	VF 8.0	VF/NM 9.0	NM- 9.2
Four Color 505-Movie, photo-c	8	16	24	55	93	130
Four Color 682-When Knighthood Was in Flower-Movie, reprint of #505; Renamed the Sword & the Rose for the novel; photo-c	7	14	21	46	76	105

SWORD IN THE STONE, THE (See March of Comics #258 & Movie Comics & Wart and the Wizard)

SWORD OF DAMOCLES
Image Comics (WildStorm Productions): Mar, 1996 - No. 2, Apr, 1996 ($2.50, limited series)

1,2: Warren Ellis scripts. 1-Prelude to "Fire From Heaven" x-over; 1st app. Sword — 3.00

SWORD OF DRACULA
Image Comics: Oct, 2003 - No. 6, Sept, 2004 ($2.95, B&W, limited series)

1-6-Tony Harris-c. 1,2-Greg Scott-a — 3.00
TPB (IDW, 2/05, $14.99) r/series — 15.00

SWORD OF RED SONJA: DOOM OF THE GODS
Dynamite Entertainment: 2007 - No. 4, 2007 ($3.50, limited series)

1-4-Lui Antonio-a; multiple covers on each — 3.50

SWORD OF SORCERY
National Periodical Publications: Feb-Mar, 1973 - No. 5, Nov-Dec, 1973 (20¢)

	GD 2.0	VG 4.0	FN 6.0	VF 8.0	VF/NM 9.0	NM- 9.2
1-Leiber Fafhrd & The Grey Mouser; Chaykin/Neal Adams (Crusty Bunkers) art; Kaluta-c	3	6	9	16	23	30
2,3: 2-Wrightson-c(i); Adams-a(i). 3-Wrightson-i(5 pgs.)	2	4	6	9	13	16
4,5: 5-Starlin-a(p); Conan cameo	2	4	6	8	10	12

NOTE: ***Chaykin*** *a-1-4p; c-2p, 3-5.* ***Kaluta*** *a-3i.* ***Simonson*** *a-3i, 4i, 5p; c-5.*

SWORD OF THE ATOM

Taffy Comics #1 © Orbit

Takion #6 © DC

Tales From the Crypt #41 © WMG

	GD 2.0	VG 4.0	FN 6.0	VF 8.0	VF/NM 9.0	NM- 9.2

DC Comics: Sept, 1983 - No. 4, Dec, 1983 (Limited series)

1-4: Gil Kane-c/a in all 4.00
Special 1-3('84, '85, '88): 1,2-Kane-c/a each 4.00
TPB (2007, $19.99) r/#1-4 and Special #1-3 20.00

SWORDS OF TEXAS (See Scout #15)
Eclipse Comics: Oct, 1987 - No. 4, Jan, 1988 ($1.75, color, Baxter paper)

1-4: Scout app. 3.00

SWORDS OF THE SWASHBUCKLERS (See Marvel Graphic Novel)
Marvel Comics (Epic Comics): May, 1985 - No. 12, Jun, 1987 ($1.50; mature)

1-12-Butch Guice-c/a (Cont'd from Marvel G.N.) 3.00

SWORN TO PROTECT
Marvel Comics: Sept, 1995 ($1.95) (Based on card game)

nn-Overpower Game Guide; Jubilee story 3.00

SYN
Dark Horse Comics: Aug, 2003 - No. 5, Feb, 2004 ($2.99, limited series)

1-5-Giffen-s/Titus-a 3.00

SYPHONS
Now Comics: V2#1, May, 1994 - V2#3, 1994 ($2.50, limited series)

V2#1-3: 1-Stardancer, Knightfire, Raze & Brigade begin 3.00
TPB (9/04, $15.95) B&W reprints #1-3; intro. by Tony Caputo 16.00

SYSTEM, THE
DC Comics (Vertigo Verite): May, 1996 - No. 3, July, 1996 ($2.95, lim. series)

1-3: Kuper-c/a 3.00
TPB (1997, $12.95) r/#1-3 13.00

TAFFY COMICS (Also see Dotty Dripple)
Rural Home/Orbit Publ.: Mar-Apr, 1945 - No. 12, 1948

1-L.B. Cole-c; origin & 1st app. of Wiggles The Wonderworm plus 7 chapter WWII funny animal adventures 60 120 180 381 653 925
2-L.B. Cole-c with funny animal Hitler; Wiggles-c/stories in #1-4 39 78 117 240 395 550
3,4,6-12: 6-Perry Como-c/story. 7-Duke Ellington, 2 pgs. 8-Glenn Ford-c/story. 9-Lon McCallister part photo-c & story. 10-Mort Leav-c. 11-Mickey Rooney-c/story 15 30 45 83 124 165
5-L.B. Cole-c; Van Johnson-c/story 21 42 63 124 202 280

TAILGUNNER JO
DC Comics: Sept, 1988 - No. 6, Jan, 1989 ($1.25)

1-6 3.00

TAILS
Archie Publications: Dec, 1995 - No. 3, Feb, 1996 ($1.50, limited series)

1-3: Based on Sonic, the Hedgehog video game 6.00

TAILS OF THE PET AVENGERS (Also see Lockjaw and the Pet Avengers)
Marvel Comics: Apr, 2010 ($3.99, one-shot)

1-Lockjaw, Frog Thor, Zabu, Lockheed and Redwing in short solo stories by various 4.00
...: The Dogs of Summer (9/10, $3.99) Eliopolous-s; see Avengers vs. the Pet Avengers 4.00

TAILSPIN
Spotlight Publishers: November, 1944

nn-Firebird app.; L.B. Cole-c 29 58 87 170 278 385

TAILSPIN TOMMY (Also see Popular Comics)
United Features Syndicate/Service Publ. Co.: 1940; 1946

Single Series 23(1940) 40 80 120 242 401 560
Best Seller (nd, 1946)-Service Publ. Co. 15 30 45 88 137 185

TAKE A CHANCE (C.E. Murphy's...)
Dabel Brothers Prods.: Dec, 2008 - No. 5, Apr, 2009 ($3.99)

1-4-C.E. Murphy-s/Ardian Syaf-a/c 4.00

TAKIO
Marvel Comics (Icon): 2011 ($9.95, HC graphic novel)

HC-Bendis-s/Oeming-a/c; Oeming sketch pages 10.00

TAKION
DC Comics: June, 1996 - No. 7, Dec, 1996 ($1.75)

1-7: Lopresti-c/a(p). 1-Origin; Green Lantern app. 6-Final Night x-over 3.00

TALENT SHOWCASE (See New Talent Showcase)

TALE OF ONE BAD RAT, THE
Dark Horse Comics: Oct, 1994 - No. 4, Jan, 1995 ($2.95, limited series)

1-4: Bryan Talbot-c/a/scripts 3.00
HC ($69.95, signed and numbered) R/#1-4 70.00

TALES CALCULATED TO DRIVE YOU BATS
Archie Publications: Nov, 1961 - No. 7, Nov, 1962; 1966 (Satire)

1-Only 10¢ issue; has cut-out Werewolf mask (price includes mask) 12 24 36 83 172 260
2-Begin 12¢ issues 8 16 24 55 93 130
3-6: 3-UFO cover 7 14 21 44 72 100
7-Storyline change 6 12 18 42 69 95
1(1966, 25¢, 44 pg. Giant)-r/#1; UFO cover 6 12 18 41 66 90

TALES CALCULATED TO DRIVE YOU MAD
E.C. Publications: Summer, 1997 - No. 8, Winter, 1999 ($3.99/$4.99, satire)

1-6-Full color reprints of Mad: 1-(#1-3), 2-(#4-6), 3-(#7-9), 4-(#10-12) 5-(#13-15), 6-(#16-18) 5.00
7,8-($4.99-c): 7-(#19-21), 8-(#22,23) 5.00

TALES FROM RIVERDALE DIGEST
Archie Publ.: June, 2005 - No. 39, Oct, 2010 ($2.39/$2.49/$2.69, digest-size)

1-39: 1-Sabrina and Josie & the Pussycats app. 11-Begin $2.49-c. 34-Begin $2.69 3.00

TALES FROM THE AGE OF APOCALYPSE
Marvel Comics: 1996 ($5.95, prestige format, one-shots)

1, ...: Sinister Bloodlines (1997, $5.95) 6.00

TALES FROM THE BOG
Aberration Press: Nov, 1995 - No. 7, Nov, 1997 ($2.95/$3.95, B&W)

1-7 4.00
Alternate #1 (Director's Cut) (1998, $2.95) 3.00

TALES FROM THE BULLY PULPIT
Image Comics: Aug, 2004 ($6.95, square-bound)

1-Teddy Roosevelt and Edison's ghost with a time machine; Cereno-s/MacDonald-a 7.00

TALES FROM THE CLERKS (See Jay and Silent Bob, Clerks and Oni Double Feature)
Graphitti Designs, Inc.: 2006 ($29.95, TPB)

nn-Reprints all the Kevin Smith Clerks and Jay and Silent Bob stories; new Clerks II story with Mahfood-a; cover gallery, sketch pages, Mallrats credits covers; Smith intro. 30.00

TALES FROM THE CRYPT (Formerly The Crypt Of Terror; see Three Dimensional...)
(Also see EC Archives • Tales From the Crypt)
E.C. Comics: No. 20, Oct-Nov, 1950 - No. 46, Feb-Mar, 1955

20-See Crime Patrol #15 for 1st Crypt Keeper 119 238 357 952 1514 2075
21-Kurtzman-r/Haunt of Fear #15(#1) 100 200 300 800 1275 1750
22-Moon Girl costume at costume party, one panel 77 154 231 616 983 1350
23-25: 24-E. A. Poe adaptation 63 126 189 504 802 1100
26-30: 26-Wood's 2nd EC-c 50 100 150 400 638 875
31-Williamson-a(1st at E.C.); B&W and color illos. in **POP**; Kamen draws himself, Gaines & Feldstein; Ingels, Craig & Davis draw themselves in his story 51 102 153 408 654 900
32,35-39: 38-Censored-c 44 88 132 352 559 765
33-Origin The Crypt Keeper 65 130 195 520 830 1140
34-Used in **POP**, pg. 83; lingerie panels 45 90 135 360 573 785
40-Used in Senate hearings & in Hartford Cournat anti-comics editorials-1954 44 88 132 352 564 775
41-45: 45-2 pgs. showing E.C. staff 43 86 129 344 547 750
46-Low distribution; pre-advertised cover for unpublished 4th horror title "Crypt of Terror" used on this book 50 100 150 400 638 875

NOTE: ***Ray Bradbury*** *adaptations-34, 36.* ***Craig*** *a-20, 22-24; c-20.* ***Crandall*** *a-38, 44.* ***Davis*** *a-24-46; c-29-46.* ***Elder*** *a-37, 38.* ***Evans*** *a-32-34, 36, 40, 41, 43, 46.* ***Feldstein*** *a-20-23; c-21-25, 28. Ingels a-in all.* ***Kamen*** *a-20, 22, 25, 27-31, 33-36, 39, 41-45.* ***Krigstein*** *a-40, 42, 45.* ***Kurtzman*** *a-21.* ***Orlando*** *a-27-30, 35, 37, 39, 41-45.* ***Wood*** *a-21, 24, 25; c-26, 27. Canadian reprints known; see Table of Contents.*

TALES FROM THE CRYPT (Magazine)
Eerie Publications: No. 10, July, 1968 (35¢, B&W)

10-Contains Farrell reprints from 1950s 6 12 18 37 59 80

TALES FROM THE CRYPT
Gladstone Publishing: July, 1990 - No. 6, May, 1991 ($1.95/$2.00, 68 pgs.)

1-r/TFTC #33 & Crime S.S. #17; Davis-c(r) 4.00
2-6: 2,3,5,6-Davis-c(r). 4-Begin $2.00-c; Craig-c(r) 4.00

TALES FROM THE CRYPT
Extra-Large Comics (Russ Cochran)/Gemstone Publishing: Jul, 1991 - No. 6 ($3.95, 10 1/4 x13 1/4", 68 pgs.)

1-Davis-c(r); Craig back-c(r); E.C. reprints 4.00
2-6 ($2.00, comic sized) 4.00

Tales of Justice #65 © MAR

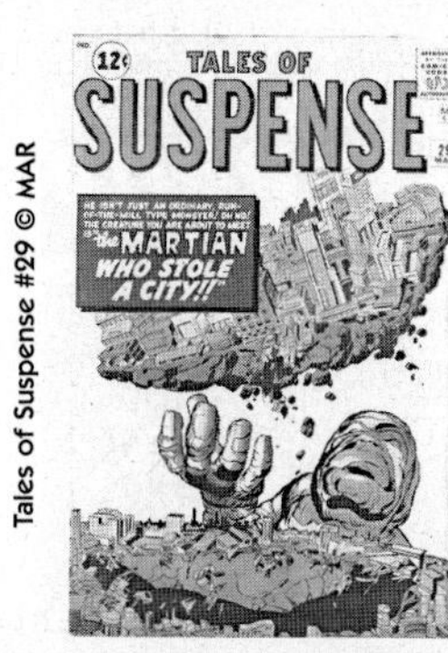

Tales of Suspense #29 © MAR

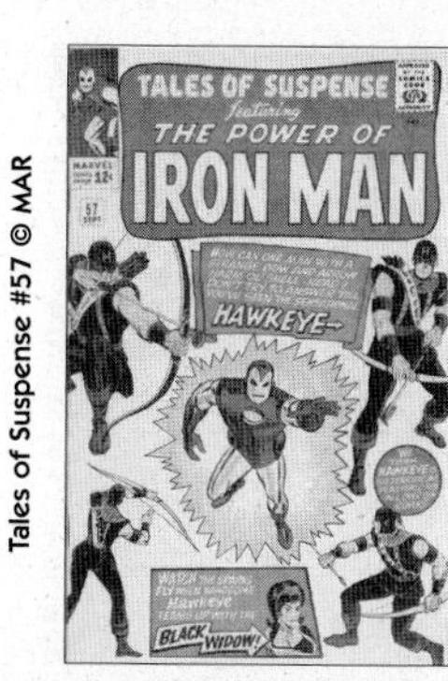

Tales of Suspense #57 © MAR

TALES FROM THE CRYPT
Russ Cochran: Sept, 1991 - No. 7, July, 1992 ($2.00, 64 pgs.)

	GD 2.0	VG 4.0	FN 6.0	VF 8.0	VF/NM 9.0	NM- 9.2
1-7						4.00

TALES FROM THE CRYPT (Also see EC Archives • Tales From the Crypt)
Russ Cochran/Gemstone: Sept, 1992 - No. 30, Dec, 1999 ($1.50, quarterly)

	GD 2.0	VG 4.0	FN 6.0	VF 8.0	VF/NM 9.0	NM- 9.2
1-4-r/Crypt of Terror #17-19, TFTC #20 w/original-c						3.00
5-30: 5-15 ($2.00)-r/TFTC #21-23 w/original-c. 16-30 ($2.50)						3.00
Annual 1-6('93-'99) 1-r/#1-5. 2- r/#6-10. 3- r/#11-15. 4- r/#16-20. 5-r/#21-25. 6- r/#26-30						14.00

TALES FROM THE CRYPT
Papercutz: July, 2007 - Present ($3.95)

	GD 2.0	VG 4.0	FN 6.0	VF 8.0	VF/NM 9.0	NM- 9.2
1-6: 1-New stories in the same vein as the originals; Cryptkeeper app. Kyle Baker-c						4.00

TALES FROM THE GREAT BOOK
Famous Funnies: Feb, 1955 - No. 4, Jan, 1956 (Religious themes)

	GD 2.0	VG 4.0	FN 6.0	VF 8.0	VF/NM 9.0	NM- 9.2
1-Story of Samson; John Lehti-a in all	9	18	27	50	65	80
2-4: 2-Joshua. 3-Joash the Boy King. 4-David	7	14	21	35	43	50

TALES FROM THE HEART OF AFRICA (The Temporary Natives)
Marvel Comics (Epic Comics): Aug, 1990 ($3.95, 52 pgs.)

	GD 2.0	VG 4.0	FN 6.0	VF 8.0	VF/NM 9.0	NM- 9.2
1						4.00

TALES FROM THE TOMB (Also see Dell Giants)
Dell Publishing Co.: Oct, 1962 (25¢ giant)

	GD 2.0	VG 4.0	FN 6.0	VF 8.0	VF/NM 9.0	NM- 9.2
1(02-810-210)-All stories written by John Stanley	13	26	39	88	189	290

TALES FROM THE TOMB (Magazine)
Eerie Publications: V1#6, July, 1969 - V7#3, 1975 (52 pgs.)

	GD 2.0	VG 4.0	FN 6.0	VF 8.0	VF/NM 9.0	NM- 9.2
V1#6	8	16	24	51	86	120
V1#7,8	6	12	18	41	66	90
V2#1-6: 4-LSD story-r/Weird V3#5. 6-Rulah-r	5	10	15	35	55	75
V3#1-Rulah-r	5	10	15	35	55	75
2-6('71),V4#1-5('72),V5#1-6('73),V6#1-6('74),V7#1-3('75)	5	10	15	30	48	65

TALES OF ASGARD
Marvel Comics Group: Oct, 1968 (25¢, 68 pgs.); Feb, 1984 ($1.25, 52 pgs.)

	GD 2.0	VG 4.0	FN 6.0	VF 8.0	VF/NM 9.0	NM- 9.2
1-Reprints Tales of Asgard (Thor) back-up stories from Journey into Mystery #97-106; new Kirby-c; Kirby-a	6	12	18	37	59	80
V2#1 (2/84)-Thor-r; Simonson-c						5.00

TALES OF ARMY OF DARKNESS
Dynamite Entertainment: 2006 ($5.95, one-shot)

	GD 2.0	VG 4.0	FN 6.0	VF 8.0	VF/NM 9.0	NM- 9.2
1-Short stories by Kuhoric, Kirkman, Bradshaw, Sablik, Ottley, Acs, O'Hare and others						6.00

TALES OF EVIL
Atlas/Seaboard Publ.: Feb, 1975 - No. 3, July, 1975 (All 25¢ issues)

	GD 2.0	VG 4.0	FN 6.0	VF 8.0	VF/NM 9.0	NM- 9.2
1-3: 1-Werewolf w/Sekowsky-a. 2-Intro. The Bog Beast; Sparling-a. 3-Origin The Man-Monster; Buckler-a(p)	2	4	6	9	13	16

NOTE: ***Grandenetti** a-1, 2. **Lieber** c-1. **Sekowsky** a-1. **Sutton** a-2. **Thorne** c-2.*

TALES OF GHOST CASTLE
National Periodical Publications: May-June, 1975 - No. 3, Sept-Oct, 1975 (All 25¢ issues)

	GD 2.0	VG 4.0	FN 6.0	VF 8.0	VF/NM 9.0	NM- 9.2
1-Redondo-a; 1st app. Lucien the Librarian from Sandman (1989 series)	3	6	9	18	27	35
2,3: 2-Nino-a. 3-Redondo-a.	2	4	6	10	14	18

TALES OF G.I. JOE
Marvel Comics: Jan, 1988 - No. 15, Mar, 1989

	GD 2.0	VG 4.0	FN 6.0	VF 8.0	VF/NM 9.0	NM- 9.2
1 ($2.25, 52 pgs.)						4.00
2-15 ($1.50): 1-15-r/G.I. Joe #1-15						3.00

TALES OF HORROR
Toby Press/Minoan Publ. Corp.: June, 1952 - No. 13, Oct, 1954

	GD 2.0	VG 4.0	FN 6.0	VF 8.0	VF/NM 9.0	NM- 9.2
1	41	82	123	256	428	600
2-Torture scenes	34	68	102	199	325	450
3-11,13: 9-11-Reprints Purple Claw #1-3	23	46	69	136	223	310
12-Myron Fass-c/a; torture scenes	24	48	72	144	237	330

NOTE: ***Andru** a-5. **Baily** a-5. **Myron Fass** a-2, 3, 12; c-1-3, 12. **Hollingsworth** a-2. **Sparling** a-6, 9; c-9.*

TALES OF JUSTICE
Atlas Comics(MjMC No. 53-66/Male No. 67): No. 53, May, 1955 - No. 67, Aug, 1957

	GD 2.0	VG 4.0	FN 6.0	VF 8.0	VF/NM 9.0	NM- 9.2
53	15	30	45	83	124	165
54-57: 54-Powell-a	11	22	33	60	83	105
58,59-Krigstein-a	12	24	36	67	94	120
60-63,65: 60-Powell-a	10	20	30	54	72	90
64,66,67: 64,67-Crandall-a. 66-Torres, Orlando-a	10	20	30	56	76	95

NOTE: ***Everett** a-53, 60. **Orlando** a-65, 66. **Severin** a-64; c-58, 60, 65. **Wildey** a-64, 67.*

TALES OF LEONARDO BLIND SIGHT (See Tales of the TMNT Vol. 2 #5)
Mirage Publishing: June, 2006 - No. 4, Sept, 2006 ($3.25, B&W, limited series)

	GD 2.0	VG 4.0	FN 6.0	VF 8.0	VF/NM 9.0	NM- 9.2
1-4-Jim Lawson-s/a						3.25

TALES OF SUSPENSE (Becomes Captain America #100 on)
Atlas (WPI No. 1,2/Male No. 3-12/VPI No. 13-18)/Marvel No. 19 on:
Jan, 1959 - No. 99, Mar, 1968

	GD 2.0	VG 4.0	FN 6.0	VF 8.0	VF/NM 9.0	NM- 9.2
1-Williamson-a (5 pgs.); Heck-c; #1-4 have sci/fi-c	164	328	492	1378	2989	4600
2,3: 2-Ditko robot-c. 3-Flying saucer-c/story	56	112	168	454	977	1500
4-Williamson-a (4 pgs.); Kirby/Everett-c/a	46	92	138	345	748	1150
5-Kirby monster-c begin	40	80	120	300	650	1000
6,8,10	36	72	108	261	568	875
7-Prototype ish. (Lava Man); 1 panel app. Aunt May (see Str. Tales #97)	38	76	114	285	618	950
9-Prototype ish. (Iron Man)	39	78	117	293	634	975
11,12,15,17-19: 12-Crandall-a.	29	58	87	210	455	700
13-Elektro-c/story	30	60	90	218	472	725
14-Intro/1st app. Colossus-c/sty	39	78	117	293	634	975
16-1st Metallo-c/story (4/61, Iron Man prototype)	35	70	105	254	552	850
20-Colossus-c/story (2nd app.)	31	62	93	225	488	750
21-25: 25-Last 10¢ issue	27	54	81	189	407	625
26,27,29,30,33,34,36-38: 33-(9/62)-Hulk 1st x-over cameo (picture on wall)	26	52	78	182	391	600
28-Prototype ish. (Stone Men)	27	54	81	189	407	625
31-Prototype ish. (Dr. Doom)	28	56	84	203	439	675
32-Prototype ish. (Dr. Strange)(8/62)-Sazzik The Sorcerer app.; "The Man and the Beehive" story, 1 month before TTA #35 (2nd Antman), came out after "The Man in the Ant Hill" in TTA #27 (1/62) (1st Antman)-Characters from both stories were tested to see which got best fan response	36	72	108	270	585	900
35-Prototype issue (The Watcher)	27	54	81	196	423	650
39 (3/63)-Origin/1st app. Iron Man & begin series; 1st Iron Man story has Kirby layouts	900	1800	2700	9000	18,000	32,000
40-2nd app. Iron Man (in new armor)	186	372	558	1562	3381	5200
41-3rd app. Iron Man; Dr. Strange (villain) app.	111	222	333	900	1950	3000
42-45: 45-Intro. & 1st app. Happy & Pepper	74	148	222	600	1300	2000
46,47: 46-1st app. Crimson Dynamo	54	108	162	437	944	1450
48-New Iron Man armor by Ditko	61	122	183	494	1072	1650
49-1st X-Men x-over (same date as X-Men #3, 1/64); also 1st Avengers x-over (w/o Captain America); 1st Tales of the Watcher back-up story & begins (2nd app. Watcher; see F.F. #13)	78	156	234	632	1366	2100
50-1st app. Mandarin	40	80	120	300	650	1000
51-1st Scarecrow	28	56	84	203	439	675
52-1st app. The Black Widow (4/64)	46	92	138	359	780	1200
53-Origin The Watcher; 2nd Black Widow app.	29	58	87	210	455	700
54,55	22	44	66	154	327	500
56-1st app. Unicorn	24	48	72	168	359	550
57-Origin/1st app. Hawkeye (9/64)	52	104	156	421	911	1400
58-Captain America battles Iron Man (10/64)-Classic-c; 2nd Kraven app. (Cap's 1st app. in this title)	46	92	138	359	780	1200
59-Iron Man plus Captain America double feature begins (11/64); 1st S.A. Captain America solo story; intro Jarvis, Avenger's butler; classic-c	42	84	126	315	683	1050
60-2nd app. Hawkeye (#64 is 3rd app.)	25	50	75	175	375	575
61,62,64: 62-Origin Mandarin (2/65)	14	28	42	97	211	325
63-1st Silver Age origin Captain America (3/65)	29	58	87	210	455	700
65-G.A. Red Skull in WWII stories(also in #66);-1st Silver-Age Red Skull (5/65).	24	48	72	168	359	550
66-Origin Red Skull	17	34	51	119	260	400
67-70: 69-1st app. Titanium Man. 70-Begin alternating-c features w/Capt. America (even #'s) & Iron Man (odd #'s)	10	20	30	67	124	180
71-78: 75-1st app. Agent 13 later named Sharon Carter; intro Batroc. 78-Col. Nick Fury app.	8	16	24	53	89	125
79-Begin 3 part Iron Man Sub-Mariner battle story; Sub-Mariner-c & cameo; 1st app. Cosmic Cube; 1st modern Red Skull	9	18	27	63	112	160
80-Iron Man battles Sub-Mariner story cont'd in Tales to Astonish #82; classic Red Skull-c	9	18	27	63	112	160
81-96,98: 82-Intro the Adaptoid by Kirby (also in #83,84). 88-Mole Man app. in Iron Man story. 92-1st Nick Fury x-over (cameo, as Agent of S.H.I.E.L.D., 8/67). 94-Intro Modok. 95-Capt. America's i.d. revealed. 98-1st brief app. new Zemo (son?); #99 is 1st full app.	7	14	21	46	76	105
97-1st Whiplash	9	18	27	61	106	150
99-Captain America story cont'd in Captain America #100; Iron Man story cont'd in Iron Man & Sub-Mariner #1	8	16	24	56	96	135
Onmibus (See Iron Man Omnibus for reprints of #39-83)						

NOTE: ***Abel** a-73-81i(as Gary Michaels), **J. Buscema** a-1; c-3. **Colan** a-39, 73-99p; c(p)-73, 75, 77, 79, 81, 83, 85-87, 89, 91, 93, 95, 97, 99. **Crandall** a-12. **Davis** a-38. **Ditko** a-1-15, 17-44, 46, 47-49p; c-2, 10i, 13i, 23i.*

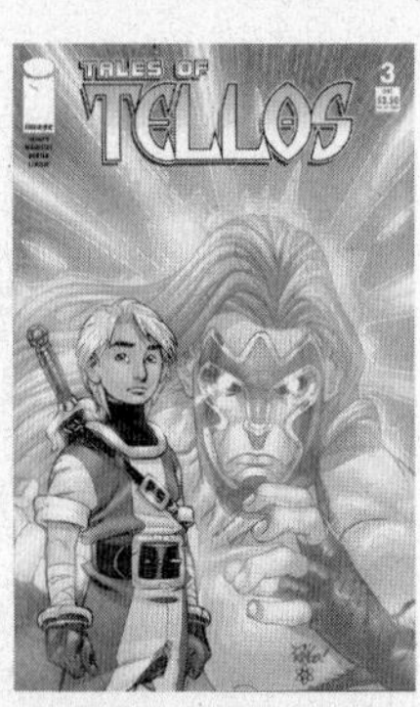
Tales of Tellos #3 © Tales of Tellos

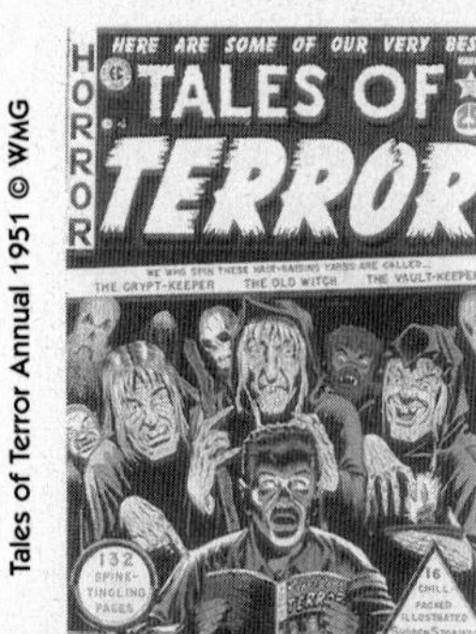

Tales of Terror Annual 1951 © WMG

Tales of the TMNT #5 © Kevin Eastman

GD VG FN VF VF/NM NM-
2.0 4.0 6.0 8.0 9.0 9.2

***Kirby/Ditko** a-7; c-10, 13, 22, 28, 34. **Everett** a-8. **Forte** a-5, 9. **Giacoia** a-82. **Heath** a-2, 10. **Gil Kane** a-88p, 89-91; c-88, 89-91p. **Kirby** a(p)-2-4, 6-35, 40, 41, 43, 59-75, 77-86, 92-99; layouts-69-75, 77; c(p)4-28(most), 29-56, 58-72, 74, 76, 78, 80, 82, 84, 86, 92, 94, 96, 98. **Leiber/Fox** a-42, 43, 45, 51. **Reinman** a-26, 44i, 49i, 52i, 53i. **Tuska** a-58, 70-74. **Wood** c/a-71i.*

TALES OF SUSPENSE
Marvel Comics: V2#1, Jan, 1995 ($6.95, one-shot)

V2#1-James Robinson script; acetate-c. 7.00

TALES OF SUSPENSE: CAPTAIN AMERICA & IRON MAN #1 COMMEMORATIVE EDITION
Marvel Comics: 2004 ($3.99, one-shot)

nn-Reprints Captain America (2004) #1 and Iron Man (2004) #1 4.00

TALES OF SWORD & SORCERY (See Dagar)

TALES OF TELLOS (See Tellos)
Image Comics: Oct, 2004 - No. 3, ($3.50, anthology)

1-3: 1-Dezago-s; art by Yates & Rousseau; Wieringo-c. 3-Porter-a 3.50

TALES OF TERROR
Toby Press Publications: 1952 (no month)

1-Fawcette-c; Ravielli-a 28 56 84 165 270 375
NOTE: *This title was cancelled due to similarity to the E.C. title.*

TALES OF TERROR (See Movie Classics)

TALES OF TERROR (Magazine)
Eerie Publications: Summer, 1964

1 6 12 18 42 69 95

TALES OF TERROR
Eclipse Comics: July, 1985 - No. 13, July, 1987 ($2.00, Baxter paper, mature)

1-13: 5-1st Lee Weeks-a. 7-Sam Kieth-a. 10-Snyder-a. 12-Vampire story 3.00

TALES OF TERROR (IDW's...)
IDW Publishing: Sept, 2004 ($16.99, hardcover)

1-Anthology of short graphic stories and text stories; incl. 30 Days of Night 17.00

TALES OF TERROR ANNUAL
E.C. Comics: 1951 - No. 3, 1953 (25¢, 132 pgs., 16 stories each)

nn(1951)(Scarce)-Feldstein infinity-c 900 1800 2700 7200 - -
2(1952)-Feldstein-c 268 536 804 1702 2926 4150
3(1953)-Feldstein bondage/torture-c 216 432 648 1372 2361 3350
NOTE: *No. 1 contains three horror and one science fiction comic which came out in 1950. No. 2 contains a horror, crime, and science fiction book which generally had cover dates in 1951, and No. 3 had horror, crime, and shock books that generally appeared in 1952. All E.C. annuals contain four complete books that did not sell on the stands which were rebound in the annual format, minus the covers, and sold from the E.C. office and on the stands in key cities. The contents of each annual may vary in the same year. Crypt Keeper, Vault Keeper, Old Witch app. on all-c.*

TALES OF TERROR ILLUSTRATED (See Terror Illustrated)

TALES OF TEXAS JOHN SLAUGHTER (See Walt Disney Presents, 4-Color #997)

TALES OF THE BEANWORLD
Beanworld Press/Eclipse Comics: Feb, 1985 - No. 19, 1991; No. 20, 1993 - No. 21, 1993 ($1.50/$2.00, B&W)

1-21 3.00

TALES OF THE BIZARRO WORLD
DC Comics: 2000 ($14.95, TPB)

nn-Reprints early Bizarro stories; new Jaime Hernandez-c 15.00

TALES OF THE DARKNESS
Image Comics (Top Cow): Apr, 1998 - No. 4, Dec, 1998 ($2.95)

1-4: 1,2-Portacio-c/a(p). 3,4-Lansing & Nocon-a(p) 3.00
1-American Entertainment Ed. 3.00
#1/2 (1/01, $2.95) 3.00

TALES OF THE DRAGON GUARD (English version of French comic title)
Marvel Comics (Soleil): Apr, 2010 - No. 3, Jun, 2010 ($5.99, limited series)

1-3: 1-Ange-s/Varanda-a. 2-Briones-a. 3-Guinebaud-a 6.00
...: Into the Veil 1-3 (11/10 - No. 3, 1/11) 1-Briones-a. 2-Paty-a. 3-Sieurac-a 6.00

TALES OF THE GREEN BERET
Dell Publishing Co.: Jan, 1967 - No. 5, Oct, 1969

1-Glanzman-a in 1-4 & 5r 4 8 12 20 30 40
2-5: 5-Reprints #1 3 6 9 16 23 30

TALES OF THE GREEN HORNET
Now Comics: Sept, 1990 - No. 2, 1990; V2#1, Jan, 1992 - No.4, Apr, 1992; V3#1, Sept, 1992 - No. 3, Nov, 1992

1,2 3.00

GD VG FN VF VF/NM NM-
2.0 4.0 6.0 8.0 9.0 9.2

V2#1-4 ($1.95) 3.00
V3#1 ($2.75)-Polybagged w/hologram trading card 4.00
V3#2,3 ($2.50) 3.00

TALES OF THE GREEN LANTERN CORPS (See Green Lantern #107)
DC Comics: May, 1981 - No. 3, July, 1981 (Limited series)

1-3: 1-Origin of G.L. & the Guardians, Annual 1 (1/85)-Gil Kane-c/a 5.00
TPB (2009, $19.99) r/#1-3 & stories from G.L. #148-151-154,161,162,164-167 ('82-'83) 20.00
Volume 2 TPB (2010, $19.99) r/Annual #1 and stories from G.L. ('83-'85) 20.00
Volume 3 TPB (2010, $19.99) r/Green Lantern #201-206 ('86) 20.00

TALES OF THE INVISIBLE SCARLET O'NEIL (See Harvey Comics Hits #59)

TALES OF THE KILLERS (Magazine)
World Famous Periodicals: V1#10, Dec, 1970 - V1#11, Feb, 1971 (B&W, 52 pg)

V1#10-One pg. Frazetta; r/Crime Does Not Pay 5 10 15 30 48 65
11-similar-c to Crime Does Not Pay #47; contains r/Crime Does Not Pay 4 8 12 26 41 55

TALES OF THE LEGION (Formerly Legion of Super-Heroes)
DC Comics: No. 314, Aug, 1984 - No. 354, Dec, 1987

314-354: 326-r-begin 3.00
Annual 4,5 (1986, 1987)-Formerly LSH Annual 4.00

TALES OF THE MARINES (Formerly Devil-Dog Dugan #1-3)
Atlas Comics (OPI): No. 4, Feb, 1957 (Marines At War #5 on)

4-Powell-a; Severin-c 11 22 33 62 86 110

TALES OF THE MARVELS
Marvel Comics: 1995/1996 (all acetate, painted-c)

...Blockbuster 1 (1995, $5.95, one-shot), ...Inner Demons 1 (1996, $5.95, one shot), ...Wonder Years 1,2 (1995, $4.95, limited series) 6.00

TALES OF THE MARVEL UNIVERSE
Marvel Comics: Feb, 1997 ($2.95, one-shot)

1-Anthology; wraparound-c; Thunderbolts, Ka-Zar app. 4.00

TALES OF THE MYSTERIOUS TRAVELER (See Mysterious...)
Charlton Comics: Aug, 1956 - No. 13, June, 1959; V2#14, Oct, 1985 - No. 15, Dec, 1985

1-No Ditko-a; Giordano/Alascia-c 50 100 150 315 533 750
2-Ditko-a(1) 41 82 123 256 428 600
3-Ditko-c/a(1) 42 84 126 265 445 625
4-7-Ditko-c/a(3-4 stories each) 48 96 144 302 514 725
8,9-Ditko-a(1-3 each). 8-Rocke-c 41 82 123 250 418 585
10,11-Ditko-c/a(3-4 each) 44 88 132 277 469 660
12 18 36 54 105 165 225
13-Baker-a (r?) 19 38 57 111 176 240
V2#14,15 (1985)-Ditko-c/a-low print run 2 3 4 6 8 10

TALES OF THE NEW GODS
DC Comics: 2008 ($19.99, TPB)

SC-Reprints from Jack Kirby's Fourth World, Orion and Mister Miracle Special 20.00

TALES OF THE NEW TEEN TITANS
DC Comics: June, 1982 - No. 4, Sept, 1982 (Limited series)

1-4 5.00

TALES OF THE PONY EXPRESS (TV)
Dell Publishing Co.: No. 829, Aug, 1957 - No. 942, Oct, 1958

Four Color 829 (#1) -Painted-c 5 10 15 30 48 65
Four Color 942-Title -Pony Express 5 10 15 30 48 65

TALES OF THE REALM
CrossGen Comics/MVCreations #4-on: Oct, 2003 - No. 5, May, 2004 ($2.95, limited series)

1-5-Robert Kirkman-s/Matt Tyree-a 3.00
Volume 1 HC (8/04, $39.95, dust jacket) r/#1-5; sketch pages and concept art 40.00

TALES OF THE SINESTRO CORPS (See Green Lantern and Green Lantern Corps x-over)
DC Comics: Nov, 2007 - Jan, 2008 ($2.99/$3.99, one-shots)

...: Cyborg-Superman (12/07, $2.99) Burnett-s/Blaine-a/VanSciver-c; JLA app. 3.00
...: Ion (1/08, $2.99) Marz-s/Lacombe-a/Benes-c; Sodam Yat app. 3.00
...: Parallax (11/07, $2.99) Marz-s/Melo-a; Kyle Rayner vs. Parallax 3.00
...: Superman-Prime (12/07, $3.99) Johns-s/VanSciver-c; origin re-told w/Ordway-a 4.00

TALES OF THE TEENAGE MUTANT NINJA TURTLES (See Teenage Mutant...)
Mirage Studios: May, 1987 - No. 7, Aug (Apr-c), 1989 (B&W, $1.50)

1-7: 2-Title merges w/Teenage Mutant Ninja... 4.00

TALES OF THE TEEN TITANS (Formerly The New Teen Titans)
DC Comics: No. 41, Apr, 1984 - No. 91, July, 1988 (75¢)

Tales of the Unexpected #17 © DC

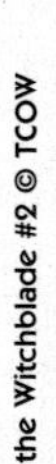
Tales of the Witchblade #2 © TCOW

Tales to Astonish #6 © MAR

	GD 2.0	VG 4.0	FN 6.0	VF 8.0	VF/NM 9.0	NM- 9.2

41,45-49: 46-Aqualad & Aquagirl join 4.00
42-44: The Judas Contract part 1-3 with Deathstroke the Terminator in all; concludes in Annual #3. 44-Dick Grayson becomes Nightwing (3rd to be Nightwing) & joins Titans; Jericho (Deathstroke's son) joins; origin Deathstroke 5.00
50-Double size; app. Betty Kane (Bat-Girl) out of costume 5.00
51,52,56-91: 52-1st brief app. Azrael (not same as newer character). 56-Intro Jinx. 57-Neutron app. 59-r/DC Comics Presents #26. 60-91-r/New Teen Titans Baxter series. 68-B. Smith-c. 70-Origin Kole 3.00
53-55: 53-1st full app. Azrael; Deathstroke cameo. 54,55-Deathstroke-c/stories 4.00
Annual 3(1984, $1.25)-Part 4 of The Judas Contract; Deathstroke-c/story; Death of Terra; indicia says Teen Titans Annual; previous annuals listed as New Teen Titans Annual #1,2 5.00
Annual 4-(1986, $1.25) 4.00

TALES OF THE TEXAS RANGERS (See Jace Pearson...)

TALES OF THE THING (Fantastic Four)
Marvel Comics: May, 2005 - No. 3, July, 2005 ($2.50, limited series)

1-3-Dr. Strange app; Randy Green-c 3.00

TALES OF THE TMNT (Also see Teenage Mutant Ninja Turtles)
Mirage Studios: Jan, 2004 - Present ($2.95/$3.25, B&W)

1-7: 1-Brizuela-a 3.25
8-70: 8-Begin $3.25-c. 47-Origin of the Super Turtles 3.25

TALES OF THE UNEXPECTED (Becomes The Unexpected #105 on)(See Adventure #75, Super DC Giant)
National Periodical Publications: Feb-Mar, 1956 - No. 104, Dec-Jan, 1967-68

Issue	GD 2.0	VG 4.0	FN 6.0	VF 8.0	VF/NM 9.0	NM- 9.2
1	104	208	312	842	1821	2800
2	44	88	132	330	715	1100
3-5	32	64	96	232	504	775
6-10: 6-1st Silver Age issue	26	52	78	182	391	600
11,14,19,20	19	38	57	128	277	425
12,13,16,18,21-24: All have Kirby-a. 16-Characters named 'Thor' (with a magic hammer) and Loki by Kirby (8/57, characters do not look like Marvel's Thor & Loki)	22	44	66	154	327	500
15,17-Grey tone-c; Kirby-a	25	50	75	175	375	575
25-30	15	30	45	104	227	350
31-39	13	26	39	90	195	300
40-Space Ranger begins (8/59, 3rd ap.), ends #82	104	208	312	842	1821	2800
41,42-Space Ranger stories	38	76	114	285	618	950
43-1st Space Ranger-c this title; grey tone-c	67	134	201	545	1173	1800
44-46	28	56	84	203	439	675
47-50	24	48	72	168	359	550
51-60: 54-Dinosaur-c/story	20	40	60	137	294	450
61-67: 67-Last 10¢ issue	16	32	48	107	234	360
68-82: 82-Last Space Ranger	11	22	33	77	144	210
83-90,92-99	7	14	21	46	76	105
91,100: 91-1st Automan (also in #94,97)	7	14	21	48	79	110
101-104	6	12	18	42	69	95

NOTE: ***Neal Adams** c-104. **Anderson** a-50. **Brown** a-50-82(Space Ranger); c-19, 40, & many Space Ranger-c. **Cameron** a-24, 27, 29; c-24. **Heath** a-49. **Bob Kane** a-24, 48. **Kirby** a-12, 13, 15-18, 21-24; c-13, 18, 22. **Meskin** a-15, 18, 26, 27, 35, 66. **Moreira** a-16, 20, 29, 38, 44, 62, 71; c-38. **Roussos** c-10. **Wildey** a-31.*

TALES OF THE UNEXPECTED (See Crisis Aftermath: The Spectre)
DC Comics: Dec, 2006 - No. 8, Jul, 2007 ($3.99, limited series)

1-8-The Spectre, Lapham-s/Battle-a; Dr. 13, Azzarello-s/Chiang-a. 4-Wrightson-c 4.00
1-Variant Spectre cover by Neal Adams 5.00
The Spectre: Tales of the Unexpected TPB (2007, $14.99) r/#4-8 15.00

TALES OF THE VAMPIRES (Also see Buffy the Vampire Slayer and related titles)
Dark Horse Comics: 2003 - No. 5, Apr, 2004 ($2.99, limited series)

1-Short stories by Joss Whedon and others. 1-Totleben-c. 3-Powell-c. 4-Edlund-c 3.00
TPB (11/04, $15.95) r/#1-5; afterword by Marv Wolfman 16.00

TALES OF THE WEST (See 3-D...)

TALES OF THE WITCHBLADE
Image Comics (Top Cow Productions): Nov, 1996 - No. 9 ($2.95)

Issue	GD 2.0	VG 4.0	FN 6.0	VF 8.0	VF/NM 9.0	NM- 9.2
1/2	1	2	3	5	7	9
1/2 Gold	2	4	6	9	12	15
1-Daniel-c/a(p)	1	3	4	6	8	10
1-Variant-c by Turner	2	4	6	9	12	15
1-Platinum Edition	3	6	9	16	23	30
2,3						6.00
4-6: 6-Green-c						5.00
7-9: 9-Lara Croft-c						4.00
7-Variant-c by Turner	1	2	3	5	6	8

	GD 2.0	VG 4.0	FN 6.0	VF 8.0	VF/NM 9.0	NM- 9.2

Witchblade: Distinctions (4/01, $14.95, TPB) r/#1-6; Green-c 15.00

TALES OF THE WITCHBLADE COLLECTED EDITION
Image Comics (Top Cow): May, 1998 - No. 2 ($4.95/$5.95, square-bound)

1,2: 1-r/#1,2. 2-($5.95) r/#3,4 6.00

TALES OF THE WIZARD OF OZ (See Wizard of OZ, 4-Color #1308)

TALES OF THE ZOMBIE (Magazine)
Marvel Comics Group: Aug, 1973 - No. 10, Mar, 1975 (75¢, B&W)

Issue	GD 2.0	VG 4.0	FN 6.0	VF 8.0	VF/NM 9.0	NM- 9.2
V1#1-Reprint/Menace #5; origin	5	10	15	32	51	70
2,3: 2-Everett biog. & memorial	4	8	12	26	41	55
V2#1(#4)-Photos & text of James Bond movie "Live & Let Die"	3	6	9	21	32	42
5-10: 8-Kaluta-a	3	6	9	19	29	38
Annual 1(Summer,'75)(#11)-B&W; Everett, Buscema-a	3	6	9	21	32	42

NOTE: *Brother Voodoo app. 2, 5, 6, 10. **Alcala** a-7-9. **Boris** c-1-4. **Colan** a-2r, 6. **Heath** a-5r. **Reese** a-2. **Tuska** a-2r.*

TALES OF THUNDER
Deluxe Comics: Mar, 1985

1-Dynamo, Iron Maiden, Menthor app.; Giffen-a 4.00

TALES OF VOODOO
Eerie Publications: V1#11, Nov, 1968 - V7#6, Nov, 1974 (Magazine)

Issue	GD 2.0	VG 4.0	FN 6.0	VF 8.0	VF/NM 9.0	NM- 9.2
V1#11	7	14	21	48	79	110
V2#1(3/69)-V2#4(9/69)	5	10	15	32	51	70
V3#1-6('70): 4- "Claws of the Cat" redrawn from Climax #1	4	8	12	26	41	55
V4#1-6('71), V5#1-7('72), V6#1-6('73), V7#1-6('74)	4	8	12	26	41	55
Annual 1	4	8	12	28	44	60

NOTE: *Bondage-c-V1#10, V2#4, V3#4.*

TALES OF WELLS FARGO (TV)(See Western Roundup under Dell Giants)
Dell Publishing Co.: No. 876, Feb, 1958 - No. 1215, Oct-Dec, 1961

Issue	GD 2.0	VG 4.0	FN 6.0	VF 8.0	VF/NM 9.0	NM- 9.2
Four Color 876 (#1)-Photo-c	9	18	27	58	99	140
Four Color 968 (2/59), 1023, 1075 (3/60), 1113 (7-9/60)-All photo-c. 1075,1113-Both have variant edition, back-c comic strip	8	16	24	55	93	130
Four Color 1167 (3-5/61), 1215-Photo-c	8	16	24	51	86	120

TALESPIN (Also see Cartoon Tales & Disney's Talespin Limited Series)
Disney Comics: June, 1991 - No. 7, Dec, 1991 ($1.50)

1-7 3.00

TALES TO ASTONISH (Becomes The Incredible Hulk #102 on)
Atlas (MAP No. 1/ZPC No. 2-14/VPI No. 15-21/Marvel No. 22 on: Jan, 1959 - No. 101, Mar, 1968

Issue	GD 2.0	VG 4.0	FN 6.0	VF 8.0	VF/NM 9.0	NM- 9.2
1-Jack Davis-a; monster-c.	164	328	492	1378	2989	4600
2-Ditko flying saucer-c (Martians); #2-4 have sci/fi-c.	63	126	189	510	1105	1700
3,4	46	92	138	352	764	1175
5-Prototype issue (Stone Men); Williamson-a (4 pgs.); Kirby monster-c begin	46	92	138	366	796	1225
6-Prototype issue (Stone Men)	37	74	111	278	602	925
7-Prototype issue (Toad Men)	37	74	111	278	602	925
8-10	35	70	105	254	552	850
11-14,17-20: 13-Swipes story from Menace #8	29	58	87	210	455	700
15-Prototype issue (Electro)	34	68	102	247	536	825
16-Prototype issue (Stone Men) named "Thorr"	31	62	93	225	488	750
21-(7/61)-Hulk prototype	31	62	93	225	488	750
22-26,28-31,33,34	26	52	78	182	391	600
27-1st Ant-Man app. (1/62); last 10¢ issue (see Strange Tales #73,78 & Tales of Suspense #32)	550	1100	1925	5500	11,000	20,000
32-Sandman prototype	27	54	81	189	407	625
35-(9/62)-2nd app. Ant-Man, 1st in costume; begin series & Ant-Man-c	214	428	642	1800	3900	6000
36-3rd app. Ant-Man	82	164	246	664	1432	2200
37,39,40	46	92	138	359	780	1200
38-1st app. Egghead	46	92	138	373	812	1250
41-43	38	76	114	285	618	950
44-Origin & 1st app. The Wasp (6/63)	52	104	156	421	911	1400
45-47	26	52	78	182	391	600
48-Origin & 1st app. The Porcupine	27	54	81	189	407	625
49-Ant-Man becomes Giant Man (11/63)	31	62	93	225	488	750
50,51,53-56,58: 50-Origin/1st app. Human Top (alias Whirlwind). 58-Origin Colossus	17	34	51	114	250	385
52-Origin/1st app. Black Knight (2/64)	21	42	63	146	311	475

Tales to Astonish #82 © MAR

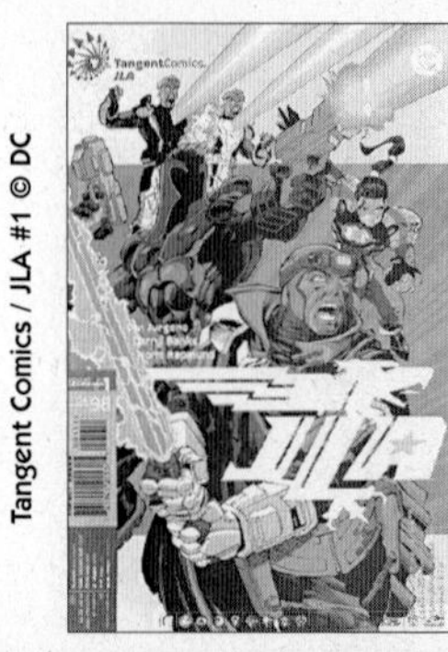

Tangent Comics / JLA #1 © DC

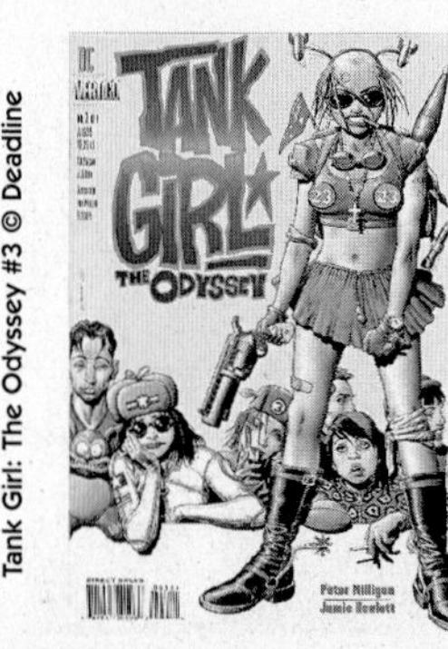

Tank Girl: The Odyssey #3 © Deadline

	GD 2.0	VG 4.0	FN 6.0	VF 8.0	VF/NM 9.0	NM- 9.2
57-Early Spider-Man app. (7/64)	36	72	108	270	585	900
59-Giant Man vs. Hulk feature story (9/64); Hulk's 1st app. this title	32	64	96	232	499	765
60-Giant Man & Hulk double feature begins	23	46	69	164	350	535
61,64-69: 61-All Ditko issue; 1st mailbag. 65-New Giant Man costume. 68-New Human Top costume. 69-Last Giant Man	12	24	36	83	172	260
62-1st app./origin The Leader; new Wasp costume; Hulk pin-up page missing from many copies	14	28	42	93	202	310
63-Origin Leader continues	13	26	39	87	186	285
70-Sub-Mariner & Incredible Hulk begins (8/65)	14	28	42	93	202	310
71-81: 72-Begin alternating-c features w/Sub-Mariner (even #'s) & Hulk (odd #'s). 79-Hulk vs. Hercules-c/story. 81-1st app. Boomerang	7	14	21	49	82	115
82-Iron Man battles Sub-Mariner (1st Iron Man x-over outside The Avengers & TOS); story cont'd from Tales of Suspense #80	9	18	27	58	99	140
83-89,94-99: 97-X-Men cameo (brief)	6	12	18	42	69	95
90-1st app. The Abomination	8	16	24	53	89	125
91-The Abomination debut continues & 1st cover	8	16	24	53	89	125
92-1st Silver Surfer x-over (outside of Fantastic Four, 6/67); 1 panel cameo only	8	16	24	53	89	125
93-Hulk battles Silver Surfer-c/story (1st full x-over)	16	32	48	111	243	375
100-Hulk battles Sub-Mariner full-length story	8	16	24	53	89	125
101-Hulk story cont'd in Incredible Hulk #102; Sub-Mariner story continued in Iron Man & Sub-Mariner #1	8	16	24	56	96	135

NOTE: ***Ayers** c(i)-9-12, 16, 18, 19. **Berg** a-1. **Burgos** a-62-64p. **Buscema** a-85-87p. **Colan** a(p)-70-76, 78-82, 84, 85, 101; c(p)-71-76, 78, 80, 82, 84, 86, 88, 90. **Ditko** a-1, 3-48, 50i, 60-67p; c-2, 7i, 8i, 14i, 17i. **Everett** a-78, 79i, 80-84, 85-90i, 94i, 95, 96; c(i)-79-81, 83, 86, 88. **Forte** a-6. **Kane** a-76, 88-91; c-89, 91. **Kirby** a(p)-1, 5-34-40, 44, 49-51, 68-70, 82, 83; layouts-71-84; c(p)-1, 3-48, 50-70, 72, 73, 75, 77, 78, 79, 81, 85, 90. **Kirby/Ditko** a-7, 8, 12, 13, 50; c-7, 8, 10, 13. **Leiber/Fox** a-47, 48, 50, 51. **Powell** a-65-69p, 73, 74. **Reinman** a-6, 36, 45, 46, 54i, 56-60i.*

TALES TO ASTONISH (2nd Series)
Marvel Comics Group: Dec, 1979 - No. 14, Jan, 1981

	GD	VG	FN	VF	VF/NM	NM-
V1#1-Reprints Sub-Mariner #1 by Buscema	2	4	6	8	11	14
2-14: Reprints Sub-Mariner #2-14	1	2	3	5	6	8

TALES TO ASTONISH
Marvel Comics: V3#1, Oct, 1994 ($6.95, one-shot)

V3#1-Peter David scripts; acetate, painted-c 7.00

TALES TO HOLD YOU SPELLBOUND (See Spellbound)

TALES TO OFFEND
Dark Horse Comics: July, 1997 ($2.95, one-shot)

1-Frank Miller-s/a, EC-style cover 3.50

TALES TOO TERRIBLE TO TELL (Becomes Terrology #10, 11)
New England Comics: Wint, 1989-90 - No. 11, Nov-Dec.1993 ($2.95/$3.50, B&W with card-stock covers)

1-($2.95) Reprints of non-EC pre-code horror; EC-style cover by Bissette 4.00
1-($3.50, 5-6/93) Second printing with alternate cover not by Bissette 4.00
2-8-($3.50) Story reprints, history of the pre-code titles and creators; cover galleries (B&W) inside & on back-c (color) 4.00
9-11-($2.95) 10,11-"Terrology" on cover 4.00

TALEWEAVER
DC Comics (WildStorm): Nov, 2001 - No. 6, Apr, 2002 ($3.50, limited series)

1-6-Philip Tan-a/Leonard Banaag-s. 2-Variant-c by Anacleto 3.50

TALKING KOMICS
Belda Record & Publ. Co.: 1947 (20 pgs, slick-c)

	GD	VG	FN	VF	VF/NM	NM-
Each comic contained a record that followed the story - much like the Golden Record sets. Known titles: Chirpy Cricket, Lonesome Octopus, Sleepy Santa, Grumpy Shark, Flying Turtle, Happy Grasshopper with records...	3	6	9	18	27	35

TALLY-HO COMICS
Swappers Quarterly (Baily Publ. Co.): Dec, 1944

	GD	VG	FN	VF	VF/NM	NM-
nn-Frazetta's 1st work as Giunta's assistant; Man in Black horror story; violence; Giunta-c	50	100	150	315	533	750

TALULLAH (See Comic Books Series I)

TAMMY, TELL ME TRUE
Dell Publishing Co.: No. 1233, 1961

	GD	VG	FN	VF	VF/NM	NM-
Four Color 1233-Movie	6	12	18	42	69	95

TANGENT COMICS
.../ THE ATOM, DC Comics: Dec, 1997 ($2.95, one-shot)
1-Dan Jurgens-s/Jurgens & Paul Ryan-a 3.00

.../ THE BATMAN, DC Comics: Sept, 1998 ($1.95, one-shot)
1-Dan Jurgens-s/Klaus Janson-a 3.00

.../ DOOM PATROL, DC Comics: Dec, 1997 ($2.95, one-shot)
1- Dan Jurgens-s/Sean Chen & Kevin Conrad-a 3.00

.../ THE FLASH, DC Comics: Dec, 1997 ($2.95, one-shot)
1-Todd Dezago-s/Gary Frank & Cam Smith-a 3.00

.../ GREEN LANTERN, DC Comics: Dec, '97 ($2.95, one-shot)
1-James Robinson-s/J.H. Williams III & Mick Gray-a 3.00

.../ JLA, DC Comics: Sept, 1998 ($1.95, one-shot)
1-Dan Jurgens-s/Banks & Rapmund-a 3.00

.../ THE JOKER, DC Comics: Dec, 1997 ($2.95, one-shot)
1-Karl Kesel-s/Matt Haley & Tom Simmons-a 3.00

.../ THE JOKER'S WILD, DC Comics: Sept, 1998 ($1.95, one-shot)
1-Kesel & Simmons-s/Phillips & Rodriguez-a 3.00

.../ METAL MEN, DC Comics: Dec, 1997 ($2.95, one-shot)
1-Ron Marz-s/Mike McKone & Mark McKenna-a 3.00

.../ NIGHTWING, DC Comics: Dec, 1997 ($2.95, one-shot)
1-John Ostrander-s/Jan Duursema-a 3.00

.../ NIGHTWING: NIGHTFORCE, DC Comics: Sept, 1998 ($1.95, one-shot)
1-John Ostrander-s/Jan Duursema-a 3.00

.../ POWERGIRL, DC Comics: Sept, 1998 ($1.95, one-shot)
1-Marz-s/Abell & Vines-a 3.00

.../ SEA DEVILS, DC Comics: Dec, 1997 ($2.95, one-shot)
1-Kurt Busiek-s/Vince Giarrano & Tom Palmer-a 3.00

.../ SECRET SIX, DC Comics: Dec, 1997 ($2.95, one-shot)
1-Chuck Dixon-s/Tom Grummett & Lary Stucker-a 3.00

.../ THE SUPERMAN, DC Comics: Sept, 1998 ($1.95, one-shot)
1-Millar-s/Guice-a 3.00

.../ TALES OF THE GREEN LANTERN, DC Comics: Sept, 1998 ($1.95, one-shot)
1-Story & art by various 3.00

.../ THE TRIALS OF THE FLASH, DC Comics: Sept, 1998 ($1.95, one-shot)
1-Dezago-s/Pelletier & Lanning-a 3.00

.../ WONDER WOMAN DC Comics: Sept, 1998 ($1.95, one-shot),
1-Peter David-s/Unzueta & Mendoza-a 3.00
... Volume One TPB (2007, $19.99) r/The Atom, Metal Men, Green Lantern, The Flash, Sea Devils one-shots; intro and new cover by Jurgens 20.00
... Volume Two TPB (2008, $19.99) r/Batman, Doom Patrol, Joker, Nightwing and Secret Six one-shots; new cover by Jurgens 20.00
... Volume Three TPB (2008, $19.99) r/The Superman, Wonder Woman, Nightwing: Nightforce, The Joker's Wild, The Trials of the Flash, Tales of the Green Lantern, Powergirl, and JLA one-shots; new cover by Jurgens 20.00

TANGENT: SUPERMAN'S REIGN
DC Comics: May, 2008 - No. 12, Apr, 2009 ($2.99, limited series)

1-12-Jurgens-s; Flash & Green Lantern app.; back-up histories of Tangent heroes 3.00
Volume 1 TPB (2009, $19.99) r/#1-6 & Justice League of America #16 20.00
Volume 2 TPB (2009, $19.99) r/#7-12 20.00

TANGLED WEB (See Spider-Man's Tangled Web)

TANK GIRL
Dark Horse Comics: May, 1991 - No. 4, Aug, 1991 ($2.25, B&W, mini-series)

1-Contains Dark Horse trading cards 6.00
2-4 4.00
...: Dark Nuggets (Image Comics, 12/09, $3.99) Martin-s/Dayglo-a 4.00
...: Dirty Helmets (Image Comics, 4/10, $3.99) Martin-s/Dayglo-a 4.00
...: Hairy Heroes (Image Comics, 8/10, $3.99) Martin-s/Dayglo-a 4.00

TANK GIRL: APOCALYPSE
DC Comics: Nov, 1995 - No. 4, Feb, 1996 ($2.25, limited series)

1-4 4.00

TANK GIRL: MOVIE ADAPTATION
DC Comics: 1995 ($5.95, 68 pgs., one-shot)

nn-Peter Milligan scripts 6.00

TANK GIRL: THE GIFTING
IDW Publishing: May, 2007 - No. 4, Aug, 2007 ($3.99, limited series)

1-4: 1-Ashley Wood-a/c; Alan Martin-s; 3 covers 4.00

TANK GIRL: THE ODYSSEYf
DC Comics: May, 1995 - No.4, Oct, 1995 ($2.25, limited series)

1-4: Peter Milligan scripts; Hewlett-a 4.00

Target Comics V2 #1 © NOVP

Tarot: Witch of the Black Rose #4 © Jim Balent

Tarzan #21 © ERB

TANK GIRL: THE ROYAL ESCAPE
IDW Publishing: Mar, 2010 - No. 4, Jun, 2010 ($3.99, limited series)

Issue	GD 2.0	VG 4.0	FN 6.0	VF 8.0	VF/NM 9.0	NM- 9.2
1-4: Alan Martin-s/Rufus Dayglo-a/c						4.00

TANK GIRL 2
Dark Horse Comics: June, 1993 - No. 4, Sept, 1993 ($2.50, lim. series, mature)

Issue	GD 2.0	VG 4.0	FN 6.0	VF 8.0	VF/NM 9.0	NM- 9.2
1-4: Jamie Hewlett & Alan Martin-s/a						4.00
TPB (2/95, $17.95) r/#1-4						18.00

TAPPAN'S BURRO (See Zane Grey & 4-Color #449)

TAPPING THE VEIN (Clive Barker's...)
Eclipse Comics: 1989 - No. 5, 1992 ($6.95, squarebound, mature, 68 pgs.)

Issue	GD 2.0	VG 4.0	FN 6.0	VF 8.0	VF/NM 9.0	NM- 9.2
Book 1-5: 1-Russell-a, Bolton-c. 2-Bolton-a. 4-Die-cut-c						7.00
TPB (2002, $24.95, Checker Book Publ. Group) r/#1-5						25.00

TARANTULA (See Weird Suspense)

TARGET: AIRBOY
Eclipse Comics: Mar, 1988 ($1.95)

Issue	GD 2.0	VG 4.0	FN 6.0	VF 8.0	VF/NM 9.0	NM- 9.2
1						3.00

TARGET COMICS (...Western Romances #106 on)
Funnies, Inc./Novelty Publications/Star Publ.: Feb, 1940 - V10#3 (#105), Aug-Sept, 1949

Issue	GD 2.0	VG 4.0	FN 6.0	VF 8.0	VF/NM 9.0	NM- 9.2
V1#1-Origin & 1st app. Manowar, The White Streak by Burgos, & Bulls-Eye Bill by Everett; City Editor (ends #5), High Grass Twins by Jack Cole (ends #4), T-Men by Joe Simon (ends #9), Rip Rory (ends #4), Fantastic Feature Films by Tarpe Mills (ends #39), & Calling 2-R (ends #14) begin; marijuana use story	459	918	1377	3350	5925	8500
2-Everett-c/a	232	464	696	1485	2543	3600
3,4-Everett, Jack Cole-a	135	270	405	864	1482	2100
5-Origin The White Streak in text; Space Hawk by Wolverton begins (6/40) (see Blue Bolt & Circus)	432	864	1296	3154	5577	8000
6-The Chameleon by Everett begins (7/40, 1st app.); White Streak origin cont'd. in text; early mention of comic collecting in letter column; 1st letter column in comics? (7/40)	226	452	678	1446	2473	3500
7-Wolverton Spacehawk-c/story (Scarce)	975	1950	2919	7100	12,550	18,000
8-Classic sci-fi cover	232	464	696	1485	2543	3600
9,12: 12-(1/41)	142	284	426	909	1555	2200
10-Intro/1st app. The Target (11/40); Simon-c; Spacehawk-s; text piece by Wolverton	258	516	774	1651	2826	4000
11-Origin The Target & The Targeteers	181	362	543	1158	1979	2800
V2#1-Target by Bob Wood; Uncle Sam flag-c	92	184	276	584	1005	1425
2-Ten part Treasure Island serial begins; Harold Delay-a; reprinted in Catholic Comics V3#1-10 (see Key Comics #5)	68	136	204	435	743	1050
3-5: 4-Kit Carter, The Cadet begins	61	122	183	390	670	950
6-9: Red Seal with White Streak in #6-10	58	116	174	371	636	900
10-Classic-c	105	210	315	667	1146	1625
11,12: 12-10-part Last of the Mohicans serial begins; Delay-a	57	114	171	362	619	875
V3#1-3,5-7,9,10: 10-Last Wolverton issue	47	94	141	296	498	700
4-V for Victory-c	60	120	180	381	658	935
8-Hitler, Tojo, Flag-c; 6-part Gulliver Travels serial begins; Delay-a.	82	164	246	528	902	1275
11,12	19	38	57	109	172	235
V4#1-4,7-12: 8-X-Mas-c	14	28	42	78	112	145
5-Classic Statue of Liberty-c	15	30	45	90	140	190
6-Targetoons by Wolverton	15	30	45	90	140	190
V5#1-8	12	24	36	69	97	125
V6#1-4,6-10	12	24	36	67	94	120
5-Classic Tojo hanging/Buy War Bonds WWII-c	20	40	60	114	182	250
V7#1-12	11	22	33	60	83	105
V8#1,3-5,8,9,11,12	10	20	30	56	76	95
2,6,7-Krigstein-a	11	22	33	62	86	110
10-L.B. Cole-c	25	50	75	150	245	340
V9#1,4,6,8,10-L.B. Cole-c	25	50	75	150	245	340
2,3,5,7,9,11, V10#1	10	20	30	56	76	95
12-Classic L.B. Cole-c	37	74	111	222	361	500
V10#2,3-L.B. Cole-c	25	50	75	150	245	340

NOTE: *Certa c-V8#9, 11, 12, V9#5, 9, 11, V10#1.* ***Jack Cole*** *a-1-8.* ***Everett*** *a-1-9; c(signed Blake)-1, 2.* ***Al Fago*** *c-V6#8.* ***Sid Greene*** *c-V2#9, 12, V3#3.* ***Walter Johnson*** *c-V5#6, V6#4.* ***Tarpe Mills*** *a-1-4, 6, 8, 11, V3#1.* ***Rico*** *a-V7#4, 10, V8#5, 6, V9#3; c-V7#6, 8, 10, V8#2, 4, 6, 7.* ***Simon*** *a-1, 2.* ***Bob Wood*** *c-V2#2, 3, 5, 6.*

TARGET: THE CORRUPTORS (TV)
Dell Publishing Co.: No. 1306, Mar-May, 1962 - No. 3, Oct-Dec, 1962
(All have photo-c)

Issue	GD 2.0	VG 4.0	FN 6.0	VF 8.0	VF/NM 9.0	NM- 9.2
Four Color 1306(#1), #2,3	6	12	18	37	59	80

TARGET WESTERN ROMANCES (Formerly Target Comics; becomes Flaming Western Romances #3)
Star Publications: No. 106, Oct-Nov, 1949 - No. 107, Dec-Jan, 1949-50

Issue	GD 2.0	VG 4.0	FN 6.0	VF 8.0	VF/NM 9.0	NM- 9.2
106(#1)-Silhouette nudity panel; L.B. Cole-c	25	50	75	150	245	340
107(#2)-L.B. Cole-c; lingerie panels	22	44	66	132	216	300

TARGITT
Atlas/Seaboard Publ.: March, 1975 - No. 3, July, 1975

Issue	GD 2.0	VG 4.0	FN 6.0	VF 8.0	VF/NM 9.0	NM- 9.2
1-3: 1-Origin; Nostrand-a in all. 2-1st in costume. 3-Becomes Man-Stalker	2	4	6	8	11	14

TAROT: WITCH OF THE BLACK ROSE
Broadsword Comics: Mar, 2000 - Present ($2.95, mature)

Issue	GD 2.0	VG 4.0	FN 6.0	VF 8.0	VF/NM 9.0	NM- 9.2
1-Jim Balent-s/c/a; at least two covers on all issues						30.00
2						15.00
3-20						10.00
21-40						5.00
41-72						3.00

TARZAN (See Aurora, Comics on Parade, Crackajack, DC 100-Page Super Spec., Edgar Rice Burroughs'..., Famous Feature Stories #1, Golden Comics Digest #4, 9, Jeep Comics #1-29, Jungle Tales of..., Limited Collectors' Edition, Popular, Sparkler, Sport Stars #1, Tip Top & Top Comics)

TARZAN
Dell Publishing Co./United Features Synd.: No. 5, 1939 - No. 161, Aug, 1947

Issue	GD 2.0	VG 4.0	FN 6.0	VF 8.0	VF/NM 9.0	NM- 9.2
Large Feature Comic 5('39)-(Scarce)-By Hal Foster; reprints 1st dailies from 1929	200	400	600	1280	2190	3100
Single Series 20('40)-By Hal Foster	129	258	387	826	1413	2000
Four Color 134(2/47)-Marsh-c/a	51	102	153	413	894	1375
Four Color 161(8/47)-Marsh-c/a	44	88	132	330	715	1100

TARZAN (...of the Apes #138 on)
Dell Publishing Co./Gold Key No. 132 on: 1-2/48 - No. 131, 7-8/62; No. 132, 11/62 - No. 206, 2/72

Issue	GD 2.0	VG 4.0	FN 6.0	VF 8.0	VF/NM 9.0	NM- 9.2
1-Jesse Marsh-a begins	96	192	288	778	1689	2600
2	42	84	126	315	683	1050
3-5	29	58	87	210	455	700
6-10: 6-1st Tantor the Elephant. 7-1st Valley of the Monsters	25	50	75	172	369	565
11-15: 11-Two Against the Jungle begins, ends #24. 13-Lex Barker photo-c begin	19	38	57	133	287	440
16-20	16	32	48	107	234	360
21-24,26-30	13	26	39	88	189	290
25-1st "Brothers of the Spear" episode; series ends #156,160,161,196-206	14	28	42	97	211	325
31-40	11	22	33	73	142	210
41-54: Last Barker photo-c	9	18	27	63	112	160
55-60: 56-Eight pg. Boy story	8	16	24	56	96	135
61,62,64-70	7	14	21	48	79	110
63-Two Tarzan stories, 1 by Manning	7	14	21	49	82	115
71-79	6	12	18	42	69	95
80-99: 80-Gordon Scott photo-c begin	6	12	18	39	62	85
100	6	12	18	42	69	95
101-109	6	12	18	37	59	80
110 (Scarce)-Last photo-c	6	12	18	42	69	95
111-120	5	10	15	35	55	75
121-131: Last Dell issue	5	10	15	32	51	70
132-1st Gold Key issue	5	10	15	35	55	75
133-138,140-154	4	8	12	26	41	55
139-(12/63)-1st app. Korak (Boy); leaves Tarzan & gets own book (1/64)	7	14	21	44	72	100
155-Origin Tarzan; text article on Tarzana, CA	5	10	15	32	51	70
156-161: 157-Banlu, Dog of the Arande begins, ends #159, 195. 169-Leopard Girl app.	4	8	12	22	34	45
162,165,168,171 (TV)-Ron Ely photo covers	4	8	12	23	36	48
163,164,166,167,169,170: 169-Leopard Girl app.	3	6	9	21	32	42
172-199,201-206: 178-Tarzan origin-r/#155; Leopard Girl app., also in #179, 190-193	3	6	9	19	29	38
200	4	8	12	22	34	45
Story Digest 1-(6/70, G.K., 148pp.)(scarce)	7	14	21	48	79	110

NOTE: *#162, 165, 168, 171 are TV issues. #1-153 all have* ***Marsh*** *art on Tarzan. #154-161, 163, 164, 166, 167, 172-177 all have* ***Manning*** *art on Tarzan. #178, 202 have* ***Manning*** *Tarzan reprints. No "Brothers of the Spear" in #1-24, 157-159, 162-195. #39-126, 128-156 all have* ***Russ Manning*** *art on "Brothers of the Spear". #196-201, 203-205 all have* ***Manning*** *B.O.T.S. reprints; #25-38, 127 all have Jesse* ***Marsh*** *art on B.O.T.S. #206 has a Marsh B.O.T.S. reprint.* ***Gollub*** *c-8-12.* ***Marsh*** *c-1-7.* ***Doug Wildey*** *a-162, 179-187. Many issues have front and back photo covers.*

TARZAN (Continuation of Gold Key series)

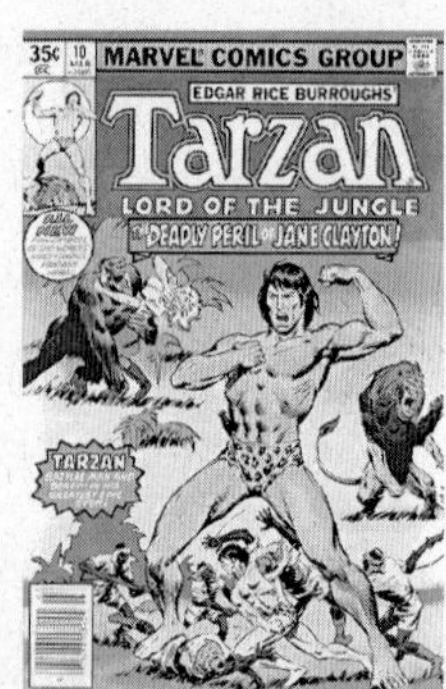

Tarzan (1977 series) #10 © ERB

Taskmaster #4 © MAR

Team America #9 © MAR

GD 2.0 VG 4.0 FN 6.0 VF 8.0 VF/NM 9.0 NM- 9.2

National Periodical Publications: No. 207, Apr, 1972 - No. 258, Feb, 1977

207-Origin Tarzan by Joe Kubert, part 1; John Carter begins (origin); 52 pg. issues thru #209 6 12 18 41 66 90
208,209-(52 pgs.): 208-210-Parts 2-4 of origin. 209-Last John Carter 4 8 12 22 34 45
210-220: 210-Kubert-a. 211-Hogarth, Kubert-a. 212-214: Adaptations from "Jungle Tales of Tarzan". 213-Beyond the Farthest Star begins, ends #218. 215-218,224,225-All by Kubert. 215-part Foster-r. 219-223: Adapts "The Return of Tarzan" by Kubert 3 6 9 14 20 25
221-229: 221-223-Continues adaptation of "The Return of Tarzan". 226-Manning-a 2 4 6 10 14 18
230-DC 100 Page Super Spectacular; Kubert, Kaluta-a(p); Korak begins, ends #234; Carson of Venus app. 4 8 12 26 41 55
231-235-New Kubert-a.: 231-234-(All 100 pgs.)-Adapts "Tarzan and the Lion Man"; Rex, the Wonder Dog r-#232, 233. 235-(100 pgs.)-Last Kubert issue. 4 8 12 24 37 50
236,237,239-258: 240-243 adapts "Tarzan & the Castaways". 250-256 adapts "Tarzan the Untamed." 252,253-r/#213 2 4 6 8 10 12
238-(68 pgs.) 2 4 6 13 18 22
Digest 1-(Fall, 1972, 50¢, 164 pgs.)(DC)-Digest size; Kubert-c; Manning-a 4 8 12 26 41 55
Edgar Rice Burroughs' Tarzan The Joe Kubert Years - Volume One HC (Dark Horse Books, 10/05, $49.95, dust jacket) recolored r/#207-214; intro. by Joe Kubert 50.00
Edgar Rice Burroughs' Tarzan The Joe Kubert Years - Volume Two HC (Dark Horse Books, 2/06, $49.95, dust jacket) recolored r/#215-224; intro. by Joe Kubert 50.00
Edgar Rice Burroughs' Tarzan The Joe Kubert Years - Volume Three HC (Dark Horse Books, 6/06, $49.95, dust jacket) recolored r/#225,227-235; Kubert intro. and sketch pages 50.00

NOTE: ***Anderson*** *a-207, 209, 217, 218.* ***Chaykin*** *a-216.* ***Finlay*** *a(r)-212.* ***Foster*** *strip-r #207-209, 211, 212, 221.* ***Heath*** *a-230i.* ***G. Kane*** *a(r)-232p, 233p.* ***Kubert*** *a-207-225, 227-235, 257r, 258r; c-207-249, 253.* ***Lopez*** *a-250-255p; c-250p, 251, 252, 254.* ***Manning*** *strip-r 230-235, 238.* ***Morrow*** *a-208.* ***Nino*** *a-231-234.* ***Sparling*** *a-230, 231.* ***Starr*** *a-233r.*

TARZAN (Lord of the Jungle)
Marvel Comics Group: June, 1977 - No. 29, Oct, 1979

1-New adaptions of Burroughs stories; Buscema-a 2 4 6 9 13 16
1-(35¢-c variant, limited distribution)(6/77) 4 8 12 24 37 50
2-29: 2-Origin by John Buscema. 9-Young Tarzan. 12-14-Jungle Tales of Tarzan. 25-29-New stories 1 2 3 5 6 8
2-5-(35¢-c variants, limited distribution)(7-10/77) 3 6 9 16 23 30
Annual 1-3: 1-(1977). 2-(1978). 3-(1979) 1 3 4 6 8 10

NOTE: ***N. Adams*** *c-11i, 12i.* ***Alcala*** *a-9i, 10i; c-8i, 9i.* ***Buckler*** *c-25-27p, Annual 3p.* ***John Buscema*** *a-1-3, 4-18p, Annual 1; c-1-7, 8p, 9p, 10, 11p, 12p, 13, 14-19p, 21p, 22, 23p, 24p, 28p, Annual 1.* ***Mooney*** *a-22i.* ***Nebres*** *a-22i.* ***Russell*** *a-29i.*

TARZAN
Dark Horse Comics: July, 1996 - No. 20, Mar, 1998 ($2.95)

1-20: 1-6-Suydam-c 3.00

TARZAN / CARSON OF VENUS
Dark Horse Comics: May, 1998 - No. 4, Aug, 1998 ($2.95, limited series)

1-4-Darko Macan-s/Igor Korday-a 3.00

TARZAN FAMILY, THE (Formerly Korak, Son of Tarzan)
National Periodical Publications: No. 60, Nov-Dec, 1975 - No. 66, Nov-Dec, 1976

60-62-(68 pgs.): 60-Korak begins; Kaluta-r 2 4 6 11 16 20
63-66 (52 pgs.) 2 4 6 9 12 15

NOTE: *Carson of Venus-r 60-65. New John Carter-62-64, 65r, 66r. New Korak-60-66. Pellucidar feature-66. Foster strip r-60(9/4/32-10/16/32), 62(6/29/32-7/31/32), 63(10/11/31-12/13/31).* ***Kaluta*** *Carson of Venus-60-65.* ***Kubert*** *a-61, 64; c-60-64.* ***Manning*** *strip-r 60-62, 64.* ***Morrow*** *a-66r.*

TARZAN/JOHN CARTER: WARLORDS OF MARS
Dark Horse Comics: Jan, 1996 - No. 4, June, 1996 ($2.50, limited series)

1-4: Bruce Jones scripts in all. 1,2,4-Bret Blevins-c/a. 2-(4/96)-Indicia reads #3 3.00

TARZAN KING OF THE JUNGLE (See Dell Giant #37, 51)

TARZAN, LORD OF THE JUNGLE
Gold Key: Sept, 1965 (Giant) (25¢, soft paper-c)

1-Marsh-r 8 16 24 55 93 130

TARZAN: LOVE, LIES AND THE LOST CITY (See Tarzan the Warrior)
Malibu Comics: Aug. 10, 1992 - No. 3, Sept, 1992 ($2.50, limited series)

1-($3.95, 68 pgs.)-Flip book format; Simonson & Wagner scripts 4.00
2,3-No Simonson or Wagner scripts 3.00

TARZAN MARCH OF COMICS (See March of Comics #82, 98, 114, 125, 144, 155, 172, 185, 204, 223, 240, 252, 262, 272, 286, 300, 332, 342, 354, 366)

TARZAN OF THE APES
Metropolitan Newspaper Service: 1934? (Hardcover, 4x12", 68 pgs.)

1-Strip reprints 25 50 75 150 245 340

TARZAN OF THE APES
Marvel Comics Group: July, 1984 - No. 2, Aug, 1984 (Movie adaptation)

1,2: Origin-r/Marvel Super Spec. 4.00

TARZAN'S JUNGLE ANNUAL (See Dell Giants)

TARZAN'S JUNGLE WORLD (See Dell Giant #25)

TARZAN: THE BECKONING
Malibu Comics: 1992 - No. 7, 1993 ($2.50, limited series)

1-7 3.00

TARZAN: THE LOST ADVENTURE (See Edgar Rice Burroughs' ...)

TARZAN-THE RIVERS OF BLOOD
Dark Horse Comics: Nov, 1999 - No. 8 ($2.95, limited series)

1-4: Korday-c/a 3.00

TARZAN THE SAVAGE HEART
Dark Horse Comics: Apr, 1999 - No. 4, July, 1999 ($2.95, limited series)

1-4: Grell-c/a 3.00

TARZAN THE WARRIOR (Also see Tarzan: Love, Lies and the Lost City)
Malibu Comics: Mar, 19, 1992 - No. 5, 1992 ($2.50, limited series)

1-5: 1-Bisley painted pack-c (flip book format-c) 3.00
1-2nd printing w/o flip-c by Bisley 3.00

TARZAN VS. PREDATOR AT THE EARTH'S CORE
Dark Horse Comics: Jan, 1996 - No. 4, June, 1996 ($2.50, limited series)

1-4: Lee Weeks-c/a; Walt Simonson scripts 3.00

TASKMASTER
Marvel Comics: Apr, 2002 - No. 4, July, 2002 ($2.99, limited series)

1-4-Udon Studio-s/a. 1-Iron Man app. 3.00

TASKMASTER
Marvel Comics: Nov, 2010 - No. 4, ($3.99, limited series)

1-4-Van Lente-s/Palo-a; Hydra & A.I.M. app. 4.00

TASMANIAN DEVIL & HIS TASTY FRIENDS
Gold Key: Nov, 1962 (12¢)

1-Bugs Bunny, Elmer Fudd, Sylvester, Yosemite Sam, Road Runner & Wile E. Coyote x-over 13 26 39 86 183 280

TATTERED BANNERS
DC Comics (Vertigo): Nov, 1998 - No. 4, Feb, 1999 ($2.95, limited series)

1-4-Grant & Giffen-s/McMahon-a 3.00

TATTERED MAN
Image Comics: May 2011 ($4.99, one-shot)

1-Justin Gray & Jimmy Palmiotti-s/Norberto Fernandez-a; covers by Fernandez & Conner 5.00

TEAM AMERICA (See Captain America #269)
Marvel Comics Group: June, 1982 - No. 12, May, 1983

1,12: 1-Origin; Ideal Toy motorcycle characters. 12-Double size 4.00
2-11: 9-Iron Man app. 11-Ghost Rider app. 3.00

NOTE: *There are 16 pg. variants known for most issues, possibly all. The only ad is on the inside front cover.*

TEAM HELIX
Marvel Comics: Jan, 1993 - No. 4, Apr, 1993 ($1.75, limited series)

1-4: Teen Super Group. 1,2-Wolverine app. 3.00

TEAM ONE: STORMWATCH (Also see StormWatch)
Image Comics (WildStorm Productions): June, 1995 - No. 2, Aug, 1995 ($2.50, lim. series)

1,2: Steven T. Seagle scripts 3.00

TEAM ONE: WILDC.A.T.S (Also see WildC.A.T.S)
Image Comics (WildStorm Productions): July, 1995 - No. 2, Aug, 1995 ($2.50, lim. series)

1,2: James Robinson scripts 3.00

TEAM 7
Image Comics (WildStorm): Oct, 1994 - No.4, Feb, 1995 ($2.50, limited series)

1-4: Dixon scripts in all, 1-Portacio variant-c 3.00

TEAM 7-DEAD RECKONING
Image Comics (WildStorm): Jan, 1996 - No. 4, Apr, 1996 ($2.50, limited series)

1-4: Dixon scripts in all 3.00

TEAM 7-OBJECTIVE HELL
Image Comics (WildStorm): May, 1995 - No. 3, July, 1995 ($1.95/$2.50, limited series)

Team X 2000 #1 © MAR

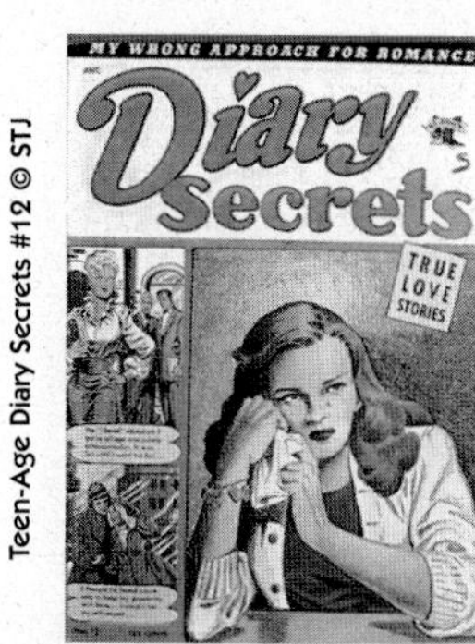

Teen-Age Diary Secrets #12 © STJ

Teenage Mutant Ninja Turtles #14 © Mirage

GD VG FN VF VF/NM NM-
2.0 4.0 6.0 8.0 9.0 9.2

1-($1.95)-Newstand; Dixon scripts in all; Barry Smith-c 3.00
1-3: 1-($2.50)-Direct Market; Barry Smith-c, bound-in card 3.00

TEAM SUPERMAN
DC Comics: July, 1999 ($2.95, one-shot)

1-Jeanty-a/Stelfreeze-c 3.00
...Secret Files 1 (5/98, $4.95)Origin-s and pin-ups of Superboy, Supergirl and Steel 5.00

TEAM TITANS (See Deathstroke & New Titans Annual #7)
DC Comics: Sept, 1992 - No. 24, Sept, 1994 ($1.75/$1.95)

1-Five different #1s exist w/origins in 1st half & the same 2nd story in each: Kilowat, Mirage, Nightrider w/Netzer/Pérez-a, Redwing, & Terra w/part Pérez-p; Total Chaos Pt. 3 4.00
2-24: 2-Total Chaos Pt 6. 11-Metallik app. 24-Zero Hour x-over 3.00
Annual 1,2 ('93, '94, $3.50, 68 pgs.): 2-Elseworlds tory 4.00

TEAM X/TEAM 7
Marvel Comics: Nov, 1996 ($4.95, one-shot)

1 5.00

TEAM X 2000
Marvel Comics: Feb, 1999 ($3.50, one-shot)

1-Kevin Lau-a; Bishop vs. Shi'ar Empire 4.00

TEAM YANKEE
First Comics: Jan, 1989 - No. 6, Feb, 1989 ($1.95, weekly limited series)

1-6 3.00

TEAM YOUNGBLOOD (Also see Youngblood)
Image Comics (Extreme Studios): Sept, 1993 - No. 22, Sept, 1995 ($1.95/$2.50)

1-22: 1-9-Liefeld scripts in all: 1,2,4-6,8-Thibert-c(i). 1-1st app. Dutch & Masada. 3-Spawn cameo. 5-1st app. Lynx. 7,8-Coupons 1 & 4 for Extreme Prejudice #0; Black and White Pt. 4 & 8 by Thibert. 8-Coupon #4 for E. P. #0. 9-Liefeld wraparound-c &(p)/a(p) on Pt. I. 16,17-Bagged w/trading card. 21-Angela & Glory-app. 3.00

TEAM ZERO
DC Comics (WildStorm Productions): Feb, 2006 - No. 6, Jul, 2006 ($2.99, limited series)

1-6-Dixon-s/Mahnke-a 3.00
TPB (2008, $17.99) r/#1-6 18.00

TECH JACKET
Image Comics: Nov, 2002 - No. 6, Apr, 2003 ($2.95)

1-6-Kirkman-s/Su-a 3.00
Vol. 1: Lost and Found TPB (7/03, $12.95, 7-3/4" x 5-1/4") B&W r/#1-6; Valentino intro. 13.00

TEDDY ROOSEVELT & HIS ROUGH RIDERS (See Real Heroes #1)
Avon Periodicals: 1950

1-Kinstler-c; Palais-a; Flag-c 18 36 54 105 165 225

TEDDY ROOSEVELT ROUGH RIDER (See Battlefield #22 & Classics Illustrated Special Issue)

TED MCKEEVER'S METROPOL (See Transit)
Marvel Comics (Epic Comics): Mar, 1991 - No. 12, Mar, 1992 ($2.95, limited series)

V1#1-12: Ted McKeever-c/a/scripts 4.00

TED MCKEEVER'S METROPOL A.D.
Marvel Comics (Epic Comics): Oct, 1992 - No. 3, Dec, 1992 ($3.50, limited series)

V2#1-3: Ted McKeever-c/a/scripts 4.00

TEENA
Magazine Enterprises/Standard Comics No. 20 on: No. 11, 1948 - No. 15, 1948; No. 20, Aug, 1949 - No. 22, Oct, 1950

A-1 #11-Teen-age; Ogden Whitney-c 10 20 30 54 72 90
A-1 #12, 15 9 18 27 47 61 75
20-22 (Standard) 7 14 21 35 43 50

TEEN-AGE BRIDES (True Bride's Experiences #8 on)
Harvey/Home Comics: Aug, 1953 - No. 7, Aug, 1954

1-Powell-a 11 22 33 62 86 110
2-Powell-a 8 16 24 44 57 70
3-7: 3,6-Powell-a 8 16 24 40 50 60

TEEN-AGE CONFESSIONS (See Teen Confessions)

TEEN-AGE CONFIDENTIAL CONFESSIONS
Charlton Comics: July, 1960 - No. 22, 1964

1 4 8 12 24 37 50
2-10 3 6 9 16 23 30
11-22 2 4 6 13 18 22

TEEN-AGE DIARY SECRETS (Formerly Blue Ribbon Comics; becomes Diary Secrets #10 on)
St. John Publishing Co.: No. 4, 9/49; nn (#5), 9/49 - No. 7, 11/49; No. 8, 2/50; No. 9, 8/50

4(9/49)-Oversized; part mag., part comic 42 84 126 265 445 625
nn(#5)(no indicia)-Oversized, all comics; contains sty "I Gave Boys the Green Light."
41 82 123 256 428 600
6,8: (Reg. size) -Photo-c; Baker-a(2-3) in each 42 84 126 265 445 625
7,9-Digest size (Pocket Comics); Baker-a(5); both have same contents; diff.-c
58 116 174 371 636 900

TEEN-AGE DOPE SLAVES (See Harvey Comics Library #1)

TEENAGE HOTRODDERS (Top Eliminator #25 on; see Blue Bird)
Charlton Comics: Apr, 1963 - No. 24, July, 1967

1 6 12 18 37 59 80
2-10 3 6 9 20 30 40
11-24 3 6 9 17 25 32

TEEN-AGE LOVE (See Fox Giants)

TEEN-AGE LOVE (Formerly Intimate)
Charlton Comics: V2#4, July, 1958 - No. 96, Dec, 1973

V2#4 4 8 12 28 44 60
5-9 3 6 9 20 30 40
10(9/59)-20 3 6 9 17 25 32
21-35 3 6 9 16 22 28
36-70 2 4 6 13 18 22
71-79,81,82,85-87,90-96: 61&62-Jonnie Love begins (origin)
2 4 6 10 14 18
80,84,88-David Cassidy pin-ups 3 6 9 14 19 24
83,89: 83-Bobby Sherman pin-up. 89-Danny Bonaduce pin-up
2 4 6 13 18 22

TEENAGE MUTANT NINJA TURTLES (Also see Anything Goes, Donatello, First Comics Graphic Novel, Gobbledygook, Grimjack #26, Leonardo, Michaelangelo, Raphael & Tales Of The...)
Mirage Studios: 1984 - No. 62, Aug, 1993 ($1.50/$1.75, B&W; all 44-52 pgs.)

1-1st printing (3000 copies)-Origin and 1st app. of the Turtles and Splinter. Only printing to have ad for Gobbledygook #1 & 2; Shredder app. (#1-4: 7-1/2x11") (Prices vary widely on this book. In Feb. 2011, a CGC 9.2 copy sold for $3,107. In May 2011, a CGC 9.8 sold for $22,752. Other recent sales include a VF copy for $1553, a CGC 9.6 copy sold for $5975 and a CGC 9.4 copy sold for $3585.)
1-2nd printing (6/84)(15,000 copies) 3 6 9 18 27 35
1-3rd printing (2/85)(36,000 copies) 2 4 6 10 14 18
1-4th printing, new-c (50,000 copies) 6.00
1-5th printing, new-c (8/88-c, 11/88 inside) 5.00
1-Counterfeit. **Note**: Most counterfeit copies have a half inch wide white streak or scratch marks across the center of back cover. Black part of cover is a bluish black instead of a deep black. Inside paper is very white & inside cover is bright white (no value)
2-1st printing (1984; 15,000 copies) 12 24 36 79 160 240
2-2nd printing 2 4 6 9 12 15
2-3rd printing; new Corben-c/a (2/85) 2 4 6 9 12 15
2-Counterfeit with glossy cover stock (no value).
3-1st printing (1985, 44 pgs.) 9 18 27 63 112 160
3-Variant, 500 copies, cover printed at different plant, has 'Laird's Photo' in white rather than light blue 12 24 36 79 160 240
3-2nd printing; contains new back-up story 1 3 4 6 8 10
4-1st printing (1985, 44 pgs.) 6 12 18 42 69 95
4,5-2nd printing (5/87, 11/87) 5.00
5-Fugitoid begins, ends #7; 1st full color-c (1985) 4 8 12 26 41 55
6-1st printing (1986) 3 6 9 17 25 32
6-2nd printing (4/88-c, 5/88 inside) 4.00
7-4 pg. Eastman/Corben color insert; 1st color TMNT (1986, $1.75-c); Bade Biker back-up story 2 4 6 11 16 20
7-2nd printing (1/89) w/o color insert 4.00
8-Cerebus-c/story with Dave Sim-a (1986) 2 4 6 9 12 15
9,10: 9 (9/86)-Rip In Time by Corben 1 3 4 6 8 10
11-15 6.00
16-18: 18-Mark Bode'-a 5.00
18-2nd printing ($2.25, color, 44 pgs.)-New-c 4.00
19-34: 19-Begin $1.75-c. 24-26-Veitch-c/a. 5.00
32-2nd printing ($2.75, 52 pgs., full color) 4.00
35-49,51: 35-Begin $2.00-c. 5.00
50-Features pin-ups by Larsen, McFarlane, Simonson, etc. 6.00
52-62: 52-Begin $2.25-c 5.00
nn (1990, $5.95, B&W)-Movie adaptation 6.00
Book 1,2($1.50, B&W): 2-Corben-c 5.00
...Christmas Special 1 (12/90, $1.75, B&W, 52 pgs.)-Cover title: Michaelangelo Christmas Special; r/Michaelangelo one-shot plus new Raphael story 5.00
... Color Special (11/09, $3.25) full color reprint of #1 4.00

Teenage Mutant Ninja Turtles (2011 series) #1 © Viacom

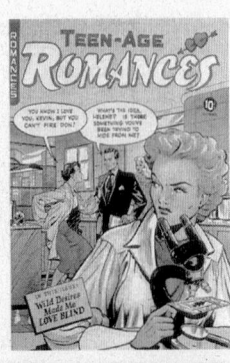

Teen-Age Romances #12 © STJ

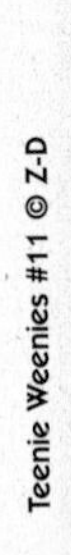
Teenie Weenies #11 © Z-D

	GD 2.0	VG 4.0	FN 6.0	VF 8.0	VF/NM 9.0	NM- 9.2
...Special (The Maltese Turtle) nn (1/93, $2.95, color, 44 pgs.)						5.00
...Special: "Times" Pipeline nn (9/92, $2.95, color, 44 pgs.)-Mark Bode-c/a						5.00
Hardcover ($100)-r/#1-10 plus one-shots w/dust jackets - limited to 1000 w/letter of authenticity						100.00
Softcover ($40)-r/#1-10						40.00

TEENAGE MUTANT NINJA TURTLES
Mirage Studios: V2#1, Oct, 1993 - V2#13, Oct, 1995 ($2.75)

	GD 2.0	VG 4.0	FN 6.0	VF 8.0	VF/NM 9.0	NM- 9.2
V2#1-13: 1-Wraparound-c						4.00

TEENAGE MUTANT NINJA TURTLES
Image Comics (Highbrow Ent.): June, 1996 - No. 23, Oct, 1999 ($1.95-$2.95)

	GD 2.0	VG 4.0	FN 6.0	VF 8.0	VF/NM 9.0	NM- 9.2
1-23: 1-8: Eric Larsen-c(i) on all. 10-Savage Dragon-c/app.						3.00

TEENAGE MUTANT NINJA TURTLES
Mirage Publishing: V4#1, Dec, 2001 - No. 28 ($2.95, B&W)

	GD 2.0	VG 4.0	FN 6.0	VF 8.0	VF/NM 9.0	NM- 9.2
V4#1-9,11-28-Laird-s/a(i)/Lawson-a(p).						3.00
10-($3.95) Splinter dies						4.00

TEENAGE MUTANT NINJA TURTLES
Dreamwave Productions: June 2003 - No. 7 ($2.95, color)

	GD 2.0	VG 4.0	FN 6.0	VF 8.0	VF/NM 9.0	NM- 9.2
1-7-Animated style; Peter David-s/Lesean-a						3.00
Vol. 1 TPB (2003, $9.95) r/#1-4; cover gallery and sketch pages						10.00

TEENAGE MUTANT NINJA TURTLES
IDW Publishing: Aug, 2011 - Present ($3.99)

	GD 2.0	VG 4.0	FN 6.0	VF 8.0	VF/NM 9.0	NM- 9.2
1-Kevin Eastman-s & layouts; four covers by Duncan (each turtle); origin flashback						5.00
1-Variant-c by Eastman						6.00
2-6-Multiple variant covers on each						4.00
... Microseries 1,2 (11/11 - No. 4) 1-Raphael. 2-Michelangelo						4.00

TEENAGE MUTANT NINJA TURTLES (Adventures)
Archie Publications: Jan, 1996 - No. 3, Mar, 1996 ($1.50, limited series)

	GD 2.0	VG 4.0	FN 6.0	VF 8.0	VF/NM 9.0	NM- 9.2
1-3						4.00

TEENAGE MUTANT NINJA TURTLES ADVENTURES (TV)
Archie Comics: 8/88 - No. 3, 12/88; 3/89 - No. 72, Oct, 1995 ($1.00/$1.25/$1.50/$1.75)

	GD 2.0	VG 4.0	FN 6.0	VF 8.0	VF/NM 9.0	NM- 9.2
1-Adapts TV cartoon; not by Eastman/Laird						5.00
2,3 (Mini-series)						4.00
1 (2nd on-going series)						5.00
1-2nd printing						3.00
2-18,20-30: 5-Begins original stories not based on TV. 14-Simpson-a(p). 22-Colan-c/a						4.00
2-11: 2nd printings						3.00
19,20,51-54: 19-1st Mighty Mutanimals (also in #20, 51-54	2	4	6	9	12	15
31-49						5.00
50-Poster by Eastman/Laird	1	2	3	5	7	9
55-60	1	2	3	4	5	7
61-70: 62-w/poster	2	3	4	6	8	10
71	2	4	6	8	10	12
72- Last issue	2	4	6	9	13	16
nn (1990, $2.50)-Movie adaptation						4.00
nn (Spring, 1991, $2.50, 68 pgs.)-(Meet Archie)						5.00
nn (Sum, 1991, $2.50, 68 pgs.)-(Movie II)-Adapts movie sequel						4.00
...Meet the Conservation Corps 1 (1992, $2.50, 68 pgs.)						4.00
...III The Movie: The Turtles are Back...In Time (1993, $2.50, 68 pgs.)						4.00
Special 1,4,5 (Sum/92, Spr/93, Sum/93, 68 pgs.)-1-Bill Wray-c						4.00
Giant Size Special 6 (Fall/93, $1.95, 52 pgs.)						4.00
Special 7-10 (Win/93-Fall//94, 52 pgs.): 9-Jeff Smith-c						4.00

NOTE: *There are 2nd printings of #1-11 w/B&W inside covers. Originals are color.*

TEENAGE MUTANT NINJA TURTLES CLASSICS DIGEST (TV)
Archie Comics: Aug, 1993 - No. 8, Mar, 1995? ($1.75)

	GD 2.0	VG 4.0	FN 6.0	VF 8.0	VF/NM 9.0	NM- 9.2
1-8: Reprints TMNT Advs.						4.00

TEENAGE MUTANT NINJA TURTLES/FLAMING CARROT CROSSOVER
Mirage Publishing: Nov, 1993 - No. 4, Feb, 1994 ($2.75, limited series)

	GD 2.0	VG 4.0	FN 6.0	VF 8.0	VF/NM 9.0	NM- 9.2
1-4: Bob Burden story						4.00

TEENAGE MUTANT NINJA TURTLES PRESENTS: APRIL O'NEIL
Archie Comics: Mar, 1993 - No. 3, June, 1993 ($1.25, limited series)

	GD 2.0	VG 4.0	FN 6.0	VF 8.0	VF/NM 9.0	NM- 9.2
1-3						4.00

TEENAGE MUTANT NINJA TURTLES PRESENTS: DONATELLO AND LEATHERHEAD
Archie Comics: July, 1993 - No. 3, Sept, 1993 ($1.25, limited series)

	GD 2.0	VG 4.0	FN 6.0	VF 8.0	VF/NM 9.0	NM- 9.2
1-3						4.00

TEENAGE MUTANT NINJA TURTLES PRESENTS: MERDUDE
Archie Comics: Oct, 1993 - No. 3, Dec, 1993 ($1.25, limited series)

	GD 2.0	VG 4.0	FN 6.0	VF 8.0	VF/NM 9.0	NM- 9.2
1-3-See Mighty Mutanimals #7 for 1st app. Merdude						4.00

TEENAGE MUTANT NINJA TURTLES/SAVAGE DRAGON CROSSOVER
Mirage Studios: Aug, 1995 ($2.75, one-shot)

	GD 2.0	VG 4.0	FN 6.0	VF 8.0	VF/NM 9.0	NM- 9.2
1						4.00

TEEN-AGE ROMANCE (Formerly My Own Romance)
Marvel Comics (ZPC): No. 77, Sept, 1960 - No. 86, Mar, 1962

	GD 2.0	VG 4.0	FN 6.0	VF 8.0	VF/NM 9.0	NM- 9.2
77-83	5	10	15	32	51	70
84-86-Kirby-c. 84-Kirby-a(2 pgs.). 85,86-(3 pgs.)	6	12	18	39	62	85

TEEN-AGE ROMANCES
St. John Publ. Co. (Approved Comics): Jan, 1949 - No. 45, Dec, 1955 (#3,7,10-18,21 are 1/2 inch taller than other issues)

	GD 2.0	VG 4.0	FN 6.0	VF 8.0	VF/NM 9.0	NM- 9.2
1-Baker-c/a(1)	66	132	198	419	722	1025
2,3: 2-Baker-c/a. 3-Baker-c/a(3)	41	82	123	249	417	585
4,5,7,8-Photo-c; Baker-a(2-3) each	32	64	96	188	307	425
6-Photo-c; part magazine; Baker-a (10/49)	34	68	102	199	325	450
9-Baker-c/a; Kubert-a	39	78	117	240	395	550
10-12,20-Baker-c/a(2-3) each	36	72	108	211	343	475
13-19,21,22-Complete issues by Baker	40	80	120	242	401	560
23-25-Baker-c/a(2-3) each	34	68	102	204	332	460
26,27,33,34,36-40,42: Baker-c/a. 33,40-Signed story by Estrada. 38-Suggestive-c. 42-r/Cinderella Love #9; Last pre-code (3/55)	24	48	72	142	234	325
28-30-No Baker-a	14	28	42	78	112	145
31,32-Baker-c. 31-Estrada-s	20	40	60	118	192	265
35-Baker-c/a (16 pgs.)	24	48	72	142	234	325
41-Baker-c; Infantino-a(r); all stories are Ziff-Davis-r	20	40	60	118	192	265
43-45-Baker-c/a	23	46	69	138	227	315

TEEN-AGE TALK
I.W. Enterprises: 1964

	GD 2.0	VG 4.0	FN 6.0	VF 8.0	VF/NM 9.0	NM- 9.2
Reprint #1	2	4	6	10	14	18
Reprint #5,8,9: 5-r/Hector #? 9-Punch Comics #?; L.B. Cole-c reprint from School Day Romances #1	2	4	6	9	13	16

TEEN-AGE TEMPTATIONS (Going Steady #10 on)(See True Love Pictorial)
St. John Publishing Co.: Oct, 1952 - No. 9, Aug, 1954

	GD 2.0	VG 4.0	FN 6.0	VF 8.0	VF/NM 9.0	NM- 9.2
1-Baker-c/a; has story "Reform School Girl" by Estrada	74	148	222	470	810	1150
2,4-Baker-c	34	68	102	199	325	450
3,5-7,9-Baker-c/a	39	78	117	240	395	550
8-Teenagers smoke reefer; Baker-c/a	42	84	126	265	445	625

NOTE: *Estrada a-1, 3-5.*

TEEN BEAM (Formerly Teen Beat #1)
National Periodical Publications: No. 2, Jan-Feb, 1968

	GD 2.0	VG 4.0	FN 6.0	VF 8.0	VF/NM 9.0	NM- 9.2
2-Superman cameo; Herman's Hermits, Yardbirds, Simon & Garfunkel, Lovin Spoonful, Young Rascals app.; Orlando, Drucker-a(r); Monkees photo-c;	15	30	45	104	227	350

TEEN BEAT (Becomes Teen Beam #2)
National Periodical Publications: Nov-Dec, 1967

	GD 2.0	VG 4.0	FN 6.0	VF 8.0	VF/NM 9.0	NM- 9.2
1-Photos & text only; Monkees photo-c; Beatles, Herman's Hermits, Animals, Supremes, Byrds app.	16	32	48	111	243	375

TEEN COMICS (Formerly All Teen; Journey Into Unknown Worlds #36 on)
Marvel Comics (WFP): No. 21, Apr, 1947 - No. 35, May, 1950

	GD 2.0	VG 4.0	FN 6.0	VF 8.0	VF/NM 9.0	NM- 9.2
21-Kurtzman's "Hey Look"; Patsy Walker, Cindy (1st app.?), Georgie, Margie app.; Syd Shores-a begins, end #23	19	38	57	111	176	240
22,23,25,27,29,31-35: 22-(6/47)-Becomes Hedy Devine #22 (8/47) on?	15	30	45	85	130	175
24,26,28,30-Kurtzman's "Hey Look"	15	30	45	88	137	185

TEEN CONFESSIONS
Charlton Comics: Aug, 1959 - No. 97, Nov, 1976

	GD 2.0	VG 4.0	FN 6.0	VF 8.0	VF/NM 9.0	NM- 9.2
1	8	16	24	51	86	120
2	4	8	12	28	44	60
3-10	4	8	12	22	34	45
11-30	3	6	9	18	27	35
31-Beatles-c	11	22	33	73	142	210
32-36,38-55	3	6	9	15	21	26
37 (1/66)-Beatles Fan Club story; Beatles-c	11	22	33	73	142	210
56-58,60-76,78-97: 89,90-Newton-c	2	4	6	10	14	18
59-Kaluta's 1st pro work? (12/69)	3	6	9	20	30	40
77-Partridge Family poster	3	6	9	14	20	24

TEENIE WEENIES, THE (America's Favorite Kiddie Comic)

Teen Titans #13 © DC

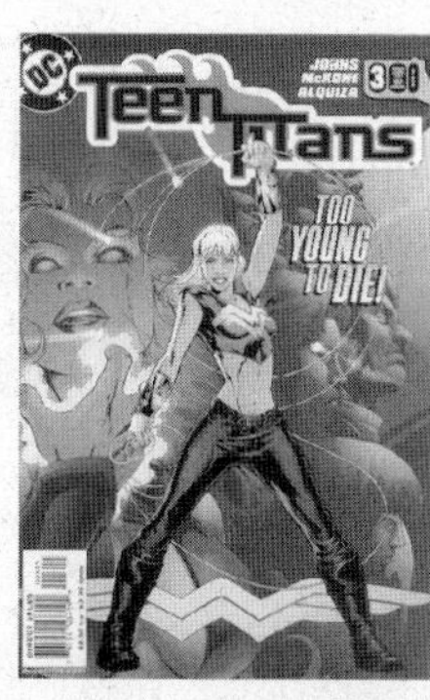

Teen Titans (2003 series) #3 © DC

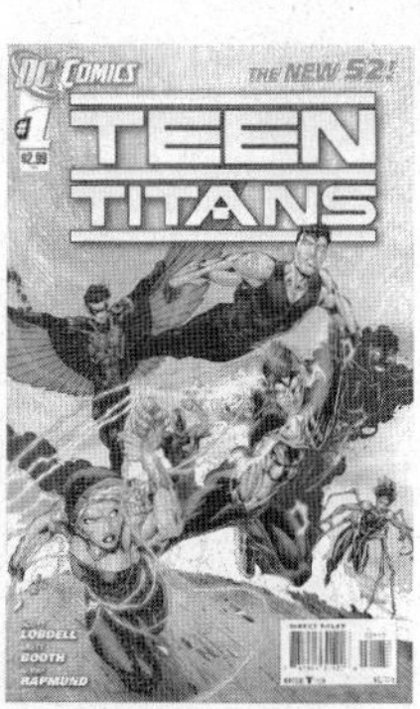

Teen Titans (2011 series) #1 © DC

GD VG FN VF VF/NM NM-
2.0 4.0 6.0 8.0 9.0 9.2

Ziff-Davis Publishing Co.: No. 10, 1950 - No. 11, Apr-May, 1951 (Newspaper reprints)
10,11-Painted-c 20 40 60 114 182 250

TEEN-IN (Tippy Teen)
Tower Comics: Summer, 1968 - No. 4, Fall, 1969
nn(#1, Summer, 1968)(25¢) Has 3 full pg. B&W photos of Sonny & Cher, Donovan and Herman's Hermits; interviews and photos of Eric Clapton, Jim Morrison and others 10 20 30 68 127 185
nn(#2, Spring, 1969),3,4 6 12 18 42 69 95

TEEN LIFE (Formerly Young Life)
New Age/Quality Comics Group: No. 3, Winter, 1945 - No. 5, Fall, 1945 (Teenage magazine)
3-June Allyson photo on-c & story 14 28 42 76 108 140
4-Duke Ellington photo on-c & story 11 22 33 64 90 115
5-Van Johnson, Woody Herman & Jackie Robinson articles; Van Johnson & Woody Herman photos on-c 14 28 42 78 112 145

TEEN LOVE STORIES (Magazine)
Warren Publ. Co.: Sept, 1969 - No. 3, Jan, 1970 (68 pgs., photo covers, B&W)
1-Photos & articles plus 36-42 pgs. new comic stories in all; Frazetta-a 8 16 24 55 93 130
2,3: 2-Anti-marijuana story 6 12 18 37 59 80

TEEN ROMANCES
Super Comics: 1964
10,11,15-17-Reprints 2 4 6 8 11 14

TEEN SECRET DIARY (Nurse Betsy Crane #12 on)
Charlton Comics: Oct, 1959 - No. 11, June, 1961; No. 1, 1972
1 5 10 15 32 51 70
2 3 6 9 21 32 42
3-11 3 6 9 18 27 35
1 (1972)(exist?) 3 6 9 15 21 26

TEEN TALK (See Teen)

TEEN TITANS (See Brave & the Bold #54,60, DC Super-Stars #1, Marvel & DC Present, New Teen Titans, New Titans, Official...Index and Showcase #59)
National Periodical Publications/DC Comics: 1-2/66 - No. 43, 1-2/73; No. 44, 11/76 - No. 53, 2/78
1-(1-2/66)-Titans join Peace Corps; Batman, Flash, Aquaman, Wonder Woman cameos 32 64 96 232 504 775
2 14 28 42 97 211 325
3-5: 4-Speedy app. 10 20 30 69 130 190
6-10: 6-Doom Patrol app.; Beast Boy x-over; readers polled on him joining Titans 8 16 24 56 96 135
11-18: 11-Speedy app. 13-X-Mas-c 7 14 21 46 76 105
19-Wood-i; Speedy begins as regular 7 14 21 48 79 110
20-22: All Neal Adams-a. 21-Hawk & Dove app.; last 12¢ issue. 22-Origin Wonder Girl 9 18 27 63 112 160
23-Wonder Girl dons new costume 6 12 18 37 59 80
24-31: 25-Flash, Aquaman, Batman, Green Arrow, Green Lantern, Superman, & Hawk & Dove guests; 1st app. Lilith who joins T.T. West in #50. 29-Hawk & Dove & Ocean Master app. 30-Aquagirl app. 31-Hawk & Dove app. 5 10 15 32 51 70
32-34,40-43: 34-Last 15¢ issue 3 6 9 20 30 40
35-39-(52 pgs.): 36,37-Superboy-r. 38-Green Arrow/Speedy-r; Aquaman/Aqualad story. 39-Hawk & Dove-r. 4 8 12 23 36 48
44-(11/76) Dr. Light app.; Mal becomes the Guardian 3 6 9 14 20 26
45,47,49,51,52 3 6 9 14 19 24
46,48: 46-Joker's daughter begins (see Batman Family). 48-Intro Bumblebee; Joker's daughter becomes Harlequin 3 6 9 17 25 32
50-1st revival original Bat-Girl; intro. Teen Titans West 3 6 9 18 27 35
53-Origin retold 3 6 9 16 22 28
... Lost Annual 1 (3/08, $4.99) Sixties-era story by Bob Haney; Jay Stephens & Mike Allred-a; President Kennedy app.; Nick Cardy-c and sketch pages 5.00

NOTE: ***Aparo** a-36. **Buckler** c-46-53. **Cardy** c-1-16. **Kane** a(p)-19, 22-24, 39r. **Tuska** a(p)-31, 36, 38, 39. DC Super-Stars #1 (3/76) was released before #44.*

TEEN TITANS (Also see Titans Beat in the Promotional Comics section)
DC Comics: Oct, 1996 - No. 24, Sept, 1998 ($1.95)
1-Dan Jurgens-c/a(p)/scripts & George Pérez-c/a(i) begin; Atom forms new team (Risk, Argent, Prysm, & Joto); 1st app. Loren Jupiter & Omen; no indicia. 1-3-Origin. 4.00
2-24: 4,5-Robin, Nightwing, Supergirl, Capt. Marvel Jr. app. 12-"Then and Now" begins w/original Teen Titans-c/app. 15-Death of Joto. 17-Capt. Marvel Jr. and Fringe join. 19-Millennium Giants x-over. 23,24-Superman app. 3.00
Annual 1 (1997, $3.95)-Pulp Heroes story 4.00

GD VG FN VF VF/NM NM-
2.0 4.0 6.0 8.0 9.0 9.2

TEEN TITANS (Also see Titans/Young Justice: Graduation Day)
DC Comics: Sept, 2003 - No. 100, Late Oct, 2011 ($2.50/$2.99/$3.99)
1-McKone-c/a;Johns-s 5.00
1-Variant-c by Michael Turner 6.00
1-2nd and 3rd printings 3.00
2-Deathstroke app. 5.00
2-2nd printing 3.00
3-15: 4-Impulse becomes Kid Flash. 5-Raven returns. 6-JLA app. 4.00
16-33: 16-Titans go to 31st Century; Legion and Fatal Five app. 17-19-Future Titans app. 21-23-Dr. Light. 24,25-Outsiders #24,25 x-over. 27,28-Liefeld-a. 32,33-Infinite Crisis 3.00
34-49,51-71: 34-One Year Later begins; two covers by Daniel and Benes. 36-Begin $2.99-c. 40-Jericho returns. 42-Kid Devil origin; Snejbjerg-a. 43-Titans East. 48,49-Amazons Attack x-over; Supergirl app. 51-54-Future Titans app. 3.00
50-($3.99) Art by Pérez (4 pgs.), McKone (6 pgs.), Nauck and Green; future Titans app. 4.00
72-88: 72-Begin $3.99-c; Ravager back-up features. 77,78-Blackest Night. 83-87-Coven of Three back-up; Naifeh-a. 88-Nicola Scott-a begins 4.00
89-99-($2.99) 89-Robin (Damian) joins. 93-Solstice app. 98 Superboy-Prime returns 3.00
100-($4.99) Nicola Scott-a; pin-ups by various 5.00
Annual 1 (4/06, $4.99) Infinite Crisis x-over; Benes-c 5.00
Annual 2009 (6/09, $4.99) Deathtrap x-over prelude; McKeever-s 5.00
... And Outsiders Secret Files and Origins 2005 (10/05, $4.99) Daniel-c 5.00
...: Cold Case (2/11, $4.99) Captain Cold and the Rogues app.; Sean Murphy-a 6.00
.../Legion Special (11/04, $3.50) (cont'd from #16) Reis-a; leads into 2005 Legion of Super-Heroes series; LSH preview by Waid & Kitson 4.00
#1/2 (Wizard mail offer) origin of Ravager; Reis-a 8.00
.../Outsiders Secret Files 2003 (12/03, $5.95) Reis & Jimenez-a; pin-ups by various 6.00
...: A Kid's Game TPB (2004, $9.95) r/#1-7; Turner-c from #1; McKone sketch pages 10.00
...: Beast Boys and Girls TPB (2005, $9.99) r/#13-15 and Beast Boy #1-4 10.00
...: Changing of the Guard TPB (2009, $14.99) r/#62-69 15.00
...: Child's Play TPB (2010, $14.99) r/#71-78 15.00
...: Deathtrap TPB (2009, $14.99) r/#70, Annual #1, Titans #12,13, Vigilante #4-6 15.00
...: Family Lost TPB (2004, $9.95) r/#8-12 & #1/2 10.00
...: Life and Death TPB (2006, $14.99) r/#29-33 and pages from Infinite Crisis x-over 15.00
...: On the Clock TPB (2008, $14.99) r/#55-61 15.00
.../ Outsiders: The Death and Return of Donna Troy (2006, $14.99) r/Titans/Young Justice: Graduation Day #1-3, Teen Titans/Outsiders Secret Files 2003 and DC Special: The Return of Donna Troy #1-4; cover gallery 15.00
.../ Outsiders: The Insiders (2006, $14.99) r/Teen Titans/ #24-26 & Outsiders #24,25,28 15.00
...: Ravager - Fresh Hell TPB (2010, $14.99) r/#71-76,79-82 & Faces of Evil: Deathstroke 15.00
... Spotlight: Cyborg TPB (2009, $19.99) r/DC Special: Cyborg #1-6 20.00
... Spotlight: Raven TPB (2008, $14.99) r/DC Special: Raven #1-5 15.00
...: The Future is Now (2005, $9.99) r/#15-23 & Teen Titans/Legion Special 10.00
...: The Hunt For Raven (2011, $17.99) r/#79-87 18.00
...: Titans Around the World TPB (2007, $14.99) r/#34-41 15.00
...: Titans of Tomorrow TPB (2008, $14.99) r/#50-54 15.00

TEEN TITANS (DC New 52)
DC Comics: Nov, 2011 - Present ($2.99)
1-7: 1-Lobdell-s/Booth-a/c; Red Robin assembles a team; Kid Flash, Wonder Girl app. 5-Superboy app. 3.00

TEEN TITANS GO! (Based on Cartoon Network series)
DC Comics: Jan, 2004 - No. 55, Jul, 2008 ($2.25)
1-12,14-55: 1,2-Nauck-a/Bullock-c/J. Torres-s. 8-Mad Mod app. 14-Speedy-c. 28-Doom Patrol app. 31-Nightwing app. 36-Wonder Girl. 38-Mad Mod app.; Clugston-a 3.00
1-(9/04, Free Comic Book Day giveaway) r/#1; 2 bound-in Wacky Packages stickers 4.00
13-($2.95) Bonus pages with Shazam! reprint 4.00
Jam Packed Action (2005, $7.99, digest) adaptations of two TV episodes 8.00
... Vol 1: Truth, Justice, Pizza! (2004, $6.95, digest-size) r/#1-5 7.00
... Vol 2: Heroes on Patrol (2005, $6.99, digest-size) r/#6-10 7.00
... Vol 3: Bring It On! (2005, $6.99, digest-size) r/#11-15 7.00
... Vol 4: Ready For Action! (2006, $6.99, digest-size) r/#16-20 7.00
... Vol 5: On The Move! (2006, $6.99, digest-size) r/#21-25 7.00
... Titans Together TPB (2007, $12.99) r/#26-32 13.00

TEEN TITANS SPOTLIGHT
DC Comics: Aug, 1986 - No. 21, Apr, 1988
1-21: 7-Guice's 1st work at DC. 14-Nightwing; Batman app. 15-Austin-c(i). 18,19-Millennium x-over. 21-($1.00-c)-Original Teen Titans; Spiegle-a 4.00

*Note: **Guice** a-7p, 8p; c-7,8. **Orlando** c/a-11p. **Perez** c-1, 17i, 19. **Sienkiewicz** c-10*

TEEN TITANS YEAR ONE
DC Comics: Mar, 2008 - No. 6, Aug, 2008 ($2.99, limited series)
1-6-The original five form a team; Wolfram-s/Kerschl-a 3.00
TPB (2008, $14.99) r/#1-6; bonus pin-up 15.00

Teen Wolf: Bite Me #1 © MTV

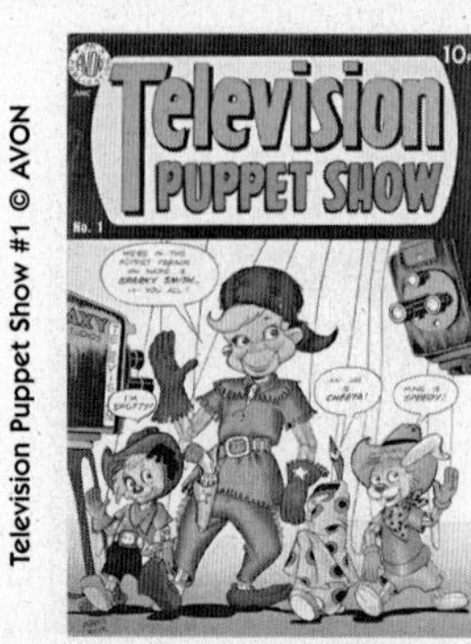

Television Puppet Show #1 © AVON

The Tenth #9 © Tony Daniel

	GD	VG	FN	VF	VF/NM	NM-
	2.0	4.0	6.0	8.0	9.0	9.2

TEEN WOLF: BITE ME (Based on the MTV series)
Image Comics (Top Cow): Sept, 2011 - No. 3, Nov, 2011 ($3.99, limited series)
1-3: 1-Tischman-s/Mooney-a/c 4.00

TEEPEE TIM (...Heap Funny Indian Boy)(Formerly Ha Ha Comics)(Also see "Cookie")
American Comics Group: No. 100, Feb-Mar, 1955 - No. 102, June-July, 1955
100-102 6 12 18 31 38 45

TEGRA JUNGLE EMPRESS (Zegra Jungle Empress #2 on)
Fox Features Syndicate: August, 1948
1-Blue Beetle, Rocket Kelly app.; used in **SOTI**, pg. 31
71 142 213 454 777 1100

TEK JANSEN (See Stephen Colbert's...)

TEKNO COMIX HANDBOOK
Tekno Comix: May, 1996 ($3.95, one-shot)
1-Guide to the Tekno Universe 4.00

TEKNOPHAGE (See Neil Gaiman's...)

TEKNOPHAGE VERSUS ZEERUS
BIG Entertainment: July, 1996 ($3.25, one-shot)
1-Paul Jenkins script 3.25

TEKWORLD (William Shatner's... on-c only)
Epic Comics (Marvel): Sept, 1992 - Aug, 1994 ($1.75)
1-Based on Shatner's novel, TekWar, set in L.A. in the year 2120 4.00
2-24 3.00

TELARA CHRONICLES (Based on the videogame Rift: Planes of Telara)
DC Comics (WildStorm): Jan, 2010; Nov, 2010 - No. 4, Feb, 2011 ($3.99, limited series)
0-(1/10, free) Preview of series 3.00
1-4-Pop Mhan-a/Drew Johnson-c 4.00
TPB (2011, $17.99) r/#0-4; background info on Telara 18.00

TELEVISION (See TV)

TELEVISION COMICS (Early TV comic)
Standard Comics (Animated Cartoons): No. 5, Feb, 1950 - No. 8, Nov, 1950
5-1st app. Willy Nilly 10 20 30 54 72 90
6-8: #6 on inside has #2 on cover 8 16 24 42 54 65

TELEVISION PUPPET SHOW (Early TV comic) (See Spotty the Pup)
Avon Periodicals: 1950 - No. 2, Nov, 1950
1-1st app. Speedy Rabbit, Spotty The Pup 20 40 60 114 182 250
2 14 28 42 82 121 160

TELEVISION TEENS MOPSY (See TV Teens)

TELL IT TO THE MARINES
Toby Press Publications: Mar, 1952 - No. 15, July, 1955
1-Lover O'Leary and His Liberty Belles (with pin-ups), ends #6; Spike & Bat begin, end #6 20 40 60 114 182 250
2-Madame Cobra-c/story 12 24 36 69 97 125
3-5 10 20 30 56 76 95
6-12,14,15: 7-9,14,15-Photo-c 8 16 24 44 57 70
13-John Wayne photo-c 15 30 45 84 127 170
I.W. Reprint #9-r/#1 above 2 4 6 8 10 12
Super Reprint #16(1964)-r/#4 above 2 4 6 8 10 12

TELLOS
Image Comics: May, 1999 - No. 10, Nov, 2000 ($2.50)
1-Dezago-s/Wieringo-a 3.00
1-Variant-c ($7.95) 8.00
2-10: 4-Four covers 3.00
...: Maiden Voyage (3/01, $5.95) Didier Crispeels-a/c 6.00
...: Sons & Moons (2002, $5.95) Nick Cardy-c 6.00
...: The Last Heist (2001, $5.95) Rousseau-a/c 6.00
Prelude ($5.00, AnotherUniverse.com) 5.00
Prologue ($3.95, Dynamic Forces) 4.00
...Collected Edition 1 (12/99, $8.95) r/#1-3 9.00
... Colossal, Vol. 1 TPB (2008, $17.99) r/#1-10, Prelude, Prologue, Scatterjack-s from Section Zero #1, cover gallery, Wieringo sketch pages; Dezago afterword 18.00
...: Kindred Spirits (2/01, $17.95) r/#6-10, Section Zero #1 (Scatterjack-s) 18.00
...: Reluctant Heroes (2/01, $17.95) r/#1-5, Prelude, Prologue; sketchbook 18.00

TEMPEST (See Aquaman, 3rd Series)
DC Comics: Nov, 1996 - No. 4, Feb, 1997 ($1.75, limited series)
1-4: Formerly Aqualad; Phil Jimenez-c/a/scripts in all 3.00

TEMPUS FUGITIVE
DC Comics: 1990 - No. 4, 1991 ($4.95, squarebound, 52 pgs.)
Book 1,2: Ken Steacy painted-c/a & scripts 6.00
Book 3,4-($5.95-c) 6.00
TPB (Dark Horse Comics, 1/97, $17.95) 18.00

TEN COMMANDMENTS (See Moses & the... and Classics Illustrated Special)

TENDER LOVE STORIES
Skywald Publ. Corp.: Feb, 1971 - No. 4, July, 1971 (Pre-code reprints and new stories)
1 (All 25¢, 52 pgs.) 5 10 15 32 51 70
2-4 4 8 12 24 37 50

TENDER ROMANCE (Ideal Romance #3 on)
Key Publications (Gilmour Magazines): Dec, 1953 - No. 2, Feb, 1954
1-Headlight & lingerie panels; B. Baily-c 20 40 60 114 182 250
2-Bernard Baily-c 12 24 36 69 97 125

TENSE SUSPENSE
Fago Publications: Dec, 1958 - No. 2, Feb, 1959
1 10 20 30 56 76 95
2 8 16 24 42 54 65

TEN STORY LOVE (Formerly a pulp magazine with same title)
Ace Periodicals: V29#3, June-July, 1951 - V36#5(#209), Sept, 1956 (#3-6: 52 pgs.)
V29#3(#177)-Part comic, part text; painted-c 15 30 45 90 140 190
4-6(1/52) 10 20 30 58 79 100
V30#1(3/52)-6(1/53) 10 20 30 56 76 95
V31#1(2/53),V32#2(4/53)-6(12/53) 10 20 30 54 72 90
V33#1(1/54)-3(5#54, #195), V34#4(7/54, #196)-6(10/54, #198)
9 18 27 52 69 85
V35#1(12/54, #199)-3(4/55, #201)-Last precode 9 18 27 50 65 80
V35#4-6(9/55, #201-204), V36#1(11/55, #205)-3, 5(9/56, #209)
9 18 27 47 61 75
V36#4-L.B. Cole-a 10 20 30 56 76 95

TENTH, THE
Image Comics: Jan, 1997 - No. 4, June, 1997 ($2.50, limited series)
1-4-Tony Daniel-c/a, Beau Smith-s 5.00
Abuse of Humanity TPB ($10.95) r/#1-4 11.00
Abuse of Humanity TPB (10/98, $11.95) r/#1-4 & 0(8/97) 12.00

TENTH, THE
Image Comics: Sept, 1997 - No. 14, Jan, 1999 ($2.50)
0-(8/97, $5.00) American Ent. Ed. 6.00
1-Tony Daniel-c/a, Beau Smith-s 6.00
2-9: 3,7-Variant-c 4.00
10-14 3.00
...Configuration (8/98) Re-cap and pin-ups 3.00
...Collected Edition 1 ('98, $4.95, square-bound) r/#1,2 5.00
...Special (4/00, $2.95) r/#0 and Wizard #1/2 3.00
Wizard #1/2-Daniel-s/Steve Scott-a 10.00

TENTH, THE (Volume 3) (The Black Embrace)
Image Comics: Mar, 1999 - No. 4, June, 1999 ($2.95)
1-4-Daniel-c/a 3.00
TPB (1/00, $12.95) r/#1-4 13.00

TENTH, THE (Volume 4) (Evil's Child)
Image Comics: Sept, 1999 - No. 4, Mar, 2000 ($2.95, limited series)
1-4-Daniel-c/a 3.00

TENTH, THE (Darkk Dawn)
Image Comics: July, 2005 ($4.99, one-shot)
1-Kirkham-a/Bonny-s 5.00

TENTH, THE : RESURRECTED
Dark Horse Comics: July, 2001 - No. 4, Feb, 2002 ($2.99, limited series)
1-4: 1-Two covers; Daniel-s/c; Romano-a 3.00

10th MUSE
Image Comics (TidalWave Studios): Nov, 2000 - No. 9, Jan, 2002 ($2.95)
1-Character based on wrestling's Rena Mero; regular & photo covers 3.00
2-9: 2-Photo and 2 Lashley covers; flip book Dollz preview. 5-Savage Dragon app.; 2 covers by Lashley and Larsen. 6-Tellos x-over 3.00

TEN WHO DARED (Disney)
Dell Publishing Co.: No. 1178, Dec, 1960
Four Color 1178-Movie, painted-c; cast member photo on back-c

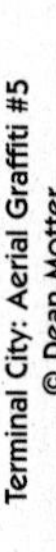
Terminal City: Aerial Graffiti #5 © Dean Motter

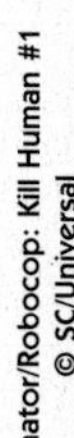
Terminator/Robocop: Kill Human #1 © SC/Universal

Terrific Comics #6 © Continental

	GD 2.0	VG 4.0	FN 6.0	VF 8.0	VF/NM 9.0	NM- 9.2
	7	14	21	48	79	110

TERMINAL CITY
DC Comics (Vertigo): July, 1996 - No. 9, Mar, 1997 ($2.50, limited series)
1-9: Dean Motter scripts, 7,8-Matt Wagner-c 3.00
TPB ('97, $19.95) r/series 20.00

TERMINAL CITY: AERIAL GRAFFITI
DC Comics (Vertigo): Nov, 1997 - No. 5, Mar, 1998 ($2.50, limited series)
1-5: Dean Motter-s/Lark-a/Chiarello-c 3.00

TERMINATOR, THE (See Robocop vs. ... & Rust #12 for 1st app.)
Now Comics: Sept, 1988 - No. 17, 1989 ($1.75, Baxter paper)
1-Based on movie 1 3 4 6 8 10
2-5 6.00
6-11,13-17 4.00
12-($2.95, 52 pgs.)-Intro. John Connor 5.00
Trade paperback (1989, $9.95) 10.00

TERMINATOR, THE
Dark Horse Comics: Aug, 1990 - No. 4, Nov, 1990 ($2.50, limited series)
1-Set 39 years later than the movie 5.00
2-4 4.00

TERMINATOR, THE
Dark Horse Comics: 1998 - No. 4, Dec, 1998 ($2.95, limited series)
1-4-Alan Grant-s/Steve Pugh-a/c 4.00
...Special (1998, $2.95) Darrow-c/Grant-s 4.00

TERMINATOR, THE: ALL MY FUTURES PAST
Now Comics: V3#1, Aug, 1990 - V3#2, Sept, 1990 ($1.75, limited series)
V3#1,2 4.00

TERMINATOR, THE: ENDGAME
Dark Horse Comics: Sept, 1992 - No. 3, Nov, 1992 ($2.50, limited series)
1-3: Guice-a(p); painted-c 4.00

TERMINATOR, THE: HUNTERS AND KILLERS
Dark Horse Comics: Mar, 1992 - No. 3, May, 1992 ($2.50, limited series)
1-3 4.00

TERMINATOR, THE: 1984
Dark Horse Comics: Sept, 2010 - No. 3, Nov, 2010 ($3.50, limited series)
1-3: Takes place during and after the 1st movie; Zack Whedon-s/Andy MacDonald-a 3.50

TERMINATOR, THE: ONE SHOT
Dark Horse Comics: July, 1991 ($5.95, 56 pgs.)
nn-Matt Wagner-a; contains stiff pop-up inside 6.00

TERMINATOR: REVOLUTION (Follows Terminator 2: Infinity series)
Dynamite Entertainment: 2008 - No. 5, 2009 ($3.50, limited series)
1-5-Furman-s/Antonio-a. 1-3-Two covers 3.50

TERMINATOR / ROBOCOP: KILL HUMAN
Dynamite Entertainment: 2011 - No. 4, 2011 ($3.99, limited series)
1-4: 1-Covers by Simonson, Lau & Feister. 2-4-Three covers on each 4.00

TERMINATOR: SALVATION MOVIE PREQUEL
IDW Publishing: Jan, 2009 - No. 4, Apr, 2009 ($3.99, limited series)
1-4: Alan Robinson-a/Dara Naraghi-s 4.00
0-Salvation Movie Preview (4/09) Mariotte-s/Figueroa-a 4.00

TERMINATOR, THE: SECONDARY OBJECTIVES
Dark Horse Comics: July, 1991 - No. 4, Oct, 1991 ($2.50, limited series)
1-4: Gulacy-c/a(p) in all 4.00

TERMINATOR, THE: THE BURNING EARTH
Now Comics: V2#1, Mar, 1990 - V2#5, July, 1990 ($1.75, limited series)
V2#1: Alex Ross painted art (1st published work) 2 4 6 9 12 15
2-5: Ross-c/a in all 1 3 4 6 8 10
Trade paperback (1990, $9.95)-Reprints V2#1-5 12.00
Trade paperback (ibooks, 2003, $17.95)-Digitally remastered reprint 18.00

TERMINATOR, THE: THE DARK YEARS
Dark Horse Comics: Aug, 1999 - No. 4, Dec, 1999 ($2.95, limited series)
1-4-Alan Grant-s/Mel Rubi-a; Jae Lee-c 4.00

TERMINATOR, THE: THE ENEMY FROM WITHIN
Dark Horse Comics: Nov, 1991 - No. 4, Feb, 1992 ($2.50, limited series)
1-4: All have Simon Bisley painted-c 4.00

TERMINATOR, THE: 2029
Dark Horse Comics: Mar, 2010 - No. 3, May, 2010 ($3.50, limited series)
1-3: Kyle Reese before his time-jump to 1984; Zack Whedon-s/Andy MacDonald-a 3.50

TERMINATOR 2: CYBERNETIC DAWN
Malibu: Nov, 1995 - No.4, Feb, 1996; No. 0. Apr, 1996 ($2.50, lim. series)
0 (4/96, $2.95)-Erskine-c/a; flip book w/Terminator 2: Nuclear Twilight 4.00
1-4: Continuation of film. 4.00

TERMINATOR 2: INFINITY
Dynamite Entertainment: 2007 - No. 7 ($3.50)
1-7: 1-Furman-s/Raynor-a; 3 covers. 6,7-Painkiller Jane x-over 3.50

TERMINATOR 2: JUDGEMENT DAY
Marvel Comics: Early Sept, 1991 - No. 3, Early Oct, 1991 ($1.00, lim. series)
1-3: Based on movie sequel; 1-3-Same as nn issues 4.00
nn (1991, $4.95, squarebound, 68 pgs.)-Photo-c 6.00
nn (1991, $2.25, B&W, magazine, 68 pgs.) 4.00

TERMINATOR 2: NUCLEAR TWILIGHT
Malibu: Nov, 1995 - No.4, Feb, 1996; No. 0, Apr, 1996 ($2.50, lim. series)
0 (4/96, $2.95)-Erskine-c/a; flip book w/Terminator 2: Cybernetic Dawn 4.00
1-4:Continuation of film. 4.00

TERMINATOR 3: RISE OF THE MACHINES (... BEFORE THE RISE on cover)
Beckett Comics: July, 2003 - No. 6, Jan, 2004 ($5.95, limited series)
1-6: 1,2-Leads into movie; 2 covers on each. 3-6-Movie adaptation 6.00

TERM LIFE
Image Comics (Shadowline): Jan, 2011 ($16.99, graphic novel)
SC-Lieberman-s/Thornborrow-a/DeStefano-l 17.00

TERRA (See Supergirl {2005 series} #12)
DC Comics: Jan, 2009 - No. 4, Feb, 2009 ($2.99, limited series)
1-4-Conner-a/c. 1,2,4-Power Girl app. 2-4-Geo-Force app. 3.00
TPB (2009, $14.99) r/#1-4 & Supergirl #12 15.00

TERRAFORMERS
Wonder Color Comics: April, 1987 - No. 2, 1987 ($1.95, limited series)
1,2-Kelley Jones-a 3.00

TERRANAUTS
Fantasy General Comics: Aug, 1986 - No. 2, 1986 ($1.75, limited series)
1,2 3.00

TERRA OBSCURA (See Tom Strong)
America's Best Comics: Aug, 2003 - No. 6, Feb, 2004 ($2.95)
1-6-Alan Moore & Peter Hogan-s/Paquette-a 3.00
TPB (2004, $14.95) r/#1-6 15.00

TERRA OBSCURA VOLUME 2 (See Tom Strong)
America's Best Comics: Oct, 2004 - No. 6, May, 2005 ($2.95)
1-6-Alan Moore & Peter Hogan-s/Paquette-a; Tom Strange app. 3.00
TPB (2005, $14.99) r/#1-6 15.00

TERRARISTS
Marvel Comics (Epic): Nov, 1993 - No. 4, Feb, 1994 ($2.50, limited series)
1-4-Bound-in trading cards in all 3.00

TERRIFIC COMICS (Also see Suspense Comics)
Continental Magazines: Jan, 1944 - No. 6, Nov, 1944
1-Kid Terrific; opium story 326 652 978 2282 3991 5700
2-1st app. The Boomerang by L.B. Cole & Ed Wheelan's "Comics" McCormick, called the world's #1 comic book fan begins 236 472 708 1499 2575 3650
3-Diana becomes Boomerang's costumed aide; L.B. Cole-c 232 464 696 1485 2543 3600
4-Classic war-c (Scarce) 423 846 1269 3046 5325 7600
5-The Reckoner begins; Boomerang & Diana by L.B. Cole; Classic Schomburg bondage & hooded vigilante-c (Scarce) 1100 2200 3300 6600 12,500 20,000
6-L.B. Cole-c/a 210 420 630 1334 2292 3250
NOTE: *L.B. Cole a-1, 2(2), 3-6. Fuje a-5, 6. Rico a-2; c-1. Schomburg c-2, 5.*

TERRIFIC COMICS (Formerly Horrific; Wonder Boy #17 on)
Mystery Publ.(Comic Media)/(Ajax/Farrell): No. 14, Dec, 1954; No. 16, Mar, 1955 (No #15)
14-Art swipe/Advs. into the Unknown #37; injury-to-eye-c; pg. 2, panel 5 swiped from Phantom Stranger #4; surrealistic Palais-a; Human Cross story; classic-c 81 162 243 518 884 1250
16-Wonder Boy-c/story (last pre-code) 29 58 87 170 278 385

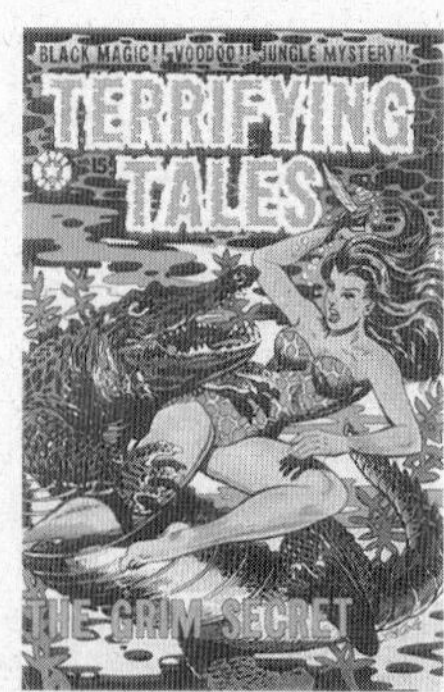

Terrifying Tales #15 © STAR

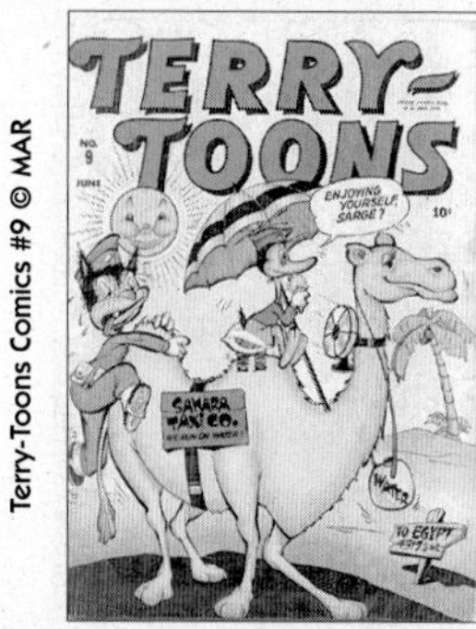

Terry-Toons Comics #9 © MAR

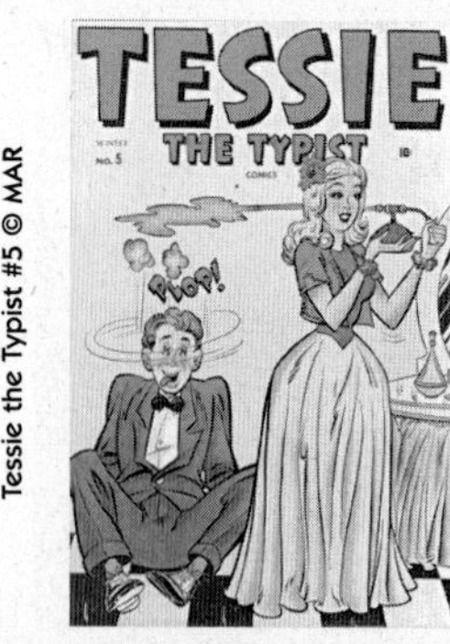

Tessie the Typist #5 © MAR

	GD 2.0	VG 4.0	FN 6.0	VF 8.0	VF/NM 9.0	NM- 9.2

TERRIFYING TALES (Formerly Startling Terror Tales #10)
Star Publications: No. 11, Jan, 1953 - No. 15, Apr, 1954

Issue	GD	VG	FN	VF	VF/NM	NM-
11-Used in **POP**, pgs. 99,100; all Jo-Jo-r	50	100	150	315	533	750
12-Reprints Jo-Jo #19 entirely; L.B. Cole splash	48	96	144	302	514	725
13-All Rulah-r; classic devil-c	54	108	162	343	574	825
14-All Rulah reprints	45	90	135	284	480	675
15-Rulah, Zago-r; used in **SOTI**-r/Rulah #22	45	90	135	284	480	675

NOTE: *All issues have* **L.B. Cole** *covers; bondage covers-No. 12-14.*

TERROR ILLUSTRATED (Adult Tales of...)
E.C. Comics: Nov-Dec, 1955 - No. 2, Spring (April on-c), 1956 (Magazine, 25¢)

Issue	GD	VG	FN	VF	VF/NM	NM-
1-Adult Entertainment on-c	21	42	63	126	206	285
2-Charles Sultan-a	15	30	45	90	140	190

NOTE: **Craig, Evans, Ingels, Orlando** *art in each.* **Crandall** *c-1, 2.*

TERROR INC. (See A Shadowline Saga #3)
Marvel Comics: July, 1992 - No. 13, July, 1993 ($1.75)

Issue	NM-
1-8,11-13: 6,7-Punisher-c/story. 13-Ghost Rider app.	3.00
9,10-Wolverine-c/story	4.00

TERROR INC.
Marvel Comics (MAX): Oct, 2007 - No. 5, Apr, 2008 ($3.99, limited series)

Issue	NM-
1-5: 1-Lapham-s/Zircher-a; origin of Mr. Terror retold	4.00

TERROR INC. - APOCALYPSE SOON
Marvel Comics (MAX): July, 2009 - No. 4, Sept, 2009 ($3.99, limited series)

Issue	NM-
1-4: 1-Lapham-s/Turnbull-a	4.00

TERRORS OF DRACULA (Magazine)
Modern Day Periodical/Eerie Publ.: Vol. 1 #3, May, 1979 - Vol. 3 #2, Sept, 1981 (B&W)

Issue	GD	VG	FN	VF	VF/NM	NM-
Vol. 1 #3 (5/79, 1st issue)	4	8	12	26	41	55
#4(8/79), #5(11/79)	3	6	9	20	30	40
Vol. 2 #1-3: 1-(2/80). 2-(5/80). 3-(8/80)	3	6	9	17	25	32
Vol. 3 #1 (5/81), #2 (9/81)	3	6	9	19	29	38

TERRORS OF THE JUNGLE (Formerly Jungle Thrills)
Star Publications: No. 17, 5/52 - No. 21, 2/53; No. 4, 4/53 - No. 10, 9/54

Issue	GD	VG	FN	VF	VF/NM	NM-
17-Reprints Rulah #21, used in **SOTI**; L.B. Cole bondage-c	49	98	147	309	522	735
18-Jo-Jo-r	38	76	114	226	368	510
19,20(1952)-Jo-Jo-r; Disbrow-a	36	72	108	216	351	485
21-Jungle Jo, Tangi-r; used in **POP**, pg. 100 & color illos.	39	78	117	234	385	535
4-10: All Disbrow-a. 5-Jo-Jo-r. 8-Rulah, Jo-Jo-r. 9-Jo-Jo-r; Disbrow-a; Tangi by Orlando10-Rulah-r	39	78	117	234	385	535

NOTE: **L.B. Cole** *c-all; bondage c-17, 19, 21, 5, 7.*

TERROR TALES (See Beware Terror Tales)

TERROR TALES (Magazine)
Eerie Publications: V1#7, 1969 - V6#6, Dec, 1974; V7#1, Apr, 1976 - V10, 1979? (V1-V6: 52 pgs.; V7 on: 68 pgs.)

Issue	GD	VG	FN	VF	VF/NM	NM-
V1#7	7	14	21	49	82	115
V1#8-11('69): 9-Bondage-c	5	10	15	32	51	70
V2#1-6('70), V3#1-6('71), V4#1-7('72), V5#1-6('73), V6#1-6('74), V7#1,4('76) (no V7#2), V8#1-3('77)	4	8	12	28	44	60
V7#3-(7/76) LSD story-r/Weird V3#5	4	8	12	28	44	60
V9#2-4, V10#1(1/79)	5	10	15	30	48	65

TERROR TITANS
DC Comics: Dec, 2008 - No. 6, May, 2009 ($2.99, limited series)

Issue	NM-
1-6: 1-Ravager and Clock King at the Dark Side Club; Bennett-a. 3-Static app.	3.00
TPB (2009, $17.99) r/#1-6	18.00

TERRY AND THE PIRATES (See Famous Feature Stories, Merry Christmas From Sears Toyland, Popular Comics, Super Book #3,5,9,16,28, & Super Comics)

TERRY AND THE PIRATES
Dell Publishing Co.: 1939 - 1953 (By Milton Caniff)

Issue	GD	VG	FN	VF	VF/NM	NM-
Large Feature Comic 2(1939)	89	178	267	565	970	1375
Large Feature Comic 6(1938)-r/1936 dailies	73	146	219	467	796	1125
Four Color 9(1940)	68	136	204	435	743	1050
Large Feature Comic 27('41), 6('42)	58	116	174	371	636	900
Four Color 44('43)	31	62	93	225	483	740
Four Color 101('45)	19	38	57	132	284	435
Family Album(1942)	20	40	60	114	182	250

TERRY AND THE PIRATES (Formerly Boy Explorers; Long John Silver & the Pirates #30 on) (Daily strip-r) (Two #26's)
Harvey Publications/Charlton No. 26-28: No. 3, 4/47 - No. 26, 4/51; No. 26, 6/55 - No. 28, 10/55

Issue	GD	VG	FN	VF	VF/NM	NM-
3(#1)-Boy Explorers by S&K; Terry & the Pirates begin by Caniff; 1st app. The Dragon Lady	39	78	117	231	378	525
4-S&K Boy Explorers	22	44	66	132	216	300
5-11: 11-Man in Black app. by Powell	13	26	39	72	101	130
12-20: 16-Girl threatened with red hot poker	10	20	30	56	76	95
21-26(4/51)-Last Caniff issue & last pre-code issue	10	20	30	54	72	90
26-28('55)(Formerly This Is Suspense)-No Caniff-a	9	18	27	47	61	75

NOTE: **Powell** *a (Tommy Tween)-5-10, 12, 14; 15-17(1/2 to 2 pgs. each).*

TERRY BEARS COMICS (TerryToons, The... #4)
St. John Publishing Co.: June, 1952 - No. 3, Mar, 1953

Issue	GD	VG	FN	VF	VF/NM	NM-
1-By Paul Terry	10	20	30	54	72	90
2,3	7	14	21	35	43	50

TERRY-TOONS ALBUM (See Giant Comics Edition)

TERRY-TOONS COMICS (1st Series) (Becomes Paul Terry's Comics #85 on; later issues titled "Paul Terry's...")
Timely/Marvel No. 1-59 (8/47)(Becomes Best Western No. 58 on?, Marvel)/ St. John No. 60 (9/47) on: Oct, 1942 - No. 86, May, 1951

Issue	GD	VG	FN	VF	VF/NM	NM-
1 (Scarce)-Features characters that 1st app. on movie screen; Gandy Goose & Sourpuss begin; war-c; Gandy Goose c-1-37	226	452	678	1446	2473	3500
2	74	148	222	470	810	1150
3-5	52	104	156	328	557	785
6,8-10: 9,10-World War II gag-c	39	78	117	240	395	550
7-Hitler, Hirohito, Mussolini-c	90	180	270	576	988	1400
11-20	27	54	81	160	263	365
21-37	20	40	60	114	182	250
38-Mighty Mouse begins (1st app., 11/45); Mighty Mouse-c begin, end #86; Gandy, Sourpuss welcome Mighty Mouse on-c	184	368	552	1168	2009	2850
39-2nd app. Mighty Mouse	57	114	171	362	619	875
40-49: 43-Infinity-c	32	64	96	188	307	425
50-1st app. Heckle & Jeckle (11/46)	50	100	150	315	533	750
51-60: 55-Infinity-c. 60-(9/47)-Atomic explosion panel; 1st St. John issue	18	36	54	103	162	220
61-86: 85,86-Same book as Paul Terry's Comics #85,86 with only a title change; published at same time?	15	30	45	84	127	170

TERRY-TOONS COMICS (2nd Series)
St. John Publishing Co./Pines: June, 1952 - No. 9, Nov, 1953; 1957; 1958

Issue	GD	VG	FN	VF	VF/NM	NM-
1-Gandy Goose & Sourpuss begin by Paul Terry	18	36	54	105	165	225
2	10	20	30	56	76	95
3-9	9	18	27	52	69	85
Giant Summer Fun Book 101,102-(Sum, 1957, Sum, 1958, 25¢, Pines)(TV) CBS Television Presents...; Tom Terrific, Mighty Mouse, Heckle & Jeckle Gandy Goose app.	14	28	42	80	115	150

TERRYTOONS, THE TERRY BEARS (Formerly Terry Bears Comics)
Pines Comics: No. 4, Summer, 1958 (CBS Television Presents...)

Issue	GD	VG	FN	VF	VF/NM	NM-
4	7	14	21	35	43	50

TESSIE THE TYPIST (Tiny Tessie #24; see Comedy Comics, Gay Comics & Joker Comics)
Timely/Marvel Comics (20CC): Summer, 1944 - No. 23, Aug, 1949

Issue	GD	VG	FN	VF	VF/NM	NM-
1-Doc Rockblock & others by Wolverton	97	194	291	621	1061	1500
2-Wolverton's Powerhouse Pepper	43	86	129	271	461	650
3-(3/45)-No Wolverton	22	44	66	132	216	300
4,5,7,8-Wolverton-a. 4-(Fall/45)	36	72	108	211	343	475
6-Kurtzman's "Hey Look", 2 pgs. Wolverton-a	36	72	108	211	343	475
9-Wolverton's Powerhouse Pepper (8 pgs.) & 1 pg. Kurtzman's "Hey Look"	38	76	114	228	369	510
10-Wolverton's Powerhouse Pepper (4 pgs.)	36	72	108	211	343	475
11-Wolverton's Powerhouse Pepper (8 pgs.)	38	76	114	228	369	510
12-Wolverton's Powerhouse Pepper (4 pgs.) & 1 pg. Kurtzman's "Hey Look"	36	72	108	211	343	475
13-Wolverton's Powerhouse Pepper (4 pgs.)	36	72	108	211	343	475
14,15: 14-Wolverton's Dr. Whackyhack (1 pg.); 1-1/2 pgs. Kurtzman's "Hey Look". 15-Kurtzman's "Hey Look" (3 pgs.) & 3 pgs. Giggles 'n' Grins	26	52	78	154	252	350
16-18-Kurtzman's "Hey Look" (?, 2 & 1 pg.)	20	40	60	114	182	250
19-Annie Oakley story (8 pgs.)	15	30	45	84	127	170
20-23: 20-Anti-Wertham editorial (2/49)	14	28	42	82	121	160

NOTE: *Lana app.-21. Millie The Model app.-13, 15, 17, 21. Rusty app.-10, 11, 13, 15, 17.*

TESTAMENT
DC Comics (Vertigo): Feb, 2006 - No. 22, Mar, 2008 ($2.99)

Issue	NM-
1-22: 1-5-Rushkoff-s/Sharp-a. 6,7-Gross & Erskine-a	3.00

The Texan #6 © STJ

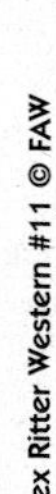
Tex Ritter Western #11 © FAW

Thanos #2 © MAR

	GD 2.0	VG 4.0	FN 6.0	VF 8.0	VF/NM 9.0	NM- 9.2
...: Akedah TPB (2006, $9.99) r/#1-5; Rushkoff intro.						10.00
...: Babel TPB (2007, $12.99) r/#11-16						13.00
...: Exodus TPB (2008, $14.99) r/#17-22						15.00
...: West of Eden TPB (2007, $12.99) r/#6-10; Rushkoff commentary						13.00

TEXAN, THE (Fightin' Marines #15 on; Fightin' Texan #16 on)
St. John Publishing Co.: Aug, 1948 - No. 15, Oct, 1951

	GD	VG	FN	VF	VF/NM	NM-
1-Buckskin Belle	16	32	48	94	147	200
2	10	20	30	58	79	100
3,10: 10-Oversized issue	10	20	30	58	79	100
4,5,7,15-Baker-c/a	21	42	63	126	206	285
6,9-Baker-c	16	32	48	94	147	200
8,11,13,14-Baker-c/a(2-3) each	24	48	72	142	234	325
12-All Matt Baker-c/a; Peyote story	30	60	90	177	289	400

NOTE: ***Matt Baker** c-4-9, 11-15. **Larsen** a-4-6, 8-10, 15. **Tuska** a-1, 2, 7-9.*

TEXAN, THE (TV)
Dell Publishing Co.: No. 1027, Sept-Nov, 1959 - No. 1096, May-July, 1960

	GD	VG	FN	VF	VF/NM	NM-
Four Color 1027 (#1)-Photo-c	8	16	24	55	93	130
Four Color 1096-Rory Calhoun photo-c	8	16	24	51	86	120

TEXAS CHAINSAW MASSACRE
DC Comics (WildStorm): Jan, 2007 - No. 6, Jun, 2007 ($2.99, limited series)

	GD	VG	FN	VF	VF/NM	NM-
1-6: 1-Two covers by Bermejo & Bradstreet; Abnett & Lanning-s						3.00
...: About a Boy #1 (9/07, $2.99) Abnett & Lanning-s/Gomez-a/Robertson-c						3.00
...: Book Two TPB (2009, $14.99) r/one shots & New Line Cinema's Tales of Horror story						15.00
...: By Himself #1 (10/07, $2.99) Abnett & Lanning-s/Craig-a/Robertson-c						3.00
...: Cut! #1 (8/07, $2.99) Pfeiffer-s/Raffaele-a/Robertson-c						3.00
...: Raising Cain 1-3 (7/08 - No. 3, 9/08, $3.50) Bruce Jones-s/Chris Gugliotti-a						3.50

TEXAS JOHN SLAUGHTER (See Walt Disney Presents, 4-Color #997, 1181 & #2)

TEXAS KID (See Two-Gun Western, Wild Western)
Marvel/Atlas Comics (LMC): Jan, 1951 - No. 10, July, 1952

	GD	VG	FN	VF	VF/NM	NM-
1-Origin; Texas Kid (alias Lance Temple) & his horse Thunder begin; Tuska-a	23	46	69	136	223	310
2	13	26	39	74	105	135
3-10	10	20	30	56	76	95

NOTE: ***Maneely** a-1-4; c-1, 3, 5-10.*

TEXAS RANGERS, THE (See Jace Pearson of... and Superior Stories #4)

TEXAS RANGERS IN ACTION (Formerly Captain Gallant or Scotland Yard?)
Charlton Comics: No. 5, Jul, 1956 - No. 79, Aug, 1970 (See Blue Bird Comics)

	GD	VG	FN	VF	VF/NM	NM-
5	8	16	24	44	57	70
6,7,9,10	6	12	18	28	34	40
8-Ditko-a (signed)	10	20	30	54	72	90
11-(68 pg. Giant) Williamson-a (5&8 pgs.); Torres/Williamson-a (5 pgs.)	10	20	30	54	72	90
12,14-20: 12-(68 pg. Giant, 6/58)	5	10	15	23	28	32
13-Williamson-a (5 pgs); Torres, Morisi-a	8	16	24	42	54	65
21-30	3	6	9	16	22	28
31-59: 32-Both 10¢-c & 15¢-c exist	2	4	6	13	18	22
60-Riley's Rangers begin	3	6	9	14	19	24
61-65,68-70	2	4	6	8	11	14
66,67: 66-1st app. The Man Called Loco. 67-Origin	2	4	6	9	13	16
71-79: 77-(4/70) Ditko-c & a (8 pgs.)	1	3	4	6	8	10
76 (Modern Comics-r, 1977)						6.00

TEXAS SLIM (See A-1 Comics)

TEX DAWSON, GUN-SLINGER (Gunslinger #2 on)
Marvel Comics Group: Jan, 1973 (20¢)(Also see Western Kid, 1st series)

	GD	VG	FN	VF	VF/NM	NM-
1-Steranko-c; Williamson-r (4 pgs.); Tex Dawson-r by Romita(3) from 1955; Tuska-r	3	6	9	18	27	35

TEX FARNUM (See Wisco)

TEX FARRELL (...Pride of the Wild West)
D. S. Publishing Co.: Mar-Apr, 1948

	GD	VG	FN	VF	VF/NM	NM-
1-Tex Farrell & his horse Lightning; Shelly-c	15	30	45	88	137	185

TEX GRANGER (Formerly Calling All Boys; see True Comics)
Parents' Magazine Inst./Commended: No. 18, Jun, 1948 - No. 24, Sept, 1949

	GD	VG	FN	VF	VF/NM	NM-
18-Tex Granger & his horse Bullet begin	12	24	36	67	94	120
19	10	20	30	54	72	90
20-24: 22-Wild Bill Hickok story. 23-Vs. Billy the Kid; Tim Holt app.	8	16	24	44	57	70

TEX MORGAN (See Blaze Carson and Wild Western)
Marvel Comics (CCC): Aug, 1948 - No. 9, Feb, 1950

	GD	VG	FN	VF	VF/NM	NM-
1-Tex Morgan, his horse Lightning & sidekick Lobo begin	28	56	84	165	270	375
2	18	36	54	105	165	225
3-6: 3,4-Arizona Annie app.	14	28	42	76	108	140
7-9: All photo-c. 7-Captain Tootsie by Beck. 8-18 pg. story "The Terror of Rimrock Valley"; Diablo app.	18	36	54	105	165	225

NOTE: *Tex Taylor app.-6, 7, 9. **Brodsky** c-6. **Syd Shores** c-2, 5.*

TEX RITTER WESTERN (Movie star; singing cowboy; see Six-Gun Heroes and Western Hero)
Fawcett No. 1-20 (1/54)/Charlton No. 21 on: Oct, 1950 - No. 46, May, 1959 (Photo-c: 1-21)

	GD	VG	FN	VF	VF/NM	NM-
1-Tex Ritter, his stallion White Flash & dog Fury begin; photo front/back-c begin	43	86	129	271	461	650
2	21	42	63	124	202	280
3-5: 5-Last photo back-c	16	32	48	94	147	200
6-10	14	28	42	80	115	150
11-19	10	20	30	58	79	100
20-Last Fawcett issue (1/54)	11	22	33	62	86	110
21-1st Charlton issue; photo-c (3/54)	14	28	42	80	115	150
22-B&W photo back-c begin, end #32	9	18	27	52	69	85
23-30: 23-25-Young Falcon app.	9	18	27	47	61	75
31-38,40-45	8	16	24	42	54	65
39-Williamson-a; Whitman-c (1/58)	9	18	27	47	61	75
46-Last issue	8	16	24	44	57	70

TEX TAYLOR (...The Fighting Cowboy on-c #1, 2)(See Blaze Carson, Kid Colt, Tex Morgan, Wild West, Wild Western, & Wisco)
Marvel Comics (HPC): Sept, 1948 - No. 9, March, 1950

	GD	VG	FN	VF	VF/NM	NM-
1-Tex Taylor & his horse Fury begin	29	58	87	170	278	385
2	15	30	45	88	137	185
3	14	28	42	82	121	160
4-6: All photo-c. 4-Anti-Wertham editorial. 5,6-Blaze Carson app.	15	30	45	92	144	195
7-9: 7-Photo-c;18 pg. Movie-Length Thriller "Trapped in Time's Lost Land!" with sabretoothed tigers, dinosaurs; Diablo app. 8-Photo-c; 18 pg. Movie-Length Thriller "The Mystery of Devil-Tree Plateau!" with dwarf horses, dwarf people & a lost miniature Inca type village; Diablo app. 9-Photo-c; 18 pg. Movie-Length Thriller "Guns Along the Border!" Captain Tootsie by Schreiber; Nimo the Mountain Lion app.	19	38	57	109	172	235

NOTE: ***Syd Shores** c-1-3.*

THANE OF BAGARTH (Also see Hercules, 1967 series)
Charlton Comics: No. 24, Oct, 1985 - No. 25, Dec, 1985

	GD	VG	FN	VF	VF/NM	NM-
24,25-Low print run						6.00

THANOS
Marvel Comics: Dec, 2003 - No. 12, Sept, 2004 ($2.99)

	GD	VG	FN	VF	VF/NM	NM-
1-12: 1-6-Starlin-s/a(p)/Milgrom-i; Galactus app. 7-12-Giffen-s/Lim-a						3.00
Vol. 4: Epiphany TPB (2004, $14.99) r/#1-6						15.00
Vol. 5: Samaritan TPB (2004, $14.99) r/#7-12						15.00

THANOS IMPERATIVE, THE
Marvel Comics: Aug, 2010 - No. 6, Jan, 2011 ($3.99, limited series)

	GD	VG	FN	VF	VF/NM	NM-
1-6-Abnett & Lanning-s/Sepulveda-a; Vision and Silver Surfer app.						4.00
...: Devastation (3/11, $3.99) Sepulveda-a; leads into The Annihilators #1						4.00
...: Ignition (7/10, $3.99) Walker-a; prequel to series						4.00
Thanos Sourcebook (8/10, $3.99) profiles/history of Thanos and Nova Corps members						4.00

THANOS QUEST, THE (See Capt. Marvel #25, Infinity Gauntlet, Iron Man #55, Logan's Run, Marvel Feature #12, Marvel Universe: The End, Silver Surfer #34 & Warlock #9)
Marvel Comics: 1990 - No. 2, 1990 ($4.95, squarebound, 52 pgs.)

	GD	VG	FN	VF	VF/NM	NM-
1,2-Both have Starlin scripts & covers (both printings)	1	2	3	4	5	7
1-(3/2000, $3.99) r/material from #1&2						4.00

THAT DARN CAT (See Movie Comics & Walt Disney Showcase #19)

THAT'S MY POP! GOES NUTS FOR FAIR
Bystander Press: 1939 (76 pgs., B&W)

	GD	VG	FN	VF	VF/NM	NM-
nn-by Milt Gross	32	64	96	192	314	435

THAT WILKIN BOY (Meet Bingo...)
Archie Publications: Jan, 1969 - No. 52, Oct, 1982

	GD	VG	FN	VF	VF/NM	NM-
1-1st app. Bingo's Band, Samantha & Tough Teddy	4	8	12	28	44	60
2-5	3	6	9	16	23	30
6-11	2	4	6	13	18	22
12-26-Giants. 12-No # on-c	3	6	9	14	20	26
27-40(1/77)	2	4	6	8	10	12
41-49	1	2	3	4	5	7
50-52 (low print)	2	4	6	8	10	12

Thief of Thieves #1 © Robert Kirkman

The Thing #20 © MAR

30 Days of Night #1 © Niles & Templesmith

THB
Horse Press: Oct, 1994 - Present ($5.50/$2.50/$2.95, B&W)

	GD 2.0	VG 4.0	FN 6.0	VF 8.0	VF/NM 9.0	NM- 9.2
1 ($5.50) Paul Pope-s/a in all	1	2	3	5	6	8
1 (2nd Printing)-r/#1 w/new material						3.00
2 ($2.50)						5.00
3-5						4.00
69 (1995, no price, low distribution, 12 pgs.)-story reprinted in #1 (2nd Printing)						3.00
Giant THB-($4.95)						5.00
Giant THB 1 V2-(2003, $6.95)						7.00
...M3/THB: Mars' Mightiest Mek #1 (2000, $3.95)						4.00
...6A: Mek-Power #1, 6B: Mek-Power #2, 6C: Mek-Power #3 (2000, $3.95)						4.00
... 6D: Mek-Power #4 (2002, $4.95)						5.00

T.H.E. CAT (TV)
Dell Publishing Co.: Mar, 1967 - No. 4, Oct, 1967 (All have photo-c)

	GD 2.0	VG 4.0	FN 6.0	VF 8.0	VF/NM 9.0	NM- 9.2
1	4	8	12	22	34	45
2-4	3	6	9	17	25	32

THERE'S A NEW WORLD COMING
Spire Christian Comics/Fleming H. Revell Co.: 1973 (35/49¢)

	GD 2.0	VG 4.0	FN 6.0	VF 8.0	VF/NM 9.0	NM- 9.2
nn	2	4	6	10	14	18

THEY ALL KISSED THE BRIDE (See Cinema Comics Herald)

THIEF OF BAGHDAD
Dell Publishing Co.: No. 1229, Oct-Dec, 1961 (one-shot)

	GD 2.0	VG 4.0	FN 6.0	VF 8.0	VF/NM 9.0	NM- 9.2
Four Color 1229-Movie, Crandall/Evans-a, photo-c	7	14	21	44	72	100

THIEF OF THIEVES
Image Comics: Feb, 2012 - Present ($2.99)

	GD 2.0	VG 4.0	FN 6.0	VF 8.0	VF/NM 9.0	NM- 9.2
1,2-Kirkman & Spencer-s/Martinbrough-a/c						3.00

THIMK (Magazine) (Satire)
Counterpoint: May, 1958 - No. 6, May, 1959

	GD 2.0	VG 4.0	FN 6.0	VF 8.0	VF/NM 9.0	NM- 9.2
1	10	20	30	58	79	100
2-6	8	16	24	40	50	60

THING!, THE (Blue Beetle #18 on)
Song Hits No. 1,2/Capitol Stories/Charlton: Feb, 1952 - No. 17, Nov, 1954

	GD 2.0	VG 4.0	FN 6.0	VF 8.0	VF/NM 9.0	NM- 9.2
1-Weird/horror stories in all; shrunken head-c	97	194	291	621	1061	1500
2,3	61	122	183	390	670	950
4-6,8,10: 5-Severed head-c; headlights	55	110	165	352	601	850
7-Injury to eye-c & inside panel	74	148	222	470	810	1150
9-Used in **SOTI**, pg. 388 & illo "Stomping on the face is a form of brutality which modern children learn early"	86	172	258	546	936	1325
11-Necronomicon story; Hansel & Gretel parody; Injury-to-eye panel; Check-a	68	136	204	435	743	1050
12-1st published Ditko-c; "Cinderella" parody; lingerie panels. Ditko-a	97	194	291	621	1061	1500
13,15-Ditko-c/a(3 & 5)	94	188	282	597	1024	1450
14-Extreme violence/torture; Rumpelstiltskin story; Ditko-c/a(4)	95	190	285	603	1039	1475
16-Injury to eye panel	36	72	108	211	343	475
17-Ditko-c; classic parody "Through the Looking Glass"; Powell-r/Beware Terror Tales #1 & recolored	84	168	252	538	919	1300

NOTE: *Excessive violence, severed heads, injury to eye are common No. 5 on.* ***Al Fago*** *c-4.* ***Forgione*** *c-1i, 2, 6, 8, 9. All* ***Ditko*** *issues #14, 15.* ***Giordano*** *a-6.*

THING, THE (See Fantastic Four, Marvel Fanfare, Marvel Feature #11,12, Marvel Two-In-One and Startling Stories:...- Night Falls on Yancy Street)
Marvel Comics Group: July, 1983 - No. 36, June, 1986

	GD 2.0	VG 4.0	FN 6.0	VF 8.0	VF/NM 9.0	NM- 9.2
1-Life story of Ben Grimm; Byrne scripts begin						5.00
2-36: 5-Spider-Man, She-Hulk app.						4.00

NOTE: ***Byrne*** *a-2i, 7; c-1, 7, 36i; scripts-1-13, 19-22.* ***Sienkiewicz*** *c-13i.*

THING, THE (Fantastic Four)
Marvel Comics: Jan, 2006 - No. 8 ($2.99)

	GD 2.0	VG 4.0	FN 6.0	VF 8.0	VF/NM 9.0	NM- 9.2
1-8: 1-DiVito-a/Slott-s. 4-Lockjaw app. 6-Spider-Man app. 8-Super-Hero poker game						3.00
...: Idol of Millions TPB (2006, $20.99) r/#1-8; Divito sketch page						21.00

THING & SHE-HULK: THE LONG NIGHT (Fantastic Four)
Marvel Comics: May, 2002 ($2.99, one-shot)

	GD 2.0	VG 4.0	FN 6.0	VF 8.0	VF/NM 9.0	NM- 9.2
1-Hitch-c/a(pg. 1-25); Reis-a(pg. 26-39); Dezago-s						3.00

THING, THE (From Another World)
Dark Horse Comics: 1991 - No. 2, 1992 ($2.95, mini-series, stiff-c)

	GD 2.0	VG 4.0	FN 6.0	VF 8.0	VF/NM 9.0	NM- 9.2
1,2-Based on Universal movie; painted-c/a						3.00

THING, THE: FREAKSHOW (Fantastic Four)
Marvel Comics: Aug, 2002 - No. 4, Nov, 2002 ($2.99, limited series)

	GD 2.0	VG 4.0	FN 6.0	VF 8.0	VF/NM 9.0	NM- 9.2
1-4-Geoff Johns-s/Scott Kolins-a						3.00
TPB (2005, $17.99) r/#1-4 & Thing & She-Hulk: The Long Night one-shot						18.00

THING FROM ANOTHER WORLD: CLIMATE OF FEAR, THE
Dark Horse Comics: July, 1992 - No. 4, Dec, 1992 ($2.50, mini-series)

	GD 2.0	VG 4.0	FN 6.0	VF 8.0	VF/NM 9.0	NM- 9.2
1-4: Painted-c						3.00

THING FROM ANOTHER WORLD: ETERNAL VOWS
Dark Horse Comics: Dec, 1993 - No. 4, 1994 ($2.50, mini-series)

	GD 2.0	VG 4.0	FN 6.0	VF 8.0	VF/NM 9.0	NM- 9.2
1-4-Gulacy-c/a						3.00

THIRD WORLD WAR
Fleetway Publ. (Quality): 1990 - No. 6, 1991 ($2.50, thick-c, mature)

	GD 2.0	VG 4.0	FN 6.0	VF 8.0	VF/NM 9.0	NM- 9.2
1-6						3.00

THIRTEEN (...Going on 18)
Dell Publishing Co.: 11-1/61-62 - No. 25, 12/67; No. 26, 7/69 - No. 29, 1/71

	GD 2.0	VG 4.0	FN 6.0	VF 8.0	VF/NM 9.0	NM- 9.2
1	6	12	18	41	66	90
2-10	5	10	15	30	48	65
11-25	4	8	12	24	37	50
26-29-r	3	6	9	18	27	35

NOTE: ***John Stanley*** *script-No. 3-29; art?*

13: ASSASSIN
TSR, Inc.: 1990 - No. 8, 1991 ($2.95, 44 pgs.)

	GD 2.0	VG 4.0	FN 6.0	VF 8.0	VF/NM 9.0	NM- 9.2
1-8: Agent 13; Alcala-a(i); Springer back-up-a						4.00

13th SON, THE
Dark Horse Comics: Nov, 2005 - No. 4, Feb, 2006 ($2.99, limited series)

	GD 2.0	VG 4.0	FN 6.0	VF 8.0	VF/NM 9.0	NM- 9.2
1-4-Kelley Jones-s/a/c						3.00

30 DAYS OF NIGHT
Idea + Design Works: June, 2002 - No. 3, Oct, 2002 ($3.99, limited series)

	GD 2.0	VG 4.0	FN 6.0	VF 8.0	VF/NM 9.0	NM- 9.2
1-Vampires in Alaska; Steve Niles-s/Ben Templesmith-a/Ashley Wood-c						30.00
1-2nd printing						10.00
2						12.00
3						10.00
Annual 2004 (1/04, $4.99) Niles-s/art by Templesmith and others						5.00
Annual 2005 (12/05, $7.49) Niles-s/art by Nat Jones						7.50
... 5th Anniversary (10/07 - No. 3, $2.99) reprints original series						3.00
... Sourcebook (10/07, $7.49) Illustrated guide to the 30 Days world						7.50
... Three Tales TPB (7/06, $19.99) r/Annual 2005, ...: Dead Space #1-3, and short story from Tales of Terror (IDW's...)						20.00
Hundred Penny Press: 30 Days of Night #1 (5/11, $1.00) r/#1						3.00
TPB (2003, $17.99) r/#1-3, foreward by Clive Barker; script for #1						18.00
The Complete 30 Days of Night (2004, $75.00, oversized hardcover with slipcase) r/#1-3; prequel; script pages for #1-3; original cover and promotional materials						75.00

30 DAYS OF NIGHT
IDW Publishing: July, 2004 (Free Comic Book Day edition)

	GD 2.0	VG 4.0	FN 6.0	VF 8.0	VF/NM 9.0	NM- 9.2
Previews CSI: Bad Rap; The Shield: Spotlight; 24: One Shot; and 30 Days of Night						3.00

30 DAYS OF NIGHT (Ongoing series)
IDW Publishing: Oct, 2011 - Present ($3.99)

	GD 2.0	VG 4.0	FN 6.0	VF 8.0	VF/NM 9.0	NM- 9.2
1-3-Niles-s/Kieth-a; covers by Kieth and Furno						4.00

30 DAYS OF NIGHT: BEYOND BARROW
IDW Publishing: Sept, 2007 - No. 3, Dec, 2007 ($3.99, limited series)

	GD 2.0	VG 4.0	FN 6.0	VF 8.0	VF/NM 9.0	NM- 9.2
1-3-Niles-s/Sienkiewicz-a/c						4.00

30 DAYS OF NIGHT: BLOODSUCKER TALES
IDW Publishing: Oct, 2004 - No. 8, May, 2005 ($3.99, limited series)

	GD 2.0	VG 4.0	FN 6.0	VF 8.0	VF/NM 9.0	NM- 9.2
1-8-Niles-s/Chamberlain-a; Fraction-s/Templesmith-a/c						4.00
HC (8/05, $49.99) r/#1-8; cover gallery						50.00
SC (8/05, $24.99) r/#1-8; cover gallery						25.00

30 DAYS OF NIGHT: DEAD SPACE
IDW Publishing: Jan, 2006 - No. 3, Mar, 2006 ($3.99, limited series)

	GD 2.0	VG 4.0	FN 6.0	VF 8.0	VF/NM 9.0	NM- 9.2
1-3-Niles and Wickline-s/Milx-a/c						4.00

30 DAYS OF NIGHT: EBEN & STELLA
IDW Publishing: May, 2007 - No. 3, July, 2007 ($3.99, limited series)

	GD 2.0	VG 4.0	FN 6.0	VF 8.0	VF/NM 9.0	NM- 9.2
1-3-Niles and DeConnick-s/Randall-a/c						4.00

30 DAYS OF NIGHT: NIGHT, AGAIN
IDW Publishing: May, 2011 - No. 4, Aug, 2011 ($3.99, limited series)

	GD 2.0	VG 4.0	FN 6.0	VF 8.0	VF/NM 9.0	NM- 9.2
1-4-Lansdale-s/Kieth-a/c						4.00

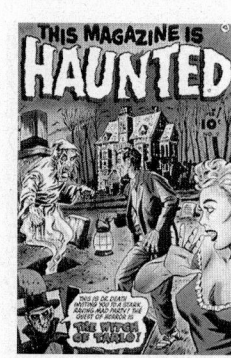

This Magazine is Haunted #9 © FAW

Thor #321 © MAR

Thor #492 © MAR

	GD 2.0	VG 4.0	FN 6.0	VF 8.0	VF/NM 9.0	NM- 9.2
30 DAYS OF NIGHT: RED SNOW						
IDW Publishing: Aug, 2007 - No. 3, Oct, 2007 ($3.99, limited series)						
1-3-Ben Templesmith-s/a/c						4.00
30 DAYS OF NIGHT: RETURN TO BARROW						
IDW Publishing: Mar, 2004 - No. 6, Aug, 2004 ($3.99, limited series)						
1-6-Steve Niles-s/Ben Templesmith-a/c						4.00
TPB (2004, $19.99) r/#1-6; cover gallery						20.00
30 DAYS OF NIGHT: SPREADING THE DISEASE						
IDW Publishing: Dec, 2006 - No. 5, Apr, 2007 ($3.99, limited series)						
1-5: 1-Wickline-s/Sanchez-a. 3-5-Sandoval-a						4.00
30 DAYS OF NIGHT: 30 DAYS 'TIL DEATH						
IDW Publishing: Dec, 2008 - No. 4, Mar, 2009 ($3.99, limited series)						
1-4-David Lapham-s/a; covers by Lapham and Templesmith						4.00
THIRTY SECONDS OVER TOKYO (See American Library)						
THIS IS SUSPENSE! (Formerly Strange Suspense Stories; Strange Suspense Stories #27 on)						
Charlton Comics: No. 23, Feb, 1955 - No. 26, Aug, 1955						
23-Wood-a(r)/A Star Presentation #3 "Dr. Jekyll & Mr. Hyde"; last pre-code issue	24	48	72	140	230	320
24-Censored Fawcett-r; Evans-a (r/Suspense Detective #1)	14	28	42	80	115	150
25,26: 26-Marcus Swayze-a	10	20	30	56	76	95
THIS IS THE PAYOFF (See Pay-Off)						
THIS IS WAR						
Standard Comics: No. 5, July, 1952 - No. 9, May, 1953						
5-Toth-a	14	28	42	82	121	160
6,9-Toth-a	11	22	33	64	90	115
7,8: 8-Ross Andru-c	9	18	27	50	65	80
THIS IS YOUR LIFE, DONALD DUCK (See Donald Duck..., Four Color #1109)						
THIS MAGAZINE IS CRAZY (Crazy #? on)						
Charlton Publ. (Humor Magazines): V3#2, July, 1957 - V4#8, Feb, 1959 (25¢, magazine, 68 pgs.)						
V3#2-V4#7: V4#5-Russian Sputnik-c parody	10	20	30	56	76	95
V4#8-Davis-a (8 pgs.)	11	22	33	60	83	105
THIS MAGAZINE IS HAUNTED (Danger and Adventure #22 on)						
Fawcett Publications/Charlton No. 15(2/54) on: Oct, 1951 - No. 14, 12/53; No. 15, 2/54 - V3#21, Nov, 1954						
1-Evans-a; Dr. Death as host begins	69	138	207	442	759	1075
2,5-Evans-a	46	92	138	290	488	685
3,4: 3-Vampire-c/story	37	74	111	222	361	500
6-9,11,12,14	28	56	84	165	270	375
10-Severed head-c	50	100	150	315	533	750
13-Severed head-c/story	48	96	144	302	514	725
15,20: 15-Dick Giordano-c. 20-Cover is swiped from panel in The Thing #16	23	46	69	136	223	310
16,19-Ditko-c. 19-Injury-to-eye panel; story-r/#1	41	82	123	256	428	600
17-Ditko-c/a(4); blood drainage story	50	100	150	315	533	750
18-Ditko-c/a(1 story); E.C. swipe/Haunt of Fear #5; injury-to-eye panel; reprints "Caretaker of the Dead" from Beware Terror Tales & recolored	42	84	126	267	451	635
21-Ditko-c, Evans-r/This Magazine Is Haunted #1	39	78	117	231	378	525

NOTE: *Baily a-1, 3, 4, 21r/#1.* ***Moldoff*** *c/a-1-13.* ***Powell*** *a-3-5, 11, 12, 17.* ***Shuster*** *a-18-20. Issues 19-21 have reprints which have been recolored from This Magazine is Haunted #1.*

	GD 2.0	VG 4.0	FN 6.0	VF 8.0	VF/NM 9.0	NM- 9.2
THIS MAGAZINE IS HAUNTED (2nd Series) (Formerly Zaza the Mystic; Outer Space #17 on)						
Charlton Comics: V2#12, July, 1957 - V2#16, May, 1958						
V2#12-14-Ditko-c/a in all	41	82	123	249	417	585
15-No Ditko-c/a	14	28	42	82	121	160
16-Ditko-a(4).	29	58	87	170	278	385
THIS MAGAZINE IS WILD (See Wild)						
THIS WAS YOUR LIFE (Religious)						
Jack T. Chick Publ.: 1964 (3 1/2 x 5 1/2", 40 pgs., B&W and red)						
nn, Another version (5x2 3/4", 26 pgs.)	2	4	6	10	14	18
THOR (See Avengers #1, Giant-Size..., Marvel Collectors Item Classics, Marvel Graphic Novel #33, Marvel Preview, Marvel Spectacular, Marvel Treasury Edition, Special Marvel Edition & Tales of Asgard)						
THOR (Journey Into Mystery #1-125, 503-on)(The Mighty Thor #413-490)						
Marvel Comics Group: No. 126, Mar, 1966 - No. 502, Sept, 1996						
126-Thor continues (#125-130 Thor vs. Hercules)	24	48	72	168	359	550
127-130: 127-1st app. Pluto	11	22	33	73	142	210
131-133,135-140: 132-1st app. Ego. 136- Intro. Sif	10	20	30	64	115	165
134-Intro High Evolutionary	10	20	30	67	124	180
141-150: 146-Inhumans begin (early app.), end #151 (see Fantastic Four #45 for 1st app.). 146,147-Origin The Inhumans. 148-1st app. Wrecker. 148,149-Origin Black Bolt in each. 149-Origin Medusa, Crystal, Maximus, Gorgon, Karnak	8	16	24	56	96	135
151-157,159,160: 159-Origin Dr. Blake (Thor) concl.	7	14	21	49	82	115
158-Origin-r/#83; origin Dr. Blake	10	20	30	64	115	165
161,167,170-179: 179-Last Kirby issue	6	12	18	39	62	85
162,168,169-Origin Galactus; Kirby-a	7	14	21	46	76	105
163,164-2nd & 3th brief app. Warlock (Him)	6	12	18	39	62	85
165-1st full app. Warlock (Him) (6/69, see Fantastic Four #67); last 12¢ issue; Kirby-a	8	16	24	55	93	130
166-2nd full app. Warlock (Him); battles Thor	7	14	21	48	79	110
180,181-Neal Adams-a	6	12	18	42	69	95
182-192: 192-Last 15¢ issue	4	8	12	28	44	60
193-(25¢, 52 pgs.); Silver Surfer x-over	11	22	33	73	142	210
194-199	4	8	12	24	37	50
200	5	10	15	30	48	65
201-206,208-224	3	6	9	14	20	25
207-Rutland, Vermont Halloween x-over	3	6	9	16	22	28
225-Intro. Firelord	3	6	9	18	27	35
226-245: 226-Galactus app.	2	4	6	10	14	18
246-250-(Regular 25¢ editions)(4-8/76)	2	4	6	10	14	18
246-250-(30¢-c variants, limited distribution)	4	8	12	24	37	50
251-280: 271-Iron Man x-over. 274-Death of Balder the Brave	1	3	4	6	8	10
260-264-(35¢-c variants, limited distribution)(6-10/77)	4	8	12	24	37	50
281-299: 294-Origin Asgard & Odin	1	2	3	5	6	8
300-(12/80)-End of Asgard; origin of Odin & The Destroyer	2	4	6	8	10	12
301-336: 316-Iron Man x-over. 332,333-Dracula app.						5.00
337-Simonson-c/a begins, ends #382; Beta Ray Bill becomes new Thor	2	4	6	10	14	18
338-340: Beta Ray Bill app. 340-Donald Blake returns as Thor						6.00
341-373,375-381,383: 341-Clark Kent & Lois Lane cameo. 373-X-Factor tie-in						4.00
374-Mutant Massacre; X-Factor app.						5.00
382-($1.25)-Anniversary issue; last Simonson-a						6.00
384-Intro. new Thor						6.00
385-399,401-410,413-428: 385-Hulk x-over. 391-Spider-Man x-over; 1st Eric Masterson. 395-Intro Earth Force. 408-Eric Masterson becomes Thor. 427,428-Excalibur x-over						4.00
400,411: 400-($1.75, 68 pgs.)-Origin Loki. 411-Intro New Warriors (appears in costume in last panel); Juggernaut-c/story						6.00
412-1st full app. New Warriors (Marvel Boy, Kid Nova, Namorita, Night Thrasher, Firestar & Speedball)	1	2	3	4	5	7
429-431,434-443: 429,430-Ghost Rider x-over. 434-Capt. America x-over. 437-Thor vs. Quasar; Hercules app.;Tales of Asgard back-up stories begin. 443-Dr. Strange & Silver Surfer x-over; last $1.00-c						3.00
432,433: 432-(52 pgs.)-Thor's 350th issue (vs. Loki); reprints origin & 1st app. from Journey into Mystery #83. 433-Intro new Thor						4.00
444-449,451-473: 448-Spider-Man-c/story. 455,456-Dr. Strange back-up. 457-Old Thor returns (3 pgs.). 459-Intro Thunderstrike. 460-Starlin scripts begin. 465-Super Skrull app. 466-Drax app. 469,470-Infinity Watch x-over. 472-Intro the Godlings						3.00
450-($2.50, 68 pgs.)-Flip-book format; r/story JIM #85 (1st Loki) plus-c plus a gallery of past-c; gatefold-c						4.00
474,476-481,483-499: 474-Begin $1.50-c; bound-in trading cards. 490-The Absorbing Man app. 491-Warren Ellis scripts begins, ends #494; Deodato-c/a begins. 492-Reintro The Enchantress; Beta Ray Bill dies. 495-Messner-Loebs scripts begin; Isherwood-c/a						3.00
475 ($2.00, 52 pgs.)-Regular edition						4.00
475 ($2.50, 52 pgs.)-Collectors edition w/foil embossed-c						5.00
482 ($2.95, 84 pgs.)-400th Thor issue						5.00
500 ($2.50)-Double-size; wraparound-c; Deodato-c/a; Dr. Strange app.						5.00
501-Reintro Red Norvell						4.00
502-Onslaught tie-in; Red Norvell, Jane Foster & Hela app.						5.00
600-up (See Thor 2007 series)						
Special 2(9/66)-(See Journey Into Mystery for 1st annual)	10	20	30	66	121	175
Special 2 (2nd printing, 1994)	2	4	6	8	10	12
King Size Special 3(1/71)	4	8	12	24	37	50
Special 4(12/71)-r/Thor #131,132 & JIM #113	3	6	9	20	30	40
Annual 5,6: 5(11/76). 6(10/77)-Guardians of the Galaxy app.	2	4	6	11	16	20
Annual 7,8: 7(1978). 8(1979)-Thor vs. Zeus-c/story	2	4	6	8	10	12

Thor V2 #39 © MAR

Thor #615 © MAR

Thor: Son of Asgard #12 © MAR

Annual 9-12: 9('81). 10('82). 11('83). 12('84) 6.00
Annual 13-19('85-'94, 68 pgs.):14-Atlantis Attacks. 16-3 pg. origin; Guardians of the Galaxy x-over.18-Polybagged w/card 4.00
...Alone Against the Celestials nn (6/92, $5.95)-r/Thor #387-389 6.00
...Legends Vol. 2: Walter Simonson Book 2 TPB (2003, $24.99) r/#349-355,357-359 25.00
...Legends Vol. 3: Walter Simonson Book 3 TPB (2004, $24.99) r/#360-369 25.00
...: The Eternals Saga TPB (2006, $24.99) r/#283-291 & Annual #7; profile pages 25.00
...: The Eternals Saga Vol. 2 TPB ('07, $24.99) r/#292-301; Thomas & Gruenwald essays 25.00
... Visionaries: Mike Deodato Jr. TPB (2004, $19.99) r/#491-494,498-500 20.00
... Visionaries: Walter Simonson (Vol. 1) TPB (5/01, $24.95) r/#337-348 25.00
... Visionaries: Walter Simonson Vol. 4 TPB (2007, $24.99) r/#371-373 & Balder the Brave #1-4 25.00
... Visionaries: Walter Simonson Vol. 5 TPB (2008, $24.95) r/#375-382 25.00
...: Worldengine (8/96, $9.95)-r/#491-494; Deodato-c/a; story & new intermission by Warren Ellis 10.00

NOTE: ***Neal Adams*** *a-180,181; c-179-181.* ***Austin*** *a-342i, 346i; c-312i.* ***Buscema*** *a(p)-178, 182-213, 215-226, 231-238, 241-253, 254r, 256-259, 272-278, 283-285, 370, Annual 6, 8, 11i; c(p)-175, 182-196, 198-200, 202-204, 206, 211, 212, 215, 219, 221, 226, 256, 259, 261, 262, 272-278, 283, 289, 370, Annual 6.* ***Everett*** *a(i)-143, 170-175; c(i)-171, 172, 174, 176, 241.* ***Gil Kane*** *a-318p; c(p)-201, 205, 207-210, 216, 220, 222, 223, 231, 233-240, 242, 243, 318.* ***Kirby*** *a(p)-126-177, 179, 194r, 254r; c(p)-126-169, 171-174, 176-178, 249-253, 255, 257, 258, Annual 5, Special 2-4.* ***Mooney*** *a(i)-201, 204, 214-216, 218, 322i, 324i, 325i, 327i.* ***Sienkiewicz*** *c-332, 333, 335.* ***Simonson*** *a-260-271p, 337-354, 357-367, 380, Annual 7p; c-260, 263-271, 337-355, 357-369, 371, 373-382, Annual 7.* ***Starlin*** *c-213.*

THOR (Volume 2)
Marvel Comics: July, 1998 - No. 85, Dec, 2004 ($2.99/$1.99/$2.25)

1-($2.99)-Follows Heroes Return; Jurgens-s/Romita Jr. & Janson-a; wraparound-c; battles the Destroyer 6.00
1-Variant-c 1 2 3 5 6 8
1-Rough Cut-($2.99) Features original script and pencil pages 3.00
1-Sketch cover 20.00
2-($1.99) Two covers; Avengers app. 4.00
3-11,13-23: 3-Assumes Jake Olson ID. 4-Namor-c/app. 8-Spider-Man-c/app. 14-Iron Man c/app. 17-Juggernaut-c 3.00
12-($2.99) Wraparound-c; Hercules appears 4.00
12-($10.00) Variant-c by Jusko 10.00
24,26-31,33,34: 24-Begin $2.25-c. 26-Mignola-c/Larsen-a. 29-Andy Kubert-a. 30-Maximum Security x-over; Beta Ray Bill-c/app. 33-Intro. Thor Girl 3.00
25-($2.99) Regular edition 4.00
25-($3.99) Gold foil enhanced cover 5.00
32-($3.50, 100 pgs.) new story plus reprints w/Kirby-a; Simonson-a 5.00
35-($2.99) Thor battles The Gladiator; Andy Kubert-a 4.00
36-49,51-61: 37-Starlin-a. 38,39-BWS-c. 38-42-Immonen-a. 40-Odin killed. 41-Orbik-c. 44-'Nuff Said silent issue. 51-Spider-Man app. 57-Art by various. 58-Davis-a; x-over with Iron Man #64. 60-Brereton-c 3.00
50-($4.95) Raney-c/a; back-ups w/Nuckols-a & Armenta-s/Bennett-a 5.00
62-84: 62-Begin $2.99-c. 64-Loki-c/app. 80-Oeming-s begins; Avengers app. 3.00
85-Last issue; Thor dies; Oeming-s/DiVito-a/Epting-c 4.00
...1999 Annual ($3.50) Jurgens-s/a(p) 4.00
...2000 Annual ($3.50) Jurgens-s/Ordway-a(p); back-up stories 4.00
...2001 Annual ($3.50) Jurgens-s/Grummett-a(p); Lightle-c 4.00
...Across All Worlds (9/01, $19.95, TPB) r/#28-35 20.00
Avengers Disassembled: Thor TPB (2004, $16.99) r/#80-85; afterword by Oeming 17.00
...Resurrection ($5.99, TPB) r/#1,2 6.00
...: The Dark Gods (7/00, $15.95, TPB) r/#9-13 16.00
...Vol. 1: The Death of Odin (7/02, $12.99, TPB) r/#39-44 13.00
...Vol. 2: Lord of Asgard (9/02, $15.99, TPB) r/#45-50 16.00
...Vol. 3: Gods on Earth (2003, $21.99, TPB) r/#51-58, Avengers #63, Iron Man #64, Marvel Double-Shot #1; Beck-c 22.00
...Vol. 4: Spiral (2003, $19.99, TPB) r/#59-67; Brereton-c 20.00
...Vol. 5: The Reigning (2004, $17.99, TPB) r/#68-74 18.00
...Vol. 6: Gods and Men (2004, $13.99, TPB) r/#75-79 14.00

THOR (Also see Fantastic Four #538)(Resumes original numbering with #600)
Marvel Comics: Sept, 2007 - No. 12, Mar, 2009; No. 600, Apr, 2009 - No. 621, May, 2011 ($2.99/$3.99) (Continues numbering as Journey Into Mystery #622) (Also see Mighty Thor #1)

1-Straczynski-s/Coipel-a/c 4.00
1-Variant-c by Michael Turner 5.00
1-Zombie variant-c by Suydam 5.00
1-Non-zombie variant-c by Suydam 5.00
1-"Marvel's Greatest Comics" edition (5/10, $1.00) r/#1 3.00
2-12: 2-Two covers by Dell'Otto and Coipel. 3-Iron Man app.; McGuinness var-c. 4-Bermejo var-c. 5-Campbell var-c. 6-Art Adams var-c. 7,8-Djurdjevic-a/c; Coipel var-c 3.00
2-Second printing with wraparound-c 3.00
7-"Marvel's Greatest Comics" edition (6/11, $1.00) r/#7 3.00

(After #12 [Mar, 2009] numbering reverted back to original Journey Into Mystery/Thor numbering with #600, Apr, 2009)

600 (4/09, $4.99) Two wraparound-c by Coipel & Djurdjevic; Coipel, Djurdjevic & Aja-a; r/Tales of Asgard from Journey Into Mystery #106,107,112,113,115; Kirby-a 5.00
601-603,611-621-($3.99) 601-603-Djurdjevic-a. 602-Sif returns. 617-Loki returns 4.00
604-610-($2.99) Tan-a. 607-609-Siege x-over. 610-Braithwaite-a; Ragnarok app. 3.00
620.1 (5/11, $2.99) Brooks-a; Grey Gargoyle app. 3.00
Annual 1 (11/09, $3.99) Suayan, Grindberg, Gaudiano-a; Djurdjevic-c 4.00
...: Ages of Thunder (6/08, $3.99) Fraction-s/Zircher-a/Djurdjevic-c 4.00
... & Hercules: Encyclopædia Mythologica (2009, $4.99) profile pages of the Pantheons 5.00
... Asgard's Avenger 1 (6/11, $4.99) profile pages of Thor characters 5.00
... Giant-Size Finale 1 (1/01, $3.99) Dr. Doom app.; r/origin from JIM #83 4.00
... God-Size Special (2/09, $3.99) story of Skurge the Executioner re-told; art by Brereton, Braithwaite, Allred and Sepulveda; plus reprint of Thor #362 (1985) 4.00
... Goes Hollywood 1 ('11, $3.99) Collection of movie-themed variant Thor covers 4.00
...: Man of War (1/09, $3.99) Fraction-s/Mann & Zircher-a/Djurdjevic-c 4.00
...: Reign of Blood (8/08, $3.99) Fraction-s/Evans & Zircher-a/Djurdjevic-c 4.00
...: Spotlight (5/11, $3.99) movie photo-c; movie preview; creator interviews 4.00
...: The Rage of Thor (10/10, $3.99) Milligan-s/Suayan-c/a 4.00
...: The Trial of Thor (8/09, $3.99) Milligan-s/Nord-c/a 4.00
...: Truth of History (12/08, $3.99) Thor and crew in ancient Egypt; Alan Davis-s/a/c 4.00
...: Whosoever Wields This Hammer 1 (6/11, $4.99) recolored r/J.I.M. #83,84,88 5.00
...: Wolves of the North (2/11, $3.99) Carey-s/Perkins-a 4.00
... By J. Michael Straczynski Vol. 1 HC (2008, $19.99) r/#1-6; variant cover gallery 20.00

THOR AND THE WARRIORS FOUR
Marvel Comics: Jun, 2010 - No. 4, Sept, 2010 ($2.99, limited series)

1-4-Thor and Power Pack team-up; Gurihiru-a; back-up with Coover-s/a 3.00

THOR: BLOOD OATH
Marvel Comics: Nov, 2005 - No. 6, Feb, 2006 ($2.99, limited series)

1-6-Oeming-s/Kolins-a/c 3.00
HC (2006, $19.99, dust jacket) r/series; afterword by Oeming 20.00
SC (2006, $14.99) r/series; afterword by Oeming 15.00

THOR CORPS
Marvel Comics: Sept, 1993 - No. 4, Jan, 1994 ($1.75, limited series)

1-4: 1-Invaders cameo. 2-Invaders app. 3-Spider-Man 2099, Rawhide Kid, Two-Gun Kid & Kid Colt app. 4-Painted-c 3.00

THOR: FIRST THUNDER
Marvel Comics: Nov, 2010 - No. 5, Mar, 2011 ($3.99, limited series)

1-5: 1-Huat-a; new retelling of origin; reprint of debut in JIM #83 4.00

THOR: FOR ASGARD
Marvel Comics: Nov, 2010 - No. 6, Apr, 2011 ($3.99, limited series)

1-6-Bianchi-a/c. 1-Frost Giants app. 4.00

THOR: GODSTORM
Marvel Comics: Nov, 2001 - No. 3, Jan, 2002 ($3.50, limited series)

1-3-Steve Rude-c/a; Busiek-s; Avengers app. 4.00

THOR: HEAVEN & EARTH
Marvel Comics: Sept, 2011 - No. 4, Nov, 2011 ($2.99, limited series)

1-4: 1-Jenkins-s/Olivetti-a/c; Loki app. 2-Texeira-a/c. 3-Alixe-a. 4-Medina-a 3.00

THORION OF THE NEW ASGODS
Marvel Comics (Amalgam): June, 1997 ($1.95, one-shot)

1-Keith Giffen-s/John Romita Jr.-c/a 3.00

THOR: SON OF ASGARD
Marvel Comics: May, 2004 - No. 12, Mar, 2005 ($2.99, limited series)

1-12: Teenaged Thor, Sif, and Balder; Tocchini-a. 1-6-Granov-c. 7-12-Jo Chen-c 3.00
... Vol. 1: The Warriors Teen (2004, $7.99, digest) r/#1-6 8.00
... Vol. 2: Worthy (2005, $7.99, digest) r/#7-12 8.00

THOR: TALES OF ASGARD BY STAN LEE & JACK KIRBY
Marvel Comics: 2009 - No. 6, 2009 ($3.99, limited series)

1-6-Reprints back-up stories from Journey Into Mystery #97-120; new covers by Coipel 4.00

THOR: THE DEVIANTS SAGA
Marvel Comics: Jan, 2012 - No. 5, ($3.99, limited series)

1-5-Rodi-s/Segovia-a; Ereshkigal app. 4.00

THOR: THE LEGEND
Marvel Comics: Sept, 1996 ($3.95, one-shot)

nn-Tribute issue 4.00

THOR THE MIGHTY AVENGER
Marvel Comics: Sept, 2010 - No. 8, Mar, 2011 ($2.99, limited series)

1-8-Re-imagining of Thor's origin; Langridge-s/Samnee-a. 1-Mr. Hyde app. 3.00

3-D-ELL #3 © DELL

3-D Romance #1 © Steriographic

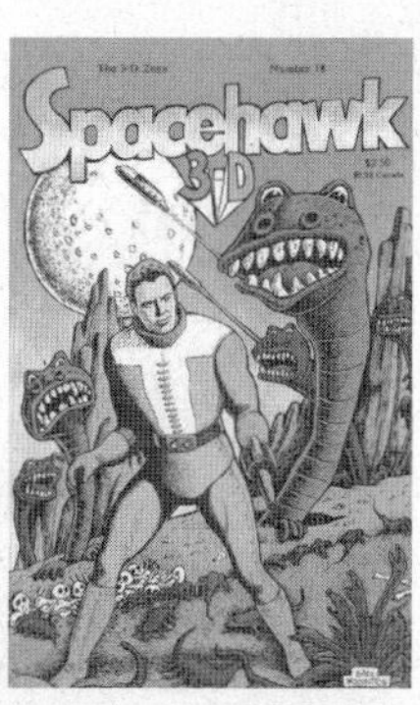

3-D Zone #18 © Renegade Press

	GD 2.0	VG 4.0	FN 6.0	VF 8.0	VF/NM 9.0	NM- 9.2

Free Comic Book Day 2011 (giveaway) Captain America app. 3.00

THOR: VIKINGS
Marvel Comics (MAX): Sept, 2003 - No. 5, Jan, 2004 ($3.50, limited series)
1-5-Garth Ennis-s/Glenn Fabry-a/c 3.50
TPB (2004, $13.99) r/series 14.00

THOSE MAGNIFICENT MEN IN THEIR FLYING MACHINES (See Movie Comics)

THRAX
Event Comics: Nov, 1996 ($2.95, one-shot)
1 3.00

THREE CABALLEROS (Walt Disney's...)
Dell Publishing Co.: No. 71, 1945
Four Color 71-by Walt Kelly, c/a 57 114 171 462 1006 1550

THREE CHIPMUNKS, THE (TV) (Also see Alvin)
Dell Publishing Co.: No. 1042, Oct-Dec, 1959
Four Color 1042 (#1)-(Alvin, Simon & Theodore) 9 18 27 58 99 140

THREE COMICS (Also see Spiritman)
The Penny King Co.: 1944 (10¢, 52 pgs.) (2 different covers exist)
1,3,4-Lady Luck, Mr. Mystic, The Spirit app. (3 Spirit sections bound together); Lou Fine-a 26 52 78 154 252 350
NOTE: *No. 1 contains Spirit Sections 4/9/44 - 4/23/44, and No. 4 is also from 4/44.*

3-D (NOTE: The prices of all the 3-D comics listed include glasses. Deduct 40-50 percent if glasses are missing, and reduce slightly if glasses are loose.)

3-D ACTION
Atlas Comics (ACI): Jan, 1954 (Oversized, 15¢)(2 pairs of glasses included)
1-Battle Brady; Sol Brodsky-c 39 78 117 240 395 550

3-D ADVENTURE COMICS
Stats, Etc.: Aug, 1986 (one shot)
1-Promo material 4.00

3-D ALIEN TERROR
Eclipse Comics: June, 1986 ($2.50)
1-Old Witch, Crypt-Keeper, Vault Keeper cameo; Morrow, John Pound-a, Yeates-c 6.00
...in 2-D: 100 copies signed, numbered(B&W) 1 3 4 8 10 12

3-D ANIMAL FUN (See Animal Fun)

THREE DAYS IN EUROPE
Oni Press: Nov, 2002 - No. 5, Apr, 2003 ($2.95, B&W, limited series)
1-5-Johnston-s/Hawthorne-a 3.00
TPB (11/03, $14.95, digest-sized) r/#1-5 15.00

3-D BATMAN (Also see Batman 3-D)
National Periodical Publications: 1953 (Reprinted in 1966)
1953-(25¢)-Reprints Batman #42 & 48 (Penguin-c/story); Tommy Tomorrow story; came with pair of 3-D Bat glasses 103 206 309 659 1130 1600
1966-Reprints 1953 issue; new cover by Infantino/Anderson; has inside-c photos of Batman & Robin from TV show (50¢) 20 40 60 137 294 450

3-D CIRCUS
Fiction House Magazines (Real Adventures Publ.): 1953 (25¢, w/glasses)
1 28 56 84 165 270 375

3-D COMICS (See Mighty Mouse, Tor and Western Fighters)

3-D DOLLY
Harvey Publications: December, 1953 (25¢, came with 2 pairs of glasses)
1-Richie Rich story redrawn from his 1st app. in Little Dot #1; shows cover in 3-D on inside 47 94 141 296 498 700

3-D-ELL
Dell Publishing Co.: No. 1, 1953; No. 3, 1953 (3-D comics) (25¢, came w/glasses)
1-Rootie Kazootie (#2 does not exist) 30 60 90 177 289 400
3-Flukey Luke 28 56 84 165 270 375

3-D EXOTIC BEAUTIES
The 3-D Zone: Nov, 1990 ($2.95, 28 pgs.)
1-L.B. Cole-c 1 2 3 5 7 9

3-D FEATURES PRESENTS JET PUP
Dimensions Publications: Oct-Dec (Winter on-c), 1953 (25¢, came w/glasses)
1-Irving Spector-a(2) 30 60 90 177 289 400

3-D FUNNY MOVIES
Comic Media: 1953 (25¢, came w/glasses)
1-Bugsey Bear & Paddy Pelican 34 68 102 199 325 450

THREE-DIMENSION ADVENTURES (Superman)
National Periodical Publications: 1953 (25¢, large size, came w/glasses)
nn-Origin Superman (new art) 103 206 309 659 1130 1600

THREE DIMENSIONAL ALIEN WORLDS (See Alien Worlds)
Pacific Comics: July, 1984 (1st Ray Zone 3-D book)(one-shot)
1-Bolton-a(p); Stevens-a(i); Art Adams 1st published-a(p) 6.00

THREE DIMENSIONAL DNAGENTS (See New DNAgents)

THREE DIMENSIONAL E. C. CLASSICS (Three Dimensional Tales From the Crypt No. 2)
E. C. Comics: Spring, 1954 (Prices include glasses; came with 2 pair)
1-Stories by Wood (Mad #3), Krigstein (W.S. #7), Evans (F.C. #13), & Ingels (CSS #5); Kurtzman-c (rare in high grade due to unstable paper) 97 194 291 621 1061 1500
NOTE: *Stories redrawn to 3-D format. Original stories not necessarily by artists listed. CSS: Crime SuspenStories; F.C.: Frontline Combat; W.S.: Weird Science.*

THREE DIMENSIONAL TALES FROM THE CRYPT (Formerly Three Dimensional E. C. Classics)(Cover title: ...From the Crypt of Terror)
E. C. Comics: No. 2, Spring, 1954 (Prices include glasses; came with 2 pair)
2-Davis (TFTC #25), Elder (VOH #14), Craig (TFTC #24), & Orlando (TFTC #22) stories; Feldstein-c (rare in high grade) 95 190 285 603 1039 1475
NOTE: *Stories redrawn to 3-D format. Original stories not necessarily by artists listed. TFTC: Tales From the Crypt; VOH: Vault of Horror.*

3-D LOVE
Steriographic Publ. (Mikeross Publ.): Dec, 1953 (25¢, came w/glasses)
1 34 68 102 199 325 450

3-D NOODNICK (See Noodnick)

3-D ROMANCE
Steriographic Publ. (Mikeross Publ.): Jan, 1954 (25¢, came w/glasses)
1 34 68 102 199 325 450

3-D SHEENA, JUNGLE QUEEN (Also see Sheena 3-D)
Fiction House Magazines: 1953 (25¢, came w/glasses)
1-Maurice Whitman-c 68 136 204 432 746 1060

3-D SUBSTANCE
The 3-D Zone: July, 1990 ($2.95, 28 pgs.)
1-Ditko-c/a(r) 5.00

3-D TALES OF THE WEST
Atlas Comics (CPS): Jan, 1954 (Oversized) (15¢, came with 2 pair of glasses)
1 (3-D)-Sol Brodsky-c 39 78 117 231 378 525

3-D THREE STOOGES (Also see Three Stooges)
Eclipse Comics: Sept, 1986 - No. 2, Nov, 1986; No. 3, Oct, 1987; No. 4, 1989 ($2.50)
1-4: 3-Maurer-r. 4-r-/"Three Missing Links" 5.00
1-3 (2-D) 5.00

3-D WHACK (See Whack)

3-D ZONE, THE
The 3-D Zone (Renegade Press)/Ray Zone: Feb, 1987 - No. 20, 1989 ($2.50)
1,3,4,7-9,11,12,14,15,17,19,20: 1-r/A Star Presentation. 3-Picture Scope Jungle Advs. 4-Electric Fear. 7-Hollywood 3-D Jayne Mansfield photo-c. 8-High Seas 3-D, 9-Redmask-r. 11-Danse Macabre; Matt Fox c/a(r). 12-3-D Presidents. 14-Tyranostar. 15-3-Dementia Comics; Kurtzman-c, Kubert, Maurer-a. 17-Thrilling Love. 19-Cracked Classics. 20-Commander Battle and His Atomic Submarine 1 2 3 5 6 8
2,5,6,10,13,16,18: 2-Wolverton-r. 5-Krazy Kat-r. 6-Ratfink. 10-Jet 3-D; Powell & Williamson-r. 13-Flash Gordon. 16-Space Vixens; Dave Stevens-c/a. 18-Spacehawk; Wolverton-r 1 2 3 5 7 9
NOTE: ***Davis** r-19. **Ditko** r-19. **Elder** r-19. **Everett** r-19. **Feldstein** r-17. **Frazetta** r-17. **Heath** r-19. **Kamen** r-17. **Severin** r-19. **Ward** r-17,19. **Wolverton** r-2,18,19. **Wood** r-1,17. Photo c-12*

3 GEEKS, THE (Also see Geeksville)
3 Finger Prints: 1996 - No. 11, Jun, 1999 (B&W)
1,2 -Rich Koslowski-s/a in all 1 2 3 5 6 8
1-(2nd printing) 3.00
3-7, 9-11 3.00
8-(48 pgs.) 4.00
10-Variant-c 3.50
...48 Page Super-Sized Summer Spectacular (7/04, $4.95) 5.00
...Full Circle (7/03, $4.95) Origin story of the 3 Geeks; "Buck Rodinski" app. 5.00
How to Pick Up Girls If You're a Comic Book Geek (color)(7/97) 4.00
When the Hammer Falls TPB (2001, $14.95) r/#8-11 15.00

300 #1 © Frank Miller

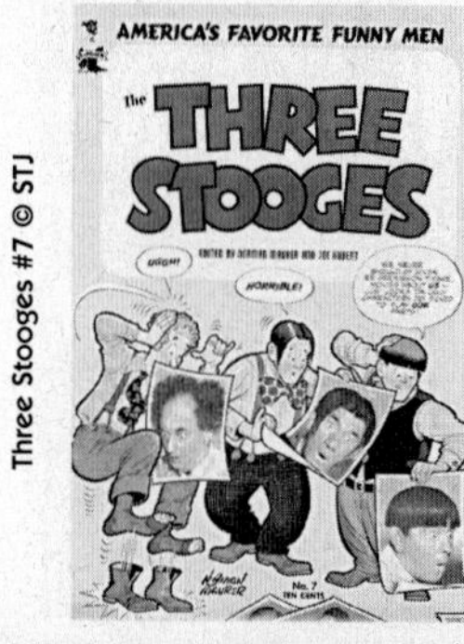

Three Stooges #7 © STJ

THRILLING COMICS
10¢
FEATURING A COMPLETE "DOC STRANGE" ACTION ADVENTURE

Thrilling Comics #15 © STD

3 GEEKS: SLAB MADNESS!
3 Finger Prints: Sept, 2008 - No. 3, Mar, 2009 ($2.99, B&W, limited series)

	GD 2.0	VG 4.0	FN 6.0	VF 8.0	VF/NM 9.0	NM- 9.2
1-3-Rich Koslowski-s/a; intro. The Cee-Gee-Cee						3.00

300 (Adapted for 2007 movie)
Dark Horse Comics: May, 1998 - No. 5, Sept, 1998 ($2.95/$3.95, limited series)

	GD 2.0	VG 4.0	FN 6.0	VF 8.0	VF/NM 9.0	NM- 9.2
1-Frank Miller-s/c/a; Spartans vs. Persians war	2	4	6	11	16	20
1-Second printing						5.00
2-4	2	4	6	8	10	12
5-($3.95-c)	2	4	6	8	10	12
HC ($30.00) -oversized reprint of series						30.00

3 LITTLE KITTENS
BroadSword Comics: Aug, 2002 - No. 3, Dec, 2002 ($2.95, limited series)

	GD 2.0	VG 4.0	FN 6.0	VF 8.0	VF/NM 9.0	NM- 9.2
1-3-Jim Balent-s/a; two covers						3.00

3 LITTLE PIGS (Disney)(...and the Wonderful Magic Lamp)
Dell Publishing Co.: No. 218, Mar, 1949

	GD 2.0	VG 4.0	FN 6.0	VF 8.0	VF/NM 9.0	NM- 9.2
Four Color 218 (#1)	10	20	30	67	124	180

3 LITTLE PIGS, THE (See Walt Disney Showcase #15 & 21)
Gold Key: May, 1964; No. 2, Sept, 1968 (Walt Disney)

	GD 2.0	VG 4.0	FN 6.0	VF 8.0	VF/NM 9.0	NM- 9.2
1-Reprints Four Color #218	3	6	9	20	30	40
2	3	6	9	15	21	26

THREE MOUSEKETEERS, THE (1st Series)(See Funny Stuff #1)
National Per. Publ.: 3-4/56 - No. 24, 9-10/59; No. 25, 8-9/60 - No. 26, 10-12/60

	GD 2.0	VG 4.0	FN 6.0	VF 8.0	VF/NM 9.0	NM- 9.2
1	20	40	60	137	294	450
2	11	22	33	71	136	200
3-5,7,9,10	8	16	24	56	96	135
6,8-Grey tone-c	10	20	30	67	124	180
11-26: 24-Cover says 11/59, inside says 9-10/59	7	14	21	48	79	110

NOTE: ***Rube Grossman** a-1-26. **Sheldon Mayer** a-1-8; c-1-7.*

THREE MOUSEKETEERS, THE (2nd Series) (See Super DC Giant)
National Periodical Publications: May-June, 1970 - No. 7, May-June, 1971 (#5-7: 68 pgs.)

	GD 2.0	VG 4.0	FN 6.0	VF 8.0	VF/NM 9.0	NM- 9.2
1-Mayer-r in all	6	12	18	41	66	90
2-4: 4-Doodles Duck begins (1st app.)	4	8	12	24	37	50
5-7:(68 pgs.). 5-Dodo & the Frog, Bo Bunny begin	5	10	15	35	55	75

THREE MUSKETEERS, THE (Also see Disney's The Three Musketeers)
Gemstone Publishing: 2004 ($3.95, squarebound, one-shot)

	GD 2.0	VG 4.0	FN 6.0	VF 8.0	VF/NM 9.0	NM- 9.2
nn-Adaptation of the 2004 DVD movie; Petrossi-c/a						4.00

THREE NURSES (Confidential Diary #12-17; Career Girl Romances #24 on)
Charlton Comics: V3#18, May, 1963 - V3#23, Mar, 1964

	GD 2.0	VG 4.0	FN 6.0	VF 8.0	VF/NM 9.0	NM- 9.2
V3#18-23	3	6	9	18	27	35

THREE RASCALS
I. W. Enterprises: 1958; 1963

	GD 2.0	VG 4.0	FN 6.0	VF 8.0	VF/NM 9.0	NM- 9.2
I.W. Reprint #1,2,10: 1-(Says Super Comics on inside)-(M.E.'s Clubhouse Rascals) DeCarlo-a. #2-(1958). 10-(1963)-r/#1	2	4	6	8	10	12

THREE RING COMICS
Spotlight Publishers: March, 1945

	GD 2.0	VG 4.0	FN 6.0	VF 8.0	VF/NM 9.0	NM- 9.2
1-Funny animal	16	32	48	94	147	200

THREE RING COMICS (Also see Captain Wizard & Meteor Comics)
Century Publications: April, 1946

	GD 2.0	VG 4.0	FN 6.0	VF 8.0	VF/NM 9.0	NM- 9.2
1-Prankster-c; Captain Wizard, Impossible Man, Race Wilkins, King O'Leary, & Dr. Mercy app.	36	72	108	211	343	475

THREE ROCKETEERS (See Blast-Off)

THREE STOOGES (See Comic Album #18, Top Comics, The Little Stooges, March of Comics #232, 248, 268, 280, 292, 304, 316, 336, 373, Movie Classics & Comics & 3-D Three Stooges)

THREE STOOGES
Jubilee No. 1/St. John No. 1 (9/53) on: Feb, 1949 - No. 2, May, 1949; Sept, 1953 - No. 7, Oct, 1954

	GD 2.0	VG 4.0	FN 6.0	VF 8.0	VF/NM 9.0	NM- 9.2
1-(Scarce, 1949)-Kubert-a; infinity-c	116	232	348	742	1271	1800
2-(Scarce)-Kubert, Maurer-a	81	162	243	518	884	1250
1(9/53)-Hollywood Stunt Girl by Kubert (7 pgs.)	68	136	204	432	746	1060
2(3-D, 10/53, 25¢)-Came w/glasses; Stunt Girl story by Kubert	41	82	123	256	428	600
3(3-D, 10/53, 25¢)-Came w/glasses; has 3-D-c	39	78	117	240	395	550
4(3/54)-7(10/54): 4-1st app. Li'l Stooge?	39	78	117	240	395	550

NOTE: *All issues have **Kubert-Maurer** art & **Maurer** covers. 6, 7-Partial photo-c.*

THREE STOOGES
Dell Publishing Co./Gold Key No. 10 (10/62) on: No. 1043, Oct-Dec, 1959 - No. 55, June, 1972

	GD 2.0	VG 4.0	FN 6.0	VF 8.0	VF/NM 9.0	NM- 9.2
Four Color 1043 (#1)	21	42	63	148	317	485
Four Color 1078,1127,1170,1187	11	22	33	77	154	230
6(9-11/61) - 10: 6-Professor Putter begins; ends #16	10	20	30	65	118	170
11-14,16,18-20	8	16	24	55	93	130
15-Go Around the World in a Daze (movie scenes)	9	18	27	58	99	140
17-The Little Monsters begin (5/64)(1st app.?)	9	18	27	58	99	140
21,23-30	7	14	21	44	72	100
22-Movie scenes from "The Outlaws Is Coming"	7	14	21	48	79	110
31-55	5	10	15	35	55	75

NOTE: *All Four Colors, 6-50, 52-55 have photo-c.*

THREE STOOGES IN 3-D, THE
Eternity Comics: 1991 ($3.95, high quality paper, w/glasses)

	GD 2.0	VG 4.0	FN 6.0	VF 8.0	VF/NM 9.0	NM- 9.2
1-Reprints Three Stooges by Gold Key; photo-c						5.00

THREE STRIKES
Oni Press: Apr, 2003 - No. 5, Oct, 2003 ($2.99, B&W, limited series)

	GD 2.0	VG 4.0	FN 6.0	VF 8.0	VF/NM 9.0	NM- 9.2
1-5-Brian Hurtt-a/DeFilippis & Weir-s						3.00
TPB (3/04, $14.95, digest-size) r/#1-5; Ed Brubaker intro.						15.00

3 WORLDS OF GULLIVER
Dell Publishing Co.: No. 1158, July, 1961 (2 issues exist with diff. covers)

	GD 2.0	VG 4.0	FN 6.0	VF 8.0	VF/NM 9.0	NM- 9.2
Four Color 1158-Movie, photo-c	7	14	21	44	72	100

THRILL COMICS (See Flash Comics, Fawcett)

THRILLER
DC Comics: Nov, 1983 - No. 12, Nov, 1984 ($1.25, Baxter paper)

	GD 2.0	VG 4.0	FN 6.0	VF 8.0	VF/NM 9.0	NM- 9.2
1-12: 1-Intro Seven Seconds; Von Eeden-c/a begins. 2-Origin. 5,6-Elvis satire						3.00

THRILLING ADVENTURES IN STAMPS COMICS (Formerly Stamp Comics)
Stamp Comics, Inc. (Very Rare): V1#8, Jan, 1953 (25¢, 100 pgs.)

	GD 2.0	VG 4.0	FN 6.0	VF 8.0	VF/NM 9.0	NM- 9.2
V1#8-Harrison, Wildey, Kiefer, Napoli-a	75	150	225	476	818	1160

THRILLING ADVENTURE STORIES (See Tigerman)
Atlas/Seaboard Publ.: Feb, 1975 - No. 2, Aug, 1975 (B&W, 68 pgs.)

	GD 2.0	VG 4.0	FN 6.0	VF 8.0	VF/NM 9.0	NM- 9.2
1-Tigerman, Kromag the Killer begin; Heath, Thorne-a; Doc Savage movie photos of Ron Ely	3	6	9	16	23	30
2-Heath, Toth, Severin, Simonson-a; Adams-c	4	8	12	22	34	45

THRILLING COMICS
Better Publ./Nedor/Standard Comics: Feb, 1940 - No. 80, April, 1951

	GD 2.0	VG 4.0	FN 6.0	VF 8.0	VF/NM 9.0	NM- 9.2
1-Origin & 1st app. Dr. Strange (37 pgs.), ends #?; Nickie Norton of the Secret Service begins	303	606	909	2121	3711	5300
2-The Rio Kid, The Woman in Red, Pinocchio begins	135	270	405	864	1482	2100
3-The Ghost & Lone Eagle begin	90	180	270	576	988	1400
4-6,8-10 (11/40): 5-Dr. Strange changed to Doc Strange. 10-1st WWII-c (Nazi)	71	142	213	454	777	1100
7-Classic-c	100	200	300	635	1093	1550
11-18,20	63	126	189	403	689	975
19-Origin & 1st app. The American Crusader (8/41), ends #39,41	71	142	213	454	777	1100
21-30: 24-Intro. Mike, Doc Strange's sidekick (1/42). 27-Robot-c. 29-Last Rio Kid	55	110	165	352	601	850
31-40: 36-Commando Cubs begin (7/43, 1st app.)	53	106	159	334	567	800
41-Classic Hitler & Mussolini WWII-c	206	412	618	1318	2259	3200
42,43,46-51: 51(12/45)-Last WWII-c (Japanese)	47	94	141	296	498	700
44-Hitler WWII-c by Schomburg	168	336	504	1075	1838	2600
45-Hitler pict. on-c	65	130	195	416	708	1000
52-Classic Schomburg hooded bondage-c; the Ghost ends	63	126	189	403	689	975
53,54: 53-The Phantom Detective begins. The Cavalier app. in both; no Commando Cubs in either	41	82	123	256	428	600
55-The Lone Eagle ends	39	78	117	233	384	535
56 (10/46)-Princess Pantha begins (not on-c), 1st app.	50	100	150	315	533	750
57-Doc Strange-c; 2nd Princess Pantha	43	86	129	271	461	650
58-66: All Princess Pantha jungle-c, w/Doc Strange #59, his last-c. 61-Ingels-a; The Lone Eagle app. 65-Last Phantom Detective & Commando Cubs. 66-Frazetta text illo	41	82	123	259	435	610
67,70,71-Last jungle-c; Frazetta-a(5-7 pgs.) in each	48	96	144	302	514	725
68,69-Frazetta-a(2), 8 & 6 pgs.; 9 & 7 pgs.	52	104	156	328	552	775

72,73: 72-Buck Ranger, Cowboy Detective c/stys begin (western theme), end #80;

Thrilling Crime Cases #42 © STAR

Thrills of Tomorrow #20 © HARV

T.H.U.N.D.E.R. Agents (2011 series) #7 © Radiant Assets

	GD 2.0	VG 4.0	FN 6.0	VF 8.0	VF/NM 9.0	NM- 9.2
Frazetta-a(5-7 ps.) in each	39	78	117	240	395	550
74-Last Princess Pantha; Tara app.	27	54	81	160	263	365
75-78: 75-All western format begins	14	28	42	81	118	155
79-Krigstein-a	15	30	45	83	124	165
80-Severin & Elder, Celardo, Moreira-a	15	30	45	83	124	165

NOTE: *Bondage c-5, 9, 13, 20, 22, 27-30, 38, 41, 52, 54, 70.* **Kinstler** *a-45.* **Leo Morey** *a-7.* **Schomburg** *(sometimes signed as* **Xela**) *c-7, 9-19, 36-80 (airbrush 62-71).* **Tuska** *a-62, 63. Woman in Red not in #19, 23, 31-33, 39-45. No. 45 exists as a Canadian reprint but numbered #48. No. 72 exists as a Canadian reprint with no* **Frazetta** *story. American Crusader c-20-24. Buck Ranger c-72-80. Commando Cubs c-37, 39, 41, 43, 45, 47, 49, 51. Doc Strange c-1-19, 25-36, 38, 40, 42, 44, 46, 48, 50, 52-57, 59. Princess Pantha c-58, 60-71.*

THRILLING COMICS (Also see All Star Comics 1999 crossover titles)
DC Comics: May, 1999 ($1.99, one-shot)

1-Golden Age Hawkman and Wildcat; Russ Heath-a 3.00

THRILLING CRIME CASES (Formerly 4Most; becomes Shocking Mystery Cases #50 on)
Star Publications: No. 41, June-July, 1950 - No. 49, July, 1952

	GD	VG	FN	VF	VF/NM	NM-
41	28	56	84	165	270	375
42-45: 42-L. B. Cole-c/a (1); Chameleon story (Fox-r)	25	50	75	147	241	335
46-48: 47-Used in **POP**, pg. 84	24	48	72	142	234	325
49-(7/52)-Classic L. B. Cole-c	45	90	135	284	480	675

NOTE: **L. B. Cole** *c-all; a-43p, 45p, 46p, 49(2 pgs.).* **Disbrow** *a-48.* **Hollingsworth** *a-48.*

THRILLING ROMANCES
Standard Comics: No. 5, Dec, 1949 - No. 26, June, 1954

	GD	VG	FN	VF	VF/NM	NM-
5	16	32	48	94	147	200
6,8	11	22	33	62	86	110
7-Severin/Elder-a (7 pgs.)	13	26	39	74	105	135
9,10-Severin/Elder-a; photo-c	12	24	36	69	97	125
11,14-21,26: 14-Gene Tierney & Danny Kaye photo-c from movie "On the Riviera". 15-Tony Martin/Janet Leigh photo-c	10	20	30	58	79	100
12-Wood-a (2 pgs.); Tyrone Power/ Susan Hayward photo-c	14	28	42	76	108	140
13-Severin-a	11	22	33	62	86	110
22-25-Toth-a	12	24	36	69	97	125

NOTE: *All photo-c.* **Celardo** *a-9, 16.* **Colletta** *a-23, 24(2).* **Toth** *text illos-19.* **Tuska** *a-9.*

THRILLING SCIENCE TALES
AC Comics: 1989 - No. 2 ($3.50, 2/3 color, 52 pgs.)

1,2: 1-r/Bob Colt #6(saucer); Frazetta, Guardineer (Space Ace), Wood, Krenkel, Orlando, WIlliamson-r; Kaluta-c. 2-Capt. Video-r by Evans, Capt. Science-r by Wood, Star Pirate-r by Whitman & Mysta of the Moon-r by Moreira 4.00

THRILLING TRUE STORY OF THE BASEBALL...
Fawcett Publications: 1952 (Photo-c, each)

	GD	VG	FN	VF	VF/NM	NM-
...Giants-photo-c; has Willie Mays rookie photo-biography; Willie Mays, Eddie Stanky & others photos on-c	68	136	204	432	746	1060
...Yankees-photo-c; Yogi Berra, Joe DiMaggio, Mickey Mantle & others photos on-c	66	132	198	419	722	1025

THRILLING WONDER TALES
AC Comics : 1991 ($2.95, B&W)

1-Includes a Bob Powell Thun'da story 3.00

THRILLKILLER
DC Comics : Jan, 1997 - No. 3, Mar, 1997($2.50, limited series)

1-3-Elseworlds Robin & Batgirl; Chaykin-s/Brereton-c/a 3.00
...'62 ('98, $4.95, one-shot) Sequel; Chaykin-s/Brereton-c/a 5.00
TPB-(See Batman: Thrillkiller)

THRILLOGY
Pacific Comics: Jan, 1984 (One-shot, color)

1-Conrad-c/a 3.00

THRILL-O-RAMA
Harvey Publications (Fun Films): Oct, 1965 - No. 3, Dec, 1966

	GD	VG	FN	VF	VF/NM	NM-
1-Fate (Man in Black) by Powell app.; Doug Wildey-a(2); Simon-c	5	10	15	35	55	75
2-Pirana begins (see Phantom #46); Williamson 2 pgs.; Fate (Man in Black) app.; Tuska/Simon-c	4	8	12	22	34	45
3-Fate (Man in Black) app.; Sparling-c	3	6	9	19	29	38

THRILLS OF TOMORROW (Formerly Tomb of Terror)
Harvey Publications: No. 17, Oct, 1954 - No. 20, April, 1955

	GD	VG	FN	VF	VF/NM	NM-
17-Powell-a (horror); r/Witches Tales #7	15	30	45	88	137	185
18-Powell-a (horror); r/Tomb of Terror #1	14	28	42	82	121	160
19,20-Stuntman-c/stories by S&K (r/from Stuntman #1 & 2); 19 has origin & is last pre-code (2/55)	31	62	93	182	296	410

NOTE: **Kirby** *c-19, 20.* **Palais** *a-17.* **Simon** *c-18?*

THROBBING LOVE (See Fox Giants)

THROUGH GATES OF SPLENDOR
Spire Christian Comics (Flemming H. Revell Co.): 1973, 1974 (36 pages) (39-49 cents)

	GD	VG	FN	VF	VF/NM	NM-
nn-1973 Edition	2	4	6	11	16	20
nn-1974 Edition	2	4	6	8	11	14

THULSA DOOM (Robert E. Howard character)
Dynamite Entertainment: 2009 - No. 4, 2009 ($3.50, limited series)

1-4-Alex Ross-c/Lui Antonio-a 3.50

THUMPER (Disney)
Dell Publishing Co.: No, 19, 1942 - No. 243, Sept, 1949

	GD	VG	FN	VF	VF/NM	NM-
Four Color 19-Walt Disney's...Meets the Seven Dwarfs; reprinted in Silly Symphonies	42	84	126	315	683	1050
Four Color 243-...Follows His Nose	11	22	33	71	136	200

THUN'DA (...King of the Congo)
Magazine Enterprises: 1952 - No. 6, 1953

	GD	VG	FN	VF	VF/NM	NM-
1(A-1 #47)-Origin; Frazetta c/a; only comic done entirely by Frazetta; all Thun'da stories, no Cave Girl	168	336	504	1075	1838	2600
2(A-1 #56)-Powell-c/a begins, ends #6; Intro/1st app. Cave Girl in filler strip (also app. in 3-6)	25	50	75	150	245	340
3(A-1 #73), 4(A-1 #78)	19	38	57	109	172	235
5(A-1 #83), 6(A-1 #86)	18	36	54	103	162	220

THUN'DA TALES (See Frank Frazetta's...)

THUNDER AGENTS (See Dynamo, Noman & Tales Of Thunder)
Tower Comics: 11/65 - No. 17, 12/67; No. 18, 9/68, No. 19, 11/68, No. 20, 11/69 (No. 1-16: 68 pgs.; No. 17 on: 52 pgs.)(All are 25¢)

	GD	VG	FN	VF	VF/NM	NM-
1-Origin & 1st app. Dynamo, Noman, Menthor, & The Thunder Squad; 1st app. The Iron Maiden	18	36	54	123	267	410
2-Death of Egghead; A-bomb blast panel	10	20	30	68	127	185
3-5: 4-Guy Gilbert becomes Lightning who joins Thunder Squad; Iron Maiden app.	8	16	24	56	96	135
6-10: 7-Death of Menthor. 8-Origin & 1st app. The Raven	7	14	21	44	72	100
11-15: 13-Undersea Agent app.; no Raven story	6	12	18	41	66	90
16-19	6	12	18	39	62	85
20-Special Collectors Edition; all reprints	4	8	12	28	44	60

...Archives Vol. 1 (DC Comics, 2003, $49.95, HC) r/#1-4, restored and recolored 50.00
...Archives Vol. 2 (DC Comics, 2003, $49.95, HC) r/#5-7, Dynamo #1 50.00
...Archives Vol. 3 (DC Comics, 2003, $49.95, HC) r/#8-10, Dynamo #2 50.00
...Archives Vol. 4 (DC Comics, 2004, $49.95, HC) r/#11, Noman #1,2 & Dynamo #3 50.00

NOTE: **Crandall** *a-1, 4p, 5p, 18, 20r; c-18.* **Ditko** *a-6, 7p, 12p, 13?, 14p, 16, 18.* **Giunta** *a-6.* **Kane** *a-1, 5p, 6p?, 14, 16p; c-14, 15.* **Reinman** *a-13.* **Sekowsky** *a-6.* **Tuska** *a-1p, 7, 8, 10, 13-17, 19.* **Whitney** *a-9p, 10, 13, 15, 17, 18; c-17.* **Wood** *a-1-11, 15(w/***Ditko***-12, 18), (inks-#9, 13, 14, 16, 17), 19i, 20r; c-1-8, 9i, 10-13(#10 w/***Williamson***(p)), 16.*

T.H.U.N.D.E.R. AGENTS (See Blue Ribbon Comics, Hall of Fame Featuring the..., JCP Features & Wally Wood's...)
JC Comics (Archie Publications): May, 1983 - No. 2, Jan, 1984

1,2: 1-New Manna/Blyberg-c/a. 2-Blyberg-c 6.00

T.H.U.N.D.E.R. AGENTS
DC Comics: Jan, 2011 - No. 10, Oct, 2011 ($3.99/$2.99)

1-3-($3.99): 1-Spencer-s/Cafu-a/Quitely-c. 3-Chaykin-a (5 pgs.) 4.00
4-10-($2.99): 4-Pérez-a (5 pgs.). 7-10-Grell & Dragotta-a 3.00
1-Variant-c by Darwyn Cooke 8.00

T.H.U.N.D.E.R. AGENTS
DC Comics: Jan, 2012 - No. 6 ($2.99, limited series)

1-5-Spencer-s/Craig-a. 1-Andy Kubert-c. 3-Craig & Simonson-a 3.00

THUNDER BIRDS (See Cinema Comics Herald)

THUNDERBOLT (See The Atomic...)

THUNDERBOLT (Peter Cannon...; see Crisis on Infinite Earths, Peter Cannon, Captain Atom and Judomaster)
Charlton Comics: Jan, 1966; No. 51, Mar-Apr, 1966 - No. 60, Nov, 1967

	GD	VG	FN	VF	VF/NM	NM-
1-Origin & 1st app. Thunderbolt	4	8	12	28	44	60
51-(Formerly Son of Vulcan #50)	3	6	9	20	30	40
52-Judomaster story	3	6	9	16	23	30
53-Captain Atom story, 2 pgs.	3	6	9	16	23	30
54-59: 54-Sentinels begin. 59-Last Thunderbolt & Sentinels (back-up story)	3	6	9	14	19	24
60-Prankster only app.	3	6	9	15	21	26

Thunderbolts #15 © MAR

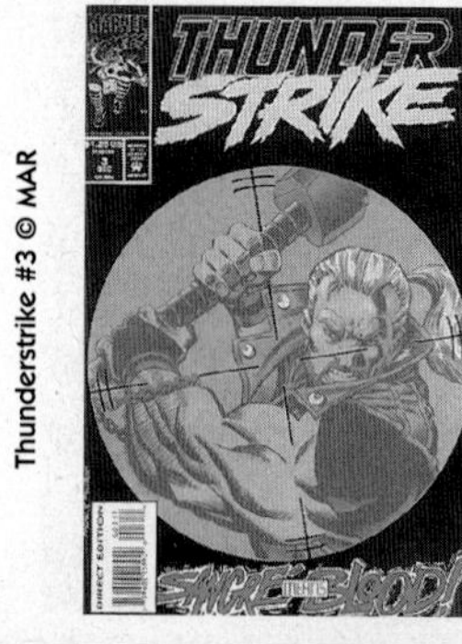

Thunderstrike #3 © MAR

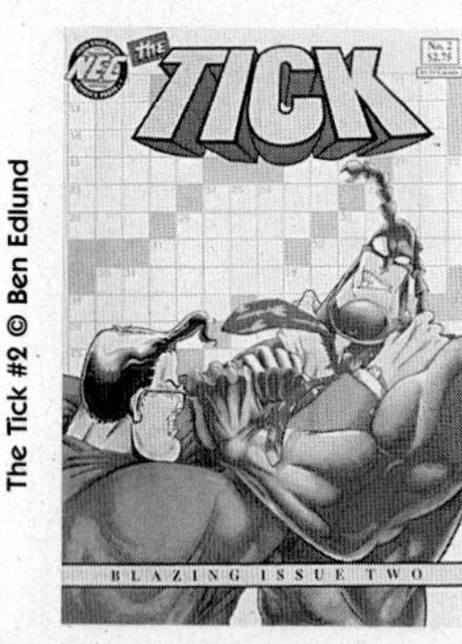

The Tick #2 © Ben Edlund

GD 2.0 | VG 4.0 | FN 6.0 | VF 8.0 | VF/NM 9.0 | NM- 9.2

57,58 ('77)-Modern Comics-r 6.00
NOTE: *Aparo a-60. Morisi a-1, 51-56, 58; c-1, 51-56, 58, 59.*

THUNDERBOLT JAXON (Revival of 1940s British comics character)
DC Comics (WildStorm): Apr, 2006 - No. 5, Sept, 2006 ($2.99, limited series)
1-5-Dave Gibbons-s/John Higgins-a 3.00
TPB (2007, $19.99) r/#1-5; intro. by Gibbons; cover gallery 20.00

THUNDERBOLTS (Also see New Thunderbolts and Incredible Hulk #449)
Marvel Comics: Apr, 1997 - No. 81, Sept, 2003; No. 100, May, 2006 - Present ($1.95-$2.99)
1-($2.99)-Busiek-s/Bagley-c/a 1 2 3 5 7 9
1-2nd printing; new cover colors 3.00
2-4: 2-Two covers. 4-Intro. Jolt 6.00
5-11: 9-Avengers app. 3.50
12-($2.99)-Avengers and Fantastic Four-c/app. 4.00
13-24: 14-Thunderbolts return to Earth. 21-Hawkeye app. 3.00
25-($2.99) Wraparound-c 4.00
26-38: 26-Manco-a 3.00
39-($2.99) 100 Page Monster; Iron Man reprints 4.00
40-49: 40-Begin $2.25-c; Sandman-c/app. 44-Avengers app. 47-Captain Marvel app. 49-Zircher-a 3.00
50-($2.99) Last Bagley-a; Captain America becomes leader 4.00
51-74,76,77,80,81: 51,52-Zircher-a; Dr. Doom app. 80,81-Spider-Man app. 3.00
75-($3.50) Hawkeye leaves the team; Garcia-a 4.00
78,79-($2.99-c) Velasco-a begins 3.00
(See New Thunderbolts for #82-99)
100 (5/06, $3.99) resumes from New Thunderbolts #18; back-up origin stories 4.00
101-109: 103-105-Civil War x-over 3.00
110-New team begins including Bullseye, Venom and Norman Osborn; Ellis-s/Deodato-a 5.00
111-136,138-149: 111-121-Ellis-s/Deodato-a. 112-Stan Lee cameo. 123-125-Secret Invasion x-over. 128-Dark Reign begins. 130,131-X-over with Deadpool #8,9. 141-143-Siege 3.00
137-(12/09, $3.99) Iron Fist and Luke Cage app. 4.00
150-(1/11, $4.99) Thunderbolts vs. Avengers; r/#1; storyline synopses of #1-150 5.00
151-158,160-163, 163.1, 164-170-($2.99) 151-153-Land-c. 155-Satana joins. 158-162-Fear Itself tie-in. 163-165-Thunderbolts in WWII; Invaders app. 3.00
159-($4.99) Fear Itelf tie-in; Juggernaut app.; short stories of escape from The Raft 5.00
Annual '97 ($2.99)-Wraparound-c 4.00
Annual 2000 ($3.50) Breyfogle-a 4.00
...: Breaking Point (1/08, $2.99, one-shot) Gage-s/Denham-a/Djurdjevic-c 3.00
... By Warren Ellis Vol. 1 HC (2007, $24.99, dustjacket) r/#150-154, ...: Desperate Measures and stories from Civil War: Choosing Sides and The Initiative 25.00
... By Warren Ellis Vol. 1: Faith in Monsters SC (2008, $19.99) same contents as HC 20.00
Civil War: Thunderbolts TPB (2007, $13.99) r/#101-105 14.00
...: Desperate Measures (9/07, $2.99, one-shot) Jenkins-s/Steve Lieber-a 3.00
...: Distant Rumblings (#-1) (7/97, $1.95) Busiek-s 5.00
First Strikes (1997, $4.99,TPB) r/#1,2 5.00
...: From the Marvel Vault (6/11, $3.99) Jack Monroe app.; Nicieza-s/Aucoin-a 4.00
...: Guardian Protocols (2007, $10.99) r/#106-109 11.00
...: International Incident (4/08, $2.99, one-shot) Gage-s/Oliver-a/Djurdjevic-c 3.00
...: Life Sentences (7/01, $3.50) Adlard-a 4.00
...: Marvel's Most Wanted TPB ('98, $16.99) r/origin stories of original Masters of Evil 17.00
...: Reason in Madness (7/08, $2.99, one-shot) Gage-s/Oliver-a/Djurdjevic-c 3.00
Wizard #0 (bagged with Wizard #89) 3.00

THUNDERBOLTS PRESENTS: ZEMO - BORN BETTER
Marvel Comics: Apr, 2007 - No. 4, July, 2007 ($2.99, limited series)
1-4-History of Baron Zemo; Nicieza-s/Grummett-a/c 3.00
TPB (2007, $10.99) r/#1-4 11.00

THUNDERBUNNY (See Blue Ribbon Comics #13, Charlton Bullseye & Pep Comics #393)
Red Circle Comics: Jan, 1984 (Direct sale only)
WaRP Graphics: Second series No. 1, 1985 - No. 6, 1985
Apple Comics: No. 7, 1986 - No. 12, 1987
1-Humor/parody; origin Thunderbunny; 2 page pin-up by Anderson 5.00
(2nd series) 1,2-Magazine size 4.00
3-12-Comic size 4.00

THUNDERCATS (TV)
Marvel Comics (Star Comics)/Marvel #22 on: Dec, 1985 - No. 24, June, 1988 (75¢)
1-Mooney-c/a begins 2 4 6 8 11 14
2-20: 2-(65¢ & 75¢ cover exists). 12-Begin $1.00-c. 18-20-Williamson-i 1 2 3 5 7 9
21-24: 23-Williamson-c(i) 1 3 4 6 8 10

THUNDERCATS (TV)
DC Comics (WildStorm): No. 0, Oct, 2002 - No. 5, Feb, 2003 ($2.50/$2.95, limited series)

GD 2.0 | VG 4.0 | FN 6.0 | VF 8.0 | VF/NM 9.0 | NM- 9.2

0-($2.50) J. Scott Campbell-c/a 3.00
1-5-($2.95) 1-McGuinness-a/c; variant cover by Art Adams; rebirth of Mumm-Ra 3.00
.../ Battle of the Planets (7/03, $4.95) Kaare Andrews-s/a; 2 covers by Campbell & Ross 5.00
...: Origins-Heroes & Villains (2/04, $3.50) short stories by various 3.50
...Reclaiming Thundera TPB (2003, $12.95) r/#0-5 13.00
... Sourcebook (1/03, $2.95) pin-ups and info on characters; art by various; A. Adams-c 3.00

THUNDERCATS: DOGS OF WAR
DC Comics (WildStorm): Aug, 2003 - No. 5, Dec, 2003 ($2.95, limited series)
1-5: 1-Two covers by Booth & Pearson; Booth-a/Layman-s. 2-4-Two covers 3.00
TPB (2004, $14.95) r/#1-5 15.00

THUNDERCATS: ENEMY'S PRIDE
DC Comics (WildStorm): Aug, 2004 - No. 5 ($2.95, limited series)
1-5-Vriens-a/Layman-s 3.00
TPB (2005, $14.99) r/#1-5 15.00

THUNDERCATS: HAMMERHAND'S REVENGE
DC Comics (WildStorm): Dec, 2003 - No. 5, Apr, 2004 ($2.95, limited series)
1-5-Avery-s/D'Anda-a. 2-Variant-c by Warren 3.00
TPB (2004, $14.95) r/#1-5 15.00

THUNDERCATS: THE RETURN
DC Comics (WildStorm): Apr, 2003 - No. 5, Aug, 2003 ($2.95, limited series)
1-5: 1-Two covers by Benes & Cassaday; Gilmore-s 3.00
TPB (2004, $12.95) r/series 13.00

THUNDER MOUNTAIN (See Zane Grey, Four Color #246)

THUNDERSTRIKE (See Thor #459)
Marvel Comics: June, 1993 - No. 24, July, 1995 ($1.25)
1-($2.95, 52 pgs.)-Holo-grafx lightning patterned foil-c; Bloodaxe returns 4.00
2-24: 2-Juggernaut-c/s. 4-Capt. America app. 4-6-Spider-Man app. 8-bound-in trading card sheet. 18-Bloodaxe app. 24-Death of Thunderstrike 3.00
Marvel Double Feature...Thunderstrike/Code Blue #13 ($2.50)-Same as Thunderstrike #13 w/Code Blue flip book 4.00

THUNDERSTRIKE
Marvel Comics: Jan, 2011 - No. 5, Jun, 2011 ($3.99, limited series)
1-5-DeFalco-s/Frenz-a. 1-Back-up origin retold; Nauck-a 4.00

TICK, THE (Also see The Chroma-Tick)
New England Comics Press: Jun, 1988 - No. 12, May, 1993 ($1.75/$1.95/$2.25; B&W, over-sized)
Special Edition 1-1st comic book app. serially numbered & limited to 5,000 copies 5 10 15 35 55 75
Special Edition 1-(5/96, $5.95)-Double-c; foil-c; serially numbered (5,001 thru 14,000) & limited to 9,000 copies 1 2 3 5 6 8
Special Edition 2-Serially numbered and limited to 3000 copies 5 10 15 30 48 65
Special Edition 2-(8/96, $5.95)-Double-c; foil-c; serially numbered (5,001 thru 14,000) & limited to 9,000 copies 1 2 3 5 6 8
1-Regular Edition 1st printing; reprints Special Ed. 1 w/minor changes 4 8 12 24 37 50
1-2nd printing 6.00
1-3rd-5th printing 3.00
2-Reprints Special Ed. 2 w/minor changes 2 4 6 13 18 22
2-8-All reprints 3.00
3-5 ($1.95): 4-1st app. Paul the Samurai 1 3 4 6 8 10
6,8 ($2.25) 5.00
7-1st app. Man-Eating Cow 6.00
8-Variant with no logo, price, issue number or company logos. 2 4 6 10 14 18
9-12 ($2.75) 4.00
12-Special Edition; card-stock, virgin foil-c; numbered edition 2 4 6 13 18 22
Pseudo-Tick #13 (11/00, $3.50) Continues story from #12 (1993) 4.00
Promo Sampler-(1990)-Tick-c/story 1 2 3 5 6 8

TICK, THE (One shots)
... Big Back to School Special 1-(10/98, $3.50, B&W) Tick & Arthur undercover in H.S. 3.50
... Big Cruise Ship Vacation Special 1-(9/00, $3.50, B&W) 3.50
... Big Father's Day Special 1-(6/00, $3.50, B&W) 3.50
... Big Halloween Special 1-(10/99, $3.50, B&W) 3.50
... Big Halloween Special 2000 (10/00, $3.50) 3.50
... Big Halloween Special 2001 (9/01, $3.95) 4.00
... Big Mother's Day Special 1-(4/00, $3.50, B&W) 3.50
... Big Red-N-Green Christmas Spectacle 1-(12/01, $3.95) 4.00

Tick Tock Tales #4 © ME

Tigress #5 © Heroic Publ.

Timecop #2 © Mark Verhaiden

GD 2.0 | VG 4.0 | FN 6.0 | VF 8.0 | VF/NM 9.0 | NM- 9.2

... Big Romantic Adventure 1-(2/98, $2.95, B&W) Candy box-c with candy map on back 3.50
... Big Summer Annual 1-(7/99, $3.50, B&W) Chainsaw Vigilante vs. Barry 3.50
... Big Summer Fun Special 1-(8/98, $3.50, B&W) Tick and Arthur at summer camp 3.50
... Big Tax Time Terror 1-(4/00, $3.50, B&W) 3.50
... Big Year 2000 Spectacle 1-(3/00, $3.50, B&W) 3.50
... Incredible Internet Comic 1-(7/01, $3.95, color) r/New England Comics website story 4.00
FCBD Special Edition (5/10) - reprints debut from 1988; Ben Edlund-s/a 3.00
Introducing the Tick 1-(4/02, $3.95, color) summary of Tick's life and adventures 4.00
The Tick's Back #0 -(8/97, $2.95, B&W) 3.50
The Tick's Comic Con Extravaganza -(6/07, $3.95, color) Wang-c 4.00
The Tick's 20th Anniversary Special Edition #1 (5/07, $5.95) short stories by various; history of the character; creator profiles; 2 covers by Suydam & Bisley 6.00

--MASSIVE SUMMER DOUBLE SPECTACLE
1,2-(7,8/00, $3.50, B&W) 3.50

TICK & ARTIE
1-(6/02, $3.50, color) prints strips from Internet comic 4.00
2-(10/02, $3.95) 4.00

TICK AND ARTHUR, THE
New England Comics: Feb, 1999 - No. 6 ($3.50, B&W)
1-6-Sean Wang-s/a 3.50

TICK BIG BLUE DESTINY, THE
New England Comics: Oct, 1997 - No. 9 ($2.95)
1-4: 1-"Keen" Ed. 2-Two covers 3.50
1-($4.95) "Wicked Keen" Ed. w/die cut-c 5.00
5-($3.50) 3.50
6-Luny Bin Trilogy Preview #0 (7/98, $1.50) 3.50
7-9: 7-Luny Bin Trilogy begins 3.50

TICK BIG BLUE YULE LOG SPECIAL, THE
New England Comics: Dec, 1997; 1999 ($2.95, B&W)
1-"Jolly" and "Traditional" covers; flip book w/"Arthur Teaches the Tick About Hanukkah" 3.50
...1999 ($3.50) 3.50
Tick Big Yule Log Special 2001-(12/00, $3.50, B&W) 3.50

TICK, THE : CIRCUS MAXIMUS
New England Comics: Mar, 2000 - No. 4, Jun, 2000 ($3.50, B&W)
1-4-Encyclopedia of characters from Tick comics 3.50
Giant No. 1 (8/03, $14.95) r/#1-4, Redux 15.00
Redux No. 1 (4/01, $3.50) 3.50

TICK, THE - COLOR
New England Comics: Jan, 2001 - Present ($3.95)
1-6: 1-Marc Sandroni-a 4.00

TICK, THE : DAYS OF DRAMA
New England Comics: July, 2005 - No. 6, June, 2006 ($4.95/$3.95, limited series)
1-($4.95) Dave Garcia-a; has a mini-comic attached to cover 5.00
2-6-($3.95) 4.00

TICK, THE - HEROES OF THE CITY
New England Comics: Feb, 1999 - Present ($3.50, B&W)
1-6-Short stories by various 3.50

TICK KARMA TORNADO (The...)
New England Comics Press: Oct, 1993 - No. 9, Mar, 1995 ($2.75, B&W)
1-($3.25) 4.00
2-9: 2-$2.75-c begins 3.50

TICK NEW SERIES (The...)
New England Comics: Dec, 2009 - Present ($4.95)
1-8 5.00

TICK'S BIG XMAS TRILOGY, THE
New England Comics: Dec, 2002 - No. 3, Dec, 2002 ($3.95, limited series)
1-3 4.00

TICK'S GOLDEN AGE COMIC, THE
New England Comics: May, 2002 - No. 3, Feb, 2003 ($4.95, Golden Age size)
1-3-Facsimile 1940s-style Tick issue; 2 covers 5.00
Giant Edition TPB (9/03, $12.95) r/#1-3 13.00

TICK'S GIANT CIRCUS OF THE MIGHTY, THE
New England Comics: Summer, 1992 - No. 3, Fall, 1993 ($2.75, B&W, magazine size)
1-(A-O). 2-(P-Z). 3-1993 Update 4.00

TICKLE COMICS (Also see Gay, Smile, & Whee Comics)
Modern Store Publ.: 1955 (7¢, 5x7-1/4", 52 pgs)
1 6 12 18 28 34 40

TICK TOCK TALES
Magazine Enterprises: Jan, 1946 - V3#33, Jan-Feb, 1951
1-Koko & Kola begin 17 34 51 98 154 210
2 11 22 33 60 83 105
3-10 10 20 30 56 76 95
11-33: 19-Flag-c. 23-Muggsy Mouse, The Pixies & Tom-Tom the Jungle Boy app. 24-X-mas-c. 25-The Pixies & Tom-Tom app. 9 18 27 50 65 80

TIGER (Also see Comics Reading Libraries in the Promotional Comics section)
Charlton Press (King Features): Mar, 1970 - No. 6, Jan, 1971 (15¢)
1 3 6 9 14 19 24
2-6: 3-Ad for life-size inflatable doll 2 4 6 8 11 14

TIGER BOY (See Unearthly Spectaculars)

TIGER GIRL
Gold Key: Sept, 1968 (15¢)
1(10227-809)-Sparling-c/a; Jerry Siegel scripts; advertising on back-c 4 8 12 26 41 55
1-Variant edition with pin-up on back cover 5 10 15 34 55 75

TIGERMAN (Also see Thrilling Adventure Stories)
Seaboard Periodicals (Atlas): Apr, 1975 - No. 3, Sept, 1975 (All 25¢ issues)
1-3: 1-Origin; Colan-c. 2,3-Ditko-p in each 2 4 6 10 14 18

TIGER WALKS, A (See Movie Comics)

TIGRA (The Avengers)
Marvel Comics: May, 2002 - No. 4, Aug, 2002 ($2.99, limited series)
1-4-Christina Z-s/Deodato-c/a 3.00

TIGRESS, THE
Hero Graphics: Aug, 1992 - No. 6?, June, 1993 ($3.95/$2.95/$3.95, B&W)
1,6: 1-Tigress vs. Flare. 6-44 pgs. 4.00
2-5: 2-$2.95-c begins 3.00

TILLIE THE TOILER (See Comic Monthly)
Dell Publishing Co.: No. 15, 1941 - No. 237, July, 1949
Four Color 15(1941) 45 90 135 284 480 675
Large Feature Comic 30(1941) 34 68 102 199 325 450
Four Color 8(1942) 21 42 63 142 304 465
Four Color 22(1943) 15 30 45 102 221 340
Four Color 55(1944), 89(1945) 12 24 36 80 163 245
Four Color 106('45),132('46): 132-New stories begin 10 20 30 65 118 170
Four Color 150,176,184 9 18 27 61 106 150
Four Color 195,213,237 7 14 21 49 82 115

TIMBER WOLF (See Action Comics #372, & Legion of Super-Heroes)
DC Comics: Nov, 1992 - No. 5, Mar, 1993 ($1.25, limited series)
1-5 3.00

TIME BANDITS
Marvel Comics Group: Feb, 1982 (one-shot, Giant)
1-Movie adaptation 4.00

TIME BEAVERS (See First Comics Graphic Novel #2)

TIME BOMB
Radical Comics: Jul, 2010 - No. 3, Dec, 2010 ($4.99, limited series)
1-3-Palmiotti & Gray-s/Gulacy-a/c 5.00

TIME BREAKERS
DC Comics (Helix): Jan, 1997 - No. 5, May, 1997 ($2.25, limited series)
1-5-Pollack-s 3.00

TIMECOP (Movie)
Dark Horse Comics: Sept, 1994 - No. 2, Nov, 1994 ($2.50, limited series)
1,2-Adaptation of film 3.00

TIME FOR LOVE (Formerly Romantic Secrets)
Charlton Comics: V2#53, Oct, 1966; Oct, 1967 - No. 47, May, 1976
V2#53(10/66) Herman-s Hermits app. 3 6 9 20 30 40
1-(10/67) 4 8 12 22 34 45
2-(12/67) -10 3 6 9 15 21 26
11,12,14-20 2 4 6 11 16 20
13-(11/69) Ditko-a (7 pgs.) 3 6 9 16 23 30
21-27 2 4 6 9 13 16

Timely Presents: All Winners #1 © MAR

Tim Holt #36 © ME

Tim Tyler Cowboy #12 © KFS

GD 2.0 VG 4.0 FN 6.0 VF 8.0 VF/NM 9.0 NM- 9.2

28,29,31: 28-Shirley Jones poster. 29-Bobby Sherman pin-up. 31-Bobby Sherman pin-up
2 4 6 11 16 20
30-(10/72)-David Cassidy full page poster 3 6 9 17 25 32
32-47 2 4 6 8 11 14

TIMELESS TOPIX (See Topix)

TIMELY PRESENTS: ALL WINNERS
Marvel Comics: Dec, 1999 ($3.99)
1-Reprints All Winners Comics #19 (Fall 1946); new Lago-c 5.00

TIMELY PRESENTS: HUMAN TORCH
Marvel Comics: Feb, 1999 ($3.99)
1-Reprints Human Torch Comics #5 (Fall 1941); new Lago-c 5.00

TIME MACHINE, THE
Dell Publishing Co.: No. 1085, Mar, 1960 (H.G. Wells)
Four Color 1085-Movie, Alex Toth-a; Rod Taylor photo-c
12 24 36 84 175 265

TIME MASTERS
DC Comics: Feb, 1990 - No. 8, Sept, 1990 ($1.75, mini-series)
1-8: New Rip Hunter series. 5-Cave Carson, Viking Prince app. 6-Dr. Fate app. 3.00
TPB (2008, $19.99) r/#1-8 and Secret Origins #43; intro. by Geoff Johns 20.00

TIME MASTERS: VANISHING POINT (Tie-in to Batman: The Return of Bruce Wayne)
DC Comics: Sept, 2010 - No. 6, Feb, 2011 ($3.99, limited series)
1-6-Jurgens-s/a/c; Rip Hunter, Superman, Green Lantern & Booster Gold app. 4.00
TPB (2011, $14.99) r/#1-6 15.00

TIMESLIP COLLECTION
Marvel Comics: Nov, 1998 ($2.99, one-shot)
1-Pin-ups reprinted from Marvel Vision magazine 3.00

TIMESLIP SPECIAL (The Coming of the Avengers)
Marvel Comics: Oct, 1998 ($5.99, one-shot)
1-Alternate world Avengers vs. Odin 6.00

TIMESTORM 2009/2099
Marvel Comics: June, 2009 - No. 4, Oct, 2009 ($3.99, limited series)
1-4-Punisher 2099 transports Spider-Man to 2099; Wolverine app.; Battle-a 4.00
...: Spider-Man One Shot (8/09, $3.99) Reed-s/Craig-a/Renaud-c 4.00
...: X-Men One Shot (8/09, $3.99) Reed-s/Irving-a/Renaud-c 4.00

TIME TO RUN (Based on 1973 Billy Graham movie)
Spire Christian Comics (Fleming H. Revell Co.): 1975 (39¢)
nn-By Al Hartley 2 4 6 10 14 18

TIME TUNNEL, THE (TV)
Gold Key: Feb, 1967 - No. 2, July, 1967 (12¢)
1-Photo back-c on both issues 7 14 21 46 76 105
2 5 10 15 35 55 75

TIME TWISTERS
Quality Comics: Sept, 1987 - No. 21, 1989 ($1.25/$1.50)
1-21: Alan Moore scripts in 1-4, 6-9, 14 (2 pg.). 14-Bolland-a (2 pg.). 15,16-Guice-c 3.00

TIME 2: THE EPIPHANY (See First Comics Graphic Novel #9)

TIMEWALKER (Also see Archer & Armstrong)
Valiant: Jan, 1994 - No. 15, Oct, 1995 ($2.50)
1-15,0(3/96): 2-"JAN" on-c, February, 1995 in indicia. 3.00
Yearbook 1 (5/95, $2.95) 3.00

TIME WARP (See The Unexpected #210)
DC Comics, Inc.: Oct-Nov, 1979 - No. 5, June-July, 1980 ($1.00, 68 pgs.)
1 2 4 6 11 16 20
2-5 2 4 6 8 11 14
NOTE: ***Aparo** a-1. **Buckler** a-1p. **Chaykin** a-2. **Ditko** a-1-4. **Kaluta** c-1-5. **G. Kane** a-2. **Nasser** a-4. **Newton** a-1-5p. **Orlando** a-2. **Sutton** a-1-3.*

TIME WARRIORS: THE BEGINNING
Fantasy General Comics: 1986 (Aug) - No. 2, 1986? ($1.50)
1,2-Alpha Track/Skellon Empire 3.00

TIM HOLT (Movie star) (Becomes Red Mask #42 on; also see Crack Western #72, & Great Western)
Magazine Enterprises: 1948 - No. 41, April-May, 1954 (All 36 pgs.)
1-(A-1 #14)-Line drawn-c w/Tim Holt photo on-c; Tim Holt, His horse Lightning & sidekick Chito begin 50 100 150 315 533 750
2-(A-1 #17)(9-10/48)-Photo-c begin, end #18 26 52 78 154 252 350
3-(A-1 #19)-Photo back-c 20 40 60 117 189 260
4(1-2/49),5: 5-Photo front/back-c 15 30 45 85 130 175
6-(5/49)-1st app. The Calico Kid (alias Rex Fury), his horse Ebony & Sidekick Sing-Song (begin series); photo back-c 22 44 66 132 216 300
7-10: 7-Calico Kid by Ayers. 8-Calico Kid by Guardineer (r-in/Great Western #10). 9-Map of Tim's Home Range 14 28 42 82 121 160
11-The Calico Kid becomes The Ghost Rider (origin & 1st app.) by Dick Ayers (r-in/Great Western I.W. #8); his horse Spectre & sidekick Sing-Song begin series
45 90 135 284 480 675
12-16,18-Last photo-c 13 26 39 74 105 135
17-Frazetta Ghost Rider-c 40 80 120 246 411 575
19,22,24: 19-Last Tim Holt-c; Bolle line-drawn-c begin; Tim Holt photo on covers #19-28, 30-41. 22-interior photo-c 11 22 33 62 86 110
20-Tim Holt becomes Redmask (origin); begin series; Redmask-c #20-on
15 30 45 86 133 180
21-Frazetta Ghost Rider/Redmask-c 36 72 108 216 351 485
23-Frazetta Redmask-c 28 56 84 165 270 375
25-1st app. Black Phantom 18 36 54 105 165 225
26-30: 28-Wild Bill Hickok, Bat Masterson team up with Redmask. 29-B&W photo-c
10 20 30 58 79 100
31-33-Ghost Rider ends 10 20 30 54 72 90
34-Tales of the Ghost Rider begins (horror)-Classic "The Flower Women" & "Hard Boiled Harry!" 14 28 42 82 121 160
35-Last Tales of the Ghost Rider 11 22 33 62 86 110
36-The Ghost Rider returns, ends #41; liquid hallucinogenic drug story
13 26 39 74 105 135
37-Ghost Rider classic "To Touch Is to Die!", about Inca treasure
13 26 39 74 105 135
38-The Black Phantom begins (not in #39); classic Ghost Rider "The Phantom Guns of Feather Gap!" 13 26 39 74 105 135
39-41: All 3-D effect c/stories 14 28 42 81 118 155
NOTE: ***Dick Ayers** a-7, 9-41. **Bolle** a-1-41; c-19, 20, 22, 24-28, 30-41.*

TIM McCOY (Formerly Zoo Funnies; Pictorial Love Stories #22 on)
Charlton Comics: No. 16, Oct, 1948 - No. 21, Aug, 1949 (Western Movie Stories)
16-John Wayne, Montgomery Clift app. in "Red River"; photo back-c
34 68 102 199 325 450
17-21: 17-Allan "Rocky" Lane guest stars. 18-Rod Cameron guest stars. 19-Whip Wilson, Andy Clyde guest star; Jesse James story. 20-Jimmy Wakely guest stars. 21-Johnny Mack Brown guest stars 24 48 72 142 234 325

TIMMY
Dell Publishing Co.: No. 715, Aug, 1956 - No. 1022, Aug-Oct, 1959
Four Color 715 (#1) 5 10 15 30 48 65
Four Color 823 (8/57), 923 (8/58), 1022 4 8 12 26 41 55

TIMMY THE TIMID GHOST (Formerly Win-A-Prize?; see Blue Bird)
Charlton Comics: No. 3, 2/56 - No. 44, 10/64; No. 45, 9/66; 10/67 - No. 23, 7/71; V4#24, 9/85 - No. 26, 1/86
3(1956) (1st Series) 12 24 36 69 97 125
4,5 8 16 24 42 54 65
6-10 3 6 9 20 30 40
11,12(4/58,10/58)-(100 pgs.) 6 12 18 42 69 95
13-20 3 6 9 18 27 35
21-45(1966): 27-Nazi story 3 6 9 14 19 24
1(10/67, 2nd series) 3 6 9 16 22 28
2-10 2 4 6 10 14 18
11-23: 23 (7/71) 1 3 4 8 10 12
24-26 (1985-86): Fago-r (low print run) 6.00

TIM TYLER (See Harvey Comics Hits #54)

TIM TYLER (Also see Comics Reading Libraries in the Promotional Comics section)
Better Publications: 1942
1 15 30 45 85 130 175

TIM TYLER COWBOY
Standard Comics (King Features Synd.): No. 11, Nov, 1948 - No. 18, Aug, 1950
11-By Lyman Young 9 18 27 50 65 80
12-18: 13-15-Full length western adventures 7 14 21 35 43 50

TINKER BELL (Disney, TV)(See Walt Disney Showcase #37)
Dell Publishing Co.: No. 896, Mar, 1958 - No. 982, Apr-June, 1959
Four Color 896 (#1)-The Adventures of... 8 16 24 55 93 130
Four Color 982-The New Advs. of... 8 16 24 51 86 120

TINY FOLKS FUNNIES
Dell Publishing Co.: No. 60, 1944

Tiny Titans #29 © DC

Tip Top Comics #25 © UFS

Titans #1 © DC

	GD 2.0	VG 4.0	FN 6.0	VF 8.0	VF/NM 9.0	NM- 9.2
Four Color 60	13	26	39	88	189	290

TINY TESSIE (Tessie #1-23; Real Experiences #25)
Marvel Comics (20CC): No. 24, Oct, 1949 (52 pgs.)

24	14	28	42	80	115	150

TINY TIM (Also see Super Comics)
Dell Publishing Co.: No. 4, 1941 - No. 235, July, 1949

Large Feature Comic 4('41)	41	82	123	249	417	585
Four Color 20(1941)	37	74	111	222	361	500
Four Color 42(1943)	14	28	42	95	205	315
Four Color 235	6	12	18	37	59	80

TINY TITANS (Teen Titans)
DC Comics: Apr, 2008 - No. 50, May, 2012 ($2.25/$2.50/$2.99)

1-29-All ages stories of Teen Titans in Elementary school; Baltazar & Franco-s/a 3.00
1-(6/08, Free Comic Book Day giveaway) r/#1; Baltazar & Franco-s/a 3.00
30-50: 30-Begin $2.99-c. 37-Marvel Family app. 44-Doom Patrol app. 3.00
...: Adventures in Awesomeness TPB (2009, $12.99) r/#7-12; pin-ups 13.00
...: Field Trippin' TPB (2011, $12.99) r/#26-32; pin-ups 13.00
...: Sidekickin' It TPB (2010, $12.99) r/#13-18; pin-ups 13.00
...: The First Rule of Pet Club... TPB (2010, $12.99) r/#19-25; pin-ups 13.00
...: Welcome To The Treehouse TPB (2009, $12.99) r/#1-6; pin-ups 13.00

TINY TITANS / LITTLE ARCHIE (Teen Titans) (Digest-size reprint in World of Archie Double Digest Magazine #5)
DC Comics: Dec, 2010 - No. 3, Feb, 2011 ($2.99)

1-3-Character crossover; Baltazar & Franco-s/a. 2-Josie and the Pussycats app. 3.00

TINY TOT COMICS
E. C. Comics: Mar, 1946 - No. 10, Nov-Dec, 1947 (For younger readers)

1(nn)-52 pg. issues begin, end #4	40	80	120	242	401	560
2 (5/46)	22	44	66	132	216	300
3-10: 10-Christmas-c	21	42	63	122	199	275

TINY TOT FUNNIES (Formerly Family Funnies; becomes Junior Funnies)
Harvey Publ. (King Features Synd.): No. 9, June, 1951

9-Flash Gordon, Mandrake, Dagwood, Daisy, etc.	8	16	24	42	54	65

TINY TOTS COMICS
Dell Publishing Co.: 1943 (Not reprints)

1-Kelly-a(2); fairy tales	39	78	117	240	395	550

TIPPY & CAP STUBBS (See Popular Comics)
Dell Publishing Co.: No. 210, Jan, 1949 - No. 242, Aug, 1949

Four Color 210 (#1)	5	10	15	32	51	70
Four Color 242	4	8	12	26	41	55

TIPPY'S FRIENDS GO-GO & ANIMAL
Tower Comics: July, 1966 - No. 15, Oct, 1969 (25¢)

1	10	20	30	67	124	180
2-5,7,9-15: 12-15 titled "Tippy's Friend Go-Go"	6	12	18	41	66	90
6-The Monkees photo-c	9	18	27	61	106	150
8-Beatles app. on front/back-c	11	22	33	73	142	210

TIPPY TEEN (See Vicki)
Tower Comics: Nov, 1965 - No. 25, Oct, 1969 (25¢)

1	11	22	33	73	142	210
2-4,6-10	7	14	21	46	76	105
5-1 pg. Beatles pin-up	8	16	24	51	86	120
11-20: 16-Twiggy photo-c	6	12	18	43	69	95
21-25	6	12	18	39	62	85
Special Collectors' Editions nn-(1969, 25¢)	6	12	18	43	69	95

TIPPY TERRY
Super/I. W. Enterprises: 1963

Super Reprint #14('63)-r/Little Groucho #1	2	4	6	8	10	12
I.W. Reprint #1 (nd)-r/Little Groucho #1	2	4	6	8	10	12

TIP TOP COMICS
United Features #1-188/St. John #189-210/Dell Publishing Co. #211 on:
4/36 - No. 210, 1957; No. 211, 11-1/57-58 - No. 225, 5-7/61

1-Tarzan by Hal Foster, Li'l Abner, Broncho Bill, Fritzi Ritz, Ella Cinders, Capt. & The Kids begin; strip-r (1st comic book app. of each)	800	1600	2400	4800	8250	11,700
2	181	362	543	1158	1979	2800
3-Tarzan-c	161	322	483	1030	1765	2500
4	94	188	282	597	1024	1450
5-8,10: 7-Photo & biography of Edgar Rice Burroughs. 8-Christmas-c	66	132	198	419	722	1025
9-Tarzan-c	84	168	252	538	919	1300
11,13,16,18-Tarzan-c: 11-Has Tarzan pin-up	63	126	189	403	689	975
12,14,15,17,19,20: 20-Christmas-c	49	98	147	309	522	735
21,24,27,30-(10/38)-Tarzan-c	52	104	156	328	552	775
22,23,25,26,28,29	39	78	117	229	375	520
31,35,38,40	36	72	108	211	343	475
32,36-Tarzan-c: 32-1st published Jack Davis-a (cartoon). 36-Kurtzman panel (1st published comic work)	53	106	159	334	567	800
33,34,37,39-Tarzan-c	48	96	144	302	514	725
41-Reprints 1st Tarzan Sunday; Tarzan-c	53	106	159	334	567	800
42,44,46,48,49	30	60	90	177	289	400
43,45,47,50,52-Tarzan-c. 43-Mort Walker panel	39	78	117	236	388	540
51,53	29	58	87	170	278	385
54-Origin Mirror Man & Triple Terror, also featured on cover	37	74	111	218	354	490
55,56,58: Last Tarzan by Foster	24	48	72	142	234	325
57,59-62-Tarzan by Hogarth	31	62	93	182	296	410
63-80: 65,67-70,72-74,77,78-No Tarzan	15	30	45	88	137	185
81-90	14	28	42	80	115	150
91-99	13	26	39	72	101	130
100	14	28	42	76	108	140
101-140: 110-Gordo story. 111-Li'l Abner app. 118, 132-No Tarzan. 137-Sadie Hawkins Day story	10	20	30	54	72	90
141-170: 145,151-Gordo stories. 153-Fritzi Ritz lingerie panels. 157-Last Li'l Abner; lingerie panels	8	16	24	44	57	70
171,172,174-183: 171-Tarzan reprints by B. Lubbers begin; end #188	9	18	27	47	61	75
173-Peanuts by Schulz	14	28	42	80	115	150
184-225-Peanuts apps.(4 pg. to 8 pg stories) in most						
Issues with Peanuts	10	20	30	54	72	90
Issues without Peanuts	8	16	24	40	50	60
Bound Volumes (Very Rare) sold at 1939 World's Fair; bound by publisher in pictorial comic boards (also see Comics on Parade)						
Bound issues 1-12	331	662	993	2317	4059	5800
Bound issues 13-24	179	358	537	1137	1956	2775
Bound issues 25-36	155	310	465	992	1696	2400

NOTE: *Tarzan by **Foster**-#1-40, 44-50; by **Rex Maxon**-#41-43; by **Burne Hogarth**-#57, 59, 62.*

TIP TOPPER COMICS
United Features Syndicate: Oct-Nov, 1949 - No. 28, 1954

1-Li'l Abner, Abbie & Slats	12	24	36	67	94	120
2	8	16	24	44	57	70
3-5: 5-Fearless Fosdick app.	8	16	24	40	50	60
6-10: 6-Fearless Fosdick app.	7	14	21	37	46	55
11-16	6	12	18	31	38	45
17(6-7/52) (2nd app. of Peanuts by Schulz in comics?) (see United Comics #22 for 5-6/52 app.)	16	32	48	94	147	200
18-26: 18-24,26-Early Peanuts (2 pgs.). 25-Early Peanuts (3 pgs.) 26-Twin Earths	13	26	39	74	105	135
27,28-Twin Earths	8	16	24	40	50	60

NOTE: *Many lingerie panels in Fritzi Ritz stories.*

TITAN A.E.
Dark Horse Comics: May, 2000 - No. 3, July, 2000 ($2.95, limited series)

1-3-Movie prequel; Al Rio-a 3.00

TITANS (Also see Teen Titans, New Teen Titans and New Titans)
DC Comics: Mar, 1999 - No. 50, Apr, 2003 ($2.50/$2.75)

1-Titans re-form; Grayson-s; 2 covers 4.00
2-11,13-24,26-50: 2-Superman-c/app. 9,10,21,22-Deathstroke app. 24-Titans from "Kingdom Come" app. 32-36-Asamiya-c. 44-Begin $2.75-c 3.00
12-($3.50, 48 pages) 4.00
25-($3.95) Titans from "Kingdom Come" app.; Wolfman & Faerber-s; art by Pérez, Cardy, Grummett, Jimenez, Dodson, Pelletier 4.00
Annual 1 ('00, $3.50) Planet DC; intro Bushido 4.00
... East Special 1 (1/08, $3.99) Winick-s/Churchill-a; continues in Titans #1 (2008) 4.00
...Secret Files 1,2 (3/99, 10/00; $4.95) Profile pages & short stories 5.00

TITANS (Also see Teen Titans)
DC Comics: Jun, 2008 - No. 38, Oct, 2011 ($3.50/$2.99)

1-($3.50) Titans re-form again; Winick-s/Churchill-a; covers by Churchill & Van Sciver 3.50
2-38: 2-4-Trigon returns. 6-10-Jericho app. 24-Deathstroke & Luthor app. 3.00
Annual 1 (9/11, $4.99) Justice League app.; Jericho returns; Richards-a 5.00
...: Villains For Hire Special 1 (7/10, $4.99) Deathstroke's team; Atom (Ryan Choi) killed 5.00
...: Fractured TPB (2010, $17.99) r/#14,16-22 18.00

T-Man #21 © QUA

Tomahawk #52 © DC

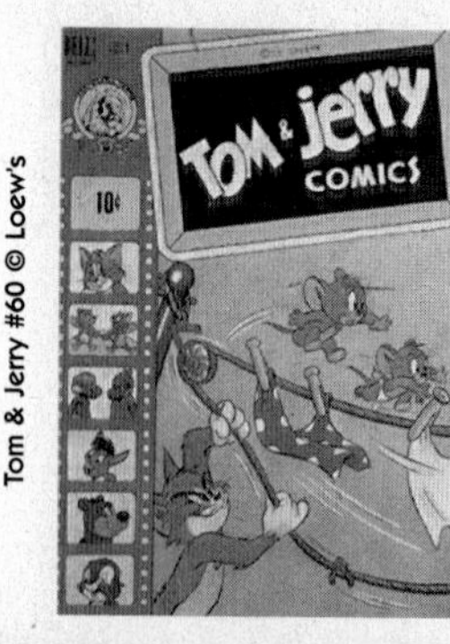

Tom & Jerry #60 © Loew's

GD VG FN VF VF/NM NM-
2.0 4.0 6.0 8.0 9.0 9.2

...: Lockdown TPB (2009, $14.99) r/#7-11 15.00
...: Old Friends HC (2008, $24.99) r/#1-6 & Titans East Special 25.00
...: Villains For Hire TPB (2011, $14.99) r/#24-27 & Villains For Hire Special 1 15.00

TITANS/ LEGION OF SUPER-HEROES: UNIVERSE ABLAZE
DC Comics: 2000 - No. 4, 2000 ($4.95, prestige format, limited series)
1-4-Jurgens-s/a; P. Jimenez-a; teams battle Universo 5.00

TITAN SPECIAL
Dark Horse Comics: June, 1994 ($3.95, one-shot)
1-($3.95, 52 pgs.) 4.00

TITANS: SCISSORS, PAPER, STONE
DC Comics: 1997 ($4.95, one-shot)
1-Manga style Elseworlds; Adam Warren-s/a(p) 5.00

TITANS SELL-OUT SPECIAL
DC Comics: Nov, 1992 ($3.50, 52 pgs., one-shot)
1-Fold-out Nightwing poster; 1st Teeny Titans 4.00

TITANS/ YOUNG JUSTICE: GRADUATION DAY
DC Comics: Early July, 2003 - No. 3, Aug, 2003 ($2.50, limited series)
1,2-Winick-s/Garza-a; leads into Teen Titans and The Outsiders series. 2-Lilith dies 3.00
3-Death of Donna Troy (Wonder Girl) 3.00
TPB (2003, $6.95) r/#1-3; plus previews of Teen Titans and The Outsiders series 7.00

T-MAN (Also see Police Comics #103)
Quality Comics Group: Sept, 1951 - No. 38, Dec, 1956
1-Pete Trask, T-Man begins; Jack Cole-a 42 84 126 265 445 625
2-Crandall-c 23 46 69 136 223 310
3,7,8: All Crandall-c 21 42 63 126 206 285
4,5-Crandall-c/a each 22 44 66 132 216 300
6-"The Man Who Could Be Hitler" c/story; Crandall-c.
28 56 84 165 270 375
9,10-Crandall-c 19 38 57 112 179 245
11-Used in **POP**, pg. 95 & color illo. 15 30 45 90 140 190
12,13,15-19,22-26: 23-H-Bomb panel. 24-Last pre-code issue (4/55).
25-Not Crandall-a 14 28 42 80 115 150
14-Hitler-c 20 40 60 117 189 260
20-H-Bomb explosion-c/story 18 36 54 103 162 220
21- "The Return of Mussolini" c/story 16 32 48 94 147 200
27-33,35-38 14 28 42 76 108 140
34-Hitler-c 18 36 54 105 165 225
NOTE: *Anti-communist stories common.* ***Crandall*** *c-2-10p.* ***Cuidera*** *c(i)-1-38. Bondage c-15.*

TMNT... (Also see Teenage Mutant Ninja Turtles and related titles)
Mirage Publishing: March 2007 ($3.25/$4.95, B&W, one-shots)
...: Raphael Movie Prequel 1; ...: Michelangelo Movie Prequel 2; ...: Donatello Movie Prequel 3;
...: April Movie Prequel 4; ...: Leonardo Movie Prequel 5; back-story for movie 3.25
...: The Official Movie Adaptation ($4.95) adapts 2007 movie; Munroe-c 5.00

TMNT MUTANT UNIVERSE SOURCEBOOK
Archie Comics: 1992 - No. 3, 1992? ($1.95, 52 pgs.)(Lists characters from A-Z)
1-3: 3-New characters; fold-out poster 4.00

TNT COMICS
Charles Publishing Co.: Feb, 1946 (36 pgs.)
1-Yellowjacket app. 32 64 96 188 307 425

TOBY TYLER (Disney, see Movie Comics)
Dell Publishing Co.: No. 1092, Apr-June, 1960
Four Color 1092-Movie, photo-c 6 12 18 42 69 95

TODAY'S BRIDES
Ajax/Farrell Publishing Co.: Nov, 1955; No. 2, Feb, 1956; No. 3, Sept, 1956; No. 4, Nov, 1956
1 9 18 27 52 69 85
2-4 7 14 21 37 46 55

TODAY'S ROMANCE
Standard Comics: No. 5, March, 1952 - No. 8, Sept, 1952 (All photo-c?)
5-Photo-c 11 22 33 62 86 110
6-Photo-c; Toth-a 11 22 33 64 90 115
7,8 9 18 27 52 69 85

TOE TAGS FEATURING GEORGE A. ROMARO
DC Comics: Dec, 2004 - No. 6, May, 2005 ($2.95/$2.99)
1-6-Zombie story by George Romaro; Wrightson-c/Castillo-a 3.00

TOKA (Jungle King)

GD VG FN VF VF/NM NM-
2.0 4.0 6.0 8.0 9.0 9.2

Dell Publishing Co.: Aug-Oct, 1964 - No. 10, Jan, 1967 (Painted-c #1,2)
1 5 10 15 30 48 65
2 3 6 9 18 27 35
3-10 3 6 9 16 22 28

TOKYO STORM WARNING (See Red/Tokyo Storm Warning for TPB)
DC Comics (Cliffhanger): Aug, 2003 - No. 3, Dec, 2003 ($2.95, limited series)
1-3-Warren Ellis-s/James Raiz-a 3.00

TOMAHAWK (Son of... on-c of #131-140; see Star Spangled Comics #69 & World's Finest Comics #65)
National Periodical Publications: Sept-Oct, 1950 - No. 140, May-June, 1972
1-Tomahawk & boy sidekick Dan Hunter begin by Fred Ray
181 362 543 1158 1979 2800
2-Frazetta/Williamson-a (4 pgs.) 66 132 198 419 722 1025
3-5 41 82 123 256 428 600
6-10: 7-Last 52 pg. issue 36 72 108 211 343 475
11-20 24 48 72 142 234 325
21-27,30: 30-Last precode (2/55) 21 42 63 126 206 285
28-1st app. Lord Shilling (arch-foe) 22 44 66 132 216 300
29-Frazetta-r/Jimmy Wakely #3 (3 pgs.) 26 52 78 154 252 350
31-40 18 36 54 107 169 230
41-50 10 20 30 68 127 185
51-56,58-60 9 18 27 62 109 155
57-Frazetta-r/Jimmy Wakely #6 (3 pgs.) 10 20 30 68 127 185
61-77: 77-Last 10¢ issue 9 18 27 58 99 140
78-85: 81-1st app. Miss Liberty. 83-Origin Tomahawk's Rangers
7 14 21 49 82 115
86-99: 96-Origin/1st app. The Hood, alias Lady Shilling
6 12 18 39 62 85
100 6 12 18 41 66 90
101-110: 107-Origin/1st app. Thunder-Man 5 10 15 30 48 65
111-115,120,122: 122-Last 12¢ issue 4 8 12 28 44 60
116-1st Neal Adams cover 7 14 21 44 72 100
117-119,121,123-130-Neal Adams-c 5 10 15 32 51 70
131-Frazetta-r/Jimmy Wakely #7 (3 pgs.); origin Firehair retold
4 8 12 22 34 45
132-135: 135-Last 15¢ issue 3 6 9 17 25 32
136-138,140 (52 pg. Giants) 3 6 9 20 30 40
139-Frazetta-r/Star Spangled #113 4 8 12 22 34 45
NOTE: ***Fred Ray*** *c-1, 2, 8, 11, 30, 34, 35, 40-43, 45, 46, 82. Firehair by* ***Kubert****-131-134, 136.* ***Maurer*** *a-138.* ***Severin*** *a-135.* ***Starr*** *a-5.* ***Thorne*** *a-137, 140.*

TOM AND JERRY (See Comic Album #4, 8, 12, Dell Giant #21, Dell Giants, Golden Comics Digest #1, 5, 8, 13, 15, 18, 22, 25, 28, 35, Kite fun Book & March of Comics #21, 46, 61, 70, 88, 103, 119, 128, 145, 154, 173, 190, 207, 224, 281, 295, 305, 321,333, 345, 361, 365, 388, 400, 444, 451, 463, 480)

TOM AND JERRY (...Comics, early issues) (M.G.M.)
(Formerly Our Gang No. 1-59) (See Dell Giants for annuals)
Dell Publishing Co./Gold Key No. 213-327/Whitman No. 328 on: No. 193, 6/48; No. 60, 7/49 - No. 212, 7-9/62; No. 213, 11/62 - No. 291, 2/75; No. 292, 3/77 - No. 342, 5/82 - No. 344, 6/84
Four Color 193 (#1)-Titled "M.G.M. Presents..." 21 42 63 148 317 485
60-Barney Bear, Benny Burro cont. from Our Gang; Droopy begins
11 22 33 76 151 225
61 10 20 30 64 115 165
62-70: 66-X-Mas-c 8 16 24 55 93 130
71-80: 77,90-X-Mas-c. 79-Spike & Tyke begin 7 14 21 44 72 100
81-99 6 12 18 41 66 90
100 6 12 18 42 69 95
101-120 5 10 15 35 55 75
121-140: 126-X-Mas-c 5 10 15 30 48 65
141-160 4 8 12 26 41 55
161-200 4 8 12 24 37 50
201-212(7-9/62)(Last Dell issue) 4 8 12 22 34 45
213,214-(84 pgs.)-Titled "...Funhouse" 6 12 18 41 66 90
215-240: 215-Titled "...Funhouse" 3 6 9 17 25 32
241-270 2 4 6 11 16 20
271-300: 286- "Tom & Jerry" 2 4 6 8 11 14
301-327 (Gold Key) 1 3 4 6 8 10
328,329 (Whitman) 2 4 6 8 11 14
330(8/80),331(10/80), 332-(3-pack only) 3 6 9 20 30 40
333-341: 339(2/82), 340(2-3/82), 341(4/82) 2 4 6 8 10 12
342-344 (All #90058, no date, date code, 3-pack): 342(6/83), 343(8/83), 344(6/84)
3 6 9 14 19 24
Mouse From T.R.A.P. 1(7/66)-Giant, G. K. 5 10 15 30 48 65

Tomb of Dracula #4 © MAR

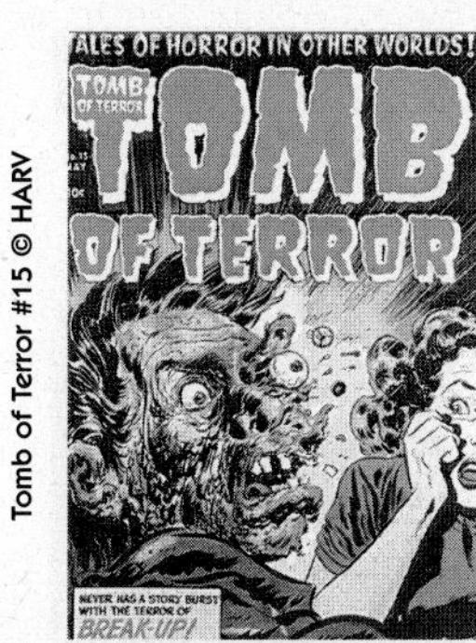

Tomb of Terror #15 © HARV

Tomb Raider: The Series #34 © Eidos

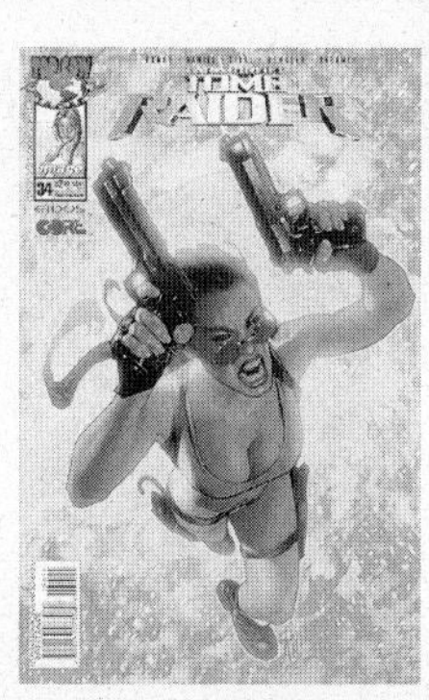

GD VG FN VF VF/NM NM-
2.0 4.0 6.0 8.0 9.0 9.2

Summer Fun 1(7/67, 68 pgs.)(Gold Key)-Reprints Barks' Droopy from Summer Fun #1
5 10 15 30 48 65

NOTE: *#60-87, 98-121, 268, 277, 289, 302 are 52 pgs.. Reprints-#225, 241, 245, 247, 252, 254, 266, 268, 270, 292-327, 329-342, 344.*

TOM & JERRY
Harvey Comics: Sept, 1991 - No. 18, Aug, 1994 ($1.25)

1-18: 1-Tom & Jerry, Barney Bear-r by Carl Barks 3.00
50th Anniversary Special 1 (10/91, $2.50, 68 pgs.)-Benny the Lonesome Burro-r by Barks (story/a)/Our Gang #9 4.00

TOMB OF DARKNESS (Formerly Beware)
Marvel Comics Group: No. 9, July, 1974 - No. 23, Nov, 1976

9 3 6 9 18 27 35
10-23: 11,16,18-21-Kirby-a. 15,19-Ditko-r. 17-Woodbridge-r/Astonishing #62; Powell-r. 20-Everett Venus-r/Venus #19. 22-r/Tales To Astonish #27; 1st Hank Pym. 23-Everett-r
2 4 6 13 18 22
20,21-(30¢-c variants, limited distribution)(5,7/76) 4 8 12 24 37 50

TOMB OF DRACULA (See Giant-Size Dracula, Dracula Lives, Nightstalkers, Power Record Comics & Requiem for Dracula)
Marvel Comics Group: Apr, 1972 - No. 70, Aug, 1979

1-1st app. Dracula & Frank Drake; Colan-p in all; Neal Adams-c
16 32 48 107 234 360
2 9 18 27 58 99 140
3-6: 3-Intro. Dr. Rachel Van Helsing & Inspector Chelm. 6-Neal Adams-c
7 14 21 46 76 105
7-9 6 12 18 41 66 90
10-1st app. Blade the Vampire Slayer (who app. in 1998 and 2002 movies)
20 40 60 140 300 460
11,14-16,20: 5 10 15 32 51 70
12-2nd app. Blade; Brunner-c(p) 9 18 27 61 106 150
13-Origin Blade 10 20 30 68 127 185
17,19: 17-Blade bitten by Dracula. 19-Blade discovers he is immune to vampire's bite. 1st mention of Blade having vampire blood in him 7 14 21 44 72 100
18-Two-part x-over cont'd in Werewolf by Night #15 6 12 18 41 66 90
21,24-Blade app. 5 10 15 32 51 70
22,23,26,27,29 3 6 9 20 30 40
25-1st app. & origin Hannibal King 4 8 12 28 44 60
25-2nd printing (1994) 2 4 6 8 10 12
28-Blade app. on-c & inside as an illusion 4 8 12 28 44 60
30,41-45-Blade app. 45-Intro. Deacon Frost, the vampire who bit Blade's mother
4 8 12 26 41 55
31-40 3 6 9 18 27 35
43-45-(30¢-c variants, limited distribution) 7 14 21 44 72 100
46,47-(Regular 25¢ editions)(4-8/76) 3 6 9 14 20 25
46,47-(30¢-c variants, limited distribution) 4 8 12 26 41 55
48,49,51-57,59,60: 57,59,60-(30¢-c) 3 6 9 14 20 25
50-Silver Surfer app. 4 8 12 24 37 50
57,59,60-(35¢-c variants)(6-9/77) 4 8 12 24 37 50
58-All Blade issue (Regular 30¢ edition) 5 10 15 30 48 65
58-(35¢-c variant)(7/77) 8 16 24 55 93 130
61-69 3 6 9 14 20 25
70-Double size 4 8 12 24 37 50

NOTE: ***N. Adams** c-1, 6. **Colan** a-1-70p; c(p)-8, 38-42, 44-56, 58-70. **Wrightson** c-43.*

TOMB OF DRACULA, THE (Magazine)
Marvel Comics Group: Oct, 1979 - No. 6, Aug, 1980 (B&W)

1,3: 1-Colan-a; features on movies "Dracula" and "Love at First Bite" w/photos. 3-Good girl cover-a; Miller-a (2 pg. sketch) 2 4 6 11 16 20
2,6: 2-Ditko-a (36 pgs.); Nosferatu movie feature. 6-Lilith story w/Sienkiewicz-a
2 4 6 8 11 14
4,5: Stephen King interview 2 4 6 13 18 22

NOTE: ***Buscema** a-4p, 5p. **Chaykin** c-5, 6. **Colan** a(p)-1, 3-6. **Miller** a-3. **Romita** a-2p.*

TOMB OF DRACULA
Marvel Comics (Epic Comics): 1991 - No. 4, 1992 ($4.95, 52 pgs., squarebound, mini-series)

Book 1-4: Colan/Williamson-a; Colan painted-c 5.00

TOMB OF DRACULA
Marvel Comics: Dec, 2004 - No. 4, Mar, 2005 ($2.99, limited series)

1-4-Blade app.; Tolagson-a/Sienkiewicz-c 3.00

TOMB OF DRACULA PRESENTS: THRONE OF BLOOD
Marvel Comics: Jun, 2011 ($3.99, one-shot)

1-Story of Raizo Kodo in 1585 Japan; Parlov-a; Hitch-c 4.00

TOMB OF LEGEIA (See Movie Classics)

GD VG FN VF VF/NM NM-
2.0 4.0 6.0 8.0 9.0 9.2

TOMB OF TERROR (Thrills of Tomorrow #17 on)
Harvey Publications: June, 1952 - No. 16, July, 1954

1 47 94 141 296 498 700
2 31 62 93 182 296 410
3-Bondage-c; atomic disaster story 31 62 93 186 303 420
4-12: 4-Heart ripped out. 8-12-Nostrand-a 29 58 87 170 278 385
13-Special S/F issue 39 78 117 240 395 550
14-Classic S/F-c; Check-a 58 116 174 371 636 900
15-S/F issue; c-shows face exploding 123 246 369 787 1344 1900
16-Special S/F issue; Nostrand-a 37 74 111 222 361 500

NOTE: ***Edd Cartier** a-13? **Elias** c-2, 5-16. **Kremer** a-1, 7; c-1. **Nostrand** a-8-12, 15r 16. **Palais** a-2, 3, 5-7. **Powell** a-1, 3, 5, 9-16. **Sparling** a-12, 13, 15.*

TOMB OF TERROR
Marvel Comics: Dec, 2010 ($3.99, B&W, one-shot)

1-Short stories of Man-Thing, Son of Satan, Werewolf By Night & The Living Mummy 4.00

TOMB RAIDER (one-shots)
Image Comics (Top Cow Prod.)

...: Arabian Nights (8/04, $5.99) Avery-s/Tan-a/c 6.00
... Cover Gallery 2006 (4/06, $2.99) artist galleries and series gallery; pin-ups 3.00
.../The Darkness Special 1 (2001, TopCowStore.com)-Wohl-s/Tan-a 3.00
Epiphany 1 (8/03, $4.99)-Jurgens-s/Banks-a/Haley-c; preview of Witchblade Animated 5.00
Takeover 1 (1/04, $2.99)-Benefiel-a/Daniel-c 3.00
... Vs. The Wolf-Men: Monster War 2005 (7/05, $2.99) 2nd part of Monster War x-over 3.00
.../Witchblade/Magdalena/Vampirella #1 (8/05, $2.99, B&W) three covers; Chin-a 3.00

TOMB RAIDER: JOURNEYS
Image Comics (Top Cow Prod.): Jan, 2002 - No. 12, May, 2003 ($2.50/$2.99)

1-12: 1-Avery-s/Drew Johnson-a. 1-Two covers by Johnson & Hughes 3.00

TOMB RAIDER: THE GREATEST TREASURE OF ALL
Image Comics (Top Cow Prod.): 2002; Oct, 2005 ($6.99)

Prelude (2002, 16 pgs., no cover price) Jusko-c/a 3.00
1-(10/05, $6.99) Jusko-a/Jurgens-s; sketch pages, reference photos, art in progress 7.00

TOMB RAIDER: THE SERIES (Also see Witchblade/Tomb Raider)
Image Comics (Top Cow Prod.): Dec, 1999 - No. 50, Mar, 2005 ($2.50/$2.99)

1-Jurgens-s/Park-a; 3 covers by Park, Finch, Turner 5.00
2-24,26-29,31-50: 21-Black-c w/foil. 31-Mhan-a. 37-Flip book preview of Stryke Force 3.00
25-Michael Turner-c/a; Witchblade app.; Endgame x-over with Witchblade #60 & Evo #1 4.00
30-($4.99) Tony Daniel-a 5.00
#0 (6/01, $2.50) Avery-s/Ching-a/c 3.00
#1/2 (10/01, $2.95) Early days of Lara Croft; Jurgens-s/Lopez-a 3.00
...: Chasing Shangri-La (2002, $12.95, TPB) r/#11-15 13.00
Free Comic Book Day giveaway - (5/02) r/#1 with "Free Comic Book Day" banner on-c 3.00
... Gallery (12/00, $2.95) Pin-ups & previous covers by various 3.00
... Magazine (6/01, $4.95) Hughes-c; r/#1,2; Jurgens interview 5.00
...: Mystic Artifacts (2001, $14.95, TPB) r/#5-10 15.00
...: Saga of the Medusa Mask (9/00, $9.95, TPB) r/#1-4; new Park-c 10.00
... Vol. 1 Compendium (11/06, $59.99) r/#1-50; variant covers and pin-up art 60.00

TOMB RAIDER/WITCHBLADE SPECIAL (Also see Witchblade/Tomb Raider)
Top Cow Prod.: Dec, 1997 (mail-in offer, one-shot)

1-Turner-s/a(p); green background cover 1 3 4 6 8 10
1-Variant-c with orange sun background 1 3 4 6 8 10
1-Variant-c with black sides 1 3 4 6 8 10
1-Revisited (12/98, $2.95) reprints #1, Turner-c 3.00
...: Trouble Seekers TPB (2002, $7.95) rep. T.R./W & W/T.R. & W/T.R. 1/2; new Turner-c 8.00

TOMBSTONE TERRITORY
Dell Publishing Co.: No. 1123, Aug, 1960

Four Color 1123 8 16 24 55 93 130

TOM CAT (Formerly Bo; Atom The Cat #9 on)
Charlton Comics: No. 4, Apr, 1956 - No. 8, July, 1957

4-Al Fago-c/a 8 16 24 44 57 70
5-8 6 12 18 31 38 45

TOM CORBETT, SPACE CADET (TV)
Dell Publishing Co.: No. 378, Jan-Feb, 1952 - No. 11, Sept-Nov, 1954 (All painted covers)

Four Color 378 (#1)-McWilliams-a 14 28 42 97 211 325
Four Color 400,421-McWilliams-a 10 20 30 66 121 175
4(11-1/53) - 11 8 16 24 53 89 125

TOM CORBETT SPACE CADET (See March of Comics #102)

TOM CORBETT SPACE CADET (TV)
Prize Publications: V2#1, May-June, 1955 - V2#3, Sept-Oct, 1955

Tom Mix Western #27 © FAW

Tom Strong #12 © ABC

Tom Terrific #4 © Terry Toons

	GD 2.0	VG 4.0	FN 6.0	VF 8.0	VF/NM 9.0	NM- 9.2
V2#1-Robot-c	33	66	99	194	317	440
2,3-Meskin-c	24	48	72	144	237	330

TOM, DICK & HARRIET (See Gold Key Spotlight)

TOM LANDRY AND THE DALLAS COWBOYS
Spire Christian Comics/Fleming H. Revell Co.: 1973 (35/49¢)

	GD	VG	FN	VF	VF/NM	NM-
nn-35¢ edition	3	6	9	16	22	28
nn-49¢ edition	2	4	6	10	14	18

TOM MIX WESTERN (Movie, radio star) (Also see The Comics, Crackajack Funnies, Master Comics, 100 Pages Of Comics, Popular Comics, Real Western Hero, Six Gun Heroes, Western Hero & XMas Comics)
Fawcett Publications: Jan, 1948 - No. 61, May, 1953 (1-17: 52 pgs.)

	GD	VG	FN	VF	VF/NM	NM-
1 (Photo-c, 52 pgs.)-Tom Mix & his horse Tony begin; Tumbleweed Jr. begins, ends #52,54,55	53	106	159	334	567	800
2 (Photo-c)	25	50	75	150	245	340
3-5 (Painted/photo-c): 5-Billy the Kid & Oscar app.	19	38	57	111	176	240
6-8: 6,7 (Painted/photo-c). 8-Kinstler tempera-c	16	32	48	94	147	200
9,10 (Paint/photo-c) 9-Used in **SOTI**, pgs. 323-325	15	30	45	90	140	190
11-Kinstler oil-c	14	28	42	82	121	160
12 (Painted/photo-c)	14	28	42	78	112	145
13-17 (Painted-c, 52 pgs.)	14	28	42	78	112	145
18,22 (Painted-c, 36 pgs.)	12	24	36	69	97	125
19 (Photo-c, 52 pgs.)	13	26	39	74	105	135
20,21,23 (Painted-c, 52 pgs.)	12	24	36	69	97	125
24,25,27-29 (52 pgs.): 24-Photo-c begin, end #61. 29-Slim Pickens app.	11	22	33	60	83	105
26,30 (36 pgs.)	10	20	30	56	76	95
31-33,35-37,39,40,42 (52 pgs.): 39-Red Eagle app.	10	20	30	56	76	95
34,38 (36 pgs. begin)	9	18	27	52	69	85
41,43-60: 57-(9/52)-Dope smuggling story	8	16	24	40	50	60
61-Last issue	9	18	27	47	61	75

NOTE: *Photo-c from 1930s Tom Mix movies (he died in 1940). Many issues contain ads for Tom Mix, Rocky Lane, Space Patrol and other premiums. Captain Tootsie by* ***C.C. Beck*** *in #6-11, 20.*

TOM MIX WESTERN
AC Comics: 1988 - No. 2, 1989? ($2.95, B&W w/16 pgs. color, 44 pgs.)

	NM-
1-Tom Mix-r/Master #124,128,131,102 plus Billy the Kid-r by Severin; photo front/back/inside-c	4.00
2-($2.50, B&W)-Gabby Hayes-r; photo covers	4.00
...Holiday Album 1 (1990, $3.50, B&W, one-shot, 44 pgs.)-Contains photos & 1950s Tom Mix-r; photo inside-c	4.00

TOMMY OF THE BIG TOP (Thrilling Circus Adventures)
King Features Synd./Standard Comics: No. 10, Sep, 1948 - No. 12, Mar, 1949

	GD	VG	FN	VF	VF/NM	NM-
10-By John Lehti	9	18	27	52	69	85
11,12	7	14	21	35	43	50

TOMMYSAURUS REX
Image Comics: Aug, 2004 ($11.95, B&W, graphic novel)

	NM-
Vol. 1 - Doug TenNapel-s/a	12.00

TOMMY TOMORROW (See Action Comics #127, Real Fact #6, Showcase #41,42,44,46,47 & World's Finest #102)

TOMOE (Also see Shi: The Way Of the Warrior #6)
Crusade Comics: July, 1995 - No. 3, June, 1996($2.95)

	GD	VG	FN	VF	VF/NM	NM-
0-3: 2-B&W Dogs o' War preview. 3-B&W Demon Gun preview						3.00
0 (3/96, $2.95)-variant-c.						3.00
0-Commemorative edition (5,000)	2	4	6	8	10	12
1-Commemorative edition (5,000)	2	4	6	9	12	15
1-($2.95)-FAN Appreciation edition						3.00
TPB (1997, $14.95) r/#0-3						15.00

TOMOE: UNFORGETTABLE FIRE
Crusade Comics: June, 1997 ($2.95, one-shot)

	NM-
1-Prequel to Shi: The Series	3.00

TOMOE-WITCHBLADE/FIRE SERMON
Crusade Comics: Sept, 1996 ($3.95, one-shot)

	NM-
1-Tucci-c	5.00
1-($9.95)-Avalon Ed. w/gold foil-c	10.00

TOMOE-WITCHBLADE/MANGA SHI PREVIEW EDITION
Crusade Comics: July, 1996 ($5.00, B&W)

	NM-
nn-San Diego Preview Edition	5.00

TOMORROW KNIGHTS
Marvel Comics (Epic Comics): June, 1990 - No. 6, Mar, 1991 ($1.50)

	NM-
1-($1.95, 52 pgs.)	4.00
2-6	3.00

TOMORROW STORIES
America's Best Comics: Oct, 1999 - No. 12, Aug, 2002 ($3.50/$2.95)

	NM-
1-Two covers by Ross and Nowlan; Moore-s	3.50
2-12-($2.95)	3.00
... Special (1/06, $6.99) Nowlan-c; Moore-s; Greyshirt tribute to Will Eisner	7.00
... Special 2 (5/06, $6.99) Gene Ha-c; Moore-s; Promethea app.	7.00
Book 1 Hardcover (2002, $24.95) r/#1-6	25.00
Book 1 TPB (2003, $17.95) r/#1-6	18.00
Book 2 Hardcover (2004, $24.95) r/#7-12	25.00
Book 2 TPB (2005, $17.99) r/#7-12	18.00

TOM SAWYER (See Adventures of... & Famous Stories)

TOM SKINNER-UP FROM HARLEM (See Up From Harlem)

TOM STRONG (Also see Many Worlds of Tesla Strong)
America's Best Comics: June, 1999 - No. 36, May, 2006 ($3.50/$2.95/$2.99)

	NM-
1-Two covers by Ross and Sprouse; Moore-s/Sprouse-a	4.00
1-Special Edition (9/09, $1.00) reprint with "After Watchmen" cover frame	3.00
2-36: 4-Art Adams-a (8 pgs.) 13-Fawcett homage w/art by Sprouse, Baker, Heath 20-Origin of Tom Stone. 22-Ordway-a. 31,32-Moorcock-s	3.00
...: Book One HC ('00, $24.95) r/#1-7, cover gallery and sketchbook	25.00
...: Book One TPB ('01, $14.95) r/#1-7, cover gallery and sketchbook	15.00
...: Book Two HC ('02, $24.95) r/#8-14, sketchbook	25.00
...: Book Two TPB ('03, $14.95) r/#8-14, sketchbook	15.00
...: Book Three HC ('04, $24.95) r/#15-19, sketchbook	25.00
...: Book Three TPB ('04, $17.95) r/#15-19, sketchbook	18.00
...: Book Four HC ('04, $24.95) r/#20-25, sketch pages	25.00
...: Book Four TPB ('05, $17.99) r/#20-25, sketch pages	18.00
...: Book Five HC ('05, $24.99) r/#26-30, sketch pages	25.00
...: Book Five TPB ('06, $17.99) r/#26-30, sketch pages	18.00
...: Book Six HC ('06, $24.99) r/#31-36	25.00
...: Book Six TPB ('08, $17.99) r/#31-36	18.00
...: The Deluxe Edition Book One (2009, $39.99, d.j.) r/#1-12; Moore intro.; sketch-a	40.00
...: The Deluxe Edition Book Two (2010, $39.99, d.j.) r/#13-24; sketch-a	40.00

TOM STRONG AND THE ROBOTS OF DOOM
DC Comics (WildStorm): Aug, 2010 - No. 6, Jan, 2011 ($3.99, limited series)

	NM-
1-6-Hogan-s/Sprouse-a. 1-Covers by Sprouse & Williams	4.00
TPB (2011, $17.99) r/#1-6	18.00

TOM STRONG'S TERRIFIC TALES
America's Best Comics: Jan, 2002 - No. 12 ($3.50/$2.95)

	NM-
1-Short stories; Moore-s; art by Adams, Rivoche, Hernandez, Weiss	3.50
2-12-($2.95) 2-Adams, Ordway, Weiss-a; Adams-c. 4-Rivoche-a. 5-Pearson, Aragonés-a 11-Timm-a	3.00
...: Book One HC ('04, $24.95) r/#1-6, cover gallery and sketch pages	25.00
...: Book One SC ('05, $17.99) r/#1-6, cover gallery and sketch pages	18.00
...: Book Two HC ('05, $24.95) r/#7-12, covers	25.00

TOM TERRIFIC! (TV)(See Mighty Mouse Fun Club Magazine #1)
Pines Comics (Paul Terry): Summer, 1957 - No. 6, Fall, 1958
(See Terry Toons Giant Summer Fun Book)

	GD	VG	FN	VF	VF/NM	NM-
1-1st app.?; CBS Television Presents...	21	42	63	126	206	285
2-6-(scarce)	16	32	48	94	147	200

TOM THUMB
Dell Publishing Co.: No. 972, Jan, 1959

	GD	VG	FN	VF	VF/NM	NM-
Four Color 972-Movie, George Pal	8	16	24	56	96	135

TOM-TOM, THE JUNGLE BOY (See A-1 Comics & Tick Tock Tales)
Magazine Enterprises: 1947 - No. 3, 1947; Nov, 1957 - No. 3, Mar, 1958

	GD	VG	FN	VF	VF/NM	NM-
1-Funny animal	12	24	36	67	94	120
2,3(1947): 3-Christmas issue	9	18	27	50	65	80
Tom-Tom & Itchi the Monk 1(11/57) - 3(3/58)	5	10	15	24	30	35
I.W. Reprint No. 1,2,8,10: 1,2,8-r/Koko & Kola #?	2	4	6	8	10	12

TONGUE LASH
Dark Horse Comics: Aug, 1996 - No. 2, Sept, 1996 ($2.95, lim. series, mature)

	NM-
1,2: Taylor-c/a	3.00

TONGUE LASH II
Dark Horse Comics: Feb, 1999 - No. 2, Mar, 1999 ($2.95, lim. series, mature)

	NM-
1,2: Taylor-c/a	3.00

TONKA (Disney)

Top Adventure Comics #2 © I.W.

Top Cat #2 © H-B

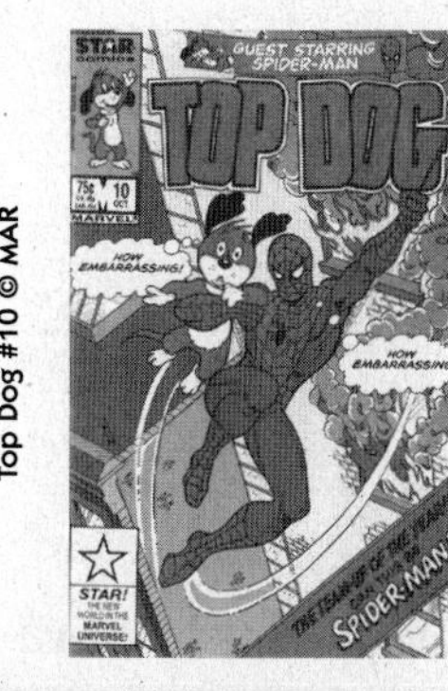

Top Dog #10 © MAR

GD 2.0 | VG 4.0 | FN 6.0 | VF 8.0 | VF/NM 9.0 | NM- 9.2

Dell Publishing Co.: No. 966, Jan, 1959
Four Color 966-Movie (Starring Sal Mineo)-photo-c 8 16 24 56 96 135

TONTO (See The Lone Ranger's Companion...)

TONY TRENT (The Face #1,2)
Big Shot/Columbia Comics Group: No. 3, 1948 - No. 4, 1949
3,4: 3-The Face app. by Mart Bailey 18 36 54 105 165 225

TOODLES, THE (The Toodle Twins with #1)
Ziff-Davis (Approved Comics)/Argo: No. 10, July-Aug, 1951; Mar, 1956 (Newspaper-r)
10-Painted-c, some newspaper-r by The Baers 13 26 39 72 101 130
...Twins 1(Argo, 3/56)-Reprints by The Baers 8 16 24 42 54 65

TOO MUCH COFFEE MAN
Adhesive Comics: July, 1993 - No. 10, Dec, 2000 ($2.50, B&W)
1-Shannon Wheeler story & art 2 4 6 9 12 15
2,3 1 2 3 5 7 9
4,5 6.00
6-10 4.00
Full Color Special-nn($2.95),2-(7/97, $3.95) 4.00

TOO MUCH COFFEE MAN SPECIAL
Dark Horse Comics: July, 1997 ($2.95, B&W)
nn-Reprints Dark Horse Presents #92-95 4.00

TOO MUCH HOPELESS SAVAGES
Oni Press: June, 2003 - No. 4, Apr, 2004 ($2.99, B&W, limited series)
1-4-Van Meter-s/Norrie-a 3.00
TPB (8/04, $11.95, digest-size) r/series 12.00

TOOTS AND CASPER
Dell Publishing Co.: No. 5, 1942
Large Feature Comic 5 20 40 60 117 189 260

TOP ADVENTURE COMICS
I. W. Enterprises: 1964 (Reprints)
1-r/High Adv. (Explorer Joe #2); Krigstein-r 2 4 6 11 16 20
2-Black Dwarf-r/Red Seal #22; Kinstler-c 2 4 6 13 18 22

TOP CAT (TV) (Hanna-Barbera)(See Kite Fun Book)
Dell Publishing Co./Gold Key No. 4 on: 12-2/61-62 - No. 3, 6-8/62; No. 4, 10/62 - No. 31, 9/70
1 (TV show debuted 9/27/61) 13 26 39 86 183 280
2-Augie Doggie back-ups in #1-4 8 16 24 55 93 130
3-5: 3-Last 15¢ issue. 4-Begin 12¢ issues; Yakky Doodle app. in 1 pg. strip.
5-Touché Turtle app. 6 12 18 42 69 95
6-10 5 10 15 32 51 70
11-20 4 8 12 24 37 50
21-31-Reprints 3 6 9 19 29 38

TOP CAT (TV) (Hanna-Barbera)(See TV Stars #4)
Charlton Comics: Nov, 1970 - No. 20, Nov, 1973
1 6 12 18 37 59 80
2-10 3 6 9 20 30 40
11-20 3 6 9 17 25 32
NOTE: *#8 (1/72) went on sale late in 1972 between #14 and #15 with the 1/73 issues.*

TOP COMICS
K. K. Publications/Gold Key: July, 1967 (All reprints)
nn-The Gnome-Mobile (Disney-movie) 2 4 6 13 18 22
1-Beagle Boys (#7), Beep Beep the Road Runner (#5), Bugs Bunny, Chip 'n' Dale, Daffy Duck (#50), Flipper, Huey, Dewey & Louie, Junior Woodchucks, Lassie, The Little Monsters (#71), Moby Duck, Porky Pig (has Gold Key label - says Top Comics on inside), Scamp, Super Goof, Tom & Jerry, Top Cat (#21), Tweety & Sylvester (#7), Walt Disney C&S (#322), Woody Woodpecker known issues; each character given own book
2 4 6 9 13 16
1-Donald Duck (not Barks), Mickey Mouse 2 4 6 13 18 22
1-Flintstones 4 8 12 22 34 45
1-Huckleberry Hound, Yogi Bear (#30) 3 6 9 14 19 24
1-The Jetsons 5 10 15 30 48 65
1-Tarzan of the Apes (#169) 3 6 9 16 22 28
1-Three Stooges (#35) 3 6 9 18 27 35
1-Uncle Scrooge (#70) 3 6 9 16 23 30
1-Zorro (r/G.K. Zorro #7 w/Toth-a; says 2nd printing) 3 6 9 14 19 24
2-Bugs Bunny, Daffy Duck, Mickey Mouse (#114), Porky Pig, Super Goof, Tom & Jerry, Tweety & Sylvester, Walt Disney's C&S (r/#325), Woody Woodpecker
2 4 6 9 12 15
2-Donald Duck (not Barks), Three Stooges, Uncle Scrooge (#71)-Barks-c, Yogi Bear (#30), Zorro (r/#8; Toth-a) 2 4 6 11 16 20
2-Snow White & 7 Dwarfs(6/67)(1944-r) 2 4 6 10 14 18
3-Donald Duck 2 4 6 11 16 20
3-Uncle Scrooge (#72) 2 4 6 13 18 22
3,4-The Flintstones 4 8 12 22 34 45
3,4: 3-Mickey Mouse (r/#115), Tom & Jerry, Woody Woodpecker, Yogi Bear.
4-Mickey Mouse, Woody Woodpecker 2 4 6 9 12 15
NOTE: *Each book in this series is identical to its counterpart except for cover, and came out at same time. The number in parentheses is the original issue it contains.*

TOP COW (Company one-shots)
Image Comics (Top Cow Productions)
... Book of Revelations (7/03, $3.99)-Pin-ups and info; art by various; Gossett-c 4.00
... Convention Sketchbook 2004 (4/04, $3.00, B&W) art by various 3.00
... Holiday Special Vol. 1 (12/10, $12.99) Flip book with Jingle Belle 13.00
... Preview Book 2005 (3/05, 99¢) Preview pages of Tomb Raider, Darkness, Rising Stars 3.00
... Productions, Inc./Ballistic Studios Swimsuit Special (5/95, $2.95) 3.00
...'s Best of: Dave Finch Vol. 1 TPB (8/06, $19.99) r/issues of Cyberforce, Aphrodite IX, Ascension and The Darkness; art & cover gallery 20.00
...'s Best of: Michael Turner Vol. 1 TPB (12/05, $24.99) r/Witchblade #1,10,12,18,19,25 & Witchblade/Tomb Raider chapters 1&3; Tomb Raider #25; art & cover gallery 25.00
... Secrets: Special Winter Lingerie Edition 1 (1/96, $2.95) Pin-ups 3.00
... 2001 Preview (no cover price) Preview pages of Tomb Raider; Jusko-a; flip cover & pages of Inferno 3.00

TOP COW CLASSICS IN BLACK AND WHITE
Image Comics (Top Cow): Feb, 2000 - Present ($2.95, B&W reprints)
...: Aphrodite IX #1(9/00) B&W reprint 3.00
...: Ascension #1(4/00) B&W reprint plus time-line of series 3.00
...: Battle of the Planets #1(1/03) B&W reprint plus script and cover gallery 3.00
...: Darkness #1(3/00) B&W reprint plus time-line of series 3.00
...: Fathom #1(5/00) B&W reprint 3.00
...: Magdalena #1(10/02) B&W reprint plus time-line of series 3.00
...: Midnight Nation #1(9/00) B&W preview 3.00
...: Rising Stars #1(7/00) B&W reprint plus cover gallery 3.00
...: Tomb Raider #1(12/00) B&W reprint plus back-story 3.00
...: Witchblade #1(2/00) B&W reprint plus back-story 3.00
...: Witchblade #25(5/01) B&W reprint plus interview with Wohl & Haberlin 3.00

TOP DETECTIVE COMICS
I. W. Enterprises: 1964 (Reprints)
9-r/Young King Cole #14; Dr. Drew (not Grandenetti) 2 4 6 10 14 18

TOP DOG (See Star Comics Magazine, 75¢)
Star Comics (Marvel): Apr, 1985 - No. 14, June, 1987 (Children's book)
1-14: 10-Peter Parker & J. Jonah Jameson cameo 5.00

TOP ELIMINATOR (Teenage Hotrodders #1-24; Drag 'n' Wheels #30 on)
Charlton Comics: No. 25, Sept, 1967 - No. 29, July, 1968
25-29 3 6 9 16 23 30

TOP FLIGHT COMICS: Four Star Publ.: 1947 (Advertised, not published)

TOP FLIGHT COMICS
St. John Publishing Co.: July, 1949
1(7/49, St. John)-Hector the Inspector; funny animal 10 20 30 54 72 90

TOP GUN (See Luke Short, 4-Color #927 & Showcase #72)

TOP GUNS OF THE WEST (See Super DC Giant)

TOPIX (...Comics) (Timeless Topix-early issues) (Also see Men of Battle, Men of Courage & Treasure Chest)(V1-V5#1,V7 on-paper-c)
Catechetical Guild Educational Society: 11/42 - V10#15, 1/28/52 (Weekly - later issues)
V1#1(8 pgs.,8x11") 24 48 72 140 230 320
2,3(8 pgs.,8x11") 14 28 42 80 115 150
4-8(16 pgs.,8x11") 11 22 33 64 90 115
V2#1-10(16 pgs.,8x11"): V2#8-Pope Pius XII 10 20 30 56 76 95
V3#1-10(16 pgs.,8x11"): V3#1-(9/44) 10 20 30 54 72 90
V4#1-10: V4#1-(9/45) 9 18 27 47 61 75
V5#1(10/46,52 pgs.,2(11/46),no #3),4(1/47)-9(6/47),10(7/47), no #13,4(10/47), 14(11/47),15(12/47) 8 16 24 40 50 60
11(8/47),12(9/47)-Life of Christ editions 10 20 30 54 72 90
V6#4(1/48),5(2/48),7(3/48),8(4/48),9(5/48),10(6/48),11(7/48)-14 (no #1-3,6)
7 14 21 35 43 50
V7#1(9/1/48)-20(6/15/49), 36 pgs. 6 12 18 29 36 42
V8#1(9/19/49)-3,5-11,13-30(5/15/50) 6 12 18 28 34 40

Top Love Stories #18 © STAR

Top Secrets #4 © S&S

Tor #2 © DC

	GD 2.0	VG 4.0	FN 6.0	VF 8.0	VF/NM 9.0	NM- 9.2
4-Dagwood Splits the Atom(10/10/49)-Magazine format	8	16	24	42	54	65
12-Ingels-a	10	20	30	54	72	90
V9#1(9/25/50)-11,13-30(5/14/51)	6	12	18	27	33	38
12-Special 36 pg. Xmas issue, text illos format	6	12	18	28	34	40
V10#1(10/1/51)-15: 14-Hollingsworth-a	6	12	18	27	33	38

TOP JUNGLE COMICS
I. W. Enterprises: 1964 (Reprint)

1(nd)-Reprints White Princess of the Jungle #3, minus cover; Kintsler-a	3	6	9	16	23	30

TOP LOVE STORIES (Formerly Gasoline Alley #2)
Star Publications: No. 3, 5/51 - No. 19, 3/54

3(#1)	21	42	63	126	206	285
4,5,7-9: 8-Wood story	18	36	54	105	165	225
6-Wood-a	22	44	66	132	216	300
10-16,18,19-Disbrow-a	18	36	54	105	165	225
17-Wood art (Fox-r)	19	38	57	112	176	240

NOTE: *All have* ***L. B. Cole*** *covers.*

TOP-NOTCH COMICS (...Laugh #28-45; Laugh Comix #46 on)
MLJ Magazines: Dec, 1939 - No. 45, June, 1944

1-Origin/1st app. The Wizard; Kardak the Mystic Magician, Swift of the Secret Service (ends #3), Air Patrol, The Westpointer, Manhunters (by J. Cole), Mystic (ends #2) & Scott Rand (ends #3) begin; Wizard covers begin, end #8	524	1048	1572	3825	6763	9700
2-(1/40)-Dick Storm (ends #8), Stacy Knight M.D. (ends #4) begin; Jack Cole-a; 1st app. Nazis swastika on-c	248	496	744	1575	2713	3850
3-Bob Phantom, Scott Rand on Mars begin; J. Cole-a	171	342	513	1086	1868	2650
4-Origin/1st app. Streak Chandler on Mars; Moore of the Mounted only app.; J. Cole-a	155	310	465	992	1696	2400
5-Flag-c; origin/1st app. Galahad; Shanghai Sheridan begins (ends #8); Shield cameo; Novick-a; classic-c	171	342	513	1086	1868	2650
6-Meskin-a	115	230	345	730	1253	1775
7-The Shield x-over in Wizard; The Wizard dons new costume	148	296	444	947	1624	2300
8-Origin/1st app. The Firefly & Roy, the Super Boy (9/40, 2nd costumed boy hero after Robin?; also see Toro in Human Torch #1 (Fall/40)	155	310	465	992	1696	2400
9-Origin & 1st app. The Black Hood; 1st Black Hood-c & logo (10/40); Fran Frazier begins (Scarce)	649	1298	1947	4738	8369	12,000
10-2nd app. Black Hood	216	432	648	1372	2361	3350
11-3rd Black Hood	135	270	405	864	1482	2100
12-15	113	226	339	718	1234	1750
16-18,20	98	196	294	622	1074	1525
19-Classic bondage-c	107	214	321	680	1165	1650
21-30: 23-26-Roy app. 24-No Wizard. 25-Last Bob Phantom. 27-Last Firefly; Nazi war-c. 28-Suzie, Pokey Oakey begin. 29-Last Kardak	68	136	204	435	743	1050
31-44: 33-Dotty & Ditto by Woggon begins (2/43, 1st app.). 44-Black Hood series ends	42	84	126	265	445	625
45-Last issue	46	92	138	290	488	685

NOTE: ***J. Binder*** *a-1-3.* ***Meskin*** *a-2, 3, 6, 15.* ***Bob Montana*** *a-30; c-28-31.* ***Harry Sahle*** *c-42-45.* ***Woggon*** *a-33-40, 42. Bondage c-17, 19. Black Hood also appeared on radio in 1944.Black Hood app. on c-9-34, 41-44. Roy the Super Boy app. on c-8, 9, 11-27. The Wizard app. on c-1-8, 11-13, 15-22, 24, 25, 27. Pokey Oakey app. on c-28-43. Suzie app. on c-44-on.*

TOPPER & NEIL (TV)
Dell Publishing Co.: No. 859, Nov, 1957

Four Color 859	5	10	15	30	48	65

TOPPS COMICS: Four Star Publications: 1947 (Advertised, not published)

TOPS
July, 1949 - No. 2, Sept, 1949 (25¢, 10-1/4x13-1/4", 68 pgs.)
Tops Magazine, Inc. (Lev Gleason): (Large size-magazine format; for the adult reader)

1 (Rare)-Story by Dashiell Hammett; Crandall/Lubbers, Tuska, Dan Barry, Fuje-a; Biro painted-c	181	362	543	1158	1979	2800
2 (Rare)-Crandall/Lubbers, Biro, Kida, Fuje, Guardineer-a	161	322	483	1030	1765	2500

TOPS COMICS
Consolidated Book Publishers: 1944 (10¢, 132 pgs.)

2000-(Color-c, inside in red shade & some in full color)-Ace Kelly by Rick Yager, Black Orchid, Don on the Farm, Dinky Dinkerton (Rare)	28	56	84	165	270	375

NOTE: *This book is printed in such a way that when the staple is removed, the strips on the left side of the book correspond with the same strips on the right side. Therefore, if strips are removed from the book, each strip can be folded into a complete comic section of its own.*

TOPS COMICS (See Tops in Humor)
Consolidated Book (Lev Gleason): 1944 (7-1/4x5", 32 pgs.)

2001-The Jack of Spades (costumed hero)	18	36	54	105	165	225
2002-Rip Raider	11	22	33	60	83	105
2003-Red Birch (gag cartoons)	6	12	18	31	38	45
2004-Gag cartoons	16	32	48	94	147	200

TOP SECRET
Hillman Publ.: Jan, 1952

1	20	40	60	114	182	250

TOP SECRET ADVENTURES (See Spyman)

TOP SECRETS (...of the F.B.I.)
Street & Smith Publications: Nov, 1947 - No. 10, July-Aug, 1949

1-Powell-c/a	36	72	108	211	343	475
2-Powell-c/a	25	50	75	147	241	335
3-6,8,10-Powell-a	22	44	66	132	216	300
9-Powell-c/a	23	46	69	136	223	310
7-Used in **SOTI**, pg. 90 & illo. "How to hurt people"; used by N.Y. Legis. Comm.; Powell-c/a	34	68	102	206	336	465

NOTE: ***Powell*** *c-1-3, 5-10.*

TOPS IN ADVENTURE
Ziff-Davis Publishing Co.: Fall, 1952 (25¢, 132 pgs.)

1-Crusader from Mars, The Hawk, Football Thrills, He-Man; Powell-a; painted-c	47	94	141	296	498	700

TOPS IN HUMOR (See Tops Comics?)
Consolidated Book Publ. (Lev Gleason)/Wise Publs.: 1944 (7-1/4x5", #2 digest size)

2001(#1)-Origin The Jack of Spades, Ace Kelly by Rick Yager, Black Orchid (female crime fighter) app.	18	36	54	103	162	220
2-Wise Publs.; WWII serviceman humor	12	24	36	69	97	125

TOP SPOT COMICS
Top Spot Publ. Co.: 1945

1-The Menace, Duke of Darkness app.	36	72	108	216	351	485

TOPSY-TURVY (Teenage)
R. B. Leffingwell Publ.: Apr, 1945

1-1st app. Cookie	18	36	54	105	165	225

TOP TEN
America's Best Comics: Sept, 1999 - No. 12, Oct, 2001 ($3.50/$2.95)

1-Two covers by Ross and Ha/Cannon; Alan Moore-s/Gene Ha-a	3.50
2-11-($2.95)	3.00
12-($3.50)	3.50
Hardcover ('00, $24.95) Dust jacket with Gene Ha-a; r/#1-7	25.00
Softcover ('00, $14.95) new Gene Ha-c; r/#1-7	15.00
Book 2 HC ('02, $24.95) Dust jacket with Gene Ha-a; r/#8-12	25.00
Book 2 SC ('03, $14.95) new Gene Ha-c; r/#8-12	15.00
...: The Forty-Niners HC (2005, $24.99, dust jacket) prequel set in 1949; Moore-s/Ha-a	25.00

TOP TEN: BEYOND THE FARTHEST PRECINCT
America's Best Comics: Oct, 2005 - No. 5, Feb, 2006 ($2.99, limited series)

1-5-Jerry Ordway-a/Paul DiFilippo-s	3.00
TPB (2006, $14.99) r/series; cover sketch pages	15.00

TOP TEN SEASON TWO
America's Best Comics: Dec, 2008 - No. 4, Mar, 2009 ($2.99, limited series)

1-4-Cannon-s/Ha-a	3.00
... Special (5/09, $2.99) Cannon-s/Daxiong-a/Ha-c	3.00

TOR (Prehistoric Life on Earth) (Formerly One Million Years Ago)
St. John Publ. Co.: No. 2, Oct, 1953; No. 3, May, 1954 - No. 5, Oct, 1954

3-D 2(10/53)-Kubert-c/a	14	28	42	76	108	140
3-D 2(10/53)-Oversized, otherwise same contents	12	24	36	67	94	120
3-D 2(11/53)-Kubert-c/a; has 3-D cover	12	24	36	67	94	120
3-5-Kubert-c/a: 3-Danny Dreams by Toth; Kubert 1 pg. story (w/self portrait)	14	28	42	76	108	140

NOTE: *The two October 3-D's have same contents and* ***Powell*** *art; the October & November issues are titled 3-D Comics. All 3-D issues are 25¢ and came with 3-D glasses.*

TOR (See Sojourn)
National Periodical Publications: May-June, 1975 - No. 6, Mar-Apr, 1976

1-New origin by Kubert	2	4	6	9	13	16
2-6: 2-Origin-r/St. John #1	1	2	3	5	6	8

NOTE: ***Kubert*** *a-1, 2-6r; c-1-6.* ***Toth*** *a(p)-3r.*

Torchwood #4 © BBC

Total Justice #2 © DC

Toy Story (2012 series) #1 © DIS & Pixar

GD 2.0 VG 4.0 FN 6.0 VF 8.0 VF/NM 9.0 NM- 9.2

TOR (3-D)
Eclipse Comics: July, 1986 - No. 2, Aug, 1987 ($2.50)
1,2: 1-r/One Million Years Ago. 2-r/Tor 3-D #2 5.00
...2-D: 1,2-Limited signed & numbered editions 1 2 3 4 5 7

TOR
Marvel Comics (Epic Comics/Heavy Hitters): June, 1993 - No. 4, 1993 ($5.95, lim. series)
1-4: Joe Kubert-c/a/scripts 6.00

TOR (Joe Kubert's...)
DC Comics: Jul, 2008 - No. 6, Dec, 2008 ($2.99, limited series)
1-6-New story; Joe Kubert-c/a/scripts 3.00
...: A Prehistoric Odyssey HC (2009, $24.99, DJ) r/#1-6; Roy Thomas intro.; sketch-a 25.00
...: A Prehistoric Odyssey SC (2010, $14.99) r/#1-6; Roy Thomas intro.; sketch-a 15.00

TOR BY JOE KUBERT
DC Comics: 2001 - 2003 ($49.95, hardcovers with dust jacket)
Volume 1 (2001) r/One Million Years Ago #1 & 3-D Comics #1&2 in flat color; script pages, sketch pages, proposals for TV and newspapers strips; intro. by Roy Thomas 50.00
Volume 2 (2002) r/Tor (St. John) #3-5; Danny Dreams; portfolio section 50.00
Volume 3 (2003) r/Tor (DC '75) #1; (Marvel '93) #1-4; portfolio section 50.00

TORCH, THE
Marvel Comics (with Dynamite Ent.): Nov, 2009 - No. 8, Jul, 2010 ($3.99, limited series)
1-8-Thinker resurrects the Golden Age Human Torch; Toro app; Alex Ross-c on all; Berkenkotter-a. 3-5-Namor app. 4.00

TORCH OF LIBERTY SPECIAL
Dark Horse Comics (Legend): Jan, 1995 ($2.50, one-shot)
1-Byrne scripts 3.00

TORCHWOOD (Based on the BBC TV series)
Titan Comics: Sept, 2010 - Present ($3.99)
1-6: 1-Barrowman-s/Edwards-a; Churchill & photo-c. 2-Art by Yeowell & Grist 4.00

TORCHY (...Blonde Bombshell) (See Dollman, Military, & Modern)
Quality Comics Group: Nov, 1949 - No. 6, Sept, 1950

	GD	VG	FN	VF	VF/NM	NM-
1-Bill Ward-c, Gil Fox-a	174	348	522	1114	1907	2700
2,3-Fox-c/a	73	146	219	467	796	1125
4-Fox-c/a(3), Ward-a (9 pgs.)	89	178	267	565	970	1375
5,6-Ward-c/a, 9 pgs; Fox-a(3) each	103	206	309	659	1130	1600
Super Reprint #16(1964)-r/#4 with new-c	8	16	24	53	89	125

TO RIVERDALE AND BACK AGAIN (Archie Comics Presents...)
Archie Comics: 1990 ($2.50, 68 pgs.)
nn-Byrne-c, Colan-a(p); adapts NBC TV movie 5.00

TORMENTED, THE (Becomes Surprise Adventures #3 on)
Sterling Comics: July, 1954 - No. 2, Sept, 1954
1,2: Weird/Horror stories 28 56 84 165 270 375

TORNADO TOM (See Mighty Midget Comics)

TORSO (See Jinx: Torso)

TOTAL ECLIPSE
Eclipse Comics: May, 1988 - No. 5, Apr, 1989 ($3.95, 52 pgs., deluxe size)
Book 1-5: 3-Intro/1st app. new Black Terror. 4-Many copies have upside down pages and are mis-cut 4.00

TOTAL ECLIPSE
Image Comics: July, 1998 (one-shot)
1-McFarlane-c; Eclipse Comics character pin-ups by Image artists 3.00

TOTAL ECLIPSE: THE SERAPHIM OBJECTIVE
Eclipse Comics: Nov, 1988 ($1.95, one-shot, Baxter paper)
1-Airboy, Valkyrie, The Heap app. 3.00

TOTAL JUSTICE
DC Comics: Oct, 1996 - No. 3, Nov, 1996 ($2.25, bi-weekly limited series) (Based on toyline)
1-3 3.00

TOTAL RECALL (Movie)
DC Comics: 1990 ($2.95, 68 pgs., movie adaptation, one-shot)
1-Arnold Schwarzenegger photo-c 4.00

TOTAL RECALL (Continuation of movie)
Dynamite Entertainment: 2011 - No. 4, 2011 ($3.99, limited series)
1-4-Quaid and Melina on Mars following the movie; Razek-a/Robertson-c 4.00

TOTAL WAR (M.A.R.S. Patrol #3 on)
Gold Key: July, 1965 - No. 2, Oct, 1965 (Painted-c)

	GD	VG	FN	VF	VF/NM	NM-
1-Wood-a in both issues	7	14	21	45	73	100
2	5	10	15	34	55	75

TOTEMS (Vertigo V2K)
DC Comics (Vertigo): Feb, 2000 ($5.95, one-shot)
1-Swamp Thing, Animal Man, Zatanna, Shade app.; Fegredo-c 6.00

TO THE HEART OF THE STORM
Kitchen Sink Press: 1991 (B&W, graphic novel)
Softcover-Will Eisner-s/a/c 15.00
Hardcover ($24.95) 25.00
TPB-(DC Comics, 9/00, $14.95) reprints 1991 edition 15.00

TO THE LAST MAN (See Zane Grey Four Color #616)

TOUCH OF SILVER, A
Image Comics: Jan, 1997 - No. 6, Nov, 1997 ($2.95, B&W, bi-monthly)
1-6-Valentino-s/a; photo-c: 5-color pgs. w/Round Table 3.00
TPB ($12.95) r/#1-6 13.00

TOUGH KID SQUAD COMICS
Timely Comics (TCI): Mar, 1942
1-(Scarce)-Origin & 1st app.The Human Top & The Tough Kid Squad; The Flying Flame app. 919 1838 2757 6709 11,855 17,000

TOWER OF SHADOWS (Creatures on the Loose #10 on)
Marvel Comics Group: Sept, 1969 - No. 9, Jan, 1971

	GD	VG	FN	VF	VF/NM	NM-
1-Romita-c, classic Steranko-a; Craig-a(p)	9	18	27	58	99	140
2,3: 2-Neal Adams-a. 3-Barry Smith, Tuska-a	5	10	15	32	51	70
4,6: 4-Marie Severin-c. 6-Wood-a	4	8	12	28	44	60
5-B. Smith-a(p), Wood-a; Wood draws himself (1st pg., 1st panel)	5	10	15	30	48	65
7-9: 7-B. Smith-a(p), Wood-a. 8-Wood-a; Wrightson-c. 9-Wrightson-c; Roy Thomas app.	5	10	15	32	51	70
Special 1(12/71, 52 pgs.)-Neal Adams-a; Romita-c	4	8	12	28	44	60

NOTE: ***J. Buscema** a-1p, 2p, Special 1r. **Colan** a-3p, 6p, Special 1. **J. Craig** a(r)-1p. **Ditko** a-6, 8, 9r, Special 1. **Everett** a-9(i)r; c-5i. **Kirby** a-9(p)r. **Severin** c-5p, 6. **Steranko** a-1p. **Tuska** a-3. **Wood** a-5-8. Issues 1-9 contain new stories with some pre-Marvel age reprints in 6-9. **H. P. Lovecraft** adaptation-9.*

TOXIC AVENGER (Movie)
Marvel Comics: Apr, 1991 - No. 11, Feb, 1992 ($1.50)
1-11: Based on movie character. 3,10-Photo-c 3.00

TOXIC CRUSADERS (TV)
Marvel Comics: May, 1992 - No. 8, Dec, 1992 ($1.25)
1-8: 1-3,8-Sam Kieth-c; based on USA Network cartoon 3.00

TOXIC GUMBO
DC Comics (Vertigo): 1998 ($5.95, one-shot, mature)
1-McKeever-a/Lydia Lunch-s 6.00

TOXIN (Son of Carnage)
Marvel Comics: June, 2005 - No. 6, Nov, 2005 ($2.99, limited series)
1-6-Milligan-s/Robertson-a; Spider-Man app. 3.00
...: The Devil You Know TPB (2006, $17.99) r/#1-6 18.00

TOYBOY
Continuity Comics: Oct, 1986 - No. 7, Mar, 1989 ($2.00, Baxter paper)
1-7 3.00
*NOTE: **N. Adams** a-1; c-1, 2,5. **Golden** a-7p; c-6,7. **Nebres** a(i)-1,2.*

TOYLAND COMICS
Fiction House Magazines: Jan, 1947 - No. 2, Mar, 1947; No. 3, July, 1947

	GD	VG	FN	VF	VF/NM	NM-
1-Wizard of the Moon begins	30	60	90	177	289	400
2,3-Bob Lubbers-c. 3-Tuska-a	17	34	51	100	158	215

NOTE: *All above contain strips by **Al Walker**.*

TOY STORY (Disney/Pixar movies)
BOOM! Entertainment (BOOM! KIDS): No. 0, Nov, 2009 - No. 7, Sept, 2010 ($2.99)
0-7: 0,1-Three covers. 2-7-Two covers 3.00
Free Comic Book Day Edition (5/10, giveaway) r/#0 The Return of Buzz Lightyear 3.00
...: The Return of Buzz Lightyear (10/10, Halloween giveaway, 8-1/2" x 5-1/4") 3.00

TOY STORY (Disney/Pixar movies)
Marvel Comics: May, 2012 - No. 4 ($2.99, limited series)
1-Master Woody 3.00

TOY STORY: MYSTERIOUS STRANGER (Disney/Pixar movies)
BOOM! Entertainment (BOOM! KIDS): May, 2009 - No. 4, July, 2009 ($2.99)

Tracker #1 © TCOW

Transformers #60 © Hasbro

Transformers Comics Magazine #2 © Hasbro

GD VG FN VF VF/NM NM-
2.0 4.0 6.0 8.0 9.0 9.2

1-4-Jolley-s/Moreno-a. 1-Three covers. 2-4-Two covers 3.00

TOY STORY: TALES FROM THE TOY CHEST (Disney/Pixar movies)
BOOM! Entertainment (BOOM! KIDS): July, 2010 - No. 4, Oct, 2010 ($2.99)

1-4-Snider-s/Luthi-a. 1-Two covers. 2-4-One cover 3.00

TOY TOWN COMICS
Toytown/Orbit Publ./B. Antin/Swapper Quarterly: 1945 - No. 7, May, 1947

1-Mertie Mouse; L. B. Cole-c/a; funny animal 39 78 117 240 395 550
2-L. B. Cole-a 22 44 66 132 216 300
3-7-L. B. Cole-a. 5-Wiggles the Wonderworm-c 20 40 60 114 182 250

TRACKER
Image Comics (Top Cow): Nov, 2009 - No. 5, Sept, 2010 ($2.99/$3.99)

1,2-Lincoln-s/Tsai-a. 1-Two covers 3.00
3-5-($3.99) 4.00

TRAGG AND THE SKY GODS (See Gold Key Spotlight, Mystery Comics Digest #3,9 & Spine Tingling Tales)
Gold Key/Whitman No. 9: June, 1975 - No. 8, Feb, 1977; No. 9, May, 1982 (Painted-c #3-8)

1-Origin 3 6 9 14 19 24
2-8: 4-Sabre-Fang app. 8-Ostellon app. 2 4 6 8 11 14
9-(Whitman, 5/82) r/#1 1 2 3 5 7 9

NOTE: ***Santos** a-1, 2, 9r; c-3-7. **Spiegel** a-3-8.*

TRAILBLAZER
Image Comics: June 2011 ($5.99, one shot, graphic novel)

nn-Gray & Palmiotti-s/Daly-a; covers by Johnson and Conner 6.00

TRAIL BLAZERS (Red Dragon #5 on)
Street & Smith Publications: 1941; No. 2, Apr, 1942 - No. 4, Oct, 1942
(True stories of American heroes)

1-Life story of Jack Dempsey & Wright Brothers 35 70 105 208 339 470
2-Brooklyn Dodgers-c/story; Ben Franklin story 22 44 66 128 209 290
3,4: 3-Fred Allen, Red Barber, Yankees stories 20 40 60 115 183 250

TRAIL COLT (Also see Extra Comics, Manhunt! & Undercover Girl)
Magazine Enterprises: 1949 - No. 2, 1949

nn(A-1 #24)-7 pg. Frazetta-a r-in Manhunt #13; Undercover Girl app.; The Red Fox by L. B. Cole; Ingels-c; Whitney-a (Scarce) 39 78 117 240 395 550
2(A-1 #26)-Undercover Girl; Ingels-c; L. B. Cole-a (6 pgs.) 31 62 93 182 296 410

TRANSFORMERS, THE (TV)(See G.I. Joe and...)
Marvel Comics Group: Sept, 1984 - No. 80, July, 1991 (75¢/$1.00)

1-Based on Hasbro Toys 3 6 9 20 30 40
2-5: 2-Golden-c. 3-(1/85) Spider-Man (black costume)-c/app. 4-Texeira-c; brief app. of Dinobots 2 4 6 11 16 20
2-10: 2nd & 3rd prints 4.00
6-10: 6-1st Josie Beller. 8-Dinobots 1st full app. 9-Circuit Breaker 1st full app. 10-Intro Constructicons 2 4 6 8 11 14
11-49: 11-1st app. Jetfire. 14-Jetfire becomes an Autobot; 1st app. of Grapple, Hoist, Smokescreen, Skids, and Tracks. 17-1st app. of Blaster, Powerglide, Cosmos, Seaspray, Warpath, Beachcomber, Preceptor, Straxus, Kickback, Bombshell, Shrapnel, Dirge, and Ramjet. 19-1st Omega Supreme. 21-1st app. of Aerialbots; 1st Slingshot; Circuit Breaker app. 22-Retells origin of Circuit Breaker, 1st Stunticons. 23-Battle at Statue of Liberty. 24-1st app. Protectobots, Combaticons; Optimus Prime killed. 25-1st Predacons. 26-Intro The Mechanic, Prime's Funeral. 27-1st Trypticon app.; Grimlock named new Autobot leader. 28-The Mechanic app. 29-Intro Scraplets, 1st app. of Triple Changers 1 2 3 5 6 8
50-60: 53-Jim Lee-c. 54-Intro Micromasters. 60-Brief 1st app. of Primus 2 4 6 8 10 12
61-70: 61-Origin of Cybertron and the Transformers, Unicron app.; app. of Primus, creator of the Transformers. 62-66 Matrix Quest 5-part series. 67-Jim Lee-c 2 4 6 10 14 18
71-77: 75-($1.50, 52 pgs.) (Low print run) 3 6 9 18 27 35
78,79 (Low print run) 4 8 12 24 37 50
80-Last issue 5 10 15 30 48 65

*NOTE: Second and third printings of most early issues (1-9?) exist and are worth less than originals. Was originally planned as a four issue mini-series. **Wrightson** a-64i(4 pgs.).*

TRANSFORMERS
IDW Publishing: No. 0, Oct, 2005 (99¢, one-shot)

0-Prelude to Transformers: Infiltration series; Furman-s/Su-a; 4 covers 3.00

TRANSFORMERS
IDW Publishing: Nov, 2009 - Present ($3.99)

1-31: Multple covers on each, 21-Chaos arc begins 4.00

GD VG FN VF VF/NM NM-
2.0 4.0 6.0 8.0 9.0 9.2

...: Continuum (11/09, $3.99) Plot synopses of recent Transformers storylines 4.00
Hundred Penny Press: Transformers Classics #1 (6/11, $1.00) r/#1 (1984 Marvel series) 1.00
...: Death of Optimus Prime (12/11, $3.99) Roche-a 4.00

TRANSFORMERS (Free Comic Book Day Editions)
Dreamwave Productions/IDW Publishing

... Animated (IDW, 5/08) Free Comic Book Day Edition; from the Cartoon Network series 3.00
... Armada (Dreamwave Prods., 5/03) Free Comic Book Day Edition 3.00
.../Beast Wars Special (IDW, 2006) Free Comic Book Day Edition; flip book 3.00
.../G.I. Joe (IDW, 2009) Free Comic Book Day Edition; flip book 3.00
... Movie Prequel (IDW, 5/07) Free Comic Book Day Edition; Figueroa-c 3.00

TRANSFORMERS: ALL HAIL MEGATRON
IDW Publishing: Jul, 2008 - No. 16, Oct, 2009 ($3.99, limited series)

1-16: 1-8,10-12-McCarthy-s/Guidi-a; 2 covers 4.00

TRANSFORMERS: ALLIANCE (Prequel to 2009 Transformers 2 movie)
IDW Publishing: Dec, 2008 - No. 4, Mar, 2009 ($3.99, limited series)

1-4-Milne-a; 2 covers 4.00

TRANSFORMERS ANIMATED: THE ARRIVAL
IDW Publishing: Sept, 2008 - No. 5, Dec, 2008 ($3.99, limited series)

1-5-Brizuela-a; 2 covers 4.00

TRANSFORMERS ARMADA (Continues as Transformers Energon with #19)
(Also see Promotional Comics section for FCBD Ed.)
Dreamwave Productions: July, 2002 - No. 18, Dec, 2003 ($2.95)

1-Sarracini-s/Raiz-a; wraparound gatefold-c 4.00
2-18 4.00
Vol. 1 TPB (2003, $13.95) r/#1-5 14.00
Vol. 2 TPB (2003, $15.95) r/#6-11 16.00

TRANSFORMERS ARMADA: MORE THAN MEETS THE EYE
Dreamwave Productions: Mar, 2004 - No. 3, May, 2004 ($4.95, limited series)

1-3-Pin-ups with tech info; art by Pat Lee & various 5.00

TRANSFORMERS, BEAST WARS: THE ASCENDING
IDW Publishing: Aug, 2007 - No. 4, Nov, 2007 ($3.99, limited series)

1-4-Furman-s/Figueroa-a; multiple covers on all 4.00

TRANSFORMERS, BEAST WARS: THE GATHERING
IDW Publishing: Feb, 2006 - No. 4, May, 2006 ($2.99, limited series)

1-4-Furman-s/Figueroa-a; multiple covers on all 4.00
TPB (8/06, $17.99) r/series; sketch pages & gallery of covers and variants 18.00

TRANSFORMERS: BUMBLEBEE
IDW Publishing: Dec, 2009 - No. 4, Mar, 2010 ($3.99, limited series)

1-4: Zander Cannon-s; multiple covers on all 4.00

TRANSFORMERS COMICS MAGAZINE (Digest)
Marvel Comics: Jan, 1987 - No. 10, July, 1988

1,2-Spider-Man-c/s 2 4 6 9 12 15
3-10 2 4 6 8 10 12

TRANSFORMERS: DARK OF THE MOON MOVIE ADAPTATION (2011 movie)
IDW Publishing: Jun, 2011 - No. 4, Jun, 2011 ($3.99, weekly limited series)

1-4-Barber-s/Jimenez-a 4.00

TRANSFORMERS: DEFIANCE (Prequel to 2009 Transformers 2 movie)
IDW Publishing: Jan, 2009 - No. 4, Apr, 2009 ($3.99, limited series)

1-4-Mowry-s; 2 covers 4.00

TRANSFORMERS: DEVASTATION
IDW Publishing: Sept, 2007 - No. 6, Feb, 2008 ($3.99, limited series)

1-6-Furman-s/Su-a; multiple covers on all 4.00

TRANSFORMERS: DRIFT
IDW Publishing: Sept, 2010 - No. 4, Oct, 2010 ($3.99, limited series)

1-4-McCarthy-s/Milne-a; multiple covers on all 4.00

TRANSFORMERS ENERGON (Continued from Transformers Armada #18)
Dreamwave Productions: No. 19, Jan, 2004 - No. 30, Dec, 2004 ($2.95)

19-30-Furman-s 4.00

TRANSFORMERS: ESCALATION
IDW Publishing: Nov, 2006 - No. 6, Apr, 2007 ($3.99, limited series)

1-6-Furman-s/Su-a; multiple covers 4.00

TRANSFORMERS: EVOLUTIONS - HEARTS OF STEEL
IDW Publishing: June, 2006 - No. 4, Sept, 2006 ($2.99, limited series)

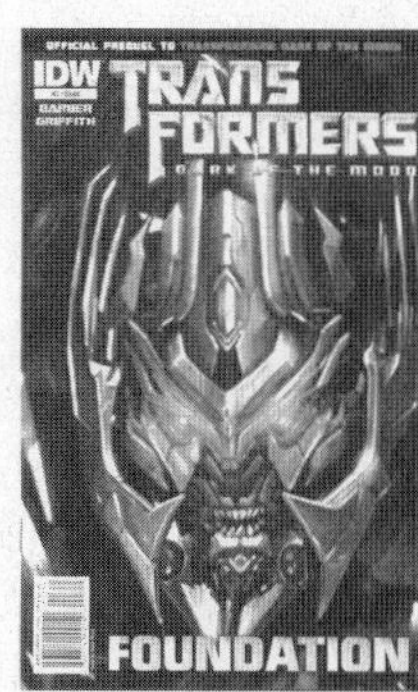

Transformers: Foundation #1 © Hasbro

Transformers: Headmasters #1 © Hasbro

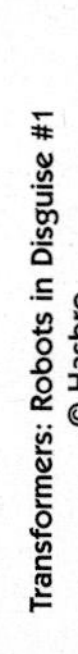
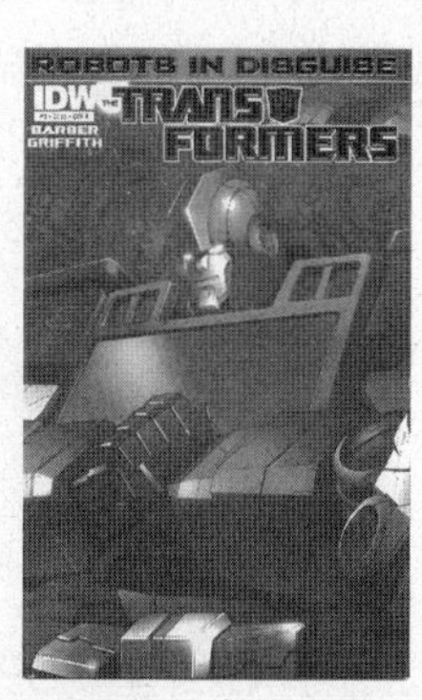

Transformers: Robots in Disguise #1 © Hasbro

GD 2.0 | VG 4.0 | FN 6.0 | VF 8.0 | VF/NM 9.0 | NM- 9.2

1-4-Bumblebee meets John Henry in 1880s railroad times 4.00

TRANSFORMERS: FOUNDATION (Prequel to 2011 Transformers: Dark of the Moon movie)
IDW Publishing: Feb, 2011 - No. 4, May, 2011 ($3.99, limited series)
1-4-Barber-s/Griffith-a; 2 covers 4.00

TRANSFORMERS: GENERATION 1
Dreamwave Productions: Apr, 2002 - No. 6, Oct, 2002 ($2.95)
Preview- 6 pg. story; robot sketch pages; Pat Lee-a 3.00
1-Pat Lee-a; 2 wraparound covers by Lee 5.00
2-6: 2-Optimus Prime reactivated; 2 covers by Pat Lee 4.00
...Vol. 1 HC (2003, $49.95) r/#1-6; black hardcover with red foil lettering and art 50.00
...Vol. 1 TPB (2002, $17.95) r/#1-6 plus six page preview; 8 pg. preview of future issues 18.00

TRANSFORMERS: GENERATION 1 (Volume 2)
Dreamwave Productions: Apr, 2003 - No. 6, Sept, 2003 ($2.95)
1-6: 1-Pat Lee-a; 2 wraparound gatefold covers by Lee 4.00
1-($5.95) Chrome wraparound variant-c 6.00
...Vol. 2 TPB (IDW Publ., 3/06, $19.99) r/#1-6 plus cover gallery 20.00

TRANSFORMERS: GENERATION 1 (Volume 3)
Dreamwave Productions: No. 0, Dec, 2003 - Present ($2.95)
0-10: 0-Pat Lee-a. 1-Figueroa-a; wrapaound-c 4.00

TRANSFORMERS: GENERATION 2
Marvel Comics: Nov, 1993 - No. 12, Oct, 1994 ($1.75)
1-($2.95, 68 pgs.)-Collector's ed. w/bi-fold metallic-c 1 3 4 6 8 10
1-11: 1-Newsstand edition (68 pgs.). 2-G.I. Joe app., Snake-Eyes, Scarlett, Cobra Commander app. 5-Red Alert killed, Optimus Prime gives Grimlock leadership of Autobots. 6-G.I. Joe app. 1 2 3 4 5 7
12-($2.25, 52 pgs.) 1 3 4 6 8 10

TRANSFORMERS: GENERATIONS
IDW Publishing: Mar, 2006 - No. 12, Mar, 2007 ($1.99/$2.49/$3.99)
1,2: 1-R/Transformers #7 (1985); preview of Transformers, Beast Wars. 2-R/#13 4.00
3-10-($2.49) 3-R/Transformers #14 (1986). 4-6-Reprint #16-18. 7-R/#24 4.00
11,12-($3.99) 4.00
Volume 1 (12/06, $19.99) r/#1-6; cover gallery 20.00

TRANSFORMERS/G.I. JOE
Dreamwave Productions: Aug, 2003 - No. 6, Mar, 2004 ($2.95/$5.25)
1-Art & gatefold wraparound-c by Jae Lee; Ney Rieber-s; variant-c by Pat Lee 4.00
1-($5.95) Holofoil wraparound-c by Norton 6.00
2-6-Jae Lee-a/c 4.00
TPB (8/04, $17.95) r/#1-6; cover gallery and sketch pages 18.00

TRANSFORMERS/G.I. JOE: DIVIDED FRONT
Dreamwave Productions: Oct, 2004 ($2.95)
1-Art & gatefold wraparound-c by Pat Lee 4.00

TRANSFORMERS: HEADMASTERS
Marvel Comics Group: July, 1987 - No. 4, Jan, 1988 ($1.00, limited series)
1-Springer, Akin, Garvey-a 6.00
2-4-Springer-c on all 5.00

TRANSFORMERS: HEART OF DARKNESS
IDW Publishing: Mar, 2011 - No. 4, Jun, 2011 ($3.99, limited series)
1-4-Abnett & Lanning-s/Farinas-a 4.00

TRANSFORMERS: INFESTATION (Crossover with Star Trek, Ghostbusters & G.I. Joe)
IDW Publishing: Feb, 2011 - No. 2, Feb, 2011 ($3.99, limited series)
1,2-Abnett & Lanning-s/Roche-a; covers by Roche & Snyder III 4.00

TRANSFORMERS: INFILTRATION
IDW Publishing: Jan, 2006 - No. 6, June, 2006 ($2.99, limited series)
1-6-Furman-s/Su-a; multiple covers on all 4.00
... Cover Gallery (8/06, $5.99) 6.00

TRANSFORMERS: IRONHIDE
IDW Publishing: May, 2010 - No. 4, Aug, 2010 ($3.99, limited series)
1-4: Mike Costa-s; multiple covers on all 4.00

TRANSFORMERS: LAST STAND OF THE WRECKERS
IDW Publishing: Jan, 2010 - No. 5, May, 2010 ($3.99, limited series)
1-5-Nick Roche-s/a; two covers 4.00

TRANSFORMERS: MAXIMUM DINOBOTS
IDW Publishing: Dec, 2008 - No. 5, Apr, 2009 ($3.99, limited series)
1-5-Furman-s/Roche-a; 2 covers for each 4.00

TRANSFORMERS: MEGATRON ORIGIN
IDW Publishing: May, 2007 - No. 4, Sept, 2008 ($3.99, limited series)
1-4-Alex Milne-a; 2 covers 4.00

TRANSFORMERS: MICROMASTERS
Dreamwave Productions: June, 2004 - No. 4 ($2.95, limited series)
1-4-Ruffolo-a; Pat Lee-c 4.00

TRANSFORMERS: MORE THAN MEETS THE EYE
Dreamwave Productions: Apr, 2003 - No. 8, Nov, 2003 ($5.25)
1-8-Pin-ups with tech info on Autobots and Decepticons; art by Pat Lee & various 5.25
Vol. 1,2 (2004, $24.95, TPB) 1-r/#1-4. 2-r/#5-8 25.00

TRANSFORMERS: MORE THAN MEETS THE EYE
IDW Publishing: Jan, 2012 - Present ($3.99)
1,2: 1-Five covers; Roche-a. 2-Three covers; Milne-a 4.00

TRANSFORMERS: MOVIE ADAPTATION (For the 2007 live action movie)
IDW Publishing: June, 2007 - No. 4, June, 2007 ($3.99, weekly limited series)
1-4: Wraparound covers on each; Milne-a 4.00

TRANSFORMERS: MOVIE PREQUEL (For the 2007 live action movie)
IDW Publishing: Feb, 2007 - No. 4, May, 2007 ($3.99, limited series)
1-4: 1-Origin of the Transformers on Cybertron; multiple covers on each 4.00
Special (6/08, $3.99) 2 covers 4.00
TPB (6/07, $19.99) r/series; gallery of covers and variants 20.00

TRANSFORMERS: NEFARIOUS (Sequel to Transformers: Revenge of the Fallen movie)
IDW Publishing: Mar, 2010 - No. 6, Aug, 2010 ($3.99, limited series)
1-6: Furman-s; multiple covers on all 4.00

TRANSFORMERS: PRIME
IDW Publishing: Jan, 2011 - No. 4, Jan, 2011 ($3.99, weekly limited series)
1-4: 1-Mike Johnson-s/E.J. Su-a 4.00

TRANSFORMERS: REVENGE OF THE FALLEN OFFICIAL MOVIE ADAPTATION
(For the 2009 live action movie sequel)
IDW Publishing: May, 2009 - No. 4, June, 2009 ($3.99, weekly limited series)
1-4: Furman-s; 2 covers on each 4.00

TRANSFORMERS: RISING STORM (Prequel to 2011 Transformers: Dark of the Moon movie)
IDW Publishing: Feb, 2011 - No. 4, May, 2011 ($3.99, limited series)
1-3-Barber-s/Magno-a; 2 covers 4.00

TRANSFORMERS: ROBOTS IN DISGUISE
IDW Publishing: Jan, 2012 - Present ($3.99)
1,2: 1-Five covers; Griffith-a. 2-Three covers 4.00

TRANSFORMERS: SAGA OF THE ALLSPARK (From the 2007 live action movie)
IDW Publishing: Jul, 2008 - No. 4, Oct, 2008 ($3.99, limited series)
1-4-Launch of the Allspark into outer space; Furman-s/Roche-c 4.00

TRANSFORMERS: SECTOR 7 (From the 2007 live action movie)
IDW Publishing: Sept, 2010 - No. 5, Jan, 2011 ($3.99, limited series)
1-5-Barber-s 4.00

TRANSFORMERS: SPOTLIGHT
IDW Publishing: Sept, 2006 - Present ($3.99, multiple covers on each)
... Arcee (2/08); ... Blaster (1/08); ... Blurr (11/08); ... Cliffjumper (6/09); ... Cyclonus (6/08); ...Doubledealer (8/08); ...Drift (4/09); ...Grimlock (3/08); ...Hardhead (7/08); Hot Rod (11/06); ... Jazz (3/09); ... Kup (4/07); ... Metroplex (7/09); ... Mirage (3/08); ... Nightbeat (10/06); ... Prowl (4/10);... Ramjet (11/07); ... Shockwave (9/06); ... Sideswipe (9/08); ... Sixshot (12/06); ... Soundwave (3/07); ... Ultra Magnus (1/07) 4.00
... Optimus Prime: 3-D (11/08, $5.99, with glasses) Furman-s/Figueroa-a 6.00

TRANSFORMERS: STORMBRINGER
IDW Publishing: Jul, 2006 - No. 4, Oct, 2006 ($2.99, limited series)
1-4-Furman-s/Figueroa-a; multiple covers on all 4.00
TPB (2/07, $17.99) r/series; cover gallery and sketch pages 18.00

TRANSFORMERS SUMMER SPECIAL
Dreamwave Productions: May, 2004 ($4.95)
1-Pat Lee-a; Figueroa-a 5.00

TRANSFORMERS: TALES OF THE FALLEN
IDW Publishing: Aug, 2009 - Present ($3.99, limited series)
1-4: 2,4-Furman-s mulitple covers on all 4.00

TRANSFORMERS: TARGET 2006
IDW Publishing: Apr, 2007 - No. 5, Aug, 2007 ($3.99, limited series)

Transmetropolitan #13 © Ellis & Robertson

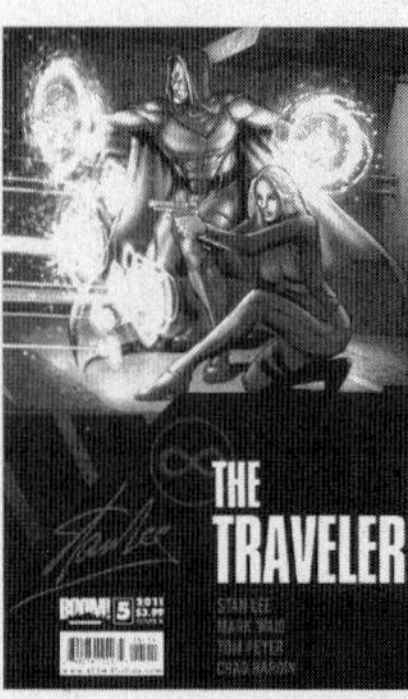

The Traveler #5 © BOOM & POW

Treasure Chest V5 #3 © George Pflaum

GD VG FN VF VF/NM NM-
2.0 4.0 6.0 8.0 9.0 9.2

1-5-Reprints from 1980s series; multiple covers on all 4.00

TRANSFORMERS: THE ANIMATED MOVIE
IDW Publishing: Oct, 2006 - No. 4, Jan, 2007 ($3.99, limited series)
1-4-Adapts animated movie; Don Figueroa-a 4.00

TRANSFORMERS, THE MOVIE
Marvel Comics Group: Dec, 1986 - No. 3, Feb, 1987 (75¢, limited series)
1-3-Adapts animated movie 5.00

TRANSFORMERS: THE REIGN OF STARSCREAM
IDW Publishing: Apr, 2008 - No. 5, Aug, 2008 ($3.99, limited series)
1-5-Continuation of the 2007 movie; Milne-a; multiple covers 4.00

TRANSFORMERS: THE WAR WITHIN
Dreamwave Productions: Oct, 2002 - No. 6, Mar, 2003 ($2.95)
1-6-Furman-s/Figueroa-a. 1-Wraparound gatefold-c 4.00
TPB (2003, $15.95) r/#1-6; plus cover gallery 16.00

TRANSFORMERS UNIVERSE
Marvel Comics Group: Dec, 1986 - No. 4, Mar, 1987 ($1.25, limited series)
1-4-A guide to all characters 6.00
TPB-r/#1-4 15.00

TRANSFORMERS WAR WITHIN: THE AGE OF WRATH
Dreamwave Productions: Sept, 2004 - No. 6 ($2.95, limited series)
1-3-Furman-s/Ng-a 4.00

TRANSFORMERS WAR WITHIN: THE DARK AGES
Dreamwave Productions: Oct, 2003 - No. 6 ($2.95)
1-6: 1-Furman-s/Wildman-a; two covers by Pat Lee & Figueroa 4.00
TPB (2004, $17.95) r/#1-6; plus cover gallery and design sketches 18.00

TRANSIT
Vortex Publ.: March, 1987 - No. 5, Nov, 1987 (B&W)
1-5-Ted McKeever-s/a 1 2 3 5 6 8

TRANSMETROPOLITAN
DC Comics (Helix/Vertigo): Sept, 1997 - No. 60, Nov, 2002 ($2.50)
1-Warren Ellis-s/Darick Robertson-a(p) 2 4 6 8 10 12
1-Special Edition (5/09, $1.00) r/#1 with "After Watchmen" cover frame 3.00
2,3 1 2 3 4 5 7
4-8 4.00
9-60: 15-Jae Lee-c. 25-27-Jim Lee-c. 37-39-Bradstreet-c 3.00
Back on the Street ('97, $7.95) r/#1-3 8.00
Back on the Street ('09, $14.99) r/#1-6; intro. by Garth Ennis 15.00
Dirge ('03/'10, $14.95/$14.95) r/#43-48 15.00
Filth of the City ('01, $5.95) Spider's columns with pin-up art by various 6.00
Gouge Away ('02/'09, $14.95/$14.99) r/#31-36 15.00
I Hate It Here ('00, $5.95) Spider's columns with pin-up art by various 6.00
Lonely City ('01/'09, $14.95/$14.99) r/#25-30; intro. by Patrick Stewart 15.00
Lust For Life ('98, $14.95) r/#4-12 15.00
Lust For Life ('09, $14.99) r/#7-12 15.00
One More Time ('04, $14.95) r/#55-60 15.00
One More Time ('11, $19.99) r/#55-60 & Filth of the City & I Hate It Here one-shots 20.00
Spider's Thrash ('02/'10, $14.95/$14.99) r/#37-42; intro. by Darren Aronofsky 15.00
Tales of Human Waste ('04, $9.95) r/Filth of the City, I Hate It Here & story from Vertigo Winter's Edge 2 10.00
The Cure ('03/'11, $14.95/$14.99) r/#49-54 15.00
The New Scum ('00, $12.95) r/#19-24 & Vertigo: Winter's Edge #3 13.00
The New Scum ('09, $14.99) r/#19-24 & Vertigo: Winter's Edge #3 15.00
Year of the Bastard ('99, $12.95)('09, $12.99) r/#13-18 13.00

TRANSMUTATION OF IKE GARUDA, THE
Marvel Comics (Epic Comics): July, 1991 - No. 2, 1991 ($3.95, 52 pgs.)
1,2 4.00

TRAPPED!
Periodical House Magazines (Ace): Oct, 1954 - No. 4, April, 1955
1 (All reprints) 10 20 30 54 72 90
2-4: 4-r/Men Against Crime #4 in its entirety 7 14 21 35 43 50
NOTE: *Colan a-1, 4. **Sekowsky** a-1.*

TRASH
Trash Publ. Co.: Mar, 1978 - No. 4, Oct, 1978 (B&W, magazine, 52 pgs.)
1,2: 1-Star Wars parody. 2-UFO-c 2 4 6 10 14 18
3-Parodies of KISS, the Beatles, and monsters 3 6 9 14 19 24
4-(84 pgs.)-Parodies of Happy Days, Rocky movies 3 6 9 14 20 26

GD VG FN VF VF/NM NM-
2.0 4.0 6.0 8.0 9.0 9.2

TRAVELER, THE (Developed by Stan Lee)
BOOM! Studios: Nov, 2010 - No. 12, Oct, 2011 ($3.99)
1-12-Waid-s/Hardin-a; three covers on each 4.00

TRAVELS OF JAIMIE McPHEETERS, THE (TV)
Gold Key: Dec, 1963
1-Kurt Russell photo on-c plus photo back-c 4 8 12 26 41 55

TREASURE CHEST (Catholic Guild; also see Topix)
George A. Pflaum: 3/12/46 - V27#8, July, 1972 (Educational comics)
(Not published during Summer)
V1#1 29 58 87 170 278 385
2-6 (5/21/46): 5-Dr. Styx app. by Baily 14 28 42 80 115 150
V2#1-20 (9/3/46-5/27/47) 11 22 33 60 83 105
V3#1-5,7-20 (1st slick cover) 10 20 30 54 72 90
V3#6-Jules Verne's "Voyage to the Moon" 12 24 36 67 94 120
V4#1-20 (9/9/48-5/31/49) 9 18 27 47 61 75
V5#1-20 (9/6/49-5/31/50) 8 16 24 44 57 70
V6#1-20 (9/14/50-5/31/51) 8 16 24 42 54 65
V7#1-20 (9/13/51-6/5/52) 8 16 24 40 50 60
V8#1-20 (9/11/52-6/4/53) 7 14 21 37 46 55
V9#1-20 ('53-'54), V10#1-20 ('54-'55) 7 14 21 35 43 50
V11('55-'56), V12('56-'57) 6 12 18 29 36 42
V13#1,3-5,7,9-20-V17#1 ('57-'63) 6 12 18 27 33 38
V13#2,6,8-Ingels-a 6 12 18 41 66 90
V17#2- "This Godless Communism" series begins(not in odd #'d issues); cover shows hammer & sickle over Statue of Liberty; 8 pg. Crandall-a of family life under communism (9/28/61) 17 34 51 114 250 385
V17#3,5,7,9,11,13,15,17,19 3 6 9 17 25 32
V17#4,6,14- "This Godless Communism" stories 13 26 39 87 186 285
V17#8-Shows red octopus encompassing Earth, firing squad; 8 pgs. Crandall-a (12/21/61) 15 30 45 104 227 350
V17#10- "This Godless Communism" - how Stalin came to power, part I; Crandall-a 14 28 42 93 202 310
V17#12-Stalin in WWII, forced labor, death by exhaustion; Crandall-a 14 28 42 93 202 310
V17#16-Kruschev takes over; de-Stalinization 14 28 42 93 202 310
V17#18-Kruschev's control; murder of revolters, brainwash, space race by Crandall 14 28 42 93 202 310
V17#20-End of series; Kruschev-people are puppets, firing squads hammer & sickle over Statue of Liberty, snake around communist manifesto by Crandall 16 32 48 111 243 375
V18#1,3,4,6-10,12-20, V19#11-20, V20#1-20(1964-65) 3 6 9 16 23 30
V18#2-Kruschev on-c (9/27/62) 3 6 9 20 30 40
V18#5- "What About Red China?" - describes how communists took over China 9 18 27 58 99 140
V18#11-Crandall draws himself & 13 other artists on cover (1/31/63) 3 6 9 20 30 40
V19#1-10- "Red Victim" anti-communist series in all 9 18 27 58 99 140
V21, V22 #1-16,18-20,V23-V25(1965-70)-(two V24#5's 11/7/68 & 11/21/68) (no V24#6): 3 6 9 14 19 24
V22#17-Flying saucer wraparound-c 3 6 9 17 25 32
V26, V27#1-8 (V26,27-68 pgs.) 3 6 9 16 22 28
Summer Edition V1#1-6('66), V2#1-6('67) 3 6 9 16 23 30
NOTE: ***Anderson** a-V18#13. **Borth** a-V7#10-19 (serial), V8#8-17 (serial), V9#1-10 (serial), V13#2, 6, 11, V14-V25 (except V22#1-3, 11-13), Summer Ed. V1#3-6. **Crandall** a-V16#7, 9, 12, 14, 16-18, 20; V17#1, 2, 4-6, 10, 12, 14, 16-18, 20; V18#1, 2, 3(2 pg.), 7, 9-20; V19#4, 11, 13, 16, 19, 20; V20#1, 2, 4, 6, 8-10, 12, 14-16, 18, 20; V21#1-5, 8-11, 13, 16-18; V22#3, 7, 9-11, 14; V23#3, 6, 9, 16, 18; V24#7, 8, 10, 13, 16; V25#8, 16; V27#1-7r, 8r(2 pg.), Summer Ed. V1#3-5, V2#3; c-V16#7, V18#2(part), 7, 11, V19#4, 19, 20, V20#15, V21#5, 9, V22#3, 7, 9, 11, V23#9, 16, V24#13, 16, V25#8, Summer Ed. V1#2 (back c-V1#2-5). **Powell** a-V10#11. V19#11, 15, V10#13, V13#6, 8 all have wraparound covers.*

TREASURE CHEST OF THE WORLD'S BEST COMICS
Superior, Toronto, Canada: 1945 (500 pgs., hard-c)
Contains Blue Beetle, Captain Combat, John Wayne, Dynamic Man, Nemo, Li'l Abner; contents can vary - represents random binding of extra books; Captain America on-c 103 206 309 659 1130 1600

TREASURE COMICS
Prize Publications? (no publisher listed): No date (1943) (50¢, 324 pgs., cardboard-c)
1-(Rare)-Contains rebound Prize Comics #7-11 from 1942 (blank inside-c) 284 568 852 1818 3109 4400

TREASURE COMICS
Prize Publ. (American Boys' Comics): June-July, 1945 - No. 12, Fall, 1947
1-Paul Bunyan & Marco Polo begin; Highwayman & Carrot Topp only app.; Kiefer-a

Treehouse of Horror #17 © Bongo

Trinity #14 © DC

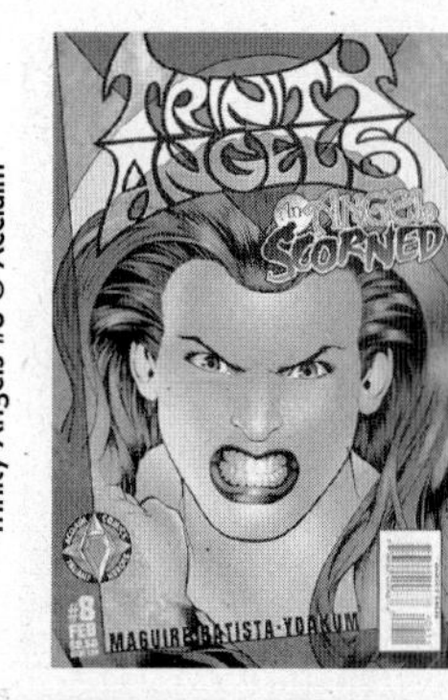

Trinity Angels #8 © Acclaim

	GD 2.0	VG 4.0	FN 6.0	VF 8.0	VF/NM 9.0	NM- 9.2
	52	104	156	328	552	775
2-Arabian Knight, Gorilla King, Dr. Styx begin	31	62	93	182	296	410
3,4,9,12: 9-Kiefer-a	24	48	72	144	237	330
5-Marco Polo-c; Krigstein-a	31	62	93	186	303	420
6,11-Krigstein-a; 11-Krigstein-c	31	62	93	182	296	410
7,8-Frazetta-a (5 pgs. each). 7-Capt. Kidd Jr. app.	41	82	123	256	428	600
10-Simon & Kirby-c/a	37	74	111	222	361	500

NOTE: *Barry a-9-11; c-12. Kiefer a-3, 5, 7; c-2, 6, 7. Roussos a-11.*

TREASURE ISLAND (See Classics Illustrated #64, Doc Savage Comics #1, King Classics, Movie Classics & Movie Comics)
Dell Publishing Co.: No. 624, Apr, 1955 (Disney)

	GD	VG	FN	VF	VF/NM	NM-
Four Color 624-Movie, photo-c	8	16	24	53	89	125

TREASURY OF COMICS
St. John Publishing Co.: 1947; No. 2, July, 1947 - No. 4, Sept, 1947; No. 5, Jan, 1948

	GD	VG	FN	VF	VF/NM	NM-
nn(#1)-Abbie an' Slats (nn on-c, #1 on inside)	14	28	42	80	115	150
2-Jim Hardy Comics; featuring Windy & Paddles	11	22	33	62	86	110
3-Bill Bumlin	10	20	30	54	72	90
4-Abbie an' Slats	11	22	33	62	86	110
5-Jim Hardy Comics #1	11	22	33	62	86	110

TREASURY OF COMICS
St. John Publishing Co.: Mar, 1948 - No. 5, 1948 (Reg. size); 1948-1950 (Over 500 pgs., $1.00)

	GD	VG	FN	VF	VF/NM	NM-
1	19	38	57	111	176	240
2(#2 on-c, #1 on inside)	12	24	36	67	94	120
3-5	10	20	30	56	76	95
1-(1948, 500 pgs., hard-c)-Abbie & Slats, Abbott & Costello, Casper, Little Annie Rooney, Little Audrey, Jim Hardy, Ella Cinders (16 books bound together) (Rare)	148	296	444	947	1624	2300
1(1949, 500 pgs.)-Same format as above	123	246	369	787	1344	1900
1(1950, 500 pgs.)-Same format as above; different-c; (also see Little Audrey Yearbook) (Rare)	123	246	369	787	1344	1900

TREASURY OF DOGS, A (See Dell Giants)

TREASURY OF HORSES, A (See Dell Giants)

TREEHOUSE OF HORROR (Bart Simpson's...)
Bongo Comics: 1995 - Present ($2.95/$2.50/$3.50/$4.50/$4.99, annual)

1-(1995, $2.95)-Groening-c; Allred, Robinson & Smith stories 5.00
2-(1996, $2.50)-Stories by Dini & Bagge; infinity-c by Groening 5.00
3-(1997, $2.50)-Dorkin-s/Groening-c 5.00
4-(1998, $2.50)-Lash & Dixon-s/Groening-c 5.00
5-(1999, $3.50)-Thompson-s; Shaw & Aragonés-s/a; TenNapel-s/a 5.00
6-(2000, $4.50)-Mahfood-s/a; DeCarlo-a; Morse-s/a; Kuper-s/a 5.00
7-(2001, $4.50)-Hamill-s/Morrison-a; Ennis-s/McCrea-a; Sakai-s/a; Nixey-s/a; Brereton back-c 5.00
8-(2002, $3.50)-Templeton, Shaw, Barta, Simone, Thompson-s/a 5.00
9-(2003, $4.99)-Lord of the Rings-Brereton-a; Dini, Naifeh, Millidge, Boothby, Noto-s/a 5.00
10-(2004, $4.99)-Monsters of Rock w/Alice Cooper, Gene Simmons, Rob Zombie and Pat Boone; art by Rodriguez, Morrison, Morse, Templeton 5.00
11-(2005, $4.99)-EC style w/art by John Severin, Angelo Torres & Al Williamson and flip book with Dracula by Wolfman/Colan and Squish Thing by Wein/Wrightson 5.00
12-(2006, $4.99)-Terry Moore, Kyle Baker, Eric Powell-s/a 5.00
13-(2007, $4.99)-Oswalt, Posehn, Lennon-s; Guerra, Austin, Barta, Rodriguez-a 5.00
14-(2008, $4.99)-s/a by Niles & Fabry; Boothby & Matsumoto; Gilbert Hernandez 5.00
15-(2009, $4.99)-s/a by Jeffrey Brown, Tim Hensley, Ben Jones and others 5.00
16-(2010, $4.99)-s/a by Kelley Jones, Evan Dorkin and others; Mars Attacks homage 5.00
17-(2011, $4.99)-s/a by Gene Ha, Jane Wiedlin and others; Nosferatu homage 5.00

TREKKER (See Dark Horse Presents #6)
Dark Horse Comics: May, 1987 - No. 6, Mar,1988 ($1.50, B&W)

1-6: Sci/Fi stories 3.00
Color Special 1 (1989, $2.95, 52 pgs.) 4.00
Collection ($5.95, B&W) 6.00
Special 1 (6/99, $2.95, color) 3.00

TRENCHCOAT BRIGADE, THE
DC Comics (Vertigo): Mar, 1999 - No. 4, Jun, 1999 ($2.50, limited series)

1-4: Hellblazer, Phantom Stranger, Mister E, Dr. Occult app. 3.00

TRENCHER (See Blackball Comics)
Image Comics: May, 1993 - No. 4, Oct, 1993 ($1.95, unfinished limited series)

1-4: Keith Giffen-c/a/scripts. 3-Supreme-c/story 3.00

TRIALS OF SHAZAM!
DC Comics: Oct, 2006 - No. 12, May, 2008 ($2.99)

1-12: 1-8-Winick-s/Porter-a. 9-11-Cascioli-a. 10-Shadowpact app. 12-JLA app. 3.00
... Volume 1 TPB (2007, $14.99) r/#1-6 and story from DCU Brave New World #1 15.00
... Volume 2 TPB (2008, $14.99) r/#7-12 15.00

TRIB COMIC BOOK, THE
Winnipeg Tribune: Sept. 24, 1977 - Vol. 4, #36, 1980 (8-1/2"x11", 24 pgs., weekly) (155 total issues)

	GD	VG	FN	VF	VF/NM	NM-
V1# 1-Color pages (Sunday strips)-Spiderman, Asterix, Disney's Scamp, Wizard of Id, Doonesbury, Inside Woody Allen, Mary Worth, & others (similar to Spirit sections)	2	4	6	10	14	18
V1#2-15, V2#1-52, V3#1-52, V4#1-33	1	3	4	6	8	10
V4#34-36 (not distributed)	2	4	6	11	16	20

NOTE: *All issues have Spider-Man. Later issues contain Star Trek and Star Wars. 20 strips in ea. The first newspaper to put Sunday pages into a comic book format.*

TRIBE (See WildC.A.T.S #4)
Image Comics/Axis Comics No. 2 on: Apr, 1993; No. 2, Sept, 1993 - No. 3, 1994 ($2.50/$1.95)

1-By Johnson & Stroman; gold foil & embossed on black-c 4.00
1-($2.50)-Ivory Edition; gold foil & embossed on white-c; available only through the creators 4.00
2,3: 2-1st Axis Comics issue. 3-Savage Dragon app. 3.00

TRIBUTE TO STEVEN HUGHES, A
Chaos! Comics: Sept, 2000 ($6.95)

1-Lady Death & Evil Ernie pin-ups by various artists; testimonials 7.00

TRICK 'R TREAT
DC Comics (WildStorm): 2009 ($19.95,SC)

nn-Short Halloween-themed story anthology; Andreyko-s; art by Huddleston & others 20.00

TRIGGER (See Roy Rogers'...)

TRIGGER
DC Comics (Vertigo): Feb, 2005 - No. 8, Sept, 2005 ($2.95/$2.99)

1-8-Jason Hall-s/John Watkiss-a/c 3.00

TRIGGER TWINS
National Periodical Publications: Mar-Apr, 1973 (20¢, one-shot)

	GD	VG	FN	VF	VF/NM	NM-
1-Trigger Twins & Pow Wow Smith-r/All-Star Western #94,103 & Western Comics #81; Infantino-r(p)	2	4	6	13	18	22

TRINITY (See DC Universe: Trinity)

TRINITY
DC Comics: Aug, 2008 - No. 52, July, 2009 ($2.99, weekly series)

1-52-Superman, Batman & Wonder Woman star; Busiek-s/Bagley-a. 52-Wraparound-c 3.00
Vol. 1 TPB (2009, $29.99) r/#1-17 30.00
Vol. 2 TPB (2009, $29.99) r/#18-35 30.00
Vol. 3 TPB (2009, $29.99) r/#36-52 30.00

TRINITY ANGELS
Acclaim Comics (Valiant Heroes): July, 1997 - No. 12, June, 1998 ($2.50)

1-12-Maguire-s/a(p):4-Copycat-c 3.00

TRINITY: BLOOD ON THE SANDS
Image Comics (Top Cow): July, 2009 ($2.99, one-shot)

1-Witchblade, The Darkness and Angelus in the 14th century Arabian desert 3.00

TRIPLE GIANT COMICS (See Archie All-Star Specials under Archie Comics)

TRIPLE THREAT
Special Action/Holyoke/Gerona Publ.: Winter, 1945

	GD	VG	FN	VF	VF/NM	NM-
1-Duke of Darkness, King O'Leary	33	66	99	194	317	440

TRIPLE-X
Dark Horse Comics: Dec, 1994 - No. 7, June, 1995 ($3.95, B&W, limited series)

1-7 4.00

TRIUMPH (Also see JLA #28-30, Justice League Task Force & Zero Hour)
DC Comics: June, 1995 - No. 4, Sept, 1995 ($1.75, limited series)

1-4: 3-Hourman, JLA app. 3.00

TRIUMPHANT UNLEASHED
Triumphant Comics: No. 0, Nov, 1993 - No. 1, Nov, 1993 ($2.50, lim. series)

0-Serially numbered, 0-Red logo, 0-White logo (no cover price; giveaway), 1-Cover is negative & reverse of #0-c 3.00

TROJAN WAR (Adaptation of Trojan war histories from ancient Greek and Roman sources)
Marvel Comics: July, 2009 - No. 5, Nov, 2009 ($3.99, limited series)

1-5-Roy Thomas-s/Miguel Sepulveda-a/Dennis Calero-c 4.00

Tron: Original Movie Adaptation #1 © DIS

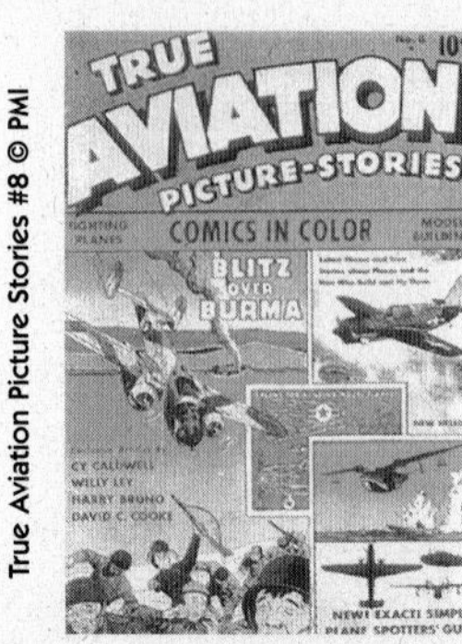

True Aviation Picture Stories #8 © PMI

True Blood #6 © HBO

GD VG FN VF VF/NM NM-
2.0 4.0 6.0 8.0 9.0 9.2

TROLL (Also see Brigade)
Image Comics (Extreme Studios): Dec, 1993 ($2.50, one-shot, 44 pgs.)
1-1st app. Troll; Liefeld scripts; Matsuda-c/a(p) 4.00
Halloween Special (1994, $2.95)-Maxx app. 4.00
...Once A Hero (8/94, $2.50) 4.00

TROLLORDS
Tru Studios/Comico V2#1 on: 2/86 - No. 15, 1988; V2#1, 11/88 - V2#4, 1989 (1-15: $1.50, B&W)
1-First printing 5.00
1-Second printing, 2-15: 6-Christmas issue; silver logo 3.00
V2#1-4 ($1.75, color, Comico) 3.00
Special 1 ($1.75, 2/87, color)-Jerry's Big Fun Bk. 3.00

TROLLORDS
Apple Comics: July, 1989 - No. 6, 1990 ($2.25, B&W, limited series)
1-6: 1-"The Big Batman Movie Parody" 3.00

TROLL PATROL
Harvey Comics: Jan, 1993 ($1.95, 52 pgs.)
1 4.00

TROLL II (Also see Brigade)
Image Comics (Extreme Studios): July, 1994 ($3.95, one-shot)
1 4.00

TRON (Based on the video game and film)
Slave Labor Graphics: Apr, 2006 - No. 6 ($3.50/$3.95)
1-4: 1-DeMartinis-a/Walker & Jones-s 4.00
5,6-($3.95) 4.00

TRON: BETRAYAL
Marvel Comics: Nov, 2010 - No. 2, Dec, 2010 ($3.99, limited series)
1,2-Prequel to Tron Legacy movie; Larroca-c 4.00

TRON: ORIGINAL MOVIE ADAPTATION
Marvel Comics: Jan, 2011 - No. 2, Feb, 2011 ($3.99, limited series)
1,2-Peter David-s/Mirco Pierfederici-a/Greg Land-c 4.00

TROUBLE
Marvel Comics (Epic): Sept, 2003 - No. 5, Jan, 2004 ($2.99, limited series)
1-5-Photo-c; Richard and Ben meet Mary and May; Millar-s/Dodson-a 3.00
1-2nd printing with variant Frank Cho-c 5.00

TROUBLED SOULS
Fleetway: 1990 ($9.95, trade paperback)
nn-Garth Ennis scripts & John McCrea painted-c/a. 10.00

TROUBLEMAKERS
Acclaim Comics (Valiant Heroes): Apr, 1997 - No. 19, June, 1998 ($2.50)
1-19: Fabian Nicieza scripts in all. 1-1st app. XL, Rebound & Blur; 2 covers. 8-Copycat-c. 12-Shooting of Parker 3.00

TROUBLE SHOOTERS, THE (TV)
Dell Publishing Co.: No. 1108, Jun-Aug, 1960
Four Color 1108-Keenan Wynn photo-c 5 10 15 35 55 75

TROUBLE WITH GIRLS, THE
Malibu Comics (Eternity Comics) #7-14/Comico V2#1-4/Eternity V2#5 on: 8/87 - #14, 1988; V2#1, 2/89 - V2#23, 1991? ($1.95, B&W/color)
1-14 ($1.95, B&W, Eternity)-Gerard Jones scripts & Tim Hamilton-c/a in all. 3.00
V2#1-23-Jones scripts, Hamilton-c/a. 3.00
Annual 1 (1988, $2.95) 4.00
Christmas Special 1 (12/91, $2.95, B&W, Eternity)-Jones scripts, Hamilton-c/a 4.00
Graphic Novel 1,2 (7/88, B&W)-r/#1-3 & #4-6 8.00

TROUBLE WITH GIRLS, THE: NIGHT OF THE LIZARD
Marvel Comics (Epic Comics/Heavy Hitters): 1993 - No. 4, 1993 ($2.50/$1.95, lim. series)
1-Embossed-c; Gerard Jones scripts & Bret Blevins-c/a in all 3.00
2-4: 2-Begin $1.95-c. 3.00

TROUT
Oni Press: Oct, 2001 - No. 2, Feb, 2002 ($2.95, B&W, limited series)
1,2-Troy Nixey-s/a 3.00

TRUE ADVENTURES (Formerly True Western)(Men's Adventures #4 on)
Marvel Comics (CCC): No. 3, May, 1950 (52 pgs.)
3-Powell, Sekowsky-a; Brodsky-c 18 36 54 103 162 220

GD VG FN VF VF/NM NM-
2.0 4.0 6.0 8.0 9.0 9.2

TRUE ANIMAL PICTURE STORIES
True Comics Press: Winter, 1947 - No. 2, Spring-Summer, 1947
1,2 10 20 30 56 76 95

TRUE AVIATION PICTURE STORIES (Becomes Aviation Adventures & Model Building #16 on)
Parents' Mag. Institute: 1942; No. 2, Jan-Feb, 1943 - No. 15, Sept-Oct, 1946
1-(#1 & 2 titled ...Aviation Comics Digest)(not digest size) 15 30 45 85 130 175
2 10 20 30 56 76 95
3-14: 3-10-Plane photos on-c. 11,13-Photo-c 9 18 27 50 65 80
15-(Titled "True Aviation Adventures & Model Building") 9 18 27 47 61 75

TRUE BELIEVERS
Marvel Comics: Sept, 2008 - No. 5, Jan, 2009 ($2.99, limited series)
1-5-Cary Bates-s/Paul Gulacy-a. 1,2-Reed Richards app. 3-Luke Cage app. 3.00

TRUE BLOOD (Based on the HBO vampire series)
IDW Publishing: Aug, 2010 - No. 6, Dec, 2010 ($3.99)
1-Messina-a; 4 covers by Messina, Campbell, Currie and Corroney 4.00
2-6-Multiple covers on each 4.00
...: Legacy Edition (1/11, $4.99) r/#1, cover gallery; full script 5.00

TRUE BLOOD: TAINTED LOVE (Based on the HBO vampire series)
IDW Publishing: Feb, 2011 - No. 6, Jul, 2011 ($3.99, limited series)
1-4: 1,2,4,5-Corroney-a; multiple covers. 3-Molnar-a 4.00
... Legacy Edition 1 (7/11, $4.99) r/#1 with full script and cover gallery 5.00

TRUE BLOOD: THE FRENCH QUARTER (Based on the HBO vampire series)
IDW Publishing: Aug, 2011 - Present ($3.99, limited series)
1-Huehner & Tischman-s; multiple covers. 3-Molnar-a 4.00

TRUE BLOOD: THE GREAT REVELATION (Prequel to the 2008 HBO vampire series)
HBO/Top Cow: July, 2008 (no cover price, one shot continued on HBO website)
1-David Wohl-s/Jason Badower-a/c 4.00

TRUE BRIDE'S EXPERIENCES (Formerly Teen-Age Brides)
(True Bride-To-Be Romances No. 17 on)
True Love (Harvey Publications): No. 8, Oct, 1954 - No. 16, Feb, 1956
8-"I Married a Farmer" 9 18 27 50 65 80
9,10: 10-Last pre-code (2/55) 7 14 21 37 46 55
11-15 6 12 18 31 38 45
16-Last issue 7 14 21 37 46 55
NOTE: *Powell a-8-10, 12, 13.*

TRUE BRIDE-TO-BE ROMANCES (Formerly True Bride's Experiences)
Home Comics/True Love (Harvey): No. 17, Apr, 1956 - No. 30, Nov, 1958
17-S&K-c, Powell-a 10 20 30 56 76 95
18-20,22,25-28,30 6 12 18 31 38 45
21,23,24,29-Powell-a. 29-Baker-a (1 pg.) 7 14 21 35 43 50

TRUE COMICS (Also see Outstanding American War Heroes)
True Comics/Parents' Magazine Press: April, 1941 - No. 84, Aug, 1950
1-Marathon run story; life story Winston Churchill 31 62 93 182 296 410
2-Red Cross story; Everett-a 15 30 45 85 130 175
3-Baseball Hall of Fame story; Chiang Kai-Shek-c/s 17 34 51 100 158 215
4,5: 4-Story of American flag "Old Glory". 5-Life story of Joe Louis 14 28 42 80 115 150
6-Baseball World Series story 15 30 45 90 140 190
7-10: 7-Buffalo Bill story. 10,11-Teddy Roosevelt 11 22 33 62 86 110
11-14,16,18-20: 11-Thomas Edison, Douglas MacArthur stories. 13-Harry Houdini story. 14-Charlie McCarthy story. 18-Story of America begins, ends #26. 19-Eisenhower-c/s 10 20 30 54 72 90
15-Flag-c; Bob Feller story 10 20 30 58 79 100
17-Brooklyn Dodgers story 11 22 33 64 90 115
21-30: 24-Marco Polo story. 28-Origin of Uncle Sam. 29-Beethoven story. 30-Cooper Brothers baseball story 9 18 27 47 61 75
31-Red Grange "Galloping Ghost" story 8 16 24 40 50 60
32-46: 33-Origin/1st app. Steve Saunders, Special Agent of the FBI, series begins. 35-Mark Twain story. 38-General Bradley-c/s. 39-FDR story. 44-Truman story. 46-George Gershwin story 7 14 21 37 46 55
47-Atomic bomb issue (c/story, 3/46) 10 20 30 56 76 95
48-54,56-65: 49-1st app. Secret Warriors. 53-Bobby Riggs story. 58-Jim Jeffries (boxer) story; Harry Houdini story. 59-Bob Hope story; pirates-c/s. 60-Speedway Speed Demon-c/story. 7 14 21 35 43 50
55-(12/46)-1st app. Sad Sack by Baker (1/2 pg.) 9 18 27 47 61 75
66-Will Rogers-c/story 7 14 21 37 46 55

True Comics #71 © PMI

True Crime Comics #2 © Magazine Village

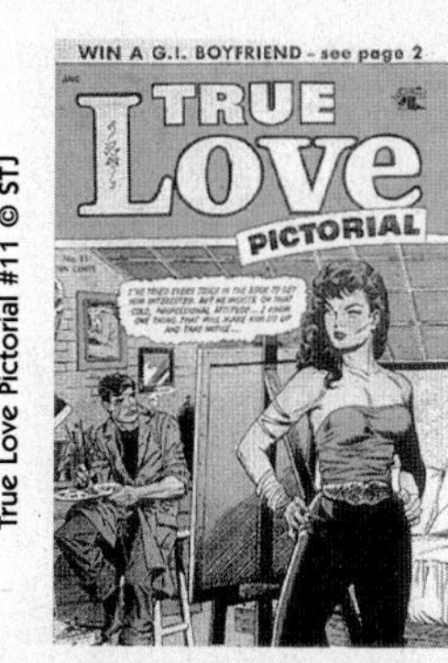

True Love Pictorial #11 © STJ

	GD 2.0	VG 4.0	FN 6.0	VF 8.0	VF/NM 9.0	NM- 9.2
67-1st oversized issue (12/47); Steve Saunders, Special Agent begins	8	16	24	42	54	65
68-70,74-77,79: 68-70,74-77-Features Steve Sanders True FBI advs. 68-Oversized; Admiral Byrd-c/s. 69-Jack Benny story. 74-Amos 'n' Andy story	6	12	18	31	38	45
71-Joe DiMaggio-c/story.	9	18	27	47	61	75
72-Jackie Robinson story; True FBI advs.	8	16	24	40	50	60
73-Walt Disney's life story	9	18	27	47	61	75
78-Stan Musial-c/story; True FBI advs.	8	16	24	40	50	60
80-84 (Scarce)-All distr. to subscribers through mail only; paper-c. 80-Rocket trip to the moon story. 81-Red Grange story. 84-Wyatt Earp app. (1st app. in comics?); Rube Marquard story	18	36	54	103	162	220

(Prices vary widely on issues 80-84)

NOTE: ***Bob Kane*** *a-7.* ***Palais*** *a-80.* ***Powell*** *c/a-80. #80-84 have soft covers and combined with Tex Granger, Jack Armstrong, and Calling All Kids. #68-78 featured true FBI adventures.*

TRUE COMICS AND ADVENTURE STORIES
Parents' Magazine Institute: 1965 (Giant) (25¢)

	GD 2.0	VG 4.0	FN 6.0	VF 8.0	VF/NM 9.0	NM- 9.2
1,2: 1-Fighting Hero of Viet Nam; LBJ on-c	3	6	9	18	27	35

TRUE COMPLETE MYSTERY (Formerly Complete Mystery)
Marvel Comics (PrPI): No. 5, Apr, 1949 - No. 8, Oct, 1949

	GD 2.0	VG 4.0	FN 6.0	VF 8.0	VF/NM 9.0	NM- 9.2
5-Criminal career of Rico Mancini	26	52	78	154	252	350
6-8: 6-8-Photo-c	20	40	60	114	182	250

TRUE CONFIDENCES
Fawcett Publications: 1949 (Fall) - No. 4, June, 1950 (All photo-c)

	GD 2.0	VG 4.0	FN 6.0	VF 8.0	VF/NM 9.0	NM- 9.2
1-Has ad for Fawcett Love Adventures #1, but publ. as Love Memoirs #1 as Marvel published the title first; Swayze-a	18	36	54	105	165	225
2-4: 3-Swayze-a. 4-Powell-a	12	24	36	67	94	120

TRUE CRIME CASES (...From Official Police Files)
St. John Publishing Co.: 1944 (25¢, 100 pg. Giant)

	GD 2.0	VG 4.0	FN 6.0	VF 8.0	VF/NM 9.0	NM- 9.2
nn-Matt Baker-c	50	100	150	315	533	750

TRUE CRIME COMICS (Also see Complete Book of...)
Magazine Village: No. 2, May, 1947; No. 3, July-Aug, 1948 - No. 6, June-July, 1949; V2#1, Aug-Sept, 1949 (52 pgs.)

	GD 2.0	VG 4.0	FN 6.0	VF 8.0	VF/NM 9.0	NM- 9.2
2-Jack Cole-c/a; used in **SOTI**, pgs. 81,82 plus illo. "A sample of the injury-to-eye motif" & illo. "Dragging living people to death"; used in **POP**, pg. 105; "Murder, Morphine and Me" classic drug propaganda story used by N.Y. Legis. Comm.	189	374	561	1197	2049	2900
3-Classic Cole-c/a; drug story with hypo, opium den & with drawing addict	126	252	378	806	1378	1950
4-Jack Cole-c/a; c-taken from a story panel in #3 (r-(2) **SOTI** & **POP** stories/#2?)	102	204	306	648	1112	1575
5-Jack Cole-c, Marijuana racket story (Canadian ed. w/cover similar to #3 exists w/out drug story)	71	142	213	454	777	1100
6-Not a reprint, original story (Canadian ed. reprints #4 w/different coloring on-c)	57	114	171	362	619	875
V2#1-Used in **SOTI**, pgs. 81,82 & illo. "Dragging living people to death"; Toth, Wood (3 pgs.), Roussos-a; Cole-r from #2	90	180	270	576	988	1400

NOTE: *V2#1 was reprinted in Canada as V2#9 (12/49); same-c & contents minus Wood-a.*

TRUE FAITH
Fleetway: 1990 ($9.95, graphic novel)

	GD 2.0	VG 4.0	FN 6.0	VF 8.0	VF/NM 9.0	NM- 9.2
nn-Garth Ennis scripts	2	4	6	12	16	20
Reprinted by DC/Vertigo ('97, $12.95)						13.00

TRUE GHOST STORIES (See Ripley's...)

TRUE LIFE ROMANCES (...Romance on cover)
Ajax/Farrell Publications: Dec, 1955 - No. 3, Aug, 1956

	GD 2.0	VG 4.0	FN 6.0	VF 8.0	VF/NM 9.0	NM- 9.2
1	11	22	33	60	83	105
2	8	16	24	40	50	60
3-Disbrow-a	8	16	24	44	57	70

TRUE LIFE SECRETS
Romantic Love Stories/Charlton: Mar-April, 1951 - No. 28, Sept, 1955; No. 29, Jan, 1956

	GD 2.0	VG 4.0	FN 6.0	VF 8.0	VF/NM 9.0	NM- 9.2
1-Photo-c begin, end #3?	15	30	45	86	133	180
2	10	20	30	54	72	90
3-11,13-19:	9	18	27	47	61	75
12-"I Was An Escort Girl" story	10	20	30	56	76	95
20-29: 25-Last precode (3/55)	8	16	24	42	54	65

TRUE LIFE TALES (Formerly Mitzi's Romances #8?)
Marvel Comics (CCC): No. 8, Oct, 1949 - No. 2, Jan, 1950 (52 pgs.)

	GD 2.0	VG 4.0	FN 6.0	VF 8.0	VF/NM 9.0	NM- 9.2
8(#1, 10/49), 2-Both have photo-c	13	26	39	72	101	130

TRUE LOVE
Eclipse Comics: Jan, 1986 - No. 2, Jan, 1986 ($2.00, Baxter paper)

	GD 2.0	VG 4.0	FN 6.0	VF 8.0	VF/NM 9.0	NM- 9.2
1,2-Love stories reprinted from pre-code Standard Comics; Toth-a(p) in both; 1-Dave Stevens-c. 2-Mayo-a						4.00

TRUE LOVE CONFESSIONS
Premier Magazines: May, 1954 - No. 11, Jan, 1956

	GD 2.0	VG 4.0	FN 6.0	VF 8.0	VF/NM 9.0	NM- 9.2
1-Marijuana story	15	30	45	84	127	170
2	9	18	27	52	69	85
3-11	9	18	27	47	61	75

TRUE LOVE PICTORIAL
St. John Publishing Co.: Dec, 1952 - No. 11, Aug, 1954

	GD 2.0	VG 4.0	FN 6.0	VF 8.0	VF/NM 9.0	NM- 9.2
1-Only photo-c	22	44	66	132	216	300
2-Baker-c/a	32	64	96	188	307	425
3-5(All 25¢, 100 pgs.): 4-Signed story by Estrada. 5-(4/53)-Formerly Teen-Age Temptations; Kubert-a in #3; Baker-c/a in #3-5	50	100	150	315	533	750
6,7: Baker-c/a; signed stories by Estrada	30	60	90	177	289	400
8,10,11-Baker-c/a	30	60	90	177	289	400
9-Baker-c	24	48	72	142	234	325

TRUE LOVE PROBLEMS AND ADVICE ILLUSTRATED (Becomes Romance Stories of True Love No. 45 on)
McCombs/Harvey Publ./Home Comics: June, 1949 - No. 6, Apr, 1950; No. 7, Jan, 1951 - No. 44, Mar, 1957

	GD 2.0	VG 4.0	FN 6.0	VF 8.0	VF/NM 9.0	NM- 9.2
V1#1	15	30	45	86	133	180
2-Elias-c	10	20	30	54	72	90
3-10: 3,4,7-9-Elias-c	8	16	24	42	54	65
11-13,15-23,25-31: 31-Last pre-code (1/55)	7	14	21	35	43	50
14,24-Rape scene	7	14	21	37	46	55
32-37,39-44	6	12	18	29	36	42
38-S&K-c	9	18	27	52	69	85

NOTE: ***Powell*** *a-1, 2, 7-14, 17-25, 28, 29, 33, 40, 41. #3 has True Love... on inside.*

TRUE MOVIE AND TELEVISION (Part teenage magazine)
Toby Press: Aug, 1950 - No. 3, Nov, 1950; No. 4, Mar, 1951 (52 pgs.)(1-3: 10¢)

	GD 2.0	VG 4.0	FN 6.0	VF 8.0	VF/NM 9.0	NM- 9.2
1-Elizabeth Taylor photo-c; Gene Autry, Shirley Temple app.	60	120	180	381	653	925
2-(9/50)-Janet Leigh/Liz Taylor/Ava Gardner & others photo-c; Frazetta John Wayne illo from J.Wayne Adv. Comics #2 (4/50)	43	86	129	271	461	650
3-June Allyson photo-c; Montgomery Cliff, Esther Williams, Andrews Sisters app; Li'l Abner featured; Sadie Hawkins' Day	31	62	93	186	303	420
4-Jane Powell photo-c (15¢)	20	40	60	117	189	260

NOTE: *16 pgs. in color, rest movie material in black & white.*

TRUE SECRETS (Formerly Our Love?)
Marvel (IPS)/Atlas Comics (MPI) #4 on: No. 3, Mar, 1950; No. 4, Feb, 1951 - No. 40, Sept, 1956

	GD 2.0	VG 4.0	FN 6.0	VF 8.0	VF/NM 9.0	NM- 9.2
3 (52 pgs.)(IPS one-shot)	15	30	45	90	140	190
4,5,7-10	11	22	33	60	83	105
6,22-Everett-a	13	26	39	72	101	130
11-20	10	20	30	56	76	95
21,23-28: 24-Colletta-c. 28-Last pre-code (2/55)	9	18	27	52	69	85
29-40: 34,36-Colletta-a	9	18	27	47	61	75

TRUE SPORT PICTURE STORIES (Formerly Sport Comics)
Street & Smith Publications: V1#5, Feb, 1942 - V5#2, July-Aug, 1949

	GD 2.0	VG 4.0	FN 6.0	VF 8.0	VF/NM 9.0	NM- 9.2
V1#5-Joe DiMaggio-c/story	37	74	111	218	354	490
6-12 (1942-43): 12-Jack Dempsey story	21	42	63	122	199	275
V2#1-12 (1943-45): 7-Stan Musial-c/story; photo story of the New York Yankees	20	40	60	115	185	255
V3#1-12 (1946-47): 7-Joe DiMaggio, Stan Musial, Bob Feller & others back from the armed service story. 8-Billy Conn vs. Joe Louis-c/story	19	38	57	111	176	240
V4#1-12 (1947-49), V5#1,2: v4#8-Joe Louis on-c	18	36	54	105	165	225

NOTE: ***Powell*** *a-V3#10, V4#1-4, 6-8, 10-12; V5#1, 2; c-V3#10-12, V4#2-7, 9-12.* ***Ravielli*** *c-V5#2.*

TRUE STORIES OF ROMANCE
Fawcett Publications: Jan, 1950 - No. 3, May, 1950 (All photo-c)

	GD 2.0	VG 4.0	FN 6.0	VF 8.0	VF/NM 9.0	NM- 9.2
1	15	30	45	83	124	165
2,3: 3-Marcus Swayze-a	11	22	33	62	86	110

TRUE STORY OF JESSE JAMES, THE (See Jesse James, Four Color 757)

TRUE SWEETHEART SECRETS
Fawcett Publs.: 5/50; No. 2, 7/50; No. 3, 1951(nd); No. 4, 9/51 - No. 11, 1/53 (All photo-c)

	GD 2.0	VG 4.0	FN 6.0	VF 8.0	VF/NM 9.0	NM- 9.2
1-Photo-c; Debbie Reynolds?	16	32	48	94	147	200
2-Wood-a (11 pgs.)	19	38	57	111	176	240

True-to-Life Romances #8 © QUA

Tuff Ghosts Starring Spooky #23 © HARV

Turok, Dinosaur Hunter #15 © VAL

GD VG FN VF VF/NM NM-
2.0 4.0 6.0 8.0 9.0 9.2

3-11: 4,5-Powell-a. 8-Marcus Swayze-a. 11-Evans-a
12 24 36 69 97 125

TRUE TALES OF LOVE (Formerly Secret Story Romances)
Atlas Comics (TCI): No. 22, April, 1956 - No. 31, Sept, 1957

22 11 22 33 60 83 105
23-24,26-31-Colletta-a in most: 9 18 27 47 61 75
25-Everett-a; Colletta-a 9 18 27 52 69 85

TRUE TALES OF ROMANCE
Fawcett Publications: No. 4, June, 1950

4-Photo-c 11 22 33 60 83 105

TRUE 3-D
Harvey Publications: Dec, 1953 - No. 2, Feb, 1954 (25¢)(Both came with 2 pair of glasses)

1-Nostrand, Powell-a 5 10 15 35 55 75
2-Powell-a 6 12 18 37 59 80
NOTE: *Many copies of #1 surfaced in 1984.*

TRUE-TO-LIFE ROMANCES (Formerly Guns Against Gangsters)
Star Publ.: #8, 11-12/49; #9, 1-2/50; #3, 4/50 - #5, 9/50; #6, 1/51 - #23, 10/54

8(#1, 1949) 24 48 72 140 230 320
9(#2),4-10 17 34 51 100 158 215
3-Janet Leigh/Glenn Ford photo on-c plus true life story of each
19 38 57 109 172 235
11,22,23 15 30 45 86 133 180
12-14,17-21-Disbrow-a 16 32 48 94 147 200
15,16-Wood & Disbrow-a in each 19 38 57 109 172 235
NOTE: *Kamen a-13. **Kamen/Feldstein** a-14. All have **L.B. Cole** covers.*

TRUE WAR EXPERIENCES
Harvey Publications: Aug, 1952 - No. 4, Dec, 1952

1 8 16 24 56 93 130
2-4 5 10 15 32 51 70

TRUE WAR ROMANCES (Becomes Exotic Romances #22 on)
Quality Comics Group: Sept, 1952 - No. 21, June, 1955

1-Photo-c 15 30 45 84 127 170
2-(10/52) 9 18 27 52 69 85
3-10: 3-(12/52). 8,9-Whitney-a 9 18 27 47 61 75
11-21: 20-Last precode (4/55). 14-Whitney-a 8 16 24 42 54 65

TRUE WAR STORIES (See Ripley's...)

TRUE WESTERN (True Adventures #3)
Marvel Comics (MMC): Dec, 1949 - No. 2, March, 1950

1-Photo-c; Billy The Kid story 16 32 48 94 147 200
2-Alan Ladd photo-c 19 38 57 112 179 245

TRUMP
HMH Publishing Co.: Jan, 1957 - No. 2, Mar, 1957 (50¢, magazine)

1-Harvey Kurtzman satire 25 50 75 150 245 340
2-Harvey Kurtzman satire 20 40 60 117 189 260
NOTE: ***Davis, Elder, Heath, Jaffee** art-#1,2; **Wood** a-1. Article by Mel Brooks in #2.*

TRUMPETS WEST (See Luke Short, Four Color #875)

TRUTH ABOUT CRIME (See Fox Giants)

TRUTH ABOUT MOTHER GOOSE (See Mother Goose, Four Color #862)

TRUTH BEHIND THE TRIAL OF CARDINAL MINDSZENTY, THE (See Cardinal Mindszenty in the Promotional Comics section))

TRUTHFUL LOVE (Formerly Youthful Love)
Youthful Magazines: No. 2, July, 1950

2-Ingrid Bergman's true life story 13 26 39 72 101 130

TRUTH RED, WHITE & BLACK
Marvel Comics: Jan, 2003 - No. 6 ($3.50, limited series)

1-Kyle Baker-a/Robert Morales-s; the testing of Captain America's super-soldier serum 3.50
2-7: 3-Isaiah Bradley 1st dons the Captain America costume 3.50
TPB (2004, $17.99) r/series 18.00

TRY-OUT WINNER BOOK
Marvel Comics: Mar, 1988

1-Spider-Man vs. Doc Octopus 5.00

TSR WORLD (...Annual on cover only)
DC Comics: 1990 ($3.95, 84 pgs.)

1-Advanced D&D, ForgottenRealms, Dragonlance & 1st app. Spelljammer 4.00

TSUNAMI GIRL

GD VG FN VF VF/NM NM-
2.0 4.0 6.0 8.0 9.0 9.2

Image Comics: 1999 - No. 3, 1999 ($2.95)

1-3-Sorayama-c/Paniccia-s/a 3.00

TUBBY (See Marge's...)

TUFF GHOSTS STARRING SPOOKY
Harvey Publications: July, 1962 - No. 39, Nov, 1970; No. 40, Sept, 1971 - No. 43, Oct, 1972

1-12¢ issues begin 11 22 33 73 142 210
2-5 7 14 21 44 72 100
6-10 5 10 15 32 51 70
11-20 4 8 12 24 37 50
21-30: 29-Hot Stuff/Spooky team-up story 3 6 9 16 23 30
31-39,43 2 4 6 13 18 22
40-42: 52 pg. Giants 3 6 9 14 20 25

TUFFY
Standard Comics: No. 5, July, 1949 - No. 9, Oct, 1950

5-All by Sid Hoff 7 14 21 37 46 55
6-9 5 10 15 24 30 35

TUFFY TURTLE
I. W. Enterprises: No date

1-Reprint 2 4 6 8 11 14

TUG & BUSTER
Art & Soul Comics: Nov, 1995 - No. 7, Feb, 1998 ($2.95, B&W, bi-monthly)

1-7: Marc Hempel-c/a/scripts 3.00
1-(Image Comics, 8/98, $2.95, B&W) 3.00

TURF
Image Comics: Apr, 2010 - No. 5 ($2.99, limited series)

1-2-Jonathan Ross-s/Tommy Lee Edwards-a 3.00

TUROK
Acclaim Comics: Mar, 1998 - No. 4, Jun, 1998 ($2.50)

1-4-Nicieza-s/Kayanan-a 3.00
..., Child of Blood 1 (1/98, $3.95) Nicieza-s/Kayanan-a 4.00
... Evolution 1 (8/02, $2.50) Nicieza-s/Kayanan-a 3.00
..., Redpath 1 (10/97, $3.95) Nicieza-s/Kayanan-a 4.00
... / Shadowman 1 (2/99, $3.95) Priest-s/Broome & Jimenez-a 4.00
...: Spring Break in the Lost Land 1 (7/97, $3.95) Nicieza-s/Kayanan-a 4.00
...: Tales of the Lost Land 1 (4/98, $3.95) 4.00
...: The Empty Souls 1 (4/97, $3.95) Nicieza-s/Kayanan-a; variant-c 4.00

TUROK, DINOSAUR HUNTER (See Magnus Robot Fighter #12 & Archer & Armstrong #2)
Valiant/Acclaim Comics: June, 1993 - No. 47, Aug, 1996 ($2.50)

1-($3.50)-Chromium & foil-c 4.00
1-Gold foil-c variant 5.00
0, 2-47: 4-Andar app. 5-Death of Andar. 7-9-Truman/Glanzman-a. 11-Bound-in trading card. 16-Chaos Effect 3.00
Yearbook 1 (1994, $3.95, 52 pgs.) 4.00

TUROK, SON OF STONE (See Dan Curtis, Golden Comics Digest #31, Space Western #45 & March of Comics #378, 399, 408)
Dell Publ. Co. #1-29(9/62)/Gold Key #30(12/62)-85(7/73)/Gold Key or Whitman #86(9/73)-125(1/80)/Whitman #126(3/81) on: No. 596, 12/54 - No. 29, 9/62; No. 30, 12/62 - No. 91, 7/74; No. 92, 9/74 - No. 125, 1/80; No. 126, 3/81 - No. 130, 4/82

Four Color 596 (12/54)(#1)-1st app./origin Turok & Andar; dinosaur-c. Created by Matthew H. Murphy; written by Alberto Giolitti 54 108 162 437 944 1450
Four Color 656 (10/55)(#2)-1st mention of Lanok 29 58 87 210 455 700
3(3-5/56)-5: 3-Cave men 21 42 63 146 311 475
6-10: 8-Dinosaur of the deep; Turok enters Lost Valley; series begins. 9-Paul S. Newman-s (most issues thru end) 14 28 42 97 211 325
11-20: 17-Prehistoric Pygmies 12 24 36 81 166 250
21-29 10 20 30 65 118 170
30-1st Gold Key. 30-33-Painted back-c. 10 20 30 66 121 175
31-Drug use story 10 20 30 65 118 170
32-40 8 16 24 53 89 125
41-50 6 12 18 42 69 95
51-57,59,60 6 12 18 39 62 85
58-Flying Saucer c/story 6 12 18 41 66 90
61-70: 62-12¢ & 15¢ covers. 63,68-Line drawn-c 5 10 15 32 51 70
71-84: 84-Origin & 1st app. Hutec 4 8 12 28 44 60
85-99: 93-r-c/#19 w/changes. 94-r-c/#28 w/changes. 97-r-c/#31 w/changes. 98-r/#58 w/o spaceship & spacemen on-c. 99-r-c/#52 w/changes.
4 8 12 22 34 45

TV Stars #4 © H-B

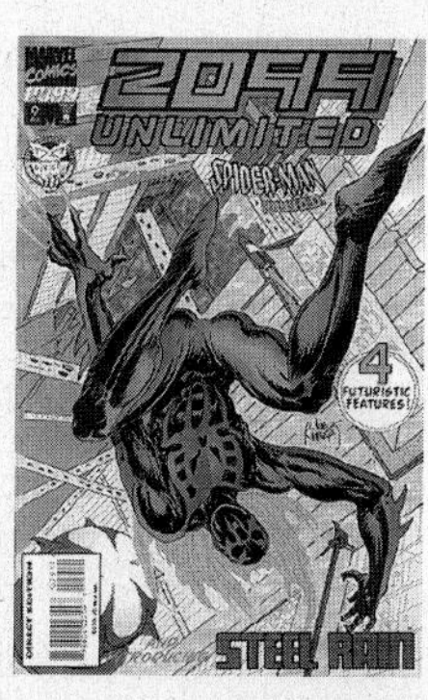

2099 Unlimited #9 © MAR

24: One Shot © 20th Century Fox

	GD 2.0	VG 4.0	FN 6.0	VF 8.0	VF/NM 9.0	NM- 9.2
100	4	8	12	28	44	60
101-129: 114,115-(52 pgs.). 129(2/82)	4	8	12	23	36	48
130(4/82)-Last issue	6	12	18	39	62	85
Giant 1(30031-611) (11/66)-Slick-c; r/#10-12 & 16 plus cover to #11	10	20	30	69	130	190
Giant 1-Same as above but with paper-c	11	22	33	73	142	210

NOTE: *Most painted-c; line-drawn #63 & 130.* ***Alberto Gioletti*** *a-24-27, 30-119, 123; painted-c No. 30-129.* ***Sparling*** *a-117, 120-130. Reprints-#36, 54, 57, 75, 112, 114(1/3), 115(1/3), 118, 121, 125, 127(1/3), 128, 129(1/3), 130(1/3), Giant 1. Cover r-93, 94, 97-99, 126(all different from original covers.*

TUROK, SON OF STONE
Dark Horse Comics: Oct, 2010 - No. 4, Oct, 2011 ($3.50)

1-4: 1-Shooter-s/Francisco-a/Swanland-c; back-up reprint of debut in Four Color 596	3.50
1-Variant-c by Francisco	3.50

TUROK THE HUNTED
Valiant/Acclaim Comics: Mar, 1995 - No. 2, Apr, 1995 ($2.50, limited series)

1,2-Mike Deodato-a(p); price omitted on #1	3.00

TUROK THE HUNTED
Acclaim Comics (Valiant): Feb, 1996 - No. 2, Mar, 1996 ($2.50, limited series)

1,2-Mike Grell story	3.00

TUROK, TIMEWALKER
Acclaim Comics (Valiant): Aug, 1997 - No. 2, Sept, 1997 ($2.50, limited series)

1,2-Nicieza story	3.00

TUROK 2 (Magazine)
Acclaim Comics: Oct, 1998 ($4.99, magazine size)

...Seeds of Evil-Nicieza-s/Broome & Benjamin-a; origin back-up story	5.00
#2 Adon's Curse -Mack painted-c/Broome & Benjamin-a; origin pt. 2	5.00

TUROK 3: SHADOW OF OBLIVION
Acclaim Comics: Sept, 2000 ($4.95, one-shot)

1-Includes pin-up gallery	5.00

TURTLE SOUP
Mirage Studios: Sept, 1987 ($2.00, 76 pgs., B&W, one-shot)

	GD	VG	FN	VF	VF/NM	NM-
1-Featuring Teenage Mutant Ninja Turtles	1	2	3	5	6	8

TURTLE SOUP
Mirage Studios: Nov, 1991 - No. 4, 1992 ($2.50, limited series, coated paper)

1-4: Features the Teenage Mutant Ninja Turtles	4.00

TV CASPER & COMPANY
Harvey Publications: Aug, 1963 - No. 46, April, 1974 (25¢ Giants)

	GD	VG	FN	VF	VF/NM	NM-
1- 68 pg. Giants begin; Casper, Little Audrey, Baby Huey, Herman & Catnip, Buzzy the Crow begin	11	22	33	73	142	210
2-5	6	12	18	432	69	95
6-10	5	10	15	30	48	65
11-20	4	8	12	24	37	50
21-31: 31-Last 68 pg. issue	3	6	9	18	27	35
32-46: All 52 pgs.	3	6	9	16	23	30

NOTE: *Many issues contain reprints.*

TV FUNDAY FUNNIES (See Famous TV...)
TV FUNNIES (See New Funnies)
TV FUNTIME (See Little Audrey)
TV LAUGHOUT (See Archie's...)

TV SCREEN CARTOONS (Formerly Real Screen)
National Periodical Publ.: No. 129, July-Aug, 1959 - No. 138, Jan-Feb, 1961

	GD	VG	FN	VF	VF/NM	NM-
129-138 (Scarce)	6	12	18	42	69	95

TV STARS (TV) (Newsstand sales only)
Marvel Comics Group: Aug, 1978 - No. 4, Feb, 1979 (Hanna-Barbera)

	GD	VG	FN	VF	VF/NM	NM-
1-Great Grape Ape app.	3	6	9	18	27	35
2,4: 4-Top Cat app.	3	6	9	16	22	28
3-Toth-c/a; Dave Stevens inks	3	6	9	17	25	32

TV TEENS (Formerly Ozzie & Babs; Rock and Rollo #14 on)
Charlton Comics: V1#14, Feb, 1954 - V2#13, July, 1956

	GD	VG	FN	VF	VF/NM	NM-
V1#14 (#1)-Ozzie & Babs	10	20	30	54	72	90
15 (#2)	6	12	18	33	41	48
V2#3(6/54) - 6-Don Winslow	6	12	18	31	38	45
7-13-Mopsy. 8(7/55). 9-Paper dolls	6	12	18	29	36	42

TWEETY AND SYLVESTER (1st Series) (TV) (Also see Looney Tunes and Merrie Melodies)
Dell Publishing Co.: No. 406, June, 1952 - No. 37, June-Aug, 1962

	GD	VG	FN	VF	VF/NM	NM-
Four Color 406 (#1)	11	22	33	71	136	200
Four Color 489,524	7	14	21	44	72	100
4 (3-5/54) - 20	6	12	18	37	59	80
21-37	5	10	15	30	48	65

(See March of Comics #421, 433, 445, 457, 469, 481)

TWEETY AND SYLVESTER (2nd Series)(See Kite Fun Book)
Gold Key No. 1-102/Whitman No. 103 on: Nov, 1963; No. 2, Nov, 1965 - No. 121, Jun, 1984

	GD	VG	FN	VF	VF/NM	NM-
1	5	10	15	32	51	70
2-10	3	6	9	18	27	35
11-30	2	4	6	13	18	22
31-50	2	4	6	9	12	15
51-70	1	3	4	6	8	10
71-102	1	2	3	5	6	8
103,104 (Whitman)	1	3	4	6	8	10
105(9/80),106(10/80),107(12/80) 3-pack only	3	6	9	20	30	40
108-116: 113(2/82),114(2-3/82),115(3/82),116(4/82)	2	4	6	8	10	12
117-121 (All # 90094 on-c; nd, nd code): 117(6/83). 118(7/83). 119(2/84)-r(1/3). 120(5/84). 121(6/84)	3	6	9	14	19	24
Digest nn (Charlton/Xerox Pub., 1974) (low print run)	3	6	9	16	23	30
Mini Comic No. 1(1976, 3-1/4x6-1/2")	1	3	4	6	8	10

TWELVE, THE (Golden Age Timely heroes)
Marvel Comics: No. 0; 2008; No. 1, Mar, 2008 - No. 12, ($2.99, limited series)

0-Rockman, Laughing Mask & Phantom Reporter intro. stories (1940s); series preview	4.00
1/2 (2008, $3.99) r/early app. of Fiery Mask, Mister E and Rockman; Weston-c	5.00
1-10-Straczynski-s/Weston-a; Timely heroes re-surface in the present	4.00
... Must Have 1 (4/12, $3.99) r/#7,8	4.00
...: Spearhead 1 (5/10, $3.99) Weston-s/a; Phantom Reporter in WW2; Invaders app.	5.00

12 O'CLOCK HIGH (TV)
Dell Publishing Co.: Jan-Mar, 1965 - No. 2, Apr-June, 1965 (Photo-c)

	GD	VG	FN	VF	VF/NM	NM-
1- Sinnott-a	6	12	18	39	62	85
2	5	10	15	30	48	65

2099 A.D.
Marvel Comics: May, 1995 ($3.95, one-shot)

1-Acetate-c by Quesada & Palmiotti	4.00

2099 APOCALYPSE
Marvel Comics: Dec, 1995 ($4.95, one-shot)

1-Chromium wraparound-c; Ellis script	5.00

2099 GENESIS
Marvel Comics: Jan, 1996 ($4.95, one-shot)

1-Chromium wraparound-c; Ellis script	5.00

2099 MANIFEST DESTINY
Marvel Comics: Mar, 1998 ($5.99, one-shot)

1-Origin of Fantastic Four 2099; intro Moon Knight 2099	6.00

2099 UNLIMITED
Marvel Comics: Sept, 1993 - No. 10, 1996 ($3.95, 68 pgs.)

1-10: 1-1st app. Hulk 2099 & begins. 1-3-Spider-Man 2099 app. 9-Joe Kubert-c; Len Wein & Nancy Collins scripts	4.00

2099 WORLD OF DOOM SPECIAL
Marvel Comics: May, 1995 ($2.25, one-shot)

1-Doom's "Contract w/America"	3.00

2099 WORLD OF TOMORROW
Marvel Comics: Sept, 1996 - No. 8, Apr, 1997 ($2.50) (Replaces 2099 titles)

1-8: 1-Wraparound-c. 2-w/bound-in card. 4,5-Phalanx	3.00

21
Image Comics (Top Cow Productions): Feb, 1996 - No. 3, Apr, 1996 ($2.50)

1-3: Len Wein scripts	3.00
1-Variant-c	3.00

21 DOWN
DC Comics (WildStorm): Nov, 2002 - No. 12, Nov, 2003 ($2.95)

1-12: 1-Palmiotti & Gray-s/Saiz-a/Jusko-c	3.00
...: The Conduit (2003, $19.95, TPB) r/#1-7; intro. by Garth Ennis	20.00

24 (Based on TV series)
IDW Publishing: July, 2004 - July, 2005 ($6.99/$7.49, square-bound, one-shots)

...: Midnight Sun (7/05, $7.49) J.C. Vaughn & Mark Haynes-s; Renato Guedes-a	7.50
...: One Shot (7/04, $6.99)-Jack Bauer's first day on the job at CTU; Vaughn & Haynes-s; Guedes-a	7.50

28 Days Later #14 © 20th Century Fox

Twilight Zone #1 © CBS

Two Gun Kid #30 © MAR

GD VG FN VF VF/NM NM-
2.0 4.0 6.0 8.0 9.0 9.2

...: Stories (1/05, $7.49) Manny Clark-a; Vaughn & Haynes-s 7.50

24: NIGHTFALL (Based on TV series)
IDW Publishing: Nov, 2006 - No. 6 ($3.99, limited series)

1-5-Two years before Season One; Vaughn & Haynes-s; Diaz-a; two covers 4.00

28 DAYS LATER (Based on the 2002 movie)
Boom! Studios: July, 2009 - No. 24, Jun, 2011 ($3.99)

1-24: 1-Covers by Bradstreet and Phillips 4.00

2020 VISIONS
DC Comics (Vertigo): May, 1997 - No. 12, Apr, 1998 ($2.25, limited series)

1-12-Delano-s: 1-3-Quitely-a. 4-"la tormenta"-Pleece-a 3.00

20,000 LEAGUES UNDER THE SEA (Movie)(See King Classics, Movie Comics & Power Record Comics)
Dell Publishing Co.: No. 614, Feb, 1955 (Disney)

Four Color 614-Movie, painted-c 8 16 24 56 96 135

TWICE TOLD TALES (See Movie Classics)

TWILIGHT
DC Comics: 1990 - No. 3, 1991 ($4.95, 52 pgs, lim. series, squarebound, mature)

1-3: Tommy Tomorrow app; Chaykin scripts, Garcia-Lopez-c/a 5.00

TWILIGHT EXPERIMENT
DC Comics (WildStorm): Apr, 2004 - No. 6, Sept, 2005 ($2.95, limited series)

1-6-Gray & Palmiotti-s/Santacruz-a 3.00
TPB (2011, $17.99) r/#1-6 18.00

TWILIGHT GUARDIAN (Also see Pilot Season: Twilight Guardian)
Image Comics (Top Cow): Jan, 2011 - No. 4, Apr, 2011 ($3.99, limited series)

1-4-Hickman-s/Kotean-a 4.00

TWILIGHT MAN
First Publishing: June, 1989 - No. 4, Sept, 1989 ($2.75, limited series)

1-4 3.00

TWILIGHT ZONE, THE (TV) (See Dan Curtis & Stories From...)
Dell Publishing Co./Gold Key/Whitman No. 92: No. 1173, 3-5/61 - No. 91, 4/79; No. 92, 5/82

Four Color 1173 (#1)-Crandall-c/a 19 38 57 133 287 440
Four Color 1288-Crandall/Evans-c/a 11 22 33 76 151 225
01-860-207 (5-7/62-Dell, 15¢) 9 18 27 61 106 150
12-860-210 on-c; 01-860-210 on inside(8-10/62-Dell)-Evans-c/a (3 stories)
9 18 27 61 106 150
1(11/62-Gold Key)-Crandall/Frazetta-a (10 & 11 pgs.); Evans-a
12 24 36 84 175 265
2 8 16 24 56 96 135
3-11: 3(11 pgs.),4(10 pgs.),9-Toth-a 6 12 18 42 69 95
12-15: 12-Williamson-a. 13,15-Crandall-a. 14-Orlando/Crandall/Torres-a
5 10 15 35 55 75
16-20 4 8 12 26 41 55
21-25: 21-Crandall-a(r). 25-Evans/Crandall-a(r); Toth-r/#4; last 12¢ issue
3 6 9 20 30 40
26,27: 26-Flying Saucer-c/story; Crandall, Evans-a(r). 27-Evans-r(2)
3 6 9 19 29 38
28-32: 32-Evans-a(r) 3 6 9 17 25 32
33-51: 43-Celardo-a. 51-Williamson-a 2 4 6 13 18 22
52-70 2 4 6 10 14 18
71-82,86-91: 71-Reprint 2 4 6 8 11 14
83-(52 pgs.) 3 6 9 14 20 25
84-(52 pgs.) Frank Miller's 1st comic book work 6 12 18 37 59 80
85-Frank Miller-a (2nd) 3 6 9 20 30 40
92-(Whitman, 5/82) Last issue; r/#1. 2 4 6 9 13 16
Mini Comic #1(1976, 3-1/4x6-1/2") 2 4 6 8 10 12

NOTE: ***Bolle*** *a-13(w/**McWilliams**), 50, 55, 57, 59, 77, 78, 80, 83, 84.* ***McWilliams*** *a-59, 78, 80, 82, 84.* ***Miller*** *a-84, 85.* ***Orlando*** *a-15, 19, 20, 22, 23.* ***Sekowsky*** *a-3.* ***Simonson*** *a-50, 54, 55, 83r.* ***Weiss*** *a-39, 79r(#39). (See Mystery Comics Digest 3, 6, 9, 12, 15, 18, 21, 24). Reprints-26(1/3), 71, 73, 79, 83, 84, 86, 92. Painted c-1-91.*

TWILIGHT ZONE, THE (TV)
Now Comics: Nov, 1990 ($2.95); Oct, 1991; V2#1, Nov, 1991 - No. 11, Oct, 1992 ($1.95); V3#1, 1993 - No. 4, 1993 ($2.50)

1-(11/90, $2.95, 52 pgs.)-Direct sale edition; Neal Adams-a, Sienkiewicz-c; Harlan Ellison scripts 5.00
1-(11/90, $1.75)-Newsstand ed. w/N. Adams-c 4.00
1-Prestige Format (10/91, $4.95)-Reprints above with extra Harlan Ellison short story 5.00
1-Collector's Edition (10/91, $2.50)-Non-code approved and polybagged; reprints 11/90 issue; gold logo, 1-Reprint ($2.50)-r/direct sale 11/90 version, 1-Reprint ($2.50)-r/newsstand 11/90 version each... 4.00
V2#1-Direct sale & newsstand ed. w/different-c 3.00
V2#2-8,10-11 3.00
V2#9-($2.95)-3-D Special; polybagged w/glasses & hologram on-c 4.00
V2#9-($4.95)-Prestige Edition; contains 2 extra stories & a different hologram on-c; polybagged w/glasses 5.00
V3#1-4, Anniversary Special 1 (1992, $2.50) 3.00
Annual 1 (4/93, $2.50)-No ads 4.00
...Science Fiction Special (3/93, $3.50) 4.00

TWINKLE COMICS
Spotlight Publishers: May, 1945

1 24 48 72 142 234 325

TWIST, THE
Dell Publishing Co.: July-Sept, 1962

01-864-209-Painted-c 4 8 12 24 37 50

TWISTED TALES (See Eclipse Graphic Album Series #15)
Pacific Comics/Independent Comics Group (Eclipse) #9,10: 11/82 - No. 8, 5/84; No. 9, 11/84; No. 10, 12/84 (Baxter paper)

1-9: 1-B. Jones/Corben-c; Alcala-a; nudity/violence in al. 2-Wrightson-c; Ploog-a 5.00
10-Wrightson painted art; Morrow-a 1 2 3 4 5 7

NOTE: ***Bolton*** *painted c-4, 6, 7; a-7.* ***Conrad*** *a-1, 3, 5; c-1i, 3, 5.* ***Guice*** *a-8.* ***Wildey*** *a-3.*

TWO BIT THE WACKY WOODPECKER (See Wacky...)
Toby Press: 1951 - No. 3, May, 1953

1 10 20 30 54 72 90
2,3 6 12 18 31 38 45

TWO FACE: YEAR ONE
DC Comics: 2008 - No. 2, 2008 ($5.99, squarebound, limited series)

1,2-Origin re-told; Sable-s/Saiz & Haun-a 6.00

TWO-FISTED TALES (Formerly Haunt of Fear #15-17)
(Also see EC Archives • Two-Fisted Tales)
E. C. Comics: No. 18, Nov-Dec, 1950 - No. 41, Feb-Mar, 1955

18(#1)-Kurtzman-c 96 192 288 768 1222 1675
19-Kurtzman-c 69 138 207 552 876 1200
20-Kurtzman-c 45 90 135 360 573 785
21,22-Kurtzman-c 37 74 111 296 473 650
23-25-Kurtzman-c 29 58 87 232 366 500
26-29,31-Kurtzman-c. 31-Civil War issue 21 42 63 168 272 375
30-Classic Davis-c 23 46 69 184 292 400
32-35: 33- "Atom Bomb" by Wood. 35-Civil War issue
21 42 63 168 272 375
36-41 16 32 48 128 207 285
Two-Fisted Annual (1952, 25¢, 132 pgs.) 107 214 321 803 1227 1650
Two-Fisted Annual (1953, 25¢, 132 pgs.) 79 158 237 593 909 1225

NOTE: ***Berg*** *a-29.* ***Colan*** *a-30,39p.* ***Craig*** *a-18, 19, 32.* ***Crandall*** *a-35, 36.* ***Davis*** *a-20-36, 40; c-30, 34, 35, 41, Annual 2.* ***Estrada*** *a-30.* ***Evans*** *a-34, 40, 41; c-40.* ***Feldstein*** *a-18.* ***Krigstein*** *a-41.* ***Kubert*** *a-32, 33.* ***Kurtzman*** *a-18-25; c-18-29, 31, Annual 1.* ***Severin*** *a-26, 28, 29, 31, 34-41 (No. 37-39 are all-**Severin** issues); c-36-39.* ***Severin/Elder*** *a-19-29, 31, 33, 36.* ***Wood*** *a-18-28, 30-35, 41; c-32, 33. Special issues: #26 (ChanJin Reservoir), 31 (Civil War), 35 (Civil War). Canadian reprints known; see Table of Contents. #25-Davis biog. #27-Wood biog. #28-Kurtzman biog.*

TWO-FISTED TALES
Russ Cochran/Gemstone Publishing: Oct, 1992 - No. 24, May, 1998 ($1.50/$2.00/$2.50)

1-24: 1-4r/Two-Fisted Tales #18-21 w/original-c 3.00

TWO-GUN KID (Also see All Western Winners, Best Western, Black Rider, Blaze Carson, Kid Colt, Western Winners, Wild West, & Wild Western)
Marvel/Atlas (MCI No. 1-10/HPC No. 11-59/Marvel No. 60 on): 3/48(No mo.) - No. 10, 11/49; No. 11, 12/53 - No. 59, 4/61; No. 60, 11/62 - No. 92, 3/68; No. 93, 7/70 - No. 136, 4/77

1-Two-Gun Kid & his horse Cyclone begin; The Sheriff begins
119 238 357 762 1306 1850
2 48 96 144 302 514 725
3,4: 3-Annie Oakley app. 39 78 117 231 378 525
5-Pre-Black Rider app. (Wint. 48/49); Anti-Wertham editorial (1st?)
39 78 117 240 395 550
6-10(11/49): 8-Blaze Carson app. 9-Black Rider app.
30 60 90 177 289 400
11(12/53)-Black Rider app.; 1st to have Atlas globe on-c; explains how Kid Colt became an outlaw 24 48 72 142 234 325
12-Black Rider app. 21 42 63 126 206 285
13-20: 14-Opium story 18 36 54 103 162 220
21-24,26-29 16 32 48 94 147 200
25,30: 25-Williamson-a (5 pgs.). 30-Williamson/Torres-a (4 pgs.)

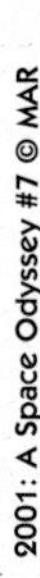
2001: A Space Odyssey #7 © MAR

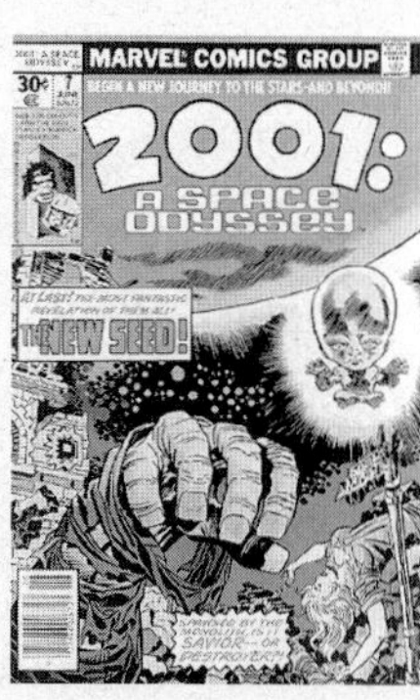

UFO & Outer Space #18 © GK

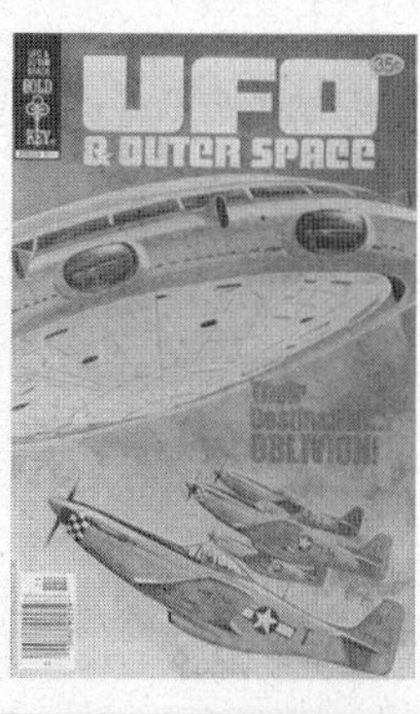

Ultimate Avengers #6 © MAR

	GD 2.0	VG 4.0	FN 6.0	VF 8.0	VF/NM 9.0	NM- 9.2
	17	34	51	98	154	210
31-33,35,37-40	9	18	27	62	109	155
34-Crandall-a	9	18	27	63	112	160
36,41,42,48-Origin in all	9	18	27	63	112	160
43,44,47	8	16	24	53	89	125
45,46-Davis-a	8	16	24	56	96	135
49,50,52,53-Severin-a(2/3) in each	7	14	21	49	82	115
51-Williamson-a (5 pgs.)	8	16	24	56	96	135
54,55,57,59-Severin-a(3) in each. 59-Kirby-a; last 10¢ issue (4/61)	7	14	21	49	82	115
56	7	14	21	46	76	105
58,60-New origin. 58-Kirby/Ayers-c/a "The Monster of Hidden Valley" cover/story (Kirby monster-c)	9	18	27	61	106	150
60-Edition w/handwritten issue number on cover	10	20	30	66	121	175
61,62-Kirby-a	7	14	21	46	76	105
63-74: 64-Intro. Boom-Boom	5	10	15	35	55	75
75-77-Kirby-a (reprint)	6	12	18	39	62	85
78-89	4	8	12	26	41	55
90,95-Kirby-a	4	8	12	28	44	60
91,92: 92-Last new story; last 12¢ issue	4	8	12	24	37	50
93,94,96-99	3	6	9	16	22	28
100-Last 15¢-c	3	6	9	16	23	30
101-Origin retold/#58; Kirby-a	3	6	9	16	23	30
102-120-reprints	2	4	6	10	14	18
121-136-reprints. 129-131-(Regular 25¢ editions)	2	4	6	10	14	18
129-131-(30¢-c variants, limited distribution)(4-8/76)	4	8	12	26	41	55

NOTE: ***Ayers** a-13, 24, 26, 27. **Davis** c-45-47. **Drucker** a-23. **Everett** a-82, 91. **Fuje** a-13. **Heath** a-3(2), 4(3), 5(2), 7; c-13, 21, 23, 53. **Keller** a-16, 19, 28, 42. **Kirby** a-54, 55, 57-62, 75-77, 90, 95, 101, 119, 120, 129; c-10, 52, 54-65, 67-72, 74-76, 116. **Maneely** a-20; c-11, 12, 16, 19, 20, 24-28, 30, 35, 41, 42, 49. **Powell** a-38, 102, 104. **Severin** a-9, 29, 51, 55, 57, 99r(3); c-9, 39, 51. **Shores** c-1-8, 11. **Trimpe** c-99. **Tuska** a-11, 12. **Whitney** a-87, 89-92, 98-113, 124, 129; c-87, 89, 91, 113. **Wildey** a-21. **Williamson** a-110r. Kid Colt in #13, 14, 16-21.*

TWO GUN KID: SUNSET RIDERS
Marvel Comics: Nov, 1995 - No. 2, Dec, 1995 ($6.95, squarebound, lim. series)

	GD 2.0	VG 4.0	FN 6.0	VF 8.0	VF/NM 9.0	NM- 9.2
1,2: Fabian Nicieza scripts in all. 1-Painted-c.						7.00

TWO GUN WESTERN (1st Series) (Formerly Casey Crime Photographer #1-4? or My Love #1-4?)
Marvel/Atlas Comics (MPC): No. 5, Nov, 1950 - No. 14, June, 1952

	GD 2.0	VG 4.0	FN 6.0	VF 8.0	VF/NM 9.0	NM- 9.2
5-The Apache Kid (Intro & origin) & his horse Nightwind begin by Buscema	26	52	78	154	252	350
6-10: 8-Kid Colt, The Texas Kid & his horse Thunder begin?	19	38	57	111	176	240
11-14: 13-Black Rider app.	14	28	42	80	115	150

NOTE: ***Maneely** a-6, 7, 9; c-6, 11-13. **Morrow** a-9. **Romita** a-8. **Wildey** a-8.*

2-GUN WESTERN (2nd Series) (Formerly Billy Buckskin #1-3; Two-Gun Western #5 on)
Atlas Comics (MgPC): No. 4, May, 1956

	GD 2.0	VG 4.0	FN 6.0	VF 8.0	VF/NM 9.0	NM- 9.2
4-Colan, Ditko, Severin, Sinnott-a; Maneely-c	15	30	45	88	137	185

TWO-GUN WESTERN (Formerly 2-Gun Western)
Atlas Comics (MgPC): No. 5, July, 1956 - No. 12, Sept, 1957

	GD 2.0	VG 4.0	FN 6.0	VF 8.0	VF/NM 9.0	NM- 9.2
5-Return of the Gun-Hawk-c/story; Black Rider app.	15	30	45	85	130	175
6,7	12	24	36	67	94	120
8,10,12-Crandall-a	13	26	39	72	101	130
9,11-Williamson-a in both (5 pgs. each)	14	28	42	76	108	140

NOTE: ***Ayers** a-9. **Colan** a-5. **Everett** c-12. **Forgione** a-5, 6. **Kirby** a-12. **Maneely** a-6, 8, 12; c-5, 6, 8, 11. **Morrow** a-9, 10. **Powell** a-7, 11. **Severin** c-10. **Sinnott** a-5. **Wildey** a-9.*

TWO MINUTE WARNING
Ultimate Sports Ent.: 2000 - No. 2 ($3.95, cardstock covers)

	GD 2.0	VG 4.0	FN 6.0	VF 8.0	VF/NM 9.0	NM- 9.2
1,2-NFL players & Teddy Roosevelt battle evil						4.00

TWO MOUSEKETEERS, THE (See 4-Color #475, 603, 642 under M.G.M.'s...;

TWO ON A GUILLOTINE (See Movie Classics)

TWO-STEP
DC Comics (Cliffhanger): Dec, 2003 - No. 3, Jul, 2004 ($2.95, limited series)

	GD 2.0	VG 4.0	FN 6.0	VF 8.0	VF/NM 9.0	NM- 9.2
1-3-Warren Ellis-s/Amanda Conner-a						3.00
TPB (2010, $19.99) r/#1-3; sketch pages; script for #1 with B&W art						20.00

2000 A.D. MONTHLY/PRESENTS (Showcase #25 on)
Eagle Comics/Quality Comics No. 5 on: 4/85 - #6, 9/85; 4/86 - #54, 1991 ($1.25-$1.50, Mando paper)

	GD 2.0	VG 4.0	FN 6.0	VF 8.0	VF/NM 9.0	NM- 9.2
1-6,1-25:1-4 r/British series featuring Judge Dredd; Alan Moore scripts begin. 1-25 ($1.25)-Reprints from British 2000 AD						3.00
26,27/28, 29/30, 31-54: 27/28, 29/30,31-Guice-c						3.00

2001, A SPACE ODYSSEY (Movie) (See adaptation in Treasury edition)
Marvel Comics Group: Dec, 1976 - No. 10, Sept, 1977 (30¢)

	GD 2.0	VG 4.0	FN 6.0	VF 8.0	VF/NM 9.0	NM- 9.2
1-Kirby-c/a in all	3	6	9	16	23	30
2-7,9,10	2	4	6	9	12	15
7,9,10-(35¢-c variants, limited distribution)(6-9/77)	3	6	9	16	23	30
8-Origin/1st app. Machine Man (called Mr. Machine)	3	6	9	16	23	30
8-(35¢-c variant, limited distribution)(6,8/77)	4	8	12	28	44	60
...Treasury 1 ('76, 84 pgs.)-All new Kirby-a	3	6	9	16	23	30

2001 NIGHTS
Viz Premiere Comics: 1990 - No. 10, 1991 ($3.75, B&W, lim. series, mature readers, 84 pgs.)

	GD 2.0	VG 4.0	FN 6.0	VF 8.0	VF/NM 9.0	NM- 9.2
1-10: Japanese sci-fi. 1-Wraparound-c						5.00

2010 (Movie)
Marvel Comics Group: Apr, 1985 - No. 2, May, 1985

	GD 2.0	VG 4.0	FN 6.0	VF 8.0	VF/NM 9.0	NM- 9.2
1,2-r/Marvel Super Special movie adaptation.						3.00

TYPHOID (Also see Daredevil)
Marvel Comics: Nov, 1995 - No. 4, Feb, 1996 ($3.95, squarebound, lim. series)

	GD 2.0	VG 4.0	FN 6.0	VF 8.0	VF/NM 9.0	NM- 9.2
1-4: Van Fleet-c/a						4.00

UFO & ALIEN COMIX
Warren Publishing Co.: Jan, 1978 (B&W magazine, 84 pgs., one-shot)

	GD 2.0	VG 4.0	FN 6.0	VF 8.0	VF/NM 9.0	NM- 9.2
nn-Toth-a, J. Severin-a(r); Pie-s	2	4	6	10	14	18

UFO & OUTER SPACE (Formerly UFO Flying Saucers)
Gold Key: No. 14, June, 1978 - No. 25, Feb, 1980 (All painted covers)

	GD 2.0	VG 4.0	FN 6.0	VF 8.0	VF/NM 9.0	NM- 9.2
14-Reprints UFO Flying Saucers #3	1	3	4	6	8	10
15,16-Reprints	1	3	4	6	8	10
17-25: 17-20-New material. 23-McWilliams-a. 24-(3 pg.-r). 25-Reprints UFO Flying Saucers #2 w/cover	1	3	4	6	8	10

UFO ENCOUNTERS
Western Publishing Co.: May, 1978 ($1.95, 228 pgs.)

	GD 2.0	VG 4.0	FN 6.0	VF 8.0	VF/NM 9.0	NM- 9.2
11192-Reprints UFO Flying Saucers	4	8	12	28	44	60
11404-Vol.1 (128 pgs.)-See UFO Mysteries for Vol. 2	4	8	12	24	37	50

UFO FLYING SAUCERS (UFO & Outer Space #14 on)
Gold Key: Oct, 1968 - No. 13, Jan, 1977 (No. 2 on, 36 pgs.)

	GD 2.0	VG 4.0	FN 6.0	VF 8.0	VF/NM 9.0	NM- 9.2
1(30035-810) (68 pgs.)	5	10	15	35	55	75
2(11/70), 3(11/72), 4(11/74)	3	6	9	18	27	35
5(2/75)-13: Bolle-a #4 on	2	4	6	13	18	22

UFO MYSTERIES
Western Publishing Co.: 1978 ($1.00, reprints, 96 pgs.)

	GD 2.0	VG 4.0	FN 6.0	VF 8.0	VF/NM 9.0	NM- 9.2
11400-(Vol.2)-Cont'd from UFO Encounters, pgs. 129-224	4	8	12	24	37	50

ULTIMAN GIANT ANNUAL (See Big Bang Comics)
Image Comics: Nov, 2001 ($4.95, B&W, one-shot)

	GD 2.0	VG 4.0	FN 6.0	VF 8.0	VF/NM 9.0	NM- 9.2
1-Homage to DC 1960's annuals						5.00

ULTIMATE... (Collects 4-issue alternate titles from X-Men Age of Apocalypse crossovers)
Marvel Comics: May, 1995 ($8.95, trade paperbacks, gold foil covers)

	GD 2.0	VG 4.0	FN 6.0	VF 8.0	VF/NM 9.0	NM- 9.2
Amazing X-Men, Astonishing X-Men, Factor-X, Gambit & the X-Ternals, Generation Next, X-Calibre, X-Man						9.00
Weapon X						10.00

ULTIMATE ADVENTURES
Marvel Comics: Nov, 2002 - No. 6, Dec, 2003 ($2.25)

	GD 2.0	VG 4.0	FN 6.0	VF 8.0	VF/NM 9.0	NM- 9.2
1-6: 1-Intro. Hawk-Owl; Zimmerman-s/Fegredo-a. 3-Ultimates app.						3.00
One Tin Soldier TPB (2005, $12.99) r/#1-6						13.00

ULTIMATE ANNUALS
Marvel Comics: 2006; 2007 ($13.99, SC)

	GD 2.0	VG 4.0	FN 6.0	VF 8.0	VF/NM 9.0	NM- 9.2
Vol. 1 (2006, $13.99) r/Ult. FF Ann. #1, Ult. X-Men Ann. #1, Ult S-M #1, Ultimates Ann #1						14.00
Vol. 2 (2007, $13.99) r/Ult. FF Ann. #2, Ult. X-Men Ann. #2, Ult S-M #2, Ultimates Ann #2						14.00

ULTIMATE ARMOR WARS (Follows Ultimatum x-over)
Marvel Comics: Nov, 2009 - No. 4, Apr, 2010 ($3.99, limited series)

	GD 2.0	VG 4.0	FN 6.0	VF 8.0	VF/NM 9.0	NM- 9.2
1-4-Warren Ellis-s/Steve Kurth-a/Brandon Peterson-c. 1-Variant-c by Kurth						4.00

ULTIMATE AVENGERS (Follows Ultimatum x-over)
Marvel Comics: Oct, 2009 - Present ($3.99)

	GD 2.0	VG 4.0	FN 6.0	VF 8.0	VF/NM 9.0	NM- 9.2
1-6-Mark Millar-s/Carlos Pacheco-a/c; Red Skull app.						4.00
1-Variant Red Skull-c by Leinil Yu						8.00
7-12-(Ultimate Avengers 2 #1-6 on cover) Yu-a; Punisher joins. 10-Origin Ghost Rider						4.00
7-Variant Ghost Rider-c by Silvestri						8.00
13-18-(Ultimate Avengers 3 #1-6 on cover) Dillon-a; Blade and a new Daredevil app.						4.00

ULTIMATE AVENGERS VS. NEW ULTIMATES (Death of Spider-Man tie-in)
Marvel Comics: Apr, 2011 - No. 6, Sept, 2011 ($3.99, limited series)

Ultimate Daredevil and Elektra #4 © MAR

Ultimate Hawkeye #1 © MAR

Ultimate Nightmare #3 © MAR

GD VG FN VF VF/NM NM-
2.0 4.0 6.0 8.0 9.0 9.2

1-6: 1-Millar-s/Yu-a/c; variant covers by Cho & Hitch. 3-6-Punisher app. 4.00

ULTIMATE CAPTAIN AMERICA
Marvel Comics: Mar, 2011 - No. 4, Jun, 2011 ($3.99)

1-4: 1-Aaron-s/Garney-a; 2 covers by Garney & McGuinness 4.00
Annual 1 (12/08, $3.99, one-shot) Origin of the Black Panther; Djurdjevic-a 4.00

ULTIMATE CIVIL WAR: SPIDER-HAM (See Civil War and related titles)
Marvel Comics: March, 2007 ($2.99, one-shot)

1-Spoof of Civil War series featuring Spider-Ham; art by various incl. Olivetti, Severin 3.00

ULTIMATE COMICS SPIDER-MAN (See Ultimate Spider-Man 2011 series)

ULTIMATE COMICS ULTIMATES (See Ultimates 2011 series)

ULTIMATE COMICS X-MEN (See Ultimate X-Men 2011 series)

ULTIMATE DAREDEVIL AND ELEKTRA
Marvel Comics: Jan, 2003 - No. 4, Mar, 2003 ($2.25, limited series)

1-4-Rucka-s/Larroca-c/a; 1st meeting of Elektra and Matt Murdock 3.00
... Vol.1 TPB (2003, $11.99) r/#1-4, Daredevil Vol. 2 #9; Larroca sketch pages 12.00

ULTIMATE DOOM (Follows Ultimate Mystery mini-series)
Marvel Comics: Feb, 2011 - No. 4, May, 2011 ($3.99, limited series)

1-4-Bendis-s/Sandoval-a; Fantastic Four, Spider-Man, Jessica Drew & Nick Fury app. 4.00

ULTIMATE ELEKTRA
Marvel Comics: Oct, 2004 - No. 5, Feb, 2005 ($2.25, limited series)

1-5-Carey-s/Larroca-c/a. 2-Bullseye app. 3.00
... : Devil's Due TPB (2005, $11.99) r/#1-5 12.00

ULTIMATE ENEMY (Follows Ultimatum x-over)(Leads into Ultimate Mystery)
Marvel Comics: Mar, 2010 - No. 4, July, 2010 ($3.99, limited series)

1-4-Bendis-s/Sandoval-a 1-Covers by McGuinness and Pearson 4.00

ULTIMATE EXTINCTION (See Ultimate Nightmare and Ultimate Secret limited series)
Marvel Comics: Mar, 2006 - No. 5, July, 2006 ($2.99, limited series)

1-5-The coming of Gah Lak Tus; Ellis-s/Peterson-a 3.00
TPB (2006, $12.99) r/#1-5 13.00

ULTIMATE FALLOUT (Follows Death of Spider-Man in Ultimate Spider-Man #160)
Marvel Comics: Sept, 2011 - No. 6, Oct, 2011 ($3.99, weekly limited series)

1-3,5,6: 1-Bendis-s/Bagley-a/c. 2,6-Hitch-c. 3,5-Andy Kubert-c 4.00
4-Debut of Miles Morales as the new Spider-Man; polybagged 4.00

ULTIMATE FANTASTIC FOUR (Continues in Ultimatum mini-series)
Marvel Comics: Feb, 2004 - No. 60, Apr, 2009 ($2.25/$2.50/$2.99)

1-Bendis & Millar-s/Adam Kubert-a/Hitch-c 5.00
2-20: 2-Adam Kubert-a/c; intro. Moleman 7-Ellis-s/Immonen-a begin; Dr. Doom app. 13-18-Kubert-a. 19,20-Jae Lee-a. 20-Begin $2.50-c 3.50
21-Marvel Zombies; begin Greg Land-c/a; Mark Millar-s; variant-c by Land 5.00
22-29,33-59: 24-26-Namor app. 28-President Thor. 33-38-Ferry-a. 42-46-Silver Surfer 3.00
30-32-Marvel Zombies; Millar-s/Land-a; Dr. Doom app. 5.00
30-32-Zombie variant-c by Suydam 6.00
50-White variant-c by Kirkham 5.00
60-($3.99) Ultimatum crossover; Kirkham-a 4.00
Annual 1 (10/05, $3.99) The Inhumans app.; Jae Lee-a/Mark Millar-s/Greg Land-c 4.00
Annual 2 (10/06, $3.99) Mole Man app.; Immonen & Irving-a/Carey-s 4.00
... MGC #1 (6/11, $1.00) r/#1 with "Marvel's Greatest Comics" logo on cover 3.00
.../Ult. X-Men Annual 1 (11/08, $3.99) Continued from Ult. X-Men/Ult. F.F. Annual #1 4.00
.../X-Men 1 (3/06, $2.99) Carey-s/Ferry-a; continued from Ult. X-Men/Fantastic Four #1 3.00
... Vol. 1: The Fantastic (2004, $12.99, TPB) r/#1-6; cover gallery 13.00
... Vol. 2: Doom (2004, $12.99, TPB) r/#7-12 13.00
... Vol. 3: N-Zone (2005, $12.99, TPB) r/#13-18 13.00
... Vol. 4: Inhuman (2005, $12.99, TPB) r/#19,20 & Annual #1 13.00
... Vol. 5: Crossover (2006, $12.99, TPB) r/#21-26 13.00
... Vol. 6: Frightful (2006, $14.99, TPB) r/#27-32; gallery of cover sketches & variants 15.00
... Vol. 7: God War (2007, $16.99, TPB) r/#33-38 17.00
... Vol. 8: Devils (2007, $12.99, TPB) r/#39-41 & Annual #2 13.00
... Vol. 9: Silver Surfer (2007, $13.99, TPB) r/#42-46 14.00
Volume 1 HC (2005, $29.99, 7x11", dust jacket) r/#1-12; introduction, proposals and scripts by Millar and Bendis; character design pages by Hitch 30.00
Volume 2 HC (2006, $29.99, 7x11", dust jacket) r/#13-20; Jae Lee sketch page 30.00
Volume 3 HC (2007, $29.99, 7x11", dust jacket) r/#21-32; Greg Land sketch pages 30.00
Volume 4 HC (2007, $29.99, 7x11", dust jacket) r/#33-41, Annual #2, Ultimate FF/X-Men and Ultimate X-Men/FF; character design pages 30.00
Volume 5 HC (2008, $34.99, 7x11", dust jacket) r/#42-53 35.00

ULTIMATE GALACTUS TRILOGY
Marvel Comics: 2007 ($34.99, hardcover, dustjacket)

GD VG FN VF VF/NM NM-
2.0 4.0 6.0 8.0 9.0 9.2

HC-Oversized reprint of Ultimate Nightmare #1-5, Ultimate Secret #1-4, Ultimate Vision #0, and Ultimate Extinction #1-5; sketch pages and cover galery 35.00

ULTIMATE HAWKEYE (Ultimate Comics)
Marvel Comics: Oct, 2011 - No. 4, Jan, 2012 ($3.99, limited series)

1-4: 1-Hickman-s/Sandoval-a/Andrews-c; polybagged. 2-4-Hulk app. 4.00
1-Variant-c by Neal Adams 6.00
1-Variant-c by Adam Kubert 8.00

ULTIMATE HULK
Marvel Comics: Dec, 2008 ($3.99, one-shot)

Annual 1 (12/08, $3.99) Zarda battles Hulk; McGuinness & Djurdjevic-a/Loeb-s 4.00

ULTIMATE HUMAN
Marvel Comics: Mar, 2008 - No. 4, Jun, 2008 ($2.99, limited series)

1-4-Iron Man vs. The Hulk; The Leader app.; Ellis-s/Nord-a 3.00
HC (2008, $19.99) r/#1-4 20.00

ULTIMATE IRON MAN
Marvel Comics: May, 2005 - No. 5, Feb, 2006 ($2.99, limited series)

1-Origin of Iron Man; Orson Scott Card-s/Andy Kubert-a; two covers 4.00
1-2nd & 3rd printings; each with B&W variant-c 3.00
2-5-Kubert-c 3.00
Volume 1 HC (2006, $19.99, dust jacket) r/#1-5; rough cut of script for #1, cover sketches 20.00
Volume 1 SC (2006, $14.99) r/#1-5; rough cut of script for #1, cover sketches 15.00

ULTIMATE IRON MAN II
Marvel Comics: Feb, 2008 - No. 5, July, 2008 ($2.99, limited series)

1-5-Early days of the Iron Man prototype; Orson Scott Card-s/Pasqual Ferry-a/c 3.00

ULTIMATE MARVEL FLIP MAGAZINE
Marvel Comics: July, 2005 - No. 26, Aug, 2007 ($3.99/$4.99)

1-11-Reprints Ultimate Fantastic Four and Ultimate X-Men in flip format 4.00
12-26-($4.99) 5.00

ULTIMATE MARVEL MAGAZINE
Marvel Comics: Feb, 2001 - No. 11, 2002 ($3.99, magazine size)

1-11: Reprints of recent stories from the Ultimate titles plus Marvel news and features. 1-Reprints Ultimate Spider-Man #1&2. 11-Lord of the Rings-c 4.00

ULTIMATE MARVEL SAMPLER
Marvel Comics: 2007 (no cover price, limited series)

1-Previews of 2008 Ultimate Marvel story arcs; Finch-c 3.00

ULTIMATE MARVEL TEAM-UP (Spider-Man Team-up)
Marvel Comics: Apr, 2001 - No. 16, July, 2002 ($2.99/$2.25)

1-Spider-Man & Wolverine; Bendis-s in all; Matt Wagner-a/c 5.00
2,3-Hulk; Hester-a 3.50
4,5,9-16: 4,5-Iron Man; Allred-a. 9-Fantastic Four; Mahfood-a. 10-Man-Thing; Totleben-a. 11-X-Men; Clugston-Major-a. 12,13-Dr. Strange; McKeever-a.14-Black Widow; Terry Moore-a. 15,16-Shang-Chi; Mays-a 3.00
6-8-Punisher; Sienkiewicz-a. 7,8-Daredevil app. 4.00
TPB (11/01, $14.95) r/#1-5 15.00
... Ultimate Collection TPB ('06, $29.99) r/#1-16 & Ult. Spider-Man Spec.; sketch pages 30.00
HC (8/02, $39.99) r/#1-16 & Ult. Spider-Man Special; Bendis afterword 40.00
...: Vol. 2 TPB (2003, $11.99) r/#9-13; Mahfood-c 12.00
...: Vol. 3 TPB (2003, $12.99) r/#14-16 & Ultimate Spider-Man Super Special; Moore-c 13.00

ULTIMATE MYSTERY (Follows Ultimate Enemy)(Leads into Ultimate Doom)
Marvel Comics: Sept, 2010 - No. 4, Dec, 2010 ($3.99, limited series)

1-4-Bendis-s/Sandoval-a; Rick Jones returns; Captain Marvel app. 1-3-Campbell-c 4.00

ULTIMATE NEW ULTIMATES (Follows Ultimatum x-over)
Marvel Comics: May, 2010 - No. 5, Mar, 2011 ($3.99)

1-5: 1-Jeph Loeb-s/Frank Cho-a; 6-page wraparound-c by Cho; Defenders app. 4.00
1-Villains variant-c by Yu 8.00

ULTIMATE NIGHTMARE (Leads into Ultimate Secret limited series)
Marvel Comics: Oct, 2004 - No. 5, Feb, 2005 ($2.25, limited series)

1-5: Ellis-s; Ultimates, X-Men, Nick Fury app. 1,2,4,5-Hairsine-a/c. 3-Epting-a 3.00
Ultimate Galactus Book 1: Nightmare TPB (2005, $12.99) r/Ultimate Nightmare #1-5 13.00

ULTIMATE ORIGINS
Marvel Comics: Aug, 2008 - No. 5, Dec, 2008 ($2.99, limited series)

1-5-Bendis-s/Guice-a. 1-Nick Fury origin in the 1940s. 2-Capt. America origin 3.00

ULTIMATE POWER
Marvel Comics: Dec, 2006 - No. 9, Feb, 2008 ($2.99, limited series)

1-9: 1-Ultimate FF meets the Squadron Supreme; Bendis-s; Land-a/c. 2-Spider-Man, X-Men

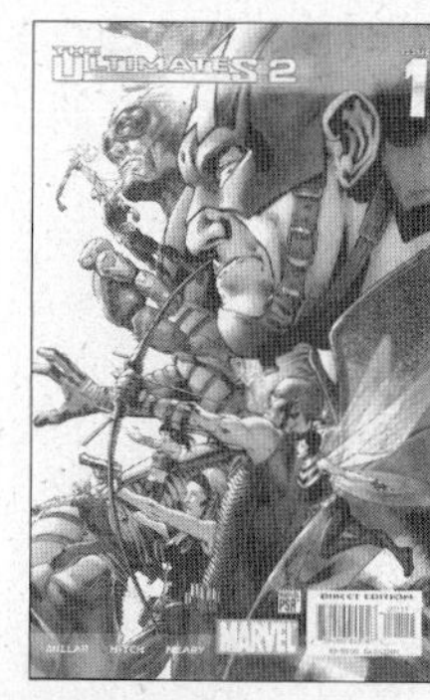

Ultimates 2 #1 © MAR

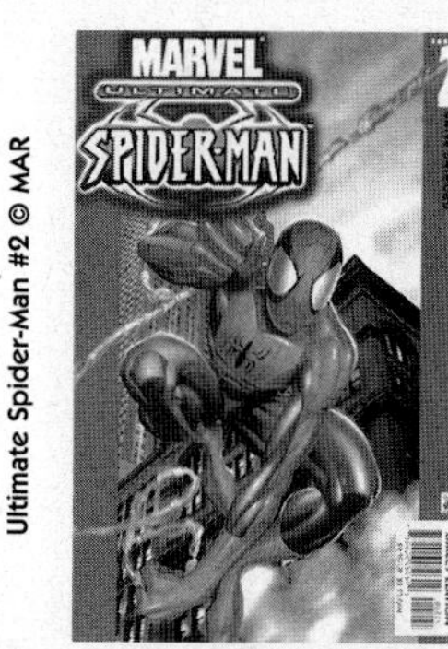

Ultimate Spider-Man #2 © MAR

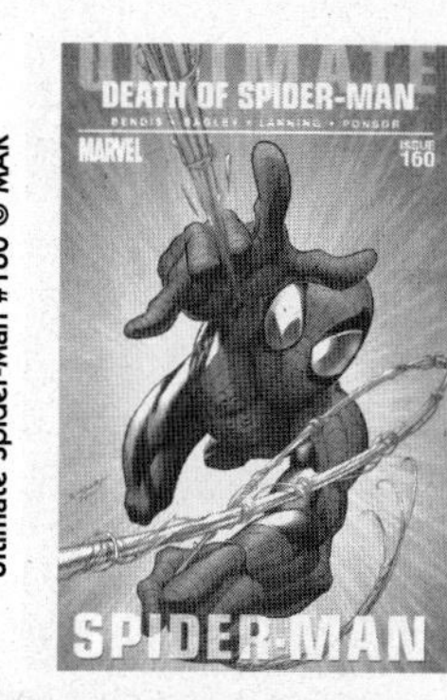

Ultimate Spider-Man #160 © MAR

	GD 2.0	VG 4.0	FN 6.0	VF 8.0	VF/NM 9.0	NM- 9.2

and the Ultimates app. 6-Doom app. 3.00
1-Variant sketch-c 5.00
1-Director's Cut (2007, $3.99) r/#1 and B&W pencil and ink pages; covers to #2,3 4.00
HC (2008, $34.99) oversized r/series; profile pages; B&W sketch art 35.00

ULTIMATES, THE (Avengers of the Ultimate line)
Marvel Comics: Mar, 2002 - No. 13, Apr, 2004 ($2.25)

1-Intro. Capt. America; Millar-s/Hitch-a & wraparound-c 6.00
2-Intro. Giant-Man and the Wasp 4.00
3-12: 3-1st Capt. America in new costume. 4-Intro. Thor. 5-Ultimates vs. The Hulk. 8-Intro. Hawkeye 3.00
13-($3.50) 4.00
... MGC #1 (5/11, $1.00) r/#1 with "Marvel's Greatest Comics" logo on cover 3.00
... Saga (2007, $3.99) Re-caps 1st 2 Ultimates series; new framing art by Charest; prelude to Ultimates 3 series; Brooks-c 4.00
... Volume 1 HC (2004, $29.99) oversized r/series; commentary pages with Millar & Hitch; cover gallery and character design pages; intro. by Joss Whedon 30.00
... Volume 1: Super-Human TPB (8/02, $12.99) r/#1-6 13.00
... Volume 2: Homeland Security TPB (2004, $17.99) r/#7-13 18.00

ULTIMATES (Ultimate Comics)
Marvel Comics: Oct, 2011 - Present ($3.99)

1-7: 1-Hickman-s/Ribic-a/Andrews-c; polybagged. 4-Reed Richards returns 4.00
1-Variant-c by Esad Ribic 6.00
Ultimate Comics Ultimates Must Have 1 (2/12, $4.99) r/#1-3 5.00

ULTIMATES 2
Marvel Comics: Feb, 2005 - No. 13, Feb, 2007 ($2.99/$3.99)

1-Millar-s/Hitch-a; Giant-Man becomes Ant-Man 4.00
2-11: 6-Intro. The Defenders. 7-Hawkeye shot. 8-Intro The Liberators 3.00
12,13-($3.99) Wraparound-c; X-Men, Fantastic Four, Spider-Man app. 4.00
13-Variant white cover featuring The Wasp 40.00
Annual 1 (10/05, $3.99) Millar-s/Dillon-a/Hitch-c; Defenders app. 4.00
Annual 2 (10/06, $3.99) Deodato-a; flashback to WWII with Sook-a; Falcon app. 4.00
HC (2007, $34.99) oversized r/series; commentary pages with Millar & Hitch; cover gallery, sketch and script pages; intro. by Jonathan Ross 35.00
... Volume 1: Gods & Monsters TPB (2005, $15.99) r/#1-6 16.00
... Volume 2: Grand Theft America TPB (2007, $19.99) r/#7-13; cover gallery w/sketches 20.00

ULTIMATES 3
Marvel Comics: Feb, 2008 - No. 5, Nov, 2008 ($2.99)

1-Loeb-s/Madureira-a; two gatefold wraparound covers by Madureira; Scarlet Witch shot 4.00
1,2-Second printings: 1-Wraparound cover by Madureira. 2-Madureira-c 3.00
2-5: 2-Spider-Man app. 3-Wolverine app. 5-Two gatefold wraparound-c (Heroes & Ultron) 3.00
2-Variant Thor cover by Turner 8.00
3-Variant Scarlet Witch cover by Cho 8.00
4-Variant Valkyrie cover by Finch 4.00

ULTIMATE SECRET (See Ultimate Nightmare limited series)
Marvel Comics: May, 2005 - No. 4, Dec, 2005 ($2.99, limited series)

1-4-Ellis-s; Captain Marvel app. 1,2-McNiven-a. 2,3-Ultimates & FF app. 3.00
Ultimate Galactus Book 2: Secret TPB (2006, $12.99) r/#1-4 13.00

ULTIMATE SECRETS
Marvel Comics: 2008 ($3.99, one-shot)

1-Handbook-styled profiles of secondary teams and characters from Ultimate universe 4.00

ULTIMATE SIX (Reprinted in Ultimate Spider-Man Vol. 5 hardcover)
Marvel Comics: Nov, 2003 - No. 7, June, 2004 ($2.25) (See Ultimate Spider-Man for TPB)

1-The Ultimates & Spider-Man team-up; Bendis-s/Quesada & Hairsine-a; Cassaday-c 5.00
2-7-Hairsine-a; Cassaday-c 3.00

ULTIMATE SPIDER-MAN
Marvel Comics: Oct, 2000 - No. 133, June, 2009 ($2.99/$2.25/$2.99/$3.99)

	GD	VG	FN	VF	VF/NM	NM-
1-Bendis-s/Bagley & Thibert-a; cardstock-c; introduces revised origin and cast separate from regular Spider-continuity	7	14	21	44	72	100
1-Variant white-c (Retailer incentive)	9	18	27	63	112	160
1-DF Edition	5	10	15	35	55	75
1-Kay Bee Toys variant edition	2	4	6	9	12	15
2-Cover with Spider-Man on car	3	6	9	18	27	35
2-Cover with Spider-Man swinging past building	3	6	9	18	27	35
3,4: 4-Uncle Ben killed	3	6	9	16	23	30
5-7: 6,7-Green Goblin app.	3	6	9	18	27	35
8-13: 13-Reveals secret to MJ	1	3	4	6	8	10

14-21: 14-Intro. Gwen Stacy & Dr. Octopus 5.00
22-($3.50) Green Goblin returns 6.00
23-32 4.00
33-1st Ultimate Venom-c; intro. Eddie Brock 5.00
34-38-Ultimate Venom 4.00
39-49,51-59: 39-Nick Fury app. 43,44-X-Men app. 46-Prelude to Ultimate Six; Sandman app. 51-53-Elektra app. 54-59-Doctor Octopus app. 3.00
50-($2.99) Intro. Black Cat 4.00
60-Intro. Ultimate Carnage on cover 4.00
61-Intro Ben Reilly; Punisher app. 3.00
62-Gwen Stacy killed by Carnage 4.00
63-92: 63,64-Carnage app. 66,67-Wolverine app. 68,69-Johnny Storm app. 78-Begin $2.50-c. 79-Debut Moon Knight. 81-85-Black Cat app. 90-Vulture app. 91-94-Deadpool 3.00
93-99: 93-Begin $2.99-c. 95-Morbius & Blade app. 97-99-Clone Saga 3.00
100-($3.99) Wraparound-c; Clone Saga; re-cap of previous issues 4.00
101-103-Clone Saga continues; Fantastic Four app. 102-Spider-Woman origin 3.00
104-($3.99) Clone Saga concludes; Fantastic Four and Dr. Octopus app. 4.00
105-132: 106-110-Daredevil app. 111-Last Bagley art; Immonen-a (6 pgs.) 112-Immonen-a; Norman Osborn app. 118-Liz Allen ignites. 123,128-Venom app. 129-132-Ultimatum 3.00
133-($3.99) Ultimatum crossover; Spider-Woman app. 4.00
(Issues #150-up, see second series)
Annual 1 (10/05, $3.99) Kitty Pryde app.; Bendis-s/Brooks-a/Bagley-c 4.00
Annual 2 (10/06, $3.99) Punisher, Moon Knight and Daredevil app.; Bendis-s/Brooks-a 4.00
Annual 3 (12/08, $3.99) Mysterio app.; Bendis-s/Lafuente-a 4.00
Collected Edition (1/01, $3.99) r/#1-3 4.00
Free Comic Book Day giveaway (5/02) - r/#1 with "Free Comic Book Day" banner on-c 3.00
... MGC #1 (5/11, $1.00) r/#1 with "Marvel's Greatest Comics" logo on cover 3.00
...Special (7/02, $3.50) art by Bagley and various incl. Romita, Sr., Brereton, Cho, Mack, Sienkiewicz, Phillips, Pearson, Oeming, Mahfood, Russell 4.00
Ultimate Spider-Man 100 Project (2007, $10.00, SC, charity book for the HERO Initiative) collection of 100 variant covers by Romita Sr. & Jr., Cho, Bagley, Quesada and more 10.00
...: Venom HC (2007, $19.99) r/#33-39 20.00
...(Vol. 1): Power and Responsibility TPB (4/01, $14.95) r/#1-7 15.00
...(Vol. 2): Learning Curve TPB (12/01, $14.95) r/#8-13 15.00
...(Vol. 3): Double Trouble TPB (6/02, $17.95) r/#14-21 18.00
Vol. 4: Legacy TPB (2002, $14.99) r/#22-27 15.00
Vol. 5: Public Scrutiny TPB (2003, $11.99) r/#28-32 12.00
Vol. 6: Venom TPB (2003, $15.99) r/#33-39 16.00
Vol. 7: Irresponsible TPB (2003, $12.99) r/#40-45 13.00
Vol. 8: Cats & Kings TPB (2004, $17.99) r/#47-53 18.00
Vol. 9: Ultimate Six TPB (2004, $17.99) r/#46 & Ultimate Six #1-7 18.00
Vol. 10: Hollywood TPB (2004, $12.99) r/#54-59 13.00
Vol. 11: Carnage TPB (2004, $12.99) r/#60-65 13.00
Vol. 12: Superstars TPB (2005, $12.99) r/#66-71 13.00
Vol. 13: Hobgoblin TPB (2005, $15.99) r/#72-78 16.00
Vol. 14: Warriors TPB (2005, $17.99) r/#79-85 18.00
Vol. 15: Silver Sable TPB (2006, $15.99) r/#86-90 & Annual #1 16.00
Vol. 16: Deadpool TPB (2006, $19.99) r/#91-96 & Annual #2 20.00
Vol. 17: Clone Saga TPB (2007, $24.99) r/#97-105 25.00
Vol. 18: Ultimate Knights TPB (2007, $13.99) r/#106-111 14.00
Vol. 19: Death of a Goblin TPB (2008, $14.99) r/#112-117 15.00
Hardcover (3/02, $34.95, 7x11", dust jacket) r/#1-13 & Amazing Fantasy #15; sketch pages and Bill Jemas' initial plot and character outlines 35.00
Volume 2 HC (2003, $29.99, 7x11", dust jacket) r/#14-27; pin-ups & sketch pages 30.00
Volume 3 HC (2003, $29.99, 7x11", dust jacket) r/#28-39 & #1/2; script pages 30.00
Volume 4 HC (2004, $29.99, 7x11", dust jacket) r/#40-45, 47-53; sketch pages 30.00
Volume 5 HC (2004, $29.99, 7x11", dust jacket) r/#46,54-59, Ultimate Six #1-7 30.00
Volume 6 HC (2005, $29.99, 7x11", dust jacket) r/#60-71; sketch page 30.00
Volume 7 HC (2006, $29.99, 7x11", dust jacket) r/#72-85; sketch & profile pages 30.00
Volume 8 HC (2007, $29.99, 7x11", dust jacket) r/#86-96 & Annual #1&2; sketch page 30.00
Volume 9 HC (2008, $39.99, 7x11", dust jacket) r/#97-111; sketch pages 40.00
Volume 10 HC (2009, $39.99, 7x11", dust jacket) r/#112-122; sketch pages 40.00

	GD	VG	FN	VF	VF/NM	NM-
Wizard #1/2	1	3	4	6	8	10

ULTIMATE SPIDER-MAN (2nd series)(Follows Ultimatum x-over)
Marvel Comics: Oct, 2009 - No. 15, Dec, 2010; No. 150, Jan, 2011 - No. 160, Aug, 2011 ($3.99)

1-15: 1-Bendis-s/Lafuente-a/c; new Mysterio. 1-Variant-c by Djurdjevic. 7,8-Miyazawa-a. 9-Spider-Woman app. 4.00
150-(1/11, $5.99) Resumes original numbering; wraparound-c by Lafuente; Bendis-s with art by Lafuente, Pichelli, Joëlle Jones, McKelvie & Young; r/Ult. S-M Special #1 6.00
150-Variant wraparound-c by Bagley 10.00
151-159: 151-154-Black Cat & Mysterio app. 157-Spider-Man shot by Punisher 4.00
153-159-Variant covers. 153-155-Pichelli. 157-McGuinness. 158-McNiven. 159-Cho 8.00
160-Black Polybagged; Bagley cover inside; Death of Spider-Man part 5 4.00
160-Red Polybagged variant; Kaluta cover inside; Death of Spider-Man part 5 20.00

ULTIMATE SPIDER-MAN (3rd series, with Miles Morales)(See Ultimate Fallout #4 for debut)
Marvel Comics: Nov, 2011 - Present ($3.99)

Ultimate Spider-Man (3rd series) #1 © MAR

Ultimate X-Men #25 © MAR

Ultimatum #4 © MAR

GD 2.0 | VG 4.0 | FN 6.0 | VF 8.0 | VF/NM 9.0 | NM- 9.2

1-Polybagged, with Kaare Andrews-c; Bendis-s/Pichelli-a; origin 4.00
1-Variant Pichelli-c with unmasked Spider-Man 10.00
1-Variant Pichelli-c with Spider-Man & city background 20.00
2-8: 4,5-Spider-Woman app. 5-Nick Fury & Ultimates app. 6-Samnee-a 4.00
Ultimate Comics Spider-Man Must Have 1 (2/12, $4.99) r/#1-3 5.00

ULTIMATE TALES FLIP MAGAZINE
Marvel Comics: July, 2005 - No. 26, Aug, 2007 ($3.99/$4.99)

1-11-Each reprints 2 issues of Ultimate Spider-Man in flip format 4.00
12-26-($4.99) 5.00

ULTIMATE THOR
Marvel Comics: Dec, 2010 - No. 4, Apr, 2011 ($3.99, limited series)

1-4: 1-Hickman-s/Pacheco-a; two covers by Pacheco & Choi; origin story 4.00

ULTIMATE VISION
Marvel Comics: No. 0, Jan, 2007 - No. 5, Jan, 2008 ($2.99, limited series)

0-Reprints back-up serial from Ultimate Extinction and related series; pin-ups 3.00
1-5: 1-(2/07) Carey-s/Peterson-a/c 3.00
TPB (2007, $14.99) r/#0-5; design pages and cover gallery 15.00

ULTIMATE WAR
Marvel Comics: Feb, 2003 - No. 4, Apr, 2003 ($2.25, limited series)

1-4-Millar-s/Bachalo-c/a; The Ultimates vs. Ultimate X-Men 3.00
Ultimate X-Men Vol. 5: Ultimate War TPB (2003, $10.99) r/#1-4 11.00

ULTIMATE WOLVERINE VS. HULK
Marvel Comics: Feb, 2006 - No. 6, July, 2009 ($2.99, limited series)

1,2-Leinil Yu-a/c; Damon Lindelof-s. 2-(4/06) 3.00
1,2-(2009) New printings 3.00
3-6: 3-(5/09) Intro. She-Hulk. 4-Origin She-Hulk 3.00

ULTIMATE X (Follows Ultimatum x-over)
Marvel Comics: Apr, 2010 - No. 5, Aug, 2011 ($3.99)

1-5: 1-Jeph Loeb-s/Art Adams-a; two covers by Adams. 5-Hulk app. 4.00

ULTIMATE X-MEN
Marvel Comics: Feb, 2001 - No. 100, Apr, 2009 ($2.99/$2.25/$2.50)

1-Millar-s/Adam Kubert & Thibert-a; cardstock-c; introduces revised origin and cast separate from regular X-Men continuity 3 6 9 14 20 25
1-DF Edition 3 6 9 16 23 30
1-DF Sketch Cover Edition 4 8 12 22 34 45
1-Free Comic Book Day Edition (7/03) r/#1 with "Free Comic Book Day" banner on-c 3.00
2 2 4 6 11 16 20
3-6 2 4 6 8 11 14
7-10 6.00
11-24,26-33: 13-Intro. Gambit. 18,19-Bachalo-a. 23,24-Andrews-a 4.00
25-($3.50) leads into the Ultimate War mini-series; Kubert-a 5.00
34-Spider-Man-c/app.; Bendis-s begin; Finch-a 5.00
35-74: 35-Spider-Man app. 36,37-Daredevil-c/app. 40-Intro. Angel. 42-Intro. Dazzler. 44-Beast dies. 46-Intro. Mr. Sinister. 50-53-Kubert-a; Gambit app. 54-57,59-63-Immonen-a. 60-Begin $2.50-c. 61-Variant Coipel-c. 66-Kirkman-s begin. 69-Begin $2.99-c 3.00
61-Retailer Edition with variant Coipel B&W sketch-c 10.00
75-($3.99) Turner-c; intro. Cable; back-up story with Emma Frost's students 4.00
76-99: 76-Intro. Bishop. 91-Fantastic Four app. 92-96-Phoenix app. 96-Spider-Man app. 99-Ultimatum x-over 3.00
100-($3.99) Ultimatum x-over; Brooks-a 4.00
Annual 1 (10/05, $3.99) Vaughan-s/Raney-a; Gambit & Rogue in Vegas 4.00
Annual 2 (10/06, $3.99) Kirkman-s/Larroca-a; Nightcrawler & Dazzler 4.00
.../Fantastic Four 1 (2/06, $2.99) Carey-s/Ferry-a; concluded in Ult. Fantastic Four/X-Men 3.00
... MGC #1 (6/11, $1.00) r/#1 with "Marvel's Greatest Comics" logo on cover 3.00
.../Ult. Fantastic Four Ann. 1 (11/08, $3.99) Continues in Ult. F.F./Ult. X-Men Annual #1 4.00
.../Fantastic Four TPB (2006, $12.99) reprints Ult X-Men/Ult. FF x-over and Official Handbook of the Ultimate Marvel Universe #1-2 13.00
... Ultimate Collection Vol. 1 (2006, $24.99) r/#1-12 & #1/2; unused Bendis script for #1 25.00
... Ultimate Collection Vol. 2 (2007, $24.99) r/#13-25; Kubert cover sketch pages 25.00
...: (Vol. 1) The Tomorrow People TPB (7/01, $14.95) r/#1-6 15.00
...: (Vol. 2) Return to Weapon X TPB (4/02, $14.95) r/#7-12 15.00
Vol. 3: World Tour TPB (2002, $17.99) r/#13-20 18.00
Vol. 4: Hellfire and Brimstone TPB (2003, $12.99) r/#21-25 13.00
Vol. 5 (See Ultimate War)
Vol. 6: Return of the King TPB (2003, $16.99) r/#26-33 17.00
Vol. 7: Blockbuster TPB (2004, $12.99) r/#34-39 13.00
Vol. 8: New Mutants TPB (2004, $12.99) r/#40-45 13.00
Vol. 9: The Tempest TPB (2004, $10.99) r/#46-49 11.00
Vol. 10: Cry Wolf TPB (2005, $8.99) r/#50-53 9.00
Vol. 11: The Most Dangerous Game TPB (2005, $9.99) r/#54-57 10.00
Vol. 12: Hard Lessons TPB (2005, $12.99) r/#58-60 & Annual #1 13.00
Vol. 13: Magnetic North TPB (2006, $12.99) r/#61-65 13.00
Vol. 14: Phoenix? TPB (2006, $14.99) r/#66-71 15.00
Vol. 15: Magical TPB (2007, $11.99) r/#72-74 & Annual #2 12.00
Vol. 16: Cable TPB (2007, $14.99) r/#75-80; sketch pages 15.00
Vol. 17: Sentinels TPB (2008, $17.99) r/#81-88 18.00
Volume 1 HC (8/02, $34.99, 7x11", dust jacket) r/#1-12 & Giant-Size X-Men #1; sketch pages and Millar and Bendis' initial plot and character outlines 35.00
Volume 2 HC (2003, $29.99, 7x11", dust jacket) r/#13-25; script for #20 30.00
Volume 3 HC (2003, $29.99, 7x11", dust jacket) r/#26-33 & Utimate War #1-4 30.00
Volume 4 HC (2005, $29.99, 7x11", dust jacket) r/#34-45 30.00
Volume 5 HC (2006, $29.99, 7x11", dust jacket) r/#46-57; Vaughan intro.; sketch pages 30.00
Volume 6 HC (2006, $29.99, 7x11", dust jacket) r/#58-65, Annual #1 & Wizard #1/2 30.00
Volume 7 HC (2007, $29.99, 7x11", dust jacket) r/#66-74, Annual #2 30.00
Wizard #1/2 2 4 6 9 12 15

ULTIMATE X-MEN (Ultimate Comics X-Men)
Marvel Comics: Nov, 2011 - Present ($3.99)

1-Spencer-s/Medina-a/Andrews-c; polybagged 4.00
1-Variant-c by Mark Bagley 6.00
2-9: 2-Rogue returns. 6-Prof. X returns 4.00
Ultimate Comics X-Men Must Have 1 (2/12, $4.99) r/#1-3 5.00

ULTIMATUM
Marvel Comics: Jan, 2009 - No. 5, July, 2009 ($3.99, limited series)

1-5-Loeb-s/Finch-a; cover by Finch & ; Ultimate heroes vs. Magneto 4.00
1-5-Variant covers by McGuinness 8.00
5-Double gatefold variant-c by Finch 4.00
March on Ultimatum Saga ('08, giveaway) text and art panel history of Ultimate universe 3.00
...: Fantastic Four Requiem 1 (9/09,$3.99) Pokaski-s/Atkins-a; Dr. Strange app. 4.00
...: Spider-Man Requiem 1,2 (8/09, 9/09,$3.99) Bendis-s/Bagley & Immonen-a 4.00
...: X-Men Requiem 1 (9/09,$3.99) Coleite-s/Oliver-a/Brooks-c 4.00
NOTE: *Numerous variant covers and 2nd & 3rd printings exist.*

ULTRA
Image Comics: Aug, 2004 - No. 8, Mar, 2005 ($2.95, limited series)

1-8: 1-Intro. Ultra/Pearl Penalosa; Luna Brothers-s/a 3.00
Vol. 1: Seven Days TPB (4/05, $17.95) r/#1-8; sketch pages 18.00

ULTRAFORCE (1st Series) (Also see Avengers/Ultraforce #1)
Malibu Comics (Ultraverse): Aug, 1994 - No. 10, Aug, 1995 ($1.95/$2.50)

0 (9/94, $2.50)-Perez-c/a. 4.00
1-($2.50, 44 pgs.)-Bound-in trading card; team consisting of Prime, Prototype, Hardcase, Pixx, Ghoul, Contrary & Topaz; Gerard Jones scripts begin, ends #6; Pérez-c/a begins 4.00
1-Ultra 5000 Limited Silver Foil Edition 5.00
1-Holographic-c, no price 1 2 3 4 5 7
2-5: Perez-c/a in all. 2 (10/94, $1.95)-Prime quits, Strangers cameo. 3-Origin of Topaz; Prime rejoins. 5-Pixx dies. 3.00
2 ($2.50)-Florescent logo; limited edition stamp on-c 4.00
6-10: 6-Begin $2.50-c, Perez-c/a. 7-Ghoul story, Steve Erwin-a. 8-Marvel's Black Knight enters the Ultraverse (last seen in Avengers #375); Perez-c/a. 9,10-Black Knight app.; Perez-c. 10-Leads into Ultraforce/Avengers Prelude 3.00
Malibu "Ashcan ": Ultraforce #0A (6/94) 3.00
.../Avengers Prelude 1 (8/95, $2.50)-Perez-c. 3.00
.../Avengers 1 (8/95, $3.95)-Warren Ellis script; Perez-c/a; foil-c 4.00

ULTRAFORCE (2nd Series)(Also see Black September)
Malibu Comics (Ultraverse): Infinity, Sept, 1995 - V2#15, Dec, 1996 ($1.50)

Infinity, V2#1-15: Infinity-Team consists of Marvel's Black Knight, Ghoul, Topaz, Prime & redesigned Prototype; Warren Ellis scripts begin, ends #3; variant-c exists. 1-1st app.Cromwell, Lament & Wreckage. 2-Contains free encore presentation of Ultraforce #1; flip book "Phoenix Resurrection" Pt. 7. 7-Darick Robertson, Jeff Johnson & others-a. 8,9-Intro. Future Ultraforce (Prime, Hellblade, Angel of Destruction, Painkiller & Whipslash); Gary Erskine-c/a. 9-Foxfire app. 10-Len Wein scripts & Deodato Studios-c/a begin. 10-Lament back-up story. 11-Ghoul back-up story by Pander Bros. 12-Ultraforce vs. Maxis (cont'd in Ultraverse Unlimited #2); Exiles & Iron Clad app. 13-Prime leaves; Hardcase returns 3.00
Infinity (2000 signed) 4.00
.../Spider-Man ($3.95)-Marv Wolfman script; Green Goblin app; 2 covers exist. 4.00

ULTRAGIRL
Marvel Comics: Nov, 1996 - No. 3 Mar, 1997($1.50, limited series)

1-3: 1-1st app. 3.00

ULTRA KLUTZ
Onward Comics: 1981; 6/86 - #27, 1/89, #28, 4/90 - #31, 1990? ($1.50/$1.75/$2.00, B&W)

1 (1981)-Re-released after 2nd #1 3.00

Ultraverse Double Feature #1 © MAL

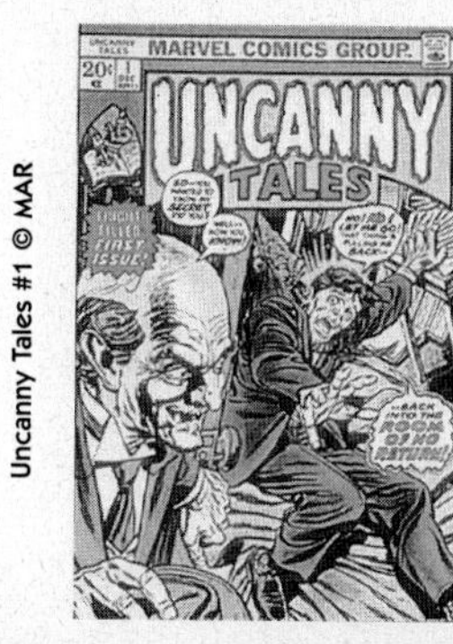

Uncanny Tales #1 © MAR

Uncanny X-Force #11 © MAR

GD 2.0 | VG 4.0 | FN 6.0 | VF 8.0 | VF/NM 9.0 | NM- 9.2

1-30: 1-(6/86). 27-Photo back-c 3.00
31-($2.95, 52 pgs.) 4.00

ULTRAMAN
Nemesis Comics: Mar, 1994 - No. 4, Sept, 1994 ($1.75/$1.95)
1-($2.25)-Collector's edition; foil-c; special 3/4 wraparound-c 4.00
1-($1.75)-Newsstand edition 3.00
2-4: 3-$1.95-c begins 3.00
#(-1) (3/93) 3.00

ULTRAMAN TIGA
Dark Horse Comics: Aug, 2003 - No. 10, June, 2004 ($3.99)
1-10-Khoo Fuk Lung-a/Tony Wong-s 4.00

ULTRAVERSE DOUBLE FEATURE
Malibu Comics (Ultraverse): Jan, 1995 ($3.95, one-shot, 68 pgs.)
1-Flip-c featuring Prime & Solitaire. 4.00

ULTRAVERSE ORIGINS
Malibu Comics (Ultraverse): Jan, 1994 (99¢, one-shot)
1-Gatefold-c; 2 pg. origins all characters 3.00
1-Newsstand edition; different-c, no gatefold 3.00

ULTRAVERSE PREMIERE
Malibu Comics (Ultraverse): 1994 (one-shot)
0-Ordered thru mail w/coupons 5.00

ULTRAVERSE UNLIMITED
Malibu Comics (Ultraverse): June, 1996; No. 2, Sept, 1996 ($2.50)
1,2: 1-Adam Warlock returns to the Marvel Universe; Rune-c/app. 2-Black Knight, Reaper & Sierra Blaze return to the Marvel Universe 3.00

ULTRAVERSE YEAR ONE
Malibu Comics (Ultraverse): 1994 ($4.95, one-shot)
nn-In-depth synopsis of the first year's titles & stories. 5.00

ULTRAVERSE YEAR TWO
Malibu Comics (Ultraverse): Aug, 1995 ($4.95, one-shot)
nn-In-depth synopsis of second year's titles & stories 5.00

ULTRAVERSE YEAR ZERO: THE DEATH OF THE SQUAD
Malibu Comics (Ultraverse): Apr, 1995 - No. 4, July, 1995 ($2.95, lim. series)
1-4: 3-Codename: Firearm back-up story. 3.00

UMBRELLA ACADEMY (Zero Killer & Pantheon City on back-c)
Dark Horse Comics: Apr, 2007
1-Free Comic Book Day Edition - previews of the upcoming series; James Jean-c 10.00

UMBRELLA ACADEMY: APOCALYPSE SUITE
Dark Horse Comics: Sept, 2007 - No. 6, Feb, 2008 ($2.99, limited series)
1-Origin of the Umbrella Aademy; Gerald Way-s/Gabriel Bá-a/James Jean-c 5.00
1-White variant-c by Bá 15.00
1-Variant-c by Gerald Way 10.00
1-2nd printing with variant-c by Bá 3.00
2-6 3.00
...: One for One (9/10, $1.00) r/#1 with red cover frame 3.00
Vol.1: Apocalypse Suite TPB (7/08, $17.95) r/#1-6, FCBD story and web shorts; design art; Grant Morrison intro.; cover gallery 18.00

UMBRELLA ACADEMY: DALLAS
Dark Horse Comics: Nov, 2008 - No. 6, May, 2009 ($2.99, limited series)
1-6-Gerald Way-s/Gabriel Bá-a/c 3.00
1-Wraparound variant-c by Jim Lee 5.00

UNBIRTHDAY PARTY WITH ALICE IN WONDERLAND (See Alice In Wonderland, Four Color #341)

UNBOUND
Image Comics (Desperado): Jan, 1998 ($2.95, B&W)
1-Pruett-s/Peters-a 3.00

UNCANNY ORIGINS
Marvel Comics: Sept, 1996 - No. 14, Oct, 1997 (99¢)
1-14: 1-Cyclops. 2-Quicksilver. 3-Archangel. 4-Firelord. 5-Hulk. 6-Beast. 7-Venom. 8-Nightcrawler. 9-Storm. 10-Black Cat. 11-Black Knight. 12-Dr. Strange. 13-Daredevil. 14-Iron Fist 3.00

UNCANNY TALES
Atlas Comics (PrPl/PPI): June, 1952 - No. 56, Sept, 1957
1-Heath-a; horror/weird stories begin 97 194 291 621 1061 1500
2 52 104 156 322 549 775
3-5 45 90 135 284 480 675
6-Wolvertonish-a by Matt Fox 47 94 141 296 498 700
7-10: 8-Atom bomb story; Tothish-a (by Sekowsky?). 9-Crandall-a 39 78 117 240 395 550
11-20: 17-Atom bomb panels; anti-communist story; Hitler story. 19-Krenkel-a. 20-Robert Q. Sale-c 31 62 93 182 296 410
21-25,27: 25-Nostrand-a? 27 54 81 158 259 360
26-Spider-Man prototype c/story 39 78 117 240 395 550
28-Last precode issue (1/55); Kubert-a; #1-28 contain 2-3 sci/fi stories each 27 54 81 162 266 370
29-41,43-49,51 20 40 60 114 182 250
42,54,56-Krigstein-a 20 40 60 117 189 260
50,53,55-Torres-a 20 40 60 114 182 250
52-Oldest Iron Man prototype (2/57) 32 64 96 188 307 425

NOTE: ***Andru** a-15, 27. **Ayers** a-14, 22, 28, 37. **Bailey** a-51. **Briefer** a-19, 20. **Brodsky** c-1, 3, 4, 6, 8, 12-16, 19. **Brodsky/Everett** c-9. **Cameron** a-47. **Colan** a-11, 16, 17, 49, 52. **Drucker** a-37, 42, 45. **Everett** a-2, 9, 12, 32, 36, 39, 48; c-7, 11, 17, 39, 41, 50, 52, 53. **Fass** a-9, 10, 15, 24. **Forte** a-18, 27, 33-35, 52, 53. **Heath** a-13, 14; c-5, 10, 18. **Keller** a-3. **Lawrence** a-14, 17, 19, 23, 27, 28, 35. **Maneely** a-4, 8, 10, 16, 29, 35; c-2, 22, 26, 33, 38. **Moldoff** a-23. **Morisi** a-48, 52. **Morrow** a-46, 51. **Orlando** a-49, 50, 53. **Powell** a-12, 18, 34, 36, 38, 43, 50, 56. **Robinson** a-3, 13. **Reinman** a-12, 36. **Romita** a-10. **Roussos** a-8. **Sale** a-34, 47, 53; c-20. **Sekowsky** a-25. **Sinnott** a-14, 15, 38, 52. **Torres** a-53. **Tothish**-a by **Andru**-27. **Wildey** a-22, 48.*

UNCANNY TALES
Marvel Comics Group: Dec, 1973 - No. 12, Oct, 1975
1-Crandall-r/Uncanny Tales #9('50s) 4 8 12 22 34 45
2-12: 7,12-Kirby-a 3 6 9 16 22 28
NOTE: ***Ditko** reprints-#4, 6-8, 10-12.*

UNCANNY X-FORCE
Marvel Comics: Dec, 2010 - Present ($3.99)
1-17: 1-Wolverine, Psylocke, Archangel, Fantomex & Deadpool team; Opeña-a; Ribic-c 4.00
1-Variant-c by Clayton Crain 10.00
5.1 (5/11, $2.99) Albuquerque-a/Bianchi-c; Lady Deathstrike app. 3.00
18-Polybagged; Dark Angel Saga conclusion 4.00
19-22: 19-Grampa-c. 20-Yu-c 4.00
19.1 (3/12, $2.99) Remender-s/Tan-a; other-dimension X-Men vs. Apocalypse 3.00
...: The Apocalypse Solution 1 (5/11, $4.99) r/#1-3 5.00

UNCANNY X-MEN, THE (See X-Men, The, 1st series, #142-on)

UNCANNY X-MEN (2nd series) (X-Men Regenesis)
Marvel Comics: Dec, 2010 - Present ($3.99)
1-8: 1-3-Gillen-s/Pacheco-a/c; Mr. Sinister app. 4-Peterson-a. 5-8-Land-a 4.00
1-Variant-c by Keown 6.00

UNCANNY X-MEN AND THE NEW TEEN TITANS (See Marvel and DC Present...)

UNCANNY X-MEN: FIRST CLASS
Marvel Comics: Sept, 2009 - No. 8, Apr, 2010 ($2.99)
1-8: 1-The X-Men #94 (1975) team; Cruz-a; Inhumans app. 3.00
... Giant-Size Special (8/09, $3.99) short stories by various; Scottie Young-c 4.00

UNCENSORED MOUSE, THE
Eternity Comics: Apr, 1989 - No. 2, Apr, 1989 ($1.95, B&W)(Came sealed in plastic bag) (Both contain racial stereotyping & violence)
1,2-Early Gottfredson strip-r in each 2 4 6 11 16 20
NOTE: *Both issues contain unauthorized reprints. Series was cancelled. **Win Smith** r-1, 2.*

UNCHARTED (Based on the video game)
DC Comics: Jan, 2012 - Present ($2.99)
1-5-Williamson-s/Sandoval-a. 1-3-Harris-c 3.00

UNCLE CHARLIE'S FABLES (Also see Adventures in Wonderland)
Lev Gleason Publ.: Jan, 1952 - No. 5, Sept, 1952 (All have Biro painted-c)
1-Peter Pester by Hy Mankin begins, ends #5. Michael the Misfit by Kida, Janice & the Lazy Giant by Maurer, Lawrence the Fortune Teller app.; has photo of Biro 15 30 45 88 137 185
2-Fuje-a; Biro photo 10 20 30 54 72 90
3-5: 5-Two Who Built a Dream, The Blacksmith & The Gypsies by Maurer, The Sleepy King by Hubbel; has photo of Biro 9 18 27 47 61 75
NOTE: ***Kida** a-1. Hubbell a- 5. **Hy Mankin** a-1-5. **Norman Maurer** a-1, 5. **Dick Rockwell** a-5.*

UNCLE DONALD & HIS NEPHEWS DUDE RANCH (See Dell Giant #52)

UNCLE DONALD & HIS NEPHEWS FAMILY FUN (See Dell Giant #38)

UNCLE JOE'S FUNNIES
Centaur Publications: 1938 (B&W)
1-Games, puzzles & magic tricks, some interior art; Bill Everett-c 77 154 231 493 847 1200

UNCLE MILTY (TV)

Uncle Sam #2 © DC

Uncle Scrooge #14 © DIS

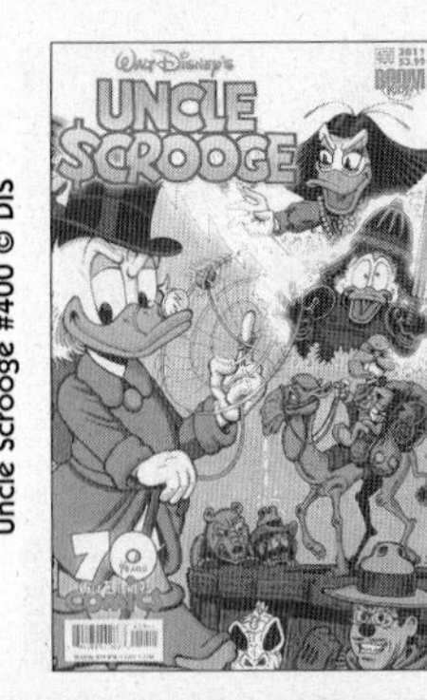

Uncle Scrooge #400 © DIS

	GD 2.0	VG 4.0	FN 6.0	VF 8.0	VF/NM 9.0	NM- 9.2

Victoria Publications/True Cross: Dec, 1950 - No. 4, July, 1951 (52 pgs.)(Early TV comic)

1-Milton Berle photo on-c of #1,2	54	108	162	343	574	825
2	35	70	105	208	339	470
3,4	29	58	87	172	281	390

UNCLE REMUS & HIS TALES OF BRER RABBIT (See Brer Rabbit, 4-Color #129, 208, 693)

UNCLE SAM
DC Comics (Vertigo): 1997 - No. 2, 1997 ($4.95, limited series)

1,2-Alex Ross painted c/a. Story by Ross and Steve Darnell 5.00
Hardcover (1998, $17.95) 18.00
Softcover (2000, $9.95) 10.00

UNCLE SAM AND THE FREEDOM FIGHTERS
DC Comics: Sept, 2006 - No. 8, Apr, 2007 ($2.99, limited series)

1-8-Acuña-a/c; Gray & Palmiotti-s. 3-Intro. Black Condor 3.00
TPB (2007, $14.99) r/#1-8 and story from DCU Brave New World #1 15.00

UNCLE SAM AND THE FREEDOM FIGHTERS
DC Comics: Nov, 2007 - No. 8, Jun, 2008 ($2.99, limited series)

1-8-Gray & Palmiotti-s/Arlem-a/Johnson-c 3.00
...: Brave New World TPB (2008, $14.99) r/#1-8 15.00

UNCLE SAM QUARTERLY (Blackhawk #9 on)(See Freedom Fighters)
Quality Comics Group: Autumn, 1941 - No. 8, Fall, 1943 (see National Comics)

1-Origin Uncle Sam; Fine/Eisner-c, chapter headings, 2 pgs. by Eisner; (2 versions: dark cover, no price; light cover with price sticker); Jack Cole-a	377	754	1131	2639	4620	6600
2-Cameos by The Ray, Black Condor, Quicksilver, The Red Bee, Alias the Spider, Hercules & Neon the Unknown; Eisner, Fine-c/a	132	264	396	838	1444	2050
3-Tuska-c/a; Eisner-a(2)	97	194	291	621	1061	1500
4	87	174	261	553	952	1350
5,7-Hitler, Mussolini & Tojo-c	119	238	357	762	1306	1850
6,8	67	134	201	426	731	1035

NOTE: ***Kotzky** (or **Tuska**) a-3-8.*

UNCLE SCROOGE (Disney) (Becomes Walt Disney's... #210 on) (See Cartoon Tales, Dell Giants #33, 55, Disney Comic Album, Donald and Scrooge, Dynabrite, Four Color #178, Gladstone Comic Album, Walt Disney's Comics & Stories #98, Walt Disney's ...)
Dell #1-39/Gold Key #40-173/Whitman #174-209: No. 386, 3/52 - No. 39, 8-10/62; No. 40, 12/62 - No. 209, 7/84

Four Color 386(#1)-in "Only a Poor Old Man" by Carl Barks; r-in Uncle Scrooge & Donald Duck #1('65) & The Best of Walt Disney Comics ('74). The 2nd cover app. of Uncle Scrooge (see Dell Giant Vacation Parade #2 (7/51) for 1st-c)	186	372	558	1562	3381	5200
1-(1986)-Reprints F.C. #386; given away with lithograph "Dam Disaster at Money Lake" & as a subscription offer giveaway to Gladstone subscribers	3	6	9	15	20	24
Four Color 456(#2)-in "Back to the Klondike" by Carl Barks; r-in Best of U.S. & D.D. #1('66) & Gladstone C.A. #4	91	182	273	737	1594	2450
Four Color 495(#3)-r-in #105	61	122	183	494	1072	1650
4(12-2/53-54)-r-in Gladstone Comic Album #11	45	90	135	338	732	1125
5-r-in Gladstone Special #2 & Walt Disney Digest #1	37	74	111	278	602	925
6-r-in U.S. #106,165,233 & Best of U.S. & D.D. #1('66)	32	64	96	232	504	775
7-The Seven Cities of Cibola by Barks; r-in #217 & Best of D.D. & U.S. #2 ('67)	29	58	87	210	455	700
8-10: 8-r-in #111,222. 9-r-in #104,214. 10-r-in #67	26	52	78	182	391	600
11-20: 11-r-in #237. 17-r-in #215. 19-r-in Gladstone C.A. #1. 20-r-in #213	21	42	63	148	317	485
21-30: 24-X-Mas-c. 26-r-in #211	17	34	51	114	250	385
31-35,37-40: 34-r-in #228. 40-X-Mas-c	13	26	39	90	195	300
36-1st app. Magica De Spell; Number one dime 1st identified by name	15	30	45	102	221	340
41-60: 48-Magica De Spell-c/story (3/64). 49-Sci/fi-c. 51-Beagle Boys-c/story (8/64)	12	24	36	79	160	240
61-63,65,66,68-71:71-Last Barks issue w/original story (#71-he only storyboarded the script)	11	22	33	73	142	210
64-(7/66) Barks Vietnam War story "Treasure of Marco Polo" banned for reprints by Disney from 1977-1989 because of its Third World revolutionary war theme. It later appeared in the hardcover Carl Barks Library set (4/89) and Walt Disney's Uncle Scrooge Adventures #42 (1/97)	15	30	45	102	221	340
67,72,73: 67,72,73-Barks-r	10	20	30	67	124	180
74-84: 74-Barks-r(1pg.). 75-81,83-Not by Barks. 82,84-Barks-r begin	8	16	24	51	86	120
85-100	7	14	21	44	72	100
101-110	6	12	18	37	59	80
111-120	4	8	12	28	44	60
121-141,143-152,154-157	4	8	12	22	34	45
142-Reprints Four Color #456 with-c	4	8	12	23	36	48
153,158,162-164,166,168-170,178,180: No Barks	3	6	9	16	22	28
159-160,165,167	3	6	9	16	23	30
161(r/#14), 171(r/#11), 177(r/#16),183(r/#6)-Barks-r	3	6	9	16	23	30
172(1/80),173(2/80)-Gold Key. Barks-a	3	6	9	18	27	35
174(3/80),175(4/80),176(5/80)-Whitman. Barks-a	4	8	12	23	36	48
177(6/80),178(7/80)	4	8	12	24	37	50
179(9/80)(r/#9)-(Very low distribution)	35	70	105	254	552	850
180(11/80),181(12/80, r/4-Color #495), pre-pack?	8	16	24	51	86	135
182-195: 182-(50¢-c). 184,185,187,188-Barks-a. 182,186,191-194-No Barks. 189(r/#5), 190(r/#4), 195(r/4-Color #386)	3	6	9	16	23	30
182(1/81, 40¢-c) Cover price error variant	4	8	12	23	36	48
196(4/82),197(5/82): 196(r/#13)	3	6	9	18	27	35
198-209 (All #90038 on-c; pre-pack; no date or date code): 198(4/83), 199(5/83), 200(6/83), 201(6/83), 202(7/83), 203(7/83), 204(8/83), 205(8/83), 206(4/84), 207(5/83), 208(6/84), 209(7/84). 198-202,204-206: No Barks. 203(r/#12), 207(r/#93,92), 208(r/U.S. #18), 209(r/U.S. #21)-Barks-r	3	6	9	20	30	40
Uncle Scrooge & Money(G.K.)-Barks-r/from WDC&S #130 (3/67)	5	10	15	35	55	75
Mini Comic #1(1976)(3-1/4x6-1/2")-r/U.S. #115; Barks-c	2	4	6	8	10	12

NOTE: ***Barks** c-Four Color 386, 456, 495, #4-37, 39, 40, 43-71.*

UNCLE SCROOGE (See Walt Disney's Uncle Scrooge for previous issues)
Boom Entertainment (BOOM! Kids): No. 384, Oct, 2009 - No. 404, Jun, 2011 ($2.99/$3.99)

384-399: 384-Magica de Spell app.; 2 covers. 392-399-Duck Tales 3.00
400-(2/11, $3.99) "Carl Barks" apps. as Scrooge story-teller; Rosa wraparound-c 4.00
400-$6.99) Deluxe Edition with Barks painted cover of Four Color #386 cover image 7.00
401-404: 401-($3.99)-Rosa-s/a 4.00
...: The Mysterious Stone Ray and Cash Flow (5/11, $6.99) reprints; Barks-s/a; Rosa-s/a 7.00

UNCLE SCROOGE AND DONALD DUCK
Gold Key: June, 1965 (25¢, paper cover)

1-Reprint of Four Color #386(#1) & lead story from Four Color #29	8	16	24	53	89	125

UNCLE SCROOGE COMICS DIGEST
Gladstone Publishing: Dec, 1986 - No. 5, Aug, 1987 ($1.25, Digest-size)

1,3	1	2	3	5	6	8
2,4						6.00
5 (low print run)	1	2	3	5	7	9

UNCLE SCROOGE GOES TO DISNEYLAND (See Dell Giants)
Gladstone Publishing Ltd.: Aug, 1985 ($2.50)

1-Reprints Dell Giant w/new-c by Mel Crawford, based on old cover	2	4	6	8	10	12
...Comics Digest 1 ($1.50, digest size)	2	4	6	8	11	14

UNCLE SCROOGE IN COLOR
Gladstone Publishing: 1987 ($29.95, Hardcover, 9-1/4"X12-1/4", 96 pgs.)

nn-Reprints "Christmas on Bear Mountain" from Four Color 178 by Barks; Uncle Scrooge's Christmas Carol (published as Donald Duck & the Christmas Carol, A Little Golden Book), reproduced from the original art as adapted by Norman McGary from pencils by Barks; and Uncle Scrooge the Lemonade King, reproduced from the original art, plus Barks' original pencils	4	8	12	24	37	50
nn-Slipcase edition of 750, signed by Barks, issued at $79.95						300.00

UNCLE SCROOGE THE LEMONADE KING
Whitman Publishing Co.: 1960 (A Top Top Tales Book, 6-3/8"x7-5/8", 32 pgs.)

2465-Storybook pencilled by Carl Barks, finished art adapted by Norman McGary	33	66	99	239	512	785

UNCLE WIGGILY (See March of Comics #19) (Also see Animal Comics)
Dell Publishing Co.: No. 179, Dec, 1947 - No. 543, Mar, 1954

Four Color 179 (#1)-Walt Kelly-c	13	26	39	88	189	290
Four Color 221 (3/49)-Part Kelly-c	9	18	27	61	106	150
Four Color 276 (5/50), 320 (#1, 3/51)	8	16	24	51	86	120
Four Color 349 (9-10/51), 391 (4-5/52)	6	12	18	42	69	95
Four Color 428 (10/52), 503 (10/53), 543	5	10	15	35	55	75

UNDEAD, THE
Chaos! Comics (Black Label): Feb, 2002 ($4.99, B&W)

1-Pulido-s/Denham-a 5.00

UNDERCOVER GIRL (Starr Flagg) (See Extra Comics, Manhunt! & Trail Colt)
Magazine Enterprises: No. 5, 1952 - No. 7, 1954

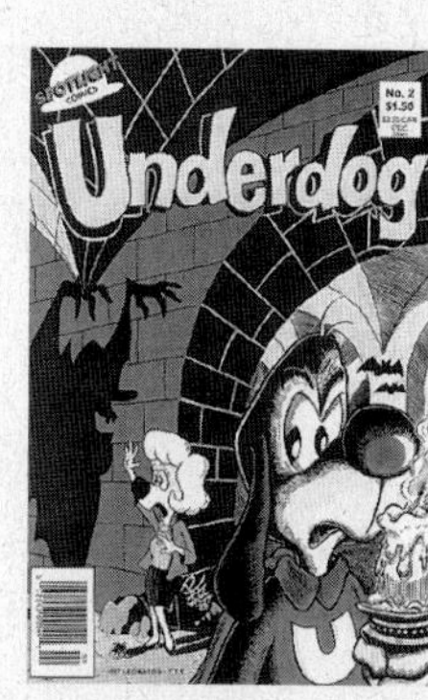

Underdog #2 © Leonardo TTV

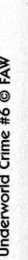

Underworld Crime #6 © FAW

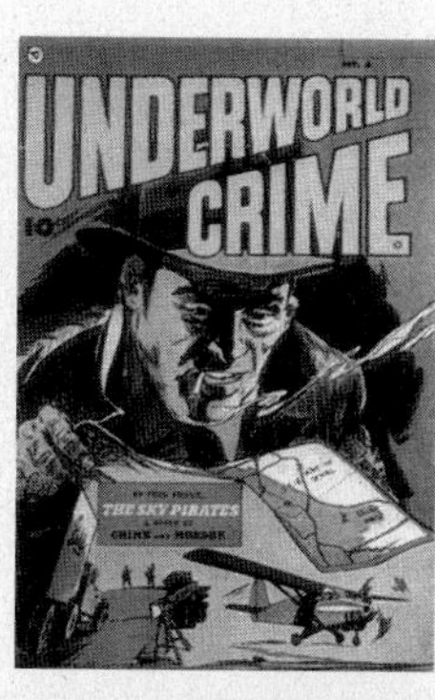

The Unexpected #191 © DC

	GD 2.0	VG 4.0	FN 6.0	VF 8.0	VF/NM 9.0	NM- 9.2
5(#1)(A-1 #62)-Fallon of the F.B.I. in all	28	56	84	165	270	375
6(A-1 #98), 7(A-1 #118)-All have Starr Flagg	26	52	78	154	252	350

NOTE: ***Powell*** *c-6, 7.* ***Whitney*** *a-5-7.*

UNDERDOG (TV)(See Kite Fun Book, March of Comics #426, 438, 467, 479)
Charlton Comics/Gold Key: July, 1970 - No. 10, Jan, 1972; Mar, 1975 - No. 23, Feb, 1979

	GD 2.0	VG 4.0	FN 6.0	VF 8.0	VF/NM 9.0	NM- 9.2
1 (1st series, Charlton)-1st app. Underdog	10	20	30	65	118	170
2-10	6	12	18	39	62	85
1 (2nd series, Gold Key)	7	14	21	44	72	100
2-10	4	8	12	24	37	50
11-20: 13-1st app. Shack of Solitude	3	6	9	19	29	38
21-23	3	6	9	20	30	40

UNDERDOG
Spotlight Comics: 1987 - No. 3?, 1987 ($1.50)

	GD 2.0	VG 4.0	FN 6.0	VF 8.0	VF/NM 9.0	NM- 9.2
1-3						4.00

UNDERDOG (Volume 2)
Harvey Comics: Nov, 1993 - No. 5, July, 1994 ($2.25)

	GD 2.0	VG 4.0	FN 6.0	VF 8.0	VF/NM 9.0	NM- 9.2
1-5						4.00
Summer Special (10/93, $2.25, 68 pgs.)						4.00

UNDERSEA AGENT
Tower Comics: Jan, 1966 - No. 6, Mar, 1967 (25¢, 68 pgs.)

	GD 2.0	VG 4.0	FN 6.0	VF 8.0	VF/NM 9.0	NM- 9.2
1-Davy Jones, Undersea Agent begins	9	18	27	58	99	140
2-6: 2-Jones gains magnetic powers. 5-Origin & 1st app. of Merman. 6-Kane/Wood-c(r)	6	12	18	39	62	85

NOTE: ***Gil Kane*** *a-3-6; c-4, 5.* ***Moldoff*** *a-2i.*

UNDERSEA FIGHTING COMMANDOS (See Fighting Undersea...)
I.W. Enterprises: 1964

	GD 2.0	VG 4.0	FN 6.0	VF 8.0	VF/NM 9.0	NM- 9.2
I.W. Reprint #1,2('64): 1-r/#? 2-r/#1; Severin-c	2	4	6	9	13	16

UNDERTAKER (World Wrestling Federation)(Also see WWE Undertaker)
Chaos! Comics: Feb, 1999 - No. 10, Jan, 2000 ($2.50/$2.95)

	GD 2.0	VG 4.0	FN 6.0	VF 8.0	VF/NM 9.0	NM- 9.2
Preview (2/99)						3.00
1-10: Reg. and photo covers for each. 1-(4/99)						3.00
1-($6.95) DF Ed.; Brereton painted-c						7.00
...Halloween Special (10/99, $2.95) Reg. & photo-c						3.00
Wizard #0						3.00

UNDERWATER CITY, THE
Dell Publishing Co.: No. 1328, 1961

	GD 2.0	VG 4.0	FN 6.0	VF 8.0	VF/NM 9.0	NM- 9.2
Four Color 1328-Movie, Evans-a	7	14	21	46	76	105

UNDERWORLD (...True Crime Stories)
D. S. Publishing Co.: Feb-Mar, 1948 - No. 9, June-July, 1949 (52 pgs.)

	GD 2.0	VG 4.0	FN 6.0	VF 8.0	VF/NM 9.0	NM- 9.2
1-Moldoff (Shelly)-c; excessive violence	48	96	144	302	514	725
2-Moldoff (Shelly)-c; Ma Barker story used in **SOTI**, pg. 95; female electrocution panel; lingerie art	43	86	129	271	461	650
3-McWilliams-c/a; extreme violence, mutilation	40	80	120	246	411	575
4-Used in Love and Death by Legman; Ingels-a	36	72	108	216	351	485
5-Ingels-a	24	48	72	142	234	325
6-9: 8-Ravielli-a. 9-R.Q. Sale-a	20	40	60	114	182	250

UNDERWORLD
DC Comics: Dec, 1987 - No. 4, Mar, 1988 ($1.00, limited series, mature)

	GD 2.0	VG 4.0	FN 6.0	VF 8.0	VF/NM 9.0	NM- 9.2
1-4						3.00

UNDERWORLD (Movie)
IDW Publishing: Sept, 2003; Dec, 2005 ($6.99)

	GD 2.0	VG 4.0	FN 6.0	VF 8.0	VF/NM 9.0	NM- 9.2
1-Movie adaptation; photo-c						7.00
... Evolution (12/05, $7.49) adaptation of movie sequel; Vazquez-a						7.50
TPB (7/04, $19.99) r/#1 and Underworld:Red in Tooth and Claw #1-3						20.00

UNDERWORLD
Marvel Comics: Apr, 2006 - No. 5, Aug, 2006 ($2.99, limited series)

	GD 2.0	VG 4.0	FN 6.0	VF 8.0	VF/NM 9.0	NM- 9.2
1-5: Staz Johnson-a. 2-Spider-Man app. 3,4-Punisher app.						3.00

UNDERWORLD CRIME
Fawcett Publications: June, 1952 - No. 9, Oct, 1953

	GD 2.0	VG 4.0	FN 6.0	VF 8.0	VF/NM 9.0	NM- 9.2
1	34	68	102	199	325	450
2	21	42	63	122	199	275
3-6,8,9 (8,9-exist?)	19	38	57	112	179	245
7-(6/53)-Red hot poker/bondage/torture-c	52	104	156	328	552	775

UNDERWORLD: RED IN TOOTH AND CLAW (Movie)
IDW Publishing: Feb, 2004 - No. 3, Apr, 2004 ($3.99, limited series)

	GD 2.0	VG 4.0	FN 6.0	VF 8.0	VF/NM 9.0	NM- 9.2
1-3-The early days of the Vampire and Lycan war; Postic & Marinkovich-a						4.00

UNDERWORLD: RISE OF THE LYCANS (Movie)
IDW Publishing: Nov, 2008 - No. 2, Nov, 2008 ($3.99, limited series)

	GD 2.0	VG 4.0	FN 6.0	VF 8.0	VF/NM 9.0	NM- 9.2
1,2-Grevioux-s/Huerta-a						4.00

UNDERWORLD STORY, THE (Movie)
Avon Periodicals: 1950

	GD 2.0	VG 4.0	FN 6.0	VF 8.0	VF/NM 9.0	NM- 9.2
nn-(Scarce)-Ravielli-c	29	58	87	172	281	390

UNDERWORLD UNLEASHED
DC Comics: Nov, 1995 - No. 3, Jan, 1996 ($2.95, limited series)

	GD 2.0	VG 4.0	FN 6.0	VF 8.0	VF/NM 9.0	NM- 9.2
1-3: Mark Waid scripts & Howard Porter-c/a(p)						3.50
...: Abyss: Hell's Sentinel 1-($2.95)-Alan Scott, Phantom Stranger, Zatanna app.						3.00
...: Apokolips-Dark Uprising 1 ($1.95)						3.00
...: Batman-Devil's Asylum 1-($2.95)-Batman app.						3.00
...: Patterns of Fear-($2.95)						3.00
TPB (1998, $17.95) r/#1-3 & Abyss-Hell's Sentinel						18.00

UNEARTHLY SPECTACULARS
Harvey Publications: Oct, 1965 - No. 3, Mar, 1967

	GD 2.0	VG 4.0	FN 6.0	VF 8.0	VF/NM 9.0	NM- 9.2
1-(12¢)-Tiger Boy; Simon-c	4	8	12	26	41	55
2-(25¢ giants)-Jack Q. Frost, Tiger Boy & Three Rocketeers app.; Williamson, Wood, Kane-a; r-1 story/Thrill-O-Rama #2	5	10	15	30	48	65
3-(25¢ giants)-Jack Q. Frost app.; Williamson/Crandall-a; r-from Alarming Advs. #1,1962	5	10	15	30	48	65

NOTE: ***Crandall*** *a-3r.* ***G. Kane*** *a-2.* ***Orlando*** *a-3.* ***Simon, Sparling, Wood*** *c-2.* ***Simon/Kirby*** *a-3r.* ***Torres*** *a-1?.* ***Wildey*** *a-1(3).* ***Williamson*** *a-2, 3r.* ***Wood*** *a-2(2).*

UNEXPECTED, THE (Formerly Tales of the...)
National Per. Publ./DC Comics: No. 105, Feb-Mar, 1968 - No. 222, May, 1982

	GD 2.0	VG 4.0	FN 6.0	VF 8.0	VF/NM 9.0	NM- 9.2
105-Begin 12¢ cover price	7	14	21	46	76	105
106-113: 113-Last 12¢ issue (6-7/69)	5	10	15	32	51	70
114,115,117,118,120-125	4	8	12	23	36	48
116 (36 pgs.)-Wrightson-a	4	8	12	24	37	50
119-Wrightson-a, 8pgs.(36 pgs.)	5	10	15	35	55	75
126,127,129-136-(52 pgs.)	4	8	12	23	36	48
128(52 pgs.)-Wrightson-a	5	10	15	35	55	75
137-156	3	6	9	16	22	28
157-162-(100 pgs.)	5	10	15	30	48	65
163-188: 187,188-(44 pgs.)	2	4	6	11	16	20
189,190,192-195 ($1.00, 68 pgs.): 189 on are combined with House of Secrets & The Witching Hour	2	4	6	13	18	22
191-Rogers-a(p) ($1.00, 68 pgs.)	3	6	9	14	19	24
196-222: 200-Return of Johhny Peril by Tuska. 205-213-Johnny Peril app. 210-Time Warp story. 222-Giffen-a	2	4	6	8	10	12

NOTE: ***Neal Adams*** *c-110, 112-115, 118, 121, 124.* ***J. Craig*** *a-195.* ***Ditko*** *a-189, 221p, 222p; c-222.* ***Drucker*** *a-107r, 132r.* ***Giffen*** *a-219, 222.* ***Kaluta*** *c-203, 212.* ***Kirby*** *a-127r, 162.* ***Kubert*** *c-204, 214-216, 219-221.* ***Mayer*** *a-217p, 220, 221p.* ***Moldoff*** *a-136r.* ***Moreira*** *a-133.* ***Mortimer*** *a-212p.* ***Newton*** *a-204p.* ***Orlando*** *a-202; c-191.* ***Perez*** *a-217p.* ***Redondo*** *a-155, 166, 195.* ***Reese*** *a-145.* ***Sparling*** *a-107, 205-209p, 212p.* ***Spiegle*** *a-217.* ***Starlin*** *c-198.* ***Toth*** *a-126r, 127r.* ***Tuska*** *a-127, 132, 134, 136, 139, 152, 180, 200p.* ***Wildey*** *a-128r, 193.* ***Wood*** *a-122i, 133i, 137i, 138i.* ***Wrightson*** *a-161r(2 pgs.). Johnny Peril in #106-114, 116, 117, 200, 205-213.*

UNEXPECTED, THE
DC Comics: Dec, 2011 ($7.99, one-shot)

	GD 2.0	VG 4.0	FN 6.0	VF 8.0	VF/NM 9.0	NM- 9.2
1-Short horror stories by various incl. Gibbons, Thompson, Lapham, Fialkov; 2 covers						8.00

UNEXPECTED ANNUAL, THE (See DC Special Series #4)

UNHOLY UNION
Image Comics (Top Cow): July, 2007 ($3.99, one-shot)

	GD 2.0	VG 4.0	FN 6.0	VF 8.0	VF/NM 9.0	NM- 9.2
1-Witchblade & The Darkness meet Hulk, Ghost Rider & Doctor Strange; Silvestri-c						4.00

UNIDENTIFIED FLYING ODDBALL (See Walt Disney Showcase #52)

UNION
Image Comics (WildStorm Productions): June, 1993 - No. 0, July, 1994 ($1.95, lim. series)

	GD 2.0	VG 4.0	FN 6.0	VF 8.0	VF/NM 9.0	NM- 9.2
0-(7/94, $2.50)						3.00
0-Alternate Portacio-c (See Deathblow #5)						5.00
1-($2.50)-Embossed foil-c; Texeira-c/a in all						4.00
1-($1.95)-Newsstand edition w/o foil-c						3.00
2-4: 4-(7/94)						3.00

UNION
Image Comics (WildStorm Prod.): Feb, 1995 - No. 9, Dec, 1995 ($2.50)

	GD 2.0	VG 4.0	FN 6.0	VF 8.0	VF/NM 9.0	NM- 9.2
1-3,5-9: 3-Savage Dragon app. 6-Fairchild from Gen 13 app.						3.00
4-($1.95, Newsstand)-WildStorm Rising Pt. 3						3.00
4-($2.50, Direct Market)-WildStorm Rising Pt. 3, bound-in card						3.00

UNION: FINAL VENGEANCE
Image Comics (WildStorm Productions): Oct, 1997 ($2.50)

	GD 2.0	VG 4.0	FN 6.0	VF 8.0	VF/NM 9.0	NM- 9.2
1-Golden-c/Heisler-s						3.00

United Comics #25 © UFS

Unity 2000 #1 © Acclaim

Unknown Soldier #212 © DC

GD 2.0 | VG 4.0 | FN 6.0 | VF 8.0 | VF/NM 9.0 | NM- 9.2

UNION JACK
Marvel Comics: Dec, 1998 - No. 3, Feb, 1999 ($2.99, limited series)
1-3-Raab-s/Cassaday-s/a 3.00

UNION JACK
Marvel Comics: Nov, 2006 - No. 4, Feb, 2007 ($2.99, limited series)
1-4-Gage-s/Perkins-c/a 3.00
...: London Falling TPB (2007, $10.99) r/#1-4; Perkins sketch page 11.00

UNITED COMICS (Formerly Fritzi Ritz #7; has Fritzi Ritz logo)
United Features Syndicate: Aug, 1940; No. 8, 1950 - No. 26, Jan-Feb, 1953
1(68 pgs.)-Fritzi Ritz & Phil Fumble 23 46 69 136 223 310
8-Fritzi Ritz, Abbie & Slats 8 16 24 44 57 70
9-21: 20-Strange As It Seems; Russell Patterson Cheesecake-a 8 16 24 40 50 60
22-(5-6/52) 2 pgs. early Peanuts by Schulz (1st in comics?) 21 42 63 122 199 275
23-26: 23-(7-8/52). 24-(9-10/52). 25-(11-12/52). 26-(1-2/53). All have 2 pgs. early Peanuts by Schulz 15 30 45 83 124 165
NOTE: *Abbie & Slats reprinted from Tip Top.*

UNITED NATIONS, THE (See Classics Illustrated Special Issue)

UNITED STATES AIR FORCE PRESENTS: THE HIDDEN CREW
U.S. Air Force: 1964 (36 pgs.)
nn-Schaffenberger-a 2 4 6 11 16 20

UNITED STATES FIGHTING AIR FORCE (Also see U.S. Fighting Air Force)
Superior Comics Ltd.: Sept, 1952 - No. 29, Oct, 1956
1 14 28 42 76 108 140
2 8 16 24 44 57 70
3-10 8 16 24 40 50 60
11-29 7 14 21 37 46 55

UNITED STATES MARINES
William H. Wise/Life's Romances Publ. Co./Magazine Ent. #5-8/Toby Press #7-11: 1943 - No. 4, 1944; No. 5, 1952 - No. 8, 1952; No. 7 - No. 11, 1953
nn-Mart Bailey-c/a; Marines in the Pacific theater 22 44 66 132 216 300
2-Bailey-a; Tojo classic-c 65 130 195 416 708 1000
3-Tojo-c 55 110 165 352 601 850
4-WWII photos; Tony DiPreta-a 15 30 45 85 130 175
5(A-1 #55)-Bailey-a, 6(A-1 #60), 7(A-1 #68), 8(A-1 #72) 11 22 33 60 83 105
7-11 (Toby) 10 20 30 54 72 90
NOTE: *Powell a-5-7.*

UNITY
Valiant: No. 0, Aug, 1992 - No. 1, 1992 (Free comics w/limited dist., 20 pgs.)
0 (Blue)-Prequel to Unity x-overs in all Valiant titles; B. Smith-c/a. (Free to everyone that bought all 8 titles that month.) 3.00
0 (Red)-Same as above, but w/red logo (5,000). 3.00
1-Epilogue to Unity x-overs; B. Smith-c/a. (1 copy available for every 8 Valiant books ordered by dealers.) 3.00
1 (Gold), 1-(Platinum)-Promotional copy. 6.00
... : The Lost Chapter 1 (Yearbook) (2/95, $3.95)-"1994" in indicia 4.00

UNITY 2000 (See preludes in Shadowman #3,4 flipbooks)
Acclaim Comics: Nov, 1999 - No. 3, Jan, 2000 ($2.50, unfinished limited series planned for 6 issues)
Preview -B&W plot preview and cover art; paper cover 3.00
1-3-Starlin-a/Shooter-s 3.00

UNIVERSAL MONSTERS
Dark Horse Comics: 1993 ($4.95/$5.95, 52 pgs.)(All adapt original movies)
Creature From the Black Lagoon nn-($4.95)-Art Adams/Austin-c/a, Dracula nn-($4.95), Frankenstein nn-($3.95)-Painted-c/a, The Mummy nn-($4.95)-Painted-c 1 2 3 4 5 7
...: Cavalcade of Horror TPB (1/06, $19.95) r/one-shots; Eric Powell intro. & cover 20.00

UNIVERSAL PRESENTS DRACULA-THE MUMMY& OTHER STORIES
Dell Publishing Co.: Sept-Nov, 1963 (one-shot, 84 pgs.) (Also see Dell Giants)
02-530-311-r/Dracula 12-231-212, The Mummy 12-437-211 & part of Ghost Stories No. 1 15 30 45 102 221 340

UNIVERSAL SOLDIER (Movie)
Now Comics: Sept, 1992 - No. 3, Nov, 1992 (Limited series, polybagged, mature)
1-3 ($2.50, Direct Sales) 1-Movie adapatation; hologram on-c (all direct sales editions have painted-c) 4.00
1-3 ($1.95, Newsstand)-Rewritten & redrawn code approved version; all newsstand editions have photo-c 3.00

UNIVERSAL WAR ONE
Marvel Comics (Soleil): 2008 - No. 3, 2008 ($5.99, limited series)
1-3-Denis Bajram-s/a; English version of French comic. 1-Bajram interview 6.00
...: Revelations 1-3 (2009 - No. 3, 2009, $5.99) Bajram-s/a 6.00

UNIVERSE
Image Comics (Top Cow): Sept, 2001 - No. 8, July, 2002 ($2.50)
1-7-Jenkins-s 3.00
8-($4.95) extra short-s by Jenkins; pin-up pages 5.00

UNIVERSE X (See Earth X)
Marvel Comics: Sept, 2000 - No. 12, Sept, 2001 ($3.99/$3.50, limited series)
0-Ross-c/Braithwaite-a/Ross & Krueger-s 4.00
1-12: 5-Funeral of Captain America 4.00
... Beasts (6/00, $3.99) Yeates-a/Ross-c 4.00
... Cap (Capt. America) (2/01, $3.99) Yeates & Totleben-a/Ross-c; Cap dies 4.00
... 4 (Fantastic 4) (10/00, $3.99) Brent Anderson-a/Ross-c 4.00
... Iron Men (9/01, $3.99) Anderson-a/Ross-c; leads into #12 4.00
... Omnibus (6/01, $3.99) Ross B&W sketchbook and character bios 4.00
Sketchbook- Wizard supplement; B&W character sketches and bios 3.00
...Spidey (1/01, $3.99) Romita Sr. flashback-a/Guice-a/Ross-c 4.00
...X (11/01, $3.99) Series conclusion; Braithwaith-a/Ross wraparound-c 4.00
Volume 1 TPB (1/02, $24.95) r/#0-7 & Spidey, 4, & Cap; new Ross-c 25.00
Volume 2 TPB (6/02, $24.95) r/#8-12 &X, Beasts, Iron Men and Omnibus 25.00

UNKNOWN, THE
BOOM! Studios: May, 2009 - No. 4, Aug, 2009 ($3.99)
1-4-Mark Waid-s/Minck Oosterveer-a; two covers on each 4.00
...: The Devil Made Flesh 1-4 (9/09 - No. 4, 12/09, $3.99) Waid-s/Oosterveer-a 4.00

UNKNOWN MAN, THE (Movie)
Avon Periodicals: 1951
nn-Kinstler-c 28 56 84 165 270 375

UNKNOWN SOLDIER (Formerly Star-Spangled War Stories)
National Periodical Publications/DC Comics: No. 205, Apr-May, 1977 - No. 268, Oct, 1982 (See Our Army at War #168 for 1st app.)
205 3 6 9 18 27 35
206-210,220,221,251: 220,221 (44pgs.). 251-Enemy Ace begins 3 6 9 14 19 24
211-218,222-247,250,252-264 2 4 6 11 16 20
219-Miller-a (44 pgs.) 3 6 9 16 23 30
248,249,265-267: 248,249-Origin. 265-267-Enemy Ace vs. Balloon Buster. 2 4 6 11 16 20
268-Death of Unknown Soldier 3 6 9 20 30 40
NOTE: ***Chaykin** a-234. **Evans** a-265-267; c-235. **Kubert** c-Most. **Miller** a-219p. **Severin** a-251-253, 260, 261, 265-267. **Simonson** a-254-256. **Spiegle** a-258, 259, 262-264.*

UNKNOWN SOLDIER, THE (Also see Brave &the Bold #146)
DC Comics: Winter, 1988-'89 - No. 12, Dec, 1989 ($1.50, maxi-series, mature)
1-12: 8-Begin $1.75-c 5.00

UNKNOWN SOLDIER
DC Comics (Vertigo): Apr, 1997 - No 4, July, 1997 ($2.50, mini-series)
1-Ennis-s/Plunkett-a/Bradstreet-c in all 6.00
2-4 4.00
TPB (1998, $12.95) r/#1-4 13.00

UNKNOWN SOLDIER
DC Comics (Vertigo): Dec, 2008 - No. 25, Dec, 2010 ($2.99)
1-25: 1-Dysart-s/Ponticelli-a; intro. Lwanga Moses; two covers by Kordey and Corben. 2-20,22-25-Ponticelli-a. 21-Veitch-a 3.00
...: Beautiful World TPB (2011, $14.99) r/#21-25; Dysart afterword; sketch/design art 15.00
...: Dry Season TPB (2010, $14.99) r/#15-20; war history 15.00
...: Easy Kill TPB (2010, $17.99) r/#7-14; war history 18.00
...: Haunted House TPB (2009, $9.99) r/#1-6; glossary 10.00

UNKNOWN WORLD (Strange Stories From Another World #2 on)
Fawcett Publications: June, 1952
1-Norman Saunders painted-c 47 94 141 296 498 700

UNKNOWN WORLDS (See Journey Into...)

UNKNOWN WORLDS
American Comics Group/Best Synd. Features: Aug, 1960 - No. 57, Aug, 1967
1-Schaffenberger-c 17 34 51 114 250 385

Unlimited Access #2 © MAR & DC

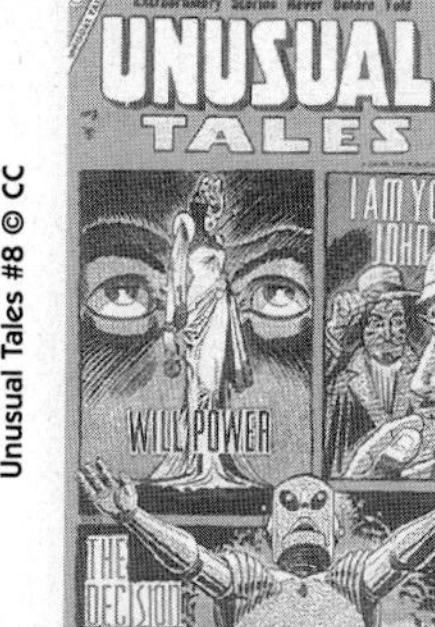

Unusual Tales #8 © CC

The Unwritten #7 © Casey & Gross

GD VG FN VF VF/NM NM-
2.0 4.0 6.0 8.0 9.0 9.2

2-Dinosaur-c/story 11 22 33 71 136 200

3-5 9 18 27 63 112 160

6-11: 9-Dinosaur-c/story. 11-Last 10¢ issue 8 16 24 53 89 125

12-19: 12-Begin 12¢ issues?; ends #57 6 12 18 42 69 95

20-Herbie cameo (12-1/62-63) 7 14 21 44 72 100

21-35: 27-Devil on-c. 31-Herbie one pagers thru #39 5 10 15 32 51 70

36- "The People vs. Hendricks" by Craig; most popular ACG story ever 5 10 15 35 55 75

37-46 4 8 12 28 44 60

47-Williamson-a r-from Adventures Into the Unknown #96, 3 pgs.; Craig-a 5 10 15 30 48 65

48-57: 53-Frankenstein app. 4 8 12 26 41 55

NOTE: ***Ditko** a-49, 50p, 54. **Forte** a-3, 6, 11. **Landau** a-56(2). **Reinman** a-3, 9, 13, 20, 22, 23, 36, 38, 54. **Whitney** c/a-most issues. John Force, Magic Agent app.-35, 36, 48, 50, 52, 54, 56.*

UNKNOWN WORLDS OF FRANK BRUNNER
Eclipse Comics: Aug, 1985 - No. 2, Aug, 1985 ($1.75)

1,2-B&W-r in color 4.00

UNKNOWN WORLDS OF SCIENCE FICTION
Marvel Comics: Jan, 1975 - No. 6, Nov, 1975; 1976 ($1.00, B&W Magazine)

1-Williamson/Krenkel/Torres/Frazetta-r/Witzend #1, Neal Adams-r/Phase 1; Brunner & Kaluta-r; Freas/Romita-c 3 6 9 16 23 30

2-6: 5-Kaluta text illos 3 6 9 14 19 24

Special 1(1976,100 pgs.)-Newton painted-c 3 6 9 16 22 28

NOTE: ***Brunner** a-2; c-4, 6. **Buscema** a-Special 1p. **Chaykin** a-5. **Colan** a(p)-1, 3, 5, 6. **Corben** a-4. **Kaluta** a-2, Special 1(ext illos); c-2. **Morrow** a-3, 5. **Nino** a-3, 6, Special 1. **Perez** a-2, 3. Ray Bradbury interview in #1.*

UNLIMITED ACCESS (Also see Marvel Vs. DC))
Marvel Comics: Dec, 1997 - No. 4, Mar, 1998 ($2.99/$1.99, limited series)

1-Spider-Man, Wonder Woman, Green Lantern & Hulk app. 4.00

2,3-($1.99): 2-X-Men, Legion of Super-Heroes app. 3-Original Avengers vs. original Justice League 3.00

4-($2.99) Amalgam Legion vs. Darkseid & Magneto 4.00

UN-MEN, THE
DC Comics (Vertigo): Oct, 2007 - No. 13, Oct, 2008 ($2.99)

1-13-Whalen-s/Hawthorne-a/Hanuka-c 3.00

...: Children of Paradox TPB (2008, $19.99) r/#6-13 20.00

...: Get Your Freak On! TPB (2008, $9.99) r/#1-5; cover gallery 10.00

UNSANE (Formerly Mighty Bear #13, 14? or The Outlaws #10-14?)(Satire)
Star Publications: No. 15, June, 1954

15-Disbrow-a(2); L. B. Cole-c 34 68 102 199 325 450

UNSEEN, THE
Visual Editions/Standard Comics: No. 5, 1952 - No. 15, July, 1954

5-Horror stories in all; Toth-a 44 88 132 277 469 660

6,7,9,10-Jack Katz-a 34 68 102 199 325 450

8,11,13,14 27 54 81 160 263 365

12,15-Toth-a. 12-Tuska-a 34 68 102 199 325 450

NOTE: ***Nick Cardy** c-12. **Fawcette** a-13, 14. **Sekowsky** a-7, 8(2), 10, 13, 15.*

UNTAMED
Marvel Comics (Epic Comics/Heavy Hitters): June, 1993 - No. 3, Aug, 1993 ($1.95, lim. series)

1-($2.50)-Embossed-c 4.00

2,3 3.00

UNTAMED LOVE (Also see Frank Frazetta's Untamed Love)
Quality Comics Group (Comic Magazines): Jan, 1950 - No. 5, Sept, 1950

1-Ward-c, Gustavson-a 27 54 81 158 259 360

2,4: 2-5-Photo-c 17 34 51 98 154 210

3,5-Gustavson-a 18 36 54 105 165 225

UNTOLD LEGEND OF CAPTAIN MARVEL, THE
Marvel Comics: Apr, 1997 - No. 3, June, 1997 ($2.50, limited series)

1-3 4.00

UNTOLD LEGEND OF THE BATMAN, THE (Also see Promotional section)
DC Comics: July, 1980 - No. 3, Sept, 1980 (Limited series)

1-Origin; Joker-c; Byrne's 1st work at DC 1 2 3 5 6 8

2,3 5.00

NOTE: ***Aparo** a-1i, 2, 3. **Byrne** a-1p.*

UNTOLD ORIGIN OF THE FEMFORCE, THE (Also see Femforce)
AC Comics: 1989 ($4.95, 68 pgs.)

1-Origin Femforce; Bill Black-a(i) & scripts 6.00

UNTOLD TALES OF BLACKEST NIGHT (Also see Blackest Night crossover titles)
DC Comics: Dec, 2010 ($4.99, one-shot)

1-Short stories by various incl. Johns, Benes, Booth; 2 covers by Kirkham & Van Sciver 5.00

UNTOLD TALES OF CHASTITY
Chaos! Comics: Nov, 2000 ($2.95, one-shot)

1-Origin; Steven Grant-s/Peter Vale-c/a 3.00

1-Premium Edition with glow in the dark cover 10.00

UNTOLD TALES OF LADY DEATH
Chaos! Comics: Nov, 2000 ($2.95, one-shot)

1-Origin of Lady Death; Cremator app.; Kaminski-s 3.00

1-Premium Edition with glow in the dark cover by Steven Hughes 10.00

UNTOLD TALES OF PURGATORI
Chaos! Comics: Nov, 2000 ($2.95, one-shot)

1-Purgatori in 57 B.C.; Rio-a/Grant-s 3.00

1-Premium Edition with glow in the dark cover 10.00

UNTOLD TALES OF SPIDER-MAN (Also see Amazing Fantasy #16-18)
Marvel Comics: Sept, 1995 - No. 25, Sept, 1997 (99¢)

1-Kurt Busiek scripts begin; Pat Olliffe-c/a in all (except #9). 4.00

2-22, -1(7/97), 23-25: 2-1st app. Batwing. 4-1st app. The Spacemen (Gantry, Orbit, Satellite & Vacuum). 8-1st app. The Headsman; The Enforcers (The Big Man, Montana, The Ox & Fancy Dan) app. 9-Ron Frenz-a. 10-1st app. Commanda. 16-Reintro Mary Jane Watson. 21-X-Men-c/app. 25-Green Goblin 3.00

...'96-(1996, $1.95, 46 pgs.)-Kurt Busiek scripts; Mike Allred-c/a; Kurt Busiek & Pat Olliffe app. in back-up story; contains pin-ups 4.00

...'97-(1997, $1.95)-Wraparound-c 4.00

...: Strange Encounters ('98, $5.99) Dr. Strange app. 6.00

UNTOLD TALES OF THE NEW UNIVERSE (Based on Marvel's 1986 New Universe titles)
Marvel Comics: May, 2006 ($2.99, series of one-shots)

...: D. P. 7 - Takes place between issues #4 & 5 of D. P. 7 series; Bright-a/Cebulski-s 3.00

...: Justice - Peter David-s/Carmine Di Giandomenico-a 3.00

...: Nightmask - Takes place between issues #4 & 5 of Nightmask series; The Gnome app. 3.00

...: Psi-Force - Tony Bedard-s/Russ Braun-a 3.00

...: Star Brand - Romita & Romita Jr.-c/Pulido-a 3.00

TPB (2006, $15.99) r/one-shots & stories from Amaz. Fantasy #18,19 & New Avengers #16 16.00

UNTOUCHABLES, THE (TV)
Dell Publishing Co.: No. 1237, 10-12/61 - No. 4, 8-10/62 (All have Robert Stack photo-c)

Four Color 1237(#1) 17 34 51 116 253 390

Four Color 1286 12 24 36 84 175 265

01-879-207, 12-879-210(01879-210 on inside) 9 18 27 61 106 150

UNTOUCHABLES
Caliber Comics: Aug, 1997 - No. 4 ($2.95, B&W)

1-4: 1-Pruett-s; variant covers by Kaluta & Showman 3.00

UNUSUAL TALES (Blue Beetle & Shadows From Beyond #50 on)
Charlton Comics: Nov, 1955 - No. 49, Mar-Apr, 1965

1 32 64 96 192 314 435

2 17 34 51 98 154 210

3-5 14 28 42 82 121 160

6-Ditko-c only 20 40 60 114 182 250

7,8-Ditko-c/a. 8-Robot-c 30 60 90 177 289 400

9-Ditko-c/a (20 pgs.) 32 64 96 192 314 435

10-Ditko-c/a(4) 34 68 102 199 325 450

11-(3/58, 68 pgs.)-Ditko-a(4) 32 64 96 192 314 435

12,14-Ditko-a 20 40 60 114 182 250

13,16-20 7 14 21 48 79 110

15-Ditko-c/a 25 50 75 150 245 340

21,24,28 6 12 18 41 66 90

22,23,25-27,29-Ditko-a 10 20 30 66 121 175

30-49 5 10 15 32 51 70

NOTE: ***Colan** a-11. **Ditko** c-22, 23, 25-27, 31(part).*

UNWRITTEN, THE
DC Comics (Vertigo): July, 2009 - Present ($1.00/$2.99)

1-($1.00) Intro. Tommy Taylor; Mike Carey-s/Peter Gross-a; two covers (white & black) 3.00

2-16,18-31,(31.5), 32, (32.5), 33, (33.5), 34, (34.5), (35.5), 36, -($2.99): 31.5-Art by Gross, Kaluta, Geary & Talbot 3.00

17-($3.99) Story printed sideways; Pick-a-Story format 4.00

35-($4.99) 5.00

...: Dead Man's Knock TPB (2011, $14.99) r/#13-18; intro. by novelist Steven Hall 15.00

...: Inside Man TPB (2010, $12.99) r/#6-12; intro. by Paul Cornell 13.00

...: Tommy Taylor and the Bogus Identity TPB (2010, $9.99) r/#1-5; sketch art; prose 10.00

UP FROM HARLEM (Tom Skinner...)

USA Comics #4 © MAR

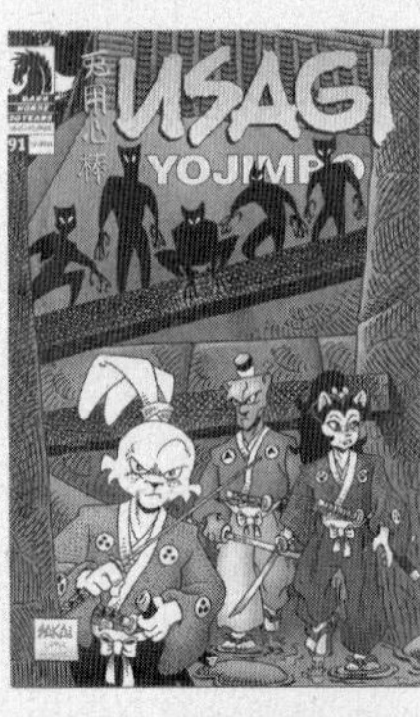

Usagi Yojimbo #91 © Stan Sakai

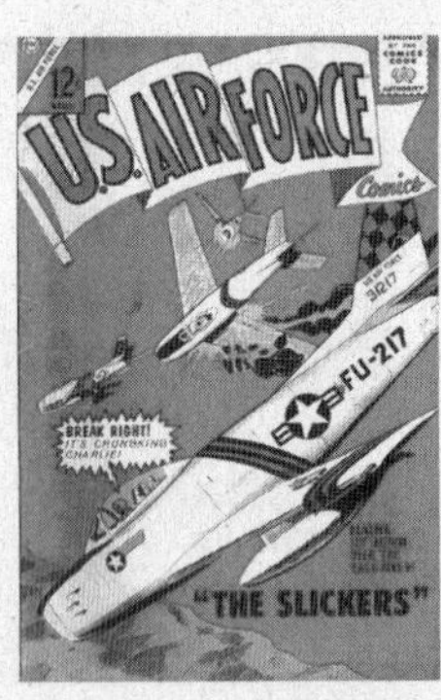

U.S. Air Force Comics #32 © CC

Spire Christian Comics (Fleming H. Revell Co.): 1973 (35/49¢)

	GD 2.0	VG 4.0	FN 6.0	VF 8.0	VF/NM 9.0	NM- 9.2
nn-(35¢ cover)	2	4	6	11	16	20
nn-(49¢ cover)	2	4	6	9	12	15

UP-TO-DATE COMICS
King Features Syndicate: No date (1938) (36 pgs.; B&W cover) (10¢)

	GD 2.0	VG 4.0	FN 6.0	VF 8.0	VF/NM 9.0	NM- 9.2
nn-Popeye & Henry cover; The Phantom, Jungle Jim & Flash Gordon by Raymond, The Katzenjammer Kids, Curley Harper & others. Note: Variations in content exist.	26	52	78	154	252	350

UP YOUR NOSE AND OUT YOUR EAR (Satire)
Klevart Enterprises: Apr, 1972 - No. 2, June, 1972 (52 pgs., magazine)

	GD 2.0	VG 4.0	FN 6.0	VF 8.0	VF/NM 9.0	NM- 9.2
V1#1,2	2	4	6	11	16	20

URTH 4 (Also see Earth 4)
Continuity Comics: May, 1989 - No. 4, Dec, 1990 ($2.00, deluxe format)

	GD 2.0	VG 4.0	FN 6.0	VF 8.0	VF/NM 9.0	NM- 9.2
1-4: Ms. Mystic characters. 2-Neal Adams-c(i)						3.00

URZA-MISHRA WAR ON THE WORLD OF MAGIC THE GATHERING
Acclaim Comics (Armada): 1996 - No. 2, 1996 ($5.95, limited series)

	GD 2.0	VG 4.0	FN 6.0	VF 8.0	VF/NM 9.0	NM- 9.2
1,2						6.00

U.S. (See Uncle Sam)

USA COMICS
Timely Comics (USA): Aug, 1941 - No. 17, Fall, 1945

	GD 2.0	VG 4.0	FN 6.0	VF 8.0	VF/NM 9.0	NM- 9.2
1-Origin Major Liberty (called Mr. Liberty #1), Rockman by Wolverton; 1st app. The Whizzer by Avison; The Defender with sidekick Rusty & Jack Frost begin; The Young Avenger only app.; S&K-c plus 1 pg. art	1000	2000	3000	7000	12,500	20,000
2-Origin Captain Terror & The Vagabond; last Wolverton Rockman; Hitler-c	423	846	1269	3000	5250	7500
3-No Whizzer	314	628	942	2198	3849	5500
4-Last Rockman, Major Liberty, Defender, Jack Frost, & Capt. Terror; Corporal Dix app.	300	600	900	2010	3505	5000
5-Origin American Avenger & Roko the Amazing; The Blue Blade, The Black Widow & Victory Boys, Gypo the Gypsy Giant & Hills of Horror only app.; Sergeant Dix begins; no Whizzer; Hitler, Mussolini & Tojo-c	300	600	900	2070	3635	5200
6-Captain America (ends #17), The Destroyer, Jap Buster Johnson, Jeep Jones begin; Terror Squad only app.	432	864	1296	3154	5577	8000
7-Captain Daring, Disk-Eyes the Detective by Wolverton app.; origin & only app. Marvel Boy (3/43); Secret Stamp begins; no Whizzer, Sergeant Dix; classic Schomburg-c	514	1028	1542	3750	6625	9500
8,10: 10-The Thunderbird only app.	354	708	1062	2478	4339	6200
9-Last Secret Stamp; Hitler-c; classic-c	400	800	1200	2800	4900	7000
11-13: 11-No Jeep Jones. 13-No Whizzer; Jeep Jones ends; Schomburg Japanese WWII-c	271	542	813	1734	2967	4200
14-17: 15-No Destroyer; Jap Buster Johnson ends	155	310	465	992	1696	2400

NOTE: ***Brodsky*** *c-14.* ***Gabrielle*** *c-4.* ***Schomburg*** *c-6, 7, 10, 12, 13, 15-17.* ***Shores*** *a-1, 4; c-9, 11.* ***Ed Win*** *a-4. Cover features: 1-The Defender; 2, 3-Captain Terror; 4-Major Liberty; 5-Victory Boys; 6-17-Captain America & Bucky.*

USA COMICS 70TH ANNIVERSARY SPECIAL
Marvel Comics: Sept, 2009 ($3.99, one-shot)

	GD 2.0	VG 4.0	FN 6.0	VF 8.0	VF/NM 9.0	NM- 9.2
1-New story of The Destroyer; Arcudi-s/Ellis-a; r/All Winners #3; two covers						5.00

U.S. AGENT (See Jeff Jordan...)

U.S. AGENT (See Captain America #354)
Marvel Comics: June, 1993 - No. 4, Sept, 1993 ($1.75, limited series)

	GD 2.0	VG 4.0	FN 6.0	VF 8.0	VF/NM 9.0	NM- 9.2
1-4						3.00

U.S. AGENT
Marvel Comics: Aug, 2001 - No. 3, Oct, 2001 ($2.99, limited series)

	GD 2.0	VG 4.0	FN 6.0	VF 8.0	VF/NM 9.0	NM- 9.2
1-3: Ordway-s/a(p)/c. 2,3-Captain America app.						3.00

USAGI YOJIMBO (See Albedo, Doomsday Squad #3 & Space Usagi)
Fantagraphics Books: July, 1987 - No. 38 ($2.00/$2.25, B&W)

	GD 2.0	VG 4.0	FN 6.0	VF 8.0	VF/NM 9.0	NM- 9.2
1	1	2	3	5	7	9
1,8,10-2nd printings						3.00
2-9						4.00
10,11: 10-Leonardo app. (TMNT). 11-Aragonés-a						6.00
12-29						3.00
30-38: 30-Begin $2.25-c						3.00
Color Special 1 (11/89, $2.95, 68 pgs.)-new & r						4.00
Color Special 2 (10/91, $3.50)						4.00
Color Special #3 (10/92, $3.50)-Jeff Smith's Bone promo on inside-c						4.00
Summer Special 1 (1986, B&W, $2.75)-r/early Albedo issues						4.00

USAGI YOJIMBO
Mirage Studios: V2#1, Mar, 1993 - No. 16, 1994 ($2.75)

	GD 2.0	VG 4.0	FN 6.0	VF 8.0	VF/NM 9.0	NM- 9.2
V2#1-16: 1-Teenage Mutant Ninja Turtles app.						3.00

USAGI YOJIMBO
Dark Horse Comics: V3#1, Apr, 1996 - Present ($2.95/$2.99/$3.50, B&W)

	GD 2.0	VG 4.0	FN 6.0	VF 8.0	VF/NM 9.0	NM- 9.2
V3#1-99,101-116: Stan Sakai-c/a						3.00
100-(1/07, $3.50) Stan Sakai roast by various incl. Aragonés, Wagner, Miller, Geary						3.50
117-144-($3.50) 136-Variant-c. 141-"200th issue"						3.50
...: One For One (8/10, $1.00) Reprints #1						3.00
Color Special #4 (7/97, $2.95) "Green Persimmon"						3.00
Daisho TPB ('98, $14.95) r/Mirage series #7-14						15.00
Demon Mask TPB ('01, $15.95)						16.00
Glimpses of Death TPB (7/06, $15.95) r/#76-82						16.00
Grasscutter TPB ('99, $16.95) r/#13-22						17.00
Gray Shadows TPB ('00, $14.95) r/#23-30						15.00
Seasons TPB ('99, $14.95) r/#7-12						15.00
Shades of Death TPB ('97, $14.95) r/Mirage series #1-6						15.00
The Brink of Life and Death TPB ('98, $14.95) r/Mirage series #13,15,16 & Dark Horse series #1-6						15.00
The Shrouded Moon TPB (1/03, $15.95) r/#46-52						16.00

U.S. AIR FORCE COMICS (Army Attack #38 on)
Charlton Comics: Oct, 1958 - No. 37, Mar-Apr, 1965

	GD 2.0	VG 4.0	FN 6.0	VF 8.0	VF/NM 9.0	NM- 9.2
1	7	14	21	44	72	100
2	4	8	12	24	37	50
3-10	3	6	9	21	32	42
11-20	3	6	9	19	29	38
21-37	3	6	9	16	23	30

NOTE: ***Glanzman*** *c/a-9, 10, 12.* ***Montes/Bache*** *a-33.*

USA IS READY
Dell Publishing Co.: 1941 (68 pgs., one-shot)

	GD 2.0	VG 4.0	FN 6.0	VF 8.0	VF/NM 9.0	NM- 9.2
1-War propaganda	41	82	123	256	428	600

U.S. BORDER PATROL COMICS (Sgt. Dick Carter of the...) (See Holyoke One Shot)

USER
DC Comics (Vertigo): 2001 - No. 3, 2001 ($5.95, limited series)

	GD 2.0	VG 4.0	FN 6.0	VF 8.0	VF/NM 9.0	NM- 9.2
1-3-Devin Grayson-s; Sean Phillips & John Bolton-a						6.00

U.S. FIGHTING AIR FORCE (Also see United States Fighting Air Force)
I. W. Enterprises: No date (1960s?)

	GD 2.0	VG 4.0	FN 6.0	VF 8.0	VF/NM 9.0	NM- 9.2
1,9(nd): 1-r/United States Fighting...#?. 9-r/#1	2	4	6	8	11	14

U.S. FIGHTING MEN
Super Comics: 1963 - 1964 (Reprints)

	GD 2.0	VG 4.0	FN 6.0	VF 8.0	VF/NM 9.0	NM- 9.2
10-r/With the U.S. Paratroops #4(Avon)	2	4	6	9	13	16
11,12,15-18: 11-r/Monty Hall #10. 12,16,17,18-r/U.S. Fighting Air Force #10,3,?&? 15-r/Man Comics #11	2	4	6	9	13	16

U.S. JONES (Also see Wonderworld Comics #28)
Fox Features Syndicate: Nov, 1941 - No. 2, Jan, 1942

	GD 2.0	VG 4.0	FN 6.0	VF 8.0	VF/NM 9.0	NM- 9.2
1-U.S. Jones & The Topper begin; Nazi-c	135	270	405	864	1482	2100
2-Nazi-c	90	180	270	576	988	1400

U.S. MARINES
Charlton Comics: Fall, 1964 (12¢, one-shot)

	GD 2.0	VG 4.0	FN 6.0	VF 8.0	VF/NM 9.0	NM- 9.2
1-1st app. Capt. Dude; Glanzman-a	4	8	12	24	37	50

U.S. MARINES IN ACTION
Avon Periodicals: Aug, 1952 - No. 3, Dec, 1952

	GD 2.0	VG 4.0	FN 6.0	VF 8.0	VF/NM 9.0	NM- 9.2
1-Louis Ravielli-c/a	11	22	33	60	83	105
2,3: 3-Kinstler-c	8	16	24	44	57	70

U.S. 1
Marvel Comics Group: May, 1983 - No. 12, Oct, 1984 (7,8: painted-c)

	GD 2.0	VG 4.0	FN 6.0	VF 8.0	VF/NM 9.0	NM- 9.2
1-12: 2-Sienkiewicz-c. 3-12-Michael Golden-c						3.00

U.S. PARATROOPS (See With the...)

U.S. PARATROOPS
I. W. Enterprises: 1964?

	GD 2.0	VG 4.0	FN 6.0	VF 8.0	VF/NM 9.0	NM- 9.2
1,8: 1-r/With the U.S. Paratroops #1; Wood-c. 8-r/With the U.S. Paratroops #6; Kinstler-c	2	4	6	9	13	16

U.S. TANK COMMANDOS
Avon Periodicals: June, 1952 - No. 4, Mar, 1953

	GD 2.0	VG 4.0	FN 6.0	VF 8.0	VF/NM 9.0	NM- 9.2
1-Kinstler-c	11	22	33	64	90	115
2-4: Kinstler-c	9	18	27	47	61	75
I.W. Reprint #1,8: 1-r/#1. 8-r/#3	2	4	6	9	13	16

NOTE: ***Kinstler*** *a-I.W. #1; c-1-4, I.W. #1, 8.*

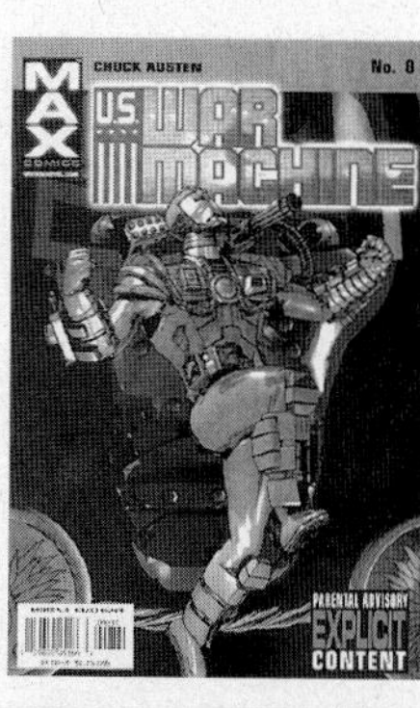

U.S. War Machine V2 #8 © MAR

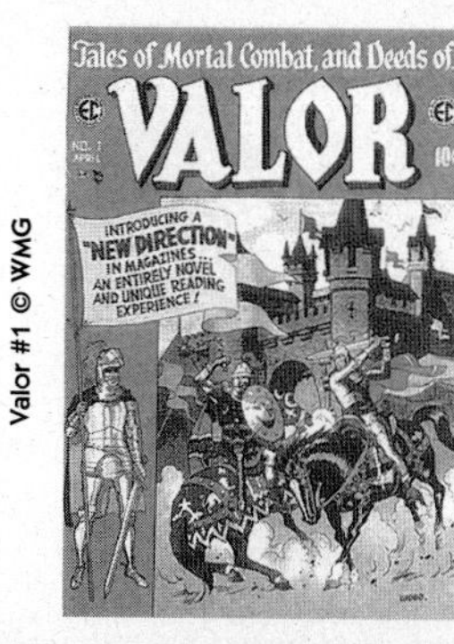

Valor #1 © WMG

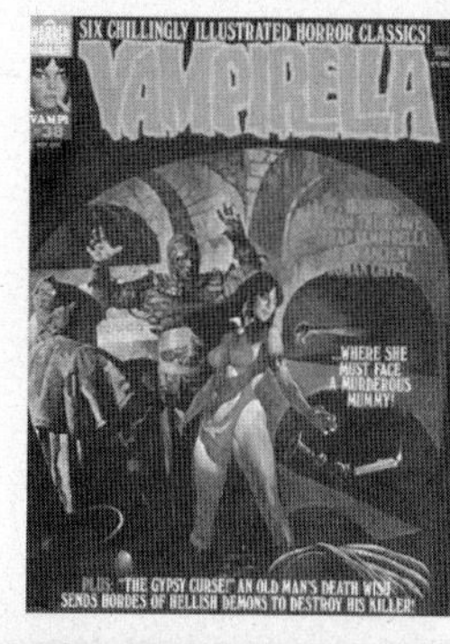

Vampirella #38 © WP

GD VG FN VF VF/NM NM-
2.0 4.0 6.0 8.0 9.0 9.2

U.S. WAR MACHINE (Also see Iron Man and War Machine)
Marvel Comics (MAX): Nov, 2001 - No. 12, Jan, 2002 ($1.50, B&W, weekly limited series)
1-12-Chuck Austen-s/a/c 3.00
TPB (12/01, $14.95) r/#1-12 15.00

U.S. WAR MACHINE 2.0
Marvel Comics (MAX): Sept, 2003 - No. 3, Sept, 2003 ($2.99, weekly, limited series)
1-3-Austen-s/Christian Moore-CGI art 3.00

"V" (TV)
DC Comics: Feb, 1985 - No. 18, July, 1986
1-Based on TV movie & series (Sci/Fi) 5.00
2-18: 17,18-Denys Cowan-c/a 4.00

VACATION COMICS (Also see A-1 Comics)
Magazine Enterprises: No. 16, 1948 (one-shot)
A-1 16-The Pixies, Tom Tom, Flying Fredd & Koko & Kola
7 14 21 35 43 50

VACATION DIGEST
Harvey Comics: Sept, 1987 ($1.25, digest size)
1 1 2 3 5 6 8

VACATION IN DISNEYLAND (Also see Dell Giants)
Dell Publishing Co./Gold Key (1965): Aug-Oct, 1959; May, 1965 (Walt Disney)
Four Color 1025-Barks-a 14 28 42 95 205 315
1(30024-508)(G.K., 5/65, 25¢)-r/Dell Giant #30 & cover to #1 ('58); celebrates Disneyland's 10th anniversary 5 10 15 35 55 75

VACATION PARADE (See Dell Giants)

VALEN THE OUTCAST
BOOM! Studios: Dec, 2011 - Present ($1.00/$3.99)
1-($1.00) Nelson-s/Scalera-a; eight covers 3.00
2-4-($3.99) Six covers on each 4.00

VALERIA THE SHE BAT
Continuity Comics: May, 1993 - No. 5, Nov, 1993
1-Premium; acetate-c; N. Adams-a/scripts; given as gift to retailers
1 2 3 5 6 8
5 (11/93)-Embossed-c; N. Adams-a/scripts 3.00
NOTE: *Due to lack of continuity, #2-4 do not exist.*

VALERIA THE SHE BAT
Acclaim Comics (Windjammer): Sept, 1995 - No.2, Oct, 1995 ($2.50, limited series)
1,2 3.00

VALKYRIE (See Airboy)
Eclipse Comics: May,1987 - No. 3, July, 1987 ($1.75, limited series)
1-3: 2-Holly becomes new Black Angel 3.00

VALKYRIE
Marvel Comics: Jan, 1997; Nov, 2010 ($2.95/$3.99, one-shots)
1-(1/97, $2.95) w/pin-ups 3.00
1-(11/10, $3.99) Origin re-told; Winslade-a/Glass-s; Anacleto-c 4.00

VALKYRIE!
Eclipse Comics: July, 1988 - No. 3, Sept, 1988 ($1.95, limited series)
1-3 3.00

VALLEY OF THE DINOSAURS (TV)
Charlton Comics: Apr, 1975 - No. 11, Dec, 1976 (Hanna-Barbara)
1-W. Howard-i 3 6 9 14 19 24
2,4-11: 2-W. Howard-i 2 4 6 8 11 14
3-Byrne text illos (early work, 7/75) 2 4 6 10 14 18

VALLEY OF THE DINOSAURS (Volume 2)
Harvey Comics: Oct, 1993 ($1.50, giant-sized)
1-Reprints 5.00

VALLEY OF GWANGI (See Movie Classics)

VALOR
E. C. Comics: Mar-Apr, 1955 - No. 5, Nov-Dec, 1955
1-Williamson/Torres-a; Wood-c/a 28 56 84 224 355 485
2-Williamson-c/a; Wood-a 21 42 63 168 272 375
3,4: 3-Williamson, Crandall-a. 4-Wood-c 16 32 48 128 207 285
5-Wood-c/a; Williamson/Evans-a 15 30 45 120 190 260
NOTE: ***Crandall** a-3, 4. **Ingels** a-1, 2, 4, 5. **Krigstein** a-1-5. **Orlando** a-3, 4; c-3. **Wood** a-1, 2, 5; c-1, 4, 5.*

VALOR
Gemstone Publishing: Oct, 1998 - No. 5, Feb, 1999 ($2.50)
1-5-Reprints 3.00

VALOR (Also see Legion of Super-Heroes & Legionnaires)
DC Comics: Nov, 1992 - No. 23, Sept, 1994 ($1.25/$1.50)
1-22: 1-Eclipso The Darkness Within aftermath. 2-Vs. Supergirl. 4-Vs. Lobo. 12-Lobo cameo. 14-Legionnaires, JLA app. 17-Austin-c(i); death of Valor. 18-22-Build-up to Zero Hour 3.00
23-Zero Hour tie-in 3.00

VALOR THUNDERSTAR AND HIS FIREFLIES
Now Comics: Dec, 1986 ($1.50)
1-Ordway-c(p) 3.00

VAMPI (Vampirella's...)
Harris Publications (Anarchy Studios): Aug, 2000 - No. 25, Feb, 2003 ($2.95/$2.99)
Limited Edition Preview Book (5/00) Preview pages & sketchbook 3.00
1-(8/00, $2.95) Lau-a(p)/Conway-s 4.00
1-Platinum Edition 20.00
2-25: 17-Barberi-a 3.00
2-25-Deluxe Edition variants ($9.95): 4-Finch-c. 5-Wieringo-c. 6-Cha-c 10.00
...Digital 1 (11/01, $2.95) CGI art; Haberlin-s 3.00
...Digital Preview (Anarchy Studios, 7/01, $2.95) preview of CGI art 3.00
Switchblade Kiss HC (2001, $24.95) r/#1-6 25.00
Vicious Preview Ed. (Apr, 2003, $1.99) Flip book w/ Xin: Journey of the Monkey King Preview Ed. 3.00
Wizard #1/2 (mail order, $9.95) includes sketch pages 10.00

VAMPIRE BITES
Brainstorm Comics: May, 1995 - No. 2, Sept, 1996 ($2.95, B&W)
1,2:1-Color pin-up 3.00

VAMPIRE LESTAT, THE
Innovation Publishing: Jan, 1990 - No. 12, 1991 ($2.50, painted limited series)
1-Adapts novel; Bolton painted-c on all 2 4 6 10 14 18
1-2nd printing (has UPC code, 1st prints don't) 3.00
1-3rd & 4th printings 3.00
2-1st printing 1 2 3 5 6 8
2-2nd & 3rd printings 3.00
3-5 5.00
3-6,9-2nd printings 3.00
6-12 4.00

VAMPIRELLA (Magazine)(See Warren Presents)(Also see Heidi Saha)
Warren Publishing Co./Harris Publications #113: Sept, 1969 - No. 112, Feb, 1983; No. 113, Jan, 1988? (B&W)
1-Intro. Vampirella in original costume & wings; Frazetta-c/intro. page; Adams-a; Crandall-a 46 92 138 345 748 1150
2-1st app. Vampirella's cousin Evily-c/s; 1st/only app. Draculina, Vampirella's blonde twin sister 14 28 42 97 211 325
3 (Low distribution) 36 72 108 270 585 900
4,6 11 22 33 76 151 225
5,7,9: 5,7-Frazetta-c. 9-Barry Smith-a; Boris/Wood-c 12 24 36 79 160 240
8-Vampirella begins by Tom Sutton as serious strip (early issues-gag line)
12 24 36 81 166 250
10-No Vampi story; Brunner, Adams, Wood-a 8 16 24 55 93 130
11-Origin & 1st app. Pendragon; Frazetta-c 9 18 27 61 106 150
12-Vampi by Gonzales begins 9 18 27 61 106 150
13-15: 14-1st Maroto-a; Ploog-a 9 18 27 58 99 140
16,22,25: 16-1st full Dracula-c/app. 22-Color insert preview of Maroto's Dracula. 25-Vampi on cocaine-s 8 16 24 56 96 135
17,18,20,21,23,24: 17-Tomb of the Gods begins by Maroto, ends #22. 18-22-Dracula-s 8 16 24 53 89 125
19 (1973 Annual) Creation of Vampi text bio 9 18 27 62 109 155
26,28,34,35,39,40: All have 8 pg. color inserts. 28-Board game inside covers. 34,35-1st Fleur the Witch Woman. 39,40-Color Dracula-s. 40-Wrightson bio
6 12 18 41 66 90
27 (1974 Annual) New color Vampi-s; mostly-r 7 14 21 46 76 105
29,38,45: 38-2nd Vampi as Cleopatra/Blood Red Queen of Hearts; 1st Mayo-a.
6 12 18 39 62 85
30-32: 30-Intro. Pantha; Corben-a(color). 31-Origin Luana, the Beast Girl. 32-Jones-a 6 12 18 41 66 90
33-Wrightson-a; Pantha ends 6 12 18 41 66 90
36,37: 36-1st Vampi as Cleopatra/Blood Red Queen of Hearts; issue has 8 pg. color insert. 37-(1975 Annual) 6 12 18 42 69 95
41-44,47,48: 41-Dracula-s 5 10 15 35 55 75
46-(10/75) Origin-r from Annual 1 6 12 18 37 59 80

Vampirella (1992 series) #1 © Harris

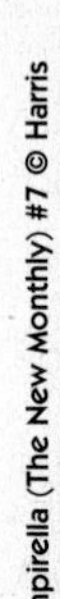
Vampirella (The New Monthly) #7 © Harris

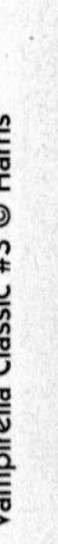
Vampirella Classic #3 © Harris

GD 2.0 | VG 4.0 | FN 6.0 | VF 8.0 | VF/NM 9.0 | NM- 9.2

49-1st Blind Priestess; The Blood Red Queen of Hearts storyline begins; Poe-s 5 10 15 35 55 75
50-Spirit cameo by Eisner; 40 pg. Vampi-s; Pantha & Fleur app.; Jones-a 5 10 15 35 55 75
51-53,56,57,59-62,65,66,68,75,79,80,82-86,88,89: 60-62,65,66-The Blood Red Queen of Hearts app. 60-1st Blind Priestess-c 4 8 12 26 41 55
54,55,63,81,87: 54-Vampi-s (42 pgs.); 8 pg. color Corben-a. 55-All Gonzales-a(r). 63-10 pgs. Wrightson-a 4 8 12 26 41 55
58,70,72: 58-(92 pgs.) 70-Rook app. 5 10 15 30 48 65
64,73: 64-(100 pg. Giant) All Mayo-a; 70 pg. Vampi-s. 73-69 pg. Vampi-s; Mayo-a 5 10 15 32 51 70
67,69,71,74,76-78-All Barbara Leigh photo-c 5 10 15 30 48 65
90-99: 90-Toth-a. 91-All-r; Gonzales-a. 93-Cassandra St. Knight begins, ends #103; new Pantha series begins, ends #108 4 8 12 26 41 55
100 (96 pg. r-special)-Origin reprinted from Ann. 1; mostly reprints; Vampirella appears topless in new 21 pg. story 8 16 24 56 96 135
101-104,106,107: All lower print run. 101,102-The Blood Red Queen of Hearts app. 107-All Maroto reprint-a issue 6 12 18 42 69 95
105,108-110: 108-Torpedo series by Toth begins; Vampi nudity splash page. 110-(100 pg. Summer Spectacular) 6 12 18 42 69 95
111,112: Low print run. 111-Giant Collector's Edition ($2.50) 112-(84 pgs.) last Warren issue 8 16 24 53 89 125
113 (1988)-1st Harris Issue; very low print run 24 48 72 168 359 550
Annual 1(1972)-New definitive origin of Vampirella by Gonzales; reprints by Neal Adams (from #1), Wood (from #9) 24 48 72 168 359 550
Special 1 (1977) Softcover (color, large-square bound)-Only available thru mail order 14 28 42 96 208 320
Special 1 (1977) Hardcover (color, large-square bound)-Only available through mail order (scarce)(500 produced, signed & #'d) 31 62 93 222 481 740
#1 1969 Commemorative Edition (2001, $4.95) reprints entire #1 5.00
...Crimson Chronicles Vol. 1 (2004, $19.95, TPB) reprints stories from #1-10 20.00
...Crimson Chronicles Vol. 2 (2005, $19.95, TPB) reprints stories from #11-18 20.00
...Crimson Chronicles Vol. 3 (2005, $19.95, TPB) reprints stories from #19-28 20.00
...Crimson Chronicles Vol. 4 (2006, $19.95, TPB) reprints stories from #29-41 20.00

NOTE: ***Ackerman*** *s-1-3.* ***Neal Adams*** *a-1, 10p, 19p(r/#10), 44(1 pg.), Annual 1.* ***Alcala*** *a-78, 90, 93i.* ***Bodé/Todd*** *c-3.* ***Bodé/Jones*** *c-4.* ***Boris/Wood*** *c-9.* ***Brunner*** *a-10, 12(1 pg.).* ***Corben*** *a-30, 31, 33, 36, 54; c-30, 31, 33, 54.* ***Crandall*** *a-1, 19(r/#1).* ***Frazetta*** *c-1, 5, 7, 11, 31.* ***Heath*** *a-58, 61, 67, 76-78, 83.* ***Infantino*** *a-57-62.* ***Jones*** *a-5, 9, 12, 27, 32 (color), 33(2 pg.), 34, 50i, 83r.* ***Ken Kelly*** *c-6, 38, 39, 40(back-c), 46, 70, 95.* ***Nebres*** *a-84, 88-90, 92-96.* ***Nino*** *a-59i, 61i, 67, 76, 85, 90.* ***Ploog*** *a-14.* ***Barry Smith*** *a-9.* ***Starlin*** *a-78.* ***Sutton*** *a-1-5, 7-11, Annual 1.* ***Toth*** *a-90i, 108, 110.* ***Wood*** *a-9, 10, 12, 19(r/#12), 27r, Annual 1; c-9(partial).* ***Wrightson*** *a-33(w/****Jones****), 40(Bio cameo) 63r. All reprint issues-19, 74, 83, 91, 105, 107, 109, 111. Annuals from 1973 on are included in regular numbering. Later annuals are same format as regular issues. Color inserts (8 pgs.) in 22, 25-28, 30-35, 39, 40, 45, 46, 49, 54, 55, 67, 72. 16 pg color insert in #36.*

VAMPIRELLA (Also see Cain/... & Vengeance of...)
Harris Publications: Nov, 1992 - No. 5, Nov, 1993 ($2.95)

0-Bagged 6.00
0-Gold 3 6 9 16 23 30
1-Jim Balent inks in #1-3; Adam Hughes c-1-3 2 4 6 11 16 20
1-2nd printing 5.00
1-(11/97) Commemorative Edition 4.00
2 2 4 6 9 12 15
3-5: 4-Snyder III-c. 5-Brereton painted-c 1 2 3 5 6 8
Trade paperback nn (10/93, $5.95)-r/#1-4; Jusko-c 1 2 3 4 5 7

NOTE: *Issues 1-5 contain certificates for free* ***Dave Stevens*** *Vampirella poster.*

VAMPIRELLA (THE NEW MONTHLY)
Harris Publications: Nov, 1997 - No. 26, Apr, 2000 ($2.95)

1-3-"Ascending Evil" -Morrison & Millar-s/Conner & Palmiotti-a. 1-Three covers by Quesada/Palmiotti, Conner, and Conner/Palmiotti 5.00
1-3-($9.95) Jae Lee variant covers 10.00
1-($24.95) Platinum Ed.w/Quesada-c 25.00
4-6-"Holy War"-Small & Stull-a, 4-Linsner variant-c 4.00
7-9-"Queen's Gambit"-Shi app. 7-Two covers. 8-Pantha-c/app. 4.00
7-($9.95) Conner variant-c 10.00
10-12-"Hell on Earth"; Small-a/Coney-s. 12-New costume 4.00
10-Jae Lee variant-c 1 3 4 6 8 10
13-15-"World's End" Zircher-p; Pantha back-up, Texeira-a 4.00
16,17: 16-Pantha-c;Texeira-a; Vampi back-up story. 17-(Pantha #2) 4.00
18-20-"Rebirth": Jae Lee-c on all. 18-Loeb-s/Sale-a. 19-Alan Davis-a. 20-Bruce Timm-a 4.00
18-20-($9.95) Variant covers: 18-Sale. 19-Davis. 20-Timm 12.00
21-26: 21,22-Dangerous Games; Small-a. 23-Lady Death-c/app.; Cleavenger-a. 24,25-Lau-a. 26-Lady Death & Pantha-c/app.; Cleavenger-a. 4.00
0-(1/99) also variant-c with Pantha #0; same contents 4.00
TPB ($7.50) r/#1-3 "Ascending Evil" 8.00
Ascending Evil Ashcan (8/97, $1.00) 3.00
...: Grant Morrison/Mark Millar Collection TPB (2006, $24.95) r/#1-6; interviews 25.00
Hell on Earth Ashcan (7/98, $1.00) 3.00
... Presents: Tales of Pantha TPB (2006, $19.95) r/stories from #13-17 & one-shots 20.00
The End Ashcan (3/00, $6.00) 6.00
...30th Anniversary Celebration Preview (7/99) B&W preview of #18-20 10.00

VAMPIRELLA
Harris Publications: June, 2001 - No. 22, Aug, 2003 ($2.95/$2.99)

1-Four covers (Mayhew w/foil logo, Campbell, Anacleto, Jae Lee) Mayhew-a; Mark Millar-s 5.00
2-22: 2-Two covers (Mayhew & Chiodo). 3-Timm var-c. 4-Horn var-c. 7-10-Dawn Brown-a; Pantha back-up w/Texeira-a. 15-22-Conner-c 4.00
Giant-Size Ashcan (5/01, $5.95) B&W preview art and Mayhew interview 6.00
...: Halloween Trick & Treat (10/04, $4.95) stories & art by various; three covers 5.00
... : Nowheresville Preview Edition (3/01, $2.95)- previews Mayhew art and photo models 3.00
...Nowheresville TPB (1/02, $12.95) r/#1-3 with cover gallery 13.00
... Summer Special #1 (2005, $5.95) Batman Begins photo-c and 2 variant-c 6.00
...: 2006 Halloween Special (2006, $2.95) Conner-c; Hester-s/Segovia-a; 4 covers 4.00

VAMPIRELLA
Dynamite Entertainment: 2010 - Present ($3.99)

1-Four covers (Campbell, Madureira, J. Djurdjevic, Alex Ross swipe of Frazetta's #1) 4.00
1-Variant-c of blood-soaked Vampirella by Alex Ross 8.00
2-14: 2-6-Trautmann-s/Wagner Reis-a; four covers. 7-Geovani-a 4.00
Annual 1 (2011, $4.99) Jerwa-s/Casalos-a; reprint with Alan Davis-a 5.00

VAMPIRELLA & PANTHA SHOWCASE
Harris Publications: Jan, 1997 ($1.50, one-shot)

1-Millar-s/Texeira-c/a; flip book w/"Blood Lust"; Robinson-s/Jusko-c/a 4.00

VAMPIRELLA & THE BLOOD RED QUEEN OF HEARTS
Harris Publications: Sept, 1996 ($9.95, 96 pgs., B&W, squarebound, one-shot)

nn-r/Vampirella #49,60-62,65,66,101,102; John Bolton-c; Michael Bair back-c 1 3 4 6 8 10

VAMPIRELLA AND THE SCARLET LEGION
Dynamite Entertainment: 2011 - Present ($3.99)

1-5: 1-Three covers (Campbell, Chen and Tucci); Malaga-a 4.00

VAMPIRELLA: BLOODLUST
Harris Publications: July, 1997 - No. 2, Aug, 1997 ($4.95, limited series)

1,2-Robinson-s/Jusko-painted c/a 5.00

VAMPIRELLA CLASSIC
Harris Publications: Feb, 1995 - No. 5, Nov, 1995 ($2.95, limited series)

1-5: Reprints Archie Goodwin stories. 4.00

VAMPIRELLA COMICS MAGAZINE
Harris Publications: Oct, 2003 - No. 9 ($3.95/$9.95, magazine-sized)

1-9-($3.95) 1-Texiera-c; b&w and color stories, Alan Moore interview; reviews. 2-KISS interview. 4-Chiodo-c. 6-Brereton-c 4.00
1-9-($9.95) 1-Three covers (Model Photo cover, Palmiotti-c, Wheatley Frankenstein-c) 10.00

VAMPIRELLA: CROSSOVER GALLERY
Harris Publications: Sept, 1997 ($2.95, one-shot)

1-Wraparound-c by Campbell, pinups by Jae Lee, Mack, Allred, Art Adams, Quesada & Palmiotti and others 4.00

VAMPIRELLA: DEATH & DESTRUCTION
Harris Publications: July, 1996 - No. 3, Sept, 1996 ($2.95, limited series)

1-3: Amanda Conner-a(p) in all. 1-Tucci-c. 2-Hughes-c. 3-Jusko-c 4.00
1-($9.95)-Limited Edition; Beachum-c 10.00

VAMPIRELLA/DRACULA & PANTHA SHOWCASE
Harris Publications: Aug, 1997 ($1.50, one-shot)

1-Ellis, Robinson, and Moore-s; flip book w/"Pantha" 4.00

VAMPIRELLA/DRACULA: THE CENTENNIAL
Harris Publications: Oct, 1997 ($5.95, one-shot)

1-Ellis, Robinson, and Moore-s; Beachum, Frank/Smith, and Mack/Mays-a Bolton-painted-c 6.00

VAMPIRELLA: INTIMATE VISIONS
Harris Publications: 2006 ($3.95, one-shots)

..., Amanda Conner 1 - r/Vampirella Monthly #1 with commentary; interview; 2 covers 4.00
..., Joe Jusko 1 - r/Vampirella; Blood Lust #1 with commentary; interview; 2 covers 4.00

VAMPIRELLA: JULIE STRAIN SPECIAL
Harris Publications: Sept, 2000 ($3.95, one-shot)

1-Photo-c w/yellow background; interview and photo gallery 4.00

Vampirella Retro #1 © Harris

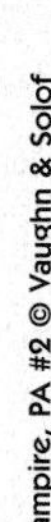
Vampire, PA #2 © Vaughn & Solof

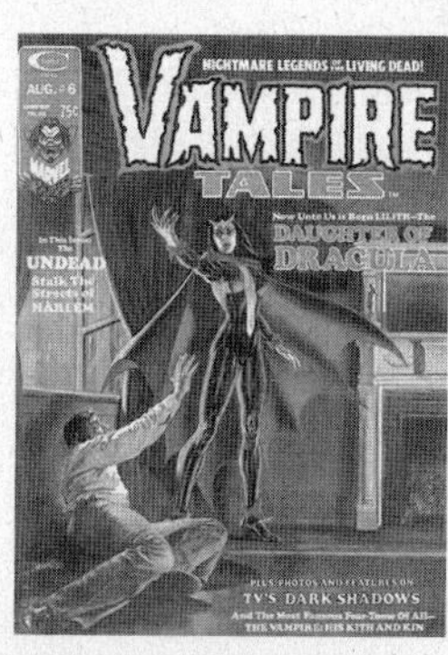

Vampire Tales #6 © MAR

GD VG FN VF VF/NM NM-
2.0 4.0 6.0 8.0 9.0 9.2

1-Limited Edition ($9.95); cover photo w/black background 10.00

VAMPIRELLA/LADY DEATH (Also see Lady Death/Vampirella)
Harris Publications: Feb, 1999 ($3.50, one-shot)
1-Small-a/Nelson painted-c 4.00
1-Valentine Edition ($9.95); pencil-c by Small 10.00

VAMPIRELLA: LEGENDARY TALES
Harris Publications: May, 2000 - No. 2, June, 2000 ($2.95, B&W)
1,2-Reprints from magazine; Cleavenger painted-c 4.00
1,2-($9.95) Variant painted-c by Mike Mayhew 10.00

VAMPIRELLA LIVES
Harris Publications: Dec, 1996 - No. 3, Feb, 1997 ($3.50/$2.95, limited series)
1-Die cut-c; Quesada & Palmiotti-c, Ellis-s/Conner-a 5.00
1-Deluxe Ed.-photo-c 5.00
2,3-($2.95)-Two editions (1 photo-c): 3-J. Scott Campbell-c 4.00

VAMPIRELLA: MORNING IN AMERICA
Harris Publications/Dark Horse Comics: 1991 - No. 4, 1992 ($3.95, B&W, lim. series, 52 pgs.)
1,2-All have Kaluta painted-c 1 2 3 5 6 8
3,4 1 3 4 6 8 10

VAMPIRELLA OF DRAKULON
Harris Publications: Jan, 1996 - No. 5, Sept, 1996 ($2.95)
0-5: All reprints. 0-Jim Silke-c. 3-Polybagged w/card. 4-Texeira-c 4.00

VAMPIRELLA/PAINKILLER JANE
Harris Publications: May, 1998 ($3.50, one-shot)
1-Waid & Augustyn-s/Leonardi & Palmiotti-a 4.00
1-($9.95) Variant-c 10.00

VAMPIRELLA PIN-UP SPECIAL
Harris Publications: Oct, 1995 ($2.95, one-shot)
1-Hughes-c, pin-ups by various 5.00
1-Variant-c 5.00

VAMPIRELLA QUARTERLY
Harris Publications: Spring, 2007 - Summer, 2008 ($4.95/$4.99, quarterly)
Spring, 2007 - Summer, 2008-New stories and re-colored reprints; five or six covers 5.00

VAMPIRELLA: RETRO
Harris Publications: Mar, 1998 - No. 3, May, 1998 ($2.50, B&W, limited series)
1-3: Reprints; Silke painted covers 4.00

VAMPIRELLA: REVELATIONS
Harris Publications: No. 0, Oct, 2005 - No. 3, Feb, 2006 ($2.99, limited series)
0-3-Vampirella's origin retold, Lilith app.; Carey-s/Lilly-a; two covers on each 4.00
... Book 1 TPB (2006, $12.95) r/series; Carey interview, script for #1, Lilly sketch pages 13.00

VAMPIRELLA: SAD WINGS OF DESTINY
Harris Publications: Sept, 1996 ($3.95, one-shot)
1-Jusko-c 5.00

VAMPIRELLA: SECOND COMING
Harris Publications: 2009 - No. 4 ($1.99, limited series)
1-4: 1-Hester-s/Sampere-a; multiple covers on each. 3,4-Rio-a 4.00

VAMPIRELLA/SHADOWHAWK: CREATURES OF THE NIGHT (Also see Shadowhawk)
Harris Publications: 1995 ($4.95, one-shot)
1 5.00

VAMPIRELLA/SHI (See Shi/Vampirella)
Harris Publications: Oct, 1997 ($2.95, one-shot)
1-Ellis-s 4.00
1-Chromium-c 6.00

VAMPIRELLA: SILVER ANNIVERSARY COLLECTION
Harris Publications: Jan, 1997 - No. 4 Apr, 1997 ($2.50, limited series)
1-4: Two editions: Bad Girl by Beachum, Good Girl by Silke 4.00

VAMPIRELLA'S SUMMER NIGHTS
Harris Publications: 1992 (one-shot)
1-Art Adams infinity cover; centerfold by Stelfreeze 3 7 10 19 27 35

VAMPIRELLA STRIKES
Harris Publications: Sept, 1995 - No. 8, Dec, 1996 ($2.95, limited series)
1-8: 1-Photo-c. 2-Deodato-c; polybagged w/card. 5-Eudaemon-c/app; wraparound-c; alternate-c exists. 6-(6/96)-Mark Millar script; Texeira-c; alternate-c exists. 7-Flip book 4.00
1-Newsstand Edition; diff. photo-c., 1-Limited Ed.; diff. photo-c 4.00

Annual 1-(12/96, $2.95) Delano-s; two covers 4.00

VAMPIRELLA: 25TH ANNIVERSARY SPECIAL
Harris Publications: Oct, 1996 ($5.95, squarebound, one-shot)
nn-Reintro The Blood Red Queen of Hearts; James Robinson, Grant Morrison & Warren Ellis scripts; Mark Texeira, Michael Bair & Amanda Conner-a(p); Frank Frazetta-c 7.00
nn-($6.95)-Silver Edition 8.00

VAMPIRELLA VS. DRACULA
Dynamite Entertainment: 2012 - Present ($3.99)
1,2-Harris-s/Rodriguez-a/Linsner-c 4.00

VAMPIRELLA VS. HEMORRHAGE
Harris Publications: Apr, 1997 ($3.50)
1 4.00

VAMPIRELLA VS. PANTHA
Harris Publications: Mar, 1997 ($3.50)
1-Two covers; Millar-s/Texeira-c/a 4.00

VAMPIRELLA/WETWORKS (See Wetworks/Vampirella)
Harris Publications: June, 1997 ($2.95, one-shot)
1 4.00
1-($9.95) Alternate Edition; cardstock-c 10.00

VAMPIRELLA/WITCHBLADE
Harris Publications: 2003; Oct, 2004; Oct, 2005 ($2.99, one-shots)
1-Brian Wood-s/Steve Pugh-a; 3 covers by Texeira, Conner and Pugh 4.00
...: The Feast (10/05, $2.99) Joyce Chin-a; covers by Chin, Conner, Rodriguez 4.00
...: Union of the Damned (10/04, $2.99, one-shot) Sharp-a; three covers 4.00
Trilogy TPB (2006, $12.95) r/one-shots; art gallery and gallery of multiple covers 13.00

VAMPIRE, PA
Moonstone: 2010 - No. 3, Oct, 2010 ($3.99)
1-3: 1-Intro. Vampire Hunter Dean; J.C. Vaughn-s/Brendon & Brian Fraim-a; three covers. 3-Zombie Proof back-up; Spencer-a 4.00

VAMPIRE'S CHRISTMAS, THE (Also see Dark Ivory)
Image Comics: Oct, 2003 ($5.95, over-sized graphic novel)
nn-Linsner-s/a; Dubisch-painted-a 6.00

VAMPIRES: THE MARVEL UNDEAD
Marvel Comics: Dec, 2011 ($3.99, one-shot)
1-Handbook-style profiles of vampire characters in the Marvel Universe; Seeley-c 4.00

VAMPIRE TALES
Marvel Comics Group: Aug, 1973 - No. 11, June, 1975 (75¢, B&W, magazine)
1-Morbius, the Living Vampire begins by Pablo Marcos (1st solo Morbius series & 5th Morbius app.) 7 14 21 48 79 110
2-Intro. Satana; Steranko-r 5 10 15 32 57 70
3,5,6: 3-Satana app. 5-Origin Morbius. 6-1st Lilith app. in this title (see Giant-Size Chillers #1 for debut) 4 8 12 28 44 60
4,7 4 8 12 22 34 45
8-1st solo Blade story (see Tomb of Dracula) 5 10 15 32 51 70
9-Blade app. 4 8 12 28 44 60
10,11 4 8 12 22 34 45
Annual 1(10/75)-Heath-r/#9 4 8 12 22 34 45
NOTE: *Alcala a-6, 8, 9i.* **Boris** *c-4, 6.* **Chaykin** *a-7.* **Everett** *a-1r.* **Gulacy** *a-7p.* **Heath** *a-9.* **Infantino** *a-3r.* **Gil Kane** *a-4, 5r.*

VAMPIRE VERSES, THE
CFD Productions: Aug, 1995 - No. 4, 1995 ($2.95, B&W, mature)
1-4 3.00

VAMPI VICIOUS
Harris Publications (Anarchy Studios): Aug, 2003 - No. 3, Nov, 2003 ($2.99)
1-3; 1-McKeever-s/Dogan-a; 3 covers by Dogan, Lau & Noto. 3-Kau-a 4.00

VAMPI VICIOUS CIRCLE
Harris Publications (Anarchy Studios): Jun, 2004 - No. 3, Sept, 2004 ($2.99/$9.95)
1-3: B. Clay Moore-s 4.00
1-3-($9.95) Limited Edition w/variant-c. 1-Noto-c. 2-Norton-c. 3-Lucas-c 10.00

VAMPI VICIOUS RAMPAGE
Harris Publications (Anarchy Studios): Feb, 2005 - No. 2, Apr, 2005 ($2.99)
1,2: Raab-s/Lau-a; two covers on each 4.00

VAMPI VS. XIN
Harris Publications (Anarchy Studios): Oct, 2004 - No. 2, Jan, 2005 ($2.99)
1,2-Faerber-s/Lau-a; two covers 4.00

Vanguard #6 © Image

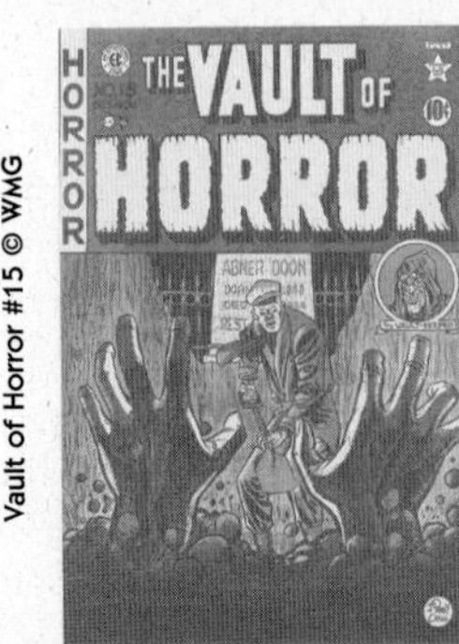

Vault of Horror #15 © WMG

Vengeance of the Moon Knight #9 © MAR

GD 2.0 | VG 4.0 | FN 6.0 | VF 8.0 | VF/NM 9.0 | NM- 9.2

VAMPS
DC Comics (Vertigo): Aug, 1994 - No. 6, Jan, 1995 ($1.95, lim. series, mature)
1-6-Bolland-c 3.00
Trade paperback ($9.95)-r/#1-6 10.00

VAMPS: HOLLYWOOD & VEIN
DC Comics (Vertigo): Feb, 1996 - No. 6, July, 1996 ($2.25, lim. series, mature)
1-6: Winslade-c 3.00

VAMPS: PUMPKIN TIME
DC Comics (Vertigo): Dec, 1998 - No. 3, Feb, 1999 ($2.50, lim. series, mature)
1-3: Quitely-c 3.00

VANGUARD (...Outpost: Earth) (See Megaton)
Megaton Comics: 1987 ($1.50)
1-Erik Larsen-c(p) 4.00

VANGUARD (See Savage Dragon #2)
Image Comics (Highbrow Entertainment): Oct, 1993 - No. 6, 1994 ($1.95)
1-6: 1-Wraparound gatefold-c; Erik Larsen back-up-a; Supreme x-over. 3-(12/93)-Indicia says December 1994. 4-Berzerker back-up. 5-Angel Medina-a(p) 3.00

VANGUARD (See Savage Dragon #2)
Image Comics: Aug, 1996 - No. 4, Feb, 1997 ($2.95, B&W, limited series)
1-4 3.00

VANGUARD: ETHEREAL WARRIORS
Image Comics: Aug, 2000 ($5.95, B&W)
1-Fosco & Larsen-a 6.00

VANGUARD ILLUSTRATED
Pacific Comics: Nov, 1983 - No. 11, Oct, 1984 (Baxter paper)(Direct sales only)
1,3-6,8-11: 1-Nudity scenes 3.00
2-1st app. Stargrazers (see Legends of the Stargrazers; Dave Stevens-c
1 2 3 4 5 7
7-1st app. Mr. Monster (r-in Mr. Monster #1); nudity scenes 5.00
NOTE: ***Evans*** *a-7.* ***Kaluta*** *c-5, 7p.* ***Perez*** *a-6; c-6.* ***Rude*** *a-1-4; c-4.* ***Williamson*** *c-3.*

VANGUARD: STRANGE VISITORS
Image Comics: Oct, 1996 - No.4, Feb, 1997 ($2.95, B&W, limited series)
1-4: 3-Supreme-c/app. 3.00

VAN HELSING: FROM BENEATH THE RUE MORGUE (Based on the 2004 movie)
Dark Horse Comics: Apr, 2004 ($2.99, one-shot)
1-Hugh Jackman photo-c; Dysart-s/Alexander-a 3.00

VANITY (See Pacific Presents #3)
Pacific Comics: Jun, 1984 - No. 2, Aug, 1984 ($1.50, direct sales)
1,2: Origin 3.00

VARIETY COMICS (The Spice of Comics)
Rural Home Publ./Croyden Publ. Co.: 1944 - No. 2, 1945; No. 3, 1946
1-Origin Captain Valiant 21 42 63 126 206 285
2-Captain Valiant 14 28 42 82 121 160
3(1946-Croyden)-Captain Valiant 13 26 39 74 105 135

VARIETY COMICS (See Fox Giants)

VARSITY
Parents' Magazine Institute: 1945
1 9 18 27 47 61 75

VAULT OF EVIL
Marvel Comics Group: Feb, 1973 - No. 23, Nov, 1975
1 (1950s reprints begin) 3 6 9 20 30 40
2-23: 3,4-Brunner-c. 11-Kirby-a 3 6 9 14 20 25
NOTE: ***Ditko*** *a-14r, 15r, 20-22r.* ***Drucker*** *a-10r(Mystic #52), 13r(Uncanny Tales #42).* ***Everett*** *a-11r(Menace #2), 13r(Menace #4); c-10.* ***Heath*** *a-5r.* ***Gil Kane*** *c-1, 6.* ***Kirby*** *a-11.* ***Krigstein*** *a-20r(Uncanny Tales #54).* ***Reinman*** *r-1.* ***Tuska*** *a-6r.*

VAULT OF HORROR (Formerly War Against Crime #1-11) (Also see EC Archives)
E. C. Comics: No. 12, Apr-May, 1950 - No. 40, Dec-Jan, 1954-55
12 (Scarce)-ties w/Crypt Of Terror as 1st horror comic
497 994 1491 3976 6338 8700
13-Morphine story 101 202 303 808 1292 1775
14 89 178 267 712 1131 1550
15- "Terror in the Swamp" is same story w/minor changes as "The Thing in the Swamp" from Haunt of Fear #15 77 154 231 616 983 1350
16 60 120 180 480 765 1050
17-Classic werewolf-c 69 138 207 552 876 1200
18,19 47 94 141 376 601 825
20-25: 22-Frankenstein-c & adaptation. 23-Used in **POP**, pg. 84; Davis-a(2); Ingels bio. 24-Craig bio. 40 80 120 320 510 700
26-B&W & color illos in **POP** 40 80 120 320 510 700
27-29,31-34,36: 31-Ray Bradbury biog. 32-Censored-c. 36- "Pipe Dream" classic opium addict story by Krigstein; "Twin Bill" cited in articles by T.E. Murphy, Wertham
34 68 102 272 436 600
30-Dismemberment-c 44 88 132 352 559 765
35-X-Mas-c 43 86 129 344 547 750
37-1st app. Drusilla, a Vampirella look alike; Williamson-a
36 72 108 288 457 625
38-39: 39-Bondage-c 33 66 99 264 425 585
40-Low distribution 40 80 120 320 510 700
NOTE: ***Craig*** *art in all but No. 13 & 33; c-12-40.* ***Crandall*** *a-33, 34, 39.* ***Davis*** *a-17-38.* ***Evans*** *a-27, 28, 30, 32, 33.* ***Feldstein*** *a-12-16.* ***Ingels*** *a-13-20, 22-40.* ***Kamen*** *a-15-22, 25, 29, 35.* ***Krigstein*** *a-36, 38-40.* ***Kurtzman*** *a-12, 13.* ***Orlando*** *a-24, 31, 40.* ***Wood*** *a-12-14. #22, 29 & 31 have Ray Bradbury adaptations. #16 & 17 have H. P. Lovecraft adaptations.*

VAULT OF HORROR, THE
Gladstone Publ.: Aug, 1990 - No. 6, June, 1991 ($1.95, 68 pgs.)(#4 on: $2.00)
1-Craig-c(r); all contain EC reprints 4.00
2-6: 2,4-6-Craig-c(r). 3-Ingels-c(r) 4.00

VAULT OF HORROR
Russ Cochran/Gemstone Publishing: Sept, 1991 - No. 5, May, 1992 ($2.00); Oct, 1992 - No. 29, Oct, 1999 ($1.50/$2.00/$2.50)
1-29: E.C reprints. 1-4r/VOH #12-15 w/original-c 4.00

V...-COMICS (Morse code for "V" - 3 dots, 1 dash)
Fox Features Syndicate: Jan, 1942 - No. 2, Mar-Apr, 1942
1-Origin V-Man & the Boys; The Banshee & The Black Fury, The Queen of Evil, & V-Agents begin; Nazi-c 135 270 405 864 1482 2100
2-Nazi bondage/torture-c 97 194 291 621 1061 1500

VECTOR
Now Comics: 1986 - No. 4, 1986? ($1.50, 1st color comic by Now Comics)
1-4: Computer-generated art 3.00

VEILS
DC Comics (Vertigo): 1999 ($24.95, one-shot)
Hardcover-($24.95) Painted art and photography; McGreal-s 25.00
Softcover ($14.95) 15.00

VELOCITY (Also see Cyberforce)
Image Comics (Top Cow Productions): Nov, 1995 - No. 3, Jan, 1996 ($2.50, limited series)
1-3: Kurt Busiek scripts in all. 2-Savage Dragon-c/app. 3.00
...: Pilot Season 1 (10/07, $2.99) Casey-s/Maguire-a 3.00
Vol. 2 #1-4 (6/10 - No. 4, 4/11, $3.99) Rocafort-a/Marz-s; multiple covers 4.00

VENGEANCE
Marvel Comics: Sept, 2011 - No. 6, Feb, 2012 ($3.99, limited series)
1-6-Casey-s/Dragotta-a. 1-Magneto and Red Skull app. 4-Loki cover 4.00

VENGEANCE OF THE MOON KNIGHT
Marvel Comics: Nov, 2009 - No. 10, Sept, 2010 ($3.99/$2.99)
1,9: 1-($3.99) Hurwitz-s/Opeña-a; covers by Yu, Ross & Finch; back-up r/Moon Knight #1 ('80) 9-Spider-Man & Sandman app.; Campbell-c 4.00
2-8,10: 2-Sentry app. 5-Spider-Man app. 7,8-Deadpool app. 10-Secret Avengers app. 3.00

VENGEANCE OF VAMPIRELLA (Becomes Vampirella: Death & Destruction)
Harris Comics: Apr, 1994 - No. 25, Apr, 1996 ($2.95)
1-($3.50)-Quesada/Palmiotti "bloodfoil" wraparound-c 1 2 3 5 6 8
1-2nd printing; blue foil-c 4.00
1-Gold 20.00
2-8: 8-Polybagged w/trading card 5.00
9-25: 10-w/coupon for Hyde -25 poster. 11,19-Polybagged w/ trading card. 25-Quesada & Palmiotti red foil-c 4.00
...: Bloodshed (1995, $6.95) 7.00

VENGEANCE OF VAMPIRELLA: THE MYSTERY WALK
Harris Comics: Nov, 1995 ($2.95, one-shot)
0 4.00

VENGEANCE SQUAD
Charlton Comics: July, 1975 - No. 6, May, 1976 (#1-3 are 25¢ issues)
1-Mike Mauser, Private Eye begins by Staton 2 4 6 9 13 16
2-6: Morisi-a in all 1 2 3 5 7 9
5,6 (Modern Comics-r, 1977) 6.00

Venom (2011 series) #2 © MAR

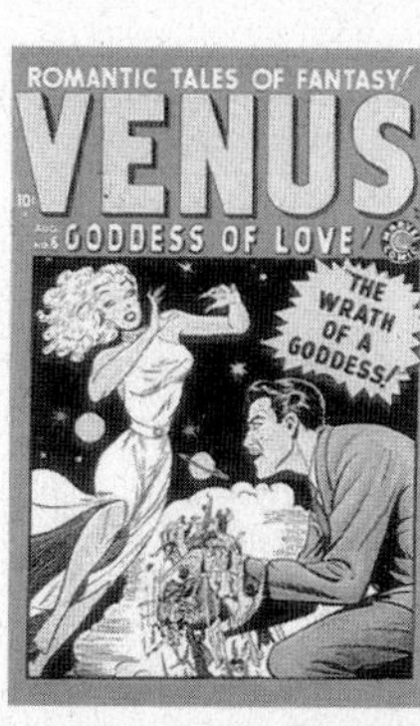

Venus #6 © MAR

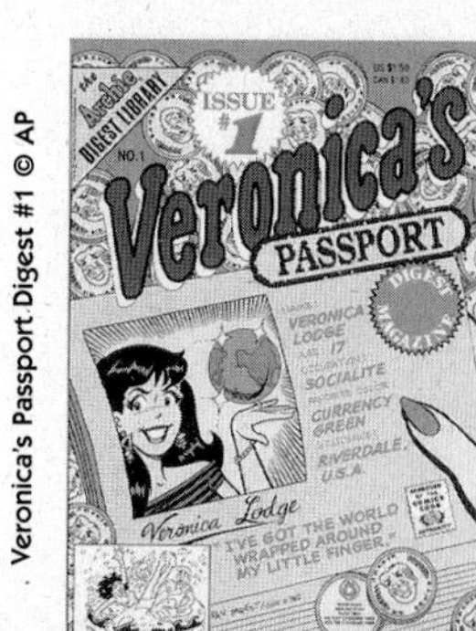

Veronica's Passport Digest #1 © AP

GD 2.0 | VG 4.0 | FN 6.0 | VF 8.0 | VF/NM 9.0 | NM- 9.2

VENOM
Marvel Comics: June, 2003 - No. 18, Nov, 2004 ($2.25)
1-7-Herrera-a/Way-s. 6,7-Wolverine app. 3.00
8-18-($2.99): 8-10-Wolverine-c/app.; Kieth-c. 11-Fantastic Four app. 3.00
... Vol. 1: Shiver (2004, $13.99, TPB) r/#1-5 14.00
... Vol. 2: Run (2004, $19.99, TPB) r/#6-13 20.00
... Vol. 3: Twist (2004, $13.99, TPB) r/#14-18 14.00

VENOM (See Amazing Spider-Man #654 & 654.1)
Marvel Comics: May, 2011 - Present ($3.99/$2.99)
1-Flash Thompson with the symbiote; Remender-s/Tony Moore-a/Quesada-c 4.00
2-12-($2.99) 2-Cover swipe of ASM #300; Kraven app. 3-Deodato-c. 6-8-Spider Island 3.00
13-($3.99) Circle of Four; Red Hulk, X-23, and Ghost Rider app. 4.00
13.1, 13.2, 13.3, 13.4, 14-($2.99) Circle of Four parts 2-6 3.00
...: Flashpoint 1 (2011, $4.99) r/Amazing Spider-Man #654, 654.1 and Venom #1 5.00

VENOM: Marvel Comics (Also see Amazing Spider-Man #298-300)
... ALONG CAME A SPIDER, 1/96 - No. 4, 4/96 ($2.95)-Spider-Man & Carnage app. 3.00
... CARNAGE UNLEASHED, 4/95 - No. 4, 7/95 ($2.95) 3.00
... DARK ORIGIN, 10/08 - No. 5, 2/09 ($2.99) 1-5-Medina-a 3.00
... /DEADPOOL: WHAT IF?, 4/11 ($2.99) Remender-s/Moll-a/Young-c; Galactus app. 3.00
... DEATHTRAP: THE VAULT, 3/93 ($6.95) r/Avengers: Deathtrap: The Vault 7.00
... FUNERAL PYRE, 8/93- No. 3, 10/93 ($2.95)-#1-Holo-grafx foil-c; Punisher app. in all 3.00

VENOM: LETHAL PROTECTOR
Marvel Comics: Feb, 1993 - No. 6, July, 1993 ($2.95, limited series)
1-Red holo-grafx foil-c; Bagley-c/a in all 5.00
1-Gold variant sold to retailers 15.00
1-Black-c (at least 58 copies have been authenticated by CGC since 2000) 9 18 27 61 106 150
NOTE: Counterfeit copies of the black-c exist and are valueless
2-6: Spider-Man app. in all 3.00
... LICENSE TO KILL, 6/97 - No. 3, 8/97 ($1.95) 3.00
... NIGHTS OF VENGEANCE, 8/94 - No. 4, 11/94 ($2.95), #1-Red foil-c 3.00
... ON TRIAL, 3/97 - No. 3, 5/97 ($1.95) 3.00
... SEED OF DARKNESS, 7/97 ($1.95) #(-1) Flashback 3.00
... SEPARATION ANXIETY, 12/94- No. 4, 3/95 ($2.95) #1-Embossed-c 3.00
... SIGN OF THE BOSS, 3/97 - No. 2, 10/97 ($1.99) 3.00
... SINNER TAKES ALL, 8/95 - No. 5, 10/95 ($2.95) 3.00
... SUPER SPECIAL, 8/95($3.95) #1-Flip book 4.00
... THE ENEMY WITHIN, 2/94 - No. 3, 4/94 ($2.95)-Demogoblin & Morbius app.
1-Glow-in-the-dark-c 3.00
... THE FINALE, 11/97 - No. 3, 1/98 ($1.99) 3.00
... THE HUNGER, 8/96- No. 4, 11/96 ($1.95) 3.00
... THE HUNTED, 5/96-No. 3, 7/96 ($2.95) 3.00
... THE MACE, 5/94 - No. 3, 7/94 ($2.95)-#1-Embossed-c 3.00
... THE MADNESS, 11/93- No. 3, 1/94 ($2.95)-Kelley Jones-c/a(p).
1-Embossed-c; Juggernaut app. 3.00
... TOOTH AND CLAW, 12/96 - No. 3, 2/97 ($1.95)-Wolverine-c/app. 3.00
... VS. CARNAGE, 9/04 - No. 4, 12/04 ($2.99)-Milligan-s/Crain-a; Spider-Man app. 3.00
TPB (2004, $9.99) r/#1-4 10.00

VENTURE
AC Comics (Americomics): Aug, 1986 - No. 3, 1986? ($1.75)
1-3: 1-3-Bolt. 1-Astron. 2-Femforce. 3-Fazers 3.00

VENTURE
Image Comics: Jan, 2003 - No. 4, Sept, 2003 ($2.95)
1-4-Faerber-s/Igle-a 3.00

VENUS (See Agents of Atlas, Marvel Spotlight #2 & Weird Wonder Tales)
Marvel/Atlas Comics (CMC 1-9/LCC 10-19): Aug, 1948 - No. 19, Apr, 1952 (Also see Marvel Mystery #91)
1-Venus & Hedy Devine begin; 1st app. Venus; Kurtzman's "Hey Look" 168 336 504 1075 1838 2600
2 90 180 270 576 988 1400
3,5 63 126 189 403 689 975
4-Kurtzman's "Hey Look" 64 128 192 406 696 985
6-9: 6-Loki app. 7,8-Painted-c. 9-Begin 52 pgs.; book-length feature "Whom the Gods Destroy!" 54 108 162 343 574 825
10-S/F-horror issues begin (7/50) 82 164 246 528 902 1275
11-S/F end of the world (11/50) 94 188 282 597 1024 1450
12-Colan-a 53 106 159 334 567 800
13-16-Venus by Everett, 2-3 stories each; covers-#13,15,16; 14-Everett part cover (Venus). 97 194 291 621 1061 1500
17-19-Classic Everett horror & skull covers; Venus app. 17-Bondage-c (scarce) 226 452 678 1446 2473 3500
NOTE: **Berg** *s/f story-13.* **Everett** *c-13, 14(part; Venus only), 15-19.* **Heath** *s/f story-11.* **Maneely** *s/f story 10(3pg.), 16.* **Morisi** *a-19.* **Syd Shores** *c-6.*

VERI BEST SURE FIRE COMICS
Holyoke Publishing Co.: No date (circa 1945) (Reprints Holyoke one-shots)
1-Captain Aero, Alias X, Miss Victory, Commandos of the Devil Dogs, Red Cross, Hammerhead Hawley, Capt. Aero's Sky Scouts, Flagman app.; same-c as Veri Best Sure Shot #1 40 80 120 246 411 575

VERI BEST SURE SHOT COMICS
Holyoke Publishing Co.: No date (circa 1945) (Reprints Holyoke one-shots)
1-Capt. Aero, Miss Victory by Quinlan, Alias X, The Red Cross, Flagman, Commandos of the Devil Dogs, Hammerhead Hawley, Capt. Aero's Sky Scouts; same-c as Veri Best Sure Fire #1 40 80 120 246 411 575

VERMILLION
DC Comics (Helix): Oct, 1996 - No. 12, Sept, 1997 ($2.25/$2.50)
1-12: 1-4: Lucius Shepard scripts. 4,12-Kaluta-c 3.00

VERONICA (Also see Archie's Girls, Betty &...)
Archie Comics: Apr, 1989 - No. 210, Feb, 2012
1-(75¢-c) 1 2 3 5 6 8
2-10: 2-(75¢-c) 5.00
11-38 4.00
39-Love Showdown pt. 4, Cheryl Blossom 6.00
40-70: 34-Neon ink-c 3.00
71-201,203-206: 134-Begin $2.19-c. 152,155-Cheryl Blossom app. 163-Begin $2.25-c 3.00
202-Intro. Kevin Keller, 1st openly gay Archie character; cover has blue background 8.00
202-Second printing; cover has black background 5.00
207-210-Kevin Keller mini-series 3.00

VERONICA'S PASSPORT DIGEST MAGAZINE (Becomes Veronica's Digest Magazine #3 on)
Archie Comics: Nov, 1992 - No. 6 ($1.50/$1.79, digest size)
1 5.00
2-6 3.00

VERONICA'S SUMMER SPECIAL (See Archie Giant Series Magazine #615, 625)

VERTICAL
DC Comics (Vertigo): 2003 ($4.95, 3-1/4" wide pages, one-shot)
1-Seagle-s/Allred & Bond-a; odd format 1/2 width pages with some 20" long spreads 5.00

VERTIGO DOUBLE SHOT
DC Comics (Vertigo): 2008 ($2.99)
1-Reprints House of Mystery (2008) #1 and Young Liars #1 in flip-book format 3.00

VERTIGO: FIRST BLOOD
DC Comics (Vertigo): Feb, 2012 ($7.99, squarebound)
TPB-Reprints first issues of American Vampire, I Zombie, The Unwritten & Sweet Tooth 8.00

VERTIGO: FIRST CUT
DC Comics (Vertigo): 2008 ($4.99, TPB)
TPB-Reprints first issues of DMZ, Army@Love, Jack of Fables, Exterminators, Scalped, Crossing Midnight, and Loveless; preview of Air 5.00

VERTIGO: FIRST OFFENSES
DC Comics (Vertigo): 2005 ($4.99, TPB)
TPB-Reprints first issues of The Invisibles, Preacher, Fables, Sandman Mystery Theater, and Lucifer 5.00

VERTIGO: FIRST TASTE
DC Comics (Vertigo): 2005 ($4.99, TPB)
TPB-Reprints first issues of Y: The Last Man, 100 Bullets, Transmetropolitan, Books of Magick: Life During Wartime, Death: The High Cost of Living, and Saga of the Swamp Thing #21 (Alan Moore's first story on that title) 5.00

VERTIGO GALLERY, THE: DREAMS AND NIGHTMARES
DC Comics (Vertigo): 1995 ($3.50, one-shot)
1-Pin-ups of Vertigo characters by Sienkiewicz, Toth, Van Fleet & others; McKean-c 4.00

VERTIGO JAM
DC Comics (Vertigo): Aug, 1993 ($3.95, one-shot, 68 pgs.)(Painted-c by Fabry)

Vertigo Pop!: London #4 © Milligan & Bond

Vext #1 © DC

V FOR VENDETTA
By Alan Moore and David Lloyd

V For Vendetta #8 © DC

GD 2.0 VG 4.0 FN 6.0 VF 8.0 VF/NM 9.0 NM- 9.2

1-Sandman by Neil Gaiman, Hellblazer, Animal Man, Doom Patrol, Swamp Thing, Kid Eternity & Shade the Changing Man 5.00

VERTIGO POP! BANGKOK
DC Comics (Vertigo): July, 2003 - No. 4, Oct, 2003 ($2.95, limited series)
1-4-Camuncoli-c/a; Jonathan Vankin-s 3.00

VERTIGO POP! LONDON
DC Comics (Vertigo): Jan, 2003 - No. 4, Apr, 2003 ($2.95, limited series)
1-4-Philip Bond-c/a; Peter Milligan-s 3.00

VERTIGO POP! TOKYO
DC Comics (Vertigo): Sept, 2002 - No. 4, Dec, 2002 ($2.95, limited series)
1-4-Seth Fisher-c/a; Jonathan Vankin-s 3.00
Tokyo Days, Bangkok Nights TPB (2009, $19.99) r/#1-4 & Vertogo Pop! Bangkok #1-4 20.00

VERTIGO PREVIEW
DC Comics (Vertigo): 1992 (75¢, one-shot, 36 pgs.)
1-Vertigo previews; Sandman story by Neil Gaiman 3.00

VERTIGO RAVE
DC Comics (Vertigo): Fall, 1994 (99¢, one-shot)
1-Vertigo previews 3.00

VERTIGO RESURRECTED: ...
DC Comics (Vertigo): Dec, 2010 - Present ($7.99, squarebound, reprints)
The Extremist 1 (1/11) r/The Extremist #1-4 8.00
Finals 1 (5/11) r/Finals #1-4; Jill Thompson-a 8.00
Hellblazer 1 (2/11) r/Hellblazer #57,58,245,246 8.00
Hellblazer - Bad Blood 1 (6/11) r/Hellblazer Special: Bad Blood #1-4 8.00
Jonny Double 1 (10/11) r/Jonny Double #1-4; Azzarello-s/Risso-a 8.00
My Faith in Frankie 1 (1/12) r/My Faith in Frankie #1-4; Carey-s 8.00
Sandman Presents - Petrefax 1 (8/11) r/Sandman Presents: Petrefax #1-4 8.00
Sgt. Rock: Between Hell and a Hard Place 1,2 (1/12, 2/12) r/the 2003 HC 8.00
Shoot 1 (12/10) r/short stories by various incl. Quitely, Sale, Bolland, Risso, Jim Lee 8.00
The Eaters 1 (12/11) r/Vertigo Visions - The Eaters and other short stories 8.00
Winter's Edge 1 (2/11) r/Vertigo's Winter Edge #1-3; Bermejo-c 8.00

VERTIGO SECRET FILES
DC Comics (Vertigo): Aug, 2000 ($4.95)
...: Hellblazer 1 (8/00, $4.95) Background info and story summaries 5.00
...: Swamp Thing 1 (11/00, $4.95) Backstories and origins; Hale-c 5.00

VERTIGO VERITE: THE UNSEEN HAND
DC Comics (Vertigo): Sept, 1996 - No. 4, Dec, 1996 ($2.50, limited series)
1-4: Terry LaBan scripts in all 3.00

VERTIGO VISIONS
DC Comics (Vertigo): June, 1993 - Present (one-shots)
Dr. Occult 1 (7/94, $3.95) 4.00
Dr. Thirteen 1 (9/98, $5.95) Howarth-s 6.00
Prez 1 (7/95, $3.95) 4.00
The Geek 1 (6/93, $3.95) 4.00
The Eaters ($4.95, 1995)-Milligan story. 5.00
The Phantom Stranger 1 (10/93, $3.50) 4.00
Tomahawk 1 (7/98, $4.95) Pollack-s 5.00

VERTIGO WINTER'S EDGE
DC Comics (Vertigo): 1998, 1999 ($7.95/$6.95, square-bound, annual)
1-Winter stories by Vertigo creators; Desire story by Gaiman/Bolton; Bolland wraparound-c 8.00
2,3-($6.95)-Winter stories: 2-Allred-c. 3-Bond-c; Desire by Gaiman/Zulli 7.00

VERTIGO X ANNIVERSARY PREVIEW
DC Comics (Vertigo): 2003 (99¢, one-shot, 48 pgs.)
1-Previews of upcoming titles and interviews; Endless Nights, Shade, The Originals 4.00

VERY BEST OF DENNIS THE MENACE, THE
Fawcett Publ.: July, 1979 - No. 2, Apr, 1980 (95¢/$1.00, digest-size, 132 pgs.)
1,2-Reprints 2 4 6 8 10 12

VERY BEST OF DENNIS THE MENACE, THE
Marvel Comics Group: Apr, 1982 - No. 3, Aug, 1982 ($1.25, digest-size)
1-3: Reprints 2 3 4 6 8 10
1,2-Mistakenly printed with DC logo on cover 2 4 6 9 12 15
NOTE: *Hank Ketcham c-all. A few thousand of #1 & 2 were printed with DC emblem.*

VERY VICKY
Meet Danny Ocean: 1993? - No. 8, 1995 ($2.50, B&W)

GD 2.0 VG 4.0 FN 6.0 VF 8.0 VF/NM 9.0 NM- 9.2

1-8, ...: Calling All Hillbillies (1995, $2.50) 3.00

VERY WEIRD TALES (Also see Slithiss Attacks!)
Oceanspray Comics Group: Aug, 2002 - No. 2, Oct, 2002 ($4.00)
1-Mutant revenge, methamphetamine, corporate greed horror stories 1 3 4 6 8 10
2-Weird fantasy and horror stories 1 2 3 5 6 8
NOTE: *Created in prevention classes taught by Jon McClure at the Oceanspray Family Center in Newport, Oregon, and paid for by the Housing Authority of Lincoln County. All books are b&w with color covers. Issues #1-2 penciled and inked by various artists. All comics feature characters created by students and are signed and numbered by Jon McClure. Issues #1-2 have print runs of 100 each.*

VEXT
DC Comics: Mar, 1999 - No. 6, Aug, 1999 ($2.50, limited series)
1-6-Giffen-s. 1-Superman app. 3.00

V FOR VENDETTA
DC Comics: Sept, 1988 - No. 10, May, 1989 ($2.00, maxi-series)
1-Alan Moore scripts in all; David Lloyd-a 1 2 3 4 5 7
2-10 5.00
HC (1990) Limited edition 60.00
HC (2005, $29.99, dustjacket) r/series; foreward by Lloyd; promo art and sketches 30.00
Trade paperback (1990, $14.95) 15.00

VIC BRIDGES FAZERS SKETCHBOOK AND FACT FILE
AC Comics: Nov, 1986 ($1.75)
1 3.00

VICE
Image Comics (Top Cow): Nov, 2005 - No. 5 ($2.99)
1-5-Coleite-s/Kirkham-a. 1-Three covers 3.00
1-Code Red Edition; variant Benitez-c 3.00

VIC FLINT(Crime Buster...)(See Authentic Police Cases #10-14 & Fugitives From Justice #2)
St. John Publ. Co.: Aug, 1948 - No. 5, Apr, 1949 (Newspaper reprints; NEA Service)
1 14 28 42 80 115 150
2 10 20 30 56 76 95
3-5 9 18 27 50 65 80

VIC FLINT (Crime Buster...)
Argo Publ.: Feb, 1956 - No. 2, May, 1956 (Newspaper reprints)
1,2 9 18 27 47 61 75

VIC JORDAN (Also see Big Shot Comics #32)
Civil Service Publ.: April, 1945
1-1944 daily newspaper-r 14 28 42 78 112 145

VICKI (Humor)
Atlas/Seaboard Publ.: Feb, 1975 - No. 4, Aug, 1975 (No. 1,2: 68 pgs.)
1,2-(68 pgs.)-Reprints Tippy Teen; Good Girl art 5 10 15 30 48 65
3,4 (Low print) 5 10 15 32 51 70

VICKI VALENTINE (...Summer Special #1)
Renegade Press: July, 1985 - No. 4, July, 1986 ($1.70, B&W)
1-4: Woggon, Rausch-a; all have paper dolls. 2-Christmas issue 3.00

VICKY
Ace Magazine: Oct, 1948 - No. 5, June, 1949
nn(10/48)-Teenage humor 8 16 24 44 57 70
4(12/48), nn(2/49), 4(4/49), 5(6/49): 5-Dotty app. 8 16 24 40 50 60

VICTORIAN UNDEAD
DC Comics (WildStorm): Jan, 2010 - No. 6, Jun, 2010 ($2.99)
1-6-Sherlock Holmes vs. Zombies; Edginton-s/Fabbri-a. 1-Two covers (Moore, Coleby) 3.00
...: Sherlock Holmes vs. Jekyll and Hyde (12/10, $4.99) Domingues-a/Van Sciver-c 5.00
...: Sherlock Holmes vs. Zombies TPB (2010, $17.99) r/#1-6; character design sketch art 18.00
... Volume 2 (1/11 - No. 5, 5/11) 1-3-($3.99) "Sherlock Holmes vs. Dracula" on-c; Fabbri-a 4.00
... Volume 2 - 4,5-($2.99) "Sherlock Holmes vs. Dracula" on-c; Fabbri-a 3.00

VIC TORRY & HIS FLYING SAUCER (Also see Mr. Monster's...#5)
Fawcett Publications: 1950 (one-shot)
nn-Book-length saucer story by Powell; photo/painted-c 69 138 207 442 759 1075

VICTORY
Topps Comics: June, 1994 ($2.50, unfinished limited series)
1-Kurt Busiek script; Giffen-c/a; Rob Liefeld variant-c exists 3.00

VICTORY
Image Comics: May, 2003 - No. 4, Feb, 2004 ($2.95, limited series)

Vic Verity Magazine #2 © Vic Verity Publ.

Vigilante #25 © DC

Villains United #6 © DC

	GD 2.0	VG 4.0	FN 6.0	VF 8.0	VF/NM 9.0	NM- 9.2

1-4: 1-Two covers; Francisco-a. 4-Two covers 3.00

VICTORY (Volume 2)
Image Comics: Aug, 2004 - No. 4, Jan, 2005 ($2.95, limited series)

1-4: 1-Three covers; Francisco-a 3.00

VICTORY COMICS
Hillman Periodicals: Aug, 1941 - No. 4, Dec, 1941 (#1 by Funnies, Inc.)

	GD	VG	FN	VF	VF/NM	NM-
1-The Conqueror by Bill Everett, The Crusader, & Bomber Burns begin; Conqueror's origin in text; Everett-c	300	600	900	2070	3635	5200
2-Everett-c/a	135	270	405	864	1482	2100
3,4	90	180	270	576	988	1400

VIC VERITY MAGAZINE
Vic Verity Publ: 1945; No. 2, Jan?, 1947 - No. 7, Sept, 1946 (A comic book)

	GD	VG	FN	VF	VF/NM	NM-
1-C. C. Beck-c/a	30	60	90	177	289	400
2-Beck-c	18	36	54	105	165	225
3-7: 6-Beck-a. 7-Beck-c	16	32	48	94	147	200

VIDEO JACK
Marvel Comics (Epic Comics): Nov, 1987 - No. 6, Nov, 1988 ($1.25)

1-5 3.00
6-Neal Adams, Keith Giffen, Wrightson, others-a 5.00

VIETNAM JOURNAL
Apple Comics: Nov, 1987 - No. 16, Apr, 1991 ($1.75/$1.95, B&W)

1-16: Don Lomax-c/a/scripts in all, 1-2nd print 4.00
...: Indian Country Vol. 1 (1990, $12.95)-r/#1-4 plus one new story 13.00

VIETNAM JOURNAL: VALLEY OF DEATH
Apple Comics: June, 1994 - No. 2, Aug, 1994 ($2.75, B&W, limited series)

1,2: By Don Lomax 4.00

VIGILANTE, THE (Also see New Teen Titans #23 & Annual V2#2)
DC Comics: Oct, 1983 - No. 50, Feb, 1988 ($1.25, Baxter paper)

1-Origin 4.00
2-16,19-49: 3-Cyborg app. 4-1st app. The Exterminator; Newton-a(p). 6,7-Origin. 20,21-Nightwing app. 35-Origin Mad Bomber. 47-Batman-c/s 3.00
17,18-Alan Moore scripts 4.00
50-Ken Steacy painted-c 3.00
Annual nn, 2 ('85, '86) 4.00

VIGILANTE
DC Comics: Nov, 2005 - No. 6, Apr, 2006 ($2.99, limited series)

1-6-Bruce Jones-s. 1,2,4-6-Ben Oliver-a 3.00

VIGILANTE
DC Comics: Feb, 2009 - No. 12, Jan, 2010 ($2.99)

1-12: 1-Wolfman-s/Leonardi-a. 3-Nightwing app. 5-X-over with Titans and Teen Titans 3.00

VIGILANTE: CITY LIGHTS, PRAIRIE JUSTICE (Also see Action Comics #42, Justice League of America #78, Leading Comics & World's Finest #244)
DC Comics: Nov, 1995 - No. 4, Feb, 1996 ($2.50, limited series)

1-4: James Robinson scripts/Tony Salmons-a/Mark Chiarello-c 3.00
TPB (2009, $19.99) r/#1-4 20.00

VIGILANTES, THE
Dell Publishing Co.: No. 839, Sept, 1957

	GD	VG	FN	VF	VF/NM	NM-
Four Color 839-Movie	7	14	21	46	76	105

VIGILANTE 8: SECOND OFFENSE
Chaos! Comics: Dec, 1999 ($2.95, one-shot)

1-Based on video game 3.00

VIKING PRINCE, THE
DC Comics: 2010 ($39.99, hardcover with dustjacket)

HC-Recolored reprints of apps. in Brave and the Bold #1-5, 7-24 & team-up with Sgt. Rock in Our Army at War #162,163; new intro. by Joe Kubert 40.00

VIKINGS, THE (Movie)
Dell Publishing Co.: No. 910, May, 1958

	GD	VG	FN	VF	VF/NM	NM-
Four Color 910-Buscema-a, Kirk Douglas photo-c	8	16	24	53	89	125

VILLAINS AND VIGILANTES
Eclipse Comics: Dec, 1986 - No. 4, May, 1987 ($1.50/$1.75, limited series, Baxter paper)

1-4: Based on role-playing game. 2-4 ($1.75-c) 3.00

VILLAINS FOR HIRE
Marvel Comics: No. 0.1, Jan, 2012; No. 1, Feb, 2012 - No. 4, May, 2012 ($2.99)

0.1-Misty Knight, Silver Sable, Black Panther app.; Arlem-a 3.00
1-4-Abnett & Lanning-s/Arlem-a; Misty Knight app. 3.00

VILLAINS UNITED (Leads into Infinite Crisis)
DC Comics: July, 2005 - No. 6, Dec, 2005 ($2.95/$2.50, limited series)

1-6-Simone-s/JG Jones-c. 1-The Secret Six and the "Society" form 3.00
...: Infinite Crisis Special 1 (6/06, $4.99) Simone-s/Eaglesham-a 5.00
TPB (2005, $12.99) r/#1-6; background info on villains 13.00

VILLAINY OF DOCTOR DOOM, THE
Marvel Comics: 1999 ($17.95, TPB)

nn-Reprints early battle with the Fantastic Four 18.00

VIMANARAMA
DC Comics (Vertigo): Apr, 2005 - No. 3, June, 2005 ($2.95, limited series)

1-3-Grant Morrison-s/Philip Bond-a 3.00
TPB (2005, $12.99) r/#1-3 13.00

VINTAGE MAGNUS (...Robot Fighter)
Valiant: Jan, 1992 - No. 4, Apr, 1992 ($2.25, limited series)

1-4: 1-Layton-c; r/origin from Magnus R.F. #22 3.00

VINYL UNDERGROUND
DC Comics (Vertigo): Dec, 2007 - No. 12, Nov, 2008 ($2.99)

1-12: 1-Spencer-s/Gane & Stewart-a/Phillips-c 3.00
...: Pretty Dead Things TPB ('08, $17.99) r/#6-12 18.00
...: Watching the Detectives TPB ('08, $9.99) r/#1-5; David Laphan intro. 10.00

VIOLATOR (Also see Spawn #2)
Image Comics (Todd McFarlane Prods.): May, 1994 - No. 3, Aug, 1994 ($1.95, lim. series)

1-Alan Moore scripts in all 5.00
2,3: Bart Sears-c(p)/a(p) 4.00

VIOLATOR VS. BADROCK
Image Comics (Extreme Studios): May, 1995 - No. 4, Aug, 1995 ($2.50, limited series)

1-4: Alan Moore scripts in all. 1-1st app Celestine; variant-c (3?) 3.00

VIOLENT MESSIAHS (...: Lamenting Pain on cover for #9-12, numbered as #1-4)
Image Comics: June, 2000 - No. 12 ($2.95)

1-Two covers by Travis Smith and Medina 4.00
1-Tower Records variant edition 5.00
2-8: 5-Flip book sketchbook 3.00
9-12-Lamenting Pain; 2 covers on each 3.00
...: Genesis (12/01, $5.95) r/'97 B&W issue, Wizard 1/2 prologue 6.00
...: The Book of Job TPB (7/02, $24.95) r/#1-8; Foreward by Gossett 25.00

VIP (TV)
TV Comics: 2000 ($2.95, unfinished series)

1-Based on the Pamela Lee (Anderson) TV show; photo-c 3.00

VIPER (TV)
DC Comics: Aug, 1994 - No. 4, Nov, 1994 ($1.95, limited series)

1-4-Adaptation of television show 3.00

VIRGINIAN, THE (TV)
Gold Key: June, 1963

	GD	VG	FN	VF	VF/NM	NM-
1(10060-306)-Part photo-c of James Drury plus photo back-c	4	8	12	28	44	60

VIRTUA FIGHTER (Video Game)
Marvel Comics: Aug, 1995 (2.95, one-shot)

1-Sega Saturn game 3.00

VIRUS
Dark Horse Comics: 1993 - No. 4, 1993 ($2.50, limited series)

1-4: Ploog-c 3.00

VISION, THE
Marvel Comics: Nov, 1994 - No. 4, Feb, 1995 ($1.75, limited series)

1-4 3.00

VISION, THE (AVENGERS ICONS: ...)
Marvel Comics: Oct, 2002 - No. 4, Jan, 2003 ($2.99, limited series)

1-4-Geoff Johns-s/Ivan Reis-a 3.00
...: Yesterday and Tomorrow TPB (2005, $14.99) r/#1-4 & Avengers #57 (1st app.) 15.00

VISION AND THE SCARLET WITCH, THE (See Marvel Fanfare)
Marvel Comics Group: Nov, 1982 - No. 4, Feb, 1983 (Limited series)

1-4: 2-Nuklo & Future Man app. 4.00

VISION AND THE SCARLET WITCH, THE

Voltron (2012 series) #1 © WEP

Voodoo (2011 series) #1 © DC

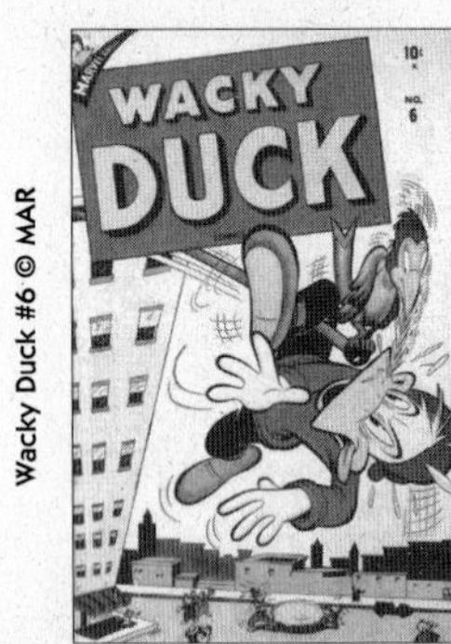

Wacky Duck #6 © MAR

GD VG FN VF VF/NM NM-
2.0 4.0 6.0 8.0 9.0 9.2

GD VG FN VF VF/NM NM-
2.0 4.0 6.0 8.0 9.0 9.2

Marvel Comics Group: Oct, 1985 - No. 12, Sept, 1986 (Maxi-series)
V2#1-12: 1-Origin; 1st app. in Avengers #57. 2-West Coast Avengers x-over 4.00

VISIONS
Vision Publications: 1979 - No. 5, 1983 (B&W, fanzine)
1-Flaming Carrot begins (1st app?); N. Adams-c 5 10 15 35 55 75
2-N. Adams, Rogers-a; Gulacy back-c; signed & numbered to 2000
5 10 15 30 48 65
3-Williamson-c(p); Steranko back-c 4 8 12 22 34 45
4-Flaming Carrot-c & info. 4 8 12 22 34 45
5-1 pg. Flaming Carrot 3 6 9 16 23 30
NOTE: ***Eisner** a-4. **Miller** a-4. **Starlin** a-3. **Williamson** a-5. After #4, Visions became an annual publication of The Atlanta Fantasy Fair.*

VISITOR, THE
Valiant/Acclaim Comics (Valiant): Apr, 1995 - No. 13, Nov, 1995 ($2.50)
1-13: 8-Harbinger revealed. 13-Visitor revealed to be Sting from Harbinger 3.00

VISITOR VS. THE VALIANT UNIVERSE, THE
Valiant: Feb, 1995 - No. 2, Mar, 1995 ($2.95, limited series)
1,2 3.00

VIXEN: RETURN OF THE LION (From Justice League of America)
DC Comics: Dec, 2008 - No. 5, Apr, 2009 ($2.99, limited series)
1-5-G. Willow Wilson-s/Cafu-a; Justice League app. 3.00
TPB (2009, $17.99) r/#1-5 18.00

VOGUE (Also see Youngblood)
Image Comics (Extreme Studios): Oct, 1995 - No.3, Jan, 1996 ($2.50, limited series)
1-3: 1-Liefeld-c, 1-Variant-c 3.00

VOID INDIGO (Also see Marvel Graphic Novel)
Marvel Comics (Epic Comics): 11/84 - No. 2, 3/85 ($1.50, direct sales, unfinished series, mature)
1,2: Cont'd from Marvel G.N.; graphic sex & violence 3.00

VOLCANIC REVOLVER
Oni Press: Dec, 1998 - No. 3, Mar, 1999 ($2.95, B&W, limited series)
1-3: Scott Morse-s/a 3.00
TPB (12/99, $9.95, digest size) r/#1-3 and Oni Double Feature #7 prologue 10.00

VOLTRON (TV)
Modern Publishing: 1985 - No. 3, 1985 (75¢, limited series)
1-3: Ayers-a in all 6.00

VOLTRON (Volume 1)
Dynamite Entertainment: 2011 - Present ($3.99)
1-3: 1-Padilla-a; covers by Alex Ross, Sean Chen & Wagner Reis. 2,3-Two covers 4.00

VOLTRON: A LEGEND FORGED (TV)
Devils Due Publishing: Jul, 2008 - No. 5, Apr, 2009 ($3.50)
1-5-Blaylock-s/Bear-a; 4 covers 3.50

VOLTRON: DEFENDER OF THE UNIVERSE (TV)
Image Comics: No. 0, May, 2003 - No. 5, Sept, 2003 ($2.50)
0-Jolley-s/Brooks-a; character pin-ups with background info 3.00
1-5-($2.95) 1-Three covers by Norton, Brooks and Andrews; Norton-a 3.00
...: Revelations TPB (2004, $11.95, digest-sized) r/#1-5; cover gallery 12.00

VOLTRON: DEFENDER OF THE UNIVERSE (TV)
Image Comics: Jan, 2004 - No. 11, Dec, 2004 ($2.95)
1-11: 1-Jolley-s; wraparound-c 3.00

VOODA (Jungle Princess) (Formerly Voodoo) (See Crown Comics)
Ajax-Farrell (Four Star Publications): No. 20, April, 1955 - No. 22, Aug, 1955
20-Baker-c/a (r/Seven Seas #6) 40 80 120 242 401 560
21,22-Baker-a plus Kamen/Baker story, Kimbo Boy of Jungle, & Baker-c(p) in all.
22-Censored Jo-Jo-r (name Powaa) 36 72 108 216 351 485
NOTE: *#20-22 each contain one heavily censored-r of South Sea Girl by **Baker** from Seven Seas Comics with name changed to Vooda. #20-r/Seven Seas #6; #21-r/#4; #22-r/#3.*

VOODOO (Weird Fantastic Tales) (Vooda #20 on)
Ajax-Farrell (Four Star Publ.): May, 1952 - No. 19, Jan-Feb, 1955
1-South Sea Girl-r by Baker 65 130 195 416 708 1000
2-Rulah story-r plus South Sea Girl from Seven Seas #2 by Baker (name changed from Alani to El'nee) 52 104 156 328 552 775
3-Bakerish-a; man stabbed in face 41 82 123 256 428 600
4,8-Baker-r. 8-Severed head panels 41 82 123 256 428 600
5-Nazi death camp story (flaying alive) 39 78 117 240 395 550
6,7,9,10: 6-Severed head panels 37 74 111 222 361 500
11-18: 14-Zombies take over America. 15-Opium drug story-r/Ellery Queen #3. 16-Post nuclear world story.17-Electric chair panels
34 68 102 199 325 450
19-Bondage-c; Baker-r(2)/Seven Seas #5 w/minor changes & #1, heavily modified; last pre-code; contents & covers change to jungle theme
40 80 120 242 401 560
Annual 1(1952, 25¢, 100 pgs.)-Baker-a (scarce) 142 284 426 909 1555 2200

VOODOO
Image Comics (WildStorm): Nov, 1997 - No. 4, Mar, 1998 ($2.50, lim. series)
1-4: Alan Moore-s in all; Hughes-c. 2-4-Rio-a 3.00
1-Platinum Ed 10.00
Dancing on the Dark TPB ('99, $9.95) r/#1-4 10.00
...-Zealot: Skin Trade (8/95, $4.95) 5.00

VOODOO (DC New 52)
DC Comics: Nov, 2011 - Present ($2.99)
1-7: 1-Marz-s/Basri-a/c. 3-Green Lantern (Kyle) app. 3.00

VOODOO (See Tales of...)

VOODOO CHILD (Weston Cage & Nicolas Cage's...)
Virgin Comics: July, 2007 - No. 6, Dec, 2007 ($2.99)
1-6: 1-Mike Carey-s/Dean Hyrapiet-a; covers by Hyrapiet & Templesmith 3.00
Vol. 1 TPB (1/08, $14.99) r/#1-6; variant covers; intro by Weston Cage & Nicolas Cage 15.00

VOODOOM
Oni Press: June, 2000 ($4.95, B&W)
1-Scott Morse-s/Jim Mahfood-a 5.00

VORTEX
Vortex Publs.: Nov, 1982 - No. 15, 1988 (No month) ($1.50/$1.75, B&W)
1 ($1.95)-Peter Hsu-a; Ken Steacy-c; nudity 1 2 3 5 7 9
2,12: 2-1st app. Mister X (on-c only). 12-Sam Kieth-a 6.00
3-11,13-15 3.00

VORTEX
Comico: 1991 - No. 2? ($2.50, limited series)
1,2: Heroes from The Elementals 3.00

VOYAGE TO THE BOTTOM OF THE SEA (Movie, TV)
Dell Publishing Co./Gold Key: No. 1230, Sept-Nov, 1961; Dec, 1964 - #16, Apr, 1970 (Painted-c)
Four Color 1230 (1961) 10 20 30 67 124 180
10133-412(#1, 12/64)(Gold Key) 8 16 24 51 86 120
2(7/65) - 5: Photo back-c, 1-5 5 10 15 35 55 75
6-14 4 8 12 28 44 60
15,16-Reprints 3 6 9 18 27 35

VOYAGE TO THE DEEP
Dell Publishing Co.: Sept-Nov, 1962 - No. 4, Nov-Jan, 1964 (Painted-c)
1 5 10 15 35 55 75
2-4 4 8 12 24 37 50

WACKO
Ideal Publ. Corp.: Sept, 1980 - No. 3, Oct, 1981 (84 pgs., B&W, magazine)
1-3 2 4 6 8 11 14

WACKY ADVENTURES OF CRACKY (Also see Gold Key Spotlight)
Gold Key: Dec, 1972 - No. 12, Sept, 1975
1 3 6 9 14 20 26
2 2 4 6 10 14 18
3-12 2 4 6 8 10 12
(See March of Comics #405, 424, 436, 448)

WACKY DUCK (...Comics #3-6; formerly Dopey Duck; Justice Comics #7 on) (See Film Funnies)
Marvel Comics (NPP): No. 3, Fall, 1946 - No. 6, Summer, 1947; Aug, 1948 - No. 2, Oct, 1948
3 25 50 75 150 245 340
4-Infinity-c 21 42 63 126 206 285
5,6(1947)-Becomes Justice comics 19 38 57 111 176 240
1(1948) 19 38 57 111 176 240
2(1948) 15 30 45 84 127 170
I.W. Reprint #1,2,7('58): 1-r/Wacky Duck #6 2 4 6 9 13 16
Super Reprint #10(I.W. on-c, Super-inside) 2 4 6 9 13 16

WACKY QUACKY (See Wisco)

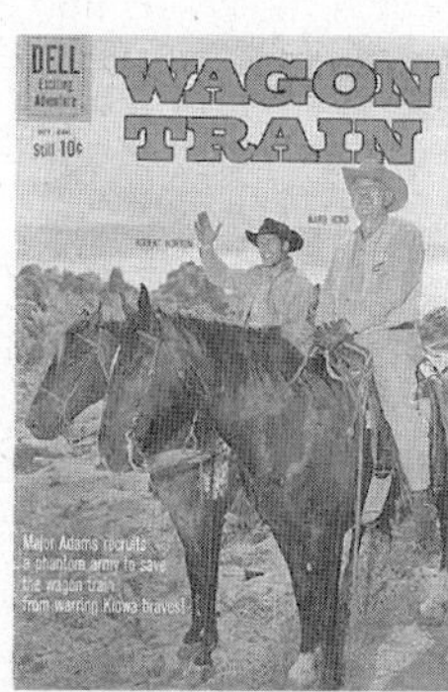

Wagon Train #7 © DELL

The Walking Dead #31 © Robert Kirkman

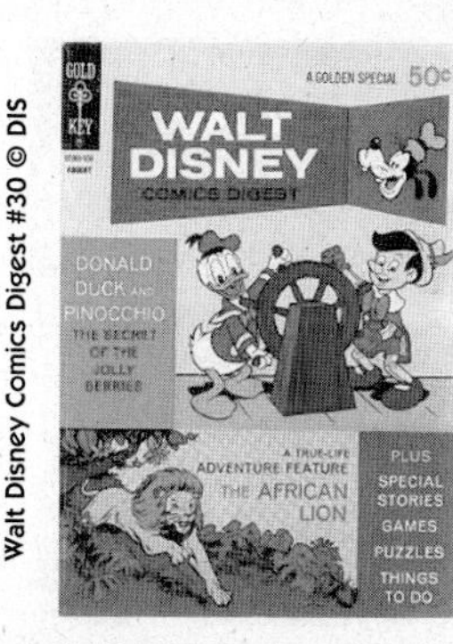

Walt Disney Comics Digest #30 © DIS

WACKY RACES (TV)
Gold Key: Aug, 1969 - No. 7, Apr, 1972 (Hanna-Barbera)

	GD 2.0	VG 4.0	FN 6.0	VF 8.0	VF/NM 9.0	NM- 9.2
1	5	10	15	35	55	75
2-7	4	8	12	22	34	45

WACKY SQUIRREL (Also see Dark Horse Presents)
Dark Horse Comics: Oct, 1987 - No. 4, 1988 ($1.75, B&W)

	GD 2.0	VG 4.0	FN 6.0	VF 8.0	VF/NM 9.0	NM- 9.2
1-4: 4-Superman parody						3.00
Halloween Adventure Special 1 (1987, $2.00)						3.00
Summer Fun Special 1 (1988, $2.00)						3.00

WACKY WITCH (Also see Gold Key Spotlight)
Gold Key: March, 1971 - No. 21, Dec, 1975

	GD 2.0	VG 4.0	FN 6.0	VF 8.0	VF/NM 9.0	NM- 9.2
1	4	8	12	24	37	50
2	3	6	9	14	20	26
3-10	2	4	6	10	14	18
11-21	2	4	6	8	10	12

(See March of Comics #374, 398, 410, 422, 434, 446, 458, 470, 482)

WACKY WOODPECKER (See Two Bit the...)
I. W. Enterprises/Super Comics: 1958; 1963

	GD 2.0	VG 4.0	FN 6.0	VF 8.0	VF/NM 9.0	NM- 9.2
I.W. Reprint #1,2,7 (nd-reprints Two Bit...): 7-r/Two-Bit, the Wacky Woodpecker #1.	2	4	6	8	11	14
Super Reprint #10('63): 10-r/Two-Bit, The Wacky Woodpecker #?	2	4	6	8	11	14

WAGON TRAIN (1st Series) (TV) (See Western Roundup under Dell Giants)
Dell Publishing Co.: No. 895, Mar, 1958 - No. 13, Apr-June, 1962 (All photo-c)

	GD 2.0	VG 4.0	FN 6.0	VF 8.0	VF/NM 9.0	NM- 9.2
Four Color 895 (#1)	10	20	30	67	124	180
Four Color 971(#2),1019(#3)	7	14	21	44	72	100
4(1-3/60),6-13	6	12	18	39	62	85
5-Toth-a	6	12	18	42	69	95

WAGON TRAIN (2nd Series)(TV)
Gold Key: Jan, 1964 - No. 4, Oct, 1964 (All front & back photo-c)

	GD 2.0	VG 4.0	FN 6.0	VF 8.0	VF/NM 9.0	NM- 9.2
1-Tufts-a in all	5	10	15	32	51	70
2-4	4	8	12	24	37	50

WAITING PLACE, THE
Slave Labor Graphics: Apr, 1997 - No. 6, Sept, 1997 ($2.95)

	GD 2.0	VG 4.0	FN 6.0	VF 8.0	VF/NM 9.0	NM- 9.2
1-6-Sean McKeever-s						3.00
Vol. 2 - 1(11/99), 2-11						3.00
12-($4.95)						5.00

WAITING ROOM WILLIE (See Sad Case of...)

WAKE THE DEAD
IDW Publ.: Sept, 2003 - No. 5, Mar, 2004 ($3.99, limited series)

	GD 2.0	VG 4.0	FN 6.0	VF 8.0	VF/NM 9.0	NM- 9.2
1-5-Steve Niles-s/Chee-a						4.00
TPB (6/04, $19.99) r/series; intro. by Michael Dougherty; embossed die cut cover						20.00

WALK IN (Dave Stewart's ...)
Virgin Comics: Dec, 2006 - No. 6, May, 2007 ($2.99)

	GD 2.0	VG 4.0	FN 6.0	VF 8.0	VF/NM 9.0	NM- 9.2
1-6: 1-5-Parker-s/Padlekar-a. 6-Parker-a						3.00

WALKING DEAD, THE (Inspired the 2010 AMC television series)
Image Comics: Oct, 2003 - Present ($2.95/$2.99, B&W)

	GD 2.0	VG 4.0	FN 6.0	VF 8.0	VF/NM 9.0	NM- 9.2
1-Robert Kirkman-s in all/Tony Moore-a	7	14	21	45	73	250
1 Special Edition (5/08, $3.99) r/#1; Kirkman afterword; original script and proposal						6.00
2-Tony Moore-a through #6	4	8	12	28	44	60
3,4	3	6	9	20	30	40
5,6: 6-Shane killed	3	6	9	16	23	30
7-12: 7-Charlie Adlard-a begins; 1st app. Tyreese	3	6	9	14	20	25
13-18,20: 13-Prison arc begins	2	4	6	9	12	15
19-1st app. Michonne	8	16	24	53	89	125
21-26,28-50: 25-Adlard covers begin. 28-Rick loses his hand. 46-Tyreese killed. 48-Lori, Herschel, others killed	2	3	4	6	8	10
27-1st app of The Governor	4	8	12	28	44	60
50-Variant wraparound superhero-style cover by Erik Larsen						100.00
51-60,62-74,76-95: 53-1st app. Abraham & Rosita. 58-Morgan returns. 66-Dale dies. 70-1st Douglas Monroe. 85-Flip book w/Witch Doctor #0. 86-Flip book w/Elephantmen. 92-Intro. Paul Monroe (Jesus)						6.00
61-Preview of Chew; 1st app. Gabriel	2	4	6	11	16	20
63-Flip book with B&W reprint of Chew #1	2	3	4	6	8	10
75-(7/10, $3.99) Orange background-c; back-up alien/sci-fi "fantasy" in color; TV series preview with cast photos						6.00
75-Variant-c homage to issue #1						15.00
Image Firsts: The Walking Dead #1 (3/10, $1.00) reprints #1						3.00
... Book 1 HC (2006, $29.99) r/#1-12; sketch pages, cover gallery; Kirkman afterword						30.00
... Book 2 HC (2006, $29.99) r/#13-24; sketch pages, cover gallery						30.00
... Book 3 HC (2007, $29.99) r/#25-36; sketch pages, cover gallery						30.00
... Book 4 HC (2008, $29.99) r/#37-48; sketch pages, cover gallery						30.00
... Book 5 HC (2010, $29.99) r/#49-60; sketch pages, cover gallery						30.00
...Vol. 1: Days Gone Bye (5/04, $9.95, TPB) r/#1-4						10.00
...Vol. 2: Miles Behind Us (10/04, $12.95, TPB) r/#7-12						13.00
...Vol. 3: Safety Behind Bars (2005, $12.95, TPB) r/#13-18						13.00
...Vol. 4: The Heart's Desire (2005, $12.99, TPB) r/#19-24						13.00
...Vol. 5: The Best Defense (2006, $12.99, TPB) r/#25-30						13.00
...Vol. 6: This Sorrowful Life (2007, $12.99, TPB) r/#31-36						13.00
...Vol. 7: The Calm Before (2007, $12.99, TPB) r/#37-42						13.00
...Vol. 8: Made to Suffer (2008, $14.99, TPB) r/#43-48						15.00
...Vol. 9: Here We Remain (2009, $14.99, TPB) r/#49-54						15.00
...Vol. 10: The Road Ahead (2009, $14.99, TPB) r/#55-60						15.00
...Vol. 11: Fear the Hunters (2010, $14.99, TPB) r/#61-66						15.00
...Vol. 12: Life Among Them (2010, $14.99, TPB) r/#67-72						15.00
...Vol. 13: Too Far Gone (2010, $14.99, TPB) r/#73-78						15.00
...Vol. 14: No Way Out (2011, $14.99, TPB) r/#79-84						15.00
...Vol. 15: We Find Ourselves (2011, $14.99, TPB) r/#85-90						15.00

WALKING DEAD SURVIVORS' GUIDE, THE
Image Comics: Apr, 2011 - No. 4 ($2.99, B&W)

	GD 2.0	VG 4.0	FN 6.0	VF 8.0	VF/NM 9.0	NM- 9.2
1-4-Alphabetical listings of character profiles, first (and last) apps. and current status						5.00

WALKING DEAD WEEKLY, THE (Reprints)
Image Comics: Jan, 2011 - No. 52, Dec, 2011 ($2.99, B&W, weekly)

	GD 2.0	VG 4.0	FN 6.0	VF 8.0	VF/NM 9.0	NM- 9.2
1-Reprints issues with original letter columns; new Kirkman afterword						40.00
1-Arizona Comic Con variant-c						30.00
2-6						8.00
7-18,20-26,28-52						5.00
19-r/1st Michonne						15.00
27-r/1st app. The Governor						10.00

WALL·E (Based on the Disney/Pixar movie)
BOOM! Studios: No. 0, Nov, 2009 - No. 7, Jun, 2010 ($2.99)

	GD 2.0	VG 4.0	FN 6.0	VF 8.0	VF/NM 9.0	NM- 9.2
0-7: 0-Prequel; J. Torres-s						3.00

WALLY (Teen-age)
Gold Key: Dec, 1962 - No. 4, Sept, 1963

	GD 2.0	VG 4.0	FN 6.0	VF 8.0	VF/NM 9.0	NM- 9.2
1	3	6	9	21	32	42
2-4	3	6	9	17	25	32

WALLY THE WIZARD
Marvel Comics (Star Comics): Apr, 1985 - No. 12, Mar, 1986 (Children's comic)

	GD 2.0	VG 4.0	FN 6.0	VF 8.0	VF/NM 9.0	NM- 9.2
1-12: Bob Bolling a-1,3; c-1,9,11,12						5.00
1-Variant with "Star Chase" game on last page and inside back-c						9.00

WALLY WOOD'S T.H.U.N.D.E.R. AGENTS (See Thunder Agents)
Deluxe Comics: Nov, 1984 - No. 5, Oct, 1986 ($2.00, 52 pgs.)

	GD 2.0	VG 4.0	FN 6.0	VF 8.0	VF/NM 9.0	NM- 9.2
1-5: 5-Jerry Ordway-c/a in Wood style						6.00

NOTE: ***Anderson** a-2i, 3i. **Buckler** a-4. **Ditko** a-3, 4. **Giffen** a-1p-4p. **Perez** a-1p, 2, 4; c-1-4.*

WALT DISNEY CHRISTMAS PARADE (Also see Christmas Parade)
Whitman Publ. Co. (Golden Press): Wint, 1977 ($1.95, cardboard-c, 224 pgs.)

	GD 2.0	VG 4.0	FN 6.0	VF 8.0	VF/NM 9.0	NM- 9.2
11191-Barks-r/Christmas in Disneyland #1, Dell Christmas Parade #9 & Dell Giant #53	4	8	12	26	41	55

WALT DISNEY COMICS DIGEST
Gold Key: June, 1968 - No. 57, Feb, 1976 (50¢, digest size)

	GD 2.0	VG 4.0	FN 6.0	VF 8.0	VF/NM 9.0	NM- 9.2
1-Reprints Uncle Scrooge #5; 192 pgs.	7	14	21	49	82	115
2-4-Barks-r	5	10	15	35	55	75
5-Daisy Duck by Barks (8 pgs.); last published story by Barks (art only) plus 21 pg. Scrooge-r by Barks	8	16	24	51	86	120
6-13-All Barks-r	4	8	12	22	34	45
14,15	3	6	9	16	23	30
16-Reprints Donald Duck #26 by Barks	3	6	9	21	32	42
17-20-Barks-r	3	6	9	18	27	35
21-31,33,35-37-Barks-r; 24-Toth Zorro	3	6	9	16	23	30
32,41,45,47-49	2	4	6	11	16	20
34,38,39: 34-Reprints 4-Color #318. 38-Reprints Christmas in Disneyland #1. 39-Two Barks-r/WDC&S #272, 4-Color #1073 plus Toth Zorro-r	3	6	9	16	23	30
40-Mickey Mouse-r by Gottfredson	2	4	6	13	18	22
42,43-Barks-r	2	4	6	13	18	22
44-(Has Gold Key emblem, 50¢)-Reprints 1st story of 4-Color #29,256,275,282	5	10	15	32	51	70

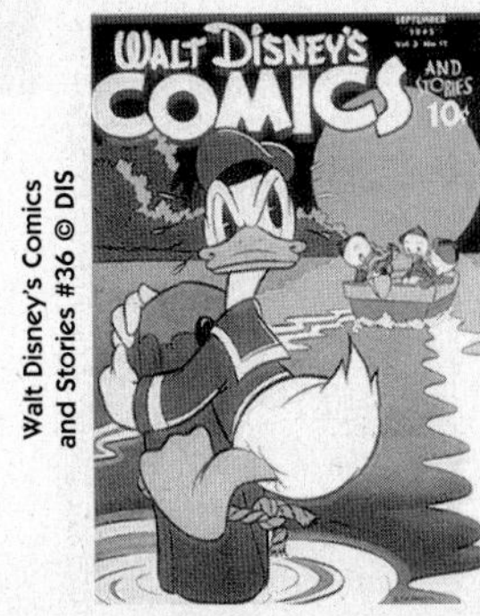

Walt Disney's Comics and Stories #36 © DIS

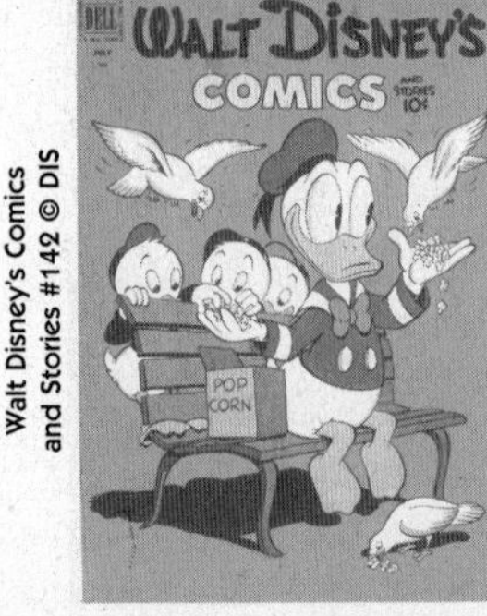

Walt Disney's Comics and Stories #142 © DIS

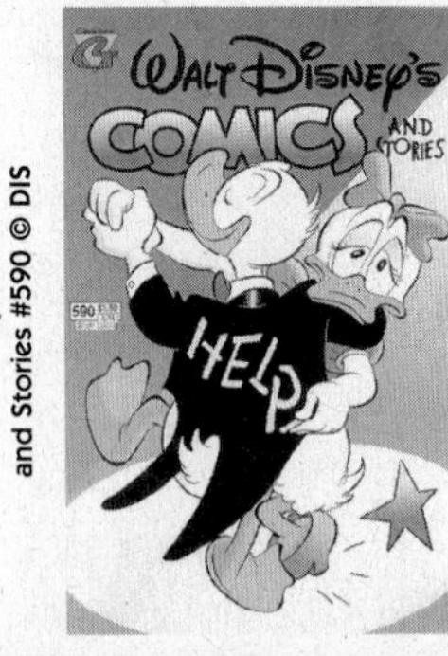

Walt Disney's Comics and Stories #590 © DIS

GD 2.0 VG 4.0 FN 6.0 VF 8.0 VF/NM 9.0 NM- 9.2

44-Republished in 1976 by Whitman; not identical to original; a bit smaller, blank back-c, 69¢ 3 6 9 16 23 30
46,50,52-Barks-r. 52-Barks-r/WDC&S #161,132 2 4 6 11 16 20
51-Reprints 4-Color #71 3 6 9 16 23 30
53-55: 53-Reprints Dell Giant #30. 54-Reprints Donald Duck Beach Party #2.
55-Reprints Dell Giant #49 2 4 6 10 14 18
56-r/Uncle Scrooge #32 (Barks) 2 4 6 13 18 22
57-r/Mickey Mouse Almanac('57) & two Barks stories 2 4 6 11 16 20
NOTE: *Toth a-52r. #1-10, 196 pgs.; #11-41, 164 pgs.; #42 on, 132 pgs. Old issues were being reprinted & distributed by Whitman in 1976.*

WALT DISNEY GIANT (Disney)
Bruce Hamilton Co. (Gladstone): Sept, 1995 - No. 7, Sept, 1996 ($2.25, bi-monthly, 48 pgs.)
1-7: 1-Scrooge McDuck in the Yukon; Rosa-c/a/scripts plus r/F.C. #218. 2-Uncle Scrooge-r by Barks plus 17 pg. text story. 3-Donald the Mighty Duck; Rosa-c; Barks & Rosa-r. 4-Mickey and Goofy; new-a (story actually stars Goofy. Mickey Mouse by Caesar Ferioli; Donald Duck by Giorgio Cavazzano (1st in U.S.). 6-Uncle Scrooge & the Jr. Woodchucks; new-a and Barks-r. 7-Uncle Scrooge-r by Barks plus new-a 4.00
NOTE: *Series was initially solicited as Uncle Walt's Collectory. Issue #8 was advertised, but later cancelled.*

WALT DISNEY PAINT BOOK SERIES
Whitman Publ. Co.: No dates; circa 1975 (Beware! Has 1930s copyright dates) (79¢-c, 52 pgs. B&W, treasury-sized) (Coloring books, text stories & comics-r)
#2052 (Whitman #886-r) Mickey Mouse & Donald Duck Gag Book 3 6 9 21 32 42
#2053 (Whitman #677-r) 3 6 9 21 32 42
#2054 (Whitman #670-r) Donald-c 4 8 12 23 36 48
#2055 (Whitman #627-r) Mickey-c 3 6 9 21 32 42
#2056 (Whitman #660-r) Buckey Bug-c 3 6 9 19 29 38
#2057 (Whitman #887-r) Mickey & Donald-c 3 6 9 21 32 42

WALT DISNEY PRESENTS (TV)(Disney)
Dell Publishing Co.: No. 997, 6-8/59 - No. 6, 12-2/1960-61; No. 1181, 4-5/61 (All photo-c)
Four Color 997 (#1) 7 14 21 48 79 110
2(12-2/60)-The Swamp Fox(origin), Elfego Baca, Texas John Slaughter (Disney TV show) begin 5 10 15 32 51 70
3-6: 5-Swamp Fox by Warren Tufts 5 10 15 30 48 65
Four Color 1181-Texas John Slaughter 6 12 18 39 62 85

WALT DISNEY'S CHRISTMAS PARADE (Also see Christmas Parade)
Gladstone: Winter, 1988; No. 2, Winter, 1989 ($2.95, 100 pgs.)
1-Barks-r/painted-c 2 4 6 8 10 12
2-Barks-r 1 2 3 5 7 9

WALT DISNEY'S CHRISTMAS PARADE
Gemstone Publishing: Dec, 2003; 2004, 2005, 2006,2008 ($8.95/$9.50, prestige format)
1-4: 1-Reprints and 3 new European holiday stories. 2-All reprints. 3-Reprints and 2 new stories, 4-Reprints and 5 new stories 9.00
5-($9.50) R/Uncle Scrooge #47 and European stories 9.50

WALT DISNEY'S COMICS AND STORIES (Cont. of Mickey Mouse Magazine) (#1-30 contain Donald Duck newspaper reprints) (Titled "Comics And Stories" #264 to #?; titled "Walt Disney's Comics And Stories" #511 on)
Dell Publishing Co./Gold Key #264-473/Whitman #474-510/Gladstone #511-547/ Disney Comics #548-585/Gladstone #586-633/Gemstone Publishing #634-698/ Boom! Kids #699-on: 10/40 - #263, 8/62; #264, 10/62 - #510, 7/84; #511, 10/86 - #633, 2/99; #634, 7/03 - #698, 11/08; #699, 10/09 - #720, 6/11

NOTE: The whole number can always be found at the bottom of the title page in the lower left-hand or right hand panel.
1(V1#1-c; V2#1-indicia)-Donald Duck strip-r by Al Taliaferro & Gottfredson's Mickey Mouse begin 2250 4500 6750 15,750 29,875 44,000
2 892 1784 2676 6512 11,756 17,000
3 389 778 1167 2723 4962 7200
4-X-Mas-c; 1st Huey, Dewey & Louie-c this title (See Mickey Mouse Magazine V4#2 for 1st-c ever) 300 600 900 1920 3460 5000
4-Special promotional, complimentary issue; cover same except one corner was blanked out & boxed in to identify the giveaway (not a paste-over). This special pressing was probably sent out to former subscribers to Mickey Mouse Mag. whose subscriptions had expired. (Very rare-5 known copies) 423 846 1269 3000 5500 8000
5-Goofy-c 245 490 735 1568 2784 4000
6-10: 8-Only Clarabelle Cow-c. 9-Taliaferro-c (1st) 206 412 618 1318 2359 3400
11-14: 11-Huey, Dewey & Louie-c/app. 155 310 465 992 1746 2500
15-17: 15-The 3 Little Kittens (17 pgs.). 16-The 3 Little Pigs (29 pgs.); X-Mas-c. 17-The Ugly Duckling (4 pgs.) 135 270 405 864 1532 2200
18-21 119 238 357 762 1356 1950
22-30: 22-Flag-c. 24-The Flying Gauchito (1st original comic book story done for WDC&S). 27-Jose Carioca by Carl Buettner (2nd original story in WDC&S) 100 200 300 635 1143 1650

GD 2.0 VG 4.0 FN 6.0 VF 8.0 VF/NM 9.0 NM- 9.2

31-New Donald Duck stories by Carl Barks begin (See F.C. #9 for 1st Barks Donald Duck) 400 800 1200 2800 4900 7000
32-Barks-a 232 464 696 1485 2543 3600
33-Barks-a; infinity-c 161 322 483 1030 1765 2500
34-Gremlins by Walt Kelly begin, end #41; Barks-a 129 258 387 826 1413 2000
35,36-Barks-a 123 246 369 787 1344 1900
37-Donald Duck by Jack Hannah 71 142 213 454 802 1150
38-40-Barks-a. 39-X-Mas-c. 40,41-Gremlins by Kelly 81 162 243 518 897 1275
41-50-Barks-a. 43-Seven Dwarfs-c app. (4/44). 45-50-Nazis in Gottfredson's Mickey Mouse Stories 68 136 204 435 755 1075
51-60-Barks-a. 51-X-Mas-c. 52-Li'l Bad Wolf begins, ends #203 (not in #55). 58-Kelly flag-c 32 64 96 232 504 775
61-70: Barks-a. 61-Dumbo story. 63,64-Pinocchio stories. 63-Cover swipe from New Funnies #94. 64-X-Mas-c. 65-Pluto story. 66-Infinity-c. 67,68-Mickey Mouse Sunday-r by Bill Wright 28 56 84 203 439 675
71-80: Barks-a. 75-77-Brer Rabbit stories, no Mickey Mouse. 76-X-Mas-c 24 48 72 168 359 550
81-87,89,90: Barks-a. 82-Goofy-c. 82-84-Bongo stories. 86-90-Goofy & Agnes app. 89-Chip 'n' Dale story 20 40 60 137 294 450
88-1st app. Gladstone Gander by Barks (1/48) 24 48 72 168 359 550
91-97,99: Barks-a. 95-1st WDC&S Barks-c. 96-No Mickey Mouse; Little Toot begins, ends #97. 99-X-Mas-c 18 36 54 123 267 410
98-1st Uncle Scrooge app. in WDC&S (11/48) 29 58 87 210 455 700
100-(1/49)-Barks-a 21 42 63 146 311 475
101-110-Barks-a. 107-Taliaferro-c; Donald acquires super powers 15 30 45 102 221 340
111,114,117-All Barks-a 13 26 39 87 186 285
112-Drug (ether) issue (Donald Duck) 13 26 39 85 180 275
113,115,116,118-123: No Barks. 116-Dumbo x-over. 121-Grandma Duck begins, ends #168; not in #135,142,146,155 10 20 30 69 130 190
124,126-130-All Barks-a. 124-X-Mas-c 11 22 33 77 154 230
125-1st app. Junior Woodchucks (2/51); Barks-a 15 30 45 102 221 340
131,133,135-137,139-All Barks-a 11 22 33 74 145 215
132-Barks-a(2) (D. Duck & Grandma Duck) 11 22 33 76 151 225
134-Intro. & 1st app. The Beagle Boys (11/51) 17 34 51 119 260 400
138-Classic Scrooge money story 14 28 42 97 211 325
140-(5/52)-1st app. Gyro Gearloose by Barks; 2nd Barks Uncle Scrooge-c; 3rd Uncle Scrooge cover app. 17 34 51 119 260 400
141-150-All Barks-a. 143-Little Hiawatha begins, ends #151,159 10 20 30 65 118 170
151-170-All Barks-a 9 18 27 58 99 140
171-199-All Barks-a 8 16 24 53 89 125
200 8 16 24 56 96 135
201-240: All Barks-a. 204-Chip 'n' Dale & Scamp begin 7 14 21 46 76 105
241-283: Barks-a. 241-Dumbo x-over. 247-Gyro Gearloose begins, ends #274. 256-Ludwig Von Drake begins, ends #274 6 12 18 41 66 90
284,285,287,290,295,296,309-311-Not by Barks 3 6 9 20 30 40
286,288,291-294,297,298,308-All Barks stories; 293-Grandma Duck's Farm Friends. 297-Gyro Gearloose. 298-Daisy Duck's Diary-r 4 8 12 24 37 50
289-Annette-c & back-c & story; Barks-s 4 8 12 28 44 60
299-307-All contain early Barks-r (#43-117). 305-Gyro Gearloose 4 8 12 26 41 55
312-Last Barks issue with original story 4 8 12 26 41 55
313-315,317-327,329-334,336-341 3 6 9 16 22 28
316-Last issue published during life of Walt Disney 3 6 9 16 22 28
328,335,342-350-Barks-r 3 6 9 16 22 28
351-360-With posters inside; Barks reprints (2 versions of each with & without posters) 4 8 12 26 41 55
351-360-Without posters... 3 6 9 14 19 24
361-400-Barks-r 3 6 9 14 20 26
401-429-Barks-r 3 6 9 14 19 24
430,433,437,438,441,444,445,466-No Barks 2 4 6 8 11 14
431,432,434-436,439,440,442,443-Barks-r 2 4 6 10 14 18
446-465,467-473-Barks-r 2 4 6 9 13 16
474(3/80),475-478 (Whitman) 3 6 9 14 19 24
479(8/80),481(10/80)-484(1/81) pre-pack only 5 10 15 32 51 70
480 (8-12/80)-(Very low distribution) 10 20 30 68 127 185
484 (1/81, 50¢-c) Cover price error variant (scarce) 6 12 18 39 62 85
485-499: 494-r/WDC&S #98 2 4 6 11 16 20
500-510 (All #90011 on-c; pre-packs): 500(4/83), 501(5/83), 502&503(7/83), 504-506(all 8/83), 507(4/84), 508(5/84), 509(6/84), 510(7/84). 506-No Barks

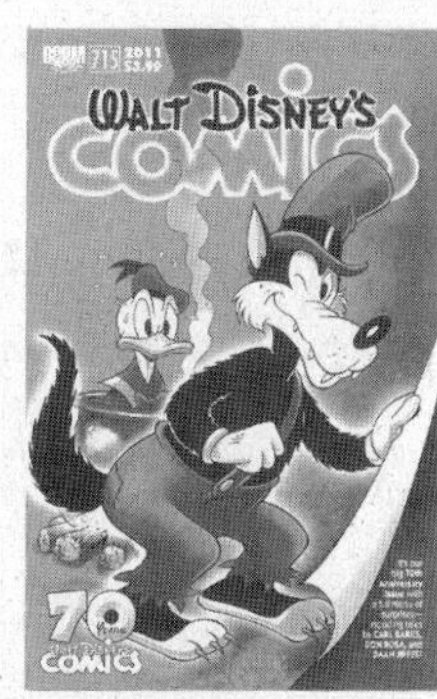

Walt Disney's Comics and Stories #715 © DIS

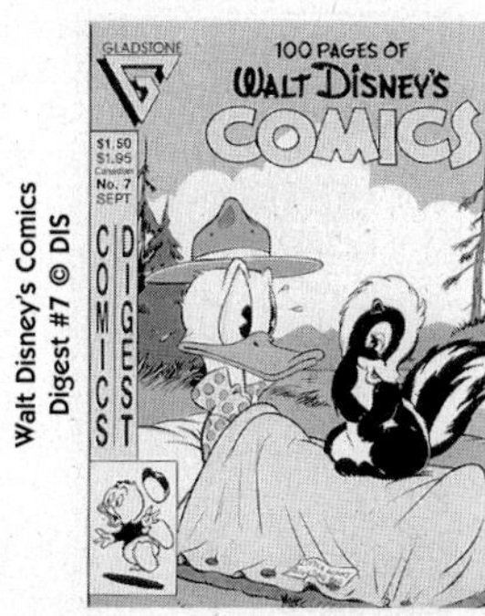

Walt Disney's Comics Digest #7 © DIS

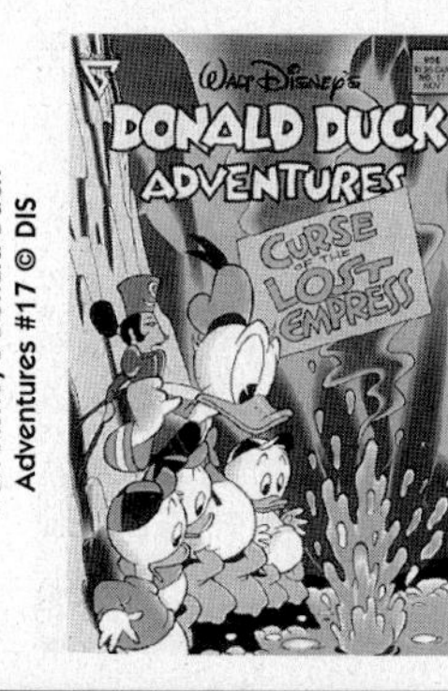

Walt Disney's Donald Duck Adventures #17 © DIS

GD 2.0 | VG 4.0 | FN 6.0 | VF 8.0 | VF/NM 9.0 | NM- 9.2

2 4 6 13 18 22
511-Donald Duck by Daan Jippes (1st in U.S.; in all through #518); Gyro Gearloose Barks-r begins (in most through #547); Wuzzles by Disney Studio (1st by Gladstone) 3 6 9 17 25 32
512,513 2 4 6 10 14 18
514-516,520 2 4 6 8 10 12
517-519,521,522,525,527,529,530,532-546: 518-Infinity-c. 522-r/1st app. Huey, Dewey & Louie from D. Duck Sunday. 535-546-Barks-r. 537-1st Donald Duck by William Van Horn in WDC&S. 541-545-52 pgs. 546,547-68 pgs. 546-Kelly-r. 547-Rosa-a 6.00
523,524,526,528,531,547: Rosa-s/a in all. 523-1st Rosa 10 pager 2 4 6 9 12 15
548-($1.50, 6/90)-1st Disney issue; new-a; no M. Mouse 1 2 3 4 5 7
549,551-570,572,573,577-579,581,584 ($1.50): 549-Barks-r begin, ends #585, not in #555, 556, & 564. 551-r/1 story from F.C. #29. 556,578-r/Mickey Mouse Cheerios Premium by Dick Moores. 562,563,568-570, 572, 581-Gottfredson strip-r. 570-Valentine issue; has Mickey/Minnie centerfold. 584-Taliaferro strip-r 4.00
550 ($2.25, 52 pgs.)-Donald Duck by Barks; previously printed only in The Netherlands (1st time in U.S.); r/Chip 'n Dale & Scamp from #204 5.00
571-($2.95, 68 pgs)-r/Donald Duck's Atom Bomb by Barks from 1947 Cheerios premium 6.00
574-576,580,582,583 ($2.95, 68 pgs.): 574-r/1st Pinocchio Sunday strip (1939-40). 575-Gottfredson-r, Pinocchio-r/WDC&S #64. 580-r/Donald Duck's 1st app. from Silly Symphony strip 12/16/34 by Taliaferro; Gottfredson strip-r begin; not in #584 & 600. 582,583-r/Mickey Mouse on Sky Island from WDC&S #1,2 5.00
585 ($2.50, 52 pgs.)-r/#140; Barks-r/WDC&S #140 5.00
586,587: 586-Gladstone issues begin again; begin $1.50-c; Gottfredson-r begins (not in #600). 587-Donald Duck by William Van Horn begins 4.00
588-597: 588,591-599-Donald Duck by William Van Horn 3.00
598,599 ($1.95, 36 pgs.): 598-r/1st drawings of Mickey Mouse by Ub Iwerks 3.00
600 ($2.95, 48 pgs.)-L.B. Cole-c(r)/WDC&S #1; Barks-r/WDC&S #32 plus Rosa, Jippes, Van Horn-r and new Rosa centerspread 4.00
601-611 ($5.95, 64 pgs., squarebound, bi-monthly): 601-Barks-c, r/Mickey Mouse V1#1, Rosa-a/scripts. 602-Rosa-c. 604-Taliaferro strip-r/1st Silly Symphony Sundays from 1932. 604,605-Jippes-a. 605-Walt Kelly-c; Gottfredson "Mickey Mouse Outwits the Phantom Blot" r/F.C. #16 6.00
612-633 ($6.95): 633-(2/99) Last Gladstone issue 7.00
634-675: 634-(7/03) First Gemstone issue; William Van Horn-c. 666-Mickey's Inferno 7.00
676-681: 676-Begin $7.50-c. 677-Bucky Bug's 75th Anniversary 7.50
682-698-($7.99) 8.00
699-714: 699-(9/09, $2.99) First BOOM! Kids issue. 700-Back-up story w/Van Horn-a 3.00
715-720: 715-(1/11, $3.99) 70th Anniverary issue; cover swipe of #1 by Van Horn; Jippes, Rosa-a. 716-Barks reprints 4.00

NOTE: *(#1-38, 68 pgs.; #39-42, 60 pgs.; #43-57, 61-134, 143-168, 446, 447, 52 pgs.; #58-60, 135-142, 169-540, 36 pgs.)*

NOTE: ***Barks** art in all issues #31 on, except where noted; c-95, 96, 104, 108, 109, 130-172, 174-178, 183, 198-200, 204, 206-209, 212-216, 218, 220, 226, 228-233, 235-238, 240-243, 247, 250, 253, 256, 260, 261, 276-283, 288-292, 295-298, 301, 303, 304, 306, 307, 309, 310, 313-316, 319, 321, 322, 324, 326, 328, 329, 331, 332, 334, 341, 342, 350, 351, 527r, 530r, 540(never before published), 546r, 557-586r(most), 596p, 601p. **Kelly** a-24p, 34-41, 43; r-522-524, 546, 547, 582, 583; covers(most)-34-118, 531r, 537r, 541r-543r, 562r, 571r, 605r. Walt Disney's Comics & Stories featured Mickey Mouse serials which were in practically every issue from #1 through #394 and #511 to date. The titles of the serials, along with the issues they are in, are listed in previous editions of this price guide. **Floyd Gottfredson** Mickey Mouse serials in issues #1-14, 18-66, 69-74, 78-100, 128, 562, 563, 568-572, 582, 583, 586-599 , 601-603 , 605-present , plus "Service with a Smile" in #13; "Mickey Mouse in a Warplant" (3 pgs.), and "Pluto Catches a Nazi Spy" (4 pgs.) in #62; "Mystery Next Door", #93; "Sunken Treasure", #94; "Aunt Marissa", #95 (r in #575); "Gangland", #98 (r in #562); "Thanksgiving Dinner", #99 (r in #567); and "The Talking Dog", #100 (r in #563); "Morty's Escapade," #128. "The Brave Little Tailor", #580; "Introducing Mickey Mouse Movies ", #581; Circus Roustabout, #585; "Rumplewatt the Giant", #604. Mickey Mouse by **Paul Murry** #152-547 except 155-57 (**Dick Moore**), 327-29 (**Tony Strobl**), 348-50 (**Jack Manning**), 533 (**Bill Wright**). **Don Rosa** story/a-523, 524, 526, 528, 531, 547, 601-present. **Al Taliaferro** Silly Symphonies in #5-"Three Little Pigs"; #13-"Birds of a Feather"; #14-"The Boarding School Mystery"; #15-"Cookieland" and "Three Little Kittens"; #16-"The Practical Pig"; #17-"The Ugly Duckling"; "The Wise Little Hen" in #580; and "Ambrose the Robber Kitten"; #19-"Penguin Isle"; and "Bucky Bug" in #20-23, 25, 26, 28 (one continuous story from 1932-34; first 2 pgs. not Taliaferro). **Gottfredson** strip r-562, 563, 568-572, 581, 585, 586, 590. **Taliaferro** strip r-584, 580. **Van Horn** a-537, 545, 561, 574, 587, 588, 591-present.*

WALT DISNEY'S COMICS DIGEST
Gladstone: Dec, 1986 - No. 7, Sept, 1987

1 1 2 3 5 6 8
2-7 6.00

WALT DISNEY'S COMICS PENNY PINCHER
Gladstone: May, 1997 - No. 4, Aug, 1997 (99¢, limited series)

1-4 3.00

WALT DISNEY'S DONALD AND MICKEY (Formerly Walt Disney's Mickey and Donald)
Gladstone (Bruce Hamilton Co.): No. 19, Sept, 1993 - No. 30, 1995 ($1.50, 36 & 68 pgs.)

19,21-24,26-30: New & reprints. 19,21,23,24-Barks-r. 19,26-Murry-r. 22-Barks "Omelet" story r/WDC&S #146. 27-Mickey Mouse story by Caesar Ferioli (1st U.S work). 29-Rosa-c; Mickey Mouse story actually starring Goofy (does not include Mickey except on title page.) 4.00
20,25-($2.95, 68 pgs.): 20-Barks, Gottfredson-r 5.00
NOTE: *Donald Duck stories were all reprints.*

WALT DISNEY'S DONALD DUCK
Gemstone Publishing: 2006

... Free Comic Book Day (5/06) r/WDC&S #531; Rosa-s/a; P&S. Block-s/a; Van Horn-s/a 3.00

WALT DISNEY'S DONALD DUCK ADVENTURES (D.D. Adv. #1-3)
Gladstone: 11/87-No. 20, 4/90 (1st Series); No. 21,8/93-No. 48, 2/98(3rd Series)

1 1 2 3 5 6 8
2-r/F.C. #308 4.00
3,4,6,7,9-11,13,15-18: 3-r/F.C. #223. 4-r/F.C. #62. 9-r/F.C. #159, "Ghost of the Grotto". 11-r/F.C. #159, "Adventure Down Under." 16-r/F.C. #291; Rosa-c. 18-r/FC #318; Rosa-c 3.00
5,8: 5-Don Rosa-c/a. 8-Rosa-a 5.00
12($1.50, 52pgs)-Rosa-c/s/a; "Return to Plain Awful" story; sequel to Four Color #223 (square egg story); Barks centerfold poster 6.00
14-r/F.C. #29, "Mummy's Ring" 4.00
19($1.95, 68 pgs.)-Barks-r/F.C. #199 (1 pg.) 4.00
20($1.95, 68 pgs.)-Barks-r/F.C. #189 & cover-r; William Van Horn-a 4.00
21,22: 21-r/D.D. #46. 22-r/F.C. #282 3.00
23-25,27,29,31,32-($1.50, 36 pgs.): 21,23,29-Rosa-c. 23-Intro/1st app. Andold Wild Duck by Marco Rota. 24-Van Horn-a. 27-1st Pat Block-a, "Mystery of Widow's Gap." 31,32-Block-c 3.00
26,28($2.95, 68 pgs.): 26-Barks-r/F.C. #108, "Terror of the River". 28-Barks-r/F.C. #199, "Sheriff of Bullet Valley" 4.00
30($2.95, 68 pgs.)-r/F.C. #367, Barks' "Christmas for Shacktown" 4.00
33($1.95, 68 pgs.)-r/F.C. #408, Barks' "The Golden Helmet;"Van Horn-c 4.00
34-43: 34-Resume $1.50-c. 34,35,37-Block-a/scripts. 38-Van Horn-c/a 3.00
44-48-($1.95-c) 3.00
NOTE: ***Barks** a-1-22r, 26r, 28r, 33r, 36r; c-3r, 8r, 10r, 14r, 20r. **Block** a-27, 30, 34, 35, 37; c-27, 30-32, 34, 35, 37; c-27, 30, 31, 32, 34, 35, 37. **Rosa** a-5, 8, 12, 43; c-13, 16, 18, 21, 23, 43.*

WALT DISNEY'S DONALD DUCK ADVENTURES (2nd Series)
Disney Comics: June, 1990 - No. 38, July, 1993 ($1.50)

1-Rosa-a & scripts 5.00
2-21,23,25,27-33,35,36,38: 2-Barks-r/WDC&S #35; William Van Horn-a begins, ends #20. 9-Barks-r/F.C. #178. 9,11,14,17-No Van Horn-a. 11-Mad #1 cover parody. 14-Barks-r. 17-Barks-r. 21-r/FC #203 by Barks. 29-r/MOC #20 by Barks 3.00
22,24,26,34,37: 22-Rosa-a (10 pgs.) & scripts. 24-Rosa-a & scripts. 26-r/March of Comics #41 by Barks. 34-Rosa-c/a. 37-Rosa-a; Barks-r 4.00
NOTE: ***Barks** r-2, 4, 9(F.C. #178), 14(D.D. #45), 17, 21, 26, 27, 29 , 35, 36(D.D #60)-38. **Taliaferro** a-34r, 36r.*

WALT DISNEY'S DONALD DUCK ADVENTURES
Gemstone Publishing: May, 2003 (giveaway promoting 2003 return of Disney Comics)

...Free Comic Book Day Edition - cover logo on red background; reprints "Maharajah Donald" & "The Peaceful Hills" from March of Comics #4; Barks-s/a; Kelly original-c on back-c 3.00
...San Diego Comic-Con 2003 Edition - cover logo on gold background 3.00
...ANA World's Fair of Money Baltimore Edition - cover logo on green background 3.00
...WizardWorld Chicago 2003 Edition - cover logo on blue background 3.00

WALT DISNEY'S DONALD DUCK ADVENTURES (Take-Along Comic)
Gemstone Publishing: July, 2003 - No. 21, Nov, 2006 ($7.95, 5" x 7-1/2")

1-21-Mickey Mouse & Uncle Scrooge app. 9-Christmas-c 8.00
... , The Barks/Rosa Collection Vol. 2 (3/08, $8.99) reprints Donald Duck's Atom Bomb, Super Snooper & The Trouble With Dimes by Barks; The Duck Who Fell to Earth, Super Snooper Strikes Again & The Money Pit by Rosa 9.00
... , The Barks/Rosa Collection Vol. 3 (9/08, $8.99) r/FC #408 "The Golden Helmet" by Barks & DDA #43 "The Lost Charts of Columbus" by Rosa; cover gallery and bonus art 9.00

WALT DISNEY'S DONALD DUCK AND FRIENDS (Continues as Donald Duck and Friends)
Gemstone Publishing: No. 308, Oct, 2003 - No. 346, Dec, 2006 ($2.95)

308-346: 308-Numbering resumes from Gladstone Donald Duck series; Halloween-c. 332-Halloween-c; r/#26 by Carl Barks 3.00

WALT DISNEY'S DONALD DUCK AND MICKEY MOUSE (Formerly Walt Disney's Donald and Mickey)
Gladstone (Bruce Hamilton Company): Sept, 1995 - No. 7, Sept, 1996 ($1.50, 32 pgs.)

1-7: 1-Barks-r and new Mickey Mouse stories in all. 5,6-Mickey Mouse stories by Caesar Ferioli. 7-New Donald Duck and Mickey Mouse x-over story; Barks-r/WDC&S #51 3.00
NOTE: *Issue #8 was advertised, but cancelled.*

WALT DISNEY'S DONALD DUCK AND UNCLE SCROOGE
Gemstone Publishing: Nov, 2005 ($6.95, square-bound one-shot)

nn-New story by John Lustig and Pat Block and r/Uncle Scrooge #59 7.00

WALT DISNEY'S DONALD DUCK FAMILY
Gemstone Publishing: Jun, 2008 ($8.99, square-bound)

GD 2.0 | VG 4.0 | FN 6.0 | VF 8.0 | VF/NM 9.0 | NM- 9.2

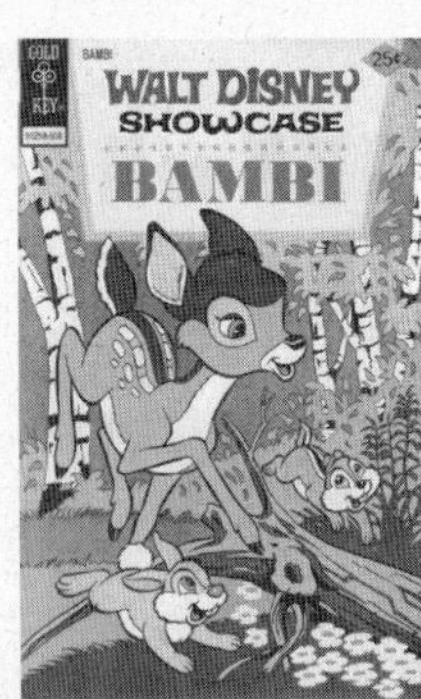

Walt Disney Showcase #31 © DIS

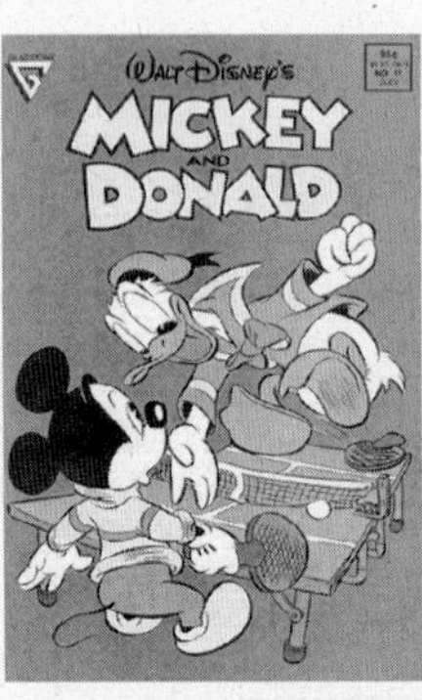

Walt Disney's Mickey and Donald #11 © DIS

Walt Disney's Spring Fever #1 © DIS

GD VG FN VF VF/NM NM-
2.0 4.0 6.0 8.0 9.0 9.2

... The Daan Jippes Collection Vol. 1 - R/Barks-s re-drawn by Jippes for Dutch comics 9.00

WALT DISNEY'S DONALD DUCK IN THE CASE OF THE MISSING MUMMY
Gemstone Publishing: Oct, 2007 ($8.99, square-bound one-shot)
nn-New story by Shelley and Pat Block and r/Donald Duck FC #29 9.00

WALT DISNEY'S GYRO GEARLOOSE
Gemstone Publishing: May, 2008
... Free Comic Book Day (5/08) short stories by Barks, Rosa, Van Horn, Gerstein 3.00

WALT DISNEY SHOWCASE
Gold Key: Oct, 1970 - No. 54, Jan, 1980 (No. 44-48: 68pgs., 49-54: 52pgs.)
1-Boatniks (Movie)-Photo-c 3 6 9 18 27 35
2-Moby Duck 3 6 9 14 19 24
3,4,7: 3-Bongo & Lumpjaw-r. 4,7-Pluto-r 2 4 6 10 14 18
5-$1,000,000 Duck (Movie)-Photo-c 3 6 9 16 22 28
6-Bedknobs & Broomsticks (Movie) 3 6 9 16 22 28
8-Daisy & Donald 2 4 6 11 16 20
9- 101 Dalmatians (cartoon feat.); r/F.C. #1183 3 6 9 17 25 32
10-Napoleon & Samantha (Movie)-Photo-c 3 6 9 17 22 28
11-Moby Duck-r 2 4 6 10 14 18
12-Dumbo-r/Four Color #668 2 4 6 11 16 20
13-Pluto-r 2 4 6 10 14 18
14-World's Greatest Athlete (Movie)-Photo-c 3 6 9 16 22 28
15- 3 Little Pigs-r 2 4 6 11 16 20
16-Aristocats (cartoon feature); r/Aristocats #1 3 6 9 16 22 28
17-Mary Poppins; r/M.P. #10136-501-Photo-c 3 6 9 16 22 28
18-Gyro Gearloose; Barks-r/F.C. #1047,1184 3 6 9 18 27 35
19-That Darn Cat; r/That Darn Cat #10171-602-Hayley Mills photo-c
3 6 9 16 22 28
20,23-Pluto-r 2 4 6 11 16 20
21-Li'l Bad Wolf & The Three Little Pigs 2 4 6 10 14 18
22-Unbirthday Party with Alice in Wonderland; r/Four Color #341
3 6 9 14 19 24
24-26: 24-Herbie Rides Again (Movie); sequel to "The Love Bug"; photo-c. 25-Old Yeller (Movie); r/F.C. #869; Photo-c. 26-Lt. Robin Crusoe USN (Movie); r/Lt. Robin Crusoe USN #10191-601; photo-c 2 4 6 11 16 20
27-Island at the Top of the World (Movie)-Photo-c 3 6 9 14 19 24
28-Brer Rabbit, Bucky Bug-r/WDC&S #58 2 4 6 11 16 20
29-Escape to Witch Mountain (Movie)-Photo-c 3 6 9 14 19 24
30-Magica De Spell; Barks-r/Uncle Scrooge #36 & WDC&S #258
3 6 9 21 32 42
31-Bambi (cartoon feature); r/Four Color #186 2 4 6 13 18 22
32-Spin & Marty-r/F.C. #1026; Mickey Mouse Club (TV)-Photo-c
3 6 9 14 19 24
33-40: 33-Pluto-r/F.C. #1143. 34-Paul Revere's Ride with Johnny Tremain (TV); r/F.C. #822. 35-Goofy-r/F.C. #952. 36-Peter Pan-r/F.C. #442. 37-Tinker Bell & Jiminy Cricket-r/F.C. #982,989. 38,39-Mickey & the Sleuth, Parts 1 & 2. 40-The Rescuers (cartoon feature)
2 4 6 9 13 16
41-Herbie Goes to Monte Carlo (Movie); sequel to "Herbie Rides Again"; photo-c
2 4 6 10 14 18
42-Mickey & the Sleuth 2 4 6 9 13 16
43-Pete's Dragon (Movie)-Photo-c 2 4 6 13 18 22
44-Return From Witch Mountain (new) & In Search of the Castaways-r (Movies)-Photo-c; 68 pg. giants begin 3 6 9 14 19 24
45-The Jungle Book (Movie); r/#30033-803 3 6 9 17 25 32
46-48: 46-The Cat From Outer Space (Movie)(new), & The Shaggy Dog (Movie)-r/F.C. #985; photo-c. 47-Mickey Mouse Surprise Party-r. 48-The Wonderful Advs. of Pinocchio-r/F.C. #1203; last 68 pg. issue 2 4 6 10 14 18
49-54: 49-North Avenue Irregulars (Movie); Zorro-r/Zorro #11; 52 pgs. begin; photo-c. 50-Bedknobs & Broomsticks-r/#6; Mooncussers-r/World of Adv. #1; photo-c. 51-101 Dalmatians-r. 52-Unidentified Flying Oddball (Movie); r/Picnic Party #8; photo-c. 53-The Scarecrow-r (TV). 54-The Black Hole (Movie)-Photo-c (predates Black Hole #1)
2 4 6 9 13 16

WALT DISNEY'S MAGAZINE (TV)(Formerly Walt Disney's Mickey Mouse Club Magazine) (50¢, bi-monthly)
Western Publishing Co.: V2#4, June, 1957 - V4#6, Oct, 1959
V2#4-Stories & articles on the Mouseketeers, Zorro, & Goofy and other Disney characters & people 7 14 21 44 72 100
V2#5, V2#6(10/57) 6 12 18 41 66 90
V3#1(12/57), V3#3-5 6 12 18 37 59 80
V3#2-Annette Funicello photo-c 10 20 30 70 133 195
V3#6(10/58)-TV Zorro photo-c 8 16 24 51 86 120
V4#1(12/58) - V4#2-4,6(10/59) 6 12 18 37 59 80
V4#5-Annette Funicello photo-c, w/ 2-photo articles 10 20 30 70 133 195

GD VG FN VF VF/NM NM-
2.0 4.0 6.0 8.0 9.0 9.2

NOTE: *V2#4-V3#6 were 11-1/2x8-1/2", 48 pgs.; V4#1 on were 10x8", 52 pgs. (Peak circulation of 400,000).*

WALT DISNEY'S MERRY CHRISTMAS (See Dell Giant #39)

WALT DISNEY'S MICKEY AND DONALD (M & D #1,2)(Becomes Walt Disney's Donald & Mickey #19 on)
Gladstone: Mar, 1988 - No. 18, May, 1990 (95¢)
1-Don Rosa-a; r/1949 Firestone giveaway 6.00
2-8: 3-Infinity-c. 4-8-Barks-r 3.00
9-15: 9-r/1948 Firestone giveaway; X-Mas-c 3.00
16($1.50, 52 pgs.)-r/FC #157 5.00
17-(68 pgs.) Barks M.M.-r/FC #79 plus Barks D.D.-r; Rosa-a; x-mas-c 6.00
18($1.95, 68 pgs.)-Gottfredson-r/WDC&S #13,72-74; Kelly-c(r); Barks-r 5.00
NOTE: ***Barks** reprints in 1-15, 17, 18. **Kelly** c-13r, 14 (r/Walt Disney's C&S #58), 18r.*

WALT DISNEY'S MICKEY MOUSE
Gemstone Publishing: May, 2007
... Free Comic Book Day (5/07) Floyd Gottfredson-s/a 3.00

WALT DISNEY'S MICKEY MOUSE ADVENTURES (Take-Along Comic)
Gemstone Publishing: Aug, 2004 - No. 12 ($7.95, 5" x 7-1/2")
1-12-Goofy, Donald Duck & Uncle Scrooge app. 8.00

WALT DISNEY'S MICKEY MOUSE AND BLOTMAN IN BLOTMAN RETURNS
Gemstone Publishing: Dec, 2006 ($5.99, squarebound, one-shot)
nn-Wraparound-c by Noel Van Horn; Super Goof back-up story 6.00

WALT DISNEY'S MICKEY MOUSE AND FRIENDS (See Mickey Mouse and Friends for #296)
Gemstone Publishing: No. 257, Oct, 2003 - No. 295, Dec, 2006 ($2.95)
257-295: 257-Numbering resumes from Gladstone Mickey Mouse series; Halloween-c. 285-Return of the Phantom Blot 3.00

WALT DISNEY'S MICKEY MOUSE AND UNCLE SCROOGE
Gemstone Publishing: June, 2004 (Free Comic Book Day giveaway)
nn-Flip book with r/Uncle Scrooge #15 and r/Mickey Mouse Four Color #79 (only Barks drawn Mickey Mouse story) 3.00

WALT DISNEY'S MICKEY MOUSE CLUB MAGAZINE (TV)(Becomes Walt Disney's Magazine)
Western Publishing Co.: Winter, 1956 - V2#3, Apr, 1957 (11-1/2x8-1/2", quarterly, 48 pgs.)
V1#1 13 26 39 86 183 280
2-4 9 18 27 58 99 140
V2#1,2 7 14 21 48 79 110
3-Annette photo-c 12 24 36 81 166 250
Annual(1956)-Two different issues; ($1.50-Whitman); 120 pgs., cardboard covers, 11-3/4x8-3/4"; reprints 13 26 39 86 183 280
Annual(1957)-Same as above 11 22 33 76 151 225

WALT DISNEY'S MICKEY MOUSE MEETS BLOTMAN
Gemstone Publishing: Aug, 2005 ($5.99, squarebound, one-shot)
nn-Wraparound-c by Noel Van Horn; Super Goof back-up story 6.00

WALT DISNEY'S PINOCCHIO SPECIAL
Gladstone: Spring, 1990 ($1.00)
1-50th anniversary edition; Kelly-r/F.C. #92 3.00

WALT DISNEY'S SPRING FEVER
Gemstone Publishing: Apr, 2007; Apr, 2008 ($9.50, squarebound)
1,2: 1-New stories and reprints incl. "Mystery of the Swamp" by Carl Barks 9.50

WALT DISNEY'S THE ADVENTUROUS UNCLE SCROOGE MCDUCK
Gladstone: Jan, 1998 - No. 2, Mar, 1998 ($1.95)
1,2: 1-Barks-a(r). 2-Rosa-a(r) 3.00

WALT DISNEY'S THE JUNGLE BOOK
W.D. Publications (Disney Comics): 1990 ($5.95, graphic novel, 68 pgs.)
nn-Movie adaptation; movie rereleased in 1990 6.00
nn-($2.95, 68 pgs.)-Comic edition; wraparound-c 4.00

WALT DISNEY'S UNCLE SCROOGE (Formerly Uncle Scrooge #1-209)
Gladstone #210-242/Disney Comics #243-280/Gladstone #281-318/Gemstone #319 on: No. 210, 10/86 - No. 242, 4/90; No. 243, 6/90 - No. 318, 2/99; No. 319, 7/03 - No. 383, 11/08
210-1st Gladstone issue; r/WDC&S #134 (1st Beagle Boys)
2 4 6 9 13 16
211-218: 216-New story ("Go Slowly Sands of Time") plotted and partly scripted by Barks. 217-r/U.S. #7, "Seven Cities of Cibola" 2 4 6 9 12 15
219-"Son Of The Sun" by Rosa (his 1st pro work) 3 6 9 14 20 25
220-Don Rosa-a/scripts 1 2 3 5 6 8
221-223,225,228-234,236-240 4.00
224,226,227,235: 224-Rosa-c/a. 226,227-Rosa-a. 235-Rosa-a/scripts 5.00
241-($1.95, 68 pgs.)-Rosa finishes over Barks-r 6.00

Walt Disney's Uncle Scrooge #383 © DIS

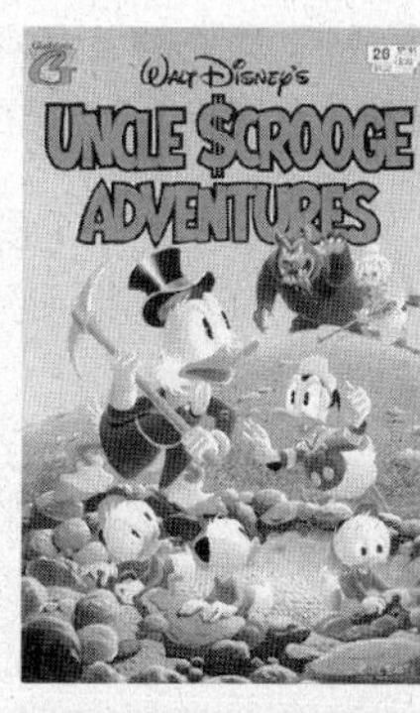

Walt Disney's Uncle Scrooge Adventures #26 © DIS

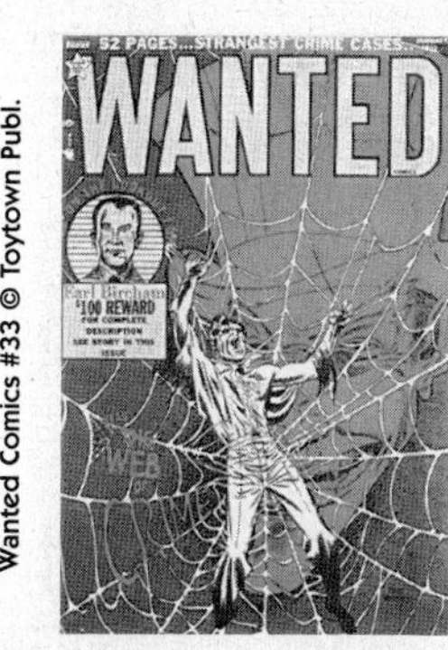

Wanted Comics #33 © Toytown Publ.

	GD 2.0	VG 4.0	FN 6.0	VF 8.0	VF/NM 9.0	NM- 9.2

242-($1.95, 68 pgs.)-Barks-r; Rosa-a(1 pg.) 6.00
243-249,251-260,264-275,277-280,282-284-($1.50): 243-1st by Disney Comics. 274-All Barks issue. 275-Contains centerspread by Rosa. 279-All Barks issue; Rosa-c. 283-r/WDC&S #98 3.00
250-($2.25, 52 pgs.)-Barks-r; wraparound-c 4.00
261-263,276-Don Rosa-c/a 5.00
281-Gladstone issues start again; Rosa-c 6.00
285-The Life and Times of Scrooge McDuck Pt. 1; Rosa-c/a/scripts 1 3 4 6 8 10
286-293: The Life and Times of Scrooge McDuck Pt. 2-8; Rosa-c/a/scripts.
293-($1.95, 36 pgs.)-The Life and Times of Scrooge McDuck Pt. 9 6.00
294-299, 301-308-($1.50, 32 pgs.): 294-296-The Life and Times of Scrooge McDuck Pt. 10-12. 296-Christmas-c. 297-The Life and Times of Uncle Scrooge Pt. 0; Rosa-c/a/scripts 3.00
300-($2.25, 48 pgs.)-Rosa-c; Barks-r/WDC&S #104 and U.S. #216; r/U.S. #220; includes new centerfold. 4.00
309-($6.95) Low print run 2 4 6 11 16 20
310-($6.95) Low print run 3 6 9 20 30 40
311-320-($6.95) 318-(2/99) Last Gladstone issue. 319-(7/03) First Gemstone issue; The Dutchman's Secret by Don Rosa 2 4 6 8 10 12
321-360 7.00
361-366: 361-Begin $7.50-c 7.50
367-383-($7.99) 8.00
... Adventures, The Barks/Rosa Collection Vol. 1 (Gemstone, 7/07, $8.50) reprints Pygmy Indians appearances in U.S. #18 by Barks and WDC&S #633 by Rosa 8.50
Walt Disney's The Life and Times of Scrooge McDuck by Don Rosa TPB (Gemstone, 2005, $16.99) Reprints #285-296, with foreword, commentaries & sketch pages by Rosa 17.00
Walt Disney's The Life and Times of Scrooge McDuck Companion by Don Rosa TPB (Gemstone, 2006, $16.99) additional chapters, with foreword & commentaries 17.00

NOTE: ***Barks*** *r-210-218, 220-223, 224(2pg.), 225-234, 236-242, 245, 246, 250-253, 255, 256, 258, 261(2 pg.), 265, 267, 268, 270(2), 272-284, 299-present; c(r)-210, 212, 221, 228, 229, 232, 233, 284. scripts-287, 293.* ***Rosa*** *a-219, 220, 224, 226, 227, 235, 261-263, 268, 275-277, 285-297; c-219, 224, 231, 261-263, 276, 278-281, 285-296; scripts-219, 220, 224, 235, 261-263, 268, 276, 285-296.*

WALT DISNEY'S UNCLE SCROOGE
Gemstone Publishing

nn-(5/05, FCBD) Reprints Uncle Scrooge's debut in Four Color Comics #386; Barks-s/a 3.00

WALT DISNEY'S UNCLE SCROOGE ADVENTURES (U. Scrooge Advs. #1-3)
Gladstone Publishing: Nov, 1987 - No. 21, May, 1990; No. 22, Sept, 1993 - No. 54, Feb, 1998

1-Barks-r begin, ends #26 1 2 3 5 6 8
2-4 4.00
5,9,14: 5-Rosa-c/a; no Barks-r. 9,14-Rosa-a 5.00
6-8,10-13,15-19: 10-r/U.S. #18(all Barks) 3.00
20,21 ($1.95, 68 pgs.) 20-Rosa-c/a. 21-Rosa-a 5.00
22 ($1.50)-Rosa-c; r/U.S. #26 5.00
23-($2.95, 68 pgs.)-Vs. The Phantom Blot-r/P.B. #3; Barks-r 4.00
24-26,29,31,32,34-36: 24,25,29,31,32-Rosa-c. 25-r/U.S. #21 3.00
27-Guardians of the Lost Library - Rosa-c/a/story; origin of Junior Woodchuck Guidebook 4.00
28-($2.95, 68 pgs.)-r/U.S. #13 w/restored missing panels 4.00
30-($2.95, 68 pgs.)-r/U.S. #12; Rosa-c 4.00
33-($2.95, 64 pgs.)-New Barks story 4.00
37-54 3.00

NOTE: ***Barks*** *r-1-4, 6-8, 10-13, 15-21, 23, 22, 24; c(r)-15, 16, 17, 21.* ***Rosa*** *a-5, 9, 14, 20, 21, 27, 51; c-5, 13, 14, 17(finishes), 20, 22, 24, 25, 27, 28, 51; scripts-5, 9, 14, 27.*

WALT DISNEY'S UNCLE SCROOGE AND DONALD DUCK
Gladstone: Jan, 1998 - No. 2, Mar, 1998 ($1.95)

1,2: 1-Rosa-a(r) 3.00

WALT DISNEY'S UNCLE SCROOGE ADVENTURES IN COLOR
Gladstone Publ.: Dec, 1995 - Present ($8.95/$9.95, squarebound, 56 issue limited series) (Polybagged w/card) (Series chronologically reprints all the stories written & drawn by Carl Barks)

1-56: 1-(12/95)-r/FC #386. 15-(12/96)-r/US #15. 16-(12/96)-r/US #16. 18-(1/97)-r/US #18 10.00

WALT DISNEY'S VACATION PARADE
Gemstone Publishing: 2004 - No. 5, July, 2008 ($8.95/$9.95, squarebound, annual)

1-3: 1-Reprints stories from Dell Giant Comics Vacation Parade 1 (July 1950) 10.00
4,5-($9.95): 4-(5/07). 5-(7/08) 10.00

WALT DISNEY'S WHEATIES PREMIUMS (See Wheaties in the Promotional section)

WALT DISNEY'S WORLD OF THE DRAGONLORDS
Gemstone Publishing: 2005 ($12.99, squarebound, graphic novel)

SC-Uncle Scrooge, Donald & nephews app.; Byron Erickson-s/Giorgio Cavazzano-a 13.00

WALT DISNEY TREASURES - DISNEY COMICS: 75 YEARS OF INNOVATION
Gemstone Publishing: 2006 ($12.99, TPB)

SC-Reprints from 1930-2004, including debut of Mickey Mouse newspaper strip 13.00

WALT DISNEY TREASURES - UNCLE SCROOGE: A LITTLE SOMETHING SPECIAL
Gemstone Publishing: 2008 ($16.99, TPB)

SC-Uncle Scrooge classics from 1954-2006, including "The Seven Cities of Cibola" 17.00

WALTER LANTZ ANDY PANDA (Also see Andy Panda)
Gold Key: Aug, 1973 - No. 23, Jan, 1978 (Walter Lantz)

1-Reprints 3 6 9 14 19 24
2-10-All reprints 2 4 6 9 12 15
11-23: 15,17-19,22-Reprints 1 2 3 5 7 9

WALT KELLY'S...
Eclipse Comics: Dec, 1987; Apr, 1988 ($1.75/$2.50, Baxter paper)

...Christmas Classics 1 (12/87)-Kelly-r/Peter Wheat & Santa Claus Funnies, ...Springtime Tales 1 (4/88, $2.50)-Kelly-r 4.00

WALTONS, THE (See Kite Fun Book)

WALT SCOTT (See Little People)

WALT SCOTT'S CHRISTMAS STORIES (See Little People, 4-Color #959, 1062)

WAMBI, JUNGLE BOY (See Jungle Comics)
Fiction House Magazines: Spr, 1942; No. 2, Win, 1942-43; No. 3, Spr, 1943; No. 4, Fall, 1948; No. 5, Sum, 1949; No. 6, Spr, 1950; No. 7-10, 1950(nd); No. 11, Spr, 1951 - No. 18, Win, 1952-53 (#1-3: 68 pgs.)

1-Wambi, the Jungle Boy begins 95 190 285 603 1039 1475
2 (1942)-Kiefer-c 40 80 120 246 411 575
3 (1943)-Kiefer-c/a 34 68 102 199 325 450
4 (1948)-Origin in text 26 52 78 154 252 350
5 (Fall, 1949, 36 pgs.)-Kiefer-c/a 20 40 60 114 182 250
6-10: 7-(52 pgs.)-New logo 15 30 45 88 137 185
11-18 14 28 42 76 108 140
I.W. Reprint #8('64)-r/#12 with new-c 3 6 9 14 20 25

NOTE: ***Alex Blum*** *c-8.* ***Kiefer*** *c-1-5.* ***Whitman*** *c-11-18.*

WANDERERS (See Adventure Comics #375, 376)
DC Comics: June, 1988 - No. 13, Apr, 1989 ($1.25) (Legion of Super-Heroes spin off)

1-13: 1,2-Steacy-c. 3-Legion app. 3.00

WANDERING STAR
Pen & Ink Comics/Sirius Entertainment No. 12 on: 1993 - No. 21, Mar, 1997 ($2.50/$2.75, B&W)

1-1st printing; Teri Sue Wood c/a/scripts in all 1 2 3 5 6 8
1-2nd and 3rd printings 3.00
2-1st printing. 4.00
2-21: 2-2nd printing. 12-(1/96)-1st Sirius issue 3.00
Trade paperback ($11.95)-r/1-7; 1st printing of 1000, signed and #'d 18.00
Trade paperback-2nd printing, 2000 signed 15.00
TPB Volume 2,3 (11/98, 12/98, $14.95) 2-r/#8-14, 3-r/#15-21 15.00

WANTED
Image Comics (Top Cow): Dec, 2003 - No. 6, Feb, 2004 ($2.99)

1-Three covers; Mark Millar-s/J.G. Jones-a; intro Wesley Gibson 3.00
1-4-Death Row Edition; r/#1-4 with extra sketch pages and deleted panels 3.00
2-6: 2-Cameos of DC villains. 6-Giordano-a in flashback scenes 3.00
...Dossier (5/04, $2.99) Pin-ups and character info; art by Jones, Romita Jr. & others 3.00
Image Firsts: Wanted #1 (9/10, $1.00) reprints #1 3.00
... Movie Edition Vol. 1 TPB (2008, $19.99) r/#1-6 & Dossier; movie photo-c; sketch pages & cover gallery; interviews with movie cast and director 20.00
HC (2005, $29.99) r/#1-6 & Dossier; intro by Vaughan, sketch pages & cover gallery 30.00

WANTED COMICS
Toytown Publications/Patches/Orbit Publ.: No. 9, Sept-Oct, 1947 - No. 53, April, 1953 (#9-33: 52 pgs.)

9-True crime cases; radio's Mr. D. A. app. 27 54 81 158 259 360
10,11: 10-Giunta-a; radio's Mr. D. A. app. 17 34 51 98 154 210
12-Used in **SOTI**, pg. 277 19 38 57 109 172 235
13-Heroin drug propaganda story 17 34 51 98 154 210
14-Marijuana drug mention story (2 pgs.) 15 30 45 90 140 190
15-17,19,20 14 28 42 80 115 150
18-Marijuana story, "Satan's Cigarettes"; r-in #45 & retitled 28 56 84 165 270 375
21,22: 21-Krigstein-a. 22-Extreme violence 14 28 42 81 118 155
23,25-34,36-38,40-44,46-48,53 13 26 39 72 101 130
24-Krigstein-a; "The Dope King", marijuana mention story 16 32 48 94 147 200

Wanted, The World's Most Dangerous Villians #1 © DC

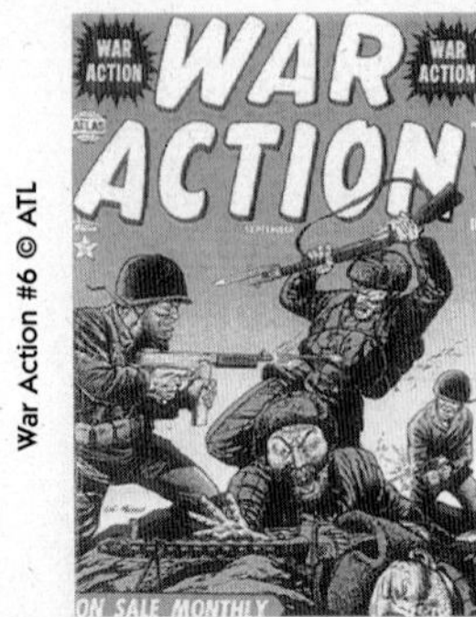

War Action #6 © ATL

Warfront #8 © HARV

	GD 2.0	VG 4.0	FN 6.0	VF 8.0	VF/NM 9.0	NM- 9.2
35-Used in **SOTI**, pg. 160	15	30	45	88	137	185
39-Drug propaganda story "The Horror Weed"	20	40	60	118	192	265
45-Marijuana story from #18	14	28	42	80	115	150
49-Has unstable pink-c that fades easily; rare in mint condition	14	28	42	82	121	160
50-Has unstable pink-c like #49; surrealist-c by Buscema; horror stories	15	30	45	85	130	175
51- "Holiday of Horror" junkie story; drug-c	17	34	51	100	158	215
52-Classic "Cult of Killers" opium use story	17	34	51	98	154	210

NOTE: ***Buscema*** *c-50, 51.* ***Lawrence*** *and* ***Leav*** *c/a most issues.* ***Syd Shores*** *c/a-48; c-37. Issues 9-46 have wanted criminals with their descriptions & drawn picture on cover.*

WANTED: DEAD OR ALIVE (TV)
Dell Publishing Co.: No. 1102, May-July, 1960 - No. 1164, Mar-May, 1961

	GD 2.0	VG 4.0	FN 6.0	VF 8.0	VF/NM 9.0	NM- 9.2
Four Color 1102 (#1)-Steve McQueen photo-c	11	22	33	76	151	225
Four Color 1164-Steve McQueen photo-c	9	18	27	61	106	150

WANTED, THE WORLD'S MOST DANGEROUS VILLAINS (See DC Special)
National Periodical Publ.: July-Aug, 1972 - No. 9, Aug-Sept, 1973 (All reprints & 20¢ issues)

	GD 2.0	VG 4.0	FN 6.0	VF 8.0	VF/NM 9.0	NM- 9.2
1-Batman, Green Lantern (story r-from G.L. #1), & Green Arrow	4	8	12	22	34	45
2-Batman/Joker/Penguin-c/story r-from Batman #25; plus Flash story (r-from Flash #121)	3	6	9	17	25	32
3-9: 3-Dr. Fate(r/More Fun #65), Hawkman(r/Flash #100), & Vigilante(r/Action #69). 4-Green Lantern(r/All-American #61) & Kid Eternity(r/Kid Eternity #15). 5-Dollman/Green Lantern. 6-Burnley Starman; Wildcat/Sargon. 7-Johnny Quick(r/More Fun #76), Hawkman(r/Flash #90), Hourman by Baily(r/Adv. #72). 8-Dr. Fate/Flash(r/Flash #114). 9-S&K Sandman/Superman	3	6	9	14	20	26

NOTE: ***B. Bailey*** *a-7r.* ***Infantino*** *a-2r.* ***Kane*** *r-1, 5.* ***Kubert*** *r-3i, 6, 7.* ***Meskin*** *r-3, 7.* ***Reinman*** *r-4, 6.*

WAR (See Fightin' Marines #122)
Charlton Comics: Jul, 1975 - No. 9, Nov, 1976; No. 10, Sept, 1978 - No. 47, 1984

	GD 2.0	VG 4.0	FN 6.0	VF 8.0	VF/NM 9.0	NM- 9.2
1-Boyette painted-c	3	6	9	14	19	24
2-10: 3-Sutton painted-c	2	4	6	8	10	12
11-20	1	2	3	5	6	8
21-40	1	2	3	4	5	7
41,42,44-47 (lower print run): 47-Reprints	1	2	3	5	6	8
43 (2/84) (lower print run) Ditko-a (7 pgs.)	2	4	6	8	10	12
7,9 (Modern Comics-r, 1977)						6.00

WAR, THE (See The Draft & The Pitt)
Marvel Comics: 1989 - No. 4, 1990 ($3.50, squarebound, 52 pgs.)

	GD 2.0	VG 4.0	FN 6.0	VF 8.0	VF/NM 9.0	NM- 9.2
1-4: Characters from New Universe						4.00

WAR ACTION (Korean War)
Atlas Comics (CPS): April, 1952 - No. 14, June, 1953

	GD 2.0	VG 4.0	FN 6.0	VF 8.0	VF/NM 9.0	NM- 9.2
1	20	40	60	117	189	270
2-Hartley-a	13	26	39	72	101	135
3-10,14: 7-Pakula-a. 14-Colan-a	10	20	30	58	79	100
11-13-Krigstein-a. 11-Romita-a	11	22	33	62	86	110

NOTE: ***Berg*** *c-11.* ***Brodsky*** *a-2; c-1-4.* ***Heath*** *a-1; c-7, 14.* ***Keller*** *a-6.* ***Maneely*** *a-1; c-12.* ***Sale*** *a-7.* ***Tuska*** *a-2, 8.*

WAR ADVENTURES
Atlas Comics (HPC): Jan, 1952 - No. 13, Feb, 1953

	GD 2.0	VG 4.0	FN 6.0	VF 8.0	VF/NM 9.0	NM- 9.2
1-Tuska-a	20	40	60	117	189	260
2	13	26	39	72	101	130
3-7,9-13: 3-Pakula-a. 7-Maneely-c. 9-Romita-a	10	20	30	58	79	100
8-Krigstein-a	11	22	33	62	86	110

NOTE: ***Brodsky*** *c-1-3, 6, 8, 11, 12.* ***Heath*** *a-2, 5, 7, 10; c-4, 5, 9, 13.* ***Reinman*** *a-13.* ***Robinson*** *a-3; c-10.*

WAR ADVENTURES ON THE BATTLEFIELD (See Battlefield)

WAR AGAINST CRIME! (Becomes Vault of Horror #12 on)
E. C. Comics: Spring, 1948 - No. 11, Feb-Mar, 1950

	GD 2.0	VG 4.0	FN 6.0	VF 8.0	VF/NM 9.0	NM- 9.2
1-Real Stories From Police Records on-c #1-9	82	164	246	528	902	1275
2,3	48	96	144	302	514	725
4-9	42	84	126	269	452	635
10-1st Vault Keeper app. & 1st Vault of Horror	206	412	618	1318	2259	3200
11-2nd Vault Keeper app.; 1st EC horror-c	142	284	426	909	1555	2200

NOTE: *All have* ***Johnny Craig*** *covers.* ***Feldstein*** *a-4, 7-9.* ***Harrison/Wood*** *a-11.* ***Ingels*** *a-1, 2, 8.* ***Palais*** *a-8. Changes to horror with #10.*

WAR AGAINST CRIME
Gemstone Publishing: Apr, 2000 - No. 11, Feb, 2001 ($2.50)

	GD 2.0	VG 4.0	FN 6.0	VF 8.0	VF/NM 9.0	NM- 9.2
1-11: E.C. reprints						4.00

WAR AND ATTACK (Also see Special War Series #3)
Charlton Comics: Fall, 1964; V2#54, June, 1966 - V2#63, Dec, 1967

	GD 2.0	VG 4.0	FN 6.0	VF 8.0	VF/NM 9.0	NM- 9.2
1-Wood-a (25 pgs.)	5	10	15	35	55	75
V2#54(6/66)-#63 (Formerly Fightin' Air Force)	3	6	9	16	22	28

NOTE: ***Montes/Bache*** *a-55, 56, 60, 63.*

WAR AT SEA (Formerly Space Adventures)
Charlton Comics: No. 22, Nov, 1957 - No. 42, June, 1961

	GD 2.0	VG 4.0	FN 6.0	VF 8.0	VF/NM 9.0	NM- 9.2
22	7	14	21	37	46	55
23-30: 26-Pearl Harbor, FDR app.	6	12	18	27	33	38
31-42: 42-Cuba's Fidel Castro story	3	6	9	17	25	32

WAR BATTLES
Harvey Publications: Feb, 1952 - No. 9, Dec, 1953

	GD 2.0	VG 4.0	FN 6.0	VF 8.0	VF/NM 9.0	NM- 9.2
1-Powell-a; Elias-c	9	18	27	63	107	150
2-Powell-a	5	10	15	34	55	75
3,4,7-9: 3,7-Powell-a	5	10	15	32	51	70
5-Flamethrower cover	14	28	42	80	115	150
6-Nostrand-a	6	12	18	39	62	85

WAR BIRDS
Fiction House Magazines: 1952(nd) - No. 3, Winter, 1952-53

	GD 2.0	VG 4.0	FN 6.0	VF 8.0	VF/NM 9.0	NM- 9.2
1	18	36	54	105	165	225
2,3	12	24	36	67	94	120

WARBLADE: ENDANGERED SPECIES (Also see WildC.A.T.S: Covert Action Teams)
Image Comics (WildStorm Productions): Jan, 1995 - No. 4, Apr, 1995 ($2.50, limited series)

	GD 2.0	VG 4.0	FN 6.0	VF 8.0	VF/NM 9.0	NM- 9.2
1-4: 1-Gatefold wraparound-c						3.00

WAR COMBAT (Becomes Combat Casey #6 on)
Atlas Comics (LBI No. 1/SAI No. 2-5): March, 1952 - No. 5, Nov, 1952

	GD 2.0	VG 4.0	FN 6.0	VF 8.0	VF/NM 9.0	NM- 9.2
1	19	38	57	111	176	240
2	12	24	36	67	94	120
3-5	10	20	30	58	79	100

NOTE: ***Berg*** *a-2, 4, 5.* ***Brodsky*** *c-1, 2, 4, 5.* ***Henkel*** *a-5.* ***Maneely*** *a-1, 4; c-3.* ***Reinman*** *a-2.*

WAR COMICS (War Stories #5 on)(See Key Ring Comics)
Dell Publishing Co.: May, 1940 (No month given) - No. 4, Sept, 1941

	GD 2.0	VG 4.0	FN 6.0	VF 8.0	VF/NM 9.0	NM- 9.2
1-Sikandur the Robot Master, Sky Hawk, Scoop Mason, War Correspondent begin; McWilliams-c; 1st war comic	71	142	213	454	777	1100
2-Origin Greg Gilday (5/41)	37	74	111	222	361	500
3-Joan becomes Greg Gilday's aide	26	52	78	154	252	350
4-Origin Night Devils	27	54	81	158	259	360

WAR COMICS
Marvel/Atlas (USA No. 1-41/JPI No. 42-49): Dec, 1950 - No. 49, Sept, 1957

	GD 2.0	VG 4.0	FN 6.0	VF 8.0	VF/NM 9.0	NM- 9.2
1	28	56	84	165	270	375
2	15	30	45	88	137	185
3-10	14	28	42	80	115	150
11-Flame thrower w/burning bodies on-c	20	40	60	114	182	250
12-20: 16-Romita-a	12	24	36	67	94	120
21,23-32: 26-Valley Forge story. 32-Last pre-code issue (2/55)	10	20	30	58	79	100
22-Krigstein-a	11	22	33	62	86	110
33-37,39-42,44,45,47,48: 40-Romita-a	10	20	30	58	79	100
38-Kubert/Moskowitz-a	11	22	33	62	86	110
43,49-Torres-a. 43-Severin/Elder E.C. swipe from Two-Fisted Tales #31	11	22	33	62	86	110
46-Crandall-a	11	22	33	62	86	110

NOTE: ***Ayers*** *a-17.* ***Berg*** *a-13.* ***Colan*** *a-4, 36, 48, 49; c-17.* ***Drucker*** *a-37, 43, 48.* ***Everett*** *a-17.* ***Heath*** *a-6-9, 16, 19, 25, 36; c-11, 16, 19, 23, 25, 26, 29-32, 36.* ***G. Kane*** *a-19.* ***Lawrence*** *a-36.* ***Maneely*** *a-7, 9, 13, 14, 20, 23; c-6, 27, 37.* ***Orlando*** *a-42, 48.* ***Pakula*** *a-26, 40.* ***Ravielli*** *a-27.* ***Reinman*** *a-11, 16, 26.* ***Robinson*** *a-15; c-13.* ***Severin*** *a-26, 27; c-48.* ***Shores*** *a-13.* ***Sinnott*** *a-37.*

WAR DANCER (Also see Charlemagne, Doctor Chaos #2 & Warriors of Plasm)
Defiant: Feb, 1994 - No. 6, July, 1994 ($2.50)

	GD 2.0	VG 4.0	FN 6.0	VF 8.0	VF/NM 9.0	NM- 9.2
1-3,5,6: 1-Intro War Dancer; Weiss-c/a begins. 1-3-Weiss-a(p). 6-Pre-Schism issue						3.00
4-($3.25, 52 pgs.)-Charlemagne app.						4.00

WAR DOGS OF THE U.S. ARMY
Avon Periodicals: 1952

	GD 2.0	VG 4.0	FN 6.0	VF 8.0	VF/NM 9.0	NM- 9.2
1-Kinstler-c/a	15	30	45	85	130	175

WAREHOUSE 13 (Based on the Syfy TV series)
Dynamite Entertainment: 2011 - Present ($3.99)

	GD 2.0	VG 4.0	FN 6.0	VF 8.0	VF/NM 9.0	NM- 9.2
1-4: 1-Raab & Hughes-s/Morse-a						4.00

WARFRONT
Harvey Publications: 9/51 - #35, 11/58; #36, 10/65; #39, 2/67

	GD 2.0	VG 4.0	FN 6.0	VF 8.0	VF/NM 9.0	NM- 9.2
1-Korean War	10	20	30	66	121	175
2	6	12	18	39	62	85
3-10	5	10	15	32	51	70

Warheads #5 © MAR

Warlands #1 © Dreamwave

Warlock and the Infinity Watch #32 © MAR

GD VG FN VF VF/NM NM-
2.0 4.0 6.0 8.0 9.0 9.2

11,12,14,16-20 4 8 12 28 44 60
13,15,22-Nostrand-a 6 12 18 39 62 85
21,23-27,31-33,35 4 8 12 28 44 60
28-30,34-Kirby-c 6 12 18 41 66 90
36-(12/66)-Dynamite Joe begins, ends #39; Williamson-a
5 10 15 32 51 70
37-Wood-a (17 pgs.) 5 10 15 32 51 70
38,39-Wood-a, 2-3 pgs.; Lone Tiger app. 4 8 12 28 44 60
NOTE: *Powell a-1-6, 9-11, 14, 17, 20, 23, 25-28, 30, 31, 34, 36.* ***Powell/Nostrand*** *a-12, 13, 15.* ***Simon*** *c-36?, 38.*

WAR FURY
Comic Media/Harwell (Allen Hardy Assoc.): Sept, 1952 - No. 4, Mar, 1953
1-Heck-c/a in all; Palais-a; bullet hole in forehead-c; all issues are very violent; soldier using flame thrower on enemy 39 78 117 240 395 550
2-4: 4-Morisi-a 21 42 63 122 199 275

WAR GODS OF THE DEEP (See Movie Classics)

WARHAWKS
TSR, Inc.: 1990 - No. 10, 1991 ($2.95, 44 pgs.)
1-10-Based on TSR game, Spiegle a-1-6 4.00

WARHEADS
Marvel Comics UK: June, 1992 - No. 14, Aug, 1993 ($1.75)
1-Wolverine-c/story; indicia says #2 by mistake 4.00
2-14: 2-Nick Fury app. 3-Iron Man-c/story. 4,5-X-Force. 5-Liger vs. Cable. 6,7-Death's Head II app. (#6 is cameo) 3.00

WAR HEROES (See Marine War Heroes)

WAR HEROES
Dell Publishing Co.: 7-9/42 (no month); No. 2, 10-12/42 - No. 10, 10-12/44 (Quarterly)
1-General Douglas MacArthur-c 27 54 81 160 263 365
2-James Doolittle and other officers-c 15 30 45 86 133 180
3,5: 3-Pro-Russian back-c 14 28 42 76 108 140
4-Disney's Gremlins app. 18 36 54 107 169 230
6-10: 6-Tothish-a by Discount 10 20 30 56 76 95
NOTE: *No. 1 was to be released in July, but was delayed. Painted c-4, 6-9.*

WAR HEROES
Ace Magazines: May, 1952 - No. 8, Apr, 1953
1 13 26 39 72 101 130
2-Lou Cameron-a 9 18 27 47 61 75
3-8: 6,7-Cameron-a 8 16 24 42 54 65

WAR HEROES (Also see Blue Bird Comics)
Charlton Comics: Feb, 1963 - No. 27, Nov, 1967
1,2: 2-John F. Kennedy story 4 8 12 26 41 55
3-10 3 6 9 18 27 35
11-26: 22-True story about plot to kill Hitler 3 6 9 14 20 26
27-1st Devils Brigade by Glanzman 3 6 9 18 27 35
NOTE: ***Montes/Bache*** *a-3-7, 21, 25, 27; c-3-7.*

WAR HEROES
Image Comics: July, 2008 - No. 6 ($2.99, limited series)
1-3-Soldiers given super powers; Mark Millar-s/Tony Harris-a/c; four covers 3.00

WAR IS HELL
Marvel Comics Group: Jan, 1973 - No. 15, Oct, 1975
1-Williamson-a(r), 5 pgs.; Ayers-a 3 6 9 17 25 32
2-8-Reprints. 6-(11/73). 7-(6/74). 7,8-Kirby-a 2 4 6 10 14 18
9-Intro Death 5 10 15 32 51 70
10-15-Death app. 3 6 9 17 25 32
NOTE: ***Bolle*** *a-3r.* ***Powell*** *a-1.* ***Woodbridge*** *a-1. Sgt. Fury reprints-7, 8.*

WAR IS HELL: THE FIRST FLIGHT OF THE PHANTOM EAGLE
Marvel Comics (MAX): May, 2008 - No. 5, Sept, 2008 ($3.99, limited series)
1-5-World War I fighter pilots; Ennis-s/Chaykin-a/Cassaday-c 4.00

WARLANDS
Image Comics: Aug, 1999 - No. 12, Feb, 2001 ($2.50)
1-9,11,12-Pat Lee-a(p)/Adrian Tsang-s 3.00
10-($2.95) Flip book w/Shidima preview 4.00
... Chronicles 1,2 (2/00, 7/00; $7.95) 1-r/#1-3. 2-r/#4-6 8.00
...Darklyte TPB (8/01, $14.95) r/#0,1/2,1-6 w/cover gallery; new Lee-c 15.00
...Epilogue: Three Stories (3/01, $5.95) includes r/Wizard #1/2 & AE #0 6.00
Another Universe #0 3.00
Wizard #1/2 5.00

WARLANDS: THE AGE OF ICE (Volume 2)
Image Comics: July, 2001 - No. 9, Nov, 2002 ($2.95)
#0-(2/02, $2.25) 3.00
#1/2 (4/02, $2.25) 3.00
1-9: 2-Flip book preview of Banished Knights 3.00
TPB (2003, $15.95) r/#1-9 16.00

WARLANDS: DARK TIDE RISING (Volume 3)
Image Comics: Dec, 2002 - No. 6, May, 2003 ($2.95)
1-6: 1-Wraparound gatefold-c 3.00

WARLOCK (The Power of...)(Also see Avengers Annual #7, Fantastic Four #66, 67, Incredible Hulk #178, Infinity Crusade, Infinity Gauntlet, Infinity War, Marvel Premiere #1, Marvel Two-In-One Annual #2, Silver Surfer V3#46, Strange Tales #178-181 & Thor #165)
Marvel Comics Group: Aug, 1972 - No. 8, Oct, 1973; No. 9, Oct, 1975 - No. 15, Nov, 1976
1-Origin by Kane 8 16 24 55 93 130
2,3 4 8 12 28 44 60
4-8: 4-Death of Eddie Roberts 3 6 9 18 27 35
9-Starlin's 2nd Thanos saga begins, ends #15; new costume Warlock; Thanos cameo only; story cont'd from Strange Tales #178-181; Starlin-c/a in #9-15
4 8 12 26 41 55
10-Origin Thanos & Gamora; recaps events from Capt. Marvel #25-34. Thanos vs.The Magus-c/story 4 8 12 28 44 60
11-Thanos app.; Warlock dies 3 6 9 20 30 40
12-14: (Regular 25¢ edition) 14-Origin Star Thief; last 25¢ issue
3 6 9 17 25 32
12-14-(30¢-c, limited distribution) 5 10 15 30 48 65
15-Thanos-c/story 3 6 9 18 27 35
NOTE: ***Buscema*** *a-2p; c-8p.* ***G. Kane*** *a-1p, 3-5p; c-1p, 2, 3, 4p, 5p, 7p.* ***Starlin*** *a-9-14p, 15; c-9, 10, 11p, 12p, 13-15.* ***Sutton*** *a-1-8i.*

WARLOCK (...Special Edition on-c)
Marvel Comics Group: Dec, 1982 - No. 6, May, 1983 ($2.00, slick paper, 52 pgs.)
1-Warlock-r/Strange Tales #178-180. 4.00
2-6: 2-r/Str. Tales #180,181 & Warlock #9. 3-r/Warlock #10-12(Thanos origin recap). 4-r/Warlock #12-15. 5-r/Warlock #15, Marvel Team-Up #55 & Avengers Ann. #7. 6-r/2nd half Avengers Annual #7 & Marvel Two-in-One Annual #2 4.00
Special Edition #1(12/83) 4.00
NOTE: ***Byrne*** *a-5r.* ***Starlin*** *a-1-6r; c-1-6(new). Direct sale only.*

WARLOCK
Marvel Comics: V2#1, May, 1992 - No. 6, Oct, 1992 ($2.50, limited series)
V2#1-6: 1-Reprints 1982 reprint series w/Thanos 3.00

WARLOCK
Marvel Comics: Nov, 1998 - No. 4, Feb, 1999 ($2.99, limited series)
1-4-Warlock vs. Drax 3.00

WARLOCK (M-Tech)
Marvel Comics: Oct, 1999 - No. 9, June, 2000 ($1.99/$2.50)
1-5: 1-Quesada-c. 2-Two covers 3.00
6-9: 6-Begin $2.50-c. 8-Avengers app. 3.00

WARLOCK
Marvel Comics: Nov, 2004 - No. 4, Feb, 2005 ($2.99, limited series)
1-4-Adlard-a/Williams-c 3.00

WARLOCK AND THE INFINITY WATCH (Also see Infinity Gauntlet)
Marvel Comics: Feb, 1992 - No. 42, July, 1995 ($1.75) (Sequel to Infinity Gauntlet)
1-Starlin-scripts begin; brief origin recap; sequel to Infinity Gauntlet 4.00
2,3: 2-Reintro Moondragon 3.00
4-24,26: 7-Reintro The Magus; Moondragon app.; Thanos cameo on last 2 pgs. 8,9-Thanos battles Gamora-c/story. 8-Magus & Moondragon app. 10-Thanos-c/story; Magus app. 13-Hulk x-over. 21-Drax vs. Thor 3.00
25-($2.95, 52 pgs.)-Die-cut & embossed double-c; Thor & Thanos app. 4.00
28-42: 28-$1.95-c begins; bound-in card sheet 3.00
NOTE: ***Austin*** *c/a-1-4i, 7i.* ***Leonardi*** *a(p)-3, 4.* ***Medina*** *c/a(p)-1, 2, 5; 6, 9, 10, 14, 15, 20.* ***Williams*** *a(i)-8, 12, 13, 16-19.*

WARLOCK CHRONICLES
Marvel Comics: June, 1993 - No. 8, Feb, 1994 ($2.00, limited series)
1-($2.95)-Holo-grafx foil & embossed-c; origin retold; Starlin scripts begin; Keith Williams-a(i) in all 4.00
2-8: 3-Thanos & Mephisto-c/story. 4-Vs. Magus-c/s. 8-Contains free 16 pg. Razorline insert 3.00

WARLOCK 5
Aircel Pub.: 11/86 - No. 22, 5/89; V2#1, June, 1989 - V2#5, 1989 ($1.70, B&W)
1-5,7-11-Gordon Derry-s/Denis Beauvais-a thru #11. 5-Green Cyborg on-c.

War Machine #6 © MAR

War of Kings #1 © MAR

Warp #11 © FC

GD VG FN VF VF/NM NM-
2.0 4.0 6.0 8.0 9.0 9.2

GD VG FN VF VF/NM NM-
2.0 4.0 6.0 8.0 9.0 9.2

5-Misnumbered as #6 (no #6); Blue Girl on-c. 3.00
12-22-Barry Blair-s/a. 18-$1.95-c begins 4.00
V2#1-5 ($2.00, B&W)-All issues by Barry Blair 3.00
Compilation 1,2: 1-r/#1-5 (1988, $5.95); 2-r/#6-9 6.00

WARLORD (See 1st Issue Special #8) (B&W reprints in Showcase Presents: Warlord)
National Periodical Publications/DC Comics #123 on: 1-2/76; No.2, 3-4/76; No.3, 10-11/76 - No. 133, Win, 1988-89

1-Story cont'd. from 1st Issue Special #8 4 8 12 24 37 50
2-Intro. Machiste 3 6 9 14 20 25
3-5 2 4 6 9 12 15
6-10: 6-Intro Mariah. 7-Origin Machiste. 9-Dons new costume 1 3 4 6 8 10
11-20: 11-Origin-r. 12-Intro Aton. 15-Tara returns; Warlord has son 6.00
21-36,40,41: 27-New facts about origin. 28-1st app. Wizard World. 32-Intro Shakira. 40-Warlord gets new costume 5.00
22-Whitman variant edition 2 4 6 13 18 22
37-39: 37,38-Origin Omac by Starlin. 38-Intro Jennifer Morgan, Warlord's daughter. 39-Omac ends. 6.00
42-48: 42-47-Omac back-up series. 48-(52 pgs.)-1st app. Arak; contains free 14 pg. Arak Son of Thunder; Claw The Unconquered app. 5.00
49-62,64-99,101-132: 49-Claw The Unconquered app. 50-Death of Aton. 51-Reprints #1. 55-Arion Lord of Atlantis begins, ends #62. 91-Origin w/new facts. 114,115-Legends x-over. 125-Death of Tara. 131-1st DC work by Rob Liefeld (9/88) 4.00
63-The Barren Earth begins; free 16pg. Masters of the Universe preview 5.00
100-($1.25, 52 pgs.) 5.00
133-($1.50, 52 pgs.) 5.00
Annual 1-6 ('82-'87): 1-Grell-c,/a(p). 6-New Gods app. 5.00
The Savage Empire TPB (1991, $19.95) r/#1-10,12 & First Issue Special #8; Grell intro. 25.00
NOTE: ***Grell** a-1-15, 16-50p, 51r, 52p, 59p, Annual 1p; c-1-70, 100-104, 112, 116, 117, Annual 1, 5.* ***Wayne Howard** a-64i.* ***Starlin** a-37-39p.*

WARLORD
DC Comics: Jan, 1992 - No. 6, June, 1992 ($1.75, limited series)

1-6: Grell-c & scripts in all 3.00

WARLORD
DC Comics: Apr, 2006 - No. 10, Jan, 2007 ($2.99)

1-10: 1-Bruce Jones-s/Bart Sears-a. 10-Winslade-a 3.00

WARLORD
DC Comics: Jun, 2009 - No. 16, Sept, 2010 ($2.99)

1-16: 1-Grell-s/Prado-a/Grell-c. 7-9,11,12,15,16-Grell-s/a/c. 10-Hardin-a 3.00
...: The Saga SC (2010, $17.99) r/#1-6; cover gallery 18.00

WARLORD OF MARS
Dynamite Entertainment: 2010 - Present ($1.00/$3.99)

1-($1.00) John Carter on Earth; Sadowski-a; covers by Ross, Campbell, Jusko. Parrillo 3.00
2-16-($3.99) Multiple covers on each. 3-Carter arrives on Mars. 4-Dejah Thoris intro. 4.00
... Annual 1 (2012, $4.99) Sadowski-a/Parrillo-c 5.00

WARLORD OF MARS: DEJAH THORIS
Dynamite Entertainment: 2011 - Present ($3.99, limited series)

1-10: 1-Five covers; Nelson-s/Rafael-a. 2-5-Four covers. 6-10-Three covers 4.00

WARLORD OF MARS: FALL OF BARSOOM
Dynamite Entertainment: 2011 - No. 5, 2012 ($3.99, limited series)

1-5-Napton-s/Castro-a/Jusko-c 4.00

WARLORDS (See DC Graphic Novel #2)

WAR MACHINE (Also see Iron Man #281,282 & Marvel Comics Presents #152)
Marvel Comics: Apr, 1994 - No. 25, Apr, 1996 ($1.50)

"Ashcan" edition (nd, 75¢, B&W, 16 pgs.) 3.00
1-($2.00, 52 pgs.)-Newsstand edition; Cable app. 4.00
1-($2.95, 52 pgs.)-Collectors ed.; embossed foil-c 5.00
2-14, 16-25: 2-Bound-in trading card sheet; Cable app. 2,3-Deathlok app. 8-red logo 3.00
8-($2.95)-Polybagged w/16 pg. Marvel Action Hour preview & acetate print; yellow logo 4.00
15 ($2.50)-Flip book 4.00

WAR MACHINE (Also see Dark Reign and Secret Invasion crossovers)
Marvel Comics: Feb, 2009 - No. 12, Feb, 2010 ($2.99)

1-12: 1-5-Pak-s/Manco-a/c; cyborg Jim Rhodes. 10-12-Dark Reign 3.00
1-Variant Titanium Man cover by Deodato 6.00

WAR MAN
Marvel Comics (Epic Comics): Nov, 1993 - No. 2, Dec, 1993 ($2.50, lim. series)

1,2 3.00

WAR OF KINGS
Marvel Comics: May, 2009 - No. 6, Oct, 2009 ($3.99, limited series)

1-6-Pelletier-a/Abnett & Lanning-s; Inhumans vs. the Shi'Ar 4.00
... Saga (2009, giveaway) synopsies of stories involving Kree, Shi'Ar, Inhumans, etc. 3.00
...: Savage World of Skaar 1 (8/09, $3.99) Gorgon & Starbolt land on Sakaar 4.00
...: Who Will Rule? 1 (11/09, $3.99) Pelletier-a; profile pages 4.00

WAR OF KINGS: ASCENSION
Marvel Comics: June, 2009 - No. 4, Sept, 2009 ($3.99, limited series)

1-4-Alves-a/Abnett & Lanning-s; Darkhawk app. 4.00

WAR OF KINGS: DARKHAWK (Leads into War Of Kings: Ascension limited series)
Marvel Comics: Apr, 2009 - No. 2, May, 2009 ($3.99, limited series)

1,2-Cebulski-s/Tolibao & Dazo-a/Peterson-c; r/Darkhawk #1,2 (1991) origin 4.00

WAR OF KINGS: WARRIORS
Marvel Comics: Sept, 2009 - No. 2, Oct, 2009 ($3.99, limited series)

1,2-Prequel to x-over; Gage-s/Asrar & Magno-a 4.00

WAR OF THE GODS
DC Comics: Sept, 1991 - No. 4, Dec, 1991 ($1.75, limited series)

1-4: Perez layouts, scripts & covers. 1-Contains free mini posters (Robin, Deathstroke). 2-4-Direct sale versions include 4 pin-ups printed on cover stock plus different-c 4.00

WAR OF THE GREEN LANTERNS: AFTERMATH
DC Comics: Sept, 2011 - No. 2, Oct, 2011 ($3.99, limited series)

1,2: 1-Bedard-s/Sepulveda & Kirkham-a. 2-Getty & Smith-a 4.00

WAR OF THE UNDEAD
IDW Publishing: Jan, 2007 - No. 3, Apr, 2007 ($3.99, limited series)

1-3-Bryan Johnson-s/Walter Flanagan-a 4.00

WAR OF THE WORLDS, THE
Caliber: 1996 - No. 5 ($2.95, B&W, 32 pgs.)(Based on H. G. Wells novel)

1-5: 1-Randy Zimmerman scripts begin 3.00

WARP
First Comics: Mar, 1983 - No. 19, Feb, 1985 ($1.00/$1.25, Mando paper)

1-Sargon-Mistress of War app.; Brunner-c/a thru #9 4.00
2-19: 2-Faceless Ones begin. 10-New Warp advs., & Outrider begin 3.00
Special 1-3: 1(7/83, 36 pgs.)-Origin Chaos-Prince of Madness; origin of Warp Universe begins, ends #3. 2(1/84)-Lord Cumulus vs. Sargon Mistress of War ($1.00). 3(6/84)-Chaos-Prince of Madness 3.00

WARPATH (Indians on the...)
Key Publications/Stanmor: Nov, 1954 - No. 3, Apr, 1955

1 11 22 33 62 86 110
2,3 8 16 24 40 50 60

WARPED
Empire Entertainment (Solson): Jun, 1990 - No. 2, Oct-Nov, 1990 (B&W mag)

1,2 3.00

WARP GRAPHICS ANNUAL
WaRP Graphics: Dec, 1985; 1988 ($2.50)

1-Elfquest, Blood of the Innocent, Thunderbunny & Myth Adventures 5.00
1 (1988) 4.00

WARREN PRESENTS
Warren Publications: Jan, 1979 - No. 14, Nov, 1981(B&W magazine)

1-Eerie, Creepy, & Vampirella-r; Ring of the Warlords; Merlin-s; Dax-s; Sanjulian-c 3 6 9 15 21 26
2-6(10/79): 2-The Rook. 3-Alien Invasions Comix. 4-Movie Aliens. 5-Dracula '79. 6-Strange Stories of Vampires Comix 2 4 6 9 13 16
8(10/80)-r/1st app. Pantha from Vamp. #30 2 4 6 11 16 20
9(11/80) Empire Encounters Comix 2 4 6 10 14 18
13(10/81),14(11/81):13-Sword and Sorcery Comix 3 6 9 14 19 24
(#7,10,11,12 may not exist, or may be a Special below)
Special-Alien Collectors Edition (1979) 3 6 9 14 19 24
Special-Close Encounters of the Third Kind (1978) 2 4 6 9 13 16
Special-Lord of the Rings (6/79) 3 6 9 19 29 38
Special-Meteor (1/80) 2 4 6 9 13 16
Special-Moonraker/James Bond (10/79) 2 4 6 9 13 16
Special-Star Wars (1977) 3 6 9 19 29 38

WAR REPORT
Ajax/Farrell Publications (Excellent Publ.): Sept, 1952 - No. 5, May, 1953

1 14 28 42 82 121 160

Warriors of Mars #1 © Savage Tales

Warstrike #4 © MAL

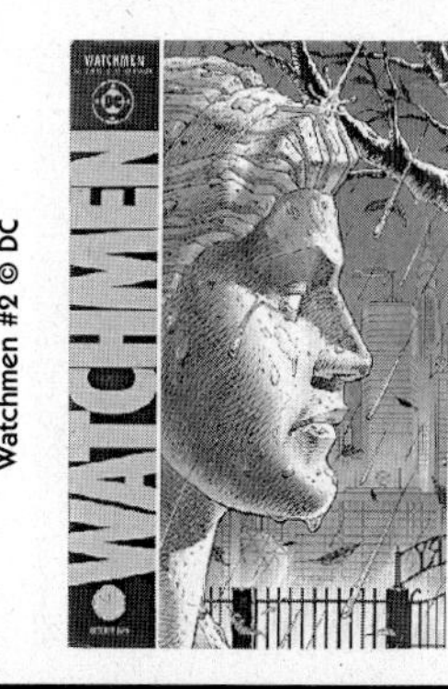
Watchmen #2 © DC

	GD 2.0	VG 4.0	FN 6.0	VF 8.0	VF/NM 9.0	NM- 9.2
2-Flame thrower w/burning bodies on-c	16	32	48	94	147	200
3,5	9	18	27	50	65	80
4-Used in **POP**, pg. 94	10	20	30	54	72	90

WARRIOR (Wrestling star)
Ultimate Creations: May, 1996 - No. 4, 1997 ($2.95)

1-4: Warrior scripts; Callahan-c/a. 3-Wraparound-c. 4-Warrior #3 in indicia; pin-ups 3.00
1-Variant-c. 5.00
X-Mas (11/96, $3.50) listed as "No. 3" in indicia; pin-ups by various; Quesada-c 4.00

WARRIOR COMICS
H.C. Blackerby: 1945 (1930s DC reprints)

1-Wing Brady, The Iron Man, Mark Markon 21 42 63 126 206 285

WARRIOR OF WAVERLY STREET, THE
Dark Horse Comics: Nov, 1996 - No. 2, Dec, 1996 ($2.95, mini-series)

1,2-Darrow-c 3.00

WARRIORS
CFD Productions: 1993 (B&W, one-shot)

1-Linsner, Dark One-a 2 4 6 10 14 18

WARRIORS, THE: OFFICIAL MOVIE ADAPTATION (Based on the 1979 movie)
Dabel Brothers Publishing/Dynamite Ent.: Feb, 2009 - No. 5, 2010 ($3.99, limited series)

1-5: 1-Three covers plus wraparound photo-c; Dibari-a. 3-Eric Powell-c 4.00
...: Jailbreak 1 (7/09, $3.99) Apon & Herman-a 4.00

WARRIORS OF MARS (Also see Warlord of Mars titles)
Dynamite Entertainment: 2012 - Present ($3.99, limited series)

1-Gullivar Jones visits Barsoom; Jusko-c 4.00

WARRIORS OF PLASM (Also see Plasm)
Defiant: Aug, 1993 - No. 13, Aug, 1995 ($2.95/$2.50)

1-4: Shooter-scripts; Lapham-c/a: 1-1st app. Glory. 4-Bound-in fold-out poster 4.00
5-7,10-13: 5-Begin $2.50-c. 13-Schism issue 3.00
8,9-($2.75, 44 pgs.) 4.00
The Collected Edition (2/94, $9.95)-r/Plasm #0, WOP #1-4 & Splatterball 10.00

WARRIORS THREE (Fandral, Volstagg, and Hogun from Thor)
Marvel Comics: Jan, 2011 - No. 4, Apr, 2011 ($3.99, limited series)

1-4-Bill Willingham-s/Neil Edwards-a. 2,4-Conner-c 4.00

WAR ROMANCES (See True...)

WAR SHIPS
Dell Publishing Co.: 1942 (36 pgs.)(Similar to Large Feature Comics)

nn-Cover by McWilliams; contains photos & drawings of U.S. war ships
18 36 54 105 165 225

WAR STORIES (Formerly War Comics)
Dell Publ. Co.: No. 5, 1942(nd); No. 6, Aug-Oct, 1942 - No. 8, Feb-Apr, 1943

5-Origin The Whistler 27 54 81 158 259 360
6-8: 6-8-Night Devils app. 8-Painted-c 20 40 60 117 189 260

WAR STORIES (Korea)
Ajax/Farrell Publications (Excellent Publ.): Sept, 1952 - No. 5, May, 1953

1 14 28 42 80 115 150
2 9 18 27 47 61 75
3-5 8 16 24 44 57 70

WAR STORIES (See Star Spangled...)

WAR STORY
DC Comics (Vertigo): Nov, 2001 - Present ($4.95, series of World War II one-shots)

...: Archangel (4/03) Ennis-s/Erskine-a 5.00
...: Condors (3/03) Ennis-s/Ezquerra-a 5.00
...: D-Day Dodgers (12/01) Ennis-s/Higgins-a 5.00
...: J For Jenny (2/03) Ennis-s/Lloyd-a 5.00
...: Johann's Tiger (11/01) Ennis-s/Weston-a 5.00
...: Nightingale (2/02) Ennis-s/Lloyd-a 5.00
...: Screaming Eagles (1/02) Ennis-s/Gibbons-a 5.00
...: The Reivers (1/03) Ennis-s/Kennedy-a 5.00
Vol. 1 (2004, $19.95) r/Johann's Tiger, D-Day Dodgers, Screaming Eagles, Nightingale 20.00
Vol. 2 (2006, $19.99) r/J For Jenny, The Reivers, Condors, Archangel; Ennis afterword 20.00

WARSTRIKE
Malibu Comics (Ultraverse): May, 1994 - No. 7, Nov, 1995 ($1.95)

1-7: 1-Simonson-c 3.00
1-Ultra 5000 Limited silver foil 4.00
Giant Size 1 (12/94, $2.50, 44pgs.)-Prelude to Godwheel 4.00

WART AND THE WIZARD (See The Sword & the Stone under Movie Comics)
Gold Key: Feb, 1964 (Walt Disney)(Characters from Sword in the Stone movie)

1 (10102-402) 4 8 12 28 44 60

WAR THAT TIME FORGOT, THE
DC Comics: Jul, 2008 - No. 12, Jun, 2009 ($2.99, limited series)

1-12: 1-Bruce Jones-s/Al Barrionuevo-a/Neal Adams-c; Enemy Ace app. 3.00
... Vol. 1 TPB (2009, $17.99) r/#1-6 18.00
... Vol. 2 TPB (2009, $17.99) r/#7-12 18.00

WARTIME ROMANCES
St. John Publishing Co.: July, 1951 - No. 18, Nov, 1953

1-All Baker-c/a 47 94 141 296 498 700
2-All Baker-c/a 34 68 102 206 336 465
3,4-All Baker-c/a 32 64 96 192 314 435
5-8-Baker-c/a(2-3) each 31 62 93 182 296 410
9,11,12,16,18: Baker-c/a each. 9-Two signed stories by Estrada
25 50 75 147 241 335
10,13-15,17-Baker-c only 20 40 60 120 195 270

WAR VICTORY ADVENTURES (#1 titled War Victory Comics)
U.S. Treasury Dept./War Victory/Harvey Publ.: Sum, 1942 - No. 3, Wint, 1943-44 (5¢/10¢)

1-(5¢)(Promotion of Savings Bonds)-Featuring America's greatest comic art by top syndicated cartoonists; Blondie, Joe Palooka, Green Hornet, Dick Tracy, Superman, Gumps, etc.; (36 pgs.); all profits were contributed to U.S.O. & Army/Navy relief funds
43 86 129 271 461 650
2-(10¢) Battle of Stalingrad story; Powell-a (8/43); flag & WWII Japanese-c
41 82 123 256 428 600
3-(10¢) Capt. Red Cross-c & text only; WWII Nazi-c; Powell-a
40 80 120 246 411 575

WAR WAGON, THE (See Movie Classics)

WAR WINGS
Charlton Comics: Oct, 1968

1 3 6 9 14 20 26

WARWORLD!
Dark Horse Comics: Feb, 1989 ($1.75, B&W, one-shot)

1-Gary Davis sci/fi art in Moebius style 3.00

WASHABLE JONES AND THE SHMOO (Also see Al Capp's Shmoo)
Toby Press: June, 1953

1- "Super-Shmoo" 19 38 57 109 172 235

WASH TUBBS (See The Comics, Crackajack Funnies)
Dell Publishing Co.: No. 11, 1942 - No. 53, 1944

Four Color 11 (#1) 24 48 72 168 359 550
Four Color 28 (1943) 16 32 48 109 237 365
Four Color 53 12 24 36 83 172 260

WASTELAND
DC Comics: Dec, 1987 - No. 18, May, 1989 ($1.75-$2.00 #13 on, mature)

1-5(4/88), 5(5/88), 6(5/88)-18: 13,15-Orlando-a 3.00
NOTE: ***Orlando** a-12, 13, 15. **Truman** a-10; c-13.*

WATCHMEN
DC Comics: Sept, 1986 - No. 12, Oct, 1987 (maxi-series)

1-Alan Moore scripts & Dave Gibbons-c/a in all 2 4 6 11 16 20
1-(2009, $1.50) Second printing 3.00
2-12 2 4 6 9 12 15
Hardcover Collection-Slip-cased-r/#1-12 w/new material; produced by Graphitti Designs 100.00
HC (2008, $39.99) recolored r/#1-12; design & promotional art; Moore & Gibbons intros 40.00
Trade paperback (1987, $14.95)-r/#1-12 25.00

WATER BIRDS AND THE OLYMPIC ELK (Disney)
Dell Publishing Co.: No. 700, Apr, 1956

Four Color 700-Movie 5 10 15 35 55 75

WATERWORLD: CHILDREN OF LEVIATHAN
Acclaim Comics: Aug, 1997 - No. 4, Nov, 1997 ($2.50, mini-series)

1-4 3.00

WAY OF THE RAT
CrossGeneration Comics: Jun, 2002 - No. 24, June, 2004 ($2.95)

1-24: 1-Dixon-s/ Jeff Johnson-a. 5-Whigham-a. 9,14-Luke Ross-a 3.00
Free Comic Book Day Special (6/03) reprints #1 w/features, interviews, CrossGen info 3.00
...: The Walls of Zhumar Vol. 1 (1/03, $15.95) r/#1-6 16.00
Vol. 2: The Dragon's Wake (2003, $15.95) r/#7-12 16.00

Weapon X #25 © MAR

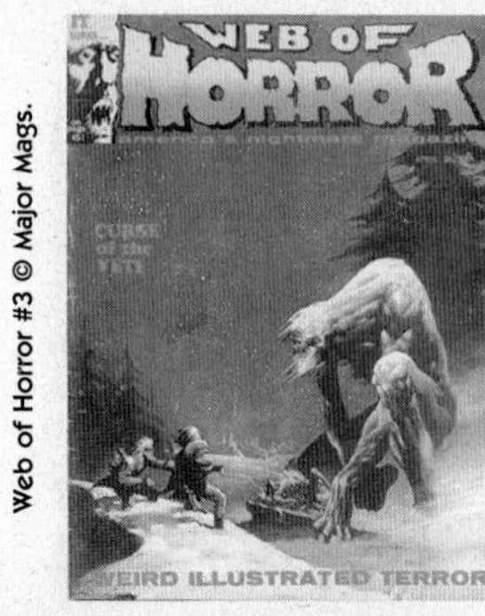

Web of Horror #3 © Major Mags.

Web of Spider-Man #12 © MAR

GD VG FN VF VF/NM NM-
2.0 4.0 6.0 8.0 9.0 9.2

GD VG FN VF VF/NM NM-
2.0 4.0 6.0 8.0 9.0 9.2

WEAPON X
Marvel Comics: Apr, 1994 ($12.95, one-shot)

nn-r/Marvel Comics Presents #72-84 13.00

WEAPON X
Marvel Comics: Mar, 1995 - No. 4, June, 1995 ($1.95)

1-Age of Apocalypse 4.00
2-4 3.00

WEAPON X
Marvel Comics: Nov, 2002 - No. 28, Nov, 2004 ($2.25/$2.99)

1-7: 1-Sabretooth-c/app.; Tieri-s/Jeanty-a 3.00
8-28: 8-Begin $2.99-c. 14-Invaders app. 15-Chamber joins. 16-18,21-25-Wolverine app. 3.00
Vol. 1: The Draft TPB (2003, $21.99) r/#1-5, #1/2 & The Draft one-shots 22.00
Vol. 2: The Underground TPB (2003, $19.99) r/#6-13 20.00
Wizard #1/2 (2002) 5.00

WEAPON X: DAYS OF FUTURE NOW
Marvel Comics: Sept, 2005 - No. 5, Jan, 2006 ($2.99, limited series)

1-5-Tieri-s/Sears-a; Chamber, Sauron & Fantomex app. 3.00
TPB (2006, $13.99) r/#1-5 14.00

WEAPON X: FIRST CLASS
Marvel Comics: Jan, 2009 - No. 3, Mar, 2009 ($3.99, limited series)

1-3:1-Sabretooth-c/app. 2-Deadpool-c/app. 4.00

WEAPON X NOIR
Marvel Comics: May, 2010 ($3.99, one-shot)

1-Dennis Calero-s/a; C.P. Smith-c 4.00

WEAPON X: THE DRAFT (Leads into 2002 Weapon X series)
Marvel Comics: Oct, 2002 ($2.25, one-shots)

...Kane 1- JH Williams-c/Raimondi-a 3.00
...Marrow 1- JH Williams-c/Badeaux-a 3.00
...Sauron 1- JH Williams-c/Kerschl-a; Emma Frost app. 3.00
...Wild Child 1- JH Williams-c/Van Sciver-a; Aurora (Alpha Flight) app. 3.00
...Zero 1- JH Williams-c/Plunkett-a; Wolverine app. 3.00

WEAPON ZERO
Image Comics (Top Cow Productions): No. T-4(#1), June, 1995 - No. T-0(#5), Dec, 1995 ($2.50, limited series)

T-4(#1): Walt Simonson scripts in all. 5.00
T-3(#2) - T-1(#4) 4.00
T-0(#5) 3.00

WEAPON ZERO
Image Comics (Top Cow Productions): V2#1, Mar, 1996 - No. 15, Dec, 1997 ($2.50)

V2#1-Walt Simonson scripts. 4.00
2-14: 8-Begin Top Cow. 10-Devil's Reign 3.00
15-($3.50) Benitez-a 4.00

WEAPON ZERO/SILVER SURFER
Image Comics/Marvel Comics: Jan, 1997($2.95, one-shot)

1-Devil's Reign Pt. 1 3.00

WEASELGUY: ROAD TRIP
Image Comics: Sept, 1999 - No. 2 ($3.50, limited series)

1,2-Steve Buccellato-s/a 3.50
1-Variant-c by Bachalo 5.00

WEASELGUY/WITCHBLADE
Hyperwerks: July, 1998 ($2.95, one-shot)

1-Steve Buccellato-s/a; covers by Matsuda and Altstaetter 3.00

WEASEL PATROL SPECIAL, THE (Also see Fusion #17)
Eclipse Comics: Apr, 1989 ($2.00, B&W, one-shot)

1-Funny animal 3.00

WEAVEWORLD
Marvel Comics (Epic): Dec, 1991 - No. 3, 1992 ($4.95, lim. series, 68 pgs.)

1-3: Clive Barker adaptation 5.00

WEB, THE (Also see Mighty Comics & Mighty Crusaders)
DC Comics (Impact Comics): Sept, 1991 - No. 14, Oct, 1992 ($1.00)

1-14: 5-The Fly x-over 9-Trading card inside 5.00
Annual 1 (1992, $2.50, 68 pgs.)-With Trading card 5.00

NOTE: ***Gil Kane** c-5, 9, 10, 12-14. **Bill Wray** a(i)-1-9, 10(part).*

WEB, THE (Continued from The Red Circle)
DC Comics: Nov, 2009 - No. 10, Aug, 2010 ($3.99)

1-10: 1-Roger Robinson-a; The Hangman back-up feature. 3-Batgirl app. 5-Caldwell-a 4.00

WEB OF EVIL
Comic Magazines/Quality Comics Group: Nov, 1952 - No. 21, Dec, 1954

1-Used in **SOTI**, pg. 388. Jack Cole-a; morphine use story
63 126 189 403 689 975
2-4,6,7: 2,3-Jack Cole-a. 4,6,7-Jack Cole-c/a 42 84 126 268 452 635
5-Electrocution-c/story; Jack Cole-c/a 52 104 156 322 549 775
8-11-Jack Cole-a 40 80 120 244 405 565
12,13,15,16,19-21 27 54 81 158 259 360
14-Part Crandall-c; Old Witch swipe 28 56 84 165 270 375
17-Opium drug propaganda story 27 54 81 162 266 370
18-Acid-in-face story 28 56 84 165 270 375

NOTE: ***Jack Cole** a(2 each)-2, 6, 8, 9. **Cuidera** c-1-21i. **Ravielli** a-13.*

WEB OF HORROR
Major Magazines: Dec, 1969 - No. 3, Apr, 1970 (Magazine)

1-Jeff Jones painted-c; Wrightson-a, Kaluta-a 9 18 27 58 99 140
2-Jones painted-c; Wrightson-a(2), Kaluta-a 8 16 24 51 86 120
3-Wrightson-c/a (1st published-c); Brunner, Kaluta, Bruce Jones-a
9 18 27 63 112 160

WEB OF MYSTERY
Ace Magazines (A. A. Wyn): Feb, 1951 - No. 29, Sept, 1955

1 58 116 174 371 636 900
2-Bakerish-a 34 68 102 199 325 450
3-10: 4-Colan-a 30 60 90 177 289 400
11-18,20-26: 12-John Chilly's 1st cover art. 13-Surrealistic-c. 20-r/The Beyond #1
26 52 78 154 252 350
19-Reprints Challenge of the Unknown #6 used in N.Y. Legislative Committee
26 52 78 154 252 350
27-Bakerish-a(r/The Beyond #2); last pre-code ish 22 44 66 132 216 300
28,29: 28-All-r 18 36 54 105 165 225

NOTE: *This series was to appear as "Creepy Stories", but title was changed before publication. **Cameron** a-6, 8, 11-13, 17-20, 22, 24, 25, 27; c-8, 13, 17. **Palais** a-28r. **Sekowsky** a-1-3, 7, 8, 11, 14, 21, 29. **Tothish** a-by **Bill Discount** #16. 29-all-r, 19-28-partial-r.*

WEB OF SCARLET SPIDER
Marvel Comics: Oct, 1995 - No. 4, Jan, 1996 ($1.95, limited series)

1-4: Replaces "Web of Spider-Man" 3.00

WEB OF SPIDER-MAN (Replaces Marvel Team-Up)
Marvel Comics Group: Apr, 1985 - No. 129, Sept, 1995

1-Painted-c (5th app. black costume?) 2 4 6 10 14 18
2,3 6.00
4-8: 7-Hulk x-over; Wolverine splash 5.00
9-13: 10-Dominic Fortune guest stars; painted-c 4.00
14-17,19-28: 19-Intro Humbug & Solo 3.00
18-1st app. Venom (behind the scenes, 9/86) 4.00
29-Wolverine, new Hobgoblin (Macendale) app. 1 2 3 5 6 8
30-Origin recap The Rose & Hobgoblin I (entire book is flashback story);
Punisher & Wolverine cameo 4.00
31,32-Six part Kraven storyline begins 1 3 4 6 8 10
33-37,39-47,49: 36-1st app. Tombstone 3.00
38-Hobgoblin app.; begin $1.00-c 4.00
48-Origin Hobgoblin II(Demogoblin) cont'd from Spectacular Spider-Man #147;
Kingpin app. 1 2 3 5 7 9
50-($1.50, 52 pgs.) 4.00
51-58 3.00
59-Cosmic Spidey cont'd from Spect. Spider-Man 4.00
60-89,91-99,101-106: 66,67-Green Goblin (Norman Osborn) app. as a super-hero. 69,70-Hulk x-over. 74-76-Austin-c(i). 76-Fantastic Four x-over. 78-Cloak & Dagger app. 81-Origin/1st app. Bloodshed. 84-Begin 6 part Rose & Hobgoblin II storyline; last $1.00-c. 86-Demon leaves Hobgoblin; 1st Demogoblin. 93-Gives brief history of Hobgoblin. 93,94-Hobgoblin (Macendale) Reborn-c/story, parts 1,2; MoonKnight app. 94-Venom cameo. 95-Begin 4 part x-over w/Spirits of Venom w/Ghost Rider/Blaze/Spidey vs. Venom & Demogoblin (cont'd in Ghost Rider/Blaze #5,6). 96-Spirits of Venom part 3; painted-c. 101,103-Maximum Carnage x-over. 103-Venom & Carnage app. 104-106-Nightwatch back-up stories 3.00
90-($2.95, 52 pgs.)-Polybagged w/silver hologram-c, gatefold poster showing
Spider-Man & Spider-Man 2099 (Williamson-i) 5.00
90-2nd printing; gold hologram-c 4.00
100-($2.95, 52 pgs.)-Holo-grafx foil-c; intro new Spider-Armor 4.00
107-111: 107-Intro Sandstorm; Sand & Quicksand app. 3.00
112-116, 118, 119, 121-124, 126-128: 112-Begin $1.50-c; bound-in trading card sheet.

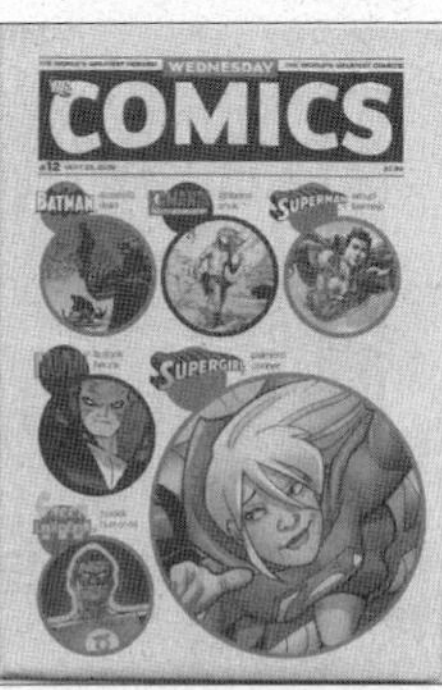

Wednesday Comics #12 © DC

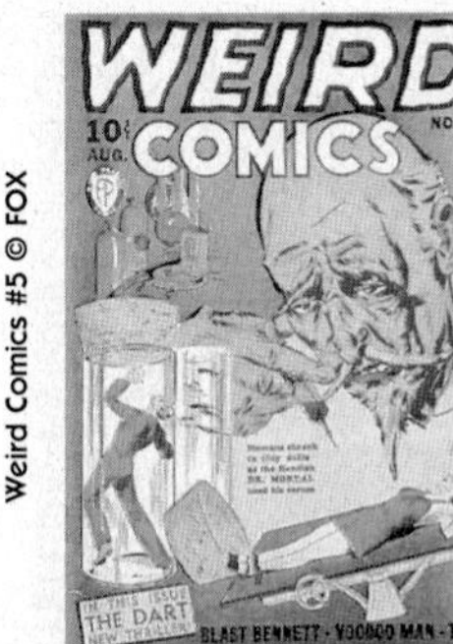

Weird Comics #5 © FOX

Weird Fantasy #16 © WMG

GD 2.0 | VG 4.0 | FN 6.0 | VF 8.0 | VF/NM 9.0 | NM- 9.2

113-Regular Ed.; Gambit & Black Cat app. 118-1st solo clone story; Venom app. 3.00
113-($2.95)-Collector's ed. polybagged w/foil-c; 16 pg. preview of Spider-Man cartoon & animation cel 4.00
117-($1.50)-Flip book; Power & Responsibility Pt.1 3.00
117-($2.95)-Collector's edition; foil-c; flip book 4.00
119-($6.45)-Direct market edition; polybagged w/ Marvel Milestone Amazing Spider-Man #150 & coupon for Amazing Spider-Man #396, Spider-Man #53, & Spectacular Spider-Man #219. 7.00
120 ($2.25)-Flip book w/ preview of the Ultimate Spider-Man 4.00
125 ($3.95)-Holodisk-c; Gwen Stacy clone 5.00
125,129: 125 ($2.95)-Newsstand. 129-Last issue 400
Annual 1 (1985) 5.00
Annual 2 (1986)-New Mutants; Art Adams-a 1 2 3 5 6 8
Annual 3-10 ('87-'94, 68 pgs.): 4-Evolutionary War x-over. 5-Atlantis Attacks; Captain Universe by Ditko (p) & Silver Sable stories; F.F. app. 6-Punisher back-up plus Capt. Universe by Ditko; G. Kane-a. 7-Origins of Hobgoblin I, Hobgoblin II, Green Goblin I & II & Venom; Larsen/Austin-c. 9-Bagged w/card 4.00
Super Special 1 (1995, $3.95)-flip book 4.00
NOTE: *Art Adams a-Annual 2. Byrne c-3-6. Chaykin c-10. Mignola a-Annual 2. Vess c-1, 8, Annual 1, 2. Zeck a-6i, 31, 32; c-31, 32.*

WEB OF SPIDER-MAN (Anthology)
Marvel Comics: Dec, 2009 - No. 12, Nov, 2010 ($3.99)
1-12: 1-Spider-Girl app. thru #7; Ben Reilly app. 2-6-Origins of villains retold. 7-Kraven origin; Paper Doll app.; Mahfood-a. 9-11-Jackpot back-up; Takeda-a. 11,12-Black Cat app. 4.00

WEBSPINNERS: TALES OF SPIDER-MAN
Marvel Comics: Jan, 1999 - No. 18, Jun, 2000 ($2.99/$2.50)
1-DeMatteis-s/Zulli-a; back-up story w/Romita Sr. art 4.00
1-($6.95) DF Edition 7.00
2,3: 2-Two covers 3.00
4-11,13-18: 4,5-Giffen-a; Silver Surfer-c/app. 7-9-Kelly-s/Sears and Smith-a. 10,11-Jenkins-s/Sean Phillips-a 3.00
12-($3.50) J.G. Jones-c/a; Jenkins-s 4.00

WEDDING BELLS
Quality Comics Group: Feb, 1954 - No. 19, Nov, 1956

	GD 2.0	VG 4.0	FN 6.0	VF 8.0	VF/NM 9.0	NM- 9.2
1-Whitney-a	16	32	48	94	147	200
2	11	22	33	60	83	105
3-9: 8-Last precode (4/55)	9	18	27	50	65	80
10-Ward-a (9 pgs.)	15	30	45	83	124	165
11-14,17	8	16	24	44	57	70
15-Baker-c	13	26	39	74	105	135
16-Baker-c/a	15	30	45	85	130	175
18,19-Baker-a each	11	22	33	64	90	115

WEDDING OF DRACULA
Marvel Comics: Jan, 1993 ($2.00, 52 pgs.)
1-Reprints Tomb of Dracula #30,45,46 4.00

WEDNESDAY COMICS (Newspaper-style, twice folded pages on 20" x 14" newsprint)
DC Comics: Sept, 2009 - No. 12, Nov, 2009 ($3.99, weekly limited series)
1-12-Superman, Batman, Kamandi, Hawkman, Deadman, Green Lantern, Flash, Teen Titans, Metamorpho, Adam Strange, Supergirl, Metal Men, Wonder Woman, The Demon with Catwoman, Sgt. Rock; s-a/ by various incl. Ryan Sook, Joe Kubert, Gaiman, Allred, Risso, Kyle Baker, Paul Pope, Conner, Simonson, Garcia-Lopez, Stelfreeze, Bermejo 4.00

WEEKENDER, THE (Illustrated...)
Rucker Pub. Co.: V1#1, Sept, 1945? - V1#4, Nov, 1945; V2#1, Jan, 1946 - V2#3, Aug, 1946 (52 pgs.)
V1#1-4: 1-Same-c as Zip Comics #45, inside-c and back-c blank; Steel Sterling, Senor Banana, Red Rube and Ginger. 2-Capt. Victory on-c. 3-Super hero-c; Mr. E, Dan Hastings, Sky Chief and the Echo. 4-Same-c as Punch Comics #10 (9/44); r/Hale the Magician (7 pgs.) & r/Mr. E (8 pgs.-Lou Fine? or Gustavson?) plus 3 humor strips & many B&W photos & r/newspaper articles plus cheesecake photos of Hollywood stars
19 38 57 111 176 240
V2#1-Same-c as Dynamic Comics #11; 36 pgs. comics, 16 in newspaper format with photos; partial Dynamic Comics reprints; 4 pgs. of cels from the Disney film Pinocchio; Little Nemo story by Winsor McCay, Jr.; Jack Cole-a 21 42 63 126 206 285
V2#2,3: 2-Same-c as Dynamic Comics #9 by Raboy; Dan Hastings (Tuska), Rocket Boy, The Echo, Lucky Coyne. 3-Humor-c by Boddington?; Dynamic Man, Ima Slooth, Master Key, Dynamic Boy, Captain Glory 19 38 57 111 176 240

WEIRD
Eerie Publications: V1#10, 1/66 - V8#6, 12/74; V9#1, 1/75 - V14#3, Nov, 1981 (Magazine) (V1-V8: 52 pgs.; V9 on: 68 pgs.)
V1#10(#1)-Intro. Morris the Caretaker of Weird (ends V2#10); Burgos-a
8 16 24 55 93 130
11,12 6 12 18 37 59 80
V2#1-4(10/67), V3#1(1/68), V2#6(4/68)-V2#7,9,10(12/68)
6 12 18 37 59 80
V2#8-r/Ditko's 1st story/Fantastic Fears #5 6 12 18 42 69 95
V3#1(2/69)-V3#4 5 10 15 32 51 70
V3#5(12/69)-Rulah reprint; "Rulah" changed to "Pulah", LSD story reprinted in Horror Tales V4#4, Tales From the Tomb V2#4, & 20 5 10 15 32 51 70
V4#1-6('70), V5#1-6('71), V6#1-7('72), V7#1-7('73), V8#1-3, V8#4(8/74), V8#4(10/74), (V8#5 does not exist), V8#6('74), V9#1-4(1/75-'76), V10#1-3('77), V11#1-4('78), V12#1(2/79)-V14#3(11/81) 5 10 15 30 48 65
NOTE: *There are two V8#4 issues (8/74 & 10/74). V9#4 (12/76) has a cover swipe from Horror Tales V5#1 (2/73). There are two V13#3 issues (6/80 & 9/80).*

WEIRD
DC Comics (Paradox Press): Sum, 1997 - No. 4 ($2.99, B&W, magazine)
1-4: 4-Mike Tyson-c 3.00

WEIRD, THE
DC Comics: Apr, 1988 - No. 4, July, 1988 ($1.50, limited series)
1-4: Wrightson-c/a in all 5.00

WEIRD ADVENTURES
P. L. Publishing Co. (Canada): May-June, 1951 - No. 3, Sept-Oct, 1951

	GD 2.0	VG 4.0	FN 6.0	VF 8.0	VF/NM 9.0	NM- 9.2
1- "The She-Wolf Killer" by Matt Baker (6 pgs.)	63	126	189	403	689	975
2-Bondage/hypodermic panel	47	94	141	298	504	710
3-Male bondage/torture-c; severed head story	41	82	123	260	435	610

WEIRD ADVENTURES
Ziff-Davis Publishing Co.: No. 10, July-Aug, 1951
10-Painted-c 40 80 120 246 411 575

WEIRD CHILLS
Key Publications: July, 1954 - No. 3, Nov, 1954
1-Wolverton-r/Weird Mysteries No. 4; blood transfusion-c by Baily
103 206 309 659 1130 1600
2-Extremely violent injury to eye-c by Baily; Hitler story
129 258 387 826 1413 2000
3-Bondage E.C. swipe-c by Baily 52 104 156 328 552 775

WEIRD COMICS
Fox Features Syndicate: Apr, 1940 - No. 20, Jan, 1942
1-The Birdman, Thor, God of Thunder (ends #5), The Sorceress of Zoom, Blast Bennett, Typhon, Voodoo Man, & Dr. Mortal begin; George Tuska bondage-c
514 1028 1542 3750 6625 9500
2-Lou Fine-c 245 490 735 1568 2684 3800
3,4: 3-Simon-c. 4-Torture-c 135 270 405 864 1482 2100
5-Intro. Dart & sidekick Ace (8/40) (ends #20); bondage/hypo-c
139 278 417 883 1517 2150
6,7-Dynamite Thor app. in each. 6-Super hero covers begin
95 190 285 603 1039 1475
8-Dynamo, the Eagle (11/40, early app.; see Science #1) & sidekick Buddy & Marga, the Panther Woman begin 94 188 282 597 1024 1450
9,10: 10-Navy Jones app. 76 152 228 486 831 1175
11-19: 16-Flag-c. 17-Origin The Black Rider. 57 114 171 362 619 875
20-Origin The Rapier; Swoop Curtis app; Churchill & Hitler-c
94 188 282 597 1024 1450
NOTE *Cover features: Sorceress of Zoom-4; Dr. Mortal-5; Dart & Ace-6-13, 15; Eagle-14, 16-20.*

WEIRD FANTASY (Formerly A Moon, A Girl, Romance; becomes Weird Science-Fantasy #23 on)
E. C. Comics: No. 13, May-June, 1950 - No. 22, Nov-Dec, 1953
13(#1) (1950) 200 400 600 1600 2550 3500
14-Necronomicon story; Cosmic Ray Bomb explosion-c/story by Feldstein; Feldstein & Gaines star 103 206 309 824 1312 1800
15,16: 16-Used in **SOTI**, pg. 144 73 146 219 584 930 1275
17 (1951) 55 110 165 440 703 965
6-10: 6-Robot-c 48 96 144 384 610 835
11-13 (1952): 11-Feldstein bio. 12-E.C. artists cameo; Orlando bio. 13-Anti-Wertham "Cosmic Correspondence" 39 78 117 312 499 685
14-Frazetta/Williamson(1st team-up at E.C.)/Krenkel-a (7 pgs.); Orlando draws E.C. staff
50 100 150 400 638 875
15-Williamson/Evans-a(3), 4,3,&7 pgs. 39 78 117 312 499 685
16-19-Williamson/Krenkel-a in all. 17-Feldstein dinosaur-c; classic sci-fi story "The Aliens". 18-Williamson/Feldstein-c; classic anti-prejudice story "Judgment Day". 19-Williamson bio.
37 74 111 296 473 650
20-Frazetta/Williamson-a (7 pgs.) 41 82 123 328 527 725
21-Frazetta/Williamson-c & Williamson/Krenkel-a 56 112 168 448 712 975

Weird Mysteries #1 © Gilmore

Weird Science #12 © WMG

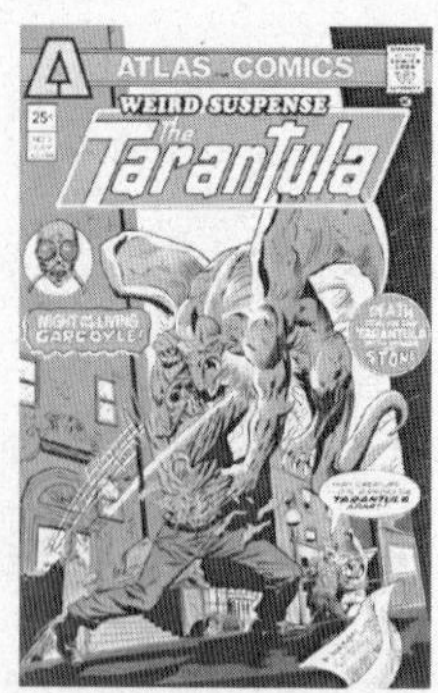

Weird Suspense #3 © Seaboard

	GD 2.0	VG 4.0	FN 6.0	VF 8.0	VF/NM 9.0	NM- 9.2
22-Bradbury adaptation	30	60	90	240	383	525

NOTE: **Crandall** *a-22.* **Elder** *a-17.* **Feldstein** *a-13(#1)-8; c-13(#1)-18 (#18 w/***Williamson***), 20.* **Harrison/Wood** *a-13.* **Kamen** *a-13(#1)-16, 18-22.* **Krigstein** *a-22.* **Kurtzman** *a-13(#1)-17(#5), 6.* **Orlando** *a-9-22 (2 stories in #16); c-19, 22.* **Severin/Elder** *a-18-21.* **Wood** *a-13(#1)-14, 17(2 stories ea. in #10-13). Ray Bradbury adaptations in #13,17-19, 22. Canadian reprints exist; see Table of Contents.*

WEIRD FANTASY
Russ Cochran/Gemstone Publ.: Oct, 1992 - No. 22, Jan, 1998 ($1.50/$2.00/$2.50)

1-22: 1,2: 1,2-r/Weird Fantasy #13,14; Feldstein-c. 3-5-r/Weird Fantasy #15-17 4.00

WEIRD HORRORS (Nightmare #10 on)
St. John Publishing Co.: June, 1952 - No. 9, Oct, 1953

	GD	VG	FN	VF	VF/NM	NM-
1-Tuska-a	63	126	189	403	689	975
2,3: 3-Hashish story	39	78	117	233	384	535
4,5	34	68	102	206	336	465
6-Ekgren-c; atomic bomb story	60	120	180	381	653	925
7-Ekgren-c; Kubert, Cameron-a	60	120	180	381	653	925
8,9-Kubert-c/a	41	82	123	256	428	600

NOTE: **Cameron** *a-7, 9.* **Finesque** *a-1-5.* **Forgione** *a-6.* **Morisi** *a-3. Bondage c-8.*

WEIRD MYSTERIES
Gillmor Publications: Oct, 1952 - No. 12, Sept, 1954

	GD	VG	FN	VF	VF/NM	NM-
1-Partial Wolverton-c swiped from splash page "Flight to the Future" in Weird Tales of the Future #2; "Eternity" has an Ingels swipe	113	226	339	718	1234	1750
2- "Robot Woman" by Wolverton; Bernard Baily-c reprinted in Mister Mystery #18; acid in face panel	155	310	465	992	1696	2400
3,6: Both have decapitation-c	77	154	231	493	847	1200
4- "The Man Who Never Smiled" (3 pgs.) by Wolverton; Classic B. Baily skull-c	168	336	504	1075	1838	2600
5-Wolverton story "Swamp Monster" (6 pgs.). Classic exposed brain-c	194	388	582	1242	2121	3000
7-Used in **SOTI**, illo "Indeed", illo "Sex and blood"	107	214	321	680	1165	1650
8-Wolverton-c panel-r/#5; used in a '54 Readers Digest anti-comics article by T. E. Murphy entitled "For the Kiddies to Read"	68	136	204	435	743	1050
9-Excessive violence, gore & torture	63	126	189	403	689	975
10-Silhouetted nudity panel	57	114	171	362	619	875
11,12: 12-r/Mr. Mystery #8(2), Weird Mysteries #3 & Weird Tales of the Future #6	54	108	162	343	574	825

NOTE: **Baily** *c-2-12. Anti-Wertham column in #5. #1-12 all have 'The Ghoul Teacher' (host).*

WEIRD MYSTERIES (Magazine)
Pastime Publications: Mar-Apr, 1959 (35¢, B&W, 68 pgs.)

	GD	VG	FN	VF	VF/NM	NM-
1-Torres-a; E. C. swipe from Tales From the Crypt #46 by Tuska "The Ragman"	11	22	33	64	90	115

WEIRD MYSTERY TALES (See DC 100 Page Super Spectacular)

WEIRD MYSTERY TALES (See Cancelled Comic Cavalcade)
National Periodical Publications: July-Aug, 1972 - No. 24, Nov, 1975

	GD	VG	FN	VF	VF/NM	NM-
1-Kirby-a; Wrightson splash pg.	6	12	18	37	59	80
2-Titanic-c/s	3	6	9	21	32	42
3,21: 21-Wrightson-c	3	6	9	18	27	35
4-10	3	6	9	14	19	24
11-20,22-24	2	4	6	11	16	20

NOTE: **Alcala** *a-5, 10, 13, 14.* **Aparo** *c-4.* **Bailey** *a-8.* **Bolle** *a-8?.* **Howard** *a-4.* **Kaluta** *a-4, 24; c-1.* **G. Kane** *a-10.* **Kirby** *a-1, 2p, 3p.* **Nino** *a-5, 6, 9, 13, 16, 21.* **Redondo** *a-9, 17.* **Sparling** *c-6.* **Starlin** *a-3?, 4.* **Wood** *a-23.*

WEIRD ROMANCE (Seduction of the Innocent #9)
Eclipse Comics: Feb, 1988 ($2.00, B&W)

1-Pre-code horror-r; Lou Cameron-r(2) 4.00

WEIRD SCIENCE (Formerly Saddle Romances) (Becomes Weird Science-Fantasy #23 on) (Also see EC Archives • Weird Science)
E. C. Comics: No. 12, May-June, 1950 - No. 22, Nov-Dec, 1953

	GD	VG	FN	VF	VF/NM	NM-
12(#1) (1950)-"Lost in the Microcosm" classic-c/story by Kurtzman; "Dream of Doom" stars Gaines & E.C. artists	200	400	600	1600	2550	3500
13-Flying saucers over Washington-c/story, 2 years before supposed UFO sighting	97	194	291	776	1238	1700
14-Robot, End of the World-c/story by Feldstein	91	182	273	728	1164	1600
15-War of Worlds-c/story (1950)	83	166	249	664	1057	1450
5-Atomic explosion-c	61	122	183	488	782	1075
6-8,10	53	106	159	424	680	935
9-Wood's 1st EC-c	57	114	171	456	728	1000
11-14 (1952) 11-Kamen bio. 12-Wood bio	39	78	117	312	499	685
15-18-Williamson/Krenkel-a in each; 15-Williamson-a. 17-Used in **POP**, pgs. 81,82. 18-Bill Gaines doll app. in story	41	82	123	328	519	710
19,20-Williamson/Frazetta-a (7 pgs. each). 19-Used in **SOTI**, illo "A young girl on her wedding night stabs her sleeping husband to death with a hatpin..." 19-Bradbury bio.	50	100	150	400	638	875
21-Williamson/Frazetta-a (6 pgs.); Wood draws E.C. staff; Gaines & Feldstein app. in story	50	100	150	400	638	875
22-Williamson/Frazetta/Krenkel-a (8 pgs.); Wood draws himself in his story (last pg. & panel)	50	100	150	400	638	875

NOTE: **Elder** *a-14, 19.* **Evans** *a-22.* **Feldstein** *a-12(#1)-8; c-12(#1)-8, 11.* **Ingels** *a-15.* **Kamen** *a-12(#1)-13, 15-18, 20, 21.* **Kurtzman** *a-12(#1)-7.* **Orlando** *a-10-22.* **Wood** *a-12(#1), 13(#2), 5-22 (#9, 10, 12, 13 all have 2* **Wood** *stories); c-9, 10, 12-22. Canadian reprints exist; see Table of Contents. Ray Bradbury adaptations in #17-22.*

WEIRD SCIENCE
Gladstone Publishing: Sept, 1990 - No. 4, Mar, 1991 ($1.95/$2.00, 68 pgs.)

1-4: Wood-c(r); all reprints in each 5.00

WEIRD SCIENCE (Also see EC Archives • Weird Science)
Russ Cochran/Gemstone Publishing: Sept, 1992 - No. 22, Dec, 1997 ($1.50/$2.00/$2.50)

1-22: 1,2: r/Weird Science #12,13 w/original-c. ,4-r/#14,15. 5-7-w/original-c 4.00

WEIRD SCIENCE-FANTASY (Formerly Weird Science & Weird Fantasy) (Becomes Incredible Science Fiction #30)
E. C. Comics: No. 23 Mar, 1954 - No. 29, May-June, 1955 (#23,24: 15¢)

	GD	VG	FN	VF	VF/NM	NM-
23-Williamson, Wood-a; Bradbury adaptation	37	74	111	296	473	650
24-Williamson & Wood-a; Harlan Ellison's 1st professional story, "Upheaval!", later adapted into a short story as "Mealtime", and then into a TV episode of Voyage to the Bottom of the Sea as "The Price of Doom"	37	74	111	296	473	650
25-Williamson dinosaur-c; Williamson/Torres/Krenkel-a plus Wood-a; Bradbury adaptation and fan letter; cover price back to 10¢	41	82	123	328	519	710
26-Flying Saucer Report; Wood, Crandall-a; A-bomb panels	39	78	117	312	494	675
27-Adam Link/I Robot series begins	37	74	111	296	473	650
28-Williamson/Krenkel/Torres-a; Wood-a	38	76	114	304	482	660
29-Classic Frazetta-c; Williamson/Krenkel & Wood-a; Adam Link/I Robot series concludes; last pre-code issue; new logo	114	228	342	912	1456	2000

NOTE: **Crandall** *a-26, 27, 29.* **Evans** *a-26.* **Feldstein** *c-24, 26, 28.* **Kamen** *a-27, 28.* **Krigstein** *a-23-25.* **Orlando** *a-in all.* **Wood** *a-in all; c-23, 27. The cover to #29 was originally intended for Famous Funnies #217 (Buck Rogers), but was rejected for being "too violent."*

WEIRD SCIENCE-FANTASY
Russ Cochran/Gemstone Publishing: Nov, 1992 - No. 7, May , 1994 ($1.50/$2.00/$2.50)

1-7: 1,2: r/Weird Science-Fantasy #23,24. 3-7 r/#25-29 4.00

WEIRD SCIENCE-FANTASY ANNUAL
E. C. Comics: 1952, 1953 (Sold thru the E. C. office & on the stands in some major cities) (25¢, 132 pgs.)

	GD	VG	FN	VF	VF/NM	NM-
1952-Feldstein-c	277	554	831	2078	3189	4300
1953-Feldstein-c	168	336	504	1260	1930	2600

NOTE: *The 1952 annual contains books cover-dated in 1951 & 1952, and the 1953 annual from 1952 & 1953. Contents of each annual may vary in same year.*

WEIRD SECRET ORIGINS
DC Comics: Oct, 2004 ($5.95, square-bound, one-shot)

nn-Reprints origins of Dr. Fate, Spectre, Congorilla, Metamorpho, Animal Man & others 6.00

WEIRD SUSPENSE
Atlas/Seaboard Publ.: Feb, 1975 - No. 3, July, 1975

	GD	VG	FN	VF	VF/NM	NM-
1-3: 1-Tarantula begins. 3-Freidrich-s	2	4	6	9	13	16

NOTE: **Boyette** *a-1-3.* **Buckler** *c-1, 3.*

WEIRD SUSPENSE STORIES (Canadian reprints of Crime SuspenStories #1-3; see Table of Contents)

WEIRD TALES ILLUSTRATED
Millennium Publications: 1992 - No. 2, 1992 ($2.95, high quality paper)

1,2-Bolton painted-c. 1-Adapts E.A. Poe & Harlan Ellison stories. 2-E.A. Poe & H.P. Lovecraft adaptations 4.00
1-($4.95, 52 pgs.)-Deluxe edition w/Tim Vigil-a not in regular #1; stiff-c; Bolton painted-c 6.00

WEIRD TALES OF THE FUTURE
S.P.M. Publ. No. 1-4/Aragon Publ. No. 5-8: Mar, 1952 - No. 8, July-Aug, 1953

	GD	VG	FN	VF	VF/NM	NM-
1-Andru-a(2); Wolverton partial-c	115	230	345	730	1253	1775
2,3-Wolverton-c/a(3) each. 2- "Jumpin Jupiter" satire by Wolverton begins, ends #5	181	362	543	1158	1979	2800
4- "Jumpin Jupiter" satire, partial Wolverton-c	145	290	435	921	1586	2250
5-Wolverton-c/a(2); "Jumpin Jupiter" satire	181	362	543	1158	1979	2800
6-Bernard Baily-c	60	120	180	381	653	925
7- "The Mind Movers" from the art to Wolverton's "Brain Bats of Venus" from Mr. Mystery #7 which was cut apart, pasted up, partially redrawn, and rewritten by Harry Kantor, the editor; Baily-c	145	290	435	921	1586	2250
8-Reprints Weird Mysteries #1(10/52) minus cover; gory cover showing heart ripped out, by B. Baily	103	206	309	659	1130	1600

WEIRD TALES OF THE MACABRE (Magazine)
Atlas/Seaboard Publ.: Jan, 1975 - No. 2, Mar, 1975 (75¢, B&W)

Weird Terror #3 © Comic Media

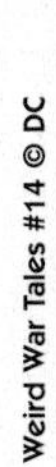
Weird War Tales #14 © DC

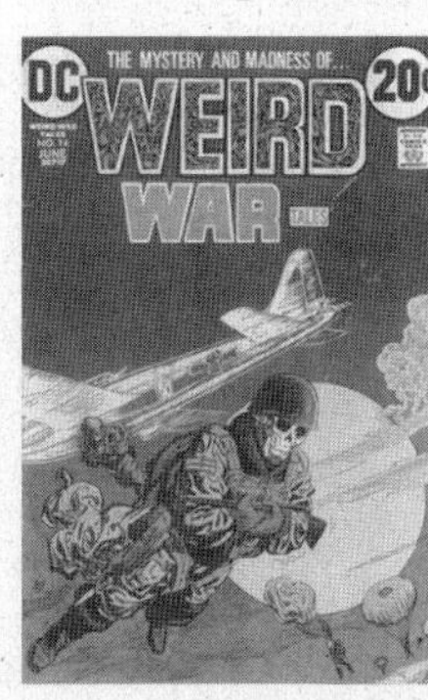

Weird Worlds (2011 series) #4 © DC

	GD 2.0	VG 4.0	FN 6.0	VF 8.0	VF/NM 9.0	NM- 9.2
1-Jeff Jones painted-c; Boyette-a	4	8	12	28	44	60
2-Boris Vallejo painted-c; Severin-a	5	10	15	32	51	70

WEIRD TERROR (Also see Horrific)
Allen Hardy Associates (Comic Media): Sept, 1952 - No. 13, Sept, 1954

	GD	VG	FN	VF	VF/NM	NM-
1- "Portrait of Death", adapted from Lovecraft's "Pickman's Model"; lingerie panels, Hitler story	61	122	183	390	670	950
2,3: 2-Text on Marquis DeSade, Torture, Demonology, & St. Elmo's Fire. 3-Extreme violence, whipping, torture; article on sin eating, dowsing	50	100	150	315	533	750
4-Dismemberment, decapitation, article on human flesh for sale, Devil, whipping	50	100	150	315	533	750
5-Article on body snatching, mutilation; cannibalism story	43	86	129	271	461	650
6-Dismemberment, decapitation, man hit by lightning	47	94	141	296	498	700
7-Body burning in fireplace-c	47	94	141	296	498	700
8,11: 8-Decapitation story; Ambrose Bierce adapt. 11-End of the world story w/atomic blast panels; Tothish-a by Bill Discount	43	86	129	271	461	650
9,10,13: 13-Severed head panels	39	78	117	234	385	535
12-Discount-a	39	78	117	234	385	535

NOTE: ***Don Heck*** *a-most issues; c-1-13.* ***Landau*** *a-6.* ***Morisi*** *a-2-5, 7, 9, 12.* ***Palais*** *a-1, 5, 6, 8(2), 10, 12.* ***Powell*** *a-10.* ***Ravielli*** *a-11.*

WEIRD THRILLERS
Ziff-Davis Publ. Co. (Approved Comics): Sept-Oct, 1951 - No. 5, Oct-Nov, 1952 (#2-5: painted-c)

	GD	VG	FN	VF	VF/NM	NM-
1-Rondo Hatton photo-c	95	190	285	603	1041	1475
2-Toth, Anderson, Colan-a	66	132	198	419	722	1025
3-Two Powell, Tuska-a; classic-c; Everett-a	94	188	282	597	1024	1450
4-Kubert, Tuska-a	63	126	189	403	689	975
5-Powell-a	57	114	171	362	619	875

NOTE: ***M. Anderson*** *a-2, 3.* ***Roussos*** *a-4. #2, 3 reprinted in Nightmare #10 & 13; #4, 5 reprinted in Amazing Ghost Stories #16 & #15.*

WEIRD VAMPIRE TALES (Comic magazine)
Modern Day Periodical Pub.: V3 #1, Apr, 1979 - V5 #3, Mar, 1982 (B&W)

	GD	VG	FN	VF	VF/NM	NM-
V3 #1 (4/79) First issue, no V1 or V2	4	8	12	26	41	55
V3 #2-4	3	6	9	20	30	40
V4 #2 (4/80), V4 #3 (7/80) (no V4 #1)	3	6	9	18	27	35
V5 #1 (1/81), V5 #2 (two issues, 4/81 & 8/81)	3	6	9	18	27	35
V5 #3 (3/82) Last issue; low print	4	8	12	22	34	45

WEIRD WAR TALES
National Periodical Publ./DC Comics: Sept-Oct, 1971 - No. 124, June, 1983 (#1-5: 52 pgs.)

	GD	VG	FN	VF	VF/NM	NM-
1-Kubert-a in #1-4,7; c-1-7	22	44	66	154	327	500
2,3-Drucker-a: 2-Crandall-a. 3-Heath-a	11	22	33	71	136	200
4,5: 5-Toth-a; Heath-a	9	18	27	61	106	150
6,7,9,10: 6,10-Toth-a. 7-Heath-a	6	12	18	42	69	95
8-Neal Adams-c/a(i)	7	14	21	48	79	110
11-20	4	8	12	23	36	48
21-35	3	6	9	17	25	32
36-(68 pgs.)-Crandall & Kubert-r/#2; Heath-r/#3; Kubert-c	3	6	9	19	29	38
37-50: 38,39-Kubert-c	2	4	6	10	14	18
51-63: 58-Hitler-c/app. 60-Hindenburg-c/s	2	4	6	9	13	16
64-Frank Miller-a (1st DC work)	4	8	12	28	44	60
65-67,69-89,91,92: 89-Nazi Apes-c/s.	2	4	6	8	10	12
68-Frank Miller-a (2nd DC work)	3	6	9	20	30	40
90-Hitler app.	2	4	6	8	11	14
93-Intro/origin Creature Commandos	2	4	6	8	11	14
94-Return of War that Time Forgot; dinosaur-c/s	2	4	6	10	14	18
95,96,98,102-123: 98-Sphinx-c. 102-Creature Commandos battle Hitler. 110-Origin/1st app. Medusa. 123-1st app. Captain Spaceman	2	4	6	8	10	12
97,99,100,101,124: 99-War that Time Forgot. 100-Creature Commandos in War that Time Forgot. 101-Intro/origin G.I. Robot	2	4	6	8	11	14

NOTE: ***Chaykin*** *a-76, 82.* ***Ditko*** *a-95, 99, 104-106.* ***Evans*** *c-73, 74, 83, 85.* ***Kane*** *c-116, 118.* ***Kubert*** *c-55, 58, 60, 62, 72, 75-81, 87, 88, 90-96, 100, 103, 104, 106, 107.* ***Newton*** *a-122.* ***Starlin*** *c-89.* ***Sutton*** *a-91, 92, 103.* ***Creature Commandos*** *-93, 97, 100, 102, 105, 108-112, 114, 116-119, 121, 124.* ***G.I. Robot*** *- 101, 108, 111, 113, 116-118, 120, 122.* ***War That Time Forgot*** *- 94, 99, 100, 103, 106, 109, 120.*

WEIRD WAR TALES
DC Comics (Vertigo): June, 1997 - No. 4, Sept, 1997 ($2.50)

1-4-Anthology by various 3.00

WEIRD WAR TALES
DC Comics (Vertigo): April, 2000 ($4.95, one-shot)

1-Anthology by various; last Biukovic-a 5.00

WEIRD WAR TALES
DC Comics: Nov, 2010 ($3.99, one-shot)

1-Anthology by various incl. Cooke, Strnad, Pugh; Cooke-c 4.00

WEIRD WESTERN TALES (Formerly All-Star Western)
National Per. Publ./DC Comics: No. 12, June-July, 1972 - No. 70, Aug, 1980

	GD	VG	FN	VF	VF/NM	NM-
12-(52 pgs.)-3rd app. Jonah Hex; Bat Lash, Pow Wow Smith reprints; El Diablo by Neal Adams/Wrightson	13	26	39	85	180	275
13-Jonah Hex-c & 4th app.; Neal Adams-a	9	18	27	63	112	160
14-Toth-a	7	14	21	48	79	110
15-Adams-c/a; no Jonah Hex	5	10	15	30	48	65
16,17,19,20	5	10	15	30	48	65
18,29: 18-1st all Jonah Hex issue (7-8/73) & begins. 29-Origin Jonah Hex	6	12	18	42	69	95
21-28,30: Jonah Hex in all	4	8	12	24	37	50
31-38: Jonah Hex in all. 38-Last Jonah Hex	3	6	9	19	29	38
39-Origin/1st app. Scalphunter & begins	2	4	6	13	18	22
40-47,50-69: 64-Bat Lash-c/story	2	4	6	8	10	12
48,49: (44 pgs.)-1st & 2nd app. Cinnamon	2	4	6	8	11	14
70-Last issue	2	4	6	9	13	16

NOTE: ***Alcala*** *a-16, 17.* ***Evans*** *inks-39-48; c-39i, 40, 47.* ***G. Kane*** *a-15, 20.* ***Kubert*** *c-12, 33.* ***Starlin*** *c-44, 45.* ***Wildey*** *a-26. 48 & 49 are 44 pgs..*

WEIRD WESTERN TALES (Blackest Night crossover)
DC Comics: No. 71, March, 2010 ($2.99, one-shot)

71-Jonah Hex, Scalphunter, Super-Chief, Firehair and Bat Lash rise as Black Lanterns 3.00

WEIRD WESTERN TALES
DC Comics (Vertigo): Apr, 2001 - No. 4, Jul, 2001 ($2.50, limited series)

1-4-Anthology by various 3.00

WEIRD WONDER TALES
Marvel Comics Group: Dec, 1973 - No. 22, May, 1977

	GD	VG	FN	VF	VF/NM	NM-
1-Wolverton-r/Mystic #6 (Eye of Doom)	4	8	12	22	34	45
2-10	3	6	9	16	22	28
11-22: 16-18-Venus-r by Everett from Venus #19,18 & 17. 19-22-r/Dr. Droom (re-named Dr. Druid) by Kirby. 22-New art by Byrne	3	6	9	14	20	25
15-17-(30¢-c variants, limited distribution)(4-8/76)	4	8	12	22	34	45

NOTE: *All 1950s & early 1960s reprints.* ***Check*** *r-1.* ***Colan*** *r-17.* ***Ditko*** *r-4, 5, 10-13, 19-21.* ***Drucker*** *r-12, 20.* ***Everett*** *r-3(Spellbound #16), 6(Astonishing #10), 9(Adv. Into Mystery #5).* ***Heath*** *a-13r.* ***Heck*** *a-1or, 14r.* ***Gil Kane*** *c-1, 2, 10.* ***Kirby*** *r-4, 6, 10, 11, 13, 15-22; c-17, 19, 20.* ***Krigstein*** *r-19.* ***Kubert*** *r-22.* ***Maneely*** *r-8.* ***Mooney*** *r-7p.* ***Powell*** *r-3, 7.* ***Torres*** *r-7.* ***Wildey*** *r-2, 7.*

WEIRD WORLD OF JACK STAFF (See Jack Staff)
Image Comics: Feb, 2010 - Present ($3.50)

1-6-Paul Grist-s/a. 2-Ian Churchill-c 3.50

WEIRD WORLDS (See Adventures Into...)

WEIRD WORLDS (Magazine)
Eerie Publications: V1#10(12/70), V2#1(2/71) - No. 4, Aug, 1971 (52 pgs.)

	GD	VG	FN	VF	VF/NM	NM-
V1#10-Sci-fi/horror	5	10	15	32	51	70
V2#1-4	4	8	12	28	44	60

WEIRD WORLDS (Also see Ironwolf: Fires of the Revolution)
National Periodical Publications: Aug-Sept, 1972 - No. 9, Jan-Feb, 1974; No. 10, Oct-Nov, 1974 (All 20¢ issues)

	GD	VG	FN	VF	VF/NM	NM-
1-Edgar Rice Burrough's John Carter Warlord of Mars & David Innes begin (1st DC app.); Kubert-c	3	6	9	16	22	28
2-4: 2-Infantino/Orlando-c. 3-Murphy Anderson-c. 4-Kaluta-a	2	4	6	10	14	18
5-7: .5-Kaluta-c. 7-Last John Carter.	2	4	6	8	11	14
8-10: 8-Iron Wolf begins by Chaykin (1st app.)	2	4	6	8	11	14

NOTE: ***Neal Adams*** *a-2i, 3i. John Carter by* ***Andersonin*** *#1-3.* ***Chaykin*** *c-7, 8.* ***Kaluta*** *a-4; c-4-6, 10.* ***Orlando*** *a-4i; c-2, 3, 4i.* ***Wrightson*** *a-2i, 4i.*

WEIRD WORLDS
DC Comics: Mar, 2011 - No. 6, Aug, 2011 ($3.99, limited series)

1-6-Short stories of Lobo, Garbage Man and Tanga; Ordway-a; Maguire-s/a; Lopresti-s/a 4.00

WELCOME BACK, KOTTER (TV) (See Limited Collectors' Edition #57 for unpublished #11)
National Periodical Publ./DC Comics: Nov, 1976 - No. 10, Mar-Apr, 1978

	GD	VG	FN	VF	VF/NM	NM-
1-Sparling-a(p)	3	6	9	16	23	30
2-10: 3-Estrada-a	2	4	6	10	14	18

WELCOME SANTA (See March of Comics #63,183)

WELCOME TO HOLSOM
Gospel Publishing House: 2005 - Present (no cover price)

1-12-Craig Schutt-s/Steven Butler-a 3.00

Wendy Witch World #39 © HARV

Werewolf By Night V2 #2 © MAR

Western Bandit Trails #3 © STJ

	GD 2.0	VG 4.0	FN 6.0	VF 8.0	VF/NM 9.0	NM- 9.2

WELCOME TO THE LITTLE SHOP OF HORRORS
Roger Corman's Cosmic Comics: May, 1995 -No. 3, July, 1995 ($2.50, limited series)

1-3						3.00

WELCOME TO TRANQUILITY
DC Comics (WildStorm): Feb, 2007 - No. 12, Jan, 2008 ($2.99)

1-12: 1-Simone-s/Googe-a; two covers by Googe and Campbell. 8-Pearson-a						3.00
...: Armageddon 1 (1/08, $2.99) Gage-s/Googe-a						3.00
...: One Foot in the Grave 1-6 (7/10 - No. 6, 2/11, $3.99) Simone-s/Domingues-a						4.00
...: One Foot in the Grave TPB (2011, $17.99) r/mini-series #1-6						18.00
... Book One TPB (2008, $19.99) r/#1-6 and variant cover gallery						20.00
... Book Two TPB (2008, $19.99) r/#7-12; sketch pages						20.00

WELLS FARGO (See Tales of...)

WENDY AND THE NEW KIDS ON THE BLOCK
Harvey Comics: Mar, 1991 - No. 3, July, 1991 ($1.25)

1-3						5.00

WENDY DIGEST
Harvey Comics: Oct, 1990 - No. 5, Mar, 1992 ($1.75, digest size)

1-5						4.00

WENDY PARKER COMICS
Atlas Comics (OMC): July, 1953 - No. 8, July, 1954

1	11	22	33	62	86	110
2	9	18	27	47	61	75
3-8	8	16	24	42	54	65

WENDY, THE GOOD LITTLE WITCH (TV)
Harvey Publ.: 8/60 - #82, 11/73; #83, 8/74 - #93, 4/76; #94, 9/90 - #97, 12/90

1-Wendy & Casper the Friendly Ghost begin	27	54	81	196	423	650
2	13	26	39	87	186	285
3-5	10	20	30	69	130	190
6-10	8	16	24	51	86	120
11-20	6	12	18	39	62	85
21-30	4	8	12	28	44	60
31-50	3	6	9	18	27	35
51-64,66-69	2	4	6	13	18	22
65 (2/71)-Wendy origin.	3	6	9	17	25	32
70-74: All 52 pg. Giants	3	6	9	16	23	30
75-93	2	4	6	9	13	16
94-97 (1990, $1.00-c): 94-Has #194 on-c						5.00

(See Casper the Friendly Ghost #20 & Harvey Hits #7, 16, 21, 23, 27, 30, 33)

WENDY THE GOOD LITTLE WITCH (2nd Series)
Harvey Comics: Apr, 1991 - No. 15, Aug, 1994 ($1.00/$1.25 #7-11/$1.50 #12-15)

1-15-Reprints Wendy & Casper stories. 12-Bunny app.						3.00

WENDY WITCH WORLD
Harvey Publications: 10/61; No. 2, 9/62 - No. 52, 12/73; No. 53, 9/74

1-(25¢, 68 pg. Giants begin)	12	24	36	84	177	270
2-5	8	16	24	51	86	120
6-10	6	12	18	37	59	80
11-20	4	8	12	28	44	60
21-30	4	8	12	22	34	45
31-39: 39-Last 68 pg. issue	3	6	9	17	25	32
40-45: 52 pg. issues	2	4	6	13	18	22
46-53	2	4	6	9	13	16

WEREWOLF (Super Hero) (Also see Dracula & Frankenstein)
Dell Publishing Co.: Dec, 1966 - No. 3, April, 1967

1-1st app.	4	8	12	24	37	50
2,3	3	6	9	16	23	30

WEREWOLF BY NIGHT (See Giant-Size..., Marvel Spotlight #2-4 & Power Record Comics)
Marvel Comics Group: Sept, 1972 - No. 43, Mar, 1977

1-Ploog-a cont'd. from Marvel Spotlight #4	12	24	36	81	166	250
2	7	14	21	46	76	105
3-5	5	10	15	35	55	75
6-10	4	8	12	26	41	55
11-14,16-20	3	6	9	19	29	38
15-New origin Werewolf; Dracula-c/story cont'd from Tomb of Dracula #18; classic Ploog-c	5	10	15	30	48	65
21-31	3	6	9	14	20	26
32-Origin & 1st app. Moon Knight (8/75)	11	22	33	76	151	225
33-2nd app. Moon Knight	7	14	21	44	72	100
34,36,38-43	3	6	9	14	19	24
35-Starlin/Wrightson-c	3	6	9	16	23	30
37-Moon Knight app; part Wrightson-c	4	8	12	24	37	50
38,39-(30¢-c variants, limited distribution)(5,7/76)	4	8	12	24	37	50

NOTE: ***Bolle** a-6i. **G. Kane** a-11p, 12p; c-21, 22, 24-30, 34p. **Mooney** a-7i. **Ploog** 1-4p, 5, 6p, 7p, 13-16p; c-5-8, 13-16. **Reinman** a-8i. **Sutton** a(i)-9, 11, 16, 35.*

WEREWOLF BY NIGHT (Vol. 2, continues in Strange Tales #1 (9/98))
Marvel Comics Group: Feb, 1998 - No. 6, July, 1998 ($2.99)

1-6-Manco-a: 2-Two covers. 6-Ghost Rider-c/app.						3.00

WEREWOLVES & VAMPIRES (Magazine)
Charlton Comics: 1962 (One Shot)

1	10	20	30	64	115	165

WEREWOLVES ON THE MOON: VERSUS VAMPIRES
Dark Horse Comics: June, 2009 - No. 3 ($3.50, limited series)

1,2-Dave Land-s & Fillbach Brothers-s/a						3.50

WEST COAST AVENGERS
Marvel Comics Group: Sept, 1984 - No. 4, Dec, 1984 (lim. series, Mando paper)

1-Origin & 1st app. W.C. Avengers (Hawkeye, Iron Man, Mockingbird & Tigra)	1	2	3	5	6	8
2-4						5.00

WEST COAST AVENGERS (Becomes Avengers West Coast #48 on)
Marvel Comics Group: Oct, 1985 - No. 47, Aug, 1989

V2#1						5.00
2-41						4.00
42-47: 42-Byrne-a(p)/scripts begin. 46-Byrne-c; 1st app. Great Lakes Avengers						4.00
Annual 1-3 (1986-1988): 3-Evolutionary War app.						5.00
Annual 4 (1989, $2.00)-Atlantis Attacks; Byrne/Austin-a						5.00

WESTERN ACTION
I. W. Enterprises: No. 7, 1964

7-Reprints Cow Puncher #? by Avon	2	4	6	8	11	14

WESTERN ACTION
Atlas/Seaboard Publ.: Feb, 1975

1-Kid Cody by Wildey & The Comanche Kid stories; intro. The Renegade	2	4	6	9	13	16

WESTERN ACTION THRILLERS
Dell Publishers: Apr, 1937 (10¢, square binding; 100 pgs.)

1-Buffalo Bill, The Texas Kid, Laramie Joe, Two-Gun Thompson, & Wild West Bill app.	84	168	252	538	919	1300

WESTERN ADVENTURES COMICS (Western Love Trails #7 on)
Ace Magazines: Oct, 1948 - No. 6, Aug, 1949

nn(#1)-Sheriff Sal, The Cross-Draw Kid, Sam Bass begin	21	42	63	122	199	275
nn(#2)(12/48)	13	26	39	74	105	135
nn(#3)(2/49)-Used in **SOTI**, pgs. 30,31	14	28	42	76	108	140
4-6	11	22	33	62	86	110

WESTERN BANDITS
Avon Periodicals: 1952 (Painted-c)

1-Butch Cassidy, The Daltons by Larsen; Kinstler-a; c-part-r/paperback Avon Western Novel #1	16	32	48	94	147	200

WESTERN BANDIT TRAILS (See Approved Comics)
St. John Publishing Co.: Jan, 1949 - No. 3, July, 1949

1-Tuska-a; Baker-c; Blue Monk, Ventrilo app.	28	56	84	165	270	375
2-Baker-c	22	44	66	128	209	290
3-Baker-c/a; Tuska-a	26	52	78	154	252	350

WESTERN COMICS (See Super DC Giant #15)
National Per. Publ: Jan-Feb, 1948 - No. 85, Jan-Feb, 1961 (1-27: 52pgs.)

1-Wyoming Kid & his horse Racer, The Vigilante in "Jesse James Rides Again" (Meskin-a), Cowboy Marshal, Rodeo Rick begin	74	148	222	470	810	1150
2	36	72	108	211	343	475
3,4-Last Vigilante	32	64	96	188	307	425
5-Nighthawk & his horse Nightwind begin (not in #6); Captain Tootsie by Beck	27	54	81	158	259	360
6,7,9,10	21	42	63	122	199	275
8-Origin Wyoming Kid; 2 pg. pin-ups of rodeo queens	34	68	102	199	325	450
11-20	18	36	54	103	162	220
21-40: 24-Starr-a. 27-Last 52 pgs. 28-Flag-c	14	28	42	82	121	160
41,42,44-49: 49-Last precode issue (2/55)	14	28	42	80	115	150

Western Fighters #3 © HILL

Western Hero #83 © FAW

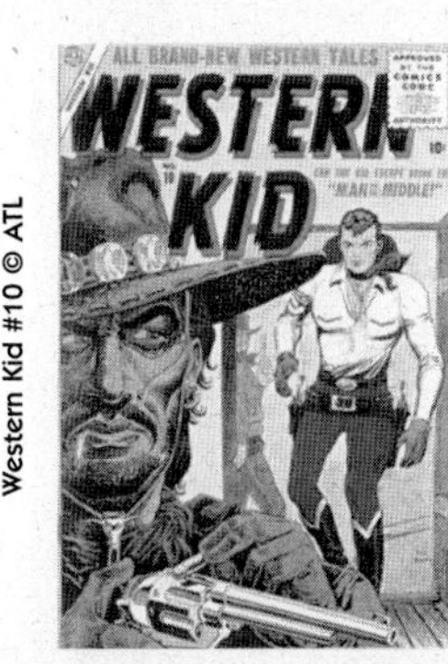

Western Kid #10 © ATL

	GD 2.0	VG 4.0	FN 6.0	VF 8.0	VF/NM 9.0	NM- 9.2
43-Pow Wow Smith begins, ends #85	14	28	42	81	118	155
50-60	12	24	36	67	94	120
61-85-Last Wyoming Kid. 77-Origin Matt Savage Trail Boss. 82-1st app. Fleetfoot, Pow Wow's girlfriend	10	20	30	56	76	95

NOTE: ***G. Kane, Infantino*** *art in most.* ***Meskin*** *a-1-4.* ***Moreira*** *a-28-39.* ***Post*** *a-3-5.*

WESTERN CRIME BUSTERS
Trojan Magazines: Sept, 1950 - No. 10, Mar-Apr, 1952

	GD	VG	FN	VF	VF/NM	NM-
1-Six-Gun Smith, Wilma West, K-Bar-Kate, & Fighting Bob Dale begin; headlight-a	36	72	108	216	351	485
2	19	38	57	111	176	240
3-5: 3-Myron Fass-c	18	36	54	105	165	225
6-Wood-a	32	64	96	188	307	425
7-Six-Gun Smith by Wood	32	64	96	188	307	425
8	18	36	54	105	165	225
9-Tex Gordon & Wilma West by Wood; Lariat Lucy app.	32	64	96	188	307	425
10-Wood-a	29	58	87	172	281	390

WESTERN CRIME CASES (Formerly Indian Warriors #7,8; becomes The Outlaws #10 on)
Star Publications: No. 9, Dec, 1951

	GD	VG	FN	VF	VF/NM	NM-
9-White Rider & Super Horse; L. B. Cole-c	21	42	63	122	199	275

WESTERNER, THE (Wild Bill Pecos)
"Wanted" Comic Group/Toytown/Patches: No. 14, June, 1948 - No. 41, Dec, 1951 (#14-31: 52 pgs.)

	GD	VG	FN	VF	VF/NM	NM-
14	15	30	45	85	130	175
15-17,19-21: 19-Meskin-a	9	18	27	52	69	85
18,22-25-Krigstein-a	11	22	33	60	83	105
26(4/50)-Origin & 1st app. Calamity Kate, series ends #32; Krigstein-a	14	28	42	78	112	145
27-Krigstein-a(2)	13	26	39	74	105	135
28-41: 33-Quest app. 37-Lobo, the Wolf Boy begins	8	16	24	40	50	60

NOTE: ***Mort Lawrence*** *a-20-27, 29, 37, 39; c-19, 22-24, 26, 27.* ***Leav*** *c-14-18, 20, 31.* ***Syd Shores*** *a-39; c-34, 35, 37-41.*

WESTERNER, THE
Super Comics: 1964

	GD	VG	FN	VF	VF/NM	NM-
Super Reprint 15-17: 15-r/Oklahoma Kid #? 16-r/Crack West. #65; Severin-c; Crandall-r. 17-r/Blazing Western #2; Severin-c	2	4	6	8	11	14

WESTERN FIGHTERS
Hillman Periodicals/Star Publ.: Apr-May, 1948 - V4#7, Mar-Apr, 1953 (#1-V3#2: 52 pgs.)

	GD	VG	FN	VF	VF/NM	NM-
V1#1-Simon & Kirby-c	36	72	108	216	351	485
2-Not Kirby-a	14	28	42	80	115	150
3-Fuje-c	12	24	36	67	94	120
4-Krigstein, Ingels, Fuje-a	13	26	39	74	105	135
5,6,8,9,12	10	20	30	54	72	90
7,10-Krigstein-a	11	22	33	62	86	110
11-Williamson/Frazetta-a	30	60	90	177	289	400
V2#1-Krigstein-a	11	22	33	62	86	110
2-12: 4-Berg-a	8	16	24	44	57	70
V3#1-11,V4#1,4-7	8	16	24	42	54	65
12,V4#2,3-Krigstein-a	11	22	33	62	86	110
3-D 1(12/53, 25¢, Star Publ.)-Came w/glasses; L. B. Cole-c	36	72	108	211	343	475

NOTE: ***Kinstlerish*** *a-V2#6, 8, 9, 12; V3#2, 5-7, 11, 12; V4#1(plus cover).* ***McWilliams*** *a-11.* ***Powell*** *a-V2#2.* ***Reinman*** *a-1-12, V4#3.* ***Rowich*** *c-5, 6i.* ***Starr*** *a-5.*

WESTERN FRONTIER
P. L. Publishers: Apr-May, 1951 - No. 7, 1952

	GD	VG	FN	VF	VF/NM	NM-
1	14	28	42	76	108	140
2	8	16	24	44	57	70
3-7	7	14	21	37	46	55

WESTERN GUNFIGHTERS (1st Series) (Apache Kid #11-19)
Atlas Comics (CPS): No. 20, June, 1956 - No. 27, Aug, 1957

	GD	VG	FN	VF	VF/NM	NM-
20	13	26	39	74	105	135
21-Crandall-a	13	26	39	74	105	135
22-Wood & Powell-a	18	36	54	103	162	220
23,24: 23-Williamson-a. 24-Toth-a	13	26	39	74	105	135
25-27	10	20	30	54	72	90

NOTE: ***Berg*** *a-20.* ***Colan*** *a-20, 26, 27.* ***Crandall*** *a-21.* ***Heath*** *a-25.* ***Maneely*** *a-24, 25; c-22, 23, 25.* ***Morisi*** *a-24.* ***Morrow*** *a-26.* ***Pakula*** *a-23.* ***Severin*** *c-20, 27.* ***Torres*** *a-26.* ***Woodbridge*** *a-27.*

WESTERN GUNFIGHTERS (2nd Series)
Marvel Comics Group: Aug, 1970 - No. 33, Nov, 1975 (#1-6: 25¢, 68 pgs.)

	GD	VG	FN	VF	VF/NM	NM-
1-Ghost Rider begins; Fort Rango, Renegades & Gunhawk app.	6	12	18	39	62	85
2,3,5,6: 2-Origin Nightwind (Apache Kid's horse)	4	8	12	22	34	45
4-Barry Smith-a	4	8	12	24	37	50
7-(52 pgs) Origin Ghost Rider retold	3	6	9	20	30	40
8-13: 10-Origin Black Rider. 12-Origin Matt Slade	3	6	9	14	20	25
14-Steranko-c	3	6	9	17	25	32
15-20	2	4	6	10	14	18
21-33	2	4	6	9	13	16

NOTE: ***Baker*** *r-2, 3.* ***Colan*** *r-2.* ***Drucker*** *r-3.* ***Everett*** *a-6i.* ***G. Kane*** *c-29, 31.* ***Kirby*** *a-1p(r), 5, 10-12; c-19, 21.* ***Kubert*** *r-2.* ***Maneely*** *r-2, 10.* ***Morrow*** *r-29.* ***Severin*** *c-10.* ***Shores*** *a-3, 4.* ***Barry Smith*** *a-4.* ***Steranko*** *c-14.* ***Sutton*** *a-1, 2i, 5, 4.* ***Torres*** *r-26('57).* ***Wildey*** *r-8, 9.* ***Williamson*** *r-2, 18.* ***Woodbridge*** *r-27('57). Renegades in #4, 5; Ghost Rider in #1-7.*

WESTERN HEARTS
Standard Comics: Dec, 1949 - No. 10, Mar, 1952 (All photo-c)

	GD	VG	FN	VF	VF/NM	NM-
1-Severin-a; Whip Wilson & Reno Browne photo-c	23	46	69	136	223	310
2-Beverly Tyler & Jerome Courtland photo-c from movie "Palomino"; Williamson/Frazetta-a (2 pgs.)	23	46	69	136	223	310
3-Rex Allen photo-c	14	28	42	80	115	150
4-7,10: 4-Severin & Elder, Al Carreno-a. 5-Ray Milland & Hedy Lamarr photo-c from movie "Copper Canyon". 6-Fred MacMurray & Irene Dunn photo-c from movie "Never a Dull Moment". 7-Jock Mahoney photo-c. 10-Bill Williams & Jane Nigh photo-c	14	28	42	78	112	145
8-Randolph Scott & Janis Carter photo-c from "Santa Fe"; Severin & Elder-a	14	28	42	80	115	150
9-Whip Wilson & Reno Browne photo-c; Severin & Elder-a	15	30	45	83	124	165

WESTERN HERO (Wow Comics #1-69; Real Western Hero #70-75)
Fawcett Publications: No. 76, Mar, 1949 - No. 112, Mar, 1952

	GD	VG	FN	VF	VF/NM	NM-
76(#1, 52 pgs.)-Tom Mix, Hopalong Cassidy, Monte Hale, Gabby Hayes, Young Falcon (ends #78,80), & Big Bow and Little Arrow (ends #102,105) begin; painted-c begin	16	32	48	94	147	200
77 (52 pgs.)	11	22	33	64	90	115
78,80-82 (52 pgs.): 81-Capt. Tootsie by Beck	11	22	33	60	83	105
79,83 (36 pgs.): 83-Last painted-c	10	20	30	54	72	90
84-86,88-90 (52 pgs.): 84-Photo-c begin, end #112. 86-Last Hopalong Cassidy	10	20	30	53	76	95
87,91,95,99 (36 pgs.): 87-Bill Boyd begins, ends #95	9	18	27	50	65	80
92-94,96-98,101 (52 pgs.): 96-Tex Ritter begins. 101-Red Eagle app.	9	18	27	52	69	85
100 (52 pgs.)	10	20	30	56	76	95
102-111: 102-Begin 36 pg. issues	9	18	27	50	65	80
112-Last issue	9	18	27	52	69	85

NOTE: *1/2 to 1 pg. Rocky Lane (Carnation) in 80-83, 86, 88, 97. Photo covers feature Hopalong Cassidy #84, 86, 89; Tom Mix #85, 87, 90, 92, 94, 97; Monte Hale #88, 91, 93, 95, 98, 100, 104, 107, 110; Tex Ritter #96, 99, 101, 105, 108, 111; Gabby Hayes #103.*

WESTERN KID (1st Series)
Atlas Comics (CPC): Dec, 1954 - No. 17, Aug, 1957

	GD	VG	FN	VF	VF/NM	NM-
1-Origin; The Western Kid (Tex Dawson), his stallion Whirlwind & dog Lightning begin	18	36	54	107	169	230
2 (2/55)-Last pre-code	11	22	33	62	86	110
3-8	10	20	30	54	72	90
9,10-Williamson-a in both (4 pgs. each)	10	20	30	56	76	95
11-17	8	16	24	44	57	70

NOTE: ***Ayers*** *a-6, 7.* ***Heck*** *a-3.* ***Maneely*** *c-2-7, 10, 13-15.* ***Romita*** *a-1-17; c-1, 12.* ***Severin*** *c-11, 16, 17.*

WESTERN KID, THE (2nd Series)
Marvel Comics Group: Dec, 1971 - No. 5, Aug, 1972 (All 20¢ issues)

	GD	VG	FN	VF	VF/NM	NM-
1-Reprints; Romita-c/a(3)	3	6	9	18	27	35
2,4,5: 2-Romita-a; Severin-c. 4-Everett-r	2	4	6	13	18	22
3-Williamson-a	3	6	9	14	20	26

WESTERN KILLERS
Fox Features Syndicate: nn, July?, 1948; No. 60, Sept, 1948 - No. 64, May, 1949; No. 6, July, 1949

	GD	VG	FN	VF	VF/NM	NM-
nn(#59?)(nd, F&J Trading Co.)-Range Busters; formerly Blue Beetle #57?	24	48	72	140	230	320
60 (#1, 9/48)-Extreme violence; lingerie panel	26	52	78	152	249	345
61-Jack Cole, Starr-a	21	42	63	122	199	275
62-64, 6 (#6-exist?)	19	38	57	111	176	240

WESTERN LIFE ROMANCES (My Friend Irma #3 on?)
Marvel Comics (IPP): Dec, 1949 - No. 2, Mar, 1950 (52 pgs.)

	GD	VG	FN	VF	VF/NM	NM-
1-Whip Wilson & Reno Browne photo-c	20	40	60	114	182	250

Western Picture Stories #3 © CM

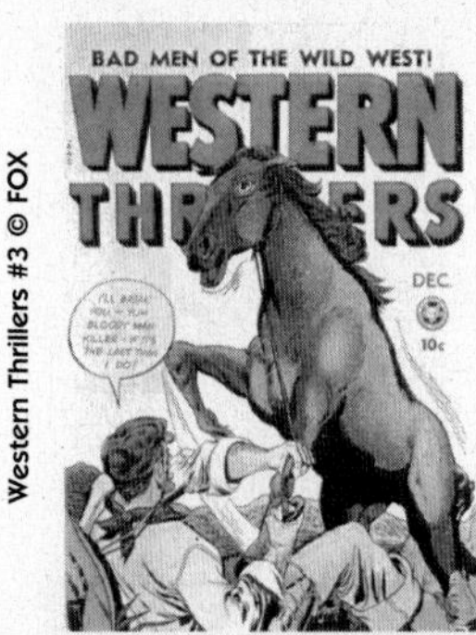

Western Thrillers #3 © FOX

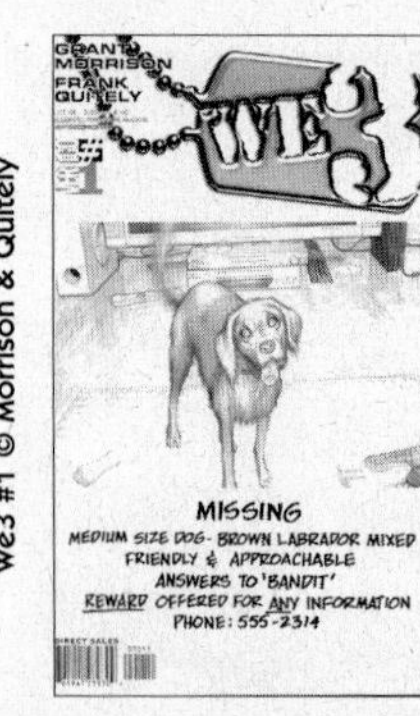

We3 #1 © Morrison & Quitely

	GD	VG	FN	VF	VF/NM	NM-
	2.0	4.0	6.0	8.0	9.0	9.2

2-Audie Murphy & Gale Storm photo-c 16 32 48 94 147 200

WESTERN LOVE
Prize Publ.: July-Aug, 1949 - No. 5, Mar-Apr, 1950 (All photo-c & 52 pgs.)
1-S&K-a; Randolph Scott photo-c from movie "Canadian Pacific" (see Prize Comics #76) 31 62 93 182 296 410
2,5-S&K-a: 2-Whip Wilson & Reno Browne photo-c. 5-Dale Robertson photo-c 23 46 69 136 223 310
3,4: 3-Pat Williams photo-c 15 30 45 85 130 175
NOTE: *Meskin & Severin/Elder a-2-5.*

WESTERN LOVE TRAILS (Formerly Western Adventures)
Ace Magazines (A. A. Wyn): No. 7, Nov, 1949 - No. 9, Mar, 1950
7 12 24 36 67 94 120
8,9 10 20 30 54 72 90

WESTERN MARSHAL (See Steve Donovan...)
Dell Publishing Co.: No. 534, 2-4/54 - No. 640, 7/55 (Based on Ernest Haycox's "Trailtown")
Four Color 534 (#1)-Kinstler-a 6 12 18 39 62 85
Four Color 591 (10/54), 613 (2/55), 640-All Kinstler-a 5 10 15 35 55 75

WESTERN OUTLAWS (Junior Comics #9-16; My Secret Life #22 on)
Fox Features Syndicate: No. 17, Sept, 1948 - No. 21, May, 1949
17-Kamen-a; Iger shop-a in all; 1 pg. "Death and the Devil Pills" r-in Ghostly Weird #122 32 64 96 188 307 425
18-21 19 38 57 111 176 240

WESTERN OUTLAWS
Atlas Comics (ACI No. 1-14/WPI No. 15-21): Feb, 1954 - No. 21, Aug, 1957
1-Heath, Powell-a; Maneely hanging-c 21 42 63 122 199 275
2 12 24 36 67 94 120
3-10: 7-Violent-a by R.Q. Sale 10 20 30 54 72 90
11,14-Williamson-a in both (6 pgs. each) 11 22 33 60 83 105
12,18,20,21: Severin covers 9 18 27 50 65 80
13,15: 13-Baker-a. 15-Torres-a 10 20 30 54 72 90
16-Williamson text illo 9 18 27 50 65 80
17,19-Crandall-a. 17-Williamson text illo 10 20 30 54 72 90
NOTE: *Ayers a-7, 10, 18, 20. Bolle a-21. Colan a-5, 10, 11, 17. Drucker a-11. Everett a-9, 10. Heath a-1; c-3, 4, 8, 16. Kubert a-9p. Maneely a-13, 16, 17, 19; c-1, 5, 7, 9, 10, 12, 13. Morisi a-18. Powell a-3, 16. Romita a-7, 13. Severin a-8, 16, 19; c-17, 18, 20, 21. Tuska a-6, 15.*

WESTERN OUTLAWS & SHERIFFS (Formerly Best Western)
Marvel/Atlas Comics (IPC): No. 60, Dec, 1949 - No. 73, June, 1952
60 (52 pgs.) 21 42 63 122 199 275
61-65: 61-Photo-c 16 32 48 94 147 200
66-Story contains 5 hangings 17 34 51 98 154 210
67-Cannibalism story 17 34 51 98 154 210
68-72 14 28 42 76 108 140
73-Black Rider story; Everett-c 15 30 45 83 124 165
NOTE: *Maneely a-62, 67; c-62, 69-73. Robinson a-68. Sinnott a-70. Tuska a-69-71.*

WESTERN PICTURE STORIES (1st Western comic)
Comics Magazine Company: Feb, 1937 - No. 4, June, 1937
1-Will Eisner-a 206 412 618 1318 2259 3200
2-Will Eisner-a 107 214 321 680 1165 1650
3,4: 3-Eisner-a. 4-Caveman Cowboy story 90 180 270 576 988 1400

WESTERN PICTURE STORIES (See Giant Comics Edition #6, 11)

WESTERN ROMANCES (See Target...)

WESTERN ROUGH RIDERS
Gillmor Magazines No. 1,4 (Stanmor Publ.): Nov, 1954 - No. 4, May, 1955
1 9 18 27 47 61 75
2-4 7 14 21 35 43 50

WESTERN ROUNDUP (See Dell Giants & Fox Giants)

WESTERN SERENADE
DC Comics: May/June, 1949
nn - Ashcan comic, not distributed to newsstands, only for in-house use (no known sales)

WESTERN TALES (Formerly Witches...)
Harvey Publications: No. 31, Oct, 1955 - No. 33, July-Sept, 1956
31,32-All S&K-a; Davy Crockett app. in each 15 30 45 86 133 180
33-S&K-a; Jim Bowie app. 15 30 45 84 127 170
NOTE: *#32 & 33 contain Boy's Ranch reprints. Kirby c-31.*

WESTERN TALES OF BLACK RIDER (Formerly Black Rider; Gunsmoke Western #32 on)
Atlas Comics (CPS): No. 28, May, 1955 - No. 31, Nov, 1955
28 (#1): The Spider (a villain) dies 19 38 57 112 179 245
29-31 14 28 42 82 121 160
NOTE: *Lawrence a-30. Maneely c-28-30. Severin a-28. Shores c-31.*

WESTERN TEAM-UP
Marvel Comics Group: Nov, 1973 (20¢)
1-Origin & 1st app. The Dakota Kid; Rawhide Kid-r; Gunsmoke Kid-r by Jack Davis 4 8 12 22 34 45

WESTERN THRILLERS (My Past Confessions #7 on)
Fox Features Syndicate/M.S. Distr. No. 52: Aug, 1948 - No. 6, June, 1949; No. 52, 1954?
1- "Velvet Rose" (Kamenish-a); "Two-Gun Sal", "Striker Sisters" (all women outlaws issue); Brodsky-c 48 96 144 302 514 725
2 24 48 72 140 230 320
3-6: 4,5-Bakerish-a; 5-Butch Cassidy app. 19 38 57 111 176 240
52-(Reprint, M.S. Dist.)-1954? No date given (becomes My Love Secret #53) 9 18 27 47 61 75

WESTERN THRILLERS (Cowboy Action #5 on)
Atlas Comics (ACI): Nov, 1954 - No. 4, Feb, 1955 (All-r/Western Outlaws & Sheriffs)
1 5 30 45 88 137 185
2-4 10 20 30 54 72 90
NOTE: *Heath c-3. Maneely a-1; c-2. Powell a-4. Robinson a-4. Romita c-4. Tuska a-2.*

WESTERN TRAILS (Ringo Kid Starring in...)
Atlas Comics (SAI): May, 1957 - No. 2, July, 1957
1-Ringo Kid app.; Severin-c 14 28 42 76 108 140
2-Severin-c 9 18 27 50 65 80
NOTE: *Bolle a-1, 2. Maneely a-1, 2. Severin c-1, 2.*

WESTERN TRUE CRIME (Becomes My Confessions)
Fox Features Syndicate: No. 15, Aug, 1948 - No. 6, June, 1949
15(#1)-Kamen-a; formerly Zoot #14 (5/48)? 32 64 96 188 307 425
16(#2)-Kamenish-a; headlight panels, violence 23 46 69 136 223 310
3-Kamen-a 25 50 75 147 241 335
4-6: 4-Johnny Craig-a 15 30 45 90 140 190

WESTERN WINNERS (Formerly All-Western Winners; becomes Black Rider #8 on & Romance Tales #7 on?)
Marvel Comics (CDS): No. 5, June, 1949 - No. 7, Dec, 1949
5-Two-Gun Kid, Kid Colt, Black Rider; Shores-c 31 62 93 182 296 410
6-Two-Gun Kid, Black Rider, Heath Kid Colt story; Captain Tootsie by C.C. Beck 26 52 78 152 249 345
7-Randolph Scott Photo-c w/true stories about the West 26 52 78 152 249 345

WEST OF THE PECOS (See Zane Grey, 4-Color #222)

WESTWARD HO, THE WAGONS (Disney)
Dell Publishing Co.: No. 738, Sept, 1956 (Movie)
Four Color 738-Fess Parker photo-c 9 18 27 61 106 150

WE3
DC Comics (Vertigo): Oct, 2004 - No. 3, May, 2005 ($2.95, limited series)
1-3-Domestic animal cyborgs: Grant Morrison-s/Frank Quitely-a 3.00
TPB (2005, $12.99) r/series 13.00

WETWORKS (See WildC.A.T.S: Covert Action Teams #2)
Image Comics (WildStorm): June, 1994 - No. 43, Aug, 1998 ($1.95/$2.50)
1-"July" on-c; gatefold wraparound-c; Portacio/Williams-c/a 4.00
1-Chicago Comicon edition 6.00
1-(2/98, $4.95) "3-D Edition" w/glasses 5.00
2-4 3.00
2-Alternate Portacio-c, see Deathblow #5 6.00
5-7,9-24: 5-($2.50). 13-Portacio-c. 16,17-Fire From Heaven Pts. 4 & 11 3.00
8 ($1.95)-Newstand, Wildstorm Rising Pt. 7 3.00
8 ($2.50)-Direct Market, Wildstorm Rising Pt. 7 3.00
25-($3.95) 4.00
26-43: 32-Variant-c by Pat Lee & Charest. 39,40-Stormwatch app. 42-Gen 13 app. 3.00
Sourcebook 1 (10/94, $2.50)-Text & illustrations (no comics) 3.00
Voyager Pack (8/97, $3.50)- #32 w/Phantom Guard preview 4.00

WETWORKS
DC Comics (WildStorm): Nov, 2006 - No. 15, Jan, 2008 ($2.99)
1-15: 1-Carey-s/Portacio-a; two covers by Portacio and Van Sciver. 2-Golden var-c 3-Pearson var-c. 4-Powell var-c 3.00
...: Armageddon 1 (1/08, $2.99) Gage-s/Badeaux-a 3.00
... Book One (2007, $14.99) r/#1-5 and stories from Eye of the storm Annual and Coup D'Etat Afterword 15.00
... Book Two (2008, $14.99) r/#6-9,13-15 15.00

Wha... Huh? #1 © MAR

What If...? #29 © MAR

What If Magneto & Professor X...? #1 © MAR

GD 2.0 VG 4.0 FN 6.0 VF 8.0 VF/NM 9.0 NM- 9.2

...: Mutations 1 (11/10, $3.99) Grevioux & Long-s/Gopez-a 4.00

WETWORKS/VAMPIRELLA (See Vampirella/Wetworks)
Image Comics (WildStorm Productions): July, 1997 ($2.95, one-shot)

1-Gil Kane-c 4.00

WHACK (Satire)
St. John Publishing Co. (Jubilee Publ.): Oct, 1953 - No. 3, May, 1954

1-(3-D, 25¢)-Kubert-a; Maurer-c; came w/glasses 24 48 72 142 234 325
2,3-Kubert-a in each. 2-Bing Crosby on-c; Mighty Mouse & Steve Canyon parodies.
3-Li'l Orphan Annie parody; Maurer-c 15 30 45 84 127 170

WHACKY (See Wacky)

WHA...HUH?
Marvel Comics: 2005 ($3.99, one-shot)

1-Humor spoofs of Marvel characters; Mahfood-a/c; Bendis, Stan Lee and others-s 4.00

WHAM COMICS (See Super Spy)
Centaur Publications: Nov, 1940 - No. 2, Dec, 1940

1-The Sparkler, The Phantom Rider, Craig Carter and his Magic Ring, Detecto, Copper Slug, Speed Silvers by Gustavson, Speed Centaur & Jon Linton (s/f) begin
168 336 504 1075 1838 2600
2-Origin Blue Fire & Solarman; The Buzzard app. 110 220 330 704 1202 1700

WHAM-O GIANT COMICS
Wham-O Mfg. Co. : April, 1967 (98¢, newspaper size, one-shot)(Six issue subscription was advertised)

1-Radian & Goody Bumpkin by Wood; 1 pg. Stanley-a; Fine, Tufts-a; flying saucer reports; wraparound-c 10 20 30 64 115 165

WHATEVER HAPPENED TO BARON VON SHOCK?
Image Comics: May, 2010 - Present ($3.99)

1-4-Rob Zombie-s/Donny Hadiwidjaja-a 4.00

WHAT IF? (1st Series) (What If? Featuring... #13 & #?-33) (Also see Hero Initiative)
Marvel Comics Group: Feb, 1977 - No. 47, Oct, 1984; June, 1988 (All 52 pgs.)

1-Brief origin Spider-Man, Fantastic Four 3 6 9 20 30 40
2-Origin The Hulk retold 2 4 6 10 14 18
3-5: 3-Avengers. 4-Invaders. 5-Capt. America 2 4 6 8 11 14
6-10,13,17: 7-Betty Brant as Spider-Girl. 8-Daredevil; Spidey parody. 9-Origins Venus, Marvel Boy, Human Robot, 3-D Man. 13-Conan app.; John Buscema-c/a(p).
17-Ghost Rider & Son of Satan app. 2 3 4 6 8 10
11,12,14-16: 11-Marvel Bullpen as F.F. 1 2 3 5 6 8
18-26,29: 18-Dr. Strange. 19-Spider-Man. 22-Origin Dr. Doom retold
1 2 3 4 5 7
27-X-Men app.; Miller-c 3 6 9 14 20 26
28-Daredevil by Miller; Ghost Rider app. 2 4 6 10 16 20
30-"What If...Spider-Man's Clone Had Lived?" 2 4 6 8 10 12
31-Begin $1.00-c; featuring Wolverine & the Hulk; X-Men app.; death of Hulk, Wolverine & Magneto 3 6 9 16 22 28
32-34,36-47: 32,36-Byrne-a. 34-Marvel crew each draw themselves. 37-Old X-Men & Silver Surfer app. 39-Thor battles Conan 5.00
35-What if Elektra had lived?; Miller/Austin-a. 2 4 6 8 10 12
Special 1 ($1.50, 6/88)-Iron Man, F.F., Thor app. 5.00
... Classic Vol. 1 TPB (2004, $24.99) r/#1-6; checklist 25.00
... Classic Vol. 2 TPB (2005, $24.99) r/#7-12 25.00
... Classic Vol. 3 TPB (2006, $24.99) r/#14,15,17-20 25.00
... Classic Vol. 4 TPB (2007, $24.99) r/#21-26; checklist of all What If? series/issues 25.00

NOTE: ***Austin*** *a-27p, 32i, 34, 35i; c-35i, 36i.* ***J. Buscema*** *a-13p, 15p; c-10, 13p, 23p.* ***Byrne*** *a-32i, 36; c-36p.* ***Colan*** *a-21p; c-17p, 18p, 21p.* ***Ditko*** *a-35, Special 1.* ***Golden*** *c-29, 40-42.* ***Guice*** *a-40p.* ***Gil Kane*** *a-3p, 24p; c(p)-2-4, 7, 8.* ***Kirby*** *a-11p; c-9p, 11p.* ***Layton*** *a-32i, 33i; c-30, 32p, 33i, 34.* ***Mignola*** *c-39i.* ***Miller*** *a-28p, 32i, 34(1), 35p; c-27, 28p.* ***Mooney*** *a-8i, 30i.* ***Perez*** *a-15p.* ***Robbins*** *a-4p.* ***Sienkiewicz*** *c-43-46.* ***Simonson*** *a-15p, 32i.* ***Starlin*** *a-32i.* ***Stevens*** *a-8, 16i(part).* ***Sutton*** *a-2i, 18p, 28.* ***Tuska*** *a-5p.* ***Weiss*** *a-37p.*

WHAT IF...? (2nd Series)
Marvel Comics: V2#1, July, 1989 - No. 114, Nov, 1998 ($1.25/$1.50)

V2#1-...The Avengers Had Lost the Evolutionary War 5.00
2-5: 2-Daredevil, Punisher app. 4.00
6-X-Men app. 5.00
7-Wolverine app.; Liefeld-c/a(1st on Wolvie?) 6.00
8,10,11,13-15,17-30: 10-Punisher app. 11-Fantastic Four app.; McFarlane-c(i).13-Prof. X; Jim Lee-c. 14-Capt. Marvel; Lim/Austin-c.15-F.F.; Capullo-c/a(p). 17-Spider-Man/Kraven. 18-F.F. 19-Vision. 20,21-Spider-Man. 22-Silver Surfer by Lim/Austin-c/a 23-X-Men. 24-Wolverine; Punisher app. 25-(52 pgs.)-Wolverine app. 26-Punisher app. 27-Namor/F.F. 28,29-Capt. America. 29-Swipes cover to Avengers #4. 30-(52 pgs.)-F.F. 4.00
9,12-X-Men 5.00
16-Wolverine battles Conan; Red Sonja app.; X-Men cameo 5.00
31-40,42-49: 31-Cosmic Spider-Man & Venom app.; Hobgoblin cameo. 32,33-Phoenix; X-Men app. 35-Fantastic Five (w/Spidey). 36-Avengers vs. Guardians of the Galaxy. 37-Wolverine; Thibert-c(i). 38-Thor; Rogers-p(part). 40-Storm; X-Men app. 42-Spider-Man. 43-Wolverine. 44-Venom/Punisher. 45-Ghost Rider. 46-Cable. 47-Magneto. 49-Infinity Gauntlet w/Silver Surfer & Thanos 3.00
41,50: 41-(52 pgs.)-Avengers vs. Galactus. 50-(52 pgs.)-Foil embossed-c; "What If Hulk Had Killed Wolverine" 4.00
51-(7/93) "What If the Punisher Became Captain America" (see it happen in 2007's Punisher War Journal #6-10) 6.00
52-99,101-104: 52-Dr. Doom. 54-Death's Head. 57-Punisher as Shield. 58-"What if Punisher Had Killed Spider-Man" w/cover similar to Amazing S-M #129. 59-...Wolverine led Alpha Flight. 60-X-Men Wedding Album. 61-Bound-in card sheet. 61,86,88-Spider-Man. 74,77,81,84,85-X-Men. 76-Last app. Watcher in title. 78-Bisley-c. 80-Hulk. 87-Sabretooth. 89-Fantastic Four. 90-Cyclops & Havok. 91-The Hulk. 93-Wolverine. 94-Juggernaut. 95-Ghost Rider 3.00
100-($2.99, double-sized) Gambit and Rogue, Fantastic Four 4.00
105-Spider-Girl (Peter Parker's daughter) debut; Sienkiewicz-a; (Betty Brant also app. as a Spider-Girl in What If? (1st series) #7) 2 4 6 12 16 20
106-114: 106-Gambit. 108-Avengers. 111-Wolverine. 114-Secret Wars 3.00
#(-1) Flashback (7/97) 3.00

WHAT IF...? (one-shots)
Marvel Comics: Feb, 2005 ($2.99)

... Aunt May Had Died Instead of Uncle Ben? - Brubaker-s/DiVito-a/Brase-c 3.00
... Dr. Doom Had Become The Thing? - Karl Kesel-s/Paul Smith-a/c 3.00
... General Ross Had Become The Hulk? - Peter David-s/Pat Olliffe-a/Gary Frank-c 3.00
... Jessica Jones Had Joined The Avengers? - Bendis-s/Gaydos-a/McNiven-c 3.00
... Karen Page Had Lived? - Bendis-s/Lark-a/c 3.00
... Magneto and Professor X Had Formed The X-Men Together? - Claremont-s/Raney-a 3.00
What If...: Why Not? TPB (2005, $16.99) r/one-shots 17.00

WHAT IF... (one-shots)
Marvel Comics: Feb, 2006 ($2.99)

... : Captain America - Fought in the Civil War?; Bedard-s/Di Giandomenico-a 3.00
... : Daredevil - The Devil Who Dares; Daredevil in feudal Japan; Veitch-s/Edwards-a 3.00
... : Fantastic Four - Were Cosmonauts?; Marshall Rogers-a/c; Mike Carey-s 3.00
... : Submariner - Grew Up on Land?; Pak-s/Lopez-a 3.00
... : Thor - Was the Herald of Galactus?; Kirkman-s/Oeming-a/c 3.00
... : Wolverine - In the Prohibition Era; Way-s/Proctor-a/Harris-c 3.00
What If: Mirror Mirror TPB (2006, $16.99) r/one-shots; design pages and Rogers sketches 17.00

WHAT IF ?... (one-shots altering recent Marvel "event" series)
Marvel Comics: Jan, 2007 - Feb, 2007 ($3.99)

... Avengers Disassembled; Parker-s/Lopresti-a/c 4.00
... Spider-Man The Other; Peter David-s/Khoi Pham-a; Venom app. 4.00
... Wolverine Enemy of the State; Robinson-s/DiGiandomenico-a/Alexander-c 4.00
... X-Men Age of Apocalypse; Remeder-s/Wilkins-a/Djurdjevic-c 4.00
... X-Men Deadly Genesis; Hine-s/Yardin-a/c 4.00
What If?: Event Horizon TPB (2007, $16.99) r/one-shots; design pages and cover sketches 17.00

WHAT IF ?... (one-shots altering recent Marvel "event" series)
Marvel Comics: Dec, 2007 - Feb, 2008 ($3.99)

... Annihilation; Nova, Iron Man and Captain America app. 4.00
... Civil War; 2 covers by Silvestri & Djurdjevic 4.00
... Planet Hulk; Pagulayan-c; Kirk, Sandoval & Hembeck-a 4.00
... Spider-Man vs. Wolverine; Romita Jr.-c; Henry-a; Nick Fury app. 4.00
... X-Men - Rise and Fall of the Shi'ar Empire; Coipel-c 4.00
What If?: Civil War TPB (2008, $16.99) r/one-shots; design pages and cover sketches 17.00

WHAT IF ?... (one-shots altering recent Marvel "event" series)
Marvel Comics: Feb, 2009 ($3.99) (Serialized back-up Runaways story in each issue)

... Fallen Son; if Iron Man had died instead of Capt. America; McGuinness-c 4.00
... House of M; if the Scarlet Witch had said "No more powers" instead; Cheung-c 4.00
... Newer Fantastic Four; team of Spider-Man, Hulk, Iron Man and Wolverine 4.00
... Secret Wars; if Doctor Doom had kept the Beyonder's power; origin re-told 4.00
... Spider-Man Back in Black; if Mary Jane had been shot instead of Aunt May 4.00

WHAT IF ?... (one-shots)
Marvel Comics: Feb, 2010 ($3.99)

... Astonishing X-Men; if Ord resurrected Jean Grey; Campbell-c 4.00
... Daredevil vs. Elektra; Kayanan-a; Klaus Janson-c swipe of Daredevil #168 4.00
... Secret Invasion; if the Skrulls succeeded; Yu-c 4.00
... Spider-Man: House of M; if Gwen Stacy survived the House of M; Dodson-c 4.00
... World War Hulk; if the heroes lost the war; Romita Jr.-c 4.00

WHAT IF ?... (one-shots) (4 part Deadpool back-up story in all but #200)
Marvel Comics: Feb, 2011 ($3.99)

... #200 ($4.99) Siege on cover; if Osborn won the Siege of Asgard; Stan Lee back-up 5.00

What The..?! #10 © MAR

Where Monsters Dwell #12 © MAR

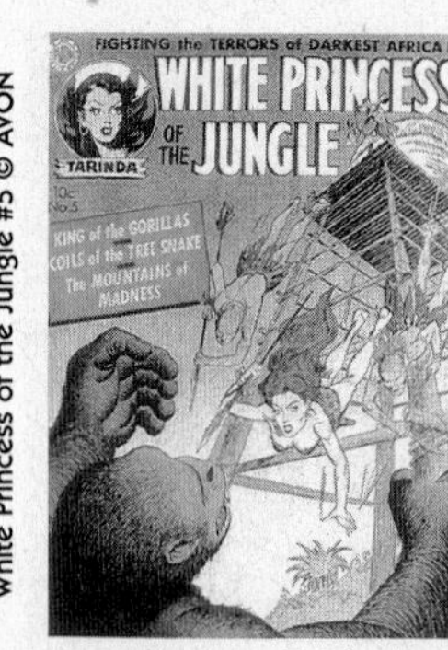

White Princess of the Jungle #5 © AVON

GD 2.0 | VG 4.0 | FN 6.0 | VF 8.0 | VF/NM 9.0 | NM- 9.2

... Dark Reign; if Norman Osborn was killed; Tanaka-a/Deodato-c 4.00
... Iron Man: Demon in an Armor; if Tony Stark became Dr. Doom; Nolan-a 4.00
... Spider-Man; if Spider-Man killed Kraven; Jimenez-c 4.00
... Wolverine: Father; if Wolverine raised Daken; Tocchini-a; Yu-a 4.00

'WHAT'S NEW? - THE COLLECTED ADVENTURES OF PHIL & DIXIE'
Palliard Press: Oct, 1991 - No. 2, 1991 ($5.95, mostly color, sq.-bound, 52 pgs.)
1,2-By Phil Foglio 6.00

WHAT THE- -?!
Marvel Comics: Aug, 1988 - No. 26, 1993 ($1.25/$1.50/$2.50, semi-annual #5 on)
1-All contain parodies 4.00
2-24: 3-X-Men parody; Todd McFarlane-a. 5-Punisher/Wolverine parody; Jim Lee-a. 6-Punisher, Wolverine, Alpha Flight. 9-Wolverine. 16-EC back-c parody. 17-Wolverine/Punisher parody. 18-Star Trek parody w/Wolverine. 19-Punisher, Wolverine, Ghost Rider. 21-Weapon X parody. 22-Punisher/Wolverine parody 3.00
25-Summer Special 1 (1993, $2.50)-X-Men parody 4.00
26-Fall Special ($2.50, 68 pgs.)-Spider-Ham 2099-c/story; origin Silver Surfer; Hulk & Doomsday parody; indica reads "Winter Special." 4.00
NOTE: ***Austin** a-6i. **Byrne** a-2, 6, 10; c-2, 6-8, 10, 12, 13. **Golden** a-22. **Dale Keown** a-8p(8 pgs.). **McFarlane** a-3. **Rogers** c-15i, 16p. **Severin** a-2. **Staton** a-21p. **Williamson** a-2i.*

WHEE COMICS (Also see Gay, Smile & Tickle Comics)
Modern Store Publications: 1955 (7¢, 5x7-1/4", 52 pgs.)
1-Funny animal 6 12 18 28 34 40

WHEEDIES (See Panic #11 -EC Comics)

WHEELIE AND THE CHOPPER BUNCH (TV)
Charlton Comics: July, 1975 - No. 7, July, 1976 (Hanna-Barbera)
1-3: 1-Byrne text illo (see Nightmare for 1st art); Staton-a. 2-Byrne-a. 2,3-Mike Zeck text illos. 3-Staton-a; Byrne-c/a 3 6 9 18 27 35
4-7-Staton-a 2 4 6 12 16 20

WHEN KNIGHTHOOD WAS IN FLOWER (See The Sword & the Rose, 4-Color #505, 682)

WHEN SCHOOL IS OUT (See Wisco in Promotional Comics section)

WHERE CREATURES ROAM
Marvel Comics Group: July, 1970 - No. 8, Sept, 1971
1-Kirby/Ayers-c/a(r) 4 8 12 28 44 60
2-8: 2-5,7,8-Kirby-c/a(r). 6-Kirby-a(r) 3 6 9 20 30 40
NOTE: ***Ditko** r-1-6, 7. **Heck** r-2, 5. All contain pre super-hero reprints.*

WHERE IN THE WORLD IS CARMEN SANDIEGO (TV)
DC Comics: June, 1996 - No. 4, Dec, 1996 ($1.75)
1-4: Adaptation of TV show 3.00

WHERE MONSTERS DWELL
Marvel Comics Group: Jan, 1970 - No. 38, Oct, 1975
1-Kirby/Ditko-r; all contain pre super-hero-r 5 10 15 30 48 65
2-10: 4-Crandall-a(r) 3 6 9 21 32 42
11,13-20: 11-Last 15¢ issue. 18,20-Starlin-c 3 6 9 18 27 35
12-Giant issue (52 pgs.) 4 8 12 23 36 48
21-Reprints 1st Fin Fang Foom app. 3 6 9 17 25 32
22-37 3 6 9 16 22 28
38-Williamson-r/World of Suspense #3 3 6 9 16 23 30
NOTE: ***Colan** r-12. **Ditko** a(r)-4, 6, 8, 10, 12, 17-19, 23-25, 37. **Kirby** r-1-3, 5-16, 18-27, 30-32, 34-36, 38; c-12? **Reinman** a-3r, 4r, 12r. **Severin** c-15.*

WHERE'S HUDDLES? (TV) (See Fun-In #9)
Gold Key: Jan, 1971 - No. 3, Dec, 1971 (Hanna-Barbera)
1 3 6 9 19 29 38
2,3: 3-r/most #1 2 4 6 11 16 20

WHIP WILSON (Movie star) (Formerly Rex Hart; Gunhawk #12 on; see Western Hearts, Western Life Romances, Western Love)
Marvel Comics: No. 9, April, 1950 - No. 11, Sept, 1950 (#9,10: 52 pgs.)
9-Photo-c; Whip Wilson & his horse Bullet begin; origin Bullet; issue #23 listed on splash page; cover changed to #9 49 98 147 309 522 735
10,11: Both have photo-c. 11-36 pgs. 28 56 84 168 274 380
I.W. Reprint #1(1964)-Kinstler-c; r-Marvel #11 3 6 9 16 22 28

WHIRLWIND COMICS (Also see Cyclone Comics)
Nita Publication: June, 1940 - No. 3, Sept, 1940
1-Origin & 1st app. Cyclone; Cyclone-c 258 516 774 1651 2826 4000
2,3: Cyclone-c 110 220 330 704 1202 1700

WHIRLYBIRDS (TV)
Dell Publishing Co.: No. 1124, Aug, 1960 - No. 1216, Oct-Dec, 1961
Four Color 1124 (#1)-Photo-c 8 16 24 55 93 130
Four Color 1216-Photo-c 8 16 24 51 86 120

WHISKEY DICKEL, INTERNATIONAL COWGIRL
Image Comics: Aug, 2003 ($12.95, softcover, B&W)
nn-Mark Ricketts-s/Mike Hawthorne-a; pin-up by various incl. Oeming, Thompson, Mack 13.00

WHISPER (Female Ninja)
Capital Comics: Dec, 1983 - No. 2, 1984 ($1.75, Baxter paper)
1,2: 1-Origin; Golden-c, Special (11/85, $2.50) 4.00

WHISPER (Vol. 2)
First Comics: Jun, 1986 - No. 37, June, 1990 ($1.25/$1.75/$1.95)
1-37 3.00

WHISPER
Boom! Studios: Nov, 2006 ($3.99)
1-Grant-s/Dzialowski-a 4.00

WHISPERS
Image Comics: Jan, 2012 - Present ($2.99)
1-Joshua Luna-s/a 3.00

WHITE CHIEF OF THE PAWNEE INDIANS
Avon Periodicals: 1951
nn-Kit West app.; Kinstler-c 16 32 48 94 147 200

WHITE EAGLE INDIAN CHIEF (See Indian Chief)

WHITE FANG
Disney Comics: 1990 ($5.95, 68 pgs.)
nn-Graphic novel adapting new Disney movie 6.00

WHITE INDIAN
Magazine Enterprises: No. 11, July, 1953 - No. 15, 1954
11(A-1 94), 12(A-1 101), 13(A-1 104)-Frazetta-r(Dan Brand) in all from Durango Kid. 11-Powell-c 20 40 60 114 182 250
14(A-1 117), 15(A-1 135)-Check-a; Torres-a-#15 14 28 42 76 108 140
NOTE: *#11 contains reprints from Durango Kid #1-4; #12 from #5, 9, 10, 11; #13 from #7, 12, 13, 16. #14 & 15 contain all new stories.*

WHITEOUT (Also see Queen & Country)
Oni Press: July, 1998 - No. 4, Nov, 1998 ($2.95, B&W, limited series)
1-4: 1-Matt Wagner-c. 2-Mignola-c. 3-Gibbons-c 3.00
TPB (5/99, $10.95) r/#1-4; Miller-c 11.00

WHITEOUT: MELT
Oni Press: Sept, 1999 - No. 4, Feb, 2000 ($2.95, B&W, limited series)
1-4-Greg Rucka-s/Steve Lieber-a 3.00
Whiteout: Melt, The Definitive Edition TPB (9/07, $13.95) r/#1-4; Rucka afterword 14.00

WHITE PRINCESS OF THE JUNGLE (Also see Jungle Adventures & Top Jungle Comics)
Avon Periodicals: July, 1951 - No. 5, Nov, 1952
1-Origin of White Princess (Taanda) & Capt'n Courage (r); Kinstler-c 57 114 171 362 619 875
2-Reprints origin of Malu, Slave Girl Princess from Avon's Slave Girl Comics #1 w/Malu changed to Zora; Kinstler-c/a(2) 41 82 123 249 417 585
3-Origin Blue Gorilla; Kinstler-c/a 37 74 111 222 361 500
4-Jack Barnum, White Hunter app.; r/Sheena #9 32 64 96 192 314 435
5-Blue Gorilla by McCann?; Kinstler inside-c; Fawcette/Alascia-a(3) 34 68 102 204 322 460

WHITE RIDER AND SUPER HORSE (Formerly Humdinger V2#2; Indian Warriors #7 on; also see Blue Bolt #1, 4Most & Western Crime Cases)
Novelty-Star Publications/Accepted Publ.: No. 4, 9/50 - No. 6, 3/51
4-6-Adapts "The Last of the Mohicans". 4(#1)-(9/50)-Says #11 on inside 16 32 48 92 144 195
Accepted Reprint #5(r/#5),6 (nd); L.B. Cole-c 9 18 27 50 65 80
NOTE: *All have **L. B. Cole** covers.*

WHITE TIGER
Marvel Comics: Jan, 2007 - No. 6, Nov, 2007 ($2.99, limited series)
1-6: 1-David Mack-c; Pierce & Liebe-s/Briones-a; Spider-Man & Black Widow app. 3.00
...: A Hero's Compulsion SC (2007,$14.99) r/#1-6; re-cap art and profile page 15.00

WHITE WILDERNESS (Disney)
Dell Publishing Co.: No. 943, Oct, 1958
Four Color 943-Movie 6 12 18 42 69 95

WHITMAN COMIC BOOK, A
Whitman Publishing Co.: Sept., 1962 (136 pgs.; 7-3/4x5-3/4; hardcover) (B&W)
1-3,5,7: 1-Yogi Bear. 2-Huckleberry Hound. 3-Mr. Jinks and Pixie & Dixie. 5-Augie Doggie &

Whiz Comics #22 © FAW

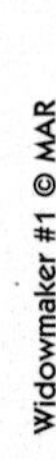
Widowmaker #1 © MAR

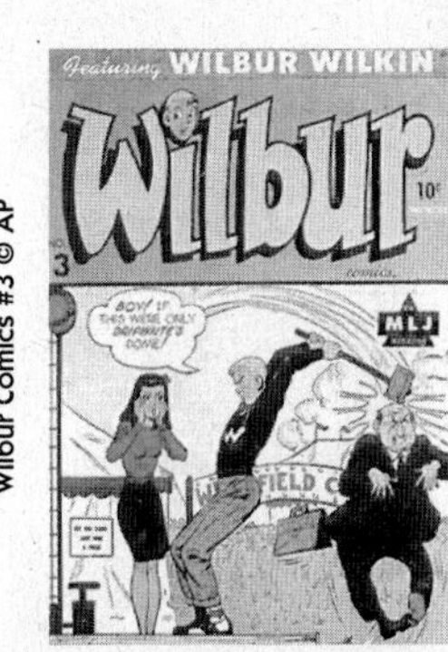

Wilbur Comics #3 © AP

GD VG FN VF VF/NM NM-
2.0 4.0 6.0 8.0 9.0 9.2

GD VG FN VF VF/NM NM-
2.0 4.0 6.0 8.0 9.0 9.2

Loopy de Loop. 7-Bugs Bunny-r from #47,51,53,54 & 55
7 14 21 44 72 100
4,6: 4-The Flintstones. 6-Snooper & Blabber Fearless Detectives/Quick Draw McGraw of the Wild West 7 14 21 48 79 110
8-Donald Duck-reprints most of WDC&S #209-213. Includes 5 Barks stories, 1 complete Mickey Mouse serial by Paul Murry & 1 Mickey Mouse serial missing the 1st episode
8 16 24 53 89 125
NOTE: *Hanna-Barbera #1-6(TV), reprints of British tabloid comics. Dell reprints-#7,8.*

WHIZ COMICS (Formerly Flash & Thrill Comics #1)(See 5 Cent Comics)
Fawcett Publications: No. 2, Feb, 1940 - No. 155, June, 1953

1-(nn on cover, #2 inside)-Origin & 1st newsstand app. Captain Marvel (formerly Captain Thunder) by C. C. Beck (created by Bill Parker), Spy Smasher, Golden Arrow, Ibis the Invincible, Dan Dare, Scoop Smith, Sivana, & Lance O'Casey begin
8000 16,000 24,000 48,000 79,000 110,000
(The only Mint copy sold in 1995 for $176,000 cash)
1-Reprint, oversize 13-1/2x10". **WARNING**: This comic is an exact duplicate reprint (except for dropping "Gangway for Captain Marvel" from-c) of the original except for its size. DC published it in 1974 with a second cover titling it as a Famous First Edition. There have been many reported cases of the outer cover being removed and the interior sold as the original edition. The reprint with the new outer cover removed is practically worthless. See Famous First Edition for value.
2-(3/40, nn on cover, #3 inside); cover to Flash #1 redrawn, pg. 12, panel 4; Spy Smasher reveals I.D. to Eve 541 1082 1623 3950 6975 10,000
3-(4/40, #3 on-c, #4 inside)-1st app. Beautia 371 748 1113 2600 4550 6500
4-(5/40, #4 on cover, #5 inside)-Brief origin Capt. Marvel retold
300 600 900 2070 3635 5200
5-Captain Marvel wears button-down flap on splash page only
284 568 852 1818 3109 4400
6-10: 7-Dr. Voodoo begins (by Raboy-#9-22) 194 388 582 1242 2121 3000
11-14: 12-Capt. Marvel does not wear cape 135 270 405 864 1482 2100
15-Origin Sivana; Dr. Voodoo by Raboy 148 296 444 947 1624 2300
16-18-Spy Smasher battles Captain Marvel 139 278 417 883 1517 2150
19-Classic shark-c 135 270 405 864 1482 2100
20 97 194 291 621 1061 1500
21-(9/41)-Origin & 1st cover app. Lt. Marvels, the 1st team in Fawcett comics. In this issue, Capt. Death similar to Ditko's later Dr. Strange 100 200 300 635 1093 1550
22-24: 23-Only Dr. Voodoo by Tuska 81 162 243 518 884 1250
25-(12/41)-Captain Nazi jumps from Master Comics #21 to take on Capt. Marvel solo after being beaten by Capt. Marvel/Bulletman team, causing the creation of Capt. Marvel Jr.; 1st app./origin of Capt. Marvel Jr. (part II of trilogy origin by CC. Beck & Mac Raboy); Captain Marvel sends Jr. back to Master #22 to aid Bulletman against Capt. Nazi; origin Old Shazam in text 514 1028 1542 3750 6625 9500
26-30 60 120 180 381 658 935
31,32: 32-1st app. The Trolls; Hitler/Mussolini satire by Beck
53 106 159 334 567 800
33-Spy Smasher, Captain Marvel x-over on cover and inside
60 120 180 381 658 935
34,36-40: 37-The Trolls app. by Swayze 41 82 123 249 417 585
35-Captain Marvel & Spy Smasher-c 49 98 147 309 522 735
41-50: 42-Classic time travel-c. 43-Spy Smasher, Ibis, Golden Arrow x-over in Capt. Marvel. 44-Flag-c. 47-Origin recap (1 pg.) 36 72 108 216 351 485
51-60: 52-Capt. Marvel x-over in Ibis. 57-Spy Smasher, Golden Arrow, Ibis cameo
29 58 87 172 281 390
61-70 27 54 81 160 263 365
71,77-80 26 52 78 152 249 345
72-76-Two Captain Marvel stories in each; 76-Spy Smasher becomes Crime Smasher
26 52 78 154 252 350
81-85,87-99: 91-Infinity-c 26 52 78 152 249 345
86-Captain Marvel battles Sivana Family; robot-c 30 60 90 177 289 400
100-(8/48)-Anniversary issue 31 62 93 186 303 420
101-106: 102-Commando Yank app. 106-Bulletman app.
26 52 78 154 252 350
107-149: 107-Capitol Building photo-c. 108-Brooklyn Bridge photo-c. 112-Photo-c. 139-Infinity-c. 140-Flag-c. 142-Used in **POP**, pg. 89
26 52 78 154 252 350
150-152-(Low dist.) 32 64 96 188 307 425
153-155-(Scarce):154,155-1st/2nd Dr. Death stories 41 82 123 256 428 600
NOTE: ***C.C. Beck** Captain Marvel-No. 25(part). **Krigstein** Golden Arrow-No. 75, 78, 91, 95, 96, 98-100. **Mac Raboy** Dr. Voodoo-No. 9-22. Captain Marvel-No. 25(part). **M.Swayze** a-37, 38, 59; c-38. **Schaffenberger** c-138-155(most). **Wolverton** 1/2 pg. "Culture Corner"-No. 65-67, 68(2 1/2 pgs), 70-85, 87-96, 98-100, 102-109, 112-121, 123, 125, 126, 128-131, 133, 134, 136, 142, 143, 146.*

WHIZ KIDS (Also see Big Bang Comics)
Image Comics: Apr, 2003 ($4.95, B&W, one-shot)

1-Galahad, Cyclone, Thunder Girl and Moray app.; Jeff Austin-a 5.00

WHOA, NELLIE (Also see Love & Rockets)
Fantagraphics Books: July, 1996 - No. 3, Sept, 1996 ($2.95, B&W, lim. series)

1-3: Jamie Hernandez-c/a/scripts 3.00

WHODUNIT
D.S. Publishing Co.: Aug-Sept, 1948 - No. 3, Dec-Jan, 1948-49 (#1,2: 52 pgs.)

1-Baker-a (7 pgs.) 24 48 72 140 230 320
2,3-Detective mysteries 13 26 39 74 105 135

WHODUNNIT?
Eclipse Comics: June, 1986 - No. 3, Apr, 1987 ($2.00, limited series)

1-3: Spiegle-a. 2-Gulacy-c 3.00

WHO FRAMED ROGER RABBIT (See Marvel Graphic Novel)

WHO IS NEXT?
Standard Comics: No. 5, Jan, 1953

5-Toth, Sekowsky, Andru-a; crime stories 20 40 60 114 182 250

WHO IS THE CROOKED MAN?
Crusade: Sept, 1996 ($3.50, B&W, 40 pgs.)

1-Intro The Martyr, Scarlet 7 & Garrison 4.00

WHO'S MINDING THE MINT? (See Movie Classics)

WHO'S WHO IN STAR TREK
DC Comics: Mar, 1987 - #2, Apr, 1987 ($1.50, limited series)

1,2 6.00
NOTE: ***Byrne** a-1, 2. **Chaykin** c-1, 2. **Morrow** a-1, 2. **McFarlane** a-2. **Perez** a-1, 2. **Sutton** a-1, 2.*

WHO'S WHO IN THE LEGION OF SUPER-HEROES
DC Comics: Apr, 1987 - No. 7, Nov, 1988 ($1.25, limited series)

1-7 4.00

WHO'S WHO: THE DEFINITIVE DIRECTORY OF THE DC UNIVERSE
DC Comics: Mar, 1985 - No. 26, Apr, 1987 (Maxi-series, no ads)

1-DC heroes from A-Z 4.00
2-26: All have 1-2 pgs-a by most DC artists 4.00
NOTE: ***Art Adams** a-4, 11, 18, 20. **Anderson** a-1-5, 7-12, 14, 15, 19, 21, 23-25. **Aparo** a-2, 3, 9, 10, 12, 13, 14, 15, 17, 18, 21, 23. **Byrne** a-4, 7, 14, 16, 18i, 19, 22i, 24; c-22. **Cowan** a-3-5, 8, 10-13, 16-18, 22-25. **Ditko** a-19-22. **Evans** a-20. **Giffen** a-1, 3,-6, 8, 13, 15, 17, 18, 23. **Grell** a-6, 9, 14, 20, 23, 25, 26. **Infantino** a-1-10, 12, 15, 17-22, 24, 25. **Kaluta** a-14, 21. **Gil Kane** a-1-11, 13, 14, 16, 19, 21-23, 25. **Kirby** a-2-6, 8-18, 20, 22, 25. **Kubert** a-2, 3, 7-11, 19, 20, 25. **Erik Larsen** a-24. **McFarlane** a-10-12, 17, 19, 25, 26. **Morrow** a-4, 7, 25, 26. **Orlando** a-1, 4, 10, 11, 21i. **Perez** a-1-5, 8-19, 22-26; c-1-4, 13-18. **Rogers** a-1, 2, 5-7, 11, 12, 15, 24. **Starlin** a-13, 14, 16. **Stevens** a-4, 7, 18.*

WHO'S WHO UPDATE '87
DC Comics: Aug, 1987 - No. 5, Dec, 1987 ($1.25, limited series)

1-5: Contains art by most DC artists 4.00
NOTE: ***Giffen** a-1. **McFarlane** a-1-4; c-4. **Perez** a-1-4.*

WHO'S WHO UPDATE '88
DC Comics: Aug, 1988 - No. 4, Nov, 1988 ($1.25, limited series)

1-4: Contains art by most DC artists 4.00
NOTE: ***Giffen** a-1. **Erik Larsen** a-1.*

WICKED, THE
Avalon Studios: Dec, 1999 - No. 7, Aug, 2000 ($2.95)

Preview-(7/99, $5.00, B&W) 5.00
1-7-Anacleto-c/Martinez-a 3.00
...: Medusa's Tale (11/00, $3.95, one shot) story plus pin-up gallery 4.00
...: Vol. 1: Omnibus (2003, $19.95) r/#0-8; Drew-c 20.00

WIDOWMAKER
Marvel Comics: Feb, 2011 - No. 4, Apr, 2011 ($3.99, limited series)

1-4-Black Widow, Hawkeye & Mockingbird app. 1,2-Jae Lee-c. 3,4-Noto-c 4.00

WIDOW WARRIORS
Dynamite Entertainment: 2010 - No. 4, 2010 ($3.99, limited series)

1-4-Pat Lee-a/c 4.00

WILBUR COMICS (Teen-age) (Also see Laugh Comics, Laugh Comix, Liberty Comics #10 & Zip Comics)
MLJ Magazines/Archie Publ. No. 8, Spring, 1946 on: Sum', 1944 - No. 87, 11/59; No. 88, 9/63; No. 89, 10/64; No. 90, 10/65 (No. 1-46: 52 pgs.) (#1-11 are quarterly)

1 58 116 174 371 636 900
2(Fall, 1944) 32 64 96 192 314 435
3,4(Wint, '44-45; Spr, '45) 23 46 69 136 223 310
5-1st app. Katy Keene (Sum, '45) & begin series; Wilbur story same as Archie story in Archie #1 except Wilbur replaces Archie 119 238 357 762 1306 1850
6-10: 10-(Fall, 1946) 26 52 78 154 252 350
11-20 16 32 48 94 147 200

Wild Bill Elliott FC #520 © DELL

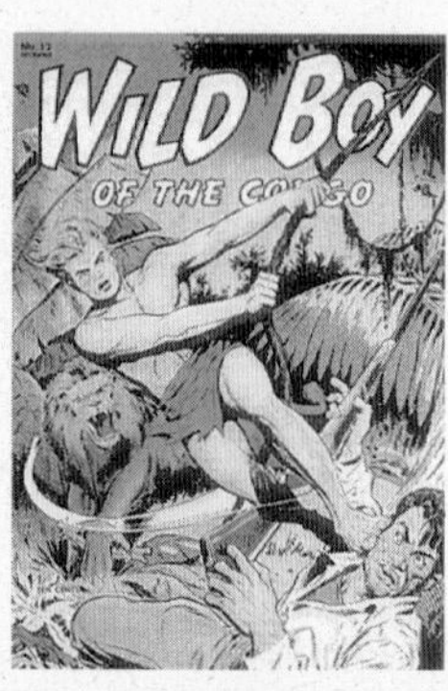

Wild Boy of the Congo #12 © Z-D

WildC.A.T.S: Covert Action Teams #47 © WSP

	GD 2.0	VG 4.0	FN 6.0	VF 8.0	VF/NM 9.0	NM- 9.2
21-30: 30-(4/50)	12	24	36	69	97	125
31-50	10	20	30	54	72	90
51-70	9	18	27	47	61	75
71-90: 88-Last 10¢ issue (9/63)	4	8	12	28	44	60

NOTE: *Katy Keene in No. 5-56, 58-61, 63-69.* ***Al Fagaly*** *c-6-9, 12-24 at least.* ***Vigoda*** *c-2.*

WILD
Atlas Comics (IPC): Feb, 1954 - No. 5, Aug, 1954

	GD	VG	FN	VF	VF/NM	NM-
1	27	54	81	158	259	360
2	17	34	51	98	154	210
3-5	15	30	45	88	137	185

NOTE: ***Berg*** *a-5; c-4.* ***Burgos*** *c-3.* ***Colan*** *a-4.* ***Everett*** *a-1-3.* ***Heath*** *a-2, 3, 5.* ***Maneely*** *a-1-3, 5; c-1, 5.* ***Post*** *a-2, 5.* ***Ed Win*** *a-1, 3.*

WILD! (This Magazine Is...) (Satire)
Dell Publishing Co.: Jan, 1968 - No. 3, 1968 (35¢, magazine, 52 pgs.)

	GD	VG	FN	VF	VF/NM	NM-
1-3: Hogan's Heroes, The Rat Patrol & Mission Impossible TV spoofs	3	6	9	16	23	30

WILD ANIMALS
Pacific Comics: Dec, 1982 ($1.00, one-shot, direct sales)

	GD	VG	FN	VF	VF/NM	NM-
1-Funny animal; Sergio Aragonés-a; Shaw-c/a						4.00

WILD BILL ELLIOTT (Also see Western Roundup under Dell Giants)
Dell Publishing Co.: No. 278, 5/50 - No. 643, 7/55 (No #11,12) (All photo-c)

	GD	VG	FN	VF	VF/NM	NM-
Four Color 278 (#1, 52pgs.)-Titled "Bill Elliott"; Bill & his horse Stormy begin; photo front/back-c begin	11	22	33	77	154	230
2 (11/50), 3 (52 pgs.)	8	16	24	51	86	120
4-10 (10-12/52)	6	12	18	41	66	90
Four Color 472 (6/53),520(12/53)-Last photo back-c	5	10	15	35	55	75
13 (4-6/54) - 17 (4-6/55)	5	10	15	32	51	70
Four Color 643 (7/55)	5	10	15	30	48	65

WILD BILL HICKOK (Also see Blazing Sixguns)
Avon Periodicals: Sept-Oct, 1949 - No. 28, May-June, 1956

	GD	VG	FN	VF	VF/NM	NM-
1-Ingels-c	24	48	72	140	230	320
2-Painted-c; Kit West app.	14	28	42	76	108	140
3-5-Painted-c (4-Cover by Howard Winfield)	10	20	30	58	79	100
6-10,12: 8-10-Painted-c. 12-Kinsler-c?	10	20	30	56	76	95
11,13,14-Kinstler-c/a (#11-c & inside-f/c art only)	11	22	33	60	83	105
15,17,18,20: 18-Kit West story. 20-Kit West by Larsen	9	18	27	50	65	80
16-Kamen-a; r-3 stories/King of the Badmen of Deadwood	9	18	27	52	69	85
19-Meskin-a	9	18	27	50	65	80
21-Reprints 2 stories/Chief Crazy Horse	9	18	27	47	61	75
22-McCann-a?; r/Sheriff Bob Dixon's...	9	18	27	47	61	75
23-27: 23-Kinstler-c. 24-27-Kinstler-c/a(r) (24,25-r?)	9	18	27	47	61	75
28-Kinstler-c/a (new); r-/Last of the Comanches	9	18	27	50	65	80
I.W. Reprint #1-r/#2; Kinstler-c	2	4	6	9	13	16
Super Reprint #10-12: 10-r/#18. 11-r/#?. 12-r/#8	2	4	6	9	13	16

NOTE: *#23, 25 contain numerous editing deletions in both art and script due to code.* ***Kinstler*** *c-6, 7, 11-14, 17, 18, 20-22, 24-28.* ***Howard Larsen*** *a-1, 2, 4, 5, 6(3), 7-9, 11, 12, 17, 18, 20-24, 26.* ***Meskin*** *a-7.* ***Reinman*** *a-6, 17.*

WILD BILL HICKOK AND JINGLES (TV)(Formerly Cowboy Western) (Also see Blue Bird)
Charlton Comics: No. 68, Aug, 1958 - No. 75, Dec, 1959

	GD	VG	FN	VF	VF/NM	NM-
68,69-Williamson-a (all are 10¢ issues)	11	22	33	60	83	105
70-Two pgs. Williamson-a	8	16	24	42	54	65
71-75 (#76, exist?)	6	12	18	28	34	40

WILD BILL PECOS WESTERN (Also see The Westerner)
AC Comics: 1989 ($3.50, 1/2 color/1/2 B&W, 52 pgs.)

	GD	VG	FN	VF	VF/NM	NM-
1-Syd Shores-c/a(r)/Westerner; photo back-c						4.00

WILD BOY OF THE CONGO (Also see Approved Comics)
Ziff-Davis No. 10-12,4-8/St. John No. 9,11 on: No. 10, 2-3/51 - No. 12, 8-9/51; No. 4, 10-11/51 - No. 9, 10/53; No. 11-#15,6/55 (No #10, 1953)

	GD	VG	FN	VF	VF/NM	NM-
10(#1)(2-3/51)-Origin; bondage-c by Saunders (painted); used in **SOTI**, pg. 189; painted-c begin thru #9 (except #7)	25	50	75	150	245	340
11(4-5/51),12(8-9/51)-Norman Saunders painted-c	14	28	42	82	121	160
4(10-11/51)-Saunders painted bondage-c	14	28	42	82	121	160
5(Winter,'51)-Saunders painted-c	14	28	42	76	108	140
6,8,9(10/53): Painted-c. 6-Saunders-c	14	28	42	76	108	140
7(8-9/52)-Kinstler-a	14	28	42	82	121	160
11-13-Baker-c. 11-r/#7 w/new Baker-c; Kinstler-a (2 pgs.)	15	30	45	88	137	185
14(4/55)-Baker-c; r-#12('51)	15	30	45	88	137	185
15(6/55)	11	22	33	64	90	115

WILDCAT (See Sensation Comics #1)

WILDC.A.T.S ADVENTURES (TV cartoon)
Image Comics (WildStorm): Sept, 1994 - No. 10, June, 1995 ($1.95/$2.50)

	GD	VG	FN	VF	VF/NM	NM-
1-10						3.00
Sourcebook 1 (1/95, $2.95)						3.00

WILDC.A.T.S: COVERT ACTION TEAMS (Also see Alan Moore's... for TPB reprints)
Image Comics (WildStorm Productions): Aug, 1992 - No. 4, Mar, 1993; No. 5, Nov, 1993 - No. 50, June, 1998 ($1.95/$2.50)

	GD	VG	FN	VF	VF/NM	NM-
1-1st app; Jim Lee/Williams-c/a & Lee scripts begin; contains 2 trading cards (Two diff versions of cards inside); 1st WildStorm Productions title						5.00
1-All gold foil signed edition						15.00
1-All gold foil unsigned edition						8.00
1-Newsstand edition w/o cards						3.00
1-"3-D Special"(8/97, $4.95) w/3-D glasses; variant-c by Jim Lee.						5.00
2-($2.50)-Prism foil stamped-c; contains coupon for Image Comics #0 & 4 pg. preview to Portacio's Wetworks (back-up)						5.00
2-With coupon missing						2.00
2-Direct sale misprint w/o foil-c						5.00
2-Newsstand ed., no prism or coupon						3.00
3-Lee/Liefeld-c (1/93-c, 12/92 inside)						4.00
4-($2.50)-Polybagged w/Topps trading card; 1st app. Tribe by Johnson & Stroman; Youngblood cameo						4.00
4-Variant w/red card						6.00
5-7-Jim Lee/Williams-c/a; Lee script						3.00
8-X-Men's Jean Grey & Scott Summers cameo						4.00
9-12: 10-1st app. Huntsman & Soldier; Claremont scripts begin, ends #13. 11-1st app. Savant, Tapestry & Mr. Majestic.						3.00
11-Alternate Portacio-c, see Deathblow #5						5.00
13-19,21-24: 15-James Robinson scripts begin, ends #20. 15,16-Black Razor story. 21-Alan Moore scripts begin, end #34; intro Tao & Ladytron; new WildC.A.T.S team forms (Mr. Majestic, Savant, Condition Red (Max Cash), Tao & Ladytron). 22-Maguire-a						3.00
20-($2.50)-Direct Market, WildStorm Rising Pt. 2 w/bound-in card						4.00
20-($1.95)-Newsstand, WildStorm Rising Part 2						3.00
25-($4.95)-Alan Moore script; wraparound foil-c.						5.00
26-49: 29-(5/96)-Fire From Heaven Pt 7; reads Apr on-c. 30-(6/96)-Fire From Heaven Pt. 13; Spartan revealed to have transplanted personality of John Colt (from Team One: WildC.A.T.S). 31-(9/96)-Grifter rejoins team; Ladytron dies						3.00
40-($3.50)Voyager Pack bagged w/Divine Right preview						5.00
50-($3.50) Stories by Robinson/Lee, Choi & Peterson/Benes, and Moore/Charest; Charest sketchbook; Lee wraparound-c						4.00
50-Chromium cover						6.00
Annual 1 (2/98, $2.95) Robinson-s						4.00
Compendium (1993, $9.95)-r/#1-4; bagged w/#0						10.00
Sourcebook 1 (9/93, $2.50)-Foil embossed-c						3.00
Sourcebook 1-($1.95)-Newsstand ed. w/o foil embossed-c						3.00
Sourcebook 2 (11/94, $2.50)-wraparound-c						3.00
Special 1 (11/93, $3.50, 52 pgs.)-1st Travis Charest WildC.A.T.S-a						4.00
...A Gathering of Eagles (5/97, $9.95, TPB) r/#10-12						10.00
.../ Cyberforce: Killer Instinct TPB (2004, $14.95) r/#5-7 & Cyberforce V2 #1-3						15.00
...Gang War ('98, $16.95, TPB) r/#28-34						17.00
...Homecoming (8/98, $19.95, TPB) r/#21-27						20.00
James Robinson's Complete Wildc.a.t.s TPB (2009, $24.99) r/#15-20,50; Annual 1, WildStorm Rising #1, Team One Wildc.a.t.s #1,2; cover and pin-up gallery						25.00

WILDCATS (3rd series)
DC Comics (WildStorm): Mar, 1999 - No. 28, Dec, 2001 ($2.50)

	GD	VG	FN	VF	VF/NM	NM-
1-Charest-a; six covers by Lee, Adams, Bisley, Campbell, Madureira and Ramos; Lobdell-s						4.00
1-($6.95) DF Edition; variant cover by Ramos						7.00
2-28: 2-Voodoo cover. 3-Bachalo variant-c. 5-Hitch-a/variant-c. 7-Meglia-a. 8-Phillips-a begins. 17-J.G. Jones-c. 18,19-Jim Lee-c. 20,21-Dillon-a						3.00
Annual 2000 (12/00, $3.50) Bermejo-a; Devil's Night x-over						4.00
...: Battery Park ('03, $17.95, TPB) r/#20-28; Phillips-c						18.00
... Ladytron (10/00, $5.95) Origin; Casey-s/Canete-a						6.00
... Mosaic (2/00, $3.95) Tuska-a (10 pg. back-up story)						4.00
...: Serial Boxes ('01, $14.95, TPB) r/#14-19; Phillips-c						15.00
...: Street Smart ('00, $24.95, HC) r/#1-6; Charest-c						25.00
...: Street Smart ('02, $14.95, SC) r/#1-6; Charest-c						15.00
...: Vicious Circles ('00, $14.95, TPB) r/#8-13; Phillips-c						15.00

WILDCATS (Volume 4)
DC Comics (WildStorm): Dec, 2006 ($2.99)

Wildcats 3.0 #6 © WSP

Wildsiderz #0 © Atomico

Wildstorm #4 © WSP

	GD 2.0	VG 4.0	FN 6.0	VF 8.0	VF/NM 9.0	NM- 9.2

1-Grant Morrison-s/Jim Lee-a; Jim Lee-c 3.00
1-Variant-c by Todd McFarlane/Jim Lee 6.00
...: Armageddon 1 (2/08, $2.99) Gage-s/Caldwell-a 3.00

WILDCATS (Volume 5) (World's End on cover for #1,2)
DC Comics (WildStorm): Sept, 2008 - No. 30, Feb, 2011 ($2.99)

1-30: 1-Christos Gage-s/Neil Googe-a. 5-Woods-a 3.00
...: Family Secrets TPB (2010, $17.99) r/#8-12 18.00
...: World's End TPB (2009, $17.99) r/#1-7 18.00

WILDC.A.T.S/ ALIENS
Image Comics/Dark Horse: Aug, 1998 ($4.95, one-shot)

	GD	VG	FN	VF	VF/NM	NM-
1-Ellis-s/Sprouse-a/c; Aliens invade Skywatch; Stormwatch app.; death of Winter; destruction of Skywatch	1	2	3	5	6	8
1-Variant-c by Gil Kane	1	3	4	6	8	10

WILDCATS: NEMESIS
DC Comics (WildStorm): Nov, 2005 - No. 9, July, 2006 ($2.99, limited series)

1-9: 1-Robbie Morrison-s/Talent Caldwell & Horacio Domingues-a/Caldwell-c 3.00
TPB (2006, $19.99) r/#1-9; cover gallery 20.00

WILDC.A.T.S: SAVANT GARDE FAN EDITION
Image Comics/WildStorm Productions: Feb, 1997 - No. 3, Apr, 1997 (Giveaway, 8 pgs.) (Polybagged w/Overstreet's FAN)

1-3: Barbara Kesel-s/Christian Uche-a(p) 3.00
1-3-(Gold): All retailer incentives 10.00

WILDC.A.T.S TRILOGY
Image Comics (WildStorm Productions): June, 1993 - No. 3, Dec, 1993 ($1.95, lim. series)

1-($2.50)-1st app. Gen 13 (Fairchild, Burnout, Grunge, Freefall) Multi-color foil-c; Jae Lee-c/a in all 5.00
1-($1.95)-Newsstand ed. w/o foil-c 3.00
2,3-($1.95)-Jae Lee-c/a 3.00

WILDCATS VERSION 3.0
DC Comics (WildStorm): Oct, 2002 - No. 24, Oct, 2004 ($2.95)

1-24: 1-Casey-s/Nguyen-a; two covers by Nguyen and Rian Hughes and Nguyen. 8-Back-up preview of The Authority: High Stakes pt. 3 3.00
...: Brand Building TPB (2003, $14.95) r/#1-6 15.00
...: Full Disclosure TPB (2004, $14.95) r/#7-12 15.00
...: Year One TPB (2010, $24.99) r/#1-12 25.00
...: Year Two TPB (2011, $24.99) r/#13-24 25.00

WILDC.A.T.S/ X-MEN: THE GOLDEN AGE (See also X-Men/WildC.A.T.S.: The Dark Age)
Image Comics (WildStorm Productions): Feb, 1997 ($4.50, one-shot)

1-Lobdell-s/Charest-a; Two covers (Charest, Jim Lee) 5.00
1-"3-D" Edition ($6.50) w/glasses 7.00

WILDC.A.T.S/ X-MEN: THE MODERN AGE
Image Comics (WildStorm Productions): Aug, 1997 ($4.50, one-shot)

1-Robinson-s/Hughes-a; Two covers (Hughes, Paul Smith) 5.00
1-"3-D" Edition ($6.50) w/glasses 7.00

WILDC.A.T.S/ X-MEN: THE SILVER AGE
Image Comics (WildStorm Productions): June, 1997 ($4.50, one-shot)

1-Lobdell-s/Jim Lee-a; Two covers(Neal Adams, Jim Lee) 5.00
1-"3-D" Edition ($6.50) w/glasses 7.00

WILDCORE
Image Comics (WildStorm Prods.): Nov, 1997 - No. 10, Dec, 1998 ($2.50)

1-10: 1-Two covers (Booth/McWeeney, Charest) 3.00
1-($3.50)-Voyager Pack w/DV8 preview 4.00
1-Chromium-c 5.00

WILD DOG
DC Comics: Sept, 1987 - No. 4, Dec, 1987 (75¢, limited series)

1-4 3.00
Special 1 (1989, $2.50, 52 pgs.) 4.00

WILDERNESS TREK (See Zane Grey, Four Color 333)

WILDFIRE (See Zane Grey, FourColor 433)

WILDFLOWER
Sirius Entertainment/Neko Press: 1996 - Present (B&W)

1-5-('96, $2.50) Billy Martinez-s/a 3.00
... Beginnings TPB (Neko Press, 2003, $14.99) r/#1-5 15.00
... Dark Euphoria 1 (2004, $2.99) Kiethan Jones-a/c; Martinez-s 3.00
... Dark Euphoria 1,2 (2004, $3.99) w/alternate-c by Martinez 4.00
... Tribal Screams 1-4 (12/00 - 2/03, $2.99) 3.00
... Tribal Screams 1 ($4.99) w/alternate-c by Dark One 5.00
... Y2K (16 pgs, edition of 2000) each contains an original Martinez sketch 10.00

WILD FRONTIER (Cheyenne Kid #8 on)
Charlton Comics: Oct, 1955 - No. 7, Apr, 1957

	GD	VG	FN	VF	VF/NM	NM-
1-Davy Crockett	10	20	30	54	72	90
2-6-Davy Crockett in all	7	14	21	37	46	55
7-Origin & 1st app. Cheyenne Kid	9	18	27	47	61	75

WILD GIRL
DC Comics (WildStorm): Jan, 2005 - No. 6, Jun, 2005 ($2.95/$2.99)

1-6-Leah Moore & John Reppion-s/Shawn McManus-a/c 3.00

WILDGUARD: CASTING CALL
Image Comics: Sept, 2003 - No. 6, Feb, 2004 ($2.95)

1-6: 1-Nauck-s/a; two covers by Nauck and McGuinness. 2-Wieringo var-c. 6-Noto var-c 3.00
... Vol. 1: Casting Call (1/05, $17.95, TPB) r/#1-6; cover gallery; Todd Nauck bio 18.00
Wildguard: Fire Power 1 (12/04, $3.50) Nauck-a; two covers 3.50
Wildguard: Fool's Gold (7/05 - No. 2, 7/05, $3.50) 1,2-Todd Nauck-s/a 3.50
Wildguard: Insider (5/08 - No. 3, 7/08, $3.50) 1-3-Todd Nauck-s/a 3.50

WILDSIDERZ
DC Comics (WildStorm): No. 0, Aug, 2005 - No. 2, Jan, 2006 ($1.99/$3.50)

0-(8/05, $1.99) Series preview & character profiles; J. Scott Campbell-a 3.00
1,2: 1-(10/05, $3.50) J. Scott Campbell-s/a; Andy Hartnell-s 3.50

WILDSTAR (Also see The Dragon & The Savage Dragon)
Image Comics (Highbrow Entertainment): Sept, 1995 - No. 3, Jan, 1996 ($2.50, lim. series)

1-3: Al Gordon scripts; Jerry Ordway-c/a 3.00

WILDSTAR: SKY ZERO
Image Comics (Highbrow Entertainment): Mar, 1993 - No. 4, Nov, 1993 ($1.95, lim. series)

1-4: 1-($2.50)-Embossed-c w/silver ink; Ordway-c/a in all 3.00
1-($1.95)-Newsstand ed. w/silver ink-c, not embossed 3.00
1-Gold variant 6.00

WILD STARS
Collector's Edition/Little Rocket Productions: Summer, 1984 - Present (B&W)

Vol. 1 #1 (Summer 1984, $1.50) 5.00
Vol. 2 #1 (Winter 1988, $1.95) Foil-c; die-cut front & back-c 5.00
Vol. 3: #1-6-Brunner-c; Tierney-s. 1,2-Brewer-a. 3-6-Simons-a 3.00
7-($5.95) Simons-a 6.00
TPB (2004, $17.95) r/Vol. 1-3 18.00

WILDSTORM
Image Comics/DC Comics (WildStorm Publishing): 1994 - Present (one-shots, TPBs)

... After the Fall TPB (2009, $19.99) r/back-up stories from Wildcats V5 #1-11, The Authority V5 #1-11; Gen 13 V4 #21-28, and Stormwatch: PHD #13-20 20.00
...Annual 2000 (12/00, $3.50) Devil's Night x-over; Moy-a 4.00
...: Armageddon TPB (2008, $17.99) r/Armageddon one-shots in Midnighter, Welcome To Tranquility, Wetworks, Gen13, Stormwatch PHD, and Wildcats titles 18.00
...Chamber of Horrors (10/95, $3.50)-Bisley-c 4.00
...Fine Arts: Spotlight on Gen13 (2/08, $3.50) art and covers with commentary 3.50
...Fine Arts: Spotlight on Jim Lee (2/07, $3.50) art and covers by Lee with commentary 3.50
...Fine Arts: Spotlight on J. Scott Campbell (5/07, $3.50) art and covers with commentary 3.50
...Fine Arts: Spotlight on The Authority (1/08, $3.50) art and covers with commentary 3.50
...Fine Arts: Spotlight on WildCATs (3/08, $3.50) art and covers with commentary 3.50
...Fine Arts: The Gallery Collection (12/98, $19.95) Lee-c 20.00
...Halloween 1 (10/97, $2.50) Warner-c 3.00
...Rarities 1(12/94, $4.95, 52 pgs.)-r/Gen 13 1/2 & other stories 5.00
...Summer Special 1 (2001, $5.95) Short stories by various; Hughes-c 6.00
...Swimsuit Special 1 (12/94, $2.95), ...Swimsuit Special 2 (1995, $2.50) 3.00
...Swimsuit Special '97 #1 (7/97, $2.50) 3.00
...Thunderbook 1 (10/00, $6.95) Short stories by various incl. Hughes, Moy 7.00
...Ultimate Sports 1 (8/97, $2.50) 3.00
...Universe Sourcebook (5/95, $2.50) 3.00
...Universe 2008 Convention Exclusive ('08, no cover price) preview of World's End x-over 3.00

WILDSTORM!
Image Comics (WildStorm Publishing): Aug, 1995 - No. 4, Nov, 1995 ($2.50, B&W/color, anthology)

1-4: 1-Simonson-a 3.00

WILDSTORM PRESENTS: ...
DC Comics (WildStorm): Jan, 2011 - Present ($7.99, squarebound, reprints)

1-(1/11) r/short stories by various incl. Pearson, Conner, Corben, Jeanty, Mahnke 8.00
Planetary: Lost Worlds (2/11) r/Planetary/Authority & Planetary/JLA: Terra Occulta 8.00

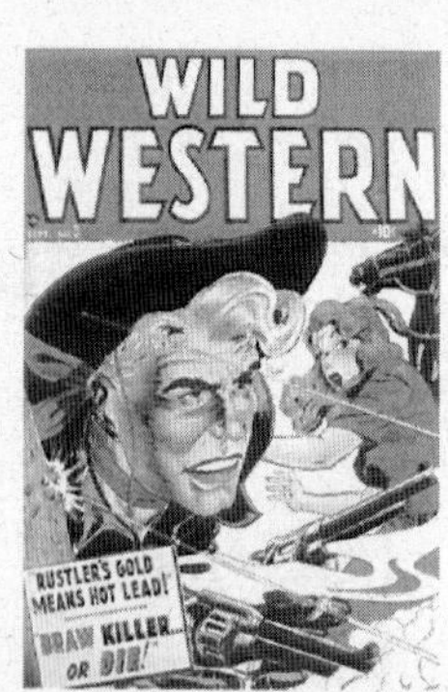

Wild Western #3 © MAR

The Wild Wild West #6 © CBS

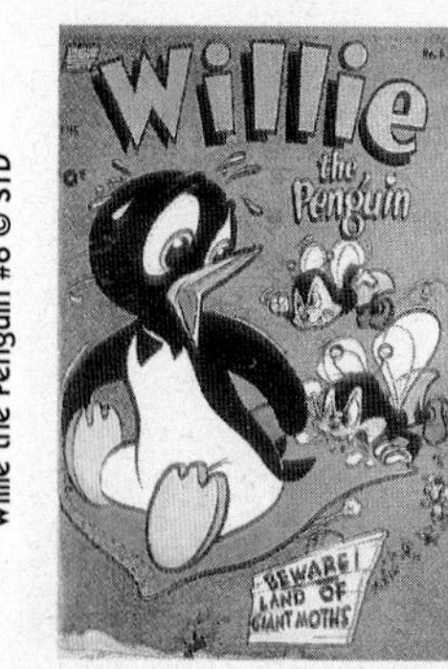

Willie the Penguin #6 © STD

GD 2.0 | VG 4.0 | FN 6.0 | VF 8.0 | VF/NM 9.0 | NM- 9.2

WILDSTORM REVELATIONS
DC Comics (WildStorm): Mar, 2008 - No. 6, May, 2008 ($2.99, limited series)
1-6-Beatty & Gage-s/Craig-a. 2-The Authority app. 3.00
TPB (2008, $17.99) r/#1-6; cover sketches 18.00

WILDSTORM RISING
Image Comics (WildStorm Publishing): May, 1995 - No.2, June, 1995 ($1.95/$2.50)
1-($2.50)-Direct Market, WildStorm Rising Pt. 1 w/bound-in card 3.00
1-($1.95)-Newstand, WildStorm Rising Pt. 1 3.00
2-($2.50)-Direct Market, WildStorm Rising Pt. 10 w/bound-in card; continues in WildC.A.T.S #21. 3.00
2-($1.95)-Newstand, WildStorm Rising Pt. 10 3.00
Trade paperback (1996, $19.95)-Collects x-over; B. Smith-c 20.00

WILDSTORM SPOTLIGHT
Image Comics (WildStorm Publishing): Feb, 1997 - No. 4 ($2.50)
1-4: 1-Alan Moore-s 3.00

WILDSTORM UNIVERSE '97
Image Comics (WildStorm Publishing): Dec, 1996 - No. 3 ($2.50, limited series)
1-3: 1-Wraparound-c. 3-Gary Frank-c 3.00

WILDTHING
Marvel Comics UK: Apr, 1993 - No. 7, Oct, 1993 ($1.75)
1-($2.50)-Embossed-c; Venom & Carnage cameo 4.00
2-7: 2-Spider-Man & Venom. 6-Mysterio app. 3.00

WILD THING (Wolverine's daughter in the M2 universe)
Marvel Comics: Oct, 1999 - No. 5, Feb, 2000 ($1.99)
1-5: 1-Lim-a in all. 2-Two covers 3.00
Wizard #0 supplement; battles the Hulk 3.00
Spider-Girl Presents Wild Thing. Crash Course (2007, $7.99, digest) r/#0-5 8.00

WILDTIMES
DC Comics (WildStorm Productions): Aug, 1999 ($2.50, one-shots)
...Deathblow #1 -set in 1899; Edwards-a; Jonah Hex app., ...DV8 #1 -set in 1944; Altieri-s/p; Sgt. Rock app., ...Gen13 #1 -set in 1969; Casey-s/Johnson-a; Teen Titans app., ...Grifter #1 -set in 1923; Paul Smith-a, ...Wetworks #1 -Waid-s/Lopresti-a; Superman app. 3.00
...WildC.A.T.s #0 -Wizard supplement; Charest-c 3.00

WILD WEST (Wild Western #3 on)
Marvel Comics (WFP): Spring, 1948 - No. 2, July, 1948
1-Two-Gun Kid, Arizona Annie, & Tex Taylor begin; Shores-c 34 68 102 199 325 450
2-Captain Tootsie by Beck; Shores-c 22 44 66 132 216 300

WILD WEST (Black Fury #1-57)
Charlton Comics: V2#58, Nov, 1966
V2#58 2 4 6 11 16 20

WILD WEST C.O.W.-BOYS OF MOO MESA (TV)
Archie Comics: Dec, 1992 - No. 3, Feb, 1993 (limited series)
V2#1, Mar, 1993 - No. 3, July, 1993 ($1.25)
1-3,V2#1-3 3.00

WILD WESTERN (Formerly Wild West #1,2)
Marvel/Atlas (WFP): No. 3, 9/48 - No. 57, 9/57 (3-11: 52 pgs, 12-on: 36 pgs)
3(#1)-Tex Morgan begins; Two-Gun Kid, Tex Taylor, & Arizona Annie continue from Wild West 27 54 81 158 259 360
4-Last Arizona Annie; Captain Tootsie by Beck; Kid Colt app. 20 40 60 114 182 250
5-2nd app. Black Rider (1/49); Blaze Carson, Captain Tootsie (by Beck) app. 23 46 69 136 223 310
6-8: 6-Blaze Carson app; anti-Wertham editorial 15 30 45 88 137 185
9-Photo-c; Black Rider begins, ends #19 19 38 57 109 172 235
10-Charles Starrett photo-c 22 44 66 128 209 290
11-(Last 52 pg. issue) 15 30 45 85 130 175
12-14,16-19: All Black Rider-c/stories. 12-14-The Prairie Kid & his horse Fury app. 15 30 45 83 124 165
15-Red Larabee, Gunhawk (origin), his horse Blaze, & Apache Kid begin, end #22; Black Rider-c/story 15 30 45 84 127 170
20-30: 20-Kid Colt-c begin. 24-Has 2 Kid Colt stories. 26-1st app. The Ringo Kid? (2/53); 4 pg. story. 30-Katz-a 12 24 36 69 97 125
31-40 10 20 30 54 72 90
41-47,49-51,53,57 9 18 27 47 61 75
48-Williamson/Torres-a (4 pgs); Drucker-a 10 20 30 56 76 95
52-Crandall-a 10 20 30 56 76 95
54,55-Williamson-a in both (5 & 4 pgs.), #54 with Mayo plus 2 text illos 10 20 30 56 76 95
56-Baker-a? 9 18 27 47 61 75
NOTE: *Annie Oakley in #46, 47. Apache Kid in #15-22, 39. Arizona Kid in #21, 23. Arrowhead in #34-39. Black Rider in #5, 9-19, 33-44. Fighting Texan in #17. Kid Colt in #4-6, 9-11, 20-47, 52, 54-56. Outlaw Kid in #43. Red Hawkins in #13, 14. Ringo Kid in #26, 39, 41, 43, 44, 46, 47, 50, 52-56. Tex Morgan in #3, 4, 6, 9, 11. Tex Taylor in #3-6, 9, 11. Texas Kid in #23-25. Two-Gun Kid in #3-6, 9, 11, 12, 33-39, 41. Wyatt Earp in #47.* **Ayers** *a-41, 42, 53, 54.* **Berg** *a-26; c-24.* **Colan** *a-49.* **Forte** *a-28, 30.* **Al Hartley** *a-16.* **Heath** *a-4, 5, 8; c-34, 44.* **Keller** *a-24, 26(2), 29-40, 44-46, 48, 52.* **Maneely** *a-10, 12, 15, 16, 28, 35, 38, 40-45; c-18-22, 33, 35, 36, 38-42, 45, 53, 54, 56, 57.* **Morisi** *a-23, 52.* **Pakula** *a-42, 52.* **Powell** *a-51.* **Romita** *a-24(2).* **Severin** *a-46, 47; c-48.* **Shores** *a-3, 5, 30, 31, 33, 35, 36, 38, 41; c-3-5.* **Sinnott** *a-34-39.* **Wildey** *a-43. Bondage c-19.*

WILD WESTERN ACTION (Also see The Bravados)
Skywald Publ. Corp.: Mar, 1971 - No. 3, June, 1971 (25¢, reprints, 52 pgs.)
1-Durango Kid, Straight Arrow-r; with all references to "Straight" in story relettered to "Swift"; Bravados begin; Shores-a (new) 3 6 9 16 23 30
2,3: 2-Billy Nevada, Durango Kid. 3-Red Mask, Durango Kid 2 4 6 11 16 20

WILD WESTERN ROUNDUP
Red Top/Decker Publications/I. W. Enterprises: Oct, 1957; 1960-'61
1(1957)-Kid Cowboy-r 5 10 15 22 26 30
I.W. Reprint #1('60-61)-r/#1 by Red Top 2 4 6 8 11 14

WILD WEST RODEO
Star Publications: 1953 (15¢)
1-A comic book coloring book with regular full color cover & B&W inside 9 18 27 47 61 75

WILD WILD WEST, THE (TV)
Gold Key: June, 1966 - No. 7, Oct, 1969 (All have Robert Conrad photo-c)
1-McWilliams-a 11 22 33 74 145 215
1-Variant edition with photo back-c (scarce) 12 24 36 79 160 240
2-Robert Conrad photo-c; McWilliams-a 9 18 27 58 99 140
2-Variant edition with Conrad photo back-c (scarce) 9 18 27 63 112 160
3-7 7 14 21 49 82 115
3-Variant edition with photo back-c (scarce) 9 18 27 58 99 140

WILD, WILD WEST, THE (TV)
Millennium Publications: Oct, 1990 - No. 4, Jan?, 1991 ($2.95, limited series)
1-4-Based on TV show 3.00

WILKIN BOY (See That...)

WILL EISNER READER
Kitchen Sink Press: 1991 ($9.95, B&W, 8 1/2" x 11", TPB)
nn-Reprints stories from Will Eisner's Quarterly; Eisner-s/a/c 10.00
nn-(DC Comics, 10/00, $9.95) 10.00

WILL EISNER'S JOHN LAW: ANGELS AND ASHES, DEVILS AND DUST
IDW Publ.: Apr, 2006 - No. 4 ($3.99, B&W, limited series)
1-New stories with Will Eisner's characters; Gary Chaloner-s/a 4.00

WILLIE COMICS (Formerly Ideal #1-4; Crime Cases #24 on; Li'l Willie #20 & 21) (See Gay Comics, Laugh, Millie The Model & Wisco)
Marvel Comics (MgPC): #5, Fall, 1946 - #19, 4/49; #22, 1/50 - #23, 5/50 (No #20 & 21)
5(#1)-George, Margie, Nellie the Nurse & Willie begin 27 54 81 158 259 360
6,8,9 15 30 45 88 137 185
7(1),10,11-Kurtzman's "Hey Look" 15 30 45 90 140 190
12,14-18,22,23 15 30 45 83 124 165
13,19-Kurtzman's "Hey Look" (#19-last by Kurtzman?) 15 30 45 84 127 170
NOTE: *Cindy app. in #17. Jeanie app. in #17. Little Lizzie app. in #22.*

WILLIE MAYS (See The Amazing...)

WILLIE THE PENGUIN
Standard Comics: Apr, 1951 - No. 6, Apr, 1952
1-Funny animal 9 18 27 52 69 85
2-6 6 12 18 31 38 45

WILLIE THE WISE-GUY (Also see Cartoon Kids)
Atlas Comics (NPP): Sept, 1957
1-Kida, Maneely-a 10 20 30 54 72 90

WILLOW
Marvel Comics: Aug, 1988 - No. 3, Oct, 1988 ($1.00)
1-3-R/Marvel Graphic Novel #36 (movie adaptation) 3.00

WILL ROGERS WESTERN (Formerly My Great Love #1-4; see Blazing & True Comics #66)

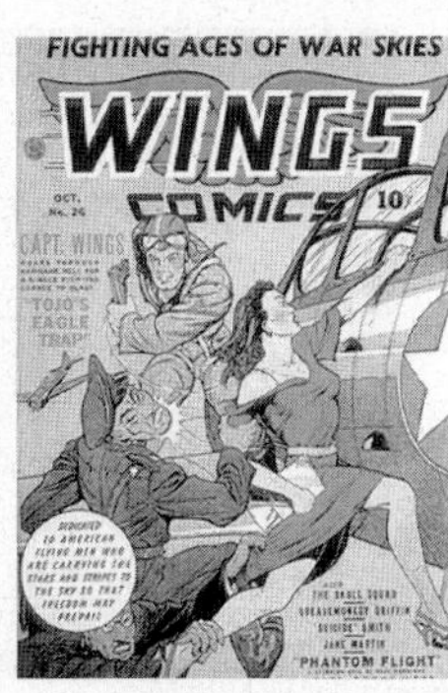

Wings Comics #26 © FH

Winter Soldier #1 © MAR

Witchblade #10 © TCOW

	GD 2.0	VG 4.0	FN 6.0	VF 8.0	VF/NM 9.0	NM- 9.2

Fox Features Syndicate: No. 5, June, 1950 - No. 2, Aug, 1950

5(#1) 31 62 93 186 303 420
2: Photo-c 26 52 78 154 252 350

WILL TO POWER (Also see Comic's Greatest World)
Dark Horse Comics: June, 1994 - No. 12, Aug, 1994 ($1.00, weekly limited series, 20 pgs.)

1-12: 12-Vortex kills Titan. 3.00

NOTE: ***Mignola** c-10-12. **Sears** c-1-3.*

WILL-YUM!
Dell Publishing Co.: No. 676, Feb, 1956 - No. 902, May, 1958

Four Color 676 (#1), 765 (1/57), 902 4 8 12 26 41 55

WIN A PRIZE COMICS (Timmy The Timid Ghost #3 on?)
Charlton Comics: Feb, 1955 - No. 2, Apr, 1955

V1#1-S&K-a; Poe adapt; E.C. War swipe 67 134 201 426 731 1035
2-S&K-a 48 96 144 302 514 725

WINDY & WILLY (Also see Showcase #81)
National Periodical Publications: May-June, 1969 - No. 4, Nov-Dec, 1969

1- r/Dobie Gillis with some art changes begin 5 10 15 35 55 75
2-4 4 8 12 22 34 45

WINGS COMICS
Fiction House Mag.: 9/40 - No. 109, 9/49; No. 110, Wint, 1949-50; No. 111, Spring, 1950; No. 112, 1950(nd); No. 113 - No. 115, 1950(nd); No. 116, 1952(nd); No. 117, Fall, 1952 - No. 122, Wint, 1953-54; No. 123 - No. 124, 1954(nd)

1-Skull Squad, Clipper Kirk, Suicide Smith, Jane Martin, War Nurse, Phantom Falcons, Greasemonkey Griffin, Parachute Patrol & Powder Burns begin
277 554 831 1759 3030 4300
2 103 206 309 659 1130 1600
3-5 71 142 213 454 777 1100
6-10: 8-Indicia shows #7 (#8 on cover) 57 114 171 362 619 875
11-15 52 104 156 328 557 785
16-Origin & 1st app. Captain Wings & begin series 55 110 165 352 601 850
17-20 45 90 135 284 480 675
21-30 42 84 126 265 445 625
31-40 39 78 117 231 378 525
41-50 32 64 96 192 314 435
51-60: 60-Last Skull Squad 30 60 90 177 289 400
61-67: 66-Ghost Patrol begins (becomes Ghost Squadron #71 on), ends #112?
27 54 81 160 263 365
68,69: 68-Clipper Kirk becomes The Phantom Falcon-origin, Part 1; part 2 in #69
27 54 81 160 263 365
70-72: 70-1st app. The Phantom Falcon in costume, origin-Part 3; Capt. Wings battles Col. Kamikaze in all 26 52 78 154 252 350
73-99: 80-Phantom Falcon by Larsen. 99-King of the Congo begins?
26 52 78 154 252 350
100-(12/48) 27 54 81 158 259 360
101-124: 111-Last Jane Martin. 112-Flying Saucer-c/story (1950). 115-Used in **POP**, pg. 89 20 40 60 114 182 250

NOTE: *Bondage covers are common. Captain Wings battles Sky Hag-#75, 76; ...Mr. Atlantis-#85-92; ...Mr. Pupin(Red Agent)-#98-103. Capt. Wings by **Elias**-#52-64, 68, 69; by **Lubbers**-#29-32, 70-111; by **Renee**-#33-46. **Evans** a-85-106, 108-111(Jane Martin); text illos-72-84. **Larsen** a-52, 59, 64, 73-77. Jane Martin by **Fran Hopper**-#68-84; Suicide Smith by **John Celardo**-#72, 74, 76, 80-104; by **Hollingsworth**-#68-70, 105-109, 111; Ghost Squadron by **Astarita**-#67-79; by **Maurice Whitman**-#80-111. King of the Congo by **Moreira**-#99, 100. Skull Squad by **M. Baker**-#52-60; Clipper Kirk by **Baker**-#60, 61; by **Colan**-#53; by **Ingels**-(some issues?). Phantom Falcon by **Larsen**-#73-84. **Elias** c-58-72. **Fawcette** c-3-12, 16, 17, 19, 22-33. **Lubbers** c-74-109. **Tuska** a-5. **Whitman** c-110-124. **Zolnerwich** c-15, 21.*

WINGS OF THE EAGLES, THE
Dell Publishing Co.: No. 790, Apr, 1957 (10¢ & 15¢ editions exist)

Four Color 790-Movie; John Wayne photo-c; Toth-a 12 24 36 82 169 255

WINKY DINK (Adventures of...)
Pines Comics: No. 75, Mar, 1957 (one-shot)

75-Marv Levy-c/a 6 12 18 31 38 45

WINKY DINK (TV)
Dell Publishing Co.: No. 663, Nov, 1955

Four Color 663 (#1) 8 16 24 51 86 120

WINNIE-THE-POOH (Also see Dynabrite Comics)
Gold Key No. 1-17/Whitman No. 18 on: January, 1977 - No. 33, July, 1984
(Walt Disney) (Winnie-The-Pooh began as Edward Bear in 1926 by Milne)

1-New art 3 6 9 18 27 35
2-5: 5-New material 2 4 6 11 16 20
6-17: 12-up-New material 2 4 6 9 13 16
18,19(Whitman) 2 4 6 11 16 20
20,21('80) pre-pack only 4 8 12 26 41 55
22('80) (scarcer) pre-pack only 5 10 15 32 51 70
23-28: 27(2/82), 28(4/82) 2 4 6 13 18 22
29-33 (#90299 on-c, no date or date code; pre-pack): 29(4/82), 30(5/83), 31(8/83), 32(4/84), 33(7/84) 3 6 9 18 27 35

WINNIE WINKLE (See Popular Comics & Super Comics)
Dell Publishing Co.: 1941 - No. 7, Sept-Nov, 1949

Large Feature Comic 2 (1941) 28 56 84 165 270 375
Four Color 94 (1945) 11 22 33 76 151 225
Four Color 174 8 16 24 56 96 135
1(3-5/48)-Contains daily & Sunday newspaper-r from 1939-1941
8 16 24 51 86 120
2 (6-8/48) 6 12 18 37 59 80
3-7 4 8 12 28 44 60

WINTER MEN, THE
DC Comics (WildStorm): Oct, 2005 - No. 5, Nov, 2006 ($2.99, limited series)

1-5-Brett Lewis-s/John Paul Leon-a 3.00
... Winter Special (2/09, $3.99) Lewis-s/Leon-a 4.00
TPB (2010, $19.99) r/#1-5 & Winter Special; original proposal, development & sketch-a 20.00

WINTER SOLDIER
Marvel Comics: Apr, 2012 - Present ($2.99)

1-3-Black Widow app.; Brubaker-s/Guice-a/Bermejo-c. 3-Dr. Doom app. 3.00

WINTER SOLDIER: WINTER KILLS (See Captain America 2005 series)
Marvel Comics: Feb, 2007 ($3.99, one-shot)

1-Flashback to Christmas Eve 1944; Toro & Sub-Mariner app.; Brubaker-s/Weeks-a 5.00

WINTERWORLD
Eclipse Comics: Sept, 1987 - No. 3, Mar, 1988 ($1.75, limited series)

1-3 3.00

WISDOM
Marvel Comics (MAX): Jan, 2007 - No. 6, July, 2007 ($3.99, limited series)

1-6: 1-Hairsine-a/c; Cornell-s. 3-6-Manuel Garcia-a 4.00
...: Rudiments of Wisdom TPB (2007, $21.99) r/#1-6; series pitch and sketch page 22.00

WISE GUYS (See Harvey...)

WISE LITTLE HEN, THE
David McKay Publ./Whitman: 1934 ,1935(48 pgs.); 1937 (Story book)

nn-(1934 edition w/dust jacket)(48 pgs. with color, 8-3/4x9-3/4") -Debut of Donald Duck (see Advs. of Mickey Mouse); Donald app. on cover with Wise Little Hen & Practical Pig; painted cover; same artist as the B&W's from Silly Symphony Cartoon, The Wise Little Hen (1934) (McKay)
Book w/dust jacket 239 478 717 1530 2615 3700
Dust jacket only 55 110 165 352 601 850
nn-(1935 edition w/dust jacket), same as 1934 ed. 139 278 417 883 1517 2150
888 (1937)(9-1/2x13", 12 pgs.)(Whitman) Donald Duck app.
34 68 102 199 325 450

WISE SON: THE WHITE WOLF
DC Comics (Milestone): Nov, 1996 - No. 4, Feb, 1997 ($2.50, limited series)

1-4: Ho Che Anderson-c/a 3.00

WIT AND WISDOM OF WATERGATE (Humor magazine)
Marvel Comics: 1973, 76 pgs., squarebound

1-Low print run 5 10 15 32 51 70

WITCHBLADE (Also see Cyblade/Shi, Tales Of The..., & Top Cow Classics)
Image Comics (Top Cow Productions): Nov, 1995 - Present ($2.50/$2.99)

0 1 2 3 5 6 8
1/2-Mike Turner/Marc Silvestri-c. 3 6 9 20 30 40
1/2 Gold Ed., 1/2 Chromium-c 3 6 9 20 30 40
1/2-(Vol. 2, 11/02, $2.99) Wohl-s/Ching-a/c 3.00
1-Mike Turner-a(p) 4 8 12 21 30 40
1,2-American Ent. Encore Ed. 1 2 3 4 5 7
2,3 2 4 6 11 16 20
4,5 2 4 6 9 13 16
6-9: 8-Wraparound-c. 9-Tony Daniel-a(p) 1 2 3 5 7 9
9-Sunset variant-c 2 4 6 8 10 12
9-DF variant-c 2 4 6 11 16 20
10-Flip book w/Darkness #0, 1st app. the Darkness 2 4 6 8 10 12
10-Variant-c 2 4 6 9 12 15
10-Gold logo 3 6 9 16 23 30
10-($3.95) Dynamic Forces alternate-c 1 2 3 5 6 8

Witchblade #144 © TCOW

Witchcraft: La Terreur #2 © DC

Witches Tales #21 © WT

	GD 2.0	VG 4.0	FN 6.0	VF 8.0	VF/NM 9.0	NM- 9.2

11-15 5.00
16-19: 18,19-"Family Ties" Darkness x-over pt. 1,4 4.00
18-Face to face variant-c, 18-American Ent. Ed., 19-AE Gold Ed.
1 2 3 5 6 8
20-25: 24-Pearson, Green-a. 25-($2.95) Turner-a(p) 4.00
25 (Prism variant) 30.00
25 (Special) 15.00
26-39: 26-Green-a begins 3.00
27 (Variant) 10.00
40-49,51-53: 40-Begin Jenkins & Veitch-s/Keu Cha-a. 47-Zulli-c/a 3.00
40-Pittsburgh Convention Preview edition; B&W preview of #40 3.00
49-Gold logo 1 2 3 5 6 8
50-($4.95) Darkness app.; Ching-a; B&W preview of Universe 5.00
54-59: 54-Black outer-c with gold foil logo; Wohl-s/Manapul-a 3.00
60-74,76-91,93-99: 60-($2.99) Endgame x-over with Tomb Raider #25 & Evo #1. 64,65-Magdalena app. 71-Kirk-a. 77,81-85-Land-c. 80-Four covers. 87-Bachalo-a 3.00
75-($4.99) Manapul-a 5.00
92-($4.99) Origin of the Witchblade; art by various incl. Bachalo, Perez, Linsner, Cooke 5.00
100-($4.99) Five covers incl. Turner, Silvestri, Linsner; art by various; Jake dies 5.00
101-124,126-143: 103-Danielle Baptiste gets the Witchblade; Linsner variant-c. 116-124,140,141-Sejic-a. 126-128-War of the Witchblades. 134-136-Aphrodite IV app. 139-Gaydos-a. 143-Matt Dow Smith-a 3.00
125-($3.99) War of the Witchblades begins; 3 covers; Sejic-a 4.00
144-($4.99) Origin retold; wraparound-c; Sejic-a; back-up w/Sablik-s; pin-up gallery 5.00
145-149-($3.99) Sejic-a/c. 149-Angelus app. 4.00
150-($4.99) Four covers; last Marz-s; Sejic-a; cover gallery & series timeline 5.00
151-153-($2.99) Altered reality after Artifacts #13; Seeley-s; multiple covers 3.00
... and Tomb Raider (4/05, $2.99) Jae Lee-c; art by Lee and Texiera 3.00
...: Animated (8/03, $2.99) Magdalena & Darkness app.; Dini-s/Bone, Bullock, Cooke-a/c 3.00
... Annual 2009 (4/09, $3.99) Basaldua-a 4.00
... Annual #1 (12/10, $4.99) the Witchblade in Stalingrad 1942, Shasteen-a; Haley-a 5.00
...: Art of the Witchblade (7/06, $2.99) pin-ups by various incl. Turner, Land, Linsner 3.00
...: Bearers of the Blade (7/06, $2.99) pin-up/profiles of bearers of the Witchblade 3.00
...: Blood Oath (8/04, $4.99) Sara teams with Phenix & Sibilla; Roux-a 5.00
...: Blood Relations TPB (2003, $12.99) r/#54-58 13.00
... Compendium Vol. 1 (2006, $59.99) r/#1-50; gallery of variant covers and art 60.00
... Compendium Vol. 2 (2007, $59.99) r/#51-100; gallery of variant covers and art 60.00
... Cover Gallery Vol. 1 (12/05, $2.99) intro. by Stan Lee 3.00
.../Darkchylde (7/00, $2.50) Green-s/a(p) 3.00
.../Dark Minds (6/04, $9.99) new story plus r/Dark Minds/Witchblade #1 10.00
.../Darkness: Family Ties Collected Edition (10/98, $9.95) r/#18,19 and Darkness #9,10 10.00
.../Darkness Special (12/99, $3.95) Green-c/a 4.00
...: Demon 1 (2003, $6.99) Mark Millar-s/Jae Lee-c/a 7.00
.../Devi (4/08, $3.99) Basaldua-a/Land-c; continues in Devi/Witchblade 4.00
...: Distinctions (See Tales of the Witchblade)
...: Due Process (8/10, $3.99) Alina Urusov-a/c; Phil Smith-s 4.00
.../Elektra (3/97, $2.95) Devil's Reign Pt. 6 4.00
... Gallery (11/00, $2.95) Profile pages and pin-ups by various; Turner-c 3.00
Image Firsts: Witchblade #1 (4/10, $1.00) reprints #1 3.00
Infinity (5/99, $3.50) Lobdell-s/Pollina-c/a 4.00
.../Lady Death (11/01, $4.95) Manapul-c/a 5.00
...: Prevailing TPB (2000, $14.95) r/#20-25; new Turner-c 15.00
...: Revelations TPB (2000, $24.95) r/#9-17; new Turner-c 25.00
.../The Punisher (6/07, $3.99) Marz-s/Melo-a/Linsner-c 4.00
.../Tomb Raider #1/2 (7/00, $2.95) Covers by Turner and Cha 4.00
...: Vol. 1 TPB (1/08, $4.99) r/#80-85; Marz intro.; cover gallery 5.00
...: Vol. 2 TPB (2/08, $14.99) r/#86-92; cover gallery 15.00
...: Vol. 3 TPB (3/08, $14.99) r/#93-100; Edginton intro.; cover gallery 15.00
... vs. Frankenstein: Monster War 2005 (8/05, $2.99) pt. 3 of x-over 3.00
...: Witch Hunt Vol. 1 TPB (2/06, $14.99) r/#80-85; Marz intro.; Choi afterward; cover gallery 15.00
Wizard #500 10.00
.../Wolverine (6/04, $2.99) Basaldua-c/a; Claremont-s 3.00

WITCHBLADE/ALIENS/THE DARKNESS/PREDATOR
Dark Horse Comics/Top Cow Productions: Nov, 2000 ($2.99)

1-3-Mel Rubi-a 4.00

WITCHBLADE COLLECTED EDITION
Image Comics (Top Cow Productions): July, 1996 - No. 8 ($4.95/$6.95, squarebound, limited series)

1-7-($4.95): Two issues reprinted in each 5.00
8-($6.95) r/#15-17 7.00
...Slipcase (10/96, $10.95)-Packaged w/ Coll. Ed. #1-4 11.00

WITCHBLADE: DESTINY'S CHILD
Image Comics (Top Cow): Jun, 2000 - No. 3, Sept, 2000 ($2.95, lim. series)

1-3: 1-Boller-a/Keu Cha-c 3.00

WITCHBLADE: MANGA (Takeru Manga)
Image Comics (Top Cow): Feb, 2007 - No. 12, Mar, 2008 ($2.99/$3.99)

1-4-Colored reprints of Japanese Witchblade manga. 1-Three covers. 2-Two covers 3.00
5-12-($3.99) 4.00

WITCHBLADE: OBAKEMONO
Image Comics (Top Cow Productions): 2002 ($9.95, one-shot graphic novel)

1-Fiona Avery-s/Billy Tan-a; forward by Straczynski 10.00

WITCHBLADE: SHADES OF GRAY
Dynamite Ent./Top Cow: 2007 - No. 4, 2007 ($3.50, lim. series)

1,2: 1-Sara Pezzini meets Dorian Gray; Segovia-a; multiple covers 3.50

WITCHBLADE/ TOMB RAIDER SPECIAL (Also see Tomb Raider/...)
Image Comics (Top Cow Productions): Dec, 1998 ($2.95)

1-Based on video game character; Turner-a(p) 4.00
1-Silvestri variant-c 6.00
1-Turner bikini variant-c 10.00
1-Prism-c 12.00
Wizard 1/2 -Turner-s 10.00

WITCHCRAFT (See Strange Mysteries, Super Reprint #18)
Avon Periodicals: Mar-Apr, 1952 - No. 6, Mar, 1953

	GD	VG	FN	VF	VF/NM	NM-
1-Kubert-a; 1 pg. Check-a	76	152	228	486	831	1175
2-Kubert & Check-a; classic skull-c	54	108	162	343	574	825
3,6: 3-Lawrence-a; Kinstler inside-c	43	86	129	271	461	650
4-People cooked alive c/story	54	108	162	343	574	825
5-Kelly Freas painted-c	58	116	174	371	636	900

NOTE: ***Hollingsworth** a-4-6; c-4, 6. **McCann** a-3?*

WITCHCRAFT
DC Comics (Vertigo): June, 1994 - No. 3, Aug, 1994 ($2.95, limited series)

1-3: James Robinson scripts & Kaluta-c in all 4.00
1-Platinum Edition 15.00
Trade paperback-(1996, $14.95)-r/#1-3; Kaluta-c 15.00

WITCHCRAFT: LA TERREUR
DC Comics (Vertigo): Apr, 1998 - No. 3, Jun, 1998 ($2.50, limited series)

1-3: Robinson-s/Zulli & Locke-a; interlocking cover images 3.00

WITCH DOCTOR (See Walking Dead #85 flip book for preview)
Image Comics: Jun, 2011 - No. 4, Nov, 2011 ($2.99, limited series)

1-4-Seifert-s/Ketner-a/c 3.00
...: The Resuscitation (12/11, $2.99) Seifert-s/Ketner-a/c 3.00

WITCHES
Marvel Comics: Aug, 2004 - No. 4, Sept, 2004 ($2.99, limited series)

1-4: 1,2-Deodato, Jr-a; Dr. Strange app. 3,4-Conrad-a 3.00
... Vol. 1: The Gathering (2004, $9.99) r/series 10.00

WITCHES TALES (Witches Western Tales #29,30)
Witches Tales/Harvey Publications: Jan, 1951 - No. 28, Dec, 1954 (date misprinted as 4/55)

	GD	VG	FN	VF	VF/NM	NM-
1-Powell-a (1 pg.)	58	116	174	371	636	900
2-Eye injury panel	37	74	111	222	361	500
3-7,9,10	29	58	87	170	278	385
8-Eye injury panels	30	60	90	177	289	400
11-13,15,16: 12-Acid in face story	27	54	81	158	259	360
14,17-Powell/Nostrand-a. 17-Atomic disaster story	28	56	84	165	270	375
18-Nostrand-a; E.C. swipe/Shock S.S.	28	56	84	165	270	375
19-Nostrand-a; E.C. swipe/ "Glutton"; Devil-c	31	62	93	182	296	410
20-24-Nostrand-a. 21-E.C. swipe; rape story. 23-Wood E.C. swipes/Two-Fisted Tales #34	28	56	84	165	270	375
25-Nostrand-a; E.C. swipe/Mad Barber; decapitation-c	50	100	150	315	533	750
26-28: 27-r/#6 with diff.-c. 28-r/#8 with diff.-c	20	40	60	114	182	250

NOTE: ***Check** a-24. **Elias** c-8, 10, 16-27. **Kremer** a-18; c-25. **Nostrand** a-17-25; 14, 17(w/**Powell**). **Palais** a-1, 2, 4(2), 5(2), 7-9, 12, 14, 15, 17. **Powell** a-3-7, 10, 11, 19-27. Bondage-c 1, 3, 5, 6, 8, 9.*

WITCHES TALES (Magazine)
Eerie Publications: V1#7, July, 1969 - V7#1, Feb, 1975 (B&W, 52 pgs.)

	GD	VG	FN	VF	VF/NM	NM-
V1#7(7/69)	7	14	21	46	76	105
V1#8(9/69), 9(11/69)	6	12	18	39	62	85
V2#1-6('70), V3#1-6('71)	5	10	15	30	48	65
V4#1-6('72), V5#1-6('73), V6#1-6('74), V7#1	4	8	12	26	41	55

NOTE: *Ajax/Farrell reprints in early issues.*

WITCHES' WESTERN TALES (Formerly Witches Tales)(Western Tales #31 on)

The Witching Hour #31 © DC

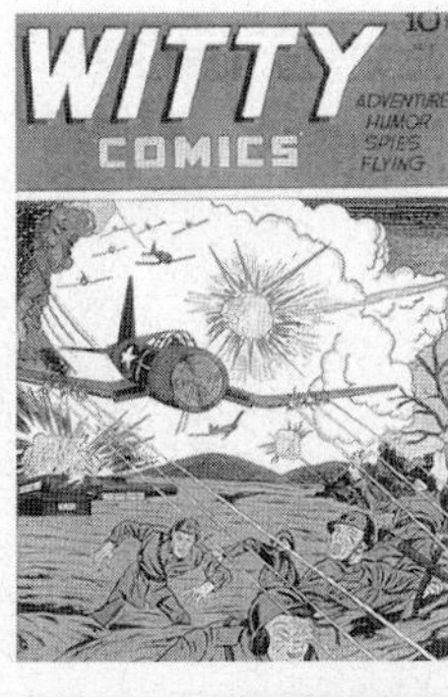
Witty Comics #1 © Irwin Rubin

Wolverine #25 © MAR

GD VG FN VF VF/NM NM-
2.0 4.0 6.0 8.0 9.0 9.2

Harvey Publications: No. 29, Feb, 1955 - No. 30, Apr, 1955
29,30-Featuring Clay Duncan & Boys' Ranch; S&K-r/from Boys' Ranch including-c.
29-Last pre-code 15 30 45 86 133 180

WITCHFINDER, THE
Image Comics (Liar): Sept, 1999 - No. 3, Jan, 2000 ($2.95)
1-3-Romano-a/Sharon & Matthew Scott-plot 3.00

WITCHFINDER: LOST AND GONE FOREVER
Dark Horse Comics: Feb, 2011 - No. 5, Jun, 2011 ($3.50, limited series)
1-5-John Severin-a; Mignola & Arcudi-s. 1-Two covers by Mignola & Severin 3.50

WITCH HUNTER
Malibu Comics (Ultraverse): Apr, 1996 ($2.50, one-shot)
1 3.00

WITCHING, THE
DC Comics (Vertigo): Aug, 2004 - No. 10, May, 2005 ($2.95/$2.99)
1-10-Vankin-s/Gallagher-a/McPherson-c. 1,2-Lucifer app. 3.00

WITCHING HOUR ("The ..." in later issues)
National Periodical Publ./DC Comics: Feb-Mar, 1969 - No. 85, Oct, 1978
1-Toth-a, plus Neal Adams-a (2 pgs.) 13 26 39 85 180 275
2,6: 6-Toth-a 7 14 21 48 79 110
3,5-Wrightson-a; Toth-p. 3-Last 12¢ issue 8 16 24 51 86 120
4,12-Toth-a 5 10 15 35 55 75
7-11-Adams-c; Toth-a in all. 8-Adams-a 7 14 21 46 76 105
13-Neal Adams-c/a, 2pgs. 7 14 21 48 79 110
14-Williamson/Garzon, Jones-a; N. Adams-c 7 14 21 49 82 115
15 3 6 9 20 30 40
16-21-(52 pg. Giants) 4 8 12 24 37 50
22-37,39,40 3 6 9 14 19 24
38-(100 pgs.) 5 10 15 35 55 75
41-60 2 4 6 10 14 18
61-83,85 2 4 6 8 11 14
84-(44 pgs.) 2 4 6 9 13 16
NOTE: *Combined with The Unexpected with #189.* ***Neal Adams*** *c-7-11, 13, 14.* ***Alcala*** *a-24, 27, 33, 41, 43.* ***Anderson*** *a-9, 38.* ***Cardy*** *c-4, 5.* ***Kaluta*** *a-7.* ***Kane*** *a-12p.* ***Morrow*** *a-10, 13, 15, 16.* ***Nino*** *a-31, 40, 45, 47.* ***Redondo*** *a-20, 23, 24, 34, 65; c-53.* ***Reese*** *a-23.* ***Sparling*** *a-1.* ***Toth*** *a-1, 3-12, 38r.* ***Tuska*** *a-11, 12.* ***Wood*** *a-15.*

WITCHING HOUR, THE
DC Comics (Vertigo): 1999 - No. 3, 2000 ($5.95, limited series)
1-3-Bachalo & Thibert-c/a; Loeb & Bachalo-s 6.00
Hardcover (2000, $29.95) r/#1-3; embossed cover 30.00
Softcover (2003, $19.95), (2009, $19.99) r/#1-3 20.00

WITHIN OUR REACH
Star Reach Productions: 1991 ($7.95, 84 pgs.)
nn-Spider-Man, Concrete by Chadwick, Gift of the Magi by Russell; X-mas stories; Chadwick-c; Spidey back-c 8.00

WITH THE MARINES ON THE BATTLEFRONTS OF THE WORLD
Toby Press: 1953 (no month) - No. 2, Mar, 1954 (Photo covers)
1-John Wayne story 29 58 87 172 281 390
2-Monty Hall in #1,2 10 20 30 58 79 100

WITH THE U.S. PARATROOPS BEHIND ENEMY LINES (Also see U.S. Paratroops...; #2-6 titled U.S. Paratroops...)
Avon Periodicals: 1951 - No. 6, Dec, 1952
1-Wood-c & inside f/c 18 36 54 103 162 220
2-Kinstler-c & inside f/c only 11 22 33 62 86 110
3-6: 6-Kinstler-c & inside f/c only 10 20 30 56 76 95
NOTE: ***Kinstler*** *c-2, 4-6.*

WITNESS, THE (Also see Amazing Mysteries, Captain America #71, Ideal #4, Marvel Mystery #92 & Mystic #7)
Marvel Comics (MjMe): Sept, 1948
1(Scarce)-Rico-c? 271 542 813 1734 2967 4200

WITTY COMICS
Irwin H. Rubin Publ./Chicago Nite Life News No. 2: 1945 - No. 2, 1945
1-The Pioneer, Junior Patrol; Japanese war-c 31 62 93 186 303 420
2-The Pioneer, Junior Patrol 15 30 45 88 137 185

WIZARD OF FOURTH STREET, THE
Dark Horse Comics: Dec, 1987 - No. 2, 1988 ($1.75, B&W, limited series)
1,2: Adapts novel by S/F author Simon Hawke 3.00

WIZARD OF OZ (See Classics Illustrated Jr. 535, Dell Jr. Treasury No. 5, First Comics Graphic Novel, Marvelous..., & Marvel Treasury of Oz)
Dell Publishing Co.: No. 1308, Mar-May, 1962 (TV)
Four Color 1308 11 22 33 71 136 200

WIZARDS OF MICKEY (Mickey Mouse)
BOOM! Studios: Jan, 2010 - No. 8, Aug, 2010 ($2.99)
1-8: 1,2-Ambrosio-s; 3 covers on each. 3-8-Two covers 3.00

WIZARD'S TALE, THE
Image Comics (Homage Comics): 1997 ($19.95, squarebound, one-shot)
nn-Kurt Busiek-s/David Wenzel-painted-a/c 20.00

WOLF & RED
Dark Horse Comics: Apr, 1995 - No. 3, June, 1995 ($2.50, limited series)
1-3: Characters created by Tex Avery 3.00

WOLFF & BYRD, COUNSELORS OF THE MACABRE (Becomes Supernatural Law with issue #24)
Exhibit A Press: May, 1994 - No. 23, Aug, 1999 ($2.50, B&W)
1-23-Batton Lash-s/a 3.00

WOLF GAL (See Al Capp's...)

WOLFMAN, THE (See Movie Classics)

WOLFPACK
Marvel Comics: Feb, 1988 ($7.95); Aug, 1988 - No. 12, July, 1989 (Lim. series)
1-1st app./origin (Marvel Graphic Novel #31) 8.00
1-12 3.00

WOLVERINE (See Alpha Flight, Daredevil #196, 249, Ghost Rider; Wolverine; Punisher, Havok &..., Incredible Hulk #180, Incredible Hulk &..., Kitty Pryde And..., Marvel Comics Presents, New Avengers, Power Pack, Punisher and..., Rampaging ..., Spider-Man vs... & X-Men #94)

WOLVERINE (See Incredible Hulk #180 for 1st app.)
Marvel Comics Group: Sept, 1982 - No. 4, Dec, 1982 (limited series)
1-Frank Miller-c/a(p) in all; Claremont-s 5 10 15 35 55 75
2-4 4 8 12 26 41 55
... By Claremont & Miller HC (2006, $19.99) r/#1-4 & Uncanny X-Men #172-173 20.00
TPB 1(7/87, $4.95)-Reprints #1-4 with new Miller-c 2 4 6 10 14 18
TPB nn (2nd printing, $9.95)-r/#1-4 2 4 6 8 10 12

WOLVERINE
Marvel Comics: Nov, 1988 - No. 189, June, 2003 ($1.50/$1.75/$1.95/$1.99/$2.25)
1 4 8 12 22 34 45
2 2 4 6 13 18 22
3-5: 4-BWS back-c 2 4 6 9 13 16
6-9: 6-McFarlane back-c. 7,8-Hulk app. 1 3 4 6 8 10
10-1st battle with Sabretooth (before Wolverine had his claws) 3 6 9 16 23 30
11-16: 11-New costume 1 2 3 5 6 8
17-20: 17-Byrne-c/a(p) begins, ends #23 1 2 3 4 5 7
21-30: 24,25,27-Jim Lee-c. 26-Begin $1.75-c 5.00
31-40,44,47 4.00
41-Sabretooth claims to be Wolverine's father; Cable cameo 6.00
41-Gold 2nd printing ($1.75) 3.00
42-Sabretooth, Cable & Nick Fury app.; Sabretooth proven not to be Wolverine's father 1 2 3 5 6 8
42-Gold ink 2nd printing ($1.75) 3.00
43-Sabretooth cameo (2 panels); saga ends 5.00
45,46-Sabretooth-c/stories 5.00
48-51: 48,49-Sabretooth app. 48-Begin 3 part Weapon X sequel. 50-(64 pgs.)-Die cut-c; Wolverine back to old yellow costume; Forge, Cyclops, Jubilee, Jean Grey & Nick Fury app. 51-Sabretooth-c & app. 5.00
52-74,76-80: 54-Shatterstar (from X-Force) app. 55-Gambit, Jubilee, Sunfire-c/story. 55-57,73-Gambit app. 57-Mariko Yashida dies (Late 7/92). 58,59-Terror, Inc. x-over. 60-64-Sabretooth storyline (60,62,64-c) 4.00
75-($3.95, 68 pgs.)-Wolverine hologram on-c 5.00
81-84,86: 81-bound-in card sheet 3.50
85-($2.50)-Newsstand edition 4.00
85-($3.50)-Collectors edition 5.00
87-90 ($1.95)-Deluxe edition 3.50
87-90 ($1.50)-Regular edition 3.00
91-99,101-114: 91-Return from "Age of Apocalypse," 93-Juggernaut app. 94-Gen X app. 101-104-Elektra app. 104-Origin of Onslaught. 105-Onslaught x-over. 110-Shaman-c/app. 114-Alternate-c 3.00
100 ($3.95)-Hologram-c; Wolverine loses humanity 1 2 3 5 7 9
100 ($2.95)-Regular-c. 4.00
102.5 (1996 Wizard mail-away)-Deadpool app.; Vallejo-c/Buckingham-a 40.00

Wolverine #169 © MAR

Wolverine V3 #1 © MAR

Wolverine (2010 series) #4 © MAR

GD 2.0 | VG 4.0 | FN 6.0 | VF 8.0 | VF/NM 9.0 | NM- 9.2

115-124: 115- Operation Zero Tolerance 3.00
125-($2.99) Wraparound-c; Viper secret 4.00
125-($6.95) Jae Lee variant-c 7.00
126-144: 126,127-Sabretooth-c/app. 128-Sabretooth & Shadowcat app.; Platt-a. 129-Wendigo-c/app. 131-Initial printing contained lettering error. 133-Begin Larsen-s/ Matsuda-a. 138-Galactus-c/app. 139-Cable app.; Yu-a. 142,143-Alpha Flight app. 3.00
145-($2.99) 25th Anniversary issue; Hulk and Sabretooth app. 4.00
145-($3.99) Foil enhanced cover (also see Promotional section for Nabisco mail-in ed.) 5.00
146-149: 147-Apocalypse: The Twelve; Angel-c/app. 149-Nova-c/app. 3.00
150-($2.99) Steve Skroce-s/a 4.00
151-174,176-182,184-189: 151-Begin $2.25-c. 154,155-Liefeld-s/a. 156-Churchill-a. 159-Chen-a begins. 160-Sabretooth app. 163-Texeira-a(p). 167-BWS-c. 172,173-Alpha Flight app. 176-Colossus app. 185,186-Punisher app. 3.00
175,183-($3.50) 175-Sabretooth app. 4.00
#(-1) Flashback (7/97) Logan meets Col. Fury; Nord-a 3.00
Annual nn (1990, $4.50, squarebound, 52 pgs.)-The Jungle Adventure; Simonson scripts; Mignola-c/a 5.00
Annual 2 (12/90, $4.95, squarebound, 52 pgs.)-Bloodlust 5.00
Annual nn (#3, 8/91, $5.95, 68 pgs.)-Rahne of Terror; Cable & The New Mutants app.; Andy Kubert-c/a (2nd print exists) 6.00
Annual '95 (1995, $3.95) 4.00
Annual '96 (1996, $2.95)- Wraparound-c; Silver Samurai, Yukio, and Red Ronin app. 4.00
Annual '97 ($2.99) - Wraparound-c 4.00
Annual 1999, 2000 ($3.50) : 1999-Deadpool app. 4.00
Annual 2001 ($2.99) - Tieri-s; JH Williams-c 4.00
...Battles The Incredible Hulk nn (1989, $4.95, squarebound, 52 pg.) r/Incr. Hulk #180,181 5.00
Best of Wolverine Vol. 1 HC (2004, $29.99) oversized reprints of Hulk #181, mini-series #1-4, Capt. America Ann, #8, Uncanny X-Men #205 & Marvel Comics Presents #72-84 30.00
...Black Rio (11/98, $5.99)-Casey-s/Oscar Jimenez-a 6.00
...Blood Debt TPB (7/01, $12.95)-r/#150-153; Skroce-c 13.00
...Blood Hungry nn (1993, $6.95, 68 pgs.)-Kieth-r/Marvel Comics Presents #85-92 w/ new Kieth-c 7.00
...: Bloody Choices nn (1993, $7.95, 68 pgs.)-r/Graphic Novel; Nick Fury app. 8.00
... Cable Guts and Glory (10/99, $5.99) Platt-a 6.00
... Classic Vol. 1 TPB (2005, $12.99) r/#1-5 13.00
... Classic Vol. 2 TPB (2005, $12.99) r/#6-10 13.00
... Classic Vol. 3 TPB (2005, $14.99) r/#11-16; The Gehenna Stone Affair 15.00
... Classic Vol. 4 TPB (2006, $14.99) r/#17-23 15.00
... Classic Vol. 5 TPB (2007, $14.99) r/#24-30 15.00
.../Deadpool: Weapon X TPB (7/02, $21.99)-r/#162-166 & Deadpool #57-60 22.00
... Doombringer (11/97, $5.99)-Silver Samurai-c/app. 6.00
... Evilution (9/94, $5.95) 6.00
...: Global Jeopardy 1 (12/93, $2.95, one-shot)-Embossed-c; Sub-Mariner, Zabu, Ka-Zar, Shanna & Wolverine app.; produced in cooperation with World Wildlife Fund 4.00
...:Inner Fury nn (1992, $5.95, 52 pgs.)-Sienkiewicz-c/a 6.00
...: Judgment Night (2000, $3.99) Shi app.; Battlebook 4.00
...: Killing (9/93)-Kent Williams-a 6.00
...: Knight of Terra (1995, $6.95)-Ostrander script 7.00
... Legends Vol. 2: Meltdown (2003, $19.99) r/Havok & Wolverine: Meltdown #1-4 20.00
... Legends Vol. 3 (2003, $12.99) r/#181-186 13.00
... Legends Vol. 4,5: 4-(See Wolverine: Xisle). 5-(See Wolverine: Snikt!)
... Legends Vol. 6: Marc Silvestri Book 1 (2004, $19.99) r/#31-34, 41-42, 48-50 20.00
.../ Nick Fury: The Scorpio Connection Hardcover (1989, $16.95) 25.00
.../ Nick Fury: The Scorpio Connection Softcover(1990, $12.95) 15.00
...: Not Dead Yet (12/98, $14.95, TPB)-r/#119-122 15.00
...: Save The Tiger 1 (7/92, $2.95, 84 pgs.)-Reprints Wolverine stories from Marvel Comics Presents #1-10 w/new Kieth-c 4.00
...Scorpio Rising ($5.95, prestige format, one-shot) 6.00
.../Shi: Dark Night of Judgment (Crusade Comics, 2000, $2.99) Tucci-a 4.00
...Triumphs And Tragedies-(1995, $16.95, trade paperback)-r/Uncanny X-Men #109,172,173, Wolverine limited series #4, & Wolverine #41,42,75 17.00
...Typhoid's Kiss (6/94, $6.95)-r/Wolverine stories from Marvel Comics Presents #109-116 7.00
...Vs. Spider-Man 1 (3/95, $2.50) -r/Marvel Comics Presents #48-50 4.00
.../Witchblade 1 (3/97, $2.95) Devil's Reign Pt. 5 4.00
Wizard #1/2 (1997) Joe Phillips-a(p) 10.00

NOTE: ***Austin*** *c-3i.* ***Bolton*** *c(back)-5.* ***Buscema*** *a-1-16,25,27p; c-1-10.* ***Byrne*** *a-17-22p, 23; c-1(back), 17-22, 23p.* ***Colan*** *a-24.* ***Andy Kubert*** *c/a-51.* ***Jim Lee*** *c-24, 25, 27.* ***Silvestri*** *a(p)-31-43, 45, 46, 48-50, 52, 53, 55-57; c-31-42p, 43, 45p, 46p, 48, 49p, 50p, 52p, 53p, 55-57p.* ***Stroman*** *a-44p; c-60p.* ***Williamson*** *a-1i, 3-8i; c(i)-1, 3-6.*

WOLVERINE (Volume 3) (Titled Dark Wolverine from #75-90)(See Daken: Dark Wolverine)
Marvel Comics: July, 2003 - No. 90, Oct, 2010 ($2.25/$2.50/$2.99)

1-Rucka-s/Robertson-a 5.00
2-19: 6-Nightcrawler app. 13-16-Sabretooth app. 3.00
20-Millar-s/Romita, Jr.-a begin, Elektra app. 4.00
20-B&W variant-c 5.00

GD 2.0 | VG 4.0 | FN 6.0 | VF 8.0 | VF/NM 9.0 | NM- 9.2

21-39: 21-Elektra-c/app. 23,24-Daredevil app. 26-28-Land-c. 29-Quesada-c; begin $2.50-c. 33-35-House of M. 36,37-Decimation. 36-Quesada-c. 39-Winter Soldier app. 3.00
40,43-48: 40-Begin $2.99-c; Winter Soldier app.; Texeira-a. 43-46-Civil War; Ramos-a. 45-Sub-Mariner app. 3.00
41,49-($3.99) 41-C.P. Smith-a/Stuart Moore-s 4.00
42-Civil War 5.00
50-($3.99) Sabretooth app.; Bianchi-a/c & Loeb-s begin; wraparound-c; McGuinness-a 4.00
50-($3.99) Variant Edition; uncolored art and cover; Bianchi pencil art page 4.00
51-55-(Regular and variant uncolored editions) Bianchi-a/Loeb-s; Sabretooth app. 3.00
55-EC-style variant-c by Greg Land 5.00
56-($3.99) Howard Chaykin-a/c 4.00
57-65: 57-61-Suydam Zombie-c; Chaykin-a. 62-65-Mystique app. 3.00
66-Old Man Logan begins; Millar-s/McNiven-a; McNiven wraparound-c 5.00
66-Variant-c by Michael Turner 1 2 3 4 5 7
66-Variant sketch-c by Michael Turner 20.00
66-2nd printing with McNiven variant-c of Logan and Hulk gang member 3.00
66-(5/10, $1.00) Reprint with "Marvel's Greatest Comics" on cover 3.00
67-74: 67-72-Old Man Logan (concludes in Wolverine: Old Man Logan Giant-Sized Special). 67-Intro. Ashley, Spider-Man's granddaughter.72-Red Skull app. 73,74-Andy Kubert-a 4.00
75-($3.99) Dark Reign, Daken as Wolverine on Osborn's team; Camuncoli-a 5.00
76-90: 76-86-Multiple covers for each. 76-Dark Reign; Yu-c. 82-84-Siege. 88,89-Franken-Castle x-over; Punisher app. 3.00
#900 (7/10, $4.99) Short stories by various incl. Finch, Rivera, Segovia, McGuinness 5.00
Annual 1 (12/07, $3.99) Hurwitz-s/Frusin-a 4.00
Annual 2 (11/08, $3.99) Swierczynski-s/Deodato-a/c 4.00
...: Blood & Sorrow TPB (2007, $13.99) r/#41,49, stories from Giant-Size Wolverine #1 and X-Men Unlimited #12 14.00
...: Chop Shop 1 (1/09, $2.99) Benson-s/Boschi-a/Hanuka-c 3.00
Civil War: Wolverine TPB (2007, $17.99) r/#42-48; gallery of B&W cover inks 18.00
... Dangerous Games 1 (8/08, $3.99) Spurrier-s/Oliver-a; Remender-s/Opena-a 4.00
...Enemy of the State HC Vol. 1 (2005, $19.99) r/#20-25; Ennis intro.; variant covers 20.00
...Enemy of the State HC Vol. 2 (2005, $19.99) r/#26-32 20.00
...Enemy of the State SC Vol. 1 (2005, $14.99) r/#20-25; Ennis intro.; variant covers 15.00
...Enemy of the State SC Vol. 2 (2006, $16.99) r/#26-32 17.00
...Enemy of the State - The Complete Edition (2006, $34.99) r/#20-32; Ennis intro.; sketch pages, variant covers and pin-up art 35.00
...: Evolution SC (2008, $14.99) r/#50-55 15.00
...: Flies to a Spider (2/09, $3.99) Bradstreet-c/Hurwitz-s/Opena-a 4.00
...: Killing Made Simple (10/08, $3.99) Yost-s/Turnbull-a 4.00
...: Enemy of the State MGC #20 (7/11, $1.00) r/#20 with "Marvel's Greatest Comics" logo 3.00
...: Mr. X (5/10, $3.99) Tieri-s/Diaz-a/Mattina-c 4.00
...: Old Man Logan Giant-Sized Special (11/09, $4.99) Continued from #72; cover gallery 5.00
...Origins & Endings HC (2006, $19.99) r/#36-40 20.00
...Origins & Endings SC (2006, $13.99) r/#36-40 14.00
...: Origin of an X-Man Free Comic Book Day 2009 (5/09) Gurihiru-a/McGuinness-c 3.00
...: Revolver (8/09, $3.99) Gischler-s/Pastoras-a 4.00
... Saga (2009, giveaway) history of the character in text and comic panels 3.00
...: Saudade (2008, $4.99) English adaptation of Wolverine story from French comic 5.00
...: Savage (4/10, $3.99) J. Scott Campbell-c; The Lizard app. 4.00
...Special: Firebreak (2/08, $3.99) Carey-s/Kolins-a; Lolos-a 4.00
...: Switchback 1 (3/09, $3.99) short stories; art by Pastoras & Doe 4.00
...: The Amazing Immortal Man & Other Bloody Tales (7/08, $3.99) Lapham short stories 4.00
...: The Anniversary (6/09, $3.99) Mariko flashback short stories; art by various 4.00
...: The Death of Wolverine HC (2008, $19.99) r/#56-61 20.00
...: The Road to Hell (11/10, $3.99) Previews new Wolverine titles and Generation Hope 4.00
...: Under the Boardwalk (2/10, $3.99) Coker-a 4.00
...Vol. 1: The Brotherhood (2003, $12.99) r/#1-6 13.00
...Vol. 2: Coyote Crossing (2004, $11.99) r/#7-11 12.00
... Weapon X Files (2009, $4.99) Handbook-style pages of Wolverine characters 5.00
...: Wendigo! 1 (3/10, $3.99) Gulacy-a; back-up with Thor 4.00

WOLVERINE (Volume 4)
Marvel Comics: Nov, 2010 - Present ($3.99)

1-5-Jae Lee-c/Guedes-a; Wolverine Goes to Hell. 1-Back-up with Silver Samurai 4.00
5.1-(4/11, $2.99) Aaron-s/Palo-a/Rivera-c 3.00
6-20: 6-Jae Lee-c/Acuña-a; X-Men & Magneto app. 20-Kingpin & Sabretooth app. 4.00
300-(3/12, $4.99) Adam Kubert-c; Sabretooth & new Silver Samurai app. 5.00
301,302-Aaron-s. 302-Art Adams-c 4.00
#1000 (4/11, $4.99) Short stories by various incl. Palmiotti, Green, Luke Ross; Segovia-c 5.00
...: Debt of Death 1 (11/11, $3.99) Lapham-s/Aja-a/c; Nick Fury app. 4.00
.../Deadpool: The Decoy 1 (9/11, $3.99) prints online story from Marvel.com; Young-c 4.00

WOLVERINE & BLACK CAT: CLAWS 2 (See Claws for 1st series)
Marvel Comics: Aug, 2011 - No. 3, Nov, 2011 ($3.99, limited series)

1-3-Linsner-a/c; Palmiotti & Gray-s; Killraven app. 4.00

Wolverine and the X-Men #1 © MAR

Wolverine: Manifest Destiny #2 © MAR

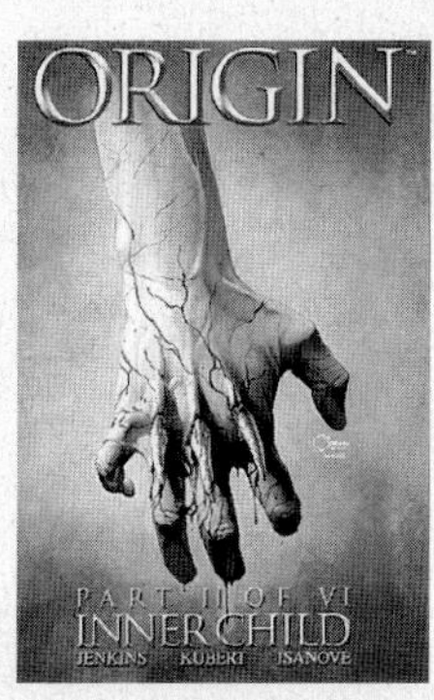

Wolverine: The Origin #2 © MAR

	GD	VG	FN	VF	VF/NM	NM-
	2.0	4.0	6.0	8.0	9.0	9.2

WOLVERINE AND JUBILEE
Marvel Comics: Mar, 2011 - No. 4, Jun, 2011 ($2.99, limited series)
1-4: 1-Vampire Jubilee; Kathryn Immonen-s/Phil Noto-a; Coipel-c 3.00

WOLVERINE AND POWER PACK
Marvel Comics: Jan, 2009 - No. 4, Apr, 2009 ($2.99, limited series)
1-4-Sumerak-s. 1,2-GuriHiru-a. 1-Sauron app. 3-Meet Wolverine as a child; Koblish-a 3.00

WOLVERINE AND THE PUNISHER: DAMAGING EVIDENCE
Marvel Comics: Oct, 1993 - No. 3, Dec, 1993 ($2.00, limited series)
1-3: 2,3-Indicia says "The Punisher and Wolverine..." 4.00

WOLVERINE & THE X-MEN (Regenesis)(See X-Men: Schism)
Marvel Comics: Dec, 2011 - Present ($3.99)
1-7: 1-3-Aaron-s/Bachalo-a/c. 3-Sabretooth app. 4-Bradshaw-a; Deathlok app. 4.00

WOLVERINE AND THE X-MEN: ALPHA & OMEGA
Marvel Comics: Dec, 2011 - Present ($3.99)
1-3-Brooks-c/Boschi & Brooks-a; Quentin Quire vs. Wolverine 4.00

WOLVERINE/CAPTAIN AMERICA
Marvel Comics: Apr, 2004 - No. 4, Apr, 2004 ($2.99, limited series)
1-4-Derenick-a/c 3.00

WOLVERINE: DAYS OF FUTURE PAST
Marvel Comics: Dec, 1997 - No. 3, Feb, 1998 ($2.50, limited series)
1-3: J.F. Moore-s/Bennett-a 4.00

WOLVERINE/DOOP (Also see X-Force and X-Statix)(Reprinted in X-Statix Vol. 2)
Marvel Comics: July, 2003 - No. 2, July, 2003 ($2.99, limited series)
1,2-Peter Milligan-s/Darwyn Cooke & J. Bone-a 3.00

WOLVERINE: FIRST CLASS
Marvel Comics: May, 2008 - No. 21, Jan, 2010 ($2.99)
1-21: 1-Wolverine and Kitty Pryde's first mission; DiVito-a. 2,9-Sabretooth app. 3.00

WOLVERINE/GAMBIT: VICTIMS
Marvel Comics: Sept, 1995 - No. 4, Dec, 1995 ($2.95, limited series)
1-4: Jeph Loeb scripts & Tim Sale-a; foil-c 4.00

WOLVERINE/HERCULES: MYTHS, MONSTERS & MUTANTS
Marvel Comics: May, 2011 - No. 4, Aug, 2011 ($2.99, limited series)
1-4-Tieri-s/Santacruz-a/Jusko-c 3.00

WOLVERINE/HULK
Marvel Comics: Apr, 2002 - No. 4, July, 2002 ($3.50, limited series)
1-4-Sam Kieth-s/a/c 4.00
Wolverine Legends Vol. 1: Wolverine/Hulk (2003, $9.99, TPB) r/#1-4 10.00

WOLVERINE: MANIFEST DESTINY
Marvel Comics: Dec, 2008 - No. 4, Mar, 2009 ($2.99, limited series)
1-4-Aaron-s/Segovia-a 3.00

WOLVERINE: NETSUKE
Marvel Comics: Nov, 2002 - No. 4, Feb, 2003 ($3.99, limited series)
1-4-George Pratt-s/painted-a 4.00

WOLVERINE: NOIR (1930s Pulp-style)
Marvel Comics: Apr, 2009 - No. 4, Sept, 2009 ($3.99, limited series)
1-4-C.P. Smith-a/Stuart Moore; covers by Smith & Calero; alternate Logan as detective 4.00

WOLVERINE: ORIGINS
Marvel Comics: June, 2006 - No. 50, Sept, 2010 ($2.99)
1-15: 1-Daniel Way-s/Steve Dillon-a/Quesada-c 3.00
1-10-Variant covers. 1-Turner. 2-Quesada & Hitch. 3-Bianchi. 4-Dell'Otto. 7-Deodato 4.00
16-($3.99) Captain America WW2 app.; preview of Wolverine #56; r/X-Men #268 4.00
16-Variant-c by McGuinness 4.00
17-24: 17-20-Capt. America & Bucky app. 21-24-Deadpool app.; Bianchi-c 3.00
25-($3.99) Deadpool app.; Bianchi-c; r/Deadpool's 1st app. in New Mutants #98 4.00
26-49: 26-Origin of Dakan; Way-s/Segovia-a/Land-c. 28-Hulk & Wendigo app. 3.00
50-($3.99) Last issue; Nick Fury app. 4.00
Annual 1 (9/07, $3.99) Way-s/Andrews-a; flashback to 1932 4.00
... Vol. 1 - Born in Blood HC (2006, $19.99, dustjacket) r/#1-5; variant covers 20.00
... Vol. 1 - Born in Blood SC (2007, $13.99) r/#1-5; variant covers 14.00
... Vol. 2 - Savior HC (2007, $19.99, dustjacket) r/#6-10; variant covers 20.00
... Vol. 2 - Savior SC (2007, $13.99) r/#6-10; variant covers 14.00
... Vol. 3 - Swift & Terrible HC (2007, $19.99, dustjacket) r/#11-15 20.00
... Vol. 3 - Swift & Terrible SC (2007, $13.99) r/#11-15 14.00
... Vol. 4 - Our War HC (2008, $19.99, dustjacket) r/#16-20 & Annual #1 20.00
... Vol. 4 - Our War SC (2008, $14.99) r/#16-20 & Annual #1 15.00

WOLVERINE/PUNISHER
Marvel Comics: May, 2004 - No. 5, Sept, 2004 ($2.99, limited series)
1-5: Milligan-s/Weeks-a 3.00
... Vol. 1 TPB (2004, $13.99) r/series 14.00

WOLVERINE, PUNISHER & GHOST RIDER: OFFICIAL INDEX TO THE MARVEL UNIVERSE
Marvel Comics: Oct, 2011 - Present ($3.99)
1-7-Each issue has chronological synopsies, creator credits, character lists for 30-40 issues of their own titles and headlining mini-series 4.00

WOLVERINE/PUNISHER REVELATIONS (Marvel Knights)
Marvel Comics: Jun, 1999 - No. 4, Sept, 1999 ($2.95, limited series)
1-4: Pat Lee-a(p) 4.00
...: Revelation (4/00, $14.95, TPB) r/#1-4 15.00

WOLVERINE SAGA
Marvel Comics: Sept, 1989 - No. 4, Mid-Dec, 1989 ($3.95, lim. series, 52 pgs.)
1-Gives history; Liefeld/Austin-c (front & back) 5.00
2-4: 2-Romita, Jr./Austin-c. 4-Kaluta-c 5.00

WOLVERINE: SNIKT!
Marvel Comics: July, 2003 - No. 5, Nov, 2003 ($2.99, limited series)
1-5-Manga-style; Tsutomu Nihei-s/a 3.00
Wolverine Legends Vol. 5: Snikt! TPB (2003, $13.99) r/#1-5 14.00

WOLVERINE: SOULTAKER
Marvel Comics: May, 2005 - No. 5, Aug, 2005 ($2.99, limited series)
1-5-Yoshida-s/Nagasawa-a/Terada-c; Yukio app. 3.00
TPB (2005, $13.99) r/#1-5 14.00

WOLVERINE: THE BEST THERE IS
Marvel Comics: Feb, 2011 - No. 12, Jan, 2012 ($3.99)
1-12: 1,2-Huston-s/Ryp-a; covers by Hitch and Djurdjevic. 3-12-Hitch-c 4.00
... - Contagion 1 (6/11, $4.99) r/#1-3, cover gallery 5.00

WOLVERINE: THE END
Marvel Comics: Jan, 2004 - No. 6, Dec, 2004 ($2.99, limited series)
1-5-Jenkins-s/Castellini-a 3.00
1-Wizard World Texas variant-c 20.00
TPB (2005, $14.99) r/#1-5 15.00

WOLVERINE: THE ORIGIN
Marvel Comics: Nov, 2001 - No. 6, July, 2002 ($3.50, limited series)
1-Origin of Logan; Jenkins-s/Andy Kubert-a; Quesada-c 40.00
1-DF edition 60.00
2 15.00
3 9.00
4-6 6.00
HC (3/02, $34.95, 11" x 7-1/2") r/#1-6; dust jacket; sketch pages and treatments 35.00
HC (2006, $19.99) r/#1-6; dust jacket; sketch pages and treatments 20.00
SC (2002, $14.95) r/#1-6; afterwords by Jemas and Quesada 15.00

WOLVERINE WEAPON X
Marvel Comics: June, 2009 - No. 16, Oct, 2010 ($3.99)
1-16: 1-5,11-Aaron-s/Garney-a. 1-Four covers. 2,3-Two covers. 11-15-Deathlok app. 4.00

WOLVERINE: XISLE
Marvel Comics: June, 2003 - No. 5, June, 2003 ($2.50, weekly limited series)
1-5-Bruce Jones-s/Jorge Lucas-a 3.00
Wolverine Legends Vol. 4 TPB (2003, $13.99) r/ #1-5 14.00

WOMEN IN LOVE (A Feature Presentation #5)
Fox Features Synd./Hero Books: Aug, 1949 - No. 4, Feb, 1950

	GD 2.0	VG 4.0	FN 6.0	VF 8.0	VF/NM 9.0	NM- 9.2
1	36	72	108	211	343	475
2-Kamen/Feldstein-c	29	58	87	170	278	385
3	20	40	60	117	189	260
4-Wood-a	24	48	72	140	230	320

WOMEN IN LOVE (Thrilling Romances for Adults)
Ziff-Davis Publishing Co.: Winter, 1952 (25¢, 100 pgs.)

	GD 2.0	VG 4.0	FN 6.0	VF 8.0	VF/NM 9.0	NM- 9.2
nn-(Scarce)-Kinstler-a; painted-c	58	116	174	371	636	900

WOMEN OF MARVEL
Marvel Comics: 2006, 2007 ($24.99, TPB)
SC-Reprints 1st apps. of Dazzler, Ms. Marvel, Shanna, The Cat plus notable stories of other female Marvel characters; Mayhew-c 25.00
Vol. 2 (2007) More stories of female Marvel characters; Mayhew-c; cover process art 25.00

Wonder Comics #13 © BP

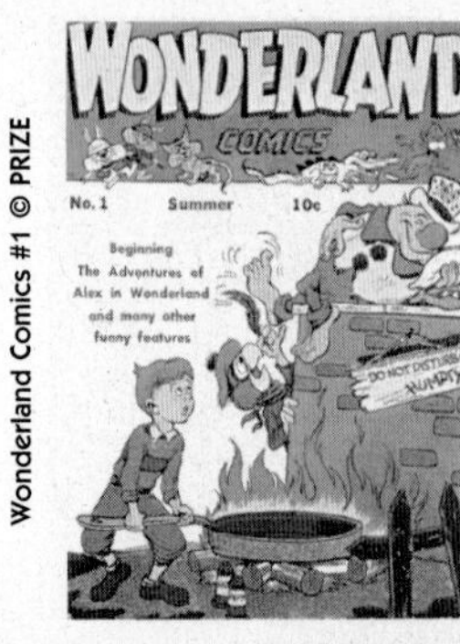

Wonderland Comics #1 © PRIZE

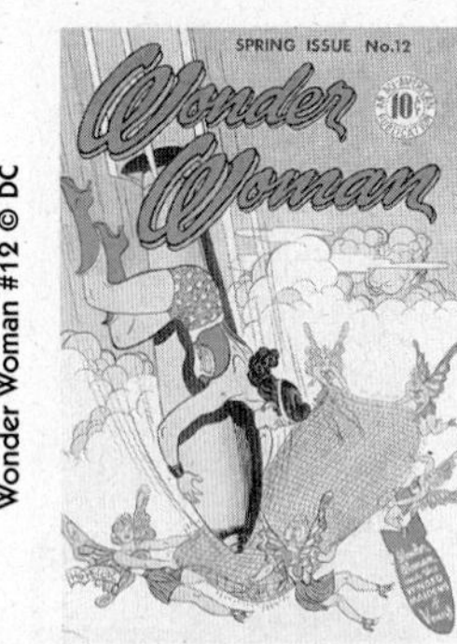

Wonder Woman #12 © DC

GD VG FN VF VF/NM NM-
2.0 4.0 6.0 8.0 9.0 9.2

GD VG FN VF VF/NM NM-
2.0 4.0 6.0 8.0 9.0 9.2

WOMEN OF MARVEL
Marvel Comics: Jan, 2011 - No. 2, Feb, 2011 ($3.99, limited series)

1,2-Short stories of female Marvel characters. 1-Pichelli-c. 2-Land-c 4.00

WOMEN OUTLAWS (My Love Memories #9 on)(Also see Red Circle)
Fox Features Syndicate: July, 1948 - No. 8, Sept, 1949

1-Used in **SOTI**, illo "Giving children an image of American womanhood"; negligee panels
81 162 243 518 884 1250
2,3: 3-Kamenish-a 60 120 180 381 653 925
4-8 47 94 141 296 498 700
nn(nd)-Contains Cody of the Pony Express; same cover as #7
22 44 66 132 216 300

WOMEN TO LOVE
Realistic: No date (1953)

nn-(Scarce)-Reprints Complete Romance #1; c-/Avon paperback #165
40 80 120 242 401 560

WONDER BOY (Formerly Terrific Comics) (See Blue Bolt, Bomber Comics & Samson)
Ajax/Farrell Publ.: No. 17, May, 1955 - No. 18, July, 1955 (Code approved)

17-Phantom Lady app. Bakerish-c/a 47 94 141 296 498 700
18-Phantom Lady app. 39 78 117 240 395 550
NOTE: *Phantom Lady not by Matt Baker.*

WONDER COMICS (Wonderworld #3 on)
Fox Features Syndicate: May, 1939 - No. 2, June, 1939 (68 pgs.)

1-(Scarce)-Wonder Man only app. by Will Eisner; Dr. Fung (by Powell), K-5 begins;
Bob Kane-a; Eisner-c 1600 3200 4800 12,000 21,000 30,000
2-(Scarce)-Yarko the Great, Master Magician (see Samson) by Eisner begins; 'Spark' Stevens by Bob Kane, Patty O'Day, Tex Mason app. Lou Fine's 1st-c; Fine-a (2 pgs.);
Yarko-c (Wonder Man-c #1) 514 1028 1542 3750 6625 9500

WONDER COMICS
Great/Nedor/Better Publications: May, 1944 - No. 20, Oct, 1948

1-The Grim Reaper & Spectro, the Mind Reader begin; Hitler/Hirohito bondage-c
232 464 696 1485 2543 3600
2-Origin The Grim Reaper; Super Sleuths begin, end #8,17
87 174 261 553 952 1350
3-5: 3-Indicia reads "Vol. 1, #2" 77 154 231 493 847 1200
6-10: 6-Flag-c. 8-Last Spectro. 9-Wonderman begins
55 110 165 352 601 850
11-14: 11-Dick Devens, King of Futuria begins, ends #14. 11,12-Ingels-c & splash pg.
14-Bondage-c 68 136 204 438 749 1060
15-Tara begins (origin), ends #20 90 180 270 576 988 1400
16,18: 16-Spectro app.; last Grim Reaper. 18-The Silver Knight begins
68 136 204 438 749 1060
17-Wonderman with Frazetta panels; Jill Trent with all Frazetta inks
71 142 213 454 777 1100
19-Frazetta panels 68 136 204 438 749 1060
20-Most of Silver Knight by Frazetta 76 152 228 486 831 1175
NOTE: ***Ingels** c-11, 12. **Roussos** a-19. **Schomburg (Xela)** c-1-10; (airbrush)-13-20. Bondage c-12, 13, 15. Cover features: Grim Reaper #1-8; Wonder Man #9-15; Tara #16-20.*

WONDER DUCK (See Wisco)
Marvel Comics (CDS): Sept, 1949 - No. 3, Mar, 1950

1-Funny animal 18 36 54 105 165 225
2,3 13 26 39 74 105 135

WONDERFUL ADVENTURES OF PINOCCHIO, THE (See Movie Comics & Walt Disney Showcase #48)
Whitman Publishing Co.: April, 1982 (Walt Disney)

nn-(#3 Continuation of Movie Comics?); r/FC #92 6.00

WONDERFUL WIZARD OF OZ (Adaptation of the original 1900 L. Frank Baum book)
(Also see the sequels Marvelous Land of Oz, Ozma of Oz, and Dorothy & The Wizard in Oz)
Marvel Comics: Feb, 2009 - No. 8, Sept, 2009 ($3.99, limited series)

1-8-Eric Shanower-a/Skottie Young-a/c 4.00
1-Variant Good Witch & Dorothy wraparound cover by J. Scott Campbell 8.00
1-Variant Scarecrow & Dorothy cover by Eric Shanower 10.00
1-(4/10, $1.00) Reprint with "Marvel's Greatest Comics" on cover 3.00
... Sketchbook (2008, giveaway) Young character design sketches; Shanower intro. 3.00
HC (2009, $29.99, dustjacket) r/#1-8; Shanower intro.; cover gallery; sketch art 30.00

WONDERFUL WORLD FOR BOYS AND GIRLS
DC Comics: May, 1964

nn - Ashcan comic, not distributed to newsstands, only for in-house use (no known sales)

WONDERFUL WORLD OF DISNEY, THE (Walt Disney)
Whitman Publishing Co.: 1978 (Digest, 116 pgs.)

1-Barks-a (reprints) 3 6 9 16 23 30
2 (no date) 2 4 6 11 16 20

WONDERFUL WORLD OF THE BROTHERS GRIMM (See Movie Comics)

WONDER GIRL (Cassandra Sandsmark from Teen Titans)
DC Comics: Nov, 2007 - No. 6, Apr, 2008 ($2.99, limited series)

1-6-Torres-s/Greene-a; Hercules app. 2-6-Female Furies app. 5,6-Wonder Woman app. 3.00
Teen Titans Spotlight: Wonder Girl TPB (2008, $17.99) r/#1-6 18.00
1-(3/11, $2.99, one-shot) Nicola Scott-c; intro. Solstice 3.00

WONDERLAND COMICS
Feature Publications/Prize: Summer, 1945 - No. 9, Feb-Mar, 1947

1-Alex in Wonderland begins; Howard Post-c 22 44 66 128 209 290
2-Howard Post-c/a(2) 14 28 42 78 112 145
3-9: 3,4-Post-c 11 22 33 62 86 110

WONDER MAN (See The Avengers #9, 151)
Marvel Comics Group: Mar, 1986 ($1.25, one-shot, 52 pgs.)

1 4.00

WONDER MAN
Marvel Comics Group: Sept, 1991 - No. 29, Jan, 1994 ($1.00)

1-29: 1-Free fold out poster by Johnson/Austin. 1-3-Johnson/Austin-c/a.
2-Avengers West Coast x-over. 4 Austin-c(i) 3.00
Annual 1 (1992, $2.25)-Immonen-a (10 pgs.) 4.00
Annual 2 (1993, $2.95)-Bagged w/trading card 4.00

WONDER MAN
Marvel Comics: Feb, 2007 - No. 5, June, 2007 ($2.99, limited series)

1-5: 1-Peter David-s/Andrew Currie-a; Beast app. 4-Nauck-a 3.00
...: My Fair Super Hero TPB (2007, $13.99) r/#1-5; Currie sketch page 14.00

WONDERS OF ALADDIN, THE
Dell Publishing Co.: No. 1255, Feb-Apr, 1962

Four Color 1255-Movie 6 12 18 42 69 95

WONDER WOMAN (See Adventure Comics #459, All-Star Comics, Brave & the Bold, DC Comics Presents, JLA, Justice League of America, Legend of..., Power Record Comics, Sensation Comics, Super Friends and World's Finest Comics #244)

WONDER WOMAN
DC Comics: Jan 1942

1-Ashcan comic, not distributed to newsstands, only for in-house use. Cover art is Sensation Comics #1 with interior being Sensation Comics #2. A CGC certified 8.5 copy sold for $17,250 in 2002.

WONDER WOMAN
National Periodical Publications/All-American Publ./DC Comics:
Summer, 1942 - No. 329, Feb, 1986

1-Origin Wonder Woman retold (more detailed than All Star #8); H. G. Peter-c/a begins
2900 5800 8700 21,750 39,875 58,000
1-Reprint, Oversize 13-1/2x10". **WARNING:** This comic is an exact reprint of the original except for its size. DC published it in 1974 with a second cover titling it as a Famous First Edition. There have been many reported cases of the outer cover being removed and the interior sold as the original edition. The reprint with the new outer cover removed is practically worthless. See Famous First Edition for value.

2-Origin/1st app. Mars; Duke of Deception app. 432 864 1296 3154 5577 8000
3 284 568 852 1818 3109 4400
4,5: 5-1st Dr. Psycho app. 219 438 657 1402 2401 3400
6-1st Cheetah app. 194 388 582 1242 2121 3000
7-Wonder Woman for President-c/sty 206 412 618 1318 2259 3200
8,9 168 336 504 1075 1838 2600
10-Invasion from Saturn classic sci-fi-c/s 174 348 522 1114 1907 2700
11-20 116 232 348 742 1271 1800
21-30: 23-Story from Wonder Woman's childhood 97 194 291 621 1061 1500
31-33,35-40: 38-Last H.G. Peter-c 81 162 243 518 884 1250
34-Robot-c 84 168 252 538 919 1300
41-44,46-48 71 142 213 454 777 1100
45-Origin retold 139 278 417 883 1517 2150
49-Used in **SOTI**, pgs. 234,236; last 52 pg. issue 73 146 219 467 796 1125
50-(44 pgs.)-Used in **POP**, pg. 97 73 146 219 467 796 1125
51-60: 60-New logo 65 130 195 416 708 1000
61-72: 62-Origin of W.W. i.d. 64-Story about 3-D movies. 70-1st Angle Man
app. 72-Last pre-code (2/55) 60 120 180 381 653 925
73-90: 80-Origin The Invisible Plane. 85-1st S.A. issue. 89-Flying
saucer-c/story 52 104 156 328 557 785
91-94,96,97,99: 97-Last H. G. Peter-a 43 86 129 271 461 650
95-A-Bomb-c 45 90 135 284 480 675

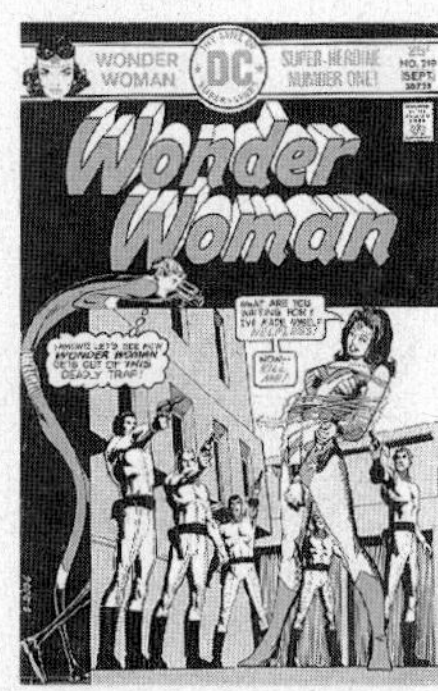

Wonder Woman #219 © DC

Wonder Woman (2nd series) #153 © DC

Wonder Woman (2006 series) #34 © DC

	GD 2.0	VG 4.0	FN 6.0	VF 8.0	VF/NM 9.0	NM- 9.2
98-New origin & new art team (Andru & Esposito) begin (5/58); origin W.W. id w/new facts	47	94	141	296	498	700
100-(8/58)	50	100	150	315	533	750
101-104,106,108-110	40	80	120	242	401	560
105-(Scarce, 4/59)-W. W.'s secret origin; W. W. appears as girl (no costume yet) (called Wonder Girl - see DC Super-Stars #1)	165	330	495	1048	1799	2550
107-1st advs. of Wonder Girl; 1st Merboy; tells how Wonder Woman won her costume	47	94	141	298	504	710
111-120	34	68	102	199	325	450
121-126: 121-1st app. Wonder Woman Family. 122-1st app. Wonder Tot. 124-Wonder Woman Family app. 126-Last 10¢ issue	27	54	81	160	263	365
127-130: 128-Origin The Invisible Plane retold. 129-3rd app. Wonder Woman Family (#133 is 4th app.)	13	26	39	86	183	280
131-150: 132-Flying saucer-c	11	22	33	76	151	225
151-155,157,158,160-170 (1967): 151-Wonder Girl solo issue	9	18	27	61	106	150
156-(8/65)-Early mention of a comic book shop & comic collecting; mentions DCs selling for $100 a copy	9	18	27	63	112	160
159-Origin retold (1/66); 1st S.A. origin?	10	20	30	69	130	190
171-176	7	14	21	48	79	110
177-W. Woman/Supergirl battle	9	18	27	61	106	150
178-1st new Wonder Woman on-c only; appears in old costume w/powers inside	9	18	27	62	109	155
179-Classic-c; wears no costume to issue #203	9	18	27	60	103	145
180-195: 180-Death of Steve Trevor. 182-Last 12¢ issue. 195-Wood inks	6	12	18	37	59	80
196 (52 pgs.)-Origin-r/All Star #8 (6 out of 9 pgs.)	6	12	18	39	62	85
197,198 (52 pgs.)-Reprints	6	12	18	39	62	85
199-Jeff Jones painted-c; 52 pgs.	9	18	27	58	99	140
200 (5-6/72)-Jeff Jones-c; 52 pgs.	9	18	27	61	106	150
201,202-Catwoman app. 202-Fafhrd & The Grey Mouser debut.	4	8	12	26	41	55
203,205-210,212: 212-The Cavalier app.	3	6	9	19	29	38
204-Return to old costume; death of I Ching.	4	8	12	26	41	55
211,214-(100 pgs.)	8	16	24	51	86	120
213,215,216,218-220: 220-N. Adams assist	3	6	9	17	25	32
217: (68 pgs.)	4	8	12	22	34	45
221,222,224-227,229,230,233-236,238-240	2	4	6	10	14	18
223,228,231,232,237,241,248: 223-Steve Trevor revived as Steve Howard & learns W.W.'s I.D. 228-Both Wonder Women team up & new World War II stories begin, end #243. 231,232: JSA app. 237-Origin retold. 240-G.A. Flash app. 241-Intro Bouncer; Spectre app. 248-Steve Trevor Howard dies (44 pgs.)	2	4	6	11	16	20
242-246,252-266,269,270: 243-Both W. Women team-up again. 269-Last Wood a(i) for DC? (7/80)	2	3	4	6	8	10
247,249-251,271: 247,249 (44 pgs.). 249-Hawkgirl app. 250-Origin/1st app. Orana, the new Wonder Woman. 251-Orana dies. 271-Huntress & 3rd Life of Steve Trevor begin	2	4	6	8	10	12
250-252,255-262,264-(Whitman variants, low print run, no issue # on cover)	2	4	6	11	16	20
267,268-Re-intro Animal Man (5/80 & 6/80)	2	4	6	8	10	12
272-280,284-286,289,290,294-299,301-325						6.00
281-283: Joker-c/stories in Huntress back-ups	2	3	4	6	8	10
287,288,291-293: 287-New Teen Titans x-over. 288-New costume & logo. 291-293-Three part epic with Super-Heroines	1	2	3	4	5	7
300-($1.50, 76 pgs.)-Anniv. issue; Giffen-a; New Teen Titans, Bronze Age Sandman, JLA & G.A. Wonder Woman app.; 1st app. Lyta Trevor who becomes Fury in All-Star Squadron #25; G.A. Wonder Woman & Steve Trevor revealed as married	1	2	3	5	7	9
326-328	1	2	3	4	5	7
329 (Double size)-S.A. W.W. & Steve Trevor wed	2	4	6	9	13	16
...: Chronicles Vol. 1 TPB (2010, $17.99) reprints debut in All Star Comics #8, apps. in Sensation Comics #1-9 and Wonder Woman #1						18.00
Diana Prince: Wonder Woman Vol. 1 TPB (2008, $19.99) r/#178-183						20.00
Diana Prince: Wonder Woman Vol. 2 TPB (2008, $19.99) r/#185-189, Brave and the Bold #87, and Superman's Girl Friend, Lois Lane #93						20.00
Diana Prince: Wonder Woman Vol. 3 TPB ('08, $19.99) r/#190-198, World's Finest #204						20.00
Diana Prince: Wonder Woman Vol. 4 TPB ('09, $19.99) r/#199-204, Brave & Bold #105						20.00
...: The Greatest Stories Ever Told TPB (2007, $19.99) intro. by Lynda Carter; Ross-c						20.00

NOTE: ***Andru/Esposito*** *c-66-160(most).* ***Buckler*** *a-300.* ***Colan*** *a-288-305p; c-288-290p.* ***Giffen*** *a-300p.* ***Grell*** *c-217.* ***Kaluta*** *c-297.* ***Gil Kane*** *c-294p, 303-305, 307, 312, 314.* ***Miller*** *c-298p.* ***Morrow*** *c-233.* ***Nasser*** *a-232p; c-231p, 232p.* ***Bob Oskner*** *c(i)-39-65(most).* ***Perez*** *c-283p, 284p.* ***Spiegle*** *a-312.* ***Staton*** *a(p)-241, 271-287, 289, 290, 294-299; c(p)-241, 245, 246. Huntress back-up stories 271-287, 289, 290, 294-299, 301-321.*

WONDER WOMAN

DC Comics: Feb, 1987 - No. 226, Apr, 2006 (75¢/$1.00/$1.25/$1.95/$1.99/$2.25/$2.50)

	GD 2.0	VG 4.0	FN 6.0	VF 8.0	VF/NM 9.0	NM- 9.2
0-(10/94) Zero Hour; released between #90 & #91						5.00
1-New origin; Perez-c/a begins	2	4	6	8	10	12
2-5						6.00
6-20: 9-Origin Cheetah. 12,13-Millennium x-over. 18,26-Free 16 pg. story						5.00
21-49: 24-Last Perez-a; scripts continue thru #62						4.00
50-($1.50, 52 pgs.)-New Titans, Justice League						5.00
51-62: Perez scripts. 60-Vs. Lobo; last Perez-c. 62-Last $1.00-c						4.00
63-New direction & Bolland-c begin; Deathstroke story continued from W. W. Special #1						5.00
64-84						4.00
85-1st Deodato-a; ends #100	3	5	7	10	12	14
86-88: 88-Superman-c & app.						6.00
89-97: 90-(9/94)-1st Artemis. 91-(11/94). 93-Hawkman app. 96-Joker-c						5.00
98,99						4.00
100 ($2.95, Newsstand)-Death of Artemis; Bolland-c ends.						4.00
100 ($3.95, Direct Market)-Death of Artemis; foil-c.						6.00
101-119, 121-125: 101-Begin $1.95-c; Byrne-c/a/scripts begin. 101-104-Darkseid app. 105-Phantom Stranger cameo. 106-108-Phantom Stranger & Demon app. 107,108-Arion app. 111-1st app. new Wonder Girl. 111,112-Vs. Doomsday. 112-Superman app. 113-Wonder Girl-c/app; Sugar & Spike app.						3.00
120 ($2.95)-Perez-c						4.00
126-149: 128-Hippolyta becomes new W.W. 130-133-Flash (Jay Garrick) & JSA app. 136-Diana returns to W.W. role; last Byrne issue. 137-Priest-s. 139-Luke-s/Paquette-a begin; Hughes-c thru #146						3.00
150-($2.95) Hughes-c/Clark-a; Zauriel app.						4.00
151-158-Hughes-c. 153-Superboy app.						3.00
159-163: 159-Begin $2.25-c. 160,161-Clayface app. 162,163-Aquaman app.						3.00
164-171: Phil Jimenez-s/a begin; Hughes-c; Batman app. 168,169-Pérez co-plot 169-Wraparound-c.170-Lois Lane-c/app.						3.00
172-Our Worlds at War; Hippolyta killed						4.00
173,174: 173-Our Worlds at War; Darkseid app. 174-Every DC heroine app.						3.00
175-($3.50) Joker: Last Laugh; JLA app.; Jim Lee-c						4.00
176-199: 177-Paradise Island returns. 179-Jimenez-c. 184,185-Hippolyta-c/app.; Hughes-c 186-Cheetah app. 189-Simonson-s/Ordway-a begin. 190-Diana's new look. 195-Rucka-s/Drew Johnson-a begin. 197-Flash-c/app. 198,199-Noto-c						3.00
200-($3.95) back-up stories in 1940s and 1960s styles; pin-ups by various						4.00
201-218,220-225: 203,204-Batman-c/app. 204-Matt Wagner-c. 212-JLA app. 214-Flash app. 215-Morales-a begins. 218-Begin $2.50-c. 220-Batman app.						3.00
219-Omac tie-in/Sacrifice pt. 4; Wonder Woman kills Max Lord; Superman app.						4.00
219-(2nd printing) Altered cover with red background						3.00
226-Last issue; flashbacks to meetings with Superman; Rucka-s/Richards-a						4.00
#1,000,000 (11/98) 853rd Century x-over; Deodato-c						3.00
Annual 1,2: 1 ('88, $1.50)-Art Adams-a. 2 ('89, $2.00, 68 pgs.)-All women artists issue; Perez-c(i)/a.						4.00
Annual 3 (1992, $2.50, 68 pgs.)-Quesada-c(p)						4.00
Annual 4 (1995, $3.50)-Year One						4.00
Annual 5 (1996, $2.95)-Legends of the Dead Earth story; Byrne scripts; Cockrum-a						4.00
Annual 6 (1997, $3.95)-Pulp Heroes						4.00
Annual 7,8 ('98,'99, $2.95)-7-Ghosts; Wrightson-c. 8-JLApe, A.Adams-c						4.00
...: Beauty and the Beasts TPB (2005, $19.95) r/#15-19 & Action Comics #600						20.00
...: Bitter Rivals TPB (2004, $13.95) r/#200-205; Jones-c						14.00
...: Challenge of the Gods TPB ('04, $19.95) r/#8-14; Pérez-s/a						20.00
...: Destiny Calling TPB (2006, $19.99) r/#20-24 & Annual #1; Pérez-c & pin-up gallery						20.00
...Donna Troy (6/98, $1.95) Girlfrenzy; Jimenez-a						3.00
...: Down To Earth TPB (2004, $14.95) r/#195-200; Greg Land-c						15.00
... 80-Page Giant 1 (2002, $4.95) reprints in format of 1960s' 80-Page Giants						5.00
...: Eyes of the Gorgon TPB ('05, $19.99) r/#206-213						20.00
Gallery (1996, $3.50)-Bolland-c; pin-ups by various						4.00
...: Gods and Mortals TPB ('04, $19.95) r/#1-7; Pérez-a						20.00
...: Gods of Gotham TPB ('01, $5.95) r/#164-167; Jimenez-s/a						6.00
...: Land of the Dead TPB ('06, $12.99) r/#214-217 & Flash #219						13.00
Lifelines TPB ('98, $9.95) r/#106-112; Byrne-c/a						10.00
...: Mission's End TPB ('06, $19.99) r/#218-226; cover gallery						20.00
...: Our Worlds at War (10/01, $2.95) History of the Amazons; Jae Lee-c						3.00
...: Paradise Found TPB ('03, $14.95) r/#171-177, Secret Files #3; Jimenez-s/a						15.00
...: Paradise Lost TPB ('02, $14.95) r/#164-170; Jimenez-s/a						15.00
Plus 1 (1/97, $2.95)-Jesse Quick-c/app.						4.00
Second Genesis TPB (1997, $9.95)-r/#101-105						10.00
Secret Files 1-3 (3/98, 7/99, 5/02; $4.95)						5.00
Special 1 (1992, $1.75, 52 pgs.)-Deathstroke-c/story continued in Wonder Woman #63						5.00
...: The Blue Amazon (2003, $6.95) Elseworlds; McKeever-a						7.00
The Challenge Of Artemis TPB (1996, $9.95)-r/#94-100; Deodato-c/a						10.00
...: The Once and Future Story (1998, $4.95) Trina Robbins-s/Doran & Guice-a						5.00

NOTE: ***Art Adams*** *a-Annual 1.* ***Byrne*** *c/a 101-107.* ***Bolton*** *a-Annual 1.* ***Deodato*** *a-85-100.* ***Perez*** *a-Annual 1; c-Annual 1(i).* ***Quesada*** *c(p)-Annual 3.*

Wonder Woman (2011 series) #7 © DC

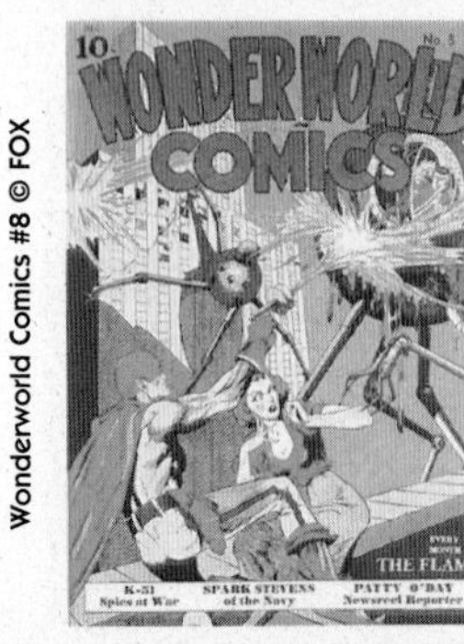

Wonderworld Comics #8 © FOX

Woody Woodpecker #34 © Walter Lantz

	GD 2.0	VG 4.0	FN 6.0	VF 8.0	VF/NM 9.0	NM- 9.2

WONDER WOMAN (Also see Amazons Attack mini-series)
DC Comics: Aug, 2006 - No. 44, Jul, 2010; No. 600, Aug, 2010 - No. 614, Oct, 2011 ($2.99)

1-Donna Troy as Wonder Woman after Infinite Crisis; Heinberg-s/Dodson-a/c 3.00
1-Variant-c by Adam Kubert 4.00
2-44: 2-4-Giganta & Hercules app. 6-Jodi Picoult-s begins. 8-Hippolyta returns. 9-12-Amazons Attack tie-in; JLA app. 14-17-Simone-s/Dodson-a/c. 20-23-Stalker app. 26-33-Rise of the Olympian. 40,41-Power Girl app. 3.00
14-DC Nation Convention giveaway edition 6.00
(Title re-numbered after #44, July 2010 to cumilative numbering of #600)
600-(8/10, $4.99) Short stories and pin-ups by various incl. Pérez, Conner, Kramer, Jim Lee; intro. by Lynda Carter; debut of new costume; cover by Pérez 5.00
600-Variant cover by Adam Hughes 8.00
600-2nd printing with new costume cover by Don Kramer 5.00
601-614: 601-606-Kramer-a; two covers by Kramer and Garner. 608-Borges-a 3.00
... Annual 1 (11/07, $3.99) Story cont'd from #4; Heinberg-s/Dodson-a/c; back-up Frank-a 4.00
...: Contagion SC (2010, $14.99) r/#40-44 15.00
...: Ends of the Earth HC (2009, $24.99) r/#20-25 25.00
...: Ends of the Earth SC (2010, $14.99) r/#20-25 15.00
...: Love and Murder HC (2007, $19.99) r/#6-10 20.00
...: Odyssey Volume One HC (2011, $22.99) r/#600-606; afterwords by Jim Lee & JMS 23.00
...: Rise of the Olympian HC (2009, $24.99) r/#26-33 & pages from DC Universe #0 25.00
...: Rise of the Olympian SC (2009, $14.99) r/#26-33 & pages from DC Universe #0 15.00
...: The Circle HC (2008, $24.99) r/#14-19; Mercedes Lackey intro.;Dodson sketch pages 25.00
...: The Circle SC (2009, $14.99) r/#14-19; Mercedes Lackey intro.;Dodson sketch pages 15.00
...: Warkiller SC (2010, $14.99) r/#34-39 15.00
...: Who is Wonder Woman? HC (2007, $19.99) r/#1-4 & Annual #1; Vaughan intro. 20.00
...: Who is Wonder Woman? SC (2009, $14.99) r/#1-4 & Annual #1; Vaughan intro. 15.00

WONDER WOMAN (DC New 52)
DC Comics: Nov, 2011 - Present ($2.99)

1-7: 1-4-Azzarello-s/Chiang-a/c. 5,6-Akins-a 3.00

WONDER WOMAN: AMAZONIA
DC Comics: 1997 ($7.95, Graphic Album format, one shot)

1-Elseworlds; Messner-Loebs-s/Winslade-a 8.00

WONDER WOMAN SPECTACULAR (See DC Special Series #9)

WONDER WOMAN: SPIRIT OF TRUTH
DC Comics: Nov, 2001 ($9.95, treasury size, one-shot)

nn-Painted art by Alex Ross; story by Alex Ross and Paul Dini 10.00

WONDER WOMAN: THE HIKETEIA
DC Comics: 2002 ($24.95, hardcover, one-shot)

nn-Wonder Woman battles Batman; Greg Rucka-s/J.G. Jones-a 25.00
Softcover (2003, $17.95) 18.00

WONDERWORLD COMICS (Formerly Wonder Comics)
Fox Features Syndicate: No. 3, July, 1939 - No. 33, Jan, 1942

	GD 2.0	VG 4.0	FN 6.0	VF 8.0	VF/NM 9.0	NM- 9.2
3-Intro The Flame by Fine; Dr. Fung (Powell-a), K-51 (Powell-a?), & Yarko the Great, Master Magician (Eisner-a) continues; Eisner/Fine-c	730	1460	2190	5329	9415	13,500
4-Lou Fine-c	343	686	1029	2400	4200	6000
5,6,9,10: Lou Fine-c	200	400	600	1280	2190	3100
7-Classic Lou Fine-c	343	686	1029	2400	4200	6000
8-Classic Lou Fine-c	300	600	900	1950	3375	4800
11-Origin The Flame	155	310	465	992	1696	2400
12-15:13-Dr. Fung ends; last Fine-c(p)	126	252	378	806	1378	1950
16-20	87	174	261	553	952	1350
21-Origin The Black Lion & Cub	81	162	243	518	884	1250
22-27: 22,25-Dr. Fung app.	63	126	189	403	689	975
28-Origin & 1st app. U.S. Jones (8/41); Lu-Nar, the Moon Man begins	87	174	261	553	952	1350
29,31,33	53	106	159	334	567	800
30-Intro & Origin Flame Girl	92	184	276	584	1005	1425
32-Hitler-c	94	188	282	597	1024	1450

NOTE: *Spies at War by* ***Eisner*** *in #13, 17. Yarko by* ***Eisner*** *in #3-11.* ***Eisner*** *text illos-3.* ***Lou Fine*** *a-3-11; c-3-13, 15(i); text illos-4.* ***Nordling*** *a-4-14.* ***Powell*** *a-3-12.* ***Tuska*** *a-5-9. Bondage-c 14, 15, 28, 31, 32. Cover features: The Flame-#3, 5-31; U.S. Jones-#32, 33.*

WONDERWORLDS
Innovation Publishing: 1992 ($3.50, squarebound, 100 pgs.)

1-Rebound super-hero comics, contents may vary; Hero Alliance, Terraformers, etc. 5.00

WOODSY OWL (See March of Comics #395)
Gold Key: Nov, 1973 - No. 10, Feb, 1976 (Some Whitman printings exist)

	GD 2.0	VG 4.0	FN 6.0	VF 8.0	VF/NM 9.0	NM- 9.2
1	2	4	6	13	18	22
2-10	2	4	6	8	10	12

WOODY WOODPECKER (Walter Lantz... #73 on?)(See Dell Giants for annuals)
(Also see The Funnies, Jolly Jingles, Kite Fun Book, New Funnies)
Dell Publishing Co./Gold Key No. 73-187/Whitman No. 188 on:
No. 169, 10/47 - No. 72, 5-7/62; No. 73, 10/62 - No. 201, 3/84 (nn 192)

	GD 2.0	VG 4.0	FN 6.0	VF 8.0	VF/NM 9.0	NM- 9.2
Four Color 169(#1)-Drug turns Woody into a Mr. Hyde	15	30	45	104	227	350
Four Color 188	11	22	33	71	136	200
Four Color 202,232,249,264,288	8	16	24	56	96	135
Four Color 305,336,350	6	12	18	41	66	90
Four Color 364,374,390,405,416,431('52)	5	10	15	35	55	75
16 (12-1/52-53) - 30('55)	4	8	12	28	44	60
31-50	4	8	12	22	34	45
51-72 (Last Dell)	3	6	9	18	27	35
73-75 (Giants, 84 pgs., Gold Key)	5	10	15	32	51	70
76-80	3	6	9	16	22	28
81-103: 103-Last 12¢ issue	3	6	9	14	19	24
104-120	2	4	6	11	16	20
121-140	2	4	6	9	12	15
141-160	1	3	4	6	8	10
161-187	1	2	3	5	7	9
188,189 (Whitman)	2	4	6	9	13	16
190(9/80),191(11/80)-pre-pack only	4	8	12	22	34	45
(No #192)						
193-197: 196(2/82), 197(4/82)	2	4	6	11	16	20
198-201 (All #90062 on-c, no date or date code, pre-pack): 198(6/83), 199(7/83), 200(8/83), 201(3/84)	3	6	9	16	22	28
Christmas Parade 1(11/68-Giant)(G.K.)	4	8	12	26	41	55
Summer Fun 1(6/66-G.K.)(84 pgs.)	5	10	15	30	48	65
nn (1971, 60¢, 100 pgs. digest) B&W one page gags	3	6	9	17	25	32

NOTE: *15¢ Canadian editions of the 12¢ issues exist. Reprints-No. 92, 102, 103, 105, 106, 124, 125, 152, 153, 157, 162, 165, 194(1/3)-200(1/3).*

WOODY WOODPECKER (See Comic Album #5,9,13, Dell Giant #24, 40, 54, Dell Giants, The Funnies, Golden Comics Digest #1, 3, 5, 8, 15, 16, 20, 24, 32, 37, 44, March of Comics #16, 34, 85, 93, 109, 124, 139, 158, 177, 184, 203, 222, 239, 249, 261, 420, 454, 466, 478, New Funnies & Super Book #12, 24)

WOODY WOODPECKER
Harvey Comics: Sept, 1991 - No. 15, Aug, 1994 ($1.25)

1-15: 1-r/W.W. #53 3.00
50th Anniversary Special 1 (10/91, $2.50, 68 pgs.) 4.00

WOODY WOODPECKER AND FRIENDS
Harvey Comics: Dec, 1991 - No. 4, 1992 ($1.25)

1-4 3.00

WORD WARRIORS (Also see Quest for Dreams Lost)
Literacy Volunteers of Chicago: 1987 ($1.50, B&W)(Proceeds donated to help literacy)

1-Jon Sable by Grell, Ms. Tree, Streetwolf; Chaykin-c 3.00

WORLD AROUND US, THE (Illustrated Story of...)
Gilberton Publishers (Classics Illustrated): Sep, 1958 -No. 36, Oct, 1961 (25¢)

	GD 2.0	VG 4.0	FN 6.0	VF 8.0	VF/NM 9.0	NM- 9.2
1-Dogs; Evans-a	9	18	27	52	69	85
2-4: 2-Indians; Check-a. 3-Horses; L. B. Cole-c. 4-Railroads; L. B. Cole-a (5 pgs.)	9	18	27	47	61	75
5-Space; Ingels-a	10	20	30	56	76	95
6-The F.B.I.; Disbrow, Evans, Ingels-a	10	20	30	56	76	95
7-Pirates; Disbrow, Ingels, Kinstler-a	9	18	27	52	69	85
8-Flight; Evans, Ingels, Crandall-a	9	18	27	52	69	85
9-Army; Disbrow, Ingels, Orlando-a	9	18	27	47	61	75
10-13: 10-Navy; Disbrow, Kinstler-a. 11-Marine Corps. 12-Coast Guard; Ingels-a (9 pgs.). 13-Air Force; L.B. Cole-c	9	18	27	47	61	75
14-French Revolution; Crandall, Evans, Kinstler-a	10	20	30	56	76	95
15-Prehistoric Animals; Al Williamson-a, 6 & 10 pgs. plus Morrow-a	10	20	30	58	79	100
16-18: 16-Crusades; Kinstler-a. 17-Festivals; Evans, Crandall-a. 18-Great Scientists; Crandall, Evans, Torres, Williamson, Morrow-a	9	18	27	52	69	85
19-Jungle; Crandall, Williamson, Morrow-a	10	20	30	58	79	100
20-Communications; Crandall, Evans, Torres-a	10	20	30	56	76	95
21-American Presidents; Crandall/Evans, Morrow-a	10	20	30	56	76	95
22-Boating; Morrow-a	8	16	24	44	57	70
23-Great Explorers; Crandall, Evans-a	9	18	27	52	69	85
24-Ghosts; Morrow, Evans-a	10	20	30	56	76	95
25-Magic; Evans, Morrow-a	10	20	30	56	76	95
26-The Civil War	11	22	33	62	86	110
27-Mountains (High Advs.); Crandall/Evans, Morrow, Torres-a	9	18	27	52	69	85

28-Whaling; Crandall, Evans, Morrow, Torres, Wildey-a; L.B. Cole-c

World of Archie #18 © AP

World of Mystery #5 © MAR

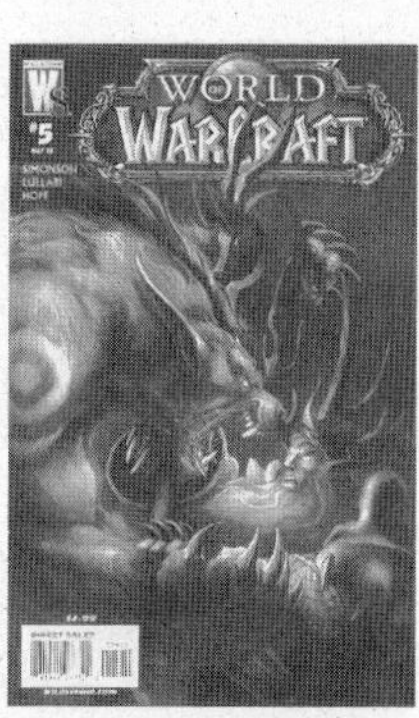

World of Warcraft #5 © Blizzard Ent.

GD VG FN VF VF/NM NM-
2.0 4.0 6.0 8.0 9.0 9.2

9 18 27 52 69 85
29-Vikings; Crandall, Evans, Torres, Morrow-a 10 20 30 58 79 100
30-Undersea Adventure; Crandall/Evans, Kirby, Morrow, Torres-a
10 20 30 56 76 95
31-Hunting; Crandall/Evans, Ingels, Kinstler, Kirby-a 9 18 27 52 69 85
32,33: 32-For Gold & Glory; Morrow, Kirby, Crandall, Evans-a. 33-Famous Teens;
Torres, Crandall, Evans-a 9 18 27 52 69 85
34-36: 34-Fishing; Crandall/Evans-a. 35-Spies; Kirby, Morrow?, Evans-a.
36-Fight for Life (Medicine); Kirby-a 9 18 27 52 69 85
NOTE: See Classics Illustrated Special Edition. Another *World Around Us* issue entitled *The Sea* had been prepared in 1962 but was never published in the U.S. It was published in the British/European *World Around Us* series. Those series then continued with seven additional WAU titles not in the U.S. series.

WORLD BELOW, THE
Dark Horse Comics: Mar, 1999 - No. 4, Jun, 1999 ($2.50, limited series)
1-4-Paul Chadwick-s/c/a 3.00
TPB (1/07, $12.95) r/#1-4; intro. by Chadwick; gallery of sketches and covers 13.00

WORLD BELOW, THE: DEEPER AND STRANGER
Dark Horse Comics: Dec, 1999 - No. 4, Mar, 2000 ($2.95, B&W)
1-4-Paul Chadwick-s/c/a 3.00

WORLD FAMOUS HEROES MAGAZINE
Comic Corp. of America (Centaur): Oct, 1941 - No. 4, Apr, 1942 (comic book)
1-Gustavson-c; Lubbers, Glanzman-a; Davy Crockett, Paul Revere, Lewis & Clark,
John Paul Jones stories; Flag-c 113 226 339 718 1234 1750
2-Lou Gehrig life story; Lubbers-a 48 96 144 302 514 725
3,4-Lubbers-a. 4-Wild Bill Hickok story; 2 pg. Marlene Dietrich story
45 90 135 284 480 675

WORLD FAMOUS STORIES
Croyden Publishers: 1945
1-Ali Baba, Hansel & Gretel, Rip Van Winkle, Mid-Summer Night's Dream
14 28 42 76 108 140

WORLD IS HIS PARISH, THE
George A. Pflaum: 1953 (15¢)
nn-The story of Pope Pius XII 6 12 18 31 38 45

WORLD OF ADVENTURE (Walt Disney's...)(TV)
Gold Key: Apr, 1963 - No. 3, Oct, 1963 (12¢)
1-Disney TV characters; Savage Sam, Johnny Shiloh, Capt. Nemo, The Mooncussers
3 6 9 21 32 42
2,3 3 6 9 15 21 26

WORLD OF ARCHIE, THE (See Archie Giant Series Mag. #148, 151, 156, 160, 165, 171, 177, 182, 188, 193, 200, 208, 213, 225, 232, 237, 244, 249, 456, 461, 468, 473, 480, 485, 492, 497, 504, 509, 516, 521, 532, 543, 554, 565, 574, 587, 599, 612, 627)

WORLD OF ARCHIE
Archie Comics: Aug, 1992 - No. 22 ($1.25/$1.50)
1 4.00
2-15: 9-Neon ink-c 3.00
16-22 3.00

WORLD OF ARCHIE DOUBLE DIGEST MAGAZINE
Archie Comics: Dec, 2010 - Present ($3.99)
1-18: 5-Reprints Tiny Titans/Little Archie #1-3 with sketch pages. 17-Archie babies 4.00

WORLD OF FANTASY
Atlas Comics (CPC No. 1-15/ZPC No. 16-19): May, 1956 - No. 19, Aug, 1959
1 50 100 150 315 533 750
2-Williamson-a (4 pgs.) 32 64 96 192 314 435
3-Sid Check, Roussos-a 29 58 87 170 278 385
4-7 23 46 69 136 223 310
8-Matt Fox, Orlando, Berg-a 25 50 75 147 241 335
9-Krigstein-a 23 26 39 136 223 310
10-15: 10-Colan-a. 11-Torres-a 20 40 60 117 189 260
16-Williamson-a (4 pgs.); Ditko, Kirby-a 30 60 90 177 289 400
17-19-Ditko, Kirby-a 30 60 90 177 289 400
NOTE: ***Ayers** a-3. **B. Baily** a-4. **Berg** a-5, 6, 8. **Brodsky** c-3. **Check** a-3. **Ditko** a-17, 19. **Everett** a-2; c-4-7, 9, 12, 13. **Forte** a-4, 8. **Infantino** a-14. **Kirby** c-15, 17-19. **Krigstein** a-9. **Maneely** c-2, 14. **Mooney** a-14. **Morrow** a-7. **Orlando** a-8, 13, 14. **Pakula** a-9. **Powell** a-4, 6. **Reinman** a-8, 10. **R.Q. Sale** a-3, 7, 9, 10. **Severin** c-1.*

WORLD OF GIANT COMICS, THE (See Archie All-Star Specials under Archie Comics)

WORLD OF GINGER FOX, THE (Also see Ginger Fox)
Comico: Nov, 1986 ($6.95, 8 1/2 x 11", 68 pgs., mature)
Graphic Novel ($6.95) 7.00
Hardcover ($27.95) 28.00

WORLD OF JUGHEAD, THE (See Archie Giant Series Mag. #9, 14, 19, 24, 30, 136, 143, 149, 152, 157, 161, 166, 172, 178, 183, 189, 194, 202, 209, 215, 227, 233, 239, 245, 251, 457, 463, 469, 475, 481, 487, 493, 499, 505, 511, 517, 523, 531, 542, 553, 564, 577, 590, 602)

WORLD OF KRYPTON, THE (World of...#3) (See Superman #248)
DC Comics, Inc.: 7/79 - No. 3, 9/79; 12/87 - No. 4, 3/88 (Both are lim. series)
1-3 (1979, 40¢; 1st comic book mini-series): 1-Jor-El marries Lara. 3-Baby Superman
sent to Earth; Krypton explodes; Mon-el app. 1 2 3 5 6 8
1-4 (75¢)-Byrne scripts; Byrne/Simonson-c 4.00

WORLD OF METROPOLIS, THE
DC Comics: Aug, 1988 - No. 4, July, 1988 ($1.00, limited series)
1-4: Byrne scripts 4.00

WORLD OF MYSTERY
Atlas Comics (GPI): June, 1956 - No. 7, July, 1957
1-Torres, Orlando-a; Powell-a? 48 96 144 302 514 725
2-Woodish-a 21 42 63 124 202 280
3-Torres, Davis, Ditko-a 24 48 72 144 237 330
4-Pakula, Powell-a 24 48 72 144 237 330
5,7: 5-Orlando-a 20 40 60 120 195 270
6-Williamson/Mayo-a (4 pgs.); Ditko-a; Colan-a; Crandall text illo
24 48 72 144 237 330
NOTE: ***Ayers** a-4. **Brodsky** c-2, 5, 6. **Colan** a-6, 7. **Everett** c-1, 3. **Pakula** a-4, 6. **Romita** a-2. **Severin** c-7.*

WORLD OF SMALLVILLE
DC Comics: Apr, 1988 - No. 4, July, 1988 (75¢, limited series)
1-4: Byrne scripts 4.00

WORLD OF SUSPENSE
Atlas News Co.: Apr, 1956 - No. 8, July, 1957
1 42 84 126 265 445 625
2-Ditko-a (4 pgs.) 24 48 72 144 237 330
3,7-Williamson-a in both (4 pgs.); #7-with Mayo 24 48 72 140 230 320
4-6,8 20 40 60 120 195 270
NOTE: ***Berg** a-6. **Cameron** a-2. **Ditko** a-2. **Drucker** a-1. **Everett** a-1, 5; c-6. **Heck** a-5. **Maneely** a-1; c-1-3. **Orlando** a-5. **Powell** a-6. **Reinman** a-4. **Roussos** a-6. **Shores** a-1.*

WORLD OF WARCRAFT (Based on the Blizzard Entertainment video game)
DC Comics (WildStorm): Jan, 2008 - No. 25, Jan, 2010 ($2.99)
1-Walt Simonson-s/Lullabi-a; cover by Samwise Didier 8.00
1-Variant cover by Jim Lee 12.00
1,2-Second printing with Jim Lee sketch cover 5.00
2-Two covers by Jim Lee and Samwise Didier 5.00
3-24: 3-14-Two covers on each 3.00
25-($3.99) Walt & Louise Simonson-s 4.00
... Special 1 (2/10, $3.99) Costa-s/Mhan-a/c 4.00
... Book One HC (2008, $19.99, dustjacket) r/#1-7; intro. by Chris Metzen of Blizzard 20.00
... Book One SC (2009, $14.99) r/#1-7; intro. by Chris Metzen of Blizzard 15.00
... Book Two HC (2009, $19.99, dustjacket) r/#8-14 20.00
... Book Two SC (2010, $14.99) r/#8-14 15.00
... Book Three HC (2010, $19.99, dustjacket) r/#15-21 20.00
... Book Three SC (2011, $17.99) r/#15-21 18.00

WORLD OF WARCRAFT: ASHBRINGER
DC Comics (WildStorm): Nov, 2008 - No. 4, Feb, 2009 ($3.99)
1-4-Neilson-s/Lullabi & Washington-a; 2 covers by Robinson & Lullabi 4.00
TPB (2010, $14.99) r/#1-4 15.00

WORLD OF WARCRAFT: CURSE OF THE WORGEN
DC Comics (WildStorm #1,2): Jan, 2011 - No. 5, May, 2011 ($3.99/$2.99)
1,2-($3.99) Neilson & Waugh-s/Lullabi & Washington-a; Polidora-c 4.00
3-5-($2.99) 3.00

WORLD OF WHEELS (Formerly Dragstrip Hotrodders)
Charlton Comics: No. 17, Oct, 1967 - No. 32, June, 1970
17-20-Features Ken King 3 6 9 18 27 35
21-32-Features Ken King 3 6 9 16 22 28
Modern Comics Reprint 23(1978) 6.00

WORLD OF WOOD
Eclipse Comics: 1986 - No. 4, 1987; No. 5, 2/89 ($1.75, limited series)
1,2: 1-Dave Stevens-c. 2-Wood/Stevens-c 1 2 3 4 5 7
3-5: 5-($2.00, B&W)-r/Avon's Flying Saucers 5.00

WORLD'S BEST COMICS
DC Comics: Feb 1940
nn - Ashcan comic, not distributed to newsstands, only for in-house use. Cover art is Action Comics #29 with interior being Action Comics #24. One copy sold for $21,000 in 2000.

World's Finest Comics #53 © DC

World's Finest Comics #172 © DC

World's Finest Comics #258 © DC

	GD	VG	FN	VF	VF/NM	NM-
	2.0	4.0	6.0	8.0	9.0	9.2

WORLD'S BEST COMICS (World's Finest Comics #2 on)
National Per. Publications (100 pgs.): Spring, 1941 (Cardboard-c)(DC's 6th annual format comic)

1-The Batman, Superman, Crimson Avenger, Johnny Thunder, The King, Young Dr. Davis, Zatara, Lando, Man of Magic, & Red, White & Blue begin; Superman, Batman & Robin covers begin (inside-c is blank); Fred Ray-c; 15¢ cover price 1475 2950 4425 10,400 17,700 25,000

WORLD'S BEST COMICS: GOLDEN AGE SAMPLER
DC Comics: 2003 (99¢, one-shot, samples from DC Archive editions)

1-Golden Age reprints from Superman #6, Batman #5, Sensation #11, Police #11 3.00

WORLD'S BEST COMICS: SILVER AGE SAMPLER
DC Comics: 2004 (99¢, one-shot, samples from DC Archive editions)

1-Silver Age reprints from Justice League #4, Adventure #247, Our Army at War #81 3.00

WORLDS BEYOND (Stories of Weird Adventure)(Worlds of Fear #2 on)
Fawcett Publications: Nov, 1951

1-Powell, Bailey-a; Moldoff-c 54 108 162 343 574 825

WORLDS COLLIDE
DC Comics: July, 1994 ($2.50, one-shot)

1-($2.50, 52 pgs.)-Milestone & Superman titles x-over 4.00
1-($3.95, 52 pgs.)-Polybagged w/vinyl clings 5.00

WORLD'S FAIR COMICS (See New York...)

WORLD'S FINEST (Also see Legends of The World's Finest)
DC Comics: 1990 - No. 3, 1990 ($3.95, squarebound, limited series, 52 pgs.)

1-3: Batman & Superman team-up against The Joker and Lex Luthor; Dave Gibbons scripts & Steve Rude-c/a. 2,3-Joker/Luthor painted-c by Steve Rude 5.00
TPB-(1992, $19.95) r/#1-3; Gibbons intro. 20.00
...: The Deluxe Edition HC (2008, $29.99) r/#1-3; Gibbons intro. from 1992; Gibbons story outline and sketches; Rude sketch pages and notes 30.00

WORLD'S FINEST
DC Comics: Dec, 2009 - No. 4, Mar, 2010 ($2.99, limited series)

1-4: Gates-s/two covers by Noto on each. 3-Supergirl/Batgirl team up. 4-Noto-a 3.00
TPB (2010, $14.99) r/#1-4, Action Comics #865 & DC Comics Presents #31 15.00

WORLD'S FINEST COMICS (Formerly World's Best Comics #1)
National Periodical Publ./DC Comics: No. 2, Sum, 1941 - No. 323, Jan, 1986 (#1-17 have cardboard covers) (#2-9 have 100 pgs.)

2 (100 pgs.)-Superman, Batman & Robin covers continue from World's Best; (cover price 15¢ #2-70) 423 846 1269 3000 5250 7500
3-The Sandman begins; last Johnny Thunder; origin & 1st app. The Scarecrow 320 640 960 2240 3920 5600
4-Hop Harrigan app.; last Young Dr. Davis 245 490 735 1568 2684 3800
5-Intro. TNT & Dan the Dyna-Mite; last King & Crimson Avenger 245 490 735 1568 2684 3800
6-Star Spangled Kid begins (Sum/42); Aquaman app.; S&K Sandman with Sandy in new costume begins, ends #7 181 362 543 1158 1979 2800
7-Green Arrow begins (Fall/42); last Lando & Red, White & Blue; S&K art 184 368 552 1168 2009 2850
8-Boy Commandos begin (by Simon(p) #12); last The King; includes "Minute Man Answers the Call" promo 171 342 513 1086 1868 2650
9-Batman cameo in Star Spangled Kid; S&K-a; last 100 pg. issue; Hitler, Mussolini, Tojo-c 213 426 639 1363 2332 3300
10-S&K-a; 76 pg. issues begin 161 322 483 1030 1765 2500
11-17: 17-Last cardboard cover issue 135 270 405 864 1482 2100
18-20: 18-Paper covers begin; last Star Spangled Kid. 19-Joker story. 20-Last quarterly issue 129 258 387 826 1413 2000
21-30: 21-Begin bi-monthly. 30-Johnny Everyman app. 89 178 267 565 970 1375
31-40: 33-35-Tomahawk app. 35-Penguin app. 84 168 252 538 919 1300
41-43,45-50: 41-Boy Commandos end. 42-The Wyoming Kid begins (9-10/49), ends #63. 43-Full Steam Foley begins, ends #48. 48-Last square binding. 49-Tom Sparks, Boy Inventor begins; robot-c 74 148 222 470 810 1150
44-Used in SOTI, ref. to Batman & Robin being gay, and a cop being shot in the face 77 154 231 493 847 1200
51-60: 51-Zatara ends. 54-Last 76 pg. issue. 59-Manhunters Around the World begins (7-8/52), ends #62 71 142 213 454 777 1100
61-64: 61-Joker story. 63-Capt. Compass app. 69 138 207 442 759 1075
65-Origin Superman; Tomahawk begins (7-8/53), ends #101 97 194 291 621 1061 1500
66-70-(15¢ issues, scarce)-Last 15¢, 68pg. issue 74 148 222 470 810 1150
71-(10¢ issue, scarce)-Superman & Batman begin as team (7-8/54); were in separate stories until now; Superman & Batman exchange identities; 10¢ issues begin 161 322 483 1030 1765 2500
72,73-(10¢ issue, scarce) 103 206 309 659 1130 1600
74-Last pre-code issue 73 146 219 467 796 1125
75-(1st code approved, 3-4/55) 71 142 213 454 777 1100
76-80: 77-Superman loses powers & Batman obtains them 55 110 165 352 601 850
81-90: 84-1st S.A. issue. 88-1st Joker/Luthor team-up. 89-2nd Batmen of All Nations (aka Club of Heroes). 90-Batwoman's 1st app. in World's Finest (10/57, 3rd app. anywhere) plus-c app. 27 54 81 196 423 650
91-93,95-99: 96-99-Kirby Green Arrow. 99-Robot-c 21 42 63 146 311 475
94-Origin Superman/Batman team retold 48 96 144 389 845 1300
100 (3/59) 32 64 96 232 504 775
101-110: 102-Tommy Tomorrow begins, ends #124 13 26 39 90 195 300
111-121: 111-1st app. The Clock King. 113-Intro. Miss Arrowette in Green Arrow; 1st Bat-Mite/Mr. Mxyzptlk team-up (11/60). 117-Batwoman-c. 121-Last 10¢ issue 12 24 36 79 160 240
122-128: 123-2nd Bat-Mite/Mr. Mxyzptlk team-up (2/62). 125-Aquaman begins (5/62), ends #139 (Aquaman #1 is dated 1-2/62) 10 20 30 68 127 185
129-Joker/Luthor team-up-c/story 11 22 33 76 151 225
130-142: 135-Last Dick Sprang story. 140-Last Green Arrow. 142-Origin The Composite Superman (villain); Legion app. 9 18 27 58 99 140
143-150: 143-1st Mailbag. 144-Clayface/Brainiac team-up. 148-Clayface/Luthor team-up; last Clayface until Action #443 7 14 21 49 82 115
151-153,155,157-160: 157-2nd Super Sons story; last app. Kathy Kane (Bat-Woman) until Batman Family #10; 1st Bat-Mite Jr. 6 12 18 41 66 90
154-1st Super Sons story; last Bat-Woman in costume until Batman Family #10. 7 14 21 44 72 100
156-1st Bizarro Batman; Joker-c/story 10 20 30 65 118 170
161,170 (80-Pg. Giants G-28,G-40) 7 14 21 46 76 105
162-165,167,168,171,172: 168,172-Adult Legion app. 5 10 15 35 55 75
166-Joker-c/story 6 12 18 41 66 90
169-3rd app. new Batgirl(9/67)(cover and 1 panel cameo); 3rd Bat-Mite/Mr. Mxyzptlk team-up 5 10 15 41 66 90
173-('68)-1st S.A. app. Two-Face as Batman becomes Two-Face in story 9 18 27 61 106 150
174-Adams-c 6 12 18 37 59 80
175,176-Neal Adams-c/a; both reprint J'onn J'onzz origin/Detective #225,226 6 12 18 41 66 90
177-Joker/Luthor team-up-c/story 6 12 18 41 66 90
178-(9/68) Intro. of Super Nova (revived in "52" weekly series); Adams-c 6 12 18 42 69 95
179-(80 Page Giant G-52) -Adams-c; r/#94 6 12 18 42 69 95
180,182,183,185,186: Adams-c on all. 182-Silent Knight-r/Brave & Bold #6. 185-Last 12¢ issue. 186-Johnny Quick-r 4 8 12 28 44 60
181,184,187: 187-Green Arrow origin-r by Kirby (Adv. #256) 4 8 12 24 37 50
188,197:(Giants G-64,G-76; 64 pages) 6 12 18 39 62 85
189-196: 190-193-Robin-r 3 6 9 21 32 42
198,199-3rd Superman/Flash race (see Flash #175 & Superman #199). 199-Adams-c 10 20 30 64 115 165
200-Adams-c 4 8 12 26 41 55
201-203: 203-Last 15¢ issue. 3 6 9 19 29 38
204,205-(52 pgs.) Adams-c: 204-Wonder Woman app. 205-Shining Knight-r (6 pgs.) by Frazetta/Adv. #153; Teen Titans x-over 4 8 12 22 34 45
206 (Giant G-88, 64 pgs.) 5 10 15 32 51 70
207,212-(52 pgs.) 3 6 9 21 32 42
208-211(25¢-c) Adams-c: 208-(52 pgs.) Origin Robotman-r/Det. #138. 209-211-(52 pgs.) 4 8 12 22 34 45
213,214,216-222,229: 217-Metamorpho begins, ends #220; Batman/Superman team-ups resume. 229-r/origin Superman-Batman team 2 4 6 13 18 22
215-(12/72-1/73) Intro. Batman Jr. & Superman Jr. (see Superman/Batman: Saga of the Super Sons TPB for all the Super Sons stories) 3 6 9 19 29 38
223-228-(100 pgs.). 223-N. Adams-r. 223-Deadman origin. 226-N. Adams, S&K, Toth-r; Manhunter part origin-r/Det. #225,226. 227-Deadman app. 5 10 15 32 51 70
230-(68 pgs.) 3 6 9 18 27 35
231-243: 231, 233, 238, 242-Super Sons 2 4 6 9 13 16
244-246-Adams-c: 244-$1.00, 84 pg. issues begin; Green Arrow, Black Canary, Wonder Woman, Vigilante begin; 246-Death of Stuff in Vigilante; origin Vigilante retold 3 6 9 14 20 26
247-252 (84 pgs.): 248-Last Vigilante. 249-The Creeper begins by Ditko, 84 pgs. 250-The Creeper origin retold by Ditko. 252-Last 84 pg. issue

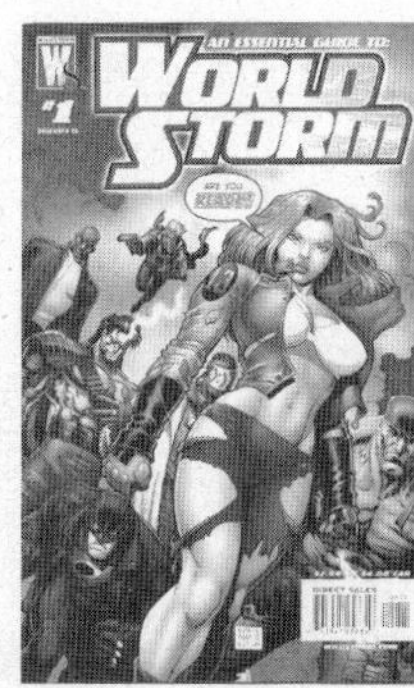

WorldStorm #1 © WSP

World War Hulk: X-Men #1 © MAR

The Worst From Mad #11 © EC

GD 2.0 VG 4.0 FN 6.0 VF 8.0 VF/NM 9.0 NM- 9.2

2 4 6 13 18 22
253-257,259-265: 253-Capt. Marvel begins; 68 pgs. begin, end #265. 255-Last Creeper. 256-Hawkman begins. 257-Black Lightning begins. 263-Super Sons. 264-Clay Face app. 2 4 6 8 11 14
258-Adams-c 2 4 6 10 14 18
266-270,272-282-(52 pgs.). 267-Challengers of the Unknown app.; 3 Lt. Marvels return. 268-Capt. Marvel Jr. origin retold. 274-Zatanna begins. 279, 280-Capt. Marvel Jr. & Kid Eternity learn they are brothers 1 3 4 6 8 10
271-(52pgs.) Origin Superman/Batman team retold 2 4 6 8 10 12
283-299: 284-Legion app. 1 2 3 4 5 7
300-($1.25, 52pgs.)-Justice League of America, New Teen Titans & The Outsiders app.; Perez-a (4 pgs.) 1 2 3 5 7 9
301-322: 304-Origin Null and Void. 309,319-Free 16 pg. story in each (309-Flash Force 2000, 319-Mask preview) 5.00
323-Last issue 6.00
NOTE: **Neal Adams** *a-230ir; c-174-176, 178-180, 182, 183, 185, 186, 199-205, 208-211, 244-246, 258.* **Austin** *a-244-246i.* **Burnley** *a-8, 10; c-7-9, 11-14, 15p?, 16-18p, 20-31p.* **Colan** *a-274p, 297, 299.* **Ditko** *a-249-255.* **Giffen** *a-322; c-284p, 322.* **G. Kane** *a-38, 174r, 282, 283; c-281, 282, 289.* **Kirby** *a-187.* **Kubert** *Zatara-40-44.* **Miller** *c-285p.* **Mooney** *c-134.* **Morrow** *a-245-248.* **Mortimer** *c-16-21, 26-71.* **Nasser** *a(p)-244-246, 259, 260.* **Newton** *a-253-281p.* **Orlando** *a-224r.* **Perez** *a-300i; c-271, 276, 277p, 278p.* **Fred Ray** *c-1-5.* **Fred Ray/Robinson** *c-13-16.* **Robinson** *a-5, 6, 9-11, 13?, 14-16; c-6.* **Rogers** *a-259p.* **Roussos** *a-212r.* **Simonson** *c-291.* **Spiegle** *a-275-278, 284.* **Staton** *a-262p, 273p.* **Swan/Moldoff** *c-126.* **Swan/Mortimer** *c-79-82.* **Toth** *a-228r.* **Tuska** *a-230r, 250p, 252p, 254p, 257p, 283p, 284p, 308p. Boy Commandos by* **Infantino** *#39-41.*

WORLD'S FINEST COMICS DIGEST (See DC Special Series #23)

WORLD'S FINEST: OUR WORLDS AT WAR
DC Comics: Oct, 2001 ($2.95, one-shot)
1-Concludes the Our Worlds at War x-over; Jae Lee-c; art by various 3.00

WORLD'S GREATEST ATHLETE (See Walt Disney Showcase #14)

WORLD'S GREATEST SONGS
Atlas Comics (Male): Sept, 1954
1-(Scarce)-Heath & Harry Anderson-a; Eddie Fisher life story plus-c; gives lyrics to Frank Sinatra song "Young at Heart" 40 80 120 242 401 560

WORLD'S GREATEST STORIES
Jubilee Publications: Jan, 1949 - No. 2, May, 1949
1-Alice in Wonderland; Lewis Carroll adapt. 32 64 96 188 307 425
2-Pinocchio 30 60 90 177 289 400

WORLDS OF ASPEN
Aspen MLT, Inc.: 2006 - 2011 (Free Comic Book Day giveaways)
...: FCBD 2006, 2007, #3, #4 Editions; Fathom, Soulfire, Shrugged short stories; Turner-c 3.00
... 2010 (5/10) Previews Fathom, Mindfield, Soulfire, Executive Assistant: Iris and Dellec 3.00
... 2011 (5/11) Previews Fathom, Soulfire, Charismagic, Lady Mechanika & others 3.00

WORLDS OF FEAR (Stories of Weird Adventure)(Formerly Worlds Beyond #1)
Fawcett Publications: V1#2, Jan, 1952 - V2#10, June, 1953
V1#2 48 96 144 302 514 725
3-Evans-a 41 82 123 256 428 600
4-6(9/52) 39 78 117 235 385 535
V2#7,8 37 74 111 222 361 500
9-Classic drowning-c (4/53) 39 78 117 231 378 525
10-Saunders painted-c; man with no eyes surrounded by eyeballs-c plus eyes ripped out story 119 238 357 762 1306 1850
NOTE: **Moldoff** *c-2-8.* **Powell** *a-2, 4, 5.* **Sekowsky** *a-4, 5.*

WORLDSTORM
DC Comics (WildStorm): Nov, 2006 (Dec on cover) - No. 2, May, 2007 ($2.99)
1,2-Previews and pin-ups for re-launched WildStorm titles.1-Art Adams-c 3.00

WORLDS UNKNOWN
Marvel Comics Group: May, 1973 - No. 8, Aug, 1974
1-r/from Astonishing #54; Torres, Reese-a 3 6 9 16 23 30
2-8 2 4 6 11 16 20
NOTE: **Adkins/Mooney** *a-5.* **Buscema** *c/a-4p. W.* **Howard** *c/a-3i.* **Kane** *a(p)-1,2; c(p)-5, 6, 8.* **Sutton** *a-2.* **Tuska** *a(p)-7, 8; c-7p. No. 7, 8 has Golden Voyage of Sinbad movie adaptation.*

WORLD WAR HULK (See Incredible Hulk #106)
Marvel Comics: Aug, 2007 - No. 5, Jan, 2008 ($3.99, limited series)
1-Hulk returns to Earth; Iron Man and Avengers app.; Romita Jr.-a/Pak-s/Finch-c 4.00
1-Variant cover by Romita Jr. 6.00
2-5: 2-Hulk battles The Avengers and FF; Finch-c. 3,4-Dr. Strange app. 5-Sentry app. 4.00
2-5-Variant cover by Romita Jr. 6.00
...: Aftersmash 1 (1/08, $3.99) Sandoval-a/Land-c; Hercules, Iron Man app. 4.00
...: Gamma Files (2007, $3.99) profile pages of Hulk characters 4.00
...Prologue: World Breaker 1 (7/07, one-shot) Rio, Weeks, Phillips, Miyazawa-a 4.00
TPB (2008, $19.99) r/#1-5 20.00

WORLD WAR HULK AFTERSMASH: DAMAGE CONTROL
Marvel Comics: Mar, 2008 - No. 3, May, 2008 ($2.99, limited series)
1-3-The clean-up; McDuffie-s. 2-Romita- Jr.-c. 3-Romita Sr.-c 3.00

WORLD WAR HULK AFTERSMASH: WARBOUND
Marvel Comics: Feb, 2008 - No. 5, Jun, 2008 ($2.99, limited series)
1-5-Kirk & Sandoval-a/Cheung-c 3.00

WORLD WAR HULK: FRONT LINE (See Incredible Hulk #106)
Marvel Comics: Aug, 2007 - No. 6, Dec, 2007 ($2.99, limited series)
1-6-Ben Urich & Sally Floyd report World War Hulk; Jenkins-s/Bachs-a 3.00
TPB (2008, $16.99) r/#1-5 & WWH Prologue: World Breaker 17.00

WORLD WAR HULK: GAMMA CORPS
Marvel Comics: Sept, 2007 - No. 4, Jan, 2008 ($2.99, limited series)
1-4-Tieri-s/Ferreira-a/Roux-c 3.00
TPB (2008, $10.99) r/#1-4 11.00

WORLD WAR HULKS
Marvel Comics: Jun, 2010; Sept, 2010 ($3.99, one-shot & limited series)
1-Short stories by various; Deadpool app.; Romita Jr.-c 4.00
...: Spider-Man vs. Thor 1,2 (9/10 - No. 2, 9/10) Gillen-s/Molina-a 4.00
...: Wolverine vs. Captain America 1,2 (9/10 - No. 2, 9/10) "Capt America vs Wolv." on-c 4.00

WORLD WAR HULK: X-MEN (See New Avengers: Illuminati and Incredible Hulk #92)
Marvel Comics: Aug, 2007 - No. 3, Oct, 2007 ($2.99, limited series)
1-3-Gage-s/DiVito-a/McGuinness-c; Hulk invades the Xavier Institute 3.00
TPB (2008, $24.99) r/#1-3, Avengers: The Initiative #4-5, Irredeemable Ant-Man #10, Iron Man #19-20, and Ghost Rider #12-13 25.00

WORLD WAR STORIES
Dell Publishing Co.: Apr-June, 1965 - No. 3, Dec, 1965
1-Glanzman-a in all 4 8 12 26 41 55
2,3 3 6 9 17 25 32

WORLD WAR II (See Classics Illustrated Special Issue)

WORLD WAR II: 1946
Antarctic Press: Oct, 1998 - No. 2 ($3.95, B&W)
1,2-Nomura-s/a 4.00

WORLD WAR III
Ace Periodicals: Mar, 1953 - No. 2, May, 1953
1-(Scarce)-Atomic bomb blast-c; Cameron-a 135 270 405 864 1482 2100
2-Used in **POP**, pg. 78 & B&W & color illos; Cameron-a 68 136 204 435 743 1050

WORLDWATCH
Wild and Wooly Press: June, 2004 - No. 3, Dec, 2004 ($2.95)
1-3-Austen-s/Derenick-a. 1-B&W. 2,3-Color 3.00

WORLD WITHOUT END
DC Comics: 1990 - No. 6, 1991 ($2.50, limited series, mature, stiff-c)
1-6: Horror/fantasy; all painted-c/a 3.00

WORLD WRESTLING FEDERATION BATTLEMANIA
Valiant: 1991 - No. 5?, 1991 ($2.50, magazine size, 68 pgs.)
1-5: 5-Includes 2 free pull-out posters 4.00

WORST FROM MAD, THE (Annual)
E. C. Comics: 1958 - No. 12, 1969 (Each annual cover is reprinted from the cover of the Mad issues being reprinted)(Value is 1/2 if bonus is missing)
nn(1958)-Bonus; record labels & travel stickers; 1st Mad annual; r/Mad #29-34 43 86 129 271 461 650
2(1959)-Bonus is small 33 1/3 rpm record entitled "Meet the Staff of Mad"; r/Mad #35-40 42 84 126 265 445 625
3(1960)-Has 20x30" campaign poster "Alfred E. Neuman for President"; r/Mad #41-46 15 30 45 104 227 350
4(1961)-Sunday comics section; r/Mad #47-54 14 28 42 98 214 330
5(1962)-Has 33-1/3 record; r/Mad #55-62 21 42 63 146 311 475
6(1963)-Has 33-1/3 record; r/Mad #63-70 21 42 63 146 311 475
7(1964)-Mad protest signs; r/Mad #71-76 10 20 30 68 127 185
8(1965)-Build a Mad Zeppelin 11 22 33 73 142 210
9(1966)-33-1/3 rpm record; Beatles on-c 14 28 42 96 208 320
10(1967)-Mad bumper sticker 7 14 21 46 76 105
11(1968)-Mad cover window stickers 6 12 18 42 69 95
12(1969)-Mad picture postcards; Orlando-a 6 12 18 42 69 95
NOTE: *Covers:* **Bob Clarke**-*#8.* **Mingo**-*#7, 9-12.*

WOTALIFE COMICS (Formerly Nutty Life #2; Phantom Lady #13 on)

Wow Comics #38 © FAW

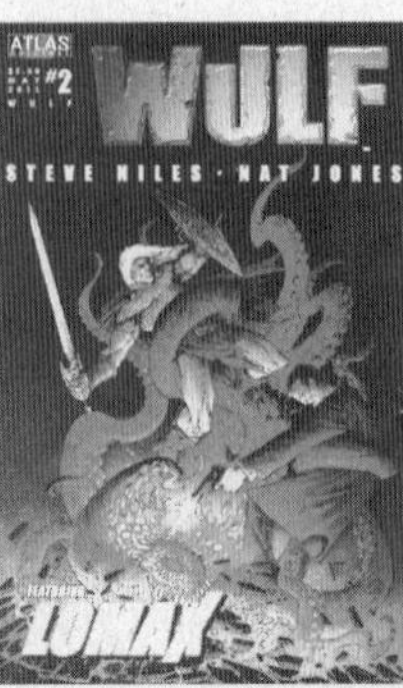

Wulf #2 © Nemesis Group

Wyatt Earp #5 © DELL

GD VG FN VF VF/NM NM-
2.0 4.0 6.0 8.0 9.0 9.2

Fox Features Syndicate/Norlen Mag.: No. 3, Aug-Sept, 1946 - No. 12, July, 1947; 1959

3-Cosmo Cat, Li'l Pan, others begin 13 26 39 72 101 130
4-12-Cosmo Cat, Li'l Pan in all 10 20 30 56 76 95
1(1959-Norlen)-Atomic Rabbit, Atomic Mouse; reprints cover to #6; reprints entire book? 8 16 24 40 50 60

WOTALIFE COMICS
Green Publications: 1957 - No. 5, 1957

1 7 14 21 35 43 50
2-5 5 10 15 22 26 30

WOW COMICS ("Wow, What A Magazine!" on cover of first issue)
Henle Publishing Co.: July, 1936 - No. 4, Nov, 1936 (52 pgs., magazine size)

1-Buck Jones in "The Phantom Rider" (1st app. in comics), Fu Manchu; Capt. Scott Dalton begins; Will Eisner-a (1st in comics); Baily-a(1); Briefer-c 303 606 909 2121 3711 5300
2-Ken Maynard, Fu Manchu, Popeye by Segar plus article on Popeye; Eisner-a 226 452 678 1446 2473 3500
3-Eisner-c/a(3); Popeye by Segar, Fu Manchu, Hiram Hick by Bob Kane, Space Limited app.; Jimmy Dempsey talks about Popeye's punch; Bob Ripley Believe it or Not begins; Briefer-a 213 426 639 1363 2332 3300
4-Flash Gordon by Raymond, Mandrake, Popeye by Segar, Tillie The Toiler, Fu Manchu, Hiram Hick by Bob Kane; Eisner-a(3); Briefer-c/a 258 516 774 1651 2826 4000

WOW COMICS (Real Western Hero #70 on)(See XMas Comics)
Fawcett Publ.: Winter, 1940-41; No. 2, Summer, 1941 - No. 69, Fall, 1948

nn(#1)-Origin Mr. Scarlet by S&K; Atom Blake, Boy Wizard, Jim Dolan, & Rick O'Shay begin; Diamond Jack, The White Rajah, & Shipwreck Roberts, only app.; 1st mention of Gotham City in comics; the cover was printed on unstable paper stock and is rarely found in fine or mint condition; blank inside-c; bondage-c by Beck 1350 2700 4050 10,400 18,700 27,000
2 (Scarce)-The Hunchback begins 174 348 522 1114 1907 2700
3 (Fall, 1941) 103 206 309 659 1130 1600
4-Origin & 1st app. Pinky 105 210 315 667 1146 1625
5 61 122 183 390 670 950
6-Origin & 1st app. The Phantom Eagle (7/15/42); Commando Yank begins 61 122 183 390 670 950
7,8 54 108 162 343 574 825
9 (1/6/43)-Capt. Marvel, Capt. Marvel Jr., Shazam app.; Scarlet & Pinky x-over; Mary Marvel-c/stories begin (cameo #9) 181 362 543 1158 1979 2800
10-Swayze-c/a on Mary Marvel 64 128 192 406 696 985
11-17,19,20: 15-Flag-c 49 98 147 309 522 735
18-1st app. Uncle Marvel (10/43); infinity-c 51 102 153 318 539 760
21-30: 23-Robot-c. 28-Pinky x-over in Mary Marvel 32 64 96 192 314 435
31-40: 32-68-Phantom Eagle by Swayze 22 44 66 132 216 300
41-50 21 42 63 124 202 280
51-58: Last Mary Marvel 20 40 60 117 189 260
59-69: 59-Ozzie (teenage) begins. 62-Flying Saucer gag-c (1/48). 65-69-Tom Mix stories (cont'd in Real Western Hero) 19 38 57 109 172 235

NOTE: *Cover features: Mr. Scarlet-#1-5; Commando Yank-#6, 7, (w/Mr. Scarlet #8); Mary Marvel-#9-56, (w/Commando Yank-#46-50), (w/Mr. Scarlet & Commando Yank-#51), (w/Mr. Scarlet & Pinky #53), (w/Phantom Eagle #54, 56), (w/Commando Yank & Phantom Eagle #58); Ozzie-#59-69.*

WRAITHBORN
DC Comics (WildStorm): Nov, 2005 - No. 6, July, 2006 ($2.99, limited series)

1-6-Marcia Chen & Joe Benitez-s/a 3.00
TPB (2007, $19.99) r/series; sketch pages and unused cover sketches 20.00

WRATH (Also see Prototype #4)
Malibu Comics: Jan, 1994 - No. 9, Nov, 1995 ($1.95)

1-9: 2-Mantra x-over. 3-Intro/1st app. Slayer. 4,5-Freex app. 8-Mantra & Warstrike app. 9-Prime app. 3.00
1-Ultra 5000 Limited silver foil 5.00
Giant Size 1 (2.50, 44 pgs.) 4.00

WRATH OF THE SPECTRE, THE
DC Comics: May, 1988 - No. 4, Aug, 1988 ($2.50, limited series)

1-3: Aparo-r/Adventure #431-440 5.00
4-Three scripts intended for Adventure #441-on, but not drawn by Aparo until 1988 1 2 3 5 6 8
TPB (2005, $19.99) r/series; Peter Sanderson intro. 20.00

WRECK OF GROSVENOR (See Superior Stories #3)

WRETCH, THE
Caliber: 1996 ($2.95, B&W)

1-Phillip Hester-a/scripts 3.00

GD VG FN VF VF/NM NM-
2.0 4.0 6.0 8.0 9.0 9.2

WRETCH, THE
Amaze Ink: 1997 - No. 4, 1998 ($2.95, B&W)

1-4-Phillip Hester-a/scripts 3.00
... Vol. 1: Everyday Doomsday (4/03, $13.95) 14.00

WRINGLE WRANGLE (Disney)
Dell Publishing Co.: No. 821, July, 1957

Four Color 821-Based on movie "Westward Ho, the Wagons"; Marsh-a; Fess Parker photo-c 8 16 24 51 86 120

WULF
Ardden Entertainment: Mar, 2011 - Present ($2.99)

1-5-Steve Niles-s/Nat Jones-a/c; Lomax app. 3-5-Iron Jaw app. 3.00

WULF THE BARBARIAN
Atlas/Seaboard Publ.: Feb, 1975 - No. 4, Sept, 1975

1,2: 1-Origin; Janson-a. 2-Intro. Berithe the Swordswoman; Janson-a w/Neal Adams, Wood, Reese-a assists 2 4 6 10 14 18
3,4: 3-Skeates-s. 4-Friedrich-s 2 4 6 8 11 14

WWE HEROES (WWE Wrestling) (#7 titled WWE Undertaker)
Titan Comics: Apr, 2010 - Present ($3.99)

1-6: 1-Two covers by Andy Smith and Liam Sharp. 5-Covers by Smith and Mayhew 4.00
7,8-"Undertaker" on cover; Rey Mysterio app. 4.00

WYATT EARP
Atlas Comics/Marvel No. 23 on (IPC): Nov, 1955 - #29, June, 1960; #30, Oct, 1972 - #34, June, 1973

1 21 42 63 122 199 275
2-Williamson-a (4 pgs.) 14 28 42 76 108 140
3-6,8-11: 3-Black Bart app. 8-Wild Bill Hickok app. 11 22 33 60 83 105
7,12-Williamson-a, 4 pgs. ea.; #12 with Mayo 11 22 33 64 90 115
13-20: 17-1st app. Wyatt's deputy, Grizzly Grant 10 20 30 54 72 90
21-Davis-c 9 18 27 50 65 80
22-24,26-29: 22-Ringo Kid app. 23-Kid From Texas app. 29-Last 10¢ issue 8 16 24 42 54 65
25-Davis-a 8 16 24 44 57 70
30-Williamson-r (1972) 2 4 6 13 18 22
31-34-Reprints. 32-Torres-a(r) 2 4 6 9 13 16

NOTE: ***Ayers** a-8, 10(2), 16(4), 17, 20(4), 26(5). **Berg** a-9. **Everett** c-6. **Kirby** c-25, 29. **Maneely** a-1; c-1-4, 8, 12, 17, 20. **Maurer** a-2(2), 3(4), 4(4), 8(4). **Severin** a-4, 9(4), 10; c-2, 9, 10, 14. **Wildey** a-5, 17, 24, 28.*

WYATT EARP (TV) (Hugh O'Brian Famous Marshal)
Dell Publishing Co.: No. 860, Nov, 1957 - No. 13, Dec-Feb, 1960-61 (Hugh O'Brian photo-c)

Four Color 860 (#1)-Manning-a 9 18 27 63 112 160
Four Color 890,921(6/58)-All Manning-a 7 14 21 48 79 110
4 (9-11/58) - 12-Manning-a. 4-Variant edition exists with back-c comic strip; Russ Manning-a. 5-Photo back-c 6 12 18 37 59 80
13-Toth-a 6 12 18 39 62 85

WYATT EARP FRONTIER MARSHAL (Formerly Range Busters) (Also see Blue Bird)
Charlton Comics: No. 12, Jan, 1956 - No. 72, Dec, 1967

12 9 18 27 47 61 75
13-19 6 12 18 31 38 45
20-(68 pgs.)-Williamson-a(4), 8,5,5,& 7 pgs. 10 20 30 54 72 90
21-(100 pgs.) Mastroserio, Maneely, Severin-a (signed LePoer) 5 10 15 32 51 70
22-30 3 6 9 16 23 30
31-50 2 4 6 12 16 20
51-72 (1967) 2 4 6 9 11 14

WYNONNA EARP
Image Comics (WildStorm Productions): Dec, 1996 - No. 5, Apr, 1997 ($2.50)

1-5-Beau Smith-s/Chin-a 3.00

WYNONNA EARP: HOME ON THE STRANGE
IDW Publishing: Dec, 2003 - No. 3, Feb, 2004 ($3.99)

1-3-Beau Smith-s/Ferreira-a 4.00

WYNONNA EARP: THE YETI WARS
IDW Publishing: May, 2011 - No. 4, Aug, 2011 ($3.99)

1-4-Beau Smith-s/Enrique Villagran-a 4.00

WYRMS
Marvel Comics (Dabel Brothers): Feb, 2007 - No. 6, Jan, 2008 ($2.99)

1-6-Orson Scott Card & Jake Black-s. 1-3-Batista-a 3.00
TPB (2008, $14.99) r/#1-6 15.00

X-Campus #3 © MAR

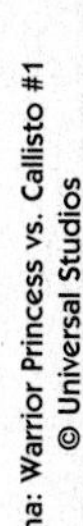

Xena: Warrior Princess vs. Callisto #1 © Universal Studios

X-Factor #62 © MAR

GD 2.0 | VG 4.0 | FN 6.0 | VF 8.0 | VF/NM 9.0 | NM- 9.2

X (Comics' Greatest World: X #1 only) (Also see Comics' Greatest World & Dark Horse Comics #8)
Dark Horse Comics: Feb, 1994 - No. 25, Apr, 1996 ($2.00/$2.50)
1-25: 3-Pit Bulls x-over. 8 -Ghost-c & app. 18-Miller-c.; Predator app. 19-22-Miller-c. 3.00
Hero Illustrated Special #1,2 (1994, $1.00, 20 pgs.) 3.00
One Shot to the Head (1994, $2.50, 36 pgs.)-Miller-c. 3.00
NOTE: *Miller c-18-22. Quesada c-6. Russell a-6.*

XANADU COLOR SPECIAL
Eclipse Comics: Dec, 1988 ($2.00, one-shot)
1-Continued from Thoughts & Images 3.00

XAVIER INSTITUTE ALUMNI YEARBOOK (See X-Men titles)
Marvel Comics: Dec, 1996 ($5.95, square-bound, one-shot)
1-Text w/art by various 6.00

X-BABIES
Marvel Comics: Dec, 2009 - No. 4, Mar, 2010 ($3.99, limited series)
1-4-Schigiel-s/Chabot-a; Skottie Young 4.00
...: Murderama (8/98, $2.95) J.J. Kirby-a 4.00
...: Reborn (1/00, $3.50) J.J. Kirby-a 4.00

X-CALIBRE
Marvel Comics: Mar, 1995 - No. 4, July, 1995 ($1.95, limited series)
1-4-Age of Apocalypse 3.00

X-CAMPUS
Marvel Comics: July, 2010 - No. 4, Nov, 2010 ($4.99, limited series)
1-4-Alternate version of X-Men; stories by European creators; Nauck-c 5.00

X-CLUB
Marvel Comics: Feb, 2012 - No. 4 ($2.99, limited series)
1-4-X-Men scientist team; Dr. Nemesis & Danger app. 1-Bradshaw-c. 2-4-Esquejo-c 3.00

XENA (TV)
Dynamite Entertainment: 2006 - 2007 ($3.50)
1-4-Three covers on each; Neves-a/Layman-s 3.50
Vol. 2 #1-4-(Dark Xena) Four covers; Salonga-a/Layman-s 3.50
Annual 1 (2007, $4.95) Three covers; Salonga-a/Champagne-s 5.00
... Vol. 2: Dark Xena TPB (2007, $14.99) r/Vol. 2 #1-4; variant cover gallery 15.00

XENA / ARMY OF DARKNESS: WHAT...AGAIN?!
Dynamite Entertainment: 2008 - No. 4, 2009 ($3.50, limited series)
1-4-Xena, Gabrielle, & Autolycus team up with Ash; Montenegro-a; two covers on each 3.50

XENA: WARRIOR PRINCESS (TV)
Topps Comics: Aug, 1997 - No. 0, Oct, 1997 ($2.95)
1-Two stories by various; J. Scott Campbell-c 1 3 4 6 8 10
1,2-Photo-c 1 3 4 6 8 10
2-Stevens-c 1 3 4 6 8 10
0-(10/97)-Lopresti-c, 0-(10/97)-Photo-c 1 2 3 5 6 8
...First Appearance Collection ('97, $9.95) r/Hercules the Legendary Journeys #3-5 and 5-page story from TV Guide 10.00

XENA: WARRIOR PRINCESS (TV)
Dark Horse Comics: Sept, 1999 - No. 14, Oct, 2000 ($2.95/$2.99)
1-14: 1-Mignola-c and photo-c. 2,3-Bradstreet-c & photo-c 3.50

XENA: WARRIOR PRINCESS AND THE ORIGINAL OLYMPICS (TV)
Topps Comics: Jun, 1998 - No. 3, Aug, 1998 ($2.95, limited series)
1-3-Regular and Photo-c; Lim-a/T&M Bierbaum-s 3.50

XENA: WARRIOR PRINCESS-BLOODLINES (TV)
Topps Comics: May, 1998 - No. 2, June, 1998 ($2.95, limited series)
1,2-Lopresti-s/c/a. 2-Reg. and photo-c 3.50
1-Bath photo-c, 1-American Ent. Ed. 4.50

XENA: WARRIOR PRINCESS / JOXER: WARRIOR PRINCE (TV)
Topps Comics: Nov, 1997 - No. 3, Jan, 1998 ($2.95, limited series)
1-3-Regular and Photo-c; Lim-a/T&M Bierbaum-s 3.50

XENA: WARRIOR PRINCESS-THE DRAGON'S TEETH (TV)
Topps Comics: Dec, 1997 - No. 3, Feb, 1998 ($2.95, limited series)
1-3-Regular and Photo-c; Teranishi-a/Thomas-s 3.50

XENA: WARRIOR PRINCESS-THE ORPHEUS TRILOGY (TV)
Topps Comics: Mar, 1998 - No. 3, May, 1998 ($2.95, limited series)
1-3-Regular and Photo-c; Teranishi-a/T&M Bierbaum-s 3.50

XENA: WARRIOR PRINCESS VS. CALLISTO (TV)
Topps Comics: Feb, 1998 - No. 3, Apr, 1998 ($2.95, limited series)
1-3-Regular and Photo-c; Morgan-a/Thomas-s 3.50

XENOBROOD
DC Comics: No. 0, Oct, 1994 - No. 6, Apr, 1995 ($1.50, limited series)
0-6: 0-Indicia says "Xenobroods" 3.00

XENON
Eclipse Comics: Dec, 1987 - No. 23, Nov. 1, 1988 ($1.50, B&W, bi-weekly)
1-23 3.00

XENOZOIC TALES (Also see Cadillacs & Dinosaurs, Death Rattle #8)
Kitchen Sink Press: Feb, 1986 - No. 14, Oct, 1996
1-Mark Schultz-s/a in all 1 3 4 6 8 10
1(2nd printing)(1/89) 3.00
2-14 5.00
Volume 1 ($14.95) r/#1-6 & Death Rattle #8 15.00
Volume 2 (5/03, $14.95, TPB) B&W r/#7-14; intro by Frank Cho 15.00

XENYA
Sanctuary Press: Apr, 1994 - No. 3 ($2.95)
1-3: 1-Hildebrandt-c; intro Xenya 3.00

XERO
DC Comics: May, 1997 - No. 12, Apr, 1998 ($1.75)
1-7 3.00
8-12 3.00

X-FACTOR (Also see The Avengers #263, Fantastic Four #286 and Mutant X)
Marvel Comics Group: Feb, 1986 - No. 149, Sept, 1998
1-($1.25, 52 pgs)-Story recaps 1st app. from Avengers #263; story cont'd from F.F. #286; return of original X-Men (now X-Factor); Guice/Layton-a; Baby Nathan app. (2nd after X-Men #201) 1 2 3 5 6 8
2-4 5.00
5-1st brief app. Apocalypse (1 page) 6.00
6-1st full app. Apocalypse 2 4 6 9 12 15
7-10: 10-Sabretooth app. (11/86, 3 pgs.) cont'd in X-Men #212; 1st app. in an X-Men comic book 5.00
11-22: 13-Baby Nathan app. in flashback. 14-Cyclops vs. The Master Mold. 15-Intro wingless Angel 4.00
23-1st brief app. Archangel (2 pages) 1 2 3 5 7 9
24-1st full app. Archangel (now in Uncanny X-Men); Fall Of The Mutants begins; origin Apocalypse 2 4 6 8 10 12
25,26: Fall Of The Mutants; 26-New outfits 5.00
27-37,39,41-49,51-59,63-70,72-83,87-91,93-99,101: 35-Origin Cyclops. 51-53-Sabretooth app. 52-Liefeld-c(p). 54-Intro Crimson; Silvestri-c/a(p). 63-Portacio/Thibert-c/a(p) begins, ends #69. 65-68-Lee co-plots. 65-The Apocalypse Files begins, ends #68. 66,67-Baby Nathan app. 67-Inhumans app. 68-Baby Nathan is sent into future to save his life. 69,70-X-Men(w/Wolverine) x-over. 77-Cannonball (of X-Force) app. 87-Quesada-c/a(p) in monthly comic begins,ends #92. 88-1st app. Random 3.00
38,50,60-62,71,75: 38,50-(52 pgs.): 50-Liefeld/McFarlane-c. 60-X-Tinction Agenda x-over; New Mutants (w/Cable) x-over in #60-62; Wolverine in #62. 61,62-X-Tinction Agenda. 62-Jim Lee-c. 71-New team begins (Havok, Polaris, Strong Guy, Wolfsbane & Madrox); Stroman-c/a begins. 75-(52 pgs.) 4.00
40-Rob Liefield-c/a (4/89, 1st at Marvel?) 5.00
60,71-2nd printings. 60-Gold ink 2nd printing. 71-2nd printing ($1.25) 3.00
84-86 -Jae Lee a(p); 85,86-Jae Lee-c. Polybagged with trading card in each; X-Cutioner's Song x-overs. 4.00
92-($3.50, 68 pgs.)-Wraparound-c by Quesada w/Havok hologram on-c; begin X-Men 30th anniversary issues; Quesada-a. 6.00
92-2nd printing 4.00
100-($2.95, 52 pgs.)-Embossed foil-c; Multiple Man dies. 6.00
100-($1.75, 52 pgs.)-Regular edition 4.00
102-105,107: 102-bound-in card sheet 3.00
106-($2.00)-Newsstand edition 3.00
106-($2.95)-Collectors edition 4.00
108-124,126-148: 112-Return from Age of Apocalypse. 115-card insert. 119-123-Sabretooth app. 123-Hound app. 124-w/Onslaught Update. 126-Onslaught x-over; Beast vs. Dark Beast. 128-w/card insert; return of Multiple Man. 130-Assassination of Grayson Creed. 146,148-Moder-a 3.00
125-($2.95)-"Onslaught"; Post app.; return of Havok 4.00
149-Last issue 4.00
#(-1) Flashback (7/97) Matsuda-a 3.00
Annual 1-9: 1-(10/86-'94, 68 pgs.) 3-Evolutionary War x-over. 4-Atlantis Attacks; Byrne/Simonson-a;Byrne-c. 5-Fantastic Four, New Mutants x-over; Keown 2 pg. pin-up. 6-New Warriors app.; 5th app. X-Force cont'd from X-Men Annual #15. 7-1st Quesada-a(p)

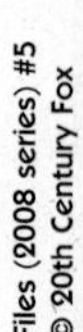

X-Factor #212 © MAR

X-Files (2008 series) #5 © 20th Century Fox

X-Force #75 © MAR

GD VG FN VF VF/NM NM-
2.0 4.0 6.0 8.0 9.0 9.2

on X-Factor plus-c(p). 8-Bagged w/trading card. 9-Austin-a(i) 4.00
...Prisoner of Love (1990, $4.95, 52 pgs.)-Starlin scripts; Guice-a 5.00
... Visionaries: Peter David Vol. 1 TPB (2005, $15.99) r/#71-75 16.00
... Visionaries: Peter David Vol. 2 TPB (2007, $15.99) r/#76-78 & Incr. Hulk #390-392 16.00
... Visionaries: Peter David Vol. 3 TPB (2007, $15.99) r/#79-83 & Annual #7 16.00
NOTE: ***Art Adams** a-41p, 42p. **Buckler** a-50p. **Liefeld** a-40; c-40, 50i, 52p. **McFarlane** c-50i. **Mignola** c-70. **Brandon Peterson** a-78p(part). **Whilce Portacio** c/a(p)-63-69. **Quesada** a(p)-87-92, Annual 7. c(p)-78, 79, 82, Annual 7. **Simonson** c/a-10, 11, 13-15, 17-19, 21, 23-31, 33, 34, 36-39; c-12, 16. **Paul Smith** a-44-48; c-43. **Stroman** a(p)-71-75, 77, 78(part), 80, 81; c(p)-71-77, 80, 81, 84. **Zeck** c-2.*

X-FACTOR (Volume 2)
Marvel Comics: June, 2002 - No. 4, Oct, 2002 ($2.50)

1-4: Jensen-s/Ranson-a. 1-Phillips-c. 2,3-Edwards-c 3.00

X-FACTOR (Volume 3)
Marvel Comics: Jan, 2006 - Present ($2.99)

1-24: 1-Peter David-s/Ryan Sook-a. 8,9-Civil War. 21-24-Endangered Species back-up 3.00
25-49: 25-27-Messiah Complex x-over; Finch-c. 26-2nd printing with new Eaton-c 3.00
50-(12/09, $3.99) Madrox in the future; DeLandro-a/Yardin-c 4.00
200-(2/10, $4.99) Resumes original series numbering; 3 covers; Fantastic Four app. 5.00
201-224,224.1, 225-232 ($2.99) 201,202-Dr. Doom & Fant. Four app. 211,212-Thor app. 230-Wolverine app.; Havok & Polaris return 3.00
... Special: Layla Miller (10/08, $3.99) David-s/DeLandro-a 4.00
...: The Quick and the Dead (7/08, $2.99) Raimondi-a; Quicksilver regains powers 3.00
...: The Longest Night HC (2006, $19.99, dust jacket) r/#1-6; sketch pages by Sook 20.00
...: The Longest Night SC (2007, $14.99) r/#1-6; sketch pages by Sook 15.00
...: Life and Death Matters HC (2007, $19.99, dust jacket) r/#7-12 20.00
...: Life and Death Matters SC (2007, $14.99) r/#7-12 15.00
...: The Many Lives of Madrox SC (2007, $14.99) r/#13-17 15.00
...: Heart of Ice HC (2007, $19.99, dust jacket) r/#18-24 20.00
...: Heart of Ice SC (2008, $17.99, dust jacket) r/#18-24 18.00

X-FACTOR (Volume 2)
Marvel Comics: June, 2002 - No. 4, Oct, 2002 ($2.50)

1-4: Jensen-s/Ranson-a. 1-Phillips-c. 2,3-Edwards-c 2.50

X-FACTOR FOREVER
Marvel Comics: May, 2010 - No. 5, Sept, 2010 ($3.99, limited series)

1-5-Louise Simonson-s/Dan Panosian-a; back-up origin of Apocalypse 4.00

X-51 (Machine Man)
Marvel Comics: Sept, 1999 - No. 12, Jul, 2000 ($1.99/$2.50)

1-7: 1-Joe Bennett-a. 2-Two covers 3.00
8-12: 8-Begin $2.50-c 3.00
Wizard #0 3.00

X-FILES, THE (TV)
Topps Comics: Jan, 1995 - No. 41, July, 1998 ($2.50)

-2(9/96)-Black-c; r/X-Files Magazine #1&2 5.00
-1(9/96)-Silver-c; r/Hero Illustrated Giveaway 5.00
0-($3.95)-Adapts pilot episode 4.00
0-"Mulder" variant-c 1 2 3 5 6 8
0-"Scully" variant-c 1 2 3 5 6 8
1/2-W/certificate 1 2 3 5 6 8
1-New stories based on the TV show; direct market & newsstand editions; Miran Kim-c on all 3 6 9 14 20 25
2 1 2 3 6 8 10
3,4 6.00
5-10 5.00
11-41: 11-Begin $2.95-c. 21-W/bound-in card. 40,41-Reg. & photo-c 4.00
Annual 1,2 ($3.95) 4.00
Afterflight TPB ($5.95) Art by Thompson, Saviuk, Kim 6.00
Collection 1 TPB ($19.95)-r/#1-6. 20.00
Collection 2 TPB ($19.95)-r/#7-12, Annual #1. 20.00
...Fight the Future ('98, $5.95) Movie adaptation 6.00
Hero Illustrated Giveaway (3/95) 1 2 3 5 6 8
Special Edition 1-5 ($4.95)-r/#1-3, 4-6, 7-9, 10-12, 13, Annual 1 5.00
Star Wars Galaxy Magazine Giveaway (B&W) 1 3 4 6 8 10
Trade paperback ($19.95) 20.00
Volume 1 TPB (Checker Books, 2005, $19.95) r/#13-17, #0, Season One: Squeeze 20.00
Volume 2 TPB (Checker Books, 2005, $19.95) r/#18-24, #1/2, Comics Digest #1 20.00
Volume 3 TPB (Checker Books, 2006, $19.95) r/#23-26, Fire, Ice, Hero Ill. Giveaway 20.00

X-FILES, THE (TV)
DC Comics (WildStorm): No. 0, Sept, 2008 - No. 6, Jun, 2009 ($3.99/$3.50)

0-($3.99) Spotnitz-s/Denham-a; photo-c 4.00
1-6-($3.50) 1-Spotnitz-s/Denham-a; 2 covers. 4-Wolfman-s 3.50

GD VG FN VF VF/NM NM-
2.0 4.0 6.0 8.0 9.0 9.2

TPB (2009, $19.99) r/#0-6 20.00

X-FILES COMICS DIGEST, THE
Topps Comics: Dec, 1995 - No. 3 ($3.50, quarterly, digest-size)

1-3: 1,2: New X-Files stories w/Ray Bradbury Comics-r. 1-Reg. & photo-c 4.00
NOTE: ***Adlard** a-1, 2. **Jack Davis** a-2r. **Russell** a-1r.*

X-FILES, THE: GROUND ZERO (TV)
Topps Comics: Nov, 1997 - No. 4, March, 1998 ($2.95, limited series)

1-4-Adaptation of the Kevin J. Anderson novel 4.00

X-FILES, THE: SEASON ONE (TV)
Topps Comics: July, 1997 - July, 1998 ($4.95, adaptations of TV episodes)

1,2,Squeeze, Conduit, Ice, Space, Fire, Beyond the Sea, Shadows 5.00

X-FILES, THE / 30 DAYS OF NIGHT
DC Comics (WildStorm)/IDW: Sept, 2010 - No. 6, Feb, 2011 ($3.99, limited series)

1-6-Steve Niles & Adam Jones-s/Tom Mandrake-a. 1-Three covers 4.00
TPB (2011, $17.99) r/#1-6; cover gallery 18.00

X-FORCE (Becomes X-Statix) (Also see The New Mutants #100)
Marvel Comics: Aug, 1991 - No. 129, Aug, 2002 ($1.00-$2.25)

1-($1.50, 52 pgs.)-Polybagged with 1 of 5 diff. Marvel Universe trading cards inside (1 each); 6th app. of X-Force; Liefeld-c/a begins 5.00
1-1st printing with Cable trading card inside 6.00
1-2nd printing; metallic ink-c (no bag or card) 3.00
2-4: 2-Deadpool-c/story. 3-New Brotherhood of Evil Mutants app. 4-Spider-Man x-over; cont'd from Spider-Man #16; reads sideways 4.00
5-10: 6-Last $1.00-c. 7,9-Weapon X back-ups. 8-Intro The Wild Pack (Cable, Kane, Domino, Hammer, G.W. Bridge, & Grizzly); Liefeld-c/a (4); Mignola-a. 10-Weapon X full-length story (part 3). 11-1st Weapon Prime; Deadpool-c/story 4.00
11-15,19-24,26-33: 15-Cable leaves X-Force 3.00
16-18-Polybagged w/trading card in each; X-Cutioner's Song x-overs 4.00
25-($3.50, 52 pgs.)-Wraparound-c w/Cable hologram on-c; Cable returns 4.00
34-37,39-45: 34-bound-in card sheet 3.00
38,40-43: 38-($2.00)-Newsstand edition. 40-43 ($1.95)-Deluxe edition 3.00
38-($2.95)-Collectors edition (prismatic) 5.00
44-49,51-67: 44-Return from Age of Apocalypse. 45-Sabretooth app. 49-Sebastian Shaw app. 52-Blob app., Onslaught cameo. 55-Vs. S.H.I.E.L.D. 56-Deadpool app. 57-Mr. Sinister & X-Man-c/app. 57,58-Onslaught x-over. 59-W/card insert; return of Longshot. 60-Dr. Strange 3.00
50 ($3.95)-Gatefold wrap-around foil-c 4.00
50 ($3.95)-Liefeld variant-c 5.00
68-74: 68-Operation Zero Tolerance 3.00
75,100-($2.99): 75-Cannonball-c/app. 4.00
76-99,101,102: 81-Pollina poster. 95-Magneto-c. 102-Ellis-s/Portacio-a 3.00
103-115: 103-Begin $2.25-c; Portacio-a thru #106. 115-Death of old team 3.00
116-New team debuts; Allred-c/a; Milligan-s; no Comics Code stamp on-c 4.00
117-129: 117-Intro. Mr. Sensitive. 120-Wolverine-c/app. 123-'Nuff Said issue. 124-Darwyn Cooke-a/c. 128-Death of U-Go Girl. 129-Fegredo-a 3.00
#(-1) Flashback (7/97) story of John Proudstar; Pollina-a 3.00
Annual 1-3 ('92-'94, 68 pgs.)-1-1st Greg Capullo-a(p) on X-Force. 2-Polybagged w/trading card; intro X-Treme & Neurtap 4.00
...And Cable '95 (12/95, $3.95)-Impossible Man app. 4.00
...And Cable '96, ...'97 ('96, 7/97) -'96-Wraparound-c 4.00
...And Spider-Man: Sabotage nn (11/92, $6.95)-Reprints X-Force #3,4 & Spider-Man #16 7.00
.../ Champions '98 ($3.50) 4.00
Annual 99 ($3.50) 4.00
...: Famous, Mutant & Mortal HC (2003, $29.99) oversized r/#116-129; foreward by Milligan; gallery of covers and pin-ups; script for #123 30.00
...New Beginnings TPB (10/01, $14.95) r/#116-120 15.00
...Rough Cut ($2.99) Pencil pages and script for #102 3.00
...Youngblood (8/96, $4.95)-Platt-c 5.00
NOTE: ***Capullo** a(p)-15-25, Annual 1; c(p)-14-27. **Rob Liefeld** a-1-7, 9p; c-1-9, 11p; plots-1-12. **Mignola** a-8p.*

X-FORCE
Marvel Comics: Oct, 2004 - No. 6, Mar, 2005 ($2.99, limited series)

1-6-Liefeld-c/a; Nicieza-s. 5,6-Wolverine & The Thing app. 3.00
X-Force & Cable Vol. 1: The Legend Returns (2005, $14.99) r/#1-6 15.00

X-FORCE (Also see Uncanny X-Force)
Marvel Comics: Apr, 2008 - No. 28, Sept, 2010 ($2.99)

1-Crain-a; Wolverine & X-23 app.; two covers (regular and bloody) by Crain on #1-5 4.00
2-21,23-28: 2,3-Bastion app. 4-6-Archangel app. 7-10-Choi-a. 9-11-Ghost Rider app. 26-28-Second Coming x-over; Granov-c. 26-Nightcrawler killed 3.00
22-($3.99) Necrosha x-over; Crain-a 4.00
...: Angels and Demons MGC #1 (5/11, $1.00) r/#1 with "Marvel's Greatest Comics" on-c 3.00

X-Infernus #1 © MAR

X-Men #34 © MAR

X-Men #139 © MAR

GD VG FN VF VF/NM NM-
2.0 4.0 6.0 8.0 9.0 9.2

...Annual 1 (2/10, $3.99) Kirkman-s/Pearson-a/c; Deadpool back-up w/Barberi-a 4.00
.../Cable: Messiah War 1 (5/09, $3.99) Choi-a; covers by Andrews and Choi 4.00
... Special: Ain't No Dog (8/08, $3.99) Huston-s/Palo-a; Dell'Edera-a; Hitch-c 4.00

X-FORCE MEGAZINE
Marvel Comics: Nov, 1996 ($3.95, one-shot)

1-Reprints 4.00

X-FORCE: SEX AND VIOLENCE
Marvel Comics: Sept, 2010 - No. 3, Nov, 2010 ($3.99, limited series)

1-3-Dell'Otto-a/Kyle & Yost-s; Domino & Wolverine vs. The Hand & The Assassins Guild 4.00

X-FORCE: SHATTERSTAR
Marvel Comics: Apr, 2005 - No. 4, July, 2005 ($2.99, limited series)

1-4-Liefeld-c/s; Michaels-a 3.00
TPB (2005, $15.99) r/#1-4 & New Mutants #99,100 16.00

X-INFERNUS
Marvel Comics: Feb, 2009 - No. 4, May, 2009 ($3.99, limited series)

1-4-Illyana Rasputin in Limbo; Cebulski-s/Camuncoli-a/Finch-c 4.00

XIN: JOURNEY OF THE MONKEY KING
Anarchy Studios: May, 2003 - No. 3, July, 2003 ($2.99)

Preview Edition (Apr, 2003, $1.99) Flip book w/ Vampi Vicious Preview Edition 3.00
1-3-Kevin Lau-a. 1-Three covers by Lau, Park and Nauck. 2-Three covers 3.00

XIN: LEGEND OF THE MONKEY KING
Anarchy Studios: Nov, 2002 - No. 3, Jan, 2003 ($2.99)

Preview Edition (Summer 2002, Diamond Dateline supplement) 3.00
1-3-Kevin Lau-a. 1-Two covers by Lau & Madureira. 2-Two covers by Lau & Oeming 3.00
TPB (10/03, $12.95) r/#1-3; cover gallery and sketch pages 13.00

X-MAN (Also see X-Men Omega & X-Men Prime)
Marvel Comics: Mar, 1995 - No. 75, May, 2001 ($1.95/$1.99/$2.25)

1-Age of Apocalypse 5.00
1-2nd print 3.00
2-4,25: 25-($2.99)-Wraparound-c 4.00
5-24, 26-28: 5-Post Age of Apocalypse stories begin. 5-7-Madelyne Pryor app. 10-Professor X app. 12-vs. Excalibur. 13-Marauders, Cable app. 14-Vs. Cable; Onslaught app. 15-17-Vs. Holocaust. 17-w/Onslaught Update. 18-Onslaught x-over; X-Force-c/app; Marauders app. 19-Onslaught x-over. 20-Abomination-c/app.; w/card insert. 23-Bishop app. 24-Spider-Man, Morbius-c/app. 27-Re-appearance of Aurora(Alpha Flight) 3.00
29-49,51-62: 29-Operation Zero Tolerance. 37,38-Spider-Man-c/app. 56-Spider-Man app. 3.00
50-($2.99) Crossover with Generation X #50 4.00
63-74: 63-Ellis & Grant-s/Olivetti-a begins. 64-Begin $2.25-c 3.00
75 ($2.99) Final issue; Alcatena-a 4.00
#(-1) Flashback (7/97) 3.00
...'96, ...'97-($2.95)-Wraparound-c; '96-Age of Apocalypse 4.00
...: All Saints' Day ('97, $5.99) Dodson-a 6.00
.../Hulk '98 ($2.99) Wraparound-c; Thanos app. 4.00

XMAS COMICS
Fawcett Publications: 12?/1941 - No. 2, 12?/1942; (50¢, 324 pgs.)
No. 7, 12?/1947 (25¢, 132 pgs.)(#3-6 do not exist)

1-Contains Whiz #21, Capt. Marvel #3, Bulletman #2, Wow #3, & Master #18; front & back-c by Raboy. Not rebound, remaindered comics; printed at same time as originals
422 844 1266 2954 5177 7400
2-Capt. Marvel, Bulletman, Spy Smasher 181 362 543 1158 1979 2800
7-Funny animals (Hoppy, Billy the Kid & Oscar) 66 132 198 419 722 1025

XMAS COMICS
Fawcett Publications: No. 4, Dec, 1949 - No. 7, Dec, 1952 (50¢, 196 pgs.)

4-Contains Whiz, Master, Tom Mix, Captain Marvel, Nyoka, Capt. Video, Bob Colt, Monte Hale, Hot Rod Comics, & Battle Stories. Not rebound, remaindered comics; printed at the same time as originals. Stocking on cover is made of green or red felt
90 180 270 576 988 1400
5-7-Same as above. 5- Red felt on-c. 7-Bill Boyd app.; stocking on cover is made of green felt (novelty cover) 68 136 204 435 743 1050

X-MEN, THE (See Adventures of Cyclops and Phoenix, Amazing Adventures, Archangel, Brotherhood, Capt. America #172, Classic X-Men, Exiles, Further Adventures of Cyclops & Phoenix, Gambit, Giant-Size..., Heroes For Hope..., Kitty Pryde & Wolverine, Marvel & DC Present, Marvel Collector's Edition:..., Marvel Fanfare, Marvel Graphic Novel, Marvel Super Heroes, Marvel Team-Up, Marvel Triple Action, The Marvel X-Men Collection, New Mutants, Nightcrawler, Official Marvel Index To..., Rogue, Special Edition..., Ultimate..., Uncanny..., Wolverine, X-Factor, X-Force, X-Terminators)

X-MEN, THE (1st series)(Becomes Uncanny X-Men at #142)(The X-Men #1-93; X-Men #94-141) (The Uncanny X-Men on-c only #114-141)
Marvel Comics Group: Sept, 1963 - No. 66, Mar, 1970; No. 67, Dec, 1970 - No. 141, Jan, 1981; Uncanny X-Men No. 142, Feb, 1981 - No. 544, Dec, 2011

GD VG FN VF VF/NM NM-
2.0 4.0 6.0 8.0 9.0 9.2

1-Origin/1st app. X-Men (Angel, Beast, Cyclops, Iceman & Marvel Girl); 1st app. Magneto & Professor X 850 1700 2550 8500 21,750 35,000
2-1st app. The Vanisher 150 300 450 1260 2730 4200
3-1st app. The Blob (1/64) 89 178 267 721 1561 2400
4-1st Quicksilver & Scarlet Witch & Brotherhood of the Evil Mutants (3/64); 1st app. Toad; 2nd app. Magneto 94 188 282 761 1656 2550
5-Magneto & Evil Mutants-c/story 61 122 183 494 1072 1650
6,7: 6-Sub-Mariner app. 7-Magneto app. 48 96 144 389 845 1300
8,9,11: 8-1st Unus the Untouchable. 9-Early Avengers app. (1/65); 1st Lucifer. 11-1st app. The Stranger. 42 84 126 315 683 1050
10-1st S.A. app. Ka-Zar & Zabu the sabertooth (3/65) 42 84 126 316 688 1060
12-Origin Prof. X; Origin/1st app. Juggernaut 46 92 138 345 748 1150
13-Juggernaut and Human Torch app. 30 60 90 218 472 725
14,15: 14-1st app. Sentinels. 15-Origin Beast 31 62 93 225 488 750
16-20: 19-1st app. The Mimic (4/66) 19 38 57 128 277 425
21-27,29,30: 27-Re-enter The Mimic (r-in #75); Spider-Man cameo
13 26 39 87 186 285
28-1st app. The Banshee (1/67)(r-in #76) 19 38 57 128 277 425
28-2nd printing (1994) 2 4 6 8 10 12
31-34,36,37,39: 34-Adkins-c/a. 39-New costumes 11 22 33 76 151 225
35-Spider-Man x-over (8/67)(r-in #83); 1st app. Changeling
23 46 69 161 343 525
38,40: 38-Origins of the X-Men series begins, ends #57. 40-(1/68) 1st app. Frankenstein's monster at Marvel 12 24 36 78 157 235
41-49: 42-Death of Prof. X (Changeling disguised as). 44-1st S.A. app. G.A. Red Raven. 49-Steranko-c; 1st Polaris 11 22 33 71 136 200
50,51-Steranko-c/a 11 22 33 73 142 210
52 10 20 30 67 124 180
53-Barry Smith-c/a (his 1st comic book work) 11 22 33 73 142 210
54,55-B. Smith-c. 54-1st app. Alex Summers who later becomes Havok. 55-Summers discovers he has mutant powers 11 22 33 73 142 210
56,57,59-63,65-Neal Adams-a(p). 56-Intro Havok w/o costume. 60-1st Sauron. 65-Return of Professor X. 11 22 33 77 154 230
58-1st app. Havok in costume; N. Adams-a(p) 13 26 39 86 183 280
62,63-2nd printings (1994) 2 4 6 8 10 12
64-1st app. Sunfire 11 22 33 74 145 215
66-Last new story w/original X-Men; battles Hulk 12 24 36 79 160 240
67-70: 67-Reprints begin, end #93. 67-70: (52 pgs.) 10 20 30 64 115 165
71-93: 71-Last 15¢ issue. 72: (52 pgs.). 73-86-r/#25-38 w/new-c. 83-Spider-Man-c/story. 87-93-r/#39-45 with covers 8 16 24 56 96 135
94 (8/75)-New X-Men begin (see Giant-Size X-Men for 1st app.); Colossus, Nightcrawler, Thunderbird, Storm, Wolverine, & Banshee join; Angel, Marvel Girl & Iceman resign
65 130 195 520 898 1275
95-Death of Thunderbird 15 30 45 104 227 350
96,97 11 22 33 71 136 200
98,99-(Regular 25¢ edition)(4,6/76) 10 20 30 70 133 195
98,99-(30¢-c variants, limited distribution) 17 34 51 116 253 390
100-Old vs. New X-Men; part origin Phoenix; last 25¢ issue (8/76)
11 22 33 77 154 230
100-(30¢-c variant, limited distribution) 20 40 60 140 300 460
101-Phoenix origin concludes 12 24 36 83 172 260
102-104: 102-Origin Storm. 104-1st brief app. Starjammers; Magneto-c/story
8 16 24 56 96 135
105-107-(Regular 30¢ editions). 106-(8/77)Old vs. New X-Men. 107-1st full app. Starjammers; last 30¢ issue 8 16 24 53 89 125
105-107-(35¢-c variants, limited distribution) 12 24 36 81 166 250
108-Byrne-a begins (see Marvel Team-Up #53) 8 16 24 56 96 135
109-1st app. Weapon Alpha (becomes Vindicator) 8 16 24 53 89 125
110,111: 110-Phoenix joins 7 14 21 44 72 100
112-116 7 14 21 44 72 100
117-119: 117-Origin Professor X 6 12 18 39 62 85
120-1st app. Alpha Flight, story line begins (4/79); 1st app. Vindicator (formerly Weapon Alpha); last 35¢ issue 8 16 24 53 89 125
121-1st full Alpha Flight story 7 14 21 49 82 115
122-128: 123-Spider-Man x-over. 124-Colossus becomes Proletarian
5 10 15 35 55 75
129-Intro Kitty Pryde (1/80); last Banshee; Dark Phoenix saga begins; intro. Emma Frost (White Queen) 6 12 18 41 66 90
130-1st app. The Dazzler by Byrne (2/80) 6 12 18 37 59 80
131-135: 131-Dazzler app.; 1st White Queen-c. 133-Wolverine app. 134-Phoenix becomes Dark Phoenix 5 10 15 35 55 75
136,138: 138-Dazzler app.; Cyclops leaves 5 10 15 30 48 65
137-Giant; death of Phoenix 6 12 18 42 69 95
139-Alpha Flight app.; Kitty Pryde joins; new costume for Wolverine

Uncanny X-Men #226 © MAR

Uncanny X-Men #324 © MAR

Uncanny X-Men #538 © MAR

GD VG FN VF VF/NM NM-
2.0 4.0 6.0 8.0 9.0 9.2

5 10 15 35 55 75
140-Alpha Flight app. 5 10 15 35 55 75
141-Intro Future X-Men & The New Brotherhood of Evil Mutants; 1st app. Rachel (Phoenix II); Death of Franklin Richards 6 12 18 37 59 80

X-MEN: Titled THE UNCANNY X-MEN No. 142, Feb, 1981 - No. 544, Dec, 2011

142-Rachel app.; deaths of alt. future Wolverine, Storm & Colossus 6 12 18 41 66 90
143-Last Byrne issue 5 10 15 32 51 70
144-150: 144-Man-Thing app. 145-Old X-Men app. 148-Spider-Woman, Dazzler app. 150-Double size 2 4 6 9 13 16
151-157,159-161,163,164: 161-Origin Magneto. 163-Origin Binary. 164-1st app. Binary as Carol Danvers 2 4 6 8 10 12
158-1st app. Rogue in X-Men (6/82, see Avengers Annual #10) 3 6 9 16 23 30
162-Wolverine solo story 2 4 6 10 14 18
165-Paul Smith-c/a begins, ends #175 2 4 6 8 11 14
166-170: 166-Double size; Paul Smith-a. 167-New Mutants app. (3/83); same date as New Mutants #1; 1st meeting w/X-Men; ties into N.M. #3,4; Starjammers app.; contains skin "Tattooz" decals. 168-1st brief app. Madelyne Pryor (last page) in X-Men (see Avengers Annual #10) 2 3 4 6 8 10
171-Rogue joins X-Men; Simonson-c/a 2 4 6 13 18 22
172-174: 172,173-Two part Wolverine solo story. 173-Two cover variations, blue & black. 174-Phoenix cameo 1 3 4 6 8 10
175-(52 pgs.)-Anniversary issue; Phoenix returns 2 4 6 8 10 12
176-185,187-192,194-199: 181-Sunfire app. 182-Rogue solo story. 184-1st app. Forge (8/84). 190,191-Spider-Man & Avengers x-over. 195-Power Pack x-over 1 2 3 5 7 9
186,193: 186-Double-size; Barry Smith/Austin-a. 193-Double size; 100th app. New X-Men; 1st app. Warpath in costume (see New Mutants #16) 1 3 4 6 8 10
200-(12/85, $1.25, 52 pgs.) 2 4 6 8 10 12
201-(1/86)-1st app. Cable? (as baby Nathan; see X-Factor #1); 1st Whilce Portacio-c/a(i) on X-Men (guest artist) 3 6 9 16 23 30
202-204,206-209: 204-Nightcrawler solo story; 2nd Portacio-a(i) on X-Men. 207-Wolverine/Phoenix story 1 2 3 5 7 9
205-Wolverine solo story by Barry Smith 2 4 6 9 13 16
210,211-Mutant Massacre begins 3 6 9 14 19 24
212,213-Wolverine vs. Sabretooth (Mutant Mass.) 3 6 9 16 22 28
214-221,223,224: 219-Havok joins (7/87); brief app. Sabretooth. 221-1st app. Mr. Sinister 1 2 3 5 6 8
222-Wolverine battles Sabretooth-c/story 3 6 9 14 20 26
225-242: 225-227: Fall Of The Mutants. 226-Double size. 240-Sabretooth app. 242-Double size, X-Factor app., Inferno tie-in 1 2 3 5 6 8
243,245-247: 245-Rob Liefeld-a(p) 1 2 3 5 6 8
244-1st app. Jubilee 3 6 9 18 27 35
248-1st Jim Lee art on X-Men (1989) 2 4 6 13 18 22
248-2nd printing (1992, $1.25) 3.00
249-252: 252-Lee-c 1 2 3 4 5 7
253-255: 253-All new X-Men begin. 254-Lee-c 1 2 3 4 5 7
256,257-Jim Lee-c/a begins 1 2 3 5 7 9
258-Wolverine solo story; Lee-c/a 1 2 3 5 7 9
259-Silvestri-c/a; no Lee-a 1 2 3 4 5 7
260-265-No Lee-a. 260,261,264-Lee-c 1 2 3 4 5 7
266-(8/90) 1st full app. Gambit (see Annual #14)-No Lee-a 4 8 12 26 41 55
267-Jim Lee-c/a resumes; 2nd full Gambit app. 2 4 6 9 13 16
268-Capt. America, Black Widow & Wolverine team-up; Lee-c/a 2 4 6 10 14 18
268,270: 268-2nd printing. 270-Gold 2nd printing 3.00
269,273,274: 269-Lee-a. 273-New Mutants (Cable) & X-Factor x-over; Golden, Byrne & Lee part pencils 1 2 3 4 5 7
270-X-Tinction Agenda begins 1 2 3 5 6 8
271,272-X-Tinction Agenda 1 2 3 5 6 8
275-(52 pgs.)-Tri-fold-c by Jim Lee (p); Prof. X 1 2 3 5 6 8
275-Gold 2nd printing 4.00
276-280: 277-Last Lee-c/a. 280-X-Factor x-over 6.00
281-(10/91)-New team begins (Storm, Archangel, Colossus, Iceman & Marvel Girl); Whilce Portacio-c/a begins; Byrne scripts begin; wraparound-c (white logo) 1 2 3 4 5 7
281-2nd printing with red metallic ink logo w/o UPC box ($1.00-c); does not say 2nd printing inside 3.00
282-1st brief app. Bishop (cover & 1 page) 2 4 6 8 10 12
282-Gold ink 2nd printing ($1.00-c) 3.00
283-1st full app. Bishop (12/91) 2 4 6 8 10 12

GD VG FN VF VF/NM NM-
2.0 4.0 6.0 8.0 9.0 9.2

284-299: 284-Last $1.00-c. 286,287-Lee plots. 287-Bishop joins team. 288-Lee/Portacio plots. 290-Last Portacio-c/a. 294-Peterson-a(p) begins (#292 is 1st Peterson-c). 294-296 ($1.50)-Bagged w/trading card in each; X-Cutioner's Song x-overs; Peterson/Austin-c/a on all 4.00
297,303,307-Gold Edition 1 2 3 4 5 7
300-($3.95, 68 pgs.)-Holo-grafx foil-c; Magneto app. 6.00
301-303,305-309,311 3.00
304-($3.95, 68 pgs.)-Wraparound-c with Magneto hologram on-c; 30th anniversary issue; Jae Lee-a (4 pgs.) 6.00
310-($1.95)-Bound-in trading card sheet 3.00
312-$1.50-c begins; bound-in card sheet; 1st Madureira 4.00
313-321 3.00
316,317-($2.95)-Foil enhanced editions 4.00
318-321-($1.95)-Deluxe editions 3.00
322-Onslaught 5.00
323,324,326-346: 323-Return from Age of Apocalypse. 328-Sabretooth-c. 329,330-Dr. Strange app. 331-White Queen-c/app. 334-Juggernaut app.; w/Onslaught Update. 335-Onslaught, Avengers, Apocalypse, & X-Man app. 336-Onslaught. 338-Archangel's wings return to normal. 339-Havok vs. Cyclops; Spider-Man app. 341-Gladiator-c/app. 342-Deathbird cameo; two covers. 343,344-Phalanx 3.00
325-($3.95)-Anniversary issue; gatefold-c 5.00
342-Variant-c 1 3 4 6 8 10
347-349:347-Begin $1.99-c. 349-"Operation Zero Tolerance" 3.00
350-($3.99, 48 pgs.) Prismatic etched foil gatefold wraparound-c; Trial of Gambit; Seagle-s begin 1 2 3 5 6 8
351-359: 353-Bachalo-a begins. 354-Regular-c. 355-Alpha Flight-c/app. 356-Original X-Men-c 3.00
354-Dark Phoenix variant-c 5.00
360-($2.99) 35th Anniv. issue; Pacheco-c 4.00
360-($3.99) Etched Holo-foil enhanced-c 5.00
360-($6.95) DF Edition with Jae Lee variant-c 7.00
361-374: 361-Gambit returns; Skroce-a. 362-Hunt for Xavier pt. 1; Bachelo-a. 364-Yu-a. 366-Magneto-c. 369-Juggernaut-c 3.00
375-($2.99) Autopsy of Wolverine 4.00
376-379: 376,377-Apocalypse: The Twelve 3.00
380-($2.99) Polybagged with X-Men Revolution Genesis Edition preview 4.00
381,382,384-389,391-393: 381-Begin $2.25-c; Claremont-s. 387-Maximum Security 3.00
383-($2.99) 4.00
390-Colossus dies to cure the Legacy Virus 4.00
394-New look X-Men begins; Casey-s/Churchill-c/a 4.00
395-399-Poptopia. 398-Phillips & Wood-a 3.00
400-($3.50) Art by Ashley Wood, Eddie Campbell, Hamner, Phillips, Pulido and Matt Smith; wraparound-c by Wood 5.00
401-415: 401-'Nuff Said issue; Garney-a. 404,405,407-409,413-415-Phillips-a 3.00
416-421: 416-Asamiya-a begins. 421-Garney-a 3.00
422-($3.50) Alpha Flight app.; Garney-a 4.00
423-(25¢-c) Holy War pt. 1; Garney-a/Philip Tan-c 3.00
424-449,452-454: 425,426,429,430-Tan-a. 428-Birth of Nightcrawler. 437-Larroca-a begins. 444-New team, new costumes; Claremont-s/Davis-a begins. 448,449-Coipel-a 3.00
450,451,455-459-X-23 app.; Davis-a 3.00
460-471: 460-Begin $2.50-c; Raney-a. 462-465-House of M. 464-468-Bachalo-a 3.00
472-499: 472-Begin $2.99-c; Bachalo-a. 475-Wraparound-c. 492-494-Messiah Complex 3.00
500-($3.99) X-Men new HQ in San Francisco; Magneto app.; Land & Dodson-a; wraparound covers by Alex Ross and Greg Land 5.00
500-Classic X-Men Dynamic Forces variant-c by Ross 8.00
500-X-Men variant-c by Michael Turner 30.00
500-X-Women variant-c by Dodson 15.00
501-511,515-521,523-525: 501-Brubaker & Fraction-s/Land-a. 523-525-Second Coming 3.00
512-514,522-($3.99). 513,514-Utopia x-over. 522-Kitty Pryde returns to Earth; Portacio-a 4.00
526-543-($3.99) 526-The Heroic Age; aftermath of Second Coming. 530-534-Land-a 540-543-Fear Itself tie-in, Juggernaut attacks; Land-a. 542-Colossus becomes the Juggernaut 4.00
534.1 (6/11, $2.99) Pacheco-a/c 3.00
544-(12/11, $3.99) Final issue; Land-a/c; Mr. Sinister app. 4.00
#(-1) Flashback (7/97) Ladronn-c/Hitch & Neary-a 3.00
Special 1(12/70)-Kirby-c/a; origin The Stranger 10 20 30 68 127 185
Special 2(11/71, 52 pgs.) 8 16 24 53 89 125
Annual 3(1979, 52 pgs.)-New story; Miller/Austin-c; Wolverine still in old yellow costume 5 10 15 30 48 65
Annual 4(1980, 52 pgs.)-Dr. Strange guest stars 3 6 9 14 20 25
Annual 5(1981, 52 pgs.) 2 4 6 8 10 12
Annual 6-8('82-'84 52 pgs.)-6-Dracula app. 1 2 3 5 6 8
Annual 9,10('85, '86)-9-New Mutants x-over cont'd from New Mutants Special Ed. #1; Art Adams-a. 10-Art Adams-a 2 4 6 8 10 12
Annual 11-13:('87-'89, 68 pgs.): 12-Evolutionary War; A.Adams-a(p). 13-Atlantis Attacks 5.00

Uncanny X-Men Annual #18 © MAR

X-Men #36 © MAR

New X-Men #153 © MAR

GD 2.0 | VG 4.0 | FN 6.0 | VF 8.0 | VF/NM 9.0 | NM- 9.2

Annual 14(1990, $2.00, 68 pgs.)-1st app. Gambit (minor app., 5 pgs.); Fantastic Four, New Mutants (Cable) & X-Factor x-over; Art Adams-c/a(p) 3 6 9 16 23 30
Annual 15 (1991, $2.00, 68 pgs.)-4 pg. origin; New Mutants x-over; 4 pg. Wolverine solo back-up story; 4th app. X-Force cont'd from New Warriors Annual #1 5.00
Annual 16-18 ('92-'94, 68 pgs.)-16-Jae Lee-c/a(p). 17-Bagged w/card 4.00
Annual '95-(11/95, $3.95)-Wraparound-c 4.00
Annual '96,'97-Wraparound-c 4.00
.../Fantastic Four Annual '98 ($2.99) Casey-s 4.00
Annual '99 ($3.50) Jubilee app. 4.00
Annual 2000 ($3.50) Cable app.; Ribic-a 4.00
Annual 2001 ($3.50, printed wide-ways) Ashley Wood-c/a; Casey-s 4.00
Annual (Vol. 2) #1 (8/06, $3.99) Storm & Black Panther wedding prelude 4.00
Annual (Vol. 2) #2 (3/09, $3.99) Dark Reign; flashback to Sub-Mariner/Emma Frost 4.00
Annual (Vol. 2) #3 (5/11, $3.99) Escape From the Negative Zone; Bradshaw-a 4.00
....At The State Fair of Texas (1983, 36 pgs., one-shot); Supplement to the Dallas Times Herald 2 4 6 9 12 15
...: The Dark Phoenix Saga TPB 1st printing (1984, $12.95) 40.00
...: The Dark Phoenix Saga TPB 2nd-5th printings 25.00
...: The Dark Phoenix Saga TPB 6th-10th printings 20.00
... Days of Future Past TPB (2004, $19.99) r/#138-143 & Annual #4 20.00
... Eve of Destruction TPB (2005, $14.99) r/#391-393 & X-Men #111-113; Churchill-c 15.00
...:Dream's End (2004, $17.99)-r/Death of Colossus story arc from Uncanny X-Men #388-390, Cable #87, Bishop #16 and X-Men #108,110; debut pages from Giant-Size X-Men #1 18.00
... From The Ashes TPB (1990, $14.95) r/#168-176 15.00
... Future History - The Messiah War Sourcebook (2009, $3.99) Cable's files on X-Men 4.00
...: God Loves, Man Kills ($6.95)-r/Marvel Graphic Novel #5 7.00
...: God Loves, Man Kills - Special Edition (2003, $4.99)-reprint with new Hughes-c 5.00
...: God Loves, Man Kills HC (2007, $19.99) reprint with Claremont & Anderson interviews; original artist Neal Adams' six sketch pages and interview 20.00
...: Hope (5/10, $2.99) Collects Cable and Hope back-ups; Dillon-a 3.00
House of M: Uncanny X-Men TPB (2006, $13.99) r/#462-465 and selections from Secrets Of The House of M one-shot 14.00
...In The Days of Future Past TPB (1989, $3.95, 52 pgs.) 6.00
...Old Soldiers TPB (2004, $19.99) r/#213,215 & Ann. #11; New Mutants Ann. #2&3 20.00
...Poptopia TPB (10/01, $15.95) r/#394-399 16.00
...: Rise & Fall of the Shi'Ar Empire HC (2007, $34.99, dustjacket) r/#475-486; bonus art 35.00
...: Rise & Fall of the Shi'Ar Empire SC (2008, $29.99) r/#475-486; bonus art 30.00
...: Sword of the Braddocks (5/09, $3.99) Psylocke vs. Slaymaster; Claremont-s 4.00
...: The Complete Onslaught Epic Book 1 TPB (2007, $29.99) r/X-Men #53-54, Uncanny X-Men #334-335, Fantastic Four #414-415, Avengers #400-401, Onslaught: X-Men, Cable #34 and Incredible Hulk #444 30.00
...: The Complete Onslaught Epic Book 2 TPB ('08, $29.99) r/Excalibur #100, Wolverine #104, X-Factor #125-126, Amazing Spider-Man #415, Green Goblin #12, Spider-Man #72, Punisher #11, X-Man #18 & X-Force #57 30.00
...: The Extremists TPB (2007, $13.99) r/#487-491 14.00
...: The Heroic Age (9/10, $3.99) Beast, Steve Rogers and Princess Powerful app. 4.00
Uncanny X-Men Omnibus Vol. 1 HC (2006, $99.99, dust jacket) r/Giant-Size X-Men #1, (Uncanny) X-Men #94-131 & Annual #3; cover gallery, promo and sketch art 100.00
Vignettes TPB (9/01, $17.95) r/Claremont & Bolton Classic X-Men #1-13 18.00
Vignettes Vol. 2 TPB (2005, $17.99) r/Claremont & Bolton Classic X-Men #14-25 18.00
... Vol. 1: Hope TPB (2003, $12.99) r/#410-415; Harris-c 13.00
... Vol. 2: Dominant Species TPB (2003, $11.99) r/#416-420; Asamiya-c 12.00
... Vol. 3: Holy War TPB (2003, $17.99) r/#421-427 18.00
... Vol. 4: The Draco TPB (2004, $15.99) r/#428-434 16.00
... Vol. 5: She Lies with Angels TPB (2004, $11.99) r/#437-441 12.00
... Vol. 6: Bright New Mourning TPB (2004, $14.99) r/#435,436,442,443 & (New) X-Men #155,156; Larroca sketch covers 15.00
...Vs. Apocalypse Vol. 1: The Twelve TPB (2008, $29.99) r/#376-377, Cable #73-76, X-Men #96,97 and Wolverine #145-147 30.00
... - The New Age Vol. 1: The End of History (2004, $12.99) r/#444-449 13.00
... - The New Age Vol. 2: The Cruelest Cut (2005, $11.99) r/#450-454 12.00
... - The New Age Vol. 3: On Ice (2006, $15.99) r/#455-461 16.00
... - The New Age Vol. 4: End of Greys (2006, $14.99) r/#466-471 15.00
... - The New Age Vol. 5: First Foursaken (2006, $11.99) r/#472-474 & Annual #1 12.00

NOTE: ***Art Adams*** *a-Annual 9, 10p, 12p, 14p; c-218p.* ***Neal Adams*** *a-56-63p, 65p; c-56-63.* ***Adkins*** *a-34, 35p; c-31, 34, 35.* ***Austin*** *a-108i, 109i, 111-117i, 119-143i, 186i, 204i, 228i, 294-297i, Annual 3i, 7i, 9i, 13; c-109-111i, 114-122i, 123, 124-141i, 142, 143, 196i, 204i, 228i, 294-297i, Annual 3i.* ***J. Buscema*** *c-42, 43, 45.* ***Buscema/Tuska*** *a-45.* ***Byrne*** *a(p)-108, 109, 111-143, 273; c(p)-113-116, 127, 129, 131-141.* ***Capullo*** *c-14.* ***Ditko*** *r-86, 89-91, 93.* ***Everett*** *c-73.* ***Golden*** *a-273, Annual 7p.* ***Guice*** *a-216p, 217p.* ***G. Kane*** *c(p)-33, 74-76, 79, 80, 94, 95.* ***Kirby*** *a(p)-1-17 (#12-17, 67r-layouts); c(p)-1-17, 25, 30 (18, 26-parts).* ***Layton*** *a-105i; c-112i, 113i.* ***Jim Lee*** *a(p)-248, 256-258, 267-277; c(p)-252, 254, 256-261, 264, 267, 270, 275-277, 286.* ***Perez*** *a-Annual 3p; c(p)-112, 128, Annual 3.* ***Peterson*** *a(p)-294-300, 304(part); c(p)-294-299.* ***Whilce Portacio*** *a(p)-281-286, 289, 290; a(i)-267; c-281-285p, 289p, 290; c(i)-267.* ***Romita, Jr.*** *a-300; c-300.* ***Roussos*** *a-84i.* ***Simonson*** *a-171p; c-171, 217.* ***B. Smith*** *a-53, 186p, 198p, 205, 214; c-53-55, 186p, 198, 205, 212, 214, 216.* ***Paul Smith*** *a(p)-165-170, 172-175, 278; c-165-170, 172-175, 278.* ***Sparling*** *a-78p.* ***Steranko*** *a-50p, 51p; c-49-51.* ***Sutton*** *a-106i.* ***Art Thibert*** *a(i)-281-286; c(i)-281, 282, 284, 285.* ***Toth*** *a-12p, 67p(r).* ***Tuska*** *a-40-42i, 43-46p, 88i(r); c-39-41, 77p, 78p.* ***Williamson*** *a-202i, 203i, 211i; c-202i, 203i, 206i.* ***Wood*** *c-14i.*

UNCANNY X-MEN AND THE NEW TEEN TITANS (See Marvel and DC Present...)

X-MEN (2nd Series)(Titled New X-Men with #114) (Titled X-Men Legacy with #210)
Marvel Comics: Oct, 1991 - Present ($1.00-$2.99)

1 a-d (four different covers, $1.50, 52 pgs.)-Jim Lee-c/a begins, ends #11; new team begins (Cyclops, Beast, Wolverine, Gambit, Psylocke & Rogue); new Uncanny X-Men & Magneto app.; 5.00
1 e ($3.95)-Double gate-fold-c consisting of all four covers from 1a-d by Jim Lee; contains all pin-ups from #1a-d plus inside-c foldout poster; no ads; printed on coated stock 6.00
1-20th Anniversary Edition-(12/11, $3.99) r/#1 with double gatefold-c; Jim Lee pin-ups 4.00
2-7: 4-Wolverine back to old yellow costume (same date as Wolverine #50); last $1.00-c. 5-Byrne scripts. 6-Sabretooth-c/story 5.00
8-10: 8-Gambit vs. Bishop-c/story; last Lee-a; Ghost Rider cameo cont'd in Ghost Rider #26. 9-Wolverine vs. Ghost Rider; cont'd/G.R. #26. 10-Return of Longshot 5.00
11-13,17-24,26-29,31: 12,13-Art Thibert-c/a. 28,29-Sabretooth app. 4.00
11-Silver ink 2nd printing; came with X-Men board game 2 4 6 9 12 15
14-16-($1.50)-Polybagged with trading card in each; X-Cutioner's Song x-overs; 14-Andy Kubert-c/a begins 5.00
25-($3.50, 52 pgs.)-Wraparound-c with Gambit hologram on-c; Professor X erases Magneto's mind 2 4 6 8 10 12
25-30th anniversary issue w/B&W-c with Magneto in color & Magneto hologram & no price on-c 2 4 6 9 12 15
25-Gold 30.00
30-($1.95)-Wedding issue w/bound-in trading card sheet 5.00
32-37: 32-Begin $1.50-c; bound-in card sheet. 33-Gambit & Sabretooth-c/story 4.00
36,37-($2.95)-Collectors editions (foil-c) 5.00
38-44,46-49,51-53, 55-65: 42,43- Paul Smith-a. 46,49,53-56-Onslaught app. 51-Waid scripts begin, end #56. 54-(Reg. edition)-Onslaught revealed as Professor X. 55,56-Onslaught x-over; Avengers, FF & Sentinels app. 56-Dr. Doom app. 57-Xavier taken into custody; Byrne-c/swipe (X-Men,1st Series #138). 59-Hercules-c/app. 61-Juggernaut-c/app. 62-Re-intro. Shang Chi; two covers. 63-Kingpin cameo. 64- Kingpin app. 4.00
45-($3.95)-Annual issue; gatefold-c 5.00
50-($2.95)-Vs. Onslaught, wraparound-c. 4.00
50-($3.95)-Vs. Onslaught, wraparound foil-c. 5.00
50-($2.95)-Variant gold-c. 3 6 9 20 30 40
50-($2.95)-Variant silver-c. 1 2 3 5 6 8
54-(Limited edition)-Embossed variant-c; Onslaught revealed as Professor X 3 6 9 16 23 30
66-69,71-74,76-79: 66-Operation Zero Tolerance. 76-Origin of Maggott 3.00
70-($2.99, 48 pgs.)-Joe Kelly-s begin, new members join 4.00
75-($2.99, 48 pgs.) vs. N'Garai; wraparound-c 4.00
80-($3.99) 35th Anniv. issue; holo-foil-c 5.00
80-($2.99) Regular-c 4.00
80-($6.95) Dynamic Forces Ed.; Quesada-c 7.00
81-93,95: 82-Hunt for Xavier pt. 2. 85-Davis-a. 86-Origin of Joseph. 87-Magneto War ends. 88-Juggernaut app. 3.00
94-($2.99) Contains preview of "X-Men: Hidden Years 4.00
96-99: 96,97-Apocalypse: The Twelve 3.00
100-($2.99) Art Adams-c; begin Claremont-s/Yu-a 4.00
100-DF alternate-c 1 3 4 6 8 10
101-105,107,108,110-114: 101-Begin $2.25-c. 107-Maximum Security x-over; Bishop-c/app. 108-Moira MacTaggart dies; Senator Kelly shot. 111-Magneto-c. 112,113-Eve of Destruction 3.00
106-($2.99) X-Men battle Domina 4.00
109-($3.50, 100 pgs.) new and reprinted Christmas-themed stories 5.00
114-(7/01) Title change to "New X-Men," Morrison-s/Quitely-c/a begins 4.00
114-(8/10, $1.00) "Marvel's Greatest Comics" reprint 3.00
115-Two covers (Quitely & BWS) 4.00
116-125,127-149: 116-Emma Frost joins. 117,118-Van Sciver-a. 121,122,135-Quitely-a. 127-Leon & Sienkiewicz-a. 128-Kordey-a. 132,139-141-Jimenez-a. 136-138-Quitely-a 142-Sabretooth app.; Bachalo-c/a thru #145. 146-Magneto returns; Jimenez-a 3.00
126-($3.25) Quitely-a; defeat of Cassanova 4.00
150-($3.50) Jean Grey dies again; last Jimenez-a 4.00
151-156: 151-154-Silvestri-c/a 3.00
157-169: 157-X-Men Reload begins 3.00
170-184: 171- Begin $2.50-c. 175,176-Crossover with Black Panther #8,9. 181-184-Apocalypse returns 3.00
185-199,201-229,231-249,251-261: 185-Begin $2.99-c. 188-190,192-194,197-199-Bachalo-a. 195,196,201-203-Ramos-a. 201-204-Endangered Species back-up. 205-207-Messiah Complex x-over. 208-Romita Jr.-a. 210-Starts X-Men: Legacy. 228,229-Acuña-a. 235-237-Second Coming x-over. 238-The Heroic Age. 245-Age of X begins 3.00
200-($3.99) Two wraparound covers by Bachalo & Finch; Bachalo & Ramos-a 4.00

X-Men (2010 series) #13 © MAR

X-Men Adventures #8 © MAR

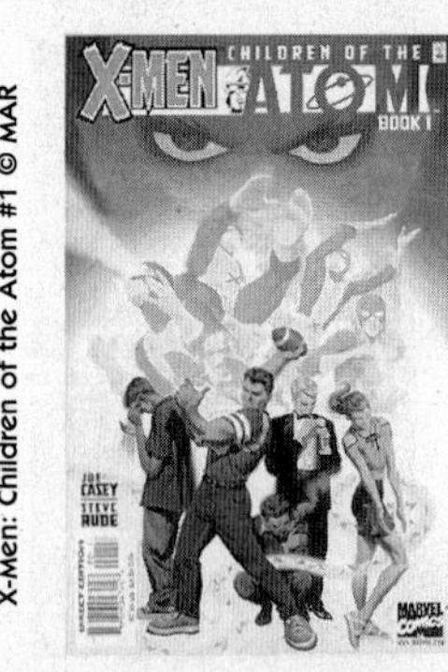
X-Men: Children of the Atom #1 © MAR

	GD 2.0	VG 4.0	FN 6.0	VF 8.0	VF/NM 9.0	NM- 9.2

230-($3.99) Acuña-a; Rogue vs. Emplate 4.00
250-($4.99) Suayan-c/Pham-a; back-up r/New Mutants #27 5.00
261.1-(3/12, $2.99) The N'Garai app.; Brooks-c 3.00
262,263-Brooks-c 3.00
#(-1) Flashback (7/97); origin of Magneto 3.00
Annual 1-3 ('92-'94, $2.25-$2.95, 68 pgs.) 1-Lee-c & layouts; #2-Bagged w/card 4.00
Special '95 ($3.95) 4.00
... '96,...'97-Wraparound-c 4.00
.../ Dr. Doom '98 Annual ($2.99) Lopresti-a 4.00
... Annual '99 ($3.50) Adam Kubert-c 4.00
Annual 2000 ($3.50) Art Adams-c/Claremont-s/Eaton-a 4.00
...2001 Annual ($3.50) Morrison-s/Yu-a; issue printed sideways 4.00
...2007 Annual #1 (3/07, $3.99) Casey-s/Brooks-a; Cable and Mystique app. 4.00
...Legacy Annual 1 (11/09, $3.99) Acuña-a; Emplate returns 4.00
Animation Special Graphic Novel (12/90, $10.95) adapts animated series 11.00
Ashcan #1 (1994, 75¢) Introduces new team members 3.00
... Archives Sketchbook (12/00, $2.99) Early B&W character design sketches by various incl. Lee, Davis, Yu, Pacheco, BWS, Art Adams, Liefeld 3.00
...: Bizarre Love Triangle TPB (2005, $9.99)-r/X-Men #171-174 10.00
.../ Black Panther TPB (2006, $11.99)-r/X-Men #175,176 & Black Panther (2005) #8,9 12.00
...: Blinded By the Light (2007, $14.99)-r/X-Men #200-204 15.00
...: Blind Science (7/10, $3.99) Second Coming x-over; Parel-c 4.00
...: Blood of Apocalypse (2006, $17.99)-r/X-Men #182-187 18.00
...: Day of the Atom (2005, $19.99)-r/X-Men #157-165 20.00
Decimation: X-Men - The Day After TPB (2006, $15.99) r/#177-181 & Decimation: House of M - The Day After 16.00
...: Declassified (10/00, $3.50) Profile pin-ups by various; Jae Lee-c 4.00
...: Earth's Mutant Heroes (7/11, $4.99) Handbook-style profiles of mutants 5.00
...: Endangered Species (8/07, $3.99) prologue to 17-part back-up series in X-Men titles 4.00
...: Endangered Species HC (2008, $24.99, d.j.) over-sized r/prologue and 17-part series 25.00
...: Evolutions 1 (12/11, $3.99) Collection of variant covers from May 2011 Marvel titles 4.00
...: Fatal Attractions ('94, $17.95)-r/x-Factor #92, X-Force #25, Uncanny X-Men #304, X-Men #25, Wolverine #75, & Excalibur #71 18.00
...: Golgotha (2005, $12.99)-r/X-Men #166-170 13.00
... Millennial Visions (8/00, $3.99) Various artists interpret future X-Men 4.00
... Millennial Visions 2 (1/02, $3.50) Various artists interpret future X-Men 4.00
...: Mutant Genesis (2006, $19.99)-r/X-Men #1-7; sketch pages and extra art 20.00
New X-Men: E is for Extinction TPB (11/01, $12.95) r/#114-117 13.00
New X-Men: Imperial TPB (7/02, $19.99) r/#118-126; Quitely-c 20.00
New X-Men: New Worlds TPB (2002, $14.99) r/#127-133; Quitely-c 15.00
New X-Men: Riot at Xavier's TPB (2003, $11.99) r/#134-138; Quitely-c 12.00
New X-Men: Vol. 5: Assault on Weapon Plus TPB (2003, $14.99) r/#139-145 15.00
New X-Men: Vol. 6: Planet X TPB (2004, $12.99) r/#146-150 13.00
New X-Men: Vol. 7: Here Comes Tomorrow TPB (2004, $10.99) r/#151-154 11.00
New X-Men: Volume 1 HC (2002, $29.99) oversized r/#114-126 & 2001 Annual 30.00
New X-Men: Volume 2 HC (2003, $29.99) oversized r/#127-141; sketch & script pages 30.00
New X-Men: Volume 3 HC (2004, $29.99) oversized r/#142-154; sketch & script pages 30.00
New X-Men Omnibus HC (2006, $99.99) oversized r/#114-154 & Annual 2001; Morrison's original pitch; sketch & script pages; variant covers & promo art; Carey intro. 140.00
...: Odd Men Out (2008, $3.99) Two unpublished stories with Dave Cockrum-a 4.00
... Original Sin 1 (12/08, $3.99) Wolverine and Daken; Deodato & Eaton-a 4.00
... Origin: Colossus (7/08, $3.99) Yost-s/Hairsine-a; Piotr Rasputin before joining X-Men 4.00
... Phoenix Force Handbook (9/10, $4.99) bios of those related to the Phoenix; Raney-c 5.00
...: Pixies and Demons Director's Cut (2008, $3.99) r/FCBD 2008 story with script 4.00
... Pizza Hut Mini-comics-(See Marvel Collector's Edition: X-Men in Promotional Comics section)
... Premium Edition #1 (1993)-Cover says "Toys 'R' Us Limited Edition X-Men" 3.00
...: Rarities (1995, $5.95)-Reprints 6.00
...: Return of Magik Must Have (2008, $3.99) r/X-Men Unlimited #14, New X-Men #37 and X-Men: Divided We Stand #2; Coipel-c 4.00
...: Road Trippin' ('99, $24.95, TPB) r/X-Men road trips 25.00
...: Supernovas ('07, $34.99, oversized HC w/d.j.) r/X-Men 188-199 & Annual #1 35.00
...: Supernovas ('08, $29.99, SC) r/X-Men 188-199 & Annual #1 30.00
...: The Coming of Bishop ('95, $12.95)-r/Uncanny X-Men #282-285, 287,288 13.00
...: The Magneto War (3/99, $2.99) Davis-a 4.00
...: The Rise of Apocalypse ('98, $16.99)-r/Rise Of Apocalypse #1-4, X-Factor #5,6 17.00
... Visionaries: Chris Claremont ('98, $24.95)-r/Claremont-s; art by Byrne, BWS, Jim Lee 25.00
... Visionaries: Jim Lee ('02, $29.99)-r/Jim Lee-a from various issues between Uncanny X-Men #248 & 286; r/Classic X-Men #39 and X-Men Annual #1 30.00
... Visionaries: Joe Madureira (7/00, $17.95)-r/Uncanny X-Men #325,326,329,330,341-343; new Madureira-c 18.00
... Vs. Hulk (3/09, $3.99) Claremont-s/Raapack-a; r/X-Men #66 4.00
...: Zero Tolerance ('00, $24.95, TPB) r/crossover series 25.00

NOTE: ***Jim Lee*** *a-1-11p; c-1-6p, 7, 8, 9p, 10, 11p.* ***Art Thibert*** *a-6-9i, 12, 13; c-6i, 12, 13.*

X-MEN
Marvel Comics: Sept, 2010 - Present ($3.99)

1-26: 1-6-"Curse of the Mutants" x-over; Medina-a. 7-10-Spider-Man app.; Bachalo-a. 12-Continued from X-Men Giant-Size #1. 16-19-FF & Skull the Slayer app. 20-23-War Machine app. 16-Deadpool app. 4.00
15.1 ($2.99) Pearson-c/Conrad-a; Ghost Rider app. 3.00
...: Curse of the Mutants - Blade 1 (10/10, $3.99) Tim Green-a 4.00
...: Curse of the Mutants - Smoke and Blood 1 (11/10, $3.99) Crain-c 4.00
...: Curse of the Mutants Spotlight 1 (1/11, $3.99) creator profiles and interviews 4.00
...: Curse of the Mutants - Storm and Gambit 1 (11/10, $3.99) Bachalo-a; 2 covers 4.00
...: Curse of the Mutants - X-Men vs. Vampires 1,2 (11/10 - No. 2, 12/10, $3.99) Bradshaw-c 4.00
... Giant-Size 1 (7/11, $4.99) Medina & Talajic-a; cover swipe of Giant-Size X-Men #1 5.00
...: Regenesis 1 (12/11, $3.99) Splits X-Men into 2 teams; Tan-a/Bachalo-c 4.00
... Spotlight 1 (7/11, $3.99) Character profiles and creator interviews 4.00
...: With Great Power 1 (2011, $4.99) r/#7-9 5.00

X-MEN (Free Comic Book Day giveaways)
Marvel Comics: 2006; May, 2008

FCBD 2008 Edition #1-(5/08) Features Pixie; Carey-s/Land-a/c 3.00
.../Runaways: FCBD 2006 Edition; new x-over story; Mighty Avengers preview; Chen-c 3.00

X-MEN ADVENTURES (TV)
Marvel Comics: Nov, 1992 - No. 15, Jan, 1994 ($1.25)(Based on animated series)

1,15: 1-Wolverine, Cyclops, Jubilee, Rogue, Gambit. 15-($1.75, 52 pgs.) 4.00
2-14: 3-Magneto-c/story. 6-Sabretooth-c/story. 7-Cable-c/story. 10-Archangel guest star. 11-Cable-c/story. 3.00

X-MEN ADVENTURES II (TV)
Marvel Comics: Feb, 1994 - No. 13, Feb, 1995 ($1.25/$1.50)(Based on 2nd TV season)

1-13: 4-Bound-in trading card sheet. 5-Alpha Flight app. 3.00
...Captive Hearts/Slave Island (TPB, $4.95)-r/X-Men Adventures #5-8 5.00
...The Irresistible Force, The Muir Island Saga (5.95, 10/94, TPB) r/X-Men Advs. #9-12 6.00

X-MEN ADVENTURES III (TV)(See Adventures of the X-Men)
Marvel Comics: Mar, 1995 - No. 13, Mar, 1996 ($1.50) (Based on 3rd TV season)

1-13 3.00

X-MEN: AGE OF APOCALYPSE
Marvel Comics: May, 2005 - No. 6, June, 2005 ($2.99, weekly limited series)

1-6-Bachalo-c/a; Yoshida-s; follows events in the "Age of Apocalypse" storyline 3.00
... One Shot (5/05, $3.99) prequel to series; Hitch wraparound-c; pin-ups by various 4.00
X-Men: The New Age of Apocalypse TPB (2005, $20.99) r/#1-6 & one-shot 21.00

X-MEN ALPHA
Marvel Comics: 1994 ($3.95, one-shot)

	GD	VG	FN	VF	VF/NM	NM-
nn-Age of Apocalypse; wraparound chromium-c	1	2	3	5	6	8
nn ($49.95)-Gold logo						50.00

X-MEN/ALPHA FLIGHT
Marvel Comics Group: Dec, 1985 - No. 2, Dec, 1985 ($1.50, limited series)

1,2: 1-Intro The Berserkers; Paul Smith-a 5.00

X-MEN/ALPHA FLIGHT
Marvel Comics Group: May, 1998 - No. 2, June, 1998 ($2.99, limited series)

1,2-Flashback to early meeting; Raab-s/Cassaday-s/a 3.00

X-MEN AND POWER PACK
Marvel Comics: Dec, 2005 - No. 4, Mar, 2006 ($2.99, limited series)

1-4-Sumerak-s/Gurihiru-a. 1-Wolverine & Sabretooth app. 3.00
...: The Power of X (2006, $6.99, digest size) r/#1-4 7.00

X-MEN AND THE MICRONAUTS, THE
Marvel Comics Group: Jan, 1984 - No. 4, Apr, 1984 (Limited series)

1-4: Guice-c/a(p) in all 5.00

X-MEN: APOCALYPSE/DRACULA
Marvel Comics: Apr, 2006 - No. 4, July, 2006 ($2.99, limited series)

1-4-Tieri-s/Henry-a/Jae Lee-c 3.00
TPB (2006, $10.99) r/series; cover gallery 11.00

X-MEN ARCHIVES
Marvel Comics: Jan, 1995 - No. 4, Apr, 1995 ($2.25, limited series)

1-4: Reprints Legion stories from New Mutants. 4-Magneto app. 3.00

X-MEN ARCHIVES FEATURING CAPTAIN BRITAIN
Marvel Comics: July, 1995 - No. 7, 1996 ($2.95, limited series)

1-7: Reprints early Capt. Britain stories 3.00

X-MEN BLACK SUN (See Black Sun:...)

X-Men Classic #78 © MAR

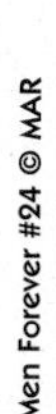

X-Men Forever #24 © MAR

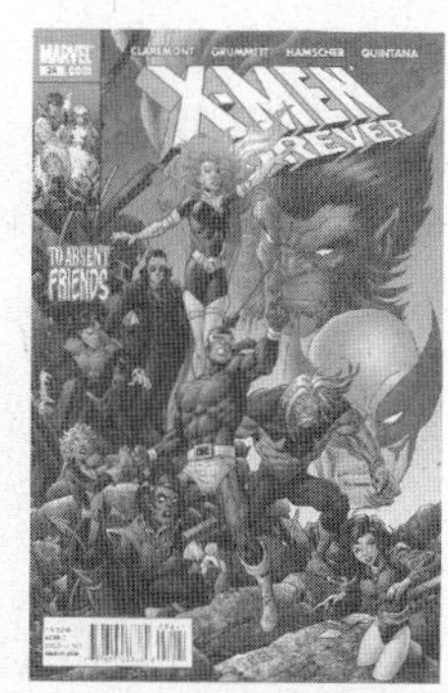

X-Men: Hidden Years #1 © MAR

GD 2.0 | VG 4.0 | FN 6.0 | VF 8.0 | VF/NM 9.0 | NM- 9.2

X-MEN BOOKS OF ASKANI
Marvel Comics: 1995 ($2.95, one-shot)
1-Painted pin-ups w/text 3.00

X-MEN: CHILDREN OF THE ATOM
Marvel Comics: Nov, 1999 - No. 6 ($2.99, limited series)
1-6-Casey-s; X-Men before issue #1. 1-3-Rude-c/a. 4-Paul Smith-a/Rude-c. 5,6-Essad Ribic-c/a 3.00
TPB (11/01, $16.95) r/series; sketch pages; Casey intro. 17.00

X-MEN CHRONICLES
Marvel Comics: Mar, 1995 - No. 2, June, 1995 ($3.95, limited series)
1,2: Age of Apocalypse x-over. 1-wraparound-c 5.00

X-MEN: CLANDESTINE
Marvel Comics: Oct, 1996 - No. 2, Nov, 1996 ($2.95, limited series, 48 pgs.)
1,2: Alan Davis-c(p)/a(p)/scripts & Mark Farmer-c(i)/a(i) in all; wraparound-c 4.00

X-MEN CLASSIC (Formerly Classic X-Men)
Marvel Comics: No. 46, Apr, 1990 - No. 110, Aug, 1995 ($1.25/$1.50)
46-110: Reprints from X-Men. 54-(52 pgs.). 57,60-63,65-Russell-c(i); 62-r/X-Men #158(Rogue). 66-r/#162(Wolverine). 69-Begins-r of Paul Smith issues (#165 on). 70,79,90,97(52 pgs.). 70-r/X-Men #166. 90-r/#186. 100-($1.50). 104-r/X-Men #200 4.00

X-MEN CLASSICS
Marvel Comics Group: Dec, 1983 - No. 3, Feb, 1984 ($2.00, Baxter paper)
1-3: X-Men-r by Neal Adams 6.00
NOTE: *Zeck c-1-3.*

X-MEN: COLOSSUS BLOODLIINE
Marvel Comics: Nov, 2005 - No. 5, Mar, 2006 ($2.99, limited series)
1-5-Colossus returns to Russia; David Hine-s/Jorge Lucas-a; Bachalo-c 3.00
TPB (2006, $13.99) r/#1-5 14.00

X-MEN: DEADLY GENESIS (See Uncanny X-Men #475)
Marvel Comics: Jan, 2006 - No. 6, July, 2006 ($3.99/$3.50, limited series)
1-($3.99) Silvestri-c swipe of Giant-Size X-Men #1; Hairsine-a/Brubaker-s 4.00
2-6-($3.50) 2-Silvestri-c; Banshee killed. 4-Intro Kid Vulcan 3.50
HC (2006, $24.99, dust jacket) r/#1-6 25.00
SC (2006, $19.99) r/#1-6 20.00

X-MEN: DIE BY THE SWORD
Marvel Comics: Dec, 2007 - No. 5, Feb, 2008 ($2.99, limited series)
1-5-Excalibur and The Exiles app.; Claremont-s/Santacruz-a 3.00
TPB (2008, $13.99) r/#1-5; handbook pages of Merlyn, Roma and Saturne 14.00

X-MEN: DIVIDED WE STAND
Marvel Comics: June, 2008 - No. 2, July, 2008 ($3.99, limited series)
1,2-Short stories by various; Peterson-c 4.00

X-MEN: EARTHFALL
Marvel Comics: Sept, 1996 ($2.95, one-shot)
1-r/Uncanny X-Men #232-234; wraparound-c 4.00

X-MEN: EMPEROR VULCAN
Marvel Comics: Nov, 2007 - No. 5, Mar, 2008 ($2.99, limited series)
1-5: 1-Starjammers app.; Yost-s/Diaz-a/Tan-c 3.00
TPB (2008, $13.99) r/#1-5 14.00

X-MEN: EVOLUTION (Based on the animated series)
Marvel Comics: Feb, 2002 - No. 9, Sept, 2002 ($2.25)
1-9: 1-8-Grayson-s/Udon-a. 9-Farber-s/J.J.Kirby-a 3.00
TPB (7/02, $8.99) r/#1-4 9.00
Vol. 2 TPB (2003, $11.99) r/#5-9; Asamiya-c 12.00

X-MEN FAIRY TALES
Marvel Comics: July, 2006 - No. 4, Oct, 2006 ($2.99, limited series)
1-4-Re-imagining of classic stories; Cebulski-s. 2-Baker-a. 3-Sienkiewicz-a. 4-Kobayashi-a 3.00
TPB (2006, $10.99) r/#1-4 11.00

X-MEN/ FANTASTIC FOUR
Marvel Comics: Feb, 2005 - No. 5, June, 2005 ($3.50, limited series)
1-5-Pat Lee-a/c; Yoshida-s; the Brood app. 3.50
HC (2005, $19.99, 7 1/2" x 11", dustjacket) oversized r/#1-5; cover gallery 20.00

X-MEN FIRST CLASS
Marvel Comics: Nov, 2006 - No. 8, Jun, 2007 ($2.99, limited series)
1-8-Xavier's first class of X-Men; Cruz-a/Parker-s. 5-Thor app. 7-Scarlet Witch app. 3.00
... Special 1 (7/07, $3.99) Nowlan-c; Nowlan, Paul Smith, Coover, Dragotta & Allred-a 4.00

GD 2.0 | VG 4.0 | FN 6.0 | VF 8.0 | VF/NM 9.0 | NM- 9.2

... - Tomorrow's Brightest HC (2007, $24.99, d.j) r/#1-8; cover & character design art 25.00
... - Tomorrow's Brightest SC (2007, $19.99) r/#1-8; cover & character design art 20.00

X-MEN FIRST CLASS (2nd series)
Marvel Comics: Aug, 2007 - No. 16, Nov, 2008 ($2.99)
1-16: 1-Cruz-a/Parker-s; Fantastic Four app. 8-Man-Thing app. 10-Romita Jr.-c 3.00
... Giant-Size Special 1 (12/08, $3.99) 5 new short stories; Haspiel-a; r/X-Men #40 4.00
... - Mutant Mayhem TPB (2008, $13.99) r/#1-5 & X-Men First Class Special 14.00

X-MEN FIRST CLASS FINALS
Marvel Comics: Apr, 2009 - No. 4, July, 2009 ($3.99, limited series)
1-4-Cruz-a/Parker-s. 1-3-Coover-a 4.00

X-MEN FIRSTS
Marvel Comics: Feb, 1996 ($4.95, one-shot)
1-r/Avengers Annual #10, Uncanny X-Men #266, #221; Incredible Hulk #181 5.00

X-MEN FOREVER
Marvel Comics: Jan, 2001 - No. 6, June, 2001 ($3.50, limited series)
1-6-Jean Grey, Iceman, Mystique, Toad, Juggernaut app.; Maguire-a 4.00

X-MEN FOREVER
Marvel Comics: Aug, 2009 - No. 24, July, 2010 ($3.99)
1-24: 1-Claremont-s/Grummett-a/c. 7-Nick Fury app. 4.00
... Alpha 1 (2009, $4.99) r/X-Men (1991) #1-3; 8 page preview of X-Men Forever #1 5.00
... Annual 1 (6/10, $4.99) Wolverine & Jean Grey romance; Sana Takeda-a/c 5.00
... Giant-Size 1 (7/10, $3.99) Grell-a/c; Lilandra & Gladiator app.; r/(Uncanny)X-Men #108 4.00

X-MEN FOREVER 2
Marvel Comics: Aug, 2010 - Present ($3.99)
1-16: 1-Claremont-s/Grummett-a/c. 2,3-Spider-Man app. 9,10-Grell-a 4.00

X-MEN: HELLBOUND
Marvel Comics: July, 2010 - No. 3, Sept, 2010 ($3.99, limited series)
1-3-Second Coming x-over; Tolibao-a/Djurdjevic-c; Majik rescued from Limbo 4.00

X-MEN: HELLFIRE CLUB
Marvel Comics: Jan, 2000 - No. 4, Apr, 2000 ($2.50, limited series)
1-4-Origin of the Hellfire Club 3.00

X-MEN: HIDDEN YEARS
Marvel Comics: Dec, 1999 - No. 22, Sept. 2001 ($3.50/$2.50)
1-New adventures from pre-#94 era; Byrne-s/a(p) 4.00
2-4,6-11,13-22-($2.50): 2-Two covers. 3-Ka-Zar app. 8,9-FF-c/app. 3.00
5-($2.75) 3.00
12-($3.50) Magneto-c/app. 4.00

X-MEN: KING BREAKER
Marvel Comics: Feb, 2009 - No. 4, May, 2009 ($3.99, limited series)
1-4-Emperor Vulcan and a Shi'ar invasion; Havok, Rachel Grey and Polaris app. 4.00

X-MEN: KITTY PRYDE - SHADOW & FLAME
Marvel Comics: Aug, 2005 - No. 5, Dec, 2005 ($2.99, limited series)
1-5-Akira Yoshida-s/Paul Smith-a/c; Kitty & Lockheed go to Japan 3.00
TPB (2006, $14.99) r/#1-5 15.00

X-MEN LEGACY (See X-Men 2nd series)

X-MEN: LIBERATORS
Marvel Comics: Nov, 1998 - No. 4, Feb, 1999 ($2.99, limited series)
1-4-Wolverine, Nightcrawler & Colossus; P. Jimenez 4.00

X-MEN LOST TALES
Marvel Comics: 1997 ($2.99)
1,2-r/Classic X-Men back-up stories 4.00

X-MEN: MAGNETO TESTAMENT
Marvel Comics: Nov, 2008 - No. 5, Mar, 2009 ($3.99, limited series)
1-5-Max Eisenhardt in 1930s Nazi-occupied Poland; Pak-s/DiGiandomenico-a. 5-Back-up story of artist Dina Babbitt with Neal Adams-a 4.00

X-MEN: MANIFEST DESTINY
Marvel Comics: Nov, 2008 - No. 5, Mar, 2009 ($3.99, limited series)
1-5-Short stories of X-Men re-location to San Francisco; s/a by various 4.00
... Nightcrawler 1 (5/09, $3.99) Molina & Syaf-a; Mephisto app. 4.00

X-MEN: MESSIAH COMPLEX
Marvel Comics: Dec, 2007 ($3.99)
1-Part 1 of x-over with X-Men, Uncanny X-Men, X-Factor and New X-Men; 2 covers 4.00
... - Mutant Files (2007, $3.99) Handbook pages of x-over participants; Kolins-c 4.00

X-Men: Phoenix - Endsong #2 © MAR

X-Men: Schism #2 © MAR

X-Men True Friends #1 © MAR

GD VG FN VF VF/NM NM-
2.0 4.0 6.0 8.0 9.0 9.2

HC (2008, $39.99, oversized) r/#1, Uncanny X-Men #492-494, X-Men #205-207, New X-Men #44-46 and X-Factor #25-27 40.00

X-MEN NOIR
Marvel Comics: Nov, 2008 - No. 4, May, 2009 ($3.99, limited series)

1-4-Pulp-style story set in 1930s NY; Van Lente-s/Calero-a 4.00
...: Mark of Cain (2/10 - No. 4, 5/10, $3.99) an Lente-s/Calero-a 4.00

X-MEN OMEGA
Marvel Comics: June, 1995 ($3.95, one-shot)

nn-Age of Apocalypse finale 1 3 4 6 8 10
nn-($49.95)-Gold edition 50.00

X-MEN: ORIGINS
Marvel Comics: Oct, 2008 - Present ($3.99, series of one-shots)

...: Beast (11/08) High school years; Carey-s; painted-a/c by Woodward 4.00
...: Cyclops (3/10) Magneto app.; Delperdang-a/Granov-c 4.00
...: Deadpool (9/10) Fernandez-a/Swierczynski-s 4.00
...: Emma Frost (7/10) Moline-a; r/excerpt from 1st app. in Uncanny X-Men #129 4.00
...: Gambit (8/09) Mr. Sinister, Sabretooth and the Marauders app.; Yardin-a 4.00
...: Iceman (1/10) Noto-a 4.00
...: Jean Grey (10/08) Childhood & early X-days; McKeever-s; Mayhew painted-a/c 4.00
...: Nightcrawler (5/10) Cary Nord-a; r/excerpt from 1st app. in Giant-Size X-Men #1 4.00
...: Sabretooth (4/09) Childhood and early meetings with Wolverine; Panosian-a/c 4.00
...: Wolverine (6/09) Pre-X-Men days and first meeting with Xavier; Texeira-a/c 4.00

X-MEN: PHOENIX
Marvel Comics: Dec, 1999 - No. 3, Mar, 2000 ($2.50, limited series)

1-3: 1-Apocalypse app. 4.00

X-MEN: PHOENIX - ENDSONG
Marvel Comics: Mar, 2005 - No. 5, June, 2005 ($2.99, limited series)

1-5-The Phoenix Force returns to Earth; Greg Land-c/a; Greg Pak-s 3.00
HC (2005, $19.99, dust jacket) r/#1-5; Land sketch pages 20.00
SC (2006, $14.99) 15.00

X-MEN: PHOENIX - LEGACY OF FIRE
Marvel Comics: July, 2003 - No. 3, Sep, 2003 ($2.99, limited series)

1-3-Manga-style; Ryan Kinnard-s/a/c; intro page art by Adam Warren 3.00

X-MEN: PHOENIX - WARSONG
Marvel Comics: Nov, 2006 - No. 5, Mar, 2007 ($2.99, limited series)

1-5-Tyler Kirkham-a/Greg Pak-s/Marc Silvestri-c 3.00
HC (2007, $19.99, dustjacket) r/#1-5; variant cover gallery and Handbook pages 20.00
SC (2007, $14.99) r/#1-5; variant cover gallery and Handbook pages 15.00

X-MEN: PIXIE STRIKES BACK
Marvel Comics: Apr, 2010 - No. 4, July, 2010 ($3.99, limited series)

1-4-Kathryn Immonen-s/Sara Pichelli-a/Stuart Immonen-c 4.00

X-MEN: PRELUDE TO SCHISM
Marvel Comics: Jul, 2011 - No. 4, Aug, 2011 ($2.99, limited series)

1-4-Jenkins-s/Camuncoli-c. 1-De La Torre-a. 2-Magneto childhood. 3-Conrad-a 3.00

X-MEN PRIME
Marvel Comics: July, 1995 ($4.95, one-shot)

nn-Post Age of Apocalyse begins 1 3 4 6 8 10

X-MEN RARITIES
Marvel Comics: 1995 ($5.95, one-shot)

nn-Reprints hard-to-find stories 6.00

X-MEN ROAD TO ONSLAUGHT
Marvel Comics: Oct, 1996 ($2.50, one-shot)

nn-Retells Onslaught Saga 3.00

X-MEN: RONIN
Marvel Comics: May, 2003 - No. 5, July, 2003 ($2.99, limited series)

1-5-Manga-style X-Men; Torres-s/Nakatsuka-a 3.00

X-MEN: SCHISM
Marvel Comics: Sept, 2011 - No. 5, Dec, 2011 ($4.99/$3.99, limited series)

1-($4.99) Aaron-s/Pacheco-a/c 5.00
2-5-($3.99) 2-Cho-a/c. 3-Acuña-a/c. 4-Alan Davis-a/c. 5-Adam Kubert-a 4.00

X-MEN: SEARCH FOR CYCLOPS
Marvel Comics: Oct, 2000 - No. 4, Mar, 2001 ($2.99, limited series)

1-4-Two covers (Raney, Pollina); Raney-a 4.00

X-MEN: SECOND COMING
Marvel Comics: May, 2010 - No. 2, Sept, 2010 ($3.99)

1-Cable & Hope return to the present; Bastion app.; Finch-a; covers by Granov & Finch 4.00
2-Conclusion to x-over; covers by Granov & Finch 4.00
...: Prepare (4/10, free) previews x-over; short story w/Immonen-a; cover sketch art 3.00

X-MEN / SPIDER-MAN ("X-Men and Spider-Man" on cover)
Marvel Comics: Jan, 2009 - No. 4, Apr, 2009 ($3.99, limited series)

1-4: 1-Team-up from pre-blue Beast days; Kraven app.; Gage-s/Alberti-a 4.00

X-MEN SPOTLIGHT ON... STARJAMMERS (Also see X-Men #104)
Marvel Comics: 1990 - No. 2, 1990 ($4.50, 52 pgs.)

1,2: Features Starjammers 5.00

X-MEN SURVIVAL GUIDE TO THE MANSION
Marvel Comics: Aug, 1993 ($6.95, spiralbound)

1 7.00

X-MEN: THE COMPLETE AGE OF APOCALYPSE EPIC
Marvel Comics: 2005 - Vol. 4, 2006 ($29.99, TPB)

Book 1-4: Chronological reprintings of the crossover 30.00

X-MEN: THE EARLY YEARS
Marvel Comics: May, 1994 - No. 17, Sept, 1995 ($1.50/$2.50)

1-16: r/X-Men #1-8 w/new-c 3.00
17-$2.50-c; r/X-Men #17,18 4.00

X-MEN: THE END
Marvel Comics: Oct, 2004 - No. 6, Feb, 2005 ($2.99, limited series)

1-6-Claremont-s/Chen-a/Land-c 3.00
... Book One: Dreamers and Demons TPB (2005, $14.99) r/#1-6 15.00

X-MEN: THE END - HEROES AND MARTYRS (Volume 2)
Marvel Comics: May, 2005 - No. 6, Oct, 2005 ($2.99, limited series)

1-6-Claremont-s/Chen-a/Land-c; continued from X-Men: The End 3.00
... Vol. 2 TPB (2006, $14.99) r/#1-6 15.00

X-MEN: THE END (MEN & X-MEN) (Volume 3)
Marvel Comics: Mar, 2006 - No. 6, Aug, 2006 ($2.99, limited series)

1-6-Claremont-s/Chen-a. 1-Land-c. 2-6-Gene Ha-c 3.00
... Vol. 3 TPB (2006, $14.99) r/#1-6 15.00

X-MEN: THE MANGA
Marvel Comics: Mar, 1998 - No. 26, June, 1999 ($2.99, B&W)

1-26-English version of Japanese X-Men comics: 23,24-Randy Green-c 4.00

X-MEN: THE MOVIE
Marvel Comics: Aug, 2000; Sept, 2000

Adaptation (9/00, $5.95) Macchio-s/Williams & Lanning-a 6.00
Adaptation TPB (9/00, $14.95) Movie adaptation and key reprints of main characters; four photo covers (movie X, Magneto, Rogue, Wolverine) 15.00
Prequel: Magneto (8/00, $5.95) Texeira & Palmiotti-a; art & photo covers 6.00
Prequel: Rogue (8/00, $5.95) Evans & Nikolakakis-a; art & photo covers 6.00
Prequel: Wolverine (8/00, $5.95) Waller & McKenna-a; art & photo covers 6.00
TPB X-Men: Beginnings (8/00, $14.95) reprints 3 prequels w/photo-c 15.00

X-MEN 2: THE MOVIE
Marvel Comics: 2003

Adaptation (6/03, $3.50) Movie adaptation; photo-c; Austen-s/Zircher-a 4.00
Adaptation TPB (2003, $12.99) Movie adaptation & r/Prequels Nightcrawler & Wolverine 13.00
Prequel: Nightcrawler (5/03, $3.50) Kerschl-a; photo cover 4.00
Prequel: Wolverine (5/03, $3.50) Mandrake-a; photo cover; Sabretooth app. 4.00

X-MEN: THE 198 (See House of M)
Marvel Comics: Mar, 2006 - No. 5, July, 2006 ($2.99, limited series)

1-5-Hine-s/Muniz-a 3.00
... Files (2006, $3.99) profiles of the 198 mutants who kept their powers after House of M 4.00
Decimation: The 198 (2006, $15.99, TPB) r/#1-5 & X-Men: The 198 Files 16.00

X-MEN: THE TIMES AND LIFE OF LUCAS BISHOP
Marvel Comics: Apr, 2009 - No. 3, June, 2009 ($3.99, limited series)

1-3-Swierczynski-s/Stroman-a. 1-Bishop's birth and childhood 4.00

X-MEN: THE ULTRA COLLECTION
Marvel Comics: Dec, 1994 - No. 5, Apr, 1995 ($2.95, limited series)

1-5: Pin-ups; no scripts 3.00

X-MEN: THE WEDDING ALBUM
Marvel Comics: 1994 ($2.95, magazine size, one-shot)

1-Wedding of Scott Summers & Jean Grey 4.00

X-Men Unlimited #33 © MAR

X-O Manowar (2012 series) #1 © VAL

X-Statix #13 © MAR

	GD	VG	FN	VF	VF/NM	NM-
	2.0	4.0	6.0	8.0	9.0	9.2

X-MEN: TO SERVE AND PROTECT
Marvel Comics: Jan, 2011 - No. 4, Apr, 2011 ($3.99, limited series)
1-4-Short story anthology by various.1-Bradshaw-c. 2-Camuncoli-c 4.00

X-MEN TRUE FRIENDS
Marvel Comics: Sept, 1999 - No. 3, Nov, 1999 ($2.99, limited series)
1-3-Claremont-s/Leonardi-a 4.00

X-MEN 2099 (Also see 2099: World of Tomorrow)
Marvel Comics: Oct, 1993 - No. 35, Aug, 1996 ($1.25/$1.50/$1.95)
1-($1.75)-Foil-c; Ron Lim/Adam Kubert-a begins 4.00
1-2nd printing ($1.75) 3.00
1-Gold edition (15,000 made); sold thru Diamond for $19.40 20.00
2-24,26-35: 3-Death of Tina; Lim-c/a(p) in #1-8. 8-Bound-in trading card sheet. 35-Nostromo (from X-Nation) app; storyline cont'd in 2099: World of Tomorrow 3.00
25-($2.50)-Double sized 4.00
Special 1 ($3.95) 4.00
...: Oasis ($5.95, one-shot) -Hildebrandt Bros.-c/a 6.00

X-MEN ULTRA III PREVIEW
Marvel Comics: 1995 ($2.95)
nn-Kubert-a 3.00

X-MEN UNIVERSE
Marvel Comics: Dec, 1999 - No. 15, Feb, 2001 ($4.99/$3.99)
1-8-Reprints stories from recent X-Men titles 5.00
9-15-($3.99) 4.00

X-MEN UNIVERSE: PAST, PRESENT AND FUTURE
Marvel Comics: Feb, 1999 ($2.99, one-shot)
1-Previews 1999 X-Men events; background info 3.00

X-MEN UNLIMITED
Marvel Comics: 1993 - No. 50, Sept, 2003 ($3.95/$2.99, 68 pgs.)
1-Chris Bachalo-c/a; Quesada-a. 6.00
2-11: 2-Origin of Magneto script. 3-Sabretooth-c/story. 10-Dark Beast vs. Beast; Mark Waid script. 11-Magneto & Rogue 5.00
12-33: 12-Begin $2.99-c; Onslaught x-over; Juggernaut-c/app. 19-Caliafore-a. 20-Generation X app. 27-Origin Thunderbird. 29-Maximum Security x-over; Bishop-c/app. 30-Mahfood-a. 31-Stelfreeze-c/a. 32-Dazzler; Thompson-c/a 33-Kaluta-c 4.00
34-37,39,40-42-($3.50) 34-Von Eeden-a. 35-Finch, Conner, Maguire-a. 36-Chiodo-c/a; Larroca, Totleben-a. 39-Bachalo-c; Pearson-a. 41-Bachalo-c; X-Statix app. 4.00
38-($2.25) Kitty Pryde; Robertson-a 3.00
43-50-($2.50) 43-Sienkiewicz-c/a; Paul Smith-a. 45-Noto-c. 46-Bisley-a. 47-Warren-s/Mays-a. 48-Wolverine story w/Isanove painted-a 3.00
X-Men Legends Vol. 4: Hated and Feared TPB (2003, $19.99) r/stories by various 20.00
NOTE: *Bachalo c/a-1. Quesada a-1. Waid scripts-10*

X-MEN UNLIMITED
Marvel Comics: Apr, 2004 - No. 14, Jun, 2006 ($2.99)
1-14: 1-6-Pat Lee-c; short stories by various. 2-District X preview; Granov-a 3.00

X-MEN VS. AGENTS OF ATLAS
Marvel Comics: Dec, 2009 - No. 2, Jan, 2010 ($3.99, limited series)
1,2-Pagulayan-a. 1-McGuinness-c. 2-Granov-c 4.00

X-MEN VS. DRACULA
Marvel Comics: Dec, 1993 ($1.75)
1-r/X-Men Annual #6; Austin-c(i) 4.00

X-MEN VS. THE AVENGERS, THE
Marvel Comics Group: Apr, 1987 - No. 4, July, 1987 ($1.50, limited series, Baxter paper)
1 5.00
2-4 4.00

X-MEN VS. THE BROOD, THE
Marvel Comics Group: Sept, 1996 - No. 2, Oct, 1996 ($2.95, limited series)
1,2-Wraparound-c; Ostrander-s/Hitch-a(p) 4.00
TPB('97, $16.99) reprints X-Men/Brood: Day of Wrath #1,2 & Uncanny X-Men #232-234 17.00

X-MEN VISIONARIES
Marvel Comics: 1995,1996,2000 (trade paperbacks)
nn-($8.95) Reprints X-Men stories; Adam & Andy Kubert-a 9.00
...2: The Neal Adams Collection (1996) r/X-Men #56-63,65 30.00
...2: The Neal Adams Col. (2nd printing, 2000, $24.95) new Adams-c 25.00

X-MEN/WILDC.A.T.S.: THE DARK AGE (See also WildC.A.T.S./X-Men...)
Marvel Comics: 1998 ($4.50, one-shot)
1-Two covers (Broome & Golden); Ellis-s 5.00

X-MEN: WORLDS APART
Marvel Comics: Dec, 2008 - No. 4, Mar, 2009 ($3.99, limited series)
1-4-Storm and the Black Panther vs. the Shadow King. 1-Campbell-c 4.00

X-NATION 2099
Marvel Comics: Mar, 1996 - No. 6, Aug, 1996 ($1.95)
1-($3.95)-Humberto Ramos-a(p); wraparound, foil-c 4.00
2-6: 2,3-Ramos-a. 4-Exodus-c/app. 6-Reed Richards app 3.00

X NECROSIA
Marvel Comics: Dec, 2009 ($3.99)
1-Beginning of X-Force/X-Men/New Mutants x-over; Crain-a; Selene returns 4.00
...: The Gathering (2/10, $3.99) Wither, Blink, Senyaka. Mortis & Eliphas short stories 4.00

X-O MANOWAR (1st Series)
Valiant/Acclaim Comics (Valiant) No. 43 on: Feb, 1992 - No. 68, Sept, 1996 ($1.95/$2.25/$2.50, high quality)
0-(8/93, $3.50)-Wraparound embossed chromium-c by Quesada; Solar app.; origin Aric (X-O Manowar) 4.00
0-Gold variant 5.00
1-Intro/1st app. & partial origin of Aric (X-O Manowar); Barry Smith/Layton-a 1 2 3 5 6 8
2-4: 2-B. Smith/Layton-c. 3-Layton-c(i). 4-1st app. Shadowman 6.00
5-15: 5-B. Smith-c. 6-Begin $2.25-c; Ditko-a(p). 7,8-Unity x-overs. 7-Miller-c. 8-Simonson-c. 12-1st app. Randy Calder. 14,15-Turok-c/stories 3.00
15-Hot pink logo variant; came with Ultra Pro Rigid Comic Sleeves box; no price on-c 4.00
16-24,26-43: 20-Serial number contest insert. 27-29-Turok x-over. 28-Bound-in trading card. 30-1st app. new "good skin"; Solar app. 33-Chaos Effect Delta Pt. 3. 42-Shadowman app.; includes X-O Manowar Birthquake! Prequel 3.00
25-($3.50)-Has 16 pg. Armorines #0 bound-in w/origin 4.00
44-68: 44-Begin $2.50-c. 50-X, 50-O, 51, 52, 63-Bart Sears-c/a/scripts. 68-Revealed that Aric's past stories were premonitions of his future 3.00
...: Birth HC (2008, $24.95) recolored reprints #0-6; script and breakdowns for #0; cover gallery; new "The Rise of Lydia" story by Layton and Leeke 25.00
Trade paperback nn (1993, $9.95)-Polybagged with copy of X-O Database #1 inside 10.00
Yearbook 1 (4/95, $2.95) 4.00
NOTE: *Layton a-1i, 2i(part); c-1, 2i, 3i, 6i, 21i. Reese a-4i(part); c-26i.*

X-O MANOWAR (2nd Series)(Also see Iron Man/X-O Manowar: Heavy Metal)
Acclaim Comics (Valiant Heroes): V2#1, Oct, 1996 - No. 21, Jun, 1998 ($2.50)
V2#1-21: 1-Mark Waid & Brian Augustyn scripts begin; 1st app. Donavon Wylie; Rand Banion dies; painted variant-c exists. 2-Donavon Wylie becomes new X-O Manowar. 7-9-Augustyn-s. 10-Copycat-c 3.00

X-O MANOWAR (3rd series)
Valiant Entertainment: May, 2012 ($3.99)
1-Robert Venditti-s/Cary Nord-a/Esad Ribic-s; origin re-told 4.00
1-Pullbox variant-c by Nord 5.00
1-Variant-c by David Aja 10.00
1-QR Voice variant-c by Jelena Kevic-Djurdjevic 30.00

X-O MANOWAR FAN EDITION
Acclaim Comics (Valiant Heroes): Feb, 1997 (Overstreet's FAN giveaway)
1-Reintro the Armorines & the Hard Corps; 1st app. Citadel; Augustyn scripts; McKone-c/a 4.00

X-O MANOWAR/IRON MAN: IN HEAVY METAL (See Iron Man/X-O Manowar: Heavy Metal)
Acclaim Comics (Valiant Heroes): Sept, 1996 ($2.50, one-shot)
(1st Marvel/Valiant x-over)
1-Pt 1 of X-O Manowar/Iron Man x-over; Arnim Zola app.; Nicieza scripts; Andy Smith-a 4.00

XOMBI
DC Comics (Milestone): Jan, 1994 - No. 21, Feb, 1996 ($1.75/$2.50)
0-($1.95)-Shadow War x-over; Simonson silver ink varnish-c 3.00
1-21: 1-John Byrne-c 3.00
1-Platinum 8.00

XOMBI
DC Comics: May, 2011 - No. 6, Oct, 2011 ($2.99)
1-6-Rozum-s/Irving-a/c 3.00

X-PATROL
Marvel Comics (Amalgam): Apr, 1996 ($1.95, one-shot)
1-Cruz-a(p) 3.00

XSE
Marvel Comics: Nov, 1996 - No. 4, Feb, 1997 ($1.95, limited series)
1-4: 1-Bishop & Shard app. 3.00

X23 #11 © MAR

Yankee Comics #1 © CHES

Yellowjacket Comics #1 © E. Levy

GD 2.0 | VG 4.0 | FN 6.0 | VF 8.0 | VF/NM 9.0 | NM- 9.2

1-Variant-c 4.00

X-STATIX
Marvel Comics: Sept, 2002 - No. 26, Oct, 2004 ($2.99/$2.25)

1-($2.99) Allred-a/c; intro. Venus Dee Milo; back-up w/Cooke-a 4.00
2-9-($2.25) 4-Quitely-c. 5-Pope-c/a 3.00
10-26: 10-Begin $2.99-c; Bond-a; U-Go Girl flashback. 13,14-Spider-Man app. 21-25-Avengers app. 26-Team dies 3.00
... Vol. 1: Good Omens TPB (2003, $11.99) r/#1-5 12.00
... Vol. 2: Good Guys & Bad Guys TPB (2003, $15.99) r/#6-10 & Wolverine/Doop #1&2 16.00
... Vol. 3: Back From the Dead TPB (2004, $19.99) r/#11-18 20.00
... Vol. 4: X-Statix Vs. the Avengers TPB (2004, $19.99) r/#19-26; pin-ups 20.00

X-STATIX PRESENTS: DEAD GIRL
Marvel Comics: Mar, 2006 - No. 5, July, 2006 ($2.99, limited series)

1-5-Dr. Strange, Dead Girl, Miss America, Tike app. Milligan-s/Dragotta & Allred-a 3.00
TPB (2006, $13.99) r/series 14.00

X-TERMINATORS
Marvel Comics: Oct, 1988 - No. 4, Jan, 1989 ($1.00, limited series)

1-1st app.; X-Men/X-Factor tie-in; Williamson-i 5.00
2-4 4.00

X, THE MAN WITH THE X-RAY EYES (See Movie Comics)

X-TREME X-MEN (Also see Mekanix)
Marvel Comics: July, 2001 - No. 46, Jun, 2004 ($2.99/$3.50)

1-Claremont-s/Larroca-c/a 4.00
2-24: 2-Two covers (Larroca & Pacheco); Psylocke killed 3.00
25-35, 40-46: 25-30-God Loves, Man Kills II; Stryker app.; Kordey-a 3.00
36-39-($3.50) 3.50
Annual 2001 ($4.95) issue opens longways 5.00
... Vol. 1: Destiny TPB (2002, $19.95) r/#1-9 20.00
... Vol. 2: Invasion TPB (2003, $19.99) r/#10-18 20.00
... Vol. 3: Schism TPB (2003, $16.99) r/#19-23; X-Treme X-Posé #1&2 17.00
... Vol. 4: Mekanix TPB (2003, $16.99) r/Mekanix #1-6 17.00
... Vol. 5: God Loves Man Kills TPB (2003, $19.99) r/#25-30 20.00
... Vol. 6: Intifada TPB (2004, $16.99) r/#24,31-35 17.00
... Vol. 7: Storm the Arena TPB (2004, $16.99) r/#36-39 17.00
... Vol. 8: Prisoner of Fire TPB (2004, $19.99) r/#40-46 and Annual 2001 20.00

X-TREME X-MEN: SAVAGE LAND
Marvel Comics: Nov, 2001 - No. 4, Feb, 2002 ($2.99, limited series)

1-4-Claremont-s/Sharpe-c/a; Beast app. 3.00

X-TREME X-POSE
Marvel Comics: Jan, 2003 - No. 2, Feb, 2003 ($2.99, limited series)

1,2-Claremont-s/Ranson-a/Migliari-c 3.00

X-23 (See debut in NYX #3)(See NYX X-23 HC for reprint)
Marvel Comics: Mar, 2005 - No. 6, July, 2005 ($2.99, limited series)

1-Origin of the Wolverine clone girl; Tan-a 4.00
1-Variant Billy Tan-c with red background 5.00
2-6-Origin continues 3.00
2-Variant B&W sketch-c 5.00
One shot 1 (5/10, $3.99) Urasov-c/Lui-s; Wolverine & Jubilee app. 4.00
...: Innocence Lost MGC 1 (5/11, $1.00) r/#1 with "Marvel's Greatest Comics" cover logo 3.00
...: Innocence Lost TPB (2006, $15.99) r/#1-6 16.00

X-23
Marvel Comics: Nov, 2010 - No. 21, May, 2012 ($3.99/$2.99)

1-Marjorie Liu-s/Will Conrad-a; three covers by Luo, Djurdjevic & Dell'Otto; origin retold 4.00
2-21-($2.99) 2-Covers by Luo and Mayhew. 3,10-12,17-19-Takeda-a. 8,9-Daken app. 13-16-Spider-Man app.; Noto-a. 20-Jubilee app.; Noto-a. 21-Silent issue; Noto-a 3.00

X-23: TARGET X
Marvel Comics: Feb, 2007 - No. 6, July, 2007 ($2.99, limited series)

1-6-Kyle & Yost-s/Choi & Oback-a. 6-Gallery of variant covers and sketches 3.00
TPB (2007, $15.99) r/#1-6; gallery of variant covers and sketches 16.00

X-UNIVERSE
Marvel Comics: May, 1995 - No. 2, June, 1995 ($3.50, limited series)

1,2: Age of Apocalypse 5.00

X-VENTURE (Super Heroes)
Victory Magazines Corp.: July, 1947 - No. 2, Nov, 1947

1-Atom Wizard, Mystery Shadow, Lester Trumble begin
110 220 330 704 1202 1700
2 54 108 162 346 591 835

GD 2.0 | VG 4.0 | FN 6.0 | VF 8.0 | VF/NM 9.0 | NM- 9.2

X-WOMEN
Marvel Comics: 2010 ($4.99, one-shot)

1-Milo Manara-a/Chris Claremont-s; a female X-Men adventure; Quesada afterword 5.00

XYR (See Eclipse Graphic Album Series #21)

YAK YAK
Dell Publishing Co.: No. 1186, May-July, 1961 - No. 1348, Apr-June, 1962

Four Color 1186 (#1)- Jack Davis-c/a; 2 versions, one minus 3 pgs.
8 16 24 56 96 135
Four Color 1348 (#2)-Davis c/a 8 16 24 51 86 120

YAKKY DOODLE & CHOPPER (TV) (See Dell Giant #44)
Gold Key: Dec, 1962 (Hanna-Barbera)

1 7 14 21 49 82 115

YANG (See House of Yang)
Charlton Comics: Nov, 1973 - No. 13, May, 1976; V14#15, Sept, 1985 - No. 17, Jan, 1986 (No V14#14, series resumes with #15)

1-Origin; Sattler-a begins; slavery-s 2 4 6 11 16 20
2-13(1976) 1 2 3 6 9 10
15-17(1986): 15-Reprints #1 (Low print run) 6.00
3,10,11(Modern Comics-r, 1977) 6.00

YANKEE COMICS
Harry 'A' Chesler: Sept, 1941 - No. 7, 1942?

1-Origin The Echo, The Enchanted Dagger, Yankee Doodle Jones, The Firebrand, & The Scarlet Sentry; Black Satan app.; Yankee Doodle Jones app. on all covers
200 400 600 1280 2190 3100
2-Origin Johnny Rebel; Major Victory app.; Barry Kuda begins
84 168 252 538 919 1300
3,4: 4-(3/42) 61 122 183 390 670 950
4 (nd, 1940s; 7-1/4x5", 68 pgs, distr. to the service)-Foxy Grandpa, Tom, Dick & Harry, Impy, Ace & Deuce, Dot & Dash, Ima Slooth by Jack Cole (Remington Morse publ.)
15 30 45 88 137 185
5-7 (nd; 10¢, 7-1/4x5", 68 pgs.)(Remington Morse publ.)-urges readers to send their copies to servicemen. 14 28 42 80 115 150

YANKEE DOODLE THE SPIRIT OF LIBERTY
Spire Publications: 1984 (no price, 36 pgs)

nn-Al Hartley-s/c/a 2 4 6 9 13 16

YANKS IN BATTLE
Quality Comics Group: Sept, 1956 - No. 4, Dec, 1956; 1963

1-Cuidera-c(i) 11 22 33 60 83 105
2-4: Cuidera-c(i) 8 16 24 40 50 60
I.W. Reprint #3(1963)-r/#?; exist? 2 4 6 9 12 15

YARDBIRDS, THE (G. I. Joe's Sidekicks)
Ziff-Davis Publishing Co.: Summer, 1952

1-By Bob Oskner 10 20 30 58 79 100

YARNS OF YELLOWSTONE
World Color Press: 1972 (50¢, 36 pgs.)

nn-Illustrated by Bill Chapman 2 4 6 9 12 15

YEAH!
DC Comics (Homage): Oct, 1999 - No. 9, Jun, 2000 ($2.95)

1-Bagge-s/Hernandez-a 3.00
2-9: 2-Editorial page contains adult language 3.00

YELLOW CLAW (Also see Giant Size Master of Kung Fu)
Atlas Comics (MjMC): Oct, 1956 - No. 4, Apr, 1957

1-Origin by Joe Maneely 113 226 339 718 1234 1750
2-Kirby-a 87 174 261 553 952 1350
3,4-Kirby-a; 4-Kirby/Severin-a 84 168 252 538 919 1300
NOTE: *Everett c-3. Maneely c-1. Reinman a-2i, 3. Severin c-2, 4.*

YELLOWJACKET COMICS (Jack in the Box #11 on)(See TNT Comics)
E. Levy/Frank Comunale/Charlton: Sept, 1944 - No. 10, June, 1946

1-Intro & origin Yellowjacket; Diana, the Huntress begins; E.A. Poe's "The Black Cat" adaptation 68 136 204 435 743 1050
2-Yellowjacket-c begin, end #10 42 84 126 265 445 625
3,5 41 82 123 256 428 600
4-E.A. Poe's "Fall of the House Of Usher" adaptation; Palais-a
42 84 126 265 445 625
6 50 100 150 315 533 750
7-Classic skull-c; Toth-a (1 pg. gag feature) 97 194 291 621 1061 1500
8-10: 1,3,4,6-10-Have stories narrated by old witch in "Tales of Terror" (1st horror series?)

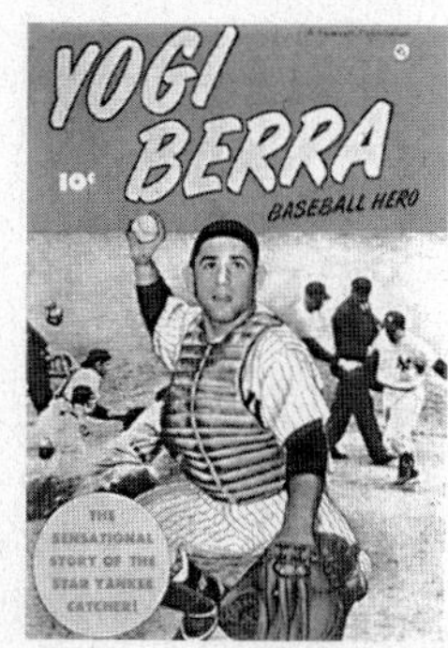

Yogi Berra nn © FAW

Young Allies Comics #12 © MAR

Young Avengers #2 © MAR

GD 2.0 | VG 4.0 | FN 6.0 | VF 8.0 | VF/NM 9.0 | NM- 9.2

48 96 144 302 514 725

YELLOWSTONE KELLY (Movie)
Dell Publishing Co.: No. 1056, Nov-Jan, 1959/60

Four Color 1056-Clint Walker photo-c 6 12 18 37 59 80

YELLOW SUBMARINE (See Movie Comics)

YEAR ONE: BATMAN/RA'S AL GHUL
DC Comics: 2005 - No. 2, 2005 ($5.99, squarebound, limited series)

1-Devin Grayson-s/Paul Gulacy-a 6.00
TPB (2006, $9.99) r/#1,2 10.00

YEAR ONE: BATMAN SCARECROW
DC Comics: 2005 - No. 2, 2005 ($5.99, squarebound, limited series)

1-Scarecrow's origin; Bruce Jones-s/Sean Murphy-a 6.00

YOGI BEAR (See Dell Giant #41, Golden Comics Digest, Kite Fun Book, March of Comics #253, 265, 279, 291, 309, 319, 337, 344, Movie Comics under "Hey There It's..." & Whitman Comic Books)

YOGI BEAR (TV) (Hanna-Barbera) (See Four Color #990)
Dell Publishing Co./Gold Key No. 10 on: No. 1067, 12-2/59-60 - No. 9, 7-9/62; No. 10, 10/62 - No. 42, 10/70

Four Color 1067 (#1)-TV show debuted 1/30/61 11 22 33 73 142 210
Four Color 1104,1162 (5-7/61) 7 14 21 49 82 115
4(8-9/61) - 6(12-1/61-62) 6 12 18 37 59 80
Four Color 1271(11/61) 6 12 18 37 59 80
Four Color 1349(1/62)-Photo-c 8 16 24 56 96 135
7(2-3/62) - 9(7-9/62)-Last Dell 6 12 18 37 59 80
10(10/62-G.K.), 11(1/63)-titled "Yogi Bear Jellystone Jollies" (80 pgs.); 11-X-Mas-c
7 14 21 48 79 110
12(4/63), 14-20 5 10 15 30 48 65
13(7/63, 68 pgs.)-Surprise Party 7 14 21 46 76 105
21-30 3 6 9 20 30 40
31-42 3 6 9 17 25 32

YOGI BEAR (TV)
Charlton Comics: Nov, 1970 - No. 35, Jan, 1976 (Hanna-Barbera)

1 5 10 15 30 48 65
2-6,8-10 3 6 9 17 25 32
7-Summer Fun (Giant, 52 pgs.) 4 8 12 28 44 60
11-20 3 6 9 16 22 28
21-35: 28-31-partial-r 2 4 6 11 16 20
Digest (nn, 1972, 75¢-c, B&W, 100 pgs.) (scarce) 3 6 9 19 29 38

YOGI BEAR (TV)(See The Flintstones, 3rd series & Spotlight #1)
Marvel Comics Group: Nov, 1977 - No. 9, Mar, 1979 (Hanna-Barbera)

1,7-9: 1-Flintstones begin (Newsstand sales only) 3 6 9 16 23 30
2-6 2 4 6 11 16 20

YOGI BEAR (TV)
Harvey Comics: Sept, 1992 - No. 6, Mar, 1994 ($1.25/$1.50) (Hanna-Barbera)

V2#1-6 3.00
...Big Book V2#1,2 ($1.95, 52 pgs): 1-(11/92). 2-(3/93) 4.00
...Giant Size V2#1,2 ($2.25, 68 pgs.): 1-(10/92). 2-(4/93) 4.00

YOGI BEAR (TV)
Archie Publ.: May, 1997

1 3.00

YOGI BEAR'S EASTER PARADE (See The Funtastic World of Hanna-Barbera #2)

YOGI BERRA (Baseball hero)
Fawcett Publications: 1951 (Yankee catcher)

nn-Photo-c (scarce) 73 146 219 468 802 1135

YOSEMITE SAM (...& Bugs Bunny) (TV)
Gold Key/Whitman: Dec, 1970 - No. 81, Feb, 1984

1 5 10 15 30 48 65
2-10 3 6 9 16 23 30
11-20 2 4 6 11 16 20
21-30 2 4 6 9 13 16
31-50 2 4 6 8 10 12
51-65 (Gold Key) 1 2 3 5 7 9
66,67 (Whitman) 2 4 6 8 10 12
68(9/80), 69(10/80), 70(12/80) 3-pack only 3 6 9 19 29 38
71-78: 76(2/82), 77(3/82), 78(4/82) 2 4 6 9 13 16
79-81 (All #90263 on-c, no date or date code; 3-pack): 79(7/83). 80(8/83). 81(2/84)-(1/3-r)
3 6 9 14 19 24
(See March of Comics #363, 380, 392)

YOSSEL
DC Comics: 2003/2011 ($14.99, B&W graphic novel)

SC-Joe Kubert-s/a/c; Nazi-occupied Poland during World War II 15.00

YOUNG ALLIES
Marvel Comics: Aug, 2010 - No. 6, Jan, 2011 ($3.99/$2.99)

1-($3.99) Wraparound-c; Nomad, Araña, Firestar, Gravity, Toro team-up; origin pages 4.00
2-6-($2.99) 2-Lafuente-c/McKeever-s/Baldeon-a. 6-Miyazawa-c; Emma Frost app. 3.00

YOUNG ALLIES COMICS (All-Winners #21; see Kid Komics #2)
Timely Comics (USA 1-7/NPI 8,9/YAI 10-20): Sum, 1941 - No. 20, Oct, 1946

1-Origin/1st app. The Young Allies (Bucky, Toro, others); 1st meeting of Captain America & Human Torch; Red Skull-c & app.; S&K-c/splash; Hitler-c; Note: the cover was altered after its preview in Human Torch #5. Stalin was shown with Hitler but was removed due to Russia becoming an ally 1300 2600 3900 9100 16,250 26,000
2-(Winter, 1941)-Captain America & Human Torch app.; Simon & Kirby-c
411 822 1233 2877 5039 7200
3-Remember Pearl Harbor issue (Spring, 1942); Stan Lee scripts; Vs. Japanese-c/full-length story; Captain America & Human Torch app.; Father Time story by Alderman
343 686 1029 2400 4200 6000
4-The Vagabond & Red Skull, Capt. America, Human Torch app. Classic Red Skull-c
470 940 1410 3431 6066 8700
5-Captain America & Human Torch app. 232 464 696 1485 2543 3600
6,7: 6-Japanese/Nazi war-c 161 322 483 1030 1765 2500
8-Classic Schomburg WWII Japanese bondage-c 181 362 543 1158 1979 2800
9-Hitler, Tojo, Mussolini-c. 239 478 717 1530 2615 3700
10-Classic Schomburg Hooded Villain bondage-c; origin Tommy Tyme & Clock of Ages; ends #19 174 348 522 1114 1907 2700
11-16: 12-Classic decapitation story; Japanese war-c. 16-Last Schomburg WWII-c
135 270 405 864 1482 2100
17-20 103 206 309 659 1130 1600

NOTE: ***Brodsky** c-15. **Ferstadt** a-3. **Gabriele** a-3; c-3, 4. **S&K** c-1, 2. **Schomburg** c-5-13, 16-19. **Shores** c-20.*

YOUNG ALLIES 70TH ANNIVERSARY SPECIAL
Marvel Comics: Aug, 2009 ($3.99, one-shot)

1-Bucky & Young Allies app.; Stern-s/Rivera-a; Terry Vance rep. from Marvel Myst. #14 5.00

YOUNG ALL-STARS
DC Comics: June, 1987 - No. 31, Nov, 1989 ($1.00, deluxe format)

1-31: 1-1st app. Iron Munro & The Flying Fox. 8,9-Millennium tie-ins 4.00
Annual 1 (1988, $2.00) 4.00

YOUNG AVENGERS
Marvel Comics: Apr, 2005 - No. 12, Aug, 2006 ($2.99)

1-Intro. Iron Lad, Patriot, Hulkling, Asgardian; Heinberg-s/Cheung-a 5.00
1-Director's Cut (2005, $3.99) r/#1 plus character sketches; original script 4.00
2-12: 3-6-Kang app. 7-DiVito-a. 9-Skrulls app. 3.00
... Special 1 (2/06, $3.99) origins of the heroes; art by various incl. Neal Adams, Jae Lee, Bill Sienkiewicz, Gene Ha, Michael Gaydos and Pasqual Ferry 4.00
... Vol. 1: Sidekicks HC (2005, $19.99, dustjacket) r/#1-6; character design sketches 20.00
... Vol. 1: Sidekicks TPB (2006, $14.99) r/#1-6; character design sketches 15.00
... Vol. 2: Family Matters HC (2006, $22.99, dustjacket) r/#7-12 & YA Special #1 23.00
... Vol. 2: Family Matters SC (2007, $17.99) r/#7-12 & YA Special #1 18.00
HC (2008, $29.99, d.j.) oversized reprint of #1-12 and Special #1; script & sketch pages 30.00

YOUNG AVENGERS PRESENTS
Marvel Comics: Mar, 2008 - No. 6, Aug, 2008 ($2.99, limited series)

1-4: 1-Patriot; Bucky app. 2-Hulkling; Captain Marvel app. 3-Wiccan & Speed. 4-Vision. 5-Stature. 6-Hawkeye; Clint Barton app.; Alan Davis-a 3.00

YOUNGBLOOD (See Brigade #4, Megaton Explosion & Team Youngblood)
Image Comics (Extreme Studios): Apr, 1992 - No. 4, Feb, 1993 ($2.50, lim. series); No. 6, June, 1994 (No #5) - No. 10, Dec, 1994 ($1.95/$2.50)

1-Liefeld-c/a/scripts in all; flip book format with 2 trading cards; 1st Image/Extreme Studios title. 5.00
1,2-2nd printing 3.00
2-(JUN-c, July 1992 indicia)-1st app. Shadowhawk in solo back-up story; 2 trading cards inside; flip book format; 1st app. Prophet, Kirby, Berzerkers, Darkthorn 4.00
3,0,4,5: 3-(OCT-c, August 1992 indicia)-Contains 2 trading cards inside (flip book); 1st app. Supreme in back-up story; 1st app. Showdown. 0-(12/92, $1.95)-Contains 2 trading cards; 2 cover variations exist, green or beige logo; w/Image #0 coupon. 4-(2/93)-Glow-in-the-dark cover w/2 trading cards; 2nd app. Dale Keown's The Pitt; Bloodstrike app. 5-Flip book w/Brigade #4 3.00
6-($3.50, 52 pgs.)-Wraparound-c 4.00
7-10: 7, 8-Liefeld-c(p)/a(p)/story. 8,9-(9/94) 9-Valentino story & art 3.00
Battlezone 1 (May-c, 4/93 inside, $1.95)-Arsenal book; Liefeld-c(p) 3.00
Battlezone 2 (7/94, $2.95)-Wraparound-c 4.00

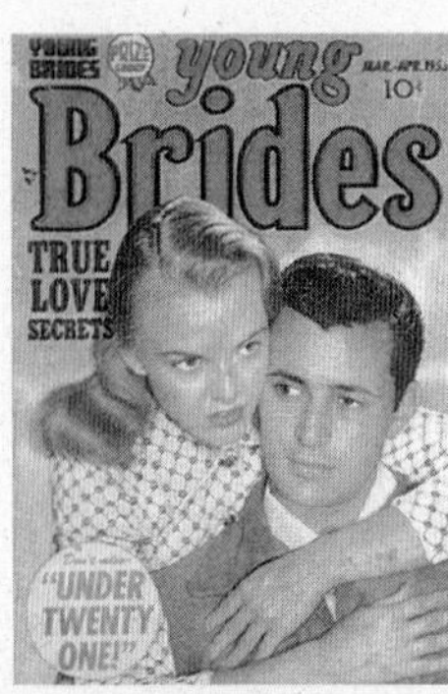

Young Brides #4 © PRIZE

Young Justice #3 © DC

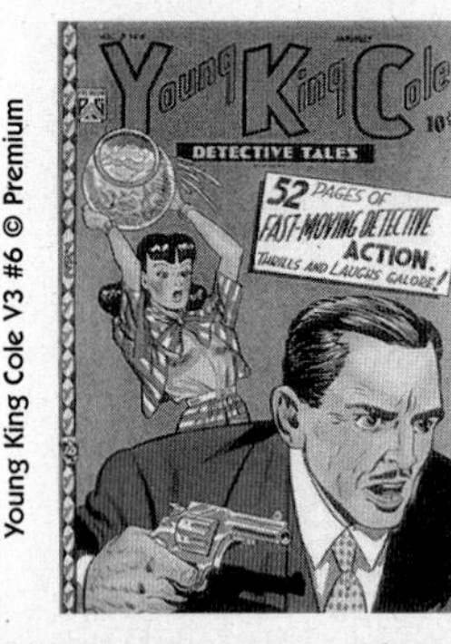

Young King Cole V3 #6 © Premium

	GD 2.0	VG 4.0	FN 6.0	VF 8.0	VF/NM 9.0	NM- 9.2

Image Firsts: Youngblood #1 (3/10, $1.00) reprints #1 3.00
...Super Special (Winter '97, $2.99) Sprouse -a 4.00
Yearbook 1 (7/93, $2.50)-Fold out panel; 1st app. Tyrax & Kanan 4.00
Vol. 1 HC (2008, $34.99) oversized r/#1-5, recolored and remastered; sketch art and cover gallery; Mark Millar intro. 35.00
TPB (1996, $16.95)-r/Team Youngblood #8-10 & Youngblood #6-8,10 17.00

YOUNGBLOOD
Image Comics (Extreme Studios)/Maximum Press No. 14: V2#1, Sept, 1995 - No. 14, Dec, 1996 ($2.50)

V2#1-10,14: Roger Cruz-a in all. 4-Extreme Destroyer Pt. 4 w/gaming card. 5-Variant-c exists. 6-Angela & Glory. 7-Shadowhunt Pt. 3; Shadowhawk app. 8,10-Thor (from Supreme) app. 10-(7/96). 14-(12/96)-1st Maximum Press issue 3.00

YOUNGBLOOD (Volume 3)
Awesome/ Awesome-Hyperwerks #2: Feb, 1998 - No. 2, Aug, 1998 ($2.50)

1-Alan Moore-s/Skroce & Stucker-a; 12 diff. covers 3.00
2-(8/98) Skroce & Liefeld covers 3.00
...Imperial 1 (Arcade Comics, 6/04, $2.99) Kirkman-sMychaels-a 3.00

YOUNGBLOOD (Volume 4)
Image Comics: Jan, 2008 - Present ($2.99/$3.99)

1-7-Casey-s/Donovan-a; two covers by Donovan & Liefeld on each 3.00
8-Obama flip cover by Liefeld; Obama app. in story 3.00
9-($3.99) Obama flip cover by Liefeld; Free Agent rejoins; Obama app. in story 4.00

YOUNGBLOOD: STRIKEFILE
Image Comics (Extreme Studios): Apr, 1993 - No. 11, Feb, 1995 ($1.95/$2.50/$2.95)

1-10: 1-($1.95)-Flip book w/Jae Lee-c/a & Liefeld-c/a in #1-3; 1st app. The Allies,Giger, & Glory. 3-Thibert-i asisst. 4-Liefeld-c(p); no Lee-a. 5-Liefeld-c(p). 8-Platt-c 3.00
NOTE: *Youngblood: Strikefile began as a four issue limited series.*

YOUNGBLOOD/X-FORCE
Image Comics (Extreme Studios): July, 1996 ($4.95, one-shot)

1-Cruz-a(p); two covers exist 5.00

YOUNG BRIDES (True Love Secrets)
Feature/Prize Publ.: Sept-Oct, 1952 - No. 30, Nov-Dec, 1956 (Photo-c: 1-4)

	GD 2.0	VG 4.0	FN 6.0	VF 8.0	VF/NM 9.0	NM- 9.2
V1#1-Simon & Kirby-a	39	78	117	240	395	550
2-S&K-a	21	42	63	126	206	285
3-6-S&K-a	20	40	60	114	182	250
V2#1-7,10-12 (#7-18)-S&K-a	19	38	57	109	172	235
8,9-No S&K-a	10	20	30	58	79	100
V3#1-3(#19-21)-Last precode (3-4/55)	10	20	30	56	76	95
4,6(#22,24), V4#1,3(#25,27)	9	18	27	52	69	85
V3#5(#23)-Meskin-c	9	18	27	54	72	90
V4#2(#26)-All S&K issue	18	36	54	105	165	225
V4#4(#28)-S&K-a	15	30	45	84	127	170
V4#5,6(#29,30)	10	20	30	56	76	95

YOUNG DR. MASTERS (See The Adventures of Young Dr. Masters)

YOUNG DOCTORS, THE
Charlton Comics: Jan, 1963 - No. 6, Nov, 1963

	GD 2.0	VG 4.0	FN 6.0	VF 8.0	VF/NM 9.0	NM- 9.2
V1#1	3	6	9	21	32	42
2-6	3	6	9	14	19	24

YOUNG EAGLE
Fawcett Publications/Charlton: 12/50 - No. 10, 6/52; No. 3, 7/56 - No. 5, 4/57 (Photo-c: 1-10)

	GD 2.0	VG 4.0	FN 6.0	VF 8.0	VF/NM 9.0	NM- 9.2
1-Intro Young Eagle	18	36	54	103	162	220
2-Complete picture novelette "The Mystery of Thunder Canyon"	10	20	30	58	79	100
3-9	9	18	27	50	65	80
10-Origin Thunder, Young Eagle's Horse	8	16	24	44	57	70
3-5(Charlton)-Formerly Sherlock Holmes?	7	14	21	35	43	50

YOUNG GUNS SKETCHBOOK
Marvel Comics: Feb, 2005 ($3.99, one-shot)

1-Sketch pages from 2005 Marvel projects by Coipel, Granov, McNiven, Land & others 4.00

YOUNG HEARTS
Marvel Comics (SPC): Nov, 1949 - No. 2, Feb, 1950

	GD 2.0	VG 4.0	FN 6.0	VF 8.0	VF/NM 9.0	NM- 9.2
1-Photo-c	16	32	48	94	147	200
2-Colleen Townsend photo-c from movie	12	24	36	67	94	120

YOUNG HEARTS IN LOVE
Super Comics: 1964

	GD 2.0	VG 4.0	FN 6.0	VF 8.0	VF/NM 9.0	NM- 9.2
17,18: 17-r/Young Love V5#6 (4-5/62)	2	4	6	9	13	16

YOUNG HEROES (Formerly Forbidden Worlds #34)
American Comics Group (Titan): No. 35, Feb-Mar, 1955 - No. 37, Jun-Jul, 1955

	GD 2.0	VG 4.0	FN 6.0	VF 8.0	VF/NM 9.0	NM- 9.2
35-37-Frontier Scout	10	20	30	54	72	90

YOUNG HEROES IN LOVE
DC Comics: June, 1997 - No. 17; #1,000,000, Nov, 1998 ($1.75/$1.95/$2.50)

1-1st app. Young Heroes; Madan-a 4.00
2-17: 3-Superman-c/app. 7-Begin $1.95-c 3.00
#1,000,000 (11/98, $2.50) 853 Century x-over 3.00

YOUNG INDIANA JONES CHRONICLES, THE
Dark Horse Comics: Feb, 1992 - No. 12, Feb, 1993 ($2.50)

1-12: Dan Barry scripts in all 3.00
NOTE: ***Dan Barry** a(p)-1, 2, 5, 6, 10; c-1-10. **Morrow** a-3, 4, 5p, 6p. **Springer** a-1i, 2i.*

YOUNG INDIANA JONES CHRONICLES, THE
Hollywood Comics (Disney): 1992 ($3.95, squarebound, 68 pgs.)

1-3: 1-r/YIJC #1,2 by D. Horse. 2-r/#3,4. 3-r/#5,6 4.00

YOUNG JUSTICE (Also see Teen Titans, Titans/Young Justice and DC Comics Presents: ...)
DC Comics: Sept, 1998 - No. 55, May, 2003 ($2.50/$2.75)

1-Robin, Superboy & Impulse team-up; David-s/Nauck-a 4.00
2,3: 3-Mxyzptlk app. 3.00
4-20: 4-Wonder Girl, Arrowette and the Secret join. 6-JLA app. 13-Supergirl x-over. 20-Sins of Youth aftermath 3.00
21-49: 25-Empress ID revealed. 28,29-Forever People app. 32-Empress origin. 35,36-Our Worlds at War x-over. 38-Joker: Last Laugh. 41-The Ray joins. 42-Spectre-c/app. 44,45-World Without YJ x-over pt. 1,5; Ramos-c. 48-Begin $2.75-c 3.00
50-($3.95) Wonder Twins, CM3 and other various DC teen heroes app. 4.00
51-55: 53,54-Darkseid app. 55-Last issue; leads into Titans/Young Justice mini-series 3.00
#1,000,000 (11/98) 853 Century x-over 3.00
...: A League of Their Own (2000, $14.95, TPB) r/#1-7, Secret Files #1 15.00
...: 80-Page Giant (5/99, $4.95) Ramos-c; stories and art by various 5.00
...: In No Man's Land (7/99, $3.95) McDaniel-c 4.00
...: Our Worlds at War (8/01, $2.95) Jae Lee-c; Linear Men app. 3.00
...: Secret Files (1/99, $4.95) Origin-s & pin-ups 5.00
...: The Secret (6/98, $1.95) Girlfrenzy; Nauck-a 3.00

YOUNG JUSTICE (Based on the 2011 Cartoon Network series)
DC Comics: No. 0, Mar, 2011 - Present ($2.99)

0-14: 1-Miss Martian joins; Joker app. 2-Joker-c/app. 5-Kid Flash & Aqualad origins 3.00
FCBD 2011 Young Justice Batman BB Super Sampler (7/11) Flash app. 3.00

YOUNG JUSTICE: SINS OF YOUTH (Also see Sins of Youth x-over issues and Sins of Youth: Secret Files)
DC Comics: May, 2000 - No. 2, May, 2000 ($3.95, limited series)

1,2-Young Justice, JLA & JSA swap ages; David-s/Nauck-a 4.00
TPB (2000, $19.95) r/#1,2 & all x-over issues) 20.00

YOUNG KING COLE (...Detective Tales)(Becomes Criminals on the Run)
Premium Group/Novelty Press: Fall, 1945 - V3#12, July, 1948

	GD 2.0	VG 4.0	FN 6.0	VF 8.0	VF/NM 9.0	NM- 9.2
V1#1-Toni Gayle begins	32	64	96	188	307	425
2	15	30	45	90	140	190
3-4	15	30	45	84	127	170
V2#1-7(8-9/46-7/47): 6,7-Certa-c	12	24	36	67	94	120
V3#1,3-6,8,9,12: 3-Certa-c. 5-McWilliams-c/a. 8,9-Harmon-c	11	22	33	64	90	115
2-L.B. Cole-a; Certa-c	15	30	45	90	140	190
7-L.B. Cole-c/a	20	40	60	120	195	270
10,11-L.B. Cole-c	18	36	54	105	165	225

YOUNG LAWYERS, THE (TV)
Dell Publishing Co.: Jan, 1971 - No. 2, Apr, 1971

	GD 2.0	VG 4.0	FN 6.0	VF 8.0	VF/NM 9.0	NM- 9.2
1	3	6	9	16	23	30
2	2	4	6	11	16	20

YOUNG LIARS (David Lapham's...)(See Vertigo Double Shot for reprint of #1)
DC Comics (Vertigo): May, 2008 - No. 18, Oct, 2009 ($2.99)

1-18: 1-Intro. Sadie Dawkins; David Lapham-s/a/c in all 3.00
...: Daydream Believer TPB (2008, $9.99) r/#1-6; Gerald Way intro. 10.00
...: Maestro TPB (2009, $14.99) r/#7-12; Peter Milligan intro. 15.00
...: Rock Life TPB (2010, $14.99) r/#13-18; Brian Azzarello intro. 15.00

YOUNG LIFE (Teen Life #3 on)
New Age Publ./Quality Comics Group: Summer, 1945 - No. 2, Fall, 1945

	GD 2.0	VG 4.0	FN 6.0	VF 8.0	VF/NM 9.0	NM- 9.2
1-Skip Homeier, Louis Prima stories	17	34	51	98	154	210
2-Frank Sinatra photo on-c plus story	19	38	57	111	176	240

YOUNG LOVE (Sister title to Young Romance)

Young Men #18 © MAR

Young Romance #172 © DC

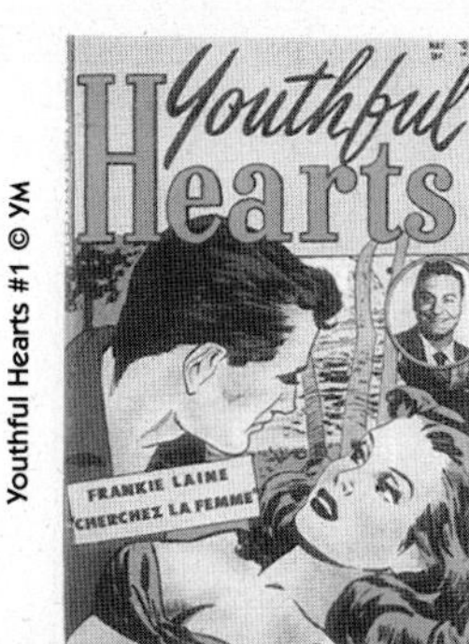

Youthful Hearts #1 © YM

Prize(Feature)Publ.(Crestwood): 2-3/49 - No. 73, 12-1/56-57; V3#5, 2-3/60 - V7#1, 6-7/63

	GD 2.0	VG 4.0	FN 6.0	VF 8.0	VF/NM 9.0	NM- 9.2
V1#1-S&K-c/a(2)	58	116	174	371	636	900
2-Photo-c begin; S&K-a	32	64	96	188	307	425
3-S&K-a	21	42	63	126	206	285
4-6-Minor S&K-a	15	30	45	90	140	190
V2#1(#7)-S&K-a(2)	21	42	63	126	206	285
2-5(#8-11)-Minor S&K-a	15	30	45	83	124	165
6,8(#12,14)-S&K-c only. 14-S&K 1 pg. art	17	34	51	98	154	210
7,9-12(#13,15-18)-S&K-c/a	21	42	63	126	206	285
V3#1-4(#19-22)-S&K-c/a	20	40	60	117	189	260
5-7,9-12(#23-25,27-30)-Photo-c resume; S&K-a	17	34	51	98	154	210
8(#26)-No S&K-a	10	20	30	58	79	100
V4#1,6(#31,36)-S&K-a	15	30	45	88	137	185
2-5,7-12(#32-35,37-42)-Minor S&K-a	14	28	42	78	112	145
V5#1-12(#43-54), V6#3,7,9(#57,61,63)-Last precode	9	18	27	54	72	90
V6#1,2,4-6,8(#55,56,58-60,62) S&K-a	11	22	33	62	86	110
V6#10-12(#64-66)	5	10	15	35	55	75
V7#1-7(#67-73)	5	10	15	30	48	65
V3#5(2-3/60),6(4-5/60)(Formerly All For Love)	4	8	12	26	41	55
V4#1(6-7/60)-6(4-5/61)	4	8	12	24	37	50
V5#1(6-7/61)-6(4-5/62)	4	8	12	24	37	50
V6#1(6-7/62)-6(4-5/63), V7#1	4	8	12	23	36	48

NOTE: ***Meskin** a-14(2), 27, 42. **Powell** a-V4#6. **Severin/Elder** a-V1#3. S&K art not in #53, 57, 61, 63-65. Photo-c most V3#5-V5#11.*

YOUNG LOVE
National Periodical Publ.(Arleigh Publ. Corp #49-61)/DC Comics: #39, 9-10/63 - #120, Wint./75-76; #121, 10/76 - #126, 7/77

	GD 2.0	VG 4.0	FN 6.0	VF 8.0	VF/NM 9.0	NM- 9.2
39	6	12	18	39	62	85
40-50	4	8	12	28	44	60
51-68,70	4	8	12	26	41	55
69-(68 pg. Giant)(8-9/68)	7	14	21	44	72	100
71,72,74-77,80	3	6	9	21	32	42
73,78,79-Toth-a	4	8	12	22	34	45
81-99: 88-96-(52 pg. Giants)	3	6	9	20	30	40
100	3	6	9	21	32	42
101-106,115-120	3	6	9	17	25	32
107 (100 pgs.)	8	16	24	56	96	135
108-114 (100 pgs.)	8	16	24	51	86	120
121-126 (52 pgs.)	4	8	12	26	41	55

NOTE: ***Bolle** a-117. **Colan** a-107r. **Nasser** a-123, 124. **Orlando** a-122. **Simonson** c-125. **Toth** a-73, 78, 79, 122-125r. **Wood** a-109r(4 pgs.).*

YOUNG LOVER ROMANCES (Formerly & becomes Great Lover...)
Toby Press: No. 4, June, 1952 - No. 5, Aug, 1952

	GD 2.0	VG 4.0	FN 6.0	VF 8.0	VF/NM 9.0	NM- 9.2
4,5-Photo-c	10	20	30	56	76	95

YOUNG LOVERS (My Secret Life #19 on)(Formerly Brenda Starr?)
Charlton Comics: No. 16, July, 1956 - No. 18, May, 1957

	GD 2.0	VG 4.0	FN 6.0	VF 8.0	VF/NM 9.0	NM- 9.2
16,17('56): 16-Marcus Swayze-a	11	22	33	60	83	105
18-Elvis Presley picture-c, text story (biography)(Scarce)	68	136	204	435	743	1050

YOUNG MARRIAGE
Fawcett Publications: June, 1950

	GD 2.0	VG 4.0	FN 6.0	VF 8.0	VF/NM 9.0	NM- 9.2
1-Powell-a; photo-c	14	28	42	78	112	145

YOUNG MEN (Formerly Cowboy Romances)(...on the Battlefield #12-20(4/53); ...In Action #21)
Marvel/Atlas Comics (IPC): No. 4, 6/50 - No. 11, 10/51; No. 12, 12/51 - No. 28, 6/54

	GD 2.0	VG 4.0	FN 6.0	VF 8.0	VF/NM 9.0	NM- 9.2
4-(52 pgs.)	20	40	60	117	189	260
5-11	14	28	42	81	118	155
12-23: 12-20-War format. 21-23-Hot Rod issues starring Flash Foster	14	28	42	78	112	145
24-(12/53)-Origin Captain America, Human Torch, & Sub-Mariner which are revived thru #28; Red Skull app.	309	618	927	2163	3782	5400
25-28: 25-Romita-c/a (see Men's Advs.). 27-Death of Golden Age Red Skull	142	284	426	909	1555	2200
25-2nd printing (1994)	2	4	6	8	10	12

NOTE: ***Berg** a-7, 14, 17, 18, 20; c-17? **Brodsky** c-4-9, 13, 14, 16, 17, 21-25. **Burgos** c-26-28. **Colan** a-14, 15, 20. **Everett** a-18-20. **Heath** a-13, 14. **Maneely** c-10-12, 15. **Pakula** a-14, 15. **Robinson** c-18. Captain America by **Romita**-#24?, 25, 26?, 27, 28. Human Torch by **Burgos**-#25, 27, 28. Sub-Mariner by **Everett**-#24-28.*

YOUNG REBELS, THE (TV)
Dell Publishing Co.: Jan, 1971

	GD 2.0	VG 4.0	FN 6.0	VF 8.0	VF/NM 9.0	NM- 9.2
1-Photo-c	3	6	9	14	19	24

YOUNG ROMANCE COMICS (The 1st romance comic)
Prize/Headline (Feature Publ.) (Crestwood): Sept-Oct, 1947 - V16#4, June-July, 1963 (#1-33: 52 pgs.)

	GD 2.0	VG 4.0	FN 6.0	VF 8.0	VF/NM 9.0	NM- 9.2
V1#1-S&K-c/a(2)	71	142	213	454	777	1100
2-S&K-c/a(2-3)	39	78	117	240	395	550
3-6-S&K-c/a(2-3) each	36	72	108	211	343	475
V2#1-6(#7-12)-S&K-c/a(2-3) each	32	64	96	188	307	425
V3#1-3(#13-15): V3#1-Photo-c begin; S&K-a	20	40	60	118	192	265
4-12(#16-24)-Photo-c; S&K-a	20	40	60	118	192	265
V4#1-11(#25-35)-S&K-a	20	40	60	114	182	250
12(#36)-S&K, Toth-a	20	40	60	118	192	265
V5#1-12(#37-48), V6#4-12(#52-60)-S&K-a	20	40	60	114	182	250
V6#1-3(#49-51)-No S&K-a	11	22	33	62	86	110
V7#1-11(#61-71)-S&K-a in most	15	30	45	88	137	185
V7#12(#72), V8#1-3(#73-75)-Last precode (12-1/54-55)-No S&K-a	10	20	30	56	76	95
V8#4(#76, 4-5/55), 5(#77)-No S&K-a	9	18	27	52	69	85
V8#6-8(#78-80, 12-1/55-56)-S&K-a	14	28	42	78	112	145
V9#3,5,6(#81, 2-3/56, 83,84)-S&K-a	14	28	42	78	112	145
4, V10#1(#82,85)-All S&K-a	14	28	42	82	121	160
V10#2-6(#86-90, 10-11/57)-S&K-a	9	18	27	60	103	145
V11#1,2,5,6(#91,92,95,96)-S&K-a	9	18	27	60	103	145
3,4(#93,94), V12#2,4,5(#98,100,101)-No S&K	5	10	15	35	55	75
V12#1,3,6(#97,99,102)-S&K-a	9	18	27	60	103	145
V13#1(#103)-Powell-a; S&K's last-a for Crestwood	9	18	27	60	103	145
2,4-6(#104-108)	5	10	15	30	48	65
V13#3(#105, 4-5/60)-Elvis Presley-c app. only	9	18	27	61	106	150
V14#1-6, V15#1-6, V16#1-4(#109-124)	4	8	12	28	44	60

NOTE: ***Meskin** a-16, 24(2), 33, 47, 50. **Robinson/Meskin** a-6. **Leonard Starr** a-11. Photo c-13-32, 34-65. Issues 1-3 say "Designed for the More **Adult** Readers of **Comics**" on cover.*

YOUNG ROMANCE COMICS (Continued from Prize series)
National Periodical Publ.(Arleigh Publ. Corp. No. 127): No. 125, Aug-Sept, 1963 - No. 208, Nov-Dec, 1975

	GD 2.0	VG 4.0	FN 6.0	VF 8.0	VF/NM 9.0	NM- 9.2
125	8	16	24	51	86	120
126-140	5	10	15	32	51	70
141-153,156-162,165-169	4	8	12	24	37	50
154-Neal Adams-c	5	10	15	35	55	75
155-1st publ. Aragonés-s (no art)	5	10	15	32	51	70
163,164-Toth-a	4	8	12	28	44	60
170-172 (68 pg. Giants): 170-Michell from Young Love ends; Lily Martin, the Swinger begins	5	10	15	32	51	70
173-183 (52 pgs.)	4	8	12	24	37	50
184-196	3	6	9	18	27	35
197-204-(100 pgs.)	8	16	24	51	86	120
205-208	3	6	9	17	25	32

YOUNG X-MEN
Marvel Comics: May, 2008 - No. 12, May, 2009 ($2.99)

1-12: 1-Cyclops forms new team; Guggenheim-s/Paquette-a/Dodson-c. 11,12-Acuña-a 3.00

YOUR DREAMS (See Strange World of...)

YOUR HIGHNESS
Dark Horse Comics: 2011 ($7.99, one-shot)

nn-Prequel to 2011 movie; Danny McBride & Jeff Fradley-s/Phillips-a/c 8.00

YOUR UNITED STATES
Lloyd Jacquet Studios: 1946

	GD 2.0	VG 4.0	FN 6.0	VF 8.0	VF/NM 9.0	NM- 9.2
nn-Used in **SOTI**, pg. 309,310; Sid Greene-a	24	48	72	142	234	325

YOUTHFUL HEARTS (Daring Confessions #4 on)
Youthful Magazines: May, 1952 - No. 3, Sept, 1952

	GD 2.0	VG 4.0	FN 6.0	VF 8.0	VF/NM 9.0	NM- 9.2
1- "Monkey on Her Back" swipes E.C. drug story/Shock SuspenStories #12; Frankie Laine photo on-c; Doug Wildey-a in al	34	68	102	199	325	450
2,3: 2-Vic Damone photo on-c. 3-Johnny Raye photo on-c	20	40	60	118	192	265

YOUTHFUL LOVE (Truthful Love #2)
Youthful Magazines: May, 1950

	GD 2.0	VG 4.0	FN 6.0	VF 8.0	VF/NM 9.0	NM- 9.2
1	15	30	45	85	130	175

YOUTHFUL ROMANCES
Pix-Parade #1-14/Ribage #15 on: 8-9/49 - No. 5, 4/50; No. 6, 2/51; No. 7, 5/51 - #14, 10/52; #15, 1/53 - #18, 7/53; No. 5, 9/53 - No. 9, 8/54

	GD 2.0	VG 4.0	FN 6.0	VF 8.0	VF/NM 9.0	NM- 9.2
1-(1st series)-Titled Youthful Love-Romances	28	56	84	165	270	375
2-Walter Johnson c-1-4	18	36	54	105	165	225
3-5	15	30	45	86	133	180

6,7,9-14(10/52, Pix-Parade; becomes Daring Love #15). 10(1/52)-Mel Torme photo-c/story.

Y: The Last Man #1 © Vaughan & Guerra

Zatanna #15 © DC

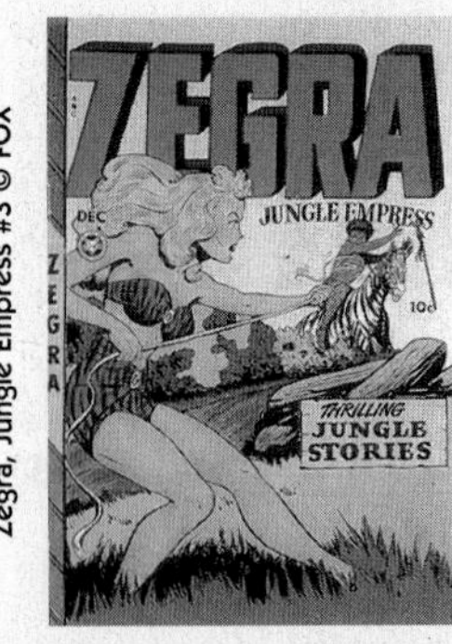

Zegra, Jungle Empress #3 © FOX

GD VG FN VF VF/NM NM-
2.0 4.0 6.0 8.0 9.0 9.2

12-Tony Bennett photo-c, 8pg. story & text bio.13-Richard Hayes (singer) photo-c/story;
Bob & Ray photo/text story. 14 28 42 82 121 160
8-Frank Sinatra photo/text story; Wood-c/a 21 42 63 122 199 275
15-18 (Ribage)-All have photos on-c. 15-Spike Jones photo-c/story. 16-Tony Bavaar photo-c
14 28 42 80 115 150
5(9/53, Ribage)-Les Paul & Mary Ford photo-c/story; Charlton Heston photo/text story
14 28 42 76 108 140
6-9: 6-Bobby Wayne (singer) photo-c/story; Debbie Reynolds photo/text story. 7(2/54)-Tony Martin photo-c/story; Cyd Charise photo/text story. 8(5/54)-Gordon McCrae photo-c/story. (8/54)-Ralph Flanagan (band leader) photo-c/story; Audrey Hepburn photo/text story
13 26 39 72 101 130

YTHAQ: NO ESCAPE
Marvel Comics (Soleil): 2009 - No. 3, 2009 ($5.99, limited series)
1-3-English language version of French comic; Arleston-s/Floch-a 6.00

YTHAQ: THE FORSAKEN WORLD
Marvel Comics (Soleil): 2008 - No. 3, 2009 ($5.99, limited series)
1-3-English language version of French comic; Arleston-s/Floch-a 6.00

Y: THE LAST MAN
DC Comics (Vertigo): Sept, 2002 - No. 60, Mar, 2008 ($2.95/$2.99)
1-Intro. Yorick Brown; Vaughan-s/Guerra-a/J.G. Jones-c
2 4 6 8 10 12
2 1 2 3 5 6 8
3-5 6.00
6-59: 16,17-Chadwick-a. 21,22-Parlov-a. 32,39-41,48,53,54-Sudzuka-a. 3.00
60-($4.99) Final issue; sixty years in the future 5.00
... Double Feature Edition (2002, $5.95) r/#1,2 6.00
... Special Edition (2009, $1.00) r/#1, "After Watchmen" trade dress on cover 3.00
... - Cycles TPB (2003, $12.95) r/#6-10; sketch pages by Guerra 13.00
... - Girl on Girl TPB (2005, $12.99) r/#32-36 13.00
... - Kimono Dragons TPB (2006, $14.99) r/#43-48 15.00
... - Motherland TPB (2007, $14.99) r/#49-54 15.00
... - One Small Step TPB (2004, $12.95) r/#11-17 13.00
... - Paper Dolls TPB (2006, $14.99) r/#37-42 15.00
... - Ring of Truth TPB (2005, $14.99) r/#24-31 15.00
... - Safeword TPB (2004, $12.95) r/#18-23 13.00
... - Unmanned TPB (2002, $12.95) r/#1-5 13.00
... - Whys and Wherefores TPB (2008, $14.99) r/#55-60 15.00
... - The Deluxe Edition Book One HC (2008, $29.99, dustjacket) oversized r/#1-10; Guerra sketch pages 30.00
... - The Deluxe Edition Book Two HC (2009, $29.99, dustjacket) oversized r/#11-23; full script to #18 30.00
... - The Deluxe Edition Book Three HC (2010, $29.99, dustjacket) oversized r/#24-36; full script to #36 30.00
... - The Deluxe Edition Book Four HC (2010, $29.99, dustjacket) oversized r/#37-48; full script to #42 30.00
... - The Deluxe Edition Book Five HC (2011, $29.99, dustjacket) oversized r/#49-60; full script to #60 30.00

Y2K: THE COMIC
New England Comics Press: Oct, 1999 ($3.95, one-shot)
1-Y2K scenarios and survival tips 4.00

YUPPIES FROM HELL (Also see Son of...)
Marvel Comics: 1989 ($2.95, B&W, one-shot, direct sales, 52 pgs.)
1-Satire 4.00

ZAGO, JUNGLE PRINCE (My Story #5 on)
Fox Features Syndicate: Sept, 1948 - No. 4, Mar, 1949
1-Blue Beetle app.; partial-r/Atomic #4 (Toni Luck) 68 136 204 435 743 1050
2,3-Kamen-a 54 108 162 343 574 825
4-Baker-c 47 94 141 296 498 700

ZANE GREY'S STORIES OF THE WEST
Dell Publishing Co./Gold Key 11/64: No. 197, 9/48 - No. 996, 5-7/59; 11/64 (All painted-c)
Four Color 197(#1)(9/48) 11 22 33 71 136 200
Four Color 222,230,236('49) 7 14 21 46 76 105
Four Color 246,255,270,301,314,333,346 5 10 15 32 51 70
Four Color 357,372,395,412,433,449,467,484 4 8 12 28 44 60
Four Color 511-Kinstler-a; Kubert-a 5 10 15 32 51 70
Four Color 532,555,583,604,616,632(5/55) 4 8 12 28 44 60
27(9-11/55) - 39(9-11/58) 4 8 12 28 44 60
Four Color 996(5-7/59) 4 8 12 28 44 60
10131-411-(11/64-G.K.)-Nevada; r/4-Color #996 3 6 9 20 30 40

ZANY (Magazine)(Satire)(See Frantic & Ratfink)
Candor Publ. Co.: Sept, 1958 - No. 4, May, 1959
1-Bill Everett-c 13 26 39 74 105 135
2-4: 4-Everett-c 9 18 27 50 65 80

ZATANNA (See Adv. Comics #413, JLA #161, Supergirl #1, World's Finest Comics #274)
DC Comics: July, 1993 - No. 4, Oct, 1993 ($1.95, limited series)
1-4 3.00
...: Everyday Magic (2003, $5.95, one-shot) Dini-s/Mays-a/Bolland-c; Constantine app. 6.00
Special 1(1987, $2.00)-Gray Morrow-c/a 4.00

ZATANNA
DC Comics: Jul, 2010 - No. 16, Oct, 2011 ($2.99)
1-16: 1-Dini-s/Roux-a/c. 4,5,7-Hardin-a. 7-Beechen-s. 8-Chang-a. 11,13-16-Hughes-c 3.00
1-6-Variant-c by Bolland 6.00
...: The Mistress of Magic TPB (2011, $17.99) r/#1-6; variant cover gallery 18.00

ZAZA, THE MYSTIC (Formerly Charlie Chan; This Magazine Is Haunted V2#12 on)
Charlton Comics: No. 10, Apr, 1956 - No. 11, Sept, 1956
10,11 12 24 36 69 97 125

ZEALOT (Also see WildC.A.T.S: Covert Action Teams)
Image Comics: Aug, 1995 - No. 3, Nov, 1995 ($2.50, limited series)
1-3 3.00

ZEGRA JUNGLE EMPRESS (Formerly Tegra)(My Love Life #6 on)
Fox Features Syndicate: No. 2, Oct, 1948 - No. 5, April, 1949
2 68 136 204 435 743 1050
3-5 53 106 159 334 567 800

ZEN (Intergalactic Ninja)
Zen Comics Publishing: No. 0, Apr, 2003 - No. 4, Aug, 2003 ($2.95)
0-4-Bill Maus-a/Steve Stern-s. 0-Wraparound-c 3.00

ZEN INTERGALACTIC NINJA
No Publisher: 1987 -1993 ($1.75/$2.00, B&W)
1 2 4 6 10 14 18
2-6: Copyright-Stern & Cote 1 3 4 6 8 10
V2#1-4-($2.00) 3.00
V3#1-5-($2.95) 3.00
... :Christmas Special 1 (1992, $2.95) 3.00
... :Earth Day Special 1 (1993, $2.95) 3.00

ZEN, INTERGALACTIC NINJA (mini-series)
Zen Comics/Archie Comics: Sept, 1992 - No. 3, 1992 ($1.25)(Formerly a B&W comic by Zen Comics)
1-3: 1-Origin Zen; contains mini-poster 3.00

ZEN INTERGALACTIC NINJA
Entity Comics: No. 0, June-July, 1993 - No. 3, 1994 ($2.95, B&W, limited series)
0-Gold foil stamped-c; photo-c of Zen model 3.00
1-3: Gold foil stamped-c; Bill Maus-c/a 3.00
0-(1993, $3.50, color)-Chromium-c by Jae Lee 4.00
...Sourcebook 1-(1993, $3.50) 4.00
...Sourcebook '94-(1994, $3.50) 4.00

ZEN INTERGALACTIC NINJA: APRIL FOOL'S SPECIAL
Parody Press: 1994 ($2.50, B&W)
1-w/flip story of Renn Intergalactic Chihuahua 3.00

ZEN INTERGALACTIC NINJA COLOR
Entity Comics: 1994 - No. 7, 1995 ($2.25)
1-($3.95)-Chromium die cut-c 4.00
1, 0-($2.25)-Newsstand; Jae Lee-c; r/...All New Color Special #0 3.00
2-($2.50)-Flip book 3.00
2-($3.50)-Flip book, polybagged w/chromium trading card 4.00
3-7 3.00
Summer Special (1994, $2.95) 3.00
Yearbook: Hazardous Duty 1 (1995) 3.00
Zen-isms 1 (1995, 2.95) 3.00
Ashcan-Tour of the Universe-(no price) w/flip cover 3.00

ZEN INTERGALACTIC NINJA COMMEMORATIVE EDITION
Zen Comics Publishing: 1997 ($5.95, color)
1-Stern-s/Cote-a 6.00

ZEN INTERGALACTIC NINJA MILESTONE
Entity Comics: 1994 - No. 3, 1994 ($2.95, limited series)

Zero Hour #3 © DC

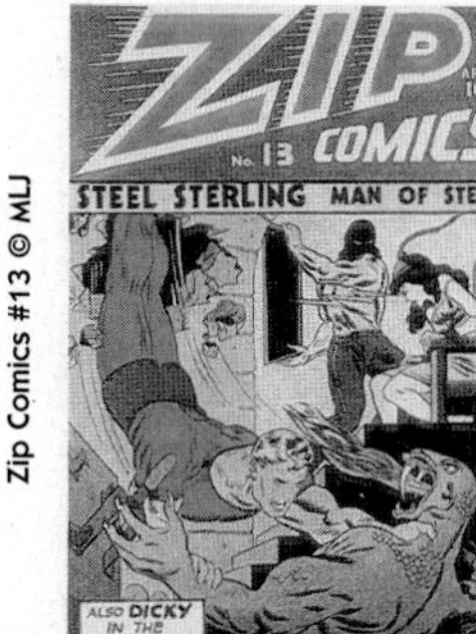

Zip Comics #13 © MLJ

Zombie King #0 © Frank Cho

1-3: Gold foil logo; r/Defend the Earth 3.00

ZEN INTERGALATIC NINJA SPRING SPECTACULAR
Entity Comics: 1994 ($2.95, B&W, one-shot)

1-Gold foil logo 3.00

ZEN INTERGALACTIC NINJA STARQUEST
Entity Comics: 1994 - No. 6, 1995 ($2.95, B&W)

1-6: Gold foil logo 3.00

ZEN, INTERGALACTIC NINJA: THE HUNTED
Entity Comics: 1993 - No. 3, 1994 ($2.95, B&W, limited series)

1-3: Newsstand Edition; foil logo 3.00
1-($3.50)-Polybagged w/chromium card by Kieth; foil logo 4.00

ZERO GIRL
DC Comics (Homage): Feb, 2001 - No. 5, Jun, 2001 ($2.95, limited series)

1-5-Sam Kieth-s/a 3.00
TPB (2001, $14.95) r/#1-5; intro. by Alan Moore 15.00

ZERO GIRL: FULL CIRCLE
DC Comics (Homage): Jan, 2003 - No. 5, May, 2003 ($2.95, limited series)

1-5-Sam Kieth-s/a 3.00
TPB (2003, $17.95) r/#1-5 18.00

ZERO HOUR: CRISIS IN TIME (Also see Showcase '94 #8-10)
DC Comics: No. 4(#1), Sept, 1994 - No. 0(#5), Oct, 1994 ($1.50, limited series)

4(#1)-0(#5) 4.00
"Ashcan"-(1994, free, B&W, 8 pgs.) several versions exist 3.00
TPB ('94, $9.95) 10.00

ZERO KILLER
Dark Horse Comics: Jul, 2007 - No.6, Oct, 2009 ($2.99)

1-6-Arvid Nelson-s/Matt Camp-a 3.00

ZERO PATROL, THE
Continuity Comics: Nov, 1984 - No. 2 ($1.50); 1987 - No. 5, May, 1989 ($2.00)

1,2: Neal Adams-c/a; Megalith begins 4.00
1-5 (#1,2-reprints above, 1987) 3.00

ZERO TOLERANCE
First Comics: Oct, 1990 - No. 4, Jan, 1991 ($2.25, limited series)

1-4: Tim Vigil-c/a(p) (his 1st color limited series) 3.00

ZERO ZERO
Fantagraphics: Mar, 1995 - No. 27 ($3.95/$4.95, B&W, anthology, mature)

1-7,9-15,17-25 5.00
8,16,26,27: 26-($4.95) Bagge-c 6.00

ZIGGY PIG-SILLY SEAL COMICS (See Animal Fun, Animated Movie-Tunes, Comic Capers, Krazy Komics, Silly Tunes & Super Rabbit)
Timely Comics (CmPL): Fall, 1944 - No. 4, Summer, 1945; No. 5, Summer, 1946; No. 6, Sept, 1946

	GD 2.0	VG 4.0	FN 6.0	VF 8.0	VF/NM 9.0	NM- 9.2
1-Vs. the Japanese	31	62	93	182	296	410
2-(Spring, 1945)	15	30	45	90	140	190
3-5	15	30	45	84	127	170
6-Infinity-c	16	32	48	92	144	195
I.W. Reprint #1(1958)-r/Krazy Komics	2	4	6	10	14	18
I.W. Reprint #2,7,8	2	4	6	10	14	18

ZIP COMICS
MLJ Magazines: Feb, 1940 - No. 47, Summer, 1944 (#1-7?: 68 pgs.)

	GD 2.0	VG 4.0	FN 6.0	VF 8.0	VF/NM 9.0	NM- 9.2
1-Origin Kalathar the Giant Man, The Scarlet Avenger, & Steel Sterling; Mr. Satan (by Edd Ashe), Nevada Jones (masked hero) & Zambini, the Miracle Man, War Eagle, Captain Valor begins	459	918	1377	3350	5925	8500
2-Nevada Jones adds mask & horse Blaze	258	516	774	1651	2826	4000
3-Biro robot-c	245	490	735	1568	2684	3800
4,5-Biro WWII-c	168	336	504	1075	1838	2600
6-8-Biro-c	155	310	465	992	1696	2400
9-Last Kalathar & Mr. Satan; classic-c	181	362	543	1158	1979	2800
10-Inferno, the Flame Breather begins, ends #13	168	336	504	1075	1838	2600
11-Inferno without costume	123	246	369	787	1344	1900
12-Biro bondage/torture-c with dwarf ghouls	129	258	387	826	1413	2000
13-Electrocution-c	148	296	444	947	1624	2300
14-Biro bondage/torture guillotine-c	123	246	369	787	1344	1900
15-Classic spider-c	152	304	456	965	1658	2350
16-Female hanging execution-c by Biro	123	246	369	787	1344	1900
17-Last Scarlet Avenger; women in bondage being cooked alive-c by Biro	155	310	465	992	1696	2400
18-Wilbur begins (9/41, 1st app.); sci-fi-c	142	284	426	909	1555	2300
19	116	232	348	742	1271	1800
20-Origin & 1st app. Black Jack (11/41); Hitler-c	206	412	618	1318	2259	3200
21,23-Nazi WWII-c	110	220	330	704	1202	1700
22-Classic Nazi Grim Reaper w/sickle, V for Victory-c	245	490	735	1568	2684	3800
24,25: 25-Last Nevada Jones	100	200	300	635	1093	1550
26-Black Witch begins; last Captain Valor; "Remember Pearl Harbor!" cover caption	142	284	426	909	1555	2200
27-Intro. Web (7/42) plus-c app.; Japanese WWII-c	213	426	639	1363	2332	3300
28-Origin Web; classic Baron Gastapo Nazi WWII-c	181	362	543	1158	1979	2800
29-The Hyena app. (scarce); Nazi WWII-c	135	270	405	864	1482	2100
30-WWII-c	77	154	231	493	847	1200
31,33-35: All WWII-c. 34-1st Applejack app. 35-Last Zambini, Black Jack	65	130	195	416	708	1000
32-Classic skeleton Nazi WWII-c	110	220	330	704	1202	1700
36-38: 38-Last Web issue	54	108	162	343	574	825
39-Red Rube begins (origin, 8/43)	55	110	165	352	601	850
40-43	48	96	144	302	514	725
44-46: WWII covers. 45-Wilbur ends	53	106	159	334	567	800
47-Last issue; scarce	55	110	165	352	601	850

NOTE: ***Biro** a-5, 9, 17; c-3-17. **Meskin** a-1-3, 5-7, 9, 10, 12, 13, 15, 16 at least. **Montana** c-29, 30, 32-35. **Novick** c-18-28, 31. **Sahle** c-37, 38, 40-46. Bondage c-8, 9, 33, 34. Cover features: Steel Sterling-1-43, 47; (w/Blackjack-20-27 & Web-27-35), 28-39; (w/Red Rube-40-43); Red Rube-44-47.*

ZIP-JET (Hero)
St. John Publishing Co.: Feb, 1953 - No. 2, Apr-May, 1953

	GD 2.0	VG 4.0	FN 6.0	VF 8.0	VF/NM 9.0	NM- 9.2
1-Rocketman-r from Punch Comics; #1-c from splash in Punch #10	81	162	243	518	884	1250
2	50	100	150	315	533	750

ZIPPY THE CHIMP (CBS TV Presents...)
Pines (Literary Ent.): No. 50, March, 1957; No. 51, Aug, 1957

	GD 2.0	VG 4.0	FN 6.0	VF 8.0	VF/NM 9.0	NM- 9.2
50,51	8	16	24	40	50	60

ZODY, THE MOD ROB
Gold Key: July, 1970

	GD 2.0	VG 4.0	FN 6.0	VF 8.0	VF/NM 9.0	NM- 9.2
1	3	6	9	16	23	30

ZOMBIE
Marvel Comics: Nov, 2006 - No. 4, Feb, 2007 ($3.99, limited series)

1-4-Kyle Hotz-a/c; Mike Raicht-s 4.00
TPB (2007, $13.99) r/#1-4 14.00
...: Simon Garth (1/08 - No. 4, 4/08) Hotz-s/a/c 4.00

ZOMBIE BOY
Timbuktu Graphics/Antarctic Press: Mar, 1988 - Nov, 1996 ($1.50/$2.50/$2.95, B&W)

1-Mark Stokes-s/a 3.00
...'s Hoodoo Tales (11/89, $1.50) 3.00
... Rises Again (1/94, $2.50) r/#1 and Hoodoo Tales 3.00
1-(Antarctic Press, 11/96, $2.95) new story 3.00

ZOMBIE KING
Image Comics: No. 0, June, 2005 ($2.95, B&W, one-shot)

0-Frank Cho-s/a 5.00

ZOMBIE PROOF
Moonstone: 2007 - Present ($3.50)

1-3: 1-J.C. Vaughn-s/Vincent Spencer-a; two covers by Spencer and Neil Vokes 4.00
1-Baltimore Comic-Con 2007 variant-c by Vokes (ltd. ed. of 500) 6.00
2-Big Apple 2008 Convention Edition; Tucci-c (ltd. ed. of 250) 6.00
3-Convention Edition; Beck-c (ltd. ed. of 100) 6.00

ZOMBIES CHRISTMAS CAROL (See Marvel Zombies Christmas Carol)

ZOMBIES!: ECLIPSE OF THE UNDEAD
IDW Publ.: Nov, 2006 - No. 4, Feb, 2007 ($3.99, limited series)

1-4-Torres-s/Herrera-a; two covers 4.00

ZOMBIES!: FEAST
IDW Publ.: May, 2006 - No. 5, Oct, 2006 ($3.99, limited series)

1-5: 1-Chris Bolton-a/Shane McCarthy-s. 3-Lorenzana-a 4.00

ZOMBIES!: HUNTERS
IDW Publ.: May, 2008 ($3.99)

1-Don Figueroa-a/c; Dara Naraghi-s 4.00

ZOMBIES VS. ROBOTS

Zoot #14 © FOX

Zorro Rides Again #4 © Zorro Productions

Zot! #12 © Scott McCloud

	GD 2.0	VG 4.0	FN 6.0	VF 8.0	VF/NM 9.0	NM- 9.2

IDW Publ.: Oct, 2006 - No. 2, Dec, 2006 ($3.99, limited series)

1-Chris Ryall-s/Ashley Wood-a; two covers by Wood						15.00
2						10.00

ZOMBIES VS. ROBOTS AVENTURE
IDW Publ.: Feb, 2010 - No. 4, May, 2010 ($3.99, limited series)

1-4-Short stories; Ryall-s; art by Matthews III, McCaffrey, & Hernandez; Wood-c						4.00

ZOMBIES VS. ROBOTS: UNDERCITY
IDW Publ.: Apr, 2011 - No. 3, Jun, 2011 ($3.99, limited series)

1-3-Chris Ryall-s/Mark Torres; two covers on each by Torres and Garry Brown						4.00

ZOMBIES VS. ROBOTS VS. AMAZONS
IDW Publ.: Sept, 2007 - No. 3, Feb, 2008 ($3.99, limited series)

1-3-Chris Ryall-s/Ashley Wood-a; two covers by Wood on each						5.00

ZOMBIE TALES THE SERIES
BOOM! Studios: Apr, 2008 - No. 12, Mar, 2009 ($3.99)

1-Niles-s; Lansdale-s/Barreto-a; two covers on each						4.00

ZOMBIE WORLD (one-shots)
Dark Horse Comics

... :Eat Your Heart Out (4/98, $2.95) Kelley Jones-c/s/a						3.00
... :Home For The Holidays (12/97, $2.95)						3.00

ZOMBIE WORLD: CHAMPION OF THE WORMS
Dark Horse Comics: Sept, 1997 - No. 3, Nov, 1997 ($2.95, limited series)

1-3-Mignola & McEown-c/s/a						3.00

ZOMBIE WORLD: DEAD END
Dark Horse Comics: Jan, 1998 - No. 2, Feb, 1998 ($2.95, limited series)

1,2-Stephen Blue-c/s/a						3.00

ZOMBIE WORLD: TREE OF DEATH
Dark Horse Comics: Jun, 1999 - No. 4, Oct, 1999 ($2.95, limited series)

1-4-Mills-s/Deadstock-a						3.00

ZOMBIE WORLD: WINTER'S DREGS
Dark Horse Comics: May, 1998 - No. 4, Aug, 1998 ($2.95, limited series)

1-4-Fingerman-s/Edwards-a						3.00

ZOO ANIMALS
Star Publications: No. 8, 1954 (15¢, 36 pgs.)

8-(B&W for coloring)	8	16	24	42	54	65

ZOO FUNNIES (Tim McCoy #16 on)
Charlton Comics/Children Comics Publ.: Nov, 1945 - No. 15, 1947

101(#1)(11/45, 1st Charlton comic book)-Funny animal; Al Fago-c	21	42	63	122	199	275
2(12/45, 52 pgs.) Classic-c	15	30	45	83	124	165
3-5	11	22	33	62	86	110
6-15: 8-Diana the Huntress app.	9	18	27	52	69	85

ZOO FUNNIES (Becomes Nyoka, The Jungle Girl #14 on?)
Capitol Stories/Charlton Comics: July, 1953 - No. 13, Sept, 1955; Dec, 1984

1-1st app.? Timothy The Ghost; Fago-c/a	11	22	33	64	90	115
2	8	16	24	42	54	65
3-7	7	14	21	37	46	55
8-13-Nyoka app.	9	18	27	52	69	85
1(1984) (Low print run)	1	2	3	4	5	7

ZOONIVERSE
Eclipse Comics: 8/86 - No. 6, 6/87 ($1.25/$1.75, limited series, Mando paper)

1-6						3.00

ZOO PARADE (TV)
Dell Publishing Co.: #662, 1955 (Marlin Perkins)

Four Color 662	5	10	15	32	51	70

ZOOM COMICS
Carlton Publishing Co.: Dec, 1945 (one-shot)

nn-Dr. Mercy, Satannas, from Red Band Comics; Capt. Milksop origin retold	39	78	117	240	395	550

ZOOT (Rulah Jungle Goddess #17 on)
Fox Features Syndicate: nd (1946) - No. 16, July, 1948 (Two #13s & 14s)

nn-Funny animal only	22	44	66	132	216	300
2-The Jaguar app.	20	40	60	114	182	250
3(Fall, 1946) - 6-Funny animals & teen-age	14	28	42	76	108	140
7-(6/47)-Rulah, Jungle Goddess (origin/1st app.)	116	232	348	742	1271	1800
8-10	74	148	222	470	810	1150
11-Kamen bondage-c	77	154	231	493	847	1200
12-Injury-to-eye panels, torture scene	57	114	171	362	619	875
13(2/48)	55	110	165	352	601	850
14(3/48)-Used in **SOTI**, pg. 104, "One picture showing a girl nailed by her wrists to trees with blood flowing from the wounds, might be taken straight from an ill. ed. of the Marquis deSade"	74	148	222	470	810	1150
13(4/48),14(5/48)-Western True Crime #15 on?	55	110	165	352	601	850
15,16	55	110	165	352	601	850

ZORRO (Walt Disney with #882)(TV)(See Eclipse Graphic Album)
Dell Publishing Co.: May, 1949 - No. 15, Sept-Nov, 1961 (Photo-c 882 on)
(Zorro first appeared in a pulp story Aug 19, 1919)

Four Color 228 (#1)	17	34	51	119	260	400
Four Color 425,617,732	11	22	33	73	142	210
Four Color 497,538,574-Kinstler-a	11	22	33	76	151	225
Four Color 882-Photo-c begin;1st TV Disney; Toth-a	13	26	39	87	186	285
Four Color 920,933,960,976-Toth-a in all	11	22	33	72	139	205
Four Color 1003('59)-Toth-a	11	22	33	72	139	205
Four Color 1037-Annette Funicello photo-c	12	24	36	84	175	265
8(12-2/59-60)	8	16	24	55	93	130
9-Toth-a	9	18	27	58	99	140
10,11,13-15-Last photo-c	8	16	24	53	89	125
12-Toth-a; last 10¢ issue	9	18	27	58	99	140

NOTE: ***Warren Tufts** a-4-Color 1037, 8, 9, 10, 13.*

ZORRO (Walt Disney)(TV)
Gold Key: Jan, 1966 - No. 9, Mar, 1968 (All photo-c)

1-Toth-a	8	16	24	51	86	120
2,4,5,7-9-Toth-a. 5-r/F.C. #1003 by Toth	5	10	15	30	48	65
3,6-Tufts-a	4	8	12	28	44	60

NOTE: *#1-9 are reprinted from Dell issues. **Tufts** a-3, 4. #1-r/F.C. #882. #2-r/F.C. #960. #3-r/#12-c & #8 inside. #4-r/#9-c & insides. #6-r/#11(all); #7-r/#14-c. #8-r/F.C. #933 inside & back-c & #976-c. #9-r/F.C. #920.*

ZORRO (TV)
Marvel Comics: Dec, 1990 - No. 12, Nov, 1991 ($1.00)

1-12: Based on TV show. 12-Toth-c						3.00

ZORRO (Also see Mask of Zorro)
Topps Comics: Nov, 1993 - No. 11, Nov, 1994 ($2.50/$2.95)

0-(11/93, $1.00, 20 pgs.)-Painted-c; collector's ed.						3.00
1,4,6-9,11: 1-Miller-c. 4-Mike Grell-c. 6-Mignola-c. 7-Lady Rawhide-c by Gulacy. 8-Perez-c. 10-Julie Bell-c. 11-Lady Rawhide-c						3.00
2-Lady Rawhide-app. (not in costume)						5.00
3-1st app. Lady Rawhide in costume, 3-Lady Rawhide-c by Adam Hughes	1	2	3	5	6	8
5-Lady Rawhide app.						4.00
10-($2.95)-Lady Rawhide-c/app.						4.00
The Lady Wears Red (12/98, $12.95, TPB) r/#1-3						13.00
Zorro's Renegades (2/99, $14.95, TPB) r/#4-8						15.00

ZORRO
Dynamite Entertainment: 2008 - No. 20, 2010 ($3.50)

1-20: 1-Origin retold; Wagner-s; three covers. 2-20-Two covers on all						3.50

ZORRO MATANZAS
Dynamite Entertainment: 2010 - No. 4, 2010 ($3.99)

1-4-Mayhew-a/McGregor-s						4.00

ZORRO RIDES AGAIN
Dynamite Entertainment: 2011 - No. 12 ($3.99)

1-8: 1-6-Wagner-s/Polls-a. 7-Snyder III-a						4.00

ZOT!
Eclipse Comics: 4/84 - No. 10, 7/85; No. 11, 1/87 - No. 36 7/91 ($1.50, Baxter-p)

1						5.00
2,3						4.00
4-10: 4-Origin. 10-Last color issue						3.00
10 1/2 (6/86, 25¢, Not Available Comics) Ashcan; art by Feazell & Scott McCloud						4.00
11-14,15-35-($2.00-c) B&W issues						3.00
14 1/2 (Adventures of Zot! in Dimension 10 1/2)(7/87) Antisocialman app.						3.00
36-($2.95-c) B&W						5.00
... The Complete Black and White Collection TPB (2008, $24.95) r/#11-36 with commentary, interviews and bonus artwork						25.00

Z-2 COMICS (Secret Agent...)(See Holyoke One-Shot #7)

ZULU (See Movie Classics)

SPECIALIZING
WANT LISTS
AND PURCHAS
COLLECTIONS.

We'll pay
TOP DOLLAR
for your
collection!

COMICS TO ASTONISH
9400 SNOWDEN RIVER PKWY
COLUMBIA, MD 21045
MONDAY-SATURDAY 12-8PM
SUNDAY 12-6PM
We also buy Magic The Gathering
WE BUY!
- ALL COMICS 30'S TO 80'S!
- ENTIRE COLLECTIONS!
- BRONZE TO GOLDEN AGE!
- GRADED BOOKS!
CONTACT:
KEEGAN F. CONRAD
410-381-2732
COMICS2U@AOL.COM
WE HAVE OVER 80,000 BACK ISSUES!
NOVA ROCKS!
Check out our new website w/h tons of CGC books
CHECK OUT OUR WEB COMIC AT:
WWW.FATGUYBLACKGUYBALDGUY.COM
WWW.COMICSTOASTONISH.COM

GARY DOLGOFF COMICS

SELLING!

800,000+ COMICS in stock!

(1940's - 2000's) 50,000+ 1960's & back • 200,000+ Bronze!

3,500+ LONG-BOXES OF THESE FOR SALE!

Action, Adventure, Amazing Spider-Man, Aquaman, Avengers, Batman, Brave and the Bold, Captain America, Classics, Conan, Daredevil, Detective, Fantastic Four, Flash, Ghost Rider, Green Lantern, Incredible Hulk, Sgt. Fury, Silver Surfer, Star Wars, Strange Adventures, Strange Tales, Sub-Mariner, Superboy, Superman, Tales of Suspense, Tales to Astonish, Tarzan, Thor, Tomb of Dracula, Wolverine, Wonder Woman, X-Men ...

& THOUSANDS MORE TITLES/ISSUES! "WE GOT 'EM ALL!"

TALES FROM THE WAREHOUSE • GARY DOLGOFF COMIC

** IF YOU STACKED ALL OUR LONG-BOXES TOGETHER ON-END, THEY'D BE ABOUT 8,000 FEET TALL! OR ABOUT 6.5 TIMES THE HEIGHT OF THE EMPIRE STATE BUILDING!*

STRICT GRADING!

FACT: Our strict grading really saves you 50%+ over 'industry-standard' grading... ASK ANYONE!

DEALERS → Buy from GD-COMICS & 'Line your pockets with a handsome-profit', every time!

WE FILL WANT-LISTS! ASK FOR DETAILS!

COLLECTORS → Wouldn't it be nice to 'Never Over-Pay' Again

TRY US OUT! WE CAN SUPPLY YOU FOR A LIFETIME.

COME VISIT OUR WAREHOUSE!

CALL OR WRITE US! OUR PLACE IS USER-FRIENDLY & EASY TO GET TO!

*** SEE NEXT PAGE FOR CONTACT INFORMATION ***

IT'S NOT MAGIC! JUST HARD WORK!
Mail Order
30% Discount
No "Handling" Charges
27 years in business
Mountain Empire Comics
Safe, Reliable Service
To learn more about our mail order service, contact us at
Oberon13@Chartertn.net or call us at 423-274-0450

Sparkle City Comics is the CGC Price Leader! Take a look at a few of our record sales...

Irrefutable facts instead of claims for a change.....

Tales of Suspense #39
CGC 9.2
$72,100 Sept/2011
(RECORD PRICE)
Sold For Less $56,763
May/2011
(Heritage)

Marvel Mystery Annual
CGC 6.5
$31,100 Dec/2011
RECORD Price)
Sold For Less $26,290
Feb/2012
(Heritage) same exact book
2 months later

Fantastic Four #12
CGC 9.4
$48,201 Oct/2011
A 9.6 sold for $43,777
2 weeks later

Avengers #4 CGC 9.2
$7,170 Nov/2011
A 9.2 sold a week earlier
for $5,750

Detective Comics #27 CGC 1.8
$116,100 Feb/2011 (RECORD PRICE)
A 2.0 Sold for $116,513 4 days earlier (Heritage)

Showcase #22 CGC 6.0
$6,200 RECORD PRICE
3 copies in 6.5 sold for less
during same period.

Tales of Suspense #59
CGC 9.6
$5,107 RECORD PRICE
sale 3 months later at $2,450

And Many More...
DETECTIVE COMICS #29 CGC 1.0 $9,600 RECORD PRICE
Tales to Astonish #44 CGC 9.6 $10,900 RECORD PRICE
Action Comics #13 CGC 1.5 $8,600 RECORD PRICE
Go to our website to view thousands of record sales at

www.sparklecitycomics.com

eBay ID – sparklecitycomics
Positive Feedback – 44,000+
Platinum Top Rated Seller with
100% rating with 0 complaints

The secret?
eBay, the #1 place to sell comic books, and we are the # 1 seller, selling a million dollars a month! We get more views, hits, and bids than every private auction website combined, not because we are great, but they cannot EVER afford to drive traffic like the billion dollar company eBay does, period.

WE WANT TO BUY YOUR COMICS!!

CALL NOW 1.800.215.4006

buyingeverything@yahoo.com

COSMIC COMICS!
LAS VEGAS, NV
4,000 SQFT. OF COMIC GOODNESS
LOCATED MINUTES FROM THE STRIP!

BUSINESS CARD ADS

THE OVERSTREET COMIC BOOK PRICE GUIDE BUSINESS CARD ADS are a great way to advertise in the Guide! Simply send us your business card and we'll reduce it and run it as is. Have your ad seen by thousands of serious comic book collectors for an entire year! If you are a comic book or collectible dealer, retail establishment, mail-order house, etc., you can reach potential customers throughout the United States and around the world in our **BUSINESS CARDS ADS**!

For more information, contact our Advertising Dept.
Gemstone Publishing, Inc., 1966 Greenspring Dr., Timonium, MD 21093
or e-mail **feedback@gemstonepub.com**.

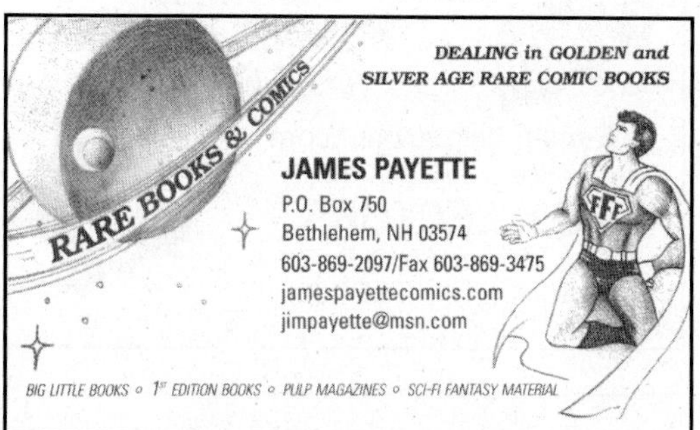

DEALING in GOLDEN and
SILVER AGE RARE COMIC BOOKS
RARE BOOKS & COMICS
JAMES PAYETTE
P.O. Box 750
Bethlehem, NH 03574
603-869-2097/Fax 603-869-3475
jamespayettecomics.com
jimpayette@msn.com
BIG LITTLE BOOKS ◦ 1ST EDITION BOOKS ◦ PULP MAGAZINES ◦ SCI-FI FANTASY MATERIAL

BUNKY BROTHERS
comics · pop culture
COMICS
Buy/Sell Vintage Comics
9155 Archibald Ave. Suite D
Rancho Cucamonga, CA
91730 USA
(Southeast Corner 7th & Archibald)
Open Mon - Fri 11:30am - 6:30pm
Sat 11:30am - 5:00pm
Sun - Call
Email: bunky@bunkybrothers.com
www.bunkybrothers.com
909.941.6402

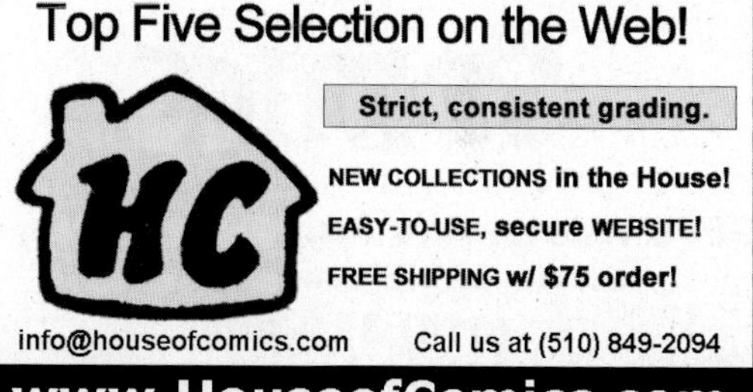

Top Five Selection on the Web!
Strict, consistent grading.
HC
NEW COLLECTIONS in the House!
EASY-TO-USE, secure WEBSITE!
FREE SHIPPING w/ $75 order!
info@houseofcomics.com
Call us at (510) 849-2094
www.HouseofComics.com

WANTED:
Jim Valentino art from "Guardians of the Galaxy"
Broome & Fox Silver Age "Flash" manuscripts
Solid prices paid!

Bill Colosimo
(716) 861-4226
wcolosimo@gmail.com
PO Box 1393
Buffalo, NY 14220

(407) 688-2768
P.O.Box 953972
Lake Mary, FL 32795
Email: pdyroff@cfl.rr.com
Ebay ID: pauldyroff
Ebay Store: Paul Dyroff Comics

Paul Dyroff
www.paulscollectibles.com
Specializing in 1930s to 1970s Comics
Buying: Comics, Magazines, Big Little Books
Pulps, Paperbacks, Sunday Comics
WWII era, Non-Sports Cards, Newspapers
Certified eBay Trading Assistant - Consignments Wanted

BUSINESS CARD ADS

BATMAN
WONDER WOMAN
COLLECTORS

E-mail: batt90@aol.com
wwali@aol.com

COLLECTORS
P.O. Box 604925
Flushing, NY 11360-4925

World's Greatest Comics

5858 Westerville Rd., Westerville, OH

Just minutes from downtown Columbus

(614) 891-3000

Monday through Saturday 12 PM to 7 PM
(Sundays by appointment)

GOLDEN AGE * SILVER AGE
BRONZE and MODERN COMICS
at prices up to

50% OFF EVERY DAY!

Get 20% off of your New Comics and Graphic Novels with our Pull Service

*****WE BUY COMICS*****

From Golden Age to Present!

www.wgcomics.com

A *REAL* Comic Shop in Central Ohio!

YOUR AD HERE!

To place your ad in the next
Overstreet Comic Book Price Guide
contact us at
feedback@gemstonepub.com

DIRECTORY LISTINGS

(PAID ADVERTISING - STORE LISTINGS)

You can have your store listed here for very reasonable rates. Send for details for next year's Guide. The following list of stores have paid to be included in this list. We cannot assume any responsibility in your dealings with these shops. This list is provided for your information only. When planning trips, it would be advisable to make appointments in advance. Remember, to get your shop included in the next edition, contact us for rates.

Gemstone Publishing, Inc., 1966 Greenspring Drive, Timonium, MD 21093.
TOLL FREE: 800-45-COMIC ext. 467
FAX: 410-252-6148
E-MAIL: feedback@gemstonepub.com

Items stocked by these shops are noted at the end of each listing and are coded as follows:

(a) Golden Age Comics
(b) Silver Age Comics
(c) Bronze Age Comics
(d) New Comics & Magazines
(e) Back Issue magazines
(f) Comic Supplies
(g) Collectible Card Games
(h) Role Playing Games
(i) Gaming Supplies
(j) Manga
(k) Anime
(l) Underground Comics
(m) Original Comic Art
(n) Pulps
(o) Big Little Books
(p) Books - Used
(q) Books - New
(r) Comic Related Posters
(s) Movie Posters
(t) Trading Cards
(u) Statues/Mini-busts, etc.
(v) Premiums (Rings, Decoders, etc.)
(w) Action Figures
(x) Other Toys
(y) Records/CDs
(z) DVDs/VHS
(1) Doctor Who Items
(2) Simpsons Items
(3) Star Trek Items
(4) Star Wars Items
(5) HeroClix

ALABAMA

Quality Comix
2751 Legends Parkway #106
Prattville, AL 36066
PH: (800) 548-3314
info@QualityComix.com
www.QualityComix.com

ARIZONA

All About Books & Comics
5060 N. Central Ave.
Phoenix, AZ 85012
PH: (602) 277-0757
FAX: (602) 678-0065
Alan@AllAboutComics.com
www.AllAboutComics.com
(a-g,i,l,q,r,t-x,2-5)

CALIFORNIA

Crush Comics
2869 Castro Valley Blvd.
Castro Valley, CA 94546
PH: (510) 581-4779
crush@crushcomics.com
www.crushcomics.com
(a-d,f,i,r,u,w,2,3)

Collectors Ink
2593 Hwy. 32
Chico, CA 95973
PH: (530) 345-0958
collectorsink@ymail.com
(a-k,r,t-x,z,1-5)

HighQualityComics.com
1106 2nd St., #110
Encinitas, CA 92024
PH: (800) 682-3936
FAX: (760) 723-0412
customerservice
@HighQualityComics.com
www.HighQualityComics.com
(a-f,j-m,p-x,1-4)

Lee's Comics
"We buy old comics!"
1020 N. Rengstorff Ave.
Suite F
Mountain View, CA 94043
PH: (650) 965-1800
Lee@Lcomics.com
www.Lcomics.com
(a-g,j,l-o,q,r,t-x,1-5)

Terry's Comics
Buying All 10¢ & 12¢
original priced comics
P.O. Box 2065
Orange, CA 92859
PH: (714) 288-8993 or
Hotline: (800) 938-0325
FAX: (714) 288-8992
info@terryscomics.com
www.terryscomics.com
(a,b,d-h,m,n,q)

ArchAngels
4629 Cass Street #9
Pacific Beach, CA 92109
PH: (310) 480-8105
rhughes@archangels.com
www.archangels.com

Bunky Brothers
9155 Archibald Ave.
Suite E
Rancho Cucamonga, CA
91730
PH: (909) 941-6402
FAX: (650) 347-2305
Bunky@BunkyBrothers.com
www.BunkyBrothers.com
(a-f,s-u,w,x,3,4)

Lee's Comics
"We buy old comics!"
2222 S. El Camino Real
San Mateo, CA 94403
PH: (650) 571-1489
Mark@Lcomics.com
www.Lcomics.com
(a-g,j,l-r,t-x,1-5)

Comic Collector Shop
574 E. El Camino Real
Sunnyvale, CA 94087
PH: (408) 732-8775
FAX: (408) 732-7131
comic.collectorshop@me.com
(a-u,w,x,1-5)

COLORADO

RTS Unlimited, Inc.
P. O. Box 150412
Lakewood, CO 80215
PH: (303) 403-1840
FAX: (303) 403-1837
RTSUnlimitedinc@gmail.com
www.RTSUnlimited.com
(a,b,c)

Cabin Fever Comics
1450 Main St. Ste. A
Longmont, CO 80517
PH: (303) 834-8183
cabinfevercomics@hotmail.com
www.cabinfevercomics.com
(a-d,f-k,n,p,r-x,3-5)

CONNECTICUT

Matt's Sportscards & Comics
169 Elm St.
Enfield, CT 06082
PH: (860) 741-2522
CardAndComicShop@cox.net
www.CardAndComicShop.com
(a-d,f-m,o,r,t,u,w,x,z,1-4)

Legends of Superheros
1655 Straits Turnpike
Middlebury, CT 06762
PH: (203) 577-2445
FAX: (203) 577-3909
E-Mail: legends
@legendsofsuperheros.com
www.legendsofsuperheros.com
(a-i,p-r,t-w,5)

Showcase New England
Dan Greenhalgh
67 Gail Drive
Northford, CT 06472
PH: (203) 484-4579
FAX: (203) 484-4837
comics@showcasene.com

FLORIDA

Emerald City Comics and Collectables, Inc.
2475 North McMullen Booth Rd.
Suite I
Clearwater, FL 33759
PH: (727) 797-0664
E-Mail: CowardlyLion
@emeraldcitycomics.com
www.emeraldcitycomics.com
(a-j,m,r,t-x,z,1-5)

Paul Dyroff Comics
P.O. Box 953972
Lake Mary, FL 32795
PH: (407) 688-2768
pdyroff@cfl.rr.com
www.paulscollectibles.com
(a-c,e,l-p,r,s,t,v,x)

Phil's Comic Shoppe
6512 West Atlantic Blvd.
Margate, FL 33063
PH: (954) 977-6947
philscomix@att.net
(b-d,f,l,m,t,u,w)

CGC
P.O. Box 4738
Sarasota, FL 34230
PH: (877) NM-COMIC
FAX: (941) 360-2558
www.CGCcomics.com

Emerald City Comics and Collectables, Inc.
9249 Seminole Boulevard
Seminole, FL 33772
PH: (727) 398-BOOK (2665)
E-Mail: CowardlyLion
@emeraldcitycomics.com
www.emeraldcitycomics.com
(a-k,m,o,r-x,z,1-5)

David T. Alexander Collectibles
P.O. Box 273086
Tampa, FL 33618
PH: (813) 968-1805
dtacollectibles@gmail.com
www.dtacollectibles.com
(a-c,e,l-o,r-t,v,x,3,4)

Pedigree Comics, Inc.
12541 Equine Lane
Wellington, FL 33414
PH/FAX: (561) 422-1120
CELL: (561) 596-9111
E-Mail: DougSchmell
@pedigreecomics.com
www.pedigreecomics.com

HAWAII

Maui Comics & Collectibles
415 Dairy Road, E322
Kahului, HI 96732
PH: (808) 446-2006
kingoil@hotmail.com
alikatime75@yahoo.com
(a-c,e-g,l-p,r-u,w,y,z,3,4)

ILLINOIS

Graham Crackers Comics Ltd.
77 E. Madison Ave.
Downtown Area
Chicago, IL 60602
PH: (312) 629-1810
E-Mail: MattStreets
@GrahamCrackers.com
GrahamCrackers.com
(b-i,r,u,w,x,1,5)

Graham Crackers Comics Ltd.
5443 N. Broadway Ave.
Edgewater Area
Chicago, IL 60640
PH: (773) 561-5010
E-Mail: ShannaBerry
@GrahamCrackers.com
GrahamCrackers.com
(b-g,i,r,u,w,5)

Graham Crackers Comics Ltd.
3162 N. Broadway Ave.
Lakeview Area
Chicago, IL 60647
PH: (773) 665-2010
E-Mail: ShaneWallace
@GrahamCrackers.com
GrahamCrackers.com
(b-g,i,r,u,w,x,1,3-5)

One Stop Comics
5734 West Belmont
Chicago, IL 60634
PH: (773) 777-9636
OneStopComics@sbcglobal.net
OneStopComic.com

Yesterday
1143 W. Addison St.
Chicago, IL 60613
PH: (773) 248-8087
(a-c,e,f,l,n-p,r-t,v,x-z,1,3,4)

The Paper Escape
205 West First Street
Dixon, IL 61021
PH: (815) 284-7567
E-Mail:paperescape@
paperescape.com
www.paperescape.com
(b-d,f-j,p-r,t,u,w,1-5)

Graham Crackers Comics Ltd.
901C Lucinda Ave.
Dekalb, IL 60115
PH: (815) 748-3883
E-Mail: CharlesFischer
@GrahamCrackers.com
GrahamCrackers.com
(b-i,r,u,w,5)

Graham Crackers Comics Ltd.
1550 Ogden Ave.
Downers Grove, IL 60515
PH: (630) 852-1810
E-Mail: JimBrozman
@GrahamCrackers.com
GrahamCrackers.com
(b-g,i,r,u,w,1,5)

Dreamland Comics
105 W. Rockland Rd.
Libertyville, IL 60048
PH: (847) 680-0727
FAX: (847) 680-4495
info@dreamland-comics.com
www.dreamland-comics.com
(a-j,r,t,u,w,3-5)

Graham Crackers Comics Ltd.
1271 Rickert Dr. 135
Naperville, IL 60540
PH: (630) 355-4310
FAX: (630) 778-0700
E-Mail: MikeWall
@GrahamCrackers.com
GrahamCrackers.com
(a-i,n,r,t,u,w,1,3-5)

One Stop Comics
111 South Ridgeland
Oak Park, IL 60302
PH: (708) 524-2287
OneStopComics@sbcglobal.net
OneStopComics.net

Graham Crackers Comics Ltd.
16030 S. Lincoln Highway
Plainfield, IL 60586
PH: (815) 254-3410
E-Mail: JoshKelly
@GrahamCrackers.com
GrahamCrackers.com
(b-i,r,u,w,5)

Graham Crackers Comics Ltd.
610 S. Randall Rd.
St. Charles, IL 60174
PH: (630) 584-0610
E-Mail: DanWeick
@GrahamCrackers.com
GrahamCrackers.com
(b-g,i,r,u,w,5)

Graham Crackers Comics Ltd.
1207 E. Butterfield Rd.
Wheaton, IL 60187
PH: (630) 668-1350
E-Mail: RickBerg
@GrahamCrackers.com
GrahamCrackers.com
(b-i,r,u,w,x,5)

INDIANA

Comics Ina Flash
P.O. Box 3611
Evansville, IN 47735-3611
PH/FAX: (812) 401-6127
comicflash@aol.com
www.comicsinaflash.com

Books Comics and Things
2212 Maplecrest Rd.
Fort Wayne, IN 46815
PH: (260) 493-6116
bct@bctcomics.com
www.bctcomics.com
(a-j,r,u,w,x,1,5)

Books Comics and Things
5808 W. Jefferson Blvd.
Suite C
Fort Wayne, IN 46804
PH: (260) 755-2425
jscott@bctcomics.com
www.bctcomics.com
(a-j,r,t,u,w,x,1,5)

Comic Carnival
7225 N. Keystone Avenue
Suite B
Indianapolis, IN 46240
PH: (317) 253-8882
ComicCarnival@yahoo.com
www.ComicCarnival.com
(a-i,m-o,q,r,t,u,w,z,2,5)

IOWA

Daydreams Comics
21 S. Dubuque St.
Iowa City, IA 52240
PH: (319) 354-6632
E-Mail: daydreamscomics
@yahoo.com
www.daydreamscomics.com
(a-d,f,j,t)

KANSAS

Prairie Dog Comics
4800 West Maple, Suite 122
Wichita, KS 67209
PH: (316) 942-3456
FAX: (316) 942-0702
pdc@pdcomics.com
www.pdcomics.com
(a-z,1-5)

KENTUCKY

Comic Book World, Inc.
7130 Turfway Rd.
Florence, KY 41042
PH: (859) 371-9562
FAX: (859) 371-6925
comicbw@one.net
www.comicbookworld.com
(a-j,l,n,o,r,u,w,1-5)

Comic Book World, Inc.
6905 Shepherdsville Rd.
Louisville, KY 40219
PH: (502) 964-5500
FAX: (502) 964-5500
cbwdoug@bellsouth.net
www.comicbookworld.com
(a-j,l,n,o,r,u,w,x,1-5)

Leroy Harper
P.O. Box 212
West Paducah, KY 42086
PH: (270) 748-9364
LHCOMICS@hotmail.com

LOUISIANA

BT & SJ Giles
P.O. Box 271
Keithville, LA 71047
PH: (318) 925-6654
billygiles@comcast.net
(a,b,d,e,n-q,z)

MAINE

Top Shelf Comics
25 Central St.
Bangor, ME 04401
PH: (207) 947-4939
TopShelf@tcomics.com
www.tcomics.com
(a-f)

MARYLAND

E. Gerber
1720 Belmont Ave.; Suite C
Baltimore, MD 21244

Esquire Comics.com
Mark S. Zaid, ESQ.
P.O. Box 3422492
Bethesda, MD 20827
PH: (202) 498-0011
esquirecomics@aol.com
www.esquirecomics.com
(b-k,r,u,w,4,5)

Alternate Worlds
Yorktowne Plaza Shopping Center
72 Cranbrook Road
Cockeysville, MD 21030
PH: (410) 666-3290
AltWorldStore@comcast.net
www.Alternateworlds.biz
(b-j,q,r,u,w,x,1-5)

Comics To Astonish Inc.
9400 Snowden River Pkwy.
Suite 112
Columbia, MD 21045
PH: (410) 381-2732
comics2u@aol.com
www.ComicsToAstonish.com
(a-k,m,r,t,u,w,z,2,3,5)

Greg Reece's Rare Comics
11028 Graymarsh Pl.
Ijamsville, MD 21754
PH: (240) 575-8600
greg@gregreececomics.com
www.gregreececomics.com
(a,b,c,e,f)

Cards Comics and Collectibles
100A Chartley Drive
Reisterstown, MD 21136
PH: (410) 526-7410
FAX: (410) 526-4006
cardscomicscollectibles@yahoo.com
www.cardscomicscollectibles.com
(a-g,j,t,w,5)

Diamond Comic Distributors
1966 Greenspring Drive
Timonium, MD 21093
PH: (800) 45-COMIC

Diamond International Galleries
1966 Greenspring Drive
Timonium, MD 21093
PH: (888) 355-9800
PH: (410) 427-9422
GalleryQuestions@DiamondGalleries.com
www.DiamondGalleries.com

MASSACHUSETTS

Gary Dolgoff Comics
116 Pleasant St.
Easthampton, MA 01027
PH: (413) 529-0326
FAX: (413) 529-9824
gary@gdcomics.com
www.gdcomics.com

That's Entertainment
56 John Fitch Highway
Fitchburg, MA 01420
PH: (978) 342-8607
Fitch@ThatsE.com
www.ThatsE.com
(a-z,1-5)

Superworld Comics, Inc.
456 Main St., Suite F
Holden, MA 01520
PH: (508) 829-2259
Ted@Superworldcomics.com
www.Superworldcomics.com
(a-c,e)

Bill Cole Enterprises Inc.
P.O. Box 60
Randolph, MA 02368-0060
PH: (781) 986-2653
FAX: (781) 986-2656
sales@bcemylar.com
www.bcemylar.com

The Outer Limits
437 Moody St.
Waltham, MA 02453
PH: (781) 891-0444
askOuterLimits@aol.com
www.eouterlimits.com
(a-h,j,l-z,1-5)

That's Entertainment
244 Park Avenue (Rt. 9)
Worcester, MA 01609-1927
PH: (508) 755-4207
Ken@ThatsE.com
www.ThatsE.com
(a-z,1-5)

MICHIGAN

Motor City Comics
33228 W. 12 Mile Rd.
PMB 286
Farmington Hills, MI 48334
PH: (248) 426-8059
FAX: (248) 426-8064
michaelg@motorcitycomics.com
www.motorcitycomics.com
(a-c,l-o,r,v,w,x)

A To Z Cards and Comics
32647 Ford Rd.
Garden City, MI 48135
PH: (734) 425-6780
Reabros@aol.com
www.YourAtoZ.com
(a-d,f,g,i,j,t,w)

Harley Yee Comics
P.O. Box 51758
Livonia, MI 48151-5758
PH: (800) 731-1029
FAX: (734) 421-7928
HarleyComx@aol.com
www.HarleyYeeComics.com

MINNESOTA

Nostalgia Zone
3006 36th Ave S.
Minneapolis, MN 55406
PH: (612) 822-2806
order@nostalgiazone.com
www.nostalgiazone.com
(a-c,e,f,l-o,s,t,v,x)

NEBRASKA

Robert Beerbohm Comic Art
P.O. Box 507
Fremont, NE 68026
PH: (402) 727-4071
Robert@BLBComics.com
www.BLBComics
(a,b,c,e,l-o,r)

Krypton Comics Inc.
2819 S. 125th Ave.
Suite 261
Omaha, NE 68144
PH: (402) 391-4131
E-Mail:Dean@KryptonComicsOmaha.com
www.KryptonComicsOmaha.com
(a-j,r,u,w,x,1-5)

NEVADA

Redbeard's Book Den
P.O. Box 217
Crystal Bay, NV 89402
PH: (775) 831-4848
FAX: (775) 831-4483
www.redbeardsbookden.com
(a,b,c,l,o,p)

Cosmic Comics!
3830 E. Flamingo Rd.
Suite F-2
Las Vegas, NV 89121
PH: (702) 451-6611
FAX: (702) 451-4609
info@CosmicComcsLV.com
www.CosmicComicsLV.com
(a-l,n,o,r,t-x,5)

NEW HAMPSHIRE

Rare Books & Comics
James F. Payette
P.O. Box 750
Bethlehem, NH 03574
PH: (603) 869-2097
FAX: (603) 869-3475
JimPayette@msn.com
www.JamesPayetteComics.com
(a,b,c,e,n,o,p)

NEW JERSEY

A Time Lost... and Found
325 E. Atlantic Avenue
Audubon, NJ 08106
PH: (856) 547-7900
ATimeLost94@aol.com
(b-f,j,l,r-u,w,x,1,3)

Nationwide Comics
Buying All 10¢ & 12¢ original priced comics
Derek Woywood
Clementon, NJ 08021
PH: (856) 217-5737 or
Hotline: (800) 938-0325
FAX: (714) 288-8992
dwoywood@yahoo.com
www.philadelphiacomic-con.com
(a,b,d-h,m,n,q)

ZAPP Comics
700 Tennent Road
Manalapan, NJ 07726
PH: (732) 617-1333
ZAPPcomics@aol.com
www.zappcomics.com
(a-g,i,j,l,r,t,u,w,x,2,4,5)

Neat Stuff Collectibles
Brian Schutzer
704 76th Street
North Bergen, NJ 07047
PH: 1-800-903-7246
E-Mail: neatstuffcollectibles@yahoo.com
www.NeatStuffCollectibles.com

All-Star Auctions
Nadia Mannarino
122 West End Avenue
Ridgewood, NJ 07450
PH: (201) 652-1305
FAX: (501) 325-6504
nadia@allstarauctions.net
www.allstarauctions.net

ZAPP Comics
574 Valley Road
Wayne, NJ 07470
PH: (973) 628-4500
ZAPPcomics@aol.com
www.zappcomics.com
(a-g,i,j,l,r,t,u,w,x,2,4,5)

JHV Associates
(By Appointment Only)
P. O. Box 317
Woodbury Heights, NJ 08097
PH: (856) 845-4010
FAX: (856) 845-3977
JHVassoc@hotmail.com
(a,b,n,s)

NEW MEXICO

Astro-Zombies
3100 Central Ave. SE
Albuquerque, NM 87106
PH: (505) 232-7800
info@astrozombies.com
astrozombies.com
(a-g,i,l,m,r,t-x,y,2,4,5)

NEW YORK

Excellent Adventures Comics
110 Milton Ave. (Rt. #50)
Ballston Spa, NY 12020
PH: (518) 884-9498
jbelskis37@aol.com
www.excellentadventurescomics.com
(a-f,l-p,r-x,1-4)

Foxprowl Collectables
440 Ellicott St.
Batavia, NY 14020
PH: (585) 415-1173
foxprowl@yahoo.com
www.foxprowl.com
(a-g,j-l,p-z,1-4)

Pinocchio Collectibles
1814 McDonald Ave.
(off Ave. P)
Brooklyn, NY 11223
PH: (718) 645-2573
a19gaba@aol.com
(b-d,f,i,w,x)

HighGradeComics.com
17 Bethany Drive
Commack, NY 11725
PH: (631) 543-1917
FAX: (631) 864-1921
BobStorms@HighGradeComics.com
www.HighGradeComics.com
(a,b,c,e)

Comicollectors.net
Marnin Rosenberg
P.O. Box 2047
Great Neck, NY 11022
PH: (516) 466-8147
www.comiccollectors.net
www.collectorsassemble.com

Mike Carbo's Comic Box
23-23 Borden Ave. Suite 100
Long Island City, NY 11101
PH: (201) 892-1212
mikecarbo@gmail.com
www.nycbm.com

Best Comics
1300 Jericho Turnpike
New Hyde Park, NY 11040
PH: (516) 328-1900
FAX: (516) 328-1909
TommyBest@aol.com
www.bestcomics.com
(a,b,d,f,m,t,u,w,3,4)

ComicConnect.com
873 Broadway
Suite 201
New York, NY 10003
PH: (212) 895-3999
FAX: (212) 260-4304
support@comicconnect.com
www.comicconnect.com
(a,b,c,m,n,s,v)

Metropolis Collectibles
873 Broadway
Suite 201
New York, NY 10003
PH: (800) 229-6387
FAX: (212) 260-4304
E-Mail: buying@
metropoliscomics.com
www.metropoliscomics.com

Midtown Comics
64 Fulton Street
New York, NY 10038
PH: (800) 411-3341
PH: (212) 302-8192
FAX: (646) 421-2033
info@midtowncomics.com
www.midtowncomics.com

Midtown Comics
459 Lexington Ave.
(Corner of 45th Street)
New York, NY 10017
PH: (800) 411-3341
PH: (212) 302-8192
FAX: (646) 421-2033
info@midtowncomics.com
www.midtowncomics.com

Midtown Comics
200 West 40th Street
New York, NY 10018
PH: (800) 411-3341
FAX: (646) 421-2033
info@midtowncomics.com
www.midtowncomics.com

Amazing Comics
12 Gillette Avenue
Sayville, NY 11782
PH: (631) 567-8069
info@amazingco.com
www.amazingco.com

Four Color Comics
Rob Rogovin
P.O. Box 1399
Scarsdale, NY 10583
PH: (914) 722-4696
FAX: (914) 722-7657
keybooks@aol.com
www.fourcolorcomics.com

NORTH CAROLINA

Heroes Aren't Hard To Find
1957 E 7th St.
Charlotte, NC 28204
PH: (704) 375-7462
FAX: (704) 375-7464
www.heroesonline.com

NORTH DAKOTA

Tom's Coin Stamp Gem Baseball & Comic Shop
#2 1st Street S.W.
Minot, ND 58701
PH: (701) 852-4522
TomsCoin@minot.com
TomsCoin.com
(a-z,1-5)

OHIO

Up Up & Away!
4016 Harrison Avenue
Cincinnati, OH 45211
PH: (513) 661-6300
E-Mail: kendall
@upupandawaycomics.com
www.upupandawaycomics.com
(a-j,m,u,w,x,2-4)

Bookery Fantasy
13,15,16 & 18 W. Main St.
Fairborn, OH 45324
PH: (937) 879-1408
BookeryFan@aol.com
www.BookeryFantasy.com
(a-j,l,n-p,r,s,u,w,x,z,1-5)

Comics and Friends
Suite 1050 Great Lakes Mall
7850 Mentor Ave.
Mentor, OH 44096
PH: (440) 255-4242
joe@comicsandfriends.com
www.comicsandfriends.com
(a-f,i-m,r,t-y,5)

Parker's Records & Comics
1222 Suite C Rt. 28
Milford, OH 45150
PH/FAX: (513) 575-3665
dkparker39@fuse.net
www.parkersrc.com
(a-i,y)

World's Greatest Comics
5858 Westerville Rd.
Westerville, OH 43081
PH: (614) 891-3000
worldsgreatestcomics
@yahoo.com
www.WGComics.com
(a-f,r,u,w,x)

OKLAHOMA

All Star Comics
6900 N. May Ave. #10
Oklahoma City, OK 73116
PH/FAX: (405) 842-7800
WGreenewood@cox.net
(a-f,l,n,o,u,w,x,1-4)

Want List Comics
(Appointment Only)
P.O. Box 701932
Tulsa, OK 74170
PH: (918) 299-0440
E-Mail: wlc777@cox.net
(a,b,c,m,n,o,s,t,x,3)

OREGON

Nostalgia Collectibles
527 Willamette Street
Eugene, OR 97401
PH: (541) 484-9202
darrell7g@comcast.net
nostalgiacollectibleseugene.com
(a-g,i-l,n-r,t,u,w,x,y,1-5)

Future Dreams
1847 East Burnside St.
Suite 116
Portland, OR 97214-1587
PH: (503) 231-8311
fdb@hevanet.com
www.futuredreamsbooks.com
(a-g,i,j,l-n,p-u,w,x,3,4)

PENNSYLVANIA

New Dimension Comics
Clearview Mall
101 Clearview Circle
Butler, PA 16001
PH: (724) 282-5283
butler@ndcomics.com
www.ndcomics.com
(a-l,n,o,r,t,u,w,x,1-5)

New Dimension Comics
Piazza Plaza
20550 Route 19 (Perry Hwy.)
Cranberry Township, PA 16066
PH: (724) 776-0433
cranberry@ndcomics.com
www.ndcomics.com
(a-l,n,o,r,t,u,w,x,1-5)

New Dimension Comics Megastore
516 Lawrence Ave.
Ellwood City, PA 16117
PH: (724) 758-2324
ec@ndcomics.com
www.ndcomics.com
(a-l,n,o,r,t,u,w,x,1-5)

Comic Universe
446 MacDade Blvd.
Folsom, PA 19033
PH: (610) 461-7960
chessflink@yahoo.com
www.ComicUniverse.net
(a-g,i-u,w,x,z,1-5)

The Comic Store
28 McGovern Ave.
Lancaster, PA 17602
PH: (717) 397-8737
FAX: (717) 397-8903
comicstore@juno.com
www.comicstorepa.com

Eide's Entertainment, LLC
1121 Penn Ave.
Pittsburgh, PA 15222
PH: (412) 261-0900
FAX: (412) 261-3102
eides@eides.com
www.eides.com
(a-g,j-z,1-5)

New Dimension Comics
Pittsburgh Mills
590 Pittsburgh Mill Circle
Tarentum, PA 15084
PH: (724) 758-1560
mills@ndcomics.com
www.ndcomics.com
(a-l,n,o,r,t,u,w,x,1-5)

New Dimension Comics
Pittsburgh Century III Mall
3075 Clairton Rd. #940
West Mifflin, PA 15213
PH: (412) 655-8661
century3@ndcomics.com
www.ndcomics.com
(a-l,n,o,r,t,u,w,x,1-5)

Hake's Americana
P.O. Box 12001
York, PA 17402
PH: (866) 404-9800
www.hakes.com

TENNESSEE

Dewayne's World - Comics & Games
459 E. Sullivan Street
Kingsport, TN 37660
PH: (423) 247-8997
dewayne@
dewaynes-world.com
www.dewaynes-world.com
(b-d,f-i,r,u,w,x,1,3-5)

TEXAS

Lone Star Comics
511 E. Abram St.
Arlington, TX 76010
PH: (817) 860-7827
FAX: (817) 860-2769
customerservice@
lonestarcomics.com
www.mycomicshop.com/
overstreet
(a-f,j,n,p,u,1-4)

Comic Heaven
P.O. Box 900
Big Sandy, TX 75755
PH: (903) 636-5555
www.comicheaven.net

Classics Incorporated
Matt Nelson
1440 Halsey Way
Suite #114
Carrollton, TX 75007
PH: (972) 980-8040
www.classicsincorporated.com
Spectre52@aol.com

Heritage Auction Galleries
3500 Maple Avenue
17th Floor
Dallas, TX 75219-3941
PH: (800) 872-6467
www.HA.com

William Hughes' Vintage Collectables
P.O. Box 270244
Flower Mound, TX 75027
PH: (972) 539-9190
FAX: (972) 691-8837
Whughes199@yahoo.com
www.VintageCollectables.net

Bedrock City Comic Co.
6517 Westheimer
Houston, TX 77057
PH: (713) 780-0675
www.bedrockcity.com
(a-g,j-o,r-x,z,1-5)

Bedrock City Comic Co.
4683 FM1960 West
Houston, TX 77069
PH: (281) 444-9763
www.bedrockcity.com
(a-g,j-o,r-x,z,1-5)

Bedrock City Comic Co.
106 W. Bay Area Blvd.
Webster, TX 77598
PH: (281) 557-2748
www.bedrockcity.com
(a-g,j-o,r-x,z,1-5)

VIRGINIA

Trilogy Shop #2
700 E. Little Creek Rd.
Norfolk, VA 23518
PH: (757) 587-2540
trilogy2@TrilogyComics.net
www.TrilogyComics.net
(d,f-j,w,5)

B & D Comic Shop
802 Elm Avenue SW
Roanoke, VA 24016
PH: (540) 342-6642
FAX: (540) 342-6694
bdcomics1@verizon.net
www.banddcomics.com
(b,c,d,f,r,w,x,5)

Trilogy Comics
5773 Princess Anne Rd.
Virginia Beach, VA 23462
PH: (757) 490-2205
trilogy1@TrilogyComics.net
www.TrilogyComics.net
(a-j,n-p,s-u,w,z,1,3-5)

WASHINGTON

DreamStrands Comics & Such
115 N. 85th St.
Seattle, WA 98103
PH: (206) 297-3737
delanor@dreamstrands.com
www.dreamstrands.com
(b-d,f,g,i,j,r,u,w,x,3-5)

Golden Age Collectables
1501 Pike Place Market
401 Lower Level
Seattle, WA 98101
PH: (206) 622-9799
FAX: (206) 622-9595
GACollect@gmail.com
www.GoldenAgeCollectables.com
(a-x,1-5)

WISCONSIN

Inner Child Collectibles and Comics
5921 Sixth Avenue A
Kenosha, WI 53140
PH: (262) 653-0400
PH: (312) 269-0189
innerchildcomics@gmail.com
innerchildcomics.com
(a-f,l-p,r-x,2-4)

Jef Hinds Comics
PO Box 44803
Madison, WI 53744-4803
PH: (608) 345-8750
jhcomics@jhcomics.com
www.jhcomics.com
(a-c,e,m-o,s,w)

CANADA

ALBERTA

Another Dimension
424 B - 10 St. NW
Calgary, Alberta T2N 1V9
PH: (403) 283-7078
FAX: (403) 283-7080
comics@another-dimension.com
www.another-dimension.com
(a-g,j,l,m,q,r,u,w,x,z,1-5)

MANITOBA

Doug Sulipa's Comic World
Box 21986
Steinbach, MB., R5G 1B5
PH: (204) 346-3674
FAX: (204) 346-1632
dsulipa@gmail.com
www.dougcomicworld.com
(a-e,h,l,n-t,y,z,3,4)

Comics America
552 Academy Road
Winnipeg, MB, R3N 03E
PH: (204) 489-0580
FAX: (204) 489-0589
comics_america@mts.net
www.comicsamerica.com

ONTARIO

Big B Comics
1045 Upper James St.
Hamilton, ONT. L9C 3A6
PH: (905) 318-9636
FAX: (905) 318-9055
mailbox@bigbcomics.com
www.bigbcomics.com
(a-g,i,j,l,m,u-x,1-5)

Vintage Comics
PO Box 25055
Kitchener, ONT. N2A 4A5
Toll Free: (888) 551-8155
info@vintagecomics.com
www.vintagecomics.com

Pendragon Comics & Books
3759 Lakeshore Boulevard West
Toronto, ONT M8W 1R1
PH: (416) 253-6974
pendragoncomics@rogers.com
www.pendragoncomics.com
(a-g,i,l,n-p,u-x)

QUEBEC

Heroes Comics
1116 Cure LaBelle
Laval, QC H7V 2V5
PH: (450) 686-9155
FAX: (450) 686-2097
heroescomics@videotron.ca
(a-j,m,r-x,1-5)

FRANCE

Editions Déesse
8, Rue Cochin
Paris, France 75005
PH: +33 1 46 34 18 31
eds@editions-deesse.com
www.editions-deesse.com
(a-f,l,m,n,r,u)

INTERNET

ComicLink Auctions & Exchange
PH: (718) 246-0300
buysell@ComicLink.com
www.ComicLink.com

Sparkle City Comics Auctions
PH: (800) 215-4006
buyingeverything@yahoo.com
www.sparklecitycomics.com

Vintage Comics
Toll Free: (888) 551-8155
info@vintagecomics.com
www.vintagecomics.com

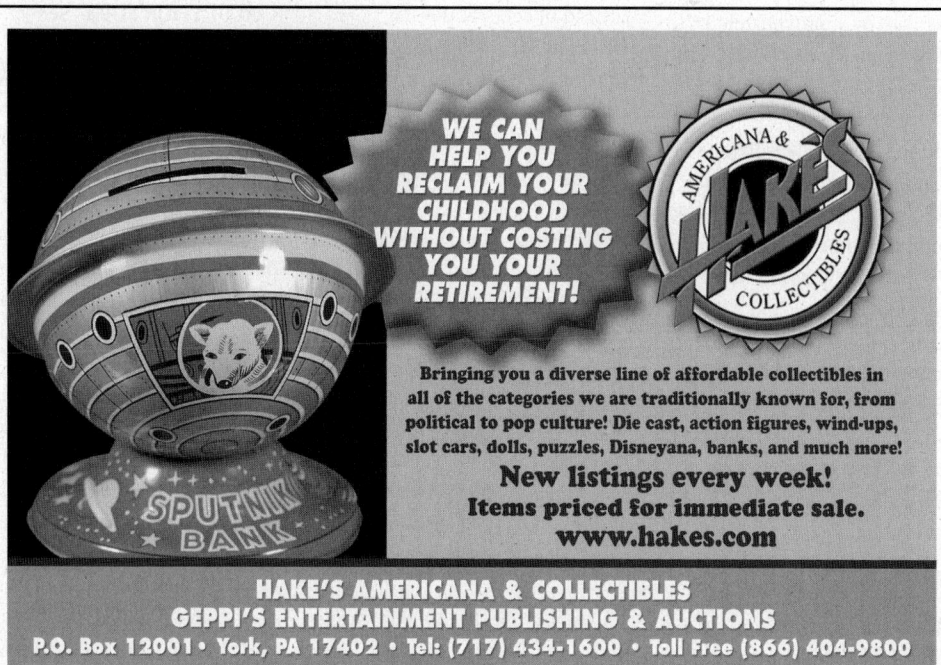

GLOSSARY

a - Story art; a(i) - Story art inks; a(p) - Story art pencils;
a(r) - Story art reprint.

ADULT MATERIAL - Contains story and/or art for "mature" readers. Re: sex, violence, strong language.

ADZINE - A magazine primarily devoted to the advertising of comic books and collectibles as its first publishing priority as opposed to written articles.

ALLENTOWN COLLECTION - A collection discovered in 1987-88 just outside Allentown, Pennsylvania. The Allentown collection consisted of 135 Golden Age comics, characterized by high grade and superior paper quality.

ANNUAL - (1) A book that is published yearly; (2) Can also refer to some square bound comics.

ARRIVAL DATE - The date written (often in pencil) or stamped on the cover of comics by either the local wholesaler, newsstand owner, or distributor. The date precedes the cover date by approximately 15 to 75 days, and may vary considerably from one locale to another or from one year to another.

ASHCAN - A publisher's in-house facsimile of a proposed new title. Most ashcans have black and white covers stapled to an existing coverless comic on the inside; other ashcans are totally black and white. In modern parlance, it can also refer to promotional or sold comics, often smaller than standard comic size and usually in black and white, released by publishers to advertise the forthcoming arrival of a new title or story.

ATOM AGE - Comics published from 1946-1956.

B&W - Black and white art.

BACK-UP FEATURE - A story or character that usually appears after the main feature in a comic book; often not featured on the cover.

BAD GIRL ART - A term popularized in the early '90s to describe an attitude as well as a style of art that portrays women in a sexual and often action-oriented way.

BAXTER PAPER - A high quality, heavy, white paper used in the printing of some comics.

BC - Abbreviation for Back Cover.

BI-MONTHLY - Published every two months.

BI-WEEKLY - Published every two weeks.

BONDAGE COVER - Usually denotes a female in bondage.

BOUND COPY - A comic that has been bound into a book. The process requires that the spine be trimmed and sometimes sewn into a book-like binding.

BRITISH ISSUE - A comic printed for distribution in Great Britain; these copies sometimes have the price listed in pence or pounds instead of cents or dollars.

BRITTLENESS - A severe condition of paper deterioration where paper loses its flexibility and thus chips and/or flakes easily.

BRONZE AGE - Comics published from 1970 to 1984.

BROWNING - (1) The aging of paper characterized by the ever-increasing level of oxidation characterized by darkening; (2) The level of paper deterioration one step more severe than tanning and one step before brittleness.

c - Cover art; c(i) - Cover inks; c(p) - Cover pencils; c(r) - Cover reprint.

CAMEO - The brief appearance of one character in the strip of another.

CANADIAN ISSUE - A comic printed for distribution in Canada; these copies sometimes have no advertising.

CCA - Abbreviation for **Comics Code Authority**.

CCA SEAL - An emblem that was placed on the cover of all CCA approved comics beginning in April-May, 1955.

CENTER CREASE - See **Subscription Copy**.

CENTERFOLD or CENTER SPREAD - The two folded pages in the center of a comic book at the terminal end of the staples.

CERTIFIED GRADING - A process provided by a professional grading service that certifies a given grade for a comic and seals the book in a protective **Slab.**

CF - Abbreviation for **Centerfold**.

CFO - Abbreviation for Centerfold Out.

CGC - Abbreviation for the certified comic book grading company, Comics Guaranty, LLC.

CIRCULATION COPY - See **Subscription Copy**.

CIRCULATION FOLD - See **Subscription Fold**.

CLASSIC COVER - A cover considered by collectors to be highly desirable because of its subject matter, artwork, historical importance, etc.

CLEANING - A process in which dirt and dust is removed.

COLOR TOUCH - A restoration process by which colored ink is used to hide color flecks, color flakes, and larger areas of missing color. Short for Color Touch-Up.

COLORIST - An artist who paints the color guides for comics. Many modern colorists use computer technology.

COMIC BOOK DEALER - (1) A seller of comic books; (2) One who makes a living buying and selling comic books.

COMIC BOOK REPAIR - When a tear, loose staple or centerfold has been mended without changing or adding to the original finish of the book. Repair may involve tape, glue or nylon gossamer, and is easily detected; it is considered a defect.

COMICS CODE AUTHORITY - A voluntary organization comprised of comic book publishers formed in 1954 to review (and possibly censor) comic books before they were printed and distributed. The emblem of the CCA is a white stamp in the upper right hand corner of comics dated after February 1955. The term "post-Code" refers to the time after this practice started, or approximately 1955 to the present.

COMPLETE RUN - All issues of a given title.

CON - A convention or public gathering of fans.

CONDITION - The state of preservation of a comic book, often inaccurately used interchangeably with **Grade**.

CONSERVATION - The European Confederation of Conservator-Restorers' Organizations (ECCO) in its professional guidelines, defines conservation as follows: "Conservation consists mainly of direct action carried out on cultural heritage with the aim of stabilizing condition and retarding further deterioration."

COPPER AGE - Comics published from 1984 to 1992.

COSMIC AEROPLANE COLLECTION - A collection from Salt Lake City, Utah discovered by Cosmic Aeroplane Books, characterized by the moderate to high grade copies of 1930s-40s comics with pencil check marks in the margins of inside pages. It is thought that these comics were kept by a commercial illustration school and the check marks were placed beside panels that instructors wanted students to draw.

COSTUMED HERO - A costumed crime fighter with "developed" human powers instead of super powers.

COUPON CUT or COUPON MISSING - A coupon has been neatly removed with scissors or razor blade from the interior or exterior of the comic as opposed to having been ripped out.

COVER GLOSS - The reflective quality of the cover inks.

COVER TRIMMED - Cover has been reduced in size by neatly cutting away rough or damaged edges.

COVERLESS - A comic with no cover attached. There is a niche demand for coverless comics, particularly in the case of hard-to-find key books otherwise impossible to locate intact.

C/P - Abbreviation for **Cleaned and Pressed**. See **Cleaning**.

CREASE - A fold which causes ink removal, usually resulting in a white line. See **Reading Crease**.

CROSSOVER - A story where one character appears prominently in the story of another character. See **X-Over**.

CVR - Abbreviation for Cover.

DEALER - See **Comic Book Dealer**.

DEACIDIFICATION - Several different processes that reduce acidity in paper.

DEBUT - The first time that a character appears anywhere.

DEFECT - Any fault or flaw that detracts from perfection.

DENVER COLLECTION - A collection consisting primarily of early 1940s high grade number one issues bought at auction in Pennsylvania by a Denver, Colorado dealer.

DIE-CUT COVER - A comic book cover with areas or edges precut by a printer to a special shape or to create a desired effect.

DISTRIBUTOR STRIPES - Color brushed or sprayed on the edges of comic book stacks by the distributor/wholesaler to code them for expedient exchange at the sales racks. Typical colors are red, orange, yellow, green, blue, and purple. Distributor stripes are not a defect.

DOUBLE - A duplicate copy of the same comic book.

DOUBLE COVER - When two covers are stapled to the comic interior instead of the usual one; the exterior cover often protects the interior cover from wear and damage. This is considered a desirable situation by some collectors and may increase collector value; this is not considered a defect.

DRUG PROPAGANDA STORY - A comic that makes an editorial stand about drug use.

DRUG USE STORY - A comic that shows the actual use of drugs: needle use, tripping, harmful effects, etc.

DRY CLEANING - A process in which dirt and dust is removed.

DUOTONE - Printed with black and one other color of ink. This process was common in comics printed in the 1930s.

DUST SHADOW - Darker, usually linear area at the edge of some comics stored in stacks. Some portion of the cover was not covered by the comic immediately above it and it was exposed to settling dust particles. Also see **Oxidation Shadow** and **Sun Shadow**.

EDGAR CHURCH COLLECTION - See **Mile High Collection**.

EMBOSSED COVER - A comic book cover with a pattern, shape or image pressed into the cover from the inside, creating a raised area.

ENCAPSULATION - Refers to the process of sealing certified comics in a protective plastic enclosure. Also see **Slabbing.**

EYE APPEAL - A term which refers

to the overall look of a comic book when held at approximately arm's length. A comic may have nice eye appeal yet still possess defects which reduce grade.

FANZINE - An amateur fan publication.

FC - Abbreviation for Front Cover.

FILE COPY - A high grade comic originating from the publisher's file; contrary to what some might believe, not all file copies are in Gem Mint condition. An arrival date on the cover of a comic does not indicate that it is a file copy, though a copyright date may.

FIRST APPEARANCE - See **Debut**.

FLASHBACK - When a previous story is recalled.

FOIL COVER - A comic book cover that has had a thin metallic foil hot stamped on it. Many of these "gimmick" covers date from the early '90s, and might include chromium, prism and hologram covers as well.

FOUR COLOR - Series of comics produced by Dell, characterized by hundreds of different features; named after the four color process of printing. See **One Shot**.

FOUR COLOR PROCESS - The process of printing with the three primary colors (red, yellow, and blue) plus black.

FUMETTI - Illustration system in which individual frames of a film are colored and used for individual panels to make a comic book story. The most famous example is DC's *Movie Comics* #1-6 from 1939.

GATEFOLD COVER - A double-width fold-out cover.

GENRE - Categories of comic book subject matter; e.g. Science Fiction, Super-Hero, Romance, Funny Animal, Teenage Humor, Crime, War, Western, Mystery, Horror, etc.

GIVEAWAY - Type of comic book intended to be given away as a premium or promotional device instead of being sold.

GLASSES ATTACHED - In 3-D comics, the special blue and red cellophane and cardboard glasses are still attached to the comic.

GLASSES DETACHED - In 3-D comics, the special blue and red cellophane and cardboard glasses are not still attached to the comic; obviously less desirable than **Glasses Attached**.

GOLDEN AGE - Comics published from 1938 (*Action Comics* #1) to 1945.

GOOD GIRL ART - Refers to a style of art, usually from the 1930s-50s, that portrays women in a sexually implicit way.

GREY-TONE COVER - A cover art style in which pencil or charcoal underlies the normal line drawing, used to enhance the effects of light and shadow, thus producing a richer quality. These covers, prized by most collectors, are sometimes referred to as **Painted Covers** but are not actually painted.

HC - Abbreviation for Hardcover.

HEADLIGHTS - Forward illumation devices installed on all automobiles and many other vehicles... OK, OK, it's a euphemism for a comic book cover prominently featuring a woman's breasts in a provocative way. Also see **Bondage Cover** for another collecting euphemism that has long since outlived its appropriateness in these politically correct times.

HOT STAMPING - The process of pressing foil, prism paper and/or inks on cover stock.

HRN - Abbreviation for Highest Reorder Number. This refers to a method used by collectors of Gilberton's *Classic Comics* and *Classics Illustrated* series to distinguish first editions from later printings.

ILLO - Abbreviation for Illustration.

IMPAINT - Another term for **Color Touch**.

INDICIA - Publishing and title information usually located at the bottom of the first page or the bottom of the inside front cover. In some pre-1938 comics and many modern comics, it is located on internal pages.

INFINITY COVER - Shows a scene that repeats itself to infinity.

INKER - Artist that does the inking.

INTRO - Same as **Debut**.

INVESTMENT GRADE COPY - (1) Comic of sufficiently high grade and demand to be viewed by collectors as instantly liquid should the need arise to sell; (2) A comic in VF or better condition; (3) A comic purchased primarily to realize a profit.

ISSUE NUMBER - The actual edition number of a given title.

ISH - Short for Issue.

JLA - Abbreviation for Justice League of America.

JSA - Abbreviation for Justice Society of America.

KEY, KEY BOOK or KEY ISSUE - An issue that contains a first appearance, origin, or other historically or artistically important feature considered especially desirable by collectors.

LAMONT LARSON - Pedigreed collection of high grade 1940s comics with the initials or name of its original owner, Lamont Larson.

LENTICULAR COVERS or "FLICKER" COVERS - A comic book cover overlayed with a ridged plastic sheet such that the special artwork underneath appears to move when the cover is tilted at different angles perpendicular to the ridges.

LETTER COL or LETTER COLUMN - A feature in a comic book that prints and sometimes responds to letters written by its readers.

LINE DRAWN COVER - A cover

published in the traditional way where pencil sketches are overdrawn with india ink and then colored. See also **Grey-Tone Cover**, **Photo Cover**, and **Painted Cover**.

LOGO - The title of a strip or comic book as it appears on the cover or title page.

LSH - Abbreviation for Legion of Super-Heroes.

MAGIC LIGHTNING COLLECTION - A collection of high grade 1950s comics from the San Francisco area.

MARVEL CHIPPING - A bindery (trimming/cutting) defect that results in a series of chips and tears at the top, bottom, and right edges of the cover, caused when the cutting blade of an industrial paper trimmer becomes dull. It was dubbed Marvel Chipping because it can be found quite often on Marvel comics from the late '50s and early '60s but can also occur with any company's comic books from the late 1940s through the middle 1960s.

MILE HIGH COLLECTION - High grade collection of over 22,000 comics discovered in Denver, Colorado in 1977, originally owned by Mr. Edgar Church. Comics from this collection are now famous for extremely white pages, fresh smell, and beautiful cover ink reflectivity.

MODERN AGE - A catch-all term applied to comics published since 1992.

MYLAR™ - An inert, very hard, space-age plastic used to make high quality protective bags and sleeves for comic book storage. "Mylar" is a trademark of the DuPont Co.

ND - Abbreviation for **No Date**.

NN - Abbreviation for **No Number**.

NO DATE - When there is no date given on the cover or indicia page.

NO NUMBER - No issue number is given on the cover or indicia page; these are usually first issues or one-shots.

N.Y. LEGIS. COMM. - New York Legislative Committee to Study the Publication of Comics (1951).

ONE-SHOT - When only one issue is published of a title, or when a series is published where each issue is a different title (e.g. Dell's *Four Color Comics*).

ORIGIN - When the story of a character's creation is given.

OVER GUIDE - When a comic book is priced at a value over *Guide* list.

OXIDATION SHADOW - Darker, usually linear area at the edge of some comics stored in stacks. Some portion of the cover was not covered by the comic immediately above it, and it was exposed to the air. Also see **Dust Shadow** and **Sun Shadow**.

p - Art pencils.

PAINTED COVER - (1) Cover taken from an actual painting instead of a line drawing; (2) Inaccurate name for a grey-toned cover.

PANELOLOGIST - One who researches comic books and/or comic strips.

PANNAPICTAGRAPHIST - One possible term for someone who collects comic books; can you figure out why it hasn't exactly taken off in common parlance?

PAPER COVER - Comic book cover made from the same newsprint as the interior pages. These books are extremely rare in high grade.

PARADE OF PLEASURE - A book about the censorship of comics.

PB - Abbreviation for Paperback.

PEDIGREE - A book from a famous and usually high grade collection - e.g. Allentown, Lamont Larson, Edgar Church/Mile High, Denver, San Francisco, Cosmic Aeroplane, etc. Beware of non-pedigree collections being promoted as pedigree books; only outstanding high grade collections similar to those listed qualify.

PENCILER - Artist that does the pencils...you're figuring out some of these definitions without us by now, aren't you?

PERFECT BINDING - Pages are glued to the cover as opposed to being stapled to the cover, resulting in a flat binded side. Also known as **Square Back or Square Bound**.

PG - Abbreviation for Page.

PHOTO COVER - Comic book cover featuring a photographic image instead of a line drawing or painting.

PIECE REPLACEMENT - A process by which pieces are added to replace areas of missing paper.

PIONEER AGE - Comics published from the 1500s to 1828.

PLATINUM AGE - Comics published from 1883 to 1938.

POLYPROPALENE - A type of plastic used in the manufacture of comic book bags; now considered harmful to paper and not recommended for long term storage of comics.

POP - Abbreviation for the anti-comic book volume, *Parade of Pleasure*.

POST-CODE - Describes comics published after February 1955 and usually displaying the CCA stamp in the upper right-hand corner.

POUGHKEEPSIE - Refers to a large collection of Dell Comics file copies believed to have originated from the warehouse of Western Publishing in Poughkeepsie, NY.

PP - Abbreviation for Pages.

PRE-CODE - Describes comics published before the **Comics Code Authority** seal began appearing on covers in 1955.

PRE-HERO DC - A term used to describe *More Fun* #1-51 (pre-Spectre), *Adventure* #1-39 (pre-

Sandman), and *Detective* #1-26 (pre-Batman). The term is actually inaccurate because technically there were "heroes" in the above books.

PRE-HERO MARVEL - A term used to describe *Strange Tales* #1-100 (pre-Human Torch), *Journey Into Mystery* #1-82 (pre-Thor), *Tales To Astonish* #1-35 (pre-Ant Man), and *Tales Of Suspense* #1-38 (pre-Iron Man).

PRESERVATION - Another term for **Conservation**.

PRESSING - A term used to describe a variety of processes or procedures, professional and amateur, under which an issue is pressed to eliminate wrinkles, bends, dimples and/or other perceived defects and thus improve its appearance. Some types of pressing involve disassembling the book and performing other work on it prior to its pressing and reassembly. Some methods are generally easily discerned by professionals and amateurs. Other types of pressing, however, can pose difficulty for even experienced professionals to detect. In all cases, readers are cautioned that unintended damage can occur in some instances. Related defects will diminish an issue's grade correspondingly rather than improve it.

PROVENANCE - When the owner of a book is known and is stated for the purpose of authenticating and documenting the history of the book. Example: A book from the Stan Lee or Forrest Ackerman collection would be an example of a value-adding provenance.

PULP - Cheaply produced magazine made from low grade newsprint. The term comes from the wood pulp that was used in the paper manufacturing process.

QUARTERLY - Published every three months (four times a year).

R - Abbreviation for Reprint.

RARE - 10-20 copies estimated to exist.

RAT CHEW - Damage caused by the gnawing of rats and mice.

RBCC - Abbreviation for Rockets Blast Comic Collector, one of the first and most prominent adzines instrumental in developing the early comic book market.

READING COPY - A comic that is in FAIR to GOOD condition and is often used for research; the condition has been sufficiently reduced to the point where general handling will not degrade it further.

READING CREASE - Book-length, vertical front cover crease at staples, caused by bending the cover over the staples. Square-bounds receive these creases just by opening the cover too far to the left.

REILLY, TOM - A large high grade collection of 1939-1945 comics with 5000+ books.

REINFORCEMENT - A process by which a weak or split page or cover is reinforced with adhesive and reinforcement paper.

REPRINT COMICS - In earlier decades, comic books that contained newspaper strip reprints; modern reprint comics usually contain stories originally featured in older comic books.

RESTORATION - Any attempt, whether professional or amateur, to enhance the appearance of an aging or damaged comic book using additive procedures. These procedures may include any or all of the following techniques: recoloring, adding missing paper, trimming, re-glossing, reinforcement, glue, etc. Amateur work can lower the value of a book, and even professional restoration has now gained a negative aura in the modern marketplace from some quarters. In all cases a restored book can never be worth the same as an unrestored book in the same condition. There is no consensus on the inclusion of pressing, non-aqueous cleaning, tape removal and in some cases staple replacement in this definition. Until such time as there is consensus, we encourage continued debate and interaction among all interested parties and reflection upon the standards in other hobbies and art forms.

REVIVAL - An issue that begins republishing a comic book character after a period of dormancy.

ROCKFORD - A high grade collection of 1940s comics with 2000+ books from Rockford, IL.

ROLLED SPINE - A condition where the left edge of a comic book curves toward the front or back; a defect caused by folding back each page as the comic was read.

ROUND BOUND - Standard saddle stitch binding typical of most comics.

RUN - A group of comics of one title where most or all of the issues are present. See **Complete Run**.

S&K - Abbreviation for the legendary creative team of Joe Simon and Jack Kirby, creators of Marvel Comics' Captain America.

SADDLE STITCH - The staple binding of magazines and comic books.

SAN FRANCISCO COLLECTION - (see **Reilly, Tom**)

SCARCE - 20-100 copies estimated to exist.

SEDUCTION OF THE INNOCENT - An inflammatory book written by Dr. Frederic Wertham and published in 1953; Wertham asserted that comics were responsible for rampant juvenile deliquency in American youth.

SET - (1) A complete run of a given title; (2) A grouping of comics for sale.

SEMI-MONTHLY - Published twice a month, but not necessarily **Bi-Weekly**.

SEWN SPINE - A comic with many spine perforations where binders' thread held it into a bound volume. This is considered a defect.
SF - Abbreviation for Science Fiction (the other commonly used term, "sci-fi," is often considered derogatory or indicative of more "low-brow" rather than "literary" science fiction, i.e. "sci-fi television."
SILVER AGE - Comics published from 1956 to 1970.
SILVER PROOF - A black and white actual size print on thick glossy paper hand-painted by an artist to indicate colors to the engraver.
SLAB - Colloquial term for the plastic enclosure used by grading certification companies to seal in certified comics.
SLABBING - Colloquial term for the process of encapsulating certified comics in a plastic enclosure.
SOTI - Abbreviation for **Seduction of the Innocent**.
SPINE - The left-hand edge of the comic that has been folded and stapled.
SPINE ROLL - A condition where the left edge of the comic book curves toward the front or back, caused by folding back each page as the comic was read.
SPINE SPLIT SEALED - A process by which a spine split is sealed using an adhesive.
SPLASH PAGE - A **Splash Panel** that takes up the entire page.
SPLASH PANEL - (1) The first panel of a comic book story, usually larger than other panels and usually containing the title and credits of the story; (2) An oversized interior panel.
SQUARE BACK or SQUARE BOUND - See **Perfect Binding**.
STORE STAMP - Store name (and sometimes address and telephone number) stamped in ink via rubber stamp and stamp pad.
SUBSCRIPTION COPY - A comic sent through the mail directly from the publisher or publisher's agent. Most are folded in half, causing a subscription crease or fold running down the center of the comic from top to bottom; this is considered a defect.
SUBSCRIPTION CREASE - See **Subscription Copy**.
SUBSCRIPTION FOLD - See **Subscription Copy**. Differs from a **Subscription Crease** in that no ink is missing as a result of the fold.
SUN SHADOW - Darker, usually linear area at the edge of some comics stored in stacks. Some portion of the cover was not covered by the comic immediately above it, and it suffered prolonged exposure to light. A serious defect, unlike a **Dust Shadow**, which can sometimes be removed. Also see **Oxidation Shadow**.
SUPER-HERO - A costumed crime fighter with powers beyond those of mortal man.
SUPER-VILLAIN - A costumed criminal with powers beyond those of mortal man; the antithesis of **Super-Hero**.
SWIPE - A panel, sequence, or story obviously borrowed from previously published material.
TEAR SEALS - A process by which a tear is sealed using an adhesive.
TEXT ILLO. - A drawing or small panel in a text story that almost never has a dialogue balloon.
TEXT PAGE - A page with no panels or drawings.
TEXT STORY - A story with few if any illustrations commonly used as filler material during the first three decades of comics.
3-D COMIC - Comic art that is drawn and printed in two color layers, producing a 3-D effect when viewed through special glasses.
3-D EFFECT COMIC - Comic art that is drawn to appear as if in 3-D but isn't.
TITLE - The name of the comic book.
TITLE PAGE - First page of a story showing the title of the story and possibly the creative credits and indicia.
TRIMMED - (1) A bindery process which separates top, right, and bottom of pages and cuts comic books to the proper size; (2) A repair process in which defects along the edges of a comic book are removed with the use of scissors, razor blades, and/or paper cutters. Comic books which have been repaired in this fashion are considered defectives.
TTA - Abbreviation for *Tales to Astonish*.
UK - Abbreviation for British edition (United Kingdom).
UNDER GUIDE - When a comic book is priced at a value less than *Guide* list.
UPGRADE - To obtain another copy of the same comic book in a higher grade.
VARIANT COVER - A different cover image used on the same issue.
VERY RARE - 1 to 10 copies estimated to exist.
VICTORIAN AGE - Comics published from 1828 to 1883.
WANT LIST - A listing of comics needed by a collector, or a list of comics that a collector is interested in purchasing.
WAREHOUSE COPY - Originating from a publisher's warehouse; similar to file copy.
WHITE MOUNTAIN COLLECTION - A collection of high grade 1950s and 1960s comics which originated in New England.
X-OVER - Short for **Crossover**.
ZINE - Short for **Fanzine**.

Archie COMICS
MAKING KIDS INTO COLLECTORS SINCE 1941
R
A

GEPPI'S ENTERTAINMENT MUSEUM PRESENTS

The OVERSTREET HALL OF FAME

The Overstreet Hall of Fame was conceived to single out individuals who have made great contributions to the comic book arts.
This includes writers, artists, editors, publishers and others who have plied their craft in insightful and meaningful ways.

While such evaluations are inherently subjective, they also serve to aid in reflecting upon those who shaped the experience of reading comic books over the years.
This year's class of inductees begins on this next page.

THE PREVIOUS INDUCTEES

Class of 2006
Murphy Anderson
Jim Aparo
Jim Lee
Mac Raboy

Class of 2007
Dave Cockrum
Steve Ditko
Bruce Hamilton
Martin Nodell
George Pérez
Jim Shooter
Dave Stevens
Alex Toth
Michael Turner

Class of 2008
Carl Barks
Will Eisner
Al Feldstein
Harvey Kurtzman
Stan Lee
Marshall Rogers
John Romita, Sr.
John Romita, Jr.
Julius Schwartz
Mike Wieringo

Class of 2009
Neal Adams
Matt Baker
Chris Claremont
Palmer Cox
Bill Everett
Frank Frazetta
Neil Gaiman
William M. Gaines
Carmine Infantino
Jack Kirby
Joe Kubert
Paul Levitz
Russ Manning
Todd McFarlane
Don Rosa
John Severin
Joe Simon
Al Williamson

Class of 2010
Sergio Aragonés
M.C. Gaines
Archie Goodwin
Winsor McCay
Mike Mignola
Frank Miller
Robert M. Overstreet
Mike Richardson
Jerry Robinson
Joe Shuster
Jerry Siegel
Jim Steranko
Wally Wood

Class of 2011
Jack Davis
Martin Goodman
Dean Mullaney
Marie Severin
Walt Simonson
Major Malcolm Wheeler-Nicholson

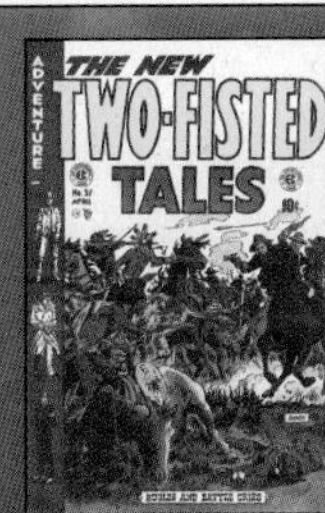

AVENGERS #58
November 1968. © MAR

Inspired by the work of Hal Foster, Alex Raymond, and Burne Hogarth, John Buscema began his career at Marvel Comics in 1948, when it was still Timely Comics. He stayed on staff there for a year and a half, afterward freelancing for a number of companies. After leaving the comics field to go into advertising in 1958, Buscema returned to comics — and Marvel in particular — in 1966, when his old boss Stan Lee brought him back to the "House of Ideas." His Silver Age output could be seen within the pages of *Avengers*, *Conan the Barbarian*, *Fantastic Four*, *Nick Fury: Agent of S.H.I.E.L.D.*, and *Silver Surfer*, among others. He also co-wrote *How to Draw Comics the Marvel Way* with Stan Lee. His final published comics work was DC Comics' *Just Imagine Stan Lee with John Buscéma Creating Superman*. His is a talent that is greatly missed, but lives on in myriad four-color tales.
- Scott Braden

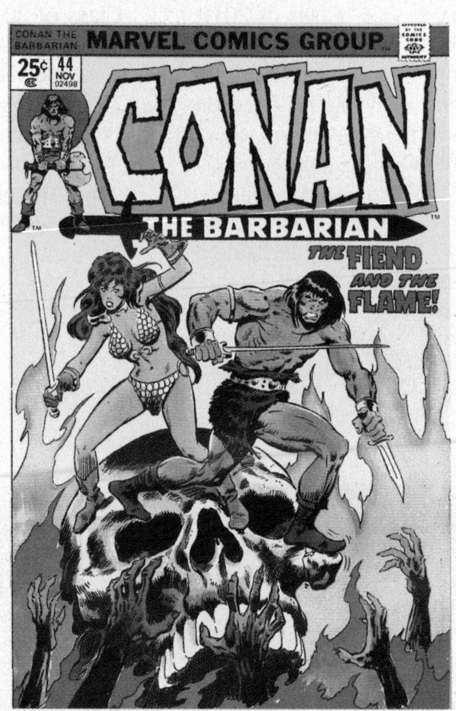

CONAN THE BARBARIAN #44
May 1979. © Conan Properties Inc.

FANTASTIC FOUR #112
July 1971. © MAR

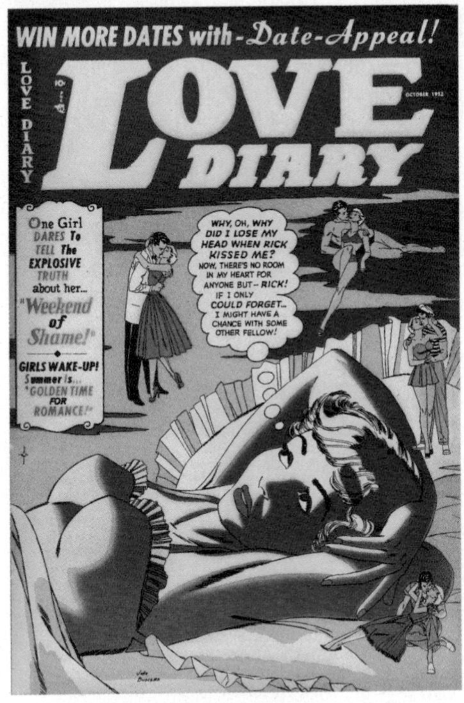

LOVE DIARY #31
October 1952. © QUA

SAVAGE SWORD OF CONAN #40
May 1979. © Conan Properties Inc.

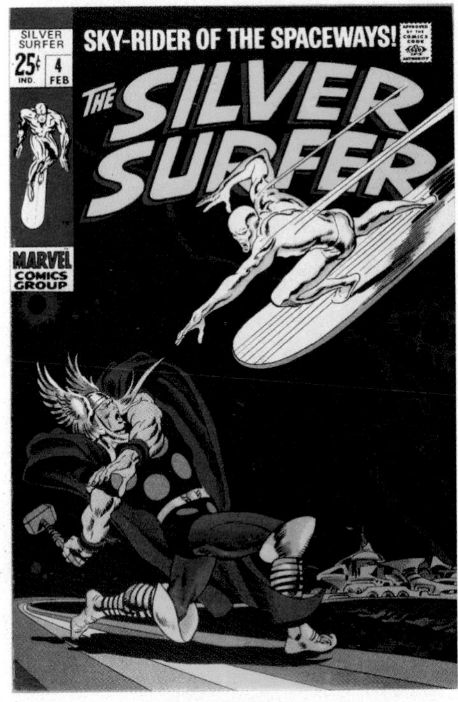

SILVER SURFER #4
February 1969. © MAR

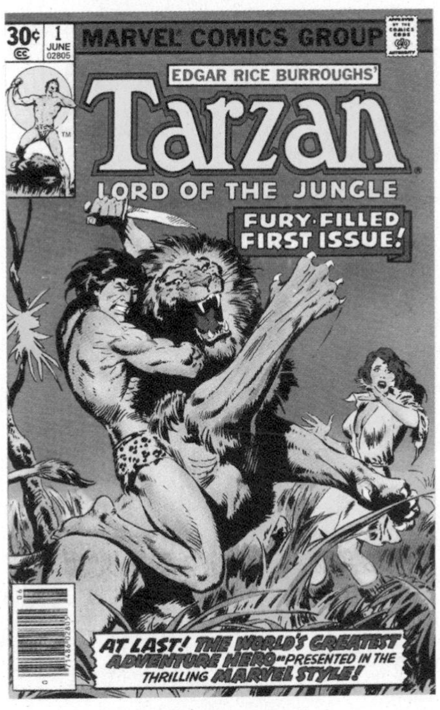

TARZAN #1
June 1977. © ERB

Born on December 12, 1919, Dan DeCarlo established the visual house style of Archie comics for the modern age. DeCarlo created Sabrina the Teenage Witch, Cheryl Blossom,and Josie and the Pussycats (he named Josie after his wife) for the company in addition to his work on the various other Archie titles.

He broke into the four-color medium working for Timely Comics in 1947, drawing such classic titles as *Millie the Model*. He also freelanced for *The Saturday Evening Post*, *Argosy*, and the Humorama line of pin-up cartoon digests. He won the National Cartoonists Society Award for Best Comic Book in 2000 for *Betty & Veronica*.

The prolific artist has also been cited to be a strong artistic influence on *Love & Rockets* creators Jaime and Gilbert Hernandez, among others, and his work can be seen in a new line of "best of" hardcovers from Archie and IDW Publishing.

- *SB*

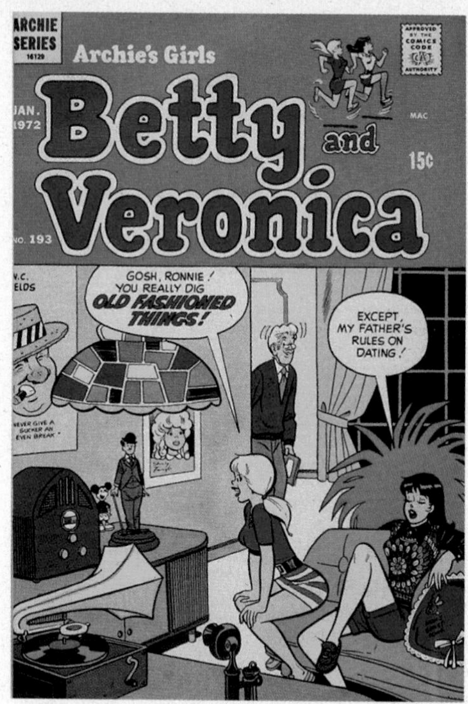

ARCHIE'S GIRLS, BETTY AND VERONICA #193
Januart 1972. © AP

CHERYL BLOSSOM #1
September 1995. © AP

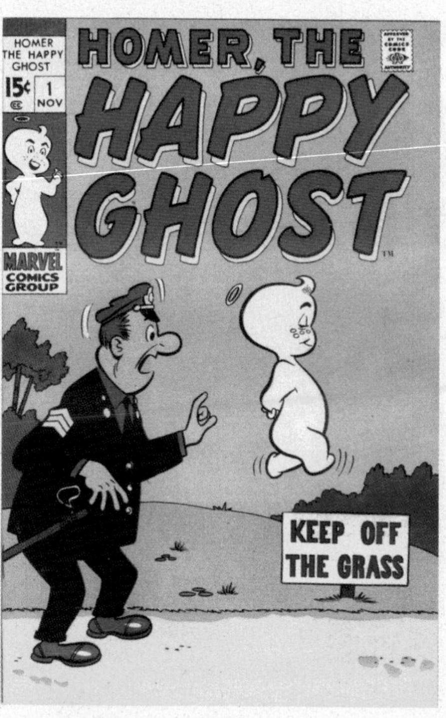

HOMER THE HAPPY GHOST #1
November 1969. © MAR

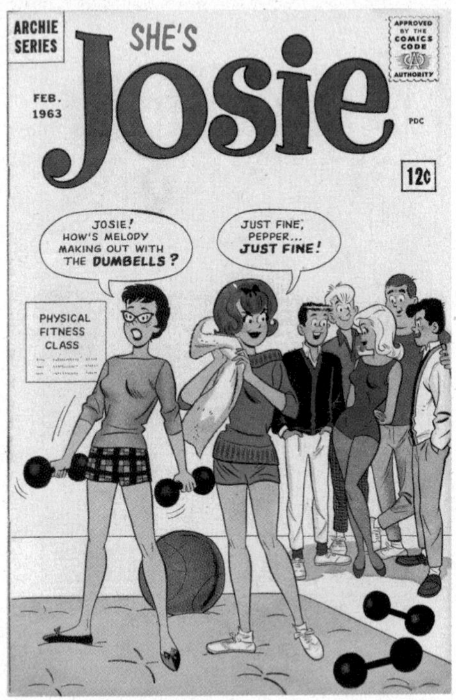

JOSIE #1
February 1963. © AP

MILLIE THE MODEL #37
November 1952. © MAR

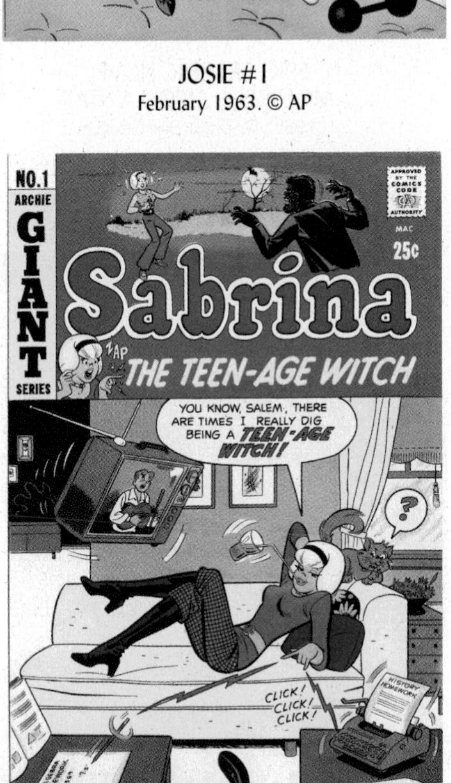

SABRINA, THE TEEN-AGE WITCH #1
April 1971. © AP

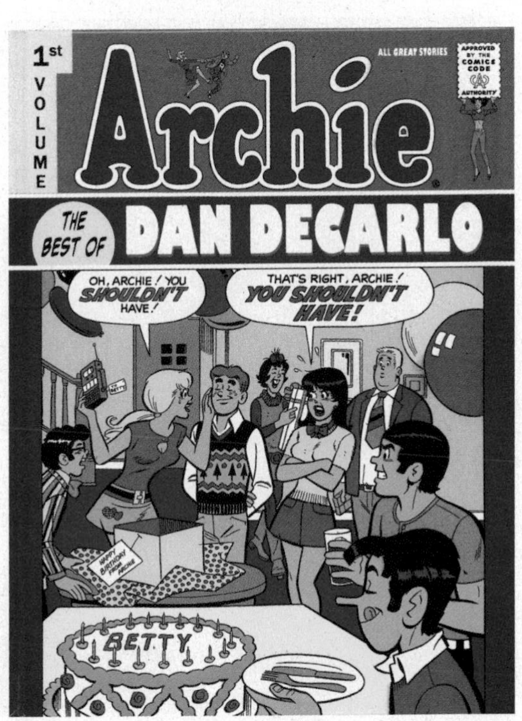

ARCHIE: THE BEST OF DAN DECARLO Vol. 1
May 2010. © AP

The term "visionary" is bandied about almost as much as the word "classic," but even in an era in which the meaning of the expression has been diluted through overuse, Jean Giraud was an edge-pushing pioneer, an artistic leader, and a true visionary. The French writer-artist passed away on Saturday, March 10, 2012 at the age of 73 after a long battle with cancer. Many American fans got to know his work through reprint collections published in the U.S. and through his collaboration with Stan Lee on *The Silver Surfer*, a two-part mini-series published in 1988-89. His range of topics was vast, and his impact equaled their scope. "The life of a storyteller like Jean Giraud cannot be evaluated simply by his prolific output or the elegance of his art or even by his commitment to his craft. Instead, in an earthly sense, we can only gauge his time among us by the impact he and his work had on others. In that sense, his effect is probably the definition of immeasurable," said Melissa Bowersox, Executive Vice-President of Geppi's Entertainment Museum.

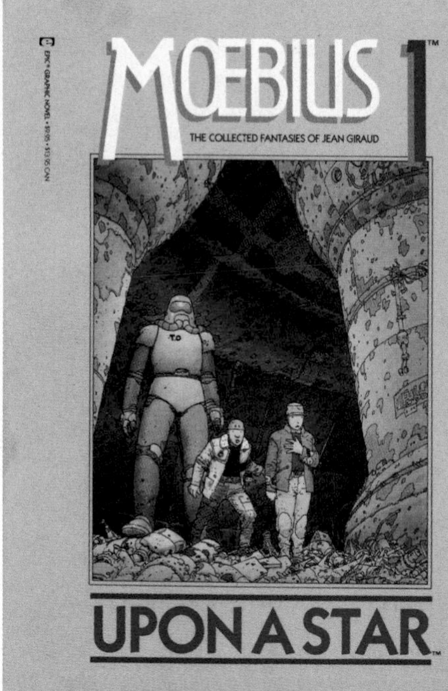

EPIC GRAPHIC NOVEL
MOEBIUS 1 - UPON A STAR
1987. © Starwatcher Graphics

IRON MAN POSTER ART
1980s. © MAR

BLUEBERRY #1
1989. © Starwatcher Graphics

GENE GIRAUD (MOEBIUS)

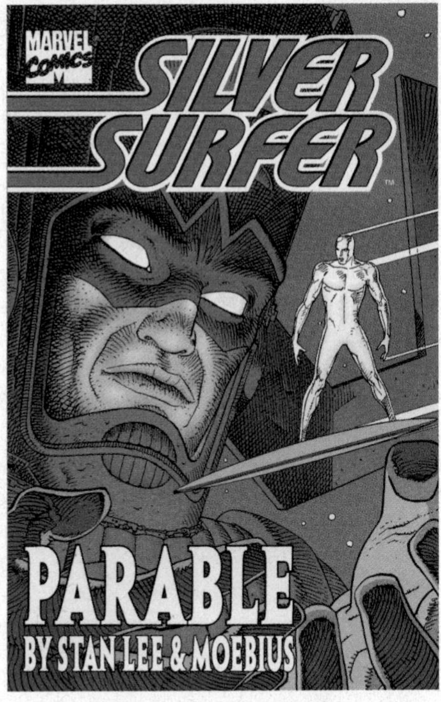

SILVER SURFER: PARABLE
February 1998. Reprint of graphic novel. © MAR

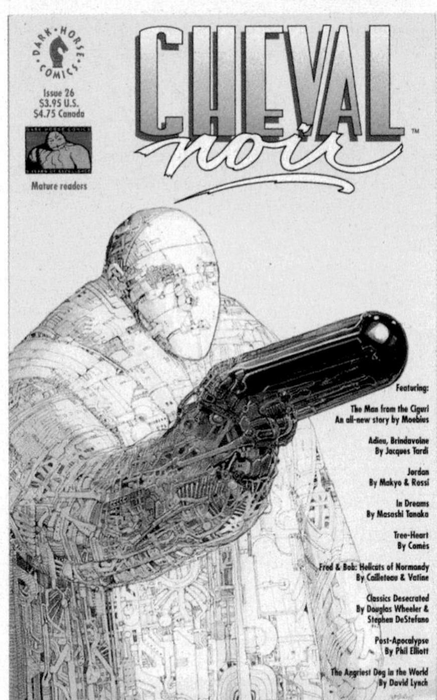

CHEVAL NOIR #26
January 1992. © DH

MOEBIUS COMICS #1
May 1996. © Starwatcher Graphics

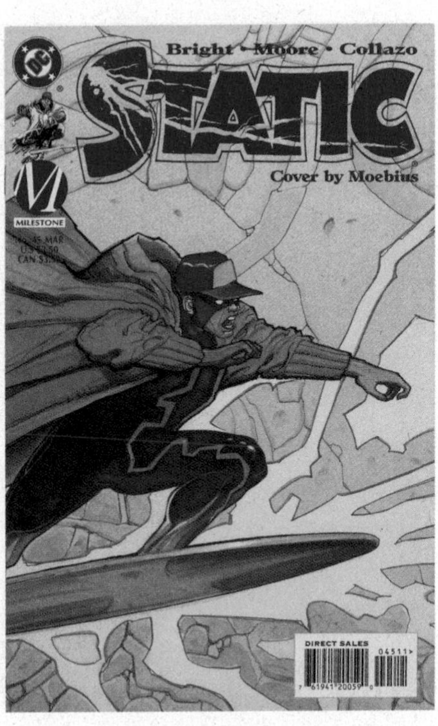

STATIC #45
March 1997. © Milestone Media

G.I. JOE, A REAL AMERICAN HERO #21
March 1984. © Hasbro

Writer-artist-editor Larry Hama began his long association with the comic book incarnation of *G.I. Joe* almost immediately following then Marvel Comics editor-in-chief Jim Shooter's meeting with Hasbro. "It was Larry's book all the way," Shooter said. And in the minds of many fans, that's how it has remained. During the title's 155-issue run at Marvel, subsequent appearance at Devil's Due Publishing, and revival at IDW Publishing, Hama's portrayal of the characters defined many of them permanently for their fans. He has, however, been far from all *G.I. Joe*. He broke into comics as an assistant for Wally Wood, served as editor for Marvel's *Conan* line and *The 'Nam*, created *Bucky O'Hare*, wrote such titles as *Kitty Pryde, Agent of SHIELD*, *Punisher: War Zone* and *Weapon X*, among others. He has also written video games, consulted for G.I Joe in feature films, and even appeared as a actor on *M*A*S*H*, but it's his work on *G.I. Joe* - including the acclaimed "Silent Interlude" in *G.I. Joe* #21, which he wrote and penciled - that continues to demand attention.

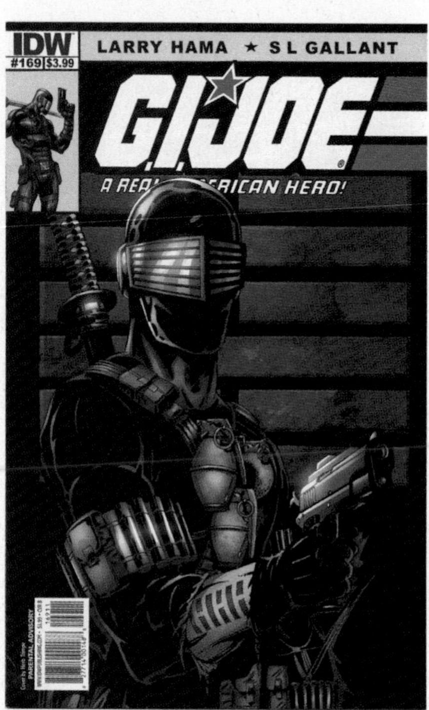

G.I. JOE, A REAL AMERICAN HERO #169
August 2011. © Hasbro

THE 'NAM #1
December 1986. © MAR

BUCKY O'HARE #1
January 1991. © Continuity

CONAN THE BARBARIAN #162
September 1984. © Conan Properties Inc.

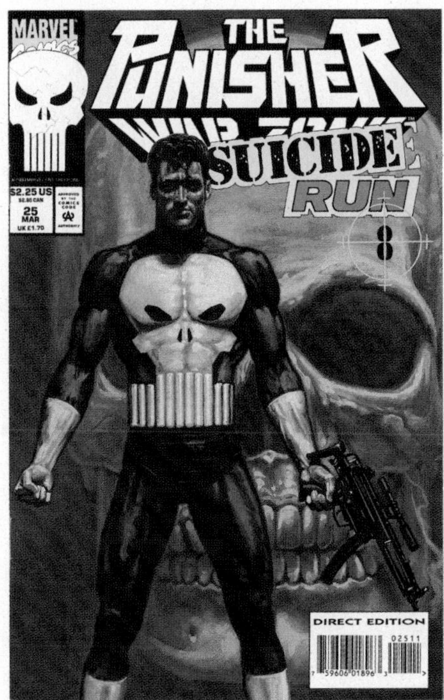

PUNISHER: WAR ZONE #25
March 1994. © MAR

WULF THE BARBARIAN #1
February 1975. © Nemesis Group

The Marvel and Superman Families seldom looked better when handled by the skilled hand of Kurt Schaffenberger. Tackling the Big Red Cheese in the Golden Age for Fawcett Comics and the Bronze Age for DC Comics, the talented artist was also recruited by Otto Binder in 1957 to work on the *Superman* family of titles. He continued to work at DC for the next three decades, where he was the lead artist on *Superman's Girl Friend, Lois Lane* for the entirety of its first decade. It's been said that Schaffenberger's rendition of Lane became the "definitive" version of the character, and the artist was often asked by DC editor Mort Weisinger to redraw other artists' depictions of her in other DC titles in which she appeared. He retired from comics in the 1980s soon after penciling the second chapter of Alan Moore's pre-*Crisis Superman* tale, "Whatever Happened to the Man of Tomorrow?" Schaffenberger passed away on January 24, 2002.
- *SB*

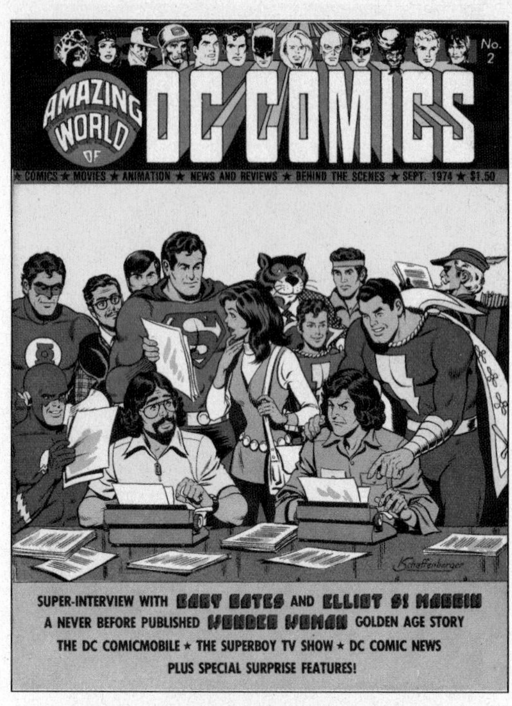

AMAZING WORLD OF DC COMICS #2
September 1974. © DC

THE MARVEL FAMILY #41
November 1949. © FAW

MASTER COMICS #120
February 1951. © FAW

ADVENTURES INTO THE UNKNOWN #165
June-July 1966. © ACG

SUPERMAN'S GIRLFRIEND LOIS LANE #73
April 1967. © DC

SHAZAM! #30
July-August 1977. © DC

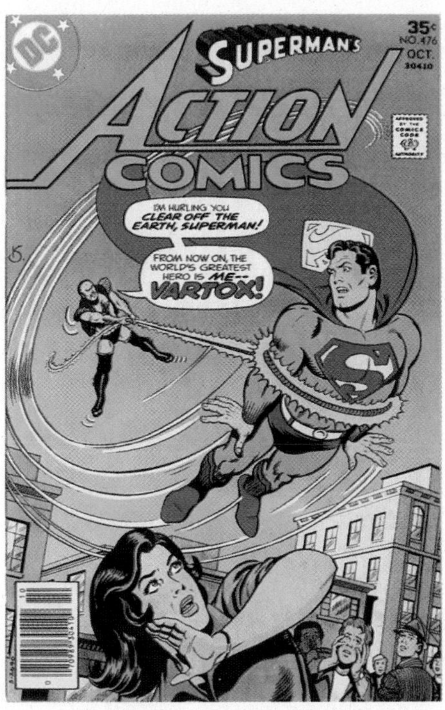

ACTION COMICS #476
October 1977. © DC

Boleslav Felix Robert "Bill" Sienkiewicz is best known for his dynamic style of comic book and graphic novel illustration beginning with Marvel's Moon Knight in the pages *The Hulk* #13, later graduating with the character from the magazine to his own comic book series. Sienkiewicz grew up in rural New Jersey, taught himself anatomy to better his sketches, and worked construction to put himself through the Newark School of Fine and Industrial Arts. Starting his career on Marvel Comics' at the age of 19, he illustrated Moon Knight for several years, including its jump being available exclusively in the Direct Market only. Initially his work showed the strong influence of Neal Adams, but as he moved from assignment to assignment, it grew more expressionistic. It continued to evolve in the pages of *New Mutants*, *Daredevil: Love and War* (*Marvel Graphic Novel* #24), and *Elektra: Assassin*, as well as his acclaimed graphic novel *Stray Toasters*. He also has created advertising material, book art, CD covers, and film designs, among other projects.
- SB & JCV

ELEKTRA: ASSASSIN HC
1987. © MAR

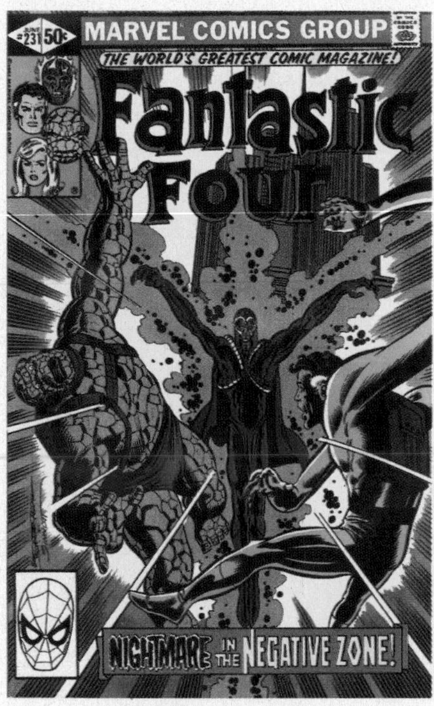

FANTASTIC FOUR #231
June 1981. © MAR

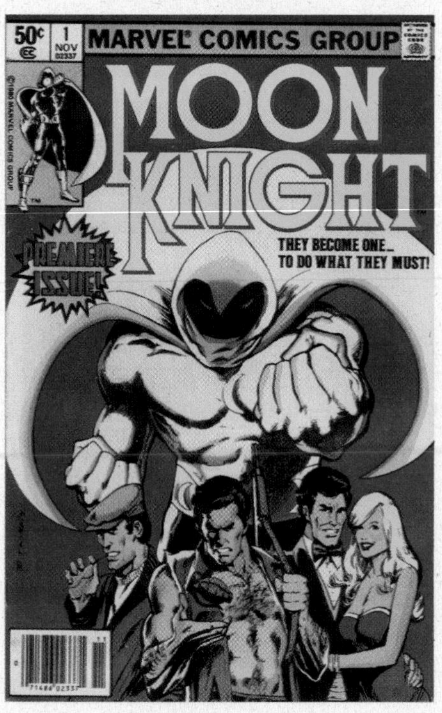

MOON KNIGHT #1
November 1980. © MAR

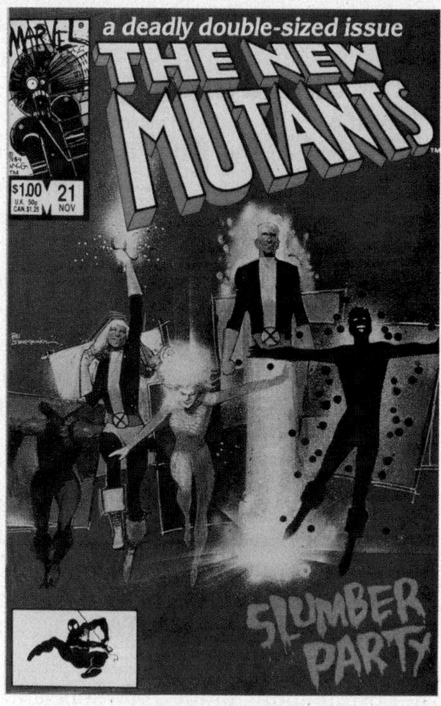

NEW MUTANTS #21
November 1984. © MAR

SAVAGE SWORD OF CONAN #102
July 1984. © Conan Properties Inc.

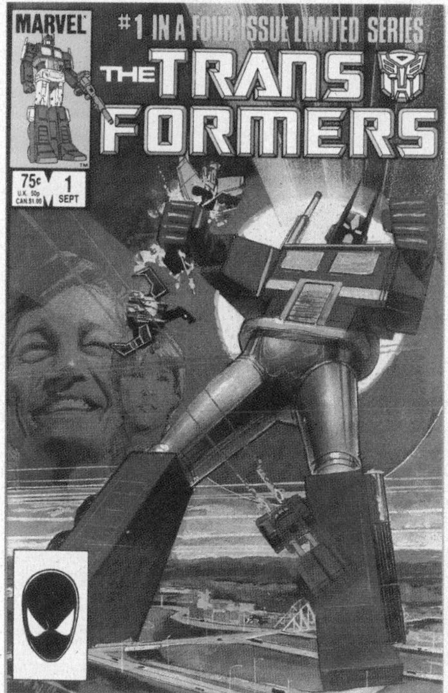

TRANSFORMERS #1
September 1984. © Hasbro

UNCANNY X-MEN #195
July 1985. © MAR

ACTION COMICS #295
December 1962. © DC

Douglas Curtis Swan, the artist most associated with Superman during the Silver Age of comics, produced hundreds of covers and stories from the 1950s through the 1980s. Following World War II and a stint on *Boy Commandos*, he began to pencil pages, leaving the inking to others, including famed inker Murphy Anderson (the pair's collaborative artwork came to be called "Swanderson" by fans). His first job pencilling the iconic character was for *Superman* #51. Swan felt, however, that his breakthrough came when he was assigned the art duties on *Superman's Pal, Jimmy Olsen*, in 1954.

Over the years, Swan was a remarkably consistent and prolific artist, often illustrating two or more titles per month. The artist illustrated the first chapter of the 1986 "last Silver Age" *Superman* story, "Whatever Happened to the Man of Tomorrow?" written by Alan Moore. Swan's last published story was five pages published posthumously in the 1996 special *Superman: The Wedding Album*.

- SB

ADVENTURE COMICS #210
March 1955. © DC

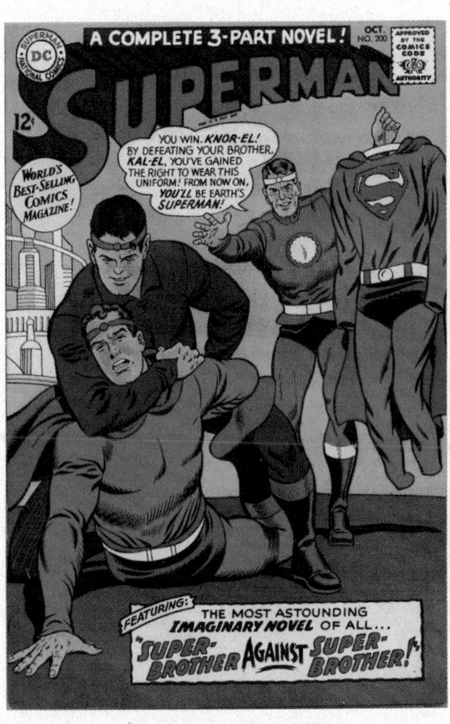

SUPERMAN #200
October 1967. © DC

SUPERMAN #423
September 1986. © DC

SUPERMAN'S GIRLFRIEND LOIS LANE #100
April 1970. © DC

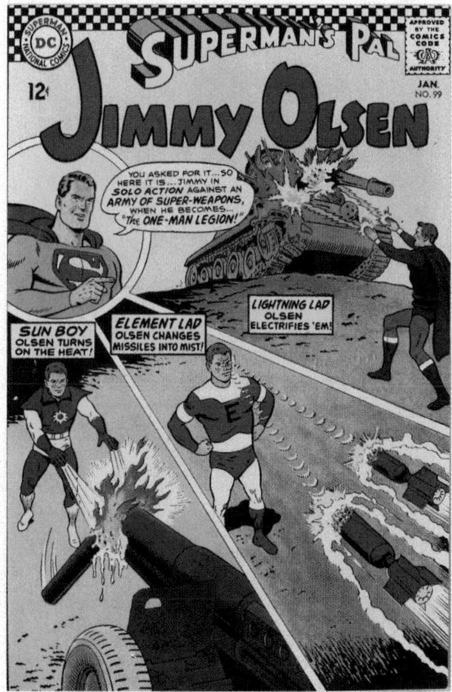

SUPERMAN'S PAL JIMMY OLSEN #99
January 1967. © DC

WORLD'S FINEST COMICS #97
October 1958. © DC

Besides being Stan Lee's first successor as Editor-in-Chief of Marvel Comics, Roy William Thomas, Jr. has made enjoyed a long career as a writer, editor and comics historian. He is possibly best known for introducing the pulp magazine hero Conan the Barbarian to American comic book audiences. With *Conan The Barbarian* and *Savage Sword of Conan*, he added to the storyline of Robert E. Howard's character and helped launch a sword and sorcery genre in comics. Thomas is also known for his championing of Golden Age superheroes to new audiences by creating *The Invaders* at Marvel and a short while later the *All-Star Squadron* and *Infinity Inc.* at DC.

Thomas also enjoyed distinctive, key runs on *The X-Men*, *The Avengers*, *Wally Wood's T.H.U.N.D.E.R. Agents* among other titles, and continues his invaluable contributions in the pages of his award-winning magazine, *Alter Ego*, which explores comics history (though generally not the history he made himself).
- SB

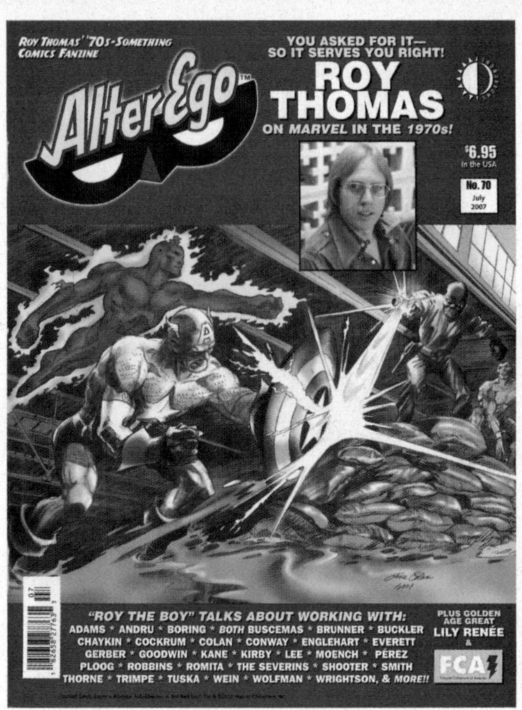

ALTER EGO #70
July 2007. © Roy Thomas

ALL-STAR SQUADRON #1
September 1981. © DC

AVENGERS #87
April 1971. © MAR

CONAN THE BARBARIAN #1
October 1970. © Conan Properties Inc.

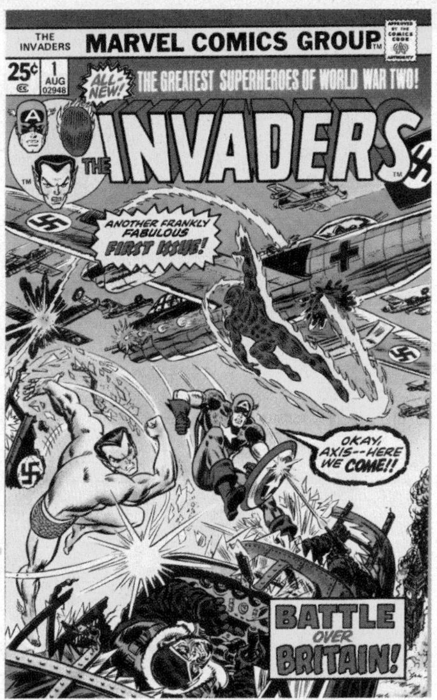

INVADERS #1
August 1975. © MAR

SAVAGE SWORD OF CONAN #2
October 1974. © Conan Properties Inc.

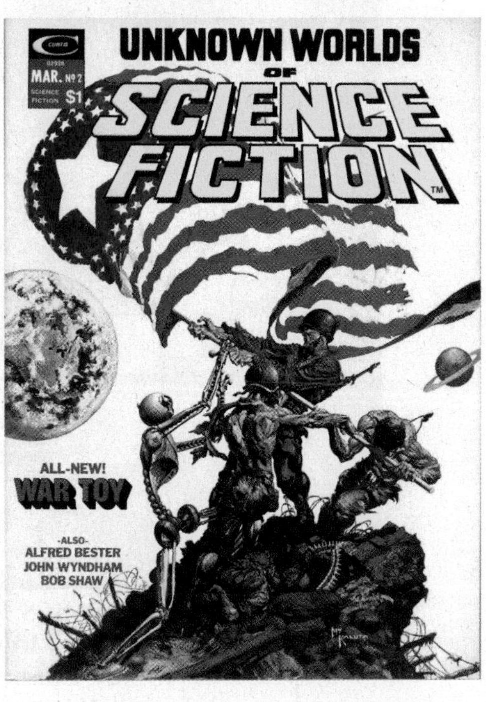

UNKNOWN WORLDS OF SCIENCE FICTION #2
March 1975. © MAR

RECORD SETTERS

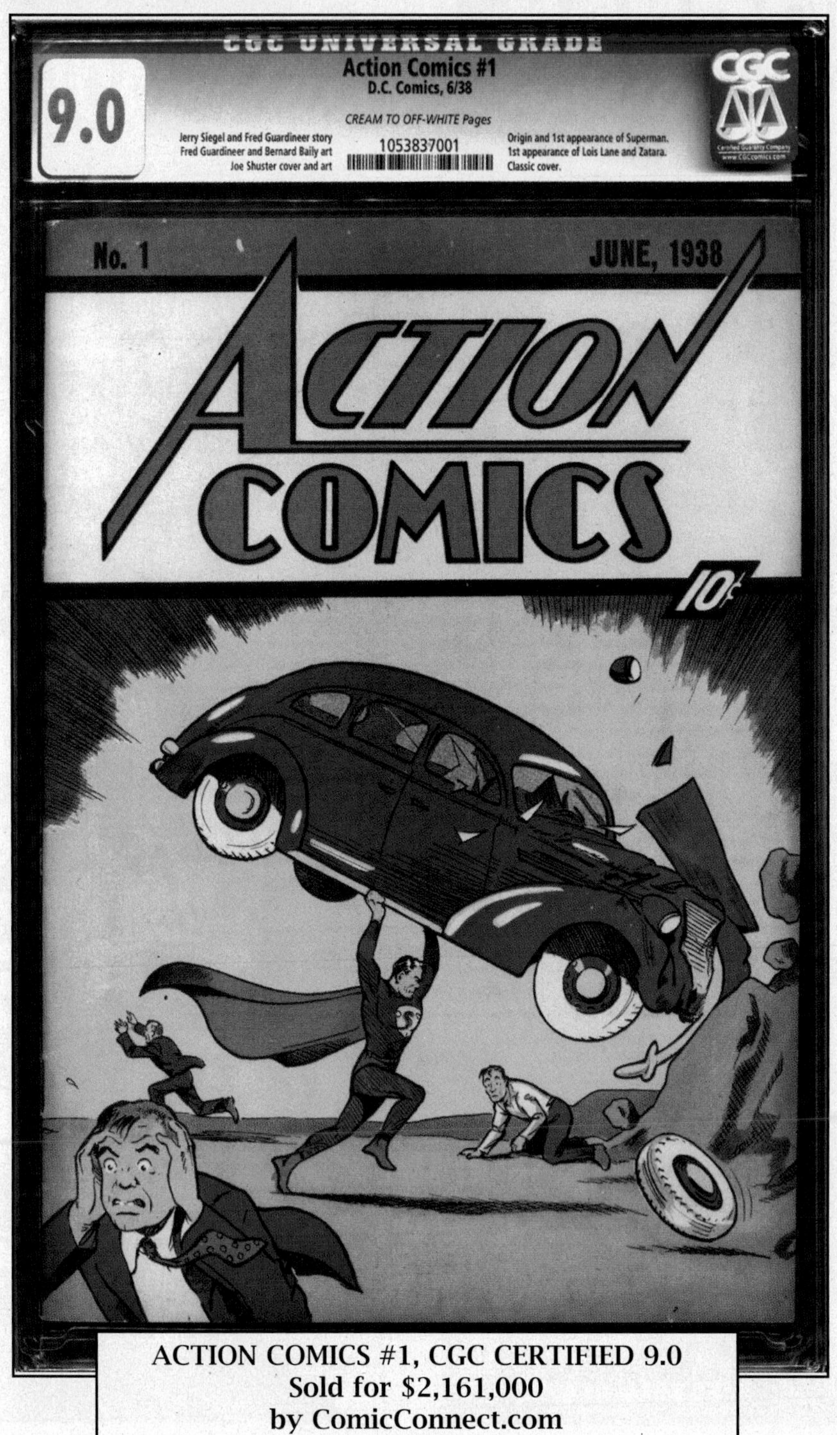

ACTION COMICS #1, CGC CERTIFIED 9.0
Sold for $2,161,000
by ComicConnect.com
in November 2011. © DC

RECORD SETTERS

TALES OF SUSPENSE #39, CGC 9.6
Sold for $375,000
by ComicLink
in April 2012. © MAR

BATMAN #1, CGC 9.2
Sold for $850,000
by Heritage Auctions
in May 2012. © DC

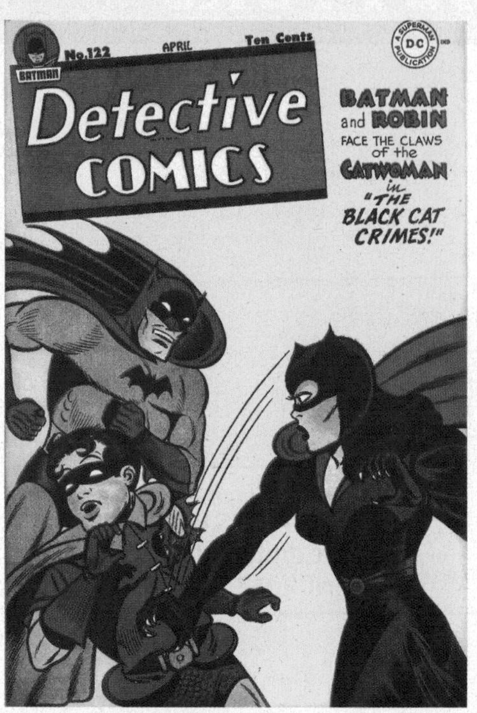

DETECTIVE COMICS #122
April 1947. First Catwoman cover. © DC

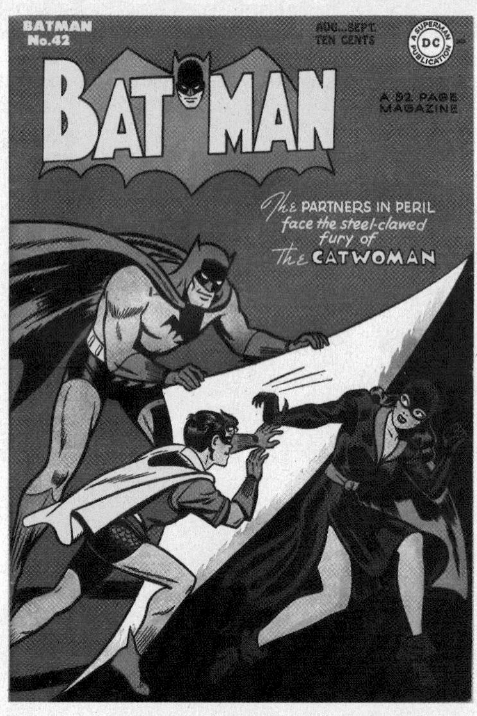

BATMAN #42
August-September 1947. © DC

SUPERMAN'S GIRL FRIEND LOIS LANE #70
November 1966. 1st Silver Age appearance. © DC

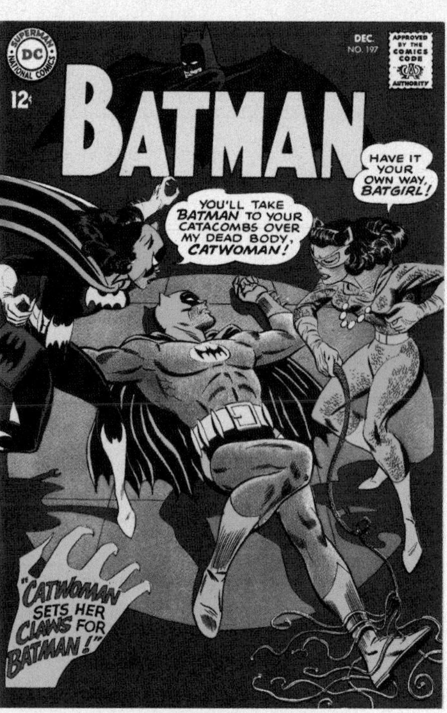

BATMAN #197
December 1967. © DC

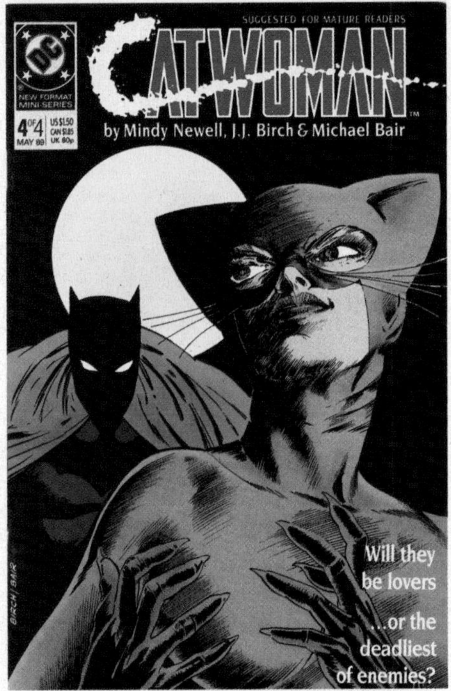

CATWOMAN #4
Four issue limited series. May 1989. © DC

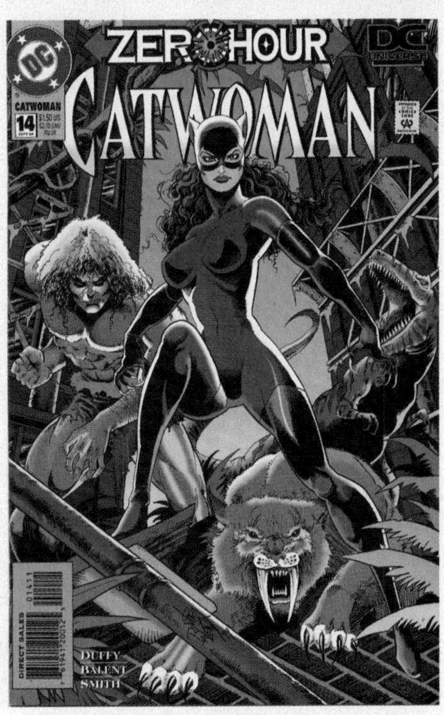

CATWOMAN #14
September 1994. Jim Balent cover. © DC

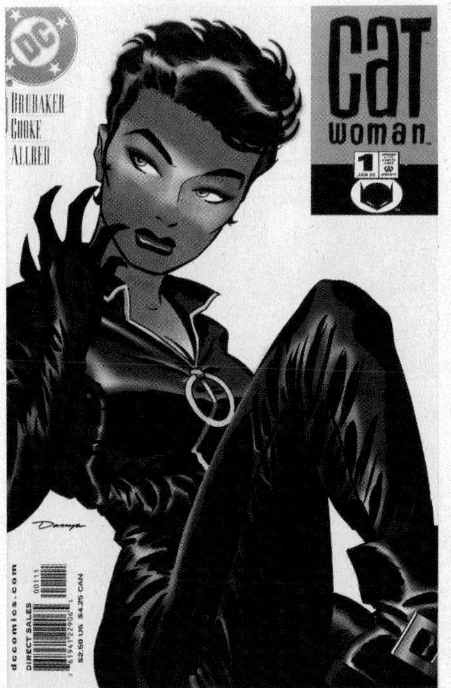

CATWOMAN #1
January 2002. Darwyn Cooke cover. © DC

CATWOMAN #74
February 2008. Adam Hughes cover. © DC

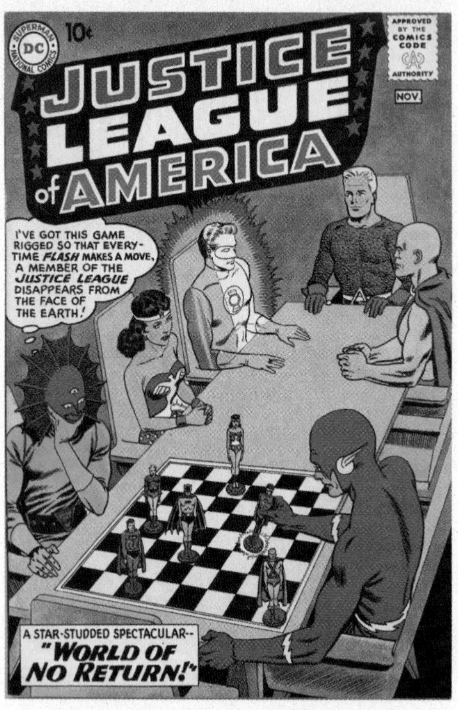

JUSTICE LEAGUE OF AMERICA #1
October-November 1960. © DC

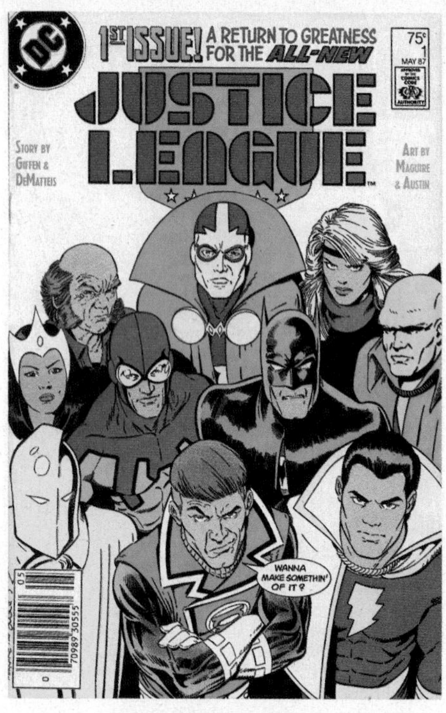

JUSTICE LEAGUE #1
May 1987. © DC

JUSTICE LEAGUE EUROPE #1
April 1989. © DC

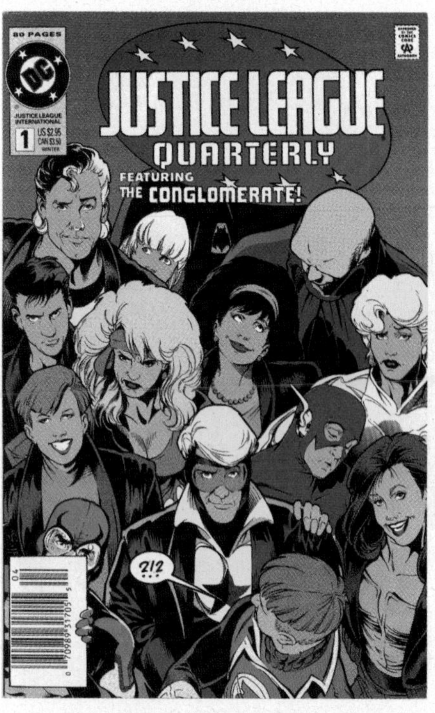

JUSTICE LEAGUE QUARTERLY #1
Winter 1990-1991. © DC

JLA #1
January 1997. © DC

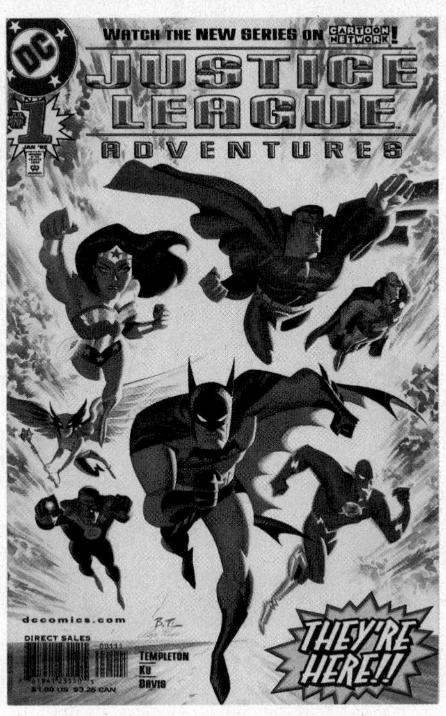

JUSTICE LEAGUE ADVENTURES #1
January 2002. © DC

JUSTICE LEAGUE OF AMERICA #1
October 2006. © DC

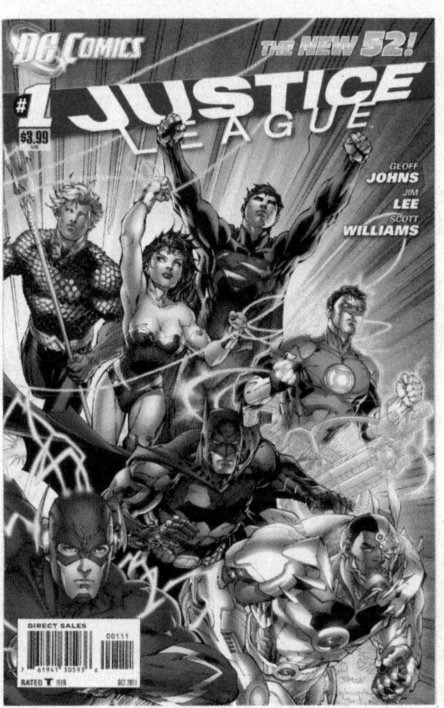

JUSTICE LEAGUE #1
October 2011. © DC

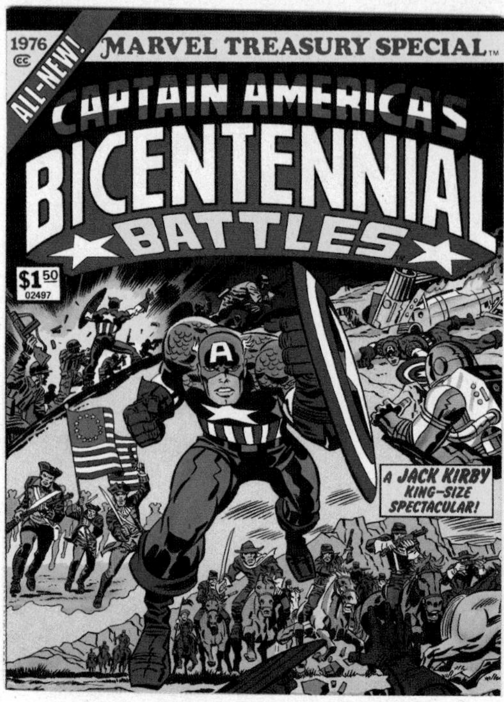

MARVEL TREASURY SPECIAL VOL. 1
June 1976. © MAR

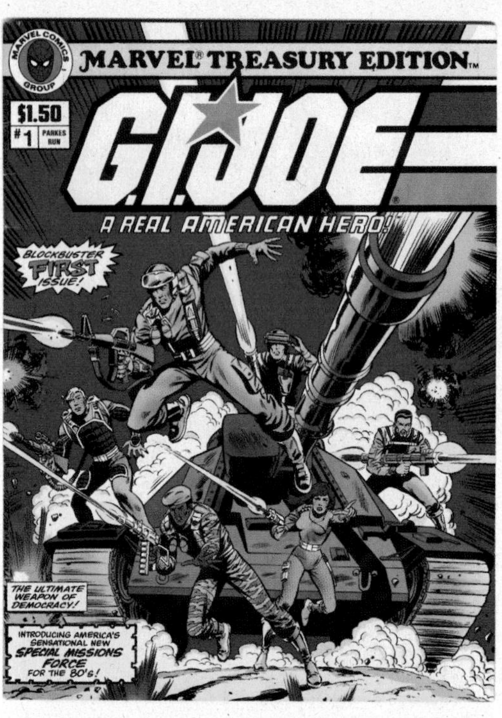

G.I. JOE SPECIAL TREASURY EDITION #1
1982. © Hasbro

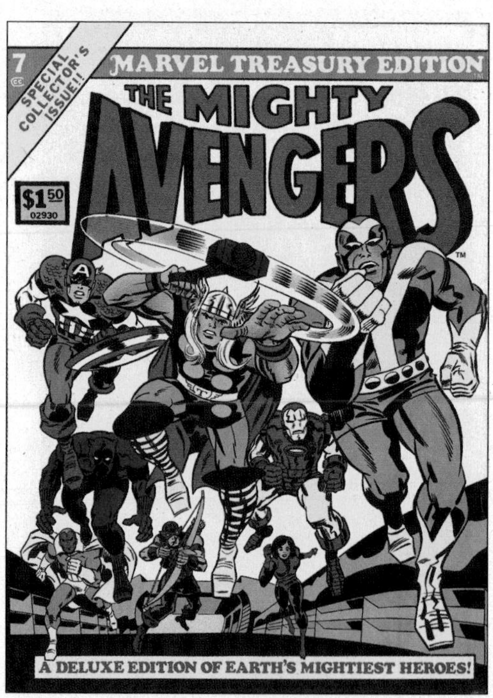

MARVEL TREASURY EDITION #7
1975. © MAR

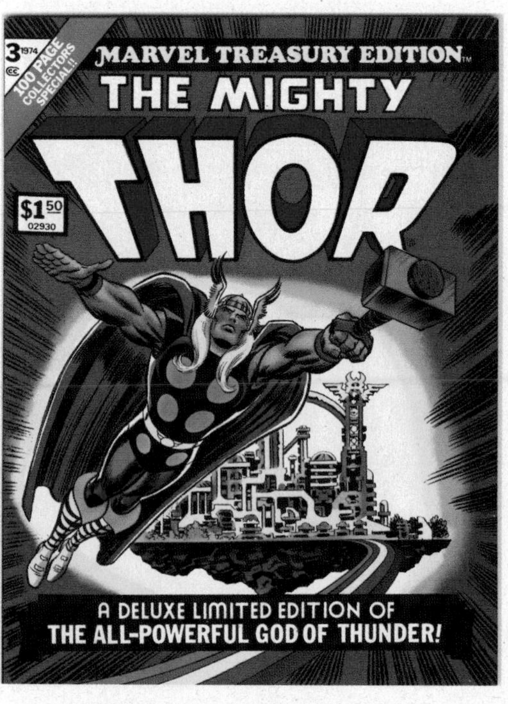

MARVEL TREASURY EDITION #3
1974. © MAR

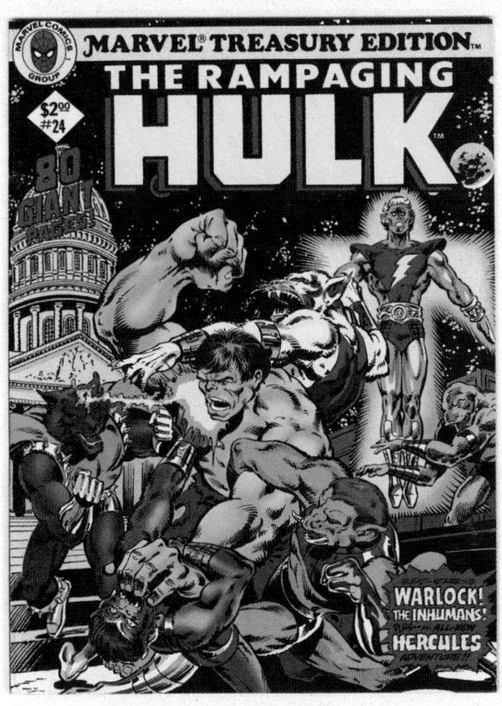

MARVEL TREASURY EDITION #24
1979. © MAR

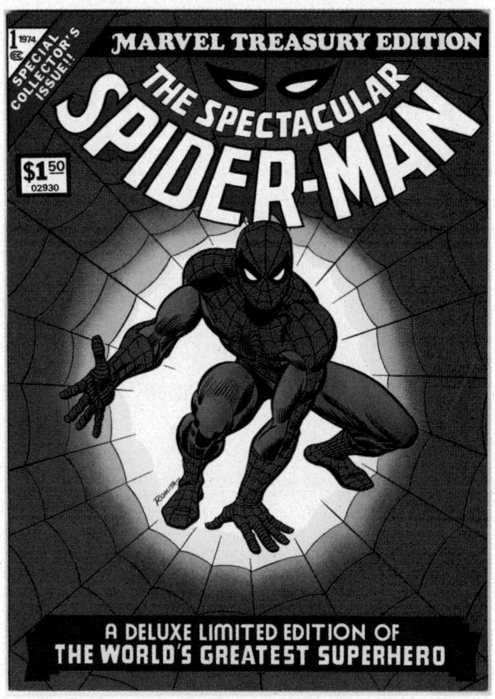

MARVEL TREASURY EDITION #1
1974. © MAR

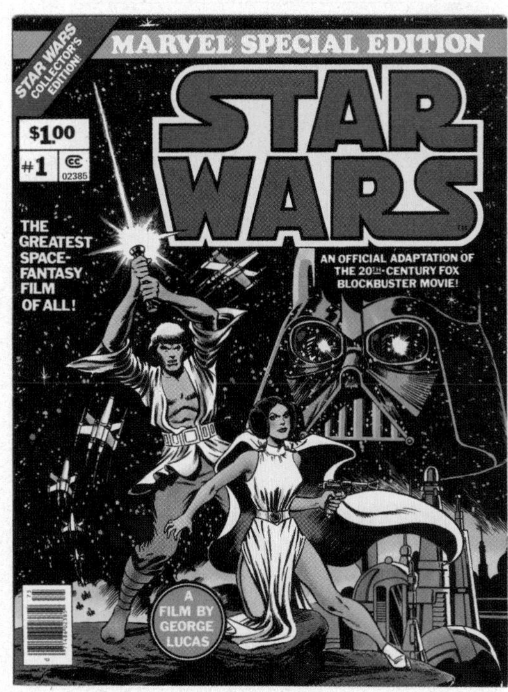

MARVEL SPECIAL EDITION STAR WARS #1
1977. © Lucasfilm

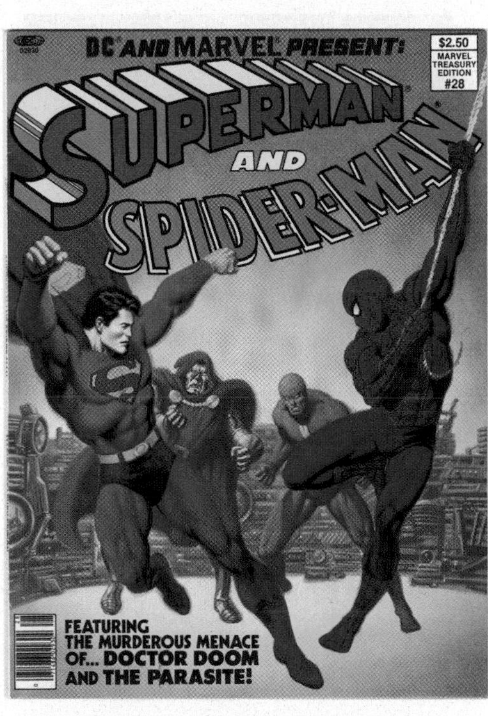

MARVEL TREASURY EDITION #28
1981. © MAR & DC

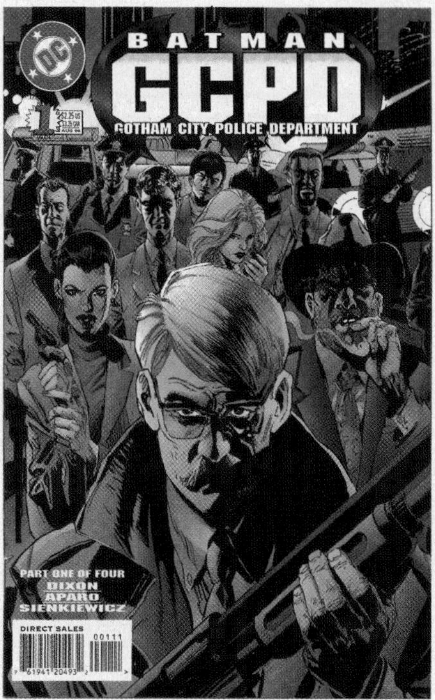

BATMAN: GCPD #1
August 1996. © DC

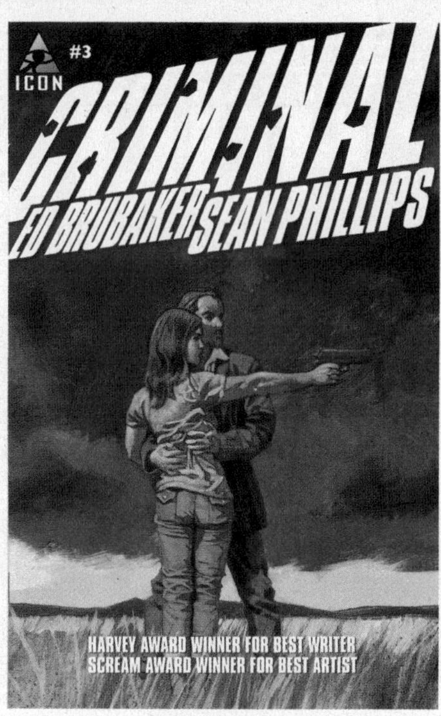

CRIMINAL #3
December 2006. © Ed Brubaker & Sean Phillips

THE MAZE AGENCY #1
December 1988. © Mike Barr

NATHANIEL DUSK II #1
October 1985. © DC

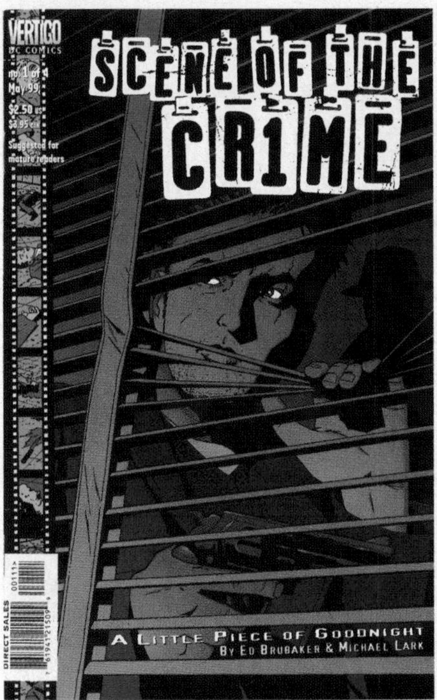

SCENE OF THE CRIME #1
May 1999. © Ed Brubaker & Michael Lark

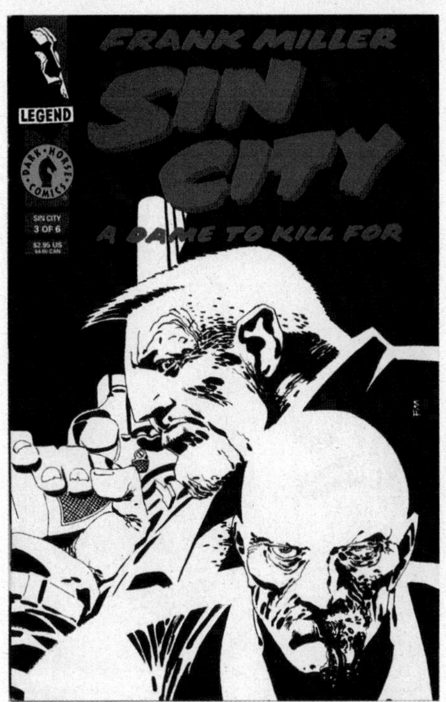

SIN CITY: A DAME TO KILL FOR #3
February 1994. © Frank Miller

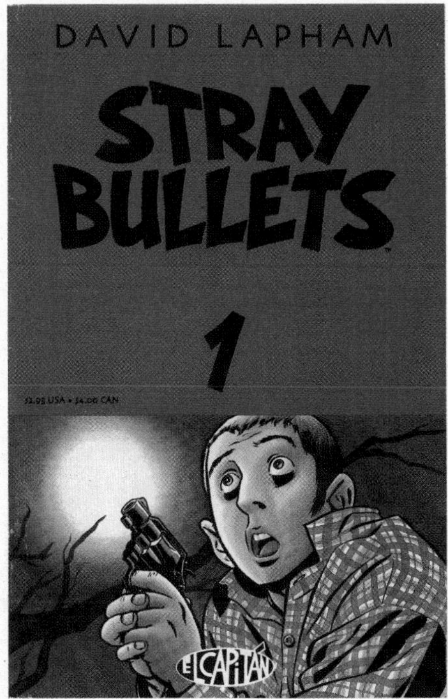

STRAY BULLETS #1
May 1995. © David Lapham

WHITEOUT #3
September 1998. © Greg Rucka

ALIEN WORLDS #2
May 1983. © Bruce Jones

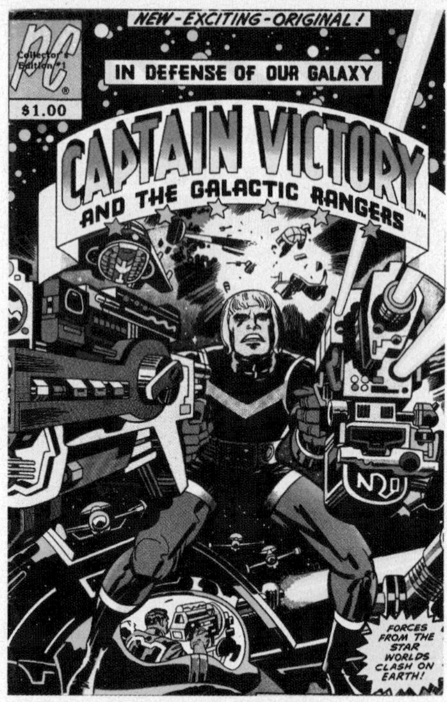

CAPTAIN VICTORY
AND THE GALACTIC RANGERS #1
November 1981. © Jack Kirby

MS. MYSTIC #1
October 1982. © Continuity Associates

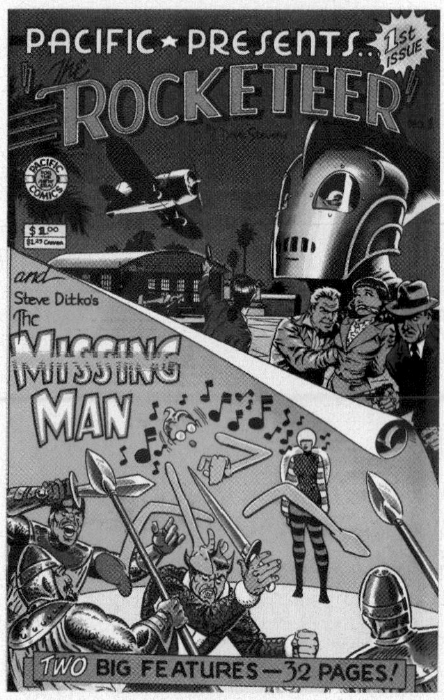

PACIFIC PRESENTS #1
October 1982. © Steve Ditko / Dave Stevens

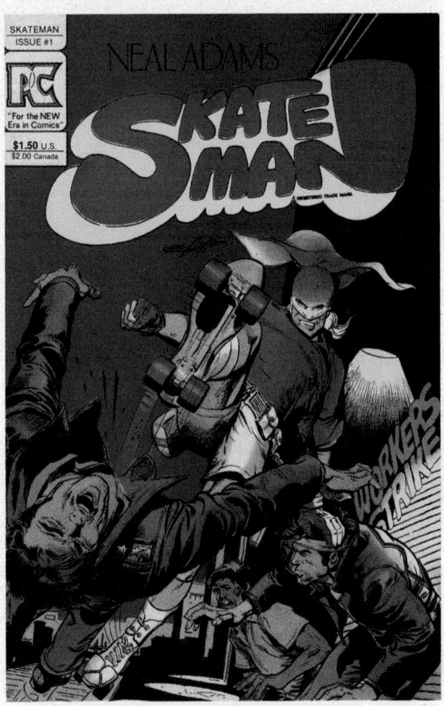

SKATEMAN #1
November 1983. © Continuity Associates

SOMERSET HOLMES #1
September 1983. © Bruce Jones

STARSLAYER #2
April 1982. © Mike Grell

VANGUARD ILLUSTRATED #2
January 1984. © Various

CREEPY #1
1964. Jack Davis cover. © WARREN

CREEPY #9
June 1966. Frank Frazetta cover. © WARREN

CREEPY #26
April 1969. Basil Gogos cover. © WARREN

CREEPY #44
March 1972. Vincente Segrelles cover. © WARREN

CREEPY #71
May 1975. Luis Bermejo cover. © WARREN

CREEPY #79
May 1976. Manuel Sanjulian cover. © WARREN

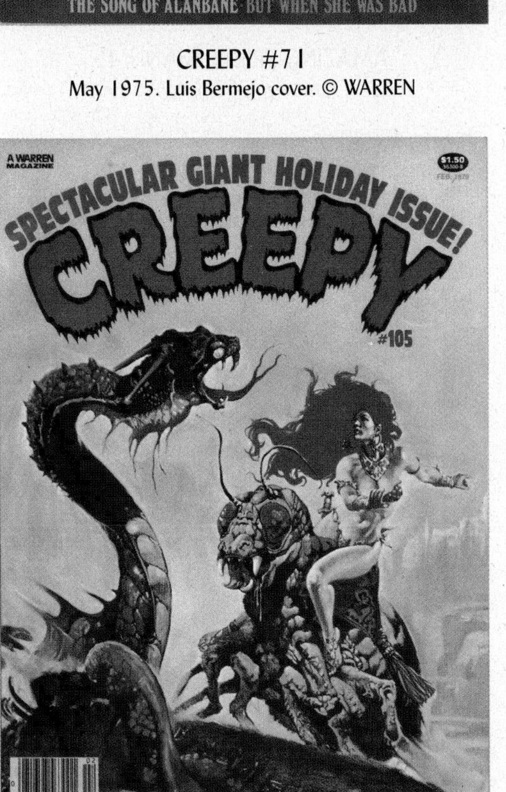

CREEPY #105
February 1979. Esteban Maroto cover. © WARREN

CREEPY 1993 FEARBOOK #1
1993. Dan Brereton cover. © HARRIS

AMAZING SPIDER-MAN #6
November 1963. © MAR

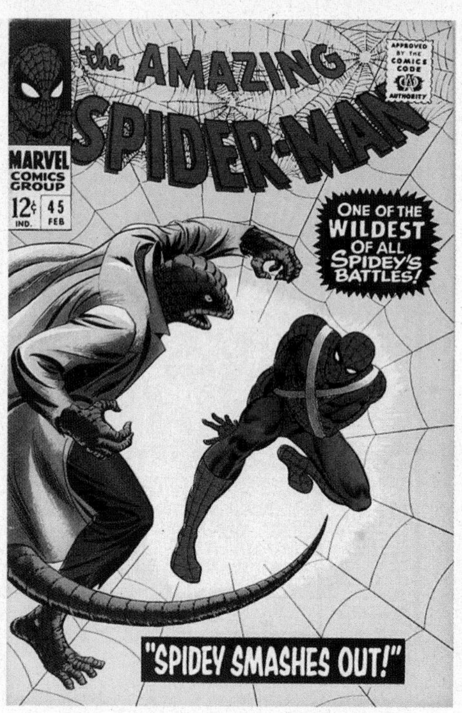

AMAZING SPIDER-MAN #45
February 1967. © MAR

AMAZING SPIDER-MAN #77
October 1969. © MAR

AMAZING SPIDER-MAN #313
March 1989. © MAR

SPIDER-MAN #2
September 1990. © MAR

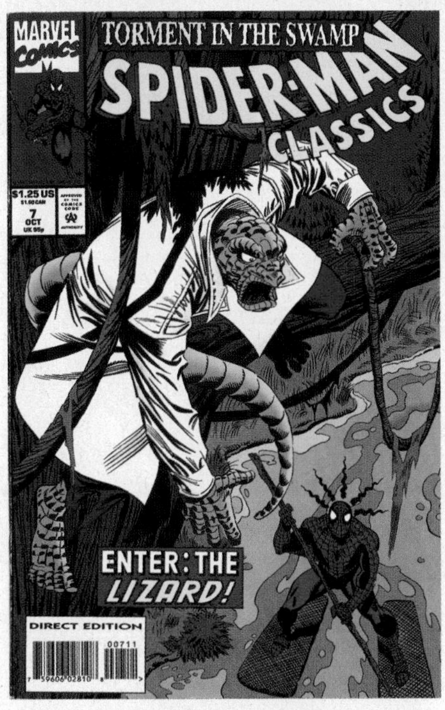

SPIDER-MAN CLASSICS #7
October 1993. © MAR

SPIDER-MAN: LIFELINE #3
June 2001. © MAR

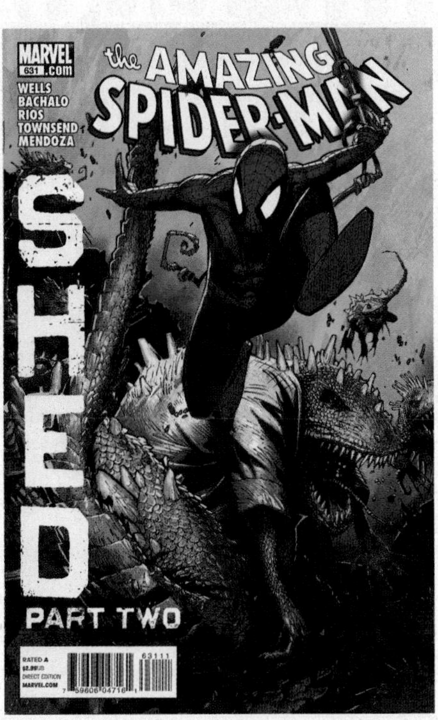

AMAZING SPIDER-MAN #631
July 2010. © MAR

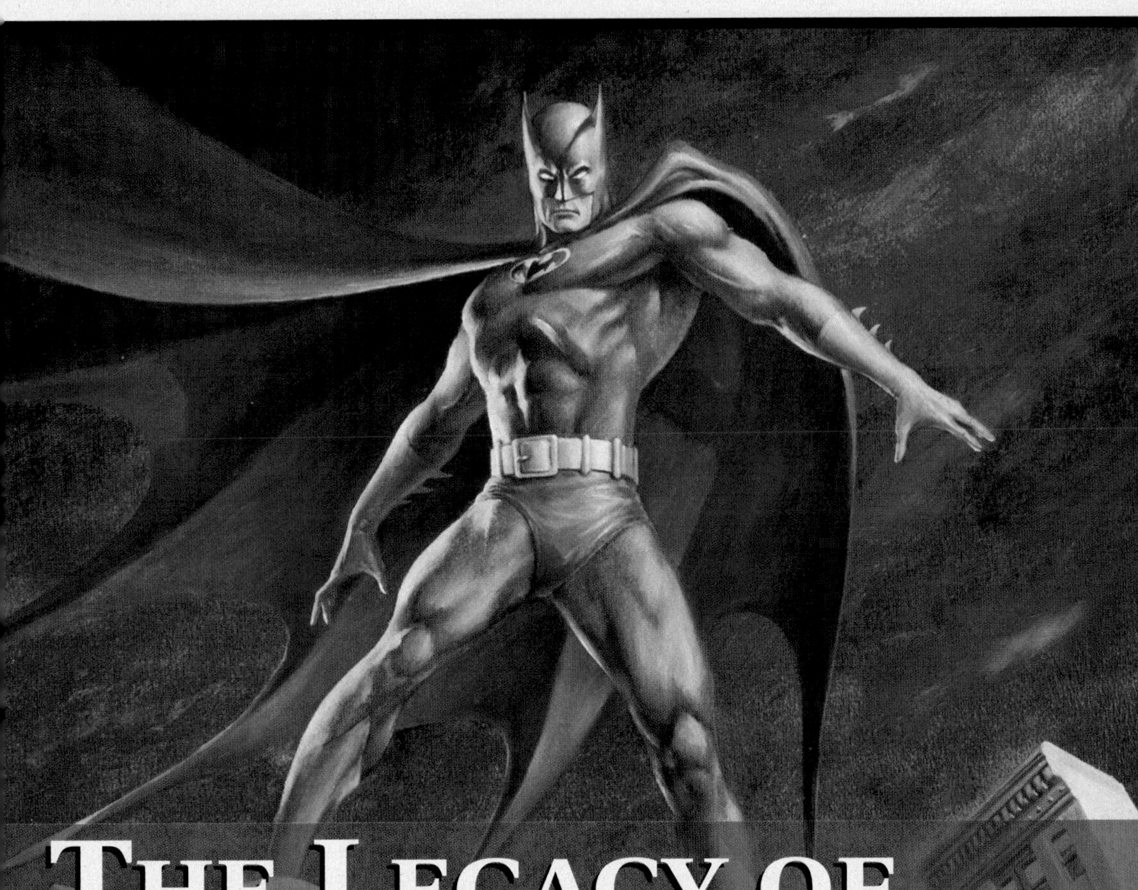

The Legacy of Batman: Son of the Demon

By Rob Hughes

*Overstreet Advisor, dealer and comics writer Rob Hughes makes the case for why 1987's **Batman: Son of the Demon**, the first Batman graphic novel, is one of the most important Batman stories ever.*

The introduction of The Bat-Man in the very first panel of Detective Comics #27, a brooding avenger of the twilight.

A darkly atmospheric, mysterious and moody presentation of the Dark Knight Detective is considered by most to be the quintessential interpretation of Batman. This was the way he was conceived more than seven decades ago by writer Bill Finger and artist Bob Kane for *Detective Comics* #27 (May, 1939).

The initial idea was Kane's, inspired by the unprecedented success of Jerry Siegel and Joe Shuster's Superman in *Action Comics #1* (June, 1938). Finger's iconic, defining details supplied made the character a grim and brooding avenger of the twilight. Batman would be a workingman's hero, a stark contrast to the bright and bold demigod from Krypton.

For a little more than a year, his creators, along with writer Gardner Fox, presented a fascinating, haunting interpretation highly influenced by film noir with heavy use of shadows and dramatic lighting.

This take on Batman, though, was soon abandoned. A lighter, more adolescent-friendly approach was soon substituted after the introduction of Robin, the Boy Wonder in *Detective Comics #38* (April, 1940). This change, though lamentable to some, was quite significant, most likely necessary for the long-term survival of the series and would last in that style for nearly 30 years.

Then came Neal Adams. It was the late 1960s and Adams was a young artist of extraordinary talent and unmatched vision, a throwback to such illustrators as Alex Raymond, Hal Foster, Frank Frazetta and Al Williamson. He had the revolutionary idea of returning Batman back to the night, just as Finger and Kane has originally created him.

He had approached DC editor Julie Schwartz for a Batman gig, but Schwartz turned him down flat. Not one to be denied, Adams then walked down the hall to Murray Boltinoff's office who was the editor of *The Brave and the Bold* comic that teamed-up Batman with other superheroes of DC's pantheon.

Soon after, an irritated Adams said Schwartz gruffly ordered him into his office demanding, "Why are all these letters saying the only [good] Batman at DC Comics is in *Brave and Bold*?" Schwartz could be cantankerous and stubborn, but he certainty wasn't stupid and he perceived that his young star artist was definitely onto something here.

He awarded Adams *Batman* and teamed him with writer Denny O'Neil, who had worked as a reporter and had experience on the police and hospital beats.

"What I thought we were doing was taking Batman back to May of 1939 and doing what Kane and Finger had done...What we were really doing was kind of remembering what we thought [Batman] should have been. What we thought it was. And that was our interpretation [beginning with] 'Secret of the Waiting Graves'" in *Detective Comics #395* [January, 1970]," O'Neil said in *Back Issue* #50.

Denny O'Neil and Neal Adams were "taking Batman back to May of 1939", starting in Detective Comics #395.

"So what Denny was doing was right. And hopefully what I was doing was right. But we all kind of got it. It was no secret that we were doing Batman right....It was fun, it was dark, it was mysterious. And you know what? It still is. It's pretty much the same as it was then. Everybody gets it," Adams said.

Reflecting on Schwartz's decision to pair them up, Adams said, "He made the best and most sound judgment you could possibly make. And revolutionized comic books. Denny and I didn't revolutionize comic books. Julie Schwartz did. We did our job."

"What comics did, and what Neal and I did, was magic realism. But then, comics and pulps had been doing it since the '30s," O'Neil said.

Then in 1971, Schwartz, O'Neil and Adams collaborated to create Ra's Al Ghul, an Anti-Christ-type of would-be world dictator whose ultimate goal was to remake mankind and planet Earth in his own image via global genocide.

Schwartz came up with the foreboding name, which is translated from the Arabic as "Head of the Demon," and Adams developed the look of Ra's entirely from his own imagination.

Ra's Al Ghul's debut would come in the classic tale "Daughter of the Demon" for *Batman #232* (June, 1971), in which he shows up unannounced in the Batcave to seek out Batman's aid to rescue his beautiful daughter, Talia from an unknown abductor who had likewise kidnapped Robin. The adventure eventually takes Batman, Ra's and his giant bodyguard Ubu to Mount Nanda Devi, situated in the remote Himalayas.

There, standing upon a ledge overlooking a deep crevice, Ra's makes a very revealing confession: "It is a beauty to which my soul responds...so stark, so pure...as untainted as my desert home! I am cursed with a love for emptiness...desolation!"

Soon after, Batman is reunited with Robin and exposes the whole journey for a ruse, a "staged and complicated quest..." but is quite baffled as to the reason why. A question to which Ra's responds, "Your admirable mind has reasoned all save the obvious...that my darling Talia loves you! My organization is vast...! I consider retiring from my activities—! I had to satisfy myself that you are a worthy successor to me!...A worthy Son-in-Law!" The tale concludes with a panel of Talia kissing a rather startled Batman ever so gently on his cheek.

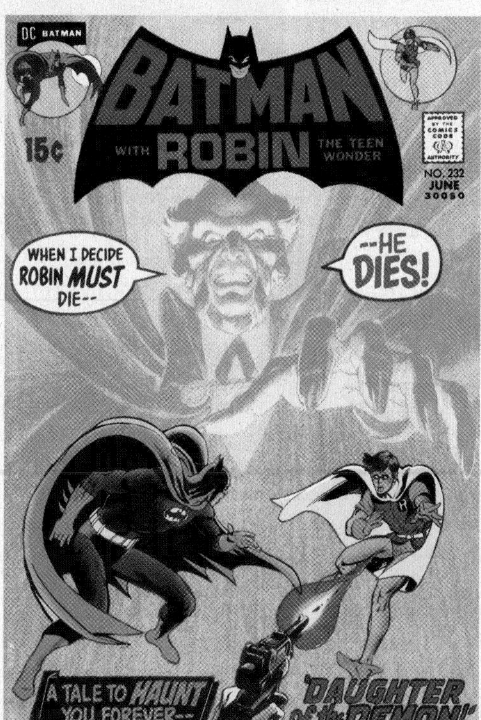

This iconic cover of **Batman #232** *introduced the "Head of the Demon" Ra's Al Ghul to the Batman mythos.*

An unexpected ending to the harrowing adventure in **Batman #232**.

Talia (created by O'Neil and artist Bob Brown) first appeared in *Detective Comics #411* (May, 1971) in the story "Into the Den of the Death-Dealers!" (cover by Adams, script by O'Neil, pencils by Brown and inks by Dick Giordano). In this tale, Batman tracks the villain Dr. Ebenezer Darrk, former president of the League of Assassins, to his lair in Asia where he meets and rescues Talia from his clutches. After a falling out with Ra's, Darrk had abducted Talia in retaliation and she ends up killing him in order to save Batman's life. An exotic beauty, Talia is perhaps a cross between the Mediterranean and the Far East, and Adams' version is considered definitive.

The story arc that introduced Ra's in *Batman #232* would continue in *Batman #242* "Bruce Wayne - R.I.P." (June, 1972), *#243* "The Lazarus Pit" (August, 1972) and conclude in *#244* "The Demon Lives Again" (September, 1972). In the climatic chapter, Ra's challenges Batman to a duel-to-the-death with scimitars.

The intense combat is unexpectedly interrupted by the sharp sting from a scorpion upon Batman's ankle, and Ra's leaves his fallen foe to his fate. Talia tarries behind long enough to secretly administer some antivenin that saves the his life. And, like a desert wraith, he rises from the dunes in the cool of the evening to re-emerge with unabashed rage at Al Ghul's tent and defeats the shocked villain who asks, "By the gods! You pursue me past your dying...! Are you man—or fiend from hell?" Batman and Talia embrace once more before he departs with Ra's slung over his shoulders into the desert night.

Flash forward 15 years.

Writer Mike W. Barr had co-created *Batman and the Outsiders* with Jim Aparo following the cancellation of *The Brave and the Bold* with issue #200 (July, 1983) and he was enjoying the

*One of the stories in **Batman Spectacular DC Special Series #15** featured a Wedding of Batman and Talia.*

success of his maxi-series *Camelot 3000* (DC, 1982-85), working with artist Brian Bolland. Barr had approached his editor, Dick Giordano, about of idea of publishing graphic novels since Marvel had already been doing so since 1982.

"I had a contract with DC to do a Batman graphic novel, and I had come up with the idea to do a Ra's al Ghul story because I had always liked the character, and Denny was over at Marvel at the time, so he had really no claim on it anymore. I came up with the idea of Talia being pregnant with Batman's child. And then later on she would lose the child," Barr said.

He believed that since this was to be the very first Batman graphic novel, published in larger prestige format on better paper stock and would carry a cover price of $14.95 - 20 times that of the then-regular 75¢ cover price — 20x that of a regular comic book (75-cents) at that time - the readers would want something more than clichéd ending. He wanted a life-changing event for Batman.

"So I said to Dick that at the end if it turns out she really has not lost the baby, that the baby's out there, that's going to be a punch that they're not going to be able to forget. And I think I was right. I don't know if anybody's been able to forget it," he said.

Giordano balked. Barr had anticipated this, though, and showed him the comic *Batman Spectacular DC Special Series #15* (Summer, 1978, written by O'Neil, penciled by Michael Golden and inked by Giordano himself) that featured the story, "I Now Pronounce You Batman and Wife!" wherein Ra's marries Batman to Talia aboard his large tanker somewhere in the Atlantic and outside U.S. jurisdiction. Satisfied, Giordano signed off.

The graphic novel would be titled *Batman Son of the Demon* (SOD), and Barr was really pushing for something special. He wanted a truly epic and more mature saga.

"The dilemma for me was how far could I push Batman past his present stories that were running in *Batman* and *Detective Comics*? In essence, how violent and how intense can I get and still remain true to the basic core of the character. I mean, Batman is

Batman: Son of the Demon was released in hardcover (shown right) and as a soft cover edition with a wraparound cover (below).

Batman: Son of the Demon begins with Ra's Al Ghul rising up from a deep crevice, as if rising from Hell itself.

not Dirty Harry who can kick down a door and start blasting away the bad guys," Barr said.

Another important hurdle to overcome finding an artist who would do the book justice.

"I initially asked Brian Bolland, with whom I had done *Camelot 3000*, but he said that he was not interested in doing a graphic novel and no one else suitable seemed to be available at the time. I then wrote an article for the *Comics Buyer's Guide* (*CBG*) that stated that I was working on the very first Batman graphic novel and was looking for an artist. Jerry [Bingham] read the article and called me up," he said.

At the time the artist was best known for his Kirby Award winning graphic novel *Beowolf* (First Comics, 1984).

After Bingham signed on, Barr completed the *SOD* plot on December 15, 1985.

"I wrote *Son of the Demon* 'Marvel style,' sending Jerry a detailed plot outline but no dialogue, nor panel breakdowns. In June of 1986, I began receiving copies of the penciled pages and began filling in the dialogue. By August of 1986, I had all the penciled pages with completed dialogue. The book was released one year later in August of 1987," Barr said.

Bingham's artwork for *SOD* took him a year and a half to finish. Each individual page required three full days to complete the pencil and ink stages on average. The black and white artwork was rendered on huge 15" x 20" sheets of heavy illustration paper supplied by DC, and then he would labor for another day or two to apply Dr. Martin's watercolors.

It's notable that that Bingham choose to ink with an old fashioned quill pen—a painstaking process of dip and apply, dip and apply - that not only demanded a great deal of skill, but time and patience as well. The exceptional detail and outstanding rendering of his work is apparent in each and every panel.

"At the time, the only options I knew were quill or brush. India ink had to be black because the printing process wasn't very forgiving and any translucency came across as muddy. A couple books tried to experiment with printing from pencils—Gene Colan drew all his comics in tone and his pencils were gorgeous but (I believe) difficult to translate for some inkers, so he was the perfect choice to try this with—but the printing process of the era didn't do it justice. Still, anything he did looked great," Bingham said.

SOD is considered Bingham's magnum opus, a true masterpiece in illustrative storytelling. His style on it is reminiscent of Hal Foster and Neal Adams.

Initially, *SOD* was intended to be printed only in soft cover format (SC), but when the editor and several of the DC executives saw the original artwork they immediately decided to produce a deluxe hard cover edition (HC) in addition. Bingham produced a full oil painting for the HC edition as well as an additional oil wrap-around cover for the SC.

Son of the Demon opens ominously with a four panel prologue in a remote desert-like region as Ra's al Ghul rises up from a deep crevice in the Earth's surface, perhaps even out of Hell itself. "The Earth screams, like a woman giving birth..." Barr wrote.

"To the best of my recollection, the original plot for *SOD* played right off of my story ['The Messiah of the Crimson Sun'] in *Batman Annual #8* (1982) with Ra's being revived from his 'death' in that story. I believe I was later told that Ra's had been used since *Annual #8*, so I just cobbled together a moody, but non-specific resurrection scene. I was able to use prose and art to hook together the theme of storms and birth that weave in and out throughout the tale," Barr said.

"I liked the layout of this page. I like geometrical compositions and was conscious of directional lines and placement of important elements, the transitions between distant, extreme close-up, close-up and receding, then to the master overhead—chopper's eye view. And the blacks circle the page to make the compositional point," Bingham said.

After the brief prologue, the tale cuts to the Gotham Chemical Plant, which has been surround by police squad cars and a SWAT unit in a tense stand off with a group of international terrorists. The insurgents hold a number of hostages, have access to deadly chemicals and are not interested in any type of negotiations with Commissioner Gordon's police force.

One of the terrorists begins to carve the letter "Q" in the cheek of one of the female hostages. Each of the terrorists already have this "Q" etched somewhere on their bodies. Later readers learn that this signified their leader, Qayin.

Was this "Mark of Qayin" branding was meant to have any connection to the infamous Mark of Cain in the Book of Genesis 4:15, where God places a mark on Cain after he had murdered his younger brother Abel?

"That was a thematic resonance I thought was too good to pass up. And if Qayin is Cain, then Batman, later in the story, becomes Abel, since they're both sons of Ra's Al Ghul," Barr said.

Batman arrives, takes on the terrorists, and resolves the situation, including rescuing a female hostage who is with child. Wounded in the process, he makes sure that both mother and child-to-be are unharmed.

"Good," comments Batman, "A child needs his parents… It's a terrible thing for a child to have to grow up alone."

Barr's dialogue here is reveals sophisticated subtext, introduces two profound themes of the story, and reflects on Batman's tragic past.

"Superman is most often mentioned when discussing Christ figures in comics, but I think Batman also qualifies. He suffered immensely by the deaths of his parents, but, rather than turning inward and becoming bitter, he made the deliberate choice to try to prevent others from suffering as he has, risking his life every day to aid people he has never met," he said.

"The father-son/parent-child relationship is expressed in many ways in *SOD*, from the pregnant woman Batman saves in the story's opening scene to the relationship between Harris Blaine Sr. to [Harris Blaine] Junior and Batman to Ra's Al Ghul. Qayin's motivation comes from the deaths of his parents. Even Batman and Qayin become Ra's' sons during the story, making them, in an odd way, brothers. This kind of parallel structure and reemphasized theme is pure gold if a writer knows how to utilize it," he said.

"That's why Robin isn't in the story. The inclusion of the Boy Wonder would seem a natural in a story dealing with father-son themes, but I felt that including Robin as Batman's symbolic son would dilute the intensity both of the relationship between Batman and Ra's Al Ghul, and the relationship between Batman and Talia when Batman learns Talia is pregnant. When Batman learns of the pregnancy, their child has to become the primary focus of any father-son relationship he might be involved in," he said.

After the action against the terrorists, a wounded Bruce Wayne dreams. He awakes with sweat pouring down his face in the Batcave and calls for Alfred, but is greeted by Talia - the second main player of *SOD* - who says, "I followed you from the factory, beloved…I knew you

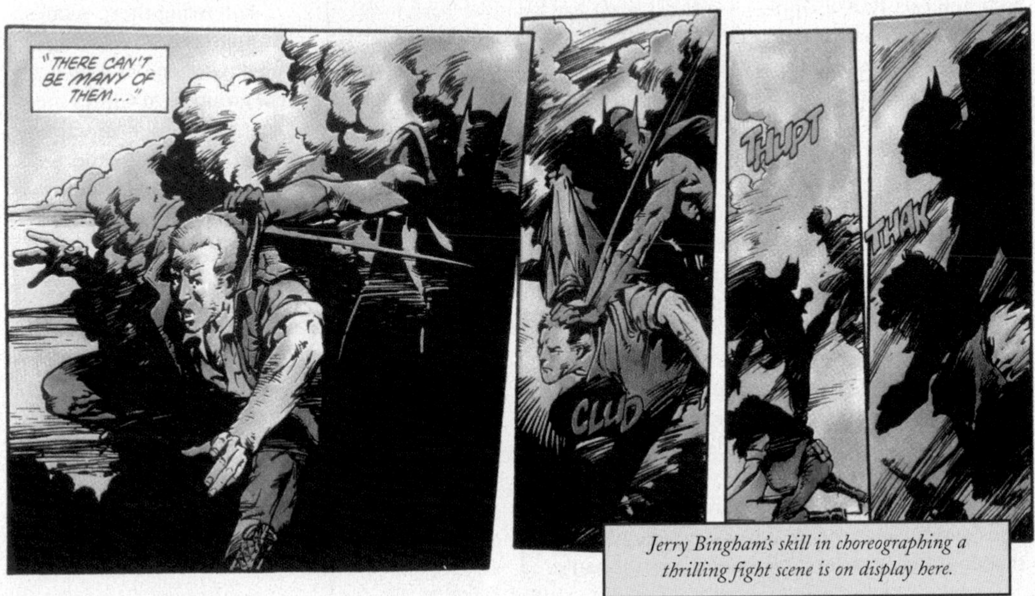

Jerry Bingham's skill in choreographing a thrilling fight scene is on display here.

would need assistance, even though you would not admit it yourself."

As always, he is reluctant to ask for aid or admit his own limitations.

"I have had many a conversation about Batman with Denny [O'Neil] and Frank [Miller]. I used to hang out with them quite often when we lived in New York. Many of these discussions have lasted for hours, but I've never seen Batman as a mentally incapacitated person nor insane. He is not a man who boarders on being psychotic. He is just very determined and fully dedicated in his mission. Batman is like a larger-than-life, religious character. Christ-like! Here to help and aid mankind in his struggles against evil and tyranny. He has chosen the road of self-sacrifice and self-denial for the betterment of mankind and benefit of us all. In short, Batman is a role model in the truest sense," Barr said.

After speaking with Commissioner Gordon and learning more about Qayin, Batman and Talia visit Blaine-Pearson Research, the company owned and run by Dr. Harris Blaine. Batman bypasses the security system to find Dr. Blaine dead on his desk, poisoned only seconds ago.

Batman and Talia then jet off of Demon's Head, a secluded mountain citadel carved into the face of the rock. The hero once again is confronted by his age-old arch nemesis, Ra's al Ghul - the third and final star player of *SOD* — who stands, along side Dr. Weltmann, supervising the construction of a new Lazarus Pit.

... AND AT LAST... THE LAZARUS PIT IS MINE.

Qayin, the man who killed Talia's mother.

At this stage, *SOD* has now taken on a much grander scope.

"Ra's was created to be a larger-than-life, James Bond style of villain. One who posed a global threat to mankind, not just a local one to Gotham City like the Joker, Penguin and Two-Face," Barr said.

"Ra's is a very powerful, very real adversary with a genius intellect that would challenge Batman to the nth degree - one who would really test his meddle. With the added element of Talia as a love interest, Batman would also have to deal with his difficult and inner most emotions and feelings for his adversary's daughter that could very well be his undoing if not handled carefully and correctly," he said.

Batman learns that Qayin murdered Talia's mother.

This is a very intriguing and enlightening origin story, the first to reveal any sort of family history of Ra's al Ghul. Talia witnessing the death of her mother struck a chord with Batman who had likewise witnessed the murder of his own parents.

In perhaps the most significant moment of *SOD*, Ra's offers an alliance with Batman to track down and bring Qayin to justice. Batman accepts. Ra's then ups the ante by saying, "...and with this position comes the hand of my daughter. To accept the first is to accept the second, there is no middle ground. Do you still accept my offer, Detective?"

Batman responds with the classic, "I do" and readily admits that he has never been able to fully forget Talia nor keep her from his thoughts.

Bingham then lays out a stunning and tasteful two-page spread love scene where Batman and Talia consummate their marriage. When Batman asks Talia about the need for a formal ceremony, she reminds him of the previous one.

Their subsequent pursuit of Qayin crosses international borders, and readers learn that Qayin is dying, with perhaps only a few weeks to live.

Following those scenes, what follows is an exciting and action-packed seven-page scene in which Batman, Talia and a small group of Al Ghul's men break into the Kennedy Space Center on Cape Canaveral by night in order to sabotage the launch of a weather satellite that the Detective is convinced Qayin will use against mankind. They fail.

Returning to Demon's Head base, Ra's is pleased that they have established a direct connection between Qayin and the nation of Golatia, but Batman is somber, disappointed at their failure to thwart the launch and concerned about losing one of Ra's soldiers named Donal. Talia interrupts their conversation to drop a bomb on her husband's world.

"Beloved, a word?" She beckons.

"Can't it wait, Talia?"

"It cannot," she insists.

A new twist to the Batman mythos.

"Now, Talia, what's so impor—"

"Beloved, I am with child. I am pregnant," she announces.

It's not often we see Batman dumbfounded.

He then embraces her saying, "That's wonderful!"

As Batman and Talia are sharing a quiet and tender moment alone, outside, there's a squadron of military helicopters approaching the mountain locale. Batman gives Talia a beautiful ornate jeweled necklace and Talia promises, "Whenever I wear it, I shall think of you...and I shall wear it always."

Asked if there any special significance to the jeweled necklace, Barr offers his insight, "To my recollection, the necklace had not appeared before. Knowing the way my mind works, I probably searched back issues for some prop to use for this purpose, but found none, and so created one."

Bingham interjects, "This is obviously after Talia has told Batman that she is pregnant and they are really beginning to connect emotionally here, as symbolized by the necklace."

The story's pace then quickens considerably by whipping up a rousing rodeo of high-paced action and intense confrontations augmented with tense and tight dialogue

Back at Demon's Head, Batman and Ra's discuss their next move when Talia faints in the arms of her father. In the medical ward, Barr and Bingham provide us with a somber scene, in which a weeping Talia informs her husband, "I am well, beloved..." She turns away from him to add, "I...I have lost the baby."

The next panel is a masterstroke of Bingham's quill pen as he draws our hero in total isolation, with no boarders or background.

"Notice how small the figure Batman is here. His whole world has just crashed down upon him. He is isolated and all alone. He feels impotent and insignificant," Bingham said.

Believing that his child is no more, Batman can resume his mission with little concern for his own safety. He joins Ra's and his men to confront Qayin.

A fierce and final fight ensues.

Barr deliberately placed the very fate of the world in the hands of Ra's al Ghul, putting the character at the very brink of achieving his lifelong goal of seeing Earth born anew out of destruction.

At this fateful moment, Ra's sides with his son-in-law. The threat is eliminated. The mission is accomplished, even if Ra's and Batman are left feeling saddened, empty.

The jeweled necklace – more than just a symbol of emotional connection.

At the end of "Messiah of the Crimson Sun" in *Batman Annual* #8, Talia sends Batman away. And likewise at the end of *SOD*, she sends him away again. Why?

"Like many star-crossed couples, they live together happily for a while, but something always comes along to spoil it. It may be that they're destined not to be together for any amount of time. But when they are together, it's

Talia sends Bruce Wayne away. Sadly, they are not destined to be together.

pretty good for each of them," Barr said.

"Talia sends Bruce Wayne away because she knows that he would never be the Batman she loves and admires so much if he were to stay with her. He's way too protective and preoccupied with her safety, especially if children were involved. She feels that it is probably best for them not to be together and is willing to sacrifice their marriage for his well being," Bingham said.

The artist provides one last profound look of our unmasked hero, standing stoically silent upon a high rooftop in sorrowful reflection as the rain descends in relentless sheets, like heavy tears from the heavenly host.

"This panel I drew with his cowl down to convey that Bruce is not the Batman here - the iconic legend of lore. No. Here, he is just a man, like you and me. A man of flesh and blood who can and is experiencing great pain and regret like any ordinary human being," he said.

The *Son of the Demon* closes at Brooksdale Orphanage with a nurse proudly presenting a newly born baby boy to an unnamed delighted couple — a baby who has a beautifully wrought necklace of ornate jewels laid across his body.

"It was a visual way of connecting the baby to Talia, letting the reader know this is the child of Bats and Talia." said Barr.

Despite little or no marketing effort, *Batman:*

Bruce Wayne in sorrowful reflection, as a man, not the Batman

Son of the Demon sold very well and it garnered a fair amount of critical acclaim as well. A landmark event as the first Batman graphic novel produced, that didn't save it from it being set aside story-wise.

"It was dropped from the canon the instant that it hit print," Barr said.

Even though DC chose to look upon *SOD* as a "black sheep," the influence and lasting impact of the book is undeniable. Batman and Talia's child has shown up in various projects under various names, depending upon the interpretation of the particular writer and artist.

The baby, with the unmistakable necklace, was not considered "in canon" until many years later.

In the Elseworlds story *Brotherhood of the Bat* (DC, 1995), the character is named Tallant Wayne who crusades against his grandfather, Ra's al Ghul.

In Alex Ross and Mark Waid's Elseworlds mini-series *Kingdom Come* (DC, 1996), the character's name is Ibn al Xu'ffasch - Arabic for "Son of the Bat" - who shows up as part of Lex

Ibn al Xu'ffasch (seated right), in league with Lex Luthor in 1996's Kingdom Come.

Luthor's Mankind Liberation Front. "Xu'ffasch is the heir to Ra's al Ghul's secret empire for one simple reason: he is Ra's grandson. The child sired by Ra's daughter Talia and his greatest enemy, The Batman, made his first appearance in the *Son of the Demon* graphic novel by Mike W. Barr and Jerry Bingham," Ross wrote.

In Grant Morrison and Andy Kubert's story arc "Batman and Son," which ran in *Batman #655-658* (DC, September–December, 2006), the boy is named Damian Wayne. Raised by Talia under the tutorship of the League of Assassins, he is a problematic protégé - narcissistic, spoiled and violent - which poses quite a challenge for Batman in his efforts to properly train and direct the boy.

It is this character that has merged into the main Batman storylines.

Young Damian Wayne is a prominent figure in current Batman lore, taking up the mantle of Robin.

An extended version of this article with additional information from Mike W. Barr and Jerry Bingham will appear in *The Overstreet Guide To Collecting Comics*, coming soon.

The Semi-Secret Origin of Comic Book Marketplace

By J.C. Vaughn

In 2011, *Comic Book Marketplace* celebrated its 20th anniversary including its first new issue in the last few years, and that provoked a lot of thought about how the publication got started in the first place. None of it would have happened without the insights, hard work and vision of Gary M. Carter, the founder of *CBM*, and the publications' longtime editor and head cheerleader.

For 83 issues (and some specials), he brought together professional writers and dedicated amateurs in pursuit of comics history. More often than not, they found it.

As longtime contributing editor Pat Calhoun saw it, *Comic Book Marketplace* was a vehicle for new attitudes.

"As the 1990s dawned, comic book collecting received a makeover and went from a fanboy hobby to investment vehicle and accepted part of pop culture," he said. The impact of the 1989 feature film *Batman* on back issue prices strongly signaled the relationship between comics books and the culture as a whole, and it occurred during a time when high grade issues were beginning to sell for premium prices.

CBM, he suggested was where these notions and other ideas came together.

"The approach was less giddy and more inclusive than previous fan publications. More attention was also paid to the non-superhero genres, and this seemed a step towards maturity, as long underwear worship was the key factor in making comic collecting a teenage thing," he said.

"This also yielded a version of comics history that was more faithful to reality, as it came to light that the biggest years in terms of number of comics sold were in the early 1950s, when superheroes were a distinct minority," he said.

"*CBM* was a window to the variety of genres that were available but maybe previously unknown to the average collector. To see examples of the work and learn about the background of the artists and writers added to the excitement of the hunt. Above all, the bricks of knowledge that *CBM* provided and the background data that was contributed by many collectors helped to lay a solid foundation for one's thorough enjoyment of the hobby," said Michael Naiman, another longtime contributor to the publication.

"Editor, publisher and founder Gary M. Carter not only manifested a vision of collecting that seemed to be just what the hobby needed (as evidenced by how completely *CBM* was embraced by said hobby) but gained him his respected position in the community," Calhoun said.

"As one of the early buyers of the Mile High Collection [Edgar Church] pedigree, he exemplified the high grade collector, and he fused that with his almost complete DC collection to blend history and research into the mix," he said. "He helped smooth the arduous politics that accompanied reshaping the hobby into an industry. There is a group of savvy Golden Age collectors in the hobby today, and when conversing with them one often gets the idea that much of their astute grasp of comic book history, art, and market position comes from having graduated from CBM University," he said.

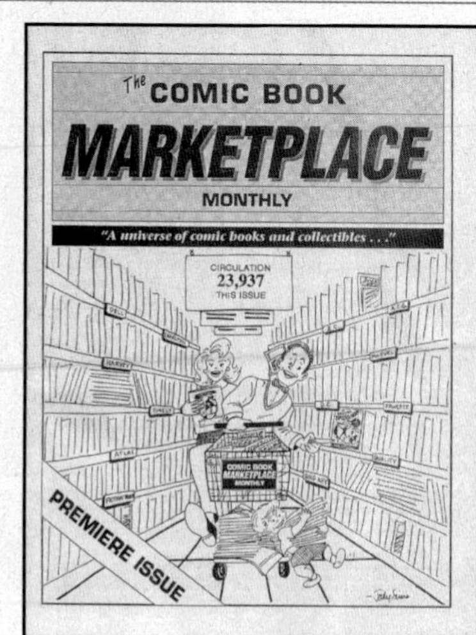

The pages of **Comic Book Marketplace #1** brought a "sheer and unadulterated love of comics and collecting." to the newsstand.

"The legacy of the original *CBM* is twofold: not only did it provide a more holistic view of the knowledge, fun, and possibilities within the hobby, but it also provided a view of the hobby that those still somewhat outside of it could better understand and appreciate," he said.

"*CBM* really started with my simple love for the medium of comic books (begun at the tender age of five) and ultimately my keen interest in collecting them (started at age seven). Credit also goes to Bob Overstreet and [Gladstone publisher] Bruce Hamilton for encouraging and helping with the initial idea early on (in early 1991) and especially my wife Lisa's amazing contribution through the first 80+ issues," Carter said.

He also credits earlier publications with sparking the embers that became the flames that *CBM* fanned.

"I suppose I should also credit the original *Rocket's Blast-Comic Collector* (Biljo White) and the *Buyer's Guide* from Alan Light for planting the 'psychic seed,' so-to-speak. I also believed that many of the original fanzines went part way towards memorizing the history of and artistic personalities associated with the medium of comics... but I wanted to take the next step combing the elements of history, rarity, value, market forces, and especially the 'sheer and unadulterated love of comics and collecting.' *CBM* was my attempt at expressing those elements. It also provided a wonderful opportunity to create community around the hobby, which I feel we did in a positive way," he said.

"I want to also credit Pat Calhoun as a (the?) key plank-holder in the *CBM* story. We had collected together since childhood, and without his influence, guidance, contributions, and support there would be no *CBM*," he said.

Carter said there wasn't a seminal moment or event that sparked him to say "I can do this!" but instead it was more a coalescing of experience, timeliness and opportunity.

"I guess it was one of those intersections of fate and event. I was ready, Lisa was ready, Pat was available... and I was kind of bursting with enthusiasm for the hobby, combined with my deep interest in the history of the medium. I kept seeing so many the early greats of the industry leaving us with no documentation of their lives and/or contributions. I felt an urgency to document while they were still around to tell us their stories. Plus I wanted to do something that might confer more credibility on a hobby that was [for decades] the object of ridicule by the mainstream. I wanted to make sure that comic historians and comic creators (especially Golden Age and Silver Age) were credited with their great accomplishments and contributions," he said.

"I also wanted to find a way to add credibility to an already-thriving marketplace. I tried to make sure every issue under my editorship clearly communicated these ideas. You may recall that I often said in those early days of *CBM*, 'When a magazine doesn't know what it is, neither do its readers.' For 80 issues or so, *CBM* pretty mush knew what it was," he said.

The magazine quickly found its voice through Carter's industry world view, which meant that tone and tenor of the publication was developed by his guiding hand working with sometimes dozens of contributors and a time in service to the notion that comic book history was worth documenting. Its impact was not lost on its supporters.

"*CBM* could not have existed without Gary's intellectual and physical involvement. He often worked late into the night to complete his projects and was the best I've ever known at networking on the telephone with his writers and advisors. He also went to the printer and walked each issue through to its finish from disc to negative to plate. He was there to take care of any problems that might arise, like a mother hen and always delivered an amazing product," said Bob Overstreet, author of *The Overstreet Comic Book Price Guide*.

The change in appreciation of comic books by the culture at large that has occurred since the publication's founding is so large and so overwhelming that many today simply will never know its scope. *CBM* both helped to record this change and to shape it. It started with the concept that those who had created the work enjoyed by so many should have their work held in high esteem and be documented.

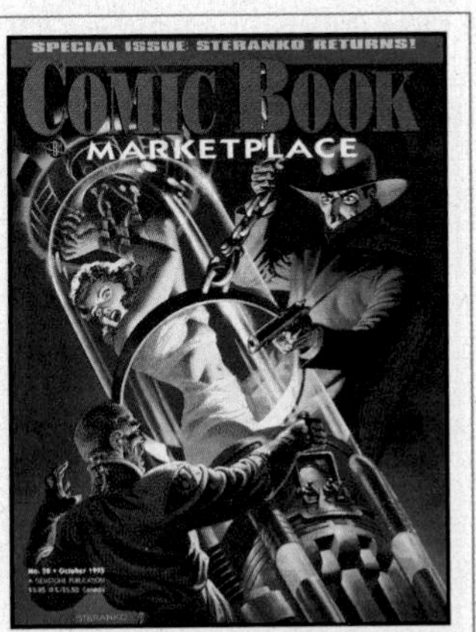

Comic Book Marketplace #28 (October 1995) featured this dynamic cover of The Shadow by the legendary Jim Steranko.

Some veteran comic book creators were startled by the attention.

Many were quite surprised, and many deeply touched by the fact that so many hobbyists and collectors held them in such high esteem. There were actually occasions when I would approach with a request for an interview and they would get a bit misty-eyed over the prospect. I was especially gratified when I would [ultimately] present them with the newly-printed *CBM* issue that featured them... they almost always wanted extra copies to send to friends and relatives. We were always happy to provide as many copies as they needed," Carter said

He said this included creators such as Creig Flessel and early DC editior Vin Sullivan.

"There were others as well. One of the more humble folks, especially considering the breath of his talent, was Murphy Anderson. What a gracious man... and what a remarkable history in the field," he said. "I also really enjoyed interviewing Gil Kane, Russ Heath, and Joe Kubert, among others. And perhaps the most exciting interview of all (at least in the top three) was Julius Schwartz. Can't say he was humble - he had a lot not to be humble about - but what a great guy, and could there be a more impressive comic book resume than Julie. I can't think of one. It was such a privilege to get to interview so many great creators over the years, I think mostly because their work meant so much to me personally," he said.

Following their start, he said it took them several issues to develop a production routine with the magazine.

"The first five issues were done on a PC. *CBM* #6 on we used a Mac, so I would say about five issues. We spent many late hours (often all night) learning software programs and doing paste-up. We also had to create half-tones of all covers and other graphics using a Hasselblad medium format camera. (I think if I recall my camera trivia correctly, it was invented by a guy from Sweden named Victor Hasselblad, which always reminded me a little of Victor Frankenstein.) Anyway, it's a giant camera. Before we used scans, we photographed everything as actual size and as a half-tones. Then we'd bring all the film home, cut it to size, and paste it on the sheets. Then we'd go back to the printer and photo all the sheets to make film of the pages and signatures. Then the strippers would set up the film to make plates. Then after plates were created, they be mounted and the presses would roll. It was quite involved but a great learning opportunity about how images and print and color make it to a printed page," he said.

"To this day, I still get a feeling of excitement when I visit a printing operation... I especially enjoy the smell of ink and the feel fresh rolls of ultrabrite newsprint. I guess publishing and printing really stay with you... I think because there's an incredible amount of work and know-how that goes into every issue, plus when you finally get to stand at the end of the bindery line and hold the completed magazine in your hand... Wow, there's just nothing like it. I used to say occasionally that it was like seeing your child born, except you got to do it once a month," he said with a laugh.

"I should also say that the real credit for most of the production goes to Lisa. She was the one with the greatest understanding of layout and color, plus she has an amazingly short learning curve on all things artistic. Pat Calhoun was also a critically important member of the early team, and usually never gets the credit he deserves. Likewise Michael Naiman," he said. "One can look at the early *CBMs* and watch the changes from issue to issue."

Carter said he believes that *CBM* really hit its stride just after #13.

"A friend, Bill Howard, put us in touch with Joe Sikoriyak, a brilliant designer and artist who had worked with Disney among others. He drastically expanded Lisa's and my thinking about content, layout, graphics, even software programs. We also began to upgrade cover stock and finish, interior stock, and ultimately added a color section... even changed the cover logo. The 'new' *CBM* lasted until #21 when I began work at Overstreet, around January of 1993," he said.

CBM would return with #22 not too long later under the banner of Gemstone Publishing after the company acquired select assets of Overstreet Publications. Carter was once again at the helm.

During his tenure at Overstreet, Carter created a *CBM*-like magazine, *Overstreet's Comic Book Quarterly*, in addition to editing *Overstreet's Comic Book Monthly* and the company's other projects.

"To this day, most collectors/readers consider those six issues of the *Quarterly* from '93 and '94 sort of like *CBM* #21a through #21f. When Overstreet Publishing became part of Gemstone, Steve Geppi was kind enough to suggest that we continue *CBM* as a Gemstone publication (back in California) and start up again with #22. That's just what we did, and that's why there's a time gap between *CBM* #21 and #22," he said.

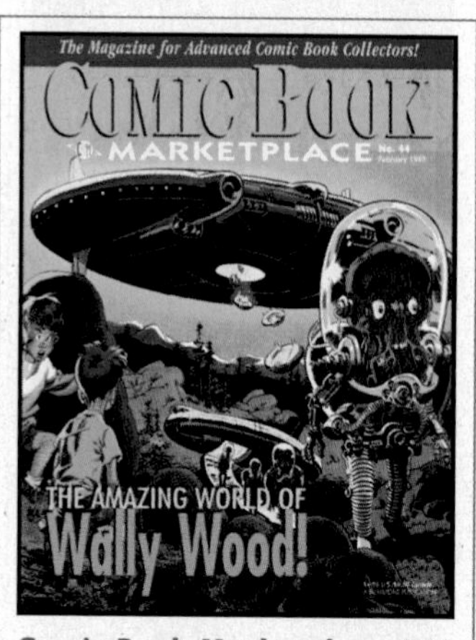

Comic Book Marketplace #44
(February 1997)
set its focus on the work of
Wally Wood.

Like any product that supports a given industry, the impact of Comic Book Marketplace on collectors and dealers may be hard to measure in succinct, practical terms, but those who were part of its audience know if for what it was. Its legacy remains one of providing information, context and insight. In addition, only in recent years have other publications caught up to its use of color sections.

"A whole lot (I mean a *whole lot*) of credit is due Pat Calhoun, Michael Naiman, and Michelle Nolan, as well as a myriad of authors/collectors who contributed their research and passion for little compensation. They wrote and researched because of their love of the medium, its artists, and its history," Carter said.

"*Comic Book Marketplace* was not the only publication which reflected on comic book history by featuring the voices of knowledgeable dealers, collectors and creators, but it was inarguably one of the best. Gary and Lisa Carter, with their skill, dedication and relationships with so many contributors, set a standard that the great fan-friendly publications have to live up to. I believe the quality of their work is why there remains such a steady market for their back issues," said Steve Geppi, President and CEO of Gemstone Publishing,

Comic Book Marketplace continues as an annual from Gemstone Publishing. The most recent issue was published on Free Comic Book Day 2012.

APPROVED BY THE COMICS CODE AUTHORITY

Comics Code Era 10¢ Batman

By Pat Calhoun

Batman entered the Comics Code era when the Comics Code Authority stamp first appeared on issues published in March 1955. The character, now the center of a multi-media empire, carried on into the Silver Age in a strong position as DC's second superstar. The signature story lines in which Batman solved puzzling crimes committed by colorful crooks had never faltered in the character's seventeen-year run to that point. Collector and historian Pat Calhoun takes a look at the defining characteristics of the Caped Crusader's tales from that period.

Since DC was never too keen on graphic violence or gore, their titles showed little change with the implementation of the Code. Interestingly, *Detective Comics* featured a couple of important Silver Age precursors. Issue #225 November 1955 replaced Captain Compass with DC's first new post-code hero, John Jones, the Manhunter from Mars, and #233 July 1956 introduced Batwoman. *Detective Comics* #235 (Sep 1956) is also noteworthy in that 'The First Batman' reveals new details of Batman's origin. DC's Silver Age began the next month with the debut of the revamped Flash in *Showcase* #4 (cover dated Oct 1956).

Although *Batman* #92 June 1955 introduced Ace, the Bat-Hound, most of the more memorable stories appeared in *Detective*, with the Bat tales there lasting 12-2/3 pages (with an ad at the bottom of a page) compared to eight pages for the lead in *Batman*. The anthology titles that had been integral to the Golden Age still held sway – for DC the other two big survivors were *Action Comics* (Superman) and *Adventure Comics* (Superboy) – and similarly those titles featured most of the major events in the saga of the Man (and Boy) of Steel.

1957 started relatively quietly; it took DC some time to realize that their Flash revival should be but the first step towards a host of GA reboots. The launch of Sputnik in October 1957 changed everything. Suddenly the space race was on and science fiction was hot, nowhere more so than at DC where science fiction had long been a way of life.

Editors Julie Schwartz, Mort Weisinger, and Jack Schiff (who was handling Batman) had all been involved in the sci-fi pulps, not to mention top writers like Gardner Fox, Edmond Hamilton, Otto Binder, and John Broome. As they brought back their old characters with new origins the Silver Age versions relied heavily on SF elements, and most of the established series were also inundated with fantastica.

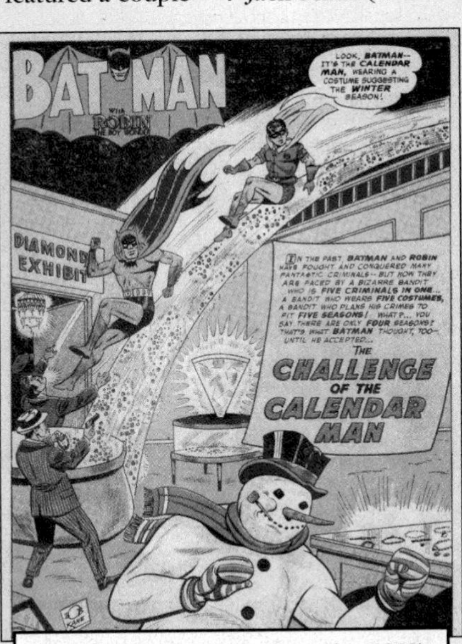

Detective Comics #259 (September 1958) Features a first rate 'puzzle crime' story by the master of such, Bill Finger, with Sheldon Moldoff's art (inked by Charles Paris) capturing the action with a clean colorful style.

So the January 1958 *Detective* and the February *Batman* both featured SF covers: as did six other *Detectives* and four other *Batmans* during the year (with *Batman* on an eight issue per year schedule).

Schiff told comics historian Will Murray that he really didn't want to go the SF route with Batman, but DC insisted. So perhaps he tried extra hard on the more down to earth issues that kept Batman a more realistic crime fighter and detective. *Detective* #253 (March) offered not one but a whole trio of colorful antagonists, "The Fox, the Shark, and the Vulture," with a cool cover by Sheldon Moldoff that nicely frames the threesome as the dynamic duo swims into their underwater trap. And September's (#259) "The Calendar Man" is a classic puzzle crime yarn committed by a concept character whose gimmick, the four, er... *five* seasons, also provides the story's framework. The first panel announces a challenge to the Caped Crusader in the morning news: he intends to stage five crimes in the next five days, each inspired by a different time of year, with the addition of a baffling 'extra' season.

The cat and mouse game that follows leaves Batman and Robin as the "despondent duo" after four days, so that the turnaround can come with the fifth season finale, and it's all brought to pass with elegantly crafted plotting- the hallmark of super Bat scribe Bill Finger.

Co-creator of Batman and Robin, chief writer for the first two decades, master of plotting puzzle crimes. Without getting into how much or how little Bob Kane was contributing, Finger contributed *a lot*. The solving of crimes that defined Batman was detective work; that's why he appeared in *Detective Comics.*

And although that first year (1958) the SF stories were fresh and fun and colorful and certainly of a piece with other DC fare, the next few years would reveal Batman as the character least suited for such stuff, with his realistic roots, his 'ratiocination' (as Poe would say), and his fight against crime getting lost in the extravagance of time travel and various interplanetary and other-dimensional adventures.

Sheldon Moldoff also contributed in a big way. His tenure on the strip doesn't quite match Finger's, but almost. He was an early assistant and went on to become the consummate Kane ghost. In this era he penciled

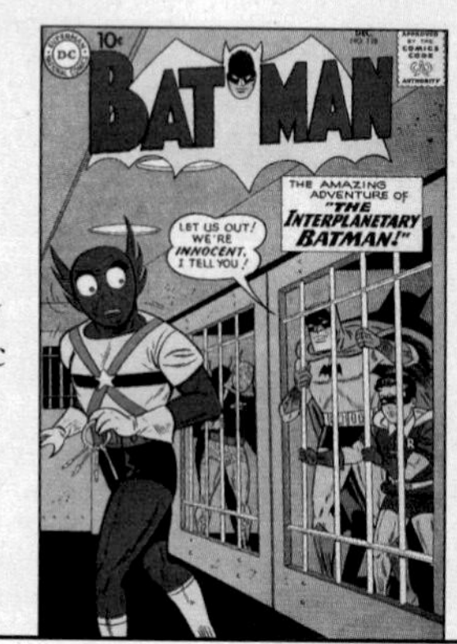

Batman #128 (December 1959)
Making the otherworld jail so much like one on Earth gives this cover some grit. It also marked Moldoff's return to cover chores after a run by Curt Swan (pencils) and Stan Kaye (inks).

Detective Comics #275 (January 1960)
Half SF story, half crime yarn, equals a pretty good blend with a vivid Moldoff cover. The two supporting features are Roy Raymond, TV Detective, and John Jones, Manhunter from Mars.

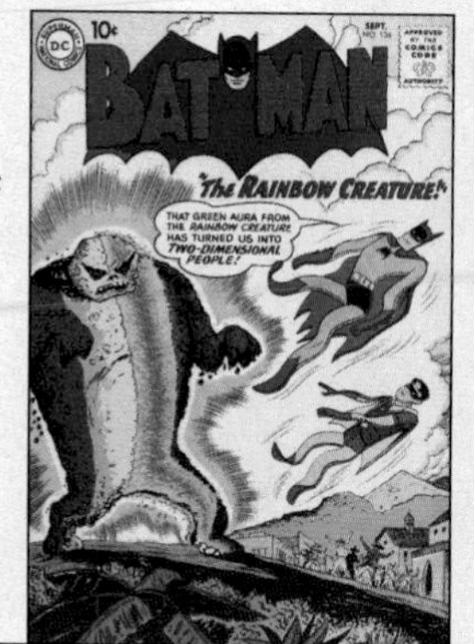

Batman #134 (September 1960)
It must be said: Batman is at his best fighting human evil, and one problem with the "SF Batman" was that the monsters were beyond good and evil.

nearly all of the stories in *Detective*, most of the stories in *Batman*, and the majority of the covers for both titles. Moldoff's take on Kane's Gouldish (*Dick Tracy*) style yields a clean no-nonsense narrative vehicle that perfectly paces the action.

Batman #121 (Feb 1959) blends the SF elements with the traditional by pitting Bats against a high-tech foe with the power to freeze in 'The Ice Crimes of Mr. Zero'. Since Superman had been tormented by an interdimensional imp since 1944 (Mr. Mxyztplk), giving Batman a similar nemesis during the sci-fi craze seemed to make sense; so Bat-Mite was introduced in *Detective* #267 (May 1959). *Detective* #272's (Oct) "Menace of the Crystal Creature" shows the SF themes already starting to take precedence over crook chasing, to Batman's detriment. Also cover-dated October, *Showcase* #22 brought back Green Lantern, completely science-fictionalized and slickly drawn by Gil Kane.

1960 definitely delivered diminishing returns, but there was still plenty of fun to be had. *Detective* #275 (Jan) struck a nice balance between crime-fighting & SF with Batman squaring off against a villain who has made himself into a super magnet in "The Zebra Batman." Finger scripted and Shelly drew, with an effective cover, too. But *Detective* #277's (March) "The Jigsaw Creature From Space" was way over-the-top with the SF goofiness that was creeping into the DC books across the board and thus threatening to turn Batman into generic DC product.

It's worth noting that March 1960 (by cover dates, actually January) marks a high point for Silver Age DC with the introduction of the Justice League of America in *The Brave and the Bold* #28. Indeed, the DC universe was running pretty well with SF for fuel. It was certainly a natural for the Superman family, the new Flash and Green Lantern were created by it and hence at home in it, Adam Strange and Space Ranger were popular new interplanetary features, only Batman was showing the stress. For Batman was a creature of the night- his present and future shaped by shadows of the past: his milieu was the dark streets of Gotham City, and his proper adversaries megalomaniac criminals as obsessed as himself.

Batman #134 (Sept) is a perfect example of the ill fit, with "The Rainbow Creature" turning (with just one of his color powers) Batman and Robin into flying pancakes. Schiff must have felt the pain of this, and he wisely responded by bringing back the Joker as cover feature for the December *Batman* (#136). No other character has helped Batman define himself more than the Clown Prince of Crime.

Batman **#136** (December 1960) Not that it's such a superb cover, but the fact that it's the first Joker cover since 1952-1953 says a lot. You've got to play your strong suits, especially when there's a Joker in the deck!

1961 was more of the same. In Batman, the two "sanest" issues were #139 (April) and #141 (Aug) that introduced Bat-Girl and brought her back teamed with Batwoman. The January *Detective* (#287) started the year off nicely as – so Moldoff's cover says – "Batman and Robin Battle an Amazing Duo - the Raven and the Wasp!" But things got zany fast with a cyclops from space, a shape-shifter, a robot Robin, and dimensional doings until the silliness almost transcends itself in #295 (Sept) "Secret of the Beast Paintings." Time Travel, aliens, monsters, this trifecta shows Finger and Moldoff's amazing abilities to turn the even the most outrageous situation into solid storytelling. Once you accept the idea that during this era the Caped Crusaders had a professor friend with a time machine, the plot percolates with admirable inevitability.

World's Finest Comics **#117** (May 1961) The rococo SF phase in full bloom on this Swan and Kaye cover – with two crazy things going on at once. Note the ominous "Still 10¢"– that means trouble ahead!

Three months later, the price change to 12¢ went into effect. When the modern comic book debuted in 1934, 10¢ cents bought 64 pages. During WWII they slimmed down to 48 pages, thus raising the price without raising the price. And the late 1940s and early 1950s brought a second shrinkage to 32 pages (This gave birth to the Superman-Batman team-up in *World's Finest*, as the book no longer had room for a separate story of each of them. That series became an entity unto itself and hence is somewhat outside the scope of this article).

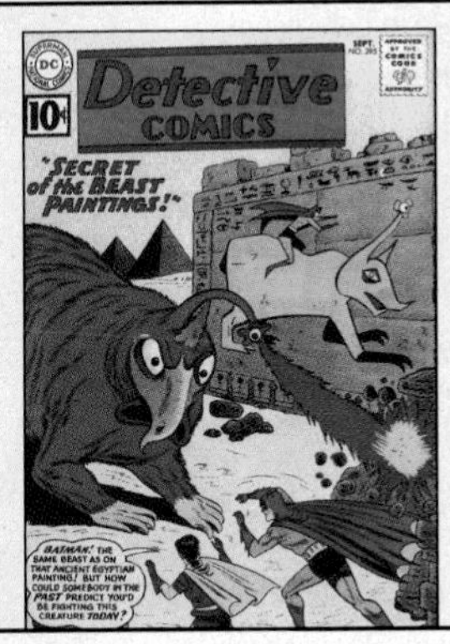

Detective Comics **#295** (September 1961) Even with the stream of curve balls the SF era pitched at Batman, Finger and Moldoff managed to knock some out of the park. This one is 12.66 pages of pure fun. Aquaman and John Jones round out the issue.

But by late 1961, taking away more pages would have resulted in an overly flimsy product, so the cover price went up for the first time. Although this change had little effect on editorial slant and content, the added hassle to both buyers and sellers in the retail marketplace was monumental, in many ways the final nail in the coffin of the old business model.

The Comics Code had above all redefined comic book readership to a younger level. And the injection of a heavy dose of SF into comics after Sputnik seemed not just an attempt to follow a trend to the marketplace but to take the image of comics from "causing juvenile delinquency" to "breeding the next generation of rocket scientists." Although this marketing strategy was somewhat successful, new comics sales had been severely truncated. Pre-Code sales were approximately 70 million copies per month, plunging to 4 million or so per month in 1961. And if Batman suffered from the "re-branding," at least it gave DC notice of the character's unique role.

The beginning of the 12¢ phase of comic books found the dynamic duo mired in the deadliest trap of their career: a 24/7 SF craze that cut the gritty heart out of Gotham City and left our heroes eviscerated as well. It is indeed testament to their heroic natures that they had the tenacity to survive it and lead the way into the cinema era, where movies of comic characters have eclipsed their paper counterparts in market share. With the transition from 12-page comic story to feature film, it is Batman's dark depths of character that have held the public's interest. He might not have super powers, but he is truly a super hero.

Pat Calhoun, an Overstreet Advisor, is a longtime collector, historian, and contributor to Comic Book Marketplace.

CGC

How the Company Has Grown and How It Works

By the CGC Grading Team

The world of comic book collecting has grown and matured since the 2000 introduction of CGC (Certified Guaranty Company). Before the founding of CGC comic book transactions were mainly face to face deals with buyers and sellers reviewing the books and negotiating the sales price. The advent of the internet changed all that. The world of the internet opened up new opportunities in that comic books from across the country were as easy to buy as those across the street. But with this new market came risk. Risk of not knowing the seller and risk of buying a book virtually sight unseen except for an online image.

CGC was created to put an end to the risk and the chaos that accompanied it, and to help bring order and stability to comic book sales. CGC is the first independent, impartial, third-party comic book grading service. A proven and respected commitment to integrity, accuracy, consistency and impartiality has made CGC the leader in its field, becoming a tool to help people with their buying and selling decisions. The universally accepted grading scale ensures consistency and gives both dealers and collectors a sense of dependability when making purchasing decisions. With CGC certification, a collector knows what he or she is getting based on an accurate and comprehensive description that can be found on the CGC certification label.

Here's a look at how CGC came together and how a book is certified.

The Formation of the Company

In January of 2000 CGC was launched under the umbrella of the Certified Collectibles Group, which includes Numismatic Guaranty Corporation (NGC), the largest third-party coin grading company in the world, Numismatic Conservation Services (NCS), the leading authority in numismatic conservation and Paper Money Guaranty (PMG), the world's leading currency certification company. The Collectibles Group sought out talented and ethical individuals to grade comic books. Experts needed a history of necessary skills to verify a comic book's authenticity and to detect restoration that can affect its value. To identify these individuals, many of the most respected individuals in the hobby were consulted, and, based on their recommendations a core grading team was selected.

The members of the CGC grading team come from diverse backgrounds, and many were comic book dealers at some time in their careers. Experience in the commercial sector can be an essential ingredient in becoming familiar with market standards. Upon joining CGC, all graders immediately cease all commercial trading. All CGC employees are prohibited from commercially buying and selling comic books to ensure they remain completely impartial, having no vested interest other than a dedication to serving clients through accurate and consistent grading.

When it was time to develop a uniform grading standard, the hobby's leaders were once again called upon. Everyone agreed that the *Overstreet Comic Book Price Guide* was the foundation of this standard, but there were a number of subjective interpretations of its published definitions. It was critical to understand how these guidelines were being applied to the everyday buying and selling of comics. To accomplish this, approximately 50 of the hobby's top experts took part in an extensive grading test. Their grades were averaged and an accurate grading standard reflecting the collective experience of the hobby's most prominent figures was thus developed. CGC now had the best standard and the best team to apply it.

With the graders in place and the grading scale established, the next step was to develop a tamper-evident holder for the long-term storage and display of certified comics. This proved to be a technical challenge. Exhaustive material tests were conducted to determine that the holders were archival safe. To create a true first line of defense, it was determined that the comic book should be sealed in a soft inner well, then sealed again inside a tamper evident hard plastic case with interlocking ridges to enable compact storage. The CGC certified grade appears on a label sealed inside the holder for an additional level of security.

Submitting your Books

Comic books may be submitted for certification in two ways - they can be submitted by authorized dealers or by Collectors Society members. The Collectors Society is an online community with direct access to certification service from CGC, and submissions can be prepared online. Both dealers and Collectors Society members typically send their comics to CGC's offices by registered mail or through an insured express company. Submissions are also accepted at many of the Comic Cons that occur around the country throughout the year.

The Comic Books are Received

Every day, CGC's Receiving Department opens newly arrived packages and immediately verifies that the number of books in each package matches the number shown on the submitted invoice. Once this is done, a more detailed comparison is made to ensure that their invoice descriptions correspond to the actual comics. This information is entered into a computer, and from this time forth, the comics will be traceable at all stages of the grading process by their invoice number and their line number within that invoice. Each book is checked to see that it is properly prepared for grading in an appropriately sized comic bag with backing board and then is labeled with a numbered barcode containing the pertinent data of invoice number and line item information for quick reading by the computer. Before any grading is performed, the book is examined by a CGC Restoration Detection Specialist. If any form of restoration work is detected, this information is entered into the computer, making it available to the grading team.

Each comic book receives a restoration check and the results appear on the label.

CGC RESTORED GRADE
Captain America Comics #1
Timely Comics, 3/41
Restoration includes: color touch, pieces added, reinforced, staples cleaned.
OFF-WHITE Pages

The Grading Begins

After being examined by a Restoration Detection Specialist, the book is then passed on to the graders. At this stage the comics have been properly sleeved and barcoded for grading and have been separated from their original invoice. This step is taken to ensure that graders do not know whose books they are grading, as a further guarantee of impartiality. The grading process begins by having the book's pages counted and entering into the computer any peculiarities or flaws that may affect a book's grade. Some examples of this would be "a tear on third page," "a corner crease – does not break color," "a 1/4" inch spine split," and so forth. This information is entered into the "Graders Notes" field and a grade is assigned.

When other graders examine the comic, they are not able to see any previous assigned grades, so as to not influence their evaluation. Graders are only able to view previous Graders Notes after determining their own grade. The Grader may then add to the existing commentary if he believes more remarks are in order. The Grading Finalizer is the last person to examine the book. He makes a final restoration check before determining his own grade, at which time he reviews the grades and notes entered by the previous graders. If all grades are in agreement or are very close, he will assign the book's final grade. The book is then forwarded to the Encapsulation Department for sealing. If there is disagreement among the graders, a discussion will ensue until a final determination is made and the book forwarded.

Encapsulating the Comics

After each comic has been graded and the necessary numbers and text entered into their respective data fields, all the comics on a particular invoice are taken from the Grading Department into the Encapsulation Department. Here, appropriately color-coded labels are printed bearing the proper descriptive text, including each book's grade and identification number. This is critical, as it serves to make each certified comic unique and is also a significant deterrent to counterfeiting CGC's valued product. All of the above information is duplicated in a barcode, which appears underneath the written text on the comic's label.

The newly-printed labels are stacked in the same sequence as the comics to be encapsulated with them, ensuring that each book and its label match one another. The comic is now ready to be fitted inside an archival-quality interior well, which is then sealed within a transparent capsule, along with the book's color-coded label. This is accomplished through a combination of compression and ultrasonic vibration.

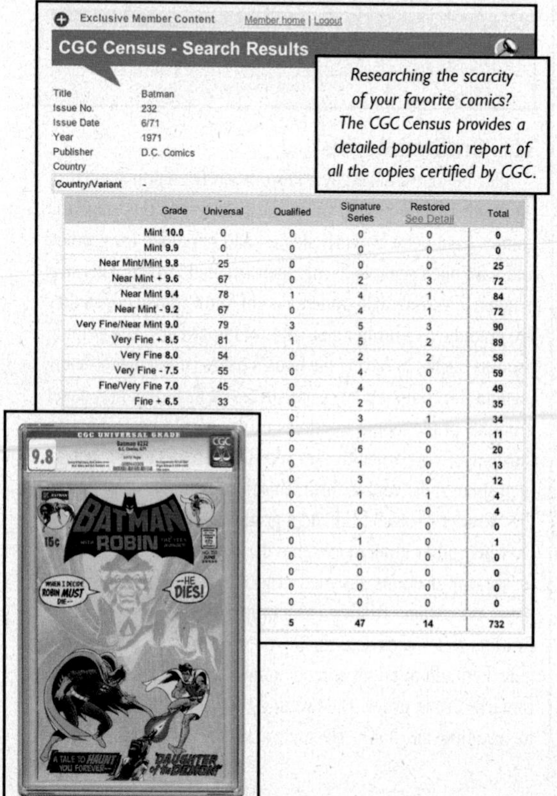

CGC Census - Search Results

Title: Batman
Issue No.: 232
Issue Date: 6/71
Year: 1971
Publisher: D.C. Comics
Country:
Country/Variant: -

Grade	Universal	Qualified	Signature Series	Restored See Detail	Total
Mint 10.0	0	0	0	0	0
Mint 9.9	0	0	0	0	0
Near Mint/Mint 9.8	25	0	0	0	25
Near Mint + 9.6	67	0	2	3	72
Near Mint 9.4	78	1	4	1	84
Near Mint - 9.2	67	0	4	1	72
Very Fine/Near Mint 9.0	79	3	5	3	90
Very Fine + 8.5	81	1	5	2	89
Very Fine 8.0	54	0	2	2	58
Very Fine - 7.5	55	0	4	0	59
Fine/Very Fine 7.0	45	0	4	0	49
Fine + 6.5	33	0	2	0	35
		0	3	1	34
		0	1	0	11
		0	5	0	20
		0	1	0	13
		0	3	0	12
		0	1	1	4
		0	0	0	4
		0	0	0	0
		0	1	0	1
		0	0	0	0
		0	0	0	0
		0	0	0	0
		0	0	0	0
		5	47	14	732

Researching the scarcity of your favorite comics? The CGC Census provides a detailed population report of all the copies certified by CGC.

The Comics are Shipped

After encapsulation, all comics are returned briefly to the Grading Department for a quality control inspection. Here, they are examined to make certain that their labels are correct for both the grade and its accompanying descriptive information. Quality control also inspects each book for any flaws in its holder, such as scuffs or nicks. While these are quite rare, CGC is careful to make certain that the comics it certifies are not only accurately graded, but attractively presented as well. When all the comics have been inspected, they're delivered to our Shipping Department for packaging. The comics are counted and their labels checked against the original invoice to make certain that no mistakes have occurred. A Shipping Department employee then verifies the method of transport as selected by the submitter on the invoice and prepares the comics for delivery or they are held in CGC's vault for in-person pick-up by the submitter.

No matter whether the US Postal Service or some private carrier is used, the method of packaging is essentially the same. The encapsulated comics are placed vertically inside sturdy cardboard boxes. In 2005, CGC developed a custom shipping box to enable the highest level of stability during shipping. A copy of the submitter's invoice is included before the box is sealed and heavy tape is used to prevent accidental or unauthorized opening of the box while it's in transit.

The barcode of every comic book is scanned before it is placed into its shipping box. The status of the book is changed to "shipped" in our tracking system, and we retain a record of what books were shipped in which box. This is the final crucial step of our detailed internal tracking system.

The CGC Label

Comic books certified by CGC bear color-coded labels that have different meanings. Whenever purchasing a CGC-certified comic, be certain to note not only the book's grade but also its label category. A Universal label is denoted by the color blue and indicates that a book was not found to have any qualifying defects or signs of restoration. There is one exception to this policy: At CGC's discretion, comics having a very minor amount of glue and/or color touch-up may still qualify for a Universal label provided that they were produced approximately 1950 or earlier and that such restoration is noted underneath the assigned grade.

As its name implies, the Restored label, identified by its purple color, is used for books found to have restoration work performed on them. The grade assigned is based on the book's appearance, with the restoration noted. A distinction is made between Amateur and Professional restoration, this judgment being based on the materials used. Since the degree of work performed is also significant with restored books, there are a total of seven possible descriptions under the Restored label. Each description is prefaced with the word

Apparent, followed by Slight, Moderate or Extensive in combination with the final descriptors Amateur or Professional. Examples of Restored labels might read Apparent Moderate Professional or Apparent Slight Amateur, both descriptions then being followed by the book's grade. Finally, comics which have had no restoration other than a trimming of their covers or edges are labeled as simply Apparent, followed by their grade.

The Qualified label is green, and this indicates that one qualifying defect is present on a book. An example of such a qualifying feature would be a missing Marvel Value Stamp that does not affect the story. While such a book technically may grade 1.5, it may appear to grade 9.6. In such instances, assigning a grade of just 1.5 does not fully represent the value of the comic to a collector. Through use of the green Qualified label, a comic buyer is able to make an informed decision as to what he is purchasing in terms of its overall desirability. Because of the complexity involved, green labels are assigned quite seldom and then only when considered absolutely necessary. In addition, comic books that have an unwitnessed signature, and therefore are not eligible for the Signature Series label (see below), get the Qualified label. This is the most common use for the Qualified label. This shows what the grade of the book would have been if the signature was not present.

A Signature Series encapsulation provides an assurance of authenticity for the signature (and in some cases a sketch as well.) **The Walking Dead** team of Robert Kirkman and Tony Moore signed this copy.

CGC encapsulation is not limited to standard size comics. Magazines and small promotional comics are included as well.

CGC's Signature Series label is yellow, and this is used when a comic book has been signed or been sketched on by a creator in the presence of a CGC representative, assuring the signature's or sketch's authenticity. Only books that meet CGC's strict criteria for authenticity are eligible for the Signature Series label. In addition to the certified grade, the yellow label includes who signed it and when it was signed. If appropriate, a Signature Series label may state where a book was signed. In 2007, CGC introduced a Signature Series Restored label. Similar to the CGC Signature Series label in color, it is differentiated by a purple bar across the top. Restoration is noted in the same fashion as on the purple CGC Restored label, and, as with the regular Signature Series label, restored books must be signed in the presence of CGC representatives in order to be eligible for signature authentication.

In October of 2003, CGC began to certify comic book related magazines. The certification process and label system for magazines is exactly the same as for comic books. Some examples of comic book related magazines CGC certifies are *MAD Magazine*, *Vampirella*, *Creepy*, *Eerie* and *Famous Monsters of Filmland*.

More recently CGC introduced grading and encapsulation for *Sports Illustrated* and *Playboy* magazines, Movie Lobby Cards and Photographs making us the first independent, impartial, expert third-party grading service for all types of collectibles.

For more information on comic book certification and CGC's many services, please visit our website at www.CGCcomics.com

FEATURE ARTICLE INDEX

Over the years, *The Overstreet Comic Book Price Guide* has grown into much more than a simple catalog of values. Almost since the very beginning, Bob has worked hard to make sure that the book reflects the latest information about the hobby, and this has resulted in some fascinating in-depth articles about aspects of the industry and the rich history of comics. Sadly, many of you may never have read a lot of these articles, or even knew they existed.

These two pages contain a comprehensive index to every feature article ever published in *The Overstreet Comic Book Price Guide*. From interviews with legendary creators to exhaustively researched retrospectives, it's all here. Enjoy this look back at the Overstreet legacy, and remember, many of these editions are still available through Gemstone and your local comic book dealer.

Note: The first three editions of *The Guide* had no feature articles, but from #4 on, a tradition was born that has carried through to the very volume. This index begins with the 4th edition and lists all articles published up to and including last year's 41st edition of *The Guide*.

AUTHOR (S)	TITLE	EDITION	PGS.
Adams, Weldon	Comics in the Schools - 1926: The Lost Comic Book History of the Lone Star State	#35 (2005)	1001-1006
Andrae, Thomas	The Enduring Magic of Disney Comics (written with Bruce Hamilton)	#17 (1987)	A-85-90
	Of Superman and Kids With Dreams: An Interview with Jerry Siegel and Joe Shuster	#18 (1988)	A-79-98
	Origins of the Dark Knight: A Conversation with Batman Artists (with Bob Kane and Jerry Robinson)	#19 (1989)	A-72-93
	Green Lantern's Light! A History by... (with Keif Fromm)	#23 (1993)	A-71-79
Bails, Jerry	Secrets Behind All-Star Comics (More Than You May Want to Know)	#04 (1974)	26-37
Barrington, Stephen	Supergirl: Back for Justice	#36 (2006)	1048-1051
Beck, C.C.	Mr. Mind and the Monster Society of Evil	#15 (1985)	A-89-93
Beerbohm, Robert L.	The American Comic Book: 1897-1932 The Beginning: The Platinum Age	#27 (1997)	1-15
	New Discoveries Beyond the Platinum Age (with Richard D. Olson, Ph.D.)	#30 (2000)	226-234
	The Golden Age and Beyond: Origins of the Modern Comic Book (written with Richard D. Olson, Ph.D.)	#30 (2000)	242-249
Blumberg, Arnold T.	Gotham Knights - A Conversation with Jerry Robinson	#27 (1997)	A-25-27
	The World of Tomorrow: How Comics of the Past Portrayed the 1990s	#28 (1998)	82-88
	Invasion of the Giant (and Not So Giant) Robots!	#28 (1998)	83-87
	One For All and All for One	#29 (1999)	107-112
	History with a Twist	#30 (2000)	18-22
	The Marketing of a Medium	#30 (2000)	195-198
	Why the Fantastic Four Made it to Forty	#31 (2001)	20-24
	Brownie Points	#31 (2001)	30-32
	Re-Creations in a Flash (Murphy Anderson profile)	#31 (2001)	39-40
	Superman: Patriotic Covers Through the Years	#32 (2002)	40-43
	Spidey Goes Hollywood	#32 (2002)	44-46
	Mutant Movie Stars: The "New" X-Men Storm the Silver Screen	#33 (2003)	854-856
	Through Waves and Flames: The Elemental Entrance of the Sub-Mariner	#33 (2003)	858-860
	Comic Book Ages: Start the Discussion (with J.C. Vaughn)	#33 (2003)	866-867
	Comic Book Ages: Defining Eras (with J.C. Vaughn)	#34 (2004)	948-951
	Going Green: The Best of the Hulk	#34 (2004)	956-959
Boatner, E. B.	Carl Barks: From Burbank to Calisota	#07 (1977)	A-37-57
	Good Lord! choke...gasp...It's EC!	#09 (1979)	A-43-76
	L. B. Cole: The Man Behind the Mask	#11 (1981)	A-55-72
Bonney, Brady	The Comic Book Legal Defense Fund	#41 (2011)	1076-1077
Borock, Steve	Comic Book Certification: An Overview of Comic Guaranty, LLC.	#35 (2005)	1007-1011
	An Insiders Look at CGC and Comic Book Certification	#36 (2006)	1044-1047
	CGC, The Art and Science of Comic Book Certification	#37 (2007)	1036-1039
	A CGC Primer: How Professional Comic Book Certification Works	#38 (2008)	1052-1055

AUTHOR (S)	TITLE	EDITION	PGS.
Braden, Scott	Strange Adventures - A Conversation with Murphy Anderson	#27 (1997)	A-30-32
	Built to Last (with J.C. Vaughn)	#28 (1998)	89-102
Brown, Nicky Wheeler-Nicholson	Major Malcolm Wheeler-Nicholson	#41 (2011)	1074-1075
Calhoun, Pat S.	Living on Borrowed Time! A Nostalgic Look at the Early Years of DC's Challengers of the Unknown (with Gary M. Carter)	#24 (1994)	A-157-164
	100 Years - A Century of Comics	#25 (1995)	A-107-123
Carter, Gary M.	DC Before Superman (written with Ken Lane Carter)	#13 (1983)	A-72-86
	The Silver Age...The Beginning: A Comparative Chronology of the First Sliver Age Comic Books	#20 (1990)	A-94-107
	Journey into the Unknown World of Atlas Fantasy (written with Pat S. Calhoun)	#22 (1992)	A-87-103
	Silver Sagas of the Scarlet Speedster: Whirlwind Adventures of the Fastest Man Alive! 1956-1960	#23 (1993)	A-80-86
CGC Grading Team	A CGC Primer: How Professional Comic Book Certification Works	#39 (2009)	1029-1032
	CGC Turns 10: A Decade of Comic Book Certification Innovation	#40 (2010)	1007-1009
	The CGC Story - How the Company was Created and Our Grading Process	#41 (2011)	1037-1040
Chesney, Landon	The Archives of the Comic Book Price Guide	#06 (1976)	44-45
Colabuono, Gary	Golden Age Ashcans - Comics' First Editions (with Mark Zaid)	#38 (2008)	1040-1045
DeFuccio, Jerry	An Interview with Will Eisner, Creator of the Spirit	#06 (1976)	31-37
	Norman Mingo and Alfred: The World's Greatest Facelift	#12 (1982)	A-45-57
	Charles Clarence Beck: The World's Second Mightiest Mortal	#15 (1985)	A-78-88
Dempsey, "Little" Jimmy	Great Old Radio Premiums	#13 (1983)	A-62-63
DeStefano, Brandon	Comics at the Movies: A Brief History of Comic Characters on the Big Screen	#39 (2009)	1033-1039
Disbrow, Jay	Confessions of a Former Comic Book Artist	#08 (1978)	A-31-38
Estrada, Jackie	Friends of Lulu Sound Off on Comics	#28 (1998)	79-81
Fulop, Scott D.	Archie Comics Publications: The Mirth of a Legend	#21 (1991)	A-77-78
Hamilton, Bruce	The Mystery of the 12 Missing EC's	#25 (1995)	A-99-106
	Special Feature: Grading - The Next Revolution for Comic Books	#29 (1999)	17-21
Hancer, Kevin B.	Edgar Rice Burroughs and the Comics	#05 (1975)	33-38
Hessee, Tim	The Pop Hollinger Story: The First Comic Book Collector/Dealer	#12 (1982)	A-58-66
Huesman, Mark	Legiondary Adventures	#29 (1999)	101-106
Hughes, Rob	When the Bat Flew Alone!	#39 (2009)	1041-1054
	The Avenger of Blood: The Spectre	#41 (2011)	1066-1073
Irons, Christopher	The Man Behind the Cover - L. B. Cole	#18 (1988)	A-77
Kronenberg, Michael	Indelible Shadows: The Spectacular Rise of Artist Jim Lee	#36 (2006)	1052-1055
	Patriot Act!!! (Captain America profile)	#37 (2007)	1024-1029
Leavitt, Craig	Katy Keene - The Overstreet Connection	#14 (1984)	A-67-78
Lee, Stan	Twenty-Five Years? I Don't Believe It!	#16 (1986)	A-82-84
Marek, Carl, et al.	Good Girl Art - An Introduction: Why it Was and What it Was (produced by the American Comic Book Co.)	#06 (1976)	38-43
	Esoteric Comics: The Ultimate Collection (produced by the American Comic Book Co. in Consultation with Scott Shaw)	#07 (1977)	A-30-35
	Women in Comics (in collaboration with Art Amsie)	#08 (1978)	A-54-75
	For Those Who Know How to Look	#09 (1979)	A-35-42
McClure, Jon Martin	A History of Publisher Experimentation and Variant Comic Books	#40 (2010)	1010-1038
Miller, John Jackson	From "A Long Time Ago" To Today's Galaxy	#38 (2008)	1046-1051
Moore, Dale	Comic Book Charites: Lifelines of the Industry	#34 (2004)	964-966
Murray, Will	Marvel's Hammer: The Mighty Thor	#36 (2006)	1028-1039
	The Untold Origin of Daredevil	#37 (2007)	1030-1035
Novinskie, Charles S.	Sixty Years of Wonder Woman	#31 (2001)	26-29
	Conan #1: When Marvel Went Barbarian	#40 (2010)	1042-1043

AUTHOR (S)	TITLE	EDITION	PGS.
Novinskie, Charles S. (cont.)	1970: Television, Animation, & Adaptations	#40 (2010)	1044-1045
	The Hero Initiative	#41 (2011)	1078-1079
Olson, Richard D. Ph.D.	The American Comic Book: 1897-1932	#26 (1996)	1-2
	The American Comic Book: 1933-Present The Modern Comic Book	#26 (1996)	10-11
	The Golden Age and Beyond: The Modern Comic Book (Revised)	#27 (1997)	23-24
	The Golden Age and Beyond: The Modern Comic Book (Revised)	#28 (1998)	211-211
	My Friend, Leonard Brown	#40 (2010)	1050-1051
Olshevsky, George	The Origin of Marvel Comics	#10 (1980)	A-46-73
Overstreet, Robert M.	Bob's Bizarre Tales	#30 (2000)	42-63
	And When The Vault Was Opened... (with Gary M. Carter)	#38 (2008)	1036-1039
Overstreet Staff	The Man Behind the Cover - Ron Dias	#17 (1987)	A-84
Rausch, Barbara A.	Katy WHO?...Never Heard of it...	#14 (1984)	A-52-56
Ray, Benn	A Brief History of Super-Teams: Top Ten Greatest Super-Teams	#29 (1999)	108-112
Robbins, Trina	Tarpe Mills - An Appreication	#08 (1978)	A-76
Saffel, Steve	Spider-Man: An Amazing Success Story	#22 (1992)	A-77-86
Schiff, Jack	Reminiscience of a Comic Book Editor (with Gene Reed)	#13 (1983)	A-64-70
Seals, John	Standing on the Shoulders of Giants: The HERO Initiative	#39 (2009)	1025-1027
Shooter, Jim	Marvel and Me	#16 (1986)	A-85-96
Taylor, Terry	Walt Disney's Snow White and the Seven Dwarfs - Fifty Years of Collectibles	#17 (1987)	A-101-111
Thomas, Harry B.	1941: Comic Books Go To War: Those fabulous comics of World War II (with Gary M. Carter)	#21 (1991)	A-79-98
Townsend, John Ph.D.	Three Uncanny Decades of X-Men	#24 (1994)	A-146-156
Vaughn, J.C.	Built to Last (with Scott Braden)	#28 (1998)	89-102
	The American Comic Book: 1897 - 1932 In the Beginning: The Platinum Age	#28 (1998)	201-203
	Avenues of Collecting: A Walk Through the Comic Book Neighborhood	#29 (1999)	91-94
	Just Another Justice League?	#29 (1999)	95-100
	EC, MAD and Beyond: Al Feldstein	#30 (2000)	24-28
	Flights to EC and Beyond with Al Williamson	#30 (2000)	36-39
	Extraordinary! (John K. Snyder III profile)	#31 (2001)	42-44
	Bendis! (Brian Michael Bendis profile)	#31 (2001)	46-48
	Archie at 60	#32 (2002)	47-49
	A Brief History of the Justice Society	#33 (2003)	850-852
	Variant Watch: Ultimate Spider-Man #1	#33 (2003)	862-863
	Comic Book Ages: Start the Discussion (with Arnold T. Blumberg)	#33 (2003)	866-867
	Comic Book Ages: Defining Eras (with Arnold T. Blumberg)	#34 (2004)	948-951
	70 Years and Still Quacking	#34 (2004)	952-955
	(Joe) Simon Says	#34 (2004)	960-963
	Enduring Duo: Wolfman & Perez (Teen Titans at 25, Crisis at 20)	#35 (2005)	993-995
	Little Lulu at 70 (and 60)	#35 (2005)	996-997
	Iron Man: Heavy Metal	#35 (2005)	998-1000
	Publisher Spotlight: Dark Horse Comics	#35 (2005)	1012-1013
	Wonder Woman: Revisited and Renewed	#36 (2006)	1041-1043
	The Semi-Secret Origins of The Overstreet Comic Book Price Guide (Bob Overstreet interview)	#37 (2007)	1016-1023
	Perspective on History: Stephen Fishler	#40 (2010)	1052-1053
Ward, Bill	The Man Behind Torchy	#08 (1978)	A-40-53
Weist, Jerry	The Golden Age and Beyond: A Short History of Comic Book Fandom & Comic Book Collecting in America	#26 (1996)	652-667
Zaid, Mark	Golden Age Ashcans - Comics' First Editions (with Gary Colabuono)	#38 (2008)	1040-1045
Zone, Ray	Anaglyphs - A Survey of 3-D Comic Books	#11 (1981)	A-44-53

OVERSTREET ADVISORS

WELDON ADAMS
Comics Historian
Fort Worth, TX

GRANT ADEY
Fats Comics
Brisbane, QLD, Australia

BILL ALEXANDER
Collector
Sacramento, CA

DAVID T. ALEXANDER
David Alexander Comics
Tampa, FL

TYLER ALEXANDER
David Alexander Comics
Tampa, FL

LON ALLEN
Heritage Comics Auctions
Dallas, TX

DAVE ANDERSON
Want List Comics
Tulsa, OK

STEPHEN BARRINGTON
Flea Market Comics
Chickasaw, AL

LAUREN BECKER
Warp 9 Comics
Clawson, MI

ROBERT BEERBOHM
Robert Beerbohm Comic Art
Fremont, NE

JON BERK
Collector
Hartford, CT

JIM BERRY
Collector
Portland, OR

JON BEVANS
Diamond Int. Galleries
Timonium, MD

PETER BILELIS, ESQ.
Collector
South Windsor, CT

BRIAN BLOCK
WB Auction Services
Adamstown, PA

DR. ARNOLD T. BLUMBERG
Collector
Baltimore, MD

STEVE BOROCK
Heritage Comics Auctions
Dallas, TX

KEVIN BOYD
Collector
Toronto, ONT Canada

MICHAEL BROWNING
Collector
Danville, WV

SHAWN CAFFREY
Finalizer/Modern Age Specialist
Certified Guaranty Co., LLC

MICHAEL CARBONARO
Mike Carbo's Comic Box
Long Island City, NY

BRETT CARRERAS
Brett's Comic Pile
Richmond, VA

GARY CARTER
Collector
Coronado, CA

JOHN CHRUSCINSKI
Tropic Comics
Lyndora, PA

GARY COLABUONO
Dealer/Collector
Arlington Heights, IL

BILL COLE
Bill Cole Enterprises, Inc.
Randolph, MA

TIM COLLINS
RTS Unlimited, Inc.
Lakewood, CO

ANDREW COOKE
Writer/Director
New York City, NY

JON B. COOKE
Editor - Comic Book Artist Magazine
West Kingston, RI

JACK COPLEY
Coliseum of Comics
Florida

JESSE JAMES CRISCIONE
Jesse James Comics
Glendale, AZ

DAN CUSIMANO
Flying Donut Trading Co.
Reston, VA

FRANK CWIKLIK
Metropolis Comics
New York, NY

OVERSTREET ADVISORS

BROCK DICKINSON
Collector
St. Catharines, ONT
Canada

PETER DIXON
Paradise Comics
Toronto, ONT
Canada

GARY DOLGOFF
Gary Dolgoff Comics
Easthampton, MA

WALTER DURAJLIJA
Big B Comics
Hamilton, ONT
Canada

KEN DYBER
Cloud 9 Comics
Portland, OR

BRUCE ELLSWORTH
Bruce's Comics and
Collectibles
Waihee, HI

CONRAD ESCHENBERG
Collector/Dealer
Cold Spring, NY

MICHAEL EURY
Author
Concord, NC

RICHARD EVANS
Bedrock City Comics
Houston, TX

D'ARCY FARRELL
Pendragon Comics
Toronto, ONT Canada

JOSEPH FIORE
ComicWiz.com
Toronto, ONT Canada

STEPHEN FISHLER
Metropolis Collectibles,
Inc.
New York, NY

DAN FOGEL
Hippy Comix, Inc.
El Sobrante, CA

STEPHEN H. GENTNER
Golden Age Specialist
Portland, OR

STEVE GEPPI
Diamond Int. Galleries
Timonium, MD

DOUG GILLOCK
ComicLink
Portland, ME

MICHAEL GOLDMAN
Motor City Comics
Farmington Hills, MI

TOM GORDON III
Collector/Dealer
Westminster, MD

JAMIE GRAHAM
Graham Crackers
Chicago, IL

DANIEL GREENHALGH
Showcase New England
Northford, CT

ERIC J. GROVES
Dealer/Collector
Oklahoma City, OK

JOHN HAINES
Dealer/Collector
Kirtland, OH

JIM HALPERIN
Heritage Comics
Auctions
Dallas, TX

JASON HAMLIN
Brett's Comic Pile
Richmond, VA

MARK HASPEL
Finalizer/
Pedigree Specialist
Certified Guaranty Co.,

JOHN HAUSER
Dealer/Collector
New Berlin, WI

JEF HINDS
Jef Hinds Comics
Madison, WI

GREG HOLLAND, Ph.D.
Collector
Alexander, AR

JOHN HONE
Collector
Silver Spring, MD

BILL HUGHES
Dealer/Collector
Flower Mound, TX

ROB HUGHES
Arch Angels
Pacific Beach, CA

ED JASTER
Heritage Comics Auctions
Dallas, TX

BRIAN KETTERER
Collector
Baltimore, MD

OVERSTREET ADVISORS

DENNIS KEUM
Fantasy Comics
Goldens Bridge, NY

PHIL LEVINE
Paperpeddler Rare and Esoteric Comics and Collectibles
Three Bridges, NJ

BEN LICHTENSTEIN
Zapp Comics
Wayne, NJ

PAUL LITCH
Primary Grader
Certified Guaranty Co., LLC

TOMMY MALETTA
Best Comics International
New Hyde Park, NY

JOE MANNARINO
All Star Auctions
Ridgewood, NJ

NADIA MANNARINO
All Star Auctions
Ridgewood, NJ

HARRY MATETSKY
Collector
Middletown, NJ

DAVE MATTEINI
Collector
Mineola, NY

JON McCLURE
Comics Historian, Writer
Portland, OR

TODD McDEVITT
New Dimension Comics
Cranberry Township, PA

MIKE McKENZIE
Alternate Worlds
Cockeysville, MD

FRED McSURLEY
Dealer/Collector
Holland, Ohio

PETER MEROLO
Collector
Sedona, AZ

JOHN JACKSON MILLER
Comics Historian, Writer
Scandinavia, WI

BRENT MOESHLIN
Quality Comix
Montgomery, AL

STEVE MORTENSEN
Miracle Comics
Santa Clara, CA

MICHAEL NAIMAN
Silver Age Specialist
Chapel Hill, NC

MARC NATHAN
Cards, Comics & Collectibles
Reisterstown, MD

JOSHUA NATHANSON
ComicLink
Portland, ME

MATT NELSON
Classics Incorporated
Carrolltown, TX

TOM NELSON
Top Notch Comics
Yankton, SD

JAMIE NEWBOLD
Southern California Comics
San Diego, CA

CHARLIE NOVINSKIE
Silver Age Specialist
Lake Havasu City, AZ

RICHARD OLSON
Collector/Academician
Poplarville, MS

TERRY O'NEILL
Terry's Comics
Orange, CA

MICHAEL PAVLIC
Purple Gorilla Comics
Calgary, AB Canada

JIM PAYETTE
Golden Age Specialist
Bethlehem, NH

JOHN PETTY
Collector/Historian
Coram, NY

JIM PITTS
Avalon Collectibles
Mountain View, CA

BILL PONSETI
Collector
Newtown Sq., PA

RON PUSSELL
Redbeard's Book Den
Crystal Bay, NV

JEFF RADER
Paperpeddler
Rare and Esoteric Comics and Collectibles
Lake Havasu, AZ

OVERSTREET ADVISORS

GREG REECE
Greg Reece's Rare Comics
Ijamsville, MD

STEPHEN RITTER
Worldwide Comics
Carrolltown, TX

DAVE ROBIE
Big Little Books
Specialist
Lancaster, PA

ROBERT ROGOVIN
Four Color Comics
Scarsdale, NY

MARNIN ROSENBERG
Collectors Assemble
Great Neck, NY

CHUCK ROZANSKI
Mile High Comics
Denver, CO

BARRY SANDOVAL
Heritage Comics Auctions
Dallas, TX

BUDDY SAUNDERS
Lone Star Comics
Arlington, TX

CONAN SAUNDERS
Lone Star Comics
Arlington, TX

MATT SCHIFFMAN
Bronze Age Specialist
Bend, OR

DOUG SCHMELL
Pedigree Comics, Inc.
Wellington, FL

BRIAN SCHUTZER
Sparkle City Comics
Neat Stuff Collectibles
North Bergen, NJ

ALIKA SEKI
Bruce's Comics and
Collectibles
Waihee, HI

DOUG SIMPSON
Paradise Comics
Toronto, ONT Canada

BEN SMITH
ComicConnect
New York, NY

MARK SQUIREK
Collector
Timonium, MD

TONY STARKS
Silver Age Specialist
Evansville, IN

AL STOLTZ
Basement Comics
Havre de Grace, MD

KEN STRIBLING
Action Island
Jackson, MS

DOUG SULIPA
"Everything 1960-1996"
Manitoba, Canada

CHRIS SWARTZ
Collector
San Diego, CA

MAGGIE THOMPSON
Comics Buyer's Guide
Iola, WI

MICHAEL TIERNEY
The Comic Book Store
Little Rock, AR

TED VAN LIEW
Superworld Comics
Worcester, MA

JOE VERENEAULT
JHV Associates
Woodbury Heights, NJ

BOB WAYNE
DC Comics
New York City, NY

LON WEBB
Dark Adventure Comics
Norcross, GA

RICK WHITELOCK
New Force Comics
Lynn Haven, FL

MIKE WILBUR
Diamond Int. Galleries
Timonium, MD

MARK WILSON
PGC Mint
Castle Rock, WA

ALEX WINTER
Hake's Americana
York, PA

HARLEY YEE
Dealer/Collector
Detroit, MI

MARK ZAID
EsquireComics.com
Bethesda, MD

VINCENT ZURZOLO, JR.
Metropolis Collectibles, Inc.
New York, NY

OVERSTREET PRICE GUIDE BACK ISSUES

The Overstreet® Comic Book Price Guide has held the record for being the longest running annual comic book publication. We are now celebrating our 42nd anniversary, and the demand for the Overstreet® price guides is very strong. Collectors have created a legitimate market for them, and they continue to bring record prices each year. Collectors also have a record of comic book prices going back further than any other source in comic fandom. The prices listed below are for NM condition only, with GD-25% and FN-50% of the NM value. Canadian editions exist for a couple of the early issues. Abbreviations: SC-softcover, HC-hardcover, L-leather bound.

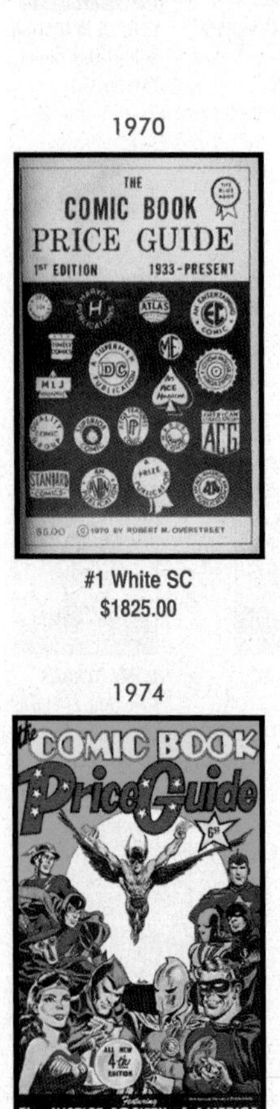

1970

#1 White SC
$1825.00

1970

#1 Blue SC
(2nd Printing)
$1550.00

1972

#2 SC $650.00
#2 HC $1100.00

1973

#3 SC $325.00
#3 HC $950.00

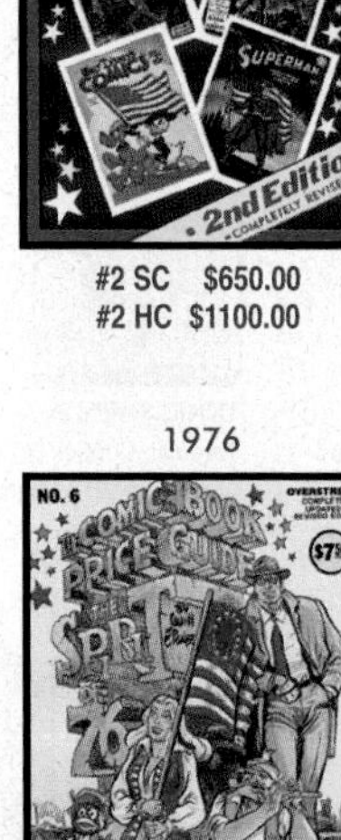

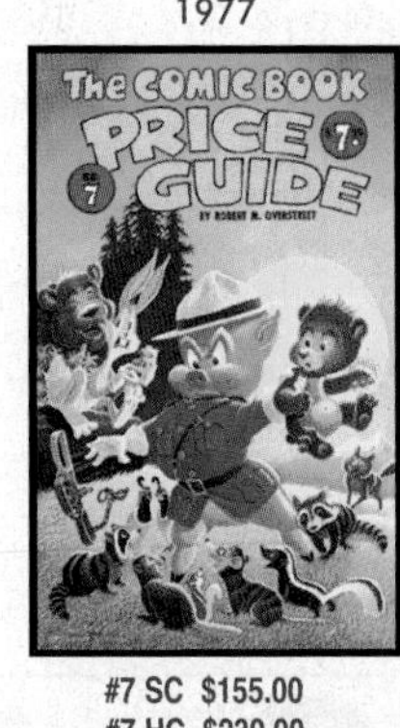

1974

#4 SC $165.00
#4 HC $475.00

1975

#5 SC $155.00
#5 HC $260.00

1976

#6 SC $105.00
#6 HC $155.00

1977

#7 SC $155.00
#7 HC $230.00

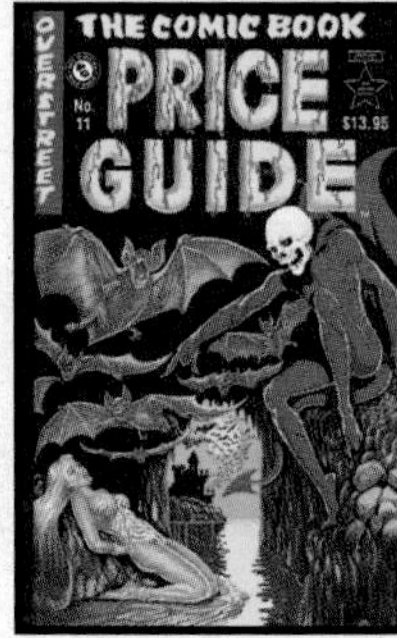

1978

#8 SC $130.00
#8 HC $180.00

1979

#9 SC $130.00
#9 HC $180.00

1980

#10 SC $140.00
#10 HC $190.00

1981

#11 SC $85.00
#11 HC $115.00

1982

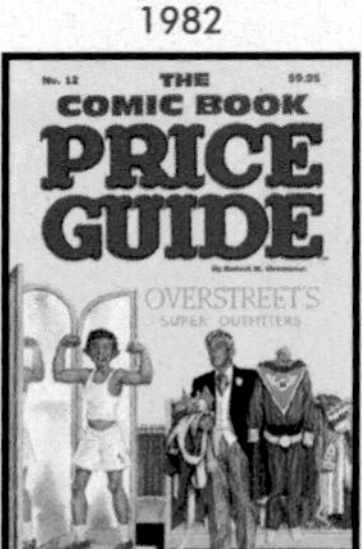

#12 SC $85.00
#12 HC $115.00

1983

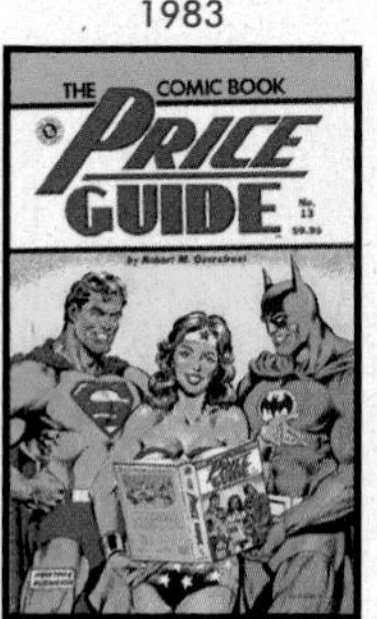

#13 SC $85.00
#13 HC $115.00

1984

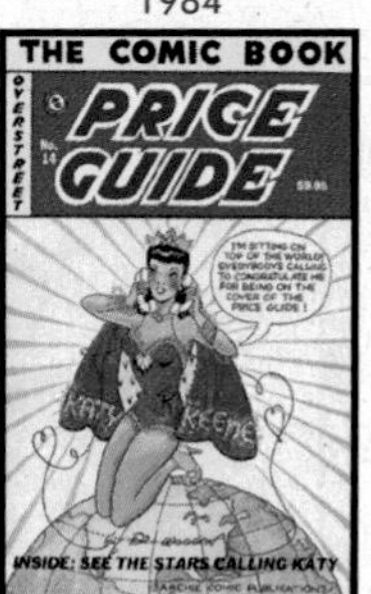

#14 SC $55.00
#14 HC $110.00
#14 L $170.00

1985

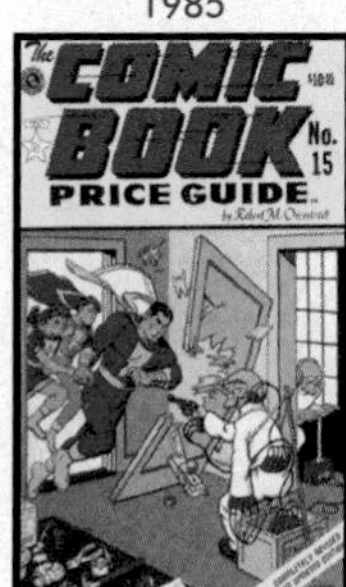

#15 SC $55.00
#15 HC $80.00
#15 L $160.00

1986

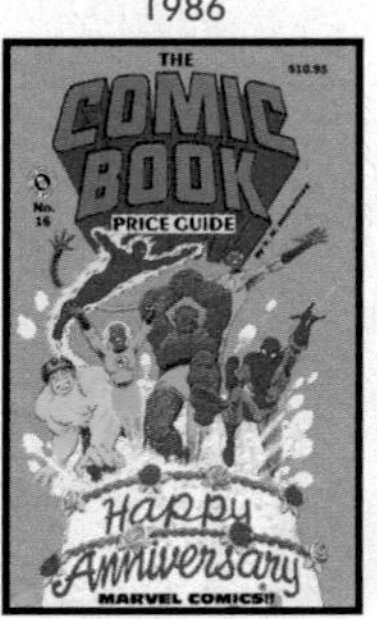

#16 SC $60.00
#16 HC $85.00
#16 L $170.00

1987

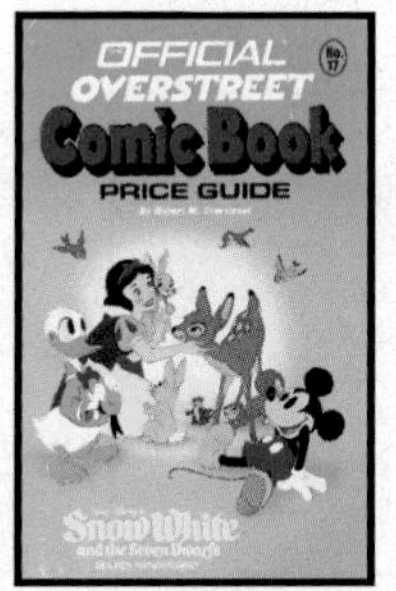

#17 SC $55.00
#17 HC $110.00
#17 L $160.00

1988

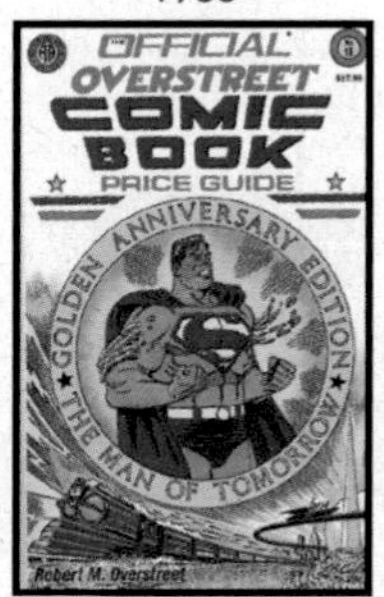

#18 SC $45.00
#18 HC $65.00
#18 L $160.00

1989

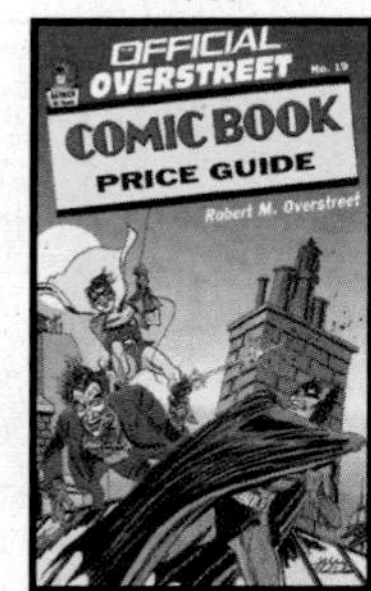

#19 SC $50.00
#19 HC $60.00
#19 L $170.00

1990

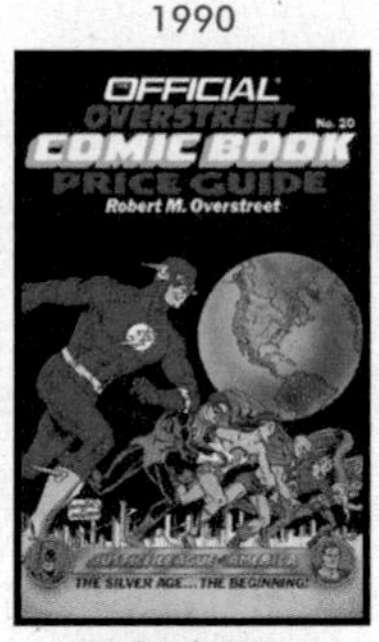

#20 SC $32.00
#20 HC $50.00
#20 L $135.00

1991

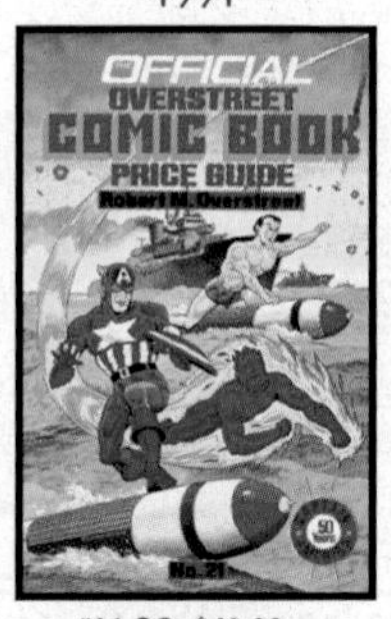

#21 SC $40.00
#21 HC $60.00
#21 L $145.00

1992

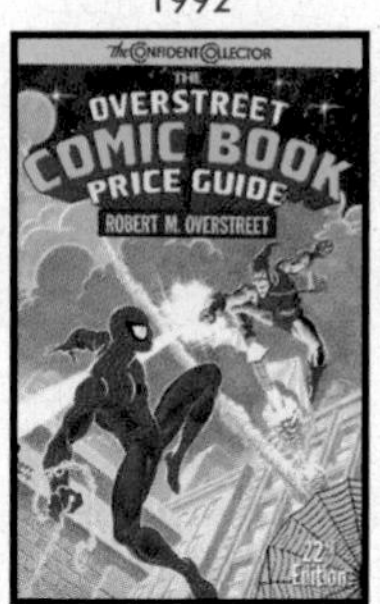

#22 SC $32.00
#22 HC $50.00

1993

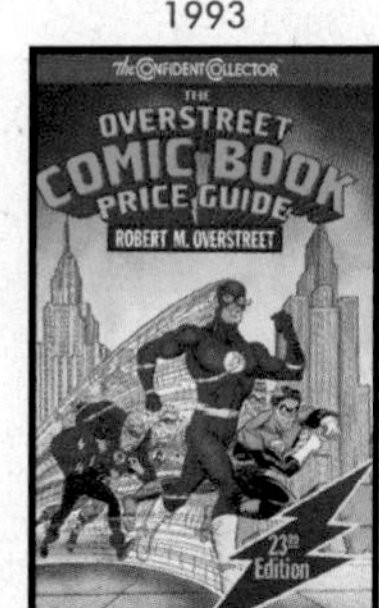

#23 SC $32.00
#23 HC $50.00

1994

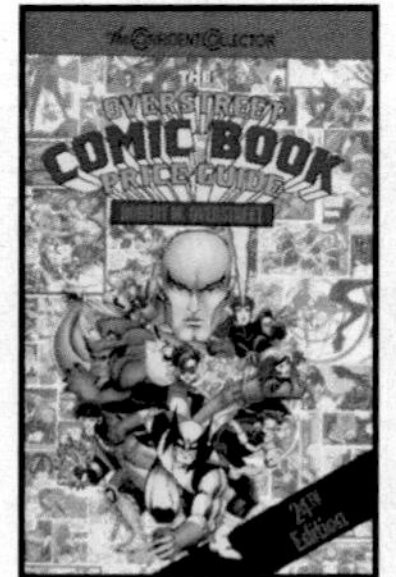

#24 SC $26.00
#24 HC $36.00

1995

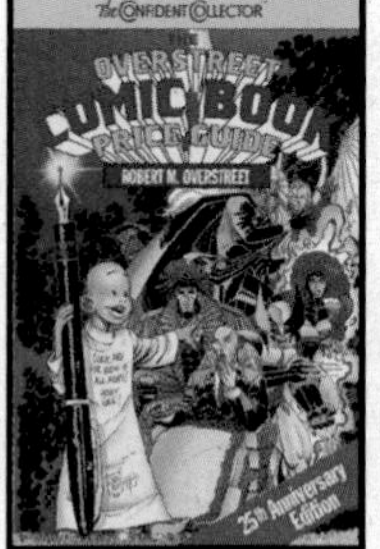

#25 SC $26.00
#25 HC $36.00
#25 L $110.00

1996

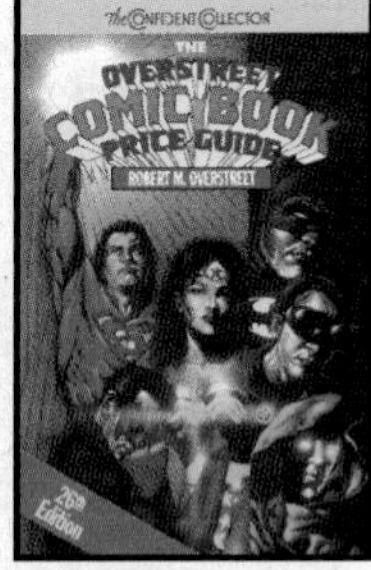

#26 SC $20.00
#26 HC $30.00
#26 L $100.00

1997

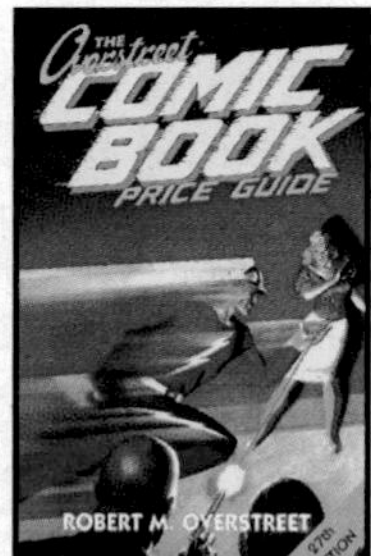

#27 SC $22.00
#27 HC $38.00
#27 L $125.00

1997

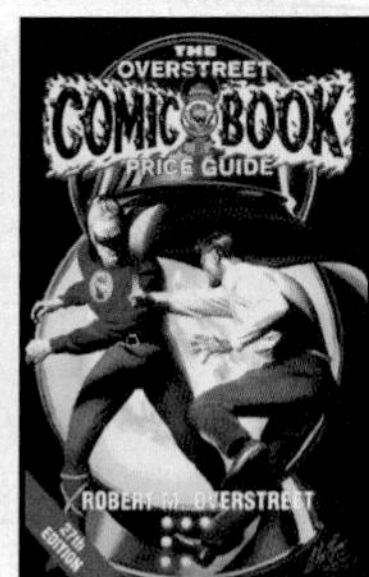

#27 SC $22.00
#27 HC $38.00
#27 L $125.00

1998

#28 SC $20.00
#28 HC $35.00

1998

#28 SC $20.00
#28 HC $35.00

1999

#29 SC $25.00
#29 HC $40.00

1999

#29 SC $20.00
#29 HC $37.00

2000

#30 SC $22.00
#30 HC $32.00

2000

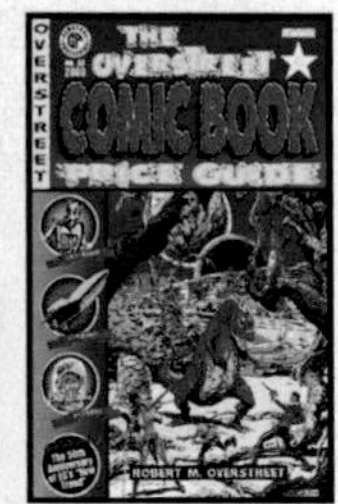

#30 SC $22.00
#30 HC $32.00

2001

#31 SC $22.00
#31 HC $32.00

2001

#31 SC $22.00
#31 HC $32.00

2001

#31 Bookstore Ed.
SC only $22.00

2002

#32 SC $22.00
#32 HC $32.00

2002

#32 SC $22.00
#32 HC $32.00

2002

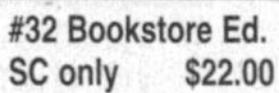

#32 Bookstore Ed.
SC only $22.00

2003

#33 SC $25.00
#33 HC $32.00

2003

#33 SC $25.00
#33 HC $32.00

2003

#33 Bookstore Ed.
SC only $25.00

2004

#34 SC $25.00
#34 HC $32.00

2004

#34 SC $25.00
#34 HC $32.00

2004

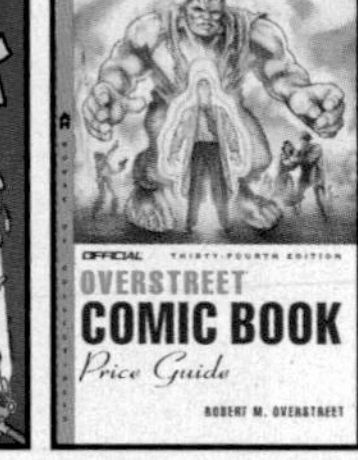

#34 Bookstore Ed.
SC only $25.00

2005

#35 SC $25.00
#35 HC $32.00

2005

#35 SC $25.00
#35 HC $55.00

2005

#35 Bookstore Ed.
SC only $25.00

2006

#36 SC $25.00
#36 HC $32.00

2006

#36 SC $25.00
#36 HC $32.00

2006

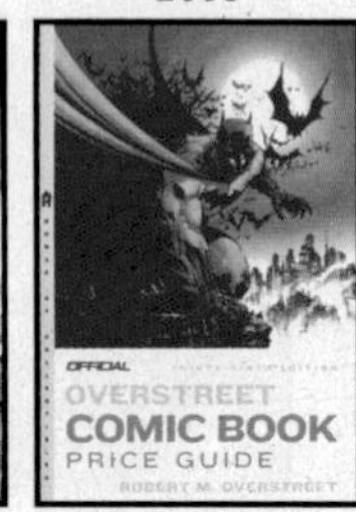

#36 Bookstore Ed.
SC only $25.00

2007

#37 SC $30.00
#37 HC $35.00

2007

#37 SC $30.00
#37 HC $35.00

2007

#37 Bookstore Ed.
SC only $30.00

2008

#38 SC $30.00
#38 HC $35.00

2008

#38 SC $30.00
#38 HC $35.00

2008

#38 Bookstore Ed.
SC only $30.00

2009

#39 SC $30.00
#39 HC $35.00

2009

#39 SC $30.00
#39 HC $35.00

2009

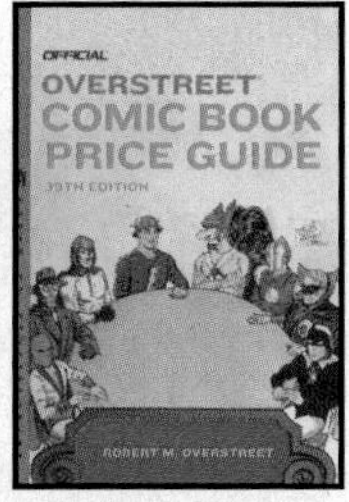

#39 Bookstore Ed.
SC only $30.00

2010

#40 SC $30.00
#40 HC $35.00

2010

#40 SC $30.00
#40 HC $35.00

2010

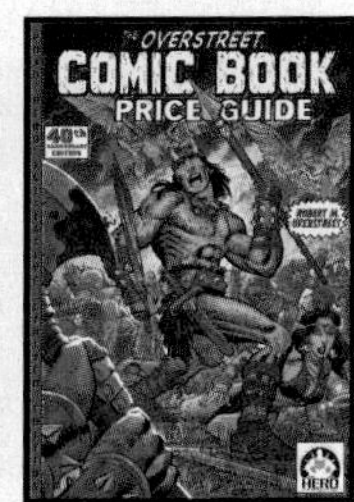

#40 HERO Initiative Ed.
HC only $35.00

2011

#41 SC $30.00
#41 HC $35.00

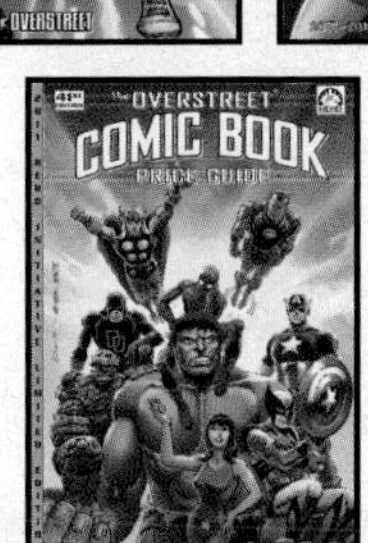

#41 HERO Initiative Ed.
HC only $35.00

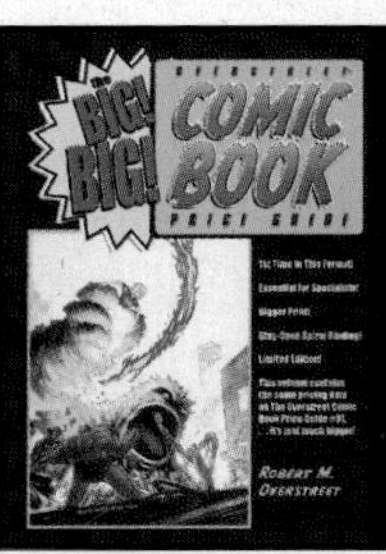

#31 Workbook - 2001
$35.00

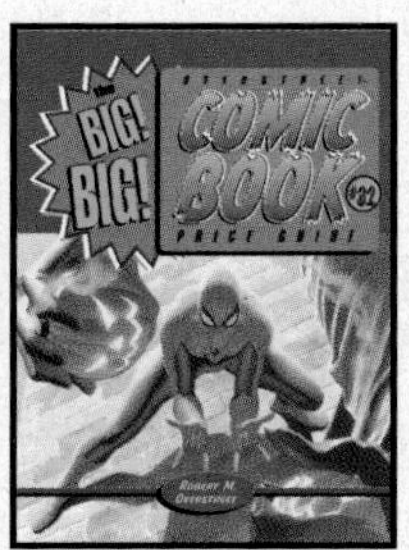

#32 Workbook - 2002
$35.00

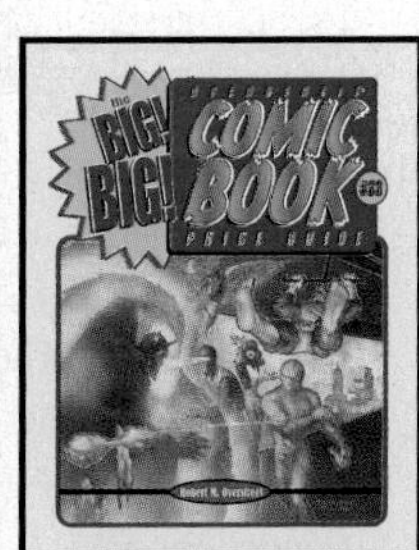

#33 Workbook - 2003
$37.00

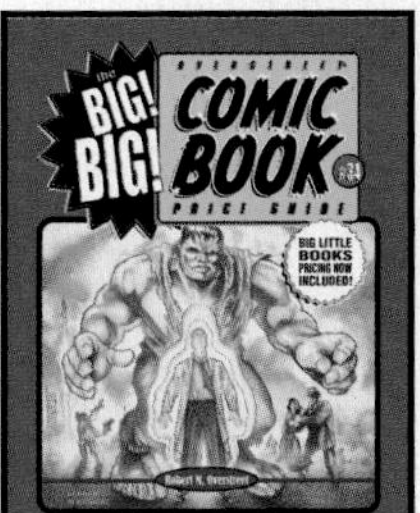

#34 Workbook - 2004
$37.00

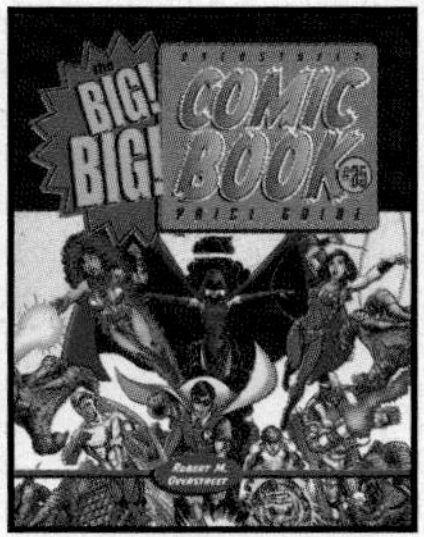

#35 Workbook - 2005
$37.00

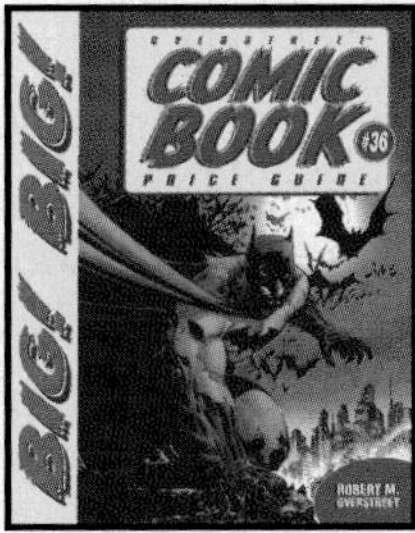

#36 Workbook - 2006
$37.00

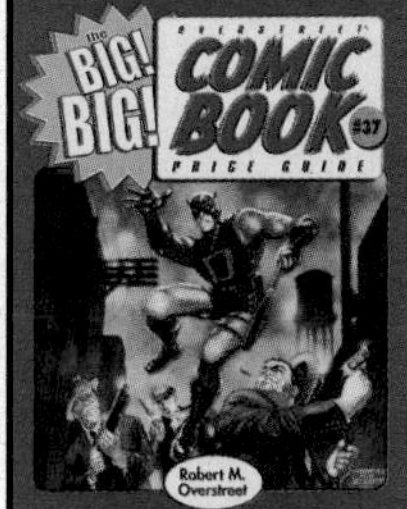

#37 Workbook - 2007
$37.00

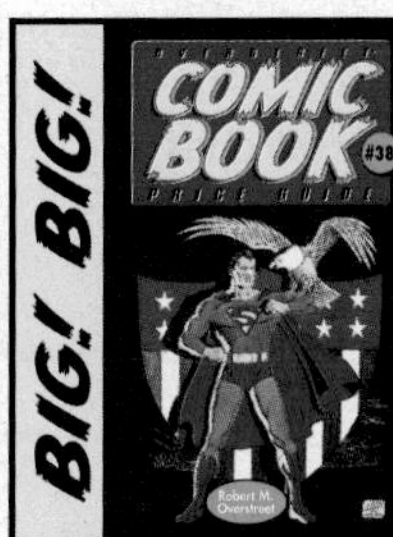

#38 Workbook - 2008
$37.00

ADVERTISERS' INDEX

A

B

C

D

E

F

G

H

7.5
MAY, 1939
No. 27
Detective COMICS
10¢
THE BATMAN!

9.6
the AMAZING SPIDER-MAN
4
NOTHING CAN STOP THE SANDMAN!

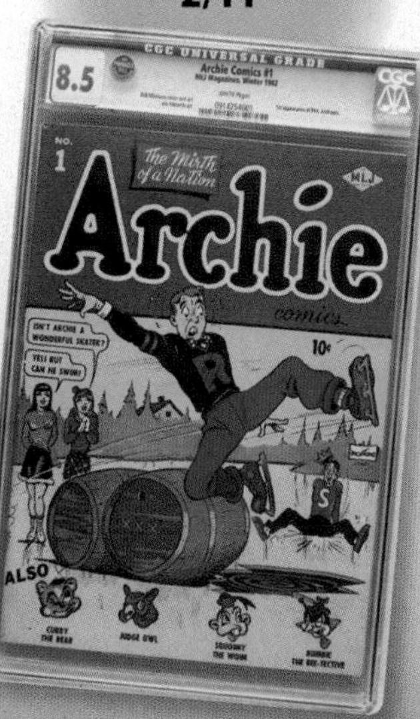
8.5
NO. 1
The Mirth of a Nation
Archie comics
10¢
ALSO